Acronyms, Initialisms & Abbreviations Dictionary

Explore your options!

Gale databases are offered in a variety of formats

 ™ The information in this Gale publication is also available in some or all of the formats described here. Your Gale Representative will be happy to fill you in. Call toll-free 1-800-877-GALE.

GaleNet

A number of Gale databases are now available on GaleNet, our new online information resource accessible through the Internet. GaleNet features an easy-to-use end-user interface, the powerful search capabilities of BRS/SEARCH retrieval software and ease of access through the World Wide Web.

Diskette/Magnetic Tape

Many Gale databases are available on diskette or magnetic tape, allowing systemwide access to your most-used information sources through existing computer systems. Data can be delivered on a variety of mediums (DOS-formatted diskettes, 9-track tape, 8mm data tape) and in industry-standard formats (comma-delimited, tagged, fixed-field).

CD-ROM

A variety of Gale titles are available on CD-ROM, offering maximum flexibility and powerful search software.

Online

For your convenience, many Gale databases are available through popular online services, including DIALOG, NEXIS, DataStar, ORBIT, OCLC, Thomson Financial Network's I/Plus Direct, HRIN, Prodigy, Sandpoint's HOOVER, the Library Corporation's NLightN and Telebase Systems.

ISSN 0270-4404

Acronyms, Initialisms & Abbreviations Dictionary

A Guide to Acronyms, Abbreviations,
Contractions, Alphabetic Symbols, and Similar Condensed Appellations

Covering: Aerospace, Associations, Banking, Biochemistry, Business, Data Processing,
Domestic and International Affairs, Economics, Education, Electronics, Genetics,
Government, Information Technology, Investment, Labor, Law, Medicine, Military Affairs,
Pharmacy, Physiology, Politics, Religion, Science, Societies, Sports, Technical
Drawings and Specifications, Telecommunications, Trade, Transportation, and Other Fields

25th Edition

Volume 1

Part 1

A-F

Mary Rose Bonk,
Editor

Pamela Dear,
Associate Editor

GALE

DETROIT · LONDON

Editor: Mary Rose Bonk

Associate Editor: Pamela Dear

Contributing Editor: Mildred Hunt

Data Entry Manager: Eleanor M. Allison
Data Entry Coordinator: Kenneth Benson

Production Director: Mary Beth Trimper
Production Assistant: Carolyn Fischer

Graphic Services Manager: Barbara J. Yarrow
Graphic Artist: Gary Leach

Manager, Technical Support Services: Theresa A. Rocklin
Programmer: Charles Beaumont

Library of Congress Catalog Card Number 84-643188
ISBN 0-7876-2423-3 (Volume 1 Complete)
ISBN 0-7876-2424-1 (Part 1: A-F only)
ISBN 0-7876-2425-X (Part 2: G-O only)
ISBN 0-7876-2426-8 (Part 3: P-Z only)
ISSN 0270-4404

Printed in the United States of America

Contents

Volume 1
Part 1 A-F

Volume 1
Part 2 G-O

Volume 1
Part 3 P-Z

Gale's publications in the acronyms and abbreviations field include:

Acronyms, Initialisms & Abbreviations Dictionary series:

Acronyms, Initialisms & Abbreviations Dictionary (Volume 1). A guide to acronyms, initialisms, abbreviations, and similar contractions, arranged alphabetically by abbreviation.

Acronyms, Initialisms & Abbreviations Dictionary Supplement (Volume 2). An interedition supplement in which terms are arranged alphabetically both by abbreviation and by meaning.

Reverse Acronyms, Initialisms & Abbreviations Dictionary (Volume 3). A companion to Volume 1 in which terms are arranged alphabetically by meaning of the acronym, initialism, or abbreviation.

Acronyms, Initialisms & Abbreviations Dictionary Subject Guide series:

Computer & Telecommunications Acronyms (Volume 1). A guide to acronyms, initialisms, abbreviations, and similar contractions used in the field of computers and telecommunications in which terms are arranged alphabetically both by abbreviation and by meaning.

Business Acronyms (Volume 2). A guide to business-oriented acronyms, initialisms, abbreviations, and similar contractions in which terms are arranged alphabetically both by abbreviation and by meaning.

International Acronyms, Initialisms & Abbreviations Dictionary series:

International Acronyms, Initialisms & Abbreviations Dictionary (Volume 1). A guide to foreign and international acronyms, initialisms, abbreviations, and similar contractions, arranged alphabetically by abbreviation.

Reverse International Acronyms, Initialisms & Abbreviations Dictionary (Volume 2). A companion to Volume 1, in which terms are arranged alphabetically by meaning of the acronym, initialism, or abbreviation.

Periodical Title Abbreviations series:

Periodical Title Abbreviations: By Abbreviation (Volume 1). A guide to abbreviations commonly used for periodical titles, arranged alphabetically by abbreviation.

Periodical Title Abbreviations: By Title (Volume 2). A guide to abbreviations commonly used for periodical titles, arranged alphabetically by title.

New Periodical Title Abbreviations (Volume 3). An interedition supplement in which terms are arranged alphabetically both by abbreviation and by title.

Highlights

Over 15,000 New Terms
Comprehensive Coverage
Subject Categories
Source Citations

The twenty-fifth edition of *Acronyms, Initialisms, and Abbreviations Dictionary (AIAD)* offers increased coverage in all fields of human endeavor. Many of the 15,000+ new terms are from the subject areas of:

- Arts
- Associations
- Business
- Education
- Internet
- Medicine
- Military affairs

Of major value to librarians and researchers is the inclusion of:

- airlines/airports
- information systems
- library symbols
- organizations
- radio/television station call letters
- research centers
- stock exchange symbols

Subject Categories Provided

Where possible, and if not already implied in the entry itself, a category or identifier follows many terms. It provides a subject context for those entries that require clarification.

Major Sources Cited

Codes are provided to indicate the source from which the information was obtained. This feature allows you to verify the entries and may, in some instances, lead to additional information. Complete bibliographic data about the publications cited can be found in the List of Selected Sources following the acknowledgments. Terms that are obtained from miscellaneous newspapers and newsmagazines, are provided by outside contributors, or are discovered through independent research by the editorial staff remain uncoded.

OUTSTANDING
REFERENCE SOURCE
ALA
RASD

Acronyms, Initialisms
& Abbreviations
Dictionary
was named an
**"Outstanding
Reference Source,"**
*the highest honor
given by the
American Library
Association Reference
and Adult Services
Division.*

Preface

The use of acronyms and similar abbreviated terms is convenient, speedy, and particularly well suited to the needs of our highly technical society. Rapid growth of this "language" and the need to eliminate guesswork in translating terms led to the publication of *Acronyms, Initialisms, and Abbreviations Dictionary (AIAD).* For over thirty years, *AIAD* has served the needs of businesspeople, students, government officials, researchers, and other interested citizens whose work requires a high degree of accuracy.

What Is Included?

Most entries in *AIAD* are specifically identified with the United States. Thousands of British and Canadian terms can also be found. Other non-U.S. acronyms most likely to be encountered in magazines and daily newspapers are included as well. For users whose principal interest is foreign and international terms, a companion volume to the *AIAD* series is available. *International Acronyms, Initialisms, and Abbreviations Dictionary* includes terms that are local to specific foreign countries (and, as such, not eligible for inclusion in *AIAD*).

No attempt is made to list acronyms of local businesses or associations, local units of government, or other terms in limited use. Obsolete terms are retained for their historical interest.

Slight Distinctions among Terms

Distinctions are not always made among the three terms used in the current title, nor are distinctions always necessary, since in many ways the definitions overlap. But the most commonly accepted, if somewhat simplified, explanations are as follows:

An *acronym* is composed of the initial letters or parts of a compound term. It is usually read or spoken as a single word, rather than letter by letter. Examples include RADAR (Radio Detection and Ranging) and LASER (Light Amplification by Stimulated Emission of Radiation).

An *initialism* is also composed of the initial letters or parts of a compound term, but is generally verbalized letter by letter, rather than as a single "word." Examples include PO (Post Office) and RPM (Revolutions per Minute).

An *abbreviation* is a shortened form of a word or words that does not follow the formation of either of the above. Examples include APR (April), Ph D (Doctor of Philosophy), BCSTG (Broadcasting), and DR (Doctor).

Also included in *AIAD* are many alphabetic symbols, in which the letters used do not necessarily correspond to the words that they represent. Included in this category are R, a missile launch environment symbol for Ship, and T, representing Meridian Angle.

Need for a Guide Evident

There have been rumblings of discontent through the years because of the overuse or misuse of acronyms, initialisms, and abbreviations. In a lecture presented before the International Congress of Pharmaceutical Sciences, Dr. Anatole Sliosberg, of the International Federation of Translators, expressed his dismay over the abuses of "abbreviomania."

> Whenever you open a scientific, technical, or economic publication, or even a daily newspaper, you are immediately struck by the number of apparently meaningless letter or syllable combinations which the most knowledgeable reader cannot decipher without the aid of a dictionary or a keen sense of divination.

The frustration of wrestling with inadequately identified designations or with the overuse of these terms is understandable. Yet, what H.L. Mencken called "the characteristic American habit of reducing complete concepts to starkest abbreviations" seems likely to continue unabated for some time. Accordingly, *AIAD* will continue to guide users through this expanding maze of linguistic shorthand.

Trends in the Field

Acronym formation often follows what might be termed the "chicken or egg" syndrome. Recent years have shown that in choosing a name or slogan, new organizations, ad hoc groups, or activist movements frequently will select a colorful acronym first—one that they hope will spotlight their philosophy and be associated easily in the public mind with their ideas or purposes. The catchy acronym will then be fleshed out with more-or-less appropriate words. This back-formation is common with political groups, fund-raising organizations, consumer-protection interests, and countless other topical coalitions.

A few editions ago, it was reported that there was a noticeable movement among corporations to abbreviate names, often because merger or expansion had rendered the original names meaningless or misleading. American District Telegraph Company changing its name to ADT, Incorporated and US Steel Corporation becoming USX Corporation are examples of this trend.

Another ongoing trend involves the creation of alternative translations to existing acronyms. These are usually facetious and sometimes quite clever. DT & I (Detroit, Toledo & Ironton Railroad) has also been translated as "Damned Tough and Independent"; IBM (International Business Machines Corp.) has been translated as "I Built a Macintosh"; PBS (Public Broadcasting Service) as "Petroleum Broadcasting Service"; and Ph D (Philosophiae Doctor) as "Piled Higher and Deeper". Proper names can be turned into acronyms in a similar process. Ford (in reference to Ford Motor Company products) has been translated as "Fix or Repair Daily".

A related type of acronym formation occurs when an existing acronym is used as inspiration for other acronyms. The association MADD (Mothers Against Drunk Driving) has led to the formation of a related group, SADD (Students Against Drunk Driving), and also to the creation of the satirical DAMM (Drinkers Against Mad Mothers). Similarly, the famous MGM (Metro-Goldwyn-Mayer) logo was the basis for MTM (Mary Tyler Moore) Productions, Inc.; and BC (Before Christ) has been updated to BV (Before Video).

Currently the most rapid proliferation of this type of spinoff formation is of the terms based on Yuppie (Young Urban Professional). Examples include Buppie (Black Urban Professional); Fuppie (Female Urban Professional); and Guppie (Gay Urban Professional). The collection of this type of acronym currently exceeds eighty terms.

"Outstanding Reference Source"

New editions are prepared by adding thousands of previously unlisted terms and updating many entries from earlier editions. Substantial editorial research is required to ensure that the most complete and current information is provided. The editors were rewarded for their diligent efforts in 1985 when the Reference and Adult Services Division of the American Library Association selected *AIAD* as one of the twenty-five most distinguished reference titles published during the past quarter century. We take great pride in this achievement.

Available in Electronic Format

AIAD is available for licensing on magnetic tape or diskette in a fielded format. Either the complete database or a custom selection of entries may be ordered. The database is available for internal data processing and nonpublishing purposes only. For more information, call 800-877-GALE.

Suggestions Are Welcome

Many suggestions concerning individual terms to be included or subjects to be covered have been received from individual users and have been most helpful. The editors invite all such comments and will make every effort to incorporate them in future editions.

Acknowledgments

For suggestions, contributions of terms, permission to take material from personal or published sources, and for other courtesies extended during the preparation of previous editions and the present one, the editors are indebted to the following:

James Aguirre, former staff writer and editor, Quality Evaluation Laboratory, United States Naval Weapons Station, Concord, California

O.T. Albertini, Plans and Policy Directorate, Joint Chiefs of Staff, Department of Defense (retired)

Irving Allen, Professor of Sociology, University of Connecticut

American Library Association (publisher of *Pugh's Dictionary of Acronyms & Abbreviations*)

Associated Press

Associated Spring Corp., B-G-R Division (publisher of *Civilian's Dictionary,* a dictionary of wartime abbreviations)

Association of American Railroads

Paul Axel-Lute

Janice Badash

Burroughs Corp. (publisher of *Computer Acronyms and Abbreviations Handbook*)

Butterworth & Co. (Publishers) Ltd. (publisher of *Index to Legal Citations and Abbreviations*)

Ethel M. Fair

John Fobian

David Glagovsky

Jack Gordon

Hoyt Hammer, Jr.

Hanley & Belfus Inc. (publisher of *Dictionary of Medical Acronyms & Abbreviations*)

William S. Hein Co. (publisher of *Bieber's Dictionary of Legal Abbreviations*)

Charles C. Hinckley, executive vice president, Union Central Life Insurance Co.

Roy Hubbard

Mildred Hunt, editorial consultant

International Business Machines Corp., Data Processing Division (publisher of *IBM Glossary for Information Processing*)

David J. Jones, compiler of *Australian Dictionary of Acronyms and Abbreviations* and *Australian Periodical Title Abbreviations*

Kogan Page Ltd. (publisher of *Dictionary of British Qualifications*)

Steven C. Krems, computer specialist, Internal Revenue Service

Ktav Publishing House, Inc. (publisher of *Biblical and Judaic Acronyms*)

Robert E. Lacey, journalist

Lund Humphries Publishers Ltd. (publisher of *Dictionary of Graphic Arts Abbreviations*)

David MacLaren

Lawrence Marwick, late editor of *Biblical and Judaic Acronyms*

David Mattison

Mamie Meredith, late Professor of English, University of Nebraska

National Association of Securities Dealers (publisher of the *NASDAQ Company Directory*)

National Library of Canada

National Library of Medicine

Morgan Oates, late librarian, *Detroit Free Press*

Charles Parsons, formerly of Translation Research Institute

Eric Partridge, late author of *A Dictionary of Slang and Unconventional English; A Dictionary of Abbreviations, with Especial Attention to War-Time Abbreviations;* and other books

James U. Rose

Janet I. Rose

Rynd Communications (publisher of *Dictionary of Health Services Management*)

Harry Schechter, late chairman, Government Printing Office Style Board

Edward A. Schmerler

Brian Scott, editor of *Dictionary of Military Abbreviations*

Peter Sikli

Standard & Poor's Corporation (publisher of *Security Owner's Stock Guide*)

Edwin B. Steen, professor emeritus of biology, Western Michigan University, author of *Abbreviations in Medicine and Dictionary of Biology*

Miriam M. Steinert, editorial consultant

A. Marjorie Taylor, editor, *Language of World War II*

Edith Thompson

Toronto Stock Exchange

David J. Trotz, editor of *Defense Weapon Systems Glossary*

Tracey Head Turbett

The University Press of Virginia (publisher of *Dictionary of Sigla and Abbreviations to and in Law Books before 1607*)

U.S. Air Force, Translation Section HQ

VCH Publishers (publisher of *Index of Acronyms and Abbreviations in Electrical and Electronic Engineering*)

Donald Weeks

Witherby & Co. Ltd. (publisher of *Aviation Insurance Abbreviations, Organisations, and Institutions; Dictionary of Commercial Terms and Abbreviations; Dictionary of Shipping International Trade Terms and Abbreviations*)

Harvey J. Wolf

User's Guide

The following examples illustrate possible elements of entries in *AIAD:*

> ①   ②   ③   ④   ⑤
>
> **FATAC...** Force Aerienne Tactique [*Tactical Air Force*] [*French*] (NATG)
>
>   ⑥   ⑦
>
> **MMT...** Multiple-Mirror Telescope [*Mount Hopkins, AZ*] [*Jointly operated by Smithsonian Institution and the University of Arizona*] [*Astronomy*]
>
>   ⑧

①   Acronym, Initialism, or Abbreviation

②   Meaning or Phrase

③   English Translation

④   Language (for non-English entries)

⑤   Source code (Allows you to verify entries or find additional information. Decoded in the List of Selected Sources)

⑥   Location or Country of origin (Provides geographic identifiers for airports, colleges and universities, libraries, military bases, political parties, radio and television stations, and others)

⑦   Sponsoring organization

⑧   Subject category (Clarifies entries by providing appropriate context)

The completeness of a listing is dependent upon both the nature of the term and the amount of information provided by the source. If additional information becomes available during future research, an entry is revised.

Arrangement of Entries

Acronyms, initialisms, and abbreviations are arranged alphabetically in letter-by-letter sequence. Spacing, punctuation, and capitalization are not considered. If the same term has more than one meaning, the various meanings are subarranged in word-by-word sequence.

Should you wish to eliminate the guesswork from acronym formation and usage, a companion volume could help. *Reverse Acronyms, Initialisms and Abbreviations Dictionary* contains essentially the same entries as *AIAD,* but arranges them alphabetically by meaning, rather than by acronym or initialism.

List of Selected Sources

Each of the sources included in the following list contributed at least 50 terms. It would be impossible to cite a source for every entry because the majority of terms are sent by outside contributors, are uncovered through independent research by the editorial staff, or surface as miscellaneous broadcast or print media references.

For sources used on an ongoing basis, only the latest edition is listed. For most of the remaining sources, the edition that was used is cited. The editors will provide further information about these sources upon request.

Unless further described in an annotation, the publications listed here contain no additional information about the acronym, initialism, or abbreviation cited.

(AABC)   *Catalog of Abbreviations and Brevity Codes.* Washington, DC: U.S. Department of the Army, 1981. [Use of source began in 1969]

(AAG)   *Aerospace Abbreviations Glossary.* Report Number AG60-0014. Prepared by General Dynamics/Astronautics. San Diego, CA: 1962.

(AAGC)   *Acronyms and Abbreviations in Government Contracting.* 2d ed. By Patricia A. Tobin and Joan Nelson Phillips. Washington, DC: George Washington University, 1997.

(AAMN)   *Abbreviations and Acronyms in Medicine and Nursing.* By Solomon Garb, Eleanor Krakauer, and Carson Justice. New York, NY: Springer Publishing Co., 1976.

(ABBR)   *Abbreviations: The Comprehensive Dictionary of Abbreviations and Letter Symbols.* Vol. 1 C. By Edward Wall. Ann Arbor, MI: The Pierian Press, 1984.

(AC)   *Associations Canada 1995/96.* Edited by Ward McBurney. Toronto, Canada: Canadian Almanac & Directory Publishing Co. Ltd., 1995.

(ACII)   *"Acronym and Initials Index."* 7 February 1996. <http://www.ioi.ie/~readout/cl.html> (7 November 1996).

(AD)   *Abbreviations Dictionary.* 8thed. By Ralph De Sola. Boca Raton, FL: CRC Press, 1992.

(ADA)   *The Australian Dictionary of Acronyms and Abbreviations.* 2nd ed. Compiled by David J. Jones. Leura, NSW, Australia: Second Back Row Press Pty. Ltd., 1981.

(ADDR)   *Army Dictionary and Desk Reference.* By Tim Zurick. Harrisburg, PA: Stackpole Books, 1992.

(AEBS)   *Acronyms in Education and the Behavioral Sciences.* By Toyo S. Kawakami. Chicago, IL: American Library Association, 1971.

(AEE)   *American Educators' Encyclopedia.* By Edward L. Dejnozka and David E. Kapel. Westport, CT: Greenwood Press, 1991.

(AF)   *Reference Aid: Abbreviations in the African Press.* Arlington, VA: Joint Publications Research Service, 1979.

(AFIT) *Compendium of Authenticated Systems and Logistics*. Washington, DC: Air Force Institute of Technology, 1984.

(AFM) *Air Force Manual of Abbreviations*. Washington, DC: U.S. Department of the Air Force, 1975. [Use of source began in 1969]

(AIA) *Aviation Insurance Abbreviations, Organisations and Institutions*. By M.J. Spurway. London, England: Witherby & Co. Ltd., 1983.

(AIE) *Acronyms and Initialisms in Education*. 6th ed. Compiled by John Hutchins. Norwich, England: Librarians of Institutes and Schools of Education, 1995.

(ANA) *"Abbreviations" - U.S. Navy Dictionary*. 3rd revision. Washington DC: DCP, 1989.

(APTA) *Australian Periodical Title Abbreviations*. Compiled by David J. Jones. Leura, NSW, Australia: Second Back Row Press Pty. Ltd., 1985.

(ARC) *Agricultural Research Centres: A World Directory of Organizations and Programmes*. 2 vols. Edited by Nigel Harvey. Harlow, Essex, England: Longman Group, 1983.
   A world guide to official, educational, industrial, and independent research centers
   which support research in the fields of agriculture, veterinary medicine, horticulture,
   aquaculture, food science, forestry, zoology, and botany.

(ARCH) *Dictionary of Architecture and Construction*. Edited by Cyril M. Harris. New York, NY: McGraw-Hill, Inc., 1975.

(ASF) *Guide to Names and Acronyms of Organizations, Activities, and Projects*. By Food and Agriculture Organization of the United Nations. Fishery Information, Data, and Statistics Service and U.S. National Oceanic and Atmospheric Administration. Aquatic Sciences and Fisheries Information System Reference Series, Number 10, 1982. n.p.

(BABM) *Bailliere's Abbreviations in Medicine*. 5th ed. By Edwin B. Steen. London, England: Bailliere Tindall, 1984.

(BARN) *The Barnhart Abbreviations Dictionary*. Edited by Robert K. Barnhart. New York, NY: John Wiley & Sons, Inc., 1995.

(BI) *British Initials and Abbreviations*. 3rd ed. By Ian H. Wilkes. London, England: Leonard Hill Books, 1971.

(BIB) *Bibliotech*. Ottawa, Canada: National Library of Canada, 1988-89.

(BJA) *Biblical and Judaic Acronyms*. By Lawrence Marwick. New York, NY: Ktav Publishing House, Inc., 1979.

(BRI) *Book Review Index*. 1997 Cumulation. Edited by Beverly Baer. Detroit, MI: Gale Research, 1998.

(BROA) *Broadcasting and Cable Yearbook 1997*. 2 vol. New Providence, NJ: R.R. Bowker, 1997.

(BTTJ) *Breaking Through Technical Jargon: A Dictionary of Computer and Automation Acronyms*. By Mark S. Merkow. New York, NY: Van Nostrand Reinhold, 1990.

(BUR) *Computer Acronyms and Abbreviations Handbook*. Tokyo, Japan: Burroughs Co. Ltd., 1978.

(BYTE)   *Byte: The Small Systems Journal.* Peterborough, NH: McGraw-Hill Information Systems, Inc., 1987-89.

(CAAL)   *CAAL COMOPTEVFOR Acronym and Abbreviation List.* Norfolk, VA: (CAAL-U) Operational Test and Evaluation Force, 1981.

(CB)   *Centres & Bureaux: A Directory of Concentrations of Effort, Information and Expertise.* Edited by Lindsay Sellar. Beckenham, Kent, England: CBD Research Ltd., 1987.
          A guide to British organizations which include the words "centre" or "bureau" in their names. Entries include name and address; telephone and telex numbers; chief official; and a description of the purposes, activities, and services of the organization.

(CDAI)   *Concise Dictionary of Acronyms and Initialisms.* By Stuart W. Miller. New York, NY: Facts on File Publications, 1988.

(CDE)   *The Computer Desktop Encyclopedia.* By Alan Freedman. New York, NY: AMACOM, 1996.

(CDI)   *The Cancer Dictionary.* By Roberta Altman and Michael Sarg, M.D. New York, NY: Facts on File, 1992.

(CED)   *Current European Directories.* 2nd ed. Edited by G.P. Henderson. Beckenham, Kent, England: CBD Research, 1981.

(CET)   *Communications-Electronics Terminology.* AFM 11-1. Vol. 3. U.S. Department of the Air Force, 1973.

(CINC)   *A CINCPAC Glossary of Commonly Used Abbreviations and Short Titles.* By Ltc. J.R. Johnson. Washington, DC: 1968.

(CMD)   *Complete Multilingual Dictionary of Computer Terminology.* Compiled by Georges Nania. Chicago, IL: National Textbook Co., 1984.
          Computer-related terms in Spanish, French, Italian, Portuguese, and English. Indexes in French, Italian, Spanish, and Portuguese are also provided.

(CNC)   *American National Standard Codes for the Representation of Names of Countries, Dependencies, and Areas of Special Sovereignty for Information Interchange.* U.S. National Bureau of Standards. Washington, DC: Government Printing Office, 1986. [Use of source began in 1977]
          These standard codes, approved by the International Organization for Standardization and the American National Standards Institute, are used in the international interchange of data in many fields.

(CPH)   *The Charles Press Handbook of Current Medical Abbreviations.* 3rd ed. Philadelphia, PA: The Charles Press Publishers, Inc., 1991.

(CRD)   *Computer-Readable Databases: A Directory and Data Sourcebook.* 6th ed. Edited by Kathleen Young Marcaccio. Detroit, MI: Gale Research, 1990.
          A guide to online databases, offline files available in various magnetic formats, and CD-ROM files. Entries include producer name, address, telephone number, description of coverage, vendors, and contact person.

(CROSS)   *Cross-Border Links: A Directory of Organizations in Canada, Mexico, and the United States.* Edited by Ricardo Hernandez and Edith Sanchez. Albuquerque, NM: Inter-Hemispheric Education Resource Center, 1992.

(CSR)	*Computer Science Resources: A Guide to Professional Literature.* Edited by Darlene Myers. White Plains, NY: Knowledge Industry Publications, Inc., 1981.
	Covers several types of computer-related literature including journals, technical reports, directories, dictionaries, handbooks, and university computer center newsletters. Five appendices cover career and salary trends in the computer industry, user group acronyms, university computer libraries, and trade fairs and shows.
(CTT)	*Corporate TrendTrac.* Edited by A. Dale Timpe. Detroit, MI: Gale Research, 1988-89.
	Covers mergers and acquisitions, stock exchange listings and suspensions, company name changes, bankruptcies, liquidations, and reorganizations.
(DA)	*Dictionary of Aviation.* By R. J. Hall and R. D. Campbell. Chicago, IL: St. James Press, 1991.
(DAS)	*Dictionary of Abbreviations and Symbols.* By Edward Frank Allen. London, England: Cassell and Co. Ltd., 1949.
(DAVI)	*The Davis Book of Medical Abbreviations: A Deciphering Guide.* By Sarah Lu Mitchell-Hatton. Philadelphia, PA: F. A. Davis Co., 1991.
(DBA)	*Directory of British Associations.* Edited by G. P. Henderson and S. P. A. Henderson. Beckenham, Kent, England: CBD Research, Ltd., 1990.
(DBQ)	*A Dictionary of British Qualifications.* London, England: Kogan Page Ltd., 1985.
(DCTA)	*Dictionary of Commercial Terms and Abbreviations.* By Alan E. Branch. London, England: Witherby & Co. Ltd., 1984.
(DD)	*The Financial Post Directory of Directors 1997.* Toronto, Canada: The Financial Post, 1996.
(DEN)	*Dictionary of Electronics and Nucleonics.* By L.E.C. Hughes, R. W. B. Stephens and L. D. Brown. New York, NY: Barnes & Noble, 1969.
(DFIT)	*Dictionary of Finance and Investment Terms.* 4th ed. Edited by John Downes and Jordan Elliot Goodman. Hauppauge, NY: Barron's Educational Series, 1995.
(DGA)	*Dictionary of Graphic Arts Abbreviations.* By L. W. Wallis. Rockport, MA: Rockport Publishers, Inc., 1986.
(DHSM)	*Dictionary of Health Services Management.* 2nd ed. By Thomas C. Timmreck. Owings Mills, MD: Rynd Communications, 1987.
(DI)	*The Dictionary of Initials-What They Mean.* Compiled and edited by Harriette Lewis. Kingswood, Surrey, England: Paper Fronts Elliot Right Way Books, 1983.
(DICI)	*The Dictionary of Initials.* By Betsy M. Parks. Secaucus, NJ: Citadel Press, 1981.
(DIT)	*Dictionary of Informatics Terms in Russian and English.* By G. S. Zhdanov, E. S. Kolobrodov, V. A. Polushkin, and A. I. Cherny. Moscow: Nauka, 1971.
(DLA)	*Bieber's Dictionary of Legal Abbreviations.* 3rd ed. By Mary Miles Prince. Buffalo, NY: William S. Hein & Co., 1988.

(DMA)   *Dictionary of Military Abbreviations: British, Empire, Commonwealth.* By B. K. C. Scott. Hastings, East Sussex, England: Tamarisk Books, 1982.

(DMAA)   *Dictionary of Medical Acronyms and Abbreviations.* 3rd ed. Edited by Stanley Jablonski. Philadelphia, PA: Hanley & Belfus, Inc., 1998.

(DMC)   *Webster's New World Dictionary of Media and Communications.* Revised ed. By Richard Weiner. New York, NY: Macmillan, 1996.

(DNAB)   *Dictionary of Naval Abbreviations.* 3rd ed. Compiled and edited by Bill Wedertz. Annapolis, MD: Naval Institute Press, 1984.

(DOAD)   *The Dictionary of Advertising.* Edited by Laurence Urdang. Lincolnwood, IL: NTC Business Books, 1986.

(DOG)   *A Dictionary of Genetics.* 5th ed. By Robert C. King and William D. Stansfield. New York, NY: Oxford University Press, 1997.

(DOGT)   *"List of Acronyms."* <http://www.em.doe.gov/rtc1994/loa.html> (5 March 1997).

(DOM)   *The Dictionary of Multimedia: Terms & Acronyms.* By Brad Hansen. Wilsonvillee, OR: Franklin, Beedle & Associates, 1997.

(DOMA)   *Dictionary of Military Abbreviations.* By Norman Polmar, Mark Warren, and Eric Wertheim. Annapolis, MD: Naval Institute Press, 1994.

(DS)   *Dictionary of Shipping International Trade Terms and Abbreviations.* 3rd ed. By Alan E. Branch. London, England: Witherby & Co. Ltd., 1986.

(DSA)   *Dictionary of Sigla and Abbreviations to and in Law Books before 1607.* By William Hamilton Bryson. Charlottesville, VA: University Press of Virginia, 1975.

(DSUE)   *A Dictionary of Slang and Unconventional English.* 8th ed. By Eric Partridge. New York, NY: Macmillan Publishing Co., 1984.

(DUND)   *Directory of United Nations Databases and Information Services.* 4th ed. Compiled by the Advisory Committee for the Coordination of Information Systems. New York, NY: United Nations, 1990.
         A guide to computerized databases and information systems/services. Entries include sponsoring organization, year established, type, scope, coverage, timespan, and contact information.

(DWSG)   *Defense Weapon Systems Glossary.* By David Trotz. Piscataway, NJ: Target Marketing, 1992.

(EA)   *Encyclopedia of Associations.* 29th ed. Vol. 1, National Organizations of the U.S. Edited by Carol A. Schwartz and Rebecca L. Turner. Detroit, MI: Gale Research, 1995 (and supplement 1995) [Use of source began in 1960]
         A guide to trade, professional, and other nonprofit associations that are national and international in scope and membership and that are headquartered in the United States. Entries include name and address; telephone and telex number; chief official; and a description of the purpose, activities, and structure of the organization.

(EAAP)   *Encyclopedia of Associations: Association Periodicals*. 3 vols. Edited by Denise M. Allard and Robert C. Thomas. Detroit, MI: Gale Research, 1987.
> A directory of publications issued by all types of national nonprofit organizations in the United States. Entries include title and organization name, address, telephone number; description of periodical, frequency of publication, and price.

(EAIO)   *Encyclopedia of Associations: International Organizations*. 29th ed. Edited by Linda Irvin. Detroit, MI: Gale Research, 1995. [Use of source began in 1985]
> A guide to trade, professional, and other nonprofit associations that are national or international in scope and membership and that are headquartered outside the United States. Entries include name and address; principal foreign language name; telephone and telex number; chief official; and a description of the purpose, activities, and structure of the organization.

(ECED)   *The European Communities Encyclopedia and Directory 1992*. London, England: Europa Publications Ltd., 1991; distributed in U.S. by Gale Research, Detroit, MI.
> A comprehensive guide to the European Communities. Entries explain widely-used acronyms and include address, telephone, telex, fax numbers and chief officers for EC-level organizations.

(ECII)   *Electronics, Computers and Industrial Instrumentation Abbreviations and Acronyms.* Edited by Sergio Sobredo. Miami, FL: Sergio Sobredo Technical Services, 1986.

(ECON)   *The Economist*. London, England: The Economist Newspaper Ltd., 1997. [Use of source began in 1988]

(EDAC)   *Dictionary of Educational Acronyms, Abbreviations, and Initialisms.* 2nd ed. Edited by James C. Palmer and Anita Y. Colby. Phoenix, AZ: Oryx Press, 1985.

(EE)   *Eastern Europe and the Commonwealth of Independent States 1992*. London, England: Europa Publications Ltd., 1992; distributed in U.S. by Gale Research, Detroit, MI.

(EECA)   *Dictionary of Electrical, Electronics, and Computer Abbreviations.* By Phil Brown. London, England: Buttersworth, 1985.

(EG)   *Environmental Glossary*. 4th ed. Edited by G. William Frick and Thomas F.P. Sullivan. Rockville, MD: Government Institutes, Inc., 1986.

(EGAO)   *Encyclopedia of Governmental Advisory Organizations*. 9th ed. Edited by Donna Batten. Detroit, MI: Gale Research, 1994-95 (and supplement, 1995). [Use of source began in 1975]
> A reference guide to permanent, continuing, and ad hoc U.S. presidential advisory committees, interagency committees, and other government-related boards, panels, task forces, commissions, conferences, and other similar bodies serving in a consultative, coordinating, advisory, research, or investigative capacity. Entries include name and address, telephone number, designated federal employee, history, recommendation and findings of the committee, staff size, publications, and subsidiaries. Also includes indexes to personnel, reports, federal agencies, presidential administration, and an alphabetical and keyword index.

(EMRF)   *The St. James Encyclopedia of Mortgage & Real Estate Finance*. By James Newell, Albert Santi, and Chip Mitchell. Chicago, IL: St. James Press, 1991.

(EPA)   *Glossary of EPA Acronyms*. Washington, DC: Environmental Protection Agency, 1987.

(ERG)   *Environmental Regulatory Glossary*. 5th ed. Edited by G. William Frick and Thomas F. P. Sullivan. Rockville, MD: Government Institutes, Inc., 1990.

(EY)   *The Europa World Year Book 1992*. London: Europa Publications Ltd., 1992. distributed in U.S. by Gale Research, Detroit, MI.
> An annual survey containing detailed information about the political, economic, statistical, and commercial situation of the regions and countries covered.

(FAAC)   *Contractions Handbook*. Changes. U.S. Department of Transportation. Federal Aviation Administration, 1993. [Use of source began in 1969]

(FAAL)   *Location Identifiers*. U.S. Department of Transportation. Federal Aviation Administration. Air Traffic Service, 1982.

(FEA)   *The Far East and Australasia 1987*. 18th ed. London, England: Europa Publications Ltd., 1986; distributed in U.S. by Gale Research, Detroit, MI.
> An annual survey containing detailed information about the political, economic, statistical, and commercial situation of the regions and countries covered.

(FFDE)   *The Facts on File Dictionary of Environmental Science*. By L. Harold Stevenson and Bruce Wyman. New York, NY: Facts on File, 1991.
> Defines terms from disciplines as diverse as biology, chemistry, geology, physics, engineering, meteorology, social science, medicine, and economics.

(GAAI)   *"Glossary of Abbreviations, Acronyms, and Initialisms."* 17 February 1998. <http://www.em.doe.gov/idb97/acropdf.html

(GAVI)   *"Glossary of Aviation Acronyms and Abbreviations."* <http://olias.arc.nasa.gov/AFO_Acronyms_.html> (5 March 1997).

(GEA)   *Government Economic Agencies of the World: An International Directory of Governmental Organisations Concerned with Economic Development and Planning*. A Keesing's Reference Publication. Edited by Alan J. Day. Harlow, Essex, England: Longman Group Ltd., 1985.
> Covers over 170 countries and territories. Two introductory sections for each area cover economic data and prevailing economic and political conditions. Individual entries provide title, address, and names of chief officials of each agency. Current activities and financial structure of each agency are also detailed. An index of agency officials is provided.

(GFGA)   *Guide to Federal Government Acronyms*. Edited by William R. Evinger. Phoenix, AZ: The Oryx Press, 1989.

(GNE)   *The Green Encyclopedia*. By Irene Franck and David Brownstone. New York, NY: Prentice Hall General Reference, 1992.

(GPO)   *Style Manual*. Washington, DC: Government Printing Office, 1984. Terms are included in Chapter 24, Foreign Languages.

(GRD)   *Government Research Directory*. 8th ed. Edited by Joseph M. Palmisano. Detroit, MI: Gale Research, 1994. (and supplement, 1994).
> A descriptive guide to U.S. government research and development centers, institutes, laboratories, bureaus, test facilities, experiment stations, data collection and analysis centers, and grants management and research coordinating offices in agriculture, business, education, energy, engineering, environment, the humanities, medicine, military science, and basic applied sciences.

(HCT)   *Health Care Terms.* 2nd ed. By Vergil N. and Debora A. Slee. St. Paul, MN: Tringa Press, 1991.

(HGAA)   *The Handy Guide to Abbreviations and Acronyms for the Automated Office.* By Mark W. Greenia. Seattle, WA: Self-Counsel Press Inc., 1986.

(IAA)   *Index of Acronyms and Abbreviations in Electrical and Electronic Engineering.* Compiled by Buro Scientia. New York, NY: VCH Publishers, 1989.

(IBMDP)   *IBM Data Processing Glossary.* 6th ed. White Plains, NY: IBM Corp., 1977.

(ICAO)   *Aircraft Type Designators.* 13th ed. International Civil Aviation Organization, August, 1981.

(ICDA)   *Designators for Aircraft Operating Agencies, Aeronautical Authorities and Services.* 49th ed. International Civil Aviation Organization, June, 1982.
         Document also includes telephony designators and postal and telegraphic addresses of government civil aviation authorities.

(ICLI)   *Location Indicators.* 51st ed. International Civil Aviation Organization, February, 1987.
         Document also contains addresses of flight information centers.

(IDOE)   *The Illustrated Dictionary of Electronics.* 6th ed. By Stan Gibilisco. New York, NY: TAB Books, 1994.

(IEEE)   *IEEE Standard Dictionary of Electrical and Electronics Terms.* Edited by Frank Jay. New York, NY: The Institute of Electrical and Electronics Engineers, Inc., 1977, 1984.
         Includes definitions for thousands of electrical and electronics terms. Each entry includes a numeric source code.

(IIA)   *Index of Initials and Acronyms.* Compiled by Richard Kleiner. New York, NY: Auerbach Publishers, 1971.

(IID)   *Information Industry Directory.* 15th ed. Edited by Annette Novallo. Detroit, MI: Gale Research, 1995. (and supplement, 1995).
         An international guide to computer-readable databases, database producers, and publishers, online vendors and time-sharing companies, telecommunications networks, and many other information systems and services. Entries include name and address, telephone number, chief official, and a detailed description of the purpose and function of the system or service.

(ILCA)   *Index to Legal Citations and Abbreviations.* By Donald Raistrick. Abingdon, Oxfordshire, England: Professional Books Ltd., 1981.

(IMH)   *International Marketing Handbook.* 2nd ed. Edited by Frank Bair. Detroit, MI: Gale Research, 1985.
         An in-depth guide to commercial and trade data on 142 countries of the world. Features include a list of European trade fairs and a report on growth markets in Western Europe.

(INF)   *Infantry.* Fort Benning, GA: U.S. Army Infantry Training School, 1996. [Use of source began in 1983]

(IRC)   *International Research Centers Directory 1992-93.* 6th ed. Edited by Annette Piccirelli. Detroit, MI: Gale Research, 1991.
         A world guide to government, university, independent, nonprofit, and commercial research and development centers, institutes, laboratories, bureaus, test facilities,

experiment stations, and data collection and analysis centers, as well as foundations, councils, and other organizations which support research.

(IRUK) *Industrial Research in the United Kingdom*. 12th ed. Harlow, Essex, England: Longman Group UK Ltd., 1987.
>A guide to all groups conducting or funding research relevant to British industrial development. Entries include name, address, telephone and telex numbers; chief officials; and scope of activities.

(IT) *Information Today: The Newspaper for Users and Producers of Electronic Information Services*. Medford, NJ: Learned Information Inc., 1988-89.

(ITD) *International Tradeshow Directory*. 5th ed. Frankfurt, Germany: M + A Publishers for Fairs, Exhibitions and Conventions Ltd., 1989.
>A guide to trade fairs and exhibitions throughout the world. Entries include event name, dates, frequency, location, description of purpose, profile of exhibitors and attendees.

(IYR) *The 1989-92 International Yacht Racing Rules*. London, England: International Yacht Racing Union, 1989.

(KSC) *A Selective List of Acronyms and Abbreviations*. Compiled by the Documents Department, Kennedy Space Center Library, 1971, 1973.

(LAIN) *Latest Intelligence: An International Directory of Codes Used by Government, Law Enforcement, Military, and Surveillance Agencies.* By James E. Tunnell. Blue Ridge Summit, PA: TAB BOOKS, 1990.

(LCCP) *MARC Formats for Bibliographic Data*. Appendix II. Washington, DC: Library of Congress, 1982.

(LCLS) *Symbols of American Libraries*. 14th ed. Edited by the Enhanced Cataloging Division. Washington, DC: Library of Congress, 1992. [Use of source began in 1980]

(LWAP) *Legal Words and Phrases: Speed Abbreviations.* By Joel Larus. Boston, MA: Aurico Publishing, 1965.

(MAE) *Medical Abbreviations and Eponyms*. By Sheila B. Sloane. Philadelphia, PA: W.B. Saunders Co., 1985.

(MAH) *Medical Abbreviations Handbook*. 2nd ed. Oradell, NJ: Medical Economics Co., Inc., 1983.

(MCD) *Acronyms, Abbreviations, and Initialisms*. Compiled by Carl Lauer. St. Louis, MO: McDonnell Douglas Corp., 1989. [Use of source began in 1969]

(MDG) *Microcomputer Dictionary and Guide*. By Charles J. Sippl. Champaign, IL: Matrix Publishers, Inc., 1975.
>A listing of definitions for over 5,000 microelectronics terms. Seven appendices.

(MEDA) *Medical Acronyms*. 2nd ed. By Marilyn Fuller Delong. Oradell, NJ: Medical Economic Books, 1989.

(MENA) *The Middle East and North Africa 1987*. 33rd ed. London, England: Europa Publications Ltd., 1986; distributed in U.S. by Gale Research, Detroit, MI.
>An annual survey containing detailed information about the political, economic, statistical, and commercial situation of the regions and countries covered.

(MHDB) *McGraw-Hill Dictionary of Business Acronyms, Initials, and Abbreviations.* By Jerry M. Rosenberg. New York, NY: McGraw-Hill, Inc., 1992.

(MHDI) *McGraw-Hill Dictionary of Information Technology and Computer Acronyms, Initials, and Abbreviations.* By Jerry M. Rosenberg. New York, NY: McGraw-Hill, Inc., 1992.

(MHDW) *McGraw-Hill Dictionary of Wall Street Acronyms, Initials, and Abbreviations.* By Jerry M. Rosenberg. New York, NY: McGraw-Hill, Inc., 1992.

(MSA) *Military Standard Abbreviations for Use on Drawings, and in Specifications, Standards, and Technical Documents.* MIL-STD-12D. U.S. Department of Defense, 1981. [Use of source began in 1975]

(MSC) *Annotated Acronyms and Abbreviations of Marine Science Related Activities.* 3rd ed. Revised by Charlotte M. Ashby and Alan R. Flesh. Washington, DC: U.S. Department of Commerce. National Oceanographic and Atmospheric Administration. Environmental Data Service. National Oceanographic Data Center, 1976, 1981.

(MUGU) *The Mugu Book of Acronyms and Abbreviations.* Missile Range, California: Management Engineering Office, 1963, 1964.

(NADA) *The New American Dictionary of Abbreviations.* By Mary A. De Vries. New York, NY: Signet, 1991.

(NASA) *Space Transportation System and Associated Payloads: Glossary, Acronyms, and Abbreviations.* Washington, DC: U.S. National Aeronautics and Space Administration, 1985.

(NATG) *Glossary of Abbreviations Used in NATO Documents.* AAP 15(B), n.p., 1979. [Use of source began in 1976]

(NCC) *NCC The National Centre for Information Technology. Guide to Computer Aided Engineering, Manufacturing and Construction Software.* Manchester, England: NCC Publications. The National Computing Centre Ltd., 1985.
  Includes software classifications and descriptions, names and addresses of suppliers, processor manufacturers, and operating systems.

(NFD) *The NSFRE Fund-Raising Dictionary.* Edited by Barbara R. Levy. New York, NY: John Wiley & Sons, Inc., 1996.

(NFPA) *Standard for Fire Safety Symbols/NFPA170.* Quincy, MA: National Fire Protection Association, 1994.

(NG) *NAVAIR Glossary of Unclassified Common-Use Abbreviated Titles and Phrases.* NAVAIRNOTE 5216 AIR-6031, n.p., July, 1969.

(NGC) *Catalogue of the National Gallery of Canada.* Compiled by National Gallery of Canada. Ottawa, Canada: National Gallery of Canada, 1998.

(NHD) *The New Hacker's Dictionary.* Edited by Eric Raymond. Cambridge, MA: MIT Press, 1991.

(NITA) *Dictionary of New Information Technology Acronyms.* 2nd ed. By Michael Gordon, Alan Singleton, and Clarence Rickards. London, England: Kogan Page, Ltd., 1986.

(NLC) *Symbols of Canadian Libraries.* 12th ed. National Library of Canada. Minister of Supply and Services Canada, 1987.

(NOAA)   *NOAA Directives Manual.* 66-13 Acronyms. 1977.

(NQ)   *NASDAQ Company Directory.* New York, NY: National Association of Securities Dealers, Inc., 1990. [Use of source began in 1983]
      Entries include company name, SIC code, contact person's name, title, address, and telephone number.

(NRCH)   *A Handbook of Acronyms and Initialisms.* Washington, DC: U.S. Nuclear Regulatory Commission. Division of Technical Information and Document Control, 1985.

(NTCM)   *NTC's Mass Media Dictionary.* R. Terry Ellmore. Lincolnwood, IL: National Textbook Co., 1991.

(NUCP)   *A Dictionary of Nuclear Power and Waste Management with Abbreviations and Acronyms.* Foo-Sun Lau. Letchworth, England: Research Studies Press, Ltd., 1987.

(NVT)   *Naval Terminology.* NWP3. Rev. B. U.S. Department of the Navy. Office of the Chief of Naval Operations, 1980. [Use of source began in 1974]
      Includes a section on definitions of naval terminology.

(OA)   *Ocran's Acronyms: A Dictionary of Abbreviations and Acronyms Used in Scientific and Technical Writing.* By Emanuel Benjamin Ocran. London, England: Routledge & Kegan Paul Ltd., 1978.

(OAG)   *Official Airline Guide Worldwide Edition.* Oak Brook, IL: Official Airlines Guide, Inc., 1984. [Use of source began in 1975]

(OCD)   *Oxford Classical Dictionary.* 2nd ed. Edited by N.G. Hammond and H.H. Scullard. London, England: Oxford University Press, 1970.

(OCLC)   *OCLC Participating Institutions Arranged by OCLC Symbol.* Dublin, OH: OCLC, 1981.

(ODBW)   *The Oxford Dictionary for the Business World.* New York, NY: Oxford University Press, Inc., 1993.

(OICC)   *Abbreviations and Acronyms.* Des Moines, IA: Iowa State Occupational Information Coordinating Committee, 1986.

(OLDSS)   *Online Database Search Services Directory.* 2nd ed. Edited by Doris Morris Maxfield. Detroit, MI: Gale Research, 1988.
      Provides detailed descriptions of the online information retrieval services offered by libraries, private information firms, and other organizations in the United States and Canada. Entries include name and address, telephone number, and key contact, as well as online systems accessed, frequently searched databases, and access hardware.

(OPSA)   *"Official Postal Service Abbreviations."* <http://www.usps.gov/ncsc/lookups/abbr_suffix.txt> (17 December 1996).

(OSI)   *OSI Standards and Acronyms.* 3rd ed. Compiled by Adrian V. Stokes. United Kingdom: Stokes, 1991.

(PAZ)   *Parenting A to Z.* By Irene M. Franck and David M. Brownstone. New York, NY: HarperCollins Publishers, Inc., 1996.

(PCM)   *PC Magazine.* New York, NY: Ziff-Davis Publishing Co., 1997. [Use of source began in 1987]

(PD) *Political Dissent: An International Guide to Dissident, Extra-Parliamentary, Guerrilla and Illegal Political Movements.* A Keesing's Reference Publication. Compiled by Henry W. Degenhardt. Edited by Alan J. Day. Harlow, Essex, England: Longman Group, 1983.
Includes the history and aims of approximately 1,000 organizations, with details of their leaderships.

(PDAA) *Pugh's Dictionary of Acronyms and Abbreviations: Abbreviations in Management, Technology and Information Science.* 5th ed. By Eric Pugh. Chicago, IL: American Library Association, 1987.

(PGP) *Peterson's Graduate Programs in the Humanities, Arts & Social Sciences.* 31st ed. Princeton, NJ: Peterson's 1997.

(PPE) *Political Parties of Europe.* 2 vols. Edited by Vincent E. McHale. The Greenwood Historical Encyclopedia of the World's Political Parties. Westport, CT: Greenwood Press, 1983.
One of a series of reference guides to the world's significant political parties. Each guide provides concise histories of the political parties of a region and attempts to detail the evolution of ideology, changes in organization, membership, leadership, and each party's impact upon society.

(PPW) *Political Parties of the World.* 2nd ed. A Keesing's Reference Publication. Compiled and edited by Alan J. Day and Henry W. Degenhardt. Harlow, Essex, England: Longman Group, 1980, 1984.
Covers historical development, structure, leadership, membership, policy, publications, and international affiliations. For each country, an overview of the current political situation and constitutional structure is provided.

(PS) *Popular Science.* New York, NY: Times-Mirror Magazines, Inc., 1995. [Use of source began in 1992]

(RCD) *Research Centers Directory.* 19th ed. Edited by Thomas J. Cichonski. Detroit, MI: Gale Research, 1994. [Use of source began in 1986]
A guide to university-related and other nonprofit research organizations carrying on research in agriculture, astronomy and space sciences, behavioral and social sciences, computers and mathematics, engineering and technology, physical and earth sciences and regional and area studies.

(RDA) *Army RD and A Magazine.* Alexandria, VA: Development, Engineering, and Acquisition Directorate, Army Materiel Command, 1997. [Use of source began in 1979]

(ROG) *Dictionary of Abbreviations.* By Walter T. Rogers. London, England: George Allen & Co. Ltd., 1913; reprinted by Gale Research, 1969.

(SAA) *Space-Age Acronyms, Abbreviations and Designations.* 2nd ed. By Reta C. Moser. New York, NY: IFI/Plenum, 1969.

(SAG) *Stock Abbreviation Guide.* New York, NY: Associated Press. [Database]

(SDI) *Report to the Congress on the Strategic Defense Initiative.* U.S. Department of Defense. Strategic Defense Initiative Organization, April, 1987.

(SEIS) *Seismograph Station Codes and Characteristics.* Geological Survey. Circular 791. By Barbara B. Poppe, Debbi A. Naab, and John S. Derr. Washington, DC: U.S. Department of the Interior, 1978.

(SLS)   *World Guide to Scientific Associations and Learned Societies/Internationales Verzeichnis Wissenschaftlicher Verbande und Gesellschaften.* 4th ed. Edited by Barbara Verrel. New York, NY: K.G. Saur, 1984.
> A directory of more than 22,000 societies and associations in all fields of science, culture, and technology. International, national, and regional organizations from 150 countries are also included.

(SPSG)   *Security Owner's Stock Guide.* New York, NY: Standard & Poor's Corp., 1994. [Use of source began in 1988]

(SRA)   *State and Regional Associations of the United States.* 9th ed. Edited by Tracey E. Chirico, Buck J. Downs and John J. Russell. Washington, DC: Columbia Books, Inc., 1997.

(SSD)   *Space Station Directory and Program Guide.* Edited and compiled by Melinda Gipson, Jane Glass, and Mary Linden. Arlington, VA: Pasha Publications Inc., 1988.

(TAG)   *Transportation Acronym Guide 1996.* U.S. Department of Transportation. Washington, DC: Bureau of Transportation Statistics, 1996.

(TDOB)   *The Dictionary of Banking.* By Charles J. Woelfel. Chicago, IL: Probus Publishing Company, 1994.

(TEL)   *Telephony's Dictionary.* 2nd ed. By Graham Langley. Chicago, IL: Telephony Publishing Corp., 1986.
> Includes definitions for U.S. and international telecommunications terms. Ten appendices.

(TNIG)   *Telecommunications, Networking and Internet Glossary.* By George S. Machovec. Chicago, IL: American Library Association, 1993.

(TOCD)   *The Official Catholic Directory 1997.* New Providence, NJ: P.J. Kenedy & Sons, 1997.

(TSPED)   *Trade Shows and Professional Exhibits Directory.* 2nd ed. Edited by Robert J. Elster. Detroit, MI: Gale Research, 1987. [Use of source began in 1986]
> A guide to scheduled events providing commercial display facilities including conferences, conventions, meetings, fairs and festivals, etc. Entries include name of trade show; sponsor name, address, and telephone number; attendance figures; principal exhibits; special features; publications; and date and location of shows.

(TSSD)   *Telecommunications Systems and Services Directory.* 4th ed. (and supplement). Edited by John Krol. Detroit, MI: Gale Research, 1989. [Use of source began in 1985]
> An international descriptive guide to telecommunications organizations, systems, and services. Entries include name and address, telephone number, chief official, and a description of the purposes, technical structure, and background of the service or system.

(USDC)   *"Glossary of Acronyms".* U.S. Department of Commerce. <http://www.pmel.noaa.gov/pubs/acronym.html> (5 March 1997).

(USGC)   *"U.S. Government Commonly Used Abbreviations and Acronyms."* <http://www.fed.gov/hptext/infohwy/gov_acro.html> (5 March 1997).

(VNW)   *Words of the Vietnam War.* By Gregory R. Clark. Jefferson, NC: McFarland and Co., Inc., 1990.

(VRA)   *VRA Special Bulletin. No. 2, 1987: Standard Abbreviaitons for Image Descriptions for Use in Fine Arts Visual Resources Collections.* Compiled by Nancy S. Schuller. Austin, TX: Visual Resources Association, 1987.

(WDAA) *Webster's New World Dictionary of Acronyms and Abbreviations.* By Auriel Douglas and Michael Strumpf. New York, NY: Webster's New World, 1989.

(WDMC) *Webster's New World Dictionary of Media and Communications.* Revised and updated ed. By Richard Weiner. New York, NY: Webster's New World, 1996.

(WGA)   *Webster's Guide to Abbreviations.* Springfield, MA: Merriam-Webster Inc., 1985.

(WYGK) *HR Words you Gotta Know!* By William R. Tracey. New York, NY: AMACOM, 1994.

Acronyms, Initialisms & Abbreviations Dictionary

A-F

Numerics
By Acronym

0I .... Zero Inventory [*Industrial engineering*]
0TLP .... Zero Transmission Level Point (IEEE)
1-A .... Selective Service Class [*for Registrant Available for Military Service*]
1-A-O .... Selective Service Class [*for a Conscientious Objector Available for Noncombatant Military Service Only*]
1B .... First Base [*or Baseman*] [*Baseball*]
1B .... One-Base Hit [*Baseball*]
1BH .... One-Base Hit [*Baseball*]
1-C .... Selective Service Class [*for a Member of Armed Forces of the US, the National Oceanic and Atmospheric Administration, or the Public Health Service*]
1/C .... Single Conductor [*Wire or cable*]
1-D .... Selective Service Class [*for Qualified Member of Reserve Component, or Student Taking Military Training, Including ROTC and Accepted Aviation Cadet Applicant*]
1-H .... Selective Service Class [*for Registrant Not Currently Subject to Processing for Induction*]
1H4 .... Henry IV, Part I [*Shakespearean work*]
1H6 .... Henry VI, Part I [*Shakespearean work*]
1 KG .... I Kings [*Old Testament book*]
1LT .... First Lieutenant [*Army*]
1/O .... First Officer [*Women's Royal Naval Service*] [*British*]
1-O .... Selective Service Class [*for Conscientious Objector Available for Alternate Service Contributing to Maintenance of National Health, Safety, or Interest*]
1p4c .... One-Page Four-Color [*Advertising*] (WDMC)
1PH .... Single-Phase
1QApoc .... [*The*] Genesis Apocryphon from Qumran. Cave One (BJA)
1QDM .... [*The*] Words of Moses from Qumran. Cave One (BJA)
1QGen .... [*The*] Genesis Apocryphon from Qumran. Cave One (BJA)
1QH .... Hodayot. Hymns of Thanksgiving from Qumran. Cave One (BJA)
1QIaIQIsa ... Complete Isaiah Scroll from Qumran. Cave One (BJA)
1QM .... Milchemet, the War of the Sons of Light and the Sons of Darkness from Qumran. C ave One (BJA)
1QpHab .... Commentary [*or Pesher on Habakkuk*] from Qumran. Cave One (BJA)
1QpHos .... Commentary on Hosea from Qumran. Cave One (BJA)
1QPhyl .... Phylacteries [*or Tefillin*] from Qumran. Cave One (BJA)
1QpMi .... Pesher [*or Commentary on Micah*] from Qumran. Cave One (BJA)
1QpNah .... Pesher [*or Commentary on Nahum*] from Qumran. Cave One (BJA)
1QPrayers.... Liturgical Fragments from Qumran. Cave One (BJA)
1QS .... Community Rule, Rule of the Congregation [*or Manual of Discipline, Serekh ha-Yahad*] from Qumran. Cave One (BJA)
1QS .... Divrei Berakhot [*or Blessings*] from Qumran. Cave One (BJA)
1QSb .... Divrei Berakhot [*or Blessings*] from Qumran. Cave One (BJA)
1S .... One Side (WDMC)
1SG .... First Sergeant [*Army*]
1stSrc .... First Source Corp. [*Associated Press*] (SAG)
1TR .... One Turn Right [*Dance terminology*]
1/U .... One Finger breadth above the Umbilicus [*Obstetrics*] (DAVI)
1/W .... One-Way
1-W .... Selective Service Class [*for Conscientious Objector Performing Alternate Service Contributing to Maintenance of National Health, Safety, or Interest*]
1WW .... Weather Wing (1st) [*California*] [*Air Force*]
2-A .... Selective Service Class [*for Registrant Deferred Because of Civilian Occupation, Other than Agriculture, or Non-Degree Study*]
2ADA .... Second Air Division Association (EA)
2-A-F .... Selective Service Class [*for Man Physically Disqualified for Military Service but Engaged in Work in the National Health, Safety, or Interest*] [*Obsolete*]
2B .... Second Base [*or Baseman*] [*Baseball*]
2-B .... Selective Service Class [*for Man Deferred or Deferrable from Military Service Because of His Necessity to War Production*] [*Obsolete*]
2B .... Two-Base Hit [*Baseball*]
2B .... Two-Box [*Oceanography*]
2-B-F .... Selective Service Class [*for Man Physically Disqualified for Military Service but Necessary to War Production*] [*Obsolete*]
2BH .... Two-Base Hit [*Baseball*]
2C .... Second Cover [*Periodicals*] (WDMC)
2-C .... Selective Service Class [*for Registrant Deferred from Military Service Because of Agricultural Occupation*]
2/C .... Two-Conductor [*Wire or cable*]
2 CO .... Second Corinthians [*New Testament book*]
2-D .... Selective Service Class [*for Registrant Deferred Because of Study for the Ministry*]

2-D .... Two-Dimensional
2-DE .... Two-Dimensional Echocardiogram [*Medicine*] (CPH)
2DES .... Two-Dimensional Electron System [*Physics*]
2-D TEE .... Two-Dimensional Transesophageal Echocardiography [*Cardiology*] (DAVI)
2F .... Two-Seater Fighter Aircraft [*Navy*]
2H4 .... Henry IV, Part II [*Shakespearean work*]
2H6 .... Henry VI, Part II [*Shakespearean work*]
2HR .... Two-Hour Pregnancy Test [*Obstetrics*] (DAVI)
2IC .... Second in Command
2 KG .... II Kings [*Old Testament book*]
2LT .... Second Lieutenant [*Army*]
2N .... Diploid Number [*Genetics*]
2/O .... Second Officer [*British military*] (DMA)
2PE .... Two-Pulse Photon Echo [*Spectroscopy*]
2PH .... Two-Phase
2-S .... Selective Service Class [*for Registrant Deferred Because of Activity in Study*]
2S .... Two Sides (WDMC)
2WD .... Two-Wheel Drive [*Automotive engineering*]
2WS .... Two-Wheel Steering [*Automotive engineering*]
2WW .... Weather Wing (2nd) [*New York*] [*Air Force*]
3-A .... Selective Service Class [*for Registrant Deferred by Reason of Extreme Hardship to Dependents; or Registrant with Child or Children*]
3AI .... Affiliated Advertising Agencies International (EA)
3-AP .... Three-Acetylpiridine [*Biochemistry*] (DAVI)
3B .... Mauritius [*Aircraft nationality and registration mark*] (FAAC)
3B .... Third Base [*or Baseman*] [*Baseball*]
3B .... Three-Base Hit [*Baseball*]
3BH .... Three-Base Hit [*Baseball*]
3B's .... Beer, Bum, and Bacca [*Nautical*] [*Slang British*] (DSUE)
3B's .... Boheme, Butterfly, and Barber of Seville [*Frequently performed operas*]
3B's .... Brief, Bright, Brotherly [*Religion*] (DSUE)
3B's .... Bull Baffles Brains [*Bowdlerized version*] (DSUE)
3C .... Catalog Card Corporation of America (NITA)
3C .... Equatorial Guinea [*Aircraft nationality and registration mark*] (FAAC)
3/C .... Three-Conductor [*Wire or cable*]
3 CI .... Three CI Complete Compliance Corp. [*Associated Press*] (SAG)
3COM .... Number 3 Common [*Lumber*]
3Com .... Three Com Corp. [*Associated Press*] (SAG)
3C's .... Character, Capacity, Capital [*Accounting*]
3-D .... Decapitation, Disembowelment, and Dismemberment [*Types of movies*]
3D .... Delayed Double Diffusion [*Test*] (DAVI)
3-D .... Selective Service Class [*for Man Deferred from Military Service Because Induction Would Cause Extreme Hardship and Privation to a Wife, Child, or Parent*] [*Obsolete*]
3D .... Swaziland [*Aircraft nationality and registration mark*] (FAAC)
3-D .... Three-Dimensional [*Pictures or films*]
3-D .... Triple-Diffusion Process (MDG)
3DEFL .... Triple Diffused Emitter-Follower Logic (MDG)
3DEG .... Three-Dimensional Electron Gas [*Physics*]
3DF .... Three-Dimensional Direction Finding [*Navigation systems*]
3DFATMIC ... 3-Dimensional Subsurface Flow and FAte and Transport of MIcrobes and Chemicals Model [*Computer science*]
3DFEMFAT ... 3-Dimensional Finite-Element Model of Flow And Transport [*Computer science*]
3DGeo .... Three D Geophysical, Inc. [*Associated Press*] (SAG)
3-DGF .... Three-Dimensional Geometry File [*Computer science*] (DOM)
3DL .... Three-Dimensional Laminate
3D Labs .... ThreeD Labs, Inc. Ltd. [*Associated Press*] (SAG)
3DO .... Three-Dimensional Optics [*Multimedia electronics corporation*] (ECON)
3DO Co .... Three Do Co. [*Associated Press*] (SAG)
3D's .... Denazification, Demilitarization, Deindustrialization [*Allied policy for Germany after World War II*]
3D Sys .... Three D Systems, Inc. [*Associated Press*] (SAG)
3DX Tch .... ThreeDX Technologies, Inc. [*Associated Press*] (SAG)
3F's .... Fashion, Features, and Fluff [*Subject assignments to which female journalists were once limited*]
3F's .... Fixity of Tenure, Fair Rents, and Free Sale [*Phrase used in Parliamentary discussions of Irish affairs, 1880-1882; opposition translated the initials as Fraud, Force, and Folly*]
3GL .... 3rd Generation Language [*Computer science*] (EERA)

3H — High, Hot, and a Helluva Lot [*Slang*] (DAVI)
3H6 — Henry VI, Part III [*Shakespearean work*]
3HO — Healthy-Happy-Holy Organization
3-I — Indiana, Illinois, Iowa [*Old baseball league*]
3I — Investors in Industry International BV
3J's — Jam, Jute, and Journalism [*3 major industries of Dundee, Scotland*]
3K's — Kingsley, Kinsella, and Keeney [*Prominent citizens of Brooklyn; all three died within a year of each other, 1884-1885*]
3LL — Lewis Lung Carcinoma [*Oncology*]
3L's — Legislators, Lawyers, and Lead [*Forces mustered by opponents of proposed nuclear-waste burial sites*]
3L's — Luxury, Leisure, Longevity [*Economics*]
3M — Maintenance and Material Management [*Navy*]
3M — Minnesota Mining & Manufacturing Co. [*Also, MMM*]
3M's — Manpower, Materials, Money
3M's — Method, Meat, and Morality [*Cure for insanity, according to Victorian medical theory*]
3/O — Third Officer [*British military*] (DMA)
3P — Third Party [*Legal shorthand*] (LWAP)
3P — Three-Pole [*or Triple Pole*] [*Switch*]
3PB — Third Party Beneficiary [*Legal shorthand*] (LWAP)
3PDT — Triple-Pole, Double-Throw [*Switch*] (MUGU)
3PH — Three-Phase
3PIE — Three-Pulse Image Photon Echo [*Spectroscopy*]
3PMM — Three-Phase Modulation Modified [*Telecommunications*] (OSI)
3PSE — Three-Pulse Stimulated Photon Echo [*Spectroscopy*]
3PST — Triple-Pole, Single-Throw [*Switch*] (MUGU)
3PTY — Three-Party Service [*Telecommunications*] (DOM)
3QInv — [*The*] Copper Treasure Inventory Scroll from Qumran. Cave Three (BJA)
3R — Request, Retrieve, and Report [*Computer science*]
3R — Resurfacing, Restoration, and Rehabilitation [*Also, RRR*] [*Later, 4R Federal Highway Administration*]
3R — Rheingold-Rotary-Reciprocating [*Motor*]
3R's — Readin', Ritin', and Rithmetic [*Also, RRR*]
3R's — Recognition, Reassurance, and Relaxation [*Military mental health technique*] (INF)
3R's — Reduction, Refinement, and Replacement [*Animal research*]
3R's — Reference and Research Library Resources Systems [*New York State Library*] [*Albany*] [*Information service or system*] (IID)
3R's — Relief, Recovery, Reform [*Elements of the New Deal*]
3S — Shoot Them, Shovel Them, Shut Up [*Ranchers way of dealing with predatory animals*]
3S — Simplification, Standardization, Specialization [*Economics*]
3S — Standard Supply System [*Army*] (RDA)
3T — Triple Throw [*Switch*]
3W — Three-Wire (MSA)
3W1 — Third World First [*An association British*]
3WC — Third Wave Civilization [*Title of record album by Ian Lloyd*]
3W's — [*The*] Who, What, or Where Game [*Also, WWW*] [*Television show*]
3W's — Worry, Want, and Wickedness [*Causes of insanity, according to Victorian medical theory*]
3WW — Weather Wing (3rd) [*Nebraska*] [*Air Force*]
3X — Guinea [*Aircraft nationality and registration mark*] (FAAC)
3YP — Three Year Plan [*From George Orwell's novel, "1984"*]
4-A — Selective Service Class [*for Registrant with Sufficient Prior Active Service to Satisfy Requirements of Law (Veteran)*]
4A's — American Association of Advertising Agencies [*New York, NY*]
4-B — Selective Service Class [*for Public Officials Deferred by Law*]
4C — Four Color [*Printing*]
4/C — Four-Conductor [*Wire or cable*]
4-C — Selective Service Class [*for Aliens Not Currently Liable for Military Service*]
4C's — Cotton, Climate, Cattle, and Citrus [*Traditional elements of Arizona's economy*]
4C's — Cut, Carat, Clarity, Color [*Factors in determining the value of a diamond*]
4-D — Dead, Dying, Diseased, Disabled [*Food processors' classification of animals unfit for use*]
4-D — Four-Dimensional (MSA)
4-D — Selective Service Class [*for a Minister of Religion*]
4DDA — Four-Dimensional Data Assimilation [*Scheme*] [*Marine science*] (OSRA)
4DDA — Four-Dimensional Data Assimilation [*Scheme*] (USDC)
4D's — Drugs, Debt, Deforestation, and Democracy [*US foreign policy concerns in Latin America*]
4E — Four Plus Edema [*Medicine*] (DAVI)
4-E — Selective Service Class [*for a Conscientious Objector Available for, Assigned to, or Released from Work of National Importance*] [*Obsolete*]
4F — Fair, Fat, Fertile, and Forty [*Medical slang describing women most susceptible to gallbladder attacks*]
4-F — Selective Service Class [*Unqualified for military service for physical reasons*]
4-G — Selective Service Class [*for Registrant Exempt from Service During Peace (Surviving Son or Brother)*]
4GL — 4th Generation Language [*Computer science*] (EERA)
4GL — Fourth-Generation Language [*Computer language*]
4G's — Glycosaminoglycans, Glycoproteins, and Glycolipids Group [*Informal name for organization that later became Society for Complex Carbohydrates*]
4H — Head, Heart, Hands, and Health [*As in 4H organizations*]
4Health — FourHealth, Inc. [*Associated Press*] (SAG)
4IS — Four-Wheel Independent Suspension [*Automotive engineering*]
4KidsEnt — For Kids Entertainment, Inc. [*Associated Press*] (SAG)

4M's — Medals, Muscles, Master's Degrees, and Marathons [*Means to advancement in the armed forces*]
4P — Four-Pole [*Switch*]
4PDT — Four-Pole, Double-Throw [*Switch*]
4PST — Four-Pole, Single-Throw [*Switch*]
4PSW — Four-Pole Switch
4QDeut32 — Manuscript of Deuteronomy 32 from Qumran. Cave 4 (BJA)
4QFlor — Florilegium. A Miscellany from Qumran. Cave Four (BJA)
4QpNah — Pesher [*or Commentary on Nahum*] from Qumran. Cave Four (BJA)
4QpPs37 — Pesher [*or Commentary on Psalm 37*] from Qumran. Cave Four (BJA)
4QPrNab — [*The*] Prayer of Nabonidus from Qumran. Cave Four (BJA)
4QTest — [*The*] Testimonia from Qumran. Cave Four (BJA)
4QTLevi — Testament of Levi from Qumran. Cave Four (BJA)
4R — Resurfacing, Restoration, Rehabilitation, and Reconstruction [*Formerly, 3R, RRR*] [*Federal Highway Administration*]
4R — Sri Lanka [*Aircraft nationality and registration mark*] (FAAC)
4RAct — Railroad, Revitalization and Regulatory Reform Act of 1976 (AAGC)
4S — Scandinavian Simvastatin Survival Study [*Cardiology*]
4S — Society for Social Studies of Science (EA)
4SDI — Four Stroke-Direct Injection [*Engine*] (RDA)
4S's — Sex, Silk, Swords, and Swash [*Elements of historical romances*]
4S's — Stealth Aircraft, Sea-Launched Cruise Missiles, SDI [*Strategic Defense Initiative*]-Like Devices, Space Systems [*High-tech weaponry*]
4S's — Sun, Sand, Sea, Sex [*Used in advertising by travel agencies*]
4to — Quarto [*An eight-page, four-leaf book*] (WDMC)
4W — Four-Wire
4-W — Selective Service Class [*for Conscientious Objector Who Has Completed Alternate Service Contributing to National Health, Safety, or Interest*]
4W — Yemen Arab Republic [*Aircraft nationality and registration mark*] (FAAC)
4WD — Four-Wheel Drive [*Vehicle*]
4WG — Weather Group (4th) [*Washington, DC*] [*Air Force*]
4WS — Four-Wheel Steering [*Automotive engineering*]
4WTS — Four-Wire Terminating Set [*Telecommunications*] (TEL)
4WW — Weather Wing (4th) [*Colorado*] [*Air Force*]
4X — Israel [*Aircraft nationality and registration mark*] (FAAC)
4Y — Selective Service classification suggested by comedian Bob Hope for himself during World War II [*Y stood for "yellow"*]
5A — Libya [*Aircraft nationality and registration mark*]
5-AC — Azacitidine [*Pharmacology*] (DAVI)
5B — Bald with Bridgework, Bifocals, Baywindow, and Bunions [*A humorous unofficial Selective Service Class*]
5BX — Five Basic Exercises [*British military*] (DMA)
5C's — Character, Capacity, Capital, Collateral, and Conditions [*Credit evaluation*] [*Banking*]
5n — Pentaploidy [*State of having five sets of chromosomes*] [*Genetics*] (DAVI)
5P's — Poet, Printer, Publisher, Publican, and Player [*Nickname given to William Oxberry (fl. 1784-1824)*]
5W — Samoa Islands [*Aircraft nationality and registration mark*] (FAAC)
5W's — Who, What, When, Where, Why [*Journalism*]
6O — Somalia [*Aircraft nationality and registration mark*] (FAAC)
6QD — Damascus Document [*or Sefer Berit Damesek*] from Qumran. Cave Six (BJA)
6R's — Remedial Readin', Remedial Ritin', and Remedial Rithmetic [*Also, RRRRRR*] [*Humorous interpretation of the three R's*]
6-TGR — Thioguanine Riboside [*Antineoplastic drug*] (DAVI)
6V — Senegal [*Aircraft nationality and registration mark*] (FAAC)
6W — Senegal [*Aircraft nationality and registration mark*] (FAAC)
6WW — Weather Wing (6th) [*Washington, DC*] [*Air Force*]
6Y — Jamaica [*Aircraft nationality and registration mark*] (FAAC)
7ATC — 7th Army Training Command (RDA)
7/C — Seven-Conductor [*Wire or cable*] (MSA)
7n — Heptaploidy [*State of having seven sets of chromosomes*] [*Genetics*] (DAVI)
7P — Lesotho [*Aircraft nationality and registration mark*] (FAAC)
7QY — Malawi [*Aircraft nationality and registration mark*] (FAAC)
7T — Algeria [*Aircraft nationality and registration mark*] (FAAC)
7th Level — Seventh Level, Inc. [*Associated Press*] (SAG)
7WW — Weather Wing (7th) [*Illinois*] [*Air Force*]
8A — Section 8(a) of the Small Business Act [*Pertaining to minority and other disadvantaged business*] (AAGC)
8CRT — Eight Card Redrawing Test [*Psychology*]
8n — Octaploidy [*State of having eight sets of chromosomes*] [*Genetics*] (DAVI)
8P — Barbados [*Aircraft nationality and registration mark*] (FAAC)
8PFAB — Eight-Parallel-Form Anxiety Battery [*Psychology*]
8Q — Maldives [*Aircraft nationality and registration mark*] (FAAC)
8R — Guyana [*Aircraft nationality and registration mark*] (FAAC)
8vo — Octavo [*A 16-page book*] (WDMC)
8X8 — EightXEight, Inc. [*Associated Press*] (SAG)
9G — Ghana [*Aircraft nationality and registration mark*] (FAAC)
9H — Malta [*Aircraft nationality and registration mark*] (FAAC)
9J — Zambia [*Aircraft nationality and registration mark*] (FAAC)
9L — Sierra Leone [*Aircraft nationality and registration mark*] (FAAC)
9M — Malaysia [*Aircraft nationality and registration mark*] (FAAC)
9N — Nepal [*Aircraft nationality and registration mark*] (FAAC)
9Q — Zaire [*Aircraft nationality and registration mark*] (FAAC)
9U — Burundi [*Aircraft nationality and registration mark*] (FAAC)
9V — Singapore [*Aircraft nationality and registration mark*] (FAAC)
9XR — Rwanda [*Aircraft nationality and registration mark*] (FAAC)

9Y .... Trinidad and Tobago [*Aircraft nationality and registration mark*] (FAAC)

10HD .... Ten High-Day [*Telecommunications*]

13L .... Insoplanar Integrated Injection Logic (NITA)

20CenInd ..... Twentieth Century Industries [*Associated Press*] (SAG)

21CLW .... Twenty-first Century Land Warrior [*Army*] (INF)

2,4D .... 2,4 Dichlorophenoxyacetic Acid (DOG)

48mo .... Fortyeightmo [*A 96-page, 48-leaf book*] (WDMC)

50-Off .... Fifty Off Stores [*Associated Press*] (SAG)

84 Charlie ... Combat Photographer [*Military*] [*Slang*] (WDMC)

99 Cents ...... Ninety-Nine Cent Only Stores [*Associated Press*] (SAG)

1838BdF ...... Eighteen Thirty Eight Bond Fund [*Associated Press*] (SAG)

2002TT .... Two Thousand Two Target Term Trust, Inc. [*Associated Press*] (SAG)

A
By Acronym

A................ A/B Astra [*Sweden*] [*Research code symbol*]
A................ Abbey
A................ Abbott Laboratories [*Research code symbol*]
A................ Abbreviation (IAA)
A................ Abitibi-Price, Inc. [*Toronto Stock Exchange symbol Vancouver Stock Exchange symbol*]
A................ Ablative [*Grammar*] (ROG)
A................ Able [*Phonetic alphabet*] [*World War II*] (DSUE)
A................ Abnormal [*Medicine*] (AAMN)
A................ About
a................ About (WDMC)
A................ Absent
A................ Absolute [*Temperature in Fahrenheit degrees*]
A................ Absolvo [*I Acquit*] [*Used by Romans in criminal trials*] [*Latin*]
A................ Absorbance [*Internal transmission density*] [*Symbol IUPAC*]
a................ Absorption Coefficient, Linear [*Symbol*] [*IUPAC*]
A................ Absorptivity
A................ Abstracts
A................ Abundant [*With respect to occurrence of species*]
A................ Academician [*or Academy*]
A................ Accelerating Contactor or Relay (IEEE)
A................ Acceleration [*or Accelerator*]
a................ Acceleration (IDOE)
A................ Accent (NTCM)
A................ Accepted
A................ Acceptor [*Physiology*]
A................ Access [*Credit card*] [*British*]
A................ Accessed BIT [*Binary Digit*] [*Computer science*]
A................ Accessory [*Protein synthesis*]
A................ Accommodation
A................ Account
A................ Accumulator [*Computer science*] (MDG)
A................ Accursius [*Deceased, 1263*] [*Authority cited in pre-1607 legal work*] (DSA)
A................ Accusative [*Grammar*] (ROG)
A................ Ace
A................ Aceite [*Acceptance*] [*Portuguese Business term*]
A................ Acetum [*Medicine*] (DMAA)
A................ Acid [*or Acidity*]
A................ Acidophil [*Medicine*] (DMAA)
A................ Ack [*Phonetic alphabet*] [*Pre-World War II*] (DSUE)
A................ Acoustic (IAA)
A................ Acquiescence (DLA)
A................ Acre
a................ Acre (IDOE)
A................ Actin [*Muscle physiology*]
A................ Acting
A................ Actinomyces (MAE)
A................ Actinomycin [*Also, act*] [*Antibiotic compound*]
A................ Action
A................ Activity
A................ Actual (ADA)
A................ Acute
A................ Ad [*To or At*] [*Latin*] (ROG)
A................ Adam's Justiciary Reports [*1893-1906*] [*Scotland*] [*A publication*] (ILCA)
A................ Adaptable
a................ Add [*Computer science*] [*Telecommunications*]
A................ Adder [*Computer device*]
A................ Address [*Computer character*] [*Computer science*]
A................ Adenine [*Also, Ade*] [*Biochemistry*]
A................ Adenosine [*One-letter symbol; see Ado*] [*A nucleoside*]
A................ Adequate
A................ Adhibendus [*To Be Used*] [*Pharmacy*] (ROG)
A................ Adjective
A................ Adjunct [*Linguistics*]
A................ Adjustment (IAA)
A................ Adjutant
A................ Administration
A................ Admiral
A................ Admittance (MAE)
A................ Adolfo [*Couturier*]
A................ Adopted From [*or Adoption Of*] [*Etymology*]
A................ Adrenaline [*Endocrinology*] (MAE)
A................ Adriamycin [*Also, ADM, ADR, D, H*] [*Antineoplastic drug*]
A................ Adult [*Film certificate*] [*British*]

A................ Adulteress [*Letter embroidered on Hester Prynne's dress in Nathaniel Hawthorne's "The Scarlet Letter"*]
A................ Advance [*Wire service code*] (NTCM)
A................ Advanced Level [*School graduating grade*] [*British*]
A................ Advanced-Level Examination [*Education*] (AIE)
A................ Aerial (IAA)
A................ Aerology [*NAO code*] (DNAB)
A................ Aeronautics (IAA)
A................ Aerospace (MCD)
A................ Affect
A................ Affirmation [*Linguistics*]
A................ Affirmed (DLA)
A................ Affix [*Linguistics*]
A................ Africa Committee [*British World War II*]
A................ Aft
A................ After
A................ Aftercooled [*Automotive engineering*]
A................ Afternoon
a................ Agar [*Biochemistry*] (DAVI)
A................ Age
A................ Agency
A................ Agglomerate [*Geology*]
A................ Agricultural Program (NTCM)
A................ Agriculture Department [*US government*]
A................ Agusta [*Construzioni Aeronautiche Giovanni Agusta SpA*] [*Italy ICAO aircraft manufacturer identifier*] (ICAO)
A................ Aided School [*British*]
A................ Air
A................ Airborne (IAA)
A................ Aircraft [*or Airplane*]
A................ Air Force Training Category [*48 inactive duty training periods and 15 days active duty training per year*]
A................ Air-Launched [*Missile launch environment symbol*]
A................ Airman
A................ Airplane (ABBR)
A................ Akinetic
A................ Alabama Public Library Service, Montgomery, AL [*Library symbol Library of Congress*] (LCLS)
A................ Alanine [*One-letter symbol; see Ala*]
A................ Alanine Nitrogen Mustard [*L-PAM*] [*Antineoplastic drug*]
A................ Alanus Anglicus [*Flourished, 1208-10*] [*Authority cited in pre-1607 legal work*] (DSA)
A................ Albedo [*Psychology*]
A................ Albericus de Porta Ravennate [*Flourished, 1165-94*] [*Authority cited in pre-1607 legal work*] (DSA)
A................ Albertus Beneventanus [*Deceased, 1187*] [*Authority cited in pre-1607 legal work*] (DSA)
a................ Albertus Longobardista [*Flourished, 12th century*] [*Authority cited in pre-1607 legal work*] (DSA)
A................ Albino Guinea Pig [*Medicine*] (DMAA)
A................ Alcohol (ADA)
A................ Alcove (ABBR)
A................ Alert Area [*Military*]
A................ Alfa [*Phonetic alphabet*] [*International*] (DSUE)
a................ Alias [*Computer science*] [*Telecommunications*]
A................ Alive
A................ Allele [*Genetics*]
A................ Allergist [*Medicine*] (DAVI)
A................ Allergologist [*Medicine*] (DMAA)
A................ Allergy
A................ Allocator
A................ Alloy Container [*Shipping*] (DCTA)
A................ Alpha
A................ Alphabetic
A................ Alternate [*Approach and landing charts*] [*Aviation*]
A................ Alternate Captain [*Sports*]
A................ Alternating Current
A................ Altezza [*Highness*] [*Italian*]
A................ Altitude Difference [*Navigation*]
A................ Alto
A................ Alveolar [*Gas*] [*Medicine*]
A................ Amateur
A................ Amber (AAG)
A................ Ambient [*Electronics*]
A................ Ambiguity [*Used in correcting manuscripts, etc.*]
A................ Ambitendency [*Psychology*]

A .... Ambulatory [Medicine]
A .... Amended (DLA)
A .... American
A .... American League [Baseball]
A .... American Stock Exchange [New York, NY]
A .... Amethopterin [Methotrexate] [Antineoplastic drug]
A .... Ammeter (MDG)
A .... Amora (BJA)
A .... Amount (ROG)
A .... Ampere [Unit of electric current] [SI symbol]
A .... Amperemeter (IAA)
A .... Amphetamine [Also, AMT, amphet] [CNS stimulant]
A .... Amphibian [or Amphibious]
A .... Ampicillin [Also, AM, AMP] [Antibacterial compound]
A .... Amplifier
A .... Amplitude [Physics]
A .... Ana [Of Each] [Pharmacy]
A .... Anaesthetics [Medical Officer designation] [British]
A .... Analog
A .... Analysis (IAA)
A .... Anaphylaxis [Medicine]
A .... Anchorite
A .... Anchor Line [Steamship] (MHDW)
A .... And (ROG)
A .... Androecium [Botany]
A .... Androsterone [Medicine] (DMAA)
A .... Anesthetic [Medicine]
A .... Angel (ROG)
A .... Angled (NTCM)
A .... Anglican
A .... Angling
A .... Angstrom [Also, AU]
A .... Animal [Psychology]
A .... Anion
A .... Anisean [Geology]
A .... Anna [Monetary unit] [India]
A .... Annealing (ABBR)
A .... Anno [or Annus] [Year] [Latin]
A .... Annual
A .... Annular
A .... Annunciator (NFPA)
A .... Anode [Technical drawings]
a .... Anode (IDOE)
A .... Anonymous
A .... Anopheles (MAE)
A .... Answer [In transcripts]
A .... Antarctic
A .... Ante [Before] [Latin]
A .... Antenna (IAA)
A .... Anterior
A .... Anther [Botany]
A .... Anthracite (ABBR)
A .... Antiaircraft [Officer's rating] [British Royal Navy]
A .... Anticlockwise
A .... Antigen [Also, a, Ag] [Immunology]
A .... Antinuclear Antibody [Medicine] (DMAA)
A .... Antiquo [I Oppose] [Used by Romans to signify a negative vote] [Latin]
a .... Antisymmetric [Chemistry]
A .... Antrum [Maxillary sinus] [Otorhinolaryngology] (DAVI)
A .... Anus
A .... Apatite Subgroup [Apatite, fluorite, calcite, pyrite, iron] [CIPW classification Geology]
A .... Apical (DAVI)
A .... Apostle [Church calendars]
A .... Apostolic
A .... Apples [Phonetic alphabet] [Royal Navy World War I] (DSUE)
A .... Applique
A .... Approach Lighting [Aviation] (DA)
A .... Approved
A .... Approximate [Rate] [Value of the English pound]
A .... April
A .... Aqua [Water] [Latin]
A .... Aqueous [Medicine] (DMAA)
A .... Arab [or Arabic] (BJA)
a .... Arabinose [One-letter symbol; see Ara] [A sugar]
A .... Aramaic [Language, etc.]
A .... Arc (ABBR)
A .... Architect
A .... Arctic [Air mass] [Meteorological symbol]
A .... Are [Also, a] [A unit of area in the metric system]
A .... Area
a .... Area (IDOE)
A .... Area Chart
A .... Argent [Money] [French]
A .... Argent [Heraldry]
A .... Argentina [IYRU nationality code] (IYR)
A .... Argon [Chemical symbol is Ar] [Chemical element]
A .... Arithmetic (IAA)
A .... Arm (IAA)
A .... Armament
A .... Armature (IAA)
A .... Armored (ADA)
A .... Army
A .... Arousal

A .... Arrive (ADA)
A .... Art (ADA)
A .... Arteria [Artery] [Latin]
a .... Arterial Blood [Medicine] (MAE)
A .... Arterial in the Blood Phase [Medicine] (DAVI)
A .... Arteriolar [Medicine] (DAVI)
A .... Article
A .... Articulated (DCTA)
A .... Artillery
A .... Asbestos (MSA)
a----- .... Asia [MARC geographic area code Library of Congress] (LCCP)
A .... Asked
A .... Asparagine [One-letter symbol; see Asn]
A .... Assault [FBI standardized term]
A .... Assembly (IAA)
A .... Assented [Investment term]
A .... Assessment [Medicine]
A .... Assignment [FCC] (NTCM)
a .... Assinado [Signed] [Portuguese Business term]
A .... Assist [Health care]
A .... Assist [Sports]
A .... Assistant [Military]
A .... Assistant Captain [Worn on assistant captains' uniforms] [Hockey]
A .... Associate [In an academic degree]
A .... Association
A .... Asta Werke AG [Germany] [Research code symbol]
A .... Astra AB [NYSE symbol] (SAG)
A .... Astra AB'A'ADS [NYSE symbol] (TTSB)
A .... Astragal (MSA)
A .... Asymmetric
A .... Asynchronous
A .... At
A .... Athletic (ADA)
A .... Atlantic [Ocean] (ABBR)
A .... Atlantic Reporter [A publication] (DLA)
A .... Atmosphere (ABBR)
A .... Atom [or Atomic]
A .... Atomic Weight
A .... Atrium [Medicine] (DMAA)
A .... Atropine (MAE)
A .... Attack [Designation for all US military aircraft]
A .... Attack [Men's lacrosse position]
A .... Attendance [Sports]
A .... Attenuation (IAA)
A .... Atto [Act] [Italian]
a .... Atto [A prefix meaning divided by 10 to the 18th power] [SI symbol]
A .... Attribute
A .... Audio (WDMC)
a .... Audio (WDMC)
A .... Audit [or Audited]
A .... Auditory (ABBR)
A .... Augmentation [Music]
A .... August (CDAI)
A .... Auricular [or Auricle] [Also, AUR] [Medicine]
A .... Auris [Ear] [Latin]
A .... Ausgabestelle [Distribution Point] [German military - World War II]
A .... Austenite (IAA)
A .... Australian
A .... Austria
A .... Authentic
A .... Authenticum [A publication] (DSA)
A .... Author
A .... Automatic (IAA)
A .... Automation (DS)
A .... Automobile
A .... Autosome [Genetics]
A .... Autotuned [NAVAID, Navigational Aid] (GAVI)
A .... Autumn-Burned [Ecology]
A .... Auxiliary (DNAB)
A .... Available [or Availability] (MCD)
A .... Avancer [Fast, as clocks] [French]
A .... Average (DAVI)
A .... Aviation [FCC] (NTCM)
A .... Axial
A .... Axis (ABBR)
A .... Azimuth (IAA)
A .... Azure (ABBR)
A .... Best of a Kind (BARN)
a .... Bright [of stars] (BARN)
A .... British Food Classification (BARN)
A .... Buchanan's Reports of the Court of Appeal, Cape [1880-1910] [South Africa] [A publication] (ILCA)
A .... Burning Surface Area of Propellant [Symbol] [Aerospace]
A .... Class "A" Preferred or Common Stock [Investment term]
A .... Codex Alexandrinus (BJA)
A .... Completely Reliable Source for Intelligence Information
A .... Eli Lilly & Co. [Research code symbol]
A .... English [Language] (BARN)
A .... Gain (IDOE)
A .... Goals Against [Hockey]
A .... Hail [Meteorological symbol]
A .... Helmholtz Energy [Symbol] [IUPAC]
A .... High Medium [Moody's bond rating] [Investment term]
A .... Includes Extra [Investment term] (DFIT)
A .... Indian Reports, Allahabad Series [A publication] (DLA)

A .... L-Asparaginase [*Also, L, L-ase, L-asnase, L-Asp*] [*An enzyme, an antineoplastic*]
A .... Louisiana Annuals [*A publication*] (DLA)
A .... Magnetic Vector Potential [*Symbol*] (DEN)
A .... Mass Number [*Symbol*]
A .... Matthew Arnold [*English poet, 1822-1888*] [*Initial used as pseudonym*]
a .... Mean Sound Absorption [*Symbol*] [*Aerospace*]
A .... Metric Paper Sizer of Standard Heights for Stationery and Printing [*International organization for standardization*] (BARN)
A .... Narrow [*Women's shoe width*] [*More than one "A" indicates increasing narrowness, up to AAAAA*]
A .... Ordinary Combustibles [*Fire classification*]
A .... Recto (ROG)
A .... Semi-Major Axis [*of a comet*] [*In astronomical units*]
A .... Series "A" Bonds or Debentures [*Investment term*]
A .... Shape Descriptor [*A-frame, for example. The shape resembles the letter for which it is named*]
A .... Shoe Width Less than B (BARN)
a .... Thermal Diffusivity [*Symbol*] [*Thermodynamics*]
a .... Thermodynamic Activity [*Chemistry*] (DAVI)
a .... Total Acidity (DAVI)
A .... Total Average Dollar Inventory
A .... United Nations General Assembly Document (ILCA)
A .... United Nations Secretariat Member [*License plate code assigned to foreign diplomats in the US*]
A .... Upper Medium [*Standard & Poor's bond rating*] [*Investment term*]
A .... Warner-Lambert Pharmaceutical Co. [*Research code symbol*]
A .... Work [*Physics*] (BARN)
A_1 .... Aortic First Heart Sound [*Cardiology*]
A1 .... First Class [*or First Quality*]
A1 .... Highest Hull [*Symbol*] [*American Bureau of Shipping*] (DS)
A-1 .... Personnel Section [*of an air staff; also, officer in charge of this section*] [*Air Force*]
A_1AT .... Alpha-1-Antitrypsin [*Protease inhibitor*] [*Serology*]
a1AT .... Alpha 1-Antitrypsin Deficiency [*Genetic disorder*] (PAZ)
A/1C .... Airman, First Class
A^2 .... Ann Arbor [*Michigan*]
A_2 .... Aortic Second Heart Sound [*Cardiology*]
A2 .... Botswana [*Aircraft nationality and registration mark*] (FAAC)
A-2 .... Intelligence Section [*of an air staff; also, officer in charge of this section*] [*Air Force*]
A2A .... Academics for the Second Amendment
A/2C .... Airman, Second Class
A^{2C2} .... Army Airspace Command and Control
A^2C^2 .... Army Airspace Command and Control (DOMA)
A2d .... Atlantic Reporter, Second Series [*West*] [*A publication*] (AAGC)
A2d .... Atlantic Reporter, Second Series [*A publication*] (DLA)
A^{2D2} .... Auxiliary Active Digital Display [*Sonar*] (DNAB)
A2LA .... American Association for Laboratory Accreditation (RCD)
A2LA .... American Association for Laboratory Accreditation (AAGC)
A^2M .... Automated Auger Microprobe
A^{2R2} .... Argonne Advanced Research Reactor (NRCH)
A^{2S2} .... Accelerated Active Search System (CAAL)
A2YSC .... Associated Two-Year Schools in Construction [*Defunct*] (EA)
A^3 .... Accelerated Acquisition Approach [*Pronounced "a-cubed"*] [*Air Force*]
A3 .... Afterburner (AFIT)
A3 .... Automatic Three Speed [*DOE*] (TAG)
A-3 .... Operations and Training Section [*of an air staff; also, officer in charge of this section*] [*Air Force*]
A^3 .... Staff Officer for Operations and Plans [*Air Force*] (DOMA)
A3 .... Tonga [*Aircraft nationality and registration mark*] (FAAC)
A/3C .... Airman, Third Class
A3I .... Ames Aircrew/Aircraft Integration Program [*NASA*] (RDA)
A3S .... Army Aircraft Avionics Study (MCD)
A4 .... Automatic Four Speed [*DOE*] (TAG)
A-4 .... Materiel and Supply Section [*of an air staff; also, officer in charge of this section*] [*Air Force*]
A^4 .... Staff Officer for Communications [*Air Force*] (DOMA)
A4HD .... Automatic 4-Speed Heavy Duty Transmission [*Automotive engineering*]
A4LD .... Automatic 4-Speed Light Duty Transmission [*Automotive engineering*]
A5 .... Automatic Five Speed [*DOE*] (TAG)
A5 .... Bhutan [*Aircraft nationality and registration mark*] (FAAC)
A5D5W .... Alcohol 5%, Dextrose 5% in Water
A5-PBA .... Alberta 5 Pin Bowlers' Association (AC)
A6 .... United Arab Emirates [*Aircraft nationality and registration mark*] (FAAC)
A7CA .... Austin Seven Clubs Association (EAIO)
A9C .... Bahrain [*Aircraft nationality and registration mark*] (FAAC)
A10 .... Crater [*Costa Rica*] [*Seismograph station code, US Geological Survey*] (SEIS)
A19 .... Article 19 - International Centre Against Censorship [*British*] (EAIO)
A-21 .... Cost Principles for Educational Institutions [*OMB Circular*] (AAGC)
A40 .... Oman [*Aircraft nationality and registration mark*] (FAAC)
A-66 .... Alpha-66 (EA)
A-76 .... Performance of Commercial Activities [*OMB Circular*] (AAGC)
A-87 .... Cost Principles for State and Local Governments (AAGC)
A-94 .... Benefit-Cost Analysis of Federal Programs: Guidelines and Discounts [*OMB Circular*] (AAGC)
A-109 .... Major Systems Acquisitions [*OMB Circular*] (AAGC)
A-120 .... Guidelines for the Use of Advisory and Assistance Services [*OMB Circular*] (AAGC)
A-125 .... Prompt Payment [*OMB Circular*] (AAGC)
A-131 .... Value Engineering [*OMB Circular*] (AAGC)

A 1938 B ..... Australia 1938 Bulletin [*A publication*]
AA .... A & A Foods Ltd. [*Vancouver Stock Exchange symbol*]
aA .... Abampere [*Also, Bi*] [*Unit of electric current*]
AA .... Abbreviated Analysis [*Military*]
AA .... Able and Available [*Unemployment insurance*] (OICC)
AA .... Abort Accept [*Telecommunications*] (OSI)
AA .... Absolute Address (AAG)
AA .... Absolute Altitude [*Navigation*]
AA .... Academic Alertness Test [*Education*] (AEBS)
AA .... Academic Alliances (EA)
AA .... Academy Award [*Academy of Motion Picture Arts and Sciences film award*]
AA .... Academy of Aphasia (EA)
AA .... Accelerated Assemblies (NASA)
AA .... Accelerometer Assembly [*NASA*]
AA .... Access America [*Commercial firm*] (EA)
AA .... Access Authorization [*Nuclear energy*]
AA .... Accommodation Address (LAIN)
AA .... Accompanied by Adult [*British Board of Film Censors*]
AA .... Accountable Activity
AA .... Accuracy in Academia (EA)
AA .... Acetic Acid [*Organic chemistry*] (MAE)
AA .... Acetylacrolein [*Organic chemistry*]
AA .... Achieved Availability (MCD)
Aa .... Achieved Availability (AAGC)
AA .... Achievement Age [*Psychology*]
AA .... Acoustics Associates (AAG)
AA .... Acrylic Acid [*Organic chemistry*]
AA .... Acting Appointment
AA .... ActionAid [*British*] (EAIO)
AA .... Activation Analysis [*Chemistry*]
AA .... Active Air Defence [*British World War II*]
AA .... Active Alkali [*Chemistry*]
AA .... Active Army
AA .... Active Assets
AA .... Active Assisted (HGAA)
AA .... Active-Assistive [*Range of motion*] [*Orthopedics*] (DAVI)
AA .... Active Attached Reserve [*Military*]
AA .... Active Avoidance [*Medicine*] (DMAA)
AA .... Activity Account
AA .... Acts of the Apostles [*New Testament book*] (BJA)
AA .... Actual Availability (MCD)
AA .... Actual Completion Date of Activity [*Business term*]
AA .... Acupuncture Analgesia [*Medicine*] (DMAA)
AA .... Acute Appendicitis [*Medicine*]
AA .... Ad Aperturam Libri [*As the Book Opens*] [*Latin*] (BARN)
AA .... Addicts Anonymous (EA)
AA .... Adenine Arabinoside [*Medicine*] (DMAA)
AA .... Adenylic Acid [*Biochemistry*]
AA .... Adhesive Active [*Tire manufacturing*]
AA .... Adjustment Assistance
AA .... Adjuvant Arthritis
AA .... Administration on Aging [*HEW*] [*Defunct*]
AA .... Administrative Agreement
AA .... Administrative Assistant
AA .... Adoption Act [*British*]
AA .... Adrenal Androgen [*Medicine*] (DMAA)
AA .... Adrenal [*or Adrenocortical*] Autoantibody
AA .... Adriamycin, ARA-C [*Cytarabine*] [*Antineoplastic drug*] (CDI)
AA .... Adriamycin, ARA-C [*Cytosine Arabinoside*] [*Antineoplastic drug*] (CDI)
AA .... Adult Accompaniment [*Restricted to age 14 and up unless accompanied by an adult*] [*Movie rating Canadian*]
AA .... Adult Authority (OICC)
AA .... Advance Airlines [*Australia*]
AA .... Advertising Agency (NTCM)
AA .... Advertising Association (EAIO)
A/A .... Advice of Allotment (AFM)
A/A .... Aerodrome to Aerodrome
AA .... Aerosol Analyzer (KSC)
AA .... Aerotronic Associate (IAA)
AA .... Affected Areas
AA .... Affiliate Artists (EA)
AA .... Affiliate Assembly [*American Association of School Librarians*]
AA .... Affirmative Action [*Employment policies for minorities*]
AA .... Africa
AA .... African Affairs [*A publication*]
AA .... After All [*Message handling*]
AA .... After Arrival
AA .... Aggregated Albumin (MAE)
AA .... Agoraphobics Anonymous (EA)
AA .... Agranulocytic Angina [*Medicine*] (DMAA)
AA .... Ah-Ah [*Lava-Flow*] [*Hawaiian*]
A/A .... Air Abort (SAA)
AA .... Air America, Inc. (CINC)
AA .... Air Armament (NATG)
AA .... Air Assault [*Military*] (DOMA)
AA .... Air Attache [*British*]
AA .... Airborne Alert (AFM)
AA .... Aircraft Artificer [*British*]
AA .... Airlift Association (EA)
AA .... Airman Apprentice [*Navy rating*]
AA .... Airplane Avionics (NASA)
A/A .... Airport and Airways (OICC)
AA .... Airship Association [*British*] (EAIO)

AA................ Airship Association - US (EA)
AA................ Air-to-Air [NASA]
aa .... Albania [MARC country of publication code Library of Congress] (LCCP)
AA................ Alcoholics Anonymous (AC)
AA................ Alcoholics Anonymous World Services (EA)
AA................ Alert Availability (MCD)
AA................ Alkalyzing Agent
AA................ All Ability School [British]
AA................ All Abnormal [Clinical hematology]
AA................ All After [Aviation] (DA)
AA................ All [Text] After [Specified Point] [Message handling]
AA................ All Along (ADA)
AA................ Alopecia Areata [Medicine]
AA................ Altesses [Highnesses] [French]
AA................ Aluminum Association (EA)
AA................ Aluminum Company of America [Wall Street slang names: "Ack Ack" and "All American"] [NYSE symbol] (SPSG)
AA................ Aluminum Co. of America [NYSE symbol] (SAG)
AA................ Alveolar-Arterial [Physiology] (MAE)
AA................ Always Afloat [Ship's charter]
AA................ Alzheimers Association [Australia]
AA................ American Airlines, Inc. [ICAO designator]
AA................ American Anthology [A publication]
AA................ American Army (DAS)
AA................ American Assembly (EA)
AA................ American Association [Baseball league]
AA................ Aminoacetone [Organic chemistry]
AA................ Amino Acid [Biochemistry]
AA................ Amino Acid Residue [Biochemistry]
AA................ Amplitude of Accommodation [Ophthalmology]
aa---- .... Amur River and Basin [MARC geographic area code Library of Congress] (LCCP)
AA................ AMVETS Auxiliary (EA)
AA................ Amyloid-Associated [Protein] [Medicine]
AA................ Amyloid-Associated Protein [Biochemistry] (DAVI)
AA................ Ana [Of Each] [Pharmacy]
AA................ Analysis Alarm [Engineering]
A/A............. Analysis/Architecture (SSD)
A/A............. Analysis of Accounts
AA................ Analytical Abstracts Online [Royal Society of Chemistry] [Information service or system] (CRD)
aa .... Ana Partes [Equal Parts] [Latin]
AA................ Andrew Public Library, Alberta [Library symbol National Library of Canada] (NLC)
AA................ Anesthesiologist's Assistant [Medicine] (DAVI)
A/A............. Angle of Attack [Military] (NG)
A/A............. Anglo-American
AA................ Angular Accelerometer [NASA] (MCD)
AA................ Angular Aperture (MCD)
AA................ Aniline Association (EA)
AA................ Anisylacetone [Organic chemistry]
AA................ Annales Africaines [A publication] (ILCA)
AA................ Annals Australia: Journal of Catholic Culture [A publication] (APTA)
AA................ Ann Arbor Railroad Co. [AAR code]
AA................ Anterior Aorta
AA................ Anterograde Amnesia [Medicine]
AA................ Ant Guard Activity [Ecology]
AA................ Anthranilic Acid [Organic chemistry]
AA................ Antiaircraft [Army]
AA................ Antibody Activity [Immunology]
AA................ Anticipatory Avoidance [Medicine]
AA................ Antioxidant Activity [Food technology]
AA................ Antiprotein Accumulator (DAVI)
AA................ Antiproton Accumulator [Particle physics]
AA................ Antonius Augustinus [Deceased, 1586] [Authority cited in pre-1607 legal work] (DSA)
A/A............. Any Acceptable
AA................ Aortic Aneurysm [Cardiology] (DAVI)
A-A............. Aortic Artery [Gradient] [Cardiology] (DAVI)
AA................ AOUON [All of Us or None] Archive [An association] (EA)
AA................ Aplastic Anemia [Medicine] (DMAA)
AA................ Apollo Applications [NASA]
AA................ Apostolicam Actuositatem [Decree on the Apostolate of the Laity] [Vatican II document]
AA................ Approach Aid [Aviation] (IAA)
AA................ Appropriate Authority [Office of Censorship] [World War II]
AA................ Appropriations and Allocations (OICC)
AA................ Approving Authority
AA................ Approximate Absolute [Temperature]
AA................ Aptitude Area
AA................ Aptitude Test for Adults [Psychoeducational test]
AA................ Arachidonic Acid [Biochemistry]
AA................ Arboricultural Association (EA)
AA................ Archaeology Abroad (EAIO)
AA................ Architect's Associate [Army research program] (RDA)
AA................ Architectural Association [British] (EA)
AA................ Arithmetic Average
AA................ Arlington Annex [Navy]
AA................ Armament Artificer [British and Canadian] [World War II]
AA................ Armature Accelerator
AA................ Armed Forces Americas
AA................ Armored Ambulance
AA................ ARMS [Action Research into Multiple Sclerosis] of America (EA)
AA................ Army Act (ILCA)

AA................ Army Air Operations (MCD)
AA................ Arrival Angle [Army]
A-A............. Arrocillo Amarillo [Race of maize] [Mexico]
AA................ Arteries [Medicine] (DMAA)
AA................ Arthrogryposis Association (EA)
AA................ Artificial Aerial (DEN)
AA................ Arts Anonymous (EA)
AA................ Asanteman Association (EA)
AA................ Asatru Alliance (EA)
AA................ Ascending Aorta [Anatomy]
AA................ Ascorbic Acid [Vitamin C] [Biochemistry]
AA................ Aspergillus Asthma
AA................ Assembly Area
AA................ Assets Accounting [Business term]
AA................ Assistant Adjutant
AA................ Assistant Administrator (GFGA)
AA................ Associate Administrator [NASA]
AA................ Associate in Accounting
AA................ Associate in Arts
AA................ Association of Anaesthetists (DAVI)
AA................ Assumptionists (TOCD)
AA................ Aster Growth with Aster [Ecology]
AA................ Astrological Association (EAIO)
AA................ Asymmetric Aminohydroxylation [Organic chemistry]
AA................ Atheist Association (EA)
AA................ Athletic Association
AA................ Atlantic Area [Services to the Armed Forces] [Red Cross]
AA................ Atlas Agena [NASA]
AA................ Atmospheric Applications (MCD)
AA................ Atomic Absorption [Environmental Protection Agency]
AA................ Atomic Absorption [Chemical analysis]
AA................ Atomic Age (IAA)
AA................ Attack Assessment [Military]
AA................ Auctores Antiquissimi [Classical studies]
AA................ Audible Alarm (IAA)
AA................ Audit Agency
AA................ Audubon Artists (EA)
AA................ Augustiniani Assumptionis [Assumptionists] [Roman Catholic men's religious order]
AA................ Ausfuehrungsanweisung [Regulatory Instructions] [German] (DLA)
AA................ Australia Antigen [Immunology] (DAVI)
AA................ Australian Airlines
AA................ Australian Army
AA................ Auswaertiges Amt [Foreign Ministry] [German]
AA................ Authorized Absence (DAVI)
AA................ Authorized Allowance
AA................ Author's Alteration [Publishing]
AA................ Autism Association [Australia]
AA................ Auto Acquisition [RADAR]
AA................ Autoanalyzer
AA................ Auto Answer (CDE)
AA................ Automatic Answer [Telecommunications] (TEL)
AA................ Automobile Accident (CPH)
AA................ Automobile Association [British]
AA................ Autonomous Area
AA................ Auxiliary Assembly [JETDS nomenclature]
AA................ Auxiliary Vessels [Navy symbol] (MUGU)
AA................ Avenue of Approach [Army] (AABC)
AA................ Average Acceleration
AA................ Average Adjuster [Insurance] (DS)
AA................ Average Audience [Television ratings]
AA................ Aviation Annex [Air Force]
AA................ Awards Almanac [A publication]
AA................ Axonal Arborization [Medicine] (DMAA)
Aa .... Biblioteca Nacional, Buenos Aires, Argentina [Library symbol Library of Congress] (LCLS)
AA................ Dry-Type Self-Cooled [Transformer] (IEEE)
AA................ High [Standard & Poor's bond rating] [Investment term]
Aa .... High [Moody's bond rating] [Investment term]
AA................ Shoe Width Less than A (BARN)
AA................ Sisters Auxiliaries of the Apostolate [Roman Catholic religious order]
AAA............. Abdominal Aortic Aneurysm [or Aneurismectomy] [Medicine]
AAA............. Acetoacetanilide [Organic chemistry]
AAA............. Acquired Aplastic Anemia [Medicine] (DMAA)
AAA............. Action Against Allergy [British] (EAIO)
AAA............. Action on Alcohol Abuse [British]
AAA............. Active Acquisition Aid
AAA............. Active Antenna Array (MCD)
AAA............. Acute Anxiety Attack [Medicine]
AAA............. Adult Album Alternative [Radio broadcasting]
AAA............. Advanced Amphibious Assault [Marine Corps] (DOMA)
AAA............. Advanced Attack Aircraft (CAAL)
AAA............. African-American Almanac [A publication]
AAA............. Agency Activity Analysis [LIMRA]
AAA............. Agnew Association of America (EA)
AAA............. Agricultural Adjustment Act [1933, 1938, 1980] [Department of Agriculture]
AAA............. Agricultural Adjustment Administration [or Agency] [Production and Marketing Administration] [Department of Agriculture]
AAA............. Agricultural Aircraft Association [Later, CAAA] (EA)
AAA............. Air-to-Air Aftercooling
AAA............. Alabama Aggregates Association (SRA)
AAA............. Alaska
AAA............. Alberta Association of Architects [1906] [Canada] (NGC)
AAA............. Alberta Association of Architects (AC)

AAA............. Album Adult Alternative [*Music classification*]
AAA............. Alianza Anticomunista Argentina [*Argentine Anti-Communist Alliance*] (PD)
AAA............. Alianza Apostolica Anticomunista [*Anti-Communist Apostolic Alliance*] [*Spain*] (PD)
AAA............. Alianza Apostolica Antigua [*Apostolic Ancient Alliance*] [*Spain Political party*] (EY)
AAA............. Alianza pour Accion Anticommunista [*Honduras*] [*Political party*] (EY)
AAA............. Allegheny Airlines [*Air carrier designation symbol*]
AAA............. Allied Airborne Association (EA)
AAA............. Allied Artists of America (EA)
AAA............. Allocation Assessment and Analysis [*Report*]
AAA............. Alma-Ata [*Former USSR Seismograph station code, US Geological Survey*] (SEIS)
AAA............. Alternative Antenna Array (MCD)
AAA............. Amalgama [*Amalgamation*] [*Pharmacy*] (ROG)
AAA............. Amateur Astronomers Association [*Later, AAANY*]
AAA............. Amateur Athletic Association [*British*]
AAA............. American Abstract Artists (EA)
AAA............. American Academy of Achievement (EA)
AAA............. American Academy of Actuaries [*Washington, DC*] (EA)
AAA............. American Academy of Addictionology (HCT)
AAA............. American Academy of Advertising [*Charleston, SC*] (EA)
AAA............. American Academy of Allergy [*Later, AAAI*] (EA)
AAA............. American Academy of Anatomists (DAVI)
AAA............. American Academy of Art [*Chicago, IL*]
AAA............. American Accordionists' Association (EA)
AAA............. American Accounting Association [*Sarasota, FL*] (EA)
AAA............. American Acupuncture Association (EA)
AAA............. American Adventurers Association (DICI)
AAA............. American Aerobics Association (EA)
AAA............. American Affenpinscher Association (EA)
AAA............. American Afghan Action [*Later, FAAA*] (EA)
AAA............. American Agents Association [*Indianapolis, IN*] (EA)
AAA............. American Airship Association [*Later, Airship Association*] (EA)
AAA............. American Albino Association [*Later, WWWCRW*]
AAA............. American Allergy Association (EA)
AAA............. American Ambulance Association (EA)
AAA............. American Angus Association (EA)
AAA............. American Antarctic Association (EA)
AAA............. American Anthropological Association (EA)
AAA............. American Aquatech International [*Vancouver Stock Exchange symbol*]
AAA............. American Arbitration Association (EA)
AAA............. American Armwrestling Association (EA)
AAA............. American Art Association [*Predecessor of Parke-Bernet, New York*]
AAA............. American Arts Alliance (EA)
AAA............. American Association of Anatomists (EA)
AAA............. American Astronomers Association (EA)
AAA............. American Australian Association (EA)
AAA............. American Automobile Association (EA)
AAA............. Americans Against Abortion (EA)
AAA............. Aminoadipic Acid [*Organic chemistry*]
AAA............. Anarchist Association of the Americas [*Defunct*] (EA)
AAA............. Androgenic Anabolic Agent [*Medicine*] (DMAA)
AAA............. Aneurysm of Ascending Aorta [*Cardiology*] (DMAA)
AAA............. Aneurysm of Ascending Aorta [*Cardiology*] (DMAA)
AAA............. Anglo-American Associates (EA)
AAA............. Ansett Airlines of Australia [*ICAO designator*] (FAAC)
AAA............. Antiaircraft Armament
AAA............. Antiaircraft Artillery (GPO)
AA-A............. Antiaircraft Assistant (SAA)
AAA............. Antique Airplane Association (EA)
AAA............. Apollo Access Arm [*NASA*] (KSC)
AAA............. Apostolic Anti-Communist Alliance [*Spain*]
AAA............. Appraisers Association of America (EA)
AAA............. Approved as Amended
AAA............. Arbitration as an Alternative (DICI)
AAA............. Archery Association of Australia
AAA............. Architectural Aluminum Association (DAC)
AAA............. Archives of American Art (EA)
AAA............. Area Agency on Aging (DHSM)
AAA............. Argentine Anticommunist Alliance [*Political party*] (LAIN)
AAA............. Army Audit Agency
AAA............. Aromatic Amino Acids [*Biochemistry*]
AAA............. Arrest after Arrival [*Medicine*] (DMAA)
AAA............. Arrival and Assembly Area [*Marine Corps*] (DOMA)
AAA............. Arts Action Australia [*An association*]
AAA............. Asian-American Almanac [*A publication*]
AAA............. Assistant Air Attache [*British*]
AAA............. Associated Actors and Artistes of America
AAA............. Associated Agents of America (EA)
AAA............. Associate in Applied Arts
AAA............. Association des Auditeurs et Anciens Auditeurs de l'Academie [*Association of Attenders and Alumni of the Hague Academy of International Law*] (EAIO)
AAA............. Association of Accounting Administrators [*Commercial firm Washington, DC*] (EA)
AAA............. Association of Administrative Assistants [*Association des Adjoints Administratifs*] (AC)
AAA............. Association of Authors' Agents (EAIO)
AAA............. Association of Average Adjusters of the United States [*New York, NY*] (EA)
aaa .... Assumptionists (TOCD)
AAA............. Assyrian Australian Association

AAA............. Astronaut-Actuated Abort [*NASA*] (MCD)
AAA............. Auburn University, Auburn, AL [*OCLC symbol*] (OCLC)
AAA............. Australia Asia Airlines [*Air carrier designation symbol*]
AAA............. Australian Academy of Anatomy
AAA............. Australian Academy of Art
AAA............. Australian Aeronautical Academy
AAA............. Australian Appliance Association
AAA............. Australian-Arab Association
AAA............. Australian Aromatherapists' Association
AAA............. Australian Asian Association
AAA............. Authorized Accounting Activity [*DoD*]
AAA............. Authors at Auction [*A publication*]
AAA............. Automated Agency Accounting
AAA............. Automated Airlift Analysis [*MTMC*] (TAG)
AAA............. Automated Amino Acid Analysis [*Food technology*]
AAA............. Auxiliary Array Antenna [*Army*]
AAA............. Awaiting Aircraft Availability
Aaa .... Best [*Moody's bond rating*] [*Investment term*]
AAA............. Highest [*Standard & Poor's bond rating*]
AAA............. Lincoln, IL [*Location identifier FAA*] (FAAL)
AAA............. Shoe width Less than AA (BARN)
AAA............. US Alcohol Testing of America [*AMEX symbol*] (SPSG)
AAAA .... Akro Agate Art Association [*Defunct*] (EA)
AAAA .... Amateur Artists Association of America [*Defunct*] (EA)
AAAA .... American Academy of Anesthesiologists' Assistants (DAVI)
AAAA .... American-African Affairs Association (EA)
AAAA .... American Association Against Addiction [*Defunct*] (EA)
AAAA .... American Association for Affirmative Action (EA)
AAAA .... American Association for the Advancement of Atheism [*Later, AA*] (EA)
AAAA .... American Association of Aardvark Aficionados (EA)
AAAA .... American Association of Advertising Agencies [*New York, NY*] (EA)
AAAA .... American Association of Audio Analgesia [*Defunct*]
AAAA .... Antique Appraisal Association of America (EA)
AAAA .... Arkansas Agricultural Aviation Association (SRA)
AAAA .... Army Aviation Association of America (EA)
AAAA .... Artists and Athletes Against Apartheid (EA)
AAAA .... Asian American Arts Alliance (EA)
AAAA .... Associated Actors and Artistes of America (EA)
AAAAA .... Shoe Width Less than AAA (BARN)
AAAAA .... Aphasia, Agnosia, Apraxia, Agraphia, Alexia [*Medicine*] (MEDA)
AAAAAA .... Association for the Alleviation of Asinine Abbreviations and Absurd Acronyms [*Satirical nonassociation*]
AAAAM .... Area Agencies on Aging Association of Michigan (SRA)
AAA & L .... American Academy of Arts and Letters [*Later, AAIAL*] (EA)
AAA & S ..... American Academy of Arts and Sciences (EA)
AAA & S ..... Associate in Arts in Arts and Science
AAAAPSF .... American Association for Accreditation of Ambulatory Plastic Surgery Facilities (EA)
AAAB .... American Association of Architectural Bibliographers
AAABA .... All-American Amateur Baseball Association (EA)
AAABC .... Advertising Agency Association of British Columbia (AC)
AAAC .... All Aluminum Alloy Conductor (MCD)
AAAC .... American-Arab Affairs Council (EA)
AAAC .... American Association of Accompanists and Coaches (EA)
AAAC .... Antiaircraft Artillery Command
AAAC .... Antimicrobial Agent Associated Colitis [*Medicine*]
AAAC .... Archival Association of Atlantic Canada
AAACC .... Association of Asian-American Chambers of Commerce [*Washington, DC*] (EA)
AAACE .... American Association for Adult and Continuing Education (EA)
AAACE .... American Association of Agricultural College Editors [*Later, ACE*] (EA)
AAACI .... American-Arab Association for Commerce and Industry [*New York, NY*] (EA)
AAACJ......... All American Association of Contest Judges (EA)
AAA-CPA...... American Association of Attorney-Certified Public Accountants [*Mission Viejo, CA*] (EA)
AAACU .... Asian Association of Agricultural Colleges and Universities [*Philippines*]
AAAD .... Airborne Antitank Armor Air Defense (MCD)
AAAD .... American Athletic Association for the Deaf (EA)
AAAD .... Aromatic Amino Acid Decarboxylase [*Also, AADC*] [*An enzyme*]
AAAD .... Association of Automotive Aftermarket Distributors (EA)
AAADC .... Alvin Ailey American Dance Center
AAADM .... American Association of Automatic Door Manufacturers
AAAE........... Alliance of Associations for the Advancement of Education [*Defunct*] (EA)
AAAE........... American Association for Agricultural Education (EA)
AAAE........... American Association of Academic Editors (EA)
AAAE........... American Association of Airport Executives (EA)
AAAE........... Amino Acid-Activating Enzyme [*Biochemistry*] (MAE)
AAAE........... Asian Automotive and Accessories Exhibition
AAAE........... Association of Arts Administration Educators (EA)
AAAEE........ American Afro-Asian Educational Exchange [*Later, AAEE*] (EA)
AAAF........... (Acetoxyacetylamino)fluorene [*Organic chemistry*]
AAAF........... Alberta Association of Agricultural Fieldmen (AC)
AAAF........... Anglo-American Air Force (DAS)
AAAF........... Anglo-American Authority File of Authors
AAAF........... Arab Amateur Athletic Federation [*See also CAA*] (EAIO)
AAAG .... Acting Assistant Adjutant-General [*Military British*] (ROG)
AA Ag .... Associate in Arts in Agriculture
AAAGA .... Association of American Geographers Annals [*A publication*] (BRI)
AAAH .... American Association for the Advancement of the Humanities

AAAHAIL...... Association of Attenders and Alumni of The Hague Academy of International Law (EA)
AAAHC .... Accreditation Association for Ambulatory Health Care (EA)
AAAHE .... American Association for the Advancement of Health Education [*Medicine*] (DMAA)
AAAHT .... [*The*] Alberta Association of Animal Health Technologists (AC)
AAAI............ Affiliated Advertising Agencies International [*Aurora, CO*] (EA)
AAAI............ Afro-American Art Institute (EA)
AAAI............ American Academy of Allergy and Immunology (EA)
AAAI............ American Association for Artificial Intelligence (EA)
AAAI............ Associate of the Institute of Administrative Accounting and Data Processing [*British*] (DCTA)
AA-AIC .... Alberta Association of the Appraisal Institute of Canada (AC)
AAAID .... Arab Authority for Agricultural Investment and Development [*Khartoum, Sudan*] (EAIO)
AAAIMH ...... American Association for the Abolition of Involuntary Mental Hospitalization [*Defunct*]
AAAIS .... Advanced Army Aircraft Instrument System (MCD)
AAAIS .... Antiaircraft Artillery Information [*or Intelligence*] Service
AAAIWD ...... American Association of Aluminum Importers and Warehouse Distributors [*Later, AMIA*] (EA)
AA/AL........... Airplane Avionics/AUTOLAND (NASA)
AAAL .... American Academy of Arts and Letters [*Later, AAIAL*] (EA)
AAAL .... American Association for Applied Linguistics (EA)
AA/AL.......... Automatic Approach/AUTOLAND (NASA)
AAALAC ...... American Association for Accreditation of Laboratory Animal Care (EA)
AAAM.......... Advanced Air-to-Air Missile [*Military*]
AAAM.......... American Association for Automotive Medicine (DAVI)
AAAM.......... Association for the Advancement of Automotive Medicine (EA)
AAAMA .... Air-to-Air Armament Mission Analyses [*Air Force*] (MCD)
AA-AMP ...... Amino Acid Adenylate [*Also called adenomonophosphate*] [*Biochemistry*] (DAVI)
AAAMS .... Advanced Antiarmor Missile Systems (MCD)
AAAN .... American Academy of Applied Nutrition [*Later, ICAN*] (EA)
AAAN .... Australian Association for Armed Neutrality
AAANA .... American Academy of Ambulatory Nursing Administration (EA)
AA & A .... Armor, Armament, and Ammunition
AA & DPD.... Appropriation Accounts and Data Processing Division [*Ministry of Agriculture, Fisheries, and Food*] [*British*]
AA & QMG... Assistant Adjutant and Quartermaster-General [*British*]
AA&S .... Advanced Aerodynamics & Structures, Inc. [*Associated Press*] (SAG)
AAANY .... Amateur Astronomers Association of New York [*Formerly, AAA*] (EA)
AAANYC ...... Amateur Astronomers Association of New York City [*Later, AAA*] (EA)
AAANZ .... Agribusiness Association of Australia and New Zealand
AAAOB .... Antiair Artillery Order of Battle (MCD)
AAAOC .... Antiaircraft Artillery Operation Center
AAAOM .... American Association for Acupuncture and Oriental Medicine (EA)
AAAP .... Action Against Armageddon Project [*Defunct*] (EA)
AAAP .... Advanced Airframe Assembly Program [*Aviation*]
AAAP .... Airborne Associative Array Processor
AAAP .... American Association of Applied Psychology [*Division of American Psychological Association*]
AAAP .... American Association of Avian Pathologists (EA)
AAAPA .... Afro-American Association of Performing Artists (EA)
AAAPEA .... Australian Association Against Painful Experiments on Animals
AAAPrA........ U.S.Alcohol Test'g 14% CI'A'Pfd [*AMEX symbol*] (TTSB)
AAAPSQ ...... Association des Animateurs et Animatrices de Pastorale de la Sante du Quebec (AC)
AAAQ .... Apparel Agents' Association of Queensland [*Australia*]
AAAR .... American Association for Aerosol Research (EA)
AAAR .... Association for the Advancement of Aeronautical Research [*France*]
AAAR .... Association for the Advancement of Aging Research [*Defunct*] (EA)
AAAR .... Regional Office, Alberta Agriculture, Airdrie, Alberta [*Library symbol National Library of Canada*] (NLC)
AAARC........ Antiaircraft Artillery Reception Center
AAARDRCRM... Antiaircraft Artillery RADAR Crewman [*Military*] (IAA)
AAARG........ American Atheist Addiction Recovery Groups [*Later, MOM*] (EA)
AAAS .... Alberta Association of Agricultural Societies (AC)
AAAS .... American Academy of Arts and Sciences (EA)
AAAS .... American Academy of Asian Studies (EA)
AAAS .... American Association for the Advancement of Science (EA)
AAAS .... Applicable Approved Accounting Standard
AAAS .... Armored Antiaircraft System (MCD)
AAAS .... Automated Attendance Accounting System [*Jet Propulsion Laboratory, NASA*]
AAASA .... Association for the Advancement of Agricultural Sciences in Africa (EAIO)
AAASA .... Association pour l'Avancement en Afrique des Sciences de l'Agriculture [*Association for the Advancement of Agricultural Sciences in Africa*] [*Addis Ababa, Ethiopia*]
AAASAD........ Armenian Assembly of America, Student Affairs Division (EA)
AAASD .... Aluminum Association Aluminum Standards and Data [*Information service or system*] (IID)
AAASM .... Associated African States and Madagascar (MHDB)
AAASS .... American Association for the Advancement of Slavic Studies (EA)
AAASUSS...... Association of Administrative Assistants and Secretaries to United States Senators (EA)
AAAT............ Anti-Aircraft Armoured Truck [*Military*] (PDAA)
AAATC .... American Association for the Advancement of Tension Control [*Later, ISTC*]
AAATC .... Association of American Air Travel Clubs [*Defunct*] (EA)
AAATP .... Asian Alliance of Appropriate Technology Practitioners (EA)
AAATP .... Association for Anesthesiologists' Assistants Training Program (DAVI)

AAATS .... Australian Advanced Air Traffic Services (GAVI)
AAAUS .... Association of Average Adjusters of the United States
AAAV .... Advanced Amphibious Assault Vehicle [*Marine Corps*]
AAAV .... American Alliance Against Violence (EA)
AAAV .... Apparel Agents' Association of Victoria [*Australia*]
AAAWA .... Apparel Agents' Association of Western Australia
AAAWC .... Alternate Antiair Warfare Commander (NVT)
AAB............ AABCO Ventures, Inc. [*Vancouver Stock Exchange symbol*]
AAB............ Abelag Aviation [*Belgium ICAO designator*] (FAAC)
AAB............ Acquisition Advisory Board (MCD)
AAB............ Action Against Burns [*Formerly, APBIC*] (EA)
AAB............ Actualizing Assessment Battery [*Personality development test*] [*Psychology*]
AAB............ Adaptive Angle Bias
AAB............ Advertising Advisory Board of the Canadian Advertising Foundation
AAB............ Air Assault Brigade (MCD)
AAB............ Aircraft Accident Board
AAB............ Aircraft Armament Bulletin [*Navy A publication*] (MCD)
AAB............ Air Force Air Base
AAB............ Alianca Anticomunista Brasileira [*Brazilian Anti-Communist Alliance*] (PD)
AAB............ All-American Boy [*Lifestyle classification*] (ECON)
AAB............ American Academy of Ballet
AAB............ American Association of Bioanalysts [*or Bioanalysis*] (DAVI)
AAB............ American Australian Business
AA/B.......... Antiaircraft Balloon [*Obsolete*]
AAB............ Anti-Aircraft Battery (DOMA)
AAB............ Army Air Base (MCD)
AAB............ Army Artillery Board (AAG)
AAB............ Army Aviation Board
AAB............ Artichoke Advisory Board (EA)
AAB............ Associate in Arts in Business
AAB............ Association of Applied Biologists [*Midlothian, Scotland*] (EA)
AAB............ Astra AB [*NYSE symbol*] (SAG)
AAB............ Astra AB'B' ADS [*NYSE symbol*] (TTSB)
AAB............ Atlantic Association of Broadcasters (AC)
AAB............ Aviation Armament Bulletin (MCD)
AAB............ Talgar [*Also, TLG*] [*Alma-Ata*] [*Former USSR*] [*Seismograph station code, US Geological Survey*] (SEIS)
AABA .... American Anorexia/Bulimia Association (EA)
AABA .... Australian Ayrshire Breeders' Association
AABAS .... Australasian Academy of Broadcast Arts and Sciences
AABB .... American Association of Blood Banks (EA)
AABB .... Association for the Advancement of British Biotechnology (EAIO)
AABC .... Access Anytime Bancorp, Inc. [*NASDAQ symbol*] (SAG)
AABC .... Accrediting Association of Bible Colleges [*Later, American Association of BibleColleges*] (EA)
AABC .... All-American Bronze Club (EA)
AABC .... American Amateur Baseball Congress (EA)
AABC .... American Association of Backgammon Clubs (EA)
AABC .... American Association of Bible Colleges (EA)
AABC .... American Association of Biofeedback Clinicians [*Defunct*] (EA)
AABC .... American Austin/Bantam Club (EA)
AABC .... Archives Association of British Columbia (AC)
AABC .... Associated Air Balance Council (EA)
AABC .... Association for Advancement of Blind Children [*Later, AABR*] (EA)
AABC .... Canadian Associated Air Balance Council (AC)
AABCC .... Alertness, Airway, Breathing, Circulation, Cervical Spine [*Medicine*] (DMAA)
AABCP .... Advanced Airborne Command Post
AABD .... Aid to the Aged, Blind, or Disabled [*Department of Health and Human Services*]
AABE .... American Association of Blacks in Energy (EA)
AABEVM .... Association of American Boards of Examiners in Veterinary Medicine [*Later, AAVSB*] (EA)
AABF .... American Australian Bicentennial Foundation [*Defunct*] (EA)
AABFS .... Amphibious Assault Bulk Fuel System [*Navy*]
AABFTFC...... Amalgamated Association of Brass Founders, Turners, Fitters, and Coppersmiths [*A union*] [*British*]
AABGA .... American Association of Botanical Gardens and Arboreta (EA)
AABGU........ American Associates, Ben-Gurion University of the Negev (EA)
AABH .... Broken Hill [*Australia ICAO location identifier*] (ICLI)
AABHC .... Arkansas Association of Bank Holding Companies (SRA)
AABHH .... American Association of Breeders of Holsteiner Horses (EA)
AABI............ Alabama Alliance of Business and Industry (SRA)
AABI............ Amateur All-Star Baseball [*An association*] (EA)
AABI............ American Association of Bicycle Importers (EA)
AABL .... Advanced Atmospheric Burst Location (MCD)
AABL .... Associated Australasian Banks in London
AABM .... Airborne Antiballistic Missiles (MCD)
AABM .... Alberta Beach Municipal Library, Alberta [*Library symbol National Library of Canada*] (NLC)
AABM .... American Academy of Behavioral Medicine (EA)
AABM .... Association of American Battery Manufacturers [*Later, BCI*] (EA)
AABN .... Anti-Apartheids Beweging Nederland [*Anti-Apartheid Movement*] [*South Africa*] [*Political party*] (EAIO)
AABNCP .... Advanced Airborne National Command Post (MCD)
AABNCP .... Advanced Airborne National Command Post (DOMA)
AABNF .... African Association for Biological Nitrogen-Fixation [*Egypt*] (EAIO)
AABP .... Acetylaminobiphenyl [*Biochemistry*] (OA)
AABP .... American Association of Bovine Practitioners (EA)
AABP .... Aptitude Assessment Battery Programming [*Computer science*] (IEEE)
AABP .... Archbishop
AABP .... Association of Area Business Publications (EA)

AABPA	American Association for Budget and Program Analysis (EA)
AABPC(Qld)...	Association of Abrasive Blastcleaners and Protective Coaters, Queensland [*Australia*]
AABR	Association for Advancement of Blind and Retarded (EA)
AABR	Australian Association of Bush Regenerators
AABS	All-Attitude Indicator Bombing System (MCD)
AABS	Association for the Advancement of Baltic Studies (EA)
AABSHIL	Aircraft Anticollision Beacon System High-Intensity Light [*Army*] (PDAA)
AABSHILL	Aircraft Anticollision Beacon System High-Intensity Light [*Army*] (MCD)
AABT	American Association of Behavioral Therapists (EA)
AABT	Association for Advancement of Behavior Therapy (EA)
AABTD	Amalgamated Association of Beamers, Twisters, and Drawers [*A union*] [*British*] (DCTA)
AABTM........	American Association of Baggage Traffic Managers [*Defunct*] (EA)
AaBU	Universidad de Buenos Aires, Buenos Aires, Argentina [*Library symbol Library of Congress*]
AaBU-C	Universidad de Buenos Aires, Facultad de Ciencias Exactas y Naturales, Buenos Aires, Argentina [*Library symbol Library of Congress*] (LCLS)
AA Bus	Associate in Arts in Business
AABW	American Association of Book Wholesalers
AABW	Antarctic Bottom Water [*Oceanography*]
AABWE	American Association of Black Women Entrepreneurs [*Silver Spring, MD*] (EA)
AABY	As Amended By [*Army*]
AAC	Aachen [*Federal Republic of Germany*] [*Seismograph station code, US Geological Survey Closed*] (SEIS)
AAC	Abort Advisory Channel [*NASA*] (KSC)
AAC	Acoustical Absorption Coefficient
AAC	Acoustical Attenuation Constant
AAC	Acquisition Advice Code [*NASA*] (KSC)
AAC	Activity Address Code [*DoD*]
AAC	Actual Acquisition Cost
AAC	Adaptive Antenna Control (MCD)
AAC	Administration above the Company (MCD)
AAC	Advanced Adaptive Control (SSD)
AAC	Advanced AERA Concepts [*FAA*] (TAG)
AAC	Aerated Autoclaved Concrete
AAC	Aerial Ambulance Co. [*Army*] (AABC)
AAC	Aeronautical Administration Communication [*A class of communication which supports administrative communication*] (GAVI)
AAC	Aeronautical Advisory Council
AAC	Aeronautical Approach Chart [*Air Force*]
AAC	Aeronca Aviators Club (EA)
AAC	African Association of Cartography (EA)
AAC	Afro-Asian Center (EA)
A/AC	Aft Across the Hatch [*Stowage*] (DNAB)
AAC	Agreement and Account of Crew (ADA)
AAC	Agricultural Advisory Council for England and Wales (BI)
AAC	Air Approach Control (MCD)
AAC	Air [*Traffic*] Area Control (DOMA)
AAC	Airborne Armament Control [*Air Force*] (MCD)
AAC	Air Carbon Arc Cutting [*Welding*]
AAC	Aircraft Armament Change
AAC	Alabama Acupuncture Council (SRA)
AAC	Al Arish [*Egypt*] [*Airport symbol*] (OAG)
AAC	Alaska Administrative Code [*A publication*] (AAGC)
AAC	Alaskan Air Command [*Elmendorf Air Force Base*]
AAC	Algonquin Arts Council (AC)
AAC	Alkyl Amines Council (EA)
AAC	All Aluminum Conductor
AAC	All-American Challenge [*Auto racing*]
AAC	Allied Longline Agency Annual Conference [*NATO*] (NATG)
AAC	Alumnae Advisory Center [*Later, CCP*] (EA)
AAC	Amateur Athletic Club
AAC	American Academy of Criminalistics (EA)
AAC	American Adoption Congress [*Later, NAAC*] (EA)
AAC	American Alligator Council [*Defunct*] (EA)
AAC	American Alpine Club (EA)
AAC	American Alumni Council [*Later, Council for the Advancement and Support of Education*] (EA)
AAC	American Archery Council (EA)
AAC	American Association of Chiropractors (EA)
AAC	American Association of Criminology (AEBS)
AAC	Aminoacetylcatechol [*or Acetamidocatechol*] [*Biochemistry*]
AAC	Amplitude Absorption Coefficient
AAC	Anacomp, Inc. [*NYSE symbol*] (SPSG)
AAC	Analytical Assessments Corp. (MCD)
AAC	Anglo-American Code [*Cataloging*] (DIT)
AAC	Anglo-American Committee [*World War II*]
AAC	Angola Air Charter Ltd. [*ICAO designator*] (FAAC)
AAC	Anno ante Christum [*In the Year before Christ*] [*Latin*]
AAC	Antarctic Circle (ROG)
AAC	Antiaircraft Cannon (KSC)
AAC	Antiaircraft Command
AAC	Antiaircraft Common [*Projectile*]
AAC	Anti-Aircraft Corps [*British military*] (DMA)
AAC	Antibiotic-Associated Colitis [*Medicine*]
AAC	Antibiotic-Associated Pseudomembranous Colitis [*Medicine*] (DMAA)
AAC	Antimicrobial Agent-Associated Colitis [*Medicine*] (DAVI)
AAC	Antimicrobial Agents and Chemotherapy
AAC	Antique Automobile Coalition [*Legislative lobbying group*]

AAC	Arabinosylazacytidine [*Biochemistry*]
AAC	Architectural Anodizers Council (EA)
AAC	Arithmetic and Controls (IAA)
AAC	Arizona Association of Chiropractic (SRA)
AAC	Armor and Arms Club (EA)
AAC	Army Acquisition Corps (RDA)
AAC	Army Air Corps [*British ICAO designator*] (FAAC)
AAC	Army Audiovisual Center
AAC	Arsenic Atmosphere Czochralski [*System for growing crystals*]
AAC	Art Advisory Committee
AAC	Assembly and Checkout [*Minuteman*] [*Military*] (AFIT)
AAC	Assembly Area Command
AAC	Assets Availability Code (MCD)
AAC	Association Africaine de Cartographie [*African Association of Cartography*] (EAIO)
AAC	Association des Amidonneries de Cereales de la CEE [*EC*] (ECED)
AAC	Association des Armateurs Canadiens [*Formerly, Dominion Marine Association*] (AC)
AAC	Association of American Choruses [*Later, Drinker Library of Choral Music*] (EA)
AAC	Association of American Colleges (EA)
AAC	Association of Analytical Chemists, Inc.
AAC	Association of Arkansas Counties (SRA)
AAC	Athletes' Advisory Council [*See also CCA*] [*Canada*]
AAC	Atomic Absorption Coefficient
AAC	Attack Aircraft Carrier (MCD)
AAC	Augmentative and Alternative Communication [*A publication*]
AAC	Australian Academy of Cricket
AAC	Australian Aerobatic Club
AAC	Australian Aircraft Consortium (LAIN)
AAC	Automatic Amplitude Control (CET)
AAC	Automatic Aperture Control
AAC	Automatic Approach Control [*Aviation*] (AAG)
AAC	Automatic Autocollimator
AAC	Automotive Advertisers Council [*Chicago, IL*] (EA)
AAC	Auxiliary Air Control [*Automotive engineering*]
AAC	Auxiliary Artillery Corps [*British military*] (DMA)
AAC	Average Annual Cost [*Business term*] (MHDB)
AAC	Aviation Administrative Communication (DA)
AAC	Aviation Armament Change (MCD)
AAC	Awami Action Committee [*India*] [*Political party*] (PPW)
AAC	Mike Monroney Aeronautical Center [*FAA*] (TAG)
AACA	Acylaminocephalosporanic Acid [*Medicine*] (DMAA)
AACA	Aircraft Airworthiness Certification Authority (DA)
AACA	Alaska Air Carriers Association (SRA)
AACA	Allied Control Commission for Austria [*World War II*]
AACA	American Apparel Contractors Association (EA)
AACA	American Association of Certified Allergists (EA)
AACA	American Association of Certified Appraisers [*Cincinnati, OH*] (EA)
AACA	American Association of Creative Artists (EA)
AACA	Amphibious Auto Club of America (EA)
AACA	Antique Automobile Club of America (EA)
AACA	Associate of the Association of Cost Accountants (ADA)
AACA	Association of Americans and Canadians for Aliyah [*Later, North American AliyahMovement*]
AACA	Association of Apex Clubs of Australia
AACA	Automotive Air Conditioning Association [*Later, IMACA*] (EA)
AACAHPO	American Association of Certified Allied Health Personnel in Ophthalmology (EA)
AAC & R	All American Cables & Radio, Inc.
AA-C & Ref Tech...	Associate in Air-Conditioning and Refrigeration Technology
AACAP	American Academy of Child and Adolescent Psychiatry (EA)
AACAR	Association for the Advancement of Central Asian Research (EA)
AACART	African-Atlantic Coast Association of Round Tables
AACB	Aeronautics and Astronautics Coordinating Board [*NASA*]
AACB	Allied Control Commission for Bulgaria [*World War II*]
AACB	American Association for Consumer Benefits (EA)
AACB	Association of African Central Banks [*Dakar, Senegal*]
AACBC	American Association of College Baseball Coaches (EA)
AACBP	American Academy of Crown and Bridge Prosthodontics (EA)
AACC	Administrative Area Control Centre [*Military British*]
AACC	Affaires des Anciens Combattants du Canada [*Department of Canadian Veterans Affairs - DVA*]
AACC	Affirmative Action Coordinating Center [*Defunct*] (EA)
AACC	Airport Associations Coordinating Council [*Geneva Airport, Switzerland*] (EAIO)
AAcC	Alexander City State Junior College, Alexander City, AL [*Library symbol Library of Congress*] (LCLS)
AACC	All-Africa Conference of Churches [*Nairobi, Kenya*] (AF)
AACC	All-Attitude Control Capability [*Aerospace*] (AAG)
AACC	American Association for Contamination Control [*Later, IES*] (EA)
AACC	American Association for Continuity of Care (EA)
AACC	American Association for Corporate Contributions [*Defunct*] (EA)
AACC	American Association of Cereal Chemists (EA)
AACC	American Association of Clinical Chemistry (EA)
AACC	American Association of Commercial Colleges [*Later, United Business Schools Association*] (AEBS)
AACC	American Association of Community Colleges (NFD)
AACC	American Association of Credit Counselors [*Defunct*] (EA)
AACC	American Automatic Control Council (EA)
AACC	Area Approach Control Center (DOMA)
AACC	Area Approach Control Centre
AACC	Army Air Corps Centre [*British military*] (DMA)
AACC	Army Aviation Control Center

AACC .... Association for the Aid of Crippled Children [*Later, Foundation for Child Development*] (EA)

AACC .... Association of Agricultrual Computer Companies (EA)

AACC .... Automatic Approach Control Coupler [*or Complex*] [*Aviation*] (MCD)

AACC .... Avicultural Advancement Council of Canada (AC)

AACCA .... Associate of Association of Certified and Corporate Accountants [*British*]

AACCC .... All-American Conference to Combat Communism (EA)

AACCI .... Australian-Arab Chamber of Commerce and Industry

AACCLA ...... Association of American Chambers of Commerce in Latin America (EA)

AACCN .... American Association of Critical Care Nurses (DAVI)

AACCP .... American Association of Colleges of Chiropody-Podiatry

AACD .... American Academy of Craniomandibular Disorders (EA)

AACD .... American Association for Counseling and Development (EA)

AACD .... Antenna Adjustable Current Distribution [*Telecommunications*] (OA)

AACD .... Arkansas Association of Conservation Districts (SRA)

AACD .... Asian American Caucus for Disarmament (EA)

AACD .... Ceduna [*Australia ICAO location identifier*] (ICLI)

AACDP .... American Association of Chairmen of Departments of Psychiatry (EA)

AACDT .... Association of Advisers, Craft, Design, and Technology [*British*] (DBA)

AACE .... Ace Cash Express [*NASDAQ symbol*] (SAG)

AACE .... Advancement of Computing in Education

AACE .... Airborne Alternate Command Echelon [*NATO*] (NATG)

AACE .... Aircraft Alerting Cockpit Equipment (DWSG)

AACE .... Aircraft Alerting Communications Electromagnetic Pulse (MCD)

AACE .... Air-to-Air Combat Environment (DOMA)

AACE .... Alabama Association of Credit Executives (SRA)

AACE .... American Association for Cancer Education (EA)

AACE .... American Association for Career Education (EA)

AACE .... American Association of Clinical Endocrinologists

AACE .... American Association of Concerned Engineers (EA)

AACE .... American Association of Cost Engineers (EA)

AACE .... Antigen-Antibody Crossed Electrophoresis [*Biochemistry*] (DAVI)

AACE .... Association des Assureurs Cooperatifs Europeens [*Association of European Cooperative Insurers - AECI*] [*Brussels, Belgium*] (EAIO)

AACE .... Association des Auteurs des Cantons de l'Est [*Association of Writers of Cantons of the East*] [*Canada*]

AACE .... Association for Adult Continuing Education [*British*]

AACEP .... Aircraft Alerting Communications Electromagnetic Pulse

AACF .... Afro-American Cultural Foundation (EA)

AACF .... Army Area Calibration Facilities (MCD)

AACFO .... American Association of Correctional Facility Officers [*Later, IACO*] (EA)

AACFT .... Army Aircraft (AABC)

AACG .... Acute Angle Closure Glaucoma [*Ophthalmology*]

AACG .... Allied Control Council for Germany [*World War II*]

AACG .... American Association for Crystal Growth (EA)

AACG .... Arrival Airfield Control Group [*Military*] (AABC)

AACGF .... All-American Collegiate Golf Foundation (EA)

AACH .... Allied Control Commission for Hungary [*World War II*]

AACHIR ...... Augusta Area Committee for Health Information Resources [*Library network*]

AACHP .... American Association for Comprehensive Health Planning [*Later, AHPA*]

AACHS .... Afro-American Cultural and Historical Society [*Later, AACHSM*]

AACHSM ...... Afro-American Cultural and Historical Society Museum (EA)

AACHT .... American Association for Clinical Histocompatibility Testing [*Later, ASHI*] (EA)

AACI .... Accredited Appraiser, Canadian Institute

AACI .... Airports Association Council International [*Switzerland*] (EAIO)

AACI .... All American Commun [*NASDAQ symbol*] (TTSB)

AACI .... All American Communications, Inc. [*NASDAQ symbol*] (SAG)

AACI .... Allied Control Commission for Italy [*World War II*]

AACI .... American Academy of Crisis Interveners (EA)

AACI .... American Association for Conservation Information [*Later, ACI*] (EA)

AACI .... American Association of Ceramic Industries (EA)

AACI .... American Association of Crop Insurers [*Washington, DC*] (EA)

AACI .... Association of American Cancer Institutes (EA)

AACI .... Association of Americans and Canadians in Israel (EA)

AACIA .... American Association for Clinical Immunology and Allergy (EA)

AACIB .... All Amer Communications'B' [*NASDAQ symbol*] (TTSB)

AACIGO ...... Association of American and Canadian Importers of Green Olives [*Later, Green Olive Trade Association*] (EA)

AACIL .... All-Articles Configuration Inspection Log [*Aerospace*] (AAG)

AACIO .... Australian Association of Chief Information Officers

AACIP .... Alberta Association of the Canadian Institute of Planners (AC)

AACIS .... Association of American CIRP [*College Internationale pour l'Etude Scientifique des Techniques de Production Mechanique*] Industrial Sponsors (EA)

AACJ .... Allied Control Council for Japan [*World War II*]

AACJC .... American Association of Community and Junior Colleges (EA)

AACL .... Affect Adjective Check List [*Psychology*]

AACL .... Alberta Association for Community Living [*Alberta Association for the Mentally Handicapped*] (AC)

AACL .... Alberta Association of College Librarians (AC)

AACL .... Anxiety Adjective Check List [*Psychology*]

AACL .... Association of American Correspondents in London [*England*] (EA)

AACLS .... Association of American Collegiate Literary Societies (EA)

AACLS .... Australian Association of Community Language Services

AACM .... Advanced Air Cycle Machine (MCD)

AACM .... Affirmative Action Compliance Manual [*BNA*] [*A publication*] (AAGC)

AACM .... African Anti-Colonial Movement of Kenya

AACM .... American Academy of Compensation Medicine [*Later, AALIM*] (EA)

AACM .... ASEAN [*Association of Southeast Asian Nations*] - Australia Consultative Meeting

AACM .... Association for the Advancement of Creative Musicians (EA)

AACM .... Automatic Armor Cluster Munition

AACM .... Average Absolute Control Movement (MCD)

AACMO .... Army Acquisition Corps Management Office (RDA)

AACN .... American Association of Colleges of Nursing (EA)

AACN .... American Association of Critical-Care Nurses (EA)

AACN .... Anno ante Christum Natum [*In the Year before the Birth of Christ*] [*Latin*] (DLA)

AACO .... Advanced and Applied Concepts Office [*MERDC*] [*Army*]

AACO .... American Association of Certified Orthoptists (EA)

AACO .... American Association of Correctional Officers [*Later, IACO*] (EA)

AACO .... Arab Air Carriers Organization (EAIO)

AACo .... Arizona Association of Counties (SRA)

AACO .... Assault Airlift Control Officer

AACOB .... Army Automation Command Operating Budget (AAGC)

AACOBE ...... Army Automation Command Operating Budget Estimate

AACOM .... American Association of Colleges of Osteopathic Medicine (EA)

AACOM .... Army Area Communications [*System*] (IAA)

AACOMS ...... Army Area Communications System (MCD)

AACOMS ...... Army Automation Communications System (AAGC)

AACP .... Advanced Airborne Command Post

AACP .... Air Carrier Contract Personnel

AACP .... Ambient Air Control Panel [*Army*]

AACP .... American Academy for Cerebral Palsy [*Later, AACPDM*] (EA)

AACP .... American Academy of Child Psychiatry [*Later, AACAP*] (EA)

AACP .... American Academy of Clinical Psychiatrists (EA)

AACP .... American Association for Correctional Psychology (EA)

AACP .... American Association of Colleges of Pharmacy (EA)

AACP .... American Association of Colleges of Podiatry [*Later, AACPM*] (EA)

AACP .... American Association of Commerce Publications [*Later, American Chamber of Commerce Executives Communications Council*] (EA)

AACP .... American Association of Community Psychiatrists (EA)

AACP .... American Association of Computer Professionals (EA)

AACP .... American Association of Convention Planners [*Defunct*] (EA)

AACP .... Anglo-American Council on Productivity [*British*] (DI)

AACP .... Army Acquisition Corps Program (INF)

AACP .... Associate of the Association of Computer Professionals [*British*] (DBQ)

AACP .... Association of American-Chinese Professionals (EA)

AACP .... Australian Association of Consulting Planners

AACPA .... Asian American Certified Public Accountants (EA)

AACPA .... Autoclaved Aerated Concrete Products Association [*British*] (DBA)

AACPDM ...... American Academy for Cerebral Palsy and Developmental Medicine (EA)

AACPM .... American Association of Colleges of Podiatric Medicine (EA)

AACPP .... Association of Asbestos Cement Pipe Producers (EA)

AACPR .... American Association for Cleft Palate Rehabilitation [*Later, ACPA*]

AACPS .... American Association of Clinic Physicians and Surgeons [*Defunct*] (EA)

AACR .... Allied Control Commission for Rumania [*World War II*]

AACR .... American Association for Cancer Research (EA)

AACR .... American Association of Conservators and Restorers (EA)

AACR .... Anglo-American Cataloguing Rules [*American Library Association A publication*]

AACR .... Association for the Advancement of Civil Rights [*Gibraltar*] [*Political party*] (PPE)

AACR2 .... Anglo-American Cataloguing Rules, Second Edition [*American Library Association A publication*]

AACRAO ...... American Association of Collegiate Registrars and Admissions Officers (EA)

AACRC .... American Association of Children's Residential Centers (12L)

AACS .... Advanced Automatic Compilation System [*Computer science*] (MHDI)

AACS .... Airborne Astrographic Camera System [*Air Force*] (MCD)

AACS .... Airspeed and Altitude Computer Set (CAAL)

AACS .... Airways and Air Communications Service [*Air Force*]

AACS .... Ambient Air Cooling System [*Military*]

AACS .... American Academy of Cosmetic Surgery (EA)

AACS .... American Antiques and Crafts Society [*Defunct*] (EA)

AACS .... American Association for Chinese Studies (EA)

AACS .... American Association of Christian Schools (EA)

AACS .... Antiaircraft Control Station (MCD)

AACS .... Antiarmor Capabilities Study (MCD)

AACS .... Army Airways Communications System

AACS .... Army Alaska Communication System [*Air Force*]

AACS .... Association of Arts Centres in Scotland [*British*]

AACS .... Asynchronous Address Communications Systems

AACS .... Attitude and Antenna Control System [*NASA*] (MCD)

AACS .... Attitude and Articulation Control Subsystem [*NASA*]

AACS .... Auxiliary Attitude Control System [*Aviation*] (MCD)

AACS .... Michigan Administrative Code Annual Supplement [*A publication*] (AAGC)

AACSB .... American Assembly of Collegiate Schools of Business (EA)

AACSC .... Army Automation and Communication Steering Committee

AACSCEDR... Associates and Advisory Committee to the Special Committee on Electronic Data Retrieval (MCD)

AACSE .... American Association of Classified School Employees (EA)

AACSH .... Adrenal Androgen Corticotropic Stimulating Hormone [*Medicine*] (DMAA)

AACSL .... American Association for the Comparative Study of Law (EA)

AACSM .... Airways and Air Communications Service Manual

AACSR.......... Airways and Air Communications Service Regulation [*Air Force*] (IAA)
AACSR.......... Aluminum Alloy Constructor Steel Reinforced (IEEE)
AACSRON ... Airways and Air Communications Service Squadron [*Air Force*] (IAA)
AACSWG..... Airways and Air Communications Service Wing [*Air Force*] (IAA)
AACT.......... Adult Assessment and Coordination Team
AACT.......... American Academy of Clinical Toxicology (EA)
AACT.......... American Association of Candy Technologists (EA)
AACT.......... American Association of Commodity Traders [*Defunct*] (EA)
AACT.......... American Association of Community Theatre (EA)
AACT.......... American Association of Crimean Turks (EA)
AACT.......... Armenian Assembly Charitable Trust (EA)
AACTE........ American Association of Colleges for Teacher Education (EA)
AACTM........ Australian Association of Ceramic Tile Merchants
AACTO........ American Association of Cable TV Owners [*Inactive*] (EA)
AACTP........ American Association of Correctional Training Personnel (EA)
AACTS .... Automatic Anechoic Chamber Test System [*Navy*] (MCD)
AACTVO...... American Association of Cable TV Owners (EA)
AACU .... American Association of Clinical Urologists (EA)
AACU .... Anti-Aircraft Co-Operation Unit [*British military*] (DMA)
AaCU .... Universidad Nacional de Cordoba, Cordoba, Argentina [*Library symbol Library of Congress*] (LCLS)
AACUBO...... American Association of College and University Business Officers [*Defunct*]
AACUO........ Association for Affiliated College and University Offices [*Later, ACUO*] (EA)
AACV .... Australian Association of Cattle Veterinarians
AACVB .... Asian Association of Convention and Visitor Bureaus (EA)
AACVPR...... American Academy of Cardiovascular and Pulmonary Rehabilitation (EA)
AACX .... Aries Air Cargo International [*Air carrier designation symbol*]
AAD .... Acetoacetate Decarboxylase [*An enzyme*]
AAD .... Active Acoustic Device
AAD .... Address Adder [*Computer science*] (IAA)
AAD .... Admission and Disposition [*Military*] (AABC)
AAD .... Advanced Academic Degree (AFM)
AAD .... Advanced Airborne Demonstrator
AAD .... Advanced Ammunition Depot
AAD .... Aero Aviation Centre Ltd. [*Canada ICAO designator*] (FAAC)
AAD .... Air Assault Division [*Army*]
AAD .... Airborne Assault Division (MCD)
AAD .... Aircraft and Armament Development
AAD .... Aircraft Assignment Directive
AAD .... Alberta Alcoholism and Drug Abuse Commission Library, Edmonton, AB, Canada [*OCLC symbol*] (OCLC)
AAD .... Alloxazine Adenine Dinucleotide [*Biochemistry*]
AAD .... American Academy of Dentists [*Defunct*] (EA)
AAD .... American Academy of Dermatology (EA)
AAD .... American Academy of Diplomacy (EA)
AAD .... American Daleco Technologies, Inc. [*Vancouver Stock Exchange symbol*]
Aad .... Aminoadipic Acid [*Biochemistry*]
AAD .... Antiaircraft Defences [*British*]
AAD .... Appropriation Account Data [*Business term*]
AAD .... Arms and Ammunition Division [*Army*]
AAD .... Army Air Defense
AAD .... Army Automation Directorate [*Formerly, DMIS*] (MCD)
AAD .... Assembly and Disassembly (IAA)
AAD .... Assigned Altitude Deviation [*Aviation*] (DA)
AAD .... Association of American Dentists
AAD .... At a Discount
AAD .... Australian-Antarctic Discordance [*Geology*]
AAD .... Average Absolute Deviation [*Statistics*]
AAD .... Deputy Associate Administrator [*NASA*]
AADA .... Abbreviated Antibiotic Drug Application [*Food and Drug Administration*]
AADA .... Advanced Air Depot Area [*Air Force*]
AADA .... American Academy of Dramatic Arts (NTCM)
AADA .... Antiaircraft Defense Area [*NATO*]
AADA .... Arizona Automobile Dealers Association (SRA)
AADA .... Arkansas Automobile Dealers Association (SRA)
AADA .... Army Adviser Discharge Affairs [*British and Canadian*] [*World War II*]
AADA .... Army Air Defense Area
AADA .... Associated Antique Dealers of America (EA)
AADA .... Association for Adult Development and Aging (EA)
AADA .... Auxiliary to the American Dental Association (EA)
AADAB........ Army Air Defense Artillery Board
AADAOPA ... American Association of Dealers in Ancient, Oriental, and Primitive Art (EA)
AADAS .... Association for the Advancement of Dutch-American Studies (EA)
AADAT .... Alberta Association of Designers & Architectural Technologists (AC)
AADB .... American Association of the Deaf-Blind (EA)
AADB .... Army Air Defense Board (KSC)
AADC .... Advanced Avionics Digital Computer [*Naval Air Systems Command*]
AADC .... Air Aide-de-Camp [*RAF*] [*British*]
AADC .... Airborne Antiarmor Defense Concept (MCD)
AADC .... All Applications Digital Computer [*Navy*]
AADC .... American Association of Dental Consultants [*Bloomington, MN*] (EA)
AADC .... American Association of Disability Communicators [*Defunct*] (EA)
AADC .... Amino Acid Decarboxylase [*An enzyme*]
AADC .... Antiaircraft Defence Commander [*British*]
AADC .... Antiaircraft Director Center (MCD)
AADC .... Approach and Departure Control [*FAA*] (TAG)
AADC .... Approach and Departure Control [*Aviation*] (FAAC)
AADC .... Area Air Defense Commander [*Military*]

AADC .... Army Air Defense Command [*or Commander*] [*Later, AADCOM*]
AADC .... Arnold Air Development Center [*Air Force*]
AADC .... Aromatic Amino Acid Decarboxylase [*Also, AAAD*] [*An enzyme*]
AADC .... Association of American Dance Companies [*Defunct*] (EA)
AADC .... Asthma and Allergic Disease Center [*Department of Health and Human Services*] (GRD)
AADC .... Australian Association for Deserted Children
AADC2 .... Army Air Defense Command and Control (MCD)
AADCCS ...... Army Air Defense Control and Coordination System (AABC)
AADCM .... Awaiting Action Deck Court-Martial
AADCOM ...... Army Air Defense Command [*or Commander*] [*Formerly, AADC, ARADCOM*] (AABC)
AADCP .... Army Air Defense Command Post
AADCS .... Automatic Air Data Calibration System [*Aerospace*]
AADD .... Auxiliary Active Digital Display [*Sonar*] (DNAB)
AADD .... Aviation and Air Defense Division [*US Army Human Engineering Laboratory, Aberdeen Proving Ground, MD*] (RDA)
AADE .... American Academy of Dental Electrosurgery (EA)
AADE .... American Association of Dental Editors (EA)
AADE .... American Association of Dental Examiners (EA)
AADE .... American Association of Diabetes Educators (EA)
AADEA .... Aminoacetaldehyde Diethyl Acetal [*Organic chemistry*]
AADEOS ...... Advanced Air Defense Electro-Optic Sensor [*Army*]
AADEP .... American Academy of Disability Evaluating Physicians (EA)
AADF .... Arab American Democratic Federation (EA)
AADF .... Association for the American Dance Festival (EA)
AADFI .... Association of African Development Finance Institutions (MHDB)
AADGE .... Allied Air Defense Ground Environment (MCD)
AADGP .... American Academy of Dental Group Practice (EA)
AADHS .... Advanced Avionics Data Handling System [*Air Force*] (MCD)
AA Dip .... Diploma of the Architectural Association School of Architecture [*British*]
AADIS .... Army Air Defense Information Service
AADLA .... Art and Antique Dealers League of America (EA)
AADM .... Airport and Airspace Delay Model (PDAA)
AADM .... American Academy of Dental Medicine [*Later, AAOM*] (EA)
A Adm .... Associate in Administration
AADMA .... Aminoacetaldehyde Dimethyl Acetal [*Organic chemistry*]
AADMC .... Army Aviation Depot Maintenance Center (MCD)
AADMS .... Advanced Academic Degree Management System (AFM)
AADN .... American Association of Doctors' Nurses (EA)
AADO .... Accepted Alternative Designation Of
A-aDO₂ ...... Alveolar-Arterial Oxygen Difference [*Physiology*]
AADOO........ Army Air Defense Operations Office [*or Officer*]
AADP .... Advanced Avionic Display Processor (MCD)
AADP .... American Academy of Dental Prosthetics (DAVI)
AADP .... Amyloid-A-Degrading Protease [*An enzyme*]
AADP .... Antiaircraft Defended Point (MUGU)
AADP .... Army Aviation Development Plan (MCD)
AADPA .... American Academy of Dental Practice Administration (EA)
AADPRT....... American Association of Directors of Psychiatric Residency Training (EA)
AADPSP ...... Activity Automatic Data Process Security Plan (MCD)
AADR .... American Academy of Dental Radiology (EA)
AADR .... American Association for Dental Research (EA)
AADS .... Access Area Digital Switching System (MCD)
AADS .... Advanced Air Defense System
AADS .... Aero/Acoustic Detection System [*Army*] (MCD)
AADS .... Airspeed and Direction Sensor (PDAA)
AADS .... American Academy of Dental Schools (DAVI)
AADS .... American Association of Dental Schools (EA)
AADS .... Antiaircraft Defense System [*Army*] (AABC)
AADS .... Area Air Defense System (MCD)
AADS .... Army Air Defense School (KSC)
AADS .... Army Air Defense Site
AADS .... Army Air Defense Staff (MCD)
AADS .... Army Air Defense System [*Formerly, FABMDS*]
AADS .... Army Aviation Decontamination Station (DOMA)
AADS .... Ascent Air Data System (NASA)
AADS .... Automated Acoustic Detection System (MCD)
AADS .... Automatic Aircraft Diagnostic System
AADSAS ...... American Association of Dental Schools Application Service (GAGS)
AADSF .... Advanced Automated Directional Solidification Furnace [*Materials processing*]
AADT .... Annual Average Daily Traffic [*on highways*]
AADT .... Average Annual Daily Traffic [*FHWA*] (TAG)
AADTS .... Association of Advisors in Design and Technical Studies [*British*]
AADV .... Acquisition Aid Vehicle [*Army*] (AABC)
AADV .... Advantage Bancorp [*NASDAQ symbol*] (TTSB)
AADV .... Advantage Bancorp, Inc. [*NASDAQ symbol*] (SAG)
AADV .... American Association of Dental Victims (EA)
AADW .... Advanced Air Defense Weapon
AAE............. Abort Advisory Equipment [*NASA*] (KSC)
AAE............. Accredited Airport Executive [*American Association of Airport Executives*] [*Designation awarded by*]
AAE............. Active Assistive Exercise [*Medicine*]
AAE............. Acute Allergic Encephalitis [*Medicine*] (MAE)
AAE............. Addis Ababa [*Ethiopia*] [*Seismograph station code, US Geological Survey*]
AAE............. Aeronautical and Astronautical Engineering (MCD)
AAE............. Aerospace Auxiliary Equipment [*NASA*]
AAE............. Affirmative Action Employer (MEDA)
AAE............. African-American English [*A dialect*]
AAE............. Alliance for Arts Education (EA)
AAE............. American Academic Environments, Inc.

AAE............ American Association of Endodontists (EA)
AAE............ American Association of Engineers [*Later, NSPE*] (EA)
AAE............ American Association of Esthetics (EA)
AAE............ American Association on Emeriti [*Later, NCE*] (EA)
AAE............ Ancillary Armament Equipment (DNAB)
AAE............ Annaba [*Algeria*] [*Airport symbol*] (OAG)
AAE............ Annuloaortic Ectasia [*Medicine*] (DMAA)
AAE............ Apparent Activation Energy
AAE............ Appointment of Agents - Excise [*Revenue Canada - Customs and Excise*] [*Information service or system*] (CRD)
AAE............ Appropriation and Expense (AFIT)
AAE............ Architectural and Engineering (AFIT)
AAE............ Arizona Air [*Aviation Services West, Inc.*] [*ICAO designator*] (FAAC)
AAE............ Armament and Electronics (AFIT)
AAE............ Army Acquisition Executive
AAE............ Army Aviation Element (AABC)
AAE............ Army Aviation Engineers
AAe............ Ars Aequi; Juridisch Studentenblad [*Netherlands*] (ILCA)
AAE............ Assembly and Equipment (IAA)
AAE............ Associate of Accountants' and Executives' Corp. of Canada
AAE............ Association for Adult Education (AIE)
AAE............ Association for Astronomy Education [*British*] (DBA)
AAE............ Association of Astronomy Educators
AAE............ Australian Antarctic Expedition [*1911-14*]
AAE............ Automatic Adaptive Equalization [*Telecommunications*]
AAE............ Automatic Answering Equipment [*Telecommunications*] (IAA)
AAE............ Automatic Assemble Editing (NTCM)
AAE............ Average Absolute Error (MCD)
AAE............ Azimuth and Elevation (IAA)
AAE............ National Association of Aeronautical Examiners
AAEA.......... African Adult Education Association [*Later, AALAE*] (EAIO)
AAEA.......... Allied African Economic Affairs Committee [*World War II*]
AAEA.......... American Academy of Equine Art (EA)
AAEA.......... American Agricultural Economics Association (EA)
AAEA.......... American Agricultural Editors' Association (EA)
AAEA.......... Arkansas Association of Educational Administrators (SRA)
AAEAEP....... American Association of Examiners and Administrators of Educational Personnel [*Later, American Association of School Personnel Administrators*] (AEBS)
AAEC.......... Association of American Editorial Cartoonists (EA)
AAEC.......... Attitude Axis Emergency Control [*Aerospace*] (MCD)
AAEC.......... Australian Atomic Energy Commission (NUCP)
AAECS........ Auxiliary Area Environmental Control System [*Nuclear energy*] (NRCH)
AAED.......... Active Airborne Expendable Decoy
AAED.......... American Academy of Esthetic Dentistry (EA)
AAED.......... American Association of Entrepreneurial Dentists (EA)
AAED.......... Arizona Association for Economic Development (SRA)
AAED.......... Edinburgh [*Australia ICAO location identifier*] (ICLI)
AAEDC........ American Agricultural Economics Documentation Center [*Department of Agriculture*] (IID)
AAEE.......... Aeroplane and Armament Experimental Establishment [*British*]
AAEE.......... American Academy of Environmental Engineers (EA)
AAEE.......... American-Asian Educational Exchange [*Defunct*] (EA)
AAEE.......... American Association of Electromyography and Electrodiagnosis [*Later, AAEM*] (EA)
A Ae E .... Associate in Aeronautical Engineering
AAEE.......... Australian Association for Engineering Education
AAEE.......... Australian Association for Environmental Education
AAEEH........ American Association of Eye and Ear Hospitals (EA)
AAEF.......... American Afghan Education Fund (EA)
AAEF.......... Automated Analytical Electrophoresis Facility [*NASA*] (MCD)
AAEFA......... Army Aviation Engineering Flight Activity
AAEGTS....... Auxiliary Area Emergency Gas Treatment System [*Nuclear energy*] (NRCH)
AAEH .... Association to Advance Ethical Hypnosis (EA)
AAEI........... American Association of Exporters and Importers [*New York, NY*] (EA)
AAEJ.......... American Association for Ethiopian Jews (EA)
AAEJN......... American Association of English Jewish Newspapers [*Later, AJPA*] (BJA)
AAE/K/N/E .... American Association of Elementary/Kindergarten/Nursery Educators [*Defunct*]
AAEL.......... American Association of Equipment Lessors (EA)
AAELSS....... Active Arm External Load Stabilization System [*Army*]
AAEM.......... Acetoacetoxyethyl Methacrylate [*Organic chemistry*]
AAEM.......... American Academy of Environmental Medicine (EA)
AAEM.......... American Association of Electrodiagnostic Medicine (EA)
AAEMIS....... Army Automated Environmental Management Information System
AAEO .... Astronomical, Atmospheric, Earth, and Ocean Sciences [*National Science Foundation*] (GRD)
AAEP.......... American Association of Equine Practitioners (EA)
AAER .... Accounting and Auditing Enforcement Releases (TDOB)
AAERP......... Australian Archives Electronic Research Project
AAERS .... Air Acoustic Echo Ranging System [*Automotive safety systems*]
AAES.......... Advanced Aircraft Electrical System [*Navy*]
AAES.......... American Association of Engineering Societies (EA)
AAES.......... American Association of Evangelical Students [*Defunct*] (EA)
AAES.......... Anti-Aircraft Experimental Section [*British military*] (DMA)
AAES.......... Association for Agricultural Education Staffs [*British*] (DBA)
AAES.......... Association of Agricultural Education Staffs [*British*]
AAES.......... Automated Aircrew Escape System (MCD)
AAESA .... American Association for the Educational Service Agencies (EDAC)
AAESA .... Army Acquisition Executive Support Agency (RDA)

AAESC .... Association pour l'Avancement des Etudes Scandinaves au Canada [*Association for the Advancement of Scandinavian Studies in Canada - AASSC*]
AAESPH .... American Association for the Education of Severely/Profoundly Handicapped (EDAC)
AAESWB .... Army Airborne Electronics and Special Warfare Board
AA-EVP .... American Association - Electronic Voice Phenomena (EA)
AAEW .... Atlantic Airborne Early Warning [*Military*]
AAEWR .... Advanced Aircraft Early Warning RADAR (MCD)
AAF............ Aboriginal Affairs Foundation [*Australia*]
AAF............ Acceptance Advice Form
AAF............ Accounting and Finance (AFIT)
AAF............ Acetic Acid, Alcohol, Formalin [*Biology*]
AAF............ Acetylaminofluorene [*Also, AcAF, AcNHFln, FAA*] [*Organic chemistry*]
a-af-- .... Afghanistan [*MARC geographic area code Library of Congress*] (LCCP)
AAF............ Agglutination Activating Factor [*Medicine*]
AAF............ Agricultural Aids Foundation
AAF............ Aigle Azur [*France ICAO designator*] (FAAC)
AAF............ Aircraft and Adventure Factory [*Mallard*]
AAF............ Alarm Association of Florida (SRA)
AAF............ Alder Flats Public Library, Alberta [*Library symbol National Library of Canada*] (NLC)
AAF............ Allied Air Forces
AAF............ Aluminum Association of Florida (SRA)
AAF............ Amer Gvt Income Portfolio [*NYSE symbol*] (TTSB)
AAF............ American Advertising Federation [*Washington, DC*] (EA)
AAF............ American Aid for Afghans (EA)
AAF............ American Air Filter Co. (MHDB)
AAF............ American Airforce [*World War II*]
AAF............ American Amputee Foundation (EA)
AAF............ American Architectural Foundation [*Later, AIAF*]
AAF............ American Astronautical Federation [*Defunct*] (EA)
AAF............ American Government Income Portfolio, Inc. [*NYSE symbol*] (CTT)
AAF............ Amino Acid Formula [*Biochemistry*]
AAF............ Ancient Arts Fellowship [*Australia*]
AAF............ Anterior Auditory Field [*Physiology*]
AAF............ Antiarmor Fuze
AAF............ Antibiotics in Animal Feeds (DICI)
AAF............ Anti-Icing Fluid [*Aviation*] (DA)
AAF............ Apalachicola, FL [*Location identifier FAA*] (FAAL)
AAF............ Arkansas Aging Foundation (SRA)
AAF............ Army Airfield
AAF............ Army Air Forces
AAF............ Ascorbic Acid Factor [*Biochemistry*]
AAF............ Association of Adventist Forums (EA)
AAF............ Atlantic Amphibious Force [*Navy*]
AAF............ Austenite and Ferrite [*Manufacturing materials*] (IAA)
AAF............ Auxiliary Air Force [*Later, R Aux AF*] [*British*]
AAF............ Average Adjustment Factor (MCD)
AAF............ Awaiting Additional Funds (AAGC)
AAFA.......... American Aid for Afghans (EA)
AAFA.......... American Alligator Farmers Association (EA)
AAFA.......... Anglo-American Families Association [*British*] (BI)
AAFA.......... Aplastic Anemia Foundation of America (EA)
AAFA.......... Assistant Auditor Freight Accounts [*Business term*]
AAFA.......... Associate in Arts in Fine Arts
AAFA.......... Asthma and Allergy Foundation of America (PAZ)
AAFAA .... Arizona Automatic Fire Alarm Association (SRA)
AAFAIS .... Army and Air Force Air Intelligence School [*British*]
AAFAR .... American Association of First Responders [*Later, National Association of First Aid Responders*] (EA)
AAFAS .... Army Air Forces Aid Society [*World War II*]
AAFAWA ...... Aluminium Fabricators' Association of Western Australia
AAFB.......... Andrews Air Force Base [*Washington, DC*]
AAFB.......... Army Air Force Board
AAFB.......... Army Air Force Bulletin [*A publication*] (MCD)
AAFB.......... Army and Air Force Base
AAFB.......... Association of Arizona Food Banks (SRA)
AAFB.......... Atypical Acid-Fast Bacilli [*Microbiology*]
AAFB.......... Auxiliary Air Force Base
AAFBD........ Army and Air Force Exchange and Motion Picture Service Board of Directors [*DoD*]
AAFBF........ Anderson Air Force Base Flightline
AAFBI......... Ara Appaloosa and Foundation Breeders International (EA)
AAFBS........ Army Air Forces Bombardier School
AAFBTC....... Army Air Forces Basic Training Center
AAFBU........ Army Air Forces Base Unit
AAFC.......... Air Accounting and Finance Center [*Air Force*]
AAFC.......... Airborne Audio Frequency Coder
AAFC.......... All-America Football Conference [*Major league 1946-49, merged with NFL 1950*]
AAFC.......... Anglo-American Food Committee [*World War II*]
AAFC.......... Antiaircraft Fire Control
AAFC.......... Army Air Forces Center
AAFC.......... Association des Artisans du Film Canadien (AC)
AAFC.......... Association of Advertising Film Companies
AAFCC........ Australian Amateur Football Council
AAFCC........ Army Air Force Classification Center
AAFCE........ Allied Air Forces, Central Europe [*Later, AIRCENT*] [*NATO*] (MCD)
AAFCFTC...... Army Air Force Central Flying Training Command
A-AF CLIC.... Army-Air Force Center for Low-Intensity Conflict [*Langley Air Force Base, VA*] (INF)
AAFCO .... Association of American Feed Control Officials (EA)

AAFCO .... Association of American Fertilizer Control Officials [*Later, AAPFCO*] (EA)
AAFCPB .... Army Air Force Clemency and Parole Board
AAFCS .... Advanced Automatic Flight Control System (MCD)
AAFCS .... American Association of Family and Consumer Sciences (PAZ)
AAFCTTC ..... Army Air Force Central Technical Training Command
AAFCWF ...... Army and Air Force Civilian Welfare Fund
AAFD .... American Association of Franchisees and Dealers
AAFDBI .... American Association of Fitness Directors in Business and Industry (EA)
AAFE .... Advanced Applications Flight Equipment (MCD)
AAFE .... Advanced Applications Flight Experiments [*NASA*] (MCD)
AAFE .... American Association of Feed Exporters [*Defunct*] (EA)
AAFE .... American Association of Forms Executives (EA)
AAFEB .... Anaerobic Attached-Film Expanded-Bed [*For treating wastewater*]
AAFEC .... Army Air Forces Engineer Command
AAFEESS ...... Automated Armed Forces Examining and Entrance Station System (MCD)
AAFEFTC ...... Army Air Force Eastern Flying Training Command
AAFEMPS .... Army and Air Force Exchange and Motion Picture Service
AAFE RADSCAT... Advanced Applications Flight Experiment Radiometer-Scatterometer Sensor [*Aviation*] (PDAA)
AAFES .... Army and Air Force Exchange Service
AAFETTC ...... Army Air Force Eastern Technical Training Command
AAFFTD .... Army Air Force Flying Training Detachment
AAFG .... All American Food Group, Inc. [*NASDAQ symbol*] (SAG)
AAFG .... Amino Acid Formula with Glutamate [*Biochemistry*]
AAFGH .... Al-Anon Family Group Headquarters (EA)
AAFGL .... Auxiliary Air Force General List [*British military*] (DMA)
AAFGS .... Army Air Forces Gunnery School
AAFH .... Academy of American Franciscan History (EA)
AAFHA .... African American Family History Association (EA)
AAFHTWF ..... Amalgamated Association of Felt Hat Trimmers and Wool Formers [*A union*] [*British*] (DCTA)
AAFI .... Air-Assisted Fuel Injection [*Automotive engineering*]
AAFI .... Allied Air Forces in Italy [*World War II*]
AAFI .... Associated Accounting Firms International [*Washington, DC*] (EA)
AAFI .... Association des Anciens Fonctionnaires Internationaux [*Association of Former International Civil Servants - AFICS*] [*Geneva, Switzerland*] (EA)
AAFI .... Australians Against Further Immigration [*An association*]
AAFIF .... Automated Air Facilities Intelligence File [*Naval Oceanographic Office*]
AAFIF .... Automated Air Facility Information File [*Defense Mapping Agency*] (MCD)
AAFIP .... Australians Against Further Immigration Party [*An association*]
AAFIR .... Army Air Force Intelligence Report (MCD)
AAFIS .... Advanced Avionic Fault Isolation System [*Navy*] (MCD)
AAFIS .... Army Air Forces Intelligence School
AAFIS .... Army and Air Force Intelligence Staff [*British*]
AAFLI .... Asian American Free Labor Institute (EA)
AAFM .... American Association of Feed Microscopists (EA)
AAFM .... Army Air Force Manual [*A publication*] (MCD)
AAFM .... Army/Air Force Motion Picture Service
AAFMAA .... Army and Air Force Mutual Aid Association (EA)
AAFMC .... American Association of Foundations for Medical Care [*Later, AMCRA*] (EA)
AAFMC .... Army Air Forces Materiel Center
AAFMC .... Australian Association of Farm Management Consultants
AAFMG .... American Association of Foreign Medical Graduates [*Defunct*] (EA)
AAFMPS .... Army and Air Force Motion Picture Service
AAFMTO .... Army Air Force Headquarters, Mediterranean Theater of Operations
AAFNE .... Allied Air Forces, Northern Europe [*Later, AIRNORTH*] [*NATO*]
AAFNS .... Army Air Forces Navigation School
AAFNTIR ...... Army Air Force Nontechnical Intelligence Report (MCD)
AAFO .... American Association for Functional Orthodontics (EA)
AAFO .... American Association of Functional Orthodontists [*Later, American Association for Functional Orthodontics*] (EA)
AAFOIC .... Army Air Force Officer-in-Charge
AAFP .... American Academy of Family Physicians [*Formerly, AAGP*] (EA)
AAFP .... American Academy of Forensic Psychology (EA)
AAFP .... American Association of Feline Practitioners (EA)
AAFP .... American Association of Financial Professionals [*Defunct*] (EA)
AAFPC .... Assistant Air Force Postal Clerk (AFM)
AAFPE .... American Association for Paralegal Education (EA)
AAFPFS(P)... Army Air Forces Pre-Flight School (Pilot)
AAFPOA .... Army Air Forces, Pacific Ocean Areas
AAFPOA (ADMIN)... Army Air Forces, Pacific Ocean Areas (Administrative)
AAFPRS .... American Academy of Facial Plastic and Reconstructive Surgery (EA)
AAFPS .... Army Air Forces Pilot School
AAFPS .... Army and Air Force Postal Service
AAFR .... Australian Armed Forces Radio
AAFR .... Auxiliary Air Force Reserve [*British*]
AAFRA .... Association of African Airlines
AAFRC .... American Association of Fund-Raising Counsel (EA)
AAFRC .... American Association of Fund-Raising Counsel, Inc.
AAFRCTP ..... American Association of Fund-Raising Counsel Trust for Philanthropy (EA)
AAFRC Trust for Philanthropy... American Association of Fund-Raising Counsel, Inc., Trust for Philanthropy (NFD)
AAFS .... Academy of Ambulatory Foot Surgery (EA)
AAFS .... American Academy of Forensic Sciences (EA)
AAFS .... American Association of Foot Specialists [*Defunct*] (EA)
AAFS .... Amphibious Assault Fire System (CAAL)

AAFS .... Amphibious Assault Fuel System [*Navy*]
AAFS .... Association for the Advancement of Family Stability [*Later, AFCO*]
AAFS .... Atomic Absorption Flame Spectrometer
AAFSAT .... Army Air Forces School of Applied Tactics [*World War II*]
AAFSC .... Additional Air Force Specialty Code (AFM)
AAFSC .... Army Air Forces Service Command
AAFSD .... American Association of Food Stamp Directors (EA)
AAFSE .... Allied Air Forces, Southern Europe [*Later, AIRSOUTH*] [*NATO*]
AAFSETC ...... Army Air Forces Southeast Training Command [*World War II*]
AAFSQ .... Association des Auxiliaires Familiales et Sociales du Quebec (AC)
AAFSS .... Advanced Aerial Fire Support System [*Army*]
AAFSSO .... Advanced Aerial Fire Support System Office [*Army*] (MCD)
AAFSW .... Association of American Foreign Service Women (EA)
AAFSWPA ..... Allied Air Forces, South West Pacific Area [*NATO*] (ADA)
AAFT .... Alliance Against Fraud in Telemarketing (EA)
AAFT .... Army Air Force Translation (MCD)
AAFTAC .... Army Air Forces Tactical Center [*World War II*]
AAFTAD .... Army Air Forces Training Aids Division [*World War II*]
AAFTC .... Army Air Forces Training Command [*World War II*]
AAFTIR .... Army Air Force Technical Intelligence Report (MCD)
AAFTO .... Army Air Force Technical Order (MCD)
AAFTS .... Advanced Automatic Film Titles System (MCD)
AAFTS .... Army Air Forces Technical School [*World War II*]
AAFTS .... Automated Adaptive Flight Training System (MCD)
AAFTTC .... Army Air Forces Technical Training Command [*World War II*]
AAFU .... Augmented Assault Fire Units [*Army*] (AABC)
AAFVL .... Australian Association of Film and Video Libraries
AAFWB .... Army and Air Force Wage Board
AAFWFTC ..... Army Air Forces Western Flying Training Command [*World War II*]
AAFWSB .... Army Air Force Weather Service Bulletin (MCD)
AAFWSM ...... Army Air Force Weather Service Manual [*A publication*] (MCD)
AAFWTTC ..... Army Air Forces Western Technical Training Command [*World War II*]
AAG .... Acquisition Advisory Group [*Business term*]
AAG .... Aeromedical Airlift Group [*Air Force*]
AAG .... Aeronautical Information Service Automation Group [*ICAO*] (DA)
AAG .... Air Adjutant-General [*Military*]
AAG .... Air Atlantique [*British ICAO designator*] (FAAC)
AAG .... Aircraft Adapter Group (DWSG)
AAG .... Airports Authority Group [*Transport Canada*] (DA)
AAG .... Alberta Agriculture Library [*UTLAS symbol*]
AAG .... All-American Girl [*Lifestyle classification*] (ECON)
AAG .... American Annuity Group [*Formerly, STI Group*] [*NYSE symbol*] (SPSG)
AAG .... American Association for the Gifted
AAG .... Area Advisory Group [*British Overseas Trade Board*] (DS)
AAG .... Army Artillery Group (AABC)
AAG .... Assistant Adjutant-General [*Military*]
AAG .... Association of American Geographers (EA)
AAG .... Atlanta Gold Corp. [*Vancouver Stock Exchange symbol Toronto Stock Exchange symbol*]
AAGB .... Auxiliary Array Guard Band [*Military*]
AAGBA .... American Angora Goat Breeder's Association (EA)
AAGC .... American Association for Gifted Children (EA)
AAGCM .... Awaiting Action General Court-Martial
AAGE .... All Aspect Gunsight Evaluation (MCD)
AAGE .... Army Advisory Group on Energy
AAGF .... Australian Avocado Growers' Association
AAGFE .... American Association of Gravity Field Energy [*Defunct*] (EA)
AAGFO .... American Academy of Gold Foil Operators (EA)
AAGI .... American Academy of Gynecologic Laparoscopists (DMAA)
AAGI .... Anglo American Gold Investment Co. Ltd. [*NASDAQ symbol*] (NQ)
AAGIWA .... American Association of Grain Inspection and Weighing Agencies (EA)
AAGIY .... Anglo Am Gold Inv ADR [*NASDAQ symbol*] (TTSB)
AAGL .... American Association of Gynecological Laparoscopists (EA)
AAGL .... Antiaircraft Gun-Laying (DEN)
AAGM .... Antiaircraft Guided Missile (AAG)
AAGMC .... Antiaircraft Artillery and Guided Missile Center
AAGMC .... Antiaircraft Guided Missile Center (SAA)
AAGMS .... Antiaircraft Guided Missile School (SAA)
AAGMS .... Antiaircraft Guided Missile System (NG)
AAGO .... American Academy of Gnathologic Orthopedics (EA)
AAGO .... Associate of American Guild of Organists
AAGP .... Active Apparel Group [*NASDAQ symbol*] (TTSB)
AAGP .... Active Apparel Group, Inc. [*NASDAQ symbol*] (SAG)
AAGp .... Aeromedical Airlift Group [*Air Force*] (AFM)
AAGP .... American Academy of General Practice [*Later, AAFP*] (EA)
AAGP .... American Association for Geriatric Psychiatry (EA)
AAGPBL .... All America Girls Professional Baseball League [*In 1992 movie, "A League of Their Own"*] [*Also, GPBL*]
AAGQ .... Association des Arts Graphiques du Quebec, Inc. (AC)
AAGR .... Air-to-Air Gunnery Range [*Army*]
AAGR .... Average Annual Growth Rate (MHDI)
A Agri .... Associate in Agriculture
AAgric .... Associate in Agriculture (NADA)
AAGS .... Adult Adrenogenital Syndrome [*Medicine*] (DAVI)
AAGS .... All-America Gladiolus Selections
AAGS .... American Antique Graphics Society (EA)
AAGS .... American Association for Geodetic Surveying (EA)
AAGS .... Army Air-Ground System
AAGS .... Association of African Geological Surveys [*See also ASGA*] (EAIO)
AAGSSCS ...... Antique and Art Glass Salt Shaker Collectors Society (EA)
AAGTTS .... Advanced Aerial Gunnery TOW Target System
AAGUS .... American Association of Genito-Urinary Surgeons (EA)

AAGW .... Air-to-Air Guided Weapons (NATG)
AAH .... Academy of Accounting Historians (EA)
AAH .... Advanced Attack Helicopter [*Army*]
AAH .... Air Arc Heater
AAH .... Aloha Airlines [*ICAO designator*] (FAAC)
AAH .... Ambassador Apartments, Inc. [*NYSE symbol*] (SAG)
AAH .... American Academy of Homiletics [*Later, AH*]
AAH .... Amphipathic Alpha Helix [*Genetics*]
AAH .... Anti-Armour Helicopter [*Military*] (PDAA)
AAH .... Apache Attack Helicopter [*Military*] (RDA)
AAH .... Association for Applied Hypnosis (EAIO)
AAH .... Association of Ancient Historians (EA)
AAH .... Association of Art Historians [*British*] (EAIO)
AAH .... Automated Attitude Hold [*Manned maneuvering unit*] [*Aerospace*] (NASA)
AAH .... Prime Residential [*NYSE symbol*] (TTSB)
AAHA .... (Acetylalanyl)histidine Aluminum [*Biochemistry*]
AAHA .... American Academy of Health Administration (EA)
AAHA .... American Academy of Hospital Attorneys (EA)
AAHA .... American All-Hobbies Association (EA)
AAHA .... American Animal Hospital Association (EA)
AAHA .... American Association of Handwriting Analysts (EA)
AAHA .... American Association of Homes for the Aging (EA)
AAHA .... American Association of Hospital Accountants [*Later, HFMA*] (EA)
AAHA .... Awaiting Action [*of*] Higher Authority [*Army*]
AAHBE .... Anglo-American-Hellenic Bureau of Education [*Defunct*]
AAHC .... American Academy of Humor Columnists (DGA)
AAHC .... American Albino Horse Club [*Later, WWWCRW*] (EA)
AAHC .... American Association of Healthcare Consultants (EA)
AAHC .... American Association of Hospital Consultants [*Later, American Association of Healthcare Consultants*] (EA)
AAHC .... Arizona Association for Home Care (SRA)
AAHC .... Association of Academic Health Centers (EA)
AAHCC .... American Academy of Husband-Coached Childbirth (EA)
AAHCM .... Association for the Advancement of Health Care Managers [*Defunct*] (EA)
AAHCPA ...... American Association of Hispanic CPA's [*Certified Public Accountants*] [*Houston, TX*] (EA)
AAHCS .... African-American Historical and Cultural Society (EA)
AAHD .... American Academy of the History of Dentistry (EA)
AAHD .... American Association of Hospital Dentists [*Formerly, AAHDC*] (EA)
AAHDC .... American Association of Hospital Dental Chiefs [*Later, AAHD*]
AAHDS .... American Association of Health Data Systems [*Defunct*] (EA)
AAHE .... American Association for Higher Education (EA)
AAHE .... American Association of Housing Educators (EA)
AAHE .... Associate in Arts in Home Economics
AAHE .... Association for the Advancement of Health Education (EA)
AAHED .... Association of Appliance and Home Entertainment Distributors [*Defunct*] (EA)
AAHFNPTO ... American Academy of Head, Facial, and Neck Pain and TMJ [*Temporomandibular Joint*] Orthopedics (EA)
AAHGS .... Afro-American Historical and Genealogical Society (EA)
AAHH .... Air Arc Heater Housing
AAHI .... Association of American Historic Inns (EA)
AAHM .... American Academy of Homeopathic Medicine (EA)
AAHM .... American Association for the History of Medicine [*University of Rochester Medical Center*] (EA)
AAHM .... Association of Architectural Hardware Manufacturers (EA)
AAHMO .... Alabama Association of Health Maintenance Organizations (SRA)
AAHN .... American Association for the History of Nursing (EA)
AAHO .... Afro-Asian Housing Organization [*Cairo, Egypt*] (EAIO)
AAHP .... American Association for Hospital Planning [*Later, The Forum for Health Care Planning*] (EA)
AAHP .... American Association for Humanistic Psychology [*Later, AHP*]
AAHP .... American Association of Health Plans (DMAA)
AAHP .... American Association of Health Plans
AAHP .... American Association of Homeopathic Pharmacists (EA)
AAHP .... American Association of Hospital Podiatrists (EA)
AAHPA .... American Association of Hospital Purchasing Agents (EA)
AAHPEAR .... American Association for Health, Physical Education, and Recreation (AEBS)
AAHPER ...... American Academy for Health, Physical Education, and Recreation (DAVI)
AAHPER ...... American Alliance for Health, Physical Education, and Recreation [*Later, AAHPERD*]
AAHPER ...... American Association for Health, Physical Education, and Recreation (DMAA)
AAHPERD .... American Alliance for Health, Physical Education, Recreation, and Dance (EA)
AAHPhA ...... American Animal Health Pharmaceutical Association [*Defunct*]
AAHP-O ...... Association of Allied Health Professionals Ontario [*Association des Professionnels Unis de la Sante, Ontario*] (AC)
AAHQ .... Advanced Allied Headquarters [*World War II*]
AAHQ .... Allied Air Headquarters [*Obsolete*]
AAHS .... Abigail Adams Historical Society (EA)
AA(HS) .... Airman Apprentice (High School)
AAHS .... American Association for Hand Surgery (EA)
AAHS .... American Aviation Historical Society (EA)
AAHS .... Australian Affiliation of Herpetological Societies
AAHS .... Children's Broadcasting [*NASDAQ symbol*] (TTSB)
AAHS .... Childrens Broadcasting Corp. [*NASDAQ symbol*] (SAG)
AAHSA .... American Association of Homes and Services for the Aging
AAHSLD .... Association of Academic Health Sciences Library Directors (EA)
AAHSLM ...... American Association of Hides, Skins, and Leather Merchants [*Later, USHSLA*]

AAHSWAA ... Arpad Academy of Hungarian Scientists, Writers, and Artists Abroad (EA)
AAHT .... Antiarmor Helicopter Troop (MCD)
AAI............. Accordion for All International [*An association*] (EAIO)
AAI............. Accountants Association of Iowa (SRA)
AAI............. Additional Authorization Item [*Military*] (INF)
AAI............. Adjusted Agreement Index (EDAC)
AAI............. Adolescent Abuse Inventory (EDAC)
AAI............. Adolescent Alienation Index [*Personality development test*] [*Psychology*]
AAI............. African-American Institute (EA)
AAI............. Age-Appropriately Immunized [*Children*]
AAI............. Agence Africaine d'Information [*African Information Agency*] [*Zaire*]
AAI............. Agribusiness Association of Iowa (SRA)
AAI............. Agricultural Ammonia Institute [*Later, The Fertilizer Institute*] (EA)
AAI............. Air Aurora, Inc. [*ICAO designator*] (FAAC)
AAI............. Airborne Alert Indoctrination (AFM)
AAI............. Aircraft Accident Investigation (DNAB)
AAI............. Aircraft Armaments, Inc. (DNAB)
AAI............. Air-to-Air Identification [*Air Force*]
AAI............. Air-to-Air Intercept (MCD)
AAI............. Air-to-Air Interrogation (MCD)
AAI............. Alfred Adler Institute (EA)
AAI............. All-Attitude Indicator
AAI............. Alliance of American Insurers [*Schaumburg, IL*] (EA)
AAI............. Allied Armies in Italy [*Obsolete*]
AAI............. Alternatives to Abortion International [*Later, AAI/WHEF*] (EA)
AAI............. Amateur Astronomers, Inc. (EA)
AAI............. Ambon [*Indonesia*] [*Seismograph station code, US Geological Survey*]
AAI............. American Association of Immunologists (EA)
AAI............. American Association of Inventors [*Defunct*] (EA)
AAI............. American Audio Institute
AAI............. Angle-of-Approach Indicator [*Aviation*] (AFM)
AAI............. Angle-of-Attack Indicator [*Military*]
AAI............. Ankle Arm Index
AAI............. Apartment Association of Indiana (SRA)
AAI............. Arab American Institute (EA)
AAI............. Architectural Association of Ireland (SLS)
AAI............. Arizona Association of Industries (SRA)
AAI............. Arm-Ankle Indices [*Cardiology*] (DAVI)
AAI............. Army Adaptation Inventory
AAI............. Army Analysis of Intelligence
AAI............. Arrival Aircraft Interval [*FAA*] (TAG)
AAI............. Associate of the Chartered Auctioneers' and Estate Agents' Institute [*British*]
AAI............. Association Actuarielle Internationale [*International Actuarial Association - IAA*] [*Brussels, Belgium*] (EAIO)
AAI............. Association Adjustment Inventory [*Psychology*]
AAI............. Association of Advertisers in Ireland (EAIO)
AAI............. Association of Art Institutions [*British*]
AAI............. Association of Australian Investigators
AAI............. Atlantic Art Institute
AAI............. Atrial Inhibited Pacemaker [*Cardiology*] (DMAA)
AAI............. Australian Air International
AAI............. Authorized Active Inventory (MCD)
AAI............. Auto Alliance International [*Joint manufacturing venture of Ford Motor Co. and Mazda*]
AAI............. AUTODIN/AUTOVON Interface (CET)
AAI............. Aviation Association of Indiana (SRA)
AAI............. Azimuth Angle Increment
AAIA.......... Acquired Artery Immune Augmentation [*Cardiology*] (DAVI)
AAIA.......... Airport and Airway Improvement Act [*OST*] (TAG)
AAIA.......... All About Issues American [*An association*] (EA)
AAIA.......... Allergy/Asthma Information Association
AAIA.......... America-Australia Interaction Association (EA)
AAIA.......... American Association for International Aging (EA)
AAIA.......... Army Area Analysis Intelligence Agency (SAA)
AAIA.......... Associate of the Association of International Accountants [*British*]
AAIA.......... Association of Asian Indians in America (EA)
AAIA.......... Association on American Indian Affairs (EA)
AAIAL .... American Academy and Institute of Arts and Letters (EA)
AAIAN .... Association for the Advancement of Instruction about Alcohol and Narcotics [*Defunct*]
AAIANSW .... Association of American Indian and Alaska Native Social Workers [*Later, NISWA*] (EA)
AAIB.......... Aircraft Accident Investigation Board
AAIB.......... Albaraka Algeria Islamic Bank (EY)
AAIB.......... American Association for the Improvement of Boxing (EA)
AAIB.......... American Association of Instructors of the Blind [*Later, AEVH*] (EA)
AAIB.......... Australian Association of Independent Businesses Ltd.
AAIB(Snr) .... Senior Associate of the Australian Institute of Bankers
AAIC.......... Allied Air Intelligence Center
AAIC.......... American Amateur Inventors Club (EA)
AAIC.......... Asian Association of Insurance Commissioners (EAIO)
AAICD .... American Association of Imported Car Dealers [*Defunct*] (EA)
AAICJ.......... American Association for the International Commission of Jurists (EA)
AAICP .... Air-to-Air Identification Control Panel [*Air Force*] (MCD)
AAICPC .... Association of Administrators of the Interstate Compact on the Placement of Children (EA)
AAICS .... Automatic Aircraft Intercept Control System
AAICU .... Alabama Association of Independent Colleges and Universities (SRA)
AAICV .... Amphibious, Armored Infantry Combat Vehicle (MCD)

AAID .... Agence Africaine d'Information et de Documentation [*African Information and Documentation Agency*]
AAID .... American Academy of Implant Dentistry (EA)
AAID .... American Association of Industrial Dentists [*Defunct*] (EA)
AAID .... Angular Accelerometer Input Device (MCD)
AAID .... Arithmetic Array Identification
AAID .... Asian Americans Information Directory [*A publication*]
AAIDS .... Adult Acquired Immunodeficiency Syndrome [*Medicine*] (DAVI)
AAIE .... American Association of Industrial Editors [*Later, IABC*] (EA)
AAIE .... American Association of Industrial Engineers
AAIE .... Association for the Advancement of International Education (EA)
AAIE .... Association of Applied Insect Ecologists (EA)
AAIEE.......... Associate of the American Institute of Electrical Engineers
AAIFF.......... Air-to-Air Identification Friend or Foe [*Air Force*] (MCD)
AAIFScT....... Associate of the Australian Institute of Food Science and Technology
AAIH .... American Academy of Industrial Hygiene (EA)
AAII .... American Association of Individual Investors [*Chicago, IL*] (EA)
AAII .... Applied Analytical Industries, Inc. [*NASDAQ symbol*] (SAG)
AAII .... Association for the Advancement of Invention and Innovation [*Patent lobby*] [*Defunct*]
AAIL .... Airborne Argon Ion LASER
AAIM .... Airdrie Municipal Library, Alberta [*Library symbol National Library of Canada*] (NLC)
AAIM .... Alliance Against Intoxicated Motorists [*An association*]
AAIM .... American Association of Industrial Management [*Springfield, MA*] (EA)
AAIMC .... All-American Indian Motorcycle Club (EA)
AAIMCo....... American Association of Insurance Management Consultants [*Houston, TX*] (EA)
AAIMME....... Associate of the American Institute of Mining and Metallurgical Engineers
AAIMS .... [*An*] Analytical Information Management System (HGAA)
AAIN .... American Association of Industrial Nurses [*Later, AAOHN*] (EA)
AAIND......... American Association of Independent News Distributors (EA)
AAIP .... Academic Administration Internship Program [*Later, AFP*] (EA)
AAIP .... Advanced Avionics Integration Program (MCD)
AAIP .... American Academy of Implant Prosthodontics (EA)
AAIP .... American Association of Independent Publishers (NTCM)
AAIP .... Associate of the American Institute of Physics
AAIP .... Association for Armenian Information Professionals (EA)
AAIP .... Association of American Indian Physicians (EA)
AAIPS .... Automated Air Information Production System (MCD)
AAIR .... Advanced Atmospheric Sounder and Imaging Radiometer [*NASA*] (NASA)
AAIR .... Airways Corp. [*NASDAQ symbol*] (SAG)
AAIRC .... Australian Amateur Ice Racing Council
A AIR SC ..... Army Air Support Control [*British and Canadian*] [*World War II*]
AAIS............ Administrative Analysis, Information, and Statistics [*Red Cross*]
AAIS............ Aircraft Accident Investigation System
AAIS............ American Association for Italian Studies (BARN)
AAIS............ American Association of Insurance Services [*Bensenville, IL*] (EA)
AAIS............ Antiaircraft Artillery Information [*or Intelligence*] Service [*Army*]
AAIS............ Army Acquisition Information System (AAGC)
AAIS............ Associate Administrator for Information Systems [*Social and Rehabilitation Service, HEW*]
AAIS............ Association of American Library Schools (BARN)
AAISW .... American Association of Industrial Social Workers (EA)
AAISW .... Association of American Indian Social Workers [*Later, NISWA*] (EA)
AAIT .... American Association of Inhalation Therapists [*Later, AART*] (EA)
AAITO .... Association of African Industrial Technology Organizations
AAITVL........ Arrival Aircraft Interval [*Aviation*] (FAAC)
AAIV .... American Association of Industrial Veterinarians (EA)
AAIVT.......... American Association of IV Therapy (EA)
AAIW .... Antarctic Intermediate Water [*Marine science*] (OSRA)
AAI/WHEF ... Alternatives to Abortion International/Women's Health and Education Foundation
AAIX............ Aeroamerica, Inc. [*Air carrier designation symbol*]
AAJ .... Air Alma, Inc. [*Canada ICAO designator*] (FAAC)
AAJ .... Alaska Administrative Journal [*A publication*] (AAGC)
AAJ .... American Association of Judges (EA)
AAJ .... Arab Airways (Jerusalem) Ltd.
AAJ .... Association of American Jurists (EA)
AAJ .... Augmented Air Jet
AAJ .... Binghamton, NY [*Location identifier FAA*] (FAAL)
AAJA .... Afro-Asian Journalists' Association (NATG)
AAJA .... Asian American Journalists Association (EA)
AAJAC......... Automatic Antijam Circuit (CET)
AAJC........... American Association of Junior Colleges [*Later, AACJC*] (EA)
AAJCS......... Anglo-American Joint Chiefs of Staff
AAJE .... American Academy of Judicial Education (DLA)
AAJE .... American Association for Jewish Education [*Later, JESNA*] (EA)
AAJE .... Anglo-American Judicial Exchange (ILCA)
AAJR........... American Academy for Jewish Research (EA)
AAJS............ American Association of Jesuit Scientists [*Defunct*] (EA)
AAJS............ Associate in Arts in Judaic Studies (BJA)
AAJSA......... American Association of Journalism School Administrators (EA)
AAJWA........ Asian Agricultural Journalists and Writers Association [*Jakarta, Indonesia*] (EAIO)
AAK............. Alaska Island Air, Inc. [*ICAO designator*] (FAAC)
AAK............. Allo-Activated Killer [*Medicine*] (DMAA)
AAK............. Aranuka [*Kiribati*] [*Airport symbol*] (OAG)
AAK............. Asiaamerica Holdings [*Vancouver Stock Exchange symbol*]
AAKF .... American Amateur Karate Federation (EA)
AAKP .... American Association of Kidney Patients (EA)
AAL............. Aalborg [*Denmark*] [*Airport symbol*] (OAG)

Aal .... Aalenian [*Geology*]
AAL............ Above Aerodrome Level
AAL............ Absolute Assembly Language [*Programming language*] (BUR)
AAL............ Academy of Art and Literature [*British*]
AAL............ Account Access Layer [*Computer science*]
AAL............ Acoustical Absorption Loss
AAL............ Additional Authorization List [*Army*] (AABC)
AAL............ Adelaide Airways Ltd. [*Australia*]
AAL............ Aeronautica and Air Label Collectors Club (EA)
AAL............ Aid Association for Lutherans (EA)
AAL............ Aircraft Approach Light (MSA)
AAL............ Aircraft Approach Limitation
AAL............ Aircraft Armament Laboratory [*Naval Air Development Center*]
AAL............ Aircraft Assignment Letter
AAL............ Alexander & Alexander Services, Inc. [*NYSE symbol*] (SPSG)
AAL............ Alexander & Alex Sv [*NYSE symbol*] (TTSB)
AAL............ Alliance Public Library, Alberta [*Library symbol National Library of Canada*] (NLC)
AAL............ American Airlines, Inc. [*Air carrier designation symbol*] (MCD)
AAL............ Ames Aeronautical Laboratory [*Air Force*]
AAL............ Angle of Attack Limiter (MCD)
AAL............ Anterior Axillary Line
AAL............ Arctic Aeromedical Laboratory [*Later, AMRL*] [*Fort Wainwright, AK*] [*Air Force*] (KSC)
AAL............ Arctic Approach Limitation (AFM)
AAL............ Artic Aerospace Laboratory [*Air Force*]
AAL............ Association of Advertising Lawyers [*Defunct*] (EA)
AAL............ Association of Architectural Librarians (EA)
AAL............ Association of Assistant Librarians
AAL............ Australasian Association for Logic
AAL............ Authorized Allowance List (MCD)
AAL............ Aviation Armament Laboratory [*Later, Naval Air Development Center*] [*Navy*]
AALA .... Alberta Association of Landscape Architects (AC)
AALA .... Alberta Association of Legal Assistants (AC)
AALA .... Ameralia, Inc. [*NASDAQ symbol*] (SAG)
AALA .... Ameralia Inc. [*NASDAQ symbol*] (TTSB)
AALA .... American Agricultural Law Association (EA)
AALA .... American Association for Laboratory Accreditation (EA)
AALA .... American Auto Laundry Association [*Later, ICA*]
AALA .... American Automobile Labeling Act of 1992
AALA .... American Automotive Leasing Association (EA)
AALA .... Asian American Librarians Association [*Defunct*] (EA)
AALA .... Associate in Arts in Liberal Arts
AALAE......... African Association for Literacy and Adult Education (EA)
AALAPSO .... Afro-Asian Latin American People's Solidarity Organization
AALAS .... American Association for Laboratory Animal Science (EA)
AALASO ...... Afro-Asian Latin-American Students' Organization (NATG)
AALB.......... Australian Administrative Law Bulletin [*A publication*]
AAL Bull ..... Australian Administrative Law Bulletin [*A publication*]
AALC.......... Advanced Airborne Launch Center (MCD)
AALC.......... African-American Labor Center (EA)
AALC.......... Afro-Asian Lawyers' Conference (NATG)
AALC.......... Amphibious Assault Landing Craft [*Navy symbol*]
AALC.......... Amplified Automatic Level Control [*Air Force*]
AALC.......... Asian American Librarians Caucus (EA)
AALC.......... Leigh Creek [*Australia ICAO location identifier*] (ICLI)
AALCC........ Aeronautica and Air Label Collectors Club (EA)
AALCI......... Ateitis Association of Lithuanian Catholic Intellectuals (EA)
A Alciat....... Andreas Alciatus [*Deceased, 1550*] [*Authority cited in pre-1607 legal work*] (DSA)
AALDEF........ Asian American Legal Defense and Education Fund (EA)
AALE.......... Associate in Arts in Law Enforcement
AALF.......... Anglican Accredited Layworkers' Federation [*British*]
AALI........... Alix Public Library, Alberta [*Library symbol National Library of Canada*] (NLC)
AALIM......... American Academy of Legal and Industrial Medicine (EA)
AALIPS .... Arthur Adaptation of the Leiter International Performance Scale [*Psychology*]
AALISA .... African-American Library and Information Science Association
AALL........... American Association for Labor Legislation (DMAA)
AALL........... American Association for Labor Legislation (DMAA)
AALL........... American Association of Law Libraries (EA)
AALM.......... Advanced Air-Launched Missile (MCD)
AALM.......... Advanced Air-Launched Motor (MCD)
AALMA........ American Association of Laban Movement Analysts (EA)
AALMG .... Antiaircraft Light Machine Gun
AALNSWBG... Australian Air League New South Wales Boys Group
AALO .... Antiaircraft Liaison Officer (SAA)
AALP........... American Association of Limited Partners (EA)
AALP........... Automated Airload Planning System
AALPA .... Associate of the Incorporated Society of Auctioneers and Landed Property Agents [*British*]
AALPP .... American Association for Legal and Political Philosophy (EA)
AALPS .... Automated Air Load Planning System [*Developed for the Army by SRI International*]
AALR .... Advanced Logic Research [*NASDAQ symbol*] (SAG)
AALR .... American Association for Leisure and Recreation (EA)
AALS........... Acoustic Artillery Location System (DNAB)
AALS........... Active Army Locator System (AABC)
AALS........... American Association of Language Specialists (BARN)
AALS........... Association for Arid Lands Studies (EA)
AALS........... Association of American Law Schools (EA)
AALT........... Alberta Association of Library Technicians (AC)
AALT........... American Association of Library Trustees [*Later, ALTA*]

AALT............	Automatic Azimuth Laying Theodolite (KSC)
AALU	Arizona Association of Life Underwriters (SRA)
AALU	Association for Advanced Life Underwriting [*Washington, DC*] (EA)
AaLU...........	Universidad Nacional de La Plata, La Plata, Argentina [*Library symbol Library of Congress*]
AaLU...........	Universidad Nacional de La Plata, La Plata, Argentina [*Library symbol Library of Congress*] (LCLS)
AALUE	Asymptotically Admissible Linear Unbiased Estimator [*Statistics*]
AALVG	Australian Air League Victorian Group
AALW	Assembled Air-Launched Weapon
AAM............	Aames Financial [*NYSE symbol*] (TTSB)
AAM............	Aames Financial Corp. [*NYSE symbol*] (SAG)
AAM............	Accident Anatomy Method [*Engineering*]
AAM............	Acme Municipal Library, Alberta [*Library symbol National Library of Canada*] (NLC)
AAM............	Acoustical Analysis Memo [*Navy*] (MCD)
AAM............	Acting Air-Marshal [*British*]
AAM............	Acupuncture Association of Minnesota (SRA)
AAM............	Advisory Agricultural Meteorologist (NOAA)
AAM............	Afro-American Museum of Detroit (EA)
AAM............	Agricultural Advisory Meteorologist (NOAA)
AAM............	Airborne Activity Monitor [*Nuclear energy*] (NRCH)
AAM............	Aircraft Availability Model (MCD)
AAM............	Airline Administrative Message (DA)
AAM............	Air-to-Air Missile [*Army*]
AAM............	Alberta Association of Midwives (AC)
AAM............	American Abolitionist Movement (EA)
AAM............	American Academy of Mechanics (EA)
AAM............	American Academy of Microbiology (EA)
AAM............	American Agriculture Movement (EA)
AAM............	American Association of Museums (EA)
AAM............	Angeborener Ausolsender Mechanismus [*Innate Release Mechanism*] [*Psychology*]
AAM............	Anglican Association of Musicians (EA)
AAM............	Anglo American Resources [*Vancouver Stock Exchange symbol*]
AAM............	Ann Arbor [*Michigan*] [*Seismograph station code, US Geological Survey*] (SEIS)
AAM............	Annual Aircraft Movements
AAM............	Antiaircraft Missile (KSC)
AAM............	Anti-Antimissile Missile
AAM............	Anti-Apartheid Movement [*South Africa*] [*Political party*] (EA)
AAM............	Army Achievement Medal (INF)
AAM............	Army Aircraft Maintenance (AABC)
AAM............	Asian and African American Materials [*Association for Library Collections and Technical Services*]
AAM............	Assembly and Maintenance (IAA)
AA/M...........	Associate Administrator for Management [*Social and Rehabilitation Service, HEW*]
AAM............	Association des Amidonneries de Mais de la CEE [*Association of the Maize Starch Industries of the European Economic Community*]
AAM............	Association of Amateur Magicians [*Defunct*] (EA)
AAM............	Association of Anglican Musicians (EA)
AAM............	Association of Assistant Mistresses in Secondary Schools [*British*] (BI)
AAM............	Atmospheric Angular Momentum [*Geophysics*]
AAM............	Auburn University at Montgomery, Montgomery, AL [*OCLC symbol*] (OCLC)
AAM............	Audio Alarm Module [*Automotive engineering*]
AAM............	Australian Anti-Apartheid Movement [*An association*]
AAM............	Auxiliary Aiming Mark [*Target*] (IAA)
AAM............	Aviation Management Corp. [*ICAO designator*] (FAAC)
AAM............	AWS Ammunition Magazine (MCD)
AAM............	Fargo, ND [*Location identifier FAA*] (FAAL)
AAMA...........	African American Museums Association (EA)
AAMA...........	American Academy of Medical Administrators (EA)
AAMA...........	American Agricultural Marketing Association (EA)
AAMA...........	American Amusement Machine Association (EA)
AAMA...........	American Apparel Manufacturers Association (EA)
AAMA...........	American Architectural Manufacturers Association (EA)
AAMA...........	American Association of Medical Assistants (EA)
AAMA...........	American Automobile Manufacturers Association
AAMA...........	American Automobile Manufacturers Association [*BTS*] (TAG)
AAMA...........	American Award Manufacturers Association [*Later, TDMA*] (EA)
AAMA...........	Arab American Medical Association (EA)
AAMA...........	Architectural Aluminum Manufacturers Association (MHDB)
AAMA...........	Asian American Manufacturers Association (EA)
AAMA...........	Australian Automotive Manufacturers' Association
AAMA...........	Automotive Accessories Manufacturers of America (MHDB)
AAMAA	Army Aviation Mission Area Analysis
AAMAP	Army Automation Master Plan
AAMAREF ...	American Academy of Medical Administrators Research and Educational Foundation (EA)
AAMB...........	Arizona Association of Mortgage Brokers (SRA)
AAMB...........	Army Automation Memorandum Budget
AAMBP	Association of American Medical Book Publishers [*Later, AMPA*] (EA)
AAMC...........	American Association of Marriage Counselors [*Later, AAMFT*] (EA)
AAMC...........	American Association of Medical Clinics [*Later, AGPA*] (EA)
AAMC...........	American Association of Medical Colleges (DAVI)
AAMC...........	American Association of Medico-Legal Consultants (EA)
AAMC...........	Army Artillery and Missile Center [*Fort Sill, OK*] (MCD)
AAMC...........	Army Aviation Materiel Command
AAMC...........	Association for Advancement of Maternity Care [*British*] (DBA)
AAMC...........	Association of American Medical Colleges (EA)
AAMCA	Army Advanced Materiel Concepts Agency (PDAA)

AAMCH	American Association for Maternal and Child Health [*Defunct*] (EA)
AAMCN	American Association of Managed Care Nurses
AAMD	Age-Associated Memory Disorder [*Medicine*] (CPH)
AAMD	American Academy of Medical Directors [*American College of Physician Exec utives*] [*Absorbed by*] (EA)
AAMD	American Association on Mental Deficiency [*Later, AAMR*] (EA)
AAMD	Association of Art Museum Directors (EA)
AAMDS	Advanced Alternative Minuteman Defense Study [*Military*]
AAME	Acetylarginine Methyl Ester [*Biochemistry*] (AAMN)
AAME	Alberta Association for Multicultural Education [*Association de l'Education Multiculturelle de l'Alberta*] (AC)
AAME	American Antarctic Mountaineering Expedition
AAME	American Association of Microprocessor Engineers
AAME	Association for the Advancement of Medical Education [*Defunct*] (EA)
AAME	Atlantic American [*NASDAQ symbol*] (TTSB)
AAME	Atlantic American Corp. [*NASDAQ symbol*] (NQ)
Aames	Aames Financial Corp. [*Associated Press*] (SAG)
AAMES	American Association for Middle East Studies [*Defunct*] (EA)
AAMESBIC ...	American Association of Minority Enterprise Small Business Investment Companies [*Washington, DC*] (EA)
AAMF	Afro-American Music Foundation (EA)
AAMF	American Association of Music Festivals [*Defunct*]
AAMFC........	American Association of Marriage and Family Counselors [*Later, AAMFT*]
AAMFT	Alberta Association for Marriage & Family Therapy (AC)
AAMFT	American Association for Marriage and Family Therapy (EA)
AAMG	Antiaircraft Machine Gun [*Army*]
AAMGA	American Association of Managing General Agents [*Washington, DC*] (EA)
AAMGE	Air-to-Air Missile Guidance Element
AAMH	American Academy of Medical Hypnoanalysts (EA)
AAMH	Australian Association of Mental Health
AAMHC	Atlantic Alliance for Maritime Heritage Conservation (EA)
AAMHPC	American Association of Mental Health Professionals in Corrections (EA)
AAMI	Age-Associated Memory Impairment [*Medicine*]
AAMI	All-Aspect Maneuvering Index (MCD)
AAMI	American Association of Machinery Importers [*Defunct*]
AAMI	American Association of Microcomputer Investors [*Defunct*] (EA)
AAMI	Amisk Public Library, Alberta [*Library symbol National Library of Canada*] (NLC)
AAMI	Association for the Advancement of Medical Instrumentation (EA)
AAMI	Association of Allergists for Mycological Investigations [*Defunct*] (EA)
AAMI	Association of Assistant Mistresses, Inc. [*British*]
AAM/ICOM ...	International Council of Museums Committee of the American Association of Museums (EA)
AAMID	Accomplishment of Assigned Mission Impeded by Deadline [*Army*] (AABC)
AAMIH	American Association for Maternal and Infant Health [*Later, AAMCH*] (EA)
AAMIH	Association des Amis du Musee International des Hussards [*Association of Friends of the International Museum of the Hussars*] [*France*] (EAIO)
AAMIM	Australian Association of Musical Instrument Makers
AAML...........	American Academy of Matrimonial Lawyers (EA)
AAML...........	Arctic Aeromedical Laboratory [*Later, AMRL*] [*Air Force*]
AAML...........	Army Aviation Materiel Laboratory (MCD)
AAMLA	American Academy of Medical-Legal Analysis (EA)
AAMLS........	Association of Accredited Medical Laboratory Schools [*Later, NAHCS*] (EA)
AAMM	AN [*Army-Navy*] and MS Manual [*Manufacturing Status*] (AAG)
AAMM	Anti-Antimissile Missile (IAA)
AAMMA	Australian Agricultural Machinery Manufacturers' Association
AAMMC	American Association of Medical Milk Commissioners (EA)
AAMMP	Active Army Military Manpower Program
AAMN	American Assembly for Men in Nursing (EA)
AAMO	Asian Association of Management Organisations [*Kuala Lumpur, Malaysia*]
AAMO	Association of Area Medical Officers [*British*]
AAMOA	Afro-American Music Opportunities Association (EA)
AAMP	Advanced Architecture Microprocessor (MCD)
AAMP	American Academy of Maxillofacial Prosthetics (EA)
AAMP	American Academy of Medical Preventics [*Later, ACAM*] (EA)
AAMP	American Association of Meat Processors (EA)
AAMP	Army Aviation Modernization Plan (MCD)
AAMPS	Arizona Association of Medical Products Suppliers (SRA)
AAMR	American Academy on Mental Retardation (EA)
AAMR	American Association on Mental Retardation (EA)
AAMRA	American Association of Medical Record Administrators [*Formerly, American Association of Medical Record Librarians*] [*Also, AMRA*] (DAVI)
AAMRDL	Army Air Mobility Research and Development Laboratories [*Army*]
AAMREP	Air-to-Air Missile Weapons System Flight Report (NG)
AAMRH	International Association of Agricultural Medicine and Rural Health (EAIO)
AAMRL	American Association of Medical Record Librarians [*Later, AMRA*] (EA)
AAMRR	Association of American Motorcycle Road Racers [*Defunct*] (EA)
AAMRS	Automated Ambulatory Medical Record System [*Medicine*] (DMAA)
AAMRT	Alberta Association of Medical Radiation Technologists (AC)
AAMS...........	Acute Aseptic Meningitis Syndrome [*Medicine*] (DMAA)
AAMS...........	Advanced Antitank Missile System (MCD)
AAMS...........	Airborne Auxiliary Memory System
AAMS...........	Alberta Arbitration & Mediation Society (AC)

AAMS......... American Academy of Medicine and Science (EA)
AAMS......... American Accordion Musicological Society (EA)
AAMS......... American Air Mail Society (EA)
AAMS......... American Association of Meta-Science (EA)
AAMS......... Arab-American Media Society (EA)
AAMS......... Army Aircraft Maintenance Shop (AABC)
AAMS......... Army Armor School (AAG)
AAMS......... Army Artillery and Missile School
AAMS......... Associate Member of the Association of Medical Secretaries, Practice Administrators, and Receptionists [British] (DBQ)
AAMS......... Attack Air Mobility System [Army]
AAMS......... Automated Azimuth Measuring System (MCD)
AAMSA....... Army Aviation Maintenance Support Activity
AA/MSB&COD... Associate Administrator for Minority Small Business and Capital Ownership Development (AAGC)
AAMSBN...... Antiaircraft Missile Battalion [Marine Corps]
AAMSE........ American Association of Medical Society Executives (EA)
AA/MSF....... Associate Administrator for Manned Space Flight [NASA] (KSC)
AAMSI .... American Association for Medical Systems and Informatics [Later, AMIA] (EA)
AAMSL........ American Association of Media Specialists and Librarians [Defunct] (EA)
AAMSU........ Army Air Movement Support Unit (MCD)
AAMSW .... American Association of Medical Social Workers [Later, National Association of Social Workers] (AEBS)
AAMT.......... American Association for Medical Transcription (EA)
AAMT.......... American Association for Music Therapy (EA)
AAMTAP ..... Army Aircraft Mobile Technical Assistance Program
AAMU .... Army Advanced Marksmanship Unit
AAMUC .... Association of American Military Uniform Collectors (EA)
AAMus........ Associate in Arts in Music
AAMV.......... American Association for Museum Volunteers (EA)
AAMVA........ American Association of Motor Vehicle Administrators (EA)
AAMW .... Amalgamated Association of Machine Workers [A union] [British]
AAMW .... Association of Advertising Men and Women [Later, Advertising and Marketing Association] (EA)
AAMX.......... Acetoacet-m-xylidide [Organic chemistry]
AAMX.......... Air America, Inc. [Air carrier designation symbol]
AAMZ.......... Association des Amis de Maurice Zundel [Paris, France] (EAIO)
AAN .... Advance Alteration Notice (MSA)
AAN .... Aeronautical Army and Navy (AAG)
AAN .... Air Ambulance Network [MTMC] (TAG)
AAN .... Aliphatic Ammonium Nitrate (MCD)
AAN .... Alpha-Amino Nitrogen (MAE)
AAN .... American Academy of Neurology (EA)
AAN .... American Academy of Nursing (EA)
AAN .... American Academy of Nutrition (EA)
AAN .... American Association of Neuropathologists (DAVI)
AAN .... American Association of Nurserymen (EA)
AAN .... Aminoacetonitrile [Organic chemistry]
AAN .... Amino Acid Nitrogen [Analytical biochemistry]
AAN .... Analgesic Abuse Nephropathy [Medicine] (DAVI)
AAN .... Analgesic-Associated Nephropathy [Medicine]
AAN .... Arnada Resources [Vancouver Stock Exchange symbol]
AAN .... Assemblee de l'Atlantique Nord [North Atlantic Assembly] [Brussels, Belgium] (EAIO)
AAN .... Assignment Action Number (AFM)
AAN .... Associate in Arts in Nursing
AAN .... Association of Alternative Newsweeklies
AAN .... Attending's Admission Notes [Medicine] (DMAA)
AAN .... Australian Association of Nematologists
AAN .... Automotive Aftermarket News [A publication]
AAN .... Oasis International Airlines [Spain ICAO designator] (FAAC)
AaNA .... Alaska Nurses Association (SRA)
AANA .... American Anorexia Nervosa Association [Later, AABA] (EA)
AANA .... American Association of Nurse Anesthetists (EA)
AANA .... [The] American Association of Nurse Attorneys (EA)
AANA .... American Association of Nursing Assistants (EA)
AANA .... Arthroscopy Association of North America (EA)
AANB .... Abigail Adams National Bancorp, Inc. [NASDAQ symbol] (SAG)
AANB .... Architects Association of New Brunswick [Association des Architectes du Nouveau-Brunswick] (AC)
AANC .... Aging Aircraft Nondestructive Inspection Development and Demonstration Center [Federal Aviation Administration]
AANC .... American Association of Nutritional Consultants (EA)
AANCP .... Advanced Airborne National Command Post [Air Force] (PDAA)
A & 0X3....... Awake and Oriented Times Three [Neurology and psychiatry] (DAVI)
A & A.......... Additions and Amendments (ADA)
A & A.......... Advertise and Award (KSC)
A & A.......... Aid and Attendance (MAE)
A & A.......... Amendments and Additions (DLA)
A & A.......... American and Australian Line [Shipping] (ROG)
A and A ...... Ancient and Accepted [Freemasonry]
A & A.......... Arbeitsschutz und Arbeitsmedizin [Industrial Safety and Medicine] [German]
A & A.......... Arcade & Attica Railroad Corp. (IIA)
A & A.......... Awake and Aware [Neurology] (DAVI)
A & A Corp... Angell and Ames on Corporations [A publication] (DLA)
A & AEE...... Aircraft and Armament Experimental Establishment [British]
A & AFA ...... Army and Air Force Act [British military] (DMA)
A & AFA ...... Asthma and Allergy Foundation of America (EA)
A & A Fd ..... A & A Foods Ltd. [Associated Press] (SAG)
A & AFES..... Army and Air Force Exchange Service
A & AP .... Arms & Armour Press [Publisher] [British]
A and AR ..... Ancient and Accepted Rite [Freemasonry]

A & ASR...... Ancient and Accepted Scottish Rite [Freemasonry] (ROG)
A & B.......... Antofagasta & Bolivia Railroad Co. (MHDB)
A & B.......... Assault and Battery
A & BRC...... Antofagasta and Bolivia Railway Co. (MHDB)
A & C.......... Abatement and Control [Environmental Protection Agency] (GFGA)
A & C.......... Addenda and Corrigenda (ADA)
A & C.......... Administrative and Clerical (ADA)
A & C.......... Antony and Cleopatra [Shakespearean drama] (BARN)
A & C.......... Arithmetic and Controls (SAA)
A & C.......... Arts and Crafts Movement [c. 1860-1920]
A & C.......... Automation and Control
A & C Cir ...... Accounts and Collection Unit Circulars [A publication] (DLA)
A & CO .... Assembly and Checkout [Minuteman] [Military] (AFIT)
A & CP .... Access and Control Point [Telecommunications] (TEL)
A & CP .... Anchors and Chains Proved [Shipping]
A & D .... Accounting and Disbursing (MCD)
A & D .... Admission and Discharge
A & D .... Admission and Disposition [Medicine] (DAVI)
A & D .... Admission and Dispositions Section [Field or evacuation hospital] (VNW)
A & D .... Alcohol and Drug [Type of addiction]
A & D .... Architects and Designers [Building] [New York City]
A & D .... Ascending and Descending (MAE)
A & D High... Angell and Durfee on Highways [A publication] (DLA)
A & DO .... Analog and Discrete Output (MCD)
A & DSL ..... Administrative and Direct Support Logistics [Company] [Army]
A & E .... Accident and Emergency [Ward, Department, or Services] [Medicine]
A & E .... Admiralty and Ecclesiastical (DLA)
A & E .... Adolphus and Ellis' English Queen's Bench Reports [A publication] (DLA)
A & E.......... Aircraft and Engineering (MCD)
A & E.......... Aircraft and Engines (AAG)
A and E....... Airframe and Engine
A & E.......... Analysis and Evaluation
A & E.......... Appeal and Error [Legal term] (DLA)
A & E.......... Appropriation and Expense (AFM)
A & E.......... Architects and Engineers
A & E.......... Architectural and Engineering [Also, A-E] (AFM)
A&E .... Architecture and Engineering (AAGC)
A & E.......... Armament and Electronics [Air Force]
A & E.......... Arts & Entertainment Network [Cable-television system]
A & E.......... Assembly and Equipment (SAA)
A & E.......... Assembly and Erection (SAA)
A & E.......... Azimuth and Elevation
A & EAC ...... American and English Annotated Cases [A publication] (DLA)
A & E Ann Cas... American and English Annotated Cases [A publication] (DLA)
A & E Anno... American and English Annotated Cases [A publication] (DLA)
A & ECA ...... Anglican and Eastern Churches Association [British] (EAIO)
A & E Cas ..... American and English Annotated Cases [A publication] (DLA)
A & ECC ..... American and English Corporation Cases [United States] [A publication] (DLA)
A & E Cor Cases... American and English Corporation Cases [United States] [A publication] (DLA)
A & E Corp Cas... American and English Corporation Cases [A publication] (DLA)
A & E Corp Cas NS... American and English Corporation Cases, New Series [A publication] (DLA)
A & E Enc .... American and English Encyclopedia of Law and Practice [A publication] (DLA)
A & E Enc L... American and English Encyclopedia of Law [A publication] (DLA)
A & E Enc L & Pr... American and English Encyclopedia of Law and Practice [A publication] (DLA)
A & E Ency.... American and English Encyclopedia of Law [A publication] (DLA)
A & E Ency Law... American and English Encyclopedia of Law and Practice [A publication] (DLA)
A & EMSq.... Armament and Electronic Maintenance Squadron [Air Force]
A & E (NS).... Adolphus and Ellis' English Queen's Bench Reports, New Series [A publication] (DLA)
A & EP & P... American and English Pleading and Practice [A publication] (DLA)
A & EP & Pr... American and English Pleading and Practice [A publication] (DLA)
A & E Pat Cas... American and English Patent Cases [A publication] (DLA)
A & ERC ..... American and English Railroad Cases [A publication] (DLA)
A & ER Cas... American and English Railroad Cases [A publication] (DLA)
A & ER Cas NS... American and English Railroad Cases, New Series [A publication] (DLA)
A & E RRC... American and English Railroad Cases [A publication] (DLA)
A & ERR Cas... American and English Railroad Cases [A publication] (DLA)
A & ERR Cas (NS)... American and English Railroad Cases, New Series [A publication] (DLA)
A & F.......... Abercrombie & Fitch [Retail stores]
A & F.......... Accounting and Finance (AFM)
A & F.......... Agriculture and Forestry Committee [US Senate]
A & F.......... Aircraft and Facilities [Navy appropriation]
A & F.......... Analysis and Forecasting, Inc. [Database producer] (IID)
A & F.......... Arming and Fusing (AFM)
A & F.......... August and February [Denotes semiannual payments of interest or dividends in these months] [Business term]
A & F 15..... August 15 and February 15 [Denotes interest payable on these dates] [Business term]
A & FC........ Armament and Fire Control (MCD)
A & F Fix..... Amos and Ferard on Fixtures [A publication] (DLA)
A & FP........ American & Foreign Power Co., Inc.
A & GW .... Atlantic & Great Western Railroad
A & H .... Accident and Health Insurance
A & H .... Agricultural and Horticultural
A & H .... Arm and Hammer [Brand of soda]

A & H .... Arnold and Hodges' English Queen's Bench Reports [*1840-41*] [*A publication*] (DLA)
A & H Bank... Avery and Hobbs' Bankrupt Law of United States [*A publication*] (DLA)
A & I .... Abstracting and Indexing
A & I .... Accident and Indemnity [*Insurance*]
A & I .... Agricultural and Industrial [*In a college name*]
A&I .... Allergy and Immunology (DMAA)
A & I .... Alteration and Improvement Program [*Navy*]
A & I .... Alteration and Inspection
A & L .... Administration and Logistics [*Military*] (INF)
A & L .... Approach and Landing [*Aviation*] (NASA)
A & LU .... Arithmetic and Logic Unit [*Computer science*]
A & M .... Agricultural and Mechanical [*In a college name*]
A and M ..... Ancient and Modern [*Hymns*]
A & M .... Andrews & McMeel [*Publisher*]
A & M .... Antitrust and Monopoly Subcommittee [*US Senate*]
A & M .... Apostle and Martyr [*Church calendars*] (ROG)
A & M .... Art and Mechanical [*Graphics*] (NTCM)
A & M .... Assembly and Maintenance (KSC)
A & MA...... Advertising and Marketing Association
A & N .... Albany & Northern Railway Co. (IIA)
A & N .... Alcock and Napier's Irish King's Bench Reports [*A publication*] (DLA)
A & N .... Army and Navy
A & NB .... Army and Navy Munitions Board [*British*] (DAS)
A & NL .... Army and Navy Life [*New York*] [*A publication*] (ROG)
A & O .... Actors and Others for Animals (EA)
A & O .... Alert and Oriented (CPH)
A & O .... April and October [*Denotes semiannual payments of interest or dividends in these months*] [*Business term*]
A & OX3 ..... Alert and Oriented Times Three [*Neurology and psychiatry*] (DAVI)
A Anth .... Alert and Oriented to Person, Place, and Time [*Neurology and psychiatry*] (DAVI)
A & OX3 ..... Awake and Oriented to Person, Place, and Time [*Neurology and psychiatry*] (DAVI)
A & OX4 ..... Alert and Oriented Times Four [*Neurology and psychiatry*] (DAVI)
A & OX4 ..... Alert and Oriented to Person, Place, Time, and Date [*Neurology and psychiatry*] (DAVI)
A & OX4 ..... Awake and Oriented Times Four [*Neurology and psychiatry*] (DAVI)
A & OX4 ..... Awake and Oriented to Person, Place, Time, and Date [*Neurology and psychiatry*] (DAVI)
A & P.......... Agricultural and Pastoral (ADA)
A & P.......... Airframe and Powerplant [*Aviation*]
A&P .... Analysis and Prediction [*Program*] [*Marine science*] (OSRA)
A&P .... Analysis and Prediction [*Program*] (USDC)
A & P.......... Anterior and Posterior [*Medicine*]
A & P.......... Attraktiv und Preiswert [*Attractive and Priced Right*] [*West German grocery products brand*]
A and P ...... Attrition and Pregnancy [*Reasons for high turnover rate among women employees*]
A & P.......... Auscultation and Palpation [*Medicine*] (AAMN)
A & P.......... Auscultation and Percussion [*Medicine*]
A & P.......... Great Atlantic & Pacific Tea Co., Inc.
A & PS .... Administration and Program Support [*George C. Marshall Space Flight Center Directorate*] [*NASA*] (NASA)
A & R .... Account and Risk [*Investment term*]
A & R .... Advised and Released [*Medicine*]
A & R .... Air and Rail [*Shipping*]
A & R .... Angus & Robertson [*Publisher*] [*Australia*]
A & R .... Approved and Removed
A & R .... Artist and Repertoire (WDMC)
A & R .... Artists and Repertory
A & R .... Assemble and Recycle (SAA)
A & R .... Assembly and Repair
A & R .... Automation and Robotics (SSD)
A & RC .... Application and Resource Control (NASA)
A & RT .... Adams & Rountree Technology, Inc. [*Information service or system*] (IID)
A & S.......... Abraham & Straus [*Retail store*]
A & S.......... Accident and Sickness Insurance
A & S.......... Alton & Southern Railroad
A & S.......... Arts and Sciences
A & S.......... Assignment and Status Chart
A & SH .... Argyll and Sutherland Highlanders [*Military unit*] [*British*]
A & S Sm .... Air & Space/Smithsonian [*A publication*] (BRI)
A & StL....... Atlantic & St. Lawrence Railroad
A & T.......... Acceptance and Transfer
A & T.......... Acquisition and Technology
A & T.......... Agricultural and Technical [*In a college name*]
A & T.......... Assemble and Test
A & TBCB .... Architectural and Transportation Barriers Compliance Board [*Office of Human Development Services*] [*Washington, DC*]
A & TE........ Acquisition and Tracking Electronics (MCD)
A & TP........ Assembly and Test Pit [*Nuclear energy*] (NRCH)
A & W .... Alive and Well
A & W .... Allen and Wright [*Root beer*] [*Initialism also used as name of franchised drive-in restaurants*]
A & W .... Atlantic & Western [*Railroad*] (MHDB)
A & W .... Atlantic & Western Railway Co. (IIA)
A & W .... Ault & Wiborg
A & W Gai ... Abdy and Walker's Gaius and Ulpian [*A publication*] (DLA)
A & WI .... Atlantic and West Indies
A & W Just... Abdy and Walker's Justinian [*A publication*] (DLA)
A & WP .... Atlanta & West Point Rail Road Co.
A & Y.......... Atlantic & Yadkin Railroad (IIA)

AANFA .... African-American Natural Foods Association (EA)
AANFM .... Association des Artistes Non Figuratifs de Montreal [*1956-61*] [*Canada*] (NGC)
AANFP .... American Academy of Natural Family Planning (EA)
AANG .... Angle between Leaf Apex and Widest Point [*Botany*]
AANM .... American Association of Nurse-Midwives [*Later, ACNM*]
AANM .... Apartment Association of New Mexico (SRA)
AAN/MA ...... Allergy and Asthma Network/Mothers of Asthmatics (PAZ)
AANN .... American Association of Neuroscience Nurses (EA)
AANN .... American Association of Neurosurgical Nurses [*Later, ABNN*] (EA)
AAnn .... Anniston Public Library, Anniston, AL [*Library symbol Library of Congress*] (LCLS)
AAnnM........ Anniston Museum of Natural History, Anniston, AL [*Library symbol Library of Congress*] (LCLS)
AANNT .... American Association of Nephrology Nurses and Technicians [*Later, ANNA*] (EA)
AAnnu .... American Annuity Group, Inc. Capital Trust I [*Associated Press*] (SAG)
AAnnuity ..... American Annuity Group, Inc. [*Associated Press*] (SAG)
AANO .... Albanian-American National Organization
AANP .... American Association of Naturopathic Physicians (EA)
AANP .... American Association of Neuropathologists (EA)
AANPI .... American Association for Nurses Practicing Independently (DAVI)
AANR .... American Association of Newspaper Representatives [*Later, NASA*] (EA)
AANS .... American Academy of Neurological Surgery (EA)
AANS .... American Association of Neurological Surgeons (EA)
AANS .... Archers Association of Nova Scotia (AC)
AANSW .... Ansett Airlines of New South Wales [*Australia*]
aant .... Aantekening [*Note*] [*Netherlands*] (ILCA)
AANT .... Argentina Association of Nuclear Technology (NUCP)
A Anth .... American Anthropologist [*A publication*] (BRI)
AAO .... AAO Aquaculture [*Vancouver Stock Exchange symbol*]
AAO .... Acetaldehyde Oxime [*Organic chemistry*]
AAO .... Administrative Arrangements Order (ADA)
AAO .... Advanced Assembly Outline (MCD)
AAO .... Am Angefuehrten Orte [*At the Place Quoted*] [*German*]
AAO .... American Academy of Ophthalmology (EA)
AAO .... American Academy of Optometry (EA)
AAO .... American Academy of Organ (EA)
AAO .... American Academy of Osteopathy (EA)
AAO .... American Academy of Otolaryngology (DAVI)
AAO .... American Academy of Ophthalmology [*Absorbed by American Academy of Ophthalmology - AAO*]
AAO .... American Association of Orthodontists (EA)
AAO .... Amino Acid Oxidase [*An enzyme*]
AAO .... Anaco [*Venezuela*] [*Airport symbol*] (OAG)
AAO .... Anglo-Australian Observatory
AAO .... Antiaircraft Officer (IIA)
AAO .... Antiair Output
AAO .... Archives Association of Ontario [*L'Association des Archives de l'Ontario*] (AC)
AAO .... Army Acquisition Objective
AAO .... Artillery Air Observer (DNAB)
AAO .... Association for the Advancement of Ophthalmology [*Defunct*] (EA)
AAO .... Astronaut Activities Office [*NASA*] (KSC)
AAO .... Atlantis Airlines [*ICAO designator*] (FAAC)
AAO .... Australian Academy of Optometry
AAO .... Authorized Acquisition Objective [*Army*] (AABC)
AAO .... AUTOVON [*Automatic Voice Network*] Assistance Operator (DNAB)
AAO .... Awake, Alert, and Oriented (HGAA)
A-AO$_2$ .... Alveolar-Arterial Oxygen Gradient [*Biochemistry*] (DAVI)
AAOA .... Acetoacet-o-anisidide [*Organic chemistry*]
AAOA .... Ambulance Association of America [*Later, AAA*] (EA)
AAOA .... American Academy of Otolaryngologic Allergy (EA)
AAOA .... Auxiliary to the American Optometric Association [*Later, AFVA*] (EA)
AAOA .... Auxiliary to the American Osteopathic Association (EA)
AAOBPPH .... American Association of Owners and Breeders of Peruvian Paso Horses (EA)
AAOC .... Acetoacet-o-chloroanilide [*Organic chemistry*]
AAOC .... American Association of Osteopathic Colleges [*Later, AACOM*] (EA)
AAOC .... Antiaircraft Operations Center [*Air Force*]
AAOD .... Army Aviation Operating Detachment
AAODC........ American Association of Oilwell Drilling Contractors [*Later, IADC*] (EA)
AAODL .... Atmospheric Aerosols and Optics Data Library (RDA)
AAOE .... Airborne Antarctic Ozone Experiment
AAOE .... Airborne Antarctic Ozone Experiment [*Marine science*] (OSRA)
AAOE .... American Association of Osteopathic Examiners (EA)
AAOE .... Arrival and Assembly Operations Element [*Navy*] (ANA)
AA of A .... Ambulance Association of America [*Later, AAA*]
AA of C .... Auctioneers Association of Canada
AAOG .... American Association of Obstetricians and Gynecologists [*Later, AGOS*] (EA)
AAOG .... Arrival and Assembly Operations Group [*Navy*] (ANA)
AAOGP........ American Academy of Orthodontics for the General Practitioner (EA)
AAOH.......... Asian Association of Occupational Health (EA)
AAOHN........ American Association of Occupational Health Nurses (EA)
AAO-HNS .... American Academy of Otolaryngology - Head and Neck Surgery (EA)
AAOI .... American Association of Inventors
AAOM .... American Academy of Occupational Medicine (EA)
AAOM .... American Academy of Oral Medicine (EA)
AAOM .... American Association of Orthomolecular Medicine (EA)
AAOM .... American Association of Orthopaedic Medicine (EA)
AAOM .... Arkansas Association of Oriental Medicine (SRA)

AAOME American Association of Osteopathic Medical Examiners (EA)

AAOMS American Association of Oral and Maxillofacial Surgeons (EA)

AAON AAON, Inc. [*NASDAQ symbol*] (SAG)

AAON American Association of Office Nurses (EA)

AAONMS Imperial Council of the Ancient Arabic Order of the Nobles of the Mystic Shrine for North America [*Freemasonry*] (EA)

AAOO American Academy of Ophthalmology and Otolaryngology (EA)

AAOP American Academy of Oral Pathology (EA)

AAOP American Academy of Oral Pathology (DMAA)

AAOP American Academy of Orthotists and Prosthetists (EA)

AAOP Antiaircraft Observation Post

AAOR American Academy of Oral Roentgenology [*Later, AADR*]

AAOR Antiaircraft Operations Room (MCD)

AAOrthMed American Association of Orthopedic Medicine (EA)

AAOS American Academy of Orthopaedic Surgeons (EA)

AAOS American Association of Osteopathic Specialists (EA)

AAOT Acetoacet-o-toluidide [*Organic chemistry*]

AAOT American Association of Orthoptic Technicians [*Later, AACO*] (EA)

AAOX3 Awake and Oriented to Time, Place, and Person [*Neurology*] (DAVI)

AAP Academy of American Poets (EA)

AAP Acquisition and Inoculation Access Period [*Immunology*]

AAP Advance Acquisition Planning (AAGC)

AAP Advance Australia Party [*Political party*]

AAP Advanced Acquisition Plan (MCD)

AAP Advanced Automation [*FAA*] (TAG)

AAP Advise if Able to Proceed [*Aviation*] (FAAC)

AAP Aerodynamics Advisory Panel [*AEC*] (MCD)

AAP Affirmative Action Plan [*or Program*] [*Equal opportunity employment*]

AAP Aggregation-Attachment Pheromone [*Entomology*]

AAP Aging Aircraft Program [*FAA*] (DA)

AAP Agribusiness Accountability Project [*Public interest research group*] [*Defunct*]

AAP Air at Atmospheric Pressure (MAE)

AAP Aircraft Actually Possessed [*Air Force*] (AFIT)

AAP Aircraft Assembly Plant

AAP Airlock Adapter Plate (MCD)

AAP Allied Administrative Publication [*NATO*]

AAP Allied Army Procedures (NATG)

AAP Allied Army Publications (NATG)

AAP Allied Authorized Publication

AAP Allowance Appendix Page

AAP Alpha Antiprotease [*Biochemistry*]

AAp Aluminum Co. of America [*AMEX symbol*] (SAG)

AAP Ambient Absolute Pressure (PDAA)

AAP Ambulance Association of Pennsylvania (SRA)

AAP American Academy of Pediatricians (PAZ)

AAP American Academy of Pediatrics (EA)

AAP American Academy of Pedodontics [*Later, AAPD*] (EA)

AAP American Academy of Periodontology (EA)

AAP American Academy of Philately [*Later, APC*] (EA)

AAP American Academy of Psychoanalysis (EA)

AAP American Academy of Psychotherapists (EA)

AAP American Association for Parapsychology (EA)

AAP American Association of Pathologists (EA)

AAP American Association of Psychiatrists (EA)

AAP American Association of the Professions (EA)

AAP Amstar American Petroleum [*Vancouver Stock Exchange symbol*]

AAP Amway Asia Pacific [*NYSE symbol*] (SPSG)

AAP Analog Antenna Positioner

AAP Analog Autopilot (KSC)

AAP Analysis and Production (MCD)

AAP Antenna Aspect Processor

AAP Anti-Air Processing Program (SAA)

AAP Antipernicious Anemia Principle [*Hematology*] (IIA)

AAP Apollo Applications Program [*NASA*]

AAP Approach Astrophysics Payload [*NASA*]

AAP Army Ammunition Plant (AABC)

AAP Army Apprenticeship Program

AAP Army Automation Program

AAP Army Avionics Program

AAP Asbestos Action Program [*Environmental Protection Agency*] (GFGA)

AAP Assessment Adjustment Pass [*Psychiatry*] (DAVI)

AAP Assessors Association of Pennsylvania (SRA)

AAP Association des Administrateurs du Personnel de la Fonction Publique [*Association of Personnel Administrators of Public Functions*] [*Canada*]

AAP Association des Arts Plastiques, Montreal [*1955*] [*Canada*] (NGC)

AAP Association for Advancement of Psychoanalysis (of the Karen Horney Psychoanalytic Institute and Center) (EA)

AAP Association for Advancement of Psychology (EA)

AAP Association for Applied Poetry (EA)

AAP Association for Applied Psychoanalysis (EA)

AAP Association for Astrological Psychology (EA)

AAP Association for the Advancement of Psychotherapy (EA)

AAP Association of Academic Physiatrists (EA)

AAP Association of Alcohol/Addictions Programs in Washington State (SRA)

AAP Association of American Physicians (EA)

AAP Association of American Publishers (EA)

AAP Association of Aviation Psychologists (EA)

AAP Association of Publishers

AAP Associative Array Processor (MCD)

AAP Astro Air International, Inc. [*Philippines*] [*ICAO designator*] (FAAC)

AAP Athlete Assistance Program [*See also PAA*] [*Canada*]

AAP Atmospheric Analysis and Prediction [*National Center for Atmospheric Research*]

AAP Attached Applications Processor

AAP Auburn University, Auburn, AL [*Library symbol Library of Congress*] (LCLS)

AAP Australia Air Publications [*A publication*]

AAP Australian Academy of Paediatrics

AAP Australian Associated Press Party Ltd.

AAP Australian Association of Philanthropy

AAP Automotive Aftermarket Professional [*AWDA University*]

AAP Auxiliary Acceleration Pump [*Automotive engineering*]

AAP Average Annual Precipitation (PDAA)

AAP Houston, TX [*Location identifier FAA*] (FAAL)

AAPA Aboriginal Areas Protection Authority [*Northern Territory, Australia*]

AAPA Advertising Agency Production Association (DGA)

AAPA Advocates Against Psychic Abuse [*Defunct*] (EA)

AAPA Alabama Asphalt Pavement Association (SRA)

AAPA American Academy of Physician Assistants (EA)

AAPA American Academy of Podiatry Administration (EA)

AAPA American Alfalfa Processors Association (EA)

AAPA American Amateur Press Association (EA)

AAPA American Art Pottery Association (EA)

AAPA American Association of Pathologists' Assistants (EA)

AAPA American Association of Physical Anthropologists (EA)

AAPA American Association of Physicians' Assistants [*Defunct*] (EA)

AAPA American Association of Port Authorities (EA)

AAPA American Association of Psychiatric Administrators (EA)

AAPA Asian American Psychological Association (EA)

AAPA Association of Accredited Practitioners in Advertising (DGA)

AAPA Association of Authorized Public Accountants (EAIO)

AAPA Association of Authorized Public Accountants [*British*] (DBA)

AAP-A Auburn University, Archives, Auburn, AL [*Library symbol*] [*Library of Congress*] (LCLS)

AAPA Australian Abalone Producers' Association

AAPAA American Academy of Psychiatrists in Alcoholism and Addictions (EA)

AAPAA Association of Asian/Pacific American Artists (EA)

AAPAP Anglo-American Press Association of Paris [*See also APAAP*] [*France*] (EA)

AAPB American Association of Pathologists and Bacteriologists [*Later, AAP*] (EA)

AAPB Association for Applied Psychophysiology and Biofeedback (EA)

AAPBA Amino(aminophenyl)benzamide [*Organic chemistry*]

AAPBC American Association of Professional Bridal Consultants (EA)

AAPBG Army Automation Program Budget Guidance

AAPC Adjusted Average per Capita Cost

AAPC Advertising Agency Production Club of New York [*Later, APC*] (EA)

AAPC Afro-American Purchasing Center (PDAA)

AAPC American Association for Protecting Children (EA)

AAPC American Association of Pastoral Counselors (EA)

AAPC American Association of Political Consultants (EA)

AAPC American Association of Professional Consultants [*Manchester, NH*] (EA)

AAPC Antibiotic-Acquired Pseudomembranous Colitis (DAVI)

AAPC Application of Autonomous Passive Classification (MCD)

AAPC Association pour l'Anthropologie Physique au Canada [*Association for Physical Anthropology in Canada*]

AAPCC Adjusted Average per Capita Cost

AAPCC American Association of Poison Control Centers (EA)

AAPCC American Association of Psychiatric Clinics for Children [*Later, AAPSC*] (EA)

AAPCHO Association of Asian/Pacific Community Health Organizations (EA)

AAPCK Acetyl(alanyl)phenylalanylchloromethyl Ketone [*Biochemistry*]

AAPCM Association of American Playing Card Manufacturers [*Defunct*] (EA)

AAPCO Association of American Pesticide Control Officials (EA)

(A-A)P CO_2 Alveolar-Arterial Carbon Dioxide Difference [*Biochemistry*] (DAVI)

AAPCYC Australian Association of Police Citizens' Youth Clubs

AAPD Absolute Average Percent Deviation [*Mathematics*]

AAPD American Academy of Pediatric Dentistry (EA)

AAPD American Academy of Physiologic Dentistry (EA)

AAPD Automated Astronomic Positioning Device [*Defense Mapping Agency*] (MCD)

AAPE American Academy of Physical Education (EA)

AAPE American Association for Paralegal Education (EA)

AAPE Average Absolute Percentage Error [*Statistics*]

AAPEI Architects Association of Prince Edward Island (AC)

AAPEP Adolescent and Adult Psychoeducational Profile [*Educational testing*]

AAPERS Active Army Personnel Reporting System [*Europe*] (MCD)

AAPERS Army Acquisition Program Executive Review System [*Army*]

AAPES Army Automation Planning, Programming, and Evaluation System (MCD)

AAPF Anti-Arteriosclerosis Polysaccharide Factor [*Medicine*] (DMAA)

AAPFCO Association of American Plant Food Control Officials (EA)

AAPFP American Association of Personal Financial Planners [*Defunct*] (EA)

AAPG Affirmative Action Planning Guide [*Executive Telecom System, Inc.*] [*Information service or system*] (CRD)

AAPG Allowance Appendix Package

AAPG American Association of Petroleum Geologists (EA)

AAPG Arab-American Press Guild (EA)

AAPG Armament and Avionics Planning Guidance (MCD)

AAPG Association of Petroleum Geologists (IID)

AAPGA Australian Apple and Pear Growers' Association

AAPH American Association for Partial Hospitalization (EA)

AAPH American Association of Professional Hypnologists [*Defunct*] (EA)

AAPH American Association of Professional Hypnotherapists (EA)

AAPH .... ASEAN [*Association of South East Asian Nations*] Association for Planning and Housing (EAIO)
AAPHD .... American Association of Public Health Dentistry (EA)
AAPHD .... American Association of Public Health Dentists (DMAA)
AAPHO .... American Association of Physician-Hospital Organization
AAPHP .... American Association of Public Health Physicians (EA)
AAPHR .... American Association of Physicians for Human Rights (EA)
AAPI .... Australian Architectural Periodicals Index (ADA)
AAPICU .... American Association of Presidents of Independent Colleges and Universities (EA)
AAPIER .... American Association for Public Information, Education and Research (AEBS)
AAPIU .... Allied Aerial Photographic Interpretation Unit [*Obsolete*]
AAPL .... Afro-American Police League (EA)
AAPL .... American Academy of Psychiatry and the Law (EA)
AAPL .... American Artists Professional League (EA)
AAPL .... American Association of Petroleum Landmen (EA)
AAPL .... Apple Computer [*NASDAQ symbol*] (TTSB)
AAPL .... Apple Computer, Inc. [*NASDAQ symbol*] (NQ)
AAPL .... [*An*] Array Processing Language [*Programming language*]
AAPLC .... Association of African American People's Legal Council (EA)
AAPLE .... American Academy for Professional Law Enforcement [*Defunct*] (EA)
AAPLOG .... American Association of Pro Life Obstetricians and Gynecologists (EA)
AAPLP .... American Academy of Pro-Life Physicians (EA)
AAPLP .... American Association of Pro-Life Pediatricians (EA)
AAPM .... American Academy of Pain Medicine (EA)
AAPM .... American Association of Physicists in Medicine (EA)
AAPM .... Army Aviation Planning Manual (AABC)
AAPMBF .... Australian Air Pilots Mutual Benefit Fund
AAPMC .... Antibiotic-Associated Pseudomembranous Colitis [*Medicine*]
AAPMR .... American Academy of Physical Medicine and Rehabilitation (EA)
AAPMR .... American Association of Physical Medicine and Rehabilitation (DAVI)
AAPNA .... Association of African Physicians in North America (EA)
AAPO .... Advanced Aircraft Programs Office
AAPO .... American Academy of Podiatry Administration (EA)
AAPO .... Apollo Applications Program Office [*NASA*] (MCD)
AAPO & S .... American Association for Pediatric Ophthalmology and Strabismus (EA)
AAPOR .... American Association for Public Opinion Research (EA)
AAPP .... Affirmative Action Program Plans [*DoD*]
AAPP .... American Association of Police Polygraphists (EA)
AAPP .... Australian Association of Pathology Practices
AAPP .... Auxiliary Airborne Power Plant
AAPPA .... Advertising Agency Print Production Association (AC)
AAPPES .... Army Automation Planning, Programming, and Evaluation System
AAPPES .... Army Auto Plan and Progress Evaluation System
AAPPO .... American Association of Preferred Provider Organizations [*Alexandria, VA*] (EA)
AAPPP .... American Association of Planned Parenthood Physicians [*Later, APPP*] (EA)
AAPPQ .... Association des Architectes en Pratique Privee du Quebec (AC)
AAPPS .... American Association of Podiatric Physicians and Surgeons (EA)
AAPPTMP .... American Association of Physicians Practicing the Transcendental Meditation Program [*Later, WMAFPH*] (EA)
AAPQ .... Association des Agences de Publicite du Quebec [*Association of Quebec Advertising Agencies*] (AC)
AAPQ .... Association des Architectes Paysagistes du Quebec (AC)
AAPr .... Alum Co. Amer $3.75 Pfd [*AMEX symbol*] (TTSB)
AAPR .... Army Aviation Program Review (MCD)
AAPR .... Average Annual Performance Rate
AAPRCO ...... American Association of Private Railroad Car Owners (EA)
AAPRD .... American Academy for Plastics Research in Dentistry [*Later, Academy of Dental Materials - ADM*]
AAPRDTW .... Association for the Advancement of Policy, Research, and Development in the Third World (EA)
AAPRM .... American Association of Passenger Rate Men [*Defunct*] (EA)
A-APRP .... All-African People's Revolutionary Party (EA)
AAPRSO .... Army Aviation Personnel Requirements of Sustained Operations Study (MCD)
AAPS .... Active Aircraft Plume Suppression (MCD)
AAPS .... Advanced Automotive Power Systems
AAPS .... Airborne Angular Position Sensor
AAPS .... Alternative Automotive Power Systems [*Environmental Protection Agency*]
AAPS .... American Academy of Plastic Surgeons (DAVI)
AAPS .... American Association for the Promotion of Science
AAPS .... American Association of Pharmaceutical Scientists (EA)
AAPS .... American Association of Phonetic Sciences (EA)
AAPS .... American Association of Physicians and Surgeons (DAVI)
AAPS .... American Association of Plastic Surgeons (EA)
AAPS .... Arizona Articulation Proficiency Scale [*Speech and language therapy*] (DAVI)
AAPS .... Associate of the Australian Psychological Society
AAPS .... Association for Ambulatory Pediatric Services [*Later, APA*] (EA)
AAPS .... Association of Alternate Postal Systems (EA)
AAPS .... Association of American Physicians and Surgeons (DAVI)
AAPS .... Australian Animal Protection Society
AAPS .... Automated Astronomic Positioning System [*Defense Mapping Agency*]
AAPSA .... Australian Apple and Pear Shippers' Association
AAPSC .... American Association of Psychiatric Services for Children (EA)
AAPSE .... American Association of Professors in Sanitary Engineering [*Later, AEEP*]
AAP/SHORAD... Air-Augmented Propulsion for Short-Range Air Defense (MCD)

AAPSM .... American Academy of Podiatric Sports Medicine (EA)
AAPSO .... Afro-Asian People's Solidarity Organization [*Cairo, Egypt*] (EAIO)
AAPSO .... Army Acquisition Pollution Prevention Support Office
AAPSO .... Australian Association of Prisoner Support Organizations
AAPSRO .... American Association of Professional Standards Review Organizations [*Later, AMPRA*] (EA)
AAPSS .... American Academy of Political and Social Science (EA)
AAPSS-A ...... American Academy of Political and Social Science. Annals [*A publication*] (BRI)
AAPT .... American Association of Philosophy Teachers (EA)
AAPT .... American Association of Physics Teachers (EA)
AAPT .... American Association of Psychiatric Technicians
AAPT .... Association of Asphalt Paving Technologists (EA)
AAPTC .... Assistant Airport Traffic Controller (IAA)
AAPTO .... American Association of Passenger Traffic Officers [*Defunct*] (EA)
AAPU .... Airborne Auxiliary Power Unit
AAPWA .... American Association of Public Welfare Attorneys (EA)
AAPWISM ..... American Association of Public Welfare Information Systems Management (EA)
AAPY .... American Association of Professors of Yiddish (EA)
AAQ .... Air Alliance, Inc. [*Canada ICAO designator*] (FAAC)
AAQ .... Armed Aircraft Qualification
AAQ .... Association des Archivistes du Quebec (AC)
AAQM .... Acting Assistant Quartermaster [*Marine Corps*]
AAQP .... Australian Association for Quality and Participation
AAQS .... Ambient Air Quality Standard (EG)
AAR .... AAR Corp. [*Associated Press*] (SAG)
AAR .... Aarhus [*Denmark*] [*Airport symbol*] (OAG)
AAR .... Accumulation Area Ratio
AAR .... Active Attached Reserve [*Royal Australian Naval Reserve*]
AAR .... Active Avoidance Reaction [*Medicine*] (DMAA)
AAR .... Acupuncture Association and Register Ltd. [*British*]
AAR .... Acute Articular Rheumatism [*Medicine*] (DMAA)
AAR .... Administrative Adjustment Report [*Supply*] [*Military*]
AAR .... Administrative Appeals Reports [*Australia A publication*]
A/AR .... Aero/Acoustic Rotor (RDA)
AAR .... After Action Report [*Military*]
AAR .... After Action Review [*Military*] (MCD)
AAR .... Against All Risks [*Insurance*]
AAR .... Aid for Afghan Refugees [*An association*] (EA)
AAR .... Air Attack RADAR
AAR .... Air-Augmented Rocket
AAR .... Airborne Attack Recorder (MCD)
AAR .... Aircraft Accident Record [*Obsolete Military*]
AAR .... Aircraft Accident Report [*Military*]
AAR .... Airport Acceptance Rate [*FAA*] (TAG)
AAR .... Air-to-Air Refueling (MCD)
AAR .... Alabama Association of Realtors (SRA)
AAR .... Alabama Department of Archives and History, Montgomery, AL [*OCLC symbol*] (OCLC)
A-Ar .... Alabama Department of Archives and History, Montgomery, AL [*Library symbol Library of Congress*] (LCLS)
AAR .... Alaska Association of Realtors (SRA)
AAR .... All-American Racers [*Automobile racing team*]
AAR .... Alliance for Aging Research (EA)
AAR .... Alternate Acquisition RADAR (MCD)
AAR .... American Academy in Rome (EA)
AAR .... American Academy of Religion (EA)
AAR .... American Association of Rabbis (EA)
AAR .... Amino Acid Racemization [*Dating process*]
AAR .... Anglo-American Racers
AAR .... Anglo Australian Resources
AAR .... Antigen-Antiglobulin Reaction [*Immunology*] (MAE)
AAR .... Applied Agricultural Research, Inc. [*Research center*] (RCD)
AAR .... Approved Auto Repair [*American Automobile Association*]
AAR .... Arabesque Resources Ltd. [*Vancouver Stock Exchange symbol*]
AAR .... Arizona Association of Realtors (SRA)
AAR .... Army Area Representative
AAR .... Asiana Airlines [*South Korea ICAO designator*] (FAAC)
AAR .... Assembly and Repair (IAA)
AAR .... Association for Automated Reasoning (EA)
AAR .... Association of American Railroads (EA)
AAR .... Association of American Rhodes Scholars
AAR .... Atlas of Australian Resources [*A publication*]
AAR .... Australia Antigen Radioimmunoassay [*Immunology*] (AAMN)
AAR .... Automatic Alternative Routing [*Telecommunications*] (TEL)
AAR .... Automotive Affiliated Representatives (EA)
AAR .... Average Annual Rainfall (PDAA)
AARA .... Access and Amendment Refusal Authority [*Army*] (AABC)
AARA .... Air-to-Air Refuelling Area (DA)
AARA .... American Amateur Racquetball Association (EA)
AARA .... American Ambulance and Rescue Association [*Defunct*] (EA)
AARA .... American Arab Relief Agency [*Defunct*]
AARA .... Antique Auto Racing Association (EA)
AARA .... Arizona Automotive Recyclers Association (SRA)
AARAD .... Aspect Angle Radiation Code (MCD)
AARB .... Advanced Air Refueling Boom [*Air Force*] (MCD)
AARC .... Alberta Association of Rehabilitation Centres (AC)
AARC .... Alliance for Acid Rain Control (EA)
AARC .... American-Arab Relations Committee (EA)
AARC .... American Association for Respiratory Care (EA)
AARC .... Army Attrition Rates Committee (NATG)
AARC .... Assassination Archives and Research Center (EA)
A Arch .... American Archivist Quarterly [*A publication*] (BRI)
A Arch .... Associate in Architecture

AARCKW......	Association of Airborne Ranger Companies of the Korean War (EA)
AARD..........	American Academy of Restorative Dentistry (EA)
AARDAC......	Army Air Reconnaissance for Damage Assessment in the Continental United States (AABC)
AARDCO......	Association of American Railroad Dining Car Officers (EA)
AARDL........	Artillery Ammunition and Rocket Development Laboratory [*Army*] (MCD)
AARE	A-Associate Response [*Computer science*] (TNIG)
AARE	ACSE [*Association Control Service Element*]-Associate-Request [*Telecommunications*] (OSI)
AAREC	Adaptive Agile RADAR ECCM [*Electronic Counter-Countermeasures*] (MCD)
AARF	Acute Alveolar Respiratory Failure [*Medicine*] (CPH)
AARF	Arab American Republican Federation [*Defunct*] (EA)
AARFA	Australian Association of Rural Fire Authorities
aarg...........	Aargang [*Annual Volume*] [*Sweden*] (BARN)
AARG..........	Association of Artist-Run Galleries (EA)
AARG	Atlantic Amphibious Ready Group (MCD)
AARGCE.......	Association of American Rod and Gun Clubs, Europe (EA)
AARI	Arctic and Antarctic Research Institute [*Russian Federation*] [*Marine science*] (OSRA)
AARI	Arctic and Antarctic Research Institute [*Russia*] (USDC)
AARL	Advanced Application Rotary Launcher (DWSG)
AARL	Advanced Automation Research Laboratory [*Purdue University*]
AARL	African-American Reference Library [*A publication*]
AARL	Army Aeromedical Research Laboratory (RDA)
AARL	Army Aeronautical Research Center [*Ames Research Center*]
AARL	Army Aircraft Radio Laboratory (IAA)
AARLMP	Afro-American Resources and Library Manpower Project [*Columbia University*] (NITA)
AARM	Advanced Antiradiation Missile (MCD)
A-ARM........	Army Armor Board (MCD)
AARM	Arrowwood Municipal Library, Alberta [*Library symbol National Library of Canada*] (NLC)
AARMA	Assistant [*US*] Army Military Attache (CINC)
AARN	Alberta Association of Registered Nurses (AC)
AARN	Association for Australian Rural Nurses
AARNet	Australian Academic and Research Network [*Computer science*] (TNIG)
AarnRt	Aaron Rents, Inc. [*Associated Press*] (SAG)
AARO	Association of Americans Resident Overseas (EA)
AAROM.......	Active Assertive Range of Motion [*Medicine*] (DMAA)
AAROM.......	Active Assistive Range of Motion [*Medicine*]
AaronRt	Aaron Rents, Inc. [*Associated Press*] (APAG)
AAROT	Alberta Association of Registered Occupational Therapists (AC)
AARP	American Association of Retired Persons (EA)
AARP	Annual Advance Retainer Pay
AARP	Atomic Air Raid Precaution (IAA)
AARPLS.......	Advanced Airborne Radio Position Location System [*Army*] (MCD)
AARPS........	Air-Augmented Rocket Propulsion System
AARPUT......	Average Aptitude Requirement per Unit Time
AARQ	ACSE [*Association Control Service Element*]-Associate-Request [*Telecommunications*] (OSI)
AARQ	Association des Amenagistes Regionaux du Quebec (AC)
AARR	Annual Allowance and Requirements Review [*Navy*]
AARR	Argonne Advanced Research Reactor
AARRC........	Army Aircraft Requirements Review Committee
AARRC........	Atlanta Aerospace Rescue and Recovery Center [*Air Force*]
AARRO........	Afro-Asian Rural Reconstruction Organization [*New Delhi, India*]
AARRS........	Air Force Aerospace Rescue and Recovery Service (SAA)
AARS	Accelerated Accounting and Reporting System
AARS	Accrual Accounting and Reporting System
AARS	Advanced Airborne RADAR System (MCD)
AARS	Aerospace Rescue and Recovery Service [*Air Force*] (PDAA)
AARS	Air Force Aerospace Rescue and Recovery Service (MCD)
AARS	Air-to-Air Refueling Squadron
AARS	All-America Rose Selections [*An association*] (EA)
AARS	American Association of Railroad Superintendents (EA)
AARS	American Association of Railway Surgeons [*Defunct*] (EA)
AARS	Anonymous Arts Recovery Society (EA)
AARS	Army Aerial Reconnaissance System
AARS	Army Aircraft Repair Ship
AARS	Army Amateur Radio System
AARS	Association of American Rhodes Scholars (EA)
AARS	Automated Attendance Reporting System (MCD)
AARS	Automatic Address Recognition System [*or Subsystem*] [*Computer science*]
AARSS........	Austere Airborne Ranging and Sighting System (MCD)
AARST........	American Association of Radon Scientists and Technologists (EA)
AART	Addressable Asynchronous Receiver Transmitter
A Art	American Artist [*A publication*] (BRI)
AART	American Association for Rehabilitation Therapy [*Defunct*] (EA)
AART	American Association for Respiratory Therapy [*Later, AARC*] (EA)
AART	American Association of Religious Therapists (EA)
A-ART	Army Artillery Board (MCD)
AART	Australian Art Index [*Database*]
AARTA	American Association of Railroad Ticket Agents [*Defunct*] (EA)
AARTE	Airport Acceptance Rate [*Aviation*] (FAAC)
AARTI	Australian Art Index [*Australian National Gallery Library*] [*Database*] (ADA)
AARTS	Army/American Council on Education Registry Transcript System (INF)
AARTS	Association of Advanced Rabbinical and Talmudic Schools (EA)
AARU	Agricultural Aviation Research Unit [*British*] (ARC)
AARU	Association of Arab Universities [*Amman, Jordan*] (EAIO)

AARV	Aerial Armored Reconnaissance Vehicle
AARV	Armored Artillery Resupply Vehicle (MCD)
AARWBA.......	American Auto Racing Writers and Broadcasters Association (EA)
AAS...........	Abort Advisory System [*NASA*]
AAS...........	Academiae Americanae Socius [*Fellow of the American Academy (Academy of Arts and Sciences)*] [*Latin*] (GPO)
AAS...........	Academy of Applied Science (EA)
AAS...........	Accredited Agents Scheme
AAS...........	Achievement Anxiety Scale [*Psychology*]
AAS...........	Activity Accreditation Schedule (MCD)
AAS...........	Acts of the Apostolic See
AAS...........	Acute Abdominal Series [*Medicine*] (MEDA)
AAS...........	Adjusted Air Speed [*Navigation*]
AAS...........	Advanced Accounting System
AAS...........	Advanced Active Sonobuoy (MCD)
AAS...........	Advanced Administrative System [*IBM Corp.*]
AAS...........	Advanced Aero-Wing Systems Corp. [*Vancouver Stock Exchange symbol*]
AAS...........	Advanced Air Station (DAS)
AAS...........	Advanced Antenna System [*Air Force*]
AAS...........	Advanced Automated System
AAS...........	Advanced Automation System
AAS...........	Advanced Avionic System (MCD)
AAS...........	Aeromedical Airlift Squadron [*Air Force*]
AAS...........	Agnostics' Adoption Society [*British*] (BI)
AAS...........	Air Armament School [*British military*] (DMA)
AAS...........	Airborne Antenna System
AAS...........	Aircraft Airworthiness Section
AAS...........	Aircraft Arresting System
AAS...........	Airport Advisory Service [*FAA*] (TAG)
AAS...........	Alabama Department of Archives and History, State Documents, Montgomery, AL [*OCLC symbol*] (OCLC)
AAS...........	Alert Area Supervisor [*Military*] (AFM)
AAS...........	Alerting Automatic Telling Status (SAA)
AAS...........	All-America Selections (EA)
AAS...........	American Academy of Sanitarians (EA)
AAS...........	American Academy of Somnology (EA)
AAS...........	American Amaryllis Society (EA)
AAS...........	American Antiquarian Society (EA)
AAS...........	American Artists Series
AAS...........	American Association of Shotgunning [*Defunct*] (EA)
AAS...........	American Association of Suicidology (EA)
AAS...........	American Astronautical Society (EA)
AAS...........	American Astronomical Society (EA)
AAS...........	American Astrophysical Society (USDC)
AAS...........	American Auditory Society (EA)
A-AS..........	American-Austrian Society (EA)
AAS...........	AmeriSource Health 'A' [*NYSE symbol*] (TTSB)
AAS...........	AmeriSource Health Corp. [*NYSE symbol*] (SAG)
AAS...........	Analog Alarm Section
AAS...........	Ancient Astronaut Society (EA)
AAS...........	Anglesey Antiquarian Society [*British*] (DBA)
AAS...........	Angular Acceleration Susceptibility [*Orientation*]
AAS...........	Annual Authorizations Service [*of the Copyright Clearance Center*]
AAS...........	Annual Automated Controls Survey [*of a ship*] (DS)
AAS...........	Annual Average Score (AABC)
AAS...........	Anthrax Antiserum [*Medicine*]
AAS...........	Aortic Arch Syndrome [*Medicine*]
AAS...........	Apollo Abort System [*NASA*] (IAA)
AAS...........	Architectural Acoustics Society (EA)
AAS...........	Area Alarm Sum (ECII)
AAS...........	Arithmetic Assignment Statement
AAS...........	Arms and Armour Society (EA)
AAS...........	Army Air Service
AAS...........	Army Attache System
AAS...........	Arnold Air Society (EA)
AAS...........	Ashmont Public Library, Alberta [*Library symbol National Library of Canada*] (NLC)
AAS...........	Asian and African Section [*Association of College and Research Libraries*]
AAS...........	Aspirator Air System [*Automotive engineering*]
AAS...........	Associate in Applied Science
AAS...........	Association for Academic Surgery (EA)
AAS...........	Association for Archery in Schools (EAIO)
AAS...........	Association for Asian Studies (EA)
AAS...........	Association of Academies of Science [*Later, NAAS*]
AAS...........	Atlantic Aviation Services (SAA)
AAS...........	Atlantoaxial Subluxation (PDAA)
AAS...........	Atomic Absorption Spectrometer [*or Spectrophotometer or Spectroscopy*]
AAS...........	Attack Assessment System (MCD)
AAS...........	Austrian Air Services [*ICAO designator*] (FAAC)
AAS...........	Automated Accounting System (BUR)
AAS...........	Automatic Addressing System [*Computer science*]
AAS...........	Automatically-Adjustable Shock-Absorber [*System*] [*Automotive engineering*]
AAS...........	Automatic Announcement Subsystem [*Telecommunications*] (TEL)
AAS...........	Auxiliary Ambulance Service (DAS)
AAS...........	Azimuth Alignment System [*Aerospace*] (AAG)
AAS...........	Campbellsville, KY [*Location identifier FAA*] (FAAL)
AASA	Academy of Arts and Sciences of the Americas (EA)
AASA	Acupuncture Association of South Australia
AASA	Administrative Assistant to the Secretary of the Army
AASA	Afro-American Student Association (EA)
AASA	Alberta Amateur Softball Association [*Also Softball Alberta*] (AC)

AASA .... American Association of School Administrators (EA)
AASA .... American Association of Surgeon's Assistants (EA)
AASA .... Ansett Airlines of South Australia
AASA .... Arkansas Association of School Administrators (SRA)
AASA .... Association of Aerial Surveyors Australia
AASACM ...... American Association of Swiss Alpine Club Members [*Defunct*] (EA)
AAS & GP..... American Association of Soap and Glycerin Producers [*Later, SDA*]
AASB .... Alabama Association of School Boards (SRA)
AASB .... American Association of Small Business [*Later, NSBU*]
AASB .... Association of Alaska School Boards (SRA)
AASB .... Auxiliary Array Signal Band [*Military*]
AASBEVM .... Association of American State Boards of Examiners in Veterinary Medicine [*Later, AAVSB*] (EA)
AASBO .... Arizona Association of School Business Officials (SRA)
AASC .... Aerospace Applications Studies Committee [*NATO*] (PDAA)
AASC .... African-American Scholars Conference [*Defunct*] (EA)
AASC .... Alliance Against Sexual Coercion (EA)
AASC .... Allied Air Support Command [*Mediterranean*]
AASC .... American Association of Small Cities (EA)
AASC .... American Association of Specialized Colleges (EA)
AASC .... American Association of State Climatologists (EA)
AASC .... Anglo-American Sporting Club
AASC .... Army Area Signal Center (AABC)
AASC .... Army Automation Steering Committee
AASC .... Association for the Advancement of Science in Canada
AASC .... Association of African Sports Confederations [*See also UCSA*] [*Yaounde, Cameroon*] (EAIO)
AASCF .... Alberta Association of Services for Children & Families [*Formerly, Alberta Association of Child Care Centres*] (AC)
Aasche......... Aasche Transportation Services [*Associated Press*] (SAG)
AascheT....... Aasche Transportation Services [*Associated Press*] (SAG)
AASCIN .... American Association of Spinal Cord Injury Nurses (EA)
AASCM .... Awaiting Action Summary Court-Martial
AASCO .... Association of American Seed Control Officials (EA)
AASCU .... American Association of State Colleges and Universities (EA)
AASD .... American Academy of Stress Disorders (EA)
AASD .... Antiaircraft Self-Destroying
AASDJ .... American Association of Schools and Departments of Journalism (EA)
AASDMCC.... American Association for Small Dredging and Marine Construction Companies (EA)
AASE........... Airborne Arctic Stratospheric Expedition
AASE........... Airborne Arctic Stratospheric Experiment [*Marine science*] (OSRA)
AASE........... American Academy of Safety Education (EA)
AASE........... American Association of Special Educators [*Defunct*] (EA)
AASE........... Army Aviation Support Element (AABC)
AASE........... Association for Applied Solar Energy [*Later, International Solar Energy Society*]
AASE........... Australian Associated Stock Exchanges (ADA)
AASEC .... American Association of Sex Educators and Counselors [*Later, AASECT*] (EA)
AASECT........ American Association of Sex Educators, Counselors, and Therapists (EA)
AASF........... Advanced Air Striking Force [*British*]
AASF........... American-Australian Studies Foundation
AASF........... Army Aviation Support Facility (MCD)
AASF........... Asian Amateur Swimming Federation [*Dhaka, Bangladesh*] (EAIO)
AASF........... Associate Administrator for Space Flight [*NASA*] (MCD)
AASFA .... Association d'Amitie et de Solidarite Franco-Algerienne [*Franco-Algerian Friendship and Solidarity Association*]
AASFE.......... American Association of Sunday and Feature Editors (EA)
AASG .... American Association of Students of German [*Defunct*] (EA)
AASG .... Association of American State Geologists [*Defunct*] (EA)
AASGP .... American Association of Sheep and Goat Practitioners [*Later, AASRP*] (EA)
AASH .... Adrenal Androgen Stimulating Hormone [*Medicine*]
AASH .... Alumni Association of Shriners Hospitals (EA)
AASH .... American Association for the Study of Headache (EA)
AASHO .... American Association of State Highway Officials [*Later, AASHTO*] (EA)
AASHTO .... American Association of State Highway and Transportation Officials (EA)
AASI............ Advanced Aerodynamics and Structures, Inc. (ECON)
AASI............ Advertising Agency Service Interchange [*Defunct*] (EA)
AASI............ Associate of the Ambulance Service Institute [*British*] (DBQ)
A'ASIA .... Australasia (ADA)
A'ASIAN .... Australasian (ADA)
AASIR .... Advanced Atmospheric Sounder and Imaging Radiometer [*NASA*] (MCD)
AASIR .... Afro-American Society for International Relations (EA)
AASK .... Adopt a Special Kid (PAZ)
AASK .... African American Study of Kidney Diseases and Hypertension Pilot Study (DMAA)
AASK .... Aid to Adoption of Special Kids [*An association*] (EA)
AASL........... American Association of School Librarians (EA)
AASL........... American Association of State Libraries [*Later, ASCLA*]
AASL........... Antiaircraft Searchlight
AASL........... Associated Aero Science Laboratories (SAA)
AASLD .... African Association for the Study of Liver Diseases (EAIO)
AASLD .... American Association for the Study of Liver Diseases (EA)
AASLH .... American Association for State and Local History (EA)
AASL NPSS... AASL [*American Association of School Librarians*] Non-Public Schools Section
AASLS .... Afro-American Studies Librarians Section [*Association of College and Research Libraries*]
AASL SLMES... AASL [*American Association of School Librarians*] School Library Media Educators Section
AASL SS ...... AASL [*American Association of School Librarians*] Supervisors Section
AASLT.......... Air Assault [*Army*] (AABC)
AASM........... Advanced Air-to-Surface Missile (MCD)
AASM........... Association of American Steel Manufacturers
AASM........... Association of Aviation and Space Museums [*Defunct*] (EA)
AASM........... Australasian Association of Secretaries and Managers
AASMA .... Advanced Avionic Systems for Multi-Mission Application (PDAA)
AASMD .... Airborne Antiship Missile Defense (MCD)
AASME......... Associate of the American Society of Mechanical Engineers
AASMM........ Associated African States, Madagascar and Mauritius [*Later, Association of African, Caribean and Pacific States*] (PDAA)
AASMMA ..... Advanced Avionic System for Multi-Mission Application (MCD)
AASMS .... Advanced Air-to-Surface Missile Seeker [*Navy*] (MCD)
AASND......... American Association for Study of Neoplastic Diseases (EA)
AASNS .... Asian-Australasian Society of Neurological Surgeons [*Kowloon, Hong Kong*] (EAIO)
AASO .... Administrative Aircraft Standardization Office [*NASA*]
AASO .... Afro-Asian Solidarity Organization (NATG)
AASO .... Assigned Activity Standardization Office [*Air Force*] (AFIT)
AASO .... Association of American Ship Owners (EA)
AASP .... Acute Atrophic Spinal Paralysis [*Medicine*] (DMAA)
AASP .... Advanced Automated Sample Processor
AASP .... American Academy of Sports Physicians (EA)
AASP .... American Aid Society of Paris [*France*] (EA)
AASP .... American Association for Social Psychiatry (EA)
AASP .... American Association of Senior Physicians (EA)
AASP .... American Association of Stratigraphic Palynologists (EA)
AASP .... American Association of Swine Practitioners (EA)
AASP .... Arizona Association of School Psychologists (SRA)
AASP .... Army Automation Security Program
AASP .... Arrival and Assembly Support Party [*Navy*] (ANA)
AASP .... Association for the Advancement of Sports Potential (EA)
AASP .... Association of African Studies Programs (EA)
AASP .... Automated Assessment Signal Processor
AASPA .... American Association of School Personnel Administrators (EA)
AASPRC....... American Association of Sheriff Posses and Riding Clubs (EA)
AASq........... Aeromedical Airlift Squadron [*Air Force*] (AFM)
AASQ .... Australian-Asian Society of Queensland
AASR .... Advanced Army System Requirements
AASR .... Airport and Airways Surveillance RADAR [*Air Force*]
AASR .... American Association of Securities Representatives
AASR .... Ancient and Accepted Scottish Rite [*Freemasonry*]
AASRC......... American Association of Small Research Companies (EA)
AASRE .... American Association of Schools of Religious Education [*Later, ATS*] (EA)
AASRI .... Arctic and Antarctic Scientific Research Institute
AASR-NMJ.... Supreme Council, Ancient Accepted Scottish Rite of Freemasonry - Northern Masonic Jurisdiction (EA)
AASROC........ Advanced Antisubmarine Rocket (SAA)
AASRP .... American Association of Small Ruminant Practitioners (EA)
AASR-SMJ ... Supreme Council, Ancient Accepted Scottish Rite of Freemasonry - Southern Masonic Jurisdiction (EA)
AASS .... Academiae Antiquarinae Societales Socius
AASS .... Advanced Acoustic Search Sensors (MCD)
AASS .... Advanced Airborne Surveillance Sensor (MCD)
AASS .... Afro-Asian Solidarity Secretariat (NATG)
AASS .... American Academy of Spinal Surgeons (EA)
AASS .... Americanae Antiquarianae Societatis Socius [*Fellow of the American Antiquarian Society*] [*Latin*]
AASS .... American Association for Social Security (EA)
AASS .... Armenian Assembly Student Services [*Later, AAASAD*] (EA)
AASS .... Army Area Signal System (IAA)
AASS .... Automatic Abort-Sensing System [*NASA*]
AASSA .... Association of American Schools in South America (EA)
AASSC .... Association for the Advancement of Scandinavian Studies in Canada GG2 [*See also AAESC*]
AASSCPA..... American Associations of Spanish Speaking CPA's (EA)
AASSP .... Arkansas Association of Secondary School Principals (SRA)
AASSREC..... Association of Asian Social Science Research Councils [*New Delhi, India*]
AASSWB...... American Association of State Social Work Boards (EA)
AAST........... American Association for the Surgery of Trauma (EA)
AASTA .... Antiaircraft Station
AASTA .... Army Aviation Systems Test Activity [*Also, USAASTA*]
A-ASTP-P..... Association of Apollo-Soyuz Test Project Philatelists (EA)
AASU .... Aeronautics and Astronautics, University of Southampton [*British*] (SAA)
AASU .... All Africa Students Union [*See also UPE*] (EAIO)
AASW .... Airborne Antisubmarine Warfare
AASW .... American Association of Scientific Workers [*Later, USFSS*] (EA)
AASW .... American Association of Social Workers
AASWI .... American Aid Society for the West Indies (EA)
AASWS .... Antimassed Armor Strike Weapon System (MCD)
AAT............. Aachen Aphasia Test [*Medicine*] (DMAA)
AAT............. Abaton Resources Ltd. [*Vancouver Stock Exchange symbol*]
AAT............. Academic Aptitude Test [*Vocational guidance test*]
AAT............. Accelerated Apprenticeship Training (ADA)
AAT............. Achievement Anxiety Text [*Psychology*] (EDAC)
AAT............. Activation Acceptance Team [*NASA*] (NASA)
AAT............. Acute Abdominal Tympany [*Medicine*] (AAMN)
AAT............. Administrative Appeals Tribunal (ADA)
AAT............. Advanced Avionics Test Bed [*The Boeing Co.*]

AAT............ Aerodynamic Accounting Technique (MCD)
AAT............. Air Abrasive Trimming (PDAA)
AAT............. Alanine Aminotransferase [Also, ALAT, ALT, GPT] [An enzyme]
AAT............. All-American Target Term Trust [NYSE symbol] (SPSG)
AAT............. All American Target Term Trust [NYSE symbol] (SAG)
AAT............. All-American Term Trust [NYSE symbol] (TTSB)
AAT............. Alpha-Antitrypsin [Biochemistry]
AAT............. Altay [China] [Airport symbol] (OAG)
AAT............. American Academy of Thermology (EA)
AAT............. American Academy of Transportation
AAT............. Analytic Approximation Theory [Physics] (OA)
AAT............. Anglo-Australian Telescope
AAT............. Antiaircraft Talker (SAA)
AAT............. Antiaircraft Tank (IAA)
AAT............. Antiaircraft Technician (MCD)
AAT............. APACHE [Active Thermal Protection for Avionics Crew and Heat-Sensitve Equipment] Action Team [Army]
AAT............. Arbitrated Access Timer [Telecommunications] (OSI)
AAT............. Army Assault Team
AAT............. Aspartate Aminotransferase [Also, ASAT, AST, GOT] [An enzyme]
AAT............. Assembly and Test (IAA)
AAT............. Association of Accounting Technicians (EAIO)
AAT............. Attitude Acquisition Technique
AAT............. Attitude Angle Transducer
AAT............. Auditory Apperception Test [Psychology]
AAT............. Australian Antarctic Territory
AAT............. Austrian Airtransport [ICAO designator] (FAAC)
AAT............. Automated Assessment Tool (MCD)
AAT............. Automatic Answer Trunk [Computer science] (IAA)
AAT............. Automatic Antenna Timer
AAT............. Average Annual Temperature (PDAA)
AAT............. Les Apocryphes de l'Ancien Testament [A publication] (BJA)
AATA............ Aboriginal Advancement Trust Account [Australia]
AATA............ African Association of Tax Administrators (EAIO)
AATA............ American Art Therapy Association (EA)
AATA............ American Association of Teachers of Arabic (EA)
AATA............ American Automobile Touring Alliance (EA)
AATA............ Animal Air Transportation Association (EA)
AATAB......... Agents' Association, Totalizator Agency Board, New South Wales
AATACB...... American Athletic Trainers Association and Certification Board (EA)
AAT & TC.... Antiaircraft Training and Test Center [Navy]
AATB........... Advanced Amphibious Training Base [Navy]
AATB........... American Association of Tissue Banks (EA)
AATB........... Army Aviation Test Board
AATBN........ Aromatic Amine Terminated Butadiene/Acrylonitrile [Organic chemistry]
AATC........... Advanced Air Training Command [Military]
AATC........... American-ASEAN [Association of South East Asian Nations] Trade Council (EA)
AATC........... Antiaircraft Training Center [Navy]
AATC........... Army Aviation Test Command [ATEC]
AATC........... Automatic Air Traffic Control [System] (IEEE)
AATCAN...... Army Air Traffic Control and Navigation System (MCD)
AATCC........ Airhead Air Traffic Coordination Center [Army] (AFIT)
AATCC........ American Association of Textile Chemists and Colorists (EA)
AATCE......... American Association of Temporary and Contract Employees (EA)
AATCLC....... American Association of Teachers of Chinese Language and Culture [Later, AACS] (EA)
AATCM........ Academy of Air Traffic Control Medicine
AATCO........ Army Air Traffic Coordinating Office (AABC)
AATCS......... [An] Automatic Test Control System (MCD)
AATD........... Aviation Applied Technology Directorate [Fort Eustis, VA] [Army] (RDA)
AATDC........ Army Air Transport Training and Development Centre [England]
AATE........... American Association of Teachers of Esperanto (EA)
AATE........... Aminoadenosine Triacid Ester [Biochemistry]
AATE........... Atlantic Association of Teacher Educators [Canada]
AATE........... Avionics Automatic Transmission Line
AATEA......... American Association of Teacher Educators in Agriculture [Later, AAAE] (EA)
AA Tech...... Associate in Automotive Technology
AATEM........ Association for the Advancement of Teacher Education in Music (AIE)
AA Ter Ed.... Associate in Arts in Terminal Education
AATESL........ American Association of Teachers of English as a Second Language
AATF........... Active Air Target Fuse (MCD)
AATF........... Air Assault Task Force [Army] (ADDR)
AATF........... American Association of Teachers of French (EA)
AATF........... Anechoic Acoustic Test Facility (MCD)
AATFC......... Air Assault Task Force [Army] (INF)
AATG........... American Association of Teachers of German (EA)
AATH........... American Association for Therapeutic Humor (EA)
AATH........... Athabasca Public Library, Alberta [Library symbol National Library of Canada] (NLC)
AAthC......... Athens College, Athens, GA [Library symbol Library of Congress] (LCLS)
AATI............ Alberta Association of Translators & Interpreters [Association des Traducteurs et Interpretes de l'Alberta] (AC)
AATI............ American Anti-Terrorism Institute [Defunct] (EA)
AATI............ American Association of Teachers of Italian (EA)
AATI............ Analysis & Technology, Inc. [NASDAQ symbol] (NQ)
AATL............ Analysis & Technology [NASDAQ symbol] (TTSB)
AATM........... American Academy of Tropical Medicine (EA)
AATMA......... Australian Association of Taxation and Management Accountants

AATMS......... Advanced Air Traffic Management System [Department of Transportation]
AATN........... Asociacion Argentina de Tecnologia Nuclear (NUCP)
AATNU......... Administration de l'Assistance Technique des Nations Unies [United Nations Technical Assistance Administration]
AATO .... All Africa Teachers' Organization (EAIO)
AATO .... Army Air Transport Organization
AATO .... Association of Architectural Technologists of Ontario (AC)
AATP........... American Academy of Tuberculosis Physicians (EA)
AATP........... American Association of Testifying Physicians (EA)
AatP........... Art and Architecture Thesaurus Program, Bennington College, Bennington, VT [Library symbol] [Library of Congress] (LCLS)
AATP........... Assembly and Test Pit [Nuclear energy] (IAA)
AATPA......... American Association of Traveling Passenger Agents [Defunct]
AATPO......... Association of African Trade Promotion Organizations [Tangier, Morocco] (EAIO)
AATR .... Apollo Applications Test Requirements [NASA] (MCD)
AATR .... Association of Auto and Truck Recyclers [Later, ADRA] (EA)
AATRACEN... Antiaircraft Training Center [Navy]
AATRI .... Army Air Traffic Regulation and Identification
AATRIS .... Army Air Traffic Regulation and Identification System (AFM)
AA-tRNA ...... Ribonucleic Acid, Transfer - Aminoacyl [or Aminoacylated] [Biochemistry, genetics]
AATS........... Alternate Aircraft Takeoff System (MCD)
AATS........... American Academy of Teachers of Singing (EA)
AATS........... American Association for Thoracic Surgery (EA)
AATS........... American Association of Theological Schools [Later, ATS] (EA)
AATS........... American Association of Trauma Specialists [Defunct] (EA)
AATS........... Armament Auxiliaries Test Set (MCD)
AATS........... Atikameg-Sovereign School, Alberta [Library symbol National Library of Canada] (BIB)
AATS........... Automatic Altitude Trim System [for helicopters] (NG)
AATS........... Automatic Antitheft System [Electronic lock]
AATSEEL...... American Association of Teachers of Slavic and East European Languages [Defunct] (EA)
AATSP .... American Association of Teachers of Spanish and Portuguese (EA)
AATT .... Aavid Thermal Technologies [NASDAQ symbol] (TTSB)
AATT .... Aavid Thermal Technologies, Inc. [NASDAQ symbol] (SAG)
AATT .... Advanced Aviation Transportation Technology (GAVI)
AATT .... American Association for Textile Technology (EA)
AATT .... American Association of Teachers of Turkish (EA)
AATTC......... American Airlines Technical Training Corp.
AATTV......... Australian Army Training Team, Vietnam (VNW)
AATTVV....... Australian Army Training Team, Vietnam (VNW)
AATU .... American Aid to Ulster (EA)
AATU .... Association of Air Transport Unions [Defunct] (EA)
AATVA......... American All-Terrain Vehicle Association (EA)
AATW .... Advanced Antitank Weapon [Army] (MCD)
AATY .... American Association of Theatre for Youth (EA)
AAU .... Acoustic Add-On Unit (MCD)
AAU .... Activation Analysis Unit [British]
AAU .... Acute Anterior Uveitis [Medicine] (MEDA)
AAU .... Add-On Audio Unit (MCD)
AAU .... Address Arithmetic Unit [Computer science]
AAU .... Administrative Area Unit [Army]
AAU .... Alta [Utah] [Seismograph station code, US Geological Survey Closed] (SEIS)
AAU .... Amanda Resources Ltd. [Vancouver Stock Exchange symbol]
AAU .... Amateur Athletic Union of the United States (EA)
AAU .... American Aid to Ulster (EA)
AAU .... Angular Accelerometer Unit
AAU .... Arua [Uganda] [Airport symbol] (AD)
AAU .... Ashland, OH [Location identifier FAA] (FAAL)
AAU .... Associated Aviation Underwriters
AAU .... Association of African Universities (EAIO)
AAU .... Association of American Universities (EA)
AAU .... Association of Atlantic Universities [Association des Universites de l'Atlantique] (AC)
AAU .... Australia Asia Airlines Ltd. [ICAO designator] (FAAC)
AAU .... Automatic Answering Unit [Telecommunications] (TEL)
AAU .... Auxiliary Air Units [Naval Reserve]
AAU .... United States Air Force, Air University Library, Maxwell AFB, AL [OCLC symbol] (OCLC)
AaUA .... Altaramaeische Urkunden aus Assur [A publication] (BJA)
AAUA .... American Association of University Administrators (EA)
AAUAP......... American Association of University Affiliated Programs for Persons with Developmental Disabilities (EA)
AAUAPDD .... American Association of University Affiliated Programs for Persons with Developmental Disabilities [Later, AAUAP] (EA)
AAU/BNA...... Association of Atlantic Universities/Blackwell North America [Project] [Information service or system] (IID)
AAUCG........ Americans Against Union Control of Government (EA)
AAUG .... Association of Arab-American University Graduates (EA)
A August...... Antonius Augustinus [Deceased, 1586] [Authority cited in pre-1607 legal work] (DSA)
AAUI .... Apple AUI [Attachment Unit Interface] (CDE)
AAUN .... American Association for the United Nations [Later, United Nations Association of the United States] (EA)
AAUNE........ Alumni Association of the University of New England [Australia]
AAUNZ........ Aus Alter und Neuer Zeit [Illustrated Addition to Israelitisches Familienblatt, Hamburg] [A publication] (BJA)
AAUP .... American Association of University Affiliated Programs for the Developmentally Disabled [Washington, DC]
AAUP .... American Association of University Professors (EA)
AAUP .... Association of American University Presses (EA)

AAUP	Association of Australian University Presses
AAUP	Australian Aviation Underwriters' Pool
AAUPF	American Association of University Professors Foundation (EA)
AAUPI	American Association of University Professors of Italian (EDAC)
AAUP-UAES	American Association of University Professors of Urban Affairs and EnvironmentalSciences (EA)
AAUS	American Association of University Students (EA)
AAUSC	American Association of University Supervisors and Coordinators (BARN)
AAUTA	Australian Association of University Teachers of Accounting
AAUTC	Army Aviation Unit Training Command (MCD)
AAUTI	American Association of University Teachers of Insurance [Later, ARIA]
AAU/USA JO	AAU [Amateur Athletic Union of the United States]/USA Junior Olympics (EA)
AAUW	American Association of University Women (EA)
AAUWEF	American Association of University Women Educational Foundation (EA)
AAV	Adeno-Associated Virus
AAV	Advanced Aerospace Vehicle (MCD)
AAV	Airborne [or Amphibious or Armored] Assault Vehicle
AAV	Alah [Philippines] [Airport symbol] (OAG)
AAV	All-Activity Vehicle
AAV	Alternative Access Vendor [Telecommunications]
AAV	Aly Aviation [British ICAO designator] (FAAC)
AAV	Amputees' Association of Victoria [Australia]
AAV	Anti-Afterburn Valve [Automotive engineering]
AAV	Antiaircraft Volunteer
AAV	Assault Amphibian Vehicle [Military]
AAV	Assessed Annual Value [Accounting] (ADA)
AAV	Association of American Vintners (EA)
AAV	Association of Avian Veterinarians (EA)
AAV	Autonomous Air Vehicle [Drone-formerly RPV] [Military] (DOMA)
AAV	Avatar Resources Corp. [Vancouver Stock Exchange symbol]
AAV	Ayrshire Artillery Volunteers [British military] (DMA)
AAVA	American Association of Veterinary Anatomists (EA)
AAVA	Army Audio-Visual Agency (PDAA)
AAVAC	Australian Association of Veterans' Athletic Clubs
AAVB	American Association of Veterinary Bacteriologists [Defunct] (EA)
AAVC	Anomalous Atrioventricular Conduction [Cardiology]
AAVC	Asian American Voters Coalition (EA)
AAVC	Association des Assureurs-Vie du Canada [Association of Life Insurers of Canada]
AAVCRS	Airborne Automatic Voice Communications System (MCD)
AAVCS	Automatic Aircraft Vectoring Control System [Air Force]
AAVCT	American Academy of Veterinary and Comparative Toxicology (EA)
AAVD	American Academy of Veterinary Dermatology (EA)
AAVD	Automatic Alternate Voice/Data [Computer science]
AavidTh	Aavid Thermal Technologies, Inc. [Associated Press] (SAG)
AAVIM	American Association for Vocational Instructional Materials (EA)
AAVLD	American Association of Veterinary Laboratory Diagnosticians (EA)
AAVM	Acting Air Vice-Marshal [British] (DAS)
AAVMC	Association of American Veterinary Medical Colleges (EA)
AAVN	American Academy of Veterinary Nutrition (EA)
AAVN	Army Aviation (AABC)
AAVNA	American Affiliation of Visiting Nurses Associations and Services [Later, VNAA] (EA)
AAvnC	Army Aviation Centre [British] (BI)
AAVP	American Association of Veterinary Parasitologists (EA)
AAVP	Association of American Volunteer Physicians (EA)
AAVPT	American Academy of Veterinary Pharmacology and Therapeutics (EA)
AAVRB	Australian Audio-Visual Reference Book [A publication] (APTA)
AAVRPHS	American Association for Vital Records and Public Health Statistics [Later, AVRHS] (EA)
AAVRS	All-Attitude Vertical Reference System [Aerospace]
AAVS	Aerospace Audiovisual Service [Air Force] (MCD)
AAVS	American Anti-Vivisection Society (EA)
AAVS	Aspirator-Assisted Vacuum System [Automotive engineering]
AAVS	Association for Administration of Volunteer Services [Later, AVA] (EA)
AAVS	Automatic Aircraft Vectoring System [Air Force] (MUGU)
AAVSB	American Association of Veterinary State Boards (EA)
AAVSC	American Association of Volunteer Services Coordinators [Later, AVA]
AAVSED	Automatic Air-Valving Surface Effects Device [Army] (MCD)
AAVSO	American Association of Variable Star Observers (EA)
AAVT	Association of Audio-Visual Technicians (EA)
A Av Tech	Associate in Aviation Technology
AAVV	Accumulated Alveolar Ventilatory Volume [Respiratory testing] (DAVI)
AAW	Aberdeen Airways [British ICAO designator] (FAAC)
AAW	Aberdeen Airways Ltd.
AAW	Advertising Association of the West [Later, AAF] (EA)
AAW	Aeromedical Airlift Wing [Air Force] (MCD)
AAW	Air Acetylene Welding
AAW	Almeta Air [Austria] [FAA designator] (FAAC)
AAW	American Academy of Wine [Defunct] (EA)
AAW	American Agri-Women (EA)
AAW	American Association of Women (EA)
AAW	American Association of Woodturners (EA)
AAW	American Atheist Women (EA)
AAW	Anterior Aortic Wall [Medicine] (DMAA)
AAW	Antiair Warfare
AAW	Antiair Weapon (SAA)
AAW	Talkeetna Mountains, AK [Location identifier FAA] (FAAL)

AAWB	American Association of Workers for the Blind [Later, AER] (EA)
AAWBOT	Aviation Antisubmarine Warfare Basic Operational Trainer
AAWC	All-African Women's Conference [or Congress]
AAWC	American Association of Workers for Children
AAWC	Antiair Warfare Center
AAWC	Antiair Warfare Commander [or Coordinator] (NVT)
AAWCJC	American Association of Women in Community and Junior Colleges (EA)
AAWD	American Association of Women Dentists (EA)
AAWDT	Annual Average Weekday Traffic [TRB] (TAG)
AAWE	Association of American Wives of Europeans (EA)
AAWEX	Antiair Warfare Exercise [Navy] (NG)
AAWEXINPT	Antiair Warfare Exercise in Port [Navy] (NVT)
AAWg	Aeromedical Airlift Wing [Air Force] (AFM)
AAWH	American Association for World Health (EA)
AAWIPT	Antiair Warfare Training in Port [Navy] (NVT)
AAWM	American Association of Waterbed Manufacturers [Later, WMA]
AAWM	American Association of Women Ministers [Later, IAWM] (EA)
AAWMIS	Army Acquisition Workforce Management Information System (RDA)
AAWO	Afro-Asian Workers' Organization (NATG)
AAWO	Association of Accommodation and Welfare Officers [British] (DBA)
AAWO	Association of American Weather Observers (EA)
AAWORD	Association of African Women for Research and Development (EAIO)
AAWP	American Association for Women Podiatrists (EA)
AAWP	American Association of Working People
AAWPA	Australian Amateur Water Polo Association
AAWPB	Afro-Asian Writers' Permanent Bureau (NATG)
AAWPC	Asian-American Women's Political Caucus (EA)
AAWPI	Association of American Wood Pulp Importers (EA)
AAWR	American Association of Women Radiologists (EA)
AAW(R)	Antiair Warfare Reporting [Navy] (NVT)
AAWR	Woomera [Australia ICAO location identifier] (ICLI)
AAWRATS	Antiair Warfare Readiness Assessment Training System (MCD)
AAWRC	American Agri-Women Resource Center (EA)
AAWS	Airborne Alert Weapon System
AAWS	Alcoholics Anonymous World Services [Canada]
AAWS	Antiair Warfare Systems [Navy] (MCD)
AAWS	Automatic Attack Warning System (AFM)
AAWS-H	Auxiliary Aircraft Warning Service
AAWS-H	Advanced Antitank Weapon System - Heavy
AAWS-M	Advance Antitank Weapon System - Medium (DWSG)
AAWS-M	Advanced Antiarmor Weapon System, Medium [Army] (INF)
AAWS-M	Advanced Antitank Weapon System - Medium [Pronounced "awesome"] (RDA)
AAWSSC	Army Atomic Weapons Systems Safety Committee [Later, DNA] (AABC)
AAWSUP	Antiair Warfare Support (NVT)
AAWTA	Advise at What Time Able [Aviation] (FAAC)
AAWTC	Assistant Airway Traffic Controller (IAA)
AAWTG	Agricultural and Allied Workers' National Trade Group [British]
AAWU	Athletic Association of Western Universities (BARN)
AAWV	American Association of Wildlife Veterinarians (EA)
AAWWS	Airborne Adverse Weather Weapons System (MCD)
AAWWW	Amalgamated Association of Wistful War Wives [World War II]
AAX	Amuraviatrans [Former USSR] [FAA designator] (FAAC)
AAX	Araxa [Brazil] [Airport symbol] (OAG)
AAXICO	American Air Export & Import Co.
AAY	Age Action Year [1976] (DI)
AAY	Air Antares Ltd. [Romania] [ICAO designator] (FAAC)
AAY	Al Ghaydah [Aden] [Airport symbol] (AD)
AAYA	Authors and Artists for Young Adults [A publication]
AAYM	American Association of Youth Museums (EA)
AAYO	All-American Youth Orchestra
AAYPL	Atlantic Association of Young Political Leaders (EA)
AAYPP	American Association of Yellow Pages Publishers [Defunct] (EA)
AAYSO	Afro-Asian Youth Solidarity Organization (NATG)
AAZ	Angus Aviation Ltd. [Canada ICAO designator] (FAAC)
AAZ	Oakland, CA [Location identifier FAA] (FAAL)
AAZK	American Association of Zoo Keepers (EA)
AAZN	American Association for Zoological Nomenclature (EA)
AAZPA	American Association of Zoological Parks and Aquariums (EA)
AAZV	American Association of Zoo Veterinarians (EA)
Ab	Abbas Antiquus [Deceased, 1296] [Authority cited in pre-1607 legal work] (DSA)
AB	Abbey [or Abbot]
AB	AB Bookman's Weekly [A publication] (BRI)
AB	Abbreviation (ROG)
AB	Abdomen [Medicine]
AB	Able-Bodied Seaman
AB	Able Seaman [Navy]
AB	Abnormal (MAE)
ab	Abortion [Medicine] (DMAA)
AB	Abortion Patient [Medicine]
Ab	Aboth (BJA)
AB	About
Ab	Abridgment (DLA)
AB	Abscess (ABBR)
AB	Absent (ROG)
AB	Abstract [Online database field identifier]
AB	Abstracting Board [International Council of Scientific Unions] [Information service or system] (IID)
Ab	Abstracts of Treasury Decisions [United States] [A publication] (DLA)
AB	Abyssinia
AB	Accessories Bulletin (MCD)
AB	Accident Benefits [Insurance]

AB	Accumulator and Buffer [*Computer science*] (IAA)
ab	Ace Bandage (HGAA)
A/B	Acid/Base [*Ratio*] (AAMN)
AB	Acquisition Beacon
AB	Acrylonitrile-Butadiene [*Organic chemistry*]
ab	Active Bilaterally (HGAA)
AB	Acute Bisectrix [*Crystallography*]
AB	Adapter Booster
AB	Adapter, Bulkhead
AB	Adaptive Behavior [*Psychology*]
AB	Additional Benefits [*Unemployment insurance*]
AB	Address Buffer (MCD)
AB	Address Bus [*Computer science*]
AB	Adjustment Bond [*Investment term*]
AB	Administrative Battalion [*British military*] (DMA)
AB	Administrative Bulletin (MCD)
AB	Admiralty Board [*British*]
AB	Advance Purchase Required [*Also, AP*] [*Airline fare code*]
AB	Advisory Board
AB	Aerial Burst Bombs
AB	Aeronautical Board [*Air Force*]
AB	Aero Talleres Boero SRL [*Argentina ICAO aircraft manufacturer identifier*] (ICAO)
AB	Africana Bulletin [*Warsaw*] [*A publication*]
AB	After Body
AB	Afterburner [*on jet engines*]
AB	Aharonov-Bohm [*Physics*]
AB	Aid to the Blind
AB	Air Bags
AB	Air Base
AB	Air Bearing (KSC)
AB	Air Berlin USA [*ICAO designator*] (ICDA)
AB	Air Blast (MSA)
AB	Air Board [*RAF*] [*British*]
AB	Air Bomber
AB	Airborne [*ICAO designator*] (FAAC)
AB	Air Brake [*Automotive engineering*]
AB	Air Break [*Mechanical engineering*] (IAA)
A/B	Air Breather [*Aerospace*]
AB	Air Brick
A/B	Aircraft Bulletin
AB	Air-Cushion Vehicle built by Air Bearings [*England*] [*Usually used in combination with numerals*]
AB	Airman Basic
AB	Aktiebolag [*or Aktiebolaget*] [*Joint-Stock Company*] [*Sweden*]
Ab	Alabamine [*Superseded by astatine*] [*Chemical element*]
AB	Alberta [*Canadian province*] [*Postal code*]
ab	Albite [*CIPW classification*] [*Geology*]
AB	Alcian Blue [*A biological stain*]
AB	Alert Building (NATG)
AB	Alexander Brown, Inc. [*NYSE symbol*] (SPSG)
AB	Alex Brown Inc. [*NYSE symbol*] (TTSB)
AB	All [*Text*] Before [*Specified Point*] [*Message handling*]
A-B	Allen-Bradley Co.
AB	Alliance Balkanique [*Balkan Alliance*]
AB	Alternative Broadcasting [*An association*] (EA)
AB	Amarillo Branch [*Military*] (SAA)
AB	Ambush
AB	American Banker [*A publication*]
AB	American Bureau of Shipping
AB	AminoAzobenzene [*Organic chemistry*]
AB	Aminobenzamide [*Organic chemistry*]
AB	Aminobenzophenone [*Organic chemistry*]
AB	Ammunition Bearer [*Military*] (INF)
AB	Anchor Bolt [*Technical drawings*]
AB	Anheuser-Busch, Inc.
AB	Ankina Breeders [*Inactive*] (EA)
A/B	Ankle/Brachial Pressure Index
AB	Announce Booth [*Soundproof room*] [*Television studio*] (NTCM)
AB	Anonymous Reports at End of Benloe [*1661*] [*England*] [*A publication*] (DLA)
AB	Antenna Supports [*JETDS nomenclature*] [*Military*] (CET)
AB	Anterior Burster [*Neuron*]
Ab	Antibody [*Also, aby*] [*Immunology*]
ab	Antibody [*Medicine*] (DMAA)
ab+	Antibody Positive
AB	Antigen-Binding [*Immunology*]
AB	Apex Beat [*Medicine*]
AB	Apnea-Bradycardia [*Spells*] [*Medicine*] (DAVI)
AB	Application Block (MSA)
AB	Applied Biosystems, Inc.
AB	Arc Brazing
AB	Archbishop (ROG)
A/B	Architectural Barriers
AB	Architecture Bulletin [*A publication*]
AB	Arctic Bibliography [*A publication*]
AB	Arithmetic Bus [*Computer science*] (IAA)
AB	Armor Board (MCD)
AB	Armour Pharmaceutical Co. [*Research code symbol*]
AB	Army Book [*British and Canadian*] [*World War II*]
AB	Array Bending (SSD)
AB	Artium Baccalaureus [*Bachelor of Arts*]
AB	As Before
AB	Asbestos Body (DAVI)
AB	Asbestos Corp. Ltd. [*Toronto Stock Exchange symbol*]
AB	Assault Breaker (MCD)
AB	Assembly Bill [*in state legislatures*]
AB	Assistance for the Blind
AB	Assistant Barrister [*British*] (ROG)
AB	Associated with Brokers [*London Stock Exchange*]
AB	Associate in Business
AB	Association of Bankrupts (EAIO)
AB	Association of Brewers [*Later, AOB*] (EA)
AB	Aster Growth with Brown Sedge [*Ecology*]
AB	Asthmatic Bronchitis [*Medicine*] (ADA)
AB	Asymmetric Balance [*Marine science*] (OSRA)
AB	Asymmetric Balance (USDC)
AB	At Bat [*Baseball*]
AB	Audio Bandwidth
AB	Auer Bodies [*Medicine*]
aB	Auf Bestellung [*On Order*] [*German*] (ILCA)
AB	Australian Ballet
AB	Australian Baptist [*A publication*] (APTA)
AB	Australian Boating [*A publication*]
AB	Australian Bridge [*A publication*]
AB	Auto Beacon (KSC)
AB	Automated Banking
AB	Automated Bibliography
AB	Automatic Blow Down (IEEE)
AB	Automatic Weather Broadcast (DA)
AB	Aviation Battalion [*Army*]
AB	Aviation Boatswain [*Navy rating*]
AB	Avionics Bay (MCD)
AB	Axiobuccal [*Dentistry*] (MAE)
AB	Bachelor of Arts (AEE)
AB	Banff Library, Alberta [*Library symbol National Library of Canada*] (NLC)
ab----	Bengal, Bay of [*MARC geographic area code Library of Congress*] (LCCP)
AB	Birmingham Public and Jefferson County Free Library, Birmingham, AL [*Library symbol Library of Congress*] (LCLS)
AB	Bond Adjustment [*Finance*]
AB	Crane Ship [*Navy symbol Obsolete*]
AB	Dainippon Pharmaceutical Co. [*Japan*] [*Research code symbol*]
AB	Falcon Airlines [*ICAO designator*] (AD)
AB	Faulty Abbreviation [*Used in correcting manuscripts, etc.*]
AB	Harbor Launch [*Coast Guard*] (DNAB)
AB	Roswell Park Memorial Institute [*Research code symbol*]
AB1	Aviation Boatswain's Mate, First Class [*Navy rating*]
AB2	Aviation Boatswain's Mate, Second Class [*Navy rating*]
AB3	Aviation Boatswain's Mate, Third Class [*Navy rating*]
ABA	Aaron Burr Association (EA)
ABA	Ababa [*Ethiopia*] [*Airport symbol*] (AD)
ABA	Abbas Air Ltd. [*British ICAO designator*] (FAAC)
ABA	Abscisic Acid [*Biochemistry*]
ABA	Achievable Benefit Achieved
ABA	Acrylonitrile-Butadiene-Acrylate [*Organic chemistry*]
ABA	Aerial Biosensing Association (EA)
ABA	African Bar Association (EAIO)
ABA	Airborne Alert (IIA)
ABA	Airborne Assault (CINC)
ABA	Air Brake Association (EA)
ABA	Aktiebolaget Aero Transport [*Swedish airline*]
ABA	Aktiebolaget Atomenergi [*Swedish nuclear development company*]
ABA	Alabama Bankers Association (SRA)
ABA	Alaska Bar Association (SRA)
ABA	Alaska Broadcasters Association (SRA)
ABA	Alger-Bouzareah [*Algeria*] [*Seismograph station code, US Geological Survey*]
ABA	Allergic Bronchopulmonary Aspergillosis [*Medicine*]
ABA	Allied Beauty Association (AC)
ABA	Amateur Boxing Association [*British*]
ABA	American Badminton Association [*Later, USBA*] (EA)
ABA	American Bakers Association (EA)
ABA	American Bandmasters Association (EA)
ABA	American Bankers Association [*Washington, DC*] (EA)
ABA	American Bantam Association (EA)
ABA	American Baptist Association
ABA	American Bar Association (EA)
ABA	American Bartenders' Association (EA)
ABA	American Basketball Association [*Later, NBA*] [*League of professional basketball players*] (EA)
ABA	American Bass Association (EA)
ABA	American Battleship Association (EA)
ABA	American Beauty Association (EA)
ABA	American Beefalo Association (EA)
ABA	American Behcet's Association (EA)
ABA	American Bell Association [*Later, ABAI*] (EA)
ABA	American Benedictine Academy (EA)
ABA	American Berkshire Association (EA)
ABA	American Bicycle Association (EA)
ABA	American Billiard Association (EA)
ABA	American Birding Association (EA)
ABA	American Board of Anesthesiology (EA)
ABA	American Boccaccio Association (EA)
ABA	American Book Awards [*Formerly, TABA*]
ABA	American Booksellers Association (EA)
ABA	American Bowhunters Association [*Defunct*] (EA)
ABA	American Bralers Association (EA)

ABA............ American Brazilian Association [*Later, Brazilian American Chamber of Commerce*] (EA)
ABA............ American Breed Association (EA)
ABA............ American Breweriana Association (EA)
ABA............ American Bridge Association (EA)
ABA............ American, British, Australian [*Military*]
ABA............ American Buddhist Academy (EA)
ABA............ American Buddhist Association (EA)
ABA............ American Buffalo Association (EA)
ABA............ American Bullmastiff Association (EA)
ABA............ American Burn Association (EA)
ABA............ American Bus Association (EA)
ABA............ American Business Association [*New York, NY*] (EA)
ABA............ Aminobutyric Acid [*Also, Abu*] [*Organic chemistry*]
ABA............ Amplifier Buffer Attenuator (MCD)
ABA............ Annual Budget Authorization (AFM)
ABA............ Antibacterial Activity [*Medicine*] (MAE)
ABA............ Antiquarian Booksellers Association [*International*]
ABA............ Antoniani Benedictini Armeni [*Mechitarists*]
ABA............ Applied Behavior Analysis [*Psychology*]
ABA............ Appropriation and Budget Activity [*Army*] (AABC)
ABA............ Arab Bankers' Association
ABA............ Architectural Barriers Act of 1968 (WYGK)
ABA............ Archives of the Canadian Rockies, Banff, Alberta [*Library symbol National Library of Canada*] (NLC)
ABA............ Area-by-Area-Allocation [*Marketing*] (DOAD)
ABA............ Arizona Bankers Association (SRA)
ABA............ Arizona Broadcasters Association (SRA)
ABA............ Arizona Builders Alliance (SRA)
ABA............ Arizona Business Association (SRA)
ABA............ Arkansas Bar Association (SRA)
ABA............ Arkansas Broadcasters Association (SRA)
ABA............ Armadillo Breeders Association [*Defunct*] (EA)
ABA............ Artem-Avia [*Ukraine*] [*FAA designator*] (FAAC)
ABA............ ASEAN [*Association of South East Asian Nations*] Bankers Association [*Singapore, Singapore*] (EAIO)
ABA............ Associate in Business Administration
ABA............ Association Belgo-Americaine [*Later, American-Belgian Association*] (EA)
ABA............ Association for Behavior Analysis (EA)
ABA............ Association of Black Anthropologists (EA)
ABA............ Ateba Mines, Inc. [*Toronto Stock Exchange symbol*]
ABA............ Australian Barefoot Association
ABA............ Australian Bicentennial Authority
ABA............ Australian Borrowers' Association
ABA............ Authorized Bond Allotment (MCD)
ABA............ Ayrshire Breeders' Association (EA)
ABA............ Azobenzenearsonate [*Also, ARS*] [*Organic chemistry*]
a-ba-- .... Bahrain [*MARC geographic area code Library of Congress*]
ABA............ Belgian-American Association (EAIO)
ABA............ Whyte Museum of the Canadian Rockies (Archives), Banff, Alberta [*Library symbol National Library of Canada*] (NLC)
ABAA .... Airman Apprentice, Aviation Boatswain's Mate, Striker [*Navy rating*]
ABAA .... American Beverage Alcohol Association [*Defunct*] (EA)
ABAA .... American Blonde d'Aquitaine Association (EA)
ABAA .... Antiquarian Booksellers Association of America (EA)
ABAA .... Associate of the British Association of Accountants and Auditors (BARN)
ABAA .... Association of Business Advertising Agencies [*British*] (DBA)
ABAAR .... Regional Office, Alberta Agriculture, Barrhead, Alberta [*Library symbol National Library of Canada*] (NLC)
ab Abr .... Ab Abraham [*The chronological reckoning from the first year of Abraham; St. Jerome's translation and enlargement of Eusebius' Chronicle*] [*Classical studies*] (OCD)
ABAC .... Abacan Resource Corp. [*NASDAQ symbol*] (SAG)
ABAC .... Abraham Baldwin Agricultural College [*Tifton, GA*]
ABAC .... Alpine Club, Banff, Alberta [*Library symbol National Library of Canada*] (NLC)
ABAC .... American Bosch Arma Corp. (AAG)
ABAC .... Antiquarian Booksellers Association of Canada
ABAC .... Appropriation and Budget Account Code
ABAC .... Association of Balloon and Airship Constructors (EA)
ABAC .... Association of British Aero Clubs (BI)
ABAC .... Association of British Aviation Consultants (DA)
ABAC .... Association of Business and Administrative Computing (MHDB)
ABAC .... Ayrshire Breeders Association of Canada (AC)
Abacan .... Abacan Resource Corp. [*Associated Press*] (SAG)
ABACCL .... ABA [*American Bar Association*] Center on Children and the Law (EA)
AbacDir........ Abacus Direct Corp. [*Associated Press*] (SAG)
ABACE .... Abacan Resource [*NASDAQ symbol*] (TTSB)
ABACIS .... Antiquarian Book and Collectibles Information Systems (IID)
ABACPD ...... American Bar Association Center for Professional Discipline (DLA)
ABACPR....... American Bar Association Center for Professional Responsibility (EA)
ABACR .... Acrylonitrile Butadiene Alternating Copolymer Rubber (PDAA)
ABACS .... Distance Education Research Centre Library, Alberta Correspondence School, Barrhead, Alberta [*Library symbol National Library of Canada*] (BIB)
ABACUS....... Agents and Brokers Automated Computer Users System (MHDI)
ABACUS....... Air Battle Analysis Center Utility System [*Air Force*]
ABACUS....... Aktiebolaget Atomenergi Computer-Based User-Oriented Service
ABACUS....... Architecture and Building Aids Computer Unit, Strathclyde University (PDAA)
ABACUS....... Arizona Basic Assessment and Curriculum Utilization System (EDAC)

ABACUS....... Association of Bibliographic Agencies of Britain, Australia, Canada, and the United States (ADA)
ABACUS....... Automatic, Block-Schematic Advanced Control User-Oriented System (PDAA)
ABACUS....... Autonetics Business & Control United Systems, Inc.
ABAD .... Air Base Air Defense [*Air Force*] (MCD)
ABAD .... Air Battle Analysis Division [*Air Force*]
ABADRL .... Arthropod-Borne Animal Diseases Research Laboratory [*Department of Agriculture*] (GRD)
ABAE .... Amateur Boxing Association of England (EAIO)
AB-AF .... Alcian Blue-Aldehyde Fuchsin [*Dyes*] (OA)
ABAF .... Brisbane/Archerfield [*Australia ICAO location identifier*] (ICLI)
ABAFA .... Association of British Adoption and Fostering Agencies (DI)
ABAFAOILSS... Association of Black Admissions and Financial Aid Officers of the Ivy League andSister Schools (EA)
ABAFLSMAC... American Bar Association, Family Law Section, Mediation and Arbitration Committee [*Defunct*] (EA)
ABAG .... Safety Components International, Inc. [*NASDAQ symbol*] (SAG)
ABAG .... Safety Components Intl. [*NASDAQ symbol*] (TTSB)
ABAH .... Alberta Horticultural Research Centre, Brooks, Alberta [*Library symbol National Library of Canada*] (NLC)
ABAH .... Australian Bureau of Animal Health
ABAI .... American Bell Association International (EA)
ABAI .... American Board of Allergy and Immunology (EA)
ABA Jour .... ABA Journal [*A publication*] (BRI)
ABAKO .... Alliance des Bakongo [*Alliance of the Bakongo People*]
ABAKWA ...... Alliance de Baboma-Bateke du Kwamouth [*Alliance of Baboma-Bateke People of Kwamouth*]
abal .... Abalone (VRA)
ABAL .... Aminobutyraldehyde [*Organic chemistry*]
ABA/LSD ...... Law Student Division - American Bar Association (EA)
ABAM .... Amberley [*Australia ICAO location identifier*] (ICLI)
ABAM .... Bawlf Municipal Library, Alberta [*Library symbol National Library of Canada*] (NLC)
ABAMP .... Absolute Ampere
ABA MPC .... American Bar Association Model Procurement Code [*A publication*] (AAGC)
ABAN .... Abandon [*Legal shorthand*] (LWAP)
ABAN .... Airman, Aviation Boatswain's Mate, Striker [*Navy rating*]
ABAN .... Amer Bancshares [*NASDAQ symbol*] (TTSB)
ABAN .... American Bancshares, Inc. (FL) [*NASDAQ symbol*] (SAG)
ABAN .... Asian Bureau Australia Newsletter [*A publication*]
ABANA .... Artist Blacksmith Association of North America (EA)
ABAND........ Abandoned
AB & C .... Atlanta, Birmingham & Coast Railroad Co.
AB & E........ Attempt Break and Enter [*Criminology*]
AB & LA ...... Australian Builder and Land Advertiser [*A publication*]
ABAND LT HO... Abandoned Lighthouse
ABANDMT..... Abandonment (ABBR)
ABANDT....... Abandonment
ABANM .... Abandonment [*Legal shorthand*] (LWAP)
ABANSW ...... Amateur Beekeepers' Association of New South Wales [*Australia*]
ABAP .... Alabama Power Co., Birmingham, AL [*Library symbol Library of Congress*] (LCLS)
AbAP........... Antibody-Against-Panel [*Immunology*] (AAMN)
ABAPSTAS ... Association of Blind and Partially-Sighted Teachers and Students [*British*]
ABAR .... Advanced [*or Alternate*] Battery Acquisition RADAR
ABAR .... Alberta RCMP Century Library, Beaverlodge, Alberta [*Library symbol National Library of Canada*] (NLC)
ABAR .... Auxiliary Battery Acquisition RADAR (MCD)
ABARE .... Australian +Bureau of Agricultural and Resource Economics (IID)
ABA Rep ...... American Bar Association Reporter [*A publication*] (DLA)
ABA Rep ...... American Bar Association Reports [*A publication*] (DLA)
ABA Rep Int'l & Comp L Sec... American Bar Association. International and Comparative Law Section. Reports [*A publication*] (DLA)
ABARHP....... American Bar Association Representation of the Homeless Project (EA)
ABARM .... Barnwell Municipal Library, Alberta [*Library symbol National Library of Canada*] (NLC)
ABARR .... Barrhead Public Library, Alberta [*Library symbol National Library of Canada*] (NLC)
ABAS .... Alice Springs [*Australia ICAO location identifier*] (ICLI)
ABAS .... Amateur Basketball Association of Scotland (BI)
ABAS .... American Board of Abdominal Surgery (EA)
ABAS .... Association of Business Administration Studies [*British*] (EAIO)
ABAS .... Bassano Public Library, Alberta [*Library symbol National Library of Canada*] (NLC)
ABASCDR .... American Bar Association Special Committee on Dispute Resolution (EA)
ABA Sec Lab Rel L... American Bar Association. Section of Labor Relations Law (DLA)
ABASG .... Abasing (ABBR)
ABASH .... Bashaw Public Library, Alberta [*Library symbol National Library of Canada*] (NLC)
ABASILP ...... American Bar Association Section of International Law and Practice (EA)
ABASNT ...... Abasement (ABBR)
ABASS .... Air Base Augmentation Support Set [*Air Force*] (AFM)
ABASS .... Assembly for Behavioral and Social Sciences [*National Research Council*]
ABAST .... Abasement (ABBR)
ABAT........... Abatement [*Legal term*] (DLA)
ABAT........... Air Base Advisory Team (CINC)
ABAT........... American Board of Applied Toxicology (DMAA)

ABATA .... Able-Bodied Seaman, Air Technical Aircraft [*Navy*]
ABATB .... Abatable (ABBR)
ABATC .... Able-Bodied Seaman, Air Technical Communications [*Navy*]
ABA/TCP ...... Traffic Court Program of the American Bar Association (EA)
ABATE........ Alliance des Bateke [*Alliance of Bateke*]
ABATE........ American Bikers Aimed toward Education
ABATE........ [*A*] Brotherhood Towards Education
ABATG........ Abating (ABBR)
Abatix........ Abatix Environmental Corp. [*Associated Press*] (SAG)
ABATMT...... Abatement (ABBR)
ABATNT...... Abatement (ABBR)
A Batt .... A Battuta [*Music*]
ABATU........ Advanced Base Aviation Training Unit [*Navy*]
ABATWL ..... Able-Bodied Seaman, Air Technical Weapons Electrical [*Navy*]
ABAU .... University of Alabama in Birmingham, Birmingham, AL [*Library symbol Library of Congress*] (LCLS)
ABAU-M...... University of Alabama in Birmingham, Lister Hill Library of the Health Sciences,Birmingham, AL [*Library symbol Library of Congress*] (LCLS)
ABAUSA...... Amateur Basketball Association of the United States of America [*Later, USA Basketball*] (EA)
ABAV .... Air Bleed Actuator Valve [*Automotive engineering*]
ABAV .... Australian Biathlon Association Victoria
ABAX .... Abaxis, Inc. [*NASDAQ symbol*] (SAG)
Abaxis .... Abaxis, Inc. [*Associated Press*] (SAG)
ABAYLD ...... American Bar Association Young Lawyers Division (EA)
ABAZI .... Alliance des Bayanzi [*Alliance of Bayanzis*]
Abb .... Abbassamento [*Music*]
Abb .... Abbey [*Record label*]
ABB .... Abbey
ABB .... Abbey Exploration, Inc. [*Toronto Stock Exchange symbol*]
Abb .... Abbildungen [*Illustration, Figure*] [*German*] (BJA)
Abb .... Abbott Laboratories
Abb .... Abbott. United States Circuit and District Court Reports [*A publication*] (DLA)
ABB .... Abbreviation (ROG)
ABBD.......... Ablating Blunt Body
ABB .... Added Belly Band [*Military*] (CAAL)
ABB .... Air Belgium [*ICAO designator*] (FAAC)
ABB .... [*The*] Akron & Barberton Belt Railroad Co. [*AAR code*]
ABB .... Albright-Butler-Bloomberg Syndrome [*Medicine*] (DMAA)
AbB .... Altbabylonische Briefe im Umschrift und Uebersetzung [*A publication*] (BJA)
ABB .... American Board of Bioanalysis (EA)
ABB .... Anterior Basal Body
ABB .... Arab-Burundi Bank SARL (EY)
ABB .... Array of Building Blocks (MHDI)
ABB .... Artificial Breeding Box
ABB .... Asea Brown Boveri [*Swedish-Swiss manufacturing company*] (ECON)
ABB .... Australian Bowls Board
ABB .... Automatic Back Bias [*RADAR*]
ABB .... Axisymmetric Blunt Body
ABB .... Nabb, IN [*Location identifier FAA*] (FAAL)
ABBA .... Able-Bodied Sick Bay Attendant [*Navy*]
ABBA .... Agnetha Faltskog, Bjorn Ulvaeus, Benny Andersson, Anni-Frid Lyngstad [*Swedish singing group; acronym formed from first letters of their first names*]
ABBA .... Amateur Basketball Association [*British*] (BI)
ABBA .... American Bail Bondsman Association (EA)
ABBA .... American Bed and Breakfast Association (EA)
ABBA .... American Bee Breeders Association (EA)
ABBA .... American Blind Bowling Association (EA)
ABB-A .... American Board of Bio-Analysis [*No connection with ABB*] [*Defunct*] (EA)
ABBA .... American Brahman Breeders Association (EA)
ABBA .... Arbejdsloshedsstatistikkens Bruger-Bank [*Danmarks Statistik*] [*Denmark Information service or system*] (CRD)
ABBA .... Australian Bloodhorse Breeders Association
ABB AB .... ABB AB [*NASDAQ symbol*] (SAG)
ABB AB .... ABB AB [*Associated Press*] (SAG)
Abb Ad........ Abbott's Admiralty Reports [*United States*] [*A publication*] (DLA)
Abb Adm..... Abbott's Admiralty Reports [*United States*] [*A publication*] (DLA)
Abb Ad R .... Abbott's Admiralty Reports [*United States*] [*A publication*] (DLA)
Abb Ap Dec... Abbott's Court of Appeals Decisions [*New York*] [*A publication*] (DLA)
Abb App Dec... Abbott's Court of Appeals Decisions [*New York*] [*A publication*] (DLA)
ABBB .... ABB AB [*NASDAQ symbol*] (SAG)
ABBB .... Association of Better Business Bureaus [*Later, CBBB*]
ABBB .... Brisbane [*Australia ICAO location identifier*] (ICLI)
Abb Beech Tr... Abbott's Reports of the Beecher Trial [*A publication*] (DLA)
ABBBMR...... Another Boring Book Bi-Monthly Rag [*Subtitle for the periodical Slightly Soiled*] [*British A publication*]
ABBBY .... ABB AB ADR [*NASDAQ symbol*] (TTSB)
ABBC .... American Baptist Black Caucus (EA)
ABBC .... Association of Bottled Beer Collectors (EAIO)
Abb CC .... Abbott's Circuit Court Reports [*United States*] [*A publication*] (DLA)
Abb Cl Ass... Abbott's Clerks and Conveyancers' Assistant [*A publication*] (DLA)
Abb Ct App... Abbott's Court of Appeals Decisions [*New York*] [*A publication*] (DLA)
Abb Ct of App Dec... Abbott's Court of Appeals Decisions [*New York*] [*A publication*] (DLA)
Abb Dec....... Abbott's Decisions [*A publication*] (DLA)
Abb Dict...... Abbott's Dictionary [*A publication*] (DLA)
Abb Dig .... Abbott's New York Digest [*A publication*] (DLA)

Abb Dig Corp... Abbott's Digest of the Law of Corporations [*A publication*] (DLA)
ABBE .... Advisory Board on the Built Environment [*Formerly, BRAB*] (EA)
Abb F.......... Abbott's Forms of Pleading [*A publication*] (DLA)
ABBF.......... Advanced Beef Breeds Federation
ABBF.......... Association of Bronze and Brass Founders [*British*] (BI)
Abb F Sup ... Abbott's Forms of Pleading, Supplement [*A publication*] (DLA)
AB (Bible).... Bachelor of Arts in Bible
ABBIM .... Association of Brass and Bronze Ingot Manufacturers (EA)
Abb Ind Dig... Abbott's Indiana Digest [*A publication*] (DLA)
Abb Int........ Abbott's Introduction to Practice under the Codes [*A publication*] (DLA)
ABBK .... Abington Savings Bank [*NASDAQ symbol*] (NQ)
Abb Law Dict... Abbott's Law Dictionary [*1879*] [*A publication*] (DLA)
Abb L Dic .... Abbott's Law Dictionary [*1879*] [*A publication*] (DLA)
Abb Leg Rem... Abbott's Legal Remembrancer [*A publication*] (DLA)
ABBM.......... Automatic Baseband Monitor (PDAA)
ABBM.......... Baptist Medical Center, School of Nursing, Birmingham, AL [*Library symbol Library of Congress*] (LCLS)
ABBMM........ Associatin of British Brush Machinery Manufacturers (MHDB)
ABBM-M...... Baptist Medical Center (Montclair), Medical Library, Birmingham, AL [*Library symbol Library of Congress*] (LCLS)
Abb Mo Ind... Abbott's Monthly Index [*A publication*] (DLA)
ABBM-P...... Baptist Medical Center (Princeton), Medical Library, Birmingham, AL [*Library symbol Library of Congress*] (LCLS)
ABBMS .... American Board of Bloodless Medicine and Surgery (EA)
ABBN.......... Brisbane [*Australia ICAO location identifier*] (ICLI)
Abb Nat Dig... Abbott's National Digest [*A publication*] (DLA)
Abb NC .... Abbott's New Cases [*New York*] [*A publication*] (DLA)
Abb N Cas ... Abbott's New Cases [*New York*] [*A publication*] (DLA)
Abb New Cas... Abbott's New Cases [*New York*] [*A publication*] (DLA)
Abb NS .... Abbott's Practice Reports, New Series [*New York*] [*A publication*] (DLA)
Abb NY App... Abbott's Court of Appeals Decisions [*New York*] [*A publication*] (DLA)
Abb NY Dig... Abbott's New York Digest [*A publication*] (DLA)
Abb NY Dig 2d... Abbott's New York Digest, Second [*A publication*] (DLA)
ABBO.......... Associate of the British Ballet Organisation
ABBOTSB..... Abbotsbury [*England*]
Abbott.......... Abbott on Merchant Ships and Seaman [*1802-1901*] [*A publication*] (DLA)
Abbott.......... Abbott's Dictionary [*A publication*] (DLA)
Abbott Civ Jur Tr... Abbott on Civil Jury Trials [*A publication*] (ILCA)
Abbott Civ Jury Trials... Abbott on Civil Jury Trials [*A publication*] (DLA)
Abbott Crim Tr Pr... Abbott on Criminal Trial Practice [*A publication*] (DLA)
Abbott PR .... Abbott's Practice Reports [*New York*] [*A publication*] (DLA)
Abbott Pract Cas... Abbott's Practice Reports [*New York*] [*A publication*] (DLA)
Abbott Pr Rep... Abbott's Practice Reports [*New York*] [*A publication*] (DLA)
Abbott's Adm... Abbott's Admiralty Reports [*United States*] [*A publication*] (DLA)
Abbott's Ad Rep... Abbott's Admiralty Reports [*United States*] [*A publication*] (DLA)
Abbott's NC... Abbott's New Cases [*New York*] [*A publication*] (DLA)
Abbott's Prac Rep... Abbott's Practice Reports [*New York*] [*A publication*] (DLA)
Abbott's Pr Rep... Abbott's Practice Reports [*New York*] [*A publication*] (DLA)
Abbott USR... Abbott's United States Circuit and District Courts Reports [*A publication*] (DLA)
Abbott US Rep... Abbott's United States Circuit and District Courts Reports [*A publication*] (DLA)
Abb PI .... Abbott's Pleadings under the Code [*A publication*] (DLA)
Abb PR .... Abbott's Practice Reports [*New York*] [*A publication*] (DLA)
Abb Prac...... Abbott's Practice Reports [*New York*] [*A publication*] (DLA)
Abb Prac NS... Abbott's Practice Reports, New Series [*New York*] [*A publication*] (DLA)
Abb Pr NS ... Abbott's Practice Reports, New Series [*New York*] [*A publication*] (DLA)
Abb Pr Rep... Abbott's Practice Reports [*New York*] [*A publication*] (DLA)
ABBR .... Abbreviation (AFM)
abbr .... Abbreviation (DMAA)
ABBR .... Brisbane [*Australia ICAO location identifier*] (ICLI)
ABBRA .... American Boat Builders and Repairers Association (EA)
ABBRD........ Abbreviated (ABBR)
abbrev .... Abbreviated (DAVI)
ABBREV ...... Abbreviation (EY)
ABBREVIO.... Abbreviomania (ABBR)
ABBRG........ Abbreviating (ABBR)
ABBRN ...... Abbreviation (ABBR)
ABBRON ...... Abbreviation (ROG)
ABBRP........ American Board of Bionic Rehabilitative Psychology (EA)
ABBR PO ..... Abbreviated Purchase Order
Abb RPS ..... Abbott's Real Property Statutes [*A publication*] (DLA)
ABBRR........ Abbreviator (ABBR)
ABBS .... American Brittle Bone Society [*Defunct*] (EA)
ABBS .... Antigua and Barbuda Broadcasting Service (EY)
ABBS .... Apple Bulletin Board System [*Pronounced "abbies"*]
ABBS .... Beaverlodge High School, Alberta [*Library symbol National Library of Canada*] (BIB)
Abb Sh........ Abbott on Shipping [*A publication*] (DLA)
Abb Ship...... Abbott on Shipping [*A publication*] (DLA)
ABBsS.......... Bellsouth Services, Birmingham, AL [*Library symbol*] [*Library of Congress*] (LCLS)
ABBT.......... Animated Backlighted Burtek Trainer
Abb Tr Ev .... Abbott's Trial Evidence [*A publication*] (DLA)
ABBU.......... Bundaberg [*Australia ICAO location identifier*] (ICLI)
Abb US .... Abbott's Circuit Court Reports [*United States*] [*A publication*] (DLA)
Abb USCC.... Abbott's United States Circuit and District Courts Reports [*A publication*] (DLA)
Abb US Pr ... Abbott's Practice in the United States Courts [*A publication*] (DLA)

ABBWA........ American Black Book Writers Association (EA)
ABBX .... Brisbane [*Australia ICAO location identifier*] (ICLI)
Abb Y Bk .... Abbott's Year Book of Jurisprudence [*A publication*] (DLA)
AbbyNtl....... Abbey Natl. [*Associated Press*] (SAG)
abC............. Abcoulomb (IDOE)
ABC............. ABC World Airways Guide [*ICAO designator*] (FAAC)
ABC............. Abeche [*Chad*] [*Seismograph station code, US Geological Survey Closed*]
ABC............. Aberford Resources Ltd. [*Toronto Stock Exchange symbol*]
ABC............. Aberrant Behavior Checklist [*Treatment effectiveness test*] [*Psychology*]
ABC............. Abridged Building Classification for Architects, Builders, and Civil Engineers
ABC............. Absolute Band Count [*Biochemistry*] (DAVI)
ABC............. Absolute Basophil Count [*Hematology*] (MAE)
ABC............. Academia Brasileira de Ciencias [*Brazil*] (MCD)
ABC............. Accent before Cooking [*Advertising slogan*]
ABC............. Acceptable Biological Catch [*Fishery management*] (MSC)
ABC............. Accounting and Budgetary Control (DNAB)
ABC............. Aconite, Belladonna, and Chloroform [*Liniment compound*]
ABC............. Acquisition Basic Course [*DSMC*] (AAGC)
ABC............. Act for Better Child Care Services
ABC............. Action Bell Canada
ABC............. Action for Brain-Handicapped Children [*Defunct*] (EA)
ABC............. Activating Event [*or Experience*], Belief System, Consequence [*Irrational behavior theory*] [*Psychotherapy*]
ABC............. Active Bioprosthetic Composition [*Artificial ligament*]
ABC............. Active Body Control [*Automotive engineering*]
ABC............. Active Body Control
ABC............. Activity-Based Cost [*Management accounting system*]
ABC............. Activity Based Costing [*Financial management*]
ABC............. Adaptable Board Computer [*Signetics*]
ABC............. Administration by Competency [*Business term*]
ABC............. Administrative, Business, and Commercial (AIE)
ABC............. Adoptee-Birthparent Center [*An association*] (EA)
ABC............. Adriamycin, BCNU [*Carmustine*], Cyclophosphamide [*Antineoplastic drug regimen*]
ABC............. Adriatic Base Command [*Military*]
ABC............. Advance Base Components [*Military*] (AFIT)
ABC............. Advance Baseline Configuration (MCD)
ABC............. Advance Booking Charter [*Airline fare*]
ABC............. Advanced Ballistics Concepts [*Air Force*] (MCD)
ABC............. Advanced Biomedical Capsule
ABC............. Advanced-Booking Charter (PDAA)
ABC............. Advancing Blade Concept [*Helicopter*]
ABC............. Advocates for Better Communication [*An association*]
ABC............. Aerated Bread Co. [*Chain of restaurants in London*]
ABC............. Affinity-Based-Collection [*Immunoassay*]
ABC............. Afghan Border Crusade [*Later, NWFF*] (EA)
ABC............. African Bibliographic Center (EA)
ABC............. After Bottom Center [*Valve position*]
ABC............. Aggregate Base Course (DAC)
ABC............. Agri-Business Council of Arizona (SRA)
ABC............. Agri-Business Council of Oregon (SRA)
ABC............. Agricultural Biotechnology Center [*University of Maryland*] [*Research center*]
ABC............. Agricultural Business and Commerce
ABC Y .... Air Balance Consultants (EA)
ABC............. Air Bath Chamber
ABC............. Air Battle Captain (INF)
ABC............. Air Battle Captain (DOMA)
ABC............. Air Blast Cooled (IAA)
ABC............. Airborne Control [*System*]
ABC............. Air Bubble Craft
ABC............. Air Business Contact [*France ICAO designator*] (FAAC)
ABC............. Aircraft Builders Council [*British*] (AIA)
ABC............. Aircraft of Bomber Command [*British*]
ABC............. Airway, Breathing, and Circulation [*Medicine*] (DAVI)
ABC............. Airway Opened, Breathing Restored, and Circulation Restored [*Cardiopulmonary resuscitation*] [*Medicine*]
ABC............. Alarms by Carrier (PDAA)
abc............. Alberta [*MARC country of publication code Library of Congress*] (LCCP)
ABC............. Alberta Ballet Co. [*Canada*]
ABC............. [*Secretary of State Madeleine*] Albright, [*National-Security Adviser Sandy*] Berger, [*and Defense Secretary William*] Cohen [*A troika known in Washington*]
ABC............. Alcobaca [*Brazil*] [*Airport symbol*] (OAG)
ABC............. Alcoholic Beverage Control [*Board*]
ABC............. Ale, Bread, and Cheese
ABC............. Alexander Bonaparte Cust [*Antagonist of Agatha Christie's novel "The ABC Murders"*]
ABC............. Alliance of British Clubs (EAIO)
ABC............. Allied Boating Association of Canada (AC)
ABC............. All-in-One Business Contactbook [*A publication*]
ABC............. Allocations for Budgetary Control
ABC............. Allowable Biological Catch
ABC............. Almond Board of California (EA)
ABC............. [*The*] Alphabet
ABC............. Alphabetical British [*Railway Guide of Timetables*] (BARN)
ABBC.......... Alpha Block Control Number [*Computer science*]
ABBX .... Already Been Chewed [*Gum*]
Abb Y .... Already Been Converted (PDAA)
AbbNtl......... Alternate Birthing Center [*Obstetrics*] (DAVI)

ABC............. Alum, Blood, and Charcoal [*A method of deodorizing by addition of a compound of these*] [*Medicine*]
ABC............. Alum, Blood, Clay Method [*Raw sewage treatment*] [*Organic chemistry*] (DAVI)
ABC............. American and British Commonwealth Association
ABC............. American Ballet Competition (EA)
ABC............. American Baptist Churches
ABC............. American Baptists Concerned (EA)
ABC............. American Barefoot Club (EA)
ABC............. American Beagle Club (EA)
ABC............. American Beveren Club
ABC............. American Bibliographical Center
ABC............. American Blade Collectors (EA)
ABC............. American Blood Commission (EA)
ABC............. American Bloodhound Club (EA)
ABC............. American Board for Certification in Orthotics and Prosthetics (EA)
ABC............. American Board of Criminalistics (EA)
ABC............. American Book Co. (AEBS)
ABC............. American Book Council [*Defunct*] (EA)
ABC............. American Book-Prices Current [*A publication*] (DGA)
ABC............. American-Born Chinese
ABC............. American Botanical Council (EA)
ABC............. American Bowling Congress (EA)
ABC............. American Boxer Club (EA)
ABC............. American Brahma Club (EA)
ABC............. American, British, and Canadian
ABC............. American-British Conversation [*as ABC-1, a 1941 report that set forth Allied worldwide strategy*] [*World War II*]
ABC............. American Brittany Club (EA)
ABC............. American Broadcasting Companies, Inc. [*Subsidiary of Capital Cities/ ABC, Inc.*]
ABC............. American Bugatti Club (EA)
ABC............. American Business Cancer [*in name "ABC Research Foundation"*]
ABC............. American Business Collaboration for Quality Dependent Care
ABC............. American Business Conference [*Washington, DC*] (EA)
ABC............. American Business Council, Malaysia (EA)
ABC............. Americans by Choice
ABC............. Americans for Better Care (EA)
ABC............. AMIGOS [*Access Method for Indexed Data Generalized for Operating System*] Bibliographic Council (EA)
ABC............. Amities Belgo-Congolaises [*Belgian-Congolese Friendship Association*]
ABC............. Analysis Bar Charting (PDAA)
ABC............. Anchor Bible Commentary [*A publication*] (BJA)
ABC............. Answer-Back Code [*Telecommunications*] (TEL)
ABC............. Anterior Bulbar Cell [*Neurobiology*]
ABC............. Antigen-Binding Capacity [*Immunology*]
ABC............. Antiquarian Booksellers' Center (EA)
ABC............. Anybody but Carter [*1976 presidential campaign*]
ABC............. Any Boy Can [*Program*] [*Defunct*] (EA)
ABC............. Apnea, Bradycardia, Cyanosis [*Medicine*] (MAE)
ABC............. Apparel Business Control [*System*] [*Computer science*]
ABC............. Applesauce, Bananas, Cereal [*Diet*] (MEDA)
ABC............. Application Builder Class [*Computer science*]
ABC............. Applied Business Telecommunications [*San Ramon, CA*] [*Information service or system Telecommunications*] (TSSD)
ABC............. Approach by Concept [*Information retrieval*]
ABC............. Approaches to Behavior Change Inventory (EDAC)
ABC............. Architectural Barriers Committee (EA)
ABC............. Argentina, Brazil, Chile
ABC............. Arizona Beef Council (SRA)
ABC............. Artificial Beta Cells [*Biochemistry*] (DAVI)
ABC............. Arts and Business Council (EA)
ABC............. Aruba, Bonaire, and Curacao [*Islands*]
ABC............. Asian Basketball Confederation (EA)
ABC............. Asian Benevolent Corps (EA)
ABC............. Asian Broadcasting Conference (NTCM)
ABC............. Asphaltenic Bottom Cracking [*Hydrocarbon processing*]
ABC............. Aspiration Biopsy Cytology [*Medicine*]
ABC............. [*Kaufman*] Assessment Battery for Children [*Diagnostic assessment test*] (PAZ)
ABC............. Assessment Biological and Chemical [*Warfare*] (NATG)
ABC............. Assessment of Basic Competencies [*Child development test*]
ABC............. Associated British Cinemas
ABC............. Associated Builders and Contractors (EA)
ABC............. Association Botanique du Canada (AC)
ABC............. Association des Banquiers Canadiens [*Canadian Bankers Association*]
ABC............. Association for Bright Children [*Societe pour Enfants Doues et Surdoues*] [*Ontario*] (AC)
ABC............. Association for Business Communication [*Urbana, IL*] (EA)
ABC............. Association of Baptist Chaplains (EA)
ABC............. Association of Bendectin Children [*Later, ABDC*] (EA)
ABC............. Association of Biotechnology Companies (EA)
ABC............. Association of Bituminous Contractors (EA)
ABC............. Association of Black Cardiologists (EA)
ABC............. Association of Black Catholics Against Abortion (EA)
ABC............. Association of Boards of Certification (EA)
ABC............. Association of Bridal Consultants (EA)
ABC............. Association of British Climatologists (EAIO)
ABC............. Association of British Counties (DBA)
ABC............. Association of Building Centres [*British*] (BI)
ABC............. Association of Business Centres [*British*] (DBA)
ABC............. Atanasoff-Berry Computer [*Early computer*]
ABC............. Atlantic Richfield [*NYSE symbol*] (TTSB)

ABC............	Atomic, Biological, and Chemical [*as, ABC Officer, ABC Warfare*] [*Obsolete*]
ABC............	ATP [*Adenosine Triphosphate*]-Binding Cassette [*Biochemistry*]
ABC............	Audit Bureau of Circulations (EA)
ABC............	Augmented Bibliographic Citation (ADA)
ABC............	Australian Bank of Commerce
ABC............	Australian Bird Count
ABC............	Australian Boys' Choir
ABC............	Australian Breeding Center
ABC............	Australian Broadcasting Co.
ABC............	Auto Backlight Control [*Photography*]
ABC............	Auto Body Computer [*Software*] [*Automotive Computer Group*] [*Automotive engineering*]
ABC............	Auto Bracketing Control [*Photography*]
ABC............	Automatic Bandwidth Control
ABC............	Automatic Bar Checker
ABC............	Automatic Bass Compensation [*Radio*]
abc............	Automatic Bass Compensation (IDOE)
ABC............	Automatic Bass Control
ABC............	Automatic Beam Control (IAA)
ABC............	Automatic Bias Compensation
ABC............	Automatic Bias Control
abc............	Automatic Bias Control (IDOE)
ABC............	Automatic Bill Calling [*Later, MCCS*] [*Telecommunications*]
ABC............	Automatic Binary Computer (ADA)
ABC............	Automatic Blip Counter
ABC............	Automatic Block Controller (MCD)
ABC............	Automatic Boiling-Column Reactor
ABC............	Automatic Branch Control (IAA)
ABC............	Automatic Bridge Control [*Navy*] (MCD)
abc............	Automatic Brightness Compensation (IDOE)
abc............	Automatic Brightness Control (IDOE)
ABC............	Automatic Brightness Control [*Telecommunications*] (TEL)
ABC............	Automation of Bibliography through Computerization [*ABC-Clio Press*]
ABC............	Automotive Booster Clubs International (EA)
ABC............	Aviation Boatswain's Mate, Chief [*Navy rating*]
ABC............	Avidin-Biotin Complex [*Immunochemistry*]
ABC............	Axiobuccocervical [*Dentistry*]
ABC............	[*A*] Better Chance (EA)
ABC............	[*A*] Brilliant Career
ABC............	Brownvale Community Library, Alberta [*Library symbol National Library of Canada*] (NLC)
ABC............	Jefferson County Court House, Birmingham, AL [*Library symbol Library of Congress*] (LCLS)
ABC............	University of Alabama in Birmingham, Birmingham, AL [*OCLC symbol*] (OCLC)
ABC3............	Airborne Battlefield Command and Control Center (SAA)
ABCA	America, Britain, Canada, Australia (ADA)
ABCA	American Baseball Coaches Association (EA)
ABCA	American Black Chiropractors Association (EA)
ABCA	American Blade Collectors Association (EA)
ABCA	American Blue Cheese Association [*Defunct*] (EA)
ABCA	American, British, Canadian, Australian (MHDB)
ABCA	American Building Contractors Association (EA)
ABCA	American Business Communication Association [*Later, ABC*]
ABCA	Antique Bicycle Club of America (EA)
ABCA	Antique Bottle Collectors Association [*Defunct*]
ABCA	Army Board of Contract Appeals (AAGC)
ABCA	Army Bureau of Current Affairs [*To encourage British soldiers to think and talk about what they were fighting for*] [*World War II*]
ABCA	Association des Banques Centrales Africaines [*Association of African Central Banks*] (EAIO)
ABCA	Association of Biological Collections Appraisers (EA)
ABCA	Australian Brangus Cattle Association
Ab Ca	Crawford and Dix's Irish Abridged Cases [*A publication*] (DLA)
ABCACT	Association of Baptist Churches of the Australian Capital Territory
ABCAIRSTD...	American-British-Canadian Air Standardization Agreement (NG)
ABC & C & C...	Airway, Breathing, Circulation, Cervical Spine, Consciousness Level [*Medicine*] (MEDA)
A-BCAS........	Active Beacon Collision Avoidance System [*Aviation*] (DA)
ABC-ASP......	American-British-Canadian Army Standardization Program
ABCA/UES ...	American Business Communication Association Unification of Engineering Standards (MHDB)
ABCB	ABC Bancorp [*NASDAQ symbol*] (SAG)
ABCB	Air Blast Circuit Breaker
ABCB	American Board of Clinical Biofeedback [*Defunct*] (EA)
ABCB	American Bottlers of Carbonated Beverages [*Later, NSDA*] (EA)
ABC Bc	ABC Bancorp [*Associated Press*] (SAG)
ABCBC........	Bear Point Community Library, Bear Canyon, Alberta [*Library symbol National Library of Canada*] (NLC)
ABCC	ABC Dispensing Technologies, Inc. [*NASDAQ symbol*] (SAG)
ABCC	Airborne Battlefield Command and Control Center (MCD)
ABCC	Airborne Command Center
ABCC	Airborne Communications Center [*Military*]
ABCC	Alternative Birth Crisis Coalition [*Defunct*] (EA)
ABCC	Amer Business Computers [*NASDAQ symbol*] (TTSB)
ABC-C	American Board of Clinical Chemistry (EA)
ABC-C	American Broadcasting Co. Contemporary Network (LAIN)
ABCC	American Business Card Club
ABCC	American Business Computers Corp. [*NASDAQ symbol*] (NQ)
ABCC	Association of British Chambers of Commerce
ABCC	Association of British Correspondence Colleges (EAIO)
ABCC	Atomic Bomb Casualty Commission [*Later, RERF*]
ABCC	Australia-Brazil Chamber of Commerce
ABCC	Australian-British Chamber of Commerce
ABCC	Australian British Chamber of Commerce (DBA)
ABCC	Circuit Court Library, Birmingham, AL [*Library symbol Library of Congress*] (LCLS)
ABCCC	Airborne Battlefield Command and Control Center [*Air Force*] (AFM)
ABCCTC	Advanced Base Combat Communication Training Center [*Pearl Harbor*]
ABCD	Able Seaman Clearance Diver
ABCD	Accelerated Business Collection and Delivery [*Postal Service*]
ABCD	Add BCD [*Binary Coded Decimal*] Number with Extend [*Computer science*]
ABCD	Adriamycin, Bleomycin, CCNU [*Lomustine*], Dacarbazine [*Antineoplastic drug regimen*]
ABCD	Advanced Base Construction Depot
ABCD	Agency for Business and Career Development (EA)
ABCD	Agrophysics Breeding Control Device [*Birth-control device for dogs*]
ABCD	Airway Opened, Breathing Restored, Circulation Restored, and Definitive Therapy [*Cardiopulmonary resuscitation*] [*Medicine*]
ABCD	America, Britain, China, and Dutch East Indies [*The ABCD Powers*] [*World War II*]
ABC-D........	American Broadcasting Co. Direction Network (LAIN)
ABCD	American Society of Bookplate Collectors and Designers (DGA)
ABCD	Apache, Black Hawk, and Chinook Self-Deployments [*Military*]
ABCD	Associacao Brasileira dos Colecionadores de Discos [*Record label*] [*Brazil*]
ABCD	Associated Baby Carriage Dealers (EA)
ABCD	Association for Bridge Construction and Design (EA)
ABCD	Association of Better Computer Dealers [*Later, ABCD: The Microcomputer Industry Association*] (EA)
ABCD	Association of Biomedical Communication Directors (EA)
ABCD	Asymmetry, Border, Color, and Diameter [*Rule*] [*Dermatology*]
ABCD	Atomic, Biological, Chemical, and Damage Control
ABCD	Australian Building Cost Database
ABCD	Australian Business Communications Directory [*A publication*]
ABCD	Automated Biological and Chemical Data [*System*]
ABCD	Awaiting Bad Conduct Discharge [*Military*]
ABCDE	Botulism Toxoid Pentavalent [*Biochemistry*] (DAVI)
ABCDEF	Allein bei Christo die Ewige Freude [*With Christ Alone Is Eternal Joy*] [*Motto of Albrecht Gunther, Count Schwarzburg (1582-1634)*] [*German*]
ABCDEF	American Boys Club in Defense of Errol Flynn [*Facetious organization*]
ABCDEF-Canada...	Association des Responsables des Bibliotheques [*Centres de Documentation Universitaires et Recherche d'Expression Francaise au Canada*] (AC)
ABCDEFGHIJ...	Automobile Builders' Combination Designed Especially for Getting Hitler including Japan [*Suggested name for Automotive Council for War Production*] [*World War II*]
ABC Dsp	ABC Dispensing Technologies, Inc. [*NASDAQ symbol*] (SAG)
ABC Dsp	ABC Dispensing Technologies, Inc. [*Associated Press*] (SAG)
ABCE...........	Adult Basic and Continuing Education (EDAC)
ABC-E	American Broadcasting Co. Entertainment Network (LAIN)
ABC-F	American Broadcasting Co. FM Network (LAIN)
ABCF...........	As-Built Configuration File (MCD)
ABCFM........	American Board of Commissioners for Foreign Missions [*Later, UCBWM*]
ABCFRC	Auke Bay Coastal Fisheries Research Center [*National Oceanic and Atmospheric Administration*] (PDAA)
ABCG	American Board of Genetic Counseling
ABCG	Coolangatta [*Australia ICAO location identifier*] (ICLI)
ABCGG	Association of British Columbia Grape Growers (AC)
ABCH	American Board of Clinical Hypnosis (EA)
ABCI...........	Advanced Business Communications, Inc. [*McLean, VA*] [*Telecommunications*] (TSSD)
ABCI...........	Airport Business Center, Inc. [*Minneapolis, MN*] [*Telecommunications*] (TSSD)
ABCI...........	Allied Bank Capital, Inc. [*NASDAQ symbol*] (SAG)
ABC-I	American Broadcasting Co. Information Network (LAIN)
ABCI...........	Appliance Recycling Ctrs Amer [*NASDAQ symbol*] (TTSB)
ABCI...........	Australian Bureau of Criminal Intelligence
ABCI...........	Automotive Booster Clubs International (EA)
ABCIA	American Board of Clinical Immunology and Allergy (EA)
ABCIC	Airway, Breathing, Circulation, Intravenous Crystalloid [*Medicine*] (DMAA)
ABCIL..........	Antibody Mediated Cell Dependent Immune Lympholysis [*Immunology*]
ABCK	Able-Bodied Seaman Cook [*Navy*]
ABCK	Alaska British Columbia Transportation Co. [*AAR code*]
ABCL	American Birth Control League
ABCL	American Board of Criminal Lawyers (EA)
ABCL	As-Built Configuration Lists
ABCLG	Absolute Ceiling
ABCM..........	Adriamycin, Bleomycin, Cyclophosphamide, Mitomycin C [*Antineoplastic drug regimen*]
ABCM..........	Air Burst Contact Maker
ABCM..........	Antilock Brake Control Module [*Automotive engineering*]
ABCM..........	Association of British Chemical Manufacturers (BARN)
ABCM..........	Association of Building Component Manufacturers (EAIO)
ABCM..........	Master Chief Aviation Boatswain's Mate [*Navy rating*]
ABCMC	Automotive Battery Charger Manufacturers Council [*Defunct*] (EA)
ABCMR	Army Board for Correction of Military Records
ABCN	Aerodrome Beacon (IAA)
ABCN	Amer Bancorp Nevada [*NASDAQ symbol*] (TTSB)
ABCN	American Bancorp of Nevada [*NASDAQ symbol*] (SAG)

ABC Newsl...   International Association of Accident Boards and Commissions. Newsletter [*A publication*] (DLA)

ABCNSW......   Association of Blind Citizens of New South Wales [*Australia*]

ABCO ....   Advanced Base Components [*Military*]

ABCO ....   Amer Buildings [*NASDAQ symbol*] (TTSB)

ABCO ....   American Baptist Churches of Oregon (SRA)

ABCO ....   American Buildings Co. [*NASDAQ symbol*] (SAG)

ABCO ....   Association of British Conference Organisers (BI)

ABCOX........   Able-bodied Seaman Coxswain [*Navy*]

ABCP ....   Airborne Command Post (MCD)

ABCP ....   American Board of Cardiovascular Perfusion (EA)

ABCP ....   Argentina, Brazil, Chile, and Peru (IIA)

ABCP ....   Association of Blind Chartered Physiotherapists

ABCP ....   Automatic Bias Compensation (MSA)

ABCPAF ......   Association of Black CPA [*Certified Public Accountant*] Firms [*Defunct*] (EA)

ABCPF ....   Association of British Columbia Professional Foresters (AC)

ABcpNV......   American Bancorp of Nevada [*Associated Press*] (SAG)

ABCQ ....   Association des Bureaux de Congres du Quebec (AC)

ABCQ ....   Association of Building Contractors of Quebec (AC)

ABCR ....   ABC Rail Products [*NASDAQ symbol*] (SAG)

ABCR ....   ABC Rail Products [*NASDAQ symbol*] (TTSB)

ABCR ....   American Bashkir Curly Registry (EA)

ABC-R..........   American Broadcasting Co. Rock Radio Network (LAIN)

ABCR ....   As-Built Configuration Record (NASA)

ABCR ....   Association of Beverage Container Recyclers (EA)

ABCR ....   Atomic, Biological, Chemical, and Radiological [*Warfare*] (NATG)

ABCRA.........   American-Byelorussian Cultural Relief Association (EA)

ABC Rail......   ABC Rail Products [*Associated Press*] (SAG)

ABCRETT .....   American Board of Certified and Registered Encephalographic Technicians and Technologists (EA)

ABCRF ....   American Business Cancer Research Foundation [*Later, ABFCR*] (EA)

ABCRS ....   American Board of Colon and Rectal Surgery (EA)

ABCS ....   Abacus

ABCS ....   Abscess (ABBR)

ABCS ....   Advanced Brake Control System (MCD)

ABCS ....   Advisory Board for Cooperative Systems [*of ICIREPAT*]

ABCS ....   American Bicentennial Commemorative Society [*Defunct*]

ABCS ....   American Board of Cosmetic Surgery (EA)

ABCS ....   American Board on Counseling Services [*Later, IACS*] (EA)

ABCS ....   American British Cab Society (EA)

ABCS ....   American Business Council of Singapore (EA)

ABCS ....   Army Battle Command System (RDA)

ABCS ....   Army Battle Command Systems [*Army*]

ABCS ....   Associated Body of Church Schoolmasters [*A union*] [*British*]

ABCS ....   Automatic Base Communication Systems (PDAA)

ABCS ....   Automatic Blip Counter System

ABCS ....   Automatic Broadcasting Control System [*Japan*]

ABCS ....   Aviation Boatswain's Mate, Senior Chief [*Navy rating*]

ABCS ....   Avionics Bay Cooling System

ABCS ....   Bear Canyon School, Alberta [*Library symbol National Library of Canada*] (BIB)

ABCS ....   Cairns [*Australia ICAO location identifier*] (ICLI)

ABCSC ....   American-British-Canadian Stores Catalogue (DEN)

ABCSD.........   Abscessed (ABBR)

ABCSG........   Abscessing (ABBR)

ABCSOA......   Australian Broadcasting Corporation Senior Executives' Association

ABCSP ....   American-British-Canadian Standardization Program

ABCST ....   Automatic Broadcast (BARN)

ABCT...........   Alabama Basic Competency Test (EDAC)

ABCT...........   American Board of Chelation Therapy (EA)

ABC-T ....   American Broadcasting Co. Talkradio Network (LAIN)

ABCT...........   Association Belgo-Congolaise du Textile [*Belgo-Congolese Textile Association*] [*Zaire*]

ABCTG ....   Administrative, Business, and Commercial Training Group (AIE)

ABCTHM ......   Anton Breini Center for Tropical Health and Medicine [*James Cook University*] [*Australia*]

ABCV ....   Artificial Breeding Center, Victoria [*Australia*]

ABCV ....   Charleville [*Australia ICAO location identifier*] (ICLI)

ABCW ....   American Bakery and Confectionery Workers' International Union [*Later, BCTWIU*]

ABCW ....   Anchor Bancorp Wisc [*NASDAQ symbol*] (TTSB)

ABCW ....   Anchor Bancorp Wisconsin, Inc. [*NASDAQ symbol*] (SAG)

ABCW ....   Atomic, Biological, Chemical Warfare

ABCWIU......   Aluminum, Brick, and Clay Workers International Union (EA)

ABCX ....   Adriamycin, Bleomycin, Cisplatin, Radiation Therapy [*Antineoplastic drug regimen*] (DAVI)

ABD ....   Abadan [*Iran*] [*Airport symbol*] (OAG)

ABD ....   Abbreviated Dial (DNAB)

ABD ....   Abdicated (ROG)

ABD ....   Abdomen [*or Abdominal*]

ABD ....   Abdominal Fluid [*Medicine*] (DAVI)

ABD ....   Abdominal Pad [*Orthopedics*] (DAVI)

abd ....   Abduct [*or Abductor*] [*Neurology and orthopedics*] (DAVI)

ABD ....   Abduction [*FBI standardized term*]

ABD ....   Aberdeen [*City and county in Scotland*] (ROG)

abd ....   Aboard (BARN)

ABD ....   Access Block Diagram

ABD ....   Acoustic Bullet Detector [*Military*] (VNW)

ABD ....   Adhesive Bonding [*Welding*]

ABD ....   Adriamycin, Bleomycin, Dacarbazine [*Antineoplastic drug regimen*]

ABD ....   Advanced Base Depot [*or Dock*] [*Obsolete Navy*]

ABD ....   Aged, Blind, or Disabled [*HEW*]

ABD ....   Aggressive Behavioral Disturbance [*Medicine*] (DMAA)

ABD ....   Airborne Ballistics Division [*NASA*] (KSC)

ABD ....   Airborne Data Marketing Ltd. [*Vancouver Stock Exchange symbol*]

ABD ....   All But the Dissertation [*PhD candidates*]

ABD ....   Alloy Bulk Diffusion (IAA)

ABD ....   American Board of Dermatology (EA)

ABD ....   Aminobenzamidine [*Biochemistry*]

ABD ....   Anchor Bible Dictionary [*A publication*]

ABD ....   Annular Base Drag

ABD ....   Apparent Bulk Density

ABD ....   Area Business Databank [*Information Access Co.*] [*Belmont, CA*] [*Information service or system*] (IID)

ABD ....   Army Budget Directive

ABD ....   Association of Blauvelt Descendants (EA)

ABD ....   Association of British Detectives (DI)

ABD ....   Atlanta [*Iceland*] [*ICAO designator*] (FAAC)

ABD ....   Australian Business Directory [*A publication*]

ABD ....   Average Body Dose [*Radiation technology*] (WDAA)

ABD ....   Average Business Day [*Bell System*]

ABD ....   Azobenzene Derivative [*Organic chemistry*]

ABDA ....   Alcohol-Related Brain Damage Association [*Australia*]

ABDA ....   American, British, Dutch, Australian (ADA)

ABDA ....   Bundesvereinigung Deutscher Apothekerverbande [*German Pharmaceutical Association Research Institute*] [*Information service or system*] (IID)

ABDACOM...   Advanced Base Depot Area Command

ABDACOM...   American-British-Dutch-Australian Supreme Command [*1942*]

ABDAFLOAT...   American-British-Dutch-Australian Naval Operational Command [*1942*]

ABDAIR........   American-British-Dutch-Australian Air Operational Command [*1942*]

ABDARM......   American-British-Dutch-Australian Army Operational Command [*1942*]

abdc............   Abduct [*or Abduction*] [*Neurology and orthopedics*] (DAVI)

ABDC ....   Adduct (ABBR)

ABDC ....   After Bottom Dead Center [*Valve position*]

ABDC ....   Association of Birth Defect Children (EA)

ABDCD........   Abducted (ABBR)

ABDCG........   Abducting (ABBR)

ABDCN........   Abduction (ABBR)

ABDCR........   Abductor (ABBR)

ABDCT........   Atrial Bolus Dynamic Computer Tomography [*Cardiology*] (DAVI)

ABDE ....   Airport Bird Detection Equipment

ABDE ....   Anfang Bedenk das Ende [*At the Beginning Consider the End*] [*Motto of Bruno II, Count of Mansfeld (1545-1615)*] [*German*]

ABDEN ....   Able-Bodied Seaman Dental, NV

ABDER ....   Abduction, External Rotation [*Physiology*]

ABDFC ....   American Bouvier des Flandres Club (EA)

Abd Hyst.....   Abdominal Hysterectomy [*Gynecology*] (CPH)

ABDI ....   Abdicate (ABBR)

ABDI ....   Administrative Board - Dress Industry (EA)

ABDI ....   Associated Beer Distributors of Illinois (SRA)

ABDIC ....   Adriamycin, Bleomycin, Dacarbazine, CCNU [*Lomustine*] [*Antineoplastic drug regimen*]

ABDID.........   Abdicated (ABBR)

ABDIN.........   Abdication (ABBR)

ABDIR.........   Abduction, Internal Rotation [*Physiology*]

ABDL ....   Automatic Binary Data Link [*Computer science*] (CET)

ABDM ....   Abdomen (ABBR)

ABDM ....   Black Diamond Municipal Library, Alberta [*Library symbol National Library of Canada*] (NLC)

ABDML ....   Abdominal (ABBR)

ABDMLY .....   Abdominally (ABBR)

ABDMS ....   American Board of Dental Medicine and Surgery (EA)

ABDMT ....   Abandonment (ABBR)

ABDMY ....   Abdominally (ABBR)

ABDND........   Abandoned (ABBR)

ABDNNT......   Abandonment (ABBR)

ABDNR........   Abandoner (ABBR)

ABDNSHP ...   Abandon Ship (MSA)

Abdnt ....   Abandonment [*Insurance*]

ABDO ....   Association of British Dispensing Opticians (DBA)

ABDOM ....   Abdomen

abdom ....   Abdomen (DMAA)

ABDOSD .....   Arbeitsgemeinschaft der Bibliotheken und Dokumentationsstellen der Osteuropa-, Sudosteuropa und DDR-Forschung [*Association of Libraries and Documentation Centres for the Study of Eastern Europe, South-Eastern Europe and the German Democratic Republic*] (PDAA)

ABDP ....   Alphabeta Pseudocoincidence Discrimination [*Analysis of radioactivity*]

ABDP ....   Association of British Directory Publishers (EAIO)

ABDPH........   American Board of Dental Public Health (EA)

abd poll......   Abductor Pollicis [*Muscle*] [*Anatomy*] (DAVI)

ABDR ....   Abacus Direct Corp. [*NASDAQ symbol*] (SAG)

ABDR ....   Aberdare [*Welsh depot code*]

ABDR ....   Army Battle Damage Repair (GFGA)

ABDR ....   Association of Blood Donor Recruiters [*Defunct*] (EA)

ABDS ....   Accounting and Budget Distribution System [*Air Force*]

ABDS ....   Associate of the British Display Society (DBQ)

ABDSA........   Association of British Dental Surgery Assistants

ABD/SCADS...   Air Base Defense/Sensor Communications and Display System [*Air Force*] (MCD)

ABDSRC.......   Sheep River Community Library, Black Diamond, Alberta [*Library symbol National Library of Canada*] (NLC)

ABDUC.........   Abduction

ABDV	Adriamycin, Bleomycin, Dacarbazine, Vinblastine [*Antineoplastic drug regimen*]
ABDV	Arrhenatherum Blue Dwarf Virus [*Plant pathology*]
Abdy & W Gai...	Abdy and Walker's Gaius and Ulpian [*A publication*] (DLA)
Abdy & W Just...	Abdy and Walker's Justinian [*A publication*] (DLA)
Abdy R Pr...	Abdy's Roman Civil Procedure [*A publication*] (DLA)
ABE	Abbotsford Air Services [*Canada ICAO designator*] (FAAC)
abe	Abequose Residue [*Medicine*] (BABM)
ABE	Aberdeen [*Scotland*] [*Seismograph station code, US Geological Survey*] (SEIS)
ABE	Abex, Inc. [*NYSE symbol*] (SPSG)
ABE	Acetone, Butanol, and Ethanol [*Fermentation products*]
ABE	Acute Bacterial Endocarditis [*Medicine*]
ABE	Adult Basic Education
ABE	Advanced Boresight Equipment [*Army*]
ABE	Aerodrome Beacon (DA)
ABE	Air-Based Electronics (MCD)
ABE	Airborne Bombing Evaluation
A/BE	Airborne Equipment (AAG)
ABE	Air-Breathing Engine (KSC)
ABE	Air Burst Effect
ABE	Allentown/Bethlehem/Easton [*Pennsylvania*] [*Airport symbol*]
ABE	Amer Body Armor & Equip [*AMEX symbol*] (TTSB)
ABE	American Board of Endodontics (EA)
ABE	Americans for Budget Equity [*Defunct*] (EA)
ABE	Antitoxin Botulism Equine Trivalent [*Biochemistry*] (DAVI)
ABE	Application Builder Editor [*Computer science*]
ABE	Arberia Airlines [*Albania*] [*FAA designator*] (FAAC)
ABE	Arithmetic Building Element [*Computer science*]
ABE	Armor Holdings, Inc. [*AMEX symbol*] (SAG)
ABE	Army Background Experiment
ABE	Associated Borrowers Endorsement [*British*]
ABEW	Association of British Editors (EAIO)
ABE	Association of Business Executives [*British*] (DBA)
ABE	Autonomous Benthic Explorer [*Oceanography*]
ABE	Aviation Boatswain's Mate, Launch and Recovery Equipment [*Navy rating*]
ABEA	American Baptist Education Association [*Defunct*] (EA)
ABEA	American Broncho-Esophagological Association (EA)
ABEAA	Aviation Boatswain's Mate, Launch and Recovery Equipment, Airman Apprentice [*Navy rating*]
ABEAG	Research Station, Agriculture Canada. Station de Recherches, Agriculture Canada, Beaverlodge, Alberta [*Library symbol National Library of Canada*] (NLC)
ABEAM	Beaumont Municipal Library, Alberta [*Library symbol National Library of Canada*] (NLC)
ABEAN	Aviation Boatswain's Mate, Launch and Recovery Equipment, Airman [*Navy rating*]
ABEC	American Baptist Extension Corp.
ABEC	Amphenol-Borg Electronics Corp. (MCD)
ABEC	Annular Bearing Engineers Committee (EA)
ABECB	Acute Bacterial Exacerbation of Chronic Bronchitis [*Medicine*]
Abe Cbl........	Adenosylcobalamin [*A vitamin*] (BABM)
A'Beckett	Judgments of the Supreme Court of New South Wales for the District of Port Philip [*1846-51*] [*A publication*] (DLA)
A'Beckett Res Judg...	A'Beckett's Reserved Judgements [*Victoria*] [*A publication*] (ILCA)
A'Beck Res Judg...	A'Beckett's Reserved Judgements [*A publication*] (ILCA)
ABECOR.......	[*The*] Associated Banks of Europe Corp. (IID)
ABED	Acid/Base Electrolyte Disorders (MHDB)
AB Ed..........	Bachelor of Arts in Education
ABEEG	Aberbeeg [*Welsh depot code*]
ABEF	Brisbane [*Australia ICAO location identifier*] (ICLI)
ABEI	(Aminobutyl)ethylisoluminol [*Biochemistry*]
ABEL	Acid/Base Electrolyte [*Disorder diagnosed by an experimental medical system of the same name*]
ABEL	Air-Breathing Electric LASER (MCD)
ABELM	Bellevue Municipal Library, Alberta [*Library symbol National Library of Canada*] (NLC)
ABEM	American Board of Emergency Medicine (EA)
ABEM	American Board of Environmental Medicine (EA)
ABEM	Beiseker Municipal Library, Alberta [*Library symbol National Library of Canada*] (NLC)
ABEN	Bentley Public Library, Alberta [*Library symbol National Library of Canada*] (NLC)
ABEND	Abnormal End [*Computer science*]
ABEP	American Board of Examiners in Psychotherapy (EA)
ABEP	Auditory Brain-Stem-Evoked Potential [*Neurology*] (DAVI)
ABEPC	American Board of Examiners in Pastoral Counseling (EA)
ABEPH	American Board of Examiners in Psychological Hypnosis [*Later, ABPH*] (EA)
ABEPP	American Board of Examiners in Professional Psychology [*Later, ABPP*]
ABEPSGP.....	American Board of Examiners of Psychodrama, Sociometry, and Group Psychotherapy (EA)
ABER	Abberrant (ABBR)
ABER	Aberdeen [*City and county in Scotland*] (ROG)
aber............	Aberrant (DMAA)
ABER	Aberration (IAA)
ABER	Aber Resources Ltd. [*NASDAQ symbol*] (NQ)
ABER	Auditory Brainstem Evoked Response [*Medicine*] (DMAA)
ABERCOR	Associated Banks of Europe Corp. (ODBW)
ABERD	Aberdeen [*City and county in Scotland*]
ABERE	Aber Resource Ltd. [*NASDAQ symbol*] (TTSB)
AberFit........	Abercrombie & Fitch Co. [*Associated Press*] (SAG)
ABERN	Aberration (ABBR)
ABERNL.......	Aberrational (ABBR)
AberRs.........	Aber Resources Ltd. [*Associated Press*] (SAG)
ABERT	Automatic BIT [*Binary Digit*] Error Rate Test [*Computer science*] (MCD)
ABERU	Airborne Emergency Reaction Unit
ABERY	Aberystwyth [*Borough in Wales*]
ABES...........	Aerospace Business Environment Simulator [*Computer-programmed management game*]
ABES...........	Air-Breathing Engine System
ABES...........	Alliance for Balanced Environmental Solutions [*Defunct*] (EA)
ABES...........	American Biblical Encyclopedia Society (EA)
ABES...........	American Broncho-Esophagological Association (EA)
ABES...........	Association for Broadcast Engineering Standards [*Defunct*] (EA)
ABES...........	Beaverlodge Elementary School, Alberta [*Library symbol National Library of Canada*] (BIB)
ABESPA	American Boards of Examiners in Speech Pathology and Audiology [*Later, COPS*] (EA)
ABESS	St. Mary's School, Beaverlodge, Alberta [*Library symbol National Library of Canada*] (BIB)
ABET...........	Accreditation Board for Engineering and Technology (EA)
ABETC	Able-Bodied Seaman Electronic Technical Communications [*Navy*]
ABETD	Abetted (ABBR)
ABETG	Abetting (ABBR)
ABETMT......	Abetment (ABBR)
ABETNT......	Abetment (ABBR)
ABETP........	Able-Bodied Seaman Electrical Technical Power [*Navy*]
ABETR	Abettor (ABBR)
ABETS	Airborne Beacon Electronic Test Set
ABETW	Able-Bodied Seaman Electrical Technical Weapons [*Navy*]
ABEV..........	Atlantic Beverage [*NASDAQ symbol*] (TTSB)
ABEV..........	Atlantic Beverage Corp. [*NASDAQ symbol*] (SAG)
ABEW	Able-Bodied Seaman Electronic Warfare [*Navy*]
ABEX	Ab Extra [*From Without*] [*Latin*]
Ab Ex	Abstract Expressionism (BARN)
ABEXed.......	Absorbance Expanded [*Spectroscopy*]
ABEZS..........	Bezanson School, Alberta [*Library symbol National Library of Canada*] (BIB)
ABF	Abaiang [*Kiribati*] [*Airport symbol*] (OAG)
abF	Abfarad (IDOE)
ABF	Absolutely Bloody Final [*Especially with reference to a drink*]
ABF	Actors' Benevolent Fund [*Australia*]
ABF	Adaptive Beam Forming (NVT)
ABF	Advance Booking Fare [*Airlines*]
ABF	Advanced Beamformer (MCD)
ABF	Advanced Bomb Family [*Navy*] (DOMA)
ABF	Air Base Flight [*Air Force*]
ABF	Airborne Freight [*NYSE symbol*] (TTSB)
ABF	Airborne Freight Corp. [*NYSE symbol*] (SPSG)
ABF	Air Burst Fuze
ABF	Aircraft Battle Force [*Obsolete Navy*]
ABF	American Bach Foundation (EA)
ABF	American Ballads and Folk Songs [*A publication*]
ABF	American Banjo Fraternity (EA)
ABF	American Bar Foundation (EA)
ABF	American Beekeeping Federation (EA)
ABF	American Behcet's Foundation (EA)
ABF	American Bikeways Foundation [*Defunct*] (EA)
ABF	American Blake Foundation (EA)
ABF	American Buyers Federation (EA)
ABF	Americas Boychoir Federation (EA)
ABF	America the Beautiful Fund (EA)
ABF	Ammonium Biflouride [*Inorganic chemistry*]
ABF	Anaerobic Bacterial Flora [*Microbiology*]
ABF	Anchor Block Foundation (EA)
ABF	Aortic Blood Flow [*Medicine*] (DMAA)
ABF	Aortobifemoral [*Medicine*] (DMAA)
ABF	Application-by-Forms (HGAA)
ABF	Army Benevolent Fund [*British*]
ABF	Asset [*or Availability*] Balance File [*Military*] (AABC)
ABF	Associated British Foods [*Commercial firm*]
ABF	Association of British Factors
ABF	Audio Bandpass Filter
ABF	Australian Bowling Federation
ABF	Australian Bridge Federation
ABF	Availability Balance File [*Military*] (AABC)
ABF	Average Branching Factor (IAA)
ABF	Aviation Boatswain's Mate, Fuel [*Navy rating*]
ABF	Belgian Flight Centre [*ICAO designator*] (FAAC)
ABF2	Aviation Boatswain's Mate, Fuel, Second Class [*Navy rating*] (DNAB)
ABF3	Aviation Boatswain's Mate, Fuel, Third Class [*Navy rating*] (DNAB)
ABFA...........	American Baseball Fans Association (EA)
ABFA...........	American Board of Forensic Anthropology (EA)
ABFA...........	Australian Business Forms Association
ABFA...........	Azobisformamide [*Organic chemistry*]
ABFAA.........	Aviation Boatswain's Mate, Fuel, Airman Apprentice [*Navy rating*]
ABFAB........	Absolutely Fabulous (DSUE)
ABFAN	Aviation Boatswain's Mate, Fuel, Airman [*Navy rating*]
A/B F & D	Airborne Fill-and-Drain (AAG)
ABFC..........	Able-Bodied Seaman Fire Control [*Navy*]
ABFC..........	Advanced Base Functional Component [*Military*]
ABFCC	American Border Fancy Canary Club (EA)
ABFCR	American Business Foundation for Cancer Research [*Defunct*] (EA)
ABFCS	Advanced Base Functional Component System [*Military*]
ABFD	Affordable Basic Floppy Disk [*Computer science*] (MHDI)

ABFD	Association of British Factors and Discounters (EAIO)
ABFDS	Aerial Bulk Fuel Delivery System [*Military*] (AFIT)
ABFE	Association of Black Foundation Executives (EA)
ABFF	Able-Bodied Seaman Firefighter [*Navy*]
ABFL	Association of British Foam Laminators (BI)
ABFLO	Association of Bedding and Furniture Law Officials (EA)
ABFM	American Board of Foreign Missions
ABFM	Association of Business Forms Manufacturers [*Defunct*] (EA)
ABFMS	American Baptist Foreign Mission Society [*Congo - Leopoldville*]
ABFOR	American-British Forces [*World War II*]
ABFP	American Board of Family Practice (EA)
ABFP	American Board of Forensic Psychiatry (EA)
ABFP	American Board of Forensic Psychology (EA)
ABF Research Reptr	American Bar Foundation. Research Reporter [*A publication*] (DLA)
ABF Research Reptr J	American Bar Foundation. Research Reporter Journal [*A publication*] (DLA)
ABF Res Newsl	American Bar Foundation. Research Newsletter [*A publication*] (DLA)
ABFS	Arkansas Best [*NASDAQ symbol*] (TTSB)
ABFS	Arkansas Best Corp. [*NASDAQ symbol*] (SAG)
ABFS	Auxiliary Building Filter System [*Nuclear energy*] (NRCH)
ABFSE	American Board of Funeral Service Education (EA)
ABFSP	Arkansas Best $2.875 'A 'Pfd [*NASDAQ symbol*] (TTSB)
ABFSWS	Associated Blacksmiths, Forge, and Smithy Workers Society [*A union*] [*British*]
ABFV	Anti-Backfire Valve [*Automotive engineering*]
ABG	Abakan-Avia [*Former USSR*] [*FAA designator*] (FAAC)
Abg	Abgeordneter [*Member of Parliament*] [*German*] (BARN)
ABG	Abingdon [*Australia Airport symbol*] (OAG)
ABG	Abington Township Public Library, Abington, PA [*OCLC symbol*] (OCLC)
ABG	Abnormal Blood Gas
abg	Addictive Behavior Group [*Psychology*] (DAVI)
ABG	Air Base Group [*Obsolete Navy*]
ABG	Alibag [*India*] [*Geomagnetic observatory code*]
ABG	American Budgetel, Inc. [*Vancouver Stock Exchange symbol*]
ABG	Antibacklash Gear
ABG	Arterial Blood Gas [*Medicine*]
ABG	Association of British Geodesists
ABG	Aural Bearing Generator
ABG	Australian Bartenders' Guild
ABG	Axiobuccogingival [*Dentistry*]
a-bg--	Bangladesh [*MARC geographic area code Library of Congress*]
ABG	Big Sandy, TX [*Location identifier FAA*] (FAAL)
ABG	Groupe AB SA [*NYSE symbol*] (SAG)
ABGA	Allied Bankshares (GA) [*NASDAQ symbol*] (TTSB)
ABGA	Allied Bankshares, Inc. [*NASDAQ symbol*] (NQ)
ABGA	American Brussels Griffon Association (EA)
ABGB	Allgemeines Buergerliches Gesetzbuch [*Austrian Civil Code*] (DLA)
ABGBI	Associated Booksellers of Great Britain and Ireland (DGA)
ABGC	Australian Banana Growers' Council
ABGCP	Association of Boys and Girls Clubs Professionals (EA)
ABGG	(Amanitinylazobenzoyl)glycylglycine
ABGK	Abgekuerzt [*Abbreviated*] [*German*]
ABGL	Gladstone [*Australia ICAO location identifier*] (ICLI)
ABGMT	Arizona Bureau of Geology and Mineral Technology [*University of Arizona*] [*Research center*] (RCD)
ABGP	Air Base Group [*Air Force*]
ABGR	American Businessmen's Group of Riyadh (EA)
ABGR	Australian Biographical and Genealogical Record [*A publication*] (ADA)
ABGSM	Association of British Generating Set Manufacturers (MHDB)
ABGTS	Auxiliary Building Gas Treatment System [*Nuclear energy*] (NRCH)
ABGW	Aluminum, Brick, and Glass Workers International Union
ABGWIU	Aluminum, Brick, and Glass Workers International Union (EA)
ABH	Aberystwyth [*Welsh depot code*]
ABH	Abhandlungen [*Transactions*] [*German Business term*]
abH	Abhenry (IDOE)
ABH	Above Burst Height (DNAB)
ABH	Advanced Base Hospital [*British*]
ABH	Air-Britain Historians [*An association*] (EAIO)
ABH	Alpha [*Australia Airport symbol*] (OAG)
ABH	Alpha Benzene Hexachloride [*Organic chemistry*] (ADA)
ABH	American Bureau of Shipping (Hellas) (DS)
ABH	Association for the Bibliography of History (EA)
ABH	Association of British Hairdressers and Hairdressing Schools
ABH	Association of British Hispanists
ABH	Association of Hispanists of Great Britain and Ireland (AIE)
ABH	Average Busy Hour [*Telecommunications*] (TEL)
ABH	Aviation Boatswain's Mate, Handler [*Navy rating*]
ABH	Samford University, Birmingham, AL [*Library symbol Library of Congress*] (LCLS)
ABH	Societe Air Bretagne Service [*France ICAO designator*] (FAAC)
ABH	University of Alabama in Birmingham, Health Sciences Library, Birmingham, AL [*OCLC symbol*] (OCLC)
ABH1	Aviation Boatswain's Mate, Handler, First Class [*Navy rating*] (DNAB)
ABH2	Aviation Boatswain's Mate, Handler, Second Class [*Navy rating*] (DNAB)
ABH3	Aviation Boatswain's Mate, Handler, Third Class [*Navy rating*] (DNAB)
ABHA	Associate of the British Hypnotherapy Association (DBQ)
ABHAA	Aviation Boatswain's Mate, Handler, Airman Apprentice [*Navy rating*]
ABHAN	Aviation Boatswain's Mate, Handler, Airman [*Navy rating*]
ABHC	American Belgian Hare Club (EA)

ABHC	American Business History Collection [*Microfiche*] (IID)
ABHC	Association of Bank Holding Companies [*Washington, DC*] (EA)
ABHC	Chief Aviation Boatswain's Mate, Handler [*Navy rating*] (DNAB)
ABHES	Accrediting Bureau of Health Education Schools (EA)
ABHH	Association of Baptist Homes and Hospitals [*Later, ABHHA*] (EA)
ABHHA	American Baptist Homes and Hospitals Association (EA)
ABHJ	Angle Bulkhead Jack
ABH-L	Samford University, Cumberland School of Law, Cordell Hull Law Library, Birmingham, AL [*Library symbol Library of Congress*] (LCLS)
ABHM	American Board of Homeopathic Medicine (EA)
ABHM	Association of Builders' Hardware Manufacturers (EAIO)
ABHM	Hamilton Island [*Australia ICAO location identifier*] (ICLI)
ABHMS	American Baptist Home Mission Society [*Later, Board of National Ministries*] (EA)
ABHP	American Board of Health Physics (EA)
ABHPBS	Blue Hills Community School, Buffalo Head Prairie, Alberta [*Library symbol National Library of Canada*] (BIB)
ABHPS	Buffalo Head Prairie School, Alberta [*Library symbol National Library of Canada*] (BIB)
ABHR	American Bay Horse Registry [*Defunct*] (EA)
ABHR	Australian Book Heritage Resources Project
ABHRD	Abhorred (ABBR)
ABHRG	Abhorring (ABBR)
ABHRNC	Abhorrence (ABBR)
ABHRNT	Abhorrent (ABBR)
ABHRNTY	Abhorrently (ABBR)
ABHRR	Abhorrer (ABBR)
ABHRT	Abhorrent (ABBR)
ABHRTY	Abhorrently (ABBR)
ABHS	American Baptist Historical Society (EA)
ABHS	American Board of Hand Surgery (EA)
Abh Sachs Ges Wiss	Abhandlungen. Saechsische Gesellschaft der Wissenschaften [*A publication*] (OCD)
ABHX	Air Blast Heat Exchanger [*Nuclear energy*] (NRCH)
Abh zu Gesch d Math	Abhandlungen zur Geschichte der Mathematischen Wissenschaften [*A publication*] (OCD)
Abh zu Gesch d Med	Abhandlungen zur Geschichte der Naturwissenschaften und der Medizin [*A publication*] (OCD)
ABI	Abilene [*Texas*] [*Airport symbol*] (OAG)
ABI	About Books, Inc. [*An association*] (EA)
ABI	Abstracted Business Information, Inc.
ABI	Advance Book Information [*Publishing*]
ABI	Advance Boundary Information (DA)
ABI	Advanced Biotechnologies, Inc.
ABI	Agile-Beam Illuminator (MCD)
ABI	Allgemeines Bucher-Lexikon [*A publication*]
ABI	American Bankruptcy Institute (EA)
ABI	American Bell, Inc.
ABI	American Beverage Institute
ABI	American-British Intelligence [*NATO*] (NATG)
ABI	American Business Information
ABI	American Butter Institute (EA)
ABI	Ankle/Brachial Pressure Index
ABI	Antigua and Barbuda Airways International Ltd. [*ICAO designator*] (FAAC)
ABI	Application Binary Interface [*Computer science*] (BYTE)
ABI	Associacao Brasileira de Imprensa [*Brazilian Press Association*]
ABI	Association of British Insurers (EAIO)
ABI	Association of British Investigators (EAIO)
ABI	Association of Business and Industry [*Iowa*] (SRA)
ABI	Atherosclerotic Brain Infarction [*Medicine*] (CPH)
ABI	Atherothrombotic Brain Infarction [*Medicine*] (DAVI)
ABI	Auditory Brainstem Implant [*Hearing technology*]
ABI	Automated Behavioral Intelligence (MCD)
ABI	Automated Broker Interface [*Customs Service*] (GFGA)
ABI	Auxiliary Building Isolation [*Nuclear energy*] (NRCH)
ABI	Aviation Billet Indicator (DNAB)
ABI	Bow Island Public Library, Alberta [*Library symbol National Library of Canada*] (NLC)
ABIA	American Boardsailing Industries Association (EA)
ABIA	Association of British Introduction Agencies (EAIO)
ABIAS	Air Bag Impact Attentuation System (MCD)
ABIC	Adaptive Behavior Inventory for Children [*Psychology*]
ABIC	Army Battlefield Interface Concept (MCD)
ABIC	Automated Battlefield Interface Concept [*Army*]
ABICC	Associate of the British Institute of Certified Carpenters
ABID	Associate of the British Institute of Interior Design (DBQ)
ABIDG	Abiding (ABBR)
ABIDGY	Abidingly (ABBR)
ABIDM	Improvement District No. 9/Banff Municipal Library, Alberta [*Library symbol National Library of Canada*] (NLC)
ABIDNC	Abidance (ABBR)
ABIG	Absence of Immunoglobulin G [*Biochemistry*] (DAVI)
ABIG	ACCESS.bus Industry Group [*Computer science*] (PCM)
ABIG	Amer Bankers Insur Grp [*NASDAQ symbol*] (TTSB)
ABIG	American Bankers Insurance Group, Inc. [*NASDAQ symbol*] (NQ)
AbigAd	Abigail Adams National Bancorp, Inc. [*Associated Press*] (SAG)
ABIH	American Board of Industrial Hygiene (EA)
ABIH	Association of British and International Hairdressers and Hairdressing Schools (DBA)
ABII	Amer Business Information [*NASDAQ symbol*] (TTSB)
ABII	American Business Information, Inc. [*NASDAQ symbol*] (SAG)
ABIIS	Automated Blood Inventory Information System (PDAA)
ABIL	Ability (ABBR)

ABIL	Airborne Beacon Interference Locator (MCD)
ABILS	Automated Bulk Items List System (MCD)
ABIM	American Board of Internal Medicine (EA)
ABIM	American Board of International Missions (EA)
ABIM	Association of British Insecticide Manufacturers (DI)
ABIM	Malaysian Youth Movement
ABIMS	American Board of Industrial Medicine and Surgery (EA)
AB in CE	Bachelor of Arts in Civil Engineering
AB in Ch E	Bachelor of Arts in Chemical Engineering
AB in EE	Bachelor of Arts in Electrical Engineering
ABINF	Airborne Infantry [*Military*] (SAA)
ABING	Abingdon [*England*]
ABingo	American Bingo & Gambling Corp. [*Associated Press*] (SAG)
AbingSB	Abington Savings Bank [*Associated Press*] (SAG)
AB in H Ec	Bachelor of Arts in Home Economics
AB INIT	Ab Initio [*From the Beginning*] [*Latin*]
AB in J	Bachelor of Arts in Journalism
AB in ME	Bachelor of Arts in Mechanical Engineering
AB in Sec Ed	Bachelor of Arts in Secondary Education
AB in TH	Bachelor of Arts in Theology
ABIO	Applied Biometrics [*NASDAQ symbol*] (TTSB)
ABIO	Applied Biometrics, Inc. [*NASDAQ symbol*] (NQ)
ABIOL	Advanced Base Initial Outfitting List [*Military*]
Abiomd	Abiomed, Inc. [*Associated Press*] (SAG)
ABIOS	Advanced Basic Input/Output System [*Computer science*] (DOM)
ABiosci	Applied Bioscience International [*Associated Press*] (SAG)
ABIPE	Association des Bibliotheques Publiques de l'Estrie (AC)
ABIPP	Associate of the British Institute of Professional Photography (DBQ)
ABIR	All-Band Intercept Receiver
ABIRA	American Biographical Institute Research Association (EA)
ABIRD	Aircraft-Based Infrared Detector
ABIS	Anglo-Brazilian Information Service [*Information service or system*] (IID)
ABIS	Apollo Bioenvironmental Information System (PDAA)
ABIS	Associate of the British Interplanetary Society (IAA)
ABIS	Association of Burglary Insurance Surveyors [*British*] (DI)
ABIS	Audit Base Inventory System [*IRS*]
ABISL	Advanced Base Initial Support Lists [*Navy*] (AFIT)
ABISS	American Bough of the International Society of Shropshires (EA)
Abit	Abitur [*School Exit Examination*] [*German*]
ABIT	Aircraft Blast Interaction Tests (MCD)
ABIT	Assertive Behavior Inventory Tool [*Psychology*] (DMAA)
Abitibi	Abitibi-Price, Inc. [*Associated Press*] (SAG)
ABIX	Abatix Environmental [*NASDAQ symbol*] (TTSB)
ABIX	Abatix Environmental Corp. [*NASDAQ symbol*] (NQ)
ABJ	Abashiri [*Japan*] [*Seismograph station code, US Geological Survey*]
ABJ	Abidjan [*Ivory Coast*] [*Airport symbol*] (OAG)
ABJ	Adhesively Bonded Joint [*or Junction*]
ABJ	Adjustable Buoyancy Jacket
ABJ	Ala Abaete Linhas Aereas, SA [*Brazil*] [*FAA designator*] (FAAC)
ABJ	American Businessmen of Jeddah (EA)
ABJ	Angle Bulkhead Jack
ABJ	Birmingham-Jefferson Library, Birmingham, AL [*OCLC symbol*] (OCLC)
ABJ	International Businessmen of Jeddah [*Saudi Arabia*] (EAIO)
ABJ	Jefferson County Law Library, Birmingham, AL [*Library symbol Library of Congress*] (LCLS)
ABJR	Abjure (ABBR)
ABJRD	Abjured (ABBR)
ABJRG	Abjuring (ABBR)
ABJRN	Abjuration (ABBR)
ABJRR	Abjurer (ABBR)
ABJS	Association of Bone and Joint Surgeons (EA)
ABJS	Australian Babji Joga Sangam [*An association*]
ABJS	Jefferson State Junior College, Birmingham, AL [*Library symbol Library of Congress*] (LCLS)
ABJT	Abject (ABBR)
ABJTN	Abjection (ABBR)
ABJTNS	Abjectness (ABBR)
ABJTY	Abjectly (ABBR)
ABK	Abisko [*Sweden*] [*Seismograph station code, US Geological Survey Closed*]
Abk	Abkurzung [*Abbreviation*] [*German*] (BARN)
ABK	Airborne Identification Kit (DEN)
ABK	Albatros Airline, Inc. [*Turkey*] [*ICAO designator*] (FAAC)
ABK	AMBAC, Inc. [*NYSE symbol*] (SPSG)
ABK	Angular Blocky Soil [*Agronomy*]
ABK	Kabri Dar [*Ethiopia*] [*Airport symbol*] (OAG)
ABKA	American Boarding Kennels Association (EA)
ABKA	Antique Bowie Knife Association (EA)
ABkCT	American Bank of Connecticut [*Associated Press*] (SAG)
ABKR	Anchor Bancorp (SPSG)
ABKT	Associated Birdkeepers and Traders [*Australia*]
ABKUFI	Abkuerzungsfimmel [*Abbreviation Craze*]
AbL	Abelson-Murine Leukemia [*Virus*]
ABL	Abetalipoproteinemia [*Medicine*] (MAE)
ABL	A-Beta-Lipoproteinemia [*Medicine*] (MAH)
ABL	Ablative
ABL	Able (ABBR)
ABL	Above Baseline
Abl	Abril [*April*] [*Spanish*] (BARN)
ABL	ABS Resources Ltd. [*Vancouver Stock Exchange symbol*]
ABL	Accepted Batch Listing [*Accounting*]
ABL	Acetylbutyrolactone [*Organic chemistry*]
ABL	Action for Better Living [*Defunct*] (EA)

ABL	Adaption Binary Load [*Program*] (CET)
ABL	Air BC Ltd. [*Canada ICAO designator*] (FAAC)
ABL	Air Blast Loading
ABL	Airborne LASER (MCD)
ABL	Alameda Belt Line [*AAR code*]
ABL	All Busy Low [*AT & T*]
ABL	Allegheny Ballistics Laboratory [*Cumberland, MD*] (MCD)
ABL	Allocated Baseline (MCD)
ABL	Allograft-Bound Lymphocytes [*Biochemistry*] (DAVI)
ABL	Ambler [*Alaska*] [*Airport symbol*] (OAG)
ABL	Amer Biltrite [*AMEX symbol*] (TTSB)
ABL	American Biltrite, Inc. [*AMEX symbol*] (SPSG)
ABL	American Biotechnology Laboratory [*A publication*]
ABL	American-British Laboratory [*Harvard University*]
ABL	American Bulgarian League [*Defunct*] (EA)
ABL	Ammunition Base Load (MCD)
ABL	Amtsblatt [*Official Gazette*] [*German*] (DLA)
ABL	Antigen-Binding Lymphocyte [*Immunology*] (AAMN)
ABL	Architectural Block Diagram Language
ABL	Armament Boresight Line
ABL	Armored Box Launcher [*Shipboard launching system*]
ABL	Armstrong Browning Library [*Baylor University*] [*Research center*] (RCD)
ABL	Army Biological Laboratory
ABL	Asian Business League [*Later, ABL-SF*] (EA)
ABL	Assembly Breakdown List
ABL	Association of Ballrooms [*British*] (EAIO)
ABL	Assyrian and Babylonian Letters Belonging to the Kouyunjik Collection(s) of the British Museum [*A publication*] (BJA)
ABL	Atlas [*Abbreviated Test Language for Avionics Systems*] Basic Language [*Computer science*]
ABL	Atmospheric Boundary Layer [*Marine science*] (OSRA)
ABL	Atmospheric Burst Locator (MCD)
ABL	Australian Bank Ltd.
ABL	Australian Baseball League
ABL	Automated Biological Laboratory [*NASA*]
ABL	Automatic Bootstrap Loader [*Computer science*]
ABL	Axiobuccolingual [*Dentistry*]
ABL	Blairmore Public Library, Alberta [*Library symbol National Library of Canada*] (NLC)
ABL	Law for the Australian Businessman [*A publication*]
ABLA	Amateur Bicycle League of America [*Later, USCF*]
ABLA	American Blind Lawyers Association (EA)
ABLA	American Business Law Association (EA)
ABLA	Blackfalds Public Library, Alberta [*Library symbol National Library of Canada*] (NLC)
ABLAT	Ablative (KSC)
ABLB	Alternate Binaural Loudness Balance [*Otorhinolaryngology*] (DAVI)
ABLB	Alternate Binaural Loudness Balancing [*Audiometry*]
ABLC	Alcohol Beverage Legislative Council (EA)
ABLC	American Brown Leghorn Club (EA)
ABLC	Amphotericin B Lipid Complex [*Antifungal*]
ABLC	Association of British Launderers and Cleaners (DI)
ABLC	Automatic Backlight Compensation [*Photography*]
ABLCHG	Airborne Launching [*Aviation*] (FAAC)
ABLCWS	Altogether Builders, Labourers, and Constructional Workers Society [*A union*] [*British*]
ABLE	Ability Based on Long Experience
ABLE	Acquisition Based on Consideration of Logistic Effects [*Air Force*]
ABLE	Activity Balance Line Evaluation [*PERT*]
ABLE	Adult Basic Learning Examination (NVT)
ABLE	Advanced Bio-Mechanical Linkage Enablement [*Rehabilitation technology*]
ABLE	Advanced Blown Lift Enhancement (MCD)
ABLE	Agricultural-Biological Literature Exploitation [*Systems study of National Agricultural Library*]
ABLE	Amazon Boundary Layer Experiment (MCD)
ABLE	Association for Biology Laboratory Education (EA)
ABLE	Asymptotically Best Linear Estimate (PDAA)
ABLE	Atmospheric Boundary Layer Experiment [*National Oceanic and Atmospheric Administration*]
ABLE	Audit Basic Learning Examination (MCD)
ABLE	Autonetics Base-Line Equipment
ABLE	Auxiliary Balance Line Evaluation [*Nuclear energy*] (NUCP)
ABLES	Airborne Battlefield Light Equipment System [*Army*]
AbleTel	Able Telcom Holding Corp. [*Associated Press*] (SAG)
ABLF	Atmosphere Boundary Layer Facility (MCD)
ABLFUW	Australian Builders' Laborers Federated Union of Workers
ABLG	Antibacklash Gear
ABLH	Abolish (ABBR)
ABLHB	Abolishable (ABBR)
ABLHNT	Abolishment (ABBR)
ABLHR	Abolisher (ABBR)
ABLI	Abraham Lincoln Birthplace National Monument
ABLISS	Association of British Library and Information Science Schools
ABLISS	Association of British Library and Information Studies Schools (DBA)
ABLJ	Adjustable Buoyancy Life Jacket
ABLK	Laverack Barracks [*Australia ICAO location identifier*] (ICLI)
ABLM	Abloom (ABBR)
ABLP	Air Bearing Lift Pad (KSC)
ABLP	Aniline Blue-Lactophenol Medium [*Botany*]
ABLR	Abler (ABBR)
ABLR	Australian Business Law Review [*A publication*]
ABLR	Longreach [*Australia ICAO location identifier*] (ICLI)
ABLS	Abelson Lymphosarcoma [*Oncology*]

ABLS...........	American Board of Laser Surgery (EA)
ABLS...........	American Bryological and Lichenological Society (EA)
ABLS...........	Association of British Library Schools
ABLS...........	Atlas Biomedical Literature System
ABLS...........	Bachelor of Arts in Library Science
ABL-SF	Asian Business League of San Francisco [California] (EA)
ABLSS	Advanced Ballistic-Type Logistic Spacecraft System (MCD)
ABLT...........	Ability (ABBR)
ABLT...........	Ablest (ABBR)
ABLTV.........	Ablative (ABBR)
ABLUE	Asymptotically Best Linear Unbiased Estimator [Statistics]
ABLUN........	Ablution (ABBR)
ABLUNRY	Ablutionary (ABBR)
ABLUNY.......	Ablutionary (ABBR)
ABLV...........	Air-Breathing Launch Vehicle [Military] (PDAA)
ABLZ...........	Ablaze (ABBR)
ABM...........	Abducens Motoneuron [Neuroanatomy]
ABM...........	Abeam
ABM...........	Abermin Corp. [Toronto Stock Exchange symbol]
ABM...........	Abingdon Mile [Newmarket Racecourse] [Horseracing] [British]
ABM...........	ABM Industries, Inc. [Associated Press] (SAG)
ABM...........	Acquisition Bus Monitor [Computer science] (MCD)
ABM...........	Acute Bacterial Meningitis [Medicine]
ABM...........	Adjusted Balance Method
ABM...........	Advanced Bill of Material [Accounting] (AAG)
ABM...........	Air Battle Management [Military]
ABM...........	Air Breathing Missile [Military] (LAIN)
ABM...........	Allen, Brady & Marsh [British advertising agency]
ABM...........	Amber Airways Ltd. [British ICAO designator] (FAAC)
ABM...........	American Buddhist Movement (EA)
ABM...........	American Building Maintenance Industries [NYSE symbol] (SPSG)
ABM...........	Amino-Form Bind Medium [Analytical biochemistry]
ABM...........	Anderson-Brinkman-Morel State [Superconductivity]
ABM...........	Antiballistic Missile [Air Force]
ABM...........	Anybody but McGovern [1972 presidential campaign]
ABM...........	Apogee Boost Motor [Aerospace] (MCD)
ABM...........	Artbibliographies Modern [Database] [Clio Press Ltd.] [Information service or system] (CRD)
ABM...........	Assistant Beach Master [British]
ABM...........	Associated Building Material Distributors of America (EA)
ABM...........	Associate in Business Management
ABM...........	Association for British Music (EAIO)
ABM...........	Association of Board Makers [British] (DBA)
ABM...........	Association of Breastfeeding Mothers (EAIO)
ABM...........	Association of Button Merchants (EAIO)
ABM...........	Asynchronous Balanced Mode [Computer science]
ABM...........	Atomic Beam Method
ABM...........	Australian Birthright Movement [An association]
ABM...........	Australian Business Monthly [A publication]
ABM...........	Automated [or Automatic] Batch Mixing [Computer science]
ABM...........	Avian Basal Medium [Culture media]
ABM...........	Aviation Boatswain's Mate [Navy rating]
ABM...........	Bamaga [Australia Airport symbol] (OAG)
ABM...........	Bonnyville Municipal Library, Alberta [Library symbol National Library of Canada] (NLC)
ABM...........	Miles College, Birmingham, AL [Library symbol Library of Congress] (LCLS)
ABMA...........	American Boiler Manufacturers Association (EA)
ABMA...........	American Brush Manufacturers Association (EA)
ABMA...........	Army Ballistic Missile Agency [Redstone Arsenal, AL]
ABMA...........	Mount Isa [Australia ICAO location identifier] (ICLI)
ABMAA	American Black Maine-Anjou Association (EA)
ABMAC	Abalone Management Advisory Committee [Australia]
ABMAC	American Bureau for Medical Advancement in China (EA)
ABMAC	Association of British Manufacturers of Agricultural Chemicals (BI)
ABMAG	Aviation Boatswain's Mate, Arresting Gear and Barriers [Navy rating]
ABMANZ	Associated Bread Manufacturers of Australia and New Zealand
ABMC...........	American Bandstand Memory Club [Later, 1950's American Bandstand Fan Club] (EA)
ABMC...........	American Battle Monuments Commission [Independent government agency]
ABMC...........	American Bike Month Committee [Defunct] (EA)
ABMC...........	American Business Media Council [Defunct] (EA)
ABMC...........	Maroochydore [Australia ICAO location identifier] (ICLI)
ABMCP........	Aviation Boatswain's Mate, Catapult [Navy rating]
ABMD...........	Abiomed, Inc. [NASDAQ symbol] (SAG)
ABMD	Advanced Ballistic Missile Defense [Army]
ABMD	Air Ballistics Missile Division [Air Force]
ABMDA	Advanced Ballistic Missile Defense Agency [Alexandria, VA] [Army]
ABMDA	Associated Building Material Distributors of America (EA)
ABME...........	American Board of Master Educators (EA)
ABME...........	Asynchronous Balanced Mode Extended [Telecommunications] (OSI)
ABME...........	Bachelor of Arts in Mechanical Engineering
ABMEC	Association of British Mining Equipment Companies (EAIO)
ABMED	Able-Bodied Seaman Medical [Navy]
ABMET........	Able-Bodied Seaman Meteorology [Navy]
ABMEWS......	Antiballistic Missile Early Warning System [Air Force]
ABMEX........	Association of British Mining Equipment Exporters (MHDB)
ABMF...........	Australian Barley Marketing Federation
ABMF...........	John E. Meyer Eye Foundation, Eye Foundation Hospital, Birmingham, AL [Library symbol Library of Congress] (LCLS)
ABMG	American Board of Medical Genetics (EA)
ABMGA	Aviation Boatswain's Mate, Gasoline System [Navy rating]
ABMI...........	Autologous Bone Marrow Transpantation [Medicine] (DMAA)
ABMIS	Airborne Ballistic Missile Intercept System

ABMIT........	American Buyers of Meeting and Incentive Travel (EA)
ABMJ..........	American Board of Missions to the Jews [Later, CPM] (EA)
ABMK	Mackay [Australia ICAO location identifier] (ICLI)
ABMLAMS ...	American Board of Medical-Legal Analysis in Medicine and Surgery (EA)
ABMLS........	Accrediting Bureau of Medical Laboratory Schools [Later, ABHES]
ABMM.........	American Board of Medical Microbiology
ABMM.........	Antiballistic-Missile Missile [Air Force] (AFM)
ABMNA	Abominate (ABBR)
ABMNAD......	Abonminated (ABBR)
ABMNAG......	Abominating (ABBR)
ABMNAN......	Abomination (ABBR)
ABMNB	Abominable (ABBR)
ABMNBY	Abominably (ABBR)
ABMP.........	American Board of Medical Psychotherapists (EA)
ABMP.........	Associated Bodywork and Massage Professionals (EA)
ABMP.........	Association of British Meat Processors (DBA)
ABM Paper...	Aminobenzyloxy Methyl Cellulose Paper (DOG)
ABMPH	Aviation Boatswain's Mate, Plane Handler [Navy rating]
ABMPM	Association of British Manufacturers of Printers' Machinery (DI)
ABMPS	Automated Business Mail Processing System [Computer science] (MHDI)
ABMPTP	Association of Black Motion Picture and Television Producers (EA)
ABMR	Academy of Behavioral Medicine Research (EA)
ABMR	Atlantic Ballistic Missile Range
ABMRC	Association of British Marketing Research Companies (DBA)
ABMRF	American Business Men's Research Foundation [Later, ARIS] (EA)
ABMS.........	Activation Ballistic Missile Site (SAA)
ABMS.........	Advanced Ballistic Missile Systems (KSC)
ABMS.........	Advisory Board for Medical Specialties (DAVI)
ABMS.........	American Board of Medical Specialties (EA)
ABMS.........	American Bureau of Metal Statistics (EA)
ABMS.........	Artillery Ballistic Meteorological System (MCD)
ABMS.........	Audit Bureau of Marketing Services (DOAD)
ABMS.........	Autologous Bone-Marrow Transplantation [Medicine] (PDAA)
ABMS.........	Automated Batch Manufacturing System [Computer science] (MHDI)
ABMS.........	Automated Breathing Metabolic Simulator [Medicine] (PDAA)
ABMT.........	American Board of Medical Toxicology (EA)
ABMT.........	Autologous Bone Marrow Transplant [Medicine]
ABMTD	Able-Bodied Seaman Motor Transport Driver [Navy]
ABMTF	Australian Bone Marrow Transplant Foundation
ABMTH	Able-Bodied Seaman Marine Technical Hull [Navy]
ABMTP	Able-Bodied Seaman Marine Technical Propulsion [Navy]
ABMU	American Baptist Missionary Union [Later, Board of International Ministries]
ABMUSN......	Able-Bodied Seaman Musician [Navy]
ABMW	Able-Bodied Seaman Mine Warfare [Navy]
ABMXA	Australian Bicycle Motocross Association
ABN	Abinger [United Kingdom] [Later, HAD] [Geomagnetic observatory code]
ABN	Abnormal [or Abnormality] [Medicine] (AAMN)
AbN	Abr-Nahrain (BJA)
Ab N	Abstracts of Treasury Decisions, New Series [A publication] (DLA)
ABN	Aerodrome Beacon [ICAO] (FAAC)
ABN	African Biosciences Network [International Council of Scientific Unions]
ABN	Air Battle Net [Military] (INF)
ABN	Airborne (AFM)
ABN	Air Fret Senegal [FAA designator] (FAAC)
ABN	Alban Exploration Ltd. [Vancouver Stock Exchange symbol]
ABN	Allied Bank of Nigeria Ltd.
ABN	Amber Boron Nitride (PDAA)
ABN	Amer Banknote [NYSE symbol] (TTSB)
ABN	American Bank Note (BARN)
ABN	American Banknote Corp. [NYSE symbol] (SAG)
ABN	American Bionetics, Inc.
ABN	American Board of Nutrition (EA)
AbN	Antibody Nitrogen (DMAA)
ABN	Aseptic Bone Necrosis [Medicine]
ABN	Associated Broadcast News [Cable-television system]
ABN	Association of British Neurologists
ABN	Auburn [Nebraska] [Seismograph station code, US Geological Survey] (SEIS)
ABN	Australian Bibliographic Network [National Library of Australia] [Information service or system] (IID)
a-bn--	Borneo Island [MARC geographic area code Library of Congress]
ABNA	Achievable Benefit Not Achieved
ABNA	Anorexia Bulimia Nervosa Association (DBA)
ABNC	Abnormal Curve [Biochemistry] (DAVI)
ABncFL	American Bancshares, Inc. (FL) [Associated Press] (SAG)
ABNCO	American Bank Note Co. (MHDW)
ABNCP........	Airborne Command Post [Air Force]
ABNCP........	Airborne National Command Force [DoD]
ABND	Abound (ABBR)
ABND	American Bank Notes Development Corporation (AAGC)
ABND	AutoBond Acceptance Corp. [NASDAQ symbol] (SAG)
ABNDASC	Airborne Direct Air Support Center
ABNDMNT	Abandonment (ABBR)
ABNDNC	Abundance (ABBR)
ABNDNT	Abundant (ABBR)
ABNDNTY	Abundantly (ABBR)
ABNED	Abnormal End [Computer science] (IAA)
ABN F%...	Abnormal Forms Percent [Sperm count] [Urology] (DAVI)
ABNF	Association of Black Nursing Faculty in Higher Education (EA)
ABNFV	Anorexia and Bulimia Nervosa Foundation of Victoria [Australia]

ABNG	Abnegate (ABBR)
ABNGA	Abnegate (ABBR)
ABNGAD	Abnegated (ABBR)
ABNGAG	Abnegating (ABBR)
ABNGD	Abnegated (ABBR)
ABNGG	Abnegating (ABBR)
ABNGN	Abnegation (ABBR)
ABNGR	Abnegator (ABBR)
ABNGS	Abnegates (ABBR)
ABNH	American Bank Note Holographics, Inc.
ABNI	Available but Not Installed
ABNINF	Airborne Infantry [*Military*]
ABnkr	American Bankers Insurance Group [*Associated Press*] (SAG)
ABNL	Abnormal (MSA)
ABNM	American Board of National Missions (EA)
ABNM	American Board of Neurological Microsurgery (EA)
ABNM	American Board of Nuclear Medicine (EA)
ABNMT	Abnormality (ABBR)
ABNMY	Abnormally (ABBR)
ABNN	American Board of Neuroscience Nursing (EA)
ABNO	All but Not Only
ABNOC	Airborne Operations Center [*NATO*] (NATG)
ABNOMS	American Board of Neurological and Orthopaedic Medicine and Surgery (EA)
ABNOR	Abnormal [*or Abnormality*]
ABNORM	Abnormal [*Medicine*] (AAMN)
ABNP	Alan R. Barton Nuclear Plant (NRCH)
Ab NS	Abstracts of Treasury Decisions, New Series [*A publication*] (DLA)
ABNS	American Board of Neurological Surgery (EA)
ABNS	American British Numismatic Society [*Defunct*] (EA)
ABNSIGBN ..	Airborne Signal Battalion (IAA)
ABNSW	Agricultural Bureau of New South Wales [*Australia*]
ABO	Aboriginal (ABBR)
ABO	Aborigine (ABBR)
ABO	Abortion [*Obstetrics*] (DAVI)
ABO	Absent Bed Occupancy [*Medicine*]
ABO	Accessory Boring Organ [*of a gastropod*]
ABO	Accumulated Benefit Obligation (TDOB)
ABO	Administration by Objectives
ABO	Advanced Byte-Oriented [*Computer science*] (HGAA)
ABO	Aeroexpreso Bogota [*Colombia*] [*ICAO designator*] (FAAC)
ABO	Affiliated Boards of Officials (EA)
ABO	Agents of Biological Origin [*Military*]
ABO	Air Board Order
ABO	American Board of Ophthalmology (EA)
ABO	American Board of Opticianry [*Later, NAO*] (EA)
ABO	American Board of Orthodontics (EA)
ABO	American Board of Otolaryngology (EA)
ABO	Antibodies [*Immunochemistry*] (DAVI)
ABO	Apparent Body Orientation (PDAA)
ABO	Arecibo, PR [*Location identifier FAA*] (FAAL)
ABO	Army Budget Office
ABO	Association of British Orchestras (DBA)
ABO	Association of British Orientalists
ABO	Association of Buying Offices [*Defunct*] (EA)
ABO	Astable Blocking Oscillator
ABO	Aviator's Breathing Oxygen [*Air Force*]
ABO	Boyle Public Library, Alberta [*Library symbol National Library of Canada*] (NLC)
ABOA	Aminobenzoic Acid [*Organic chemistry*]
ABOA	Bon Accord Public Library, Alberta [*Library symbol National Library of Canada*] (NLC)
ABOB	Anhydrobis(beta-hydroxyethyl)biguanide [*Antiviral agent*]
ABoC	Agricultural Bank of China
ABOC	Arnolt-Bristol Owners Club [*Later, ABR*] (EA)
ABOCF	Association of British Organic and Compound Fertilisers Ltd. (BI)
Abo Child School ...	Aboriginal Child at School [*A publication*]
ABOD	Abode (ABBR)
ABOF	American Berlin Opera Foundation (EA)
ABOG	American Board of Obstetrics and Gynecology (EA)
Abogada Int'l. ..	Abogada Internacional [*A publication*] (DLA)
ABOGNY	Associated Builders and Owners of Greater New York (SRA)
ABOHN	American Board for Occupational Health Nurses (EA)
ABOI	Association of British Oceanic Industries (DS)
ABOI	Association of British Offshore Industries (DBA)
ABOIP	Amended Basis of Issue Plan [*DoD*]
ABOIPFD	Amended Basis of Issue Plan, Feeder Data [*DoD*]
Abo Island Forum ...	Aboriginal and Islander Forum [*A publication*]
ABOJK	[*A*] Bunch of Jewish Kids [*Slang*] (BJA)
ABOK	Oakey [*Australia ICAO location identifier*] (ICLI)
ABOL	Abolished
abol	Abolitionist
ABOL	Adviser Business Oriented Language [*Programming language*]
ABOLD	Abolished (ABBR)
ABOLG	Abolishing (ABBR)
ABOLN	Abolition (ABBR)
ABOLNM	Abolitionism (ABBR)
ABOLNST	Abolitionist (ABBR)
ABOLNT	Abolitionist (ABBR)
ABOLT	Abolishment (ABBR)
ABOM	Abominate (ABBR)
ABOM	American Board of Orthopaedic Microneurosurgery (EA)
ABOM	Assistant Base Operations Manager [*NASA*] (KSC)
ABOM	Australian Bureau of Meteorology [*Marine science*] (OSRA)

ABOM	Bowden Pioneer Museum, Alberta [*Library symbol National Library of Canada*] (BIB)
Abomac	[*A*] Bit of Money and a Cat [*Lifestyle classification*]
A (Bomb)	Atom Bomb
A-bomb	Atomic Bomb (ODBW)
ABOMD	Abominated (ABBR)
ABOMG	Abominating (ABBR)
ABOML	Abominable (ABBR)
ABOMN	Abomination (ABBR)
ABOMS	American Board of Oral and Maxillofacial Surgery (EA)
AB ONE	Air Bases Command, 1st Naval District
ABOOW	Assistant Battalion Officer-of-the-Watch (DNAB)
ABOP	American Board of Oral Pathology (EA)
ABOPS	Association of Business Officers of Preparatory Schools (EA)
ABOR	Aborigine
ABOR	Abortion [*Medicine*]
Abor	Abortion (DMAA)
ABORIGINE ..	Aircooled Beryllium Oxide with Integrated Gas Turbine
ABORL	Aboriginal (ABBR)
ABORLY	Aboriginally (ABBR)
Abortion L Rep ...	Abortion Law Reporter [*A publication*] (DLA)
ABOS	Advanced Banking On-Line System (BUR)
ABOS	American Board of Oral Surgery [*Later, ABOMS*] (EA)
ABOS	American Board of Orthopedic Surgery (EA)
ABOS	Bonaza School, Alberta [*Library symbol National Library of Canada*] (BIB)
ABOSS	Advanced Bombardment System
ABOT	Aluminum Beaker Oxidation Test [*Lubricant testing*]
ABOTA	American Board of Trial Advocates (EA)
ABOW	Bowden Public Library, Alberta [*Library symbol National Library of Canada*] (NLC)
ABP	Abra De Llog [*Philippines*] [*Seismograph station code, US Geological Survey Closed*]
ABP	Absolute Boiling Point
ABP	Account Balance Pension (WYGK)
ABP	Acetyl Benzoyl Peroxide [*Organic chemistry*]
ABP	Actin-Binding Protein [*Cytology*]
ABP	Active Band-Pass [*Electronics*] (IAA)
ABP	Actual Block Processor [*IBM Corp.*] [*Computer science*] (BUR)
ABP	Adapter, Binding Post
ABP	Adriamycin, Bleomycin, Prednisone [*Antineoplastic drug regimen*]
ABP	Advanced Business Processor [*Datapoint Corp.*]
ABP	Air Bearing Platform
ABP	Airborne Beacon Processor
ABP	Aldosterone-Binding Protein [*Endocrinology*]
ABP	Amer Business Prod [*NYSE symbol*] (TTSB)
ABP	American Board of Pathology (EA)
ABP	American Board of Pediatrics (EA)
ABP	American Board of Pedodontics [*Later, ABPD*] (EA)
ABP	American Board of Periodontology (EA)
ABP	American Board of Prosthodontics (EA)
ABP	American Business Press [*Later, American Business Publishers*]
ABP	American Business Products, Inc. [*NYSE symbol*] (SPSG)
ABP	Aminobiphenyl [*Biochemistry*] (OA)
ABP	Androgen Binding Protein [*Endocrinology*]
ABP	Approval to Build Prototype [*Automotive project management*]
ABP	Arabinose Binding Protein [*Biochemistry*]
ABP	Archbishop
ABP	Arterial Blood Pressure [*Medicine*]
ABP	Asociacion Bancaria de Panama (EY)
ABP	Associated Book Publishers [*Subsidiary of International Thomson Organisation*]
ABP	Associated British Ports (DS)
ABP	Associated Business Papers (NTCM)
ABP	Association for Birth Psychology (EA)
ABP	Association of Black Psychologists (EA)
ABP	Association of Business Publishers (EA)
ABP	Asteroid Belt Probe
ABPA	Acoustical and Board Products Association
ABPA	Acute Bronchopulmonary Asthma [*Medicine*] (MEDA)
ABPA	Advanced Base Personnel Administration
ABPA	Aftermarket Body Parts Association (EA)
ABPA	Allergic Bronchopulmonary Aspergillosis [*Medicine*]
ABPA	American Backgammon Players Association [*Defunct*] (EA)
ABPA	American Board Products Association [*Later, AHA*] (EA)
ABPA	American Book Producers Association (EA)
ABPA	Association des Bibliotheques des Provinces de l'Atlantique [*Atlantic Provinces Association of Libraries*] [*Canada*]
ABPAC	Association des Bibliothecaires Parlementaires au Canada [*Association of Parliamentary Librarians of Canada*]
ABPAH	Autobody and Paint Association of Hawaii (SRA)
ABPANC	American Board of PostAnesthesia Nursing Certification (EA)
AB-PAS-Pbh ...	Alcian Blue-Periodic Acid Schiff-Lead Hematoxylin Procedure [*Biotechnology*]
ABPBC	Association of Book Publishers of British Columbia (AC)
ABPC	Abaxial Leaflet Pubescence - Curly [*Botany*]
ABPC	Abelson Plasmacytoma [*Oncology*]
ABPC	American Book Prices Current [*A publication*]
ABPC	American Book Publishers Council [*Later, AAP*]
ABPC	Antibody-Producing Cell [*Medicine*] (DMAA)
ABPC	Association of British Packing Contractors (BI)
ABPC	Association of British Pewter Craftsmen
ABPC	Au Bon Pain [*NASDAQ symbol*] (SPSG)
ABPC	Australian Beef Promotion Committee
ABPCA	Aluminum Building Products Credit Association [*Defunct*]

ABPCA	Au Bon Pain 'A' [*NASDAQ symbol*] (TTSB)
ABPD	American Board of Pediatric Dentistry (EA)
ABPD	American Board of Podiatric Dermatology [*Defunct*] (EA)
ABPDA	Aftermarket Body Parts Distributors Association [*Later, ABPA*] (EA)
ABPDC	American Board of Professional Disability Consultants (EA)
ABPE	Acute Bovine Pulmonary Emphysema [*Cattle disease*]
ABPF	Audio Bandpass Filter
ABPG	Advanced Base Proving Ground
ABPH	Able-Bodied Seaman Photography [*Navy*]
ABPH	American Board of Psychological Hypnosis (EA)
ABPI	Ankle/Brachial Pressure Index
ABPI	Association of the British Pharmaceutical Industry
ABPL	Abelson Plasmacytoid Lymphosarcoma [*Oncology*]
ABPLA	American Board of Professional Liability Attorneys [*Chicago, IL*] (EA)
ABPLM	Asynchronous Bipolar Pulse Length Modulation [*Electronics*] (IAA)
ABPM	Ambulatory Blood Pressure Monitoring [*Medicine*]
ABPM	American Board of Preventive Medicine (EA)
ABPM	Association of Business Product Manufacturers (EA)
ABPM	Authorized in Accordance with Bureau of Naval Personnel Manual
ABPMR	American Board of Physical Medicine and Rehabilitation (EA)
ABPN	American Board of Psychiatry and Neurology (EA)
ABPN	Association of British Paediatric Nurses
ABPN	Proserpine [*Australia ICAO location identifier*] (ICLI)
ABPNB	Association des Bibliothecaires Professionel du Nouveau-Brunswick (AC)
ABPO	Advanced Base Personnel Officer
ABPO	American Board of Podiatric Orthopedics (EA)
ABPP	American Board of Professional Psychology (EA)
ABPP	Amino(bromo)(phenyl)pyrimidinone [*Antiherpes compound*]
ABPP	Amyloid Beta Protein Precursor [*Biochemistry*]
ABPPAC	American Book Publishers Political Action Committee (EA)
ABPR	American Book Publishing Record [*A publication*]
ABPR	Association of Baptist Professors of Religion
ABPR	Association of British Picture Restorers
ABPRBC	American Barred Plymouth Rock Bantam Club [*Defunct*] (EA)
ABPRC	American Barred Plymouth Rock Club [*Later, Plymouth Rock Fanciers Club*] (EA)
ABPRC	American Buff Plymouth Rock Club (EA)
ABPS	Airborne Beacon Processing System
A/BPS	Airborne Propellant System (AAG)
ABPS	Air-Breathing Propulsion System [*or Subsystem*] [*NASA*]
ABPS	American Baptist Publishing Society (BARN)
ABPS	American Board of Plastic Surgery (EA)
ABPS	American Board of Podiatric Surgery (EA)
ABPsi	Association of Black Psychologists (EA)
AB Ps S	Associate of the British Psychological Society
ABPSTS	Association of Blind and Partially Sighted Teachers and Students [*British*]
ABPT	Able-Bodied Seaman Physical Training [*Navy*]
AB-PT	American Broadcasting-Paramount Theatres, Inc. (NTCM)
ABPT	Association of Blind Piano Tuners [*British*] (BI)
ABPTS	Advanced Boost Phase Track Satellite
ABPU	Advanced Base Personnel Unit
ABPVM	Association of British Plywood and Veneer Manufacturers (BI)
ABPW	Agency Broadcast Producers Workshop [*Defunct*] (EA)
ABPWC	Association of Business and Professional Women in Construction (EA)
ABPWG	Whyte Museum of the Canadian Rockies (Gallery), Banff, Alberta [*Library symbol National Library of Canada*] (NLC)
ABQ	Admiralty Berthing Officer [*British*]
ABQ	Albuquerque [*New Mexico*] [*Seismograph station code, US Geological Survey*] (SEIS)
ABQ	Albuquerque [*New Mexico*] [*Airport symbol*] (OAG)
ABQ	Association Beton Quebec (AC)
ABQ	Association des Bibliothecaires du Quebec (AC)
ABQAUR	American Board of Quality Assurance and Utilization Review (EA)
ABQAURP	American Board of Quality Assurance and Utilization Review Physicians [*Later, ABQAUR*] (EA)
ABQI	Antipyrylbenzoquinoneimine [*Organic chemistry*]
ABQMG	Able-Bodied Seaman Quartermaster Gunner [*Navy*]
ABQSJ	Associes Benevoles Qualifies au Service des Jeunes (AC)
ABR	Abaterra Energy Ltd. [*Toronto Stock Exchange symbol Vancouver Stock Exchange symbol*]
ABR	Abbreviation (IAA)
ABR	Aberdeen [*South Dakota*] [*Airport symbol*] (OAG)
ABR	Aberrant Banding Region [*Genetics*]
ABR	Abnormal Banding Region [*Genetics*]
ABR	Abortus Bang Ringprobe [*Test*] [*Medicine*]
ABR	Abraham (ABBR)
ABR	Abrasion (DAVI)
ABR	Abrasive (ABBR)
ABR	Abrasive
abr	Abridged (WDMC)
ABR	Abridged
abr	Abridgment (WDMC)
ABR	Absolute Bed Rest [*Medicine*]
ABR	Acceptable Biological Removal [*Fishery management*]
ABR	Acrylate-Butadiene Rubber
ABR	Active Business Records [*Bell & Howell Co.*]
ABR	Additional Billet Requirements [*Military*]
ABR	Adhesive Bonding Repair
ABr	Agglutination Test for Brucellosis [*Immunology*] (DMAA)
ABR	Airborne Resupply (CINC)
ABR	American Bankruptcy Reports [*A publication*] (DLA)
ABR	American Board of Radiology (EA)
ABR	American Book Review [*A publication*] (BRI)
ABR	Amphibian Boat Reconnaissance Aircraft
aBR	Anti-Beevers-Ross [*Beta-alumina crystallography*]
ABR	Arbor Property Tr [*NYSE symbol*] (TTSB)
ABR	Arbor Property Trust Co. [*Formerly, EQK Green Acres Trust*] [*NYSE symbol*] (SAG)
ABR	Arnolt-Bristol Registry (EA)
ABR	Association for Biomedical Research (EA)
ABR	Auditory Brain Response [*Neurology*] (DAVI)
ABR	Auditory Brainstem Response [*Neurophysiology*]
ABR	AutoBaud Rate [*Detect*] (CDE)
ABR	Automatic Backup and Recovery [*Computer science*] (IAA)
ABR	Automatic Band Rate (IEEE)
ABR	Brooks Public Library, Alberta [*Library symbol National Library of Canada*] (NLC)
a-br--	Burma [*MARC geographic area code Library of Congress*] (LCCP)
Abr	De Abrahamo [*Philo*] (BJA)
ABR	Hunting Cargo Airlines Ltd. [*British ICAO designator*] (FAAC)
ABR	Real-Aerovias Brasil [*Brazilian international airline*]
ABRA	Abraham (ABBR)
ABRA	Advanced Biophysical Research Accelerator (BARN)
ABRA	American Blood Resources Association (EA)
ABRA	American Buckskin Registry Association (EA)
ABRAC	Abracadabra (DSUE)
ABRAC	Agriculture Biotechnology Research Advisory Committee [*Department of Agriculture*] (EGAO)
ABRAC	Australian Biological Resources Advisory Committee
ABRACADABRA	Abbreviations and Related Acronyms Associated with Defense, Astronautics, Business, and Radio-Electronics [*Raytheon Co. publication*]
ABRAD	Abrade (ABBR)
ABRADD	Abraded (ABBR)
ABRADG	Abrading (ABBR)
ABRALOC	Acoustic Beacon Ranging and Location (PDAA)
ABRAM	Abraham (ABBR)
Abrams	Abrams Industries, Inc. [*Associated Press*] (SAG)
ABRAN	Aberration (ABBR)
ABRAN	Abrasion (ABBR)
ABrand	American Brands, Inc. [*Associated Press*] (SAG)
ABRANL	Aberrational (ABBR)
ABRAS	Abrasion (ABBR)
ABRAV	Abrasive (ABBR)
Abraxas	Abraxas Petroleum Corp. [*Associated Press*] (SAG)
ABRB	Advanced Base Receiving Barracks
ABRC	[*The*] Advisory Board for the Research Councils [*British*]
ABRC	Association des Bibliotheques de Recherche du Canada [*Canadian Association of Research Libraries*] (EAIO)
ABRC	Auto Body Representatives Council (EA)
Abr Ca Eq	Abridgment of Cases in Equity [*1667-1744*] [*A publication*] (DLA)
Abr Cas	Crawford and Dix's Irish Abridged Cases [*A publication*] (DLA)
Abr Cas Eq	Equity Cases Abridged [*2 vols.*] [*21, 22 English Reprint*] [*A publication*] (DLA)
ABRD	Aboard (ABBR)
ABRD	Abrade (ABBR)
ABRD	Abroad (ABBR)
ABRD	Abroad
ABRD	Advanced Base Receiving Depot
ABRD	Advanced Base Repair Depot
ABRD	Advanced Base Reshipment Depot
ABrd	American Brands, Inc. [*Associated Press*] (SAG)
ABRDA	American Bill of Rights Day Association [*Defunct*] (EA)
ABRDD	Abraded (ABBR)
ABRDG	Abrading (ABBR)
ABRE	Adoptive Bit Rate Encoding [*Computer science*]
ABRE	Air Battalion Royal Engineers [*Later, Royal Aircraft Establishment*] [*British*]
ABRE	American Craft Brewing International [*NASDAQ symbol*] (SAG)
ABRE	Army Board of Review for Eliminations
AB (Rel)	Bachelor of Arts with Religious Major
AB Rep	American Bankruptcy Reports [*A publication*] (DLA)
Abr Eq Cas	Equity Cases Abridged [*2 vols.*] [*21, 22 English Reprint*] [*A publication*] (DLA)
ABRES	Advanced Ballistic Reentry System
ABRET	American Board of Registration of EEG [*Electroencephalographic*] Technologists (EA)
AB Rev	American Bankruptcy Review [*A publication*] (DLA)
ABRF	Brisbane [*Australia ICAO location identifier*] (ICLI)
ABRFM	Association of British Roofing Felt Manufacturers Ltd. (BI)
ABRG	Abridge (ABBR)
ABRGA	Abrogate (ABBR)
ABRGAD	Abrogated (ABBR)
ABRGAN	Abrogation (ABBR)
ABRGB	Abridgeable (ABBR)
ABRGD	Abridged (ABBR)
ABRGG	Abridging (ABBR)
ABRGN	Aborigine (ABBR)
ABRGNL	Aboriginal (ABBR)
ABRGNT	Abridgment (ABBR)
ABRGR	Abridger (ABBR)
ABRGT	Abridgment (ABBR)
ABRI	Abrams Industries [*NASDAQ symbol*] (TTSB)
ABRI	Abrams Industries, Inc. [*NASDAQ symbol*] (NQ)
ABRI	Rust International Rust International, Birmingham, AL [*Library symbol*] [*Library of Congress*] (LCLS)
ABRID	Abridged (ABBR)

ABR Inf	ABR Information Services, Inc. [*Associated Press*] (SAG)
ABRK	Rockhampton [*Australia ICAO location identifier*] (ICLI)
ABRL	Army Ballistic Research Laboratory (SAA)
ABRL	Aviation Base Responsibility List (AFIT)
ABRM	Anterior Byssus Retractor Muscle [*Mollusk anatomy*]
ABRM	Breton Municipal Library, Alberta [*Library symbol National Library of Canada*] (NLC)
ABRMS	American Board of Ringside Medicine and Surgery (EA)
ABRN	Aberrance (ABBR)
ABRNC	Aberrancy (ABBR)
ABRNS	American Bankruptcy Reports, New Series [*A publication*] (DLA)
ABRNT	Aberrant (ABBR)
ABRNTY	Aberrantly (ABBR)
ABRO	Able-Bodied Seaman Radio Operator [*Navy*]
ABRO	Animal Breeding Research Organisation [*British*]
ABRO	Army in Burma Reserve of Officers [*British military*] (DMA)
ABRO	Brocket Public Library, Alberta [*Library symbol National Library of Canada*] (NLC)
ABROD	Abroad (ABBR)
ABROG	Abrogate (ABBR)
ABROGAG	Abrogating (ABBR)
ABROGD	Abrogated (ABBR)
ABROGG	Abrogating (ABBR)
ABROGN	Abrogation (ABBR)
Ab Rom Proc	Abdy's Roman Civil Procedure [*A publication*] (DLA)
ABROW	Brownfield Public Library, Alberta [*Library symbol National Library of Canada*] (NLC)
ABRP	Able-Bodied Seaman RADAR Plotter [*Navy*]
ABRP	Abrupt (ABBR)
ABRPNS	Abruptness (ABBR)
ABRRM	Association of British Reclaimed Rubber Manufacturers (BI)
ABRS	Adolescent Behavior Rating Scale [*Devereaux*] [*Also, DAB*] [*Psychology*]
ABRS	Aquatic Based Recreation Survey [*Environmental Protection Agency*]
ABRS	Association of British Riding Schools (BI)
ABRS	Automated Book Request System [*Computer science*]
ABRSM	Associated Board of the Royal Schools of Music [*British*] (BI)
ABRSN	Abrasion (ABBR)
ABRST	Abreast (ABBR)
ABRSV	Abrasive (MSA)
ABRT	Abort (MCD)
ABRT	A/B Rederi Transatlantic [*Pacific Australia Direct Line*] (MHDB)
ABRT	Assyrian and Babylonian Religious Texts [*A publication*] (BJA)
ABRTD	Aborted (ABBR)
ABRTG	Aborting (ABBR)
ABRTN	Abortion (ABBR)
ABRTNST	Abortionist (ABBR)
ABRTNT	Abortionist (ABBR)
ABRTREQ	Abort Request (MCD)
ABRTV	Abortive (ABBR)
ABRTVNS	Abortiveness (ABBR)
ABRTVY	Abortively (ABBR)
ABRUM	Bruderheim Municipal Library, Alberta [*Library symbol National Library of Canada*] (NLC)
ABRV	Advanced Ballistic Reentry Vehicle (MCD)
ABRW	American Craft Brewing International [*NASDAQ symbol*] (SAG)
ABRX	ABR Information Services [*NASDAQ symbol*] (TTSB)
ABRX	ABR Information Services, Inc. [*NASDAQ symbol*] (SAG)
ABS	ABAC Resources [*Vancouver Stock Exchange symbol*]
ABS	Abastumani [*Former USSR Seismograph station code, US Geological Survey Closed*]
ABS	Abbess
AB's	Abdominal Muscles
ABS	Abdominal Surgery [*Medical specialty*] (DHSM)
ABS	Abitibi Asbestos Mining Co. Ltd. [*Vancouver Stock Exchange symbol*]
ABS	Able-Bodied Seaman
Abs	Absatz [*Paragraph*] [*German*] (ILCA)
ABS	Abscesses (ABBR)
Abs	Abschnitt [*Section, Part, Chapter, or Division*] [*German*] (BARN)
ABS	Absent (AFM)
ABS	Absent Subscriber, Office Closed (WDMC)
abS	Absiemens (IDOE)
ABS	ABS Industries [*Associated Press*] (SAG)
ABS	Absolute [*Flowchart*]
ABS	Absonant (ABBR)
ABS	Absorb [*or Absorption*]
Abs	Absorption (DMAA)
Abs	Abstain (ILCA)
ABS	Abstract
Abs	Abstracts of Treasury Decisions [*A publication*] (DLA)
ABS	Abstrene (ABBR)
ABS	Abuse (ABBR)
ABS	Abu Simbel [*Egypt*] [*Airport symbol*] (OAG)
ABS	Acid and Base Washed and Silanized (SAA)
ABS	Acrylonitrile-Butadiene-Styrene [*Organic chemistry*]
ABS	Active Boom Suspension [*Engineering*]
ABS	Acute Brain Syndrome [*Medicine*]
ABS	Adaptive Behavior Scale [*American Association on Mental Deficiency*] [*Psychology*]
ABS	Additional Budget Submissions [*DoD*]
ABS	Admitting Blood Sugar [*Medicine*]
ABS Inf	Adult Bovine Serum [*Medicine*] (DMAA)
ABS	Advanced Battlefield Simulation (RDA)
ABS	Affects Balance Scale [*Personality development test*] [*Psychology*]
ABS	Air Base Simulator [*Air Force*]

ABS	Air Base Squadron [*Air Force*]
ABS	Air Base Survivability
ABS	Airborne Backing Store
ABS	Air-Brake Switch
ABS	Air-Breathing System
ABS	Albertson's, Inc. [*NYSE symbol*] (SPSG)
ABS	Albumin-Buffered Saline [*Clinical chemistry*]
ABS	Alkyl Benzenesulfonate [*Organic chemistry*]
ABS	Aloin, Extract of Belladonna, and Strychnine Pill [*A laxative*] [*Pharmacology*] (DAVI)
ABS	Altitude Barometric Switch [*Automotive engineering*]
ABS	Amalgamated Book Services [*British*]
ABS	American Backgammon Society
ABS	American Ballads and Songs [*A publication*]
ABS	American Bamboo Society (EA)
ABS	American Beethoven Society (EA)
ABS	American Begonia Society (EA)
ABS	American Bible Society (EA)
ABS	American Biological Society (EA)
ABS	American Bladesmith Society (EA)
ABS	American Board of Surgery (EA)
ABS	American Bonanza Society (EA)
ABS	American Bonsai Society (EA)
ABS	American Boxwood Society (EA)
ABS	American Breeder Service
ABS	American Broadcasting System (IAA)
ABS	American Bryological Society [*Later, ABLS*] (EA)
ABS	American Budgerigar Society (EA)
ABS	American Bureau of Shipping (EA)
AbS	Analysis by Synthesis (PDAA)
ABS	Anglo-Belgian Society (DBA)
ABS	Anheuser-Busch, Inc., Corporation Library, St. Louis, MO [*OCLC symbol*] (OCLC)
ABS	Animal Behavior Society (EA)
ABS	Antenna Base Spring
ABS	Antiblocking System (IAA)
ABS	Antilock Braking System [*Automotive engineering*]
ABS	Antique Boat Society (EA)
ABS	Antiseptic Biological Suppository [*Medicine*] (IIA)
ABS	Antiskid Braking System [*General Motors Corp.*]
ABS	Approved to British Standard [*British Standards Institution*]
ABS	Architects' Benevolent Society [*British*] (BI)
ABS	Armoured Boarding Steamer [*British military*] (DMA)
ABS	Army Broadcasting Service (GFGA)
AB's	Asbestos Bodies
ABS	Asset-Backed Security [*Finance*]
ABS	Associated Biomedic Systems, Inc.
ABS	Associated Blacksmiths of Scotland [*A union*]
ABS	Associate in Business Science
ABS	Associate of the Building Societies [*Institute*] [*British*] [*German*] (BARN)
ABS	Association for Baha'i Studies (EAIO)
ABS	Association of Black Sociologists (EA)
ABS	Association of Black Storytellers (EA)
ABS	Association of British Sailmakers (DBA)
ABS	Association of British Spectroscopists (DBA)
ABS	Association of Broadcasting Staff [*A union*] [*British*] (DCTA)
ABS	Association on Broadcasting Standards [*Later, Association for Broadcast Engineering Standards*]
ABS	At Bed Side [*Medicine*]
ABS	Athabaska Airways Ltd. [*Canada ICAO designator*] (FAAC)
ABS	Atlantic Base Section
ABS	ATLAS Block Structure (MCD)
ABS	Australia Braford Society
ABS	Australia-Britain Society
ABS	Australian Ballet School
ABS	Automated Bioassay System (MCD)
ABS	Automated Bond System [*Investment term*] (DFIT)
ABS	Automatic Beam Current Stabilizing (IAA)
ABS	Automatic Black Signal [*TRB*] (TAG)
ABS	Automatic Braking System (MCD)
ABS	Aux Bons Soins De [*Care Of, c/o*] [*Correspondence*] [*French*]
ABS	Auxiliaries of the Blessed Sacrament (TOCD)
ABS	Auxiliary Building Sump [*Nuclear energy*] (IEEE)
ABS	Average Busy Season [*Telecommunications*] (TEL)
ABS	Average Busy Stream [*Computer science*] (ACRL)
ABS	Birmingham Southern College, Birmingham, AL [*Library symbol Library of Congress*] (LCLS)
Abs	Ohio Law Abstract [*A publication*] (DLA)
ABSA	Agricultural Bureau of South Australia
ABSA	Association for Business Sponsorship of the Arts [*British*] (EAIO)
ABSA	Association of British Secretaries in America
ABSAM	Association of British Solid Fuel Appliance Manufacturers (DBA)
ABSAME	Association for Behaviorial Sciences and Medical Education (EA)
ABSAP	Airborne Search and Attack Plotter
ABSAT	American Broadcasting Co. Television Satellite (NTCM)
ABSAUM	Association des Bibliotheques de la Sante Affiliee a l'Universite de Montreal (AC)
ABSB	Absorb (ABBR)
ABSB	Air Burst/Surface Burst (MCD)
ABSBA	Australian Brown Swiss and Braunvieh Association
ABSBB	Absorbable (ABBR)
ABSBBT	Absorbability (ABBR)
ABSBCY	Absorbency (ABBR)
ABSBD	Absorbed (ABBR)

ABSBG......... Absorbing (ABBR)
ABSBH........ Average Busy Season Busy Hour [*Telecommunications*] (TEL)
ABSBN........ Absorption (ABBR)
ABSBNC...... Absorbance (ABBR)
ABSBNC...... Absorbency (ABBR)
ABSBR........ Absorber (ABBR)
ABSBT........ Absorbent (ABBR)
ABSC.......... Abscissa [*Mathematics*] (AAMN)
ABSC.......... Abscond (ABBR)
ABSC.......... Absence (ABBR)
ABSC.......... Associate of the British Society of Commerce
ABSC.......... Association des Bibliotheques de la Sante du Canada [*Canadian Association of Health Libraries*]
ABSC.......... Association of Boiler Setters, Chimney and Furnace Constructors [*British*] (BI)
ABSC.......... Australian Billiards and Snooker Council
ABSC.......... Automatic Bass Compensation [*Radio*] (MSA)
ABSC.......... Automatic Blip-Scan Counter
ABSCD........ Abscond (ABBR)
Abschn....... Abschnitt [*Paragraph, Chapter*] [*German*] (ILCA)
ABS CLG..... Absolute Ceiling [*Aviation*]
ABSCM........ Association of Boys and Students Clothing Manufacturers (EA)
ABsCpt........ American Business Computers Corp. [*Associated Press*] (SAG)
ABSCS........ Automatic Blip-Scan Counter System
ABSCT........ Autologous Peripheral Blood Stem Cell Transplantation [*Medicine*]
ABSD.......... Absented (ABBR)
ABSD.......... Abused (ABBR)
ABSD.......... Advance Base Section Dock [*Floating drydock, first used in World War II*]
ABSD.......... Advanced Base Supply Depot
ABSDA........ Atlantic Building Supply Dealers Association (AC)
ABSDATA..... Australian Bureau of Statistics Database
ABSDT........ Absurdity (ABBR)
ABSE.......... Able-Bodied Seaman Survival Equipment [*Navy*]
ABSE.......... Absolute Error (IAA)
ABSEL......... Association for Business Simulation and Experiential Learning [*Tulsa, OK*] (EA)
ABSE RE..... Absente Reo [*The Defendant Being Absent*] [*Legal term Latin*] (ADA)
ABSF........ American Blind Skiing Foundation (EA)
ABSF.......... Australian Blind Sports Federation
ABSFA........ Banff Centre Library, Alberta [*Library symbol National Library of Canada*] (NLC)
ABS FEB..... Absente Febre [*In the Absence of Fever*] [*Pharmacy*]
ABS FEBR.... Absente Febre [*In the Absence of Fever*] [*Pharmacy*] (ROG)
ABSG.......... Absenting (ABBR)
ABSG.......... Abusing (ABBR)
ABSHP........ Archbishop
ABSI.......... ABS Industries, Inc. [*NASDAQ symbol*] (NQ)
ABSI.......... Adaptive Behavior Scale for Infants and Early Childhood [*Child development test*]
ABSIE......... American Broadcasting Station in Europe [*OWI*]
ABSIG........ Able-Bodied Seaman Signalman [*Navy*]
ABSIG........ Anti-Bureaucracy Special Interest Group [*Mensa*] (EA)
Abs Iur....... Absolutus Iuris [*Absolute Jurisdiction*] [*Latin*]
ABSJM........ Amicable and Brotherly Society of Journeymen Millwrights [*A union*] [*British*]
ABSLA........ Approved Basic Stock Level of Ammunition (MCD)
ABSLDR..... Absolute Loader [*Computer science*]
ABSLT........ Absolute (ABBR)
ABSLT........ Absolute
ABSLTM...... Absolutism (ABBR)
ABSLTN...... Absolution (ABBR)
ABSLTST..... Absolutist (ABBR)
ABSLTY...... Absolutely (ABBR)
ABSLV....... Absolve (ABBR)
ABSLVB...... Absolvable (ABBR)
ABSLVD...... Absolved (ABBR)
ABSLVG...... Absolving (ABBR)
ABSLVR...... Absolver (ABBR)
ABSLY....... Absolutely (ROG)
ABSM.......... Associate of the Birmingham and Midland Institute School of Music [*British*]
ABSM.......... Association of British Steriliser Manufacturers (EAIO)
ABSMA....... American Bleached Shellac Manufacturers Association (EA)
ABSML........ Abysmal (ABBR)
ABSN.......... Able-Bodied Seaman Stores Naval [*Navy*]
ABSN.......... Adoptee-Birthparent Support Network (EA)
ABSNC........ Absence (ABBR)
Abs (NS)..... Abstracts of Treasury Decisions, New Series [*A publication*] (DLA)
ABSNT........ Absent (ABBR)
ABSNTE....... Absentee (ABBR)
ABSNTEM ... Absenteeism (ABBR)
ABSOL........ Absolute
ABSOLN...... Absolution (ABBR)
ABSOLNS.... Absoluteness (ABBR)
Absoluo...... Absolution (BARN)
ABSOLY...... Absolutely (ABBR)
ABSORB...... Absorption
absorp........ Absorption (DMAA)
ABSORS...... American Bureau of Shipping Information Retrieval System (MSC)
ABSP.......... About Buttonhooks, Spoons, and Patents [*An association Defunct*] (EA)
ABSPN........ Absorption (ABBR)
ABSPT........ Absorptivity (ABBR)
ABSPV........ Absorptive (ABBR)

ABSq.......... Air Base Squadron [*Air Force*]
AbSR.......... Abnormal Skin Reflex [*Medicine*] (DMAA)
ABSR.......... Abuser (ABBR)
ABSR.......... Southern Research Institute, Birmingham, AL [*Library symbol Library of Congress*] (LCLS)
ABSRD........ Absurd (ABBR)
ABSRDNS.... Absurdness (ABBR)
ABSRDT...... Absurdity (ABBR)
ABSRDY...... Absurdly (ABBR)
ABS RE....... Absente Reo [*The Defendant Being Absent*] [*Legal term Latin*] (ADA)
ABSS.......... Advanced Beach Signal Station (IAA)
ABSS.......... Air Bag Skid System (MCD)
ABSS.......... American Board of Spinal Surgery (EA)
ABSSA........ Amateur Beekeepers' Society of South Australia
ABS/SAN..... Acrylonitrile-Butadiene-Styrene and Styrene-Acrylonitrile [*Organic chemistry*] (ERG)
ABS-SE....... Adaptive Behavior Scale, School Edition [*Child development test*]
ABSSOP...... Committee for the Application of the Behavioral Sciences to the Strategies of Peace (EA)
ABST.......... Absentee (ABBR)
ABST.......... Abstract
ABST.......... Adult Basic Skill Training (NVT)
ABST.......... Auxiliary Building Sump Tank [*Nuclear energy*] (NRCH)
Abst.......... De Abstinentia [*of Porphyry*] [*Classical studies*] (OCD)
ABSTA........ Abstain (ABBR)
ABSTAD...... Abstained (ABBR)
ABSTAG...... Abstaining (ABBR)
ABSTD........ Able-Bodied Seaman Steward [*Navy*]
ABSTD........ ABS [*Australian Bureau of Statistics*] Time-Series Database [*Information service or system*] (CRD)
ABSTECH ... American Bureau of Shipping Worldwide Technical Services (MHDB)
ABSTEE...... Absentee
ABSTM........ Absenteeism (ABBR)
ABSTMS...... Abstemious (ABBR)
ABSTMSNS. Abstemiousness (ABBR)
ABSTMSY.... Abstemiously (ABBR)
ABSTN........ Abstention (ABBR)
ABSTNC...... Abstinence (ABBR)
ABSTNT...... Abstinent (ABBR)
ABSTR........ Abstract
ABSTRCT.... Abstract
ABSTRD...... Abstracted (ABBR)
ABSTRN...... Abstraction (ABBR)
ABSTRNS.... Abstractness (ABBR)
ABSTRR...... Abstracter (ABBR)
ABSTRS...... Abstruse (ABBR)
Abstr T....... Abstracts of Title [*A publication*] (DLA)
ABSTRU...... Abstruse (ABBR)
ABSTRUNS.. Abstruseness (ABBR)
ABSTRUY.... Abstrusely (ABBR)
ABSTRY...... Abstractly (ABBR)
ABSTT........ Abstract [*Legal*] [*British*] (ROG)
ABSTURN ... Absence and Turnover Rates [*Database*]
ABSU.......... Aid to Believers in the Soviet Union [*See also ACU*] [*Paris, France*] (EAIO)
ABS U N ..... Absque Ulla Nota [*Without Any Marking or Note*] [*Latin*] (ROG)
ABSV.......... Able-Bodied Seaman Stores Victualling [*Navy*]
ABSV.......... Absolute Value (IAA)
ABSV.......... Abusive (ABBR)
ABSVM....... Absolute Voltmeter (IAA)
ABSVNS...... Abusiveness (ABBR)
ABSVS........ Auxiliary Building Special Ventilation System [*Nuclear energy*] (NRCH)
ABSVY........ Abusively (ABBR)
ABSW......... Air-Brake Switch
ABSW......... Association of British Science Writers
ABSY.......... Absently (ABBR)
ABT.......... Abbot Energy Corp. [*Vancouver Stock Exchange symbol*]
ABT.......... Abbott Laboratories [*NYSE symbol*] (SPSG)
ABT.......... Abort
ABT.......... Abort Timer (HGAA)
ABT.......... About (MUGU)
abt.......... About [*Internet language*] [*Computer science*]
ABT.......... Abstract Planning Tool
ABT.......... Abstracts of Bioanalytic Technology [*Council of American Bioanalysts*] [*A publication*] (AEBS)
ABT.......... Abteilung [*Department, Division, Section*] [*German*]
abT.......... Abtesla [*Unit of magnetic induction*]
ABT.......... Abundant (ABBR)
ABT.......... Actual Bottom Time
ABT.......... Advanced Booster Technology (MCD)
ABT.......... Air Blast Transformer (MSA)
ABT.......... Airborne Tracking (MCD)
ABT.......... Air-Breathing Target [*Military*]
ABT.......... Air-Breathing Threat [*Military*]
ABT.......... Air Brousse, Inc. [*Canada ICAO designator*] (FAAC)
ABT.......... All Body Type [*Army*] (AABC)
ABT.......... Allied Board of Trade
ABT.......... American Ballet Theater
ABT.......... American Board of Toxicology (EA)
ABT.......... American Board of Trade
ABT.......... Animated Burtek Trainer
ABT.......... Answer-Back Tone [*Telecommunications*] (HGAA)
ABT.......... Applied Business Technology Corp.
ABT.......... Arabian Bank Trade [*Saudi Arabia*]

ABT.............	Arabian Bulk Trade [Saudi Arabia] [Commercial firm]
ABT.............	Associate in Business Technology
ABT.............	Association of Banking Teachers [British] (DBA)
ABT.............	Association of Beauty Teachers [British]
ABT.............	Association of Book Travelers (EA)
ABT.............	Association of Building Technicians [A union] [British]
ABT.............	Atlantic Booster Test (KSC)
ABT.............	Australian Board of Translators
ABT.............	Autologous Blood Transfusion [Medicine] (DMAA)
ABT.............	Automatic Battery Test
ABT.............	Automatic Braking Technology [Rollerblade, Inc.] (PS)
ABT.............	Automatic Bus Terminal [Computer science] (MCD)
ABT.............	Automatic Bus Transfer (NVT)
ABT.............	Auxiliary Ballast Tank
a-bt--	Bhutan [MARC geographic area code Library of Congress]
ABTA.............	Allied Brewery Traders' Association [British] (DI)
ABTA.............	American Board of Trial Advocates
ABTA.............	American Brain Tumor Association [Formerly Association for Brain Tumor Research (AFBTR)] (PAZ)
ABTA.............	American Bridge Teachers' Association (EA)
ABTA.............	Association of British Travel Agents
ABTA.............	Australia-British Trade Association
ABTA.............	Australian Baton Twirling Association
ABTA Bull	Australian-British Trade Association. Bulletin [A publication]
ABTAPL.......	Association of British Theological and Philosophical Libraries
ABTB.............	Association of Bank Travel Bureaus [Defunct] (EA)
ABT Bld	ABT Building Products Corp. [Associated Press] (SAG)
ABTC.............	ABT Building Products [NASDAQ symbol] (TTSB)
ABTC.............	ABT Building Products Corp. [NASDAQ symbol] (SAG)
ABTC.............	American Belgian Tervuren Club (EA)
ABTCA	American Black and Tan Coonhound Association (EA)
ABTD	Abutted (ABBR)
ABTD	American Book Trade Directory [A publication]
ABTD	Australian Book Trade Directory [A publication] (APTA)
ABTD	Automatic Bulk Tape Degausser
ABTD	Thursday Island [Australia ICAO location identifier] (ICLI)
ABTE.............	Able Telcom Holding Corp. [NASDAQ symbol] (SAG)
ABTE.............	Able Telecom Holding [NASDAQ symbol] (TTSB)
ABTEF...........	Australian Boot Trade Employees' Federation
ABTF.............	Airborne Task Force
ABTF.............	Assault Battalion Task Force (MCD)
ABT-FC	About-Face (ABBR)
ABTG	Abutting (ABBR)
ABTI.............	Alpha-Beta Technology [NASDAQ symbol] (TTSB)
ABTI.............	Alpha-Beta Technology, Inc. [NASDAQ symbol] (SAG)
ABTICS	Abstract and Book Title Index Card Service [United Kingdom]
ABTL.............	Townsville [Australia ICAO location identifier] (ICLI)
AbtLab	Abbott Laboratories Ltd. [Associated Press] (SAG)
ABTM...........	American Board of Tropical Medicine [Inactive] (EA)
ABTM...........	Association of British Transport Museums
ABTNOMS....	American Board of Thoracic Neurological Orthopaedic Medicine and Surgery (EA)
ABTNT	Abutment (ABBR)
ABTOAD.......	Air Blast Time-of-Arrival Detector (PDAA)
ABTR	Association for Brain Tumor Research (EA)
ABTS...........	American Board of Thoracic Surgery (EA)
ABTSA.........	Association for the Behavioral Treatment of Sexual Abusers (EA)
ABTSA.........	Association of British Tree Surgeons and Arborists (DI)
ABTSS	Airborne Transponder Subsystem
ABTT.............	Associate of British Theatre Technicians
ABTT.............	Townsville [Australia ICAO location identifier] (ICLI)
ABTTA..........	American Bridge, Tunnel, and Turnpike Association [Later, IBTTA] (EA)
ABTU	Advanced Base Torpedo Unit [Navy]
ABTU	Advanced Base Training Unit [Navy]
ABTU	Air Bombers Training Unit [Navy]
ABTU	Army Basic Training Unit [British military] (DMA)
ABTV...........	Townsville [Australia ICAO location identifier] (ICLI)
ABTX...........	AgriBioTech, Inc. [NASDAQ symbol] (SAG)
ABU	ABO Resource Corp. [Vancouver Stock Exchange symbol]
abu	Aburra (VRA)
ABU	Abuyama [Japan] [Seismograph station code, US Geological Survey]
ABU	Administrative Base Unit [British military] (DMA)
ABU	Aerovias Bueno Ltd. [Colombia] [ICAO designator] (FAAC)
ABU	Alliance Biblique Universelle
ABU	American Board of Urology (EA)
Abu	Aminobutyric Acid [Also, ABA] [Biochemistry]
ABU	Amphibious Beach Unit [Military]
ABU	Antibody Unit
ABU	Asia Pacific Broadcasting Union (EAIO)
ABU	Asymptomatic Bacteriuria [Medicine] (DMAA)
ABU	Australian Brushmakers' Union
ABUAHP.......	American Board of Urologic Allied Health Professionals (EA)
ABUC...........	Able-Bodied Seaman Underwater Control [Navy]
ABUIC...........	Association des Bureaux de l'Information des Universites [Association of University Information Bureaus] [Canada]
ABUL	Abulia (ABBR)
ABUL	Abuliomania (ABBR)
abund	Abundant (BARN)
ABUNDNC.....	Abundance (ABBR)
ABUNDT	Abundant (ABBR)
ABUNDTY	Abundantly (ABBR)
ABUS	Abuse (ABBR)
ABus	Associate in Business Administration
ABUSD.........	Abused (ABBR)
ABUSG.........	Abusing (ABBR)
ABusnP........	American Business Products, Inc. [Associated Press] (SAG)
ABusnPd	American Business Products, Inc. [Associated Press] (SAG)
ABUSR.........	Abuser (ABBR)
ABUSV.........	Abusive (ABBR)
ABUSVNS	Abusiveness (ABBR)
ABUSVY.......	Abusively (ABBR)
ABUT	Abutment (ABBR)
ABUTD.........	Abutted (ABBR)
ABUTG.........	Abutting (ABBR)
ABUTMT.......	Abutment (ABBR)
ABV.............	Above (MSA)
ABV.............	Above
ABV.............	Abschnittsbevollmaechtiger [Section Deputy] [German]
ABV.............	Absolute Value [BUR]
ABV.............	Absorptive Technology, Inc. [Vancouver Stock Exchange symbol]
ABV.............	Abuja [Nigeria] [Airport symbol] (OAG)
abV.............	Abvolt (IDOE)
ABV.............	Actinomycin D, Bleomycin, Vincristine [Antineoplastic drug regimen]
ABV.............	Adriamycin, Bleomycin, Vinblastine [Antineoplastic drug regimen]
ABV.............	Air Blast Valve
ABV.............	Air Bubble Vehicle
ABV.............	Air Bypass Valve [Automotive engineering]
ABV.............	Anegada [Virgin Islands] [Seismograph station code, US Geological Survey] (SEIS)
ABV.............	Armed Boarding Vessel
ABV.............	Arthropod-Borne Virus [Medicine] (DMAA)
ABV.............	Auxiliary Building Ventilation [Nuclear energy] (NRCH)
ABV.............	Repeat the Figures in Abbreviated Form [Aviation code]
ABVA	Association of British Veterinary Acupuncture (DBA)
ABVA	United States Veterans Administration Hospital, Birmingham, AL [Library symbol Library of Congress] (LCLS)
ABV-BRD	Above-Board (ABBR)
ABVD...........	Adriamycin, Bleomycin, Vinblastine [Oncovin], Dacarbazine [Antineoplastic drug regimen]
ABVE...........	American Board of Vocational Experts (EA)
ABVS...........	Advisory Board on Veterinary Specialties (EA)
ABVT...........	American Board of Veterinary Toxicology (EA)
ABW.............	Abau [Papua] [Airport symbol] (AD)
ABW.............	ABC Technology, Inc. [Vancouver Stock Exchange symbol]
abW.............	Abwatt (IDOE)
ABW.............	Actual Body Weight (DAVI)
ABW.............	Advise by Wire (MHDB)
ABW.............	Air Base Wing [Air Force] (MCD)
ABW.............	Albanian Airways [ICAO designator] (FAAC)
ABW.............	American Baptist Women (EA)
ABW.............	Antarctic Bottom Water [Marine science] (OSRA)
ABW.............	Anybody but Wallace [Political slogan referring to Alabama governor George Wallace]
ABW.............	Arberia Airways [Albania] [FAA designator] (FAAC)
ABW.............	Aruba [ANSI three-letter standard code] (CNC)
ABW.............	Autobond Welder
ABW.............	Automated Batch Weighing
ABW.............	Average Body Weight (DMAA)
ABW.............	St. Louis, MO [Location identifier FAA] (FAAL)
ABWA	American Bottled Water Association [Later, IBWA] (EA)
ABWA	American Business Women's Association (EA)
ABWA	American Business Writing Association [Later, ABCA] (EA)
ABWA	Architects' Board of Western Australia
ABWA	Associated Business Writers of America (EA)
ABWAK	Association of British Wild Animal Keepers (DBA)
abWb	Abweber [Also, Mx] [Unit of magnetic flux]
ABWC...........	American Buff Wyandotte Club [Defunct] (EA)
ABWC...........	Automatic Bandwidth Control (MSA)
ABWE...........	Association of Baptists for World Evangelism (EA)
ABWG...........	Air Base Wing [Air Force]
ABWH...........	Association of Black Women Historians (EA)
ABWHE.........	Association of Black Women in Higher Education (EA)
ABWIK	Assault and Battery with Intent to Kill
ABWM...........	Berwyn WI Municipal Library, Alberta [Library symbol National Library of Canada] (NLC)
ABWM	Women's Missionary Union, SBC Library, Birmingham, AL [Library symbol] [Library of Congress] (LCLS)
ABWP...........	Weipa [Australia ICAO location identifier] (ICLI)
ABWR..........	Advanced Boiling Water Reactor
ABWR..........	American Beefalo World Registry (EA)
ABWRC.........	American Blue and White Rabbit Club (EA)
ABWRC.........	Army Biological Warfare Research Center
ABWS	Able-bodied Seaman Work Study [Navy]
ABWS	Berwyn School, Alberta [Library symbol National Library of Canada] (BIB)
ABWTR	Able-Bodied Seaman Writer [Navy]
ABX.............	Airborne Express, Inc. [ICAO designator] (FAAC)
ABX.............	Albury [Australia Airport symbol] (OAG)
ABX.............	Albury [New South Wales] [Airport symbol] (AD)
ABX.............	American Barrick Resources Corp. [LA Barrick Gold] [NYSE symbol Toronto Stock Exchange symbol] (SPSG)
ABx.............	Antibiotics [Pharmacology] (DAVI)
ABX.............	Barrick Gold [NYSE symbol] (TTSB)
ABX.............	Barrick Gold Corp. [NYSE symbol] (SAG)
a-bx--	Brunei [MARC geographic area code Library of Congress]
ABXL...........	Abaxial (MSA)
ABY.............	Abby Investment [Vancouver Stock Exchange symbol]
ABY.............	Abitibi-Price [NYSE symbol] (TTSB)
ABY.............	Abitibi-Price, Inc. [NYSE symbol] (SPSG)

Aby	Abyssinia
ABY	Abyssinian [*Cat species*]
ABY	Acid Bismuth Yeast [*Agar*] (MAE)
ABY	Albany [*Georgia*] [*Airport symbol*] (OAG)
aby	Antibody [*Also, Ab*] [*Immunology*]
ABYA	Association of British Yacht Agents (BI)
ABYA	Association of Brokers and Yacht Agents [*British*] (DBA)
ABYC	American Boat and Yacht Council (EA)
ABYC	Antique Boat and Yacht Club (EA)
ABYNC........	Abeyance (ABBR)
ABYNT........	Abeyant (ABBR)
ABYS	Abyss (ABBR)
ABYSM	Abysmal (ABBR)
ABYSS	Abyssinia
ABZ	Aberdeen [*Scotland*] [*Airport symbol*] (OAG)
ABZ	Aber Resources Ltd. [*Toronto Stock Exchange symbol*]
AbZ	Aboda Zara (BJA)
ABZ	Aero Belize Ltd. [*FAA designator*] (FAAC)
ABZ	Albendazole [*Anthelmintic*]
ABZ	Association of British Zoologists (BI)
AbZar..........	Aboda Zara (BJA)
AbzG	Abzahlungsgesetz [*Law on hire purchase agreements*] [*German*] (ILCA)
aC	Abcoulomb [*Unit of electric charge*]
AC.............	Abdominal Circumference [*Neonatology and pediatrics*] (DAVI)
AC.............	Able Chief (MCD)
AC.............	Absolute Ceiling [*Aviation*]
AC.............	Acceded to Throne (ROG)
AC.............	Acceleration Command
AC.............	Accelerator (AAG)
Ac.............	Acceptance Number [*Business term*]
AC.............	Accepted (ROG)
AC.............	Access [*Telecommunications*] (TEL)
AC.............	Access Control (SAA)
AC.............	Access Cycle (IAA)
AC.............	Accessory Cells [*Histology*]
Ac.............	Accident
AC.............	Accommodation Convergence [*Ophthalmology*]
AC.............	Account
AC.............	Accountants and Controllers
AC.............	Account Control (AFM)
A/C	Account Current [*Business term*]
AC.............	Accounting Computer (IAA)
AC.............	Accounting Program [*Association of Independent Colleges and Schools specialization code*]
AC.............	Accredited Center [*Youth Training Scheme*] [*British*] (AIE)
AC.............	Accumulator [*Computer science*]
Ac.............	Accursius [*Deceased, 1263*] [*Authority cited in pre-1607 legal work*] (DSA)
AC.............	Acetate [*Also, ACTT*] [*Organic chemistry*]
AC.............	Acetic Acid [*Organic chemistry*] (OA)
ac.............	Acetyl [*As substituent on nucleoside*] [*Biochemistry*]
AC.............	Acetylcholine [*Biochemistry*] (IIA)
AC.............	Acetylcysteine [*Biochemistry*] (AAMN)
AC.............	A. Christiaens [*Belgium*] [*Research code symbol*]
AC.............	Acid (AAMN)
AC.............	Acidus [*Acid*] [*Latin*] (ROG)
ac.............	Acmite [*CIPW classification*] [*Geology*]
AC.............	Acoustical [*Technical drawings*]
AC.............	Acoustic Coupler [*Computer MODEM*]
AC.............	Acquisition Circular (AAGC)
AC.............	Acquisition Costs
AC.............	Acre
AC.............	Acromioclavicular [*Joint*] [*Medicine*] (DHSM)
Ac.............	Acryl Group [*Organic chemistry*] (DAVI)
AC.............	Acting (ROG)
Ac.............	Actinium [*Chemical element*]
AC.............	Action Civile [*Civil Action*] [*French*] (ILCA)
AC.............	Activated Carbon
AC.............	Activation Coefficient
AC.............	Activator [*Genetics*]
AC.............	Active Capital [*Investment term*]
AC.............	Active Cirrhosis [*Medicine*]
AC.............	Active Component
AC.............	Activity (WDAA)
AC.............	Activity Captain (MCD)
AC.............	Activity Code [*DoD*]
Ac.............	Acts of the Apostles [*New Testament book*] (BJA)
AC.............	Actual Cost [*Accounting*]
AC.............	Actual Count (MHDI)
AC.............	Acupuncture Clinic [*British*]
AC.............	Acute [*Medicine*]
Ac.............	Acyl [*Organic chemistry*]
AC.............	Adapter Cable
AC.............	Adaptive Control [*Manufacturing term*]
AC.............	Additional Claim [*Unemployment insurance*] (OICC)
AC.............	Address Carry [*Computer science*] (IAA)
AC.............	Address Coding [*Business term*]
AC.............	Address Counter [*Computer science*] (MHDI)
AC.............	Adenylate Cyclase [*An enzyme*]
AC.............	Adherent Cell (AAMN)
AC.............	Adirondack Council (EA)
AC.............	Adjacent Channel (IAA)
AC.............	Adjustment-Calibration
AC.............	Admiral Commanding

AC.............	Admiral's Club [*American Airlines' club for frequent flyers*] [*Dallas/Ft. Worth Airport Texas*] (EA)
AC.............	Adopted Child
AC.............	Adrenal Cortex [*Medicine*]
AC.............	Adrenocorticoid [*Medicine*]
AC.............	Adriamycin, Carmustine [*Antineoplastic drug*] (CDI)
AC.............	Adriamycin, CCNU [*Lomustine*] [*Antineoplastic drug regimen*]
AC.............	Adriamycin, Cyclophosphamide [*Antineoplastic drug regimen*]
AC.............	Adult-Contemporary [*Music*]
A-C............	Adult-Versus-Child [*Medicine*] (DMAA)
AC.............	Advanced Certificate (PGP)
AC.............	Advanced Certification [*Canadian Society of Radiological Technicians*]
AC.............	Advertising Council (EA)
AC.............	Advice of Charge [*Telecommunications*] (TEL)
AC.............	Advisory Circular
AC.............	Advisory Committee (NRCH)
AC.............	Advisory Council on Scientific Research and Technical Development [*British*]
AC.............	Aerial Current (IAA)
ac.............	Aerodynamic Center (IDOE)
AC.............	Aerodynamics Center [*NASA*]
AC.............	Aeronautical Approach Chart [*Air Force*]
AC.............	Aeronautical Center [*FAA*]
AC.............	Aeronca Club (EA)
AC.............	Aerospace Center [*Defense Mapping Agency*]
AC.............	Aerospace Corp. (AAG)
AC.............	Aesculapian Club (EA)
AC.............	Affinity Chromatography [*Biopharmaceutical Purification*]
AC.............	African Coasters [*Steamship*] (MHDB)
AC.............	After Christ
AC.............	Aging, Federal Council (OICC)
AC.............	Agribusiness Council (EA)
AC.............	Aided Card (LAIN)
AC.............	Air Canada [*ICAO designator*] (OAG)
AC.............	Air Canada Corp. [*Vancouver Stock Exchange symbol Toronto Stock Exchange symbol*]
AC.............	Aircarrier (DA)
AC.............	Air Command (ADA)
A/C	Air Commodore [*RAF, RCAF*]
AC.............	Air Compressor (AAG)
AC.............	Air Conditioning (KSC)
a/c	Air Conditioning (IDOE)
AC.............	Air Conditioning
AC.............	Air Conditioning Equipment Room [*NFPA pre-fire planning symbol*] (NFPA)
AC.............	Air Conduction
AC.............	Air Congo [*Zaire*]
AC.............	Air Controller (NVT)
AC.............	Air Controlman [*Navy rating*]
AC.............	Air Cooled (IAA)
AC.............	Air Corps [*Obsolete*]
AC.............	Air Council (ADA)
AC.............	Aircraft [*Public-performance tariff class*] [*British*]
A/C	Aircraft [*FAA*] (TAG)
a/c	Aircraft (IDOE)
AC.............	Aircraft Carrier Flag [*Navy British*]
AC.............	Aircraft Commander
AC.............	Aircraft Control (MUGU)
AC.............	Aircraftman [*British*]
AC.............	Aircraftwoman [*Military*]
AC.............	Aircrewman
AC.............	Airdrome Control [*British*] (SAA)
AC.............	Airframe Change
AC.............	Airfreight Container [*Shipping*] (DCTA)
A/C	Air-to-Cloth [*Air pollution control*] (FFDE)
AC.............	Airworthiness Certificate (MCD)
AC.............	Airworthiness Circular (DA)
AC.............	Airworthiness Committee
AC.............	Alaska Coalition (EA)
AC.............	Alaskan Command [*Discontinued, 1975*] [*Military*]
AC.............	Albert Champion [*Automotive industrialist whose company is now part of General Motors*]
A/C	Albumin-Coagulin Ratio [*Biochemistry*] (MAE)
AC.............	Alcohol Concentration (TAG)
AC.............	Alcuin Club (EAIO)
AC.............	Alfalfa Club (EA)
AC.............	Algoma Central Railway [*AAR code*]
ac.............	Alicyclic [*Chemistry*]
AC.............	Alien Cell
AC.............	Alkali Cellulose [*Chemistry*]
AC.............	All Culture [*Broth*] [*Biochemistry*] (DAVI)
AC.............	Allens Creek [*Nuclear power plant*] (NRCH)
AC.............	Allergic Conjunctivitis [*Ophthalmology*]
AC.............	Alliance Capital Management LP [*NYSE symbol*] (SPSG)
AC.............	Alliance Cap Mgmt L.P. [*NYSE symbol*] (TTSB)
AC.............	Allied Commission [*World War II*]
A-C............	Allied Corp. [*Initialism is trademark*]
AC.............	Allis-Chalmers Corp.
AC.............	Allocation Counter [*Computer science*] (IAA)
AC.............	Allowable Cost (OICC)
A/C	All the Conveniences
AC.............	Allyl Chloride [*Organic chemistry*]
AC.............	Alpine Club [*British*]
A/C	Alter Course [*Navigation*]

AC.............. Alternate Call Listing [*Telecommunications*] (TEL)
AC.............. Alternating Current
ac.............. Alternating Current (IDOE)
AC.............. Altitude Compensator [*Automotive engineering*]
AC.............. Altocumulus [*Cloud*] [*Meteorology*]
AC.............. Ambassador's Club [*TWA's club for frequent flyers*] (EA)
AC.............. Ambulance Corps (ADA)
A/C.............. Ambulatory Care [*Medicine*] (DAVI)
AC.............. American Can Co. (CDAI)
AC.............. American Cause [*An association*] (EA)
AC.............. American Cheese (IIA)
AC.............. American Conditions [*Insurance*]
AC.............. Ammonium Citrate [*Organic chemistry*] (OA)
AC.............. Amphibious Car [*British*]
AC.............. Amphibious Corps [*Marine Corps*]
AC.............. Amygdaloid Complex (PDAA)
AC.............. Analog Computer (AAG)
AC.............. Analysis Console (MCD)
AC.............. Analytic [*or Analytical*] Chemist
A/C.............. Anchored Catheter [*Medicine*]
AC.............. Ancilla College [*Formerly, Ancilla Domini College*] [*Donaldson, IN*]
AC.............. Andre and Coquelin [*Often used as a pattern on clothes designed by Courreges, the initials represent the first names of the couturier and his wife*]
AC.............. Anglican Communion
AC.............. Annee Courante [*Of the Current Year*] [*French*]
AC.............. Anni Currentis [*Of the Current Year*] [*Latin*] (ROG)
AC.............. Anno Christi [*In the Year of Christ*] [*Latin*]
AC.............. Anno Corrente [*In the Current Year*] [*Latin*] (ADA)
AC.............. Annotated Card Program
AC.............. Annual Conference (ADA)
AC.............. Annual Cycle of Readings from Torah and Prophets (BJA)
AC.............. Annulment of Certification
AC.............. Anodal Closure [*Physiology*]
AC.............. Anodal Contraction [*Physiology*]
AC.............. Anode Circuit
AC.............. Another Copy (ROG)
AC.............. Answer Complete [*Telecommunications*] (TEL)
AC.............. Answer Construct
AC.............. Ante Christum [*Before Christ*] [*Latin*]
AC.............. Ante Cibum [*Before Meals*] [*Pharmacy*]
AC.............. Ante-Communion
AC.............. Antecubital [*Anatomy*]
AC.............. Antenna Current (IAA)
AC.............. Anterior Chamber [*Ophthalmology*]
AC.............. Anterior Colporrhaphy [*Gynecology*] (CPH)
AC.............. Anterior Commissure [*Neuroanatomy*]
AC.............. Anterior Connective [*Anatomy*]
AC.............. Anterior Cortical [*Anatomy*]
AC.............. Anterior Cruciate [*Ligament*] [*Anatomy*] (DAVI)
AC.............. Anthracenecarboxylic Acid [*Organic chemistry*]
AC.............. Antibiotic Concentrate [*Medicine*] (DMAA)
AC.............. Anticenter
AC.............. Anticlutter (NATG)
AC.............. Anticoagulant [*or Anticoagulation*]
AC.............. Anticoincidence Counter (OA)
A-C.............. Anti-Communist (ADA)
AC.............. Anticomplementary [*Immunology*]
AC.............. Anticorrosive
AC.............. Anti-Crime (LAIN)
AC.............. Anti-Inflammatory Corticoid [*Pharmacology*] (DAVI)
AC.............. Antiphlogistic-Corticoid [*Medicine*] (AAMN)
AC.............. Aortic Closure [*Cardiology*]
AC.............. Apical Cell [*Botany*]
AC.............. Apostolic Church
AC.............. Appalachian Consortium (EA)
AC.............. Appeal Cases [*Canada*] [*A publication*] (DLA)
AC.............. Appeal Court [*Legal*] [*British*] (ROG)
AC.............. Appeals Council [*Social Security Administration*] (OICC)
AC.............. Appellate Court (DLA)
AC.............. Application Control [*or Controller*] [*Computer science*] (NASA)
AC.............. Apprenticeship Committee [*Department of Labor*]
AC.............. Approach Chart
A/C.............. Approach Control [*Aviation*]
AC.............. Approved Cult
AC.............. Arc Cutting [*Welding*]
AC.............. Archaeological Conservancy (EA)
AC.............. Arch-Chancellor
AC.............. Architect of the Capitol [*US*]
AC.............. Archonist Club (EA)
AC.............. Archons of Colophon (EA)
AC.............. Arctic Circle
AC.............. Area Code
AC.............. Area Commander [*British military*] (DMA)
AC.............. Area Coverage
AC.............. Arithmetic Computation Test [*Military*]
AC.............. Arkansas College [*Batesville*]
AC.............. Armament Control
AC.............. Armaments Command [*Formerly, Munitions Command*] [*Rock Island, IL*] [*Army*]
AC.............. Arm Circumference
AC.............. Armored Cable
AC.............. Armoured Car [*Military British*]
AC.............. Army Circular [*British military*] (DMA)
AC.............. Army Co-Operation [*British military*] (DMA)

AC.............. Army Corps
AC.............. Army Council (ADA)
AC.............. Art Complete (MCD)
AC.............. Arthritis Care [*An association*] (EAIO)
AC.............. Artillery Controller (NATG)
AC.............. Arts Council (EAIO)
AC.............. Arts Council of Great Britain (EAIO)
AC.............. Arts of the Church [*A publication*]
AC.............. Asbestos Cement [*Technical drawings*]
ac.............. Ashmore and Cartier Islands [*at (Australia) used in records cataloged after January 1978*] [*MARC country of publication code Library of Congress*] (LCCP)
ac----.......... Asia, Central [*MARC geographic area code Library of Congress*] (LCCP)
AC.............. Asian CineVision [*Later, ACV*] [*An association*] (EA)
AC.............. Asparagus Club (EA)
AC.............. Asphalt Composition (KSC)
AC.............. Asphalt Concrete [*FHWA*] (TAG)
AC.............. Asphaltic Concrete
A/C.............. Assemble and Checkout (MCD)
AC.............. Assessment Center [*Business term*]
AC.............. Assigned Contractor (SAA)
AC.............. Assistant Cameraman
AC.............. Assistant Cashier [*Banking*]
AC.............. Assistant Clerk [*Navy British*] (ROG)
AC.............. Assistant Commandant [*Army/Marine Corps*]
AC.............. Assistant Commissioner
AC.............. Assistant Controller (DCTA)
AC.............. Assist Control (DAVI)
AC.............. Assisted Control (MEDA)
AC.............. Associate Contractor
AC.............. [*The*] Associated Clubs (EA)
AC.............. Associate in Commerce
AC.............. Association of Cosmetologists [*Later, ACH*] (EA)
AC.............. Astronomical Constant
AC.............. Athletic Club [*Usually in combination with proper noun, as, DAC, Detroit Athletic Club*]
AC.............. Atlantic Charter
AC.............. Atlantic Congress
AC.............. Atlantic Council [*Later, ACUS*] [*NATO*] (NATG)
A-C.............. Atlas-Centaur [*Missile*]
AC.............. Atomicity Controller
AC.............. Atriocarotid [*Medicine*]
AC.............. Attack Center
AC.............. Attack Characterization (MCD)
AC.............. Attack Console
AC.............. Attitude Control [*System*] [*Aerospace*]
ac.............. Attitude Control (IDOE)
AC.............. Audio Center [*Command and Service Module*] [*NASA*]
AC.............. Audit Compliance (MCD)
AC.............. Auditor Camerae [*Auditor of the Papal Treasury*]
AC.............. Auditory Cortex [*Neurology*]
AC.............. Augmentation Concentration [*Biochemistry*]
AC.............. Auriculocarotid [*Medicine*] (MAE)
AC.............. Australian Christian [*A publication*] (APTA)
AC.............. Australian Cruiser (DMA)
AC.............. Author Catalogue (ROG)
AC.............. Authorization and Consent (OICC)
AC.............. Authorization under Consideration (DCTA)
AC.............. Author's Correction [*Publishing*]
AC.............. Autistics and Cousins
AC.............. Auto/Axial Compression [*Chromatography*]
AC.............. Autocarrier [*Predecessor of British auto maker, AC Cars*]
AC.............. Auto-Cite [*VERALEX, Inc.*] [*Information service or system*] (CRD)
AC.............. Autocollimator
AC.............. Autocontext [*Freight-forwarding company*] [*British*]
AC.............. Autodecoder (IAA)
AC.............. Automatic Checkout (BUR)
AC.............. Automatic Computer
ac.............. Automatic Computer (IDOE)
AC.............. Automatic Control
AC.............. Automobile Club
AC.............. Auxiliary Command
AC.............. Auxiliary Console (SAA)
AC.............. Availability Code
AC.............. Average Consumer
AC.............. Average Cost
AC.............. Aviation Cadet [*Air Force*]
AC.............. Awaiting Connection [*Telecommunications*] (TEL)
AC.............. Awareness Center [*Defunct*] (EA)
AC.............. Axial Centrifugal (AAG)
AC.............. Axiocervical [*Dentistry*]
AC.............. Axiom of Choice [*Logic*]
AC.............. Azacytidine [*or Azacitidine*] [*Also, AZA, Aza-C*] [*Antineoplastic drug*]
AC.............. Azimuth Comparator
AC.............. Blood Gas [*US Chemical Corps symbol*]
AC.............. Buchanan. Cape Colony Court of Appeal Reports [*South Africa*] [*A publication*] (DLA)
AC.............. Calgary Public Library, Alberta [*Library symbol National Library of Canada*] (NLC)
AC.............. Canadian Reports, Appeal Cases [*1828-1913*] [*A publication*] (DLA)
AC.............. Case on Appeal (DLA)
AC.............. Collier [*Navy symbol Obsolete*]
AC.............. Hercules, Inc. [*Research code symbol*]
AC.............. Hydrogen Cyanide [*Also, HCN*] [*Poison gas Army symbol*]

AC............	Law Reports, Appeal Cases [*England*] [*A publication*] (DLA)
AC............	Michigan Administrative Code (AAGC)
AC............	Quebec dans le Monde [*An association*] (EAIO)
AC............	Rockwell International Corp. [*ICAO aircraft manufacturer identifier*] (ICAO)
AC1..........	Air Controlman, First Class [*Navy rating*]
AC1..........	Aircraftman, First Class [*Canadian*]
AC2..........	Air Controlman, Second Class [*Navy rating*]
AC2..........	Aircraftman, Second Class [*Canadian*]
AC2MP.......	Army Command and Control Master Plan
AC2S.........	Army Command and Control System (MCD)
AC3..........	Air Controlman, Third Class [*Navy rating*]
ACA...........	Acapulco [*Mexico*] [*Airport symbol*]
ACA...........	Accession Compensatory Account (DCTA)
AC/A.........	Accomodative Convergence/Accomodation (Ratio) [*Ophthalmology*]
ACA...........	Accounts Control Area (AFM)
ACA...........	Accreditation Council for Accountancy [*Later, ACAT*] (EA)
ACA...........	Acute Care Admission [*Medicine*]
ACA...........	Acyclovir [*Pharmacology*] (DAVI)
ACA...........	Adenocarcinoma [*Medicine*] (MAE)
ACA...........	Adjacent Channel Attenuation
ACA...........	Administrative Committee on Administration [*United Nations*]
ACA...........	Adult Children Anonymous (EA)
ACA...........	Adult Children of Alcoholics [*Support group*]
ACA...........	Advance Change Authorization (SAA)
ACA...........	Advanced Cargo Aircraft
ACA...........	Advanced Combat Aircraft (MCD)
ACA...........	Advanced Contract Administrator
ACA...........	Advertisement Contractors' Association [*British*] (BI)
ACA...........	Advertising Council of America, Inc. (NTCM)
ACA...........	Advisory Committee on Allotments [*New Deal*]
ACA...........	Advisory Committee on the Arts [*Terminated, 1973*] (EGAO)
ACA...........	Aero Club of America [*Later, National Aeronautic Association of the USA*]
ACA...........	Affenpinscher Club of America [*Later, AAA*]
ACA...........	Afghan Community in America (EA)
ACA...........	Afro-Caribbean Alliance [*British*]
ACA...........	Aged Care Australia [*An association*]
ACA...........	Agence Centrale des Approvisionnements [*Central Supplies Agency*] (NATG)
ACA...........	Agile Combat Aircraft [*Proposed*]
ACA...........	Agricultural Computer Association [*Defunct*] (EA)
ACA...........	Agricultural Council of Arkansas (SRA)
ACA...........	Agriculture Council of America (EA)
ACA...........	Air Canada [*ICAO designator*] (FAAC)
ACA...........	Air Canada Library [*UTLAS symbol*]
ACA...........	Air Clearance Authority
ACA...........	Air Combat Analysis
ACA...........	Air Commando Association (EA)
ACA...........	Aircraft Change Analysis (AAG)
ACA...........	Aircrew Association (EAIO)
ACA...........	Airflow Club of America (EA)
ACA...........	Airlift Clearance Authority (AFM)
ACA...........	Airspace Control Authority [*Air Force*] (DOMA)
ACA...........	Airspace Coordination Area (MCD)
ACA...........	Akita Club of America (EA)
ACA...........	Alabama Cattlemen's Association (SRA)
ACA...........	Alabama Coal Association (SRA)
ACA...........	Alaska Carriers Association, Inc., Anchorage AK [*STAC*]
ACA...........	Alaska Coal Association (SRA)
ACA...........	Alaska Coastal Airlines
ACA...........	Alberta Camping Association (AC)
ACA...........	Alberta Chess Association (AC)
ACA...........	Alberta Construction Association (AC)
ACA...........	Alberta Council on Aging (AC)
ACA...........	All Composite Aircraft (MCD)
ACA...........	Alley Cat Allies [*An association*] (EA)
ACA...........	Alliance for Capital Access [*Defunct*] (EA)
ACA...........	Alliance for Communities in Action (EA)
ACA...........	Allied Command Atlantic (EAIO)
ACA...........	Allied Commission, Austria [*World War II*]
ACA...........	Allied Control Authority [*Allied German Occupation Forces*]
ACA...........	Allocated Configuration Audit (MCD)
ACA...........	Alternate Competition Advocate (AAGC)
ACA...........	Altitude Controller Assembly (MCD)
ACA...........	Aluminium Coatings Association [*British*] (DBA)
ACA...........	Amchitka Central A [*Alaska*] [*Seismograph station code, US Geological Survey Closed*] (SEIS)
ACA...........	American Cadet Alliance (EA)
ACA...........	American Camping Association (EA)
ACA...........	American Canoe Association (EA)
ACA...........	American Carnivals Association (EA)
ACA...........	American Cartographic Association (EA)
ACA...........	American Casting Association (EA)
ACA...........	American Cat Association (EA)
ACA...........	American Cement Alliance (EA)
ACA...........	American Cemetery Association (EA)
ACA...........	American Chain Association (EA)
ACA...........	American Chaplain's Association (EA)
ACA...........	American Cheerleader Association
ACA...........	American Chess Academy [*Commercial firm*] (EA)
ACA...........	American Chianina Association (EA)
ACA...........	American Chiropractic Association (EA)
ACA...........	American Citizens Abroad (EA)
ACA...........	American Civic Association (EA)
ACA...........	American Collection Association [*Orem, UT*] (EA)
ACA...........	American Collectors Association [*Minneapolis, MN*] (EA)
ACA...........	American College of Allergists (EA)
ACA...........	American College of Anesthesiologists (EA)
ACA...........	American College of Angiology (EA)
ACA...........	American College of Apothecaries (EA)
ACA...........	American Color Association (EA)
ACA...........	American Communications Association
ACA...........	American Commuters Association
ACA...........	American Compensation Association (EA)
ACA...........	American Composers Alliance (EA)
ACA...........	American Congregational Association (EA)
ACA...........	American Conservation Association, Inc. (EPA)
ACA...........	American Consumers Association [*Chicago, IL*] (EA)
ACA...........	American Coptic Association (EA)
ACA...........	American Correctional Association (EA)
ACA...........	American Corriedale Association (EA)
ACA...........	American Council for the Arts (EA)
ACA...........	American Council on Alcoholism (EA)
ACA...........	American Counseling Association [*NACFT*] [*Absorbed by*] (EA)
ACA...........	American Counter-Trade Association (EA)
ACA...........	American Creativity Association (EA)
ACA...........	American Crossbow Association (EA)
ACA...........	American Cryptogram Association (EA)
ACA...........	American Crystallographic Association (EA)
ACA...........	American Culture Association (EA)
ACA...........	American Cyanamid Co., Princeton, NJ [*OCLC symbol*] (OCLC)
ACA...........	Americans for Constitutional Action (EA)
ACA...........	Amerifax Cattle Association (EA)
ACA...........	Aminocaproic Acid [*Organic chemistry*]
ACA...........	Aminocephalosporanic Acid [*Pharmacology*]
ACA...........	Ammoniacal Copper Arsenate [*Wood preservative*]
ACA...........	Ammoniacal Copper Arsenite (OA)
ACA...........	Amusement Caterers' Association [*British*] (BI)
ACA...........	Analytica Chimica Acta [*A publication*]
ACA...........	Anglers' Co-Operative Association [*British*] (EAIO)
ACA...........	Annunciator Control Assembly (MCD)
ACA...........	Anterior Cerebral Artery [*Anatomy*] (AAMN)
ACA...........	Anterior Communicating Aneurysm (HGAA)
ACA...........	Anterior Coronary Artery (HGAA)
ACA...........	Anticardiolipin Antibody [*Immunochemistry*]
ACA...........	Anticentromere Antibody [*Immunology*]
ACA...........	Anticollagen Antibody [*Immunology*]
ACA...........	Anticomplement Activity [*Medicine*] (DMAA)
ACA...........	Anti-Corruption Agency
ACA...........	Anticytoplasmic Antibody [*Medicine*] (DMAA)
ACA...........	Apex Clubs of Australia
ACA...........	Application Control Architecture [*Computer science*]
ACA...........	Arcadian Corp. [*NYSE symbol*] (SAG)
ACA...........	Architectural Cladding Association [*British*] (DBA)
ACA...........	Arctic Control Area [*Aviation*] (FAAC)
ACA...........	Arizona Cattlemen's Association (SRA)
ACA...........	Arkansas Chiropractic Association (SRA)
ACA...........	Armaments Control Agency [*Western European Union*] (NATG)
ACA...........	Armistice Terms and Civil Administration [*British World War II*]
ACA...........	Arms Control Association (EA)
ACA...........	Arthritis Care Association [*British*]
ACA...........	Artists Confronting AIDS [*An association*] (EA)
ACA...........	Arts Council of Australia
ACA...........	Arts Councils of America [*Later, American Council for the Arts*]
ACA...........	Asian Christian Association [*Taiwan*] (EAIO)
ACA...........	Assembly Coordination Advice (MCD)
ACA...........	Assignment Control Authority [*Military*] (NVT)
ACA...........	Assignment of Claims Act [*1940*] (OICC)
ACA...........	Assistant Catering Accountant [*British military*] (DMA)
ACA...........	Assistant Clerks Association [*A union*] [*British*]
ACA...........	Assistant County Architect [*British*]
ACA...........	Associacao Civica Angolana [*Political party*] (EY)
ACA...........	Associate Contractor Agreement (MCD)
ACA...........	Associated Chiropodists of America
ACA...........	Associated Collection Agencies [*Colorado*] (SRA)
ACA...........	Associated Councils of the Arts [*Later, American Council for the Arts*]
ACA...........	Associate in Commercial Arts
ACA...........	Associate of the Institute of Chartered Accountants [*British*] (EY)
ACA...........	Association Canadienne d'Archaeologie [*Canadian Archaeological Association - CAA*]
ACA...........	Association Canadienne d'Athletisme [*Canadian Athletics Association*]
ACA...........	Association Canadienne de l'Acoustique [*Canadian Acoustics Association*]
ACA...........	Association Canado-Americaine (EA)
ACA...........	Association for Communication Administration (EA)
ACA...........	Association for the Care of Asthma (EA)
ACA...........	Association of Canadian Advertisers, Inc. (WDMC)
ACA...........	Association of Canadian Archivists
ACA...........	Association of Certified Accountants (EAIO)
ACA...........	Association of Child Advocates (EA)
ACA...........	Association of Commuter Airlines [*Later, NATA*]
ACA...........	Association of Consultant Architects (EAIO)
ACA...........	Association of Consulting Actuaries (EA)
ACA...........	Association of Correctional Administrators
ACA...........	Association of County Archivists [*British*] (DBA)
ACA...........	Asynchronous Communication Adapter [*Computer science*] (IAA)
ACA...........	Attitude Controller Assembly [*NASA*] (KSC)
ACA...........	Australasian Corrosion Association (EAIO)

ACA............. Australia Canada Association (ADA)
ACA............. Australian Cardiacs' Association
ACA............. Australian Committee on Africa
ACA............. Australian Consumers' Association (ODBW)
ACA............. Australian Council for Aeronautics
ACA............. Australian Cricket Association
ACA............. Australian Croatian Association
ACA............. Australian Croquet Association
ACA............. Australian Curling Association
ACA............. Autobody Craftsman Association (SRA)
ACA............. Automatic Circuit Analyzer
ACA............. Automatic Clinical Analyzer [Medicine] (MAE)
ACA............. Automatic Conference Arranger (CET)
ACA............. Awaiting Combat Assignment (MUGU)
ACA............. Azimuth Control Amplifier
ACA............. Camrose Public Library, Alberta [Library symbol National Library of Canada] (NLC)
ACAA......... Agricultural Conservation and Adjustment Administration [New Deal]
ACAA......... Airman Apprentice, Air Controlman, Striker [Navy rating]
ACAA......... Alberta Crown Attorneys' Association (AC)
ACAA......... American Coal Ash Association (EA)
ACAA......... Army Concepts Analysis Agency
ACAA......... Association of Canadian Alumni Administrators (NFD)
ACAA......... Association of Canadian Alumni Administrators
ACAA......... Association of Consulting Architects Australia
ACAA......... Asthma Care Association of America [Defunct] (EA)
ACAA......... Automatic Chemical Agent Alarm [Military] (RDA)
ACAA......... Aviation Cadet Alumni Association (EA)
ACAAC....... American College Admissions Advisory Center [Later, ACAACCC] (EA)
ACAACCC..... American College Admissions Advisory and Career Counseling Center (EA)
ACAAD....... Authorized Commanders Atomic Air Defense (CINC)
ACAAI....... American College of Allergy, Asthma, and Immunology (DMAA)
ACAAK....... Association of Community Arts Agencies of Kansas (SRA)
ACAAM....... Air Courses of Action Assessment Model [Navy]
ACAAP....... Arab Canadian Association of the Atlantic Provinces (AC)
ACAAR....... Action Committee on American-Arab Relations [Later, AARC]
ACAAS....... Automatic Chemical Agent Alarm System (MCD)
ACAATO....... Association of Colleges of Applied Arts & Technology of Ontario [Association des Colleges d'Arts Appliquees et de Technologie de l'Ontario] (AC)
ACAB.......... Air Cavalry Attack Brigade (MCD)
ACAB.......... Allied Central Air Bureau [World War II]
ACAB.......... Army Contract Adjustment Board
ACAB.......... Association Canadienne des Arbitres de Badminton [Canadian Association of Badminton Referees]
ACABQ....... Advisory Committee on Administrative and Budgetary Questions [United Nations]
ACABRIT....... Allied Commission, Austria, British Element [World War II]
ACABUG....... American, Canadian, Australian, British Urban Game [Computer-assisted simulation wargame] [Army] (INF)
ACAC.......... Acacia [Gum Arabic] [Chemistry] (ROG)
Acac........... Acetylacetonate [Organic chemistry]
ACAC.......... Acetylacetone [Organic chemistry]
ACAC.......... Admiral Commanding Aircraft-Carriers [Navy British]
ACAC.......... Air Control Area Commander (NVT)
ACAC.......... Air Crew Association Canada
ACAC.......... Allied Container Advisory Committee [Obsolete]
ACAC.......... American Christian Action Council [Later, NCBBC] (EA)
ACAC.......... American College Admissions Center [Later, ACAAC]
ACAC.......... American Croatian Academic Club [Later, ACAS]
ACAC.......... AMOCO Canada Petroleum Co. Ltd., Calgary, Alberta [Library symbol National Library of Canada] (NLC)
ACAC.......... Anti-Communist Advisory Committee (EA)
ACAC.......... Association Canadienne de Fabricants d'Armoires de Cuisine (AC)
ACAC.......... Association of College Admissions Counselors [Later, NACAC] (EA)
ACAC.......... Australian Cinema Advertising Council
ACACA....... Army Command and Administration Communication Agency (NATG)
ACACA....... Australasian Conference of Assessment and Certification Agencies
ACACC....... Advisory Council, Allied Control Commission [Italy] [World War II]
ACACC....... Association des Cartothecaires et des Archives Cartographiques du Canada [Association of Canadian Map Libraries and Archives] (EAIO)
ACACE....... Advisory Council for Adult and Continuing Education [British]
ACACH....... Alberta Children's Hospital, Calgary, Alberta [Library symbol National Library of Canada] (NLC)
AcaciaR....... Acacia Research Corp. [Associated Press] (SAG)
ACACJC....... Genealogical Society Library, Church of Jesus Christ of Latter-Day Saints, Cardston, Alberta [Library symbol National Library of Canada] (NLC)
ACACN....... American Council of Applied Clinical Nutrition (EA)
AcAcOH....... Acetoacetic Acid [Biochemistry] (DAVI)
ACACP....... Americans Concerned about Corporate Power [Defunct] (EA)
ACACP....... Canadian Park Service, Environment Canada [Service Canadien des Parcs, Environnement Canada], Canmore, Alberta [Library symbol National Library of Canada] (BIB)
ACACS........ Air Cycle Air-Conditioning System (MCD)
ACACT........ Associate Committee on Air Cushion Technology [Canada] (HGAA)
ACACW....... Athletic Conference of American College Women [Later, ARFCW]
ACAD........ Academic (ABBR)
Acad........... Academicae Quaestiones [of Cicero] [Classical studies] (OCD)
ACAD........ Academician [or Academy] (EY)
Acad........... Academy [Record label]
acad............. Academy (VRA)

ACAD......... Acadia (ABBR)
ACAD......... Acadia National Park
ACAD......... Advanced Computer-Aided Design
ACAD......... Air Containment Atmosphere Dilution [Nuclear energy] (NRCH)
ACAD......... Alarm Communications and Display System (MCD)
ACAD......... Alcoholism and Drug Abuse Commission, Calgary, Alberta [Library symbol National Library of Canada] (NLC)
ACAD......... American Conference of Academic Deans (EA)
ACAD......... Atmospheric Containment Atmosphere Dilution (PDAA)
ACAD......... Autodesk, Inc. [Sausalito, CA] [NASDAQ symbol] (NQ)
ACAD......... Automotive Committee for Air Defense [World War II]
ACADA......... Advanced Chemical Agent Detector Alarm (MCD)
ACADA......... Automatic Chemical Agent Alarm [Military] (RDA)
acad bd...... Academy Board (VRA)
ACADC......... Academic (ABBR)
ACADCLY..... Academically (ABBR)
ACAD CL YR... Academic Class Year (DNAB)
ACADCN......... Academician (ABBR)
ACADE......... Association for Computer Art and Design Education [Defunct] (EA)
Acadiana..... Acadiana Bancshares, Inc. [Associated Press] (SAG)
ACADL........ Academical (ABBR)
Acad Nat Sci... Academy of Natural Science (BARN)
ACADOP......... Association Canadienne de Documentation Professionnelle (AC)
Acad Post.... Academica Posteriora [of Cicero] [Classical studies] (OCD)
Acad Pr...... Academica Priora [of Cicero] [Classical studies] (OCD)
ACAD PR...... Academic Press (DGA)
ACADPR......... U.S. Arms Control and Disarmament Agency Procurement Regulation [A publication] (AAGC)
ACADS........ Alarm Communications and Display Segment (MCD)
ACADS........ Australian Computer-Aided Design Systems
ACAE......... Alabama Council of Association Executives (SRA)
ACAE......... Alberta Energy Co., Calgary, Alberta [Library symbol National Library of Canada] (NLC)
ACAE......... American Council for the Arts in Education [Defunct] (EA)
ACAE......... Association of Chinese and American Engineers
ACAE......... Association of Cuban Architects in Exile (EA)
ACAE......... Ateliers et Chantiers de l'Afrique Equatoriale [Equatorial Africa Shipyards] [Gabon]
ACAE......... Canada Awards for Business Excellence
ACAEL......... Library & Records Centre, Alsands Energy Ltd., Calgary, Alberta [Library symbol National Library of Canada] (NLC)
ACAEN........ Association Canadienne pour l'Avancement des Etudes Neerlandaises [Canadian Association for the Advancement of Netherlandic Studies - CAANS]
A CAES........ Anni Caesar [Era of the Caesars] [Latin] (ROG)
AcAF........... Acetylaminofluorene [Also, AAF, AcNHFln, FAA] [Organic chemistry]
ACAF........... Amphibious Corps, Atlantic Fleet [Marine Corps]
ACAF........... Asphalt Contractors Association of Florida (SRA)
ACAF........... Association Canadienne de l'Ataxie de Friedreich [Canadian Association of Friedreich's Ataxia]
ACAF........... Automatic Circuit Assurance Feature (CET)
ACAFDCS..... Autograph Chapter of the American First Day Cover Society [Defunct] (EA)
ACAG......... Afro-Caribbean Action Group [British]
ACAG......... Alberta Gas Ethylene Co., Calgary, Alberta [Library symbol National Library of Canada] (NLC)
ACAG......... Anti-Counterfeit Action Group [Australia]
ACAGR......... Allied Commission, Agriculture Subcommission [World War II]
ACAH......... Accreted Crystaline Anthropoid Homologue
ACAH......... Acylcholine Acyl-Hydrolase [Same as PCE] [An enzyme]
ACAH......... Autoimmune Chronic Active Hepatitis [Medicine]
ACAH......... Horse Industry Branch, Alberta Agriculture, Calgary, Alberta [Library symbol National Library of Canada] (NLC)
ACAHA........ Association of Chief Administrators of Health Authorities [British]
ACAHR......... American Council for the Advancement of Human Rights (EA)
ACAI........... Alkali and Clean Air Inspectorate [British] (DCTA)
ACAI........... American Christian Association for Israel [Later, American-Israel Cultural Foundation] (EA)
ACAI........... Atlantic Coast Airlines [NASDAQ symbol] (TTSB)
ACAI........... Atlantic Coast Airlines, Inc. [NASDAQ symbol] (SAG)
ACAID......... Anterior Chamber-Associated Immune Deviation [For study of foreign tissue grafts] (TAG)
ACAIS......... Air Carrier Activity Information System [BTS] [FAA] (TAG)
ACAJ........... Association Canadienne des Adjoints Juridiques (AC)
ACAJ........... Pacific Coast Apparel Co., Inc. [NASDAQ symbol] (SAG)
ACAL........... Aircraft Change Application List (MCD)
ACAL........... Aircraft Configuration Allowance List (DNAB)
ACAL........... Association for Computer Assisted Learning (AIE)
ACAL........... Camrose Lutheran College, Alberta [Library symbol National Library of Canada] (NLC)
ACALA........ Administration for Civil Affairs in Liberated Areas [World War II]
ACALA........ Armament and Chemical Acquisition and Logistics Agency [Army] (INF)
ACALD........ Association for Children and Adults with Learning Disabilities [Later, LDA] (EA)
ACALJ......... Association Canadienne pour l'Avancement de la Litterature de Jeunesse [Canadian Association for the Advancement of Children's Literature]
ACALLS....... Calling Lake School, Alberta [Library symbol National Library of Canada] (BIB)
ACALM........ American College of Animal Laboratory Medicine (RDA)
ACALM........ Calmar Public Library, Alberta [Library symbol National Library of Canada] (NLC)
ACALP......... Advisory Council on Australia's Languages Policy
ACALS......... Army Computer-Aided Acquisition and Logistics Support

ACALS .... Cadotte Lake School, Alberta [*Library symbol National Library of Canada*] (BIB)
ACAM .... American College of Advancement in Medicine (EA)
ACAM .... Apollo Computer Address Matrix [*NASA*]
ACAM .... Augmented Content-Addressed Memory
ACAM .... Autocam Corp. [*NASDAQ symbol*] (SAG)
ACAM .... Canmore Municipal Library, Alberta [*Library symbol National Library of Canada*] (NLC)
ACAMAR ...... Asociacion Centroamericana de Armadores [*Central American Association of Shipowners*] [*Guatemala, Guatemala*] (EAIO)
ACAmp .... AC [*Alternating Current*] Amperometric [*Electromagnetics*]
ACAMP .... Allied Camouflage and Concealment Publication [*NATO*] (NATG)
ACAMPS ...... Automated Communications and Message Processing System [*Army*] (RDA)
ACAMR .... Associate Committee on Aviation Medical Research [*Canada*]
ACAMS .... Automatic Continuous Air Monitoring System (MCD)
ACAN .... Acanthrocytes [*Hematology*] (DAVI)
ACAN .... Action Committee Against Narcotics
ACAN .... Advisory Committee on Antarctic Feature Names [*Board on Geographic Names*] (NOAA)
ACAN .... Agencia Centroamericana de Noticias SA [*Press agency*] [*Panama*]
ACAN .... Airman, Air Controlman, Striker [*Navy rating*]
ACAN .... Army Communications Administrative Network [*Domestic and overseas integrated system of fixed radio, wire, cable, and associated communications facilities*]
ACAN .... Media Resource Centre, Access Network, Calgary, Alberta [*Library symbol National Library of Canada*] (NLC)
AC & BC ...... Air Conduction and Bone Conduction [*Otorhinolaryngology*] (DAVI)
AC & CAT .... Africa Circle and Correspondence Association for Thematicists (EAIO)
AC & EC ...... Army Communications and Equipment Coordination
AC & HB ...... Algoma Central & Hudson Bay Railroad (IIA)
AC & HS ...... Before Meals and At Bedtime [*Pharmacy*] (DAVI)
AC & I .... Acquisition, Construction, and Improvement (DNAB)
AC & QT ...... Acceptance, Conforming, and Qualification Test
AC & R .... American Cable & Radio Corp.
AC & RC ...... Active Components and Reserve Components
AC & S .... Atlantic City & Shore Railroad
AC & SC ...... Air Command and Staff College [*Maxwell AFB, AL*] [*Air Force*]
AC & SS ...... Aerial Combat and Surveillance System (SAA)
AC & SS ...... Air Command and Staff School [*Air Force*]
AC & TWU ... Atlantic Communication and Technical Workers Union
AC & W .... Air Communications and Weather [*Group*] [*Navy*]
AC & W .... Air [*or Aircraft*] Control and Warning [*Military*]
AC & WS ...... Aircraft Control and Warning Stations [*Military*]
AC & WSq .... Aircraft Control and Warning Squadron [*Air Force*]
AC & Y .... [*The*] Akron, Canton & Youngstown Railroad Co. (IIA)
ACANSW ...... After Care Association of New South Wales [*Australia*]
ACANSW ...... Australian Czech Association of New South Wales
acant .... Acanthus (VRA)
ACANTH ...... Acanthrocytes [*Hematology*] (DAVI)
ACAO .... Acyl Coenzyme A Oxidase (DMAA)
ACAO .... Allied Civil Affairs Office [*World War II*]
ACAO .... Association of Chief Ambulance Officers [*British*] (DBA)
ACAO .... Official Committee on Armistice Terms and Civil Administration [*British World War II*]
ACAODA ...... Australian Council of Alcohol and Other Drug Associations
ACAP .... Aboriginal Community Affairs Panel [*Australia*]
ACAP .... Acapulco [*Mexico*] (ABBR)
ACAP .... Advanced Combat Air Patrol (MCD)
ACAP .... Advanced Composite Airframe Program [*Air Force*]
ACAP .... Advanced Computer for Array Processing
ACAP .... Aeronautical Chart Automation Project [*Military*] (DA)
ACAP .... Agence Camerounaise de Presse [*Cameroon Press Agency*]
ACAP .... American Committee for Aid to Poland (EA)
ACAP .... American Council on Alcohol Problems (EA)
ACAP .... Analysis of Critical Actions Program (SAA)
ACAP .... Analyst Capability
ACAP .... Annapurna Conservation Area Project [*Nepal*]
ACAP .... Army Career and Alumni Program (INF)
ACAP .... Army Child Advocacy Program (MCD)
ACAP .... Army Combat Artist Program
ACAP .... Army Contract Appeals Panel
ACAP .... Army Cost Analysis Paper
ACap .... Australian Capitol [*Record label*]
ACAP .... Automatic Circuit Analysis Program
ACAP .... Aviation Consumer Action Project (EA)
ACAPA .... American Concrete Agricultural Pipe Association [*Defunct*]
ACapBd .... American Capital Bond Fund, Inc. [*Associated Press*] (SAG)
ACapCv .... American Capital Convertible Securities, Inc. [*Associated Press*] (SAG)
ACapIn .... American Capital Income Trust [*Associated Press*] (SAG)
ACAPN .... Association of Child and Adolescent Psychiatric Nurses
A CAPO .... A Capriccio [*At One's Fancy*] [*Music*] (ROG)
A Capp .... A Cappella [*Unaccompanied*] [*Music*]
ACAPQ .... Association des Courtiers d'Assurances de la Province de Quebec [*Insurance Brokers Association of Quebec*] (AC)
ACAPrA .... Arcadian Corp. Mand Cv Pfd [*NYSE symbol*] (TTSB)
ACAPS .... Analog Circuit Analysis and Partitioning System [*Computer science*]
ACAPS .... Automated Chemical Analysis for Process Solutions System [*Hughes Aircraft Co.*] (ECON)
ACAPS .... Automated Costing and Planning System (DNAB)
ACAQ .... Advisory Committee on Air Quality [*Australia*]
ACAQ .... Autistic Children's Association of Queensland [*Australia*]

ACAQE .... Aquatic Environments Ltd., Calgary, Alberta [*Library symbol National Library of Canada*] (NLC)
ACAR .... Aegis Consumer Funding [*NASDAQ symbol*] (TTSB)
ACAR .... Aegis Consumer Funding Group [*NASDAQ symbol*] (SAG)
ACAR .... Aero Car (SAA)
ACAR .... Aluminum Conductor Alloy Reinforced (MCD)
ACAR .... Angular Correlation of Annihilation Radiation [*Spectroscopy*]
ACAR .... Annihilation Radiation [*Physics*]
ACAR .... Army Contract Adjustment Region (MCD)
ACAR .... Cardston Public Library, Alberta [*Library symbol National Library of Canada*] (NLC)
ACARC .... Arctec Canada Ltd., Calgary, Alberta [*Library symbol National Library of Canada*] (NLC)
ACARD .... Advisory Council for Applied Research and Development [*British government*]
ACARDA ...... British-Romanian Association (EAIO)
ACARM .... Association of Commonwealth Archivists and Records Managers (EAIO)
ACARM .... Carbon Municipal Library, Alberta [*Library symbol National Library of Canada*] (NLC)
ACARMA ...... Carmanguay Public Library, Alberta [*Library symbol National Library of Canada*] (NLC)
ACARO .... Caroline Public Library, Alberta [*Library symbol National Library of Canada*] (NLC)
ACARRE ...... Australian Centre for Advanced Risk and Reliability Engineering
ACARS .... Aircraft Communications Addressing and Reporting System (IEEE)
ACARS .... ARINC [*Aeronautical Radio, Inc.*] Communications Addressing and Reporting System (USDC)
ACARS .... ARINC [*Aeronautical Radio, Inc.*] Communications Addressing and Reporting System
ACARS .... ARINC [*Aeronautical Radio Inc.*] Communications Addressing and Reporting Systems [*Marine science*] (OSRA)
ACARS .... ARINC [*Aeronautical Radio Incorporated*] Communications and Address Reporting System [*Digital communications system used primarily for aircraft-to-airline messages*] (GAVI)
ACARS .... Automatic Communications Addressing and Reporting System [*FAA*] (TAG)
ACARS .... Carstairs Public Library, Alberta [*Library symbol National Library of Canada*] (NLC)
ACARS MU... ACARS [*ARINC Communications and Address Reporting System*] Management Unit (GAVI)
ACARTSD ..... African Centre for Applied Research and Training in Social Development (EAIO)
ACARU .... Association Canadienne d'Administrateurs de Recherche Universitaire [*Canadian Association of University Research Administrators - CAURA*]
ACAS .... Advisory, Conciliation, and Arbitration Service [*London, England*]
ACAS .... African Commission on Agricultural Statistics (EA)
ACAS .... Agatha Christie Appreciation Society: Postern of Murder (EA)
ACAS .... Airborne Collision-Avoidance System [*Later, TCAS*]
ACAS .... Aircraft Collision Avoidance System (PDAA)
ACAS .... Air Cycle Air-Conditioning System (MCD)
ACAS .... American Computer Appraisal Service (MHDI)
ACAS .... American Croatian Academic Society [*Formerly, ACAC*] (EA)
ACAS .... Analytical Chemistry and Applied Spectroscopy (MUGU)
ACAS .... Anchored Cell Analysis and Sorting [*Cell culture*]
ACAS .... Application Control Architecture Service [*Computer science*]
ACAS .... Army Commissary Automation System (GFGA)
ACAS .... Army Crisis Action System
ACAS .... Assistant Chief of Air Staff [*Army British*]
ACAS .... Associate of the Casualty Actuarial Society [*Designation awarded by Casualty Actuarial Society*]
ACAS .... Association Canadienne des Administrateurs et des Administratrices Scolaires (AC)
ACAS .... Association Canadienne des Administrateurs Scolaires [*Canadian Association of Academic Administrators*]
ACAS .... Association for Central Asian Studies (EA)
ACAS .... Association of Casualty Accountants and Statisticians [*Later, SIA*]
ACAS .... Association of College Auxiliary Services [*Later, NACAS*] (EA)
ACAS .... Association of Concerned African Scholars (EA)
ACAS .... Atlantic Coast Air Service
ACAS .... AUTOVON Centralized Alarm System
ACAS .... Caslan Public Library, Alberta [*Library symbol National Library of Canada*] (NLC)
ACASA .... Autistic Children's Association of South Australia
ACASD .... Air Clutch Antislack Device (CAAL)
ACASE .... Academie Canadienne des Arts et des Sciences de l'Enregistrement (AC)
ACASG .... Alberta & Southern Gas Co. Ltd., Calgary, Alberta [*Library symbol National Library of Canada*] (BIB)
ACAS(I) .... Assistant Chief of Air Staff (Intelligence) [*Army British*]
ACASLA .... Association of Chief Architects of Scottish Local Authorities (EAIO)
ACAS(O) ...... Assistant Chief of Air Staff (Operations) [*Army British*]
A/CASP .... Air Conditioning Analytical Simulation Package (PDAA)
ACAS(P) ...... Assistant Chief of Air Staff (Policy) [*Army British*]
ACASPP .... American Committee to Advance the Study of Petroglyphs and Pictographs (EA)
ACAST .... Advisory Committee on the Application of Science and Technology to Development [*Also, ACASTD, ACST*] [*United Nations*]
ACAS(T) ...... Assistant Chief of Air Staff (Technical) [*Army British*]
ACAST .... Castor Public Library, Alberta [*Library symbol National Library of Canada*] (NLC)
ACASTD ...... Advisory Committee on the Application of Science and Technology to Development [*Also, ACAST, ACST*] [*United Nations*]
ACAS(TR) .... Assistant Chief of Air Staff (Technical Requirements) [*Army British*]

ACAT........... Accreditation Council for Accountancy and Taxation (EA)
ACAT........... Acetocoenzyme A Acetyltransferase (DMAA)
ACAT........... Acquisition Category (AAGC)
ACAT........... Acquisition Category (CAAL)
ACAT........... Action des Chretiens pour l'Abolition de la Torture [*Action by Christians for the Abolition of Torture*] (EAIO)
ACAT........... Advanced Computer Audit Techniques [*Arthur Andersen & Co.*]
ACAT........... Advanced Conformal Antenna Technique
ACAT........... Air Conditioner Air Transportable (MCD)
ACAT........... American Center for the Alexander Technique (EA)
ACAT........... Arctco, Inc. [*NASDAQ symbol*] (SAG)
ACAT........... Ashore Coordinated ASW [*Antisubmarine Warfare*] Training [*Navy*] (DOMA)
ACAT........... Automated Computerized Axial Tomography [*Radiology*] (DAVI)
ACAT........... Christian Action for the Abolition of Torture [*Defunct*] (EA)
ACATA......... American College of Addiction Treatment Administrators (EA)
ACATEI........ American Committee for the Advancement of Torah Education in Israel [*Later, OTII*] (EA)
ACATS......... Advanced Digital Television Service
ACATS .... Advisory Committee on Advanced Television Service [*FCC high-definition television*] (NTCM)
ACATS .... Airborne Chromatograph for Atmospheric Trace Species [*Instrumentation*]
ACATT........ Aviation Combined Arms Team Trainer
ACAU .... Australian Civil Affairs Unit (VNW)
ACAU .... Automatic Calling and Answering Unit [*Telecommunications*] (OA)
ACAUS .... Association of Chartered Accountants in the United States (EA)
ACAV .... Armored Cavalry Assault Vehicle
ACAVA .... Association of Cultural Advancement through Visual Art [*British*] (DBA)
ACAVS .... Advanced Cab and Visual System [*Army*] (RDA)
ACAW .... Air Communications and Weather Group [*Navy*] (IAA)
ACAW .... Aircraft Control and Warning (MCD)
ACAWA .... Amateur Canoe Association of Western Australia
ACAX .... Air California [*Air carrier designation symbol*]
ACB............. ABC [*Air Business Contact*] [*France ICAO designator*] (FAAC)
ACB............. Acceptance and Certification Branch [*Social Security Administration*]
ACB............. Access Method Control Block [*Computer science*] (BUR)
ACB............. Adapter Control Block [*Computer science*] (IBMDP)
ACB............. Advertising Checking Bureau
ACB............. African Continental Bank Ltd.
ACB............. Air Circuit Breaker
ACB............. Air Corps Board [*Obsolete*] (MCD)
ACB............. Air Crew System Bulletin (MCD)
ACB............. Air-Cushion Barge (MCD)
ACB............. Airfield Construction Branch [*British military*] (DMA)
ACB............. Airmen Classification Battery [*Military tests*]
ACB............. Amchitka Central B [*Alaska*] [*Seismograph station code, US Geological Survey Closed*] (SEIS)
ACB............. American Biodynamics, Inc. [*Vancouver Stock Exchange symbol*]
ACB............. American Capital Bond Fund, Inc. [*NYSE symbol*] (SPSG)
ACB............. American City Bureau [*An association*] (EA)
ACB............. American Council of the Blind (EA)
ACB............. Aminochlorobenzophenone [*Organic chemistry*]
ACB............. Amphibious Construction Battalion [*Also, PHIBCB*]
ACB............. Annoyance Call Bureau [*Telephone-pest control*]
ACB............. Antibody-Coated Bacteria [*Immunology*]
ACB............. Antrum-Corpus Boundary [*Anatomy*]
ACB............. Aortocoronary Bypass [*Cardiology*]
ACB............. Aortocoronary Saphenous Vein Bypass [*Cardiology*] (AAMN)
ACB............. Application Control Block [*Computer science*] (NITA)
ACB............. Army Classification Battery [*Military tests*]
ACB............. Army Communications Board
ACB............. Arterialized Capillary Blood [*Medicine*] (AAMN)
ACB............. Asbestos-Cement Board [*Technical drawings*]
ACB............. Associated Credit Bureaus [*Houston, TX*] (EA)
ACB............. Association Canadienne de Badminton [*Canadian Badminton Association*]
ACB............. Association Canadienne des Bibliotheques [*Canadian Library Association - CLA*]
ACB............. Association of Certification Bodies [*British*] (DBA)
ACB............. Association of Clinical Biochemists [*British*]
ACB............. Association of Concert Bands (EA)
ACB............. Association of Customers' Brokers [*Later, AIB*] (EA)
ACB............. Association of the Customs Bar [*Later, CITBA*] (EA)
ACB............. Asymptomatic Carotid Bruit [*Medicine*] (DMAA)
ACB............. Ateliers et Chantiers de Bretagne [*France*] (NUCP)
ACB............. Australian Casemix Bulletin [*A publication*]
ACB............. Bellaire, MI [*Location identifier FAA*] (FAAL)
ACB............. Brascon Resources Ltd., Calgary, Alberta [*Library symbol National Library of Canada*] (NLC)
a-cb--......... Cambodia [*Democratic Kampuchea*] [*MARC geographic area code Library of Congress*] (LCCP)
ACB............. University of South Alabama, Biomedical Library, Mobile, AL [*OCLC symbol*] (OCLC)
ACB............. Van Kam Am Cap Bd [*NYSE symbol*] (TTSB)
ACBA .... Academy of Comic Book Artists
ACBA .... Aggregate Concrete Block Association [*British*] (DBA)
ACBA .... Aircrew Body Armor [*System*] [*Army*]
ACBA .... American Cavy Breeders Association (EA)
ACBA .... American Charbray Breeders Association [*Later, AICA*] (EA)
ACBA .... Appaloosa Color Breeders Association (EA)
ACBA .... Associate of the Canadian Bankers Association (DD)
ACBA .... Association of Concert Bands of America [*Later, ACB*] (EA)

ACBAR .... Agency Coordinating Body for Afghan Relief [*Afghanistan/Pakistan*] (ECON)
ACBB .... American Council for Better Broadcasts (EA)
ACBB .... Foothills Christian College, Calgary, Alberta [*Library symbol Obsolete National Library of Canada*] (NLC)
ACBC .... Achenbach Child Behavior Checklist (EDAC)
ACBC .... Anthony Colin Bruce Chapman [*British auto industrialist and engineer, founder of Lotus Cars*]
ACBC .... Association of Canadian Bible Colleges (AC)
ACBC .... Australia-China Business Council
ACBC .... Australian Catholic Bishops' Conference
ACBC .... Biotechnica Canada, Calgary, Alberta [*Library symbol National Library of Canada*] (BIB)
ACBCC .... Advisory Committee to the Board and to the Committee on Commodities [*UNCTAD*]
ACBCC .... Australia-China Business Co-Operation Committee
ACBCT .... Automatic Circuit Board Card Tester
AC/BD .... Acrylonitrile/Butadiene [*Organic chemistry*]
ACBD .... Active Commission Base Date [*Military*]
ACBD .... Association Canadienne des Bibliotheques de Droit [*Canadian Association of Law Libraries - CALL*]
ACBDP .... Burnet, Duckworth & Palmer, Calgary, Alberta [*Library symbol National Library of Canada*] (BIB)
ACBE........... Air Contrast Barium Enema [*Medicine*]
ACBE........... Association for Community Based Education (EA)
ACB-EC .... Association of Cooperative Banks of the EC [*Economy Community*] [*Belgium*] (EAIO)
ACBEI.......... Association for Community Based Educational Institutions [*Later, ACBE*] (EA)
ACBEP .... Calgary Board of Education Professional Library, Alberta [*Library symbol National Library of Canada*] (NLC)
ACBES .... American Council of the Blind Enterprises and Services (EA)
ACBF .... African Capacity Building Foundation (ECON)
ACBFC .... Academy of Comic-Book Fans and Collectors [*Defunct*]
ACBFC .... American Church Building Fund Commission [*Later, Episcopal Church Building Fund*] (EA)
ACBFE .... American Council of the Blind Federal Employees (EA)
ACBG .... Aortacoronary Bypass Graft [*Cardiology*]
ACBGEN ...... Application Control Block Generation [*Computer science*] (MHDI)
ACBGS .... Aortocoronary Bypass Graft Surgery [*Cardiology*] (CPH)
ACBIS .... Academic Collective Bargaining Information Service (EA)
A/C BK .... Account Book (DGA)
ACBL........... American Commercial Barge Lines, Inc. [*AAR code*]
ACBL........... American Contract Bridge League (EA)
ACBL........... American Council of Blind Lions (EA)
ACBLF......... Association Canadienne des Bibliothecaires de Langue Francaise [*Later, ASTED*]
ACBLT......... Airlift Contingency Battalion Landing Team (NVT)
ACBM.......... Advisory Committee for Biology and Medicine [*AEC*]
ACBM.......... Asbestos-Containing Building Material (ERG)
ACBM.......... Associated Corset and Brassiere Manufacturers (EA)
ACBM.......... Association Canadienne des Bibliotheques Musicales [*Canadian Association of Music Libraries*]
ACBM.......... Association of Canadian Biscuit Manufacturers [*Association Canadienne des Manufacturiers de Biscuits*] (AC)
ACBM.......... Association of Cartonboard Makers [*British*] (DBA)
ACBM.......... Atomic Cesium Beam MASER
ACBMAG ..... Aviation Chief Boatswain's Mate, Arresting Gear and Barriers [*Navy rating*]
ACBMCP ..... Aviation Chief Boatswain's Mate, Catapult [*Navy rating*]
ACBMGA ..... Aviation Chief Boatswain's Mate, Gasoline System [*Navy rating*]
ACBMPH ..... Aviation Chief Boatswain's Mate, Plane Handler [*Navy rating*]
ACBNM .... Acute Care Bed Need Methodology [*Hospital management*]
ACBO .... Army Central Budget Office
ACBOA .... American Citizens Band Operators Association (EA)
ACBP .... American Council of the Blind Parents [*Later, CFVI*] (EA)
ACBPE .... BP Exploration Canada Ltd., Calgary, Alberta [*Library symbol National Library of Canada*] (NLC)
ACBR .... Accumulator Buffer Register [*Computer science*] (MHDI)
ACBR .... Association Canadienne des Boursiers Rhodes [*Canadian Association of Rhodes Scholars - CARS*]
ACBRA .... ACB [*American Council of the Blind*] Radio Amateurs [*An association*] (EA)
ACBRA .... American CB Radio Association (EA)
ACBS .... Accrediting Commission for Business Schools (EA)
ACBS .... Alert Crew Billet Security (AFM)
ACBS .... Antique and Classic Boat Society (EA)
ACBS .... Aortocoronary Bypass Surgery [*Cardiology*] (CPH)
ACBSI......... Associate of the Chartered Building Societies Institute [*British*] (DBQ)
ACBSP .... Association of Collegiate Business Schools and Programs (PGP)
ACBT.......... Automatic Circuit Board Tester
ACBTBL....... Arnold Cook Braille and Talking Book Library [*Australia*]
ACBWG .... Apollo Reentry Communications Blackout Working Group [*NASA*]
ACBWS .... Automatic Chemical Biological Warning System
ACC............. Aboriginal Coordinating Council [*Australia*]
ACC............. Academic Computation Center [*Georgetown University*] [*Research center*] (RCD)
ACC............. Academic Computer Center [*University of Washington*] [*Research center*] (RCD)
ACC............. Academic Computing Center [*University of California, Riverside*] [*Research center*] (RCD)
ACC............. Academic Computing Center [*University of Vermont*] [*Research center*] (RCD)
ACC............. Academy of Canadian Cinema [*Academie du Cinema Canadien*]
Acc............. Accademia [*Academy*] [*Italian*] (BJA)

ACC	ACC Corp. [*Associated Press*] (SAG)
ACC	Accelerando [*Quickening the Pace*] [*Music*]
ACC	Acceleration
acc	Acceleration (IDOE)
ACC	Acceptable Container Condition [*Shipping*] (DS)
ACC	Acceptance [*Banking*]
ACC	Access
ACC	Access Control Committee
ACC	Accessory
ACC	Accessory
ACC	Accident
Acc	Accidental [*Injury Insurance*] (BARN)
ACC	Accident Compensation Commission (BARN)
ACC	Accident Reconstruction Criminology (LAIN)
ACC	Accommodation
ACC	Accompagnamento [*Accompaniment*] [*Music*]
ACC	Accompanied
Acc	Accord (DLA)
ACC	According (To)
Acc	Account (EY)
acc	Account [*Internet language*] [*Computer science*]
ACC	Accounting Careers Council [*Later, AICPA*]
ACC	Accounting Classification Code (AFM)
ACC	Accounting Controllers Committee
ACC	Accra [*Ghana*] [*Airport symbol*] (OAG)
ACC	Accumulator [*Flowchart*] (MSA)
Acc	Accursius [*Deceased, 1263*] [*Authority cited in pre-1607 legal work*] (DSA)
ACC	Accusative
ACC	Acetyl-CoA Carboxylase [*An enzyme*]
ACC	Acetylcysteine [*Biochemistry*]
ACC	Acid Copper Chromate [*Wood preservative*]
ACC	Acinic Cell Carcinoma [*Medicine*]
ACC/C	Acknowledge Control (IAA)
ac/c	Acrylic on Canvas (VRA)
ACC	Action Change Card
ACC	Active Citizenship Campaign
ACC	Active Clearance Control (PDAA)
ACC	Acute Care Center [*Medicine*] (DAVI)
ACC	Adaptive Control Constrained [*Manufacturing term*]
ACC	Additives and Containments Committee [*British*]
ACC	Adenoid Cystic Carcinoma [*Medicine*]
ACC	Adjustable Chain Clutch (PDAA)
ACC	Administrative Committee on Coordination [*of the United Nations*] [*Aviation*]
ACC	Admiralty Corrosion Committee [*British*] (KSC)
ACC	Adrenocortical Carcinoma [*Medicine*]
ACC	Advanced Carbon-Carbon (MCD)
ACC	Advanced Computer Communications [*Santa Barbara, CA*]
ACC	Advanced Concepts Center [*General Motors Corp.*] [*Automotive engineering*]
ACC	Advertising Creative Circle (DGA)
ACC	Advisory Council on Camps (EA)
ACC	Aerocharter Midlands Ltd. [*British ICAO designator*] (FAAC)
ACC	African-Canadian Council (AC)
ACC	Aft Cargo Carrier (IEEE)
ACC	Aft Cargo Compartment (MCD)
ACC	Agricultural Council of California (SRA)
ACC	Agricultural Credit Corp. Ltd. [*British*] (BI)
ACC	Airborne Control Computer
ACC	Air Center Commander
ACC	Air Chief Commandant [*British*]
ACC	Air Combat Command [*Air Force*]
ACC	Air Component Command [*Military*] (MCD)
ACC	Air Component Commander [*Air Force*] (DOMA)
ACC	Air Conditioning Clutch Compressor [*Automotive engineering*]
ACC	Air Control Center [*Military*]
ACC	Air Control Commission (AAG)
ACC	Air Controlman, Chief [*Navy rating*]
ACC	Air Coordinating Committee [*Governmental policy body for civil aviation in US; terminated, 1960*]
A/CC	Aircraft Carrier
ACC	Aircraft Commander [*MTMC*] (TAG)
ACC	Aircraft Controlling Custodian (MCD)
ACC	Air Crew Change
ACC	Airlift Coordination Center [*Air Force*] (DOMA)
ACC	Airport Consultants Council (EA)
ACC	Airspace Control Center (MCD)
ACC	Airspace Coordination Center [*NATO*] (DOMA)
ACC	Alarm Control Center (NVT)
ACC	Alaska Coastal Current [*Marine science*] (OSRA)
ACC	Alaskan Collectors Club (EA)
ACC	Alberta Craft Council (AC)
ACC	Allahabad Criminal Cases [*India*] [*A publication*] (DLA)
ACC	Allied Chemical Corp. [*Later, Allied Corp.*] (MCD)
ACC	Allied Chief Commissioner [*World War II*]
ACC	Allied Commander-in-Chief [*World War II*]
ACC	Allied Control Center [*NATO*] (NATG)
ACC	Allied Control Commission [*World War II*]
ACC	Allied Control Council [*World War II*]
ACC	Alpena Community College [*Michigan*]
ACC	Alpine Club of Canada (EA)
ACC	Alternate Command Center [*Navy*] (CINC)
ACC	Alternating Current Circuit
ACC	Altocumulus Castellanus [*Cloud*] [*Meteorology*]
ACC	Aluminum Co. of Canada Ltd. [*Toronto Stock Exchange symbol Vancouver Stock Exchange symbol*]
ACC	Alveolar Cell Carcinoma [*Oncology*] (AAMN)
ACC	Amarillo College, Amarillo, TX [*OCLC symbol*] (OCLC)
ACC	Ambulatory Care Clinic [*or Center*] [*Medicine*]
ACC	Amchitka Central C [*Alaska*] [*Seismograph station code, US Geological Survey Closed*] (SEIS)
ACC	American Catholic Committee (EA)
ACC	American Catholic Conference [*Defunct*] (EA)
ACC	American Chamber of Commerce (DCTA)
ACC	American Chesapeake Club (EA)
ACC	American Cimflex Corp. [*Pittsburgh, PA*]
ACC	American Citizenship Center (EA)
ACC	American College of Cardiology (EA)
ACC	American College of Chemosurgery (EA)
ACC	American College of Counselors (EA)
ACC	American College of Cryosurgery (EA)
ACC	American Communications Consultants, Inc. [*Telecommunications service*] (TSSD)
ACC	American Concert Choir [*Defunct*] (EA)
ACC	American Conference of Cantors (EA)
ACC	American Continental Corp.
ACC	American Copper Council (EA)
ACC	American Copyright Council (EA)
ACC	American Corporation Cases, by Withrow [*1868-87*] [*A publication*] (DLA)
ACC	American Craft Council (EA)
ACC	American Craftsmen's Council (BARN)
ACC	American Crystallographic Community
ACC	American Cyanamid Co. (KSC)
ACC	Aminocyclopropane-Carboxylic Acid [*Organic chemistry*]
ACC	Amphibious Command Car (NATG)
ACC	Analytical Calibration Curve
ACC	Anglican Church of Canada
ACC	Anglican Consultative Council [*British*] (EAIO)
ACC	Annual Capital Charge
ACC	Annual Contributions Contract [*Public housing development*]
ACC	Annual Course Contribution
ACC	Anodal Closure Contraction [*Also, AnCC*] [*Physiology*]
ACC	Antarctic Circumpolar Current [*Oceanography*]
ACC	Antenna Control Console
ACC	Anthropogenic Climate Change [*Marine science*] (OSRA)
ACC	Antibody-Containing Cell [*Immunology*]
ACC	Anti-Communist Committee (EA)
A-CC	Antiphlogistic-Corticoid Conditioning Effect [*Medicine*]
ACC	Antique Collectors' Club [*British*] (DBA)
ACC	Aortic Cross Clamping [*Cardiology*]
ACC	Aplasia Cutis Congenita [*Medicine*] (MEDA)
ACC	Appleton-Century-Crofts [*Publisher*]
ACC	Approach Control Center (MCD)
ACC	Approved Capital Costs [*Canada*]
ACC	Arab Co-Operation Council (ECON)
ACC	Area Consultative Committee
ACC	Area Control Center (DA)
ACC	Area Coordination Center
ACC	Argonne Code Center [*Department of Energy*] (IID)
ACC	Armament Control Computer (MCD)
ACC	Armored Column Cover (MCD)
ACC	Army Catering Corps [*British*]
ACC	Army Chemical Center
ACC	Army Commanders' Conference
ACC	Army Communications Command [*Fort Huachuca, AZ*]
ACC	Army Competitive Category (RDA)
ACC	Army Component Command (CINC)
ACC	Army Cooperation Command [*British*]
ACC	Artillery Control Console [*British*]
ACC	Asbestos Claims Council (EA)
ACC	Asbestos Compensation Coalition (EA)
ACC	Ashland Community College [*Ashland, KY*]
ACC	Asian Coconut Community [*Later, APCC*]
ACC	Asian Cultural Council (EA)
ACC	Assault Crisis Center
ACC	Assistant Camp Commandant [*British*]
ACC	Associated Communications Corp.
ACC	Association Canadienne de Cross (AC)
ACC	Association Canadienne de la Construction [*Canadian Construction Association*]
ACC	Association Canadienne de la Courtepointe (AC)
ACC	Association Canadienne des Communications [*Canadian Communication Association - CCA*]
ACC	Association Chiropratique Canadienne [*Canadian Chiropractic Association*]
ACC	Association des Camps du Canada (AC)
ACC	Association des Consommateurs du Canada [*Consumers' Association of Canada - CAC*]
ACC	Association for Creative Change within Religious and Other Social Systems (EA)
ACC	Association of Chiropractic Colleges (EA)
ACC	Association of Choral Conductors (EA)
ACC	Association of Computer Consultants (EA)
ACC	Association of Conservative Clubs [*British*] (DBA)
ACC	Association of County Councils [*British*]
ACC	Astronaut Control Console [*NASA*]
ACC	Astronomical Great Circle Course
ACC	Asynchronous Communications Control

ACC............ Asynchronous Computer Conferencing
ACC............ Atlantic Christian College [*Wilson, NC*]
ACC............ Atlantic Coast Conference (EA)
ACC............ Atlantic Council of Canada (EAIO)
ACC............ Attack Control Concept
ACC............ Attack Control Console
ACC............ Auburn Community College [*New York*]
ACC............ Audio Control Center
ACC............ Aural Comprehension Course (DNAB)
ACC. .... Auto Camping Club Ltd. [*British*] (BI)
ACC............ Automatic Carrier Control [*Telecommunications*] (TEL)
ACC............ Automatic Chrominance Control (DEN)
acc............ Automatic Chrominance Control (IDOE)
ACC............ Automatic Climate Control [*Automotive engineering*]
acc............ Automatic Color Compensation (IDOE)
ACC............ Automatic Color Control
ACC............ Automatic Combustion Control
ACC............ Automatic Contrast Control
ACC............ Automatic Control Center [*Purdue University*]
ACC............ Automatic Control Certified (DCTA)
ACC............ Automatic Control Console (NASA)
ACC............ Automatic Course Control [*Air Force*]
ACC............ Automotive Climate Control
ACC............ Automotive Composites Consortium
ACC............ Automotive Composites Consortium [*General Motors Corp., Ford Motor Co., and Chrysler Corp.*]
ACC............ Auxiliary Crew Compartment (MCD)
ACC............ Average Correlation Coefficient (PDAA)
ACC............ Aviation Control Center
ACC............ Aviation Credit Corps
ACC............ Cessford Community Library, Alberta [*Library symbol National Library of Canada*] (NLC)
a-cc--.......... China, Mainland [*MARC geographic area code Library of Congress*] (LCCP)
ACC............ Classic Record Club [*Record label*]
ACC............ L'Association Canadienne du Camionnage (AC)
ACCA .... Accelerated Capital Cost Allowance [*Accounting*]
ACCA .... Ad Hoc Crypto-Coordination Agency (MUGU)
ACCA .... Aeronautical Chamber of Commerce of America [*Later, AIA*]
ACCA .... Agricultural Central Cooperative Association Ltd. [*British*] (BI)
ACCA .... Agricultural Credit Corp. Act [*1932*]
ACCA .... Air Charter Carriers Association (MHDB)
ACCA .... Air Conditioning Contractors of America (EA)
ACCA .... Air Courier Conference of America (EA)
ACCA .... American Cave Conservation Association (EA)
ACCA .... American Chamber of Commerce in Australia
ACCA .... American Chamber of Commerce in Austria (EA)
ACCA .... American Child Custody Alliance (EA)
ACCA .... American Clinical and Climatological Association (EA)
ACCA .... American College of Cardiovascular Administrators (EA)
ACCA .... American College of Clinic Administrators [*Defunct*] (EA)
ACCA .... American Commercial Collectors Association (EA)
ACCA .... American Corporate Counsel Association (EA)
ACCA .... American Correctional Chaplains Association (EA)
ACCA .... American Cotton Cooperative Association (EA)
ACCA .... American Council for Coordinated Action [*Defunct*] (EA)
ACCA .... Angel Collectors Club of America (EA)
ACCA .... Antenna Counterbalance Cylinder Assembly
ACCA .... Arizona Concrete Contractors Association (SRA)
ACCA .... Armed Career Criminal Act of 1984
ACCA .... Art Collectors Club of America (EA)
ACCA .... Associated Colleges of the Chicago Area
ACCA .... Association of Canadian Courts Administrators (AC)
ACCA .... Association of Certified and Corporate Accountants [*British*]
ACCA .... Association of County Commissions of Alabama (SRA)
ACCA .... Asynchronous Communications Control Attachment
ACCA .... Australian Cultural Center Association
ACCA .... Australian Current Case Annotator [*A publication*]
ACCACA...... Advisory Council on Clean Air Compliance Analysis [*Environmental Protection Agency*]
ACCACA...... Air Conditioning Trade Association of California (SRA)
ACC-ACO.... Army Communications Command Advanced Concepts Office [*Fort Huachuca, AZ*]
ACCAD........ Accademia
ACCAD........ Advanced Computing Center for the Arts and Design [*Ohio State University*] [*Research center*] (RCD)
ACCAD........ Advisory Committee on Climate Applications and Data [*Marine science*] (OSRA)
a-cc-an .... Anhwei Province [*China, Mainland*] [*MARC geographic area code Library of Congress*] (LCCP)
ACC & CE .... Association of Consulting Chemists and Chemical Engineers (EA)
ACCANSW.... Australian Chinese Community Association of New South Wales
ACCAP .... Autocoder-to-COBOL Conversion Aid Program [*IBM Corp.*] [*Computer science*]
ACCART ...... Australian Council for the Care of Animals in Research and Teaching
ACCAS .... Altocumulus Castellanus [*NWS*] (FAAC)
ACCAS .... Association of Crossroads Care Attendant Schemes (EAIO)
ACCase........ Acetyl-CoA Carboxylase [*An enzyme*]
ACCASP........ Air Coordinating Committee [*Terminated*] Airspace Subcommittee
ACCAT........ Advanced Command and Control Architectural Testbed (MCD)
ACCB .... Access Beyond, Inc. [*NASDAQ symbol*] (SAG)
ACCB .... Air Cavalry Combat Brigade [*Army*]
ACCB .... Aircraft Change Control Board [*DoD*]
ACCB .... Aircraft Configuration Change Board
ACCB .... Aircraft Configuration Control Board [*DoD*]

ACCB .... Airframe Change Control Board (MCD)
ACCB .... American Chamber of Commerce of Bolivia (EA)
ACCB .... Atlas Configuration Control Board [*Aerospace*] (AAG)
ACCB .... Library Services, Colonel Belcher Hospital, Calgary, Alberta [*Library symbol National Library of Canada*] (BIB)
ACCBD........ Association Canadienne du Contreplaqué de Bois Dur (AC)
ACCB/TRICAP... Air Cavalry Combat Brigade/Triple Capability Division [*Army*] (MCD)
AccBynd...... Access Beyond, Inc. [*Associated Press*] (SAG)
ACCC .... ACC Corp. [*NASDAQ symbol*] (NQ)
ACCC .... Advisory Committee to the Canada Centre for Inland Waters (PDAA)
ACCC .... Advisory Council on College Chemistry
ACCC .... Alternate Central Computer Complex (MCD)
ACCC .... Alternate Command and Control Center [*Air Force*] (MCD)
ACCC .... American Council of Christian Churches (EA)
ACCC .... Antique Comb Collectors Club (EA)
ACCC .... Area Chemist Contractors' Committee [*National Health Service*] [*British*] (DI)
ACCC .... Area Control Computer Complex (AAGC)
ACCC .... Area Control Computer Complex [*FAA*] (TAG)
ACCC .... Association of Canadian Choral Conductors [*Association des Chefs des Choeurs Canadiens*]
ACCC .... Association of Canadian Community Colleges [*Association des Colleges Communautaires du Canada*]
ACCC .... Association of Community Cancer Centers (EA)
ACCC .... Australia-China Chamber of Commerce
ACCCA .... Advisory and Coordinating Committee on Child Abuse [*Western Australia*]
ACCCA .... American Catholic Correctional Chaplains Association (EA)
ACCCA .... American Community Cultural Center Association (EA)
ACC-CCC .... Action Coordinating Council for Comprehensive Child Care
ACCCE .... Allied Commission, Commerce Subcommission, Exports [*World War II*]
ACCCEL....... Assessing the Cognitive Consequences of Computer Environments for Learning Project (EDAC)
ACCCF .... American Concert Choir and Choral Foundation [*Later, ACF*]
a-cc-ch .... Chekiang Province [*China, Mainland*] [*MARC geographic area code Library of Congress*] (LCCP)
ACCCI .... American Coke and Coal Chemicals Institute (EA)
ACC Cns ...... ACC Consumer Finance Corp. [*NASDAQ symbol*] (SAG)
ACC Cns ...... ACC Consumer Finance Corp. [*Associated Press*] (SAG)
ACCCNSW.... Association of Child Care Centers in New South Wales [*Australia*]
ACC/COM.... Air Coordinating Committee [*Terminated*] Communications Subcommittee
ACC Cp .... ACC Corp. [*Associated Press*] (SAG)
ACCCS .... Crooked Creek Colony School, Alberta [*Library symbol National Library of Canada*] (BIB)
AccCSci....... Accent Color Sciences, Inc. [*Associated Press*] (SAG)
ACCD .... Accelerated Construction Completion Date (NATG)
ACCD .... Accident
ACCD .... Advance Corporate Contract Directive (MCD)
ACCD .... Aerospace Communication and Controls Division [*NASA*] (KSC)
ACCD .... Aircraft Compatibility Control Drawing (MCD)
ACCD .... Alberta Committee of Citizens with Disabilities (AC)
ACCD .... American Coalition of Citizens with Disabilities [*Defunct*] (EA)
ACCDCE ...... Accordance (ROG)
ACCE .... Acceptance [*Banking*]
ACCE .... Advisory Committee on Chemicals in the Environment [*Australia*]
ACCE .... American Chamber of Commerce Executives (EA)
ACCE .... American College for Continuing Education (EA)
ACCE .... American Council for Construction Education (EA)
ACCE .... American Council on Cosmetology Education [*Defunct*] (EA)
ACCE .... Association Canadienne des Chercheurs en Education [*Canadian Educational Researchers Association - CERA*]
ACCE .... Association of Christian Church Educators (EA)
ACCE .... Association of County Chief Executives [*British*] (EAIO)
ACCE .... Atlantic Circulation and Climate Experiment [*Marine science*] (OSRA)
ACCE .... Canterra Energy Ltd., Calgary, Alberta [*Library symbol National Library of Canada*] (NLC)
ACCEd........ Associate of the College of Craft Education [*British*] (DI)
AC-CEF .... Allis-Chalmers Critical Experimental Facility
ACCEH .... Access Committee Centre on Environment for the Handicapped [*British*]
ACCEL........ Accelerando [*Quickening the Pace*] [*Music*]
ACCEL........ Accelerate (AABC)
ACCEL........ Accelerator [*Automotive engineering*]
ACCEL........ Accelerometer
Accel .... Accel International Corp. [*Associated Press*] (SAG)
ACCEL........ Automated Circuit Card Etching Layout [*Computer science*]
ACCEL........ Canuck Engineering Ltd., Calgary, Alberta [*Library symbol National Library of Canada*] (NLC)
ACCELO........ Accelerando [*Quickening the Pace*] [*Music*] (ROG)
Accelr8........ Accelr8 Technology Corp. [*Associated Press*] (SAG)
ACCEM........ Advanced Composite Cost Estimating Model (MCD)
Accent .... Accent Software International Ltd. [*Associated Press*] (SAG)
ACCENT........ Autogenetically-Controlled Cesium Electro-Nuclear Thrust System (MCD)
AccentS ...... Accent Software International Inc. [*Associated Press*] (SAG)
ACCEPN...... Acceptation [*Acceptance*] [*French Banking*]
ACCEPT...... Access Electronic Payment Terminals [*for credit cards*] [*British*]
ACCEPT...... Addictions Community Centres for Education, Prevention, Treatment, and Research [*British*] (AIE)
ACCEPT........ Alcohol Community Centre for Education, Prevention, and Treatment [*British*] (DI)

ACCEPT........ Automated Cargo Clearance and Enforcement Processing Technique [*US Customs Service*]
ACCEPTCE ... Acceptance [*Banking*] (ROG)
ACCEPTN ..... Acceptance
ACCES .... Accessory
ACCES .... Alantic Canada Centre for Environmental Science (AC)
ACCES .... American Chamber of Commerce of El Salvador (EA)
ACCES .... Army Civilian Career Evaluation System
ACCES .... Cenlor Services Ltd., Calgary, Alberta [*Library symbol National Library of Canada*] (NLC)
AccesH .... Access HealthNet, Inc. [*Associated Press*] (SAG)
AccesHlt ...... Access Health, Inc. [*Associated Press*] (SAG)
ACCESS ...... Academic Consortium for Economic and Social Surveys [*Australia*]
ACCESS ...... Access Characteristics Estimation System [*Computer science*] (MHDI)
ACCESS ...... Accessory (KSC)
ACCESS ...... ACMD [*Advanced Concepts and Missions Division*] Combined Control and EnergyStorage System (SSD)
ACCESS ...... Action Center for Educational Service and Scholarships
ACCESS ...... Action Coordinating Committee to End Segregation in the Suburbs
ACCESS ...... Afloat Consumption Cost and Effectiveness Surveillance System [*Navy*]
ACCESS ...... Aircraft Communication Control and Electronic Signaling System [*Air Force*]
ACCESS ...... Alliance des Communautes Culturelles pour l'Egalite dans la Sante et les Services Sociaux (AC)
ACCESS ...... American and Canadian Connection for Efficient Securities Settlement [*Canada*]
ACCESS ...... American College of Cardiology Extended Study Services
ACCESS ...... American Coordinating Committee for Equality in Sport and Society (EA)
ACCESS ...... AMOCO Chemicals Customer Service System
ACCESS ...... Architects' Central Constructional Engineering Surveying Service [*British*] (NITA)
ACCESS ...... Architects, Construction and Consulting Engineers, Specialist Service (MHDB)
ACCESS ...... Argonne Code Center Exchange and Storage System (MHDB)
ACCESS ...... Army Commissary Computer Entry Store System (AABC)
ACCESS ...... Assembly Concept for Construction of Erectable Space Structures [*Space shuttle experiment*] [*NASA*]
ACCESS ...... Assessment for Community Care Services [*Health Care Financing Administration*]
ACCESS ...... Association of Community Colleges for Excellence in Systems and Services [*Consortium*]
ACCESS ...... Automated Catalog of Computer Equipment and Software Systems [*Army*] (NITA)
ACCESS ...... Automated Command Control Executive Support System [*Air Force*] (DOMA)
ACCESS ...... Automated Computer Controlled Editing Sound System
ACCESS ...... Automated CONARC Command Echelon Standard Systems (MCD)
ACCESS ...... Automated Control and Checking of Electrical Systems Support (MCD)
ACCESS ...... Automatic Card Control Entrance Security System [*Computer science*]
ACCESS ...... Automatic Central Communications Electronic Switching System
ACCESS ...... Automatic Computer-Controlled Electronic Scanning System [*National Institute of Standards and Technology*]
ACCESS ...... Automatic Crane Control Storage System
ACCESS ...... [*A*] Complete Computerized Examination System [*Anatomy and physiology*]
AccessAny ... Access Anytime Bancorp, Inc. [*Associated Press*] (SAG)
ACCF............ Actuarial Common Claims File [*Health insurance*] (GHCT)
ACCF............ Agence Centrafricaine des Communications Fluviales [*Central African Agency for River Communications*] (AF)
ACCF............ American Committee for Cultural Freedom
ACCF............ American Council for Capital Formation (EA)
ACCF............ Area Communications Control Function [*Defense Communications System*] (DNAB)
ACCFA.......... Association des Citoyens de Culture Francaise d'Amerique [*American Association of Citizens of French Culture*] [*Canada*]
ACCFTV....... Australian Council for Children's Films and Television
a-cc-fu .... Fukien Province [*China, Mainland*] [*MARC geographic area code Library of Congress*] (LCCP)
ACC/FWC .... Automatic Combustion Control and Feedwater Control (DNAB)
ACCG .... Agricultural Chemicals Consultative Group [*Australia*]
ACCG .... Association Canadienne des Chirurgiens Generaux [*Canadian Association of General Surgeons - CAGS*]
ACCG .... Association County Commissioners of Georgia (SRA)
ACCG .... Clarkson Gordon Library, Calgary, Alberta [*Library symbol National Library of Canada*] (BIB)
a-ccg- .... Yangtze River and Basin [*China, Mainland*] [*MARC geographic area code Library of Congress*] (LCCP)
ACCGAT ...... Accumulator Gating [*Naval Space Surveillance System*] (DNAB)
ACCGET ...... American Council on Capital Gains and Estate Taxation [*Later, ACCF*] [*Tax lobbying organization*]
ACCGS .... Air Cadet Central Gliding School [*British*]
AcCh .... Acetylcholine [*Biochemistry*] (AAMN)
ACCH .... American College of Clinical Hypnosis [*Defunct*] (EA)
ACCH .... Association for the Care of Children's Health (EA)
ACCH .... Calgary Herald, Alberta [*Library symbol National Library of Canada*] (NLC)
ACCHAN...... Allied Command Channel [*NATO*]
a-cc-he .... Heilungkiang Province [*China, Mainland*] [*MARC geographic area code Library of Congress*] (LCCP)

a-cc-hh .... Hupeh Province [*China, Mainland*] [*MARC geographic area code Library of Congress*] (LCCP)
ACCHO........ Association Canadienne des Communications entre l'Homme et l'Ordinateur [*Canadian Association of Communications between Man and Computers*]
a-cc-ho .... Honan Province [*China, Mainland*] [*MARC geographic area code Library of Congress*] (LCCP)
a-cc-hp .... Hopeh Province [*China, Mainland*] [*MARC geographic area code Library of Congress*] (LCCP)
AcChR......... Acetylcholine Receptor [*Also, AChR*] [*Biochemistry*]
AcCHS .... Acetylcholinesterase [*An enzyme*] (MAE)
a-cc-hu .... Hunan Province [*China, Mainland*] [*MARC geographic area code Library of Congress*] (LCCP)
ACCI............ ACC Consumer Finance [*NASDAQ symbol*] (TTSB)
ACCI............ ACC Consumer Finance Corp. [*NASDAQ symbol*] (SAG)
ACCI............ Accident Injury
ACCI............ Adult Career Concerns Inventory [*Test*]
ACCI............ Amer Complex Care [*NASDAQ symbol*] (TTSB)
ACCI............ American Corporate Counsel Institute [*Washington, DC*] (EA)
ACCI............ American Cottage Cheese Institute [*Later, ACDPI*] (EA)
ACCI............ American Council on Consumer Interests (EA)
ACCI............ Apportionment of Close Companies' Income [*Business term*] (NITA)
ACCI............ Association of Chambers of Commerce of Ireland (DI)
ACCI............ Association of Crafts and Creative Industries (EA)
ACCID .... Accident (AAMN)
ACCID .... Approach to Command and Control Implementation and Design (SAA)
ACCID .... Initial Notification of an Aircraft Accident [*Aviation code*]
ACCIDSUB ... Subsequent Notification of an Aircraft Accident [*Aviation code*]
a-cc-im........ Inner Mongolia Autonomous Region [*China, Mainland*] [*MARC geographic area code Library of Congress*] (LCCP)
ACC/INC...... Accident/Incident [*FRA*] (TAG)
ACCION....... Americans for Community Cooperation in Other Nations (AEBS)
ACCIS .... Advisory Committee for the Co-Ordination of Information Systems [*Database producer*] [*Geneva, Switzerland*] [*United Nations*]
ACCIS .... Air Command and Control Improvement System [*NATO*]
ACCJ........... American Chamber of Commerce in Japan (EA)
ACCJC......... Genealogical Society Library, Church of Jesus Christ of Latter-Day Saints, Calgary, Alberta [*Library symbol National Library of Canada*] (NLC)
a-cck- .... Kunlun Mountain Region [*China, Mainland*] [*MARC geographic area code Library of Congress*] (LCCP)
ACCK .... Librarians Committee of the Associated Colleges of Central Kansas [*Library network*]
a-cc-ka .... Kansu Province [*China, Mainland*] [*MARC geographic area code Library of Congress*] (LCCP)
a-cc-kc........ Kwangsi Chuang Autonomous Region [*China, Mainland*] [*MARC geographic area code Library of Congress*] (LCCP)
a-cc-ki .... Kiangsi Province [*China, Mainland*] [*MARC geographic area code Library of Congress*] (LCCP)
a-cc-kn .... Kwangtung Province [*China, Mainland*] [*MARC geographic area code Library of Congress*] (LCCP)
ACCKP .... Aboriginal Cultural Centre and Keeping Place [*University of New England*] [*Australia*]
a-cc-kr .... Kirin Province [*China, Mainland*] [*MARC geographic area code Library of Congress*] (LCCP)
a-cc-ku .... Kiangsu Province [*China, Mainland*] [*MARC geographic area code Library of Congress*] (LCCP)
a-cc-kw .... Kweichow Province [*China, Mainland*] [*MARC geographic area code Library of Congress*] (LCCP)
ACCKWA ..... AIDS Committee of Cambridge, Kitchener/Waterloo & Area (AC)
ACCL........... All Canadian Congress of Labour
ACCL........... American Citizens Concerned for Life Education Fund/ACCL Communications Center [*Defunct*] (EA)
ACCL........... American College of Computer Lawyers [*Defunct*] (EA)
ACCL........... American Council of Christian Laymen [*Later, LCACCC*] (EA)
ACCL........... American Council of Commercial Laboratories [*Later, ACIL*] (KSC)
ACCl............ Anodal Closure Clonus [*Physiology*] (MAE)
ACCL........... Army Coating and Chemical Laboratory (MCD)
ACCL........... Calgary Library Service Centre, Alberta [*Library symbol National Library of Canada*] (NLC)
Acclaim .... Acclaim Entertainment, Inc. [*Associated Press*] (SAG)
ACCLAIM .... Automated Circuit Card Lay-Out and Implementation [*Computer science*] (PDAA)
ACCLAIMS ... Army COMSEC [*Communications Security*] Commodity, Logistical, and Accounting Information Management System (AABC)
a-cc-lp .... Liaoning Province [*China, Mainland*] [*MARC geographic area code Library of Congress*] (LCCP)
ACCLRM ..... Accelerometer
ACCM......... Acoustic Counter-Countermeasures [*Navy*] (NG)
ACCM......... Advanced Concept Cost Model (MCD)
ACCM......... Advisory Council for the Church's Ministry [*Church of England*]
ACCM......... Advisory Council on Calibration and Measurement (ACII)
ACCM......... AIDS Community Care Montreal [*Sida Benevoles Montreal*] (AC)
ACCM......... Air Controlman, Master Chief [*Navy rating*]
ACCM......... American College of Clinic Managers [*Later, ACMGA*] (EA)
ACCM......... Associated Concrete Contractors of Michigan (SRA)
ACCMB .... Aircraft Crewman Badge [*Military decoration*] (GFGA)
ACCME .... Accreditation Council for Continuing Medical Education (EA)
ACC/MET.... Air Coordinating Committee [*Terminated*] Meteorological Subcommittee
ACCMIS ...... Army Command and Control Management Information System
ACCML........ Army Chemical Corps Medical Laboratories (KSC)
ACCMPLSMNT... Accomplishment
ACCMS .... American Center for Chinese Medical Sciences (EA)

ACCN .... Accommodation
ACCN .... American Court and Commercial Newspapers (EA)
ACCN .... Arms Control Computer Network [Defunct] (EA)
ACCN .... Associated Court and Commercial Newspapers (DGA)
ACCN .... Audit Central Control Network (MCD)
ACCNET .... Army Command and Control Network (AABC)
a-cc-nn .... Ningsia Hui Autonomous Region [China, Mainland] [MARC geographic area code Library of Congress] (LCCP)
ACCNR .... Library and Records Center, Crows Nest Resources Ltd., Calgary, Alberta [Library symbol National Library of Canada] (NLC)
ACCNT .... Accountant
ACCO .... Agricultural Cooperative Council of Oregon (SRA)
ACCO .... American College of Chiropractic Orthopedists (EA)
ACCO .... American Cyanamid Co.
ACCO .... Aminocyclopropanecarboxylicacid Oxidase [An enzyme]
ACCO .... [The] Associated Christian Colleges of Oregon [Library network]
ACCO .... Associate of the Canadian College of Organists
ACCO .... Association of Child Care Officers [British] (DI)
ACCO .... Association of County Commissioners of Oklahoma (SRA)
ACCO .... Coors [Adolph] Co. [NASDAQ symbol] (NQ)
AcCoA .... Acetyl Coenzyme A [Biochemistry]
ACCOB .... Coors (Adolph)CI'B' [NASDAQ symbol] (TTSB)
Accom .... Accom, Inc. [Associated Press] (SAG)
ACCOM .... Accommodate [or Accommodation] (AFM)
ACCOM .... Accompaniment [Music]
ACCOM .... Accompany (AFM)
ACCOM .... Aircraft Communicator [Signaling device] [Aviation] (IAA)
Accom ad Lib... Accompaniment ad Libitum [Music]
ACCOMMODON... Accommodation (ROG)
Accom Oblto... Accompaniment Obligato [Music]
ACCOMP ..... Academic Computing Group
ACCOMP ..... Accompaniment [Music]
ACCOMP ..... Accomplish (AFM)
ACCOMPL ... Accomplish (MUGU)
ACCON........ Acoustic Control (NVT)
ACCOP .... Canadian Occidental Petroleum Ltd., Calgary, Alberta [Library symbol National Library of Canada] (NLC)
ACCOR........ Army COMSEC [Communications Security] Central Office of Record (AABC)
ACCORD ..... According
Accord .... Accordion [Music]
ACCORD ..... American Citizens Committee on Reducing Debt (EA)
ACCORD ..... Army Computer Capabilities Online Repository and Disseminator (PDAA)
ACCORD ..... Association for Co-Ordinated Rural Development [Government body] [British]
ACCORDCE... Accordance (ROG)
ACCORDG ... According (ROG)
ACCORDS .... Acoustic Correlation and Detection System
ACCOS .... Automatic Computer Calculation of Optical Systems (MCD)
ACCOS .... Canstar Oil Sands Ltd., Calgary, Alberta [Library symbol National Library of Canada] (NLC)
ACCOSCA..... African Confederation of Cooperative Savings and Credit Associations [See also ACECA] [Nairobi, Kenya] (EAIO)
Accountancy L Rep... Accountancy Law Reporter [A publication] (DLA)
ACCOVAM.... Association Canadienne des Courtiers en Valeurs Mobilieres [Investment Dealers' Association of Canada - IDA]
ACCOW .... Assistant Combat Cargo Officer, Well Deck (CAAL)
ACCOY .... Accompany (ROG)
ACCP .... Advisory Committee on Civilian Policy [World War II]
ACCP .... American Chamber of Commerce of the Philippines (EA)
ACCP .... American College of Chest Physicians (EA)
ACCP .... American College of Clinical Pharmacology (EA)
ACCP .... American College of Clinical Pharmacy (EA)
ACCP .... American Council on Chiropractic Physiotherapy [Later, CCPT] (EA)
ACCP .... Army Correspondence Course Program
ACCP .... Association Canadienne des Chefs de Pompiers [Canadian Association of Fire Chiefs]
ACCP .... Association of Casualty Care Personnel [Canada]
ACCP .... Atlantic Climate Change Program (USDC)
ACCP .... Atlantic Climate Change Program [Marine science] (OSRA)
ACCP .... Canadian Petroleum Association, Calgary, Alberta [Library symbol National Library of Canada] (NLC)
a-ccp- .... Pohai Sea and Area [China, Mainland] [MARC geographic area code Library of Congress] (LCCP)
ACCPA .... Army Chemical Center Procurement Agency
a-cc-pe .... Peking Municipality [China, Mainland] [MARC geographic area code Library of Congress] (LCCP)
ACCPFF........ Anti-Communist Confederation of Polish Freedom Fighters in USA (EA)
ACCPL .... Accomplice [FBI standardized term]
ACCPT .... Accept [or Acceptance] [Banking] (KSC)
ACCPT .... Accompaniment (WGA)
ACCQ .... Association des Cadres des Colleges du Quebec (AC)
ACCR .... Accrete (ABBR)
ACCR .... Accrued (AFM)
ACCR .... American Christian Committee for Refugees [Post-World War II, Europe]
ACCR .... American Council on Chiropractic Roentgenology [Later, Council on Roentgenologyof the American Chiropractic Association] (EA)
ACC-R.......... Area Control-RADAR (DA)
ACCR .... Association Canadienne du Canotage Recreatif [Canadian Association of Recreational Boating]
ACCRA .... American Chamber of Commerce Researchers Association (EA)
ACCRCY....... Accuracy

ACCRD......... Accreted (ABBR)
Accrd .... Accrued
accrd int ...... Accrued Interest [Finance] (BARN)
ACCRDTN..... Accreditation
ACCRDTRD... Accredited
ACCRED........ Accredited (EY)
ACCRES .... Accrescinto [Increased] [Music] (ROG)
ACCRG .... Accreting (ABBR)
ACCRN .... Accretion (ABBR)
ACC-ROC ..... American Chamber of Commerce in Republic of China (EA)
ACCRS .... Ridgevalley School, Crooked Creek, Alberta [Library symbol National Library of Canada] (BIB)
ACCRT .... Accurate
ACCRU .... American Constitutional and Civil Rights Union [Defunct] (EA)
ACCRV .... Accretive (ABBR)
ACCRY .... Accessory (KSC)
ACCRY .... Accuracy (AFM)
ACCS .... Access Health [NASDAQ symbol] (TTSB)
ACCS .... Access Health Marketing, Inc. [NASDAQ symbol] (SAG)
ACCS .... Active Contamination Control Subsystem (SSD)
ACCS .... Advanced Communications Control System (CAAL)
ACCS .... Aerospace Command and Control System (SAA)
ACCS .... Afloat Command and Control System (CAAL)
ACCS .... Airborne Command and Control System
ACCS .... Airborne Command Control Squadron [Air Force] (CINC)
ACCS .... Air Command and Control System [NATO]
ACCS .... Air Controlman, Senior Chief [Navy rating]
ACCS .... Aircraft Communications System
ACCS .... American Child Care Services [Defunct] (EA)
ACCS .... American Christmas Crib Society [Defunct] (EA)
ACCS .... Amphibious Command and Control System (MCD)
ACCS .... Armored Crashworthy Crew Set (MCD)
ACCS .... Army Command and Control Study (MCD)
ACCS .... Army Command and Control System (RDA)
ACCS .... Associate of the Corporation of Secretaries [Associate of the Corp. of Certified Secretaries] [Acronym is based on former name, British] (DI)
ACCS .... Association Canadienne du Commerce des Semences (AC)
ACCS .... Association Catholique Canadienne de la Sante [Canadian-Catholic Health Association]
ACCS .... Association of Connecticut Career Schools (SRA)
ACCS .... Attitude Coordinate Converter System (AAG)
ACCS .... Automated Circulation Control System [Library management]
ACCS .... Automated Command and Control System (MCD)
ACCS .... Automated Communications and Control System [Navy] (MCD)
ACCS .... Automatic Calling Card Service [Telecommunications] (TEL)
ACCS .... Automatic Case Control System
ACCS .... Automatic Checkout and Control System
a-ccs- .... Sikiang River and Basin [China, Mainland] [MARC geographic area code Library of Congress] (LCCP)
ACC/SCN ..... Administrative Committee on Coordination - Subcommittee on Nutrition [United Nations] (EAIO)
ACCSEATO ... Air Component Commander, Southeast Asia Treaty Organization (CINC)
AccSEC .... Accounting Standards Executive Committee
ACCSFNB ..... Association des Conseillers et Conseilleres Scolaires Francophones du Nouveau-Brunswick (AC)
AccSftl .... Accent Software Intl. Ltd. [Associated Press] (SAG)
a-cc-sh .... Shansi Province [China, Mainland] [MARC geographic area code Library of Congress] (LCCP)
ACCSIC .... Atomic Collision Cross Sections Information Center [ORNL]
ACCSL .... Accessorial (AABC)
a-cc-sm .... Shanghai Municipality [China, Mainland] [MARC geographic area code Library of Congress] (LCCP)
AccSol .... Access Solutions International, Inc. [Associated Press] (SAG)
a-cc-sp .... Shantung Province [China, Mainland] [MARC geographic area code Library of Congress] (LCCP)
ACCSq .... Airborne Command Control Squadron [Air Force] (AFM)
ACCSS .... Access
a-cc-ss......... Shensi Province [China, Mainland] [MARC geographic area code Library of Congress] (LCCP)
a-cc-su .... Sinkiang Uighur Autonomous Region [China, Mainland] [MARC geographic area code Library of Congress] (LCCP)
a-cc-sz .... Szechuan Province [China, Mainland] [MARC geographic area code Library of Congress] (LCCP)
ACCT........... Academy of Canadian Cinema & Television [Academie Canadienne du Cinema et de la Television] (AC)
ACCT........... Accent
ACCT........... Accompaniment [Music]
ACCT........... Account [or Accountant] (AFM)
ACCT........... Account
acct............. Account (WDMC)
ACCT........... Accountancy
ACCT........... Accountant (ABBR)
ACCT........... Agence de Cooperation Culturelle et Technique [Agency for Cultural and Technical Cooperation] (EAIO)
ACCT........... Alliance for Coal and Competitive Transportation
ACCT........... American Chamber of Commerce in Thailand (EA)
ACCT........... American Council for Competitive Telecommunications [Formerly, Ad Hoc Committee for Competitive Telecommunications] (EA)
ACC-T.......... Association Canadienne de Cinema-Television [Canada]
ACCT.......... Association of Community College Trustees (EA)
ACCTA .... Association Canadienne du Controle du Trafic Aerien [Canadian Air Traffic Control Association - CATCA]
ACCTANT..... Accountant (DLA)

ACCTB .... Accountable (ABBR)
ACCTBNS ..... Accountableness (ABBR)
ACCTBT .... Accountability (ABBR)
ACCTBY .... Accountably (ABBR)
ACCTCY .... Accountancy
ACCTD .... Accented (WDAA)
ACCTD .... Accounted (ABBR)
ACCTG .... Accounting
ACCTG .... Accounting
acctg .... Accounting (DD)
ACCTG & FINO... Accounting and Finance Officer [*Air Force*]
a-cc-ti .... Tibetan Autonomous Region [*China, Mainland*] [*MARC geographic area code Library of Congress*] (LCCP)
ACCTID .... Account Identifier [*Computer science*]
ACCTLC .... Association of Canadian Commercial Testing Laboratories and Consultants
Acct L Rep... Accountant Law Reports [*England*] [*A publication*] (DLA)
ACCTNCY ..... Accountancy
ACCTNG ...... Accounting
ACCTNT .... Accountant (ABBR)
ACCTS .... Accounts [*Secondary school course*] [*British*]
a-cc-ts .... Tsinghai Province [*China, Mainland*] [*MARC geographic area code Library of Congress*] (LCCP)
ACCTSTR ..... Accountable Strength (AABC)
ACCTV .... Academy of Canadian Cinema and Television [*Canada*] (WWLA)
ACCTVS .... Association of CCTV [*Closed Circuit Television*] Surveyors (EAIO)
ACCTY .... Accountancy (ABBR)
ACCU .... Accugraph Corp. [*NASDAQ symbol*] (SAG)
ACCU .... Asian Confederation of Credit Unions [*of the World Council of Credit Unions*] [*Bangkok, Thailand*] (EAIO)
ACCU .... Asian Cultural Centre for UNESCO
ACCU .... Association of Catholic Colleges and Universities (EA)
ACCU .... Audio Central Control Unit (NASA)
ACCU .... Automatic Combustion Control Unmanned (PDAA)
ACCU .... Automatic Control Certified for Unattended Engine Room (DS)
ACCU .... Award Central Control Unit [*NASA*] (NASA)
ACCUCC .... Association des Coordonnateurs de Congres des Universites et des Colleges du Canada (AC)
ACCUF .... Accugraph Corp. [*NASDAQ symbol*] (TTSB)
Accugph...... Accugraph Corp. [*Associated Press*] (SAG)
Accugrph ..... Accugraph Corp. [*Associated Press*] (SAG)
AccuM .... AccuMed International, Inc. [*Associated Press*] (SAG)
ACCUM .... Accumulate (KSC)
ACCUM .... Accumulations [*Finance*]
ACCUM .... Accumulator [*Computer science*]
AccuMed...... AccuMed International, Inc. [*Associated Press*] (SAG)
ACCUMULON... Accumulation (ROG)
ACCU-OS ..... Automatic Control Certified for Unattended Engine Room - Open Seas (DS)
ACCUR......... Accurate [*or Accurately*] (MSA)
accur .... Accuratissime [*Most Carefully*] [*Pharmacy*] (DAVI)
Accur .... Accursius [*Deceased, 1263*] [*Authority cited in pre-1607 legal work*] (DSA)
ACCUS .... Accusative
ACCUS .... Automobile Competition Committee for the United States FIA [*Federation Internationale de l'Automobile*] (EA)
ACC-USA...... American Comet Club - United Spoilers of America [*Later, MERCPAC*] (EA)
AccuStff...... AccuStaff, Inc. [*Associated Press*] (SAG)
ACCUTF .... Association of Canadian College and University Teachers of French
ACCV .... Armored Cavalry Cannon Vehicle (MCD)
ACCVA .... Association Canadienne des Centres de Vie Autonome (AC)
ACCVOL .... Canadian Alliance Against Software Theft [*Alliance Canadienne Contre le vol de Logiciels*] (AC)
ACCW .... Alternating Current Continuous Wave
ACCW .... American Council for Career Women [*New Orleans, LA*] (EA)
ACCWM .... Air Cleaner Cold Weather Modulator [*Automotive engineering*]
ACCWP .... Acquisition, Cataloguing, and Circulation Working Party of the Aslib Computer Applications Group [*Banking*] (NITA)
ACCWS .... Assistant Chief, Chemical Warfare Service
ACCWS .... Auxiliary Component Cooling Water System [*Nuclear energy*] (NRCH)
ACCX .... Atchison Casting [*NASDAQ symbol*] (TTSB)
ACCX .... Atchison Casting Corp. [*NASDAQ symbol*] (SAG)
ACCY .... Accessory (AFM)
ACCY .... Accountancy (AFM)
a-ccy- .... Yellow River and Basin [*China, Mainland*] [*MARC geographic area code Library of Congress*] (LCCP)
a-cc-yu .... Yunnan Province [*China, Mainland*] [*MARC geographic area code Library of Congress*] (LCCP)
ACD .... Absolute Cardiac Dullness [*Medicine*]
ACD .... Acandi [*Colombia*] [*Airport symbol*] (OAG)
ACD .... Accede (ABBR)
ACD .... Access Control Document [*NASA*] (NASA)
ACD .... Accord (AABC)
ACD .... Accuracy Control Document (NASA)
ACD .... Accuracy Control Document (NASA)
ACD .... Acid-Citrate-Dextrose [*Hematology*]
ACD .... Actinomycin D [*Medicine*] (DMAA)
ACD .... Action-Chart Diagramer [*Computer science*]
ACD .... Active Control Device (SSD)
ACD .... Acute Coronary Disease [*Medicine*] (PDAA)
ACD .... Adapter Control Detector [*Computer science*]
ACD .... Addressed Cable Delivery (IAA)
ACD .... Adelaide College of Divinity
ACD .... Adjournment in Contemplation of Dismissal [*Law*]

ACD .... Administrative Commitment Document
ACD .... Administrative Contract Document (MCD)
ACD .... Admiralty Chart Datum (PDAA)
ACD .... Adult Celiac Disease [*Medicine*] (CPH)
ACD .... Advanced Chemistry Development
ACD .... Advanced Copies Delivered
ACD .... Aerial Control Display (IAA)
ACD .... Aerodynamic Configuration Drivers (MCD)
ACD .... Air Cavalry Division [*Army*]
ACD .... Air Condensate Drain [*Aerospace*] (AAG)
ACD .... Aircraft Damage (ADA)
ACD .... Airlift Communications Division [*Military*]
ACD .... Airline Aviation Academy, Inc. [*ICAO designator*] (FAAC)
ACD .... Alarm Control and Display (TEL)
ACD .... Allergic Contact Dermatitis [*Dermatology*]
ACD .... Alliance Centriste et Democrate [*Algeria*] [*Political party*] (EY)
ACD .... Alliance for Cultural Democracy (EA)
ACD .... Allied Civil Defense [*World War II*]
ACD .... Allied-Signal, Inc. [*Toronto Stock Exchange symbol*]
ACD .... Allocated Configuration Documentation (AAGC)
ACD .... Alternating Current Dump
ACD .... Amchitka Central D [*Alaska*] [*Seismograph station code, US Geological Survey Closed*] (SEIS)
ACD .... American Capital Income Trust [*NYSE symbol*] (SPSG)
ACD .... American Center for Design (EA)
ACD .... American College of Dentists (EA)
ACD .... Analysis and Computation Division [*National Range Operations Directorate*] [*White Sands Missile Range, NM*]
ACD .... Anamilo Club of Detroit [*Michigan*] (EA)
ACD .... Antenna Control Display
ACD .... Anterior Chamber Diameter [*Ophthalmology*] (DAVI)
ACD .... Anterior Chest Diameter
ACD .... Anticoagulant Citrate Dextrose [*Hematology*]
ACD .... Archaeologiae Christianae Doctor [*Doctor of Christian Archeology*]
ACD .... Architectural Control Document (SSD)
ACD .... Area of Cardiac Disease (MEDA)
ACD .... Area of Cardiac Dullness [*Cardiology*] (DAVI)
ACD .... Arms Control and Disarmament [*A publication*]
ACD .... Army Chaplains Department [*British military*] (DMA)
ACD .... Army Communications Division
ACD .... Assistant Command Director [*Military*] (MCD)
ACD .... Associate Creative Director [*Advertising*] (WDMC)
ACD .... Associated Construction Distributors International (EA)
ACD .... Association Canadienne des Dietetistes [*Canadian Association of Dietitians*]
ACD .... Association of Canadian Distillers [*Association des Distallateurs Canadiens*] (AC)
ACD .... Associative Computer Device
ACD .... Asymptotic Conical Dipole (PDAA)
ACD .... Attack Center Display
ACD .... Attitude Control Development [*Aerospace*] (SSD)
ACD .... Attitude Control Document (SSD)
ACD .... Attitude toward Caring for the Dying Scale
ACD .... Aulus Caius Decimus [*Coin inscription*] (ROG)
ACD .... Authorised Computer Distributors (NITA)
ACD .... Automatic Call Director [*Telecommunications*]
ACD .... Automatic Call Distribution [*Switching system*] [*Telecommunications*]
ACD .... Automatic Call Distributor [*Datapoint Corp.*] (NITA)
ACD .... Automatic Closing Device (DAC)
ACD .... Automatic Contour Digitizer
ACD .... Automatic Control Distribution (IAA)
ACD .... Aviation Commission Date (DNAB)
ACD .... Engineering, Research and Development Service [*FAA*] (TAG)
ACD .... Van Kam Am Cap Inc.Tr [*NYSE symbol*] (TTSB)
ACDA .... Afan Cooperative Development Agency [*British*]
ACDA .... Affiliate of the Company Directors' Association of Australia
ACDA .... American Choral Directors Association (EA)
ACDA .... American Commodity Distribution Association (EA)
ACDA .... American Component Dealers Association (EA)
ACDA .... Arms Control and Disarmament Act [*1961*]
ACDA .... Arms Control and Disarmament Agency [*Washington, DC*]
ACDA .... [*United States*] Arms Control and Disarmament Agency (USGC)
ACDA .... Association Canadienne de Direction D'Artists (AC)
ACDA .... Association Canadienne pour le Droit a l'Avortement [*Canadian Abortion Rights Action League - CARAL*]
ACDA .... Association of Catholic Diocesan Archivists (EA)
ACDA .... Aviation Combat Development Agency [*CDC*]
ACDA/MEA... Arms Control and Disarmament Agency Military and Economic Affairs Bureau [*Washington, DC*]
ACDAR......... Acoustic Detection and Ranging [*Geophysics*]
ACDA/WEC... Arms Control and Disarmament Agency Weapons Evaluation and Control Bureau [*Washington, DC*]
ACDA/WEC/FO... Arms Control and Disarmament Agency Weapons Evaluation and Control Bureau Field Operations Division [*Washington, DC*]
ACDB .... Airport Characteristics Data Bank [*International Civil Aviation Organization*] [*Information service or system*] (IID)
ACDB .... Army Corporate Database (GFGA)
ACDC .... Administrative Communications Distribution Center [*Air Force*] (AFM)
ACDC .... Advanced Coherent Deception Countermeasure (MCD)
A-C/D-C..... Alternating Current/Direct Current
ACDC .... Army Combat Development Committee [*British*]
ACDC .... Army Combat Developments Command
ACDC .... Assessment and Career Development Centre [*Australia*]
ACDC .... Auburn-Cord-Duesenberg Club (EA)
AC-DC .... Bisexual [*Psychiatry and infectious disease*] (DAVI)

ACDCA .... Australian Cattle Dog Club of America (EA)
ACDCS .... Automated Classified Document Control System
ACDD .... Acceded (ABBR)
ACDD .... Accreditation Council on Services for People with Developmental Disabilities (EA)
ACDDS .... Advanced Cartographic Data Digitizing System (MCD)
A CDE .... Air Commodore [RAF, RCAF]
ACDE .... American Council for Drug Education (EA)
ACDE .... Association Canadienne des Dessinateurs Editoriaux (AC)
ACDE .... Association Canadienne du Droit de l'Environnement [Canadian Association of Environmental Law]
ACDE .... Association of Commercial Diving Educators (EA)
ACDEA .... Association Canadienne des Etudes Avancees (AC)
ACDEC .... Army Combat Development Experimental Center (AAG)
ACDEPO .... Association of Civil Defence and Emergency Planning Officers [British] (DBA)
ACD-ESS ...... Automatic Call Distributor - Electronic Switching System [Telecommunications] (TEL)
ACDF .... Adult Child of a Dysfunctional Family [Psychology] (DAVI)
ACDF .... Anterior Cervical Diskectomy and Fusion [Medicine] (DAVI)
ACDFA .... American College Dance Festival Association (EA)
ACDFG .... American Committee for Democracy and Freedom in Greece (EA)
ACDG .... Acceding (ABBR)
ACDG .... Devonian Group of Charitable Foundations, Calgary, Alberta [Library symbol National Library of Canada] (NLC)
ACDH .... Deloitte, Haskins & Sells, Calgary, Alberta [Library symbol National Library of Canada] (BIB)
ACDHA .... American Cream Draft Horse Association (EA)
ACDI .... Agence Canadienne de Developpement International [Canadian International Development Agency - CIDA]
ACDI .... Agricultural Cooperative Development International (EA)
ACDI .... Associated Construction Distributors, International
ACDIFDEN .... Active Duty under Instruction in a Flying Status, Not Involving Flying [Navy] (DNAB)
ACDIFDENIS... Active Duty under Instruction in a Flying Status, Not Involving Flying [Navy] (DNAB)
ACDIFINOPS... Active Duty under Instruction in a Flying Status, Involving Operational or Training Flights [Navy] (DNAB)
ACDIFINSPRO... Active Duty under Instruction in a Flying Status, Involving Proficiency Flying [Navy] (DNAB)
ACDIFOPS.... Active Duty in a Flying Status, Involving Operational or Training Flights [Navy] (DNAB)
ACDIFOT ...... Active Duty in a Flying Status, Operational and Training Flights [Navy]
ACDIFOTCREW... Active Duty in a Flying Status, Operational and Training Flights as Crewmember [Navy]
ACDIFOTINS... Active Duty under Instruction in a Flying Status, Operational and Training Flights [Navy]
ACDIFOTINSCREW... Active Duty under Instruction in a Flying Status, Operational and Training Flights as Crewmember [Navy]
ACDIFOTINSNONCREW... Active Duty under Instruction in a Flying Status, Operational and Training Flights as Noncrewmember [Navy]
ACDIFOTNONCREW... Active Duty in a Flying Status, Operational and Training Flights as Noncrewmember [Navy]
ACDIFPRO ... Active Duty in a Flying Status, Involving Proficiency in Flying [Navy] (DNAB)
ACDIV .... Assault Craft Division (DNAB)
ACDL .... Association for Constitutional Democracy in Liberia (EA)
ACDL .... Asynchronous Circuit Design Language [Computer science] (PDAA)
ACDM .... Academe (ABBR)
ACDM .... Assessment of Career Decision Making [Vocational guidance test]
ACDM .... Association Canadienne pour les Deficients Mentaux [Canadian Association for the Mentally Retarded]
ACDM .... Association of Chairmen of Departments of Mechanics (EA)
ACDMC .... Academic
ACDMK .... Academic (ABBR)
ACDMKL .... Academical (ABBR)
ACDMKY .... Academically (ABBR)
ACDMN .... Academician (ABBR)
ACDMS .... Automated Control of a Document Management System [Computer science] (DIT)
ACDMY .... Academy (ABBR)
ACDMY .... Academy
ACDN .... Alaska Census Data Network [Alaska State Department of Labor] [Juneau] [Information service or system] (IID)
ACDNC .... Accedence (ABBR)
ACDNT .... Accident (AFM)
ACDNT .... Accident
ACDNTL .... Accidental (ABBR)
ACDNTLY ..... Accidentally (ABBR)
ACDO .... Air Carrier District Office
ACDO .... Assistant Command Duty Officer [Military] (MCD)
ACDP .... Advisory Committee on Dangerous Pathogens [British]
ACDP .... Antenna Control and Display Panel (MCD)
ACDP .... Armament Control and Display Panel (PDAA)
ACDP .... Association of Compact Disk Publishers (EA)
ACDP .... Dome Petroleum Ltd., Calgary, Alberta [Library symbol National Library of Canada] (NLC)
ACDPI .... American Cultured Dairy Products Institute (EA)
ACDPS .... Automated Cartographic Drafting and Photogrammetric System (HGAA)
ACDQ .... Association Canadienne des Detaillants en Quincaillerie (AC)
ACDR .... Acceder (ABBR)
ACDR .... Alpha-Cedrene
ACDRB .... Active Contract Data Review Board [Air Force] (AFIT)
A Cdre .... Air Commodore [RAF, RCAF] (DMA)

ACDRU .... Arms Control and Disarmament Research Unit [British]
ACDS .... Accept Data State [Computer science] (IAA)
ACDS .... Advanced Combat Direction System (MCD)
ACDS .... Advanced Command Data System (NG)
ACDS .... Advisory Committee on Dangerous Substances [British]
ACDS .... Anglo-Continental Dental Society [British]
ACDS .... Assistant Chief of Defence Staff [British Australia] (NATG)
ACDS .... Associated Chain Drug Stores (EA)
ACDS .... Association Canadienne Droit et Societe [Canadian Law and Society Association - CLSA]
ACDS .... Association for Children with Down Syndrome (EA)
ACDS .... Attitude Control and Determination Subsystem (MCD)
ACDS .... Automated Cargo Document System
ACDS .... Automatic Comprehensive Display System [Computer science]
ACDS .... Automatic Countermeasures Dispensing System (PDAA)
ACDSNSW ..... Australian Cattle Dog Society of New South Wales
Ac Ds System... Activator-Dissociation System (DOG)
ACDT .... Accident (AABC)
A CDT .... Air Commandant [British]
ACDTL .... Accidental (ABBR)
ACDTR .... Airborne Central Data Tape Recorder (MCD)
ACDU .... Active Duty
ACDUINS ...... Active Duty under Instruction [Navy]
ACDUOBLI ... Active Duty Obligation [DoD]
ACDUTRA ..... Active Duty for Training [Army] (MCD)
ACE .... Above Client Expectations [Program]
ACE .... Absorption of Conversion Electrons (IAA)
ACE .... Academic Courseware Exchange [Combined Apple University Consortium and Kinko's project] [Software distributor]
ACE .... Academie Canadienne d'Endodontie [Canadian Academy of Endodontics] (EAIO)
ACE .... Accelerated Cathode Excitation [Electricity] (IAA)
ACE .... Accelerated Christian Education [An association]
ACE .... Accelerated College Examination Board (PAZ)
ACE .... Accelerated Co-Pilot Enrichment [Program]
ACE .... Acceptance Checkout Equipment [NASA]
ACE .... Accounting, Cost, Estimating
ACE .... Acetic (ABBR)
ACE .... Acetonitrile [Organic chemistry] (BABM)
ACE .... Acknowledge Enable [Computer science] (IAA)
ACE .... Acme Electric [NYSE symbol] (TTSB)
ACE .... Acme Electric Corp. [NYSE symbol] (SPSG)
ACE .... Acquisition Career Enhancement
ACE .... Acquisition Enhancement [Program] (DOMA)
ACE .... Actinium Emanation [Chemistry] (MAE)
ACE .... Action by the Community Relating to the Environment [EC] (ECED)
ACE .... Active Color Enhancement [Proxima Corp.] [Computer science] (PCM)
ACE .... Active Corps of Executives [Maintained by the Service Corps of Retired Executives Association]
ACE .... Activity Civil Engineer (DNAB)
ACE .... Adjusted Current Earnings
ACE .... Adrenal Cortical Extract [Endocrinology]
ACe .... Adriamycin, Cyclophosphamide [Antineoplastic drug regimen]
ACE .... Adriamycin [Doxorubicin], Cyclophosphamide, Etoposide [VP-16] [Antineoplastic drug regimen] (DAVI)
ACE .... Adult and Community Education
ACE .... Adult Continuing Education (OICC)
ACE .... Advanced Certificate in Education (GAGS)
ACE .... Advanced Certificate of Education (AIE)
ACE .... Advanced Clean Emission [Automotive engineering]
ACE .... Advanced Combustion Engineering
ACE .... Advanced Communication Enhancement [Multimedia modem] [Telecommunications] (PCM)
ACE .... Advanced Compilation Equipment (MCD)
ACE .... Advanced Composition Explorer
ACE .... Advanced Composition Explorer [Satellite] [Marine science] (OSRA)
ACE .... Advanced Composition Explorer [Satellite] [NASA] (USDC)
ACE .... Advanced Compound Engine
ACE .... Advanced Computational Element (MCD)
ACE .... Advanced Computing Environment [Personal computer standard] (ECON)
ACE .... Advanced Computing Environment (CDE)
ACE .... Advanced Control Experiments (MCD)
ACE .... Advancing Careers in Engineering
ACE .... Adverse Channel Enhancement
ACE .... Advisory Centre for Education [British]
ACE .... Advocacy Centre for the Elderly (AC)
ACE .... Aerial Combat Evaluator (MCD)
ACE .... Aerobic Chair Exercise (MEDA)
ACE .... Aerosol Characterization Experiment [Marine science] (OSRA)
ACE .... Aerosol Characterization Experiment (USDC)
ACE .... Aerosol Climatic Effects [NASA]
ACE .... Aerospace Contract Engineers (MCD)
ACE .... Aerospace Control Environment [Air Force]
ACE .... Affinity Capillary Electrophoresis [An enzyme]
ACE .... After the Christian Era (BJA)
ACE .... Age Concern England [An association British]
ACE .... Agricultural Communicators in Education (EA)
ACE .... Agricultural, Construction, and Earthmoving Equipment [Acronym is the name of ametal coating painting product] [Imperial Chemical Industries Ltd.] [British]
ACE .... Aid for Commonwealth English Scheme [British]
ACE .... Aids to Communication in Education (AIE)
ACE .... Airborne Command Element [Air Force] (DOMA)

ACE............. Airborne Communications and Electronics (MCD)
ACE............. Airborne Cooperational Equipment
ACE............. Air Cargo Exhibition [*British*] (ITD)
ACE............. Air Collection and Enrichment
ACE............. Air Combat Element (MCD)
ACE............. Air Combat Emulator [*Computer game*]
ACE............. Air Combat Engagement (MCD)
ACE............. Air-Conditioning Equipment (AAG)
ACE............. Aircraft Catering Equipment [*British airlines*]
ACE............. Aircraft Condition Evaluation [*Navy*] (MCD)
ACE............. Air Crew Error (MCD)
ACE............. Air Cushion Equipment (MHDB)
ACE............. Airport Capacity Enhancement [*FAA*] (TAG)
ACE............. Airspace Control [*or Coordination*] Element [*Army*]
ACE............. Alcohol, Chloroform, Ether [*An early anesthetic mixture*]
ACE............. Alliance for Clean Energy [*Defunct*] (EA)
ACE............. Allied Command Europe [*NATO*]
ACE............. Allied Forces Central Europe [*NATO*] (MCD)
ACE............. Alternate Command Elements [*Navy*] (CINC)
ACE............. Alternating Current Electrocoagulation [*Chemical engineering*]
ACE............. Altimeter Control Equipment [*Aviation*]
ACE............. Altitude Control Electronics
ACE............. Amateur Cartoonist Extraordinary [*National Cartoonists' Society award*]
ACE............. Ambush Communication Equipment [*Military*]
ACE............. Amchitka Central E [*Alaska*] [*Seismograph station code, US Geological Survey Closed*] (SEIS)
ACE............. American Chemical Exchange
ACE............. American Cinema Editors (EA)
ACE............. American Coaster Enthusiasts (EA)
ACE............. American College of Ecology [*Defunct*] (EA)
ACE............. American College of Epidemiology (EA)
ACE............. American Council on Education (EA)
ACE............. American Council on the Environment (EA)
ACE............. AMEX [*American Stock Exchange*] Commodities Exchange
ACE............. Ammunition, Casualties, and Equipment (INF)
ACE............. Amplification Controlling Element [*Genetics*]
ACE............. Amplifier-Controlled Euphonic [*Electronics*] (IAA)
ACE............. Analysis and Control Element [*Army*]
ACE............. Analysis Coordination Element
ACE............. An Chomhairle Ealaion [*Arts Council*] (EAIO)
ACE............. Ancillary Composing Equipment (DGA)
ACE............. Angiotensin Converting Enzyme [*Medicine*] (MEDA)
ACE............. Angiotensin Converting Enzyme [*Biochemistry*]
ACE............. Animated Computer Education
ACE............. Annals of Collective Economy [*Later, Annals of Public and Co-Operative Economy*] [*A publication*]
ACE............. Anno Christianis Aerae [*In the Year of the Christian Era*] [*Latin*]
ACE............. Anode Current Efficiency [*Environmental science*]
ACE............. Antarctic Current Experiment [*Global Atmospheric Research Program*] (USDC)
ACE............. Antarctic Current Experiment [*Marine science*] (OSRA)
ACE............. April Computing Executive [*Commercial firm British*]
ACE............. Architects Council of Europe (DAC)
ACE............. Area Control Error (OA)
ACE............. Armored Combat Earthmover [*Army*]
ACE............. Armored Combat Equipment (DOMA)
ACE............. Army/American Council on Education (INF)
ACE............. Army Combat Engineers (CINC)
ACE............. Army Corps of Engineers
ACE............. Army Corps of Engineers (AAGC)
ACE............. Arrecife [*Canary Islands*] [*Airport symbol*] (OAG)
ACE............. Assessment of Combat Effectiveness [*Army*] (AABC)
ACE............. Assistant Chief of Engineers [*Military*]
ACE............. Associate Credit Executive [*Society of Certified Consumer Credit Executives*] [*Designation awarded by*]
ACE............. Associated Corpuscular Emission
ACE............. Associate of the College of Engineering [*British*] (ROG)
ACE............. Association Canadienne d'Economique [*Canadian Economics Association - CEA*]
ACE............. Association Canadienne d'Education [*Canadian Education Association - CEA*]
ACE............. Association Canadienne de l'Electricite (AC)
ACE............. Association Canadienne des Entraineurs [*Canadian Association of Coaches*]
ACE............. Association Canadienne d'Exportation [*Canadian Export Association*]
ACE............. Association for Childhood Education International
ACE............. Association for Christian Ethics [*Vatican*] (EA)
ACE............. Association for Comparative Economics [*Later, ACES*]
ACE............. Association for Continuing Education (EA)
ACE............. Association for Cooperation in Engineering [*Defunct*]
ACE............. Association for Cultural Exchange
ACE............. Association for the Conservation of Energy [*British*] (IRUK)
ACE............. Association of Clandestine Radio Enthusiasts (EA)
ACE............. Association of Collegiate Entrepreneurs (EA)
ACE............. Association of Comics Enthusiasts (EAIO)
ACE............. Association of Communication Engineers [*Charlotte, NC*] (TSSD)
ACE............. Association of Conservation Engineers (EA)
ACE............. Association of Consulting Engineers [*British*] (DI)
ACE............. Association of Consulting Engineers of Great Britain
ACE............. Association of Cooperative Educators
ACE............. Association of Cost Engineers [*British*] (DBA)
ACE............. Association of Country Entertainers (EA)
ACE............. Association of Cultural Executives [*Canada*]
ACE............. Association of Cycle Exhibitors [*Later, NABEA*] (EA)

ACE............. Asynchronous Communication Element (MHDB)
ACE............. Atlantic Center for the Environment (EA)
ACE............. Atmospheric Collection Equipment (USDC)
ACE............. Atmospheric Collection Equipment [*Marine science*] (OSRA)
ACE............. Atmospheric Control Experimentation
ACE............. Attendant Care Evaluation
ACE............. Attitude Control Electronics [*Aerospace*]
ACE............. Attorneys, Certified Public Accountants, and Enrolled Agents [*In "Operation ACE," IRS investigation of these occupations as sources of income tax evasion*]
ACE............. Audit, Control, and Evaluation (PDAA)
ACE............. Aurally Coded English [*in The ACE Spelling Dictionary*] [*British*]
ACE............. Australian Centre for Egyptology
ACE............. Australian Choreographic Ensemble
ACE............. Automated Computing Engine (PDAA)
ACE............. Automated Cost Estimates
ACE............. Automated Credit Enquiry [*British Information service or system*] (IID)
ACE............. Automatic Calling Equipment [*Telecommunications*] (BUR)
ACE............. Automatic Checkout Equipment
ACE............. Automatic Circuit Exchange
ACE............. Automatic Clutter Eliminator [*FAA*]
ACE............. Automatic Computer Evaluation (BUR)
ACE............. Automatic Computing Engine [*Early computer*] [*National Physical Laboratory*]
ACE............. Automatic Computing Equipment (IAA)
ACE............. Automatic Continuity Equipment
ACE............. Automatic Continuous Evaporation
ACE............. Automatic Control Equipment
ACE............. Automatic Controlled Exposure
ACE............. Automatic Cross-Connection Equipment [*Computer science*]
ACE............. Autumn Circulation Experiment [*Denmark, Great Britain, Norway, West Germany*] [*1987-88 Oceanography*]
ACE............. Auxiliary Conversion Equipment
ACE............. Avenger Control Electronics [*Navy*]
ACE............. Average Consumer Extraodinaire .
ACE............. Average Cumulative Error (PDAA)
ACE............. Aviation and Computer Enthusiasts [*Defunct*] (EA)
ACE............. Aviation Combat Element [*Marine Corps*] (DOMA)
ACE............. Aviation Construction Engineers [*Military*]
ACE............. Awards for Cablecasting Excellence
a-ce--.......... Ceylon [*Sri Lanka*] [*MARC geographic area code Library of Congress*] (LCCP)
ACE............. Engineering Library, City of Calgary, Alberta [*Library symbol National Library of Canada*] (BIB)
ACE............. Homer, AK [*Location identifier FAA*] (FAAL)
ACE............. Race Cargo Airlines [*Ghana*] [*ICAO designator*] (FAAC)
ACE............. World Association of Commercial and Special Vehicle Editors
ACE-11......... Adriamycin [*Doxorubicin*], Cyclophosphanide, and Etoposide in High Dose Infusion [*Vepeside*] [*Antineoplastic drug regimen*] (DAVI)
ACEA........... Air Line Communication Employees Association
ACEA........... American Cotton Exporters' Association (EA)
ACEA........... Arizona Consulting Engineers Association (SRA)
ACEA........... Assistant Civil Engineer Adviser [*Military British*]
ACEA........... Association Canadienne des Etudes Africaines [*Canadian Association of African Studies*] (EAIO)
ACEA........... Association Canadienne des Etudes Asiatiques [*Canadian Asian Studies Association - CASA*]
ACEA........... Association des Constructeurs Europeens d'Automobiles [*Association of European Car Manufacturers*] [*EC*] (ECED)
ACEA........... Association of Cost and Executive Accountants [*British*] (EAIO)
ACEA........... Australian Citrus Exporters' Association
ACEAA......... Advisory Committee on Electrical Appliances and Accessories
ACE-ACCIS... Allied Command Europe Automated Command Control and Information System [*Proposed*] [*NATO*]
ACEARTS..... Airborne Countermeasures Environment and RADAR Target Simulation
ACEAS .... Association Canadienne pour l'Etude de l'Administration Scolaire [*Canadian Association for the Study of Academic Administration*]
ACEB........... Advisory Council on Exhibition Birds [*Australia*]
ACEB........... Army Classification Evaluation Board
ACEB........... Army Clothing and Equipment Board (MCD)
ACEB........... Association Canadienne d'Entraineurs de Badminton [*Canadian Association of Badminton Coaches*]
ACEB........... Association Canadienne des Ecoles de Bibliothecaires [*Canadian Association of Library Schools*]
ACEBAC ...... Association Catholique des Etudes Bibliques au Canada [*Catholic Association of Bible Studies in Canada*]
ACEBD......... Airborne and Communications-Electronics Board [*Army*] (RDA)
ACEC........... Advisory Council on Energy Conservation [*British*]
ACEC........... American Consulting Engineers Council (EA)
ACEC........... Area of Critical Environmental Concern [*Bureau of Land Management designation*]
ACEC........... Army Communications and Electronic Command
ACEC........... Association Canadienne des Entrepreneurs en Couverture [*Canadian Association of Bedding Entrepreneurs*]
ACEC........... Association Canadienne des Etudes Cinematographiques [*Canadian Association of Film Studies*]
ACEC........... Association Canadienne pour les Etudes en Cooperation [*Canadian Association for Studies in Cooperation - CASC*]
ACEC........... Association of Canadian Editorial Cartoonists (AC)
ACEC........... Association of Consulting Engineers of Canada
ACEC........... Ateliers de Constructions Electriques de Charleroi [*SA, Belgium*] (NUCP)

ACEC............	Ateliers de Constructions Electriques de Charleroi [*Telecommunications equipment manufacturers*] [*Belgium*] (NITA)
ACECA	Association des Cooperatives d'Epargne et de Credit d'Afrique [*African Confederation of Cooperative Savings and Credit Associations - ACCOSCA*] [*Nairobi, Kenya*] (EAIO)
ACECO	Allied Commission, Economic Section [*World War II*]
ACEC/RMF ...	ACEC [*American Consulting Engineers Council*] Research and Management Foundation (EA)
AceCsh	Ace Cash Express [*Associated Press*] (SAG)
ACED	Accede (ABBR)
ACED	Advanced Communications Equipment Depot (NATG)
ACED	Aerospace Crew Equipment Development
ACED	Agnostic Christians for Equality for Dignity (EA)
ACED	Anhydrotic Congenital Ectodermal Dysplasia [*Medicine*] (DMAA)
ACED	Anticompromise Emergency Destruction (MCD)
AC Ed	Associate in Commercial Education
ACED	Association Canadienne de l'Enseignement a Distance [*Canadian Association for Distance Education - CADE*]
ACEDI	American Central European Dental Institute
ACED-I........	Association of Conference and Events Directors-International (EA)
ACEE...........	Adult Cost per Entered Employment [*Job Training and Partnership Act*] (OICC)
ACEE	Air Combat Engagement Experiment
ACEE	Aircraft Emission Estimator (MCD)
ACEE	Aircraft Energy Efficiency (MCD)
ACEE	Air Craft Energy Efficiency
ACEE	Area Council for Economic Education (EA)
ACEE	Association Canadienne des Etudes Ecossaises [*Canadian Association for Scottish Studies - CASS*]
ACEEA.........	Association Canadienne pour l'Etude de l'Education des Adultes [*Canadian Association for the Study of Adult Education - CASAE*]
ACEEE.........	American Council for an Energy Efficient Economy (EA)
ACEF...........	Adult Children Educational Foundation (EA)
ACEF	Adult Christian Education Foundation (EA)
ACEF	Asian Cultural Exchange Foundation (EA)
ACEF	Association Canadienne d'Etudes Fiscales (AC)
ACEF	Association Canadienne pour les Etudes du Folklore [*Canadian Folklore Studies Association*]
ACEF	Association Canadienne pour les Etudes sur les Femmes [*Canadian Women's Studies Association - CWSA*]
ACEF	Association of Commodity Exchange Firms [*Later, Futures Industry Association*] (EA)
ACEF	Australian Council of Employers' Federations
ACEF du Nord...	Association Cooperative d'Economie Familiale - Montreal (Nord) (AC)
ACEFEL.......	Arctic Construction and Frost Effects Laboratory [*Army*] (PDAA)
ACEFO	Association Canadienne des Etudes Finno-Ougriennes [*Finno-Ugrian Studies Association - FUSAC*]
ACEGB	Association of Consulting Engineers of Great Britain
ACEH	Acid Cholesteryl Ester Hydrolase [*An enzyme*]
ACEH	Association Canadienne des Etudes Hongroises [*Canadian Association of Hungarian Studies - CAHS*]
ACEHSA......	Accrediting Commission on Education for Health Services Administration (EA)
ACEI...........	Association for Childhood Education International (EA)
ACEI...........	Association of Consulting Engineers of Ireland (EAIO)
ACEJ..........	American Council on Education for Journalism [*Later, ACEJMC*] (EA)
ACEJMC......	Accrediting Council on Education in Journalism and Mass Communications (EA)
ACEL..........	Accelerate (ABBR)
ACEL..........	Aerospace Crew Equipment Laboratory [*Philadelphia, PA*] (MCD)
ACEL..........	Air Crew Equipment Laboratory (MCD)
ACEL..........	Alfacell Corp. [*NASDAQ symbol*] (SAG)
ACELA........	Association Canadienne des Etudes Latino-Americaines [*Canadian Association of Latin American Studies - CALAS*]
ACELAC......	Association Canadienne des Etudes Latino-Americaines et Caraibes [*Canadian Association of Latin American and Caribbean Studies*]
ACE/LACE	Air Cycle Engine / Liquid Air Cycle Engine (SAA)
ACELD........	Accelerated (ABBR)
ACELF........	Association Canadienne d'Education de Langue Francaise (AC)
ACELG	Accelerating (ABBR)
ACELLC.......	Association Canadienne pour l'Etude de la Litterature et des Langues du Commonwealth [*Canadian Association for Commonwealth Literature and Language Studies - CACLALS*]
ACELN	Acceleration (ABBR)
ACELP........	Algebraic Code-Excited Linear Prediction (ACRL)
ACELR........	Accelerator (ABBR)
ACELS........	Accelerates (ABBR)
ACE Ltd.	ACE Ltd. [*Associated Press*] (SAG)
ACELV........	Accelerative (ABBR)
ACEM..........	Actinium Emanation [*Chemistry*] (IAA)
ACEM..........	Association Canadienne des Editeurs de Musique [*Canadian Music Publishers Association - CMPA*]
ACEM..........	Association of Consulting Engineers of Manitoba (AC)
ACEM..........	Aviation Chief Electrician's Mate [*Navy*]
ACEM..........	Southern Materials Resource Centre, Alberta Education, Calgary, Alberta [*Library symbol National Library of Canada*] (NLC)
ACEMA........	Australian Computer Equipment Manufacturers' Association
A Cemb........	A Cembalo [*Music*]
ACEMB.......	Annual Conference on Engineering in Medicine and Biology (HGAA)
ACEMIS.......	Automated Communications and Electronics Management Information System [*Army*]
ACEN	Academy of Chief Executive Nurses of Teaching Hospitals (AC)
ACEN	Alberta Environment, Calgary, Alberta [*Library symbol National Library of Canada*] (NLC)

ACEN	Assembly of Captive European Nations (EA)
ACEN	Association Canadienne des Enseignants Noirs [*Canadian Association of Black Teachers*]
ACENET.......	Allied Command Europe Communications Network [*NATO*] (NATG)
ACENOE......	Assistance aux Createurs d'Entreprises du Nord-Ouest Europeen [*Multinational organization*] (EAIO)
ACEO	Association of Chief Education Officers [*British*] (BI)
ACE-OCE	Army Corps of Engineers, Office of the Chief Engineer (AAGC)
ACEORP.......	Automotive and Construction Equipment Overhaul and Repair Plant [*Navy*]
ACEP..........	Advisory Committee on Export Policy [*Department of Commerce*]
ACEP..........	American College of Emergency Physicians (EA)
ACEP..........	American Council for Emigres in the Professions [*Defunct*] (EA)
ACEP..........	Arms Control Education Project [*Defunct*] (EA)
ACEP..........	Asahi Chemical Exchange Process [*Nuclear energy*] (NUCP)
ACEP...........	Association Canadienne des Etudes Patristiques [*Canadian Society of Patristic Studies - CSPS*]
ACEP..........	Association Canadienne des Etudes Prospectives [*Canadian Association for Future Studies - CAFS*]
ACEP..........	Associations Canadienne pour l'Education Pastorale (AC)
ACEP..........	Australian Council of Egg Producers
ACEP..........	Parts Source [*NASDAQ symbol*] (TTSB)
ACEP..........	Parts Source, Inc. (The) [*NASDAQ symbol*] (SAG)
ACEPD.........	Automotive and Construction Equipment Parts Depot [*Navy*]
ACEPU........	Association Canadienne des Eaux Potables et Usees (AC)
ACEQ	Association Canadienne des Editeurs de Quotidiens [*Canadian Association of Newspaper Editors*]
ACEQ	Association des Conseillers en Environnement du Quebec (AC)
ACER	Afro-Caribbean Educational Resource Centre [*British*]
ACER	Afro-Caribbean Educational Resource Project (AIE)
ACER	Alberta Energy Resources Conservation Board, Calgary, Alberta [*Library symbol National Library of Canada*] (NLC)
ACER	American Council of Executives in Religion [*Defunct*] (EA)
ACER	Ancient Classics for English Readers [*A publication*]
ACER	Association Canadienne pour les Etudes Rurales [*Canadian Association of Rural Studies - CARS*]
ACER	Association for Canada Educational Resources (AC)
ACERA	Air Carrier Economic Regulation Act
ACERC	Army Coastal Engineering Research Center
ACEREP	Allied Command Europe Report (AFM)
ACERM	Cereal Municipal Library, Alberta [*Library symbol National Library of Canada*] (NLC)
ACERP	Advanced Communications-Electronics Requirements Plan [*Air Force*]
ACERR........	Energy Resources Research, Calgary, Alberta [*Library symbol National Library of Canada*] (NLC)
ACERS	Allied Command Europe Reporting System
ACerS	American Ceramic Society (EA)
ACERT	Advisory Committee for the Education of Romany and Other Travellers
ACertCM	Archbishop of Canterbury's Certificate in Church Music [*British*] (DBQ)
A certificate...	Adult Certificate [*Board of Film Censors*] [*British*] (WDMC)
ACES...........	Acceptance Checkout and Evaluation System [*NASA*] (NASA)
ACES...........	Acceptance Control Equipment Section [*or System*] [*NASA*] (NASA)
ACES...........	(Acetamidol)Aminoethanesulfonic Acid [*A buffer*]
ACES...........	Acoustic Containerless Experiment System [*Materials processing*]
ACES...........	Action Chretienne pour l'Eglise du Silence [*Belgium*]
ACES...........	Advanced Concept Ejection Seat [*Aviation*] (MCD)
ACES...........	Advanced Concept Escape System (MCD)
ACES...........	Advisory Council on Education Statistics [*Department of Education*] (GFGA)
ACES...........	Aerolineas Centrales de Colombia [*Airline*] [*Colombia*]
ACES...........	Air Carrier Engineering Service
ACES...........	Air Collection and Enrichment System
ACES...........	Air Collection Engine System
ACES...........	Air Combat Expert Simulation [*Military*] (RDA)
ACES...........	Alert Citizens for Environmental Safety [*Formed to protect West Texas and the US/Mexico border region's natural resources*] (CROSS)
ACES...........	Amer Casino Enterprises [*NASDAQ symbol*] (TTSB)
ACES...........	American Casino Enterprises, Inc. [*NASDAQ symbol*] (NQ)
ACES...........	American Catholic Esperanto Society (EA)
ACES...........	Americans for the Competitive Enterprise System [*Later, ACEE*] (EA)
ACES...........	Annual Cycle Energy System [*Energy Research and Development Adminintration*]
ACES...........	Antisubmarine Composite Engineering Squadron
ACES...........	Area Cooperative Educational Services [*Information service or system*]
ACES...........	ARMMS [*Automated Reliability and Maintenance Management System*] Control Executive System [*NASA*]
ACES...........	Army Career Education System
ACES...........	Army Communications Electronics School (MCD)
ACES...........	Army Communications Equipment Support (MCD)
ACES...........	Army Continuing Education System
ACES...........	Army Continuing Evaluation Services
ACES...........	Army Controlling Education Service
ACES...........	Associated Collectors of El Salvador (EA)
ACES...........	Association for Children for Enforcement of Support (EA)
ACES...........	Association for Comparative Economic Studies [*Notre Dame, IN*] (EA)
ACES...........	Association for Counselor Education and Supervision (EA)
ACES...........	Association of Consulting Engineers of Saskatchewan (AC)
ACES...........	Assurance Control Economics System (MUGU)
ACES...........	Automated Camera Effects System

ACES............ Automated Circulation and Enquiry System [*University of Aberdeen*] [*British*] (NITA)
ACES............ Automated Code Evaluation System
ACES............ Automatically Controlled Electrical System [*NASA*] (MCD)
ACES............ Automatic Checkout and Evaluation System [*Air Force*]
ACES............ Automatic Checkout Equipment Sequencer (NASA)
ACES............ Automatic Control Evaluation Simulator [*Spaceflight training machine*]
ACES............ Resource Centre, City of Calgary Electric System, Alberta [*Library symbol National Library of Canada*] (NLC)
ACE-S/C ...... Acceptance Checkout Equipment - Spacecraft [*NASA*] (KSC)
ACESG .... American Council on Educational Simulation and Gaming
AcesHlt .... Access Health Marketing, Inc. [*Associated Press*] (SAG)
ACESIA .... American Council for Elementary School Industrial Arts [*Later, TECC*] (EA)
ACESIS .... Army Corps of Engineers Socioeconomic Information System [*Information service or system*] (IID)
ACESS .... Accessory (IAA)
ACESS .... Advanced Cabin Entertainment and Services System [*Aircraft*]
ACESS .... Association Canadienne des Ecoles du Service Social [*Canadian Association of Schools of Social Work - CASSW*]
ACESW .... Association of Chief Education Social Workers [*British*] (DBA)
acet............. Acetate (VRA)
ACET/.......... Aceto Corp. [*NASDAQ symbol*] (NQ)
Acet............. Acetone [*Medicine*]
ACET........ Acetylene (MSA)
ACET........ Advisory Committee on Electronics and Telecommunications [*International Electrotechnical Commission*] [*ISO*] (DS)
ACET........ Advisory Council for the Elimination of Tuberculosis
ACET........ Advisory Council on Education and Training (AIE)
ACET........ Association Canadienne des Ecoles de Traduction
ACET........ Association Canadienne des Employes de Telephone [*Canadian Telephone Employees' Association - CTEA*]
ACET........ Association Canadienne des Entreprises de Telecommunications [*Canadian Association of Telecommunication Businesses*]
ACET........ Association for Educational Communications and Technology (NTCM)
ACET........ Automatic Cancellation of Extended Targets (AABC)
ACETA......... Association Canadienne des Employes du Transport Aerien [*Canadian Air Line Employees' Association - CALEA*]
ACETL.......... Acetylene (ABBR)
Aceto .... Aceto Corp. [*Associated Press*] (SAG)
ACETS......... Air-Cushion Equipment Transportation System
ACETS......... Association of California Enhanced Telemessaging Services (SRA)
acetyl-CoA ... Acetylcoenzyme A [*Biochemistry*] (DAVI)
ACEU .... Aerocontrol Electronics Unit [*NASA*] (NASA)
ACEUM .... Association Canadienne des Ecoles Universitaires de Musique [*Canadian Association of University Schools of Music - CAUSM*]
ACEUN .... Association Canadienne des Ecoles Universitaires de Nursing [*Canadian Association of University Schools of Nursing - CAUSN*]
ACEUR .... Allied Command Europe [*NATO*]
ACEVAL....... Air Combat Evaluation (MCD)
ACEVAL/AIMVAL... Air Combat Evaluation / Air Intercept Missile Evaluation (PDAA)
ACEWA .... American Committee on East-West Accord [*Later, ACUSSR*] (EA)
ACF............. Abbreviated Cost Form (MCD)
ACF............. Aboriginal Cultural Foundation [*Australia*]
ACF............. Academic Computer Facility [*Roosevelt University*] [*Research center*] (RCD)
ACF............. Academie Canadienne Francaise [*French-Canadian Academy*] [*French*] (BARN)
ACF............. Access Control Facility
ACF............. Access Control Field [*Computer science*] (ACRL)
ACF............. Access Cost Factor [*Telecommunications*] (TEL)
ACF............. Accessory Clinical Findings [*Medicine*]
ACF............. Acid Concentrator Feed [*Nuclear energy*] (NRCH)
ACF............. Acid-Fast Culture [*Biochemistry*] (DAVI)
ACF............. ACM Government Opportunity Fund [*NYSE symbol*] (SAG)
ACF............. Acquisition Career Field [*Army*] (RDA)
ACF............. Activated Carbon Fiber
ACF............. Active Citizen Force [*British military*] (DMA)
ACF............. Active Contract File [*DoD*]
ACF............. Acute Care Facility [*Medicine*]
ACF............. Address Census [*or Control*] File [*Bureau of the Census*] (GFGA)
ACF............. Address Control File [*US Census Bureau*]
ACF............. Administration for Children and Families [*Department of Health and Human Services*]
ACF............. Advanced Collaborative Filtering [*Firefly Network*] [*Computer science*]
ACF............. Advanced Communication Facility
ACF............. Advanced Communications Function [*IBM Corp.*] [*Computer science*]
ACF............. African Colonial Forces [*British military*] (DMA)
ACF............. African Cultural Foundation (EA)
ACF............. Air California (MCD)
ACF............. Air Charter [*France ICAO designator*] (FAAC)
ACF............. Air Combat Fighter (MCD)
ACF............. Airlift Contingency Forces [*Marine Corps*] (DOMA)
ACF............. Alberta Choral Federation (AC)
ACF............. Alberta Curling Federation (AC)
ACF............. All-Craft Foundation (EA)
ACF............. All for the Children Foundation [*Defunct*] (EA)
ACF............. Alternate Command Facility [*Navy*] (NVT)
ACF............. Alternate Communications Facility [*Military*]
ACF............. Amchitka Central F [*Alaska*] [*Seismograph station code, US Geological Survey Closed*] (SEIS)
ACF............. American Car and Foundry
ACF............. American Checker Federation (EA)

ACF............. American Chess Foundation (EA)
ACF............. American Chestnut Foundation (EA)
ACF............. American Choral Foundation (EA)
ACF............. American Coal Foundation (EA)
ACF............. American Conservatives for Freedom (EA)
ACF............. American Crime Fighters (EA)
ACF............. American Crossword Federation (EA)
ACF............. American Culinary Federation (EA)
ACF............. Americans for Constitutional Freedom [*Later, MC/ACF*] (EA)
ACF............. Americredit Corp. [*NYSE symbol*] (SAG)
ACF............. AmeriCredit Corp. [*NYSE symbol*] (TTSB)
ACF............. Analog Computer Facility
ACF............. APE [*Automatic Processing Equipment*] Control Facility
ACF............. Appeal of Conscience Foundation (EA)
ACF............. Area Computing Facilities (CET)
ACF............. Area Confinement Facility [*Military*] (AABC)
ACF............. Area Control Facility [*FAA*] (TAG)
ACF............. Area Control Facility (GAVI)
ACF............. Area Coverage File (MCD)
ACF............. Army Cadet Force [*Military unit*] [*British*]
ACF............. Army Club Fund
ACF............. Army College Fund
ACF............. Asian Club Federation (EAIO)
ACF............. Association of Connecticut Fairs (SRA)
ACF............. Association of Consulting Foresters (EA)
ACF............. Australian Calisthenics Federation
ACF............. Australian Children's Foundation
ACF............. Australian Commission for the Future
ACF............. Australian Cotton Foundation
ACF............. Authorization Control Facility [*Computer access security software*] (NITA)
ACF............. Autocorrelation Function [*Statistics*]
ACF............. Automatic Control Features (NRCH)
ACF............. Automatic Cop Feeder (PDAA)
ACF............. Axisymmetrical Conical Flow
ACF............. Foothills Pipe Lines (Yukon) Ltd., Calgary, Alberta [*Library symbol National Library of Canada*] (NLC)
ACF............. Les Arrets de la Cour Federale [*Legal database, Department of Justice*] [*Canada*] (NITA)
ACFA .... American Cat Fanciers Association (EA)
ACFA .... American Council for Free Asia (EA)
ACFA .... Army Cadet Force Association [*British military*] (DMA)
ACFA .... Association Canadienne de Football Amateur [*Canadian Association of Amateur Football*]
ACFA .... Association Canadienne des Femmes Arabes (AC)
ACFA .... Association Canadienne-Francaise de l'Alberta (AC)
ACFA .... Association of Commercial Finance Attorneys (EA)
ACFA .... Association of Consulting Foresters of Australia
ACFA .... Australian Cane Farmers' Association
ACFAF......... Australian Cystic Fibrosis Associations Federation
ACFAO .... American College of Foot and Ankle Orthopedics and Medicine (DMAA)
ACFARS .... Advisory Committee on Fisheries Applications of Remote Sensing [*Australia*]
ACFAS .... American College of Foot and Ankle Surgeons (DMAA)
ACFAS .... Association Canadienne-Francaise pour l'Avancement des Sciences
ACFAT......... Aircraft Carrier Firefighting Assistance Team (DNAB)
ACFB .... Association Canadienne Fournisseurs Bibliotheque [*Canadian Association of Library Suppliers*]
ACFC........... Abbott and Costello Fan Club (EA)
ACFC........... American Center of Films for Children (EA)
ACFC........... Anne Christy Fan Club (EA)
ACFC........... Archie Campbell Fan Club [*Defunct*] (EA)
ACFC........... Association of Canadian Film Craftspeople (AC)
ACFC........... Association of Canadian Financial Corporations (AC)
ACFC........... Association of Commercial Finance Companies of New York [*Later, NCFA*] (EA)
ACFC........... Aviation Chief Fire Controlman [*Navy*]
ACFC........... Fluor Canada Ltd., Calgary, Alberta [*Library symbol National Library of Canada*] (NLC)
ACFD........... Association of Canadian Faculties of Dentistry
ACFE........... American Car and Foundry, Electronics
ACFE........... Association Canadienne des Fondements de l'Education (AC)
ACFE........... Association Canadienne pour la Formation des Enseignants (AC)
ACFEA......... Air Carrier Flight Engineers Association
ACFEL......... Arctic Construction and Frost Effects Laboratory [*Boston, MA*] [*Army*]
ACFF........... Affinity Cross-Flow Filtration
ACFF........... Air Cargo Fast Flow (DA)
ACFF........... Alternating Current Flip-Flop (IAA)
ACFF........... Australian Cranio-Facial Foundation
ACFFTU....... All Ceylon Federation of Free Trade Unions
ACFG .... Automatic Continuous Function Generation [*Computer science*]
ACFH .... Foothills Hospital, Calgary, Alberta [*Library symbol National Library of Canada*] (NLC)
ACFHE .... Association of Colleges for Further and Higher Education [*British*] (EAIO)
ACFI........... Advisory Committee on Flight Information [*FAA*]
ACFI........... American Car and Foundry Industries
ACFIA......... Associated Committee of Friends on Indian Affairs (EA)
ACFL........... Access Floor [*Technical drawings*]
ACFL........... Association Canadienne de Financement et de Location (AC)
ACFL........... Atlantic Coast Football League
ACFM.......... Actual Cubic Feet per Minute (NRCH)
ACFM.......... Association Culturelle Franco-Manitobaine (AC)
ACFM.......... Association of Cereal Food Manufacturers (EAIO)

ACFM-FC ..... Association of Canadian Fire Marshals & Fire Commissioners [*L'Association Canadienne des Directeurs et Commissaires des Incendies*] (AC)
ACF-MR .... Accreditation Council for Facilities for the Mentally Retarded
ACFN .... American Committee for Flags of Necessity [*Later, FACS*] (EA)
ACFNA .... Anarchist-Communist Federation of North America [*Canada*]
ACFNSW ...... Accountants' Fellowship of New South Wales [*Australia*]
ACFNY .... Asthmatic Children's Foundation of New York (EA)
ACFO .... American College of Foot Orthopedists (EA)
ACFO .... Assistant Chief Fire Officer [*British*]
ACFO .... Association Canadienne-Francaise de l'Ontario (AC)
ACFO .... Association of Car Fleet Operators [*British*] (DBA)
ACFOD-USA... Asian Cultural Forum on Development - USA [*Defunct*] (EA)
ACFOR .... Association Canadienne des Cadres en Informatique [*Canadian Association of Information Officials*]
ACFP.......... Advanced Computer Flight Plan [*Air Force*] (GFGA)
ACFP.......... Association Candienne de la Formation Professionelle (AC)
ACFPC .... Arms Control and Foreign Policy Caucus (EA)
ACFPP .... Association Canadienne des Fabricants de Panneaux de Particules (AC)
ACFQ .... Association Cooperative Feminine du Quebec (AC)
ACFR .... Advisory Council on Federal Reports
ACFR .... American College of Foot Roentgenologists [*Later, American College of Podiatric Radiologists*] (EA)
ACFR .... Association Canadienne des Femmes en Radio et Television (AC)
ACFRE .... Advanced Certified Fund-Raising Executive (NFD)
ACFRE .... Advanced Certified Fund Raising Executive [*National Society of Fund Raising Executives*]
ACFS.......... Advanced Concepts Flight Simulator (GAVI)
ACFS.......... American College of Foot Specialists [*Later, ACCE*] (EA)
ACFS.......... American College of Foot Surgeons (EA)
ACFS.......... Assistant Chief of Fleet Support [*Navy British*]
ACFS.......... Australia-China Friendship Society
ACFSA .... American Correctional Food Service Association (EA)
AC FT.......... Acre Foot (ABBR)
ACFT........... Aircraft (AFM)
ACFT........... Aircraft Flying Training
ACFTC......... Aircraft Carrier (ABBR)
AcftCrmnBad... Aircraft Crewman Badge [*Military decoration*] (AABC)
ACFTTBI....... Aircraft to Be Identified [*Aviation*] (AIA)
ACFTU........ All-China Federation of Trade Unions [*Communist China*]
ACFUCY .... Actinomycin D, Fluorouracil, Cyclophosphamide [*Antineoplastic drug regimen*]
ACFUSA....... Anti-Cancer Foundation of the Universities of South Australia
ACFVI......... Australian Chamber of Fruit and Vegetable Industries
ACF/Vtam..... Advanced Control Function/Virtual Telecommunications Access Method [*IBM Corp.*] (NITA)
ACFWI-EC .... Association of the Cider and Fruit Wine Industry of the EC [*Economic Community*] [*Belgium*] (EAIO)
ACG .... Academie Canadienne du Genie [*Canadian Academy of Engineering*] (EAIO)
AcG............. Accelerator Globulin [*Medicine*]
ACG .... ACM Government Income Fund [*NYSE symbol*] (SPSG)
ACG .... ACM Gvt Income Fund [*NYSE symbol*] (TTSB)
ACG .... Activated Charcoal Granule (PDAA)
ACG .... Acycloguanosine [*Also, ACV, Acyclovir*] [*Antiviral compound*]
ACG .... Address Coding Guide
ACG .... Adjacent Charging Group [*Telecommunications*] (TEL)
ACG .... Advanced Computing Group (USDC)
ACG .... Advanced Computing Group [*Marine science*] (OSRA)
ACG .... Advanced Concepts Group
ACG .... African Cavalry Guard [*British military*] (DMA)
ACG .... Airborne Coordinating Group
ACG .... Air Cargo Express, Inc.
ACG .... Air Cargo Glider
ACG .... Air-Core Gauge (RDA)
ACG .... Airline Carriers of Goods
ACG .... Air London [*British ICAO designator*] (FAAC)
ACG .... Alpha Control Guidance
ACG .... Alphanumeric Character Graphic [*Computer science*] (ECII)
ACG .... Alternating Current Generator
ACG .... Aluminium Can Group [*Australia An association*]
ACG .... American College of Gastroenterology (EA)
ACG .... American Council on Germany (EA)
ACG .... An Comunn Gaidhealach [*The Highland Association*] (EA)
ACG .... Angiocardiography [*Medicine*]
ACG .... Angle Closure Glaucoma [*Ophthalmology*]
ACG .... Annual Capital Grant [*Education*] (AIE)
ACG .... Aortocoronary Graft [*Cardiology*] (DMAA)
ACG .... Apex Cardiogram [*Medicine*]
ACG .... Area Coordination Group [*Air Force*] (AABC)
ACG .... Arts Centre Group (EAIO)
ACG .... Assistant Chaplain-General [*British*]
ACG .... Assistant Commissary General
ACG .... Association Canadienne des Geographes [*Canadian Association of Geographers*]
ACG .... Association for Corporate Growth [*Deerfield, IL*] (EA)
ACG .... Atlantic Energy [*Vancouver Stock Exchange symbol*]
ACG .... Atmospheric Composition Payload Group [*NASA*] (SSD)
ACG .... Auto Car Guard
ACG .... Automatic Code Generator
ACG .... Automatic Correlation Guidance
ACG .... Automotive Component Group [*Automotive engineering*]
ACG .... Auxiliary Coastguard [*British*]

ACG .... Glenbow-Alberta Institute, Calgary, Alberta [*Library symbol National Library of Canada*] (NLC)
ACGA .... American Carnival Glass Association (EA)
ACGA .... American Community Gardening Association (EA)
ACGA .... American Council on Gift Annuities (NFD)
ACGA .... American Cranberry Growers' Association [*Defunct*] (EA)
ACGA .... American Cricket Growers Association [*Defunct*] (EA)
ACGA .... American Cut Glass Association (EA)
ACGA .... Arizona Cotton Growers Association (SRA)
ACGA .... Association Canadienne de Gestion des Achats [*Purchasing Management Association of Canada - PMAC*]
ACGA .... Australian Cashmere Growers' Association
ACGA .... Australian Coffee Growers Association
ACGB .... Aircraft Corp. of Great Britain (OA)
ACGB .... Arts Council of Great Britain
ACGBI .... Automobile Club of Great Britain and Ireland [*Later, Royal Automobile Club*]
ACGC .... American Checkered Giant Club [*Later, ACGRC*]
ACGC .... American Custard Glass Collectors (EA)
ACGC .... Angurugu Community Government Council [*Australia*]
ACGC .... Association of Country Greyhound Clubs [*Australia*]
ACGC .... Australian Chicken Growers' Council
ACGCA .... Advent Christian General Conference of America (EA)
ACGD .... Association for Corporate Growth and Diversification [*Later, ACG*] (EA)
ACGE .... Association Canadienne du Genie Eolien [*Canada*]
ACGF .... American Child Guidance Foundation [*Defunct*] (EA)
ACGF .... Australian Cherry Growers' Federation
ACGF .... Autocovariance Generating Function [*Statistics*]
ACGG .... American Custom Gunmakers Guild (EA)
ACGG .... Associate Committee of Geodesy and Geophysics [*Canada*]
ACGH .... Calgary General Hospital, Alberta [*Library symbol National Library of Canada*] (NLC)
ACGI .... Associate of the City and Guilds of London Institute [*British*]
ACGIH......... American Conference of Governmental Industrial Hygienists (EA)
ACGM .... Advisory Committee on Genetic Manipulation [*Health and Safety Executive*] [*British*]
ACGM .... Aircraft Carrier General Memorandum
ACGME .... Accreditation Council for Graduate Medical Education [*American Medical Association*]
AC GN SCH... Acidic Gneisses and Schists [*Agronomy*]
ACGO .... Gulf Canada Ltd., Calgary, Alberta [*Library symbol National Library of Canada*] (NLC)
ACGP .... American College of General Practice [*Later, ACM*] (EA)
ACGp .... Area Coordination Group [*Air Force*] (AFM)
ACGP .... Army Career Group
ACGPOMS.... American College of General Practitioners in Osteopathic Medicine and Surgery (EA)
ACGPS .... Association Canadienne pour la Gestion de la Production et let Stocks [*Also, APICS Region VIII*] (AC)
ACGPSP....... Association Canadienne de la Gestion du Personnel des Services Publics [*Canadian Association of Public Service Personnel Management*]
ACGR .... Associate Committee on Geo-Technical Research [*Canada*] (HGAA)
ACGR .... Association Canadienne des Gerants de la Redaction [*Canadian Association of Editorial Directors*]
ACGRA........ Australian Cotton Growers' Research Association
ACGRC........ American Checkered Giant Rabbit Club (EA)
ACGS .... Acting Commissary General of Subsistence [*Army*]
ACGS .... Aerospace Cartographic and Geodetic Service
ACGS .... American-Canadian Genealogical Society (EA)
ACGS .... American Council on German Studies
ACGS .... Assistant Chief of the General Staff [*Military British*]
ACGSC .... Army Command and General Staff School
ACGS(OR).... Assistant Chief of the General Staff (Operational Requirements) [*British*] (RDA)
ACGSq .... Aerial Cartographic and Geodetic Squadron [*Air Force*] (AFM)
ACGT .... Antibody-Coated Grid Technique [*Medicine*] (DMAA)
ACGTL .... Alberta Gas Trunk Line Co. Ltd., Calgary, Alberta [*Library symbol National Library of Canada*] (NLC)
ACGWC........ AIDS Committee of Guelph & Wellington County (AC)
ACH .... Acetone Cyanohydrin [*Organic chemistry*] (PDAA)
ACh .... Acetylcholine [*Biochemistry*]
ACH .... Acetylcholinesterase [*An enzyme*] (PDAA)
Ach .... Acharnenses [*Acharnians*] [*of Aristophanes*] [*Classical studies*] (OCD)
Ach .... Achiasaph (BJA)
ach............. Acholi [*MARC language code Library of Congress*] (LCCP)
ACH .... Achondroplasia [*Medicine*]
ACH .... Acknowledge Hold [*Computer science*] (IAA)
ACH .... Acquisition Command Headquarters (AFIT)
ACH .... Active Chronic Hepatitis [*Medicine*] (DMAA)
ACH .... Adrenal Cortical Hormone [*Endocrinology*]
ACH .... Advanced Chain Home [*RADAR*]
ACH .... Aftercoming Head [*Obstetrics*]
ACH .... Air Change per Hour [*Ventilation and infiltration rates*]
ACH .... Air Cleaner Housing [*Automotive engineering*]
ACH .... Aircrafthand [*British*]
ACH .... Aircraft Hangar (MCD)
ACH .... Alexander Haagen Properties [*AMEX symbol*] (TTSB)
ACH .... Alexander Haagen Property, Inc. [*AMEX symbol*] (SPSG)
ACH .... Aluminum Chlorohydrate [*Inorganic chemistry*]
ACH .... American Center for Homeopathy (EA)
ACH .... American College of Heraldry (EA)
ACH .... Amyotrophic Cerebellar Hypoplasia [*Medicine*] (DMAA)

ACH .... Anglican Church Handbooks [*A publication*]
A Ch............ Ante Christum [*Before Christ*] [*Latin*]
ACH .... Anton Chico, NM [*Location identifier FAA*] (FAAL)
ACH .... Area Combined Headquarters [*World War II*] (DMA)
ACH .... Arm Girth, Chest Depth, and Hip Width [*Anatomical index*]
ACh .... Associate of the Institute of Chiropodists [*British*] (DBQ)
ACH .... Association Canadienne des Hispanistes [*Canadian Association of Hispanists - CAH*]
ACH .... Association Canadienne des Humanites [*Humanities Association of Canada - HAC*]
ACH .... Association for Computers and the Humanities (EA)
ACH .... Association of Caribbean Historians [*Nassau, Bahamas*] (EAIO)
ACH .... Association of Comparative Haematology [*British*] (DBA)
ACH .... Association of Contemporary Historians (EA)
ACH .... Association of Cosmetologists and Hairdressers (EA)
ACH .... Attempts per Circuit per Hour [*Telecommunications*] (TEL)
ACH .... Autocorrelation Histogram [*Statistics*]
ACH .... Automated Clearinghouse [*Banking*]
ACH .... Barcklay Flying Service [*ICAO designator*] (FAAC)
a-ch--.......... China, Republic of [*Taiwan*] [*MARC geographic area code Library of Congress*] (LCCP)
a-ch--.......... Formosa [*MARC geographic area code Library of Congress*] (LCCP)
ACH .... Home Oil Co. Ltd., Calgary, Alberta [*Library symbol National Library of Canada*] (NLC)
ACh .... L'Astrologie Chaldeenne [*A publication*] (BJA)
ACHA .... Accion Chilena Anticomunista [*Chilean Anticommunist Action*] [*Political party*] (EY)
ACHA .... American Catholic Historical Association (EA)
ACHA .... American College Health Association (EA)
ACHA .... American College of Hospital Administrators [*Later, ACHE*] (EA)
ACHA .... American Coon Hunters Association (EA)
ACHA .... American Council of Highway Advertisers (EA)
ACHA .... Arizona Clearing House Association (SRA)
ACHA .... Association Canadienne de Hockey Amateur [*Canadian Amateur Hockey Association - CAHA*]
ACHA .... Hardy Associates, Calgary, Alberta [*Library symbol National Library of Canada*] (NLC)
ACHAB .... Association des Centres Hospitaliers et Centres d'Accueil Prives du Quebec (AC)
ACHAM .... Champion Public Library, Alberta [*Library symbol National Library of Canada*] (NLC)
ACHAS .... Haverlift Systems Ltd., Calgary, Alberta [*Library symbol National Library of Canada*] (NLC)
ACHC .... Association to Combat Huntington's Chorea [*British*] (EAIO)
ACHC .... Holy Cross Hospital, Calgary, Alberta [*Library symbol National Library of Canada*] (NLC)
ACHCA .... American College of Health Care Administrators (EA)
ACHCA .... Australian Catholic Health Care Association
ACHCL .... Academy for Catholic Health Care Leadership [*Defunct*] (EA)
ACHCR .... American Council for Health Care Reform (EA)
ACHCU .... Canadian Union College, College Heights, Alberta [*Library symbol National Library of Canada*] (NLC)
ACHD .... Ached (ABBR)
ACHD .... Association of California Hospital Districts (SRA)
Achdny........ Archdeanery
ACHDU .... Association Canadienne de l'Habitation et du Developpement Urbain [*Canadian Association of Housing and Urban Development*]
ACHDWU .... All-Ceylon Harbor and Dock Workers' Union
AChE .... Acetylcholinesterase [*An enzyme*] (OA)
ACHE .... Action Committee for Higher Education [*Defunct*] (EA)
ACHE .... American College of Healthcare Executives (EA)
ACHE .... American Council for Headache Education [*Medicine*]
ACHE .... American Council of Hypnotist Examiners (EA)
ACHE .... Association for Continuing Higher Education (EA)
ACHE .... Canadian Hunter Exploration Ltd., Calgary, Alberta [*Library symbol National Library of Canada*] (NLC)
A Chem .... Associate in Chemistry
ACHEMA ...... Air Cooled Heat Exchanger Manufacturers Association [*Defunct*] (EA)
ACHEMA ...... Ausstellungs-Tegung fuer Chemisches Apparatewesen [*Triennial international chemical engineering exhibition*]
AChemS ...... Association for Chemoreception Sciences (EA)
ACHET .... Asociacion Chilena de Empresas de Turismo [*Chile*] (EY)
ACHEX .... Aerosol Characterization Experiment (PDAA)
ACHFS .... Father R. Perin School, Chard, Alberta [*Library symbol National Library of Canada*] (BIB)
ACHG .... Aching (ABBR)
ACHG .... American Citizens for Honesty in Government [*Defunct*] (EA)
ACHI .... Application Channel Interface (TEL)
ACHI .... Association for Childbirth at Home, International (EA)
ACHIEV .... Achievement (ABBR)
Achil .... Achilleis [*of Statius*] [*Classical studies*] (OCD)
ACHL .... American Council for Healthful Living (EA)
ACHM .... Chauvin Municipal Library, Alberta [*Library symbol National Library of Canada*] (BIB)
ACHN .... Army Community Health Nursing [*Army*]
ACHO .... American College of Home Obstetrics (EA)
ACHO .... Husky Oil Operations, Calgary, Alberta [*Library symbol National Library of Canada*] (NLC)
ACHOBS ...... Assistant Chief Observer [*Navy*] (NVT)
ACHOD........ Acoustic Helicopter Overflight Detector (MCD)
ACHOO........ Autosomal-Dominant Compelling Helioophthalmic Outburst
ACHP .... Advisory Committee On Highway Policy [*MTMC*] (TAG)
ACHP .... Advisory Council on Historic Preservation (NRCH)

ACHP .... Association Canadienne d'Hygiene Publique [*Canadian Association of Public Health*]
ACHQ .... Area Combined Headquarters [*World War II*]
AChR .... Acetylcholine Receptor [*Also, AcChR*] [*Biochemistry*]
ACHR .... Achromatic (ABBR)
ACHR .... American Committee for Human Rights (EA)
ACHR .... American Council of Human Rights [*Later, PHR*] (EA)
AChr .... Ante Christum [*Before Christ*] [*Latin*]
ACHR .... Argentine Commission for Human Rights (EA)
AChRAb .... Acetylcholine Receptor Antibody [*Immunology*]
ACHRC .... Alberta Children's Hospital Research Centre [*Canada*] (IRC)
ACHRE .... Advisory Committee on Human Radiation Experiments
ACHRM .... Achromatism (ABBR)
ACHRMTK.... Achromatic (ABBR)
AChrn .... Ante Christum Natum [*Before Christ's Birth*] [*Latin*]
ACHROM...... Achromatism (ABBR)
ACHRT .... Achromaticity (ABBR)
ACHRU .... Association Canadienne d'Habitation et de Renovation Urbaine (AC)
ACHRY .... Achromatically (ABBR)
ACHS .... Aches (ABBR)
ACHS .... American Camp and Hospital Service
ACHS .... American Catholic Historical Society (EA)
AChS .... Associate of the Society of Chiropodists [*British*]
ACHS .... Association of College Honor Societies (EA)
ACHS .... Association of Community Home Schools [*British*]
ACHS .... Automatic Checkout System [*NASA*] (AAG)
ACHS .... Chevron Canada Resources Ltd., Calgary, Alberta [*Library symbol National Library of Canada*] (NLC)
ACHSA .... American Correctional Health Services Association (EA)
ACHSWW.... American Committee on the History of the Second World War (EA)
ACHU .... Aircrew Holding Unit [*British military*] (DMA)
ACHUD........ Advisory Committee to the Department of Housing and Urban Development
ACHV .... Achieve (ABBR)
ACHVB .... Achievable (ABBR)
ACHVD .... Achieved (ABBR)
ACHVE .... Achieve (ABBR)
ACHVG .... Achieving (ABBR)
ACHVIT .... Achievement
ACHVMNT.... Achievement
ACHVNT....... Achievement (ABBR)
ACHVR .... Achiever (ABBR)
ACHVT .... Achievement (ABBR)
ACI............. Accelerated Capabilities Initiative [*Office of naval research*]
ACI............. Accrued Comprehensive Income (DICI)
ACI............. Acid [*Pharmacy*] (ROG)
ACI............. Acoustic Comfort Index
ACI............. Actual Cost Incurred [*Accounting*] (MCD)
ACI............. Acute Coronary Insufficiency (HGAA)
ACI............. Adenylate Cyclase Inhibitor [*Biochemistry*]
ACI............. Adjacent Channel Interference
ACI............. Adjusted Calving Interval [*Dairy science*] (OA)
ACI............. Adrenal Cortical Insufficiency [*Endocrinology*] (MAE)
ACI............. Adult-Child Interaction [*Test*]
ACI............. Advanced Chip Interconnect [*Computer science*]
ACI............. Advanced Communications Interface [*Computer science*] (DGA)
ACI............. Advancing the Consumer Interest [*A publication*]
ACI............. [*The*] Advertising Council, Inc. (NTCM)
ACI............. After-Care Instructions [*Medicine*] (DAVI)
ACI............. Age Controlled Item (NASA)
ACI............. Agence Congolaise d'Information [*Congolese Information Agency*] (AF)
ACI............. Airborne Controlled Intercept [*Air Force*]
ACI............. Air Caledonie International [*France ICAO designator*] (FAAC)
ACI............. Air Combat Information
ACI............. Air Combat Intelligence [*Obsolete Navy*]
ACI............. Air Control Intercept
ACI............. Air Council Instruction [*World War II*]
ACI............. Air Couriers International, Inc. [*Defunct*] (TSSD)
ACI............. Aircraft Condition Inspection (MCD)
ACI............. Air Curtain Incinerator (MCD)
ACI............. Alderney [*Channel Islands*] [*Airport symbol*] (OAG)
ACI............. Alderney [*United Kingdom*] [*Airport symbol*] (AD)
ACI............. Alliance Co-Operative Internationale [*International Co-Operative Alliance*] (EAIO)
ACI............. Allocated Configuration Identification [*NASA*] (KSC)
ACI............. Allocated Configuration Item [*Navy*]
ACI............. Alloy Casting Institute [*Later, SFSA*] (EA)
ACI............. Altered Commercial Item (MCD)
ACI............. Alternating Current Input (MHDI)
ACI............. Altitude Command Indicator
ACI............. American Canvas Institute
ACI............. American Carpet Institute [*Later, CRI*] (EA)
ACI............. American Concrete Institute (EA)
ACI............. American Conference Institute (AAGC)
ACI............. Amplifier-Control Intercommunications (MCD)
ACI............. Analytical Condition Inspection [*Air Force*] (MCD)
ACI............. Anticlonus Index [*Neurology*] [*Medicine*] (DAVI)
ACI............. Anti-Communism International (EAIO)
ACI............. Anti-Communist International (EA)
ACI............. Approved Consumer Information
ACI............. Arcavacata [*Italy*] [*Seismograph station code, US Geological Survey*] (SEIS)
ACI............. Arlen Communications, Inc. [*Bethesda, MD*] [*Information service or system Telecommunications*] (TSSD)

ACI	Army Council Instruction [*World War II*]
ACI	Ashland Coal [*NYSE symbol*] (SPSG)
ACI	Aspiryl Chloride [*Organic chemistry*] (MAH)
ACI	Assist Card International (EA)
ACI	Associate of the Institute of Commerce [*British*] (DCTA)
ACI	Association Canadienne de l'Immeuble [*Canadian Real Estate Association - CREA*]
ACI	Association Canadienne de l'Imprimerie (EAIO)
ACI	Association Canadienne de l'Informatique [*Canadian Information Processing Society - CIPS*]
ACI	Association for Conservation Information (EA)
ACI	Association for Cultural Interchange (EA)
ACI	Association of Canadian Interpreters
ACI	Association of Chinese from Indochina [*Later, SEAC*] (EA)
ACI	Association of Commerce and Industry (EA)
ACI	Assure Contre l'Incendie [*Insured Against Fire*] [*French*]
ACI	Asynchronous Communications Interface [*Computer science*] (HGAA)
ACI	Attitude Control Indicator [*Aerospace*] (IAA)
ACI	Austrian Cultural Institute (EA)
ACI	Author Comfort Index [*Publishing*]
ACI	Automated Car Identification [*Railroads*]
ACI	Automatic Card Identification
ACI	Automatic Closure and Interlock [*Nuclear energy*] (NRCH)
ACI	Automatic Control Instrumentation
ACI	Automobile Club of Italy (BARN)
ACI	Awana Clubs International (EAIO)
ACI	ESSO [*Standard Oil*] Resources Canada Ltd., Calgary, Alberta [*Library symbol National Library of Canada*] (NLC)
ACIA	Agricultural Construction Industry Association [*British*] (EAIO)
ACIA	Alabama Concrete Industries Association (SRA)
ACIA	Alabama Crop Improvement Association (SRA)
ACIA	Alternative Center for International Arts (EA)
ACIA	Arizona Construction Industry Association (SRA)
ACIA	Arizona Crop Improvement Association (SRA)
ACIA	Associated Cooperage Industries of America (EA)
ACIA	Associate of the Corporation of Insurance Agents (ODBW)
ACIA	Asynchronous Communications Interface Adapter [*Computer science*] (MDG)
ACIA	Australian Chemical Industry Council
ACIA	Aviation Career Incentive Act [*1974*] (AABC)
ACIA	Western Regional Office, Parks Canada [*Bureau Regional de l'Quest, Parcs Canada*] Calgary, Alberta [*Library symbol National Library of Canada*] (NLC)
ACIArb	Associate of the Chartered Institute of Arbitrators [*British*] (DBQ)
ACIAS	American Council of Industrial Arts Supervisors (EA)
ACIAS	Association des Cadres Intermediaires des Affaires Sociales (AC)
ACIASAO	American Council of Industrial Arts State Association Officers [*Later, CTEA*] (EA)
ACIATE	American Council on Industrial Arts Teacher Education [*of the International Technology Education Association*] [*Later, CTTE*] (EA)
ACIB	Air Characteristic Improvement Board [*Navy*] (DOMA)
ACIB	Associate of the Corporation of Insurance Brokers [*Canada*] (DD)
ACIB	Associate of the Corporation of Insurance Brokers [*British*]
ACIB	Association Canadienne de l'Industrie du Bois (AC)
ACIBD	Association des Createurs et Intervenants de la Bande Dessinee (AC)
ACIBM	American Center for Immuno-Biology and Metabolism
ACIBS	Australian Council of Independent Business Schools
ACIC	Acicular (ABBR)
ACIC	Aeronautical Chart and Information Center [*St. Louis, MO*] [*Later, DMAAC*] [*Air Force*]
ACIC	Aeronautical Charting and Information Center [*Marine science*] (OSRA)
ACIC	Air Corps Information Circular [*Obsolete*]
ACIC	Albanian Catholic Information Center (EA)
ACIC	Allied Captured Intelligence Center [*US and Britain*]
ACIC	American Committee for International Conservation (EA)
ACIC	Apollo Contractor Information Center [*NASA*] (KSC)
ACIC	Associate of Canadian Institute of Chemistry
ACIC	Association Canadienne pour l'Integration Communautaire [*Canadian Association for Community Living*] (EAIO)
ACIC	Association des Cadres d'Institutions Culturelles (AC)
ACIC	Association of California Insurance Companies (SRA)
ACIC	Australian Citrus Industry Council
ACIC	Automatic Combat Intelligence Center (MCD)
ACIC	Auxiliary Combat Information Center
ACICAFE	Association du Commerce et de l'Industrie du Cafe dans la CEE [*Association for the Coffee Trade and Industry in the EEC*]
ACICO	Assistant Combat Information Center Officer (MUGU)
ACICO	Association of Community Information Centres in Ontario (AC)
ACICS	Accrediting Council for Independent Colleges and Schools (PGP)
ACIC-TC	Aeronautical Chart and Information Center Technical Translation Section [*Air Force*]
ACID	Acceleration, Cruising, Idling, Deceleration (MHDI)
ACID	Acidus [*Acid*] [*Latin*] (ROG)
ACID	Adriamycin, Cyclophosphamide, Dacrabazine [*DTIC*], Actinomycin D [*Antineoplastic drug regimen*] (DAVI)
ACID	Aircraft Identification (KSC)
ACID	Arithmetic, Coding, Information, and Digit Symbols [*Psychometrics*]
ACID	Association of Canadian Industrial Designers
ACID	Association of Colleges Implementing the Diploma of Higher Education [*British*]
ACID	Atomicity, Consistency, Isolation, and Durability
ACID	Attempted Corporate Integration of Dividends [*Economics*]

ACID	Automatic Classification and Interpretation of Data (BUR)
ACIDO	Association of Chartered Industrial Designers of Ontario (AC)
ACID test	Atomicity, Consistency, Isolation, and Durability Test (DOM)
ACIDY	Allied Commission, Industry Subcommission [*World War II*]
ACIF	Abell Cluster Inertial Frame [*Cosmology*]
ACIF	All Canada Insurance Federation
ACIF	American Collectors of Infant Feeders (EA)
ACIF	Anticomplement Immunofluorescence Test [*Immunochemistry*]
ACIF	Artillery Counterfire Information [*Army*] (ADDR)
ACIF	Associacao Catolica Interamericana de Filosofia (EAIO)
ACIFIC	Aspartame Committee of the International Food Information Council (EA)
ACIG	Advanced Computer Image Generator (MCD)
ACIG	Information Group West Corp., Calgary, Alberta [*Library symbol National Library of Canada*] (BIB)
ACIGS	Assistant Chief of the Imperial General Staff [*British*]
ACIGY	Advisory Council of the International Geophysical Year
ACII	Associate of the Chartered Insurance Institute [*British*] (EY)
ACII	Association Canadienne des Implantes Intraoculaires [*Canadian Implant Association*] (EAIO)
ACIIB	American Civilian Internee Information Bureau [*Army*] (AABC)
ACIIB(Br)	American Civilian Internee Information Bureau (Branch) (GFGA)
ACIID	[*A*] Critical Insight into Israel's Dilemmas [*Jewish student newspaper*]
ACIIP	Association Canadienne des Infirmieres et Infirmiers Pediatriques (AC)
ACIIST	Association Canadienne des Infirmieres et Infirmiers en Sante du Travail [*Formerly, National Association of Occupation Health Nurses*] (AC)
ACIIW	American Council of the International Institute of Welding (EA)
ACIL	Aberration-Compensated Input Lens [*Optics*]
ACIL	American Center for International Leadership (EA)
ACIL	American Council of Independent Laboratories (EA)
ACIL	Automatic Controlled Instrument Landing (NASA)
ACILA	Associate of the Chartered Institute of Loss Adjustors [*Insurance*]
ACILL	Australian Construction Industry Law Letter [*A publication*]
ACIM	Accident Cost Indicator Model [*US Bureau of Mines*]
ACIM	Advanced Common Intercept Missile (MCD)
ACIM	American Committee on Italian Migration (EA)
A-CIM	Apparel-Computer Integrated Manufacturing Center [*Research center*] (RCD)
ACIM	Auxiliary Computer Input Multiplexer
ACIM	Availability Centered Inventory Model (MCD)
ACIM	Axis Crossing Interval Meter [*SONAR*]
ACIMD	Advanced Common Intercept Missile Demonstration (MCD)
ACIMO	Association de Coureurs Internationaux en Multicoques Oceaniques [*Association of International Competitors on Oceanic Multihulls*] (EAIO)
ACIMS	Aerial Color Infrared Management System (MCD)
ACIMS	Aircraft Component Intensive Management System [*Military*] (AABC)
ACINF	Advisory Committee on Irradiated and Novel Foods [*Government body*] [*British*]
ACINF	Airborne Acoustic Information System (Intelligence)
ACI-NM	Association of Commerce and Industry of New Mexico (SRA)
ACINT	Acoustic Intelligence [*Military*] (NG)
ACINTEL	Assistant Chief of Staff, Intelligence (NATG)
ACIO	Aeronautical Chart and Information Office [*Air Force*] (SAA)
ACIO	Air Combat Intelligence Office [*or Officer*] [*Navy*]
ACIOA	Advisory Committee on International Oceanographic Affairs [*British*]
ACIOP	Atlantic Command Intelligence Operating Procedures (MCD)
ACIOPJF	Association Catholique Internationale des Oeuvres de Protection de la Jeune Fille [*Later, ACISJF*]
ACIP	Active Certificate Information Program [*for stock certificates*] [*Computer science*]
ACIP	Acute Canine Idiopathic Polyneuropathy [*Veterinary science*] (DMAA)
ACIP	Advisory Committee on Immunization Practices [*Public Health Service*]
ACIP	Advisory Committee on Immunization Practices
ACIP	Aerodynamic Coefficient Identification Package (NASA)
ACIP	Aerodynamic Coefficient Instrumentation Package (NASA)
ACIP	Airport Capital Improvement Program [*OST*] (TAG)
ACIP	American College of International Physicians (EA)
ACIP	American Council on International Personnel [*New York, NY*] (EA)
ACIP	Analytical Condition Inspection Program [*Air Force*] (MCD)
ACIP	Attack Center Indicator Panel
ACIP	Aviation Career Incentive Pay [*Air Force*] (AFM)
ACIPH	Agence de Cooperation Internationale Pour l'Integration Economique et Sociale des Personnes Handicapees (AC)
ACIPRD	Production Research Division, Esso Resources Canada Ltd., Calgary, Alberta [*Library symbol National Library of Canada*] (NLC)
ACIPS	Accoustic Information Processing System [*Navy*] (DOMA)
ACIQ	Association des Commissaires Industriels du Quebec (AC)
ACIR	Advisory Commission on Intergovernmental Relations [*Washington, DC*]
ACIR	Association Culturelle Internationale: Reliance [*Leucate, France*] (EAIO)
ACIR	Automotive Crash Injury Research
ACIR	Aviation Crash Injury Research (MUGU)
ACIRC	Air Circulating
AC/IREF	American Chapter, International Real Estate Federation (EA)
ACIS	Acoustic Control Induction System [*Automotive engineering*]
ACIS	Acoustic Control Induction System
ACIS	Advanced Credit Information System
ACIS	Aeronautical Chart and Information Squadron [*Air Force*] (DNAB)
ACIS	Africa Church Information Service (EAIO)

ACIS............ Air Cargo Integrated System (MCD)
ACIS............ Aircraft Crew Interphone System (MCD)
ACIS............ American Committee for Irish Studies (AEBS)
ACIS............ American Conference for Irish Studies (EA)
ACIS............ American Council for International Studies (EA)
ACIS............ American Council on International Sports (EA)
ACIS............ Armament Control Indicator Set (DWSG)
ACIS............ Arms Control Impact Statement (MCD)
ACIS............ Army Combat Identification Systems
ACIS............ Associate of the Chartered Institute of Secretaries [Later, Institute of Chartered Secretaries and Administrators] [British] (EY)
ACIS............ Association pour la Cooperation Islamique [Senegal] (EY)
ACIS............ Automated Claims Information System [Air Force] (DNAB)
ACIS............ Avionics, Control, and Information Systems (MCD)
ACIS............ Infocon Information Services Ltd., Calgary, Alberta [Library symbol National Library of Canada] (NLC)
ACIS............ US Army Combat Identification System (RDA)
ACISJF......... Association Catholique Internationale des Services de la Jeunesse Feminine [International Catholic Society for Girls] [Geneva, Switzerland] (EAIO)
ACISQ .... Aeronautical Chart and Information Squadron [Air Force]
ACISSSQ....... Association des Cadres Intermediaires de la Sante et des Services Sociaux du Quebec (AC)
AcIT .... Academie Internationale du Tourisme [International Academy of Tourism] (EAIO)
ACIT............ ACI Telecentrics, Inc. [NASDAQ symbol] (SAG)
ACIT............ Adaptive Subbands Excited Transform [Telecommunications] (OSI)
ACIT............ Association des Chimistes de l'Industrie Textile [Association of Chemists of the Textile Industry] (EAIO)
ACIT............ Association of Chemical Industry of Texas (SRA)
ACI TIcn....... ACI Telecentrics, Inc. [Associated Press] (SAG)
ACITS.......... Advisory Committee on Information Technology Standardization [Commission of the European] (NITA)
ACITT.......... Association for Computers and Information Technology in Teaching (AIE)
ACIU .... Allied Central Interpretation Unit [World War II]
ACIU .... ASAP and Computer Interface Unit
ACIWLP .... American Committee for International Wild Life Protection [Later, ACIC] (EA)
ACJ............. Acromioclavicular Joint [Anatomy] (DAVI)
ACJ............. Air Correction Jet [Automotive engineering]
ACJ............. American Citizens for Justice [An association] (EA)
ACJ............. American Committee on Japan (EA)
ACJ............. American Council for Judaism (EA)
ACJ............. Americus, GA [Location identifier FAA] (FAAL)
ACJ............. Ancillae Sacri Cordis Jesu [Handmaids of the Sacred Heart of Jesus] [Roman Catholic religious order]
ACJ............. Andean Commission of Jurists [See also CAJ] (EAIO)
ACJ............. Asociacion Cristiana de Jovenes [Young Men's Christian Association] (EAIO)
ACJ............. Associate in Criminal Justice
ACJ............. Attitude Control Jet [Aerospace]
ACJ............. Handmaids of the Sacred Heart of Jesus (TOCD)
ACJ............. Sacred Heart College, Cullman, AL [Library symbol Library of Congress] (LCLS)
ACJA.......... American Congregation of Jews from Austria (EA)
ACJA.......... American Criminal Justice Association [A publication] (DLA)
ACJA-LAE .... American Criminal Justice Association - Lambda Alpha Epsilon (EA)
ACJC.......... Association Catholique de la Jeunesse Canadienne-Francaise [Catholic Association of Francophone Youth] [Canada]
ACJI........... A Coeur Joie International [An association] (EAIO)
ACJ (Mad Pr)... Accident Compensation Journal [Madhya Pradesh, India] [A publication] (DLA)
ACJP .... Air Correction Jet-Primary [Automotive engineering]
ACJS.......... Academy of Criminal Justice Sciences (EA)
ACJS.......... Air Correction Jet-Secondary [Automotive engineering]
ACJS.......... Alliance Carpenters and Joiners Society [A union] [British]
ACJSS......... Associated Carpenters and Joiners Society of Scotland [A union]
ACK........... Acklands Ltd. [Toronto Stock Exchange symbol]
ACK........... Acknowledge (AFM)
ACK........... Acknowledgement [Telecommunications] (OSI)
ack............ Acknowledgment (WDMC)
ACK........... Acknowledgment Character [Keyboard] [Computer science]
ACK........... Affirmative Acknowledge [Computer Science] (NITA)
ACK........... Air Cape [ICAO designator] (FAAC)
ACK........... Altitude Conversion Kit
ACK........... American Committee for KEEP (EA)
ACK........... Armstrong World Indus [NYSE symbol] (TTSB)
ACK........... Armstrong World Industries, Inc. [Formerly, Armstrong Cork Co.] [NYSE symbol] (SPSG)
ACK........... Assistant Cook [British military] (DMA)
ACK........... Automatic Color Killer [Video recording]
ACK........... Automatic Course Keeping (IAA)
ACK........... Nantucket [Massachusetts] [Airport symbol] (OAG)
ACK0.......... Even Positive Acknowledgment [Computer science] (IBMDP)
ACK1.......... Odd Positive Acknowledgment [Computer science] (IBMDP)
ACKB.......... Acknowledgeable (ABBR)
AckCom .... Ackerley Communications, Inc. [Associated Press] (SAG)
ACK'D .... Acknowledged [Business term]
ACKD.......... Acquired Cystic Kidney Disease [Medicine] (DMAA)
ACKG .... Acknowledging (ABBR)
AckGrp .... Ackerley Group [Associated Press] (SAG)
ACKGT .... Acknowledgment
ACKI........... Acknowledge Input [Computer science] (IAA)
ackl............ Acknowledgement (WDMC)

ACKNE........ Acknowledge
ACKNOWL.... Acknowledgement (DLA)
ACKNT........ Acknowledgment (ROG)
ACKO.......... Acknowledge Output [Computer science] (IAA)
ACKT.......... Acknowledgment (ABBR)
ACKTX........ Automatic Circuit Exchange (MSA)
ACL........... Access Control List [Computer science] (HGAA)
ACL........... Accion Ciudadana Liberal [Liberal Citizens' Action] [Spain Political party] (PPE)
ACL........... Accumulated Leading (DGA)
ACL........... ACE Limited [NYSE symbol] (TTSB)
ACL........... ACE Ltd. [NYSE symbol] (SPSG)
ACL........... Achilles Resources [Vancouver Stock Exchange symbol]
ACL........... Acromioclavicular Line [Anatomy] (DAVI)
ACL........... Action-Centered Leadership [Management term]
ACL........... Add and Carry Logical Word (SAA)
ACL........... Adjective Check List [Psychology]
ACL........... Advanced CMOS Logic [Texas Instruments, Inc.]
ACL........... Aeronautical Computers Laboratory [Johnsville, PA] [Navy]
ACL........... Agent Collaboration Language [Computer science] (RDA)
ACL........... Air Capitol [Italy ICAO designator] (FAAC)
ACL........... Air Cleaner Gasket [Automotive engineering]
ACL........... Aircraft Cargo Loader (DWSG)
ACL........... Aircraft Circular Letter (MCD)
ACL........... Aircraft Control Link
ACL........... Aircraft Load
ACL........... Alberta Case Locator [University of Alberta] [Canada Information service or system] (CRD)
ACL........... Alberta Education Libraries [Professional collection] [UTLAS symbol]
ACL........... Alicudi [Lipari Islands] [Seismograph station code, US Geological Survey] (SEIS)
ACL........... Allen Cognitive Levels Test
ACL........... Allowable Cabin Load [in an aircraft]
ACL........... Allowable Cargo Load [Air Force] (AFIT)
ACL........... Allowable Cleanliness Level [Industrial maintenance and engineering]
ACL........... Allowable Container Load [in an aircraft] (NASA)
ACL........... Alternaria Citri (Lemon race) [A toxin-producing fungus]
ACL........... Alternate Concentration Limit [Nuclear energy] (NRCH)
ACL........... Alternative Concentration Limits [Environmental Protection Agency] (EPA)
ACL........... Altimeter Check Location [Aviation] (FAAC)
ACL........... Ambassador College, Pasadena, CA [OCLC symbol] (OCLC)
ACL........... American Classical League (EA)
ACL........... American Coalition for Life (EA)
ACL........... American Collegians for Life (EA)
ACL........... American Commercial Lines, Inc.
ACL........... American Committee for Liberation [Later, RFE/RL]
ACL........... American Consultants League (EA)
ACL........... Aminocaprolactam [Organic chemistry]
ACL........... Analytical and Computer Laboratory
ACL........... Analytical Chemistry Laboratory [Department of Energy]
ACL........... Anterior Cruciate Ligament [Anatomy]
ACL........... Anti-Catholic League (EA)
ACL........... Antigen-Carrier Lipid [Immunology]
ACL........... Application Control Language [Computer science] (BUR)
ACL........... Ascent Closed Loop (MCD)
ACL........... Associated California Loggers (SRA)
ACL........... Association Canadienne Linguistique [Canadian Linguistic Association - CLA]
ACL........... Association for Community Living (SRA)
ACL........... Association for Computational Linguistics (EA)
ACL........... Association of Certified Liquidators (EA)
ACL........... Association of Christian Librarians (EA)
ACL........... Association of Cinema Laboratories [Later, ACVL] (EA)
ACL........... Atlantic Coast Line R. R. [AAR code]
ACL........... Atlantic Container Line [British]
ACL........... Atlas Commercial Language [Computer science] (BUR)
ACL........... Attained Competency Level
ACL........... Audit Command Language
ACL........... Australian Companies Legislation [A publication]
ACL........... Authorized Consumption List [Military] (AABC)
ACL........... Automated Coagulation Laboratory
ACL........... Automatic Carrier Landing System [Military]
ACL........... Automator Control Language [Computer science]
ACL........... Aviation Circular Letter
ACL........... Avionics Cooling Loop (MCD)
ACL........... Law Society of Alberta, Calgary, Alberta [Library symbol National Library of Canada] (NLC)
ACL........... Monsanto Chemical Co. [Research code symbol]
ACLA.......... American Citizens and Lawmen Association (EA)
ACLA.......... American Clinical Laboratory Association (EA)
ACLA.......... American Comparative Literature Association (EA)
ACLA.......... American Cotton Linter Association [Defunct] (EA)
ACLA.......... American Country Life Association (EA)
ACLA.......... Anti-Communist League of America (EA)
ACLA.......... Association Canadienne de Linguistique Appliquee [Canadian Association of Applied Linguistics - CAAL]
ACLA.......... Australian Commercial Law Association
ACLA.......... Australian Criminal Lawyers' Association
ACLA.......... Lavalin Services, Inc., Calgary, Alberta [Library symbol National Library of Canada] (NLC)
ACLAE........ Association Canadienne des Laboratoires d'Analyse Environmenmentale (AC)
AClaim......... American Claims Evaluators [Associated Press] (SAG)

ACLALS........	Association for Commonwealth Literature and Language Studies (EAIO)
ACLAM........	American College of Laboratory Animal Medicine (EA)
ACLANT.......	Allied Command Atlantic [*NATO*]
ACLANTREP...	Allied Command Atlantic Reporting System [*NATO*] (MCD)
ACLAR.........	Claresholm Public Library, Alberta [*Library symbol National Library of Canada*] (NLC)
AClasVoy.....	American Classic Voyages, Inc. [*Associated Press*] (SAG)
ACL AT........	Australian Current Law Articles [*A publication*]
ACLB...........	Aircraft Launching Bulletin
ACLB...........	Association of Christians in Local Broadcasting [*British*]
ACLB...........	Australian Corporation Law Bulletin [*A publication*]
ACLBIMET.....	Air Cleaner Bi-Metal Sensor [*Automotive engineering*]
ACLC..........	Adaptive Communication Live Controller (MCD)
ACLC..........	Air Cadet League of Canada [*World War II*]
AC/LC.........	Anti-Axial Compression/Liquid Chromatography
ACLC..........	Assessment of Children's Language Comprehension [*Education*]
ACLC..........	Association Canadienne de Litterature Comparee [*Canadian Comparative Literature Association - CCLA*]
AC/LC.........	Auto/Axial Compression/Liquid Chromatography
ACLCP........	Associated College Libraries of Central Pennsylvania [*Library network*]
ACLCP........	Australian Community Languages and Cultural Program
ACLCS........	Airborne Command-Launch Control Subsystem (CAAL)
ACLD..........	Above Clouds [*Aviation*] (FAAC)
ACLD..........	Accolade (ABBR)
ACLD..........	Aircooled (MSA)
ACLD..........	Association for Children with Learning Disabilities [*Later, LDA*] (EA)
ACLDB........	Army Central Logistics Data Bank (AABC)
AcLDL........	Acetylated Low-Density Lipoprotein [*Biochemistry*]
ACLDV........	Air Cleaner Duct and Valve [*Automotive engineering*]
ACLE..........	Accel International Corp. [*Formerly, Acceleration Corp.*] [*NASDAQ symbol*] (NQ)
ACLE..........	Accel Intl. [*NASDAQ symbol*] (TTSB)
ACLE..........	Association Canadienne des Laboratoires d'Essais [*Canadian Testing Association*] (AC)
ACLE..........	Automatic Clutter Eliminator (MSA)
ACLEA........	Association of Continuing Legal Education Administrators (EA)
ACLF..........	Adult Congregate Living Facilities [*Military*]
ACLF..........	Advisory Committee on Live Fish [*Australia*]
ACLG..........	Air-Cushion Landing Gear
ACLI..........	Adrian C. and Leon Israel [*in company name "ACLI International"*]
ACLI..........	American Council of Life Insurance [*Washington, DC*] (EA)
ACLI..........	Clive Public Library, Alberta [*Library symbol National Library of Canada*] (NLC)
ACLIC.........	Association of California Life Insurance Companies (SRA)
ACLICS.......	Airborne Communications Location Identification and Collection System
ACLID.........	Australian Corporate Law [*Database*]
ACLIM........	Acclimate (ABBR)
ACLIMD.......	Acclimated (ABBR)
ACLIMG.......	Acclimating (ABBR)
ACLIMN.......	Acclimation (ABBR)
ACLIMZ.......	Acclimatize (ABBR)
ACLIMZD.....	Acclimatized (ABBR)
ACLIMZG.....	Acclimatizing (ABBR)
ACLIMZN.....	Acclimatization (ABBR)
ACLIQ........	Association de Climatologie du Quebec (AC)
ACLJ..........	American Center for Law and Justice [*Located on Pat Robertson's estate*] [*Virginia Beach, VA*] (ECON)
ACLJ..........	American Civil Law Journal [*A publication*] (DLA)
ACLLS........	Association for Commonwealth Literature and Languages Studies
ACLLS........	Little Buffalo School, Cadotte Lake, Alberta [*Library symbol National Library of Canada*] (BIB)
ACLM.........	Acclaim (ABBR)
ACLM.........	American College of Legal Medicine (EA)
ACLM.........	Antigua Caribbean Liberation Movement [*Political party*] (EAIO)
ACLM.........	Association of Contact Lens Manufacturers [*British*] (DBA)
ACLM.........	Cold Lake Municipal Library, Alberta [*Library symbol National Library of Canada*] (NLC)
ACLMA........	Acclimate (ABBR)
ACLMAD......	Acclimated (ABBR)
ACLMAG......	Acclimating (ABBR)
ACLMAN......	Acclamation (ABBR)
ACLMATZ.....	Acclimatize (ABBR)
ACLMATZD...	Acclimatized (ABBR)
ACLMATZG...	Acclimatizing (ABBR)
ACLMATZN...	Acclimatization (ABBR)
ACLMN.......	Acclamation (ABBR)
ACLMRS......	Advisory Committee for Land-Mobile Radio Services (NTCM)
ACLMS........	Menno Simons Community School, Cleardale, Alberta [*Library symbol National Library of Canada*] (BIB)
ACLMY.......	Acclamatory (ABBR)
ACLN.........	Australian Construction Law Newsletter [*A publication*]
A/CLNR.......	Air Cleaner [*Automotive engineering*]
ACLO..........	Aboriginal Community Liaison Officer [*Australia*]
ACLO..........	Agena Class Lunar Orbiter [*NASA*]
ACLO..........	Association of Cooperative Library Organizations [*Later, ASCLA*]
ACLOG........	Assistant Chief of Staff, Logistics (NATG)
ACLOS........	Advisory Committee on the Law of the Sea [*Department of State*] [*Terminated, 1983*] (NOAA)
ACLOS........	Automatic Command to Line of Sight [*Military British*]
ACLP..........	Above Core Load Pad [*Nuclear energy*] (NRCH)
ACLP..........	Above Core Load Plane [*Nuclear energy*] (NRCH)
ACLP..........	Air Cushion Launch Platform (MCD)

ACLP..........	Association of Contact Lens Practitioners [*British*] (BI)
ACLPS........	Academic Clinical Laboratory Physicians and Scientists
ACLR..........	Accent Color Sciences, Inc. [*NASDAQ symbol*] (SAG)
ACLR..........	Access Control-Logging and Reporting [*Computer science*] (MHDI)
ACLRA........	Accelerate (ABBR)
ACLRAD.......	Accelerated (ABBR)
ACLRAG.......	Accelerating (ABBR)
ACLRAN.......	Acceleration (ABBR)
ACLRAV.......	Accelerative (ABBR)
ACLRD........	Australian Center for Leadership Research and Development
ACLRR........	Atlantic Coast Line R. R.
ACLRTR.......	Accelerator (ABBR)
ACLS..........	Advanced Cardiac Life Support System
ACLS..........	African Communications Liaison Service (EA)
ACLS..........	Aircraft Carrier Landing System (PDAA)
ACLS..........	Air-Cushion Landing System
ACLS..........	All-Weather Carrier Landing System [*Navy*]
ACLS..........	American Council of Learned Societies (EA)
ACLS..........	Analog Concept Learning System (PDAA)
ACLS..........	Automated Carrier Landing System [*Military*]
ACLS..........	Automated Control and Landing System [*Aerospace*]
ACLS..........	Automatic Carrier Landing System [*FAA*] (TAG)
ACLS..........	Auxiliary Contractor Logistic Support [*Military*]
ACLSP........	Automated Carrier Landing Systems Project [*Military*]
ACLSV........	Armored Combat Logistics Support Vehicle [*Army*]
ACLSVF.......	Armored Combat Logistics Support Vehicle Family
ACLT..........	Accelerate (BARN)
ACLT..........	Actual Calculated Landing Time [*FAA*] (TAG)
ACLT..........	Association of Canadian Law Teachers
ACLTR........	Accelerator (MSA)
ACLU..........	Always Causing Legal Unrest [*An association*] (EA)
ACLU..........	American Civil Liberties Union (EA)
ACLU..........	American College of Life Underwriters [*Later, The American College*] (EA)
ACLUF........	American Civil Liberties Union Foundation (EA)
ACLU Leg Act Bull...	American Civil Liberties Union. Legislative Action Bulletin [*A publication*] (ILCA)
ACLU Leg Action Bull...	American Civil Liberties Union. Legislative Action Bulletin [*A publication*] (DLA)
ACLV..........	Accrued Leave [*Military*]
ACLV..........	Air-Cushion Logistic Vehicle [*Helicopter*]
ACLV..........	Apple Chlorotic Leafspot Virus [*Plant pathology*]
ACLY..........	Accelr8 Technology Corp. [*NASDAQ symbol*] (SAG)
ACLYT........	Acolyte (ABBR)
ACM..........	Abatement Council of the Midwest (SRA)
ACM..........	Abrasive Ceramic Mosaic (DICI)
ACM..........	Academy of Country Music (EA)
ACM..........	Accelerated Claimant Match
ACM..........	Accumulator (DNAB)
ACM..........	Acoustic Countermeasures [*Navy*] (NG)
ACM..........	Acquisition and Control Module (MCD)
ACM..........	Active Countermeasures
ACM..........	Activity Control Number
ACM..........	Acute Cerebrospinal Meningitis [*Medicine*] (DMAA)
ACM..........	Additional Crew Member [*Military*] (AFM)
ACM..........	Address Calculation Machine [*Compagnie Honeywell Bull*] (NITA)
ACM..........	Address Complete Message [*Telecommunications*] (ACRL)
ACM..........	Adriamycin, Cyclophosphamide, Methotrexate [*Antineoplastic drug regimen*]
ACM..........	Advanced Circuit Module
ACM..........	Advanced Concepts Missile (MCD)
ACM..........	Advanced Consumer Marketing
ACM..........	Advanced Conventional Munitions
ACM..........	Advanced Cruise Missile
ACM..........	Aerodynamic Configured Missile (MCD)
ACM..........	Aerospun Cluster Munitions (MCD)
ACM..........	Air Caledonia, Inc. [*Canada ICAO designator*] (FAAC)
ACM..........	Air Chief Marshal [*RAF*] [*British*]
ACM..........	Air Combat Maneuvering (AFM)
ACM..........	Air Commerce Manual
ACM..........	Air Court-Martial
ACM..........	Aircraft Coloring and Marking (NATG)
AC/M.........	Aircraft Meteorological (NATG)
ACM..........	Air Cycle Machine [*Aerospace*]
ACM..........	Alarm Control Module [*Telecommunications*] (TEL)
ACM..........	Albumin-Calcium-Magnesium [*Biochemistry*] (MAE)
ACM..........	Alkaline Contaminant Material [*In used frying oils*]
ACM..........	Allocated Configuration Management [*NASA*] (NASA)
ACM..........	Alterable Control Memory
ACM..........	Alternative Communities Movement [*British*]
ACM..........	American Campaign Medal [*Military decoration*]
ACM..........	American College of Medicine (EA)
ACM..........	American College of Musicians (EA)
ACM..........	American Conservatory of Music [*Chicago, IL*]
ACM..........	American Council on Marijuana and Other Psychoactive Drugs [*Later, ACDE*] (EA)
ACM..........	Amplitude Comparison Monopulse [*Electronics*] (IAA)
ACM..........	Amsterdam Center for Mathematics and Computer Sciences
ACM..........	Analog Command Module [*Computer science*] (NITA)
ACM..........	Annual Corrective Maintenance (CAAL)
ACM..........	Another Chicago Magazine [*A publication*] (BRI)
ACM..........	Antiarmor Cluster Munition (MCD)
ACM..........	Anticruise Missile (MCD)
ACM..........	Arab Common Market [*United Arab Republic, Iraq, Jordan, Kuwait, and Syria*]

ACM............ Archconfraternity of Christian Mothers (EA)
ACM............ Area Club Management [*Military*]
ACM............ Area Composition Machine (DGA)
ACM............ Arnold-Chiari Malformation [*Medicine*]
ACM............ Artificial Compression Method
ACM............ Asbestos-Containing Material
ACM............ Asbestos-Covered Metal [*Technical drawings*]
ACM............ Assistant Chief of Mission [*Foreign Service*]
ACM............ Assistant Cub Master [*Scouting*]
ACM............ Associated Colleges of the Midwest (EA)
ACM............ Association for Classical Music [*Later, MA*] (EA)
ACM............ Association for Computing Machinery (EA)
ACM............ Association of Canadian Manufacturers (BARN)
ACM............ Association of College Management [*British*] (DBA)
ACM............ Association of Crane Makers [*British*] (BI)
ACM............ Associative Communication Multiplexer
ACM............ Astral Bellevue Pathe, Inc. [*Toronto Stock Exchange symbol*]
ACM............ Astrocyte-Conditioned Medium [*Analytical biochemistry*]
ACM............ Asynchronous Communication Control Module (MHDI)
ACM............ Audible Current Meter [*Electronics*] (DICI)
ACM............ Audio Center Module [*NASA*] (IAA)
ACM............ Australian College of Midwives
ACM............ Authorized Controller Material
ACM............ Authorized Control Material Order (AAGC)
ACM............ Automated Cost Model
ACM............ Automatic Clutter Mapping
ACM............ Automatic Coating Machine
ACM............ Automatic Control Module
ACM............ Auxiliary Core Memory [*Computer science*] (MCD)
ACM............ Auxiliary Minelayer [*Navy symbol*]
ACM............ Aviation Chief Metalsmith [*Navy*]
ACM............ Axon Cylinder Membrane
ACM............ Court Martial Reports, Air Force Cases [*A publication*] (DLA)
ACM............ Drill Minelaying and Recovery Vessel [*Navy symbol*] (DNAB)
ACM............ Mobil Oil Canada Ltd., Calgary, Alberta [*Library symbol National Library of Canada*] (NLC)
ACM............ Natchitoches, LA [*Location identifier FAA*] (FAAL)
ACM............ University of South Alabama, Mobile, AL [*OCLC symbol*] (OCLC)
ACMA.......... Acidproof Cement Manufacturers Association [*Defunct*] (EA)
ACMA.......... Acquisition Career Management Advocate [*Army*] (RDA)
ACMA.......... Advanced Civil/Military Aircraft (MCD)
ACMA.......... Air Carrier Mechanic Association
ACMA.......... Alliance Cabinet Makers Association [*A union*] [*British*]
ACMA.......... Alumina Ceramic Manufacturers Association [*Defunct*] (EA)
ACMA.......... American Cast Metals Association (EA)
ACMA.......... American Catfish Marketing Association (EA)
ACMA.......... American Certified Morticians Association [*Defunct*] (EA)
ACMA.......... American Circus Memorial Association (EA)
ACMA.......... American Comedy Museum Association [*Defunct*] (EA)
ACMA.......... American Cutlery Manufacturers Association (EA)
ACMA.......... Army Class Manager Activity (AABC)
ACMA.......... Asbestos Cement Manufacturers Association [*British*] (BI)
ACMA.......... Associate of the Institute of Cost and Management Accountants [*British*]
ACMA.......... Athletic Clothing Manufacturers' Association [*British*] (BI)
ACMA.......... Australian Conveyor Manufacturers Association
ACMA.......... Australian Council of Manufacturing Associates
ACMA.......... Australian Country Music Awards
ACMA.......... Average Current-Mantle Adiabat [*Geochemistry*]
ACMA.......... [*A*] Contractor Managed Account (AAG)
ACMAC .... ACM [*Association for Computing Machinery*] Accreditation Committee
ACMAF........ Association des Classes Moyennes Africaines [*African Middle Classes Association*]
ACMAPS ..... Advanced Computer Program Multiple Array Processor System
ACMAS .... Automated Classified Material Accountability System
ACMB.......... Applications Configuration Management Board [*NASA*] (NASA)
ACMC.......... Advanced Cruise Missile Combustor (MCD)
ACMC.......... American and Common Market Club (EAIO)
ACMC.......... American Cemetery-Mortuary Council (EA)
ACMC.......... Area Combined Movements Center [*Army*] (AABC)
ACMC.......... Assistant Commandant of the [*US*] Marine Corp (DOMA)
ACMC.......... Association des Chantiers Maritimes Canadiens [*Association of Canadian Maritime Shipyards*]
ACMC.......... Association of Canadian Medical Colleges (AC)
ACMC.......... Association of Church Missions Committees (EA)
ACMC.......... Australian Council of Marriage Counselling
ACMC.......... Automotive Chemical Manufacturers Council (EA)
ACMC.......... Information Centre, Manalta Coal Ltd., Calgary, Alberta [*Library symbol National Library of Canada*] (NLC)
ACMCAQ ..... Air Conditioning and Mechanical Contractors' Association of Queensland [*Australia*]
ACMCASA .... Air Conditioning and Mechanical Contractors' Association of South Australia
ACMCAV ...... Air Conditioning and Mechanical Contractors' Association of Victoria [*Australia*]
ACMD .... Accommodate (ABBR)
ACMD .... Advanced Concepts and Missions Division [*NASA*]
ACMD .... African Cassanova Mosaic Disease [*Botany*]
ACMD .... Assistant Chief Medical Director
ACMD .... Associate Chief Medical Director (DMAA)
ACMD .... Association Canadienne du Marketing Direct (AC)
ACMD .... Macleod Dixon Library, Calgary, Alberta [*Library symbol National Library of Canada*] (NLC)
ACMDD .... Accommodated (ABBR)
ACMDG .... Accommodating (ABBR)

ACMDN........ Accommodation (ABBR)
ACMDOSq.... Air Commando Squadron [*Air Force*]
ACMDV .... Accommodative (ABBR)
ACME.......... Academy of Country Music Entertainment [*Canada*]
ACME.......... Acme Metals [*NASDAQ symbol*] (SAG)
ACME.......... Adult Community Movement for Equality [*Civil rights*]
ACME.......... Advanced Computer for Medical Research [*Stanford University*]
ACME.......... Advisory Committee on the Marine Environment [*Marine science*] (OSRA)
ACME.......... Advisory Council for Minority Enterprise [*Department of Commerce*]
ACME.......... Advisory Council on Medical Education
ACME.......... Aircraft Component Mating Evaluation (MCD)
ACME.......... American Council on the Middle East [*Defunct*] (EA)
ACME.......... Antenna Contour Measuring Equipment
ACME.......... Application Creation Made Easy [*Watcom International Corp.*] [*Computer science*] (PCM)
ACME.......... Application of Computers to Manufacturing Engineering
ACME.......... Association for Couples in Marriage Enrichment (EA)
ACME.......... Association of Consulting Management Engineers (EA)
ACME.......... Attitude Control and Maneuvering Electronics [*Aerospace*] (MCD)
ACME.......... Automated Classification of Medical Entities [*National Center for Health Statistics*] (GFGA)
ACME.......... Monenco Consultants Ltd., Calgary, Alberta [*Library symbol National Library of Canada*] (NLC)
AcmeC .... Acme-Cleveland Corp. [*Associated Press*] (SAG)
AcmeE .... Acme Electric Corp. [*Associated Press*] (SAG)
AcmeMet..... Acme Metals [*Associated Press*] (SAG)
AcmeMt...... Acme Metals [*Associated Press*] (SAG)
ACMES .... Army Countermine Mobility Equipment System (MCD)
ACMES .... Attitude Control and Maneuvering Electronics System [*Aerospace*] (MCD)
AcmeU........ Acme United Corp. [*Associated Press*] (SAG)
ACMF.......... Air Corps Medical Forces [*Obsolete*]
ACMF.......... Allied Central Mediterranean Force [*Later, AAI*] [*World War II*]
ACMF.......... American Corn Millers' Federation (EA)
ACMF.......... Arachnoid Cyst of the Middle Fossa [*Medicine*] (DMAA)
ACMF.......... Australian Chicken Meat Federation
ACMFP........ Association Canadienne des Manufacturiers de Fenetres et Portes [*Canadian Association of Window and Door Manufacturers*]
ACMFS........ Automated Combat Mission Folder System (MCD)
ACMG .... Allied Commission, Military Government Subcommission [*World War II*]
ACMG .... Association of Canadian Mountain Guides [*Association des Guides de Montagne Canadiens*] (AC)
ACMGA....... American College of Medical Group Administrators (EA)
ACMH .... Advisory Committee on Major Hazards [*British*]
ACMHA....... American College of Mental Health Administration (EA)
ACMHCK..... Association of Community Mental Health Centers of Kansas (SRA)
ACMI........... AccuMed International, Inc. [*NASDAQ symbol*] (SAG)
ACMI........... AccuMed Intl. [*NASDAQ symbol*] (TTSB)
ACMI........... Advisory Committee on Medical Uses of Isotopes [*Nuclear energy*] (NRCH)
ACMI........... Aircraft Combat Maneuvering Instrument (DWSG)
ACMI........... American College of Medical Informatics (DMAA)
ACMI........... American Cotton Manufacturers Institute [*Later, ATMI*]
ACMI........... Art and Craft Materials Institute (EA)
ACMI........... Atypical Chronic Myeloid Leukemia [*Medicine*] (DMAA)
ACMIn......... ACM Government Income Fund, Inc. [*Associated Press*] (SAG)
ACMIP .... Army Force/Materiel Cost Methodology Improvement Project
ACMIS .... Air Combat Maneuvering Instrumentation System [*Air Force*] (DWSG)
ACMIS .... Automated Career Management Information System
ACMIW .... AccuMed Intl. Wrrt [*NASDAQ symbol*] (TTSB)
ACML .... Anti-Common Market League [*British*] (BI)
ACMLA .... Accumulate (ABBR)
ACMLA .... Association of Canadian Map Libraries and Archives (EAIO)
ACMLAD ..... Accumulated (ABBR)
ACMLAG ..... Accumulating (ABBR)
ACMLAN ..... Accumulation (ABBR)
ACMLATR ... Accumulator (ABBR)
ACMLAV ..... Accumulative (ABBR)
ACMLC........ Army Chemical Center
ACMM.......... Accom, Inc. [*NASDAQ symbol*] (SAG)
ACMM.......... Association Canadienne de Maisons Mobiles [*Canadian Association of Mobile Homes*]
ACMM.......... Aviation Chief Machinist's Mate [*Navy*]
ACMM.......... I. N. McKinnon Memorial Library, Calgary, Alberta [*Library symbol National Library of Canada*] (NLC)
ACMMB....... Association Canadienne des Manufacturiers de Maconnerie en Beton (AC)
ACMMC....... Aviation Chief Machinist's Mate, Carburetor Mechanic [*Navy*]
ACMMD ...... ACM Managed Dollar Income Fund, Inc. [*Associated Press*] (SAG)
ACMMF....... Aviation Chief Machinist's Mate, Flight Engineer [*Navy*]
ACMMH ...... Aviation Chief Machinist's Mate, Hydraulic Mechanic [*Navy*]
ACM MI ...... ACM Managed Income Fund, Inc. [*Associated Press*] (SAG)
ACMMI .... Aviation Chief Machinist's Mate, Instrument Mechanic [*Navy*]
ACMMP....... Aviation Chief Machinist's Mate, Propeller Mechanic [*Navy*]
ACMMT....... Aviation Chief Machinist's Mate, Gas Turbine Mechanic [*Navy*]
ACMMu....... ACM Municipal Securities Income [*Associated Press*] (SAG)
ACMN.......... Acumen (ABBR)
ACMN.......... Aircrewman [*British military*] (DMA)
ACMNG....... Allied Commission, Mining Subcommission [*World War II*]
ACMNP....... [*A*] Christian Ministry in the National Parks (EA)
ACMNPV ..... Autographa Californica Multipnucleocapsid Nuclear Polyhedrosis Virus [*Entomology*]

ACMO .... ACE [*Allied Command Europe*] Communication Management Organization [*NATO*] (NATG)
ACMO .... Afloat Communications Management Office [*Naval Ship Engineering Center*] (IEEE)
ACMO .... Alaska Coastal Management Office
ACMO .... Assistant Chief of Mission Operations [*NASA*]
ACMO .... Association of Condominium Managers of Ontario (AC)
ACMO .... Authorized Controlled Material Order [*Military*] (AFIT)
ACM Op ...... ACM Government Opportunity Fund, Inc. [*Associated Press*] (SAG)
ACMP .... Accompany (AABC)
ACMP .... Advanced Cruise Missile Program [*Navy*]
ACMP .... Alveolar-Capillary Membrane Permeability [*Medicine*] (DMAA)
ACMP .... Amateur Chamber Music Players (EA)
ACMP .... Anthropology Case Materials Project [*National Science Foundation*]
ACMP .... Assistant Commissioner of the Metropolitan Police [*British*] (DAS)
ACMPA .... Association Canadienne des Maitres de Poste et Adjoints [*Canadian Postmasters and Assistants Association - CPAA*]
ACMPC .... Association Canadienne des Manufacturiers de Palettes et Contenants [*Canadian Wood Pallet and Container Association*] (EAIO)
ACMPD .... Accompanied (ABBR)
ACMPG .... Accompanying (ABBR)
ACMPL .... Accomplice (ABBR)
ACMPLH ..... Accomplish (ABBR)
ACMPLHB ... Accomplishable (ABBR)
ACMPLHD ... Accomplished (ABBR)
ACMPLHNT... Accomplishment (ABBR)
ACMPLS ...... Accomplice (ABBR)
ACMPM .... Air Combat Maneuvering Performance Measurement (MCD)
ACMPNT ...... Accompaniment (ABBR)
ACMPS .... Automated Communications and Message Processing System [*Army*] (MCD)
ACMPST ...... Accompanist (ABBR)
ACMPT .... Accompaniment (ABBR)
ACMPY .... Accompany (ABBR)
ACMPYD ..... Accompanied (ABBR)
ACMQ .... Association des Communicateurs Municipaux du Quebec (AC)
ACMR .... Advisory Committee on Marine Resources Research (USDC)
ACMR .... Air Combat Maneuvering Range (DOMA)
ACMR .... Air Combat Maneuvering Range
ACMR .... Attitude Control and Maneuver Rate [*Aerospace*]
ACMR .... Mount Royal College, Calgary, Alberta [*Library symbol National Library of Canada*] (NLC)
ACMRA .... Association of Commercial Mail Receiving Agencies [*Defunct*] (EA)
AC/MRDD .... Accreditation Council for Services for Mentally Retarded and Other Developmentally Disabled Persons [*Later, ACDD*] (EA)
ACMRR .... Advisory Committee of Experts on Marine Resources Research [*Marine science*] (OSRA)
ACMRR .... Advisory Committee on Marine Resources Research
ACMRU .... Audio Commercial Message Repeating Unit [*Device delivering a recorded commercial from cigarette vending machines*]
ACMS .... Academie Canadienne de Medecine Sportive (AC)
ACMS .... Advanced Configuration Management System
ACMS .... Advanced Cost Management System (AAGC)
ACMS .... Advanced CounterMeasure Systems [*Commercial firm*] (RDA)
ACMS .... Air Call Medical Services [*British*]
ACMS .... Air Combat Maneuvering Simulator (MCD)
ACMS .... Air Conditioned Microclimate System [*Army*] (RDA)
ACMS .... Aircraft Condition Monitoring System (GAVI)
ACMS .... Airplane Condition Monitoring System [*Aviation*]
ACMS .... American Chinese Medical Society [*Later, CAMS*] (EA)
ACMS .... American Coordinated Medical Society (EA)
ACMS .... Application Control Management System (MCD)
ACMS .... Army Command Management System
ACMS .... Australian Chamber Music Society
ACMS .... Australian College of Metaphysical Studies
ACMS .... Automated Career Management System
ACMS .... Automated Configuration Management System [*NASA*] (NASA)
ACMS .... Special Court-Martial, Air Force [*United States*] (DLA)
ACM Sc ...... ACM Government Securities Fund, Inc. [*Associated Press*] (SAG)
ACMSC .... ACM [*Association for Computing Machinery*] Standards Committee
ACMSp .... ACM Government Spectrum Fund, Inc. [*Associated Press*] (SAG)
ACMT .... ACMAT Corp. [*NASDAQ symbol*] (NQ)
ACMT .... Advanced Cruise Missile Technology (MCD)
ACMT .... Aerial Combat Maneuvering Training (MCD)
ACMT .... American College of Medical Technologists (EA)
ACMT .... American Commission on Ministerial Training (EA)
ACMT .... Artificial Circus Movement Tachycardia [*Medicine*] (DMAA)
ACMT .... Automatic Configuration Management Tool
ACMTA .... ACMAT Corp'A' [*NASDAQ symbol*] (TTSB)
ACMTC .... Australian Coal Marketing and Technology Council
ACMU .... American Canoe Manufacturers Union [*Defunct*] (EA)
ACMV .... Assist-Control Mechanical Ventilation [*Medicine*]
ACMVS .... Air Combat Maneuvering Visual System (MCD)
ACN .... Academia Cosmologica Nova [*International Free Academy of New Cosmology - IFANC*] (EAIO)
ACN .... Accession Number [*Online database field identifier*]
ACN .... Access Network, Media Resource Center [*UTLAS symbol*]
ACN .... Acetone Cyanohydrin [*Organic chemistry*]
ACN .... Acetonitrile [*Organic chemistry*]
ACN .... Acrylonitrile [*Organic chemistry*]
ACN .... Action Canada Network [*Coalition formed in 1987 opposed to free trade*] (CROSS)
ACN .... Action Control Number [*Army*] (MCD)
ACN .... Activity Classification Number [*NASA*] (GFGA)

ACN .... Activity Control Number [*Navy*]
ACN .... Acuson Corp. [*NYSE symbol*] (CTT)
ACN .... Acute Conditioned Neurosis
ACN .... Advance Change Notice (AAG)
ACN .... Aerolineas Centroamericanas SA [*Central American Airlines*] [*Nicaragua*] [*ICAO designator*] (FAAC)
ACN .... Agricultural Communications Network [*Purdue University*] [*Telecommunications service*] (TSSD)
ACN .... Aid to the Church in Need (EA)
ACN .... Air Commander, Norway [*NATO*] (NATG)
ACN .... Air Consignment Note (ADA)
ACN .... Aircraft Classification Number [*Aviation*] (FAAC)
ACN .... All Concerned Notified
ACN .... American Cable Network, Inc. (NTCM)
ACN .... American College of Neuropsychiatrists (EA)
ACN .... American College of Nutrition (EA)
ACN .... American Council on NATO [*Later, Atlantic Council of the United States*]
ACN .... Ante Christum Natum [*Before the Birth of Christ*] [*Latin*]
ACN .... Anthocyanin [*Fruit pigment*]
ACN .... Artificial Cloud Nucleation [*Rainmaking*]
ACN .... Asbestos Cloth Neck (OA)
ACN .... Ascension Island Tracking Station [*NASA*] (NASA)
ACN .... Assignment Control Number [*Army*]
ACN .... Australian Customs Notice [*A publication*]
ACN .... Authorized Code Number (AFM)
ACN .... Auto Chek Centres [*Vancouver Stock Exchange symbol*]
ACN .... Automatic Celestial Navigation [*Air Force*]
ACN .... Mbala [*Zambia*] [*Airport symbol*] (AD)
ACN .... Nielsen [*A. C.*] Co. [*Commercial firm*] (WDMC)
ACNA .... Advisory Council on Naval Affairs
ACNA .... Air Canada Corp. [*NASDAQ symbol*] (SAG)
ACNA .... Atlantic Community Newspapers Association (AC)
ACNA .... Nova, An Alberta Corp., Calgary, Alberta [*Library symbol National Library of Canada*] (NLC)
ACNAC .... Anglican Council of North America and the Caribbean
ACNAF .... Air Canada'A' [*NASDAQ symbol*] (TTSB)
ACNAM ...... Associations Council of the National Association of Manufacturers (EA)
ACNAS .... Admiral Commanding North Atlantic Station [*Navy British*] (DMA)
ACNAS .... Advanced Cableship Navigation Aid System (TEL)
ACNBA .... AIDS Committee of North Bay & Area [*Comite du Sida de North Bay et de la Region*] (AC)
ACNBC .... Associate Committee on the National Building Code [*National Research Council Canada*]
ACNC .... Novacor Chemicals Ltd., Calgary, Alberta [*Library symbol National Library of Canada*] (NLC)
ACNCT .... Technical Library, Novacor Chemicals Ltd., Calgary, Alberta [*Library symbol National Library of Canada*] (BIB)
ACND .... Advisory Committee on Northern Development [*Canada*]
ACNE .... Northern Engineering Services Co. Ltd., Calgary, Alberta [*Library symbol National Library of Canada*] (NLC)
ACNEE .... Action Committee for Narcotics Education and Enforcement
ACNER .... Norcen Energy Resources Ltd., Calgary, Alberta [*Library symbol National Library of Canada*] (NLC)
ACNET .... AC Network (MCD)
ACNET .... Alternating Current Network
AcNeu .... Acetylneuraminic Acid [*Also, NAN, NANA*] [*Biochemistry*]
ACNF .... American Central NOTAM [*Notice to Airmen*] Facility [*Military*]
ACNFP .... Advisory Committee on Novel Foods and Processes [*British*]
ACNGS .... Allens Creek Nuclear Generating Station (NRCH)
ACNH .... Nova/Husky Research Corp. Ltd., Calgary, Alberta [*Library symbol National Library of Canada*] (NLC)
ACNHA .... American College of Nursing Home Administrators [*Later, ACHCA*]
AcNHFln ..... Acetylaminofluorene [*Also, AAF, AcAF, FAA*] [*Organic chemistry*]
ACNI .... All Chiefs, No Indians [*Slang*] (AAG)
ACNI .... Automatic Call Number Identification [*Telecommunications*] (IAA)
ACNM .... American College of Nuclear Medicine (EA)
ACNM .... American College of Nurse-Midwives (EA)
ACNM .... American Cordage and Netting Manufacturers (EA)
ACNMP .... Alliance for Canadian New Music Projects [*Alliance pour des Projets de Musique Canadienne Nouvell*] [*Also Contemporary Showcase*] (AC)
ACNMR .... Alternating Current Normal Mode Rejection [*Electronics*] (IAA)
ACNMS .... Advisory Committee on Nuclear Materials Safeguards
ACNN .... Air Commander, North Norway [*NATO*] (NATG)
ACNO .... Advisory Council of National Organizations [*Corporation for Public Broadcasting*] (NTCM)
ACNO .... Assistant Chief of Naval Operations
ACNO .... Association des Comites Nationaux Olympiques [*Association of National Olympic Committees - ANOC*] [*Paris, France*] (EAIO)
ACNOA .... Association de Comites Nationaux Olympiques d'Afrique [*Association of National Olympic Committees of Africa - ANOCA*] (EA)
ACNOC .... Technical Library, Novatel Communications Ltd., Calgary, Alberta [*Library symbol National Library of Canada*] (NLC)
ACNOCOMM... Assistant Chief of Naval Operations for Communications and Cryptology (IAA)
ACNO(COMM)/DNC... Assistant Chief of Naval Operations (Communications)/ Director, Naval Communications (DNAB)
ACNOE .... Association des Comites Nationaux Olympiques d'Europe [*Association of the European National Olympic Committees - ENOC*] [*Brussels, Belgium*] (EAIO)
ACNOR .... Association Canadienne de Normalisation [*Canadian Association of Standardization*]
ACNOT .... Assistant Chief of Naval Operations (Transportation)

ACNP .... American College of Neuropsychopharmacology (EA)
ACNP .... American College of Nuclear Physicians (EA)
ACNP .... Northern Pipeline Agency, Calgary, Alberta [*Library symbol National Library of Canada*] (NLC)
ACN/PCN ..... Aircraft Classification Number/Pavement Classification Number (DA)
AcNPV .... Autographa Californica Nuclear Polyhedrosis Virus
ACNS .... Academic Computing and Network Services [*Northwestern University*] [*Information service or system*] (IID)
ACNS .... Advanced Communications Network Service (MHDI)
ACNS .... Advisory Committee on Nuclear Safety [*Canada*]
ACNS .... Amer Communications Svcs [*NASDAQ symbol*] (TTSB)
ACNS .... American Communications Services, Inc. [*NASDAQ symbol*] (SAG)
ACNS .... American Council for Nationalities Service (EA)
ACNS .... American Council of Nanny Schools (EA)
ACNS .... Assistant Chief of the Naval Staff [*British*]
ACNS .... Associated Correspondents News Service
ACNS(A) ...... Assistant Chief of the Naval Staff (Air) [*British*]
ACNSA .... Association Canadienne de Nage Synchronisee Amateur [*Canadian Association of Amateur Synchronized Swimmers*]
ACNSFI .... American Committee for the National Sick Fund of Israel (EA)
ACNT .... Accent (ABBR)
ACNT .... Accent Software International Ltd. [*NASDAQ symbol*] (SAG)
ACNTD .... Accented (ABBR)
ACNTF .... Accent Software Intl. [*NASDAQ symbol*] (TTSB)
ACNTG .... Accenting (ABBR)
ACNTL .... Accentual (ABBR)
ACNTU .... Accentuate (ABBR)
ACNTUD .... Accentuated (ABBR)
ACNTUG .... Accentuating (ABBR)
ACNTUN .... Accentuation (ABBR)
ACNU .... Accent Software Intl. Ltd. [*NASDAQ symbol*] (SAG)
ACNU .... Association Canadienne pour les Nations-Unies [*United Nations Association in Canada*] (EAIO)
ACNU .... Association Congolaise pour les Nations Unies [*United Nations Association of the Congo*] (EAIO)
ACNUR .... Alto Comisionado de las Naciones Unidas para los Refugiados [*Office of the United Nations High Commissioner for Refugees*] [*Spanish*] (DUND)
ACNW .... Accent Software International Ltd. [*NASDAQ symbol*] (SAG)
ACNW .... Advisory Committee on Nuclear Waste [*United States Nuclear Regulatory Commission*]
ACNWLG ...... Acknowledge (ABBR)
ACNWLGB ... Acknowledgeable (ABBR)
ACNWLGD ... Acknowledged (ABBR)
ACNWLGG ... Acknowledging (ABBR)
ACNWLGNT... Acknowledgment (ABBR)
ACNWLGR ... Acknowledger (ABBR)
ACNWS .... Nowsco Well Service Ltd., Calgary, Alberta [*Library symbol National Library of Canada*] (NLC)
ACNX .... Automatic Cancellation (CAAL)
ACNY .... Adventurers Club of New York [*Defunct*] (EA)
ACNY .... Advertising Club of New York [*New York, NY*] (EA)
ACNY .... Advertising Club of New York (SRA)
ACO .... Abell-Corwin-Olowin Clusters [*Galaxy cluster*]
ACO .... Abort Once around Cutoff (MCD)
ACO .... Acceptance Checkout [*NASA*] (NASA)
AcO .... Acetoxy [*Biochemistry*]
ACO .... Acordia, Inc. [*NYSE symbol*] (SPSG)
ACO .... Action Cut-Out
ACO .... Acute Coronary Occlusion [*Medicine*] (DMAA)
ACO .... Adaptive Control Optimized [*Manufacturing term*]
ACO .... Administrative Consent Order [*Environmental Protection Agency*]
ACO .... Administrative Contracting Office [*or Officer*]
ACO .... Admiralty Compass Observatory [*British*] (DEN)
ACO .... Advance Centennial Officer (AAG)
ACO .... Adviser on Combined Operations [*British*]
ACO .... Aero Sierra Eco SA de CV [*Mexico ICAO designator*] (FAAC)
ACO .... African Curriculum Organisation (AIE)
ACO .... Agricultural Climatological Office [*Department of Commerce*]
ACO .... Air Colombia [*ICAO designator*] (FAAC)
ACO .... Air Communication Officer [*Military*] (IAA)
ACO .... Air [*or Airborne*] Control Officer [*or Contract*] [*Military British*]
ACO .... Air Control Officer [*Navy*] (DOMA)
ACO .... Aircraft Control Operator (MUGU)
ACO .... Akron, OH [*Location identifier FAA*] (FAAL)
ACO .... Alabaster Cavern State Park [*Oklahoma*] [*Seismograph station code, US Geological Survey*] (SEIS)
ACO .... Alert, Cooperative, and Oriented (HGAA)
ACO .... Alpha Cutoff
ACO .... Alternating Current Output (MHDI)
ACO .... American College of Orgonomy (EA)
ACO .... American College of Otorhinolaryngologists (EA)
ACO .... American Composers Orchestra
ACO .... American Council of Otolaryngology [*Later, ACO-HNS*] (EA)
ACO .... Anglican Communion Office [*British*] (EAIO)
ACO .... Annual Cost of Ownership
ACO .... Anodal Closing Odor [*Physiology*]
ACO .... Area Clearance Officer (MUGU)
ACO .... Armament Concepts Office [*Army*] (RDA)
ACO .... Assistant Customs Officer
ACO .... Association Canadienne des Optometristes [*Canadian Association of Optometrists*]
ACO .... Association Canadienne d'Orthopedie (AC)
ACO .... Association de la Construction de l'Outaouais [*Outaouais Construction Association*] (AC)

ACO .... Association of Canadian Orchestras
ACO .... Association of Charity Officers (EAIO)
ACO .... Association of Children's Officers [*British*] (DI)
ACO .... Association of Commissioned Officers (USDC)
ACO .... Association of Conservation Officers (EAIO)
ACO .... Associaton of Commissioned Officers [*Marine science*] (OSRA)
ACO .... Atco Ltd. [*Toronto Stock Exchange symbol*]
ACO .... Atomic Coordination Office [*British*]
ACO .... Attack Cut Out [*Military*] (NG)
ACO .... Austin Community College, Austin, MN [*OCLC symbol*] (OCLC)
ACO .... Authorized Contracting Officer (SAA)
ACO .... Automatic Call Origination [*Telecommunications*]
ACO .... Automatic Cutout [*Valve*] [*Aviation*] (AIA)
ACO .... Coaldale Public Library, Alberta [*Library symbol National Library of Canada*] (NLC)
ACOA .... Adult Child of Alcoholic [*Psychology*] (DAVI)
ACoA .... Adult Children of Alcoholics [*Bestseller by Janet Geringer Woititz*]
ACOA .... Adult Children of Alcoholics
ACOA .... AIDS [*Acquired Immune Deficiency Syndrome*] Council of Central Australia
ACOA .... American Committee on Africa (EA)
ACOA .... American Construction Owners Association [*Defunct*] (EA)
ACOA .... Associate Committee on Aerodynamics [*National Research Council*] [*Canada*]
ACOA .... Atlantic Canada Opportunities Agency
ACOA(F & A)... Assistant Comptroller of the Army for Finance and Accounting
ACOA JI .... ACOA [*Administrative and Clerical Officers Association*] Journal [*A publication*]
ACOAP .... Adriamycin, Cyclophosphamide, Vincristine, Cytosine Arabinoside, Prednisone [*Antineoplastic drug regimen*] (DAVI)
ACOB .... Actual Current on Board (DNAB)
ACOB .... ASCII COBOL [*Computer science*]
ACOC .... A. C. Owners Club - American Centre (EA)
ACOC .... Air Command Operations Center [*NATO*] (NATG)
AC/OC .... Air Cooperation Command [*RAF*] [*British*]
ACOC .... Allied Command Operations Center
ACOC .... American Clipper Owners Club (EA)
ACOC .... America's Cup Organizing Committee
ACOC .... Area Communications Operations Center [*Telecommunications*] (TEL)
ACOC .... Associated Contractor Originated Change (AAG)
ACOC .... Australian Council of Churches
ACOC .... Automatic Control Operations Center (DNAB)
ACOCA .... Army Communication Operations Center Agency
ACOCC .... Atlantic [*Fleet*] Commander Operational Control Center [*Navy*]
ACOCS .... Army Customer Order Control System
ACOD .... Adjournment in Contemplation of Dismissal [*Law*]
ACODAC .... Acoustic Data Capsule [*Oceanography*] (MSC)
ACODS .... Army Container-Oriented Distribution Systems
ACOE .... Army Common Operating Environment (RDA)
ACOE .... Army Communities of Excellence
ACOE .... Automatic Checkout Equipment
ACOEP .... American College of Osteopathic Emergency Physicians (EA)
ACOF .... Attendant Control of Facilities [*Western Electric Co.*]
AC of AS ...... Assistant Chief of Air Staff [*Army British*]
AC of N .... Assistant Controller of the Navy [*British*]
ACOFS .... Assistant Chief of Staff (MCD)
AC of S .... Assistant Chief of Staff
AC of T .... Assistant Chief of Transportation [*Army*]
ACOG .... Advanced Combat Optical Gunsight [*Military*] (INF)
ACOG .... Agence Civile OTAN [*Organisation du Traite de l'Atlantique Nord*] du Temps de Guerre [*NATO Civil Wartime Agency*] (NATG)
ACOG .... Aircraft on Ground [*Navy*]
ACOG .... American College of Obstetricians and Gynecologists (EA)
ACOG .... Atlanta Centennial Olympic Games
ACOG .... Atlanta Committee for the Olympic Games
ACOH .... Advisory Committee for Operational Hydrology [*WMO*] (MSC)
ACOHA .... American College of Osteopathic Hospital Administrators [*Later, COHE*] (EA)
ACO-HNS ..... American Council of Otolaryngology - Head and Neck Surgery [*Later, AAO-HNS*] (EA)
ACOHS .... Occupational Health and Safety Library, Alberta Workers' Health, Safety and Compensation, Calgary, Alberta [*Library symbol National Library of Canada*] (NLC)
ACOI .... American College of Osteopathic Internists (EA)
ACOJ .... Association Canadienne des Orchestres de Jeunes [*Canadian Association of Youth Orchestres - CAYO*]
ACOL .... AIDS Committee of London (AC)
ACOL .... Amcol International Corp. [*NASDAQ symbol*] (SAG)
ACOL .... AMCOL Intl. [*NASDAQ symbol*] (TTSB)
ACOL .... Analytical Chemistry by Open Learning [*A publication*]
ACOL .... Annualized Cost of Living Model
ACOL .... Antiproton Collector [*Particle physics*]
ACOL .... Application Control Language [*Computer science*] (MHDI)
ACOL .... Crowsnest Public Library, Coleman, Alberta [*Library symbol National Library of Canada*] (NLC)
ACOLI .... Advance Circuit Order and Layout Information [*Telecommunications*] (TEL)
ACOM .... A+ Network [*NASDAQ symbol*] (TTSB)
ACOM .... A Plus Communications, Inc. [*NASDAQ symbol*] (SAG)
ACOM .... Area Cutover Manager (DNAB)
ACOM .... Asian Communist [*Later, B Group*] [*Division of National Security Agency*]
A Com .... Associate in Commerce
ACOM .... Association for Computer Operations Management (EA)

ACOM	Association for Convention Operations Management (EA)
ACOM	Automatic Circuit Quality Monitoring (PDAA)
ACOM	Automatic Coding Machine [Computer science] (CET)
ACOM	Aviation Chief Ordnanceman [Navy]
ACOM	Cochrane Municipal Library, Alberta [Library symbol National Library of Canada] (NLC)
ACOMARS	Association of Centers of Medieval and Renaissance Studies [Later, CARA] (EA)
ACO/MGE	Acceptance and Checkout / Maintenance Ground Equipment (SAA)
A-Com-in-C	Air-Commodore-in-Chief [RAF, RCAF] (DAS)
A Comm	Air Commodore [RAF, RCAF] (DAS)
A Comm A	Associate of the Society of Commercial Accountants [British]
ACOMMW	Aerospace Communications Wing [Air Force]
ACOMP	Accompaniment (ABBR)
ACOMP	Accompany (ABBR)
ACOMP	Accomplish (ABBR)
ACOMPB	Accomplishable (ABBR)
ACOMPD	Accomplished (ABBR)
ACOMPG	Accomplishing (ABBR)
ACOMPLINE	A Computerised London Information System Online [Greater London Council Research Library Bibliographic database] [British]
ACOMPLIS	A Computerised London Information Service [Greater London Council Research Library] [British]
ACOMPR	Accomplisher (ABBR)
ACOMPT	Accomplishment (ABBR)
ACOMR	Advisory Committee on Oceanic Meteorological Research (USDC)
ACOMR	Advisory Committee on Oceanic Meteorological Research [Marine science] (OSRA)
ACOMS	American College of Oral and Maxillofacial Surgeons (EA)
AComS	American Communications Services, Inc. [Associated Press] (SAG)
ACOMS	Army Communications Objectives Measurement Survey [or System] (GFGA)
ACOMS	Automated Collection Management System
ACOMT	Aviation Chief Ordnanceman, Turret Mechanic [Navy]
ACONA	Advisory Council on Naval Affairs of the Navy League
A/COND	Air Conditioning [Automotive engineering]
ACONDA	Activities Committee on New Directions for ALA [American Library Association]
ACONet	Akademisches Computer Netz [Academic Computer Network] [Computer science] [Austria] (TNIG)
ACONM	Consort Municipal Library, Alberta [Library symbol National Library of Canada] (NLC)
ACONS	Aerospace Control Squadron [Air Force]
ACONS	Conklin Community School, Alberta [Library symbol National Library of Canada] (BIB)
ACONT	Account (ABBR)
ACONTB	Accountable (ABBR)
ACONTBLY	Accountably (ABBR)
ACONTBT	Accountability (ABBR)
ACONTG	Accounting (ABBR)
ACONTNC	Accountancy (ABBR)
ACOOG	American College of Osteopathic Obstetricians and Gynecologists (EA)
ACOP	Adriamycin, Cyclophosphamide, Oncovin [Vincristine], Prednisone [Antineoplastic drug regimen]
ACOP	Airborne Corps Operation Plan [Military] (AABC)
ACOP	American College of Optometric Physicians (EA)
ACOP	American College of Osteopathic Pediatricians (EA)
ACOP	Analysis of Capabilities, Opportunities, and Prospects
ACOP	Approved Code of Practice (DS)
ACOP	Army Customer Order Program
ACOP	Association of Chief Officers of Police [British] (DI)
ACOP	Association of Chief Officers of Probation [British] (DBA)
ACOP	Atlantic Centennial Olympic Properties
A-COPE	Adolescent-Coping Orientation for Problem Experiences [Psychology]
ACOPP	Abbreviated COBOL Preprocessor [Computer science] (IEEE)
ACOPP	Adriamycin, Cyclophosphamide, Oncovin [Vincristine], Procarbazine, Prednisone [Antineoplastic drug regimen]
ACOPS	Advisory Committee on Pollution of the Sea (EAIO)
ACOPS	Advisory Committee on Protection of the Sea [Marine science] (OSRA)
ACOR	American Center of Oriental Research
ACOR	Coronation Public Library, Alberta [Library symbol National Library of Canada] (NLC)
ACORBAT	Association for Cooperation in Banana Research in the Caribbean and Tropical America [Guadeloupe, French West Indies] (EAIO)
ACORD	Action through Creative Organization, Research, and Discussion [An association] (EA)
ACORD	Advanced Concepts for Ordnance
ACORD	Advisory Committee on Energy Research and Development [British government]
ACORD	Advisory Council on Research and Redevelopment for Fuel and Power (NUCP)
ACORD	Agency for Cooperation and Research in Development [International consortium on Africa] (ECON)
ACORD	Automotive Consortium on Recycling and Disposal [Industry research group]
ACORDD	Action Council of Regional Dissemination Directors
ACORDD	Advisory Committee for the Research and Development Department [British Library] (AIE)
ACORDE	[A] Corsortium on Restorative Dentistry Education [Medicine] (DMAA)
Acordia	Acordia, Inc. [Associated Press] (SAG)
ACORE	Advisory Council for Orthopaedic Resident Education (EA)
ACORN	A Classification of Residential Neighborhoods [Database CACI] [Information service or system] (CRD)

ACORN	Acronym-Oriented Nut
ACORN	Association for Community Organizations for Refaring Now
ACORN	Association of Community Organizations for Reform Now (EA)
ACORN	Associative Content Retrieval Network [A. D. Little, Inc.] [Information service or system]
ACORN	Automated Coder of Report Narrative [Computer science] (DIT)
ACORN	Automatic Checkout and Recording Equipment
ACOS	Accost (ABBR)
ACOS	A Computer Series [Nippon Electric Co. Japan]
ACOS	Advanced Computer Oriented System (BUR)
ACOS	Advisory Committee on Safety [International Electrotechnical Commission] [ISO] (DS)
ACOS	American College of Osteopathic Surgeons (EA)
ACOS	Arms Control Observation Satellite
ACOS	Assistant Chief of Staff
ACOS	Automated Cloud Observation System (MCD)
ACOS	Automatic Checkout Set (AAG)
ACOS	[A] Common Operational Software (MCD)
ACOSA	AIDS [Acquired Immune Deficiency Syndrome] Council of South Australia
ACOSCA	African Cooperative Savings and Credit Association [See also ACECA] [Later, ACCOSCA] (EAIO)
ACOSD	Accosted (ABBR)
ACOSG	Accosting (ABBR)
ACOSIM	Air Warfare Simulation [Military]
ACOSS	Active Control of Space Structures
ACOST	Advisory Committee on Science and Technology [British]
ACOT	Apple Classroom of Tomorrow
ACOT	Assistant Chief of Staff, Organization and Training Division (NATG)
ACOU	Coutts Public Library, Alberta [Library symbol National Library of Canada] (NLC)
ACOUS	Acoustic [or Acoustical] (KSC)
ACOUSID	Acoustic-Seismic Intrusion Detector (MCD)
ACOU-SID	Acoustic Sound Intrusion Device [Military] (VNW)
ACOUST	Acoustic (ABBR)
ACOUST	Acoustics (ROG)
ACOUSTINT	Acoustical Intelligence [Military] (AABC)
ACO(W)	Atomic Coordinating Office (Washington, DC) [British Defense Staff]
ACP	Abnormal Control Plasma [Clinical chemistry]
ACP	Acceptance Checkout Procedure (KSC)
ACP	Acceptance Message [Aviation code]
ACP	Accessory Conduction Pathway [Medicine] (DMAA)
ACP	Accion Democratica Popular [Popular Democratic Action] [Costa Rica] [Political party]
ACP	Accomplishment/Cost Procedure
ACP	Acepromazine
ACP	Acetophenone [Organic chemistry]
ACP	Acetoxycyclopentenone [Organic chemistry]
ACP	Acid Phosphatase [Also, ACPH, AP] [An enzyme]
ACP	Acoustic Communication Program
ACP	Action Congress Party [Ghana] [Political party] (PPW)
ACP	Action Control Point [Telecommunications]
ACP	Action Current Potential (IAA)
ACP	Action for Child Protection (EA)
ACP	Acyl Carrier Protein [Biochemistry]
ACP	Adaptive Control Process
ACP	Additional Conditional Purchase [Business term] (ADA)
ACP	Additive Color Process
ACP	Advance Command Post (NATG)
ACP	Advanced Composite Products, Inc.
ACP	Advanced Computational Processor
ACP	Advanced Cooperative Project [NASA]
ACP	Advisory Caution Panel (MCD)
ACP	Advisory Committee on Pesticides [British]
ACP	Aerial Communications Point [Military] (DOMA)
ACP	Aerial Control Point [Military] (DOMA)
ACP	Aerospace Computer Program [Air Force]
ACP	African, Caribbean, and Pacific Countries [Associated with the EEC] (AF)
ACP	African Comprehensive Party [Jamaica] [Political party] (EY)
ACP	After Conning Position [British military] (DMA)
ACP	Agence Centrale Parisienne de Presse [Parisian Central Press Agency] [French] (AF)
ACP	Agence Congolaise de Presse [Congolese Press Agency]
ACP	Agricultural Conservation Program [Department of Agriculture]
ACP	Airborne Command Post [Air Force]
ACP	Air Cape [South Africa ICAO designator] (FAAC)
ACP	Air Carcinogen Policy [Environmental Protection Agency] (GFGA)
ACP	Air-Conditioning Pack
ACP	Air Control Point
ACP	Aircraft Communication Procedures [Navy] (MCD)
ACP	Aircraft Performance (SAA)
ACP	Airlift Command Post [Military]
ACP	Airline Carriers of Passengers
ACP	Airlines Control Program [IBM Corp.]
ACP	Airman Commissioning Program [Air Force] (AFM)
ACP	Alarm Control Panel
ACP	Albanian Communist Party [Political party]
ACP	Alignment Control Panel
ACP	Allied Collection Point [World War II]
ACP	Allied Communications Publications [Military]
ACP	Alternate Care Plan [Health Care Financing Administration]
ACP	Alternate Command Post [Military] (CET)
ACP	Alternative Coated Paper
ACP	Alternative Complement Pathway [Hematology]

ACP	AMERCO [*NYSE symbol*] (SAG)
ACP	American Club of Paris (EA)
ACP	American College of Pathologists (DAVI)
ACP	American College of Pharmacists (EA)
ACP	American College of Physicians (EA)
ACP	American College of Podopediatrics (EA)
ACP	American College of Prosthodontists (EA)
ACP	American College of Psychiatrists (EA)
ACP	American Collegiate Press
ACP	American Real Estate Partnership [*NYSE symbol*] (SPSG)
ACP	Amer R.E.Ptnrs L.P. [*NYSE symbol*] (TTSB)
Acp	Aminocaproic Acid [*Biochemistry*]
ACP	Amino(chloro)Pentenoic Acid [*Organic chemistry*]
ACP	Ammunition Control Point (AFM)
ACP	Amorphous Hydrous Calcium Phosphate [*Inorganic chemistry*]
ACP	Analytical Computer Program
ACP	Ancillary Control Processor
ACP	Animal Care Panel [*Later, AALAS*]
ACP	Anodal Closing Picture [*Physiology*]
ACP	Anthology of Catholic Poets [*A publication*]
ACP	Anti-Comintern Pact
A-CP	Anti-Concorde Project (EA)
ACP	Apparent Candle Power
ACP	Arab Communist Party [*Political party*]
ACP	Archiv fuer die Civilistische Praxis [*A publication*] (ILCA)
ACP	Area Command Post (FAAC)
ACP	Area Concept Papers [*Military*]
ACP	Area Coordinating Paper
ACP	Arithmetic and Control Processor
ACP	Armament Control Panel
ACP	Armored Command Post [*Army*] (RDA)
ACP	Army Capabilities Plan
ACP	Army Controllership Program
ACP	Army Cost Position
ACP	Asbestos-Cement Pressure [*Construction*] (DICI)
ACP	Asphaltic Concrete Pavement
ACP	Aspirin, Caffeine, Phenacetin [*Medicine*] (AAMN)
ACP	Asset Capitalization Program [*Air Force*] (DOMA)
ACP	Associate Client Program [*Business International Corp.*] [*Information service or system*] (IID)
ACP	Associate Collegiate Players
ACP	Associate Computer Professional
ACPB	Attack Church Press (EA)
ACP	Associated Collegiate Press (EA)
ACP	Associated Construction Publications (EA)
ACP	Associated of Correctors of the Press [*Later, NGA*] (DGA)
ACP	Associate of the College of Preceptors [*British*]
ACP	Associates of Clinical Pharmacology (EA)
ACP	Association Canadienne de Philosophie [*Canadian Philosophical Association - CPA*]
ACP	Association Canadienne des Paiements (AC)
ACP	Association Canadienne des Physiciens et Physiciennes (AC)
ACP	Association for Child Psychiatrists (DAVI)
ACP	Association for Child Psychoanalysis (EA)
ACP	Association of Canadian Publishers
ACP	Association of Child Psychotherapists (EAIO)
ACP	Association of Circus Proprietors of Great Britain (BI)
ACP	Association of Clinical Pathologists
ACP	Association of Computer Professionals (EA)
ACP	Association of Correctional Psychologists
ACP	Association of Correctors of the Press (BARN)
ACP	Association of Coupon Processors (EA)
ACP	Astronaut Control Panel [*NASA*] (NASA)
ACP	Atlantic City Free Public Library, Atlantic City, NJ [*OCLC symbol*] (OCLC)
ACP	Atmospheric Contamination Potential
ACP	Attack Center Panel
ACP	Atypical Chest Pain [*Medicine*]
ACP	Audio Center Equipment (SAA)
ACP	Audio Control Panel (NASA)
ACP	Audit Control Point
ACP	Australia Council Press Clips [*Database*]
ACP	Australian Christian Party [*Political party*]
ACP	Australian Company Law and Practice [*A publication*]
ACP	Australian Country Party [*Political party*] (BARN)
ACP	Automated Calibration Procedure
ACP	Automated Chemistry Program [*Computer science*]
ACP	Automated Communications Publications (AFIT)
ACP	Automated Computer Program
ACP	Automatic Cartridge, Pistol [*Military*] (VNW)
ACP	Automatic Check Personalization (DGA)
ACP	Automatic Colt Pistol (DICI)
ACPS	Automatic Communications Program (DWSG)
ACP	Auxiliary Checkpoint
ACP	Auxiliary Command Post (SAA)
ACP	Auxiliary Control Panel [*Aerospace*] (AAG)
ACP	Aviation Continuation Pay [*Navy*] (DOMA)
ACP	Azimuth Change Pulse
ACP	Groupe des Sept pour la Cooperation du Secteur Prive Europeen avec l'Afrique, les Caribes et le Pacific [*Group of Seven for European Private Sector Cooperation with Africa, the Caribbean, and the Pacific*] (EAIO)
ACP	University Animal Care Program [*Arizona State University*] [*Research center*] (RCD)
ACP 80	Air Cargo Processing in the 80's [*British Telecom*]

ACPA	ACPA [*Affiliated Conference of Practicing Accountants*] International (EA)
ACPA	Activated Carbons Producers' Association [*European Council of Chemical Manufacturers Federations*] [*Brussels, Belgium*] (EAIO)
ACPA	Adaptive Controlled Phased Array (CAAL)
ACPA	Adjusted Compensation Payment Act [*1936*]
ACPA	Advisory Commission on Parliamentary Accommodation [*Canada*]
ACPA	Affiliated Chiropodists-Podiatrists of America (EA)
ACPA	Agriculture and Consumer Protection Act of 1973
ACPA	American Capon Producers Association (EA)
ACPA	American Catholic Philosophical Association (EA)
ACPA	American Catholic Psychological Association [*Later, PIRI*] (EA)
ACPA	American Chronic Pain Association (EA)
ACPA	American Citizens for Political Action (EA)
ACPA	American Cleft Palate Association [*Later, ACPCA*] (EA)
ACPA	American College of Physicians Assistants [*Defunct*] (EA)
ACPA	American College Personnel Association (EA)
ACPA	American Concrete Pavement Association (EA)
ACPA	American Concrete Pipe Association (EA)
ACPA	American Concrete Pumping Association (EA)
ACPA	Amino(chloro)pentenedioic Acid [*Organic chemistry*]
ACPA	Arizona Crop Protection Association (SRA)
ACPA	Arkansas Crop Protection Association (SRA)
A-CPA	Asbestos-Cement Products Association [*Defunct*] (EA)
ACPA	Associate of the Institution of Certified Public Accountants [*British*]
ACPA	Association Canadienne de Patinage Artistique [*Canada*]
ACPA	Association des Collaboratrices et Partenaires en Affaires (AC)
ACPA	Association of Computer Programmers and Analysts (EA)
ACPA	Audio Capture and Playback Adapter (PCM)
ACPA	Australian Citrus Processors' Association
ACPA	L'Association Canadienne des Producteurs d'Acier (AC)
ACPAC	Annual Conference Program Advisory Committee [*American Occupational Therapy Association*]
ACPAE	Association of Certified Public Accountant Examiners [*Later, NASBA*] (EA)
ACPAI	Affiliated Conference of Practicing Accountants International [*Later, ACPA*] (EA)
ACPANDP	Assistant Chief of Staff, Plans and Policy Division (NATG)
ACPATT	All Commands Process as Attached [*Army*] (AABC)
ACPAU	Association Canadienne du Personnel Administratif Universitaire [*Canadian Association of University Administration Personnel*]
ACPAV	Association Cooperative de Productions Audio-Visuelles (AC)
ACPB	Attack Class Patrol Boat [*Navy*]
ACPC	Air Control Component
ACPC	Aircraft Camera Parameter Control
ACPC	All Canada Poetry Contests
ACPC	American Christian Palestine Committee [*Defunct*]
ACPC	American College of Probate Counsel [*Later, ACTEC*] (EA)
ACPC	American College Personnel Accreditation (OICC)
ACPC	American Council for Polish Culture (EA)
ACPC	American Council of Parent Cooperatives [*Later, PCPI*] (EA)
ACPC	Aminocyclopentane Carboxylic [*Acid*] (DMAA)
ACPC	Association Canadienne des Periodiques Catholiques [*Canadian Association of Catholic Periodicals*]
ACPC	Association Canadienne des Professeurs de Comptabilite [*Canadian Association of Professors of Accounting*]
ACPC	Petro-Canada, Calgary, Alberta [*Library symbol National Library of Canada*] (NLC)
ACPCA	American Cleft Palate-Craniofacial Association (EA)
ACPCA	Association Cinematographique Professionnelle de Conciliation et d'Arbitrage (EAIO)
ACPCC	American Council of Polish Cultural Clubs [*Later, ACPC*] (EA)
ACPCQJ	Australian Crime Prevention Council. Quarterly Journal [*A publication*]
ACPD	Alternating Current Plasma Detector [*Spectrometry*]
ACPD	Amino(cyclopentyl)dicarboxylate [*Organic chemistry*]
ACPD	Army Control Program Directive
ACPD	Association Canadienne des Professeurs de Droit [*Canadian Association of Law Teachers - CALT*]
ACPDA	Association Canadienne des Presidents de Departements d'Anglais [*Canadian Association of Chairmen of English Departments - CACE*]
ACPDP	Alternating Current Plasma Display Panel [*Electronics*] (IAA)
ACPDS	Advisory Committee on Personal Dosimetry Services [*National Science Foundation*] (NRCH)
ACPE	American College of Physician Executives (EA)
ACPE	American Council on Pharmaceutical Education (EA)
ACPE	Association Canadienne des Pigistes de l'Edition [*Canada*]
ACPE	Association for Clinical Pastoral Education (EA)
ACPE	Association for Continuing Professional Education [*Formerly, AFSTE*] (EA)
ACPEN	Aircraft Penetration Model (MCD)
ACPERS	Army Civilian Personnel System
ACPET	Australian Council for Private Education and Training
ACPF	Acoustic Containerless Processing Facility
ACPF	Amphibious Corps, Pacific Fleet [*Marine Corps*]
ACPF	Asia Crime Prevention Foundation (EAIO)
ACPF	Asociacion del Congreso Panamericano de Ferrocarriles [*Pan American Railway Congress Association*] (EAIO)
ACPF	Averaged-Coupled Pair Functional [*Quantum chemistry*]
ACPF	Plasti-Fab Ltd., Calgary, Alberta [*Library symbol National Library of Canada*] (NLC)
ACPFA	Association Canadienne des Producteurs de Films d'Animation [*Canada*]
ACPH	Acid Phosphatase [*Also, ACP, AP*] [*An enzyme*]

ACPH .... Air Change per Hour [*Ventilation and infiltration rates*]
ACPHOB....... Acrophobia (ABBR)
ac phos....... Acid Phosphatase [*An enzyme*] (CPH)
ACPI............ Advanced Configuration and Power Interface (PCM)
ACPI............ American City Planning Institute
ACPI............ Assistant Chief Patrol Inspector [*Immigration and Naturalization Service*]
ACPI............ Association Canadienne des Professeurs d'Immersion (AC)
ACPI............ Automatic Cable Pair Identification [*Computer science*] (IAA)
ACPI............ Aviation Crime Prevention Institute (EA)
ACPIC .... American Council for Private International Communications, Inc. [*Proposed corporation to replace Radio Free Europe*]
ACPL........... Acoustical Plaster [*Technical drawings*]
ACPL........... Assistant Controller, Personnel and Logistics [*Navy British*]
ACPL........... ATLAS Crew Procedures Laboratory [*NASA*] (MCD)
ACPL........... Atmospheric Cloud Physics Laboratory [*Spacelab*] [*NASA*]
ACPL........... Planning Library & Resource Centre, Calgary, Alberta [*Library symbol National Library of Canada*] (NLC)
ACPLC .... Peter Lougheed Centre, Calgary General Hospital, Alberta [*Library symbol National Library of Canada*] (BIB)
ACPLS .... Association Canadienne des Professeurs de Langue Seconde (AC)
ACPM.......... Acoustic Containerless Processing Module (MCD)
ACPM.......... Activity Career Program Manager [*Military*]
ACPM.......... Advisory Committee on Program Management (MHDB)
ACPM.......... Aerospace Computer Program Model [*Air Force*] (IAA)
ACPM.......... American College of Pain Medicine
ACPM.......... American College of Preventive Medicine (EA)
ACPM.......... Associate Contractor Program Manager [*NASA*] (NASA)
ACPM.......... Associate of the Confederation of Professional Management [*British*] (DBQ)
ACPM.......... Association of Canadian Pension Management
ACPM.......... Association of Corrugated Papermakers [*British*] (BI)
ACPM.......... Attitude Control Propulsion Motor [*Aerospace*]
ACPMA .... Australian Clay Pipe Manufacturers' Association
ACPMC .... Alberta Petroleum Marketing Commission, Calgary, Alberta [*Library symbol National Library of Canada*] (NLC)
ACPMME...... Association of Concentrated and Powdered Milk Manufacturers of the EEC (EAIO)
ACPMR .... American Congress of Physical Medicine and Rehabilitation [*Later, ACRM*] (EA)
ACPn........... American College of Psychoanalysts (EA)
ACPNCTR..... Acupuncture
ACPO .... Associate Contractor Projects Office [*NASA*] (NASA)
ACPO .... Association of Chief Police Officers [*British*]
ACPO .... Association of the Chemical Profession of Ontario (AC)
ACPO .... PanArctic Oils Ltd., Calgary, Alberta [*Library symbol National Library of Canada*] (NLC)
ACPOC .... Association of Children's Prosthetic-Orthotic Clinics (EA)
ACPP .... Adrenocorticopolypeptide [*Endocrinology*]
ACPP .... Advisory Committee on Polar Programs [*National Science Foundation*] (MSC)
ACPP .... Advisory Council on Personnel Policy [*Canada*]
ACPP .... Aircraft Crashworthiness Program Plan (MCD)
ACPP .... American Concrete Pressure Pipe Association (EA)
ACPP .... Asian Center for the Progress of Peoples [*Hong Kong*] (EAIO)
ACPP .... Association Canadienne des Patineurs Professionnels [*Canadian Association of Professional Skaters*]
ACPP .... Association for Child Psychology and Psychiatry [*British*]
ACPP .... Pan Canadian Petroleum Ltd., Calgary, Alberta [*Library symbol National Library of Canada*] (NLC)
ACPPA .... American Concrete Pressure Pipe Association (EA)
ACPPD........ Average Cost per Patient Day [*Medicine*]
ACPP PF ..... Acid Phosphatase Prostatic Fluid [*Biochemistry*] (DAVI)
ACPPr .... Amer R.E. Ptnrs 5%'PIK'Pfd [*NYSE symbol*] (TTSB)
ACPPU .... Association Canadienne des Professeures et Professeurs d'Universite (AC)
ACPR .... Advanced Core Performance Reactor (NRCH)
ACPR .... Advanced Core Pulsed Reactor (NRCH)
ACPR .... Advanced Critical Pulse Reactor [*Nuclear energy*]
ACPR .... American College of Podiatric Radiologists (EA)
ACPR .... American Crossbred Pony Registry (EA)
ACPR .... Annular Core Pulsed Reactor
ACPRA .... American College Public Relations Association [*Later, Council for the Advancement and Support of Education*]
ACPROG ...... Assistant Chief of Staff, Programs Division (NATG)
ACPRS .... Ames Cubic Precision Ranging System [*NASA*]
ACPRTS .... Association Canadienne des Professeurs de Redaction Technique et Scientifique [*Canadian Association of Teachers of Technical Writing - CATTW*]
ACPS .... Acrocephalopolysyndactyly (DMAA)
ACPS .... Air-Conditioning and Pneumatic System (MCD)
ACPS .... Alkaline Calcium Petroleum Sulfonate
ACPS .... American Coalition of Patriotic Societies [*Defunct*] (EA)
ACPS .... American Color Print Society (EA)
ACPS .... American Connemara Pony Society (EA)
ACPS .... Armament Control Processor Set (CAAL)
ACPS .... Association Canadienne de la Presse Syndicale [*Canadian Syndicated Press Association*]
ACPS .... Attitude Control Propulsion System [*or Subsystem*] [*NASA*]
ACPS .... Planning Section Library, Calgary Police Service, Alberta [*Library symbol National Library of Canada*] (NLC)
ACPSAHMWA... American Commission for Protection and Salvage of Artistic and Historical Monuments in War Areas [*World War II Defunct*]
ACPSEM ...... Australasian College of Physical Scientists and Engineers in Medicine

ACPSF .... Australian Cerebral Palsy Sports Federation
ACPSM .... Association of Chartered Physiotherapists in Sports Medicine (EAIO)
ACPT........... Accept (AABC)
acpt .... Acceptance (WDMC)
ACPT........... Acid Phosphatase with Tartrate [*Clinical chemistry*]
ACPT........... Air Command Post [*Military*]
ACPT........... Asian Confederation of Physical Therapy (EAIO)
ACPTB .... Acceptable (ABBR)
ACPTBT .... Acceptability (ABBR)
ACPTBY .... Acceptability (ABBR)
ACPTC .... Association of College Professors of Textiles and Clothing (EA)
ACPTD .... Accepted (ABBR)
ACPTEC........ Action Committee of Public Transport of the European Communities GG2 [*See also CATPCE*] (EAIO)
ACP/TF........ Airline Control Program Transaction Processing Facility [*IBM Corp.*] (NITA)
ACPTG .... Accepting (ABBR)
Acpt Ins ...... Acceptance Insurance Companies, Inc. [*Associated Press*] (SAG)
ACPTNC .... Acceptance (ABBR)
ACPTNS .... Acceptableness (ABBR)
ACP/TPF ...... Airline Control Program / Transaction Processing Facility [*Computer science*] (BTTJ)
ACPTR .... Acceptor (MSA)
ACPTT......... Air Combat Part Task Trainer
ACPTY .... Acceptably (ABBR)
ACPU .... Association Canadienne des Professeurs d'Universite [*Canadian Association of University Professors*]
ACPU .... Auxiliary Computer Power Unit
ACPY .... Accompany (FAAC)
ACQ .... Acquest Enterprises Ltd. [*Vancouver Stock Exchange symbol*]
ACQ .... Acquire (ROG)
ACQ .... Acquisition (AFM)
ACQ .... Acquittal (AFM)
ACQ .... Admiral Commanding Battlecruisers [*Obsolete Navy British*]
ACQ .... Aero Continente [*Peru*] [*ICAO designator*] (FAAC)
ACQ .... Annual Contracted Quantity (ADA)
ACQ .... Areas of Change Questionnaire
ACQ .... Association Canadienne des Quotidiens (AC)
ACQ .... Association de la Construction du Quebec [*Construction Association of Quebec*] (AC)
ACQ .... Association des Cablodistributeurs du Quebec Inc. (AC)
ACQ .... Association des Consommateurs du Quebec (AC)
ACQ .... Association du Camionnage du Quebec, Inc. [*Quebec Trucking Association Inc.*] (AC)
ACQ .... Waseca, MN [*Location identifier FAA*] (FAAL)
ACQADJ .... Acquisition Adjustment (IAA)
ACQDA......... Arkansas County Quality Deer Association
ACQE .... Acquisition and Control Query Executive [*Programming language*]
ACQE .... Association Candienne sur la Qualite de l'Eau [*Also, Canadian National Committee of the Internation Association on Water Quality*] [*Formerly, Canadian Association on Water Pollution Research & Control*] (AC)
ACQIS .... Acquisition (ABBR)
ACQL .... Association for Canadian and Quebec Literatures
ACQM .... Automatic Circuit Quality Monitoring (MHDI)
ACQN .... Acquisition (IAA)
ACQNT .... Acquaint (ABBR)
ACQNTD .... Acquainted (ABBR)
ACQNTG .... Acquainting (ABBR)
ACQNTNC .... Acquaintance (ABBR)
ACQNTNCSP... Acquaintanceship (ABBR)
ACQR .... Acquire (ABBR)
ACQRB .... Acquirable (ABBR)
ACQRD........ Acquired (ABBR)
ACQRG .... Acquiring (ABBR)
ACQRNT .... Acquirement (ABBR)
ACQRR .... Acquirer (ABBR)
ACQRT .... Acquirement (ABBR)
ACQS .... Acquiesce (ABBR)
ACQS .... Association of Consultant Quantity Surveyors (MHDI)
ACQSD........ Acquiesced (ABBR)
ACQSEL........ Acquisition Select Switch (MCD)
ACQSG .... Acquiescing (ABBR)
ACQSN .... Acquisition (ABBR)
ACQSNC....... Acquiescence (ABBR)
ACQSNT .... Acquiescent (ABBR)
ACQSNTY ..... Acquiescently (ABBR)
ACQSTN....... Acquisition
Acq/Strat..... Acquisition Strategy (AAGC)
ACQT .... Acquit (ABBR)
ACQT .... Aviation Cadet Qualifying Test [*Military*]
ACQTD .... Acquitted (ABBR)
ACQTG .... Acquitting (ABBR)
ACQTL .... Acquittal (ABBR)
ACQTNC....... Acquittance (ABBR)
ACQUIRE..... Aquatic Information Retrieval (GNE)
ACQUIS .... Acquisition
ACQWL........ American Center for the Quality of Work Life (EA)
ACR .... Abandon Call and Retry [*Telecommunications*]
ACR .... Absolute Catabolic Rate [*Medicine*] (DMAA)
ACR .... Abstracts of Classified Reports [*A publication*]
ACR .... Accelerated Cost Recovery [*Accounting*] (ADA)
ACR .... Access Control Register [*Computer science*]
ACR .... Accumulator Register [*Computer science*] (IAA)
ACR .... Accura Resources [*Vancouver Stock Exchange symbol*]

ACR	Achromatic Color Removal (DGA)
ACR	Acreage Conservation Reserve
ACR	ACR Group [*Associated Press*] (SAG)
Acr	Acriflavine [*Anti-infective mixture*]
ACR	Across (MSA)
ACR	Across
Acr	Acrylic [*Organic chemistry*]
ACR	Active Cavity Radiometer
ACR	Actual Cost Report (NASA)
ACR	Address Control Register [*Computer science*] (MHDI)
ACR	Address Correction Requested
ACR	Adenomatosis of the Colon and Rectum [*Medicine*]
ACR	Adjacent Channel Rejection
ACR	Administrative Communications Requirement (IAA)
AC(R & D)	Admiral Commanding Reserves [*Navy British*]
ACR	Advanced Capabilities RADAR
ACR	Advanced Cargo Rotorcraft [*Later, Advanced Cargo Aircraft - ACA*]
ACR	Advanced Combat Rifle [*Military*] (INF)
ACR	Advanced Confidential Report (MCD)
ACR	Advanced Converter Reactor [*Atomic energy*]
ACR	Advanced Cracking Reactor [*Fuel technology*]
ACR	Aerial Combat Reconnaissance
ACR	Aerodrome Control RADAR (IAA)
ACR	Aeroelastically Conformable Rotor (RDA)
ACR	Air Cavalry Regiment
ACR	Air Control and Reporting (NATG)
ACR	Air Control RADAR
ACR	Air Control Room (MUGU)
ACR	Air-Cooled Compact Reactor (SAA)
ACR	Air Corps Reserve [*Obsolete*]
ACR	Aircraft Checker's Report (AAG)
ACR	Aircraft Control Room
ACR	Air Crew Rescue (CINC)
ACR	Airfield Control RADAR [*Air Force*]
ACR	Alaskan Communications Region [*Air Force*]
ACR	Alliance for Consumer Rights (EA)
ACR	Allied Commission on Reparations
ACR	Allowance Change Request
ACR	Alternate CPU [*Central Processing Unit*] Recovery [*IBM Corp.*] [*Computer science*] (BUR)
ACR	American College of Radiology (EA)
ACR	American College of Rheumatology (EA)
ACR	American Computer Referral (NITA)
ACR	American Council for Romanians (EA)
ACR	American Criminal Reports, Edited by Hawley [*A publication*] (DLA)
ACR	Americans for Children's Relief [*Defunct*] (EA)
ACR	Ammunition Condition Report
ACR	Ancient Conserved Region [*Genetics*]
ACR	Annual Confidential Report
ACR	Annual Curriculum Review [*Education*] (AIE)
ACR	Anomalous Cosmic Ray
ACR	Antarctic Cold Reversal [*Climatology*]
ACR	Antenna Coupler Receiver (MCD)
ACR	Antenna Coupling Regulator (IEEE)
ACR	Anti-Camout Ribbed Bit [*Screwdriving tool*]
ACR	Anticircling Run [*Navy*] (NG)
ACR	Anticonstipation Regimen [*Medicine*]
ACR	Appeal Court Reports [*Ceylon*] [*A publication*] (DLA)
ACR	Applied Communication Research, Inc. [*Information service or system*] (IID)
ACR	Applied Computer Research [*Information service or system*] (IID)
ACR	Approach Control RADAR [*Aviation*]
ACR	Araracuara [*Colombia*] [*Airport symbol*] (OAG)
ACR	Area Coordination Review
ACR	Armored Cavalry Regiment
ACR	Armored Cruiser [*Navy symbol Obsolete*]
ACR	ASA, Air Starline, AG [*Switzerland ICAO designator*] (FAAC)
ACR	Assistant Chief for Research
ACR	Associate Contractor (SAA)
ACR	Association Canadienne des Radiodiffuseurs (AC)
ACR	Association for Conflict Resolution [*Defunct*] (EA)
ACR	Association for Consumer Research (EA)
ACR	Association of Clinical Research [*British*] (DBA)
ACR	Association of College Registrars [*British*]
ACR	Association of Computer Retailers (EA)
ACR	Audio Cartridge (WDMC)
ACR	Audio Cassette Recorder (RDA)
acr	Audio Cassette Recorder (IDOE)
acr	Audio Cassette Recording (IDOE)
ACR	Australian and New Zealand Conveyancing Report [*A publication*]
ACR	Australian Council of Recyclers
ACR	Automatic Call Recording [*Telecommunications*] (CMD)
ACR	Automatic Card Reader
ACR	Automatic Carriage Return
ACR	Automatic Compression Regulator (IEEE)
ACR	Automatic Compression - Release
ACR	Auxiliary Computer Room [*Apollo*] [*NASA*]
ACR	Avalanche Controlled Rectifier (PDAA)
ACR	AVCAL Change Request (MCD)
ACR	Calgary Research Centre, Alberta [*Library symbol National Library of Canada*] (NLC)
ACRA	Accurate (ABBR)
ACRA	Airlift Concepts and Requirements Agency
ACRA	American Car Rental Association (EA)
ACRA	American Collegiate Retailing Association (EA)

ACRA	American Commercial Rabbit Association [*Defunct*] (EA)
ACRA	American Constitutional Rights Association (EA)
ACRA	American Cotswold Record Association (EA)
ACRA	American Craft Retailers Association (EA)
ACRA	American Cultural Resources Association
ACRA	Anti-Char Rapide Autopropulse [*French antitank weapon system*]
ACRA	Approved Conference Rate and Interconference Agreement [*of Steamship Lines in the Foreign Commerce of the United States*]
ACRA	Association Canadienne des Redacteurs Agricoles de Langue Francaise (AC)
ACRA	Association of College Registrars and Administrators [*British*]
ACRA	Association of Company Registration Agents [*British*] (DBA)
ACRA	Auto Collision Repair Association
ACRAF	Artists Civil Rights Assistance Fund [*Defunct*]
AC(R & D)	Assistant Controller, Research and Development [*Admiralty*] [*British*]
ACRANS	Accurateness (ABBR)
ACRAY	Accurately (ABBR)
ACRB	Army Council of Review Boards
ACRB	Royal Bank of Canada, Calgary, Alberta [*Library symbol Obsolete National Library of Canada*] (NLC)
ACRBA	American Chinchilla Rabbit Breeders Association (EA)
ACRBT	Acerbity (ABBR)
ACRBT	Acrobatic (FAAC)
ACRBTC	Acrobatic (ABBR)
ACRBTCY	Acrobatically (ABBR)
ACRC	Air Compressor Research Council [*Defunct*]
A Cr C	Allahabad Criminal Cases [*India*] [*A publication*] (DLA)
ACRC	American City Racing League [*Auto racing*]
ACRC	Arkansas Cancer Research Center [*Little Rock*]
ACRC	Association of Commercial Records Centers (EA)
ACRC	Audio Center - Receiver (KSC)
ACRC	Calgary Branch Library, Alberta Research Council, Alberta [*Library symbol National Library of Canada*] (NLC)
ACRCLTL	Agricultural
ACRCP	Reid Crowther & Partners Ltd., Calgary, Alberta [*Library symbol National Library of Canada*] (BIB)
ACRCY	Accuracy (ABBR)
ACRD	Accord (ABBR)
ACRD	Accredit (ABBR)
ACRD	Accrued (ABBR)
ACRD	Airfield and Carrier Requirements Department (SAA)
ACRD	Army Chief of Research and Development (SAA)
ACRD	Automatic Compression - Release Device
ACRDD	Accorded (ABBR)
ACRDG	According (ABBR)
ACRDGY	Accordingly (ABBR)
ACRDL	Army Chemical Research and Development Labs (MCD)
ACRDM	Centre for Research & Development in Masonry [*Centre de Recherche et de Developpement en Maconnerie*] Calgary, Alberta [*Library symbol National Library of Canada*] (NLC)
ACRDN	Awaiting Contract Record Disposition Notice (AAGC)
ACRDNC	Accordance (ABBR)
ACRDT	Accordant (ABBR)
ACRDT	Acridity (ABBR)
ACRE	Action Committee for Rural Electrification (EA)
ACRE	Advanced Chemical Rocket Engine [*Air Force*]
ACRE	Advanced Cryogenic Rocket Engineering (PDAA)
ACRE	Advisory Committee on Releases to the Environment [*British*]
ACRE	Air Cushion Relief Equipment (PDAA)
ACRE	Alliance for a Clean Rural Environment (EA)
ACRE	American Cannabis Research Experiment (EA)
ACRE	Associate Citizens for Responsible Education [*Group opposing sex education in schools*]
ACRE	Atlantic City Remodelers Exposition [*Remodeling Contractors Association*] (TSPED)
ACRE	Automatic Call Recording Equipment [*Telecommunications*]
ACRE	Automatic Checkout and Readiness Equipment
ACRE	Automatic Climatological Recording Equipment [*Meteorology*] (PDAA)
ACRE	Cremona Public Library, Alberta [*Library symbol National Library of Canada*] (NLC)
A/C Rec	Accounts Receivable [*Business term*] (MHDB)
ACREC	American College of Real Estate Consultants [*Later, RECP*] (EA)
acred	Accreditation
ACREF	Alliance Canadienne des Responsables et Enseignants en Francais [*Canadian Association for the Teachers of French as a First Language*] (AC)
ACREF	Association Canadienne pour la Recherche en Economie Familiale [*Canadian Association for Research in Home Economics - CARHE*]
ACRE-FT/D	Acre-Feet per Day
AcreG	Acres Gaming, Inc. [*Associated Press*] (SAG)
ACREIT	American Conference of Real Estate Investment Trusts [*Defunct*] (EA)
ACREL	Alternating Current Relay [*Electronics*] (IAA)
ACREND	Association Canadienne de Recherche en Evaluation Nondestructifs (AC)
ACREP	Association Canadienne de Recherche et d'Education pour la Paix [*Canadian Peace Research and Education Association - CPREA*]
ACREQ	Allied Commission, Requisitions Subcommittee [*World War II*]
ACRES	Airborne Communication Relay Station [*Air Force*]
ACRES	American Council on Rural Special Eduction
ACRES	Association Canadienne pour la Recherche en Economie de Sante [*Canadian Health Economics Research Association - CHERA*]
ACRES	Australian Centre for Remote Sensing
AcresGm	Acres Gaming, Inc. [*Associated Press*] (SAG)

ACREW	Aircrew
ACRF	Ambulatory Care Research Facility [*Medicine*] (DMAA)
ACRF	Ambulatory Care Research Facility (DMAA)
ACRFAET	Aircraft Crash Rescue Field Assistance and Evaluation Team [*Air Force*] (AFM)
ACRFLT.......	Across Flats
ACRFT	Aircraft
ACRG	Acreage (ABBR)
ACRG	ACR Group [*NASDAQ symbol*] (SAG)
ACRGTQ......	Association des Constructeurs de Routes et Grands Travaux du Quebec [*Quebec Road Builders & Heavy Construction Association*] (AC)
ACRH	Argonne Cancer Research Hospital [*Illinois*]
ACRH	Association Canadienne des Resources Hydriques [*Canadian Water Resources Association*] (EAIO)
ACRHSC......	Aboriginal Community Recreation Health Services Centre [*Australia*]
ACRHSCSA...	Aboriginal Community Recreation Health Services Centre of South Australia
ACRHU........	Association Canadienne des Responsables de l'Habitation et de l'Urbanisme [*Canada*]
ACRI	Acacia Research Corp. [*NASDAQ symbol*] (SAG)
ACRI	Acrid (ABBR)
ACRI	Air-Conditioning and Refrigeration Institute (MSA)
ACRI	American Cocoa Research Institute (EA)
ACRI	Applied Computer Research Institute [*La Trobe University*] [*Australia*]
ACRI	Association Canadienne des Relations Industrielles [*Canadian Industrial Relations Association - CIRA*]
ACRI	Industrial Development Department, Alberta Research Council, Calgary, Alberta [*Library symbol National Library of Canada*] (BIB)
ACRIM	Active Cavity Radiometer Irradiance Monitor
ACRIM	Association for Correctional Research and Information Management (EA)
ACRIP	Adrenocortical Renin Inhibitory Peptide [*Biochemistry*]
ACRIS	AID [*Agency for International Development*] Consultant Registry InformationSystem (IID)
ACRIS	Aperture Card Raster Image Scanner [*Versatec Co.*] (NITA)
ACRIT	Acridity (ABBR)
ACRIT	Advisory Committee for Research on Information Transfer [*Netherlands*] (NITA)
ACRL	Aero-Chem Research Laboratories, Inc. (KSC)
ACRL	Alternaria citri Rough Lemon-specific Toxins
ACRL	American City Racing League [*Auto racing*]
ACRL	Association of College and Research Libraries [*American Library Association*] (EA)
ACRL AAS....	ACRL [*Association of College and Research Libraries*] Asian and African Section
ACRL ANSS...	ACRL [*Association of College and Research Libraries*] Anthropology and Sociology Section
ACRL ARTS...	ACRL [*Association of College and Research Libraries*] Art Section
ACRL AS.....	ACRL [*Association of College and Research Libraries*] Art Section
ACRL ASS....	ACRL [*Association of College and Research Libraries*] Anthropology and Sociology Section
ACRL BIS....	ACRL [*Association of College and Research Libraries*] Bibliographic Instruction Section
ACRL CJCLS...	ACRL [*Association of College and Research Libraries*] Community and Junior College and Research Libraries
ACRL CLS....	ACRL [*Association of College and Research Libraries*] College Libraries Section
ACRL EBSS...	ACRL [*Association of College and Research Libraries*] Education and Behavioral Sciences Section
ACRL LPSS...	ACRL [*Association of College and Research Libraries*] Law and Political Science Section
ACRL RBMS...	ACRL [*Association of College and Research Libraries*] Rare Books and Manuscripts Section
ACRL SEES...	ACRL [*Association of College and Research Libraries*] Slavic and East European Section
ACRL STS....	ACRL [*Association of College and Research Libraries*] Science and Technology Section
ACRL ULS....	ACRL [*Association of College and Research Libraries*] University Libraries Section
ACRL WESS...	ACRL [*Association of College and Research Libraries*] Western European Specialists Section
ACRL WSS...	ACRL [*Association of College and Research Libraries*] Women's Studies Section
ACRM	Acrimony (ABBR)
AC/RM	Air-Conditioning Room (AAG)
ACRM	Air Cushion Rig Mover (PDAA)
ACRM	American College of Radio Marketing (EA)
ACRM	American Congress of Rehabilitation Medicine (EA)
ACRM	Aviation Chief Radioman [*Navy*]
ACRM	Crossfield Municipal Library, Alberta [*Library symbol National Library of Canada*] (NLC)
ACRMA	Air-Conditioning and Refrigerating Machinery Association [*Later, ARI*] (KSC)
A/CRMD	Association for Children with Retarded Mental Development (EA)
ACRMNIS.....	Acrimonious (ABBR)
ACRMNY......	Acrimony (ABBR)
ACRMP	Automation Communication Resource Management Plan [*Army*]
ACRMPIA	Alliance of Canadian Regional Motion Picture Industry Associations
ACRMS	Acrimonious (ABBR)
ACRN	Accounting Classification Reference Number (MCD)
ACRN	Accounting Code Reference Number
ACRN	Accretion (ABBR)
ACRNM........	Acronym (ABBR)

AcrnVn........	Acorn Venture Capital Corp. [*Associated Press*] (SAG)
ACRO	Acrobat (DSUE)
ACRO	Acrodyne Communications [*NASDAQ symbol*] (TTSB)
ACRO	Acrodyne Communications, Inc. [*NASDAQ symbol*] (SAG)
ACRO	Acrodyne Holdings, Inc. [*NASDAQ symbol*] (SAG)
ACRO	Acrophobe [*or Acrophobia*] (ABBR)
ACRO	Aircraft Control Room Officer [*British military*] (DMA)
ACRO	American College of Radiation Oncology
ACRO	Association Canadienne de la Recherche Operationnelle [*Canadian Association of Operational Research*]
ACRODABA...	Acronym Data Base [*Defunct*]
Acrody	Acrodyne Holdings, Inc. [*Associated Press*] (SAG)
Acrodyne	Acrodyne Communications, Inc. [*Associated Press*] (SAG)
ACROL........	Acrolect (ABBR)
ACRON........	Acronym (WDAA)
ACRONYM...	Anti-Cronyism Movement [*Philippines*]
ACRONYM...	[*A*] Contrived Reduction of Nomenclature Yielding Mnemonics [*Humorous interpretation of the term*]
ACROS........	Acrostic (ABBR)
Across	Across Data Systems, Inc. [*Associated Press*] (SAG)
ACROW.......	Acrodyne Communicns Wrrt [*NASDAQ symbol*] (TTSB)
ACROWE......	Association of Cooperative Retailers-Owned Wholesalers of Europe (EAIO)
ACRP	Advisory Committee on Radiological Protection [*Canada*]
ACRP	Airborne Communications Reconnaissance Platform
ACRP	Airborne Communications Reconnaissance Program (AFM)
ACRP	Armament Control Relay Panel (MCD)
ACRP	Army Cost Reduction Program (AABC)
ACRP	Asian Conference on Religion and Peace [*Singapore, Singapore*] (EAIO)
ACRP	Association Canadienne des Restaurateurs Professionnels [*Canadian Association of Professional Conservators - CAPC*]
ACRPI	Association of Clinical Research Pharmaceutical Industries [*British*] (DBA)
acrpl	Acropolis (VRA)
ACRPP	Association pour la Conservation et la Reproduction Photographique de la Presse,Paris, France [*Library symbol Library of Congress*] (LCLS)
A Cr R	Allahabad Criminal Reports [*India*] [*A publication*] (DLA)
ACRR	American Council on Race Relations
ACRR	Annular Core Research Reactor [*Nuclear energy*] (NRCH)
ACRRSV......	Autistic Citizens' Residential and Resources Society of Victoria [*Australia*]
ACRRT	American Chiropractic Registry of Radiologic Technologists (EA)
ACRS	Abbreviated Conners Parent/Teacher Rating Scale (EDAC)
ACRS	Accelerated Capital Recovery System [*Accounting*]
ACRS	Accelerated Cost Recovery Schedule [*Accounting*]
ACRS	Accelerated Cost Recovery System [*Accounting*]
ACRS	Acceleration Curve Restraint Seat [*Automotive safety systems*]
acrs	Across (BARN)
ACRS	Across Data Systems [*NASDAQ symbol*] (TTSB)
ACRS	Across Data Systems, Inc. [*NASDAQ symbol*] (SAG)
ACRS	Active Contrast Reduction System (MCD)
ACRS	Advisory Committee on Reactor Safeguards [*Nuclear Regulatory Commission*]
ACRS	Air Cushion Recovery System (MCD)
ACRS	Air-Cushion Restraint System [*General Motors*]
ACRS	Association for Correctional Research and Statistics (OICC)
ACRS	Australian Camellia Research Society
ACRS	Automatic Chemical Reaction System
ACRS	Southern Branch Library, Alberta Research Council, Calgary, Alberta [*Library symbol National Library of Canada*] (NLC)
ACRSA	Association Canadienne de Recherches Sociales Appliquees [*Canadian Association of Applied Social Research - CAASR*]
ACRSD........	Accursed (ABBR)
ACRSDNS...	Accursedness (ABBR)
ACRSDY......	Accursedly (ABBR)
ACRSE........	American Council on Rural Special Education (EA)
ACRSM........	Air Cushion Restraint System Module
ACRSP........	Association for Canadian Registered Safety Professionals [*Association des Professionnels en Securite Agrees du Canada*] (AC)
ACRSS	Association for Children with Russell-Silver Syndrome (EA)
ACRST	Accurst (ABBR)
ACRT	Accredit (ABBR)
acrt............	Acroteria (VRA)
ACRT	Actrade International Ltd. [*NASDAQ symbol*] (SAG)
ACRT	Actrade Intl Ltd. [*NASDAQ symbol*] (TTSB)
ACRT	Analysis Control Routine [*Computer science*] (OA)
ACRT	Aviation Chief Radio Technician [*Navy*]
ACRTC	Advanced CRT Controller [*Computer chip*]
ACRTD........	Accredited (ABBR)
ACRTG........	Accrediting (ABBR)
ACRU	Accrue (ABBR)
ACRUD........	Accrued (ABBR)
ACRUG........	Accruing (ABBR)
ACRUT........	Accruement (ABBR)
ACRV	Accretive (ABBR)
ACRV	Armored Command and Reconnaissance Vehicle [*Former USSR*] (AABC)
ACRV	Artillery Command Reconnaissance Vehicle [*Former USSR*]
ACRV	Association Canadienne des Regulateurs des Vols [*Canadian Air Line Dispatchers' Association - CALDA*]
ACRV	Assured Crew Return Vehicle [*Aerospace*]
ACRV	Audio Center - Receiver (KSC)

ACRV .... Automated Command Response Verification (MCD)
ACRV .... Rocky View School Division, Calgary, Alberta [*Library symbol National Library of Canada*] (NLC)
ACRVH .... Library Services, Rocky View General Hospital, Calgary, Alberta [*Library symbol National Library of Canada*] (BIB)
ACRW .... Aircrew (AFM)
ACRW .... American Council of Railroad Women (EA)
ACRY .... Acrylic
ACRY .... Australian Council of Rural Youth
ACRYL .... Acrylic (MSA)
ACRYL-BIS... Acrylamide Bis-Acrylamide
ACS............. Aberdeen Cable Services [*Cable TV*] (NITA)
ACS............. Aboriginal Children's Services [*Australia*]
ACS............. Academic Computer Service [*Generic*] [*Research center*] (RCD)
ACS............. Accelerated Climatic Simulator (PDAA)
ACS............. Access [*Telecommunications*] (MSA)
ACS............. Accounting Control System
ACS............. Accumulator Switch [*Computer science*]
ACS............. Acetylstrophanthidin [*Organic chemistry*]
ACS............. Acquisition and Command Support (MCD)
ACS............. Acrocephalosyndactyly [*Medicine*] (DMAA)
ACS............. Acting Commissary of Subsistence
ACS............. Active Communications Satellite
ACS............. Activity Characteristics Sheet [*Agency for International Development*]
ACS............. Acute Confusional State [*Medicine*] (MEDA)
ACS............. Adaptive Control System
ACS............. Additional Curates' Society [*British*]
ACS............. Address Change Service [*Postal Service*] [*United States*] (WDMC)
ACS............. Adhesive Component System (PDAA)
ACS............. Administrative Computing Service
ACS............. Administrative Control System [*Telecommunications*] (TEL)
ACS............. Admiralty Computing Service [*British*] (SAA)
ACS............. Adrenocorticosteroid [*Medicine*] (OA)
ACS............. Advance Count Switch
ACS............. Advanced Cardiovascular Systems
ACS............. Anodal Ceramic System
ACS............. Advanced Civil Schooling [*Army*] (INF)
ACS............. Advanced Clothing Subsystem [*SIPE*] [*Military*] (RDA)
ACS............. Advanced Communications Service [*Later, AIS*] [*AT & T*]
ACS............. Advanced Communication System [*Computer science*] (TNIG)
ACS............. Advanced Computer Services [*Honeywell Information Systems*] (IEEE)
ACS............. Advanced Computer System [*IBM Corp.*] (IEEE)
ACS............. Advanced Control System [*IBM Corp.*] (NITA)
ACS............. Advanced Course Studentships [*British*]
ACS............. Advanced Cryptographic System [*Air Force*] (MCD)
ACS............. Advertisers Casting Service
AC(S) .... Advisory Committee, Statistics [*British*]
ACS............. Aegis Combat System [*Navy*] (LAIN)
ACS............. Aerial Common Sensor [*Military*] (RDA)
ACS............. Aerodrome Control Service
ACS............. Aeronautical Command Systems [*Air Force*]
ACS............. Affiliated Computer Systems [*Later, MPEC Co.*] [*Telecommunications*] (TSSD)
ACS............. Affinely Connected Space
ACS............. Afloat Correlation System [*Navy*]
ACS............. African Coastal Security (DOMA)
ACS............. Aft Crew Station [*NASA*] (MCD)
ACS............. Age Concern Scotland [*An association*] (EAIO)
ACS............. Agena Control System [*NASA*]
ACS............. Agricultural Cooperative Service [*Washington, DC Department of Agriculture*] (GRD)
ACS............. Airbag Central Sensor [*Automotive safety*]
ACS............. Air Capable Ship (MCD)
ACS............. Air Coating System (PDAA)
ACS............. Air Commando Squadron (CINC)
ACS............. Air Commerce [*Yugoslavia*] [*ICAO designator*] (FAAC)
ACS............. Air Conditioning Sensor [*Automotive engineering*]
ACS............. Air Conditioning System
ACS............. Aircraft Carrier Squadron [*British military*] (DMA)
ACS............. Aircraft Communications System
ACS............. Aircraft Control and Surveillance [*Air Force*]
ACS............. Aircraft Control System (MUGU)
A/CS .... Aircraft Security Vessel
ACS............. Air Force Communications Service, Scott AFB, IL [*OCLC symbol*] (OCLC)
ACS............. Airline Charter Service
ACS............. Airman Classification Squadron [*Air Force*]
ACS............. Airplane Configuration System
ACS............. Airways Communication Station (NATG)
ACS............. Alarm and Control System [*Telecommunications*] (TEL)
ACS............. Alaska Conservation Society (EA)
ACS............. Alaskan Communications System [*Air Force*]
ACS............. Alcohol Counselling Service [*British*] (DI)
A-CS .... Alignment Countdown Set [*Aerospace*] (AAG)
ACS............. Allied Chiefs of Staff [*World War II*]
ACS............. Alternate Core Spray [*Nuclear energy*] (NRCH)
ACS............. Alternating Current, Synchronous
ACS............. Alternating Current Synthesizer [*Exxon Corp.*]
ACS............. Alternative Curriculum Strategies [*Education*] (AIE)
ACS............. Altertext Conversion System (DGA)
ACS............. Altitude Control System
ACS............. Altos Computer Systems (NITA)
ACS............. Amalgamated Conservation Society (AC)
ACS............. American Camellia Society (EA)

ACS............. American Canal Society (EA)
ACS............. American Cancer Society (EA)
ACS............. American Capital Convertible Securities, Inc. [*NYSE symbol*] (SPSG)
ACS............. American Carbon Society (EA)
ACS............. American Carnation Society (EA)
ACS............. American Carousel Society (EA)
ACS............. American Celiac Society [*Later, ACS/DSC*] (EA)
ACS............. American Ceramic Society (EA)
ACS............. American Cetacean Society (EA)
ACS............. American Cheese Society (EA)
ACS............. American Chemical Society (EA)
ACS............. American Cockatiel Society (EA)
ACS............. American College of Surgeons (EA)
ACS............. American College of Switzerland
ACS............. American Colonization Society
ACS............. American Committee of Slavists (EA)
ACS............. American Communication Services [*Evanston, IL*] [*Telecommunications*] (TSSD)
ACS............. American Community Schools [*In foreign countries*]
ACS............. American Conifer Society (EA)
ACS............. American Contemplative Society [*Defunct*] (EA)
ACS............. American Copyright Society [*Defunct*] (EA)
ACS............. American Cryonics Society (EA)
ACS............. American Crystal Sugar Co. (MHDW)
ACS............. American Cultural Society [*Defunct*]
ACS............. American Czechoslovak Society (EA)
ACS............. Americans for Common Sense [*Defunct*] (EA)
ACS............. Analog Computer System
ACS............. Analysis Computer System
ACS............. Analysis of Coping Style [*Test*]
ACS............. Ancillary Communications Services [*Australia*]
ACS............. Anglo-Chilean Society (EAIO)
ACS............. Anglo-Continental Society [*British*]
ACS............. Anisotropically Conductive Silicone [*Rubber*] [*Robotics*]
ACS............. Annealed Copper-Covered Steel
ACS............. Anodal Closing Sound [*Physiology*]
ACS............. Anterior Convex Side
ACS............. Anti-Communist Society [*Belize*] (PD)
ACS............. Anti-Curl System [*Intellifax*] [*Brother Industries USA, Inc.*] [*Telecommunications*]
ACS............. Antireticular Cytotoxic Serum
ACS............. Aperture Current Setting [*In Coulter counter*] [*Microbiology*]
ACS............. Apollo Command [*or Communications*] System [*NASA*]
ACS............. Applied Computer Science (IAA)
ACS............. Applied Computer Solution
ACS............. Approximate Cubic Search [*Mathematics*]
ACS............. Armament Control System [*Air Force*]
ACS............. Armored Crew Seat
ACS............. Army Calibration System
ACS............. Army Commanding Service
ACS............. Army Communicative Systems [*Provisional*] (RDA)
ACS............. Army Community Service
ACS............. ARPA Calibration Satellite (MCD)
ACS............. Art Center School
ACS............. Arterial Cannulation Support [*Cardiology*] (DAVI)
ACS............. Artillery Computer System
ACS............. Asbestos Cement Sheet (ADA)
ACS............. Assembly Control System [*IBM Corp.*] (BUR)
ACS............. Assessment of Cognitive Skills
ACS............. Asset Control System [*or Subsystem*] [*Army*] (AABC)
ACS............. Assistant Chief of Staff
ACS............. Assistant Chief of Supplies [*British military*] (DMA)
ACS............. Assistant Chief Statistician
ACS............. Associated Computer System (MHDI)
ACS............. Associate in Commercial Science
ACS............. Associate in Customer Service [*Canada*] (DD)
ACS............. Association Canadienne de Semiotique [*Canadian Semiotic Association - CSA*]
ACS............. Association Canadienne des Slavistes [*Canadian Association of Slavists - CAS*]
ACS............. Association for Canadian Studies [*See also AEC*]
ACS............. Association for Christian Schools [*Defunct*] (EA)
ACS............. Association of Caribbean Studies
ACS............. Association of Certified Servers (EA)
ACS............. Association of Clinical Scientists (EA)
ACS............. Association of Commonwealth Students [*British*] (BI)
ACS............. Association of Contemplative Sisters (EA)
ACS............. Association of Council Secretaries [*Later, NAES*] (EA)
ACS............. Association of Cricket Statisticians (EAIO)
ACS............. Astro Communications System [*NASA*] (KSC)
ACS............. Asynchronous Communications Server [*Computer science*] (IT)
ACS............. Atmosphere Climate Study [*National Science Foundation*] (MSC)
ACS............. Atmosphere Control System [*NASA*] (KSC)
ACS............. Attack Center Switchboard
ACS............. Attendant Care Scheme
ACS............. Attitude Command System (IEEE)
ACS............. Attitude Configuration System (SSD)
ACS............. Attitude Control and Stabilization [*NASA*] (KSC)
ACS............. Attitude Control System [*or Subsystem*] [*Aerospace*]
ACS............. Audio Communications System
ACS............. Audio Conducted Susceptibility (IAA)
ACS............. Autograph Card Signed [*Manuscript descriptions*]
ACS............. Automated Circulation System [*Computer science*]
ACS............. Automated Commercial System [*US Customs Service computerized system*]

ACS............	Automated Communications Set (BUR)
ACS............	Automated Communications System (PCM)
ACS............	Automatic Cartographic System
ACS............	Automatic Checkout System [NASA]
ACS............	Automatic Clutch System [Powertrain] [Automotive engineering]
ACS............	Automatic Coding System [Computer science] (IAA)
ACS............	Automatic Control System
ACS............	Automatic Counter System
ACS............	Automation Composition System (MCD)
ACS............	Autonomous Replication Core-Consensus Sequence [Genetics]
ACS............	Auxiliary Code Storage [Computer memory] (NITA)
ACS............	Auxiliary Cooling System [Nuclear energy] (NRCH)
ACS............	Auxiliary Core Storage [Computer science] (BUR)
ACS............	Azimuth Control System
ACS............	J. C. Sproule & Associates Ltd., Calgary, Alberta [Library symbol National Library of Canada] (NLC)
ACS............	Las Acacias [Argentina] [Geomagnetic observatory code]
ACS............	Les Arrets de la Cour Supreme [Legal database] [Canada] (NITA)
ACS............	Smith [A.O.] Corp. [NYSE symbol] (SAG)
ACS............	Van Kam Am Cap Cv Sec [NYSE symbol] (TTSB)
ACSA..........	Acoustical Society of America
ACSA..........	Adenylate Cyclase-Stimulating Activity [Medicine] (DMAA)
ACSA..........	Affiliated Computer Services'A' [NASDAQ symbol] (TTSB)
ACSA..........	Affiliated Computer Services, Inc. [NASDAQ symbol] (SAG)
ACSA..........	Alaska Council of School Administrators (SRA)
ACSA..........	Allied Communications Security Agency [Brussels, Belgium] [NATO]
ACSA..........	Allied Communications Support Area
ACSA..........	American Center for Students and Artists (EA)
ACSA..........	American Cormo Sheep Association (EA)
ACSA..........	American Cotton Shippers Association (EA)
ACSA..........	American Council of Spotted Asses (EA)
ACSA..........	Americans Concerned about Southern Africa (EA)
ACSA..........	Aqua-Cat Catamaran Sailing Association (EA)
ACSA..........	Association Canadienne de Sociologie et d'Anthropologie [Canadian Sociology and Anthropology Association - CSAA]
ACSA..........	Association Canadienne de Softball Amateur [Canadian Association of Amateur Softball]
ACSA..........	Association of California School Administrators (SRA)
ACSA..........	Association of California State Attorneys (SRA)
ACSA..........	Association of Cambodian Survivors of America (EA)
ACSA..........	Association of Collegiate Schools of Architecture (EA)
ACSA..........	Australian Carpetmaster Sheepbreeders' Association
ACSA..........	Australian Customer Service Association
ACSA..........	Ayrshire Cattle Society of Australia
ACSA..........	Southern Alberta Institute of Technology, Calgary, Alberta [Library symbol National Library of Canada] (NLC)
ACSAA........	Alberta College of Art, Calgary, Alberta [Library symbol National Library of Canada] (NLC)
ACSAA........	American Committee for South Asian Art [Defunct Defunct] (EA)
ACSAC........	Assistant Chief of Staff for Automation and Communications [Military] (AABC)
ACSAD........	Arab Center for the Study of Arid Zones and Dry Lands [of the League of Arab States] [Syria] [Research center] (IRC)
AC/SAF.......	Assistant Chief of Staff, Air Force
ACSALF.......	Association Canadienne des Sociologues et Anthropologues de Langue Francaise [Canadian Association of French-Language Sociologists and Anthropologists]
ACSAP........	Automated Cross-Section Analysis Program [Computer science]
ACSAS........	Advanced Conformal Submarine Acoustic Sensor
ACSAS........	Alabama Council for School Administration and Supervision (SRA)
ACSAS........	Automated Configuration Status Accounting System [Navy]
ACSB..........	Accessible (ABBR)
ACSB..........	Americans for a Common Sense Budget [Inactive Defunct] (EA)
ACSB..........	Amplitude Companded Single Sideband [Electronics]
ACSB..........	Apollo Crew Systems Branch [NASA] (KSC)
ACSB..........	Aviation Command Screening Board (DNAB)
ACSBNS......	Accessibleness (ABBR)
ACSBT........	Accessibility (ABBR)
ACSBY........	Accessibly (ABBR)
ACSC..........	Accrediting Commission for Specialized Colleges [Defunct] (EA)
ACSC..........	AIDS Committee of Simcoe County (AC)
ACSC..........	Air Carrier Service Corp.
ACSC..........	Air Command and Staff College [Maxwell AFB, AL] [Air Force] (MCD)
ACSC..........	Ambulatory Care - Sensitive Condition
ACSC..........	American Cocker Spaniel Club (EAIO)
ACSC..........	American Council on Schools and Colleges (EA)
ACSC..........	AMTRAK Commuter Services Corp. [Later, CSC]
ACSC..........	Anglican Community Services Council [Australia]
ACSC..........	Applied Communications Systems Center [AT & T]
ACSC..........	Armament Control System Checkout [Air Force] (SAA)
ACSC..........	Armaments Cooperation Steering Committee
ACSC..........	Army Computer Systems Command [Also, CSC]
ACSC..........	Association of California Surety Companies (SRA)
ACSC..........	Association of Casualty and Surety Companies [Later, AIA] (EA)
ACSC..........	Atlanta Cancer Surveillance Center [Emory University] [Research center] (RCD)
ACSC..........	Automated Contingency Support Capability (AFM)
ACSC..........	Technical Library, Shell Canada Resources Ltd., Calgary, Alberta [Library symbol National Library of Canada] (NLC)
ACSCA........	Australian Cable and Subscription Communications Association
ACSCC........	Australian Consumer Sales and Credit Law Cases [A publication]
ACSCCIM.....	Assistant Chief of Staff for Command and Control Information Management

ACSC-E.......	Assistant Chief of Staff for Communications - Electronics [Army] (AABC)
ACSCI.........	Association for Computer-Based Systems for Career Information (OICC)
ACSCL........	Calgary Research Centre Library, Shell Canada Ltd., Alberta [Library symbol National Library of Canada] (NLC)
ACSCOT......	American College of Surgeons Committee on Trauma
ACSD..........	Academic Computer Services Division [Milwaukee School of Engineering] [Research center] (RCD)
ACSD..........	Army Communications - Service Division
ACSD..........	Automatic Color-Scanned Device (MCD)
ACSDI........	Sulphur Development Institute of Canada, Calgary, Alberta [Library symbol National Library of Canada] (NLC)
ACSDO........	Air Carrier Safety District Office
ACS/DSC.....	American Celiac Society/Dietary Support Coalition (EA)
ACSE..........	Application Control Service Element (ACII)
ACSE..........	Association Control Service Element [Telecommunications] (OSI)
ACSEA........	Air Command, Southeast Asia
ACSEA........	Allied Command Southeast Asia [World War II]
ACSEB........	Aviation Clothing and Survival Equipment Bulletin (MCD)
AcSEC........	Accounting Standards Executive Committee (TDOB)
ACSED........	Automated Computer Science Education
ACSENSW....	Association of Consulting Structural Engineers of New South Wales [Australia]
ACSEP........	Aircraft Certification Systems Evaluation Program [FAA] (TAG)
ACSES........	Automated Computer Science Education System
ACSET........	Advisory Committee on the Supply and Education of Teachers [British]
ACSET(FE)...	Advisory Committee for the Supply and Education of Teachers, Further Education Sub-Committee (AIE)
ACSF..........	Aircraft Storage Facility (SAA)
ACSF..........	Artificial Cerebrospinal Fluid [Medicine]
ACSF..........	Association of French Host Centers [Paris] [Information service or system] (IID)
ACSF..........	Attack Carrier Striking Force
ACSFOR......	Assistant Chief of Staff for Force Development [Army]
ACSFQ........	Association des Centres de Ski de Fond du Quebec (AC)
AC-SG........	Alternating Current Signal Generator
ACSG..........	Area Coordination Subgroup [Air Force] (AFM)
ACSGC........	Association Canadienne des Sciences Geodesiques et Cartographiques [Canadian Institute of Surveying and Mapping] (EAIO)
ACSGp........	Area Coordination Subgroup [Air Force] (AFM)
ACSGRP......	Area Coordination Subgroup [Air Force]
ACSH..........	American Council on Science and Health (EA)
ACSHRD......	Atlantic Canada Society for Human Resource Development
ACSI..........	American Cinemastores [NASDAQ symbol] (SAG)
ACSI..........	American Communication Services, Inc. [Evanston, IL] (TSSD)
ACSI..........	Assistant Chief of Staff for Intelligence [Washington, DC] [Army]
ACSI..........	Association Canadienne des Sciences de l'Information [Canadian Association for Information Science]
ACSI..........	Association of Christian Schools International (EA)
ACSI..........	Automotive Cooling Systems Institute (EA)
ACSICR......	Association Canadienne des Societes d'Investissement en Capital de Risque
ACSIEC	[The] Suicide Information and Education Centre, Calgary, Alberta [Library symbol National Library of Canada] (NLC)
ACSIF.........	Alaska Communication System Industrial Fund (AFM)
ACSIG.........	Alignment Countdown Set Inertial Guidance [Aerospace] (AAG)
ACSIL.........	Admiralty Centre for Scientific Information and Liaison [British]
ACSIM........	Accelerated Constrained Simplex Technique (PDAA)
ACSIM........	Arms Control Simulation (SAA)
ACSIM........	Assistant Chief of Staff for Information Management [Army]
ACSIM-C4....	Assistant Chief of Staff for Information Management-Command, Control, Communications, and Computers [Military] (GFGA)
ACSIQ........	Association des Chefs de Service d'Incendie du Quebec [Quebec Fire Chief Association] (AC)
Acsius.........	Accursius [Deceased, 1263] [Authority cited in pre-1607 legal work] (DSA)
ACSIW........	American Cinemastores Wrrt [NASDAQ symbol] (TTSB)
ACSJ..........	Academic Committee on Soviet Jewry (EA)
ACSL..........	Advanced Continuous Simulation Language [Pronounced "axle"] [Computer science] (CSR)
ACSL..........	Advanced Continuous System Language (MCD)
ACSL..........	American Computer Science League (EA)
ACSL..........	Australian Co. Secretary's Letter [A publication]
ACSL..........	Standing Lenticular Altocumulus [Meteorology]
AcSM..........	Academy Sergeant-Major [British military] (DMA)
ACSM..........	Acoustic Warfare Support Measures (NVT)
ACSM..........	Advanced Conventional Standoff Missile (MCD)
ACSM..........	Alkylated Chlorsulfonated Polyethylene [Plastics technology]
ACSM..........	American College of Sports Medicine (EA)
ACSM..........	American Congress on Surveying and Mapping (EA)
ACSM..........	Apollo Command and Service Module [NASA] (IAA)
ACSM..........	Assemblies, Components, Spare Parts, and Materials [NATO] (NATG)
ACSM..........	Associate of the Camborne School of Mines [British]
ACSM..........	Stockmen's Memorial Foundation, Calgary, Alberta [Library symbol National Library of Canada] (NLC)
ACSMA.......	American Canine Sports Medicine Association (EA)
ACSMA.......	American Cloak and Suit Manufacturers Association (EA)
ACSMAC......	Association Canadienne pour les Structures et Materiaux Composites (AC)
ACSMH.......	Association of Clerks and Stewards in Mental Hospitals [A union] [British]

ACSN .... Accession (ABBR)
ACSN .... Advanced Change Study Notice [*Aerospace*]
ACSN .... Appalachian Community Service Network [*Cable-television system*]
ACSN .... Association for Citizens with Special Needs [*Australia*]
ACSN .... Association of Collegiate Schools of Nursing [*Later, NLN*]
ACSND .... Accessioned (ABBR)
ACSNG .... Accessioning (ABBR)
ACSNI .... Advisory Committee on the Safety of Nuclear Installations [*British*] (NUCP)
ACSNL .... Accessional (ABBR)
ACSNSW ..... Arts and Crafts Society of New South Wales [*Australia*]
ACS-O .... Access Opening (AAG)
ACSO .... Aircraft Capable of Satellite Operations
ACSO .... Association of County Supplies Officers [*British*] (DBA)
ACSO .... SUNCOR Inc., Calgary, Alberta [*Library symbol National Library of Canada*] (NLC)
ACSOC .... Acoustical Society of America
ACSP .... Advanced Control Signal Processor [*For spacecraft*]
ACSP .... Advisory Council on Scientific Policy
ACSP .... Aged Care Support Program [*Australia*]
ACSP .... Aircraft Cross-Servicing Program [*Military*]
ACSP .... Alternating Current Spark Plug (IAA)
ACSP .... Army Central Service Point
ACSP .... Association Canadienne de Sante Publique (AC)
ACSP .... Association Canadienne de Science Politique [*Canadian Political Science Association - CPSA*]
ACSP .... Association Canadienne des Soins Palliatifs (AC)
ACSP .... Association of Catholic School Principals [*Australia*]
ACSP .... Association of Collegiate Schools of Planning (EA)
ACSP .... Institute of Sedimentary and Petroleum Geology, Calgary, Alberta [*Library symbol National Library of Canada*] (NLC)
ACSPA .... Australian Canvas and Synthetic Products Association
A/csPay .... Accounts Payable (HGAA)
ACSPFT .... Asian Committee for Standardization of Physical Fitness Tests [*Obu-Shi, Japan*] (EAIO)
ACSPNL ...... Access Panel [*Technical drawings*] (IAA)
ACSQ .... Airborne Communications Squadron [*Air Force*]
ACSQ .... Association des Communicateurs Scientifiques du Quebec (AC)
AC Sqn .... Army Co-Operation Squadron [*British and Canadian*] [*World War II*]
ACSR .... Advanced Combat Surveillance RADAR
ACSR .... Aluminum Cable Steel Reinforced
ACSR .... Aluminum Conductor Steel Reinforced
ACSR .... Arizona Cactus and Succulent Research (EA)
ACSR .... Association Canadienne des Sciences Regionales [*Canadian Regional Science Association - CRSA*]
ACSR .... Australian Corporations and Securities Reports [*A publication*]
ACSRC .... Assistant Chief of Staff for Reserve Components [*Army*]
A/CS REC .... Accounts Receivable [*Accounting*]
ACSRNAS .... Armoured Car Section, Royal Naval Air Service [*British military*] (DMA)
ACSRY .... Accessory (ABBR)
ACSS .... Advanced Communications Support System [*Sytek, Inc.*] [*Computer science*] (TNIG)
ACSS .... Air Combat and Surveillance System (MCD)
ACSS .... Air Command and Staff School [*Air Force*]
ACSS .... American Catholic Sociological Society [*Later, ASR*] (EA)
ACSS .... American Cheviot Sheep Society (EA)
ACSS .... Analog Computer Subsystem
ACSS .... Army Chief of Support Services
ACSS .... Associated Carters Society of Scotland [*A union*]
ACSS .... Association Canadienne des Sciences Sportives [*Canadian Association of Sports Sciences*]
ACSS .... Association of Colleges and Secondary Schools [*Later, SACS*] (EA)
ACSS .... Augmented Contact Support Set [*TOW*]
ACSS .... Australian Council of Social Service
ACSS .... Automated Color Separation System (PDAA)
ACSS .... Automated Contingency Support System
ACSS .... Automated Contract Specification System
ACS/S & A ... Assistant Chief of Staff, Studies and Analysis [*Air Force*] (MCD)
ACSSAVO ..... Association of Chief State School Audio-Visual Officers [*Defunct*] (EA)
ACSSB .... Amplitude-Companded Single Sideband (DA)
ACSSN .... Association of Colleges and Secondary Schools for Negroes [*Later, ACSS*]
ACSSP .... Air Carrier Standard Security Programs [*FAA*] (TAG)
ACSSR .... Ammunition Consolidated Stock Status Report
ACST .... Access Time
ACST .... Accost (ABBR)
ACST .... Acoustic (MSA)
ACST .... Advisory Committee on the Application of Science and Technology to Development [*Also, ACAST, ACASTD*] [*United Nations*]
ACST .... Army Clerical Speed Test
ACST .... Association Canadienne pour le Soustitrage (AC)
ACST .... Association of Correspondence School Teachers (AEBS)
ACSTA .... American Center for Stanislavski Theatre Art (EA)
ACSTA .... Society for Treatment of Autism, Calgary, Alberta [*Library symbol National Library of Canada*] (NLC)
ACSTC .... Acoustic
ACSTCW ..... Association of Civil Service Temporary Clerks and Writers [*A union*] [*British*]
ACSTFA .... Advisory Committee on Science and Technology and Foreign Affairs [*Terminated, 1975*] [*Department of State*] (EGAO)
ACSTH .... Artistic Crafts Series of Technical Handbooks [*A publication*]
ACSTI .... Advisory Committee for Scientific and Technical Information [*British*]

ACSTIA .... Advisory Committee for Scientific, Technological, and International Affairs [*National Science Foundation*] (EGAO)
ACSTIS .... Advanced Circular Scan Thermal Imaging System (MCD)
ACSTL .... Acoustical (ABBR)
ACSTLY .... Acoustically (ABBR)
ACSTM .... Accustom (ABBR)
ACSTMD ...... Accustomed (ABBR)
ACSTMG ...... Accustoming (ABBR)
ACSTT .... Advisory Committee of the Supply and Training of Teachers [*British*]
ACSTV .... Accusative (ABBR)
ACSU .... Army Civil Services' Union [*Singapore*]
ACSUS .... Association for Canadian Studies in the United States (EA)
ACSV .... Aortocoronary Saphenous Vein [*Cardiology*] (MAE)
ACSV .... Arts and Crafts Society of Victoria [*Australia*]
ACSW .... Academy of Certified Social Workers
ACSW .... Advanced Conventional Standoff Weapon
ACSW .... Advanced Crew-Served Weapon [*Army*] (INF)
ACSW .... Advisory Council on the Status of Women [*Canada*]
ACSWC .... American Committee of the Slovak World Congress (EA)
ACSWC .... American Council of the Slovak World Congress [*Defunct*] (EA)
ACSWS .... Admiralty Civilian Shore Wireless Service [*British*] (IAA)
ACSYNT ...... Aircraft Synthesis [*Computer science*]
ACSYS .... Accounting Computer System [*Burroughs Corp.*]
ACSYS .... Arctic Climate System Study (ECON)
ACSZJ .... American Committee for Shaare Zedek in Jerusalem (EA)
ACT .... Acceleration Time
ACT .... Accounting Control Table (CMD)
ACT .... Accumulation Time
ACT .... Accumulator, Temporary
ACT .... Acetate Cloth Tape
ACT .... Achievement through Counselling and Treatment
ACT .... Acoustical Tile [*Technical drawings*]
ACT .... Acoustic Charge Transport [*Computer science*]
ACT .... Acquisition, Control of Test [*Units*] (NASA)
ACT .... Act in Crisis Today [*Fund sponsored by the Lutheran Church in America*]
ACT .... Acting
ACT .... Actinidin
act .... Actinomycin [*Also, A*] [*Generic form Antibiotic compounds*]
ACT .... Action [*NATO*]
ACT .... Action by Christians Against Torture (EAIO)
ACT .... Action for Children in Trouble (EA)
ACT .... Action for Children's Television [*Defunct*] (EA)
ACT .... Action Library, Washington, DC [*OCLC symbol*] (OCLC)
ACT .... Activated Clotting [*or Coagulation*] Time [*Medicine*]
ACT .... Activation (NVT)
ACT .... Active (AFM)
act .... Active (VRA)
ACT .... Active Cleaning Technique [*Optical surface*]
ACT .... Active Control Technique [*or Technology*]
ACT .... Activity (MSA)
ACT .... Activity Completion Technique [*Personality development test*] [*Psychology*]
Act .... Acton's Prize Cases, Privy Council [*A publication*] (DLA)
ACT .... Actor's Conservatory Theater
ACT .... Actual (KSC)
ACT .... Actuarial Data Base [*I. P. Sharp Associates*] [*Database*]
ACT .... Actuary [*Insurance*]
ACT .... Actuate (KSC)
ACT .... Adaptive Computer Technologies [*San Jose, CA*]
ACT .... Adaptive Control of Thought [*Psychology*]
ACT .... Adjuvant Chemotherapy [*Oncology*]
ACT .... Administrative Clerical and Technical Programs [*Department of Labor*]
ACT .... Adrenocorticotrophin (PDAA)
ACT .... Advance Corporation Tax [*British*]
ACT .... Advanced Capability Tanker (MCD)
ACT .... Advanced Career Training
ACT .... Advanced Chassis Technology [*Automotive engineering*]
ACT .... Advanced Color Technology, Inc. [*Chelmsford, MA*] [*Printer manufacturer*]
ACT .... Advanced Communications Technology [*Tymshare, Inc.*]
ACT .... Advanced Composite Technology [*Materials science*]
ACT .... Advanced Computer Techniques (MCD)
ACT .... Advanced Concepts and Technology Program [*Army*] (RDA)
ACT .... Advanced Concepts Team [*Army*] (RDA)
ACT .... Advanced Concepts Test (MCD)
ACT .... Advanced Concept Tire [*Firestone Tire & Rubber Co.*]
ACT .... Advanced Concept Train [*Aerospace*]
ACT .... Advanced Conversion Technology (MCD)
ACT .... Advanced Core Test [*Nuclear energy*]
ACT .... Advanced Coronary Treatment [*Cardiology*] (DAVI)
ACT .... Advanced Coronary Treatment Foundation
ACT .... Advanced Corporation Tax Act [*British*] (ECON)
ACT .... Advertised Computer Technologies [*Data Courier, Inc.*] [*Information service or system Defunct*] (IID)
ACT .... Advertising Control for Television [*Advertising testing service*] (WDMC)
ACT .... Advisory Council on Technology [*British*]
ACT .... Advocates for Communication Technology for Deaf/Blind People
ACT .... Aerial Combat Tactics (SAA)
ACT .... Agricultural Central Trading [*British*]
ACT .... AIDS Committee of Toronto (AC)
ACT .... Aid to Children with Tracheostomies [*British*] [*An association*] (DBA)
ACT .... Air Cavalry Troop (DOMA)

ACT	Air-Charged Temperature [*Automotive engineering*]
ACT	Air Combat Tactics (AFM)
A Ct	Air Commandant [*British*] (DMA)
ACT	Air Control Team [*Air Force*]
ACT	Air Cooled Triode [*Chemistry*] (IAA)
ACT	Air Council for Training [*British*] (DAS)
ACT	Aircraft Commander Time
ACT	Aircrew Classification Test (AFM)
ACT	Air-Cushion Trailer [*or Transporter*]
ACT	Airport Control Tower
ACT	Algebraic Compiler and Translator [*Computer science*]
ACT	Allergen Challenge Test [*Medicine*] (DAVI)
ACT	Alliance for Cannabis Therapeutics (EA)
ACT	[*The*] Alliance for Children & Television [*The Children's Broadcast Institute*] (AC)
ACT	Allied Chemical Technology [*Trademark*]
ACT	Alpha Counter Tube
ACT	Alternaria citri (Tangerine race) [*A toxin-producing fungus*]
ACT	Alternative Control Technology [*Environmental science*]
ACT	Alumina Ceramic Test
ACT	American Association of Agricultural Communicators of Tomorrow (EA)
ACT	American-Canadian Tour [*Auto racing*]
ACT	American Citizens Together [*An association*]
ACT	American College of Theriogenologists (EA)
ACT	American College of Toxicology (EA)
ACT	American College Testing Program (EA)
ACT	American Conference of Therapeutic Selfhelp/Selfhealth Social Action Clubs [*Defunct*] (EA)
ACT	American Conservative Trust (EA)
ACT	American Conservatory Theatre
ACT	American Council for Turfgrass [*Defunct*] (EA)
ACT	American Council of Taxpayers [*Formerly, COST*] (EA)
ACT	American Council on Transplantation [*Defunct*] (EA)
ACT	Americans Combatting Terrorism [*Commercial firm*] (EA)
ACT	Americans for Constitutional Training (EA)
ACT	Analog Control Technology [*Computer science*]
ACT	Analogical Circuit Technique (PDAA)
ACT	Anglo-Canadian Telephone Co. [*Toronto Stock Exchange symbol*]
ACT	Annual Change Traffic
ACT	Antenna Cross Talk
ACT	Anticar Theft [*Campaign or Committee*]
ACT	Antichymotrypsin [*Biochemistry*]
ACT	Anticoagulant Therapy [*Medicine*]
ACT	Anticomet Tail (IAA)
ACT	Anti-Comet Tail Gun [*Television*] (WDMC)
ACT	Anticompromise Technique
ACT	Apparatus Carrier Telephone [*British military*] (DMA)
ACT	Applied Computer Techniques (TEL)
ACT	Area Composition Terminal (DGA)
ACT	Area Correlation Tracker [*Air Force*]
ACT	Armored Cavalry Trainer [*Army*] (AABC)
ACT	Army Communicative Technology (RDA)
ACT	Artists in Christian Testimony (EA)
ACT	Asset Control Techniques [*TRW, Inc.*]
ACT	Assignment Control Trainee (MCD)
ACT	Associated Container Transportation
ACT	Associate of the College of Technology [*British*]
ACT	Association for Commuter Transportation (EA)
ACT	Association for Composite Tanks (EA)
ACT	Association of Career Teachers [*British*]
ACT	Association of Catholic Teachers [*Defunct*]
ACT	Association of Charter Trustees [*British*]
ACT	Association of Christian Teachers [*British*] (EAIO)
ACT	Association of Civilian Technicians (EA)
ACT	Association of Classroom Teachers [*Defunct*]
ACT	Association of Communications Technicians (EA)
ACT	Association of Consumers and Taxpayers [*Political Group*] [*New Zealand*]
ACT	Association of Corporate Treasurers (EAIO)
ACT	Association of Cycle Traders (EAIO)
ACT	Association of Cytogenetic Technologists (EA)
ACT	Assure Competitive Transportation [*Truckers' lobby*]
ACT	Asthma Care Training (MEDA)
ACT	Attention Control Training
ACT	At the Center of Things [*Slang*]
ACT	Augmented Catalytic Thruster (MCD)
ACT	Australian Capital Territory (PPW)
ACT	Australian Community Theatre
ACT	Auto-Lock Channel Tuning [*Television technology*]
ACT	Automated Computerized Tomography [*Radiology*] (DAVI)
ACT	Automated Contingency Translator [*Computer science*]
ACT	Automated Control and Distribution of Trainees [*Army*] (MCD)
ACT	Automatically Controlled Transportation [*Airport passenger shuttle*] [*Ford Motor Co.*]
ACT	Automatic Cable Tester
ACT	Automatic Cannon Technology (MCD)
ACT	Automatic Capacitor Tester
ACT	Automatic Channel and Time [*Toshiba Corp.*] [*Programmable television set*]
ACT	Automatic Checkout Technician [*or Technique*] (MCD)
ACT	Automatic Circuit Tester
ACT	Automatic Code Translation [*Computer science*]
ACT	Automatic Code Translator (NITA)
ACT	Automatic Component Tester
ACT	Automatic Coulometric Titration (PDAA)
ACT-D	Automatic Credit Transfer (CDAI)
ACT	Aviation Classification Test
ACT	Azimuth Control Torquer
ACT	Flight Line, Inc. [*ICAO designator*] (FAAC)
ACT	Treehouse Books, Calgary, Alberta [*Library symbol National Library of Canada*] (NLC)
ACT	Waco [*Texas*] [*Airport symbol*] (OAG)
ACTA	Acetate (ABBR)
ACTA	Activate Test Article [*Military*] (NASA)
ACTA	Active Test Article (MCD)
ACTA	Adelaide Convention and Tourism Authority [*Australia*]
ACTA	Advanced Cargo/Tanker Aircraft
ACTA	Advanced Civilian Technology Agency (AAGC)
ACTA	Advanced Combat Training Academy [*Army*] (AABC)
ACTA	Air Coach Transport Association
ACTA	Alabama Cable Telecommunications Association (SRA)
ACTA	Alliance of Canadian Travel Associations
ACTA	Alternative Carrier Telecommunications Association (EA)
ACTA	American Cardiology Technologists Association [*Later, NSCPT*] (EA)
ACTA	American Cement Trade Alliance [*Later, ACA*] (EA)
ACTA	American Colon Therapy Association (EA)
ACTA	American Community Theatre Association (EA)
ACTA	American Corrective Therapy Association [*Later, AKA*] (EA)
ACTA	Arizona Cable Telecommunications Association (SRA)
ACTA	Association Canadienne des Techniques de l'Asphalte [*Canadian Technical AsphaltAssociation*] (EAIO)
ACTA	Association Canadienne de Technologie Avancee [*Canadian Association of Advanced Technology*]
ACTA	Association Canadienne de Therapie Animale [*Canadian Animal Therapy Association*]
ACTA	Association Canadienne pour la Technologie des Animaux de Laboratoire [*Canadian Association for Laboratory Animals Technology*]
ACTA	Association of Chart and Technical Analysts [*British*]
ACTA	Australian Capital Territory Athletics [*An association*]
ACTA	Australian Catholic Theological Association
ACTA	Australian Clay Target Association
ACTA	Automated Calibration Temperature Activated [*Electronic balance*]
ACTA	Automatic Centrifugal Tinning Apparatus
ACTA	Automatic Computerized Transverse Axial [*Computer X-ray system*]
ACTAC	Association of Community Technical Aid Centres (EAIO)
ACTAD	Actuated (ABBR)
ACTAG	Actuating (ABBR)
ACTAN	Actuation (ABBR)
ActAndr	Acts of Andrew (BJA)
ACT & UPC	Association of Charter Trustees and Urban Parish Councils [*British*] (DBA)
ActApp	Active Apparel Group, Inc. [*Associated Press*] (SAG)
ACTA-Quebec	Association des Agents de Voyages du Quebec (AC)
ACTAR	Acoustics of the Target
ACTAR	Actuator (ABBR)
ACTAS	Army Consideration of Tactical Air Support
Act Ass	Acts of the General Assembly, Church of Scotland [*1638-1842*] [*A publication*] (DLA)
ACTATE	Australian Capital Territory Association for the Teaching of English
ACTAWA	Australian Capital Territory Amateur Weightlifting Association
ACT-B	AIDS Committee of Thunder Bay (AC)
ACTB	Aircrew Classification Test Battery
ACTB	Association Canadienne des Fabricants de Tuyaux de Beton (AC)
ACTB	Australian Capital Territory Basketball
ACTBA	Australian Capital Territory Bridge Association
ACTBC	Medical Library, Tom Baker Cancer Center, Calgary, Alberta [*Library symbol National Library of Canada*] (NLC)
act-C	Actinomycin-C [*Antineoplastic drug*]
ACTC	Applied Cellular Technology [*NASDAQ symbol*] (SAG)
ACTC	Art Class Teacher's Certificate [*British*]
ACTC	Association Candienne de Television par Cable [*Formerly, National Community Antenna Television Association of Canada*] (AC)
ACTC	Association Culturelle et Touristique des Cantons [*Cultural and Tourist Association of Cantons*] [*Canada*]
ACTC	Association of Community Travel Clubs (EA)
ACTC	Bureau of Air Commerce Type Certificate
ACTC	CSIRO [*Commonwealth Scientific and Industrial Research Organisation*] Activities Archive [*Database*]
ACTC	TCPL Resources Ltd., Calgary, Alberta [*Library symbol National Library of Canada*] (NLC)
Act Can	Acta Cancellariae, by Monroe [*England*] [*A publication*] (DLA)
ACT Canada	Advanced Card Technology Association of Canada (AC)
ACTCCS	Australian Capital Territory Council of Cultural Societies
ACTCOM	Army Authority for Major Commands to Disseminate Information and Take Appropriate Action
ACT/CONV	Activation/Conversion (DNAB)
ACTCP	Trans-Canada Pipelines, Calgary, Alberta [*Library symbol National Library of Canada*] (NLC)
ACTCPG	Australian Capital Territory Continence Promotion Group
ACTCR	Texaco Canada Resources Ltd., Calgary, Alberta [*Library symbol National Library of Canada*] (NLC)
ACTCS	Active Thermal Control System [*NASA*] (MCD)
ACTCS	Air Conditioning and Temperature Control System [*Aerospace*]
ACTCUAC	Australian Capital Territory Credit Union Association Cooperative
ACTD	Acted (ABBR)
act-D	Actinomycin-D [*Also, AMD, DACT*] [*Antineoplastic drug*]
ACT-D	Activated Clotting Time for Dactinomycin [*Clinical medicine*]
ACTD	Advanced Concept and Technology Demonstration [*Military*] (RDA)

ACTD .... Advanced Concepts and Technology Demonstration [*Military*] (INF)
ACTD .... Advanced Concept Technology Demonstration
ACTD .... Attitude Control Torquing Device [*Aerospace*]
ACTD .... Automatic Telephone Call Distribution (PDAA)
ACTDP .... Air Conditioner Technical Data Package (DWSG)
ACTDS .... Automatically Cued Target Detecting System (MCD)
ACTDU .... Active Duty (DNAB)
ACTE .... Actuate
ACTE .... Agkistrodon Contortrix Thrombin-Like Enzyme
ACTe .... Anodal Closure Tetanus [*Physiology*]
ACTE .... Association of Corporate Travel Executives (EA)
ACTE .... Automatic Checkout Test Equipment (AAG)
ACTE .... Techman Engineering Ltd., Calgary, Alberta [*Library symbol National Library of Canada*] (NLC)
ACTEA .... Accrediting Council for Theological Education in Africa [*of the Association of Evangelicals of Africa and Madagascar*] [*See also COHETA*] (EAIO)
ACTEC .... American Coalition on Trade Expansion with Canada (EA)
ACTEC .... American College of Trust and Estate Counsel (EA)
ACTEDS .... Army Civilian Training, Education, and Development System
ACTEIN .... Australian Capital Territory Education Information Network
Actel .... Actel Corp. [*Associated Press*] (SAG)
ACTEL .... Alternating Current Thin-Film Electroluminescence (MHDI)
ACTEMS ...... Advisory Committee for Teacher Education in the Mid-South (AIE)
ACTER .... Anticountermeasures Trainer
ACTERS .... ADD-H [*Attention Deficit Disorder with Hyperactivity*] Comprehensive Teachers Rating Scale
ACTES .... Annual Cycle Thermal Energy Storage (PDAA)
ACTEW .... Advocates for Community Based Training & Education for Women (AC)
Act Ex .... Active Exercise [*Rehabilitation*] (DAVI)
ACTF .... Activities File [*CSIRO database*] (ADA)
ACTF .... Altitude Control Test Facility
ACTF .... American College Theater Festival
ACTF .... American Conservatory Theatre Foundation (EA)
ACTF .... CSIRO [*Commonwealth Scientific and Industrial Research Organisation*] Activities File [*Database*]
ACTFL .... American Council on the Teaching of Foreign Languages (EA)
ACTFL .... Australian Council for Teaching Foreign Languages
ACTG .... Acting (AFM)
ACTG .... Actuating (KSC)
ACTG .... Advance Carrier Training Group [*Navy*]
ACTG .... AIDS [*Acquired Immune Deficiency Syndrome*] Clinical Trials Group (EA)
ACTG .... [*A*] Chance to Grow (EA)
ACTGS .... Australian Capital Territory Geographical Society
Actg Sec ..... Acting Secretary (BARN)
ACTGTA ...... Australian Capital Territory Geography Teachers' Association
ACTH .... Adrenocorticotrophic Hormone [*Endocrinology*]
ACTH .... Arbitrary Correction to Hit [*Gunnery term*] [*Navy*]
ACTH .... Association for Canadian Theatre History
ACTH .... Association of Canadaian Teaching Hospitals (AC)
ACTH .... Australian College of Travel and Hospitality
ACTH .... Automated Computerized Transverse [*Axial scanner*] [*Radiology*] (DAVI)
ACTHA .... Australian Capital Territory Hockey Association
ACTH-LI ...... Adrenocorticotrophin-Like Immunoreactivity [*Immunochemistry*]
ACTHR .... Adrenocorticotropic Hormone Receptor [*Medicine*] (DMAA)
ACTH-RF ..... Adrenocorticotropic Hormone-Releasing Factor [*Endocrinology*] (MAE)
ACTI .... Acacia Confusa Trypsin Inhibitor [*Biochemistry*]
ACTI .... Advanced Computer Training Institute [*Springfield, VA*]
ACTI .... Advisory Committee on Technology Innovation [*Board on Science and Technology for International Development*] [*Office of International Affairs National Research Council*] (EGAO)
ACTI .... Air Combat Tactics Instructor (DOMA)
ACTI .... Applied Computer Tech [*NASDAQ symbol*] (TTSB)
ACTI .... Applied Computer Technology, Inc. [*NASDAQ symbol*] (SAG)
ACTIAC .... Arms Control Technical Information and Analysis Center [*Department of State*]
ACT/IC .... Active in Commission [*Vessel status*] [*Navy*]
ACTICE .... Authority Coordinating the Transport of Inland Continental Europe [*NATO*]
ACTIFD .... Actifed [*Burroughs-Wellness, Inc.*] [*Pharmacology*] (DAVI)
ACTIFS .... Active Control for Total In-Flight Simulator (MCD)
ACTIME .... Agency for the Coordination of Transport in the Mediterranean [*NATO*] (MCD)
ACTIMED ..... Agency for the Coordination of Transport in the Mediterranean [*NATO*] (NATG)
ACTIN-D ...... Actinomycin Dactinomycin [*Antineoplastic drug regimen*] (DAVI)
Action .... Action Industries, Inc. [*Associated Press*] (SAG)
ACTION .... Action International Ministries (EAIO)
ACTION .... American Council to Improve Our Neighborhoods [*Later, NUC*]
ACTION .... [*A*] Commitment to Improve Our Nation [*Canada*]
ACTIRF .... Association Canadienne de Traitement d'Images et Reconnaissance des Formes [*Canada*]
ACT/IS .... Active in Service [*Vessel status*] [*Navy*]
ACTIS .... Advanced Circular Scan Thermal Imaging System (MCD)
ACTIS .... AIDS [*Acquired Immune Deficiency Syndrome*] Clinical Trials Information Service (IID)
ACTISPP ...... Australian Capital Territory Injury Surveillance and Prevention Project
ACTISUD ...... Authority for the Coordination of Inland Transport in Southern Europe [*NATO*]
ACTITFE .... Australian Capital Territory Institute of Technical and Further Education

ACTIV .... Activation (NASA)
ACTIV .... Activity (ABBR)
ACTIV .... Advisory Centre on Technology for Industry in Victoria [*Australia*]
ACTIV .... Army Concept Team in Vietnam
ACTIVE .... Advance Components through Increased Volumetric Efficiency (SAA)
Activisn ...... Activision, Inc. [*Associated Press*] (SAG)
ACTIW .... Applied Computer Tech Wrrt [*NASDAQ symbol*] (TTSB)
ActJn .... Acts of John (BJA)
ACTL .... Actel Corp. [*NASDAQ symbol*] (SAG)
ACTL .... Actual (MSA)
ACTL .... American College of Trial Lawyers (EA)
Act Lawt Ct... Acts of Lawting Court [*Scotland*] [*A publication*] (DLA)
Act Ld Aud C... Acts of Lords Auditors of Causes [*Scotland*] [*A publication*] (DLA)
Act Ld Co CC... Acts of Lords of Council in Civil Causes [*1478-1501*] [*Scotland*] [*A publication*] (DLA)
Act Ld Co Pub Aff... Acts of Lords of Council in Public Affairs [*Scotland*] [*A publication*] (DLA)
ACTLS .... Australian Capital Territory Lieder Society
ACTLT .... Actuality (ABBR)
ACTLU .... Activate Logical Unit [*IBM Co.*] (ACRL)
ACTLY .... Actually (ABBR)
ACTLZ .... Actualize (ABBR)
ACTLZAN .... Actualization (ABBR)
ACTLZD .... Actualized (ABBR)
ACTLZG .... Actualizing (ABBR)
ACTLZN .... Actualization (ABBR)
ACTM .... ACT Manufacturing [*NASDAQ symbol*] (TTSB)
ACTM .... ACT Manufacturing, Inc. [*NASDAQ symbol*] (SAG)
ACTM .... Ashridge Centre for Transport Management [*Ashridge Management College*] [*British*] (CB)
ACTM .... Association of Cotton Textile Merchants of New York [*Later, ATMI*] (EA)
ACTM .... Audio Center - Transmitter (KSC)
ACTMA .... Australian Capital Territory Marching Association
ACTMC .... Army Clothing, Textile, and Materiel Center
ACT Mf .... ACT Manufacturing, Inc. [*Associated Press*] (SAG)
ACTMJA .... Australian Capital Territory Master Joiners' Association
ACTMR .... Association Canadienne Contre la Tuberculose et les Maladies Respiratoires [*Canadian Association Against Tuberculosis and Respiratory Diseases*]
ACTN .... Action
ACTN .... Action
ACTN .... Action Performance Companies [*NASDAQ symbol*] (SAG)
ACTN .... Action Performance Cos. [*NASDAQ symbol*] (TTSB)
ACTN .... Adrenocorticotropin [*Endocrinology*] (MAE)
ACTNB .... Actionable (ABBR)
ACTNB .... Australian Capital Territory Nurses' Board
ACTNE .... Acetone (ABBR)
ACT Net ...... ACT Networks, Inc. [*Associated Press*] (SAG)
ACTNG .... Accounting
ActnPr........ Action Products International, Inc. [*Associated Press*] (SAG)
ACTNRG...... Auctioneering
ACTNS .... Acuteness (ABBR)
ACTNT .... Accountant (MUGU)
ACTO .... Action Officer [*Army*] (AABC)
ACTO .... Advanced Control Test Operation [*Oak Ridge National Laboratory*]
ACTO .... Army Communicative Technology Office
ACTO .... Association of Chief Technical Officers (EAIO)
ACTO .... Automatic Computing Transfer Oscillator (IEEE)
ACT/OC .... Active out of Commission [*Vessel status*] [*Navy*]
Act of Sed .. Act of Sederunt (DLA)
ACTOJ .... Active Correlation Track-on-Jam
ACTOL .... Air Cushion Take-Off and Landing [*Aviation*] (PDAA)
Acton .... Acton's Prize Cases, Privy Council [*A publication*] (DLA)
ACTOR .... Askania Cine-Theodolite Optical-Tracking Range
ACT/OS .... Active out of Service [*Vessel status*] [*Navy*]
ACTOV .... Accelerated Turn-Over to Vietnamese [*Military*]
ACTP .... Adrenocorticotrophic Polypeptide [*Endocrinology*]
ACTP .... Advanced-Composite Thermoplastic [*Materials engineering*]
ACTP .... Advanced Computer Techniques Project (KSC)
ACTP .... Advanced Computer Technology Project [*British*] (EECA)
ACTP .... Advanced Control Technology Program [*Oak Ridge National Laboratory*]
ACTP .... Total Petroleum (North America) Ltd., Calgary, Alberta [*Library symbol National Library of Canada*] (NLC)
ACTPA .... Australian Capital Territory Pistol Association
ActPaul .... Acts of Paul (BJA)
ACTPC .... Acting Pay Clerk [*Navy*]
Act PC .... Acts of the Privy Council (Dasent) [*England*] [*A publication*] (DLA)
Act PC NS... Acts of the Privy Council, New Series (Dasent) [*England*] [*A publication*] (DLA)
ActPerf........ Action Performance Companies [*Associated Press*] (SAG)
ActPet......... Acts of Peter (BJA)
ACTPN .... Advisory Committee for Trade Policy and Negotiations [*US Trade Representative*] (EGAO)
ACTPO .... Accountable Property Officer [*Military*] (AABC)
Act Pr C ...... Acton's Reports, Prize Cases [*England*] [*A publication*] (DLA)
Act Pr C Col S... Acts of the Privy Council, Colonial Series [*England*] [*A publication*] (DLA)
ACTPU .... Activate Physical Unit [*IBM Co.*] (ACRL)
ACTR .... Actor
ACTR .... Actuator (KSC)
ACTR .... Air Corps Technical Report [*Obsolete*]
ACTR .... American Council of Teachers of Russian (EA)
ACTR .... Association for Canadian Theatre Research (AC)

ACTR .... Touche Ross & Co., Calgary, Alberta [*Library symbol National Library of Canada*] (NLC)

ACTRA .... Alliance of Canadian Cinema, Television & Radio Artists [*Alliance des Artistes Canadiens du Cinema, de la Television et de la Radio*] [*Formerly, Association of Canadian Television & Radio Artists*] (AC)

ACTRA .... Alliance of Canadian Cinema, Television and Radio Artists [*Canada*] (WWLA)

ACTRA .... Association of Canadian Television and Radio Artists

ACTRAC .... Accurate Tracking (MUGU)

Actrade .... Actrade International Ltd. [*Associated Press*] (SAG)

ACTRAM .... Advisory Committee on the Transport of Radioactive Materials [*British*]

ACTRAN .... Analog Computer Translator

ACTRAN .... Autocoder-to-COBOL Translating Service [*Computer science*] (IEEE)

ACTRC .... Australian Capital Territory Racing Club

ACTRE .... Actress (ABBR)

ACTREP .... Activities Report [*Shipping*]

ACTRL .... Acoustic Trials (NVT)

ACTRL .... Actuarial

ACTRM .... Association Canadienne des Techniciens en Radiation Medicale [*Canadian Association of Medical Radiation Technologists*] (EAIO)

ACTRS .... Actress (ABBR)

ACTRS .... Association of Catholic TV and Radio Syndicators (EA)

ACTRUS .... Automatically Controlled Turbine Run-Up System [*Navigation*]

ACTRY .... Actuary (ABBR)

ACTRY .... Actuary

ACTS .... Academic and Creative Thinking Skills

ACTS .... Accounts, Collection, and Taxpayer Service [*Internal Revenue Service*]

ACTS .... Acoustic Control and Telemetry System

ACTS .... Acquisitions, Cataloguing, Technical Systems [*Library service*]

ACTS .... Action for Child Transportation Safety [*Defunct*] (EA)

ACTS .... Activated Carbon Treatment System (MCD)

ACTS .... Active Control Torque System [*Automotive engineering*] (PS)

ACTS .... Advanced Communication Technology Satellite Program [*Office of Space Scie nce and Applications*] [*Washington, DC NASA*] (GRD)

ACTS .... [*The*] Advanced Construction Technology Show [*British*] (ITD)

ACTS .... Advanced Contingency Theater Sensor [*Military*] (DOMA)

ACTS .... Advisory Commission on Textbook Specifications

ACTS .... Advisory Committee on Toxic Substances [*British*]

ACTS .... Africa Community Technical Service [*Formerly, Red Sea Desert Development*] (AC)

ACTS .... African Centre for Technology Studies [*Kenya*] (EAIO)

ACTS .... Aid for Commonwealth Teaching of Science Scheme [*British*]

ACTS .... Air Combat Training System [*Army*]

ACTS .... Air Corps Tactical School [*Obsolete*]

ACTS .... Air Crew Training System

ACTS .... Air-Cushion Takeoff System (MCD)

ACTS .... Airlines Computer Tracing System [*Luggage retrieving system*]

ACTS .... Alberta Conservation Tillage Society (AC)

ACTS .... All-Channel Television Society [*UHF interest group*] (NTCM)

ACTS .... American Catholic Truth Society [*Defunct*] (EA)

ACTS .... American Christian Television Service [*Cable-television system*]

ACTS .... American Coalition for Traffic Safety (EA)

ACTS .... American College Testing Service (HCT)

ACTS .... Analog Conditioning and Test System

ACTS .... Application Control and Teleprocessing System (MHDI)

ACTS .... Arc Current Time Simulator

ACTS .... Area Communications Terminal Subsystem [*Ground Communications Facility, NASA*]

ACTS .... Army Criteria Tracking System

ACTS .... Asbestos Contractor Tracking System [*Environmental Protection Agency*] (ERG)

ACTS .... Assignment Control and Tracking System [*Computer science*]

ACTS .... Association Canadienne des Travailleurs Sociaux [*Canadian Association of Social Workers - CASW*]

ACTS .... Association for Christian Training and Service (EA)

ACTS .... Association of Cable Television Suppliers (EA)

ACTS .... Association of Career Training Schools [*Defunct*] (EA)

ACTS .... Association of Clerical, Technical, and Supervisory Staffs [*British*] (DCTA)

ACTS .... Association of Community Tribal Schools (EA)

ACTS .... Association of Competitive Telecommunications Suppliers (AC)

ACTS .... Attitude Control and Translation System [*Aerospace*] (MCD)

ACTS .... Automated Commitment Tracking System [*Nuclear energy*] (NRCH)

ACTS .... Automated Component Trading System

ACTS .... Automated Computer Time Service

ACTS .... Automated Configuration Tracking System (MCD)

ACTS .... Automated Custom Terminal System

ACTS .... Automatic Clutch and Throttle System [*Automotive powertrain*]

ACTS .... Automatic Coin Telephone Service

ACTS .... Automatic Computer Telex Services

ACTS .... Aviation Combat Training System [*Military*]

ACTSA .... American Carpal Tunnel Syndrome Association (EA)

ACTSA .... Australian Capital Territory Softball Association

Acts & Ords Interreg... Acts and Ordinances of the Interregnum [*1642-60*] [*British A publication*] (ILCA)

Acts & Ords Interregnum... Acts and Ordinances of the Interregnum [*1642-60*] [*United Kingdom*] [*A publication*] (DLA)

Acts Austl Parl... Acts of the Australian Parliament [*A publication*] (ILCA)

ActSc .... Actuarial Science (DD)

ACTSEB .... Anterior Chamber Tube Shunt Encircling Band [*Ophthalmology*] (DAVI)

ACTSECDEF... Acting Secretary of Defense (SAA)

ACTSECNAV... Acting Secretary of the Navy

ACTSF.......... Australian Capital Territory Soccer Federation

ACT-SO .... Afro-American Cultural Technological Scientific Olympics

ACTS/PROP... Attitude Control and Translation System/Propulsion [*Aerospace*]

ACTSRC .... Australian Capital Territory Smallbore Rifle Club

ACTSRFC .... Australian Capital Territory Sport and Recreational Fishing Council

ACTS/SCE .... Attitude Control and Translation System/Stabilization and Control Electronics [*Aerospace*]

ACTSU .... Association of Computer Time-Sharing Users

ACTT .... Accountant (ABBR)

ACTT .... Acetate [*Also, AC*] [*Organic chemistry*] (MSA)

ACTT .... Act Teleconferencing [*NASDAQ symbol*] (TTSB)

ACTT .... Act Teleconferencing, Inc. [*NASDAQ symbol*] (SAG)

ACTT .... Advanced Communication and Timekeeping Technology [*Seiko Telecommunications Systems*] [*FM data receiver chip set*] (PCM)

ACTT .... Association of Cinematograph, Television, and Allied Technicians [*Canada*]

ACTT .... [*A*] Christmas Trains and Trucks Program [*Marine Corps program in Vietnam*]

ACTTA .... Australian Capital Territory Touch Association

ACTTC........ Advanced Composites Technology Transfer Consortium

ACTTC........ Australian Coal Trade and Technology Committee

ACTTCL .... Association for Clinical Theological Training and Care [*British*] (EAIO)

ActTele .... Act Teleconferencing, Inc. [*Associated Press*] (SAG)

ACTTOA .... Australian Courier and Taxi Truck Operators' Association

ACTTS .... Automatic Closed Transition Transfer Switch

ACTTSA .... Association Canadienne des Techniciens et Technologistes en Sante Animale (AC)

ACTTU .... Act Teleconferencing Unit [*NASDAQ symbol*] (TTSB)

ACTTW .... Act Teleconferencing Wrrt [*NASDAQ symbol*] (TTSB)

ACTU .... Actuate (ABBR)

ACTU .... Association of Catholic Trade Unionists (EA)

ACTU .... Automatic Control of Training Unit (IAA)

ACTU .... Transalta Utilities, Calgary, Alberta [*Library symbol National Library of Canada*] (NLC)

ACTUAL .... American Council of Teachers of Uncommonly Taught Asian Languages [*Defunct*] (EA)

ACTUD........ Actuated (ABBR)

ACTUG........ Actuating (ABBR)

ACTUN .... Actuation (ABBR)

ACT UP .... AIDS [*Acquired Immune Deficiency Syndrome*] Coalition to Unleash Power

ACTUR .... Actuary (ABBR)

ACTV .... Activate (AFM)

ACTV .... Active (FAAC)

ACTV .... Activity (AABC)

ACTV .... ACTV, Inc. [*Associated Press*] (SAG)

ACTV .... Advanced Compatible Television [*Wide-screen, high-resolution system utilizing standard broadcast channels*] [*RCA Corp.*]

ACTV .... American Coalition for Traditional Values (EA)

ACTVA .... Activate (ABBR)

ACTVAD ...... Activated (ABBR)

ACTVAG ...... Activating (ABBR)

Act Val....... Actual Value [*Business term*] (MHDB)

ACTVAN ...... Activation (ABBR)

ACTVF........ Australian Childrens Television Foundation

ACTVNANAL... Activation Analysis (MSA)

ACTVNS ...... Activeness (ABBR)

ActVoic .... Active Voice Corp. [*Associated Press*] (SAG)

ACTVOR ...... Activator (ABBR)

ACTVT........ Activate (MSA)

ACTVTD ...... Activated (ABBR)

ACTVTG ...... Activating (ABBR)

ACTVTN ...... Activation (ABBR)

ACTVTR ...... Activator (MSA)

ACTVTY ...... Activity

ACTVTY....... Activity

ACTVY .... Actively (ABBR)

ACTWU .... Amalgamated Clothing and Textile Workers Union (EA)

ACTY .... Activity (AFM)

ACTY .... Actuary (ROG)

ACTY .... Acutely (ABBR)

ACTYF........ Applied Carbon Technology [*NASDAQ symbol*] (TTSB)

ACTYLN ...... Acetylene (ABBR)

ACU .... Acceleration Compensation [*or Control*] Unit [*Aviation*]

ACU .... AC [*Alternating Current*] Control Unit

ACU .... Accugraph Corp. [*Toronto Stock Exchange symbol*]

Acu .... Accursius [*Deceased, 1263*] [*Authority cited in pre-1607 legal work*] (DSA)

ACU .... Achutupo [*Panama*] [*Airport symbol*] (OAG)

ACU .... Acknowledgement Unit [*Telecommunications*] (TEL)

ACU .... Acme United [*AMEX symbol*] (TTSB)

ACU .... Acme United Corp. [*AMEX symbol*] (SPSG)

ACU .... Activity Credit Unit (DNAB)

ACU .... Actors' Church Union [*Episcopalian*]

ACU .... Acute Care Unit [*Medicine*]

ACU .... Address Control Unit [*Computer science*] (MDG)

ACU .... Administration of the Customs Union [*EEC*] (DS)

ACU .... Advanced Connector Unit [*Telecommunications*] (TSSD)

ACU .... Aerocancun [*Mexico ICAO designator*] (FAAC)

ACU .... Airborne Control Unit [*Telecommunications*] (TSSD)

ACU .... Air Cleanup Unit [*Nuclear energy*] (NRCH)

ACU .... Air-Conditioning Unit
ACU .... Aircraft Control Unit (NVT)
ACU .... Alarm Control Unit [*Bell System*] [*Telecommunications*]
ACU .... Altocumulus [*Cloud*] [*Meteorology*] (MUGU)
ACU .... American Catholic Union (EA)
ACU .... American Church Union (EA)
ACU .... American Congregational Union
ACU .... American Conservative Union (EA)
ACU .... American Cycling Union (EA)
ACU .... Analysis Control Unit
ACU .... Annunciator Control Unit [*Military*] (MCD)
ACU .... Antenna Control Unit
ACU .... Anticrime Unit
ACU .... Arithmetic and Control Unit (BUR)
ACU .... Arithmetic Computer
ACU .... Armament Control Unit (DNAB)
ACU .... Asian Clearing Union
ACU .... Asian Currency Unit
ACU .... Assault Craft Unit (NVT)
ACU .... Association Canadienne d'Urbanisme [*Canadian City Planning Association*]
ACU .... Association for Communist Unity [*Australia*]
ACU .... Association of College Unions [*Later, ACU-I*] (EA)
ACU .... Association of Commonwealth Universities [*British*] (EAIO)
ACU .... Association of Computer Users (EA)
ACU .... Association of Cricket Umpires (EAIO)
ACU .... Autocycle Union [*British*]
ACU .... Automatic Call [*or Calling*] Unit [*Telecommunications*] (TEL)
ACU .... Automatic Control Unit (IAA)
ACU .... Auxiliary Conditioning Unit
ACU .... Availability Control Unit (IAA)
ACU .... Avionics Cooling Unit [*Aerospace*] (NASA)
ACU .... East Kurupa, AK [*Location identifier FAA*] (FAAL)
ACU .... University of Calgary, Alberta [*Library symbol National Library of Canada*] (NLC)
ACUA .... Airline Credit Union Association (EA)
ACUA .... Association of College and University Auditors [*Madison, WI*] (EA)
ACUA .... University of Calgary Archives, Alberta [*Library symbol National Library of Canada*] (BIB)
ACUAI .... Arctic Institute of North America, University of Calgary, Alberta [*Library symbol National Library of Canada*] (NLC)
ACU Aq .... Australian Catholic University Aquinas Campus
ACUBO........ Association of College and University Business Officers (NFD)
ACUBS .... Association of College and University Broadcasting Stations (NTCM)
ACUC .... American Coalition of Unregistered Churches (EA)
ACUC .... Association of Canadian Underwater Councils
ACUCA .... Association of Christian Universities and Colleges in Asia (EA)
ACUCAA ...... Association of College, University, and Community Arts Administrators [*Later, APAP*] (EA)
ACUCES ...... Research Centre for Canadian Ethnic Studies, University of Calgary, Alberta [*Library symbol National Library of Canada*] (NLC)
ACU CH....... Australian Catholic University Castle Hill Campus
ACU Christ... Australian Catholic University Christ Campus
ACUCM .... Association of College and University Concert Managers [*Later, ACUCAA*]
ACUCTF ...... Association of Canadian University and College Teachers of French
ACUE .... American Committee of United Europe
ACU-ERI...... American Conservative Union Education and Research Institute (EA)
ACUF .... Advisory Committee on Undersea Feature Names [*Board on Geographic Names*] (NOAA)
ACUFE .... Faculty of Education, University of Calgary, Alberta [*Library symbol National Library of Canada*] (NLC)
ACUG .... Atex Commercial Users Group (EA)
ACUHO........ Association of College and University Housing Officers [*Later, ACUHO-I*] (EA)
ACUHO-I ..... Association of College and University Housing Officers - International (EA)
ACU-I .... Association of College Unions - International (EA)
ACUI .... Automatic Calling Unit Interface [*Telecommunications*] (IEEE)
ACUIB .... Association of Canadian University Information Bureaus [*See also ABUIC*]
ACUIIS .... Association of Colleges and Universities for International-Intercultural Studies [*Defunct*] (EA)
ACUJ........... American Committee for Ulster Justice (EA)
ACUL .... Alabama Credit Union League (SRA)
ACUL .... Alaska Credit Union League (SRA)
ACUL .... Arizona Credit Union League (SRA)
ACUL .... Arkansas Credit Union League (SRA)
ACUL .... Law Library, University of Calgary, Alberta [*Library symbol National Library of Canada*] (BIB)
ACULE .... Association of Credit Union League Executives (EA)
ACUM .... Accumulate (ABBR)
ACUM .... Medical Library, University of Calgary, Alberta [*Library symbol National Library of Canada*] (NLC)
ACUMA .... Map Library, University of Calgary, Alberta [*Library symbol National Library of Canada*] (NLC)
ACU MacK ... Australian Catholic University Mackillop Campus
ACUMB........ Accumulable (ABBR)
ACUMC .... Materials Centre Library, University of Calgary, Alberta [*Library symbol National Library of Canada*] (NLC)
ACU McA .... Australian Catholic University McAuley Campus
ACUMD........ Accumulated (ABBR)
ACU Mercy... Australian Catholic University Mercy Campus
ACUMG........ Accumulating (ABBR)
ACUMG........ Association of College and University Museums and Galleries (EA)

ACUMN........ Accumulation (ABBR)
ACUMR........ Accumulator (ABBR)
ACU MSM ... Australian Catholic University Mount St. Mary Campus
ACUMV........ Accumulative (ABBR)
ACUNO........ Union Oil Co. of Canada Ltd., Calgary, Alberta [*Library symbol National Library of Canada*] (NLC)
ACUNS........ Academic Council on the United Nations System
ACUNS........ Association of Canadian Universities for Northern Studies
ACUNY........ Associated Colleges of Upper New York
ACUO .... Association of College and University Offices (EA)
ACUO .... Avionics Cooling Unit Operator (MCD)
ACUP .... Acupuncture (ABBR)
ACUP .... Association of Canadian University Presses
ACUP .... Association of College and University Printers (EA)
ACUPAE .... American Council for University Planning and Academic Excellence (EA)
ACUR .... Accurate (ABBR)
ACURA .... Ambulatory Care Utilization Review [*Insurance*] (WYGK)
ACURA .... Association for the Coordination of University Religious Affairs (EA)
ACURAD ...... Acoustic Underwater Range Determination Systems
ACURC........ Accuracy (ABBR)
ACURIL .... Association of Caribbean University and Research Institute Libraries
ACURM........ Association of Concern for Ultimate Reality and Meaning (EA)
ACURNS ..... Accurateness (ABBR)
ACURP........ American College of Utilization Review Physicians (EA)
ACURY........ Accurately (ABBR)
ACUS .... Accuse (ABBR)
ACUS .... Administrative Conference of the United States [*Independent government agency*] [*Washington, DC*]
ACUS .... Amendment to the Constitution of the United States (DLA)
ACUS .... Association Canadienne des Utilisateurs SAS (AC)
ACUS .... AT & T College and University System [*Bedminster, NJ*] [*Telecommunications service*] (TSSD)
ACUS .... Atlantic Council of the United States (EA)
ACUSA........ Australian Colleges and Universities Staff Association
ACUSD........ Accused (ABBR)
ACUSE........ Action Committee for a United States of Europe [*EC*] (ECED)
ACUSG........ Accusing (ABBR)
ACUSGY....... Accusingly (ABBR)
ACU Sign..... Australian Catholic University Signadou Campus
ACUSN........ Accusation (ABBR)
Acuson........ Acuson Corp. [*Associated Press*] (SAG)
ACUSR........ Accuser (ABBR)
ACUSSR....... American Committee on US-Soviet Relations [*Defunct*] (EA)
ACUSTL ...... Accusatorial (ABBR)
ACUSTRY..... Accusatory (ABBR)
ACUSTY ...... Accusatory (ABBR)
ACUSV .... Accusative (ABBR)
ACUSYST.... Automated Culture System
ACUT .... Acute Phase [*Laboratory*] (DAVI)
ACUTA .... Association of College and University Telecommunications Administrators (EA)
ACUTE .... Accountants Computer Users Technical Exchange (EA)
ACUTE .... Association of Canadian University Teachers of English
ACUTENS .... Acupuncture and Transcutaneous Electrical Nerve Stimulation [*Orthopedics and neurology*] (DAVI)
ACUTF .... Association of Canadian University Teachers of French
ACUTNS ...... Acuteness (ABBR)
ACV............. Access Control Verification [*Computer science*] (HGAA)
ACV............. Acellular Vaccine [*Medicine*]
ACV............. Acinetobacter Calcoaceticus Varanitratus [*Microbiology*]
ACV............. ACTION Cooperative Volunteer Program
ACV............. Actual Cash Value [*Accounting*]
ACV............. Acyclovir [*Also, ACG, Acycloguanosine*] [*Antiviral compound*]
ACV............. Advertising Club of Victoria [*Australia*]
ACV............. Air Control Valve (MCD)
ACV............. Air-Cushion Vehicle
ACV............. Airline Cargo Services, Inc. [*British*] [*FAA designator*] (FAAC)
ACV............. Alarm Check Valve (MSA)
ACV............. Alberto Culver [*NYSE symbol*] (SAG)
ACV............. Alberto-Culver CI'B' [*NYSE symbol*] (TTSB)
ACV............. Alfalfa Cryptic Virus [*Plant pathology*]
ACV............. All-Commodity Volume [*Marketing*] (WDMC)
ACV............. Alternating Current Volts
ACV............. Amount of Critical View
ACV............. Anthology of Commonwealth Verse [*A publication*]
ACV............. Arcata-Eureka [*California*] [*Airport symbol*] (AD)
ACV............. Armored Cannon Vehicle (MCD)
ACV............. Armored Cavalry Vehicle
ACV............. Armored Combat Vehicle
ACV............. Armored Command Vehicle [*Army*]
ACV............. Armoured Control Vehicle [*Military*]
ACV............. Army Air Cushioned Vehicle (VNW)
ACV............. Asian CineVision (EA)
ACV............. Associate, College of Violinists
ACV............. Association Canadienne des Veterinaires [*Canadian Veterinary Medical Association*] (EAIO)
ACV............. Atria/Carotid/Ventricular [*Anatomy*]
ACV............. Austin Concept Vehicle
ACV............. Auxiliary Aircraft Carrier [*Navy symbol*]
ACV............. Eureka/Arcata [*California*] [*Airport symbol*] (OAG)
ACVA .... Advisory Committee on Voluntary Foreign Aid [*Department of State*]
ACVA .... Alberto-Culver CI'A' [*NYSE symbol*] (TTSB)
ACVAFS .... American Council of Voluntary Agencies for Foreign Service [*Later, I/ACVIA*] (EA)

ACVB .... Aortocoronary Venous Bypass [*Cardiology*] (DMAA)
ACVC .... Active Voice [*NASDAQ symbol*] (TTSB)
ACVC .... Active Voice Corp. [*NASDAQ symbol*] (SAG)
ACVC .... Ada Compiler Validation Capacity [*Computer science*]
ACVC .... Alberta Vocational Centre, Calgary, Albert [*Library symbol National Library of Canada*] (NLC)
ACVC .... American Council of Venture Clubs (EA)
ACVC .... Armament and Combat Vehicle Center (MCD)
ACVC .... Arms Control Verification Committee [*Pronounced "acey-veecee"*]
ACVC .... Army Commercial Vehicle Code (AABC)
ACVCC .... Association of Canadian Venture Capital Companies
ACVD .... Acute Cardiovascular Disease [*Medicine*] (AAMN)
ACVD .... American College of Veterinary Dermatology (EA)
A-CVD .... Autoimmune Collagen Vascular Disease [*Medicine*] (CPH)
ACV-DP .... Acyclovir Diphosphate [*Antiviral compound*]
ACVE .... Accelerometer Calibration Vibration Exciter
ACVE .... Advisory Committee on Voter Education [*Defunct*] (EA)
ACVF .... Advanced Composite Vertical Fin (MCD)
ACVFA .... Advisory Committee on Voluntary Foreign Aid [*Department of State*]
ACVH .... Association Canadienne des Veterans du Hockey [*Canadian Association of Hockey Veterans*]
ACVIM .... American College of Veterinary Internal Medicine (EA)
ACVL .... Association of Cinema and Video Laboratories (EA)
ACVM .... American College of Veterinary Microbiologists (EA)
ACVMC .... Armored Combat Vehicle Material Center (MCD)
ACV-MP .... Acyclovir Monophosphate [*Antiviral compound*]
ACVO .... American College of Veterinary Ophthalmologists (EA)
ACVP .... Additive Color Viewer Printer
ACVP .... American College of Veterinary Pathologists (EA)
ACVR .... American College of Veterinary Radiology (EA)
ACVRD .... Arteriosclerotic Cardiovascular Renal Disease [*Medicine*] (DAVI)
ACVS .... American College of Veterinary Surgeons (EA)
ACVS .... (Aminoadipyl)cysteinylvaline Synthetase [*An enzyme*]
ACVS .... Automatic Computer Voltage Stabilizer (MHDI)
ACVT .... Advisory Committee for Vocational Training (AIE)
ACVT .... American College of Veterinary Toxicologists [*Later, AAVCT*] (EA)
ACVT .... Armored Combat Vehicle Technology (RDA)
ACVTP .... Acyclovir Triphosphate [*Antiviral compound*]
ACVTP .... Armored Combat Vehicle Technology Program
ACVTVM ...... Alternating Current Vacuum Tube Voltmeter (IAA)
ACVV .... Association Canadienne de Vol a Voile [*Canada*]
ACVVC .... Armored Cavalry's Veterans of Vietnam and Cambodia
ACVWS .... Armoured Combat Vehicle Weapon System [*Military*] (PDAA)
ACVZS .... V. Zay, Smith Associates Ltd., Calgary, Alberta [*Library symbol National Library of Canada*] (NLC)
ACW .... Access Control Word [*Computer science*] (MHDI)
ACW .... Accumaster Consolidated Workstation [*Computer science*] (TNIG)
AC/W .... Acetone/Water [*Medicine*] (AAMN)
A-CW .... Aerophysics - Curtiss-Wright (SAA)
ACW .... AIDS Committee of Windsor (AC)
ACW .... Airborne Collision Warning
ACW .... Air Cadets School [*RAF*] [*British ICAO designator*] (FAAC)
ACW .... Air [*or Aircraft*] Control and Warning [*Military*]
ACW .... Aircraft Control and Warning (SAA)
ACW .... Aircraftwoman [*British*]
ACW .... Alcoholism Center for Women (EA)
ACW .... Alternating Continuous Wave [*Radio*]
ACW .... American Canadian Systems, Inc. [*Vancouver Stock Exchange symbol*]
ACW .... American Chain of Warehouses (EA)
ACW .... Anticarrier Warfare (MCD)
ACW .... Anticlockwise
ACW .... Apostolate of Christ the Worker
ACW .... Association of Community Workers [*British*]
ACW .... Automated Keyed Continuous Wave (DNAB)
ACW .... Western Canada High School, Calgary, Alberta [*Library symbol National Library of Canada*] (NLC)
ACWA .... Amalgamated Clothing Workers of America [*Later, ACTWU*] (EA)
ACWA .... American Civil War Association (EA)
ACWA .... American Clean Water Association (EA)
ACWA .... Associate of the Institute of Cost and Works Accountants [*British*]
ACWA .... Association of California Water Agencies (SRA)
ACWA .... Association of Civilian Widows of Australia
ACWA .... Automatic Car Wash Association International [*Later, ICA*]
ACWB .... Williams Brothers Canada Ltd., Calgary, Alberta [*Library symbol National Library of Canada*] (NLC)
ACWBBS ..... American Civil War Bulletin Board System [*Information service or system*] (IID)
ACWC .... Advisory Committee on Weather Control [*Terminated, 1957*]
ACWC .... American Council of Women Chiropractors [*Later, Council of Women Chiropractors*] (EA)
ACWC .... Association of Canadian Women Composers
ACWC .... Australian Carpet Wool Council
ACWCN .... Action Will Be Cancelled (NOAA)
ACWE .... American Cotton Waste Exchange [*Defunct*] (EA)
ACWF .... Actual Cost of Work Flow [*Accounting*]
ACWF .... American Council for World Freedom (EA)
ACWF .... Army Central Welfare Fund
ACWG .... Aircraft Control and Warning Group [*Air Force*]
ACWIS .... American Committee for the Weizmann Institute of Science (EA)
ACWL .... American Crime Writers League [*An association*]
ACWL .... Army Chemical Warfare Laboratory
ACWM .... Americans for Customary Weight and Measure (EA)
ACWO .... Aircraft Control and Warning Officer [*Military*]
ACWP .... Actual Cost for Work Performed [*Accounting*]

ACWP .... Applied Cost for Work Performed (SSD)
ACWR .... William Roper Hull Home, Calgary, Alberta [*Library symbol National Library of Canada*] (NLC)
ACWRD .... Western Research & Development Ltd., Calgary, Alberta [*Library symbol National Library of Canada*] (NLC)
ACWRON .... Aircraft Control and Warning Squadron [*Military*]
ACWRRE ...... American Cargo War Risk Reinsurance Exchange (EA)
ACWRT .... American Civil War Round Table (EAIO)
ACWS .... Aircraft Control and Warning Squadron [*Air Force*]
ACWS .... Aircraft Control and Warning System [*Military*]
ACWS .... All-Canada Weekly Summaries [*Canada Law Book Ltd.*] [*Database*]
ACWS .... Amalgamated Carriage and Wagon Society [*A union*] [*British*]
ACWS .... Assistant Casework Supervisor [*Red Cross*]
ACWSS .... Aircraft Control and Warning System Station [*Military*] (IAA)
ACWT .... Average Customer Wait Time
ACWW .... Associated Country Women of the World [*British*]
ACX .... Action Industries, Inc. [*AMEX symbol*] (SPSG)
ACX .... ACX Technologies [*NYSE symbol*] (TTSB)
ACX .... ACX Technologies [*NYSE symbol*] (SAG)
ACX .... Air Charters, Inc. [*Canada ICAO designator*] (FAAC)
ACX .... American Can Canada [*Toronto Stock Exchange symbol*]
ACx .... Anomalous Cirumflex [*Coronary Artery*] (DMAA)
Acxiom .... Acxiom Corp. [*Associated Press*] (SAG)
ACXM .... Acxiom Corp. [*NASDAQ symbol*] (NQ)
AC/XRT .... Adriamycin, Cyclophosphamide/X-Ray Therapy [*Antineoplastic drug regimen*]
ACXT .... ACX Technologies [*NASDAQ symbol*] (SAG)
ACX Tc .... ACX Technologies [*Associated Press*] (SAG)
ACY .... Acoyapa [*Nicaragua*] [*Seismograph station code, US Geological Survey*] (SEIS)
ACY .... Air City SA [*Switzerland ICAO designator*] (FAAC)
ACY .... [*The*] Akron, Canton & Youngstown Railroad Co. [*AAR code*]
ACY .... Amcan Cyphermaster Ltd. [*Vancouver Stock Exchange symbol*]
ACY .... Archana Airways Ltd. [*India*] [*FAA designator*] (FAAC)
ACY .... Armed Combat Youth [*Government of South Vietnam training program*] (VNW)
ACY .... Atlantic City [*New Jersey*] [*Airport symbol*] (OAG)
ACY .... Average Crop Yield [*Agriculture*] (WDAA)
a-cy-- .... Cyprus [*MARC geographic area code Library of Congress*] (LCCP)
ACYC .... Anticyclonic [*Meteorology*] (BARN)
ACYC .... Association of Combined Youth Clubs [*British*] (DBA)
ACYD .... Association of Cotton Yarn Distributors [*Later, AYD*]
A-CY-DIC .... Adriamycin, Cyclophosphamide, Dacarbazine [*Antineoplastic drug regimen*]
ACYF .... Administration for Children, Youth, and Families [*Office of Human Development Services*]
Acyl-Co A .... Organic Compound - Coenzyme A Ester [*Biochemistry*] (DAVI)
ACYOA .... Armenian Church Youth Organization of America (EA)
ACYP .... Australian Coalition of Young People
ACYPL .... American Council of Young Political Leaders (EA)
ACZ .... Acheron Resources Ltd. [*Vancouver Stock Exchange symbol*]
ACZ .... Action Indus [*AMEX symbol*] (TTSB)
ACZ .... Action Industries [*AMEX symbol*] (SAG)
ACZ .... Czar Public Library, Alberta [*Library symbol National Library of Canada*] (NLC)
ACZ .... Wallace, NC [*Location identifier FAA*] (FAAL)
ACZA .... Ammoniacal Copper Zinc Arsenate [*Wood preservative*]
ACZCS .... Advanced Coastal Zone Color Scanner (MCD)
AD .... Abdominal Diameter [*Roentgenology*]
AD .... Above Deck [*of a ship*] (DS)
AD .... Abwehrdienst [*Counterintelligence Service*] [*German military - World War II*]
AD .... Access Door
AD .... Accessions Document [*Air Force*]
AD .... Accidental Damage (WDAA)
AD .... Accidental Discharge [*Firearms*]
AD .... Accident Dispensary [*Medicine*]
AD .... Accion Democratica [*Democratic Action*] [*Venezuela Political party*] (PPW)
AD .... Accion Democratica [*Democratic Action*] [*El Salvador*] [*Political party*] (PD)
AD .... Account Directory [*Computer science*] (OA)
AD .... Accounting and Disbursing (MCD)
AD .... Accrued Dividend
AD .... Achievement Drive [*Psychology*] (AAMN)
AD .... Acknowledgment Due
AD .... Acoustic Decoupler (DNAB)
AD .... Acquisition Director
AD .... Action Directe [*Direct Action*] [*Terrorist group*] [*French*] (PD)
AD .... Action Driver [*Computer science*]
AD .... Action for Development [*FAO*] [*United Nations*]
AD .... Activation Domain [*Biochemistry*]
AD .... Active Dosimeter
AD .... Active Duty
AD .... Actuator Drive (SAA)
AD .... AD 2000: a Journal of Religious Opinion [*A publication*] (APTA)
AD .... Adamantane [*Organic chemistry*]
AD .... Adapt
AD .... Adaptation Of [*Etymology*]
Ad .... Addams' Ecclesiastical Reports [*A publication*] (DLA)
AD .... Adde [*Add or Up To*] [*Pharmacy*]
AD .... Addendum
AD .... Addict [*Drug*] [*Slang*]
AD .... Address (IAA)
AD .... Address Data

Ad...............	Adelphoe [*of Terence*] [*Classical studies*] (OCD)
AD...............	Aden Airways
AD...............	Adenoid Degenerative [*Viruses*]
AD...............	Adenovirus [*Also, ADV*]
AD...............	Adipose Fin [*Fish anatomy*]
AD...............	Adjective (ROG)
Ad...............	Administration (DLA)
Ad...............	Administrative (DLA)
AD...............	Administrative Department (ADA)
AD...............	Administrative Directive (MCD)
AD...............	Administrative Discharge [*Military*] (VNW)
AD...............	Administrative District (ADA)
AD...............	Administrative Operation and Support Services [*Kennedy Space Center*] [*NASA*] (NASA)
Ad...............	Administrator (DLA)
AD...............	Administrator, Deputy (SAA)
AD...............	Admitting Diagnosis [*Medicine*] (MAE)
ad...............	Adnexa [*Medicine*] (CPH)
AD...............	Adopted By
AD...............	Adoption Directory [*A publication*]
Ad...............	Adrenal [*Medicine*]
AD...............	A Drink
AD...............	Adult (WGA)
AD...............	Advanced Deployability Posture [*Military*] (DOMA)
AD...............	Advanced Design (IEEE)
AD...............	Advanced Development
A/D...............	Advance/Decline (MCD)
A-D...............	Advance-Decline Line [*Investment term*]
AD...............	Advanced Ruling Expiration Date [*IRS*]
AD...............	Advantage (WGA)
AD...............	Adverb (ROG)
AD...............	Advertisement
AD...............	Advertisement
ad...............	Advertisement (WDMC)
AD...............	Advertisement Digest [*A publication*]
ad...............	Advertising (WDMC)
AD...............	Advice (AABC)
AD...............	Advisory Direction (NATG)
AD...............	Advo, Inc. [*NYSE symbol*] (SAG)
AD...............	ADVO Inc. [*NYSE symbol*] (TTSB)
AD...............	Aerial Delivery (MCD)
AD...............	Aerodrome
AD...............	Aerodynamic Decelerator (AAG)
AD...............	Aeronautical Data
AD...............	Africa Diary [*A publication*]
AD...............	African Law Reports, Appellate Division [*A publication*] (DLA)
AD...............	After Date [*Business term*]
AD...............	After Digital [*Post-computer revolution*]
AD...............	Afterdischarge [*Electrophysiology*]
AD...............	After the Dish [*Description of TV viewing via satellite transmission vs traditional or cable TV*] (PS)
AD...............	Aggregate Demand
AD...............	Agnus Dei [*Lamb of God*] [*Latin*]
AD...............	Agricultural Decisions [*A publication*]
AD...............	Ahead Flag [*Navy British*]
AD...............	Aid to the Disabled
AD...............	Airborne Designator (MCD)
AD...............	Aircraft Depot [*British military*] (DMA)
AD...............	Aircraft Depth [*Bomb*] (DNAB)
AD...............	Aircraft Division (MCD)
AD...............	Air Data (MCD)
AD...............	Air Defense [*Air Force*]
AD...............	Air Density [*Explorer satellite*] [*NASA*]
AD...............	Air Department of the Admiralty [*British*]
AD...............	Air Depot
AD...............	Air Despatch [*British military*] (DMA)
AD...............	Air Director (DAS)
AD...............	Air Distance (SAA)
AD...............	Air Division [*Air Force*]
AD...............	Air-Dried [*Lumber*]
AD...............	Airdrome
AD...............	Air Duct (MSA)
AD...............	Airframe Design Division [*Bureau of Aeronautics; later, NASC*] [*Navy*]
AD...............	Air-Start Diesel Engine (DNAB)
AD...............	Airworthiness Directive
AD...............	Albrecht Durer [*German artist, 1471-1528*]
AD...............	Alcohol Dehydrogenase [*Also, ADH*] [*An enzyme*]
AD...............	Aleutian Disease [*of mink*] [*Veterinary medicine*]
AD...............	Alexandra [*Newport and South Wales*] Docks & Railway [*Wales*]
AD...............	Alianca Democratica [*Democratic Alliance*] [*Brazil Political party*] (EY)
AD...............	Alianca Democratica [*Democratic Alliance*] [*Portugal Political party*] (PPE)
AD...............	Alianza Democratica [*Democratic Alliance*] [*Chile*] [*Political party*] (PPW)
AD...............	Allergic Disease
AD...............	Allied Distribution [*An association*] (EA)
AD...............	Allowable Deficiency (MCD)
AD...............	Alloy Diffused (IAA)
AD...............	Alpha Delta [*Society*]
A/D...............	Alternate Definition of Accident [*Insurance*]
AD...............	Alternate Drop [*Electroanalysis*]
AD...............	Alternis Diebus [*Alternate Days*] [*Pharmacy*]
AD...............	Altitude Deviation

AD...............	Alzheimer's Disease [*Medicine*]
AD...............	Ambulance Driver
AD...............	American Decisions [*A publication*] (DLA)
AD...............	American Defenders [*Defunct*] (EA)
AD...............	Ampere Demand Meter (MSA)
AD...............	Amplifier Detector
AD...............	Amplifier Discriminator [*Instrumentation*]
AD...............	Analgesic Dose
AD...............	Analog Device [*Computer science*] (IAA)
A/d...............	Analog Divider [*Electronics*] (ECII)
a/d...............	Analog-to-Digital (IDOE)
A/D...............	Analog-to-Digital (IDOE)
AD...............	Analog-to-Digital [*Converter*] [*Computer science*] (AFM)
AD...............	Analysis Division (ACII)
AD...............	Anderson - Darling Test [*Statistics*]
AD...............	Andorra [*ANSI two-letter standard code*] (CNC)
AD...............	Androstenedione [*Endocrinology*]
AD...............	Angelus Domini [*Angel of the Lord*] [*Latin*] (BARN)
AD...............	Anima Dulcis [*Sweet Soul*] [*Latin*]
Ad...............	Animal Detail [*Rorschach*] [*Psychology*]
AD...............	Anno Domini [*In the Year of Our Lord*] [*Latin*] (GPO)
AD...............	Annual Digest and Reports of Public International Law Cases [*A publication*] (DLA)
AD...............	Anodal Deviation [*Physiology*]
AD...............	Anodal Duration [*Physiology*] (MAE)
AD...............	Anode (MSA)
ad...............	Ante Diem [*Before the Day*] [*Latin*] (GPO)
AD...............	Anterior Deltoid [*Myology*]
AD...............	Antidiarrhea [*Medicine*]
AD...............	Anti-Disturbance (MCD)
AD...............	Anti-Dumping [*International trade*] (GFGA)
AD...............	Antigenic Determinant [*Medicine*]
AD...............	Antilles Air Boats (MHDB)
AD...............	Apollo Development [*NASA*] (KSC)
AD...............	Appellate Division [*Legal term*]
AD...............	Applied Dynamics (IAA)
AD...............	Approximate Digestibility
AD...............	Archdeaconry
AD...............	Archduke
AD...............	Area Dean [*Church of England in Australia*]
AD...............	Area Director
AD...............	Area Discriminator [*SAGE*]
AD...............	Area Drain [*Technical drawings*]
AD...............	Arithmetic Device
AD...............	Armament Depot [*Military British*]
AD...............	Armament Division [*Air Force Systems Command*] [*Eglin Air Force Base, FL*]
A/D...............	Arm/Destruct (KSC)
AD...............	Armored Division [*Military*] (MCD)
AD...............	Army Dental Corps [*British*]
AD...............	Army Department [*British*] (RDA)
AD...............	Army Depot (AABC)
AD...............	Art Director [*Films, television, etc.*]
AD...............	Arthritic Dose [*Medicine*] (BABM)
AD...............	Artificer Diver [*British military*] (DMA)
AD...............	Artillery Division [*Military*] (MCD)
AD...............	Artist Direct [*Record label*]
AD...............	Artist's Diploma (PGP)
AD...............	As Drawn (MSA)
A/D...............	Assembly/Disassembly Facility
AD...............	Assembly District
AD...............	Assembly Drawing
A/D...............	Assets and Depreciation [*Accounting*]
AD...............	Assignment Date [*Telecommunications*] (TEL)
AD...............	Assistant Director
AD...............	Associate Degree
AD...............	Associate Director
AD...............	Associated with Dual Capacity Firms [*London Stock Exchange*]
AD...............	Assured Destruction [*Capability*] [*of missiles*]
AD...............	ASTIA [*Armed Services Technical Information Agency*] Document
AD...............	Asymmetric Dihydroxylation [*Organic chemistry*]
AD...............	Athletic Director
AD...............	Atomic Drive (AAG)
AD...............	Attack Director [*Military*] (MCD)
AD...............	Attendant [*Telecommunications*] (TEL)
AD...............	Attention Display [*Communications device*]
A/D...............	Audimeter/Diary System [*A. C. Nielson Co.*] (NTCM)
AD...............	Auris Dextra [*Right Ear*] [*Latin*]
AD...............	Australian Democrats [*Political party*] (EAIO)
AD...............	Auto-Diesel Technician Program [*Association of Independent Colleges and Schools specialization code*]
AD...............	Autograph Document [*Manuscript descriptions*]
AD...............	Automatic Depositor [*Banking*] (BUR)
AD...............	Automatic Detection [*Air Force*]
AD...............	Automatic Display [*Computer science*]
AD...............	Autonomic Dysreflexia [*Neurology*] (DAVI)
AD...............	Autosomal Dominant [*Genetics*]
AD...............	Availability Date [*Banking*]
AD...............	Avalanche Diode (KSC)
AD...............	Average Depth (IAA)
AD...............	Average Deviation [*Statistics*]
AD...............	Average Diameter
AD...............	Avia [*Francis Lombardi eC*] [*Italy ICAO aircraft manufacturer identifier*] (ICAO)
AD...............	Aviation Daily

AD	Aviation Detachment [*Military*] (VNW)
AD	Aviation Division [*Forecast Systems Laboratory*] (USDC)
AD	Aviation Division [*Marine science*] (OSRA)
AD	Aviation Machinist's Mate [*Navy rating*]
AD	Aviatsionnaya Diviziya [*Air Division*] [*Former USSR*]
AD	Avoidable Delay
A/D	Awaiting Delivery (MCD)
AD	Awaiting Disconnection [*Telecommunications*] (TEL)
AD	Axiodistal [*Dentistry*]
AD	Axis Deviation (MAE)
AD	Axle Detector
AD	Azimuth Drive (GFGA)
Ad	C. H. Boehringer Sohn, Ingelheim [*Germany*] [*Research code symbol*]
AD	Cytosine Arabinoside Daunomycin [*Also, DA*] [*Antineoplastic drug regimen*] (DAVI)
AD	Deputy Administrator [*NASA*]
AD	Destroyer Tender [*Navy symbol*]
AD	Devon Public Library, Alberta [*Library symbol National Library of Canada*] (NLC)
AD	Diphenylchlorarsine [*Toxic smoke used in warfare, also called Clark I*] (DAVI)
AD	Doctor of Arts
AD	Exec Express [*ICAO designator*] (AD)
AD	Lab. Miquel [*Spain*] [*Research code symbol*]
AD	New York Supreme Court, Appellate Division Reports [*A publication*] (DLA)
AD	Norfolk, Franklin & Danville Railway Co. [*The Atlantic & Danville Railway Co.*] [*AAR code*]
AD	Servantes de l'Agneu Divin [*Sisters of the Lamb of God*] [*Roman Catholic religious order*]
AD	Sisters of the Lamb of God (TOCD)
AD	South African Supreme Court Appellate Division Reports [*A publication*] (DLA)
AD	Travel-Agent Discount [*For air travel*]
AD1	Great Sitkin [*Alaska*] [*Seismograph station code, US Geological Survey*] (SEIS)
AD2	Umak [*Alaska*] [*Seismograph station code, US Geological Survey*] (SEIS)
AD 2d	New York Supreme Court, Appellate Division Reports, Second Series [*A publication*] (DLA)
AD 2 VIC	Ad Duas Vices [*For Two Doses*] [*Pharmacy*]
AD3	Kagalaska [*Alaska*] [*Seismograph station code, US Geological Survey*] (SEIS)
AD4	Hidden Bay [*Alaska*] [*Seismograph station code, US Geological Survey*] (SEIS)
AD5	Yakak [*Alaska*] [*Seismograph station code, US Geological Survey*] (SEIS)
AD6	South Kanaga [*Alaska*] [*Seismograph station code, US Geological Survey*] (SEIS)
AD7	North Kanaga [*Alaska*] [*Seismograph station code, US Geological Survey*] (SEIS)
AD8	Adagdak [*Alaska*] [*Seismograph station code, US Geological Survey*] (SEIS)
AD 86	Accion Democratica 86 [*Democratic Action 1986*] [*Aruba*] [*Political party*] (EY)
AD 2000	Areas of Development International Conference and Exhibition [*British*] (ITD)
ADA	Academy of Dispensing Audiologists (EA)
ADA	(Acetamidol)Iminodiacetic Acid [*A buffer*]
ADA	Acetone-Dicarboxylic Acid (WDAA)
ADA	Action Data Automation [*British*] (NATG)
A/D	Action for Dysphasic Adults [*British*]
ADA	Active Duty Agreement
Ada	Ada [*Byron*] [*The name of a computer language*] (BARN)
ADA	Adak Island [*Alaska*] [*Seismograph station code, US Geological Survey Closed*] (SEIS)
ADA	Adana [*Turkey*] [*Airport symbol*] (OAG)
ADA	Address Adder (IAA)
ADA	Adenosine Deaminase [*An enzyme*]
ADA	Adjusted Daily Average (ADA)
ADA	Adola Mining Corp. [*Vancouver Stock Exchange symbol*]
ADA	Adult Children of Alcoholics [*Chemical dependency*] [*Psychology*] (DAVI)
ADA	Advanced Development Analysis
ADA	Advanced Disk Array [*Computer science*]
ADA	Aerojet Differential Analyzer
ADA	After Date of Award of Contract [*Telecommunications*] (TEL)
ADA	Agrupament Democratic d'Andorra [*Andorran Democratic Association*] [*Political party*] (PPW)
ADA	Aiken Dynamic Algebra (MCD)
ADA	Airborne Data Automation (AFM)
ADA	Aircraft Defense Analysis (MCD)
ADA	Air Data Assembly (NASA)
ADA	Air Defense Area [*Army*]
ADA	Air Defense Artillery [*Military*]
AD-A	Air Density A [*Explorer satellite*] [*NASA*]
ADA	Air Division Advisor [*Air Force*] (SAA)
ADA	Airlines Deregulation Act [*1978*]
ADA	Aluminum Dihydroxyaminoacetate [*Also, ALGLYN*] [*Pharmacology*]
ADA	American Dairy Association (EA)
ADA	American Dance Asylum
ADA	American Dart Association [*Defunct*] (EA)
ADA	American Dehydrators Association [*Later, AAPA*] (EA)
ADA	American Dental Association (EA)

ADA	American Dermatological Association (EA)
ADA	American Diabetes Association (EA)
ADA	American Dietetic Association (EA)
ADA	American Dove Association (EA)
ADA	American Down Association (EA)
ADA	Americans for Democratic Action (EA)
ADA	Americans with Disabilities Act [*An association*] (EA)
ADA	Americans with Disabilities Act [*of 1990*] (USGC)
ADA	AmeriData Technol [*NYSE symbol*] (TTSB)
ADA	Ameridata Technologies, Inc. [*Formerly, Sage Technologies*] [*NYSE symbol*] (SAG)
ADA	Ammonia Double-Alkali [*Organic chemistry*] (DICI)
ADA	Ammonium Dihydrogen Arsenate [*Inorganic chemistry*]
ADA	Amplifier Detector Assembly
ADA	Analog-Digital-Analog (IAA)
ADA	Analog Drive Assembly (MCD)
ADA	Andover Distributors Association (EA)
ADA	Angle Data Assembly
ADA	Angular Differentiating-Integrating Accelerometer
ADA	Anterior Descending Artery [*Anatomy*] (MAE)
ADA	Anthraquinone Disulfonic Acid [*Organic chemistry*]
ADA	Anti-Deficiency Act (AAGC)
ADA	Anti-Discrimination Act [*Australia*]
ADA	Anti-Dumping Authority
ADA	Antiques Dealers' Association of America (EA)
ADA	Applied Decision Analysis
ADA	Arming Device Assemblies [*Army*] (MCD)
ADA	Art Directors Annual [*A publication*]
ADA	Arts Development Association [*British*] (DBA)
ADA	Assistant Defence Advisor [*British military*] (DMA)
ADA	Assistant Director of Artillery [*British*]
ADA	Assistant District Attorney
ADA	Association des Detaillants en Alimentation du Quebec [*Quebec Food Retailers Association*] (AC)
ADA	Association of Dairymen's Assistants [*A union*] [*British*]
ADA	Association of Drainage Authorities [*British*] (DCTA)
ADA	Atomic Development Authority [*Proposed by Bernard Baruch to exercise control over those aspects of atomic energy inimical to global security; never organized*]
ADA	Audio Distribution Amplifier
ADA	Australian Civil Aviation Authority, Flying Unit [*ICAO designator*] (FAAC)
ADA	Australian Digest [*A publication*]
ADA	Australian Diving Association
ADA	Authority Directing Arrest or Confinement [*Military*]
ADA	Auto Directional Antenna
ADA	Automated Differential Agglutination (PDAA)
ADA	Automated Dispensing Analyzer (PDAA)
ADA	Automatic Damper Arm (KSC)
ADA	Automatic Data Acquisition [*Programming language named for Augusta Ada Byron*]
ADA	Automatic Data Aids (MCD)
ADA	Automatic Document Analysis (DIT)
ADA	Automobile Dealers Association
ADA	Average Daily Allowance (ADA)
ADA	Average Daily Attendance
ADA	Aviation Data and Analysis System [*BTS*] (TAG)
ADA	Azimuth Drive Assembly (MCD)
ADA	Azodicarbonamide (OA)
ADA	Daysland Public Library, Alberta [*Library symbol National Library of Canada*] (NLC)
ADA	Troy State University, Troy, AL [*OCLC symbol*] (OCLC)
ADAA	Aboriginal Development Assistance Association [*Australia*]
ADAA	Air Defense Action Area [*Military*]
ADAA	Air-Driven Air Amplifier
ADAA	Alabama District Attorneys Association (SRA)
ADAA	Alberta Dental Assistants Association [*Formerly, Alberta Dental Nurses & Assistants Association*] (AC)
ADAA	American Dental Assistants Association (EA)
ADAA	Anxiety Disorders Association of America (EA)
ADAA	Art Dealers Association of America (EA)
ADAA	Australian Dictionary of Acronyms and Abbreviations [*A publication*]
AdA&S	Advanced Aerodynamics & Structures, Inc. [*Associated Press*] (SAG)
ADAB	Assistant Director of the Army Budget
ADABAS	Adaptable Database System [*Database management system*] [*Registered trademark of Software AG, Darmstadt, Germany*]
ADABD	Air Defense Artillery Board [*Army*]
ADAB (FSM)	Assistant Director of the Army Budget (Financial Systems Management)
ADABP	Adenosine Deceminase Binding Protein [*Biochemistry*]
ADAC	Acoustic Data Analysis Center
ADAC	ADAC Laboratories [*NASDAQ symbol*] (NQ)
ADAC	Airborne Data Requisition Center (SAA)
ADAC	Air Defence Artillery Commander [*Military British*]
AD/AC	Air Defense Aircraft (MCD)
ADAC	Air Defense Artillery Complex (MCD)
ADAC	Airfoil Design and Analysis Center [*Ohio State University*] (MCD)
ADAC	All-Digital Attack Center (MCD)
ADAC	Allgemeiner Deutscher Automobil Club [*German Automobile Association*]
ADAC	Analog-to-Digital-to-Analog Converter (IAA)
ADAC	Association Danse au Canada [*Dance Association of Canada*]
AD/AC	Automatic Detection/Automatic Classification [*Antisubmarine warfare*] (MCD)
ADAC	Automatic Direct Analog Computer (BUR)

ADACC......... Automatic Data Acquisition and Computer Complex [*Air Force*]
A/DACG........ Arrival/Departure Airfield Control Group (DOMA)
ADACIOM..... Associated Drug and Chemical Industries of Missouri
AdacLb........ ADAC Laboratories [*Associated Press*] (SAG)
ADACS........ Air Defense Artillery Control Station [*Army*]
ADACS........ Attitude Determination and Control Software [*Orbital satellites*]
ADACS........ Attitude Determination and Control System (MCD)
ADACS........ Automated Data Acquisition and Control System (MCD)
A-DACT........ Adriamycin, Dactinomycin [*Antineoplastic drug regimen*]
ADACT........ Advise Action Taken (NOAA)
ADACVM...... Association of Deans of American Colleges of Veterinary Medicine
              [*Later, Association of American Veterinary Medical Colleges*]
              (AEBS)
ADAD.......... After Date of Award (MCD)
ADAD.......... Air Defense Alerting Device [*Military*]
ADAD.......... Air Defense Artillery, Director [*Air Force*]
ADADA........ Advise Approximate Date (NOAA)
ADADC........ American Dairy Association and Dairy Council (SRA)
ADADS........ Army Depot Automatic Diagnostic System (RDA)
ADAE.......... Advanced Diploma in Art Education [*British*]
ADAE.......... Association pour le Developpement de l'Administration de l'Education
              [*Association for the Development of Educational Administration*]
              [*Canada*]
ADAEA........ Alcohol and Drug Abuse Education Act (GFGA)
AdaEx......... [*The*] Adams Express Co. [*Associated Press*] (SAG)
ADAEX........ Automatic Data Acquisition and Computer Complex [*Computer
              science*] (MHDB)
ADAF.......... Advection-Dominated Accretion Flow [*Planetary science*]
ADAF.......... Australian Drug and Alcohol Foundation
ADAG.......... Adagio [*Slow*] [*Music*]
ADAG.......... American Dairy Association of Georgia and Alabama (SRA)
Adage......... Adage, Inc. [*Associated Press*] (SAG)
ADAGE........ Air Defense Air-to-Ground Engagement [*Simulation*]
ADAGO........ Adagio [*Slow*] [*Music*] (ROG)
ADAH.......... Assistant Director of Army Health [*British*]
ADAHF........ American Dental Association Health Foundation
ADAI.......... Adenosine Deaminase Inhibitor (PDAA)
ADAI.......... Apollo Documentation Administration Instruction [*NASA*] (KSC)
ADAI.......... Assistance Dogs of America [*An association*] (EA)
ADAI.......... Automobile Dealers Association of Indiana (SRA)
ADaiM........ Marine Environmental Sciences Consortium, Dauphin Island, AL
              [*Library symbol*] [*Library of Congress*] (LCLS)
Adair Lib..... Adair on Law Libels [*A publication*] (DLA)
ADAIS......... Aerodynamic Data Analysis and Integration System [*Computer
              science*]
ADAKSARCOORD... Adak [*Alaska*] Search and Rescue Coordinator [*Coast Guard*]
              (DNAB)
ADAL.......... Action Data Automation Language [*Computer science*] (MHDB)
ADAL.......... Authorized Dental Allowance List [*Military*] (DNAB)
ADALCON..... Advise All Concerned
ADALINE...... Adaptive Linear (KSC)
AD/ALT........ Advanced Destroyer/Aircraft Lightweight Torpedo (MCD)
ADAM.......... Adamantine (ABBR)
ADAM.......... Adams National Historic Site
ADAM.......... A.D.A.M. Software [*NASDAQ symbol*] (TTSB)
ADAM.......... ADAM Software, Inc. [*NASDAQ symbol*] (SAG)
ADAM.......... Adaptive Arithmetical Method
ADAM.......... Adaptive Digital Avionics Module
ADAM.......... Adaptive Dynamic Analysis and Maintenance (MHDI)
ADAM.......... A Data Management System (NITA)
ADAM.......... Advanced Data Access Method [*Computer science*] (IAA)
ADAM.......... Advanced Data Management
ADAM.......... Advanced Direct-Landing Apollo Mission [*NASA*] (IEEE)
ADAM.......... Advanced Dynamic Anthropomorphic Manikin [*Air Force*]
ADAM.......... Agriculture Department's Automated Manpower
ADAM.......... Air Base Damage Assessment Model (MCD)
ADAM.......... Air Defense Antimissile
ADAM.......... Air Defense Area Monthly Report [*Army*]
ADAM.......... Air Deflection and Modification [*NASA*] (KSC)
ADAM.......... Air Deflection and Modulation [*Air Force*] (MCD)
ADAM.......... Air-Delivered Attack Marker [*Air Force*] (MCD)
ADAM.......... All-Digital Answering Machine [*PhoneMate, Inc.*]
ADAM.......... American Defenders Against Animal Mistreatment [*Inactive*] (EA)
ADAM.......... American Divorce Association for Men
ADAM.......... Amniotic Deformity, Adhesion, Mutilation [*Syndrome*] [*Medicine*]
              (DMAA)
ADAM.......... Analog Data Acquisition Module
ADAM.......... Angular Distribution Auger Microscopy
ADAM.......... Animated Dissection of Anatomy for Medicine [*Interactive Multimedia
              Program*]
ADAM.......... Aperture Distribution and Maintenance [*System*]
ADAM.......... Area Denial Artillery Munition (AABC)
ADAM.......... Artillery-Delivered Antipersonnel Mine (RDA)
ADAM.......... Artillery Delivered Antipersonnel Munitions (MCD)
ADAM.......... Association des Directeurs d'Agence-Vie de Montreal (AC)
ADAM.......... Association of Distributors of Advertising Material (EAIO)
ADAM.......... Associometrics Data Management System (IEEE)
ADAM.......... Automated Deposition of Advanced Materials [*Materials technology*]
ADAM.......... Automated Design and Manufacturing (SAA)
ADAM.......... Automatic Distance and Angle Measurement
ADAM.......... Automatic Document Abstracting Method (NITA)
ADAM.......... Axisymmetric Duct Aeroacoustic Modeling (MCD)
Adam.......... Justiciary Reports [*1893-1916*] [*Scotland*] [*A publication*] (DLA)
ADA/MH....... Alcohol, Drug Abuse, and Mental Health [*Block grant*]

ADAMHA...... Alcohol, Drug Abuse, and Mental Health Administration [*Formerly,
              HSMHA*] [*Department of Health and Human Services Rockville,
              MD*]
ADAM II...... Aerial Port Documentation and Management System
Adam Jur Tr... Adam on Trial by Jury [*A publication*] (DLA)
ADAML....... Advise by Airmail [*Army*]
Adams........ Adams County Legal Journal [*Pennsylvania*] [*A publication*] (DLA)
Adams........ Adams' Reports [*41, 42 Maine*] [*A publication*] (DLA)
Adams........ Adams' Reports [*1 New Hampshire*] [*A publication*] (DLA)
ADAMS....... Advanced Action Manipulator System
ADAMS....... Advanced Design Aluminum Metal Shelter [*A prefabricated building
              known as an ADAMS hut*]
ADAMS....... Airborne Data Acquisition Multifunction System (MCD)
ADAMS....... Airborne Data Analysis and Monitoring System (MCD)
ADAMS....... Automated Dynamic Analysis of Mechanical Systems [*Mechanical
              Dynamics, Inc.*] [*Automotive engineering*]
Adams Eq ... Adams' Equity [*A publication*] (DLA)
AdamSft...... ADAM Software, Inc. [*Associated Press*] (SAG)
Adam Sl...... Adam on the Law of Slavery in British India [*A publication*] (DLA)
Adams Leg J (PA)... Adams' Legal Journal [*Pennsylvania*] [*A publication*] (DLA)
Adams LJ .... Adams County Legal Journal [*Pennsylvania*] [*A publication*] (DLA)
Adams Rom Ant... Adams' Roman Antiquities [*A publication*] (DLA)
Adams St C... Adams State College (GAGS)
ADAMT....... Adamant (ABBR)
ADAMTY...... Adamantly (ABBR)
AD AN........ Ad Annum [*Up to the Year*] [*Latin*]
ADaN........ Alabama State Normal School, Daphne, AL [*Library symbol Library of
              Congress Obsolete*] (LCLS)
ADAND....... Automobile Dealers Association of North Dakota (SRA)
ADANDAC.... Administrative and Accounting Purposes
AD and C.... Advise Duration and Charge [*British telephone term*]
AD & C....... Ammunition Distribution and Control [*Military*] (NG)
AD and D.... Accidental Death and Dismemberment [*Insurance*]
AD & D....... Advanced Dungeons and Dragons
AD & Dur RP... Adams and Durham on Real Property [*A publication*] (DLA)
Ad & E....... Adolphus and Ellis' English King's Bench Reports [*A publication*]
              (DLA)
Ad & El....... Adolphus and Ellis' English King's Bench Reports [*A publication*]
              (DLA)
Ad & El (Eng)... Adolphus and Ellis' English King's Bench Reports [*A publication*]
              (DLA)
Ad & Ell NS... Adolphus and Ellis' English Queen's Bench Reports, New Series
              [*A publication*] (DLA)
Ad & El NS... Adolphus and Ellis' Reports, New Series [*A publication*] (ILCA)
ADANET....... ADABAS [*Adaptable Database System*] network software
              [*Computer*] (NITA)
Ad Ang Sax L... Adams' Essay on Anglo-Saxon Law [*A publication*] (DLA)
ADAO......... Air Defense Artillery Officer (SAA)
ADAOD........ Air Defense Artillery Operations Detachment
ADAOO........ Air Defense Artillery Operations Office [*or Officer*]
ADAP.......... Active Duty Assistance Program (DNAB)
ADAP.......... Adaptive Intercommunication Requirement (MCD)
ADAP.......... Adaptor (KSC)
ADAP.......... Aerodynamic Data Analysis Program [*Computer science*] (SSD)
ADAP.......... AIDS [*Acquired Immuno-Deficiency Syndrome*] Drug Assistance
              Program
ADAP.......... Airport Development Aid Program [*FAA*]
ADAP.......... Alzheimer's Disease-Associated Protein [*Medicine*]
ADAP.......... American Dental Assistant's Program
ADAP.......... Analog-Digital Automatic Program (DNAB)
ADAP.......... Assistant Director of Administrative Planning [*Military British*]
ADAP.......... Assistant Director of Army Psychiatry [*British*]
ADAP.......... Assistant Director of Psychiatry [*British*] (DAVI)
ADAPB........ Adaptable (ABBR)
ADAPCP...... Alcohol and Drug Abuse Prevention and Control Program [*Military*]
              (AABC)
ADAPD....... Adapted (ABBR)
ADAPG....... Adapting (ABBR)
ADAPN....... Adaptation (ABBR)
ADAPN....... Adaption (ABBR)
ADAPR....... Adapter (ABBR)
ADAPS....... Armament Delivery Analysis Programming System (PDAA)
ADAPS....... Automatic Display and Plotting System (BUR)
AdapSl....... Adaptive Solutions, Inc. [*Associated Press*] (SAG)
ADAPSO...... Association of Data Processing Service Organizations [*Later, CSSIA*]
              [*US and Canada*] (EA)
AdapSol...... Adaptive Solutions, Inc. [*Associated Press*] (SAG)
ADAPSP...... Association of Data Processing Service Organizations Panels
ADAPT........ Accent on Developing Abstract Processes of Thought
ADAPT........ Active Duty Assistance Program Team
ADAPT........ Adaptation
ADAPT........ Adapter
ADAPT........ Adoption of Automatically Programmed Tools [*Computer science*]
              (IEEE)
ADAPT........ Advanced Development Aims Processor Transponder [*Military*]
              (MCD)
ADAPT........ Alcohol and Drug Abuse Prevention Treatment
ADAPT........ American Disabled for Accessible Public Transit (EA)
ADAPT........ Analog-Digital Automatic Program Tester [*Computer science*]
ADAPT........ Automated Data Analysis and Presentation Techniques (MCD)
ADAPT........ Automatic Data Acquisition and Processing Techniques [*Army*] (RDA)
ADAPT........ Avco Data Analysis and Prediction Technique [*for sunspot prediction*]
ADAPT........ [*A*] Diagnostic and Prescriptive Technique [*Teaching process*]
Adaptec...... Adaptec, Inc. [*Associated Press*] (SAG)
ADAPTICOM... Adaptive Communication (MHDB)

ADAPTS	Air-Deliverable Antipollution Transfer System
ADAPTS	Analogue/Digital/Analogue Process and Test System (PDAA)
ADAPTTN	Adaptation (ABBR)
ADAPTV	Adaptive (ABBR)
ADAPV	Adaptive (ABBR)
ADAPY	Adaptably (ABBR)
ADAR	Advanced Data Acquisition Routine [Computer science] (OA)
ADAR	Advanced Design Array RADAR
ADAR	Airborne Data Acquisition Registration [Digital mapping]
ADAR	Air Defense Area [Army]
ADAR	Air Deployable Active Reservoir [Military] (DOMA)
ADAR	Analog Data Reduction System (CAAL)
ADAR	Army Defense Acquisition Regulation [Superseded by AFARS in 1984] (AAGC)
ADAR	Darwell Public Library, Alberta [Library symbol National Library of Canada] (NLC)
ADARA	American Deafness and Rehabilitation Association (EA)
ADARC	Aaron Diamond AIDS Research Center
ADARCO	Advise Date of Reporting in Compliance with Orders [Navy]
ADARD	Acid Deposition and Atmospheric Research Division [Environmental Protection Agency] (GFGAG)
ADARE	Advise Date of Receipt (NOAA)
ADARS	Adaptive Antenna Receiver System
ADARS	Airborne Data Acquisition and Recording System
ADARS	Army Defense Acquisition Regulation Supplement (AABC)
ADARUQ	Association des Administrateurs de Recherches Universitaires du Quebec (AC)
ADAS	Acid Deposition Assessment Staff [Environmental Protection Agency] (GFGA)
ADA-S	Action Data Automation - Small (SAA)
ADAS	Advanced Digital Avionics System (MCD)
ADAS	Agricultural Development and Advisory Service [British] (ARC)
ADAS	Airborne Data Acquisition System
ADAS	Airborne Dynamic Alignment System (MCD)
ADAS	Alzheimer's Disease Assessment Scale
ADAS	American Dental Association Specifications
ADAS	Analog Data Aquisition System
ADAS	Architecture Design and Assessment System [Software package]
ADAS	Army Digital Avionics System (MCD)
ADAS	Automated Data Acquisition System [GCA Corp.]
ADAS	Automatic Dialing Alarm System (PDAA)
ADAS	Auxiliary Data Annotation Set [or System]
ADAS	AWOS Data Acquisition System [FAA] (TAG)
ADaS	United States Sports Academy, Daphne, AL [Library symbol] [Library of Congress] (LCLS)
ADAS-Cog	Alzheimer's Disease Assessment Scale Cognitive Subscale
ADase	Adenosine Deminase [An enzyme] (DMAA)
ADASH	Advise Date of Shipment (NOAA)
ADASP	Air Defense Annual Service Practice (AABC)
ADASP	Automatic Data and Select Program (KSC)
ADASSA	Aerodynamic Design and Analysis System for Supersonic Aircraft (MCD)
ADAT	Army Dependents' Assurance Trust [British] (DI)
ADAT	Artificially Intelligent Devices and Techniques (NITA)
ADAT	Automatic Data Accumulation and Transfer
ADATE	Association pour le Developpement de l'Audiovisuel et de la Technologie en Education [Canada]
ADATE	Automatic Digital Assembly Test Equipment (MCD)
ADATM	Artillery-Delivered Antitank Mine (MCD)
ADatP	Allied Data Processing Publications (NATG)
ADATS	Advanced Anti-Aircraft and Anti-Tank Guided-Missile System (ECON)
ADATS	Air Defense Antitank System
ADATS	Air Defense Artillery Threat Simulator (MCD)
ADATS	Army Development and Acquisition of Threat Simulators
ADATS	Assistant Director, Auxiliary Territorial Service [British military] (DMA)
ADATT	Advise Action to Be Taken by This Office (NOAA)
ADAU	Adolescent Drug Abuse Unit [Medicine] (DMAA)
ADAU	Auxiliary Data Acquisition Unit [Computer science] (MHDI)
ADAV	American Dairy Association of Virginia (SRA)
ADAV	Animal Defense/Anti-Vivisection Society of BC (AC)
ADAVAL	Advise Availability [Army]
ADAWS	Action Data Automation Weapons System (MCD)
ADAWS	Assistant Director of Army Welfare Services [British]
ADAX	Applied Digital Access [NASDAQ symbol] (SAG)
A (Day)	Act Day [Financial Services] [British]
A (Day)	Announcement Day [Military] (DNAB)
ADB	Accidental Death Benefit [Insurance]
ADB	Acoustic Distribution Box (CAAL)
ADB	Adjusted Debit Balance [Accounting]
adb	Adobe (VRA)
ADB	Aerodynamic Data Book (NASA)
ADB	African Development Bank [Also, AfDB]
ADB	Air Defense Board [Army] (AAG)
ADB	American Design Bicentennial [An association Defunct] (EA)
adb	Another Debugger [Computer science] (BYTE)
ADB	Antonov Design Bureau [Former USSR ICAO designator] (FAAC)
ADB	Apollo Data Bank [NASA] (MCD)
ADB	Apple Desktop Bus [Computer science]
ADB	Applications Database [Environmental Protection Agency] (GFGA)
ADB	Arctic Drift Barge
ADB	Asian Development Bank
ADB	Asian Development Bank (GNE)
ADB	Association [or Associate] of Drama Boards [British]
ADB	Average Daily Balance
ADB	Bachelor of Domestic Arts

ADB	United States Army Ballistic Research Laboratories, Aberdeen Proving Grounds, MD [OCLC symbol] (OCLC)
ADBA	American Dog Breeders Association [Defunct] (EA)
ADBC	Adriamycin, Dacarbazine, Bleomycin, CCNU [Lomustine] [Antineoplastic drug regimen]
ADBC	American Defenders of Bataan and Corregidor (EA)
ADBD	Active Duty Base Date [Later, PSD] [Navy]
ADBE	Adobe Systems [NASDAQ symbol] (TTSB)
ADBE	Adobe Systems, Inc. [NASDAQ symbol] (NQ)
ADB(Ed)	Associate of the Drama Board (Education) [British] (DI)
ADBF	Azurophil-Derived Bactericidal Factor
ADBM	Apple Desktop Bus Microcontroller [Computer processor]
ADBMS	Available Database Management System
ad Brut	Epistulae ad Brutum [of Cicero] [Classical studies] (OCD)
ADBS	Advanced Database System
ADB(S)	Associate of the Drama Board (Special) [British] (DI)
ADBSS	Arizona Desert Bighorn Sheep Society (SRA)
ADBT	Access Decision Binding Time (MHDI)
ADC	Accretion Disk Corona [Astrophysics]
ADC	Acoustic Device, Countermeasure (CAAL)
ADC	Acquisition, Development, and Construction [Real estate loan]
ADC	Acta Dominorum Concilii [3 vols.] [1839-1943 Scotland] [A publication] (DLA)
ADC	Action for Disabled Customers [British Telecom]
ADC	Active Diffusion Control (MCD)
ADC	Active Duty Commitment
ADC	Actuation Data Communication [Naval Ordnance Laboratory]
ADC	Adaptive Data Compression [Computer science]
ADC	Adaptive Noise Control [Automotive engineering]
ADC	Address Complete, Charge [Telecommunications] (TEL)
ADC	Adduce (ABBR)
ADC	Add with Carry
AdC	Adenylate Cyclase (DMAA)
ADC	Adopted Child [Legal shorthand] (LWAP)
AdC	Adrenal Cortex [Medicine]
ADC	Advanced Data Communications [Computer science] (ECII)
ADC	Advanced Data Connector [Computer science]
ADC	Advanced Design [or Drawing] Change
ADC	Advanced Development Concept (CAAL)
ADC	Advance Delivery of Correspondence [Military]
ADC	Advancing Developing Countries [Economics]
ADC	Advice of Duration and Charge (ODBW)
ADC	Advisory Defense Committee
ADC	Aerodrome Control [British]
ADC	Aerodrome Defence Corps [British]
ADC	Aerodynamic Data Correlation (MCD)
ADC	Aerophysics Development Corp.
ADC	Aerospace Defense Command [Formerly, Air Defense Command] [Air Force]
ADC	Agree Reality Corp. [NYSE symbol] (SAG)
ADC	Agree Realty [NYSE symbol] (TTSB)
ADC	Agricultural Development Council [Later, WIIAD] (EA)
ADC	Aide-de-Camp [Military French]
ADC	AIDS [Acquired Immune Deficiency Syndrome] Dementia Complex [Medicine]
ADC	Aid to Dependent Children
ADC	Airborne Digital Computer [Air Force]
ADC	Aircraft Directives Configuration [Navy] (NG)
ADC	Air Data Computer [or Computing] (MCD)
ADC	Air Data Converter
ADC	Air Defense Center (AAG)
ADC	Air Defense Command [Peterson Air Force Base, CO]
ADC	Air Defense Computer (AAG)
ADC	Air Development Center [Air Force]
ADC	Air Diffusion Council (EA)
ADC	Air Direction Center
ADC	Airdrome Defense Corps [Air Force]
ADC	Airline of Adriatic [Croatia] [ICAO designator] (FAAC)
ADC	Alaska Defense Command [Known to many of the soldiers who served in it as "All Damn Confusion"] [World War II]
ADC	Albumin, Dextrose, Catalase [Media]
ADC	Alloy Data Center [National Institute of Standards and Technology]
ADC	Allyl Diglycol Carbonate [Organic chemistry]
ADC	Almost-Developed Country
ADC	Amateur Dramatic Club [British]
ADC	Ambulance Design Criteria [National Highway Transportation Safety Administration]
ADC	American-Arab Anti-Discrimination Committee (EA)
ADC	American Deserters Committee, France (EA)
ADC	American Digital Cartography
ADC	Ampere Direct Current (MCD)
ADC	Ampex Disk Controller [Computer science] (IAA)
ADC	Analog-to-Digital Computer [Computer science] (MCD)
ADC	Analog-to-Digital Converter [Computer science] (MUGU)
adc	Analog-to-Digital Converter (IDOE)
ADC	Analytical Development Corp.
ADC	Analytic Decisions Corp. [Information service or system] (IID)
ADC	Analytic Drag Control [Aviation] (NASA)
ADC	Anchorage Dependent Cell [Culture technology]
ADC	Animal Damage Control [Department of Agriculture]
ADC	Anodal Duration Contraction [Physiology]
ADC	Antenna Dish Control
ADC	Anthracenedicarboxaldehyde [Biochemistry]
ADC	Anti-Drug Coalition [Later, NADC] (EA)
ADC	Apollo Display Console [NASA]

ADC .... Apparent Depth of Compensation [*Geology*]
ADC .... Appeal Cases, District of Columbia [*A publication*] (DLA)
ADC .... Applied Data Communication [*Computer science*] (IAA)
ADC .... Ardeer Double Cartridge Test [*Sensitivity to propagation test of an explosive*]
ADC .... Area Damage Control (MCD)
ADC .... Area Data Center
ADC .... Area Defense Counsel [*Military*]
ADC .... Areas of Deeper Convection (PDAA)
ADC .... Arginine Decarboxylase [*An enzyme*]
ADC .... Armament Development Center [*Army*]
ADC .... Army Dental Corps [*British*]
ADC .... Art Directors Club (EA)
ADC .... Asian Development Center
ADC .... Assistant Defense Counsel
ADC .... Assistant Director, Curatorial
ADC .... Assistant Director of Ceremonies [*Freemasonry*]
ADC .... Assistant Director of Contracts [*Military British*]
ADC .... Assistant District Commission (MCD)
ADC .... Assistant Division Commander [*Military*]
ADC .... Assistive Device Center [*Research center*] (RCD)
ADC .... [*The*] Associated Daimler Co. [*British*] (DCTA)
ADC .... Associated Designers of Canada (AC)
ADC .... Associate Diploma in Computing
ADC .... Association of Defense Counselors (EA)
ADC .... Association of District Councils [*British*]
ADC .... Association of Diving Contractors (EA)
ADC .... Asynchronous Data Channel (MCD)
ADC .... Asynchronous Digital Combiner (MCD)
ADC .... Atlantic Dairy Council (AC)
ADC .... Auburn Dam [*California*] [*Seismograph station code, US Geological Survey*] (SEIS)
ADC .... Audio Data Communication [*Computer science*] (IAA)
ADC .... Australian Design Council
ADC .... Authorized Data Chain (AFM)
ADC .... Automated Data Collection [*Computer science*] (BTTJ)
ADC .... Automatic Damping Control [*Automotive suspensions*]
ADC .... Automatic Data Center (ECII)
ADC .... Automatic Data Collector [*National Weather Service*]
ADC .... Automatic Data Computing [*Computer science*] (IAA)
ADC .... Automatic Depth Control (MCD)
ADC .... Automatic Deviation Control (MCD)
ADC .... Automatic Digital Calculator [*Computer science*] (ADA)
ADC .... Automatic Drift Control (AFM)
ADC .... Automatic Drip Coffee [*Brand name*]
ADC .... Automatic Drive Control (IAA)
ADC .... Average Daily Census
ADC .... Aviation Development Council (EA)
ADC .... Axiodistocervical [*Dentistry*]
ADC .... Chief Aviation Machinist's Mate (Reciprocating) [*Navy rating*]
ADC .... Debolt Community Library, Alberta [*Library symbol National Library of Canada*] (NLC)
ADCA .... Advanced Design Composite Aircraft (MCD)
ADCA .... Aerospace Department Chairmen's Association (EA)
ADCA .... American Dexter Cattle Association (EA)
ADCA .... Aminodecephalosporanic Acid [*Biochemistry*]
ADCA .... Aminodeoxyclavulanic Acid [*Organic chemistry*]
ADCA .... Antique Doorknob Collectors of America (EA)
ADCA .... Australian Die Casting Association
ADCAA .... Age Discrimination Claims Assistance Act [*1988*]
ADCAD .... Airways Data Collection and Distribution [*Computer science*]
ADCAP .... Advanced Capability
Ad Capt ...... Ad Captandum [*For the Purpose of Captivating*] [*Latin*]
ADCAR .... Automated Document Control and Retrieval System [*Computer science*] (GFGA)
ADCAS .... Automatic Data Collection and Analysis System [*Fort Huachuca, AZ*] [*United States Army Electronic Proving Ground*] (GRD)
ADCASHAL ... Advance Cash Allowance Authorized
ADCAT .... Air Defense Control and Targets Office [*Army*]
ADCATT ...... Air Defense Combined Arms Tactical Trainer [*Army*]
ADCC .... Actual Development Cost Certification [*HUD*]
ADCC .... Air Defence Cadet Corps [*Military British*]
ADCC .... Air Defense Command and Control [*MICOM*] (RDA)
ADCC .... Air Defense Command Center
ADCC .... Air Defense Command Computer [*Military*] (IAA)
ADCC .... Air Defense Control Center [*Air Force*]
ADCC .... American Devon Cattle Club [*Later, Devon Cattle Association*] (EA)
ADCC .... Andean Development Corp. [*NASDAQ symbol*] (SAG)
ADCC .... Antibody-Dependent Cell-Mediated Cytotoxicity [*Immunology*]
ADCC .... Antibody-Dependent Cellular Cytotoxicity [*DOG*]
ADCC .... Area Damage Control Center [*Army*]
ADCC .... Associated Day Care Centers
ADCC .... Asynchronous Data Communications Channel
ADCC .... Atlantic Development Council Canada
ADCCC .... Air Defense Command Commendation Certificate
ADCCCS ...... Air Defense Command, Control, and Coordination System (AABC)
ADCCM .... Advanced Cooperative Countermeasure (MCD)
ADCCOMNET ... Air Defense Command Communications Network [*Military*] (IAA)
AdccoSA ..... Adecco SA [*Associated Press*] (SAG)
ADCCP .... Advanced Data Communications Control Procedure [*American National Standards Institute*]
ADCCQ .... ANZAC [*Australia-New Zealand Army Corps*] Day Commemoration Committee, Queensland
ADCCS .... Air Defense Command and Control System (MCD)
ADCCSA .... Air Diffusion and Components Council of South Australia

ADCE .... Air Defense Communication Equipment [*Military*]
ADCEO .... Assistant Division Communications Electronics Officer [*Military*] (AABC)
ADCEP .... Advanced Structural Concept and Evaluation Program [*Military*] (DNAB)
ADCF .... Air Defense Control Facility (FAAC)
ADCGEN ...... Aide-de-Camp General [*Appointment to the Queen*] [*British*]
ADCI .... American Die Casting Institute (EA)
ADCII .... American Die Casting Institute, Inc.
ADCIR .... Administrative Circular
ADCIS .... Association for Development of Computer-Based Instructional Systems (EA)
ADCJ .... Air Defense Communications Jammer [*Military*] (PDAA)
ADCL .... Accredited Dosimetry Calibration Laboratories
ADCLS .... Advanced Data Collection and Location System
ADCM .... Air Defense Command Manual (SAA)
ADCM .... Archbishop of Canterbury's Diploma in Church Music [*British*]
ADCM .... Art Directors Club of Montreal [*1950*] [*Canada*] (NGC)
ADC(M) .... Assistant Division Commander for Maneuver [*Military*] (INF)
ADCMC .... Antibody-Dependent Cell-Mediated Cytotoxicity [*Immunology*]
ADCN .... Advanced Design [*or Drawing*] Change Notice
ADCN .... Aeronautical Data Communication Network (DA)
ADCNM .... Assistant Deputy Chief of Naval Material (MCD)
ADCNO .... Assistant Deputy Chief of Naval Operations (DNAB)
ADCNO(CP/EEO) ... Assistant Deputy Chief of Naval Operations (Civilian Personnel/Equal Employment Opportunity) (DNAB)
ADCO .... Adco Technologies [*NASDAQ symbol*] (TTSB)
ADCO .... Adco Technologies, Inc. [*NASDAQ symbol*] (SAG)
ADCO .... Air Defense Communications Office (AABC)
ADCO .... Alcohol and Drug Control Office [*Military*] (AABC)
ADCO .... As Design Changes Occur (MCD)
ADCO .... Association of Day Care Operators of Ontario (AC)
ADC-OA .... Air Defense Command-Office of Operations Analysis [*Peterson Air Force Base, CO*]
ADCOC .... Area Damage Control Center [*Army*]
ADCOH .... Appalachian Ultradeep Core Hole [*Project of seismic profiling*]
ADCOINS ..... Air Defense Command Interoperability System [*Army*]
ADCOM .... Administrative Command
ADCOM .... Advance Command
ADCOM .... Advanced Communications (DNAB)
ADCOM .... Advanced Cooperative Countermeasure (MCD)
ADCOM .... Air Defense Command [*Army*]
ADCOMD ...... Administrative Command [*Navy British*]
ADCOMINPAC ... Administrative Command, Minecraft, Pacific Fleet
ADCOMPHIBSPAC ... Administrative Command, Amphibious Forces, Pacific Fleet
ADCOMR .... Aerospace Defense Command Region [*Military*]
ADCOMSUBORDCOMPHIBSPAC ... Administrative Command, Amphibious Forces, Pacific Fleet, Subordinate Command
Ad Con .... Addison on Contracts [*A publication*] (DLA)
ADCON .... Address Constant [*Computer science*]
ADCON .... Administrative Control
ADCON .... Advance Concepts for Terrain Avoidance
ADCON .... Advise [*or Issue Instructions to*] All Concerned
ADCON .... Analog-to-Digital Converter [*Computer science*]
ADCON .... Archdeacon
ADCONFU ..... Adriamycin, Cyclophosphamide, 5-Fluorouracil, Actinomycin D [*Antineoplastic drug regimen*] (DAVI)
ADCONFU ..... Adriamycin, Cyclophosphamide, Vincristine, 5-Fluorouracil, [*Antineoplastic drug regimen*] (DAVI)
Ad Cont ...... Addison on Contract [*A publication*] (ILCA)
A/D converter ... Analog-to-Digital Converter [*Computer science*] (DOM)
ADCOP .... Acquisition and Distribution of Commercial Products [*Also, ADCP*] [*Department of Defense program*]
ADCOP .... Air Defense Command Post
ADCOP .... Area Damage Control Party [*Army*]
ADCOP .... Associate Degree Completion Program [*Navy*] (NG)
AdcoTc .... Adcom Technologies, Inc. [*Associated Press*] (SAG)
ADCP .... Acoustic Doppler Current Profiler [*Oceanography*]
ADCP .... Acquisition and Distribution of Commercial Products [*Also, ADCOP*] [*Department of Defense program*] (MCD)
ADCP .... Adenosine Deaminase Complexing Protein (DMAA)
ADCP .... Advanced [*Flight*] Control Programmer
ADCP .... Advanced Data Communication Protocol [*Computer science*]
ADC(P) .... Aide-de-Camp Personal [*Appointment to the Queen*] [*British*]
ADCP .... Air Defense Command Post (AABC)
ADC/PL .... Advanced Data Collection - Position Location (MCD)
ADCPM .... Adaptive Differential Pulse Code Modulation [*Computer science*]
ADCR .... Aerospace Division Commitment Record (SAA)
ADCR .... Air Defense Command Regulation (SAA)
ADCR .... Applicable Document Contractual Record [*Military*]
ADCR .... Devon Coal Research Centre, Alberta [*Library symbol National Library of Canada*] (NLC)
ADCS .... ADA Design and Coping Standards [*DoD*]
ADCS .... Advanced Defense Communications Satellite [*Air Force*] (AFM)
ADCS .... Air Data Computer Set
ADCS .... Air Data Computing System
ADCS .... Air Defense Control System [*Military*]
ADCS .... Argonz del Castillo Syndrome [*Medicine*] (DMAA)
ADCS .... AUTODIN Coordination Station (CET)
ADCS .... Automated Document Control System [*Computer science*] (MCD)
ADCS .... Automatic Data Collection System (RDA)
ADCS .... Automatic Data Correlation System (MCD)
ADCS .... Senior Chief Aviation Machinist's Mate [*Navy rating*]
ADCSCD ...... Assistant Deputy Chief of Staff for Combat Developments [*Army*]
ADCSLOG .... Assistant Deputy Chief of Staff for Logistics [*Army*]

ADCSLOG-SA... Assistant Deputy Chief of Staff for Logistics for Security Assistance [*Military*]
ADCSOPS .... Assistant Deputy Chief of Staff for Operations and Plans [*Military*]
ADCSOPS (JA)... Assistant Deputy Chief of Staff for Operations and Plans (Joint Affairs) [*Military*]
ADCSP........ Advanced Defense Communications Satellite Program [*Air Force*]
ADCSPC....... Air Data Computer Static Pressure Compensator (MCD)
ADCSRDA..... Assistant Deputy Chief of Staff for Research, Development, and Acquisition [*Military*]
ADCSTE....... Assistant Deputy Chief of Staff, in Test and Evaluation [*Army*]
ADCT .... ADC Telecommunications [*NASDAQ symbol*] (TTSB)
ADCT .... ADC Telecommunications, Inc. [*NASDAQ symbol*] (NQ)
ADCT .... Adduct (ABBR)
ADCT .... Art Directors Club of Toronto [*1947*] [*Canada*] (NGC)
ADCT .... Assisted-Draught Crossflow Tower (PDAA)
ADCT .... Association of District Council Treasurers [*British*]
Ad Ct Dig.... Administrative Court Digest [*A publication*] (DLA)
ADCTel........ ADC Telecommunications, Inc. [*Associated Press*] (SAG)
ADCTN........ Adduction (ABBR)
ADCTV........ Adductive (ABBR)
ADCU .... Air Vehicle Digital Computer Unit
ADCU .... Alarm Display and Control Unit [*Telecommunications*] (TEL)
ADCU .... Alternate Detection and Control Unit (MCD)
ADCU .... Association of Data Communications Users [*Defunct*] (EA)
ADCUS .... Advise Customs [*Aviation*] (FAAC)
ADCVR........ Analog-Digital Converter (NITA)
ADCWT........ Adipose Fin Clip with Coded Wire Tag [*Pisciculture*]
ADD .... Abstracts of Declassified Documents [*A publication*]
ADD .... Accidental Death and Disability [*Insurance*]
ADD .... Acoustic Deception Device (CAAL)
ADD .... Acoustic Detection Device (MCD)
ADD .... Acoustic Discrimination of Decoys
ADD .... Activated Dough Development (OA)
ADD .... Adastra Aviation Ltd. [*Canada ICAO designator*] (FAAC)
Add .... Addams' Ecclesiastical Reports [*A publication*] (DLA)
add .... Addantur [*Let Them Be Added*] [*Latin*]
ADD .... Adde [*Add or Up To*] [*Pharmacy*]
ADD .... Addendum (KSC)
add .... Addendum (WDMC)
ADD .... Addis Ababa [*Ethiopia*] [*Airport symbol*] (OAG)
Add .... Addison's Pennsylvania Supreme Court Reports [*A publication*] (DLA)
ADD .... Addition (AABC)
ADD .... Address
ADD .... Adduction [*or Adductor*] [*Medicine*]
ADD .... Adenosine Deaminase [*An enzyme*] (DMAA)
ADD .... Administration on Developmental Disabilities [*Human Development Services*]
ADD .... Advanced Development Design (CAAL)
ADD .... Aerospace Defense Division [*Air Force*]
ADD .... Aerospace Design and Development, Inc. (AAGC)
ADD .... Aerospace Digital Development
ADD .... After Diversity Demand (IAA)
ADD .... Against Drunk Driving [*Also, The Neil Gray Memorial Fund*] (AC)
ADD .... Airborne Deception Device
ADD .... Air Defense Development
ADD .... Air Defense District (NATG)
ADD .... Air Defense Division [*NATO*] (SAA)
ADD .... Airstream Direction Detector (PDAA)
ADD .... Alcohol and Drug Dependency Clinic (DAVI)
ADD .... Alphanumeric Digital Display (CAAL)
ADD .... American Doctoral Dissertations [*A publication*]
ADD .... Amino(dimethyl)dihydrobenzofuran [*Organic chemistry*]
ADD .... Analog Data Digitizer
ADD .... Analog-Digital-Designer [*Trademark*]
ADD .... Androstanediene [*Biochemistry*] (DAVI)
ADD .... Androstanediene-Dione (BABM)
ADD .... Armaments Design Department [*Ministry of Supply*] [*British World War II*]
ADD .... Arming Decision Device (MUGU)
ADD .... Army Data Dictionary (RDA)
ADD .... Ascent Descent Director (PDAA)
ADD .... Attention Deficit Disorder [*Psychology*]
ADD .... Auditory Discrimination in Depth [*Program*] [*Education*]
ADD .... Authorized Data Distributor (HGAA)
ADD .... Automated Design and Documentation (SAA)
ADD .... Automated Diagram Drafting (SAA)
ADD .... Automatic Data Descriptor
ADD .... Automatic Digital Depth (IAA)
ADD .... Automatic Dish Detergent
ADD .... Automatic Distribution of Documents [*DoD*]
ADD .... Automatic Document Distribution (MCD)
ADD .... Automatic Drawing Device (DIT)
ADD .... Average Daily Dose [*Pharmacy*] (DAVI)
ADD .... Aviatsiia Dalnego Deistviia [*Long-Range Aviation*] [*Strategic bombing force of USSR*]
ADD .... Awaiting Delivery of Data (AAGC)
add .... Journalism addition (WDMC)
ADD .... United States Army ARRADCOM - STINFO Division, Dover, NJ [*OCLC symbol*] (OCLC)
ADDA.......... Air Defense Defended Area [*Army*]
ADDA.......... Air Defense Operations Area [*Army*] (ADDR)
ADDA.......... Alaska Detroit Diesel Allison [*Commercial firm*]
ADDA.......... American Design Drafting Association (EA)
AD/DA......... Analog Digital/Digital Analog (RDA)

ADDA.......... Attention-Deficit Disorder Association (EA)
ADDA.......... Darwin [*Australia ICAO location identifier*] (ICLI)
ADDABASE... Australian Database Development Association Database
Add Abr ...... Addington's Abridgment of Penal Statutes [*A publication*] (DLA)
ADDAC........ Analog Data Distributor and Control [*Computer science*] (KSC)
Add Agr Act... Addison on the Agricultural Holdings Act [*A publication*] (DLA)
ADDAM....... Adaptive Dynamic Decision-Aiding Method
Addams ...... Addams' Ecclesiastical Reports [*A publication*] (DLA)
ADDAMS...... Automated Dredging and Disposal System [*U.S. Army Corps of Engineers*]
Addams Ecc (Eng)... Addams' Ecclesiastical Reports [*A publication*] (DLA)
ADDAR........ Automatic Digital Data Acquisition and Recording [*Computer science*]
ADDAS........ Automatic Digital Data Assembly System [*Computer science*]
ADDB.......... Australian Drug Database
ADDBLEC... Australian Drug Database (Law Enforcement Component)
ADDC.......... Addict (ABBR)
Add C......... Addison on Contracts [*A publication*] (DLA)
ADDC.......... Air Defense Direction Center [*Air Force*]
ADDC.......... Alignment and Diagnostic Display Console
ADDC.......... Ammonium Diethyldithiocarbamate [*Organic chemistry*]
ADDC.......... Analog-Discrete Data Converter [*Computer science*] (MCD)
ADDC.......... Analog-to-Digital Data Converter [*Computer science*] (MCD)
ADDC.......... Association of Desk and Derrick Clubs (EA)
ADDCD........ Addicted (ABBR)
ADDCG........ Addicting (ABBR)
Add Ch........ Addison Charges [*Addison's Pennsylvania Reports*] [*A publication*] (DLA)
ADDCN........ Addiction (ABBR)
Add Con...... Addison on Contracts [*A publication*] (DLA)
Add Cont..... Addison on Contracts [*A publication*] (DLA)
ADDCS........ Aircraft Decontaminating, Deicing, Cleaning System (MCD)
ADD c TRIT... Adde cum Tritu [*Add Trituration*] [*Pharmacy*]
add C Trit.... Adde Cum Tritu [*Add Triturition*] [*Pharmacology*] (DAVI)
ADDD......... Darwin [*Australia ICAO location identifier*] (ICLI)
ADDD/H...... Attention Deficit and Distractability Disorder with Hyperactivity [*Medicine*] (DAVI)
ADDDS........ Automatic Direct-Distance Dialing System [*Telecommunications*] (IEEE)
Add Ecc ...... Addams' Ecclesiastical Reports [*A publication*] (DLA)
Add Eccl ...... Addams' Ecclesiastical Reports [*A publication*] (DLA)
Add Eccl Rep... Addams' Ecclesiastical Reports [*A publication*] (DLA)
ADDED........ Additional Education
ADDEE .... Addressee (NVT)
AD DEF AN... Ad Defectionem Animi [*To the Point of Fainting*] [*Pharmacy*]
ad Deliq ...... Ad Deliquium [*To Fainting*] [*Pharmacy*] (DAVI)
ADDELREP... Additional Delay in Reporting [*Military*] (DNAB)
ADDEND...... Addendus [*To Be Added*] [*Pharmacy*]
Add ER .... Addams' Ecclesiastical Reports [*A publication*] (DLA)
ADDER........ Automatic Digital-Data-Error Recorder [*Computer science*]
AddEsther .... Additions to Esther [*Apocrypha*] (BJA)
ADDEV .... Advanced Development [*Army*] (AABC)
ADDF .... Automated Deferred Discrepancy File
ADDG.......... Adding (ABBR)
ADD-H .... Attention Deficit Disorder with Hyperactivity [*Medicine*]
ADD-HA ...... Attention Deficit Disorder with Hyperactivity [*Medicine*]
ADDI .... Airborne Dual Detector Indicator (MCD)
ADDIC......... Alcohol and Dependency Intervention Council [*Military*] (AABC)
Addict .... Addiction [*Chemical dependency*] (DAVI)
Addis .... Addison's County Court Reports [*Pennsylvania*] [*A publication*] (DLA)
Addison (PA)... Addison's County Court Reports [*Pennsylvania*] [*A publication*] (DLA)
ADDISS........ Advanced Deployable Digital Imagery Support System [*Military*] (DOMA)
addit........... Additional (DLA)
ADDIV........ Air Defense of the Division (MCD)
ADDL.......... Additional (KSC)
AD/DL........ Aircraft Division/Department List [*Air Force*]
ADDL.......... Aircraft Dummy Deck Landing [*Navy*]
ADDL.......... American Double Dutch League (EA)
ADDL.......... Anti-Digit Dialing League (EA)
ADDLASS.... Air Deployable Drifting Linear Array SONAR System (MCD)
ADDM .... Addendum to Monthly Collection [*IRS*]
ADDM .... Automated Documentation Development and Maintenance [*FAA*] (TAG)
ADDM .... Automated Drafting and Digitizing Machine [*Computer science*] (RDA)
ADDMS........ Automatic Depth/Deployed Moored Sweep (MCD)
ADDN.......... Addition
ADDN.......... Darwin [*Australia ICAO location identifier*] (ICLI)
ADDNDM..... Addendum (ABBR)
ADDNL........ Additional
ADDNLY...... Additionally (ABBR)
ADDNR .... Assistant and Deputy Director of Naval Recruiting [*British*]
ADDO/MA .... Associate Deputy Director for Operations/Military Affairs
ADDP.......... Air Defense Defended Point [*Army*]
Add PA .... Addison's County Court Reports [*Pennsylvania*] [*A publication*] (DLA)
ADDPEP....... Aerodynamic Deployable Decelerator Performance Evaluation Program
ADDPLA...... Additional Places
Add Poll ..... Adductor Pollicis [*Muscle*] [*Anatomy*] (DAVI)
ADDR.......... Adder [*Computer device*]
ADDR.......... Addington Resources [*NASDAQ symbol*] (TTSB)
ADDR.......... Addington Resources, Inc. [*NASDAQ symbol*] (NQ)
ADDR.......... Address [*Computer character*] [*Computer science*]
ADDR.......... Address

ADDR............ Address Register
ADDRD......... Addressed (ABBR)
ADDRE.......... Addressee (ABBR)
Add Rep....... Addison's County Court Reports [*Pennsylvania*] [*A publication*] (DLA)
ADDRESOR... Analog-to-Digital Data Reduction System for Oceanographic Research
ADDRESS .... Automated Design of Damage Resistant Structures (MCD)
ADDRG .... Addressing (ABBR)
ADDRG .... American Deep Drawing Research Group (DICI)
ADDRI......... Apollo Document Distribution Requirements Index [*NASA*] (KSC)
ADD-RT........ Attention Deficit Disorder-Residual Type
adds............ Additions (WDMC)
ADDS .... Advanced Data Display System (DNAB)
ADDS .... Advanced Deep Diving Submersible
ADDS .... Advanced Display and Debriefing Subsystem (DWSG)
ADDS .... Airborne Detection Discrimination Sensor
ADDS .... Air Defense Demonstration System (MCD)
ADDS .... Air Deployment Delivery System [*Military*] (NVT)
ADDS .... Air Development Delivery System (DNAB)
ADDS .... American Digestive Disease Society (EA)
ADDS .... American Diopter and Decibel Society (EA)
ADDS .... American Diversified Dog Society [*Defunct*] (EA)
ADDS .... Apollo Data [*or Document*] Descriptions Standards [*NASA*] (MCD)
ADDS .... Applied Digital Data Systems [*Commercial firm*] (NITA)
ADDS .... Area Data Distribution System [*Army*] (ADDR)
ADDS .... Army Data Distribution System
ADDS .... Army DEIS [*Defense Energy Information System*] Data Entry System
ADDS .... Assistant Director of Dental Services
ADDS .... Astrodigital Doppler Speedometer [*Electronics*]
ADDS .... ASW [*Antisubmarine Warfare*] Acoustic Deception Device (MCD)
ADDS .... Automated Digital Data System
ADDS .... Automated Digital Design System [*Raytheon Co.*]
ADDS .... Automatic Data Digitizing System [*Air Force*]
ADDS .... Automatic Data Distribution System [*Army*] (AABC)
ADDSC......... Association des Directeurs de Departements de Sante Communautaire [*Association of Public Health Department Directors*] [*Canada*]
ADDSD......... Addressed (ABBR)
ADDSRTS .... Automated Digitized Document Storage, Retrieval and Transmission System [*Computer science*] (MHDB)
ADDSS......... Address (ECII)
ADDSSEE...... Addressee (ECII)
Add T.......... Addison on Torts [*A publication*] (DLA)
ADDT .... Additive (MSA)
ADDT .... All-Digital Data Tape (KSC)
ADDT .... Angular Distribution Data Tape
ADDTL......... Additional
ADDTN......... Addition
Add Tor....... Addison on Torts [*A publication*] (DLA)
Add Torts..... Addison on Torts [*A publication*] (DLA)
Add Torts Abr... Addison on Torts, Abridged [*A publication*] (DLA)
Add Torts D & B.. Addison on Torts, Dudley and Baylies' Edition [*A publication*] (DLA)
Add Torts Woods... Addison on Torts, Woods Edition [*A publication*] (DLA)
ADDU .... Additional Duty
ADDU .... Alcohol and Drug Dependency Unit [*Medicine*] (DAVI)
A-D-Duct...... Adduction [*Neurophysiology*] (DAVI)
ADDUNIFALW... Additional Uniform Allowance [*Military*]
ADDV .... Additive (ABBR)
ADD W H...... Attention Deficit Disorder with Hyperactivity [*Psychology*] (DAVI)
ADDX .... Darwin [*Australia ICAO location identifier*] (ICLI)
ADDY .... Alcohol, Drugs, Driving, and You [*An association*]
ADE............. Accion Democratica Ecuatoriana [*Ecuadorean Democratic Action*] [*Political party*] (PPW)
ADE............. Acute Disseminated Encephalitis [*Neurology*] (DAVI)
ADE............. Acute Disseminated Encephalomyelitis [*Medicine*]
ADE............. ADA Air [*Albania*] [*FAA designator*] (FAAC)
ADE............. Address Enable [*Computer science*] (IAA)
ADE............. Address Error (NITA)
ADE............. Adelaide [*Mount Bonython*] [*Australia Seismograph station code, US Geological Survey*] (SEIS)
ADE............. Aden [*People's Democratic Republic of Yemen*] [*Airport symbol*] (OAG)
Ade............. Adenine [*Also, A*] [*Biochemistry*]
ADE............. Advanced Data Entry
ADE............. Adverse Drug Event [*Medicine*]
ADE............. Adverse Drug Event [*Food and Drug Administration*]
ADE............. Aerial Delivery Equipment (MCD)
ADE............. After Delivery Economies
ADE............. Aircraft Data Entry (DNAB)
ADE............. Air Defense Element (AABC)
ADE............. Air Defense Emergency [*Military*] (AABC)
ADE............. Air Defense Evaluation
ADE............. Air Density [*Explorer satellite*] [*NASA*]
ADE............. Alpha Disintegration Energy
ADE............. Alphanumeric Display Equipment
ADE............. American Dance Ensemble
ADE............. Anglo Dominion Gold Exploration Ltd. [*Toronto Stock Exchange symbol*]
ADE............. Animal Disease Eradication Division [*of ARS, Department of Agriculture*]
ADE............. Antibody-Dependent Enhancement [*of viral infection*]
ADE............. Apparent Digestible Energy [*Nutrition*]
ADE............. Application Development Environment [*Computer science*] (BTTJ)
ADE............. Applications Development Environment [*Computer science*]

ADE............. Approved Data Element (AFM)
ADE............. Armament Design Establishment [*British*]
ADE............. Armored Division Equivalent [*Military*]
ADE............. Army Department Establishments [*British*]
ADE............. Army Development and Employment Agency [*Fort Lewis, WA*]
ADE............. Arrhythmogenic Dose of Epinephrine [*Medicine*]
ADE............. Assessor's Data Exchange [*A publication*] (EAAP)
ADE............. Assistant Division Engineer [*Army*] (AABC)
ADE............. Association Europeenne pour l'Etude de l'Alimentation et Developpement de l'Enfant [*European Association of Nutrition and Child Development*] (EAIO)
ADE............. Association for Documentary Editing (EA)
ADE............. Association of Departments of English (EA)
ADE............. Association of Directors of Education (AIE)
ADE............. Atomic Defense Engineering (MUGU)
ADE............. Audible Doppler Enhancer [*Telecommunications*] (TEL)
ADE............. Authorized Data Element
ADE............. Automated Debugging Environment [*Applied Data Research, Inc.*]
ADE............. Automated Design Engineering [*Telecommunications*] (TEL)
ADE............. Automatic Data Entry [*Air Force*]
ADE............. Automatic Data Evaluation
ADE............. Automatic Drafting Equipment (IEEE)
ADE............. Chemical System Laboratory, Aberdeen Proving Grounds, MD [*OCLC symbol*] (OCLC)
ADE............. Delburne Public Library, Alberta [*Library symbol National Library of Canada*] (NLC)
ADEA .... Age Discrimination in Employment Act [*1967*] [*Department of Labor*]
ADEA .... American Driver Education Association [*Later, ADTSEA*] (EA)
ADEA .... Army Development and Employment Agency [*Fort Lewis, WA*] (INF)
ADEA .... Assistant Director of Expense Accounts [*Navy British*]
ADEA .... Association Belge pour le Developpement Pacifique de l'Energie Atomique [*Belgium Association for the Peaceful Development of Atomic Energy*] (NUCP)
ADEAA........ Alcohol-Drug Education Association in Alberta (AC)
ADEAR........ Alzheimers Disease Education and Referral [*Center*]
A de Ba .... Andreas Bonellus de Barulo [*Flourished, 1260-71*] [*Authority cited in pre-1607 legal work*] (DSA)
ADEC .... Address Decoding [*Computer science*] (IAA)
ADEC .... Adecco SA [*NASDAQ symbol*] (SAG)
ADEC .... Aiken Dahlgren Electronic Calculator (MCD)
ADEC .... Association for Death Education and Counseling (EA)
Ade Cbl .... Adenosylcobalamin [*Biochemistry*] (DAVI)
ADeCC........ Morgan County Court House, Decatur, AL [*Library symbol*] [*Library of Congress*] (LCLS)
ADECp .... ADE Corp. [*Associated Press*] (SAG)
ADED .... Air Defense Effectiveness Demonstration [*Army*] (MCD)
ADED .... Air Delivery Equipment Division [*Natick Laboratories*] [*Army*]
ADED .... Association of Driver Educators for the Disabled (EA)
ADeD .... Decatur Daily, Decatur, AL [*Library symbol Library of Congress*] (LCLS)
ADEDA........ Advise Effective Date (NOAA)
Ad Ed Act.... Adams on the Education Act [*A publication*] (DLA)
ADEDS........ Advanced Digital Electronic Displays
ADEDS........ Advanced Electronic Display System [*FAA*]
ADEDU........ Assistant Director for Education [*Vietnam*]
ADEE.......... Addressee (CINC)
ADEE.......... Age-Dependent Epileptic Encephalopathy [*Medicine*] (DMAA)
ADEE.......... Air Defence Experimental Establishment [*Later, ADRDE, RRE*] [*British*]
ADEE.......... Air Defense Electronic Environment (SAA)
ADEF.......... [*French Rating Agency*] Agence d'Evaluation Financiere (ODBW)
AD EFFECT... Ad Effectum [*Until Effectual*] [*Pharmacy*]
ADEFSq....... Air Defense Squadron [*Air Force*]
ADEFUCC..... Association des Directeurs de Departements d'Etudes Francaises des Universites et Colleges du Canada [*Association of Directors of Departments of French Studies of Canadian Universities and Colleges*]
ADEG .... Auxiliary Display Equipment Group (KSC)
Ad Ej .... Adams on Ejectment [*A publication*] (DLA)
ADEKS........ Advanced Design Electronic Key System [*Telecommunications*]
Adel........... Adelaide [*South Australia*] (BARN)
ADELA .... Atlantic Community Development Group for Latin America [*Joint US-European private investment company*]
ADELF........ Association des Distributeurs Exclusifs de Livres en Langue Francaise [*Association of Exclusive Distributors of French-Language Books*] [*Canada*]
ADELF........ Association des Ecrivains de Langue Francaise [*Association of French-Language Writers*] (EAIO)
ADELL......... Adult Education and Lifelong Learning
Adelph .... Adelphia Communications Corp. [*Associated Press*] (SAG)
Adelphi U ... Adelphi University (GAGS)
Adel R .... Adelaide Review [*A publication*]
ADELT......... Automatically Deployable Emergency Locator Transmitter [*Aviation*] (DA)
ADEM.......... Acute Disseminated [*or Disseminating*] Encephalomyelitis [*Medicine*]
ADEM.......... Adaptively Data Equalized MODEM
ADEM.......... Air Defences, Eastern Mediterranean [*British military*] (DMA)
ADEM.......... Association des Directeurs d'Ecole de Montreal (AC)
ADEM.......... Automatically Data Equalized MODEM [*Computer science*] (IAA)
ADEMA-PPLSJ... Alliance pour la Democratie au Mali - Parti Pan-Africain pour la Liberte, la Solidarite, et la Justice [*Political party*] (EY)
ADEMQA...... Office of Acid Deposition, Environmental Monitoring, and Quality Assurance [*Washington, DC Environmental Protection Agency*] (GRD)

ADEMRCM... CANMET [*Canada Centre for Mineral and Energy Technology*] Library, Energy, Mines, and Resources Canada, Devon, Alberta [*Bibliotheque CANMET, Energie, Mines, et Ressources Canada*] [*Library symbol National Library of Canada*] (NLC)

ADEMS .... Advanced Diagnostic Engine Monitoring System [*Air Force*]

ADEMS .... Airborne Display Electrical Management System (MCD)

ADEMS .... Automated Data Entry Measurement System [*Computer science*] (IAA)

ADEN .... Armament Development, Enfield

AD/EN .... Armament Division, Deputy for Engineering [*Eglin Air Force Base, FL*]

ADEN .... Augmented Deflector Exhaust Nozzle [*Aviation*]

ADEN/DEFA... Armament Development, Enfield/Direction Etude Fabrication [*Military*] (MCD)

Aden LR ...... Aden Law Reports [*A publication*] (ILCA)

adenoca....... Adenocarcinoma [*Medicine*]

Adeno-SCC... Adenocarcinoma-Squamous Cell Carcinoma [*Oncology*]

ADEO .... Advance Development Engineering Order

ADEOS .... Advanced Earth Observing Satellite [*Japan*]

ADEOS .... Air Droppable, Expendable Ocean Sensor [*Oceanography*] (MSC)

ADEP .... Air Depot [*Army*]

A DEP .... Anno Depositionis [*In the Year of the Deposit*] [*Freemasonry*] [*Latin*]

ADEP .... Authorized Direct Expenditure Plan (SAA)

ADEPA .... Association d'Entraide pour les Agoraphobes (AC)

ADEPNS ...... Adeptness (ABBR)

ADEPO .... Automatic Dynamic Evaluation by Programmed Organizations

ADEPREP..... Army Deployment Reporting System (AABC)

ADEPS .... Antisubmarine Warfare Automated Detection Prediction System (MCD)

ADEPT .... Acoustic Directed Energy Pulse Train (BARN)

ADEPT .... ADA Development Environment Portable Tools [*A programming language*] (NITA)

ADEPT .... Adult Diabetes Education Program and Training

ADEPT .... Advanced Development Prototype (MHDI)

ADEPT .... Aerospace Draftsman's Education and Proficiency Training (MCD)

ADEPT .... Agricultural and Dairy Educational Political Trust

ADEPT .... Air Force Depot Equipment Performance Tester (AAG)

ADEPT .... Antibody-Directed Enzyme Prodrug Therapy [*Oncology*]

ADEPT .... Association d'Etudes Politiques Transeuropeennes [*Trans European Policy Studies Association - TEPSA*] (EA)

ADEPT .... Automated Direct Entry Packaging Technique

ADEPT .... Automatic Data Extractor and Plotting Table

ADEPT .... Automatic Debiting and Electronic Payment for Transport [*Automotive engineering*] (ECON)

ADEPT .... Automatic Dynamic Evaluation by Programmed Test

ADEPT .... [*A*] Distinctly Empirical Prover of Theorems

AdeptT .... Adept Technology, Inc. [*Associated Press*] (SAG)

Ad Eq .... Adams' Equity [*A publication*] (DLA)

ADEQ .... Adequate (DAVI)

adeq .... Adequate (DMAA)

ADER .... Automatic Data Extraction Routine (CAAL)

ADER .... Derwent Public Library, Alberta [*Library symbol National Library of Canada*] (NLC)

ADERC .... Alzheimer's Disease Education Referral Center (BARN)

ADERI .... American Disability Evaluation Research Institute [*Research center*] (RCD)

A DES .... A Destra [*To the Right*] [*Italian*] (ADA)

ADES .... Advanced Diagnostic Executive System

ADEs.......... Adverse Drug Event

ADES .... Air Defense Engagement System (MCD)

ADES .... Air Defense Engineering Service (MCD)

ADES .... Alliance pour la Democratie et l'Emancipation Sociale [*Burkina Faso*] [*Political party*] (EY)

ADES .... Analysis, Design, and Evaluation System (MCD)

ADES .... Angle-Dispersed Electron Spectroscopy (MCD)

ADES .... Association of Directors of Education, Scotland (DI)

ADES .... Automated Data Entry System [*Computer science*] (IAA)

ADES .... Automatic Digital Encoding System [*Computer science*]

ADESMS ...... Mistassiny School, Desmarais, Alberta [*Library symbol National Library of Canada*] (BIB)

ADESPS ...... Pelican Mountain School, Desmarais, Alberta [*Library symbol National Library of Canada*] (BIB)

ADETOM ..... Association pour le Developpement de l'Enseignement Technique d'Outre-Mer [*Association for the Development of Overseas Technical Education*] [*French*] (AF)

ADEU .... Automatic Data Entry Unit

AD EUND ..... Ad Eundem Gradum [*To the Same Degree*] [*Of the admission of a graduate of one university to the same degree at another without examination*] [*Latin*]

ADEW .... Air Defense Early Warning (NATG)

ADeW .... Wheeler Basin Regional Library, Decatur, AL [*Library symbol Library of Congress*] (LCLS)

ADEWS .... Air Defense Electronic Warfare System (MCD)

ADEX .... ADE Corp. [*NASDAQ symbol*] (SAG)

AD EX .... Ad Extremum [*To the Extreme, To the End*] [*Latin*]

ADEX .... Advanced Antisubmarine Warfare Exercise (NVT)

ADEX .... Air Defense Exercise (NVT)

ADEXJAM .... Artillery-Delivered Expendable Jammer [*Army*]

ADF............. Acid-Detergent Fiber [*Food analysis*]

ADF............. ACM Managed Dollar Income [*NYSE symbol*] (TTSB)

ADF............. ACM Managed Dollar Income Fund [*NYSE symbol*] (SPSG)

ADF............. Acoustic Depth Finder

ADF............. Acquisition Data Facility (MCD)

ADF............. Adapter Definition File (BYTE)

ADF............. Adapter Description File [*Computer science*] (PCM)

ADF............. Adera Financial Corp. Ltd. [*Vancouver Stock Exchange symbol*]

ADF............. A Direction Finder

ADF............. Administrative Determination of Fault

ADF............. Administrator's Discretionary Fund [*Marine science*] (OSRA)

ADF............. Administrators's Discretionary Fund (USDC)

ADF............. Advanced Development Facility [*Branch*] [*Marine science*] (OSRA)

ADF............. Advanced Development Facility Branch [*Forecast Systems Laboratory*] (USDC)

ADF............. Advanced Disposal Fee

ADF............. Aerial Direction Finding

ADF............. Aeronutronics Division, Ford Motor Co. (AAG)

ADF............. African Development Foundation (EGAO)

ADF............. After Deducting Freight [*Billing*]

ADF............. Airborne Direction Finder (MCD)

ADF............. Air Defense Fighter (DOMA)

ADF............. Air Defense Force

ADF............. Air Development Force

ADF............. Air Direction Finder

ADF............. Aktion Demokratischer Fortschritt [*Action for Democratic Progress*] [*Germany*] (PPE)

ADF............. Alaska Defense Frontier [*Military*]

ADF............. Algorithm Development Facility [*for spacecraft data*] [*Jet Propulsion Laboratory*]

ADF............. All Dielectric Filter

ADF............. Alliance pour la Democratie et la Federation [*Burkina Faso*] [*Political party*] (EY)

ADF............. American Dance Festival [*Later, AADF*] (EA)

ADF............. American Defense Foundation (EA)

ADF............. American Ditchley Foundation (EA)

ADF............. American Duty Free [*Freight*]

ADF............. Anterior Dendritic Field [*Neurology*]

ADF............. Application Development Facility [*IBM Corp.*] [*Computer science*]

ADF............. Approved Deposit Fund (ADA)

ADF............. Approximate Degrees of Freedom [*Statistics*]

ADF............. Arab Deterrent Force [*Palestine*] (PD)

ADF............. Archdiocesan Development Fund [*Catholic*]

ADF............. Arkadelphia, AR [*Location identifier FAA*] (FAAL)

ADF............. Army Distaff Foundation (EA)

ADF............. Asian Development Fund [*Asian Development Bank*]

ADF............. Assured Destruction Force [*Military*]

ADF............. Atmosphere Defense Initiative (LAIN)

ADF............. Australian Dance Foundation

ADF............. Australian Deerstalkers' Federation

ADF............. Australian Defence Force (ADA)

ADF............. Australian Diabetes Foundation

ADF............. Automated Design Facility (MCD)

ADF............. Automatic Direction Finder [*Military*]

ADF............. Automatic Display Finder [*Computer science*] (NASA)

ADF............. Automatic Document Feeder [*For copying machines*]

ADF............. Automotive Diesel Fuel

ADF............. Auxiliary Detonation Fuze (NG)

ADF............. Biomedical Laboratory, Aberdeen Proving Grounds, MD [*OCLC symbol*] (OCLC)

ADFA.......... Automatic Direction Finding Approach (SAA)

ADFAB........ Australian Dairy Foods Advisory Bureau

ADFAP........ Automatic Direction Finding Approach

ADFC.......... Adiabatic Film Cooling

ADFC.......... Air Defense Filter Center [*Military*]

ADFC.......... Alliance for a Drug-Free Canada [*Alliance pour un Canada sans Drogues*] (AC)

ADFC.......... Association des Femmes Collaboratrices [*Association of Feminine Collectives*] [*Canada*]

ADFE.......... Association Democratique des Francais de l'Etranger [*Democratic Association of French Citizens Abroad*] (PPW)

AD FEB........ Adstante Febre [*When Fever Is Present*] [*Pharmacy*]

Ad-Fed........ Advertising Federation of Minnesota (SRA)

ADFF........... Australian Deer Farmers' Federation

ADFHQ........ Air Defense Force Headquarters (SAA)

ADFI........... American Dog Feed Institute [*Defunct*] (EA)

ADFIAP .... Association of Development Financing Institutions in Asia and the Pacific [*Manila, Philippines*] (EA)

AD FIN........ Ad Finem [*At or To the End*] [*Latin*]

ADFL.......... Association of Departments of Foreign Languages (EA)

ADFlex........ ADFlex Solutions [*Associated Press*] (SAG)

ADF-N......... Acid Detergent Fiber Nitrogen [*Organic chemistry*] (DICI)

ADFN.......... Albinism-Deafness [*Syndrome*] [*Medicine*] (DMAA)

ADFO.......... Assistant Director, Flight Operations [*NASA*] (KSC)

ADFOA........ Australian Duty Free Operators' Association

ADFOR........ Adriatic Force [*Military*]

ADFORMS..... Australian Defense Formatted Message System [*Military*]

ADFORS....... Advertisement Format Selection [*Marketing*]

ADFP.......... Atroxin-Defibrinated Plasma [*Clinical chemistry*]

ADFR.......... Automatic Direction Finder, Remote Control (AAG)

ADFS.......... Alternative Delivery and Financing System [*Medicine*] (HCT)

ADFS.......... American Dentists for Foreign Service (EA)

ADFS.......... Automatic Direction Finding System

ADFSC........ Automatic Data Field Systems Command [*Fort Belvoir, VA*] [*Army*]

ADFT.......... Artillery Direct Fire Trainer (AABC)

ADFU.......... Air Defense Firing Unit (MCD)

ADFV.......... Alcohol and Drug Foundation of Victoria [*Australia*]

ADFW .... Assistant Director of Fortifications and Works [*Military British*]

ADFWC........ Australian Defense Force Warfare Center [*Military*]

ADG........... Accessory Drive Gear Box (MCD)

ADG........... Action Democratique Guyanaise [*French Guiana*] [*Political party*] (EY)

ADG	Adage (ABBR)
ADG	Adrian, MI [*Location identifier FAA*] (FAAL)
ADG	Advance Development Group [*Army*] (AABC)
ADG	Advantage Enterprises, Inc. [*Vancouver Stock Exchange symbol*]
ADG	Aeronautical Development Group [*Military*] (AFIT)
ADG	Aircraft Delivery Group [*Air Force*]
ADG	Air Defense Group [*Air Force*] (MCD)
ADG	Air Defense Guard [*Military*]
ADG	Air Density Gauge [*Aviation*]
ADG	Air-Driven Generator (MCD)
ADG	Ambulatory Diagnostic Group [*Medicine*] (DMAA)
ADG	American Dance Guild (EA)
ADG	Antenna Directive Gain
ADG	Assistant Director-General [*British*]
ADG	Atmospheric Dynamic Payload Group [*NASA*] (SSD)
ADG	Atrial Diastolic Gallop [*Cardiology*] (MAE)
ADG	Attack Display Group (MCD)
ADG	Automatic Degaussing (IAA)
ADG	Automotive Development Group [*LTV Steel Corp.*]
ADG	Auxiliary Deception Generator (MCD)
ADG	Average Daily Gain [*of weight*] [*Cattle*]
ADG	Aviation Depot Group (AAG)
ADG	Aviones y Servicios del Golfo SA de CV [*Mexico ICAO designator*] (FAAC)
ADG	Axiodistogingival [*Dentistry*]
ADG	Degaussing Ship [*Navy symbol*]
ADGA	American Dairy Goat Association (EA)
ADGB	Accessory Drive Gear Box (MCD)
ADGB	Air Defense of Great Britain
ADGE	Adage, Inc. [*NASDAQ symbol*] (NQ)
ADGE	Air Defense Ground Environment [*NATO*] (MCD)
ADGEN	Address Generator
ADGILE	Air Defense Gun Missile Experiment [*Army*]
ADGINT	Advanced GPS/Inertial Integration (MCD)
ADGL	Adrenal Gland [*Anatomy*]
ADGM	Address Generator Module
ADGMS	Assistant Director-General of Medical Services [*Military British*]
ADGO	Adagio [*Slow*] [*Music*]
ADGp	Air Defense Group [*Air Force*] (AFM)
ADGPA	American Dairy Goat Products Association (EA)
AD GR ACID	Ad Gratum Aciditatem [*To an Agreeable Sourness*] [*Pharmacy*]
Ad Grat Acid	Ad Gratum Aciditatem [*To an Agreeable Sourness*] [*Pharmacy*]
AD GR GUST	Ad Gratum Gustum [*To an Agreeable Taste*] [*Pharmacy*]
ADGRU	Advisory Group [*Military*]
ADGT	Assistant Director-General of Transportation [*British military*] (DMA)
ADGV	Gove [*Australia ICAO location identifier*] (ICLI)
ADH	Academy of Dentistry for the Handicapped (EA)
ADH	Ada [*Oklahoma*] [*Airport symbol*] (AD)
ADH	Ada, OK [*Location identifier FAA*] (FAAL)
ADH	Adhere (MSA)
adh	Adhesion [*Medicine*] (DMAA)
ADH	Adhesive (KSC)
ADH	Adhibendus [*To Be Used*] [*Pharmacy*] (ROG)
ADH	Advanced Development Hardware (SSD)
ADH	Alcohol Dehydrogenase [*Also, AD*] [*An enzyme*]
ADH	Angra Do Heroismo [*Azores*] [*Seismograph station code, US Geological Survey*] (SEIS)
ADH	Antidiuretic Hormone [*Vasopressin*] [*Endocrinology*]
ADH	Assistant Director of Hygiene [*Military British*]
ADH	Association of Delaware Hospitals (SRA)
ADH	Association of Dental Hospitals of Great Britain and Northern Ireland (BI)
ADH	Automatic Data Handling [*Computer science*]
ADH	Societa' Adriatica [*Italy ICAO designator*] (FAAC)
ADHA	American Dental Hygienists' Association (EA)
ADHA	Analog Data Handling Assembly (IAA)
ADHC	Adult Day Health Care (GFGA)
ADHC	Advantage Health Corp. [*NASDAQ symbol*] (SAG)
ADHC	Air Defense Hardware Committee [*NATO*] (NATG)
ADHCA	Advise This Headquarters of Complete Action [*Army*]
ADHCS	Amalgamated Drillers and Hole Cutters Society [*A union*] [*British*]
ADHD	Attention Deficit Hyperactivity Disorder [*Medicine*]
ADHEL	Air Defense High Energy LASER (MCD)
ADHEVE	Adhesive (ROG)
ADHGB	Allgemeines Deutsches Handelsgesetzbuch von 1861 [*German commercial code*] (ILCA)
ADHI	Area Defense Homing Interceptor
ADHIB	Adhibendus [*To Be Administered*] [*Pharmacy*] (DAVI)
ADHIBEND	Adhibendus [*To Be Used*] [*Pharmacy*]
AD HL	Ad Hunc Locum [*To (or At) This Place*] [*Latin*]
AdHlthC	Advanced Health Corp. [*Associated Press*] (SAG)
AdHM	Adler. Handbuch der Musikgeschichte [*A publication*]
ADHN	Adhesion (ABBR)
ADHOC	Association of Department Heads of Catering [*British*] (DBA)
ad hom	Ad Hominem [*To the man*] [*A debating technique that attacks the person not his ideas*] [*Latin*] (BARN)
ADHOS	Alternative to Dedicated Hospital Ship (CAAL)
ADHP	Association for the Development of Human Potential (EA)
ADHR	Adhere (ABBR)
ADHRD	Adhered (ABBR)
ADHRG	Adhering (ABBR)
ADHRNC	Adherence (ABBR)
ADHRNT	Adherent (ABBR)
ADHRT	Adherent (ABBR)
ADHRTY	Adherently (ABBR)

ADHS	Analog Data Handling System (AAG)
ADHSV	Adhesive (ABBR)
ADHSV	Adhesive
ADHSVNS	Adhesiveness (ABBR)
ADHSVY	Adhesively (ABBR)
ADHVNS	Adhesiveness (ABBR)
ADI	Academy of Dentistry International (EA)
ADI	Acceptable Daily Intake [*Toxicology*]
ADI	Accounting Department Instructions
ADI	Aciodistoincisal [*Medicine*] (MEDA)
ADI	Acoustical Door Institute [*Defunct*] (EA)
ADI	Adaptronics, Inc.
ADI	Ad-Dome International Ltd. [*Vancouver Stock Exchange symbol*]
ADI	Address Incomplete [*Telecommunications*] (TEL)
ADI	Aircraft De-Ice and Inhibitor [*MTMC*] (TAG)
ADI	Air Defense Initiative [*DoD*]
ADI	Air Defense Institute
ADI	Air Defense Intercept [*Air Force*]
AD/I	Air Density/Injun [*Explorer satellite*]
ADI	Air Distribution Institute (EA)
ADI	Alien Declared Intention
AdI	Alliance des Independants [*Independent Party*] [*Switzerland Political party*] (PPE)
ADI	Allied Distribution (EA)
ADI	Allowable Daily Intake [*Toxicology*]
ADI	Alternate Digit Inversion [*Computer science*] (IAA)
ADI	Alternating Direction Implicit [*Algorithm*]
ADI	Alternating Direction Iterative (PDAA)
ADI	Altitude Direction Indicator (AFM)
ADI	Alzheimer's Disease International (EA)
ADI	American Defense Institute (EA)
ADI	American Directors Institute (EA)
ADI	American Documentation Institute [*Later, American Society for Information Science*]
ADI	American Dressage Institute
ADI	Analog Devices [*NYSE symbol*] (SAG)
ADI	Analog Display Indicator (MCD)
ADI	Antidetonation Injection
ADI	Apollo Document Index [*NASA*] (KSC)
ADI	Application Data Interchange [*Telecommunications*] (OSI)
ADI	Applied Dynamics International
ADI	Approved Driving Instructor [*British*] (DBQ)
ADI	Aquarian Digest International [*A publication*]
ADI	Area of Dominant Influence [*Mapmaking*] [*Telecommunications*]
ADI	Art Dreco Institute (EA)
ADI	Assembly Decay Indicator
ADI	Assistance Dogs International (EA)
ADI	Assistant Director of Intelligence [*British military*] (DMA)
ADI	Association for Direct Instruction (EA)
ADI	Atlantodens Interval [*Neurosurgery and orthopedics*] (DAVI)
ADI	Attitude Direction Indicator [*Aerospace*]
ADI	Attitude Display Indicator [*Aerospace*] (MCD)
ADI	Audeli Air Express [*Spain ICAO designator*] (FAAC)
ADI	Austempered Ductile Iron [*Metallurgy*]
ADI	Automatic Derivation of Invariants (MCD)
ADI	Automatic Direction Indicator (AFM)
ADI	Axiodistoincisal [*Dentistry*]
ADI	Didsbury Public Library, Alberta [*Library symbol National Library of Canada*] (NLC)
ADI	Doyon, AK [*Location identifier FAA*] (FAAL)
ADIA	Adia Services, Inc. [*NASDAQ symbol*] (NQ)
ADIA	American Diamond Industry Association (EA)
AdiaSA	Adia SA [*Associated Press*] (SAG)
ADIAY	Adia S.A. ADS [*NASDAQ symbol*] (TTSB)
ADIB	Abu Dhabi International Bank, Inc.
A-DIC	Adriamycin, Dacarbazine [*Antineoplastic drug regimen*]
ADIC	Advanced Digital Information Corp. (PCM)
ADIC	American Dental Interfraternity Council (EA)
ADIC	Analog-to-Digital Conversion System [*Computer science*]
ADIC	Automated Digital Interior Communications (MCD)
A-DIC-DACT	Adriamycin, Dacarbazine, Dactinomycin [*Antineoplastic drug regimen*]
ADICEP	Association des Directeurs des Centres Europeens des Plastiques [*Association of Directors of European Centres for Plastics*] (EAIO)
ADIDAS	Adi Dassler [*Founder of German sporting goods company; acronym used as brand name of shoes manufactured by the firm*]
ADIDS	Aeronautical Digital Information Display System (DA)
ADIE	Acquisition Data Input Equipment (AABC)
ADIE	Automatic Dialing and Indicating Equipment [*Telecommunications*] (IAA)
A Dies Tech	Associate in Diesel Technology
ADIF	Autocrine Differentiation-Inhibiting Factor [*Biochemistry*]
ADIF	Avionics Development and Integration Facility (MCD)
ADIG	Tax Action Digest [*Australia A publication*]
ADIGE	Archivio Dati Italiani di Geologia [*Italian Geological Data Archive*] [*National Research Council Database*] (IID)
ADIGECS	Association des Directeurs Generaux des Commissions Scolaires du Quebec (AC)
ADI(K)	Assistant Director of Intelligence, Department K [*Air Ministry*] [*British*]
ADIL	Air Defense Identification Line [*Air Force*]
Adil	Angkatan Democratic Liberal Sabah [*Malaysia*] [*Political party*] (EY)
ADIL	Annual Digest of International Law [*A publication*]
ADILP	Lone Pine Public Library, Didsbury, Alberta [*Library symbol National Library of Canada*] (NLC)

ADILR	Annual Digest and Reports of Public International Law Cases [*A publication*] (DLA)
ADIMD	Advise Immediately by Dispatch (NOAA)
ADIN	AUSLANG [*Australian Supply Language*] Dictionary of Item Names [*A publication*]
ADIN	Aviation Distributors, Inc. [*NASDAQ symbol*] (SAG)
ADINA	Automatic Dynamic Incremental Nonlinear Analysis (MCD)
AD INF	Ad Infinitum [*To Infinity*] [*Latin*]
Adingtn	Addington Resources, Inc. [*Associated Press*] (SAG)
AD INIT	Ad Initium [*At the Beginning*] [*Latin*]
ADINSP	Administrative Inspection [*Military*] (NVT)
AD INT	Ad Interim [*In the Meantime*] [*Latin*]
ADINTELCEN...	Advanced Intelligence Center [*Navy*]
ADIOC	Archdiocese (ABBR)
ADIOCN	Archdiocesan (ABBR)
ADIOS	Advanced Digital Inertial Optical Sensor
ADIOS	Analog-Digital Input/Output System [*Computer science*]
ADIOS	Asian Dust Input to the Oceanic System [*Research project*]
ADIOS	Automatic Diagnostic Input/Output System [*Computer science*]
ADIOS	Automatic Digital Input/Output System [*Computer science*]
ADIP	Advanced Developing Institutions Program
ADIP	Air Defense, Interdiction, and Photographic
ADIP	Alloy Development for Irradiation Performance (MCD)
ADIP	Association des Distributeurs Independants de Produits Petroliers (AC)
ADIP	Automated Data Interchange Systems Panel [*Computer science*] (MHDB)
ADipA	Associate Diploma in Arts (ADA)
ADIPA	Association of Development Institutes for the Pacific and Asia
ADipAborStud...	Associate Diploma in Aboriginal Studies
A Dip ARM...	Advanced Diploma, Australian Risk Management
ADIPE	Aircraft Design-Induced Pilot Error [*National Transportation Safety Board*]
ADipFA	Associate Diploma in Fine Arts
ADipGeol	Associate Diploma in Geology
ADipLibStud...	Associate Diploma in Library Studies
ADIPM	Air Defense Inspector Provost Marshall (SAA)
ADipME	Associate Diploma in Mechanical Engineering
ADipPhot	Associate Diploma in Photography
ADipPhysio...	Associate Diploma in Physiotherapy
ADipProWri...	Associate Diploma in Professional Writing
ADipRec	Associate Diploma in Recreation
ADipSocWel...	Associate Diploma in Social Welfare
ADipSW	Associate Diploma in Social Work
ADIPU	Advise Whether Individual May Be Properly Utilized in Your Installation [*Army*] (AABC)
ADipVal	Associate Diploma in Valuation
ADIQ	Association des Designers Industriels du Quebec (AC)
ADIRS	ADIS [*Australasian Drug Information Services*] Drug Information Retrieval System [*ADIS Press Ltd.*] [*Auckland, New Zealand*]
ADIRS	Air Data Inertial Reference System (DA)
ADIRU	Air Data Inertial Reference Unit
ADIS	Advanced Driver Information System [*Automotive engineering*]
ADIS	Airborne Digital Instrumentation System
ADIS	Air Defense Integrated System [*Military*]
ADIS	Airport Data Information System (DA)
ADIS	Association for Development of Instructional Systems [*Later, ADCIS*] [*Western Washington University Bellingham, WA*] (BUR)
ADIS	Attitude Director Indicator System (PDAA)
ADIS	Australasian Drug Information Services
ADIS	Automatic Data Interchange System [*International Civil Aviation Organization*]
ADIS	Automatic Diffemic Identification of Speakers [*University of Bonn*]
ADISOK	Ananeotiko Demokratiko Socialistiko Kinema [*Democratic Socialist Reform Movement*] [*Cyprus*] [*Political party*] (EY)
ADISP	Aeronautical Data Interchange System Panel (OA)
ADISQ	Association du Disque et de l'Industrie du Spectacle Quebecoise [*Quebec Association of the Record and Entertainment Industry*] [*Canada*]
ADISS	Advanced Defense Intelligence Support System (MCD)
ADIT	Alien Documentation, Identification, and Telecommunications [*Immigration and Naturalization Service*]
ADIT	Alliance Defense Industry and Technology (NATG)
ADIT	Analog-Digital Integrating Translator [*Computer science*]
ADIT	Automated Data on Instructional Technology
ADIT	Automatic Detection and Integrated Tracking (MCD)
ADITS	Aircraft Diagnostics and Integrated Test System (MCD)
ADIU	Airborne Data Insertion Unit (DNAB)
ADIU	Armament and Disarmament Information Unit [*British*]
A DIV	Air Division [*Air Force*]
ADIZ	Air Defense Identification Zone [*Air Force, FAA*]
ADJ	Adjacent
ADJ	Adjal [*Former USSR*] [*FAA designator*] (FAAC)
ADJ	Adjective
ADJ	Adjoining
ADJ	Adjoint (ABBR)
ADJ	Adjornator [*British*]
ADJ	Adjourned
ADJ	Adjudged (ROG)
ADJ	Adjunct
adj	Adjunto [*Enclosure*] [*Spanish Business term*]
ADJ	Adjust
ADJ	Adjustable
ADJ	Adjuster [*Finance*]
ADJ	Adjustment (AFM)
ADJ	Adjutant (AFM)
ADJ	Angle Deception Jamming
ADJ	Aviation Machinist's Mate, Jet Engine Mechanic [*Navy rating*]
ADJ	Improper Use of Adjective [*Used in correcting manuscripts, etc.*]
ADJ1	Aviation Machinist's Mate, Jet Engine Mechanic, First Class [*Navy rating*] (DNAB)
ADJ2	Aviation Machinist's Mate, Jet Engine Mechanic, Second Class [*Navy rating*] (DNAB)
ADJ3	Aviation Machinist's Mate, Jet Engine Mechanic, Third Class [*Navy rating*] (DNAB)
ADJA	Adjacent (ABBR)
Adj A	Adjunct in Arts
ADJAA	Airman Apprentice, Jet Striker [*Navy rating*]
ADJAC	Adjacens [*Adjacent*] [*Pharmacy*] (ROG)
ADJAG	Assistant Deputy Judge Advocate General [*Military British*]
ADJAN	Airman, Jet Striker [*Navy rating*]
ADJAY	Adjacently (ABBR)
ADJBLE	Adjustable
ADJC	Adjacency (ABBR)
ADJC	Aviation Machinist Mate Jet, Chief [*Navy rating*]
ADJCNC	Adjacency (ABBR)
ADJCNT	Adjacent (ABBR)
ADJCNTY	Adjacently (ABBR)
ADJD	Adjourned (ROG)
ADJD	Adjudicated (ADA)
ADJDCA	Adjudicate (ABBR)
ADJDCAD.....	Adjudicated (ABBR)
ADJDCAG......	Adjudicating (ABBR)
ADJDCAN	Adjudication (ABBR)
ADJDCR	Adjudicator (ABBR)
ADJDG	Adjudge (ABBR)
ADJDGD	Adjudged (ABBR)
ADJDGG	Adjudging (ABBR)
adjd sumns...	Adjourned Summons (BARN)
ADJF	Adjustment File [*IRS*]
ADJFCUSA...	Adjusted on Basis of Photostat or Reviewed Copy of Temporary Pay Record from Finance Center, United States Army (AABC)
ADJFP	Adjacent Fire Platoon [*Army*]
ADJG	Adjutant General (DNAB)
Adj-Gen	Adjutant-General (DAS)
ADJ L	Adjoining Landowner (DLA)
ADJM	Aviation Machinist Mate Jet, Master Chief [*Navy rating*]
ADJMOM	Adjoint Gamma-Ray Moments [*Computer code*]
ADJMT	Adjustment
ADJN	Adjoin (ABBR)
ADJN	Adjourn (ROG)
ADJNC	Adjunct (ABBR)
ADJNCV	Adjunctive (ABBR)
ADJNG	Adjoining (ABBR)
ADJOING	Adjoining (ROG)
ADJ/PPR	Adjusted Permanent Pay Record [*Military*] (DNAB)
ADJR	Adjure (ABBR)
ADJRAN	Adjuration (ABBR)
ADJRAY	Adjuratory (ABBR)
ADJ/RCT	Adjusted Reviewed Copy of Temporary Pay Record [*Military*] (DNAB)
ADJRD	Adjured (ABBR)
ADJRG	Adjuring (ABBR)
ADJRN	Adjourn (ABBR)
ADJRND	Adjourned (ABBR)
ADJRNG	Adjourning (ABBR)
ADJRNNT.....	Adjournment (ABBR)
ADJRNT	Adjournment (ABBR)
ADJRR	Adjurer (ABBR)
ADJS	Adjust (ABBR)
ADJS	Angle Deception Jamming System
ADJS	Aviation Machinist Mate Jet, Senior Chief [*Navy rating*]
ADJSB	Adjustable (ABBR)
ADJSBY	Adjustably (ABBR)
ADJSD	Adjusted (ABBR)
Adj Sess	Adjourned Session (DLA)
ADJSG	Adjusting (ABBR)
ADJSNT	Adjustment (ABBR)
ADJSPD	Adjustable Speed (IAA)
ADJSR	Adjuster (ABBR)
ADJST	Adjustment (ABBR)
ADJSTB	Ajustable (ABBR)
ADJSTER	Adjuster
ADJSTR	Adjuster (ABBR)
ADJT	Adjustable [*Technical drawings*]
ADJT	Adjutant
ADJT	Adjutant
ADJ/TDA	Adjusted Transcript Deserter's Account [*Military*] (DNAB)
ADJ/TDA	Adjusted Transcript Deserter's Account [*Military*] (DNAB)
Adjt-Gen	Adjutant-General [*British military*] (DMA)
ADJTNC	Adjutancy (ABBR)
ADJTOR	Adjustor
ADJTS	Adjutants (ABBR)
ADJUD	Adjudicate (ABBR)
ADJUDD	Adjudicated (ABBR)
ADJUDG	Adjudicating (ABBR)
ADJUDN	Adjudication (ABBR)
ADJUDR	Adjudicator (ABBR)
ADJUDRY	Adjudicatory (ABBR)
ADJUN	Adjudication (ROG)
Ad Jus	Adams' Justiciary Reports [*Scotland*] [*A publication*] (DLA)

ADJV............ Adjective (ABBR)
ADJVL.......... Adjectival (ABBR)
ADK............ Adak Island [Alaska] [Airport symbol] (OAG)
ADK Lib........ Adak Island [Alaska] [Seismograph station code, US Geological Survey] (SEIS)
ADK............ Adenosine Kinase (DMAA)
ADK............ Adenylate Kinase [An enzyme]
ADK............ Adirondack Mountain Club (EA)
ADK............ Alliance for Democracy in Korea [Defunct] (EA)
ADK............ Allied Digital Tech [AMEX symbol] (TTSB)
ADK............ Allied Digital Technologies [Formerly, AMG Digital Technologies] [AMEX symbol] (SAG)
ADK............ Attach-Detach Kit
ADK............ Automatic Depth Keeping (IAA)
ADK............ Aviation Development Co. Nigeria Ltd. [ICAO designator] (FAAC)
Adk............ Awning Deck [of a ship] (DS)
ADKM.......... Antoko Demokraty Kristiana Malagasy [Malagasy Christian Democratic Party] (AF)
Adk Town..... Adkinson on Township and Town Law in Indiana [A publication] (DLA)
ADL............ Acceptable Defect Level
ADL............ Acid-Detergent Lignin [Food analysis]
ADL............ Acoustic Delay Line
ADL............ Active Duty List [Army] (INF)
ADL............ Activities of Daily Living [Medicine]
ADL............ Activities of Daily Living (WYGK)
ADL............ Activities of Daily Living
ADL............ Ada Design Language [Computer science] (ODBW)
ADL............ Adelaide [Australia Airport symbol] (OAG)
AdL............ A. de Lara Limited Edition Recordings [Now Orfeo with same numbers] [Record label Great Britain]
AD L............ Ad Libitum [At Pleasure, As Desired] [Music] (ROG)
Ad L............ Administrative Law (DLA)
ADL............ Adolescent Medicine [Medical specialty] (DHSM)
ADL............ Adrian Resources [Vancouver Stock Exchange symbol]
ADL............ Aerobic Dive Limit [Psysiology]
ADL............ Aeronautical Data-Link [FAA] (TAG)
ADL............ Aids Distribution List [Military] (SAA)
ADL............ Airborne Data Link
ADL............ Airborne Data Loader [Aviation]
ADL............ Aircraft Data Line (MCD)
ADL............ Air-Dale Ltd. [Canada ICAO designator] (FAAC)
ADL............ Amateur Drama League [Republic of Ireland] (BI)
ADL............ Antenna Dummy Load
ADL............ Anti-Defamation League of B'nai B'rith (EA)
ADL............ Apollo Documentation List [NASA] (MCD)
ADL............ Architecture Description Language [Computer science] (CSR)
ADL............ Area Dental Laboratory [Military]
ADL............ Armament Data Line [Military] (NVT)
ADL............ Armament Datum Line (MCD)
ADL............ Arthur D. Little [Commercial firm] (NITA)
ADL............ Arthur D. Little, Inc. [Cambridge, MA] [Research code symbol]
ADL............ Arthur D. Little, Inc., Cambridge, MA [OCLC symbol] (OCLC)
ADL............ Artificial Delay Line (IAA)
ADL............ Associated Deliveries Limited [British]
ADL............ Atmospheric Devices Laboratory [Cambridge, MA] (AAG)
ADL............ Authorized Data List [DoD]
ADL............ Automatic Data Link [Computer science]
ADL............ Automatic Data Logger (PDAA)
ADL............ Average Decreasing Line
ADL............ Avionics Development Laboratory [Rockwell International-Space Division] [NASA] (NASA)
ADL............ Societe de Gestion de l'Aeroport de Libreville [Airline] [Gabon] (EY)
Ad L 2d........ Pike and Fischer's Administrative Law Reporter, Second Series [A publication] (DLA)
Ad L 2d(P & F)... Pike and Fischer's Administrative Law Reporter, Second Series [A publication] (ILCA)
ADLA.......... Adulate (ABBR)
ADLA.......... Assistant Director for Legal and Legislative Affairs [National Security Agency] [Obsolete]
ADLAC........ Adelphia Communic'A' [NASDAQ symbol] (TTSB)
ADLAC........ Adelphia Communications Corp. [NASDAQ symbol] (SAG)
ADLAD........ Adulated (ABBR)
ADLAG........ Adulating (ABBR)
ADLAN........ Adulation (ABBR)
ADLAR........ Adaptive Lens Array (MCD)
ADLAR........ Adulator (ABBR)
ADLARY...... Adulatory (ABBR)
ADLAT........ Advanced Low-Altitude Technique
ADLAT........ Advanced Low Altitude Terrain [Missile] (DOMA)
ADLAT........ Advanced Low-Altitude Terrain System (MCD)
ADLATAD..... Advise Latest Address [Military] (AABC)
Ad LB.......... Administrative Law Bulletin [A publication] (DLA)
Ad L Bull..... Administrative Law Bulletin [A publication] (ILCA)
ADL Bull..... Australian Administrative Law Bulletin [A publication]
ADLC.......... Advanced Data Link Control [Computer science]
ADLC.......... Animal Defence League of Canada (AC)
ADLC.......... Antibody-Dependent Lymphocyte-Mediated Cytotoxicity [Clinical chemistry]
ADLC.......... Asynchronous DataLink Control [IBM Corp.]
ADLC.......... Azimuth Drive Local Control
ADLI.......... Advanced Deck-Launched Interceptor (MCD)
ADLI.......... Amer Dental Technologies [NASDAQ symbol] (TTSB)
ADLI.......... American Dental LaserAm [NASDAQ symbol] (SAG)
Ad Lib.......... Adair on Libels [A publication] (DLA)

ADLIB......... Adaptive Library Management System [Lipman Management Resources Ltd.] [Information service or system] (IID)
AD LIB........ Ad Libitum [At Pleasure, As Desired] [Music]
ADLIB......... [A] Design Language for Indicating Behavior [1967] [Computer science] (CSR)
AD LIBIT.... Ad Libitum [At Pleasure, As Desired] [Music]
ADLIPS....... Automatic Data Link Plotting System
ADLM......... Aerial Delivered Land Mine (AFM)
ADLMS....... Air-Delivered Land Mine System [Military]
Ad L News.... Administrative Law News [A publication] (DLA)
Ad L Newsl... Administrative Law Newsletter [A publication] (DLA)
ADLO......... Air Defense Liaison Officer
ADLO......... Association of Direct Labour Organisations [British]
AD LOC........ Ad Locum [To (or At) the Place] [Latin]
ADLOG........ Advance Logistical Command [Army]
ADLP......... Adipose Fin and Left Pectoral Fin Clips [Pisciculture]
ADLP......... Aircraft Data Link Processor [Mode S subnetwork function onboard the aircraft that implements OSI network layer protocols] (GAVI)
ADLP......... Australian Democratic Labor Party [Political party] (PPW)
ADLR......... Adrian Resources Ltd. [NASDAQ symbol] (SAG)
ADLR......... Assistant Director of Light Railways [British military] (DMA)
ADLR......... Automated Direct Labor Reporting (MCD)
Ad L Rep 2d (P & F)... Administrative Law Reporter, Second (Pike and Fischer) [A publication] (DLA)
ADLRF........ Adrian Resources [NASDAQ symbol] (TTSB)
ADLS .... Airborne Data Link System
ADLS .... Air Dispatch Letter Service [Navy]
ADLS .... Anterior Dorsolateral Scale Count
ADLSNC...... Adolescence (ABBR)
ADLSNT...... Adolescent (ABBR)
ADLST....... Adolescent (ABBR)
ADLT.......... Adult (ABBR)
ADLT.......... Adult
ADLT.......... Advanced Lighting Technol [NASDAQ symbol] (TTSB)
ADLT.......... Advanced Lighting Technologies, Inc. [NASDAQ symbol] (SAG)
ADLTA........ Adulterate (ABBR)
ADLTAD...... Adulterated (ABBR)
ADLTAG...... Adulterating (ABBR)
ADLTDE...... Association of Dark Leaf Tobacco Dealers and Exporters (EA)
ADLTHD...... Adulthood (ABBR)
ADLTNT...... Adulterant (ABBR)
ADLTR........ Adulterer (ABBR)
ADLTRA...... Adulterate (ABBR)
ADLTRAD.... Adulterated (ABBR)
ADLTRAG.... Adulterating (ABBR)
ADLTRAN.... Adulteration (ABBR)
ADLTRES.... Adulteress (ABBR)
ADLTRNT.... Adulterant (ABBR)
ADLTRR...... Adulterer (ABBR)
ADLTRS...... Adulteress (ABBR)
ADLTRU...... Adulterous (ABBR)
ADLTRY...... Adultery (ABBR)
ADLTUS...... Adulterous (ABBR)
ADLTUSY.... Adulterously (ABBR)
ADLTY........ Adultery [FBI standardized term]
ADLV......... Adipose Fin and Left Ventral Fin Clips [Pisciculture]
ADLY......... Arrival Delay [Air Traffic Control] (FAAC)
ADM.......... Abductor Digiti Minimi [Muscles of Hands or Feet] [Anatomy] (DAVI)
ADM.......... Academy of Dental Materials (EA)
ADM.......... Acoustic Digital Memory
ADM.......... Acquisition Decision Memorandum (MCD)
ADM.......... Activity Data Method (IEEE)
ADM.......... Adams Exploration Ltd. [Vancouver Stock Exchange symbol]
ADM.......... Adaptable Data Manager [Hitachi Ltd.] [Japan]
ADM.......... Adaptive Delta Modulation [Electronics]
ADM.......... Add/Drop Multiplexer [Telecommunications] (ACRL)
ADM.......... Additional Dealer Markup [Automobile retailing]
ADM.......... Add Magnitude [Computer science] (IAA)
ADM.......... Administration [or Administrator] (EY)
ADM.......... Administrative Medicine (AAMN)
ADM.......... Admiral (EY)
ADM.......... Admiral
ADM.......... Admiralty [British]
ADM.......... Admission
ADM.......... Admit (WGA)
Adm.......... Admitted [Medicine] (DAVI)
ADM.......... Admove [Apply] [Pharmacy]
AdM.......... Adrenal Medulla [Anatomy]
ADM.......... Adriamycin [Also, A, ADR, D, H] [Antineoplastic drug]
ADM.......... Advanced Data Management [Information service or system] (IID)
ADM.......... Advanced Deployment Model (MCD)
ADM.......... Advanced Development Memory (MCD)
ADM.......... Advanced Development Model
ADM.......... Advanced Diploma in Midwifery [British]
ADM.......... Advance Decoy Missile (MCD)
ADM.......... Advanced Microdevices, Inc. (NITA)
ADM.......... Aerolineas Dominicanas SA [Dominican Republic] [ICAO designator] (FAAC)
ADM.......... Aeronaves de Mexico SA [Mexican airline] (MCD)
ADM.......... Affiliated Dress Manufacturers (EA)
ADM.......... Agarose Diffusion Method [Medical device safety test]
ADM.......... Air Decoy Missile (AFM)
ADM.......... Air Defense Missile
ADM.......... Air Defense Mission [Army]
ADM.......... Alcohol, Drug or Mental Disorder

ADM............ American Dance Machine
ADM............ Ammonium Dimolybdate [Inorganic chemistry]
ADM............ Annual Delegate Meeting [British] (DCTA)
ADM............ Apollo Data Manager [NASA] (KSC)
ADM............ Application Data Management (IAA)
ADM............ Arc Data Monitor [Welding] [Automotive engineering]
ADM............ Archer Daniels Midland [Commercial firm]
ADM............ Archer-Daniels-Midland Co. [NYSE symbol] (SPSG)
ADM............ Ardmore [Oklahoma] [Airport symbol Obsolete] (OAG)
ADM............ Area Defense Missile
ADM............ Area Denial Munition (MCD)
ADM............ Arrow Diagramming Method (MCD)
ADM............ Assistant Deputy Minister [Canada]
ADM............ Assistant District Manager (DCTA)
ADM............ Association of Drum Manufacturers [British] (DBA)
ADM............ Asynchronous Disconnected Mode
ADM............ Atomic Demolition Munition
ADM............ Austro-Daimler Motoren AG [Automobile manufacturer]
ADM............ Authorized Data Item Description Manual [A publication] (MCD)
ADM............ Automated Data Management (IAA)
ADM............ Automated Depot Maintenance
ADM............ Automated Drafting Machine
ADM............ Automatic Degreasing Machine
ADM............ Automatic Detection Mark (NVT)
ADM............ Automatic Display Mode [Computer science] (BUR)
ADM............ Automatic Distribution of Microfiche
ADM............ Automatic Drivetrain Management [Automotive engineering]
ADM............ Average Daily Membership
ADM............ Delia Municipal Library, Alberta [Library symbol National Library of Canada] (NLC)
Adm............ High Court of Admiralty [England] (DLA)
ADM............ NRDS [Nevada] [Seismograph station code, US Geological Survey Closed] (SEIS)
AdmA.......... Administrateur Agree [Canada] (DD)
ADMA .... Advanced Direct Memory Access [Siemens Corp.] (NITA)
ADMA .... Agricultural Development and Marketing Authority [Northern Territory, Australia]
ADMA .... Alkyldimethylamine [Acronym is a trademark of Ethyl Corp. for its brand of alkyldimethylamine products]
ADMA .... American Drug Manufacturers' Association [Later, PMA]
ADMA .... Area-Dominant Military Aircraft
ADMA .... Association of Direct Marketing Agencies [Defunct] (EA)
ADMA .... Automatic Damper Manufacturers Association [Defunct] (EA)
ADMA .... Automatic Drafting Machine (DIT)
ADMA .... Aviation Distributors and Manufacturers Association (EA)
ADMAC .... Austrian Documentation Centre for Media and Communication Research [Information service or system] (IID)
ADMACQ...... Association des Detaillants de Materiaux de Construction du Quebec [Quebec Building Materials Dealers Association] (AC)
ADMAD .... Advise Method and Date of Shipment (NOAA)
AD MAN ...... Advertising Manager (DGA)
Adm & Ecc... English Law Reports, Admiralty and Ecclesiastical [A publication] (DLA)
Adm & Eccl... English Law Reports, Admiralty and Ecclesiastical [A publication] (DLA)
AD MAN MED... Ad Manus Medici [To Be Delivered into the Hands of the Physician] [Pharmacy]
ADMAP .... Advise by Air Mail as Soon as Possible (FAAC)
Admar......... Admar Group, Inc. [Associated Press] (SAG)
ADMAT .... Administrative-Material Inspection [Military] (NVT)
ADMATCH.... Address Matching Software Package [Bureau of the Census] (GFGA)
ADMB .... Adumbrate (ABBR)
ADMB .... Agricultural Development and Marketing Board [Northern Territory Australia]
ADMB .... Air Defense Missile Base (SAA)
ADMBD .... Adumbrated (ABBR)
ADMBG....... Adumbrating (ABBR)
ADMBRA .... Adumbrate (ABBR)
ADMBRAD ... Adumbrated (ABBR)
ADMBRAG ... Adumbrating (ABBR)
ADMC .... Air Defense Missile Command (AABC)
ADMC .... Antibody-Dependent Macrophage-Mediated Cytotoxicity [Clinical chemistry]
ADMCEN ...... Administration Center
ADMCS .... Allyl(dimethyl)chlorosilane [Organic chemistry]
Adm Ct .... Admiralty Court (BARN)
ADMD .:...... Adjust Mode [Computer science]
ADMD .... Administration Management Domain [Telecommunications] (TEL)
ADMD .... Administrative Division [Municipality] [Board on Geographic Names]
AdMd .... Advanced Medical, Inc. [Associated Press] (SAG)
ADME......... Absorption, Distribution, Metabolism, Excretion [Medicine]
ADME......... Assistant Director of Mechanical Engineering [British military] (DMA)
AdMEd .... Advanced Master of Education (GAGS)
ADMG .... Admitting (MSA)
ADMG .... Advance Devices and Material Committee [British]
ADMG .... Advanced Materials Group, Inc. [NASDAQ symbol] (SAG)
ADMG .... Advanced Matts Group [NASDAQ symbol] (TTSB)
ADMG .... Air Defense Machine Gun (MCD)
ADMG .... Assistant Deputy Military Governor [US Military Government, Germany]
ADMHA........ Alcohol, Drug Abuse, and Mental Health Administration [Formerly, HSMHA] [Department of Health and Human Services] (OICC)
ADMI .... American Dry Milk Institute [Later, ADPI] (EA)
admin.......... Administer (CPH)
ADMIN .... Administration [or Administrator] (EY)

admin.......... Administration (DD)
Admin.......... Administration (DMAA)
ADMIN .... Administratrix [Business term] (ADA)
ADMIN .... Automated Document Management Information Network (NITA)
Admin Bull.... Administrators' Bulletin [A publication]
Admin Cd..... Administrative Code [A publication] (DLA)
ADMINCEN... Army Administration Center, Fort Benjamin Harrison (AABC)
Admin Dec.... Administrative Decisions [A publication] (DLA)
ADMINI........ Administrative Instructions
ADMINID...... Administrative Identification (MHDI)
ADMININSP... Administrative Inspection [Military] (NVT)
ADMININST... Administrative Instructions
Administrn.... Administration (DLA)
ADMIN L...... Administrative Law (DLA)
Admin LJ..... [The] Administrative Law Journal of The American University [A publication] (AAGC)
Admin L Rev... Administrative Law Review [A publication] [ABA] (AAGC)
ADMIN MOD... Administration Module (MCD)
ADMINO....... Administrative Office [or Officer] (CINC)
ADMINO....... Administrative Order
ADMINORD... Administrative Order (NVT)
ADMINPLAN... Administrative Plan (NVT)
Admin pub.... Administration Publique [A publication] (ILCA)
ADMINR....... Administrator
ADMINREP.... Administrative Report (NVT)
Admin Rev.... Administrative Review [A publication]
AdminSc...... Administrative Science (DD)
Admin SO ... Administrative Staff Officer
Adminstr....... Administrator (DLA)
Adminstrv .... Administrative (DLA)
ADMINSUP... Administrative Support (NVT)
ADMINSUPP... Administrative Support Unit (DNAB)
Adm Interp... Administrative Interpretations [A publication] (DLA)
ADMINV....... Administrative
Admir.......... Admiralty Division (DLA)
ADMIR........ Automatic Diagnostic Maintenance Information Retrieval [Computer science] (IAA)
ADMIRAL..... Automatic and Dynamic Monitor with Immediate Relocation, Allocation, and Loading (IEEE)
ADMIRE .... Adaptive Decision Maker in an Information Retrieval Environment [Stanford University] (NITA)
ADMIRE .... Automatic Diagnostic Maintenance Information Retrieval System [Computer science] (MCD)
ADMIS .... Admissions
ADMIS .... Automated Data Management Information System
admit.......... Admission [Medicine] (DAVI)
ADMIT .... Aeronautical Depot Maintenance Industrial Technology [Navy] (AFIT)
ADMIT .... Alcohol Drug Motorsensory Impairment Test [Pharmometrics Corp.]
ADMIV .... Administrative (FAAC)
ADMIX .... Administratrix [Business term] (ROG)
ADMK .... All-India Anna Dravida Munnetra Kazhagam [Political party] (PPW)
AdMkSv .... Advanced Marketing Systems [Associated Press] (SAG)
ADML......... Adenovirus Major Late [Medicine]
Adml .... Admiral (BARN)
ADML......... Advanced Design Methods Laboratory [Ohio State University] [Research center] (RCD)
ADML......... Average Daily Member Load
ADMLP .... Adenovirus Major Late Promoter [Genetics]
ADMLP .... ASCII COBOL Data Manipulation Language-Preprocessor [Computer science]
AdMLS .... Advanced Master of Library Science (GAGS)
ADMLT .... Admiralty (ABBR)
ADMM .... Administrative Memo (NATG)
ADMM .... Association of Dandyroll and Mould Makers (DGA)
ADMN .... Administer (ABBR)
ADMN .... Administration
ADMN .... Administration
ADMN .... Administrative Appeals Tribunal Decisions [Australia A publication]
ADMN .... Atmospheric Deposition Monitoring Program [Environmental Protection Agency]
ADMND....... Administered (ABBR)
ADMNG....... Administering (ABBR)
ADMNH .... Admonish (ABBR)
ADMNHR .... Admonisher (ABBR)
ADMNN .... Admonition (ABBR)
ADMNSTR.... Administrator
ADMNSTRV... Administrative
ADMNT .... Adamant (ABBR)
ADMNT .... Administrate (ABBR)
ADMNTD...... Administrated (ABBR)
ADMNTG...... Administrating (ABBR)
ADMNTN...... Administration (ABBR)
ADMNTNS... Admonitions (ABBR)
ADMNTR...... Administrator (ABBR)
ADMNTS...... Administrates (ABBR)
ADMNTV...... Administrative (ABBR)
ADMNTVY... Administratively (ABBR)
ADMNTX...... Administratrix (ABBR)
ADMNTY...... Adamantly (ABBR)
Admo.......... Administrative Officer [Army]
Admo.......... Administrative Order [Army]
ADMO.......... Air Defense Management Office (MCD)
ADMON....... Administration (ROG)
ADMON....... Admission (ROG)
ADMON....... Admonish (ABBR)

ADMOND ..... Admonished (ABBR)
ADMONG ..... Admonishing (ABBR)
ADMONGY .. Admonishingly (ABBR)
ADMONR ..... Admonisher (ABBR)
ADMONT ..... Admonishment (ABBR)
ADMONTN ... Admonition (ABBR)
ADMOR .... Administrator (ROG)
ADMOS .... Automatic Device for Mechanical Order Selection
ADMOV .... Admove [Apply] [Pharmacy]
ADMP .... Aerodynamic Damping Moment in Pitch [Helicopter rotor]
ADMR .... Absorbance-Detected Magnetic Resonance [Physics]
ADMR .... [The] Admar Group, Inc. [NASDAQ symbol] (NQ)
ADMR .... Administrator
ADMR .... Admire (ABBR)
ADMR .... Adult Daily Minimum Requirement (HGAA)
AD-MRA ...... American and Delaine-Merino Record Association (EA)
ADMRAN...... Admiration (ABBR)
ADMRB........ Admirable (ABBR)
ADMRCS...... Administratrices [Legal shorthand] (LWAP)
ADMRD........ Admired (ABBR)
ADMRG........ Admiring (ABBR)
ADMRGY...... Admiringly (ABBR)
ADMRL .... Application Data Material Readiness List [DoD]
ADMRL .... Automatic Data Material Requirements List
ADMRLT ...... Admiralty (ABBR)
ADMRN........ Admiration (ABBR)
ADMRR .... Admirer (ABBR)
AdmRsc .... Adams Resources & Energy, Inc. [Associated Press] (SAG)
ADMRX........ Administratrix [Business term] (ROG)
ADMRY........ Admirably (ABBR)
ADMRY........ Admirably (ABBR)
ADMS .... Administrator (WGA)
ADMS .... Advanced Marketing Services, Inc. [NASDAQ symbol] (NQ)
ADMS .... Advanced Marketing Svcs [NASDAQ symbol] (TTSB)
ADMS .... Air Defense Missile Squadron [Air Force]
ADMS .... American Donkey and Mule Society (EA)
ADMS .... Analog and Digital Monitoring System [Computer science] (MCD)
ADMS .... Application Data Management Services (MCD)
ADMS .... Assistant Director of Medical Services
ADMS .... Asynchronous Data Multiplexer Synchronizer
ADMS .... Atmospheric Diffusion Measuring System
ADMS .... Automated Document Management Systems (DGA)
ADMS .... Automatic Digital Message Switching
ADMSB .... Admissible (ABBR)
ADMSBLT ..... Admissibility (ABBR)
ADMSBT ...... Admissibility (ABBR)
ADMSC .... Automatic Digital Message Switching Center [AUTODIN]
ADMSE .... Automatic Digital Message Switch Equipment (MCD)
ADMSG .... Advise by [Electronically Transmitted] Message [Army] (AABC)
ADMSLBN ..... Air Defense Missile Battalion [Army] (AABC)
ADMSN........ Admission (AFM)
ADMSPT ...... Administrative Support (MCD)
AD-MSS .... Anaerobically Digested Municipal Sewage Solids [Culture medium]
ADMSTR ...... Administer (ABBR)
ADMSTR ...... Administrator
ADMSTRA .... Administrate (ABBR)
ADMSTRAN... Administration (ABBR)
ADMSTRATR... Administrator (ABBR)
ADMSTRAV... Administrative (ABBR)
ADMSV .... Admissive (ABBR)
ADMT .... Admit (ABBR)
ADMT .... ADM Tronics Unlimited [NASDAQ symbol] (TTSB)
ADMT .... ADM Tronics Unltd. [NASDAQ symbol] (SAG)
ADMT .... Agena Detailed Maneuver Table [NASA] (SAA)
ADMT .... Association for Dance Movement Therapy (EAIO)
ADMTD .... Admitted (ABBR)
ADMTDY ...... Admittedly (ABBR)
ADMTG .... Admitting (ABBR)
ADMTNC ...... Admittance (ABBR)
ADMTR .... Administrator
ADM Tr .... ADM Tronics Unlimited [Associated Press] (SAG)
ADMTRX...... Administratrix [Business term] (ROG)
ADMTY .... Admiralty (NATG)
ADMU .... Air Data Measuring Unit (NATG)
ADMX .... Administratrix [Business term] (ROG)
ADMXR .... Admixture (ABBR)
ADMY .... Admiralty [British]
ADN .... Accession Designation Number [Military]
ADN .... Accion Democratica Nacionalista [Nationalist Democratic Action] [Bolivia] [Political party] (PPW)
ADN .... Accion Democratico Nacional [National Democratic Action] [Aruba] [Political party] (EY)
ADN .... Adams [New York] [Seismograph station code, US Geological Survey Closed] (SEIS)
ADN .... Adanac Mining & Exploration Ltd. [Toronto Stock Exchange symbol Vancouver Stock Exchange symbol]
ADN .... Address Complete, No-Charge [Telecommunications] (TEL)
ADN .... Aden [People's Democratic Republic of Yemen]
adn .... Adenoid [Otorhinolaryngology] (DAVI)
adn .... Adenoidectomy [Otorhinolaryngology] (DAVI)
ADN .... Adiponitrile [Organic chemistry]
ADN .... Aerodienst GmbH [Germany ICAO designator] (FAAC)
ADN .... AgriData Network [AgriData Resources, Inc.] [Milwaukee, WI] [Telecommunications service] (TSSD)

ADN .... Allgemeiner Deutscher Nachrichtendienst [German General News Service] [Germany] (EG)
ADN .... Ammonium Dinitramide [Potential rocket fuel component] [Inorganic chemistry]
ADN .... Antideoxyribonuclease [Medicine] (DMAA)
ADN .... Archdeacon
ADN .... Ashley, Drew & Northern Railway Co. [AAR code]
ADN .... Assistant Director of Nursing (BARN)
ADN .... Associate Degree in Nursing
ADN .... Automatic Data Network
ADN .... Avionics Decision Notice (MCD)
ADN .... Aydin [Turkey] [Airport symbol] (AD)
ADNA .... Assistant Director of Naval Accounts [British]
ADNAC .... Air Defense of North American Continent [Army] (AABC)
Ad Nat .... Ad Nationes [of Tertullian] [Classical studies] (OCD)
AD NAUS .... Ad Nauseum [To the Extent of Producing Nausea] [Latin]
ADNC .... Air Defense National Center (NATG)
ADNC .... Air Defense Notification Center (NATG)
ADNC .... Assistant Director of Naval Construction [British]
ADND .... Addend (ABBR)
ADNDA......... Addenda (ABBR)
ADNDM .... Addendum (ABBR)
ADNE .... Alden Electronics, Inc. [NASDAQ symbol] (NQ)
ADNEA......... Alden Electronics 'A' [NASDAQ symbol] (TTSB)
ADNET .... Action Data Network (MCD)
ADNET .... Administrative Distributed Network (GFGA)
ADNET .... Anti-Drug Network (DOMA)
AD NEUT...... Ad Neutralizandum [To Neutralization] [Pharmacy]
ADNI .... Additional (DA)
ADNI .... Assistant Director of Naval Intelligence [British]
ADNL TFC .... Additional Traffic [Air Traffic Control] (FAAC)
AdNMR .... Advanced NMR Systems [Associated Press] (SAG)
ADNOC........ Abu Dhabi National Oil Co. (ODBW)
ADNOK........ Advise if Not Correct [Aviation] (FAAC)
ADNOMOVPEN... Advised Not to Move Dependents until Suitable Quarters Located [Military]
ADNS .... Automated Data Network System [Army]
ADNV .... Adhesive (ABBR)
ADO .... ActiveX Data Objects [Computer science]
ADO .... ActiveX Data Objects [Computer science]
ADO .... Adagio [Slow] [Music]
ADO .... Ad Com Marketing, Inc. [Vancouver Stock Exchange symbol]
ADO .... Additional Day Off
ADO .... Address Out [Computer science] (IAA)
Ado .... Adenosine [Also, A] [A nucleoside]
ADO .... Administration Duty Officer (NATG)
ADO .... Adolescent Medicine [Medicine] (DMAA)
ADO .... Advanced Development Objective [Military]
ADO .... Air Defence Officer [Navy British]
ADO .... Air Defense Operations (NATG)
ADO .... Air Drop Operator
ADO .... Alleged Discrimination Official (MCD)
ADO .... American Darts Organization (EA)
ADO .... Ampex Digital Optics [Telecommunications] (WDMC)
ADO .... Andamooka [Australia Airport symbol] (OAG)
ADO .... Animal Disease Occurrence [Database] [Commonwealth Agricultural Bureaux] [Information service or system] (CRD)
ADO .... Army Digitalization Office
ADO .... Army Distribution Objective (MCD)
ADO .... Associated Disbursing Officer [Military] (DNAB)
ADO .... Association of Dispensing Opticians [British] (DBQ)
ADO .... Audio Decode Oscillator
ADO .... Auto Defense Ordinance (CINC)
ADO .... Automatic Dial-Out (NITA)
ADO .... Automotive Diesel Oil (ADA)
ADO .... Automotive Distillate Oil (ADA)
ADO .... Avalanche Diode Oscillator
ADO .... Axiodisto-Occlusal [Dentistry]
ADO .... Data Automation Design Office [Air Force]
ADO .... Donalda Public Library, Alberta [Library symbol National Library of Canada] (BIB)
ADo .... George S. Houston Memorial Library, Dothan, AL [Library symbol Library of Congress] (LCLS)
ADO .... Louisville, KY [Location identifier FAA] (FAAL)
Ado .... Much Ado about Nothing [Shakespearean work]
ADOA .... American Dog Owners Association (EA)
ADOAP........ Adriamycin [Doxorubicin], Cytosine Arabinoside , Vincristine, Prednisone [Cytarabine] [Antineoplastic drug regimen] (DAVI)
ADOAP........ Adriamycin, Oncovin, ara-C, Prednisone [Antineoplastic drug regimen]
ADOBE........ Atmospheric Diffusion of Beryllium Program [NASA] (KSC)
AdobeSy ..... Adobe Systems [Associated Press] (SAG)
ADOC.......... Abu Dhabi Oil Co. [United Arab Emirates] (EY)
ADOC.......... Agora/Documentaire [Agence France-Presse] [French Information service or system] (CRD)
ADOC.......... Air Defense Operations Center [Air Force]
ADOC.......... Alianza Democratica de Oposicion Civilista [Panama] [Political party] (EY)
ADOC.......... Automatic Defense Operation Center
ADoC.......... Houston County Court House, Dothan, AL [Library symbol Library of Congress] (LCLS)
ADOCBL....... Adenosylcobalamin [Also, DBC] [A vitamin]
ADOCo........ After Dinner Opera Co.
ADOCS........ Advanced Digital/Optical Control System
ADOD.......... Arthrodentosteodysplasia [Medicine] (DMAA)

ADOD.........	Assistant Director of Operations Division [*British military*] (DMA)
ADOD.........	Donalda and District Museum, Donalda, Alberta [*Library symbol National Library of Canada*] (BIB)
ADODM......	Adult-Onset Diabetes Mellitus [*Medicine*] (DAVI)
ADOF.........	Arbitrary Degree of Freedom (MCD)
ADOF.........	Assistant Director of Ordnance Factories [*Ministry of Supply*] [*British World War II*]
ADOGA.......	American Dehydrated Onion and Garlic Association (EA)
AdoHcy......	Adenosylhomocysteine [*Biochemistry*]
ADOIT........	Automatically Directed Outgoing Intertoll Trunk [*Bell System*]
adol..........	Adolescence (DMAA)
ADOL.........	Adolescent
ADOL.........	American Directory of Organized Labor [*A publication*]
Adol & El....	Adolphus and Ellis' English King's Bench Reports [*A publication*] (DLA)
Adol & El NS...	Adolphus and Ellis' English Queen's Bench Reports, New Series [*A publication*] (DLA)
Adoles.......	Adolescence [*A publication*] (BRI)
A (Dolly).....	Articulating Dolly [*Trailer engineering*]
Adolph & E...	Adolphus and Ellis' English King's Bench Reports [*A publication*] (DLA)
ADOM........	Acid Deposition and Oxidant Model [*for acid rain*] [*Canada and Federal Republic of Germany*]
ADOM.........	Administration
ADOM.........	Air Deployed Oceanographic Mooring (PDAA)
ADOM.........	Army Depot Operations Management (MCD)
ADOM.........	Donnelly Municipal Library, Alberta [*Library symbol National Library of Canada*] (NLC)
AdoMet......	Adenosylmethionine [*Also, SAM, SAMe*] [*Biochemistry*]
ADONIS.......	Acoustic-Daylight, Ambient-Noise Imaging System
ADONIS.......	Automated Document Delivery Over Networked Information Service (NITA)
ADONIS.......	Automatic Digital On-Line Instrumentation System
ADONIS.......	Automatic Document Online Information System [*Document delivery system*] [*Association of European Publishers*] (NITA)
ADOP.........	Additive Operational Project [*Army*]
ADOP.........	Adoption (ABBR)
ADOP.........	Adriamycin, Oncovin [*Vincristine*], Prednisone [*Antineoplastic drug regimen*]
ADOP.........	Advanced Distributed Onboard Processor (SDI)
ADOPB.......	Adoptable (ABBR)
ADOPD.......	Adopted (ABBR)
ADOPE.......	Automatic Decisions Optimizing Predicted Estimates
ADOPG.......	Adopting (ABBR)
ADOPN.......	Adoption (ABBR)
ADOPR.......	Adopter (ABBR)
ADOPT.......	Adoption (DLA)
ADOPT.......	Advanced Optics Technology (MCD)
ADOPT.......	Approach to Distributed Processing Transaction [*Computer science*] (MHDB)
ADOPT.......	Automatic Design Optimization Techniques (MCD)
ADOPV.......	Adoptive (ABBR)
ADOR........	Active Duty Dates of Rank [*Army*] (INF)
ADORAN.....	Adoration (ABBR)
ADORB.......	Adorable (ABBR)
ADORBL.....	Adorably (ABBR)
ADORBNS...	Adorableness (ABBR)
ADORBT.....	Adorability (ABBR)
ADORBY.....	Adorably (ABBR)
ADORD.......	Adored (ABBR)
ADORG.......	Adoring (ABBR)
ADORGY.....	Adoringly (ABBR)
ADORNT.....	Adornment (ABBR)
ADORTN.....	Adoration (ABBR)
ADOS........	Advanced Diskette Operating System
ADOS.........	Area Distribution Officers [*Military British World War II*]
ADOS.........	Assistant Director of Ordnance Services [*British*]
ADOS.........	Astronautical Defensive-Offensive System
ADOS.........	Authorization for Disposal of Overhead Supplies (MCD)
ADOSOM.....	Association pour le Developpement des Oeuvres Sociales d'Outre-Mer [*Association for the Development of Social Welfare Projects Overseas*] [*French*] (AF)
ADOT.........	Automatically Directed Outgoing Trunk [*Bell System*]
ADOT.........	Automatic Digital Optical Tracker [*Army*] (AABC)
ADoT..........	Troy State University at Dothan, Dothan, AL [*Library symbol*] [*Library of Congress*] (LCLS)
ADOW.........	Automatic Dial Order Wire [*Military*] (NVT)
ADoW.........	George C. Wallace Community College, Dothan, AL [*Library symbol Library of Congress*] (LCLS)
ADP..........	Academy of Denture [*or Dental*] Prosthetics (EA)
ADP..........	Acceptance Data Package (KSC)
ADP..........	Accountability Data Package (MCD)
ADP..........	Acid Dew Point
ADP..........	Acme Aviation Ltd. [*British ICAO designator*] (FAAC)
ADP..........	Acoustic Data Processor (MCD)
adp..........	Adapter [*MARC relator code*] [*Library of Congress*] (LCCP)
ADP..........	Adaptive Learn Processor [*Fuel systems*] [*Automotive engineering*]
ADP..........	Additional Dealer Profit [*Automobile retailing*]
ADP..........	Adenosine Diphosphate [*Biochemistry*]
ADP..........	Administrative Data Processing (KSC)
ADP..........	Advanced Data Processing (NITA)
ADP..........	Advanced Development Plan [*Air Force*] (MCD)
ADP..........	Advanced Passenger Train [*British*]
ADP..........	African Democratic Party [*Political party*]
ADP..........	After-Depolarization [*Neurophysiology*]

ADP............	Agence Dahomeene de Presse [*Dahomean Press Agency*]
ADP............	Agence Dahomeenne de Presse [*Dahomean Press Agency*]
ADP............	Agence Djiboutienne de Presse (EY)
ADP............	Agent Development Program [*LIMRA*]
ADP............	Aggregate Demand Potential (PDAA)
ADP............	Agricultural Development Project [*London, England*]
ADP............	Airborne Data Processor [*Air Force*]
ADP............	Air Data Package
ADP............	Air Data Probe [*Aerospace*] (MCD)
ADP............	Air Defense Position [*Military*]
ADP............	Air Delivery Platoon (DNAB)
ADP............	Air Driven Pump
ADP............	Airport Development Program
ADP............	Alclometasone Dipropionate [*Glucocorticoid*]
ADP............	Alliance pour la Democratie et le Progres [*Benin*] [*Political party*] (EY)
ADP............	Allied Defense Publications (NATG)
ADP............	Allied Products [*NYSE symbol*] (TTSB)
ADP............	Allied Products Corp. [*NYSE symbol*] (SPSG)
ADP............	Alpha Delta Phi [*Fraternity*]
ADP............	Alpha Delta Pi [*Sorority*]
ADP............	Alternative Defense Posture (DNAB)
ADP............	Americans for Due Process (EA)
ADP............	Aminodiphenyl [*Organic chemistry*]
ADP............	Ammonium Dihydrogen Phosphate [*Inorganic chemistry*]
adp............	Ammonium Dihydrogen Phosphate (IDOE)
ADP............	Anatuberculina Diagnostica Petragnani [*Petragnani Diagnostic Anatuberculin*] [*Medicine*]
ADP............	Anguilla Democratic Party [*Political party*] (EY)
ADP............	Angular Distribution Pattern [*Surface analysis*]
ADP............	Animal Disease and Parasite Research Division [*of ARS, Department of Agriculture*]
ADP............	Anuradhapura [*Ceylon*] [*Airport symbol*] (AD)
ADP............	Apollo Dynamic Programs [*NASA*] (KSC)
ADP............	Approach Deterioration Parameter (MCD)
ADP............	Approved Drug Product [*Medicine*] (DMAA)
ADP............	Area Diastolic Pressure [*Cardiology*] (DAVI)
ADP............	Area Distribution Panel
ADP............	Armor Development Corp. [*Vancouver Stock Exchange symbol*]
ADP............	Army Depot Police [*British military*] (DMA)
ADP............	Artillery Destruction Program
ADP............	Artist's Diploma (PGP)
ADP............	Ascorbyl Dipalmitate [*Organic chemistry*]
ADP............	Assistant Director of Pathology [*Military British*]
ADP............	Assistant District Postmaster [*British*] (DCTA)
ADP............	Association for Denture Prosthesis (EAIO)
ADP............	Association of Database Producers (IID)
ADP............	Association of Directors and Producers [*British*]
ADP............	Association of Disabled Professionals (EAIO)
ADP............	Atmospheric Dynamics Program [*National Oceanic and Atmospheric Administration*]
ADP............	Australian Democratic Party [*Political party*] (PPW)
ADP............	Automated Data Processing [*FAA*] (TAG)
ADP............	Automatic Data Plotter
ADP............	Automatic Data Processing
adp............	Automatic Data Processing (IDOE)
ADP............	Automatic Data Processing, Inc. [*Trademark for data processing services*]
ADP............	Automatic Deletion Procedure (DNAB)
ADP............	Automatic Destruct Program (MUGU)
ADP............	Automatic Die Positioner [*Electronics*] (EECA)
ADP............	Automatic Digital Processor (MCD)
ADP............	Average Deferral Percentage
ADP............	Azerbaijan Democratic Party [*Iran*] [*Political party*]
ADP............	United States Army ARRADCOM - PLASTEC Division, Dover, NJ [*OCLC symbol*] (OCLC)
ADPA..........	Air Data Probe Assemblies [*Aerospace*] (NASA)
ADPA..........	Alcohol and Drug Problems Association of North America (EA)
ADPA..........	American Defense Preparedness Association (EA)
ADPA..........	Automobile Dealers Parts Association
ADPAC.......	American Democratic Political Action Committee (EA)
AD-PAC.......	American Druze Public Affairs Committee (EA)
ADPACS......	Automated Data Processing and Communications Service (MHDI)
Ad Part Dol...	Ad Partes Dolentes [*To the Painful Parts*] [*Pharmacy*]
ad part dolent...	Ad Partes Dolentes [*To the Painful Parts*] [*Pharmacy*]
ADPase.......	Adenosine Diphosphatase [*An enzyme*]
ADPASS......	Advanced Patrol Sensor System (MCD)
ADPB..........	Adaptable (ABBR)
ADPB..........	Air Defense Planning Board (MCD)
ADPBCT.....	Automatic Data Processing Budget Control Totals
ADP/BISG....	ADP [*Automatic Data Processing, Inc.*] Brokerage Information Services Group [*Also, an information service or system*] (IID)
ADPBT.......	Adaptability (ABBR)
ADPBUD.....	Automatic Data Processing Budget (DNAB)
ADPC..........	Adaxial Leaflet Pubescence - Curly [*Botany*]
ADPC..........	Agricultural Development Planning Center [*ASEAN*] [*Thailand*] [*Research center*] (IRC)
ADPC..........	Alliance Democratique pour le Progres du Cameroun [*Political party*] (EY)
ADPC..........	Automatic Data Processing Center
ADP/CIS.......	Automation of Data Processing/Computerization of Information Systems [*Food Stamp Program*] [*Department of Agriculture*] (GFGA)
ADPCM......	Adaptive Differential Pulse Code Modulation [*Telecommunications*] (MCD)

ADPCM .... Association for Data Processing and Computer Management (NITA)
ADPCMT ...... Adaptive Differential Pulse Code Modulated Transcoder [*Telecommunications*]
ADPD .... Angular Dependent Photoelectron Diffraction (PDAA)
ADPE .... ADP [*American Defense Preparedness*] Equipment (DOMA)
ADPE .... Alliance Democratique pour le Progres et l'Emancipation [*Cameroon*] [*Political party*] (EY)
ADPE .... Automatic Data Processing Engineering
ADPE .... Automatic Data Processing Equipment
ADPE .... Auxiliary Data Processing Equipment
ADPE/DS ...... Automatic Data Processing Equipment/Data System (AAGC)
ADP-EFS ...... ADP [*Automatic Data Processing, Inc.*] Electronic Financial Services [*Telecommunications service*] (TSSD)
ADPEP .... Automated Data Preparation by Electronic Photocomposition (MCD)
ADPEP .... Automated Data Preparation Evaluation Program (MCD)
ADPERSACT... Advise by Message of Action the Following Individual Is Taking [*Military*]
ADPES .... Angle-Dispersed Photoelectron Spectroscopy
ADPES .... Automatic Data Processing by Equipment Systems
ADPESO ...... Automatic Data Processing Equipment Selection Office [*Navy*]
ADPEV .... Aid to Displaced Persons and Its European Villages (EAIO)
ADPF .... Australian Dairy Products Federation
ADPFB .... Automatic Data Processing Field Branch [*BUPERS*]
ADP/FIS ...... ADP [*Automatic Data Processing, Inc.*] Financial Information Services, Inc. [*Later, ADP/BISG*] [*Information service or system*] (IID)
ADPG .... Air Defense Planning Group (MCD)
ADPI .... Air Diffusion Perfomance Index [*Of room ventilation*]
ADPI .... American Dairy Products Institute (EA)
ADPI .... Analog & Digital Peripherals, Inc. (PCM)
ADPI .... Association Internationale d'Etudes pour la Protection des Investissements
ADPKD .... Audlt Polycystic Kidney Disease [*Medicine*] (CPH)
ADPKD .... Autosomal Dominant Polycystic Kidney Disease [*Medicine*]
ADPL .... Assistant Director for Policy and Liaison [*National Security Agency*] [*Obsolete*]
ADPL .... Automated Drawing Parts List (MCD)
ADPL .... Average Daily Patient Load [*Medicine*]
ADPLAN .... Advanced Planning (ODBW)
ADPLL .... All-Digital Phase-Locked Loop (KSC)
ADPLO .... Automatic Data Processing Liaison Officer [*Military*] (MCD)
ADPLS .... Automated Drawing Parts List System (MCD)
ADPM .... Automatic Data Processing Machine
ADPMG .... Assistant Deputy Postmaster-General [*Canada*]
ADPMIS .... Automatic Data Processing Management Information System (AABC)
ADPMO .... Automatic Data Processing Modification Order
ADPNS .... Adeptness (ABBR)
ADPO .... Advanced Development Program Office
AD POND OM... Ad Pondus Omnium [*To the Weight of the Whole*] [*Pharmacy*]
ADPP .... ACTION Drug Prevention Program
ADPP .... Assembly Detail Purchased Parts (AAG)
ADPP & DB... Automatic Data Processing Planning and Development Branch [*BUPERS*]
ADPP & PB... Automatic Data Processing Programming and Processing Branch [*BUPERS*]
ADPPB .... Automatic Data Processing Production Branch [*BUPERS*]
ADPPRS....... Automatic Data Processing Program Reporting System [*Military*] (MCD)
ADPR .... ADP [*Adenosine Diphosphate*] Ribosylated Enzyme
ADPR .... Assistant Director for Plans and Resources [*National Security Agency*] [*Obsolete*]
ADPR .... Assistant Director of Public Relations [*Military British*]
ADPREP .... Automatic Data Processing Resource Estimating Procedures
ADPRID........ Advanced Degree Program for ROTC Instructor Duty (MCD)
ADPRO........ Automatic Data Processing Requirements Office [*Jet Propulsion Laboratory, NASA*]
ADPRORED... Advise by Message Why Individual Is Being Reduced [*Military*]
ADPRT .... Adenosine Diphosphate Ribosyltransferase [*An enzyme*]
ADPS .... Acid Deposition Planning Staff [*Environmental Protection Agency*] (GFGA)
ADPS .... Active Delayed Phase Shift (IAA)
ADP(S) .... Advanced Development Plan (System)
ADPS .... Advanced Digital Processing System
ADPS .... Apollo Document Preparation Standards [*Handbook*] [*NASA*] (KSC)
ADPS .... Assistant Director, Army Postal Services [*British military*] (DMA)
ADPS .... Automatic Data Processing Security [*Military*] (MCD)
ADPS .... Automatic Data Processing Services
ADPS .... Automatic Data Processing System [*or Subsystem*]
ADPS .... Automatic Display Plotting System (MCD)
ADPSC .... Automatic Data Processing Service Center [*Service of the US military*] (AABC)
ADPSE .... Automatic Data Processing Systems and Equipment (GFGA)
ADPSO .... Association of Data Processing Service Organizations [*Includes American and Canadian companies*] [*Later, ADAPSO - The Computer Software and Services Industry Association*] (EA)
ADPSO .... Australian Dairy Products Standards Organization
ADPSO .... Automatic Data Processing Selection Office [*Military*] (MCD)
ADPSR .... Architects/Designers/Planners for Social Responsibility (EA)
ADPSS .... Archivio Dati e Programmi per le Scienze Sociali [*Data and Program Archive for the Social Sciences*] [*University of Milan*] [*Italy*] [*Information service or system*] (IID)
ADPSSEP ..... Automated Data Processing System Security Enhancement Program (GFGA)
ADPSSO....... Automated Data Processing System Security Officer (MCD)
ADPT .... Adaptec, Inc. [*NASDAQ symbol*] (NQ)

ADPT .... Adapter (KSC)
ADPT .... Adenosine Phosphoribosyltransferase [*An enzyme*]
ADPT .... Adept (ABBR)
ADP-T .... Automated Data Processing Telecommunications (MCD)
ADPTC .... Automatic Data Processing Training Center [*Military*] (MCD)
ADP/TCS ..... ADP [*Automatic Data Processing, Inc.*] Telephone Computing Services, Inc. [*Telecommunications service*] (TSSD)
ADPTN .... Adoption
ADPTOS....... Automatic Data Processing Tactical Operation System (DNAB)
ADPTR .... Adapter (MSA)
ADPU .... Airborne Digital Processing Unit
ADPU .... Automatic Data Processing Unit (IAA)
ADPUB......... Advertising and Publicity (WDMC)
ad-pub .... Advertising and Publicity [*Theater*] (WDMC)
ADPY .... Adeptly (ABBR)
ADQ .... Abductor Digiti Quinti [*Muscles of Hands or Feet*] [*Anatomy*] (DAVI)
ADQ .... Almost Differential Quasiternary Code [*Telecommunications*] (TEL)
ADQ .... Association des Denturologistes du Quebec (AC)
ADQ .... Association des Dermatologistes du Quebec [*Association of Dermatologists of Quebec*] (AC)
ADQ .... Avion Taxi Canada, Inc. [*ICAO designator*] (FAAC)
ADQ .... Kodiak [*Alaska*] [*Airport symbol*] (OAG)
ADQA .... Adequate (ABBR)
ADQAY......... Adequately (ABBR)
ADQC .... Adequacy (ABBR)
ADQC .... Almost Difference Quasiternary Code (PDAA)
ADQCY......... Adequacy (ABBR)
ADQT .... Adequate (FAAC)
ADQTNS....... Adequateness (ABBR)
ADQTY......... Adequately (ABBR)
ADR .... Accepted Dental Remedies [*A publication*]
ADR .... Accepted Dental Remedy (DAVI)
ADR .... Accident Data Recorder [*Aviation*] (AIA)
ADR .... Accord Dangereuse Routier [*European agreement on the carriage of dangerous goods by road*]
ADR .... Accord European Relative au Transport International par Route des Marchandises Dangereuses par Route [*European Agreement on the International Transport of Dangerous Goods by Road*] (PDAA)
ADR .... Achievable Data Rate (MCD)
ADR .... Acid-Detergent Residue [*Food analysis*]
ADR .... Acute Dystonic Reaction [*Neurology*] (DAVI)
ADR .... Adder [*Computer device*] (MDG)
ADR .... Additional Dialogue Replacement
ADR .... Address [*Computer character*] [*Computer science*]
ADR .... Address Register (BUR)
Adr............. Adrenaline [*Endocrinology*]
ADR .... Adria Airways [*Yugoslavia*] [*ICAO designator*] (FAAC)
ADR .... Adriamycin [*Also, A, ADM, D, H*] [*Antineoplastic drug*]
Adr............. Adriamycin (DMAA)
ADR .... Adriatic (ABBR)
ADR .... Advanced Dated Remittances [*IRS*]
ADR .... Advanced Development Report [*NASA*] (KSC)
ADR .... Advance Deviations Report (AAG)
ADR .... Adverse Drug Reaction [*Medicine*]
ADR .... Advisory Route [*Aviation*] (FAAC)
ADR .... Advisory Rule (DA)
ADR .... Aerodrome Damage Repair [*NATO*]
ADR .... Aeronautical Data Report [*Navy*]
ADR-T .... Agrement Dangereuse Routier [*Agreement on the International Carriage of Dangerous Goods by Road*] [*1968*]
ADR .... Airborne Data Recorder (MCD)
ADR .... Airborne Digital Recorder
ADR .... Aircraft Design Research Division [*Navy*]
ADR .... Aircraft Destination Record (MCD)
ADR .... Aircraft Direction Room [*Navy*]
ADR .... Aircraft Discrepancy Report
ADR .... Air Defense Region (NATG)
ADR .... Air Defense Requirement (SAA)
ADR .... Air Design Review (MCD)
ADR .... Airfield Damage Repair [*Military*]
ADR .... Alianza Democratica Revolucionaria [*Democratic Revolutionary Alliance*] [*Bolivia*]
ADR .... Alternative Dispute Resolution
ADR .... Alternative Dispute Resolution (WYGK)
ADR .... Alzheimer's Disease Research
ADR .... American Depositary Receipt
ADR .... Ammunition Disposition Request [*or Report*]
ADR .... Analog-Digital Recorder [*Computer science*]
ADR .... Anderson Reservoir [*California*] [*Seismograph station code, US Geological Survey*] (SEIS)
ADR .... Angle Data Recorder
ADR .... Aperture Direct Read-Out
ADR .... Appellate Division Reports [*Massachusetts*] [*A publication*] (DLA)
ADR .... Applied Data Research [*Commercial firm*] (NITA)
ADR .... Applied Data Research, Inc. [*Princeton, NJ*] (TSSD)
ADR .... Army Density Report
ADR .... Asia Data Research, Inc. [*Database producer*] (IID)
ADR .... Asset Depreciation Range [*IRS*]
ADR .... Audit Discrepancy Report (NRCH)
ADR .... Austin Data Recorder [*Military*] (SAA)
ADR .... Australian De Facto Relationships Law [*A publication*]
ADPT .... Australian Design Rule [*Automotive technology*]
ADR .... Australian Disabilities Review [*A publication*]
ADR .... Automated Demand Resolution [*FAA*] (TAG)

ADR .... Automated Durability Road
ADR .... Automatical Digital Relay (PDAA)
ADR .... Automatic Data Relay
ADR .... Automatic Dialogue Replacement
ADR .... Automatic Distortion Reduction (IAA)
ADR .... Automatic Dividend Reinvestment [Investment term]
ADR .... Average Daily Rate [Hotels]
ADR .... Aviation Design Research [Navy]
ADR .... Aviation Machinist's Mate, Reciprocating Engine Mechanic [Navy rating]
ADR .... Award Resources [Vancouver Stock Exchange symbol]
ADR1 .... Aviation Machinist's Mate, Reciprocating Engine Mechanic, First Class [Navy rating]
ADR2 .... Aviation Machinist's Mate, Reciprocating Engine Mechanic, Second Class [Navy rating]
ADR3 .... Aviation Machinist's Mate, Reciprocating Engine Mechanic, Third Class [Navy rating]
ADRA .... Administrative Dispute Resolution Act (AAGC)
ADRA .... Administrative Dispute Resolution Act of 1996 (AAGC)
ADRA .... Adventist Development and Relief Agency, International (EA)
ADRA .... American Drag Racing Association [Commercial firm] (EA)
ADRA .... Animal Diseases Research Association [Moredun Institute] [British] (ARC)
ADRA .... Army Dollar Resource Allocation
ADRA .... Automatic Dynamic Response Analyzer (PDAA)
ADRA .... Automotive Dismantlers and Recyclers Association (EA)
ADRA .... Automotive Dismantlers and Recyclers Association (EA)
ADRAA .... Airman Apprentice, Aviation Machinist's Mate, Reciprocating Engine Mechanic, Striker [Navy rating]
ADRAC .... Automatic Digital Recording and Control
ADRAMS ...... Air Droppable Measurement System [Oceanography] (MSC)
ADRAN .... Advanced Digital Ranging System [NASA] (KSC)
ADRAN .... Airman, Aviation Machinist's Mate, Reciprocating Engine Mechanic, Striker [Navy rating]
A Dr & Dgn .. Associate in Drafting and Design
ADRAO .... Association pour le Developpement de la Riziculture en Afrique de l'Ouest [West Africa Rice Development Association - WARDA] (EAIO)
ADRAT .... Advanced Deep-Running Acoustic Torpedo (MCD)
ADRB .... Army Disability Review Board
ADRB .... Army Discharge Review Board
ADRC .... Alzheimer's Disease and Related Conditions [Medicine]
ADRC .... Alzheimer's Disease Research Center [Bronx, NY] [Department of Health and Human Services] (GRD)
ADRC .... American Dutch Rabbit Club (EA)
ADRC .... Animal Drug Research Center [Denver, CO] [Department of Health and Human Services] (GRD)
ADRC .... Association du Droit de Retransmission Canadien (AC)
ADRC .... Association of Drug Referral Centers [Australia]
ADRC .... Automatic Data Rate Changer
ADRC .... Aviation Machinist's Mate, Reciprocating Engine Mechanic, Chief [Navy rating]
ADRCM .... Aviation Machinist's Mate, Reciprocating Engine Mechanic, Master Chief [Navy rating]
ADRCS .... Aviation Machinist's Mate, Reciprocating Engine Mechanic, Senior Chief [Navy rating]
ADRDA .... Alzheimer's Disease and Related Disorders Association (EA)
ADRDE .... Advise Reason for Delay [Aviation] (FAAC)
ADRDE .... Air Defence Research and Development Establishment [Later, RRE] [British]
ADRECS ...... Advanced Recovery System (MCD)
ADREDPRED... Advise by Message Reduction Current Period of Active Duty [Military]
ADREN .... Adrenal [Gland] (ABBR)
Adrenex ...... Adrenalectomy [Medicine] (DAVI)
ADREP .... Aircraft Accident/Incident Reporting System [International Civil Aviation Organization] [Information service or system] (IID)
ADREP .... Automatic Data Processing Resource Estimating Procedures
ADRES .... Aircraft Data Recording Evaluation System (PDAA)
ADRES .... Army Data Retrieval Engineering System (MCD)
ADRES .... Army Data Retrieval System (NITA)
ADRF .... Australian Dental Research Fund
ADRG .... Applied Demographic Research Group [Database producer] (IID)
ADRG .... Assistant Deputy Registrar General [Canada]
ADRG .... Automatic Data Routing Group (AAG)
ADRI .... Animal Diseases Research Institute [Canada] (IRC)
ADRI .... Automatic Dead-Reckoning Instrument [Aviation] (PDAA)
ADRIA .... Adriamycin [Also called doxorubicin] [Antineoplastic drug] (DAVI)
Adria-L-PAM... Adriamycin, L-Phenylalanine Mustard [Antineoplastic drug regimen]
AdrianR .... Adrian Resources Ltd. [Associated Press] (SAG)
ADRIES .... Advanced Digital RADAR Imagery Exploitation System
ADRIQ .... Association des Directeurs de Recherche Industrielle du Quebec (AC)
ADRIS .... Association for the Development of Religious Information Systems (EA)
ADRIS .... Automatic Dead Reckoning Instrument Systems [Navigation] [Canada]
ADRJ .... Australian Dispute Resolution Journal [A publication]
ADRK .... Auxiliary Display Request Keyboard
ADRLT .... Association of Directors of Recreation, Leisure, and Tourism [British] (DBA)
ADRM .... Aerodrome
ADRM .... Darwin [Australia ICAO location identifier] (ICLI)
ADRM .... Drumheller Municipal Library, Alberta [Library symbol National Library of Canada] (NLC)

ADRMP .... Automatic Dialer with Recorded Message Player [Telecommunications]
ADRMPS ...... Auto-Dialed Remote Message Players [Telecommunications]
ADRN.......... Adrenaline (ABBR)
ADRN .... Advanced Document Revision Notice [NASA] (KSC)
ADRN .... Advance Drawing Release Notice (KSC)
ADRNDCK .... Adirondack (FAAC)
ADRNT........ Adornment (ABBR)
ADROBN ...... Airdrome Battalion
Ad Rom ...... Expositio of Epistulae ad Romanos [of Augustine] [Classical studies] (OCD)
Ad Rom Ant... Adams' Roman Antiquities [A publication] (DLA)
ADRP .... Acoustic Data Reduction Program (CAAL)
ADRP .... Adipose Differentiation-Related Protein [Medicine] (DMAA)
ADRP .... Adipose Fin and Right Pectoral Fin Clips [Pisciculture]
ADRP .... Airdrop [Military] (AABC)
ADRP .... Autosomal Dominant Retinitis Pigmentosa [Ophthalmology]
ADRPM .... Acoustic Detection Range Prediction Model (MCD)
ADRRB........ Army Disability Rating Review Board (AABC)
ADRS .... Address [Computer character] [Computer science] (AFM)
ADRS .... Airborne Digital Recording System
ADRS .... Analog-to-Digital Data Recording System [Computer science] (IEEE)
ADRS .... Asset Depreciation Range System [Accounting]
ADRS .... Automated Data Retrieval System (NRCH)
ADRS .... Automatic Data Reporting System (NATG)
ADRS .... Automatic Document Request (AIE)
ADRS .... Automatic Document Request Service [or System]
ADRS .... [A] Departmental Reporting System [IBM Corp.]
ADRSA .... Assistant Data Recording System Analyst (MUGU)
ADRSE .... Addressee (ABBR)
ADRSS .... Automated Data Reports Submission System
ADRT .... Adroit (ABBR)
ADRT .... Adroit
ADRT .... Alternate Departure Route [Air Traffic Control] (FAAC)
ADRT .... Analog Data Recorder Transcriber
ADRT .... Assistant Director of Railway Transport [British military] (DMA)
ADRTNS........ Adroitness (ABBR)
ADRTY .... Adroitly (ABBR)
ADRUSAR ..... Army Density Report, United States Army Reserve
ADRV .... Adipose Fin and Right Ventral Fin Clips [Pisciculture]
A-DRV .... Atomic Drive
ADRX .... Andrx Corp. [NASDAQ symbol] (SAG)
ADS .... Academie des Sciences [Academy of Science] [French]
ADS .... Accelerated Declassification System (NVT)
ADS .... Accessory Drive System (NG)
ADS .... Accident Documentation System [Safety research] [Automotive engineering]
ADS .... Accounting Data System
ADS .... Accurately Defined System [Computer science]
ADS .... Acoustic Doppler Sounder (MCD)
ADS .... Active Deferral Service (MCD)
ADS .... Activity Data Sheet (IEEE)
ADS .... Acute Diarrheal Syndrome [Medicine] (DMAA)
ADS .... Additive Delivery System
ADS .... Address (FAAC)
ADS .... Address Data Strobe [Electronics]
ADS .... Address Display System [or Subsystem]
ADS .... Administration of Designed Services (TEL)
ADS .... Administrative Data Systems
Ads .... Ad Sectam [At the Suit Of] [Legal term Latin]
Ads .... Adsorption
ADS .... Advanced Data Scalar
ADS .... Advanced Data System [DoD]
ADS .... Advanced Debugging System
ADS .... Advanced Declassification Schedule (MCD)
ADS .... Advanced Deep-Dive System (NVT)
ADS .... Advanced Digital Systems [Commercial firm] (NITA)
ADS .... Advanced Display System
ADS .... Advanced Distributed Simulation [Army]
ADS .... Advanced Diving System
ADS .... Advanced Dosimetry System (PDAA)
ADS .... Advanced Dressing Station [British]
ADS .... Adversus [Against] [Latin] (ROG)
ADS .... Advertising Dimensions Standards [American Newspaper Publishers Association]
ADS .... AEGIS Display System (DNAB)
ADS .... Aerial Delivery System
ADS .... Aerial Demonstration Squadron (MCD)
ADS .... Aeronautical Design Standard [Army]
ADS .... Aerospace Data Systems (MCD)
ADS .... Affiliated Drug Stores (EA)
ADS .... Agent Distributor Service [Departments of State and Commerce]
ADS .... Aircraft Development Service [Air Force]
ADS .... Air Data Sensor [Aerospace] (MCD)
ADS .... Air Data System [or Subsystem] (RDA)
ADS .... Air Defense Sector [Air Force]
ADS .... Air Defense Ship (NATG)
ADS .... Air Defense Squadron [Air Force]
ADS .... Air Defense System
ADS .... Air Deployable Airborne Deception Device System
ADS .... Air Development Service (MCD)
ADS .... Air Development Station [Navy]
ADS .... Air Drop System [Army]
ADS ...... Airport Data System [FAA]
ADS .... Alaska Dental Society (SRA)

ADS	All-Digital Simulator
ADS	Alliance Democratique Senegalaise [*Allied Democratic Party of Senegal*] [*Political party*]
AD(S)	Allied Demands, Supplies [*World War II*]
ADS	Alpha Delta Sigma [*Fraternity*] (NTCM)
ADS	Alternate Delivery System [*Medicine*] (DHSM)
ADS	Alternate Device Support [*NASA*]
ADS	Alternative Delivery System [*Health care service*]
ADS	Alzheimer's Disease Society [*British*]
ADS	Amateur Dramatic Society [*Cambridge, England*]
ADS	America Defense Society (SAA)
ADS	American Daffodil Society (EA)
ADS	American Dahlia Society (EA)
ADS	American Denture Society
ADS	American Depositary Share (ECON)
ADS	American Dialect Society (EA)
ADS	American Driving Society (EA)
ADS	American Druze Society (EA)
ADS	Ammunition Distribution System
ADS	Anatomical Dead Space (DAVI)
ADS	Angle Data Subsystem
ADS	Anker Data Systems (IAA)
ADS	Annual Demographic Survey [*Bureau of the Census*] (GFGA)
ADS	Anomaly Dynamics Study [*NORPAX*]
ADS	Anonymous Donor's Sperm [*Obstetrics*] (DAVI)
ADS	Antex Data Systems (HGAA)
ADS	Antibody Deficiency Syndrome [*Immunology*] (MAE)
ADS	Anticipate Discharge Tomorrow [*Medicine*] (DAVI)
ADS	Anticoincidence Detection System
ADS	Antidiuretic Substance
ADS	Anti-Ice/De-Ice System [*or Subsystem*] (MCD)
ADS	Applicant Data System [*Department of Labor*]
ADS	Application Design Service [*IBM Corp.*]
ADS	Application Development Systems [*Computer science*]
ADS	Applied Decision Systems [*Information service or system*] (IID)
ADS	Arctic Drift Station
ADS	Arctic Drilling System
ADS	Area Detection System [*Military*] (LAIN)
ADS	Army Dental Service
ADS	Assault Data System (DNAB)
ADS	Association for Dressings and Sauces (EA)
ADS	Association of Diesel Specialists (EA)
ADS	Association of District Secretaries [*British*]
ADS	Aston Dark Space [*Physics*]
ADS	Astrophysics Data System
ADS	Atmospheric Diving Suit [*Deep sea diving*]
ADS	Atmospheric Diving System
ADS	Attitude Display System (MCD)
A/DS	Audio/Digital Systems [*Telecommunications service*] (TSSD)
ADS	Audio Distribution System (NASA)
ADS	August Derleth Society (EA)
ADS	Australian Driving Society
ADS	AutoCAD [*Computer-Aided Design*] Development System (PCM)
ADS	Autodesk Development System [*Computer science*] (PCM)
ADS	Autograph Document Signed [*Manuscript descriptions*]
ADS	Automated Declassification System (MCD)
ADS	Automated Design System (MCD)
ADS	Automated Dispatch System [*Telecommunications*]
ADS	Automated Documentation Systems [*Computer science*]
ADS	Automated Drafting System
ADS	Automatic Data System [*Computer science*]
ADS	Automatic Defense System (MCD)
ADS	Automatic Degaussing System (DWSG)
ADS	Automatic Dependence Surveillance System [*International Civil Aviation Organisation*]
ADS	Automatic Dependent Surveillance [*FAA*] (TAG)
ADS	Automatic Depressurization System [*Nuclear energy*] (NRCH)
ADS	Automatic Development System (MCD)
ADS	Automatic Digital Switch
ADS	Automatic Dispatch System [*Nuclear energy*] (NRCH)
ADS	Automatic Door Seal [*Technical drawings*]
ADS	Autopilot Disengage Switch (MCD)
ADS	Aviation Data Service, Inc. [*Information service or system*] (IID)
ADS	Aviation Depot Squadron [*Air Force*]
ADS	Aviones de Sonora SA [*Mexico ICAO designator*] (FAAC)
ADS	Azimuth Determining System [*Army Space Technology and Research Office*] (RDA)
ADS	Azione Dinamico-Specifico [*Dynamic-Specific Action*] [*Italian Medicine*]
ADS	Dallas, TX [*Location identifier FAA*] (FAAL)
ADSA	Air-Derived Separation Assurance [*Aviation*]
ADSA	Alberta Deaf Sports Association (AC)
ADSA	Alberta Debate & Speech Association (AC)
ADSA	American Dairy Science Association (EA)
ADSA	American Dental Society of Anesthesiology (EA)
ADSA	Art Deco Societies of America (EA)
ADSA	Associated Driving Schools of Australia
ADSA	Atomic Defense Support Agency
ADSA	Australian Down Syndrome Association
ADSA	Australian Drama Studies Association
AD SAEC	Ad Saeculum [*To the Century*] [*Latin*] (ADA)
ADSAF	Automatic Data System within the Army in the Field
ADSAI	American Dermatologic Society of Allergy and Immunology (EA)
AD/SAM	Air Defense - Surface-to-Air Missile
ADS & T	Assistant Director of Supplies and Transport [*Military British*]

ADSAP	Advise as Soon as Possible (NOAA)
ADSAQ	Association des Distributeurs Aux Services Alimentaires du Quebec (AC)
ADSARM	Advanced Defense Suppression Antiradiation Missile
ADSAS	Air-Derived Separation Assurance System [*Aviation*]
AD SAT	Ad Saturandum [*To Saturation*] [*Pharmacy*]
ADSAT	Anomalous Dispersion Spherical Array Target [*for increasing radio reflectivity*]
AD SATUR	Ad Saturandum [*To Saturation*] [*Pharmacy*]
ADSB	Adsorb (ABBR)
ADSBNT	Adsorbent (ABBR)
ADSBT	Adsorbent (ABBR)
ADSC	Active Duty Service Commitment [*Military*] (AFM)
ADSC	Advanced Section Communication Zone [*World War II*]
ADSC	Air Defense Software Committee (NATG)
ADSC	Air Defense Systems Command
ADSC	Association of Drilled Shaft Contractors (EA)
ADSC	Automatic Data Service Center
ADSC	Automatic Digital Switching Center (IEEE)
ADSC	Average Daily Service Charge [*Hospitals*]
ADSCOM	Advanced Shipboard Communications (MCD)
ADSCS	Aided Display Submarine Control System [*Navy*] (MCD)
ADSD	Active Duty Service Date [*Military*] (DNAB)
ADSD	Addressed [*Computer science*] (IAA)
ADSD	Air Defense Systems Directorate (NATG)
ADSDA	Advise Earliest Date (NOAA)
ADSDP	Automated Data System Development Plan [*Military*] (MCD)
ADSE	Addressee
ADSE	Alternative Delivery Schedule Evaluator (MHDB)
ADSE	American Dental Society of Europe (EA)
AD SEC	Advance Section [*Military*]
ADSEC	Air Defense System Engineering Committee
ADSEL	Address-Selective [*British*] (MCD)
ADSEP	Automatic Data Set Editing Program [*NASA*] (KSC)
ADSF	Australian Deaf Sports Federation
ADSF	Australian Disabled Skiers' Federation
ADSF	Automated Directional Solidification Furnace [*Materials processing*]
ADSG	Atomic Defense and Space Group [*Westinghouse Electric Corp.*] (MCD)
Ad Sh	Advance Sheet (DLA)
ADSH	Audio Stream Handler (PCM)
ADSHIPDA	Advise Shipping Data (AABC)
ADSHIPDA	Advise Shipping Date
ADSHPDAT	Advise Shipping Date
ADSI	Active Directory Service Interface [*Computer science*]
ADSI	Adapted Delivered Source Instruction
ADSI	American Disposal Services, Inc. [*NASDAQ symbol*] (SAG)
ADSI	Analog Display Services Interface [*Interactive television technology*] (PS)
ADSIA	Allied Data System Interoperability Agency [*Brussels, Belgium*] [*NATO*]
ADSID	Air Defense Systems Integration Division [*Air Force*]
ADSID	Air-Delivered Seismic Intrusion Detectors
ADSIGS	Assistant Director of Signals (IAA)
ADSIM	Advanced Simulation [*Missions project*]
ADSIM	Airfield Delay Simulation Model [*FAA*] (TAG)
ADSK	Autodesk, Inc. [*NASDAQ symbol*] (SAG)
ADSK	Autodesk, Inc. [*NASDAQ symbol*] (TTSB)
ADSL	Assembly Department Shortage List
ADSL	Asymmetrical Digital Single Line (DMAA)
ADSL	Asymmetric Digital Subscriber Line [*Telecommunications*]
ADSL	Asynchronous Digital Subscriber Loop [*Computer science*]
ADSL	Authorized Depot Stockage List [*Army*]
ADSL	Auxiliary of the Decalogue Society of Lawyers (EA)
ADSM	Air Defense Service Medal [*Military decoration*] (GFGA)
ADSM	Air Defense Suppression Missile (AABC)
ADSM	American Defense Service Medal (BARN)
ADSM	Automated Data Systems Manual [*Military*] (GFGA)
ADSMO	Air Defense System Management Office [*Air Force*]
ADSN	Accounting and Disbursing Station Number [*Air Force*] (AFM)
ADSO	Adaptive Solutions [*NASDAQ symbol*] (TTSB)
ADSO	Adaptive Solutions, Inc. [*NASDAQ symbol*] (SAG)
ADSO	Aerospace Defense Systems Officer [*Air Force*] (AFM)
ADS/O	Application Development System/Online [*Computer science*] (HGAA)
ADSO	Assistant Division Supply Officer [*Army*]
ADSO	Automatic Display Switching Oscilloscope
ADSOC	Administrative Support Operations Center [*Army*]
ADSOD	Air Defense Systems Operation Division (SAA)
ADSOL	Analysis of Dynamical Systems Online [*Computer science*] (MHDI)
ADSORB	Adsorbent
ADSOS	Advance Services of Supply [*Army*]
ADSOT	Automatic Daily System Operability Test
ADSOW	Adaptive Solutions Wrrt [*NASDAQ symbol*] (TTSB)
ADSP	Adaptive Digital Signal Processor (MCD)
ADSP	Advanced Design Special Processor (LAIN)
ADSP	Advanced Digital SAR Processor (MCD)
ADSP	Advanced Digital Signal Processor
ADSP	AppleTalk Data Stream Protocol [*Apple Computer, Inc.*] (PCM)
ADSP	Ariel Corp. [*NASDAQ symbol*] (SAG)
ADSP	Automatic Dispatching Stick Repeater
ADSPEC	Additional Specialty [*Military*] (INF)
ADSPN	Adsorption (ABBR)
ADSPN	Advise Disposition [*Aviation*] (FAAC)
ADSPSE	Assistance for Disabled Students in Post-Secondary Education [*Australia*]

ADSPU	Ariel Corp. Unit 2000 [*NASDAQ symbol*] (TTSB)
ADSPW	Ariel Corp. Wrrt [*NASDAQ symbol*] (TTSB)
ADSq	Air Defense Squadron [*Vietnam*] [*Air Force*] (AFM)
ADSQ	Audio Data Sequence [*Telecommunications*] (NTCM)
ADSR	Attack/Decay/Sustain/Release [*Audio programming parameters*]
ADSS	Advanced Digital Simulation System (MCD)
ADSS	Aerospace Data Systems Standard (SSD)
ADSS	Aircraft Damage Sensing System
ADSS	Air Data Screening System [*Environmental Protection Agency*] (GFGA)
ADSS	Air Defense Suppression System (MCD)
ADSS	Analysis of Digitized Seismic Signals [*Computer science*]
ADSS	Army Decision Support System
ADSS	Association of Directors of Social Services (EAIO)
ADSS	Automated Data Subsystem (AABC)
ADSS	Automated Dictionary Support System [*Army*] (RDA)
ADSS	Automatic Data Switching System [*Deep Space Network*]
ADST	Advanced Distributed Simulation Technology [*Army*] (RDA)
ADST	Approved Deferred Share Trust (ODBW)
ADST	Association for the Development of Social Therapy [*Defunct*] (EA)
ADST	AUTODIN Digital Subscriber Terminal (AABC)
ADSTADIS	Advise Status and/or Disposition [*Army*]
ADSTAP	Advancement, Strength, and Training Plan System
ADSTAR	Advance Document Storage and Retrieval
ADSTAR	Automatic Document Storage and Retrieval [*Computer science*]
ADST FEB	Adstante Febre [*When Fever Is Present*] [*Pharmacy*]
ADSTKOH	Advise Stock on Hand [*Army*]
ADS-TP	Administrative Data Systems - Teleprocessing (IEEE)
ADSU	Advanced Direct Support Unit (NATG)
ADSU	Air Data Sensor Unit (MCD)
ADSU	Airstream Direction Sensing Unit (MCD)
ADSU	Albrecht Durer Study Unit [*American Topical Association*] (EA)
ADSU	Automatic Dependent Surveillance Unit [*ICAO designator*] (FAAC)
ADSUP	Automatic Data System Uniform Practices [*A programming language*]
ADSVAL	Air Defense Simulator Evaluation (MCD)
ADSW	Advanced Defense Suppression Weapon
ADSW	Association of Directors of Social Work (EAIO)
ADSWSO	Air Defense Special Weapons Support Organization
ADSYM	Automobile Defog/Defrost System Model (PDAA)
ADSYS	Air Device Systems [*Honda Motor Co.*] [*Automotive air conditioning*]
ADT	Abstract Data Type [*Computer science*]
ADT	Accelerated Deactivation Test [*Chemistry*]
ADT	Accelerated Development Test (MUGU)
ADT	Accepted Dental Therapeutics
ADT	Access Developer's Toolkit [*Microsoft Corp.*] (PCM)
ADT	Active Disk Table [*Computer science*] (IBMDP)
ADT	Active Duty for Training [*Army*] (AABC)
ADT	Actual Departure Time (CINC)
ADT	Actual Dive Time
ADT	Adaptive Technologies (Canada) [*Vancouver Stock Exchange symbol*]
ADT	Adenosine Triphosphate [*Biochemistry*] (AAMN)
ADT	Admission/Discharge/Transfer [*Hospital records*] (DHSM)
ADT	ADT Limited [*NYSE symbol*] (TTSB)
ADT	ADT Ltd. [*NYSE symbol*] (SPSG)
ADT	Adult Diphtheria and Tetanus Virus
ADT	Advanced Design Team
ADT	Advanced Development Technology (KSC)
ADT	Advanced Dispenser Technology (MCD)
ADT	Advanced Driver Training [*British military*] (DMA)
ADT	Aerated Drain Tank [*Nuclear energy*] (NRCH)
ADT	Aerial Demonstration Team
ADT	Agar-Gel Diffusion Test [*Clinical chemistry*] (MAE)
ADT	Aided Tracking
ADT	Airborne Data Terminal (MCD)
ADT	Airborne Digital Timer
ADT	Air Data Transducer [*Aerospace*] (MCD)
AD/T	Air Detector/Tracker (CAAL)
ADT	Air Dorval Ltd. [*Canada ICAO designator*] (FAAC)
ADT	Air-Dried Ton
ADT	Alaskan Daylight Time
ADT	Alternate-Day Treatment [*Medicine*]
ADT	American District Telegraph
ADT	Amphibious Training Demonstrator
ADT	Androgen-Deprivation Therapy [*Medicine*]
ADT	Anethole Dithiolthione [*Biochemistry*]
ADT	Anti-Dumping Tribunal [*Canada*]
ADT	Antigen Detection Test [*Clinical chemistry*]
ADT	Any Desired Thing [*Notation in a placebo prescription*] [*Medicine*]
ADT	Application Dedicated Terminal [*Computer science*] (IAA)
ADT	Approved Departure Time (MCD)
ADT	Arizona Dance Theatre
ADT	Articulated Dump Truck [*Caterpillar Tractor Co.*]
ADT	Assistant Director for Training [*National Security Agency*]
ADT	Assistant Director of Torpedoes [*Navy British*]
ADT	Assured Depot Task
ADT	Asynchronous Data Transceiver
ADT	Asynchronous Data Transfer [*Transmission technique*] (CDE)
ADT	Atlantic Daylight Time
ADT	Atomic Damage Template [*Military drafting*]
ADT	Attribute Distributed Tree (MHDI)
ADT	Atwood, KS [*Location identifier FAA*] (FAAL)
ADT	Auditory Discrimination Test ["*Wepman*"] [*Education*]
ADT	Australian Dance Theatre [*Adelaide*]
ADT	Automated Dithionate Test (AAMN)

ADT	Automatic Data Translator [*or Transmitter*]
ADT	Automatic Debit Transfer [*Banking*]
ADT	Automatic Detection and Tracking (MCD)
ADT	Autonomous Data Transfer
ADT	Average Daily Traffic
AdT	Die Agada der Tannaiten (BJA)
ADTA	Aircraft Development Test Activity [*Army*] (MCD)
ADTA	Air Data Transducer Assembly [*Aerospace*] (NASA)
ADTA	American Dance Therapy Association (EA)
ADTA	American Dental Trade Association (EA)
ADTA	Association of Defense Trial Attorneys (EA)
ADTA	Australian Driver Trainers' Association
ADTA	Aviation Development Test Activity [*Test and Evaluation Command*] [*Army*] (RDA)
ADTAC	Air Defense Tactical Air Commander [*Air Force*]
ADTAC	Tactical Air Command, Deputy Commander for Air Defense (MCD)
ADTAKE	Action Decision [*or Determination*] Taken
ADTAKE	Advice Decision [*or Determination*] Taken
ADTAKE	Advise What Action Has Been Taken [*Military*] (NVT)
ADTAM	Air-Delivered Target-Activated Munitions (AFM)
ADTC	Advanced Deposition Tech [*NASDAQ symbol*] (TTSB)
ADTC	Advanced Deposition Technologies [*NASDAQ symbol*] (SAG)
ADTC	Air Defense Technical Center (NATG)
ADTC	Armament Development and Test Center [*Eglin Air Force Base, FL*] (MCD)
ADTC	Tennant Creek [*Australia ICAO location identifier*] (ICLI)
ADTCW	Advanced Deposition Tech Wrrt [*NASDAQ symbol*] (TTSB)
ADTD	Apollo Docking Test Device [*NASA*]
ADTD	Association of Data Terminal Distributors
ADTD	Association of Disciples for Theological Discussion (EA)
ADTDS	Air Defense Tactical Data Systems [*Missile minder*] (RDA)
ADTe	Anodal Duration Tetanus [*Physiology*] (DMAA)
ADTe	Tetanic Contraction [*Neurology*] (DAVI)
ADTEC	Advanced Decoy Technology (SAA)
ADTECH	Advanced Decoy Technology (MCD)
AD TERT VIC	Ad Tertiam Vicem [*Three Times*] [*Pharmacy*]
ADTF	Australian Dairy Traders' Federation
ADTF	Aviation Development Test Facility (MCD)
ADTG	Application Development Task Group [*Navy*]
ADTI	American Dinner Theatre Institute (EA)
ADTI	Association pour le Developpement du Tourisme International [*Louveciennes, France*] (EAIO)
ADTIC	Arctic-Desert-Tropic Information Center [*Air University*] [*Maxwell Air Force Base, AL*]
ADTK	Adept Technology [*NASDAQ symbol*] (TTSB)
ADTK	Adept Technology, Inc. [*NASDAQ symbol*] (SAG)
ADTLP	Army-Wide Doctrinal and Training Literature Program
AD/TMD	Air Defense/Theater Missile Defense
ADTMP	Tyrrell Museum of Palaeontology, Drumheller, Alberta [*Library symbol National Library of Canada*] (NLC)
ADTN	Addition (ABBR)
ADTN	Adminstrative Data Transmission Network [*FAA*] (TAG)
ADTN	Adtran, Inc. [*NASDAQ symbol*] (SAG)
ADTN	Aminodihydroxytetrahydronaphthalene [*Organic chemistry*]
ADTn	Assistant Director of Transportation [*British military*] (DMA)
ADTN	Tindal [*Australia ICAO location identifier*] (ICLI)
ADTNG	Auditing
ADTNL	Additional (ABBR)
ADTNLY	Additionally (ABBR)
Ad Torts	Addison on Torts [*A publication*] (DLA)
ADTP	Accelerated Development Test Program (AAG)
ADTP	Alcohol Dependency Treatment Program (DAVI)
ADTR	Alcohol and Drug Treatment and Rehabilitation Block Grant [*Department of Health and Human Services*] (GFGA)
AD-TR	Armament Development Technical Report
Adtran	Adtran, Inc. [*Associated Press*] (SAG)
Ad Tr M	Adams on Trade Marks [*A publication*] (DLA)
ADTRM	Auditorium
ADTS	Airborne Data Transfer System (MCD)
ADTS	Air Data Test System
ADTS	Automated Data and Telecommunications Service [*Later, Office of Information andResources Management*]
ADTS	Automatic Data Test System [*Bell System*]
ADTS	Automatic Data Transfer System (MCD)
ADTS	Avionics Depot Test Station (MCD)
ADTSC	Auto Dealers Traffic Safety Council [*HUF*] [*Absorbed by*] (EA)
ADTSEA	American Driver and Traffic Safety Education Association (EA)
ADTU	Automatic Digital Test Unit
ADTU	Auxiliary Data Translator Unit
ADTV	Additive (ABBR)
ADU	Acceleration-Deceleration Unit
ADU	Accumulation Distribution Unit [*Computer science*]
ADU	Adapter Unit (NG)
ADU	Aircraft Delivery Unit [*Air Force*]
ADU	Air Distribution Unit [*Portable cooling system*] [*Air Force*]
ADU	Americans for Democracy in Ukraine (EA)
ADU	Ammonium Diuranate [*Inorganic chemistry*]
ADU	Analog Delay Unit
ADU	Analog Display Unit
ADU	Angular Display Unit (IAA)
ADU	Angular Display Unit (IAA)
ADU	Annunciator Display Unit (MCD)
ADU	Arc Detector Unit
ADU	Audubon, IA [*Location identifier FAA*] (FAAL)
ADU	Automatic Data Unit

ADU .... Automatic Dialing Unit [*Telecommunications*]
adu .... Automatic Dialing Unit (IDOE)
ADU .... Auxiliary Display Unit
ADU .... Duchess Public Library, Alberta [*Library symbol National Library of Canada*] (NLC)
ADUC .... Adduce (ABBR)
ADUCB........ Adducable (ABBR)
ADUCD........ Adduced (ABBR)
ADUCG........ Adducing (ABBR)
ADUCTD...... Adducted (ABBR)
ADUCTG...... Adducting (ABBR)
ADUCTN...... Adduction (ABBR)
ADUCTV...... Adductive (ABBR)
ADUF .... Duffield Public Library, Alberta [*Library symbol National Library of Canada*] (NLC)
ADUL .... Adulate (ABBR)
ADULD........ Adulated (ABBR)
ADULG........ Adulating (ABBR)
ADULN .... Adulation (ABBR)
ADULR........ Adulator (ABBR)
ADULT .... Adulterant (ABBR)
ADULT .... Adulterate (ABBR)
ADULT .... Adulteration (ABBR)
ADULT .... Adultery (DLA)
Adult L........ Adult Learning [*A publication*] (BRI)
adult progressive SMA... Spinal Muscular Atrophy [*Aran-Duchenne type*] (PAZ)
ADULY........ Adulatory (ABBR)
ADUM .... Automated Data Unit Movement (AABC)
Ad Us......... Ad Usum [*According to Custom*] [*Pharmacy*]
AD US EXTER... Ad Usum Externum [*For External Use*] [*Pharmacy*]
ADUT .... Advanced Development Unit Test [*Army*]
ADUY .... Arduously (ABBR)
ADV .... Acid Degree Value [*Food technology*]
ADV .... Acoustic Doppler Velocimeter [*Instrumentation*]
ADV .... Acreage Diversion [*Agriculture*]
ADV .... Actinomycin-D, Dacarbazine, Vincristine [*Antineoplastic drug regimen*]
ADV .... Adenovirus [*Also, AD*]
ADV .... Ad Valorem [*According to the Value*] [*Latin Business term*]
ADV .... Advance [*Flowchart*] (AFM)
ADV .... Advance Air Charters [*Canada ICAO designator*] (FAAC)
ADV .... Advanced
ADV .... Advanced Development Vehicle
ADV .... Advanced Micro Devices, Inc.
ADV .... Advantage
ADV .... Advent
ADV .... Adverb [*or Adverbial*]
ADV .... Adversus [*or Adversum*] [*Against*] [*Latin*]
ADV .... Advertisement
adv............. Advertising (WDMC)
ADV .... Advest Group [*NYSE symbol*] (TTSB)
ADV .... [*The*] Advest Group, Inc. [*NYSE symbol*] (SPSG)
ADV .... Advice (ROG)
ADV .... Advise [*Legal term*]
ADV .... Advisory
adv............. Advisory (DD)
adv............. Advocaat [*Barrister*] [*Netherlands*] (ILCA)
Adv .... Advocate [*Ife, Nigeria*] [*1968*] [*A publication*] (ILCA)
Adv .... Advocate [*Cleveland*] [*1929*] [*A publication*] (ILCA)
Adv .... Advocate [*Canada*] [*1943*] [*A publication*] (ILCA)
ADV .... Airborne Digital Voltmeter
ADV .... Air Defense Variant
ADV .... Air Diverter Valve [*Automotive engineering*]
ADV .... Aleutian Disease Virus [*of mink*]
ADV .... Anti-Diesel Device [*Automotive engineering*]
ADV .... Anti-Drainback Valve [*Automotive engineering*]
ADV .... Arc Drop Voltage
ADV .... Archer International Developments Ltd. [*Vancouver Stock Exchange symbol*]
A/DV .... Arterio/Deep Venous [*Medicine*]
ADV .... Atmospheric Dump Valves [*Nuclear energy*] (NRCH)
ADV .... Drayton Valley Public Library, Alberta [*Library symbol National Library of Canada*] (NLC)
ADV .... Improper Use of Adverb [*Used in correcting manuscripts, etc.*]
ADVA .... Advanced Digital Systems, Inc. [*NASDAQ symbol*]
ADVA .... Advanced Soviet [*Combined with GENS to form A Group*] [*Division of National Security Agency*]
ADVA .... American Division Veterans Association (EA)
ADVA .... American Deaf Volleyball Association (EA)
AdvA&S .... Advanced Aerodynamics & Structures, Inc. [*Associated Press*] (SAG)
ADVAC........ Advise Acceptance (NOAA)
Adv (Adel) ... Advertiser (Adelaide) [*A publication*]
ADVAILTRANS... Advise Appropriate Command Having Cognizance of Transportation when Available for Transportation [*Military*] (DNAB)
ADVAILTRANSCONUS... Advise Appropriate Command Having Cognizance of Transportation when Available for Transportation to Continental United States [*Military*]
ADVAILTRANSPOE... Advise [*Command Designated*] Date Available for Transportation from Port ofEmbarkation [*Military*]
AD VAL .... Ad Valorem [*According to the Value*] [*Latin Business term*]
ADVAL .... Advise Availability [*Army*]
ADVAL .... Air Defense Evaluation Tests (MCD)
ADVALT .... Allotment Advice (FAAC)
ADVANC....... Advanced Driver and Vehicle Advisory Navigation Concept

ADVANCE..... Advanced Driver And Vehicle Advisory Navigation Concept [*FHWA*] (TAG)
ADVANCE.... Advanced Driver and Vehicle Navigation Concept
ADVANCE.... Advanced Driver and Vehicle Navigation Concept
ADVANCE.... Airborne Doppler Velocity Altitude Navigation Compass Equipment (MCD)
ADVANCE..... Army Data Validation and Netting Capabilities Establishment
Advance Aust... Advance Australia [*A publication*]
ADVANCEM... Advancement (DLA)
Advant .... Advanta Corp. [*Associated Press*] (SAG)
Advanta .... ADVANTA Corp. [*Associated Press*] (SAG)
AdvantB .... Advanta Corp. [*Associated Press*] (SAG)
ADVAST .... Advanced Station (MHDI)
ADVATG .... Advantage (ABBR)
ADVATGUS... Advantageous (ABBR)
ADVATGUSY... Advantageously (ABBR)
ADVB .... Adverbial
AdvBcp .... Advantage Bancorp, Inc. [*Associated Press*] (SAG)
ADVBL .... Adverbial (ABBR)
Adv Bl......... Advokatbladet [*Denmark*] [*1921-*] [*A publication*] (ILCA)
ADV-BR....... Advanced Branch [*Training*] [*Military*] (DNAB)
Adv C .... Advanced Certificate (PGP)
ADVCA .... Advocate (ABBR)
ADVCAD...... Advocated (ABBR)
ADVCAG...... Advocating (ABBR)
ADVCAN...... Advocation (ABBR)
ADVCAP....... Advance Capability (MCD)
AdvCert........ Advanced Certificate
AdvCertApplMgtComm... Advanced Certificate in Applied Management Communication
AdvCertBankFin... Advanced Certificate in Banking and Finance
AdvCertBuildCons... Advanced Certificate in Building Construction
AdvCertBuildInsp... Advanced Certificate in Building Inspection
AdvCertCustomsAgProc... Advanced Certificate in Customs Agent Procedures
AdvCertEstateAg... Advanced Certificate in Estate Agency
AdvCertFurnProd... Advanced Certificate in Furniture Production
Adv Cert in Ed... Advanced Certificate in Education
Adv Cert in Mus Ed... Advanced Certificate in Music Education
AdvCertMgt... Advanced Certificate in Management
AdvCertOffMgt... Advanced Certificate in Office Management
AdvCertPers... Advanced Certificate in Personnel
AdvCertSalesMgt... Advanced Certificate in Sales Management
ADVCHG ...... Advance Change (DNAB)
Adv Chron... Advocates' Chronicle [*India*] [*A publication*] (DLA)
ADVCTN....... Advection [*NWS*] (FAAC)
ADVCY .... Advocacy (ABBR)
AdvD .... Advanced Deposition Technologies [*Associated Press*] (SAG)
AdvDep........ Advanced Deposition Technologies [*Associated Press*] (SAG)
ADV DEV..... Advanced Development [*Army*]
AdvDIn........ Advanced Digital Information Corp. [*Associated Press*] (SAG)
AdvDip........ Advanced Diploma
AdvDipEd..... Advanced Diploma in Education (ADA)
AdvDipT....... Advanced Diploma in Teaching
ADVDISC...... Advance Discontinuance of Allotment
ADVDLA-DEP... Advance Payment of Dislocation Allowance to Dependents [*Air Force*] (AFM)
AdvDp .... Advanced Deposition Technologies [*Associated Press*] (SAG)
ADVEC .... Advection (ABBR)
ADVECT .... Advection (ABBR)
adven.......... Adventurer
AdvEnId .... Advanced Energy Industries, Inc. [*Associated Press*] (SAG)
ADVENT .... Ada Development Environment (SSD)
Advent .... Advent Software, Inc. [*Associated Press*] (SAG)
AdvEnv........ Advanced Environ Recycling Technologies, Inc. [*Associated Press*] (SAG)
advers .... Advertisement (BARN)
ADVERSAT... Adversative (ABBR)
ADVERT .... Advertisement
ADVERTIS..... Advertising (DLA)
Advert L Anth... Advertising Law Anthology [*A publication*] (ILCA)
ADVERTNC... Advertence (ABBR)
Advest .... [*The*] Advest Group, Inc. [*Associated Press*] (SAG)
ADVET .... Australian Directory of Vocational Education and Training [*A publication*]
AdvFCm ...... Advanced Fibre Communications [*Associated Press*] (SAG)
AdvFin .... Advanced Financial, Inc. [*Associated Press*] (SAG)
AdvFn .... Advanced Financial, Inc. [*Associated Press*] (SAG)
AdvFnlB .... Advance Financial Bancorp [*Associated Press*] (SAG)
Adv Frt........ Advance Freight [*Shipping*] (MHDW)
ADVG .... Advancing (IAA)
ADVG .... Advantage (MSA)
ADVG .... Advantage Companies, Inc. [*NASDAQ symbol*] (SAG)
advg............ Advertising
Adv Gd........ Advanced Guard [*British military*] (DMA)
ADVGP........ Advisory Group
ADVH .... Advanced Health Corp. [*NASDAQ symbol*] (SAG)
ADVHED....... Advanced Headquarters (MUGU)
AdvHlt.......... Advantage Health Corp. [*Associated Press*] (SAG)
ADVICE .... Analytical Determination of the Values of Information to Combat Effectiveness (PDAA)
advid .... Advertising Video (WDMC)
ADVID.......... Advertising Videotape
ADV INTEL CEN... Advanced Intelligence Center [*Navy*]
Adv Iovinian... Adversus Iovinianum [*of St. Jerome*] [*Classical studies*] (OCD)
ADVIRC........ Autosomal Dominant Vitreo-Retinochoroidopathy [*Medicine*] (DMAA)

ADVISE........ Area Denial Visual Indication Security Equipment (MCD)
ADVISER..... Airborne Dual-Channel Variable Input Severe Environmental Recorder/Reproducer [*Air Force*] (MCD)
ADVISOR..... Advanced Integrated Safety and Optimizing Computer
ADV/L .... Advance Leave [*Military*]
ADVL .... Adverbial (ABBR)
AdvLfe .... Advantage Life Products [*Associated Press*] (SAG)
AdvLight ...... Advanced Lighting Technologies, Inc. [*Associated Press*] (SAG)
AdvLog .... Advanced Logic Research, Inc. [*Associated Press*] (SAG)
ADVLOGSYSCEN... Advanced Logistics Systems Center [*Air Force*]
ADVM .... Adaptive Delta Voice Modulation [*Air Force*]
Adv M .... Advanced Master (PGP)
AdvMag .... Advanced Magnetics [*Associated Press*] (SAG)
AdvMam ...... Advanced Mammography Systems [*Associated Press*] (SAG)
AdvMat .... Advanced Materials Group, Inc. [*Associated Press*] (SAG)
AdvMed .... Advanced Medical, Inc. [*Associated Press*] (SAG)
ADVMNT ...... Advancement
ADVMOS ...... Advanced Military Occupational Specialty [*Army*] (AABC)
ADV MTR ..... Advertising Matter [*Freight*]
ADVN .... Advance (FAAC)
ADVN .... Advanta Corp. [*NASDAQ symbol*] (SAG)
ADVNA......... ADVANTA Corp. Cl'A' [*NASDAQ symbol*] (TTSB)
ADVNB......... ADVANTA Corp. Cl'B' [*NASDAQ symbol*] (TTSB)
ADVNC........ Advance
ADVNC .... Advance (ABBR)
ADVNCD ...... Advanced (ABBR)
ADVNCD ...... Advanced
ADVNCG ...... Advancing (ABBR)
ADVNCNT .... Advancement (ABBR)
ADVNCT ...... Advancement (ABBR)
ADVNT .... Advent (ABBR)
AdvntCos ..... Advantage Companies, Inc. [*Associated Press*] (SAG)
ADVNTG ...... Advantage (ABBR)
ADVNTGD ... Advantaged (ABBR)
ADVNTGG ... Advantaging (ABBR)
ADVNTGU ... Advantageous (ABBR)
ADVNTGUY... Advantageously (ABBR)
ADVNTR...... Adventure (ABBR)
ADVNTR...... Adventure
ADVNTRD .... Adventured (ABBR)
ADVNTRES... Adventuress (ABBR)
ADVNTRG .... Adventuring (ABBR)
ADVNTRR .... Adventurer (ABBR)
ADVNTRSM... Adventuresome (ABBR)
ADVNTRU .... Adventurous (ABBR)
ADVNTRUS... Adventurous (ABBR)
ADVNTRUSY... Adventurously (ABBR)
ADVNZ........ ADVANTA Corp. Dep Shrs [*NASDAQ symbol*] (TTSB)
Adv O.......... Advance Opinions in Lawyers' Edition of United States Reports [*A publication*] (DLA)
ADVO .... Advocate (ABBR)
ADVOC........ Advocate (DLA)
Advocat........ Advocat, Inc. [*Associated Press*] (SAG)
ADVOCNET... Adult and Vocational Educational Electronic Mail Network [*National Center for Research in Vocational Education*] [*Columbus, OH*] [*Telecommunications*] (TSSD)
ADVOD........ Advocated (ABBR)
ADVOF........ Advise This Office (NOAA)
ADVOG........ Advocating (ABBR)
AdVoic........ Advanced Voice Technologies, Inc. [*Associated Press*] (SAG)
Advo Inc ...... Advo, Inc. [*Associated Press*] (SAG)
ADVON........ Advanced Echelon [*Marine Corps*]
ADVON........ Advanced Operations Unit [*Navy*]
ADVON........ Advocation (ABBR)
Adv Ops........ Advance Opinions [*A publication*] (DLA)
ADVOR........ Advocator (ABBR)
AdvOrtho..... Advanced Orthopedic Technologies, Inc. [*Associated Press*] (SAG)
ADVOS........ Advocates (ABBR)
ADV/P .... Advanced Pay
ADVP .... Advance Paradigm, Inc. [*NASDAQ symbol*] (SAG)
AdvPara....... Advance Paradigm, Inc. [*Associated Press*] (SAG)
AdvPhot....... Advanced Photonix, Inc. [*Associated Press*] (SAG)
ADVPMT...... Advance Payment [*Finance*]
AdvPoly....... Advanced Polymer Systems, Inc. [*Associated Press*] (SAG)
ADV POSS ... Adverse Possession [*Legal term*] (DLA)
advp oz........ Avoirdupois Ounce
AdvPro........ Advanced Promotion Technologies, Inc. [*Associated Press*] (SAG)
ADVR .... Advance Release [*Military*]
ADVR .... Advisor (AABC)
AdvRdio....... Advanced Radio Telecom Corp. [*Associated Press*] (SAG)
Adv Rep NJ... New Jersey Advance Reports and Weekly Law Review [*A publication*] (DLA)
AdvRoss ...... Advance Ross Corp. [*Associated Press*] (SAG)
ADVRS........ Adverse (ABBR)
ADVRS........ Assistant Director of Veterinary and Remount Services [*British military*] (DMA)
ADVRSNS.... Adverseness (ABBR)
ADVRSRY.... Adversary (ABBR)
ADVRST...... Adversity (ABBR)
ADVRSY...... Adversely (ABBR)
ADVRTNT..... Advertent (ABBR)
ADVRTZG.... Advertising (ABBR)
ADVRTZNT... Advertisement (ABBR)
ADVRTZR.... Advertiser (ABBR)
ADVRY........ Advisory

ADVS .... Advent Software [*NASDAQ symbol*] (TTSB)
ADVS .... Advent Software, Inc. [*NASDAQ symbol*] (SAG)
ADVS .... Advise (AFM)
ADVS .... Assistant Director of Veterinary Services [*Military British*]
ADVS .... Dixonville School, Alberta [*Library symbol National Library of Canada*] (BIB)
ADVSB .... Advisable (ABBR)
ADVSBT ...... Advisability (ABBR)
ADVSBY...... Advisably (ABBR)
ADVSCOL.... Advanced Schools (MUGU)
ADVSD........ Advised (ABBR)
ADVSDY...... Advisedly (ABBR)
AdvSem .... Advanced Semiconductor Materials International NV [*Associated Press*] (SAG)
ADVSG .... Advising (ABBR)
Adv Sh .... Advance Sheet (DLA)
ADVSNT...... Advisement (ABBR)
ADVSR........ Advisor (AFM)
ADVSR........ Advisor
ADVSRY...... Advisory (ABBR)
ADVST .... Advance Stoppage (MUGU)
ADVST .... Advisement (ABBR)
AdvSu .... Advanced Surgical, Inc. [*Associated Press*] (SAG)
AdvSurg....... Advanced Surgical, Inc. [*Associated Press*] (SAG)
ADVSY........ Adversary (ABBR)
ADVSY........ Advisory (AFM)
ADVT .... Advanced Development Verification Test (RDA)
ADVT .... Advantage Life Products [*NASDAQ symbol*] (NQ)
ADVT .... Advertise
advt .... Advertisement (ODBW)
advt .... Advertisement (WDMC)
advt .... Advertisement (VRA)
ADVT .... Advertisement (AABC)
ADVT .... Advertiser
advt .... Advertising (WDMC)
ADVT-C .... Advanced Development Verification Test - Coordinator (MCD)
AdvTch .... Advanced Technology Materials [*Commercial firm Associated Press*] (SAG)
ADVTD .... Advertised (ABBR)
ADVT-G .... Advanced Development Verification Test - Government (MCD)
ADVTG .... Advantage
ADVTG .... Advertising (ABBR)
advtg .... Advertising (DD)
ADVTGE ...... Advantage (ROG)
AdvThr .... Advanced Therapeutic Systems Ltd. [*Associated Press*] (SAG)
AdvTiss....... Advanced Tissue Sciences, Inc. [*Associated Press*] (SAG)
AdvTLb .... Advanced Technology Laboratories, Inc. [*Associated Press*] (SAG)
ADVTM .... Advisory Team
ADVTMT ...... Advertisement (ABBR)
ADVTNG ...... Advanced Training [*Military*] (NVT)
ADVTR........ Advertiser (ABBR)
ADVTSNG .... Advertising
ADVUL .... Air Defense Vulnerability Simulation [*Simulation game*]
ADVUSWS ... Naval Advanced Undersea Weapons School
ADVV .... Adverbs (ADA)
Adv Valent... Adversus Valentinianos [*of Tertullian*] [*Classical studies*] (OCD)
AdvVoic .... Advanced Voice Technologies, Inc. [*Associated Press*] (SAG)
ADVY .... Advisory [*NWS*] (FAAC)
ADW .... Aerial Distribution Wire [*Telecommunications*] (TEL)
ADW .... Air Defense Warning [*Air Force*]
ADW .... Air Defense Weapon
ADW .... Air Defense Wing [*Air Force*]
ADW .... Andres Wines Ltd. [*Toronto Stock Exchange symbol Vancouver Stock Exchange symbol*]
ADW .... Application Development Workbench [*Sterling Software, Atlanta, GA*] (CDE)
ADW .... Assault with Deadly Weapon
ADW .... Automated Data Wiring
ADW .... Camp Springs, MD [*Location identifier FAA*] (FAAL)
ADWA .... Atlantic Deeper Waterways Association (EA)
ADWAR........ Advanced Directional Warhead (MCD)
ADWC......... Air Defense Weapons Center [*Tyndall Air Force Base, FL*] (MCD)
ADWCP .... Automated Digital Weather Communications Program [*Air Force*] (AFM)
ADWCR....... Air Defense Weapons Center Regulation (MCD)
ADWE & M... Assistant Director of Works, Electrical and Mechanical [*Military British*]
ADWEPS ..... Air Defense Weapons Cost Effectiveness Study (AABC)
ADWKP....... Air Defense Warning Key Point [*Air Force*]
ADWS .... Air Defense Weapon System (MCD)
ADWS .... Automatic Digital Weather Switch [*Air Force*] (AFM)
ADWS .... Deadwood School, Alberta [*Library symbol National Library of Canada*] (BIB)
ADWSS .... Air Defense Weapon Simulation System (MCD)
ADX .... Adams Express [*NYSE symbol*] (TTSB)
ADX .... [*The*] Adams Express Co. [*NYSE symbol*] (SPSG)
ADX .... Add Index Register [*Computer science*] (IAA)
ADX .... Address Complete, Coin-Box [*Telecommunications*] (TEL)
ADX .... Adrenalectomized [*Medicine*]
ADX .... Advanced Development Experimental [*Army*] (AABC)
ADX .... Aerial (IAA)
ADX .... Air Defense Exercise [*Army/Air Force*] (AABC)
ADX .... Anderson Aviation, Inc. [*FAA designator*] (FAAC)
ADX .... Asymmetric Data Exchange
ADX .... Automatic Data Exchange

ADX	Automatic Digital Exchange [*Telecommunications*] (ODBW)
ADXR	Association of DX [*Distance*] Reporters (EA)
ADY	Additional Duty (AABC)
ADY	Aerodyne Executive Aviation Services [*ICAO designator*] (FAAC)
ADY	Audre Recognition Systems, Inc. [*Vancouver Stock Exchange symbol*]
Adye CM	Adye on Courts-Martial [*A publication*] (DLA)
ADYN	Amplidyne [*Electricity*] (KSC)
ADYN	Andyne Computing Ltd. [*NASDAQ symbol*] (SAG)
ADYNF	Andyne Computing [*NASDAQ symbol*] (TTSB)
ADZ	Advise
ADZ	Air Defense Zone [*Army/Airforce*] (NATG)
ADZ	San Andres Island [*Colombia*] [*Airport symbol*] (OAG)
ADZAR	Advise Arrival [*Aviation*] (FAAC)
ADZI	Advise Intentions [*Aviation*] (FAAC)
ADZOF	Advise This Office (FAAC)
ADZY	Advisory (FAAC)
AE	Abort Electronics [*Apollo*] [*NASA*]
AE	Above Elbow [*Medicine*]
A/E	Above Elbow [*Amputation*] [*Medicine*] (DMAA)
AE	Absolute Error
A/E	Absorptivity-Emissivity [*Ratio*]
AE	Academia Europaea
AE	Academic English
AE	Acceleration Enrichment [*Automotive fuel systems*]
AE	Accion Espanola [*Spanish Action*] [*Political party*] (PPE)
AE	Accommodation Endorsement [*Banking*]
AE	Account Executive [*Advertising, securities*]
AE	Accrued Expenditure [*Accounting*] (AFM)
AE	ACE Developments [*Vancouver Stock Exchange symbol*]
AE	Acid Equivalent (GNE)
AE	Acoustic Emission
AE	Acousto-Electric (PDAA)
AE	Acquisition Executive [*Military*] (DOMA)
AE	Acrodermatitis Enteropathica [*Medicine*]
AE	Activation Energy (MAE)
AE	Active Enhancement (MCD)
A/E	Activity Elements (MCD)
AE	Adam and Eve (EA)
AE	Adams Res & Energy [*AMEX symbol*] (TTSB)
AE	Adams Resources & Energy, Inc. [*AMEX symbol*] (SPSG)
AE	Added Entry [*Online database field identifier*]
AE	Additional Expenses
AE	Address Effective [*Computer science*] (IAA)
AE	Administrative Entity [*Job Training and Partnership Act*] (OICC)
AE	Adult Education
AE	Adult Education Quarterly [*A publication*] (BRI)
AE	Adult Erythrocyte [*Medicine*] (DMAA)
AE	Advance Engineering Memorandum (AAGC)
AE	Adverse Effects [*Medicine*]
AE	Aeon [*10^9 years*] [*Geology*]
Ae	Aerodrome Report [*Aviation*] (DA)
AE	Aeroelectronic (IEEE)
AE	Aero Flugzeugbau [*Germany ICAO aircraft manufacturer identifier*] (ICAO)
AE	Aeromedical Evacuation [*Later, AME*] (AFM)
AE	Aeronautical (ABBR)
AE	Aeronautical Engineer
AE	Aerospace Education
AE	Aerospace Engineer (PGP)
AE	Aerospace Environment (MCD)
AE	Aes [*Obverse*] [*Numismatics*]
AE	Aetatis [*Age*] [*Latin*]
AE	Affect Elaboration [*Scale*] [*Psychology*]
A(E)	Africa (Ethiopia) Committee [*British World War II*]
AE	After End [*Naval engineering*] (DAS)
AE	Age Equivalent [*Development level*] [*Education*]
AE	Age Exemption (WDAA)
AE	Aggregate Expenditure [*Economics*]
AE	Agricultural Engineer
AE	Agricultural Engineering Research Division [*of ARS, Department of Agriculture*]
AE	Airborne Electronics (MCD)
AE	Airborne Equipment Division [*Bureau of Aeronautics; later, NASC*] [*Navy*]
AE	Aircraft Equipment
AE	Air Ecosse Ltd. [*British*]
AE	Air Efficiency Award [*RAF*] [*British*] (DMA)
AE	Air Ejector
AE	Air Electrical [*NATO*] (NATG)
AE	Air Engineering [*British*]
AE	Air Entry [*Respiration*] (DAVI)
AE	Air Escape [*Technical drawings*]
AE	Air Europe [*ICAO designator*] (AD)
AE	Air Mechanic (Engines) [*British military*] (DMA)
AE	Alergic Encephalomyelitis [*Medicine*] (BARN)
ae	Algeria [*MARC country of publication code Library of Congress*] (LCCP)
AE	All England
AE	Almost Everywhere
AE	Alpha Epsilon (EA)
AE	Alternative Energy
AE	American Embassy
AE	American Express Co. (CDAI)
AE	Ammunition Examiner [*British and Canadian*] [*World War II*]
AE	Ammunition Ship [*Navy symbol*]
ae	And Elsewhere [*Mathematics*]
AE	Angled End [*Outdoor advertising*] (NTCM)
AE	Angle of Elevation
AE	Angstromeinheit [*Angstrom Unit*] [*German*]
A/E	Annular Expansion Column [*Chromatography*]
AE	Anoxic Encephalopathy [*Medicine*]
AE	Antarctic Expedition
AE	Antitoxineinheit [*Antitoxin Unit*] [*German*]
AE	Apoenzyme [*Clinical chemistry*] (MAE)
AE	Apollo Engineering [*NASA*] (SAA)
AE	Apostle and Evangelist [*Church calendars*]
AE	Appearance Energy [*Surface ionization*]
AE	Application Engineering
AE	Application-Entity [*Telecommunications*] (OSI)
AE	Applications Explorer [*NASA*]
AE	Applied Entomology
AE	Applied Entomology Group [*Natick Labs, MA*] [*Army*]
AE	Apportioned Effort (MCD)
AE	Arbeitseinheit [*Work Unit*] [*German*]
A-E	Architect-Engineer
A-E	Architectural and Engineering [*Also, A & E*] (KSC)
A/E	Architectural Engineering (OICC)
AE	Arithmetic Element (BUR)
AE	Arithmetic Expression (IEEE)
AE	Armed Experimental [*British military*] (DMA)
AE	Armed Forces Europe
AE	Armor, Artillery, and Engineers Aptitude Area [*Army*]
AE	Army Education
AE	Army in Europe
AE	Artificial Erythrocyte [*Hematology*]
AE	Aryepiglottic [*Medicine*] (DAVI)
ae----	Asia, East [*MARC geographic area code Library of Congress*] (LCCP)
AE	Assault Echelon (NVT)
AE	Assault Engineer [*British military*] (DMA)
AE	Assimilation Efficiency
AE	Assistant Editor [*Publishing*]
AE	Assistant Engineer
AE	Associate Editor [*Publishing*]
AE	Associate Engraver [*British*] (ROG)
AE	Associate in Education
AE	Associate in Engineering
AE	Association Europeenne des Officiers Professionnels de Sapeurs-Pompiers [*European Association of Professional Fire Brigade Officers - EAPFBO*] (EAIO)
AE	Association of Entertainers (EA)
AE	Astrology Encyclopedia [*A publication*]
AE	Astronomische Einheit [*Astronomical Unit*] [*German*]
AE	Asymmetric Epoxidation [*Organic chemistry*]
AE	Atlas Explorer [*Computer geography tutorial*] (PCM)
AE	Atmospheric Entry
AE	Atmospheric Explorer [*Satellite*] [*NASA*]
AE	Atomic Emission
AE	Atomic Energy (ADA)
AE	Attenuation Equalizer (IAA)
AE	Audit Entry [*Accounting, finance*] (BUR)
AE	Auroral Electrojet [*Index*]
AE	Autoclave Engineers, Inc.
AE	Autoimmune Encephalomyelitis [*Hematology*]
AE	Automatic Electric (MCD)
AE	Automatic Exposure Camera
AE	Automation Device (IAA)
AE	Autumnal Equinox
AE	Auxiliary Equation [*Mathematics*] (OA)
AE	Auxiliary Equipment (KSC)
AE	Average Error (MCD)
AE	Aviation Electrician's Mate [*Navy rating*]
AE	Aviation Engineer (IAA)
A-E	Dow Chemical Co. [*Research code symbol*]
AE	Dubai [*IYRU nationality code*] (IYR)
AE	Edmonton Public Library, Alberta [*Library symbol National Library of Canada*] (NLC)
AE	Energy of Activation [*Medicine*] (DAVI)
AE	George William Russell [*Irish poet, 1867-1935*] [*Pseudonym*]
AE	L'Annee Epigraphique [*A publication*] (OCD)
AE	Third-Class Ship in Lloyd's Register (BARN)
AE	United Arab Emirates [*ANSI two-letter standard code*] (CNC)
AE1	Anion Exchanger 1 [*Biochemistry*]
AE1	Aviation Electrician's Mate, First Class [*Navy rating*]
AE2	Aviation Electrician's Mate, Second Class [*Navy rating*]
AE3	Aviation Electrician's Mate, Third Class [*Navy rating*]
AEA	Abemama [*Kiribati*] [*Airport symbol*] (OAG)
AEA	Aboriginal Electoral Assistant [*Australia*]
AEA	Abort Electronics Assembly [*Apollo*] [*NASA*]
AEA	Above-Elbow Amputation [*Orthopedics*] (DAVI)
AEA	Accountable Entertainment Allowance [*British*]
AEA	Action Error Analysis [*Engineering*]
AEA	Active Element Array
AEA	Actors' Equity Association (EA)
AEA	Actors' Equity of Australia
AEA	Actual Expenses Allowable [*Military*] (AFM)
AEA	Adult Education Association of the USA (EA)
AEA	Advanced Engine Aerospace
AEA	Aerospace Education Association (EA)

AEA............ African Economic Affairs Committee [London] [World War II]
AEA............ Aft End Assembly
AEA............ Agence Europeenne d'Approvisionnement
AEA............ Aggregate Expense Analysis [Insurance]
AEA............ Agricultural Education Association [British]
AEA............ Agricultural Engineers Association [British] (DS)
AEA............ Aircraft Electronics Association (EA)
AEA............ Aircraft Engineers Association
AEA............ Air Efficiency Award [RAF] [British]
AEA............ Air Entraining Agent [Freight]
AEA............ Air Europa [Spain ICAO designator] (FAAC)
AEA............ Alabama Education Association (SRA)
AEA............ Alberta Historical Resources, Alberta Culture and Multiculturalism, Edmonton, Alberta [Library symbol National Library of Canada] (NLC)
AEA............ Alcohol, Ether, Acetone [Solvent mixture]
AEA............ All-Electric Aircraft [Aviation] (PDAA)
AEA............ Aluminum Extruders Association (DAC)
AEA............ American Economic Association (EA)
AEA............ American Education Association (EA)
AEA............ American Electrology Association (EA)
AEA............ American Electronics Association (EA)
AEA............ American Engineering Association [Defunct] (EA)
AEA............ American Enterprise Association [Later, AEI]
AEA............ American Entrepreneurs Association [Defunct] (EA)
AEA............ American Equine Association (EA)
AEA............ American Eskimo Association (EA)
AEA............ American Evaluation Association (EA)
AEA............ American Export Airlines
AEA............ Americans of European Ancestry [Psychometrics]
AEA............ Annus Erat Augusti [It Was in the Year of Augustus] [Coin inscription] [Latin] (ROG)
AEA............ Antenna Elevation Angle
AEA............ Aquatic Exercise Association (EA)
AEA............ Area Education Agency (OICC)
AEA............ Argenta Systems [Vancouver Stock Exchange symbol]
AEA............ Arizona Education Association (SRA)
AEA............ Arkansas Education Association (SRA)
AEA............ Art Exhibitions Australia
AEA............ Artists Equity Association [Later, NAEA] (EA)
AEA............ [The] Arts, Education, and Americans (EA)
AEA............ Assignment Eligibility and Availability [Military] (AABC)
AEA............ Associate in Engineering Administration
AEA............ Association Europeenne d'Athletisme [European Athletic Association - EAA] (EA)
AEA............ Association Europeenne de l'Asphalte [European Mastic Asphalt Association - EMAA] (EAIO)
AEA............ Association Europeenne des Audioprothesistes [European Association of Hearing Aid Dispensers] (EAIO)
AEA............ Association of Enrolled Agents [Later, NAEA] (EA)
AEA............ Association of Environmental Authorities (SRA)
AEA............ Association of European Airlines (EAIO)
AEA............ Association of Seventh-Day Adventist Engineers and Architects (EA)
AEA............ Atlantic Education Association [Canada]
AEA............ Atlantic Episcopal Assembly (AC)
AEA............ Atomic Energy Act [1954]
AEA............ Atomic Energy Authority [British]
AEA............ Auger Electron Analysis
AEA............ Augustinian Educational Association [Defunct] (EA)
AEA............ Autoerotic Asphyxiation [Medicine]
AEA............ Automatic Error Analysis
AEA............ Automation Economic Analysis
AEA............ Automotive Electric Association [ASIA] [Absorbed by] (EA)
AEA............ United States Army, Corps of Engineers, South Atlantic Division, Atlanta, GA [OCLC symbol] (OCLC)
AEAA.......... Airman Apprentice, Aviation Electrician, Striker [Navy rating]
AEAA.......... Ascent Engine Arming Assembly [NASA] (KSC)
AEAC.......... Agricultural Equipment Advisory Committee [Australia]
AEAC.......... Alternate Emergency Action Center (CINC)
AEACC .... East Coulee Community Library, Alberta [Library symbol National Library of Canada] (NLC)
AEACP .... Airborne Emergency Alternate Command Post (CINC)
AEAD .... Alcoholism and Drug Abuse Commission, Edmonton, Alberta [Library symbol National Library of Canada] (NLC)
AEADST .... Advanced Electronic and Digital Sensor Technology
AEAE.......... Alberta Advanced Education, Edmonton, Alberta [Library symbol National Library of Canada] (NLC)
AEAE.......... Americans for the Enforcement of Attorney Ethics
AEAF.......... Allied Expeditionary Air Force
AEAF.......... Australian Educational Allowance Fund
AEAG .... Alberta Agriculture, Edmonton, Alberta [Library symbol National Library of Canada] (NLC)
AEagIG........ American Eagle Group [Associated Press] (SAG)
AEAGL .... Laboratory, Alberta Agriculture, Edmonton, Alberta [Library symbol Obsolete National Library of Canada] (NLC)
AEagleO....... American Eagle Outfitters, Inc. [Associated Press] (SAG)
AEAGLS .... Eaglesham School, Alberta [Library symbol National Library of Canada] (BIB)
AEAGS .... Operating and Maintenance Division, Alberta Government Services, Edmonton, Alberta [Library symbol National Library of Canada] (NLC)
AEAH .... Alberta Hospital, Edmonton, Alberta [Library symbol National Library of Canada] (BIB)
AEAHA .... Resource Library, Alberta Hospital Association, Edmonton, Alberta [Library symbol National Library of Canada] (NLC)

AEAI........... Association Europeenne des Assures de l'Industrie [European Association of Industrial Insurers] [Brussels, Belgium] (EAIO)
AEAM .... Adaptive Environmental Assessment and Management
AEAM .... Association des Evangeliques d'Afrique et Madagascar [Association of Evangelicals of Africa and Madagascar] (EAIO)
AEAM .... Eaglesham Municipal Library, Alberta [Library symbol National Library of Canada] (NLC)
AEAME........ Allsopp, Morgan Engineering Ltd., Edmonton, Alberta [Library symbol National Library of Canada] (NLC)
AEAN.......... Airman, Aviation Electrician, Striker [Navy rating]
AE & M .... Apostle, Evangelist, and Martyr [Church calendars] (ROG)
AE & P .... Ambassador Extraordinary and Plenipotentiary [Diplomacy]
AE & S........ Air Equipment and Support [Army] (AABC)
AEAO.......... Airborne Emergency Actions Officer [SAC]
AEAONMS .... Ancient Egyptian Arabic Order Nobles of the Mystic Shrine (EA)
AEAOS .... Alberta Oil Sands Information Centre, Edmonton, Alberta [Library symbol National Library of Canada] (NLC)
AEAP.......... Alliance Europeenne des Agences de Presse
AEAPA .... Alberta Personnel Administration, Edmonton, Alberta [Library symbol National Library of Canada] (NLC)
AEAPS .... Auger Electron Appearance Potential Spectroscopy
AEAQ .... Association des Entomologistes Amateurs du Quebec (AC)
AEAR .... American Ear Association for Research (EA)
AEAR .... Committee on American East Asian Relations [Defunct] (EA)
AEARC .... Army Equipment Authorizations Review Center (AABC)
AEARN .... Alberta Association of Registered Nurses, Edmonton, Alberta [Library symbol National Library of Canada] (NLC)
AEAS.......... Air Equipment and Support [Army] (AFIT)
AEAS.......... Association of Educational Advisers Scotland (DBA)
AEAS.......... Automatic Equalization/Analyzation System
AEASA........ Automotive Exhibitors' Association of South Australia
AEASC .... Alberta Securities Commission, Edmonton, Alberta [Library symbol National Library of Canada] (NLC)
AEAT.......... Ambulance Employees' Association of Tasmania [Australia]
AEATG .... Alberta Attorney General, Edmonton, Alberta [Library symbol National Library of Canada] (NLC)
AEAU .... Athabasca University, Alberta [Library symbol National Library of Canada] (NLC)
AEAUC .... Alberta Government Libraries Union Catalogue, Edmonton, Alberta [Library symbol National Library of Canada] (NLC)
AEAV.......... Adult Education Association of Victoria [Australia]
AEAV.......... Ambulance Employees' Association of Victoria [Australia]
AEB........... Accident Evolution and Barrier [Engineering]
AEB........... Acquired Epidermolysis Bullosa [Medicine]
AEB........... Active Electronic Buoy (DWSG)
AEB........... Advanced Engine Bell
AEB........... Aerial Exploitation Battalion (MCD)
AEB........... Aft Equipment Bay [NASA] (KSC)
AEB........... Airborne and Electronics Board [Army] (MCD)
AEB........... Air, Emergency Breathing System (DNAB)
AEB........... Amchitka [Alaska] [Seismograph station code, US Geological Survey Closed] (SEIS)
AEB........... American Egg Board (EA)
AEB........... American Ethnology Bureau [British] (DAS)
AEB........... Apollo Engineering Bulletin [NASA] (SAA)
AEB........... Arctic [Iceland] [ICAO designator] (FAAC)
AEB........... Arctic Environmental Buoy System (NOAA)
AEB........... Art Exhibitions Bureau
AEB........... Associated Examining Board [British]
AEB........... Association d'Etudes Baha'ies [Association for Baha'i Studies] (EAIO)
AEB........... Association Europeenne de la Boyauderie [European Natural Sausage Casings Association - ENSCA] (EA)
AEB........... Association of Editorial Businesses (EA)
AE-B.......... Atmosphere Explorer B [Satellite] [NASA]
AEB........... Atomic Energy Bureau [Korea] (NUCP)
AEB........... Atomic Energy Bureau [Japan] (NUCP)
AEB........... Australian Business and Estate Planning Reporter [A publication]
AEB........... Auto Exposure Bracketing [Photography]
AEB........... Auxiliary Equipment Building [Nuclear energy] (NRCH)
AEB........... Average Extent of Burning
AEB........... Avian Erythroblastosis [Medicine] (DMAA)
AEB........... United States Army, Corps of Engineers, Coastal Engineering Research Center, Fort Belvoir, VA [OCLC symbol] (OCLC)
AEBA.......... Agricultural Economics Bulletin for Africa [A publication]
AEBA.......... Automatic Emergency Broadcast Alert [Telecommunications] (IAA)
AEBCNSW.... Association of Ethnic Broadcasters and Coordinators of New South Wales [Australia]
AEBE.......... Approach End Barrier Engagement (MCD)
AEBIG .... Aslib Economics and Business Information Group (NITA)
AEBR .... Airborne Electron Beam Recorder
AEBS.......... Anti-Estrogen Binding Site [Biochemistry]
AEBSF........ Aminoethyl Benzene Sulfonyl Fluoride [Organic chemistry]
AEBSTA....... Atomic Energy Bureau of Science and Technics Agency [Japan]
AEC........... Academy of Electrical Contracting (EA)
AEC........... Adaptive Echo Cancellation [Navy] (MCD)
AEC........... Additional Extended Coverage [Insurance]
AEC........... Adelaide Entertainment Centre [Australia]
AEC........... Adenylate Energy Charge (BARN)
AEC........... Adult Education Centre [British]
AEC........... Aerocesar, Aerovias del Cesar [Colombia] [ICAO designator] (FAAC)
AEC........... Affaires Exterieures Canada [External Affairs Canada]
AEC........... Affiliated Employers of California (SRA)
AEC........... Aft End Cone [NASA] (NASA)
AEC........... Aft Events Controller [NASA] (MCD)
AEC........... Agricultural Economics Division [of AMS, Department of Agriculture]

AEC............ Agricultural Executive Council [*British*]
AEC............ Air Eligibility Code
AEC............ Air Emplaced Classifier (MCD)
AEC............ Airship Experimental Center [*Navy*]
AEC............ Alaska Engineering Commission [*Later, the Alaska Railroad*]
AEC............ Alberta Department of Culture Library [*UTLAS symbol*]
AEC............ Alberta Energy Co. Ltd. [*Toronto Stock Exchange symbol Vancouver Stock Exchange symbol*]
AEC............ Alcohol Education Centre [*British*] (DI)
AEC............ Altitude Engine Control (AAG)
AEC............ Aluminum Extruders Council (EA)
AEC............ Amelia Earhart Collectors Club (EA)
AEC............ American Economic Council (EA)
AEC............ American Education Coalition [*Defunct*] (EA)
AEC............ American Election Commission [*Defunct*] (EA)
AEC............ American Electrical Cases [*A publication*] (DLA)
AEC............ American Engineering Council
AEC............ American Express Card [*Credit card*]
AEC............ Americans for Educational Choice (EA)
AEC............ Amino(ethyl)carbazole [*Organic chemistry*]
AEC............ Aminoethyl Cellulose [*Organic chemistry*] (OA)
AEC............ Aminoethyl Cysteine [*Biochemistry*] (OA)
AEC............ Analog Electronic Computer
AEC............ Architects' Emergency Committee
AEC............ Architectural and Engineering Construction (BYTE)
AEC............ Area Equipment Compounds [*Military*] (AABC)
AEC............ Arizona Employers Council (SRA)
AEC............ Arkansas Electric Cooperatives (SRA)
AEC............ Army Educational Corps [*Later, RAEC*] [*British*]
AEC............ Army Education Center
AEC............ Army Electronics Command
AEC............ Army Engineer Center (SAA)
AEC............ Army Environmental Center [*Aberdeen Proving Ground, MD*] (RDA)
AEC............ Assembled Electronic Component
AEC............ Associated Estates Realty [*NYSE symbol*] (SPSG)
AEC............ Associated Estates Realty [*NYSE symbol*] (SPSG)
AEC............ Associate Enforcement Counsel [*Environmental Protection Agency*] (GFGA)
AEC............ Association des Editeurs Canadiens [*Association of Canadian Editors*]
AEC............ Association des Enducteurs, Calandreurs et Fabricants de Revetements de Sols Plastiques de la CEE [*Association of Coated Fabrics, Plastic Films and Plastic and Synthetic Floor Coverings of the European Economic Community*] (PDAA)
AEC............ Association des Etudes Canadiennes [*Association for Canadian Studies - ACS*]
AEC............ Association Europeenne de Ceramique [*European Ceramic Association*] [*France*]
AEC............ Association Europeenne des Conservatoires [*European Association of Conservatories - EAC*] (EAIO)
AEC............ Association Europeenne des Contribuables [*European Taxpayers Association - ETA*] (EA)
AEC............ Association Europeenne pour la Cooperation [*European Association for Cooperation*]
AEC............ Association of Education Committees [*British*]
AEC............ Association of Electronic Cottagers [*Defunct*] (EA)
AEC............ Association of Episcopal Colleges (EA)
AEC............ At Earliest Convenience [*Medicine*] (AAMN)
AEC............ Atlantic & East Carolina Railway Co. [*AAR code*]
AEC............ Atlas Educational Center (EA)
AEC............ Atomic Energy Commission [*Functions divided, 1975, between Nuclear Regulatory Commission and Energy Research and Development Administration*]
AEC............ Atomic Energy Commission. Reports [*A publication*] (DLA)
AEC............ Atomic Energy Corporation [*South Africa*] [*Research center*]
AEC............ Automatic Engine Control [*Heavy-duty diesel engines*]
AEC............ Automatic Exciter Control
AEC............ Automatic Exposure Control [*In reprographic systems*]
AEC............ Average Electrode Current
AEC............ Aviation Electrician's Mate, Chief [*Navy rating*]
AEC............ Aviation Electronic Combat [*Army*] (RDA)
AEC............ Concordia College, Edmonton, Alberta [*Library symbol National Library of Canada*] (NLC)
AEC............ United States Army, Corps of Engineers, Los Angeles District, Los Angeles, CA [*OCLC symbol*] (OCLC)
AECA........... Alberta Consumer and Corporate Affairs, Edmonton, Alberta [*Library symbol National Library of Canada*] (NLC)
AECA........... American Edge Collectors Association (EA)
AECA........... Arms Export Control Act
AECA........... Association Europeenne des Centres d'Audiophonologie [*European Association of Audiophonological Centres - EAAC*] (EAIO)
AEC-AFSWP-TP... Atomic Energy Commission - Armed Forces Special Weapons Project Technical Publication (MCD)
AECAH........ Association Europeenne des Conservatoires, Academies de Musique, et Musikhochschulen [*European Association of Music Conservatories, Academies, and High Schools*] (EAIO)
AECAL......... Audio Enhanced Computer Aided Learning (AIE)
AECAWA...... Association of Episcopal Conferences of Anglophone West Africa (EAIO)
AECB.......... Arms Export Control Board
AECB.......... Association for the Export of Canadian Books [*Association pour l'Exportation du Livre Canadien*] (AC)
AECB.......... Association of Environmental Conscious Builders [*British*] (DBA)
AECB.......... Atomic Energy Control Board [*Canada*]

AECBCA ...... Atomic Energy Commission Board of Contract Appeals [*Replaced by the Energy Research and Development Administration Board of Contract Appeals in 1975*] (AAGC)
AECC .... Aeromedical Evacuation Control Center [*Military*] (MCD)
AECC .... Alberta Cancer Clinic, Edmonton, Alberta [*Library symbol National Library of Canada*] (NLC)
AECC .... Amelia Earhart Collectors Club (EA)
AECC .... Australian Export Commodity Classification
AECCE .... Association Educative et Culturelle Canada Egypte (AC)
AECCG .... African Elephant Conservation Coordinating Group
AECCH .... Peter Wilcock Library, Charles Camsell General Hospital, Edmonton, Alberta [*Library symbol National Library of Canada*] (NLC)
AECCI.......... Cross Cancer Institute, Edmonton, Alberta [*Library symbol National Library of Canada*] (NLC)
AECCP .... Alaska Early Childhood Certification Process (EDAC)
AECD .... Allergic Eczematous Contact Dermatitis [*Dermatology*] (DMAA)
AECD .... Atomic Energy Commission Declassified Report (NUCP)
AECD .... Auxiliary Emission Control Device [*Automotive engineering*]
AEC-DASA-TP... Atomic Energy Commission - Defense Atomic Support Agency Technical Publication (MCD)
AEC-DASA-TP... Atomic Energy Commission - Defense Atomic Support Agency Technical Publication (MCD)
AEC-DNA-TP... Atomic Energy Commission - Defense Nuclear Agency Technical Publication (MCD)
AECE .... Airborne Engineer Contraction Equipment (MCD)
AECEA .... Australian Early Childhood Education Association
AECEO .... Association of Early Childhood Educators, Ontario (AC)
AECF .... American Egyptian Cooperation Foundation (EA)
AECG .... Ambulatory Electrocardiogram (MCD)
AECGIS .... Automated Electrocardiograph Interpretive System [*Veterans Administration*]
AECGV .... Association Europeenne du Commerce en Gros des Viandes [*European Association Wholesale Trade in Meat*] [*EC*] (ECED)
AECI .... American Electronic Components, Inc. [*NASDAQ symbol*] (SAG)
AECI .... Associate Member of the Institute of Employment Consultants [*British*] (DBQ)
AECI .... Association of Electrical Contractors Ireland (EAIO)
AECI .... Association of European Conjuncture Institutes (EA)
AECI .... Association of European Cooperative Insurers [*Brussels, Belgium*] (EAIO)
AECJC .... Genealogical Society Library, Church of Jesus Christ of Latter-Day Saints, Edmonton, Alberta [*Library symbol National Library of Canada*] (NLC)
AECK .... Eckville Public Library, Alberta [*Library symbol National Library of Canada*] (NLC)
AECL .... Aircraft and Equipment Configuration List (MCD)
AECL .... Alberta Culture, Edmonton, Alberta [*Library symbol National Library of Canada*] (NLC)
AECL .... Atomic Energy Centre - Lahore (MCD)
AECL .... Atomic Energy of Canada Ltd.
AECLP .... Alliance to End Childhood Lead Poisoning (PAZ)
AECLS......... Alberta Culture Library Services, Edmonton, Alberta [*Library symbol National Library of Canada*] (NLC)
AECM .... Active Electronic Counter-Measure (PDAA)
AECM .... Association of European Candle Manufacturers (EA)
AECM .... Atomic Energy Commission Manual
AECM .... Aviation Electrician's Mate, Master Chief [*Navy rating*]
AECMA........ Association Europeenne des Constructeurs de Materiel Aerospatial [*European Association of Aerospace Manufacturers*] (EAIO)
AECMQ .... Association des Enseignants de la Construction et du Meuble du Quebec (AC)
AECNP .... Association Europeenne des Centres Nationaux de Productivite [*European Association for National Productivity Centers - EANPC*] (EAIO)
AEC(NSW) ... Aboriginal Education Council (New South Wales) [*Australia*]
AECO .... Aeromedical Evacuation Control Officer [*Military*] (AABC)
AECO .... Agora-Economie [*Agence France-Presse*] [*French Information service or system*] (CRD)
AECO .... Concordia Lutheran Seminary, Edmonton, Alberta [*Library symbol National Library of Canada*] (BIB)
AECOM .... Army Electronics Command (MUGU)
AECP .... Advance Engineering Change Proposal (MSA)
AECP .... Airman Education and Commissioning Program
AECP .... Altitude Engine Control Panel (AAG)
AECP .... Army Extension Course Program (AABC)
AECPR .... Atomic Energy Commission Procurement Regulations [*Obsolete*]
AECPrA .... Assoc Estates Rlty 9.75% Dep Pfd [*NYSE symbol*] (TTSB)
AECPSUPC... Association for the Encouragement of Correct Punctuation, Spelling, and Usage inPublic Communications (EA)
AECQ .... Association des Entrepreneurs en Construction du Quebec (AC)
AECQ .... Association des Entrepreneurs en Couture du Quebec (AC)
AECR .... Association des Employes du Conseil de Recherches [*Research Council Employees' Association - RCEA*] [*Canada*]
AECS.......... Advanced Entry Control System [*Air Force*]
AECS.......... Advanced Environmental Control System (MCD)
AECS.......... Alberta Union of Provincial Employees, Edmonton, Alberta [*Library symbol National Library of Canada*] (NLC)
AECS.......... Apollo Environmental Control System [*NASA*] (IAA)
AECS.......... Association of European Correspondence Schools (EA)
AECS.......... Automated Environmental Control System (MCD)
AECS.......... Aviation Electrician's Mate, Senior Chief [*Navy rating*]
AECT.......... Association for Educational Communications and Technology [*Washington, DC*]
AECT.......... Association of Electric Companies of Texas (SRA)
AECT.......... Automatic Exposure Control Technique

AEC/TIC....... Atomic Energy Commission/Technical Information Center (MCD)
AECTR .... American Emergency Committee for Tibetan Refugees [*Defunct*] (EA)
AECTRC .... Advanced Environmental Control Technology Research Center [*University of Illinois*] [*Environmental Protection Agency Research center*] (RCD)
AECU .... Atomic Energy Commission Unclassified Report (NUCP)
AECU .... Canadian Utilities Ltd., Edmonton, Alberta [*Library symbol National Library of Canada*] (NLC)
AED............. Academy for Educational Development (EA)
AED............. Active Electronic Decoy (CAAL)
AED............. Advanced Electronic Design
AED............. Advanced Electronics Design [*Commercial firm*] [*British*] (NITA)
AED............. Advanced Engine Development [*Automotive industry supplier*]
AED............. Advanced Gravis [*Vancouver Stock Exchange symbol*]
AED............. Advance Electronic Diagnostics [*Automotive industry supplier*]
AED............. AE Developments Ltd. [*Research center British*]
aed .... Aedicula (VRA)
AED............. Aerodynamic Equivalent Diameter (PDAA)
AED............. Aeromedical Education Division [*FAA*]
AED............. Aeronautical Engineering Department [*NASA*] (KSC)
AED............. Aeronautical Engineering Division [*Air Force*] (DOMA)
AED............. Aeronautical Engineering Duty [*Navy*]
AED............. Aerospace Electrical Division (SAA)
AED............. Agena Ephemeris Data [*NASA*] (SAA)
AED............. Aircraft Explosive Device (MCD)
AED............. Air Enforcement Division [*Office of Enforcement and Compliance Monitoring*] [*Environmental Protection Agency*] (EPA)
AED............. Air Equipment Department [*British military*] (DMA)
AED............. Air Experienc Flight [*British ICAO designator*] (FAAC)
AED............. ALGOL Extended for Design [*1967*] [*Computer science*]
AED............. Alphanumeric Entry Device
AED............. Ammunition Engineering Directorate [*Army*] (MCD)
AED............. Anaelectrodiabatic [*Nuclear wave*]
AED............. Analog Event Distributor [*Computer science*] (MCD)
AED............. Analysis and Evaluation Division [*Environmental Protection Agency*] (GFGA)
AED............. Antiepileptic Drug
AED............. Armament Engineering Directorate [*Dover, NJ*] [*Army*] (GRD)
AED............. Artium Elegantium Doctor [*Doctor of Fine Arts*]
AED............. Associated Equipment Distributors (EA)
A Ed............ Associate in Education
AED............. Association Europeene des Decafeineurs [*European Association of Decaffeinators*] [*France*] (EAIO)
AED............. Association for Educational Development (EA)
AED............. Association of Electronic Distributors (EA)
AED............. Association of Engineering Distributors [*British*] (BI)
AED............. Association of Equipment Distributors (MHDB)
AED............. Assurance Engineering [*or Effectiveness*] Division [*Military*] (DNAB)
AED............. Astro-Electronics Division [*RCA*]
AED............. Atomic Emission Detector [*Instrumentation*]
AED............. Australian Education directory [*A publication*]
AED............. Australian Ethnic Democrats [*Political party*]
AED............. Automated Engineering Design [*Programming language*] [*1960*] [*Computer science*]
AED............. Automatic External Defibrillator (PDAA)
AED............. Average and Excess Demand (IAA)
AED............. Avionics Electrical Distribution (MCD)
AED............. Bancode A Edwards [*NYSE symbol*] (SAG)
AED............. Banco de A Edwards ADS [*NYSE symbol*] (TTSB)
Aed............. De Aedificiis [*of Procopius*] [*Classical studies*] (OCD)
AED............. Edson Public Library, Alberta [*Library symbol National Library of Canada*] (NLC)
AED............. United States Army, Corps of Engineers, Office of the Chief of Engineers, Washington, DC [*OCLC symbol*] (OCLC)
AEDA .... Ammunition, Explosives, and Other Dangerous Articles
AEDA .... Associated Equipment Distributors of Arizona (SRA)
AED & LC .... Advanced Airborne Expendable Decoy and Launcher Control (DWSG)
AEDAP .... Aboriginal Education Direct Assistance Program [*Australia*]
AEDB .... Apollo Engineering Documentation Board [*NASA*] (MCD)
AEDBCS ...... Association Europeenne des Directeurs de Bureaux de Concerts et Spectacles [*European Association of Directors of the Bureau of Concerts and Events*] [*France*] (EAIO)
AEDC .... American Economic Development Council (EA)
AEDC .... Arnold Engineering Development Center [*Arnold Air Force Base, TN*]
AEDCAP ...... Automated Engineering Design Circuit Analysis Program (MHDB)
AEDCM .... Advanced Electrochemical Depolarized Concentrator Module [*NASA*]
AEDD .... Air Engineering Development Division [*Air Force*]
AEDE .... Airplane Economic Design Evaluator [*Boeing Co.*]
AEDEC .... Association Europeenne d'Etudes Chinoises [*European Association of Chinese Studies - EACS*] (EAIO)
AEDG .... Edgerton Public Library, Alberta [*Library symbol National Library of Canada*] (NLC)
AEDH .... Association Europeenne des Directeurs d'Hopitaux [*Later, EAHM*] (EA)
AEDI .... Association pour l'Etude du Developpement International [*Association for the Study of International Development ASID*] [*Canada*]
AEDM.......... Edberg Municipal Library, Alberta [*Library symbol National Library of Canada*] (NLC)
AEDN .... African Economic Development News [*Kenya*] [*A publication*] (EY)
AEDN .... Distribution Networks, Edmonton, Alberta [*Library symbol National Library of Canada*] (NLC)
AEDNET ...... Automated Engineering Design of Networks [*Computer science*] (IAA)

AEDO .... Aeronautical Engineering Duty Officer [*Navy*] (DOMA)
AEDO .... Aircraft Engineering District Office
AEDP .... Advanced Electrical Development Package (MCD)
AEDP .... Association for Educational Data Processing
AEDP .... Automated External Defibrillator-Pacemaker [*Cardiology*]
AEDPS .... Automated Engineering Document Preparation System (MCD)
AEDR .... Avionics Equipment Design Review
AED/R & S... Associated Equipment Distributors' Research and Services Operation
AEDS .... Advanced Electric Distribution System
AEDS .... Airport Engineering Data Sheet [*FAA*] (MCD)
AEDS .... Analog Event Distribution System [*Computer science*] (MCD)
AEDS .... Association for Educational Data Systems (EA)
AEDS .... Association for Electronic Data Systems [*Database producer*] (ECII)
AEDS .... Atmospheric Electric Detection System (KSC)
AEDS .... Atomic Energy Detection System [*Nuclear energy*]
AEDST .... Australian Eastern Daylight Saving Time (ADA)
AEDT .... Association Europeenne des Organisations Nationales des Commercants Detaillants en Textiles [*European Association of National Organizations of Textile Manufacturers*]
AEDU .... Admiralty Experimental Diving Unit [*British*]
AEE .... Absolute Essential Equipment
AEE .... Abstract Evolution Equation (PDAA)
AEE .... Additional Expediting Expense [*Insurance*]
AEE .... Adverse Environment Effect
AEE .... Aegean Aviation [*Greece*] [*ICAO designator*] (FAAC)
AeE .... Aeronautical Engineer
AEE .... Aileen, Inc. [*NYSE symbol*] (SPSG)
AEE .... Airborne Evaluation Equipment (IEEE)
AEE .... Alberta Education, Edmonton, Alberta [*Library symbol National Library of Canada*] (NLC)
AEE .... Alliance for Environmental Education (EA)
AEE .... American-European Express [*Railway*]
AEE .... Ancillary Education Establishment
AEE .... Anomalously Enriched Element [*Environmental chemistry*]
AEE .... Antlers, OK [*Location identifier FAA*] (FAAL)
AEE .... Assistant Executive Engineer [*British*] (DCTA)
AEE .... Associate in Engineering
AEE .... Association des Eglises Evangelique (AC)
AEE .... Association for Experiential Education (EA)
AEE .... Association of Energy Engineers (EA)
AEE .... Association of Engineering Employees of Oregon (SRA)
AE-E .... Atmosphere Explorer E [*Satellite*] [*NASA*]
AEE .... Atomic Energy Establishment [*Libya*] (NUCP)
AEE .... Atomic Energy Establishment [*British*]
AEE .... Average Excitation Energy [*Physics*]
AEE .... United States Army, Corps of Engineers, New England Division, Waltham, MA [*OCLC symbol*] (OCLC)
AEEA .... Aminoethylethanolamine [*Organic chemistry*]
AEEA .... Association Europeenne des Editeurs d'Annuaires [*European Association of Directory Publishers - EADP*] (EA)
AEEA .... City of Edmonton Archives, Alberta [*Library symbol National Library of Canada*] (NLC)
AEEAE .... Atmospheric Environment Service, Environment Canada [*Service de l'Environnement Atmospherique, Environnement Canada*] Edmonton, Alberta [*Library symbol National Library of Canada*] (NLC)
AEEC .... Airlines Electronic Engineering Committee
AEEC .... Association of European Express Carriers (DA)
AEEC .... Australian Export Statistics [*Database*]
AEECA .... Environment Council of Alberta, Edmonton, Alberta [*Library symbol National Library of Canada*] (NLC)
AEECEEC...... Association des Etudes de l'Europe Centrale et de l'Europe de l'Est du Canada [*Central and East European Studies Association of Canada - CEESAC*]
AEECW........ Conservation and Protection-Western and Northern Region, Environment Canada [*Conservation et Protection-Region de l'Ouest et du Nord, Environnement Canada*], Edmonton, Alberta [*Library symbol National Library of Canada*] (NLC)
AEED .... Alberta Economic Development and Trade, Edmonton, Alberta [*Library symbol National Library of Canada*] (NLC)
AEED .... Association Europeenne des Enseignants Dentaires [*European Association of Teachers of Dentistry*] (PDAA)
AEED .... Association Europeenne pour l'Etude du Diabete [*European Association for the Study of Diabetes - EASD*] (EAIO)
AEEDO .... Aboriginal Economic and Employment Development Officer [*Australia*]
AEEE .... Army Equipment Engineering Establishment
AEEF .... Association Europeenne des Exploitations Frigorifiques [*European Association of Refrigeration Enterprises*] [*Common Market*] [*Belgium*]
AEEFWT....... Aqua Europa - European Federation for Water Treatment [*British*] (EAIO)
AEEGS .... American Electroencephalographic Society (EA)
AEEI .... Employment and Immigration Canada [*Emploi et Immigration Canada*] Edmonton, Alberta [*Library symbol National Library of Canada*] (NLC)
AEEL .... Aeronautical Engineering and Electronic Laboratory [*Johnsville, PA*] [*Navy*]
AEEL .... Arctic Environmental Engineering Laboratory [*University of Alaska*]
AEELS .... Airborne ELINT Emitter Location System (MCD)
AEEM .... Airborne Electronic Equipment Modification
AEEM .... Northern Materials Resource Centre, Alberta Education, Edmonton, Alberta [*Library symbol National Library of Canada*] (NLC)
AEEMS .... Automatic Electric Energy Management System [*Aviation*] (OA)
AEEN........... Agence Europeenne pour l'Energie Nucleaire [*France*] (NUCP)

AEEN............ Agenzia Europea per L'Energia Nucleare (NUCP)

AEEN............ Alberta Environment, Edmonton, Alberta [*Library symbol National Library of Canada*] (NLC)

AeEng......... Aeronautical Engineer (IEEE)

AEE(NSW).... Association for Environmental Education (New South Wales) [*Australia*]

AEEP........... Association Europeenne pour l'Etude de la Population [*European Association for Population Studies - EAPS*] (EAIO)

AEEP........... Association of Environmental Engineering Professors (EA)

AEEP........... Automotive Energy Efficiency Program [*Department of Transportation*]

AEEP........... Edmonton Power Co., Alberta [*Library symbol National Library of Canada*] (NLC)

AEEPCW...... Epec Consulting Western Ltd., Edmonton, Alberta [*Library symbol National Library of Canada*] (NLC)

AEEPM........ Association pour l'Etude des Etats Proches de la Mort [*International Association for Near-Death Studies*] (EAIO)

AEER........... Adult Entered Employment Rate [*Job Training and Partnership Act*] (OICC)

AEERB .... Army Enlisted Education Review Board (MCD)

AEERL......... Air and Energy Engineering Research Laboratory [*Research Triangle Park, NC*] [*Environmental Protection Agency*] (GRD)

AEES........... Association for the Evaluation of the Elementary School (AEBS)

AEET........... Atomic Energy Establishment, [*Trombay, India*] (NUCP)

AEETF......... Army's Electronic Environmental Test Facility [*Military*] (IAA)

AEEW.......... Atomic Energy Establishment, Winfrith [*England*]

AEF............. Advanced Electronics Field

AEF............. Advertising Educational Foundation (EA)

AEF............. Aero Lloyd Flugreisen GmbH [*Germany ICAO designator*] (FAAC)

AEF............. Aeromedical Evacuation Flight [*Air Force*]

AEF............. Aerospace Education Foundation (EA)

AEF............. Africa Evangelical Fellowship (EA)

AEF............. Afrique Equatoriale Francaise [*French Equatorial Africa*] [*French*] (AF)

AEF............. After England Failed [*Soldier slang for American Expeditionary Force in World War I*]

AEF............. Airborne Equipment Failure [*Air Force*]

AEF............. Aircraft Engineering Foundation

AEF............. Aircraft Equipment Failure

AEF............. Air Experience Flight [*British military*] (DMA)

AEF............. Airfields Environment Federation (EAIO)

AEF............. Alberta Equestrian Federation (AC)

AEF............. Alliance Global Enviro Fd [*NYSE symbol*] (TTSB)

AEF............. Alliance Global Environmental Fund, Inc. [*NYSE symbol*] (SPSG)

AEF............. Allied Expeditionary Force

AEF............. Allogeneic Effect Factor [*Immunochemistry*]

AEF............. Alternative Environmental Futures [*An association*]

AEF............. American Economic Foundation (EA)

AEF............. American Education Fellowship [*Defunct*] (AEBS)

AEF............. American European Foundation [*Later, SFMJF*] (EA)

AEF............. American Euthanasia Foundation (EA)

AEF............. American Expeditionary Force [*World War I*]

AEF............. Americans for Economic Freedom (EA)

AEF............. America's Ekiden Federation [*Defunct*] (EA)

AEF............. Amyloid Enhancing Factor [*Biochemistry*] (DMAA)

AEF............. Architectural Engineering Firm (IAA)

AEF............. Arkansas Environmental Federation (SRA)

AEF............. Armenian Educational Foundation (EA)

AEF............. Artists Equity Fund [*of the National Artists Equity Association*] (EA)

AEF............. Asia Education Foundation

AEF............. Association de l'Evangelisation des Enfants (AC)

AEF............. Association Europeenne des Festivals [*European Association of Festivals*] [*Switzerland*] (EAIO)

AEF............. Auditory-Evoked Magnetic Field [*Neurophysiology*]

AEF............. Australian Employers' Federation

AEF............. Aviation Engineer Force

AEF............. Centre d'Action Europeenne Federaliste [*European Center for Federalist Action*]

AEF............. Northern Forest Research Centre, Environment Canada [*Centre de Recherches Forestieres du Nord, Environnement Canada*] Edmonton, Alberta [*Library symbol National Library of Canada*] (NLC)

AEF............. United States Army, Corps of Engineers, Buffalo District, Buffalo, NY [*OCLC symbol*] (OCLC)

AEFA........... Aboriginal Evangelical Fellowship of Australia

AEFA........... American Education Finance Association (EA)

AEFA........... Army Experimental Flight Activity (MCD)

AEFA........... Association of European Federations of Agro-Engineers [*EC*] (ECED)

AEFA........... Aviation Engineering Flight Activity [*Formerly, ASTA*] [*Edwards Air Force Base, CA*] [*Army*]

AEFC........... Alkaline Electrolyte Fuel Cell

AEFC........... Atlantic Estuarine Fisheries Center [*National Oceanic and Atmospheric Administration*] (MSC)

AEFDV .... Acute Encephalography and Fatty Degeneration of the Viscera [*Reye's syndrome*] [*Medicine*]

AEFEO......... Automotive Emissions and Fuel Economy Office [*Division of automaker certifying compliance with government exhaust emission and fuel economy standards*]

AEFF........... Assurance Engineering Field Facility (DNAB)

AEFIA.......... Alberta Federal and Intergovernmental Affairs, Edmonton, Alberta [*Library symbol National Library of Canada*] (NLC)

AEFLLC .... Allied Expeditionary Force Long Lines Control [*British military*] (DMA)

AEFM.......... Association Europeenne des Festivals de Musique [*European Association of Music Festivals - EAMF*] (EAIO)

AEFO........... Association des Enseignantes et des Enseignants Franco-Ontariens [*Franco-Ontarien Teachers' Association*] (AC)

AEFQ........... Association d'Economie Familiale du Quebec (AC)

AEFR........... Aurora, Elgin & Fox River Electric R. R. [*AAR code*]

AEFS........... Antiexposure Flight Suit

AEFS........... Arctic Environmental Field Station [*Environmental Protection Agency*] (GFGA)

AEFSA......... Aboriginal Education Foundation of South Australia

AEG............. Active Element Group [*QCR*]

AEG............. Acute Erosion Gastritis [*Medicine*]

AEG............. Ad Eundem Gradum [*To the Same Degree*] [*Of the admission of a graduate of one university to the same degree at another without examination*] [*Latin*]

AEG............. AEGON N.V. [*NYSE symbol*] (SPSG)

AEG............. Aegrus [*or Aegra*] [*The Patient*] [*Medicine*]

AEG............. Aerial Enterprises Ltd. [*British ICAO designator*] (FAAC)

AEG............. Aeromedical Evacuation Group [*Air Force*]

AEG............. Aircraft Evaluation Group [*FAA*] (TAG)

AEG............. Air Encephalogram [*Medicine*]

AEG............. All Edges Gilt [*Bookbinding*] (ADA)

AEG............. Allegemeine Elektrizitats Gesellschaft [*Federal Republic of Germany*]

AEG............. Allgemaine Elektizitaetsgesellschaft [*Automotive industry supplier*]

AEG............. Analytic Ephemeris Generator

AEG............. Applied Energy, Inc. [*Vancouver Stock Exchange symbol*]

AEG............. Association of Engineering Geologists (EA)

AEG............. Association of Exploration Geochemists [*ICSU*] (EAIO)

AEG............. Atlantic Environmental Group [*National Marine Fisheries Service*]

AEG............. Atrialectrogram [*Cardiology*]

AEG............. [*The*] Egyptian Era [*Beginning 747BC*] (ROG)

AEG............. Staff Library, Glenrose Provincial General Hospital, Edmonton, Alberta [*Library symbol National Library of Canada*] (NLC)

AEG............. United States Army, Corps of Engineers, Detroit District, Detroit, MI [*OCLC symbol*] (OCLC)

AEGH .... Edmonton General Hospital, Alberta [*Library symbol National Library of Canada*] (NLC)

AEGIS .... Active Electronic Gimballess Inertial System

Aegis .... Aegis Consumer Funding Group [*Associated Press*] (SAG)

AEGIS .... Agricultural, Ecological, and Geographical Information System

AEGIS .... Aid for the Elderly in Government Institutions [*British*]

AEGIS .... Airborne Early Warning/Ground Integration Segment

AEGIS .... [*An*] Existing Generalized Information System [*Computer science*]

AEGL .... Acute Emergency Guideline Levels [*EPA*]

AEGM.......... Anglican Evangelical Group Movement (BARN)

AEGM.......... Association of Electronic Guard Manufacturers [*British*]

AEGMCR...... Grant MacEwan Cromdale Campus LRC, Edmonton, Alberta [*Library symbol National Library of Canada*] (NLC)

AEGMJP....... Grant MacEwan Jasper Place Campus LRC, Edmonton, Alberta [*Library symbol National Library of Canada*] (NLC)

AEGMMW .... Grant MacEwan Mill Woods Campus LRC, Edmonton, Alberta [*Library symbol National Library of Canada*] (NLC)

AEGMSS ...... Grant MacEwan Seventh Street Plaza Campus, Edmonton, Alberta [*Library symbol National Library of Canada*] (NLC)

Aegon .... AEGON NV [*Associated Press*] (SAG)

AEGp.......... Aeromedical Evacuation Group [*Air Force*] (AFM)

AEGPL .... Association Europeenne des Gaz de Petrole Liquefies [*European Liquefied Petroleum Gas Association - ELPGA*] (EAIO)

AEGRAFLEX... Association Europeenne des Graveurs et des Flexographes [*European Association of Engravers and Flexographers*] (EAIO)

AEG S .... Aegean Sea

AEGS .... Alberta Public Works, Supply and Services, Edmonton, Alberta [*Library symbol National Library of Canada*] (NLC)

AEGSA .... Good Samaritan Auxiliary Hospital, Edmonton, Alberta [*Library symbol National Library of Canada*] (NLC)

AEGT........... Alberta Government Telephones, Edmonton, Alberta [*Library symbol National Library of Canada*] (NLC)

AEGTS .... Annulus Exhaust Gas Treatment System [*Nuclear energy*] (NRCH)

AEH............. Abecher [*Chad*] [*Airport symbol*] (AD)

AEH............. Academie Europeenne d'Histoire [*European Academy of History - EAH*] (EAIO)

AEH............. Allegiance Corp. [*NYSE symbol*] (SAG)

AEH............. Anhydroenneahepitol [*Organic chemistry*]

AEH............. Antenna Effective Height

AEH............. Avia Express Ltd. [*Hungary*] [*ICAO designator*] (FAAC)

AEH............. United States Army, Corps of Engineers, Huntington District, Huntington, WV [*OCLC symbol*] (OCLC)

AEHA .... Anuario Espanol e Hispano-Americano [*A publication*]

AEHA .... Army Environmental Health Agency

AEHA .... Army Environmental Hygiene Agency

AEHA .... Australian Early Holden Association

AEHA .... Hardy Associates Ltd., Edmonton, Alberta [*Library symbol National Library of Canada*] (NLC)

AEHC .... Aminoethylhomocysteine [*Biochemistry*]

AEHC .... Assembly of Episcopal Hospitals and Chaplains (EA)

AEHC .... Housing Library, Alberta Housing and Public Works, Edmonton, Alberta [*Library symbol National Library of Canada*] (NLC)

AEHCI .... Health Care Insurance Commission, Edmonton, Alberta [*Library symbol National Library of Canada*] (NLC)

AEHE........... Library Services Branch, Alberta Department of Health, Edmonton, Alberta [*Library symbol National Library of Canada*] (BIB)

AEHF........... Association for Employee Health and Fitness (EA)

AEHH .... Handicapped Housing Society of Alberta, Edmonton, Alberta [*Library symbol National Library of Canada*] (NLC)

AEHHC......... Association of Educators of Homebound and Hospitalized Children [*Later, DPH*] (EA)

AEHL........... Army Environmental Health Laboratory

AEHO .... Alberta Hospital Library, Oliver, Alberta [*Library symbol National Library of Canada*] (NLC)

AEHP .... Atmospheric Electricity Hazards Protection

AEHRC....... Association Executives Human Rights Caucus (EA)

AEHSC .... Alberta Hospitals & Medical Care, Edmonton, Alberta [*Library symbol National Library of Canada*] (NLC)

AEHSD .... Alberta Social Services and Community Health, Edmonton, Alberta [*Library symbol National Library of Canada*] (NLC)

AEHT........... Alberta Transportation, Edmonton, Alberta [*Library symbol National Library of Canada*] (NLC)

AEHW .... Aboriginal Environmental Health Worker [*Australia*]

AEI .... Acclimatization Experiences Institute [*Later, IEE*] (EA)

AEI .... Acrylic Eye Illustrator [*Medicine*]

AEI .... Adult Education Institute (AIE)

AEI .... Advanced Education Institution

AEI .... Aerial Exposure Index

AEI .... Aeroexpreso Interamerican [*Colombia*] [*ICAO designator*] (FAAC)

AEI .... Aerospace Education Instructor (AFM)

AEI .... Air Express International Corp.

AEI .... Albert Einstein Institution (EA)

AEI .... Allow Enable Intercept [*Military*] (CAAL)

AEI .... Alternate Energy Institute [*Defunct*] (EA)

AEI .... American Enterprise Institute for Public Policy Research (EA)

AEI .... American Express International (ODBW)

AEI .... Annual Efficiency Index [*Army*]

AEI .... Application-Entity Invocation [*Telecommunications*] (OSI)

AEI .... Arbitrary Evolution Index (DMAA)

AEI .... Armament Enhancement Initiative [*DoD*]

AEI .... Armor Enhancement Initiative [*Army*]

AEI .... Associated Electrical Industries [*British*]

AEI .... Associated Enterprises, Inc. (TSSD)

AEI .... Association des Ecoles Internationales

AEI .... Association of Escort/Interpreters (EA)

AEI .... Atrial Emptying Index [*Medicine*] (DMAA)

AEI .... Audio End Instrument (MCD)

AEI .... Australian Economic Indicators [*A publication*]

AEI .... Auto Enthusiasts International [*Defunct*] (EA)

AEI .... Automated Equipment Identification (BTTJ)

AEI .... Automatic Error Interrogation [*Telecommunications*] (OA)

AEI .... Average Efficiency Index

AEI .... Azimuth Error Indicator

AEI .... United States Army, Corps of Engineers, Mobile District, Mobile, AL [*OCLC symbol*] (OCLC)

AEIA .... American Excess Insurance Association [*East Hartford, CT*] (EA)

AEIAF.......... Albert Einstein International Academy Foundation (EA)

AEIAR .... Association Europeenne des Institutions d'Amenagement Rural [*European Association of Country Planning Institutions*] (EAIO)

AEIB .... Activation Engineering Information Bulletin (AAG)

AEIB .... Association for Education in International Business [*Later, AIB*] (EA)

AEIC .... Advanced Earned Income Credit [*IRS*]

AEIC .... Air Express International Corp. [*NASDAQ symbol*] (SAG)

AEIC .... Air Express Intl. [*NASDAQ symbol*] (TTSB)

AEIC .... Alberta Tourism and Small Business, Edmonton, Alberta [*Library symbol National Library of Canada*] (NLC)

AEIC .... Association of Edison Illuminating Companies (EA)

AEICP.......... Association of Entertainment Industry Computer Professionals (EA)

AEIDC .... Arctic Environmental Information and Data Center [*University of Alaska, Fairbanks*] [*Research center*] (IID)

AEIE .... Agence d'Examen de l'Investissement Etranger [*Foreign Investment Review Agency - FIRA*] [*Canada*]

AEIH........... Association Europeenne des Industries de l'Habillement [*European Association of Clothing Industries*] (EA)

AEIL .... American Export Isbrandtsen Lines [*Later, American Export Industries Co.*]

AEIM .... Association of Evangelicals for Italian Missions (EA)

AEIMS......... Administrative Engineering Information Management System

AEINE.......... Engineering and Architecture, Indian and Northern Affairs Canada [*Genie et Architecture, Affaires Indiennes et du Nord Canada*], Edmonton, Alberta [*Library symbol National Library of Canada*] (BIB)

AEIOU .... Albertus Electus Imperator Optimus Vivat [*Inscription used by Albert II, 15th-century German king*]

AEIOU .... Aller Ehren Ist Oesterreich Voll [*Austria Is Crowned with All Honor*] [*Variation of 15th-century inscription*]

AEIOU .... Aller Erst Ist Oesterreich Verdorben [*Variation of 15th-century inscription*]

AEIOU .... Alles Erdreich Ist Oesterreich Unterthan [*Variation of 15th-century inscription*]

AEIOU .... Austriae Est Imperare Orbi Universo [*It Is Given to Austria to Rule the Whole World*] [*Variation of 15th-century inscription*]

AEIOU .... Austria Erit In Orbe Ultima [*Austria Will Be The Last in the World*] [*Variation of 15th-century inscription*]

AEIOU .... Austria's Empire Is Obviously Upset [*Variation of 15th-century inscription*]

AEIOU .... Austria's Empire Is Overall Universal [*Variation of 15th-century inscription*]

AEIPPR .... American Enterprise Institute for Public Policy Research (EA)

AEIQ........... Association des Enseignants en Imprimerie du Quebec (AC)

AEIROF .... Anodically Electrodeposited Iridium Oxide Film [*Electrochemistry*]

AEIS .... Aboriginal Electoral Information Service [*Australia*]

AEIS........... Advanced Energy Industries [*NASDAQ symbol*] (TTSB)

AEIS........... Advanced Energy Industries, Inc. [*NASDAQ symbol*] (SAG)

AEIS........... Aeronautical Enroute Information Service (DA)

AEIS........... Associate of the Educational Institute of Scotland

AEJ .... Air Affaires EJA France [*ICAO designator*] (FAAC)

AEJ .... Aluminum Extension Jacket

AEJ .... Association for Education in Journalism [*Later, AEJMC*] (EA)

AEJ .... Canada Department of Justice [*Ministere de la Justice*] Edmonton, Alberta [*Library symbol National Library of Canada*] (NLC)

AEJE .... Americans for the Enforcement of Judicial Ethics

AEJGAE....... John Graham Architect Engineer Ltd., Edmonton, Alberta [*Library symbol National Library of Canada*] (NLC)

AEJI .... Association of European Jute Industries

AEJMC .... Association for Education in Journalism and Mass Communication (EA)

AEJR .... Adult Education Journal Review [*A publication*] (ADA)

AEK .... Aero Costa Rica [*ICAO designator*] (FAAC)

AEK .... Aircraft Ejection Kit

AEK .... Aseki [*Papua New Guinea*] [*Airport symbol Obsolete*] (OAG)

AEK .... Salomon, Inc. [*AMEX symbol*] (SPSG)

AEK .... Salomon Inc. 6.50% AMGN'ELKS' [*AMEX symbol*] (TTSB)

AEK .... United States Army, Corps of Engineers, Rock Island District, Rock Island, IL [*OCLC symbol*] (OCLC)

AEKC........... [*The*] King's College, Edmonton, Alberta [*Library symbol National Library of Canada*] (NLC)

AEL .... Acceptor Energy Level

AEL .... Actuarial Engine Life (AFIT)

AEL .... Acute Erythroleukemia [*Oncology*]

AEL .... Admiralty Engineering Laboratory [*British*] (MCD)

Ael............. Aelianus [*c. 170-235AD*] [*Classical studies*] (OCD)

AEL .... AEL Industries, Inc. [*Associated Press*] (SAG)

AEL .... Aerobiology and Evaluation Laboratory [*Army*] (KSC)

AEL .... Aeronautical Engineering Laboratory [*NASA*] (KSC)

AEL .... Aeronautical Engine Laboratory [*Later, NAPC*] [*Navy*]

AEL .... Aerospace Electronics Laboratories (MCD)

AEL .... Aircraft Engine Laboratory

AEL .... Aircraft Equipment List (MCD)

AEL .... Air Europe SpA [*Italy ICAO designator*] (FAAC)

AEL .... Alberta Environment Library [*UTLAS symbol*]

AEL .... Albert Lea, MN [*Location identifier FAA*] (FAAL)

AEL .... Allowable Expense Level [*Department of Housing and Urban Development*] (GFGA)

AEL .... Allowance Equipage List

AEL .... Aluminum Electrical Lead

AEL .... American Electronic Laboratories, Inc.

AEL .... American Electronics Laboratory (AAGC)

AEL .... Americanism Educational League [*Buena Park, CA*] (EA)

AEL .... American Emigrants' League (EA)

AEL .... Ameritel Management, Inc. [*Vancouver Stock Exchange symbol*]

AEL .... Animal Educational League [*Defunct*]

AEL .... Appalachia Educational Laboratory [*Department of Education*] [*Charleston, WV*]

AEL .... Appalachian Environmental Laboratory [*University of Maryland Center for Environmental and Estuarine Studies*] [*Research center*] (RCD)

AEL .... Armament and Electronics Laboratory

AEL .... Army Electronics Laboratories (KSC)

AEL .... Association Europeenne du Laser [*European Laser Association - ELA*] (EA)

AEL .... Association of Equipment Lessors [*Later, AAEL*]

AEL .... Atomic Energy Level

AEL .... Audit Entry Language [*Burroughs Corp.*]

AEL .... Audit Error List

AEL .... Australian Employment Legislation [*A publication*]

AEL .... Authorized Equipment Listing (AABC)

AEL .... Auto Exposure Lock [*Photography*]

AEL .... Automation Engineering Laboratory

AEL .... Average Effectiveness Level (IAA)

AEL .... Luscar Ltd., Edmonton, Alberta [*Library symbol National Library of Canada*] (NLC)

AEL .... Small Ammunition Ship [*Navy symbol*] (DNAB)

AEL .... United States Army, Corps of Engineers, Louisville District, Louisville, KY [*OCLC symbol*] (OCLC)

AELC........... Accident-Experience Learning Curve (PDAA)

AELC........... Acquisition Education Learning Center [*Army*]

AELC........... Aerospace Engine Life Committee [*Air Force*] (AFIT)

AELC........... Agricultural Equipment Liaison Committee [*Victoria, Australia*]

AELC........... Architect-Engineers Liaison Commission

AELC........... Association of Evangelical Lutheran Churches

AEICmp....... American Electronic Components, Inc. [*Associated Press*] (SAG)

AELD .... Ascent Engine Latching Device [*NASA*] (KSC)

AELDC .... Atomic Energy Levels Data Center

AELE .... Americans for Effective Law Enforcement (EA)

AELE .... Association Europeenne de Libre-Echange [*European Free Trade Association - EFTA*] [*Geneva, Switzerland*]

AELECTECH... Associate in Electrical Technology (IAA)

AELECTRTECHN... Associate in Electronics Technology (IAA)

A El Ed .... Associate in Elementary Education

Aelf C .... Canons of Aelfric [*A publication*] (DLA)

AELIA .... Association d'Etudes Linguistiques Interculturelles Africaines [*Canada*]

AELJ .... Association pour l'Etude des Langues Juives [*Association for the Study of Jewish Languages*] (EAIO)

AELJ .... Atomic Energy Law Journal [*A publication*] (DLA)

AELK.......... Elk Point Public Library, Alberta [*Library symbol National Library of Canada*] (NLC)

AELL .... Province of Alberta Law Library System, Edmonton, Alberta [*Library symbol National Library of Canada*] (NLC)

AELMRP ...... Atomic Energy Labor Management Relations Panel

AELMS........ Elmworth School, Alberta [*Library symbol National Library of Canada*] (BIB)

AELN............ AEL Industries, Inc. [*NASDAQ symbol*] (NQ)

AELN............ Australian Environmental Law News [*A publication*]

AELN............ Local Networks, Edmonton, Alberta [*Library symbol National Library of Canada*] (NLC)

AELNO........ Elnora Public Library, Alberta [*Library symbol National Library of Canada*] (NLC)

AELO............ Aeromedical Evacuation Liaison Officer [*Air Force*] (AFM)

AELP............ Allied Electrical Publication [*Military*]

AEIP............. Allied Electrical Publications (NATG)

AEIPw......... American Electric Power Co., Inc. [*Associated Press*] (SAG)

AELRO........ Army Electronics Logistics Research Office (KSC)

AELS........... Airborne Electronic LASER System

AELT............ Association Europeenne de Laboratoires de Teledetection [*European Association of Remote Sensing Laboratories - EARSEL*] (EA)

AELTC........ All England Lawn Tennis Club

AELW.......... Airborne Electronics Warfare Course (DNAB)

AEM............ Accelerated Evaluation Method

AEM............ Acoustical Emission Monitoring (NASA)

AEM............ Active Engine Mount [*Automotive engineering*]

AEM............ Advance Engineering Memorandum

Aem............ Aemilius Paulus [*of Plutarch*] [*Classical studies*] (OCD)

AEM............ Aero Madrid [*Spain ICAO designator*] (FAAC)

AEM............ Aeronautical Mobile

AEM............ Agnico Eagle Mines [*NASDAQ symbol*] (TTSB)

AEM............ Agnico-Eagle Mines, Inc. [*NYSE symbol*] (SAG)

AEM............ Aircraft and Engine Mechanic

AEM............ Air Efficiency Medal [*RAF*] [*British*]

AEM............ American Energy Month [*Defunct*] (EA)

AEM............ Analytical Electron Microscope [*or Microscopy*] (DAVI)

AEM............ Analytical Electron Microscopy

AEM............ Analytic Element Method

AEM............ Application Explorer Mission [*NASA*]

AEM............ Arabian Exhibition Management WLL [*Manama, Bahrain*]

AEM............ Architect-Engineer-Manager [*Plan*]

AEM............ Arsenal Exchange Model (MCD)

AEM............ Associated Employers of Montana (SRA)

AEM............ Association Europeenne des Metaux [*European Association of Metals*] [*Belgium*] (EAIO)

AEM............ Association Europeenne du Moulinage [*European Throwsters Association - ETA*] (EA)

AEM............ Association of Electronic Manufacturers [*Later, EIA*] (EA)

AEM............ Attack Evaluation Model (MCD)

AEM............ Augmented Energy Management (MCD)

AEM............ Australian Employment Law Guide [*A publication*]

AEM............ Automatic Environment Monitoring (BUR)

AEM............ Automobile Engineering and Manufacturing [*Commercial firm British*]

AEM............ Aviation Electrician's Mate [*Navy rating*]

AEM............ Empress Municipal Library, Alberta [*Library symbol National Library of Canada*] (NLC)

AEM............ European Mills Association [*EC*] (ECED)

AEM............ Missile Support Ship (NATG)

AEM............ United States Army, Corps of Engineers, Lower Mississippi Valley Division, Vicksburg, MS [*OCLC symbol*] (OCLC)

AEMA........... Alberta Municipal Affairs, Edmonton, Alberta [*Library symbol National Library of Canada*] (NLC)

AEMA........... Asphalt Emulsion Manufacturers Association (EA)

AEMA........... Athletic Equipment Managers Association (EA)

AEMAN........ Alberta Manpower, Edmonton, Alberta [*Library symbol National Library of Canada*] (NLC)

AEMB.......... Airborne Electromechanical Bombing

AEMB.......... Alliance for Engineering in Medicine and Biology [*Defunct*] (EA)

AEMB.......... Association Europeenne des Marches aux Bestiaux [*European Association of Livestock Markets - EALM*] [*Brussels, Belgium*] (EAIO)

AEMB.......... Multilingual Biblioservice, Edmonton, Alberta [*Library symbol National Library of Canada*] (NLC)

AEMBA........ Advanced Executive Master of Business (PGP)

AEMC.......... Acryloyloxyethyl N-Methylcarbamate [*Organic chemistry*]

AEMC.......... Albert Einstein Medical Center

AEMC.......... American Electro Metal Corp.

AEMC.......... Arizona Energy Management Council (SRA)

AEMC.......... Auger and Elevator Manufacturers Council (EA)

AEMC.......... Australian Egg Marketing Council

AEMCC........ Air and Expedited Motor Carriers Conference (EA)

AEMCO........ Aircraft Engineering Maintenance Co.

AEMD.......... Albert Einstein Medical College (DAVI)

AEME.......... American Executives for Management Excellence [*An association*] (EA)

AEME.......... Association of International Marketing (EAIO)

AEME.......... Association pour l'Enseignement Medical en Europe [*Association for Medical Education in Europe - AMEE*] (EA)

AEM-ED...... Association of Electronic Manufacturers, Eastern Division (EA)

A-EMEPB.... Aviation-Electromagnetic Efects Policy Board [*Military*]

AEMH.......... Misericordia Hospital, Edmonton, Alberta [*Library symbol National Library of Canada*] (NLC)

AEMHSM..... Association Europeenne des Musees de l'Histoire des Sciences Medicales [*European Association of Museums of the History of Medical Sciences - EAMHMS*] (EAIO)

Aemil Ferret... Aemilius Ferretus [*Deceased, 1552*] [*Authority cited in pre-1607 legal work*] (DSA)

Aemil Pap ... Aemilius Papinianus [*Deceased, 212*] [*Authority cited in pre-1607 legal work*] (DSA)

AEMIS.......... Aerospace and Environmental Medicine Information System (IID)

AEML.......... Alberta Labour, Edmonton, Alberta [*Library symbol National Library of Canada*] (NLC)

AEMN.......... Australian Energy Management News [*A publication*]

AEMNA........ Association des Etudiants Musulmans Nord-Africains [*North African Muslim Students Association*] (AF)

AEMO.......... Advance Engineering Material Order

AEMO.......... African Elected Members Organization

AEMP.......... Atmospheric Electromagnetic Pulse

AEMR.......... Myrias Research Corp., Edmonton, Alberta [*Library symbol National Library of Canada*] (NLC)

AEMS.......... Agro-Environmental Monitoring System [*Computerized Data Collection*]

AEMS.......... Aircraft Engine Management System (MCD)

AEMS.......... Airline Economic Modeling System (HGAA)

AEMS.......... American Engineering Model Society (EA)

AEMS.......... Aminoethyl(methyl)sulfone [*Biochemistry*]

AEMS.......... Armament Electronic Maintenance Squadron

AEMS.......... Arts Education for a Multicultural Society (AIE)

AEMS.......... Automated Edge Match System (MCD)

AEMS.......... Automated Electrophoresis Microscope System (MCD)

AEMS.......... Milner & Steer, Edmonton, Alberta [*Library symbol National Library of Canada*] (BIB)

AEMSA........ Army Electronics Material Support Agency

AEMSAT...... Association of European Manufacturers of Self-Adhesive Tapes (EA)

AEMSM........ Association of European Metal Sink Manufacturers (EAIO)

AEM/SME.... Association for Electronics Manufacturing of the Society of Manufacturing Engineers (EA)

A-EMT........ Advanced Emergency Medical Technician (HCT)

AEMT.......... Association of Electrical Machinery Trades (EAIO)

AEMT.......... Association of Emergency Medical Technicians [*British*] (DBA)

AEMT.......... Automated Electronic Maintenance Training (MCD)

AEMT.......... Automatically Erectable Modular Torus

AEMT.......... Regional Library, Transport Canada [*Bibliotheque Regionale de Transports Canada*] Edmonton, Alberta [*Library symbol National Library of Canada*] (NLC)

AEMTC........ Western Region, Engineering and Architecture Library, Transport Canada [*Region de l'Ouest, Bibliotheque d'Ingenierie et d'Architecture, Transports Canada*], Edmonton, Alberta [*Library symbol National Library of Canada*] (NLC)

AEMTCA...... Civil Aviation Branch, Canadian Air Transportation Administration, Transport Canada [*Direction Generale de l'Aviation Civile, Administration Canadienne des Transports Aeriens, Transports Canada*] Edmonton, Alberta [*Library symbol National Library of Canada*] (NLC)

AEMTM........ Association of European Machine Tool Merchants [*Berkhamsted, Hertfordshire, England*] (EAIO)

AEMUM........ Association des Etudiants et Etudiantes en Medecine de l'Universite de Montreal (AC)

AEMVQ........ Association des Enseignants des Metiers du Vetement du Quebec (AC)

AEN............. Adaption Error Note

AEN............. Address Enable [*Computer science*]

AEN............. Advance Evaluation Note

Aen............. Aeneid [*of Vergil*] [*Classical studies*] (OCD)

AEN............. Agence de l'OCDE pour l'Energie Nucleaire [*OECD Nuclear Energy Agency - NEA*] (EAIO)

AEN............. Air Enterprise [*France ICAO designator*] (FAAC)

AEN............. Alberta Environmental Centre Library [*UTLAS symbol*]

AEN............. Alberta Environmental Network (AC)

AEN............. AMC Entertainment [*AMEX symbol*] (TTSB)

AEN............. AMC Entertainment, Inc. [*AMEX symbol*] (SPSG)

AEN............. Aseptic Epiphyseal Necrosis [*Medicine*] (DMAA)

A En........... Associate in English

AEN............. Association of Educational Negotiators [*Later, NAEN*] (EA)

AEN............. Enchant Public Library, Alberta [*Library symbol National Library of Canada*] (NLC)

AEN............. United States Army, Corps of Engineers, New Orleans District, New Orleans, LA [*OCLC symbol*] (OCLC)

AENA.......... All England Netball Association (EAIO)

AENA.......... Northern Alberta Institute of Technology, Edmonton, Alberta [*Library symbol National Library of Canada*] (NLC)

AENABC...... North American Baptist College and Divinity School, Edmonton, Alberta [*Library symbol National Library of Canada*] (NLC)

AENAC........ Nova, an Alberta Corp., Edmonton, Alberta [*Library symbol National Library of Canada*] (BIB)

AENC.......... Association Executives of North Carolina (SRA)

AENC.......... Avian Embryo Nutrient Cartridge

AEnC.......... Enterprise State Junior Colleg, Enterprise, AL [*Library symbol*] [*Library of Congress*] (LCLS)

AENF.......... Network Facilities-Development, Edmonton, Alberta [*Library symbol National Library of Canada*] (NLC)

AENG.......... Airways Engineer

A Eng.......... Associate in Engineering

A Eng Elect... Associate in Engineering Electronics

A Engr .... Associate in Engineering

AENI........... Technical Data Control Centre, Edmonton, Alberta [*Library symbol National Library of Canada*] (NLC)

AENM.......... Archenemy (ABBR)

AENORS...... Anticipated Engine Not Operationally Ready Supply [*Military*] (AFIT)

AENPR........ Aggregate Estimated Net Pool Return [*Business term*]

AENPr......... AMC Entertain't $1.75 Cv Pfd [*AMEX symbol*] (TTSB)

AENR.......... Alberta Energy and Natural Resources, Edmonton, Alberta [*Library symbol National Library of Canada*] (NLC)

AENT........... Entwistle Public Library, Alberta [*Library symbol National Library of Canada*] (NLC)

AEO............ Acoustoelectric Oscillator (IEEE)

AEO............ Advance Engineering Order

AEO............ Aeroservicios Ejecutivos del Occidente SA de CV [*Mexico ICAO designator*] (FAAC)

AEO............ Aioun El Atrouss [*Mauritania*] [*Airport symbol*] (OAG)

AEO............ Airborne Electronics Operator (IAA)

AEO............ Air Electronics Officer [*British*]

AEO............ Air Engineer Officer

AEO............ All Engines Operating [*Aviation*]

AEO............ American Eagle Petroleums Corp. [*Toronto Stock Exchange symbol*]

AEO............ Ammunition Executive Office [*Military British*]

AEO............ Appeals Examining Office [*CSC*]

AEO............ Area Education Officer [*Military British*]

AEO............ Area Engineering Officer [*Army Corps of Engineers*] (AAG)

AEO............ Army Energy Office

AEO............ Assistant Experimental Officer [*Ministry of Agriculture, Fisheries, and Food*] [*Also, AExO, AXO*] [*British*]

AEO............ Association of Education Officers [*British*]

AEO............ Association of Exhibition Organisers [*British*] (DBA)

AEO............ ATM [*Apollo Telescope Mount*] Experiments Officer [*NASA*]

AEO............ Atomic Energy Organisation [*Iran*] (NUCP)

AEO............ Author Earn-Out [*Publishing*]

AEO............ Oblate Archives of Alberta-Saskatchewan, Edmonton, Alberta [*Library symbol National Library of Canada*] (NLC)

AEO............ United States Army, Corps of Engineers, Ohio River District, Cincinnati, OH [*OCLC symbol*] (OCLC)

AEOB.......... Advanced Engine Overhaul Base

AEOC.......... Aminoethylhomocysteine [*Biochemistry*] (OA)

AEOC.......... Aquatic Ecosystem Objectives Committee [*Great Lakes Science Advisory Board*] [*Canada*]

AEOD.......... Office for Analysis and Evaluation of Operational Data [*Nuclear Regulatory Commission*]

AEODP........ Allied Explosive Ordnance Disposal Publication (MCD)

AEOE.......... Association for Environmental and Outdoor Education (EA)

AEOG.......... Air Ejection Off Gas (IEEE)

AEOH.......... Alberta Occupation Health and Safety, Edmonton, Alberta [*Library symbol National Library of Canada*] (NLC)

AEOK.......... Alexander Energy [*NASDAQ symbol*] (TTSB)

AEOK.......... Alexander Energy Corp. [*NASDAQ symbol*] (NQ)

AEOM.......... Alberta Office of the Ombudsman, Edmonton, Alberta [*Library symbol National Library of Canada*] (NLC)

AEON.......... Advanced Electronics Network [*British*] (NITA)

AEOO.......... Aeromedical Evacuation Operations Office [*or Officer*] [*Military*] (MCD)

AEoP.......... Allied Explosive Ordnance Disposal Publications (NATG)

AEOP.......... Amend Existing Orders Pertaining To

AEOP.......... Australian and New Zealand Equal Opportunity Law and Practice [*A publication*]

AEOS.......... Advanced Earth Observation Satellite

AEOS.......... Aft Engineering Operating Station (DNAB)

AEOS.......... After Engineering Operating Station (CAAL)

AEOS.......... Amer Eagle Outfitters [*NASDAQ symbol*] (TTSB)

AEOS.......... American Eagle Outfitters, Inc. [*NASDAQ symbol*] (SAG)

AEOS.......... Ancient Egyptian Order of Sciots (EA)

AEOSS........ Advanced Electro-Optical Sensor Simulation

AEOTR........ Advanced Electro-Optical Tracker/Ranger (MCD)

AEOW.......... Air Engineer Officer's Writer [*British military*] (DMA)

AEP............ Abstract Enterprise [*Vancouver Stock Exchange symbol*]

AEP............ Accrued Expenditure Paid [*Accounting*] (AFM)

AEP............ Acoustic Evoked Potential [*Physiology*]

AEP............ Adaptive Escalator Predictor (MCD)

AEP............ Adult Education Program

AEP............ Advanced Energy Projects [*Department of Energy*]

AEP............ A. E. Lepage Capital Prop. [*Limited Partnership Units*] [*Toronto Stock Exchange symbol*]

AEP............ Aggregate Exercise Price [*Investment term*]

AEP............ Aircraft Equipment Procedures (MCD)

AEP............ Air Evacuation Patients (AFIT)

AEP............ Airports Economic Panel [*ICAO*] (DA)

AEP............ Alberta Legislature Library, Edmonton, Alberta [*Library symbol National Library of Canada*] (NLC)

AEP............ Allied Engineering Publications (NATG)

AEP............ Allied Equipment Publications

AEP............ Alternative Education Project (EA)

AEP............ Amer Electric Pwr [*NYSE symbol*] (TTSB)

AEP............ American Electric Power

AEP............ American Electric Power Co., Inc. [*NYSE symbol*] (SAG)

AEP............ Aminoethylphosphonic Acid [*Organic chemistry*]

AEP............ Aminoethylpiperazine [*Organic chemistry*]

AEP............ Annual Engineering Plan (AFIT)

AEP............ Annual Execution Plan (RDA)

AEP............ Anterior Extreme Position [*Medicine*]

AEP............ Apollo Experiment Pallet [*NASA*]

AEP............ Apollo Extension Program [*NASA*]

AEP............ AppleTalk Echo Protocol [*Apple Computer, Inc.*] (PCM)

AEP............ Appropriateness Evaluation Protocol [*Medicine*] (MEDA)

AEP............ Aqueous Extraction Process

AEP............ Army Equipment Policy [*British military*] (DMA)

AEP............ Artificial Endocrine Pancreas [*Medicine*]

AEP............ Association d'Economie Politique [*Political Economic Association*] [*Canada*]

AEP............ Association of Educational Psychologists [*British*]

AEP............ Association of Embroiderers and Pleaters [*British*] (BI)

AEP............ Atomic Energy Project

AEP............ Auditory-Evoked Potential [*Neurophysiology*]

AEP............ AUTODIN Enhancement Program [*Computer science*] (MCD)

AEP............ Automated Environmental Prediction (CAAL)

AEP............ Automatic Electronic Production (IAA)

AEP............ Automatic End Point

AEP............ Automatic Extracting Program

AEP............ Average Evoked Potential [*Neurophysiology*]

AEP............ Buenos Aires [*Argentina*] Jorge Newbery Airport [*Airport symbol*] (OAG)

AEP............ Compania Aero Transportes Panamenos SA [*Panama*] [*ICAO designator*] (FAAC)

AEP............ United States Army, Corps of Engineers, Memphis District, Memphis, TN [*OCLC symbol*] (OCLC)

AEPA.......... Aminoethylphosphonic Acid [*Organic chemistry*] (PDAA)

AEPA.......... Bibliography Section, Alberta Public Affairs Bureau, Edmonton, Alberta [*Library symbol National Library of Canada*] (NLC)

AEPAA .... Provincial Archives of Alberta, Edmonton, Alberta [*Library symbol National Library of Canada*] (NLC)

AEPB.......... Active Enlisted Plans Branch [*BUPERS*]

AEPC.......... Alberta Provincial Courts, Edmonton, Alberta [*Library symbol National Library of Canada*] (NLC)

AEPC.......... Army Equipment Policy Committee (AAG)

AEPCF........ Premier's Commission on Future Health Care for Albertans, Edmonton, Alberta [*Library symbol National Library of Canada*] (BIB)

AEPCO........ American Elsevier Publishing Co. (DGA)

AEPD.......... Amino(ethyl)propanediol [*Organic chemistry*]

AEPDS........ Automated EAM Processing and Dissemination System (MCD)

AEPE.......... Association Europea de Profesores de Espanol (AIE)

AEPEM........ Association of Electronic Parts and Equipment Manufacturers [*Later, EIA*]

AEPFC........ Associates of Elvis Presley Fan Clubs (EA)

AEPG.......... Army Electronic Proving Ground

AEPI.......... AEP Industries [*NASDAQ symbol*] (TTSB)

AEPI.......... AEP Industries, Inc. [*Moonachie, NJ*] [*NASDAQ symbol*] (NQ)

AEPI.......... Aerospace Engineering Process Institute

AEPI.......... American Educational Publishers Institute [*Later, AAP*]

AEPI.......... Atmospheric Emissions Photometric Imaging [*Plasma physics*]

AEPIC........ Architecture and Engineering Performance Information Center [*University of Maryland*] [*College Park*] [*Information service or system*] (IID)

AEP Ind........ AEP Industries [*Associated Press*] (SAG)

AEPL.......... Approved Equivalent Parts List

AEPL.......... Professional Library, Edmonton Catholic School District, Edmonton, Alberta [*Library symbol National Library of Canada*] (NLC)

AEPM.......... Association of Evangelical Professors of Missions (EA)

AEPOM .... Association pour l'Etude des Problemes d'Outre-Mer [*Association for the Study of Overseas Problems*] [*French*] (AF)

AEPP.......... Association of Existential Psychology and Psychiatry [*Defunct*] (EA)

AEPP.......... Southeast/East Asian English Publications in Print [*Japan Publications Guide Service*] [*Japan Information service or system*] (CRD)

AEPPF........ Albert Einstein Peace Prize Foundation (EA)

AEPQ.......... Association d'Education Prescolaire du Quebec (AC)

AEPR.......... American Exmoor Pony Registry (EA)

AEPR.......... Resource Center, City of Edmonton Personnel Department, Alberta [*Library symbol National Library of Canada*] (NLC)

AEPRD........ Planning, Research and Development Division, Alberta Attorney General, Edmonton, Alberta [*Library symbol National Library of Canada*] (NLC)

AEPRT .... All Equipment Production Reliability Tests (MCD)

AEPS.......... Advanced Electronic Publishing System (NITA)

AEPS.......... Advanced Extravehicular Protective System [*NASA*]

AEPS.......... Aircraft Electrical Power System

AEPS.......... Aircrew Escape Propulsion System [*Navy*]

AEPS.......... Alfred E. Packer Society (EA)

AEPS.......... Aminoethylaminopropylsilane

AEPS.......... Asphalt Employees Protection Society [*A union*] [*British*]

AEPS.......... ATM [*Apollo Telescope Mount*] Electrical Power System [*NASA*]

AEPS.......... Automated Environmental Prediction System (MCD)

AEPU.......... Alberta Public Utilities Board, Edmonton, Alberta [*Library symbol National Library of Canada*] (NLC)

AEPUC .... Association pour l'Education Permanente dan les Universites du Canada (AC)

AEPW.......... Aircraft Emergency Procedures over Water

AEPW.......... College Plaza Resource Centre, Alberta Public Works, Supply and Services, Edmonton, Alberta [*Library symbol National Library of Canada*] (NLC)

AEPWW .... Western Region Library, Public Works Canada [*Bibliotheque de la Region de l'Ouest, Travaux Publics Canada*] Edmonton, Alberta [*Library symbol National Library of Canada*] (NLC)

AEQ............ Aequales [*Equal*] [*Latin*]

AEq .... Age Equivalent (MAE)

AEQ............ Asiamerica Equities Ltd. [*Vancouver Stock Exchange symbol*]

AEQ............ Association des Electrolystes du Quebec (AC)

AEQI.......... Agricultural Environmental Quality Institute [*Department of Agriculture*] [*Beltsville, MD*]

AEqP.......... Allied Equipment Publications (NATG)

Aequtrn........ Aequitron Medical, Inc. [*Associated Press*] (SAG)

AER............ Abbreviated Effectiveness Report [*Air Force*]

AER............ Academic Evaluation Report [*Military*] (INF)

AER............ Ace Air Cargo Express, Inc. [*ICAO designator*] (FAAC)

AER............ Acoustic Evoked Response [*Neurophysiology*] (DMAA)

AER............ Address Extension Register [*Computer science*] (IAA)

AER............ Adler/Sochi [*Former USSR Airport symbol*] (OAG)

AER............ Aerial (IAA)

AER............ Aerodrome (IAA)
AER............ Aerodynamic (IAA)
AER............ Aerolift, Inc. [Vancouver Stock Exchange symbol]
AER............ Aeronautical Engineering Report
AER............ Aeronautical Equipment Reference (SAA)
AER............ Aeronautics (MCD)
AER............ Aeroplane (ADA)
AER............ After Engine Room
AER............ Agricultural Economic Reports
AER............ Agri-Energy Roundtable (EA)
AER............ Airborne Extended Range
AER............ Air Equivalence Ratio [For hydrocarbon combustion]
AER............ Airman Effectiveness Report [Air Force]
AER............ Alberta Research Council, Edmonton, Alberta [Library symbol National Library of Canada] (NLC)
AER............ Albumin Excretion Rate [Physiology]
AER............ Aldosterone Excretion Rate [Endocrinology]
AER............ All England Law Reports [A publication]
AER............ Alliance to End Repression (EA)
AER............ Alpha Epsilon Rho [Also, AERho] [Fraternity] (NTCM)
AER............ Alteration Equivalent to a Repair
AER............ Aluminum Efficient Radiator [General Motors Corp.] [Automotive engineering]
AER............ Americans for Economic Reform (EA)
AER............ Antenna Effective Resistance
AER............ Apical Ectodermal Ridge [Embryology, genetics]
AER............ Approach End Runway [Aviation] (FAAC)
AER............ Army Emergency Relief (EA)
AER............ Army Emergency Reserve [British]
AER............ Association Europeenne de Radiologie [European Association of Radiology - EAR] (EA)
AER............ Association for Education and Rehabilitation of the Blind and Visually Impaired (EA)
AER............ Auditory-Evoked Response [Neurophysiology]
AER............ Average Evoked Response [Neurophysiology]
AER............ Azimuth Elevation Range (KSC)
AER............ Thai-American Treaty of Amity and Economic Relations (IMH)
AER............ United States Army, Corps of Engineers, Omaha District, Omaha, NE [OCLC symbol] (OCLC)
AERA .... Aeration (ABBR)
AERA .... Airborne Electronics Research Activity [Lakehurst, NJ] [United States Army Communications-Electronics Command] (GRD)
AERA .... American Educational Research Association (EA)
AERA .... Ancient Egypt Research Associates
AERA .... Associate Engraver, Royal Academy [British]
AERA .... Automated En-Route Air Traffic Control [Proposed] [FAA]
AERA .... Automotive Engine Rebuilders Association (EA)
AERA .... Royal Alexandra Hospital, Edmonton, Alberta [Library symbol National Library of Canada] (NLC)
AERASN....... School of Nursing, Royal Alexandra Hospital, Edmonton, Alberta [Library symbol National Library of Canada] (NLC)
AERB .... Army Educational Requirements Board
AERB .... Army Education Review Board
AERB .... Atomic Energy Regulatory Board [India]
AERC .... African Economic Research Consortium
AERC .... African Economic Research Consortium
AERC .... Aircraft Engine Record Card (DNAB)
AERC .... Amelia Earhart Research Consortium (EA)
AERC .... American Endurance Ride Conference (EA)
AERC .... Association of Ecosystem Research Centers (EA)
AERC .... Association of Executive Recruiting Consultants [Later, AESC] (EA)
AERC .... Atlantic Educational Research Council [Canada]
AERC .... Clover Bar Branch, Alberta Research Council, Edmonton, Alberta [Library symbol National Library of Canada] (NLC)
AERCAB ...... Advanced [or Aircrew] Escape/Rescue Capability [Navy - Air Force]
AERCQ .... Association des Enseignants en Refrigeration et Climatisation du Quebec (AC)
AERCW .... Auxiliary Essential Raw Cooling Water [Nuclear energy] (NRCH)
AERD .... Agricultural Engineering Research and Development [Canada]
AERD .... Alpha Energy Range Discrimination [Analysis of radioactivity]
AERD .... Atomic Energy Research Department [NASA] (KSC)
AERDA .... Army Electronics Research and Development Activity [White Sands Missile Range, NM]
AERDC .... Agricultural Extension and Rural Development Centre [University of Reading] [British] (CB)
AERDL .... Army Electronics Research and Development Laboratory (AABC)
AERDL .... Army Engineer Research and Development Laboratories [Fort Belvoir, VA]
AERDO .... Association of Evangelical Relief and Development Organizations (DICI)
AERDYN........ Aerodynamic (ABBR)
AerE............ Aeronautical Engineer (ADA)
AERE............ Association of Environmental and Resource Economists (EA)
AERE............ Atomic Energy Research Establishment [of United Kingdom Atomic Energy Authority]
AER En .... AER Energy Resources [Associated Press] (SAG)
AERF............ Atlas Economic Research Foundation (EA)
AERF............ Australian Equine Research Foundation
AERG .... Advanced Environmental Research Group [Commercial firm]
AERG .... Army Engineer Reactors Group [Fort Belvoir, VA]
AERI .... Agricultural Economics Research Institution [British]
AERI............ Automotive Exhaust Research Institute [Defunct] (EA)
AerialC .... Aerial Communications, Inc. [Associated Press] (SAG)
AERIC .... Applied Economic Research and Information Centre [Conference Board of Canada] [Ottawa, ON]

AERIS .... Airborne Electronic Ranging Instrumentation System
AERIS .... Airways Environmental RADAR Information System (IEEE)
AERIS .... Automatic Electronic Range Instrumentation System (MCD)
AERIS .... Industrial Information, Alberta Research Council, Edmonton, Alberta [Library symbol National Library of Canada] (NLC)
AERL......... Aerial (AFM)
AERL......... Aerial Communications, Inc. [NASDAQ symbol] (SAG)
AERL......... Aero-Elastic Research Laboratory [MIT] (MCD)
AERL......... Arctic Environmental Research Laboratory [Environmental Protection Agency] (NOAA)
AERL......... Australian Energy Research Laboratory
AERL......... Avco-Everett Research Laboratory (MCD)
AERLS .... Agricultural Extension and Research Liaison Service [Nigeria] (IRC)
AERLT........ Aerialist (ABBR)
AERM......... Aerographer's Mate [Navy rating]
Aer M......... Aerosol Mask [Medicine] (DAVI)
AERM......... R. M. Hardy & Associates Ltd., Edmonton, Alberta [Library symbol National Library of Canada] (NLC)
AERN......... AER Energy Resources [NASDAQ symbol] (SAG)
AERN......... Aeronaut (ABBR)
AERNC........ Aeronautics (ABBR)
AERNL........ Aeronautical (ABBR)
AERNLY........ Aeronautically (ABBR)
AERNO........ Aeronautical Equipment Reference Number [Military]
Aero......... Aerobacter [Microbiology]
AERO .... Aeroballistics (SAA)
AERO .... Aerodynamic (NASA)
AERO .... Aerographer
AERO .... Aeronautics (AFM)
Aero......... Aeronautics (DD)
AERO .... Aerospace
AERO .... Aerosurfaces (NASA)
AERO .... Air Education Recreation Organization [British] (DA)
AERO .... Alternative Energy Resources Organization (EA)
AERO .... Association of Educational Research Officers of Ontario [Association Ontarienne des Agents de Recherche en Education] (AC)
AERO .... Automatic Earnings Recomputation Operation [Social Security]
AERO .... Azimuth, Elevation, and Range Overtake (SAA)
AERO-A........ Aeroballistics - Aerodynamics Analysis (SAA)
AEROBEE ..... Aerojet/Bumblebee [Navy missile]
AEROCE .... Atmosphere/Ocean Chemistry Experiment [Marine science] (OSRA)
AEROCE .... Atmosphere/Ocean Chemistry Experiment (USDC)
AEROCOM.... Aeronautical Communications Equipment Corp.
AEROCONDOR... Aerovias Condor de Colombia Ltda. [Condor Airlines of Colombia Ltd.]
AEROCOR .... Aerolineas Cordillera Ltda. [Chile] [ICAO designator] (FAAC)
AERO-D........ Aeroballistics - Dynamics Analysis (SAA)
AERODF .... Aerospace Defense Flight [Air Force]
AERO-DIR .... Aeroballistics - Director (SAA)
AERODS...... Aerospace Defense Squadron [Air Force]
AERODW...... Aerospace Defense Wing [Air Force]
AERODYN...... Aerodynamic (KSC)
AERO-E........ Aeroballistics - Experimental Aerodynamics (SAA)
AERO-F........ Aeroballistics - Flight Evaluation (SAA)
AER OF........ Aerological Officer
Aeroflex....... Aeroflex, Inc. [Associated Press] (SAG)
AEROFLOT... Aero Flotilla [Airline] [Former USSR]
AEROG........ Aerologist
AEROHEAT..... Aerodynamic Heating (NG)
AEROIS........ Aerospace Intelligence Squadron [Air Force]
AEROL........ Aerological
AEROMED..... Aeromedical
AEROMOD..... Aerodynamic Modeling [Module]
AERON........ Aeronautical
AERONICA .... Aerolineas Nicaraguenses [Nicaragua Airlines] (EY)
AERONL........ Aeronautical
AERO-P........ Aeroballistics - Future Projects (SAA)
AERO-PCA..... Aeroballistics - Program Coordination and Administration (SAA)
AEROPERU.... Linea Aerea Peruana [Peruvian State Airlines]
AEROPOST.... Aerodynamic Post-Processing [Module]
AERO-PS..... Aeroballistics - Project Staff (SAA)
AERO R Bn... Aeronautical Radiobeacon [Nautical charts]
AERO R Rge... Aeronautical Radio Range [Nautical charts]
AEROS .... Advanced Earth Resources Observation System
AEROS .... Aerometric and Emissions Reporting System [Environmental Protection Agency]
AEROS .... Artificial Earth Research and Orbiting Satellite (NATG)
AEROSAT.... Aeronautical Communications Satellite System
AEROSAT.... Aeronautical Satellite
AEROSG ...... Aerospace Support Group [Air Force]
AEROS-NATE... Aeronomy Satellite - Neutral Atmosphere Temperature Experiment
AEROSOL.... Aerospace Spin-Off Laboratory
Aeroson...... Aerosonic Corp. [Associated Press] (SAG)
AEROSP...... Aerospace (MSA)
AEROSPACE... Aeronautics and Space
AEROSPACECOM... Aerospace Communications
AEROSPRSCHPLTSCH... Aerospace Research USAF Test Pilot School [Later, USAFTESTPLTSCH]
AEROSS....... Aerospace Support Squadron [Air Force]
AEROSSq....... Aerospace Support Squadron [Air Force]
AERO-TS..... Aeroballistics - Technical and Scientific Staff (SAA)
AEROVENCA... Aeronautica Venezolana CA [Venezuela] [ICAO designator] (FAAC)
Aerovx........ Aerovox, Inc. [Associated Press] (SAG)
AERP .... Advanced Equipment Repair Program [Military] (DNAB)
AERP .... Aircrew Eyes Respiratory System (DWSG)

AERPW .... Alberta Recreation and Parks, Edmonton, Alberta [*Library symbol National Library of Canada*] (NLC)

AERREFRON... Aerial Refueling Squadron (DNAB)

AER Rep ...... All England Law Reports (Reprint) [*1558-1935*] [*A publication*] (DLA)

AER Rep Ext... All England Law Reports (Reprint) Australian Extension Volumes [*A publication*] (DLA)

AERS .... Aero Sys Engr [*NASDAQ symbol*] (TTSB)

AERS .... Aero Systems Engineering, Inc. [*NASDAQ symbol*] (NQ)

AERS .... Airborne Environmental Reporting System

AERS .... Airborne Equipment Repair Squadron (MCD)·

AERS .... Airborne Expendable Rocket System (MCD)

AERS .... Aircraft Equipment Requirement Schedule

AERS .... Army Education Requirement System (DOMA)

AERS .... Atlantic Estuarine Research Society (EA)

AERSG .... African Elephant and Rhino Specialist Group [*of the International Union for Conservation of Nature and Natural Resources*] (EA)

AERSL .... Aerosol (ABBR)

AERSPC ...... Aerospace (ABBR)

AERSWE ..... Solar and Wind Energy Research Program Information Centre, Alberta Research Council, Edmonton, Alberta [*Library symbol Obsolete National Library of Canada*] (NLC)

AerSyE........ Aero Systems Engineering, Inc. [*Associated Press*] (SAG)

AERT.......... Acceptable Environmental Range Test

AERT.......... Advanced Environmental Recycling Technology, Inc. [*NASDAQ symbol*] (NQ)

AERT.......... Advanced Environmental Research and Technology (MCD)

AERT.......... Advanced Environ Recycling Technologies, Inc. [*NASDAQ symbol*] (SAG)

Aer T .... Aerosol Tent [*Medicine*] (DAVI)

AERT.......... Association for Education by Radio-Television [*Defunct*] (AEBS)

AERTA .... Advanced Envirn Recycl Tech [*NASDAQ symbol*] (TTSB)

AERTC .... Association pour les Etudes sur la Radio-Television Canadienne [*Association for the Study of Canadian Radio and Television - ASCRT*]

AERTEL....... Association Europeenne Rubans, Tresses, Tissus Elastiques [*European Ribbon, Braid, and Elastic Material Association*]

AERTP .... Terrace Plaza Branch Library, Alberta Research Council, Edmonton, Alberta [*Library symbol National Library of Canada*] (NLC)

AERTZ......... Advanced Environm'l Recyclg Wrrt [*NASDAQ symbol*] (TTSB)

AERU .... University Branch, Alberta Research Council, Edmonton, Alberta [*Library symbol National Library of Canada*] (NLC)

AERX .... Aero Spacelines [*Air carrier designation symbol*]

AES............. Aalesund [*Norway*] [*Airport symbol*] (OAG)

AES............. Abrasive Engineering Society (EA)

AES............. Acrylonitrile Ethylene Styrene [*Organic chemistry*]

AES............. Active Electromagnetic System [*Electronics*] (IAA)

AES............. Active Employment Strategy

AES............. Adult Emergency Service [*In TV series "A.E.S. Hudson Street"*]

AES............. Advanced Engineering Services [*General Motors Corp.*] [*Automotive engineering*]

AES............. Advanced Extravehicular Suit [*NASA*]

AES............. Aerodrome Emergency Service (DA)

AES............. Aerolineas Centrales de Colombia [*ICAO designator*] (FAAC)

AES............. Aeromedical Evacuation Squadron [*Air Force*]

AES............. Aeronautical Earth Station (DA)

AES............. Aerospace Electrical Society (EA)

AES............. Aerospace Electronics System (IAA)

AES............. AES Corp. [*NYSE symbol*] (SAG)

Aes............. Aesop (BARN)

AES............. Agricultural Economics Society (EAIO)

AES............. Agricultural Estimates Division [*of AMS, Department of Agriculture*]

AES............. Agricultural Extension Service (OICC)

AES............. Air and Earth Shock (MCD)

AES............. Air and Energy Staff [*Environmental Protection Agency*] (GFGA)

AES............. Aircraft Earth Station [*ICAO designator*] (FAAC)

AES............. Aircraft Ejection Seat

AES............. Aircraft Electrical Society (SAA)

AES............. Aircraft Engineering Squadron (SAA)

AES............. Airways Engineering Society [*Defunct*] (EA)

AES............. Alkylethoxylated Sulfate [*Surfactant*] [*Organic chemistry*]

AES............. All-England Series

AES............. Allyl Elthenesulphonate (PDAA)

AES............. Alternative Economic Strategy

AES............. Amateur Entomologists' Society (EA)

AES............. American Ecology Services (EA)

AES............. American Educational Society (EA)

AES............. American Electrochemical Society [*Later, ECS*]

AES............. American Electroencephalographic Society (EA)

AES............. American Electromechanical Society

AES............. American Electronical Society

AES............. American Electroplaters' Society (EA)

AES............. American Encephalographic Society [*Neurophysiology*] (DAVI)

AES............. American Endocrine Society (DAVI)

AES............. American Endodontic Society (EA)

AES............. American Entomological Society (EA)

AES............. American Epidemiological Society (EA)

AES............. American Epilepsy Society (EA)

AES............. American Equilibration Society (EA)

AES............. American Ethnological Society (EA)

AES............. American Eugenics Society [*Later, SSSB*] (EA)

AES............. Analog Event System [*Computer science*] (MCD)

AES............. Analysis and Evaluation Staff [*Environmental Protection Agency*] (GFGA)

AES............. Anterior Ectosylvian Sulcus [*Neuroanatomy*]

AES............. Anti-Embolic Stockings [*Medicine*] (DMAA)

AES............. Antral Ethmoidal Sphenoidectomy [*Otorhinolaryngology*] (DAVI)

AES............. Apollo Earth-Orbiting Station [*NASA*]

AES............. Apollo Experiment Support [*NASA*]

AES............. Apollo Extension System [*NASA*]

AES............. Applications Environment System

AES............. Applied Energy Services [*Commercial firm*] (ECON)

AES............. Area Electronic Supervisor

AES............. Army Excess Property (AABC)

AES............. Army Exchange Service [*Centralized the control of PX's in US*] [*World War II*]

AES............. Array Element Study

AES............. Artificial Earth Satellite [*NASA*]

AES............. Artillery Equipment School [*British*] (DAS)

AES............. Astronomical Explorer Satellite

AES............. Atlantic Economic Society (EA)

AES............. Atlantic Estuarine Society

AES............. Atmospheric Environment Service [*Canada*]

AES............. Atomic Emission Spectroscopy

AES............. Attenuation Efficiency Score (PDAA)

AES............. Audio Engineering Society (EA)

AES............. Auger Electron Spectrometry [*or Spectroscopy*]

AES............. Automatic Emission Spectroscopy (MCD)

AES............. Automatic External Standard [*or Standardization*] [*Radioactivity measurement*]

AES............. Automatic Extraction System [*Computer science*] (MHDI)

AES............. Auxiliary Encoder System

AES............. Avionics Expert System (MCD)

AES............. Guam Agricultural Experiment Station [*University of Guam*] [*Research center*] (RCD)

AES............. Missouri Agricultural Experiment Station [*University of Missouri - Columbia*] [*Research center*] (RCD)

AES............. Northway, AK [*Location identifier FAA*] (FAAL)

AES............. Statistics Canada [*Statistique Canada*] Edmonton, Alberta [*Library symbol National Library of Canada*] (NLC)

AES............. United States Army, Corps of Engineers, Southwest Division, Dallas, TX [*OCLC symbol*] (OCLC)

AESA.......... Aerolineas de El Salvador [*Airline*] [*El Salvador*]

AESA.......... American Educational Studies Association (EA)

AESA.......... Association of Environmental Scientists and Administrators [*Defunct*] (EA)

AESA.......... Association pour l'Enseignement Social en Afrique [*Association for Social Work Education in Africa - ASWEA*] (EAIO)

AESAE........ Stanley Associates Engineering Ltd., Edmonton, Alberta [*Library symbol National Library of Canada*] (NLC)

AESAL........ Academie Europeenne des Sciences, des Arts, et des Lettres [*European Academy of Arts, Sciences, and Humanities*] (EAIO)

AES/ALSS/LESA... Apollo Extension System / Apollo Logistics Support System / Lunar Exploration System for Apollo [*NASA*] (SAA)

AES & S ...... Association of English Singers and Speakers [*British*] (DBA)

AESAP .... Army Entertainment Scholarships and Awards Program (AABC)

AESB.......... Architect-Engineers - Spanish Bases

AESBNW ..... Association of Engineers and Scientists of the Bureau of Naval Weapons [*Later, ASE*]

AESC.......... Aerojet Electrosystems Co. (MCD)

AESC.......... Aerospace and Electronic Systems Society (NITA)

AESC.......... AES Corp. [*NASDAQ symbol*] (SAG)

AESC.......... American Engineering Standards Committee [*Later, ANSI*]

AESC.......... Association of Executive Search Consultants (EA)

AESC.......... Automatic Electronic Switching Center

AESC.......... Canadian Steel Environmental Association [*Association Environnemental de la Siderurgie Canadienne*] (AC)

AESC.......... Syncrude Canada Ltd., Edmonton, Alberta [*Library symbol National Library of Canada*] (NLC)

AESCH........ Aeschylus [*Greek poet, 525-456BC*] [*Classical studies*] (ROG)

Aeschin....... Aeschines [*c. 397-322BC*] [*Classical studies*] (OCD)

AES Chn ..... AES China Generating Co. [*Associated Press*] (SAG)

AESCO .... Association Europeenne des Ecoles et Colleges d'Optometre [*European Association of Schools and Colleges of Optometry - EASCO*] (EA)

AESCOT ...... Aircraft Electrical System Component Tester (DWSG)

AES Cp .... AES Corp. [*Associated Press*] (SAG)

AESD .... Acoustic Environmental Support Detachment [*Office of Naval Research*] [*Arlington, VA*]

AESD .... AIDS Education/Services for the Deaf [*An association*]

AESD .... Alberta School for the Deaf, Edmonton, Alberta [*Library symbol National Library of Canada*] (NLC)

AESE.......... Association of Earth Science Editors (EA)

AES/EBU ..... Audio Engineering Society/European Broadcast Union (DOM)

AESEQ .... Association des Entrepreneurs de Services en Environnement du Quebec (AC)

AESES........ Association of Employees Supporting Education Services [*Canada*]

AESF.......... American Electroplaters & Surface Finishers Society [*Association des Galvanoplastes d'Amerique*] [*Formerly, American Electroplaters Society*] (AC)

AESFS........ American Electroplaters' and Surface Finishers Society (EA)

AESG .... Alberta Solicitor General, Edmonton, Alberta [*Library symbol National Library of Canada*] (NLC)

AESG .... Australian Employee Survey Group

AESGP .... Association Europeenne des Specialites Pharmaceutiques Grand Public [*European Proprietary Association*] (EA)

AES(I).......... Association of Engineers and Scientists (Independent)

AESI........... Australian Earth Sciences Information System [*Database on AUSINET*] (NITA)

AESIAC .... Air Education Section of the Irish Aviation Council (EAIO)

AESIR .... Aerospace Instrumentation Range Station

AESIS.......... Schick Information Systems, Edmonton, Alberta [*Library symbol Obsolete National Library of Canada*] (NLC)
AESJ............ Atomic Energy Society of Japan (NUCP)
AESL........... Associated Engineering Services [*Canada*]
AESM.......... Association for Equine Sports Medicine (EA)
AESMC........ Automotive Exhaust Systems Manufacturers Council (EA)
AESMD .... Aircraft Escape System Maintenance Data (MCD)
AESN........... Association of Export Subscription Newsagents (DGA)
AESNW .... Art Education Society of New South Wales [*Australia*]
AESO .... Airborne Electronic Sensor Operator [*Canadian Navy*]
AESO .... Aircraft Environmental Support Office [*Naval Air Rework Facility*] [*North Island, CA*]
AESOP .... Accounts Enquiry Sales and Order Processing (ADA)
AESOP .... Airborne Experiment to Study Ozone Production (USDC)
AESOP .... Airborne Experiment to Study Ozone Production [*Marine science*] (OSRA)
AESOP .... Artificial Earth Satellite Observation Program [*Navy*]
AESOP .... Automated Educational Services On-Line Processing (MCD)
AESOP .... Automated Endoscopic System for Optimal Positioning [*Medicine*]
AESOP .... Automated Engineering and Scientific Optimization Program [*NASA*]
AESOP .... [*An*] Evolutionary System for On-Line Processing [*Computer science*]
AESOPS ...... AMSAA [*Army Materiel Systems Analysis Agency*] Evade Sustained Operations Performance Simulation (MCD)
AESP .... Applied Extrasensory Projection [*Psychology*] (DAVI)
AESP .... Auxiliary Engineering Signal Processor
AESQ .... Aeromedical Evacuation Squadron [*Air Force*] (DAVI)
AESQ .... Air Explorer Squadron
AESR .... Aeronautical Equipment Service Record (MCD)
AESR .... Army Equipment Status Report
AESRC .... American English Spot Rabbit Club (EA)
AESRS .... Army Equipment Status Reporting System (AABC)
AESRS .... Automatic Electronic Switching System
AESS .... Aerospace and Electronics Systems (IEEE)
AESS .... Aircraft Ejection Seat System
AESS .... Appraisals, Evaluation, and Sectoral Study
AESS .... Association des Economistes, Sociologues, et Statisticiens [*Economists', Sociologists', and Statisticians' Association ESSA*] [*Canada*]
AESS .... Automatic Electronic Switching System (MCD)
AESS .... IEEE Aerospace and Electronics Systems Society (EA)
AEST .... Aeromedical Evacuation Support Team
AESTH .... Aesthete (ABBR)
AESTH .... Aesthetics
AESTHY ...... Aesthetically (ABBR)
AESU .... Absolute Electrostatic Unit (IAA)
AESU .... Aerospace Environmental Support Unit [*Air Weather Service*] (IID)
AESV.......... Association Europeene de Saint Vladimir (EAIO)
AET .... Absorption Equivalent Thickness
AET .... Acoustic Emission Testing (MHDB)
AET .... Actual Elapsed Time
AET .... Actual Equipment Trainer (MCD)
AET .... Actual Evapotranspiration [*Biology*]
AET .... Actual Exposure Time (MUGU)
AET .... Advanced Energy Technology
AET .... Aerlinte Eireann Teoranta [*Irish Air Lines*]
AET .... Aeromedical Evacuation Technician
AET .... Aero-Palma SA [*Spain ICAO designator*] (FAAC)
AET .... Aerosurface End-to-End Test (MCD)
aet .... Aetas [*or Aetatis*] [*Age or Aged*] [*Latin*]
Aet .... Aetia [*of Callimachus*] [*Classical studies*] (OCD)
aet .... Aetiology [*or Etiology*] [*Medicine*] (DAVI)
AET .... Aetna Capital LLC [*NYSE symbol*] (SAG)
AET .... Aetna, Inc. [*NYSE symbol*] (SAG)
AET .... Aetna Life & Casualty [*NYSE symbol*] (TTSB)
AET .... Aetna Life & Casualty Co. [*NYSE symbol*] (SAG)
AET .... Africa Educational Trust [*British*]
AET .... Aircraft Equipment Trainer (MCD)
AET .... Aircrew Egress Trainer (MCD)
AET .... Airfields Environment Trust [*British*]
AET .... Alberta Treasury, Edmonton, Alberta [*Library symbol National Library of Canada*] (NLC)
AET .... Allakaket [*Alaska*] [*Airport symbol*] (OAG)
AET .... Alliance for Environmental Technology
AET .... Alliance pour l'Enfant et la Television [*The Children's Broadcast Institute*] (AC)
Aet .... Aminoethyl [*Biochemistry*]
AET .... Aminoethylisothiuronium [*Radiology*]
AET .... Apparent Elastic Thickness [*Geoscience*]
AET .... Approximate Exposure Time
AET .... Army Extension Training (GFGA)
AET .... Associate in Electrical Technology
AET .... Associate in Engineering Technology
AET .... Association des Employes du Trafic [*Association of Traffic Employees*] [*Canada*]
AET .... Association Europeenne Thyroide [*European Thyroid Association - ETA*] (EAIO)
AET .... Association of Autoelectrical Technicians Ltd. [*British*] (BI)
AET .... Atrial Ectopic Tachycardia [*Medicine*]
AET .... Auto Exhaust Testing
Aet .... De Aeternitate Mundi [*Philo*] (BJA)
AET .... United States Army, Corps of Engineers, North Atlantic Division, New York, NY [*OCLC symbol*] (OCLC)
AETA .... Adult Education Tutors' Association [*Australia*]
AETA .... Amatex Export Trade Association [*Defunct*] (EA)
AETA .... American Educational Theatre Association [*Later, ATA*] (EA)

AETA .... American Embryo Transfer Association (EA)
AETA .... Antique Engine and Thresher Association (EA)
AETA .... Australian Equestrian Trade Association
AETAC........ Aviation Electronic Technician's Mate, Combat Aircrewman [*Navy*]
AETAT .... Aetatis [*Age*] [*Latin*]
AETATE .... Facility Engineering and Systems Development Library, Transport Canada [*Bibliotheque de l'Ingenierie des Installations et de la Mise au Point des Systemes, Transports Canada*], Edmonton, Alberta [*Library symbol National Library of Canada*] (NLC)
AETATE........ Telecommunications and Electronics, Canadian Air Transportation Administration, Transport Canada [*Telecommunications et Electronique, Administration Canadienne des Transports Aeriens, Transports Canada*] Edmonton, Alberta [*Library symbol National Library of Canada*] (NLC)
AETATES...... Facility Engineering and Systems Development Sub-Library, Edmonton InternationalAirport, Transport Canada [*Succursale de la Bibliotheque de l'Ingenierie des Installations et de la Mise au Point des Systemes, Aeroport International d'Edm onton, Transports Canada*], Alberta [*Library symbol National Library of Canada*] (NLC)
AeTBD .... Aerobically Thioglycolate Broth Disk (PDAA)
AETBS......... Bureau of Statistics, Alberta Treasury, Edmonton, Alberta [*Library symbol National Library of Canada*] (NLC)
AETC.......... Accessory and Equipment Technical Committee (KSC)
AETC.......... Air Education and Training Command [*Air Force*] (DOMA)
AETC.......... Applied Extrusion Tech [*NASDAQ symbol*] (TTSB)
AETC.......... Applied Extrusion Technologies [*NASDAQ symbol*] (SPSG)
AETC.......... ARCO Exploration and Technology Co.
AETCT .... Corporate Tax Administration, Alberta Treasury, Edmonton, Alberta [*Library symbol National Library of Canada*] (NLC)
AETD.......... Aero-Electronic Technology Department [*Navy*] (MCD)
AETDA .... Aminoethyltricosadiynamide [*Organic chemistry*]
AETE .... Aerospace Engineering Test Establishment [*Canada*]
AETF .... Association des Etudiants Tchadiens en France [*Association of Chadian Students in France*] [*Chad*] (AF)
AETF .... Azimuth Error Test Feature
AETF .... Azimuth Error Test Fixture (MCD)
AETFAT........ Association pour l'Etude Taxonomique de la Flore d'Afrique Tropicale [*Association for the Taxonomic Study of Tropical African Flora*] [*French*] (AF)
AETH........... Aether [*Ether*] (ROG)
AETI .... Apollo Engineering and Technology Index [*NASA*] (KSC)
aetiol........... Aetiology [*or Etiology*] [*Medicine*] (DAVI)
AETIS .... Army Extension Training Information System
AETL .... Approved Engineering Test Laboratory [*Military*] (CAAL)
AETL .... Armament and Electronics Test Laboratory [*NATO*]
AETL .... Army Engineer Topographic Laboratories (RDA)
A et M .... Arts et Metiers [*Arts and Crafts*] [*French*]
AETM.......... Aviation Electronic Technician's Mate [*Navy*]
AETMS........ Airborne Electronic Terrain Map System (MCD)
AETM(SA).... Australian Electric Transport Association (South Australia)
AETN.......... Alberta Tree Nursery and Horticultural Centre, Edmonton, Alberta [*Library symbol National Library of Canada*] (BIB)
AETN.......... American Educational Television Network [*Cable-television system*]
AetnaC........ Aetna Capital LLC, Inc. [*Associated Press*] (SAG)
Aetna Inc.... Aetna, Inc. [*Associated Press*] (SAG)
AetnLf......... Aetna Life & Casualty Co. [*Associated Press*] (SAG)
AETO.......... Active Employment Training Organization
AEtP........... Allied Electronics Publications (NATG)
AETPrA .... Aetna Capital 9.50%'MIPS' [*NYSE symbol*] (TTSB)
AETR.......... Advanced Electronically Tuned Radio [*Automotive accessory*]
AETR.......... Advanced Engineering Test Reactor
AETR.......... Advanced Epithermal Thorium Reactor
Aetrium....... Aetrium, Inc. [*Associated Press*] (SAG)
AETS .... Army Extension Training System
AETS .... Association for the Education of Teachers in Science (EA)
AETT .... Acetyl Ethyl Tetramethyl Tetralin [*Musk fragrance, neuro-toxic compound*]
AETT .... Association for Educational and Training Technology (EAIO)
AETTN......... Association of Engineering Technicians & Technologists of Newfoundland (AC)
AEU .... Accrued Expenditure Unpaid [*Accounting*] (AFM)
AEU .... Air Evacuation Unit [*Military*]
AEU .... Altitude Encoder Unit (MCD)
AEU .... Amalgamated Engineering Union [*United Kingdom*]
AEU .... American Ethical Union (EA)
AEU .... Annual Estimated Usage
AEU .... Army Exhibit Unit
AEU .... United States Army, Corps of Engineers, St. Louis District, St. Louis, MO [*OCLC symbol*] (OCLC)
AEU .... University of Alberta, Edmonton, Alberta [*Library symbol National Library of Canada*] (NLC)
AEUA .... University of Alberta Archives, Edmonton, Alberta [*Library symbol National Library of Canada*] (NLC)
AEUAG .... Department of Agricultural Engineering, University of Alberta, Edmonton, Alberta [*Library symbol National Library of Canada*] (NLC)
AEUAH........ Learning Resource Centre, Agnes Macleod Memorial Library, University of Alberta Hospitals, Edmonton, Alberta [*Library symbol National Library of Canada*] (BIB)
AEUB .... Boreal Institute for Northern Studies, University of Alberta, Edmonton, Alberta [*Library symbol National Library of Canada*] (NLC)
AEUC .... Association des Employes d'Universites et de Colleges [*Association of University and College Employees - AUCE*] [*Canada*]

AEUCA	Ukrainian Canadian Archives and Museum, Edmonton, Alberta [*Library symbol National Library of Canada*] (BIB)
AEUIA	Alleluia [*An old abbreviation, formed from the vowels of the word*]
AEUL	Law Library, University of Alberta, Edmonton, Alberta [*Library symbol National Library of Canada*] (NLC)
AEULS	Faculty of Library Science, University of Alberta, Edmonton, Alberta [*Library symbol National Library of Canada*] (NLC)
AEUM	University Map Collection, University of Alberta, Edmonton, Alberta [*Library symbol National Library of Canada*] (NLC)
AEUN	Unifarm, Edmonton, Alberta [*Library symbol National Library of Canada*] (NLC)
AEUS	Absolute Electrical Unit Scale
AEUS	Bruce Peel Special Collections Library, University of Alberta, Edmonton, Alberta [*Library symbol National Library of Canada*] (NLC)
AEUSJ	Faculte Saint-Jean, University of Alberta, Edmonton, Alberta [*Library symbol National Library of Canada*] (NLC)
AEUT	Alberta Utilities and Telephones, Edmonton, Alberta [*Library symbol National Library of Canada*] (NLC)
AEV	Aerothermodynamic Elastic Vehicle
AEV	Aeroventas SA [*Mexico ICAO designator*] (FAAC)
AEV	Anthology of English Verse [*A publication*]
AEV	Armored Engineer Vehicle (MCD)
AEV	Avian Erythroblastosis Virus
AEV	Evansburg Public Library, Alberta [*Library symbol National Library of Canada*] (NLC)
AEV	United States Army, Corps of Engineers, Savannah District, Savannah, GA [*OCLC symbol*] (OCLC)
AEVA	Australian Equine Veterinary Association
AEVAC	Air Evacuation
AEVC	Alberta Vocational Centre, Edmonton, Alberta [*Library symbol National Library of Canada*] (NLC)
AEVH	Association for Education of the Visually Handicapped [*Later, AER*] (EA)
AEVMOST	Angle Evaporated Vertical Channel Power MOSFET [*Metal-Oxide-Semiconductor Field-Effect Transistor*] (IAA)
AEVPC	Association Europeenne de Vente par Correspondance [*European Mail Order Traders' Association*] [*Belgium*] (ECED)
AEVS	Automated Eligibility Verification System (MEDA)
AEVS	Automatic Electronic Voice Switch (RDA)
AEW	Aboriginal Education Worker [*Australia*]
AEW	Admiralty Experiment Works [*British*]
AEW	Airborne [*or Aircraft*] Early Warning Station
AEW	Airborne Electronic Warfare (NG)
AEW	American Education Week
AEW	American Energy Week [*Later, AEM*] [*An association*] (EA)
AEW	Appalachian Power Co. [*NYSE symbol*] (SPSG)
AEW	Association of Electrical Wiremen [*A union*] [*British*]
AEW	United States Army, Corps of Engineers, Fort Worth District, Fort Worth, TX [*OCLC symbol*] (OCLC)
AEWA	Airborne Early Warning Aircraft
AEW & C	Airborne Early Warning and Control [*Army*] (AFM)
AEW & CSq	Airborne Early Warning and Control Squadron [*Air Force*]
AEWB	Army Electronic Warfare Board (MCD)
AEWC	Airborne Early Warning and Control [*Army*] (AABC)
AEWC	Alaska Eskimo Whaling System (USDC)
AEWCAP	Airborne Early Warning Combat Air Patrol (NVT)
AEWCON	Airborne Early Warning and Control [*Air Force*] (IAA)
AEWES	Army Engineer Waterways Experiment Station [*Vicksburg, MS*]
AEWF	Airborne Early Warning Fighter
AEWHA	All England Women's Hockey Association (EAIO)
AEWIB	Army Electronic Warfare and Intelligence Board
AEWICS	Airborne Early Warning and Interceptor Control System
AEWIS	Army Electronic Warfare Information System
AEWLA	All England Women's Lacrosse Association (EAIO)
AEWM	Acoustic Emission Weld Monitor (PDAA)
AEWP	Aerospace Education Workshop Project
AEWPC	Army Electronic Warfare Policy Committee (IAA)
AEWPrC	Appal Pwr,7.40% Pfd [*NYSE symbol*] (TTSB)
AEWR	Adverse Effect Wage Rate (GFGA)
AEWRADAR	Airborne Early Warning RADAR [*Air Force*] (IAA)
AEWRON	Airborne Early Warning Squadron
AEWS	Advanced Earth Satellite Weapon System [*Air Force*]
AEWS	Advanced Electronic Warfare System (MCD)
AEWSP	Aircraft Electronics Warfare Self-Protection System [*Army*]
AEWSPS	Aircraft Electronics Warfare Self-Protection System [*Army*]
AEWTF	Aircrew Electronic Warfare Tactics Facility (NATG)
AEWTS	Advanced Electronic Warfare Test Set (MCD)
AEWTU	Airborne Early Warning Training Unit
AEWVH	[*The*] Association for the Education and Welfare of the Visually Handicapped [*British*]
AEWW	Airborne Early Warning Wing (MUGU)
AEX	Agreement to Extend Enlistment [*Military*]
AEX	Alexandria, LA [*Location identifier FAA*] (FAAL)
AEX	Automated Execution [*FAA*] (TAG)
AEX	Avco Airway Express, Inc. [*FAA designator*] (FAAC)
AEX	United States Army, Corps of Engineers, North Central Division, Chicago, IL [*OCLC symbol*] (OCLC)
AEXC	Exshaw Community Library, Alberta [*Library symbol National Library of Canada*] (NLC)
AExO	Assistant Experimental Officer [*Ministry of Agriculture, Fisheries, and Food*] [*Also, AEO, AXO*] [*British*]
AExp	American Express Co. [*Associated Press*] (SAG)
AEXP	Applications Experience
AExp 96	American Express Co. [*Associated Press*] (SAG)
AExpl	American Exploration Co. [*Associated Press*] (SAG)
AEY	Aero Energy Ltd. [*Toronto Stock Exchange symbol*]
AEY	Akureyri [*Iceland*] [*Airport symbol*] (OAG)
AEY	Alcohol Education for Youth (EA)
AEY	Annual Effective Yield [*Finance*]
AEY	United States Army, Corps of Engineers, Jacksonville District, Jacksonville, FL [*OCLC symbol*] (OCLC)
AEY	Waverly, TN [*Location identifier FAA*] (FAAL)
AEYC	Alcohol Education for Youth and Community [*Defunct*] (EA)
AEZ	Aerial Transit Co. [*ICAO designator*] (FAAC)
AEZ	United States Army Engineer District, Nashville, Nashville, TN [*OCLC symbol*] (OCLC)
aF	Abfarad [*Unit of capacitance*]
AF	Abnormal Frequency
AF	Abortion Fund (EA)
AF	About Face [*An association*] (EAIO)
AF	Accokeek Foundation (EA)
AF	Accumulation Factor (DEN)
AF	Accuracy Figure [*British and Canadian*] [*World War II*]
AF	Acid-Fast [*Microbiology*]
AF	Acre-Foot
AF	Across Flats
AF	Activating Factor [*Biochemistry*]
AF	Actum Fide [*Done in Faith*] [*Latin*] (WGA)
AF	Addison Foster [*Record label*]
AF	Ad Finem [*At or To the End*] [*Latin*]
AF	Admiral of the Fleet [*British*]
AF	Adult Female (HGAA)
AF	Advance Freight [*Shipping*]
AF	Aeronautically Fixed
AF	A Favor [*In Favor*] [*Spanish*]
AF	Affiliation of Author [*Online database field identifier*]
AF	Affiliation of First Author [*Used to define searchable field*] (NITA)
AF	Affirmative Flag [*Navy British*]
AF	Affix [*Linguistics*]
AF	Afghani [*Monetary unit*] [*Afghanistan*]
AF	Afghanistan [*ANSI two-letter standard code*] (CNC)
af	Afghanistan [*MARC country of publication code Library of Congress*] (LCCP)
AF	Aflatoxin [*A toxic factor*] [*Biochemistry*] (DAVI)
AF	Africa
AF	[*The*] Africa Fund (EA)
Af	African [*Derogatory nickname for blacks in Zimbabwe and South Africa*]
AF	After Ford [*Calendar used in Aldous Huxley's novel, "Brave New World;" refers to Henry Ford*]
AF	Aft Fuselage (NASA)
AF	Agape Force (EA)
AF	Aggregation Factor [*Biochemistry*]
AF	Agricultural Forecaster (NOAA)
AF	Agriservices Foundation (EA)
A/F	Airfield (NATG)
AF	Air Filter
AF	Air Forager [*Ornithology*]
AF	Air Force
AF	Air Foundation
AF	Airframe (KSC)
AF	Air Frame (MCD)
AF	Air France [*ICAO designator*]
A/F	Air/Fuel [*Mixture ratio*]
AF	Air-to-Fuel Ratio (MCD)
AF	Airway Facilities [*FAA*] (TAG)
AF	Albumin-Free [*Medicine*]
AF	Aldehyde Fuchsin [*A dye*]
AF	Ale Firkin [*Unit of measurement*] (ROG)
AF	Al Fine [*To the End*] [*Music*]
AF	Alternating Field
AF	Alternating Flow
AF	Alternative Fertility [*Demography*]
AF	Alternative Forum [*An association*] (EAIO)
AF	Aluminium Federation
AF	Amaurosis Fugax [*Medicine*] (DMAA)
AF	Ambassadors for Friendship (EA)
AF	America First (EA)
AF	American Forests [*A publication*] (BRI)
AF	Americanism Foundation [*Norwalk, OH*] (EA)
AF	Americares Foundation (EA)
AF	America's Foundation (EA)
AF	America's Future [*New Rochelle, NY*] (EA)
AF	Amerind Foundation (EA)
AF	Aminofluorene [*Also, FA*] [*Carcinogen*]
AF	Amniotic Fluid [*Obstetrics*]
AF	Amphiphilic Flavin [*Chemistry*]
AF	Amplification Factor
AF	Anarchist Federation [*British*]
AF	Anchoring Fibril [*Anatomy*]
AF	Angelini Francesco [*Italy*] [*Research code symbol*]
AF	Angiogenesis Factor [*Biochemistry*]
AF	Angle Frame (OA)
AF	Anglo-French [*Language, etc.*]
AF	Anglo-Frisian [*Language, etc.*]
A-F	Ankle-Foot [*Orthosis*] [*Orthopedics*] (DAVI)
AF	Anno Futuro [*In the Next Year*] [*Latin*] (ADA)
AF	Anterior Fontanelle [*Neonatology and pediatrics*] (DAVI)
AF	Anterior [*Part of*] Foot

AF	Antibody-Forming [*Immunology*] (MAE)
AF	Antiferromagnetic
A-F	Antifibrinogen [*Hematology*] (DAVI)
AF	Anti-Fouling Paint (DNAB)
AF	Anti-Friction [*Lubricants*]
AF	Aortic Flow [*Cardiology*]
AF	Appalachian Forum [*An association*] (EA)
AF	Apply Force [*Industrial engineering*]
AF	Appropriated Funds
AF	Area Weapon Forward (MCD)
AF	Argentina Fund [*NYSE symbol*] (SPSG)
AF	Aristos Foundation (EA)
AF	Arithmetic Flag Aspect Factor (MHDI)
AF	Armed Forces
AF	Army Force
AF	Army Form
AF	Arpad Federation (EA)
AF	Arthritis Foundation (EA)
AF	Artificially Fed
AF	Artilleriefuehrer [*Division artillery commander*] [*German military - World War II*]
AF	Artists' Fellowship (EA)
Af	Aruban Florin [*Monetary unit*] (ODBW)
A/F	As Found (ODBW)
AF	Asiatic Fleet [*Obsolete Navy*]
AF	Aspect Factor (PDAA)
Af	Aspergillus fumigatus [*A fungus*]
AF	Assembly and Fabrication
AF	Assembly Fixture (MCD)
AF	Associate Fellow (ADA)
AF	Associational Fluency [*Personality research*] [*Psychology*]
AF	Asymmetry Factor [*Mathematics*]
af	At Fault (DI)
AF	Atmospheric Flight
AF	Atomic Fluorescence
AF	Atomic Forum (IEEE)
AF	Atrial Fibrillation [*Cardiology*]
Af	Atrial Flutter [*Cardiology*]
AF	Attiyeh Foundation (EA)
aF	Attofarad (IDOE)
AF	Audio Fidelity (NTCM)
AF	Audio Frequency [*Data transmission*]
AF	Augmented Final Fade (SAA)
AF	Auranofin [*An organogold*]
AF	Auricular Fibrillation [*Medicine*]
AF	Aurora Foundation (EA)
AF	Australia First [*Political party*]
AF	Austrian Forum [*Defunct*] (EA)
AF	Auto-Fiche (MCD)
AF	Autofocus [*Cameras*]
AF	Automatic Filter (ADA)
AF	Automatic Focusing [*Photography*]
AF	Automatic Following [*RADAR*]
AF	Automation Foundation
AF	Auxiliary Feed [*Nuclear energy*] (NRCH)
AF	Auxiliary Feedwater [*Nuclear energy*] (NRCH)
AF	Auxiliary Field (MUGU)
AF	Availability Factor [*Generating time ratio*] (IEEE)
AF	Aviation Forum [*British*]
AF	Award Fee
AF	Axial Flow (AAG)
AF	Axle Flange Gasket [*Automotive engineering*]
AF	Flug & Fahrzeugwerke AG Altenrhein [*Switzerland ICAO aircraft manufacturer identifier*] (ICAO)
AF	Forestburg Public Library, Alberta [*Library symbol National Library of Canada*] (NLC)
Af	Frontal Area [*Automotive engineering*]
AF	Office of Alcohol Fuels [*Department of Energy*]
af----	Siam, Gulf of [*MARC geographic area code Library of Congress*] (LCCP)
AF	Store Ship [*Navy symbol*]
AFA	Access Flooring Association [*British*] (DBA)
AFA	Actors' Fund of America (EA)
AFA	Acute Focal Appendicitis [*Medicine*]
AFA	Adams Family Association (EA)
AFA	Adelaide Festival of Arts [*Australia*]
AFA	Adoptive Families of America [*Formerly, OURS (Organization for United Response)*] (PAZ)
AFA	Adoptive Families of America [*An association*]
AFA	Advanced Fuel Assembly [*Nuclear energy*] (NUCP)
AFA	Advertising Federation of America [*Later, AAF*]
AFA	Aerial Field Artillery (MCD)
AFA	Aerophilatelic Federation of the Americas (EA)
afa	Afro-Asiatic [*MARC language code Library of Congress*] (LCCP)
AFA	Agribusiness Foundation of Australia
AFA	AIDS Follow-Up Assessment Questionnaire [*Department of Health and Human Services*] (GFGA)
AFA	Aircraft Finance Association [*Later, NAFA*] (EA)
AFA	Air Force Academy
AFA	Air Force Act [*British military*] (DMA)
AFA	Air Force Advisory
AFA	Air Force Association (EA)
AFA	Air Force Auxiliary [*British*]
AFA	Air Frame Assembly (MCD)
AFA	Air Freight Association of America (EA)

AFA	Alabama Forestry Association (SRA)
AFA	Alaska Forest Association (SRA)
AFA	Alcohol-Formaldehyde-Acetic [*Fixative*] [*Medicine*] (DMAA)
AFA	Alfa Air [*Czechoslovakia*] [*ICAO designator*] (FAAC)
AFA	Alien Firearms Act
AFA	Allergy Foundation of America [*Later, A & AFA*]
AFA	Allied Financial Agency [*World War II*]
AFA	Allied Fiscal Administration [*World War II*]
AFA	Amateur Fencing Association (EAIO)
AFA	Amateur Football Alliance [*British*] (BI)
AFA	American Family Association (EA)
AFA	American Fan Association (EA)
AFA	American Farriers Association (EA)
AFA	American Fashion Association (EA)
AFA	American Federation of Arts (EA)
AFA	American Federation of Astrologers (EA)
AFA	American Federation of Aviculture (EA)
AFA	American Finance Association (EA)
AFA	American Firearm Association (EA)
AFA	American Firewalking Association (EA)
AFA	American Fitness Association (EA)
AFA	American Flag Association [*Defunct*] (EA)
AFA	American Flock Association (EA)
AFA	American Florists Association (EA)
AFA	American Flyers Airline (MCD)
AFA	American Forces in Action [*Military*]
AFA	American Forensic Association (EA)
AFA	American Forest Adventures [*Defunct*] (EA)
AFA	American Forestry Association (EA)
AFA	American Formalwear Association [*Later, IFA*] (EA)
AFA	American Foundrymen's Association [*Later, AFS*]
AFA	American Fracture Association (EA)
AFA	American Franchise Association (EA)
AFA	American Freedom Association
AFA	American Freeman Association (EA)
AFA	Amfonelic Acid [*Biochemistry*]
AFA	Analog Filter Assembly (MCD)
AFA	Anorexic Family Aid and National Information Centre [*British*] (CB)
AFA	Anthology Film Archives (EA)
AFA	Aphanizomenon Flos-Aquae [*Blue green algae*]
AFA	Application Fit Analysis
AFA	Application for Federal Assistance (OICC)
AFA	Arkansas Forestry Association (SRA)
AFA	Armed Forces Act
AFA	Army Finance Association [*Defunct*] (EA)
AFA	Army Flight Activity
AFA	Art For All
AFA	Asatru Free Assembly [*Later, AA*] (EA)
AFA	Aspirin Foundation of America (EA)
AFA	Assemblee des Franco-Americains/Association of Franco-Americans (EA)
AFA	Assembly Fixture Accessory (MCD)
AFA	Assistant Freight Agent
AFA	Associated Fraternities of America
AFA	Associate in Fine Arts
AFA	Associate of the Faculty of Actuaries [*British*]
AFA	Association of Federal Appraisers [*Later, Association of Governmental Appraisers*]
AFA	Association of Federal Architects
AFA	Association of Flight Attendants (EA)
AFA	Association of Fraternity Advisors (EA)
AFA	Atheist Foundation of Australia
AFA	Athletic Footwear Association (EA)
AFA	Atlanta, GA [*Location identifier FAA*] (FAAL)
AFA	Audio Frequency Amplifier
AFA	Audio Frequency Apparatus
AFA	Auditor Freight Accounts
AFA	Australian Family Association
AFA	Australian Flute Association
AFA	Australian Folklore Association
AFA	Automatic Field Assistant (MCD)
AFA	Autry Family Association
AFA	Avicultural Federation of Australia
AFA	Azimuth Follow-Up Amplifier
AFA	Fort Assiniboine Public Library, Alberta [*Library symbol National Library of Canada*] (NLC)
AFA	San Rafael [*Argentina*] [*Airport symbol*] (OAG)
AFA	United States Army, Corps of Engineers, Wilmington District, Wilmington, NC [*OCLC symbol*] (OCLC)
AFAA	Adult Film Association of America (EA)
AFAA	Aerobics and Fitness Association of America (EA)
AFAA	Air Force Audit Agency
AFAA	Airline Flight Attendants Association [*Defunct*] (EA)
AFAA	American Fighter Aces Association (EA)
AFAA	Application for Federal Assistance and Assurances (OICC)
AFAA	Automatic Fire Alarm Association (EA)
AFAAC	Air Force Comptroller
AFA(ACT)	Arthritis Foundation of Australia (Australian Capital Territory)
AFAADS	Advanced Forward Area Air Defense System
AFAADW	Advanced Forward Area Air Defense Weapon
AFAAEC	Air Force Academy and Aircrew Examining Center
AFAAR	American Fund for Alternatives to Animal Research (EA)
AFAAR	Automated Forward Area Alerting RADAR [*Army*]
AFAAR	Regional Office, Alberta Agriculture, Fairview, Alberta [*Library symbol National Library of Canada*] (NLC)

AFA Art	Associate in Fine Arts in Art		**AFAP**	Army Family Action Planning
AFAAV	Veterinary Laboratory, Alberta Agriculture, Fairview, Alberta [*Library symbol National Library of Canada*] (NLC)		**AFAP**	Artillery-Fired Atomic Projectile
			AFAPL	Air Force Aero-Propulsion Laboratory [*Wright-Patterson Air Force Base, OH*] (AFM)
AFAB	Air Force Academy Board		**AFAPO**	Air Force Accountable Property Officer (AAG)
AFAB	Air Force Audit Branch (AFM)		**AFAPS**	Air Force Air Pictorial Service (SAA)
AFABA	Association des Federations Africaines de Basketball Amateur [*African Association of Basketball Federations*] [*Egypt*]		**AFAQ**	Arthritis Foundation of Australia, Queensland
			AFAQ	Association des Femmes d'Affaires du Quebec (AC)
AFABBN	American Friends of the Anti-Bolshevik Bloc of Nations (EA)		**AFAR**	Advanced Field Array RADAR
AF-ABN	American Friends of the Anti-Bolshevik Bloc of Nations (EA)		**AFAR**	Aid for Afghan Refugees [*An association*] (EA)
AFABS	Air Force Arctic Broadcasting Squadron [*New York, NY*] (EY)		**AFAR**	Airborne Fixed Array RADAR (MSA)
AFAC	Airborne Forward Air Controller		**AFAR**	American Federation for Aging Research (EA)
AFAC	Air Force Acquisition Circular (MCD)		**AFAR**	American Foundation for Aging Research (EA)
AFAC	Air Force Armament Center [*Eglin Air Force Base, FL*]		**AFAR**	American Foundation for AIDS Research (EA)
AFAC	Alabama Food and Agriculture Council (SRA)		**AFAR**	American Friends of Afghan Refugees (EA)
AFAC	Allied Finance Adjusters Conference [*Greensboro, NC*] (EA)		**AFAR**	Attorneys for Animal Rights (EA)
AFAC	American Fisheries Advisory Committee		**AFAR**	Automatic False Alarm Rate
AFAC	Army Finance and Accounting Center (MCD)		**AFAR**	Azores Fixed Acoustic Range [*NATO*]
AFAC	Automatic Field Analog Computer		**AFARD**	Association des Femmes Africaines pour la Recherche sur le Developpement [*Association of African Women for Research and Development - AAWORD*] (EAIO)
AFACAL	Associate Fellow of American College of Allergists (DHSM)			
AFAC & IC	Air Force Aeronautical Chart and Information Center (MUGU)			
AFACE	Army Field Artillery Combat Effectiveness Model (MCD)		**AFARE**	Arctic Forward Area Refueling Equipment (DWSG)
AFACG	Army Air Forces Commanding General [*World War II*]		**AFARS**	Army Federal Acquisition Regulations Supplement
AFAD	Air Force Acquisition Document (MCD)		**AFARV**	Armored Forward Area Rearm Vehicle (MCD)
AFAD	Air Force Authorization Document (MCD)		**AFARV**	Armored Forward Area Resupply Vehicle (MCD)
AFAD	Armed Forces Acquisition Document (NASA)		**AFAS**	Advanced Field Artillery System
AFAD	Association of Fatty Acid Distillers [*British*] (BI)		**AFAS**	Afro-American Studies Librarians Section [*Association of College and Research Libraries*]
AFA Dance	Associate in Fine Arts in Dance			
AFADGRU	Air Force Advisory Group (CINC)		**AFAS**	Air Flow Actuated Switch
AFA Drama	Associate in Fine Arts in Drama		**AFAS**	Air Force Aid Society (EA)
AFADS	Advanced Field Artillery Tactical Data System [*Army*]		**AFAS**	American Fine Arts Society (EA)
AFADS	Advanced Forward Air Defense System [*Missiles*] (IEEE)		**AFAS**	Aontas Fiontair Agus Spoirt [*Association for Adventure Sports*] [*British*] (EAIO)
AFADTC	Air Force Armament Development and Test Center (MCD)			
AFADVMC	Air Force Advanced Management Class		**AFAS**	Arden Industrial Products [*NASDAQ symbol*] (SAG)
AFAE	Air Force Acquisition Executive (MCD)		**AFAS**	Area Fire Armor System
AFAE	American Foundation on Automation and Employment [*Later, CNB-TV*] (EA)		**AFAS**	Army Field Artillery School
			AFAS	Associate of the Faculty of Architects and Surveyors [*British*]
AFAEP	Association of Fashion Advertising and Editorial Photographers (EAIO)		**AFAS**	Associate of the Faculty of Astrological Studies [*British*]
			AFAS	Automated Frequency Assignment System [*Telecommunications*]
AFAES	Air Force Acquisition Executive System (AAGC)		**AFAS**	Automotive Fine Arts Society
AFAF	Air Force Assistance Fund		**AFAS**	Auxiliary Feedwater Actuating System [*Nuclear energy*] (NRCH)
AFAF	Air Force Auxiliary Field		**AFAS-ARM**	Advanced Field Artillery System - Armaments [*Army*] (RDA)
AFAF	Air Force Director of Accounting and Financing (AAG)		**AFAS-C**	Advanced Field Artillery System - Cannon
AFAF	Atlantic Fleet Amphibious Force [*Navy*]		**AFASC**	Air Force Aeronautical Systems Command
AFAF	Autonomous Fire and Forget [*Military*]		**AFASD**	Air Force Aeronautical Systems Division
AFAFC	Air Force Accounting and Finance Center		**AFASE**	Association for Applied Solar Energy [*Later, International Solar Energy Society*]
AFAFC	American Friends of Anne Frank Center (EA)			
AFAFF	Australian Federation of Air Freight Forwarders		**AFASED**	African Association of Education for Development (EAIO)
AFAFFO	Air Force Aerospace Fuels Field Office (AFM)		**AFA-SEF**	Air Force Association - Space Education Foundation
AFAFPSO	Air Force Aerospace Fuel Petroleum Supply Office		**AFAS-FARV**	Advanced Field Artillery System - Future Armored Resupply Vehicle [*Army*] (RDA)
AFAG	Air Force Advisory Group			
A-FA-H	Aniline-Furfuryl Alcohol-Hydrazine (SAA)		**AFASIC**	Association for All Speech Impaired Children (EAIO)
AFAHC	American Foundation for Alternative Health Care [*Later, AFAHCRD*] (EA)		**AFAS-MOB**	Advanced Field Artillery System - Mobility [*Army*] (RDA)
			AFASPO	Air Force Automated Systems Project Office
AFAHCRD	American Foundation for Alternative Health Care, Research, and Development (EA)		**AF/ASPR**	Air Force/Armed Service Procurement Regulation
			AFAST	Army Field Assistance and Technology
AFAI	Air Force Agent Installation (AFM)		**AFAT**	Air Force Acceptance Team (MCD)
AFAIAA	Associate Fellow of the American Institute of Aeronautics and Astronautics [*Formerly, AFIAS*]		**AFAT**	Air Force Advisory Team
			AFAT	Association Forestiere de l'Abitibi-Temiscamingue, Inc. (AC)
AFAIK	As Far As I Know [*Internet language*] [*Computer science*]		**AFATDS**	Advanced Field Artillery Tactical Data System
AFAITC	Armed Forces Air Intelligence Training Center		**AFATL**	Air Force Armament Technology Laboratory [*Eglin Air Force Base, FL*] (AFM)
AFAIU	American Friends of the Alliance Israelite Universelle (EA)			
AFAK	Armed Forces Assistance to Korea [*Military*]		**AFATL**	Air Force Armament Testing Laboratory (DOMA)
AFAL	Air Force Astronautics Laboratory [*Edwards Air Force Base, CA*] (GRD)		**AFATR**	Air Force Atlantic Test Range (SAA)
			AFATS	Advanced Fuel Accessories Test System (DWSG)
AFAL	Air Force Avionics Laboratory [*Wright-Patterson Air Force Base, OH*]		**AFAUD**	Air Force Auditor General
			AFAUSSS	Association of Former Agents of the US Secret Service (EA)
AFAL	Association Francophone d'Amitie et de Liaison (EA)		**AFAUX**	Air Force Auxiliary Field
AFALC	Air Force Acquisition Logistics Center (MCD)		**AFAV**	Anti-Fluoridation Association of Victoria [*Australia*]
AFALD	Air Force Acquisition Logistics Division [*Wright Patterson Air Force Base*] (MCD)		**AFAVC**	Atlantic Fleet Audio-Visual Center [*Navy*] (DNAB)
			AFAW	Fawcett Public Library, Alberta [*Library symbol National Library of Canada*] (NLC)
AFALLS	Air Force Alaskan Long Line System [*Communications*] (MCD)			
AFALT	Air Force Alternate Headquarters		**AFaxA**	American Facsimile Association [*Later, IFAXA*] (EA)
AFAM	Air Field Attack Munition (MCD)		**AFB**	Acid-Fast Bacillus [*Microbiology*]
AFAM	Air Force Achievement Medal [*Military decoration*]		**AFB**	Affable (ABBR)
AFAM	Air Force Acquisition Model (AAGC)		**AFB**	Aflatoxin B [*Mycotoxin*]
AFAM	Air Force Armament Museum		**AF/B**	After Bulkhead in Hatch [*Stowage*] (DNAB)
AFAM	Ancient Free and Accepted Masons [*Freemasonry*]		**AFB**	Aircooled Fluidized Bed [*Chemical engineering*]
AFAM	Australian Family Law Guide [*A publication*]		**AFB**	Air Force Base
AFAM	Australian Family Studies Database		**AFB**	Air Force Bulletin
AFAM	Automatic Frequency Assignment Model [*Telecommunications*]		**AFB**	Airframe Bulletin (MCD)
AFAMA	Air Force Air Materiel Area		**AFB**	Air Freight Bill [*Shipping*]
AFAMF	American Fighter Aces Museum Foundation (EA)		**AFB**	All Former Buyers
AFAMM	Aerial Field Artillery Multi-Mode (MCD)		**AFB**	Aluminum Four Barrel Carburetor [*Automotive engineering*] (DICI)
AFamR	American Family Restaurants, Inc. [*Associated Press*] (SAG)			
AFAMRL	Air Force Aerospace Medical Research Laboratory [*Wright-Patterson Air Force Base, OH*]		**AFB**	American Farm Bureau
			AFB	American Festival Ballet
AFA Mus	Associate in Fine Arts in Music		**AFB**	American Fibre Corp. [*Vancouver Stock Exchange symbol*]
AFAN	Association for Astrological Networking (EA)		**AFB**	American Foulbrood [*Honeybee disease*]
AF & AM	Ancient Free and Accepted Masons [*Freemasonry*]		**AFB**	American Foundation for the Blind (EA)
AFANG	American Friends of the Australian National Gallery		**AFB**	Anal Fin Base [*Fish anatomy*]
AFANG	American Friends of the Australian National Gallery Foundation (EA)		**AFB**	Anarchist Federation of Britain
AFANPERA	African National People's Empire Re-Established (EA)		**AFB**	Antifriction Bearing
AFANT	Amateur Fishermen's Association of the Northern Territory		**AFB**	Aorto-Femoral Bypass [*Medicine*]
AFAO	Air Force Administrative Order [*Canada, 1946-1964*]		**AFB**	Atmospheric Fluidized Bed [*Chemical engineering*]
AFAO	Approved Force Acquisition Objective [*Army*] (AABC)		**AFB**	Australian Fringe Benefits Tax Guide for Employers [*A publication*]
AFAP	Air Forces, Arabian Peninsula [*British military*] (DMA)			

AFB	Force Aerienne Belge [*Belgium ICAO designator*] (FAAC)	
AFBA	Armed Forces Benefit Association	
AFBA	Armed Forces Broadcasters Association (EA)	
AFBAA	Armed Forces Benefit and Aid Association (EA)	
AFBALTAP	Allied Forces Baltic Approaches [*NATO*] (MCD)	
AFBANK	African Bank [*South Africa*]	
AFBC	Advance Financial Bancorp [*NASDAQ symbol*] (SAG)	
AFBC	Atmospheric Fluidized Bed Coal [*Energy technology*]	
AFBC	Atmospheric Fluidized-Bed Combustion [*Fuel technology*]	
AFBCMR	Air Force Board for Correction of Military Records (GFGA)	
AFBD	Association of Futures Brokers and Dealers (EAIO)	
AFBDA	Air Force Base Disposal Agency (DOMA)	
AFBDA	Anti-Friction Bearing Distributors Association [*Later, BSA*] (EA)	
AFBF	American Farm Bureau Federation (EA)	
AFBF	Arizona Farm Bureau Federation (SRA)	
AFBF	Arkansas Farm Bureau Federation (SRA)	
AFBFAR	Air Force Bent Fin Artillery Rocket (MCD)	
AFBG	Aortofemoral Bypass Graft [*Cardiology*] (DMAA)	
AFBG	Arteriofemoral Bypass Graft [*Medicine*]	
AFBH	American Friends of Beit Halochem (EA)	
AFBH	American Friends of Beth Hatefutsoth (EA)	
AFBIS	Associate Fellow of the British Interplanetary Society (DI)	
AFBITS	Air Force Base Information Transfer System (MCD)	
AFBM	Air Force Ballistic Missile (KSC)	
AFBM	Association of Fancy Box Makers [*A union*] [*British*]	
AFBMA	Air Force Ballistic Missile Arsenal	
AFBMA	Anti-Friction Bearing Manufacturers Association (EA)	
AFBMC	Air Force Ballistic Missile Center	
AFBMC	Air Force Ballistic Missile Committee	
AFBMD	Air Force Ballistic Missile Division [*Inglewood, CA*]	
AFBMD-FO	Air Force Ballistic Missile Division - Field Operations (SAA)	
AFBMIR	Air Force Ballistic Missile Installation Regulation	
AFBMTC	Air Force Ballistic Missile Training Center	
AFBO	Approved Force Budget Objective [*Army*] (AABC)	
AFBP	Air Force Bailment Property	
AFBR	Air Force Board of Review	
AFBRF	American Farm Bureau Research Foundation (EA)	
AFBRMC	Air Force Business Research Management Center [*Wright-Patterson Air Force Base, OH*]	
AFBS	Air Force Board Structure (MCD)	
AFBS	Air Force Broadcasting Service (DOMA)	
AFBS	American and Foreign Bible Society	
AFBSD	Air Force Ballistic Systems Division [*Later, Space and Missile Systems Operations*]	
AFBT	Affability (ABBR)	
AFBTR	Association for Brain Tumor Research (EA)	
AFBU	Air Force Base Unit	
AFBW	Analog Fly by Wire [*Aviation*]	
AFBY	Affably (ABBR)	
AFC	Acadian Friendship Committee [*See also CAA*] (EAIO)	
AFC	Acupuncture Foundation of Canada	
AFC	Adjustable Focus Control (MCD)	
AFC	Adult Foster Care	
AFC	Advanced Fighter Capability (MCD)	
AFC	Advanced Fire Control (MCD)	
AFC	Aerodynamic Flight Control (MCD)	
AFC	Affiliation Code [*IRS*]	
AFC	African Farmers Committee [*See also CPA*] (EAIO)	
AFC	African Football Confederation (EAIO)	
AFC	African Forestry Commission [*UN Food and Agriculture Organization*]	
AFC	African West Air [*Senegal*] [*ICAO designator*] (FAAC)	
AFC	Agoraphobic Foundation of Canada Inc. [*Fondation Canadienne pour les Agoraphobes Inc.*] (AC)	
AFC	Air-Filled Cushion [*Medicine*] (DAVI)	
AFC	Airflex Clutch (DS)	
AFC	Air Flow Control [*Automotive engineering*]	
AFC	Air Force Change (AAGC)	
AFC	Air Force Circulars	
AFC	Air Force Component	
AFC	Air Force Comptroller (AAG)	
AFC	Air Force Council [*Advisory board to Air Force*]	
AFC	Air Force Cross [*US and British*] [*Military decoration*]	
AFC	Airframe Change (MCD)	
AFC	Airman, First Class (IIA)	
AFC	Airworthiness and Flight Characteristics (MCD)	
AFC	Alabama Fan Club (EA)	
AFC	ALIBI Fan Club (EA)	
AFC	Alkaline Fuel Cell	
AFC	Alliance for Fair Competition [*Falls Church, VA*] (EA)	
AFC	Allmerica Financial [*NYSE symbol*] (TTSB)	
AFC	Allmerica Financial Corp. [*NYSE symbol*] (SAG)	
AFC	Aluminum Field Coil	
AFC	American Filtrona Corp.	
AFC	American Finance Conference [*Later, NCFA*] (EA)	
AFC	American Flag Committee (EA)	
AFC	American Folklife Center [*Library of Congress*]	
AFC	American Football Conference [*of NFL*]	
AFC	American Forest Council (EA)	
AFC	American Foxhound Club (EA)	
AFC	American Freedom Center (EA)	
AFC	American Freedom Coalition (EA)	
AFC	Amplitude-Frequency Characteristic [*Telecommunications*] (OA)	
AFC	Analog Function Control [*Electronics*] (ECII)	
AFC	Analog to Frequency Converter	
AFC	Antenna for Communications	

AFC	Antibody-Forming Cell [*Immunology*]	
AFC	Apollo Flight Control [*NASA*] (MCD)	
AFC	Apostolate for Family Consecration (EA)	
AFC	Application Foundation Classes [*Microsoft Corp.*] [*Computer science*]	
AFC	April Fan Club (EA)	
AFC	Aquatic Federation of Canada	
AFC	Area Forecast Center [*Meteorology*] (BARN)	
AFC	Area Frequency Coordinator (MUGU)	
AFC	Armament and Fuel Coordinator (MCD)	
AFC	Armed Forces Council	
AFC	Army Field Commands	
AFC	Army Finance Center	
AFC	Army Flying Corps [*British*] (AIA)	
AFC	Asian Football Confederation (EAIO)	
AFC	Assimilation and Fractional Crystallization [*Geology*]	
AFC	Association Football Club [*British*] (DI)	
AFC	Association for Colleges (AIE)	
AFC	Association Forestiere Canadienne [*Canadian Forestry Association*] (EAIO)	
AFC	Association of Feminine Collectives [*Canada*]	
AFC	Association of Film Commissioners (EA)	
AFC	Association of Fish Canners [*British*] (DBA)	
AFC	Association of Flooring Contractors [*British*] (BI)	
AFC	Athletic Footwear Council [*Later, AFA*] (EA)	
AFC	Atomic Fluid Cell (OA)	
AFC	Atomic Fuel Corp. [*Japan*]	
AFC	Audio Frequency Change	
AFC	Audio Frequency Choke	
AFC	Audio Frequency Coder	
AFC	Audiofrequency Control [*Electronics*] (ECII)	
AFC	Auditor Freight Claims	
AFC	Australia Fan Club (EA)	
AFC	Australian Film Corp.	
AFC	Automated Fare Collection	
AFC	Automatic Fare Collection [*TRB*] (TAG)	
AFC	Automatic Fidelity Control	
AFC	Automatic Field Control (MHDB)	
AFC	Automatic Fire Control	
AFC	Automatic Flight Control	
AFC	Automatic Flow Control	
AFC	Automatic Frequency Control [*Electronics*]	
AFC	Automatic Frequency Control (IDOE)	
AFC	Average Fixed Cost [*Economics*]	
AFC	Aviation Fire Controlman [*Navy*]	
AFC	Axial Flow Compressor	
AFC	Faust Community Library, Alberta [*Library symbol National Library of Canada*] (NLC)	
AFC	Fayette County Court House, Fayette, AL [*Library symbol Library of Congress*] (LCLS)	
AFC	United States Army, Concepts Analysis Agency, Bethesda, MD [*OCLC symbol*] (OCLC)	
AFCA	American Fan Collectors Association (EA)	
AFCA	American Fastener and Closure Association [*Defunct*] (EA)	
AFCA	American Football Coaches Association (EA)	
AFCA	Anadromous Fish Conservation Act [*1965*]	
AFCA	Area Fuel Consumption Allocation [*Environmental Protection Agency*] (GFGA)	
AFCA	Armed Forces Chemical Association [*Later, ADPA*] (EA)	
AFCA	Armed Forces Chemical Association [*Later, ADPA*] (EA)	
AFCA	Armed Forces Communications Association [*Later, AFCEA*] (MCD)	
AFCA	Armed Forces Cycling Association	
AFCA	Assistant Freight Claim Agent	
AFCA	Atom Flourescence for Chemical Analysis (PDAA)	
AFCA	Australian Football Coaches Association	
AFCAA	Air Force Cost Analysis Agency (DOMA)	
AFCAB	Air Force Contract Adjustment Board (AAGC)	
AFCAC	African Civil Aviation Commission [*See also CAFAC*] (EAIO)	
AFCAC	Air Force Computer Acquisition Center	
AFCAI	Associate Fellow of the Canadian Aeronautical Institute	
AFCAM	Air Force Coated Aluminum Metal (MCD)	
AFCAM	Association of Fluorocarbon Consumers and Manufacturers [*Australia*]	
AFCAN	Analog Factor Calibration Network	
AFC & TO	Air Force Clothing and Textile Office (AFIT)	
AFCAO	Air Force Computer Acquisition Office	
AFCAP	Air Force Capability Assessment Program (GFGA)	
AFCAPS	Air Force Civilian Automated Pay System (GFGA)	
AFCAPS	Air Force Coronary Atherosclerosis Prevention Study	
AFCARA	Air Force Civilian Appellate Review Agency	
AFCARA	Air Force Civilian Appellate Review Agency (DOMA)	
AFCAS	Advanced Flight Control Actuation System [*Navy*] (MCD)	
AFCAS	African Commission on Agricultural Statistics [*Ghana*] (EAIO)	
AFCAS	Army Air Forces Chief of the Air Staff [*World War II*]	
AFCAS	Athabaska Delta Community School, Fort Chipewyan, Alberta [*Library symbol National Library of Canada*] (BIB)	
AFCAS	Automatic Flight Control and Augmentation System (DA)	
AFCAS-AE	Advanced Flight Control Actuation System - All Electric (MCD)	
AFCASI	Associate Fellow of the Canadian Aeronautic and Space Institute (DD)	
AFCASOLE	Association des Fabricants de Cafe Soluble des Pays de la CEE [*Association of Soluble Coffee Manufacturers of the Countries of the European Economic Community*]	
AFCAT	Alert Force Capability Test (MCD)	
AFC-AU	American Friends of Chung-Ang University (EA)	
AFCB	Affiliated Community Bancorp [*NASDAQ symbol*] (TTSB)	

AFCB.......... Affiliated Community Bancorp, Inc. [*NASDAQ symbol*] (SAG)
AFCB.......... Armed Forces Combat Bulletin
AFCC.......... Air Force Combat Command
AFCC.......... Air Force Communication Center
AFCC.......... Air Force Communications Command
AFCC.......... Air Force Component Commander (AFM)
AFCC.......... Arsenal Family and Children's Center [*Research center*] (RCD)
AFCC.......... Assault Fire Command Console [*Army*]
AFCC.......... Association of Family and Conciliation Courts (EA)
AFCC.......... Association of Federal Communications Consulting Engineers (NITA)
AFCCB .... Air Force Configuration Control Board (AAG)
AFC Cbl ..... AFC Cable Systems [*Associated Press*] (SAG)
AFCCDC ..... Air Force Command and Control Development Center
AFCCDD....... Air Force Command and Control Development Division [*Bedford, MA*] (AAG)
AFCCE .... Air Force Cost Center
AFCCE .... Association of Federal Communications Consulting Engineers (EA)
AFCCG .... Atlantic Fleet Combat Camera Group [*Obsolete*]
AFCCP .... Air Force Command and Control Post
AFCCP .... Air Force Component Command Post (AFM)
AF-CCP .... Air Force Consolidation and Containerization Point (DOMA)
AFCCPC ..... Air Force Communications Computer Programming Center
AFCCS .... Air Force Command and Control System
AFCD .... Advanced Fighter Capability Demonstrator (MCD)
AFCD .... Air Force Cryptologic Depot (AFM)
AFCD .... Association of Florida Community Developers (SRA)
AFCE.......... Air Force Civil Engineering Unit (MCD)
AFCE.......... Allied Forces Central Europe [*NATO*] (MCD)
AFCE.......... American Foundation for Continuing Education (EA)
AFCE.......... Automatic Flight Control Equipment
AFCEA....... Armed Forces Communications and Electronics Association (EA)
AFCEC....... Air Force Civil Engineering Center [*Tyndall Air Force Base, FL*]
AFCEE....... Air Force Center for Environmental Excellence (DOMA)
AFCEL....... Air Force Contractor Experience List (AFM)
AFCENT....... Allied Forces Central Europe [*NATO*]
AFCESA....... Air Force Civil Engineering Support Agency (DOMA)
AFCET......... Association Francaise pour la Cybernetique Economique et Technique [*French Association for Economic and Technical Cybernetics*]
AFCF.......... Anthropology Film Center Foundation (EA)
AFCF.......... Armed Forces Christian Fellowship
AFCFP....... Arab Federation of Chemical Fertilizer Producers (EA)
AFCFS......... Advanced Fighter Control Flight Simulator [*Military*] (PDAA)
AFCG.......... American Fine China Guild (EA)
AFCGRB ...... American Friends of Covent Garden and the Royal Ballet (EA)
AFCH .... Air Force Component Headquarters
AF Ch Sch ... Air Force Chaplain School [*Maxwell Air Force Base, AL*]
AFCI........... Acute Focal Cerebral Ischemia [*Medicine*] (DMAA)
AFCI........... Advanced Fibre Communications [*NASDAQ symbol*] (SAG)
AFCI........... American Foot Care Institute [*Defunct*] (EA)
AFCI........... Associate of the Faculty of Commerce and Industry [*British*] (DBQ)
AFCIA......... Armed Forces Civilian Instructors Association (EA)
AFCIA......... Associate Fellow of the Catering Institute of Australia
AFCIP......... Air Force Center for International Programs
AFCIS-L ...... Armor Full Crew Research Simulator Center - Laboratory
AFCK.......... Antenna Field Charge Kit
AFCL.......... Agreed, Cease Fire Line [*Military*] (INF)
AFCL.......... Associate of the Farriers Co. of London [*British*] (DI)
AFCLC......... Air Force Contract Law Center
AFCM.......... Air Force Commendation Medal [*Military decoration*] (AFM)
AFCM.......... ASEAN [*Association of South East Asian Nations*] Federation of Cement Manu facturers [*Indonesia*] (EAIO)
AFCM.......... Association for Classical Music [*Later, MA*] (EA)
AFCM.......... Association of First Class Mailers
AFCM.......... Automatic Fine Cull Machine (MHDB)
AFCM.......... Fox Creek Municipal Library, Alberta [*Library symbol National Library of Canada*] (NLC)
AFCM.......... Master Chief Aircraft Maintenanceman [*Navy rating*]
AFCMA........ Aluminum Foil Container Manufacturers Association (EA)
AFCMC........ Air Force Contract Maintenance Center (AFM)
AFCMD .... Air Force Contract Management Division [*Los Angeles, CA*]
AFCMD/QA... Air Force Contract Management Division Directorate of Quality Assurance [*Los Angeles, CA*]
AFCMO....... Air Force Contract Management Office
AFCMR .... Armed Forces Central Medical Registry [*School of Aerospace Medicine*] (PDAA)
AFCN .... American Friends of the Captive Nations [*Defunct*] (EA)
AFCNF .... Air Force Central Notice to Airmen Facility
AFCO .... Admiralty Fleet Confidential Order [*British*] (DMA)
AFCO .... Air Force Contracting Officer
AFCO .... Air Force Control Office (AAG)
AFCO .... American Family Communiversity (EA)
AFCO .... Automatic Fuel Cutoff [*NASA*] (KSC)
AFCOA....... Air Force Chief of Operations Analysis (MUGU)
AFCOA....... Air Force Contracting Office Approval
AFCOLR ...... Air Force Coordinating Office for Logistics Research (MCD)
AFCOM .... Air Force Commendation Medal [*Military decoration*]
AFCOM .... Air Force Communications [*Satellite*]
AFCOMAC.... Air Force Combat Ammunitions Center
AFCOMMSTA... Air Force Communications Station
AFCOMPMET... Air Force Comptroller Management Engineering Team
AFCOMS ...... Air Force Commissary Service
AFCOMSEC... Air Force Communications Security
AFCOMSECCEN... Air Force Communications Security Center (AFM)
AFCOMSECM... Air Force Communications Security Manual

AFCON .... Air Force Contractor (SAA)
AFCON .... Air Force Controlled [*Units*]
AFCOOP....... Atlantic Filmmakers' Co-Operative (AC)
AFCORS ...... Advanced Fire Control RADAR System (MCD)
AFCOS .... Air Force Combat Operations Staff
AFCOS .... Armed Forces Courier Service
AFCP.......... Advanced Flight Control Programmer
AFCP.......... Air Force Command Post
AFCP.......... Automatic Flight Control Panel (MCD)
AFCPL .... Air Force Computer Program Library (SAA)
AFCPMC ...... Air Force Civilian Personnel Management Center
AFCR.......... American Federation for Clinical Research (EA)
AFCR.......... American Foster Care Resources (EA)
AFCR.......... American Fund for Czechoslovak Refugees (EA)
AFCRB......... Air Force Central Review Board (EA)
AFCRC......... Air Force Cambridge Research Center [*Obsolete*]
AFCRL......... Air Force Cambridge Research Laboratories [*Later, AFGL*] [*Hanscom Air Force Base, MA*]
AFCRL......... Air Force Cambridge Research Library (MCD)
AFCRP......... Air Force Cost Reduction Program (AFM)
AFCRS .... Airborne Fire Control RADAR Set (MCD)
AFCS.......... Active Federal Commissioned Service
AFCS.......... Adaptive Flight Control System
AFCS.......... Advanced Flight Control System (MCD)
AFCS.......... Air Force Chief of Staff (SAA)
AFCS.......... Air Force Coding System (SAA)
AFCS.......... Air Force Communications Service [*or System*] [*Scott Air Force Base, IL*]
AFCS.......... Air Force Communications Squadron (MCD)
AFCS.......... Armament and Flight Control System (SAA)
AFCS.......... Army Facilities Components System (AABC)
AFCS.......... Army Functional Component System
AFCS.......... Automatic Fare Collection System
AFCS.......... Automatic Fire Control System (AAG)
AFCS.......... Automatic Flight Control System [*Aerospace*]
AFCS.......... Avionic Flight Control System
AFCS.......... Fox Creek School, Alberta [*Library symbol National Library of Canada*] (BIB)
AFCSA .... Air Force Center for Studies and Analyses [*Washington, DC*]
AFCSA .... Air Force Chief of Staff, Studies and Analysis (SAA)
AFCSC .... Air Force Command and Staff College
AFCSC .... Air Force Cryptologic Support Center
AFCSCP .... Automatic Flight Control System Control Panel (MCD)
AFCSDG ...... Air Force Container System Development Group
AFCSDO...... Air Force Communications-Computer Systems Doctrine Office
AFCS E & I... Air Force Communications Service, Engineering and Installation (CET)
AFCSL......... Air Force Communications Security Letter
AFCSM......... Air Force Communications Security Manual
AFCSM......... Air Force Communications Service Manual
AFCSP......... Air Force Communications Security Pamphlet (MCD)
AFCSS......... Air Force Communications Support System
AFCSS......... Army in the Field Containers System Study (MCD)
AFCT.......... Affect
AFCT.......... Alert Force Capability Test (MCD)
AFCTAN .... Affectation (ABBR)
AFCTCP........ Air Force Combat Theater Communications Program (AFIT)
AFCTD........ Affected (ABBR)
AFCTDY .... Affectedly (ABBR)
AFCTG .... Affecting (ABBR)
AFCTGY .... Affectingly (ABBR)
AFCTN .... Affection (ABBR)
AFCTNA .... Affectionate (ABBR)
AFCTNAY ..... Affectionately (ABBR)
AFCTNT....... Affectionate (ABBR)
AFCTNTY ..... Affectionately (ABBR)
AFCTS .... Air Force Combined Tomography System (MCD)
AFCTV.......... Action for Children's Television
AFCU .... American and Foreign Christian Union (EA)
AFCU .... American Friends of Cambridge University (EA)
AFCU .... Association of Federal Computer Users [*Defunct*] (EA)
AFCU .... Australian Federation of Credit Unions
AFCVC........ Vice Chief of Staff [*Air Force*]
AFCW......... Association of Family Case-Workers [*British*] (BI)
AFCWB .... American Federation of Catholic Workers for the Blind [*Later, CAPVI*] (EA)
AFCWBVH.... American Federation of Catholic Workers for the Blind and Visually Handicapped [*Later, CAPVI*] (EA)
AFCWF........ Air Force Civilian Welfare Fund (AFM)
AFCX........... AFC Cable Systems [*NASDAQ symbol*] (SAG)
AFD............ Accelerated Freeze-Drying [*Food processing*]
AFD............ Acid Fractionator Distillate (GFGA)
AFD............ Acoustic Firing Device (CAAL)
AFD............ Active Filter Design
AFD............ Admiralty Floating Dock [*British*]
AFD............ African Development [*A publication*]
AFD............ Aft Flight Deck (NASA)
AFD............ Airborne Frequency Doubler
AFD............ Air Force Depot
AFD............ Air Force Detachment
AFD............ Air Force Directive (AAG)
AFD............ Airport Facility Directory [*FAA*] (TAG)
AFD............ Alliance of Free Democrats [*Hungary Political party*] (EY)
A/FD............ Altered from a Detail (SAA)
AFD............ Alternating Field Demagnetization

AFD.............	Americans for Decency (EA)
AFD.............	Ammunition Ship
AFD.............	Amplitude-Frequency Distortion
AFDH...........	Appointed Factory Doctor (PDAA)
AFD.............	April Fools' Day
AFD.............	Arithmetic Function Designator
AFD.............	Armed Forces Day
AFD.............	Arm/Fire Device (MCD)
AFD.............	Arming and Fusing Device
AFD.............	Assistant Field Director [*Red Cross*]
AFD.............	Assistant Flight Director [*NASA*] (KSC)
AFD.............	Associated Film Distribution (BARN)
AFD.............	Associated Food Dealers of Michigan (SRA)
AFD.............	Association of Food Distributors [*Later, AFI*] (EA)
AFD.............	Association of Footwear Distributors [*Defunct*] (EA)
AFD.............	Australian Faculty Directory [*A publication*]
AFD.............	Australian Foundation for the Disabled
AFD.............	Automated Flaw Detector
AFD.............	Automated Frequency Deconfliction [*Telecommunications*] (LAIN)
AFD.............	Automatic Fast Demagnetization
AFD.............	Automatic File Distribution [*Computer science*] [*Telecommunications*]
AFD.............	Automatic Fire Detection (NITA)
AFD.............	Auxiliary Floating Dry Dock [*Navy symbol*]
AFD.............	Axial Flux Density (IEEE)
AFD.............	Axial Flux Difference [*Nuclear energy*] (NRCH)
AFD.............	Bibliotheque Dentinger [*Dentinger Library*] Falher, Alberta [*Library symbol National Library of Canada*] (NLC)
AFD.............	Doctor of Fine Arts
AFD.............	Panorama Flight Service [*ICAO designator*] (FAAC)
AFD.............	Watford City, ND [*Location identifier FAA*] (FAAL)
AFDA	Air Force Distribution Agency
AFDA	Alabama Funeral Directors Association (SRA)
AFDA	American Fish Decoy Association (EA)
AFDA	Arizona Funeral Directors Association (SRA)
AFDA	Axial Flux Difference Alarm (IEEE)
AFDAA	Air Force Data Automation Agency (AFM)
AFDAG	Airborne Forward Delivery Airfield Group
AFDAMET	Air Force Data Automation Management Engineering Team
AFDAP	Advanced Fiber Optic Digital Autopilot [*Military*]
AFDAP	Air Force Data Automation Planning Concepts [*Manual*]
AFDAP	Air Force Designated Acquisition Program
AFDAP	Air Force Director of Development and Planning (SAA)
AFDAP	Assistant for Development Planning [*Air Force*]
AFDAR	Air Force Defense Acquisition Regulations (MCD)
AFDARS	Air Force Defense Acquisition Regulation Supplement [*Superseded by AFFARS in 1984*] (AAGC)
AFDAS	Aircraft Fatigue Data Analysis System (ADA)
AFDAS	Airframe Fatigue Data Analysis System (MCD)
AFDASTA	Air Force Data Station
AFDAT	Air Force Directorate of Advanced Technology
AFDATACOM...	Air Force Data Communications System
AFDATASTA...	Air Force Data Station (CET)
AfDB	African Development Bank [*Also, ADB*] (EY)
AFDB	African Development Bank (USGC)
AFDB	Air Force Decorations Board
AFDB	Alternative Fuel Data Bank [*Bartlesville Energy Technology Center*] [*Database*]
AFDB	Armed Forces Development Board
AFDB	Auxiliary Floating Dry Dock (Big) [*Non-self-propelled*] [*Navy symbol*]
AFDBS	Association Francaise des Documentalistes et des Bibliothecaires Specialises (NITA)
AFDC	Agriculture and Fishery Development Corp. [*South Korea*]
AFDC	Aid to Families with Dependent Children
AFDC	Air Force Department Constabulary [*British military*] (DMA)
AFDC	Artillery Fire Data Computer (PDAA)
AFDC	Association des Facultes Dentaires du Canada [*Association of Dentistry Faculties in Canada*]
AFDC	Australian Folkloric Dance Company [*An association*]
AFDC	Automatic Formation Drone Control
AFDC	Auxiliary Floating Dry Dock (Concrete) [*Non-self-propelled*] [*Navy symbol*]
AFDCB	Armed Forces Disciplinary Control Board
AFDCCO	Air Force Departmental Catalog Coordinating Office
AFDCF	American First Day Cover Foundation [*Defunct*] (EA)
AFDCMI	Air Force Policy on Disclosure of Classified Military Information (SAA)
AFDCO	Air Force Distribution Control Office
AFDCP	Aft Flight Deck Control Panel (MCD)
AFDCP	Air Force Decision Coordinating Paper (MCD)
AFDCS	American First Day Cover Society (EA)
AFDCS	Association of First Division Civil Servants [*British*]
AFDCS	Automatic Film Data Collection System (MCD)
AFDCUF	Aid to Families with Dependent Children of Unemployed Fathers
AFDC-UP......	Aid to Families with Dependent Children - Unemployed Parents
AFDD	Aeroflightdynamics Directorate [*Army and NASA joint operation*] (RDA)
AFDDA........	Air Force Director of Data Automation (IEEE)
AFDDC	Deputy Chief of Staff, Development, Air Force
AFDE...........	American Fund for Dental Education [*Later, AFDH*] (EA)
AFDE...........	Arctic Fuel Dispensing Equipment (MCD)
AFDE...........	Association of Forensic Document Examiners (EA)
AFDEA	American Funeral Directors and Embalmers Association (EA)
AFDEC	Association of Franchised Distributors of Electronic Components [*British*]
AFDEN	Adult Females, Density Of [*Ecology*]
AFDF...........	African Development Fund
AFDFO	Development Field Office [*Air Force*]
AFDFR	Air Force Development Field Representative (AAG)
AFDFS	Air Force Department Fire Service [*British military*] (DMA)
AFDH	American Fund for Dental Health (EA)
AFDICQ	Association des Fabricants et Distributeurs de l'Industrie de la Cuisine du Quebec (AC)
AFDIER	Air Force Departmental Industrial Equipment Reserve (SAA)
AFDIERSS....	Air Force Departmental Industrial Equipment Reserve Storage Site
AFDIS	Air Force Director of Inspection Services (MUGU)
AFDIT..........	Associazione Italiana dei Fornitori e Distributori di Informazione Telematica [*Italian Association for the Production and Distribution of Online Information*] [*Rome*] [*Information service or system*] (IID)
AFDK	After Dark [*NWS*] (FAAC)
AFDL	Abstract Family of Deterministic Languages (PDAA)
AFDL	Auxiliary Floating Dry Dock (Little) [*Non-self-propelled*] [*Navy symbol*]
AFDL(C)......	Auxiliary Floating Dry Dock (Little, Concrete) [*Non-self-propelled*] [*Navy symbol*]
AFDM..........	Ash-Free Dry Mass [*Analytical chemistry*]
AFDM..........	Auxiliary Floating Dry Dock (Medium) [*Non-self-propelled*] [*Navy symbol*]
AFDMP	Air Force Directorate of Materials and Processes (KSC)
AFDMS	Airborne Flight Detection Measurement System (MCD)
AFDO	Aft Flight Deck Operator (MCD)
AFDO	Air Force Duty Officer
AFDO	Assistant Fighter Director Office [*Navy*]
AFDO	Assistant Flight Dynamics Officer [*NASA*]
AFDO	Association of Food and Drug Officials (EA)
AFDO	Award Fee Determining Official (AAGC)
AFDOA	Armed Forces Dental Officers Association (EA)
AFDOUS.......	Association of Food and Drug Officials of the United States [*Later, AFDO*] (EA)
AFDP	Army Force Development Plan
AFDP	Award Fee Determination Plan (AAGC)
AFDPDB	Aft Flight Deck Power Distribution Box (MCD)
AFDPP	Air Force Director of Personnel Planning (SAA)
AFDPRC	Air Force Disaster Preparedness Resource Center
AFDR	Air Force Directorate of Requirement (AAG)
AFDRB	Air Force Disability Review Board
AFDRB	Air Force Discharge Review Board
AFDRD	Air Force Director [*or Directorate*] of Research and Development
AFDRIF	Air Force Directory of Resident Inspection Facilities (AAG)
AFDRQ	Air Force Director of Requirements
AFDRT	Air Force Director of Research and Technology (SAA)
AFDRTF	Alberta Forest Development Research Trust Fund [*Also Forest Research Program - Environmental Protection & Enhancement Fund*] (AC)
AFDS	Advanced Fighter Diagnostic System (MCD)
AFDS	Advanced Flight Deck Simulator [*Aviation*] (PDAA)
AFDS	Air Foil Design System [*Automotive engineering*]
AFDS	Amphibious Flagship Data System [*Military*] (NVT)
AFDS	Associated Funeral Directors Service (EA)
AFDS	Association for the Free Distribution of the Scriptures [*British*]
AFDS	Automatic Flight Director System (MCD)
AFDS	Autonomous Free-Flight Dispenser System [*Air Force*]
AFDS	Autopilot Flight Director System (GAVI)
AFDS	Auxiliary Fighter Director Ship [*Navy*]
AFDSC	Air Force Data Services Center
AFDSDC	Air Force Data Systems Design Center [*Gunter Air Force Station, AL*] (AFM)
AFDSEC	Air Force Data Systems Evaluation Center
AFDSI	Air Force Director of Special Investigations (SAA)
AFDSI	Associated Funeral Directors Service International (EA)
AFDT...........	AEELS [*Airborne ELINT Emitter Location System*] Fixed Downlink Terminal (MCD)
AFDT...........	Air Freight Decision Tool (MCD)
AFDTC	Air Force Development Test Center (DOMA)
AFDTL.........	Air Force Drug Testing Laboratory [*Brooks Air Force Base, TX*] (GRD)
AFDU	Air Fighting Development Unit [*British*]
AFDU	Alternative Fuels Development Unit [*La Porte, TX*] [*Department of Energy*]
AFDVT	Affidavit
AFDW	Air Force District of Washington
AFDW	Ash-Free Dry Weight (DMAA)
AFDWAFO	Air Force District of Washington Accounting and Finance Office
AFE.............	Accredited Financial Examiner [*Society of Financial Examiners*] [*Designation awarded by*]
AFE.............	Advanced Fuel Electronics [*Automotive engineering*]
AFE.............	Aerospace Facilities Engineer
AF/E...........	After End of the Hatch [*Stowage*] (DNAB)
AFE.............	Agricultural Futures Exchange [*London, England*]
AFE.............	Airfast Service Indonesia PT [*ICAO designator*] (FAAC)
AFE.............	Air Force Experiment
AFE.............	Air Force in Europe
AFE.............	Allowed Failure Effect
AFE.............	Alternate Fighter Engine (MCD)
AFE.............	Alternative Fuel Electronics [*Fuel systems*] [*Automotive engineering*]
AFE.............	Americans for the Environment (EA)
AFE.............	Amniotic Fluid Embolism [*Obstetrics*]
AFE.............	Apple File Exchange [*Computer science*]
AFE.............	Authority for Expenditure
AFE.............	Automatic Fire Extinguisher (MCD)
AFE.............	Royal Air Force Establishments [*British*]
AFEA	American Farm Economic Association [*Later, AAEA*] (EA)

AFEA............	American Film Export Association (EA)
AFEA............	Automobile Fuel Efficiency Act [1980]
AFEA............	Aviation Facilities Energy Association [Defunct] (EA)
AFEAS..........	Alternative Fluorocarbon Environmental Acceptability Study [World Meteorological Organization]
AFEAS..........	Association Feminine d'Education et d'Action Sociale [Women's Association of Education and Social Action] [Canada]
afeb	Afebrile [Free from fever] [Medicine] (DAVI)
AFEB............	Armed Forces Epidemiological Board [Washington, DC]
AFEB............	Award Fee Evaluation Board [NASA] (NASA)
AFEBS..........	Air Force European Broadcasting Squadron
AFEC............	Association Francaise des Etudes Canadiennes [French Association of Canadian Studies]
AFEC............	Association Francophone d'Education Comparee [French-Speaking Comparative Education Association - FSCEA] (EAIO)
AFEC............	Award Fee Evaluation Committee [NASA] (NASA)
AFECI..........	Association des Fabricants Europeens de Chauffe-Bains et Chauffe-Eau Instantaneset de Chaudieres Murales au Gaz [Association of European Manufacturers of Instantaneous Gas Water Heaters and Wall-Hung Boilers] (EA)
AFECOGAZ...	Association des Fabricants Europeens d'Appareils de Controle [European Control Manufacturers Association] (EAIO)
AFECOR	Association des Fabricants Europeens d'Appareils de Controle et de Regulation [European Control Device Manufacturers' Association] [EC] (ECED)
AFECTI........	Association Francaise d'Experts de la Cooperation Technique Internationale [French Association of Experts Assigned to International Technical Cooperation] (AF)
AFED...........	Afsala Bancorp, Inc. [NASDAQ symbol] (SAG)
AFEDEF........	Association des Fabricants Europeens d'Equipements Ferroviaires [Association of European Railway Equipment Manufacturers] (EAIO)
AFEDPC	Air Force Electronic Data Processing Center (AAG)
AFEE...........	Association for Evolutionary Economics [Lincoln, NE] (EA)
AFEE...........	Association Francaise des Entreprises pour l'Environnement [French Environmentalist Association]
AFEE...........	Association Francaise pour l'Etude des Eaux [French Water Study Association] [Paris] [Information service or system] (IID)
AFEES..........	Air Forces Escape and Evasion Society (EA)
AFEES..........	Armed Forces Examining and Entrance Stations (AFM)
AFEES..........	Automated Armed Forces Examining and Entrance Station
AFEF...........	Air Force Emergency Force
AFEFL..........	Andelin Foundation for Education in Family Living (EA)
AFEFR..........	Air Force Electronic Failure Report (SAA)
AFEI............	Americans for Energy Independence (EA)
AFEI............	Association of Finnish Electric Industries
AFEIS..........	Armed Forces Examining and Induction Stations
AFELIS.........	Air Force Engineering and Logistics Information System (IEEE)
AFEM...........	Armed Forces Expeditionary Medal [Military decoration] (AFM)
AFEMMIS.....	Air Force Equipment Maintenance Management Information System (MCD)
AFEMS.........	Air Force Equipment Management System (AFM)
AFEMST.......	Air Force Equipment Management Survey Team
AFEMT........	Air Force Equipment Management Team (AFIT)
AFEO...........	ASEAN [Association of South East Asian Nations] Federation of Engineering Organizations (EAIO)
AFEOAR	Air Force European Office of Aerospace Research (KSC)
AFEOC.........	Air Force Emergency Operations Center (CET)
AFEOS	Air Force Electro-Optical Site (CET)
AFEP...........	Army Facilities Energy Program (MCD)
AFEPBA........	Armed Forces Enlisted Personnel Benefit Association [Later, MBA]
AFEPC.........	Australian Flour Export Promotion Committee
AFEPI..........	Air Force Equipment Procurement Instruction
AFEPIC........	Air Force Electronic Properties Information Center (PDAA)
AFEQ..........	Association des Fabricants d'Engrais du Quebec (AC)
AFER...........	Air Force Engineering Responsibility (CET)
AFERA	Association des Fabricants Europeens de Rubans Auto-Adhesifs [Association of European Manufacturers of Self-Adhesive Tapes - AEMSAT] (EAIO)
AFERB	Air Force Educational Requirements Board (AFM)
AFERC.........	Air Force Edwards Research Center
AFERSS........	Air Force Environmental Rocket-Sounding System [Meteorology]
AFES...........	Admiralty Fuel Experimental Station [British]
AFES...........	Aggregate Field Expense Study [LIMRA]
AFES...........	Air Force Exchange Service (AFM)
AFES...........	American Far Eastern Society (EA)
AFES...........	Armed Forces Examining Station
AFES...........	Armed Forces Exchange Service (DNAB)
AFES...........	Automatic Feature Extraction System (MCD)
AFESC.........	Air Force Electronic Security Command
AFESC.........	Air Force Engineering and Services Center [Tyndall Air Force Base, FL]
AFESC/ESL...	Air Force Engineering and Services Center/Engineering and Services Laboratory [Tyndall Air Force Base, FL]
AFESD	Air Force Electronic Systems Division
AFESMET.....	Air Force Engineering and Services Management Engineering Team
AFest	Australian Festival [Record label]
AFETAC.......	Air Force Environmental Technical Applications Center (MCD)
AFETO.........	Air Force Engineering Technology Office [Tyndall Air Force Base, FL]
AFETR.........	Air Force Eastern Test Range [Later, ESMC] [Patrick Air Force Base, FL]
AFETRM.......	Air Force Eastern Test Range Manual [A publication] (MCD)
AFETS..........	Air Force Engineering and Technical Service (AFM)

AFEU...........	Association France-Etats-Unis [France-United States Association] (EA)
AFEWC........	Air Force Electronic Warfare Center (CAAL)
AFEWES.......	Air Force Electronic Warfare Evaluation Simulator
AFEX...........	Air Forces Europe Exchange
AFEX...........	Ammonia-Fiber Explosion [Agricultural engineering] (PS)
AFEX...........	Ammonia Freeze Explosion [Chemical engineering]
AFF.............	Above Finished Floor [Technical drawings]
AFF.............	Accelerator Free Fall [Parachuting]
AFF.............	Acceptance and Ferry Flight [NASA] (NASA)
AFF.............	Advanced Firefighter [Military]
AFF.............	Affairs (AFM)
AFF.............	Affecting (ROG)
AFF.............	Affectionately [Correspondence]
AFF.............	Afferent [Medicine]
AFF.............	Affiliated (ADA)
aff...............	Affinis [Having an Affinity with but Not Identical To] [Latin] (MAE)
Aff...............	Affinity Column [Chromatography]
AFF.............	Affirmative
AFF.............	Affirming (ROG)
AFF.............	Agriculture, Forestry, Fishing [Department of Employment] [British]
AFF.............	Alabama Farmers Federation (SRA)
AFF.............	American Family Foundation (EA)
AFF.............	American Farm Foundation [Defunct] (EA)
AFF.............	An Foras Forbartha [National Institute for Physical Planning and ConstructionResearch] [Ireland] [Research center] (IRC)
AFF.............	Anne Frank Fund [Basel, Switzerland] (EAIO)
AFF.............	Armenian Film Foundation (EA)
AFF.............	Army Field Forces
AFF.............	Asociacion Filatelica de Filipinas [Philatelic Association of the Philippines] (EA)
AFF.............	Associated Fresh Foods [British]
AFF.............	Association of Family Farmers (EA)
AF/F...........	Atrial Fibrillation and/or Flutter [Cardiology] (DAVI)
AFF.............	Atrial Filling Fraction [Cardiology]
AFF.............	Auditory-Flutter Fusion (PDAA)
AFF.............	Australian Fencing Federation
AFF.............	Australian Futsal Federation
AFF.............	Automated Field Fire
AFF.............	Automatic Fast Feed (NITA)
AFF.............	Automatic Frequency Follower
AFF.............	Automatic Front Feed (ECII)
AFF.............	Axisymmetrical Flow Field
AFF.............	Colorado Springs, CO [Location identifier FAA] (FAAL)
AFF.............	Morgan Stanley Africa Investment Fund [NYSE symbol] (SAG)
AFF.............	Morgan Stanley Africa Inv Fd [NYSE symbol] (TTSB)
AFFA...........	Actors' Feature Film Award [Australia]
AFFA...........	Aerobics and Fitness Foundation of America (EA)
AFFA...........	Air Freight Forwarders Association of America [Later, AFA] (EA)
AFFA...........	Association for Field Archaeology [Defunct] (EA)
AFFARS	Air Force Federal Acquisition Regulation Supplement [Replaced AFDARS in 1984] (AAGC)
AFFAS..........	Armed Forces Financial Advisory Services [British]
AFFB...........	Army Field Forces Board
AFFBC.........	Ahrens-Fox Fire Buffs Club [Defunct] (EA)
AFFC...........	Advanced Fire/Flight Control System (MCD)
AFFC...........	Air Force Finance Center
AFFC...........	Air Forces Ferry Command
AFFC...........	Alan Feinstein Fan Club (EA)
AFFC...........	Aluminum Foil Field Coil
AFFC...........	Annette Funicello Fan Club (EA)
AFFC...........	Atlanta Flames Fan Club (EA)
AFFC...........	Australian Film Finance Corp.
AffCmpS.......	Affiliated Computer Services, Inc. [Associated Press] (SAG)
AFFCO	Alaska Forest Fire Council
AffCom........	Affiliated Community Bancorp, Inc. [Associated Press] (SAG)
AFFCS.........	Advanced Fuze Function Control System (MCD)
AFFD...........	Affirmed
AFFDL.........	Air Force Flight Dynamics Laboratory [Wright-Patterson Air Force Base, OH] (AFM)
AFFE...........	Airborne Fire Fighting Equipment [Air Force] (MCD)
AFFE...........	Air Force Far East
AFFE...........	Army Forces Far East
AFFEC.........	Affectionate (ADA)
AFFECTLY...	Affectionately [Correspondence] (ROG)
AFFET	Affettuoso [With Expression] [Music]
AFFETT	Affettuoso [With Expression] [Music]
AFFETTO.....	Affettuoso [With Expression] [Music]
AFFF...........	America First Financial Fund 1987 [NASDAQ symbol] (NQ)
AFFF...........	America First Financial Fund Ltd. [Associated Press] (SAG)
AFFF...........	American Family Farm Foundation (EA)
AFFF...........	American Fish Farmers Federation [Defunct] (EA)
AFFF...........	Aqueous Film-Forming Foam [Firefighting chemical for ships]
AFFFA.........	American Forged Fitting and Flange Association [Defunct] (EA)
AFFFT.........	Academy of Family Films and Family Television (EA)
AFFFZ.........	Amer First Finl 1987-A Fd [NASDAQ symbol] (TTSB)
AFFG...........	Affirming
AFFHF.........	American Freedom from Hunger Foundation [Later, MFM/FFH]
AFFI...........	Affidavit [Legal term] (DLA)
AFFI...........	Affinity Technology Gp [NASDAQ symbol] (TTSB)
AFFI...........	Affinity Technology Group, Inc. [NASDAQ symbol] (SAG)
AFFI...........	American Frozen Food Institute (EA)
AFFI...........	Arab Federation for Food Industries (EA)
AFFIE.........	Affirmation Book [Self-help advice]
AFFIL.........	Affiliate

Affil RSH ..... Affiliate of the Royal Society of Health [*British*]
AffilSLAET ... Affiliate of the Society of Licensed Aircraft Engineers and Technologists [*British*] (DBQ)
AFFILTN....... Affiliation
Affin............ Affinity [*Laboratory analysis*]
AffinEnt........ Affinity Entertainment, Inc. [*Associated Press*] (SAG)
AffInstSM...... Affiliate of the Institute of Sales Management [*British*] (DI)
AffinTel........ Affinitty Teleproductions, Inc. [*Associated Press*] (SAG)
AffIP............ Affiliate of the Institute of Plumbing [*British*] (DBQ)
AFFIRM........ Analyzer for FORTRAN [*Formula Translation*] Incremental Reengineering Methodology
AFFIRM........ Association for Federal Information Resources Management (EA)
AffIWHTE ..... Affiliate of the Institution of Works and Highways Technician Engineers [*British*] (DBQ)
AFFJ .... American Fund for Free Jurists (EA)
AFFL............ Affiliate (MUGU)
AFFL............ Affluent
AFFLC.......... Air Force Film Library Center
AFFLIZ......... Afflizione [*Afflictedly*] [*Music*] (ROG)
AFFLT.......... Affiliate
AFFLTD........ Affiliated
AFFLY.......... Affectionately [*Correspondence*] (ROG)
AFFM........... Association of Folding Furniture Manufacturers [*British*] (BI)
AFFM........... Australian Financial Futures Market
AFFMA......... Air Force Frequency Management Agency (DOMA)
AF(F)MMIU... Amphibious Forces Ordnance Material Mobile Instruction Unit [*Obsolete Navy*]
AFFMO......... Affezionatissimo [*Very Tenderly, Pathetically*] [*Music*] (ROG)
AFFOM......... Air Force Field Office Manager (AAG)
AFFOR .... Air Force Forces [*Element of a joint task force*]
AFFOR .... All Faiths for One Race (AIE)
AFFORD........ Analysis for Forces Objectives and Resources Determination (MCD)
AFFOR/DC.... Air Force Forces Deputy [*or Director*] Communications-Electronics (AFIT)
AFFPC.......... Air Force Financial Postal Clerk (AFM)
AFFR............ Affair
AFFR............ Affair
AFFR............ Affray [*FBI standardized term*]
AFFRA.......... American Family Farm and Ranch Association (EA)
Aff Reh .... Affirmed [*or Affirming*] on Rehearing [*Legal term*] (DLA)
AFFRET........ Affrettando [*Hurrying the Pace*] [*Music*]
affrett.......... Affrettando [*Tenderly*] [*Music*] [*Italian*] [*Music*] (BARN)
AFFRETTO ... Affrettando [*Hurrying the Pace*] [*Music*]
AFFRI........... Armed Forces Radiobiology Institute
AFFRMN....... Affirmation (ROG)
AFFS............ American Federation of Film Societies [*Defunct*] (EA)
AFFS............ Army Field Feeding System (INF)
AFFSA......... Air Force Flight Standards Agency (DOMA)
AFFSIM........ Airborne Formation Flight Simulator (MCD)
AFFT............ Affidavit
AFFT............ Association of Federal Fiscal Technicians (EA)
AFFT............ Auditory-Flutter Fusion Threshold (PDAA)
AFFTC.......... Air Force Field Technical Center [*Edwards Air Force Base, CA*] (MCD)
AFFTC.......... Air Force Flight Test Center [*Edwards Air Force Base, CA*]
AFFTD.......... Air Force Foreign Technology Division (KSC)
AFFTE.......... Affectionate [*Correspondence*] (ROG)
AffTech........ Affinity Technology Group, Inc. [*Associated Press*] (SAG)
AFFTIS......... Air Force Flight Test Instrumentation System
AFFTU.......... Augmentor Fuel Flow Test Unit (MCD)
AFFUS .... Association of Free French in the US (EA)
AFFX........... Affymetrix, Inc. [*NASDAQ symbol*] (SAG)
AFFX........... Air Freight [*Air carrier designation symbol*]
AFFY........... Affectionately [*Correspondence*] (ROG)
Affymet........ Affymetrix, Inc. [*Associated Press*] (SAG)
AFG............. Afghani
AFG............. Afghanistan [*ANSI three-letter standard code*] (CNC)
AFG............. Afghanite [*A zeolite*]
AFG............. Aflatoxin G [*Mycotoxin*]
AFG............. ALANON Family Group Headquarters (EA)
AFG............. Allied Freighter Guard (NATG)
AFG............. Alpha Fetal Globulin [*Biochemistry*] (DAVI)
AFG............. Alternative Force Generator (MCD)
AFG............. Amer Finl Group [*NYSE symbol*] (TTSB)
AFG............. American Federation of Guards (EA)
AFG............. American Financial Group, Inc. [*NYSE symbol*] (SAG)
AFG............. American Friends of Greece (EA)
AFG............. Americans for God (EA)
AFG............. Amniotic Fluid Glucose [*Obstetrics*]
AFG............. Analog Function Generator
AFG............. Antenna Field Gain
AFG............. Arbitrary Function Generator (MUGU)
AFG............. Argyrophil, Fluorescent, Granulated [*Cells*] [*Anatomy*]
AFG............. Ariana Afghan Airlines [*Afganistan*] [*ICAO designator*] (FAAC)
AFG............. Army Force Guidance
AFG............. Association des Fabricants de Glucose de la CEE [*Association of the Glucose Producers in the European Economic Community*]
AFG............. Audio Function Generator (MCD)
AFG............. Australian Factors' Guild
AFG............. Australian Fruit Growers [*An association*]
AFG............. Auto Force Generator [*Military*] (DOMA)
AFG............. Automatic Function Generator (HGAA)
AFGC........... American Forage and Grassland Council [*Lexington, KY*]
AFGCM .... Air Force Good Conduct Medal [*Military decoration*] (AFM)
AFGE.......... American Federation of Government Employees (EA)

AFGE............ American Forum for Global Education (IID)
AFGF........... Acidic Fibroblast Growth Factor [*Biochemistry*]
AFGH........... Afghanistan
Afgh............ Afghanistan (VRA)
AFGIS.......... Aerial Free Gunnery Instructions School [*Obsolete*]
AFGL........... AFGL International, Inc. [*NASDAQ symbol*] (SAG)
AFGL........... AFGL Intl. [*NASDAQ symbol*] (TTSB)
AFGL........... Air Force Geophysics Laboratory [*Formerly, AFCRL*] [*Hanscom Air Force Base, MA*]
AFGM.......... American Federation of Grain Millers (EA)
AFGM.......... American Friends of the Gutenberg Museum (EA)
AFGO.......... Air Force General Order
AFGOM........ Air Force Command and Control System Graphic Operator Macros (MCD)
AFGP .... Air Force Advisory Group
AFGP .... Antifreeze Glycoprotein [*Biochemistry*]
AFGR.......... Approved Force Gross Requirement [*Army*] (AABC)
AFGRAD...... African Graduate Fellowship Program [*African-American Institute*] (AEBS)
AFGS........... Air Force Guide Specification (MCD)
AFGS........... American-French Genealogical Society (EA)
AFGU.......... Aerial Free Gunnery Unit
AFGW.......... American Flint Glass Workers' Union of North America [*Later, AFGWU*]
AFGWC .... Air Force Global Weather Center (DOMA)
AFGWC .... Air Force Global Weather Central [*or Control*] [*Offutt Air Force Base, NE*]
AFGWRP...... Air Force Global Weather Reconnaissance Program
AFGWU........ American Flint Glass Workers Union (EA)
AFH............. Acceptance for Honor [*Business term*]
afh.............. Afrihili [*MARC language code Library of Congress*] (LCCP)
AFH............. Air Fecteau Ltd. [*Canada ICAO designator*] (FAAC)
AFH............. Air Force Hospital
AFH............. American Foundation for Health (EA)
AFH............. American Foundation for Homeopathy (EA)
AFH............. Angiofollicular (Lymph Node) Hyperplasia [*Oncology*]
AFH............. Antenna Feed Horn
AFH............. Anterior Facial Height
AFH............. Army Family Housing
AFH............. Australian Federation of Homeopaths
AFH............. Away from Home
AFH............. United States Army, Cold Regions Research and Engineering Laboratory Library, Hanover, NH [*OCLC symbol*] (OCLC)
AFHA .... Armed Forces Hostess Association (EA)
AFHB .... Auxiliary and Fuel Handling Building [*Nuclear energy*] (NUCP)
AFHC .... Air Force Headquarters Command
AFHC .... Association of Fair Housing Committees [*Defunct*]
AFHC .... Australian Freedom from Hunger Campaign
AFHF .... Air Force Historical Foundation (EA)
AFHF .... American Foot Health Foundation (EA)
AFHG .... Additive-Free Hard Gold [*Metallurgy*]
AFHHA .... American Federation of Home Health Agencies (EA)
AFHM .... Affirmative Fair Housing Marketing Regulations [*Department of Housing and Urban Development*] (GFGA)
AFHMM....... American Friends of the Haifa Maritime Museum (EA)
AFHP .... Anonymous Families History Project (EA)
AFHPSP ...... Air Force Health Professions Scholarship Program
AFHPSP ...... Armed Forces Health Profession Scholarship Program
AFHQ .... African Force Headquarters [*World War II*]
AFHQ .... Air Force Headquarters
AFHQ .... Allied Forces Headquarters [*Might refer to any theater of war*] [*World War II*]
AFHQ .... Army Field Headquarters
AFHQ (CIC)... Allied Forces Headquarters (Counter Intelligence Corps) [*World War II*]
AFHQPS ...... Allied Forces Headquarters Petroleum Section [*World War II*]
AFHR .... Association des Fournisseurs d'Hotels et Restaurants Inc. (AC)
AFHRA .... Air Force Historical Research Agency (DOMA)
AFHRL .... Air Force Human Resources Laboratory [*Brooks Air Force Base, TX*] (AFM)
AFHRL .... Australian Fish Health Reference Laboratory
AFHRL/FT .... Air Force Human Resources Laboratory/Flying Training Division [*Williams Air Force Base, AZ*]
AFHRL/MD... Air Force Human Resources Laboratory/Manpower Development Division [*Alexandria, VA*]
AFHS .... Alberta Family Histories Society (AC)
AFHS .... American Family Heritage Society [*Defunct*] (EA)
AFHS .... Average Flying Hours per Sortie [*Air Force*] (AFIT)
AFHSC .... American Fashion Homesewing Council
AFHTWF ..... Amalgamated Association of Felt Hat Trimmers and Wool Formers [*A union*] [*British*] (DCTA)
AFHU .... American Friends of the Hebrew University (EA)
AFHV .... America's Funniest Home Videos [*Television program*]
AFHW .... American Federation of Hosiery Workers [*Later, ACTWU*]
AFI.............. Adjusted Family Income (GFGA)
AFI.............. Aero Filipanas Ltd. [*Philippines*] [*ICAO designator*] (FAAC)
AFI.............. Afiamalu [*Samoa Islands*] [*Seismograph station code, US Geological Survey*] (SEIS)
AFI.............. African/Indian Ocean [*Aviation*]
AFI.............. African India Ocean Region [*USTTA*] (TAG)
AFI.............. Aid for India [*An association British*] (EAIO)
AFI.............. Air Filter Institute [*Later, ARI*] (EA)
AFI.............. Air Flow Indicator
AFI.............. Air Forces, Iceland (MCD)
AFI.............. Amalfi [*Colombia*] [*Airport symbol*] (AD)

AFI .... Amaurotic Familial Idiocy
AFI .... American Fiber Institute
AFI .... American Film Institute (EA)
AFI .... American Firearms Industry [*A publication*] (EAAP)
AFI .... American Flag Institute [*Defunct*] (EA)
AFI .... American Forest Institute [*Later, AFC*]
AFI .... American Friends of Israel (EA)
AFI .... American Fur Industry (EA)
AFI .... Ancient Forest International [*An association*]
AFI .... Anthropology Film Institute [*Later, AFCF*] (EA)
AFI .... Armed Forces Institute
AFI .... Armed Forces Insurance
AFI .... Assistant Flying Instructor (DA)
AFI .... Association of Federal Investigators (EA)
AFI .... Association of Food Industries (EA)
AFI .... Association of Futures Investment [*British*] (DBA)
AFI .... [*The*] Atlantic Fertilizer Institute (AC)
AFI .... Audio Frequency Interference
AFI .... Australians against Further Immigration [*Political party*]
AFI .... Authority and Format Identifier [*Telecommunications*] (OSI)
AFI .... Automatic Fault Isolation
AFI .... Auxiliary Force, India [*British military*] (DMA)
AFI .... Awaiting Final Invoice (AAGC)
AFI .... United States Army, Corps of Engineers, Philadelphia District, Philadelphia, PA [*OCLC symbol*] (OCLC)
AFIA .... Air Force Inspection Agency (DOMA)
AFIA .... American Feed Industry Association (EA)
AFIA .... American Female Impersonators Association (EA)
AFIA .... American Footwear Industries Association [*Later, FIA*]
AFIA .... American Foreign Insurance Association (EA)
AFIA .... Apparel and Fashion Industry's Association [*British*] (BI)
AFIA .... Associate of the Federal Institute of Accountants [*Australia*] (ODBW)
AFIAAWW .... American Film Institute Alumni Association Writers Workshop (EA)
AFIAS .... Army Air Forces Deputy Chiefs of Air Staff [*World War II*]
AFIAS .... Associate Fellow of the Institute of Aeronautical Sciences [*Later, AFAIAA*]
AFIB .... Atrial Fibrillation [*Cardiology*]
AFIC .... Air Force Intelligence Center
AFIC .... Air Force Intelligence Command [*Established 1991*] (DOMA)
AFIC .... American Forces Information Council (DOMA)
AFIC .... Approved Force Inventory Objective [*Military*]
AFIC .... Asian Finance/Investment Corp. [*Proposed*] (ECON)
AFIC .... Association of Fashion and Image Consultants (EA)
AFIC .... Australian Feeds Information Centre [*Database*]
AFICCS .... Air Force Integrated Command and Control System (AFM)
AFICD .... Associate Fellow of the Institute of Civil Defence [*British*]
AFICE .... Air Forces, Iceland
AFICE .... Association for International Cotton Emblem [*Brussels, Belgium*] (EAIO)
AFID .... Alkali Flame Ionization Detector [*Instrumentation*]
AFID .... Anti-Fratricide Identification Device [*Military*] (DOMA)
AFID .... Arithmetic Function Identifier
AFID .... Australian Film Institute Distribution
AFIDA .... Agricultural Foreign Investment Disclosure Act [*1978*]
AFIDA .... Asociacion de Ferias Internacionales de America [*Association of International Trade Fairs of America*] (EAIO)
AFIDES .... Association Francophone Internationale des Directeurs d'Etablissements Scolaires [*International Association of French-Speaking Directors of Educational Institutions*] [*Anjou, PQ*]
AFIDS .... Advanced Facility Intrusion Detection System (DWSG)
AFIDS .... Ami Frame Interface Development System [*Lotus Development Corp.*] (PCM)
AFIDS .... Automatic Firearms Identification System [*Jet Propulsion Laboratory, NASA*]
AFIE .... Abnormal Fluctuation in the Economy (MCD)
AFIE .... American Federation of Italian Evangelicals [*Later, AEIM*] (EA)
AFIE .... Armed Forces Information and Education (MCD)
AFIEC .... Armed Forces Information and Education Center (SAA)
AFIED .... Armed Forces Information and Education Division
AFIF .... Air Force Industrial Fund (AFM)
AFIF .... Armed Forces Information Film (AFM)
AFIF .... Associated Fraternity of Iron Forgers [*A union*] [*British*]
AFIF .... Association of Foremen Iron Founders [*A union*] [*British*]
AFIFIO .... Air Force Information for Industry Office (DOMA)
AFIG .... Air Force Inspector General (SAA)
AFIGAC .... Air Force Inspector General Activities Center
AFIGAP .... Association Francophone Internationale des Groupes d'Animation de la Paraplegie [*International French-Speaking Association of Paraplegic Therapy Groups*] [*Brie-Comte-Robert, France*] (EAIO)
AFII .... American Federation of International Institutes [*Later, ACNS*]
AFIIM .... Associate Fellow of the Institute of Industrial Managers [*British*]
AFIL .... Amer Filtrona [*NASDAQ symbol*] (TTSB)
AFIL .... American Filtrona Corp. [*NASDAQ symbol*] (NQ)
AFIL .... Flight Plan Filed in the Air [*Aviation code*]
A-FILE .... Adolescent-Family Inventory of Life Events and Changes [*Psychology*]
AFILR .... Approved Force Investment Level Requirement (AFIT)
AFiltrn .... American Filtrona Corp. [*Associated Press*] (SAG)
AFIM .... Air Force Inventory Manager
AFIM .... American Friends of the Israel Museum (EA)
AFIMA .... Associate Fellow of the Institute of Mathematics and Its Applications [*British*] (DBQ)
AFIMS .... Air Force Information Management Study
AFIN .... Assistant Chief of Staff, Intelligence [*Air Force*] (MCD)
AFIN .... Australian Finance Availability Guide [*A publication*]
AFIN .... Australia-Wide Funeral Information [*Database*]
AFINS .... Airways Flight Inspector
AFINSPATH ... Armed Forces Institute of Pathology [*DoD*] (DNAB)
AF Inst .... Air Force Institute of Technology (GAGS)
AF Inst Pet ... Associate Fellow of the Institute of Petroleum [*British*]
AFINTELMET ... Air Force Intelligence Management Engineering Team
AFIO .... Agreement for Fighter Interceptor Operations
AFIO .... Approved Force Inventory Objective [*Army*] (AABC)
AFIO .... Association of Former Intelligence Officers (EA)
AFIO .... Association of Former Intelligence Officers (DOMA)
AFIO .... Authorization for Interceptor Operations (MCD)
AFIP .... Air Force Information Program (SAA)
AFIP .... Air Force Institute of Pathology (DAVI)
AFIP .... Air Force Intelligence Publication (SAA)
AFIP .... American Federation of Information Processing [*Formerly, AFIPS*]
AFIP .... Anne Frank Institute of Philadelphia [*Formerly, NIH*] (EA)
AFIP .... Armed Forces Information Program
AFIP .... Armed Forces Institute of Pathology [*DoD*] (EA)
AFIP .... Automated Financial Improvement Program [*Navy*] (GFGA)
AFIPS .... American Federation of Information Processing Societies [*Later, AFIP*] (EA)
AFIR .... Air Force Installation Representative
Afir .... Firkin of Ale [*Unit of measurement*] (DAS)
AFIRB .... Armed Forces Identification Review Board [*US Total Army Personnel Agency*] (EGAO)
AFIRE .... Association of Foreign Investors in US Real Estate (EA)
AFIRE .... Association of Fundamental Institutions of Religious Education
AFIRM .... Affirmative (AABC)
AFIRO .... Air Force Installation Representative Officer
A-FIRST .... Advanced - Far Infrared Search/Track
AFIS .... Aerodrome Flight Information Service
AFIS .... Aircraft Fault Indentification System [*Aviation*] (PDAA)
AFIS .... Air Force Intelligence Service
AFIS .... Air Force Intelligence Study
AFIS .... American Forces Information Service [*DoD*]
AFIS .... Armed Forces Induction Station
AFIS .... Armed Forces Information School
AFIS .... Armed Forces Information Service [*DoD*]
AFIS .... Army Force Integration Study
AFIS .... Australian Firms Information System
AFIS .... Automated Field Interview System
AFIS .... Automated Financial Information System [*Computer science*] (MHDI)
AFIS .... Automated Fingerprint Identification System [*NEC Corp.*]
AFIS .... Automatic Flight Inspection (DA)
AFISA .... Air Force Intelligence Support Agency (DOMA)
AFISC .... Air Force Inspection and Safety Center
AFISM .... Aluminum-Free Inorganic Suspended Material
AFIS(O) .... Aerodrome Flight Information Service (Officer) (DA)
AFISOL .... Aerodrome Flight Information Service Officer's Licence [*British*] (DBQ)
AFISR .... Air Force Industrial Security Regulations
AFIT .... Airblast Fuel Injection Tube [*Gas turbine engine*]
AFIT .... Air Force Institute of Technology [*Wright-Patterson Air Force Base, OH*]
AFIT .... American Fabricating Institute of Technology [*Defunct*] (EA)
AFIT .... Armed Forces Institute of Technology
AFIT .... Automatic Fault Isolation Test
AFIT .... University of North Alabama, Florence, AL [*Library symbol Library of Congress*] (LCLS)
AFITC .... Armed Forces Intelligence Training Center
AFIT(RS) ...... Air Force Institute of Technology, Residence School
AFIT/SL .... Air Force Institute of Technology School of Systems and Logistics [*Wright-Patterson Air Force Base, OH*]
AFIX .... Air Freighters [*Air carrier designation symbol*]
AFJ .... Air Force Jet
AFJ .... Alliance [*Uganda*] [*FAA designator*] (FAAC)
AFJA .... Australian Fresh Juice Association
AFJAG .... Air Force Judge Advocate General
AF JAG Bull ... Air Force JAG Bulletin [*A publication*] (AAGC)
AFJAGS .... Air Force Judge Advocate General School
AFJCC .... American Forum for Jewish-Christian Cooperation (EA)
AFJCE .... American Federation of Jews from Central Europe (EA)
AFJCMA .... Australian Fresh Juice and Cordial Manufacturers' Association
AFJFCINV .... American Federation of Jewish Fighters, Camp Inmates and Nazi Victims [*Defunct*] (EA)
AFJITR .... American Friends of the Jerusalem Institute for Talmudic Research (EA)
AFJKT .... Air Force Job Knowledge Test
AFJMG .... American Friends of the Jewish Museum of Greece (EA)
AFJMSNS .... Air Force Justification for Major System New Start (MCD)
AFJN .... Africa Faith and Justice Network (EA)
AFJPO .... Air Force Joint Project Office (SAA)
AFJROTC ..... Air Force Junior Reserve Officers Training Corps (AFM)
AFJSWF .... American Friends of the Jerusalem Society for World Fellowship (EA)
AFK .... Africa Air Links [*Sierra Leone*] [*ICAO designator*] (FAAC)
AFK .... Armed Forces of the Republic of Korea (CINC)
AFK .... Away from Keyboard [*Computer hacker terminology*] (NHD)
AFK .... Fort Kent Public Library, Alberta [*Library symbol National Library of Canada*] (NLC)
AFKAC .... Air Force Cryptographic Code System (CET)
AFKAG .... Air Force Cryptographic Aid, General
AFKAI .... Air Force Cryptographic Aid, Recognition and Identification Systems (CET)
AFKAM .... Air Force Cryptographic Maintenance Manual (CET)
AFKAP .... Air Force Cryptographic One Time Pads (CET)

AFKN	American Forces Korea Network [*Military*] (GFGA)
AFKT	Air Force Knowledge Test (SAA)
AFL	Above Field Level [*Aerospace*] (AAG)
AFL	Abstract Family of Languages [*Computer science*]
AFL	Active Fuel Length [*Nuclear energy*] (NRCH)
AFL	Actresses' Franchise League [*British*]
AFL	Adolescent Family Life Program [*Department of Health and Human Services*]
AFL	Advanced Flow LASER (MCD)
AFL	Aeroflot - Russian International Airlines [*Russian Federation*] [*ICAO designator*] (FAAC)
AFL	AFLAC, Inc. [*NYSE symbol*] (SPSG)
AFL	Aflatoxicol [*Metabolite of AFB*] [*Biochemistry*]
AFL	Air Force Letter
AFL	Air Force Liaison
AFL	Air Force List [*British military*] (DMA)
AFL	Alberta Federation of Labour [*Federation du Travail de l'Alberta*] (AC)
AFL	American Federation of Labor [*Later, AFL-CIO*] (GPO)
AFL	American Football League [*Reorganized as part of AFC and NFC*] (EA)
AFL	American Friends of Lafayette (EA)
AFL	Americans for Life (EA)
AFL	Animated Film Language (BUR)
AFL	Antifatty Liver [*Medicine*]
AFL	Artificial Limb (HGAA)
AFL	Association for Family Living [*Defunct*] (EA)
AFL	Association for Library Information, Pittsburgh, PA [*OCLC symbol*] (OCLC)
AFL	Atrial Flutter [*Cardiology*] (MAE)
AFL	Australian Family Lawyer [*A publication*]
AFL	Australian Festival of Life
AFL	AUTOLAND [*Automatic Landing*] Flight Tests [*NASA*] (MCD)
AFL	Automatic Fault Location
AFL	Aviation Foot Lockers [*Army*] (RDA)
AFL	Flatbush Public Library, Alberta [*Library symbol National Library of Canada*] (NLC)
AFL	French Institute/Alliance Francaise Library [*UTLAS symbol*]
AFLA	Adolescent Family Life Act [*of 1981*]
AFLA	Amateur Fencers League of America [*Later, USFA*] (EA)
AFLA	American Foreign Law Association (EA)
AFLA	Armed Forces Leave Act of 1946
AFLA	Asian Federation of Library Associations [*Japan*]
AFLA	Automotive Fleet and Leasing Association (EA)
AFLAC	AFLAC, Inc. [*Associated Press*] (SAG)
AFLANT	Air Forces, Atlantic
AFLAS	Aviation Fuels Logistical Area Summary [*Air Force*] (AFIT)
AFLAT	Air Force Language Aptitude Test
AFLB	Australian Family Law Bulletin [*A publication*]
AFLC	Air Force Logistics Center (MCD)
AFLC	Air Force Logistics Command [*Formerly, Air Materiel Command*] [*Wright-Patterson Air Force Base, OH*]
AFLC	Association of Free Lutheran Congregations
AFLCA	American Fur Liner Contractors Association (EA)
AFLCF	Air Force Logistics Command Form
AFLCG	Air Force Logistics Control Group
AFL-CIO	American Federation of Labor and Congress of Industrial Organizations
AFL-CIO	American Federation of Labor-Congress of Industrial Organizations (AAGC)
AFLCL	Air Force Logistics Command Letter (MCD)
AFLCM	Air Force Logistics Command Manual (MCD)
AFLC-OA	Air Force Logistics Command Operations Analysis Office [*Wright-Patterson Air Force Base, OH*]
AFLCON	Air Force Logistics Command Operations Network (MCD)
AFLCON	Air Force Logistics Communications Network (AFM)
AFLCP	Air Force Logistics Command Pamphlets
AFLCR	Air Force Logistics Command Regulations
AFLD	Airborne Fraunhofer Line Discriminator
AFLD	Airfield (AFM)
AFLD	Air Force Acquisition Logistics Division (AAGC)
AFLD	American Foundation for Learning Disabilities
AF/LE	Air Force, Logistics and Engineering (DOMA)
AFLE	Association of French Language Epidemiologists (EAIO)
AFLETS	Air Force Law Enforcement Terminal System
AFLEX	Automatic-Landing Flight Experiment [*Space program*] [*Japan*]
AFLFI	About Face/Let's Face It (EA)
AFLI	African Library [*Belgium Ministry of Foreign Affairs*] [*Information service or system*] (CRD)
AFLI	Air Force Legislative Item
AFLI	Association for Library Information [*Duquesne University Library*] [*Information service or system*] (IID)
AFLICO	OAU [*Organization of African Unity*] Coordinating Committee for the Liberation of Africa [*Tanzania*] (EAIO)
AFLIR	Advanced Forward-Looking Infrared
AFLL	Army Fuels and Lubricants Laboratory
AFLL	Association of French-Language Leprologists [*Paris, France*] (EAIO)
AFLM	Association Francaise De Lutte Contre La Mucoviscidose [*French Cystic Fibrosis Association*]
AFLMC	Air Force Logistics Management Center [*Gunter Air Force Station, AL*] (AFM)
AFLO	Advocates for Library Outreach [*Office for Literacy and Outreach*] [*American Library Association*]
AFLOGMET	Air Force Logistics Management Engineering Team
AFLP	Acute Fatty Liver of Pregnancy [*Medicine*]

AFLP	Amplified Fragment Length Polymorphism [*Also, Ampli FLP*] [*Genetics*]
AFLP	Armed Forces Language Program
AFLR	Armed Forces Liaison Representative [*Red Cross*]
AFLRL	Army Fuels and Lubricants Research Laboratory
AFLRS	Allied Forces Local Resources Section [*World War II*]
AFLRT	Armed Forces Librarians Round Table [*American Library Association*]
AFLS	Active Flight Load System (MCD)
AFLS	Armed Forces Librarians Section [*Public Library Association*]
AFLSA	Air Force Legal Services Agency (DOMA)
AFLSA	Air Force Longevity Service Award [*Military decoration*] (AFM)
AFLSC	Air Force Legal Services Center
Af L Studies	African Law Studies [*A publication*] (DLA)
AFLU	Available for Local Use (MCD)
AFLX	ADFlex Solutions [*NASDAQ symbol*] (SAG)
AFLX	Air Florida [*Air carrier designation symbol*]
AFM	Abrasive Flow Machining [*Mechanical engineering*]
AFM	Academy of Family Mediators (EA)
AFM	Accredited Farm Manager [*Designation given by American Society of Farm Managers and Rural Appraisers*]
AFM	Acting Fort Major [*Military British*] (ROG)
AFM	Adhesive Film Mechanism
AFM	Affirmative [*ICAO designator*] (FAAC)
AFM	Affretair [*Zimbabwe*] [*ICAO designator*] (FAAC)
AFM	Aflatoxin M [*Mycotoxin*]
AFM	After Full Moon [*Freemasonry*] (ROG)
AFM	Air Flow Meter [*Automotive engineering*]
AFM	Air Force Manual [*A publication*]
AFM	Air Force Medal [*British*]
AFM	Air Force Museum
AFM	Air Freight Motor Carriers Conference, Inc., Arlington VA [*STAC*]
AFM	Airplane Flight Manual [*Federal Aviation Administration*]
AFM	Alex von Falkenhausen Motorenwerke [*Automobile manufacturer*]
AFM	Alternate Financial Mechanisms [*Health insurance*] (GHCT)
AFM	American Family Member
AFM	American Federation of Musicians of the United States and Canada [*Later, THFC*] (EA)
AFM	Analysis and Forecasting Mode
AFM	Ancient Freemasons
AFM	Annular Fire Missile
AFM	Antiferromagnet [*Physics*]
AFM	Antifriction Metal
AFM	Apollo Follow-On Missions [*NASA*] (SAA)
AFM	Application Functions Module [*Computer science*]
AFM	Approved Flight Manual [*FAA A publication*] (MCD)
AFM	Arbeitsgruppe fuer Menschenrechte [*Germany*]
AFM	Armed Forces Management (AABC)
AFM	Armed Forces Movement [*Portugal*]
A/FM	Arm/Firing Mechanism (MCD)
AFM	Associated Foam Manufacturers (EA)
AFM	Associated Fur Manufacturers (EA)
AFM	Association of Free Magazines (DGA)
AFM	Atomic Force Microscope
AFM	Audio Frequency Modulation
AFM	Automatic Fault-Finding and Maintenance (SAA)
AFM	Automatic Flight Management
AFM	Aviation Fleet Maintenance (NVT)
AFM	Fort McMurray Public Library, Alberta [*Library symbol National Library of Canada*] (NLC)
AFM	United States Army, Corps of Engineers, Waterways Experiment Station, Vicksburg,MS [*OCLC symbol*] (OCLC)
AFMA	Access Floor Manufacturing Association (EA)
AFMA	American Federation of Medical Accreditation (EA)
AFMA	American Feed Manufacturers Association [*Later, AFIA*] (EA)
AFMA	American Fiber Manufacturers Association (EA)
AFMA	American Film Marketing Association (EA)
AFMA	American Footwear Manufacturers' Association [*Later, FIA*]
AFMA	American Fur Merchants' Association (EA)
AFMA	American Furniture Manufacturers Association (EA)
AFMA	Armed Forces Management Association [*Later, ADPA*] (EA)
AFMA	Artificial Flower Manufacturers' Association of Great Britain (BI)
AFMA	Association of Food Marketing Agencies in Asia and the Pacific (EA)
AFMA	Australian Film Making Association
AFMA	Australian Folk Music Associates
AFMA	Australian Foodservice Manufacturers' Association
AFMA	Autobody Filler Manufacturers Association [*ASEMC*] [*Absorbed by*] (EA)
AFMA	Fort Macleod Public Library, Alberta [*Library symbol National Library of Canada*] (NLC)
AFMAB	Atmospheric Forcings for the Mid-Atlantic Bight [*Oceanography*] (MSC)
AFMAG	Air Force Management Analysis Group (MCD)
AFMAG	Army Air Forces Air Adjutant General [*World War II*]
AFMAG	Audiofrequency Magnetic Fields [*Prospecting technique*]
AFMAINMET	Air Force Maintenance Management Engineering Team
AFMAQ	Association des Fabricants de Material Agricole du Quebec (AC)
AFMAS	Anzac Community School, Fort McMurray, Alberta [*Library symbol National Library of Canada*] (BIB)
AFMBT	Artificial Flower Manufacturers Board of Trade [*Defunct*] (EA)
AFMC	Air Force Material Command
AFMC	American Floral Marketing Council (EA)
AFMC	Armed Forces Mail Call [*Defunct*] (EA)
AFMC	Armed Forces Marketing Council (EA)
AFMC	Association des Facultes de Medecine du Canada [*Association of Medical Faculties of Canada*]

AFMC.........	Association of Former Members of Congress [Formerly, FMC] (EA)
AFMC.........	Australian Fertilizer Manufacturers' Committee
AFMC.........	Automotive Filter Manufacturers Council [Later, FMC] (EA)
AFMC.........	Auxiliary Force Medical Corps [British military] (DMA)
AFMCC......	Air Freight Motor Carriers Conference [Later, AEMCC] (EA)
AFMCH	American Foundation for Maternal and Child Health (EA)
AFMCO	Army Force Modernization Coordination Office
AFMD	Accounting and Financial Management Division [GAO] (AAGC)
AFMD	Air Force Missile Division (SAA)
AFMDC	Air Force Machinability Data Center (MCD)
AFMDC	Air Force Missile Development Center [AFSC]
AFME.........	Airframe
AFME.........	American Friends of the Middle East [Later, AMIDEAST] (EA)
AFMEA........	Air Force Management Engineering Agency
AFMED.......	Allied Forces Mediterranean [NATO]
AFMEDMET..	Air Force Medical Management Engineering Team
AFMEI........	Association of Free Methodist Educational Institutions (EA)
AFMENS	Air Force Mission Element Need Statement
AFMF........	Air Fleet Marine Force
AFMFIC........	Associated Factory Mutual Fire Insurance Companies [Later, FMS] (EA)
AFM File.....	Adobe Font Metrics File (CDE)
AFMFP........	Aircraft, Fleet Marine Force, Pacific [Obsolete]
AFMH........	American Foundation for Mental Hygiene
AFMH........	Association for Faculty in the Medical Humanities (EA)
AFMH........	Fort McMurray Regional Hospital, Alberta [Library symbol National Library of Canada] (NLC)
AFMI........	Association of French Mechanical Industries (EA)
AFMIC........	Air Force Materials Information Center (DIT)
AFMIC........	Armed Forces Medical Intelligence Center [Fort Detrick] [Frederick, MD]
AF-MIPR	Air Force - Military Interdepartmental Purchase Requests
AFMIS........	Army Food Management Information System (GFGA)
AFMK.........	Keyano College, Fort McMurray, Alberta [Library symbol National Library of Canada] (NLC)
AFMKS.........	Fort McKay School, Alberta [Library symbol National Library of Canada] (BIB)
AFML.........	Air Force Materials Laboratory [Wright-Patterson Air Force Base, OH]
AFML.........	Armed Forces Medical Library [Later, National Library of Medicine, 1956]
AFMLC........	Aeronautical Frequency Management Committee [British] (DA)
AFMLO........	Air Force Medical Logistics Office
AFMM........	American Festival of Microtonal Music (EA)
AFMM........	Association of Fish Meal Manufacturers [British] (DBA)
AFMM.........	Heritage Park, Fort McMurray, Alberta [Library symbol National Library of Canada] (BIB)
AFMMFO......	Air Force Medical Materiel Field Office (AFM)
AFMML.......	Air Force Medical Materiel Letter
AFMMO.......	Air Force MIPR [Military Interdepartmental Purchase Request] Management Office (AFIT)
AFmMP.......	United States Army, Military Police School, Fort McClellan, AL [Library symbol Library of Congress] (LCLS)
AFMOA	Air Force Medical Operations Agency (DOMA)
AFMP.........	Association of Free Magazines and Periodicals [British] (EAIO)
AFMPA........	Air Force Medical Publications Agency
AFMPA........	Armed Forces Medical Procurement Agency
AFMPC........	Air Force Manpower and Personnel Center (MCD)
AFMPC........	Air Force Military Personnel Center [Randolph Air Force Base, TX]
AFMPC........	Assistant for Materiel Program Control [Air Force]
AFMPMET....	Air Force Manpower and Personnel Management Engineering Team
AFMPP........	Air Force Manual of Procurement and Productions [A publication] (AAGC)
AFMR.........	American Foundation for Management Research [Later, AMA] (EA)
AFMR.........	Antiferromagnetic Resonance
AFMR.........	Armed Forces Master Records [Solicited phonograph records, and money to buy records, for the armed forces] [See also RFOFM] [World War II]
AFMR.........	Armed Forces Military Report [DoD]
AFMR.........	Asian Federation for the Mentally Retarded [Singapore] (EAIO)
AFMR.........	Assistant Firemaster [British]
AFMRB........	Air Force Material Review Board (MCD)
AFMRS........	ASW [Antisubmarine Warfare] Formatted Message Reporting System
AFMS.........	Advanced Flight Management System (DA)
AFMS.........	Airborne Frequency Multiplexing System
AFMS.........	Air Force Manpower Standards
AFMS.........	Air Force Medical Service
AFMS.........	Airlift Field Maintenance Section
AFMS.........	American Federation of Mineralogical Societies (EA)
AFMS.........	Operations Library, Syncrude Canada Ltd., Fort McMurray, Alberta [Library symbol National Library of Canada] (NLC)
AFMSA........	Air Force Medical Support Agency (DOMA)
AFMSC........	Air Force Medical Service Center (MCD)
AFMSC........	Air Force Medical Specialist Corps
AFMSC........	Armed Forces Menu Service Committee (AABC)
AFMSI........	Information Centre, SUNCOR Inc. Resources Group, Fort McMurray, Alberta [Library symbol National Library of Canada] (NLC)
AFMSL........	Air Force Measurement Standards Laboratories (AFIT)
AFMSMET....	Air Force Maintenance and Supply Management Engineering Team [Wright-Patterson Air Force Base, OH]
AFMSO	Air Force Mortuary Services Office
AFMSP........	Air Force Meteorological Satellite Program (NOAA)
AFMSS........	Air Force Material Supply and Services (SAA)
AFMSS........	Air Force Mission Support System (DOMA)
AFMT.........	Air Force Manufacturing Technology
AFMTC.......	Air Force Military Training Center (AFM)
AFMTC........	Air Force Missile Test Center [Later, AFETR] [Patrick Air Force Base, FL]
AFMU.........	Acetylamino(formylamino)methyluracil [Biochemistry]
AFMUSC	American Federation of Musicians of the United States and Canada [Later, THFC]
AFMW........	Action for Former Military Wives [Later, NAFMW] [An association] (EA)
AFMWRA.....	Air Force Morale, Welfare, and Recreation Agency (DOMA)
AFN...........	Active Filter Network
AFN...........	Address Complete, Subscriber Free, No-Charge [Telecommunications] (TEL)
AFN...........	Adoptive Family Network [Formerly, Families Adopting Children Everywhere (FACE)] (PAZ)
AFN...........	African International Airlines [Lesotho] [ICAO designator] (FAAC)
AFN...........	Afunctional Neutrophil (DMAA)
AFN...........	Air Force Finance Center
AF/N.........	Air Force/Navy (AAG)
AFN...........	Alaska Federation of Natives (EA)
AFN...........	Alfin Fragrances, Inc. [AMEX symbol] (SPSG)
AFN...........	Alfin Inc. [AMEX symbol] (TTSB)
AFN...........	All Figure Number [Telecommunications] (TEL)
AFN...........	American Forces Network (AABC)
AFN...........	Archie Frazer-Nash [British auto industrialist and founder of AFN Cars]
AFN...........	Armed Forces Network [Military]
AFN...........	Armed Forces Network [TV-radio] (DOMA)
AFN...........	Assembly of First Nations [Canadian Indian organization]
AFN...........	Association of Free Newspapers [British] (EAIO)
AFN...........	Automatic Feature Negotiation [Computer science]
AFN...........	Average Failure Number
AFN...........	Jaffrey, NH [Location identifier FAA] (FAAL)
AFN...........	United States Army, Corps of Engineers, New York District, New York, NY [OCLC symbol] (OCLC)
AFNA	Accordion Federation of North America (EA)
AFNA	Air Force - Navy
AF/NA	Air Force/Navy Aeronautical
AFNA	American Foundation for Negro Affairs (EA)
AFNAB	Air Force - Navy Aeronautical Bulletin
AFNAG........	Air Force NATO Agreement (MCD)
AFNAS	Air Force - Navy Aeronautical Standard
AFNB	Armed Forces News Bureau [Later, AFPS]
AFNC	Air Force Nurse Corps
AFnclGp......	American Financial Group, Inc. [Associated Press] (SAG)
AFNCOAR ...	Air Force Noncommissioned Officer Academy [Graduate] Ribbon [Military decoration] (AFM)
AFND	Acute Febrile Neutrophilic Dermatosis [Medicine] (DMAA)
AFNE	Allied Forces Northern Europe [NATO]
AFNE	American Forces Network, Europe (AABC)
AFNE	Americans for Nuclear Energy (EA)
AFNEA	Air Force NOTAM [Notice to Airmen] Exchange Area
AFNEO	Air Force NOTAM [Notice to Airmen] Exchange Office
AF NETF	Air Force Nuclear Engineering Test Facility [Reactor]
AFNETR	Air Force Nuclear Engineering Test Reactor (SAA)
AFNETSTA ...	Air Force Networks Station
AFNEWS	Air Force News Agency (DOMA)
AFNFICM	Atlantic Fleet Naval Forces Intelligence Collection Manual (MCD)
AFNON........	Allied Forces North Norway [NATO] (MCD)
AFNOR........	Association Francaise de Normalisation [French Association for Standardization] [Database producer] (IID)
AFNORTH ...	Allied Forces Northern Europe [NATO]
AfNPV	Anagrapha Falcifera Nuclear Polyhedrosis
AFNRC	Armed Forces National Research Council [National Academy of Sciences]
AFNRD	Air Force National Range Division
AFNS	Air Force - Navy Standard (SAA)
AFNS	Air Force News Service
AFNSW	Arthritis Foundation of New South Wales [Australia]
AFNT	Air Force Negotiation Team (AAGC)
AFNY	Alliance Francaise de New York [Later, FIAF]
AFNZRB	American Federation of New Zealand Rabbit Breeders (EA)
AFO...........	Accounting and Finance Office [or Officer]
AFO...........	Admiralty Fleet Order [Obsolete British]
AFO...........	Advanced File Organization
AFO...........	Aero Empresa Mexicana SA [Mexico ICAO designator] (FAAC)
AFO...........	Afton, WY [Location identifier FAA] (FAAL)
AFO...........	Airport Fire Officer (DA)
AFO...........	Airports Field Office
AFO...........	Ankle-Foot Orthosis [Orthopedics]
AFO...........	Announced [or Announcement of] Flight Opportunity [NASA] (KSC)
AFO...........	Anti-Fascist Organization [Later, AFPFL] [Burma] [World War II]
AFO...........	Army Forwarding Officer [British]
AFO...........	Artillery Forward Observer
AFO...........	Assaulting Federal Officer [FBI standardized term]
AFO...........	Association des Fermieres de l'Ontario (AC)
AFO...........	Association of Field Ornithologists (EA)
AFO...........	Atlantic Fleet Organization
AFO...........	Auto-Free Ottawa (AC)
AFO...........	Axial Flux Offset (IEEE)
AFOA	Alabama Forest Owners' Association (SRA)
AFOA	Antiques Fairs Organisers Association [British] (DBA)
AFOAO	Air Force Operations Analysis Office (KSC)
AFOAR	Air Force Office of Aerospace Research [AFSC]
AFOAS	Air Force Office of Aerospace Sciences [AFOAR]
AFOAT	Air Force Office of Atomic Energy
AFOAT-1	Office of the Air Force Assistant for Atomic Energy, Section 1 (LAIN)

AFOB	Air Force Operations Base
AFOB	American Foundation for Overseas Blind [*Later, HKI*] (EA)
AFOBIC	Alliance of Female Owned Businesses Involved in Construction (EA)
AFOC	Air Force Comptroller
AFOC	Air Force Operations Center
AFOC	Alaska Field Operations Center [*Anchorage, AK*] [*Department of the Interior*] (GRD)
AFOC	Auditor Freight Overcharge Claim
AFOC	Automatic Flight Operation Center [*Army*] (RDA)
AFOCC	Air Force Director of Command Control and Communications
AFOCE	Air Force Office of Civil Engineering (SAA)
AFOD	Arab Federation for the Organs of the Deaf [*Damascus, Syria*] (EAIO)
AFODC	Deputy Chief of Staff for Operations, Air Force
AFOE	Amphibious Follow-on-Echelon [*Navy*] (MCD)
AFOE	Assault Follow-On Echelon [*Marine Corps*] (MCD)
AFOEHL	Air Force Occupational and Environmental Health Lab
AFOEP	Air Force Officer Education Program (AFM)
AF of L	American Federation of Labor [*Later, AFL-CIO*]
AFOG	Asian Federation of Obstetrics and Gynaecology (PDAA)
AFOIC	Air Force Officer in Charge
AFOJP	American Fans of Jon Pertwee (EA)
AFOLDS	Air Force On-Line Data System
AFOM	Foremost Municipal Library, Alberta [*Library symbol National Library of Canada*] (NLC)
AFOMO	Air Force Office of Manpower and Organization
AFOMS	Air Force Office of Medical Support
AFOMS	Air Force Office of Medical Support (DOMA)
AFOP	Association of Farmworker Opportunity Programs (EA)
AFOPA	Air Force Office of Public Affairs
AFOQT	Air Force Officer Qualifying Test
AFOR	Air Force Operations Room [*British military*] (DMA)
AFOR	Automated Forces [*Air Force*] (RDA)
AFORA	Air Force Office of Research Analysis (AFM)
AFORD	Air Force Overseas Replacement Depot [*World War II*]
AFORD	Alliance for Democracy [*Malawi*] [*Political party*] (ECON)
AFOREP	Air Force Operational Report (AFM)
AFORG	Air Force Overseas Replacement Group [*World War II*]
AFORMS	Air Force Operations Resource Management Systems
A FORT	A Fortiori [*With More Reason*] [*Latin*] (ROG)
AFOS	Advanced Field Operating System [*National Weather Service*]
AFOS	Air Force Objective Series [*Papers*]
AFOS	Air Force Operational Service (SAA)
AFOS	Armed Forces Optometric Society (EA)
AFOS	Automation of Field Observations and Services
AFOS	Automation of Field Operations and Services [*National Weather Service*] (MSC)
AFO(S)	Auxiliary Fuel Oil (System) [*Nuclear energy*] (NRCH)
AFOSCR	Air Force Organization Status Change Report
AFOSH	Air Force Occupational Safety and Health [*Standards*]
AFOSI	Air Force Office of Special Investigation
AFOSP	Air Force Office of Security Police
AFOSR	Air Force Office of Scientific Research [*Bolling Air Force Base*] [*Washington, DC*]
AFOT	American Friends of Turkey (EA)
AFOTC	Air Force Operational Test Center (MCD)
AFOTEC	Air Force Operational Test and Evaluation Center [*Kirtland Air Force Base, NM*]
AFOUA	Air Force Outstanding Unit Award [*Military decoration*] (AFM)
AFOUAR	Air Force Outstanding Unit Award Ribbon [*Military decoration*]
AFOUE	Air Force Outstanding Unit Emblem [*Military decoration*]
AFP	Abstract Family of Processors [*Computer science*] (PDAA)
AFP	ACE [*American Council on Education*] Fellows Program (EA)
AFP	Acute Flaccid Paralysis [*Medicine*]
AFP	Adiabatic Fast Passage (OA)
AFP	Administradoras de Fondos de Pensione [*Chile*] (ECON)
AFP	Advanced Fileable Processor
AFP	Advanced Flexible Processor (MCD)
AFP	Advanced Function Printing (IAA)
AFP	Aflatoxin P [*Mycotoxin*]
AFP	AFP Imaging Corp. [*Associated Press*] (SAG)
AFP	Agence France-Presse [*French Press Agency*] (IID)
AFP	Air Force Pamphlet
AFP	Air Force Plan (MCD)
AFP	Air Force Police (NATG)
AFP	Alpha-Fetoprotein [*Clinical chemistry*]
AFP	Alternate Flight Plan
AFP	Alternative Fertility Proportion [*Demography*]
AFP	American Federation of Police (EA)
AFP	American Federation of Priests
AFP	Americans for Peace [*Defunct*] (EA)
AFP	Amniotic Alphafetoprotein [*Obstetrics*]
AFP	Anglican Fellowship of Prayer (EA)
AFP	Annual Financial Plan
AFP	Annual Funding Program [*Army*]
AFP	Anterior Faucial Pillar [*Anatomy*] (MAE)
AFP	Antifreeze Polypeptide [*Biochemistry*]
AFP	Antifreeze Protein
AFP	Aperture File Protocol [*Computer science*]
AFP	AppleTalk Filing Protocol [*Apple Computer, Inc.*] (BYTE)
AFP	Approval for Full Production [*Navy*] (DOMA)
AFPB	Armed Forces Police
AFP	Army Force Program
AFP	Army Fuze Program (MCD)
AFP	Associated Fantasy Publishers

AFP	Association des Familles Paguin [*Association of the Paguin Family*] [*Canada*]
AFP	Association for Finishing Processes of SME [*Society of Manufacturing Engineers*] (EA)
AFP	Association of Federal Photographers [*Defunct*] (EA)
AFP	Association of Flock Processors [*Defunct*] (EA)
AFP	Associative File Processors (NITA)
AFP	Atrial Filling Pressure [*Cardiology*] (DAVI)
AFP	Attached FORTRAN Processor [*Burroughs Corp.*] [*Computer science*] (BUR)
AFP	Audio Flat Panel [*Speaker system*]
AFP	Authority for Purchase
AFP	Portugese Air Force [*ICAO designator*] (FAAC)
AFP	United Capital Corp. [*AMEX symbol*] (SAG)
AFP	United States Army, Corps of Engineers, Portland District, Portland, OR [*OCLC symbol*] (OCLC)
AFP	Wadesboro, NC [*Location identifier FAA*] (FAAL)
AFPA	Advertising Film Producers Association [*British*] (BI)
AFPA	Agricultural Fair Practices Act of 1967
AFPA	Airborne Flat Plate Array
AFPA	Alberta Forest Products Association (AC)
AFPA	American Fisheries Protection Act
AFPA	American Folklife Preservation Act [*1976*]
AFPA	American Forest and Paper Association (ECON)
AFPA	Automatic Flow Process Analysis (IEEE)
AFPAM	Air Force Pamphlet
AFPAM	Automatic Flight Planning and Monitoring
AFPAV	Airfield Pavement [*Air Force*]
AFPB	Air Force Personnel Board
AFPBA	Australian Federation of Pipe Band Associations
AFPBS	Air Force Pacific Broadcasting Squadron
AFPC	AFP Imaging [*NASDAQ symbol*] (TTSB)
AFPC	AFP Imaging Corp. [*NASDAQ symbol*] (NQ)
AFPC	Agricultural and Food Policy Center [*Texas A & M University*] [*Research center*] (RCD)
AFPC	Air Force Personnel Council
AFPC	Air Force Policy Council (AAG)
AFPC	Air Force Postal Clerk (AFM)
AFPC	Air Force Procurement Circulars
AFPC	Alliance de la Fonction Publique du Canada [*Public Service Alliance of Canada - PSAC*]
AFPC	American Federation for the Pueri Cantores (EA)
AFPC	American Food for Peace Council [*Defunct*] (EA)
AFPC	Armed Forces Policy Council
AFPC	Association des Facultes de Pharmacie du Canada [*Association of Faculties of Pharmacy of Canada*]
AF/PC	Automatic Frequency/Phase-Controlled [*Loop*] (IEEE)
AFPCA	Air Force of the People Chinese Liberation Army
AFPCB	Armed Forces Pest Control Board [*Washington, DC*]
AFPCH	Army Force Planning Cost Handbook
AFPCP	Air Force Potential Contractor Program (MCD)
AFPCS	Association for Fair Play for Children in Scotland (EAIO)
AFPCS	Automatic Flight Path Control System [*Aviation*] (PDAA)
AFPD	Armed Forces Police Department [*or Detachment*]
AFPD	Authorization for Program Development [*NASA*] (NASA)
AFPDA	Army Force Planning Data and Assumptions (AABC)
AFPDAB	Air Force Physical Disability Appeal Board
AFPDC	Deputy Chief of Staff, Personnel [*Air Force*]
AFPDS	Armed Forces Production Distribution Service (DNAB)
AFPE	Air Force Planning Element
AFPE	Air Force Preliminary Evaluation (MCD)
AFPE	American Foundation for Pharmaceutical Education (EA)
AFPE	American Foundation for Political Education
AFPE	Association for Progressive Education (EA)
AFPEA	Air Force Packaging Evaluation Agency (MCD)
AFPEB	Air Force Professional Entertainment Branch
AFPEC	Armed Forces Product Evaluation Committee (AABC)
AFPEDA	Alabama Farm and Power Equipment Dealers Association (SRA)
AFPEO	Air Force Program Executive Office (DOMA)
AFPEO	Air Force Program Executive Offices (BARN)
AFPEO	Armed Forces Professional Entertainment Office
AFPF	America First Preferred Equity Mortgage Ltd. [*NASDAQ symbol*] (NQ)
AFPFL	Anti-Fascist People's Freedom League [*Formerly, AFO*] [*Burma*] [*World War II*]
AFPFZ	Amer First Ptc/Pfd Eqty Mtg [*NASDAQ symbol*] (TTSB)
AFPG	Air Force Personnel Processing Group
AFPG	Air Force Planning Guide
AFPH	American Federation of the Physically Handicapped
AFPhys	Associate of the Faculty of Physiatrics [*British*]
AFPI	Air Force Procurement Instructions
AFPI	American Foreign Policy Institute [*Defunct*] (EA)
AFPI	American Forest Products Industries [*Later, AFC*]
AFPID	Air Force Purchase Item Description
AFPJ	American Federation of Polish Jews (EA)
AFPL	Air Force Packaging Laboratory
AFPL	Alianza Federal des Pueblos Libres [*An association*] (NTCM)
AFPLC	Air Force Policy Letter for Commanders
AFPM	Aircraft Force Projection Model [*Computer*] [*Navy*]
AFPMB	Armed Forces Pest Management Board (RDA)
AFPMO	Air Force Polaris Material Office
AFPMP	Army Air Forces Military Personnel [*World War II*]
AFPMPMS ...	Air Force Professional Manpower and Personnel Management School
AFPO	Air Force Property Officer (MCD)

AFPO	Air Force Purchasing Office (MUGU)
AFPOB	American Friends of the Paris Opera and Ballet (EA)
AFPOM	Air Force Program Objectives Memorandum (MCD)
AFPP	Acute Fibrinopurulent Pneumonia [*Medicine*]
AFPP	Air Force Procurement Procedures
AFPPA	American Federation of Poultry Producers Associations [*Defunct*] (EA)
AFPPF	Automatic Fluorescent Penetrant Processing Facility (MCD)
AFPPG	American Foundation for Psychoanalysis and Psychoanalysis in Groups (EA)
AFPPS	American Forces Press and Publications Service
AFPR	Air Force Plant Representative
AFPR	Air Force Procurement Regulation
AFPR	Air Force Procurement Representative
AF/PR	Air Force, Programs, and Evaluation (DOMA)
AFPR	Air Force Project Representative
AFPR	Armed Forces Procurement Regulation
AFPRC	Armed Forces Provisional Ruling Council [*Gambia*] [*Political party*]
AFPRD	Association of Family Practice Residency Directors (EA)
AFPRDS	Air Force Petroleum Retail Distribution Station (AFM)
AFPRL	Air Force Personnel Research Lab (MCD)
AFPRO	Air Force Plant Representative Office
AFPRO	Air Force Program Representative Office (MCD)
AFProv	Administradora de Fondos de Pensiones Provida SA [*Associated Press*] (SAG)
AFPRP	Air Force Production Reserve Policy
AFPS	American Forces Press Service [*Formerly, AFNB*]
AFPS	Army Film and Photographic Section [*British military*] (DMA)
AFPS	Aseptic Food Processing System
AFPS	AWIPS [*Advanced Weather Interactive Processing System*] Forecast Preparation System [*Marine science*] (OSRA)
AFPS	AWIPS [*Advanced Weather Interactive Processing System*] Forecast Preparation System (USDC)
AFPSC	Armed Forces Philippines Supply Center (CINC)
AFP/SME	Association for Finishing Processes of the Society of Manufacturing Engineers (EAIO)
AFPSP	Australian Foundation for the Peoples of the South Pacific
AFPT	Air Force Personnel Test (AFM)
AFPT	Auxiliary Feed Pump Turbine (IEEE)
AFPTRC	Air Force Personnel and Training Research Center [*Later, Air Force Personnel Research Laboratory*] [*Lackland Air Force Base, TX*]
AFPU	Air Force Postal Unit
AFPU	Army Film and Photographic Unit [*British military*] (DMA)
AFPVD	American Foundation for the Prevention of Venereal Disease (EA)
AFQ	Aflatoxin Q [*Mycotoxin*]
AFQ	Air Afrique (MCD)
AFQ	Airframe Flight Qualification
AFQ	Association Forestiere Quebecoise Inc. [*Quebec Forestry Association Inc.*] (AC)
AFQA	Air Force Quality Assurance (KSC)
AFQAR	Air Force Quality Assurance Representative
AFQC	Air Force Quality Control
AFQCR	Air Force Quality Control Representative
AFQQPRI	Amendment to the Final Qualitative and Quantitative Personnel Requirements Information (MCD)
AFQT	Armed Forces Qualification Test
AFQTVA	Armed Forces Qualification Test, Verbal Arithmetic Subtest
AFR	Absolute Filtration Rating
AFR	Abstract Family of Relations (PDAA)
AFR	Acceptable Failure Rate
AFR	Access Function Register
AFR	Accident Frequency Rate [*Employment*] (ODBW)
AFR	Acid Fractionator Recycle [*Nuclear energy*] (NRCH)
AFR	Advanced Fault Recognition [*Computer science*] (NITA)
AFR	Advanced Fleet Reactor [*Navy*] (DOMA)
AFR	Afareaitu [*Society Islands*] [*Seismograph station code, US Geological Survey*] (SEIS)
AFR	Afore [*Papua New Guinea*] [*Airport symbol*] (OAG)
AFR	Africa
Afr	Africa (VRA)
afr	Afrikaans [*MARC language code Library of Congress*] (LCCP)
AFR	Aircraft Flight Report (AAG)
AFR	Air Force Regulation
AFR	Air Force Reserve
AFR	Air Force Reserve (DOMA)
AFR	Air Force Route (DA)
AFR	Airframe
AFR	Air France [*ICAO designator*] (FAAC)
AFR	Air-Fuel Ratio (ADA)
A-FR	Algerian-Franc (ABBR)
AFR	Alternating Frequency Rejection [*Automotive technology*]
AFR	American Friends of Refugees [*Defunct*]
AFR	America's Freedom Ride [*Defunct*] (EA)
AFR	Amplitude-Frequency Response [*Telecommunications*] (OA)
AFR	Anglo-French [*Language, etc.*]
AFR	Aqueous Flare Response [*Physiology*]
AfR	Archiv foer Retsvidenskaben og dens Anvendelse [*Denmark*] [*A publication*] (ILCA)
AFR	Armed Forces Radio (ADA)
AFR	Armed Forces Radiobiology Research Institute, Bethesda, MD [*OCLC symbol*] (OCLC)
AFR	Arterial Flow Rate
AFR	Artillery Flash Ranging [*Army*] (AABC)
AFR	Ascorbic Free Radical [*Biochemistry*]
AFR	Atrial Filling Rate [*Cardiology*]
AFR	Auditor Freight Receipts
AFR	Australians for Reconciliation [*An association*]
AFR	Automatic Field/Format Recognition [*Computer science*] (NITA)
AFR	Automatic Format Recognition [*Computer science*] (ADA)
AFR	Available for Release (MCD)
AFR	Awaiting Forward Release [*Telecommunications*] (TEL)
AFR	Away from Reactor [*Storage facilities*]
AFR	Axial Flow Reactor [*Chemical engineering*]
AFRA	American Family Records Association (EA)
AFRA	American Farm Research Association [*Superseded by AFBRF*] (EA)
AFRA	American Federation of Radio Artists
AFRA	Armed Forces Reserve Act of 1952, as Amended
AFRA	Average Freight Rate Assessment [*Shipping*]
AFRAA	African Airlines Association [*Kenya*] (AF)
AFRACA	African Regional Agricultural Credit Association (EAIO)
AFRADBIORSCHINST	Armed Forces Radiobiology Research Institute
AF/RADC	Air Force Rome Air Development Center
AFR Ae S	Associate Fellow of the Royal Aeronautical Society [*British*]
AFRAIDS	Acute Fear Regarding AIDS
AFRAM	Air Force Recoverable Assembly Management (PDAA)
Afr Am R	African American Review [*A publication*] (BRI)
AFRAMS	Air Force Recoverable Assembly Management System (AFM)
AFRANE	Amitie Franco-Afghane [*French Afghan Friendship Committee*]
AFRAP	Air Force Recruiter Assistance Program (MCD)
AFRAP	American Foundation of Religion and Psychiatry [*Later, Institutes of Religion and Health*] (EA)
AFRAPT	Air Force Research in Aircraft Propulsion Technology Program [*West Lafayette, IN*] (GRD)
AFRAS	Associate Fellow of the Royal Aeronautical Society [*British*]
AFrAS	United States Army Aviation School, Fort Rucker, AL [*Library symbol Library of Congress*] (LCLS)
AFRASEC	Afro-Asian Organization for Economic Cooperation
AFRASIA	Africa and Asia
AFRB	Air Force Retiring Board
AFRB	Australian Family Research Bulletin [*A publication*] (ADA)
AFRB	Award Fee Review Board
AFRBA	Air Force Review Boards Agency (DOMA)
AFRBA	Armed Forces Relief and Benefit Association (EA)
AFRBO	Air Force Review Boards Office
AFRBSGP	Air Force Reserve Base Support Group
AFRC	Adoption and Family Reunion Center (EA)
AFRC	Agricultural and Food Research Council [*Research center British*] (IRC)
AFRC	Air Force Records Center
AFRC	Area Frequency Response Characteristic (PDAA)
AFRC	Armed Forces Recreation Center
AFRC	Armed Forces Reserve Center (AABC)
AFRC	Armed Forces Revolutionary Council [*Ghana*] (PPW)
AFRC	Automatic Frequency Ratio Controller (MHDB)
AFRCC	Air Force Rescue Coordination Center
AFRCC	Air Force Reserve Coordination Center (AFM)
AFRCD	Air-Fuel Ratio Control Device [*Automotive engineering*]
AFRCE	Air Force Regional Civil Engineers
AFRCN	African
AFRCSTC	Air Force Reserve Combat Support Training Center
AFRCTC	Air Force Reserve Combat Training Center
AFRD	Acute Febrile Respiratory Disease [*Medicine*]
AFRD	Air Force Research Directorate (KSC)
AFRD	Air Force Research Division
AFRD	Air Force Reserve Division
AFRDB	Air Force Research and Development Branch
AFRDR	Air Force Director of Reconnaissance and Electronic Warfare (IEEE)
AFRDS	Association of Fund Raisers and Direct Sellers (EA)
AFREDCOM	Armed Forces Readiness Command (MCD)
AF Rep	Alaska Federal Reports [*A publication*] (DLA)
AFREQ	Army Air Forces Requirements Division [*World War II*]
AFRES	Air Force Reserve
AFRESBSGP	Air Force Reserve Regions Base Support Group
AFRESM	Armed Forces Reserve Medal [*Military decoration*]
AFRESNAVSQ	Air Force Reserve Navigation Squadron
AFRESR	Air Force Reserve Regions
AFRESRGP	Air Force Reserve Regions Group
AFRESS	Air Force Reserve Sectors
AFREXIMBANK	African Export Import Bank
AFRF	American Freedom of Residence Fund [*Defunct*] (EA)
AFRF	American Friends of Russian Freedom [*Later, AFR*] (EA)
AFRFI	American Friends of Religious Freedom in Israel [*Defunct*] (EAIO)
AFRFTC	Air Force Reserve Flying Training Center
AFRH	Armed Forces Retirement Home
AFRI	Action from Ireland [*An association*] (EAIO)
AFRI	Acute Febrile Respiratory Illness [*Medicine*]
AfrI	African Imprint Library Services, Bedford, NY [*Library symbol Library of Congress*] (LCLS)
AFRI	American Foundation for Resistance International (EA)
AFRI	American Fur Resources Institute [*Defunct*] (EA)
AFRI	Applied Forest Research Institute [*Syracuse University*]
Africana	Africana Bulletin [*Warsaw*] [*A publication*]
AFRICA NEWS	Africa News Service (EA)
African LD	African Law Digest [*A publication*] (ILCA)
African LR Comm	African Law Reports, Commercial Series [*A publication*] (DLA)
African LR Mal	African Law Reports, Malawi Series [*A publication*] (DLA)
African LRSL	African Law Reports, Sierra Leone Series [*A publication*] (DLA)
Africa T	Africa Today [*A publication*] (BRI)
AFRICOBRA	African Commune of Bad Relevant Artists [*Chicago*]
AFRID	Automatic Fuze Radiograph Inspection Device (PDAA)

AFRIK	Afrikaans
AFRIMS	Armed Forces Research Institute of Medical Sciences [*Bangkok - collaboration of Thailand and United States*]
AFRKB	American Federation of Retail Kosher Butchers (EA)
Afr LR	African Law Reports [*A publication*] (DLA)
Afr LR Mal Ser	African Law Reports, Malawi Series [*A publication*] (DLA)
Afr LR Sierre L Ser	African Law Reports, Sierra Leone Series [*A publication*] (DLA)
AFRM	Advanced Flight Research Model (SAA)
AFRM	Airframe (AABC)
AFRM	Armed Forces Reserve Medal [*Military decoration*]
AFRMA	American Fancy Rat and Mouse Association (EA)
AFRO	Air Force Research Objectives
AFRO	Air Force Reserve Orders
AFRO	Air Force Routine Order [*Canada, 1920-1945*]
AFROASI	Authority for Removal of Accepted Spacecraft Installations (MCD)
AFROC	Air Force Retired Officer's Community
AFROC	Association of Freestanding Radiation Oncology Centers (EA)
AFROIC	Air Force Resident Officer in Charge
AFRom	American Friends of Romania (EA)
AFROSAI	African Organization of Supreme Audit Institutions [*Lome, Togo*] (EAIO)
AFROSAT	African Satellite
AFROTC	Air Force Reserve Officers Training Corps [*Washington, DC*]
AFRP	Air Force Recurring Publication (AFM)
AFRP	American Foundation of Religion and Psychiatry [*Later, Institutes of Religion and Health*]
AFRP BC	Association of Fund Raising Professionals of British Columbia [*Canada*]
AFRPC	Air Force Reserve Policy Committee
AFRPL	Air Force Rocket Propulsion Laboratory [*Later, AFAL*] [*Edwards Air Force Base, CA*]
AFRR	Air Force Reserve Regions (AFM)
AFRR	Air Force Resident Representative (AAG)
Afr Rep	Africa Report [*A publication*] (BRI)
AFRRGp	Air Force Reserve Recovery Group (AFM)
AFRRI	Armed Forces Radiobiology Research Institute [*Bethesda, MD*] [*DoD*]
Afr Rpt	Africa Report [*A publication*]
AFRS	Advanced Fighter RADAR System
AFRS	Agricultural and Food Research Service [*Ministry of Agriculture, Fisheries, and Food*] [*British*] (IRUK)
AFRS	Air Force Rescue Service
AFRS	Air Force Reserve Sectors (AFM)
AFRS	American Forces Radio Station [*Vietnam*] (VNW)
AFRS	Approved Force Retention Stock [*Air Force*] (AFIT)
AFRS	Armed Forces Radio Service [*Military*]
AFRS	Armed Forces Radio Service [*United States military*] [*Established during World War II*] [*Later, Armed Forces Radio and Television Service*] (WDMC)
AFRS	Armed Forces Recruiting Stations [*DoD*]
AFRS	Automatic Flight Reference System (DNAB)
AFRS	Auxiliary Flight Reference System
AFRS	Away from Reactor Storage [*Nuclear energy*] (NUCP)
AFRSC	Armed Forces Recipe Service Committee (AABC)
AFRSF	Air Force Range Support Facility
AFRSF	Atlantic Fleet Range Support Facility [*Navy*] (DNAB)
AFRSI	Advanced Flexible Reusable Surface Insulation [*For space shuttles*]
AFRST	American Friends of the Royal Shakespeare Theatre (EA)
AFRST	Automatic Focusing Random Scene Tracker (MCD)
AFRSTC	Air Force Reserve Specialist Training Center
AFRT	Air Freight (FAAC)
AFRT	American [*formerly, Armed*] Forces Radio and Television [*DoD*]
AFrT	Troy State University at Fort Rucker, Fort Rucker, AL [*Library symbol Library of Congress*] (LCLS)
AFRTC	Air Force Research Training Center
AFRTC	Air Force Reserve Training Center
AFRTD	Air Force Research and Technology Division
AFRTLA	Australian Federation of Right to Life Associations
AFRTS	American [*formerly, Armed*] Forces Radio and Television Service [*or System*]
AFRTS	American Forces Radio and Television Service [*Network of broadcast stations*] [*United States military*] [*Formerly, Armed Forces Radio Service*] (WDMC)
AFRTS	Armed Forces Radio and Telegraph Service
AFRTS	Armed Forces Radio-Television [*Cable-television system*]
AFRTS-BC	Armed Forces Radio and Television Service-Broadcast Center (GFGA)
AFRTS-PC	American Forces Radio and Television Service-Programming Center [*See also AFIS*] [*DoD*] (WDMC)
AFRU	Armed Forces Reporting Unit [*Red Cross*]
AFS	Acid-Fast Smear [*Biochemistry*] (DAVI)
AFS	Active Federal Service (DOMA)
AFS	Active Fuzing System
AFS	Adirondack Forty-Sixers (EA)
AFS	Administrative Fact Sheet [*Vocational education*] (OICC)
AFS	Advanced Fermentation System
AFS	Advanced Figure Sensor (KSC)
AFS	Advanced Firing Systems (MSA)
AFS	Advanced Flying School [*British military*] (DMA)
AFS	Aerial Film Speed
AFS	Aerial Fire Support
AFS	Aerodrome Fire Service [*British*] (AIA)
AFS	Aeronautical Fixed Service
AFS	AFloat Prepositioning Ship (DOMA)
AFS	African Studies [*Johannesburg*] [*A publication*]
AFS	Agriculture and Forestry Secretariat
AFS	Air Data Ltd. [*British*] [*FAA designator*] (FAAC)
AFS	Air Flow Sensor [*Automotive engineering*]
AFS	Air Force Specialty
AFS	Air Force Standard (NASA)
AFS	Air Force Station
AFS	Air Force Stock (AAG)
AFS	Air Force Supply
AFS	Airline Feed System
AFS	AIRS [*Aerometric Information Retrieval System*] Facility Subsystem [*Environmental Protection Agency*] (GFGA)
AFS	Airways Facilities Sector (FAAC)
AFS	Alternative Financing System [*Health care*] (HCT)
AFS	American Family Society (EA)
AFS	American Feline Society (EA)
AFS	American Fern Society (EA)
AFS	American Fertility Society (EA)
AFS	American Field Service [*Later, AFSIIP*]
AFS	American Fisheries School (USDC)
AFS	American Fisheries Society (EA)
AFS	American Flywheel Systems [*Research center*] (ECON)
AFS	American Folklore Society (EA)
AFS	American Foundrymen's Society (EA)
AFS	American Fuchsia Society (EA)
AFS	Andrew File System [*Computer science*] (TNIG)
AFS	Anne Frank Stichting [*Anne Frank Foundation*] [*Netherlands*] (EAIO)
AFS	Antenna Feed System
AFS	Applicant File Search [*US Employment Service*] [*Department of Labor*]
AFS	Arming and Fusing System (MSA)
AFS	Army Fire Service
AFS	Asian Fisheries Society [*Marine science*] (OSRA)
AFS	Associate of the Faculty of Architects and Surveyors [*British*] (DBQ)
AFS	Associates First Capital Corp. [*NYSE symbol*] (SAG)
AFS	Associates First Captial'A' [*NYSE symbol*] (TTSB)
AFS	Association for Food Self-Sufficiency (EAIO)
AFS	Association for Stammerers (EAIO)
AFS	Association of Football Statisticians [*British*] (DBA)
AFS	Association of Foremen and Supervisors [*Australia*]
AFS	Atlantic Ferry Service [*World War II*]
AFS	Atomic Fluorescence Spectroscopy
AFS	Atomic Frequency Standard
AFS	Audio Frequency Shift (IEEE)
AFS	Australian Fabian Society
AFS	Australian Fisheries Service [*Marine science*] (OSRA)
AFS	Australian Friesian Sahiwal [*Cattle terminology*]
AFS	Automatic Fault Simulator
AFS	Automatic Firing Sequencer
AFS	Automatic Flight System [*Aviation*] (AIA)
AFS	Automatic Flight System (GAVI)
AFS	Automatic Frequency Stabilization
AFS	Auxiliary Feedwater System [*Nuclear energy*] (NRCH)
AFS	Auxiliary Fire Service [*British*]
AFS	Aviation Facilities Service [*of FAA*]
AFS	Azimuth Follow-Up System
AFS	Combat Store Ship [*Navy symbol*]
AFS	Combat Support Ship [*Military*]
AFS	United States Army, Corps of Engineers, Seattle District, Seattle, WA [*OCLC symbol*] (OCLC)
AFSA	Air Force Safety Agency (DOMA)
AFSA	Air Force Senior Advisory
AFSA	Air Force Sergeants Association (EA)
AFSA	Alabama Financial Services Association (SRA)
AFSA	American Federation of School Administrators (EA)
AFSA	American Financial Services Association [*Washington, DC*] (EA)
AFSA	American Fire Sprinkler Association (EA)
AFSA	American Flagship Available
AFSA	American Flight Strips Association (EA)
AFSA	American Foreign Service Association (EA)
AFSA	Application for Federal Student Aid (GFGA)
AFSA	Arizona Financial Services Association (SRA)
AFSA	Armed Forces Security Agency [*Obsolete*]
AFSA	Arthritis Foundation of South Australia
AFSA	Association for Spiritual Awareness (EA)
AFSA	Association of Former Senate Aides (EA)
AFSA	Australian Friendly Societies' Association
AFSA	Automated Fire Support Artillery (MCD)
AFSA	Aviation Force Structure for the Army (MCD)
AFSAA	Air Force Studies and Analyses Agency (DOMA)
AFSAB	Air Force Scientific Advisory Board (MCD)
AFSAC	Air Force Special Activities Center
AFSAC	Armed Forces Security Agency Council [*Abolished, 1952*]
AFSAC/IRC	Armed Forces Security Agency Council Intelligence Requirements Committee [*Obsolete*]
AFSAG	Armed Forces Security Agency [*Obsolete*]
AFSA-JB	Air Force Senior Advisory - Jefferson Barracks
AfsalaBc	Afsala Bancorp, Inc. [*Associated Press*] (SAG)
AFSAM	Air Force School of Aviation Medicine
AFSAMSO	Air Force Space and Missile Systems Organization (KSC)
AFSARC	Air Force System Acquisition Review Council
AFSARI	Automation for Storage and Retrieval of Information
AFSAS	Academy for Friends of Secretarial Arts and Sciences [*Defunct*] (EA)
AFSAS	Advanced Fire Support Avionics System

AFSAS	American Federation of School Administrators and Supervisors [*AFL-CIO*]
AFSATCOM	Air Force Satellite Communications System (AFM)
AFSATLCF	Air Force Satellite Control Facility
AFSAW	Air Force Special Activities Wing
AFSAWC	Air Force Special Air Warfare Center (MCD)
AFSB	Air Force Specification Bulletin
AFSB	Air Force Support Base (SAA)
AFSB	American Federation of Small Business [*Chicago, IL*] (EA)
AFSBC	Assembly of Free Spirit Baptist Churches (EA)
AFSC	Air Force Service Center [*or Command*]
AFSC	Air Force Skill Code
AFSC	Air Force Space Command (DOMA)
AFSC	Air Force Specialty Code
AFSC	Air Force Supply Catalog
AFSC	Air Force Supply Code
AFSC	Air Force Systems Command [*Andrews Air Force Base, MD*]
AFSC	American Federation of Soroptimist Clubs [*Later, Soroptimist International of the Americas*]
AFSC	American Friends Service Committee (EA)
AFSC	Anchor Financial Corp. [*NASDAQ symbol*] (SAG)
AFSC	Armed Forces Sports Committee (EA)
AFSC	Armed Forces Staff College
AFSC	Assessment of Fluency in School-Age Children [*Speech evaluation test*]
AFSC	Automatic Flight Stabilization and Control System (SAA)
AFSC	Automatic Frame Scan Control (PDAA)
AFSC	Automic Fire Control System [*Army*]
AFSCA	Amalgamated Flying Saucer Clubs of America (EA)
AFSCAG	Air Force Service Contract Advisory Group (MCD)
AFSCC	Air Force Satellite Control Center (CET)
AFSCC	Air Force Security Communications Center (MCD)
AFSCC	Air Force Special Communications Center (CET)
AFSCC	Armed Forces Supply Control Center [*DoD*]
AFSC-DH	Air Force Systems Command Design Handbooks
AFSC/DL	Air Force Systems Command Director of Laboratories
AFSCE	American Fertility Society Classification of Endometriosis
AFSCE	Association of Former Students of the College of Europe (EAIO)
AFSCF	Air Force Satellite [*or Spacecraft*] Control Facility [*Sunnyvale Air Force Station, CA*] (AFM)
AFSCF	Air Force Systems Command Form
AFSCI	American Foundation for the Science of Creative Intelligence (EA)
AFSCIC	Air Force Systems Command Inspection Center
AFSCL	Air Force Systems Command Letter
AFSCM	Air Force Systems Command Manual
AFSCME	American Federation of State, County, and Municipal Employees (EA)
AFSCN	Air Force Satellite Control Network (MCD)
AFSCO	Air Force Security Clearance Office
AFSCOORD	Assistant Fire Support Coordinator [*Military*] (AABC)
AFSCP	Air Force Systems Command Pamphlet
AFSCP	Air Force Systems Concept Paper (MCD)
AFSCPP	Air Force Systems Command Procurement Production (MCD)
AFSCR	Air Force Systems Command Regulation
AFSCS	Air Force Satellite Communications System (MCD)
AFSCS	Army Field Stock Control System
AFSC/SSD	Air Force Systems Command Space Systems Division
AFSC/STLO	Air Force Systems Command, Scientific Technical Liaison Office (MUGU)
AFSD	Aforesaid
AFSD	Air Force Space Division (MCD)
AFSD	Air Force Stock Data (SAA)
AFSD	Air Force Supply Date
AFSD	Air Force Supply Depot
AFSD	Air Force Supply Directive (MCD)
AFSD	Central Library, Dow Chemical of Canada Ltd., Fort Saskatchewan, Alberta [*Library symbol National Library of Canada*] (NLC)
AFSE	Allied Forces Southern Europe [*NATO*] (NATG)
AFSEA	Air Force Special Elements Activity [*American Embassy security*] (VNW)
AFSec	Air Force Section (AFM)
AFSEC	Armed Forces Stamp Exchange Club (EA)
AFSEEE	Association of Forest Service Employees for Environmental Ethics (EA)
AFSEM	Army Food Service Energy Management (AABC)
AFSERT	Associate Fellow of the Society of Electronic and Radio Technicians [*British*] (DBQ)
AFSF	Advanced Field Site Facility
AFSF	Air Force Satellite Facility
AFSF	Air Force Stock Fund
AFSF	Air Force Supply Force
AFSFO	Airways Facilities Sector Field Office (FAAC)
AFSFOU	Airways Facilities Sector Field Office Plus Unit (FAAC)
AFSG	Asian Folklore Studies Group [*Later, ISA*] (EA)
AFSHP	Association of Federal Safety and Health Professionals [*Defunct*] (EA)
AFSHRC	Albert F. Simpson Historical Research Center (AFM)
AFSI	Americans for a Safe Israel (EA)
AFSI	Architectural Fabric Structures Institute (EA)
AFSI	Association of Suppliers to the Furniture Industries Show [*Wood Work Industrial Exhibition*] (TSPED)
AFSI	Aviation Financial Services, Inc.
AFSIE	Air Force Standard Items and Equipment (SAA)
AFSIG	Ascent Flight Systems Integration Group [*NASA*] (NASA)
AFSIIP	AFS [*American Field Service*] International-Intercultural Programs (CDAI)
AFSINC	Air Force Service Information and News Center
AFSIP	Air Force Standard Intelligence Publication (AFM)
AFSIR	Air Force Salary Impact Report
AFSK	Audio Frequency Shift Key
AFSK	Audio Frequency Shift Keying (NITA)
AFSL	Approved Fastener Substitution List (MCD)
AFSL	Association Forestiere Saguenay-Lac St-Jean Inc. (AC)
AFSLAET	Associate Fellow of the Society of Licensed Aircraft Engineers and Technologists [*British*] (DBQ)
AFSM	Artillery Forces Simulation Model (MCD)
AFSM	Association for Food Service Management [*Later, SFM*] (EA)
AFSM	Association for Service Management
AFSM	Association of Field Service Managers [*Later, ASMI*] (EA)
AFSM	Augmented Finite State Machine [*Computer science*]
AFSM	Fort Saskatchewan Municipal Library, Alberta [*Library symbol National Library of Canada*] (NLC)
AFSMAAG	Air Force Section, Military Assistance Advisory Group
AFSMAS	Association Francophone de Spectrometrie de Masse de Solides [*French-Speaking Association of Solids Mass Spectrometry*] (EAIO)
AFSMI	Association of Field Service Managers, International [*Later, ASMI*] (EA)
AFSN	Air Force Serial Number
AFSN	Air Force Service Number
AFSN	Air Force Stock Number
AFSNCOA	Air Force Senior Noncommissioned Officers' Academy (AFM)
AFSO	Aerial Fire Support Officer [*Army*] (INF)
AFSO	Air Force Service Office (AFM)
AFSO	Airways Facilities Sector Office (FAAC)
AFSO	American Friends of Scottish Opera (EA)
AFSOB	Air Force Special Operation Base (MCD)
AFSOC	Air Force Special Operations Command
AFSOC	Air Force Special Operations Command (DOMA)
AFSONOR	Allied Forces South Norway [*NATO*] (MCD)
AFSOON	Air Force Solar Observing Optical Network (MCD)
AFSOUTH	Allied Forces Southern Europe [*NATO*]
AFSOUTHCOM	Air Forces Southern Europe Command [*NATO*]
AFSP	Acute Fibrinoserous Pneumonia [*Medicine*]
AFSP	Air Force Security Police (VNW)
AFSP	Air Force Space Plane (AAG)
AFSP	Air Force Space Program
AFSP	Air Force Spare (SAA)
AFSP	Air Force Standard Practice
AFSP	Anglo-French Supply and Purchases [*World War II*]
AFSPA	Air Force Security Police Agency (DOMA)
AFSPA	American Foreign Service Protective Association [*Washington, DC*] (EA)
AFSPACECOM	Air Force Space Command (DOMA)
AFSPBRSIO	Armed Forces Surplus Property Bidders Registration and Sales Information Office [*Later, Defense Surplus Bidders Control Office*]
AFSPCOMMCEN	Air Force Special Communications Center (AFM)
AFSPD	Air Force Systems Project Division (MCD)
AFSPMET	Air Force Security Policy Management Engineering Team
AFSR	Advanced Foreign System Requirements
AFSR	Air Force Staff Requirement
AFSR	American Fund for Slovak Refugees [*Defunct*] (EA)
AFSR	Argonne Fast Source Reactor
AFSR	Armed Forces Screen Reports
AFSRAN	Air Force Stock Record Account Number (AAG)
AFSS	Africa South of the Sahara [*A publication*]
AFSS	Air Force Security Service [*Later, AFESC*] (AFM)
AFSS	Air Force Service Statement
AFSS	Air Force Supply Services System
AFSS	Automated Flight Service Station (FAAC)
AFSS	Automated Flight Service Station [*FAA*] (TAG)
AFSSA	Army Financial Stock Summary Analysis
AFSSC	Armed Forces Supply Support Center [*Merged with Defense Logistics Services Center*]
AFSSD	Air Force Space Systems Division
AFSSG	Sherritt Gordon Mines Ltd., Fort Saskatchewan, Alberta [*Library symbol National Library of Canada*] (NLC)
AFSSMET	Air Force Special Staff Management Engineering Team
AFSSO	Air Force Special Security Office [*or Officer*] (AFM)
AFSSOP	Air Force Security Service Office of Production
AFST	Assured Field Shop Task
AFST	Auxiliary Feedwater Storage Tank [*Nuclear energy*] (IEEE)
AFstApt	America First Apartment Investors LP [*Associated Press*] (SAG)
AFSTC	Air Force Satellite Test Center (MCD)
AFSTC	Air Force Space Technology Center [*Kirtland Air Force Base, NM*] (MCD)
AFSTC	Air Force Space Test Center [*Later, Western Test Range*]
AFSTC	Army Foreign Science and Technology Center
AFSTE	Association for Field Services in Teacher Education [*Later, ACPE*]
AFstP2	America First PREP [*Preferred Real Estate Participation*] Fund 2 Ltd. [*Associated Press*] (SAG)
AFSTRIKE	Air Force Strike Command (MCD)
AFSU	American Fraternal Snowshoe Union (EA)
AFSU	Auxiliary Ferry Service Unit
AFSUB	Army Air Forces Antisubmarine Command
AFSV	American Franciscan Society for Vocations [*Later, FVC*] (EA)
AFSWA	Armed Forces Special Weapons Agency
AFSWA	Army Air Forces Assistant Secretary of War for Air [*World War II*]
AFSWB	American Friends of Scottish War Blinded [*Defunct*] (EA)

AFSWC .... Air Force Special Weapons Center [*AFSC*] [*Kirtland Air Force Base, NM*]
AFSWP .... Armed Forces Special Weapons Project [*Later, DASA*]
AFT .... Acetate Film Tape
AFT .... Active File Table [*Computer science*] (IBMDP)
AFT .... Adapter Fault Tolerance [*Intel*] [*Computer science*]
AFT .... Adaptive Ferroelectric Transformer (OA)
AFT .... Aerodynamic Flight Test (NASA)
AFT .... Aflatoxin [*Mycotoxin*] [*Generic form*]
AFT .... After (KSC)
aft .... After (VRA)
aft .... Afternoon (WDMC)
AFT .... Afternoon
AFT .... Agglutination-Flocculation Test [*Immunology*] (DMAA)
AFT .... Air Freight Terminal
AFT .... American Farmland Trust (EA)
AFT .... American Federation of Teachers (EA)
AFT .... American Film Theater
AFT .... American Fluid Technology
AFT .... American Friends of Turkey (EA)
AFT .... Analog Facility Terminal [*Computer science*] (TEL)
AFT .... An Foras Taluntais [*Agricultural Institute*] [*Ireland*] [*Research center*] (IRC)
AFT .... Animal-Facilitated Therapy
AFT .... Annual Field Training [*Army*] (AABC)
AFT .... Annual Financial Target [*DoD*]
AFT .... Anterior Fold from Typhlosole
AFT .... Arthritis Foundation of Tasmania [*Australia*]
AFT .... Assembly Facility Tool (MCD)
AFT .... Association of Family Therapy [*British*] (DBA)
AFT .... Asynchronous Framing Technique [*Computer science*]
AFT .... Atmospheric Flight Test (NASA)
AFT .... Audio Frequency Transformer
AFT .... Auditor Freight Traffic
AFT .... Autogenic Feedback Training (MCD)
AFT .... Automated Flow Technology
AFT .... Automatic Fine Tuning
AFT .... Automatic Flight Termination
AFT .... Automatic Frequency Tuner
AFT .... Automatic Funds Transfer
AFT .... Fort Smith, AR [*Location identifier FAA*] (FAAL)
AFT .... United States Army, Corps of Engineers, Tulsa District, Tulsa, OK [*OCLC symbol*] (OCLC)
AFTA .... Acoustic Fatigue Test Article (NASA)
AFTA .... Advanced First-Term Avionics (DNAB)
AFTA .... Aft Frame Tilt Actuator [*Aviation*] (NASA)
AFTA .... Air Force Telecom Association (AC)
AFTA .... American Family Therapy Association (EA)
AFTA .... Arab Fund for Technical Assistance to Arab and African Countries
AFTA .... ASEAN [*Association of South East Asian Nations*] Free Trade Area (ECON)
AFTA .... Association of French Teachers in Africa [*See also AFPA*] [*Khartoum, Sudan*] (EAIO)
AFTA .... Atlantic Free Trade Area
AFTA .... Australian Federation of Travel Agents (BARN)
AFTA .... Automated Fault Tree Analyzer (MCD)
AFTA .... Avionics Fault Tree Analyzer (MCD)
AFTAAS .... Advanced Fast Time Acoustic Analysis System (MCD)
AFTAC .... Air Forces Tactical Center
AFTAC .... Air Force Tactical Air Command (MCD)
AFTAC .... Air Force Technical Applications Center [*Patrick Air Force Base, FL*]
AFTAC .... American Fiber, Textile, Apparel Coalition (EA)
AFTAD .... Analysis - Forcast Transport and Diffusion [*Marine science*] (OSRA)
AFTAI .... Analysis-Forecast Transport and Diffusion (USDC)
AFTAM .... Association Francaise pour l'Accueil des Travailleurs Africains et Malgaches [*French Association for the Reception of African and Malagasy Workers*] (AF)
AFTAT .... Air Force Technical Approval Team (AAG)
AFTAU .... American Friends of the Tel Aviv University (EA)
AFTB .... Afterburner [*on jet engines*]
AFTB .... Air Force Test Base
AFTB .... Army Family Term Building
AFTB .... Association for the Blind [*Australia*]
AFTBC .... Air Flow Thermal Balance Calorimeter
AFTBQ .... Association for the Blind, Queensland [*Australia*]
AFTBWA ...... Association for the Blind of Western Australia
AFTC .... Air Force Flight Training Command
AFTC .... American Fox Terrier Club (EA)
AFTC .... Apparent Free Testosterone Concentration [*Clinical chemistry*]
AFTCA .... Amateur Field Trial Clubs of America (EA)
AFTCC .... Air Force Troop Carrier Command [*British military*] (DMA)
AFTCLR .... After Cooler
AFTCM .... American Foundation of Traditional Chinese Medicine (EA)
AFTCom .... Associate of the Faculty of Teachers in Commerce [*British*] (DBQ)
AFTD .... Air Force Test Director (MCD)
AFTDS .... Automated Flight Test Data System (MCD)
AFTE .... American Federation of Technical Engineers [*Later, International Federation of Professional and Technical Engineers*] (EA)
AFTE .... Arab Federation for Technical Education [*Baghdad, Iraq*] (EAIO)
AFTE .... Association of Firearm and Tool Mark Examiners (EA)
AFTE .... Authority for Tooling Expenditures
AFTEC .... Air Force Flight Test Center [*Edwards Air Force Base, CA*] (MCD)
AFTEC .... Air Force Test and Evaluation Center [*Kirtland Air Force Base, NM*] (AFM)
AFTENCAP ... Air Force Tactical Exploitation of National Capability [*Air Force*]

AFTER .... Air Force Thermionic Engineering and Research [*Stanford University*] (PDAA)
AFTER .... Ask a Friend to Explain Reconstruction [*An association*] (EA)
AFTER .... Automatic Functional Test and Evaluation Routine [*Raytheon Co.*]
AFTERM .... Association Francaise de Terminologie [*French Association of Terminology*] [*Canada*]
AFTEX .... Australia-France Technological Exchange Scheme
AFTF .... Air Force Task Force (AFM)
AFTFWC .... Air Force Tactical Fighter Weapons Center (MCD)
AFTHBA .... American Fox Trotting Horse Breed Association (EA)
AFTI .... Advanced Fighter Technology Integration [*Air Force*]
AFTIA .... Armed Forces Technical Information Agency (NATG)
AFTIC .... Air Force Technical Intelligence Center
AFTIQ .... Association des Firmes-Conseils en Technologie de l'Information de Quebec (AC)
AFTJ .... Airborne Fuze Test Jammer (CAAL)
AFTL .... Academy of Florida Trial Lawyers (SRA)
AFTLI .... Association Feeling Truth and Living It
AFTM .... Additive Full-Time Manning (MCD)
AFTM .... American Foundation for Tropical Medicine (EA)
AFTM .... Assistant Freight Traffic Manager
AFTMA .... American Fishing Tackle Manufacturers Association (EA)
AFTMA .... Australian Federation of Timber Merchants' Associations
Aftmarkt ...... Aftermarket Technology Corp. [*Associated Press*] (SAG)
AFTN .... Aeronautical Fixed Telecommunication Network [*United Kingdom*]
AFTN .... Afternoon (FAAC)
AFTN .... Autonomously Functioning Thyroid Nodule [*Endocrinology*]
AFTO .... Air Force Technical Order
AFTO .... Association of Flight Training Organizations [*British*] (DBA)
AFTO .... Australian Foreign Trade Office
AFTOC .... Air Force Technical Order Management Center (MCD)
AFTOD .... Air Force Technical Objectives Documents
AFTOSB .... Air Force Technical Order Standardization Board
A/FTP .... Acceptance Functional Test Procedure [*NASA*] (KSC)
AFTP .... Additional Flight Training Period (AABC)
AFTP .... Advanced Fault Tree Analysis Program [*SIA Computer Services*] [*Software package*] (NCC)
AFTP .... Aircrew Flight Training Period (AABC)
AFTPS .... Air Force Test Pilot School (MCD)
AFTR .... Air Force Technical Report
AFTR .... American Federal Tax Reports [*Prentice-Hall, Inc.*] [*A publication*] (DLA)
AFTR .... Army Flying Time Report (MCD)
AFTR .... Association of Foreign Trade Representatives (EA)
AFTR2d .... American Federal Tax Reports, Second Series [*Prentice-Hall, Inc.*] [*A publication*] (DLA)
AFTRA .... American Federation of Television and Radio Artists (EA)
AFTRANSMET... Air Force Transportation Management Engineering Team
AFTRC .... Air Force Training Command
AFTRCC .... Aerospace and Flight Test Radio Coordinating Council (MCD)
AFTRRC .... Animal Feed and Tissue Residue Research Center [*Department of Health and Human Services*] (GRD)
AFTS .... Adaptive Flight Training System (MCD)
AFTS .... Aeronautical Fixed Telecommunications Service
AFTS .... Airborne Flight Test System (MCD)
AFTS .... Air Force Tactical Shelter (MCD)
AFTS .... Armed Forces Television Service (NTCM)
AFTS .... Aseptic Fluid Transfer System [*NASA*]
AFTS .... Automatic Flexible Test Station
AFTS .... Automatic Frequency Tone Shift (NVT)
AFTSC .... Air Force Technical Service Command
AFTTH .... Air Force Technical Training Headquarters
AFTU .... Air Force Test Unit (MCD)
AFTU .... Association of Free Trade Unions [*Former USSR*]
AFTU-V .... Air Force Test Unit, Vietnam
AFTVA .... American Federation of Teachers in Virginia (SRA)
AFTWDS ...... Afterwards (ROG)
AFTWUA ...... Amalgamated Footwear and Textile Workers' Union of Australia
AFTX .... America First Tax Exempt Mortgage [*NASDAQ symbol*] (NQ)
AFTxE .... America First Tax Exempt Mortgage Fund [*Associated Press*] (SAG)
AFTXZ .... Amer First Tax Exempt Mtg L.P. [*NASDAQ symbol*] (TTSB)
AFTY .... Affinity Entertainment, Inc. [*NASDAQ symbol*] (SAG)
AFTY .... Affinity Teleproductions, Inc. [*NASDAQ symbol*] (SAG)
AFU .... Advanced Flying Unit [*Air Force*]
AFU .... Afro Unity Airways [*Benin*] [*ICAO designator*] (FAAC)
AFU .... Air Force Units
AFU .... All Fouled-Up [*Bowdlerized version*] (AAG)
AFU .... American Fraternal Union [*Ely, MN*] (EA)
AFU .... Arkansas Farmers Union (SRA)
AFU .... Assault Fire Unit [*Army*]
AFU .... Auxiliary Functional Unit [*Data link*] (NG)
AFU .... University of Arkansas, Fayetteville, Fayetteville, AR [*OCLC symbol*] (OCLC)
AFUA .... ARMS/FIRMS Users Association (EA)
AFUD .... American Foundation for Urologic Disease (EA)
AFUDC .... Allowance for Funds Used during Construction
AFUDE .... Asociacion de Familiares de Uruguayos Desaparecidos [*France*]
AFUE .... Annual Fuel Utilization Efficiency [*Furnaces*]
AFUG .... AIRS [*Aerometric Information Retrieval System*] Facility Users Group [*Environmental Protection Agency*] (GFGA)
AFUPO .... Air Force Unit Post Office
AFUR .... Amplified Failure or Unsatisfactory Report
AFUS .... Air Force of the United States
AFUS .... Armed Forces of the United States
AFV .... Aerospace Flight Vehicle

AFV............	Afluidal Variant [*Bacteriology*]
AFV............	Air Afrique Vacances [*Ivory Coast*] [*FAA designator*] (FAAC)
AFV............	Alliance for Volunteerism [*Defunct*] (EA)
AFV............	Alternative Fuel Vehicle
AFV............	American Friends of Vietnam (EA)
AFV............	Amnionic Fluid Volume [*Obstetrics*] (DAVI)
AFV............	Anti-Flood Valve (MCD)
AFV............	Area Full Value (ECII)
AFV............	Armored Family of Vehicles [*Military*] (RDA)
AFV............	Armored Fighting Vehicle [*Marine Corps*]
AFV............	Armored Force Vehicle
AFV............	Arthritis Foundation of Victoria [*Australia*]
AFV............	Audio Follow Video [*Tape editing*] (NTCM)
AFV............	Fairview Public Library, Alberta [*Library symbol National Library of Canada*] (NLC)
AFVA..........	Air Force Visual Aid
AFVA..........	American Film and Video Association (EA)
AFVA..........	American Foundation for Vision Awareness (EA)
AFVBM........	American Federation of Violin and Bow Makers (EA)
AFVC..........	Auxiliary Force Veterinary Corps [*British military*] (DMA)
AFVC..........	Fort Vermilion Community Library, Alberta [*Library symbol National Library of Canada*] (NLC)
AFVCS........	Automatic Fingerprint Verification Computer System
AFVD..........	Area Full Value Display (ECII)
AFVES........	E. E. Oliver School, Fairview, Alberta [*Library symbol National Library of Canada*] (BIB)
AFVG..........	Anglo-French Variable-Geometry [*Combat aircraft*]
AFVHS........	Hillcrest Community School, Fort Vermilion, Alberta [*Library symbol National Library of Canada*] (BIB)
AFVL..........	American Friends of the Vatican Library (EA)
AFVN..........	American [*formerly, Armed*] Forces Vietnam Network
AFVP..........	Aviation Forecast Verification Program (USDC)
AFVP..........	Aviation Forecast Verification Program [*Marine science*] (OSRA)
AFVPA........	Advertising Film and Videotape Producers' Association [*British*]
AFVPS........	Fort Vermilion Public School, Alberta [*Library symbol National Library of Canada*] (BIB)
AFVRLS.......	Rocky Lane School, Fort Vermilion, Alberta [*Library symbol National Library of Canada*] (BIB)
AFVS..........	Fairview High School, Alberta [*Library symbol National Library of Canada*] (BIB)
AFVSM........	Association Forestiere de la Vallee du St-Maurice Inc. (AC)
AFVSMS......	St. Mary's School, Fort Vermilion, Alberta [*Library symbol National Library of Canada*] (BIB)
AFVSS........	Afebrile, Vital Signs Stable [*Medicine*] (DAVI)
AFVSTS.......	St. Thomas More School, Fairview, Alberta [*Library symbol National Library of Canada*] (BIB)
AFVTG........	Armed Forces Vocational Testing Group [*Randolph Air Force Base, TX*] (AFM)
AFW...........	Advocates for Women [*Defunct*] (EA)
AFW...........	Afriwest Airlines Ltd. [*Nigeria*] [*FAA designator*] (FAAC)
AFW...........	Air Force Weapon
AFw...........	Akkadische Fremdwoerter als Beweis fuer Babylonischen Kultureinfluss [*A publication*] (BJA)
AFW...........	Army Field Workshop
AFW...........	Auxiliary Feedwater [*Nuclear energy*] (NRCH)
AFW...........	Auxiliary Fresh Water (DNAB)
AFW...........	Axial Flow Wheel
AFW...........	United States Army, Corps of Engineers, Walla Walla District, Walla Walla, WA [*OCLC symbol*] (OCLC)
AFWA..........	Air Force with Army
AFWA..........	Arthritis Foundation of Western Australia
AFWAB........	Army Fixed Wing Aptitude Battery (AABC)
AFWAL........	Air Force Wright Aeronautical Laboratories [*Wright-Patterson Air Force Base, OH*]
AFWAL/ML...	Air Force Wright Aeronautical Laboratories Materials Laboratory [*Wright-Patterson Air Force Base, OH*]
AFWAR........	Air Force Personnel on Duty with Army
AFWAR........	Association of Federal Woman's Award Recipients [*Defunct*] (EA)
AFWAS........	Auxiliary Feedwater Actuating System [*Nuclear energy*] (NRCH)
AFWB.........	Air Force Welfare Board (AFM)
AFWC..........	Affiliated Woodcarvers Ltd. (EA)
AFWC..........	American Federation of World Citizens [*Later, Fellowship of World Citizens*] (EA)
AFWC..........	Auxiliary Feedwater Control [*Nuclear energy*] (NRCH)
AFWE..........	Air Forces, Western Europe [*NATO*] (NATG)
AFWE..........	Average Female Weekly Earnings
AFWET........	Air Force Weapons Effectiveness Testing (AFM)
AFWETS.......	Air Force Weapons Effectiveness Testing System
AFWG.........	AFPS Forecast Working Group (USDC)
AFWIS.........	Air Force WWMCCS [*Worldwide Military Command and Control System*] Information System (GFGA)
AFWIZO.......	Australian Federation of the Women's International Zionist Organization
AFWL.........	Air Force Weapons Laboratory [*Kirtland Air Force Base, NM*]
AFWL.........	Armed Forces Writers League [*Later, NAGC*] (EA)
AFWL/LEAPS...	AFWL [*Air Force Weapons Laboratory*] LASER Engineering and Applications to Prototype Systems (MCD)
AFWMAA.....	Air Force Wide Mission Area Analysis (MCD)
AFWN.........	Air Force Personnel on Duty with Navy
AFWOFS......	Air Force Weather Observing and Forecasting System
AFWR.........	Approved Force War Reserves (AFM)
AFWR.........	Atlantic Fleet Weapons Range [*Later, AFRSF*] [*Navy*]
AFWS.........	Advanced Filament Wound Structure
AFWS.........	Air Force Weapon Supply [*or System*] (SAA)
AFWS.........	Automated Fiber Winner System

AFWS.........	Auxiliary Feedwater System [*Nuclear energy*] (NRCH)
AFWST........	Armed Forces Women's Selection Test
AFWTF........	Atlantic Fleet Weapons Training Facility [*Navy*]
AFWTR	Air Force Western Test Range [*Later, Space and Missile Test Center*] [*Vandenberg Air Force Base, CA*]
AFWTRM	Air Force Western Test Range Manual (MCD)
AFWW	Air Force Weather Wing (SAA)
AFWWMCCS...	Air Force World Wide Military Command and Control System (MCD)
AFWY.........	Amer Freightways [*NASDAQ symbol*] (TTSB)
AFWY.........	American Freightways Corp. [*NASDAQ symbol*] (NQ)
AFWYU.......	American Foundation for World Youth Understanding (EA)
AFX...........	Address Complete, Subscriber Free, Coin-Box [*Telecommunications*] (TEL)
AFX...........	Air Freight Express, Inc. [*ICAO designator*] (FAAC)
AFX...........	Application Frameworx [*Microsoft Corp.*]
AFXF..........	Advanced Flash X-Ray Facility
AFY...........	Afyon [*Turkey*] [*Airport symbol*] (AD)
AFY...........	Air Facility (DNAB)
AFY...........	Air Foyle (Executive) Ltd. [*British ICAO designator*] (FAAC)
AFY...........	Association Franco-Yukonnaise (AC)
AFYDP	Army's Five-Year Defense Program
AFYMOSAP...	Additional Fiscal Year Money Is Authorized by the Secretary of the Army (AABC)
AFZ...........	Auto-Free Zone [*TRB*] (TAG)
AFZA..........	Australian Fishing Zone Authority
AG............	Abbott Laboratories [*Research code symbol*]
AG............	Above Grade (DAC)
AG............	Accessory Gland
AG............	Accountant General
AG............	Acid Generator [*Chemistry*]
AG............	Acting (ADA)
AG............	Action Group [*United National Independence Party Alliance of Nigeria*] [*Political party*]
AG............	Acts of the Gods (BJA)
AG............	Ad Gentes [*Decree on the Church's Missionary Activity*] [*Vatican II document*]
AG............	Adjutant General
AG............	Advanced Guard
AG............	Adventurers' Guild [*British*] (DBA)
AG............	Advisory Group [*Military*]
AG............	Aerographer's Mate [*Navy rating*]
AG............	Aerojet-General Corp.
AG............	Aeronautical Standards Group [*Military*]
AG............	Aerospace Group
AG............	Aerospace Guidance and Metrology Center [*Air Force*] (AFIT)
AG............	Africa Guild [*Defunct*] (EA)
AG............	After Goetz [*A reference to "vigilante" Bernhard Goetz, who shot four youths on a New York subway in 1984 after allegedly being threatened by them*] [*See also BG*]
Ag............	Agada (BJA)
AG............	Again [*Telecommunications*] (TEL)
AG............	Against (ROG)
AG............	Against Grain
AG............	Against Gravity (HGAA)
Ag............	Agamemnon [*of Aeschylus*] [*Classical studies*] (OCD)
AG............	Agate [*Typography*] (DGA)
ag............	Agate (VRA)
AG............	AGCO Corp. [*NYSE symbol*] (SAG)
AG............	Agency (EY)
ag............	Agent (ODBW)
AG............	Agent General
AG............	Age of Primary Taxpayer [*IRS*]
AG............	Aggressive Growth [*Investment term*]
AG............	Agitate (MSA)
Ag............	Agnus Dei [*Lamb of God*] [*Latin*]
AG............	Agorot [*Monetary unit*] [*Israel*]
Ag............	Agree (ILCA)
AG............	Agreement (ADA)
ag............	Agreement (ODBW)
AG............	Agriculture
Ag............	Agriculture Department (US) (AAGC)
AG............	Air Bridge Carriers [*ICAO designator*] (AD)
A/G...........	Aircraft Arresting Gear (NG)
AG............	Air Gap
AG............	Air Gauge
A/G...........	Airgraph (ADA)
AG............	Air Group
AG............	Air Gunner [*British*]
AG............	Airplane Group (MCD)
AG............	Air-to-Ground [*Photos, missiles, etc.*]
A/G...........	Air-to-Ground [*FAA*]
AG............	Aktiengesellschaft [*Corporation*] [*German*]
A/G...........	Albumin/Globulin [*Medicine*]
AG............	Alignment Group
AG............	Alternating Gradient
AG............	Americans for God (EA)
AG............	Aminoglycoside [*Endocrinology*] (DAVI)
AG............	Aminoguanosine [*Biochemistry*]
AG............	Amtsgericht [*Inferior Court*] [*German*]
AG............	Analytical Grade [*Organic chemistry*]
AG............	Anastomosis Group [*Plant pathology*]
AG............	Anatomische Gesellschaft [*Anatomical Society*] [*Germany*] (EAIO)
AG............	Andean Group

A-G .... Anders Gaan Leven-Geweldloos, Rechtvaardig, Open Ecologisch Netwerk [*Belgium*] [*Political party*] (ECED)
AG .... Anderson Galleries
AG .... And Gate [*Logic element*] [*Computer science*]
AG .... Anion Gap [*Medicine*] (DAVI)
AG .... Annual Goal [*Education*]
AG .... Antigas [*Military*]
Ag .... Antigen [*Also, A, a*] [*Immunology*]
AG .... Antiglobulin [*Clinical chemistry*]
AG .... Antigravity
AG .... Antigua-Barbuda [*ANSI two-letter standard code*] (CNC)
AG .... Apparel Guild (EA)
AG .... Arbeitsgericht [*Labor Court*] [*German*]
ag .... Argentina [*MARC country of publication code Library of Congress*] (LCCP)
Ag .... Argentum [*Silver*] [*Chemical element*]
AG .... Aristos Guild (EA)
AG .... Armed Guard
AG .... Armor Grating [*Technical drawings*]
AG .... Army Group (NATG)
AG .... Army Guidance
A-G .... Arresting Gear [*Aviation*]
AG .... Art Gallery
AG .... Artificial Gravity (NASA)
AG .... Artists Guild
AG .... Assault Gun (MCD)
AG .... Assicurazioni Generali [*General Assurance*] [*Commercial firm Italy*]
AG .... Association for Gnotobiotics (EA)
AG .... Assumption Guild (EA)
AG .... Atlas Gemini [*NASA*] (KSC)
AG .... Atrial Gallop [*Cardiology*]
AG .... Attached Gingiva [*Medicine*] (DMAA)
AG .... Attention Getting [*by the hearing-impaired*]
AG .... Attitude Gyro (MCD)
AG .... Attorney General
Ag .... Attorney General (AAGC)
AG .... Attorney General's Opinions [*A publication*] (DLA)
AG .... Auditor General [*Military*]
AG .... Aufklaerungsgruppe [*Air Forces Reconnaissance Unit*] [*German military - World War II*]
AG .... August
Ag .... Augustine [*Deceased, 430*] [*Authority cited in pre-1607 legal work*] (DSA)
AG .... Authors Guild (EA)
AG .... Autoleather Guild (EA)
AG .... Automatic Gauge
AG .... Availability Guarantee [*Military*]
AG .... Axiogingival [*Dentistry*]
AG .... Galahad Public Library, Alberta [*Library symbol National Library of Canada*] (NLC)
ag---- .... Mekong River and Basin [*MARC geographic area code Library of Congress*] (LCCP)
AG .... Miscellaneous Auxiliary Ship [*Navy ship symbol*]
Ag .... Silver [*Chemical element*] (DOG)
AG .... Try Again [*Telecommunications*] (TEL)
AG1 .... Aerographer's Mate, First Class [*Navy rating*]
AG2 .... Aerographer's Mate, Second Class [*Navy rating*]
Ag₂0 .... Silver Oxide [*Chemistry*] (DAVI)
AG3 .... Aerographer's Mate, Third Class [*Navy rating*]
AGA .... Abrasive Grain Association (EA)
AGA .... Accelerated Growth Area [*Embryology*]
AGA .... Accredited Gemologists Association (EA)
AGA .... Aceglutamide Aluminum [*Biochemistry*]
AGA .... Acute Gonococcal Arthritis [*Medicine*] (CPH)
AGA .... Adjutants General Association of the United States [*Later, AGAUS*] (EA)
AGA .... Aerodromes, Air Routes, and Ground Aid (DA)
AGA .... Aerodromes, Air Routes, and Ground Aids [*Aviation*]
AGA .... Aeronaves del Centro [*Venezuela*] [*ICAO designator*] (FAAC)
AGA .... Agadir [*Morocco*] [*Airport symbol*] (OAG)
AGA .... Air Routes and Ground Aids (SAA)
AGA .... Air-to-Ground-to-Air
AGA .... Alliance of Gay Artists (EA)
AGA .... Amalgamated Gas Accumulation [*Stove designed by Gustaf Dalen in 1922*]
AGA .... Amateur Golfers' Association of America (EA)
AGA .... Amateur Gymnastics Association (WDAA)
AGA .... American Galvanizers Association (EA)
AGA .... American Gas Association (EA)
AGA .... American Gastroenterological Association (EA)
AGA .... American Gay Atheists (EA)
AGA .... American Gelbvieh Association (EA)
AGA .... American Genetic Association (EA)
AGA .... American Geriatrics Association (DAVI)
AGA .... American Girl Resources [*Vancouver Stock Exchange symbol*]
AGA .... American Glassware Association [*Defunct*]
AGA .... American Go Association (EA)
AGA .... American Goiter Association [*Later, American Thyroid Association*]
AGA .... American Gold Association [*Defunct*] (EA)
AGA .... American Grand Prix Association (EA)
AGA .... American Graniteware Association (EA)
AGA .... American Guernsey Association (EA)
AGA .... American Guides Association [*Defunct*] (EA)
AGA .... American Guppy Association [*Later, IFGA*] (EA)
AGA .... Animal Guild of America (EA)

AGA .... Antigliadin Antibodies [*Immunology*]
AGA .... Appropriate for Gestational Age [*Medicine*]
AGA .... Arizona Golf Association (SRA)
AGA .... Art Galleries Association [*British*] (DBA)
AGA .... Artists' Guild of Australia
AGA .... As Good As
AGA .... Associated Geographers of America
AGA .... Association of Gaugers and Appraisers Ltd. [*British*] (BI)
AGA .... Association of Government Accountants [*Arlington, VA*] (EA)
AGA .... Association of Governmental Appraisers [*American Society of Appraiser*] [*Absorbed by*] (EA)
AGA .... Association of Government Auditors (AAGC)
AGA .... Association of the Graphic Arts (EA)
AGA .... Astrologers' Guild of America (EA)
AGA .... At Gestational Age [*Medicine*] (DAVI)
AGA .... Attitude Gyro Assembly (MCD)
AGA .... Australian Garlic Association
AGA .... Automated Genetic Analyzer [*Instrumentation*]
AGA .... Automatic Gas Analyzer [*Nuclear energy*] (NRCH)
AGA .... Average for Gestational Age [*Medicine*] (DAVI)
AGA .... Average Global Automobile [*Emissions to atmosphere*]
AGA .... Azimuth Gimbal Assembly (MCD)
AGA .... United States National Arboretum, Washington, DC [*OCLC symbol*] (OCLC)
AGAA .... Airman Apprentice, Aerographer's Mate, Striker [*Navy rating*]
AGAA .... Amateur Golfers' Association of America [*Defunct*] (EA)
AGAA .... American Guild of Animal Artists (EA)
AGAA .... Association des Groupes d'Astronomes Amateurs [*Association of Amateur Astronomy Groups*] [*Canada*]
AGAA .... Attitude Gyro Accelerometer Assembly (MCD)
AGAA .... Automatic Gain Adjusting Amplifier [*Telecommunications*]
Ag-AB .... Antigen-Antibody [*Complex*] [*Immunology*]
AGAC .... Aero Geo Astro Corp.
AGAC .... American Guild of Authors and Composers (EA)
AGAC .... Association of Graphic Arts Consultants (EA)
AGACS .... Air-Ground-Air Communications System
AGACS .... Automatic Ground-to-Air Communications System
AGADS .... Advanced Graphics Avionics Display System (MCD)
AGAFBO ...... Atlantic and Gulf American Flag Berth Operators
AGAG .... Acidic Glycoaminoglycan [*Biochemistry*]
AGAH .... Association for Government Assisted Housing [*Defunct*] (EA)
AGAHD .... Action Group Against Harassment & Discrimination in the Workplace [*Groupe d'Action Contre le Harcelement et Discrimination au Travail*] [*Action Against Harassment*] (AC)
AGAHM .... Association des Gens d'Affaires Haitiens de Montreal [*Haitian Businessmen's Association of Montreal*] (AC)
AGAI .... AG Associates [*NASDAQ symbol*] (TTSB)
AGAI .... AG Associates, Inc. [*NASDAQ symbol*] (SAG)
AGAL .... American Gas Association Laboratories
AGALA .... Authors Guild of the Authors League of America (EA)
AGALEV ...... Anders Gaan Leven [*Live Differently*] [*Belgium Political party*] (PPW)
AGAM .... Acres Gaming [*NASDAQ symbol*] (TTSB)
AGAM .... Acres Gaming, Inc. [*NASDAQ symbol*] (SAG)
AGAMP .... Automatic Gain Adjusting Amplifier [*Telecommunications*] (TEL)
AGAMW ...... Acres Gaming Wrrt [*NASDAQ symbol*] (TTSB)
AGAN .... Airman, Aerographer's Mate, Striker [*Navy rating*]
AG & MC .... Aerospace Guidance and Metrology Center [*Newark Air Force Station, OH*]
AG & QMG ... Adjutant-General and Quartermaster-General [*British*]
AGANGVC .... American Gas Association Natural Gas Vehicle Coalition
AGANI .... Apollo Guidance and Navigation Information [*NASA*]
AgAp .... Against Apion [*Josephus*] (BJA)
AGAP .... Attitude Gyro Accelerometer Package (KSC)
AGAP .... Australian Genome Research Facility
AGAP .... Automated Graphics Application Program (MCD)
AGAR .... Department of Agriculture Acquisition Regulation [*Superseded AGPR in 1984*] (AAGC)
AGARD .... Advisory Group for Aerospace Research and Development [*NATO*]
AGAS .... Aviation Gasoline [*Navy*]
AG Asc .... AG Associates, Inc. [*Associated Press*] (SAG)
AGASIA .... Asian Agriculture, Agrotechnology, and Agribusiness Exhibition and Conference
AGASP .... Arctic Gas and Aerosol Sampling Program [*Marine science*] (OSRA)
AGASP .... Arctic Gas and Aerosol Sampling Program (USDC)
AGASS .... Automated Geomagnetic Airborne Survey System [*Aviation*] (PDAA)
AGAT .... Ability Grouped Active Teaching (EDAC)
AGATE .... Accessibility to Gate Arrays through Technology and Engineering (PDAA)
AGATE .... Advanced General Aviation Transport Experiments (GAVI)
AGATE .... Air-to-Ground Acquisition and Tracking Equipment
AGAUS .... Adjutants General Association of the United States (EA)
AGAV .... Asociacion Guatemalteca de Agentes de Viajes [*Guatemalan Association of Travel Agents*] (EY)
AGAVE .... Automatic Gimbaled-Antenna Vectoring Equipment [*Air Force*]
AGAWA .... Avocado Growers' Association of Western Australia
AGB .... Aboveground Biomass [*Of vegetation*]
AGB .... Accessory Gear Box
AGB .... Advanced Geometry Blade [*Military*] (RDA)
AGB .... Afton, OK [*Location identifier FAA*] (FAAL)
A/GB .... Agriculture (Great Britain). Ministry of Agriculture, Fisheries, and Food [*A publication*]
AGB .... Air-Service-Gabon [*ICAO designator*] (FAAC)
AGB .... Allgemeine Geschaftsbedingungen [*General Conditions of Contracts, Transactions, Etc.*] [*German*] (DLA)
AGB .... Any Good Brand

AGB .... Assault Gun Battalion (INF)
AGB .... Association of German Broadcasters (EA)
AGB .... Association of Governing Boards (NFD)
AGB .... Association of Governing Boards of Universities and Colleges (EA)
AGB .... Asymptotic Giant Branch [Astronomy]
AGB .... Audits of Great Britain
AGB .... Canadian Angus Resources [Vancouver Stock Exchange symbol]
AGB .... Icebreaker [Navy ship symbol]
AGB .... United States Department of Agriculture, Food and Nutrition
                  Information Center, Beltsville, MD [OCLC symbol] (OCLC)
AGBA .... Alexander Graham Bell Association for the Deaf (EA)
AGBA .... American Galloway Breeders' Association (EA)
AGBAD .... Alexander Graham Bell Association for the Deaf (EA)
AGBag .... AG-Bag International Ltd. [Associated Press] (SAG)
AGBC .... Avocado Growers Bargaining Council [Defunct] (EA)
AGBCA .... Agriculture Board of Contract Appeals (AAGC)
AGBG .... AG-Bag International Ltd. [NASDAQ symbol] (SAG)
AGBG .... Ag-Bag Intl. Ltd. [NASDAQ symbol] (TTSB)
AGBGB .... Ausfuehrungsgesetz zur Burgerlichen Gesetzbuch [Implementing law
                  to the civil code] [German] (ILCA)
AGBI .... Artists' General Benevolent Institution [British]
AgBioTech ... Center for Agricultural Molecular Biology [Rutgers University]
                  [Research center] (RCD)
AGBIZ .... Agribusiness Information [G. V. Olsen Associates] [Information
                  service or system] (CRD)
AGBM .... Antiglomerular Basement Antibody Test
AGBM .... Association of Grey Board Makers [British] (DBA)
AGBS .... Artillery Ground Burst Simulator (MCD)
AGBU .... Armenian General Benevolent Union (EA)
AGBUA .... Armenian General Benevolent Union of America [Later, AGBU] (EA)
AGBUS .... Analog Ground Bus
AGC .... Absolute Granulocyte Count [Medicine] (DMAA)
AGC .... Adjutant General's Corps
AGC .... Advanced Gas Centrifuge
AGC .... Advanced Graduate Certificate
AGC .... Aerographer's Mate, Chief [Navy rating]
AGC .... Aerojet-General Corp.
AGC .... African Groundnut Council [See also CAA] [Nigeria]
AGC .... Agricultural Genetics Co. Ltd. [British] (IRUK)
AGC .... Agriculture Canada
AGC .... Air-Ground Chart (AFM)
AGC .... Air-Ground Communications (CET)
AGC .... Alaska Game Commission [Terminated, 1959]
AGC .... Amer General [NYSE symbol] (TTSB)
AGC .... American General Corp. Capital LLC [Associated Press] (SAG)
AGC .... American General Life Insurance Co. [NYSE symbol] (SPSG)
AGC .... American Grassland Council [Later, AFGC] (EA)
AGC .... Amphibious Force Flagship [Later, LCC] [Navy symbol]
AGC .... Amphibious Group Command [NATO] (NATG)
AGC .... Amplitude Gain Control
AGC .... Ancient Gneiss Complex [Geology]
AGC .... Angel Island [California] [Seismograph station code, US Geological
                  Survey] (SEIS)
AGC .... Apollo Guidance Computer [NASA]
AGC .... Arab Agricultural Aviation [Egypt] [ICAO designator] (FAAC)
AGC .... Armed Guard Center
AGC .... Army Advisory Group, China
AGC .... Army General Council
AGC .... Artists Guild of Chicago [Defunct] (EA)
AGC .... Assessment Guidance Centre [British]
AGC .... Associated General Contractors of America (EA)
AGC .... Association of Graphic Communications (SRA)
AGC .... Athena Gold Corp. [Vancouver Stock Exchange symbol]
AGC .... Atlantic-Gulf Coastwise Steamship Freight Bureau, Elizabeth NJ
                  [STAC]
AGC .... Automatech Graphics Corp. [Information service or system] (IID)
AGC .... Automatic Gain Control [Electronics]
AGC .... Automatic Gauge Control [or Controller]
AGC .... Automatic Generation Control (ACII)
AGC .... Avocado Growers Council [Later, AGBC] (EA)
AGC .... General Communications Vessel [Navy ship symbol] [World War II]
AGC .... Grande Cache Public Library, Alberta [Library symbol National
                  Library of Canada] (NLC)
AGC .... Pittsburgh, PA [Location identifier FAA] (FAAL)
AGC .... United States Department of Agriculture, Forest Service, North
                  Central Forest Experiment Station, St. Paul, MN [OCLC
                  symbol] (OCLC)
AGCA .... Altitude Gyroscope Control Assembly [Military] (CAAL)
AGCA .... American Game Collectors Association (EA)
AGCA .... Associated General Contractors of America
AGCA .... Australian Greeting Card Association
AGCA .... Automatic Ground-Controlled Approach [RADAR]
AGCAP .... Automated Generic Case Analysis Program (MCD)
AGCAS .... Association of Graduate Careers Advisory Services [British] (DBA)
AGCB .... Association Geologique Carpatho-Balkanique [Carpathian Balkan
                  Geological Association - CBGA] (EA)
AGCC .... Airborne and Ground Communications Central (MCD)
AGCC .... Air-Ground Communications Channel
AGCC .... American Guernsey Cattle Club [Later, AGA] (EA)
AGCC .... Associated General Contractors of California (AAGC)
AGCC .... Association of Gifted-Creative Children (EA)
AGC/CFAR ... Automatic Gain Control/Constant False Alarm Rate
AGCCS .... Army Global Command and Control System (RDA)
AGCCS .... Army Global Command and Control System [Army]
AGCD .... Association of Green Crop Driers [British] (BI)

AGCE .... Atmosphere General Circulation Experiment (MCD)
AGCF .... Air-Ground Correlation Factor (AABC)
AGCG .... Associated Granite Craftsmen's Guild (EA)
AGCH .... AG-Chem Equipment [NASDAQ symbol] (TTSB)
AGCH .... Ag-Chem Equipment Co., Inc. [NASDAQ symbol] (SAG)
Ag-Chm ...... Ag-Chem Equipment Co. Inc. [Associated Press] (SAG)
AGCI .... Automatic Ground-Controlled Intercept (MCD)
AGCIC .... Association of German Chambers of Industry and Commerce (EA)
AGCL .... Associate Member of the Guild of Cleaners and Launderers
                  [British] (DBQ)
AGCL .... Automatic Ground-Controlled Landing
AGCL .... Small Communications Ship [Navy symbol] (DNAB)
AGCLA .... Alberta Government Civil Lawyers Association (AC)
AGCM .... Aerographer's Mate, Master Chief [Navy rating]
AGCM .... Army Good Conduct Medal
AGCM .... Atmospheric General Circulation Model [Meteorology]
AGCM .... Grand Centre Municipal Library, Alberta [Library symbol National
                  Library of Canada] (NLC)
AGCMDL ..... Army Good Conduct Medal
AGCO .... AGCO Corp. [Associated Press] (SAG)
AGCO .... Air-Ground Cooperation Officer
AG Corps .... Adjutant General's Corps (AAGC)
AGCP .... Automatic Gain Calibration Program
AGCPrC ...... Amer Gen'l Del LLC 6% Cv'MIPS' [NYSE symbol] (TTSB)
AGCPrD ...... Amer Genl 7% Cv Pfd [NYSE symbol] (TTSB)
AGCPrM ...... Amer Gen 8.45% 'MIPS' [NYSE symbol] (TTSB)
AGCPrN ...... Amer Gen 8.125% 'MIPS' [NYSE symbol] (TTSB)
AGCRS .... Army Gas-Cooled Reactor System (SAA)
AGCRSP ...... Army Gas-Cooled Reactor Systems Program
AGCS .... Advanced Guidance and Control System (MCD)
AGCS .... Aerographer's Mate, Senior Chief [Navy rating]
AGCS .... Air-Ground Communications System (SAA)
AGCS .... Association of Golf Club Secretaries (EAIO)
AGCS .... Automatic Ground Checkout System (KSC)
AGCS .... Automatic Ground Computer System (KSC)
AGCS .... Automatic Ground Control Station (KSC)
AGCS .... Automatic Guidance and Control System
AGCSA .... Australian Golf Course Superintendents' Association
AGCSB .... Atlantic-Gulf Coastwise Steamship Freight Bureau
AGCSC .... Automatic Ground Control System Computer (KSC)
AGCT .... Adenine-Guanine-Cytosine-Thymine (PDAA)
AGCT .... Army General Classification Test [Measurement of intelligence]
AGCTS .... Armed Guard Center Training School [Obsolete]
AGCU .... Air-Ground Cooling Unit (MCD)
AGCU .... Attitude Gyro Coupling Unit (KSC)
AGCU .... Autopilot Ground Control Unit (AAG)
AGCW .... Autonomous Guidance for Conventional Weapons [Air Force]
AGCY .... Agency (AFM)
AGCY .... Agency
agcy .... Agency (WDMC)
AGD .... Academy of General Dentistry (EA)
AGD .... Adjutant General's Department [Army]
AGD .... Agar-Gel Diffusion [Clinical chemistry]
AGD .... Agarose Diffusion [Method] [Cardiology] (DAVI)
AGD .... Agderfly AS [Norway ICAO designator] (FAAC)
AGD .... Agreed
AGD .... Aircraft Gunfire Detector
AGD .... American Gauge Design Committee
AGD .... Associated Gas Distributors
AGD .... Association of Graphic Designers (DGA)
AGD .... Attack Geometry Display (DNAB)
AGD .... Attorney General's Department (ADA)
AGD .... Auditor General's Department [Air Force]
AGD .... Axial Gear Differential (OA)
AGD .... Seagoing Dredge [Navy symbol]
AGD .... United States Department of Agriculture, Forest Service, Engineering-
                  TIC, Washington, DC [OCLC symbol] (OCLC)
AGDA .... American Gasoline Dealers Association (EA)
AGDA .... American Gun Dealers Association (EA)
AGDATA .... Agricultural Commodities Data Base [Alberta Department of
                  Agriculture] [Information service or system] (IID)
AGDC .... American Gauge Design Committee (MCD)
AGDC .... Assistant Grand Director of Ceremonies [Freemasonry]
AGD/CSD .... Axial Gear Differential/Constant-Speed Drive (DNAB)
AGDD .... Agar Gel Double Diffusion [Medicine] (DMAA)
AGDE .... Escort Research Ship [Navy symbol]
AG Dec .... Attorney General's Decisions [A publication] (DLA)
AGDEX .... Agricultural Index [Edinburgh School of Agriculture] [Information
                  service or system] [British] (NITA)
AGDIC .... Astro Guidance Digital Computer (IEEE)
A-GDL .... Army Gas Dynamic LASER (MCD)
AGDL .... Attorney General of the Duchy of Lancaster (ILCA)
AGDM .... Americana Gold&Diamond Hldgs [NASDAQ symbol] (TTSB)
AGDM .... Americana Gold & Diamond Holdings [NASDAQ symbol] (SAG)
AG/DR .... Assistant Gunner/Driver [Military] (INF)
AGDS .... American Gauge Design Standard
AGDS .... Auxiliary Deep Submergence Support Ship [Navy symbol] (NVT)
AGE .... Acrylamide Gel Electrophoresis (MAE)
AGE .... Acute Gastroenteritis [Medicine] (DAVI)
AGE .... Admiralty Gunnery Establishment [British]
AGE .... Adult Growth Examination [Test]
AGE .... Advanced Glycosylated End-Product [Biochemistry]
AGE .... Advisory Group on Energy [Army] (RDA)
AGE .... Aerospace Ground Equipment [NASA]
AGE .... Aerospace Guidance and Metrology Center [Air Force]

AGE............ Affiliated Government Employees' Distributing Co. [*California*]
AGE............ Agarose Gel Zone Electrophoresis
AGE............ Agenahambo [*Papua New Guinea*] [*Seismograph station code, US Geological Survey Closed*] (SEIS)
AGE............ Agnico-Eagle Mines Ltd. [*Toronto Stock Exchange symbol*]
AgE............ Agricultural Engineer
AGE............ Air Ground Engagement [*Military*] (DOMA)
AGE............ Air-Ground Equipment
AGe............ Akkadische Goetterepitheta [*A publication*] (BJA)
AGE............ Allyl Glycidyl Ether [*Organic chemistry*]
AGE............ Amarillo Grain Exchange (EA)
AGE............ Amazon Ground Emissions (MCD)
AGE............ Americans for Generational Equity (EA)
AGE............ Angle of Greatest Extension [*Orthopedics*]
AgE............ Antigen E
AGE............ Apollo Guidance Equipment [*NASA*] (KSC)
AGE............ Arterial Gas Embolism
AGE............ Asian Geotechnical Engineering Information Center [*Information service or system*] (IID)
AGE............ Asian Geotechnology Engineering Database [*Asian Institute of Technology*] [*Information service or system*] (CRD)
AGE............ Assembly of Governmental Employees [*Defunct*] (EA)
AGE............ Associated Ground Equipment (CINC)
AGE............ Associate in General Education
AGE............ Attorney General of England (ROG)
AGE............ Auditory Gross Error
AGE............ Automatic Ground Equipment
AGE............ Automatic Guidance Electronics
AGE............ Auxiliary Ground Equipment
AGE............ Aviation Ground Equipment (AAGC)
AGE............ Edwards [*A. G.*] & Sons, Inc. [*NYSE symbol*] (SPSG)
AGE............ Gem Public Library, Alberta [*Library symbol National Library of Canada*] (NLC)
AGE............ Servicios Aereos de Los Angeles SA de CV [*Mexico ICAO designator*] (FAAC)
AGE............ United States Department of Agriculture, Eastern Regional Research Center, Philadelphia, PA [*OCLC symbol*] (OCLC)
AGE............ Wangerooge [*Germany Airport symbol*] (OAG)
AGEA......... Australian Grain Exporters' Association
AGEAA........ An Gluaiseacht Eireannach in Aghaidh Apartheid [*Irish Anti-Apartheid Movement*] (EAIO)
AGEAS........ Automatic Ground Effect Augmentation System (MCD)
AGEC.......... Arbeitsgemeinschaft Europaeischer Chorverbaende [*Federation of European Choirs*] [*Utrecht, Netherlands*] (EAIO)
AGEC.......... Army General Equipment Command
AGEC.......... Australian Grape Exporters' Committee
AGECON....... Agricultural Economics [*Database*] [*Department of Agriculture Washington, DC*]
AGED......... Advisory Group on Electron Devices [*Army Washington, DC*]
AGED .... Aerospace Ground Equipment Department
AGED .... Army Group Effects Department
AGEd......... Associate in General Education
AGED .... Association des Grandes Entreprises de Distribution de Belgique [*Trade organization*] [*Belgium*] (EY)
AGED .... Automated General Experimental Device [*Animal performance testing*]
AGEED........ Association Generale des Eleves et Etudiants du Dahomey en France [*General Association of Dahomean Pupils and Students in France*] [*Dahomey*]
AGEH......... Hydrofoil Research Ship [*Navy symbol*]
AGEHR........ American Guild of English Handbell Ringers (EA)
AGEI.......... Aerospace Ground Equipment Illustration [*Air Force*] (SAA)
AGEI.......... Aerospace Ground Equipment Installation
AGEI.......... Associates of the Graymoor Ecumenical Institute [*Defunct*] (EA)
Age MR ...... Age Monthly Review [*A publication*]
AGenCp...... American General Corp. [*Associated Press*] (SAG)
AGENT........ Advanced Graphite Experiments Testing [*Military*]
AGEOCP...... Aerospace Ground Equipment Out of Commission for Parts [*Air Force*]
AGEOP........ Aerospace Ground Equipment Out of Commission for Parts [*Air Force*] (SAA)
AGEP.......... Advisory Group on Electronic Parts [*Military*]
AGEP.......... Agence Generale d'Editions Professionnelles [*Agency General of Professional Publishing*] [*Canada*]
AGEPC........ Acetyl-Glyceryl-Ether Phosphorylcholine
AGEPI......... Association Guineenne des Editeurs de la Presse Independente [*Press association*] [*Guinea*] (EY)
AGER.......... Auxiliary General for Environmental Research [*Ship*] [*Military*] (LAIN)
AGER .... Environmental Research Ship [*Navy symbol*]
AGERD........ Aerospace Ground Equipment Requirements Data
AGERM........ Association Generale des Etudiants Reunionnais en Metropole [*General Association of Reunionese Students in France*] (AF)
AGERS........ Auxiliary General Electronics Research Ship [*Navy*]
AGES .... Advocacy Group for the Environmentally Sensitive [*Association Groupant les Malades de l'Environnement*] (AC)
Ages .... Agesilaus [*of Plutarch*] [*Classical studies*] (OCD)
Ages .... Agesilaus [*of Xenophon*] [*Classical studies*] (OCD)
AGES .... Aircrew Gliding Escape System (MCD)
AGES .... Air-Ground Engagement Simulation (RDA)
AGES .... Air-to-Ground Engagement System (MCD)
AGES .... American Gas and Electric Services
AGES .... American Greek Exchange Society (EA)
AGES/AD ..... Air-to-Ground Engagement System - Air Defense (DWSG)
AGE/SE ...... Aerospace Ground Equipment/Support Equipment (MCD)
AGET.......... Advisory Group on Electron Tubes

AGETS .... Automated Ground Engine Test System (MCD)
AGEX......... Address Generation/Execute Cycle [*Computer science*]
AGF............ Adjutant-General to the Forces [*British*]
AGF............ Agen [*France*] [*Airport symbol*] (OAG)
AGF............ AGF Management Ltd. [*Toronto Stock Exchange symbol*]
AGF............ Alternating Gradient Focusing
AGF............ American Government Income Fund [*NYSE symbol*] (SPSG)
AGF............ Angle of Greatest Flexion [*Orthopedics*]
AGF............ Army Ground Forces
AGF............ Assurances Generales de France
AGF............ Atlantic Gulf Airlines, Inc. [*ICAO designator*] (FAAC)
AGF............ Automatic Guided Flight (MUGU)
AGF............ Aviation Guided Flight (MUGU)
AGF............ Forest Product Laboratory, Madison, WI [*OCLC symbol*] (OCLC)
AGF............ Miscellaneous Command Ship [*Navy symbol*]
AGFA .... Aktiengesellschaft fuer Anilinfabriken [*German photographic manufacturer*]
AGFA .... Assistant General Freight Agent
AGFA .... Avant-Garde Francaise d'Amerique [*French Avant-Garde of America*] [*Canada*]
AGFCS......... Automatic Gunfire Control System (DNAB)
AG FEB .... Aggrediente Febre [*When the Fever Increases*] [*Pharmacy*]
AGFF.......... Research Frigate [*Navy symbol*] (NVT)
AGFIS .... Assemblee Generale des Federations Internationales Sportives [*General Assembly of International Sports Federations*]
AGFIS .... Association Generale des Federations Internationales de Sports [*General Association of International Sports Federations - GAISF*] (EA)
AGFK .... Association Quebecoise de la Fibrose Kystique [*Quebec Cystic Fibrosis Association*] (AC)
AGFL .... Airborne Ground Fire Locator
AGFLS .... Airborne Ground Fire Locating System
AGFNET ...... Arbeitsgemeinschaft der Grossfochungseinrichtungen [*The Association of National Research Centers of the Federal Republic of Germany*] [*Computer science*] (TNIG)
AGFRTS ...... Air and Ground Forces Resources and Technical Staff [*Army*]
AGFS .... Aviation Gridded Forecast System (USDC)
AGFS .... Aviation Gridded Forecast System [*Marine science*] (OSRA)
AGFSA .... American Ground Flat Stock Association (EA)
AGFSR .... Aircraft Ground Fire Suppression and Rescue [*Air Force*] (MCD)
AGFSRS .... Aircraft Ground Fire Suppression and Rescue Systems [*Wright-Patterson Air Force Base, OH*] [*Air Force*]
AGG .... Agammaglobulinemia [*Medicine*]
AGG .... Agammaglobulinemia Leukemia [*Medicine*] (DAVI)
AGG .... Agent to the Governor-General [*British*]
Agg .... Aggadah (BJA)
Agg .... Aggadic (BJA)
AGG .... Agglutination [*Immunology*]
agg .... Aggravated (MAE)
AGG .... Aggregate
AGG .... Algoma Airways, Inc. [*Canada ICAO designator*] (FAAC)
AGG .... American Groomer's Guild (EA)
AGG .... Angoram [*Papua New Guinea*] [*Airport symbol*] (OAG)
AGG .... United States Department of Agriculture, Plum Island Animal Disease Center, Greenport, NY [*OCLC symbol*] (OCLC)
AGGAFT ...... American Grape Growers Alliance for Fair Trade [*Defunct*] (EA)
AGGD .... Apollo Guidance Ground Display [*NASA*] (MCD)
AGGD .... Automatic Gravity Gradient
AGGDSSD ..... Astro-Geodetic Geoid Data Station Spacing and Distribution (SAA)
AGGE .... Balalae, Shortland Islands [*Solomon Islands*] [*ICAO location identifier*] (ICLI)
AGGG .... Advisory Group on Greenhouse Gases [*Australia*]
AGGG .... Honiara [*Solomon Islands*] [*ICAO location identifier*] (ICLI)
AGGH .... Honiara/Henderson, Guadalcanal Island [*Solomon Islands*] [*ICAO location identifier*] (ICLI)
AGGL .... Agglutination [*Immunology*]
aggl .... Agglutination (DMAA)
AGGL .... Graciosa Bay/Luova, Santa Cruz Islands [*Solomon Islands*] [*ICAO location identifier*] (ICLI)
AGGLUT ...... Agglutination [*Immunology*] (AAMN)
agglut .... Agglutination (DMAA)
AGGM .... Munda, New Georgia Islands [*Solomon Islands*] [*ICAO location identifier*] (ICLI)
AGGN.......... Gizo/Nusatupe, Gizo Island [*Solomon Islands*] [*ICAO location identifier*] (ICLI)
AGGR.......... Aggregate (AABC)
AGGR.......... Air-to-Ground Gunnery Range
Aggred Feb.. Aggrediente Febre [*When the Fever Increases*] [*Pharmacy*]
AGGREG ...... Aggregation [*Medicine*] (AAMN)
AGGRGT ...... Aggregate
AGGRO .... Aggravation (DSUE)
AGGS .... American Gloxinia and Gesneriad Society (EA)
AGGS .... American Good Government Society [*Defunct*] (EA)
AGGS .... Antigas Gangrene Serum [*Medicine*]
AGGSNA Rept... Aerial Geological and Geophysical Survey of Northern Australia. Report [*A publication*]
AGH .... American Guild of Hypnotherapists (EA)
AGH .... Angelholm/Helsingbord [*Sweden*] [*Airport symbol*] (OAG)
AGH .... Antihemophilic Globulin [*Factor VIII*] [*Hematology*] (DAVI)
AGH .... Arc Gas Heater
AGH .... Army Group Headquarters
AGH .... Atlantis Group, Inc. [*AMEX symbol*] (SPSG)
AGH .... Atlantis Plastics, Inc. [*Formerly, Atlantis Group*] [*AMEX symbol*] (SAG)

AGH .... United States Department of Agriculture, APHIS [*Animal and Plant Health Inspection Service*], Plant Protection and Quarantine, Hyattsville, MD [*OCLC symbol*] (OCLC)
AGHA .... Acadian Genealogical and Historical Association [*Defunct*] (EA)
AGHA .... American Gotland Horse Association (EA)
AGHDEA .... Association of General Heating and Domestic Engineer Assistants [*A union*] [*British*]
AGHE .... Association for Gerontology in Higher Education (EA)
AGHS .... Australian Garden History Society
AGHS .... Patrol Combatant Support Ship [*Navy symbol*]
AGHTM .... Association Generale des Hygienistes et Techniciens Municipaux [*General Association of Municipal Health and Technical Experts*] (EAIO)
AGHW .... Association of Gardening and Hardware Wholesalers [*British*] (DBA)
AGHWG .... Arctic Goose Habitat Working Group
AGI .... Adjusted Gross Income [*Income taxes*]
AGI .... Adjutant General Inspection (DNAB)
AGI .... Agence Gabonaise d'Information [*Gabonese Information Agency*] (AF)
AGI............ Agenzia Giornalistica Italia [*Press agency*] [*Italy*]
AGI............ Agio Resources Corp. [*Vancouver Stock Exchange symbol*]
AGI............ Agrar-Aviacion SA [*Spain ICAO designator*] (FAAC)
AGI............ Agreement Item (MCD)
AGI............ Air Gunnery Instructor [*British military*] (DMA)
AGI............ Alan Guttmacher Institute (EA)
AGI............ Alliance Graphique Internationale [*International League of Graphic Artists*] [*Zurich, Switzerland*] (EAIO)
AGI............ Alpine Group, Inc. [*AMEX symbol*] (SPSG)
AGI............ American Geographical Institute
AGI............ American Geological Institute (EA)
AGI............ Annual General Inspection [*Army*]
A/GI............ Anti-Gas Instructor [*British military*] (DMA)
AGI............ Associate of the Greek Institute [*British*] (DI)
AGI............ Associate of the Institute of Certificated Grocers [*British*]
AGI............ Augustine Island [*Alaska*] [*Seismograph station code, US Geological Survey*] (SEIS)
AGI............ Auxiliary Intelligence Collection Ship [*Navy*] (CAAL)
AGI............ Gibbons Public Library, Alberta [*Library symbol National Library of Canada*] (NLC)
AGI............ Intelligence Gathering Vessel [*Military*]
AgI............ Silver Iodide [*Pharmacology*] (DAVI)
AGI............ United States Department of Agriculture, Forest Service, Intermountain Forest and Range Experiment Station, Ogden, UT [*OCLC symbol*] (OCLC)
AGIC .... Air-Ground Information Center
AGIC .... Andrus Gerontological Information Center [*University of Southern California*] (IID)
AGIC .... Auto Glass Industry Council (EA)
AGIC .... Automatically-Generated Integrated Circuit (DNAB)
AGICHS .... Auto Glass Industry Committee for Highway Safety [*Later, AGIC*] (EA)
AGICOA .... Association de Gestion Internationale Collective des Oeuvres Audiovisuelles [*Association for the International Collective Management of Audiovisual Works*] [*Geneva, Switzerland*] (EAIO)
AGID .... Agar Gell Immunodiffusion [*Veterinary medicine*]
AGID .... Association of Geoscientists for International Development [*Bangkok, Thailand*] (EAIO)
AGIF........... American GI Forum (OICC)
AGIFORS...... Airline Group of International Federation of Operational Research Societies [*Denmark*] (MCD)
AGII .... Argonaut Group, Inc. [*NASDAQ symbol*] (NQ)
AGIL........... Airborne General Illumination Light
AGILE......... Aspects of Gymnastics and Independent Learning Experience (AIE)
AGILE......... Auto-Graphics Interactive Library Exchange [*Auto-Graphics, Inc.*] [*Information service or system*] (IID)
AGILE......... Autonetics General Information Learning Equipment
AG IMPS HND... Agricultural Implements Hand [*Freight*]
AG IMPS O T HND... Agricultural Implements Other Than Hand [*Freight*]
AGIN .... Action Group on Immigration and Nationality [*British*] (DI)
AGIO .... Armed Guard Inspection Officer
AGIP .... Agence d'Illustrations pour la Presse [*Press Illustrations Agency*] [*French*] (AF)
AGIP .... American Government Income Portfolio, Inc. [*Associated Press*] (SAG)
AGIPA .... Adaptive Ground-Implemented Phased Array [*NASA*]
AGIR .... Ateliers de Gestion Integree des Ressources Limitees [*Canada*]
AGIS .... Acoustographic Imaging System (PDAA)
AGIS .... Air-Ground Integration System
AGIS .... Apex Global Information Services
AGIS .... Apex Global Information Services [*Computer science*]
AGIS .... Apex Global Internet Service [*Computer science*]
AGIS .... Apex Global Internet Services
AGIS .... Armed Guard Inspection Service
AGIS .... Association of Ground Investigation Specialists [*British*] (DBA)
AGIS .... Associazione Generale Italiana dello Spettacolo [*General Italian Entertainments Association*] [*Italy*] (EY)
AGIT........... Agita [*Shake*] [*Pharmacy*]
Agit........... Agitato [*Agitatedly*] [*Music*]
AGIT ANTE SU... Agita Ante Sumendum [*Shake Before Taking*] [*Latin Pharmacy*] (WDAA)
AGIT A US ... Agita ante Usum [*Shake before Using*] [*Pharmacy*]
AGIT BENE... Agita Bene [*Shake Well*] [*Pharmacy*]
AGITO......... Agitato [*Agitatedly*] [*Music*]
AGIT-PROP... Agitation and Propaganda [*Military*]

Agit Vas...... Agitato Vase [*The Vessel Being Shaken*] [*Pharmacy*]
AGJ............ Aguni [*Japan*] [*Airport symbol*] (OAG)
AGJ............ Air Greece SA [*FAA designator*] (FAAC)
AGJ............ Australian Guitar Journal [*A publication*] (APTA)
AGJHS .... American Gathering of Jewish Holocaust Survivors (EA)
AGK .... Roman L. Hruska United States Meat Animal Research Center, Clay Center, NE [*OCLC symbol*] (OCLC)
AGKO .... Arginine, Glutamate, alpha-Ketoglutarate Oxalacetate
AGL............ Above Ground Level
AGL............ Absolute Ground Level (MCD)
AGL............ Acute Granulocytic Leukemia [*Medicine*]
AGL............ Agricultural (ROG)
AGL............ Air Angouleme [*France ICAO designator*] (FAAC)
AGL............ Airborne Gun-Laying
AGL............ American Guild of Luthiers (EA)
AGL............ Aminoglutethimide [*Organic chemistry*] (MAE)
AGL............ Angelica Corp. [*NYSE symbol*] (SPSG)
AGL............ Anglesey [*Welsh island and county*] (ROG)
AGL............ Argon Gas LASER
AGL............ Argon Glow Lamp
AGL............ Argrel Resources Ltd. [*Formerly, Sundance Gold Ltd.*] [*Vancouver Stock Exchange symbol*]
AGL............ Automated Group Learning (PDAA)
AGL............ Automatic Gun-Laying (DEN)
AGL............ Computation Center-Advanced Graphics Laboratory [*University of Texas at Austin*] [*Research center*] (RCD)
AGL............ Glenwood Public Library, Alberta [*Library symbol National Library of Canada*] (NLC)
AGL............ Lighthouse Tender [*Navy symbol Obsolete*]
AGL............ National Agricultural Library, Beltsville, MD [*OCLC symbol*] (OCLC)
AGL............ Wanigela [*Papua New Guinea*] [*Airport symbol*] (OAG)
AGLA .... AGLA [*Australian Government Lawyers' Association*] Bulletin [*A publication*]
AGLA .... Alliance for Gay and Lesbian Artists in the Entertainment Industry [*Defunct*] (EA)
AGLAA .... Association of German Language Authors in America [*Defunct*] (EA)
AGLBIC .... Association for Gay, Lesbian, and Bisexual Issues in Counseling (EA)
AGLC .... Air-to-Ground Liaison Code [*Air Force*]
AGLC .... Alberta Government Libraries' Council (AC)
AGLF.......... Association for Governmental Leasing and Finance [*Washington, DC*] (EA)
AGLF.......... Atlantic Gulf Communities Corp. [*NASDAQ symbol*] (SAG)
AGLIC .... Association for Gay and Lesbian Issues in Counseling [*Later, AGLBIC*] (EA)
AGLINE .... Agriculture Online [*Doane Western, Inc.*] (NITA)
AGLINET ...... Agricultural Libraries Information Network [*Department of Agriculture*] [*Library network*]
AGLINET ...... Agricultural Library Networks [*IAALD*] [*United Kingdom*]
AGLME........ (Acetylglycyl)lysine Methyl Ester Acetate [*Biochemistry*]
AGLO .... Air-Ground Liaison Officer [*Marine Corps*]
AGLOW .... Association of Great Lakes Outdoor Writers (SRA)
AGLP .... Association of Gay and Lesbian Psychiatrists (EA)
AGLR .... Airborne Gun-Laying RADAR (AFM)
AGLS .... Association for General and Liberal Studies (EA)
AGLS .... Gift Lake School, Alberta [*Library symbol National Library of Canada*] (BIB)
AGLSP .... Association of Graduate Liberal Studies Programs (EA)
AGLT.......... Acidified Glycerol Lysis Test [*Clinical chemistry*]
AGLT.......... Airborne Gun-Laying for Turrets
AGLT.......... Automatic Gun-Laying Turrets [*World War II British*]
AGL(T)TRG... Automated Gun Laying (Turret) Training [*British military*] (DMA)
AGM........... Acting Grand Master [*Freemasonry*]
AGM........... Admiralty General Message [*Obsolete British*]
AGM........... Advanced Glass Melter
AGM........... African Green Monkeys [*Virology*]
AGM........... Aircraft Ground Mishap (DOMA)
AGM........... Air Guam [*ICAO designator*] (FAAC)
AGM........... Air-to-Ground Missile
AGM........... Allagash [*Maine*] [*Seismograph station code, US Geological Survey*] (SEIS)
AGM........... Alternative Generator Model (DNAB)
AGM........... American Green Movement (EA)
AGM........... American Guild of Music (EA)
AGM........... Annual General Meeting
AGM........... Assistant General Manager [*AEC*]
AGM........... Associated Grantmakers of Massachusetts (SRA)
AGM........... Association of Good Motorists [*British*] (BI)
AGM........... At Gage Marks (SAA)
AGM........... Attack Guidance Matrix [*Military*] (INF)
AGM........... Attorney General's Ministry [*Canada*]
AGM........... Auxiliary General Missile
AGM........... Avalon Resources, Inc. [*Vancouver Stock Exchange symbol*]
AGM........... Gleichen Municipal Library, Alberta [*Library symbol National Library of Canada*] (NLC)
AGM........... Missile Range Instrumentation Ship [*Navy symbol*]
AGM........... United States Department of Agriculture, Forest Service, Rocky Mountain Station, Fort Collins, CO [*OCLC symbol*] (OCLC)
AGMA .... American Gear Manufacturers Association (EA)
AGMA .... American Guild of Musical Artists (EA)
AGMA .... Amusement Game Manufacturers Association [*Later, AAMA*] (EA)
AGMA .... Assistant General Manager for Administration [*AEC*]
AGMA .... Athletic Goods Manufacturers Association [*Later, SGMA*] (EA)
AGMAP .... Agricultural and Food Products Market Development Assistance Program [*Canada*]

AGMAS .... Association of Government Marketing Assistance Specialists (EA)
AGMAzine .... American Guild of Musical Artists Magazine [*A publication*] (EAAP)
AGMC .... Adelaide Gem and Mineral Club [*Australia*]
AGMC .... Aerospace Guidance and Metrology Center [*Newark Air Force Station, OH*] (AFM)
AGMC .... Association of General Merchandise Chains [*NMRI*] [*Absorbed by*] (EA)
AGMEF........ Ana G. Mendez Educational Foundation
AGMEPS ..... Advisory Group on Management of Electronic Parts Specifications
AGMF .... Agents Master File [*IRS*]
AGMIA .... Assistant General Manager for International Activities [*AEC*]
AgMIL .... Agricultural Materials in Libraries [*Later, Agriculture Library*] [*Online Computer Library Center, Inc.*] [*Information service or system*] (CRD)
AGMIS .... Adjutant General Management Information System
AGMIV .... African Green Monkey Immunodeficiency Virus
AGMK .... African Green Monkey Kidney [*Type of cell line*]
AGMkK .... African Green Monkey Kidney [*Type of cell line*] [*Medicine*] (DMAA)
AGMO .... Assistant General Manager for Operations [*AEC*]
AGMPP .... Assistant General Manager for Plans and Production [*AEC*]
AGMR .... Major Communications Relay Ship [*Navy symbol*]
AGMRD .... Assistant General Manager for Research and Development [*AEC*]
AGMS .... Aircraft Ground Mobility System (MCD)
AGMS .... Air-to-Ground Missile System (RDA)
AGMS .... American Gem Market System [*Information service or system*] (IID)
AGMS .... Australian Guild of Music and Speech
AGMSA .... American Gem and Mineral Suppliers Association (EA)
AGMT .... Agreement (ROG)
AGMT .... Augment (MSA)
AGMTI .... Air-to-Ground Moving Target Indicator
AGMV .... Agropyron Mosaic Virus [*Plant pathology*]
AGN .... Active Galactic Nucleus [*Astronomy*]
AGN .... Acute Glomerulonephritis [*Medicine*]
AGN .... Additive Gaussian Noise
AGN .... Aerojet-General Nucleonics [*of Aerojet-General Corp.*]
AGN .... Again
AGN .... Agana [*Diocesan abbreviation*] [*Guam*] (TOCD)
AGN .... Agincourt [*Canada*] [*Later, OTT*] [*Geomagnetic observatory code*]
AGN .... Agnosia [*Medicine*]
AGN .... Allergan, Inc. [*NYSE symbol*] (SPSG)
AGN .... Angoon [*Alaska*] [*Airport symbol*] (OAG)
AGN .... Argcen Holdings [*Vancouver Stock Exchange symbol*]
AGN .... Articles for the Government of the Navy [*Obsolete*]
AGN .... Augmentation
AGN .... Compagnie Nationale Air Gabon [*ICAO designator*] (FAAC)
AGN .... United States Department of Agriculture, Northern Regional Research Center, Peoria, IL [*OCLC symbol*] (OCLC)
AGNBC........ Advisory Group on National Bibliographic Control
AGNCS......... Nose Creek School, Grovedale, Alberta [*Library symbol National Library of Canada*] (BIB)
AGNCY .... Agency
AGnDE .... American General Delaware LLC [*Associated Press*] (SAG)
Agn Fr .... Agnew on the Statute of Frauds [*A publication*] (DLA)
AGNG .... Aging
AGnHosp..... American General Hospitality Corp. [*Associated Press*] (SAG)
AGNIB.......... Association des Groupements de Negoce Interieur du Bois et des Produits Derives dans les Pays de la CEE [*Association of National Trade Groups for Wood and Derived Products in Countries of the European Economic Community*]
Agnico .... Agnico-Eagle Mines, Inc. [*Associated Press*] (SAG)
AGNIS......... Apollo Guidance and Navigation Industrial Support [*NASA*]
AGNIS......... Azimuth Guidance Nose in Stands (MCD)
AgNO3......... Silver Nitrate [*Pharmacology*] (DAVI)
AgNOR........ Silver-Staining Nucleolar Organizer Region [*Biochemistry*] (DAVI)
AGNOS........ Agnostic
Agn Pat....... Agnew on Patents [*A publication*] (DLA)
AGNPP........ Aboveground Net Primary Production [*Of biomass*]
AGNQ.......... Apollo/GOSS [*Ground Operations Support System*] Navigation Qualifications [*NASA*]
AGNS .... Allied-General Nuclear Services (NRCH)
AGNS .... Automated Ground Network System
AGNS .... Grouard Northland School, Alberta [*Library symbol National Library of Canada*] (BIB)
AGNST........ Against (ROG)
AGNT .... Agent
AGNU .... Agri-Nutrition Group Ltd. [*NASDAQ symbol*] (SAG)
AGNU .... Asociacion Guatemalteca Pro Naciones Unidas [*Guatemala*] (EAIO)
AGNY .... Artists Guild of New York (EA)
AGO .... Adjutant General's Office [*Washington, DC*] [*Army*]
AGO .... Administration Group Office
AGO .... Agitato [*Agitatedly*] [*Music*] (ROG)
AGO .... Air Gunnery Officer
AGO .... Algo Resources Ltd. [*Vancouver Stock Exchange symbol*]
AGO .... American Guild of Organists (EA)
AGO .... Angola [*ANSI three-letter standard code*] (CNC)
AGO .... Angola Air Charter Ltd. [*ICAO designator*] (FAAC)
AGO .... Arresting Gear Officer [*Military*] (MCD)
AGO .... Art Gallery of Ontario [*UTLAS symbol*]
AGO .... Associated Gospel Churches of Canada (AC)
AGO .... Association of Gypsy Organizations [*British*] (DBA)
AGO .... Atmospheric Gas Oil [*Petroleum technology*]
AGO .... Attorney General's Opinions
AGO .... Auditor General's Office
AGO .... Magnolia, AR [*Location identifier FAA*] (FAAL)
AGO .... Santiago, Chile, Tracking Station [*NASA*] (NASA)

AGODDS ..... AGOR [*Auxiliary General Oceanographic Research*] Oceanographic Digital DataSystem (MCD)
AGOE .... Advisory Group for Ocean Engineering [*Society of Naval Architects and Marine Engineers*] (DNAB)
AGOES .... Advanced Geosynchronous Observation Environment Satellite [*NASA*] (NASA)
AGOR .... Auxiliary General Oceanographic Research Ship [*Navy*] (MSC)
AGor .... Gordo Public Library, Gordo, AL [*Library symbol Library of Congress*] (LCLS)
AGOR .... Oceanographic Research Ship
AGOS .... Air-Ground Operations Section [*or School or System*]
AGOS .... American Gynecological and Obstetrical Society (EA)
AGOS .... Aviation Gunnery Officers School
AGOS .... Ocean Surveillance Ship [*Navy*] (CAAL)
AGOSP........ Ad Hoc Advisory Group on Science Programs [*Terminated, 1976*] [*National Science Foundation*] (EGAO)
AGOSS........ Automated Ground Operations Scheduling System [*Also, AUTO-GOSS*] (MCD)
AGOTUOC ... [*A*] Gentleman of the University of Cambridge [*Pseudonym used by Owen Manning*]
Agourn .... Agouron Pharmaceuticals, Inc. [*Associated Press*] (SAG)
AGP .... Accelerated Graphics Port [*Computer science*]
AGP .... Accelerated Graphics Port [*Computer science*]
AGP .... Acid Glycoprotein [*Biochemistry*]
AGP .... Adjutant General Pool [*for Army officers*]
AGP .... Advanced Graphics Port [*Intel*] [*Computer science*]
AGP .... Advanced Guided Projectile (MCD)
AGP .... Agar Gel Precipitation [*Biochemistry*] (DMAA)
AGP .... Agence Gabonaise de Presse [*Gabonese Press Agency*] (AF)
AGP .... Agence Guineenne de Presse [*Guinean Press Agency*] (AF)
AGP .... Agreement on Government Procurement (AAGC)
AGP .... Aircraft Grounded for Lack of Parts
AGP .... Aircraft Gun Pod (NG)
AGP .... Air Tara Ltd. [*Republic of Ireland*] [*ICAO designator*] (FAAC)
AGP .... American Life Group, Inc. [*NYSE symbol*] (SAG)
AGP .... American Pad & Paper [*NYSE symbol*] (SAG)
AGP .... American Pad & Paper [*Stock exchange term*]
AGP .... Anthology of German Poetry through the Nineteenth Century [*A publication*]
AGP .... Antisymmetrized Geminal Power [*Chemical physics*]
AGP .... Arabinogalactan Protein [*Biochemistry*]
AGP .... Argonaut Resources Ltd. [*Vancouver Stock Exchange symbol*]
AGP .... Army Ground Pool [*for officers*]
AGP .... Army Group
AGP .... Asom Gana Parishad [*Assam People's Council*] [*India*] [*Political party*] (FEA)
AGP .... Association of Gay Psychologists [*Later, ALGP*] (EA)
AGP .... Association of Gut Processors [*British*] (BI)
AGP .... Australian Gruen Party [*Political party*]
AGP .... Automatic Guidance Programming (NATG)
AGP .... Auxiliary Generating Plant [*Aviation*] (AIA)
AGP .... Average Goals Against per Period [*Hockey*]
AGP .... Grande Prairie Public Library, Alberta [*Library symbol National Library of Canada*] (NLC)
AGP .... Malaga [*Spain*] [*Airport symbol*] (OAG)
AGP .... Motor Torpedo Boat Tender [*Navy symbol Obsolete*]
AGP .... Pacific Southwest Forest and Range Experiment Station, Berkeley, CA [*OCLC symbol*] (OCLC)
AGP .... Patrol Craft Tender [*Navy symbol*]
AGPA .... American Group Practice Association (EA)
AGPA .... American Group Psychotherapy Association (EA)
AGPA .... Ammunition Group - Picatinny Arsenal (MCD)
AGPAEA ...... Association de Gestion Portuaire de l'Afrique de l'Est et de l'Afrique Australe [*Port Management Association of Eastern and Southern Africa - PMAESA*] (EAIO)
AGPAM .... American Guild of Patient Account Management (EA)
AGP & Co ... AGP & Company, Inc. [*Associated Press*] (SAG)
AGPB .... Advanced General Purpose Bomb (MCD)
AGPC .... Adjutant General Publications Center [*Army*]
AGPC .... AGP & Co., Inc. [*NASDAQ symbol*] (SAG)
AGPC .... Grande Prairie College, Alberta [*Library symbol National Library of Canada*] (NLC)
AGPCH........ Association of General Practitioner Community Hospitals [*British*] (EAIO)
AGP-CNO .... Assemblee Generale Permanente des Comites Nationaux Olympiques [*Permanent General Assembly of National Olympic Committees*]
AGPDC........ Aeronutronic General Perturbations Differential Correction Program
AGPES .... Penson Elementary School, Grovedale, Alberta [*Library symbol National Library of Canada*] (BIB)
AGPGS........ Grandview Colony School, Grande Prairie, Alberta [*Library symbol National Library of Canada*] (BIB)
AGPH .... Agouron Pharmaceuticals, Inc. [*NASDAQ symbol*] (NQ)
AGPH .... Grande Prairie Regional Hospital, Alberta [*Library symbol National Library of Canada*] (NLC)
AGPHBS...... Harry Balfour School, Grande Prairie, Alberta [*Library symbol National Library of Canada*] (BIB)
AGPHS......... Holy Cross School, Grande Prairie, Alberta [*Library symbol National Library of Canada*] (BIB)
AGPI .... Agar Gel Precipitin Inhibition (DMAA)
AGPI .... Automatic Ground Position Indicator [*Military*]
AGPKS .... Kateri Mission School, Grande Prairie, Alberta [*Library symbol National Library of Canada*] (BIB)
AGPM .... Associated Glass and Pottery Manufacturers (EA)
AGPMR .... Agricultural Property Management Regulations

AgPp............ Aggregates of P-Protein [*Botany*]
AGPP.......... Association for Group Psychoanalysis and Process (EA)
AGPPI........ American Grain Products Processing Institute [*Defunct*] (EA)
AGPR.......... Agricultural Procurement Regulations
AGPR.......... Department of Agriculture Procurement Regulation [*A publication*] (AAGC)
AGPS.......... Automatic Gun Positioning System
AGPS.......... St. Patrick Community School, Grande Prairie, Alberta [*Library symbol National Library of Canada*] (BIB)
AGPSCS...... St. Clement School, Grande Prairie, Alberta [*Library symbol National Library of Canada*] (BIB)
AGPSGS...... St. Gerard School, Grande Prairie, Alberta [*Library symbol National Library of Canada*] (BIB)
AGPSJS ...... St. Joseph School, Grande Prairie, Alberta [*Library symbol National Library of Canada*] (BIB)
AGPT .... Agar-Gel Precipitation Test [*Clinical chemistry*]
AGPTT .... Aerial Gunnery Part Task Trainer (MCD)
AGPU.......... Aviation Ground Power Unit (MCD)
AGQ .... Agrinion [*Greece*] [*Airport symbol*] (AD)
AGQ .... Ambergate Exploration [*Vancouver Stock Exchange symbol*]
AGQ .... Association de Golf du Quebec (AC)
AGQ .... Association des Graveurs du Quebec [*1971, CGQ from 1978, CQE from 1984*] [*Canada*] (NGC)
AGQ .... United States Department of Agriculture, Southern Forest Experiment Station, N ew Orleans, LA [*OCLC symbol*] (OCLC)
AGQT .... Attorney General of the Queen's Troop [*Military British*] (ROG)
AGR .... Active Guard and Reserve [*Military*] (DOMA)
AGR .... Active Guard Reserve [*DoD*]
AGR .... Additional Government Requirement (AAGC)
AGR .... Advanced Gas-Cooled Reactor [*British*]
agr.............. Aggregate (VRA)
AGR .... Agra [*India*] [*Airport symbol*] (OAG)
AGR .... Agra [*India*] [*Seismograph station code, US Geological Survey Closed*] (SEIS)
AGR .... Agra Industries Ltd. [*Toronto Stock Exchange symbol*]
AGR .... Agree (FAAC)
Agr............. Agricola [*of Tacitus*] [*Classical studies*] (OCD)
AGR .... Agricultural [*or Agriculture*]
Agr............. Agricultural (DD)
AGR .... Agricultural Research Services, Animal Health Division [*Department of Agriculture ICAO designator*] (FAAC)
Agr.............. Agriculture (DD)
AGR .... Agriculture Division [*Census*] (OICC)
AGR .... Air-to-Ground Ranging
AGR .... Air-to-Ground Rocket (MCD)
AGR .... Alien Grange
AGR .... Amiridia, Genitourinary Abnormalities, and Mental Retardation [*Medicine*] (DMAA)
AGR .... Annual Growth Rate
AGR .... Anticipatory Goal Response [*Medicine*]
AGR .... Association of Graduate Recruiters [*British*] (DBA)
AGR .... Auditor General's Report [*Canada Information service or system*] (IID)
AGR .... Autonetics Generalized Reset
AGR .... Avon Park, FL [*Location identifier FAA*] (FAAL)
AGR .... Corporacion Bancaria de Espana [*NYSE symbol*] (SAG)
Agr............. De Agricultura [*Philo*] (BJA)
AGR .... Faulty Agreement [*Used in correcting manuscripts, etc.*]
AGR .... Granum Public Library, Alberta [*Library symbol National Library of Canada*] (NLC)
AGR .... RADAR Picket Ship [*Navy symbol*]
AGR .... United States Department of Agriculture, Russell Agricultural Research Center, Athens, GA [*OCLC symbol*] (OCLC)
AGRA.......... AGORA-GENERAL [*Agence France-Presse*] [*Information service or system*] (CRD)
Agra.......... Agra High Court Reports [*India*] [*A publication*] (ILCA)
AGRA.......... Army Group Royal Artillery [*British*]
AGRA.......... Association of Genealogists and Record Agents [*British*] (EAIO)
AGRA.......... Automatic Gain Ranging Amplifier (MCD)
Agra FB ...... Agra Full Bench Rulings [*India*] [*A publication*] (ILCA)
Agra HC...... Agra High Court Reports [*India*] [*A publication*] (DLA)
Agrartud Egy Kozl... Agrartudomanyi Egyetem Koezlemenyei [*A publication*]
AGRAS........ Antiglare, Antireflective, Antistatic [*Cathode ray tube treatment*] (PCM)
AGRAS........ Grassland Public Library, Alberta [*Library symbol National Library of Canada*] (NLC)
AGR C.......... Agreed Case [*Legal term*] (DLA)
AGRC.......... American Graves Registration Command [*Military*]
AGRCLT...... Agriculture
AGRCO........ American Graves Registration Command [*Military*]
AGRE.......... American Greetings Corp. [*NASDAQ symbol*] (NQ)
AGRE.......... Army Group, Royal Engineers [*British and Canadian*] [*World War II*]
AGRE.......... Atlantic Gas Research Exchange
AGRECE...... Agrupacion de Exportadores del Centro de Espana [*Trade association*] [*Spain*] (EY)
AGREE........ Advanced Ground Receiving Equipment Experiment [*NASA*] (PDAA)
AGREE........ Advisory Group on Reliability of Electronic Equipment [*Military*] (MHDB)
AgreeRit...... Agree Realty Corp. [*Associated Press*] (SAG)
AGREET ...... Agreement (ROG)
AGreet........ American Greetings Corp. [*Associated Press*] (SAG)
AGREMC...... Assemblee des Gestionnaires de Reseaux Electriques Municipalises et Cooperatives [*Assembly of Managers of Municipal and Cooperative Electrical Systems*] [*Canada*]
AgrEng........ Agricultural Engineering (DD)
Ag Rep .... Agricultural Representative [*Canada*]

AGRF .... American Geriatric Research Foundation [*Later, ARI*]
AGRI .... Agriculture (DLA)
AGRI .... AgriDyne Technologies, Inc. [*NASDAQ symbol*] (SAG)
AGRI .... American Genealogical Research Institute
AgriBio........ AgriBioTech, Inc. [*Associated Press*] (SAG)
AGRIC......... Agriculture
AGRIC......... Agriculture Canada
Agric & Mkts... Agriculture and Markets [*A publication*] (DLA)
Agric C .... Agricultural Code [*A publication*] (DLA)
AGRICC........ Automatic Generation and Retrieval of Information on Chemical Components (PDAA)
Agric Dec..... Agricultural Decisions [*A publication*] (DLA)
AGRICOLA ... Agricultural On-Line Access [*Formerly, CAIN*] [*National Agricultural Library, Information Systems Division Bibliographic database*] [*Information service or system*] (IID)
Agric Tech ... Agricultural Technologist [*A publication*]
AgriDyn........ AgriDyne Technologies, Inc. [*Associated Press*] (SAG)
AGRIMATION... Agricultural Automation
AGRINDEX... Agricultural Research Information Index [*United Nations*]
AgriNutr...... Agri-Nutrition Group [*Associated Press*] (SAG)
AGRIS.......... International Information System for the Agricultural Sciences and Technology [*Food and Agriculture Organization*] [*United Nations Information service or system*] (IID)
AGRISTARS... Agriculture and Resources Inventory Surveys through Aerospace (MCD)
AgRISTARS... Agriculture and Resources Inventory Survey through Aerospace Remote Sensing
Agrium........ Agrium, Inc. [*Associated Press*] (SAG)
AGRL .... Agricultural
AGRM .... Adjutant-General of the Royal Marines [*British*]
AGRM .... Agreement (AABC)
AGRMT .... Agreement (FAAC)
AGRO.......... Americas Growth Fund, Inc. [*NASDAQ symbol*] (SAG)
AGROINFORM... Agricultural Information Services [*HUD Information service or system*] (IID)
AGROINFORM... Information Center of the Ministry of Agriculture and Food [*Ministry of Agriculture and Food*] [*Information service or system*] (IID)
AGROMASH... Mezhdunarodnoe Obshchestvo po Mashinam dlja Ovoshchevodstva, Sadovodstva, i Vinogradstva [*International Association for Vine, Fruit, and Vegetable-Growing Mechanization*] (EAIO)
AGROMEK... International Exhibition for Agricultural Mechanization and Breeding Stock
AGRON .... Agronomy
AGROSTAT... Food and Agriculture Organization Statistical Division Information System (GFGA)
AGROT........ Agrotikon Komma [*Agrarian Party*] [*Greek Political party*] (PPE)
AGRP.......... [*The*] Associated Group, Inc. [*NASDAQ symbol*] (SAG)
AGRR.......... Angora Goat Record and Registry (EA)
Agr Rust Orig... De Agricultura or De Re Rustica Origines [*of Cato*] [*Classical studies*] (OCD)
AGRS .... Acid Gas Removal System [*Chemical engineering*]
AGRS .... American Graves Registration Service [*Military*]
AGRT .... Agreement
AGRT .... Automatic Guard Receiver Terminals [*Navy*] (MCD)
AGS .... Abort Guidance Section [*NASA*] (KSC)
AGS .... Abort Guidance System [*or Subsystem*] [*Apollo*] [*NASA*]
AGS .... Acoustic Guidance SONAR (HGAA)
AGS .... Adipic, Glutaric, and Succinic [*Acids for flue-gas cleaning*]
AGS .... Adrenogenital Syndrome [*Medicine*]
AGS .... Advanced Genetic Sciences, Inc.
AGS .... Advanced Graduate Specialist (GAGS)
AGS .... Advanced Graphics Software, Inc. (PCM)
AGS .... Advanced Guidance System
AGS .... Aero Gun Sights
AGS .... Agencies (EY)
AGS .... Airborne Gunsight
AGS .... Aircraft General Standards [*British*]
AGS .... Aircraft Generation Squadron (MCD)
AGS .... Air Gambia [*ICAO designator*] (FAAC)
AGS .... Air Grease System (PDAA)
AGS .... Air-Ground System
AGS .... Air Gunnery School [*British*] (OA)
AGS .... [*The*] Alabama Great Southern Railroad Co. [*AAR code*]
AGS .... Alberta Genealogical Society (AC)
AGS .... Allied Geographic Section [*Southwest Pacific*] [*Obsolete*]
AGS .... Alpine Garden Society (EA)
AGS .... Alternating Gradient Synchrotron
AGS .... Alternating Guidance Section
AGS .... American Gem Society (EA)
AGS .... American Geographical Society (EA)
AGS .... American Geriatrics Society (EA)
AGS .... American Gesneria Society [*Later, GSI*] (EA)
AGS .... American Glovebox Society (EA)
AGS .... American Gloxinia Society [*Later, AGGS*] (EA)
AGS .... American Goat Society (EA)
AGS .... American Golf Sponsors (EA)
AGS .... American Gourd Society (EA)
AGS .... American Graphological Society (EA)
AGS .... American Gynecological Society [*Later, AGOS*] (EA)
AGS .... Anesthetic Gas Standards
AGS .... Angus [*County in Scotland*] (ROG)
AGS .... Angus Resources Ltd. [*Vancouver Stock Exchange symbol*]
AGS .... Animated Graphics System (WDMC)
AGS .... Annulus Gas System [*Nuclear energy*] (NRCH)

AGS	Antigravity Suit [*NASA*] (MCD)
AGS	Armed Guard School
AGS	Armored Gun System [*Army*]
AGS	Army General Staff
AGS	Arnold's Geological Series
AGS	Artificial Gravity Structure
AGS	Ascent Guidance and Control System [*NASA*] (KSC)
AGS	Assistant General Secretary (DCTA)
AGS	Assistant Grand Sojourner [*Freemasonry*]
AGS	Associate in General Studies
AGS	Association for Gravestone Studies (EA)
AGS	Association of Graduate Schools in Association of American Universities (EA)
AGS	Atlantic Generating Station [*Nuclear energy*] (NRCH)
AGS	Atlantic Geoscience Association
AGS	Augusta [*Georgia*] [*Airport symbol*]
AGS	Australian Geographical Studies [*A publication*]
AGS	Australian Geriatrics' Society
AGS	Automatic Gain Stabilization
AGS	Auxiliary General Survey [*Navy*] (MSC)
AGS	Gadsden State Junior College, Gadsden, AL [*Library symbol Library of Congress*] (LCLS)
AGS	Surveying Ship [*Navy symbol*]
AGS	United States Department of Agriculture, Southern Regional Research Center, New Orleans, LA [*OCLC symbol*] (OCLC)
AGSA	American Grooming Shop Association (EA)
AGSA	Art Gallery of South Australia
AGSA	Art Glass Suppliers Association (EA)
AGSA	Australasian Genetic Support Group Association
AGSAN	Astronomical Guidance System for Air Navigation (OA)
AGS ARMT.	Armored Gun System, Armament [*Army*] (RDA)
AGSAS	Andy Griffith Show Appreciation Society (EA)
AGSC	Advanced Graduate Specialist Certificate (PGP)
AGSC	Australian Guild of Screen Composers
AGSC	Coastal Surveying Ship
AGSCC	Army General Supplies Commodity Center
AGSCPO	Army General Staff Civilian Personnel Office, Office of the Chief of Staff
AGSD	Advanced Ground Segment Design (SSD)
AGSD	Association for Glycogen Storage Disease (EA)
AGSE	Aerospace Ground Support Equipment
AGSE	Aircraft Ground Support Equipment (MCD)
AGSES	Association of Girl Scout Executive Staff (EA)
AGSG	Alliance of Genetic Support Groups (EA)
AGSI	Automatic Government Source Inspection
AGSIDC	Arab Gulf States Information Documentation Center [*Information service or system*] (IID)
AGSIM	American Graduate School of International Management [*Formerly, Thunderbird Graduate School of International Management*] [*Glendale, AZ*]
AGSL	Satellite Launching Ship [*Navy symbol Obsolete*]
AGSM	American Gold Star Mothers (EA)
AGSM	Anti-G [*Gravity*] Straining Maneuver (DOMA)
AGSM	Associate of the Guildhall School of Music [*British*]
AGSM	Australian Graduate of the School of Management (ODBW)
AGSN	Ambiguous Genitalia Support Network (PAZ)
AGSO	Australian Geological Survey Organisation
AGSO	Australian Geological Survey Organisation [*Formerly, BMR - Bureau of Mineral Resources*]
AGSO	Australian Government Solicitors' Office
AGSP	Alignment Group Sensing Platform (AAG)
AGSP	Atlas General Survey Program (IEEE)
AGSPW	Association of Girl Scout Professional Workers [*Later, AGSES*] (EA)
AGSq	Aircraft Generation Squadron [*Air Force*]
AGSR	Advanced Ground Surveillance RADAR (MCD)
AGSR	All-Weather Ground Surveillance RADAR
AGSRO	Association of Government Supervisors and Radio Officers [*British*]
AGS-RTO	Automatic Ground Spoiler - Rejected Takeoff (MCD)
AGSS	American Geographical and Statistical Society
AGSS	Attitude Ground Support System (MCD)
AGSS	Auxiliary Submarine [*Navy symbol*]
AGST	Against
AGSV	Ag Services of America, Inc. [*NASDAQ symbol*] (SAG)
AgSvcs	Ag Services of America, Inc. [*Associated Press*] (SAG)
AGSW	Air-to-Ground Standoff Weapon (MCD)
AGT	Above Ground Test [*Defense Nuclear Agency*]
AGT	Adage Graphics Terminal
AGT	Additional Gunner Training (MCD)
AGT	Adrenoglomerulotrophin [*Medicine*] (MEDA)
AGT	Advanced Gas Turbine
AGT	Advanced Ground Transport
AGT	Advanced Guidance Technology [*SAMSO*] [*Air Force*] (MCD)
AGT	Advanced Gun Technology (DOMA)
AGT	Against
AGT	Agent (AABC)
agt	Agent (WDMC)
agt	Agreement (WDMC)
AGT	Agreement
AGT	Aircraft Gas and Turbine
AGT	Alberta Government Telephones [*Part of Telecom Canada*] [*Calgary, AB*] [*Telecommunications service*] (TSSD)
AGT	Allison Gas Turbine [*Engine*]
AGT	Amadeus Global Travel Distrution SA [*Spain ICAO designator*] (FAAC)
AGT	American General Hospitality Corp. [*NYSE symbol*] (SAG)

AGT	American Government Term Trust [*NYSE symbol*] (SPSG)
AGT	Aminoglutethimide [*Antineoplastic drug*] (CDI)
AGT	Antiglobulin Test [*Hematology*]
AGT	Army Gunner Training (MCD)
AGT	Arresting Gear Tester
AGT	Audiographic Teleconference
AGT	Automated Guideway Transit [*TRB*] (TAG)
AGT	Aviation Gas Turbine (KSC)
AGT	Target Service Ship [*Navy symbol*] (DNAB)
AGT	United States Department of Agriculture, Food Safety and Quality Service Library- Agricultural South Building, Washington, DC [*OCLC symbol*] (OCLC)
AGTA	Agence Generale de Transit en Afrique [*General Transit Agency in Afica*] [*Congo*]
AGTA	Airline Ground Transportation Association [*Defunct*] (EA)
AGTA	Airport Ground Transportation Association (EA)
AGTA	American Gem Trade Association (EA)
AGTC	Airport Ground Traffic Control [*Department of Transportation*]
AGTD	Athletic Goods Team Distributors (EA)
AGTDC	Accord General sur les Tarifs Douaniers et le Commerce [*General Agreement on Tariffs and Trade*] [*Switzerland*] (EAIO)
AGTE	Association of Group Travel Executives
AGTELIS	Army Ground Transportable Emitter Location Identification System
AGTELIS	Automatic Ground Transportable Emitter Location and Identification System [*Army*]
AGTH	Adrenoglomerulotropin Hormone [*Endocrinology*] (MAE)
AGTI	Allein Gott Traue Ich [*I Trust in God Alone*] [*Motto of Dorothee, Duchess of Braunschweig-Lunebert (1546-1617)*] [*German*]
AGTI	Association of Geography Teachers of Ireland (AIE)
AGTOA	American Greyhound Track Operators Association (EA)
AGTP	Automatically Generated Test Analysis and Programs (MCD)
AGTr	Adrenoglomerulotrophin [*Also, ASH*] [*Endocrinology*]
AGTR	Agitator [*FBI standardized term*]
AGTR	Technical Research Ship [*Navy symbol*]
AGTS	Advanced Gunnery Target Systems (MCD)
AGTS	Aerial Gunnery Target System (MCD)
AGTS	Association for Gifted and Talented Students (EA)
AGTS	Automated Gyro Test Set
AGTT	Abnormal Glucose Tolerance Test [*Medicine*]
AGTT	Aerial Gunnery TOW Target (MCD)
AGTT	American Government Term Trust [*Associated Press*] (SAG)
AGTV	Active-Gated Television (PDAA)
AGTV	Advanced Ground Transportation Vehicle (PDAA)
AGTX	Applied Graphics Technologies, Inc. [*NASDAQ symbol*] (SAG)
AGU	Address-Generation Unit [*Computer science*]
AGU	Aerospace Ground Unit
AGU	Agrium, Inc. [*NYSE symbol*] (SAG)
AGU	Aguascalientes [*Mexico*] [*Airport symbol*] (OAG)
AGU	All Got Up (ADA)
AGU	American Agricultural Economics Documentation Center, Washington, DC [*OCLC symbol*] (OCLC)
AGU	American Geophysical Union (EA)
AGU	Angle Resources Ltd. [*Vancouver Stock Exchange symbol*]
AGU	Anhydroglucose Unit [*Biochemistry*]
AGU	Automatic Ground Unit
AGU	Aviation Ground Unit [*Naval Reserve*]
AGU	Societe Anonyme de Transports Aeriens Air-Guadeloupe [*France ICAO designator*] (FAAC)
AGUS	Atypical Glandular Cells of Undetermined Significance [*Gynecology*]
AGV	Acarigua [*Venezuela*] [*Airport symbol*] (OAG)
AGV	Air Glaciers SA [*Switzerland ICAO designator*] (FAAC)
AGV	Alkali-Gravity-Viscosity [*Glass technology*]
AGV	Aniline Gentian Violet
AGV	Argyle Ventures [*Vancouver Stock Exchange symbol*]
AGV	Automatic Guided Vehicle [*Robotic manufacturing equipment*]
AGV	Avion a Grande Vitesse [*French high-speed train*]
AGV	United States Department of Agriculture, Cooperative Information System Agriculture Canada Library, Ontario, ON, Canada [*OCLC symbol*] (OCLC)
AGVA	American Guild of Variety Artists (EA)
AGVC	Alberta Vocational Centre, Grouard, Alberta [*Library symbol National Library of Canada*] (NLC)
AGVC	Automatic Governing Valve Control [*Nuclear energy*] (NRCH)
AGVG	Anglo-German Variable Geometry [*Avaition*] (PDAA)
AGVGA	American Greenhouse Vegetable Growers Association (EA)
AGVM	Girouxville Public Library, Alberta [*Library symbol National Library of Canada*] (NLC)
AGVS	Air-to-Ground Voice System [*or Subsystem*] (MCD)
AGVS	Automatic Guided Vehicle System [*Robotics*]
AGVS	Automatic Guided Vehicle Systems (EA)
AGVT	Advanced Ground Vehicle Technology Project [*Army*]
AGW	Acoustic-Gravity Wave
AGW	Actual Gross Weight [*Railroads*]
agw	Actual Gross Weight (ODBW)
AGW	Adjusted Gross Weight (MCD)
AGW	Advanced Graphics Workstation [*Auto-trol Technology Corp.*] (NITA)
AGW	Air Gap Width
AGW	Allowable [*Takeoff*] Gross Weight [*for an aircraft*]
AGW	Alternate Gross Weight
AGW	Association of Golf Writers (EAIO)
AGW	Autonomous Guided Weapon (DOMA)
AGW	Avia Airlines [*South Africa*] [*FAA designator*] (FAAC)
AGW	United States Department of Agriculture, Western Regional Research Center, Berkeley, CA [*OCLC symbol*] (OCLC)
AGWAR	Adjutant General, War Department [*Obsolete*]

AGWHS........ Holy Family School, Grimshaw, Alberta [*Library symbol National Library of Canada*] (BIB)
AGWI .... American Gulf West Indies Co.
AGWI .... Atlantic, Gulf, West Indies [*Marine insurance*] (ODBW)
AGWKS....... Kennedy Elementary School, Grimshaw, Alberta [*Library symbol National Library of Canada*] (BIB)
AGWM .... Grimshaw WI Municipal Library, Alberta [*Library symbol National Library of Canada*] (NLC)
agwr .... Agateware (VRA)
AGWS .... Advanced Gun Weapon System (MCD)
AGWS .... Australian-German Welfare Society
AGWS .... Australian-Greek Welfare Society
AGWS .... Grimshaw Junior/Senior High School, Alberta [*Library symbol National Library of Canada*] (BIB)
AGWSE .... Association of Ground Water Scientists and Engineers (EA)
AGWT .... American Ground Water Trust (EA)
AGWU .... Australian Glass Workers' Union
AGX .... Agincourt Exploration, Inc. [*Vancouver Stock Exchange symbol*]
AGX .... Araguacema [*Brazil*] [*Airport symbol*] (AD)
AGX .... Aviogenex [*Yugoslavia*] [*ICAO designator*] (FAAC)
AGY .... Aero Flight Service, Inc. [*FAA designator*] (FAAC)
AGY .... Aeroguayacan [*Chile*] [*ICAO designator*] (FAAC)
AGY .... Agency (ADA)
AGY .... Argosy Gaming Co. [*NYSE symbol*] (SAG)
AGY .... Argosy Mining Corp. Ltd. [*Toronto Stock Exchange symbol*]
AGZ .... Actual Ground Zero [*Nuclear explosions*]
AGZ .... Actual Ground Zone (MUGU)
AGZ .... Agassiz Resources Ltd. [*Toronto Stock Exchange symbol*]
AGZ .... Aggeneys [*South Africa*] [*Airport symbol*] (OAG)
AGZ .... Agri [*Turkey*] [*Airport symbol*] (AD)
AGZ .... Agrolet-Mci Ltd. [*Slovakia*] [*FAA designator*] (FAAC)
AH .... Abdominal Hysterectomy [*Medicine*]
aH .... Abhenry [*Unit of inductance*]
AH .... Absorptive Hypercalciuria [*Medicine*] (DMAA)
AH .... Academy of Homiletics (EA)
AH .... Accelerated Hypertension [*Medicine*]
AH .... Acceptor Handshake (MHDI)
AH .... Access for the Handicapped [*Defunct*] (EA)
AH .... Accidental Hypothermia [*Medicine*]
AH .... Accumulator High [*Computer science*]
AH .... Acetohexamide [*Pharmacology*] (DAVI)
AH .... Adenomatous Hyperplasia [*Medicine*]
AH .... Adult Heart
AH .... After Hatch [*Shipping*]
AH .... After Hours (ADA)
AH .... After-Hyperpolarization [*Also, AHP*] [*Neurophysiology*]
AH .... Agriculture Handbook
AH .... Agudas Haraborim [*Union of Orthodox Rabbis of the United States and Canada*]
Ah .... Ahikar (BJA)
Ah .... Ahilot (BJA)
AH .... Air Algerie [*ICAO designator*] (AD)
AH .... Aircraft Handler [*British*]
AH .... Air-Cushion Vehicle built by Ajax Hovercraft [*England*] [*Usually used in combination with numerals*]
AH .... Airfield Heliport
A/H .... Air Handling [*Nuclear energy*] (NRCH)
A/H .... Air Over Hydraulic (AAG)
AH .... Alan Hutchison Publishing Ltd. [*British*]
AH .... Alcoholic Hepatitis [*Medicine*]
AH .... Alfred Holt [*Blue Funnel Line*] [*Steamship*] (MHDB)
AH .... Allen & Hanburys [*Great Britain*] [*Research code symbol*]
AH .... Allied Health Program [*Association of Independent Colleges and Schools specialization code*]
AH .... Allowance Holder [*Environmental Protection Agency*] (GFGA)
AH .... Alter Heading [*Navigation*]
AH .... Alternate Headquarters [*Military*] (NVT)
AH .... Amenorrhea and Hirsutism [*Endocrinology*] (MAE)
A/H .... Amenorrhea/Hyperprolactinemia [*Endocrinology*]
AH .... American Hebrew (BJA)
AH .... American Heritage [*A publication*] (BRI)
AH .... American Horizons [*Defunct*] (EA)
AH .... American Humanics (EA)
AH .... Aminohippurate (MAE)
A H .... Ampere Hour
Ah .... Ampere Hour (IDOE)
AH .... Analog Hybrid (OA)
AH .... Anhydrous Hydrazine [*Rocket propellant*]
AH .... Animal Husbandry Research Division [*of ARS, Department of Agriculture*]
AH .... Anno Hebraico [*In the Hebrew Year*] [*Since 3761 BC*] [*Latin*]
AH .... Anno Hegirae [*In the Year of the Hegira*] [*The flight of Mohammed from Mecca AD 622*] [*Latin*]
AH .... Anterior Hypothalamic Nucleus [*Brain anatomy*]
AH .... Antihalation
AH .... Antihunt [*Circuit*] [*Electronics*]
AH .... Antihyaluronidase [*Clinical chemistry*]
A/H .... Antwerp/Hamburg [*Range of ports between and including these two cities*] [*Shipping*] (DS)
AH .... Apache Helicopter [*Anti-armor attack helicopter*]
AH .... Aqueous Humor [*Anatomy*] (CPH)
AH .... Army Helicopter [*British military*] (DMA)
AH .... Army Hospital
AH .... Arterial Hypertension [*Medicine*]
AH .... Artificial Heart [*Medicine*]

AH .... Artificial Horizon (MCD)
AH .... Arts and Humanities
AH .... Ascites Hepatoma [*Medicine*]
AH .... Asia House [*An association*] (EA)
AH .... Association of Headmistresses [*British*] (DI)
AH .... Association of Hispanists [*British*]
AH .... Astigmatism, Hypermetropic [*Also, AsH*] [*Ophthalmology*]
AH .... At Home
AH .... Atrial His-Bundle [*Cardiology*]
AH .... Attack Heavy (DNAB)
AH .... Attack Helicopter (CINC)
AH .... Attitude Hold (MCD)
aH .... Attohenry (IDOE)
AH .... Authentication Header [*Computer science*]
AH .... Autonomic Hyperreflexia [*Medicine*]
AH .... Available Hours [*Electronics*] (IEEE)
ah--- .... Himalaya Mountain Region [*MARC geographic area code Library of Congress*] (LCCP)
AH .... Hinton Public Library, Alberta [*Library symbol National Library of Canada*] (NLC)
AH .... Hospital Ship [*Navy symbol*]
AH .... Huntsville Public Library, Huntsville, AL [*Library symbol Library of Congress*] (LCLS)
AHA .... Acetohydroxamic Acid [*Medicine*] (DMAA)
AHA .... Acquired Hemolytic Anemia [*Medicine*] (MAE)
AHA .... Additive Histologic Assessment [*Medicine*]
AHA .... Adirondack Historical Association (EA)
AHA .... Agricultural and Horticultural Engineering Abstracts [*A publication*]
AHA .... AHA Automotive Technologies Corp. [*Toronto Stock Exchange symbol*]
AHA .... Ahua [*Hawaii*] [*Seismograph station code, US Geological Survey*] (SEIS)
AHA .... Air Alpha, AS [*Denmark*] [*ICAO designator*] (FAAC)
AHA .... Alabama Hospitality Association (SRA)
AHA .... Alberta Healthcare Association [*Formerly, Alberta Hospital Association*] (AC)
AHA .... Alberta Hospital Association [*Edmonton*]
AHA .... Alert Holding Area [*Military*] (DOMA)
AHA .... All Hope Abandoned [*Union*] [*British*] (DGA)
AHA .... Alpha-Hydroxy Acid [*Organic chemistry*]
AHA .... Alpha Industries, Inc. [*AMEX symbol*] (SPSG)
AHA .... American Habonim Association [*Later, Labor Zionist Alliance*]
AHA .... American Hardboard Association (EA)
AHA .... American Healing Association [*Defunct*] (EA)
AHA .... American Health Association (EA)
AHA .... American Heart Association (EA)
AHA .... American Hellenic Alliance (EA)
AHA .... American Hepatitis Association (EA)
AHA .... American Herb Association (EA)
AHA .... American Hereford Association (EA)
AHA .... American Herens Association (EA)
AHA .... American Historical Association (EA)
AHA .... American Hitchhiker Association
AHA .... American Hobbit Association (EA)
AHA .... American Homebrewers Association (EA)
AHA .... American Homeowners Association [*Defunct*] (EA)
AHA .... American Hominological Association (EA)
AHA .... American Hospital Association (EA)
AHA .... American Hotel Association [*Later, AH & MA*]
AHA .... American Hound Association
AHA .... American Hovercraft Association [*Superseded by HA*] (EA)
AHA .... American Humane Association (EA)
AHA .... American Humanist Association (EA)
AHA .... American Hydrogen Association (EA)
AHA .... American Hypnosis Association (EA)
AHA .... American Hypnotists' Association (EA)
AHA .... Anterior Hypothalamic Area
AHA .... Anti-Heart Antibody [*Medicine*] (DMAA)
AHA .... Antihistone Antibody [*Medicine*] (DMAA)
AHA .... Area Health Authority
AHA .... Arkansas Hospital Association (SRA)
AHA .... Arkansas Hospitality Association (SRA)
AHA .... Aspartyl-Hydroxamic Acid (MAE)
AHA .... Associate, Institute of Hospital Administrators [*or Administration*] (DAVI)
AHA .... Associate of the Australian College of Health
AHA .... Associate of the Institute of Health Service Administrators [*British*] (DCTA)
AHA .... Association of Handicapped Artists (EA)
AHA .... Association of Hispanic Arts (EA)
AHA .... Association of Housing Aid [*British*] (DBA)
AHA .... Australian Hepatitis Antigen [*Biochemistry*] (DAVI)
AHA .... Australian Heritage Award
AHA .... Autoimmune Hemolytic Anemia [*Hematology*]
AHA .... Aylmer Heritage Association (AC)
AHA .... Hardisty Public Library, Alberta [*Library symbol National Library of Canada*] (NLC)
AHA .... United States Army Environmental Hygiene Agency, Aberdeen Proving Grounds, MD [*OCLC symbol*] (OCLC)
AHaagen ..... Alexander Haagen Property, Inc. [*Associated Press*] (SAG)
AHAB .... Attacking Hardened Air Bases [*Air Force*] (PDAA)
AHAB .... First Alabama Bank of Huntsville, Huntsville, AL [*Library symbol*] [*Library of Congress*] (LCLS)
AHAC .... Adelaide Harriers Athletic Club [*Australia*]
AHACM .... Ancient and Honorable Artillery Co. of Massachusetts (EA)

AHAF .... American Handwriting Analysis Foundation (EA)
AHAF .... American Health Assistance Foundation (EA)
AHAG .... Affordable Housing Action Group (AC)
AHAL .... Hay Lakes Public Library, Alberta [*Library symbol National Library of Canada*] (NLC)
AHAM .... Association of Home Appliance Manufacturers (EA)
AHAMS .... Advanced Heavy Antitank Missile System [*Army*] (MCD)
AH & MA .... American Hotel & Motel Association
AHAP .... Apartment House Addressing Program [*US Postal Service*]
AHAPQ........ Association des Hommes d'Affaires et Professionnels du Quebec (AC)
AHAR .... Advanced Highway Advisory Radio [*FHWA*] (TAG)
AHAR .... Australian Heraldic Archival Record
AHAS .... Acetohydroxyacidsynthase [*An enzyme*]
AHAS .... Association of Heritage Approved Specialists [*An association*] (EAIO)
AHAS .... Automatic Helicopter Approach System [*Army*]
AHASC........ Airport Handling Agreements Sub-Committee [*IATA*] (DS)
AHA(T) .... Area Health Authority (Teaching) [*British*]
AHAT .... Arylhydroxamic(acyltransferase) [*An enzyme*]
AHAU .... University of Alabama in Huntsville, Huntsville, AL [*Library symbol Library of Congress*] (LCLS)
AHAUS .... Amateur Hockey Association of the United States (EA)
AHAWA ...... Australian Hungarian Association of Western Australia
AHAWS ...... Advanced Heavy Antitank Weapon System (MCD)
AHB .... Abha [*Saudi Arabia*] [*Airport symbol*] (OAG)
AHB .... Aboriginal Heritage Branch [*South Australia*]
AHB .... Aerolineas de Honduras, SA [*Honduras*] [*FAA designator*] (FAAC)
AHB .... Africanized Honey Bee
AHB .... Air Heater Blower
AHB .... Air Historical Branch [*Air Ministry*] [*British*]
AHB .... Alpha-Hydroxybutyric Acid (DMAA)
AHB .... Alpha-Hydroxybutyric Dehydrogenase [*An enzyme*] (MAH)
AHB .... American Highways and Byways [*A publication*]
AHB .... Assault Helicopter Battalion [*Military*]
AHB .... Athabaska Gold [*Vancouver Stock Exchange symbol*]
AHB .... Attack Helicopter Battalion
AHB .... Automatic Half Barrier
AHBA .... Acadian Home Builders Association (SRA)
AHBA .... Alabama Home Builders Association (SRA)
AHBA .... American Home Business Association [*Greenwich, CT*] (EA)
AHBA .... Arkansas Home Builders Association (SRA)
AHBA .... Association of Hotel Booking Agents [*British*] (BI)
AHBAI .... American Health and Beauty Aids Institute (EA)
AHBC .... Adelaide Historical Bottle Club [*Australia*]
AHBD .... Alpha-Hydroxybutyric Dehydrogenase [*An enzyme*]
AHC .... Academic Health Center
AHC .... Academic Health Center
AHC .... Academy of Hospital Counselors [*Later, AHCC*] (EA)
AHC .... Accepting Houses Committee [*Banking*] [*British*]
AHC .... Achilles Heel Cleavage (DOG)
AHC .... Acute Hemorrhagic Conjunctivitis [*Ophthalmology*] (AAMN)
AHC .... Acute Hemorrhagic Cystitis [*Urology*] (AAMN)
AHC .... Ad-Hoc Committee
AHC .... Adrenal Hypoplasia Congenita [*Metabolic disease*]
AHC .... Adrenal Hypoplasia Congenita [*Medicine*]
AHC .... Airport Handling Committee [*IATA*] (DS)
AHC .... Allan Hancock College [*Santa Maria, CA*]
AHC .... Allied High Commission [*Germany*] (NATG)
AHC .... Amerada Hess Corp. [*NYSE symbol Toronto Stock Exchange symbol*] (SPSG)
AHC .... American Health Consultants [*Information service or system*] (IID)
AHC .... American Helicopter Company [*Air Force*] (MCD)
AHC .... American Hellenic Congress [*Defunct*] (EA)
AHC .... American Horse Council (EA)
AHC .... American Horticultural Council [*Later, AHS*]
AHC .... American Hospital Corps
AHC .... American Hostage Committee [*Defunct*] (EA)
AHC .... Ampere-Hour Capacity
AHC .... Anthropogenic Hydrocarbons
AHC .... Appaloosa Horse Club (EA)
AHC .... Army Hospital Corps
AHC .... Assault Helicopter Company [*Army*] (AABC)
AHC .... Association des Hopitaux du Canada [*Association of Hospitals of Canada*]
AHC .... Association for the History of Chiropractic (EA)
AHC .... Association Henri Capitant (EA)
AHC .... Association of Hebrew Catholics (EA)
AHC .... Atlas Historique du Canada [*Historical Atlas of Canada*] [*Project*]
AHC .... Attack Helicopter Company [*Military*]
AHC .... Australian Handball Council
AHC .... Auto Headway Control [*Mitsubishi*] [*Automotive engineering*]
AHC .... Automatic Headway Control
AHC .... Herlong, CA [*Location identifier FAA*] (FAAL)
AHCA .... Afghan Hound Club of America (EA)
AHCA .... American Health Care Association (EA)
AHCA .... American Hockey Coaches Association (EA)
AHCA .... Arizona Health Care Association (SRA)
AHCA .... Arkansas Health Care Association (SRA)
AHCA .... Austin-Healey Club of America (EA)
AHCAA .... American Health Care Advisory Association (EA)
AHCADM ...... African Heritage Center for African Dance and Music (EA)
AHCAS .... Ad Hoc Committee for American Silver (EA)
AHCBSU ...... Ad Hoc Committee on the Baltic States and the Ukraine (EA)
AHCC .... Academy of Health Care Consultants [*Defunct*] (EA)
AHCC .... Arbor Health Care Co. [*NASDAQ symbol*] (SAG)

AHCC .... Association des Hopitaux Catholiques du Canada [*Association of Catholic Hospitals of Canada*]
AHCCBSU .... Ad Hoc Congressional Committee on the Baltic States and the Ukraine (EA)
AHCCIA .... Ad Hoc Congressional Committee for Irish Affairs (EA)
AHCCL .... Ad Hoc Committee on Copyright Law (EA)
AHCD .... Acquired Hepatocellular Degeneration [*Medicine*] (DMAA)
AHCEI .... Ad Hoc Committee on Equipment Interoperability [*NATO*] (NATG)
AHCEI .... American Histadrut Cultural Exchange Institute [*Defunct*] (EA)
AHCF .... Alternate Headquarters Command Facility [*Military*] (MCD)
AHCFSI .... Ad Hoc Committee on Freedom of Scholarly Inquiry [*Defunct*] (EA)
AHCGS .... Grace Shepherd School, Hines Creek, Alberta [*Library symbol National Library of Canada*] (BIB)
AHCI .... Ambanc Holding Co., Inc. [*NASDAQ symbol*] (SAG)
AHCIET .... Asociacion Hispanoamericana de Centros de Investigacion y Estudios de Telecomunicaciones (EA)
AHCIMA ...... Associate of the Hotel, Catering, and Institutional Management Association [*British*] (DBQ)
AHCIS .... Ambulatory Health Care Information System
AHCL .... Almaguin Highlands Community Living (AC)
AHCLF .... Ad Hoc Committee for Lebanese Freedom [*Defunct*] (EA)
AHCM .... Academy of Hazard Control Management (EA)
AHCM .... Hines Creek Municipal Library, Alberta [*Library symbol National Library of Canada*] (NLC)
AHCo .... Assault Helicopter Company [*Air Force*] (AFM)
AHCPR .... Agency for Health Care Policy and Research [*Department of Health and Human Services*]
AHCQ .... Association de l'Huile a Chauffage du Quebec (AC)
AHCRA .... Arabian Horse Club Registry of America [*Later, AHR*]
AHCS .... Aboriginal Home Care Service [*Australia*]
AHCS .... Advanced Hybrid Computer System
AHCS .... American Historic and Cultural Society (EA)
AHCS .... American Hungarian Catholic Society [*Later, William Penn Association*] (EA)
AHCS .... Australian Horticultural Correspondence School
AHCS .... Hines Creek High School, Alberta [*Library symbol National Library of Canada*] (BIB)
AHCT .... Ascending Horizon Crossing Time (OA)
AHCTL .... Acetylhomocysteinethiolactone [*Citiolone*] [*Organic chemistry*]
AHCy .... Adenosyl Homocysteine (DMAA)
AHD .... Advanced Helicopter Development (DNAB)
AHD .... Ahead (FAAC)
AHD .... Airborne and Helicopter Division [*Aeroplane and Armament Experimental Establishment*] [*British*]
AHD .... Airhead [*Army*] (AABC)
AHD .... Airport Hotel Directory [*National Association of Business Travel Agents*] [*A publication*]
AHD .... American Health Decisions (EA)
AHD .... American Heritage Dictionary [*A publication*]
AHD .... Anti-Helicopter Device
AHD .... Antihypertensive Drug [*Medicine*]
AHD .... Arc Heating Device
AHD .... Ardmore [*Oklahoma*] [*Airport symbol Obsolete*] (OAG)
Ahd .... Arrowhead [*Military decoration*] (AABC)
AHD .... Arteriosclerotic Heart Disease [*Cardiology*]
AHD .... Association of Household Distributors [*British*] (EAIO)
AHD .... Atherosclerotic Heart Disease [*Cardiology*] (DAVI)
AHD .... Audio High Density
AHD .... Autoimmune Hemolytic Disease [*Medicine*]
AHD .... Czech Air Handling [*Czechoslovakia*] [*ICAO designator*] (FAAC)
AHDA .... Animal Health Distributors Association [*British*] (DBA)
AHDB .... Automated Historical Data Base
AHDC .... Aboriginal Housing Development Committee [*Australia*]
AHDG .... Aboriginal Health Development Group [*Australia*]
AHDGA .... American Hot Dip Galvanizers Association [*Later, AGA*] (EA)
AHDME .... Association of Hospital Directors of Medical Education [*Later, AHME*] (EA)
AHDMS .... Automated Hospital Data Management System [*Medicine*] (DMAA)
AHDP .... Azacycloheptane Diphosphonate [*Organic chemistry*]
AHDPA .... Association of House Democratic Press Assistants (EA)
AHDR .... Air Header
AHDRC .... Ancient History Documents Research Center [*Macquarie University*] [*Australia*]
AHDS .... Anthrahydroquinone Disulfonate [*Organic chemistry*]
AHE........... Acute Hemorrhagic Encephalomyelitis [*Medicine*] (MAE)
AHE........... Air to Heat Exchanger [*Aerospace*] (AAG)
AHE........... Alternatives in Higher Education [*Program*] [*National Science Foundation*]
AHE........... American Health Properties [*NYSE symbol*] (SPSG)
AHE........... Ammunition Handling Equipment
AHE........... Armament Handling Equipment (MCD)
AHE........... Associate in Home Economics
AHE........... Association for Higher Education [*of the NEA*] [*Later, AAHE*] (EA)
AHE........... Association for Human Emergence [*Defunct*] (EA)
AHE........... Association for Humanistic Education (EA)
AHE........... Heinsburg Public Library, Alberta [*Library symbol National Library of Canada*] (NLC)
AHE........... University of Arkansas for Medical Sciences, Area Health Education Center, Little Rock, AR [*OCLC symbol*] (OCLC)
AHEA .... American Home Economics Association (EA)
AHEA .... American Hungarian Educators' Association (EA)
AHEA .... Area Health Education Activity (DMAA)
AHEA .... Australian Horticultural Exporters Association
AHEAD .... Army Help for Education and Development
AHEAD .... Association for Humanistic Education and Development (EA)

AHEAD	Association of Higher Education and Disabilities
AHEC	Acadia Health Education Coalition (SRA)
AHEC	American Hardwood Export Council (EA)
AHEC	Appropriate Home Energy Cooperative [Canada]
AHEc	Area Health Education Center [Veterans Administration] (DHSM)
AH Ec	Associate in Home Economics
AHEC	Australian Health Ethics Committee
AHEC	Australian Horticultural Export Council
AHEIHE	Association of Higher Educational Institutions Concerned with Home Economics [British] (DBA)
AHEL	Army Human Engineering Laboratory (MCD)
AHEM	Association of Hydraulic Equipment Manufacturers
AHEO	Area Health Education Officer [National Health Service] [British] (DI)
AHEP	American Health Properties [NASDAQ symbol] (SAG)
AHEPA	American Hellenic Educational Progressive Association
AHERA	Asbestos Hazard Emergency Response Act of 1986
AHeritge	American Heritage Life Investment Corp. [Associated Press] (SAG)
AHES	American Humane Education Society (EA)
AHES	Artificial Heart Energy System
AHESC	Airport Handling Equipment Sub-Committee [IATA] (DS)
AHEY	Army Handicapped Employe of the Year (RDA)
AHF	Active History File [Army]
AHF	Acute Heart Failure [Medicine]
AHF	American Health Foundation (EA)
AHF	American Hepatic Foundation (EA)
AHF	American Heritage Foundation (EA)
AHF	American Hobby Federation [Defunct] (EA)
AHF	American Homeowners Foundation (EA)
AHF	American Hospital Formulary [A publication]
AHF	American Host Foundation (EA)
AHF	American Humanics Foundation [Later, AH] (EA)
AHF	American Hungarian Federation (EA)
AHF	American Hungarian Foundation (EA)
AHF	Anhydrous Hydrogen Fluoride [Inorganic chemistry]
AHF	Animal Health Foundation (EA)
AHF	Antihemophilic Factor [Factor VIII] [Also, AHG, PTF, TPC Hematology]
AHF	Architectural Heritage Foundation (EA)
AHF	Architectural History Foundation (EA)
AHF	Area Health Authority Full Time [Chiropody] [British]
AHF	Argentinian Hemorrhagic Fever [Medicine] (DMAA)
AHF	Army Historical Foundation (EA)
AHF	Associated Health Foundation (EA)
AHF	Australian Handball Federation
AHF	Auto Hold Fire (KSC)
AHF	Azad Hind Fauj [Indian National Army]
AHFA	African Heritage Federation of the Americas [Defunct] (EA)
AHFC	American Hungarian Folklore Centrum (EA)
AHFLCD	Association of Health Facility Licensure and Certification Directors (EA)
AHFMR	Alberta Heritage Foundation for Medical Research [Canada]
AHFR	Argonne High-Flux Reactor (NRCH)
AHFRAC	Army Human Factors Research Advisory Committee
AHFRDC	Army Human Factors Research and Development Committee (AABC)
AHFS	American Hospital Formulary Service
AHG	Aerochago [Dominican Republic] [ICAO designator] (FAAC)
AHG	Aggregated Human Globulin [Biochemistry] (DAVI)
AHG	American Herbalists Guild (EA)
AHG	American High-Density Gradient
AHG	Anchor Gold Corp. [Vancouver Stock Exchange symbol]
AHG	Anhydroglucose [Biochemistry]
AHG	Antihemophilic Globulin [Factor VIII] [Also, AHF, PTF, TPC Hematology]
AHG	Antihuman Globulin [Consumption test] [Medicine]
AHG	Apria Healthcare Group, Inc. [NYSE symbol] (SAG)
AHG	Archconfraternity of the Holy Ghost (EA)
AHG	Australian Historical Geography [A publication]
AHGBS	Association of Heads of Girls Boarding Schools [British]
AHGC	Advanced Hardened Guidance Computer (MCD)
AHGF	Antique and Historical Glass Foundation (EA)
AHGMR	Ad Hoc Group on Missile Reliability (SAA)
AHGMRF	Ad Hoc Group for Medical Research Funding (EA)
AHGO	AIDS Housing Group of Ottawa (AC)
AHGO	Americans for Hope, Growth, & Opportunity
AHGS	Acute Herpetic Gingival Stomatitis [Dentistry]
AHGS	Advanced Harpoon Guidance System (MCD)
AHGS	Attitude Heading Gyroscope System
AHGS	Church of Jesus Christ of Latter-Day Saints, Genealogical Society Library, Huntsville Branch, Huntsville, AL [Library symbol Library of Congress] (LCLS)
AHGTC	Ancient and Honourable Guild of Town Criers (EAIO)
AHGUSPTUN...	Ad Hoc Group on US Policy toward the UN [Defunct] (EA)
AHH	Alpha-Hydrazine Analogue of Histidine (MAE)
AHH	Amery, WI [Location identifier FAA] (FAAL)
AHH	Arc Heater Housing
AHH	Aromatic Hydrocarbon Hydroxylase [An enzyme]
AHH	Aryl Hydrocarbon Hydroxylase [An enzyme]
AHH	Association for Hispanic Handicapped of New Jersey (EA)
AHH	Association for Holistic Health [Defunct] (EA)
AHH	Hairy Hill Public Library, Alberta [Library symbol National Library of Canada] (NLC)
AHHA	American Holstein Horse Association (EA)
AHHAP	Association of Halfway House Alcoholism Programs of North America (EA)
AHHS	American Hackney Horse Society (EA)

AHHSA	American Holistic Health Sciences Association [Defunct] (EA)
AHI	Active Hostility Index [Psychology]
AHI	Aerodynamic Heating Indicator (MCD)
AHI	Afro-Hispanic Institute (EA)
AHI	Agrupacion Herrena Independiente [Spain Political party] (EY)
AHI	Amahai [Indonesia] [Airport symbol] (OAG)
AHI	American Healthcare Institute [Later, AMHS Institute] (EA)
AHI	American Healthcare Management, Inc. [NYSE symbol] (SPSG)
AHI	American Hellenic Institute (EA)
AHI	American Honey Institute [Later, HICA] (EA)
AHI	Animal Health Institute (EA)
AHI	Antihyaluronidase [Bacteriology] (DAVI)
AHI	Apnea-Plus-Hypopnea Index [Medicine] (DMAA)
AHI	Approach, Horizon Indicator [Aviation] (PDAA)
AHI	Artificial Horizon Indicator [Aerospace] (MCD)
AHI	Augmented Human Intellect (KSC)
AHI	Axel Heiberg Island [Canada]
AHI	Servicios Aeros de Chihuahua Aerochisa SA de CV [Mexico ICAO designator] (FAAC)
AHIC	American HealthChoice, Inc. [NASDAQ symbol] (SAG)
AHIC	Art Hazards Information Center (EA)
AHIDC	Australian Housing Industry Development Council
AHIDGS	Association of Heads of Independent and Direct Grant Girls Schools [British]
AHIHA	American Hearing Impaired Hockey Association (EA)
AHIHlth	AHI Healthcare Systems, Inc. [Associated Press] (SAG)
AHII	American Health Industries Institute (EA)
AHIL	Association of Hospital and Institution Libraries [of ALA] [Later, ASCLA]
AHIP	Advanced Helicopter Improvement Program [Army] (RDA)
AHIP	Army Helicopter Improvement Program
AHIP	Assisted Health Insurance Plan
AHIPAC	American Hellenic Institute Public Affairs Committee (EA)
AHIS	AGILE [Autonetics General Information Learning Equipment] Homing Interceptor Simulation
AHIS	AHI Healthcare Systems, Inc. [NASDAQ symbol] (SAG)
AHIS	Alternative Health Insurance Services [An association] (EA)
AHIS	American Hull Insurance Syndicate [New York, NY] (EA)
AHIS	Association of Heads of Independent Schools [British]
AHIS	Automated Hospital Information System [Veterans Administration] (IID)
AHIT	Attack Helicopter Instrument Test (MCD)
AHJ	Artificial Hip Joint (DMAA)
AHJCP	Association of Hillel/Jewish Campus Professionals (EA)
AHK	Air Hong Kong Ltd. [ICAO designator] (FAAC)
AHK	Aktiv Hinten Kinematik [Active Rear-Axle Movement] [German]
AHK	Amhawk Resources Corp. [Vancouver Stock Exchange symbol]
a-hk--	Hong Kong [MARC geographic area code Library of Congress] (LCCP)
AHKGA	Australian Hayward Kiwifruit Growers Association
AHL	Acetate Halftone Litho [Du Pont]
AHL	Adam, Harding & Lueck [Commercial firm British]
AHL	Adaptive Head Lamp
AHL	Ad Hunc Locum [To (or At) This Place] [Latin]
AHL	AHL Group [Formerly, Automotive Hardware Ltd.] [Toronto Stock Exchange symbol]
AHL	Air Hanson Ltd. [British ICAO designator] (FAAC)
AHL	Alcohol-Induced Hyperlipidemia [Medicine] (PDAA)
AHL	America: History and Life [ABC-Clio Information Services] [Database] [A publication]
AHL	American Heritage Life Investment Corp. [NYSE symbol] (SPSG)
AHL	American Hockey League (EA)
AHL	Apparent Half-Life (DMAA)
AHL	Associated Humber Lines [Steamship] (MHDB)
AHL	Association for Holistic Living (EA)
AHL	Auroral Hydrogen Line
AHL	Average Hearing Level
AHL	High Level Municipal Library, Alberta [Library symbol National Library of Canada] (NLC)
AHLC	American Hair Loss Council (EA)
AHLE	Acute Hemorrhagic Leukoencephalitis [Medicine] (MAE)
AHLE	Auroral Hydrogen Line Emission
AHLFS	Florence MacDougall Community School, High Level, Alberta [Library symbol National Library of Canada] (BIB)
AHLG	Antihuman Lymphocyte Globulin [Medicine] (DMAA)
A-HLH	Amphipathic Helix-Loop-Helix [Genetics]
AHLHS	American Hungarian Library and Historical Society (EA)
AHLI	American Home Lighting Institute (EA)
AHLMA	American Home Laundry Manufacturers Association [Later, AHAM] (EA)
AHLPS	High Level Public School, Alberta [Library symbol National Library of Canada] (BIB)
AHLS	Antihuman Lymphocyte Serum [Immunochemistry] (MAE)
AHltCh	American HealthChoice, Inc. [Associated Press] (SAG)
AHlthcp	American Healthcorp, Inc. [Associated Press] (SAG)
AHltMg	American Healthcare Management, Inc. [Associated Press] (SAG)
AHltPr	American Health Properties [Associated Press] (SAG)
AHLV	American Hop Latent Virus [Plant pathology]
AHLZS	Zama City School, High Level, Alberta [Library symbol National Library of Canada] (BIB)
AHM	Aaronson, Huchra, and Moruld [Method of determining age of the universe]
AHM	Acutely Hazardous Material
AHM	Ahmanson [H. F.] & Co. [NYSE symbol] (SPSG)
AHM	Airport Handling Manual [IATA] (DS)

AHM............ Allowance Holder Monthly [*Environmental Protection Agency*] (GFGA)
AHM............ Ambulatory Holter Monitoring [*Medicine*] (CPH)
AHM............ Ammonium Heptamolybdate [*Inorganic chemistry*]
AHM............ Ampere-Hour Meter
AHM............ Anterior Hyaloid Membrane [*Ophthalmology*]
AHM............ Anti-Helicopter Mine [*Military*]
AHM............ Association of Headmistresses [*British*] (BI)
AHM............ Auxiliary Handling Machine [*Nuclear energy*] (NRCH)
AHM............ Garrison Aviation Ltd. [*Canada ICAO designator*] (FAAC)
AHM............ Hanna Municipal Library, Alberta [*Library symbol National Library of Canada*] (NLC)
AHMA .... Advanced Hypersonic Manned Aircraft
AHMA .... Allied Hat Manufacturers Association (EA)
AHMA .... American Hardware Manufacturers Association (EA)
AHMA .... American Holistic Medical Association (EA)
Ahmans ...... Ahmanson [*H.F.*] & Co. [*Associated Press*] (SAG)
AHMA-PSW... Affordable Housing Management Association - Pacific Southwest (SRA)
AHMB .... American Hotel and Motel Brokers [*Formerly, MBAA*] (EA)
AHMC .... American Horticultural Marketing Council (EA)
AHMC .... Association of Hospital Management Committees
AHMD .... Airborne Helmet Mounted Display
AHme........... American Home Products Corp. [*Associated Press*] (SAG)
AHME .... Association for Hospital Medical Education (EA)
AHMF .... American Holistic Medical Foundation (EA)
AHMGSA..... Ad Hoc Monitoring Group on Southern Africa [*Defunct*] (EA)
AHMH .... Association of High Medicare Hospitals (EA)
AHMI .... American Holistic Medical Institute [*of the American Holistic Medical Association*] [*Formerly, BIA Later, AHMF*] (EA)
AHMI .... Appalachian Hardwood Manufacturers, Inc. (EA)
AHMI .... Association of Head Mistresses, Inc. [*British*]
AHMJ .... Arc-Heated Materials Jet [*Langley Research Center*]
Ahmn .... Ahmanson [*H.F.*] & Co. [*Associated Press*] (SAG)
AHMOM ...... Association of Health Management Organizations in Michigan (SRA)
AHMPS .... Association of Headmistresses of Preparatory Schools [*British*]
AHMS .... American Home Mission Society
AHMWG....... Ad Hoc Mixed Working Group (SAA)
AHN .... Adventist Health Network of North America [*Defunct*] (EA)
AHN .... Air Hainaut [*France ICAO designator*] (FAAC)
AHN .... Army Health Nurse (AABC)
AHN .... Assistant Head Nurse (AAMN)
AHN .... Athens [*Georgia*] [*Airport symbol*] (OAG)
AHNA......... Accredited Home Newspapers of America [*Later, SNA*]
AHNA......... American Holistic Nurses Association (EA)
AHNC .... Anisotropic Hypernetted Chain [*Chemical physics*]
AHNO......... Association of Head and Neck Oncologists of Great Britain
AHNT......... Access HealthNet, Inc. [*NASDAQ symbol*] (SAG)
A/H/O.......... Abort/Hold/Orbit [*NASA*]
AHO .... Ahold Ltd. [*NYSE symbol*] (SAG)
AHO .... Albright's Hereditary Osteodystrophy [*Medicine*]
AHO .... Alghero [*Italy*] [*Airport symbol*] (OAG)
AHO .... Applicant Holding Office [*Employment*]
AHO .... Assisted Hydrothermal Oxidation [*Of hazardous wastes*]
AHO .... Association of Holocaust Organizations (EA)
AHO .... Attack Helicopter Operations (CAAL)
AHO .... Oakwood College, Huntsville, AL [*Library symbol Library of Congress*] (LCLS)
AHOAG........ Attack Helicopter Operations and Analysis Group
AHOC......... Australian Home Owners' Club
AHOD......... Areal Hypolimnetic Oxygen Deficit [*Hydrobiology*]
AHOEC....... Association of Heads of Outdoor Education Centres [*British*] (DBA)
AHOF .... Arabian Horse Owners Foundation (EA)
AHOF .... Automotive Hall of Fame
Ahold.......... Ahold Ltd. [*Associated Press*] (SAG)
AHOM .... American HomePatient Care [*NASDAQ symbol*] (SAG)
AHOM .... Holden Municipal Library, Alberta [*Library symbol National Library of Canada*] (BIB)
AHome........ American Home Products Co. [*Associated Press*] (SAG)
AHomPat ..... American HomePatient Care [*Associated Press*] (SAG)
AHomstr ..... American Homestar Corp. [*Associated Press*] (SAG)
AHONDA ...... Ad Hoc Committee on New Directions of the Research and Technical Services Division of the ALA [*American Library Association*] (NITA)
AHOP .... Assisted Home-Ownership Program [*Canada*]
AHOPSS..... Association of Heads of Polytechnic Student Services [*British*] (AIE)
AHOS.......... Automatic Hydrologic Observing System [*National Weather Service*]
AHOTE .... Association of Health Occupations Teacher Educators (EA)
AHP .... Absorption Heat Pumping [*Engineering*]
AHP .... Accelerator Heel Point [*Automotive engineering*]
AHP .... Accelerator Heel Point
AHP .... Accountable Health Partnership [*Medicine*]
AHP .... Accountable Health Plan [*Medicine*]
AHP .... Acute Hemorrhagic Pancreatitis [*Medicine*] (MAE)
AHP .... Aerochiapas SA de CV [*Mexico ICAO designator*] (FAAC)
AHP .... Affordable Housing Program [*Federal Home Loan Bank*]
AHP .... Afterhyperpolarization [*Also, AH*] [*Neurophysiology*]
AHP .... Air, High Pressure (DNAB)
AHP .... Air Horsepower [*Air Force*]
AHP .... Allied Health Professionals
AHP .... Allied Hydrographic Publication [*NATO*]
AHP .... Alternating Hamiltonian Path
AHP .... Alternative Health Plans [*Department of Health and Human Services*] (GFGA)
AHP .... American Health Professionals

AHP .... American Homeopathic Pharmacopoeia [*Last published in 1920*]
AHP .... American Home Products Corp. [*NYSE symbol*] (SPSG)
AHP .... American Horse Publications (EA)
AHP .... Americans for Historic Preservation (EA)
AHP .... Analytic Hierarchy Process
AHP .... Aniline Hydrogen Phthalate (OA)
AHP .... Approved Health Plan [*Medicine*]
AHP .... Army Heliport (AABC)
AHP .... Assistant Head Postmaster (DCTA)
AHP .... Assistant House Physician
AHP .... Association for Healthcare Philanthropy (NFD)
AHP .... Association for Healthcare Philanthropy
AHP .... Association for Humanistic Psychology (EA)
AHP .... Association of Health Professionals [*Australia*]
AHP .... Attitude Hold Pitch [*Axis*]
AHP .... Awards, Honors, and Prizes [*A publication*]
AHP .... Evacuation Hospital Ship [*Navy symbol Obsolete*]
AHPA .... Accumulator High-Pressure Air
AHPA .... (Adeninyl)hydroxypropanoic Acid [*Antiviral*]
AHPA .... Almond Hullers and Processors Association (SRA)
AHPA .... American Half-Paso Association [*Defunct*] (EA)
AHPA .... American Health Planning Association (EA)
AHPA .... American Herbal Products Association (EA)
AHPA .... American Honey Producers Association (EA)
AHPA .... American Horse Protection Association (EA)
AHPA .... Arthritis Health Professions Association (EA)
AHPA .... Australian Health Professionals Association
AHPAT .... Allied Health Professions Admissions Test [*Admissions and selection test*]
AHPB .... Association for Humanistic Psychology in Britain (EAIO)
AHPBS .... Bishop Routhier School, High Prairie, Alberta [*Library symbol National Library of Canada*] (BIB)
AHPC .... Aging Health Policy Center [*Research center*] (RCD)
AHPC .... Arizona Heat Pump Council (SRA)
AHPCRC..... Army High-Performance Computing Research (RDA)
AHPCRC....... Army High Performance Computing Research Center [*University of Minnesota*] [*Research center*] (RCD)
AHPCS .... American Historical Print Collectors Society (EA)
AHPD .... High Prairie and District Centennial Museum, High Prairie, Alberta [*Library symbol National Library of Canada*] (BIB)
AHP Foundation... Association for Healthcare Philanthropy Foundation (NFD)
AHPGSMBS... Amalgamated Hackle Pin Grinders Sick and Mutual Benefit Society [*British*]
AHPI .... Allied Healthcare Products, Inc. [*NASDAQ symbol*] (SAG)
AHPI .... American Health Professions Institute (DAVI)
AHPL .... [*A*] Hardware Programming Language [*1971*] [*Computer science*] (CSR)
AHPM .... High Prairie Municipal Library, Alberta [*Library symbol National Library of Canada*] (NLC)
AHPNAS..... Advanced High-Performance Nuclear Attack Submarine
AHPO......... Anterior Hypothalamic Preoptic (DMAA)
AHPOA........ Anterior Hypothalamus, Preoptic Area [*Brain anatomy*]
AHPP .... Association of Humanistic Psychology Practitioners (EAIO)
AHPQ......... L'Association des Hoteliers de la Province de Quebec [*Province of Quebec Hotel Keepers' Association*] (AC)
AHPR .... Academy of Hospital Public Relations [*Later, Hospital Academy - HA*]
AHPRT .... Aboriginal Health Policy Review Team [*Australia*]
AHPS .... American Helvetia Philatelic Society (EA)
AHPS .... American Historical Philatelic Society [*Formerly, AHPS-CWPS*] (EA)
AHPS .... Association of Headmistresses of Preparatory Schools [*British*] (BI)
AHPS .... Auxiliary Hydraulic Power Supply
AHPSAS ..... St. Andrew's School, High Prairie, Alberta [*Library symbol National Library of Canada*] (BIB)
AHPSC .... Airport Handling Procedures Sub-Committee [*IATA*] (DS)
AHPS-CWPS... American Historical Philatelic Society - Civil War Philatelic Society [*Later, AHPS*]
AHPV .... Association of Hospital Pharmacists of Victoria [*Australia*]
AHQ .... Air Headquarters
AHQ .... Allied Headquarters
AHQ .... Anthrahydroquinone [*Organic chemistry*]
AHQ .... Area Headquarters (NATG)
AHQ .... Army Headquarters
AHQ .... Association des Hopitaux du Quebec [*Quebec Hospital Association*] (AC)
AHQ .... Association for Healthcare Quality [*Defunct*] (EA)
AHQ .... Wahoo, NE [*Location identifier FAA*] (FAAL)
AHQC......... Australian Hardwood Quality Council
AHR .... Ablative Heat Rate (MCD)
AHR .... Academy of Human Rights
AHR .... Acceptable Hazard Rate (IEEE)
ahr............. Acceptable Hazard Rate (ODBW)
AHR .... Acier Haut Resistance [*Bicycling*] (DICI)
AHR .... Active High Resolution (MCD)
AHR .... Adsorptive Heat Recovery [*Chemical engineering*]
AHR .... A. H. Robins Co. [*Research code symbol*]
AHR .... Air Holland Regional (AHR) [*ICAO designator*] (FAAC)
AHR .... Americana Hotels & Realty Corp. [*NYSE symbol*] (SPSG)
AHR .... American Hair Restoration
AHR .... American Historical Review [*A publication*] (BRI)
A/HR........... Ampere/Hour (MCD)
AHR .... Anchor (MSA)
AHR .... Andalusian Horse Registry (EA)
AHR .... Annual History Review (MCD)
AHR .... Annual Hospital Report [*Program of the Department of Health and Human Services*]

AHR .... Aqueous Homogeneous Reactor
AHR .... Arabian Horse Registry of America (EA)
AHR .... Arnhem Resources, Inc. [Vancouver Stock Exchange symbol]
AHR .... Aryl Hydrocarbon Receptor [Biochemistry]
AHR .... Association for Health Records [Later, AHQ] (EA)
AHR .... Association for Human Rights (EA)
AHR .... Association of Humanistic Rabbis (EA)
AHR .... Attitude Hold Roll [Axis] (NASA)
AHR .... Autonomic Hyperreflexia [Medicine] (MEDA)
AHR .... Provincial Archives of Alberta, Historical Resource Library [UTLAS symbol]
AHRA .... Advanced Helmet Sight Reticle Assembly [Air Force] (MCD)
AHRA .... African Human Rights Research Association [Formerly, African Human Rights Study Group] (EA)
AHRA .... Alberta Health Record Association (AC)
AHRA .... American Hair Replacement Association [Inactive] (EA)
AHRA .... American Healthcare Radiology Administrators (EA)
AHRA .... American Himalayan Rabbit Association (EA)
AHRA .... American Hospital Radiology Administrators (DAVI)
AHRA .... American Hot Rod Association (EA)
AHRC .... Alister Hardy Research Centre [Manchester College] [British] (CB)
AHRC .... American Harlequin Rabbit Club (EA)
AHRC .... Australian Harness Racing Council
AHRF .... Alberta Historical Resources Foundation (AC)
AHRF .... American Hearing Research Foundation (EA)
AHRL .... Arctic Health Research Laboratory [HEW]
AHRM .... High River Municipal Library, Alberta [Library symbol National Library of Canada] (NLC)
AHRMA .... American Historic Racing Motorcycle Association (EA)
AHRP .... Academy on Human Rights and Peace (EA)
AHRR .... Australian Historic Records Register [Database]
AHRRN .... Automatic Hydrologic Radio Reporting Network (DNAB)
AHRS .... Altitude Heading Reference System (GAVI)
AHRS .... Attitude Heading Reference System (NG)
AHRS .... Automatic Heading Reference System
AHRSJ .... Americans for Human Rights and Social Justice (EA)
AHRTAG .... Appropriate Health Resources and Technologies Action Group [London, England]
AHRU .... Americans for Human Rights in Ukraine (EA)
AHRU .... Attitude Heading Reference Unit
AHRU .... Aviation Human Research Unit [Army]
AHS .... Ablative Heat Shield
AHS .... Aboriginal Health Service [Australia]
AHS .... Academy of Health Sciences [Health Services Command] [Fort Sam Houston, TX] [Army]
AHS .... Acute Hospital Syndrome [Used facetiously to explain the popularity of a West German soap opera]
AHS .... Advanced Homing Sensor
AHS .... African Horse Sickness [Medicine] (DMAA)
AHS .... Agricultural History Society (EA)
AHS .... Aigner Holdings [Vancouver Stock Exchange symbol]
AHS .... Airborne Hardware Simulator (MCD)
AHS .... Alternate Health Services
AHS .... Alveolar Hypoventilation Syndrome [Medicine] (DMAA)
AHS .... American Hanoverian Society (EA)
AHS .... American Harp Society (EA)
AHS .... American Hearing Society [Later, NAHSA] (EA)
AHS .... American Heartworm Society (EA)
AHS .... American Helicopter Society (EA)
AHS .... American Hemerocallis Society (EA)
AHS .... American Heritage Society [Defunct] (EA)
AHS .... American Hibiscus Society (EA)
AHS .... American Hiking Society (EA)
AHS .... American Horticultural Society (EA)
AHS .... American Hospital Society
AHS .... American Hosta Society (EA)
AHS .... American Housing Survey [Department of Housing and Urban Development] (GFGA)
AHS .... American Humane Society
AHS .... American Hypnodontic Society (EA)
AHS .... Ammonium Hydrogen Sulfate [Inorganic chemistry]
AHS .... Ammunition Handling System (MCD)
AHS .... Amtrak Historical Society (EA)
AHS .... Anno Humanae Salutis [In the Year of Human Salvation] [Latin]
AHS .... Annual Housing Survey [Department of Housing and Urban Development] (GFGA)
AHS .... Annual Hull Survey (DS)
AHS .... Antenna Homing System
AHS .... Antiquarian Horological Society (EA)
AHS .... Arab Horse Society (EAIO)
AHS .... Arlington Hall Station [Virginia] [Army] (AABC)
AHS .... Assistant Head of Section (DCTA)
AHS .... Assistant House Surgeon
AHS .... Associated Heat Services [Energy management contractor] [British]
AHS .... Associated Humane Societies (EA)
AHS .... Association for Humanist Sociology (EA)
AHS .... Association of Hungarian Students in North America [Defunct] (EA)
AHS .... At Home Series [Baseball]
AHS .... Attack Heading Slot (SAA)
AHS .... Attack Helicopter Support (MCD)
AHS .... Attitude Horizon Sensor (IIA)
AHS .... Augustana Historical Society (EA)
AHS .... Australian Health Services
AHS .... Australian Historical Statistics [A publication]
AHS .... Australian Historical Studies [A publication] (APTA)

AHS .... Automated Highway System
AHS .... Automated Highway System
AHS .... Automated Highway Systems [FHWA] (TAG)
AHS .... Autonomous Helicopter System [Military] (LAIN)
AHS .... Aviation Historical Society (EA)
AHS .... Azores Hot Spot [Geology]
AHS .... Berry Aviation, Inc. [ICAO designator] (FAAC)
AHS .... Harding College, Searcy, AR [OCLC symbol] (OCLC)
AHS .... International Association of Hydrological Sciences [See also AISH] [British]
AHSA .... African Heritage Studies Association (EA)
AHSA .... American Hampshire Sheep Association (EA)
AHSA .... American Health Security Act [Medicine]
AHSA .... American Home Satellite Association [Defunct] (EA)
AHSA .... American Home Sewing Association [Later, AHSCA] (EA)
AHSA .... American Horse Shows Association (EA)
AHSA .... American Humor Studies Association (EA)
AHSA .... Armorial and Heraldry Society of Australasia
AHSA .... Association of Hospital Security Administrators
AHSA .... Association of Human Services in Alberta (AC)
AHSC .... American Home Sewing Council [Later, AHSCA] (EA)
AHSC .... American Hospital Supply Corp (BABM)
AHSC .... Australian Health Services Commission
AHSCA .... American Home Sewing and Craft Association (EA)
AHSCo .... Assault Helicopter Support Company [Air Force] (AFM)
AHSCP .... African Household Survey Capability Programme [United Nations] (EY)
AHSCP .... Army High School Completion Program (MCD)
AHSE .... Assembly, Handling, and Shipping Equipment
AHSF .... American Hungarian Studies Foundation [Later, AHF] (EA)
AHSG .... Alpha-2HS-Glycoprotein (DMAA)
AHSGE .... Alabama High School Graduation Examination (EDAC)
AHSGR .... American Historical Society of Germans from Russia (EA)
AHSI .... Advanced Human Systems Institute [San Jose State University] [Research center] (RCD)
AHSLEA .... Australian Hides, Skins, and Leather Exports Association
AHSM .... Academy for Health Services Marketing [Chicago, IL] (EA)
AHSM .... Alpha Hand and Shoe Monitor [Radiation detection]
AHSME .... Annual High School Mathematics Examination [Educational test]
AHS-MS .... American Housing Survey-Metropolitan Sample [Department of Housing and Urban Development] (GFGA)
AHSN .... Assembly of Hospital Schools of Nursing (EA)
AHSP .... Association for High Speed Photography [British] (BI)
AHSPI .... Actions Having Significant Personnel Implications (MCD)
AHSR .... Airborne Height-Surveillance RADAR (IAA)
AHSR .... Air Height Surveillance RADAR
AHSR .... Association for Health Services Research (EA)
AHSRC .... Arctic Health Services Research Center [HEW]
AHSS .... Association of Home Study Schools [Later, ACTS] (EA)
AHSS .... Augusta Huiell Seaman Society [Defunct] (EA)
AHSSPPE ..... Association on Handicapped Student Service Programs in Postsecondary Education (EA)
AHST .... Alaska-Hawaii Standard Time (WGA)
AHST .... Anchor Handling Salvage Tug (DS)
AHST .... Association of Health Service Treasurers [British]
AHST .... Association of Highway Steel Transporters (EA)
AHST .... Attack Helicopter Self Test (MCD)
AHSTC .... Association pour l'Histoire de la Science et de la Technologies au Canada (AC)
AHSTC .... Austin-Healey Sports and Touring Club (EA)
AHSV .... African Horsesickness Virus [Veterinary medicine]
AHT............ Absorbtion Heat Transformer
AHT............ Acoustic Homing Torpedo
AHT............ Adaptive Hough Transform [Computer science]
AHT............ Aggregation Half Time [Medicine] (DMAA)
AHT............ AIRCOA Hotel Ltd. [AMEX symbol] (SPSG)
AHT............ Alaska Hydro-Train [AAR code]
AHT............ Amchitka, AK [Location identifier FAA] (FAAL)
AHT............ Anchor Handling Tug (DS)
AHT............ Animal Health Trust [British] (BI)
AHT............ Antihyaluronidase Titer [Clinical chemistry] (MAE)
AHT............ Arabian Horse Trust (EA)
AHT............ Assembly History Tag
AHT............ Attack Helicopter Team
AHT............ Augmented Histamine Test [Medicine] (MAE)
AHT............ Autoantibodies to Human Thyroglobulin [Endocrinology] (DAVI)
AHT............ Average Holding Time [Telecommunications] (TEL)
AHTAE .... American Hotel Trade Association Executives (EA)
AHTA of BC... Animal Health Technologists Association of BC (AC)
AHTC .... Association d'Histoire du Theatre du Canada [Association for Canadian Theatre History - ACTH]
AHTD .... Association of High Tech Distributors (EA)
AHTE .... Australian Horticultural Trades Exhibition
AHTG .... Antihuman Thymocytic Globulin [Clinical chemistry] (MAE)
AHTGG........ Antihuman Thymocyte Gamma Globulin [Immunochemistry]
AHTN .... Association of Hospital Television Networks (EA)
AHTP .... Aerodynamic Heat Test Plans
AHTP .... Antihuman Thymocytic Plasma [Clinical chemistry] (MAE)
AHTR .... Acute Hemolytic Transfusion Reaction [Medicine]
AHTS .... American Health and Temperance Society (EA)
AHTS .... Anchor Handling Tug Supply Vessel (DS)
AHTS .... Antihuman Thymus Serum (DMAA)
AHU .... Accumulated Heat Unit (OA)
AHU .... Ahuachapan [El Salvador] [Seismograph station code, US Geological Survey] (SEIS)

AHU	Air-Handling Unit [*Mechanical engineering*] (OA)
AHU	Al Hoceima [*Morocco*] [*Airport symbol*] (OAG)
AHU	Antihalation Undercoat [*Photography*] (OA)
AHU	Hughenden Public Library, Alberta [*Library symbol National Library of Canada*] (NLC)
AHUD	Austere Heads-Up Display [*Aviation*] (MCD)
AHUM	Hussar Municipal Library, Alberta [*Library symbol National Library of Canada*] (NLC)
AHV	Accelerator, High Voltage (SAA)
AHV	Ad Hanc Vocem [*At This Word*] [*Latin*]
AHV	Aircraft Handling Vehicle (MCD)
AHV	Alters- und Hinterlassenen-Versicherung [*Old Age and Dependents Insurance*] [*State insurance company Liechtenstein*] (EY)
AHV	Avian Herpes Virus (DMAA)
AHVMA	American Holistic Veterinary Medical Association (EA)
AHVN	American Hospital Video Network [*Satellite television system*]
AHW	[*The*] Ahnapee & Western Railway Co. [*Formerly, AW*] [*AAR code*]
AHw	Akkadisches Handwoerterbuch [*A publication*] (BJA)
AHW	Atomic Hydrogen Welding
AHW	Australian Hard Wheat [*Agriculture*]
AHWA	American Hazardous Waste Association (EA)
AHWA	Association of Hospital and Welfare Administrators [*British*] (BI)
AH-WC	Associate of Heriot-Watt College, Edinburgh
AHWEP	Aboriginal Health Worker Education Program [*Australia*]
AHWG	Ad Hoc Working Group [*Army*]
AHWHEF	Australian Hairdressers, Wigmakers, and Hairworkers Employees Federation
AHWT	Ames Dimensional Hypersonic Wind Tunnel (SAA)
Ahx	Aminohexanoic Acid [*Biochemistry*]
AHX	Athens, TX [*Location identifier FAA*] (FAAL)
AHX	Azahypoxanthine [*Biochemistry*]
AHY	Architectural Heritage Year [*1975*] [*British*] (DI)
AHY	Azalavia-Azerbaijan Hava Yollari [*ICAO designator*] (FAAC)
AHYD	Aromatics Hydrogenation [*Fuel technology*]
AHYDO	Applicable High-Yield Discount Obligation [*Finance*]
AHYM	Hythe Municipal Library, Alberta [*Library symbol National Library of Canada*] (NLC)
AI	Aaland Islands
AI	Accent on Information (EA)
AI	Access/Information [*Information service or system*] (IID)
AI	Accidental Injury
AI	Accidentally Incurred
A/I	Accident/Incident
AI	Accident Intelligence [*British police term*]
AI	ACCION International (EA)
AI	Accrued Interest [*Investment term*]
AI	Accumulated Interest [*Banking*]
AI	Acquisition Institute [*Defunct*] (EA)
AI	Action Item (NASA)
AI	Active Ingredient
AI	Activity Index
AI	Actuator/Indicator
AI	Adas [*or Adath*] Israel (BJA)
AI	Address Incomplete [*Telecommunications*] (TEL)
AI	Ad Interim [*In the Meantime*] [*Latin*] (EY)
AI	Adjustment Inventory [*Psychology*]
AI	Administrative Instructions
AI	Admiralty Instruction [*A publication*] (DLA)
AI	Admiralty Islands
AI	Adobe Illustrator [*Computer science*] (PCM)
AI	Adsorption Isotherm Test [*Environmental chemistry*] (FFDE)
AI	Advocacy Institute (EA)
AI	Aeronautica Industrial SA [*Spain ICAO aircraft manufacturer identifier*] (ICAO)
AI	After Image [*Psychology*]
AI	Aged Individual [*Title XVI*] [*Social Security Administration*] (OICC)
AI	Aged Intact Animal [*Endocrinology*]
AI	Agenda Item (MCD)
AI	AGILE [*Autonetics General Information Learning Equipment*] Interceptor
AI	Agricultural Index
AI	Agudath Israel [*Union of Israel*] [*World organization of Orthodox Jews*]
AI	Airborne Intercept [*RADAR*] [*Air Force*] (AFM)
AI	Aircraft Identification (AAG)
AI	Aircraft Industry (AAG)
AI	Aircraft Instruments and Aircrew Stations [*NATO*] (NATG)
AI	Aircraft Interceptor (MCD)
AI	Airfield Index
AI	Air India [*ICAO designator*] (AD)
AI	Air Injection [*Automotive engineering*]
AI	Air Inspector
AI	Air Installations
AI	Air Intelligence (NVT)
AI	Air Interdiction (MCD)
AI	Airship Industries Ltd. [*British*]
AI	Airspeed Indicator (MSA)
AI	Airways Inspector
AI	Alban Institute (EA)
AI	Alianza Interamericana [*Defunct*] (EA)
AI	Allergy and Immunology [*Medical specialty*] (DHSM)
AI	Allergy Index [*Medicine*] (DAVI)
AI	All Inertial (SAA)
AI	All Iron
AI	Alloys Index [*METADEX*] (NITA)

AI	Alpines International (EA)
AI	Altesse Imperiale [*Imperial Highness*] [*French*]
AI	Altimeter Indicator (MCD)
AI	Altitude Indicator [*Aviation*] (DA)
AI	Altitude Indoctrination (MCD)
AI	Altrusa International (EA)
AI	Amcot, Inc. (EA)
AI	American Indian
AI	American Institute
AI	American Israelite (BJA)
AI	Amity International (EAIO)
AI	Amnesty International [*London, England*] (EAIO)
AI	Amorphous Inclusion [*Cytology*]
AI	Amplifier Input
AI	Analog Input
AI	Angiogenesis Inhibitor [*Physiology*]
AI	Angiotensin I [*Biochemistry*] (MAE)
AI	Angle Iron [*Freight*]
AI	Anglo-Indian [*Language, etc.*]
AI	Anglo-Irish [*Language, etc.*]
AI	Anglo-Israelism [*or Anglo-Israelite*]
AI	Anguilla [*ANSI two-letter standard code*] (CNC)
AI	Anno Inventionis [*In the Year of the Discovery*] [*Latin*]
AI	Annoyance Index [*Aviation*] (OA)
AI	Antecedent Index (NOAA)
AI	Antenna Impedance
AI	Anthracite Institute [*Absorbed by PCMA*]
AI	Anthropological Institute (BARN)
AI	Anti-Icing [*Technical drawings*]
AI	Anxiety Index [*Psychology*]
AI	Aortic Incompetence [*or Insufficiency*] [*Medicine*]
AI	Apical Impulse [*Medicine*] (AAMN)
AI	Applications and Industry (MCD)
AI	Appraisal Institute (EA)
AI	Appreciation Index [*Television ratings*] [*British*]
AI	Aprovecho Institute (EA)
AI	Aptitude Index
AI	Arctic Institute
AI	Area Inspector [*British railroad term*]
AI	Arica Institute (EA)
AI	Army Intelligence
AI	Arrow Automotive Industries, Inc. [*AMEX symbol*] (SPSG)
AI	Articulation Index
AI	Artificial Insemination [*Medicine*]
AI	Artificial Intelligence [*Computer science*]
AI	Arts International (EA)
AI	Asbestos Institute (EA)
AI	Asphalt Institute (EA)
AI	Assignment Instructions
AI	Assistance and Instructions (MCD)
AI	Assistant Inspector (DCTA)
AI	Assistant Instructor
AI	Association Institute (EA)
AI	Assurex International (EA)
AI	Astrologers International [*Defunct*] (EA)
AI	Atherogenic Index [*By ultracentrifugation*] [*Cardiology*] (DAVI)
AI	Athletic Institute (EA)
AI	Atomics International (NRCH)
AI	Atrial Insufficiency [*Cardiology*] (AAMN)
AI	Attenuation Index
AI	Attitude Indicator [*NASA*] (KSC)
AI	Auditory Induction
AI	Australian Internationals (EA)
AI	Australian Investor [*A publication*] (ADA)
AI	Austrian Institute [*Later, ACI*] (EA)
AI	Authority for Issue Indicator (AFIT)
AI	Authorized Inspector
AI	Autographics International (EA)
AI	Automated Instruction (DNAB)
AI	Automatic Input [*Computer science*] (BUR)
AI	Automation Institute (MCD)
AI	Automotive Industries [*A publication*]
AI	Auto-Oxidation Inhibitor (BARN)
AI	Avian Influenza
AI	Aviation Investigator (LAIN)
AI	Avionic Instrument (MCD)
AI	Avionics Integration
AI	Awaiting Instruction [*Military*] (DNAB)
AI	Axioincisal [*Dentistry*]
AI	Azimuth Indicator
ai----	Indochina [*MARC geographic area code Library of Congress*] (LCCP)
AI	Inherent Availability
AI	Inherent Availability (AAGC)
AI	Interpreter, Second Class [*British*]
AI	Irricana Municipal Library, Alberta [*Library symbol National Library of Canada*] (NLC)
AIA	Abrasive Industries Association (MHDB)
AIA	Academie Internationale d'Astronautique [*France*] (EAIO)
AIA	Academy of Irish Art
AIA	Accident/Incident Analysis (PDAA)
AIA	Accuracy in Academia
AIA	Acquired Artery Immune Augmentation [*Medicine*] (DAVI)
AIA	Acronyms, Initials, and Abbreviations (DAVI)
AIA	Action Item Assignment (DNAB)
AIA	Acupuncture International Association (EA)

AIA.............. Advise if Able [Aviation] (FAAC)
AIA.............. Aerialift Industries Association [Defunct] (EA)
AIA.............. Aerospace Industries Association of America (EA)
AIA.............. Aestheticians International Association (EA)
AIA.............. Aging in America (EA)
AIA.............. Agudath Israel of America (EA)
AIA.............. AIDS Initial Assessment Questionnaire [Department of Health and Human Services] (GFGA)
AIA.............. Airborne Integration Area (MCD)
AIA.............. Aircraft Industries Association (BARN)
AIA.............. Air Intelligence Agency [Air Force]
AIA.............. Allergy Information Association [Canada]
AIA.............. Alliance [Nebraska] [Airport symbol] (OAG)
AIA.............. Allylisopropylacetamide [Biochemistry]
AIA.............. American Imagery Association [Defunct] (EA)
AIA.............. American Importers Association [Later, AAEI]
AIA.............. American Institute of Architects (EA)
AIA.............. American Institute of Architects, Washington, D.C. [1867] (NGC)
AIA.............. American Insurance Association [New York, NY] (EA)
AIA.............. American Insured Mortgage Investors. Series 84 Ltd. [AMEX symbol] (SPSG)
AIA.............. American International Academy [Defunct] (EA)
AIA.............. American International Association for Economic and Social Development [Defunct] (EA)
AIA.............. American International Assurance Co., Ltd. [Commercial firm] (ECON)
AIA.............. American Inventors Association
AIA.............. Americans for International Aid (EA)
AIA.............. Amylase Inhibitor Activity [Food technology]
AIA.............. Anglo-Irish Agreement [1985]
AIA.............. Anglo-Israel Association [British] (BI)
AIA.............. Anthracite Industry Association (EA)
AIA.............. Anti-Icing Additive (NATG)
AIA.............. Anti-Immunoglobulin Antibodies (DOG)
AIA.............. Anti-Inflation Act [Canada]
AIA.............. Anti-Injunction Act of 1932 (WYGK)
AIA.............. Anti-Intrusion Alarm
AIA.............. Anything Invented Anywhere [As opposed to NIH, Not Invented Here, an acronym indicating refusal to accept foreign technology]
AIA.............. Apiary Inspectors of America (EA)
AIA.............. Archaeological Institute of America (EA)
AIA.............. Argentine Interplanetary Association
AIA.............. Argentine Island [Antarctica] [Seismograph station code, US Geological Survey] (SEIS)
AIA.............. Army Information Architecture
AIA.............. Army Institute of Administration (MCD)
AIA.............. Army Intelligence Agency
AIA.............. Artificially Induced Aurora
AIA.............. Asbestos International Association [British] (EAIO)
AIA.............. Aspirin-Induced Asthma [Medicine]
AIA.............. Assistant Inspector Armourer [British and Canadian] [World War II]
AIA.............. Associate in Arts (ROG)
AIA.............. Associate of the Institute of Actuaries [British]
AIA.............. Association Internationale d'Allergologie [International Association of Allergology]
AIA.............. Association Internationale des Arbitres de Water Polo [International Association of Water Polo Referees - IAWPR] (EAIO)
AIA.............. Association of Immigration Attorneys (EA)
AIA.............. Association of Indians in America (EA)
AIA.............. Association of Industrial Advertisers [Later, B/PAA] (EA)
AIA.............. Association of Industrial Archaeology (EAIO)
AIA.............. Association of Insolvency Accountants [Chicago, IL] (EA)
AIA.............. Association of Insurance Advertisers [Defunct] (EA)
AIA.............. Association of Insurance Attorneys [Later, ADTA] (EA)
AIA.............. Association of International Accountants [British] (EAIO)
AIA.............. Athletes in Action (EA)
AIA.............. Australian Institute of Archaeology
AIA.............. Authors Institute of America (EA)
AIA.............. Auto Internacional Association (EA)
AIA.............. Automated Image Analysis [Instrumentation]
AIA.............. Automated Imaging Association (EA)
AIA.............. Automobile Importers of America [Later, AIAM] (EA)
AIA.............. Automotive Industries Association of Canada
AIA.............. Avies [Estonia] [FAA designator] (FAAC)
AIAA.............. Aerospace [formerly, Aircraft] Industries Association of America (MCD)
AIAA.............. Agricultural Information Association for Australasia
AIAA.............. American Industrial Arts Association (EA)
AIAA.............. American Institute of Aeronautics and Astronautics (EA)
AIAA.............. Apparel Importers' Association of Australia
AIAA.............. Architect Member of the Incorporated Association of Architects and Surveyors [British] (DI)
AIAA.............. Area of Intense Air Activity (DA)
AIAA.............. Association of International Advertising Agencies (EA)
AIAAM.............. Advanced Interceptor Air-to-Air Missile (MCD)
AIAA-TIS.............. Technical Information Service - of American Institute of Aeronautics and Astronautics (EA)
AI-Ab.............. Anti-Insulin Antibody [Endocrinology] (DAVI)
AIAB.............. Associate of the International Association of Book-Keepers (DCTA)
AIAC.............. Aerospace Industries Association of Canada [Association des Industries Aerospatiales du Canada] [Formerly, Air Industries Association of Canada] (AC)
AIAC.............. American Indian Arts Council (EA)
AIAC.............. Associate of the Institute of Company Accountants [British]

AIAC.............. Association Internationale des Aeroports Civils [International Civil Airports Association - ICAA] (EAIO)
AIAC.............. Associazione Internazionale di Archeologia Classica [International Association for Classical Archaeology - IACA] (EAIO)
AIAC.............. Automotive Industries Association of Canada
AIACR.............. Association Internationale des Automobile Clubs Reconnus [International Automobile Federation]
AIAD.............. Academic Individual Advanced Development [Military] (RDA)
AIAD.............. Acronyms, Initialisms, and Abbreviations Dictionary [Formerly, AID] [A publication]
AIADA.............. Alabama Independent Automobile Dealers Association (SRA)
AIADA.............. American International Automobile Dealers Association (EA)
AIADA.............. Arizona Independent Auto Dealers Association (SRA)
AIADA.............. Arkansas Independent Automobile Dealers Association (SRA)
AIADMK.............. All-India Anna Dravida Munnetra Kazhagam [Tamil Nadu] [Political party]
AIAE.............. Associate of the Institute of Automobile Engineers [British] (MCD)
AIA/EAC.............. European Advisory Council of the Asbestos International Association [EC] (ECED)
AIAEE.............. Association for International Agricultural and Extension Education (EA)
AIAF.............. American Institute of Architects Foundation (EA)
AIAG.............. Association Internationale des Assureurs Contre la Grele [International Association of Hail Insurers]
AIAG.............. Automotive Industry Action Group (EA)
AIAgrE.............. Associate of the Institution of Agricultural Engineers [British] (DBQ)
AIAI.............. American Indian Archaeological Institute (EA)
AIAI.............. Artificial Intelligence Applications Institute [British]
AIAIS.............. American In-Vitro Allergy/Immunology Society (EA)
AIAKS.............. American Institute of Architects in Kansas (SRA)
AIAL.............. American Indian Assistance League (OICC)
AIAL.............. Associate Member of the International Institute of Arts and Letters
AIAL.............. Association of International Institute of Arts and Letters
AIAM.............. Association of International Automobile Manufacturers (EA)
AIAMC.............. Association of International Automobile Manufacturers of Canada [Association des Fabricants Internationaux d'Automobiles du Canada] (AC)
AI/AN.............. American Indian and Alaska Native
AIAN.............. Association Internationale des Approvisionneurs de Navires [British] (EAIO)
AIA/NA.............. Asbestos Information Association/North America (EA)
AI & O.............. Annual Inspection and Overhaul [Nuclear energy] (NRCH)
AI & T.............. Assembly Integration and Test
AIANNA.............. American Indian/Alaska Native Nurses Association (EA)
AIAOS.............. Academic Instructor and Allied Officer School [Military] (AFM)
AIAP.............. Army's Incentive Awards Program (RDA)
AIAP.............. Association Internationale des Arts Plastiques [International Association of Art - IAA] (EAIO)
AIAPQ.............. Association des Intermediaires en Assurance de Personnes du Quebec (AC)
AIAQ.............. Association de l'Industrie de l'Aluminium du Quebec (AC)
AIAR.............. American Institute for Aerological Research (MCD)
AIAR.............. American Institute for Archaeological Research (EA)
AI Arb.............. Associate of the Institute of Arbitrators [British]
AIArbA.............. Associate of the Institute of Arbitrators Australia
AIARD.............. Association for International Agriculture and Rural Development (EA)
AIAS.............. American Institute of Architecture Students (EA)
AIAS.............. Anti-Intrusion Alarm Set
AIAS.............. Army Institute of Advanced Studies
AIAS.............. Associate Surveyor Member of the Incorporated Association of Architects and Surveyors [British]
AIASA.............. American Industrial Arts Student Association [Later, TSA] (EA)
AIASA.............. Annual Integrated Assessment of Security Assistance [Military] (DOMA)
AIA/SC.............. American Institute of Architects Service Corp. [Information service or system] (IID)
AIASS.............. American-Israel Anti-Smoking Society (EA)
AIAT.............. Anti-Inflation Appeal Tribunal [Canada]
AIAT.............. Associate of the Institute of Animal Technicians [British] (DI)
AIAT.............. Association of the Institute of Asphalt Technology [British] (DBQ)
AIAT.............. Attitude-Interest Analysis Test [Psychology]
AIAT.............. Auditory Integrative Abilities Test
AIATSC.............. All International Air Traffic Switching Centers (FAAC)
AIAV.............. Australian Indonesian Association of Victoria [Australia]
AIAVA.............. Amino(iodoacetamido)valeric Acid [Organic acid]
AIAW.............. Association for Intercollegiate Athletics for Women (EA)
AIAX.............. Alaska International Air, Inc. [Air carrier designation symbol]
AIB.............. Academy of International Business [Cleveland, OH] (EA)
AIB.............. Accidents Investigation Branch [Air Force British]
AIB.............. Admiralty Interview Board [British]
AIB.............. Agency Investigation Board
AIB.............. Agricultural Information Bulletin
AIB.............. Airbus Industrie [France ICAO designator] (FAAC)
AIB.............. Aircraft Instrument Bulletin [Navy] (NG)
AIB.............. Allied Intelligence Bureau (ADA)
AIB.............. Allied Irish Banks ADS [NYSE symbol] (SPSG)
AIB.............. American Institute of Baking (EA)
AIB.............. American Institute of Banking (EA)
AIB.............. Aminoisobutyrate (DMAA)
AIB.............. Aminoisobutyric Acid [Biochemistry]
AIB.............. Analog Input/Output Board [Computer science] (NITA)
AIB.............. Analysis and Information Branch [Climate Analysis Center] [National Weather Service]
AIB.............. Anthracite Information Bureau [Defunct]
AIB.............. Anti-Inflation Board

AIB............ Aptitude Index Battery [*LIMRA*]
AIB............ Arab Information Bank [*Information service or system*] (IID)
AIB............ Armored Infantry Battalion
AIB............ Army Infantry Board (RDA)
AIB............ Assassination Information Bureau [*An association*] (EA)
AIB............ Associate Insurance Broker (DD)
AIB............ Associate of the Institute of Bankers [*British*] (EY)
AIB............ Association Internationale de Bibliophile [*International Association of Bibliophiles - IAB*] [*Paris, France*] (EAIO)
AIB............ Association Internationale de Bryozoologie [*International Bryozoology Association - IBA*] [*Paris, France*] (EAIO)
AIB............ Association of Independent Businesses (EAIO)
AIB............ Association of Insurance Brokers Ltd. [*British*] (BI)
AIB............ Association of Investment Brokers [*New York, NY*] (EA)
AIB............ Athlete Information Bureau [*Canada*]
AIB............ Australian Insolvency Bulletin [*A publication*]
AIB............ Australian Institute of Bankers
AIB............ Automatic Intercept Bureau [*Telecommunications*] (TEL)
AIB............ Avian Infectious Bronchitis [*Medicine*] (DMAA)
AIB............ Avionics Integration Bench (MCD)
AIB............ Community College of Allegheny County, Boyce Campus, Monroeville, PA [*OCLC symbol*] [*Ina ctive*] (OCLC)
AIBA............ Agricultural Information Bank for Asia [*Southeast Asian Regional Center for Graduate Study and Research in Agriculture*] [*Information service or system*] (IID)
AIBA............ Air Intercept Battle Analysis
AIBA............ Alpha-Aminoisobutyric Acid [*Organic chemistry*]
AIBA............ American Industrial Bankers Association [*Later, NCFA*] (EA)
AIBA............ Aminoisobutyric Acid [*Biochemistry*] (AAMN)
AIBA............ Associate of the Institution of Business Agents [*British*] (DBQ)
AIBA............ Association Internationale de Boxe Amateur [*International Amateur Boxing Association*] (EA)
AIBA............ Association of International Border Agencies (EA)
AIBAA............ Artists in Bark Association of Australia
AIBBC .... Australian Indoor Bias Bowls Council
AIBC............ American Irish Bicentennial Committee (EA)
AIBC............ Architectural Institute of British Columbia [*1914*] [*Canada*] (NGC)
AIBC............ Architectural Institute of British Columbia (AC)
AIBC............ Australia-Indonesia Business Council
AIBCM .... Association of Industrialized Building Component Manufacturers Ltd. [*British*] (BI)
AIBD .... American Institute of Building Design (EA)
AIBD .... Asia-Pacific Institute for Broadcasting Development (EAIO)
AIBD .... Associate of the Institute of British Decorators
AIBD .... Association of International Bond Dealers [*Zurich, Switzerland*] (EAIO)
AIBD .... International Securities Market Association [*Switzerland*] (EAIO)
AIBDA .... Asociacion Interamericana de Bibliotecarios y Documentalistas Agricolas [*Inter-American Association of Agricultural Librarians and Documentalists*] (EAIO)
AIBDQ............ Association of International Bond Dealers Quotation [*Stock exchange term*]
AIBF............ Advanced Internally Blown Jet Flag (MCD)
AIBI............ Association Internationale de la Boulangerie Industrielle [*International Association of the Bread Industry*] (EAIO)
AIBICC .... Associate of the Incorporated British Institute of Certified Carpenters (DI)
AIBiol............ Associate Member of the Institute of Biology [*British*] (DI)
AIBM............ Association Internationale des Bibliotheques, Archives, et Centres de Documentation Musicaux [*International Association of Music Libraries, Archives, and Documentation Centres - IAML*] (EAIO)
AIBN .... Azobisisobutyronitrile [*Organic chemistry*]
AIBNRM .... American Institute of Bolt, Nut, and Rivet Manufacturers [*Later, Industrial Fasteners Institute*]
AIBP............ Anglo-Irish Beef Processors Ltd. [*Northern Ireland*]
AIBP............ Associate of the Institute of British Photographers
AIBS............ Active Isolation/Balance System [*for aircraft*] (RDA)
AIBS............ American Institute of Biological Sciences (EA)
AIB(Scot) ..... Associate of the Institute of Bankers in Scotland (DBQ)
AIC............ Academie Internationale de la Ceramique [*International Academy of Ceramics - IAC*] (EAIO)
AIC............ Accelerator Information Center [*ORNL*]
AIC............ Accretion-Induced Collapse [*Astrophysics*]
AIC............ Acoustic Isolation Chamber
AIC............ Activity Identification Code [*Navy*]
AIC............ Adaptive Inferential Control [*Control technology*]
AIC............ Address Information Center [*Memphis, TN*] [*US Postal Service*]
AIC............ Adriatic Resources Corp. [*Vancouver Stock Exchange symbol*]
AIC............ Advanced Image Compression (MCD)
AIC............ Advanced Intelligence Center [*Navy*]
AIC............ Advertising Inquiry Council (DGA)
AIC............ Aerodynamic-Influence Coefficient
AIC............ Aeronautical Information Circular (FAAC)
AIC............ Afghanistan Information Center [*Later, ASAP*] (EA)
AIC............ Agent in Charge [*Criminology*] (LAIN)
AIC............ Agricultural Improvement Council [*British*]
AIC............ Agricultural Institute of Canada
AIC............ Agrupaciones Independientes de Canarias [*Spain Political party*] (EY)
AIC............ Airborne Information Correlation (MCD)
AIC............ Aircraft Identification Control (SAA)
AIC............ Aircraft in Commission
AIC............ Aircraft Industries Center (AAG)
AIC............ Aircraft Industry Conference [*Navy*]
AIC............ Aircraft Information Correlator (CAAL)

AIC............ Air India [*ICAO designator*] (FAAC)
AIC............ Air Information Center (NATG)
AIC............ Air Information Codification (NATG)
AIC............ Air Inlet Controller (MCD)
AIC............ Air Intelligence Command (SAA)
AIC............ Air Intercept [*or Interception*] Control [*or Controller*]
AIC............ Air Interception Committee [*Air Ministry*] [*British*]
AIC............ Allied Intelligence Committee [*London*]
AIC............ Allowance Item Code
AIC............ Alternative Information Center [*Israeli news organization*]
AIC............ American Institute for Conservation of Historic and Artistic Works (EA)
AIC............ American Institute of Chefs [*Later, ACF*]
AIC............ American Institute of Chemists (EA)
AIC............ American Institute of Constructors (EA)
AIC............ American Institute of Cooperation [*Defunct*] (EA)
AIC............ American International College [*Springfield, MA*]
AIC............ American International Communications Corp. [*Boulder, CO*]
AIC............ American Italian Congress (EA)
AIC............ Americans for Immigration Control (EA)
AIC............ Aminoimidazolecarboxamide [*Also, AICA*] [*Organic chemistry*]
AIC............ Ammunition Identification Code
AIC............ Anacapa Island [*California*] [*Seismograph station code, US Geological Survey*] (SEIS)
AIC............ Apollo Intermediate Chart [*NASA*] (MCD)
AIC............ Appraisal Institute of Canada
AIC............ Apprenticeship Information Center [*Department of Labor*]
AIC............ Aquaculture Information Center [*Department of Agriculture Information service or system*] (IID)
AIC............ Arizona International Campus [*University of Arizona*]
AIC............ Army Industrial College
AIC............ Army Intelligence Center
AIC............ Arthritis Information Clearinghouse [*Public Health Service*] (EA)
AIC............ Artificial Insemination Centre [*Australia*]
AIC............ Art Information Center (EA)
AIC............ Art Institute of Chicago
AIC............ Asbestos Information Centre Ltd. [*British*] (CB)
AIC............ Asociacion Interamericana de Contabilidad [*Interamerican Accounting Association - IAA*] [*Mexico City, Mexico*] (EAIO)
AIC............ Asset Investors Corp. [*NYSE symbol*] (SPSG)
AIC............ Associate of the Institute of Chemistry [*Later, ARIC*] [*British*]
AIC............ Association des Industries des Carrieres [*Federations of Quarrying Industries*] [*Belgium*] (EY)
AIC............ Association des Infirmieres Canadiennes [*Canadian Nurses' Association - CNA*]
AIC............ Association Internationale de Cybernetique [*International Association for Cybernetics - IAC*] (EAIO)
AIC............ Association Internationale de la Couleur [*International Color Association*] [*Soesterberg, Netherlands*] (EA)
AIC............ Association Internationale des Charites [*International Association of Charities - IAC*] (EAIO)
AIC............ Association Internationale des Charites de St. Vincent De Paul [*International Association of Charities of St. Vincent De Paul*] (EAIO)
AIC............ Association Internationale des Cordeliers [*International Songwriters' Association - ISA*] (EAIO)
AIC............ Association of Idaho Cities (SRA)
AIC............ Association of Image Consultants (EA)
AIC............ Association of Independent Camps (EA)
AIC............ Association of Independent Cinemas [*British*]
AIC............ Association of Independent Consultants (AC)
AIC............ Association of Interstate Motor Carriers, Newark NJ [*STAC*]
AIC............ Astrology Information Centre (AC)
AIC............ Asymmetric Illumination Contrast [*Microscopy*]
AIC............ Atlantic Intelligence Center [*Navy*]
AIC............ Attack Information Center (AFM)
AIC............ Automatic Initiation Circuit (IEEE)
AIC............ Automatic Intercept Center [*Bell System*]
AIC............ Automatic Iris Control (PDAA)
AIC............ Automotive Information Council (EA)
AIC............ Awaiting Incoming Continuity [*Telecommunications*] (TEL)
AIC............ Ayer Information Center [*Information service or system*] (IID)
AIC............ Community College of Allegheny County, Pittsburgh, PA [*OCLC symbol*] (OCLC)
AICA............ Alliance of Independent Colleges of Art (EA)
AICA............ American Institute of Commemorative Art (EA)
AICA............ American-International Charolais Association (EA)
AICA............ Aminoimidazolecarboxamide [*Also, AIC*] [*Organic chemistry*]
AICA............ Aminoimidazolecarboxylic Acid [*Organic chemistry*]
AICA............ Anterior Inferior Cerebellar Artery [*Anatomy*]
AICA............ Anterior Inferior Communicating Artery [*Anatomy*]
AICA............ Anterior Internal Cerebral Artery [*Anatomy*] (DAVI)
AICA............ Associate Member of the Commonwealth Institute of Accountants [*British*] (ODBW)
AICA............ Association Internationale des Critiques d'Art [*International Association of Art Critics*] (EAIO)
AICA............ Association Internationale pour le Calcul Analogique [*International Association for Analogue Computation*] [*Later, IMACS*]
AICA............ Associazione degli Industriali delle Conserve Animali [*Meat Products Manufacturers Association*] [*Italy*]
AICA............ Associazione Italiana per il Calcolo Automatico [*Italian Association for Automatic Data Processing*]
AICA............ Australasian Institute of Chartered Accountants
AICA............ Automobile Importers Compliance Association [*Defunct*] (EA)
AICAE............ American Indian Council of Architects and Engineers (EA)

AICAP .... American Institute of Computerized Accounting Professionals [Defunct] (EA)
AICAR .... Aminoimidazolecarboxamide Ribonucleotide [Also, AICR] [Biochemistry]
AICB .... Associate of the Institute of Canadian Bankers (DD)
AICB .... Association Internationale Contre le Bruit [International Association Against Noise] [ICSU] (EAIO)
AICBM .... Anti-Intercontinental Ballistic Missile
AICC .... Action Item Control Card (MCD)
AICC .... Air Intercept Control Command (SAA)
AICC .... All-India Congress Committee
AICC .... American Immigration and Citizenship Conference (EA)
AICC .... American Indonesian Chamber of Commerce (EA)
AICC .... Antibody-Induced Cell-Mediated Cytoxicity [Medicine] (PDAA)
AICC .... Asian Indian Chamber of Commerce (EA)
AICC .... Association des Ingenieurs-Conseils du Canada [Association of Canadian Engineer-Councils]
AICC .... Association Internationale de Chimie Cerealiere [International Association for Cereal Chemistry] [Also, ICC]
AICC .... Association of Independent Corrugated Converters (EA)
AICC .... Association of Independent Crop Consultants [British] (DBA)
AICC .... Australia-India Chamber of Commerce
AICC .... Automated Intelligent Cruise Control [FHWA] (TAG)
AICC .... Automatic Interactive Computer Control (MCD)
AICC .... Autonomous Intelligent Cruise Control [Automotive engineering]
AICCA .... Aboriginal and Islander Child Care Agencies [Australia]
AICCC .... Alarm Industry Committee for Combating Crime [Defunct] (EA)
AICCC .... American Institute of Child Care Centers [Defunct]
AICCF .... Association Internationale du Congres des Chemins de Fer [International Railway Congress Association - IRCA] (EAIO)
AICCI .... Australia-Israel Chamber of Commerce and Industry
AICCP .... Association of Interstate Commerce Commission Practitioners (EA)
AICCP .... Association of the Institute for Certification of Computer Professionals (EA)
AICCT .... Association for the Improvement of Community College Teaching [Defunct] (EA)
AICCU .... Association of Independent California Colleges and Universities (SRA)
AICD .... Accelerated Individual and Company Development (PDAA)
AICD .... Activation-Induced Cell Death [Immunology]
AICD .... Automatic Implantable Cardiovascular Defibrillator [Unit] [Cardiology] (DAVI)
AICD .... Automatic Implantable Cardioverter-Defibrillator [Cardiology]
AICE .... American Institute for Character Education [Later, CEI] (EA)
AICE .... American Institute of Chemical Engineers [New York, NY]
AICE .... American Institute of Consulting Engineers [Later, ACEC] (EA)
AICE .... American Institute of Crop Ecology (EA)
AICE .... Angiotensin I Converting Enzyme (DMAA)
AICE .... Associate of the Institute of Civil Engineers [British]
AICE .... Association of Independent Commercial Editors (NTCM)
AI-CE .... Atomic International - Combustion Engineering
AI Ceram ..... Associate of the Institute of Ceramics [British]
AICES .... Association of International Courier and Express Services (EAIO)
AICF .... Action Internationale Contre la Faim [International Action Against Hunger] [Paris, France] (EAIO)
AICF .... America-Israel Cultural Foundation (EA)
AICF .... American Immigration Control Foundation (EA)
AICF .... American Inns of Court Foundation (EA)
AICF .... Australian Indoor Cricket Federation
AICF .... Autoimmune Complement Fixation [Immunochemistry]
AICGS .... American Institute for Contemporary German Studies (EA)
AICH .... American Indian Community House
AICH .... Automatic Integrated Container Handling (PDAA)
AIChE .... American Institute of Chemical Engineers (EA)
AIChor .... Associate of the Benesh Institute of Choreology [British] (DBQ)
AICI .... Apparel Industry Committee on Imports (EA)
AIC/INT .... Aerodynamic Influence Coefficients with Interference (PDAA)
AICIPP .... America-Israel Council for Israeli-Palestinian Peace (EA)
AICITLO ...... Army Instructor Cadre Interceptor Transporter Loader Operations [Course]
AICITLOM .... Army Instructor Cadre Interceptor Transporter / Loader Operations Maintenance Course
AICL .... Association Internationale des Critiques Litteraires [International Association of Literary Critics] (EAIO)
AICLC .... American Israeli Civil Liberties Coalition (EA)
AICM .... Association d'Ileostomie & Colostomie de Montreal [Colostomy Association of Montreal] (AC)
AICM .... Association of Independent Colleges of Music (EA)
AICMA .... Association Internationale des Constructeurs de Materiel Aerospatial [International Association of Aerospace Equipment Manufacturers]
AICMDM ...... Association of Independent Copy Machine Dealers and Manufacturers (EA)
AICMIP .... All-India Coordinated Millet Improvement Programme
AICMR .... Association Internationale des Constructeurs de Materiel Roulant [International Association of Rolling Stock Builders - IARSB] (EAIO)
AICO .... Action Information Control Officer [Navy]
AICO .... American Insulator Corp.
AICO .... Asociacion Iberoamericana de Camaras de Comercio [Ibero-American Association of Chambers of Commerce - IAACC] [Bogota, Colombia] (EAIO)
AICP .... American Institute of Certified Planners (EA)
AICP .... Army Internal Control Program (RDA)
AICP .... Army Inventory Control Point

AICP............ Artificially Intelligent Computer Performer
AICP............ Asian Infrastructure Consortia Program [Australia]
AICP............ Associate of the International Council of Psychologists
AICP............ Association Internationale des Circuits Permanents [Circuits International] [Germany] (EAIO)
AICP............ Association of Independent Commercial Producers [New York, NY] (EA)
AICP............ Association of Independent Composers and Performers (EA)
AICP............ Atomic Incident Control Plan
AICPA .... American Institute of Certified Public Accountants [New York, NY] (EA)
AICPA-Prof Stand (CCH)... American Institute for Certified Public Accountants - Professional Standards (Commerce Clearing House) [A publication] (DLA)
AIC/PMG ...... Photographic Materials Specialty Group of the American Institute for Conservation of Historic and Artistic Works (EA)
AICPOA .... Advanced Intelligence Center, Pacific Ocean Areas [Navy]
AICQ .... Association des Ingenieurs-Conseils du Quebec [Consulting Engineers of Quebec] (AC)
AIC(Q) .... Australian Institute of Cartographers (Queensland)
AICR .... Adaptive Intercommunication Requirement
AICR .... American Institute for Cancer Research [Research center] (RCD)
AICR .... Aminoimidazolecarboxamide Ribonucleotide [Also, AICAR] [Biochemistry]
AICR .... Association for International Cancer Research (EAIO)
AICRC .... American Indian Culture Research Center (EA)
AICRC .... Association of Independent Clinical Research Contractors [British] (DBA)
AI Cr D .... All India Criminal Decisions [A publication] (DLA)
AICRIP .... All-India Coordinated Rice Improvement Program
AICRO .... Association of Independent Contract Research Organisations [British]
AICS .... Aboriginal Independent Community Schools [Australia]
AICS .... Action Item Closeout Sheet (MCD)
AICS .... Adaptive Interference Cancellation System (CAAL)
AICS .... Advanced Imaging Communications System (MCD)
AICS .... Advanced Interior Communication System
AICS .... Air Induction Control System [Air Force]
AICS .... Air Inlet Control System
AICS .... Air Intercept Controller Supervisor (NVT)
AICS .... Air Intercept Control School
AICS .... American Institute of Ceylonese Studies (EA)
AICS .... American International Checkers Society (EA)
AICS .... Amnesty International Canadian Section
AICS .... Army Intelligence Center and School (MCD)
AICS .... Associate of the Institute of Chartered Shipbrokers [British]
AICS .... Association Internationale du Cinema Scientifique [International Scientific Film Association]
AICS .... Association of Independent Church Schools (AC)
AICS .... Association of Independent Colleges and Schools (EA)
AICS .... Association of Independent Computer Specialists (EAIO)
AICS .... Association of Industrial Colleges and Schools (OICC)
AICS .... Australian Inventory of Chemical Substances
AICS .... Automated Industrial Control System [Computer science] (MHDB)
AICS .... Automatic Inlet Control System (NG)
AICS .... Automatic Intersection Control System
AICSC .... Aircraft Integrated Crew Station Concepts (MCD)
AICSTS .... Air Inlet Control System Test Set
AICT .... Association Internationale Contre la Torture [International Association Against Torture] [Milan, Italy] (EAIO)
AICT .... Association Internationale des Critiques de Theatre [International Association of Theatre Critics]
AICT .... Atlantic Information Centre for Teachers [Defunct] (EA)
AICT .... Automatic Integrated Circuit Tester
AICTA .... Associate of the Imperial College of Tropical Agriculture [British]
AICU .... Association of International Colleges and Universities (EA)
AICU .... AUTODIN Interface Control Unit (MCD)
AICUZ .... Air Installation Compatible Use Zoning [Air Force]
AICV .... Amphibious Infantry Combat Vehicle [Army] (ADDR)
AICV .... Armored Infantry Combat Vehicle
AICV .... Association des Industries des Cidres et Vins de Fruits de la CEE [Association of the Cider and Fruit Wine Industries of the EEC] (ECED)
AICV .... Australian Institute of Consultant Valuers
AICVF-CE .... Association des Industries de Cidre et Vins de Fruits de la CE [Belgium] (EAIO)
AICVS .... Association Internationale Contre la Violence dans le Sport [International Association for Non-Violent Sport - IANVS] [Monte Carlo, Monaco] (EAIO)
AICW .... Advanced Individual Combat Weapon [Army] (INF)
AICW .... Associate of the Institute of Clerks of Works [British] (DI)
AICX........... Applied Imaging Corp. [NASDAQ symbol] (SAG)
AICY .... Association for International Children and Youth (EA)
AICYEE........ Association of the International Christian Youth Exchange in Europe (EAIO)
AID.............. Abbreviated Item Description (NASA)
AID.............. Abortion Information Data Bank [of Zero Population Growth, Inc.] [Defunct]
AID.............. Acceptable Intake Daily [of foods and additives]
AID.............. Accepting Individual Differences Curriculum (EDAC)
AID.............. Accident, Incident, Deficiencies (AFM)
AID.............. Accident/Injury/Damages (DLA)
AID.............. Acquired Immunodeficiency [Also, AIDS, GRID] [Medicine]
AID.............. Acquisition Integrated Data Base [Army] (RDA)
AID.............. Acronyms and Initialisms Dictionary [Later, AIAD] [A publication]
AID.............. Action in Distress [British] (DI)

AID.............. Action Item Directive (AAG)
AID.............. Active Integral Defense (AFM)
AID.............. Acute Infectious Disease [*Medicine*]
AID.............. Acute Ionization Detector [*Medicine*] (DMAA)
AID.............. Adaptive Intelligent Dialog (PDAA)
AID.............. Adriamycin, Ifosfamide, Dacarbazine [*Antineoplastic drug regimen*]
AID.............. Adult Information on Drugs [*Referral service*]
AID.............. Advanced Integrated Diagnostics (BUR)
AID.............. Advanced Interactive Draughting [*McGrane Computer Systems Ltd.*] [*Software package*] (NCC)
AID.............. Advanced Ionization Detector
AID.............. Advanced Ionization Development (MCD)
AID.............. Advance Information Document (MCD)
AID.............. Advertising Investigation Department [*British*]
AID.............. Aeronautical Inspection Directorate [*British*] (MCD)
AID.............. Aerospace Information Division [*Library of Congress*]
AID.............. Agency for International Development [*State Department*] [*Also, USAID US International Development Cooperation Agency*]
AID.............. Agency for International Development, Washington, DC [*OCLC symbol*] (OCLC)
AID.............. AGILE [*Autonetics General Information Learning Equipment*] Interceptor Defense
AID.............. Agricultural, Industrial, and Development [*Bank*] [*Dominica*] (EY)
AID.............. Aided
AID.............. Aidu [*Inawashiro*] [*Seismograph station code, US Geological Survey Closed*] (SEIS)
AID.............. Ailing-In Difficulty
AID.............. Airborne Intelligent Display (MCD)
AID.............. Aircraft & Instrument Demisting Ltd. [*British*]
AID.............. Aircraft Identification Determination (SAA)
AID.............. Aircraft Installation Delay (DA)
AID.............. Aircraft Interface Device (DWSG)
AID.............. Air Information Division [*Library of Congress*] (MCD)
AID.............. Air Inlet Damper (NRCH)
AID.............. Air Inspection Directorate [*British*]
AID.............. Air Intake Duct (DNAB)
AID.............. Airline Interline Development
AID.............. Airport Information Desk
AID.............. Algebraic Interpretive Dialogue [*Computer science*] (BUR)
AID.............. Alliance Internationale de la Distribution par Cable [*International Alliance for Distribution by Cable*] (EAIO)
AID.............. All-Ireland Distress (DI)
AID.............. Altered Item Drawing (SSD)
AID.............. America-India Dispensary [*Pharmacology*] (DAVI)
AID.............. American Institute of Interior Designers [*Later, ASID*]
AID.............. American Instructors of the Deaf [*Also known as CAID*] (EA)
AID.............. Americans of Italian Descent (EA)
AID.............. Amphibious Inhaul Device (PDAA)
AID.............. Analog Input Differential (MCD)
AID.............. Analytical Instrument Development, Inc.
AID.............. Anderson, IN [*Location identifier FAA*] (FAAL)
AID.............. Anti-Inflammatory Drug [*Pharmacology*] (DAVI)
AID.............. Apogee Intercept Defense (MCD)
AID.............. Applied Information and Documentation [*Database producer*] (IID)
AID.............. Arbitron Information on Demand [*Marketing service*] (DOAD)
AID.............. Arbitron's Information on Demand [*Arbitron Co.*] [*Information service or system*] (NTCM)
AID.............. Area Imaging Device (MCD)
AID.............. Argon Ionization Detector [*Medicine*] (DMAA)
AID.............. Argonne Interactive Display
AID.............. Army Information Digest
AID.............. Army Intelligence Department [*British*]
AID.............. Artificial Insemination by Donor [*Medicine*]
AID.............. Artikkel-Indeks Database [*Norwegian Center for Informatics*] [*Information service or system*]
AID.............. Arts in Danger [*An association British*] (DI)
AID.............. Assembly Instruction Device (DNAB)
AID.............. Assistance and Independence for the Disabled [*British*]
AID.............. Assistance in Divorce [*British*] (DI)
AID.............. Associated Independent Distributors [*Later, IDA*] (EA)
AID.............. Associated In-Group Donors
AID.............. Association for International Development [*Defunct*] (EA)
AID.............. Association Internationale des Debardeurs [*International Longshoremen's Association - ILA*] [*Canada*]
AID.............. Association Internationale des Documentalistes et Techniciens de l'Information [*International Association of Documentalists and Information Officers*]
AID.............. Association Internationale des Documentaristes [*International Association of Documentary Filmmakers*]
AID.............. Association of Institutional Distributors [*Later, FOOD*] (EA)
AID.............. Associative Interactive Dictionary [*for databases*] [*National Library of Medicine*]
AID.............. Atherectomy Imaging Device [*Medicine*]
AID.............. Atomics International Division
AID.............. Attached Inflatable Decelerator [*Aerodynamics*]
AID.............. Attached Inflatable Detector
AID.............. Audit Item Disposition (MCD)
AID.............. Auditory Information Display
AID.............. Augmented Index and Digest [*Information Retrieval Ltd.*] [*British*] (NITA)
AID.............. Autoimmune Deficiency [*or Disease*] [*Immunology*]
AID.............. Auto-Instructional Device (AEBS)
AID.............. Auto-Interactive Design [*Combines operator-executed and automatic features*] [*Computer science*]
AID.............. Automated Industrial Drilling (MHDI)

AID.............. Automatic Implantable Defibrillator [*Cardiology*]
AID.............. Automatic Incident Detector (DI)
AID.............. Automatic Information Distribution [*Computer science*] (MHDI)
AID.............. Automatic Initial Distribution (DNAB)
AID.............. Automatic Interaction Detection [*or Detector*] [*Computer science*]
AID.............. Automatic Interrogation Distortion [*Telecommunications*] (OA)
AID.............. Automotive Industry Data [*British*]
AID.............. Avalanche Injection Diode
AIDA .... Advanced Integrated Circuit Design Aids [*ESPRIT*] (NITA)
AIDA .... Aid Auto Stores, Inc. [*NASDAQ symbol*] (SAG)
AIDA .... Air Base Damage Assessment Model (MCD)
AIDA .... American Independent Designers Association (EA)
AIDA .... American Indian Development Association [*Defunct*] (EA)
AIDA .... American Indicator Digest Average [*American Stock Exchange*]
AIDA .... American International Dragon Association (EA)
AIDA .... Analysis of Interconnected Decision Areas [*Business term*] (PDAA)
AIDA .... Asociacion Internacional de Derecho de Aguas [*International Association for Water Law - IAWL*] [*Spain*] (EAIO)
AIDA .... Associated Independent Dairies of America (EA)
AIDA .... Association Internationale de Defense des Artistes [*International Association for the Defence of Artists*] (EAIO)
AIDA .... Association Internationale de Droit des Assurances [*International Association for Insurance Law*] [*Belgium*] (EAIO)
AIDA .... Association Internationale de la Distribution [*International Association of Distribution*] [*Belgium*] (EAIO)
AIDA .... Association Internationale de la Distribution des Produits Alimentaires et des Produits de Grande Consommation [*International Association for the Distribution of Food Products and General Consumer Goods*] (EAIO)
AIDA .... Associazione Italiana per la Documentazione Avanzata [*Italian Association forAdvanced Documentation*] [*Information service or system*] (IID)
AIDA .... Attention-Interest-Desire-Action [*Formula*] [*Marketing*]
AIDA .... Australian Irish Dancing Association
AIDA .... Automated Inspection of Data
AIDA .... Automatic Instrumented Diving Assembly
AIDA .... Automatic Intruder Detector Alarm [*Military British*]
AIDAB .... Automobile Information Disclosure Act [*1958*]
AIDAB .... Australian International Development Assistance Bureau
AIDAC .... Assistance Information and Data Acquisition Center [*Navy*]
AIDAC .... Association Internationale de Developpement et d'Action Communautaires [*International Association for Community Development*] [*Marcinelle, Belgium*] (EAIO)
AIDAP .... Automatic Inspection, Diagnostic, and Prognostic [*System*] [*Army*]
AIDAPS .... Automatic Inspection, Diagnostic, and Prognostic System [*Army*]
AIDAR .... Agency for International Development Acquisition Regulation [*A publication*] (AAGC)
AIDAS .... Advanced Instrumentation and Data Analysis System
AIDAS .... Agricultural Industry Development Advisory Service (ODBW)
AIDASA .... Association Internationale pour le Developpement en Afrique des Sciences Humaines Appliquees [*International Association for the Development of Applied Human Sciences in Africa*] (AF)
AIDAT .... Automatic Integrated Dynamic Avionics Tester
AIDATS .... Army In-Flight Data Transmission System (MCD)
AIDA-USA .... Association Internationale de Defense des Artistes [*International Associationfor the Defense of Artists*] - USA (EA)
AidAut......... Aid Auto Stores, Inc. [*Associated Press*] (SAG)
AidAuto........ Aid Auto Stores, Inc. [*Associated Press*] (SAG)
AIDBA .... Association Internationale pour le Developpement des Bibliotheques en Afrique [*International Association for the Development of Libraries in Africa*]
AIDC .... Alliance Internationale de la Distribution par Cable [*International Alliance for Distribution by Cable - IADC*] (EAIO)
AIDC .... American Industrial Development Council [*Later, AEDC*] (EA)
AIDC .... Association Internationale de Droit Constitutionnel [*International Association of Constitutional Law - IACL*] (EAIO)
AIDC .... Automatic Image Density Control [*Photocopying toning technique*] (NITA)
AIDCAS .... Attention, Interest, Desire, Conviction, Action, and Satisfaction [*Sales*] (WDMC)
AIDD .... American Institute for Design and Drafting [*Later, ADDA*] (EA)
AIDD .... Association of Insulin-Dependent Diabetics [*Defunct*] (EA)
AIDDE .... AMES Interactive Dynamic Display Editor (MCD)
AIDE............ Action Internationale pour les Droits de l'Enfant [*International Action for the Rights of the Child - IARC*] [*Paris, France*] (EAIO)
AIDE............ Adapted Identification Decision Equipment
AIDE............ Adaptive and Integrated Decision Expeditor (MCD)
AIDE............ Aerospace [*or Aircraft*] Installation Diagnostic Equipment (KSC)
AIDE............ Agence Internationale pour le Developpement [*Paris, France*] (EAIO)
AIDE............ Aide Informatisee pour le Developpement des Entreprises [*Automated Information for Management - AIM*]
AIDE............ Airborne Insertion Display Equipment
AIDE............ Aircraft Installation Diagnostic Equipment (MCD)
AIDE............ Association Internationale des Distributions d'Eau
AIDE............ Automated Image Device Evaluator [*Electronics*]
AIDE............ Automated Integrated Design Engineering (IEEE)
AIDE............ Automated Integrative Design Engineering (NITA)
AIDE............ Automatic Integrated Director Equipment
AIDECS .... Automatic Inspection Device for Explosive Charge Shell (AABC)
AIDELF......... Association Internationale des Demographes de Langue Francaise (EAIO)
AIDES .... Airborne Infrared Decoy Evaluation System (MCD)
AIDES .... American Independent Designers and Engineers Society
AIDES .... Analyst [*Information or Intelligence*] Display and Exploitation System
AIDES .... Automated Image Data Extraction System (MCD)

AIDE/TPS ..... Advanced Interactive Data Entry / Transaction Processing System [*Computer science*] (PDAA)

AIDEX .... Australia International Defence Equipment Exhibition

AIDI .... Associazione Italiana per la Documentazione e l'Informazione [*Italian Association for Documentation and Information*] (NITA)

AIDIS .... Asociacion Interamericana de Ingeniera Sanitaria [*Inter-American Association of Sanitary and Environmental Engineering*] (EA)

AIDJEX......... Arctic Ice Dynamics Joint Experiment [*National Science Foundation - Canada*]

AIDL........... Asociacion Interamericana pro Democracia y Libertad [*Interamerican Association for Democracy and Freedom*]

AIDLCM .... Association Internationale pour la Defense des Langues et Cultures Menacees [*International Association for the Defence of Threatened Languages and Cultures*]

AIDLD .... Architects, Interior Designers, Landscape Designers [*British*]

AIDLUPA...... Association Internationale des Docteurs (Lettres et Sciences Humaines) de l'Universite de Paris et des Autres Universites de France [*International Association of Doctors (Letters and Liberal Studies) of the University of Paris and Other Universities of France*] [*Canada*]

AIDMS .... Applied Information and Data Management Systems Section [*Battelle Memorial Institute*] [*Information service or system*] (IID)

AIDN .... Association Internationale du Droit Nucleaire [*International Nuclear Law Association - INLA*] (EA)

AIDO .... Air Intelligence Duty Officer (DNAB)

AIDO .... Arab Industrial Development Organization (EA)

AIDO .... International Association of Opera Directors [*Sweden*] (EAIO)

AIDOAO........ Association Internationale des Diffuseurs d'Oeuvres d'Art Originales [*International Association of Original Art Diffusors - IAOAD*] (EAIO)

AIDP .... Acute Idiopathic Demyelinating Polyneuropathy [*Medicine*] (DMAA)

AIDP .... Advanced Institutional Development Program [*Under Title III of the Higher Education Act*]

AIDP .... Association Internationale de Droit Penal [*International Association of Penal Law*]

AID/PEP .... Agency for International Development/Private Enterprise Promotion

AIDPM .... Associate of the Institute of Data Processing Management [*British*] (DCTA)

AIDPR.......... Agency for International Development, Procurement Regulations

AIDR .... Aerospace Internal Data Report [*Air Force*] (MCD)

AIDR .... Army Institute of Dental Research (RDA)

AIDR .... International Association for Rural Development Overseas (AIE)

AIDRB .... Army Investigational Drug Review Board (AABC)

AIDRF .... Australian Intellectual Disabilities Research Foundation

AIDS .... Abort Inertial Digital System [*NASA*] (KSC)

AIDS .... Abstract Information Digest Service [*Forest Products Research Society*] [*Information service or system*] (IID)

AIDS .... Academy of International Dental Studies (EAIO)

AIDS .... Accident/Incident Data System [*Database*] [*FAA*]

AIDS .... Account Identification and Description Services [*Dun & Bradstreet*] (IID)

AIDS .... Accretive Industrial Development Syndrome [*Real estate phenomenon*]

AIDS .... Acoustic Intelligence Data System [*Navy*]

AIDS .... Acquired Immune Deficiency Syndrome [*Also, AID, GRID*] [*Medicine*]

AIDS .... Acquired Immune Deficiency Syndrome [*Internet language*] [*Computer science*]

Aids .... Acquired Immune Deficiency Syndrome [*Medicine*] (ODBW)

AIDS .... Acquired Immunodeficiency Syndrome [*Medicine*] (DAVI)

AIDS .... Action Information Display System

AIDS .... Acute Infectious Disease Series [*Medicine*] (DAVI)

AIDS .... Adaptive Intrusion Data System (MCD)

AIDS .... Administrative Information Data System (AFM)

AIDS .... Advanced Impact Drilling System (HGAA)

AIDS .... Advanced Integrated Data System (AFM)

AIDS .... Advanced Integrated Display System [*Military*]

AIDS .... Advanced Interactive Debugging System

AIDS .... Aerospace Intelligence Data System [*IBM Corp.*] (DIT)

AIDS .... Agricultural Information and Documentation Section [*Royal Tropical Institute*] [*Netherlands Information service or system*] (IID)

AIDS .... Agricultural Information Development Scheme (EAIO)

AIDS .... Airborne Integrated Data System

AIDS .... Aircraft Integrated Data System (MCD)

AIDS .... Aircraft Integrated Design System (MCD)

AIDS .... Aircraft Interface Data Summaries (MCD)

AIDS .... Aircraft Intrusion Detection System [*RADAR*]

AIDS .... Air Force Intelligence Data Handling System [*ESD*]

AIDS .... All Individuals Deserve Support [*Alternative translation of AIDS, Acquired Immune Deficiency Syndrome, used as a slogan by AWARE*]

AIDS .... Almost Ideal Demand System [*Agriculture*]

AIDS .... Amdahl Internally Developed Software

AIDS .... American Institute for Decision Sciences [*Later, DSI*] (EA)

AIDS .... Analyst Intelligence Data System (MCD)

AIDS .... Apple [*Computer*] Infected Disk Syndrome (NHD)

AIDS .... Architectural Interaction Design System

AIDS .... Area Intrusion Detection System (MCD)

AIDS .... Army Inventory Data Systems

AIDS .... Artwork-Interactive Design System (MCD)

AIDS .... Assessment of Intelligibility of Dysarthric Speech [*Speech and language therapy*] (DAVI)

AIDS .... Association for Independent Disabled Self-Sufficiency [*British*]

AIDS .... Association of Interior Decor Specialists [*Later, ASCR*]

AIDS .... Attitudinal Information Data System (NVT)

AIDS .... Augmented Ignition Delay Sensor (CAAL)

AIDS .... Automated Identification Division System [*FBI*]

AIDS .... Automated Information Data System

AIDS .... Automated Information Dissemination System (NITA)

AIDS .... Automated Integrated Debugging System (MCD)

AIDS .... Automated Intelligence Data System [*Air Force*]

AIDS .... Automated Inventory Distribution System

AIDS .... Automatic Illustrated Documentation System [*Information International, Inc.*]

AIDS .... Automatic Integrated Debugging System [*Computer science*] (BUR)

AIDS .... Automation Instrument Data Service [*Computer-based industrial information system*] [*Indata Ltd.*] [*British*]

AIDS .... North Atlantic Institute for Defense Study [*NATO*] (NATG)

AIDSCOM ..... Army Information and Data Systems Command

AIDSEARCH... American International Data Search, Inc. [*Information service or system Defunct*] (IID)

AIDS-KS .... Acquired Immune Deficiency Syndrome with Kaposi's Sarcoma [*Medicine*] (DMAA)

AIDSM .... Academie Internationale de Droit et de Sante Mentale (AC)

AID/TA .... Agency for International Development, Bureau for Technical Assistance [*Department of State*]

AIDTA .... Associate of the International Dance Teachers' Association [*British*] (DBQ)

AIDUIM .... Association Internationale pour le Developpement des Universites Internationaleset Mondiales [*International Association for the Development of International and World Universities - IADIWU*] [*Aulnay-Sous-Bois, France*] (EAIO)

AIDUM .... Association Internationale pour le Developpement des Universites Internationaleset Mondiales [*International Association for the Development of International and World Universities - IADIWU*]

AIDUS.......... Automated Information Directory Update System (PDAA)

AIDUS.......... Automated Input and Document Update Service [*International Data Corp.*]

AIE .... Acceptance Inspection Equipment [*Army*] (AABC)

AIE .... Acute Inclusion Body Encephalitis [*Medicine*] (DMAA)

AIE .... Acute Infectious Endocarditis [*Medicine*] (DMAA)

AIE .... Aiome [*Papua New Guinea*] [*Airport symbol*] (OAG)

AIE .... Airborne Interceptor Equipment

AIE .... Air Inuit Ltd. [*Canada ICAO designator*] (FAAC)

AIE .... American Institute of Engineers

AIE .... Application Interface Engine [*Computer science*]

AIE .... Aries Resources [*Vancouver Stock Exchange symbol*]

AIE .... Army Information Engineering (GFGA)

AIE .... Association Internationale de l'Etancheite [*International Waterproofing Association - IWA*] (EAIO)

AIE .... Association Internationale des Entreprises d'Equipement Electrique [*International Association of Electrical Contractors - IAEC*] (EAIO)

AIE .... Authorized "In Excess"

AIEA .... Agence Internationale de l'Energie Atomique

AIEA .... Association Internationale des Etudiants en Agriculture [*International Association of Agriculture Students - IAAS*] (EAIO)

AIEA .... Association of International Education Administrators (EA)

AIEAS.......... Association Internationale des Etudes de l'Asie du Sud-Est [*Paris, France*] (EAIO)

AIEB .... Association Internationale des Etudes Byzantines [*International Association for Byzantine Studies - IABS*] (EAIO)

AIEC........... Advanced Ion Exchange Cellulose [*Analytical biochemistry*]

AIEC........... All-Industry Electronics Conference

AIEC........... American Indian Environmental Council (EA)

AIEC........... American Indian Ethnohistorical Conference [*Later, American Society for Ethnohistory*] (EA)

AI-EC .... Amnesty International EC Representation [*Belgium*] (EAIO)

AIEC........... Association of Illinois Electric Cooperatives (SRA)

AIECA .... Associated Independent Electrical Contractors of America [*Later, IEC*] (EA)

AIECE......... Association d'Instituts Europeens de Conjoncture Economique [*Association of European Conjuncture Institutes*] (EAIO)

AIECF.......... American Indian and Eskimo Cultural Foundation [*Defunct*]

AIECM......... Association Internationale d'Etude des Civilisations Mediterraneennes [*International Association of Studies on Mediterranean Civilizations*] (EAIO)

AIED............ American Institute for Economic Development (EA)

AI Ed........... Associate in Industrial Education

AIED............ Association Internationale des Etudiants Dentaires [*International Association of Dental Students - IADS*] [*British*] (EA)

AI EDAM ...... Artificial Intelligence for Engineering Design, Analysis, and Manufacturing [*A publication*]

AIEDP .... Asian Institute for Economic Development and Planning

AIEE .... American Institute of Electrical Engineers [*Later, IEEE*]

AIEE .... Associate of the Institute of Electrical Engineers [*British*]

AIEE .... Associate of the Institute of Electrical Engineers of Canada (DD)

AIEE .... Association des Instituts d'Etudes Europeennes [*Association of Institutes for European Studies*]

AIEE .... Australia's International Engineering Exhibition

AIEEA.......... Association Internationale pour l'Etude de l'Economie de l'Assurance [*Switzerland*] (EAIO)

AIEEE .... American Institute of Electrical and Electronics Engineers [*Also, IEEE*] (NTCM)

AIEF .... Association Internationale des Etudes Francaises [*Paris, France*] (EAIO)

AIEF .... Association Internationale pour l'Etude du Foie [*International Association for the Study of the Liver*] (EAIO)

AIEGA .... Association Internationale d'Eutonie Gerda Alexander [*International Association for Gerda Alexander Eutony*] [*Switzerland*] (EAIO)

AIEGL.......... Association Internationale d'Epigraphie Grecque et Latine [*International Association for Greek and Latin Epigraphy*] (EAIO)

AIEI .... Association Internationale pour l'Education Integrative [*International Association for Integrative Education - IAIE*] (EAIO)
AIEID .... Asociacion Internacional de Estudio Integral del Deporte [*International Association of Sport Research*]
AIEJI .... Association Internationale des Educateurs de Jeunes Inadaptes [*International Association of Workers for Troubled Children and Youth*] (EAIO)
AIEKF .... Adaptive Iterated Extended Kalman Filtering (MCD)
AIEL .... Asociacion Internacional de Estructuras Laminares y Espaciales [*International Association for Shell and Spatial Structures*]
AIEL .... Association Internationale d'Epigraphie Latine [*International Association for Latin Epigraphy*]
AIEM .... Associate of the Institute of Executives and Managers [*British*] (DBQ)
AIEMA .... Association Internationale pour l'Etude de la Mosaique Antique [*International Association for the Study of Ancient Mosaics*]
AIENDF .... Atomics International Evaluated Nuclear Data Files (KSC)
AIEP .... Amount of Insulin Extractable from the Pancreas (MAE)
AIEP .... Asociacion Internacional de Escritores Policiacos [*International Association of Crime Writers*] (EAIO)
AIEP .... Association Internationale des Usagers d'Embranchements Particuliers [*International Association of Users of Private Sidings*]
AIEP .... Association Internationale d'Etudes Patristiques [*International Association for Patristic Studies*] (EAIO)
AIEP .... Association of Independent Electricity Producers [*British*] (DBA)
AIEPE .... Association Internationale des Ecoles Privees Europeennes
AIEQ .... Association Internationale pour l'Etude du Quaternaire [*International Association for the Study of the Quaternary*] [*Canada*]
AIER .... American Institute for Economic Research [*Great Barrington, MA*] (EA)
AIERE .... Associate of the Institution of Electronic and Radio Engineers [*British*]
AIERI .... Association Internationale des Etudes et Recherches sur l'Information [*International Association of Mass Communications Research*]
AIERS .... Association Internationale pour l'Evaluation du Rendement Scolaire [*International Association for the Valuation of Educational Achievement*] (EAIO)
AIES .... Accreditation and Institutional Eligibility Staff [*Office of Education*]
AIES .... Artificial Intelligence Expert System
AIES .... Association des Institutions d'Enseignement Secondaire (AC)
AIES .... Association Internationale pour les Etudes Sanskrites [*France*] (EAIO)
AIESEC .... Association Internationale des Etudiants en Sciences Economiques et Commerciales [*International Association of Students in Economics and Commerce*] [*Brussels, Belgium*] (EAIO)
AIESEC .... Association Internationale des Etudiants en Sciences Economiques et Commerciales (AIE)
AIESEE .... Association Internationale d'Etudes du Sud-Est Europeen [*International Association of South-East European Studies - IASEES*] (EAIO)
AIESEP .... Association Internationale des Ecoles Superieures d'Education Physique [*International Association for Physical Education in Higher Education*] (EAIO)
AIESI .... Association Internationale des Ecoles des Sciences de l'Information [*International Association of Information Sciences Schools*] [*Canada*] (EAIO)
AIESS .... Association Internationale des Ecoles de Service Social [*International Association of Schools of Social Work - IASSW*] (EA)
AIEST .... Association Internationale d'Experts Scientifiques du Tourisme [*International Association of Scientific Experts in Tourism*] (EAIO)
AIET .... American International Exhibition for Travel (ITD)
AIET .... Average Instruction Execution Time [*Computer parameter*]
AIETA .... Airborne Infrared Equipment for Target Analysis
AIEWROC .... Army Intelligence/Electronic Warfare Reorganization Overwatch Committee (MCD)
AIExpE .... Associate of the Institute of Explosives Engineers [*British*] (DBQ)
AIF .... Acceptance Insurance Companies [*NYSE symbol*] (SPSG)
AIF .... Additional Information Form
AIF .... Aerospace Intelligence File (CINC)
AIF .... Affiliated Inventors Foundation (EA)
AIF .... Agenzia Internazionale Fides [*News agency*] [*Vatican City*] (EY)
AIF .... Air Ile de France [*ICAO designator*] (FAAC)
AIF .... Air Intelligence Force
AIF .... Air Interceptor Fuze
AIF .... Alliance Internationale des Femmes [*International Alliance of Women - IAW*] [*Valetta, Malta*] (EAIO)
AIF .... Allied Invasion Forces [*World War II*]
AIF .... Altitude Instrument Flying (DA)
AIF .... American Institute of France [*Defunct*] (EA)
AIF .... American Ireland Fund (EA)
AIF .... American Issues Forum [*American bicentennial project*]
AIF .... Amphibian Imperial Forces
AIF .... Amsterdam Institute of Finance
AIF .... Animal Industry Foundation (EA)
AIF .... Annual Improvement Factor (MCD)
AIF .... Anti-Invasion Factor [*In bone resorption*]
AIF .... Apoptosis-Inducing Factor [*Biochemistry*]
AIF .... Apoptosis-Inducing Factor [*Cytology*]
AIF .... Army Industrial Fund
AIF .... Asociacion Internacional de Fomento [*International Development Association*]
AIF .... Associated Industries of Florida (SRA)
AIF .... Association Internationale Futuribles [*Futuribles International*] (EAIO)
AIF .... Association of Invoice Factors [*British*] (DBA)
AIF .... Association of Iowa Fairs (SRA)
AIF .... Atomic Industrial Forum [*Later, USCEA*] (EA)
AIF .... Audience Interest Factor
AIF .... Australasian Institute of Fundraising
AIF .... Australian Infrastructure Fund
AIF .... Automated Installation File (MCD)
AIF .... Automated Intelligence File [*Military*] (AABC)
AIFA .... American International Freight Association
AIFA .... Association Internationale Francophone des Aines [*Canada*] (EAIO)
AIFAN .... Association Internationale des Femmes d'Affaires Noires [*Black Business Women - International - BBWI*] [*France*] (EAIO)
AIFB .... American Institute of Financial Brokers (EA)
AIFC .... American Indemnity Financial Corp. [*NASDAQ symbol*] (NQ)
AIFCS .... Airborne Interception Fire Control System [*Air Force*]
AIFD .... Alaska Institute for Fisheries Development
AIFD .... American Institute of Floral Designers (EA)
AIFD .... American Institute of Food Distribution (EA)
AIFE .... American Institute for Exploration (EA)
AIFEE .... All-India Federation of Electricity Employees
AIFF .... Audio Interchange File Format [*Computer science*] (BTTJ)
AIFI .... American Indian Film Institute
AIFI .... Automatic In-Flight Insertion (NG)
AIFireE .... Associate of the Institution of Fire Engineers [*British*]
AIFL .... America Israel Friendship League (EA)
AIFLD .... American Institute for Free Labor Development (EA)
AIFLD .... Association des Industries des Fruits et Legumes Deshydrates de la CEE [*European Organization of the Dehydrated Fruit and Vegetable Industries*] [*EC*] (ECED)
AIFLV .... Association de l'Industrie des Fruits et Legumes au Vinaigre, en Saumure, a l'Huile et des Produits Similaires des CE [*Association of the Industry of Fruit and Vegetables in Vinegar, Brine, Oil and Similar Products of the EC*] (ECED)
AIFM .... Associate of the Institute of Factory Managers [*British*] (DI)
AIFM .... Association Internationale des Femmes Medecins [*Medical Women's International Association - MWIA*] [*Germany*] (EAIO)
AIFM .... Automatic Integrating Fluctuation Meter
AIFOS .... Academic Instructor and Foreign Officer School [*Military*]
AIFP .... Association Internationale de la Fonction Publique [*Avignon, France*] (EAIO)
AIFR .... American Institute of Family Relations
AIFRB .... American Institute of Fishery Research Biologists (EA)
AIFS .... Advanced Indirect Fire System
AIFS .... Advanced Instruction Flying School
AIFS .... Advanced Integrated Flight System (MCD)
AIFS .... American Institute for Foreign Study (EA)
AIFSA .... American Institutions Food Service Association (EA)
AIFSM .... Association of Industrial Filter and Separator Manufacturers [*British*] (DBA)
AIFSS .... Automated International Flight Service Station [*FAA*] (TAG)
AIFSSF .... American Institute for Foreign Study Scholarship Foundation (EA)
AIFST .... Associate of the Institute of Food Science and Technology [*British*] (DBQ)
AIFT .... Ackerman Institute for Family Therapy (EA)
AIFT .... American Institute for Foreign Trade
AIFT .... Audio Input Frequency Tolerance
AIFTA .... Anglo-Irish Free Trade Area [*British*]
AIFTA .... Associate of the Institute of Freight Trades Association (DS)
AIFTAA .... Anglo-Irish Free Trade Area Agreement (PDAA)
AIFTDS .... Airborne Integrated Flight Test Data System [*NASA*]
AIFU .... Automated Instruction Fetch Unit [*Computer science*] (MHDI)
AIFURC .... Assignment Instructions Were Furnished Your Command [*Military*]
AIFV .... Armored Infantry Fighting Vehicle (NATG)
AIFVA .... Atlantic Independent Film & Video Association (AC)
AIG .... Accident Investigation [*Aviation*]
AIG .... Address Indicating Group [*Computer science*]
AIG .... Adjutant Inspector General [*Military*]
AIG .... Airbus Industries Group [*FAA*] (TAG)
AIG .... Air Inspector General (MCD)
AIG .... Air Intelligence Group [*Military*] (MCD)
AIG .... Air Inter Gabon [*ICAO designator*] (FAAC)
AIG .... Alliance of Individual Grocers [*British*] (BI)
AIG .... All Inertial Guidance [*Aerospace*] (AAG)
AIG .... Alltransport International Group
AIG .... American Insurance Group [*Commercial firm*]
AIG .... American International Group, Inc. [*NYSE symbol*]
AIG .... Angle of Inner Gimbal
AIG .... Antigo, WI [*Location identifier FAA*] (FAAL)
AIG .... Anti_Immunoglobulin [*Medicine*] (DMAA)
AIG .... Architectural Inventory Group [*Association of Canadian Archivists*]
AIG .... Army Inspector General (MCD)
AIG .... Artificial Intelligence Group [*MIT*]
AIG .... Assistant Inspector General [*Military*]
AIG .... Assistant Instructor in Gunnery [*British military*] (DMA)
AIG .... Association Internationale de Geodesie [*International Association of Geodesy*]
AIGA .... Absence of Immunoglobulin [*Immunology*] (DAVI)
AIGA .... American Institute of Graphic Arts (EA)
AIG(A) .... Assistant Inspector General for Auditing (DNAB)
AIGA .... Association Internationale de Geomagnetisme et d'Aeronomie [*International Association of Geomagnetism and Aeronomy*]
AIGC .... American Indian Graduate Center (EA)
AIGC .... American Institute of Group Counseling [*Defunct*] (EA)
AIGCM .... Associate of the Incorporated Guild of Church Musicians [*British*]
AIGE .... Asociacion Interamericana de Gastroenterologia [*Interamerican Association of Gastroenterology*] [*Guatemala*]
AIGE .... Association for Individually Guided Education (EA)
AIGE .... Astroinertial Guidance Equipment

AIGI .... Association Internationale de Geologie de l'Ingenieur [*International Association of Engineering Geology*]
AIGM .... Absence of Immunoglobulin M [*Immunology*] (DAVI)
AIGM .... Association Internationale de Grands Magasins [*International Association of Department Stores - IADS*] (EAIO)
AIGP .... Association Internationale de la Gestion du Personnel [*International Association of Personnel Administration*] [*Canada*]
AIGRIC........ Assistant Inspector-General, Royal Irish Constabulary (ROG)
AIGS .... Acoustic Intelligence Gathering System [*Military*] (CAAL)
AIGS .... All Inertial Guidance System [*Aerospace*]
AIGS .... Auxiliary Inerting Gas Subsystem [*Nuclear energy*] (NRCH)
AIGSS .... Annual Inert Gas System Survey (DS)
AIH. .... Academie Internationale d'Heraldique [*Bridel, Luxembourg*] (EAIO)
AIH. .... Agmatine Iminohydrolase [*An enzyme*]
AIH. .... Airtours International Airways Ltd. [*British ICAO designator*] (FAAC)
AIH. .... All in Hand (ADA)
AIH. .... American Income Holding, Inc. [*NYSE symbol*] (SPSG)
AIH. .... American Institute of Homeopathy (EA)
AIH. .... American Institute of Hydrology (EA)
AIH. .... Artificial Insemination by Husband [*Medicine*]
AIH. .... Artificial Insemination, Homologous [*Medicine*] (MAE)
AIH. .... Asociacion Internacional de Hispanistas [*International Association of Hispanists*] [*Aalst, Belgium*] (EA)
AIH. .... Association Internationale des Hydrogeologues [*International Association of Hydrogeologists - IAH*]
AIH. .... Association Internationale d'Hotellerie [*International Hotel Association - IHA*] (EAIO)
AIH. .... Association Internationale d'Hydrologie Scientifique
AIH. .... Association of Independent Hospitals and Kindred Organisations [*British*] (BI)
AIH. .... Australian Institute of Homeopathy
AIHA .... American Indian Historical Association (EA)
AIHA .... American Industrial Hygiene Association (EA)
AIHA .... American Italian Historical Association (EA)
AIHA .... Associate of the Institute of Hospital Almoners [*British*]
AIHA .... Autoimmune Hemolytic Anemia [*Hematology*]
AIHC .... American Industrial Health Council (EA)
AIHCA .... American Indian Health Care Association (EA)
AIHCE .... Association Internationale d'Histoire Contemporaine de l'Europe [*International Association for Contemporary History of Europe*] [*Defunct*] (EAIO)
AIHD .... Acquired Immune Hemolytic Disease [*Medicine*] (DMAA)
AIHE........... Asociacion Interamericana de Hombres de Empresa [*Inter-American Businessmen's Association*]
AIHE........... Association for Innovation in Higher Education [*Defunct*] (EA)
AIHEC .... American Indian Higher Education Consortium (EA)
AIHED .... American Institute for Human Engineering and Development (EA)
AIHEX .... Asian International Hardware Exposition
AIHF........... American Indian Heritage Foundation (EA)
AIHJA.......... Association Internationale des Hautes Juridictions Administratives [*International Association of Supreme Administrative Jurisdictions*] (EAIO)
AIHP .... Academie Internationale d'Histoire de la Pharmacie [*International Academy of the History of Pharmacy*] (EAIO)
AIHP .... American Institute of the History of Pharmacy (EA)
AIHP .... Authority for Intellectually Handicapped Persons [*Western Australia*]
AIHR .... African Institute of Human Rights (EAIO)
AIHR .... American Indian Horse Registry (EA)
AIHR .... Association of International Health Researchers (EA)
AIHS .... American Indian Historical Society [*Defunct*] (EA)
AIHS .... American Irish Historical Society (EA)
AIHS .... Aspen Institute for Humanistic Studies (EA)
AIHS .... Australian International Hotel School
AIHSA .... American Insurers Highway Safety Alliance (EA)
AIHSC .... Auto Industries Highway Safety Committee [*Later, DSMC*] (EA)
AIHSS .... American Institute for Hollow Structural Sections (EA)
AIHV .... Association Internationale pour l'Histoire du Verre [*International Association for the History of Glass*] (EA)
AIHX .... Auxiliary Intermediate Heat Exchanger [*Nuclear energy*] (NRCH)
AII............... Acceptance Inspection Instruction
AII............... Acquired Intelligence, Inc. [*Information service or system*] (IID)
AII............... Acute Intestinal Infection [*Medicine*] (DMAA)
AII............... Aerial Inspection Instrument
AII............... Air India International
AII............... Air Integra, Inc. [*Canada ICAO designator*] (FAAC)
AII............... Allocable Installment Indebtedness (MHDB)
AII............... American Indian Institute (EA)
AII............... American Institute, Inc. (EA)
AII............... American Insured Mortgage Investors - Series 85 Ltd. [*AMEX symbol*] (SPSG)
AII............... American Interprofessional Institute [*Defunct*] (EA)
AII............... Angiotensin [*Biochemistry*]
AII............... Anthes Industries, Inc. [*Toronto Stock Exchange symbol*]
AII............... Apollo Implementing Instructions [*NASA*] (KSC)
AII............... Army Intelligence Interpreter
AII............... Automatic Imagery Interpretation
a-ii-- .... India [*MARC geographic area code Library of Congress*] (LCCP)
AIIA .... Alabama Independent Insurance Agents (SRA)
AIIA .... American Institute for Islamic Affairs (EA)
AIIA .... Associate of the Insurance Institute of America
AIIA .... Association of International Insurance Agents [*Later, Intersure*] (EA)
AIIA .... Atlantic Institute for International Affairs [*France*] (EA)
AIIAB .... Alaska Independent Insurance Agents and Brokers (SRA)
AIIAL .... Associate of the International Institute of Arts and Letters [*British*] (DI)

AIIB............. Allied Irish Investment Bank
AIIBP .... Association Internationale de l'Industrie des Bouillions et Potages [*International Association of the Manufacture of Soups and Broths*] (EAIO)
AIIC............. Apparel Industries Inter-Association Committee [*Defunct*] (EA)
AIIC............. Army Imagery Intelligence Corps
AIIC............. Associate of the Insurance Institute of Canada
AIIC............. Association des Infirmieres et Infirmiers du Canada (EAIO)
AIIC............. Association Internationale des Interpretes de Conference [*International Association of Conference Interpreters*] (EAIO)
AIID .... American Institute of Interior Designers [*Later, ASID*] (AEBS)
AIIDAP .... Association Internationale d'Information et de Documentation en Administration Publique [*International Association for Information and Documentation in Public Administration*] (EAIO)
AIIDC .... Authorized Item Identification Data Collaborator Code
AIIDR .... Authorized Item Identification Data Receiver Code
AIIDS .... Authorized Item Identification Data Submitter Code
AIIE .... American Institute of Industrial Engineers [*Later, IIE*] (EA)
AIIEA .... All-India Insurance Employees' Association
AIIF .... Automated Installation Intelligence File
AIII .... Association Internationale d'Irradiation Industrielle [*Association of International Industrial Irradiation*] (EAIO)
AIII .... Autologic Information International, Inc. [*NASDAQ symbol*] (SAG)
AIIM........... Associate of the Institution of Industrial Managers [*British*] (DCTA)
AIIM........... Association for Information and Image Management (EA)
AIIM........... Association of Independent Investment Managers [*Formerly, National Micrographics Association*] (EAIO)
AIIN............ Associated Industries of the Inland Northwest (SRA)
AI Inf Sc ...... Associate of the Institute of Information Scientists [*British*]
AIIP............. Asociacion Internacional de Investigacion para la Paz [*International Peace Research Association*] (EAIO)
AIIP............. Associate of the Institute of Incorporated Photographers [*British*] (DI)
AIIP............. Association of Independent Information Professionals (EA)
AIIPA .... Associazione Italiana Industriali Prodotti Alimentari [*Food manufacturers association*] [*Italy*] (EY)
AIIRM .... Association Internationale des Interets Radio-Maritimes
AIIS .... Advanced IR Imaging Seeker (MCD)
AIIS .... American Institute for Imported Steel (EA)
AIIS .... American Institute for International Steel (EA)
AIIS .... American Institute of Indian Studies (EA)
AIIS .... American Institute of Iranian Studies (EA)
AIIS .... American Institute of Islamic Studies (EA)
AIIS .... Automated Import Inspection System [*Department of Agriculture*] (GFGA)
AIISTQ .... Association des Infirmieres et Infirmiers en Sante du Travail du Quebec (AC)
AIISUP .... Association Internationale d'Information Scolaire, Universitaire, et Professionelle [*International Association for Educational and Vocational Information - IAEVI*] (EAIO)
AIIT............. Amiodarone-Iodine-Induced Thyrotoxicosis [*Medicine*] (DMAA)
AIITech .... Associate of the Institute of Incorporated Technologists [*British*] (DI)
AIIU .... Australian Institute for International Understanding
AIJ.............. Activities Implemented Jointly [*Between nations*]
AIJ.............. AIL Absorbent Industry [*Vancouver Stock Exchange symbol*]
AIJ.............. Air Jet [*ICAO designator*] (FAAC)
AIJ.............. American Insured Mortgage Investors - Series 86 Ltd. [*AMEX symbol*] (SPSG)
AIJ.............. Ampullary-Isthmic Junction [*Anatomy*]
AIJA .... Alliance Internationale Jeanne d'Arc [*Saint Joan's International Alliance - SJIA*] (EAIO)
AIJA .... Association Internationale des Jeunes Avocats [*Young Lawyers' International Association*] (EAIO)
AIJA .... Australian Institute of Jewish Affairs
AIJD .... Association Internationale des Juristes Democrates [*International Association of Democratic Lawyers*]
AIJE .... Association des Industries du Jute Europeennes [*Association of European Jute Industries*]
AIJE .... Association Internationale des Juges des Enfants
AIJE .... Association Internationale des Magistrats de la Jeunesse [*International Association of Youth Magistrates*]
AIJN............ Association de l'Industrie des Just et Nectars de Fruits et de Legumes de la CEE [*Association of the Industry of Juices and Nectars from Fruits and Vegetables of the EEC*] (ECED)
AIJP............ Association Internationale des Journalistes Philateliques [*International Association of Philatelic Journalists*] [*Germany*]
AIJPA .... Artificial Intelligence Job Performance Aid [*Army*]
AIJPF .... Association Internationale des Journalistes de la Presse Feminine et Familiale [*International Association of Women and Home Page Journalists - IAWHPJ*] (EAIO)
AIJWF .... All-India Jute Textile Workers' Federation
AIK............. African Airlines International Ltd. [*Kenya*] [*ICAO designator*] (FAAC)
AIK............. Aikawa [*Japan*] [*Seismograph station code, US Geological Survey*] (SEIS)
AIK............. Aiken, SC [*Location identifier FAA*] (FAAL)
Aik .... Aikens' Vermont Supreme Court Reports [*1825-28*] [*A publication*] (DLA)
AIK............. American Insured Mortgage Investors - Series 88 Ltd. [*AMEX symbol*] (SPSG)
AIK............. Assistance-in-Kind [*Funds*]
AIK............. Associated Industries of Kentucky (SRA)
AIKCU .... Association of Independent Kentucky Colleges and Universities (SRA)
AIKD .... American Institute of Kitchen Dealers
Aik Dig .... Aiken's Digest of Alabama Statutes [*A publication*] (DLA)
Aikens' Rep... Aikens' Vermont Reports [*A publication*] (DLA)

Aikens (VT)...	Aikens' Vermont Reports [*A publication*] (DLA)
AIKR	Artificial Intelligence Knowledge Representation [*Computer science*] (NITA)
Aik Rep	Aikens' Vermont Reports [*A publication*] (DLA)
Aik Stat	Aiken's Digest of Alabama Statutes [*A publication*] (DLA)
Aik (VT) Rep...	Aikens' Vermont Reports [*A publication*] (DLA)
AIL	Absolute Interferometric LASER (SAA)
AIL	Action Item List (MCD)
AIL	Acute Infectious Lymphocytosis [*Medicine*] (DMAA)
AIL	Adams International Ltd.
AIL	Administrative/Intelligence/Logistics [*Military*]
AIL	Advance Information Letter [*Military*] (AABC)
AIL	Aeronautical Instruments Laboratory [*Military*]
AIL	Aerospace Instrumentation Laboratory [*Air Force*] (MCD)
AIL	Aileen, Inc. (IIA)
AIL	Aileron [*Aviation*]
AIL	Aileron [*Martinique*] [*Seismograph station code, US Geological Survey*] (SEIS)
AIL	Airborne Instruments Laboratory [*Mineola, NY*]
AIL	Aircraft Instrument Laboratory [*Navy*] (AAG)
AIL	Air Illinois, Inc. [*ICAO designator*] (FAAC)
AIL	Air Intelligence Liaison [*British*]
AIL	American Institute of Laundering [*Later, IFI*] (EA)
AIL	American Institute of Leisuretime (EA)
AIL	American Israeli Lighthouse (EA)
AIL	Angioimmunoblastic Lymphadenopathy [*Medicine*]
AIL	Argon Ion LASER
AIL	Arithmetic Input Left [*Computer science*] (MHDI)
AIL	Array Interconnection Logic [*Computer science*]
AIL	Artificial Intelligence Laboratory [*Massachusetts Institute of Technology*] [*Research center*] (RCD)
AIL	Art Institute of Light (EA)
AIL	Associate of the Institute of Linguists [*British*]
AIL	Association Internationale pour la Lecture (EAIO)
AIL	Audio Input Level
AIL	Automatic Interference Limiter [*Automotive sound systems*]
AIL	Average Inventory Level
AIL	Aviation Instrument Laboratory [*Navy*]
AIL	Avionics Integration Laboratories [*NASA*] (NASA)
AILA	Airborne Instruments Laboratory Approach
AILA	American Immigration Lawyers Association (EA)
AILA	American Indian Library Association (EA)
AILA	American Indian Lore Association (EA)
AILA	American Institute of Landscape Architects [*Later, ASLA*] (EA)
AILA	Asociacion de Industriales Latinoamericanos [*Latin American Industrialists Association - LAIA*] [*Uruguay*]
AILA	Associate of the Institute of Land Agents [*British*] (DI)
AILA	Associate of the Institute of Landscape Architects [*British*]
AILA	Association Internationale de Linguistique Appliquee [*International Association of Applied Linguistics*] (EA)
AILA	Australian Institute of Loss Adjusters
AILACT	Association for Informal Logic and Critical Thinking (EA)
AILACTE	Association of Indepedent Liberal Arts Colleges for Teacher Education (EDAC)
AILAM	Associate of the Institute of Leisure and Amenity Management [*British*] (DBQ)
AILAS	Airborne Integrated Light Avionics System
AILAS	Automatic Instrument Landing Approach System [*Aviation*]
AILC	American Indian Law Center (EA)
AILC	American Indian Liberation Crusade (EA)
AILC	American International Law Cases [*1783-1968*] [*A publication*] (DLA)
AILC	Association Internationale de Litterature Comparee [*International Comparative Literature Association*]
AILCNY	Association of Independent Living Centers in New York (SRA)
AILD	Angioimmunoblastic Lymphadenopathy with Dysproteinemia [*Medicine*]
AILE	Arterial Insufficiency of the Lower Extremities [*Medicine*]
AILE	Association Internationale des Lotteries d'Etat [*International Association of State Lotteries*] [*Canada*] (EAIO)
Aileen	Aileen, Inc. [*Associated Press*] (SAG)
AILGA	Associate of the Institute of Local Government Administrators [*British*] (DI)
AILN	Australian International Law News [*A publication*]
AIL/NA	Association of International Libraries/North America
AILO	Air Intelligence Liaison Officer [*British*]
AI Loco E	Associate of the Institution of Locomotive Engineers [*British*]
AILOT	Allowance in Lieu of Overtime
AILP	Alpnet, Inc. [*NASDAQ symbol*] (NQ)
AILP	Automated Language Processing Systems, Inc. (MHDW)
AILR	Australian International Law Review [*A publication*]
AILS	Advanced Impact Location System (SAA)
AILS	Advanced Integrated Landing System
AILS	Airborne Infrared Live Scanner
AILS	Angular Intensity Light Scattering [*Physics*]
AILS	Automatic Instrument Landing System (FAAC)
AILSA	Aerospace Industrial Life Sciences Association [*of Aerospace Medical Association*] (MCD)
AILSA	American Indian Law Students Association [*Later, NALSA*] (EA)
AILSS	Advanced Integrated Life-Support System
AILT	Amiloride Inhibitable Lithium Transport [*Biochemistry*] (DAVI)
AILV	Artichoke Italian Latent Virus [*Plant pathology*]
AILX	Air Illinois, Inc. [*Air carrier designation symbol*]
AIM	Academy for Interscience Methodology (EA)
AIM	Academy Introduction Mission [*Military*]
AIM	Accelerated Investment Mortgage

AIM	Access Isolation Mechanism [*Computer science*] (NITA)
AIM	Access to Information for Medicine [*Allegheny General Hospital, Health Sciences Library*] [*Information service or system*] (IID)
AIM	Accident Investigation Methodology [*Engineering*]
AIM	Accuracy in Media (EA)
AIM	Achievement Identification Measure [*Educational test*]
AIM	Acquisition Information Management Program [*Army*]
AIM	Acronyms in Moderation [*Term coined by Ralph Slovenko*]
AIM	Action for Independent Maturity [*Later, AARP*]
AIM	Active Inert Missile
AIM	Active Integrated Module
AIM	ADA Integrated Methodology (MCD)
AIM	Adaptive Injection Molding [*Engineering*]
AIM	Adaptive Internetwork Management System [*Ungermann-Bass, Inc.*]
AIM	ADCOM [*Air Defense Command*] Intelligence Memorandum (MCD)
AIM	Add, Initial, Multiprecision
AIM	Adhesive Insulation Material
AIM	Adoption Identity Movement (EA)
AIM	Advanced Industrial Management
AIM	Advanced Informatics in Medicine [*British*]
AIM	Advanced Information in Medicine
AIM	Advanced Information Management [*Information service or system*] (IID)
AIM	Advanced Information Manager [*Fujitsu Ltd.*] [*Japan*]
AIM	Advanced Intercept Missile
AIM	Advance Information Memo (MCD)
AIM	Adventures in Movement for the Handicapped (EA)
AIM	Aerial Independent Model (OA)
AIM	Aerial Intercept Missile
AIM	Aeronautical Information Manual [*FAA*] (TAG)
AIM	Aerosol Inhalation Measurement [*Medicine*]
AIM	Aerosonic Corp. [*AMEX symbol*] (SPSG)
AIM	Aerospace Industrial Modernization
AIM	Aerothermodynamic Integration Model
AIM	Aesculapius International Medicine (EA)
AIM	Africa Inland Mission International (EAIO)
AIM	Agency for Industrial Mission [*Canada*]
AIM	Agile Intelligent Manufacturing [*Computer-assisted manufacturing*]
AIM	Agoraphobics in Motion [*An association*] (EA)
AIM	Aid for International Medicine (EA)
AIM	Aid to Improved Marksmanship [*Army training aid*] (INF)
AIM	Aid to Incarcerated Mothers (EA)
AIM	Ailuk [*Marshall Islands*] [*Airport symbol*] (OAG)
AIM	Airborne Infrared Mapper
AIM	Airborne Interceptor Missile (SAA)
AIM	Aircraft Intermediate Maintenance [*Detachment*] [*Navy*] [*Marine Corps*] (DOMA)
AIM	Aircraft Inventory Management Group [*Military*] (AFIT)
AIM	Air Incident Message
AIM	Air Intercept Missile (AFM)
AIM	Air Isolated Monolithic [*Circuit*]
AIM	Air-Launched Interceptor Missile (MCD)
AIM	Airman's Information Manual [*FAA*]
AIM	Alarm Indicating Monitor
AIM	Alliance Internationale pour le Merite (EA)
AIM	Ambassadors in Mission [*Religious organization*] [*Canada*]
AIM	Ambulancias Insulares SA [*Spain ICAO designator*] (FAAC)
AIM	American Indian Movement (EA)
AIM	American Innerspring Manufacturers (EA)
AIM	American Institute of Maintenance (EA)
AIM	American Institute of Management [*Quincy, MA*] (EA)
AIM	American Interactive Media, Inc. [*Software manufacturer*]
AIM	American International Media [*Joint venture of Philips International and PolyGram BV International*]
AIM	Amputees in Motion (EA)
AIM	Analog Input Module [*Computer science*]
AIM	AOL [*America Online*] Instant Messenger [*Computer science*]
AIM	Apogee Injection Module [*NASA*]
AIM	Apple/IBM/Motorola (CDE)
AIM	Application Integration Module [*Telecommunications*] (TSSD)
AIM	Architectural and Industrial Maintenance [*Coatings*]
AIM	Area Interdiction Mine [*Air Force*] (MCD)
AIM	Armored-Infantry-Mechanized (AABC)
AIM	Army Installation Management
AIM	Army Integrated Meteorological Systems (NOAA)
AIM	Articulated Instructional Media (SAA)
AIM	Artificial Intelligence in Medicine
AIM	Asian Institute of Management [*Philippines*]
AIM	Assembly Instruction Mnemonics [*Computer science*]
AIM	Assistance in Ministries (EA)
AIM	Assistant Industrial Manager [*of Naval District*] (MUGU)
AIM	Associated Industries of Massachusetts
AIM	Associated Industries of Missouri (SRA)
AIM	Associated Information Managers (EA)
AIM	Associate in Industrial Management
AIM	Associate of the Institution of Metallurgists [*British*]
AIM	Association Europeenne des Industries de Produits de Marque [*European Association of Industries of Branded Products*] (EAIO)
AIM	Association for Infant Massage (EA)
AIM	Association for Information Management [*Aslib*] (NITA)
AIM	Association for Innovative Marketing (EA)
AIM	Association for the Integration of Management [*New York, NY*] (EA)
AIM	Association Internationale de la Meunerie [*International Milling Association - IMA*] (EAIO)

AIM............ Association Internationale de la Mutualite [*International Association for Mutual Assistance*] [*Switzerland*] (EAIO)
AIM............. Association Internationale de Mycologie [*International Mycological Association*] (EAIO)
AIM............ Association Internationale du Mohair [*International Mohair Association*] (EAIO)
AIM............ Association of Independent Microdealers [*Later, CMC*] (EA)
AIM............ Association of Independent Museums [*British*] (EAIO)
AIM............ Association of Indian Muslims (EA)
AIM............ Association of Information Managers (NITA)
AIM............ Association of Information Managers for Financial Institutions [*Defunct*] (EA)
AIM............ Association of Inplant Managers (DGA)
AIM............ Association of International Marketing [*British*] (EAIO)
AIM............ Association of Interracial Marriages
AIM............ Association of Iowa Merchants (SRA)
AIM............ Association of Mary Immaculate (EA)
AIM............ Associative Index Method
AIM............ Astrometric Interferometry Mission [*to determine locations of stars*] (ECON)
AIM............ Atlantic International Marketing Committee [*Maryland, Virginia, North Carolina, and South Carolina*]
AIM............ Audio Institutional Membership [*Telecommunications*]
AIM............ Authoring of Instructional Materials
AIM............ Automated Information Management (NASA)
AIM............ Automated Integrated Manufacturing (MCD)
AIM............ Automated Intelligent Microscope
AIM............ Automated Interactive Microscope
AIM............ Automatic Identification Manufacturers (EA)
AIM............ Automatic Inflation Module
AIM............ Automation of Interlending by Microcomputer [*British*] (NITA)
AIM............ Automotive Industrial Motor
AIM............ Automotive Industry Matters [*A publication*] (ADA)
AIM............ Autonomous Infantry Mortar [*Military*] (INF)
AIM............ Avalanche-Induced Migration (MCD)
AIM............ Awaiting Incoming Message [*Telecommunications*] (TEL)
AIM............ Inherent Mobile Availability
AIM............ Irvine Municipal Library, Alberta [*Library symbol National Library of Canada*] (NLC)
AIM............. L-Asparaginase, Ifosfamide, and Methotrexate [*Antineoplastic drug regimen*] (DAVI)
AIM............. Salima [*Malawi*] [*Airport symbol*] (AD)
AIM 84........ American Insured Mortgage Investors Ltd. [*Associated Press*] (SAG)
AIM 85........ American Insured Mortgage Investors - Series 85 Ltd. [*Associated Press*] (SAG)
AIM 86........ American Insured Mortgage Investors - Series 86 Ltd. [*Associated Press*] (SAG)
AIM 88........ American Insured Mortgage Investors 1988 [*Associated Press*] (SAG)
AIMA............ Aborigines Inland Mission of Australia
AIMA............ Acoustical and Insulating Materials Association [*Later, ABPA*] (EA)
AIMA............ American Incense Manufacturers Association (EA)
AIMA............ American Industrial Music Association (EA)
AIMA............ As Interest May Appear [*Insurance*]
AIMA............ Association Internationale des Musees d'Agriculture [*International Association of Agricultural Museums*] (EAIO)
AIMA............ Association of Incorporated Managers and Administrators [*British*] (EAIO)
AIMACC .... Air Material Command [*later, Air Force Logistics Command*] Compiling [*System*]
AIMACO .... Air Material Command [*Later, Air Force Logistics Command*] [*Air Force*]
AIMACO .... Air Material Computer (MCD)
Al Mar E ..... Associate of the Institute of Marine Engineers [*British Australia*]
AIM/ARM ..... Abstracts of Instructional Materials/Abstracts of Research Materials
AIMAS .... Academie Internationale de Medecine Aeronautique et Spatiale [*International Academy of Aviation and Space Medicine IAASM*] [*Canada*] (EA)
AIMAV .... Association Internationale pour la Recherche et la Diffusion des Methodes Audio-Visuelles et Structuro-Globales [*International Association for Research and Diffusion of Audio-Visual and Structural-Global Methods*] (EA)
AIMAV .... International Association for Crosscultural Communication [*State University of Ghent*] [*Research center Belgium*] (IRC)
AIMB........... American Institute of Mortgage Brokers [*Washington, DC*] (EA)
AIMBE......... American Institute of Medical and Biological Engineering
AIMBE......... Association Internationale de Medecine et de Biologie de l'Environnement [*International Association of Medicine and Biology of Environment - IAMBE*] [*France*] (EA)
AIMBI.......... Associate Member of the Institute of Medical and Biological Illustration [*British*] (DBQ)
AIMBM........ Associate of the Institute of Municipal Building Management [*British*] (DBQ)
AIMBW .... American Institute of Men's and Boys' Wear [*Later, MFA*]
AIMC........... Academic Information Management Center (NITA)
AIMC........... American Institute of Medical Climatology (EA)
AIMC........... Army Installation Management Course
AIMC........... Association Internationale pour la Mobilisation de la Creativite [*International Association for the Mobilization of Creativity*] [*Canada*]
AIMC........... Association of Insurance Managers in Industry and Commerce [*British*] (BI)
AIMC........... Association of Internal Management Consultants [*East Bloomfield, NY*] (EA)
AIMC........... Association of Interstate Motor Carriers [*Defunct*]

AIMC........... Associazione Internazionale Mosaicisti Contemporanei [*International Association of Contemporary Mosaicists*] (EAIO)
AIMC........... Auto-Initiate Manual-Confirm (CAAL)
AIMCAL....... Association of Industrial Metallizers, Coaters, and Laminators (EA)
AIMCC .... Audi International Motor Car Club (EA)
AIMCS .... African International Movement of Catholic Students (EA)
AIMD........... Abnormal Involuntary Movement Disorder [*Medicine*] (DMAA)
AIMD........... Aircraft Intermediate Maintenance Department [*Navy*] (NVT)
AIME........... American Institute of Mining, Metallurgical, and Petroleum Engineers (EA)
AIME........... American Invitational Mathematics Examination [*Educational test*]
AIME........... Associate of the Institute of Marine Engineers [*British*]
AIME........... Associate of the Institute of Mechanical Engineers
AIME........... Associate of the Institute of Mining Engineers
AIME........... Association for Indiana Media Educators (SRA)
AIME........... Association for Informational Media and Equipment (EA)
AIME........... Automatic In-Process Microcircuit Evaluation (MCD)
AIME........... Average Indexed Monthly Earnings [*Social Security Administration*]
AIMEA......... Applied Immunoenzymometric Assay [*Clinical chemistry*]
AIMEA......... Association Internationale des Metiers et Enseignements d'Art [*International Association for Crafts and the Teaching of Art*]
Al Mech E .... Associate of the Institution of Mechanical Engineers [*British*]
AIMED......... Association of Independent Mailing Equipment Dealers (EA)
AIMEE......... Associate of the Institution of Mechanical Engineers [*British*]
AIMER .... Access to Information on Multicultural Educational Resources (AIE)
AIMES........ Association of Independent Medical Equipment Suppliers (EA)
AIMES........ Automated Information and Management Systems (MCD)
AIMES........ Automated Inventory Management Evaluation System (IEEE)
AIMES........ Avionics Integrated Maintenance Expert System (MCD)
AIMEVAL..... Airborne Intercept Missile Evaluation (MCD)
AIMF.......... American International Music Fund [*Defunct*] (EA)
AIMF.......... Association Internationale des Maires et Responsables des Capitales et Metropoles Partiellement ou Entierement Francophones [*International Association of Mayors Responsible for Capital Cities or Metropolises Partially or Entirely French-Speaking*] (EA)
AIMF.......... Association Internationale des Maires Francophones - Bureau a Quebec (AC)
AIMF.......... Audit Information Management-Systems File [*IRS*]
AIMG.......... Amnesty International Medical Group
AIMH.......... Academy of International Military History [*Later, IMA*] (EA)
AIM-HI........ Applications In Mathematics for High Schools
AIMI.......... Airborne Infrared Measurement Instrument
AIMI.......... Aircraft Intensively Managed Items
AIMI.......... Associacao Internacional de Missoes dos Israelitas [*International Board of Jewish Missions*] (EAIO)
AIMI.......... Aviation Intensive Management Items (AABC)
AIMIA......... Australian Interactive Multimedia Industry Association
AIMILO....... Army/Industry Materiel Information Liaison Office [*or Officer*]
AIMIS......... Advanced Integrated Modular Instrumentation System (MCD)
AIMIT......... Associate of the Institute of Musical Instrument Technology [*British*] (DBQ)
AIMLC......... Association of Island Marine Laboratories of the Caribbean (EA)
AIMLO .... Auto-Instructional Media for Library Orientation [*Colorado University Library*] (NITA)
AIMLS......... Associate of the Institute of Medical Laboratory Sciences [*British*] (DBQ)
AIMM......... Associate of the Institution of Mining and Metallurgy [*British*]
AIMM......... Association of Importers-Manufacturers for Muzzleloading (EA)
AIMM......... Australian Institute of Materials Management
AIMM......... Australian Institute of Mining and Metallurgy (NUCP)
AIMM......... Autoimmune, Inc. [*NASDAQ symbol*] (SAG)
AIMME........ American Institute of Mining and Metallurgical Engineers (NUCP)
AIMMPE....... American Institute of Mining, Metallurgical, and Petroleum Engineers (BARN)
AIMO.......... Association of Industrial Medical Officers [*British*] (BI)
AIMO.......... Associazione Italiana Manufatture Ombrelli [*Umbrella manufacturers association*] [*Italy*] (EY)
AIMO.......... Audibly Instructed Manufacturing Operations [*Military*]
AIMOSACGP... Assignment Instructions Will Include MOS [*Military Occupational Specialty*]within Army Career Group (AABC)
AIMP.......... Air Intercept Missile Package
AIMP.......... Anchored Interplanetary Monitoring Platform
AIMP.......... Association of Independent Music Publishers (EA)
AIMP.......... Association of International Meeting Planners (EA)
AIMPA .... Associate of the Institute of Personnel Management of Australia
AIMPAP ...... Asbestos Inspection and Management Plan Assistance Program [*Environmental Protection Agency*]
AIMPES....... Associazione Italiana Manufatturieri Pelli-Cuoio e Succedanei [*Leather and Imitation Skins Association*] [*Italy*] (EY)
AIMPG........ American Importers Meat Products Group
AIMQ .... Association des Ingenieurs Municipaux du Quebec [*Association of Quebec Municipal Engineers*] (AC)
AIMR .... Association for Investment Management and Research (EA)
AIMR .... Association for the Improvement of the Mississippi River (EA)
AIM/R .... Association of Industry Manufacturers Representatives (EA)
AIMRA .... Agricultural and Industrial Manufacturers' Representatives Association (EA)
AIMRT .... American Institute for the Medical Research of Trauma (EA)
AIMS.......... Abnormal Involuntary Movement Scale [*Medicine*]
AIMS.......... Academic Instructional Measurement System [*Academic achievement and aptitude test*]
AIMS.......... Activities Integrating Math and Science
AIMS.......... Advanced Image Management Software [*Computer science*]
AIMS.......... Advanced Imagery Manipulation System
AIMS.......... Advanced Impact Management System [*Padding for sportswear*]

AIMS............ Advanced Inertial Measurement System

AIMS............ Advanced Inert Missile Simulator (DWSG)

AIMS............ Advanced Information and Management Systems (NITA)

AIMS............ Advanced Integrated Magnetic Anomaly Detection System (MCD)

AIMS............ Advanced Interceptor Missile Subsystem [Military]

AIMS............ Advanced Intercontinental Missile System

AIMS............ Agency-Wide Information Management System [Department of Agriculture] (GFGA)

AIMS............ Agricultural Information and Marketing Services [Department of Agriculture] [Information service or system] (IID)

AIMS............ Airborne Identification, Mark XII System

AIMS............ Airborne Identification, Mobile System [Military] (NVT)

AIMS............ Airborne Integrated Maintenance System

AIMS............ Aircraft Inflight Monitoring System (MCD)

AIMS............ Aircraft Integrated Munition System (MCD)

AIMS............ Air Infiltration Measurement Service [National Association of Home Builders National Research Center]

AIMS............ Air-Launched Intercept Missile Record System

AIMS............ Airplane Information Management System [Honeywell, Inc.]

AIMS............ Air Traffic Control RADAR Beacon/Identification Friend or Foe/Mark XII/System

AIMS............ Airways Integrating and Monitoring System (MCD)

AIMS............ Allied Indian Metis Society [Canada]

AIMS............ All-India Institute of Medial Sciences

AIMS............ Altitude Identification Military System (MCD)

AIMS............ Amalgamated Instrument Makers Society [A union] [British]

AIMS............ American Institute for Maghrib Studies (EA)

AIMS............ American Institute for Marxist Studies [Defunct] (EA)

AIMS............ American Institute for Mental Studies [Later, AITSV] (EA)

AIMS............ American Institute of Maritime Services

AIMS............ American Institute of Merchant Shipping [Washington, DC] (EA)

AIMS............ American Institute of Musical Studies (EA)

AIMS............ American International Managers Society

AIMS............ American International Marchigiana Society (EA)

AIMS............ Analysis of Internal Management Systems

AIMS............ Annual Improvement, Maintenance, and Support (MHDI)

AIMS............ Applications Interface Message Set

AIMS............ Applied Information Management System [Computer science] (DIT)

AIMS............ Army Information Management System

AIMS............ Army Insecticide Measuring System (RDA)

AIMS............ Army Integrated Decision Equipment

AIMS............ Army Integrated Meteorological Systems

AIMS............ Army Integrated Microfilm System

AIMS............ Arson Information Management System [Developed by National Fire Administration] [Emmitsburg, MD]

AIMS............ Arthritis Impact Measurement Scales [Medicine]

AIMS............ Asociacion Internacional de Mercadotecnia Social [Social Marketing International Association - SMIA] [Defunct Mexico] (EAIO)

AIMS............ Assessment, Improvement, and Monitoring System [School milk programs]

AIMS............ Assessments for Integration into Mainstream Settings

AIMS............ Associated Iron Moulders of Scotland [A union]

AIMS............ Association for Improvements in the Maternity Services (EAIO)

AIMS............ Association for Improving Moral Standards [British] (BI)

AIMS............ Association for International Medical Study [Defunct] (EA)

AIMS............ Association of Illinois Middle-Level Schools (SRA)

AIMS............ Association of Independent Maryland Schools (EDAC)

AIMS............ Association of Independent Merchant Stockists (DGA)

AIMS............ Association of Independent Metropolitan Stations (NTCM)

AIMS............ Association of Independent Motor Stores [British] (DBA)

AIMS............ Association of International Marathons and Road Races [New Zealand] (EAIO)

AIMS............ Association of Irish Musical Societies (EAIO)

AIMS............ Audit Information Management System [Department of the Treasury]

AIMS............ Australian Institute of Medical Scientists

AIMS............ Automated Industrial Management System

AIMS............ Automated Information and Management System (BUR)

AIMS............ Automated Instructional Management System [Army]

AIMS............ Automated Instructional Materials Services [Developed by the System Development Corp.] (IID)

AIMS............ Automatic Interference Measurement System (MCD)

AIMS............ Automotive Information Management System [Computer software] [Automotive engineering]

AIMS............ AVSCOM [Aviation Systems Command] Integrated Microfilm Systems [Army]

AIMSO......... Aircraft Intermediate Maintenance Support Office (DNAB)

AIM Str....... AIM Strategic Income Fund [Associated Press] (SAG)

AIMT........... Association for Integrated Manufacturing Technology [Later, NCS/AIMTECH] (EA)

AIMT........... Association Internationale de Musees de Transports [International Association of Transport Museums - IATM] (EAIO)

AIMTA......... Associate of the Institute of Municipal Treasurers and Accountants [British]

AIMTC......... Association Internationale de Medecine Traditionnelle Chinoise [International Association of Traditional Chinese Medicine] [Canada]

AIM Tech..... Association for Integrated Manufacturing Technology [Later, NCS/AIMTECH] (EAAP)

AIM-TWX.... Abridged Index Medicus Accessed by Teletypewriter Exchange Service [National Library of Medicine]

AIMU.......... American Institute of Marine Underwriters [New York, NY] (EA)

AIMVAL....... Air Intercept Missile Evaluation (MCD)

AIMVTE....... Abstracts of Instructional Materials in Vocational and Technical Education (OICC)

AIMXS .... Aircraft IFF [Identification, Friend or Foe] Mark XII System (AABC)

AIN............. Acute Interstitial Nephritide [or Nephritis] [Medicine] (MAE)

AIN............. Advanced Intelligent Network

AIN............. Advanced Intelligent Network [Computer science] (ACRL)

AIN............. African International Airways [Swaziland] [ICAO designator] (FAAC)

AIN............. Ainahou [Hawaii] [Seismograph station code, US Geological Survey] (SEIS)

AIN............. Airframe Integrated Nozzle (MCD)

AIN............. Albany International Corp. [NYSE symbol] (CTT)

AIN............. Albany Intl. 'A' [NYSE symbol] (TTSB)

AIN............. Alternative Information Network (EA)

AIN............. American Information Network (EA)

AIN............. American Information Network Ltd. [Information service or system] (IID)

AIN............. American Institute of Nutrition (EA)

AIN............. Anal Intraepithelial Neoplasia [Oncology]

AIN............. Analog Input [Electronics] (ECII)

AIN............. Anterior Interpositus Nucleus [Anatomy]

AIN............. Approved Item Name

AIN............. Army Interoperability Network (RDA)

AIN............. Assembly Identification Number (NG)

AIN............. Assistant in Nursing

AIN............. Association of Interpretive Naturalists [Later, NAI] (EA)

AIN............. Atlantis Resources Ltd. [Toronto Stock Exchange symbol]

AIN............. Auditory Interneuron [Neurology]

AIN............. Australian and New Zealand Insurance Reporter [A publication]

AIN............. Community College of Allegheny County, Center North, Pittsburgh, PA [OCLC symbol] (OCLC)

AIN............. Innisfail Public Library, Alberta [Library symbol National Library of Canada] (NLC)

AIN............. Wainwright [Alaska] [Airport symbol] (OAG)

AINA .... American Institute of Nautical Archaeology [Later, INA] (EA)

AINA .... American-Israel Numismatic Association (EA)

AINA .... Arctic Institute of North America (EA)

AINA .... Associate of the Institute of Naval Architects

AINA .... Automated Immunonephelometric Assay [Medicine] (DMAA)

AINBA........ Asociacion Internacional de Beisbol Amateur [International Association of Amateur Baseball] (EA)

AINBN......... Association for the Introduction of New Biological Nomenclature [Belgium] (EAIO)

AINC .... Ministere des Affaires Indiennes et du Nord Canadien [Department of Indian Affairs and Northern Development] [Canada]

A-Ind.......... Anglo-Indian (BARN)

AIND .... Arnold Indus [NASDAQ symbol] (TTSB)

AIND .... Arnold Industries, Inc. [NASDAQ symbol] (NQ)

AIndF......... American Indemnity Financial Corp. [Associated Press] (SAG)

AIndPrp....... American Industrial Properties Real Estate Investment Trust [Associated Press] (SAG)

AINDTN....... Air Induction

A-INF.......... Army Infantry Board (MCD)

A in G Ed.... Associate in General Education

A/INL .... Air Inlet [Automotive engineering]

AINL........... Analog Interlock [Electronics] (ECII)

AINL........... Association of Immigration and Nationality Lawyers [Later, AILA] (EA)

AINLF......... Association Internationale des Navigants de Langue Francaise (EAIO)

AINM .... Assistant Inspector of Naval Materiel

AINN .... Applied Innovation [NASDAQ symbol] (TTSB)

AINN .... Applied Innovation, Inc. [NASDAQ symbol] (SAG)

AINO .... Assistant Inspector of Naval Ordnance

AINP .... Association Internationale des Numismates Professionnels [International Association of Professional Numismatists - IAPN] [Switzerland] (EAIO)

AINRP......... Approved Item Name Reclassification Program [DoD] (AFIT)

AINS .... Advanced Inertial Navigation System (MCD)

AINS .... Anti-Inflammatory Nonsteroidal [Agent or drug] [Pharmacology] (DAVI)

AINS .... Area-Inertial Navigation System (PDAA)

AINS .... Automotive Information Network Service

AINSE .... Argonne Institute of Nuclear Science and Engineering [AEC]

AINSMAT .... Assistant Inspector of Naval Materiel

A Ins R .... American Insolvency Reports [A publication] (DLA)

A Inst AM .... Associate of the Institute of Administrative Management [British] (DCTA)

AInstBB....... Associate of the Institute of British Bakers (DBQ)

AInstBCA..... Associate of the Institute of Burial and Cremation Administration [British] (DBQ)

AInstFF .... Associate of the Institute of Freight Forwarders [British] (DBQ)

A Inst M ...... Associate of the Institute of Marketing [British] (DCTA)

AInstMO...... Associate of the Institute of Market Officers [British] (DI)

A Inst MSM... Associate of the Institute of Marketing and Sales Management [British]

AInstP .... Associate of the Institute of Physics and the Physical Society [British] (EY)

AInstPet...... Associate of the Institute of Petroleum [British] (DI)

AInstPI........ Associate of the Institute of Patentees and Inventors [British] (EY)

A Inst PS .... Associate of the Institute of Purchasing and Supply [British] (DCTA)

AInstSMM.... Associate of the Institute of Sales and Marketing Management [British] (DBQ)

AInstTA....... Associate of the Institute of Transport Administration [British] (DBQ)

AInsuf .... Aortic Insufficiency [Cardiology] (DAVI)

Ainsw......... Ainsworth's Lexicon [A publication] (DLA)

Ainsworth Lex... Ainsworth's Latin-English Dictionary [1837] [A publication] (DLA)

AINTELG ...... Air Intelligence Group [Military] (MCD)

AINTELO ...... Air Intelligence Officer [Air Force]

AINTELS	Air Intelligence Squadron [Air Force]
AINTM	American Institute of Nail and Tack Manufacturers (EA)
AINTSEC	Air Intelligence Section [Army]
A INV	Anno Inventionis [In the Year of the Discovery] [Freemasonry] [Latin]
AIO	Academie Internationale Olympique [International Olympic Academy] [Athens, Greece] (EAIO)
AIO	Action Information Organization
AIO	Activity, Interest, and Opinion [Factor scores] [Marketing]
AIO	Airborne Infrared Observatory [NASA]
AIO	Airborne Interceptor Officer (MCD)
AIO	Airborne Ionospheric Observatory (MCD)
AIO	Air Installation Office
AIO	Air Intelligence Officer [Navy] (NVT)
AIO	Air Intelligence Organization (NATG)
AIO	Air Intercept Officer (MCD)
AIO	Allied Interrogating Organization
AIO	American Institute of Organbuilders (EA)
AIO	Americans for Indian Opportunity (EA)
AIO	Amyloid of Immunoglobulin Origin [Medicine]
AIO	Analog Input/Output Board [Computer science] (NITA)
AIO	Arakan Independence Organization [Myanmar] [Political party]
AIO	Arecibo Ionospheric Observatory [Later, National Astronomy and Ionospheric Observatory] [Puerto Rico]
AIO	Arion Resources, Inc. [Vancouver Stock Exchange symbol]
AIO	Army Inventory Objective (AABC)
AIO	Artillery Intelligence Officer [Army]
AIO	Assistant Information Officer (DCTA)
AIO	Atlantic, IA [Location identifier FAA] (FAAL)
AIO	Australia's Independent Optometrists [An association]
a-io--	Indonesia [a-pt (Portuguese Timor) used in records cataloged before April 1980] [MARC geographic area code Library of Congress] (LCCP)
AIOA	American Iron Ore Association (EA)
AIOA	Aviation Insurance Officers Association (DA)
AIOB	American Institute of Oral Biology (EA)
AIOB	Associate of the Institute of Builders [British]
AIOB	Association Internationale pour l'Oceanographie Biologique [International Association of Biological Oceanography - IABO] (EAIO)
AIOC	Assistant Instrumentation Operations Coordination (KSC)
AIOC	Associate of the Institute of Carpenters [British] (DBQ)
AIOCC	Associate Infantry Officer Career Course [Army]
AIOCC	Association Internationale des Organisateurs de Courses Cyclistes [International Association of Organizers of Cycle Competitions] [France] (EAIO)
AIOD	Aorto-Iliac Occlusive Disease [Medicine]
AIOD	Automatic Identified Outward Dialing [Telecommunications]
AIOEC	Association of Iron Ore Exporting Countries
AIOF	American Israel Opera Foundation (EA)
AIO Inventory	Attitudes, Interests, and Opinions of Individuals [Psychographics] (WDMC)
AIOIS	American Intra-Ocular Implant Society [Later, ASCRS] (EA)
AIOK of M	Ancient and Illustrious Order Knights of Malta [East Canton, OH] (EA)
AION	Alphabetical Index of Names
AION	Anterior Ischemic Optic Neuropathy [Neurology and ophthalmology] (DAVI)
AIOP	Analog Input/Output Package [Computer science]
AIOP	Association Internationale d'Orientation Professionnelle
AIOPI	Association of Information Officers in the Pharmaceutical Industry [British]
AIOSP	Association Internationale d'Orientation Scolaire et Professionnelle [International Association for Educational and Vocational Guidance - IAEVG] (EAIO)
AIOTT	Action Information Operations Tactical Trainer (ADA)
AIOW	Association of Independent Optical Wholesalers [Later, OLA]
AIP	Ablative Insulative Plastic
AIP	Acceptance Inspection Package (KSC)
AIP	Accident Insurance Policy (MHDB)
AIP	Acute Idiopathic Pericarditis [Medicine] (DMAA)
AIP	Acute Infectious Polyneuritis [Medicine] (DMAA)
AIP	Acute Intermittent Porphyria [Medicine]
AIP	Advanced Interceptor Propulsion (MCD)
AIP	Aeronautical Information Publication [FAA] (TAG)
AIP	Aeronautical Information Publication (FAAC)
AIP	Agence Ivoirienne de Presse [Ivory Coast] (AF)
AIP	Airborne Instrumentation Platform
AIP	Air Independent Propulsion [Submarine] (DOMA)
AIP	Air-Independent Propulsion System [Navy]
AIP	Air Intake Panel
AIP	Airport Improvement Program [FAA] (TAG)
AIP	Aldosterone-Induced Protein [Biochemistry]
AIP	Allied Intelligence Publications [NATO] (NATG)
AIP	Alphanumeric Impact Printer
AIP	Alpine Aviation Inc. [ICAO designator] (FAAC)
AIP	Alternate Inspection Policy
AIP	Aluminum Isopropoxide [or Isopropylate] [Organic chemistry]
AIP	American Independent Party
AIP	American Institute of Parliamentarians (EA)
AIP	American Institute of Physics (EA)
AIP	American Institute of Planners [Later, American Planning Association] (EA)
AIP	American International Pictures, Inc.
AIP	American Israeli Paper Mills Ltd. [AMEX symbol] (SPSG)
AIP	Amer Israeli Paper Ord [AMEX symbol] (TTSB)

AIP	Anatuberculin, Pertragnani's Integral [Pharmacology] (DAVI)
AIP	Anatuberculin, Petragnani's Integral [Medicine] (BABM)
AIP	Annual Implementation Plan [Health Planning and Resource Development Act of 1974]
AIP	Anti-Inflammatory Protein (PDAA)
AIP	Approval in Principle (NRCH)
AIP	Army Information Program
AIP	Arylene Isopropylidene Polymers [Organic chemistry]
AIP	Ascot Investment Corp. [Toronto Stock Exchange symbol Vancouver Stock Exchange symbol]
AIP	Assault on Illiteracy Program (EA)
AIP	Associate of the Institute of Physicians [British]
AIP	Associate of the Institute of Physics (ADA)
AIP	Associate of the Institute of Plumbing [British] (DBQ)
AIP	Association Internationale de Papyrologues [International Association of Papyrologists] (EAIO)
AIP	Association Internationale de Pediatrie [International Pediatric Association - IPA] [Paris, France] (EAIO)
AIP	Association Internationale de Photobiologie [International Photobiology Association] [Epalinges, Switzerland] (EA)
AIP	Association Internationale des Ports [International Association of Ports and Harbors - IAPH] [Tokyo, Japan] (EAIO)
AIP	Association of Independent Producers [British]
AIP	Associazione Italiana Pellicceria [Furriers association] [Italy] (EY)
AIP	Astronomy Institute Potsdam
AIP	Australia in Print [Book distributor]
AIP	Australian Intellectual Property Cases [A publication]
AIP	Australia's Indigenous Peoples Party [Political party]
AIP	Auto-Igniting Propellant (SAA)
AIP	Automated Imagery Processing (PDAA)
AIP	Automated Immunoprecipitin [System] [Clinical chemistry]
AIP	Automated Implementation Plan
AIP	Automated Information Processing [Computer science] (MCD)
AIP	Automatic Input Processing [Computer science] (MCD)
AIP	Average Instructions per Second [Computer science]
AIP	Average Intravascular Pressure [Medicine] (MAE)
AIP	Aviation Indoctrination Program [Military] (DNAB)
AIP	Avionics Integration Plan [NASA] (NASA)
AIPA	Alberta Irrigation Projects Association (AC)
AIPA	American Indian Press Association [Defunct] (EA)
AIPA	American Ionospheric Propagation Association
AIPA	Associate of the Institute of Incorporated Practitioners in Advertising (DGA)
AIPA	Association Internationale de la Psychologie Adlerienne [International Association of Adlerian Psychology]
AIPA	Association Internationale de Psychologie Appliquee [International Association of Applied Psychology]
AIPA	Association of Importers and Producers of Admixtures [Belgium] (EAIO)
AIPAC	American Israel Public Affairs Committee (EA)
AIPAD	Association of International Photography Art Dealers (EA)
AIPASA	Aged and Invalid Pensioners' Association of South Australia
AIPBS	American Institute for Patristic and Byzantine Studies (EA)
AIPC	Advanced Programmable Interrupt Controller
AIPC	Agar Immersion, Plating, and Contact (PDAA)
AIPC	All Indian Pueblo Council (EA)
AIPC	American Institute for Political Communication
AIPC	American Institute of Polish Culture (EA)
AIPC	Army Installations Planning Committee (AABC)
AIPC	Association Internationale de Prophylaxie de la Cecite [International Association for the Prevention of Blindness]
AIPC	Association Internationale des Palais des Congres [International Association of Congress Centers] [Zagreb, Yugoslavia] (EA)
AIPC	Association Internationale des Ponts et Charpentes [International Association of Bridges and Construction] [Switzerland]
AIPC	Australian Intellectual Property Cases [A publication]
AIPCEE	Associations des Industries du Poisson de la CEE [Association of the Fish Industries of the European Economic Community]
AIPCR	Association Internationale Permanente des Congres de la Route [Permanent International Association of Road Congresses - PIARC] (EAIO)
AIPCS	Aspen Institute Program on Communications and Society (NTCM)
AIPD	Army Institute for Professional Development (EA)
AIPD	Associated Industrial Photographic Dealers [Defunct]
AIPDPS	Association Internationale de Philosophie du Droit et de Philosophie Sociale [See also IAPLSP]
AIPDWF	All-India Port and Dock Workers' Federation
AIPE	American Institute for Professional Education (EA)
AIPE	American Institute of Park Executives [Later, APRS] (EA)
AIPE	American Institute of Plant Engineers (EA)
AIPE	Associate of the Institution of Production Engineers [British]
AIPE	Association Internationale de la Presse Echiqueenne [International Association of Chess Press] [Kerteminde, Denmark] (EAIO)
AIPEA	Association Internationale pour l'Etude des Argiles [International Association for the Study of Clays] (EAIO)
AIPEDD	American Institute for the Prevention and Eradication of Dental Disease
AIPELF	Association Internationale de Pedagogie Experimentale de Langue Francaise [International Association of Experimental French Language Education] [Canada]
AIPEPO	Association Internationale de Presse pour l'Etude des Problemes d'Outre-Mer [International Press Association for Studying Overseas Problems]
AIPEQ	Association des Institutions de Niveaux Prescolaire et Elementaire du Quebec (AC)

AIPEU .... American Institute on Problems of European Unity [*Later, AFPI*] (EA)
AIPF............. American Indian Projects Foundation [*Defunct*] (EA)
AIPF............. Asociacion Internacional de Planificacion Familiar [*Social Marketing International Association - SMIA*] (EAIO)
AIPG .... American Institute of Professional Geologists (EA)
AIPG .... Amnesty International Parliamentary Group
AIPH .... Aged and Invalid Pensioners' Home
AIPH .... Agricultural and Industrial Process Heat (MCD)
AIPH .... Association Internationale de Paleontologie Humaine (EAIO)
AIPH .... Association Internationale des Producteurs de l'Horticulture [*International Association of Horticultural Producers*] [*Netherlands*]
AIPH .... International Association of Horticultural Producers [*The Hague, Netherlands*] (EA)
AIPI .... Associazione Internazionale dei Professori d'Italiano [*International Association of Teachers of Italian*] (EAIO)
AIPIL........... Australasians in Property in London
AIPIO .... Australian International Pilots' Industrial Organisation
AIPL............ Animal Improvement Programs Laboratory [*Formerly, DHIA*] (EA)
AIPLA.......... American Intellectual Property Law Association (EA)
AIPLB.......... Australian Intellectual Property Law Bulletin [*A publication*]
AIPLF.......... Assemblee Internationale des Parlementaires de Langue Francaise (AC)
AIPLF.......... Association Internationale des Parlementaires de Langue Francaise [*International Association of French-Speaking Parliamentarians*] (EAIO)
AIPLU .... American Institute for Property and Liability Underwriters [*Malvern, PA*] (EA)
AIPM .... Associate of the Institute of Personnel Management (ADA)
AIPMI.......... Acute Infero-Posterior Myocardial Infarction [*Medicine*]
AIPN .... American International Petroleum Corp. [*NASDAQ symbol*] (NQ)
AIPN .... Amer Intl. Petroleum [*NASDAQ symbol*] (TTSB)
AIPNW........ American Intl. Pete Wrrt [*NASDAQ symbol*] (TTSB)
AIPO .... American Institute of Public Opinion [*Also, ARI*] (NTCM)
AIPO .... Artificial Intelligence Project Office (SSD)
AIPO .... ASEAN [*Association of South East Asian Nations*] Inter-Parliamentary Organisation
AIPP .... American Institute of Pollution Prevention
AIPP............ Arctic Islands Pipeline Program [*Canada*]
AIPP............ Army Industrial Preparedness Program
AIPPh.......... Association Internationale des Professeurs de Philosophie [*International Association of Teachers of Philosophy*] (EAIO)
AIPPI .... Association Internationale pour la Protection de la Propriete Industrielle [*International Association for the Protection of Industrial Property*] [*Zurich, Switzerland*] (EA)
AIPR .... American Institute of Pacific Relations [*Defunct*]
AIPR .... Applied Imagery Pattern Recognition
AIPR .... Australian Institute of Parapsychological Research
AIPR .... Automated Information Processing Request (MCD)
AIPS .... Advanced Integrated Power Supply
AIPS .... Advanced Integrated Propulsion System [*Aerospace*]
AIPS .... Advanced Interactive Presentation System
AIPS .... American Institute for Public Service (EA)
AIPS .... American Institute of Pathologic Science [*Defunct*] (EA)
AIPS............ Applications Information Processing System (MCD)
AIPS............ Army Information Processing Standards (MCD)
AIPS............ Association Internationale de la Presse Sportive [*International Sport Press Association*] (EAIO)
AIPS............ Association Internationale pour la Prevention du Suicide [*International Association for Suicide Prevention*]
AIPS............ Association Internationale pour le Progres Social
AIPS............ Astronomical Image Processing System
AIPS............ Astronomical Information Processing System [*Computer program*]
AIPS............ Automated Intelligence Processing System (MCD)
AIPS............ Automatic Indexing and Proofreading System
AIPSM .... Australian Institute of Purchasing and Supply Management
AIPSO .... Auto Insurance Plans Services Office [*A rule and rate-making association*]
AIPT .... Assistant Inspector of Physical Training [*Military British*]
AIPT .... Association for International Practical Training (EA)
AIPTS.......... Active Imaging Pointer-Tracker System (MCD)
AIPU .... Arab Inter-Parliamentary Union [*Syrian Arab Republic*] (EAIO)
AIPU .... Associative Information Processing Unit (PDAA)
AIPULF .... Association Internationale des Presses Universitaires de Langue Francaise [*International Association of French Language University Presses*] [*Canada Defunct*]
AIQ.............. Animal Inspection and Quarantine Division [*of ARS, Department of Agriculture*]
AIQ.............. Association des Entrepreneurs en Isolation de la Province du Quebec (AC)
a-iq-- .... Iraq [*MARC geographic area code Library of Congress*] (LCCP)
AIQPS .... Associate of the Institute of Qualified Private Secretaries [*British*] (DI)
AIQS .... Associate of the Institute of Quantity Surveyors [*British*]
AIR.............. AAR Corp. [*NYSE symbol*] (SPSG)
AIR.............. Abitibi Resources Ltd. [*Vancouver Stock Exchange symbol*]
AIR.............. Accelerated Idioventricular Rhythm [*Cardiology*] (DAVI)
AIR.............. Accelerated Item Reduction [*Military*]
AIR.............. Accountable Indirect Representational Supplement [*British*]
AIR.............. Acoustic Intercept Receiver [*Navy*]
AIR.............. Action for Industrial Recycling [*An association*]
AIR.............. Action Item Report (NASA)
AIR............. Action of Instant Recording [*Video technology*]
AIR............. Acute Insulin Response [*Endocrinology*]
AIR............. Adaptive Intercommunication Requirement (NASA)

AIR............ Additional Information Request (MCD)
AIR............ Advanced Integration Research [*PC motherboard*] [*Computer science*] (PCM)
AIR............ Aeronautical [*or Aerospace*] Information Report (MCD)
AIR............ Aerospace Information Report [*SAE*] (AAGC)
AIR............ After Initial Release (MCD)
AIR............ Airborne Interceptor RADAR
AIR............ Airborne Interceptor Rocket (AFM)
AIR............ Aircraft Incident Report [*Navy*] (NG)
AIR............ Aircraft Inspections and Repair
AIR............ Aircraft Inventory Record (NVT)
AIR............ Aircraft Recovery (CINC)
AIR............ Air Incident Report
AIR............ Air Inflatable Retarder [*for bombs*] (MCD)
AIR............ Air Injection Reactor
AIR............ Air Intercept Rocket (IEEE)
AIR............ Airlift International, Inc. [*ICAO designator*] (FAAC)
AIR............ Airline Industrial Relations Conference (EA)
AIR............ Airworthiness
AIR............ Alliance of Independent Retailers (EAIO)
AIR............ All India Law Reporter [*Usually followed by a province abbreviation*] [*as AIR All., for Allahabad, Bom. for Bombay, Dacca for Dacca, HP for Himachal Pradesh, Hyd. for Hyderabad, etc.*] [*A publication*] (DLA)
AIR............ All-India Radio
AIR............ American Indian Refugees (EA)
AIR............ American Industrial Real Estate Association (EA)
AIR............ American Institute of Reciprocators [*Defunct*] (EA)
AIR............ American Institute of Refrigeration [*Defunct*]
AIR............ American Institute of Research (OICC)
AIR............ American Institutes for Research [*Information service or system*] (IID)
AIR............ American Institutes for Research in the Behavioral Sciences (EA)
AIR............ Aminoimidazole Ribonucleotide [*Biochemistry*]
AIR............ Annals of Improbable Research [*A publication*]
AIR............ Antenna Input Resistance
AIR............ Applied Information Resources [*Research center*] (RCD)
AIR............ Arithmetic Input Right [*Computer science*] (MHDI)
air............ Armenian Soviet Socialist Republic [*MARC country of publication code Library of Congress*] (LCCP)
AIR............ Army Intelligence Reserve
AIR............ Artificial Intelligence Research [*Computer science*] (DAVI)
AIR............ Artist in Residence (BARN)
AIR............ Asociacion Interamericana de Radiodifusion [*Inter-American Association of Broadcasters - IAAB*] [*Montevideo, Uruguay*] (EA)
AIR............ Asociacion Internacional de Radiodifusion [*International Association of Broadcasting - IAB*] (EAIO)
AIR............ Assembly Inspection Record (SAA)
AIR............ Association for Institutional Research (EA)
AIR............ Association of Independent Railways [*British*] (DBA)
AIR............ Assumed Investment Return [*Business term*] (DICI)
AIR............ Australian Institute of Radiography (EAIO)
AIR............ Aviation Item Reports
AIR............ Avionics Integration Research (SSD)
AIR............ Axiom Information Resources
AIR............ Bellaire, OH [*Location identifier FAA*] (FAAL)
a-ir-- .... Iran [*MARC geographic area code Library of Congress*] (LCCP)
AIR............ Iron River Public Library, Alberta [*Library symbol National Library of Canada*] (NLC)
AIR............ Naval Air Systems Command Headquarters (AAGC)
AIRA............ Air Attache [*Air Force*]
AIRA............ All India Reporter, Allahabad Series [*A publication*] (ILCA)
AIRA............ American Independent Refiners Association (EA)
AIRA............ American-International Reiki Association (EA)
AIRA............ Anti-Insulin Receptor Antibody [*Medicine*] (DMAA)
AIRAC .... Aeronautical Information Regulation and Control
AIRAC .... All-Industry Research Advisory Council [*Later, IRC*] (EA)
AIRAC .... Atmospheric Infrared Attenuation Coefficient
AIRACCDT.... Air Accident
AIRACLIS..... Air Activities Logistic Information System (MCD)
AIRACS........ Aircraft Acquisition and Support (NG)
AIRAD .... Air Administrative Net [*Army*] (AABC)
AIRAF .... Aircraft, Asiatic Fleet
AIR Aj .... All India Reporter, Ajmer Series [*A publication*] (ILCA)
AIR All........ All India Reporter, Allahabad Series [*A publication*] (ILCA)
AIR And ...... All India Reporter, Andhra Series [*A publication*] (ILCA)
AIR Andh ..... All India Reporter, Andhra Series [*A publication*] (ILCA)
AIR Andh Pra... All India Reporter, Andhra Pradesh Series [*A publication*] (ILCA)
Air & Space Law... Air and Space Lawyer [*A publication*] (DLA)
AIRANTISUBRON... Air Antisubmarine Squadron [*Navy*]
AIRARMUNIT... Aircraft Armament Unit
AIRASDEVLANT... Aircraft Antisubmarine Development Detachment, Atlantic Fleet
AIRASLT ...... Air Assault Badge [*Military decoration*] (GFGA)
AIR Asm ...... All India Reporter, Assam Series [*A publication*] (ILCA)
AIRASRON ... Aircraft Antisubmarine Squadron (DNAB)
AIR Assam ... All India Reporter, Assam Series [*A publication*] (ILCA)
AIRB .... All India Reporter, Bombay Series [*A publication*] (ILCA)
AIRB .... Aviation Insurance Rating Bureau [*Defunct*] (EA)
AIRBALTAP... Allied Air Forces, Baltic Approaches [*NATO*] (NATG)
AIRBAREX.... Air Barrier Exercise [*Military*] (NVT)
AIRBASECOM... Air Base Commander
AIRBATFORPAC... Aircraft Battle Force, Pacific Fleet [*Navy*]
AIR Bhop .... All India Reporter, Bhopal Series [*A publication*] (ILCA)
AIR Bilas .... All India Reporter, Bilaspur Series [*A publication*] (ILCA)
AIRBM .... Anti-Intermediate Range Ballistic Missile

AIRBO	Association Internationale pour les Recherches au Bas Fourneau d'Ougree
AIRBOC	Airborne Rapid-Blooming Off-Board Chaff (DOMA)
AIR Bom	All India Reporter, Bombay Series [*A publication*] (ILCA)
airbr	Airbrush (VRA)
AIRBR	Association Internationale du Registre des Bateaux du Rhin [*International Association of the Rhine Ships Register*]
AIRBS	American Institute for Research in the Behavioral Sciences
AIRBUT	Automatic Resupply and Buildup Time [*Air Force*] (AFIT)
AIRC	All India Reporter, Calcutta Series [*A publication*] (ILCA)
AIRC	American Indian Research Center
AIRC	Association of Independent Radio Contractors [*British*]
AIRC	Association of International Relations Clubs (EA)
AIRC	Australian Immigration Research Center
AIRC	Irma Community Library, Alberta [*Library symbol National Library of Canada*] (NLC)
AIR Cal	All India Reporter, Calcutta Series [*A publication*] (ILCA)
AIR CAN	Air Canada (MHDW)
AirCan	Air Canada Corp. [*Associated Press*] (SAG)
Aircav	Air Cavalry (BARN)
AIRCENT	Air Forces, [*US*] Central Command (DOMA)
AIRCENT	Allied Air Forces, Central Europe [*Formerly, AAFCE*] [*NATO*]
AIRCEY	Air Ceylon Ltd.
Aircft	Aircraft
AIRCLNR	Air Cleaner
AIRCO	Air Coordinator [*Air Force*]
Aircoa	Aircoa Hotel Partners Ltd. [*Associated Press*] (SAG)
AIRCOM	Aerospace Communications Complex [*Air Force*]
AIRCOM	Air Command (MCD)
AIRCOM	Air Force Communications Program
AIRCOM	Airways Communications System
AIRCOMD	Air Command Net [*Army*] (AABC)
AIRCOMNET	Air Communications Network
AIRCON	Automated Information and Reservation Computer Operated Network
AIR COND	Air Condition [*Technical drawings*] (DAC)
AIRCSC	Air Command and Staff College [*Air Force*]
AirCure	Air-Cure Technologies, Inc. [*Associated Press*] (SAG)
AIRD	American Indian Research and Development [*An association*] (EA)
AIR Dacca	All India Reporter, Dacca Series [*A publication*] (ILCA)
Aird Black	Aird. Blackstone Economised [*1873*] [*A publication*] (ILCA)
Aird Civ Law	Aird's Civil Laws of France [*A publication*] (DLA)
AIRDEF	Air Defense Division [*NATO*] (NATG)
AIRDEFCOM	Air Defense Commander
AIRDELOPS	Air Delivery Operations [*Aerial resupply*] [*Military*] (NVT)
AIRDELPLT	Air Delivery Platoon
AIRDEP	Air Deputy [*NATO*] (NATG)
AIRDEVRON	Air Development Squadron [*Navy*]
AIRDIV	Air Division [*Air Force*]
AIRDIVDEF	Air Division Defense [*Air Force*] (MUGU)
AIRE	Acute Infarction Ramipril Efficacy [*Cardiology study*]
AIRE	Air-Cure Environmental [*NASDAQ symbol*] (SPSG)
AIRE	American Institute of Radio Engineers [*Telecommunications*] [*An association*] (ECII)
AIREA	American Institute of Real Estate Appraisers [*Later, AI*] (EA)
AIREASTLANT	Naval Air Forces East Atlantic Area [*NATO*] (NATG)
AIR East Punjab	All India Reporter, East Punjab Series [*A publication*] (ILCA)
AIREDIV	Aircraft Repair Division (SAA)
AIRELO	Air Electrical Officer
AIREN	American Institute for Research and Education in Naturopathy (EA)
AIRENGPROPACCOVERHAUL	Airplane Engine, Propeller, and Accessory Overhaul [*Navy*]
AIREO	Air Engineer Officer
AIREP	Aircraft Report
AIREP	Air Report [*Aviation ICAO designator*] (FAAC)
AIREPDIV	Aircraft Repair Division [*Military*]
AIREPDN	Aircraft Repair Division [*Military*]
AIRES	Advanced Imagery Requirements and Exploitation System (MCD)
AIRET	Australian Institute for Rational Emotive Therapy
AIREVAC	Air Evacuation
AIREVACWING	Air Evacuation Wing
AIREW	Airborne Infrared Early Warning
AirExp	Air Express International Corp. [*Associated Press*] (SAG)
AIRF	Aircraft Instrument Repair Facility
AIRF	All-India Railwaymen's Federation
AIRF	Alterations in Respiratory Function [*Medicine*] (DMAA)
AIRF	Assignment Instructions Remain Firm [*Army*]
AIRFA	American Indian Religious Freedom Act [*1978*]
AIRFAM	Aircraft Familiarization
AIRFC	All India Reporter, Federal Court Series [*A publication*] (ILCA)
AIRFERRON	Air Ferry Squadron [*Navy*]
AIR FIL	Air Filter [*Freight*]
AIRFL	Air Refueling [*Aviation*] (FAAC)
AIRFMF	Air Fleet Marine Force (AFIT)
AIRFMFLANT	Aircraft, Fleet Marine Force, Atlantic [*Obsolete*]
AIRFMFPAC	Aircraft, Fleet Marine Force, Pacific [*Obsolete*]
AIRFORWARD	Shore-Based Air Force, Forward Area, Central Pacific
AirFrt	Airborne Freight Corp. [*Associated Press*] (SAG)
Airgas	Airgas, Inc. [*Associated Press*] (SAG)
AIRGI	Airman's Guide [*A publication*]
AIRGLO	Airborne Infrared Gunfire Locator
AIRGRP	Air Group
AIRHC	Alaska International Rail and Highway Commission [*Terminated, 1961*]
AIR Him Pra	All India Reporter, Himachal Pradesh Series [*A publication*] (ILCA)
AIRHP	All India Reporter, Himachal Pradesh Series [*A publication*] (ILCA)

AIRHPER	Alberta Information Retrieval for Health, Physical Education and Recreation (NITA)
AIR Hy	All India Reporter, Hyderabad Series [*A publication*] (ILCA)
AIR Hyd	All India Reporter, Hyderabad Series [*A publication*] (ILCA)
AIRI	Associate of the Institute of the Rubber Industry [*British*]
AIRI	Association of Independent Research Institutes (EA)
AIRIA	Adult Inventory of Reading Interests and Attitudes (EDAC)
AIRIMP	Air Reservations Interline Message Procedure
AIR Ind Dig	All India Reporter, Indian Digest [*A publication*] (ILCA)
AIRIS	Advanced Infrared Imaging Seeker (MCD)
AIRIS	Air Store Issuing Ship
AIRJ & K	All India Reporter, Jammu and Kashmir Series [*A publication*] (ILCA)
AIR Kerala	All India Reporter, Kerala Series [*A publication*] (ILCA)
AIR Kutch	All India Reporter, Kutch Series [*A publication*] (ILCA)
AIRL	Aeronautical Icing Research Laboratory
AIRL	Automation Industries Research Laboratory (KSC)
AIR Lahore	All India Reporter, Lahore Series [*A publication*] (ILCA)
AIRLANT	Air Forces, Atlantic Fleet [*Navy*]
Airlease	Airlease Ltd. [*Associated Press*] (SAG)
AIRLEX	Air Landing Exercise [*Military*] (NVT)
AIRLIGHT	Airborne Lighting System [*Air Force*] (MCD)
AIRLMAINT	Airline-Like Maintenance (DNAB)
AIRLO	Air Liaison Officer [*Air Force*]
AIRLOC	Air Lines of Communication
AIRLORDS	Airlines Load Optimization Recording and Display System [*Airport passenger-moving sidewalk*]
AIRM	Airborne Infrared Mapper
AIRM	Air Methods [*NASDAQ symbol*] (TTSB)
AIRM	Air Methods Corp. [*NASDAQ symbol*] (SAG)
AIRM	All India Reporter, Madras Series [*A publication*] (ILCA)
AIR Mad	All India Reporter, Madras Series [*A publication*] (ILCA)
AIR Madh Pra	All India Reporter, Madhya Pradesh Series [*A publication*] (ILCA)
AIR Manip	All India Reporter, Manipur Series [*A publication*] (ILCA)
AIRMAP	Air Monitoring Analysis and Prediction [*System*]
AIRMB	All India Reporter, Madhya Bharat Series [*A publication*] (ILCA)
AIRME	Apollo Initiator Resistance Measuring Equipment [*NASA*] (NASA)
AIRMEC	Association Internationale pour la Recherche Medicale et les Echanges Culturels [*International Association for Medical Research and Cultural Exchange*] [*Paris, France*] (EAIO)
AIRMET	Airman's Meteorological Information [*FAA*] (TAG)
AirMeth	Air Methods Corp. [*Associated Press*] (SAG)
AIRMG	Aircraft Machine Gunner
AIRMIC	Association of Insurance and Risk Managers in Industry and Commerce (EAIO)
AIRMICS	Army Institute for Research in Management Information and Computer Science [*Atlanta, GA*] (IEEE)
AIRMILMIS	Aircraft Military Mission
AIRMLC	All-Industry Radio Music Licensing Committee (NTCM)
AIR/MMH	Acoustic Intercept Receiver/Multimode Hydrophone System [*Navy*]
AIRMoN	Atmospheric Integrated Research Monitoring Network (OSRA)
AIRMoN	Atmospheric Integrated Research Monitoring Network (USDC)
AIRMOVE	Air Movement [*Message*] (NVT)
AIRMOVEX	Air Movement Exercise [*Military*] (NVT)
AIRMP	All India Reporter, Madhya Pradesh Series [*A publication*] (ILCA)
AIRMSN	Air Mission [*Air Force*]
AIR My	All India Reporter, Mysore Series [*A publication*] (ILCA)
AIRN	All India Reporter, Nagpur Series [*A publication*] (ILCA)
AIR Nag	All India Reporter, Nagpur Series [*A publication*] (ILCA)
AIRNAVAID	Air Navigational Aid [*Navy*] (NG)
AIRNAVO	Air Navigation Office [*Navy*]
AIRNET	Airport Network Simulation Model [*FAA*] (TAG)
AirNetS	AirNet Systems, Inc. [*Associated Press*] (SAG)
AIRNON	Allied Air Forces, North Norway [*NATO*] (NATG)
AIRNORSOLS	Aircraft, Northern Solomons [*Military*]
AIRNORTH	Allied Air Forces, Northern Europe [*Formerly, AAFNE*] [*NATO*]
Air NZ	Air New Zealand Ltd. [*Airline*]
AIROF	Anodic Iridium Oxide Film (PDAA)
AIROPNET	Air Operational Network [*Air Force*]
AIROPNSO	Air Operations Officer [*Air Force*]
AIROPS	Air Operations [*Military*]
AIR Oris	All India Reporter, Orissa Series [*A publication*] (ILCA)
AIR Oudh	All India Reporter, Oudh Series [*A publication*] (ILCA)
AIRP	All India Reporter, Patna Series [*A publication*] (ILCA)
AIRP	Association Internationale de Relations Professionnelles [*International Industrial Relations Association - IIRA*] (EAIO)
AIRPA	American Indian Registry for the Performing Arts (EA)
AIRPAC	Air Forces, Pacific Fleet
AIRPAC	Air Pacific [*ICAO designator*] (AD)
AIRPAC(ADV)	Air Forces Pacific Advanced
AIRPAC(PEARL)	Air Forces Pacific, Pearl Harbor
AIRPACSUBCOMFORD	Air Forces Subordinate Command, Forward Area
AIRPAP	Air Pressure Analysis Program [*Bell System*]
AIRPASS	Airborne Interception RADAR and Pilot's Attack Sight System
AIR Pat	All India Reporter, Patna Series [*A publication*] (ILCA)
AIRPAX	Aircraft Expendable Bathythermograph Program in the Pacific [*National Science Foundation*] (MSC)
AIRPC	All India Reporter, Privy Council [*A publication*] (ILCA)
AIR PEP	All India Reporter, Patiala and East Punjab States Union Series [*A publication*] (ILCA)
AIR PEPSU	All India Reporter, Patiala and East Punjab States Union Series [*A publication*] (ILCA)
AIR Pesh	All India Reporter, Peshawar Series [*A publication*] (ILCA)
AIRPL	Airplane [*Freight*]
AirProd	Air Products & Chemicals, Inc. [*Associated Press*] (SAG)
AIRPS	Air Postal Squadron [*Air Force*]

airpt	Airport (VRA)
AIR Pun	All India Reporter, Punjab Series [*A publication*] (ILCA)
AIRR	All India Reporter, Rajasthan Series [*A publication*] (ILCA)
AIR Raj	All India Reporter, Rajasthan Series [*A publication*] (ILCA)
AIRRES	Air Rescue (CINC)
AIRS	Ablator Insulated Ramjet Study [*NASA*] (KSC)
AIRS	Access to Information and Reading Service (AIE)
AIRS	Accident/Incident Reporting System [*National Transportation Safety Board*] [*Information service or system*] (IID)
AIRS	Accident Information Retrieval System (RDA)
AIRS	Accounting Incomplete Records System [*Software package*] (NCC)
AIRS	Advanced Inertial Reference Sphere [*ICBM technology*]
AIRS	Advanced Infrared Sounder (GAVI)
AIRS	Advanced Instrumentation for Reflood Studies [*Nuclear energy*] (NRCH)
AIRS	Aerobics International Research Society (EA)
AIRS	Aerometric Information Retrieval System [*Environmental Protection Agency Information service or system*] (CRD)
AIRS	African International Reservation System (PDAA)
AIRS	Airborne Infrared Radiometer System
AIRS	Airborne Integrated Reconnaissance System (MCD)
AIRS	Aircraft Inventory Reporting System (AABC)
AIRS	Airport Information Retrieval System [*FAA*]
AIRS	Alarm Identification Reporting System (ACRL)
AIRS	Alliance of Information and Referral Systems (EA)
AIRS	American Information Retrieval Service [*Document delivery service*] (NITA)
AIRS	Army Information Radio Service (MCD)
AIRS	Artificial Intelligence Research Support [*Program*] [*Computer science*]
AIRS	Atmospheric Infrared Sounder (SSD)
AIRS	Audit Integrated Reporting System [*IRS*]
AIRS	Automated Information Reference Systems, Inc. [*Information service or system*] (IID)
AIRS	Automatic Image Retrieval System (MCD)
AIRS	Automatic Information Retrieval System [*Information service or system*] (BUR)
AirSA	Air South Australia
AIRSAR	Airborne Synthetic Aperture RADAR [*Instrumentation*]
AIR Sau	All India Reporter, Saurashtra Series [*A publication*] (ILCA)
AIRSC	All India Reporter, Supreme Court [*A publication*] (ILCA)
AIRSCOFORPAC	Aircraft Scouting Force, Pacific Fleet
AirSen	Air Sensors, Inc. [*Associated Press*] (SAG)
AIRSHIPGR	Airship Group
AIRSHIPRON	Airship Squadron
AIRSHTR	Air Shutter
AIR Simla	All India Reporter, Simla Series [*A publication*] (ILCA)
AIR Sind	All India Reporter, Sind Series [*A publication*] (ILCA)
AIRSKEDELFLT	Aircraft Schedule for Delivery to Fleet
AIRSO	Association of Industrial Road Safety Officers [*British*] (DBA)
AIRSOLS	Air Solomons Command [*US*]
AIRSONOR	Allied Air Forces, South Norway [*NATO*] (NATG)
AIRSOPAC	Aircraft, South Pacific Force [*Navy*]
AIRSOUTH	Allied Air Forces, Southern Europe [*Formerly, AAFSE*] [*NATO*]
AIRSOWESPAC	Aircraft, Southwest Pacific Force [*Navy*]
AIRSS	ABRES [*Advanced Ballistic Reentry System*] Instrumentation Range Safety Systems [*Air Force*] (MCD)
AIR-STD	Air Force International Standard
AIRSTORDEP	Air Stores Depot [*Navy*]
AIRSVC	Air Services [*Military*] (NVT)
AirSys	Airport Systems International, Inc. [*Associated Press*] (SAG)
AIRSYSCOM	Air Systems Command [*Navy*]
AIRT	Air Transn Hldgs [*NASDAQ symbol*] (TTSB)
AIRT	Air Transportation Holding Co., Inc. [*NASDAQ symbol*] (NQ)
AIRT	Australian Institute of Radio and Television
AIRTAS	Air-Deployed Towed-Array Surveillance System (MCD)
AIRTASS	Airborne Towed Array SONAR System (MCD)
AIRTC	All India Reporter, Travancore-Cochin Series [*A publication*] (ILCA)
AirTch	AirTouch Communications [*Associated Press*] (SAG)
AIRTE	Associate of the Institute of Road Transport Engineers (DBQ)
AIRTO	Association of Independent Research and Technology Organizations [*British*] (DBA)
AirTouch	AirTouch Communications Co. [*Formerly, PacTel Corp.*] [*Associated Press*] (SAG)
airtps	Airborne Troops [*British and Canadian*] [*World War II*]
AIRTRAINRON	Air Training Squadron (MUGU)
AIRTRANS	Airport Transportation
AirTrans	Air Transportation Holding Co., Inc. [*Associated Press*] (SAG)
AIRTRANSEX	Air Transportation Exercise [*Military*] (NVT)
AIRTRANSRON	Air Transport Squadron
AIRTRANSRONLANT	Air Transport Squadron, Atlantic
AIRTRANSRONPAC	Air Transport Squadron, Pacific
AIRTRANSRONWESTCOAST	Air Transport Squadron, West Coast
AIRTRARON	Air Training Squadron
AIR Trip	All India Reporter, Tripura Series [*A publication*] (ILCA)
AIRU	Air University (MCD)
Air UK	United Kingdom Airlines [*ICAO designator*] (AD)
Air U Rev	Air University. Review [*A publication*] (DLA)
AIRV	Air Injection Relief Valve [*Automotive engineering*]
AIRVAN	Air Mobile Van [*Trailer unit for use on ground or in air*] [*Military*]
AIRVP	All India Reporter, Vindhya Pradesh Series [*A publication*] (ILCA)
AirWat	Air & Water Technologies Corp. [*Associated Press*] (SAG)
Airways	Airways Corp. [*Associated Press*] (SAG)
AIRWC	Air War College [*Air Force*]
AIRXRS	American Industrial Radium and X-Ray Society [*Later, ASNT*]
AIRYX	Air Express Division of the Railway Express Agency

AIS	Abbreviated Injury Scale [*Medicine*] (PDAA)
AIS	Ablating Inner Surface
AIS	Academic Instructors School [*Air Force*]
AIS	Academy of Independent Scholars [*Defunct*] (EA)
AIS	Accelerated Inspection System (DNAB)
AIS	Accounting Information System (BUR)
AIS	Acctex Information Systems (NITA)
AIS	Accumulator Injection System [*Nuclear energy*] (NRCH)
AIS	Acorn Interactive System [*Videodisc control system*] (NITA)
AIS	Action Item Sheet (MCD)
AIS	Adoptees in Search [*An association*] (EA)
AIS	Advanced Imaging Software (DGA)
AIS	Advanced Indications Structure (MCD)
AIS	Advanced Indications System (MCD)
AIS	Advanced Information System/Net 1 Service [*Formerly, ACS*] [*American Bell, Inc.*]
AIS	Advanced Instructional System (MCD)
AIS	Advanced Interactive Software (DGA)
AIS	Advanced Ionospheric Sounder [*A ground-based instrument*]
AIS	Advanced Isotope Separation [*Process*] [*Nuclear energy*]
AIS	Advance in Schedule (KSC)
AIS	Adversary Information System [*Military*] (RDA)
AIS	Advertising Information Services
AIS	Aeronautical Information Section
AIS	Aeronautical Information Service
AIS	Aeronautical Information Specialist (FAAC)
AIS	Airborne Imaging Spectrometer
AIS	Airborne Infrared Spectrometer
AIS	Airborne Initiation System
AIS	Airborne Instrumentation Subsystem (MCD)
AIS	Aircraft Inspection System
AIS	Aircraft Instrument Subsystem [*Navy*] (MCD)
AIS	Air Intelligence Service
AIS	Airlock Illumination Subassembly (MCD)
AIS	Airport in Sight (FAAC)
AIS	Air Tranport School [*Former USSR ICAO designator*] (FAAC)
AIS	AIS Resources Ltd. [*Vancouver Stock Exchange symbol*]
AIS	Akademio Internacia de la Sciencoj [*International Academy of Sciences - IAS*] (EAIO)
AIS	Alarm Indication Signal [*Telecommunications*] (TEL)
AIS	Alarm Inhibit Signal [*Telecommunications*] (TEL)
AIS	Alcohol Insoluble Solids [*Food analysis*]
AIS	Alternate Interim Successor [*Military*] (NVT)
AIS	Altitude Indication System
AIS	Altman Information Systems, Inc. [*Information service or system*] (IID)
AIS	America-Italy Society (EA)
AIS	American Indian Scholarships [*Later, AIGC*] (EA)
AIS	American Indians for Sobriety (EA)
AIS	American Indian Sign Language (BYTE)
AIS	American Indycar Series [*Auto racing*]
AIS	American Information Services [*Information service or system*] (IID)
AIS	American Institute of Stress (EA)
AIS	American Iris Society (EA)
AIS	American Ivy Society (EA)
AIS	Ampal-Amer Israel Corp. [*AMEX symbol*] (SPSG)
AIS	Amron Information Services (IID)
AIS	Analog Input System
AIS	Analog-In Single-Ended (MCD)
AIS	Analog Instrumentation Subsystem
AIS	Androgen Insensitivity Syndrome [*Endocrinology*]
AIS	Anglo-Italian Society [*British*] (DBA)
AIS	Anglo-Ivorian Society [*British*] (DBA)
AIS	Annual Inspection Summary (MCD)
AIS	Answer in Sentence [*Computer science*] (MHDB)
AIS	Antenna Interface Subsystem (CAAL)
AIS	Anterior Interosseous Nerve Syndrome [*Medicine*] (DMAA)
AIS	Anti-Icing System [*Aircraft*]
AIS	Anti-Insulin Serum [*Biochemistry*] (MAE)
AIS	APCE [*Automated Product Control Environment*] Interface Set (SSD)
AIS	Apollo Instrumentation Ships [*NASA*] (MCD)
AIS	Applicant Information Service [*Institute of International Education*] (AEBS)
AIS	Arabidopsis Information Service
AIS	Argonne National Laboratory Illinois Site (AAGC)
AIS	Army Infantry School (KSC)
AIS	Army Information Systems (RDA)
AIS	Army Intelligence and Security
AIS	Army Intelligence School
AIS	Army Intelligence Survey [*ITAC*] (MCD)
AIS	Arorae [*Kiribati*] [*Airport symbol*] (OAG)
AIS	Artists in the Schools Program (EDAC)
AIS	Ascension Island Station [*NASA*] (SAA)
AIS	Associate of the Institute of Statisticians [*Later, MIS*] [*British*]
AIS	Association for Integrative Studies (EA)
AIS	Association Internationale de la Savonnerie et de la Detergence [*International Association of the Soap and Detergent Industry*] (EAIO)
AIS	Association Internationale de la Soie [*International Silk Association - ISA*] (EAIO)
AIS	Association Internationale de Sociologie [*International Sociological Association - ISA*] (EAIO)
AIS	Attitude Indicating System (MCD)
AIS	Audio Integrating System (DA)
AIS	Australian-Indian Society

AIS............. Automated Cell-Injection System
AIS............. Automated Identification System [*FBI*]
AIS............. Automated Imaging System (DGA)
AIS............. Automated Indicator System (MCD)
AIS............. Automated Information System
AIS............. Automated Instrumentation System
AIS............. Automated Insurance Service
AIS............. Automatic Idle Speed [*Automotive engineering*]
AIS............. Automatic Image Screening
AIS............. Automatic Intercept System [*Bell System*]
AIS............. Automatic Intercity Station [*Telecommunications*] (OA)
AIS............. Automatic Intermediate Station (MCD)
AIS............. Avionics Intermediate Shop (MCD)
AIS............. Community College of Allegheny County, South Campus, West
            Mifflin, PA [*OCLC symbol*] (OCLC)
a-is--.......... Israel [*MARC geographic area code Library of Congress*] (LCCP)
AIS............. Italian Instrument Society (ACII)
AISA......... Acquired Idiopathic Sideroblastic Anemia [*Medicine*] (DMAA)
AISA......... Alabama Independent School Association (SRA)
AISA......... American Indoor Soccer Association (EA)
AISA......... American Institute for Shippers' Associations (EA)
AISA......... American Institute of Supply Associations [*Later, ASA*] (EA)
AISA......... Analytical Isoelectrofocusing Scanning Apparatus [*Analytical
            chemistry*]
AISA......... Associate of Incorporated Secretaries Association
AISA......... Association Internationale pour la Securite Aerienne [*International Air
            Safety Association*]
AISA......... Association Internationale pour le Sport des Aveugles [*International
            Blind Sports Association - IBSA*] [*Farsta, Sweden*] (EAIO)
AISA......... Association of International Schools in Africa (EA)
AISACT....... Association of Independent Schools of the Australian Capital Territory
AISAG......... Aeronautical Information Service Automation Group [*ICAO*] (DA)
AISAM........ Association Internationale des Societes d'Assurance Mutuelle
            [*International Association of Mutual Insurance Companies*] [*Paris,
            France*] (EAIO)
AISAP......... Aeronautical Information Service Automation Specialist Panel
            [*ICAO*] (DA)
AISAR......... Accidental Incident Sabotage Assistance Request (MCD)
AISB............ Association Internationale de Standardisation Biologique
            [*International Association of Biological Standardization - IABS*]
            (EAIO)
AISB............ Society for the Study of Artificial Intelligence and the Simulation of
            the Brain (MHDI)
AISC........... American Indian Studies Center [*Research center*] (RCD)
AISC........... American Institute of Steel Construction (EA)
AISC........... Amnistie Internationale Section Canadienne [*Amnesty International
            Canadian Section*]
AISC........... Argentine Information Service Center (EA)
AISC........... Army Information Systems Command
AISC........... Assessment and Information Services Center [*National Oceanic and
            Atmospheric Administration Information service or system*] (IID)
AISC........... Association Internationale des Skal Clubs [*International Association
            of Skal Clubs*] (EAIO)
AISC........... Association of Independent Software Companies [*Later, ADAPSO*]
            (EA)
AISC........... Association of Informed Senior Citizens [*Defunct*] (EA)
AISC........... Associazione Italiana di Studi Canadesi [*Italian Association of
            Canadian Studies*]
AISCA .... Association of Independent Schools & Colleges in Alberta (AC)
AISD .... Abstracting and Indexing Services Directory [*A publication*]
AISD .... Army Intelligence School, Fort Devens (MCD)
AISDT .... Australian Institute of Surgical and Dental Technicians
AISE........... American Intercultural Student Exchange (EA)
AISE........... Association Internationale des Sciences de l'Education [*International
            Association for the Advancement of Educational Research*]
AISE........... Association Internationale des Sciences Economiques [*International
            Economic Association - IEA*] [*Paris, France*] (EAIO)
AISE........... Association Internationale des Statisticiens d'Enquetes [*International
            Association of Survey Statisticians*] (EAIO)
AISE........... Association of Iron and Steel Engineers (EA)
AISE........... Average Integral Square Error (PDAA)
AISEIT......... Association of Institute and School of Education In-Service Tutors
            [*British*]
AISES.......... American Indian Science and Engineering Society (EA)
AISF............ Airlift Industrial Services Flight [*Military*]
AISF........... Australian Indoor Soccer Federation
AISF........... Avionic Integration Support Facility (MCD)
AISG .... Accountants International Study Group [*Later, International
            Federation of Accountants*]
AISG .... American Insurance Services Group [*New York, NY*] (EA)
AISG .... Artists in Stained Glass [*Canada*]
AISHWC....... Australian Industrial Safety, Health, and Welfare Cases
            [*A publication*]
AISI............ Advanced International Studies Institute (EA)
AISI............ Airborne Instrumentation Subsystem Internal (MCD)
AISI............ American Iron and Steel Institute (EA)
AISI............ American-Italy Society, Inc.
AISI............ Associate of the Iron and Steel Institute
AISIS .... Advanced Icing Severity Indication System [*Military*] (RDA)
AIS/ISMA .... Army Information Systems / Information Systems Management
            Activity (RDA)
AISJ........... Association Internationale des Sciences Juridiques [*International
            Association of Legal Science - IALS*] (EAIO)
AISL........... Aviation Information Services Ltd. (IID)
AISLE.......... [*An*] Intersociety Liaison Committee on the Environment

AISLF.......... Association Internationale des Sociologues de Langue Francaise
            [*International Association of French Language Sociologists*]
            (EAIO)
AISLLI.......... Associazione Internazionale per gli Studi di Lingua e Letteratura
            Italiane [*International Association for the Study of the Italian
            Language and Literature - IASILL*] (EAIO)
AISME........ Australian Institute of Sales and Marketing Executives
AIS-MEBA .... Association of Industrial Scientists [*affiliated with*] Marine Engineers
            Beneficial Association [*A union*]
AISMF......... Avionics Intermediate Shop Mobile Facility Support (DWSG)
AISMO........ Afloat Intelligence System Manager Overview (DOMA)
AIS/MR........ Alternative Intermediate Services for the Mentally Retarded
AISNSW....... Association of Independent Schools of New South Wales [*Australia*]
AISOB .... Associate of the Incorporated Society of Organ Builders [*British*]
            (DBQ)
AISP........... Association Internationale de Science Politique [*International Political
            Science Association - IPSA*] [*Canada*]
AISP........... Association Internationale des Secretaires Professionnelles
            [*International Association of Professional Secretaries*] [*Canada*]
AISP........... Association of Information Systems Professionals [*Defunct*] (EA)
AISP........... Australian Insolvency Management Practice [*A publication*]
AISq........... Aerospace Intelligence Squadron [*Air Force*]
AISQ........... Association of Independent Schools of Queensland [*Australia*]
AISR .... Army Institute of Surgical Research (RDA)
AIsrael........ American Israeli Paper Mills Ltd. [*Associated Press*] (SAG)
AISS........... Airborne Infrared Surveillance Set
AISS........... Air Intelligence Services Squadron [*Defunct Air Force*]
AISS........... Association Internationale de la Science du Sol [*International Society
            of Soil Science - ISSS*] (EAIO)
AISS........... Association Internationale de la Securite Sociale [*International Social
            Security Association*]
AISS........... Automatic Intercom Switching System
AIST........... Agency of Industrial Science and Technology
AIST........... Association for Intelligent Systems Technology (EA)
AIST........... Automatic Information Station [*or System*] (BUR)
AISTC.......... Associate of the International Institute of Sports Therapy [*British*]
            (DBQ)
AISTD .... Associate of the Imperial Society of Teachers of Dancing [*British*]
            (DBQ)
AISTM......... Associate of the Institute of Sales Technology and Management
            [*British*] (DBQ)
AI Struct E ... Associate of the Institute of Structural Engineers [*British*]
AISV........... Amphibious Infantry Support Vehicle
AISWA .... Association of Independent Schools of Western Australia
AISWG .... Advieskomitee vir Internasionale Samewerking op Wetenskaplike
            Gebied [*International Council of Scientific Unions*]
AISWG .... Air Interface Sub-Working Group [*NATO*] (NATG)
AISX........... Applied Immune Sciences, Inc. [*NASDAQ symbol*] (SAG)
AIT............. Academy for Implants and Transplants (EA)
AIT............. Acoustic Impact Technique [*Test*] (PDAA)
AIT............. Acute Intensive Treatment [*Medicine*] (DMAA)
AIT............. Advanced Identification Techniques (MCD)
AIT............. Advanced Individual Training [*Army*]
AIT............. Advanced Infantry Training
AIT............. Advanced Information Technology (NITA)
AIT............. Advanced Instruction Technique (DA)
AIT............. Advanced Intelligent Tape [*Sony Corp.*] (PCM)
AIT............. Advanced Interceptor Technology (MCD)
AIT............. Adventures in Travel [*Oakland, CA*] [*Information service or system*]
            (IID)
A(IT) .... Africa Inland Transport [*British World War II*]
AIT............. Agency for Instructional Technology (EA)
AIT............. Agency for Instructional Television (NTCM)
AIT............. Agglutination-Inhibition Test [*Clinical chemistry*]
AIT............. Air Injection Tube [*Automotive engineering*]
AIT............. Aitkin, MN [*Location identifier FAA*] (FAAL)
AIT............. Aitutaki [*Cook Islands*] [*Airport symbol*] (OAG)
AIT............. Allanco Iolite Monitor Corp. [*Vancouver Stock Exchange symbol*]
AIT............. Alliance Internationale de Tourisme [*International Touring Alliance*]
            (EAIO)
AIT............. Aluminum Tartrate (DMAA)
AIT............. American Industrial Transport, Inc.
AIT............. American Institute in Taiwan
AIT............. American Institute of Technology (MCD)
AIT............. American Institution in Thailand
AIT............. American International Airways, Inc. [*ICAO designator*] (FAAC)
AIT............. Ameritech Corp. [*NYSE symbol*] (SPSG)
AIT............. Analytic Intelligence Test [*Psychology*]
AIT............. Architect-in-Training (OA)
AIT............. Army Ammunition in Thailand (MCD)
AIT............. Army Intelligence Translator
AIT............. Asian Institute of Technology [*Bangkok, Thailand*] (MCD)
AIT............. Assessment of Instructional Terms (EDAC)
AIT............. Association Internationale des Travailleurs [*International Association
            of Workers*] [*France*]
AIT............. Association of Inspectors of Taxes [*British*]
AIT............. Association of Insurance Teachers [*British*] (DBA)
AIT............. Association of Investment Trusts [*British*] (BI)
AIT............. Assured Intermediate Task (MCD)
AIT............. Autogenous Ignition Temperature (DNAB)
AIT............. Autoignition Temperature
AIT............. Automated Information Transfer [*FAA*] (TAG)
AIT............. Automatic Identification Technology [*Army*] (RDA)
AIT............. Automatic Information Test [*Military*]
AIT............. Automotive Information Test (AABC)

AIT	Inter-American Translators Association [*Defunct*] (EA)
AIT[3]	Advanced IT [*Information Technology*] Transfer [*British*]
AITA	Act Inside the Army [*European antiwar group*]
AITA	Advanced Individual Training Available [*Military*]
AITA	Air Industries and Transports Association (MCD)
AITA	Association Internationale du Theatre Amateur [*International Amateur Theatre Association - IATA*] (EAIO)
AITAA	Advanced Individual Training Attrition Analysis (MCD)
AITAA	Asian Institute of Technology Alumni Association [*Thailand*] (EAIO)
AITC	Action Information Training Center
AITC	Advocates of International Trade and Comity [*Defunct*] (EA)
AITC	Air Intelligence Training Center (MCD)
AITC	Alabama International Trade Center [*University of Alabama*] [*Research center*] (RCD)
AITC	Allyl Isothiocyanate [*Organic chemistry*]
AITC	American Indian Travel Commission [*Defunct*] (EA)
AITC	American Institute of Timber Construction (EA)
AITC	Association de l'Industrie Touristique du Canada [*Travel (later, Tourism) Industry Association of Canada - TIAC*]
AITC	Association Internationale des Traducteurs de Conference [*International Association of Conference Translators*] (EAIO)
AITC	Association of Investment Trust Companies (ODBW)
AITCT	Alabama Initial Teacher Certification Test (EDAC)
AITD	All-Inclusive Trust Deed [*Insurance*]
AITD	Autoimmune Thyroid Disease [*Endocrinology*]
AITE	Advanced Indication Technology Experiment (MCD)
AITE	Aircraft Integrated Test Equipment
AITE	Australian International Technology Exhibition
AITE	Automatic Intercity Telephone Exchange [*Telecommunications*] (OA)
AITEP	Aboriginal and Islander Teacher Education Program [*Australia*]
AITEP	Association for International Technical Promotion
AITES-ITA	Association Internationale des Travaux en Souterrain - International Tunneling Association [*Bron, France*] (EA)
AITF	All in the Family [*TV program*]
AITF	Ammunition Initiatives Task Force (MCD)
AITF	Army in the Field (MCD)
AITG	Australian Income Tax Guide [*A publication*]
AITI	Aero Industries Technical Institute
AITI	Artikkel-Indeks Tidsskrifter [*Norwegian Center for Informatics*] [*Database*]
AITIA	American Institute of Technical Illustrators Association [*Defunct*] (EA)
AITIT	Association Internationale de la Teinture et de l'Impression Textiles [*International Association of Textile Dyers and Printers*] (EAIO)
AITME	Association des Instituts de Theologie du Moyen-Orient [*Association of Theological Institutes in the Middle East - ATIME*] (EAIO)
AITO	Association of Independent Tour Operators [*British*] (DBA)
AITO	Australian Institute of Tourism Officers
AITP	Allergy, Immunology, and Transplantation Program [*NIH*]
AITP	American Institute of Tax Practice (EA)
AITP	Association of Information Technology Professionals
AITP	Association of Information Technology Professionals
AITQ	Association des Intervenants en Toxicomanie du Quebec (AC)
AITRC	Applied Information Technologies Research Center [*Information service or system*] (IID)
AITS	Acknowledged Information Transfer Service [*Telecommunications*] (ACRL)
AITS	Action Item Tracking System [*Radiation measurement*] (NRCH)
AITS	American International Travel Service (IIA)
AITS	Association of Independent Television Stations, Inc. (NTCM)
AITS	Automated Information Transfer System [*Department of Commerce*] [*Database*]
AITS	Automatic Integrated Telephone System [*Telecommunications*] (OA)
AITSA	Associate of the Institute of Trading Standards Administration [*British*] (DBQ)
AITSA	Association of Interpreters and Translators of South Australia
AI-TSL	Artificial Intelligence-Transaction Security Ltd. [*British*] (NITA)
AITSV	American Institute - the Training School at Vineland [*Later, TTS*] (EA)
AITT	Arginine Insulin Tolerance Test [*Endocrinology*] (MAE)
AITT	Association of Industrial Truck Trainers [*British*] (DBA)
AITT	Australian Institute of Travel and Tourism
AITU	Alliance of Independent Telephone Unions [*Later, TIU*] (EA)
AITUC	All-India Trade Union Congress
AIU	Aboriginal Issues Unit [*Australia*]
AIU	Abort Interface Unit [*NASA*]
AIU	Absolute Iodine Uptake [*Medicine*]
AIU	Action for Interracial Understanding [*Defunct*] (EA)
AIU	Advanced Instrumentation Unit [*National Physical Laboratory*] (PDAA)
AIU	Aero Insurance Underwriters
AIU	Alarm Interface Unit [*Telecommunications*] (TEL)
AIU	Alliance Israelite Universelle [*Universal Israelite Alliance*]
AIU	Allied Independent Unions [*Lebanon*]
AIU	American International Underwriters
AIU	Antigen-Inducing Unit [*Medicine*] (DMAA)
AIU	Array Interface Unit [*Computer science*] (CAAL)
AIU	ASAP Interface Unit
AIU	Association Internationale des Universites [*International Association of Universities - IAU*] (EAIO)
AIU	Association Internationale des Urbanistes [*International Society of City and Regional Planners - ISOCARP*] (EAIO)
AIU	Atiu [*Cook Islands*] [*Airport symbol*] (OAG)
AIU	Atlantic Independent Union
AIU[3]	Attack Helicopter Interface Unit (MCD)
AIU	Auxiliary Interface Unit [*NASA*]
AIU	Avionics Interface Unit (MCD)

AIUAS	Australian Industrial Union of Academic Staff
AIUC	American Irish Unity Committee (EA)
AIUFFAS	Association Internationale des Utilisateurs de Files de Fibres Artificielles et Synthetiques [*International Association of Users of Yarn of Man-Made Fibers*]
AIUFOR	Australian International UFO [*Unidentified Flying Object*] Research
AIUM	American Institute of Ultrasound in Medicine (EA)
AIUPS	Angle-Integrated Ultraviolet Photoelectron Spectroscopy
AIUR	Adjusted Insured Unemployment Rate
AIURA	American Institute of Urban and Regional Affairs
AIUSA	Amnesty International of the USA (EA)
AIUTA	Association Internationale des Universites du Troisieme Age [*International Association of Universities of the Third Age*] (EAIO)
AIV	Accelerated Inverse Voltage
AIV	Advanced Interactive Video
AIV	Airvias SA Linhas Aereas [*Brazil*] [*FAA designator*] (FAAC)
AIV	Alcina Development Corp. [*Vancouver Stock Exchange symbol*]
AIV	Aliceville, AL [*Location identifier FAA*] (FAAL)
AIV	Aluminum Intensive Vehicle [*Auto industry*]
AIV	Apartment Investment & Management Co. [*NYSE symbol*] (SAG)
AIV	Apartment Investment & Mgmt'A' [*NYSE symbol*] (TTSB)
AIV	Armored Infantry Vehicle (MSA)
AIV	Associated Industries of Vermont (SRA)
AIV	Association Internationale de Volcanologie [*International Association of Volcanology*]
AIV	Aviation Impact Variable (OSRA)
AIV	Aviation Impact Variable (USDC)
AIVA	Association Internationale des Villes d'Avenir [*International Association of Cities of the Future*] (EA)
AIVF	Association of Independent Video and Filmmakers (EA)
AIVFC	Association Internationale des Villes Francophones des Congres [*International Association of French-Speaking Congress Towns - IAFCT*]
AIVM	Association Internationale pour les Voiles Minces [*en Beton*] [*International Association for Shell Structures*]
AIVP	American Institute of Vocal Pedagogy (EA)
AIVPA	Association Internationale Veterinaire de Production Animale [*International Veterinary Association for Animal Production - IVAAP*] [*Brussels, Belgium*] (EAIO)
AIVR	Accelerated Idioventricular Rhythm [*Cardiology*]
AIVS	American Institute for Verdi Studies (EA)
AIVV	Anterior Informal Vertebral Vein [*Medicine*] (DMAA)
AIW	Ardmore, OK [*Location identifier FAA*] (FAAL)
AIW	Asbestos Insulated Wire
AIW	Atlantic-Intercoastal Waterway (WDAA)
AIW	Auroral Infrasonic Wave [*Substorm*]
AIW	Auroral Intrasonic Wave [*Substorm*] (PDAA)
AIW	International Union, Allied Industrial Workers of America (EA)
AIWA	Asian-Indian Women in America (EA)
AiWb	Altiranisches Woerterbuch [*A publication*] (BJA)
AIWB	Australian Irish Welfare Bureau
AIWC	Intelligence Watch Condition [*NATO*] (NATG)
AIWEC	Advanced/Innovative Wind Energy Concept (MCD)
AIWF	American Institute of Wine and Food (EA)
AIWF	Association of the International Winter Sports Federations [*Switzerland*] (EAIO)
AIWHTE	Associate of the Institution of Works and Highways Technician Engineers [*British*] (DBQ)
AIWI	American Industrial Writing Institute
AIWM	American Institute of Weights and Measures [*Defunct*] (EA)
AIWO	Agudas Israel World Organization [*Jerusalem, Israel*]
AIWPHSA	American Institute of Wholesale Plumbing and Heating Supply Associations [*Later, AISA*]
AIWRS	Arctic International Wildlife Range Society (EA)
AIWS	Advanced Interdiction Weapon System
AIWSc	Associate Member of the Institute of Wood Science [*British*] (DBQ)
AIWSF	Association of the International Winter Sports Federations [*Berne, Switzerland*] (EAIO)
AIWSP	Associate Member of the Institute of Work Study Practitioners [*British*]
AIX	Advanced Interactive Executive [*IBM RT Personal Computer*] (BYTE)
AIX	Air International [*British ICAO designator*] (FAAC)
AIX	Astrotech International Corp. [*AMEX symbol*] (SPSG)
AIX	Astrotech Intl. [*AMEX symbol*] (TTSB)
AIX	Australian International Tax Agreements [*A publication*]
AIX	Mekoryuk, AK [*Location identifier FAA*] (FAAL)
AIY	Atlantic City [*New Jersey*] [*Airport symbol*] (OAG)
AIY	Ayrshire Imperial Yeomanry [*British military*] (DMA)
Aiyar	Aiyar's Company Cases [*India*] [*A publication*] (DLA)
Aiyar CC	Aiyar's Company Cases [*India*] [*A publication*] (DLA)
Aiyar LPC	Aiyar's Leading Privy Council Cases [*India*] [*A publication*] (DLA)
Aiyar Unrep D	Aiyar's Unreported Decisions [*India*] [*A publication*] (DLA)
AIYE	Average Indexed Yearly Earnings (GFGA)
AIYEP	Australia-Indonesia Youth Exchange Program
AIZ	Amcast Industrial [*NYSE symbol*] (SPSG)
AIZ	Arkia Israel Inland Airlines [*ICAO designator*] (FAAC)
AIZ	Lake Of The Ozarks [*Missouri*] [*Airport symbol*] (OAG)
AJ	Acta Juridica [*South Africa*] [*A publication*] (ILCA)
AJ	Acting Judge (ADA)
AJ	Acting Justice (ADA)
AJ	Actualite Juridique [*A publication*] (ILCA)
AJ	Adas [*or Adath*] Jeshurun (BJA)
AJ	Adherens Junction [*Cytology*]
AJ	Adjustment [*Accounting*]
AJ	Advanced Jaguar [*Jaguar PLC*] [*Automotive engineering*]

AJ .... After Japan [*Industry*]
AJ .... Air Jordan [*Airline*]
Aj .... Ajax [*of Sophocles*] [*Classical studies*] (OCD)
AJ .... Ajoutez [*Add*] [*Music*]
AJ .... Alliance for Justice (EA)
Aj .... All India Reporter, Ajmer Series [*A publication*] (ILCA)
AJ .... All Island Air [*ICAO designator*] (AD)
AJ .... Alloy Junction
AJ .... [*The*] Alma & Jonquieres Railway Co. [*AAR code*]
AJ .... American Jurist [*A publication*] (DLA)
AJ .... Analog Junction (TEL)
AJ .... Andrew Jackson [*US general and president, 1767-1845*]
AJ .... Ankle Jerk [*Neurology*]
AJ .... Antijamming [*RADAR*]
AJ .... Antiquitates Judaicae [*Jewish Antiquities*] [*of Josephus*] [*Classical studies*] (OCD)
AJ .... Applejack
AJ .... Applied Journalism
AJ .... Arc Jet
AJ .... Area Junction [*Telecommunications*] (OA)
AJ .... Assembly Jig
AJ .... Associated with Jobbers [*London Stock Exchange*]
AJ .... Associate in Journalism
AJ .... Associate Jewelers [*Defunct*] (EA)
AJ .... Associate Justice [*US Supreme Court*]
AJ .... Attack Jet
AJ .... Australian Jaycees
AJ .... Australian Journalist [*A publication*]
AJ .... British Guiana Supreme Court, Appellate Jurisdiction (DLA)
AJ .... Jasper Public Library, Alberta [*Library symbol National Library of Canada*] (NLC)
AJA .... Adjacent (AFM)
AJA .... Ajaccio [*Corsica*] [*Airport symbol*] (OAG)
AJA .... AJ Services Ltd. [*British ICAO designator*] (FAAC)
AJA .... American Jail Association (EA)
AJA .... American Jazz Alliance [*Formerly, CJOA*] (EA)
AJA .... American Jewish Archives [*An association*] (EA)
AJA .... American Jobs Abroad [*A publication*]
AJA .... American Journal of Archaeology [*A publication*] (BRI)
AJA .... American Judges Association (EA)
AJA .... American Judo Association (EA)
AJA .... Americans of Japanese Ancestry [*Psychometrics*]
AJA .... Anglo-Jewish Association [*British*]
AJA .... Arizona Jewelers Association (SRA)
a-ja-- .... Japan [*MARC geographic area code Library of Congress*] (LCCP)
AJA .... Jarvie Public Library, Alberta [*Library symbol National Library of Canada*] (NLC)
AJAC .... Automatic Jamming Avoidance Circuitry (AABC)
AJAC .... Automovile Journalists Association of Canada [*Association des Journalistes Automobile du Canada*] (AC)
AJacT .... Jacksonville State University, Jacksonville, AL [*Library symbol Library of Congress*] (LCLS)
AJAD .... Automated Joint Application Development [*Computer science*] (BTTJ)
AJAG .... Assistant Judge Advocate General [*Army*]
AJAG/CIV .... Assistant Judge Advocate General for Civil Law [*Army*] (AABC)
AJAG/MIL .... Assistant Judge Advocate General for Military Law [*Army*] (AABC)
AJ/AI .... Antijamming/Anti-Interference (CET)
AJAN .... Australian Journal of Advanced Nursing [*A publication*] (APTA)
AJAO .... American Juvenile Arthritis Organization (EA)
AJAPW .... Association of Jewish Anti-Poverty Workers [*Superseded by ECJF*]
AJAQ .... Army Job Activities Questionnaire
AJAR .... Association des Juifs Anciens Resistants [*Association of Jews in the Resistance*] [*Acronym is pseudonym of writer Romain Gary*]
AJAS .... American Junior Academy of Sciences
AJAS .... Associated Japan-America Societies of the United States (EA)
AJASS .... African Jazz Art Society Studios
AJAX .... Association of Journalists Against Extremism [*British*] (DI)
AJAY .... Ajay Sports [*NASDAQ symbol*] (TTSB)
AJAY .... Ajay Sports, Inc. [*NASDAQ symbol*] (NQ)
AJAYP .... Ajay Sports 10% Cv Pfd [*NASDAQ symbol*] (TTSB)
AJAYW .... Ajay Sports Wrrt [*NASDAQ symbol*] (TTSB)
AJAZ .... American Jewish Alternatives to Zionism (EA)
AJB .... Administration of Justice Branch [*US Military Government, Germany*]
AJB .... Associated Japanese Bank (International) Ltd.
AJB .... Audio Junction Box (MCD)
AJB .... Jacksonville State University, Jacksonville, AL [*OCLC symbol*] (OCLC)
AJBA .... American Junior Brahman Association (EA)
AJBA .... Australian Jersey Breeders' Association
AJBC .... American Junior Bowling Congress (EA)
AJBIC .... Arlin J. Brown Information Center (EA)
AJBO .... Antijamming Blackout
AJBP .... Association of Jewish Book Publishers (EA)
AJC .... Alvin Junior College [*Texas*]
AJC .... American Jewish Committee (EA)
AJC .... American Jewish Conference
AJC .... American Jewish Congress (EA)
AJC .... American Joint Committee for Cancer Staging and End Results Reporting [*Later, AJCC*] (EA)
AJC .... Arabian Jockey Club (EA)
AJC .... Arizona Job Colleges [*An association Defunct*] (EA)
AJC .... Atlanta Journal-Constitution
AJC .... Austin Junior College [*Later, Austin Community College*] [*Minnesota*]
AJC .... Bar Harbor Airlines [*ICAO designator*] (FAAC)
AJCA .... American Junior Chianina Association (EA)

AJCAF .... Association of Jewish Chaplains of the Armed Forces (EA)
AJCARF .... Office of Animal Care and the A. J. Carlson Animal Research Facility [*University of Chicago*] [*Research center*] (RCD)
AJCC .... Adelaide Junior Chamber of Commerce [*Australia*]
AJCC .... Alternate Joint Command Center (MCD)
AJCC .... Alternate Joint Communications Center
AJCC .... American Jersey Cattle Club (EA)
AJCC .... American Joint Committee on Cancer (EA)
AJCC .... Australian Junior Chamber of Commerce
AJCCA .... American Jewish Correctional Chaplains Association (EA)
AJCCS .... American Joint Committee on Cancer Staging [*Oncology*] (DAVI)
AJCCS & ER... American Joint Committee for Cancer Staging and End Results [*Oncology*] (DAVI)
AJCE .... Australian Joint Citrus Exporters [*An association*]
AJCH .... American Jewish Commission on the Holocaust (EA)
AJCH .... American Journal of Clinical Hypnosis [*A publication*]
AJCM .... Anti-Jam Control Modem [*Military*] (DOMA)
AJCRW .... Association of Jewish Community Relations Workers (EA)
AJCU .... Air Jet Control Unit
AJCU .... Association of Jesuit Colleges and Universities (EA)
AJCW .... Association of Jewish Center Workers (EA)
AJD .... Antijam Display
AJDC .... American Joint Distribution Committee
AJDE .... Alperin Jet-Diffuser Ejector (MCD)
AJDF .... ASEAN [*Association of South East Asian Nations*] Japan Development Fund
AJDG .... Air Jet Distortion Generator (MCD)
AJDS .... Association of Jewish Day Schools [*Association des Ecoles Juives*] (AC)
AJE .... Adjusting Journal Entry [*Accounting*]
AJE .... Adult Jewish Education
AJE .... Alfa Jet [*Spain ICAO designator*] (FAAC)
AJE .... American Journal of Education [*A publication*] (BRI)
AJE .... Antijam Equipment
AJEA .... Australian Journal of Experimental Agriculture [*A publication*]
AJ Ecol .... Australian Journal of Ecology [*A publication*]
AJ Ed .... Australian Journal of Education [*A publication*]
AJEFO .... Association des Juristes d'Expression Francaise de l'Ontario (AC)
AJEI .... Anglo-Japanese Economic Institute [*British*] (EAIO)
AJET .... Australian Journal of Educational Technology [*A publication*]
AJEUNAL .... Alliance de Jeunesse Angolaise pour la Liberte [*Alliance of Angolan Youth for Freedom*]
AJEX .... Association of Jewish Ex-Servicemen [*British*] (DI)
AJF .... American Justice Federation [*An association*]
AJF .... Antijam Frequency
AJF .... Association Jeunesse Fransaskoise [*Canada*]
AJF .... Jouf [*Saudi Arabia*] [*Airport symbol*] (OAG)
AJFCA .... Association of Jewish Family and Children's Agencies (EA)
AJFH .... Antijam Frequency Hopper
AJFL .... Australian Journal of Family Law [*A publication*]
AJFLD .... Association des Industries des Fruits et Legumes Deshydrates de la CEE [*European Organization of the Dehydrated Fruit and Vegetable Industries*] (EAIO)
AJG .... Gallagher [*Arthur J.*] & Co. [*NYSE symbol*] (SPSG)
AJGA .... American Junior Golf Association (EA)
AJGA .... Arizona Jojoba Growers Association (EA)
AJGS .... Association of Jewish Genealogical Societies (EA)
AJH .... Antijam Hopper
AJHA .... American Junior Hereford Association (EA)
AJHC .... American Jewish Heritage Committee (EA)
AJHC .... American Jewish History Center of the Jewish Theological Seminary [*Defunct*] (EA)
AJHPER .... Australian Journal for Health, Physical Education, and Recreation [*A publication*]
AJHS .... African Journal of the Health Sciences [*A publication*]
AJHS .... American Jewish Historical Society (EA)
AJHSNME .... American Junior High School National Mathematics Exam
AJI .... Ajiro [*Japan*] [*Seismograph station code, US Geological Survey*] (SEIS)
AJI .... American Jewish Institute [*Later, JIB*] (EA)
AJI .... American Justice Institute (EA)
AJI .... Antijamming Improvements (AABC)
AJIL .... American Journal of International Law [*A publication*]
AJIQ .... Association des Journalistes Independants du Quebec [*Quebec Association of Independent Journalists*] (AC)
AJIS .... Automated Jail Information System
AJJ .... Akjoujt [*Mauritania*] [*Airport symbol*] (AD)
AJJ .... Americans for Justice on the Job [*Defunct*] (EA)
AJJ .... Angel, Jerald J., Los Angeles CA [*STAC*]
AJJ .... Arizona Jojoba, Inc. [*Vancouver Stock Exchange symbol*]
AJJA .... Australian Ju Jitsu Association
AJJAF .... Association des Jeunes Juristes Africains [*France*]
AJJDC .... American Jewish Joint Distribution Committee (EA)
AJL .... Aero Jalisco SA de CV [*Mexico ICAO designator*] (FAAC)
AJL .... AJL Peps Trust [*Associated Press*] (SAG)
AJL .... Amway Japan Ltd. [*NYSE symbol*] (SAG)
AJL .... Amway Japan LtduADS [*NYSE symbol*] (TTSB)
AJL .... Association of Jewish Libraries (EA)
AJL .... Association of Junior Leagues (EA)
AJL .... Australian Journal of Linguistics [*A publication*]
AJL .... Australian Journal of Liturgy [*A publication*] (APTA)
AJLA .... Association of the Junior Leagues of America [*Later, AJL*] (EA)
AJLA .... Automated Juvenile Law Archive [*National Center for Juvenile Justice*] [*Information service or system*] (CRD)
AJLAC .... American Jewish League Against Communism (EA)

AJLC .... American Jewish Leadership Conference (EA)
AJLI .... American Jewish League for Israel (EA)
AJLL .... Australian Journal of Labour Law [*A publication*]
AJLO .... Avalanching Junction Light Output
AJLSPC .... Australian Joint Lamb and Sheepmeat Promotion Committee
AJM .... Abrasive Jet Machining (PDAA)
AJM .... Air Jamaica [*ICAO designator*] (FAAC)
ajm .... Aljamia [*MARC language code Library of Congress*] (LCCP)
AJM .... Analog Junction Module (TEL)
AJM .... Arthur Johnson Memorial Library, Raton, NM [*OCLC symbol*] (OCLC)
AJM .... Australian Journal of Mining [*A publication*]
AJMA .... American Jesuit Missionary Association [*Later, JM*] (EA)
AJMA .... American Jewelry Marketing Association [*Defunct*] (EA)
AJMA .... Antijam Manpack Antenna (MCD)
AJM/C .... Anti-Jam Modem Controller [*Computer science*] (LAIN)
AJME .... Americans for Justice in the Middle East [*Lebanon*] (EAIO)
Ajmer-Merwara LJ... Ajmer-Merwara Law Journal [*India*] [*A publication*] (DLA)
AJMP .... African Journal of Medical Practice [*A publication*]
AJMR .... American Journal on Mental Retardation [*A publication*] (BRI)
AJ/MRDN ...... AND-JEF/Mouvement Revolutionnaire pour la Democratie Nouvelle [*AND-JEF/New Democratic Revolutionary Movement*] [*Senegal*] [*Political party*]
AjN .... Adjective Noun [*Used in correcting manuscripts, etc.*]
AJN .... American Journal of Nursing (IIA)
AJN .... Anjouan [*Comoro Islands*] [*Airport symbol*] (OAG)
AJNR .... American Journal of Neuroradiology [*A publication*]
AJO .... Aero Ejecutivo SA de CV [*Mexico ICAO designator*] (FAAC)
AJO .... American Jazz Orchestra
AJO .... Antijam Operator (CET)
AJO .... Association of Jensen Owners (EA)
a-jo-- .... Jordan [*MARC geographic area code Library of Congress*] (LCCP)
AJOHN .... Australian Journal of Holistic Nursing [*A publication*]
AJOIA .... American Jews Opposed to Israeli Aggression (EA)
AJOJ .... April, July, October, and January [*Denotes quarterly payments of interest or dividends in these months*] [*Business term*]
AJP .... Aero Jets Corporativos, SA de C.V. [*Mexico*] [*FAA designator*] (FAAC)
AJP .... AJL Peps Trust [*NYSE symbol*] (SAG)
AJP .... Alarm and Jettison Panel
AJP .... American Journal of Philology [*A publication*] (BRI)
AJP .... American Journal of Psychiatry [*A publication*]
AJP .... Annales des Justices de Paix [*France*] [*A publication*] (ILCA)
AJP .... Australasian Journal of Philosophy [*A publication*] (APTA)
AJP .... Australian Journal of Pharmacy [*A publication*]
AJPA .... American Jewish Press Association (EA)
AJ-PADS ...... AND JEF - Parti Africain pour la Democratie et le Socialisme [*Senegal*] [*Political party*] (EY)
AJPC .... American Jewish Periodical Center (EA)
AJPC .... American Jewish Physicians' Committee [*Later, AFHU*] (EA)
AJPF .... American Jewish Philanthropic Fund (EA)
AJPHA .... American Junior Paint Horse Association (EA)
AJPHA .... American Junior Polled Hereford Association [*Later, NJPHA*] (EA)
AJPM .... Ad Jesum per Mariam [*To Jesus through Mary*] [*Latin*]
AJPO .... Ada Joint Program Office [*Later, Ada Board*] [*DoD*] (RDA)
AJPRS .... American Jewish Public Relations Society (EA)
A J Psy .... American Journal of Psychology [*A publication*] (BRI)
AJPsych .... American Journal of Psychiatry [*A publication*] (BRI)
AJQ .... Army Job Questionnaire
AJQHA .... American Junior Quarter Horse Association (EA)
AJR .... Abdominojugular Reflux Maneuver [*Medicine*] (DMAA)
AJR .... Agent Job Review [*LIMRA*]
AJR .... Ajax Resources Ltd. [*Vancouver Stock Exchange symbol*]
AJR .... AJR: American Journalism Review [*A publication*] (BRI)
AJR .... American Journalism Review [*A publication*] [*Formerly, WJR Washington Journalism Review*] (WDMC)
AJR .... Assembly Joint Resolution [*Congress*]
AJR .... Association of Jewish Refugees in Great Britain
AJR .... Australian Journalism Review [*A publication*] (APTA)
AJR .... Automatic "J" Relay (MCD)
ajr .... Azerbaijan Soviet Socialist Republic [*MARC country of publication code Library of Congress*] (LCCP)
AJRC .... American Junior Red Cross
AJRC .... Australia-Japan Research Centre [*Australian National University*]
AJRFU .... Australian Junior Rugby Football Union
AJRQ .... Association de la Jeunesse Rurale du Quebec (AC)
AJRQ .... Association des Journaux Regionaux du Quebec (AC)
AJRT .... Adaptive Jam-Resistant Tranceiver (PDAA)
AJS .... Acute Joint Syndrome [*Medicine*] (DMAA)
AJS .... Aeroejecutivos, Aeroservicios Ejecutivos [*Colombia*] [*ICAO designator*] (FAAC)
AJS .... Alliance des Jeunes pour le Socialisme [*Alliance of Youth for Socialism*] [*France Political party*] (PPE)
AJS .... American Journal of Sociology [*A publication*] (BRI)
AJS .... American Judicature Society (EA)
AJS .... Angle Jamming System
AJS .... Anti-Jackknife System [*Automotive engineering*]
AJS .... Antijam Synthesizer
AJS .... Association for Jewish Studies (EA)
AJS .... Axisymmetric Jet Stretcher
AJSA .... American Junior Shorthorn Association (EA)
AJSA .... American Junior Simmental Association [*Later, ASA*] (EA)
AJSC .... Association of Jewish Sponsored Camps (EA)
AJSH .... Journal of Occupational Health and Safety - Australia and New Zealand [*A publication*]
AJSM .... Association of Jute Spinners and Manufacturers [*British*] (DBA)

AJSMF .... Australian Journal of Sex, Marriage, and Family [*A publication*] (APTA)
AJSMOC ...... AJS [*Albert John Stevens*] and Matchless Owners Club [*Mount Sorrel, Leicestershire, England*] (EAIO)
AJ Soc Is ..... Australian Journal of Social Issues [*A publication*]
AJSS .... American Jewish Society for Service (EA)
AJT .... Advanced Jet Trainer
AJT .... Amerijet International [*ICAO designator*] (FAAC)
AJT .... Antijam Technique
AJTC .... American Japanese Trade Committee (EA)
AJTI .... Association on Japanese Textile Imports [*Defunct*] (EA)
AJTR .... Allowance Prescribed in Joint Travel Regulations [*Military*] (AABC)
AJT(UK) .... Association of Jamaican Trusts (United Kingdom) [*British*]
AJTWC .... Alternate Joint Typhoon Warning Center (DNAB)
AJU .... Aracaju [*Brazil*] [*Airport symbol*] (OAG)
AJU .... Washington, DC [*Location identifier FAA*] (FAAL)
AJVD .... Abrupt Junction Varactor Doubler
AJW .... Alexandria, MN [*Location identifier FAA*] (FAAL)
AJWDFP ...... Arab-Jewish Women's Dialogue for Peace [*Defunct*] (EA)
AJWO .... Association of Jewish Women's Organisations [*British*] (DI)
AJWR .... Alternate Joint War Room [*Later, ANMCC*] (CINC)
AJWS .... American Jewish World Service (EA)
AJX .... Ajax Magnethermic (IIA)
AJY .... Agades [*Niger*] [*Airport symbol*] (OAG)
AJY .... Ajay Resources, Inc. [*Vancouver Stock Exchange symbol*]
AJY .... Ashland, KY [*Location identifier FAA*] (FAAL)
AJY .... Association for Jewish Youth [*British*]
AK .... Above Knee [*Medicine*]
A/K .... Above Knee [*Amputation*] [*Medicine*] (DMAA)
AK .... Ackerley Communications [*AMEX symbol*] (TTSB)
AK .... Ackerley Communications, Inc. [*AMEX symbol*] (SPSG)
AK .... Actinic Keratosis [*Ophthalmology*] (DAVI)
AK .... Adapter Kit (MCD)
AK .... Adaption Kit
AK .... Adenosine Kinase [*An enzyme*]
AK .... Adenylate Kinase [*An enzyme*]
AK .... Afterpiece Kisser [*Slang Bowdlerized version*]
Ak .... Akademie [*Academy*] [*German*] (BJA)
AK .... Alaska [*Postal code*]
Ak .... Alaska State Library, Juneau, AK [*Library symbol Library of Congress*] (LCLS)
AK .... Albright-Knox Art Gallery [*Buffalo, NY*]
AK .... Allied Kommandatura
AK .... Altair [*Airline*] (MHDB)
AK .... Alte Kaempfer [*Old Fighters*] [*German*]
AK .... Alternaria kikuchiana [*A toxin-producing fungus*]
AK .... Amplitude Keyed
AK .... Antediluvian Knight [*Old actor*] (IIA)
AK .... Anterior [*Wall of*] Kidney
AK .... Apogee Kick [*NASA*] (KSC)
AK .... Apple's Kin [*An association Defunct*] (EA)
AK .... Arbeitskraft
Ak .... Arkansas Reports [*A publication*] (DLA)
AK .... Armee Korps [*Army Corps*] [*German*]
AK .... 'Arse over Kettle [*Head over heels*] [*Slang British*] (DSUE)
AK .... Aviation Storekeeper [*Navy rating*]
AK .... Avtomat Kalashnikov [*Submachine Gun*] [*Commonwealth of Independent States*]
AK .... Cargo Ship [*of any type*] [*Navy symbol*]
ak---- .... Caspian Sea and Area [*MARC geographic area code Library of Congress*] (LCCP)
AK .... E. Merck AG [*Germany*] [*Research code symbol*]
AK .... Kitscoty Public Library, Alberta [*Library symbol National Library of Canada*] (NLC)
AK1 .... Aviation Storekeeper, First Class [*Navy rating*]
AK1 .... West Kanaga [*Alaska*] [*Seismograph station code, US Geological Survey*] (SEIS)
AK2 .... Aviation Storekeeper, Second Class [*Navy rating*]
AK2 .... South Tanaga [*Alaska*] [*Seismograph station code, US Geological Survey*] (SEIS)
AK3 .... Aviation Storekeeper, Third Class [*Navy rating*]
AK3 .... North Tanaga [*Alaska*] [*Seismograph station code, US Geological Survey*] (SEIS)
AK5 .... North Tanaga [*Alaska*] [*Seismograph station code, US Geological Survey*] (SEIS)
AKA .... Above Knee Amputation [*Medicine*]
AKA .... Air Korea Co. Ltd. [*South Korea*] [*ICAO designator*] (FAAC)
AKA .... Alaska (ROG)
AKA .... Albert Kahn Associates [*Founded in 1895, one of the oldest architectural firms in the US*]
AKA .... Alcoholic Ketoacidosis [*Endocrinology and gastroenterology*] (DAVI)
AKA .... Alkyl Ketene Dimer [*Organic chemistry*]
AKA .... All Known Allergies [*Medicine*] (DAVI)
AKA .... Also Known As
aka .... Also Known As [*Pseudonym*] (WDMC)
AKA .... American Killifish Association (EA)
AKA .... American Kinesiotherapy Association (EA)
AKA .... American Kitefliers Association (EA)
AKA .... Ankang [*China*] [*Airport symbol*] (OAG)
AKA .... Annals of the Kings of Assyria [*A publication*] (BJA)
AKA .... Arkansas Arts Center, Little Rock, AR [*OCLC symbol*] (OCLC)
AKA .... Attack Cargo Ship [*Navy symbol*]
AKA .... Australian Kite Association
AKA .... Australian Korfball Association

AkA	Z. J. Loussac Public Library, Anchorage, AK [*Library symbol Library of Congress*] (LCLS)
AKAA	Airman Apprentice, Aviation Storekeeper [*Navy rating*]
AkAAH	Alaska Health Sciences Library, Anchorage, AK [*Library symbol Library of Congress*] (LCLS)
AkAAP	United States Department of the Interior, Alaska Pipeline Office, Anchorage, AK [*Library symbol Library of Congress*] (LCLS)
AkAAPU	Alaska Pacific University, Anchorage, AK [*Library symbol*] [*Library of Congress*] (LCLS)
AkAAR	United States Department of the Interior, Alaska Resources Library, Anchorage, AK [*Library symbol Library of Congress*] (LCLS)
AkAArA	ARCO-Alaska, Inc., Anchorage, AK [*Library symbol*] [*Library of Congress*] (LCLS)
AkAAS	ASK Information Search, Anchorage, AK [*Library symbol*] [*Library of Congress*] (LCLS)
AkAAVS	UAITC/CIT/Audio Visual Services, Anchorage, AK [*Library symbol Library of Congress*] (LCLS)
AkAbF	United States National Marine Fisheries Service, Auke Bay Fisheries Laboratory, Auke Bay, AK [*Library symbol Library of Congress*] (LCLS)
AkABP	BP Exploration Information Resource Center, Anchorage, AK [*Library symbol*] [*Library of Congress*] (LCLS)
AkAbU	University of Alaska, Juneau-Douglas Southeastern College, Auke Bay, AK [*Library symbol Library of Congress*] (LCLS)
AkAC	Anchorage Community College, Anchorage, AK [*Library symbol Library of Congress*] (LCLS)
AkACon	Anchorage Higher Education Consortium Library, Anchorage, AK [*Library symbol Library of Congress*] (LCLS)
AKADCOMRGN	Alaskan ADCOM Region [*Military*]
AkAEG	Alaska Department of Fish and Game Habitat, Anchorage, AK [*Library symbol*] [*Library of Congress*] (LCLS)
AkAF	United States National Marine Fisheries Service, Area Office, Anchorage, AK [*Library symbol Library of Congress*] (LCLS)
AKAGA	A Kinder and Gentler America
AkAGS	Church of Jesus Christ of Latter-Day Saints, Genealogical Society Library, Anchorage Branch, Anchorage, AK [*Library symbol Library of Congress*] (LCLS)
AkAH	United States Public Health Service, Arctic Health Research Center, Anchorage, AK [*Library symbol Library of Congress*] (LCLS)
AkAM	Alaska Methodist University, Anchorage, AK [*Library symbol Library of Congress*] (LCLS)
AK Amp	Above-Knee Amputation [*Orthopedics*] (DAVI)
AK Amp	At-the-Knee Amputation (VNW)
AKAN	Airman, Aviation Storekeeper [*Navy rating*]
AkAOS	Center for Oil Spill, Oil Spill Public Information Center, Anchorage, AK [*Library symbol*] [*Library of Congress*] (LCLS)
AKAR	Angkatan Keadilan Rakyat [*People's Justice Movement*] [*Malaysia*] [*Political party*] (EY)
AkAS	Anchorage School District, Library Resources, Anchorage, AK [*Library symbol Library of Congress*] (LCLS)
AkAU	University of Alaska, Anchorage, AK [*Library symbol Library of Congress*] (LCLS)
AkB	Kuskokwin Consortium Library, Bethel, AK [*Library symbol Library of Congress*] (LCLS)
AKB	University of Arkansas at Pine Bluff, Pine Bluff, AR [*OCLC symbol*] (OCLC)
AkBarH	Barrow High School, Barrow, AK [*Library symbol*] [*Library of Congress*] (LCLS)
AkBarN	North Slope Borough School District, Barrow, AK [*Library symbol*] [*Library of Congress*] (LCLS)
AkBarNA	United States Navy, Naval Arctic Research Laboratory, Barrow, AK [*Library symbol Library of Congress*] (LCLS)
AKBC	Australian Korea Business Council
AkBIA	United States Bureau of Indian Affairs, Bethel Regional Library, Bethel, AK [*Library symbol Library of Congress*] (LCLS)
AKBS	Advanced Kinematic Bombing System
AkBSD	Lower Kuskokwim School District, Media Center, Bethel, AK [*Library symbol*] [*Library of Congress*] (LCLS)
AKC	American Kennel Club (EA)
AKC	Anchor Machine & Manufacturing Ltd. [*Toronto Stock Exchange symbol*]
AKC	Arca Aerovias Colombians Ltda. [*Colombia*] [*ICAO designator*] (FAAC)
AKC	Army Kinematograph Corp. [*British military*] (DMA)
AKC	Associate of King's College [*London*]
AKC	Australia Kangaroo Club [*Defunct*] (EA)
AKC	Aviation Storekeeper, Chief [*Navy rating*]
AkC	Cordova Public Library, Cordova, AK [*Library symbol Library of Congress*] (LCLS)
AKC	Keg River Community Library, Alberta [*Library symbol National Library of Canada*] (NLC)
AKC	University of Central Arkansas, Conway, AR [*OCLC symbol*] (OCLC)
AKCA	Associated Koi Clubs of America (EA)
AKCCI	Australia-Korea Chamber of Commerce and Industry
AKCL	Associate of King's College London
AKCLIS	Australian Key Center in Land Information Studies
AKCM	Aviation Storekeeper, Master Chief [*Navy rating*]
AKCNSW	Australian Kelpie Club of New South Wales
AKCORD	Aviation Kamchatka-California Organization for Reconstruction and Development (ECON)
AKCS	Aviation Storekeeper, Senior Chief [*Navy rating*]
AKD	Akdeniz Hava Tasimacilik TIC, Ve San A.S. [*Turkey*] [*FAA designator*] (FAAC)
AKD	Alkylketene Dimer [*Organic chemistry*]
AKD	Automatic Key Distribution
AKD	Cargo Ship, Dock [*Navy symbol*]
AKD	Central Arkansas Library System, Little Rock, AR [*OCLC symbol*] (OCLC)
AkDFG	Alaska Fish and Game Library, Douglas, AK [*Library symbol*] [*Library of Congress*] (LCLS)
AkDil	Dillingham Public Library, Dillingham, AK [*Library symbol Library of Congress*] (LCLS)
AkDj	Delta Community Library, Delta Junction, AK [*Library symbol Library of Congress*] (LCLS)
AkDJHS	Juneau-Douglas High School, Douglas, AK [*Library symbol*] [*Library of Congress*] (LCLS)
AKE	Acrokeratoelastoidosis (DMAA)
AKE	Agrotikon Komma Ellados [*Agrarian Party of Greece*] [*Political party*]
AKE	Akers Medical Technology Ltd. [*Vancouver Stock Exchange symbol*]
AKE	Akieni [*Gabon*] [*Airport symbol*] (OAG)
AKE	Ammunition Transport
AKE	Hendrix College, Conway, AR [*OCLC symbol*] (OCLC)
AKEC	Keephills Community Library, Alberta [*Library symbol National Library of Canada*] (NLC)
AkEiel	United States Air Force, Base Library, Eielson AFB, AK [*Library symbol Library of Congress*] (LCLS)
AKEL	Anorthotiko Komma Ergazomenou Laou [*Progressive Party of the Working People*] [*Cyprus*] [*Political party*] (PPW)
AkElm	United States Air Force, Base Library, Elmendorf AFB, AK [*Library symbol Library of Congress*] (LCLS)
AkElmM	United States Air Force, Hospital Medical Library/SGAL, Elmendorf Air Force Base, AK [*Library symbol Library of Congress*] (LCLS)
AKERR	Allied Kinetic Energy Recovery Rope [*Army*] (INF)
AKES	Automatic Kinetic Enzyme System (PDAA)
AKF	Aga Khan Foundation [*Switzerland*] (EAIO)
AKF	American Kidney Fund (EA)
AKF	American-Korean Foundation [*Later, IHAP*] (EA)
AKF	Arkansas Library Commission, Little Rock, AR [*OCLC symbol*] (OCLC)
AKF	Australia-Korea Foundation
AKF	Australian Karate Federation
AKF	Australian Kendo Federation
AkF	Fairbanks North Star Borough Library, Fairbanks, AK [*Library symbol Library of Congress*] (LCLS)
AKF	Kufrah [*Libya*] [*Airport symbol*] (OAG)
AKF	Refrigerated Cargo Ship [*World War II*]
AK-FBM	Polaris Cargo Resupply Ship [*Navy symbol*] (DNAB)
AKFED	Aga Khan Fund for Economic Development
AkFg	United States Army, Recreational Services Post Library, Fort Greeley, AK [*Library symbol Library of Congress*] (LCLS)
AkFGS	Church of Jesus Christ of Latter-Day Saints, Genealogical Society Library, Fairbanks Alaska District Branch, Fairbanks, AK [*Library symbol Library of Congress*] (LCLS)
AkFL	Fairbanks Law Library, Fairbanks, AK [*Library symbol Library of Congress*] (LCLS)
AkFLHS	Lathrop High School, Fairbanks, AK [*Library symbol*] [*Library of Congress*] (LCLS)
AkFLJS	Howard Luke Junior-Senior High School, Fairbanks, AK [*Library symbol*] [*Library of Congress*] (LCLS)
AKFM	Antokon'ny Kongresin'ny Fahaleovantenan'i Madagasikara [*Congress Party for Malagasy Independence*] [*Political party*] (AF)
AKFM	Association of Knitted Fabrics Manufacturers (EA)
AkFM	Fairbanks Memorial Hospital, Fairbanks, AK [*Library symbol Library of Congress*] (LCLS)
AkFr	United States Army, Recreational Services Post Library, Fort Richardson, AK [*Library symbol Library of Congress*] (LCLS)
AkFSD	Fairbanks North Star Borough School District, Fairbanks, AK [*Library symbol*] [*Library of Congress*] (LCLS)
AKFSR	American Karakul Fur Sheep Registry [*Later, AKSR*] (EA)
AkFw	United States Army, Recreational Services Post Library, Fort Wainwright, AK [*Library symbol Library of Congress*] (LCLS)
AkFWHS	West Valley High School, Fairbanks, AK [*Library symbol*] [*Library of Congress*] (LCLS)
AkFwP	Alaskan Projects Office, Fort Wainwright, AK [*Library symbol Library of Congress*] (LCLS)
AkFy	Fort Yukon Community/School Library, Fort Yukon, AK [*Library symbol Library of Congress*] (LCLS)
AKG	Alaskagold Mines Ltd. [*Vancouver Stock Exchange symbol*]
AKG	Alkoxyglycerol [*Organic chemistry*]
AKG	Anguganak [*Papua New Guinea*] [*Airport symbol*] (OAG)
AKG	Arkansas Louisiana Gas Co. (IIA)
AKG	Auxiliary Killing Ground [*British and Canadian*] [*World War II*]
AKGA	American Knit Glove Association (EA)
AKGA	Association of Kew Gardeners in America [*Defunct*] (EA)
AKGA	Australian Kiwifruit Growers' Association
AKGD	Acknowledged (ROG)
AKH	Adipokinetic Hormone [*Endocrinology*]
AKH	Akhal [*Turkmenistan*] [*ICAO designator*] (FAAC)
AKH	Akhalkalaki [*Former USSR Seismograph station code, US Geological Survey Closed*] (SEIS)
AKH	Akhisar [*Turkey*] [*Airport symbol*] (AD)
AKH	Allgemeines Krankenhaus [*Austria*] [*Largest hospital in Europe*]
AkH	Haines Borough Public Library, Haines, AK [*Library symbol Library of Congress*] (LCLS)
AKH	Henderson State University, Arkadelphia, AR [*OCLC symbol*] (OCLC)
AkHi	Alaska Historical Library and Museum, Juneau, AK [*Library symbol Library of Congress*] (LCLS)
AKHMA	Alaska Hotel and Motel Association (SRA)
AkHom	Homer Public Library, Homer, AK [*Library symbol Library of Congress*] (LCLS)

AKI............. Aircraft Kill Indicator

AKI............. Akiak [*Alaska*] [*Airport symbol*] (OAG)

AKI............. Akiko-Lori Gold [*Vancouver Stock Exchange symbol*]

AKI............. Akita [*Japan*] [*Seismograph station code, US Geological Survey*] (SEIS)

AKI............. Anti-Knock Index [*Automotive industry*]

AKI............. Automix Keyboards, Inc.

AKI............. General Stores Issue Ship [*Navy symbol*]

AKI............. Killam Public Library, Alberta [*Library symbol National Library of Canada*] (NLC)

AKJ............. Asahikawa [*Japan*] [*Airport symbol*] (OAG)

AkJ............. Juneau Memorial (Public) Library, Juneau, AK [*Library symbol Library of Congress*] (LCLS)

AkJBM........ United States Bureau of Mines, Alaska Field Operation Center, Juneau, AK [*Library symbol Library of Congress*] (LCLS)

AkJEC......... Alaska Department of Environmental Conservation, Juneau, AK [*Library symbol*] [*Library of Congress*] (LCLS)

AkJFG......... Alaska Department of Fish and Game, Juneau, AK [*Library symbol Library of Congress*] (LCLS)

AkJFS......... Forestry Science Laboratory, Juneau, AK [*Library symbol Library of Congress*] (LCLS)

AkJL........... Alaska Legislative Affairs Agency, Legislative Reference Library, Juneau, AK [*Library symbol*] [*Library of Congress*] (LCLS)

AkJU........... University of Alaska, Juneau Library, Juneau, AK [*Library symbol Library of Congress*] (LCLS)

AKK............. Akhiok [*Alaska*] [*Airport symbol*] (OAG)

akk............. Akkadian [*MARC language code Library of Congress*] (LCCP)

AKK............. Aklak Air Ltd. [*Canada ICAO designator*] (FAAC)

AKK............. Alpha Kappa Kappa [*Fraternity*]

AKK............. Antifaschistischer Kampf Kaiserslautern [*Kaiserslautern Antifascist Struggle*] [*Germany*] (PD)

AKK............. John Brown University, Siloam Springs, AR [*OCLC symbol*] (OCLC)

AkK............. Ketchikan Public Library, Ketchikan, AK [*Library symbol Library of Congress*] (LCLS)

Akkad......... Akkadian (BJA)

AkKC.......... Ketchikan Community College, Ketchikan, AK [*Library symbol*] [*Library of Congress*] (LCLS)

AkKe.......... Kenai Community Library, Inc., Kenai, AK [*Library symbol Library of Congress*] (LCLS)

AkKeH........ Kenai Central High School, Kenai, AK [*Library symbol Library of Congress*] (LCLS)

AkKeHi........ Kenai Historical, Inc., Fort Kenai Museum, Kenai, AK [*Library symbol Library of Congress*] (LCLS)

AkKeK........ Kenai Peninsula Libraries, Kenai, AK [*Library symbol Library of Congress*] (LCLS)

AkKF.......... United States Bureau of Commercial Fisheries, Technological Laboratory Library, Ketchikan, AK [*Library symbol Library of Congress Obsolete*] (LCLS)

AkKo.......... Kodiak Public Library (A. Holmes Johnson Memorial Library), Kodiak, AK [*Library symbol Library of Congress*] (LCLS)

AKKO.......... Turkish Communist Party - Marxist-Leninist [*Political party*] (PD)

AkKoC........ Kodiak Community College, Kodiak, AK [*Library symbol*] [*Library of Congress*] (LCLS)

AkKoH........ Kodiak High School Library, Kodiak, AK [*Library symbol Library of Congress*] (LCLS)

AkKoHi....... Kodiak Historical Society, Kodiak, AK [*Library symbol Library of Congress*] (LCLS)

AkKSD........ Ketchikan Gateway Borough School District, Ketchikan, AK [*Library symbol*] [*Library of Congress*] (LCLS)

AkKSISD...... Southeast Island School District, Ketchikan, AK [*Library symbol*] [*Library of Congress*] (LCLS)

AkKTHi........ Tongass Historical Society Museum, Ketchikan, AK [*Library symbol Library of Congress*] (LCLS)

AkKzMHS..... Kotzebue Middle-High School, Kotzebue, AK [*Library symbol*] [*Library of Congress*] (LCLS)

AKL............. Air Kilroe Ltd. [*British ICAO designator*] (FAAC)

Ak-L............ Alaska State Court System, Law Library, Anchorage, AK [*Library symbol Library of Congress*] (LCLS)

AKL............. Ark-La-Tex Industries [*Vancouver Stock Exchange symbol*]

AKL............. Auckland [*New Zealand*] [*Airport symbol*] (OAG)

AKL............. Haskell, TX [*Location identifier FAA*] (FAAL)

AKL............. Light Cargo Ship [*Navy symbol*]

AKL............. University of Akron, Law Library, Akron, OH [*OCLC symbol*] (OCLC)

AkLA........... Alaska Library Association

AKLM.......... Acclaim Entertainment [*NASDAQ symbol*] (TTSB)

AKLM.......... Acclaim Entertainment, Inc. [*NASDAQ symbol*] (NQ)

AKM............. Acme [*Spain ICAO designator*] (FAAC)

AKM............. Apogee Kick Motor [*NASA*] (KSC)

AKM............. Kinuso Municipal Library, Alberta [*Library symbol National Library of Canada*] (NLC)

AKM............. University of Arkansas Medical Science Campus, Little Rock, AR [*OCLC symbol*] (OCLC)

AKMC.......... Azad Kashmir Muslim Conference [*Pakistan*] [*Political party*] (FEA)

AKML.......... Aladdin Knights of the Mystic Light (EA)

AKMS.......... Army Key Management System

AKN............. Alaskon Resources [*Vancouver Stock Exchange symbol*]

AKN............. Alkan Air Ltd. [*Canada ICAO designator*] (FAAC)

AkN............. Kegoayah Kozga Public Library, Nome, AK [*Library symbol Library of Congress*] (LCLS)

AKN............. King Salmon [*Alaska*] [*Airport symbol*] (OAG)

AKN............. King Salmon-Naknek [*Alaska*] [*Airport symbol*] (AD)

a-kn--.......... Korea, North [*MARC geographic area code Library of Congress*] (LCCP)

AKN............. Net Cargo Ship [*Navy symbol Obsolete*]

AkNak........ Martin Monsen Regional Library, Naknek, AK [*Library symbol Library of Congress*] (LCLS)

AkNakBS..... Bristol Bay School, Media Center, Naknek, AK [*Library symbol*] [*Library of Congress*] (LCLS)

AKNF.......... Adair-Koshland-Nemethy-Filmer [*Enzyme model*]

AkNNC........ Northwest Community College, Nome, AK [*Library symbol*] [*Library of Congress*] (LCLS)

AkNpHS...... North Pole High School, North Pole, AK [*Library symbol*] [*Library of Congress*] (LCLS)

AKO .... Akron, CO [*Location identifier FAA*] (FAAL)

AKO .... Embotelladora Andina ADS [*NYSE symbol*] (TTSB)

AKO .... Embotelladora Andina SA [*NYSE symbol*] (SAG)

AKO .... [*A*] Kind Of (MHDI)

a-ko--.......... Korea, South [*MARC geographic area code Library of Congress*] (LCCP)

AKO .... Ouachita Baptist University, Arkadelphia, AR [*OCLC symbol*] (OCLC)

Akorn........ Akorn, Inc. [*Associated Press*] (SAG)

AKP............. Agence Khmere de Presse [*Cambodian Press Agency*]

AKP............. Alkaline Phosphatase (DMAA)

AKP............. Alpha Kappa Psi [*Fraternity*]

AKP............. Alzhirskaia Kommunisticheskaia Partia [*Albanian Communist Party*] [*Political party*]

AKP............. Anaktuvuk Pass [*Alaska*] [*Airport symbol*] (OAG)

AKP............. Arbeidernes Kommunistiske Parti [*Workers' Communist Party*] [*Norway Political party*] (PPE)

AKP............. Argentinian Communist Party [*Political party*]

AKP............. Arkansas Power & Light [*NYSE symbol*] (SAG)

AKP............. Arkansas Power and Light Co. (IIA)

AKP............. Arkansas Technical University, Russellville, AR [*OCLC symbol*] (OCLC)

AKP............. Austrian Communist Party [*Political party*]

AkP............. Petersburg Public Library, Petersburg, AK [*Library symbol Library of Congress*] (LCLS)

AkPal......... Palmer Public Library, Palmer, AK [*Library symbol Library of Congress*] (LCLS)

AkPalA........ Alaska Agricultural Experiment Station, Palmer, AK [*Library symbol Library of Congress*] (LCLS)

AkPalU........ University of Alaska, Matanuska-Susitna Community College, Palmer, AK [*Library symbol Library of Congress*] (LCLS)

AKPIRG....... Alaska Public Interest Research Group [*Research center*] (RCD)

AKP (M-L)... Arbeidernes Kommunistparti (Marxist-Leninistene) [*Workers Communist Party (Marxist-Leninist)*] [*Norway Political party*]

AkPP.......... Petersburg Press, Petersburg, AK [*Library symbol Library of Congress*] (LCLS)

AKPPr......... Entergy Arkansas $2.40cmPfd [*NYSE symbol*] (TTSB)

AkPT.......... Tongass National Forest, Petersburg, AK [*Library symbol Library of Congress*] (LCLS)

AKQ .... Wakefield, VA [*Location identifier FAA*] (FAAL)

AKR .... Address Key Register

AKR .... Aerolik [*Former USSR*] [*FAA designator*] (FAAC)

AKR .... Akron, OH [*Location identifier FAA*] (FAAL)

AKR .... Auroral Kilometric Radiation [*Planetary science*]

a-kr--.......... Korea [*MARC geographic area code Library of Congress*] (LCCP)

AKR .... University of Akron, Akron, OH [*OCLC symbol*] (OCLC)

AKR .... Vehicle Cargo Ship [*Navy symbol*]

AKRN.......... Akorn, Inc. [*NASDAQ symbol*] (NQ)

AKRO.......... Acknowledge Receipt Of [*Telecommunications*] (TEL)

AKS............. Advanced Kick Stage [*Missile launching*] (MCD)

AKS............. Akhmos-I [*Belarus*] [*FAA designator*] (FAAC)

AKS............. AK Steel Holding [*NYSE symbol*] (TTSB)

AKS............. AK Steel Holding [*NYSE symbol*] (SAG)

AKS............. Arakis Capital [*Vancouver Stock Exchange symbol*]

AKS............. Associated Knowledge Systems [*Imperial Chemical Industries Ltd.*] [*Information service or system*] (IID)

AKS............. Association for Korean Studies (EA)

AKS............. Auki [*Solomon Islands*] [*Airport symbol*] (OAG)

AKS............. General Stores Issue Ship [*Navy symbol*]

AkS............. Kettleson Memorial Library, Sitka, AK [*Library symbol Library of Congress*] (LCLS)

AkSB.......... Blatchley Junior High School, Sitka, AK [*Library symbol Library of Congress*] (LCLS)

AkSC........... Sitka Council on Alcoholism and Other Drug Abuse, Sitka, AK [*Library symbol*] [*Library of Congress*] (LCLS)

AKSE.......... Arakis Energy Corp. [*NASDAQ symbol*] (SAG)

AKSEF........ Arakis Energy [*NASDAQ symbol*] (TTSB)

AkSeld........ Seldovia Public Library, Seldovia, AK [*Library symbol Library of Congress*] (LCLS)

AkSew .... Seward Community Library, Seward, AK [*Library symbol Library of Congress*] (LCLS)

AkSew .... Seward Community Library, Seward, AK [*Library symbol*] [*Library of Congress*] (LCLS)

AkSJ........... Sheldon Jackson College, Sitka, AK [*Library symbol Library of Congress*] (LCLS)

AkSk.......... Skagway Public Library, Skagway, AK [*Library symbol Library of Congress*] (LCLS)

AkSMH........ Mount Edgecumbe High School, Sitka, AK [*Library symbol*] [*Library of Congress*] (LCLS)

AkSol......... Soldotna Public Library (Joyce Carver Memorial Library), Soldotna, AK [*Library symbol Library of Congress*] (LCLS)

AkSolK........ Kenai Peninsula Community College, Soldotna, AK [*Library symbol*] [*Library of Congress*] (LCLS)

AKSPr......... AK Steel Hldg 7%'SAILS' [*NYSE symbol*] (TTSB)

AKSR.......... American Karakul Sheep Registry (EA)

AK(SS)........ Cargo Submarine [*Navy symbol Obsolete*]

AkSSD .... Sitka School District, Sitka, AK [*Library symbol*] [*Library of Congress*] (LCLS)
AK Steel ...... AK Steel Holding Corp. [*Associated Press*] (SAG)
AK Stl ...... AK Steel Holding Corp. [*Associated Press*] (SAG)
AKSY .... Aksys Ltd. [*NASDAQ symbol*] (SAG)
AKSYS .... AKsys Ltd [*NASDAQ symbol*] (TTSB)
AksysL .... Aksys Ltd. [*Associated Press*] (SAG)
AKT .... Aircompany Karat [*Former USSR*] [*FAA designator*] (FAAC)
akt .... Aktiv [*Active*] [*German*]
AKT .... Applied Knowledge Test [*Vocational guidance test*]
AKT .... Auditory, Kinesthetic, Tactile Approach [*Teaching method*]
AktG .... Aktiengesetz [*Law governing public companies*] [*German*] (ILCA)
AKU .... Aga Khan University [*Karachi, Pakistan*]
AKU .... Aksu [*China*] [*Airport symbol*] (OAG)
AKU .... Akulik, AK [*Location identifier FAA*] (FAAL)
AKU .... Akureyri [*Iceland*] [*Seismograph station code, US Geological Survey*] (SEIS)
aku .... Alaska [*MARC country of publication code Library of Congress*] (LCCP)
AKU .... Algemene Kunstzijde Unie [*Later, AKZO*] [*Netherlands*] [*Commercial firm*]
a-ku-- .... Kuwait [*MARC geographic area code Library of Congress*] (LCCP)
AkU .... University of Alaska, Fairbanks, AK [*Library symbol Library of Congress*] (LCLS)
AKU .... University of Arkansas at Little Rock, Little Rock, AR [*OCLC symbol*] (OCLC)
AkU-AB .... University of Alaska, Institute of Arctic Biology, Fairbanks, AK [*Library symbol Library of Congress*] (LCLS)
AkU-AE .... University of Alaska, Artic Environmental Information and Data Center, Anchorage, AK [*Library symbol*] [*Library of Congress*] (LCLS)
AkU-G .... University of Alaska, Geophysical Institute Library, Fairbanks, AK [*Library symbol*] [*Library of Congress*] (LCLS)
AkU-M .... University of Alaska, Bio-Medical Library, Fairbanks, AK [*Library symbol Library of Congress*] (LCLS)
AkU-Mu .... University of Alaska Museum Library, Fairbanks, AK [*Library symbol*] [*Library of Congress*] (LCLS)
AkU-NL .... University of Alaska, Alaska Native Language Center, Fairbanks, AK [*Library symbol*] [*Library of Congress*] (LCLS)
AKUP .... Association of Korean University Presses
AKURON ...... Autonetics Kalman Utilization of Reference for Optimal Navigation (MCD)
AkU-W .... University of Alaska, Wildlife Library, Fairbanks, AK [*Library symbol*] [*Library of Congress*] (LCLS)
AKV .... Akulivik [*Canada*] [*Airport symbol*] (OAG)
AKV .... Cargo Ship and Aircraft Ferry [*Navy symbol*]
AkV .... Valdez Public Library, Valdez, AK [*Library symbol Library of Congress*] (LCLS)
AkW .... Wrangell Public Library, Wrangell, AK [*Library symbol Library of Congress*] (LCLS)
AKWAS .... Author and Keywords in Alphabetical Sequence (ADA)
AkWas .... Wasilla Public Library, Wasilla, AK [*Library symbol Library of Congress*] (LCLS)
AKWIC .... Author and Keyword in Context
AkWill .... Willow Public Library, Willow, AK [*Library symbol Library of Congress*] (LCLS)
AKY .... Akaitcho Yellowknife Gold Mines Ltd. [*Toronto Stock Exchange symbol*]
AKY .... Akyab [*Myanmar*] [*Airport symbol*] (OAG)
AKY .... Akyab [*Burma*] [*Airport symbol*] (AD)
AKY .... San Antonio, TX [*Location identifier FAA*] (FAAL)
AKY .... YAK-Service [*Former USSR*] [*FAA designator*] (FAAC)
AKYFW .... Albanian Kosovar Youth in the Free World (EA)
AKZ .... Aerokuznetsk, Joint Stock Company [*Former USSR*] [*FAA designator*] (FAAC)
AKZ .... Antiarmor Kill Zone [*Military*] (INF)
AKZA .... Aktiekomitee Zuidelyk Afrika [*Belgium*]
AKZO .... Akzo NV [*NASDAQ symbol*] (NQ)
Akzo .... Akzo NV [*Associated Press*] (SAG)
AKZOY .... Akzo Nobel N.V. ADS [*NASDAQ symbol*] (TTSB)
AL .... Abnormal Lungs [*Medicine*]
AL .... Abraham Lincoln [*US president, 1809-1865*]
AL .... Absolute Limen [*Psychophysics*]
AL .... Acceptable Level (GNE)
AL .... Accession List
AL .... Accidental Loss [*Nuclear energy*]
AL .... Accrued Liability [*Accounting*]
AL .... Accumulator Low [*Computer science*]
AL .... Acoustics Laboratory
AL .... Acquisition and Logistics (MCD)
AL .... Acquisition Letter [*Replaced PIL*] (AAGC)
AL .... Acquisition Logistician (NG)
AL .... Acquisition of Land Act [*Town planning*] [*British*]
A/L .... Acting Lieutenant [*Navy British*]
AL .... Action for Life (EA)
AL .... Action Learning (PDAA)
AL .... Action [*Indicator*] Level [*Radiation measurement*] (NRCH)
AL .... Action Linkage [*An association*] (EA)
AL .... Acute Leukemia [*Medicine*]
AL .... Adaptation Level
AL .... Additional Listing [*Telecommunications*] (TEL)
AL .... Adductor Longus [*Anatomy*]
A/L .... Administration/Logistics (INF)
AL .... Administrative Leave (GFGA)
AL .... Admiralty Letter [*British military*] (DMA)

AL .... Advisory Leaflet
AL .... Aerodynamics Laboratory [*Naval Ship Research and Development Center*]
AL .... Aeromechanics Laboratory [*Army*] (GRD)
AL .... Aeronautical Laboratory
AL .... Aeronautical Radionavigation Land Station [*ITU designation*]
AL .... Aeronomy Laboratory [*National Institute of Standards and Technology*]
AL .... Aerophysics Laboratory (MCD)
AL .... Afar Locality [*Paleoanthropology*]
AL .... Aft Left (MCD)
AL .... Agricultural Labourer
AL .... Aircraft Logistics Division [*Bureau of Aeronautics*] [*Later, NASC*] [*Navy*]
AL .... Air Electrical [*Special duties officer*] [*Military British*]
A/L .... Air-Landing [*British military*] (DMA)
A/L .... Air Launch [*or Lift*] (SAA)
AL .... Air League [*An association*] (EAIO)
AL .... Air Letter
AL .... Air Liaison
AL .... Airlift (AABC)
AL .... Air Lock [*Technical drawings*]
AL .... Alabama [*Postal code*]
Al .... Alanus Anglicus [*Flourished, 1208-10*] [*Authority cited in pre-1607 legal work*] (DSA)
AL .... Alarm [*Telecommunications*] (TEL)
AL .... Albania [*ANSI two-letter standard code*] (CNC)
Al .... Albericus de Porta Ravennate [*Flourished, 1165-94*] [*Authority cited in pre-1607 legal work*] (DSA)
Al .... Albertus Beneventanus [*Deceased, 1187*] [*Authority cited in pre-1607 legal work*] (DSA)
Al .... Albertus Longobardista [*Flourished, 12th century*] [*Authority cited in pre-1607 legal work*] (DSA)
Al .... Albertus Magnus [*Teutonicus*] [*Deceased, 1280*] [*Authority cited in pre-1607 legal work*] (DSA)
Al .... Albertus Ranconis [*Flourished, 1369-72*] [*Authority cited in pre-1607 legal work*] (DSA)
AL .... Albumin [*Also, ALB*] [*Biochemistry*]
AL .... Albuquerque Operations Office (DOGT)
AL .... Alcan Aluminium Ltd [*NYSE symbol*] (TTSB)
AL .... ALCAN Aluminium Ltd. [*NYSE symbol Toronto Stock Exchange symbol Vancouver Stock Exchange symbol*] (SPSG)
AL .... Alcoholism [*Chemical dependency and psychiatry*] (DAVI)
Al .... Aleyn's English King's Bench Reports [*A publication*] (DLA)
Al .... Alfven Number [*IUPAC*]
AL .... Algeria [*IYRU nationality code*] (IYR)
AL .... Alia [*Others*] [*Latin*]
AL .... Alias [*Otherwise*] [*Latin*]
AL .... Alibi [*Elsewhere*] [*Latin*] (ROG)
AL .... Alignment Lab
AL .... Alignment Mark [*On cardiography*] [*Cardiology*] (DAVI)
Al .... Alinea [*Paragraph*] [*Italian*] (ILCA)
Al .... Alinea [*Paragraph*] [*Dutch*] (ILCA)
AL .... Alkane [*Organic chemistry*]
AL .... Allegheny (GAVI)
AL .... Allegheny Airlines [*ICAO designator*] (AD)
AL .... Alley (WGA)
AL .... All Lengths [*Lumber*]
Al .... Allosteric [*Biochemistry*]
AL .... Allowance List
AL .... Almanor Railroad Co. [*AAR code*]
Al .... Alpavia [*France ICAO aircraft manufacturer identifier*] (ICAO)
AL .... Alternaria alternata f lycopersici [*A toxin-producing fungus*]
Al .... Alternating Light [*Navigation signal*]
AL .... Alternative List [*Sweden Political party*]
AL .... Alternative Liste [*Alternative List*] [*Austria Political party*]
Al .... Aluminum [*Chemical element*]
AL .... Amber Light (MSA)
AL .... American League [*Baseball*]
AL .... American Legend (EA)
AL .... American Legion (EA)
AL .... American Literature [*A publication*] (BRI)
A/L .... Ammunition Loading (SAA)
AL .... Amoebocyte Lysate [*Biochemistry*]
AL .... Amplitude Limiter [*Electronics*] (OA)
AL .... Analog Link [*Telecommunications*] (TEL)
AL .... Analog Loop-Back [*Telecommunications*] (TEL)
AL .... Analytical Laboratory (NRCH)
AL .... Analytical Letters [*A publication*]
AL .... Analytical Limits (NRCH)
AL .... Andersen Laboratories, Inc.
AL .... Angle Lock
AL .... Angler's Library [*A publication*]
AL .... Anglo-Latin [*Language, etc.*]
AL .... Animal Liberation (EA)
AL .... Annee de Lumiere [*Light Year*] [*French*]
AL .... Anno Lucis [*In the Year of Light*] [*Latin*]
AL .... Annual Lease [*Business term*] (MHDB)
AL .... Annual Leave [*US Civil Service*]
AL .... Antenna Laboratory (MCD)
AL .... Antennule Length [*of Crustacea*]
AL .... Anterior Pituitary Lobe [*Anatomy*]
AL .... Approach & Landing [*MTMC*] (TAG)
A/L .... Approach/Landing
AL .... Apres Livraison [*After Delivery of Goods*] [*French*]

AL .... Arab League
AL .... Architectural League of New York (EA)
AL .... Area Weapon Left (MCD)
AL .... Argininosuccinate Lyase [Also, ASL] [An enzyme]
AL .... Argyrophil
AL .... Arm Length
AL .... Army List [British military] (DMA)
AL .... Arrival Locator
AL .... Artificial Life [Computer science]
AL .... Artificial Line [Electricity] (OA)
AL .... Artificial Luminance [Theory proposed by James Clerk Maxwell in 1864]
AL .... Artistic License (EA)
A/L .... Assemble/Load [Computer science]
AL .... Assembly Language [Computer science]
AL .... Asset/Locating (LAIN)
AL .... Assets Less Than (NITA)
AL .... Assignment of License [FCC] (NTCM)
AL .... Associated Laboratories (EA)
AL .... Assumed Latitude [Navigation]
AL .... Astronomical League (EA)
AL .... Astronuclear Laboratory [Westinghouse Electric Corp.] (MCD)
AL .... Astropower Laboratory [Douglas Aircraft Corp.] (MCD)
AL .... Auris Laeva [Left Ear] [Medicine]
AL .... Autograph Letter [Manuscript descriptions]
A/L .... AUTOLAND [Automatic Landing] (NASA)
AL .... Automobile Liability [Insurance]
AL .... Aviation Electronicsman [Military]
AL .... Avionics Laboratory [Air Force]
AL .... Awami League [Bangladesh] [Political party] (FEA)
AL .... Axiolingual [Dentistry]
AL .... Ayian Leukosis [Medicine] (DMAA)
AL .... Azure Laid [Paper] (DGA)
AL .... Intoxicated [Airline notation]
AL .... Laureate of Arts
AL .... Lethbridge Public Library, Alberta [Library symbol National Library of Canada] (NLC)
AL .... Lightship [Navy symbol Obsolete]
ALA .... Abraham Lincoln Association (EA)
ALA .... Academy of Lighting Arts
ALA .... Actual Leaf Area [Botany]
ALA .... Adult Learning Association (EA)
ALA .... African Literature Association (EA)
ALA .... Air-Land Assault (CINC)
ALA .... Alabama
ALA .... Alabama Lenders Association (SRA)
Ala .... Alabama Reports [A publication] (DLA)
Ala .... Alabama Supreme Court Reports [A publication] (DLA)
ALA .... Alamethicin [An antibiotic]
ALA .... Alamo [Nevada] [Seismograph station code, US Geological Survey] (SEIS)
Ala .... Alanine [Also, A] [An amino acid]
Ala .... Alanus Anglicus [Flourished, 1208-10] [Authority cited in pre-1607 legal work] (DSA)
ALA .... Alberta Limousin Association (AC)
ALA .... Alcatel Alsthom ADS [NYSE symbol] (TTSB)
ALA .... Alcatel Alsthom Compagnie General d'Electricite [NYSE symbol] (SPSG)
ALA .... Alighting Area [Aviation]
ALA .... Alina International Industries [Vancouver Stock Exchange symbol]
ALA .... Allegheny Airlines (IIA)
ALA .... Alliance for Labor Action [1968-1971]
ALA .... Alma-Ata [Former USSR Airport symbol] (OAG)
AIA .... Aluminum Association
ALA .... Amalgamated Lithographers of America [Later, GAIU]
ALA .... American Laminators Association (EA)
ALA .... American Land Alliance [Defunct] (EA)
ALA .... American Landrace Association (EA)
ALA .... American Laryngological Association (EA)
ALA .... American Latvian Association in the United States (EA)
ALA .... American Lawyers Association [Later, TAG] (EA)
ALA .... American Lawyers Auxiliary (EA)
ALA .... American League of Anglers (EA)
ALA .... American Legion Auxiliary (EA)
ALA .... American Liberal Association (EA)
ALA .... American Library Association (EA)
ALA .... American Lighting Association (EA)
ALA .... American Literary Anthology
ALA .... American Logistics Association (EA)
ALA .... American Longevity Association (EA)
ALA .... American Lung Association (EA)
ALA .... Aminolaevulinate [or Aminolaevulinic] Acid [Biochemistry]
ALA .... Antenna Lightning Arrester
ALA .... Arab Liberation Army
ALA .... Arakan Liberation Army [Myanmar] [Political party] (EY)
ALA .... Arc Lamp Assembly
ALA .... Area Letter of Acceptance [Department of Housing and Urban Development] (GFGA)
ALA .... Army Launch Area
ALA .... Army Logistics Assessment
ALA .... Arts Law Australia [A publication]
ALA .... Arussi Liberation Army [Ethiopia] (AF)
ALA .... Asociacion Latinoamericana de Archivos [Latin American Association of Archives - LAAA] (EAIO)
ALA .... Assembly of Librarians of the Americas [Defunct] (EA)

ALA .... Associated Locksmiths of America
ALA .... Associate in Liberal Arts
ALA .... Associate of the Library Association [British] (EY)
ALA .... Association for Laboratory Automation
ALA .... Association of Legal Administrators (EA)
ALA .... Australian Lighthouse Association
ALA .... Austral Lineas Aereas [Airline] [Argentina] (EY)
ALA .... Authorized Landing Area (ADA)
ALA .... Authors League of America (EA)
ALA .... Automobile Legal Association [Defunct] (EA)
ALA .... Avis Licensee Association (EA)
ALa .... Axiolabial [Dentistry]
ALA .... Delta-Amino Levulinic Acid [Biochemistry] (DAVI)
ALA .... International Association of Latin American Air Carriers [ICAO designator] (FAAC)
ALAA .... African Law Association in America [Later, INTWORLSA] (EA)
Ala A .... Alabama Appellate Court (DLA)
ALAA .... American Labor Arbitration Awards [Prentice-Hall, Inc.] [A publication] (DLA)
ALAA .... Associate of the London Association of Certified and Corporate Accountants [British] (EY)
ALAA .... Association of Legal Aid Attorneys of the City of New York (EA)
Ala A&M U ... Alabama Agricultural and Mechanical University (GAGS)
ALAAC .... Lakedell and Area Community Library, Westerose, Alberta [Library symbol National Library of Canada] (NLC)
Ala Acts ...... Acts of Alabama [A publication] (DLA)
Ala Admin Month... Alabama Administrative Monthly [A publication] (AAGC)
ALAAF .... Field Crops Branch, Alberta Agriculture, Lacombe, Alberta [Library symbol National Library of Canada] (NLC)
ALAAG .... Research Station, Agriculture Canada [Station de Recherches, Agriculture Canada] Lacombe, Alberta [Library symbol National Library of Canada] (NLC)
ALAAP .... Alabama Army Ammunition Plant (AABC)
Ala App .... Alabama Appellate Court Reports [A publication] (DLA)
Ala App .... Alabama Court of Appeals (DLA)
ALAB .... Alabama National Bancorporation [NASDAQ symbol] (SAG)
ALAB .... Alabama Natl Bancorp [NASDAQ symbol] (TTSB)
ALAB .... American League of Anglers and Boaters (EA)
AL-Ab .... Antilymphocyte Antibody [Medicine] (DMAA)
Alabama Rep... Alabama Reports [A publication] (DLA)
ALABM .... Air-Launched Antiballistic Missile
Alab (NS) .... Alabama Reports, New Series [A publication] (DLA)
ALABOL .... Algorithmic and Business Oriented Language [Computer science]
Alab Rep .... Alabama Reports [A publication] (DLA)
ALAC .... Alaska Air Command [Air Force]
ALAC .... American Lhasa Apso Club (EA)
ALAC .... Artificial Limb and Appliance Centre [British]
ALAC .... Association de la Librairie Ancienne du Canada [Association of Antique Bookstores of Canada]
ALAC .... Lacombe Public Library, Alberta [Library symbol National Library of Canada] (NLC)
ALACAT .... Asociacion Latinoamericana de Agentes de Carga Aerea y Transporte [Latin American Association of Freight and Transport Agents - LAFTA] (EA)
ALACE .... Association of Local Authority Chief Executives [British] (DBA)
ALACE .... Autonomous Lagrangian Circulation Explorer (OSRA)
ALACE .... Autonomous Lagrangian Circulation Explorer [Oceanography]
ALACF .... Asociacion Latinoamericana de Ciencias Fisiologicas [Latin American Association of Physiological Sciences] [ICSU] (EAIO)
ALACFO .... All Air Carrier Field Offices (FAAC)
ALACHA .... Alabama Automated Clearinghouse Association (SRA)
Ala Civ App... Alabama Civil Appeals [A publication] (DLA)
Ala Code ..... Alabama Code [A publication] (AAGC)
Ala Code ..... Code of Alabama [A publication] (DLA)
Ala Const .... Alabama Constitution [A publication] (DLA)
ALACP .... American League to Abolish Capital Punishment [Defunct] (EA)
Ala Cr App ... Alabama Criminal Appeals [A publication] (DLA)
ALAD .... Abnormal Left Axis Deviation (MAE)
ALAD .... Academic Librarians Assisting the Disabled Discussion Group [Association of Specialized and Cooperative Library Agencies]
ALAD .... Aminolaevulinate Dehydratase [Also, ALD] [An enzyme]
ALAD .... Arid Lands Agricultural Development [Program] [Later, ICARDA Middle East]
ALAD .... Automatic Liquid Agent Detector (AABC)
ALADA .... Asociacion Latinoamericana de Derecho Aeronautico y Espacial
ALADA .... Associacao Latino-Americana de Direito Agrario
ALADAA .... Asociacion Latinoamericana de Estudios Afroasiaticos [Latin American Association for Afro-Asian Studies - LAAAS] (EAIO)
ALADDIN ...... Atmospheric Layer and Density Distribution of Ions and Neutrals [Rocket] [NASA]
ALADH .... Delta-Aminolevulinate Dehydratase (DMAA)
ALADI .... Latin American Integration Association [Trade association of Argentina, Bolivia, Brazil, Chile, Colombia, Ecuador, Mexico, Paraguay, Peru, Uruguay, and Venezuela] (BARN)
ALADIM .... Asociacion Latinoamericana para el Desarrollo y la Integracion de la Mujer [Latin American Association for the Development and Integration of Women - LAADIW] [Santiago, Chile] (EAIO)
ALADIN .... Advanced LASER-Aided Defect Inspection in Nondestructive Testing (IAA)
ALADIN .... Algebraic Automated Digital Iterative Network [Computer science] (MHDI)
ALADIN .... Automated Laboratory Diagnostic Instrument

ALADIN	Automatisering Landbouwkundige Dokumentatie-En Informatievespreiding in Nederland [*Automation of Agricultural Documentation and Information in the Netherlands*] [*Centre for Agricultural Publishing and Documentation*] (NITA)
ALADLO	All Air Defense Liasion Officers in Region (FAAC)
AladnKn	Aladdin Knowledge Systems [*Commercial firm Associated Press*] (SAG)
ALADR	Animal Diseases Research Institute (West), Agriculture Canada [*Institut de Recherches Veterinaires (Ouest), Agriculture Canada*] Lethbridge, Alberta [*Library symbol National Library of Canada*] (NLC)
ALAE	Association of Licensed Aircraft Engineers [*A union*] [*British*]
ALAF	Asociacion Latinoamericana de Ferrocarriles [*Latin American Railways Association - LARA*] [*Argentina*]
ALAF	Australian Literary Awards and Fellowships [*A publication*]
ALAF	Lafond Public Library, Alberta [*Library symbol National Library of Canada*] (NLC)
ALAFEM	Asociacion Latinoamericana de Facultades y Escuelas de Medicina de America Latina [*Latin American Association of Medical Schools and Faculties - LAAMSF*] [*Quito, Ecuador*] (EAIO)
ALAFFO	All Airway Facilities Sector and Field Offices (FAAC)
ALAG	Agriculture Canada, Lethbridge, Alberta [*Library symbol National Library of Canada*] (NLC)
ALaG	Axiolabiogingival [*Dentistry*]
AlaHA	Alabama Hospital Association (SRA)
ALAHUA	Associacion Latino Americana para la Promocion de l'Habitat la Arquitectura y elUrbanismo [*Latin American Association for the Promotion of the Habitat, Architecture and Town Planning*] [*Ecuador*] (PDAA)
ALAI	Agencia Latinoamericana de Informacion [*Latin American Information Agency*] [*Canada*]
ALAI	Association Litteraire et Artistique Internationale [*International Literary and Artistic Association*]
ALAI	Irrigation Division, Alberta Agriculture, Lethbridge, Alberta [*Library symbol National Library of Canada*] (NLC)
ALAIRC	Alaskan Air Command [*Elmendorf Air Force Base*] [*Air Force*]
ALAIRS	Advanced Low-Altitude Infrared Reconnaissance Sensor
ALA/ISAD	American Library Association Information Science and Automation Division (NITA)
ALaL	Axiolabiolingual [*Dentistry*]
AlaLA	Alabama Library Association (SRA)
ALALC	Asociacion Latinoamericana de Libre Comercio [*Also, LAFTA*] [*Latin American Free Trade Association*]
ALALY	Aluminum Alloy (MCD)
ALAM	Association of Licensed Automobile Manufacturers
ALAM	Association of Lightweight Agggregate Manufacturers (MHDB)
ALAM	Atlas LISP [*Library and Information Software Packaging*] Algebraic Manipulator (PDAA)
ALAM	Lamont Public Library, Alberta [*Library symbol National Library of Canada*] (NLC)
Alamar	Alamar Biosciences, Inc. [*Associated Press*] (SAG)
ALAMAR	Asociacion Latinoamericana de Armadores [*Latin American Shipowners' Association*] (EAIO)
Alamco	Alamco, Inc. [*Associated Press*] (SAG)
ALAMOC	Asociacion Latinoamericana de Analisis y Modificacion del Comportamiento [*Latin American Association of Behavior Analysis and Modification*] (EAIO)
AlamoGp	Alamo Group, Inc. [*Associated Press*] (SAG)
Alamr	Alamar Biosciences, Inc. [*Associated Press*] (SAG)
ALAN	Adult Literacy and Numeracy Scale
ALAN	Alanco Environmental Res [*NASDAQ symbol*] (TTSB)
ALAN	Alanco Resources Corp. [*NASDAQ symbol*] (SAG)
ALANAM	Latin American Association of National Academies of Medicine (EA)
AlaNBcp	Alabama National Bancorporation [*Associated Press*] (SAG)
Alanco	Alanco Resources Corp. [*Associated Press*] (SAG)
Al & N	Alcock and Napier's Irish King's Bench Reports [*A publication*] (DLA)
Al & Nap	Alcock and Napier's Irish King's Bench Reports [*A publication*] (DLA)
ALANET	American Library Association's Electronic Information Service
ALANF	Army Land Forces
ALANO	All Accident Notice Offices (FAAC)
ALANON	Alcoholics Anonymous Family Groups (ADA)
Ala NS	Alabama Reports, New Series [*A publication*] (DLA)
Alantec	Alantec Corp. [*Associated Press*] (SAG)
ALAO	Association of Life Agency Officers [*Later, LIMRA*]
ALAOLPR	American Library Association Office for Library Personnel Resources (EA)
AlaP	Alabama Power Co. [*Associated Press*] (SAG)
ALAP	AppleTalk Link Access Protocol [*Apple Computer, Inc.*] (BYTE)
ALAP	As Late as Possible (PCM)
ALAP	As Low as Possible [*or Practical*] (NRCH)
ALAP	Asociacion Latinoamericana de Administracion Publica
ALAP	Associative Linear Array Processor [*Computer science*]
ALAP	Parkland Regional Library, Lacombe, Alberta [*Library symbol National Library of Canada*] (NLC)
AlaPC	Alabama Power Capital Trust I [*Associated Press*] (SAG)
ALAPCO	Association of Local Air Pollution Control Officials (EA)
ALAPO	Association of Local Air Pollution Control Officers [*Environmental Protection Agency*] (ERG)
Ala R	Alabama Reports [*A publication*] (DLA)
ALAR	Association of Light Alloy Refiners and Smelters Ltd. [*British*] (BI)
ALAR	Regional Office, Alberta Agriculture, Lethbridge, Alberta [*Library symbol National Library of Canada*] (NLC)
ALARA	As Low as Reasonably Achievable [*Radiation exposure*] [*Nuclear Regulatory Commission*]
ALARACT	All Army Activities (AABC)

Ala Rep	Alabama Reports [*A publication*] (DLA)
Ala Rep NS	Alabama Reports, New Series [*A publication*] (DLA)
Ala Reps	Alabama Reports [*A publication*] (DLA)
ALARM	Adjustable Leg and Ankle Repositioning Mechanism (DMAA)
ALARM	Advanced Low-Altitude RADAR Model (MCD)
ALARM	Airborne LASER Receiver Module (MCD)
ALARM	Air-Launched Advanced Ramjet Missile (KSC)
ALARM	Air-Launched Antiradiation Missile
ALARM	Alerting Long-Range Airborne RADAR for MTI [*Moving Target Indicator*]
ALARM	Anaesthesia Literature Abstracting Retrieval Method [*American Society of Anesthesiologists*] (NITA)
ALARM	Assessment of Language and Reading Maturity Test (EDAC)
ALARM	Automatic Light Aircraft Readiness Monitor
ALARM	[*A*] Logistics Assessment of the Readiness to Mobilize [*Military*]
Ala RNS	Alabama Reports, New Series [*A publication*] (DLA)
ALARP	As Low as Reasonably Practicable [*Radiation exposure*] [*Nuclear Regulatory Commission*]
ALARR	Air-Launched, Air-Recoverable Rocket
ALART	Army Low-Speed Air Research Tasks
ALARTC	All Air Route Traffic Control Centers in Region (FAAC)
ALAS	Accident Legal Advise Service [*British*]
ALAS	Alaska (AFM)
ALAS	Alliance of Latin Artistes Society [*Defunct*] (EA)
ALAS	Aminolaevulinate Synthase [*An enzyme*]
ALAS	Approach Landing Autopilot System [*or Subsystem*] [*Aviation*] (MCD)
ALAS	Army Library Automated Systems (IID)
ALAS	Arthropods of La Selva [*Costa Rica*]
ALAS	Artillery Location Acoustic System (MCD)
ALAS	Artists' Legal Advice Services (AC)
ALAS	Associate in Letters, Arts, and Sciences
ALAS	Associate of the Chartered Land Agents' Society [*British*]
ALAS	Association for Latin American Studies [*Defunct*]
ALAS	Association of Latvian Academic Societies [*Defunct*] (EA)
ALAS	Asynchronous Look-Ahead Simulator (IEEE)
ALAS	Atmospheric Laboratory for Applications and Science [*Satellite mission*]
ALAS	Automated Labor and Attendance Subsystem (SAA)
ALAS	Automated Library Acquisitions System [*Suggested name for the Library of Congress computer system*]
ALAS	Automated Literature Alerting System [*Computer science*] (DIT)
ALAS	Automatic Landing Autopilot Subsystem (NASA)
ALAS	Automatic Load Alleviation System (MCD)
ALAS	Auxiliary Loans to Assist Students
ALAS	Delta-Aminolevulinate Synthase (DMAA)
ALASAM	Advanced Low-Altitude SAM (MCD)
ALASC	Aircraft Launching Accessory Service Change (MCD)
Ala Sel Cas	Alabama Select Cases (Supreme Court), by Shepherd [*37, 38, 39*] [*A publication*] (DLA)
Alaska	Alaska Airlines [*ICAO designator*] (AD)
Alaska	Alaska Reporter [*A publication*] (DLA)
Alaska	Alaska Reports [*A publication*] (AAGC)
Alaska Admin Code	Alaska Administrative Code [*A publication*] (DLA)
Alaska B Brief	Alaska Bar Brief [*A publication*] (DLA)
Alaska BJ	Alaska Bar Journal [*A publication*] (DLA)
Alaska Co	Alaska Codes (Carter) [*A publication*] (DLA)
Alaska Const	Alaska Constitution [*A publication*] (DLA)
Alaska Fed	Alaska Federal Reports [*A publication*] (DLA)
Alaska Fed Rep	Alaska Federal Reports [*A publication*] (DLA)
Alaska Sess Laws	Alaska Session Laws [*A publication*] (DLA)
Alaska Stat	Alaska Statutes [*A publication*] (DLA)
ALA/SRRT/GLTF	American Library Association/Social Responsibilities Round Table/Gay and LesbianTask Force (EA)
ALASRU	Asociacion Latinoamericana de Sociologia Rural [*Latin American Rural Sociological Association - LARSA*] (EAIO)
ALAST	Advanced LASER Spot Tracker (MCD)
Ala St B Found Bull	Alabama State Bar Foundation. Bulletin [*A publication*] (DLA)
Ala St Found Bull	Alabama State Foundation Bulletin [*A publication*] (ILCA)
ALAT	Aircraft Latitude (MCD)
ALAT	Alanine Aminotransferase [*Formerly, SGPT*] [*Pharmacology*] (DAVI)
ALAT	Alanine Transaminase [*Also, AAT, ALT, GPT*] [*An enzyme*]
ALAT	All Air Traffic Service Personnel in Region (FAAC)
ALAT	Army Language Aptitude Test [*Later, DLAT*]
ALATA	As Low as Technically Achievable (NUCP)
ALATAS	All Air Traffic (Area) Supervisors in Region (FAAC)
Alateen	Alcoholics Anonymous Teens (BARN)
Alaten	Alatenn Resources, Inc. [*Associated Press*] (SAG)
ALATF	All Air Traffic Field Facilities (FAAC)
ALATFO	All Air Traffic Field Offices (FAAC)
Ala-tRNA	Ribonucleic Acid, Transfer - Alanyl [*Biochemistry, genetics*]
ALAU	Union of Latin American Universities (EA)
ALAW	Advanced Light Antitank Weapon (RDA)
ALB	Academic Libraries of Brooklyn [*Library network*]
ALB	Aero Albatros [*Mexico ICAO designator*] (FAAC)
ALB	Airborne LASER Bathymeter (PDAA)
ALB	Aircraft Launching Bulletin (MCD)
ALB	Air-Land Battle (MCD)
ALB	Air-Launched Booster (MCD)
ALB	Albania [*ANSI three-letter standard code*] (CNC)
Alb	Albania (VRA)
alb	Albanian [*MARC language code Library of Congress*] (LCCP)
ALB	Albany [*New York*] [*Airport symbol*] (OAG)
Alb	Albericus de Porta Ravennate [*Flourished, 1165-94*] [*Authority cited in pre-1607 legal work*] (DSA)

Alb.............	Albericus de Rosate [*Deceased, 1360*] [*Authority cited in pre-1607 legal work*] (DSA)
ALB.............	Albermarle Corp. [*NYSE symbol*] (SAG)
ALB.............	Alberni [*British Columbia*] [*Seismograph station code, US Geological Survey*] (SEIS)
ALB.............	Alberta [*Canadian province*]
Alb.............	Albertus de Saliceto [*Authority cited in pre-1607 legal work*] (DSA)
Alb.............	Albertus Longobardista [*Flourished, 12th century*] [*Authority cited in pre-1607 legal work*] (DSA)
alb.............	Album (VRA)
ALB.............	Albumin [*Also, AL*] [*Biochemistry*]
ALB.............	Albus [*White*] [*Pharmacy*]
ALB.............	American Legion Baseball (EA)
ALB.............	Anticipated Level of Business
ALB.............	Antilock Brake [*Automotive engineering*]
ALB.............	Automatic Loc-Bottom [*Packaging*]
ALB.............	Automobile Labor Board
ALB.............	Avian Lymphoblastosis [*Medicine*] (DMAA)
ALB.............	University of Alberta Library [*UTLAS symbol*]
ALBA.............	Alberta [*Canadian province*]
ALBA.............	American Lawn Bowls Association (EA)
ALBA.............	American Leather Belting Association [*Later, NIBA*]
ALBA.............	Arizona Licensed Beverage Association (SRA)
AL-BAAB......	Al Bahrain Arab African Bank
Alban..........	Albania
Albank........	Albank Financial Corp. [*Associated Press*] (SAG)
Albany Med C...	Albany Medical College (GAGS)
Alb Arb........	Albert Arbitration [*Lord Cairns' Decisions*] [*A publication*] (DLA)
AlbaW..........	Alba-Waldensis, Inc. [*Associated Press*] (SAG)
Alb Brun......	Albertus Brunus [*Deceased, 1541*] [*Authority cited in pre-1607 legal work*] (DSA)
ALBC............	Albion Banc Corp. [*NASDAQ symbol*] (SAG)
ALBC............	Albumin Clearance (DMAA)
ALBC............	AntiLASER Beam Coating
AlBCap.........	Allied Bank Capital, Inc. [*Associated Press*] (SAG)
AlBD	All the Best Dog Poems [*A publication*]
Alb de Odofre...	Albertus Denarii de Odofredo [*Deceased, 1300*] [*Authority cited in pre-1607 legal work*] (DSA)
Alb de Ros...	Albericus de Rosate [*Deceased, 1360*] [*Authority cited in pre-1607 legal work*] (DSA)
ALBE............	Adult Literacy and Basic Education
ALBE............	Air/Land Battlefield Environment [*Army*] (RDA)
Albe.............	Albericus de Rosate [*Deceased, 1360*] [*Authority cited in pre-1607 legal work*] (DSA)
Albemar.......	Albermarle Corp. [*Associated Press*] (SAG)
Albemr........	Albemarle Corp. [*Associated Press*] (SAG)
ALBEN	Aerodynamic Load Balanced Elliptical Nozzle (MCD)
Alber...........	Albericus de Rosate [*Deceased, 1360*] [*Authority cited in pre-1607 legal work*] (DSA)
Alber Bru.....	Albertus Brunus [*Deceased, 1541*] [*Authority cited in pre-1607 legal work*] (DSA)
Alber de Malet...	Albericus de Maletis [*Flourished, 1431-33*] [*Authority cited in pre-1607 legal work*] (DSA)
Alberic de Rosat...	Albericus de Rosate [*Deceased, 1360*] [*Authority cited in pre-1607 legal work*] (DSA)
Alberta LRR...	Alberta Institute of Law Research and Reform [*Canada*] (ILCA)
Alberto........	Alberto Culver Co. [*Associated Press*] (SAG)
Albertsn.......	Albertson's, Inc. [*Associated Press*] (SAG)
Albertson C (ID)...	Albertson College of Idaho (GAGS)
ALBES.........	Association of London Borough Engineers and Surveyors [*British*] (BI)
ALB-F..........	Air-Land Battle-Future [*Army*] (INF)
ALB/GLOB....	Albumin/Globulin Ratio [*Gastroenterology*] (DAVI)
ALBI............	Air-Launched Ballistic Intercept
ALBI............	Air-Launched Boost Intercept (MSA)
AlbionBc......	Albion Banc Corp. [*Associated Press*] (SAG)
ALBIS..........	Air-Launched Ballistic Intercept System (MCD)
ALBIS..........	Australian Library-Based Information System [*National Library of Australia*] (NITA)
ALBK...........	Albank Financial Corp. [*NASDAQ symbol*] (SAG)
ALBK...........	ALBANK Finl [*NASDAQ symbol*] (TTSB)
Alb LJ........	Albany Law Journal [*A publication*] (DLA)
Alb LQ........	Alberta Law Quarterly [*A publication*] (DLA)
Alb LS Jour...	Albany Law School Journal [*A publication*] (DLA)
ALBM..........	Air-Land Battle Management
ALBM..........	Air-Launched Ballistic Missile
AlbnyIn........	Albany International Corp. [*Associated Press*] (SAG)
ALBO..........	Automatic Line Buildout [*Bell Laboratories*]
ALBP...........	Adipocyte Lipid-Binding Protein
Alb Pp.........	Albertus Papiensis [*Flourished, 1211-40*] [*Authority cited in pre-1607 legal work*] (DSA)
ALBR	Academic Library Book Review [*A publication*] (BRI)
Albri...........	Albericus de Porta Ravennate [*Flourished, 1165-94*] [*Authority cited in pre-1607 legal work*] (DSA)
Albri de Rosa...	Albericus de Rosate [*Deceased, 1360*] [*Authority cited in pre-1607 legal work*] (DSA)
AlbrtE.........	Alberta Energy Co. Ltd. [*Associated Press*] (SAG)
ALBS...........	African Love Bird Society (EA)
ALBS...........	Air-Launched Balloon System (MCD)
ALBS...........	Australian Limousin Breeders' Society
ALBSAC.......	Adult Literacy and Basic Skills Action Coalition [*Australia*]
ALBSU.........	Adult Literacy and Basic Skills Unit [*British*]
ALBTCX.......	Airborne Lidar Bathymetry Technical Center of Expertise [*US Army Corps of Engineers*]
Albuquerque BJ...	Albuquerque Bar Journal [*A publication*] (DLA)

ALBUS	All Bureaus [*Navy*]
ALC.............	Aboriginal Lands Council [*Australia*]
ALC.............	Aboriginal Loans Commission [*Australia*]
ALC.............	Absolute Lymphocyte Count [*Medicine*]
ALC.............	Acquisition Life Cycle
ALC.............	Active Lane Control [*Image control and lane positioning*] [*Automotive engineering*]
ALC.............	Acute Lethal Catatonia [*Neurology and psychiatry*] (DAVI)
ALC.............	Adaptive Linear Combiner [*Computer science*]
ALC.............	Adaptive Logic Circuit
ALC.............	Adjusted Liquid Capital
ALC.............	Administrative/Logistics Center [*Military*] (INF)
ALC.............	Advanced Library Concepts, Inc. [*Later, ALI'I*] [*Information service or system*] (IID)
ALC.............	Aeronca Lovers Club (EA)
ALC.............	Aft Load Controller (MCD)
ALC.............	Agricultural Land Commission [*British*] (BI)
ALC.............	Air Launchable Concept
ALC.............	Airline Link Control (HGAA)
ALC.............	Air Lines Circuit (SAA)
ALC.............	Air Logistics Center [*McClellan Air Force Base, CA*] (MCD)
ALC.............	Air Logistics Command [*Air Force*]
ALC.............	Alabama Central R. R. [*AAR code*]
ALC.............	A la Carte [*According to the Menu, each item ordered individually*] [*French*] (ADA)
Alc.............	Alcaeus [*Seventh century BC*] [*Classical studies*] (OCD)
Alc.............	Alcestis [*of Euripides*] [*Classical studies*] (OCD)
Alc.............	Alcibiades [*of Plutarch*] [*Classical studies*] (OCD)
Alc.............	Alcibiades [*of Plato*] [*Classical studies*] (OCD)
Alc.............	Alcock's Registry Cases [*1832-41*] [*Ireland*] [*A publication*] (DLA)
ALC.............	Alcohol (KSC)
alc.............	Alcoholism [*Chemical dependency*] (DAVI)
ALC.............	Alcove [*Classified advertising*] (ADA)
ALC.............	Alexanders, Laing & Cruickshank [*Broker*] [*British*]
ALC.............	Algoma Central Railway [*Toronto Stock Exchange symbol*]
ALC.............	Alicante [*Spain*] [*Airport symbol*] (OAG)
ALC.............	Alkali-Extractable Light Chain [*Biochemistry*]
ALC.............	Alternative Level of Care [*Medicine*] (MEDA)
ALC.............	Alternative Lifestyle Checklist
ALC.............	Amercian League Championship
ALC.............	American Labor Cases [*Prentice-Hall, Inc.*] [*A publication*] (DLA)
ALC.............	American LaMancha Club (EA)
ALC.............	American Lamb Council (EA)
ALC.............	American Lancia Club (EA)
ALC.............	American Langshan Club (EA)
ALC.............	American Language Course [*Military*] (DNAB)
ALC.............	American Leading Cases [*A publication*] (DLA)
ALC.............	American Life Convention [*Later, ACLI*]
ALC.............	American Lutheran Church [*Later, ELCA*]
ALC.............	Amoeba-Less Life Cycle (PDAA)
ALC.............	Analytical Liquid Chromatograph
ALC.............	Antenna Loading Coil
ALC.............	Approximate Lethal Concentration [*Medicine*] (DMAA)
ALC.............	Area Logistics Command
ALC.............	Armament Logistics Command [*Army*] (PDAA)
ALC.............	Army Legal Corps [*British military*] (DMA)
ALC.............	Army Logistics Center
ALC.............	Army-Wide Library Council (RDA)
ALC.............	Artificial Luminous Cloud
ALC.............	Asian Law Centre [*University of Melbourne*] [*Australia*]
ALC.............	Assembly Language Coding [*Computer science*]
ALC.............	Associated Lutheran Charities [*Later, Lutheran Social Welfare Conference of America*] (EA)
ALC.............	Astro Launch Circuit [*NASA*] (KSC)
ALC.............	Audio Load Compensator (MCD)
ALC.............	Australian Lithuanian Community
ALC.............	Australian Loan Council
ALC.............	Automatic Landing Control (SAA)
ALC.............	Automatic Level Control [*Camera*] [*Aviation*]
alc.............	Automatic Level Control (IDOE)
ALC.............	Automatic Light Control (KSC)
ALC.............	Automatic Load Control
ALC.............	Avian Leukosis Complex (MAE)
ALC.............	Axiolinguocervical [*Dentistry*]
ALC.............	Lethbridge College, Alberta [*Library symbol National Library of Canada*] (NLC)
ALC.............	Southern Jersey Airways, Inc. [*ICAO designator*] (FAAC)
ALCA............	Aft Load Control Assembly (MCD)
ALCA............	Aircraft Loaders Control Assembly
ALCA............	Alabama Counseling Association (SRA)
ALCA............	Aluminum Chlorohydroxyallantoinate [*Organic chemistry*]
ALCA............	American Leather Chemists Association (EA)
ALCA............	American Lock Collectors Association (EA)
ALCA............	Anomalous Left Coronary Artery [*Cardiology*] (DMAA)
ALCA............	Arizona Landscape Contractors Association (SRA)
ALCA............	Associated Landscape Contractors of America (EA)
ALCA............	Automatic Level Control Assembly (MCD)
ALCA............	Automotive Legislative Council of America (EA)
ALCAC	Airlines Communications Administrative Council
AL CAC	Alla Cacia [*In the Hunting Style*] [*Music*] (ROG)
ALCA/ILD......	Interior Landscape Division of ALCA [*Later, ALCA/IPD*] (EA)
ALCA/IPD......	Interior Plantscape Division of ALCA (EA)
ALCAL	Alloy-Coated Aluminum (KSC)
ALCAN	Alaska-Canada [*Highway*]
Alcan	ALCAN Aluminum Ltd. [*Associated Press*] (SAG)

ALCAN .... Aluminum Co. of Canada Ltd.
Alc & N....... Alcock and Napier's Irish King's Bench Reports [*A publication*] (ILCA)
Alc & Nap.... Alcock and Napier's Irish King's Bench Reports [*A publication*] (DLA)
ALCANUS..... Alaska, Canada, United States (AABC)
AL CAP .... Alla Capella [*In Church Style*] [*Music*] (ROG)
ALCAP .... Aluminocalcium Phosphorous Oxide [*Inorganic chemistry*]
ALCAPP .... Automatic List Classification and Profile Production
ALCAR .... Phosphoribosyl-5 Amino-Imidazole-Carboxamide (BABM)
ALCARS .... Airborne Launch Control and Recovery System (MCD)
ALCAS .... Air Logistics Center Augmentation Squadron [*Air Force*]
Alcatel .... Alcatel Alsthom Compagnie General d'Electricite [*Associated Press*] (SAG)
ALCATS....... Automated Lines of Communications and Target System (MCD)
ALCC .... Acetyl Levo-Carnitine Chloride [*Biochemistry*]
ALCC........... Airborne Launch Control Center
ALCC........... Airlift Control Center (AFM)
ALCC........... Allied Capital Commercial [*NASDAQ symbol*] (TTSB)
ALCC........... Allied Capital Commercial Corp. [*NASDAQ symbol*] (SAG)
ALCC........... Associated Landscape Contractors of Colorado (SRA)
ALCC........... Association of London Computer Clubs (NITA)
ALCC........... La Crete Community Library, Alberta [*Library symbol National Library of Canada*] (NLC)
ALCCAM ...... Army Life Cycle Cost Analysis Model (MCD)
ALCCM .... Army Life Cycle Cost Model (MCD)
ALCD .... Alcide Corp. [*NASDAQ symbol*] (NQ)
ALCD .... Alclad [*Metallurgy*]
ALCD .... Aluminum-Clad (MSA)
ALCD .... Associate of the London College of Divinity [*British*]
ALCD .... Association of Law Costs Draftsmen [*British*] (DBA)
ALCE .... Airlift Control Element (AFM)
ALCEA .... Air Line Communication Employees Association
ALCENT....... Airlift Center [*Air Force*] (MCD)
ALCES .... Association of Lecturers in Colleges of Education in Scotland
ALCF .... Association of Lutheran College Faculties (EA)
ALCF .... Australian Lithuanian Catholic Federation
ALCFA........ American Lithuanian Catholic Federation Ateitis [*Later, LCFA*] (EA)
ALCH .... Alchemy
alch .... Alchemy (VRA)
ALCH .... Alcohol
ALCH .... Approach Light Contact Height
ALCHLC....... Alcoholic
ALCHLSM..... Alcoholism
ALCHRNI...... American Labor Committee for Human Rights in Northern Ireland (EA)
ALCI .... Allcity Insurance [*NASDAQ symbol*] (TTSB)
ALCI .... Allcity Insurance Co. [*NASDAQ symbol*] (NQ)
ALCI .... Appliance Leakage Current Interrupter (BARN)
Alcide .... Alcide Corp. [*Associated Press*] (SAG)
ALCJ .... Army Logistics Command Japan (CINC)
ALCJC .... Genealogical Society Library, Church of Jesue Christ of Latter-Day Saints, Lethbridge, Alberta [*Library symbol National Library of Canada*] (NLC)
ALCKT......... All Offices Having Send-Receive Teletypewriter Service on Circuit (FAAC)
ALCL .... Allied Capital Lending [*NASDAQ symbol*] (TTSB)
ALCL .... Allied Capital Lending Corp. [*NASDAQ symbol*] (SAG)
ALCL .... Assembly Line Communications Link [*General Motors computerized automotive production*]
ALCL .... Association of London Chief Librarians
ALCLAN ...... Air Logistics Command Local Area Network
ALCM .... Air-Launched Cruise Missile
Alcm .... Alcman [*Seventh century BC*] [*Classical studies*] (OCD)
ALCM .... All-Comm Media [*NASDAQ symbol*] (TTSB)
ALCM .... All-Comm Media Corp. [*NASDAQ symbol*] (SAG)
ALCM .... American Lutheran Church Men (EA)
ALCM .... Associated Landscape Contractors of Massachusetts (SRA)
ALCM .... Associate of the London College of Music [*British*]
ALCM .... Association of Liquidpaperboard Carton Manufacturers
ALCMGS ...... Air-Launched Cruise Missile Guidance Set (MCD)
ALCMI......... Asociacion Latinoamericana y del Caribe de Mundazas Internacionales [*Latin American and Caribbean International Moving*] [*Panama*] (EAIO)
ALCO .... Airlift Coordinating Office [*or Officer*] (AFIT)
ALCO .... Airlift Launch Control Officer [*Air Force*] (AFM)
ALCO .... Airlift Liaison Coordination Officer [*Air Force*]
ALCO .... Alico, Inc. [*NASDAQ symbol*] (NQ)
ALCO .... Alico, Inc. [*NASDAQ symbol*] (TTSB)
ALCO .... American Locomotive Co.
ALCO .... Asset-Liability Committee [*Banking*]
Alcoa .... Aluminum Co. of America [*Associated Press*] (SAG)
Alco Bev ..... Alcoholic Beverage (DLA)
Alco Bev Cont... Alcoholic Beverage Control (DLA)
Alcock & N... Alcock and Napier's Irish King's Bench Reports [*A publication*] (DLA)
ALCOGS....... Advanced Low-Cost G-Cueing System
ALCOH .... Alcohol
ALCOL .... Alcohol
ALCOLIC ...... Alcoholic [*Freight*]
ALCOM .... Alaskan Command [*Discontinued, 1975*] [*Military*]
ALCOM .... Algebraic Compiler [*or Computer*] [*Computer science*]
ALCOM .... ALGOL Compiler [*Computer science*] (DIT)
ALCOM .... All Commands [*A dispatch to all commands in an area*] [*Navy*]
ALCOMLANT... All Commands, [*US*] Atlantic Fleet [*Navy*] (NVT)
ALCOMPAC... All Commands, [*US*] Pacific Fleet [*Navy*] (NVT)
ALCON .... All Concerned [*Army*] (AABC)

ALCONH ...... Alianza Campesina de Organizaciones Nacionales de Honduras [*Peasant Alliance of National Organizations of Honduras*] [*Political party*] (PD)
ALcons........ Articulation Loss of Consonants [*Audiology*]
ALCOP .... Alternate Command Post [*Military*] (AFM)
ALCOR .... ARPA [*Advanced Research Projects Agency*]/Lincoln C-Band Observable RADAR [*Army*] (AABC)
ALCORCEN... Air Logistic Coordination Center
ALCOS .... Advanced Land Combat Systems [*Army*] (RDA)
AlcoSt.......... Alco Standard Corp. [*Associated Press*] (SAG)
ALCP .... Alternate Command Post
ALCP .... Area Local Control Panel (NRCH)
Alc Per Prop... Alcock on Personal Property [*A publication*] (DLA)
ALCPT......... American Language College Placement Test (DNAB)
ALCQ .... Association des Litteratures Canadiennes et Quebecoises [*Association for Canadian and Quebec Literatures - ACQL*]
AlcR............ Alcohol Rub [*Medicine*]
AL CR .... Aluminum Crown [*Dentistry*]
Alc Reg........ Alcock's Registry Cases [*Ireland*] [*1832-41*] [*A publication*] (ILCA)
Alc Reg C .... Alcock's Registry Cases [*1832-41*] [*Ireland*] [*A publication*] (DLA)
Alc Reg Cas... Alcock's Registry Cases [*1832-41*] [*Ireland*] [*A publication*] (DLA)
ALCS.......... Airborne Launch Control System [*Air Force*] (MCD)
ALCS.......... American League Championship Series [*Baseball*]
ALCS.......... Authors' Lending and Copyright Society [*British*]
ALCS.......... Authors' Licensing and Collecting Society [*British*] (DBA)
ALCS.......... Author's Licensing and Correcting Society [*British*]
ALCS.......... Automatic Launch Control System (DNAB)
ALCT.......... Arts and Letters Club, Toronto [*1908*] [*Canada*] (NGC)
ALCT.......... Attempt to Locate (FAAC)
ALCTS........ Association for Library Collections and Technical Services
ALCTS CCS... ALCTS [*Association for Library Collections and Technical Services*] Cataloging and Classification Section
ALCTS RLMS... ALCTS [*Association for Library Collections and Technical Services*] Reproduction of Library Materials Section
ALCTS RS .... ALCTS [*Association for Library Collections and Technical Services*] Resources Section
ALCU .... Agricultural Librarians in Colleges and Universities (AIE)
ALCU .... Altocumulus [*Cloud*] [*Meteorology*]
ALCU .... Arithmetic Logic and Control Unit [*Computer science*]
ALCU .... Asynchronous Line Control Unit [*Telecommunications*]
AlCulA .... Alberto Culver Co. [*Associated Press*] (SAG)
ALCUS .... Association of Ladies of Charity of the United States (EA)
ALCW .... American Lutheran Church Women [*Defunct*] (EA)
ALCWA .... Association of Licensed Clubs of Western Australia
ALD .... Acceptable Limit for Dispersion
ALD .... Acoustic Locating Device (SAA)
ALD .... Acral Lick Dermatitis [*Medicine*]
ALD .... Activity Level Dependent (KSC)
ALD .... Adrenoleukodystrophy [*Medicine*]
ALD .... Advanced LASER Designator
ALD .... Advanced Logic Design (MHDB)
ALD .... Advanced Logistics Development
ALD .... Aeronavs La Dprada SA [*Spain ICAO designator*] (FAAC)
ALD .... Airborne Line Discriminator
ALD .... Airlift Division [*Air Force*]
ALD .... Alcoholic Liver Disease [*Medicine*]
Ald .... Alden's Condensed Reports [*Pennsylvania*] [*A publication*] (DLA)
ALD .... Alderman
ALD .... Aldine [*of Aldus Manutius*] (DGA)
ALD .... Aldolase [*An enzyme*]
Ald .... Aldricus [*Flourished, 1154-72*] [*Authority cited in pre-1607 legal work*] (DSA)
Ald .... Aldridge. History and Jurisdiction of the Courts of Law [*1835*] [*A publication*] (ILCA)
ALD .... Allendale, SC [*Location identifier FAA*] (FAAL)
ALD .... Alliance for Leadership Development [*Defunct*] (EA)
ALD .... Allied-Lyons [*Toronto Stock Exchange symbol*]
Ald .... Allied Record Sales [*Record label*]
ALD .... Allied-Signal, Inc. [*NYSE symbol*] (SPSG)
ALD .... Altadena Library District, Altadena, CA [*OCLC symbol*] (OCLC)
ALD .... Alter Ridge [*Washington*] [*Seismograph station code, US Geological Survey*] (SEIS)
ALD .... American Library Directory [*R. R. Bowker Co.*] [*Online database*]
ALD .... American Lobbyists Directory [*A publication*]
ALD .... Aminolaevulinate Dehydratase [*Also, ALAD*] [*An enzyme*]
ALD .... Analog Line Driver [*Computer science*] (BUR)
ALD .... Anterior Lateral Dendrites [*Neurology*]
ALD .... Anterior Latissimus Dorsi [*Anatomy*]
ALD .... Appraisal of Language Disturbance [*Test*]
ALD .... Approximate Lethal Dose
ALD .... Asbestos Lung Disease
ALD .... Asian Literature Division - of MLA [*Modern Language Association of America*] (EA)
ALD .... Assistant Laboratory Director
ALD .... Assistant Local Director (DCTA)
ALD .... Assistive Listening Device (WYGK)
ALD .... Asynchronous Line Driver [*Prentice Corp.*]
ALD .... At a Later Date
ALD .... Automated Logic Diagram [*Computer science*] (IBMDP)
ALD .... Automatic Locking Differential
ALD .... Automatic Louver Damper (OA)
ALD .... Available-to-Load Date (AABC)
ALDA .... Air Line Dispatchers Association [*Defunct*]
ALDA .... Alabama Dental Association (SRA)
ALDA .... Aldila, Inc. [*NASDAQ symbol*] (SAG)

ALDA	Allied Linens and Domestics Association [*Defunct*] (EA)
ALDA	Aluminum(dihydroxy)allantoinate [*Organic chemistry*]
ALDA	American Land Development Association (EA)
ALDA	American Luggage Dealers Association [*Later, ALDC*] (EA)
ALDA	Analytic Learning Disability Assessment [*Child development test*]
ALDA	Aqua Lung Dealers Association [*Defunct*] (EA)
ALDA	Association of Late-Deafened Adults (EA)
ALDA	Association of Learning Disabled Adults [*Defunct*] (EA)
Ald Abr	Alden's Abridgment of Law [*A publication*] (DLA)
Ald & VH	Alden and Van Hoesen's Digest of Mississippi Laws [*A publication*] (DLA)
Ald Ans Cont...	Aldrich's Edition of Ansen on Contracts [*A publication*] (DLA)
ALDBAS	Army Logistics Data Base and Access System
ALDC	Acetolactate Decarboxylase [*An enzyme*]
ALDC	American Luggage Dealers Cooperative (EA)
ALDC	Army Logistic Development Committee [*British*] (RDA)
ALDC	Army Logistics Data Center
ALDC	Asociacion Latinoamericana de Derecho Constitucional [*Latin American Constitutional Law Association - LACLA*] (EAIO)
AldCAdv	Allied Capital Advisers, Inc. [*Associated Press*] (SAG)
AldCall	Allied Capital Corp II [*Associated Press*] (SAG)
AldCap	Allied Capital Lending Corp. [*Associated Press*] (SAG)
AldCapC	Allied Capital Commercial Corp. [*Associated Press*] (SAG)
ALDCS	Active Lift Distribution Control System [*Aerospace*]
ALDD	Alidade [*Engineering*]
AldD	Allied Digital Technologies [*Formerly, AMG Digital Technologies*] [*Associated Press*] (SAG)
AldDevic	Allied Devices Corp. [*Associated Press*] (SAG)
Alden	Alden Electronics, Inc. [*Associated Press*] (SAG)
ALDEP	Automated Layout Design Program [*IBM Corp.*]
ALDF	Animal Legal Defense Fund (EA)
ALDH	Aldehyde Dehydrogenase [*An enzyme*]
Ald Hist	Aldridge. History and Jurisdiction of the Courts of Law [*A publication*] (DLA)
AldHIPd	Allied Healthcare Products, Inc. [*Associated Press*] (SAG)
ALDHU	Latin American Human Rights Association (EA)
ALDI	Associated Long-Distance Interstate Message [*Telecommunications*] (TEL)
Al Dieb	Alterius Diebus [*Every Other Day*] [*Pharmacy*]
Aldila	Aldila, Inc. [*Associated Press*] (SAG)
Ald Ind	Alden's Index of United States Reports [*A publication*] (DLA)
AldIrish	Allied Irish Banks Ltd. [*Associated Press*] (SAG)
AldIrish	Allied Irish Banks PLC [*Associated Press*] (SAG)
ALDL	Assembly Line Diagnostic Link [*Automotive engineering*]
AldLife	Allied Life Financial [*Commercial firm Associated Press*] (SAG)
ALDM	Alderman (WGA)
ALDM	Alderman
ALDMN	Alderman (ROG)
ALDN	Aladdin Knowledge Systems [*NASDAQ symbol*] (SAG)
ALDNF	Aladdin Knowledge Systems [*NASDAQ symbol*] (TTSB)
ALDO	Activity Level Dependent Operations (NASA)
ALDO	Aldosterone [*Endocrinology*]
ALDOC	League of Arab States Documentation and Information Center [*Information service or system*] (IID)
ALDOL	Aldolase [*An enzyme*] (DAVI)
ALDONYS	Associated Licensed Detectives of New York State (SRA)
ALDOST	Aldosterone [*Endocrinology*] (DAVI)
ALDP	Adrenoleukodystrophy Protein [*Biochemistry*]
ALDP	Automatic Language Data Processing
ALDPS	Automated Logistics Data Processing System
Ald Ques	Aldred's Questions on the Law of Property [*A publication*] (DLA)
Aldra	Aldracus [*Flourished, 13th century*] [*Authority cited in pre-1607 legal work*] (DSA)
Aldri	Aldricus [*Flourished, 1154-72*] [*Authority cited in pre-1607 legal work*] (DSA)
ALDRI	Automatic Low Date Rate Input
Aldridge	History and Jurisdiction of the Courts of Law [*1835*] [*A publication*] (DLA)
ALDS	Analysis of Large Data Sets [*Computer science*] (MHDB)
ALDS	Apollo Launch Data System [*NASA*]
ALDs	Assistive Listening Devices (PAZ)
ALDS	Automatic Lightning Detection System [*To aid in the prevention of forest fires*]
Aldsignl	Allied Signal, Inc. [*Associated Press*] (SAG)
ALDT	Administrative and Logistics Delay [*or Down*] Time (MCD)
ALDT	Argon LASER Discharge Tube
ALDU	Association of Lawyers for the Defence of the Unborn (EAIO)
ALDV	Allied Devices Corp. [*NASDAQ symbol*] (SAG)
AldWste	Allied Waste Industries, Inc. [*Associated Press*] (SAG)
ALE	Actuarial Life Expectancy (AFIT)
ALE	Adaptive Line Enhancer [*Telecommunications*] (CAAL)
ALE	Additional Living Expense [*Insurance*]
ALE	Address Latch Enable [*Computer science*]
ALE	Admixture-Lathe-Cut + Eutectic [*Dental alloy*]
ALE	Aerolineas Especiales de Colombia [*ICAO designator*] (FAAC)
ALE	Airborne LASER Experiment [*Strategic Defense Initiative*]
ALE	Airport Landing Equipment (MCD)
ALE	Airport Lighting Equipment (NASA)
ALE	Alert [*Northwest Territories*] [*Seismograph station code, US Geological Survey*] (SEIS)
ale	Aleut [*MARC language code Library of Congress*] (LCCP)
AL E	Alia Editione [*Another Edition*] [*Latin*] (ROG)
ALE	Alliance Libre Europeenne [*European Free Alliance - EFA*] [*Political party Brussels, Belgium*] (EAIO)
ALE	Alliance Resources Ltd. [*Vancouver Stock Exchange symbol*]
ALE	Alternate Low Energy (CAAL)
ALE	American Lives Endowment [*Defunct*] (EA)
ALE	Arid Land Ecology [*AEC project*]
ALE	Arid Lands Ecology Reserve
ALE	Army Liaison Element (MCD)
ALE	Association for Liberal Education [*British*]
ALE	Association of Leadership Educators (EA)
ALE	Atmospheric Lifetime Experiment [*Environmental science*]
ALE	Atmospheric Lifetime Experiment Station [*Adrigole, Ireland*]
ALE	Atomic Layer Epitaxy [*Physical chemistry*]
ALE	Automated Large Experiment [*NASA*]
ALE	Automatic LASER Encoder
ALE	Automatic Link Establishment (DOMA)
a-le--	Lebanon [*MARC geographic area code Library of Congress*] (LCCP)
ALE	Leduc Public Library, Alberta [*Library symbol National Library of Canada*] (NLC)
ALEA	Airborne Law Enforcement Association (EA)
ALEA	AirLine Employees Association, International (EA)
ALEA	Air Line Employees Association, International (EA)
ALEA	American Lutheran Education Association [*Later, ELEA*] (EA)
ALEA	Australian Livestock Exporters' Association
ALEAA	American Lithuanian Engineers' and Architects' Association (EA)
ALEAS	Asociacion Latinoamericana de Educacion Agricola Superior
ALEBCI	Asociacion Latinoamericana de Escuelas de Bibliotecologia y Ciencias de la Informacion
ALEC	American Labor Education Center (EA)
ALEC	American Legislative Exchange Council (EA)
ALEC	Analysis of Linear Electronic Circuits (MHDI)
ALEC	Arid Lands Environment Centre [*Australia*]
ALEC	Artificial Lung-Expanding Compound [*Medicine*] (DMAA)
ALEC	Assembly Line Effectiveness Center
ALEC	Association of Louisiana Electric Cooperatives (SRA)
ALEC	Australian Industrial and Intellectual Property [*A publication*]
ALECS	Air Force - Los Alamos EMP [*Electromagnetic Pulse*] Calibration Simulator
ALECSO	Arab League Educational, Cultural, and Scientific Organization [*Tunisia*]
AL ED	Alia Editione [*Another Edition*] [*Latin*] (ADA)
ALED	Australian Libraries: the Essential Directory [*A publication*]
ALEDC	Associate Logistics Executive Development Course
ALEF	Alcor Life Extension Foundation (EA)
ALEF	Food Processing Development Center, Leduc, Alberta [*Library symbol National Library of Canada*] (NLC)
ALEG	Legal Public Library, Alberta [*Library symbol National Library of Canada*] (NLC)
ALEGEO	Asociacion Latinoamericana de Editores en Geociencias
ALEHU	Advanced Legal Education, Hamline University School of Law (DLA)
ALEM	Adaptive Learning Environments Model (EDAC)
ALEM	Apollo Lunar Exploration Mission [*NASA*]
ALEM	Association of Loading and Elevating Equipment Manufacturers [*British*] (EAIO)
ALEMS	Apollo Lunar Excursion Module Sensors [*NASA*]
AL/EMU	Airlock/Extravehicle Mobility Unit [*NASA*] (MCD)
ALEN	Alberta Environment, Lethbridge, Alberta [*Library symbol National Library of Canada*] (NLC)
ALEOA	American Law Enforcement Officers Association (EA)
ALEP	Atypical Lymphoepitheloid Cell Proliferation [*Medicine*]
ALEP	Audio Lingual Education Press (KSC)
ALEPH	Automated Library Expandable Program, Hebrew University of Jerusalem [*Israel*] [*Information service or system*] (IID)
ALERFA	Alert Phase [*Aviation code*]
Alergn	Allergan, Inc. [*Associated Press*] (SAG)
ALERT	Acute Launch Emergency Reliability Tip [*NASA*] (KSC)
ALERT	Adaptive LASER Resonator Technique (MCD)
ALERT	Alberta League for Environmentally Responsible Tourism (AC)
ALERT	Alcohol Level Evaluation Road Tester
ALERT	Alternatives for Learning through Educational Research and Technology (DICI)
ALERT	American Library for Education, Research, and Training
ALERT	American Life Education and Research Trust (EA)
ALERT	American Lifesaving Emergency Response Team (EA)
ALERT	Automated Law Enforcement Response Team (DICI)
ALERT	Automated Linguistic Extraction and Retrieval Technique
ALERT	Automated Local Evaluations in Real Time [*National Oceanic and Atmospheric Administration*]
ALERT	Automatic Logging Electronic Reporting and Telemetering System [*Maintains surveillance over petroleum wells and pipelines*]
ALERT	Automatic Logical Equipment Readiness Tester
ALERT	[*A*] Law Enforcement Roundtable [*Information service or system*] (IID)
AlertC	Alert Centre, Inc. [*Associated Press*] (SAG)
ALERTCONS...	Alert Conditions (MCD)
AlertCt	Alert Centre, Inc. [*Associated Press*] (SAG)
ALERTS	Airborne LASER Equipment Real-Time Surveillance
ALES	Aboriginal Languages Education Strategy [*Australia*]
ALES	American Labor Education Service [*Defunct*]
AL/ES	Artificial Intelligence and Expert System
ALES	Nor'Wester Brewing [*NASDAQ symbol*] (TTSB)
ALESA	American League for Exports and Security Assistance [*Washington, DC*] (EA)
ALESC	Amiral Commandant l'Escadre [*Admiral, French Fleet*] (NATG)
ALESCO	American Library and Educational Services Co.
ALESEP	Airfoil Leading Edge Separation (MCD)
ALESW	Australian League of Ex-Servicemen and Women
ALET	Aloette Cosmetics [*NASDAQ symbol*] (TTSB)

ALET	Aloette Cosmetics, Inc. [*NASDAQ symbol*] (NQ)
A level	Advanced Level (ODBW)
ALEX	Alert Exercise (NATG)
Alex	Alexander [*of Plutarch*] [*Classical studies*] (OCD)
Alex	Alexander [*of Lucian*] [*Classical studies*] (OCD)
ALEX	Alexander & Baldwin [*NASDAQ symbol*] (TTSB)
ALEX	Alexander & Baldwin, Inc. [*NASDAQ symbol*] (NQ)
Alex	Alexander Tartagna de Imola [*Deceased, 1477*] [*Authority cited in pre-1607 legal work*] (DSA)
Alex	Alexandra [*of Lycophron*] [*Classical studies*] (OCD)
Alex	Alexipharmaca [*of Nicander*] [*Classical studies*] (OCD)
ALEX	Automatic Label Exchange
AlexAlx	Alexander & Alexander Services, Inc. [*Associated Press*] (SAG)
Alexan	Alexander Tartagna de Imola [*Deceased, 1477*] [*Authority cited in pre-1607 legal work*] (DSA)
Alexand	Alexander Tartagna de Imola [*Deceased, 1477*] [*Authority cited in pre-1607 legal work*] (DSA)
Alexander	Alexander's Reports [*66-72 Mississippi*] [*A publication*] (DLA)
Alexanderreich	Das Alexanderreich aus Prosopographischer Grundlage [*A publication*] (OCD)
AlexBld	Alexander & Baldwin, Inc. [*Associated Press*] (SAG)
AlexBr	Alex Brown, Inc. [*Associated Press*] (SAG)
AlexBrn	Alex Brown, Inc. [*Associated Press*] (SAG)
AlexBrn	Brown [*Alex*], Inc. [*Associated Press*] (SAG)
Alex Br Stat	Alexander's British Statutes in Force in Maryland [*A publication*] (DLA)
Alex Cas	Report of the "Alexandra" Case, by Dudley [*A publication*] (DLA)
Alex Ch Pr	Alexander's Chancery Practice in Maryland [*A publication*] (DLA)
Alex Com Pr	Alexander's Practice of the Commissary Courts, Scotland [*A publication*] (DLA)
Alex Dig	Alexander's Texas Digest [*A publication*] (DLA)
Alexdr	Alexander's, Inc. [*Associated Press*] (SAG)
AlexEng	Alexander Energy Corp. [*Associated Press*] (SAG)
Alex Ins	Alexander on Life Insurance in New York [*A publication*] (DLA)
Alexion	Alexion Pharmaceuticals, Inc. [*Associated Press*] (SAG)
Alex Sev	Alexander Severus [*of Scriptores Historiae Augustae*] [*Classical studies*] (OCD)
ALEXSHIP	Alexandria Shipping & Navigation Co. [*Egypt*] (IMH)
Aleyn	Aleyn's Select Cases, English King's Bench [*82 English Reprint*] [*A publication*] (DLA)
Aleyn (Eng)	Aleyn's Select Cases, English King's Bench [*82 English Reprint*] [*A publication*] (DLA)
ALF	Absorption Limiting Frequency (DEN)
ALF	Accelerated Loading Facility (ADA)
ALF	Afar Liberation Front [*Ethiopia*] (PD)
ALF	Airlift [*International*]
ALF	Alberta Law Foundation (AC)
ALF	Alfred [*New York*] [*Seismograph station code, US Geological Survey*] (SEIS)
ALF	Alien Life Force [*Acronym is name of title character in television series*]
ALF	Allied Command Europe [*ICAO designator*] (FAAC)
ALF	Allied Land Forces
ALF	Aloft (FAAC)
ALF	Alpha-Omega Industries, Inc. [*Vancouver Stock Exchange symbol*]
ALF	Alta [*Norway*] [*Airport symbol*] (OAG)
ALF	American Land Forum [*Later, ALRA*] (EA)
ALF	American Leadership Forum (EA)
ALF	American Legal Foundation [*WLF*] [*Absorbed by*] (EA)
ALF	American Life Foundation [*Press*]
ALF	American Liver Foundation (EA)
ALF	American Loan Fund
ALF	Animal Liberation Front (EA)
ALF	Annual License Fee [*FCC*] (NTCM)
ALF	Application Library File [*Computer science*]
ALF	Approach Light Facility (PDAA)
ALF	Arab Liberation Front
ALF	Assisted Living Concepts [*AMEX symbol*] (TTSB)
ALF	Assisted Living Concepts, Inc. [*AMEX symbol*] (SAG)
ALF	Assisted-Living Facility [*Health care*]
ALF	Association of Libertarian Feminists (EA)
ALF	Australian Lecture Foundation
ALF	Australian Liberation Front [*Political party*]
ALF	Australian Library Fair
ALF	Automatic Lead Former
ALF	Automatic Letter Facer
ALF	Automatic Line Feed [*Telecommunications*]
ALF	Auxiliary Landing Field
ALF	Average Load Factor
ALF	Azania Liberation Front [*South Africa*]
ALFA	Access to Learning for Adults (AIE)
ALFA	Advanced LASER Flow Analysis (MCD)
ALFA	Advanced Liaison Forward Area
ALFA	Aerolinea Federal Argentina [*Argentine Federal Airline*] (EY)
ALFA	Air-Land Forces Agency [*Air Force Army*] (MCD)
ALFA	Air-Land Forces Applications
ALFA	Air Lubricated Free Attitude [*NASA*] (KSC)
ALFA	Alfa Corp. [*NASDAQ symbol*] (NQ)
ALFA	Anonima Lombarda Fabbrica Automobili
ALFA	Automatic Line Fault Analysis (MHDB)
ALFAA	Air-Land Forces Applications Agency [*TAC-TRADOC*] (MCD)
ALFAA	Assisted Living Facilities Association of America
Alfacell	Alfacell Corp. [*Associated Press*] (SAG)
AlfaCp	Alfa Corp. [*Associated Press*] (SAG)
ALFAD	Acoustic Low-Flying-Aircraft Detector (MCD)
ALFAL	Asociacion de Linguistica y Filologia de America Latina
ALFAR	American Law Firms for African Relief [*Defunct*] (EA)
ALFC	Aboriginal Land Fund Commission [*Australia*]
ALFC	Allied Life Financial [*NASDAQ symbol*] (SAG)
ALFC	Automatic Local Frequency Control
ALFCE	Allied Land Forces Central Europe [*NATO*] (NATG)
ALFGL	Automatic Low-Frequency Gain-Limiting Circuit (RDA)
ALFI	Air-Land Forces Integration (MCD)
ALFI	Air-Land Forces Interface
ALFI	American League of Financial Institutions [*Washington, DC*] (EA)
Alfin	Alfin, Inc. [*Associated Press*] (SAG)
ALFLEX	Automatic Landing Flight Experiment [*Japan*]
ALFLEX	Automatic-Landing Flight Experiment [*Space program*] [*Japan*]
ALFMED	Apollo Light-Flash Moving-Emulsion Detector [*NASA*]
ALFOODACT	All Food Activities [*DoD*]
ALFOR	Allied Forces
ALFORD	Appalachian Laboratory for Occupational Respiratory Diseases
ALFRAC	Aluminum Fracture Toughness Database [*Information service or system*] (IID)
ALFRED	Associative Learning from Relative Environmental Data
Alfred U	Alfred University (GAGS)
ALFS	Airborne Low-Frequency SONAR [*Sound Navigation and Ranging*] [*Navy*]
ALFS	Alaska Landscape Flux Study (USDC)
ALFS	Alaska Landscape Flux Study (OSRA)
ALFSE	Allied Land Forces Southern Europe [*NATO*]
ALFSEA	Allied Land Forces Southeast Asia [*NATO*]
ALFSEE	Allied Land Forces Southeastern Europe [*NATO*]
ALFSFO	All Flight Standards Field Offices (FAAC)
ALFSH	Allied Land Forces Schleswig-Holstein [*NATO*] (NATG)
ALFSS	All Flight Service Stations in Region (FAAC)
ALFT	Abnormal Liver Function Test [*Medicine*] (DMAA)
ALFT	Airlift
ALFT	Approach and Landing Flight Test [*Aviation*] (MCD)
ALFTRAN	ALGOL-to-FORTRAN Translator [*Computer science*] (MCD)
ALFY	[*A*] New Life for You, Inc.
ALG	Advanced Landing Ground [*Air Force*]
ALG	Aircraft Landing Gear
ALG	Airlift Group [*Military*]
ALG	Alamo Group [*NYSE symbol*] (TTSB)
ALG	Alamo Group, Inc. [*NYSE symbol*] (SAG)
ALG	Algebra
ALG	Algeria
Alg	Algeria (VRA)
ALG	Algiers [*Algeria*] [*Seismograph station code, US Geological Survey*] (SEIS)
ALG	Algiers [*Algeria*] [*Airport symbol*] (OAG)
ALG	Algoma Steel Corp. Ltd. [*Toronto Stock Exchange symbol Vancouver Stock Exchange symbol*]
alg	Algonquian [*MARC language code Library of Congress*] (LCCP)
ALG	Along (FAAC)
ALG	Annapolis Lymphoblast Globulin [*Biochemistry*] (MAH)
ALG	Antilymphocyte [*or Antilymphocytic*] Globulin [*Immunology*]
ALG	Asbestos Litigation Group (EA)
ALG	Australian Lace Guild
ALG	Axiolinguogingival [*Dentistry*]
ALG	Offshore Logistics, Inc. [*ICAO designator*] (FAAC)
ALG	University of Alabama, Graduate School of Library Science, University, AL [*OCLC symbol*] (OCLC)
ALGA	Associate in Local Government Administration (ADA)
ALGA	Australian Lychee Growers' Association
AlGaAs	Aluminum Gallium Arsenide (IEEE)
ALGASM	Amiral Commandant le Groupe Anti-Sous-Marin [*Commander, Antisubmarine Force*] [*French*] (NATG)
AlgAU	Universite d'Alger, Algiers, Algeria [*Library symbol Library of Congress*] (LCLS)
ALGC	La Glace Community Library, Alberta [*Library symbol National Library of Canada*] (NLC)
ALGCU	Association of Land Grant Colleges and Universities [*Later, NASULGC*]
ALGDGADLU	A la Gloire du Grand Architecte de l'Univers [*Freemasonry*] [*French*] (ROG)
ALGEB	Algebra
ALGEC	Algorithmic Language for Economic Calculations [*Computer science*]
ALGEE	ABN AMRO Holdings N.V. [*AM Symbol*] (TTSB)
Alger's Law Promoters & Prom Corp	Alger's Law in Relation to Promoters and Promotion of Corporations [*A publication*] (DLA)
ALGES	Association of Local Government Engineers and Surveyors [*British*] (DI)
ALGFO	Association of Local Government Financial Officers [*British*] (DI)
ALGH	Allegheny & Western Energy Corp. [*NASDAQ symbol*] (NQ)
ALGHNY	Allegheny (FAAC)
ALGI	American Locker Group, Inc. [*NASDAQ symbol*] (NQ)
ALGI	Amer Locker Group [*NASDAQ symbol*] (TTSB)
AlgLud	Allegheny Ludlum Corp. [*Associated Press*] (SAG)
ALGLYN	Aluminum Glycinate [*Also, ADA*] [*Pharmacology*]
ALGM	Air-Launched Guided Missile [*Military*]
Algma	Algoma Steel, Inc. [*Associated Press*] (SAG)
ALGN	Alignment (KSC)
ALGNNG	Aligning
ALGNR	Aligner
ALGO	Algos Pharmaceutical Corp. [*NASDAQ symbol*] (SAG)
ALGOL	Algorithmic Language [*1958*] [*Formerly, IAL*] [*Computer science*]
AlgosPh	Algos Pharmaceutical Corp. [*Associated Press*] (SAG)
ALGP	Association of Lesbian and Gay Psychologists (EA)

ALGR .... Allied Group [NASDAQ symbol] (SAG)
ALGS .... Algoma Steel, Inc. [NASDAQ symbol] (SAG)
ALGSE .... Algoma Steel [NASDAQ symbol] (TTSB)
ALH .... Advanced Light Helicopter [Air Force] (PDAA)
ALH .... Albany [Australia Airport symbol] (OAG)
ALH .... Aleta Resource Industries [Vancouver Stock Exchange symbol]
Alh .... Alhambra (BARN)
ALH .... Alicahue [Chile] [Seismograph station code, US Geological Survey] (SEIS)
ALH .... Allan Hills [Antarctic meteorology]
ALH .... Alpha Aviation, Inc. [ICAO designator] (FAAC)
ALH .... Anterior Lobe Hormone [Endocrinology] (MAE)
ALH .... Anterior Lobe of Hypophysis [Anatomy] (AAMN)
ALH .... Atypical Lymphoid Hyperplasia [Medicine]
ALHA .... American Labor Health Association [Later, GHAA]
ALHA .... American Landscape Horticulture Association (EA)
ALHARD ...... Air-Launched High-Altitude Reconnaissance Drone (MCD)
ALHC .... American Life Holding Co. [NASDAQ symbol] (SAG)
ALHE .... Association of London Housing Estates [British] (DI)
ALHFA .... Association of Local Housing Finance Agencies (EA)
ALHFAM ...... Association for Living Historical Farms and Agricultural Museums (EA)
ALHHS .... Association of Librarians in the History of the Health Sciences (EA)
ALHRT .... American Library History Round Table
ALHT .... Apollo Lunar Hand Tool [NASA]
ALHTC .... Apollo Lunar Hand Tool Carrier [NASA]
ALHY .... Alpha Hospitality [NASDAQ symbol] (TTSB)
ALHY .... Alpha Hospitality Corp. [NASDAQ symbol] (SAG)
ALHYW .... Alpha Hospitality Wrrt [NASDAQ symbol] (TTSB)
ALHZ .... Houlihan Lokey Howard & Zukin [Financial advisors] (ECON)
ALI .... Activity Level Independent (KSC)
ALI .... Acute Lung Injury [Medicine] (DMAA)
ALI .... Aetna Life Insurance Co. of Canada [Toronto Stock Exchange symbol]
ALI .... Agricultural Limestone Institute
ALI .... Airborne LASER Illuminator
ALI .... Air Liberia [ICAO designator] (FAAC)
ALI .... Airlift International, Inc. (IIA)
ALI .... Alberta Legislation Information [Alberta Public Affairs Bureau] [Canada Information service or system] (CRD)
Ali .... Alibi [Elsewhere] [Latin]
ALI .... Alicante [Spain] [Seismograph station code, US Geological Survey] (SEIS)
ALI .... Alice, TX [Location identifier FAA] (FAAL)
ALI .... Alimony [Legal shorthand] (LWAP)
ALI .... ALITALIA [Aerolinee Italiane Internazionali] [Italian airline] (MCD)
ALI .... Alternative Living Services [AMEX symbol] (SAG)
ALI .... American Ladder Institute (EA)
ALI .... American Law Institute (EA)
ALI .... Annual Limit of Intake (MHDB)
ALI .... Arc Lamp Igniter
ALI .... Argyll Light Infantry [Military unit] [British]
ALI .... Arm Length Index
ALI .... Arthur D. Little, Inc.
ALI .... Associate of the Landscape Institute [British] (DBQ)
ALI .... Association Lyrique Internationale [Toulouse, France] (EAIO)
ALI .... Asynchronous Line Interface [Telecommunications]
ALI .... Australian Leisure Index [Information service or system A publication]
ALI .... Australian Literature Index [A publication]
ALI .... Automated Logic Implementation [Computer science] (IEEE)
ALI .... Automatic Language Identification (MCD)
ALI .... Automatic Line Integration (NVT)
ALI .... Automatic Location Identification [Street crime locator]
ALI .... Automotive Lift Institute (EA)
ALI .... Autonomous Learner Index
ALI .... Awaiting Laboratory Input
ALI .... Linaria Public Library, Alberta [Library symbol National Library of Canada] (NLC)
ALIA .... American Life Insurance Association [Later, ACLI] (EA)
ALIA .... Association of Lecturers in Accountancy [British]
ALIA .... Royal Jordanian Airlines (IMH)
ALI-ABA ...... ALI-ABA [American Law Instutute - American Bar Association] Committee on Continuing Professional Education (EA)
ALI-ABA CLE Rev... American Law Institute - American Bar Association Council of Legal Education Review [A publication] (DLA)
ALI-ABA Course MJ... American Law Institute - American Bar Association. Course Materials Journal [A publication] (DLA)
ALIADS .... Alaskan Integrated Air Defense System
AlianPh........ Alliance Pharmaceutical Corp. [Associated Press] (SAG)
AlianPh........ Alliance Pharmaceuticals [Associated Press] (SAG)
ALIANSA ...... Alimentos para Animales, SA [Feed plant] [Guatemala]
AliantCm...... Aliant Communications, Inc. [Associated Press] (SAG)
ALIAS.......... Algebraic Logic Investigation of Apollo Systems (MCD)
ALIAS.......... Australia's Library, Information and Archives Services: an Encyclopaedia of Practice and Practitioners [A publication]
ALIATCS ...... All International Air Traffic Communications Stations [FAA]
ALIAZO .... Alliance of Natives of Zombo [Angola]
A Lib .... American Libraries [A publication] (BRI)
ALIB............ Army Library
ALIC............ Arid Lands Information Center [University of Arizona] [Tucson]
ALIC............ Association of Life Insurance Counsel (EA)
ALICAT........ Advanced Long-Wave IR Circuit and Array Technology (MCD)
ALICE.......... Ada/Lattice ICE [Integrated Conceptual Environment] [Computer science]
ALICE.......... Adaptive Line Canceller and Enhancer (CAAL)

ALICE......... Adiabatic Low-Energy Injection and Capture Experiment
ALICE......... Advance Light Imaging with Computer Enhancement [First projection television that houses a computer system]
ALICE......... Alaskan Integrated Communications Exchange
ALICE......... All-Purpose Lightweight Individual Carrying Equipment [Army] (RDA)
ALICE......... Applicative Language Idealized Computing Engine [Imperial College] [British]
ALICE......... Archivio dei Libri Italiani, su Calcolatore Elettronica [Editrice Bibliografica] [Italian Information service or system] (CRD)
ALICE......... Artisoft LAN [Linked Access Network] Interface Chip for Ethernet [Artisoft, Inc.] [Computer science] (PCM)
ALICE......... Automated Location of Isolation and Continuity Error [Module] [Raytheon Co.]
Alico......... Alico, Inc. [Associated Press] (SAG)
ALICO......... American Life Insurance Co. [Surinam] (EY)
ALICS......... Advanced Logistics Information and Control System [Air Force]
ALICW .... All-Purpose Lightweight Individual Carrying Equipment [Army]
ALID......... Automated Library Issue Document (NVT)
ALIDE......... Asociacion Latinoamericana de Instituciones Financieras de Desarrollo [Latin American Association of Development Financing Institutions] [Lima, Peru] (EAIO)
ALIFAR .... Asociacion Latinoamericana de Industrias Farmaceuticas [Latin American Association of Pharmaceutical Industries - LAAPI] (EAIO)
ALI Fed Income Tax Project... American Law Institute Federal Income Tax Project [A publication] (DLA)
ALIFO......... All International Field Offices (FAAC)
ALIFSS......... All International Flight Service Stations in Region (FAAC)
ALIGN......... Alignment
ALIGN......... Alignment
AligrR......... Align-Rite International, Inc. [Associated Press] (SAG)
ALII............ Advanced Libraries & Information, Inc. [Information service or system] (IID)
ALII............ Allied Capital Corp II [NASDAQ symbol] (TTSB)
ALIM......... Air-Launched Intercept Missile
ALIMDA...... Association of Life Insurance Medical Directors of America (EA)
ALIMPREPS... Alert Implementation Reports (NATG)
ALIMREP ...... Alert Implementation Report (MCD)
ALIMS......... Automatic LASER Instrumentation Measuring System (MCD)
ALIN......... Agricultural Libraries Information Network [Department of Agriculture] [Library network]
ALing......... Archivum Linguisticum [A publication] (BARN)
ALIO......... Activity Level Independent Operations (NASA)
ALIP......... Abnormal Localization of Immature P recursors [Clinical hematology]
ALIP......... Annular Linear Induction Pump [Nuclear energy] (NRCH)
ALIP......... Australian Library and Information Professionals [A publication]
ALIR......... Advanced LASER Intercept Receiver (MCD)
ALIRATS...... Airborne LASER Illuminator Ranging and Tracking System
ALIrish......... Allied Irish Banks PLC [Associated Press] (SAG)
ALIRT......... Adaptive Long-Range Infrared Tracker
ALIS......... Advanced Life Information System [Computer science]
ALIS......... Arid Lands Information System [University of Arizona] [Tucson] (IID)
ALIS......... Auroral Large Imaging System
ALIS......... Automated Library Information System [National Technological Library of Denmark] [Lyngby] (IID)
ALIS......... Automated Library Information System [Dataphase Systems, Inc.] (IID)
ALISA......... Moscow Exchange of Building Materials [Russian Federation] (EY)
ALISE......... Association for Library and Information Science Education (EA)
Alison Pr .... Alison's Practice [Scotland] [A publication] (DLA)
Alis Princ Scotch Law... Alison's Principles of the Criminal Law of Scotland [A publication] (DLA)
Alis Princ Scot Law... Alison's Principles of the Criminal Law of Scotland [A publication] (ILCA)
A Lit............ Associate in Literature
ALIT............ Australian Literature [A database] (NITA)
ALIT............ Automatic Line Insulation Test [or Tester] [Bell System]
ALITALIA..... Aerolinee Italiane Internazionali [Italian International Airline] [Facetious translation: Always Late in Takeoffs, Always Late in Arrivals]
A Litt .... Associate in Letters
ALIVE......... Air-Launched Instrumented Vehicle Evaluation (MCD)
ALJ .... Administrative Law Judge [Also, HE] [Federal trial examiner]
ALJ .... Aero Leasing Italiana SpA [Italy ICAO designator] (FAAC)
ALJ .... Albany Law Journal [A publication] (DLA)
ALJ .... Alexander Bay [South Africa] [Airport symbol] (OAG)
ALJ .... Association for Legal Justice [Northern Ireland]
ALJD......... Administrative Law Judge of the Department [Department of Labor] (OICC)
ALJH......... Association of Libraries of Judaica and Hebraica in Europe
ALK......... Air Lanka [Sri Lanka] [ICAO designator] (FAAC)
ALK......... Alaska Air Group [NYSE symbol] (TTSB)
ALK......... Alaska Air Group, Inc. [NYSE symbol] (SPSG)
ALK......... Alaska Airlines, Inc. (IIA)
Alk .... Alaska Reports [A publication] (DLA)
ALK......... Alkaline (KSC)
Alk......... Alkyl [Chemistry]
ALK......... Almanac (ROG)
ALK......... Altero Technology [Vancouver Stock Exchange symbol]
ALK......... Anaplastic Lymphoma Kinase [An enzyme]
ALK......... Automated Lamellar Keratoplasty [Medicine]
Al Kada...... Native Tribunals' Reports [Egypt] [A publication] (DLA)
ALKAPT...... Homogentisic Acid [In urine] [Genetics] (DAVI)
Alkerm...... Alkermes, Inc. [Associated Press] (SAG)
ALKISO....... Alkaline Phosphatase Isoenzymes [Biochemistry] (DAVI)

ALK-P .... Alkaline Phosphatase [*An enzyme*] (DAVI)
alk phos ...... Alkaline Phosphatase [*An enzyme*] (CPH)
alk ptase ..... Alkaline Phosphatase [*An enzyme*] (CPH)
ALKS .... Alkermes, Inc. [*NASDAQ symbol*] (SPSG)
ALKY .... Alkalinity (MSA)
ALL .... Accelerated Learning of Logic
ALL .... Acute Lymphatic [*or Lymphoblastic or Lymphocytic*] Leukemia [*Medicine*]
ALL .... Address Locator Logic [*Computer science*]
ALL .... Admiralty List of Lights [*British*]
ALL .... Affiliated Leadership League of and for the Blind of America (EA)
ALL .... Airborne LASER Laboratory [*Air Force*]
ALL .... Aircraft Landing Lamp
ALL .... AirLifeLine (EA)
ALL .... Albenga [*Italy*] [*Airport symbol*] (AD)
Al L .... Alia Lectio [*Another Reading*] [*Latin*]
ALL .... Aliserio [*Italy ICAO designator*] (FAAC)
All .... Allative (BJA)
all .... Allegata [*Schedules, Enclosures*] [*Italian*] (ILCA)
ALL .... Allegheny Airlines (MCD)
ALL .... Allegro [*Quick*] [*Music*] (ROG)
ALL .... Alleluia
All .... Allen's Massachusetts Reports [*A publication*] (DLA)
All .... Allen's New Brunswick Reports [*Canada*] [*A publication*] (DLA)
ALL .... Allentown College of Saint Francis De Sales, Center Valley, PA [*OCLC symbol*] (OCLC)
ALL .... Allergy (AAMN)
ALL .... Alley
ALL .... Allowance Load List (AFIT)
ALL .... Allstate Corp. [*NYSE symbol*] (SPSG)
ALL .... American League of Lobbyists (EA)
ALL .... American Lebanese League (EA)
ALL .... American Liberation League
ALL .... American Life League (EA)
ALL .... American Life Lobby (EA)
ALL .... Anchor Line Ltd. [*Steamship*] (MHDB)
ALL .... Application Language Liberator (MCD)
ALL .... Arc LASER Light
ALL .... Argon LASER Lining
ALL .... Ariel Resources Ltd. [*Vancouver Stock Exchange symbol*]
ALL .... Association for Latin Liturgy (EA)
ALL .... Association of Language Learning [*British*] (DBA)
ALL .... Augustana Luther League [*Later, ILLL*]
All .... Indian Law Reports, Allahabad Series [*A publication*] (DLA)
All .... Liberal Alliance [*Political party*] [*British*]
ALLA .... Acute Lymphocytic Leukemia Antigen [*Medicine*] (DMAA)
ALLA .... Allied Capital Advisers [*NASDAQ symbol*] (TTSB)
ALLA .... Allied Capital Advisers, Inc. [*NASDAQ symbol*] (SAG)
ALLA .... Allied Longline Agency [*NATO*]
ALLACM .... Air-Launched Low-Altitude Cruise Missile (MCD)
AllACm .... All American Communications, Inc. [*Associated Press*] (SAG)
AllAFG .... All American Food Group, Inc. [*Associated Press*] (SAG)
AllAmTar ..... All American Target Term Trust [*Associated Press*] (SAG)
All & Mor Tr... Allen and Morris' Trial [*A publication*] (DLA)
AllASem .... All American Semiconductor, Inc. [*Associated Press*] (SAG)
ALLB .... Lac La Biche Public Library, Alberta [*Library symbol National Library of Canada*] (NLC)
ALLBVC .... Alberta Vocational Centre, Lac La Biche, Alberta [*Library symbol National Library of Canada*] (NLC)
ALLC .... Allied Capital Corp. [*NASDAQ symbol*] (SAG)
ALLC .... Association for Literary and Linguistic Computing [*University College of North Wales*] [*Gwynedd*] (EA)
ALLCE .... Allowance (ROG)
AllChemE ..... Alliance for Chemical Sciences & Technologies in Europe
AllCity .... Allcity Insurance Co. [*Associated Press*] (SAG)
AllCom .... All-Comm Media Corp. [*Associated Press*] (SAG)
AllCom .... Alliance Communications Corp. [*Associated Press*] (SAG)
All Cr Cas .... Allahabad Criminal Cases [*India*] [*A publication*] (DLA)
ALLCT .... Allocate
ALLCTN .... Allocation
ALLD .... Airborne LASER Locator Designator (MCD)
ALLD .... Allied
ALLD .... Allied
Alld .... Allied Record Sales [*Record label*]
ALLD .... Allowed
AlldBk .... Allied Bankshares, Inc. [*Associated Press*] (SAG)
AlldBksh ...... Allied Bankshares [*Associated Press*] (SAG)
AlldCap .... Allied Capital Corp. [*Associated Press*] (SAG)
AlldDgtl .... Allied Digital Technologies [*Formerly, AMG Digital Tchnologies*] [*Associated Press*] (SAG)
AlldHldg ...... Allied Holdings, Inc. [*Associated Press*] (SAG)
AlldPd .... Allied Products Corp. [*Associated Press*] (SAG)
AlldRsh .... Allied Research Associates, Inc. [*Associated Press*] (SAG)
ALLE .... Allegiant Bancorp [*NASDAQ symbol*] (TTSB)
ALLE .... Allegiant Bancorp, Inc. [*NASDAQ symbol*] (SAG)
ALLEE .... Alley [*Commonly used*] (OPSA)
ALLEG .... Allegiance
ALLEG .... Allegory (ADA)
alleg .... Allegory (VRA)
AllegCp .... Allegheny Corp. [*Associated Press*] (SAG)
AllegCp .... Allegheny Corp. [*Associated Press*] (SAG)
Allegheny C... Allegheny College (GAGS)
Allegian .... Allegiance Banc Corp. [*Associated Press*] (SAG)
Allegiant ...... Allegiant Bancorp, Inc. [*Associated Press*] (SAG)
Allegnc .... Allegiance Corp. [*Associated Press*] (SAG)

AllegPhy ...... Allegiant Physician Services, Inc. [*Associated Press*] (SAG)
Allegro .... Allegro New Media, Inc. [*Associated Press*] (SAG)
Allegro .... Allergro New Media, Inc. [*Associated Press*] (SAG)
ALLEGTO .... Allegretto [*Moderately Quick*] [*Music*]
Allen .... Aleyn's English King's Bench Reports [*A publication*] (DLA)
Allen .... Allen's Massachusetts Supreme Judicial Court Reports [*1861-67*] [*A publication*] (DLA)
Allen .... Allen's New Brunswick Reports [*Canada*] [*A publication*] (DLA)
Allen .... Allen's Washington Territory Reports [*1854-85*] [*A publication*] (DLA)
AllenGp .... [*The*] Allen Group, Inc. [*Associated Press*] (SAG)
Allen NB ...... Allen's New Brunswick Reports [*Canada A publication*] (DLA)
Allen Tel Cas... Allen's Telegraph Cases [*A publication*] (DLA)
All ER Rep... All England Law Reports (Reprint) [*1558-1935*] [*A publication*] (DLA)
All ER Rep Ext... All England Law Reports (Reprint), Australian Extension Volumes [*A publication*] (DLA)
All ER Repr... All England Law Reports (Reprint) [*1558-1935*] [*A publication*] (DLA)
ALLG .... Allegiance Banc [*NASDAQ symbol*] (TTSB)
ALLG .... Allegiance Banc Corp. [*NASDAQ symbol*] (SAG)
Allgem .... Allgemein [*General*] [*Music*]
Allgett .... Allegretto [*Moderately Quick*] [*Music*]
Allg Gesch Bed... Allgemeine Geschaftsbedingungen [*General conditions of contracts, transactions, etc.*] [*German*] (ILCA)
AllGIE .... Alliance Global Environmental Fund, Inc. [*Associated Press*] (SAG)
AllgPow .... Allegheny Power System, Inc. [*Associated Press*] (SAG)
ALLGTTO .... Allegretto [*Moderately Quick*] [*Music*] (ROG)
Allg VersBed... Allgemeine Versicherungsbedingungen [*General conditions of insurance*] [*German*] (ILCA)
ALLHAT .... Antihypertensive and Lipid-Lowering Heart Attack Trial [*Clinical trial*]
ALLI .... Alliance Communications Corp. [*NASDAQ symbol*] (SAG)
ALLI .... Allied Capital Corp. II [*NASDAQ symbol*] (SAG)
ALLI .... Allowance for Loan and Lease Losses (TDOB)
AlliAM .... Alliance All Market Advantage Fund, Inc. [*Associated Press*] (SAG)
AlliAMkt .... Alliance All Market Advantage Fund, Inc. [*Associated Press*] (SAG)
ALLIBAKAT... Alliance des Bahemba au Katanga [*Alliance of the Bahemba in Katanga*] [*Zaire*]
All ICR .... All Indian Criminal Reports [*A publication*] (DLA)
AlliedGp .... Allied Group [*Associated Press*] (SAG)
ALLIF .... Alliance Communic 'B' [*NASDAQ symbol*] (TTSB)
AlliGam .... Alliance Gaming Corp. [*Associated Press*] (SAG)
Allin .... Allinson's Pennsylvania Superior and District Court Reports [*A publication*] (DLA)
AllinCm .... Allin Communications Corp. [*Associated Press*] (SAG)
All Ind Crim Dec... All India Criminal Decisions [*A publication*] (ILCA)
All Ind Cr R... All Indian Criminal Reports [*A publication*] (DLA)
All Ind Cr T... All India Criminal Times [*A publication*] (DLA)
All India Crim Dec... All India Criminal Decisions [*A publication*] (DLA)
All India Rep... All India Reporter, Nagpur [*A publication*] (DLA)
All Ind Rep NS... All India Reporter, New Series [*A publication*] (DLA)
all'ingr .... All'Ingrosso [*wholesale*] [*Italian*] (ODBW)
Allinson .... Allinson's Pennsylvania Superior and District Court Reports [*A publication*] (DLA)
All IR .... All India Reports [*A publication*] (DLA)
Allison's Am Dict... Allison's American Dictionary [*A publication*] (DLA)
All LD of Mar... Alleyne. Legal Decrees of Marriage [*1810*] [*A publication*] (DLA)
AllLig .... Allergan Ligand Retinoid Therapeutics [*Associated Press*] (SAG)
All LJ .... Allahabad Law Journal [*India*] [*A publication*] (DLA)
All LR .... Allahabad Law Review [*India*] [*A publication*] (DLA)
All LT .... Allahabad Law Times [*India*] [*A publication*] (DLA)
ALL-MBE .... Atomic Layer-by-Layer Molecular Beam Epitaxy
AllmerPr .... Allmerica Property & Casualty [*Associated Press*] (SAG)
ALLMIS .... Army Lessons Learned Management Information System (INF)
AllmrFn .... Allmerica Financial Corp. [*Associated Press*] (SAG)
AllmrFn .... Allmerican Financial Corp. [*Associated Press*] (SAG)
AllmrST .... Allmerica Securities Trust [*Formerly, State Mutual Securities Trust*] [*Associated Press*] (SAG)
ALLN .... Allin Communications Corp. [*NASDAQ symbol*] (SAG)
ALLN .... Anterior Lateral Line Nerve [*Fish anatomy*]
ALLNAVSTAS... All Naval Stations [*A dispatch to all Naval stations in an area*]
All NB .... Allen's New Brunswick Reports [*Canada*] [*A publication*] (DLA)
ALLNCE .... Alliance
All Nig LR .... All Nigeria Law Reports [*A publication*] (DLA)
AllnImg .... Alliance Imaging, Inc. [*Associated Press*] (SAG)
All NLR .... All Nigeria Law Reports [*A publication*] (DLA)
Alln Part ...... Allnat. Law of Partition [*1820*] [*A publication*] (DLA)
Alln Wills .... Allnat on Wills [*A publication*] (DLA)
ALLO .... Allegro [*Quick*] [*Music*]
ALLO .... Allegro-Elite [*Formerly, Allegro*] [*Record label*]
ALLO .... All Others [*Later, G Group*] [*Division of National Security Agency*]
ALLO .... Atypical Legionella-Like Organism
ALLOC .... Allocate [*or Allocation*] (AFM)
ALLOT .... Allocated
ALL'OTT .... All'Ottava [*At the Octave*] [*Music*]
AllouH .... Allou Health & Beauty Care, Inc. [*Associated Press*] (SAG)
All'Ova .... All'Ottava [*At the Octave*] [*Music*]
ALLOW .... Allowance
ALLP .... Adaptive Lattice Linear Prediction (PDAA)
ALLP .... Alliance Pharmaceutical [*NASDAQ symbol*] (TTSB)
ALLP .... Alliance Pharmaceutical Corp. [*NASDAQ symbol*] (NQ)
ALLP .... Arc LASER Light Pump
ALLP .... Audiolingual Language Programming [*Computer science*]
ALLPIE .... Alliance for Parental Involvement in Education (PAZ)
AllQt .... All Quotes, Inc. [*Associated Press*] (SAG)
AllQuote ...... All Quotes, Inc. [*Associated Press*] (SAG)
ALLRGST ..... Allergist
ALLRGY .... Allergy

ALLS	Adult Life Long Learning Section [*Public Library Association*]
ALLS	Apollo Lunar Landing System [*NASA*] (SAA)
ALLS	Apollo Lunar Logistic Support [*NASA*]
AllSeasG	All Seasons Global Fund [*Associated Press*] (SAG)
All Ser	Allahabad Series, Indian Law Reports [*A publication*] (DLA)
All Sher	Allen on Sheriffs [*A publication*] (DLA)
Allst98	Allstate Corp. [*Associated Press*] (SAG)
Allstate	Allstate Corp. [*Associated Press*] (SAG)
AllstFn	Allstate Financial Corp. [*Associated Press*] (SAG)
AllTch	Alliant Techsystems [*Associated Press*] (SAG)
Alltel	ALLTEL Corp. [*Formerly, Allied Telephone Co.*] [*Associated Press*] (SAG)
All Tel Cas	Allen's Telegraph Cases [*A publication*] (DLA)
ALLTO	Allegretto [*Moderately Quick*] [*Music*] (ROG)
Alltrista	Alltrista Corp. [*Associated Press*] (SAG)
ALLTV	Active Low-Light-Level Television [*Night vision device*] [*Air Force*] (MCD)
ALLUS	Allusion
ALLVRJ	Air-Launched Low-Volume Ramjet (MCD)
Allwaste	Allwaste, Inc. [*Associated Press*] (SAG)
All WN	Allahabad Weekly Notes (and Supplement) [*India*] [*A publication*] (DLA)
Allwood	Allwood's Appeal Cases under the Weights and Measures Act [*England*] [*A publication*] (DLA)
All WR	Allahabad Weekly Reporter [*India*] [*A publication*] (DLA)
AllWrld	Alliance World Dollar Government Fund [*Associated Press*] (SAG)
AllWrld2	Alliance World Dollar Government Fund 2 [*Associated Press*] (SAG)
ALLY	Alley [*Commonly used*] (OPSA)
ALLY	Alliance Gaming [*NASDAQ symbol*] (TTSB)
ALLY	Alliance Gaming Corp. [*NASDAQ symbol*] (SAG)
ALLY	Alloy
ALM	Acral Lentiginous Melanoma [*Medicine*]
ALM	Advanced List of Materials
ALM	Aerial Lentiginous Melanoma [*Medicine*] (DMAA)
ALM	Aerophysics Laboratory Memorandum [*NASA*] (KSC)
ALM	Aircraft Limited Model
ALM	Air-Launched Missile
ALM	Airlift Loading Model
ALM	Alabama League of Municipalities (SRA)
ALM	Alamogordo [*New Mexico*] [*Airport symbol*] (OAG)
ALM	Alarm (MSA)
ALM	Alice Lake Mines [*Vancouver Stock Exchange symbol*]
ALM	Allmerica Sec Tr [*NYSE symbol*] (TTSB)
ALM	Allmerica Securities Trust [*Formerly, State Mutual Securities Trust*] [*NYSE symbol*] (SAG)
Alm	Almagest [*of Ptolemy*] [*Classical studies*] (OCD)
ALM	Almeria [*Spain*] [*Seismograph station code, US Geological Survey*] (SEIS)
alm	Almost [*Philately*]
ALM	Alveolar Lining Material [*Medicine*] (DAVI)
ALM	American Leprosy Missions (EA)
ALM	Antillaanse Luchtvaart Maatschappij [*Airline*] [*Netherlands Antilles*]
ALM	Antilliaanse Luchtvaart Maatschappij [*Netherlands ICAO designator*] (FAAC)
ALM	Apollo Lunar Module [*NASA*]
ALM	Applied Laboratory Method (OA)
ALM	AppWare Loadable Module [*Computer science*] (PCM)
ALM	Arkansas & Louisiana Missouri Railway Co. [*AAR code*]
ALM	Arm Lock Magnet
ALM	Artium Liberalium Magister [*Master of the Liberal Arts*]
ALM	Assembler Language for MULTICS
ALM	Asset/Liability Management [*Banking*]
ALM	Association of Lloyd's Members [*British insurers' organization*] (ECON)
ALM	Association of Lutheran Men (EA)
ALM	Asynchronous Line Module
ALM	Asynchronous Line Multiplexer [*Telecommunications*]
ALM	Audio Level Meter
ALM	Augmented Lunar Module (MCD)
ALM	Linden Municipal Library, Alberta [*Library symbol National Library of Canada*] (NLC)
ALM	Master of Liberal Arts (PGP)
ALM	University of Alabama, University, AL [*OCLC symbol*] (OCLC)
ALMA	Adoptees Liberty Movement Association (EA)
ALMA	Aircraft Locknut Manufacturers Association (EA)
ALMA	Allyl Methacrylate [*Organic chemistry*]
ALMA	Alphanumeric Code for Music Analysis [*Input code for music notation*] (NITA)
ALMA	Alphanumeric Language for Music Analysis
ALMA	Alternative Living Manager's Association [*Defunct*] (EA)
ALMA	American Lace Manufacturers Association
ALMA	American Lithuanian Musicians Alliance (EA)
ALMA	American Loudspeaker Manufacturers Association (EA)
ALMA	Analytical Laboratory Managers Association (EA)
ALMA	Association of Labor Mediation Agencies [*Later, ALRA*] (EA)
ALMA	Association of Library Magazines of America (DGA)
ALMA	Association of Literary Magazines of America [*Later, CCLM*] (EA)
ALMACA	Association of Labor-Management Administrators and Consultants on Alcoholism (EA)
ALMAJCOM	All Major Commands
ALMAR	All Marine Corps Activities (NVT)
ALMA Society	Adoptees' Liberty Movement Association (PAZ)
ALMB	Air-Launched Missile Ballistics (MCD)
ALMC	Air-Launched Missile Change (DNAB)
ALMC	Almanac (ROG)

ALMC	Army Logistics Management College [*Fort Lee, VA*]
ALMDA	Airlock Multiple Docking Adapter [*NASA*] (MCD)
ALME	Acetyllysine Methyl Ester [*Biochemistry*]
ALMI	Alpha Microsystems [*NASDAQ symbol*] (NQ)
ALMI	Anterior Lateral Myocardial Infarct [*or Infarction*] [*Cardiology*]
ALMICS	Automated Logistics Management and Inventory Control System (MCD)
ALMIDO	Amplitude and Latency Measuring Instrument with Digital Output (MCD)
ALMIDS	Army Logistics Management Integrated Data Systems (AABC)
AL MIL	Alla Militaire [*In Military Style*] [*Music*] (ROG)
ALMILACT	All Military Activities (AFM)
ALMIMSIP	Air-Launched Missile Intermediate Maintenance System Program [*Navy*] (MCD)
ALMIOS	Air-Launched Missile Inventory Objectives Study (MCD)
ALMIRBM	Air-Launched Medium-Intermediate Range Ballistic Missile (MCD)
ALMIW	Alpha Microsystems Wrrt [*NASDAQ symbol*] (TTSB)
ALMO	Army Logistics Manpower Office [*Merged with Operations Personnel Office*]
AL MOD	Alla Moderna [*In Modern Style*] [*Music*] (ROG)
ALMOND	Almondsbury [*England*]
ALMP	Aboriginal Language Maintenance Project [*Australia*]
ALMPT	Air-Launched Missile Propulsion Technology (MCD)
ALMR	Advanced Liquid Metal Reactors [*Nuclear energy*]
ALMR	Alamar Biosciences, Inc. [*NASDAQ symbol*] (SAG)
ALMRS	Automated Land and Minerals Records System [*Department of the Interior*] (GFGA)
ALMS	Aircraft Landing Measurement System (MCD)
ALMS	Air-Launched Missile System
ALMS	Air-Lift Management System [*Air Force*] (PDAA)
ALMS	Analytic Language Manipulation System
ALMS	Atomic Line Molecular Spectroscopy
ALMS	Automated Logic Mapping System (PDAA)
ALMS	Automated Logistics Management System (SSD)
ALMS	Auxiliary Liquid Metal System [*Nuclear energy*] (NRCH)
ALMSA	Army Logistics Management Systems Activity
ALMSA	Automated Logistics Management Systems Agency [*DoD*]
ALMV	Air-Launched Miniature Vehicle
ALMV	Anterior Leaflet of Mitral Valve [*Cardiology*] (AAMN)
ALN	Acao Libertadora Nacional [*Brazilian Action for National Liberation*] [*Political party*] (LAIN)
ALN	Accounting Line Number (CINC)
ALN	Adaptive Learning Network [*Computer science*]
ALN	Administrative Law Notes [*Australia A publication*]
ALN	Advanced Land Navigation (MCD)
ALN	Air Lincoln, Inc. [*ICAO designator*] (FAAC)
ALN	Albany & Northern Railway Co. [*AAR code*]
ALN	Alianca Libertadora Nacional [*National Liberation Alliance*] [*Brazil Political party*] (PD)
ALN	Align
ALN	Allen Group [*NYSE symbol*] (TTSB)
ALN	[*The*] Allen Group, Inc. [*NYSE symbol*] (SPSG)
ALN	Allentown [*Diocese abbreviation*] [*Pennsylvania*] (TOCD)
ALN	Alton, IL [*Location identifier FAA*] (FAAL)
ALN	American Law Network [*Telecommunications service*] (TSSD)
ALN	Ameroil Energy Corp. [*Vancouver Stock Exchange symbol*]
ALN	Ammunition Lot Number
ALN	Anterior Lateral Nerve
ALN	Anterior Lymph Node [*Medicine*] (MAE)
ALN	Armee de Liberation Nationale [*National Liberation Army*] [*Algeria*] [*Political party*] (AF)
ALN	Armee de Liberation Nationale [*National Liberation Army*] [*Guadeloupe*] [*Political party*] (PD)
ALNA	Armee de Liberation Nationale de l'Angola [*Angolan Army of National Liberation*]
ALNAV	All Navy Activities [*A dispatch to all activities in an area*]
ALNAV	All-Navy Message
ALNAVSTA	All Naval Stations [*A dispatch to all Naval stations in an area*]
AlnCap	Alliance Capital Management Ltd. [*Associated Press*] (SAG)
AlnEnt	Alliance Entertainment Corp. [*Associated Press*] (SAG)
ALNICO	Aluminum, Nickel, Cobalt [*Alloy*]
ALNK	AmeriLink Corp. [*NASDAQ symbol*] (SAG)
ALNK	Armee de Liberation Nationale Kamerounaise [*Cameroonese National Liberation Army*]
ALNK	Armee de Liberation Nationale Kamerunaise [*Cameroonian Army of National Liberation*] (AF)
ALNMT	Alignment (AAG)
ALNN	Air-Launched Nonnuclear Ordnance (DNAB)
ALNNO	Air-Launched Nonnuclear Ordnance
AlnOrg	Allen Organ Co. [*Associated Press*] (SAG)
ALNOT	Alert Notice
AlnSem	Alliance Semiconductor Corp. [*Associated Press*] (SAG)
ALNT	Aliant Communications, Inc. [*NASDAQ symbol*] (SAG)
ALNTS	Automatic Liquid Nitrogen Transfer System
ALNW	Air-Launched Nuclear Weapon (DNAB)
ALNY	Architectural League of New York [*Later, AL*] (EA)
ALO	Accredited Leasing Officer [*Canada*] (DD)
ALO	Administrative Liaison Officer
ALO	Admiralty Liaison Officer [*British*]
ALO	Advanced Lunar Operation
ALO	Air Liaison Officer
ALO	Air Logistics Officer (AAGC)
ALO	Alamo Developments [*Vancouver Stock Exchange symbol*]
ALO	Albuquerque Operations Office [*Department of Energy*]
ALO	Allied Liaison Office [*Military*]

AI'O	A l'Orient [At the East] [Freemasonry] [French] (ROG)
ALO	AL Pharmaceuticals, Inc. [Later, AL Labs] [NYSE symbol] (SAG)
ALO	ALPHARMA INC.'A' [NYSE symbol] (TTSB)
ALO	Alpharm, Inc. [NYSE symbol] (SAG)
ALO	Alternate Launch Officer [Air Force]
ALO	Alternate Liaison Officer
ALO	Alternative Liste Oesterreich [Austrian Alternative List] [Political party] (PPW)
ALO	Amalgamated Lace Operatives of America
ALO	American Liaison Office
ALO	Apollo Lunar Orbit [NASA]
ALO	Appropriate Labor Organization (OICC)
ALO	Arm Length Order
ALO	Army Liaison Officer
ALO	Authorized Level of Organization (AABC)
ALO	Automatic Lock-On (MCD)
ALO	Axiolinguo-Occlusal [Dentistry]
ALO	Lougheed Public Library, Alberta [Library symbol National Library of Canada] (NLC)
ALO	Pennsylvania Commuter Airlines, Inc. [ICAO designator] (FAAC)
ALO	Waterloo [Iowa] [Airport symbol] (OAG)
ALOA	Alabama Optometric Association (SRA)
ALOA	Amalgamated Lace Operatives of America [Defunct] (EA)
ALOA	Amalgamated Lithographers of America (DGA)
ALOA	Assembly of Librarians of the Americas [Defunct]
ALOA	Associated Locksmiths of America (EA)
ALOAL	Autonomous Lock-On After Launch (MCD)
ALoaLHi	Lee County Historical Society, Museum Library, Loachapoka, AL [Library symbol Library of Congress] (LCLS)
ALOC	Administrative and Logistics Operations Center [Military] (INF)
ALOC	Air Line of Communication [Air Force]
ALOC	Air Logistics Chain (MCD)
ALOC	Allocate [or Allocation] (AABC)
ALOC	Alternate Launch Officer Console [Air Force]
ALOC	Apollo Launch Operations Committee [NASA] (KSC)
ALOC	Aviation Logistics and Operations Center [Military] (DOMA)
ALOE	Analysis of Local Oriented Edges [Cancer technology]
ALOE	[A] Lady of England [Pseudonym used by Charlotte Maria Tucker, 19th-century author of children's books]
Aloette	Aloette Cosmetics, Inc. [Associated Press] (SAG)
AL of H	American Legion of Honor
ALOFT	Airborne Light Optical Fiber Technology
ALOFT	[A] Language Oriented to Flight Engineering and Testing [NASA] (KSC)
ALOG	Administration-Logistics [Military] (INF)
ALOG	Analogic Corp. [NASDAQ symbol] (NQ)
ALOG	Analogic Corp. [NASDAQ symbol] (TTSB)
Al(OH)₃	Aluminum Hydroxide [Antacid] [Pharmacology] (DAVI)
ALOHA	Aboriginal Lands of Hawaiian Ancestry [Hawaiian group seeking compensation for land]
ALOHA	Association of Local Official Health Agencies (AC)
ALOM	Air-Land Operations Manual (MCD)
ALOM	Longview Municipal Library, Alberta [Library symbol National Library of Canada] (NLC)
ALOMA	American Lithuanian Organist - Musicians Alliance [Formerly, ALRCOA] (EA)
ALOMAD	Adriamycin, Leukeran [Chlorambucil], Oncovin , Methotrexate, Actinomycin D, Dacarbazine [Vincristine] [Antineoplastic drug regimen]
ALOMO	Lomond Public Library, Alberta [Library symbol National Library of Canada] (NLC)
ALON	Aircraft Longitude (MCD)
ALON	Air Liaison Officer Net (NATG)
ALOO	Albuquerque Operations Office [Department of Energy] (GRD)
ALOP	Apollo Launch Operation Panel [NASA] (KSC)
ALOP	Army Logistics Objectives Program
ALOPE	Airborne LIDAR [Light Detection and Ranging] Oceanographic Probing Experiment [NASA]
ALOR	Advanced Lunar Orbital Rendezvous (IEEE)
A l'OR	A l'Orient [At the East] [Freemasonry] [French]
ALOREP	Airlift Operational Report
ALOS	Apollo Lunar Orbital Science [NASA] (KSC)
ALOS	Average Length of Stay [of patients in a health care institution]
ALOSH	Appalachian Laboratory for Occupational Safety and Health [Department of Health and Human Services] (GFGA)
ALOSYN	Alouette Topside Sounder Synoptic [NASA]
ALOT	Adaptive LASER Optics Techniques (MCD)
ALOT	Adsorption Layer Open Tubular Column [Chromatography]
ALOT	Airborne Lightweight Optical Tracking [Air Force]
ALOT	Allotment (AABC)
ALOT	Astro-Med [NASDAQ symbol] (TTSB)
ALOT	Astro-Med, Inc. [NASDAQ symbol] (NQ)
ALOTM	Allotment (AFM)
ALOTMT	Allotment (DNAB)
ALOTS	Airborne Lightweight Optical Tracking System [Air Force]
ALOW	Air Electrical Officer's Writer [British military] (DMA)
ALO WS	ALPHARMA Inc.Wrrt [NYSE symbol] (TTSB)
ALOX	Aluminium Oxide
ALOXCON	Aluminum-Oxide Electrolytic Capacitor (MUGU)
ALP	Acute Lupus Pericarditis [Medicine] (AAMN)
ALP	Adaptive Light Pattern
ALP	Administration Laboratory Project File [University of Alberta] [Canada Information service or system] (CRD)
ALP	Advanced Language Program [Institute for Defense Analysis]
ALP	Advanced Lunar Projects

ALP	Advisory Light Panel (MCD)
ALP	Agence Lao Presse [Laos Press Agency]
ALP	Airborne Line Printer
ALP	Air-Launched Platform (NVT)
ALP	Air Liaison Party
ALP	Air Logistics Pipeline Study (MCD)
ALP	Air, Low Pressure (DNAB)
ALP	Airport Layout Plan [FAA] (TAG)
ALP	Airport Layout Plan (FAAC)
ALP	Alabama Power Capital Trust I [NYSE symbol] (SAG)
ALP	Alabama Power Co. [NYSE symbol] (SPSG)
ALP	Aleppo [Syria] [Airport symbol] (OAG)
ALP	Alkaline Phosphatase [Also, AP] [An enzyme]
ALP	Alkyl Lysophospholipid [Biochemistry]
ALP	Allied Liaison and Protocol [Military]
ALP	Allied Logistics Publication [Military]
ALP	Alphalytic Protease [An enzyme]
ALP	Alpliner AG [Switzerland ICAO designator] (FAAC)
ALP	Alprazolam [Tranquilizer]
ALP	Alternative Loan Program
ALP	Alternatives Loan Program [Humane Society of the United States]
ALP	Ambulance Loading Post [Military]
ALP	American Labor Party
ALP	Anterior Lobe of Pituitary [Gland]
ALP	Antigua Labour Party [Political party] (PPW)
ALP	Antilymphocyte Plasma [Immunology] (MAE)
ALP	Approved for Limited Production (MCD)
ALP	Arakan Liberation Party [Myanmar] [Political party]
ALP	Arithmetic Logic Processor
ALP	Articulated Leg Platform [Drilling technology]
ALP	Assembly Language Preprocessor [Computer science] (IEEE)
ALP	Assembly Language Program [Computer science]
ALP	Association of Little Presses (DGA)
ALP	Australian Labour Party [Political party] (PPW)
ALP	Authorization for Local Purchase
ALP	Automated Language Processing (NITA)
ALP	Automated Learning Process
ALP	Automated Library Program [Computer science] (DIT)
ALP	Elmira, NY [Location identifier FAA] (FAAL)
ALPA	Air Line Pilots Association, International (EA)
ALPA	Alaskan Long-Period Array
Al Pa	Albertus Papiensis [Flourished, 1211-40] [Authority cited in pre-1607 legal work] (DSA)
ALPA	American Legion Press Association [Later, NALPA] (EA)
ALPA	Amiral Commandant les Porte-Avions [Admiral, Aircraft Carriers] [French] (NATG)
ALPA	Asociacion Latinoamericana de Produccion Animal
ALPAC	Automatic Language Processing Advisory Committee [National Research Council]
ALPAG	All London Parents' Action Group [British] (AIE)
ALPAI	Air Line Pilots Association, International (EA)
ALPAK	Algebra Package [Computer science]
ALPAL	Algeria - Palma, Spain [Submarine cable] [Telecommunications]
ALPANSA	Alas Panamenas SA [Panama] [ICAO designator] (FAAC)
ALPB	Aircraft Logistics Planning Board (MCD)
ALPB	American Lutheran Publicity Bureau (EA)
ALPBC	American League of Professional Baseball Clubs (EA)
ALPBP	Assessment of Language Proficiency of Bilingual Persons Project (EDAC)
ALPC	Adaptive Linear Predictive Coding (TEL)
ALPC	Army Logistics Policy Council (AABC)
ALPCA	Automobile License Plate Collectors Association (EA)
ALPCyT	Asociacion Latinoamericana de Politica Cientifica y Tecnologica [Latin American Association for Science and Technology] [Mexico] (EAIO)
ALPE	Airborne LASER Propagation Experiment (MCD)
ALPEC	Ammunition Loading Production Engineering Center [Army]
ALPERSCOM	All Personnel Communication [Military] (AFM)
ALPES	Advanced Logical Programming Environments Support [ESPRIT project] (NITA)
ALPETH	Aluminum and Polyethylene [Components of a type of telecommunications cable]
ALPEX	Alpine Experiment [International Council of Scientific Unions]
ALPH	Alpha
ALPH	Alphabetical (WDAA)
ALPH	Alphabetic Phonogram [Egyptology] (ROG)
ALPH	AlphaNet Solutions [NASDAQ symbol] (TTSB)
ALPH	AlphaNet Solutions, Inc. [NASDAQ symbol] (SAG)
ALPHA	Action League of Physically Handicapped Adults [Canada]
ALPHA	Alkali Plasma Hall Accelerator (MCD)
ALPHA	Alphabetical [Flowchart]
alpha	Alphabetical (WDMC)
ALPHA	Alternative Learning Program for High School Age
ALPHA	AMC [Army Materiel Command] Logistics Program - Hardcore Automated
ALPHA	Automatic Literature Processing, Handling, and Analysis
AlphaBta	Alpha-Beta Technology, Inc. [Associated Press] (SAG)
AlphaIn	Alpha Industries, Inc. [Associated Press] (SAG)
ALPHANUM	Alphanumeric
AlpharI	Alpharel, Inc. [Associated Press] (SAG)
Alpharma	AL Pharmaceuticals, Inc. [Associated Press] (SAG)
Alpharma	Alpharm, Inc. [Associated Press] (SAG)
AlphaSo	Alpha Solarco, Inc. [Associated Press] (SAG)
AlphaTch	Alpha Technology Group, Inc. [Associated Press] (SAG)

ALPHGR......	Average Linear Planar Heat Generation Rate [*Nuclear energy*] (NRCH)
AlphH..........	Alpha Hospitality Corp. [*Associated Press*] (SAG)
AlphHsp......	Alpha Hospitality Corp. [*Associated Press*] (SAG)
Alphm.........	AI Pharmaceuticals, Inc. [*Associated Press*] (SAG)
Alphm.........	Alpharm, Inc. [*Associated Press*] (SAG)
AlphNet......	AlphaNet Solutions, Inc. [*Associated Press*] (SAG)
Alphr..........	Alpharel, Inc. [*Associated Press*] (SAG)
ALPID.........	Analysis of Large Plastic Incremental Deformation (MCD)
AlpineGr.....	Alpine Group [*Associated Press*] (SAG)
AlpinGr	Alpine Group, Inc. [*Associated Press*] (SAG)
ALPL..........	Advanced Lunar Projects Laboratory
ALPLASMA...	Aluminum Plasma Model (MCD)
AlpLce	Alpine Lace Brands, Inc. [*Associated Press*] (SAG)
ALPM..........	Assembly-Line Preventive Maintenance [*Automotive engineering*]
ALPM..........	Augmented Lunar Payload Module
AlpMic.........	Alpha Microsystems [*Associated Press*] (SAG)
ALPNA	American Licensed Practical Nurses Association (EA)
Alpnet........	Alpnet, Inc. [*Associated Press*] (SAG)
ALPO..........	Air-Land Programs Office
ALPO..........	Allegheny Portage Railroad National Historic Site
ALPO..........	Aluminophosphate [*Inorganic chemistry*]
ALPO..........	Anterolateral Pre-Olivary Nucleus [*Neuroanatomy*]
ALPO..........	Apollo Lunar Polar Orbiter [*NASA*]
ALPO..........	Association of Land and Property Owners
ALPO..........	Association of Lunar and Planetary Observers (EA)
ALPOS........	Avionics Laboratory Predictive Operations and Support (MCD)
Al Pp	Albertus Papiensis [*Flourished, 1211-40*] [*Authority cited in pre-1607 legal work*] (DSA)
ALPPA	Agriculture and Livestock Professional Photographers Association (EA)
ALPPrA	Alabama Pwr 7.60%'A'Pfd [*NYSE symbol*] (TTSB)
ALPPrB	Alabama Pwr 6.80% 'A'Pfd [*NYSE symbol*] (TTSB)
ALPPrC	Alabama Pwr 6.40% 'A'Pfd [*NYSE symbol*] (TTSB)
ALPPrH	Alabama Pwr 7.60% 2nd'A'Pfd [*NYSE symbol*] (TTSB)
ALPPrQ	Ala Pwr Cap 17.375% Tr Pfd Sec [*NYSE symbol*] (TTSB)
Al Pr	Alison's Principles of the Criminal Law of Scotland [*A publication*] (DLA)
ALPR	Argonne Low-Power Reactor [*Obsolete*]
ALPRA........	American Lithuanian Press and Radio Association
ALPRA-V......	American Lithuanian Press and Radio Association - Viltis (EA)
ALPRO........	Alianza para el Progreso [*Alliance for Progress*] [*Washington, DC*]
ALPS..........	Accidental Launch Prevention System (DOMA)
ALPS..........	Accidental Launch Protection System [*Military*]
ALPS..........	Accountancy & Legal Professions Selection Ltd. [*British*] (ECON)
ALPS..........	Advanced Linear Programming System [*Operational research technique*]
ALPS..........	Advanced Liquid Propulsion System [*NASA*]
ALPS..........	Air-Launched Probe System (MCD)
ALPS..........	Air-Launched Projected Sonobuoy (MCD)
ALPS..........	Allegiant Physician Services, Inc. [*NASDAQ symbol*] (SAG)
ALPS..........	Alternative Launch-Point System
ALPS..........	Analysis of Longwall Pillar Stability [*Computer program*] [*US Bureau of Mines*]
ALPS..........	Aphasia Language Performance Scale [*Speech and language therapy*] (DAVI)
ALPS..........	Applied LASER Projects Staff
ALPS..........	Approach and Landing Procedures Simulator [*Aviation*] (MCD)
ALPS..........	Army Linguist Personnel Study
ALPS..........	Asociacion Latinoamericana de Psicologia Social [*Latin American Association for Social Psychology - LAASP*] (EAIO)
ALPS..........	Assembly Line Planning System (MHDB)
ALPS..........	Associated Logic Parallel System (BUR)
ALPS..........	Association for Loss Prevention and Security (EA)
ALPS..........	Automated Language Processing Systems [*Electronic translation of foreign languages*] [*Commercial firm*] (NITA)
ALPS..........	Automated Leave and Pay System [*Military*] (DNAB)
ALPS..........	Automated Library Processing Services [*System Development Corp.*] (IID)
ALPS..........	Automated Logistics Planning System (MCD)
ALPS..........	Automatic Landing Positioning System
ALPS..........	Automatic License Plate Scanning
ALPS..........	Automatic Linear Positioning System
ALPSP	Association of Learned and Professional Society Publishers [*British*]
ALPSS	Army Life-Support Power Source System (MCD)
ALPT..........	Albumen (VRA)
ALPTA.........	American Low Power Television Association [*Defunct*] (EA)
ALPURCOMS...	All-Purpose Communications System
ALQ............	Adolescent Language Quotient (PAZ)
ALQ............	Albuquerque [*New Mexico*] [*Seismograph station code, US Geological Survey*] (SEIS)
ALQ............	Alegrete [*Brazil*] [*Airport symbol Obsolete*] (OAG)
ALQ............	Almost Letter Quality [*Refers to the quality of print or of a printer*] (NITA)
ALQ............	Altair Aviation Ltd. [*Canada ICAO designator*] (FAAC)
ALQ............	Association des Libraires du Quebec (AC)
ALQAS	Aircraft-Landing Quality Association Scheme (OA)
ALQDS	All Quadrants (FAAC)
ALQS	Aliquippa & Southern Railroad Co. [*AAR code*]
ALQT..........	All Quotes, Inc. [*NASDAQ symbol*] (SAG)
ALR............	Active Line Rotation [*Telecommunications*] (TEL)
ALR............	Actual Loss Ratio [*Insurance*]
ALR............	Administrative License Revocation [*Laws*]
ALR............	Advanced Logic Research Access 386 [*Microcomputer*]
ALR............	Advanced Logic Research, Inc. (PCM)

ALR............	African Language Review [*A publication*]
ALR............	Airborne LASER Range-Finder
ALR............	Air-Land Resupply (CINC)
ALR............	Aldehyde Reductase (DMAA)
ALR............	Alden's Law Reports [*A publication*] (DLA)
ALR............	Alerting Message [*Aviation code*]
ALR............	Alexandra [*New Zealand*] [*Airport symbol*] (OAG)
ALR............	Algarvilara Transportes Aereos Algarvios SA [*Portugal ICAO designator*] (FAAC)
ALR............	Aliter [*Otherwise*] [*Latin*] (ADA)
ALR............	Allied Research Corp. [*AMEX symbol*] (SPSG)
ALR............	Amagat-Leduc Rule [*Physics*]
ALR............	American Labor Cases [*Prentice-Hall, Inc.*] [*A publication*] (DLA)
ALR............	American Law Register [*A publication*] (DLA)
ALR............	American Law Reports
ALR............	American Law Reports Annotated, 1st-5th Series [*Lawyers Co-op*] [*A publication*] (AAGC)
ALR............	Arachidonic Linoleic Acid Ratio [*Clinical chemistry*]
ALR............	Artillery-Locating RADAR
ALR............	Augmentor of Liver Regeneration [*Biochemistry*]
ALR............	Authors' Lending Royalty
ALR............	Automatic Level Recorder
ALR............	Automatic License Revocation
ALR............	Automatic Load Regulator
ALR............	University of Arkansas at Little Rock, Law Library, Little Rock, AR [*OCLC symbol*] (OCLC)
ALR 2d	American Law Reports, Annotated, Second Series [*A publication*] (DLA)
ALR 3d	American Law Reports, Annotated, Third Series [*A publication*] (DLA)
ALR 4th	American Law Reports, Annotated, Fourth Series [*A publication*] (DLA)
ALRA	Abortion Law Reform Association (EAIO)
ALRA	Academy of Live and Recorded Arts [*British*]
ALRA	Advanced LASER Requirements Assessment (MCD)
ALRA	American Land Resource Association [*Defunct*] (EA)
ALRA	Army Long-Range Appraisal
ALRA	Associated Legislative Rabbinate of America (EA)
ALRA	Association of Labor Relations Agencies (EA)
ALRAAM	Air-Launched Long-Range Air-to-Air Missile (MCD)
ALRAFAC.....	All RADAR Air Traffic Control Facilities in Region [*FAA*]
ALRANL	Abortion Law Reform Association. News Letter [*A publication*] (DLA)
ALRA(WA) ...	Association for the Legal Right to Abortion (Western Australia)
ALRAWI......	Advanced Long-Range All-Weather Interceptor (MCD)
ALRC	Aerojet Liquid Rocket Co. (KSC)
ALRC	Alternative Resources [*NASDAQ symbol*] (TTSB)
ALRC	Alternative Resources Corp. [*NASDAQ symbol*] (SAG)
ALRC	Anti-Locust Research Centre [*Later, Centre for Overseas Pest Research*] [*British*] (MCD)
ALRC	Area Learning Resource Center
ALRCOA......	American Lithuanian Roman Catholic Organist Alliance [*Later, ALOMA*] (EA)
ALRCP	Army Long-Range Capabilities Plan
ALRCWA......	American Lithuanian Roman Catholic Women's Alliance [*Later, LCW*] (EA)
ALRD	Army Logistics Research and Development
ALRE..........	Aircraft Launch and Recovery Equipment [*Navy*] (MCD)
AL Rec........	American Law Record [*Cincinnati*] [*A publication*] (DLA)
AL Reg	American Law Register [*Philadelphia*] [*A publication*] (DLA)
AL Reg (NS)...	American Law Register, New Series [*A publication*] (DLA)
AL Reg (OS)...	American Law Register, Old Series [*A publication*] (DLA)
ALREMP	Aircraft Launch and Recovery Equipment Maintenance Program [*Navy*] (NG)
Alrenco........	Alrenco, Inc. [*Associated Press*] (SAG)
ALREP	Air-Launched Report [*Navy*] (NG)
AL Rep	Alabama Reports [*A publication*] (DLA)
AL Rep	American Law Reporter [*Davenport, IA*] [*A publication*] (DLA)
ALRES	Army Logistics Readiness Evaluation System
ALR Fed	American Law Reports, Annotated, Federal [*A publication*] (DLA)
ALRGN........	All Regional Offices (FAAC)
ALRH..........	Apollo Lunar Radioisotopic Heater [*NASA*] (MCD)
ALRI..........	Acute Lower Repiratory Infection [*Medicine*] (CPH)
ALRI..........	Advanced Lithography Research Initiative [*British*]
ALRI..........	Advanced Long-Range Interceptor
ALRI..........	Airborne Long-Range Input (KSC)
ALRI..........	Airborne Long-Range Intercept
ALRI..........	Allergan Ligand Retinoid Therapeutics [*NASDAQ symbol*] (SAG)
ALRI..........	Anterolateral Rotatory [*or Rotational*] Instability [*Orthopedics*]
ALRIS	Airborne Long-Range Input System (SAA)
ALRIZ.........	Allergan Ligand Retinoid (Unit) [*NASDAQ symbol*] (TTSB)
ALRLCS	American Law Reports Later Case Service [*A publication*] (DLA)
ALRM.........	Alarm
ALRM.........	Alarm System [*Automotive advertising*]
ALRM.........	Protection One [*NASDAQ symbol*] (TTSB)
ALRM.........	Protection One, Inc. [*NASDAQ symbol*] (SAG)
ALR Mal	African Law Reports, Malawi Series [*A publication*] (DLA)
ALR (Malawi Ser)...	African Law Reports, Malawi Series [*A publication*] (DLA)
ALRN.........	Altron, Inc. [*NASDAQ symbol*] (NQ)
ALRNS........	American Law Register, New Series [*A publication*] (ILCA)
ALROS........	American Laryngological, Rhinological, and Otological Society (EA)
ALRPG........	Army Long-Range Planning Guidance
ALRR.........	Ames Laboratory Research Reactor
ALRRI........	Airborne Long-Range RADAR Input (MUGU)
ALRS	Admiralty List of Radio Signals [*British*]
ALRS	Altitude Report Status (SAA)
ALRS	Arithmetic Logic Register Stack [*Computer science*] (MHDI)

ALR (Sierra L Ser)... African Law Reports, Sierra Leone Series [*A publication*] (DLA)
ALRSL .... African Law Reports, Sierra Leone Series [*A publication*] (DLA)
ALRT........... Advanced Light Rapid Transit
ALRT........... First Alert [*NASDAQ symbol*] (TTSB)
ALRT........... First Alert, Inc. [*NASDAQ symbol*] (SAG)
ALRTF.......... Army Long-Range Technological Forecast (AABC)
ALRTP .... Army Long-Range Training Plan (RDA)
ALRU .... Automated Line Record Update [*Telecommunications*] (TEL)
ALS............. Accumulator Left Shift (SAA)
ALS............. Acetolactate Synthase [*An enzyme*]
ALS............. Acquisition Law Specialist (AAGC)
ALS............. Active LASER Seeker (MCD)
ALS............. Acute Lateral Sclerosis [*Medicine*]
ALS............. ADA Language System (MCD)
ALS............. Advanced Landing System
ALS............. Advanced Launch System [*Rocketry*]
ALS............. Advanced Legal Software [*Computer science*] (HGAA)
ALS............. Advanced Library Systems, Inc. [*Information service or system*] (IID)
ALS............. Advanced Life Support [*System*]
ALS............. Advanced Light Source [*For Synchrotron radiation*] [*High-energy physics*]
ALS............. Advanced Limb Scanner (MCD)
ALS............. Advanced Logistics Spacecraft
ALS............. Advanced Logistic System (AFM)
ALS............. Advanced Low-Power Schottky (MCD)
ALS............. Advanced Lunar Studies
ALS............. Agricultural Land Service [*Later, ADAS*] [*British*]
ALS............. Air Alsie, AS [*Denmark ICAO designator*] (FAAC)
ALS............. Airborne LASER System
ALS............. Airborne Live Scanner
ALS............. Aircraft Landing System
ALS............. Airfield Lighting System
ALS............. Air Lock System (MCD)
ALS............. Air Logistics Service [*or System*] [*Military*]
ALS............. Alabama Supreme Court and State Law Library, Montgomery, AL [*OCLC symbol*] (OCLC)
ALS............. Alamosa [*Colorado*] [*Airport symbol*] (OAG)
ALS............. Alclare Resources [*Vancouver Stock Exchange symbol*]
ALS............. Aldolase [*An enzyme*]
ALS............. Alerting and Status (SAA)
ALS............. Alias [*Otherwise*] [*Latin*]
ALS............. Alishan [*Republic of China*] [*Seismograph station code, US Geological Survey*] (SEIS)
ALS............. Allegheny Ludlum [*NYSE symbol*] (TTSB)
ALS............. Allegheny Ludlum Corp. [*NYSE symbol*] (SPSG)
ALS............. Allegheny Ludlum Steel Company
ALS............. All-Language Services, Inc.
ALS............. All-Weather Landing System [*Also, AWLS*]
ALS............. Almond Leaf Scorch [*Plant pathology*]
ALS............. Alternate Landing Site [*NASA*] (NASA)
ALS............. Alternate Life Style
ALS............. [*The*] Alton & Southern Railway Co. [*AAR code*]
ALS............. American Lessing Society [*Later, LS*] (EA)
ALS............. American Library Society [*Defunct*]
ALS............. American Liszt Society (EA)
ALS............. American Literary Society [*Defunct*] (EA)
ALS............. American Lithotripsy Society (EA)
ALS............. American Littoral Society (EA)
ALS............. American Lumber Standards
ALS............. American Lunar Society (EA)
ALS............. American Luxembourg Society (EA)
ALS............. Ammonium Lauryl Sulfate [*Organic chemistry*]
ALS............. Ammunition Loading System (MCD)
ALS............. Amphibious Logistics Systems [*Navy*]
ALS............. Amyotrophic Lateral Sclerosis [*Medicine*]
ALS............. Angiotensin-Like Substance [*Biochemistry*] (MAE)
ALS............. Anterolateral Sclerosis [*Neurology*] (DAVI)
ALS............. Anticipated Life Span [*Statistics*] (DAVI)
ALS............. Anti-Collision Light System [*or Subsystem*] (MCD)
ALS............. Antilymphocyte [*or Antilympholytic*] Serum [*Immunology*]
ALS............. Application Layer Structure [*Telecommunications*] (OSI)
ALS............. Approach and Landing Simulator [*Aviation*]
ALS............. Approach Landing System [*Aviation*] (MCD)
ALS............. Approach Light System [*Aviation*]
ALS............. Arithmetic Logic Section [*Computer science*]
ALS............. Armenian Literary Society (EA)
ALS............. Arrowhead Library System [*Library network*]
AlS............. Asia Library Services, Auburn, NY [*Library symbol Library of Congress*] (LCLS)
ALS............. Associate of the Linnaean Society [*British*]
ALS............. Association of Legal Secretaries [*British*] (DBA)
ALS............. Associative Light Searcher (SAA)
ALS............. Associative List Selection
ALS............. Augmented Logistics Support (MCD)
ALS............. Australian LANDSAT [*Land Satellite*] Station
ALS............. Autograph Letter Signed [*Manuscript descriptions*]
als .... Autograph Letter Signed [*Manuscript description*] (ODBW)
ALS............. Automated Library System [*Foundation for Library Research, Inc.*] [*Information service or system*] (IID)
ALS............. Automated Light Survey
ALS............. Automated Liquid Sampler [*Instrumentation*]
ALS............. Automated Litigation Support [*Department of Justice*] (GFGA)
ALS............. Automated Loans System [*Library science*]
ALS............. Automatic Landing System
ALS............. Automatic Leveling Seat [*Automotive engineering*]
ALS............. Automatic Level Setting
ALS............. Automatic Lubrication System
ALS............. Autonomic Lability Score [*In ion detection*]
ALS............. Autonomous Listening Stations [*Instrumentation*]
ALS............. Auxiliary Lighter Ship (DNAB)
ALS............. Azimuth Laying Set (AABC)
a-ls-- .... Laos [*MARC geographic area code Library of Congress*] (LCCP)
ALSA........... Alberta Land Surveyors' Association (AC)
ALSA........... American Law Student Association [*Later, Law Student Division - American Bar Association*] (EA)
ALSA........... American Legal Studies Association (EA)
ALSA........... Amphibious Logistics Support Ashore [*Marine Corps*] (MCD)
ALSA........... Amyotrophic Lateral Sclerosis Association (EA)
ALSA........... Area Library Services Authority [*Indiana*]
ALSA........... Arkansas Livestock Show Association (SRA)
ALSA........... Astronaut Life Support Assembly [*NASA*]
ALSA........... Australasian Law Students Association
ALSA........... Four Rivers Area Library Services Authority [*Library network*]
ALSA 2 .... Area II Library Services Authority [*Library network*]
ALSA 6 .... Area VI Library Services Authority [*Library network*]
ALSAA.......... Americans (of Lebanese-Syrian Ancestry) for America (EA)
ALSAC .... Aiding Leukemia Stricken American Children [*Later, ALSAC - St. Jude Children's Research Hospital*] [*Fund-raising organization*]
ALSAC .... American Lebanese Syrian Association Charities (EA)
ALSAFECOM... All Safety Commands [*Air Force*] (AFM)
Alsager........ Alsager's Dictionary of Business Terms (DLA)
ALSAM......... Air-Launched Ship-Attack Missile
ALSAM......... Air-Launched Surface Attack Missile
ALSAML....... Ahvenanmaan Kokoomus; Alaendsk Samling [*Aland Coalition*] [*Finland*] (PPE)
ALSB........... Advanced Logistics Support Base [*Navy*]
ALSB........... Almond Leaf Scorch Bacterium [*Plant pathology*]
ALSC........... Alliance Semiconductor [*NASDAQ symbol*] (TTSB)
ALSC........... Alliance Semiconductor Corp. [*NASDAQ symbol*] (SAG)
ALSC........... Aluminum Linear Shaped Charge (PDAA)
ALSC........... American Lumber Standards Committee (EA)
ALSC........... Army Logistics Specialty Committee (MCD)
ALSC........... Association for Library Service to Children (EA)
ALSC........... Auxiliary Library Service Collections
ALSCA......... Australian Leather and Suede Clothing Association
ALSCC .... Apollo Lunar Surface Closeup Camera [*Apollo 11*] [*NASA*]
Al Sc CrL..... Alison's Principles of the Criminal Law of Scotland [*A publication*] (DLA)
ALSCI.......... Association of Lecturers in Scottish Central Institutions (AIE)
ALSCP .... Appalachian Land Stabilization and Conservation Program
ALSCS .... Admixture-Lathe-Cut + Single Composition Spherical [*Dental alloy*]
ALSD .... Alzheimer-Like Senile Dementia [*Medicine*] (DMAA)
ALSD .... Ames Life Sciences Directorate (DNAB)
ALSD .... Apollo Lunar Surface Drill [*NASA*]
ALSE........... Aircraft Life Support Equipment [*Military*] (DOMA)
ALSE........... Apollo Lunar Sounder Experiment [*NASA*]
ALSE........... Astronaut Life Support Equipment [*NASA*] (MCD)
ALSE........... Availability of Logistics Support Elements (MCD)
ALSE........... Aviation Life Support Equipment (AABC)
AL SEA FRON... Alaskan Sea Frontier [*Navy*]
AL Sec......... Air Liaison Section [*British and Canadian*] [*World War II*]
AL SEC......... Alaskan Sector
ALSEC......... All Sectors (FAAC)
AL SEG .... Al Segno [*At the Sign*] [*Music*]
AlSens......... Alcohol Sensors Intl. Ltd. [*Associated Press*] (SAG)
ALSEP.......... Apollo Lunar Surface Experiments Package [*NASA*]
Al Ser.......... Indian Law Reports, Allahabad Series [*A publication*] (DLA)
ALSF........... Abundant Life Seed Foundation (EA)
ALSF........... Approach Lighting System with Sequenced Flashers [*Aviation*]
ALSF........... Approach Lighting System With Sequenced Flashing Lights [*FAA*] (TAG)
ALSFA.......... Asa Lafitte Stark Family Association [*Defunct*] (EA)
ALSF-I .... Approach Light System with Sequenced Flashing Lights in ILS CAT-I Configuration [*FAA*] (TAG)
ALSF-II .... Approach Light System with Sequenced Flashing Lights in ILS CAT-II Modification [*FAA*] (TAG)
ALSI............ Aluminum Silicon [*An alloy*]
ALSI............ Analogue Large Scale Integration (NITA)
ALSI............ Arkansas League of Savings Institutions (SRA)
ALSIP.......... Approach Lighting System Improvement Program [*FAA*] (TAG)
ALSISS .... Association of Learned Societies in Social Sciences [*British*] (DBA)
AlskAir......... Alaska Air Group, Inc. [*Associated Press*] (SAG)
AlskAplo ...... Alaska Apollo Gold Mines [*Associated Press*] (SAG)
ALSL........... Assembly Line Shortages Log
ALSL........... Assembly List Shortage Log (AAG)
ALSM.......... Air-Launched Strategic Missile
ALSM.......... Association of Litigation Support Managers [*Australia*]
ALS/N .... Ada Language System/Navy (SSD)
ALSNRF .... ALS [*Amyotrophic Lateral Sclerosis*] and Neuromuscular Research Foundation (EA)
AlSns.......... Alcohol Sensors Intl. Ltd. [*Associated Press*] (SAG)
ALS-NSDI .... Actual Loss Sustained - No Specified Daily Indemnity [*Insurance*]
ALSO .... Auxiliary Library Service Organization
ALSOR .... Air Launch Sounding Rocket
ALSP........... Adkins Life Skills Program (EDAC)
ALSP........... Aggregate Level Simulation Protocol
ALSP........... Army Logistics Study Program
ALSP........... Atmosphere and Land Surface Processes (OSRA)
ALSP........... Atmosphere and Land Surface Processes (USDC)

ALSPAC .... Advanced Logistics System Project Advisory Committee [*Terminated, 1977*] [*DoD*] (EGAO)
ALS/P-D .... Amyotrophic Lateral Sclerosis/Parkinsonism-Dementia [*Medicine*]
ALSPEC ...... Automated LASER Seeker Performance Evaluation System (MHDI)
ALSPES ...... Automated LASER Seeker Performance Evaluation System (MCD)
ALSPT .... Associateship of the London School of Polymer Technology [*British*] (DBQ)
ALSR .... Automated Logistics Systems Review (MCD)
ALSRC .... Apollo Lunar Sample Return Container [*NASA*]
ALSS .... Acoustic Lens SONAR System (MCD)
ALSS .... Adult Learning Satellite Service [*Public Broadcasting Service*] [*Telecommunications service*] (TSSD)
ALSS .... Advanced LASER System Study
ALSS .... Advanced Life Support System (MCD)
ALSS .... Advanced Location Strike System [*Formerly, Airborne Location and Strike System*] [*Air Force*]
ALSS .... Airborne Location and Strike System (MCD)
ALSS .... Aircrew Life Support System (CAAL)
ALSS .... Airline System Simulator
ALSS .... Airlock Support System [*or Subsystem*] [*NASA*] (MCD)
ALSS .... Apollo Logistic Support System [*NASA*]
ALSS .... Association of Lutheran Secondary Schools (EA)
ALSS .... Aviation Life Support Systems (MCD)
ALSSA .... Air Line Stewards and Stewardesses Association (EA)
ALSSF .... Adult Literacy Support Services Fund (AIE)
ALSS/LESA .. Apollo Logistic Support System / Lunar Explorations System for Apollo [*NASA*] (SAA)
ALSSOA ...... Amyotrophic Lateral Sclerosis Society of America (EA)
ALSSOC ...... Amyotrophic Lateral Sclerosis Society of Canada
ALST .... Adolescent Language Screening Test [*Speech development test*]
ALST .... Alaska Standard Time
ALST .... Altostratus [*Also, AS*] [*Meteorology*]
ALSTA .... All Stations (KSC)
ALSTACON .. All Stations, Continental United States (MUGU)
ALSTAR .... Altitude Layer Surveillance Terminal Area RADAR
ALSTAR .... Automated Logistics System for Tracking, Analysis, and Reporting
ALSTG .... Altimeter Setting (FAAC)
ALSU .... Autonomous Line Scanning Unit (MCD)
ALSV .... Air-Launched Sortie Vehicle [*Aviation*] (AIA)
ALSWA .... Aboriginal Legal Service of Western Australia
ALT .... Above Local Terrain (MCD)
ALT .... Accelerated Life Testing
ALT .... Acquisition Lead Time
ALT .... Administrative Lead Time
ALT .... Aer Lingus Teoranta [*Ireland*]
ALT .... Agricultural Laboratory Technology
ALT .... Airborne LASER Tracker [*System*]
ALT .... Alabama Trucking Association, Montgomery AL [*STAC*]
ALT .... Alanine Aminotransferase [*Also, AAT, ALAT, GPT*] [*An enzyme*]
ALT .... Alanine Transaminase [*Biochemistry*] (DAVI)
ALT .... Albatrosz Ltd. [*Hungary ICAO designator*] (FAAC)
ALT .... Alert Centre, Inc. [*AMEX symbol*] (SAG)
ALT .... All Leisure Aviation Ltd. [*British*] [*FAA designator*] (FAAC)
ALT .... Altar Gold & Resources [*Vancouver Stock Exchange symbol*]
ALT .... Alteration
ALT .... Altered (DCTA)
ALT .... Altering [*FBI standardized term*]
Alt .... Alternaria [*A fungus*]
ALT .... Alternate
alt .... Alternate (VRA)
alt .... Alternating [*Polymer*] [*Organic chemistry*]
Alt .... Alternating Light [*Navigation signal*]
ALT .... Alternative (ROG)
ALT .... Alternative Lengthening of Telomeres [*Genetics*]
ALT .... Alternative Local Telephone Company (ECON)
ALT .... Alternator (KSC)
ALT .... Altesse [*Highness*] [*French*]
ALT .... Altimeter (NG)
ALT .... Altintas [*Turkey*] [*Seismograph station code, US Geological Survey*] (SEIS)
ALT .... Altitude (AFM)
ALT .... Alto
ALT .... Altoona [*Pennsylvania*]
ALT .... Altoona-Johnstown [*Diocesan abbreviation*] [*Pennsylvania*] (TOCD)
ALT .... Altus, OK [*Location identifier FAA*] (FAAL)
ALT .... Amber Light (IAA)
ALT .... American Law Times [*A publication*] (DLA)
ALT .... Approach and Landing Test [*Aviation*] (MCD)
ALT .... Argon LASER Trabeculoplasty [*Ophthalmology*] (DAVI)
ALT .... Assistant Language Teacher
ALT .... [*The*] Association of Law Teachers [*British*]
ALT .... Autolymphocyte Therapy [*Oncology*]
ALT .... Automatic Layshaft Transmission [*Automotive engineering*]
ALT .... Automatic Line Testing [*Telecommunications*] (TEL)
ALT .... Automotive Layshaft Transmission
ALT .... Livingston University, Livingston, AL [*Library symbol Library of Congress*] (LCLS)
ALT .... RADAR Altimeter (TEL)
ALTA .... Adventist Language Teachers Association [*Defunct*] (EA)
ALTA .... Airline Traffic Association
ALTA .... Alberta [*Canadian province*]
Alta .... Alberta [*Canada*] (DD)
ALTA .... Alberta Library Trustees' Association (AC)
ALTA .... Alta Gold Co. [*NASDAQ symbol*] (NQ)
ALTA .... American Land Title Association (EA)

ALTA .... American Library Trustee Association (EA)
ALTA .... American Literary Translators Association (EA)
ALTA .... Association of Local Transport Airlines [*Defunct*] (EA)
ALTA .... Australian Logic Teachers' Association
ALTA .... Automatic Line Test and Administrative System [*Taiwan International Standard Electronics Ltd., a subsidiary of ITT*] (NITA)
ALTAC .... Algebraic Translator and Compiler [*Computer science*] (MCD)
Alta Gaz ..... Alberta Gazette [*A publication*] (DLA)
AltaGld .... Alta Gold Co. [*Associated Press*] (SAG)
ALTAIR .... ARPA [*Advanced Research Projects Agency*] Long-Range Tracking and Instrument RADAR
ALTAIR .... Automatic Logical Translation and Information Retrieval [*Computer science*] (DIT)
Alta L .... Alberta Law [*A publication*] (DLA)
Alta LQ .... Alberta Law Quarterly [*A publication*] (DLA)
ALTAN .... Alternate Alerting Network [*Air Force*]
ALT & S ...... [*The*] Alton & Southern Railway Co.
ALTAPE .... Automatic Line Tracer and Programming Equipment
ALTARE .... Automatic Logic Testing and Recording Equipment
Alta Rev Stat .. Alberta Revised Statutes [*Canada*] [*A publication*] (DLA)
ALTARF .... All London Teachers Against Racism and Fascism [*British*] (AIE)
ALTA SOSC .. ALTA [*American Library Trustee Association*] Specialized Outreach Services Committee [*American Library Association*]
ALT/AST ...... Ratio of Serum Alanine Aminotransferase to Serum Aspartate Aminotransferase [*Medicine*] (MEDA)
Alta Stat ..... Alberta Statutes [*Canada*] [*A publication*] (DLA)
ALTB .... Acute Laryngotracheobronchitis [*Virus*]
ALT Bankr .... American Law Times, Bankruptcy Reports [*A publication*] (DLA)
ALTBR .... Law Times Bankruptcy Reports [*United States*] [*A publication*] (DLA)
ALTC .... Alantec Corp. [*NASDAQ symbol*] (SAG)
ALTCGC ...... Arizona Long Term Care Gerontology Center [*University of Arizona*] [*Research center*] (RCD)
ALTCOM ...... Alternate Command [*or Commander*] [*Navy*] (NVT)
ALTCOM ...... Alternate Command, Atlantic Fleet (MCD)
ALTCOMCEN ... Alternate Command Center [*Navy*] (NVT)
ALTCOMLANT ... Alternate Commander, Atlantic [*Navy*] (NVT)
ALTCOMLANTFLT ... Alternate Command, Atlantic Fleet
ALTCOMPAC ... Alternate Commander, Pacific [*Navy*] (NVT)
Alt County Gov't ... Alternative County Government [*A publication*] (DLA)
Alt Criminol J .. Alternative Criminology Journal [*A publication*]
ALTD .... Alternate Postal Delivery [*NASDAQ symbol*] (TTSB)
ALTD .... Alternate Postal Delivery, Inc. [*NASDAQ symbol*] (SAG)
ALTD .... Australian Land Transport Development Program
ALT DIEB ..... Alternis Diebus [*Every Other Day*] [*Pharmacy*]
ALTDS .... Apollo Launch Trajectory Data System [*NASA*] (KSC)
ALTDS .... Army LASER Target Designator System
ALTE .... Altitude Error
ALTE .... Altitude Transmitting Equipment [*FAA*] (MSA)
ALTE .... Apparent Life-Threatening Episode [*Medicine*]
ALTech .... Applied Language Technology
ALTEE .... Acetyl-L-Tyrosine Ethyl Ester [*Biochemistry*] (MAE)
Alt Eg .... Alter Ego [*My Other Self*] [*Latin*]
ALTEL .... Artillery-Launched Television System (PDAA)
ALTEL .... Association of Long Distance Telephone Companies (EA)
Al Tel Ca ..... Allen's Telegraph Cases [*A publication*] (DLA)
ALTEN .... Articulated Linear Thrust Engine [*Submarine technology*]
Alteon .... Alteon, Inc. [*Associated Press*] (SAG)
ALTER .... Alteration (ROG)
ALTER .... Alternate
Altera .... Altera Corp. [*Associated Press*] (SAG)
ALTERN HOR ... Alternis Horis [*Every Other Hour*] [*Pharmacy*]
ALTERON ..... Alteration
ALTF .... Airlift Task Force [*Air Force*] (AFM)
ALTFFL .... Alternating Fixed and Flashing [*Lights*]
ALTFGFL ...... Alternating, Fixed, and Group-Flashing [*Lights*] (DNAB)
ALTFGPGL ... Alternating Fixed and Group Flashing [*Lights*]
ALTFL .... Alternating Flashing [*Lights*]
ALTG .... Association of Little Theatre Groups [*Australia*]
ALTGA .... Ark-La-Tex Genealogical Association (EA)
ALTGPOCC ... Alternating Group Occulting [*Lights*]
ALTH .... Althaea [*Rose of Sharon*] [*Pharmacology*] (ROG)
ALTH .... Alumina Trihydrate [*Inorganic chemistry*]
ALT HOLD .... Altitude Hold Mode (GAVI)
ALT HOR ..... Alternis Horis [*Every Other Hour*] [*Pharmacy*]
ALTHQ .... Alternate Headquarters [*Military*] (AABC)
ALTID .... Alteration Identification
Alt Id .... Alter Idem [*Another Self*] [*Latin*]
ALTIHP .... Avionics Laboratory Technical Information Handling Profile
ALTINSAR ... Alternate Instruction Address Register [*Computer science*] (MHDI)
ALT INST ..... Alteration of Instruments [*Legal term*] (DLA)
AL/TL .... Antennule Length to Total Body Length Ratio [*of Crustacea*]
ALTLIB .... Alternate Library [*Computer program*] [*NASA*]
AltLivng ...... Alternative Living Services [*Associated Press*] (SAG)
ALTM .... Altimeter (KSC)
ALTN .... Alteon, Inc. [*NASDAQ symbol*] (SPSG)
ALTN .... Alteration [*Technical drawings*] (DAC)
ALTN .... Alternate (AFM)
ALTN .... Alternative (IEEE)
alt noc .... Alternis Nocibus [*Every Other Night*] [*Pharmacy*] (BARN)
ALT NOCT ... Alternis Nocte [*Every Other Night*] [*Pharmacy*]
ALTNR .... Alternator
ALTNTR .... Alternator (MSA)
ALTNV .... Alternative (MSA)
ALTOCC ...... Alternating Occulting [*Lights*]
ALTOGR ...... Altogether (ROG)

AltOrAT............ Alter Orient und Altes Testament [*Kevelaer/Neukirchen*] [*A publication*] (BJA)
AltosHrn .... Altos Hornos de Mexico SA de CV [*Associated Press*] (SAG)
ALTP............ Airline Transport Pilot's Licence [*British*] (AIA)
ALTP............ American Legion Transportation Post
ALTP............ Automatic Linear Temperature Programmer
altpc .... Altarpiece (VRA)
AltPosD............ Alternate Postal Delivery, Inc. [*Associated Press*] (SAG)
ALT PROG ... Alternate Program (DNAB)
Alt Pr R .... Alternative Press Review [*A publication*] (BRI)
ALTPT.......... Alternate Airport (FAAC)
ALTR............ Alter
ALTR............ Altera Corp. [*NASDAQ symbol*] (NQ)
ALTR............ Alteration (AABC)
ALTR............ Alternate (KSC)
ALTR............ Alternator [*Automotive engineering*]
ALTR............ American Law Times Reports [*A publication*] (DLA)
ALTR............ Approach and Landing Test Requirement [*NASA*] (NASA)
ALTRA............ Association of Licensed Trade Relief Agencies [*British*] (DBA)
ALTRAN......... Algebraic Translator [*Programming language*] [*1969*]
ALTRAN......... Assembly Language Translator [*Xerox Corp.*]
ALTRD............ Altered (MSA)
ALTREC.......... Automatic Life Testing and Recording of Electronic Components [*Canada*]
AltResc......... Alternative Resources Corp. [*Associated Press*] (SAG)
Altris............ Altris Software, Inc. [*Associated Press*] (SAG)
ALTRN .... Alteration
ALTRN .... Alteration (MSA)
ALTRNS .... American Law Times Reports, New Series [*United States*] [*A publication*] (DLA)
ALTRNTR...... Alternator
ALTRNTV ..... Alternative
ALTRON .... Advanced (ROG)
Altron......... Altron, Inc. [*Associated Press*] (SAG)
ALTRV .... Altitude Reservation [*Air Force*] (AFM)
ALTS............ Acute Lumbar Traumatic Sprain (HGAA)
ALTS............ Advanced Lunar Transportation Systems
ALTS............ Aided LASER Tracking System (RDA)
ALTS............ Alterations (ROG)
ALTS............ Altris Software, Inc. [*NASDAQ symbol*] (SAG)
ALTS............ Amerikos Lietuviu Tautine Sajunga [*National Lithuanian Society of America*] (EA)
ALTS............ Analog Line Termination Subsystem [*Telecommunications*] (TEL)
ALTS............ Automated Land Titles System (ADA)
ALTS............ Automated Library Technical Services [*Program*] [*Los Angeles Public Library*]
ALTS............ Automatic LASER Test Set [*Hughes Aircraft Co.*]
ALTS............ Automatic Line Test Set [*Telecommunications*] (TEL)
ALTTD.......... Altitude
ALTU............ Adder, Logical, and Transfer Unit [*Computer*]
ALTU............ Association of Liberal Trade Unionists [*British*] (DI)
ALU............ Adult Literacy Unit [*British*]
ALU............ Advanced Levitation Unit [*Materials processing*]
ALU............ Advanced Logical Utility (PDAA)
ALU............ Air-Launched Unit
alu .... Alabama [*MARC country of publication code Library of Congress*] (LCCP)
ALU............ Allou Health&Beauty'A' [*AMEX symbol*] (TTSB)
ALU............ Allou Health & Beauty Care, Inc. [*AMEX symbol*] (SPSG)
ALU............ Alpine Luft-Transport AB [*Switzerland ICAO designator*] (FAAC)
ALU............ Alula [*Somalia*] [*Airport symbol*] (OAG)
ALU............ Aluminium [*British*] (ADA)
ALU............ Alushta [*Former USSR Seismograph station code, US Geological Survey Closed*] (SEIS)
ALU............ Amble Resources Ltd. [*Vancouver Stock Exchange symbol*]
ALU............ Annual Life Unit (MCD)
ALU............ Arab Lawyers Union [*See also UAA*] [*Cairo, Egypt*] (EAIO)
ALU............ Arithmetic Logic Unit [*Computer science*]
ALU............ Association for the Liberation of Ukraine [*Defunct*] (EA)
ALU............ Association of Life Underwriters of South Dakota (SRA)
ALU............ Asynchronous Line Unit [*Telecommunications*]
ALU............ University of Lethbridge, Alberta [*Library symbol National Library of Canada*] (NLC)
ALU............ University of Lethbridge Library [*UTLAS symbol*]
ALUCARD .... Aircraft Loss, Utilization, Combat, and Repair Damage (MCD)
ALUE............ Admissible Linear Unbiased Estimator [*Statistics*]
ALUG .... Department of Geography, University of Lethbridge, Alberta [*Library symbol National Library of Canada*] (NLC)
ALUIA .... Automated Living User Intervention Anarchy [*Computer science*]
ALUM............ Aluminum [*Chemical symbol is Al*]
alum............ Aluminum (VRA)
ALUM.......... Alumnus (ROG)
ALUM.......... Underwood McLellan Ltd., Lethbridge, Alberta [*Library symbol National Library of Canada*] (NLC)
Alumax .... Alumax, Inc. [*Associated Press*] (SAG)
ALUMINAUT... Aluminium Submarine for Deep-Ocean Research [*Navy symbol British*]
ALUMN .... Aluminum [*Chemical symbol is Al*]
ALUMN .... Aluminum
Alum Yalen... Alumni Yalensia [*Alumni of Yale College*] [*Latin*]
ALURE .... Alternative Land Uses and the Rural Economy [*Ministry of Agriculture*] [*British*]
ALUS .... Adult Language Use Survey (AIE)
ALUSLO .... American Legation, United States Naval Liaison Officer
ALUSNA........ American Legation, United States Naval Attache (MUGU)

ALUSNLO..... American Legation, United States Naval Liaison Officer (MCD)
ALUSNOB .... American Legation, United States Naval Observer
ALUT........... Aluta [*Leather*] [*Pharmacy*] (ROG)
ALUT........... Associateship of Loughborough University of Technology [*British*] (DBQ)
ALUTN .... Aleutian (FAAC)
ALUTS .... Aleutian Islands
ALV .... Abelson Leukemia Virus
ALV .... Acadia Mineral Ventures Ltd. [*Toronto Stock Exchange symbol*]
ALV .... Adeno-Like Virus [*Medicine*] (DMAA)
ALV .... Air-Launched Vehicle (AFM)
ALV .... Alarm Valve (DAC)
ALV .... Alsavia, Societe [*France ICAO designator*] (FAAC)
alv .... Alveolar [*Anatomy*]
ALV .... Alvus [*Stomach*] [*Medicine*] (ROG)
ALV .... Anthology of Light Verse [*A publication*]
ALV .... Autonomous Land Vehicle [*Military*] (RDA)
ALV .... Avian Leukosis Virus
ALV .... Gaylord, MI [*Location identifier FAA*] (FAAL)
ALV ADST .... Alvo Adstricta [*When the Bowels Are Constipated*] [*Pharmacy*]
Alv Adstrict... Alvo Adstricta [*When the Bowels Are Constipated*] [*Pharmacy*]
ALV DEJECT.. Alvi Dejectiones [*Discharge from the Bowels*] [*Pharmacy*]
ALVE........... Australian Leave and Holidays Practice Manual [*A publication*]
Alves .... Dampier and Maxwell's British Guiana Reports [*A publication*] (DLA)
ALVF........... Acute Left Ventricular Failure [*Cardiology*] (DMAA)
ALVIN .... Alex [*Aarons*] and Vinton [*Freedley*] [*Theatrical producers of the 1920's and 1930's, after whom the Alvin Theatre in New York City was named*]
ALVIN .... Antenna Lobe for Variable Ionospheric Nimbus (IEEE)
ALVINN......... Autonomous Land Vehicle in a Neural Network [*Military*]
ALVIS.......... Atomic Vapor LASER Isotope Separation (NUCP)
ALVM.......... Alveolar Mucosa [*Medicine*] (DMAA)
ALVRJ.......... Advanced Low-Volume Ramjet
ALVRJ.......... Air-Launched Low-Volume Ramjet
Alvx .... Alveolectomy [*Dentistry and maxillofacial surgery*] (DAVI)
ALVX .... Alveolectomy [*Medicine*] (DMAA)
ALW .... Air-Launched Weapon
ALW .... Alas Nacionales SA [*Dominican Republic*] [*ICAO designator*] (FAAC)
ALW .... Alawas Gold Corp. [*Vancouver Stock Exchange symbol*]
ALW .... Allowance (AFM)
ALW .... Allowance Race [*Horse racing*]
ALW........... Allwaste, Inc. [*NYSE symbol*] (SAG)
ALW........... Arch-Loop-Whorl [*Basis of Galton's System of Fingerprint Classifications*]
ALW .... Association of Lithuanian Workers (EA)
ALW........... Walla Walla [*Washington*] [*Airport symbol*] (OAG)
ALWF........... Actual Wind Factor [*NWS*] (FAAC)
ALWL .... Army Limited War Laboratory
ALWLA......... American Lithuanian Workers Literary Association (EA)
ALWMI......... Anterolateral Wall Myocardial Infarction [*Cardiology*]
ALWOS......... Automated Low-Cost Weather Observation System (MCD)
ALWS......... Advanced Lightweight SONAR [*Military*]
ALWS......... Australian Lutheran World Service
ALWT......... Advanced Lightweight Torpedo [*Navy*]
ALX........... Albany Resources [*Vancouver Stock Exchange symbol*]
ALX........... Alexander Bay [*New York*] [*Seismograph station code, US Geological Survey*] (SEIS)
ALX........... Alexander City, AL [*Location identifier FAA*] (FAAL)
ALX........... Alexander's, Inc. [*NYSE symbol*] (SPSG)
ALX........... Alexandria [*Diocesan abbreviation*] [*Louisiana*] (TOCD)
ALX........... Alitaxi SRL [*Italy ICAO designator*] (FAAC)
ALXN........... Alexion Pharmaceuticals [*NASDAQ symbol*] (TTSB)
ALXN........... Alexion Pharmaceuticals, Inc. [*NASDAQ symbol*] (SAG)
ALY........... Alexandria [*Egypt*] [*Airport symbol*] (OAG)
ALY........... Alley (MCD)
ALY........... Alley
ALY........... Allied Cellular [*Vancouver Stock Exchange symbol*]
ALY........... Alloy
aly........... Alloy (VRA)
ALY........... Alyeska Air Service [*ICAO designator*] (FAAC)
ALYA........... Army Laboratory of the Year Award (RDA)
A-LYM .... Atypical Lymphocyte [*Hematology*] (DAVI)
ALYN........... Alyn Corp. [*NASDAQ symbol*] (SAG)
AlynCp........ Alyn Corp. [*Associated Press*] (SAG)
ALZ........... Alitak [*Alaska*] [*Airport symbol*] (OAG)
ALZ........... Alta Flights Ltd. [*Canada ICAO designator*] (FAAC)
Alz........... Alzamento [*Raising, Lifting*] [*Music*]
ALZ........... Assault Landing Zone (AFM)
ALZ........... Lazy Bay, AK [*Location identifier FAA*] (FAAL)
ALZA........... ALZA Corp. [*Associated Press*] (SAG)
ALZDA........ Australian Lead/Zinc Development Association
AM........... Above Mentioned
AM........... Abrasive Machining (IAA)
AM........... Academy of Management [*Mississippi State, MS*] (EA)
AM........... Access Manager [*Computer science*]
AM........... Access Method [*Computer science*]
AM........... Accounts Maintenance [*IRS*]
AM........... Acetoxymethyl Ester
AM........... Acoustic-Magnetic (NVT)
AM........... Acquisition Manager
AM........... Action Monegasque [*Monegasque Action*] [*Political party*] (PPE)
A-M........... Active Mariner Program [*Military*] (DNAB)
AM........... Active Market [*Investment term*]
AM........... Active Monitor [*Telecommunications*]
AM........... Actomyosin [*Biochemistry*]

AM	Actual Miss [*Distance*]
AM	Actuator Mechanism (NASA)
AM	Adaptive Multiplexer (CAAL)
AM	Address Mark [*Microprocessors*]
AM	Address Mode [*Computer science*]
AM	Address Modifier
AM	Addressograph Multigraph [*Later, AM International*] (DGA)
AM	Administration and Management Operations [*Kennedy Space Center*] [*NASA*] (NASA)
AM	Administrative Manual
AM	Administrative Module [*AT&T*] (ACRL)
AM	Adrenal Medulla [*Anatomy*]
AM	Advancement of Management (SAA)
AM	Aeromedical Monitor (SAA)
AM	Aeromexico [*Airline*] (DS)
AM	Aeronautical Radionavigation Mobile Station [*ITU designation*]
AM	Aeronaves de Mexico SA [*Mexico ICAO designator*] (ICDA)
AM	Aerospace Medicine (MCD)
AM	After Market [*Investment term*]
AM	Agricultural Marketing
AM	Agricultural Missions (EA)
AM	Aircooled Motor
AM	Airlock Module [*NASA*]
AM	Airmail
AM	Air Marshal [*British*]
AM	Air Mass [*Solar energy research*]
AM	Air Mattress [*Medicine*]
AM	Air Mechanician
AM	Air Medal [*Military decoration*]
AM	Air Ministry [*British*]
AM	Air Mobile
AM	Air Movements (SAA)
Am	Alabamine [*Chemical element*] (BARN)
AM	Alberta Medal [*Canada*] (DD)
AM	Albert Medal [*British*]
AM	Alert Message (CINC)
AM	Algonquin Mercantile Corp. [*Toronto Stock Exchange symbol*]
AM	Alice Meynell [*British poet, 1847-1922*]
AM	Alpes Maritimes [*French*]
AM	Alpha Meter (MCD)
AM	Alternaria mali [*A toxin-producing fungus*]
AM	Alternate Mode (CAAL)
AM	Aluminum Matting [*Military*]
AM	Alveolar Macrophage [*Hematology*]
AM	Amacrine Cell [*of the retina*] [*Optics*]
AM	Amalgam [*Dentistry*]
AM	Amatol [*Materials*]
AM	Ambassadors of Mary (EA)
AM	Amber
AM	Ambient (KSC)
AM	Amendment
AM	America (ROG)
Am	America [*A publication*] (BRI)
AM	American
AM	American Motors Corp.
Am	Americium [*Chemical element*]
AM	Amethopterin [*Methotrexate*] [*Also, A, M, MTX*] [*Antineoplastic drug*] (AAMN)
AM	Ametropia [*Ophthalmology*]
AM	Aminophylline [*A drug*]
AM	AM International [*AMEX symbol*] (TTSB)
AM	AM International, Inc. [*Formerly, Addressograph-Multigraph Corp.*] [*AMEX symbol*] (SPSG)
AM	Ammeter
AM	Ammunition (ADA)
Am	Amnion (DMAA)
Am	Amores [*of Ovid*] [*Classical studies*] (OCD)
AM	Amorphous Material [*Agronomy*]
Am	Amos [*Old Testament book*]
AM	Amperemeter (MAE)
AM	Ampere Minute (IAA)
A/M	Ampere per Meter [*Unit of magnetic field strength*]
AM	Ampicillin [*Also, A, AMP*] [*Antibacterial compound*]
AM	Amplifier [*JETDS nomenclature*] [*Military*] (CET)
AM	Amplitude Modulation [*Electronics*]
AM	Amplitude Modulator (IDOE)
AM	Ampoule
Am	Amyl [*Organic chemistry*]
AM	Analog Module [*Telecommunications*] (TEL)
AM	Analog Monolithic [*Electronics*] (OA)
AM	Ananda Marga (EA)
AM	Ancient Monuments Act [*Town planning*] [*British*]
AM	Anderson Model [*Physics*]
AM	Angle, Meter (DAVI)
AM	Angular Momentum
AM	Anno Mundi [*In the Year of the World*] [*Since 4004 BC*] [*Latin*] (GPO)
AM	Annus Mirabilis [*The Wonderful Year (1666)*] [*Latin*] (GPO)
AM	Anovular Menstruation
AM	Ante Meridiem [*Before Noon*] [*Latin*] (GPO)
AM	Antenna Management (NASA)
AM	Anterior-Median [*Ophthalmology*]
AM	Anterior Mitochondrion [*Cytology*]
AM	Anterior Mitral Leaflet [*Cardiology*]
AM	Anteromeatal [*Anatomy*] (DAVI)

AM	Antibodies to Cardiac Myosin [*Immunology*] (DAVI)
AM	Antimateriel [*Munitions*]
AM	Apostolatus Maris [*Apostleship of the Sea - AOS*] (EA)
AM	Appalachian Mountains
AM	Applications Management [*Computer science*]
AM	Approved Market [*Business term*]
AM	Archipelago Mundi [*An international association*] (EA)
AM	Archives des Murasu [*A publication*] (BJA)
AM	Arctic Missions [*Later, IM*] (EA)
AM	Area Multiplexer (CAAL)
AM	Arithmetic Mean [*Statistics*] (DCTA)
AM	Armillaria mellea [*A fungus*]
AM	Arms Material (AABC)
AM	Arms Memorandum
AM	Army Manual
AM	Arousal Mechanism [*Medicine*]
AM	Art and Mechanical [*Graphic arts*] (WDMC)
AM	Artium Magister [*Master of Arts*]
AM	Asamblea Majorera [*Spain Political party*] (EY)
AM	Aseptic Meningitis [*Medicine*]
AM	Assignment Memorandum [*Army*] (AABC)
A/M	Assignment of Mortgage [*Business term*] (EMRF)
AM	Assistant Manager
AM	Associate Member
AM	Association of Management (EA)
AM	Associative Memory [*Computer science*]
AM	Assumed Mean
AM	Astigmatism, Myopic [*Also, AsM*] [*Ophthalmology*]
AM	Asynchronous MODEM
AM	Atomic Migration
AM	Atrial Myxoma [*Medicine*] (DAVI)
A-M	Austin-Moore [*Prosthesis*] [*Medicine*]
AM	Australian Ministry [*A publication*] (APTA)
AM	Automated Mapping [*Cartography*]
A/M	Automatic/Manual (MDG)
AM	Automatic Monitoring (CET)
AM	Automedica Corp. [*An association Defunct*] (EA)
AM	Auxiliary Marker [*Telecommunications*] (TEL)
AM	Auxiliary Memory
AM	Auxiliary Minesweeper [*NATO*]
AM	Ave Maria
AM	Aviamilano [*Construzioni Aeronautiche SpA*] [*Italy ICAO aircraft manufacturer identifier*] (ICAO)
AM	Aviation Medicine
A/M	Aviation Medicine [*Medical officer designation*] [*British*]
AM	Aviation Metalsmith
AM	Aviation Structural Mechanic [*Navy rating*]
AM	Awaiting Maintenance
AM	Award of Merit [*Royal Horticultural Society*] [*British*]
AM	Axiomesial [*Dentistry*]
AM	Magrath Public Library, Alberta [*Library symbol National Library of Canada*] (NLC)
am----	Malaya [*MARC geographic area code Library of Congress*] (LCCP)
AM	Master of Arts (NADA)
AM	Mine Countermeasure Tender [*Navy symbol*]
AM	Mistress of Arts
AM	Montgomery Public Library, Montgomery, AL [*Library symbol Library of Congress*] (LCLS)
AM	Yaw Analysis Methodology
AM1	Aviation Structural Mechanic, First Class [*Navy rating*]
AM2	Air Mail Route Number 2
A/M²	Amperes per Square Meter
AM2	Aviation Structural Mechanic, Second Class [*Navy rating*]
AM3	Aviation Structural Mechanic, Third Class [*Navy rating*]
AMA	Abstaining Motorists' Association (EA)
AMA	Academy of Model Aeronautics (EA)
AMA	Accessory Meningeal Artery [*Anatomy*]
AMA	Accumulator Makers' Association [*British*] (BI)
AMA	Acoustical Materials Association [*Later, ABPA*] (EA)
AMA	Actual Mechanical Advantage [*Physics*]
AMA	Adaptive Multifunction Antenna (MCD)
AMA	Adhesives Manufacturers Association (EA)
AMA	Advanced Medical, Inc. [*AMEX symbol*] (SPSG)
AMA	Advanced Minuteman Accelerometer
AMA	Aerial Manufacturers Association [*British*] (DBA)
AMA	Aerospace Medical Association (MCD)
AMA	Affirmative Marketing Agreement [*Business term*] (EMRF)
AMA	Against Medical Advice
AMA	Agricultural Manufacturers' Association [*Australia*]
AMA	Agricultural Marketing Administration [*World War II*]
AMA	Ahmadiyya Muslim Association (EAIO)
AMA	Aircraft Manufacturers Association [*Superseded by MAA*] (EA)
AMA	Airhead Maintenance Area [*Military British*]
AMA	Air Materiel Area [*Later, Air Logistics Centers*] [*Air Force*]
AMA	Alaska Miners Association (SRA)
AMA	Alternative Medical Association (EA)
Ama	Amadeo [*Record label*] [*Austria, etc.*]
AMA	Amalgamated Mining [*Vancouver Stock Exchange symbol*]
AMA	Amarillo [*Texas*] [*Airport symbol*] (OAG)
AMA	Amateur Martial Association [*British*] (DBA)
AMA	Amateur Music Association [*British*] (DBA)
AMA	Amatignak Island [*Alaska*] [*Seismograph station code, US Geological Survey Closed*] (SEIS)
AMA	Ambulance Manufacturers Association [*Later, TBEA*] (EA)
AMA	American Machinery Association

AMA............	American Maltese Association (EA)
AMA............	American Management Association [*New York, NY*] (EA)
AMA............	American Maritain Association (EA)
AMA............	American Maritime Association (EA)
AMA............	American Marketing Association [*Chicago, IL*] (EA)
AMA............	American Matthay Association (EA)
AMA............	American McAll Association (EA)
AMA............	American Mead Association [*Inactive*] (EA)
AMA............	American Medical Association (EA)
AMA............	American Medical Association, Division of Library and Archival Services, Chicago, IL [*OCLC symbol*] (OCLC)
AMA............	American Metaphysical Association (EA)
AMA............	American Military Association
AMA............	American Ministerial Association (EA)
AMA............	American Missionary Association
AMA............	American Mobilehome Association (EA)
AMA............	American Monument Association (EA)
AMA............	American Motel Association (EA)
AMA............	American Motivational Association (EA)
AMA............	American Motorcyclist Association (EA)
AMA............	American Mule Association (EA)
AMA............	American Municipal Association [*Later, NLC*] (EA)
AMA............	American Mustang Association (EA)
AMA............	American Mutual Alliance [*Insurance association*] [*Later, Alliance of American Insurers*]
AMA............	Aminomalonic Acid [*Organic chemistry*]
AMA............	Aminomethyl Anthracene [*Organic chemistry*]
AMA............	Amyl Acetate [*Organic chemistry*]
AMA............	Analog Major Alarm (MCD)
AMA............	Angular Measurement Accuracy
AMA............	Antimalarial Agent
AMA............	Antimitochondral Antibody [*Immunology*]
AMA............	Antimyosin Antibody [*Medicine*] (DMAA)
AMA............	Apparel Manufacturers Association (EA)
AMA............	Apple Management Association (EA)
AMA............	Archery Manufacturers Association [*Later, AMO*]
AMA............	Area Minimum Altitude [*Aviation*] (FAAC)
AMA............	Arena Managers Association [*Defunct*] (EA)
AMA............	Arizona Mining Association (SRA)
AMA............	Arizona Multihousing Association (SRA)
AMA............	Army Mounteering Association [*British military*] (DMA)
AMA............	ASROC [*Antisubmarine Rocket*] Missile Assembly
AMA............	Asset Management Account
AMA............	Assistant Masters' Association [*British*]
AMA............	Associate Missionaries of the Assumption (EA)
AMA............	Associate of the Museums Association [*British*] (EY)
AMA............	Association of Metropolitan Authorities [*British*]
AMA............	Association of Model Agents [*British*] (DBA)
AMA............	Association of Municipal Authorities [*British*] (DCTA)
AMA............	Associative Memory Address [*Computer science*]
AMA............	Associative Memory Array [*Computer science*]
AMA............	Australian Marching Association
AMA............	Australian Monopoly Association
AMA............	Automated Modification Analyzer [*Computer science*]
AMA............	Automatic Malfunction Analysis (KSC)
AMA............	Automatic Memory Allocation [*Computer science*] (BUR)
AMA............	Automatic Message Accounting [*Bell Laboratories*] [*Telecommunications*]
AMA............	Automobile Manufacturers' Association [*Later, MVMA*] (EA)
AMA............	Axa Midi Assurances [*Commercial firm France*]
AMA............	Mayerthorpe Public Library, Alberta [*Library symbol National Library of Canada*] (NLC)
AMAA..........	Adhesives Manufacturers Association of America [*Later, AMA*] (EA)
AMAA..........	Airman Apprentice, Aviation Structural Mechanic, Striker [*Navy rating*]
AMAA..........	American Maine-Anjou Association (EA)
AMAA..........	American Medical Association Auxiliary (EA)
AMAA..........	American Medical Athletic Association (EA)
AMAA..........	Armenian Missionary Association of America (EA)
AMAA..........	Army Mutual Aid Association [*Later, AAFMAA*] (EA)
AMAA..........	Art Museum Association of America (EA)
AMAA..........	Association of Medical Advertising Agencies (EA)
AMAAN.......	Associate Member of the Australian Association of Neurologists
AMAB..........	Air Ministry's Accident Branch [*British*]
AMAB..........	Air Mobile Assault Brigade (MCD)
AMABE........	Associate Member of the Association of Business Executives [*British*] (DCTA)
AMAC..........	Aircraft Monitor and Control (NG)
AMAC..........	Alabama Christian School of Religion, Montgomery, AL [*Library symbol*] [*Library of Congress*] (LCLS)
AMAC..........	American Medical Alert Corp. [*NASDAQ symbol*] (NQ)
AMAC..........	Arlington Memorial Amphitheater Commission [*Abolished 1960, functions transferred to Department of Defense*]
AMAC..........	Armament Monitor and Control (CAAL)
AMAC..........	Arner Medical Alert [*NASDAQ symbol*] (TTSB)
AMAC..........	Assistance Medicale a l'Afrique Centrale [*Medical Assistance to Central Africa*] [*Belgium*] (AF)
AMAC..........	Automated Multiparameter Analyzer for Cells
AMACAB......	Allied Military Administration Civil Affairs Branch [*World War II*]
Am Acad Matri Law J...	American Academy of Matrimonial Lawyers. Journal [*A publication*] (DLA)
Am Acad Pol & Soc Sci...	American Academy of Political and Social Science (DLA)
AMA-CIPP....	American Medical Association Committee on Insurance and Prepayment Plans (EA)

AMACS........	Automatic Message Accounting Collecting System [*Telecommunications*] (TEL)
AMACU.......	Adults Molested as Children United (EA)
AMACUS.....	Automated Microfilm Aperture Card Updating System [*Army*]
AMAD.........	Activity Median Aerodynamic Diameter
AMAD.........	Airframe-Mounted Accessory Drive (MCD)
AMAD.........	Association Mondiale des Arts Divinatoires [*Divinatory Arts World Association - DAWA*] [*Rillieux-La-Pape, France*] (EAIO)
AMAD.........	Auxilium Meum a Deo [*My Help Cometh from the Lord*] [(*Ps., CXXI. 2*) Motto of Christian, Margrave of Brandenburg-Baireuth (1581-1655)]
AMADA.......	Alle Macht aan de Arbeiders [*All Power to the Workers*] [*Belgium Political party*] (PPW)
AMADA.......	Archery Manufacturers and Dealers Association [*Later, AMO*] (EA)
AMADAC.....	Aminomethylalizarindiacetic [*Organic chemistry*]
AMA-DE......	American Medical Association Drug Evaluation
AMADE.......	Association Mondiale des Amis de l'Enfance [*World Association of Children's Friends*] [*Monaco*] (EAIO)
AMADS.......	Airframe-Mounted Accessory Drive System
AMAE.........	Air Member for Aeronautical Engineering [*British and Canadian*] [*World War II*]
AMAE.........	Association of Mexican-American Educators (OICC)
AMA-ERF....	American Medical Association Education and Research Foundation (EA)
AMAF.........	Air Member for Accounts and Finance [*British and Canadian*] [*World War II*]
AMAF.........	Associated Manitoba Arts Festivals, Inc. (AC)
AMAF.........	Automatic Merchandising Association of Florida (SRA)
AMAFA.......	Air Mass and Frontal Analysis [*Meteorology*]
AMAFE.......	Association of Manufacturers of Animal-Derived Food Enzymes [*EC*] (ECED)
AMAG.........	American Mission for Aid to Greece
AMAG.........	Army Materiel Acquisition Guidance
AMAI..........	Aero-Medical Acceleration Laboratory (DMAA)
AMA/I.........	AMA [*American Management Association*]/International [*New York, NY*] (EA)
AMAI..........	Arena Managers Association, Inc. [*Defunct*]
AMAIS........	Agricultural Materials Analysis Information Service [*Laboratory of the Government Chemist*] [*British*] (NITA)
AMaJ..........	Judson College, Marion, AL [*Library symbol Library of Congress*] (LCLS)
AMAL..........	Aeronautical Medical Acceleration Laboratory [*Air Force*]
AMAL..........	Afwaj al-Muqawimah al-Lubnaniyah [*Lebanese Resistance Battalions*]
AMAL..........	Amalgamated (ADA)
Amal..........	Amalvius de Claris Aquis [*Flourished, 14th century*] [*Authority cited in pre-1607 legal work*] (DSA)
AMAL..........	Authorized Medical Allowance List (CAAL)
AMAL..........	Aviation Medical Acceleration Laboratory (MCD)
AMAL..........	Mallaig Public Library, Alberta [*Library symbol National Library of Canada*] (NLC)
Amal Engng Union Mon J...	Amalgamated Engineering Union. Monthly Journal [*A publication*]
AMALG........	Amalgamated (EY)
AMALG........	Associated Multiplier Agency Liaison Group [*Australia*]
AM-ALRI......	Anteromedial-Anterolateral Rotatory Instability [*Medicine*]
Amalvis.......	Amalvius de Claris Aquis [*Flourished, 14th century*] [*Authority cited in pre-1607 legal work*] (DSA)
AMAM........	Army Materiel Command Mission Area Manager
AMAM........	Manning Municipal Library, Alberta [*Library symbol National Library of Canada*] (NLC)
AMAMP.......	Army Multibus Avionics Multi-Process (MCD)
AMAMS.......	Advanced Medium Antitank Missile (MCD)
AM Am Soc CE...	Associate Member of the American Society of Civil Engineers
AMA/MTR....	Automatic Message Accounting / Magnetic Tape Recording [*Computer science*] (MHDB)
AMAN.........	Airman, Aviation Structural Mechanic, Striker [*Navy rating*]
AMAN.........	Mannville Public Library, Alberta [*Library symbol National Library of Canada*] (NLC)
AMANDA.....	Antarctic Muon and Neutrino Detector Array [*Astronomy*] (ECON)
AMANDA.....	Automized Medical Anamnesis Dialog Assistant [*Computer*]
AM & CA.....	Air Movement and Control Association (EA)
Am & E Corp Cas...	American and English Corporation Cases [*A publication*] (DLA)
Am & E Corp Cas NS...	American and English Corporation Cases, New Series [*A publication*] (DLA)
Am & E Eq D...	American and English Decisions in Equity [*A publication*] (DLA)
Am & Eng Ann Cas...	American and English Annotated Cases [*A publication*] (DLA)
Am & Eng Corp Cas...	American and English Corporation Cases [*A publication*] (DLA)
Am & Eng Dec Eq...	American and English Decisions in Equity [*A publication*] (DLA)
Am & Eng Enc Law...	American and English Encyclopedia of Law [*A publication*] (DLA)
Am & Eng Enc Law & Pr...	American and English Encyclopedia of Law and Practice [*A publication*] (DLA)
Am & Eng Enc Law Sup...	American and English Encyclopedia of Law. Supplement [*A publication*] (DLA)
Am & Eng Ency Law...	American and English Encyclopedia of Law [*A publication*] (DLA)
Am & Eng Eq D...	American and English Decisions in Equity [*A publication*] (DLA)
Am & Engl RC...	American and English Railway Cases [*A publication*] (DLA)
Am & Eng Pat Cas...	American and English Patent Cases [*A publication*] (DLA)
Am & Eng R Cas...	American and English Railroad Cases [*A publication*] (DLA)
Am & Eng R Cas NS...	American and English Railroad Cases, New Series [*A publication*] (DLA)

Am & Eng RR Ca... American and English Railroad Cases [*A publication*] (DLA)
Am & Eng RR Cas... American and English Railroad Cases [*A publication*] (DLA)
Am & Eng RR Cases... American and English Railroad Cases [*A publication*] (DLA)
Am & Eng Ry Cas... American and English Railway Cases [*A publication*] (DLA)
Am & Eng Ry Cas NS... American and English Railroad Cases, New Series [*A publication*] (DLA)
Am & ER Cas... American and English Railroad Cases [*A publication*] (DLA)
Am & ER Cas NS... American and English Railroad Cases, New Series [*A publication*] (DLA)
Am & Fer.... Amos and Ferard on Fixtures [*A publication*] (DLA)
AM & O....... Armstrong, Macartney, and Ogle's Irish Nisi Prius Reports [*A publication*] (DLA)
AM & P....... Andrews, McMeel & Parker [*Later, A & M*] [*Publisher*]
AMA/NET....... American Medical Association Network (NITA)
AMANET....... Atlantic Antisubmarine Warfare Communication Net (NVT)
Am Ann Cas... American Annotated Cases [*A publication*] (DLA)
AMANS....... Association of Municipal Administrators, Nova Scotia (AC)
Am Ant....... American Antiquity [*A publication*] (BRI)
AMAP....... Adaptive Mobile Access Protocol (MCD)
AMAP....... Aerojet Mass Analyzer Program (MCD)
AMAP....... As Much As Possible [*Medicine*]
AMAP....... Atelier de Modelisation de l'Architecture des Plantes [*Software manufacturer*] [*Paris, France*]
AMAPAC..... American Medical Association Political Action Committee
AMAPr........ Advanced Med'l 10% cm Pfd [*AMEX symbol*] (TTSB)
AMAPS....... Advanced Manufacturing, Accounting, and Production System (MCD)
AMAPS....... Apogee Motor Assembly with Paired Satellites [*NASA*]
AMAPS/G..... Advanced Manufacturing, Accounting, and Production System for Government Contractors (MCD)
Am A Psych L Bull... American Academy of Psychiatry and the Law. Bulletin [*A publication*] (DLA)
AmApt......... American Apartment Communities, Inc. [*Associated Press*] (SAG)
AMAQ......... Association des Mines d'Aminante du Quebec (AC)
AMAR........ Alvin, Mid-Atlantic Ridge [*Oceanography*]
AMAR........ Amarillo Biosciences, Inc. [*NASDAQ symbol*] (SAG)
AMAR........ Antimissile Array RADAR
AMAR........ Marwayne Public Library, Alberta [*Library symbol National Library of Canada*] (NLC)
AmarBio...... Amarillo Biosciences, Inc. [*Associated Press*] (SAG)
AMARC...... Aerospace Maintenance and Regeneration Center [*Air Force*]
AMARC...... Army Material Acquisition Reorganization Committee (MCD)
AMARC...... Army Materiel Acquisition Review Committee [*Terminated, 1974*]
AMARC...... Automatic Message Accounting Recording Center [*Telecommunications*] (TEL)
AMARS....... Air Mobile Aircraft Refueling System
AMARS....... Automatic Message Accounting Recording System [*Bell System*]
AMARS....... Automatic Message Address Routing System (AABC)
AMARS....... Autonetics Modular Airborne RADAR System
AMARTS..... American Arts Documentation Centre (EA)
AMARV...... Advanced Maneuvering Reentry Vehicle (MCD)
AMAS........ Advanced Midcourse Active System (MCD)
AMAS........ Air Member for Air Staff [*British and Canadian*] [*World War II*]
AMAS........ American Military Assistance Staff
AMAS........ Automatic Maneuvering Attack System [*Air Force*]
AMAS........ Automatic Message Accounting System (MCD)
AMASCP..... Air Material Area Stock Control Point (NG)
AMASD....... Airport Managers Association of South Dakota (SRA)
AMASE....... Advanced Mapping and Surveying Equipment (IIA)
AMASEE..... Associate Member of the Association of Supervisory and Executive Engineers [*British*] (DBQ)
AMASLG..... Association of Management Analysts in State and Local Government (EA)
AMASM....... Air Materiel Area System Management [*Air Force*]
AMASME..... Associate Member of the American Society of Mechanical Engineers
AMASS........ Airport Movement Area Safety System [*FAA*] (TAG)
AMASS....... Amplitude Miss Distance Acoustical Scoring System (MCD)
AMASS....... Automatic Multiaddress Segregation System (MCD)
AMAT........ Airborne Moving Attack Target (SAA)
Amat.......... Amatorius [*of Plutarch*] [*Classical studies*] (OCD)
AMAT........ American Mission for Aid to Turkey
A-MAT........ Amorphous Material [*Clinical medicine*]
AMAT........ Applied Materials [*NASDAQ symbol*] (TTSB)
AMAT........ Applied Materials, Inc. [*NASDAQ symbol*] (NQ)
AMATC........ Air Material Armament Test Center
Amati......... Amati Communications Corp. [*Associated Press*] (SAG)
AMATIS....... Automated Meteorological and Terminal Information Service
Amat Narr... Narrationum Amatoriarum Libellus [*of Parthenius*] [*Classical studies*] (OCD)
AMATYC...... American Mathematical Association of Two Year Colleges (EA)
AMAU......... United States Air University, Maxwell Air Force Base, Montgomery, AL [*Library symbol Library of Congress*] (LCLS)
AMAV........ Avalon [*Australia ICAO location identifier*] (ICLI)
AMAVS....... Advanced Metallic Air Vehicle Structure (MCD)
AMAVU....... Advanced Modular Audio Visual Unit (MHDI)
AMAW........ Advanced Medium Antitank Weapon (MCD)
Amax......... Amax Gold [*Associated Press*] (SAG)
AMAX........ American Metal Climax, Inc. [*Later, AMAX, Inc.*]
AmaxG........ Amax Gold, Inc. [*Associated Press*] (SAG)
AMAY......... Albury [*Australia ICAO location identifier*] (ICLI)
AMB.......... Active Magnetic Bearing [*Mechanical engineering*]
AMB.......... Adjusted Monetary Base [*Economics*]
AMB.......... Administrative Machine Branch [*Army*] (AABC)
AMB.......... Admiralty Medical Board [*British military*] (DMA)
AMB.......... Aerospace Medicine and Biology
AMB.......... AIDS Malignancy Bank [*National Cancer Institute*]

AMB.......... Aircraft Maintenance Base
AMB.......... Aircraft Mishap Board (DNAB)
AMB.......... Air-Launched Missile Bulletin (MCD)
AMB.......... Air Ministry Bulletin [*British military*] (DMA)
AMB.......... Air Mission Brief [*Air Force*] (INF)
AMB.......... Airways Modernization Board [*Functions transferred to FAA*]
AMB.......... Ambassador
AMB.......... Ambassador
amb.......... Amber (VRA)
AMB.......... Amber (MSA)
AMB.......... Amberquest Resources Ltd. [*Vancouver Stock Exchange symbol*]
AMB.......... Ambient (MSA)
AMB.......... Ambiguous [*Used in correcting manuscripts, etc.*]
AMB.......... Ambilobe [*Madagascar*] [*Airport symbol*] (OAG)
Amb.......... Ambler's Reports, Chancery [*27 English Reprint*] [*A publication*] (DLA)
AMB.......... Ambulance (AFM)
AMB.......... Ambulatory [*or Ambulation*] [*Also, AMBUL*] [*Medicine*]
AMB.......... Ambulong [*Philippines*] [*Seismograph station code, US Geological Survey Closed*] (SEIS)
AMB.......... Ambush
AMB.......... American Brands, Inc. [*NYSE symbol*] (SPSG)
AmB.......... American Brunswick [*Record label*]
AMB.......... Amphotericin B [*Antifungal agent*]
AMB.......... Antarctic Meteorite Bibliography [*Lunar and Planetary Institute*] [*Database*]
AMB.......... Antimotorboat
AMB.......... Armament Material Bulletin (NG)
AMB.......... Armoured Motor Battery [*British military*] (DMA)
AMB.......... Army Maintenance Board
AMB.......... Asbestos Mill Board [*Technical drawings*]
AMB.......... Astronomy Missions Board [*NASA*]
AMB.......... Australian Market Basket Survey
AMB.......... Auto-Manual Bridge Control [*Telecommunications*] (TEL)
AMB.......... Avian Myeloblastosis [*Medicine*] (DMAA)
AMB.......... Bachelor of Mechanic Arts
AMB.......... Blount, Inc., Montgomery, AL [*Library symbol Library of Congress*] (LCLS)
AMB.......... Deutsche Rettungsflugwacht EV [*Germany ICAO designator*] (FAAC)
AMB.......... Minesweeper, Harbor [*Navy symbol Obsolete*]
AMBA........ Accounting Master of Business Administration (GAGS)
Am BA........ American Bar Association (DLA)
AMBA........ American Malting Barley Association (EA)
AMBA........ American-Mideast Business Association (EA)
AMBA........ American Mold Builders Association (EA)
AMBA........ American Mustang and Burro Association (EA)
AMBA........ Amino(methoxy)benzanilide [*Organic chemistry*]
AMBA........ Arizona Mortgage Bankers Association (SRA)
AMBA........ Associate Member of the British Arts Association (DBQ)
AMBA........ Association of Military Banks of America [*Bethesda, MD*] (EA)
AMBA........ Australian Mohair Breeders' Association
AMBA........ Australian Mountain Bike Association
Ambac........ Ambac, Inc. [*Associated Press*] (SAG)
AMBAC........ American Bosch Arma Corp. (MCD)
AMBAC........ American Municipal Bond Assurance Corp.
AMBAC........ Asociacion Mexicana de Bibliotecarios, Asociacion Civil [*Spanish*]
AMBAE........ Association of Master of Business Administration Executives [*New York, NY*] (EA)
Ambanc...... Ambanc Corp. [*Associated Press*] (SAG)
AmbancH...... Ambanc Holding Co., Inc. [*Associated Press*] (SAG)
Am Bankr.... American Bankruptcy [*A publication*] (DLA)
Am Bank R.... American Bankruptcy Reports [*A publication*] (DLA)
Am Bank Rev... American Bankruptcy Review [*A publication*] (DLA)
Am Bankr NS... American Bankruptcy, New Series [*A publication*] (DLA)
Am Bankr R... American Bankruptcy Reports [*A publication*] (DLA)
Am Bankr Reg... American Bankruptcy Register [*A publication*] (DLA)
AMBANKRREP... American Bankruptcy Reports
Am Bankr Rep NS... American Bankruptcy Reports, New Series [*A publication*] (DLA)
Am Bankr Rev... American Bankruptcy Review [*A publication*] (DLA)
Am Bankr R (NS)... American Bankruptcy Reports, New Series [*A publication*] (DLA)
Am Bankruptcy Reps... American Bankruptcy Reports [*A publication*] (DLA)
AMBAQ........ Association des MBA du Quebec (AC)
Ambar........ Ambar, Inc. [*Associated Press*] (SAG)
Am Bar Asso Rep... American Bar Association Reports [*A publication*] (DLA)
Ambass........ Ambassador
AMBBA........ Associated Master Barbers and Beauticians of America [*Later, HI/AMBBA*] (EA)
AMBC.......... Amer Bancorp Ohio [*NASDAQ symbol*] (TTSB)
AMBC.......... American Bancorp [*NASDAQ symbol*] (NQ)
AMBC.......... American Bancorp Ohio [*NASDAQ symbol*] (SAG)
AMBC.......... American Minor Breeds Conservancy (EA)
AMBCp........ Association des Medecins Biochimistes du Canada (AC)
AmBcp........ American Bancorp Ohio [*Associated Press*] (SAG)
AMBCS........ Associate Member of the British Computer Society (DBQ)
AMBD........ Aminomethyl(methyl)benzothiadiazinedioxide [*Biochemistry*]
AMBD........ Automatic Multiple Blade Damper (OA)
Amb de Vig... Ambrosius de Vignate [*Flourished, 15th century*] [*Authority cited in pre-1607 legal work*] (DSA)
AMBE.......... Association of Management and Business Education (AIE)
AMBEI........ Associate Member of the Institution of Body Engineers [*British*] (DBQ)
AMBEL........ Ambiguity Eliminator [*Electronics*]

AMBER .... Acquisition of Monographs and Bibliographical Enquiry Remotely [*Computer software*] (NITA)

AMBER .... Advanced Multiple-Beam Equalization Radiography [*Medicine*] (DMAA)

AMBERS ..... A. M. Best Electronic Retrieval Services [*A. M. Best Co.*] [*Database*]

AMBF.......... Asset Master Balance File [*Military*] (AABC)

AMBFinl........ AMB Financial Corp. [*Associated Press*] (SAG)

Am B Found Res J... American Bar Foundation Research Journal [*A publication*] (AAGC)

AMBI.......... AMBI, Inc. [*NASDAQ symbol*] (SAG)

AMBI.......... AMBI, Inc. [*Associated Press*] (SAG)

AMBI.......... Ambitious (DSUE)

AMBI.......... Applied Microbiology [*NASDAQ symbol*] (TTSB)

AMBI.......... Applied Microbiology, Inc. [*NASDAQ symbol*] (SAG)

AMBIENS ..... Atmospheric Mass Balance of Industrially Emitted and Natural Sulfur [*Environmental Protection Agency*] (GFGA)

AMBIG .... Ambiguity [*or Ambiguous*] (MCD)

AmBiltrt ...... American Biltrite, Inc. [*Associated Press*] (SAG)

AMBIM .... Associate Member of the British Institute of Management

AmbIn.......... Ambassadors International, Inc. [*Associated Press*] (SAG)

AmBiogn....... American Biogenetic Sciences, Inc. [*Associated Press*] (SAG)

AMBIT.......... Algebraic Manipulation by Identity Translation

AMBIT.......... Augmented Built-In Test

AMBIT/L....... Acronym May Be Ignored Totally [*Computer science*] (CSR)

AMBIW .... Applied Microbiology Wrrt [*NASDAQ symbol*] (TTSB)

AMBK.......... Ambanc Corp. [*NASDAQ symbol*] (SAG)

Am B'kc'y Rep... American Bankruptcy Reports [*A publication*] (DLA)

AmBknt........ American Banknote Corp. [*Associated Press*] (SAG)

AMBL.......... Acute Myeloblastic Leukemia [*Hematology and oncology*] (DAVI)

AMBL.......... Airmobile (AABC)

Ambl........... Ambler's Reports, Chancery [*27 English Reprint*] [*A publication*] (DLA)

AMBL.......... Ambulance

AMBLADS ... Advise Method, Bill of Lading, and Date Shipped

AmBldg........ American Buildings Co. [*Associated Press*] (SAG)

AMBM .... Association of Men's Belt Manufacturers [*BA*] [*Absorbed by*] (EA)

AMBNC .... Ambiance

Am B News... American Bar News [*A publication*] (DLA)

Am B (NS)... American Bankruptcy, New Series [*A publication*] (DLA)

AMBOP....... American Board of Oral Pathology [*Later, ABOP*] (EA)

AMBOV .... Association of Members of Boards of Visitors [*British*] (DI)

AMBPrA ...... AMER BRANDS $2.67 CV Pfd [*NYSE symbol*] (TTSB)

AMBQ .... Association des Marchands de Bois en Gros du Quebec [*Quebec Wholesale Lumber Association*] (AC)

AMBR .... Ambar, Inc. [*NASDAQ symbol*] (SAG)

AMBR .... Amber (DAVI)

Am BR .... American Bankruptcy Reports [*A publication*] (DLA)

Ambra......... Alhambra [*Record label*] [*Spain*]

AMBRDL ...... Army Medical Bioengineering Research and Development Laboratory (RDA)

AM Brit IRE... Associate Member of the British Institution of Radio Engineers [*Later, AMIERE*]

AMBRL .... Army Medical Biomechanical Research Laboratory

Am BR (NS)... American Bankruptcy Reports, New Series [*A publication*] (DLA)

Ambr Opizo... Ambrosius Opizonus [*Flourished, 15th century*] [*Authority cited in pre-1607 legal work*] (DSA)

AMBSQ .... Association des Manufacturiers de Bois de Sciage du Quebec [*Quebec Lumber Manufacturers Association*] (AC)

AmbssApt .... Ambassador Apartments, Inc. [*Associated Press*] (SAG)

AMBT.......... Ambulatory (AABC)

AMBTAC ...... Acrylamidomethylbutyl Trimethylammonium Chloride [*Organic chemistry*]

AMBUCS...... National Association of American Business Clubs (EA)

AMBUL .... Ambulatory [*or Ambulation*] [*Also, AMB*] [*Medicine*]

ambul .... Ambulatory (VRA)

AMBUSH...... Advanced Model Builder Shell [*Programming language*] [*1970*] (CSR)

AmBusn .... American Business Information, Inc. [*Associated Press*] (SAG)

AMBV.......... Auxiliary Mexican Border Veterans (EA)

AMC............ Absent-Minded Club [*Defunct*] (EA)

AMC............ Acceptable Means of Compliance (DA)

AMC............ Account Manager Code (TEL)

AMC............ Acquisition Method Coding (MCD)

AMC............ Activity Mission Code (DNAB)

AMC............ Adenoma Malignum of the Cervix [*Oncology*]

AMC............ Advanced Medical Communications [*Commercial firm*] [*British*] (NITA)

AMC............ Advanced Memory Concepts (MCD)

AMC............ Advanced Minuteman Computer

AMC............ Advanced Motor Case (MCD)

AMC............ Aerodrome Surface Movement Control

AMC............ Aerodynamic Maneuver Capability (SAA)

AMC............ Aerodynamic Mean Chord (DA)

AMC............ Aeromedical Monitor Console

AMC............ Aerospace Manufacturers Council [*Defunct*] (EA)

AMC............ Aerospace Medical Command [*Air Force*]

AMC............ Agency Management Conference [*LIMRA*]

AMC............ Agricultural Mortgage Corp. [*Finance British*]

AMC............ Airborne Mode Control

AMC............ Aircraft Manufacturer's Council

AMC............ Aircraft Manufacturing Co. (MCD)

AMC............ Aircraft Model Change

AMC............ Aircraft Motion Compensation

AMC............ AiResearch Manufacturing Co.

AMC............ Air-Launched Missile Change (MCD)

AMC............ Air Mail Center

AMC............ Air Malta Co. Ltd. [*ICAO designator*] (FAAC)

AMC............ Air Materiel Command [*Later, Air Force Logistics Command*]

AMC............ Air Ministry Constabulary [*British military*] (DMA)

AMC............ Air Mission Commander [*Military*] (INF)

AMC............ Air Mobility Command [*Air Force*]

AMC............ Air Monitoring Center [*Rockwell International Corp.*]

AMC............ Air Monitoring Center [*Rockwell International Corp.*]

AMC............ Air Mounting Centre [*British military*] (DMA)

AMC............ Airspace Management and Control (MCD)

AMC............ Airspace Management Center (MCD)

AMC............ Alarm Monitor Computer

AMC............ Alberta Microelectronic Centre [*University of Alberta*] [*Research center*] (RCD)

AMC............ Albertus Magnus College [*New Haven, CT*]

AMC............ Alkyd Moulding Compound (PDAA)

AMC............ Allied Mediterranean Commission [*World War II*]

AMC............ All Major Commands (MCD)

AMC............ Almaden [*California*] [*Seismograph station code, US Geological Survey*] (SEIS)

AMC............ Alternate Media Center [*New York University*] [*New York, NY Telecommunications*]

AMC............ Amador Central Railroad Co. [*AAR code*]

AMC............ AMCA Resources Ltd. [*Vancouver Stock Exchange symbol*]

AMC............ AMC Entertainment, Inc. [*Associated Press*] (SAG)

AmC............ American Catalogue [*A bibliographic publication*]

AMC............ American College, Bryn Mawr, PA [*OCLC symbol*] (OCLC)

AmC............ American Columbia [*Record label*]

AMC............ American Maritime Cases

AMC............ American Mining Congress (EA)

AMC............ American Mission to the Chinese [*Later, American Mission to the Chinese and Asian*] (EA)

AMC............ American Monitor Corp. (MCD)

AMC............ American Mothers Committee (EA)

AMC............ American Motors Corp.

AMC............ American Movers Conference (EA)

AMC............ American Movie Classics [*Cable-television network*]

AMC............ American Multi Cinema [*Third largest theatre chain in America*]

AMC............ American Music Center (EA)

AMC............ American Music Conference (EA)

AMC............ Amino-Methyl-Coumarin

AMC............ Am-Timan [*Chad*] [*Airport symbol*] (AD)

AMC............ Angular Motion Compensator

AMC............ Animal Medical Center (EA)

AMC............ Antimalaria Campaign

AMC............ Appalachian Mountain Club (EA)

AmC............ Arcata Microfilm Corp., Winston-Salem, NC [*Library symbol Library of Congress*] (LCLS)

AMC............ Archival and Manuscripts Control [*USMARC format*] [*Computer science*]

AMC............ Armament Material Change (NG)

AMC............ Armed Merchant Cruiser [*Obsolete Navy British*]

AMC............ Arm Muscle Circumference

AMC............ Army Materiel Command [*Formerly, DARCOM*] [*Alexandria, VA*]

AMC............ Army Medical Center

AMC............ Army Medical Corps

AMC............ Army Missile Command

AMC............ Army Mobility Command

AMC............ Army Munitions Command [*Later merged with Army Weapons Command*]

AMC............ Arthrogryposis Multiplex Congenita [*Medicine*] (MEDA)

AMC............ Art Master's Certificate

AMC............ Art Material Club [*Later, AMMA*] (EA)

AMC............ Asian Media Coalition [*Inactive*] (EA)

AMC............ Associated Merchandising Corp.

AMC............ Associated Minority Contractors of America (EA)

AMC............ Associated Motor Carriers Tariff Bureau, Saint Paul MN [*STAC*]

AMC............ Association Management Centre (AC)

AMC............ Association Medicale Canadienne [*Canadian Medical Association - CMA*]

AMC............ Association of Management Consultants (EA)

AMC............ Association of Mature Canadians (AC)

AMC............ Association of Mercy Colleges (EA)

AMC............ Association of Minnesota Counties (SRA)

AMC............ Association of Municipal Corporationss [*British*]

AMC............ Associative Memory Computer [*Computer science*]

AMC............ ATI Multimedia Channel [*Computer science*]

AMC............ Atlantic Marine Center [*National Oceanic and Atmospheric Administration*]

AMC............ Australian Media Contacts [*A publication*] (ADA)

AMC............ Auto-Manual Center [*Telecommunications*] (TEL)

AMC............ Automatic Maneuvering Control (DNAB)

AMC............ Automatic Message Counting

AMC............ Automatic Mission Control

AMC............ Automatic Mixture Control

AMC............ Automatic Modulation Control (DEN)

AMC............ Automatic Monitoring Circuit [*Telecommunications*] (OA)

AMC............ Autonomous Multiplexer Channel

AMC............ Auxiliary Coastal Minesweepers [*Navy symbol*]

AMC............ Average Monthly Consumption (MCD)

AMC............ Aviation Maintenance Costs

AMC............ Aviation Material Change (SAA)

AMC............ Aviation Structural Mechanic, Chief [*Navy rating*]

AMC............ Avionics Maintenance Conference (EA)

AMC............ Axial Magma Chamber [*Geology*]

AMC............ Axiomesiocervical [*Dentistry*]

AMC............ Millarville Community Library, Alberta [*Library symbol National Library of Canada*] (NLC)

AMCA.......... Advanced Materiel Concepts Agency [*Alexandria, VA*] [*Army*]

AMCA.......... Aft Motor Control Assembly (NASA)

AMCA.......... Air Movement and Control Association (EA)

AMCA.......... Air Moving and Conditioning Association (SAA)

AMCA.......... Alaskan Malamute Club of America (EA)

AMCA.......... Amateur Motor Cycle Association [*British*] (DBA)

AMCA.......... American Medical Curling Association (EA)

AMCA.......... American Mission to the Chinese and Asian [*Defunct*] (EA)

AMCA.......... American Mosquito Control Association (EA)

AMCA.......... Amino(methyl)coumarinacetate [*Organic chemistry*]

AMCA.......... Aminomethylcyclohexanecarboxylic Acid [*Pharmacology*] (AAMN)

AMcA.......... Antimicrosomal Antibody [*Clinical chemistry*]

AMCA.......... Antique Motorcycle Club of America (EA)

AMCA.......... Architectural Metal Craftsmen's Association [*British*] (BI)

AMCA.......... Arkansas Motor Carriers Association (SRA)

AMCA.......... Australian Migration Consultants' Association

AMCADC...... Army Materiel Command Administrative Data Center

AMCADS...... Army Materiel Command Announcement Distribution System (RDA)

AMC-AF....... Air Materiel Command [*later, Air Force Logistics Command*] - Air Force

AMCAL........ Americal Division [*Army*] (VNW)

AMCALMSA... Army Materiel Command Automated Logistics Management Systems Agency (AABC)

AMCAP....... Advanced Microwave Circuit Analysis Programme (HGAA)

AMCAPS...... Automatic Multiple-Parameter Collection Processing System [*Air Force*] (MCD)

AMCARS...... Automated Maintenance Control and Records System (MCD)

AMCAS....... American Medical College Application Service

AmCAS....... Centre for American and Commonwealth Arts and Studies [*British*] (CB)

AmCasn...... American Casino Enterprises, Inc. [*Associated Press*] (SAG)

Amcast....... Amcast Industrial [*Associated Press*] (SAG)

AMCAWS...... Advanced Medium-Caliber Aircraft Weapon System (MCD)

AMCB.......... Aluminum Manufacturers Credit Bureau [*Defunct*] (EA)

AMCB.......... American Medical Center for Burma [*Defunct*] (EA)

AMCB.......... Army Materiel Command Board [*Aberdeen Proving Ground, MD*] (MCD)

AMCBMC..... Air Materiel Command [*later, Air Force Logistics Command*] Ballistic Missile Center (IEEE)

AMCBO....... Association of Major City Building Officials (EA)

AMCBPS...... Avoidable Mortality from Cancer in Black Populations Survey [*Department of Health and Human Services*] (GFGA)

AMCBW....... Amalgamated Meat Cutters and Butcher Workmen of North America [*Later, UFCWIU*] (EA)

AMCC.......... American Mexican Claims Commission [*Terminated, 1947*]

AMCC.......... Army Material Command Circular (MCD)

AMCC.......... Army Metrology and Calibration Center

AMCC.......... ARTCC Maintenance Control Center [*FAA*] (TAG)

AMCC.......... Association of Manufacturers of Confectionery and Chocolate (EA)

AMCC.......... Australia-Malaysia Chamber of Commerce

AMCCDO...... Army Materiel Command Catalog Data Office (AABC)

AMCC-MM... Army Metrology and Calibration Center Metrology Development and Engineering Division

AMCCN....... Army Materiel Command Deputy Chief of Staff for Chemical and Nuclear Matters

AMCCOM..... US Army Armament, Munitions, and Chemical Command [*Pronounced "a-m-c-com"*] [*Rock Island, IL*] (RDA)

AMCCOMR... Armament, Munitions, and Chemical Command Regulation [*Military*]

AMCD.......... Addressograph-Multigraph Copier Duplicator

AMCD.......... American Medical Center at Denver (AAMN)

AMCD.......... Annular Momentum Control Device [*NASA*]

AMCD.......... Association for Multicultural Counseling and Development (EA)

AMCD.......... Audit and Management Consulting Division [*United Nations*] (ECON)

AMCDC....... Army Materiel Command Data Center

AMCDDC...... Army Materiel Command Depot Data Center

AMCDE....... Army Materiel Command Deputy Chief of Staff for Developments Engineering and Acquisition

AMCE.......... Amer Claims Evaluation [*NASDAQ symbol*] (TTSB)

AMCE.......... American Claims Evaluation, Inc. [*NASDAQ symbol*] (NQ)

AMCE.......... Arena Meetings, Conventions and Exhibitions Proprietary Ltd.

AMCEA........ Advertising Media Credit Executives Association [*Toledo, OH*] (EA)

AMCEC........ Allied Military Communications-Electronics Committee (AABC)

AMCEE........ Association for Media-Based Continuing Education for Engineers (EA)

Am Cent Dig... American Digest (Century Edition) [*A publication*] (DLA)

AMCF.......... Air Materiel Command [*later, Air Force Logistics Command*] Forms

AMCF.......... Alkali Metal Cleaning Facility [*Nuclear energy*] (NRCH)

AMCFASC.... Army Materiel Command Facilities and Services Center (AABC)

AMC-FAST ... Army Materiel Command Field Assistance for Science and Technology Program (RDA)

AMCFO .... Army Materiel Command Field Office (RDA)

AMCFSA ...... Army Materiel Command Field Safety Agency (AABC)

AMCGO........ Army Materiel Command General Order

AMCH.......... Crescent Heights High School, Medicine Hat, Alberta [*Library symbol National Library of Canada*] (NLC)

AMCHA........ Aminomethylcyclohexanecarboxylic Acid [*Pharmacology*]

AMCHAM...... American Chamber of Commerce in Australia

AmCham...... American Chamber of Commerce of Mexico (CROSS)

AmCham HK.. American Chamber of Commerce in Hong Kong (EA)

AMCHCCP... Association for Maternal and Child Health and Crippled Children's Programs (EA)

Am Ch Dig... American Chancery Digest [*A publication*] (DLA)

AMCHQ........ Air Materiel Command [*later, Air Force Logistics Command*] Headquarters

AMCI.......... American Medserve Corp. [*NASDAQ symbol*] (SAG)

AMCI.......... Ameritech Mobile Communications, Inc. [*Schaumburg, IL*] [*Telecommunications*] (TSSD)

AMCI & SA... Army Materiel Command Installations and Service Agency (AABC)

AMCIB .... Associate Member of the Corporation of Insurance Brokers [*British*] (DI)

AMCIC .... Army Materiel Command Information Center

AMCID .... Accumulation Mode Charge Injection Device (MCD)

AMCID .... Army Materiel Command Installation Division

AMCIGW ...... Army Materiel Command Inspector General, Western Inspection Activity

AMCIL .... Army Materiel Command International Logistics Directorate (MCD)

AmCin .... American Cinemastores [*Associated Press*] (SAG)

AmCine........ American Cinemastores [*Associated Press*] (SAG)

AMCIT........ Associate Member of the Chartered Institute of Transport [*British*] (DI)

AMCITS........ American Citizens [*Military*] (ADDR)

AMCL.......... Air Materiel Command [*later, Air Force Logistics Command*] Letter

AMCL.......... Amended Clearance [*Aviation*] (FAAC)

A-MCL .... Anterior Portion - Medial Collateral Ligament [*Anatomy*]

AMCL.......... Approval MILSTRIP [*Military Standard Requisition and Issue Procedures*] Change Letter [*DoD*]

AMCL.......... Approved MAPAD [*Military Assistance Program Address File*] Change Letter (AAGC)

AMCL.......... Association of Metropolitan Chief Librarians [*London*]

AMCLDC...... Army Materiel Command Logistic Data Center (AABC)

Am CLJ........ American Civil Law Journal [*A publication*] (DLA)

AMCLO........ Air Materiel Command [*later, Air Force Logistics Command*] Liaison Office [*or Officer*]

AMCLO........ Air Materiel Command [*later, Air Force Logistics Command*] Logistics Office [*or Officer*]

AMCLSSA .... Army Materiel Command Logistics Systems Support Agency (AABC)

AMCM........ Advanced Mine Countermeasures (MCD)

AMCM........ Airborne Mine Countermeasure Equipment

AMCM........ Air Materiel Command [*later, Air Force Logistics Command*] Manual

AMCM........ Anti-Mine Countermeasure (MCD)

AMCM........ Army Materiel Command Memorandum

AMCM........ Aviation Structural Mechanic, Master Chief [*Navy rating*]

AMCMEA..... Australian Management College Mount Eliza Association

AMCMFO .... Air Materiel Command [*later, Air Force Logistics Command*] Missile Field Office

AMCMR....... Army Materiel Command Materiel Requirements Directorate (MCD)

AMCMS........ Airborne Mine Countermeasure System (NG)

AMCN........ Amer Coin Merchandising [*NASDAQ symbol*] (TTSB)

AMCN........ American Coin Merchandising, Inc. [*NASDAQ symbol*] (SAG)

AMCNSW.... Arms and Militaria Collectors' Association of New South Wales [*Australia*]

AMCO .... Aerojet Manufacturing Co.

AMCO .... Afro-Mauritian Common Organization

AmCo .... American Micro Co., Kansas City, MO [*Library symbol Library of Congress*] (LCLS)

AMCO .... Associated Oklahoma Trucking Association (SRA)

AMCO .... Association of Major Charitable Associations

AMCODE...... AMEX [*American Stock Exchange*] Computerized Order Display and Execution System

AMC of A...... Associated Male Choruses of America (EA)

AmCoin....... American Coin Merchandising, Inc. [*Associated Press*] (SAG)

AMCOL........ Amcol International Corp. [*Associated Press*] (SAG)

Amcol Int...... Amcol International Corp. [*Associated Press*] (SAG)

AMCOM....... AMEX [*American Stock Exchange*] Communications [*Network*]

AMCON....... AMCON Distributing [*Associated Press*] (SAG)

AMCON....... American Consul

AMCONGEN.. American Consulate General (CINC)

AMCONREPO.. American Consular Reporting Officer

Amcor......... Amcor Capital Ltd. [*Associated Press*] (SAG)

AMCOR....... Atlantic Margin Coring Project

AmcorFn...... Amcore Financial [*Associated Press*] (SAG)

Am Corp Cas... American Corporation Cases, by Withrow [*A publication*] (DLA)

AMCORR..... American Committee for Rescue and Resettlement of Iraqi Jews (EA)

AMCOS....... Aldermaston Mechanised Cataloging and Ordering System [*British*] (DIT)

AMCOS....... Aldermaston Mechanized Cataloguing and Ordering Systems [*British*] (DIT)

AMCOS....... Army Manpower Cost System (RDA)

AMCP.......... ADL [*Avionics Development Laboratory*] Master Control Program [*NASA*] (NASA)

AMCP.......... Allied Military Communications Panel

AMCP.......... Amcor Ltd. [*NASDAQ symbol*] (SAG)

AMCP.......... Anhydrous Monocalcium Phosphate [*Inorganic chemistry*]

AMCP.......... Army Materiel Command Pamphlet (MCD)

AMCPA .... American Managed Care Pharmacy Association (EA)

AMCPI .... Army Materiel Command Procurement Instructions

AMCPP .... Army Materiel Command Procurement and Production Directorate

AMCPSCC .... Army Materiel Command Packaging, Storage, and Containerization Center [*Tobyhanna, PA*]

AMCQ.......... Association des Maitres Couvreurs du Quebec [*Quebec Master Roofers Association*] (AC)

AMCR.......... Air Materiel Command [*later, Air Force Logistics Command*] Regulations

AMCR.......... Amcor Ltd. [*NASDAQ symbol*] (SAG)

Am Cr .... American Criminal Reports [*A publication*] (DLA)

AMCR.......... Army Materiel Command Regulations

AMCRA .... American Managed Care and Review Association (EA)

AMCRA	Atlantic Motorcycle Competition Riders' Association (AC)
Am Craft	American Craft [*A publication*] (BRI)
AmCraft	American Craft Brewing International [*Associated Press*] (SAG)
AMCRC	AMC [*American Motors Corp.*] Rambler Club (EA)
AMCRD	Army Materiel Command Research and Development
AmCrft	American Craft Brewing International [*Associated Press*] (SAG)
AMCRIC	Aviation Material Combat Ready In-Country (MCD)
AMCROSS....	American Red Cross
Am Cr R	American Criminal Reports [*A publication*] (DLA)
Am Cr Rep...	American Criminal Reports, Edited by Hawley [*A publication*] (DLA)
Am Cr R (Hawley)...	American Criminal Reports, Edited by Hawley [*A publication*] (DLA)
Am Cr Tr.....	American Criminal Trials (Chandler) [*A publication*] (DLA)
AMCRY	Amcor Limited ADR [*NASDAQ symbol*] (TTSB)
AMCS..........	Advanced Mail Coding System (MCD)
AMCS..........	Advanced Missile Control System (SAA)
AMCS..........	Airborne Missile Control System
AMCS..........	Aircraft Mounted Control System
AMCS..........	Aircrew Microclimate Cooling System [*Military*] (DOMA)
AMCS..........	AMISYS Managed Care Sys [*NASDAQ symbol*] (TTSB)
AMCS..........	Army Mobilization Capabilities Study
AMCS..........	Association for Mexican Cave Studies (EA)
AMCS..........	Association of Marine Catering and Supply [*British*] (DBA)
AMCS..........	Association of Military Colleges and Schools of the US (EA)
AMCS..........	Automatic Motion Control System
AMCS..........	Aviation Structural Mechanic, Senior Chief [*Navy rating*]
AMCSA	Army Materiel Command Support Activity
AMCSI	Associate Member of the Construction Surveyor's Institute [*British*] (DBQ)
AMCSS	Advanced Materials Cargo Sling System (MCD)
AMCSS	Airborne Missile Control Subsystem
AMCSS	Army Military Clothing Sales Store (DOMA)
AMCT..........	Associate of Manchester College of Technology [*British*]
AMCTB........	Associated Motor Carriers Tariff Bureau (EA)
AMCTC	Army Materiel Command Technical Committee
AMCTO	Association of Municipal Clerks & Treasurers of Ontario (AC)
AMCTSO	Air Materiel Command [*later, Air Force Logistics Command*] Test Site Office
AMCU	Adults Molested as Children United (EA)
AMC(U).......	Minesweeper, Coastal (Underwater Locator) [*Navy symbol*]
AM CUR.......	Amicus Curiae [*Friend of the Court*] [*Latin Legal term*] (ADA)
AMCV..........	Amer Classic Voyages [*NASDAQ symbol*] (TTSB)
AMCV..........	American Classic Voyages, Inc. [*NASDAQ symbol*] (SAG)
AMCV..........	Armoured Mine Clearing Vehicle [*Military*]
AMCV..........	Artichoke Mottled Crinkle Virus [*Plant pathology*]
AMCWC	Adelaide Medical Centre for Women and Children [*Australia*]
AMD...........	Acacia Mineral [*Vancouver Stock Exchange symbol*]
AMD...........	Accident Model Document [*NASA*] (KSC)
AMD...........	Acid Mine Drainage [*Mining technology*]
AMD...........	Actinomycin-D [*Also, act-D, DACT*] [*Antineoplastic drug*]
AMD...........	Actinomycin-D [*Also, act-D, DACT*] [*Antineoplastic drug*]
AMD...........	Administrative and Miscellaneous Duties [*RAF*] [*British*]
AMD...........	Administrative Machine Division [*Army*] (AABC)
AMD...........	Advanced Micro Dev [*NYSE symbol*] (TTSB)
AMD...........	Advanced Micro Devices, Inc. [*NYSE symbol*] (SPSG)
AMD...........	Advance Manufacturing Directive
AMD...........	Aerolineas Medellin [*Colombia*] [*ICAO designator*] (FAAC)
AMD...........	Aero-Mechanics Department [*Navy*] (MCD)
AMD...........	Aeromedical Data
AMD...........	Aerospace Materials Document (MCD)
AMD...........	Aerospace Medical Division [*Brooks Air Force Base, TX*] [*Air Force*]
AMD...........	Against Manufacturing Defects [*Automotive engineering*]
AMD...........	Age-Related Macular Degeneration [*Ophthalmology*]
AMD...........	Ahmedabad [*India*] [*Airport symbol*] (OAG)
AMD...........	Aircraft Maintenance Department [*Military*] (AFIT)
AMD...........	Air Management Division [*Environmental Protection Agency*] (GFGA)
AMD...........	Air Movement Data [*Air Force*]
AMD...........	Air Movement Designator [*Army*]
AMD...........	Air-Moving Device [*Technical drawings*] (DAC)
AMD...........	Alliance pour Une Mauritanie Democratique [*Alliance for One Democratic Mauritania*] (PD)
AMD...........	Allied Masonic Degrees [*Freemasonry*]
AMD...........	Alpha Activity Median Diameter [*Nuclear energy*] (NRCH)
AMD...........	Alpha-Methyldopa [*Also, MD*] [*Antihypertensive compound*]
AMD...........	Alternating Monocular Deprivation [*Optics*]
AMD...........	Ambulance Manufacturers Division [*An association*] (EA)
AMD...........	Amderma [*Former USSR Seismograph station code, US Geological Survey Closed*] (SEIS)
AMD...........	Amend
AmD...........	American Decca [*Record label*]
Am D	American Decisions [*A publication*] (DLA)
AmD...........	American Diagnostics Corp.
AMD...........	America's Manifest Destiny [*An association*] (EA)
AMD...........	Applied Mechanics Division [*American Society of Mechanical Engineers*]
AMD...........	Approved Marine Devices Co. (MCD)
AMD...........	Army Medical Department
AMD...........	Association for Macular Diseases (EA)
AMD...........	Associative Memory Device [*Computer science*] (DIT)
AMD...........	Asteroid Meteoroid Detector
AMD...........	Atomic and Molecular Physical Data Program [*American Society for Testing and Materials*] (IID)
AMD...........	Automated Maintenance Depot
AMD...........	Automated Mooney Decay [*Chemical engineering*]
AMD...........	Automated Multiple Development [*Chromatography*]

AMD...........	Automatic Map Display (MCD)
AMD...........	Auxiliary Memory Drum
AMD...........	Average Monthly Demand
AMD...........	Axiomesiodistal [*Dentistry*]
AMD...........	Bozeman, MT [*Location identifier FAA*] (FAAL)
AMDA	Advanced Maneuvering Demonstrator Aircraft (MCD)
AMDA	Advances for Mutual Defense Assistance
AMDA	Airline Medical Directors Association (EA)
AMDA	American Medical Directors Association (EA)
AMDA	American Microcomputer Dealers Association (EA)
AMDA	American Milking Devon Association (EA)
AMDA	Anglo-Malaysian Defence Agreement
AMDA	Art Museum Development Association (NFD)
AMDA	Associated Minicomputer Dealers of America (EA)
AMDAC	Amdahl Diagnostics Assistance Center
AMDAG	American Decartelization Agency [*Post-World War II*]
AMdAlt........	American Medical Alert Corp. [*Associated Press*] (SAG)
AMDAPS	Automatic Meteorological Data Acquisition and Processing System (MCD)
AMDAR	Automated Manpower Data Department of the Navy Reports (MCD)
AMDAS	Airborne Mine Detection and Surveillance System [*Navy*] (DOMA)
AMDAS	Automatic Magnetic Data Acquisition System (MCD)
AMDB	Arab Malaysian Development Bank
AM-DBS	Amplitude Modulation, Double Sideband [*Electronics*] (HGAA)
AMDC	American Modern Dance Caucus
AMDC	Army Missile Defense Command (AABC)
AMDC	Army Missile Development Center (MCD)
AMDC	Assistant Marshal of the Diplomatic Corps [*British*]
AMDCL	Association of Metropolitan District Chief Librarians [*British*]
AMDE	Association of Medical Deans in Europe (EAIO)
AMDEA	Association of Manufacturers of Domestic Electric Appliances [*British*] (DI)
Am Dec.......	American Decisions, Select Cases [*San Francisco, CA*] [*A publication*] (DLA)
AMDECL	Association of Metropolitan District Education and Children's Librarians [*British*] (DBA)
Am Dec's.....	American Decisions [*A publication*] (DLA)
AMDEN	Adult Males, Density Of [*Ecology*]
AmDentl	American Dental LaserAm [*Associated Press*] (SAG)
AMDEX	Automated Maintenance Data Exchange (MCD)
AMDF..........	Absolute Magnitude Difference Function (PDAA)
AMDF..........	Army Master Data File (AABC)
AMDFRMS	Army Master Data File Reader Microfilm System [*Later, ARMS*] (AABC)
AMDG	Ad Majorem Dei Gloriam [*To the Greater Glory of God*] [*Latin*] (WGA)
AMDGF	Alveolar-Macrophage-Derived Growth Factor [*Biochemistry*]
AMDH	Academia Mexicana de Derechos Humanos [*The Mexican Academy for Human Rights*] (CROSS)
AMDHL	Amdahl Corp. [*Associated Press*] (SAG)
AMDI	Acoustic Miss Distance Indicator (PDAA)
AMDI	Admiralty Merchant Ship Defense Instructions [*British*]
AMDI	Automatic Miss Distance Indicator
Amdia.........	American Media, Inc. [*Formerly, Enquirer/Star Group*] [*Associated Press*] (SAG)
Am Dig	American Digest [*A publication*] (DLA)
Am Dig Cent Ed...	American Digest (Century Edition) [*A publication*] (DLA)
Am Dig Dec Ed...	American Digest (Decennial Edition) (West) [*A publication*] (DLA)
Am Dig Decen Ed...	American Digest (Decennial Edition) (West) [*A publication*] (DLA)
Am Dig Eighth Dec Ed...	American Digest (Eighth Decennial Edition) (West) [*A publication*] (DLA)
Am Dig Fifth Dec Ed...	American Digest (Fifth Decennial Edition) (West) [*A publication*] (DLA)
Am Dig Fourth Dec Ed...	American Digest (Fourth Decennial Edition) (West) [*A publication*] (DLA)
Am Dig Key No Ser...	American Digest (Key Number Series) (West) [*A publication*] (DLA)
Am Dig Secd Dec Ed...	American Digest (Second Decennial Edition) (West) [*A publication*] (DLA)
Am Dig Seventh Dec Ed...	American Digest (Seventh Decennial Edition) (West) [*A publication*] (DLA)
Am Dig Sixth Dec Ed...	American Digest (Sixth Decennial Edition) (West) [*A publication*] (DLA)
Am Dig Third Dec Ed...	American Digest (Third Decennial Edition) (West) [*A publication*] (DLA)
AMDIS	Australian Marine Data Information Service
AmDisp........	American Disposal Services, Inc. [*Associated Press*] (SAG)
AMDL..........	Abstract Machine Description Language [*1977*] [*Computer science*] (CSR)
AMDL..........	Air Munitions Development Laboratory (MUGU)
AMDLEVAC...	Aeromedical Evacuation [*Later, AME*]
AMDLS	Agricultural Meteorological Data Logging System (NOAA)
AMDM	Association of Microbiological Diagnostic Manufacturers (EA)
AMDMA	American Metal Detector Manufacturers Association (EA)
AMDO	Aeronautical Maintenance Duty Officer
AMDO	American Merchandise Display Osaka [*Department of Commerce Japan*] (IMH)
AMDOC	American Doctors [*Later, PCOS*] (EA)
AMDP	Aircraft Maintenance Delayed for Parts [*Military*]
AMDP	Air Member for Development and Production [*Air Ministry*] [*British*]
AMDR	Advance Missile Deviation Report
AMDRA	American Motorcycle Drag Racing Association [*of the National Hot Rod Association*] [*Later, NMRA*] (EA)
AMDS	Advanced Mine Detection System [*Navy*] (DOMA)

AMDS .... Advanced Missions Docking System [*or Subsystem*] [*NASA*] (NASA)
AMDS .... Agri-Markets Data Service [*Capitol Publications, Inc.*] [*Database*] [*Defunct*]
AMDS .... Airborne Mine Detection System (MCD)
AMDS .... Arctic Mobile Drilling Structure (PDAA)
AMDS .... Association of Military Dental Surgeons
AMDS .... Australian MARC [*Machine Readable Catalogue*] Distribution Service (NITA)
AMDS .... Automatic Message Distribution System (CET)
AMDSB .... Amplitude Modulation, Double Sideband [*Electronics*]
AMDSB/SC... Amplitude Modulation, Double Sideband, Suppressed Carrier [*Electronics*] (CET)
AMDSYS ..... AMEDISYS, Inc. [*Associated Press*] (SAG)
AMDT .... Active Maintenance Downtime
AMDT .... Adjusted Maximum Dive Time
AMDT .... Amendment (AABC)
AMDT .... ASCII [*American Standard Code for Information Interchange*] Message De finition Table (NITA)
AMDU .... Aerospace Maintenance and Development Unit (MCD)
AMDUCA ..... Animal Medicinal Drug Use Clarification Act of 1994
Amdura .... Amdura Corp. [*Associated Press*] (SAG)
AMDV .... Devonport [*Australia ICAO location identifier*] (ICLI)
AME .... Acoustic-Magneto-Electric (PDAA)
AME .... Admiralty Mining Establishment [*British*] (MCD)
AME .... Adult Migrant Education [*Department of Labor*]
AME .... Advanced Master of Education
AME .... Advanced Modeling Extension [*Computer science*] (PCM)
AME .... Aeromedical Evacuation [*Formerly, AE, AMDLEVAC*] (AABC)
AME .... Aeronave Militar Espanola, Ministerio de Defensa [*Spain*] [*FAA designator*] (FAAC)
AME .... African Methodist Episcopal [*Church*]
AME .... Agreed Medical examiner (DAVI)
AME .... Aircraft Mission Equipment (MCD)
AME .... Aircraft Movement Element (MCD)
AME .... Airspace Management Element (MCD)
AME .... Alberta Materials Exchange [*Formerly, Alberta Waste Materials Exchange*] (AC)
AME .... Alliance for Monetary Education (EA)
AME .... Alliance Missionnaire Evangelique [*Missionary Evangelical Alliance - MEA*] [*Renens, Switzerland*] (EAIO)
AME .... Alternariol Methyl Ether [*Biochemistry*]
AME .... Alternate Mission Equipment (MCD)
AME .... Alveolar Mixing Efficiency [*Physiology*]
AME .... Amchitka East [*Alaska*] [*Seismograph station code, US Geological Survey Closed*] (SEIS)
AME .... American (BARN)
AmE .... American English [*Language*] (WGA)
AME .... Ametek, Inc. [*NYSE symbol*] (SPSG)
AME .... Amphotericin B Methyl Ester [*A drug*]
AME .... Amplitude Modulation Equivalent [*Telecommunications*] (TEL)
AME .... Angle Measuring Equipment
AME .... Antimultipath Equipment
AME .... Apparent Metabolisable Energy
AME .... Apparent Mineralocorticoid Excess [*Medicine*]
A-ME .... Arcuate-Median Eminence [*Anatomy*]
AME .... Associated Memory Equipment
AME .... Associate Managing Editor (WDMC)
AME .... Association for Management Excellence [*Later, AAIM*] (EA)
AME .... Association for Manufacturing Excellence (EA)
AME .... Association of Marriage Enrichment [*British*] (DBA)
AME .... Association of Membership Executives (EA)
AME .... Astronaut Maneuvering Equipment [*NASA*] (MCD)
AME .... Authorized Medical Examiner (DA)
AME .... Automatic Microfiche Editor
AME .... Automatic Monitoring Equipment
AME .... Automotive Mechanical and Electrical [*Test*]
AME .... Average Monthly Earnings
AME .... Aviation Medical Examiner
AME .... Aviation Structural Mechanic, Safety Equipment [*Navy rating*]
AME .... Fuerzas Aereas Espanolas [*Spain ICAO designator*] (FAAC)
AME .... Medley Public Library, Alberta [*Library symbol National Library of Canada*] (NLC)
AME .... MERADCOM [*Mobility Equipment Research and Development Command*] Technical Library, Fort Belvoir, VA [*OCLC symbol*] (OCLC)
AME1 .... Aviation Structural Mechanic, Safety Equipment, First Class [*Navy rating*] (DNAB)
AME2 .... Aviation Structural Mechanic, Safety Equipment, Second Class [*Navy rating*] (DNAB)
AME3 .... Aviation Structural Mechanic, Safety Equipment, Third Class [*Navy rating*] (DNAB)
AMEA .... American Medical Electroencephalographic Association (DAVI)
AMEA .... American Medical Equestrian Association (EA)
AMEA .... Apparel Manufacturing Executives Association (EA)
AMEA .... Association of Machinery and Equipment Appraisers (EA)
AMEAA .... Aviation Structural Mechanic, Safety Equipment, Airman Apprentice [*Navy rating*]
AmEagl .... American Eagle Group [*Associated Press*] (SAG)
AMEAMS..... Adaptive Multibeam Experiment for Aeronautical and Maritime Services (MCD)
AMEAN .... Aviation Structural Mechanic, Safety Equipment, Airman [*Navy rating*]
AMEB .... American Embassy (DNAB)
AMEBIA....... Amebiasis [*Medicine*] (DAVI)
AMEC .... Acoustic Model Evaluation Committee [*Woods Hole Oceanographic Institution*] (MSC)

AMEC.......... Advanced Manufacturing Engineering Council
AMEC.......... Aft Master Events Controller [*NASA*] (NASA)
AMEC.......... Airframe Manufacturing Equipment Committee
AMEC.......... Army Management Engineering College (RDA)
AMEC.......... Army Mobility Equipment Center (SAA)
AMEC.......... Artic Military Environmental Cooperation [*U.S., Russia, and Norway study of radioactive waves*]
AMEC.......... Association des Malentendants Canadiens (AC)
AMEC.......... Association of Management Education Centres [*British*]
AMEC.......... Association of Missouri Electric Cooperatives (SRA)
AMECD .... Association for Measurement and Evaluation in Counseling and Development (EA)
AMECFA...... Aerospace Engineering Test Establishment, Canadian Forces Base Coal Lake, Medley, Alberta [*Library symbol National Library of Canada*] (NLC)
AMECH .... Account Mechanical
AmEcol .... American Ecology Corp. [*Associated Press*] (SAG)
AMECOS ..... Automatic Measuring, Computing, and Sorting
AME/COTAR. Angle Measuring Equipment, Correlation Tracking and Ranging
AMECQ .... Association des Medias Ecrits Communautaires du Quebec (AC)
AMECUSD... Association of Manufacturers and Exporters of Concentrated and Unconcentrated Soft Drinks [*British*] (BI)
AMECZ........ Antimechanized [*Army*] (AABC)
AMED.......... AMEDISYS, Inc. [*NASDAQ symbol*] (SAG)
Am Ed .... American Edition (DLA)
AMED.......... Association of Management Education and Development [*British*] (DBA)
AMEDA .... Automatic Microscope Electronic Data Accumulator (MHDB)
AMEDD .... Army Medical Department (AABC)
AMED/DC .... Army Medical Corps/Dental Corps
AMEDDPAS.. Army Medical Department Property Accounting System (AABC)
AMedH........ American Medical Holdings, Inc. [*Associated Press*] (SAG)
AMedia........ American Media, Inc. [*Formerly, Enquirer/Star Group*] [*Associated Press*] (SAG)
AMed P....... Allied Medical Publications (NATG)
AMEDPC ..... Automotive Manufacturers EDP [*Electronic Data Processing*] Council (EA)
AMEDS .... Army Medical Science
AMEDS .... Army Medical Service
AMEDS .... Automated Measurement Evaluator and Director System (MHDB)
AmEduc ...... American Educational Products, Inc. [*Associated Press*] (SAG)
AMEE .... Admiralty Marine Engineering Establishment [*British*]
AMEE .... Association for Medical Education in Europe [*Scotland*]
AMEE .... Association of Managerial Electrical Executives [*British*] (BI)
AMEEGA ..... American Medical Electroencephalographic Association (EA)
AMEEMR...... Association for Medical Education in the Eastern Mediterranean Region [*United Arab Emirates*] (EAIO)
AMEG.......... Ambient Multimedia Environmental Goals [*Environmental Protection Agency*]
AMEG.......... Association for Measurement and Evaluation in Guidance [*Later, AMECD*] (EA)
AMEGL........ Acute Megakaryoblastic Leukemia [*Medicine*] (DMAA)
AMEGS .... AMSAA [*Army Materiel Systems Analysis Agency*] Missile End Game Simulation (MCD)
AMEHTS ..... Adult Migrant Education Home Tutor Scheme
AMEIC .... Associate Member of Engineering Institute of Canada
AMEL.......... Active Matrix Electroluminescent (RDA)
AMEL.......... Aero-Mechanical Engineering Laboratory [*Army*] (RDA)
AMEL.......... Aeromedical Equipment Laboratory
AMEL.......... Aircraft Multiengine Land [*Pilot rating*] (IEEE)
AMEL.......... Amer Brands [*AMB*] (TTSB)
Am El Ca .... American Electrical Cases [*A publication*] (ILCA)
Am Elec Ca... American Electrical Cases [*A publication*] (ILCA)
Am Elect Cas.. American Electrical Cases [*A publication*] (DLA)
Am Electl Cas... American Electrical Cases [*A publication*] (ILCA)
Am Electr Cas... American Electrical Cases [*A publication*] (DLA)
AME LNO .... Airspace Management Element Liaison Officer
AMEM.......... African Methodist Episcopal Mission
AMEM.......... Association of Marine Engine Manufacturers (EA)
AMEM.......... Association of Miniature Engine Manufacturers [*British*] (DBA)
AMEMB....... American Embassy (AFM)
AMEME .... Association of Mining, Electrical, and Mechanical Engineers [*British*] (DI)
AMEMIC...... Association of Mill and Elevator Mutual Insurance Companies (EA)
AMEN.......... Association Mondiale pour l'Energie Non-Polluante [*Planetary Association for Clean Energy - PACE*]
AMEN.......... Melbourne/Essendon [*Australia ICAO location identifier*] (ICLI)
Am Enc Dict.. American Encyclopedic Dictionary [*A publication*] (DLA)
AMEND .... Abusive Men Exploring New Directions [*In association name AMEND Network*]
AMEND .... Aiding Mothers Experienceing Neonatal Death [*Medicine*] (MEDA)
AMEND .... Amendment
AMEND .... Association for Relatives of the Mentally, Emotionally, and Nervously Disturbed [*British*] (BI)
AMENDT ...... Amendment
Am-Eng Ann Cases... American and English Annotated Cases [*A publication*] (DLA)
AmEagl .... Amer Educational Prd [*NASDAQ symbol*] (TTSB)
AMEP .... American Educational Products [*NASDAQ symbol*] (SAG)
AMER.......... Amer Federal Bank [*NASDAQ symbol*] (TTSB)
AMER.......... America
Amer.......... America (VRA)
AMER.......... America [*or American*]
AMER.......... American Middle East Rehabilitation (EA)
AMER.......... America Online [*NASDAQ symbol*] (TTSB)
AMER.......... America Online, Inc. [*NASDAQ symbol*] (SAG)

Amer........... Amerman's Reports [*111-115 Pennsylvania*] [*A publication*] (DLA)
AMER.......... Amersham [*England*]
AMERA........ American Arabic Association (EA)
Amer Acad Rome... Memoirs. American Academy at Rome [*A publication*] (OCD)
AMERADC.... Army Mobility Equipment Research and Development Center (MCD)
Ameral......... Ameralia, Inc. [*Associated Press*] (SAG)
Amer & Eng Enc Law... American and English Encyclopedia of Law [*A publication*] (DLA)
Amerasia J... Amerasia Journal [*A publication*] (BRI)
Amerc......... Amerco, Inc. [*Associated Press*] (SAG)
AmerCas...... Ameristar Casinos, Inc. [*Associated Press*] (SAG)
AMERCN...... American
AMERCO...... AMERCO [*Associated Press*] (SAG)
Amer Corp Cas... American Corporation Cases [*A publication*] (DLA)
Amercrd...... Americredit Corp. [*Associated Press*] (SAG)
Amer Dec ... American Decisions [*A publication*] (DLA)
AmerEco...... American Eco Corp. [*Associated Press*] (SAG)
Amer Elec Ca... American Electrical Cases [*A publication*] (DLA)
Amer Fed Tax Rep... American Federal Tax Reports [*Prentice-Hall, Inc.*] [*A publication*] (DLA)
Ameriana...... Ameriana Bancorp [*Associated Press*] (SAG)
AMERICAL ... Americans in New Caledonia [*Army's 23rd infantry; acronym used as name of division. Active in World War II, disbanded 1945; reactivated 1967-71*]
American Repts... American Reports [*A publication*] (DLA)
American State Rep... American State Reports [*A publication*] (DLA)
Ameridta...... Ameridata Technologies, Inc. [*Formerly, Sage Technologies*] [*Associated Press*] (SAG)
AMERIEZ...... Antarctic Marine Ecosystem Research at the Ice Edge Zone
Amerigas..... Amerigas Partners LP [*Associated Press*] (SAG)
Amerign...... Amerigon, Inc. [*Associated Press*] (SAG)
amerik........ Amerikanisch [*American*] [*German*]
AMERIMIC .. American Military Industrial Complex
Amerin........ Amerin Corp. [*Associated Press*] (SAG)
AMERIND..... American Indian
AmeriqTc..... Ameriquest Technology, Co. [*Formerly, CMS Enhancements*] [*Associated Press*] (SAG)
AmeriSrc ..... AmeriSource Health Corp. [*Associated Press*] (SAG)
Ameritch..... Ameritech Corp. [*Associated Press*] (SAG)
AMERITECH... American Information Technologies Corp. [*Telecommunications Chicago, IL*]
Ameriwd..... Ameriwood Industries International [*Associated Press*] (SAG)
Amer Jur .... American Jurist [*A publication*] (DLA)
Amer Law Reg (NS)... American Law Register, New Series [*A publication*] (DLA)
Amer Law Reg (OS)... American Law Register, Old Series [*A publication*] (DLA)
Amer Lea Cas... American Leading Cases [*A publication*] (DLA)
AmerOn ...... America Online, Inc. [*Associated Press*] (SAG)
Ameron........ Ameron, Inc. [*Associated Press*] (SAG)
AMEROSE.... American Committee of OSE [*Defunct*]
AmerPag...... American Paging, Inc. [*Associated Press*] (SAG)
Amer R........ Americas Review: A Review of Hispanic Literature and Art of the USA [*A publication*] (BRI)
Amer Rep .... American Reports [*A publication*] (DLA)
Amer Reports... American Reports [*A publication*] (DLA)
Amer Reps... American Reports [*A publication*] (DLA)
Amer Rev E-W Tr... American Review of East-West Trade [*A publication*] (DLA)
Amer R'y Rep... American Railway Reports [*A publication*] (DLA)
AMERSA...... Association of Medical Education and Research in Substance Abuse (EA)
AmersGF..... [*The*] Americas Growth Fund, Inc. [*Associated Press*] (SAG)
Amer State Reps... American State Reports [*A publication*] (DLA)
AMER STD... American Standard (WDAA)
Amer St Rep... American State Reports [*A publication*] (DLA)
Amer U....... [*The*] American University (GAGS)
AMERWAX... American Wax Importers and Refiners Association (EA)
AMES.......... Adult Migrant English Services [*New South Wales, Australia*]
AMESca...... Aeromedical Evacuation System [*Air Force*] (AFM)
AMES.......... Aircraft Maintenance Effectiveness Simulation (MCD)
AMES.......... Aircraft Multiengine Sea [*Pilot rating*] (AIA)
AMES.......... Air Member for Engineering and Supply [*British and Canadian*] [*World War II*]
AMES.......... Air Ministry Experimental Station [*British*]
Ames.......... Ames Department Stores [*Associated Press*] (SAG)
AMES.......... Ames Department Stores [*NASDAQ symbol*] (TTSB)
AMES.......... Ames Department Stores, Inc. [*NASDAQ symbol*] (SAG)
Ames.......... Ames' Reports [*4-7 Rhode Island*] [*A publication*] (DLA)
Ames.......... Ames' Reports [*1 Minnesota*] [*A publication*] (DLA)
AMES.......... Association of Marine Engineering Schools [*Liverpool, Merseyside, England*] (EAIO)
AMES.......... Australian Major Energy Statistics [*Database*]
AMES.......... Automated Medical Examination System (PDAA)
AMES.......... Automatic Message Entry System [*Computer science*] (MCD)
AMES.......... East Sale [*Australia ICAO location identifier*] (ICLI)
Ames Cas B & N... Ames' Cases on Bills and Notes [*A publication*] (DLA)
Ames Cas Par... Ames' Cases on Partnership [*A publication*] (DLA)
Ames Cas Pl... Ames' Cases on Pleading [*A publication*] (DLA)
Ames Cas Sur... Ames' Cases on Suretyship [*A publication*] (DLA)
Ames Cas Trusts... Ames' Cases on Trusts [*A publication*] (DLA)
Ames DS ..... Ames Department Stores [*Associated Press*] (SAG)
Ames K & B... Ames', Knowles', and Bradley's Reports [*8 Rhode Island*] [*A publication*] (DLA)
AMESLAN .... American Sign Language [*for the deaf*]
AMESP........ Administration des Mesures d'Encouragement du Secteur Petrolier [*Petroleum Incentives Administration*] [*Canada*]
AmEsq .... American Esquire [*Record label*]

AMESW........ Ames Dept Stores Wrrt 'C' [*NASDAQ symbol*] (TTSB)
AMET .... Accelerated Mission Endurance Test (MCD)
AMET .... Africa - Middle East Theater [*World War II*]
A Met......... Associate in Metallurgy [*British*]
AMETA........ Army Management Engineering Training Agency (RDA)
AMETA........ Army Materiel Education and Training Activity [*School of Engineering at Red River Army Depot*] [*Texarkana, TX*] (RDA)
Ametek....... Ametek, Inc. [*Associated Press*] (SAG)
Am Ethnol... American Ethnologist [*A publication*] (BRI)
AMETS........ Artillery Meteorological System (NATG)
AMEU......... Americans for Middle East Understanding (EA)
AMEU......... Automotive, Metal, and Engineering Union
AMEVN........ Fortis AMEV [*AM Symbol*] (TTSB)
AMEX......... Agencia Mexicana de Noticias SA [*Press agency*] [*Mexico*]
AMEX......... Airletter Mail Service [*American Express Co.*]
AMEX......... American Exiles
AMEX......... American Express Co.
AMEX......... American Stock Exchange [*New York, NY*] (EA)
AMEXCO ..... American Express Co.
AmExp .... American Express Co. [*Associated Press*] (SAG)
AMEZ......... African Methodist Episcopal Zion [*Church*]
AMF .... Abort Motor Facility [*NASA*] (NASA)
AMF .... ACE [*Allied Command Europe*] Mobile Force [*NATO*]
AMF .... Acid-Modified Flour (OA)
AMF .... ACM Managed Income Fund [*NYSE symbol*] (TTSB)
AMF .... ACM Managed Income Fund, Inc. [*NYSE symbol*] (CTT)
AMF .... Acoustic Match Filter
AMF .... Actuarial Mail File [*IRS*]
AMF .... Advanced Maneuvering FLAP [*Flight Application Software*] (MCD)
AMF .... Air Mail Facility [*Post Office*]
AMF .... Air Mail Field
AMF .... Airman Memorial Foundation (EA)
AMF .... Air Materiel Force
AMF .... Airport Mail Facility (AFM)
AMF .... Algonquin Minerals [*Vancouver Stock Exchange symbol*]
AMF .... Allied Mobile Force [*NATO*]
AMF .... Ama [*Papua New Guinea*] [*Airport symbol*] (OAG)
AMF .... Ambler, AK [*Location identifier FAA*] (FAAL)
AMF .... American Messianic Fellowship (EA)
AMF .... American Missionary Fellowship (EA)
AMF .... Americans for Medical Freedom [*Defunct*] (EA)
AMF .... Ameriflight, Inc. [*ICAO designator*] (FAAC)
Amf.......... Amfion [*Record label*] [*Mexico*]
AMF .... Amparafaravola [*Malagasy*] [*Airport symbol*] (AD)
AMF .... Analog Matched Filter
AMF .... Annual Material Forecast [*Military*] (AFM)
AMF .... Antimuscle Factor [*Immunology*]
AMF .... Apogee Motor Fire [*Aerospace*]
AMF .... Applicant Master File [*State Employee Security Agency*] (OICC)
AMF .... Arab Monetary Fund
AMF .... Arc Melting Furnace
AMF .... Area Maintenance Facility
AMF .... Army Management Fund
AMF .... Assembly Machine Fixture (MCD)
AMF .... Autocrine Mobility Factor [*Oncology*]
AMFA......... Aircraft Mechanics Fraternal Association (EA)
AMFA......... Allied Military Financial Agency [*World War II*]
AMF(A)....... Allied Mobile Force (Air) [*NATO*]
AMFA......... Alternative Motor Fuels Act
AMFA......... American Music Festival Association (EA)
AMFA......... Association Medicale Franco-Americaine (EA)
AmFAR....... American Foundation for AIDS Research [*New York, NY*] (EA)
AMFAX........ Aviation Meteorological Facsimile [*National Weather Service*]
AMFB......... American Federal Bank [*NASDAQ symbol*] (CTT)
AMFC......... AMB Financial [*NASDAQ symbol*] (TTSB)
AMFC......... AMB Financial Corp. [*NASDAQ symbol*] (SAG)
AMFC......... Andrea McArdle Fan Club (EA)
AMFC......... Anne Murray Fan Club (EA)
AMFC......... Australian Meatworks Federal Council
AMFDP........ Army Master Force Development Plan (MCD)
AMFEA........ Air Materiel Force, European Area
Amfed........ Amfed Financial, Inc. [*Associated Press*] (SAG)
Am Fed Tax R... American Federal Tax Reports [*Prentice-Hall, Inc.*] [*A publication*] (DLA)
Am Fed Tax R 2d... American Federal Tax Reports, Second Series [*Prentice-Hall, Inc.*] [*A publication*] (DLA)
AMFEP........ Association of Microbial Food Enzyme Producers (EA)
AMFF .... Advanced Materials Fabrication Facility [*Manufacturing*] (MCD)
AMFF .... Amfed Financial, Inc. [*NASDAQ symbol*] (SAG)
AMFFA........ American Medical Fly Fishing Association (EA)
AMFGC........ Association of Midwest Fish and Game Commissioners [*Later, AMFWA*]
AMFH......... Association of Memoirists and Family Historians (EA)
AMFHSTFU... Association of Members and Friends of the Historic Southern Tenant Farmers Union [*Defunct*] (EA)
AMFI.......... Amcore Financial [*NASDAQ symbol*] (SAG)
AMFI.......... Aviation Maintenance Foundation, Inc. (EA)
AMFIA........ Associate Member of the Fundraising Institute-Australia, Inc. (NFD)
AMFIE........ Association of Mutual Fire Insurance Engineers [*Later, ILCA*]
AMFINFOS... American Forces Information Service [*DoD*] (AABC)
AMFIS........ American Microfilm Information Society [*An association*] (ECII)
AMFIS........ Automatic Microfilm Information System
AMF(L)....... Allied Mobile Force (Land) [*NATO*]
AMF-L......... Faulkner University, Jones School of Law, Montgomery, AL [*Library symbol*] [*Library of Congress*] (LCLS)

AMFM.......... Advisory Panel of Alternative Means of Financing and Managing Radioactive Waste Facilities [*Terminated, 1984*] [*Department of Energy*] (EGAO)

AM-FM........ Algorithm Mass-Factoring Method (MCD)

AMFM.......... Association Mondiale des Federalistes Mondiaux [*World Association of World Federalists - WAWF*] (EA)

AMFM.......... Automated Mapping/Facility Management [*Computer science*]

AMFO.......... Association of Manpower Franchise Owners (EA)

Am For L Ass'n Newsl... American Foreign Law Association. Newsletter [*A publication*] (DLA)

AMFPA........ Air Materiel Force, Pacific Area

AmFPr......... America First Part Preferred Equity Mortgage Fund Ltd. [*Associated Press*] (SAG)

AMFPS........ Association of Mutual Fund Plan Sponsors [*Later, ICI*] (EA)

AMFR.......... Aerospace Mechanical Fastening Requirements (MCD)

AmFrght...... American Freightways Corp. [*Associated Press*] (SAG)

AMFS.......... Airframe Mechanical and Fluid Subsystems (MCD)

AMFSO........ Assistant Missile Flight Safety Officer (MUGU)

AMFT.......... Association of Migrants from Turkey [*Australia*]

AMFUR........ Amplified Failure or Unsatisfactory Report [*Obsolete*]

AMFV.......... A Mind Forever Voyaging [*Infocom Computer gaming*]

AMFWA........ Association of Midwest Fish and Wildlife Agencies (EA)

AMFWC........ Association of Midwest Fish and Wildlife Commissioners [*Later, AMFWA*] (EA)

AMFWSCA ... AMF Windflite Sailboard Class Association (EA)

AMG.......... Acoustic Myography [*Otorhinolaryngology*] (DAVI)

AMG.......... Acquisition Management Guide [*Military*] (AFIT)

AMG.......... Acreage Marketing Guide

AMG.......... Activation Management Group [*NASA*] (NASA)

AMG.......... Aircraft Machine Gunner

AMG.......... Air Material AG [*Switzerland ICAO designator*] (FAAC)

AMG.......... Alarm Monitor Group [*Army*]

AMG.......... Albertus Magnus Guild (EA)

AMG.......... Algebraic Multigrid [*Computation method*]

AMG.......... Alles mit Gott [*Everything with God*] [*Motto of Georg Albrecht, Margrave of Brandenburg-Baireuth (1619-66)*] [*German*]

AMG.......... Allied Medical Group [*British*]

AMG.......... Allied Military Government [*of occupied territory*] [*Formerly, AMGOT Post-World War II*]

AMG.......... Alma, GA [*Location identifier FAA*] (FAAL)

AMG.......... Alpha-Macroglobulin [*Biochemistry*]

AMG.......... Amboin [*Papua New Guinea*] [*Airport symbol*] (OAG)

AMG.......... American Military Government

AMG.......... American Mission to Greeks [*Later, AMG International*] (EA)

AMG.......... Americus [*Georgia*] [*Seismograph station code, US Geological Survey*] (SEIS)

AMG.......... Among

AMG.......... Amplitude Modulation Generator

AMG.......... Amyloglucosidase [*An enzyme*] (KSC)

AMG.......... Angle of Middle Gimbal

AMG.......... Antenna Mast Group [*PATRIOT*] [*Army*] (RDA)

AMG.......... Antimacrophage Globulin (MAE)

AMG.......... Applied Mathematics Group [*Brown University*] (MCD)

AMG.......... Applied Microbiology Group [*Natick Laboratories*] [*Army*] (RDA)

AMG.......... Arizona Masonry Guild (SRA)

AMG.......... Armor Machine Gun (MCD)

AM-G.......... Assistant Major-General [*Military British*] (ROG)

AMG.......... Ausfrech-Melcher-Grossapach [*Mercedes-Benz cars*] [*High-performance parts supplier*]

AMG.......... Australian Musicians' Guild

AMG.......... Automatic Magnetic Guidance

AMG.......... Axiomesiogingival [*Dentistry*]

AMG.......... Medicine Hat General Hospital, Alberta [*Library symbol National Library of Canada*] (NLC)

AMGA......... American Medical Golf Association (EA)

AMGA......... American Modified Golf Association (EA)

AMGA......... American Murray Grey Association (EA)

AMGA......... Award of Merit for Group Achievement [*Military*] (DNAB)

AMGBA........ American MGB Association (EA)

AMGCR........ American MGC Register (EA)

AMGD......... American Vanguard Corp. [*NASDAQ symbol*] (NQ)

AMGD......... Amer Vanguard [*NASDAQ symbol*] (TTSB)

AMGE.......... Association Mondiale des Guides et des Eclaireuses [*World Association of Girl Guides and Girl Scouts - WAGGGS*] [*London, England*] (EAIO)

AMGE.......... Association of Marine and General Engineers [*A union*] [*British*]

Amgen......... Amgen, Inc. [*Associated Press*] (SAG)

Am Geneal... American Genealogist [*A publication*] (BRI)

AMGLU........ Amalgamated Machine and General Labourers Union [*British*]

AMGM......... Airmailgram

AMGN......... Amgen, Inc. [*NASDAQ symbol*] (NQ)

AMGO......... Assistant Master-General of Ordnance [*British*]

AmGold........ Americana Gold & Diamond Holdings [*Associated Press*] (SAG)

AMGOT........ Allied Military Government of Occupied Territory [*Later, AMG*] [*Post-World War II*]

AMGP......... Association of Medical Group Psychoanalysts (EA)

AMGR......... Airport Manager (FAAC)

AMGRA........ American Milk Goat Record Association [*Later, ADGA*] (EA)

AMGS......... Acceleration Monitoring Guidance System (MCD)

AMGS......... Association for Maintained Girls' Schools (AIE)

AMGS......... Australian Macadamia Growers' Society

AMGSSS...... Air Mobile Ground Security and Surveillance System [*Army*]

AMGST........ Amongst (ROG)

AmGvl......... American Government Income Fund [*Associated Press*] (SAG)

AMH.......... Alan Mann Helicopters Ltd. [*British*] [*FAA designator*] (FAAC)

AMH.......... Alaska Military Highway

AMH.......... Almaden Resources Corp. [*Vancouver Stock Exchange symbol*]

AMH.......... Amdahl Corp. [*AMEX symbol*] (SPSG)

amh.......... Amharic [*MARC language code Library of Congress*] (LCCP)

AMH.......... Amherst College, Amherst, MA [*OCLC symbol*] (OCLC)

AMH.......... Anti-Muellerian Hormone [*Also, MIS*] [*Embryology*] [*Biochemistry*]

AMH.......... Arba Minch [*Ethiopia*] [*Airport symbol*] (AD)

AMH.......... Association Mondiale de Hockey [*World Hockey Association - WHA*] [*Canada*]

AMH.......... Association of Marian Helpers (EA)

AMH.......... Automated Medical History

AMH.......... Aviation Structural Mechanic, Hydraulic Mechanic [*Navy rating*]

AMH.......... Harbor Minesweepers [*Navy symbol*]

AMH.......... Huntingdon College, Montgomery, AL [*Library symbol Library of Congress*] (LCLS)

a-mh--.......... Macao [*MARC geographic area code Library of Congress*] (LCCP)

AMH.......... Mixed Astigmatism with Exceeding Myopia [*Ophthalmology*]

Amh.......... Mixed Astigmatism with Myopia Predominating [*Ophthalmology*] (DAVI)

AMH1.......... Aviation Structural Mechanic, Hydraulics, First Class [*Navy rating*] (DNAB)

AMH2.......... Aviation Structural Mechanic, Hydraulics, Second Class [*Navy rating*] (DNAB)

AMH3.......... Aviation Structural Mechanic, Hydraulics, Third Class [*Navy rating*] (DNAB)

AMHA......... Alaska Manufactured Housing Association (SRA)

AMHA......... American Miniature Horse Association (EA)

AMHA......... American Morab Horse Association (EA)

AMHA......... American Morgan Horse Association (EA)

AMHA......... American Motor Hotel Association (EA)

AMHA......... Arizona Mobile Housing Association (SRA)

AMHA......... Arkansas Manufactured Housing Association (SRA)

AMHA......... Army Management Headquarters Activity (MCD)

AMHA......... Association of Mental Health Administrators (EA)

AMHAA........ Aviation Structural Mechanic, Hydraulics, Airman Apprentice [*Navy rating*]

AMHAI........ Association for Mental Health Affiliation with Israel (EA)

AMHAN........ Aviation Structural Mechanic, Hydraulics, Airman [*Navy rating*]

AMHA-TP.... Automated Microhemagglutination Assay for Antibodies to Treponema pallidum [*Serology*]

AMHAZ........ Ammunition and Hazardous Materials Handling Review Board (MCD)

AMHB......... Hobart [*Australia ICAO location identifier*] (ICLI)

AMHC......... Amer Healthcorp [*NASDAQ symbol*] (TTSB)

AMHC......... American Healthcorp [*NASDAQ symbol*] (SPSG)

AMHC......... Association of Mental Health Clergy (EA)

AMHC......... Aviation Structural Mechanic, Hydraulics, Chief [*Navy rating*] (DNAB)

AMHCA........ American Mental Health Counselors Association (EA)

AMHD......... Average Man-Hours per Day (DNAB)

AMHE......... Association des Medecins Haitiens a l'Etranger [*Association of Haitian Physicians Abroad*] (EA)

AmHes......... Amerada-Hess Corp. [*Associated Press*] (SAG)

AMHF......... American Mental Health Foundation (EA)

AMHF......... American Mental Health Fund (EA)

AMHF......... American Motorcycle Heritage Foundation (EA)

AMHF......... Hobart [*Australia ICAO location identifier*] (ICLI)

AMHI.......... Alabama Manufactured Housing Institute (SRA)

AMHI.......... American Morgan Horse Institute (EA)

Am Hist...... American History [*A publication*] (BRI)

AMHL......... Association of Mental Health Librarians (EA)

AMHN......... Aboriginal Mental Health Network [*Western Australia*]

AmHotl......... Americana Hotels & Realty Corp. [*Associated Press*] (SAG)

AMHPD........ Association of Mental Health Practitioners with Disabilities [*Defunct*] (EA)

AMHPS........ Association of Minority Health Professions Schools (EA)

AMHR......... American Miniature Horse Registry (EA)

AMHS......... American Material Handling Society [*Later, IMMS*] (EA)

AMHS......... Association of Mental Health Specialties (EA)

AMHS......... Association of Methodist Historical Societies [*Later, General Commission on Archives and History of the United Methodist Church*] (EA)

AMHS......... Automated Materials Handling System [*Computer science*]

AMHS......... Automated Message Handling System

AMHS......... Medicine Hat High School, Alberta [*Library symbol National Library of Canada*] (NLC)

AMHS......... Melbourne [*Australia ICAO location identifier*] (ICLI)

AMHSA........ Association of Massachusetts Homes and Services for the Aging (SRA)

AMHSA........ Automated Materials Handling Systems Association [*British*] (DBA)

AMHT......... Automated Multiphasic Health Testing

AMHTS........ Automated Multiphasic Health Testing and Services (KSC)

AMHTTA...... Associate Member of the Highway and Traffic Technicians' Association [*British*] (DBQ)

AMI.......... Absolute Memory Image (MCD)

AMI.......... Access Methods, Inc. (NITA)

AMI.......... Acme Metals [*NYSE symbol*] (TTSB)

AMI.......... Acme Metals [*NYSE symbol*] (SAG)

AMI.......... Acquired Monosaccharide Intolerance [*Medicine*] (DMAA)

AMI.......... Active Microwave Instrument

AMI.......... Acute Mesenteric Ischemia [*Medicine*]

AMI.......... Acute Myocardial Infarction [*Medicine*]

AMI.......... Advanced Manned Interceptor [*US Air Force Artillery Spotting Division interceptor*]

AMI.......... Advanced Manufacturing Initiative [*Department of Energy*]

AMI.......... Advertising and Marketing Intelligence [*The New York Times Co.*] [*Information service or system*] (CRD)

AMI	Aerospace Materials Information
AMI	Africa Music International [*Lorient, France*] (EAIO)
AMI	Agence Maritime Internationale [*International Maritime Agency*]
AMI	Agence Mauritanienne de l'Information [*News Agency*] (EY)
AMI	Aircraft Multiplex Intercommunications
AMI	Airline Mutual Insurance [*International Air Transport Association*]
AMI	Air Maldives [*ICAO designator*] (FAAC)
AMI	Air Mercury International [*Belgium ICAO designator*] (FAAC)
AMI	Air Mileage Indicator [*Navigation*]
AMI	Air Movement Institute (EA)
AMI	Airspeed Mach Indicator (MCD)
AMI	Alliance of Metalworking Industries (EA)
AMI	Alpha/Mach Indicator (NASA)
AMI	Alternate Mark Inversion [*Telecommunications*] (IEEE)
AMI	Alternative Mark Inversion Signal (NITA)
AMI	Alternative Mortgage Instrument
AMI	Amalgamated Military and Technical Improvement Plan (DNAB)
AMI	American Management Institute (IIA)
AMI	American Meat Institute (EA)
AMI	American Megatrends, Inc. (PCM)
AMI	American Methanol Institute
AMI	American Microsystems, Inc. (MCD)
AMI	American Military Institute (EA)
AMI	American Mothers, Inc. (EA)
AMI	American Motorsport International (EA)
AMI	American Museum of Immigration (EA)
AMI	American Mushroom Institute (EA)
AMI	American Reserve Mining Corp. [*Vancouver Stock Exchange symbol*]
Ami	Amiga [*Record label*] [*Germany*]
AMI	Amitriptyline [*Also, AT*] [*Antidepressant compound*]
AMI	Ampenan [*Indonesia*] [*Airport symbol*] (AD)
AMI	Analytical Methods, Inc.
AMI	Annual Military Inspection
AMI	Anterior Myocardial Infarction [*Medicine*] (DMAA)
AMI	Antimateriel Incendiary
AMI	Apogee Motor Igniter [*NASA*]
AMI	Applied Materials, Inc.
AMI	Applied Mathematics Institute [*University of Delaware*] [*Research center*] (RCD)
AMI	Arginine Maturity Index [*For prediction of peanut harvest date*]
AMI	Assistance Medicale Internationale [*International Medical Assistance*] [*Canada*]
AMI	Association des Manoeuvres Interprovinciaux [*Interprovincial Labourers Association*] (AC)
AMI	Association for Multi-Image (EA)
AMI	Association Media Independents Ltd. [*British*] (DBA)
AMI	Association Montessori Internationale [*International Montessori Association*] [*Amsterdam, Netherlands*] (EAIO)
AMI	Association of Meat Inspectors [*British*]
AMI	Association of Medical Illustrators (EA)
AMI	Australasian Medical Index [*A publication*]
AMI	Austria Microsystems International (NITA)
AMI	Automatic Motion Inhibit [*Nuclear energy*] (NRCH)
AMI	Auxiliary Inshore Minesweeper [*NATO*]
AMI	Average Mutual Information (PDAA)
AMI	Axiomesioincisal [*Dentistry*]
AMI	Handmaids of Mary Immaculate [*Roman Catholic religious order*]
AMI	Mataram [*Indonesia*] [*Airport symbol*] (OAG)
AMI	Millet Public Library, Alberta [*Library symbol National Library of Canada*] (NLC)
AMIA	American Medical Informatics Association (EA)
AMIA	American Metal Importers Association [*Defunct Defunct*] (EA)
AMIA	American Mutual Insurance Alliance [*Later, Alliance of American Insurers*] (EA)
AMIA	Angular Magnetic-Hydrodynamic Integrating Accelerometer
AMIA	Australian Management Industrial Association
AMIADB	Army Member, Inter-American Defense Board (AABC)
AMIAE	Associate Member of the Institute of Aeronautical Engineers [*British*] (DI)
AMIAE	Associate Member of the Institute of Automobile Engineers [*British*] (ROG)
AMI Ae E	Associate Member of Institution of Aeronautical Engineers [*British*]
AMIAgrE	Associate Member of the Institution of Agricultural Engineers [*British*]
AMIAMA	Associate Member of the Incorporated Advertising Managers' Association (DGA)
AMIAP	Associate of the Institution of Analysts and Programmers [*British*] (DBQ)
AMIAT	Associate Member of the Institute of Asphalt Technology [*British*] (DBQ)
AMIB	Army Military Intelligence Battalion (MCD)
AMIC	Aerospace Materials Information Center [*Air Force*] (MCD)
AMIC	Air Movement Information Center [*NATO*] (NATG)
AMIC	American Marine Insurance Clearinghouse [*New York, NY*] (EA)
AMIC	Analytical Methodology Information Center [*Environmental Protection Agency*]
AMIC	Arbitration & Mediation Institute of Canada Inc. [*Institut d'Arbitrage et de Mediation du Canada Inc.*] [*Formerly, Arbitrators' Institute of Canada*] (AC)
AMIC	Army Methods of Instruction Centre [*British military*] (DMA)
AMIC	Asian Mass Communication Research and Information Centre [*Singapore*] (EAIO)
AMIC	Automated Management Information Center (SSD)
Amic	De Amicitia [*of Cicero*] [*Classical studies*] (OCD)
AMICA	Automatic Module for Industrial Control Analysis
AMICA	Automatic Musical Instrument Collectors Association (EA)

AMICA	Automobile Mutual Insurance Co. of America
AMICE	Associate Member of the Institution of Civil Engineers [*Later, MICE*] [*British*]
AMI Chem E	Associate Member of the Institution of Chemical Engineers [*British*]
AMICOM	Army Missile Command
AMICorrST	Associate Member of the Institution of Corrosion Science and Technology [*British*] (DBQ)
AMICS	Aircraft Maintenance Irregularity Control System (PDAA)
AMICUS	Automated Management Information Civil Users System [*Department of Justice*] (GFGA)
AMICW	Associate Member of the Institute of Clerks of Works [*British*] (DI)
AMIDEAST	America-Mideast Educational and Training Services [*Acronym is now organization's official name*] (EA)
AMIDS	Advanced Multispectral Image Descriptor System [*Photography*]
AMIDS	Airborne Minefield Detector System (MCD)
AMIDS	Airport Management and Information Display System (DA)
AMIDS	Area Manpower Instructional Development Systems
AMIE	Ambassadors International, Inc. [*NASDAQ symbol*] (SAG)
AMIE	Ambassadors Intl. [*NASDAQ symbol*] (TTSB)
AMIE	Association of Mutual Insurance Engineers [*Later, ILCA*] (EA)
AMIED	Associate Member of the Institution of Engineering Designers [*British*]
AMIEE	Associate Member of the Institution of Electrical Engineers [*Later, MIEE*] [*British*] (EY)
AMIElecIE	Associate Member of the Institution of Electrical and Electronics Incorporated Engineers [*British*] (DBQ)
AMIERE	Associate Member of the Institution of Electronic and Radio Engineers [*Formerly, AM Brit IRE*] [*British*]
AMIEV	Association Medicale Internationale pour l'Etudes des Conditions de Vie et de Sante [*International Medical Association for the Study of Living Conditions and Health*] [*Sofia, Bulgaria*] (EAIO)
AMIEx	Associate Member of the Institute of Export [*British*]
AMIF	American Marine Insurance Forum [*New York, NY*] (EA)
AMIF	American Meat Institute Foundation (EA)
AMIF	Associate Member of the Institute of Fuel [*British*]
AMIF	Automated Map Information File [*DoD*] (PDAA)
AMIFireE	Associate Member of the Institution of Fire Engineers [*British*]
AMIGasE	Associate Member of the Institution of Gas Engineers [*British*]
AMIGeol	Associate of the Geological Society [*British*] (DBQ)
AMIGO	Ants, Mice, and Gophers [*Electromagnetic antipest device*]
AMIGOS	Access Method for Indexed Data Generalized for Operating System [*Computer science*]
AMIGOS	Americans Mutually Interested in Giving Others a Start [*Defunct*] (EA)
AMIH	Association for Middle-Income Housing [*Later, MMHA*] (EA)
AMIHT	Associate Member of the Institution of Highway Engineers [*British*] (DBQ)
AMIHVE	Associate Member of the Institute of Heating and Ventilating Engineers [*British*] (DI)
AMII	Association of Musical Instrument Industries [*British*] (BI)
AMIIA	Army Medical Intelligence and Information Agency (MCD)
AMIISE	Associate Member of the International Institute of Social Economics [*British*] (DBQ)
AMIK	American Mission in Korea
AMIK	(Amino)(Iodo)ketanserin [*Biochemistry*]
AMILM	Milo Municipal Library, Alberta [*Library symbol National Library of Canada*] (NLC)
AMILocoE	Associate Member of the Institution of Locomotive Engineers [*British*]
AMIM	Army Modernization Information Memorandum (RDA)
AMIM	Associate Member of the Institute of Metallurgists [*British*] (DBQ)
AMIManf	Associate Member of the Institute of Manufacturing [*British*] (DBQ)
AMI Mar E	Associate Member of the Institute of Marine Engineers [*British*]
AMIME	Associate Member of the Institution of Marine Engineers [*British*] (DS)
AMIME	Associate Member of the Institution of Mining Engineers [*British*]
AMIMechE	Associate Member of the Institution of Mechanical Engineers [*Later, MIMechE*] [*British*] (EY)
AMIMGTechE	Associate Member of the Institution of Mechanical and General Technician Engineers [*British*] (DBQ)
AMIMH	Associate Member of the Institute of Materials Handling [*British*] (DBQ)
AMIMI	Associate Member of the Institute of the Motor Industry [*British*]
AMIMinE	Associate Member of the Institution of Mining Engineers [*British*] (EY)
AMIMM	Associate Member of the Institution of Mining and Metallurgy [*British*]
AMIMS	Associate Member of the Institute of Management Specialists [*British*] (DBQ)
AMI Mun E	Associate Member of the Institution of Municipal Engineers [*British*]
AMIN	Advertising and Marketing International Network [*Stamford, CT*] (EA)
AM In	AM International [*Associated Press*] (SAG)
AMINA	Associate Member of the Institution of Naval Architects [*British*]
AMINA	Association Mondiale des Inventeurs [*World Association of Inventors and Researchers*] (EAIO)
AmInc	American Income Holdings, Inc. [*Associated Press*] (SAG)
AMINCO	American Instrument Co.
AMIND	American Indian
Am Ind CRJ	American Indian Culture and Research Journal [*A publication*] (BRI)
Am Ind J	American Indian Journal [*A publication*] (DLA)
Am Ind L Newsl	American Indian Law Newsletter [*A publication*] (DLA)
Am Ind L Rev	American Indian Law Review [*A publication*] (DLA)
AMINOIL	American Independent Oil Co.
AmInPt	American International Petroleum Corp. [*Associated Press*] (SAG)
Am Insolv Rep	American Insolvency Reports [*A publication*] (DLA)
Am Ins Rep	American Insolvency Reports [*A publication*] (DLA)
AMInstAEA	Associate Member of the Institute of Automotive Engineer Assessors [*British*] (DBQ)
AMInstBE	Associate Member of the Institution of British Engineers

AMInstBTM... Associate Member of the Institute of Business and Technical Management [*British*] (DBQ)
AMInstCE..... Associate Member of the Institution of Civil Engineers [*British*] (EY)
AM Inst CM... Associate Member of the Institute of Commercial Management [*British*] (DCTA)
AM Inst E... Associate Member of the Institute of Electronics [*British*]
AmInstEE..... American Institute of Electrical Engineers [*Later, IEEE*]
AM Inst F.... Associate Member of the Institute of Fuel [*British*]
AM INST GE... Associate Member of the Institute of Gas Engineers [*British*] (ROG)
AMInstHE.... Associate Member of the Institution of Highway Engineers [*British*]
AMInstPC.... Associate Member of the Institute of Public Cleansing [*British*] (DI)
AMInstR..... Associate Member of the Institute of Refrigeration [*British*]
AMInstSM... Associate Member of the Institution of Sales Management [*British*] (DI)
AMInstT....... Associate Member of the Institute of Transport [*British*] (EY)
AM Inst TA... Associate Member of the Institute of Transport Administration [*British*] (DCTA)
AM Inst W ... Associate Member of the Institute of Welding [*British*]
AM in T .... Master of Arts in Teaching
AMINTAPHIL... International Association for Philosophy of Law and Social Philosophy, American Section (EA)
AmIntG .... American International Group [*Associated Press*] (SAG)
AM Intl .... AM International [*Associated Press*] (SAG)
AmIntPt....... American International Petroleum [*Associated Press*] (SAG)
AmIntPt....... American International Petroleum [*Associated Press*] (SAG)
AMIO .... Amiodarone [*Coronary vasodilator*] [*Cardiology*]
AMIOP .... Associate Member of the Institute of Printing (DGA)
AMIOSH....... Associate Member of the Institution of Occupational Safety and Health [*British*] (DCTA)
AMIP........... Allied Minimum Imports Program [*World War II*]
AMIP........... American Market for International Program [*Telecommunications*]
AMIP........... Army Management Information Program (AABC)
AMIP........... Army Management Intern Program (RDA)
AMIP........... Army Model Improvement Program (RDA)
AMIP........... Atmospheric Model Intercomparison Project (OSRA)
AMIP........... Atmospheric Model Intercomparison Project (USDC)
AMIPA .... Associate Member of the Institute of Practitioners in Advertising [*British*] (DI)
AMIPAC ...... Americans in Israel Political Action Committee (EA)
AMIPC .... Associate Member of the Institute of Production Control [*British*] (DBQ)
AMIPE......... Associate Member of the Institution of Production Engineers [*British*]
AMI Plant E... Associate Member of the Institute of Plant Engineers [*British*]
AMI-ProdE ... Associate Member of the Institution of Production Engineers [*British*] (DBQ)
AMI PTG M... Associate Member of the Institute of Printing Management (DGA)
AMIQ .... Associate Member of the Institute of Quarrying [*British*] (DBQ)
AMIQ .... Association pour l'Avancement de la Micro-Informatique [*Association for the Advancement of Micro-Information*] [*Canada*]
AMIQM .... Associate Member of the Institute of Quality Assurance (ODBW)
AMIR .... Mirror Public Library, Alberta [*Library symbol National Library of Canada*] (NLC)
AMIRA .... Amplified Immunoradiometric Assay
AMIREE (Aust)... Associate Member of the Institute of Radio and Electronic Engineers (Australia)
AMIRTE....... Associate Member of the Institute of Road Transport Engineers [*British*] (DBQ)
AMIS........... Acquisition Management Information System [*Air Force*]
AMIS........... Adult Migrant Information System [*Australia*]
AMIS........... Advanced Management Information Service [*or System*] [*Air Force*]
AMIS........... Agency Management Information Systems [*DCAA*] (AAGC)
AMIS........... Agricultural Management Information System [*European Economic Community*] (ADA)
AMIS........... Airborne Modular Integrated System (MCD)
AMIS........... Aircraft Movement Information Service [*Air Force*]
AMIS........... Aircraft Multiplex Intercommunications System
AMIS........... Air Movements Information Section
AMIS........... Airport Management Information System
AMIS........... American Musical Instrument Society (EA)
AMIS........... Amistad Recreation Area [*National Park Service designation*]
AMIS........... Arbitration & Mediation Institute of Saskatchewan Inc. (AC)
AMIS........... Army Management Information System
AMIS........... Aspirin Myocardial Infarction Study [*Medicine*]
AMIS........... Audio Media Integration Standard [*Telecommunications*] (BARN)
AMIS........... Automated Incendiary Submunition (MCD)
AMIS........... Automated Maintenance Information System (MCD)
AMIS........... Automated Management Information System (DIT)
AMIS........... Automated Mask Inspection System (PDAA)
AMIS........... Automated Minerals Information System [*Bureau of Mines*] [*Database*]
AMISC .... Army Management Information Systems Course
AMISIBR ...... American Marine Insurance Syndicate for Insurance of Builder's Risks [*Defunct*] (EA)
AMISM......... Associate Member of the Institute of Supervisory Management [*British*] (DBQ)
Amistar........ Amistar Corp. [*Associated Press*] (SAG)
AMIStruct E... Associate Member of the Institute of Structural Engineers [*British*]
AMITA......... American-Italian Women of Achievement
AMITD .... Associate Member of the Institute of Training and Development [*British*] (DBQ)
AMI-USA...... Association Montessori International - USA (EA)
AMIW.......... Associate Member of the Institute of Welding [*British*]
AMI Water E... Associate Member of the Institute of Water Engineers [*British*]
AMIWES ...... Associate Member of the Institution of Water Engineers and Scientists [*British*] (DI)

AMIWHTE .... Associate Member of the Institution of Works and Highways Technician Engineers [*British*] (DBQ)
AMIWM....... Associate Member of the Institution of Works Managers [*British*]
AMIWPC .... Associate Member of the Institute of Water Pollution Control [*British*] (DBQ)
AMIX........... American Information Exchange [*Information service or system*] (ECON)
AMJ .... Almenara [*Brazil*] [*Airport symbol Obsolete*] (OAG)
AMJ .... Assemblee Mondiale de la Jeunesse [*World Assembly of Youth*]
AMJ .... Augustines de la Misericorde de Jesus [*Religious order*] [*Canada*]
AMJ .... Aviation Amos [*M et J*], Inc. [*Canada ICAO designator*] (FAAC)
Am J 2d...... American Jurisprudence, Second Series [*A publication*] (DLA)
AMJA .... American Medical Joggers Association [*Later, AMAA*]
AMJAMS..... Automated Military Justice Analysis and Management System
Am J For Psych... American Journal of Forensic Psychiatry [*A publication*] (DLA)
Am J Juris... American Journal of Jurisprudence [*Lawyers Co-op*] [*A publication*] (AAGC)
Am J Leg Forms Anno... American Jurisprudence Legal Forms, Annotated [*A publication*] (DLA)
Am J L Rev... American Journal Law Review [*A publication*] (DLA)
Am Jour Soc... American Journal of Sociology [*A publication*] (DLA)
AMJP.......... [*A*] Messianic Jewish Perspective (EA)
Am J Pl & Pr Forms Anno... American Jurisprudence Pleading and Practice Forms, Annotated [*A publication*] (DLA)
Am J Police Sci... American Journal of Police Science [*A publication*] (DLA)
Am J Proof of Facts... American Jurisprudence Proof of Facts [*A publication*] (DLA)
Am Jr.......... American Jurisprudence [*A publication*] (DLA)
Am Jr.......... American Jurist [*A publication*] (DLA)
Am J Tax Pol'y... American Journal of Tax Policy [*A publication*] (DLA)
Am J Trial Advoc... American Journal of Trial Advocacy [*A publication*] (DLA)
Am J Trials... American Jurisprudence Trials [*A publication*] (DLA)
Am Jur........ American Jurisprudence [*A publication*] (DLA)
Am Jur........ American Jurist [*A publication*] (DLA)
Am Jur 2d ... American Jurisprudence, Second Series [*A publication*] (DLA)
Am Jurist..... American Jurist [*A publication*] (DLA)
Am Jur Legal Forms... American Jurisprudence Legal Forms [*A publication*] (DLA)
Am Jur Legal Forms 2d... American Jurisprudence Legal Forms, Second Series [*A publication*] (DLA)
Am Jur Leg Forms Anno... American Jurisprudence Legal Forms, Annotated [*A publication*] (DLA)
Am Jur Pl & Pr Forms... American Jurisprudence Pleading and Practice Forms, Annotated [*A publication*] (DLA)
Am Jur Pl & Pr Forms (Rev Ed)... American Jurisprudence Pleading and Practice Forms, Revised Editions [*A publication*] (DLA)
Am Jur Proof of Facts... American Jurisprudence Proof of Facts [*A publication*] (DLA)
Am Jur Proof of Facts Anno... American Jurisprudence Proof of Facts, Annotated [*A publication*] (DLA)
Am Jur Trials... American Jurisprudence Trials [*A publication*] (DLA)
AMJV .... Alexander Marx Jubilee Volume [*A publication*] (BJA)
AMK........... Aeromak [*Yugoslavia*] [*ICAO designator*] (FAAC)
AMK........... Amark Explorations Ltd. [*Vancouver Stock Exchange symbol*]
AMK........... American Technical Ceramics [*AMEX symbol*] (SPSG)
AMK........... Amer Techl Ceramics [*AMEX symbol*] (TTSB)
AMK........... Antimisting Kerosene [*Aviation*]
a-mk-- .... Muscat and Oman [*Oman*] [*MARC geographic area code Library of Congress*] (LCCP)
AMK........... University of Arkansas at Monticello, Monticello, AR [*OCLC symbol*] (OCLC)
AMKI.......... King Island [*Australia ICAO location identifier*] (ICLI)
AMKITU ...... Amalgamated Moulders and Kindred Industries Trade Union [*British*]
AMKO .... American Mothers of Korean Orphans (EA)
AMKTU ...... Army Marksmanship Training Unit [*CONARC*] (AABC)
AML........... Abandoned Mine Land [*Department of the Interior*]
AML........... Aberdeen Marine Laboratory
AML........... Absolute Maximum Loss
AML........... Acanthiomeatal Line [*Medicine*] (MEDA)
AML........... Acquisition Material List (MCD)
AML........... Actual Measured Loss [*Telecommunications*] (TEL)
AML........... Acute Monocytic Leukemia [*Medicine*] (DAVI)
AML........... Acute Myelogenous Leukemia [*Medicine*]
AML........... Acute Myeloid [*or Myeloblastic or Myelocytic*] Leukemia [*Medicine*]
AML........... Adaptive Maneuvering Logic (MCD)
AML........... Adjustable Mortgage Loan [*Business term*] (EMRF)
AML........... Admiralty Materials Laboratory [*British*]
AML........... Advanced Math Library [*Computer science*] (MHDI)
AML........... Advance Material List (DNAB)
AML........... Aeromedical Laboratory
AML........... Aeronautical Materials Laboratory
AML........... Airfield Marking and Lighting (NATG)
AML........... Air Malawi [*ICAO designator*] (FAAC)
AML........... Air Mobile, Light Helicopter [*Army*] (VNW)
AML........... Alaska Municipal League (SRA)
AML........... Allied Military Liaison [*Balkans*] [*World War II*]
AML........... Amberley [*New Zealand*] [*Later, EYR*] [*Geomagnetic observatory code*]
AML........... American Mail Line
AML........... American Men of Letters [*A publication*]
AML........... American Meteorite Laboratory
AML........... Amli Residential Prop [*NYSE symbol*] (TTSB)
AML........... AMLI Residential Properties [*NYSE symbol*] (SAG)
AML........... Amplitude-Modulated Link [*Electronics*]
AML........... Animated Movie Language (BUR)
AML........... Anterior Mitral Leaflet [*Cardiology*]
AML........... Application Macro Language (PCM)

AML............	Application Module Library [IBM Corp.]
AML............	Applied Mathematics Laboratory
AML	Approved Materials List [NASA]
AML............	Arctic Marine Locomotive [An icebreaker used in oil exploration in the Arctic]
AML............	Area Medical Laboratory [Military] (AABC)
AML............	Arkansas Municipal League (SRA)
AML............	Armee-Munitionslager [Army ammunition depot] [German military - World War II]
AML............	Army Medical Library [Became Armed Forces Medical Library, 1952; later, NLM]
AML............	Army Missile Laboratory (RDA)
AML............	Array Machine Language [Computer science]
AML............	Association of Master Lightermen and Barge Owners [British] (BI)
AML............	Automated MEDICARE Log (MEDA)
AML............	Automated Multitest Laboratory
AML............	Automatic Machine Loading
AML............	Automatic Magazine Loading
AML............	Auxiliary Minelayer
AML............	Aviation Materiel Laboratories [Army]
AML............	[A] Manufacturing Language [Computer science]
AML............	Puerto Armuellas [Panama] [Airport symbol] (AD)
AML............	Washington, DC [Location identifier FAA] (FAAL)
AMLA..........	Airplane Model List of America
AMLA..........	American Mutual Life Association (EA)
Am Lab Arb Awards (P-H)...	American Labor Arbitration Awards (Prentice-Hall, Inc.) [A publication] (DLA)
Am Lab Arb Cas...	American Labor Arbitration Cases [Prentice-Hall, Inc.] [A publication] (DLA)
Am Lab Arb Serv...	American Labor Arbitration Services [A publication] (DLA)
Am Lab Cas...	American Labor Cases [Prentice-Hall, Inc.] [A publication] (DLA)
Am Law Inst...	American Law Institute. Restatement of the Law [A publication]
Am Law Rec...	American Law Record [Cincinnati] [A publication] (DLA)
Am Law Rec...	American Law Record (Reprint) [Ohio] [A publication] (DLA)
Am Law Record...	American Law Record (Reprint) [Ohio] [A publication] (DLA)
Am Law Reg...	American Law Register [Philadelphia] [A publication] (DLA)
Am Law Reg NS...	American Law Register, New Series [A publication] (DLA)
Am Law Reg (Old Ser)...	American Law Register (Reprint) [Ohio] [A publication] (DLA)
Am Law Reg OS...	American Law Register, Old Series [A publication] (DLA)
Am Law S Rev...	American Law School Review [A publication] (DLA)
Am Law T Rep...	American Law Times Reports [A publication] (DLA)
AMLB..........	Advertising and Marketing Law Bulletin [Australia A publication]
AMLB..........	Alternate Monoaural Loudness Balance Test [Medicine] (DMAA)
AMLC..........	Aerospace Medical Laboratory (Clinical) [Lackland Air Force Base, TX] (MCD)
Am LC........	American Leading Cases [A publication] (DLA)
AMLC..........	Association of Marine Laboratories of the Caribbean (EAIO)
AMLC..........	Asynchronous Multiline Controller [Telecommunications]
Am L Cas...	American Leading Cases [A publication] (DLA)
AMLCC........	Asynchronous Multiline Communications Coupler [Telecommunications] (NITA)
AMLCD	Active Matrix Liquid Crystal Display
AmLck	American Locker Group, Inc. [Associated Press] (SAG)
AML Com...	AML Communications, Inc. [Associated Press] (SAG)
Am LCRP.....	Sharswood and Budd's Leading Cases on Real Property [A publication] (DLA)
AMLE..........	Aviation Maintenance and Logistics Evaluation (MCD)
Am Lead Ca (Ed of 1871)...	American Leading Cases (Edition of 1871) [A publication] (DLA)
Am Lead Cas...	American Leading Cases, Edited by Hare and Wallace [A publication] (DLA)
Am Lead Cases...	American Leading Cases [A publication] (DLA)
Am Lead Cas (H & W)...	American Leading Cases, Edited by Hare and Wallace [A publication] (DLA)
Am Leading Cas...	American Leading Cases [A publication] (DLA)
Am Leg........	American Legislator [A publication] (DLA)
Am Leg N ...	American Legal News [A publication] (DLA)
Am L Elec...	American Law of Elections [A publication] (DLA)
AmLev.........	Aminolaevulinic Acid [Biochemistry]
AMLF..........	Association des Medecins de Langue Francaise [Canada] (EAIO)
AmLfe.........	American Life Holding Co. [Associated Press] (SAG)
AMLG..........	Allied Military Liaison, Greece [World War II]
AMLG..........	Amalgam [Metallurgy]
AMLI..........	Americans for a Music Library in Israel [Defunct] (EA)
AMLICP........	[A] Monthly Lesson in Criminal Politics [Center for Financial Freedom and Accuracy in Financial Reporting] [A publication]
AmLife.........	American Life Group, Inc. [Associated Press] (SAG)
Am L Ins......	American Law Institute. Restatement of the Law [A publication] (DLA)
Am L Inst...	American Law Institute. Restatement of the Law [A publication] (DLA)
AMLI Rs	AMLI Residential Properties [Associated Press] (SAG)
AmList.........	American List Corp. [Associated Press] (SAG)
AMLJ..........	Ajmer-Merwara Law Journal [India] [A publication] (DLA)
AMLJ..........	AML Communication, Inc. [NASDAQ symbol] (SAG)
AMLJ..........	AML Communications [NASDAQ symbol] (TTSB)
AMLLV........	Advanced Multipurpose Large Launch Vehicle (MCD)
AMLM..........	McLennan Municipal Library, Alberta [Library symbol National Library of Canada] (NLC)
Am L Mag ...	American Law Magazine [A publication] (DLA)
AMLN..........	Amylin Pharmaceuticals [NASDAQ symbol] (SPSG)
AMLO..........	Aeromedical Liaison Office [or Officer] [Air Force] (AFM)

AMLO..........	Assistant Military Landing Officer [British and Canadian] [World War II]
AmLP..........	American Lyric Poems: from Colonial Times to the Present [A publication]
AMLP..........	Amplitude Modulation Link Program
AMLR..........	Abandoned Mine Land Reclamation [Department of the Interior]
AMLR..........	Autologous Mixed Lymphocyte Reaction [Immunochemistry]
Am L Rec...	American Law Record [Ohio] [A publication] (DLA)
Am L Rec (Ohio)...	American Law Record (Reprint) (Ohio) [A publication] (DLA)
Am L Reg...	American Law Register [Philadelphia] [A publication] (DLA)
Am L Reg & Rev...	American Law Register and Review [A publication] (DLA)
Am L Reg (NS)...	American Law Register, New Series [A publication] (DLA)
Am L Reg (OS)...	American Law Register, Old Series [A publication] (DLA)
Am L Rep...	American Law Reporter [Davenport, IA] [A publication] (DLA)
AMLRTN......	Amelioration
AMLS..........	Adaptive Maneuvering Logic Score (MCD)
AMLS..........	Advanced Manned Launch System [NASA]
AMLS..........	Airspace Management Liaison Section (MCD)
AMLS..........	Antimouse Lymphocyte Serum [Immunology] (MAE)
AMLS..........	Master of Arts in Library Science
AMLS..........	Master of Arts in Library Science (NADA)
Am L School Rev...	American Law School Review [A publication] (DLA)
Am L Sch Rev...	American Law School Review [A publication] (DLA)
Am LS Rev...	American Law School Review [A publication] (DLA)
AMLSU........	Air Ministry Local Staff Union [Singapore]
Am LT........	American Law Times [A publication] (DLA)
AMLT..........	Launceston [Australia ICAO location identifier] (ICLI)
Am LT Bankr...	American Law Times, Bankruptcy Reports [A publication] (DLA)
Am LT Bankr Rep...	American Law Times, Bankruptcy Reports [A publication] (DLA)
Am LTR	American Law Times Reports [A publication] (DLA)
Am LT Rep...	American Law Times Reports [A publication] (DLA)
Am LTRNS...	American Law Times Reports, New Series [A publication] (DLA)
AmLum........	American Lumen [Record label]
AMLV..........	Laverton [Australia ICAO location identifier] (ICLI)
AMM..........	Adaptive Mathematical Model
AMM..........	Additional Memory Module
AMM..........	Advanced Manufacturing Methods (MHDB)
AMM..........	Advanced Multipurpose Missile (MCD)
AMM..........	Advance Manned Mission (SAA)
AMM..........	Agnogenic Myeloid Metaplasia [Medicine]
AMM..........	Air 2000, Ltd, [British ICAO designator] (FAAC)
AMM..........	Aircraft Maintenance Manual
AMM..........	Air-Mining Mission [Military]
AMM..........	Allied Military Mission [World War II]
AMM..........	Alpha-Methylmannoside [Biochemistry]
AMM..........	Alternative Method of Management (MHDB)
AMM..........	Alternative Music Market
AMM..........	American Money Management Association [Barrington, IL] (EA)
Am M	American Music [A publication]
Am M	American Music [A publication] (BRI)
AMM..........	Amir Mines Ltd. [Toronto Stock Exchange symbol]
AMM..........	Amman [Jordan] [Airport symbol] (OAG)
AMM..........	Ammeter
AMM..........	Ammonia (MAE)
AMM..........	Ammunition (KSC)
AMM..........	AMRE, Inc. [NYSE symbol] (SPSG)
AMM..........	Analog Monitor Module [Computer science]
AMM..........	Anomalous Magnetic Moment
AMM..........	Antibodies to Murine Cardiac Myosin [Immunology] (DAVI)
AMM..........	Antimissile Missile [Air Force]
AMM..........	Army Maintenance Management (MCD)
AMM..........	Army Mobility Model (RDA)
AMM..........	Associated Maintenance Module [Telecommunications] (TEL)
AMM..........	Associated Millinery Men (EA)
AMM..........	Associate Mercantile Market (DICI)
AMM..........	Association Medicale Mondiale [World Medical Association - WMA] [Ferney-Voltaire, France]
AMM..........	Association of Manipulative Medicine [British] (BI)
AMM..........	Association of Manitoba Museums (AC)
AMM..........	Australian Meteorological Magazine [A publication]
AMM..........	Automatic Maintenance Monitor
AMM..........	Aviation Machinist's Mate [Navy rating]
AMM..........	Master of Mechanic Arts
AMM..........	Medicine Hat College, Alberta [Library symbol National Library of Canada] (NLC)
AMM..........	United States Army Material and Mechanics Research Center, Watertown, MA [OCLC symbol] (OCLC)
AMMA..........	Acrylonitrile Methyl Methacrylate [Organic chemistry]
AMMA..........	Advanced Memory Management Architecture [Computer science] (BYTE)
AMMA..........	American Mail-Order Merchants Association (EA)
AMMA..........	American Military Music Association (EA)
AMMA..........	American Millinery Manufacturers Association [Defunct]
AMMA..........	American Museum of Marine Archaeology
AMMA..........	Army Medical Material Agency (MCD)
AMMA..........	Art Material Manufacturers Association [Defunct] (EA)
AMMA..........	Art Metalware Manufacturers' Association [British] (DBA)
AMMA..........	Assistant Masters and Mistresses Association (EAIO)
AMMA..........	Australian Macadamia Manufacturers' Association
AMMAC.......	Aviation Machinist's Mate, Combat Aircrewman [Navy rating]
AMMAN	Ammanford [District in Wales]
AmMatT......	American Materials & Technologies Corp. (The) [Associated Press] (SAG)
AMMB..........	AMRESCO INC. [NASDAQ symbol] (TTSB)

AMMB......... Amresco, Inc. [NASDAQ symbol] (SAG)
AMMB......... Association des Manufacturiers de Maconnerie de Beton (AC)
AMMB......... Melbourne/Moorabbin [Australia ICAO location identifier] (ICLI)
AmMbSat..... American Mobile Satellite Corp. [Associated Press] (SAG)
AMMC......... Aircraft Material Management Center [Air Force]
AMMC......... Army Maintenance Management Center
AMMC......... Association of Map Memorabilia Collectors (EA)
AMMC......... Aviation Machinist's Mate, Carburetor Mechanic [Navy rating]
AMMC......... Aviation Materiel Management Center (AABC)
AMMC......... Melbourne [Australia ICAO location identifier] (ICLI)
AMMCG....... Acquisition Management Mission Cluster Group [Army] (RDA)
AM/MDA..... Airlock Module and Multiple Docking Adapter (PDAA)
AMMDEL...... American Military Mission, Delhi [World War II]
AmMdRs...... American Medical Response [Associated Press] (SAG)
AmMdsv...... American Medserve Corp. [Associated Press] (SAG)
AmMdTc...... American Medical Technologies, Inc. [Associated Press] (SAG)
AMME......... Automated Multimedia Exchange [Communications] [Army] (MCD)
AMMF......... Association Mondiale des Medecins Francophones [Ottawa, ON]
      (EAIO)
AMMF......... Aviation Machinist's Mate, Flight Engineer [Navy rating]
AMMG......... American Magnetics Corp. (MHDW)
AMMG......... Mount Gambier [Australia ICAO location identifier] (ICLI)
AMMH........ Annual Maintenance Manhours [Military] (AABC)
AMMH........ Aviation Machinist's Mate, Hydraulic Mechanic [Navy rating]
AMMI......... American Merchant Marine Institute [Later, AIMS] (EA)
AMMI......... American Museum of the Moving Image [New York City] (ECON)
AMMI......... Aviation Machinist's Mate, Instrument Mechanic [Navy rating]
AMMI......... Mildura [Australia ICAO location identifier] (ICLI)
AMMIC........ Armament Maintenance Management Information Center [Navy]
      (NG)
AMMINET .... Automated Mortgage Management Information Network [Computer
      science] (MHDI)
AMMIP........ Aviation Materiel Management Improvement Program [Military] (NG)
AMMIS........ Aircraft Maintenance Management Information System
AMMIS........ Aircraft Maintenance Manpower Information System [Air Force]
AMMIS........ Automated Manpower Management Information System
AMMISCA .... American Military Mission to China [World War II]
AMMISSq .... Ammunition Supply Squadron [Air Force]
AMML......... Acute Myelomonocytic Leukemia [Medicine]
AMML......... Automated Microbial Metabolism Laboratory [NASA]
AMML......... Melbourne [Australia ICAO location identifier] (ICLI)
AMMLA........ American Merchant Marine Library Association (EA)
AMMM......... Melbourne [Australia ICAO location identifier] (ICLI)
Amm Marc... Ammianus Marcellinus [c. 330-395AD] [Classical studies] (OCD)
AMMN .... Ammonia
AMMO .... Alliance of Manufacturing and Management Organizations (MHDB)
AMMO .... Ammunition (AFM)
AMMO .... Army Mobile Missile Operation
AMMO .... Army Model Improvement Program Management Office (RDA)
AMMO .... Audience Measurement by Market for Outdoor (NTCM)
AMMOBR...... Ammunition Bearer [Military] (AABC)
AMMOL....... Acute Myelomonoblastic Leukemia [Medicine]
AMMOLOG... Ammunition Logistics [Army] (RDA)
ammon ...... Ammonia
AMMORK..... Ammunition Rack
AMMP......... Aboriginal Middle Management Program [Australia]
AMMP......... Advanced Manned Missions Program [NASA] (MCD)
AMMP......... Apollo Master Measurements Program [NASA] (KSC)
AMMP......... Approved Modernization Maintenance Program (AFM)
AMMP......... Aviation Machinist's Mate, Propeller Mechanic [Navy rating]
AMMQ .... Macquarie Island [Australia ICAO location identifier] (ICLI)
AMMR .... Advanced Multimission RADAR
AMMR .... Aircraft Maintenance Manpower Requirement [Air Force] (AFM)
AMMR .... Melbourne [Australia ICAO location identifier] (ICLI)
AMMRC....... Army Materials and Mechanics Research Center [Watertown, MA]
AMMRES ..... Advanced Missile Materials Research Technical Advisory Group
      [Terminated, 1975] [DoD] (EGAO)
AMMRL....... Aircraft Maintenance Material Readiness List [Navy] (NG)
AMMRS .... Advanced Multimission Reconnaissance System [Military] (MCD)
AMMS......... Acquisition Management Milestone System [DoD]
AMMS......... Advanced Magnetic Minesweeping (MCD)
AMMS......... Advanced Microwave Moisture Sensor (MCD)
AMMS......... Army Maintenance Management System (MCD)
AMMS......... Army Management Milestone System
AMMS......... Automated Message Management System (MCD)
AMMS......... Automated Multi-Media Switch (PDAA)
AMMSA........ Automatic Multimode Mass Spectrometry
AMMSA........ Aboriginal Multi-Media Society of Alberta (AC)
AMMSDO...... Antimissile Missile and Space Defense Office
AMMSq....... Airborne Missile Maintenance Squadron [Air Force]
AMM SYS .... Ammonia System (DS)
AMMT......... Advanced Multimission Torpedo (MCD)
Am MT .... American Music Teacher [A publication] (BRI)
AMMT......... Aviation Machinist's Mate, Turret Mechanic [Navy rating]
AMMTR....... Antimissile Missile Test Range [Military]
AMMUN ...... Ammunition
AmMuT2...... American Municipal Term Trust II [Associated Press] (SAG)
AmMuT3...... American Municipal Term Trust III [Associated Press] (SAG)
AmMuTr...... American Municipal Term Trust [Associated Press] (SAG)
AMMV .... American Merchant Marine Veterans (EA)
AMMX......... Melbourne [Australia ICAO location identifier] (ICLI)
AMN........... Adrenomyeloneuropathy [Neurology]
AMN........... Aircraft Mechanician [British military] (DMA)
AMN........... Airman (AFM)
AMN........... Air Montenegro [Yugoslavia] [ICAO designator] (FAAC)

AMN........... All Malignant Neoplasm [Medicine]
AMN........... Alloxazine Mononucleotide [Pharmacology]
AMN........... Alma, MI [Location identifier FAA] (FAAL)
AMN........... Amanu [Tuamotu Archipelago] [Seismograph station code, US
      Geological Survey] (SEIS)
AMN........... Ameron, Inc. [NYSE symbol] (SPSG)
AMN........... Ameron Intl. [NYSE symbol] (TTSB)
AMN........... Aminomethyl Naphthalene [Organic chemistry]
AMN........... Ammunition
AMN........... Atomic Mass Number
AMNA......... Ammonia (MSA)
AMNB......... Association des Municipalities du Nouveau-Brunswick (AC)
AMNB......... Association Museums New Brunswick [Association des Musees du
      Nouveau-Brunswick] (AC)
AMNCS....... Advanced Multiplatform Navy Computer System (MCD)
AMND......... Amend [or Amendment] (AFM)
AMNE......... Airborne Mine Neutralization Equipment (DWSG)
Am Neg Ca... American Negligence Cases [A publication] (DLA)
Am Neg Cas... American Negligence Cases [A publication] (DLA)
Am Neg Cases... American Negligence Cases [A publication] (DLA)
Am Neg Dig... American Negligence Digest [A publication] (DLA)
Am Negl Cas... American Negligence Cases [A publication] (DLA)
Am Negl R... American Negligence Reports [A publication] (DLA)
Am Negl Rep... American Negligence Reports [A publication] (DLA)
Am Neg Rep... American Negligence Reports [A publication] (DLA)
AMNET........ American Network, Inc. [Portland, OR] (TSSD)
Amnex .... Amnex, Inc. [Associated Press] (SAG)
AMNI......... Associate Member of the Nautical Institute [British]
amnio .... Amniocentesis [Obstetrics] (DAVI)
AMNIP........ Adaptive Man-Machine Nonarithmetic Information Processing
      [Documentation]
AMNIPS ...... Adaptive Man/Machine Non-Numeric Information Processing System
      [IBM Corp.] (NITA)
AMNJ......... Academy of Medicine of New Jersey (SRA)
AMNL......... Amplitude-Modulation Noise Level (IDOE)
AMNL......... Army Medical Nutrition Laboratory (MCD)
AmnM........ Airman's Medal [Military decoration] (AFM)
Am Notary .. American Notary [A publication] (DLA)
AmNP........ American Negro Poetry [A publication]
AMNPA .... Australian Monthly Newspapers and Periodicals Association
A-MNR........ Alianza del Movimiento Nacionalista Revolucionario [Bolivia] (PPW)
AMNS .... Aminonucleoside (DMAA)
AMNSWP..... Acoustic Minesweeping
AMNSYS ..... Airborne Mine Neutralization System (DOMA)
AMNT......... Amount
AmNtEn....... American Natural Energy Corp. [Associated Press] (SAG)
AMNU......... Asociacion Mexicana para las Naciones Unidas [United Nations
      Association of Mexico] (EAIO)
AMO........... Accredited Management Organization [Institute of Real Estate
      Management] [Designation awarded by]
AMO........... Administrative Medical Officer [British]
AMO........... Admiralty Monthly Order [British military] (DMA)
AMO........... Advance Material Order [Manufacturing]
AMO........... Aircraft Material Officer
AMO........... Air Mass Zero
AMO........... Air Material Office [Military] (DNAB)
AMO........... Air Member for Organization [British and Canadian] [World War II]
AMO........... Air Ministry Order [British]
AMO........... Air Montreal, Inc. [Canada ICAO designator] (FAAC)
AMO........... Air Movement Officer [Military]
AMO........... Alamogordo Public Library, Alamogordo, NM [OCLC symbol] (OCLC)
AMO........... Alliance All Market Advantage Fund, Inc. [NYSE symbol] (SAG)
AMO........... Alliance All-Mkt Adv Fd [NYSE symbol] (TTSB)
AMO........... Allied Meteorological Office (NATG)
AMO........... Alternant Molecular Orbital [Physical chemistry]
AMO........... Amboina [Indonesia] [Seismograph station code, US Geological
      Survey] (SEIS)
AMO........... Amco Industrial Holdings Ltd. [Toronto Stock Exchange symbol]
AMO........... American Medical Optics [Commercial firm] (DAVI)
AMO........... American Medical Technology, Inc. [Vancouver Stock Exchange
      symbol]
AMO........... American Motors Owners Association (EA)
AM/O......... A Mon Ordre [To My Order] [French Business term] (ROG)
AMO........... Answering Machine Owner
AMO........... Archery Manufacturers Organization (EA)
AMO........... Architectural Millworkers of Ontario (AC)
AMO........... Area Monitoring Office [Military] (DNAB)
AMO........... Assistant Medical Officer
AMO........... Association of Magisterial Officers [British] (DBA)
AMO........... Association of Municipalities of Ontario (AC)
AMO........... Atomic, Molecular, and Optical Physics
AMO........... Automation Management Office [Military] (AABC)
AMO........... Aviation Maintenance Officer [Military] (NVT)
AMO........... Aviation Marine-Outillage
AMO........... Aviation Material Office [Military] (AFIT)
AMO........... Aviation Medical Officer [Military] (AABC)
AMO........... Axiomesio-Occlusal [Dentistry]
AMO........... Mao [Chad] [Airport symbol] (AD)
AMO........... Morinville Public Library, Alberta [Library symbol National Library of
      Canada] (NLC)
AMOA .... American Mailorder Association (EA)
AMOA .... Amusement and Music Operators Association (EA)
AMOA .... Amusement Machine Operators' Association [Australia]
AMOA .... Arkansas Music Operators Association (SRA)
AMOA .... Atmospheric Monitor Oxygen Analyzer (IEEE)

AMOAC .... Automatic Multiloop Optimal Approach Controller [*Navy*]
AMOAP .... Associated Marine Officers Association of the Philippines
AMOAS .... Administrative Management by Objectives Appraisal System (EDAC)
AMOB .... Ancient Mystic Order of Bagmen of Bagdad Imperial Guild [*Roanoke, VA*] (EA)
AMOB .... Automatic Meteorological Oceanographic Buoy [*Marine science*] (MSC)
AMob .... Mobile Public Library, Mobile, AL [*Library symbol Library of Congress*] (LCLS)
AMobB .... Bishop State Junior College, Mobile, AL [*Library symbol Library of Congress*] (LCLS)
AMobC .... Mobile College, Mobile, AL [*Library symbol*] [*Library of Congress*] (LCLS)
AMobHi .... Historic Mobile Preservation Society Headquarters, Mobile, AL [*Library symbol Library of Congress*] (LCLS)
AMobM .... Museum of the City of Mobile, Mobile, AL [*Library symbol Library of Congress*]
AMobS .... Spring Hill College, Mobile, AL [*Library symbol Library of Congress*] (LCLS)
AMobU .... University of South Alabama, Mobile, AL [*Library symbol Library of Congress*] (LCLS)
AMobU-M .... University of South Alabama, Biomedical Library, Mobile, AL [*Library symbol Library of Congress*] (LCLS)
AMOC .... American Mission for Opening Churches (EA)
AMOC .... Aston Martin Owners Club (EA)
AMOC .... Australian Mathematics Olympiad Committee
AMOC .... [*A*] Matter of Crime [*Novel by Matthew Bruccoli*]
AMOCC .... American Mission for Opening Closed Churches [*Later, AMOC*] (EA)
AMOCO .... American Oil Co. [*Later, Amoco Oil Co.*]
Amoco .... AMOCO Corp. [*Associated Press*] (SAG)
AMOCOM ..... Army Mobility Command
AMOD .... Army's Mobility Opportunity Development Program
AMOD .... Behavior Modification [*Psychology*] (DAVI)
AMOF .... [*A*] Matter of Fact [*Pierian Press, Inc.*] [*Information service or system*] (IID)
AMOG .... Adhesion Molecule on Glia (DMAA)
AMOHST ...... Ammunition Hoist
AMOHSTDR.. Ammunition Hoist Drive
AmOilfDv .... American Oilfield Divers, Inc. [*Associated Press*] (SAG)
AMOK .... Aerochemical Metal-Oxide Kinetics [*Program*] (MCD)
AMOL.......... Acute Monoblastic Leukaemia [*Medicine*] (BABM)
AMoL.......... Acute Monocytic Leukemia [*Also, AMonoL*] [*Medicine*]
AMOL.......... Automated Measurement of Lineups [*A. C. Nielsen Co.*] (WDMC)
AMOL-FD ..... Acousto-Optic Mode Locker and Frequency Doubler (MCD)
AMOM .... Morrin Municipal Library, Alberta [*Library symbol National Library of Canada*] (NLC)
AMonA .... University of Montevallo, Montevallo, AL [*Library symbol Library of Congress*] (LCLS)
AMonoL .... Acute Monoblastic Leukemia [*Also, AMoL*] [*Medicine*]
AMON ZINGIB... Amonium Zingiber [*Ginger*] [*Pharmacology*] (ROG)
AMOO .... Aerospace Medical Operations Office [*NASA*] (KSC)
AMOO .... Amerco [*NASDAQ symbol*] (SAG)
AMOO .... AMERCO [*NASDAQ symbol*] (TTSB)
A Moo.......... Moore's Reports [*Bosanquet and Puller*] [*England*] [*A publication*] (DLA)
AMOOS .... Advanced Maneuvering Orbit-to-Orbit Shuttle [*NASA*] (NASA)
AMOP .... Arctic and Marine Oil Spill Program [*Environment Canada*]
AMOP .... Association of Mail Order Publishers (DGA)
AMO PC .... American Medical Optics Posterior Chamber [*Lens*] [*Ophthalmology*] (DAVI)
AMOPS .... Army Mobilization and Operations Planning System
AMOR .... Amorphous (AAMN)
AMOR .... Army Mortar Requirements Study
AMORC .... Ancient Mystical Order Rosae Crucis [*Rosicrucian Order*] (EA)
AMORE .... Analysis of Military Organizational Effectiveness (MCD)
AMORP .... Amorphous [*Sediment*] [*Biochemistry*] (DAVI)
amorph........ Amorphous
AMORS .... Atomic Magneto-Optic Resonance Spectrometry
AMO(R)S ..... Automatic Meteorological, Oceanographic, (and Radiation) Station
AMOS .... Acoustic, Meteorological, and Oceanographic Survey
AMOS .... Additionally Awarded Military Occupational Specialty
AMOS .... Adjustable Multi-Class Organizing System (MHDI)
AMOS .... Advanced Mortgage Online System [*Computer science*] (HGAA)
AMOS .... Aerospace Maintenance and Operational Status (AFM)
AMOS .... Afro-Mediterranean Orbital System [*Israel*]
AMOS .... Air Force Maui Optical Station
AMOS .... Alpha Microsystems Operating System
AMOS .... Alternate Military Occupational Specialty (MUGU)
AMOS .... American Maritime Officers Service (EA)
AMOS .... American Meteorological Observation Station (HGAA)
AMOS .... AMEX [*American Stock Exchange*] Options Switching System
AMOS .... Ancient Mystic Order of Samaritans (EA)
AMOS .... Antireflection Coated Metal-Oxide Semiconductor (MCD)
AMOS .... ARPA [*Advanced Research Projects Agency*] Maui Optical Station (MUGU)
AMOS .... Assembly Management Operating System (MCD)
AMOS .... Associated Migrant Opportunity Services
AMOS .... Associative Memory Organizing System
AMOS .... Australian Meteorological and Oceanographic Society
AMOS .... Automated Meteorogical Observing System (USDC)
AMOS .... Automated Military Outpatient System (RDA)
AMOS .... Automatic Computer, Ministry of Supply [*British*] (DEN)
AMOS .... Automatic Meteorological Observation [*or Observing*] Station [*or System*]
AMOS .... Avalanche Injection Metal-Oxide Semiconductor

AMOSA .... Association of Aviation Maintenance Organizations (EAIO)
Amos & F.... Amos and Ferard on Fixtures [*A publication*] (DLA)
Amos & F Fixt... Amos and Ferard on Fixtures [*A publication*] (DLA)
AMOSC .... Authorized Military Occupational Specialty Code (AABC)
Amos Eng Code... Amos on an English Code [*A publication*] (DLA)
Amos Engl Const... Amos' Primer of the English Constitution [*A publication*] (DLA)
Amos Fifty Years... Amos' Fifty Years of the English Constitution [*A publication*] (DLA)
Amos Int Law... Amos on International Law [*A publication*] (DLA)
AMOSIST..... Automated Military Outpatient System Specialist (MCD)
Amos Jur...... Amos' Science of Jurisprudence [*A publication*] (DLA)
Amos Reg Vice... Amos on Laws for Regulation of Vice [*A publication*] (DLA)
AMOSS .... Adaptive Mission-Oriented Software System (MCD)
AMOSS .... Additional Mobile SAM [*Surface-to-Air Missile*] Site (NATG)
AMOT.......... Air Member for Organization and Training [*British and Canadian*] [*World War II*]
AMP............ Accelerated Mental Process (MEDA)
AMP............ Accelerometer Monitoring Program [*NASA*] (KSC)
AMP............ Acetaldehyde Monoperacetate (PDAA)
AMP............ Acid Mucopolysaccharide [*Biochemistry*]
AMP............ Acquisition Management Plan [*Navy*]
AMP............ Active Medium Propagation [*Amplifier*]
AMP............ Active Monitor Present (ACRL)
AMP............ Adaptation Mathematical Processor
AMP............ Adaptive Microwave Proximity [*Military*] (MCD)
AMP............ Additional Military Production
AMP............ Add, Multiprecision
AMP............ Adenosine Monophosphate [*Biochemistry*]
AMP............ Administrative Module Processor (ACRL)
AMP............ Advanced Management Program
AMP............ Advanced Manned Penetrator
AMP............ Advanced Microstructure Profiler [*Instrumentation, oceanography*]
AMP............ Advanced Minuteman Platform
AMP............ Advance Market Protection (MCD)
AMP............ Aero Transporte SA [*Peru*] [*ICAO designator*] (FAAC)
AMP............ Agence Madagascar - Presse [*Press agency*] [*Malagasy Republic*]
AMP............ Agence Malgache de Presse [*Malagasy Press Agency*] (AF)
AMP............ Agricultural Marketing Project [*Defunct*] (EA)
AMP............ Aircraft/Missile Project (AFM)
AMP............ Air Mail Pioneers (EA)
AMP............ Air Member for Personnel [*Air Ministry*] [*British*]
AMP............ Alliances for Minority Participation [*National Science Foundation*]
AMP............ Allied Mining and Mine Countermeasures Publications [*NATO*] (NATG)
AMP............ Altitude Manned Penetrator (MCD)
AMP............ Ambar [*Pakistan*] [*Seismograph station code, US Geological Survey*] (SEIS)
AMP............ American Majority Party (EA)
AMP............ American Mathematics Project (EA)
AMP............ American Melting Point
AmP............ American Poetry [*A publication*]
AMP............ Amino(methyl)propanol [*Organic chemistry*]
AMP............ Aminomonophosphate [*Organic chemistry*] (DAVI)
AMP............ Ammonium Molybdophosphate [*Inorganic chemistry*]
AMP............ Ampac Petroleum Resources, Inc. [*Vancouver Stock Exchange symbol*]
AMP............ Ampanihy [*Madagascar*] [*Airport symbol*] (OAG)
AMP............ Ampere [*or Amperage*] [*Unit of electric current*] (AFM)
amp .... Ampere (IDOE)
amp .... Ampere (ODBW)
amp .... Ampere (DMAA)
Amp .... Amperometric [*Electromagnetics*]
AMP............ Amphenol Corp. (SAA)
AMP............ Amphetamine [*Pharmacology*] (DAVI)
AMP............ Ampicillin [*Also, A, AM*] [*Antibacterial compound*]
AMP............ AMP, Inc. [*NYSE symbol*] (SPSG)
AMP............ Amplidyne [*Electricity*] (SAA)
amp .... Amplification [*Medicine*] (DAVI)
AMP............ Amplifier (KSC)
amp .... Amplifier (ODBW)
amp .... Amplifier [*Electronic*] (WDMC)
AMP............ Amplitude
AMP............ Amplus [*Large*] [*Pharmacy*] (ROG)
AMP............ Ampule [*Pharmacy*]
amp .... Ampule (DMAA)
AMP............ Amputation [*Medicine*]
amp .... Amputee [*Orthopedics and rehabilitation*] (DAVI)
AMP............ Analytical Maintenance Program [*Navy*] (NVT)
AMP............ Ancient and Modern Palestine [*A publication*] (BJA)
AMP............ Another Mother for Peace [*Defunct*] (EA)
AMP............ Anteromedial Puncture [*Medicine*]
AMP............ Apollo Mission Programs [*NASA*] (KSC)
AMP............ Applied Mathematics Panel [*DoD*]
AMP............ Area Mail Processing [*US Postal Service*]
AMP............ Argonne Microprocessor
AMP............ Army Materiel Plan (AABC)
AMP............ Army Mine Planter
AMP............ Army Modernization Plan (RDA)
AMP............ Aseptic Maintenance by Pressurization [*NASA*]
AMP............ Asset Management Performance (HGAA)
AMP............ Assisted Maintenance Period [*British military*] (DMA)
AMP............ Associated Music Publishers (NTCM)
AMP............ Association for Media Psychology (EA)
AMP............ Association for Men in Psychology
AMP............ Association of Maryland Pilots (SRA)

AMP	Association of Media Producers [*ICIA*] [*Absorbed by*] (EA)
AMP	Association of Multiracial Playgroups
AMP	Associative Memory Processor [*Computer science*] (BUR)
AMP	Asymmetric Multiprocessing [*Computer science*] (PCM)
AMP	Atlantic Monthly Press
A-MP	Austin-Moore Prosthesis [*Medicine*]
AMP	Australian Molasses Pool [*An association*]
AMP	Automated Molding Plant [*Manufacturing*]
AMP	Automatic Message Processor (MCD)
AMP	Automatic Multipattern Metering [*Photography*]
AMP	Avalanche Mode Photodiode
AMP	Average Mean Pressure
AMP	Average Month Program [*Air Force*] (AFIT)
AMP	Avionics Modernization Program [*Air Force*] (DOMA)
AMP	Axially Magnetized Plasma
AMP	Medicine Hat Public Library, Alberta [*Library symbol National Library of Canada*] (NLC)
AMP	Mobile Public Library, Mobile, AL [*OCLC symbol*] (OCLC)
a-mp--	Mongolia [*MARC geographic area code Library of Congress*] (LCCP)
AMP	Tampa, FL [*Location identifier FAA*] (FAAL)
AMPA	Adaptive Multibeam Phased Array [*RADAR*] (MCD)
AMPA	Advanced Maritime Patrol Aircraft (PDAA)
AMPA	American Manganese Producers Association [*Defunct*] (EA)
AMPA	American Medical Publishers' Association (EA)
AMPA	Aminomethyl Phosphonic Acid [*Organic chemistry*]
AMPA	Arkansas Municipal Police Association (SRA)
AMPA	Associated Motion Picture Advertisers (EA)
AMPA	Associate Member of the Master Photographers Association [*British*] (DBQ)
AMPA	Automotive Machine & Parts Association
AMPA	Azimuth Mark Pulse Amplifier
AMPAC	American Medical Political Action Committee (EA)
AMPAC	American Motorcyclist Political Action Committee
AmPac	American Pacific Corp. [*Associated Press*] (SAG)
Ampace	Ampace Corp. [*Associated Press*] (SAG)
Ampal	Ampal-American Israel Corp. [*Associated Press*] (SAG)
AMPAQ	Association des Manufacturiers de Produits Alimentaires du Quebec [*Quebec Food Processors Association*] (AC)
AMPAS	Academy of Motion Picture Arts and Sciences (EA)
Am Pat LA Bull	American Patent Law Association. Bulletin [*A publication*] (DLA)
Am Pat L Assoc Bull	American Patent Law Association. Bulletin [*A publication*] (DLA)
AMPB	American Pacific Bank [*NASDAQ symbol*] (SAG)
AMPBA	Amer Pac Bk Aumsville OR [*NASDAQ symbol*] (TTSB)
AMPC	Advanced Management Program for Clinician (PGP)
AmPC	American Poems; a Contemporary Collection [*A publication*]
AMPC	American Publishing Co. [*NASDAQ symbol*] (SAG)
AMPC	Area Mail Processing Center [*US Postal Service*]
AMPC	Associated Mail and Parcel Centers (EA)
AMPC	Automatic Message Processing Center
AMPC	Auxiliary Military Pioneer Corps [*British*]
AMPC	Point Cook [*Australia ICAO location identifier*] (ICLI)
AMPCC	Australian Manufacturing Production Commodity Classification
Ampco	Ampco-Pittsburgh Corp. [*Associated Press*] (SAG)
AMPCO	Associated Missile Products Corp.
AMPCO	Association of Major Power Consumers in Ontario (AC)
AMPD	Amino(methyl)propanediol [*Organic chemistry*]
AMPD	Army Mobilization Program Directive
AMPD	Average Miles Driven Per Day [*DOE*] (TAG)
AMPD	Aza(methyl)pregnanedione [*Biochemistry*]
AMPDA	Adenosine Monophosphate Deaminase [*An enzyme*]
AMPDS	Advanced Missile Propulsion Definition Study [*NASA*] (KSC)
AMPDS	Automated Message Processing Dissemination System (MCD)
AMPEC	American Motion Picture Export Co. (EA)
AMPECA	American Motion Picture Export Co./Africa [*Later, AMPEC*] [*An association*] (EA)
AMPEF	Americans for Medical Progress Educational Foundation (EA)
AMPERE	APL [*Applied Physics Laboratory*] Management Planning and Engineering Resource Evaluation [*Navy*]
AMPEREDOC	Association Multinationale des Producteurs et Revendeurs d'Electricite-Documentation [*Multinational Association of Producers and Retailers of Electricity-Documentation*] [*Electricity Supply Board*] [*Information service or system*] (IID)
AMPES	Automated Message Processing Exchange System [*Military*] (GFGA)
AMPEX	Alexander M. Poniatoff, Excellence [*Acronym is name of electronics company and brand name of its products; formed from name of firm's founder, plus "excellence"*]
Ampex	Ampex Corp. [*Associated Press*] (SAG)
AMPFION	Auto-Magnetic Plasma-Filled Ion Diode (MCD)
AMPFTA	American Military Precision Flying Teams Association (EA)
AMPFUR	Amplifying Failure, Unsatisfactory, or Removal Report (MCD)
AMPG	Air Material Proving Ground
AMPGATP	Advanced Multipurpose Gas Turbine Program
AMPH	American Physicians Service Group, Inc. [*NASDAQ symbol*] (NQ)
AMPH	Amer Physicans Svc Gr [*NASDAQ symbol*] (TTSB)
AMPH	Amphetamine [*Pharmacology*] (DAVI)
AMPH	Amphibious (AFM)
Amph	Amphibole [*A mineral*]
Amph	Amphion [*Record label*] [*France*]
Amph	Amphitruo [*of Plautus*] [*Classical studies*] (OCD)
amph	Amphoric [*Sound*] [*Medicine*] (DAVI)
AMPH	Association of Management in Public Health [*Later, AAHA*] (EA)
AMPHBS	Amphibious
AMPHENOL	American Phenolic Corp. (KSC)
amphet	Amphetamine [*Also, A, AMT*] [*CNS stimulant*]

AMPHETAMINE	Alpha-Methylphenethylamine [*CNS stimulant*]
AMPHFORLANT	Amphibious Forces, Atlantic
AMPHFORMED	Amphibious Forces, Mediterranean
AMPHFORPAC	Amphibious Forces, Pacific
AMPHI	Aerial Mission Photographic Indoctrination (MCD)
AMPHI	Amphitheatre (ROG)
AMPHIB	Amphibious
AMPHIBEX	Amphibious Exercise [*Navy, Marine Corps*]
AMPHIBFOR	Amphibious Forces
AMPHIBFORCENPAC	Amphibious Forces, Central Pacific
AMPHIBFORLANT	Amphibious Forces, Atlantic (MUGU)
AMPHIBFORMED	Amphibious Forces, Mediterranean (MUGU)
AMPHIBFORPAC	Amphibious Forces, Pacific (MUGU)
AMPHIBIND	Amphibious [*Warfare*] Indoctrination (DOMA)
AMPHIBINT	Amphibious Intelligence (DOMA)
AMPHIBPLN	Amphibious Planning (DOMA)
Am Phil	American Philatelist [*A publication*]
Am Phil	American Philatelist [*A publication*] (BRI)
Amphnl	Amphenol Corp. [*Associated Press*] (SAG)
AmPhoeG	American Phoenix Group, Inc. [*Associated Press*] (SAG)
AMPHOTO	American Photographic Book Publishing Co.
AMP-HR	Ampere-Hour (MDG)
amp-hr	Ampere Hour (IDOE)
AMPI	Adolescent Multiphasic Personality Inventory [*Personality development test*] [*Psychology*]
AMPI	Amplicon, Inc. [*NASDAQ symbol*] (NQ)
AMPI	Annual Military Personnel Inspection
AMPI	Associated Milk Producers, Inc.
AMPIA	Alberta Motion Picture Industries Association (AC)
AMPIA	Alberta Motion Picture Industries Association [*Canada*] (WWLA)
AMPIC	Atomic and Molecular Processes Information Center [*ORNL*]
AMPIE	[*The*] American Psycho/Info Exchange [*Information service or system*] (IID)
AMPIM	Animal Models of Protecting Ischemic Myocardium [*Cardiology project*]
AMPL	Advanced Microprocessor Programming Language [*Texas Instruments, Inc.*]
AMPL	Advanced Microprocessor Prototyping Laboratory [*Texas Instruments, Inc.*]
AMPL	Alaskan Malamute Protection League (EA)
AMPL	Ampal American Israel Corp. [*NASDAQ symbol*] (SAG)
AMPL	Amplifier (AAG)
AMPL	Amplitude
AMPL	Amplus [*Large*] [*Pharmacy*]
AMPL	[*A*] Macro Programming Language [*Computer science*]
AMPLAS	Apparatus Mounted in Plastic
Am Pl Ass	American Pleader's Assistant [*A publication*] (DLA)
Amplcn	Amplicon, Inc. [*Associated Press*] (SAG)
AMPLDN	Amplidyne [*Electricity*]
AMPLE	Analytical Mode for Performing Logistic Evaluation (DNAB)
AMPLFD	Amplified
AMPLG	Amplidyne Generator [*Electricity*]
AmpliFLP	Amplified Fragment Length Polymorphism [*Genetics*]
AMPLMG	Amplidyne Motor Generator [*Electricity*]
AMPLO	Administrators of Medium Public Libraries of Ontario (AC)
AMPLP	Ampal-Amer Israel 6.50% Pfd [*NASDAQ symbol*] (TTSB)
AMPLTD	Amplitude (FAAC)
AMPM	Association of Malt Products Manufacturers [*British*] (BI)
AMPME	Assemblee Mondiale des Petites et Moyennes Entreprises [*World Assembly of Small and Medium Enterprises - WASME*] [*See also AMEPM New Delhi, India*] (EAIO)
AMPMOD	Army Materiel Plan Modernization
AmPo	American Poetry [*A publication*]
AMPO	Amount to Make the Property Operational [*Business term*] (EMRF)
AMPOL	[*The*] Almanac of American Politics [*National Journal Inc.*] [*Database*] [*A publication*]
AMPP	Advanced Microprogrammable Processors (MCD)
AMPP	Advance Materials Process Program [*Department of Energy*]
AmPP	American Poetry and Prose [*A publication*]
AMPP	Arctic Meteorology Photographic Probe
AMPP	Association of Makers of Packaging Papers [*British*] (DBA)
AMPP	Association of Motion Picture Producers [*Later, AMPTP*] (EA)
AMPPD	Army Mobilization Planning and Programming Directive (AABC)
AMPPE	Acute Multifocal Placoid Pigment Epitheliopathy [*Ophthalmology*]
AMPPGD	Army Mobilization Planning and Programming Guidance Document (AABC)
AMPPPE	Acute Multifocal Posterior Placoid Pigment Epitheliopathy [*Dermatology*] (DAVI)
AMPPS	Automated Modular Preplanner Programming System (MCD)
AMPQ	Association des Medecins Psychiatres du Quebec [*Quebec Psychiatrists' Association*] (AC)
AMPR	Aeronautical Manufacturers Planning Report (AAGC)
AMPR	Aeronautical Manufacturers' Planning Report [*NASA*]
AMPR	Aeronautical Manufacturers Progress Report [*NASA*]
Am Pr	American Practice [*A publication*] (DLA)
A-M Pr	Austin-Moore Prosthesis [*Medicine*] (DMAA)
AMPR	Automatic Manifold Pressure Regulator [*Aviation*]
AMPRA	American Medical Peer Review Association (EA)
AMPRI	Association Member of the Plastics and Rubber Institute [*British*] (DBQ)
Am Prob	American Probate Reports [*A publication*] (DLA)
Am Prob NS	American Probate, New Series [*A publication*] (DLA)
Am Prob Rep	American Probate Reports [*A publication*] (DLA)
Am Property	American Law of Property [*A publication*] (DLA)
Am Pro Rep	American Probate Reports [*A publication*] (DLA)

AM Pros	Austin Moore Prosthesis [Medicine] (DAVI)
Am Pr Rep...	American Practice Reports [Washington, DC] [A publication] (DLA)
Am Pr Rep NS...	American Practice Reports, New Series [A publication] (DLA)
AMPRS	Automated Material Parts Request System (MCD)
AMPRS	Automated Military Construction Progress Reporting System (GFGA)
AMPRT	Asymptotically Most Powerful Rank Test [Statistics]
AMPS........	Abnormal Mucopolysacchariduria [Medicine] (MAE)
AMPS........	Accrued Military Pay System (AFM)
AMPS........	Acid Mucopolysaccharide [Biochemistry]
AMPS........	(Acrylamido)methylpropanesulfonic Acid [Trademark of Lubrizol] [Organic chemistry]
AMPS........	Adaptive Mode Planning System [Computer program]
AMPS........	Adenosine Monophosphate Succinate [Biochemistry]
AMPS........	Advanced Maneuvering Propulsion System
AMPS........	Advanced Manned Penetrator System
AMPS........	Advanced Mobile Phone Service [Bell System]
AMPS........	Advanced Mobile-Phone System
AMPS........	Advanced Mobile Phone System (ACRL)
AMPS........	Advanced Mobile Phone System
AMPS........	Aircraft Multispectral Photographic System [NASA]
AMPS........	Amazing Magic Pivot Swing [Training device for baseball batter's rear foot]
AMPS........	American Metered Postage Society [Defunct] (EA)
AMPS........	Americans for More Power Sources [Defunct] (EA)
AMPS........	Amperes (KSC)
AMPS........	Analog Mobile Phone System (PS)
AMPS........	Arctic Marine Pipelaying System
AMPS........	Army Mine Planter Service
AMPS........	Army Motion Picture Service
AMPS........	Assembly Manufacturing Payroll System (MHDB)
AMPS........	Assembly of Mathematical and Physical Sciences [National Research Council]
AMPS........	Assessment of Motor and Process Skills [Occupational therapy]
AMP/S	Associated Milk Producers/Southern Region [Texas] (SRA)
AMPS........	Associated Music Publishers [Musical slang]
AMPS........	Association Mondiale de Prospective Sociale [World Social Prospects Study Association] [Geneva, Switzerland] (EAIO)
AMPS........	Association of Management and Professional Staffs [British] (DBA)
AMPS........	Atmosphere, Magnetosphere, and Plasmas in Space [Space shuttle payload] [NASA]
AMPS........	Atmospheric Magnetospheric Plasma System (NASA)
AMPS........	Auction-Market Preferred Stock
AMPS........	Automated Material Processing System [Computer science]
AMPS........	Automated Merchandise Processing System [US Customs Service]
AMPS........	Automated Program Search [Tape recorder feature]
AMPS........	Automatic Mapping and Planning System [Environmental Protection Agency] (ERG)
AMPS........	Automatic Message Processing System [USAERDL]
AMPS........	Automatic Multi-Program Selection [Photography] [Minolta Corp.]
AMPS........	Autonomous Marine Power Source [Navy]
AMPS........	Auxiliary Marine Power Source [For submarines] (DOMA)
AMPS........	[A] Marriage Prediction Schedule [Premarital relations test]
AMPSIN......	Adaptive Mode Planning System Input [Computer program]
AMPSS	Advanced Manned Precision Strike System [Proposed Air Force plane]
AMPSS	Airlift Mission Planning and Scheduling System [Air Force] (MCD)
AMPT........	Advanced Maneuvering Propulsion Technology [NASA] (KSC)
AMPT........	Alpha-Methyl-p-tyrosine [Also, MPT] [Pharmacology]
AMPT........	Aminopterin [Antineoplastic drug regimen] (DAVI)
AMPT........	Ampthill [England]
AMPT........	Association for Medical Physics Technology [British]
AMPTD.......	Amplitude (MSA)
AMPTE........	Active Magnetospheric Particle Tracer Explorer [Project] [NASA/West Germany]
AMPTE........	Active Mesospheric Particle Tracer Explorer (MCD)
AMPTF........	Apollo Mission Planning Task Force [NASA] (KSC)
ampth	Amphitheater (VRA)
AMPTP.......	Alliance of Motion Picture and Television Producers (EA)
AMPU........	Australian Modern Pentathlon Union
AMPUL	Ampulla [Ampule] [Pharmacy]
AMPW	Association of Makers of Printing and Writing Papers (DGA)
AMPW	Association of Makers of Printings and Writings [British] (DBA)
AMQ...........	Academie de Musique du Quebec (AC)
AMQ...........	Aeromedicare Ltd. [British ICAO designator] (FAAC)
AMQ...........	Ambon [Indonesia] [Airport symbol] (OAG)
AMQ...........	American Medical Qualification [British]
Am Q	American Quarterly [A publication] (BRI)
AMQ...........	Analog Multiplexer Quantitizer [Computer science] (KSC)
AMQ...........	Apparent Molar Quantity
AMQ...........	Association de Manutention du Quebec (AC)
AMQ...........	Association des Microbiologistes du Quebec (AC)
AMQ...........	Association Mathematique du Quebec (AC)
AMQ...........	Association Medicale du Quebec (AC)
AMQ...........	Association Miniere du Quebec (AC)
AMQUA........	American Quaternary Association (EA)
AMR...........	Abnormal Mission Routine
AMR...........	Activity Metabolic Rate
AMR...........	Ada, OK [Location identifier FAA] (FAAL)
AMR...........	Advanced Management Research [A publication] (DLA)
AMR...........	Advanced Meat Recovery [Food Technology]
AMR...........	Advanced Medium Rocket (MCD)
AMR...........	Advanced Microwave Radiometer (SSD)
AMR...........	Advanced Missile Receiver (MCD)
AMR...........	Advanced Modular RADAR (MCD)
AMR...........	Advance Material Request
AMR...........	Aerospace Medical Research
AMR...........	Affiliated Medical Research, Inc. [Research code symbol]
AMR...........	Airborne Magnetic Recorder
AMR...........	Airborne Microwave Refractometer (CAAL)
AMR...........	Airman Military Record [Air Force]
AMR...........	Air Movement Recorder
AMR...........	Airport Movement RADAR (DA)
AMR...........	Air Specialties Corp. [ICAO designator] (FAAC)
AMR...........	Alberta Education Materials Resource Centre [UTLAS symbol]
AMR...........	Alternating Motion Rate
AMR...........	Alternating Motion Reflex [Neurology] (DAVI)
AMR...........	Alternating Motion Reflexes [Medicine] (BABM)
AMR...........	Altitude Marking Range (KSC)
Am R	American Reports [A publication] (DLA)
AMR...........	AMR Corp. [NYSE symbol] (SPSG)
AMR...........	Amrinone [Cardiotonic]
AMR...........	Analytic Mission Reliability (MCD)
AMR...........	Anisotropic Magnetoresistance
AMR...........	Annee Mondiale du Refugie
AMR...........	[The] Arcata & Mad River Rail Road Co. [AAR code]
AMR...........	Area Manpower Review [Department of Labor]
AMR...........	Arithemetic Mask Register (MHDI)
AMR...........	Assign Missile RADAR (CAAL)
AMR...........	Associate of the Association of Health Care Information and Medical Record Officers [British] (DBQ)
AMR...........	Association Marketing Roundtable (EA)
AMR...........	Aston Martin Racing [British]
AMR...........	Astro Musical Research (EA)
AMR...........	Atlantic Missile Range [Later, Eastern Test Range]
AMR...........	Automated Management Reports (BUR)
AMR...........	Automatic Message Recording
AMR...........	Automatic Message Registering
AMR...........	Automatic Message Routing (BUR)
AMR...........	Automatic Meter Reading
AMR...........	Auxiliary Machinery Room (CAAL)
AMR...........	Aviation Medical Reports
AM(R)........	Master of Arts in Research
AMR...........	Milk River Public Library, Alberta [Library symbol National Library of Canada] (NLC)
AMR...........	Reffton Corp., Montgomery, AL [Library symbol Library of Congress] (LCLS)
AMRA	Abandoned Military Reservations Act [1884]
AMRA	Accessory Manufacturers Racing Association [British] (BI)
AMRA	Advertising Media Representation Agency (DGA)
AMRA	Alabama Marine and Recreation Association (SRA)
AMRA	American Mechanical Rights Agency
AMRA	American Medical Record Association (EA)
AMRA	American Metal Repair Association [Defunct]
AMRA	American Military Retirees Association (EA)
AMRA	Ancient Mediterranean Research Association (EA)
AMRA	Army Materials Research Agency [Later, AMMRC] [Watertown, MA]
AMRA	Association of Medical Rehabilitation Administrators (EA)
AMRA	Automatic Meter Reading Association (EA)
AMRA	Automotive Maintenance and Repair Association
AMRAAM	Advanced Medium-Range Air-to-Air Missile (MCD)
AMRAC	Anti-Missile Research Advisory Council
AMRAD........	Air Munitions Requirements and Development Committee [DoD] (MCD)
AMRAD........	Amateur Radio Research and Development Corp. (IID)
AMRAD........	Armament/Munitions Requirements, Acquisition and Development Committee [Military Washington, DC]
AMRAD........	ARPA [Advanced Research Projects Agency] Measurements RADAR [Raytheon]
Am Rail Cas...	American Railway Cases [A publication] (DLA)
Am Rail R ...	American Railway Reports [A publication] (DLA)
Am Railw Cas...	American Railway Cases [A publication] (DLA)
Am R & Corp...	American Railroad and Corporation Reports [A publication] (DLA)
Am R & C Rep...	American Railroad and Corporation Reports [A publication] (DLA)
AMR & DL...	Air Mobility Research and Development Laboratory [Also, USAMR & DL] [Army]
AMRAP	Alaska Mineral Resource Assessment Program [Department of the Interior]
AMRC	Advanced Metals Research Corp.
AMRC	American Recreation Centers, Inc. [NASDAQ symbol] (NQ)
AMRC	Amer Recreation Ctrs [NASDAQ symbol] (TTSB)
AMRC	Army Mathematics Research Center [Madison, Wisconsin]
AMRC	Army Mobility Research Center
AMRC	Association of Medical Record Consultants [Defunct] (EA)
AMRC	Association of Medical Research Charities [British]
AMRC	Association of Municipal Recycling Coordinators (AC)
AMRC	Automotive Market Research Council (EA)
AMRCA	American Miniature Racing Car Association
Am R Ca ...	American Railway Cases [A publication] (DLA)
AMRCFO	Additional Material Required to Complete Fabrication Order
AMRCO	Association of Motor Racing Circuit Owners [British] (DBA)
AMRCUS	Alternative Marriage and Relationship Council of the United States
AMRD	Aircraft Maintenance and Repair Department [British military] (DMA)
AMRD	Air Member for Research and Development [Later, TRE] [Air Ministry] [British]
AMRD	Air Mobility Research and Development Laboratory [Also, AMR & DL, USAMR & DL] [Army] (MCD)
AMRD	American Radio Systems Corp. [NASDAQ symbol] (SAG)
AMRD	Amer Radio Systems'A' [NASDAQ symbol] (TTSB)
AMRD	Army Missile and Rockets Directorate
AMRD	Automatic Message Routing Device

AMRDC........ Army Medical Research and Development Command
AMRDC........ Army Missile Research and Development Command (MCD)
AMRDC........ Army Mobility Research and Development Center
AMRDC........ Association of Medical Rehabilitation Directors and Coordinators [Later, AMRA] (EA)
AMRD-NASC... Army Missile and Rockets Division - NATO Supply Center
AMRE.......... Air Ministry Reconnaissance Department [British] (DAS)
AMRE.......... Air Ministry Research Establishment [British military] (DMA)
AMRE.......... American Recreation Co. Holdings [NASDAQ symbol] (SAG)
Amre.......... AMRE, Inc. [Associated Press] (SAG)
AmReC........ American Re Capital [Associated Press] (SAG)
AMRECOM... Armament Material Readiness Command
AmReCp....... American Re Corp. [Associated Press] (SAG)
AMREE........ American Medical Research Expedition to Mount Everest
AMREF........ African Medical and Research Foundation, USA (EA)
AMREP........ Aircraft/Missile Maintenance - Production Compression Report
Am Rep ...... American Reports [A publication] (DLA)
Amrep......... Amrep Corp. [Associated Press] (SAG)
Am Reports... American Reports [A publication] (DLA)
Am Repts.... American Reports [A publication] (GFGA)
AmResc....... American Resources, Inc. [Associated Press] (SAG)
Amresco...... Amresco, Inc. [Associated Press] (SAG)
AmResCp..... American Resource Corp., Inc. [Associated Press] (SAG)
AMREX .... American Real Estate Exchange
AMRF........ African Medical and Research Foundation (EA)
AMRF........ Amended Route of Flight [Aviation]
AMRF........ American Medical Resources Foundation (DMAA)
AMRF........ Automated Manufacturing Research Facility [Gaithersburg, MD] [Department of Commerce] (GRD)
AMRF........ Automated Research Facility [National Bureau of Standards] (NITA)
AMRF........ Melbourne [Australia ICAO location identifier] (ICLI)
Amrhost...... Amerihost Properties, Inc. [Associated Press] (SAG)
AMRI........ Amrion, Inc. [NASDAQ symbol] (SAG)
AMRI .... Anteromedial Rotatory Instability [Medicine]
AMRI .... Association of Missile and Rocket Industries
Amriana....... Ameriana Bancorp [Associated Press] (SAG)
AMRICD...... Army Medical Research Institute of Chemical Defense (RDA)
AmRice....... American Rice, Inc. [Associated Press] (SAG)
Amrigs........ Amerigas Partners LP [Associated Press] (SAG)
AmriHlt....... AmeriSource Health Corp. [Associated Press] (SAG)
AMRIID...... Army Medical Research Institute of Infectious Diseases (RDA)
AMRINA...... Associate Member of the Royal Institution of Naval Architects [British]
Amrion....... Amrion, Inc. [Associated Press] (SAG)
AMRIP .... Avionics Module Repair Improvement Program [Navy]
AMRIR .... Advanced Medium-Resolution Imaging Radiometer
Amrisfe....... Amerisafe, Inc. [Associated Press] (SAG)
AmRiverO.... American River Oil Co. [Associated Press] (SAG)
AmriVst....... AmeriVest Properties, Inc. [Associated Press] (SAG)
AMRL......... Above Modern River Level [Geology]
AMRL......... Aerospace Medical Research Laboratory [Later, MRL] [Wright-Patterson Air Force Base, OH]
AMRL......... Air Medical Research Laboratory [Later, MRL] (MCD)
AMRL......... Applied Marine Research Laboratory [Old Dominion University] [Research center] (RCD)
AMRL......... Army Medical Research and Nutrition Laboratory (DAVI)
AMRL......... Army Medical Research Laboratory
AMRLA....... Army Medical Research Laboratory, Alaska (RDA)
AmrLink..... AmeriLink Corp. [Associated Press] (SAG)
AmRlt .... American Realty Trust [Associated Press] (SAG)
AMRN .... Amerin Corp. [NASDAQ symbol] (SAG)
AMRNL ...... Army Medical Research and Nutrition Laboratory
AMRO .... Amsterdam-Rotterdam Bank
AMRO .... Association of Health Care Information and Medical Records Officers (EAIO)
AMRO .... Association of Medical Record Officers [British] (BI)
AMRO .... Atlantic Missile Range [later, Eastern Test Range] Operations
Amrobank.... Amsterdam-Rotterdam Bank [Netherlands]
AMROO....... Atlantic Missile Range [later, Eastern Test Range] Operations Office
AMRPD ...... Applied Manufacturing Research and Process Development
AMRPV ...... Advanced Multimission Remotely Piloted Vehicle (MCD)
AMRR .... Army Materials Research Reactor
Am RR & C Rep... American Railroad and Corporation Reports [A publication] (DLA)
Am RR Ca ... American Railway Cases [A publication] (DLA)
Am RR Cas... American Railway Cases [A publication] (DLA)
Am R Rep... American Railway Reports [A publication] (DLA)
Am RR Rep... American Railway Reports [A publication] (DLA)
AMRS .... Australian Machine Readable Cataloguing Record Service [National Library of Australia] (NITA)
AMRS .... Automated Management and Reporting System [Department of Housing and Urban Development] (GFGA)
AMRS .... Automated Medical Record System (AAMN)
AMRS .... Master of Arts in Religious Studies (PGP)
AmRsc........ American Resources, Inc. [Associated Press] (SAG)
AMRSH....... Associate Member of the Royal Society of Health [Formerly, ARSH] [British]
AMRSHF ...... Adrenal Metabolic Research Society of the Hypoglycemia Foundation (EA)
AMRTS .... Atlantic Missile Range [Later, Eastern Test Range] Telemetry Submodule (SAA)
AMRV .... Astronaut Maneuvering Research Vehicle [NASA]
AMRV .... Atmospheric Maneuvering Reentry Vehicle (IEEE)
AmrVst....... AmeriVest Properties, Inc. [Associated Press] (SAG)
Am Ry Ca ... American Railway Cases [A publication] (DLA)

Am Ry Cases... American Railway Cases [A publication] (DLA)
Am Ry Rep... American Railway Reports [A publication] (DLA)
AMS.......... Abortus, Militensis, Suis [Microbiology]
AMS.......... Academy of Marketing Science [Coral Gables, FL] (EA)
AMS.......... Accelerator Mass Spectrometry
AMS.......... Access Method Service [Computer science] (BUR)
AMS.......... Accident Mitigation System [Industrial engineering]
AMS.......... Accommodation and Messenger Service, Admiralty [Obsolete British]
AMS.......... Acoustic Material Signature (MCD)
AMS.......... Acoustic Measurement System (KSC)
AMS.......... Actuation Mechanism Subsystem (MCD)
AMS.......... Actuation Mine Simulator (MCD)
AMS.......... Acute Mountain Sickness
AMS.......... Additional Member System [Electoral reform] [British]
AMS.......... Adjustable Muzzle Stabilizer [Rifles] [Army] (INF)
AMS.......... Administrative and Management Services (OICC)
AMS.......... Administrative Management Society [Willow Grove, PA] (EA)
AMS.......... Administrative Management Staff [Environmental Protection Agency] (GFGA)
AMS.......... Admission Multiphasic Screening [Medicine] (CPH)
AMS.......... Advanced Manned Spacecraft
AMS.......... Advanced Manufacturing System (MCD)
AMS.......... Advanced Manufacturing Systems Exposition and Conference (ITD)
AMS.......... Advanced Mapping System [Geography]
AMS.......... Advanced Marketing Services [Book supplier]
AMS.......... Advanced Masking Systems [Automotive engineering] [3M Co.]
AMS.......... Advanced Memory Specification [Computer science]
AMS.......... Advanced Memory Systems, Inc. (IEEE)
AMS.......... Advanced Metallic Structures [Program] [Air Force]
AMS.......... Advanced Meteorological System (MCD)
AMS.......... Advanced Minuteman System
AMS.......... Advanced Missile System
AMS.......... Advanced Mission Studies [NASA] (KSC)
AMS.......... Advanced Monopulse Seeker
AMS.......... Aerial Monitoring System [Nuclear energy] (NRCH)
AMS.......... Aeronautical [or Aerospace] Material Specification
AMS.......... Aeronautical Military Standards
AMS.......... Aerospace Material Specification (MCD)
AMS.......... Aerospace Materials Specifications (AAGC)
AMS.......... Agency Manager Survey [LIMRA]
AMS.......... Aggravated in Military Service (MAE)
AMS.......... Aggregate Measure of Support [International trade] (ECON)
AMS.......... Agricultural Manpower Society [British] (EAIO)
AMS.......... Agricultural Marketing Service [Formerly, CMS] [Washington, DC Department of Agriculture]
AMS.......... Airborne Maintenance System
AMS.......... Aircraft Material Specifications [Society of Automotive Engineers]
AMS.......... Airlock Module Station [NASA] (MCD)
AMS.......... Air Mail Service
AMS.......... Air Management Station
AMS.......... Air Mass (FAAC)
AMS.......... Air Member for Supply [British and Canadian] [World War II]
AMS.......... Air Missile System (NG)
AMS.......... Air Muskoka [Canada ICAO designator] (FAAC)
AMS.......... Alabama State University, Montgomery, AL [Library symbol Library of Congress] (LCLS)
AMS.......... Alarm Monitoring System
AMS.......... Alma Mater Society [Canada]
AMS.......... Alpha Magnetic Spectrometer
AMS.......... Alpha-Methylstyrene [Organic chemistry]
AMS.......... Alteration Management System (NVT)
AMS.......... Altered Mental Status (MEDA)
AMS.......... Altitude Measurement System
AMS.......... Ambassador Industries Ltd. [Vancouver Stock Exchange symbol]
AMS.......... American Magnolia Society [Later, TMS] (EA)
AMS.......... American Management Systems [Associated Press] (SAG)
AMS.......... American Management Systems, Inc. [Information service or system] (IID)
AMS.......... American Market Selection [Cigars]
AMS.......... American Mathematical Society (EA)
AMS.......... American Medical Security Group, Inc.
AMS.......... American Medical Systems [Commercial firm] (DAVI)
AMS.......... American Meteorological Society [Boston, MA]
AMS.......... American Meteor Society (EA)
AMS.......... American Microchemical Society (EA)
AMS.......... American Microscopical Society (EA)
AMS.......... American Military Society (EA)
AMS.......... American Mohammedan Society [Later, MM] (EA)
AMS.......... American Montessori Society (EA)
AMS.......... American Motility Society (EA)
AMS.......... American Museum of Safety (EA)
AMS.......... American Musicological Society (EA)
AMS.......... American Shared Hospital Services [AMEX symbol] (SPSG)
Ams.......... Americas: A Quarterly Review of Inter-American Cultural History [A publication] (BRI)
AMS.......... Amer Shared Hosp Sv [AMEX symbol] (TTSB)
AMS.......... Ammonium Sulfamate [Inorganic chemistry]
AMS.......... Amos [California] [Seismograph station code, US Geological Survey] (SEIS)
ams .... Amount of Substance [Molecular quantity] (MAE)
AMS.......... Amplifier Subsystem (NASA)
AmS.......... AMS Press, Inc., New York, NY [Library symbol Library of Congress] (LCLS)
AMS.......... Amsterdam [Netherlands] [Airport symbol] (OAG)
AMS.......... Amylase [An enzyme] (MAE)

AMS............	Ancient Monuments Society (EAIO)
AMS............	Anglo-Mongolian Society (EAIO)
AMS............	Angular Motion Simulator (MCD)
AMS............	Anisotropy of Magnetic Susceptibility [*Geophysics*]
AMS............	Annual Machinery Survey [*American Bureau of Shipping*] (DS)
AMS............	Antenna Mast Set (MCD)
AMS............	Antimacrophage Serum (MAE)
AMS............	Apogee and Maneuvering Stage [*Space flight*]
AMS............	Apollo Mission Simulator [*NASA*]
AMS............	Applications Management System [*Computer application*] (PCM)
AMS............	Applied Mathematics Series
AMS............	Arab-American Media Society (EA)
AMS............	Arbetsmarknadsstyrelsen [*National Labor Market Board*] [*Sweden*]
AMS............	Arkansas Medical Society (SRA)
AMS............	Army Management School (KSC)
AMS............	Army Management Structure
AMS............	Army Management System
AMS............	Army Map Service [*Later, Defense Mapping Agency Topographic Center*] [*Washington, DC*]
AMS............	Army Medical Service [*British*]
AMS............	Army Medical Staff
AMS............	Array Motion Sensor
AMS............	Arthritis and Musculoskeletal and Skin Diseases Database [*National Arthritis and Musculoskeletal and Skin Diseases Information Clearinghouse*] [*Information service or system*] (CRD)
AMS............	Arthur Machen Society [*Defunct*] (EA)
AMS............	Articulated Mirror System [*Astronomy*]
AMS............	Artillery and Missile School [*Army*] (MCD)
AMS............	Assembly, Maintenance, and Servicing (SSD)
AMS............	Assets Management System
AMS............	Assistant Military Secretary [*British*]
AMS............	Associated Mariners' Society [*A union*] [*British*]
AMS............	Associate of the Institute of Management Services [*British*] (DBQ)
AMS............	Association of Marshall Scholars (EA)
AMS............	Association of Medical Secretaries [*British*] (BI)
AMS............	Association of Messenger Services
AMS............	Association of Metal Sprayers [*British*] (EAIO)
AMS............	Association of Military Surgeons of the United States (RDA)
AMS............	Association of Museum Stores (EA)
AMS............	Associative Memory System [*Computer science*] (DIT)
AMS............	Assurance Medical Society [*British*]
AMS............	Asymmetric Multiprocessing System [*IBM Corp.*]
AMS............	Atlanta Motor Speedway
AMS............	Atmospheric Monitor System (IEEE)
AMS............	Attitude Maneuvering System (SAA)
AMS............	Atypical Measles Syndrome [*Medicine*]
AMS............	Atypical Mole Syndrome
AMS............	Auditory Memory Span [*Psychometrics*]
AMS............	Australian Macadamia Society
AMS............	Australian Malaysian Society
AMS............	Australian Minesweeper [*A publication*]
AMS............	Australian Museum Society
AMS............	Authority for Material Substitution (MCD)
AMS............	Autographed Manuscript [*Manuscript description*] (WGA)
AMS............	Automated Manifest System (DA)
AMS............	Automated Material System (SAA)
AMS............	Automated Microbial Systems (MCD)
AMS............	Automated Minefield System (MCD)
AMS............	Automated Multiphasic Screening [*Medicine*] (MAH)
AMS............	Automatic Management Switch [*Communication Devices, Inc.*]
AMS............	Automatic Meteorological System (RDA)
AMS............	Automatic Mode Status (CAAL)
AMS............	Automatic Monitoring System [*Aviation*]
AMS............	Automicrobic System
AMS............	Autopilot Mode Selector
AMS............	Auxiliary Machinery Space (DNAB)
AMS............	Auxiliary Memory Set (MCD)
AMS............	Auxiliary Minesweeper [*NATO*]
AMS............	Average Monthly Sales (MCD)
AMS............	Aviation Structural Mechanic, Structures [*Navy rating*]
AMS............	Avionics Maintenance Shop
AMS............	Avionics Maintenance Squadron [*Air Force/Navy*] (MCD)
AMS............	Avonics Management System
AMS............	Chandler, AZ [*Location identifier FAA*] (FAAL)
AMS............	[*A*] Minehunting SONAR (MCD)
AMS............	Motor Minesweeper [*Navy symbol Obsolete*]
AMS............	National Arthritis and Musculoskeletal and Skin Diseases Information Clearinghouse [*US Public Health Service*] [*Information service or system*] (IID)
AMS1..........	Aviation Structural Mechanic, Structures, First Class [*Navy rating*] (DNAB)
AMS2..........	Aviation Structural Mechanic, Structures, Second Class [*Navy rating*] (DNAB)
AMS3..........	Aviation Structural Mechanic, Structures, Third Class [*Navy rating*] (DNAB)
AMSA..........	(Acridinylamino)methanesulfon-m-anisidide [*Antineoplastic drug regimen*]
AMSA..........	Advanced Manned Strategic Aircraft [*Facetious translation: "America's Most Studied Aircraft"*] [*Air Force*]
AMSA..........	Advanced Mutual Security Act
AMSA..........	Aerospace Multiple Station Analysis (MCD)
AMSA..........	American Meat Science Association (EA)
AMSA..........	American Medallic Sculpture Association (EA)
AMSA..........	American Medical Society on Alcoholism
AMSA..........	American Medical Student Association (EA)

AMSA..........	American Metal Stamping Association [*Later, PMA*] (EA)
AMSA..........	American Music Scholarship Association (EA)
AMSA..........	Amsacrine [*Medicine*] (BABM)
AMSA..........	Amsacrine [*Also, M-AMSA*] [*Antineoplastic drug*] (CDI)
AMSA..........	Anglican Men's Society in Australia
AMSA..........	Anterior Middle Suprasylvian Association [*Area of cat cortex*]
AMSA..........	Anti-Metric Society of America [*An association*]
AMSA..........	Area Maintenance Support Activity (AABC)
AMSA..........	Association of Metropolitan Sewerage Agencies (EA)
AMSA..........	Australian Malaysian Singaporean Association
AMSA..........	Australian Marine Sciences Association
AMSA..........	Australian Maritime Safety Authority
AMS-A.........	Automatic Meteorological System - Artillery (MCD)
AMSAA	Ambulance and Medical Service Association of America [*Later, AAA*] (EA)
AMSAA	Army Materiel Systems Analysis Activity [*or Agency*] [*Aberdeen Proving Ground, MD*] (MCD)
AMSAA	Aviation Structural Mechanic, Structures, Airman Apprentice [*Navy rating*]
AMSAC	Advanced Multi-Stage Axial-Flow Compresor Program [*NASA*] (PDAA)
AMSAC	American Society of African Culture [*Defunct*] (EA)
AMSAC	ATWS [*Anticipated Transient without Scram*] Mitigating System Actuation Circuitry [*Nuclear energy*] (NRCH)
AMS(Aff)......	Affiliate, Association of Medical Secretaries, Practice Administrators, and Receptionists [*British*] (DBQ)
AmSafRz.....	American Safety Razor Co. [*Associated Press*] (SAG)
AM SAM	American Samoa
AMSAM.......	Antimissile Surface-to-Air Missile
Am Samoa....	American Samoa Code [*A publication*] (DLA)
Am Samoa Code Ann...	American Samoa Code. Annotated [*A publication*] (DLA)
AMSAN	Aviation Structural Mechanic, Structures, Airman [*Navy rating*]
AMSAODD ...	American Medical Society on Alcoholism and Other Drug Dependencies [*Later, ASAM*] (EA)
AMSAT........	American Satellite (MCD)
AMSAT........	Radio Amateur Satellite Corp. (EA)
AMSC..........	Acquisition Management System Control (AAGC)
AMSC..........	Acquisition Management Systems Control Aviation Structural Mechanic, Structures, Chief [*Navy rating*] (DNAB)
AMSC..........	Acquisition Method Suffix Code (AAGC)
AMSC..........	Advanced Military Spaceflight Capability
AMSC..........	Alliance des Moniteurs de Ski du Canada [*Canadian Ski Instructors' Alliance*]
AMSC..........	Allied Military Staff Conference [*Quebec, Yalta, etc.*] [*World War II*]
AMSC..........	American Miniature Schnauzer Club (EA)
AMSC..........	American Superconductor Corp. [*NASDAQ symbol*] (SPSG)
AMSC..........	Amer Superconductor [*NASDAQ symbol*] (TTSB)
AMSC..........	Archives, Manuscripts, and Special Collections [*Research Libraries Group project*] (IT)
AMSC..........	Army Management Staff College (RDA)
AMSC..........	Army Material Supply Command (KSC)
AMSC..........	Army Mathematics Steering Committee
AMSC..........	Army Medical Specialist Corps
AMSC..........	Army Mobility Support Center
AMSC..........	Automatic Message Switching Center (NOAA)
AMSC..........	Averaged Magnitude Squared Coherence (MCD)
Amscan.......	Amscan Holdings, Inc. [*Associated Press*] (SAG)
AMSCAT	Airborne Microwave Scattermeter [*For measuring wind speed and direction*]
Am Sci.......	American Scientist [*A publication*] (BRI)
AMSCN	Advance Master Schedule Change Notice (SAA)
AMscNA.......	National Aeronautics and Space Administration, Marshall Space Flight Center, AL [*Library symbol*] [*Library of Congress*] (LCLS)
AMSCO	Access Method Services Cryptographic Option (MHDI)
AMSCO	Acquisition Management System Control Officer (MCD)
AMSCO	American Mineral Spirits Co.
AMSCO	American Sterilizer Co.
Amsco	AMSCO International [*Associated Press*] (SAG)
AMSCO	Army Management Structure Code
AMSCO	Army Medical Supply Control Officer
AMSCP	Associate Member of the Society of Certified Professionals [*British*] (DBQ)
AMSD	Administrative and Management Services [*DoD*] (GFGA)
AMSDCL	Acquisition Management Systems and Data Control List
AMSDEP	Asian Manpower Skill Development Program [*United Nations*]
AMSDL	Acquisition Management System Data List [*Military*] (DOMA)
AMSDL	Acquisition Management Systems and Data Control List
AMSDL	Acquisition Management Systems and Data Requirements Control List [*A publication*] (AAGC)
AMSDRP.....	Acquisition Management Systems and Data Requirements Control Program [*Navy*]
AMSE	Aeronautical Material Support Equipment (DNAB)
AMSE	Aircraft Maintenance Support Equipment (MCD)
AMSE..........	Associate Member of the Society of Engineers, Inc. [*British*] (DBQ)
AMSE..........	Association for Advancement of Modelling and Simulation Techniques in Enterprises [*France*] (EAIO)
AMSE..........	Association Mondiale des Sciences de l'Education [*World Association for Educational Research - WAER*] (EAIO)
AMSE..........	Association of Media Sales Executives [*British*] (BI)
AMSE..........	Association of Muslim Scientists and Engineers (EA)
AMSEC........	Analytic Methodology for System Evaluation and Control [*Army*]
AmSECT.......	American Society of Extra-Corporeal Technology (EA)
AMSEF........	Antiminesweeping Explosive Float
AMSEL.........	Aeronautical Maintenance Support Equipment List [*Military*] (AFIT)

AMSERT ...... Associate Member of the Society of Electronic and Radio Technicians [*British*] (DBQ)
Amserv .... AMSERV Healthcare, Inc. [*Associated Press*] (SAG)
AMSF .... Area Maintenance Supply Facility [*Army*] (AABC)
AMSF .... Army Morale Support Fund (AABC)
AMSF .... Australian Marathon Swimming Federation
AMSFT .... American Medical Support Flight Team [*Later, Operation Angel Plane*] (EA)
AMSGA .... Association of Manufacturers and Suppliers for the Graphic Arts (DGA)
AMSGS .... Army Medical Service Graduate School
AMS-H .... Advanced Missile System - Heavy (MCD)
AMS-H .... Antiarmor Missile System - Heavy [*Army*] (INF)
AMSH .... Association for Moral and Social Hygiene [*British*] (BI)
AMSHAA ..... Associate Member of the Society of Hearing Aid Audiologists [*British*] (DI)
AMSHAH ..... Assessment Models in Support of Hazard Assessment Handbook (MCD)
AmShrd .... American Shared Hospital Services [*Associated Press*] (SAG)
AMSI .... Admiralty Merchant Shipping Instructions [*British*]
AMSI .... Apache Medical Systems, Inc. [*NASDAQ symbol*] (SAG)
AMSI .... Atlantic Merchant Shipping Instructions
AMSIF .... International Fertilizer Development Center, Muscle Shoals, Alberta [*Library symbol National Library of Canada*] (NLC)
AmsInco ...... Americas Income Trust [*Associated Press*] (SAG)
AmSIP .... American Strategic Income Portfolio [*Associated Press*] (SAG)
AmSIP2 .... American Strategic Income Portfolio II [*Associated Press*] (SAG)
AmSIP3 .... American Strategic Income Portfolio III [*Associated Press*] (SAG)
AMSIS .... Air Ministry Secret Intelligence Summary [*British military*] (DMA)
AMSIT .... Appearance, Mood, Sensorium, Intelligence, and Thought Processes [*Mental status examination*] [*Medicine*] (DAVI)
AMSJS .... American Milking Shorthorn Junior Society (EA)
AMS-K .... Army Management System - Korea
AMSL .... Above Mean Sea Level [*Navigation*]
AMSL .... Acquisition Management System List (MCD)
AMSL .... Applied Mathematics and Statistics Laboratory [*Stanford University*] (MCD)
AMSL .... Approved Material Substitution List
AMSLAET .... Associate Member of the Society of Licensed Aircraft Engineers and Technologists [*British*] (DBQ)
AMSM .... Access Methods Service Macros [*Computer science*] (HGAA)
AMSMH .... Association of Medical Superintendents of Mental Hospitals [*Later, AAPA*] (EA)
AMSMS .... Airborne Mechanical Special Mission System (MCD)
AMSN .... Amscan Holdings, Inc. [*NASDAQ symbol*] (SAG)
AMSO .... Air Member for Supply and Organisation [*Air Ministry*] [*British*]
AMSO .... Ammunition Shipment Order [*Army*]
AMSO .... Association of Major Symphony Orchestra Volunteers (EA)
AMSO .... Association of Market Survey Organisations [*British*]
AMSO .... Automated Microform Storage and Retrieval [*Computer science*] (MHDI)
AMSOC .... American Miscellaneous Society (EA)
AmSoc .... American Society of Peru (EAIO)
AM SOC CE... American Society of Civil Engineers (WDAA)
Am Soc Int L... American Society of International Law (DLA)
Am Soc ME... American Society of Mechanical Engineers (WDAA)
Am Soc'y Int'l Proc... American Society of International Law. Proceedings [*A publication*] (DLA)
AMSoE .... Southeast Alabama Multitype System, Montgomery, AL [*Library symbol*] [*Library of Congress*] (LCLS)
AMSOG .... Army Molecular Sieve Oxygen Generator (RDA)
AMSOL .... American Soldier
AMSORB ...... Analysis of Multiple Source Obscurants on Realistic Battlefield (MCD)
AmSouth ...... AmSouth Bancorp [*Associated Press*] (SAG)
AMSP .... Advanced Magnetic Silencing Project [*Military*] (DNAB)
AMSP .... Advanced Military Studies Program [*DoD*]
AMSP .... Allied Military Security Publication
AMSP .... Army Maintenance and Supply Procedures [*or Publications*] (NATG)
AMSP .... Army Master Study Program (AABC)
AMSP .... Asbestos Medical Surveillance Program [*Military*] (DNAB)
AMS P & S... Agricultural Marketing Service, P and S Docket [*United States*] [*A publication*] (DLA)
AMSPAR ...... Association of Medical Secretaries, Practice Administrators, and Receptionists [*British*] (DBA)
AMSPDC ...... Association of Medical School Pediatric Department Chairmen (EA)
Am Spect ..... American Spectator [*A publication*] (BRI)
AMSq .... Avionics Maintenance Squadron [*Air Force*] (AFM)
AMSR .... Advanced Microwave Scanning Radiometer (MCD)
AMSR .... Air Member for Supply and Research [*Air Ministry*] [*British*]
AMSR .... Alternate Management Summary Report (MCD)
Am SR .... American State Reports [*A publication*] (DLA)
AMSR .... Amserv Healthcare [*NASDAQ symbol*] (TTSB)
AMSR .... Amserv Healthcare, Inc. [*NASDAQ symbol*] (NQ)
AMSR .... Annotated Manual of Statutes and Regulations [*of the Federal Home Loan Bank Board*]
AMSR .... Automated Microfilm Storage and Retrieval [*Army*] (IID)
AMSR .... Autonomous Missile Site RADAR (AABC)
AMSRDC ...... Army Medical Service Research and Development Command
AMSS .... Advanced Manned Space Simulator
AMSS .... Advanced Meteorological Sounding System
AMSS .... Advanced Mine-Hunting SONAR System (MCD)
AMSS .... Advanced Multimission Sensor System
AMSS .... Advanced Multipurpose Surfacing System (MCD)
AMSS .... Aeronautical Mobile Satellite Service [*ICAO designator*] (FAAC)
AMSS .... American Milking Shorthorn Society (EA)

AmSS .... American Sea Songs and Chanteys [*A publication*]
AMSS .... Army Medical Service School [*Later, Medical Field Service School*]
AMSS .... Association of Muslim Social Scientists (EA)
AMSS .... Autograph Manuscript Signed [*Manuscript descriptions*]
AMSS .... Automated Multistage Substructuring (MCD)
AMSS .... Automatic Master Sequence Selector
AMSS .... Automatic Multiaddress Segregation System
AMSSA .... Affiliation of Multicultural Societies & Service Agencies of BC (AC)
AMSSA .... Army Medical Supply Support Activity
AMSSB .... Amplitude Modulation, Single Sideband [*Electronics*]
AMSSB/SC... Amplitude Modulation, Single Sideband, Suppressed Carrier [*Electronics*] (CET)
AMSSP .... Aeronautical Mobile Satellite Service Panel [*ICAO*] (DA)
AMSSS .... Actron Microprocessor Softwear Support System (MCD)
AMSST .... Associate of the Society of Surveying Technicians [*British*] (DBQ)
AMST .... Advanced Medium STOL [*Short Takeoff and Landing*] Transport
AMST .... Advanced Military Spaceflight Technology (MCD)
AMST .... American Studios, Inc. [*NASDAQ symbol*] (SAG)
AMST .... Amer Studios [*NASDAQ symbol*] (TTSB)
Amst .... Amsterdam (BARN)
AMST .... Association of Maximum Service Telecasters
AMSTAN ...... American Radiator & Standard Sanitary Corp. [*Later, American Standard, Inc.*]
Am Sta Rep... American State Reports [*A publication*] (DLA)
Am State Papers... American State Papers [*A publication*] (DLA)
Am State Rep... American State Reports [*A publication*] (DLA)
AmStd .... American Standard Cos., Inc. [*Associated Press*] (SAG)
AmStFn .... American States Financial Corp. [*Associated Press*] (SAG)
Am Stock Exch Rules... Rules of the American Stock Exchange [*A publication*] (DLA)
Am Stock Ex Guide... American Stock Exchange Guide [*Commerce Clearing House*] [*A publication*] (DLA)
AmStores..... American Stores Co. [*Associated Press*] (SAG)
Am St P...... American State Papers [*A publication*] (DLA)
AMSTP .... Association of Makers of Soft Tissue Papers [*British*] (DBA)
Am St Papers... American State Papers [*A publication*] (DLA)
AMStPapyr... American Studies in Papyrology [*New Haven, CT*] [*A publication*] (BJA)
Am St R ..... American State Reports [*1886-1911*] [*A publication*] (DLA)
Am St RD .... American Street Railway Decisions [*A publication*] (DLA)
Am St Rep... American State Reports [*A publication*] (DLA)
Am St Reports... American State Reports [*A publication*] (DLA)
Am St Ry Dec... American Street Railway Decisions [*A publication*] (DLA)
Am St Ry Rep... American Street Railway Reports [*A publication*] (DLA)
AMSTS .... Automatic Multiparameter Semiconductor Test Set
AMSU .... Access Methods Services Utilities [*Computer science*] (HGAA)
AMSU .... Advanced Microwave Sounding Unit [*Satellite instrument for meteorology*]
AMSU .... Aeronautical Material Screening Unit (AFIT)
AMSU .... Air Motor Servo Unit (MCD)
AMSU .... Amphibious Maintenance Support Unit (DNAB)
AMSU .... Attitude Monitor Switching Unit (MCD)
AMSU .... Auto-Manual Switching Unit [*Telecommunications*] (DCTA)
AMSULANT... Amphibious Maintenance Support Unit, Atlantic (DNAB)
AMSUPAC... Amphibious Maintenance Support Unit, Pacific (DNAB)
AmSupr........ American Superconductor Corp. [*Associated Press*] (SAG)
AMSUS .... Association of Military Surgeons of the United States (EA)
AmSvce .... America Service Group, Inc. [*Associated Press*] (SAG)
AMSW .... American Software [*NASDAQ symbol*] (SAG)
AMSW .... Artium Magister [*Master of Arts*] in Social Work (IIA)
AMSWA .... Amer Software'A' [*NASDAQ symbol*] (TTSB)
AMSWAG .... AMSAA [*Army Materiel Systems Analysis Agency*] Simulation Wargame (MCD)
AMSWU .... Amalgamated Metal Workers and Shipwrights' Union [*Australia*]
AMSY .... American Management Systems, Inc. [*NASDAQ symbol*] (NQ)
AMSY .... Amer Mgmt Systems [*NASDAQ symbol*] (TTSB)
AMT .... Accelerated Mission Testing (IEEE)
AMT .... Acme-Cleveland [*NYSE symbol*] (TTSB)
AMT .... Acme-Cleveland Corp. [*NYSE symbol*] (SPSG)
AMT .... Active Maintenance Time
AMT .... Active Memory Technology (ECON)
AMT .... Acute Military Tuberculosis [*Medicine*] (DMAA)
AMT .... Advanced Manufacturing Techniques (NITA)
AMT .... Advanced Manufacturing Technology [*Technical Insights, Inc.*] [*Information service or system*] (CRD)
AMT .... Advanced Materials Technology [*Information service or system*] (IID)
AMT .... Aerial Mail Terminal (AFM)
AMT .... Air Mail Transfer (ADA)
amt .... Air Mail Transfer (ODBW)
AMT .... Air Mail Transmission
AMT .... Air Member for Training [*British and Canadian*] [*World War II*]
AMT .... Air Movements Talker (SAA)
AMT .... Alkali-Metal Turbine
AMT .... Alpha-Methyltyrosine [*Pharmacology*] (MAE)
AMT .... Altercate Minimum Tax (TDOB)
AMT .... Alternative Mating Technique [*Zoology*]
AMT .... Alternative Minimum Tax
AMT .... Amalgamated Military Technical (DNAB)
AMT .... Amatsia [*Israel*] [*Geomagnetic observatory code*]
AMT .... American Medical Technologists (EA)
AMT .... American Medical Television
AMT .... American Mime Theatre (EA)
AMT .... American Telecommunications Corp. [*Vancouver Stock Exchange symbol*]
AMT .... American Trans Air, Inc. [*ICAO designator*] (FAAC)

AMT............ Amethopterin [*Methotrexate*] [*Antineoplastic drug*] (MAE)
AMT............ Aminomethyltrimethylpsoralen [*Cytology*]
AMT............ Aminomethyltrioxsalen [*Organic chemistry*]
AMT............ Aminopterin [*Antiviral compound*]
AMT............ Ammonium Metatungstate [*Inorganic chemistry*]
AMT............ Amount (AFM)
AMT............ Amphetamine [*Also, A, amphet*] [*CNS stimulant*]
AMT............ Amplitude-Modulated Transmitter [*Electronics*]
AMT............ Angular Mapping Transformation [*Computer science*]
AMT............ Apogee Motor Timer [*NASA*]
AMT............ Army Modernization Training
AMT............ Assistance Militaire Technique [*Military Technical Assistance*] [*Niger*] (AF)
AMT............ Associate in Mechanical Technology
AMT............ Associate in Medical Technology
AMT............ Association for Manufacturing Technology (EA)
AMT............ Association of Marine Traders [*British*] (BI)
AMT............ Association of Massage Therapists [*Australia*]
AMT............ Association of Medical Technologists [*British*] (DBA)
AMT............ Assyrian Medical Texts [*A publication*] (BJA)
AMT............ Astrograph Mean Time [*Navigation*]
AMT............ Audio Frequency Magnetotelluric
AMT............ AUTODIN Multimedia Terminal (NVT)
AMT............ Automated Mechanical Transmission [*Automotive engineering*]
AMT............ Automated Microfiche Terminal (PDAA)
AMT............ Automatic Moon Tracking
AMT............ Automatic Motor Tester
AMT............ Available Machine Time
AMT............ Master of Arts in Teaching
AMT............ Troy State University at Montgomery, Montgomery, AL [*Library symbol Library of Congress*] (LCLS)
AMT............ West Union, OH [*Location identifier FAA*] (FAAL)
AMTA......... Airborne Moving Target Attack
AMTA......... Alabama-Mississippi Telephone Association (SRA)
AMTA......... Alberta Marine Trades Association (AC)
AMTA......... American Massage Therapy Association (EA)
AMTA......... American Medical Tennis Association (EA)
AMTA......... Amistar Corp. [*NASDAQ symbol*] (NQ)
AMTA......... Antenna Measurement Techniques Association (EA)
AMTA......... Arizona Motor Transport Association (SRA)
AMTA......... Audio-Monitored Talk Amplifier (DNAB)
AMTANK...... Amphibious Tank [*Military*]
AMTAS........ Army Modernization Training Automation System
AMTAS........ Automatic Modal Tuning and Analysis System (NASA)
Am Tax Q.... American Taxpayers' Quarterly [*A publication*] (DLA)
AMTB......... Antimotor Torpedo Boat [*Navy*]
AMTC......... Advanced Manufacturing Technology Centre [*University of Manchester*] [*British*] (NITA)
AMTC......... Air Material Armament Test Center [*Air Force*] (MCD)
AMTC......... American Fair Trade Council [*Sausalito, CA*] (EA)
AMTC......... American Manchester Terrier Club (EA)
AMTC......... Amtech Corp. [*NASDAQ symbol*] (NQ)
AMTC......... Apparel Manufacturing Technology Center [*Research center*] (RCD)
AMTC......... Army Missile Test Center [*White Sands Missile Range, NM*]
AMTC......... Art Master's Teaching Certificate [*British*]
AMTC......... Association for Mechanical Translation and Computation Linguistics (NITA)
Amtch......... Amtech Systems [*Associated Press*] (SAG)
AmtchCp...... Amtech Corp. [*Associated Press*] (SAG)
AMTCL........ Association for Machine Translation and Computational Linguistics [*Later, Association for Computational Linguistics*] (EA)
AMTCS........ Amyltrichlorosilane [*Organic chemistry*]
AMTD......... Adaptive Mobile Torpedo Decoy [*Navy*] (MCD)
AMTD......... Amino(mercapto)thiodiazole [*Organic chemistry*]
AMTD......... Amino(mercopto)thiadiazole [*Organic chemistry*]
AMTD......... Automatic Magnetic Tape Dissemination [*Defense Documentation Center*]
AMTD......... Automatic Magnetic Tape Distribution [*Program*]
AMTDA....... Agricultural Machinery and Tractor Dealers Association (HGAA)
AMTDA....... American Machine Tool Distributors Association (EA)
AMTE......... Adjusted Megaton Equivalent (MCD)
AMTE......... Admiralty Marine Technology Establishment [*Research center British*] (IRC)
AMTE......... Association des Media et de la Technologie en Education au Canada [*Association for Media and Technology in Education in Canada - AMTEC*]
AMTEA....... American Machine Tool Export Associates (EA)
AMTeC........ Advanced Manufacturing Technology Centre [*Research center British*] (CB)
AMTEC....... Alkali Metal Thermoelectric Converter [*Power source*]
AMTEC....... American Metalworking Technology for the European Community (SAA)
AMTEC....... Association for Media and Technology in Education in Canada [*See also AMTE*]
AMTEC....... Automatic Time Element Compensator (SAA)
Amtech....... Amtech Systems, Inc. [*Associated Press*] (SAG)
AmTele....... American Telecasting, Inc. [*Associated Press*] (SAG)
AMTEP....... Automobile Mechanic Training Evaluation Project [*Southern Association of Colleges and Schools*] (EDAC)
AMTE(PL) .... Admiralty Marine Training Establishment (Physiological Laboratory) [*Research center British*]
AMTESS...... Army Maintenance Training and Evaluation Simulation System (MCD)
AMTESS...... Army Training Effectiveness and Simulation System (MCD)
AMTEX....... Air-Mass Transformation Experiment [*National Science Foundation/Japan*]

AMTEX....... Air Mass Transportation Experiment [*Global Atmospheric Research Program*] (USDC)
AMTF......... Acoustic Model Test Facility [*NASA*] (NASA)
AMTF......... Aerobic-Media Trickling Filter (PDAA)
AMTF......... Air Mobile Task Force
AMTF......... Air Movements Training Flight
AMTF......... American Music Theater Festival
Am Theat.... American Theatre [*A publication*] (BRI)
Am Them.... American Themis [*A publication*] (DLA)
AMTI......... Adaptive Moving Target Indicator [*Military*]
AMTI......... Airborne Moving Target Indicator (CAAL)
AMTI......... Alternative Minimum Taxable Income
AMTI......... Ameican Medical Technologies, Inc. [*NASDAQ symbol*] (SAG)
AMTI......... American Medical Technologies [*NASDAQ symbol*] (SAG)
AMTI......... American Med Technologies [*NASDAQ symbol*] (TTSB)
AMTI......... Area Moving Target Indicator [*NASA*] (KSC)
AMTI......... Automatic Moving Target Indicator (MSA)
AMTICS....... Advanced Mobile Traffic Information and Communications System [*Automotive engineering*]
AMTIDE...... Aircraft Multipurpose Test Inspection and Diagnostic Equipment
AMTIR....... Advanced Moving Target Indicator, RADAR
AMTIS....... Arts Management Training Initiative, Scotland (AIE)
AMTK......... American Materials & Technologies Corp. (The) [*NASDAQ symbol*] (SAG)
AMTK......... Amphibious Tank [*Military*]
AMTL......... Amtrol, Inc. [*NASDAQ symbol*] (SAG)
AMTL......... AMTROL, Inc. [*NASDAQ symbol*] (TTSB)
AMTL......... Army Materials Technology Laboratory [*Watertown, MA*]
AMTMA...... American Measuring Tool Manufacturers Association [*Defunct*] (EA)
Am T-M Cas... American Trade-Mark Cases (Cox) [*A publication*] (DLA)
AMTOR...... Amateur Microprocessor Teleprinter Over Radio
AMTORG..... American Trade Organization [*Commonwealth of Independent States*]
AmToys....... American Toys, Inc. [*Associated Press*] (SAG)
AMTP........ Aerodynamic Model Test Plan (SAA)
AMTP........ ARTEP [*Army Training and Evaluation Program*] Mission Training Plan (INF)
AMTPI........ Associate Member of the Town Planning Institute [*British*] (EY)
AMTR........ Aerodynamic Model Test Report (SAA)
AMTR........ Amateur
AMTR........ Ammeter
AMTR........ Amtran, Inc. [*NASDAQ symbol*] (SAG)
AMTR........ Atlantic Missile Test Range (KSC)
AMTRA....... Australian Motorcycle Trailriders' Association
AMTRAC..... Amphibian [*or Amphibious*] Tractor [*or Truck*]
AMTRACBN... Amphibian [*or Amphibious*] Tractor Battalion [*or Truck*]
Am Trade Mark Cas... American Trade-Mark Cases (Cox) [*A publication*] (DLA)
AMTRAK...... American Track [*National Railroad Passenger Corp.; formerly, Railpax*]
AMTRALEASE... American Truck Leasing Network, Inc.
Amtran....... Amtran, Inc. [*Associated Press*] (SAG)
AMTRAN...... Automatic Mathematical Translator [*Programming language*] [*1970*]
AMTRANS..... Army Missile Transport Systems (KSC)
AmTrans...... [*The*] Complete Bible, An American Translation [*A publication*] (BJA)
AMTREX...... Amphibious Training Exercise [*Navy*] (NVT)
AMTRI........ Advanced Manufacturing Technology Research Institute [*Research center British*] (IRC)
Am Tr M Cas... Cox's American Trade-Mark Cases [*A publication*] (DLA)
AmTrnz...... AmerTranz Worldwide Holding Corp. [*Associated Press*] (SAG)
Amtrol........ Amtrol, Inc. [*Associated Press*] (SAG)
AmTrst....... AmTrust Capital Corp. [*Associated Press*] (SAG)
AMTS........ Active Maintenance Training Simulator [*Military*]
AMTS........ Advanced Meteorological Temperature Sounder (MCD)
AMTS........ Advanced Mobile Telephone System (MCD)
AMTS........ AGE [*Air-Ground Equipment*] Module Test Set (MCD)
AMTS........ Association Mondiale des Travailleurs Scientifiques [*Scientific Workers World Association*] (NATG)
AMTT........ Automated Mixed Traffic Transit (PDAA)
AMTU........ Army Marksmanship Training Unit [*CONARC*] (INF)
AMTU........ Melbourne [*Australia ICAO location identifier*] (ICLI)
AMTX........ Amati Communications [*NASDAQ symbol*] (TTSB)
AMTX........ Amati Communications Corp. [*NASDAQ symbol*] (SAG)
AMTZ........ AmerTranz Worldwide Holding Corp. [*NASDAQ symbol*] (SAG)
AMU.......... ACM [*Association for Computing Machinery*] Municipal Securities Income [*NYSE symbol*] (SPSG)
AMU.......... ACM Muni Securities Income [*NYSE symbol*] (TTSB)
AMU.......... African Mathematical Union (EA)
AMU.......... Air Mileage Unit [*Navigation*]
AMU.......... Air Mission Unit [*Air Force*]
AMU.......... Alabama State University, Montgomery, AL [*OCLC symbol*] (OCLC)
AMU.......... Alarm Monitor Unit [*Telecommunications*] (TEL)
AMU.......... Alaska Methodist University
AMU.......... Alternate Master Unit (MCD)
AMU.......... Amadeusair GmbH [*Austria ICAO designator*] (FAAC)
AMU.......... Amanab [*Papua New Guinea*] [*Airport symbol*] (OAG)
AMU.......... American Malacological Union (EA)
AMU.......... American Military University
AMU.......... American Musicians Union (EA)
AMU.......... Analog Multiplier Unit (ECII)
AMU.......... Anchorage [*Alaska Methodist University*] [*Alaska*] [*Seismograph station code, US Geological Survey*] [*Closed*] (SEIS)
AMU.......... Antenna Matching Unit
AMU.......... Aqueous Makeup [*Room*] [*Nuclear energy*] (NRCH)
AMU.......... Arab Maghreb Union [*Morocco, Algeria, Mauritania, Tunisia, and Libya*]

AMU.............. Army Marksmanship Unit
AMU.............. Army Medical Unit
AMU.............. Asian Monetary Unit
AMU.............. Associated Metalworkers' Union [British] (DCTA)
AMU.............. Associated Midwestern Universities, Inc.
AMU.............. Association of Master Upholsterers [British] (BI)
AMU.............. Association of Minicomputer Users (EA)
AMU.............. Astronaut Maneuvering Unit [Gemini] [NASA]
AMU.............. Atomic Mass Unit
amu............... Atomic Mass Unit (IDOE)
AMU.............. Auburn University at Montgomery, Montgomery, AL [Library symbol Library of Congress] (LCLS)
AMU.............. Auxiliary Memory Unit
AMU.............. Average Monthly Usage (KSC)
AMU.............. Avionics Module Unit
AMUBC........ Association of Marine Underwriters of British Columbia (AC)
AMUCOM..... Army Munitions Command [Later merged with Army Weapons Command]
AMUDB........ African and Mauritian Union of Development Banks (EAIO)
AMUE.......... Association for the Monetary Union of Europe
AMUFOC..... Association des Etablissements Multiplicateurs de Semences Fourrageres des Communautes Europeennes [Association of Forage Seed Breeders of the European Community] [Brussels, Belgium]
AMUG.......... Arizona Macintosh Users Group
AMuI............ International Fertilizer Development Center, Muscle Shoals, AL [Library symbol Library of Congress] (LCLS)
Am U Int L Rev... American University Intramural Law Review [A publication] (DLA)
Am U Intra L Rev... American University Intramural Law Review [A publication] (DLA)
Am U L......... American University Law Review [A publication] (DLA)
A-MuLV......... Abelson-Murine Leukemia Virus
AmuLV......... Amphotrophic Murine Leukemia Virus [Medicine] (DMAA)
AMUN.......... Air Munitions
AMUNC........ Army Munitions Command [Later merged with Army Weapons Command]
AMunInc...... American Municipal Income Portfolio, Inc. [Associated Press] (SAG)
AMURT........ Ananda Marga Universal Relief Team [India]
AMUS.......... Alpha Micro Users Society (EA)
AMus........... Associate in Music
AMusD......... Doctor of Musical Arts (GAGS)
AMUSE........ Amusement
A MUS LCM... Associate in Music of the London College of Music (ROG)
AMusTCL..... Associate in Music of Trinity College of Music, London [British] (DBQ)
AMUUS....... Association of Marine Underwriters of the United States (EA)
AMUX.......... Avionics Multiplex
AMV.............. Abbott Mead Vickers [Commercial firm British]
AMV.............. Adjusted Market Value [Automobile retailing]
AMV.............. Aircraft Maintenance Co. [Egypt] [ICAO designator] (FAAC)
AMV.............. Alfalfa Mosaic Virus
AMV.............. Ammonium Metavanadate [Inorganic chemistry]
AMV.............. Amstar Venture Corp. [Vancouver Stock Exchange symbol]
AMV.............. AmVestors Financial Co. [NYSE symbol] (SAG)
AMV.............. AmVestors Finl [NYSE symbol] (TTSB)
AMV.............. Area of Mutual Visibility [Aviation] (PDAA)
AMV.............. Armored Maintenance Vehicle
AMV.............. Articulated-Frame Mechanical-Drive Vehicle [Automotive engineering]
AMV.............. Assisted Mechanical Ventilation [Medicine] (DAVI)
AMV.............. Association Mondiale Veterinaire [World Veterinary Association - WVA] [Madrid, Spain] (EAIO)
AMV.............. Astable Multivibrator
AMV.............. Australian Merchant Vessel [Shipping] (ADA)
AMV.............. Average Magnitude for Velocity [Military]
AMV.............. Avian Myeloblastosis Virus
AMVA........... Asociacion Mundial Veterinaria de Avicola [World Veterinary Poultry Association - WVPA] [Huntingdon, Cambridgeshire, England] (EAIO)
AMVA........... United States Veterans Administration Hospital, Montgomery, AL [Library symbol Library of Congress] (LCLS)
AMVANSW... Amalgamated Milk Vendors' Association of New South Wales [Australia]
AMvB........... Algemene Maatregel van Bestuur [Order in Council] [Netherlands] (ILCA)
AMVB........... Association of Music Video Broadcasters [Defunct] (EA)
AMVC........... Australian Milk Vendors' Council
AMVER .... Automated [formerly, Atlantic] Merchant Vessel Report [Coast Guard]
AMVER .... Automated Mutual-Assistance Vessel Rescue System (DS)
AMVERS ..... Automated [formerly, Atlantic] Merchant Vessel Report System [Coast Guard]
AmvestF...... AmVestors Financial Co. [Associated Press] (SAG)
Am Vets....... American Law of Veterans [A publication] (DLA)
AMVETS....... American Veterans of World War II, Korea, and Vietnam (GPO)
AMVG .... Anciens Moudjahidine et Victimes de la Guerre [War Veterans and Victims] [Algeria]
AMVHA........ Asociacion Mundial de Veterinarios Higienistas de los Alimentos [World Association of Veterinary Food-Hygienists - WAVFH] [Berlin, Federal Republic of Germany] (EAIO)
AMVI........... Acute Mesenteric Vascular Insufficiency [Medicine] (AAMN)
AmVien........ American Viennola [Record label]
Am Vis........ American Visions [A publication]
Am Vis........ American Visions [A publication] (BRI)
aMVL.......... Anterior Mitral Valve Leaflet [Cardiology] (AAMN)
AMVM......... Administrative Motor Vehicle Management

AMVMI........ Association Mondiale des Veterinaires Microbiologistes, Immunologistes, et Specialistes des Maladies Infectieuses [World Association of Veterinary Microbiologists, Immunologists, and Specialists in Infectious Diseases - WAVMI] [Maisons-Alfort, France] (EAIO)
AmVox........ American Vox [Record label]
AMVP.......... AmeriVest Properties, Inc. [NASDAQ symbol] (SAG)
AMVPA .... Asociacion Mundial Veterinaria de Pequenos Animales [World Small Animal Veterinary Association - WSAVA] [Hatfield, Hertfordshire, England] (EAIO)
AMVRT .... Avian Myeloblastic Virus Reverse Transcription [Genetics]
Amvst......... AmVestors Financial [Associated Press] (SAG)
AMVT.......... Acute Mesenteric Venous Thrombosis [Medicine]
AMVTA........ Association of Motor Vehicle Training Agents [British] (DBA)
AMVWW ..... AmVestors Fin'l Wrrt [NASDAQ symbol] (TTSB)
AMW.......... Active Microwave Workshop
AMW.......... Actual Measurement Weight [Railroads]
AMW.......... Air Midwest, Inc. [ICAO designator] (FAAC)
AMW.......... Air Ministry Warden [British military] (DMA)
AMW.......... American Mizrachi Women [Formerly, MWOA] (EA)
AMW.......... America's Most Wanted [Television program]
AMW.......... Ames, IA [Location identifier FAA] (FAAL)
AMW.......... Amphibious Warfare [Navy] (NVT)
AMW.......... Amwest Insurance Group, Inc. [AMEX symbol] (SPSG)
AMW.......... Amwest Insur Group [AMEX symbol] (TTSB)
AMW.......... Angular Momentum Wheel (KSC)
AMW.......... Antimateriel Warhead
AMW.......... Antimissile Warfare
AMW.......... Association of Married Women (EA)
AMW.......... Average Monthly Wage
AMWA........ American Medical Women's Association (EA)
AMWA........ American Medical Writers' Association (EA)
AMWA........ Area Microwave Assembly [Ground Communications Facility, NASA]
AMWA........ Association of Metropolitan Water Agencies (EA)
AMWAC....... America/West Africa Conference [Shipping]
AmWagr...... American Wagering, Inc. [Associated Press] (SAG)
AMWAR ...... Application of the 1973 Middle East War to CAA [Concepts Analysis Agency] War Games, Models, and Simulations
AMWBPD.... Alliance of Minority Women for Business and Political Development (EA)
AMWC........ Ananda Marga Women's Center [Australia]
AMWD......... Advanced Millimeter Wave Device
AMWD......... American Woodmark Corp. [NASDAQ symbol] (NQ)
AMWD .... Amer Woodmark [NASDAQ symbol] (TTSB)
AMWE......... Average Male Weekly Earnings
AMWES........ Associate Member of the Women's Engineering Society [British] (DBQ)
AmWest...... America West Airlines, Inc. [Associated Press] (SAG)
AMwest...... Amwest Insurance Group, Inc. [Associated Press] (SAG)
AMWG........ Academy of Master Wine Growers (EA)
AMWG........ American Movement for World Government (EA)
AMWH .... Antimateriel Warhead
AmWhite...... American White Cross [Associated Press] (SAG)
AmWhte...... American White Cross [Associated Press] (SAG)
AMWL......... Amphibious Warfare Lift Capability [Navy] (MCD)
AMWO......... Attrition and Modification Work Order
AMWR .... Air Ministry War Room [British World War II]
AMWS .... Advanced Manportable Weapons System (Provisional) [Army] (RDA)
AMWS .... American Men and Women of Science [R. R. Bowker Co.] [Information service or system A publication] (IID)
AM WS .... AM Intl Wrrt [AMEX symbol] (TTSB)
AMWS .... Associated Metal Workers Society [A union] [British]
AmWtr .... American Water Works [Associated Press] (SAG)
AMWU .... Associated Metal Workers Union [British]
AMWWA ...... Association of Medical Women in Western Australia
AMWY .... Wynyard [Australia ICAO location identifier] (ICLI)
AmwyAs...... Amway Asia Pacific [Associated Press] (SAG)
AmwyJ........ Amway Japan Ltd. [Associated Press] (SAG)
AMX........... Aerovias de Mexico SA de CV [ICAO designator] (FAAC)
AMX........... Alumax, Inc. [NYSE symbol] (SAG)
AMX........... Alumax Inc. [NYSE symbol] (TTSB)
AMX........... AMAX, Inc. [Formerly, Alumax, Inc., American Metal Climax, Inc.] [NYSE symbol Toronto Stock Exchange symbol] (SPSG)
AMX........... Amoxicillin [Medicine] (DMAA)
AMX........... Automatic Message Exchange
AMXCo........ AMX Corp. [Associated Press] (SAG)
AMXI........... AMNEX, Inc. [Formerly, NYCOM Information Services] [NASDAQ symbol] (SPSG)
AMXX........ AMX Corp. [NASDAQ symbol] (SAG)
AMY........... Academy Resources Ltd. [Vancouver Stock Exchange symbol]
AMY........... Ambassador Airways Ltd. [British ICAO designator] (FAAC)
AMY........... Ambatomainty [Madagascar] [Airport symbol] (OAG)
AMY........... Amylas [An enzyme] (DAVI)
AMY........... Amylase [An enzyme]
a-my--........ Malaysia [MARC geographic area code Library of Congress] (LCCP)
AMY............ Mynarski Public Library, Alberta [Library symbol National Library of Canada] (NLC)
AMYA......... American Model Yachting Association (EA)
AMYGD....... Amygdalus [Almond] [Pharmacology] (ROG)
AMYLAS ..... Amylase [An enzyme] (DAVI)
Amylin........ Amylin Pharmaceuticals, Inc. [Associated Press] (SAG)
AMYR......... Myrnam Public Library, Alberta [Library symbol National Library of Canada] (NLC)
AMY-SP...... Amylas Urine Spot [Test] [Gastroenterology] (DAVI)
AMZ............ Air Meuse - Dat Wallonie [Belgium ICAO designator] (FAAC)

AMZ	Amazon Petroleum Corp. [*Vancouver Stock Exchange symbol*]
AMZ	American List Corp. [*AMEX symbol*] (SPSG)
AMZ	Amer List [*AMEX symbol*] (TTSB)
AMZ	Ardmore [*New Zealand*] [*Airport symbol*] (OAG)
AMZ	Association Mondiale de Zootechnie [*World Association for Animal Production*]
AMZB	Australian Milking Zebu Breed [*Agriculture*]
AN	Abbott's New Cases [*New York*] [*A publication*] (DLA)
AN	Above-Named
AN	Abr-Nahrain (BJA)
AN	Abstract Number [*Database terminology*] (NITA)
AN	Acanthosis Nigricans [*Medicine*]
AN	Accession Number [*Online database field identifier*]
AN	Accion Nacional [*National Action*] [*Spain Political party*] (PPE)
AN	Account Number
AN	Acetonitrile [*Organic chemistry*]
AN	Acide Nucleique [*French Medicine*]
A/N	Acidic and Neutral [*Chemical analysis*]
AN	Acid Number [*Chemistry*]
AN	Acne Neonatorum [*Medicine*] (DMAA)
AN	Acoustic Neuroma [*Medicine*] (DMAA)
AN	Acrylonitrile [*Organic chemistry*]
An	Actinon (MAE)
AN	Action Nationale [*National Action for People and Homeland*] [*Switzerland Political party*] (PPE)
AN	Acuerdo Nacional [*Paraguay*] [*Political party*] (EY)
AN	Administrative Note
AN	Adult Normal [*Medicine*] (DMAA)
AN	Advanced Navigator [*Air Force*]
AN	Advice Note (ADA)
AN	Aerodynamics Note
AN	Africa Network [*An association*] (EA)
AN	African Notes [*Ibadan*] [*A publication*]
AN	Agencia Nacional [*National Agency*] [*Press agency*] [*Brazil*]
AN	Agency Name [*Database terminology*] (NITA)
AN	Aids to Navigation
AN	Air Force - Navy
AN	Airman [*Nonrated enlisted man*] [*Navy*]
AN	Air Navigation
AN	Alianza Nacional [*National Alliance*] [*Spain Political party*] (PPE)
A/N	Allied/Neutral [*Military*]
AN	All Normal [*Hematology*]
AN	Alphanumeric
AN	Ambient Noise [*Composite of sounds present at a given spot in the ocean*] (NVT)
AN	Ambulances for Nicaragua (EA)
AN	American Newspapers, 1821-1936 [*A bibliographic publication*]
AN	Ammonium Nitrate [*Inorganic chemistry*]
AN	Amoco Corp. [*NYSE symbol*] (SAG)
AN	Amoco Corp. [*NYSE symbol*] (TTSB)
An	Anabasis [*of Xenophon*] [*Classical studies*] (OCD)
An	Anaesthetic
an	Anatomic [*Anatomy*] (DAVI)
an	Andorra [*MARC country of publication code Library of Congress*] (LCCP)
An	Andreas Bonellus de Barulo [*Flourished, 1260-71*] [*Authority cited in pre-1607 legal work*] (DSA)
An	Andreas de Capua [*Flourished, 1242-57*] [*Authority cited in pre-1607 legal work*] (DSA)
An	Andria [*of Terence*] [*Classical studies*] (OCD)
AN	Anemone [*Botany*]
AN	Anesthesia [*or Anesthetic*] [*Medicine*] (DAVI)
AN	Anesthesiology [*Medical specialty*] (DHSM)
AN	Aneurysm
An	Angelus de Ubaldis [*Deceased, 1407*] [*Authority cited in pre-1607 legal work*] (DSA)
AN	Anglo-Norman [*Language, etc.*]
AN	Anhydrous
AN	Animal
AN	Animate (WGA)
AN	Anisometropia [*Ophthalmology*]
an	Anisoyl [*As substituent on nucleoside*] [*Biochemistry*]
AN	Annex
AN	Anno [*or Annus*] [*Year*] [*Latin*]
AN	Anode
AN	Anonymous (WGA)
An	Anonymous Reports at End of Benloe [*1661*] [*England*] [*A publication*] (DLA)
AN	Anorexia Nervosa [*Medicine*]
an	Anorthite [*CIPW classification*] [*Geology*]
AN	Ansett Airlines of Australia [*ICAO designator*] (AD)
AN	Answer
AN	Answering Flag [*Navy British*]
an	Ante [*Before*] [*Latin*]
AN	Antenatal [*Medicine*]
A/N	Antenatal [*Medicine*] (DMAA)
AN	Anther [*Botany*]
An	Antonius de Butrio [*Deceased, 1408*] [*Authority cited in pre-1607 legal work*] (DSA)
AN	Antonov [*Former USSR ICAO aircraft manufacturer identifier*] (ICAO)
AN	Apalachicola Northern Railroad Co. [*AAR code*]
AN	Appeals Notes [*A publication*] (DLA)
AN	Archdeacon Nares [*Pseudonym used by Robert Nares*]
AN	Arcuate Nucleus [*In the medulla oblongata*]
AN	Argentaffin [*Cytology*]

AN	Army and Navy
AN	Army-Navy Joint Type Ordnance
A/N	Army/Navy Number
AN	Army - Navy Retractor [*Surgery*] (DAVI)
A/N	Arrival Notice [*Shipping*]
A/N	Artery and Nerve [*Cardiology*] (DAVI)
AN	Ascending Neuron [*Neurology*]
AN	Aseptic Necrosis [*Medicine*]
A/N	As Needed (NRCH)
AN	Aspergillus niger [*Factor*]
AN	Assignee Name [*Database terminology*] (NITA)
AN	Associate in Nursing
AN	Astronautics Notice (AAG)
AN	Astronavigation (NATG)
An	Atmosphere, Normal (MAE)
AN	Atomic Number
AN	Autograph Note (BARN)
AN	Autonetics (KSC)
AN	Avascular Necrosis [*Medicine*] (AAMN)
AN	Axle Nut (DICI)
AN	Die Akkadische Namengebung [*A publication*] (BJA)
an----	East China Sea and Area [*MARC geographic area code Library of Congress*] (LCCP)
AN	National Agreement [*Paraguay*] (PD)
AN	National Alliance [*Italy Political party*] (ECON)
AN	Neerlandia Public Library, Alberta [*Library symbol National Library of Canada*] (NLC)
AN	Netherlands Antilles [*ANSI two-letter standard code*] (CNC)
AN	Net Laying Ship [*Later, ANL*] [*Navy symbol*]
A_n	Normal Atmosphere (DAVI)
AN	Rhone-Poulenc [*France*] [*Research code symbol*]
AN1	Anna [*Ohio*] [*Seismograph station code, US Geological Survey*] (SEIS)
AN3	Anna [*Ohio*] [*Seismograph station code, US Geological Survey*] (SEIS)
ANA	Acadiana Bancshares, Inc. [*AMEX symbol*] (SAG)
ANA	Acetylneuraminic Acid [*Biochemistry*] (MAE)
ANA	Acoustic Neuroma Association (EA)
A/NA	Activated/Non-Activated [*Cytology*]
ANA	Adaptive Null Antenna
ANA	Aden News Agency [*People's Democratic Republic of Yemen*] (MENA)
ANA	Administration for Native Americans [*Office of Human Development Services*]
ANA	Aerojet Network Analyzer
ANA	Air Force - Navy Aeronautical
ANA	Air Force - Navy Aeronautical Bulletin (NASA)
ANA	Air Navigation Act [*British*]
ANA	Alabama Agricultural and Mechanical University, Normal, AL [*Library symbol Library of Congress*] (LCLS)
ANA	Alabama Nurserymen's Association (SRA)
ANA	Alanine Nitroanilide [*Biochemistry*]
ANA	All Nippon Airways Co. Ltd. [*Japan ICAO designator*] (FAAC)
ANA	Alpha-Naphthyl Acetate [*Organic chemistry*]
ANA	Amchitka [*Alaska*] [*Seismograph station code, US Geological Survey Closed*] (SEIS)
ANA	American Naprapathic Association (EA)
ANA	American Narcolepsy Association (EA)
ANA	American National Archives (DIT)
ANA	American Nature Association [*Defunct*]
ANA	American Neurological Association (EA)
ANA	American Newspaper Association
ANA	American Normande Association (EA)
ANA	American Numismatic Association (EA)
ANA	American Nurses' Association (EA)
ANA	American Nutritionists Association (EA)
ANA	Anaheim, CA [*Location identifier FAA*] (FAAL)
ANA	Analcime [*A zeolite*]
ANA	Anatech International Corp. [*La Jolla, CA*]
ANA	Anguilla National Alliance (PPW)
ANA	Antibodies to Nuclear Antigen [*Immunology*]
ANA	Antinuclear Antibody [*Immunology*]
ANA	Appropriate National Authorities [*NATO*] (NATG)
ANA	Arab Network of America (BARN)
ANA	Arab News Agency
ANA	Arizona Newspapers Association (SRA)
ANA	Arizona Nursery Association (SRA)
ANA	Arkansas Nurserymen's Association (SRA)
ANA	Arlington Naval Annex (MCD)
ANA	Armenian National Army [*Guerrilla force*] [*Former USSR*] (ECON)
ANA	Army-Navy Aeronautical (KSC)
ANA	Army-Navy-Air Force (MCD)
ANA	Article Number Association (EAIO)
ANA	Article Numbering Association [*Retailing*] [*British*] (NITA)
ANA	Aspartyl Naphthylamide (MAE)
ANA	Assigned Night Answer [*Telecommunications*] (TEL)
ANA	Assistant Naval Attache [*British*]
ANA	Associate, National Academician
ANA	Associate of the National Academy of Design
ANA	Associate of the National Academy of Design, New York (NGC)
ANA	Association of National Advertisers (EA)
ANA	Association of Naval Aviation (EA)
ANA	Association of Nordic Aeroclubs (EA)
ANA	Association of Nurse Administrators [*British*] (DBA)
ANA	Athenagence [*News agency*] [*Greece*] (EY)

ANA .... Athens News Agency [*Greece*]
ANA .... Atlantic Nutritional Association (EA)
ANA .... Australian National Airways
ANA .... Autoantibodies to Nuclear Antigens (MCD)
ANA .... Automated Naval Architecture (PDAA)
ANA .... Automatic Network Analyzer
ANA .... Automatic Number Analysis (NITA)
ANA .... Automatic Number Announcer [*Telecommunications*] (TEL)
ANA .... Nanton Public Library, Alberta [*Library symbol National Library of Canada*] (NLC)
ANA .... Northern Arkansas Regional Library, Harrison, AR [*OCLC symbol*] (OCLC)
ANA .... Program Director for Automation [*FAA*] (TAG)
ANAA .... Acoustic Neuroma Association of Australasia
ANAA .... American Nursing Assistants' Association (EA)
ANAB .... Alameda Naval Air Base [*California*] (SAA)
Anab .... Anabasis [*of Arrian*] [*Classical studies*] (OCD)
ANAC .... Aboriginal Nurses Association of Canada [*Association des Infirmieres et Infirmiers Autochtones du Canada*] [*Indian & Inuit Nurses of Canada*] (AC)
ANAC .... Acoustic Neuroma Association of Canada [*Association pour les Neurinomes Acoustiques du Canada*] (AC)
ANAC .... Alaska Native Arts and Crafts Cooperative Association
ANAC .... American Nobel Anniversary Committee (EA)
ANAC .... Anachronism
Anac .... Anacreon [*Greek poet, 527-488BC*] [*Classical studies*] (OCD)
AN AC .... Anno ante Christum [*In the Year before Christ*] (ROG)
ANAC .... Association of Nurses in AIDS [*Acquired Immune Deficiency Syndrome*] Care (EA)
ANACDUTRA... Annual Active Duty for Training [*Army*]
ANACE .... Army Net Assessment, Central Europe
Anach .... Anacharsis [*of Lucian*] [*Classical studies*] (OCD)
ANACHEM... Association of Analytical Chemists, Inc. (EA)
ANACITEC.... Asociacion Argentino-Norteamericana para el Avance de la Ciencia, Technologia, yCultura [*Argentine-North American Association for the Advancement of Science, Technology, and Culture*] (EA)
Anacmp .... Anacomp, Inc. [*Associated Press*] (SAG)
ANACOM...... Analog Computer
ANACONDA... Analytical Control and Data (MHDB)
ANACR.......... Anacreon [*Greek poet, 572-488BC*] [*Classical studies*] (ROG)
ANACS .... American Numismatic Association Certification Service
ANAD .... ANAADIGICS Inc. [*NASDAQ symbol*] (TTSB)
ANAD .... Anadigics, Inc. [*NASDAQ symbol*] (SAG)
ANAD .... Anniston Army Depot [*Alabama*] (AABC)
ANAD .... Anorexia Nervosa and Associated Disorders [*Later, ANAD-National Association of Anorexia Nervosa and Associated Disorders*] (EA)
ANAD .... National Association of Anorexia Nervosa and Associated Disorders (PAZ)
Anadigc .... Anadigics, Inc. [*Associated Press*] (SAG)
ANADIR........ Association Nationale des Anciens Detenus et Internes Resistants [*National Association of Former Resistance Prisoners and Internees*] [*Algeria*] (AF)
ANADP.......... Association of North American Directory Publishers (EA)
Anadrk.......... Anadarko Petroleum [*Associated Press*] (SAG)
ANADS.......... Ambient Noise and Data System [*Pacific Missile Range*] (MCD)
ANAEA.......... Associate of the National Association of Estate Agents [*British*] (DBQ)
ANAEC .... All Naval Activities Employing Civilians (MCD)
ANAERO...... Anaerobe [*Biochemistry*] (DAVI)
ANAES .... Anaesthesia [*or Anaesthetic*] (ADA)
ANAES .... Anaesthetist (ADA)
ANAESTH .... Anaesthesia [*or Anaesthetic*] (ADA)
ANAESTH .... Anaesthetist (ADA)
ANAF .... A & A Foods Ltd. [*NASDAQ symbol*] (SAG)
ANAF .... Army-Navy-Air Force
ANAFF .... A & A Foods Ltd [*NASDAQ symbol*] (TTSB)
ANA-FL .... Antinuclear Antibody Fluid [*Medicine*] (DAVI)
ANAFTA ...... Army-Navy-Air Force Times Alliance [*A publication*]
ANAG .... Abstracts of North American Geology [*A publication*]
ANAG .... Acute Narrow Angle Glaucoma [*Opthamology*] (DMAA)
ANAG .... Anagram (ADA)
ANAH .... Association Nationale d'Aide aux Handicapes [*National Association of Aids to Handicapped Persons*] [*Canada*]
ANAI .... African Network of Administrative Information [*Information service or system*] (IID)
ANAI .... Article Numbering Association of Ireland (EAIO)
ANAL .... Analgesic [*Medicine*]
ANAL .... Analogy
ANAL .... Analysis (AABC)
anal .... Analyst (DAVI)
An Albg .... Antonius Albergati [*Deceased, 1634*] [*Authority cited in pre-1607 legal work*] (DSA)
ANALIT .... Analysis of Automatic Line Insulation Test [*Bell System*]
ANALIT .... Analysis of Intelligence (MCD)
Analog.......... Analog Devices, Inc. [*Associated Press*] (SAG)
Analog.......... Analog Science Fiction and Fact [*A publication*] (BRI)
Analogy.......... Analogy, Inc. [*Associated Press*] (SAG)
ANALY .... Analyze (MSA)
ANALYS...... Analysis
Analysts.......... Analysts International Corp. [*Associated Press*] (SAG)
AnalyTc.......... Analysis & Technology, Inc. [*Associated Press*] (SAG)
ANAM .... Association of North American Missions (EA)
ANAMMG...... Association Nationale des Anciens Moudjahidine et Mutiles de Guerre [*National Association of War Veterans and War Wounded*] [*Algeria*]

Anangel........ Anangel American Shipholdings Ltd. [*Associated Press*] (SAG)
ANAP .... Agglutination Negative, Absorption Positive [*Medicine*] (MAE)
ANAP .... Airport Noise Abatement Plan (PDAA)
ANAPAC...... Analysis Package (MHDI)
ANAPO........ Alianza Nacional Popular [*National Popular Alliance*] [*Colombia*] (PD)
ANAPROP ... Anomalous Propagation [*Telecommunications Electronics*] (NVT)
ANAR .... Approach, Naval Aviation Safety Review [*A publication*]
ANARA........ Alcoholic and Narcotic Addict Rehabilitation Amendments
ANARAP...... Administration for Native Americans Research Analysis Project (EDAC)
ANARC .... Association of North American Radio Clubs (EA)
Anarch .... [*The*] Anarchiad [*American satirical epic poem, 1786-1787*]
Anaren.......... Anaren Microwave, Inc. [*Associated Press*] (SAG)
ANARESAT... Australian National Antarctic Research Satellite
ANAS .... Auditory Nerve Activating Substance [*Physiology*]
ANASP .... Advanced Nuclear Attack Submarine Program (MCD)
anast .... Anastomosis [*Medicine*] (MAE)
ANAT .... American National Insurance Co. [*NASDAQ symbol*] (NQ)
ANAT .... Amer Natl Insur [*NASDAQ symbol*] (TTSB)
Anat.......... Anatomie [*Anatomy*] [*German*]
ANAT .... Anatomy [*or Anatomical*]
ANatBc.......... American National Bancorp [*Associated Press*] (SAG)
ANATC .... Air Navigation and Traffic Control
ANATRAN ... Analog Translator [*Computer science*]
ANAU .... Nauru Island [*ICAO location identifier*] (ICLI)
ANAUC .... Anno Ab Urbe Condita [*In the Year from the Building of the City (Rome)*] [*Latin*] (ROG)
ANAV .... Area Navigation
ANAVETS...... Army, Navy & Air Force Veterans in Canada [*Les Anciens Combattants de l'Armee, de la Marine et des Forces Aeriennes au Canada*] (AC)
ANAVIT .... Asociacion Nicaraguense de Agencias de Viajes (EY)
ANB .... Abbey Natl. [*NYSE symbol*] (SAG)
ANB .... Aids to Navigation Boat
ANB .... Air Navigation & Trading Co. Ltd. [*British ICAO designator*] (FAAC)
ANB .... Air Navigation Board [*Military*] (SAA)
ANB .... Air Navigation Bureau [*British*] (AIA)
ANB .... Alpha-Naphthyl Butyrate [*Organic chemistry*]
ANB .... Ambient Noise Background
ANB .... Amchitka [*Alaska*] [*Seismograph station code, US Geological Survey Closed*] (SEIS)
ANB .... ANB Corp. [*Associated Press*] (SAG)
ANB .... Anglo-Bomarc Mines [*Vancouver Stock Exchange symbol*]
ANB .... Anniston [*Alabama*] [*Airport symbol*] (OAG)
An B .... Anonymous Reports at End of Benloe [*1661*] [*England*] [*A publication*] (DLA)
ANB .... Army-Navy-British
ANB .... Athletics New Brunswick [*Athletisme du Nouveau-Brunswick*] (AC)
ANB .... Avascular Necrosis of Bone [*Medicine*] (DMAA)
ANBACIS...... Automated Nuclear, Biological, and Chemical Information System [*Military*] (DOMA)
ANB & TC .... American National Bank & Trust Co. (MHDB)
ANBC .... ANB Corp. [*NASDAQ symbol*] (SAG)
ANB Corp .... ANB Corp. [*Associated Press*] (SAG)
AnBD .... Anaerobic Broth Disk (PDAA)
ANBE .... Alpha-Naphthyl Butyrate Esterase [*An enzyme*]
ANBFM .... Adaptive Narrowband FM [*Frequency Modulation*] MODEM [*Telecommunications*] (TEL)
ANBK .... American National Bancorp [*NASDAQ symbol*] (SAG)
ANBK .... American National Savings Bank [*NASDAQ symbol*] (SAG)
ANBK .... Amer Natl Bancorp [*NASDAQ symbol*] (TTSB)
ANBLS .... Association of New Brunswick Land Surveyors [*Association des Arpenteurs-Geometres du Nouveau-Brunswick*] (AC)
ANBS .... Air Navigation and Bombing School
ANBS .... Armed Nuclear Bombardment Satellite
ANBS .... Army-Navy-British Standard (SAA)
ANBUG........ Australian Neutron Beam Users' Group
ANC .... Abbott's New Cases [*New York*] [*A publication*] (DLA)
ANC .... Absolute Neutrophil Count [*Hematology*]
ANC .... Academy of the New Church
ANC .... Acid-Neutralizing Capacity [*Chemistry*]
ANC .... Acoustic Noise Canceling [*Headsets*] [*Bose Corp.*]
ANC .... Active Noise Control [*Noise pollution technique*]
ANC .... Active Noise Control
ANC .... Active Nutation Control
ANC .... Adaptive Noise Cancelling (MCD)
ANC .... Advanced Nozzle Concepts (MCD)
ANC .... African National Congress [*South Africa*] (PD)
ANC .... African National Council [*Later, UANC*] [*Zimbabwe*] [*Political party*] (PPW)
ANC .... African Nations' Cup [*Soccer*]
ANC .... Airborne Navigation Computer
ANC .... Air Force-Navy-Civil Committee on Aircraft Requirements
ANC .... Air Navigation Charge (ADA)
ANC .... Air Navigation Committee [*NATO*] (NATG)
ANC .... Air Navigation Conference [*ICAO*]
ANC .... Alianza Nacional Cristiana [*Costa Rica*] [*Political party*] (EY)
ANC .... All Nationals Congress [*Fiji*] [*Political party*] (EY)
ANC .... All Numbers Calling [*Telephone*]
ANC .... American National Cowbelles [*Later, ANCW*] (EA)
ANC .... American Nationalities Council (EA)
ANC .... American Negligence Cases [*A publication*] (DLA)
ANC .... American News Co. (DGA)
ANC .... Anchorage
ANC .... Anchorage [*Alaska*] [*Airport symbol*] (OAG)

ANC	Ancient
anc	Ancient (VRA)
ANC	Ancillary (MCD)
ANC	Anglo Cargo Ltd. [British ICAO designator] (FAAC)
AN C	Anno Christi [In the Year of Christ] [Latin] (ROG)
ANC	Antarctic [Marguerite Bay] [Antarctica] [Seismograph station code, US Geological Survey] [Closed] (SEIS)
ANC	Antenatal Care
ANC	Antenatal Clinic
ANC	Ante Nativitatem Christi [Before the Birth of Christ] [Latin] (ROG)
ANC	Anti-Nuclear Campaign [British]
ANC	Antioch College, Yellow Springs, OH [OCLC symbol] (OCLC)
ANC	Area Naval Commander [NATO] (NATG)
ANC	Arlington National Cemetery
ANC	Armee Nationale Congolaise [Congolese National Army]
ANC	Armenian National Committee (EA)
ANC	Army-Navy Anticorrosion Compound
ANC	Army-Navy-Civil (MSA)
ANC	Army-Navy-Commerce
ANC	Army Nurse Corps
ANC	Asahi New Cast [Metal fabrication]
ANC	Asian Canadian Resources Ltd. [Vancouver Stock Exchange symbol]
ANC	Asociacion Nacional Campesina Pro-Tierra [National Peasant Association for Land] [Guatemala] [Political party]
ANC	Assistant Network Controller [NASA] (KSC)
ANC	Association Nucleaire Canadienne [Canadian Nuclear Association - CNA]
ANC	Association of Neighbourhood Councils [British]
ANC	Association of Noise Consultants [British]
ANC	Australian Nutgrowers' Council
ANC	Average Net Cost [Insurance]
ANCA	Allied Naval Communications Agency [London, England] [NATO]
ANCA	American National Cattlemen's Association [Later, NCA] (EA)
ANCA	American Nickel Collectors' Association (EA)
ANCA	Antineutrophil Cytoplasmic Antibody [Immunology]
ANCA	Armenian National Council of America (EA)
ANCAA	Association of Nebraska Community Action Agencies (SRA)
ANCAB	Alaska Native Claims Appeals Board (in United States Interior Decisions) [A publication] (DLA)
ANCACU	American National Commission for the Accreditation of Colleges and Universities (EA)
ANCAI	Association Nationale des Camionneurs Artisans (AC)
ANCAM	Association of Newspaper Classified Advertising Managers (EA)
ANCAP	Ammonium Nitrate, Copper, Aluminum, and Plywood [Proposed currency]
ANCAT	Abatement of Nuisances Caused by Air Transport
ANCB	American National Cowbelles [Later, ANCW] (EA)
AncBWI........	Anchor Bancorp Wisconsin, Inc. [Associated Press] (SAG)
ANCC	Affiliated National Coaches Council (EA)
ANCC	All Nations Christian College [British]
AnCC	Anodal Closure Contraction [Also, ACC] [Physiology]
ANCC	Army-Navy Country Club
ANCC	Australian Netherlands Chamber of Commerce
ANCC	Automated Network Control Center [Military] (DOMA)
Anc Charters...	Ancient Charters [1692] [A publication] (DLA)
ANCCSA	American North Country Cheviot Sheep Association (EA)
ANCD	Australian National Capital Dancers [An association]
Anc Dial Exch...	Ancient Dialogue upon the Exchequer [A publication] (DLA)
ANCE	Assemblee des Nations Captives d'Europe [Assembly of Captive European Nations]
ANCE	Attitude Nutation Control Electronics (NASA)
ANCET	Analytical Nuclear Casualty Estimation Technique (PDAA)
ANCF	Account Number Change File [IRS]
ANCFIL	Anchored Filament
ANCG	Announcing (MSA)
ANCH	Anches [Reeds] [Music]
ANCH	Anchorage [Maps and charts]
ANCH	Anchored
ANCH	Anechoic (MSA)
ANCHA.........	American National Committee to Aid Homeless Armenians (EA)
ANCHEP	American National Council for Health Education of the Public (EA)
AnchFin	Anchor Financial Corp. [Associated Press] (SAG)
AnchGm	Anchor Gaming [Associated Press] (SAG)
ANCHOR	Alpha-Numeric Character Generator [Computer science] (MHDB)
Anch Prohib...	Anchorage Prohibited [Nautical charts]
ANCHR.........	Anchor
ANCIB	Army-Navy Communications Intelligence Board [Later, STANCIB]
ANCICC	Army-Navy Communications Intelligence Coordinating Committee [Later, ANCIB]
ANCIDF........	Australian National Committee of the International Dairy Federation
ANCIF	Automated Nautical Chart Index File [System] [DoD]
ANCIL	Ancillary (MCD)
ANC-in-C.....	Allied Naval Commander-in-Chief [World War II]
AnClsr	Ancient Israel: Its Life and Institutions [A publication] (BJA)
AnCL	Anthology of Contemporary Latin-American Poetry [A publication]
ANCLAV	Automatic Navigation Computer for Land and Amphibious Vehicles
AnClemOchr...	Annuaire. Academie Theologique (S. Clement D'Ochride) [A publication] (BJA)
Ancmp	Anacomp, Inc. [Associated Press] (SAG)
ANCNT	Ancient
ANCO	Alternate Net Control Officer [Navy] (NVT)
ANCO	Anacomp, Inc. [NASDAQ symbol] (SAG)
AnCO	An Comhairle Oiliuna (ACII)
ANCO	Anderson Co.
ANCO	Annual Customer Order [Air Force] (AFIT)

ANCOA.........	Aerial Nurse Corps of America
ANCOC........	Advanced Noncommissioned Officer Course [Army] (INF)
ANCOES.......	Advanced Noncommissioned Officer Education System (MCD)
ANCOM........	Andean Common Market (EAIO)
ANCOR........	American-Netherlands Club of Rotterdam
AncorCm.......	Ancor Communications [Associated Press] (SAG)
ANCOVA.......	Analysis of Covariance
ANCOVS.......	Active Night Covert Viewing [or Vision] System
ANCPA........	Amino-(nitro)cyclopentanecarboxylic Acid [Organic chemistry]
ANCPCJ	Alliance of NGOs [Nongovernmental Organizations] on Crime Prevention and Criminal Justice (EA)
ANCPEA	Army-Navy Communications Production Expediting Agency
ANCPT	Anticipate (FAAC)
ANCR	Aircraft Not Combat Ready (MCD)
ANCR	Ancor Communicatons [NASDAQ symbol] (SAG)
ANCRT	Associate of the National College of Rubber Technology [British] (DI)
ANCS	Airborne Night Classification System (MCD)
ANCS	Alternate Net Control Station (CET)
ANCSA........	African National Congress of South Africa
ANCSA........	Alaska Native Claims Settlement Act [1971]
ANCS-II.......	Automated Nautical Charting System (OSRA)
ANCS-II.......	Automated Nautical Charting System (USDC)
ANCT	Ancient
ANCU	Air Navigation Computer Unit (MCD)
ANCW	American National Cattle Women (EA)
ANCWA.......	American Naturalized Citizen Welfare Association [Later, US Naturalized CitizenAssociation] (EA)
ANCWEC......	Australian National Committee, World Energy Council
ANCXF	Allied Naval Commander Expeditionary Forces
ANCYL	African National Congress Youth League [South Africa] (PD)
AND	Active Nutation Damper
AND	Admiralty Net Defence [Antitorpedo nets] [British World War II]
AND	Air Force-Navy Design
AND	Air Navigation Device
AND	Air Navigation Directions
AND	Airplane Nose Down
AND	Algoneurodystrophy [Medicine] (DMAA)
And	All India Reporter, Andhra Series [A publication] (DLA)
AND	Alphanumeric Display
AND	Amchitka [Alaska] [Seismograph station code, US Geological Survey Closed] (SEIS)
AND	Andalusite [Mineralogy]
AND	Andaman Islands
AND	Andante [Slow] [Music]
and	Andere [Other] [German]
AND	Anderson [South Carolina] [Airport symbol] (OAG)
And	Anderson's Agriculture Cases [England] [A publication] (DLA)
And	Anderson's English Common Pleas Reports [1534-1605] [A publication] (DLA)
AND	Andorra [ANSI three-letter standard code] (CNC)
And	Andorra (VRA)
AND	Andrea Electronics [AMEX symbol] (TTSB)
AND	Andrea Electronics Corp. [AMEX symbol] (SPSG)
And	Andreas Bonellus de Barulo [Flourished, 1260-71] [Authority cited in pre-1607 legal work] (DSA)
And	Andrews' English King's Bench Reports [95 English Reprint] [A publication] (DLA)
And	Andrews' Reports [63-73 Connecticut] [A publication] (DLA)
And	Androgen [Antineoplastic drug] (DAVI)
And	Andromeda [Constellation]
AND	Androne Resources Ltd. [Vancouver Stock Exchange symbol]
AND	Antenatal Diagnosis
AND	Anterior Nasal Discharge [Medicine] (DMAA)
AND	Army-Navy Design Standards
AND	Artists for Nuclear Disarmament [Defunct] (EA)
AND	Associate Administrator for NAS Development [FAA] (TAG)
AND	Association for the Neurologically Disabled of Canada (AC)
AND	Australian National Dictionary [A publication]
AND	Automatic Network Dialing [Telecommunications] (TEL)
AND	National Jet Service, Inc. [ICAO designator] (FAAC)
ANDA	Abbreviated New Drug Application [FDA]
ANDA	Auxiliary to the National Dental Association (EA)
ANDAC........	Air Navigation Data Center (SAA)
And Agr Dec...	Anderson's Agricultural Decisions [Scotland] [A publication] (DLA)
And & Ston JA...	Andrews and Stoney's Supreme Court of Judicature Acts [A publication] (DLA)
ANDAS........	Automatic Navigation and Data Acquisition System
ANDB	Air Navigation Development Board [Functions absorbed by the FAA]
ANDB	Andover Bancorp [NASDAQ symbol] (TTSB)
ANDB	Andover Bancorp, Inc. [NASDAQ symbol] (NQ)
And Ch W	Anderson on Church Wardens [A publication] (DLA)
And Com.......	Anderson's History of Commerce [A publication] (DLA)
And Cr Law...	Andrews on Criminal Law [A publication] (DLA)
And de Baro...	Andreas Bonellus de Barulo [Flourished, 1260-71] [Authority cited in pre-1607 legal work] (DSA)
And de Ca ...	Andreas de Capua [Flourished, 1242-57] [Authority cited in pre-1607 legal work] (DSA)
And Dig	Andrews' Digest of the Opinions of the Attorneys-General [A publication] (DLA)
ANDE	Active Nutation Damper Electronics
ANDE	Alphanumeric Display Equipment
ANDE	Andersons Inc. [NASDAQ symbol] (TTSB)
Andean	Andean Development Corp. [Associated Press] (SAG)
AndeanD......	Andean Development Corp. [Associated Press] (SAG)

An de Bu ..... Antonius de Butrio [*Deceased, 1408*] [*Authority cited in pre-1607 legal work*] (DSA)

ANDEF .... Action for Nuclear Disarmament Education Fund (EA)

An de Iser ... Andreas de Isernia [*Deceased circa 1316*] [*Authority cited in pre-1607 legal work*] (DSA)

An de Peru ... Angelus de Ubaldis de Perusio [*Deceased, 1407*] [*Authority cited in pre-1607 legal work*] (DSA)

Ander (Eng) ... Anderson's Reports, English Court of Common Pleas [*A publication*] (DLA)

Anders .... Anderson's Reports, English Court of Common Pleas [*A publication*] (DLA)

Anderson ..... Anderson's Reports, English Court of Common Pleas [*A publication*] (DLA)

Anderson UCC ... Anderson's Uniform Commercial Code [*A publication*] (DLA)

ANDES .... Aerolineas Nacionales del Ecuador [*Airline*]

ANDF .... Architecture Neutral Distributed Format (CDE)

Andh .... All India Reporter, Andhra Series [*A publication*] (DLA)

Andh Pra ..... All India Reporter, Andhra Pradesh Series [*A publication*] (DLA)

ANDI .... Automated Non-Destructive Inspector [*Robotics*] (PS)

ANDIPS .... American National Dictionary for Information Processing Systems [*A publication*]

ANDL .... Army Nuclear Defense Laboratory (MCD)

And L & Cts .. Andrews on United States Laws and Courts [*A publication*] (DLA)

And Law Dict ... Anderson's Law Dictionary [*A publication*] (DLA)

And Man Const ... Andrews' Manual of the United States Constitution [*A publication*] (DLA)

ANDMS .... Advanced Network Design and Management System [*Computer science*] (MHDB)

ANDNO .... Andantino [*Slow*] [*Music*]

ANDO .... Andantino [*Slow*] [*Music*]

AN DO .... Anno Domini [*In the Year of Our Lord*] [*Latin*]

Andoc .... Andocides [*Fifth century BC*] [*Classical studies*] (OCD)

ANDP .... Alliance Nationale pour la Democratie et le Progres [*Haiti*] [*Political party*] (EY)

And Pr Lea ... Andrews' Precedents of Leases [*A publication*] (DLA)

And Pr Mort ... Andrews' Precedents of Mortgages [*A publication*] (DLA)

ANDPVA .... Association for Native Development in the Performing and Visual Arts [*Canada*]

And Q & A ... Anderson's Examination Questions and Answers [*A publication*] (DLA)

ANDR .... Andersen Group [*NASDAQ symbol*] (TTSB)

ANDR .... Andersen Group, Inc. [*NASDAQ symbol*] (NQ)

Andr .... Andreas Bonellus de Barulo [*Flourished, 1260-71*] [*Authority cited in pre-1607 legal work*] (DSA)

Andr .... Andreas de Isernia [*Deceased circa 1316*] [*Authority cited in pre-1607 legal work*] (DSA)

Andr .... Andrews' English King's Bench Reports [*95 English Reprint*] [*A publication*] (DLA)

Andr .... Andromache [*of Euripides*] [*Classical studies*] (OCD)

Andr .... Andromeda [*Constellation*]

Andr Acza .... Andreas Acconzaioco de Ravello [*Flourished, 1294-1300*] [*Authority cited in pre-1607 legal work*] (DSA)

Andr Alciat ... Andreas Alciatus [*Deceased, 1550*] [*Authority cited in pre-1607 legal work*] (DSA)

Andr Azaio ... Andreas Acconzaioco de Ravello [*Flourished, 1294-1300*] [*Authority cited in pre-1607 legal work*] (DSA)

ANDRB .... Active Duty Nondisability Retirement Branch [*BUPERS*] [*Navy*]

Andr de Bar ... Andreas Bonellus de Barulo [*Flourished, 1260-71*] [*Authority cited in pre-1607 legal work*] (DSA)

Andr de Ca ... Andreas de Capua [*Flourished, 1242-57*] [*Authority cited in pre-1607 legal work*] (DSA)

Andr de Cap ... Andreas de Capua [*Flourished, 1242-57*] [*Authority cited in pre-1607 legal work*] (DSA)

Andr de Isern ... Andreas de Isernia [*Deceased circa 1316*] [*Authority cited in pre-1607 legal work*] (DSA)

Andr de Ra ... Andreas Acconzaioco de Ravello [*Flourished, 1294-1300*] [*Authority cited in pre-1607 legal work*] (DSA)

Andre .... Andreas Bonellus de Barulo [*Flourished, 1260-71*] [*Authority cited in pre-1607 legal work*] (DSA)

Andre .... Andreas de Isernia [*Deceased circa 1316*] [*Authority cited in pre-1607 legal work*] (DSA)

Andrea .... Andrea Electronics Corp. [*Associated Press*] (SAG)

ANDREE ...... Association for Nuclear Development and Research in Electrical Engineering (MCD)

And Rev Law ... Andrews on the Revenue Law [*A publication*] (DLA)

Andrew .... Andrew Corp. [*Associated Press*] (SAG)

Andrews (Eng) ... Andrews' English King's Bench Reports [*95 English Reprint*] [*A publication*] (DLA)

Andrews U ... Andrews University (GAGS)

Andr Fachin ... Andreas Fachineus [*Deceased, 1622*] [*Authority cited in pre-1607 legal work*] (DSA)

AndrGr .... Andersen Group, Inc. [*Associated Press*] (SAG)

ANDRO .... Androsterone [*Pharmacology*] (DAVI)

Andros .... Andros, Inc. [*Associated Press*] (SAG)

ANDROS ...... Androsterone [*Pharmacology*] (DAVI)

Andr Pomat ... Andreas Pomates [*Authority cited in pre-1607 legal work*] (DSA)

Andr Tiraq ... Andreas Tiraquellus [*Deceased, 1558*] [*Authority cited in pre-1607 legal work*] (DSA)

AndrxCp ...... Andrx Corp. [*Associated Press*] (SAG)

ANDS .... Advanced Navy Display System

ANDS .... Automated Newspaper Delivery System (PDAA)

ANDSOOHA ... Association of Nursing Directors & Supervisors of Ontario Official Health Agencies (AC)

ANDTC .... Association Nationale des Distributeurs de Tabac et de Confiserie (AC)

ANDTE .... Andante [*Slow*] [*Music*]

AnDTe .... Anodal Duration Tetanus [*Physiology*]

And Tiraq .... Andreas Tiraquellus [*Deceased, 1558*] [*Authority cited in pre-1607 legal work*] (DSA)

ANDTS .... Associate of the Non-Destructive Testing Society [*British*]

ANDTSNSW ... Australian Native Dog Training Society of New South Wales [*Australia*]

ANDUS .... Anglo-Dutch-United States

AndvBc .... Andover Bancorp, Inc. [*Associated Press*] (SAG)

ANDVT .... Advanced Narrowband Digital Voice Terminal (MCD)

AndvTog ...... Andover Togs, Inc. [*Associated Press*] (SAG)

ANDW .... Andrew Corp. [*NASDAQ symbol*] (NQ)

ANDY .... Andros, Inc. [*NASDAQ symbol*] (NQ)

Andyne .... Andyne Computing Ltd. [*Associated Press*] (SAG)

ANDZ .... Anodize (MSA)

ANDZNG ...... Anodizing

ANE .... Acoustic Noise Environment

ANE .... Aeronautical and Navigational Electronics (MCD)

ANE .... Aerospace and Navigational Electronics (MCD)

ANE .... Alto Exploration [*Vancouver Stock Exchange symbol*]

ANE .... Americans for Nuclear Energy (EA)

ANE .... Ancient Near East (BJA)

AnE .... Expression of Anger [*Psychology*]

ANE .... Minneapolis, MN [*Location identifier FAA*] (FAAL)

ANE .... Newbrook Public Library, Alberta [*Library symbol National Library of Canada*] (NLC)

ANE .... Nora-2000 [*Bulgaria*] [*ICAO designator*] (FAAC)

ANEA .... Associate of New Era Academy of Dance [*British*]

ANEC .... American Natural Energy Corp. [*NASDAQ symbol*] (SAG)

ANEC .... American Nuclear Energy Council (EA)

AnEC .... Ancient English Christmas Carols [*A publication*]

ANEC .... Armenian National Education Committee (EA)

ANEC .... Association Nordique des Etudes Canadiennes [*Nordic Association for Canadian Studies*]

ANECInst ..... Associate of the Northeast Coast Institution of Engineers and Shipbuilders [*British*]

ANED .... Associazione Nazionale Ex-Deportati Politici nei Campi Nazisti [*National Association of Political Ex-Deportees of the Nazi Camps*] [*Italy Political party*] (EAIO)

ANEDA .... Association Nationale d'Etudes pour la Documentation Automatique [*National Association for Studies in Automatic Documentation*] [*French*] (NITA)

ANEEG .... Army, Navy Electronics Evaluation Group

ANEF .... American-Nepal Education Foundation (EA)

ANEI .... Australian Noise Exposure Index

Anekd .... Anekdote [*Anecdote*] [*German*]

ANEL .... Association Nationale des Editeurs de Livres (AC)

ANEN .... African NGOs [*Nongovernmental Organizations*] Environment Network (EAIO)

ANEN .... Anaren Microwave [*NASDAQ symbol*] (TTSB)

ANEN .... Anaren Microwave, Inc. [*NASDAQ symbol*] (NQ)

AnEnPo .... Anthology for the Enjoyment of Poetry [*A publication*]

ANEP .... Agence Nationale d'Edition et de Publicite [*National Publication and Advertising Agency*] [*Algeria*] (AF)

ANEP .... Airport Noise Evaluation Process (PDAA)

ANEP .... [*The*] Ancient Near East in Pictures [*A publication*] (BJA)

ANEPA .... Army-Navy Electronics Production Agency

ANER .... Aneroid (MSA)

ANERA .... American Near East Refugee Aid (EA)

Anera .... Asia-North America Eastbound Rate Agreement [*Shipping*]

ANERAC ...... Annual Northeast Regional Antipollution Conference

Anergen ...... Anergen, Inc. [*Associated Press*] (SAG)

ANES .... Anesthesiology (AABC)

ANES .... Australian National Eisteddfod Society

ANESG .... Atomic/Nuclear Energy Study Group (EA)

ANESR .... Apparent Norepinephrine Secretion Rate [*Medicine*] (DMAA)

Anesta .... Anesta Corp. [*Associated Press*] (SAG)

ANESTH ...... Anesthesia [*or Anesthetic*] [*Medicine*]

ANESTHLGY ... Anesthesiology

ANET .... ACT Networks [*NASDAQ symbol*] (TTSB)

ANET .... ACT Networks, Inc. [*NASDAQ symbol*] (SAG)

ANET .... Ancient Near Eastern Texts Relating to the Old Testament [*A publication*] (BJA)

ANET .... Association of Nurses Endorsing Transplantation (EA)

ANETH .... Anethum [*Dill Seed*] [*Pharmacology*] (ROG)

ANEX .... Analyst-to-Analyst Exchange Message Format (MCD)

ANEX .... Annex [*Commonly used*] (OPSA)

an ex .... Anode Excitation (MAE)

ANEXGOVT ... At No Expense to the Government

ANF .... Abercrombie & Fitch Co. [*NYSE symbol*] (SAG)

ANF .... Account Number File [*Integrated Data Retrieval System*] [*IRS*]

ANF .... Actinide Nitride-Fueled Reactor (NRCH)

ANF .... Aero North Icelandic, Inc. [*ICAO designator*] (FAAC)

ANF .... Agriculture, Nutrition, and Forestry (DLA)

ANF .... Air Navigation Facility

ANF .... Allied Naval Forces [*NATO*]

ANF .... Alpha-Naphthoflavone [*Biochemistry*]

ANF .... American Nurses' Foundation (EA)

ANF .... America's New Foundations [*A publication*]

ANF .... Anchored Filament

Anf .... Anfang [*Beginning*] [*German*]

AnF .... Angel Flight (EA)

ANF .... Antinuclear Factor [*Immunology*]

ANF .... Anti-Nuclear Force (DNAB)

ANF .... Antofagasta [*Chile*] [*Airport symbol*] (OAG)

ANF	Armenian National Federation (AC)
ANF	Army News Features
ANF	Arrived Notification Form [British] (DCTA)
ANF	Associazione la Nostra Famiglia [Ponte Lambro, Italy] (EAIO)
ANF	Atlantic Nuclear Force [NATO]
ANF	Atrial Natriuretic Factor [Biochemistry]
ANF	Australian National Formulary
ANF	Automatic Number Identification Failure [Telecommunications] (TEL)
ANF	Aviation News Features
ANFA	Allied Non-Theatrical Film Association (AEBS)
ANFC	Association des Numismates Francophones du Canada (AC)
ANFC	Association Nationale des Forblantiers et Couvreurs, Section Locale 2020 [National Association of Tinsmiths & Tilers, Local 2020] (AC)
AN/FCC	Army Navy/Fixed Communications Cabinet (MCD)
ANFCE	Allied Naval Forces Central Europe [NATO]
ANFD	Australian National Field Days
ANFDC	Australian National Field Days Committee
ANFE	Aircraft Nonflying-Electronics (CINC)
ANFE	Aircraft Not Fully Equipped
AnFE	Anthology for Famous English and American Poetry [A publication]
ANFI	Automatic Noise Figure Indicator (MCD)
ANFICM	Atlantic Fleet Naval Forces Intelligence Collection Manual
ANFLOW	Anaerobic Upflow Fixed-Film Process [For treating wastewater]
ANFM	August, November, February, and May [Denotes quarterly payments of interest or dividends in these months] [Business term]
ANFO	Ammonium Nitrate and Fuel Oil [Explosive]
AnFP	Anthology of French Poetry [A publication]
ANFQ	L'Association de la Neurofibromatose du Quebec (AC)
ANFRIDI	Annuaire Francais de Droit International [A publication]
ANFS	Airport Network Flow Simulator (MCD)
ANFSA	Australian Nuffied Farming Scholars' Association
AN/FSC	Army Navy/Fixed Satellite Communication (MCD)
ANFSOC	Australian National Flower Show Organising Committee
ANFTES	Archives Nationales du Film, de la Television, et de l'Enregistrement Sonore [National Film, Television, and Sound Archives] [NFTSA] [Canada]
ANFWDC	Australian National Four Wheel Drive Council
ANG	Acoustic Noise Generator
ANG	Air National Guard
ANG	Air Niugini [Papua New Guinea] [ICAO designator] (FAAC)
ANG	Alarm Network Group
ANG	Alberta Natural Gas Co. Ltd. [Toronto Stock Exchange symbol Vancouver Stock Exchange symbol]
ANG	Alliance for Neighborhood Government [Later, NAN] (EA)
ANG	American Needlepoint Guild (EA)
ANG	American Newspaper Guild [Later, TNG] (EA)
ANG	American Nominalist Group (EA)
ANG	A New Genesis (TOCD)
Ang	Angell and Durfee's Reports [1 Rhode Island] [A publication] (DLA)
Ang	Angell's Rhode Island Reports [A publication] (DLA)
Ang	Angelus de Gambilionibus de Aretio [Flourished, 1422-51] [Authority cited in pre-1607 legal work] (DSA)
Ang	Angelus de Ubaldis [Deceased, 1407] [Authority cited in pre-1607 legal work] (DSA)
ANG	Angiogram [Cardiology]
ANG	Angiotensin [Biochemistry]
ANG	Angle (MSA)
ANG	Anglesey [Welsh island and county]
ANG	Anglican
ang	Anglo-Saxon [MARC language code Library of Congress] (LCCP)
ANG	Angola
Ang	Angolia (VRA)
ANG	Antigua [Antigua] [Seismograph station code, US Geological Survey] (SEIS)
ANG	Applied Naturalist Guild [Defunct]
ANG	Army National Guard
ANG	Association of National Grasslands (EA)
ANg	Die Akkadische Namengebung [A publication] (BJA)
ANGA	Australian Nashi Growers' Association
Ang Adv Enj	Angell on Adverse Enjoyment [A publication] (DLA)
AngAG	Anglo American Gold [Associated Press] (SAG)
Ang & A Corp	Angell and Ames on Corporations [A publication] (DLA)
Ang & D High	Angell and Durfee on Highways [A publication] (DLA)
Ang & Dur	Angell and Durfee's Reports [1 Rhode Island] [A publication] (DLA)
Ang Are	Angelus de Gambilionibus de Aretio [Flourished, 1422-51] [Authority cited in pre-1607 legal work] (DSA)
Ang Ass	Angell on Assignment [A publication] (DLA)
ANGB	Air National Guard Base
Ang BT	Angell on Bank Tax [A publication] (DLA)
Ang Car	Angell on Carriers [A publication] (DLA)
Ang Corp	Angell and Ames on Corporations [A publication] (DLA)
Ang de Perigl	Angelus de Periglis [Deceased, 1446] [Authority cited in pre-1607 legal work] (DSA)
Ange	Angelus de Gambilionibus de Aretio [Flourished, 1422-51] [Authority cited in pre-1607 legal work] (DSA)
Ange	Angelus de Ubaldis [Deceased, 1407] [Authority cited in pre-1607 legal work] (DSA)
Ange Aret	Angelus de Gambilionibus de Aretio [Flourished, 1422-51] [Authority cited in pre-1607 legal work] (DSA)
Angeion	Angeion Corp. [Associated Press] (SAG)
Angel	Angelus de Gambilionibus de Aretio [Flourished, 1422-51] [Authority cited in pre-1607 legal work] (DSA)
Angel de Clavas	Angelus Carletus de Clavasio [Deceased, 1492] [Authority cited in pre-1607 legal work] (DSA)

Angelegenh	Angelegenheit [Affair] [German]
Angelic	Angelica Corp. [Associated Press] (SAG)
ANGELL	Associated Nursery Guides Emphatically Lacking in Leisure
Angelo St U	Angelo State University
Angest	Angestellter [Clerk, Employee] [German]
ANG-FWO	Air National Guard Fighter Weapons Office [Tucson, AZ]
Ang GR	Angiotensin Generation Rate [Biochemistry] (MAE)
Ang High	Angell and Durfee on Highways [A publication] (DLA)
Ang Highw	Angell and Durfee on Highways [A publication] (DLA)
Angim	Epic Angim Dimma (BJA)
Ang Ins	Angell on Insurance [A publication] (DLA)
angio	Angiocatheter [or Angiocatheterization] [Cardiology] (DAVI)
angio	Angiogram [Cardiology]
angio	Angiography [Cardiology] (DAVI)
ANGL	Angle
ANGL	Anglican
ANGL	Anglice [In English] [Latin]
Angl	Anglistik [Study of English language and literature] [German]
ANGL	Anglo American Corp. of South Africa Ltd. [NASDAQ symbol] (NQ)
ANGLCN	Anglican
ANGLE	Access Now for Gay and Lesbian Equality [An association]
ANGLICO	Air and Naval Gunfire Liaison Company [Military]
Ang Lim	Angell on Limitation of Actions [A publication] (DLA)
ANGLR	Angler
ANGLY	Anglo Amer So Afr ADR [NASDAQ symbol] (TTSB)
AngMtg	Angeles Mortgage Partners [Associated Press] (SAG)
ANGN	Angeion Corp. [NASDAQ symbol] (NQ)
An Go	Antonius Gomez [Flourished, 16th century] [Authority cited in pre-1607 legal work] (DSA)
ANGO	Association du Negoce des Grains Oleagineuses, Huiles, et Graisses Animales et Vegetales et Leurs Derives de la CEE [Trade Association for Oilseeds, Oil, Vegetable and Animal Fats, and Their Derivatives of the European Economic Community]
ANGOC	Asian NonGovernmental Organizations Coalition for Agrarian Reform and Rural Development [Philippines] (EAIO)
ANGOP	Angolan News Agency
ANGOS	Air National Guard Optometric Society (EA)
ANGOSA	Air National Guard Operational Support Aircraft [Air Force] (DOMA)
AnGP	Anthology of German Poetry [A publication]
AngPar	Angeles Participating Mortgage Trust [Associated Press] (SAG)
ANGPC	Air National Guard Policy Council
ANGR	Air Navigation (General) Regulation [British] (DA)
AN/GRA	Air Force-Navy Ground RADAR (SAA)
AN/GRC	Army-Navy Ground Radio Communications
ANGRY	Anti-Nuclear Group Representing York (NRCH)
AngSA	Anglo American Corp. of South Africa Ltd. [Associated Press] (SAG)
Ang-Sax	Anglo-Saxon
ANGSC	Air National Guard Support Center
ANGTA	Alaska Natural Gas Transportation Act of 1976
Ang Tide Waters	Angell on Tide Waters [A publication] (DLA)
ANGTS	Alaska Natural Gas Transportation System
Ang TW	Angell on Tide Waters [A publication] (DLA)
ANGUS	Acoustically Navigated Geological Underwater Survey [Unmanned vehicle]
ANGUS	Air National Guard of the United States
ANGV	Advanced Natural Gas Vehicle
ANGW	Alles nach Gottes Willen [Everything According to the Will of God] [Motto for a number of members of German and Bavarian royalty during the 16th and 17th centuries]
Ang Wat	Angell on Water Courses [A publication] (DLA)
Ang Water Courses	Angell on Water Courses [A publication] (DLA)
ANGWS	Advanced Naval Gun Weapon System (MCD)
ANH	Academic Nursing Home (DMAA)
ANH	All-North Resources Ltd. [Vancouver Stock Exchange symbol]
ANH	Anair - Anich Airways [Croatia] [ICAO designator] (FAAC)
ANH	Anhang [Appendix] [German] (EG)
ANH	Anhydrous
ANH	Artificial Nutrition and Hydration [Medicine]
ANH	Associated Newspaper Holdings [British]
ANH	Association of Neighbourhood Houses of Greater Vancouver (AC)
ANH	Nhill [Victoria, Australia] [Airport symbol] (AD)
ANHA	Alabama Nursing Home Association (SRA)
ANHA	American National Heritage Association (EA)
ANHA	American Nursing Home Association [Later, AHCA] (EA)
ANHC	Army Native Hospital Corps [British military] (DMA)
ANHECA	Australian Nursing Homes and Extended Care Association
Anheus	Anheuser-Busch Companies, Inc. [Associated Press] (SAG)
AN(HS)	Airman (High School) (DNAB)
ANHS	American Natural Hygiene Society (EA)
ANHSA	Aeronias Nacionales de Honduras Sociedad Anonima [Airline] [Honduras]
ANHSCSR	Association of National Health Service Corps Scholarship Recipients [Defunct] (EA)
ANHSO	Association of National Health Service Officers [British]
ANHSSO	Association of National Health Service Supplies Officers [British] (DBA)
ANHY	Anhydrous
ANHYD	Anhydride (MSA)
ANHYD	Anhydrous
anhydr	Anhydrous (BARN)
ANI	Acute Nerve Irritation (HGAA)
ANI	Adizes Network International [Santa Monica, CA] (EA)
ANI	Advanced Network Integration (TEL)
ANI	Agencia Nacionale de Informacoes [National Information Agency] [Portugal]

ANI.............. Ambient Noise Index (CAAL)
ANI.............. American National Insurance Co.
ANI.............. American Nuclear Insurers [Farmington, CT] (EA)
ANI.............. Americans for the National Interest [Defunct] (EA)
ANI.............. Analog Number Identification [Electronics] (ECII)
ANI.............. Aniak [Alaska] [Airport symbol] (OAG)
ANI.............. Animal
ANI.............. Anina Resources, Inc. [Vancouver Stock Exchange symbol]
ANI.............. Apprentices National Insurance [British]
ANI.............. Army-Navy-Industry (MCD)
ANI.............. Association Nationale pour l'Infographie [National Computer Graphics Association of Canada]
ANI.............. Associazione Nazionalista Italiana [Italian Nationalist Association] [Political party] (PPE)
ANI.............. Atmosphere Normale Internationale [International Normal Atmosphere]
ANI.............. Authorized Nuclear Inspector (NRCH)
ANI.............. Autism Network International (EA)
ANI.............. Automatic Number Identification [Telecommunications]
ANIA.......... Automated Nephelometric Immunoassay [Medicine] (DMAA)
ANIC.......... Anicom, Inc. [NASDAQ symbol] (SAG)
ANICA........ Atmospheric Nutrient Input to Coastal Areas [Project] (OSRA)
ANICA........ Atmospheric Nutrient Input to Coastal Areas [Project] (USDC)
ANICO........ American National Insurance Co.
Anicom........ Anicom, Inc. [Associated Press] (SAG)
ANICS........ Alaskan NICS [FAA] (TAG)
ANIH.......... Associate of the National Institute of Hardware [British] (DBQ)
ANIK.......... Anika Research [NASDAQ symbol] (TTSB)
ANIK.......... Anika Research, Inc. [NASDAQ symbol] (SAG)
AnikaRs........ Anika Research, Inc. [Associated Press] (SAG)
anil.............. Aniline [Philately]
AnIL.............. Anthology of Irish Literature [A publication]
ANILCA........ Alaska National Interest Land Conservation Act [1980]
ANIM.......... Acute Necrosis of Intestinal Mucosa [Gastroenterology]
ANIM.......... Agence Internationale d'Information du Mali [Press agency] [Mali]
ANIM.......... Agence Nationale d'Information Malienne [Malian National Information Agency] (AF)
ANIM.......... Animal
ANIM.......... Animation [Films, television, etc.]
ANIM.......... Association of Nuclear Instrument Manufacturers [Later, SAMA]
Animal Rights L Rep... Animal Rights Law Reporter [A publication] (DLA)
ANIMO........ Animato [Lively, Animated] [Music]
ANIP.......... Army-Navy Instrumentation Program
ANIP.......... Army Navy Integrated Presentation
ANIRC.......... Annual National Information Retrieval Colloquium
ANIS.......... Anisocytosis [Hematology] (DAVI)
ANIS.......... Anisum [Anise Seed] [Pharmacology] (ROG)
aniso.......... Anisocytosis [Hematology]
Anisometr.... Anisometropia [Ophthalmology]
ANIT.......... Alpha-Naphthylisothiocyanate [Organic chemistry]
ANITA.......... [A] New Inspiration to Arithmetic
AnIV.......... Anthology of Irish Verse [A publication]
ANix.......... Australian Nixa [Record label]
Anixter........ Anixter International, Inc. [Associated Press] (SAG)
ANJ.............. Aero-Alentejo, Servicos Aereos Lda. [Portugal ICAO designator] (FAAC)
ANJ.............. Aintree Resources [Vancouver Stock Exchange symbol]
ANJ.............. Atlantic Community College, Mays Landing, NJ [OCLC symbol] (OCLC)
ANJ.............. Australian Nurses' Journal [A publication] (APTA)
ANJ.............. Zanaga [Congo] [Airport symbol] (OAG)
ANJEC.......... Association of New Jersey Environmental Commissions (SRA)
ANJGG........ Green Grove Community Library, Nilton Junction, Alberta [Library symbol National Library of Canada] (NLC)
ANJSB........ Army-Navy Joint Specifications Board
ANK.......... Air Nippon Co. Ltd. [Japan ICAO designator] (FAAC)
ANK.......... Alphanumeric Keyboard
ANK.......... American Neturei Karta [Friends of Jerusalem] (EA)
ANK.......... Ankara [Turkey] [Seismograph station code, US Geological Survey] (SEIS)
ANK.......... Ankara [Turkey] [Airport symbol] (OAG)
ank.......... Ankle (MAE)
ANK.......... Automatic Navigation Kit (MCD)
ANKB.......... Alphanumeric Keyboard
ANKC.......... Australian National Kennel Council
ANKFF.......... Australian National Kung Fu Federation
ANL.............. Above Normal Loss [Insurance]
ANL.............. Acute Nonlymphoblastic Leukemia [Medicine]
ANL.............. American National Standard Labels (BUR)
ANL.............. Amplitude Noise Limiting
ANL.............. Analog (NASA)
ANL.............. Andalgala [Argentina] [Seismograph station code, US Geological Survey Closed] (SEIS)
ANL.............. Animal (WGA)
ANL.............. Anneal (KSC)
ANL.............. Annoyance Level [Aircraft noise]
ANL.............. Annual (AABC)
ANL.............. Argonne National Laboratory [Argonne, IL] [Department of Energy] (GRD)
ANL.............. Argonne National Laboratory, Argonne, IL [OCLC symbol] (OCLC)
ANL.............. Army Natick Laboratory
ANL.............. Automatic Noise-Landing (DNAB)
ANL.............. Automatic Noise Limiter [Electronics]
ANL.............. Nacoia Lda. [Angola] [FAA designator] (FAAC)
ANL.............. Net Laying Ship [Formerly, AN] [Navy symbol]

ANLA.......... Association of Newfoundland & Labrador Archivists [L'Association des Archivistes de Terre-Neuve et de Labrador] (AC)
ANLC.......... Alaska Native Language Center [Research center] (RCD)
ANLC.......... Army-Navy Liquidation Commission [World War II]
ANL-E.......... Argonne National Laboratory-East [Argonne, IL] (GAAI)
ANL-E.......... Argonne National Laboratory-East
ANL-E.......... Argonne National Laboratory-East (DOGT)
ANL/EES...... Argonne National Laboratory Energy and Environmental Systems Division
ANL/ES........ Argonne National Laboratory Division of Environmental Impact Studies
ANL/ETD...... Argonne National Laboratory Engineering and Technology Division [Illinois]
ANLF.......... Afghanistan National Liberation Front
ANLG.......... Analog (MSA)
ANLG.......... Analog
ANLG.......... Analogy, Inc. [NASDAQ symbol] (SAG)
ANLG.......... Analogy Inc. [NASDAQ symbol] (TTSB)
ANLG.......... Antilogarithmic Function
ANLGS.......... Analogous (MSA)
ANLI.......... Antibody-Negative Mice with Latent Infection [Immunology]
ANL ID.......... Argonne National Laboratory, Idaho Division
ANLL.......... Acute Nonlymphoblastic Leukemia [Medicine] (DAVI)
ANLL.......... Acute Nonlymphocytic Leukemia [Medicine]
Anlogic.......... Analogic Corp. [Associated Press] (SAG)
ANLOR.......... Angle Order (IEEE)
ANLP.......... Alpha-Numeric Logic Package [Computer science] (MHDI)
ANLR.......... Angular
ANLR.......... Annular
ANLS.......... Analyst
ANLSC.......... Additive Noise Linear Sequential Circuit
ANLT.......... Analytical Surveys [NASDAQ symbol] (TTSB)
ANLT.......... Analytical Surveys, Inc. [NASDAQ symbol] (NQ)
ANL-W.......... Argonne National Laboratory-West
ANL-W.......... Argonne National Laboratory-West
ANL-W.......... Argonne National Laboratory-West [Idaho Falls, ID] (GAAI)
ANL-W.......... Argonne National Laboratory-West (DOGT)
ANLX.......... New South Wales Land Tax [Australia A publication]
ANLY.......... Analysis
ANLY.......... Analysts International Corp. [NASDAQ symbol] (NQ)
ANLY.......... Analysts Intl. [NASDAQ symbol] (TTSB)
ANLYS.......... Analysis (FAAC)
ANLYS.......... Analysis
ANLYST.......... Analyst
AnlySur........ Analytical Surveys, Inc. [Associated Press] (SAG)
ANLYTC........ Analytic
ANLYTCL........ Analytical
ANLYZ.......... Analyzer
ANM.......... Acoustic Noise Making (CAAL)
ANM.......... Acute Necrotic Myelopathy [Medicine]
ANM.......... Admiralty Notice to Mariners [British] (DI)
ANM.......... After New Moon [Freemasonry] (ROG)
ANM.......... Alliance of Nonprofit Mailers (EA)
ANM.......... Ambient Noise Measurement (CAAL)
ANM.......... Ameritech Network Management (ACRL)
ANM.......... Angeles Mortgage Partners [AMEX symbol] (SPSG)
ANM.......... Angeles Mtge Inv Tr L.P. [AMEX symbol] (TTSB)
ANM.......... (Anilinonaphthyl)maleimide [Organic chemistry]
ANM.......... Anmerkung [Note] [German]
ANM.......... Antalaha [Madagascar] [Airport symbol] (OAG)
ANM.......... Artesia Public Library, Artesia, NM [OCLC symbol] (OCLC)
ANM.......... Nampa Municipal Library, Alberta [Library symbol National Library of Canada] (NLC)
ANM.......... New Music (Australia) [Record label]
ANMA.......... American Naturopathic Medical Association (EA)
ANMA.......... Auxiliary to the National Medical Association (EA)
ANMB.......... Army-Navy Munitions Board [Later, Munitions Board]
ANMC.......... American National Metric Council (EA)
ANMC.......... Assistant Navy Mail Clerk
ANMCC........ Alternate National Military Command Center [Formerly, AJWR] (AFM)
ANMCS........ Anticipated Not Mission Capable, Supply [Military] (NVT)
ANMD.......... Association of Neuro-Metabolic Disorders (EA)
ANMI.......... Airborne Navigational Multiple Indicators (MCD)
ANMI.......... Air Navigation Multiple Indicator (PDAA)
ANMI.......... Allegro New Media [NASDAQ symbol] (TTSB)
ANMI.......... Allegro New Media, Inc. [NASDAQ symbol] (SAG)
ANMI.......... Allied Naval Maneuvering Instructions [NATO] (NATG)
ANMIC.......... Alternate National Military Intelligence Center (MCD)
ANML.......... Animal
AnML.......... Anthology of Medieval Lyrics [A publication]
ANMO.......... Albuquerque [New Mexico] [Seismograph station code, US Geological Survey] (SEIS)
AnMoPo...... Anthology of Modern Poetry [A publication]
ANMP.......... Afghan National Movement Party [Political party] (EY)
AnMP.......... Anthology of Mexican Poetry [A publication]
ANMPO...... Army-Navy Medical Procurement Office (DNAB)
ANMR.......... Advanced NMR Systems [Associated Press] (SAG)
ANMR.......... Advanced NMR Systems, Inc. [NASDAQ symbol] (NQ)
ANMRW...... Advanced NMR Sys Wrrt [NASDAQ symbol] (TTSB)
ANMS.......... Automated Notices to Mariners System
ANMTD........ Animated
ANN.......... Agencia Nicaraguense de Noticias [News agency] (EY)
ANN.......... Airports National Network [British Airports Authority] (NITA)
Ann.......... Annales [of Tacitus] [Classical studies] (OCD)
ann.......... Annales [Annals] [Latin] (GPO)

ANN .... Annals
Ann .... Annaly's Lee Tempore Hardwicke [*7-10 George II, King's Bench*] [*1733-38*] [*A publication*] (DLA)
ANN .... Annamalainagar [*India*] [*Geomagnetic observatory code*]
ANN .... Annealed
ANN .... Annette Island [*Alaska*] [*Airport symbol Obsolete*] (OAG)
ANN .... Annex
ann .... Anni [*Years*] [*Latin*] (GPO)
ANN .... Anno [*Year*] [*Latin*]
Ann .... Annotated (DLA)
ann .... Annotator [*MARC relator code*] [*Library of Congress*] (LCCP)
ANN .... Announce (AABC)
ANN .... Announcer (NTCM)
ANN .... Ann Taylor Stores [*NYSE symbol*] (SPSG)
Ann .... Annuaire (BJA)
ANN .... Annual
ANN .... Annuity (ROG)
ANN .... Annunciator [*Electronically controlled signal board*] (KSC)
ANN .... Annus [*Year*] [*Latin*]
ANN .... Answer, No-Charge [*Telecommunications*] (TEL)
ANN .... Artificial Neural Network
ANN .... Artificial Neural Network
ANN .... Arts for a New Nicaragua (EA)
ANN .... Asia-Pacific News Network
Ann .... Cases in King's Bench [*7-10 George II Tempore*] [*A publication*] (DLA)
Ann .... Cunningham's English King's Bench Reports [*A publication*] (DLA)
ANN .... Program Director for Navigation and Landing [*FAA*] (TAG)
Ann .... Queen Anne (DLA)
ANNA .... American Nephrology Nurses' Association (EA)
ANNA .... Army, Navy, NASA, Air Force Geodetic Satellite
ANNADIV ..... Annapolis Division [*Maryland*] [*Navy*] (DNAB)
Annals .... Annals of the American Academy of Political and Social Science [*A publication*] (AAGC)
Annaly .... Lee's English King's Bench Reports Tempore Hardwicke, Annaly Edition [*1733-38*] [*A publication*] (DLA)
AnnapB .... Annapolis Bancshares, Inc. [*Associated Press*] (SAG)
ANNB .... Annapolis Bancshares, Inc. [*NASDAQ symbol*] (TTSB)
ANNB .... Annapolis Bancshares, Inc. [*NASDAQ symbol*] (SAG)
Ann C .... Annals of Congress [*A publication*] (DLA)
ANNC .... Announce (FAAC)
Ann Cal Codes... West's Annotated California Codes [*A publication*] (DLA)
Ann Cas ...... American and English Annotated Cases [*A publication*] (DLA)
Ann Cas ...... American Annotated Cases [*A publication*] (DLA)
Ann Cas ...... New York Annotated Cases [*A publication*] (DLA)
Ann Code..... Annotated Code [*A publication*] (DLA)
Ann Codes & St... Bellinger and Cotton's Annotated Codes and Statutes [*Oregon*] [*A publication*] (DLA)
Ann Cong..... Annals of Congress [*A publication*] (DLA)
ANNCR........ Announcer
anncr .... Announcer (WDMC)
Ann de la Fac de Droit et des Sci Econ (Beyrouth)... Annales. Faculte de Droit et des Sciences Economiques [*Beyrouth, Lebanon*] [*A publication*] (DLA)
Ann de la Fac de Droit et des Sci Econ de Lille... Annales. Faculte de Droit et des Sciences Economiques de Lille, France [*A publication*] (DLA)
Ann de la Pro... Annales de la Propriete Industrielle, Artistique, et Litteraire [*A publication*] (DLA)
Ann de Leg... Annuaire de Legislation Francaise et Etrangere [*A publication*] (DLA)
Ann Dig .... Annual Digest and Reports of Public International Law Cases [*A publication*] (DLA)
Ann Dig ILC... Annual Digest and Reports of Public International Law Cases [*A publication*] (DLA)
Ann Dir Int... Annali di Diritto Internazionale [*Milan*] [*A publication*] (DLA)
Ann Dr Com Fr Etr Int... Annales de Droit Commercial Francais, Etranger, et International [*A publication*] (DLA)
Ann Dr Com Ind Fr Etr... Annales de Droit Commercial et Industriel Francais, Etranger, et International [*A publication*] (DLA)
AnNE .... Anthology of New England Poets [*A publication*]
Anne .... Queen Anne (DLA)
Ann Ec Fr Dr Beyrouth... Annales. Faculte de Droit. Ecole Francaise de Droit de Beyrouth [*A publication*] (DLA)
Ann Econ ..... Annales de Droit Economique [*A publication*] (DLA)
Ann Econ ..... Annales Economiques [*A publication*] (DLA)
Ann Fac Bari... Annali. Facolta di Giurisprudenza. Universita di Bari [*A publication*] (DLA)
Ann Fac Beyrouth... Annales. Faculte de Droit et des Sciences Economiques de Beyrouth. Faculte de Droit [*A publication*] (DLA)
Ann Fac Lyon... Annales. Faculte de Droit et des Sciences Economiques de Lyon [*A publication*] (DLA)
Ann Hitotsubashi Acad... Annals. Hitotsubashi Academy [*A publication*] (DLA)
Ann Ins........ Annesley on Insurance [*A publication*] (DLA)
Ann Ist........ Annali. Istituto di Corrispondenza Archeologica [*A publication*] (OCD)
ANNIV .... Anniversary
Ann JP........ Annales des Justices de Paix [*France*] [*A publication*] (DLA)
Ann Jud ...... Annuaire Judiciaire. [*A publication*] (DLA)
ANNL .... Annual (ROG)
ANNL .... Annual
Ann Law Review... Annual Law Review [*Australia A publication*]
Ann Leg Bibliog... Annual Legal Bibliography [*Harvard Law School Library*] [*A publication*] (DLA)
Ann Leg Fr... Annuaire de Legislation Francaise [*A publication*] (DLA)
Ann L Reg US... Annual Law Register of the United States [*A publication*] (DLA)
Ann L Rep... Annotated Law Reporter [*1932-35*] [*India*] [*A publication*] (DLA)
Annls .... Annals (DAVI)

ANNLY........ Annually (ROG)
Ann Malg.... Annales Malgaches [*A publication*] (DLA)
Ann Malg.... Annales. Universite de Madagascar [*A publication*] (DLA)
ANNNI........ Axial Next-Nearest-Neighbor Interactions [*Crystallography*]
ANN NO ...... Announcement Number (DNAB)
Anno .... Annotated (DLA)
Anno Cases... American Annotated Cases [*A publication*] (DLA)
AnNoLy .... Anthology of Norwegian Lyrics [*A publication*]
ANNOT........ Annotated
ANNPAC...... Association of National Non-Profit Artists' Centres [*Canada*]
Ann Parl .... Annales Parlementaires [*Belgium*] [*A publication*] (DLA)
Ann Pr....... Annual Practice [*A publication*] (DLA)
Ann Proc Nat Asso R Coms... Annual Proceedings. National Association of Railway Commissions [*A publication*] (DLA)
Ann Reg ..... Annual Register [*London*] [*A publication*] (DLA)
Ann Reg NS... Annual Register, New Series [*A publication*] (DLA)
Ann Rep ..... Annual Report [*A publication*] (DLA)
Ann Rep & Op Ind Att'y Gen... Annual Report and Official Opinions of the Attorney General of Indiana [*A publication*] (DLA)
Ann Rep & Op MD Att'y Gen... Annual Report and Official Opinions of the Attorney General of Maryland [*A publication*] (DLA)
Ann Rep Fla Att'y Gen... Annual Report of the Attorney General of Florida [*A publication*] (DLA)
Ann Rep SC Att'y Gen... Annual Report of the Attorney General of South Carolina to the General Assembly [*A publication*] (DLA)
ANNREPT..... Annual Report (DNAB)
Ann Rept Dept Mines NSW... Annual Report. Department of Mines. New South Wales [*Australia A publication*] (DLA)
Ann Rev Int'l Aff... Annual Review of International Affairs [*A publication*] (DLA)
Ann Sem Giur... Annali. Seminario Giuridico. Universita di Palermo [*A publication*] (ILCA)
Ann Sem Giur Catania... Annali. Seminario Giuridico. Universita Catania [*A publication*] (ILCA)
Ann St .... Annotated Statutes [*A publication*] (DLA)
Ann Stat Guid... Annuario di Statistiche Guidiziarie [*A publication*] (ILCA)
Ann St Dir ... Annali di Storia del Diritto [*A publication*] (ILCA)
Ann St Ind T... Annotated Statutes of Indian Territory [*A publication*] (DLA)
Ann Surv Afr L... Annual Survey of African Law [*A publication*] (DLA)
Ann Surv Am... Annual Survey of American Law [*A publication*] (DLA)
Ann Surv Banking L... Annual Survey of Banking Law [*A publication*] (DLA)
Ann Surv Colo L... Annual Survey of Colorado Law [*A publication*] (DLA)
Ann Survey... Annual Survey of Massachusetts Law [*A publication*] (DLA)
Ann Surv Ind L... Annual Survey of Indian Law [*A publication*] (DLA)
Ann Surv of Aust Law... Annual Survey of Australian Law [*A publication*]
Ann Surv S Afr L... Annual Survey of South African Law [*A publication*] (DLA)
Ann Tax Cas... Annotated Tax Cases [*England*] [*A publication*] (DLA)
AnnTayl .... Ann Taylor Stores [*Associated Press*] (SAG)
Annual R ..... Louisiana Annual Reports [*A publication*] (DLA)
Annu de la Fac de Droit de Skopje... Annuaire. Faculte de Droit de Skopje [*A publication*] (DLA)
ANNUI......... Annuity (DLA)
ANNUIT........ Annuitant (ROG)
ANNUL........ Annulment (DLA)
ANNUN .... Annunciation
ANNUN .... Annunciator
ANNUNC........ Annunciation [*or Annunciator*] (ROG)
ANNX.......... Annex [*Commonly used*] (OPSA)
annx.......... Annexure [*British and Canadian*] [*World War II*]
ANNY .... Annuity
AnNZ.......... Anthology of New Zealand Verse [*A publication*]
ANO .... Above-Named Officer [*Army orders*]
ANO .... Air Navigation Office [*Navy*]
ANO .... Air Navigation Order
ANO .... Air North Ltd. [*Australia ICAO designator*] (FAAC)
ANO .... Alphanumeric Output
ANO .... Anodyne [*Medicine*] (ROG)
AnO .... Anordnung [*Direction, Instruction*] [*German*] (ILCA)
ANO .... Another
ANO .... Antipolo [*Philippines*] [*Later, MUT*] [*Geomagnetic observatory code*]
ANO .... Antonio Enes [*Mozambique*] [*Airport symbol*] (AD)
ANO .... Aricana Resources [*Vancouver Stock Exchange symbol*]
ANO .... Arkansas Nuclear One (NRCH)
ANO .... Capiteq Ltd., Trading as Air North Regional [*Australia*] [*FAA designator*] (FAAC)
ANO .... Nordegg Public Library, Alberta [*Library symbol National Library of Canada*] (NLC)
ANO .... University of North Alabama, Florence, AL [*OCLC symbol*] (OCLC)
ANoA .... Antinucleolar Antibodies [*Immunology*] (AAMN)
ANOBCT-EC... Association of National Organizations in the Bakery and Confectionery Trade in the EC [*European Community*] [*Belgium*] (EAIO)
ANOC .... Advanced Noncommissioned Officer Course [*Army*]
AnOC .... Anodal Opening Contraction [*Also, AOC*] [*Physiology*]
ANOC .... Association of National Olympic Committees [*See also ACNO*] [*Paris, France*] (EAIO)
ANOC .... Authorized Notice of Change
ANOCA .... Association of National Olympic Committees of Africa (EA)
ANOCL .... Anodal Opening Clonus [*Medicine*] (DMAA)
ANOD .... Airborne Night Observation Device (MCD)
ANOD .... Anodize (MSA)
anod alum... Anodized Aluminum (VRA)
ANODE........ Ambient Noise Directionality Estimator (MCD)
ANODE........ Analytic Orbit Determination Program (MCD)
ANODYN ...... Anodynum [*A Soothing Medicament*] [*Pharmacy*] (ROG)
AnOE........... Anthology of Old English Poetry [*A publication*]

ANOM......... Analysis of Means (PDAA)
ANOM......... Assistant Network Operations Manager [*NASA*] (KSC)
ANON......... Anonymous
anon .... Anonymous (VRA)
anon .... Anonymous (WDMC)
ANON......... Anonymous
ANOP......... Anophthalmia (DMAA)
ANOPO....... Aircraft Noise Prediction Office [*NASA*]
ANOPP....... Aircraft Noise Prediction Program [*NASA*]
ANOPS....... Aircraft Not Operationally Ready Supply (AFIT)
ANOR......... Another (ROG)
ANORE....... Aircraft Not Operationally Ready Due to Lack of Equipment (SAA)
ANORM....... Anticipated Not Operationally Ready, Maintenance (NVT)
ANORP....... Aircraft Not Operationally Ready Due to Lack of Parts (SAA)
ANORS....... Anticipated Not Operationally Ready, Supply (AFM)
ANOT......... Annotate
ANOV......... Analysis of Variance
ANOVA....... Analysis of Variance
ANP .... Accao Nacional Popular [*National Popular Action*] [*Angola*] [*Political party*] (AF)
ANP .... Adult Nurse Practitioner (DAVI)
ANP .... Advanced Nurse Practitioner (MEDA)
ANP .... Agence Nigerienne de Presse [*News Agency*] [*Niger*] (EY)
ANP .... Aircraft Nuclear Power [*or Propulsion*]
ANP .... Air Navigation Plan (DA)
ANP .... Albert Rolland [*France*] [*Research code symbol*]
ANP .... Algemeen Nederlandisch Persbureau [*Press agency*] [*Netherlands*]
ANP .... Allied Navigation Publications [*NATO*] (NATG)
ANP .... Alpha-Atrial Natriuretic Polypeptide [*Biochemistry*] (DAVI)
ANP .... American NAZI Party [*Later, NSWWP*]
ANP .... Anglo Canadian Mining Corp. [*Toronto Stock Exchange symbol Vancouver Stock Exchange symbol*]
ANP .... Annapolis, MD [*Location identifier FAA*] (FAAL)
ANP .... Anpu [*Republic of China*] [*Seismograph station code, US Geological Survey*] (SEIS)
ANP .... Associated Negro Press (IIA)
ANP .... Atrial Natriuretic Peptide [*Biochemistry*]
ANP .... Australian National Party [*Political party*]
ANP .... Awami National Party [*Pakistan*] [*Political party*] (FEA)
ANP .... Lab. Anphar [*France*] [*Research code symbol*]
a-np-- .... Nepal [*MARC geographic area code Library of Congress*] (LCCP)
ANPA .... American Newspaper Publishers Association (EA)
ANPAC....... Animal Political Action Committee (EA)
ANPAF .... American Newspaper Publishers Association Foundation (EA)
ANPA/RI...... American Newspaper Publishers' Association/Research Institute (DGA)
ANPASC...... [*A*] National Plan for Arts in Small Communities (EA)
ANPAT....... American Newspaper Publishers Abstracting Technique
ANPA/TEC.... American Newspaper Publishers' Association Technical Exposition and Conference (ITD)
ANPB .... Army-Navy Petroleum Board
ANPBC....... Association of Naturopathic Physicians of British Columbia (AC)
ANPC .... Air-Nitrogen Pressurization Control
ANPC .... Alberta Native Plants Council (AC)
ANPC .... American Nail Producers Council
ANPD .... Aircraft Nuclear Propulsion Department [*Navy*]
ANPEI .... Association of Nurses of Prince Edward Island (AC)
ANPEO....... Assembly of National Postsecondary Educational Organizations (EDAC)
ANPERA...... American National Postal Employees Retirees Association (EA)
ANPL .... Adoptee/Natural Parent Locators [*Later, ANPLI*] (EA)
ANPLI .... Adoptee/Natural Parent Locators - International [*Formerly, ANPL*] [*Later, MPI*] (EA)
ANPM .... African Nationalist Pioneer Movement [*Defunct*]
ANPO .... Adoptees and Natural Parents Organization (EA)
ANPO .... Aircraft Nuclear Propulsion Office [*of AEC*] [*Defunct*]
ANPO .... Association of National Park Officers [*British*]
ANPOD....... Antenna Positioning Device
An Post....... Analytica Posteriora [*of Aristotle*] [*Classical studies*] (OCD)
ANPP .... Above Ground Net Primary Production [*Ecology*]
A-NPP .... Adsorbed Normal Pool Plasma [*Clinical chemistry*]
ANPP .... Aircraft Nuclear Propulsion Program
ANPP .... Allied Nuclear Power Program [*Military*] (GFGA)
ANPP .... Army Nuclear Power Program
ANPP .... Association of Negro Press Photographers
ANPP .... Azidonitrophenyl Phosphate [*Also, ACN*] [*Organic chemistry*]
ANPPF .... Aircraft Nuclear Power Plant Facility
ANPPM .... Asociacion Nacional pro Personas Mayores [*National Association for Hispanic Elderly*] (EA)
ANPPPC...... Army-Navy Petroleum Pool, Pacific Coast
ANPR .... Advance Notice of Proposed Rulemaking [*Also, ANPRM*] [*US Government agencies*]
An Pr .... Analytica Priora [*of Aristotle*] [*Classical studies*] (OCD)
ANPRA....... American Native Press Research Association [*Defunct*] (EA)
ANPRM....... Advance Notice of Proposed Rulemaking [*Also, ANPR*] [*US Government agencies*]
ANPSI .... Animal Psi [*Parapsychology*]
ANPT .... Aeronautical National Taper Pipe Threads
ANPV .... Adjusted Net Present Value (MCD)
ANQ .... Angola, IN [*Location identifier FAA*] (FAAL)
ANQ:QJ....... ANQ: A Quarterly Journal of Short Articles, Notes, and Reviews [*A publication*] (BRI)
ANR .... Active Noise Reduction (MCD)
ANR .... Advanced Negative Resist [*Materials science*]
ANR .... Advanced Non-Rigid Airship [*British*]

ANR .... Aeronorte SA [*Colombia*] [*ICAO designator*] (FAAC)
ANR .... Agricultural and Natural Resources
ANR .... Air Navigation Regulations (ADA)
ANR .... Alaskan NORAD Region
ANR .... Alberta Energy and Natural Resources Library [*UTLAS symbol*]
ANR .... American Negligence Reports, Current Series [*A publication*] (DLA)
ANR .... Americans for Nonsmokers' Rights (EA)
ANR .... Andizhan [*Former USSR Seismograph station code, US Geological Survey*] (SEIS)
ANR .... Andrews, TX [*Location identifier FAA*] (FAAL)
ANR .... Angelina & Neches River Railroad Co. [*AAR code*]
ANR .... Another (ROG)
ANR .... Antwerp [*Belgium*] [*Airport symbol*] (OAG)
ANR .... Association of Nursing Religious [*British*] (DBA)
ANR .... Audio News Release (WDMC)
ANR .... Australian Naval Reserve
ANR .... Automatic Network Routing [*Telecommunications*] (ACRL)
ANR .... Awaiting Number Received [*Telecommunications*] (TEL)
ANR .... National Economic and Legislative Report [*Commerce Clearing House*] [*A publication*] (DLA)
ANRA .... Affiliated Nutritional Retailers Association [*Commercial firm*] (EA)
ANRA .... Air Navigation Radio Aids
ANRAC....... Aids to Navigation Radio Control [*Military*]
ANRC .... Affiliated National Riding Commission (EA)
ANRC .... American National Red Cross [*Later, ARC*]
ANRC .... Animal Nutrition Research Council (EA)
ANRC .... Automatic Noise Reduction Circuit [*Electronics*]
ANRCP....... Additional Nonresidential Conditional Purchase (ADA)
ANRED .... Anorexia Nervosa and Related Eating Disorders (EA)
ANREP .... Annual Report
ANREP .... Appraisal of the Navy RDT & E [*Research, Development, Test, and Evaluation*] Program
ANRET .... Association of Natural Resource Enforcement Trainers (EA)
ANRG .... Anergen, Inc. [*NASDAQ symbol*] (SPSG)
ANRHRD..... Air, Noise, and Radiation Health Research Division [*Environmental Protection Agency*] (GFGA)
ANRI .... Acute Nerve Root Irritation (HGAA)
ANRI .... Australian Neurological Research Institute
ANRL .... Antihypertensive Neural Renomedullary Liquid
ANRL .... Antihypertensive Neutral Renomedullary Lipids [*Cardiology*] (DAVI)
ANRORC..... Addition Nucleophile Ring Opening Ring Closure [*Organic chemistry*]
ANRP .... Association for a National Recycling Policy (EA)
ANRPC....... Association of Natural Rubber Producing Countries [*Kuala Lumpur, Malaysia*] (EAIO)
ANRT .... Association Nationale de la Recherche Technique [*National Association of Technical Research - NATR*] [*France Information service or system*] (IID)
AnRts .... Writers for Animal Rights [*Defunct*] (EA)
ANRU .... New South Wales Revenue Rulings [*Australia A publication*]
ANS .... Academy of Natural Sciences of Philadelphia, Philadelphia, PA [*OCLC symbol*] (OCLC)
ANS .... Active Network Synthesis
ANS .... Admiralty Naval Staff [*British*]
ANS .... Advanced Navigation School [*British military*] (DMA)
ANS .... Advanced Network & Services, Inc. [*Nonprofit company formed to manage the National Science Foundation Network*] (IID)
ANS .... Advanced Network System [*Computer science*] (ECON)
ANS .... Advanced Neutron Source [*Proposed nuclear reactor*]
ANS .... Agencia Noticiosa Saporiti [*Press agency*] [*Argentina*]
ANS .... Airborne Navigation Sensor
ANS .... Air Navigation School [*British*]
ANS .... Alternate [*or Alternative*] News Service (ADA)
ANS .... American Name Society (EA)
ANS .... American National Standard [*ANSI*] (MCD)
ANS .... American Navion Society (EA)
ANS .... American Neurotology Society (EA)
ANS .... American Newcomen Society
ANS .... American Norwich Society [*Defunct*] (EA)
ANS .... American Nuclear Society (EA)
ANS .... American Numismatic Society (EA)
ANS .... American Nutrition Society (EA)
ANS .... Andahuaylas [*Peru*] [*Airport symbol Obsolete*] (OAG)
ANS .... Anilinonaphthalenesulfonic Acid [*Also, ANSA*] [*Organic chemistry*]
ANS .... Ansco Resources (BC) [*Vancouver Stock Exchange symbol*]
Ans .... Anselmus de Baggio de Lucca [*Deceased, 1086*] [*Authority cited in pre-1607 legal work*] (DSA)
ANS .... Answer (AFM)
ans............ Answer (WDMC)
Ans .... Ansyl [*Organic radical*]
ANS .... Anterior Nasal Spine [*Medicine*] (DMAA)
ANS .... Antineutrophilic Serum [*Hematology*] (DAVI)
ANS .... Antirat Neutrophil Serum [*Medicine*] (DMAA)
ANS .... Apollo Network Simulations [*NASA*] (KSC)
ANS .... Aquatic Nuisance Species [*Oceanography*]
ANS .... Arabian-Nubian Shield [*Geology*]
ANS .... Armenian Numismatic Society (EA)
ANS .... Army Network Station
ANS .... Army Newspaper Service
ANS .... Army News Service
ANS .... Army Nursing Service [*British*]
ANS .... Arteriolonephrosclerosis [*Urology*]
ANS .... Associated Nuclear Services [*British*] (IRUK)
ANS .... Associate in Nursing Science (DAVI)
ANS .... Astronomical Netherlands Satellite
ANS .... Autograph Note Signed [*Manuscript descriptions*]

ANS .... Automatic Navigation System
ANS .... Autonomic Nervous System [Medicine]
ANS .... Autonomous Navigation System
ANS .... NAS Transition Implementation Service [FAA] (TAG)
ANS .... New Sarepta Public Library, Alberta [Library symbol National Library of Canada] (NLC)
ANS .... Symbol, SA [Spain] [FAA designator] (FAAC)
ANS .... Transportes Aereos Norte-Sur Ltda. [Chile] [ICAO designator] (FAAC)
ANSA .... Advanced Network System Architecture (BUR)
ANSA .... Agenzia Nazionale Stampa Associata [Associated National Press Agency] [Italy]
ANSA .... Aminohydroxynaphthalenesulfonic Acid [Organic chemistry]
ANSA .... Aminonaphtholsulfonic Acid [Organic chemistry]
ANSA .... (Anilino)naphthalenesulfonic Acid [Also, ANS] [Organic chemistry]
ANSA .... Association of Norwalk School Administration
ANSA .... Australian National Sportfishing Association (EAIO)
ANSABLE .... Answerable (ROG)
ANSAC .... American Natural Soda Ash Corp. (EA)
Ansaldo ...... Ansaldo Signal [Associated Press] (SAG)
Ansan .... Ansan, Inc. [Associated Press] (SAG)
ANSAS .... Automatic Null Steering/Surveillance Array System (MCD)
ANSC .... American National Standards (Institute) Committee [Later, NISO]
ANSC .... American Nuclear Science Corp. (MCD)
ANSC .... Andover Service Center [IRS]
ANSC .... Army and Navy Staff College [Redesignated National War College, 1946]
ANSC .... Autonomous Navigation System Concept (MCD)
anschl........ Anschliessend [Following, Subsequent] [German]
ANSCII .... American National Standard Code for Information Interchange (MCD)
ANSCOL...... Army and Navy Staff College [See ANSC]
Ans Con ...... Anson on Contracts [A publication] (DLA)
ANSCR........ Alphanumeric System for Classification of Recordings
ANSCS OCR... American National Standard Character Set for Optical Character Recognition (MCD)
ANSD .... Answered (ROG)
An Seni....... An Seni Respublica Gerenda Sit [of Plutarch] [Classical studies] (OCD)
ANSER .... Agricultural Network Serving Extension and Research [University of Kentucky] [Lexington] [Information service or system] [Research center] (IID)
ANSER .... Analytic Services, Inc.
ANSETT....... Ansett Airlines of Australia
ANSG .... Answering (ROG)
ANSH .... Association of Nova Scotia Hairdressers (AC)
ANSI .... American National Standards Institute (EA)
ANSI .... American Nuclear Standards Institute
ANSI .... Application for New Stock Item
ANSI .... Assistant Naval Science Instructor (DNAB)
ANSIA .... Army-Navy Shipping Information Agency
ANSI/ASQC... American National Standards Institute/American Society for Quality Control (RDA)
ANSIC .... Aerospace Nuclear Safety Information Center (MCD)
ANSIM .... Analog Simulator (MHDB)
AnSL .... Anthology of Swedish Lyrics [A publication]
ANSLICS ..... Aberdeen and North Scotland Library and Information Cooperative Services (NITA)
ANSMET ...... Antarctic Search for Meteorites
ANSN .... Ansan, Inc. [NASDAQ symbol] (SAG)
ANSNU........ Ansan Inc. Unit [NASDAQ symbol] (TTSB)
ANSNW....... Ansan Inc. Wrrt'A' [NASDAQ symbol] (TTSB)
ANSNZ........ Ansan Inc. Wrrt'B' [NASDAQ symbol] (TTSB)
AnSO .... Annual Service Order
ANSO .... Assistant Naval Stores Officer
Ansoft .... Ansoft Corp. [Associated Press] (SAG)
Anson Cont... Anson on Contracts [A publication] (DLA)
ANSP .... Academy of Natural Sciences [Academy of Natural Sciences of Philadelphia] [Acronym is based on former name,] (EA)
AnSP.......... Anthology of Spanish Poetry from Garsilaso to Garcia [A publication]
ANSP .... Association of Navy Safety Professionals [Defunct] (EA)
ANSR .... Add-On Non-Stop Reliability (PDAA)
ANSR .... Advanced Naval System Requirements
ANSR .... Answer (ROG)
ANSR .... Association of Nonsmokers' Rights [British] (DBA)
ANSS .... Advanced Network Support System [Computer science] (PCM)
ANSS .... American Nature Study Society (EA)
ANSS .... Ansys, Inc. [NASDAQ symbol] (SAG)
ANSS .... Anthropology and Sociology Section [Association of College and Research Libraries]
ANSS .... Associate of the Normal School of Science
ANSSIR........ [A] Network of Social Security Information Resources [Health and Welfare Canada] [Defunct] (IID)
ANSSR........ Aerodynamically Neutral Spin-Stabilized Rocket (MCD)
ANSSRAS .... Aerodynamically Neutral Spin-Stabilized Rocket Artillery System [Army] (MCD)
ANST .... Ansoft Corp. [NASDAQ symbol] (SAG)
ANST .... Ansoft Corp. [NASDAQ symbol] (TTSB)
Anst .... Anstruther's English Exchequer Reports [145 English Reprint] [A publication] (DLA)
ANST .... New South Wales Strata Title Law and Practice [Australia A publication]
Anst Eng Law... Anstey's Guide to the English Law and Constitution [A publication] (DLA)
ANSTHS ...... Anesthesia
ANSTHSLGY... Anesthesiology

ANSTI .... African Network of Scientific and Technological Institutes [Kenya] [Research center]
ANSTO........ Australian Nuclear Science and Technology Organisation
Anst Pl Gui... Anstey's Pleader's Guide [A publication] (DLA)
Anstr........... Anstruther's English Exchequer Reports [145 English Reprint] [A publication] (DLA)
Anstr (Eng)... Anstruther's English Exchequer Reports [145 English Reprint] [A publication] (DLA)
ANSUR........ Anthropometric Survey [Human figure simulation] [Army] (RDA)
ANSVIP .... American National Standard Vocabulary for Information Processing
ANSW .... Antinuclear Submarine Warfare [Navy]
ANSWER...... Algorithm for Non-Synchronized Waveform Error Reduction (MHDB)
ANSWER...... Automated Network Schedule with Evaluation of Resources (MCD)
ANSWERS.... Antisurface Weapons Exchange and Reaction Simulation (MCD)
ANSWRNG... Answering
ANSY .... AirNet Systems [NASDAQ symbol] (TTSB)
ANSY .... AirNet Systems,Inc. [NASDAQ symbol] (SAG)
ANSYS .... Analysis System for Static and Dynamic Problems (MCD)
Ansys......... Ansys, Inc. [Associated Press] (SAG)
ANT........... Acoustic Noise Test
ANT........... Active Name Table (HGAA)
ANT........... Adenine Nucleotide Translocator [Genetics]
ANT........... Advanced Nosetip Test [AEC] (MCD)
ANT........... Air North Charter [Canada ICAO designator] (FAAC)
ANT........... American National Theater [Kennedy Center for the Performing Arts]
ANT........... Aminonitrothiazole [Biochemistry] (DAVI)
ANT........... Antarctic
ANT........... Antenna (AFM)
ant............ Antenna (IDOE)
ANT........... Antenna Noise Temperature
ANT........... Anterior
ANT........... Anthony Indus [NYSE symbol] (TTSB)
ANT........... Anthony Industries, Inc. [NYSE symbol] (SPSG)
ANT........... Anticipated (WGA)
ANT........... Antient [Archaic variation of "ancient"] (ROG)
Ant............ Antigone [of Sophocles] [Classical studies] (OCD)
ANT........... Antigua (ROG)
ANT........... Antimonium [Antimony] [Symbol is Sb] [Chemical element] (ROG)
Ant............ Antimycin (DAVI)
ANT........... Antiphon
Ant............ Antiquitates Judaicae [Jewish Antiquities] [of Josephus] [Classical studies] (BJA)
ANT........... Antiquities
Ant............ Antlia [Constellation]
ANT........... Antofagasta [Chile] [Seismograph station code, US Geological Survey] (SEIS)
Ant............ Antonius [of Plutarch] [Classical studies] (OCD)
Ant............ Antony and Cleopatra [Shakespearean work]
ANT........... Antonym
ANT........... Antrim [County in Ireland] (ROG)
ANT........... A. N. Tupolev [Initialism used as designation for Russian aircraft designed by Tupolev]
ANT........... [The] Apocryphal New Testament [A publication] (BJA)
ANT........... Association Nationale des Telespectateurs [National Association of Telespectators] [Canada]
ANT........... Autonomous Navigation Technology (MCD)
ANT........... Netherlands Antilles [ANSI three-letter standard code] (CNC)
ANT........... San Antonio, TX [Location identifier FAA] (FAAL)
ANTA .... American National Theatre and Academy [Defunct] (EA)
AntA.......... Antimycin A (DMAA)
ANTAC .... Air Navigation and Tactical Control
ANTACCS.... Advanced Navy Tactical Command and Control System (NG)
ANTAG .... Antagonist (AAMN)
antag .... Antagonistic (DAVI)
Ant & Cl ..... Antony and Cleopatra [Shakespearean drama] (BARN)
Ant & CM... Antiques & Collecting Magazine [A publication] (BRI)
Antar......... Antarctica (VRA)
Antarc......... Antarctic
Antarc......... Antarctic (BARN)
ANTARCTICSUPPORT... Antarctic Support Activities
Antares....... Antares Resources Corp. [Associated Press] (SAG)
ANTARES..... Antenna Tracking Altitude, Azimuth, and Range by Electronic Scan (PDAA)
Ant Aug....... Antonius Augustinus [Deceased, 1586] [Authority cited in pre-1607 legal work] (DSA)
Ant August... Antonius Augustinus [Deceased, 1586] [Authority cited in pre-1607 legal work] (DSA)
Ant Ax....... Anterior Axillary Line [Anatomy] (DAVI)
AnTBD .... Anaerobically Thioglycolate Broth Disk (PDAA)
Ant Boid ...... Antonius Boidus [Flourished, 16th century] [Authority cited in pre-1607 legal work] (DSA)
ANTC .... Air Navigation Technical Committee (SAA)
ANTC .... Air Navigation Traffic Control
ANTC .... Antec Corp. [NASDAQ symbol] (SAG)
ANTC .... ANTEC Corp. [NASDAQ symbol] (TTSB)
ANT-C......... Antennapedia Complex [Gene cluster in fruit fly]
ANTC .... Antichaff Circuit (IEEE)
ANTC .... Association of Nursery Training Colleges [British]
Ant Class..... Antiquite Classique [A publication] (OCD)
ANTCOMDUSARCARIB... Antilles Command, United States Army Caribbean
Ant Corse..... Antonius Corsettus [Flourished, 15th century] [Authority cited in pre-1607 legal work] (DSA)
ANTCP .... Anticipate (AABC)
Ant de But ... Antonius de Butrio [Deceased, 1408] [Authority cited in pre-1607 legal work] (DSA)

Ant de Rosell... Antonius de Rosellis [*Deceased, 1466*] [*Authority cited in pre-1607 legal work*] (DSA)
ANTE........... Adjoint Neutron Transport Equation (PDAA)
ANTEC......... Annual Technical Conference [*Society of Plastics Engineers*]
Antec.......... Antec Corp. [*Associated Press*] (SAG)
Ant Fab........ Antonius Faber [*Deceased, 1624*] [*Authority cited in pre-1607 legal work*] (DSA)
ant frt.......... Anticipated Freight [*Commerce*] (BARN)
Ant Gab Rom... Antonius Gabrielius (Romanus) [*Deceased, 1555*] [*Authority cited in pre-1607 legal work*] (DSA)
ANTGWDPEC... Association of National Trade Groups of Wood and Derived Products in the EEC [*European Economic Community*] Countries [*Denmark*] (EAIO)
ANTH .... Anthelmintic [*Expelling Worms*] [*Medicine*] (ROG)
ANTH .... Anthology
Anth .... Anthon's New York Nisi Prius Reports [*A publication*] (DLA)
Anth Black... Anthon's Abridgment of Blackstone [*A publication*] (DLA)
Anth Lat...... Anthologia Latina [*A publication*] (OCD)
Anth LS....... Anthon's Law Student [*A publication*] (DLA)
Anth Lyr Graec... Anthologia Lyrica Graeca [*A publication*] (OCD)
Anth NP .... Anthon's New York Nisi Prius Reports [*A publication*] (DLA)
Anth NPR...... Anthon's New York Nisi Prius Reports [*A publication*] (DLA)
Anthol......... Anthologie [*Anthology*] [*German*]
ANTHOL....... Anthology
Anthon NP (NY)... Anthon's New York Nisi Prius Reports [*A publication*] (DLA)
Anthon Rep.... Anthon's New York Nisi Prius Reports [*A publication*] (DLA)
Anthon's NP... Anthon's New York Nisi Prius Reports [*A publication*] (DLA)
Anthon's NP (2d Ed)... Anthon's Nisi Prius Reports [*2nd ed.*] [*A publication*] (DLA)
Anthon's Rep... Anthon's New York Nisi Prius Reports [*A publication*] (DLA)
Anthony....... Anthony Industries, Inc. [*Associated Press*] (SAG)
Anth Pal....... Anthologia Palatina [*Classical studies*] (OCD)
Anth Plan..... Anthologia Planudea [*Classical studies*] (OCD)
Anth Prec..... Anthon's New Precedents of Declarations [*A publication*] (DLA)
ANTHR......... Anthropological [*or Anthropology*]
ANTHRO .... Anthropology
Anthro......... Anthropology (DD)
ANTHROP ...... Anthropology
anthrop........ Anthropology (VRA)
ANTHROPOL... Anthropological
Anthropol..... Anthropologie [*Anthropology*] [*German*]
Anth RR Cons... Anthony on Consolidation of Railroad Companies [*A publication*] (DLA)
Anth Shep.... Anthony's Edition of Shephard's Touchstone [*A publication*] (DLA)
Anth St .... Anthon's Study of Law [*A publication*] (DLA)
ANTI........... Acetoxy-N-trimethylanilinium Iodide [*Organic chemistry*]
ANTI........... Antibody [*Biochemistry*] (DAVI)
ANTI........... Antietam National Battlefield Site
ANTI........... Automated Near-Term Improvement (MCD)
ANTICOAG..... Anticoagulant [*or Anticoagulation*] (AAMN)
Antid......... Antidotum [*Antidote*] [*Latin*]
anti-DNA...... Antibody to Deoxyribonucleic Acid Test [*Rheumatology*] (DAVI)
anti-ENA...... Antibody to Extractable Nuclear Antigen Test [*Rheumatology*] (DAVI)
ANTIG......... Antigua (ROG)
anti-GMB..... Antiglomerular Basement Membrane [*Antibodies*] [*Cardiology*] (DAVI)
anti-HAA..... Antibody Hepatitis-Associated Antigen [*Immunology*] (MAE)
anti-HAV..... Antibody to Hepatitis A Virus [*Medicine*] (MEDA)
anti-HB$_5$Ag... Antibody to Hepatitis B Surface Antigen [*Immunology*] (DAVI)
anti-HBc..... Antibody to Hepatitis B Core Antigen [*Medicine*] (MEDA)
anti-HBs..... Antibody to Hepatitis B Surface Antigen [*Medicine*] (MEDA)
ANTILOG...... Antilogarithm
ANTIM .... Antimonium [*Antimony*] [*Symbol is Sb*] [*Chemical element*] (ROG)
ANTIns......... American National Insurance Co. [*Associated Press*] (SAG)
ANTIOPE...... L'Acquisition Numerique et Televisualisation d'Images Organisees en Pages d'Ecriture [*French videotex system*]
ANTIQ .... Antiquarian [*or Antiquities*]
ANTIQ .... Antique [*Bookbinding*] (ROG)
Antiq J .... Antiquaries Journal [*A publication*] (BRI)
anti-RNP...... Antiribonucleoprotein [*Genetics*] (DAVI)
anti-S......... Antisulfanilic Acid [*Biochemistry*] (DAVI)
anti-Sm...... Anti-Smith [*Antibody*] [*Hematology*] (DAVI)
anti-SM/RNP... Antibody Smooth Muscle-Ribonucleoprotein [*Genetics*] (DAVI)
ANTI-SOC .... Anti-Socialist Party (ADA)
ANTISUBFITRON... Antisubmarine Fighter Squadron [*Navy*]
Antitrust Bull... Antitrust Bulletin (AAGC)
Antitrust L & Trade Reg Rep... Antitrust Law and Trade Regulations Report [*Bureau of National Affairs*] [*A publication*] (ILCA)
ANTIVOX...... Antivoice-Operated Transmission (CET)
ANT JENTAC... Ante Jentaculum [*Before Breakfast*] [*Pharmacy*]
Ant Journ..... Antiquaries Journal [*A publication*] (OCD)
Ant Kunstpr... Die Antike Kunstprosa [*A publication*] (OCD)
Antl........... Antlia [*Constellation*]
ANTLAT....... Antique Latin (ADA)
ANTLD .... Antique Laid [*Paper*] (ADA)
Ant Luc....... Ante Lucem [*Before Daylight*] [*Latin*]
AntM......... Antarctic Medal
Anto .... Antonius de Butrio [*Deceased, 1408*] [*Authority cited in pre-1607 legal work*] (DSA)
ANTO .... Austrian National Tourist Office (EA)
Anto de But... Antonius de Butrio [*Deceased, 1408*] [*Authority cited in pre-1607 legal work*] (DSA)
Anto de Trem... Antonius de Tremolis [*Flourished, 16th century*] [*Authority cited in pre-1607 legal work*] (DSA)
Anto Fab...... Antonius Faber [*Deceased, 1624*] [*Authority cited in pre-1607 legal work*] (DSA)
ANTON......... Antonym (ADA)

Anton Burg... Antonius Burgos [*Deceased, 1525*] [*Authority cited in pre-1607 legal work*] (DSA)
Anton Costan... Antonius Guibertus Costanus [*Flourished, 16th century*] [*Authority cited in pre-1607 legal work*] (DSA)
Anton Fab.... Antonius Faber [*Deceased, 1624*] [*Authority cited in pre-1607 legal work*] (DSA)
Anton Gabr... Antonius Gabrielius (Romanus) [*Deceased, 1555*] [*Authority cited in pre-1607 legal work*] (DSA)
Anton Gabr Roman... Antonius Gabrielius (Romanus) [*Deceased, 1555*] [*Authority cited in pre-1607 legal work*] (DSA)
Anto Nice..... Antonius Nicellus [*Flourished, 15th century*] [*Authority cited in pre-1607 legal work*] (DSA)
Anto Nice..... Antonius Nicenus [*Authority cited in pre-1607 legal work*] (DSA)
ANTOPS...... Antarctic Operations [*Military*] (NVT)
ANTOR......... Assembly of National Tourist Office Representatives in New York [*Defunct*] (EA)
ANTOS........ Antique Old Style [*Paper*] (ADA)
ANTOSTRAT... Antarctic Offshore Seismic Stratigraphy Project [*Australia*]
ANTOX........ Antitoxin (MSA)
ANTP .... Army Nozzle Technology Program (MCD)
ANT PIT ...... Anterior Pituitary [*Endocrinology*]
ANT PRAND... Ante Prandium [*Before Dinner*] [*Pharmacy*]
ANTQ .... Antique
antq .... Antique (VRA)
ANTR .... Antares Resources [*NASDAQ symbol*] (TTSB)
ANTR .... Antares Resources Corp. [*NASDAQ symbol*] (SAG)
Ant R .... Antioch Review [*A publication*] (BRI)
ANTR .... Apparent Net Transfer Rate (MAE)
ANTRAC...... Andrulis Tracker [*Military*] (CAAL)
Ant Rom ...... Antiquitates Romanae [*of Dionysius Halicarnassensis*] [*Classical studies*] (OCD)
Ant Rosel.... Antonius de Rosellis [*Deceased, 1466*] [*Authority cited in pre-1607 legal work*] (DSA)
ANTS .... Advanced Naval Training School
ANTS .... Airborne Night Television System [*Obsolete Army*] (MCD)
ANTS .... Amino-naphthalene-trisulfonic Acid [*Organic chemistry*]
ANTS .... Andover Newton Theological School [*Newton Center, MA*]
ANTS .... Anglo-Norman Text Society [*British*]
ANTS .... Any Tape Search [*Computer program*] (KSC)
ANTS .... ARPA [*Advanced Research Projects Agency*] Network Terminal System
ANTS .... ATM [*Apollo Telescope Mount*] Navigation and Timing Summary [*NASA*]
ANTS .... Automatic Nitrogen Transfer System
ANTSPT .... Antiseptic (MSA)
Ant Sup Spine... Anterior Superior Spine [*Of ilium*] [*Anatomy*] (DAVI)
ANTT.......... Aboriginal National Theatre Trust [*Australia*]
ANTU .... Air Navigation Training Unit
ANTU .... Alpha-Naphthylthiourea [*Organic chemistry*]
ANTUF .... All-Nigeria Trade Union Federation
ANTWO........ Antique Wove [*Paper*] (ADA)
ANU .... Airplane Nose Up (NG)
ANU .... Antelope Island [*Utah*] [*Seismograph station code, US Geological Survey*] (SEIS)
ANU .... Antigua [*IYRU nationality code*] [*Airport symbol*]
ANU .... Anuhco, Inc. [*AMEX symbol*] (SPSG)
ANU .... Army and Navy Union, USA (EA)
ANU .... Australian National University
ANU .... Avionair, Inc. [*Canada ICAO designator*] (FAAC)
ANuA .... Antinuclear Antibody [*Medicine*] (DMAA)
Anude .... Asamblea Nicaraguense de Unidad Democratica [*Nicaraguan Assembly Democratic Unity*] (PD)
ANUDS....... Army Nuclear Data System [*Study*] (AABC)
ANUF .... Account Number Update File [*IRS*]
ANUG .... Acute Necrotizing Ulcerative Gingivitis [*Dentistry*]
ANUG .... Atex Newspaper Users Group (EA)
ANUGA........ Allgemeine Nahrungs und Genussmittel Ausstellung [*General Food and Delicacies Fair*] [*West Germany*]
Anuhco....... Anuhco, Inc. [*Associated Press*] (SAG)
ANUIES....... Asociacion Nacional de Universidades e Institutos de Ensenanza Superior [*The Mexican Association of Universities and Public Institutes of Higher Education*] (CROSS)
ANULAE...... Amalgamated National Union of Local Authorities Employees' Federation of Malaya
ANULIS....... Australian National University Library and Information Service
ANUP .... Antineoplastic Urinary Protein
ANUSA........ Australian National University Staff Association
ANUVIBHA... Anuvrat Vishva Bharati [*Anuvrat Global Organization*] [*India*] (EAIO)
ANV .... Accion Nacional Vasca [*Basque National Action*] [*Spain Political party*] (PPE)
ANV .... Advanced Naval Vehicle (CAAL)
ANV .... Air Nevada Airlines, Inc. [*ICAO designator*] (FAAC)
ANV .... Angle Neovascularization [*Opthalmology*]
AnV .... Anisidine Value [*Food science*]
ANV .... Anticipatory Nausea and Vomiting [*Medicine*]
ANV .... Anvik [*Alaska*] [*Airport symbol*] (OAG)
ANV .... Anvil Mountain [*Alaska*] [*Seismograph station code, US Geological Survey*] (SEIS)
ANV .... Army of Northern Virginia [*Civil War*]
ANV .... Avian Nephritis Virus [*Medicine*] (DMAA)
ANVAR........ Agence Nationale de Valorisation de la Recherche [*National Agency for the Promotion of Research*] [*Information service or system*] (IID)
ANVCE....... Advanced Naval Vehicle Concepts Evaluation (MCD)
ANVIA........ Americans for the National Voter Initiative Amendment (EA)

ANVIL	Action for Non-Violence in Learning [*British*] (DI)
ANVIS	Advanced Night Vision [*Goggles*]
ANVIS	Aviator's Night Vision Imaging System (RDA)
ANVM	Association of United States Night Vision Manufacturers (EA)
ANVO	Accept No Verbal Orders
AN/VRC	Army-Navy Vehicular Radio Communications
ANVS	Advanced Night Viewer Subsystem (MCD)
ANW	Ainsworth, NE [*Location identifier FAA*] (FAAL)
ANW	American West Capital [*Vancouver Stock Exchange symbol*]
A/N/W	Andrews/Nelson/Whitehead [*Commercial firm*]
ANW	Apollo Network [*NASA*] (KSC)
ANW	Aviacion del Noroeste SA de CV [*Mexico ICAO designator*] (FAAC)
a-nw--	New Guinea Island [*MARC geographic area code Library of Congress*] (LCCP)
ANW	Program Director for Weather and Flight Service Stations [*FAA*] (TAG)
ANWA	Abstracts of New World Archaeology [*A publication*]
ANWC	American News Women's Club (EA)
ANWC	Association for Non-White Concerns in Personnel and Guidance (EA)
ANWCG	Army Nuclear Weapon Coordination Group
ANWD	Alphanumeric Warning Display (MCD)
ANWES	Association of Naval Weapons, Engineers, and Scientists [*Later, ASE*]
ANWF	Australian National Word Festival
ANWG	Apollo Navigation Working Group [*NASA*] (MCD)
ANWL	All Nations Women's League (EA)
ANWPP	Accidental Nuclear War Prevention Project [*Nuclear Age Peace Foundation*] (EA)
ANWR	Arctic National Wildlife Refuge [*Alaska*]
ANWS	Association of Northwest Steelheaders (EA)
AN-WSC-3	Whiskey-3 [*Shipboard radio*]
ANWSRP	Army Nuclear Weapons Stockpile Reliability Program
ANX	Anax Aviation [*France ICAO designator*] (FAAC)
ANX	Andenes [*Norway*] [*Airport symbol*] (OAG)
ANX	Annex (AABC)
ANX	Annex
anx	Anxiety [*Psychology*] (DAVI)
ANX	Napoleon, MO [*Location identifier FAA*] (FAAL)
ANXF	Allied Naval Expeditionary Force [*British military*] (DMA)
anx Neur	Anxiety Neurosis [*Psychology*] (DAVI)
anx reac	Anxiety Reaction [*Psychology*] (DAVI)
ANY	Ancom ATM International, Inc. [*Toronto Stock Exchange symbol*]
ANY	Anthony, KS [*Location identifier FAA*] (FAAL)
ANY	Architecture New York [*A publication*]
ANYSFP	Associated New York State Food Processors (SRA)
ANYTC	Alternative to the New York Times Committee (EA)
ANZ	Air New Zealand Ltd. [*ICAO designator*] (FAAC)
ANZ	Anzar Road [*California*] [*Seismograph station code, US Geological Survey*] (SEIS)
Anz.	Anzeiger [*or Anzeigen*] [*German*] (OCD)
ANZ	Australia & New Zealand Bank [*NYSE symbol*] (SPSG)
ANZ	Australia & N.Z. Bk ADS [*NYSE symbol*] (TTSB)
ANZA	Australia-New Zealand Association [*Also, The ANZA Club*] (AC)
ANZA	Australian, New Zealand, African [*Radio network*]
ANZAC	Australian-New Zealand Army Corps (VNW)
ANZACS	Australian and New Zealand Association for Canadian Studies
ANZAM	Australia, New Zealand, and Malaysia [*Defense pact*] (BARN)
ANZBC	Australia-New Zealand Business Council
ANZCAN	Australian-New Zealand-Canada [*Cable*]
ANZCERTA	Australia-New Zealand Closer Economic Relations Trade Agreement (BARN)
ANZC Hals	Australian and New Zealand Commentary on Halsbury's Laws of England [*A publication*]
ANZDL	Australia-New Zealand Direct Line
ANZECC	Australian and New Zealand Environment and Conservation Council
ANZFAS	Australian and New Zealand Federation of Animal Societies
ANZFM	Australia and New Zealand Funds Management [*Banking*]
ANZHES JI	ANZHES [*Australian and New Zealand History of Education Society*] Journal [*A publication*]
ANZIC	Associate of the New Zealand Institute of Chemistry
ANZITR	Australian and New Zealand Income Tax Reports [*A publication*] (DLA)
ANZJ of Crim	Australian and New Zealand Journal of Criminology [*A publication*]
ANZMSA	Australian and New Zealand Merchants' and Shippers' Association (DS)
ANZPr	Aust&N.ZealandBk9.125%Pfd [*NYSE symbol*] (TTSB)
ANZSC	Australia-New Zealand Studies Centre [*Pennsylvania State University*]
A-NZSNY	Australian-New Zealand Society of New York (EA)
ANZTAC	Australia and New Zealand Trade Advisory Committee [*British Overseas Trade Board*] (DS)
ANZUK	Australia, New Zealand, and United Kingdom
ANZUS	Australia, New Zealand, and the United States [*Signatories to the Tripartite Security Treaty of 1951*]
AO	Abnormal Occurrence (NRCH)
A/O	About or On (MCD)
AO	Absolute Output [*Computer science*]
AO	Abwehroffizier [*Counterintelligence Officer*] [*German military - World War II*]
AO	Access Opening [*Technical drawings*]
AO	Accountant [*or Accounting*] Officer
AO	Account Of [*Business term*]
AO	Accounts Office [*Army*] (AABC)
AO	Achievement Orientation [*Psychology*] (AAMN)

AO	Acid Output [*Physiology*]
A-O	Acoustic-Optic [*Ophthalmology and otorhinolaryngology*] (DAVI)
A-O	Acousto-Optic (MCD)
AO	Acridine Orange [*Dye*]
AO	Action Officer [*Air Force*] (AFM)
AO	Adjusted Output [*Computer science*]
AO	Administration Office
AO	Administrative and Overhead [*Costs*] (KSC)
AO	Administrative Officer (GFGA)
AO	Administrative Operations
AO	Administrative Order (DLA)
AO	Admiralty Office [*Navy British*] (ROG)
AO	Adult Operculum
AO	Adults Only (ADA)
AO	Aerial Observer [*Military*] (NVT)
AO	Aeromere SpA [*Italy ICAO aircraft manufacturer identifier*] (ICAO)
AO	Aeronautical Order (AFM)
AO	Aerosol Obscurant (MCD)
AO	Affiliation Officer [*British*]
AO	After Orders (MCD)
AO	Airborne Observer [*Military*] (VNW)
AO	Aircraft Operator (DA)
AO	Airdrome Officer
AO	Airlock Outfitting (SSD)
AO	Air Observer [*Military British*]
AO	Air Officer [*RAF*] [*British*]
AO	Air Operator (NRCH)
AO	Air Ordnance [*Special duties officer*] [*British*]
AO	Air Over (MSA)
AO	Aldehyde Oxidase [*An enzyme*]
AO	Algo Group, Inc. [*Toronto Stock Exchange symbol*]
AO	Alliance for Opportunity [*Defunct*] (EA)
A/O	All Over the Hatch [*or Hold*] [*Stowage*] (DNAB)
AO	Ambulance Officer
AO	AMERCO [*NYSE symbol*] (SAG)
AO	American Optical Corp.
AO	Among Others
AO	Amplifier Output [*Computer science*]
AO	Analog Output [*Computer science*] (NASA)
A/O	Analog/Output
AO	And Others
ao	Angola [*MARC country of publication code Library of Congress*] (LCCP)
AO	Angola [*ANSI two-letter standard code*] (CNC)
AO	Anno Ordinis [*In the Year of the Order*] [*Used by the Knights Templar Freemasonry*] (ROG)
AO	Announcement of Opportunity [*NASA*] (MCD)
AO	Anodal Opening [*Physiology*]
AO	Answer Only (TEL)
AO	Answer Originate (IAA)
AO	Anterior Oblique (MAE)
Ao	Aorta [*Cardiology*] (AAMN)
AO	Aortic Valve Opening [*Cardiology*]
AO	Appointing Order
A/O	Aqueous to Organic [*Ratio*]
AO	Arcane Order [*Defunct*] (EA)
AO	Archives Office (ADA)
AO	Area Office
AO	Area of Operation [*Military*] (VNW)
AO	Area of Operations [*Military*] (AABC)
AO	Arkansas & Ozarks Railway [*AAR code*]
AO	Army Order [*British*]
AO	Artillery/Ordnance (MCD)
AO	Assembly Order
AO	Assembly Outline
AO	Assist Order
AO	Astronomical Observatory
AO	At Occupation [*An underwriting designation for an occupational accident*] [*Insurance*]
AO	Atomic Orbital
AO	Atrioventricular Valve Opening (DAVI)
AO	Atypical Odontalgia [*Dental pain that has no apparent organic cause*]
AO	Audio-Only
AO	Audio Operator (NTCM)
AO	Audio Oscillator
AO	Audit Organization (DNAB)
AO	Auramine-O [*A biological stain*]
AO	Authenticator Organization (MCD)
AO	Authorized Order
AO	Autoimmune Oophoritis [*Medicine*]
AO	Automatic Observer
AO	Autonomous Oblast [*Former USSR*]
AO	Auxiliary Oiler (MCD)
AO	Auxiliary Oscillator
AO	Avanguardia Operaia [*Worker's Vanguard*] [*Italy Political party*] (PPE)
AO	Average Out [*Business term*]
AO	Aviation Officer [*MTMC*] (TAG)
AO	Aviation Ordnanceman [*Navy rating*]
AO	Avisco [*ICAO designator*] (AD)
AO	Awards and Obligations (GFGA)
AO	Axio-Occlusal [*Dentistry*]
AO	Axis of Orientation (WDMC)
A/O	Axis of Orientation [*Imaginary vertical line at the left of a block of text*] [*Also, mental margin*] (WDMC)

AO .... Oiler [Fuel tanker] [Navy ship symbol]
AO .... Onoway Public Library, Alberta [Library symbol National Library of Canada] (NLC)
Ao .... Operational Availability
Ao .... Operational Availability (AAGC)
ao---- .... South China Sea and Area [MARC geographic area code Library of Congress] (LCCP)
AO1 .... Aviation Ordnanceman, First Class [Navy rating]
AO2 .... Aviation Ordnanceman, Second Class [Navy rating]
AO3 .... Aviation Ordnanceman, Third Class [Navy rating]
AOA .... Abnormal Oxygen Affinity [Hematology] (DAVI)
AOA .... Abort Once Around [NASA]
AOA .... Accident Officers Association (AIE)
AOA .... Accident Offices Association [British] (BI)
AOA .... Administration on Aging [Defunct Department of Health and Human Services]
AOA .... Advanced Optical Adjunct (LAIN)
AOA .... Aerodrome Owners Association [British] (BI)
AOA .... Aerostar Owners Association (EA)
AOA .... Airborne Optical Adjunct [Army] (RDA)
AOA .... Air Officer in Charge of Administration [RAF] [British]
AOA .... Airport Operation Area (DA)
AOA .... Alabaster, AL [Location identifier FAA] (FAAL)
AOA .... Alberta Orienteering Association (AC)
AOA .... American Ontoanalytic Association (EA)
AOA .... American Optometric Association (EA)
AOA .... American [or Army] Ordnance Association [Later, ADPA] (EA)
AOA .... American Orthopedic Association (EA)
AOA .... American Orthopsychiatric Association (EA)
AOA .... American Osteopathic Association (EA)
AOA .... American Ostrich Association (EA)
AOA .... American Outreach Association (EA)
AOA .... American Overseas Airlines
AOA .... American Overseas Association [Later, ARCOA] (EA)
AOA .... Amphibious Objective Area [Navy]
AOA .... Amphibious Operating Area
AOA .... Angle of Arrival
AOA .... Angle of Attack [Military] (MCD)
AOA .... Any One Accident [Insurance] (AIA)
AOA .... Any One Aircraft [Insurance] (AIA)
AOA .... Apollo Airlines [Greece] [FAA designator] (FAAC)
AOA .... Arkansas Optometric Association (SRA)
AOA .... Ascending Order Arrangement (MHDB)
AOA .... Aspira of America (EA)
AOA .... Association of Official Architects [British]
AOA .... Association of Otolaryngology Administrators (EA)
AOA .... Atlantic Ocean Area
AOA .... Atlantic Operating Area [Military] (DNAB)
AOA .... At or Above [Aviation]
AOA .... Australian Onion Association
AOA .... Australian Osteopathic Association
AOA .... Authorized Ordering Agency (MCD)
AOAA .... Aminooxyacetic Acid [Biochemistry]
AOAA .... Aviation Ordnanceman, Airman Apprentice, Striker [Navy rating]
AOA/AACS .... Alabama Oilmen's Association and Alabama Association of Convenience Stores (SRA)
AOABH .... Assault Occasioning Actual Bodily Harm [Criminology]
AOAC .... Army Ordnance Ammunition Command [Merged with Munitions Command]
AOAC .... Association of Official Agricultural Chemists (DAVI)
AOAC .... Association of Official Analytical Chemists (EA)
AOAC .... Automobile Owners Action Council [Defunct] (EA)
AOAC .... Calibrated Angle of Attack (MCD)
AOAC .... Olds College, Alberta [Library symbol National Library of Canada] (NLC)
AOACB .... Aviation Ordnanceman, Combat Aircrewman, Air Bomber [Navy rating Obsolete]
AOAcc .... Any One Accident [Insurance] (AIA)
AOAC Europe... Association of Official Analytical Chemists - Europe [Bennekom, Netherlands] (EAIO)
AOAD .... Arab Organization for Agricultural Development (EAIO)
AOAD .... Army Operating Availability Data
AOAF .... At or After (FAAC)
AOAF .... Farm Business Management Branch, Alberta Agriculture, Olds, Alberta [Library symbol National Library of Canada] (NLC)
AOAI .... Amateur Organist Association International (EA)
AOAI .... Angle-of-Attack Indicator [Military]
AOAI .... Avanti Owners Association International (EA)
AOAL .... Local Angle of Attack (MCD)
AO AMPL ..... And-Or Amplifier (HGAA)
AOAN .... Aviation Ordnanceman, Airman, Striker [Navy rating]
AOAO .... Advanced Orbiting Astronautical Observatory
AOAO .... American Osteopathic Academy of Orthopedics (EA)
AOAP .... Army Oil Analysis Program (MCD)
AOAP .... As Often As Possible (DAVI)
AOARRF .... Archbishop Oscar Arnulfo Romero Relief Fund (EA)
AOAS .... American Osteopathic Academy of Sclerotherapy (EA)
AOAS .... Angle-of-Attack Sensor [Military] (MCD)
AOAS .... Arab Organization of Administrative Sciences (EAIO)
AOAS .... Selected Angle of Attack (MCD)
AOASM .... American Osteopathic Academy of Sports Medicine (EA)
AOAT .... Allowed-Off Aircraft Time
AOAT .... Alter Orient und Altes Testament. Veroeffentlichungen zur Kultur und Geschichte des Alten Orients und des Alten Testaments [Kevelaer/Neukirchen/Vluyn] [A publication] (BJA)

AOAT .... Angle of Attack Transmitter [Military]
AOAT .... True Angle of Attack (MCD)
AOATC .... Atlantic Ocean Air Traffic Control [NATO] (NATG)
AOB .... Accessory Olfactory Bulb [Anatomy]
AOB .... Administrative Operations Branch [NTIS]
AOB .... Advanced Operational Base [Navy]
AOB .... Airborne Optical Beacon
AOB .... Air Order of Battle (AFM)
AOB .... Alcohol on Breath [Police term]
AOB .... Angle of Bank
AOB .... Angle of Beam
AOB .... Angle on the Bow [Navy] (NVT)
AOB .... Annual Operating Budget [Army]
AOB .... An Old Bachelor [Pseudonym used by William Lloyd Garrison Acronym also facetiously translated as "Ass, Oaf, and Blockhead"]
AOB .... Antediluvian Order of Buffaloes [British]
AOB .... Any One Bottom [Marine insurance] (DS)
AOB .... Any Other Business (ADA)
AOB .... Approved Operating Budget [Army] (AABC)
AOB .... Association of Brewers (EA)
AOB .... Atmospheric Observation Bell (PDAA)
AOB .... At or Below [Aviation]
AOB .... Automated Office Battery [Selection and career development test]
AOB .... Automatic Optical Bench [Hughes Aircraft Co.]
AOBA .... Apartment and Office Building Association [of Metro Washington, DC] (SRA)
AOBAT .... Altorientalische Bilder zum Alten Testament [A publication] (BJA)
AOBC .... American Overseas Book Co.
AOBC .... Army Officer Basic Course [Army] (RDA)
AOBD .... Acousto-Optic Beam Deflector [Instrumentation]
AOBEM .... American Osteopathic Board of Emergency Medicine (EA)
AOBF .... At or Before (FAAC)
AOBF .... Australian Outward Bound Foundation
AOBGP .... American Osteopathic Board of General Practice (EA)
AOBMO .... Army Ordnance Ballistic Missile Office
AOBP .... American Osteopathic Board of Pediatrics (EA)
AOBS .... Acute Organic Brain Syndrome [Medicine] (DMAA)
AOBS .... Annual Officer Billet Summary (DNAB)
AOBS .... Army Outward Bound School [British military] (DMA)
AOBS .... Association of Oldtime Barbell and Strongmen (EA)
AOBSR .... Air Observer [Military] (AFM)
AOBTS .... Air Order of Battle Textual Summary (MCD)
AOC .... Abnormal Operating Condition (GFGA)
AOC .... Abridged Ocular Chart [Ophthalmology] (DAVI)
AOC .... Administrative Order on Consent [Environmental Protection Agency] (ERG)
AOC .... Adult Opportunity Center [State employment service]
AOC .... Advanced Office Computer [Northern Telecom, Inc.] (NITA)
AOC .... Advanced Office Concepts Corp. [Defunct Information service or system] (IID)
AOC .... Advanced Officer's Course [Army]
AOC .... Advice of Charge [Telecommunications] (DOM)
AOC .... Aerodrome Obstruction Chart
AOC .... Aeronautical Operational Control
AOC .... Aeronautical Operation Control [Communications which support safety and regularity of flight that normally take place between aircraft and the operator] (GAVI)
AOC .... Agreed Operational Characteristics (DNAB)
AOC .... Aircraft Operational Capability (DNAB)
AOC .... Aircraft Operations Center (OSRA)
AOC .... Aircraft Operations Center (USDC)
AOC .... Air Officer Commanding [RAF] [British]
AOC .... Air Oil Cooler
AOC .... Air Operations Center [Air Force]
AOC .... Air Operators Certificate [British] (AIA)
AOC .... Airport Operators Council [Later, AOCI] (EA)
AOC .... Alianca Operaria Camponesa [Peasants and Workers Alliance] [Portugal Political party] (PPE)
AOC .... Allard Owners Club [British] (EAIO)
AOC .... Altered Oceanic Crust [Geology]
AOC .... Alvis Owners Club [North Droitwich, Worcestershire, England] (EAIO)
AOC .... American Oceans Campaign [An association] (EA)
AOC .... American Ophthalmological Color [Chart]
AOC .... American Optical Corp. (DAVI)
AOC .... American Orthoptic Council (EA)
AOC .... Amphicar Owners Club (EA)
AOC .... Anno Orbis Conditi [In the Year of the Creation] [Latin]
AOC .... Anodal Opening Contraction [Also, AnOC] [Physiology]
AOC .... Aon Corp. [NYSE symbol] (SPSG)
AOC .... Aortic Valve Closure [Medicine]
AOC .... Appellation d'Origine Controle [Official place name for wine]
AOC .... Architect of the Capitol [US]
AOC .... Area of Concentration (RDA)
AOC .... Area of Concern (MCD)
AOC .... [The] Army Operations Center
AOC .... Army Ordnance Corps [Later, RAOC] [British]
AOC .... Assimilable Organic Carbon [Environmental chemistry]
AOC .... Associated Overseas Countries of the European Economic Community
AOC .... Association of Old Crows (EAIO)
AOC .... Association of Oregon Counties (SRA)
AOC .... Association of Orthopaedic Chairmen (EA)
AOC .... Association Olympique Canadienne [Canadian Olympic Association - COA]

AOC	Assumption of Control Message [*Aviation*]
AOC	Attached to Other Correspondence [*Business term*]
AOC	Attention Operating Characteristic [*Psychometrics*]
AOC	Auditor Overcharge Claims
AOC	Australian Ordnance Council
AOC	Automatic Operation Control
AOC	Automatic Output Control
AOC	Automatic Overload Circuit
AOC	Automatic Overload Control (IEEE)
AOC	Average Operating Cost (KSC)
AOC	Aviation Officer Candidate [*Navy*]
AOC	Aviation Ordnanceman, Chief [*Navy rating*]
AOC	Awaiting Outgoing Continuity [*Telecommunications*] (TEL)
AOC	Award of Contract
AOC	JV Avcom [*Russian Federation*] [*ICAO designator*] (FAAC)
AOCA	American Osteopathic College of Anesthesiologists (EA)
AOCA	Australian Oilseed Crushers' Association
AOCA	Australian Owned Companies Association
AOCAI	American Osteopathic College of Allergy and Immunology (EA)
AOCAN	Aviation Officer Candidate Airman [*Navy*] (DNAB)
AOCB	Any Other Competent Business (ODBW)
AOCBAF	Air Officer Commanding Base Air Forces [*RAF*] [*British*]
AOCC	Advanced Office Concepts Corp. [*Defunct*] (TSSD)
AOCC	ARIA [*Apollo Range Instrumentation Aircraft*] Operations Control Center [*NASA*]
AOCC	Australian Overseas Construction Council
AOCD	American Osteopathic College of Dermatology (EA)
AOCDO	Association of Oregon Community Development Organizations (SRA)
AOCE	Apple Open Collaboration Environment [*Computer science*] (PCM)
AOCE	Attitude and Orbit Control Electronics [*Aerospace*] (NASA)
AOCEO	Army Ordnance Combat Equipment Office
AOCEUR	Alternative Operational Concepts in Europe [*Military*]
AOCF	Alliance for Our Common Future (EA)
AOCF	Association of Outplacement Consulting Firms (EA)
AOCH	Association of Ohio Children's Hospitals (SRA)
AOCI	Accredited Off-Campus Instruction
AOCI	Airport Operators Council International (EA)
AOCI	Anodal Opening Clonus [*Medicine*] (DMAA)
AOCIC	Air Officer Commanding-in-Chief [*RAF*] [*British*]
AOCINC	Air Officer Commanding-in-Chief [*RAF*] [*British*] (NATG)
AOC-in-C	Air Officer Commanding-in-Chief [*RAF*] [*British*]
AOC in CBAFO	Air Officer Commanding-in-Chief British Air Force Occupation [*RAF*]
AOCJ	Association of Obedience Clubs and Judges (EA)
AOCL	Anodal Opening Clonus [*Physiology*]
AOCM	Advanced Optical Countermeasures (MCD)
AOCM	Aircraft Out of Commission for Maintenance [*Military*]
AOCM	Aircraft out of Commission for Parts [*MTMC*] (TAG)
AOCM	Aviation Ordnanceman, Master Chief [*Navy rating*]
AOCN	Assembly Order Control Number
AOC Newsl.	Administrative Office of the Courts. Newsletter [*A publication*] (DLA)
AOCNM	American Osteopathic College of Nuclear Medicine [*Defunct*] (EA)
AOCO	Atomic Ordnance Cataloging Office
AOCP	Airborne Operational Computer Program (MCD)
AOCP	Aircraft Out of Commission for [*Lack of*] Parts [*Obsolete Military*]
AOCP	American Osteopathic College of Pathologists
AOCP	American Osteopathic College of Proctology (EA)
AOCP	Aviation Officer Continuation Pay [*Navy*]
AOCPA	American Osteopathic College of Pathologists
AOCPM	American Osteopathic College of Preventive Medicine (EA)
AOCPMR	American Osteopathic College of Physical Medicine and Rehabilitation [*Later, AOCRM*] (EA)
AOCPR	American Osteopathic College of Proctology
AOCPrA	Aon Cp 8% Perpetual Pfd [*NYSE symbol*] (TTSB)
AOCPrB	Aon Cp 6.25% Cv Ex Pfd [*NYSE symbol*] (TTSB)
AOCR	Advanced Optical Character Reader
AOCR	Aircraft Operating Cost Report (NG)
AOCR	American Osteopathic College of Radiology (EA)
AOCR	American Osteopathic College of Rheumatology (EA)
AOCRD	Acceptance and Operational Checkout Requirements Document [*NASA*] (NASA)
AOCRM	American Osteopathic College of Rehabilitation Medicine (EA)
AOCRZ	Aqua Care Sys Wrrt'B' [*NASDAQ symbol*] (TTSB)
AOCS	Airline Operational Control Society [*Defunct*] (EA)
AOCS	Alpha Omega Computer System (IEEE)
AOCS	American Oil Chemists' Society (EA)
AOCS	Atlantic Outer Continental Shelf
AOCS	Attitude and Orbit Control System [*or Subsystem*] (MCD)
AOCS	Automated Orbit Control System (MCD)
AOCS	Aviation Officer Candidate School [*Navy*]
AOCS	Aviation Ordnanceman, Senior Chief [*Navy rating*]
AOCT	Associated Overseas Countries and Territories (DS)
AOCU	Arithmetic Output Control Unit
AOCU	Associative Output Control Unit [*Computer science*]
AOC-USA	Allard Owners Club USA (EA)
AOD	Abou Deia [*Chad*] [*Airport symbol*] (AD)
AOD	Above Ordnance Datum [*Military*] (DA)
AOD	Absent On Duty [*Military*]
AOD	Academy of Operative Dentistry (EA)
AOD	Academy of Oral Dynamics (EA)
AOD	Acousto-Optics Device
AOD	Administrative Officer of the Day (DAVI)
AOD	Administrative Officer on Duty
AOD	Administrative Organs Department (LAIN)
AOD	Adult Onset Diabetes [*Medicine*] (DMAA)

AOD	Advanced Ordnance Department [*British*]
AOD	Advanced Ordnance Depot
AOD	Aerodrome Officer-of-the-Day (DNAB)
AOD	Aerosol Optical Depth (USDC)
AOD	Aerosol Optical Depth (OSRA)
AOD	Aircraft Operations Division [*Johnson Space Center*] [*NASA*] (NASA)
AOD	Airfield Operations Designator [*Air Force/Army*]
AOD	Airlift Operations Directive (AFM)
AOD	Air Officer of the Day [*Air Force*] (AFM)
AOD	Alleged Onset Date [*of disability*] [*Social Security Administration*] (OICC)
AOD	Allocate on Demand [*Computer science*] (BYTE)
AOD	Analog Output Differential [*Computer science*] (MCD)
AOD	Ancient Order of Druids
AOD	Angle of Descent
AOD	Apollo Operations Director [*NASA*] (SAA)
AOD	Area Office Director [*OFCCP*] (AAGC)
AOD	Area-Oriented Depots [*Military*] (RDA)
AOD	Area-Oriented Distribution [*DoD*]
AOD	Argon-Oxygen Decarburization [*Steelmaking*]
AOD	Argon Oxygen Decarburization
AOD	Arithmetic Output Data [*Computer science*]
AOD	Army Ordnance Department [*British*]
AOD	Arsenal Operations Directorate [*Rock Island Arsenal*] [*Army*]
AOD	Arterial Occlusive Disease [*Medicine*]
AOD	As-Of Date (AFM)
AOD	Assistant Operations Director [*Air Force/Army*] (MCD)
AOD	Auriculo-Osteodysplasia [*Medicine*]
AOD	Automatic Overdrive
AOD	Aviation Officer of the Day [*MTMC*] (TAG)
AOD	Aviation Operating Detachment (CINC)
AOD	Ontario, CA [*Location identifier FAA*] (FAAL)
AODAP	Office of Alcohol and Other Drug Abuse Programming [*University of Minnesota*] [*Research center*]
AODB	American Stock Exchange Option Display Book
AODC	Age of Date, Clock (SSD)
AODC	Allowance Officer Desk Code (DNAB)
AODC	Association of Offshore Diving Contractors [*British*] (DBA)
AODC	Australian Oceanographic Data Centre
AODC	Automobile Objets d'Art Club (EA)
AODE	Age of Date, Ephermis (SSD)
AO/DI	Always On/Dynamic ISDN [*Integrated Services Digital Network*] [*Telecommunications*]
AODM	Adult-Onset Diabetes Mellitus [*Endocrinology*]
AODME	Academy of Osteopathic Directors of Medical Education (EA)
AODP	Acquisition Orbit Determination Program Assembly [*Space Flight Operations Facility, NASA*]
AODP	Advanced Ocean Drilling Program [*National Science Foundation*]
AODRA	American Oxford Down Record Association [*Later, AOSA*] (EA)
AODRM	Academy of Oral Diagnosis, Radiology, and Medicine (EA)
AODS	All-Ordnance Destruct System
AODS	Atlas [*Missile*] Operational Data Summary
AOE	Abbreviated Operational Evaluation (MCD)
AOE	ACM Gvt Opportunity Fd [*NYSE symbol*] (TTSB)
AOE	Advanced Order Entry [*Investment system*] (ECON)
AOE	Aerodrome [*or Airport*] of Entry
AOE	Aerososel [*Chile*] [*FAA designator*] (FAAC)
AOE	Airborne Operational Equipment
AOE	Airport of Entry (DA)
AOE	Alcoholic Onion Extract
AOE	Army of Excellence [*Military program*] (INF)
AOE	Association of Optometric Educators (EA)
AOE	Association of Overseas Educators [*Defunct*] (EA)
AOE	Auditing Order Error
AOE	Fast Combat Support Ship [*Navy symbol*]
AOE	Multipurpose Stores Ship [*Navy*]
AOEC	Airways Operations Evaluation Center
AOEHI	American Organization for the Education of the Hearing Impaired [*Later, IOEHI*] (EA)
AOEL	Advanced Ocean Engineering Laboratory [*Scripps Institution of Oceanography*]
AOEM	Automotive Original Equipment Manufacturers
AOEO	American Overseas Educators Organization [*Later, Association of Overseas Educators*] (AEBS)
AOER	Arab Oil and Economic Review [*A publication*]
AOER	Army Officers' Emergency Reserve [*British*]
AOERP	Automated Overseas Employment Referral Program
AOES	Advanced Orbit/Ephemeris Subsystem
AOES	Air-Ocean Environmental Specialist (DNAB)
AOES	Arctic Ocean Environment Simulator
AOET	Allowed Off-Engine Time (AFIT)
AOEW	Airplane Operating Empty Weight (OA)
AOF	ACM Government Opportunity Fund, Inc. [*NYSE symbol*] (CTT)
AOF	Active Optical Fuze
AOF	Advanced Operating Facility [*Computer Technology, Inc.*]
AOF	Afrique Occidentale Francaise [*French West Africa*] [*French*]
AOF	Aircraft Operating Fee (ADA)
AOF	Air Objective Folder (SAA)
AOF	American Opportunity Foundation [*Washington, DC*] (EA)
AOF	American Optometric Foundation (EA)
AOF	[*The*] Ancient Order of Foresters
AOF	Australian Oilseeds Federation
AOFA	Atlantic Offshore Fishermen's Association (EA)
AOFAS	American Orthopedic Foot and Ankle Society (EA)
AOFB	Ancient Order of Frothblowers [*British*]

AOFC .... Ancient Order of Foresters of California [*Later, AOFPCJ*] (EA)
AOFC .... Apple Octopus Fan Club (EA)
AOFCG .... American Order of the French Croix de Guerre (EA)
AOFLA .... Artlantic Offshore Fish and Lobster Association (USDC)
AOFLA .... Atlantic Offshore Fish and Lobster Association (OSRA)
AOFPCJ .... Ancient Order of Foresters of the Pacific Coast Jurisdiction [*Hilo, HI*] (EA)
AOFS .... Active Optical Fuzing System
AOFS .... American Orthopedic Foot Society [*Later, AOFAS*] (EA)
AOG .... Acid Fractionator Off-Gas [*Nuclear energy*] (NRCH)
AOG .... Aircraft on Ground [*Navy*]
AOG .... Alberta Energy [*NYSE symbol*] (TTSB)
AOG .... Alberta Energy Co. Ltd. [*NYSE symbol*] (SAG)
AOG .... All-Over Good (IIA)
AOG .... Amino(octyl)guanidine [*Organic chemistry*]
AOG .... Arrival of Goods (WDMC)
AOG .... Assemblies of God (ADA)
AOG .... Association of Graduates of the United States Air Force Academy (EA)
AOG .... Augmented Off-Gas System [*Nuclear energy*] (NRCH)
AOG .... Automated Onboard Gravimeter
AOG .... Gasoline Tanker [*Navy symbol*]
AOGA .... Aircraft Operations Group Association
AOGA .... Alaska Oil and Gas Association (SRA)
AOGA .... Assembly of God in Australia
AOGBH .... Assault Occasioning Grievous Bodily Harm [*Criminology*]
AOGC .... Association of Oklahoma General Contractors (SRA)
AOGM .... Army of Occupation of Germany Medal [*Military decoration*]
AOGMS .... Army Ordnance Guided Missile School (MCD)
AOGO .... Advanced Orbiting Geophysical Observatory
AOH .... Accepted on Hire
AOH .... Acid Open Hearth (PDAA)
AOH .... Aircraft Requiring Overhaul (AFIT)
AOH .... Air Over Hydraulic [*Automotive engineering*]
AOH .... Alternariol [*Biochemistry*]
AOH .... Ancient Order of Hibernians in America (EA)
AOH .... Annual Operating Hours (MCD)
AOH .... Apollo Operations Handbook [*NASA*]
AOH .... Aviator's Oxygen Helmet (NG)
AOH .... Awaiting Office Hours
AOH .... Awaiting Overhaul (NG)
AOH .... Lima, OH [*Location identifier FAA*] (FAAL)
AOH .... North Coast Aviation, Inc. [*ICAO designator*] (FAAC)
AOHA .... American Osteopathic Hospital Association (EA)
AOHC .... Association of Ontario Health Centres [*Association des Centres de Sante de l'Ontario*] (AC)
AOHI .... After Overhaul Inspection
AOHREF .... American Osteopathic Hospital Research and Education Foundation (EA)
AOHS .... American Osteopathic Historical Society [*Defunct*] (EA)
AOI .... Academia Ophthalmologica Internationalis (EAIO)
AOI .... Accent on Information [*Databank for the handicapped and rehabilitation professionals*] [*Accent on Living*] (IID)
AOI .... Acousto-Optical Imaging
AOI .... Advance Ordering Information
AOI .... Ancona [*Italy*] [*Airport symbol*] (OAG)
AOI .... And-Or Invert (IEEE)
AOI .... Apnea of Infancy [*Also, AOP (Apnea of Prematurity)*] (PAZ)
AOI .... Area of Interest (AABC)
AOI .... Associated Oregon Industries (SRA)
AOI .... Automated Optical Inspection
AOI .... Avionics Operating Instruction (MCD)
AOIC .... Assistant Officer in Charge [*DoD*]
AOIF .... American Opportunity Income Fund, Inc. [*Associated Press*] (SAG)
ao-il .... Aorta-Iliac [*Cardiology*] (DAVI)
A OIL .... Aviation Oil [*Military*]
AOINST .... Administrative Office Instruction
AOIP .... Assault on Illiteracy Program (EA)
AOIP .... Australian Organizations Industrial Policy
AOIPS .... Atmospheric and Oceanographic Information Processing System [*Satellite image enhancing system*] (MCD)
AOIR .... Assembly Operation and Inspection Report
AOIV .... Automatically Operated Inlet Valve
AOIVM .... Angiographically Occult Intracranial Vascular Malformation [*Neurosurgery*] (DAVI)
AOJ .... Acquire on Jam
AOJ .... Aero-Jet SA [*Switzerland ICAO designator*] (FAAC)
AOJ .... Angle on Jam (MCD)
AOJ .... Aomori [*Japan*] [*Airport symbol*] (OAG)
AO(J) .... Jumbo Oiler (DNAB)
AOJC .... Association des Orchestres de Jeunes du Canada [*Canadian Association of Youth Orchestras*]
AOJC .... Association of Orthodox Jews in Communications (EA)
AOJS .... Association of Orthodox Jewish Scientists (EA)
AOJT .... Association of Orthodox Jewish Teachers (EA)
AOK .... Aerovias del Atlantico Ltd. [*Colombia*] [*ICAO designator*] (FAAC)
A-OK .... All Equipment OK [*Expression meaning "in perfect working order." Popularized during early development of NASA's space program*]
AOK .... All Out-of-Kilter [*Slang*]
AOK .... Karpathos [*Greece*] [*Airport symbol*] (OAG)
AOKAI .... Amateur Organists and Keyboard Association International (EA)
AOL .... Absent over Leave [*Navy*]
AOL .... Acro-Osteolysis [*Medicine*]
AOL .... Admiralty Office, London (ROG)
AOL .... Admiralty Oil Laboratory [*British*]

AOL .... Airborne Oceanographic LIDAR [*Light Detection and Ranging*] (PDAA)
AOL .... Air Exel Executive [*France ICAO designator*] (FAAC)
AOL .... All Operator Letter (MCD)
AOL .... America Online [*Online Service*] (PCM)
AOL .... Any One Loss [*Insurance*] (AIA)
AOL .... Application Oriented Language [*Computer science*] (BUR)
AOL .... Artist-Owned Label [*Music*]
AOL .... Associated Oregon Loggers (SRA)
AOL .... Association of Illustrators [*British*] (DBA)
AOL .... Atlantic Oceanographic Laboratories [*of Environmental Science Services Administration*]
AOL .... Olds Public Library, Alberta [*Library symbol National Library of Canada*] (NLC)
AOL .... Paso De Los Libres [*Argentina*] [*Airport symbol*] (OAG)
AOL .... Small Oiler [*Navy symbol*] (DNAB)
AOLA .... Atlantic Offshore Lobstermen's Association (SRA)
AOLC .... Auxiliaries of Our Lady of the Cenacle (EA)
AOLIC .... Association of Ohio Life Insurance Companies (SRA)
AOLM .... Apollo Orbiting Laboratory Module [*NASA*]
AOLO .... Advanced Orbital Launch Operations
AOLOC .... Any One Location [*Marine insurance*] (DS)
AOLR .... Amplifier Open Loop Response
AOLRC .... Association of Ohio Longrifle Collectors (EA)
AOLS .... Association of Our Lady of Salvation [*Defunct*]
AOM .... Aaron Mining Ltd. [*Vancouver Stock Exchange symbol*]
AOM .... Academy of Orthomolecular Medicine
AOM .... Acousto-Optic Modulator
AOM .... Active Oxygen Method [*Food fat stability test*]
AOM .... Acute Otitis Media [*Medicine*]
AOM .... Add One to Memory [*Computer science*]
AOM .... Aircraft Operating Manual (GAVI)
AOM .... All Officers Meeting [*Military*] (DNAB)
AOM .... Altos Office Manager [*Altos Computer Systems*]
AOM .... Ancient Order of Maccabeans (BJA)
AOM .... AOM-Minerve, SA [*France*] [*FAA designator*] (FAAC)
AOM .... Aomori [*Japan*] [*Seismograph station code, US Geological Survey*] (SEIS)
AOM .... Army of Occupation Medal [*Military decoration*]
AOM .... Association of Ontario Midwives [*Association des Sages-Femmes de l'Ontario*] [*Formerly, Ontario Association of Midwives*] (AC)
AOM .... Association of Operative Millers (EA)
AOM .... Aviation Ordnanceman [*Navy rating Obsolete*]
AOM .... Master of Obstetric Art (DAVI)
AOM .... Okotoks Municipal Library, Alberta [*Library symbol National Library of Canada*] (NLC)
AOMA .... American Occupational Medical Association (EA)
AOMA .... Apartment Owners and Managers Association of America (EA)
AOMA .... Arizona Osteopathic Medical Association (SRA)
AOMA .... Arkansas Oil Marketers Association (SRA)
AOMA .... Arkansas Osteopathic Medical Association (SRA)
AOMAC .... Aviation Ordnanceman, Combat Aircrewman [*Navy rating Obsolete*]
AOMB .... Aviation Ordnanceman, Bombsight Mechanic [*Navy rating Obsolete*]
AOMC .... Ariel Owners' Motorcycle Club (EA)
AOMC .... Army Ordnance Missile Center (MCD)
AOMC .... Army Ordnance Missile Command [*Later, Missile Command*] [*Redstone Arsenal, AL*]
AOMD .... Amended Operator and Maintenance Decision [*Army*]
AOME .... Assistant Ordnance Mechanical Engineer [*British military*] (DMA)
AOMJ .... Aomori Outpost [*Japan*] [*Seismograph station code, US Geological Survey*] (SEIS)
AOML .... Atlantic Oceanographic and Meteorological Laboratory [*Miami, FL*] [*National Oceanic and Atmospheric Administration*]
AOML/FD ..... Acousto-Optic Mode-Locker / Frequency Doubles (PDAA)
AOMP .... Artisans Order of Mutual Protection [*Philadelphia, PA*] (EA)
AOMPS .... Automatic Outgoing Message Processor System (NVT)
AOMS .... Association of Organisers of Music, Scotland
AOMSA .... Army Ordnance Missile Support Agency
AOMSC .... Army Ordnance Missile Support Center (NATG)
AOMT .... Aviation Ordnanceman, Turret Mechanic [*Navy rating*]
AON .... Accessory Optic Nucleus [*Neuroanatomy*]
AO-N .... Administrative Office - Navy
AON .... Aero Trade International [*Romania*] [*ICAO designator*] (FAAC)
AON .... All or None [*Investment, securities*]
AON .... Anterior Octaval Nucleus [*Neuroanatomy*]
Aon .... Aon Corp. [*Associated Press*] (SAG)
AON .... Arona [*New Guinea*] [*Airport symbol*] (AD)
AON .... Automated Optical Navigation (MCD)
AON .... Average Octane Number
AON .... Average of Normals
AONB .... Area of Outstanding Natural Beauty [*Great Britain*]
AONBP-CE ... Association des Organisations Nationales de la Boulangerie et de la Patisserie de la CE [*Association of National Organizations in the Bakery and Confectionary Trade in the European Community*] [*Belgium*] (EAIO)
AOncol .... American Oncology Resources, Inc. [*Associated Press*] (SAG)
Aon Cp .... Aon Corp. [*Associated Press*] (SAG)
AOND .... Administrative Office, Navy Department
AONE .... American Organization of Nurse Executives (EA)
AONET .... American Osteopathic Network [*American Osteopathic Association*] [*Information service or system*] (IID)
AONS .... Air Observers Navigation School [*Military*] (OA)
AONTAS .... Aos-Oideachas Naisiunta Tri Aontu Saorlach [*National Association of Adult Education*] (EAIO)
AOO .... Altoona [*Pennsylvania*] [*Airport symbol*] (OAG)

AOO	Altoona-Martinsburg [Pennsylvania] [Airport symbol] (AD)
AOO	American Oceanic Organization (EA)
AOO	Amphibious Operations Officer [British military] (DMA)
AOO	Anodal Opening Odor [Physiology]
AOO	Anticipated Operational Occurrence [Nuclear energy] (NRCH)
AOO	Area Operations Office [Employment and Training Administration] (OICC)
AOO	Aviation Ordnance Officer
AOOC	Albertville Olympic Organizing Committee [Albertville, France] (EAIO)
AOOcc	Any One Occurrence [Insurance] (AIA)
AOP	Abnormal Operating Procedure (NRCH)
AOP	Academy of Orthomolecular Psychiatry [Later, AOM] (EA)
AOP	Accuracy of Position (MCD)
AOP	Acetoxypregnenolone [Pharmacology]
AOP	Acidity Oxidation Potential [Chemistry]
A-OP	Acylated Octapeptide [Biochemistry]
AOP	Additive Operational Project [Army] (MCD)
AOP	Administrative and Operational Procedure (MCD)
AOP	Advanced On-Board Processor [Computer]
AOP	Advanced Oxidation Process [Chemistry]
AOP	Aerodrome Operation (DA)
AOP	Aeropiloto-Sociedade Exploradora de Servicos Aereos Lda. [Portugal ICAO designator] (FAAC)
AOP	Aerospace Observation Platform
AOP	Airborne Optical Platform
AOP	Aircraft Out for Parts (MCD)
AOP	Air Observation Post
AOP	Allied Ordnance Publications (NATG)
AOP	All Other Perils [Insurance]
AOP	All Over Pattern [Quilting]
AOP	Altoona Area Public Library, Altoona, PA [OCLC symbol] (OCLC)
AOP	Amino-Oligopeptidase [An enzyme]
AOP	Ammonia Oxidation Plant (MCD)
AOP	Annual Operating Program [Army]
AOP	Anodal Opening Picture [Physiology]
AOP	Anomalistic Observational Phenomena [In study of UFO's]
AOP	Any One Person [Insurance] (AIA)
AoP	Aortic Pressure [Medicine]
AOP	Apnea of Prematurity [Also, AOI (Apnea of Infancy)] (PAZ)
AOP	Applicant Outreach Program [Department of Labor]
AOP	Apprenticeship Outreach Program [Bureau of Apprenticeship and Training] (OICC)
AOP	Arctic Offshore Program [National Science Foundation] (GFGA)
AOP	Area of Probability (NVT)
AOP	Armoured Observation Post [British and Canadian] [World War II]
AOP	Army Observation Post [British military] (DMA)
AOP	Artillery Observation Post [British military] (DMA)
AOP	Assembly and Operations Plan
AOP	Association of Online Professionals
AOP	Association of Optical Practitioners [British] (BI)
AOP	Association of Optometrists [British] (DBA)
AOP	Association of Osteopathic Publications [Defunct]
AOP	Atomic Ordnance Platoon (NG)
AOP	Automatic Operations Panel
AOP	Environmental Protection Agency Analytical Operations Branch
AoP	Left Ventricle to Aorta Pressure Gradient [Cardiology] (DAVI)
AoP	Rock Springs, WY [Location identifier FAA] (FAAL)
AOPA	Aircraft Owners and Pilots Association (EA)
AOPA	American Orthotic and Prosthetic Association (EA)
AOPA	Automotive Occupant Protection Association (EA)
AOPB	Active Officer Promotion Branch [BUPERS]
AOPC	Adult Outpatient Psychotherapy Clinic (DMAA)
AOPE	Associated Organizations for Professionals in Education [Defunct] (EA)
AOPEC	Arab Organization of Petroleum Exporting Countries
AOPES	Association of Organisers of Physical Education, Scotland
AOPF	Air Observation Post Flight [British military] (DMA)
aopf--	Paracel Islands [MARC geographic area code Library of Congress] (LCCP)
AOPHA	Association of Ohio Philanthropic Homes and Housing for the Aging (SRA)
AOPL	Association of Oil Pipe Lines (EA)
AOPM	Airline Operations Planning Model (NASA)
AOPrA	AMERCO Sr'A'Pfd [NYSE symbol] (TTSB)
AOPS	Air Operations [Military] (NVT)
AOPSA	Advanced Optical Power Spectrum Analyzer (MCD)
AOPU	Asian Oceanic Postal Union [Later, APPU] [China, Korea, Philippines, Thailand]
AOPV	Air-Operated Plastic Valve
AOPW	Aortic Posterior Wall [Cardiology] (DMAA)
AoPW	Aortic Posterior Wall [Cardiology] (DMAA)
AOQ	Alliance, NE [Location identifier FAA] (FAAL)
AOQ	Association des Optometristes du Quebec (AC)
AOQ	Average Outgoing Quality [Quality control]
AOQ	Aviation Officers' Quarters
AOQL	Average Outgoing Quality Laboratory
AOQL	Average Outgoing Quality Level [or Limit] [Quality control]
AOR	Abnormal Occurrence Report
AOR	Accumulated Operating Results
AOR	Add One to the Right (SAA)
AOR	Adult Oriented Rock [Music]
AOR	Advance List of Oversea-Returnees for Reassignment [Army]
AOR	Advice of Rights [Legal term] (BARN)
AOR	Afro International Ent. Ltd. [Nigeria] [FAA designator] (FAAC)
AOR	Agency of Record [An advertising agency] (WDMC)

AOR	Agency Owners Roundtable [Formerly, Canadian Association of Professional Advertising Agencies] (AC)
AOR	Airborne Overland RADAR
AOR	Aircraft Operating Report (MCD)
AOR	Air Operations Room
AOR	Album-Oriented Radio [Radio station format] (WDMC)
AOR	Album Oriented Rock [Facetious translation: Another Old Record] [Broadcasting]
AOR	Aldehyde Ferredoxin Oxidoreductase [An enzyme]
AOR	Allowance Override Requirement (CAAL)
AOR	Alor Setar [Malaysia] [Airport symbol] (OAG)
AOR	Anchor Order (MSA)
A/OR	And/Or
AOR	Angle of Reflection
AOR	Annual Operating Requirements
AOR	Antenna Ohmic Resistance
AOR	Aorist [Grammar] (ROG)
AOR	Apollo Owners Register (EA)
AOR	Arbor Resources, Inc. [Vancouver Stock Exchange symbol]
AOR	Area of Responsibility (MCD)
AOR	Argon Oxygen Refining (DNAB)
AOR	Army Operational Research
AOR	Assembly Operations Record
AOR	Association of Rehabilitation Ltd.
AOR	Atlantic Ocean Region [INTELSAT]
AOR	At Own Risk [Medicine] (BARN)
AOR	Auxiliary Oil Replenisher [or Replenishment] [Navy British]
AOR	Operational Replenishment Ship [Canadian Navy]
AOR	Operations Research Service [FAA] (TAG)
AOR	Replenishment Oiler [Navy ship symbol]
AORA	Atlantic Ocean Recovery Area [NASA]
AORC	Association of Official Racing Chemists (EA)
AORC	Automotive Occupant Restraints Council (EA)
AORD	Astronaut Operations Requirement Document [NASA] (KSC)
AORE	Army Operational Research Establishment [British]
AORF	Amplifier Oscillator, Radiofrequency
AORF	Arctic Ocean Radiative Fluxes [Data set] (OSRA)
AORG	Allen Organ Co. [NASDAQ symbol] (NQ)
AORG	Army Operational Research Group [British]
AORGB	Allen Organ CI'B' [NASDAQ symbol] (TTSB)
AORI	American Oncology Resources, Inc. [NASDAQ symbol] (SAG)
AORI	Amer Oncology Res [NASDAQ symbol] (TTSB)
AORL	Apollo Orbital Research Laboratory [NASA]
AORN	Association of Operating Room Nurses (EA)
AOR REGURG	Aortic Regurgitation [Medicine] (MEDA)
AORS	Abnormal Occurrence Reporting System (MHDB)
AORS	Advanced Optical Rate Sensor
AORS	Army Operations Research Symposia (RDA)
AORS	Association of Ontario Road Superintendents (AC)
AORT	Association of Operating Room Technicians [Later, AST] (EA)
aort regurg	Aortic Regurgitation [Medicine] (CPH)
AORT STEN	Aortic Stenosis [Medicine] (MEDA)
AOS	Acceptance of Others Scale [Psychology] (EDAC)
AOS	Accessory Optic System [Neuroanatomy]
AOS	Acousto-Optical Spectrograph (ADA)
AOS	Acquisition of Satellite [Telecommunications]
AOS	Acquisition of Signal [Telecommunications]
AOS	Active Optical Sensor (MCD)
AOS	Active Oxygen Species [Biochemistry]
AOS	Activity Operating Schedule
AOS	Add-On Stabilization (MCD)
AOS	Add or Subtract
AOS	Advanced Operating System [Data General Corp.]
AOS	Agency Officers School [Formerly, FOS] [LIMRA]
AOS	Airborne Optical Sensor [Military] (SDI)
AOS	Airborne Optical Surveillance (MCD)
AOS	Airborne Optical System (LAIN)
AOS	Airlift Operations School Library, Scott AFB, IL [OCLC symbol] (OCLC)
AOS	Air Observer School [British]
AOS	Air Oil Separator
AOS	Air Operations Specialist
AOS	Airways Operations Specialist (SAA)
AOS	Algebraic Operating System [Texas Instruments, Inc.] [Computer science]
AOS	All Over Set [Quilting]
AOS	Alotta Resources Ltd. [Vancouver Stock Exchange symbol]
AOS	Alpha-Olefin Sulfonate [Surfactant] [Organic chemistry]
AOS	Alternative Operator Services [Telecommunications]
AOS	American Ophthalmological Society (EA)
AOS	American Orchid Society (EA)
AOS	American Oriental Society (EA)
AOS	American Orthodontic Society (EA)
AOS	American Osler Society (EA)
AOS	American Otological Society (EA)
AOS	Amook [Alaska] [Airport symbol] (OAG)
AOS	Amphibious Objective Study [Navy]
AOS	Amplifier Output Stage
AOS	Analog Output Submodule (SAA)
AOS	Ancient Order of Shepherds
AOS	Angle of Site
AOS	Announcement and Order Sheet (SAA)
AOS	Anodal Opening Sound [Physiology]
AOS	Any One Steamer [Marine insurance] (DS)

AOS	Apostleship of the Sea [*See also AM*] [*Vatican City, Vatican City State*] (EAIO)
AOS	Army Optical Station
AOS	Army Ordnance Stores [*British*]
AOS	Association in Occupational Studies [*Associate degree*] (PAZ)
AOS	Astronomical Observatory Satellite (KSC)
AOS	Atlantic Ocean Ship [*INTELSAT*]
AOS	Audit Operations Staff [*Environmental Protection Agency*] (GFGA)
AOS	Author Organization Source [*Database terminology*] (NITA)
AOS	Automated Office System (HGAA)
AOS	Average Oxidation State [*Physical chemistry*]
AOS	Azimuth Orientation System [*Military*]
AOS	Servicios Aereos del Sol SA de CV [*Mexico ICAO designator*] (FAAC)
AOS	Smith(A.O.) [*NYSE symbol*] (TTSB)
AOS	Smith AO Corp. [*NYSE symbol*] (SAG)
AOS	Special Liquids Tanker [*Navy*] (MCD)
AOSA	Alden Ocean Shell Association (EA)
AOSA	American Optometric Student Association (EA)
AOSA	American Orff-Schulwerk Association (EA)
AOSA	American Oxford Sheep Association (EA)
AOSA	Association of Official Seed Analysts (EA)
AOSAP	Airway Operations Specialist [*Airport*]
AOSB	Acquisition Officer Selection Board [*Army*] (INF)
AOSB	Arctic Ocean Science Board (OSRA)
AOSC	Association of Oilwell Servicing Contractors (EA)
AOSC	Association of Student Councils [*Canada*]
AOSC	Astro Sciences Corp. [*NASDAQ symbol*] (SAG)
AOSCA	Association of Official Seed Certifying Agencies (EA)
AOSD	Adult-Onset Still's Disease [*Medicine*] (DAVI)
AOSD	Aeronautical Operating Systems Division [*NASA*]
AOSE	American Order of Stationary Engineers
AOSEA	American Office Supply Exporters Association [*Defunct*] (EA)
AOSED	Association of Osteopathic State Executive Directors (EA)
AOSG	Airways Operations Specialist (General)
AOSI	Alberta Oil Sands Index [*Alberta Oil Sands Technology and Research Authority*] [*Information service or system*]
AOSIS	Alliance of Small Island States
AOSL	Authorized Organizational Storage List [*Army*]
AOSM	Airline Operations Simulation Model (MCD)
AOSM	Annual Ordinary Shareholders' Meeting [*Investment term*]
AOSML	Army Ordnance Submarine Mine Laboratory (KSC)
AOSO	Advanced Orbiting Solar Observatory [*NASA*]
AOSP	Active Optics Simulation Program [*NASA*] (KSC)
AOSP	Army Occupational Survey Program [*Formerly, MODB*]
AOSP	Atmospheric and Ocean Sciences Program (OSRA)
AOSP	Atmospheric and Ocean Sciences Program (USDC)
AOSP	Automatic Operating and Scheduling Program [*Computer science*]
AOSPS	American Otorhinologic Society for Plastic Surgery [*Later, AAFPRS*] (EA)
AOSPV	Airways Operations Supervisor
AOSQ	Activity Order and Shipping Quantity (AFIT)
AO-SR	Assembly Over-Ships Records
AOSS	Active Optics Simulation System [*NASA*]
AOSS	Airborne Oil Surveillance System
AOSS	Airways Operations Specialist
AOSS	Americanae Orientalis Societatis Socius [*Fellow of the American Oriental Society*]
AOSS	Automated Office Support System [*Department of Energy*]
AO(SS)	Submarine Oiler [*Navy ship symbol*] [*Obsolete*]
AOSSM	American Orthopaedic Society for Sports Medicine (EA)
AOSTRA	Alberta Oil Sands Technology and Research Authority (IID)
AOSUS	Apostleship of the Sea in the United States (EA)
AOS/VS	Advanced Operating System/Virtual Storage [*Data General Corp.*]
AOT	Abbottabad [*Pakistan*] [*Airport symbol*] (AD)
AOT	Acquisition on Target
AOT	Active on Target
AOT	Actual Operating Time (MCD)
AOT	Aerosol Optical Thickness [*Climatology factor*]
AOT	Alignment-Off-Time [*Instrumentation*]
AOT	Alignment Optical Telescope
AOT	Angle-Only Track
AOT	Angle on Target
AOT	Antarctic Observation Team
AOT	Anti-Ovotransferrin [*Biochemistry*]
AOT	Any Old Time [*Journalism*] (WDMC)
AOT	[*The*] Aramaic of the Old Testament [*A publication*] (BJA)
AOT	Army Orientation Training (MCD)
AOT	'Arse over Top [*Head over Heels*] [*Bowdlerized version*] (ADA)
AOT	Ascot Resources Ltd. [*Vancouver Stock Exchange symbol*]
AOT	Askania Optical Tracker
AOT	Assembly Outline Tooling
AOT	Assignment Oriented Training
AOT	Association of Occupational Therapists [*British*] (BI)
AOT	Association of Tutors [*British*]
AOT	Automotive Organization Team (EA)
AOT	Auxiliary Output Tester
AOT	Average Operation Time
AOT	Avionics Operating Time (MCD)
AOT	Avionics Overall Test [*NASA*]
AOT	Deutsche Forschungs-and Versuchsanstalt fur Luft EV [*Germany ICAO designator*] (FAAC)
AOT	Transport Oiler [*Navy*] (MCD)
AOTA	Absorber Open Test Assembly [*Nuclear energy*] (NRCH)
AOTA	All-Optical Towed-Array SONAR [*Navy*] (DOMA)

AOTA	American Occupational Therapy Association (EA)
AOTC	Aviation Officers Training Corps
AOTCB	American Occupational Therapy Certification Board [*AOTA*]
AOTD	Active Optical Target Detector (NVT)
AOTD	Air Organisation and Training Division [*British military*] (DMA)
AOTE	Amphibious Operational Training Element
AOTe	Anodal Opening Tetanus [*Medicine*] (MAE)
AOTE	Associated Organizations for Teacher Education [*Later, AOPE*]
AOTF	Acousto-Optic Tunable Filter [*Instrumentation*]
AOTF	American Occupational Therapy Foundation (MEDA)
AOTFA	American Old Time Fiddlers Association (EA)
AOTH	Active Optical Target Housing (MCD)
AOTI	Advanced Orthopedic Tech [*NASDAQ symbol*] (TTSB)
AOTI	Advanced Orthopedic Techs [*NASDAQ symbol*] (SAG)
AOTM	Association of Occupational Therapists of Manitoba [*Association des Ergotherapeutes du Manitoba*] (AC)
AOTN	ACE Operational Telegraph Network (MCD)
AOTOI	American Organization of Tour Operators to Israel [*Defunct*] (EA)
AOTOP	Advent Orbital Test and Operation Plan (SAA)
AOTOS	Admiral of the Ocean Sea [*Annual award of US Merchant Marine; title originally bestowed on Christopher Columbus by the Spanish government*]
AOTP	Abbreviated Outline Test Plan [*DoD*]
AOTPAC	American Occupational Therapy Political Action Committee [*AOTA*]
AOTS	Acousto-Optic Tunable Scanning [*Instrumentation*]
AOTS	Advanced On-the-Job Training System (MCD)
AOTS	Advanced Orbital Test Satellite [*European Space Agency*]
AOTT	All-Ordnance Thrust Termination (KSC)
AOTT	Automatic Outgoing Trunk Test [*Bell System*]
AOTU	Amphibious Operational Training Unit [*Military*] (DNAB)
AOTV	Aeroassisted Orbital Transfer Vehicle
AOU	Air-Operated Unit
AOU	American Open University [*Computer science*]
AOU	American Ornithologists' Union (EA)
AOU	Apparent Oxygen Utilization
AOU	Area of Uncertainty (CAAL)
AOU	Arithmetic Output Unit
AOU	Associative Output Unit [*Computer science*]
AOU	Automated Offset Unit [*Air Force*]
AOU	Azimuth Orientation Unit [*Military*] (AABC)
AOUF	Area of Uncertainty Factor
AOUSC	Administrative Office of United States Courts
A/OUT	Air Outlet [*Automotive engineering*]
AOUW	Ancient Order United Workmen [*Seattle, WA*] (EA)
AOV	Air-Operated Valve (NRCH)
AOV	Analysis of Variance (OA)
AOV	Any One Vessel [*Marine insurance*] (DS)
AOV	Ava, MO [*Location identifier FAA*] (FAAL)
AOVC	Automatic Overload Circuit (MSA)
AOVDQS	Appellation d'Origine Vin de Qualite Superieure [*Trademark for Vintage Wine of Superior Quality*]
AOVI	Agent Orange Victims International [*Later, VVAOVI*] (EA)
AOW	Army Ordnance Workshop [*British military*] (DMA)
AOW	Articles of War
AOW	Asia-Oceania Workshop [*Computer science*] (TNIG)
Aow	Wartime Operational Availability [*DoD*]
AOWC	Army Ordnance Weapons Command
AOWG	Agent Orange Working Group [*Cabinet Council on Human Resources*]
AOWP	Automated Order Writing Process (MCD)
AOWS	Aircraft Overhaul Work Stoppage (NG)
AOWS	Automated Order Writing System (MCD)
AOWSFM	Association of Optical Workers and Spectacle Frame Makers [*A union*] [*British*]
AOX	Aerotaxi del Valle [*Colombia*] [*ICAO designator*] (FAAC)
aoxp--	Spratley Island [*MARC geographic area code Library of Congress*] (LCCP)
AOYM	Oyen Municipal Library, Alberta [*Library symbol National Library of Canada*] (NLC)
A-P	Abdominal Perineal [*Medicine*] (CPH)
AP	Abingdon Press [*Publisher*]
AP	About Proof (WDAA)
AP	Above Proof
AP	Abrasive Paver (DICI)
AP	Absolute Pardon (ADA)
AP	Absolute Pitch [*Physiology*]
AP	Academic Press, Inc. [*Publishers*]
AP	Accelerometer Package (KSC)
AP	Accessory Pathway [*Medicine*] (DMAA)
AP	Access Panel [*Technical drawings*]
AP	Access Permit [*or Permittee*] [*Nuclear energy*]
AP	Access Point [*Telecommunications*] (TEL)
AP	Accion del Pueblo [*Costa Rica*] [*Political party*] (EY)
AP	Accion Popular [*Popular Action*] [*Peru*] [*Political party*] (PPW)
AP	Accion Popular [*Popular Action*] [*Spain Political party*] (PPE)
AP	Accounting Point (GFGA)
AP	Account Paid
A/P	Account-Purchase (ADA)
AP	Accounts Payable
AP	Acid Phosphatase [*Also, ACP, ACPH*] [*An enzyme*]
AP	Acidproof
AP	Acoustic-Pressure (NVT)
AP	Acquisition Plan
AP	Acquisition Point (MUGU)
AP	Acquisition Policy

AP	Action Potential [of auditory nerve]
AP	Activator Protein
AP	Acute Proliferative [or Proliferation] (MAE)
AP	Adapter Panel
AP	Additional Premium [Insurance]
AP	Add Packed [Computer science]
AP	Adenosis Pattern [Medicine]
AP	Adhesion Proteoglycan [Biochemistry]
AP	Adjective Phrase [Linguistics]
AP	Adjustment and Preventative (MCD)
AP	Administrative Procedure (NRCH)
AP	Administrative Processor (TEL)
AP	Administrative Publication [Navy]
AP	Admiralty Pattern [The right procedure, the correct thing to do] [British]
AP	Adoratrici Perpetuae del Santissimo Sacramento [Nuns of the Perpetual Adoration of the Blessed Sacrament] [Roman Catholic religious order]
AP	Adriamycin Cisplatin [Antineoplastic drug] (CDI)
AP	Advanced Placement [Education]
AP	Advanced Post [Military]
AP	Advanced Pressurized [In name of nuclear reactor, AP 600, developed by Westinghouse Electric Corp.]
AP	Advanced Processor [Honeywell, Inc.] (NITA)
AP	Advanced Procurement (NG)
AP	Advanced Purification [Chromatography]
AP	Advance Pay (MCD)
AP	Advance Purchase Required [Also, AB] [Airline fare code]
AP	Advertising Provider (WDMC)
AP	Advice of Payment
AP	Aerial Port
AP	Aeropelican
AP	Aeroplane Flag [Navy British]
AP	Aerosol Protective (DICI)
AP	Aero Spacelines [ICAO aircraft manufacturer identifier] (ICAO)
AP	After Peak (MSA)
AP	Aft Perpendicular [Naval engineering]
AP	Agency Procedure
AP	Agrarian Party [Albania] [Political party] (EY)
AP	Aiming Point
AP	Airborne Platform (DWSG)
AP	Air Passage (MSA)
AP	Air Patrol (DNAB)
AP	Air Pilot
AP	Airplane
AP	Airplane Pilot
AP	Air Plot (DNAB)
AP	Air Police [By extension, a person who is a member of the Air Police]
AP	Air Pollution (KSC)
AP	Airport
A/P	Airport
AP	Air Position
AP	Air Pressure (MCD)
AP	Air Processing Subsystem (MCD)
AP	Air Publication [Navy]
AP	Airway Pressure [Pulmonary ventilation]
AP	Alianza para el Progreso [Alliance for Progress] [Washington, DC]
AP	Alianza Patriotica [Bolivia] [Political party] (EY)
AP	Alianza Popular [Popular Alliance] [Madrid, Spain] (PPW)
AP	Alignment Periscope
AP	Alignment Procedures
AP	Alkaline Permanganate [Nuclear energy] (NUCP)
AP	Alkaline Phosphatase [Also, ALP] [An enzyme]
AP	Alliance for Progress [OAS]
AP	Alliance Party [Fiji] [Political party] (EY)
A/P	Allied Papers
AP	Allied Publication (RDA)
AP	Allophycocyanin [Also, APC] [Biochemistry]
AP	All-Purpose
AP	Alpha Particle Spectrometer (KSC)
AP	Alphaprodine [Anesthesiology]
AP	Alternative Poland [Defunct] (EA)
AP	Aluminum Perchlorate (MCD)
AP	Alum Precipitated [Medicine]
AP	Ambush Patrol
AP	American Paper Co.
AP	American Pharmacopeia
AP	American Pioneer Lines [Steamship] (MHDW)
AP	American Plan [Hotel room rate]
AP	American Platinum, Inc. [Vancouver Stock Exchange symbol]
AP	American Poetry [A publication]
AP	Aminopeptidase [An enzyme] (MAE)
AP	Aminopurine [Biochemistry]
AP	Aminopyrine [An antipyretic and anesthetic]
AP	Ammonium Perchlorate [Inorganic chemistry]
AP	Ammunition Point
AP	Ampco-Pittsburgh [NYSE symbol] (TTSB)
AP	Ampco-Pittsburgh Corp. [NYSE symbol] (SPSS)
AP	Amphibian Papilla [An auditory organ]
AP	Amusement Parks and Arcades [Public-performance tariff class] [British]
AP	Amyloid Protein [Biochemistry]
AP	Anal Pore
AP	Analytical Psychology
AP	Anaphylactoid Purpura [Medicine]
AP	Anavatan Partisi [Motherland Parties] (EAIO)
AP	Ancient Parish
AP	Ancient Petition
AP	Andhra Pradesh [State in southeast India]
AP	[The] Angel Planes [An association] (EA)
AP	Angina Pectoris [Medicine]
AP	Angle Point
AP	Aniline Point [Measure of solvency]
AP	Annals of Philosophy [A publication] (BARN)
AP	Annealing Point (MCD)
AP	Annie People (EA)
ap	Anni Praesentis [In the Present Year] [Latin]
AP	Annual Plan
AP	Annual Practice [A publication] (DLA)
AP	Anomalous Propagation [Telecommunications Electronics] (TEL)
AP	Answer Print (NTCM)
AP	Antarctica Project (EA)
A/P	Antennas and Propagation (MCD)
AP	Ante Partum [Obstetrics]
AP	Ante Prandium [Before Dinner] [Pharmacy]
AP	Anterior Pituitary [Endocrinology]
AP	Anteroposterior [Projection] [Radiology] (DAVI)
AP	Anther Primordium [Botany]
AP	Antidromic Potential [Medicine] (DMAA)
ap	Antiperiplanar [Chemistry]
AP	Antipersonnel [Projectile]
AP	Antiplasmin [Hematology]
AP	Antipyrine [Analgesic] (AAMN)
AP	Aortic Plexus [Anatomy]
AP	Aortic Pressure [Medicine]
AP	Aortopulmonary [Cardiology]
ap	Apatite [CIPW classification] [Geology]
AP	Aperture
Ap	Apex [Medicine] (DMAA)
AP	Apical Meristem [Botany]
AP	Apical Pulse [Medicine]
Ap	Apocalypse (BJA)
AP	Apollo Program [NASA]
Ap	Apologia [of Plato] [Classical studies] (OCD)
Ap	Apologia Socratis [of Xenophon] [Classical studies] (OCD)
AP	Apostle
ap	Apostle (VRA)
AP	Apostleship of Prayer (EA)
Ap	Apostolic (BJA)
AP	Apothecary (WGA)
AP	Apparent (ADA)
AP	Appearance Potential [Physics]
AP	Appendectomy [Medicine]
AP	Appendicitis [Medicine] (DAVI)
AP	Appendix [Anatomy] (DAVI)
ap	Apple [Philately]
AP	Application Process [Telecommunications] (OSI)
AP	Application Program [Computer science] (BUR)
AP	Applications Processor (IEEE)
AP	Applied Physics (IEEE)
AP	Apply Pressure [Industrial engineering]
AP	Apprenticeship Program (DD)
AP	Approach [Database terminology] (NITA)
AP	Approaches (NATG)
AP	Approach Lights [Aviation] (AIA)
AP	April
AP	A Protester [To Be Protested] [French Business term]
AP	Apud [At, In the Works Of, According To] [Latin]
AP	Aquagenic Pruritus [Medicine]
AP	Aquatic Plant
AP	Aramaic Papyri Discovered at Assuan [A publication] (BJA)
AP	[The] Archaeology of Palestine [A publication] (BJA)
AP	Archaeus Project (EA)
AP	Architectural Psychology Newsletter [British]
AP	Area Planning
AP	Argument Programming (MSA)
AP	Argyre Plamitia [A filamentary mark on Mars]
AP	Arithmetic Processor
AP	Arithmetic Progression
AP	Arithmetic Project [National Science Foundation]
AP	Armageddon Project [Later, AAAP] (EA)
AP	Armed Forces Pacific
AP	Armor-Piercing [Ammunition]
AP	Army Pensions
AP	Array Processor [Computer science] (BUR)
AP	Arterial Presssure [Medicine] (DHSM)
AP	Artificial Personality
AP	Artificial Pneumothorax [Medicine]
AP	Artificial Pupil (SAA)
AP	Artist's Proof
AP	Ascent Phase
A/P	Ascites-Plasma Ratio [Medicine] (MAE)
AP	Ashpit [British] (ROG)
AP	Asking Price
AP	Aspen Airways [ICAO designator] (AD)
AP	As Prescribed (AFM)
AP	As Purchased
AP	Assembly of Parties [INTELSAT]
AP	Assessment and Plans [Medicine]
AP	Assessment Paid [Billing]

AP	Asset Position
AP	Assignment of (Construction) Permit [FCC] (NTCM)
AP	Assistance Payments [Social Security Administration]
AP	Assistant Paymaster
AP	Associated Parishes (EA)
AP	Associated Period [Medicine] (DAVI)
AP	Associated Person [Stock exchange term]
AP	Associated Presbyterian [British] (ROG)
AP	Associated Press [News agency and wire service] (EA)
AP	Associated Publishers (EA)
AP	Associate Presbyterian (IIA)
AP	Associate Producer
AP	Association for Psychotheatrics [Defunct] (EA)
AP	Association Period (MAE)
AP	Associative Processor [Computer science] (BUR)
AP	Assumed Position [Navigation]
AP	Assurance Problem
AP	Atmospheric and [Space] Physics
AP	Atmospheric Pressure
AP	Atomic Powered
AP	Atriopeptin [Biochemistry]
AP	Atrium Pace [Cardiology]
AP	Attached Processor [Computer science] (BUR)
AP	Attachment Plaque
ap	Attachment Point [Genetics] (DOG)
AP	Attack Plan (MCD)
AP	Attack Plotter (NVT)
AP	Attitude and Pointing (MCD)
AP	Attitude Processor (NASA)
AP	Audemars Piguet [Trademark for line of watches] (ECON)
A/P	Authority to Pay [or Purchase]
AP	Author's Proof [Publishing]
ap	Author's Proof [Publishing] (WDMC)
A/P	Automatic Pilot (MCD)
AP	Automatic Programming [Computer science]
AP	Automotive Products [Commercial firm British]
AP	Auto Part (NRCH)
A/P	Autopilot (GAVI)
AP	Auxiliary Patrol [British military] (DMA)
AP	Auxiliary Police (LAIN)
AP	Auxiliary Power (CAAL)
AP	Auxiliary Printer (ECII)
AP	Average Price
AP	Average Product [Economics]
AP	Aviapolk [Russian term for an air regiment]
AP	Aviation Pilot [Navy]
AP	Awaiting Parts
AP	Award Processing [Social Security Administration] (OICC)
AP	Axiopulpal [Dentistry]
AP	Ciba-Geigy [France] [Research code symbol]
Ap	Contra Apionem [Against Apion] [Josephus] (BJA)
Ap	Hymnus in Apollinem [of Callimachus] [Classical studies] (OCD)
Ap	New York Supreme Court, Appellate Division Reports [A publication] (DLA)
AP	Nuns of Perpetual Adoration of Blessed Sacrament (TOCD)
AP	Penhold Public Library, Alberta [Library symbol National Library of Canada] (NLC)
ap----	Persian Gulf [MARC geographic area code Library of Congress] (LCCP)
AP	Transport [Navy ship symbol]
AP0	Autopilot Zero
Ap 2d	New York Appellate Division Reports, Second Series [A publication] (DLA)
APA	Abort Programmer Assembly [NASA] (KSC)
APA	Accreditation of Prior Achievement [Education] (AIE)
APA	Acetone Producers Association [Belgium] (EAIO)
APA	Acquired Pattern Addiction [Telecommunications] (PCM)
APA	Acrylamide Producers Association (EA)
APA	Action Potential Amplitude [Physiology]
APA	Additional Personal Allowance (DLA)
APA	Administrative Procedures Act [1946]
APA	Advanced Programs Authorization
APA	Advance of Pay and Allowances (AABC)
APA	Advertising Photographers of America (EA)
APA	Aerovias Panama Airways
APA	Agricultural Pilots Association [Defunct] (EA)
APA	Agricultural Publishers Association (EA)
APA	Airborne Power Adapter
APA	Aircraft Plume Analysis
APA	Aircraft Procurement, Army (AABC)
APA	Air Park Aviation Ltd. [Canada ICAO designator] (FAAC)
APA	Air Pathway Analyses [Environmental chemistry]
APA	Air Patrol Area (NVT)
APA	Air Products & Chemicals, Inc., Allentown, PA [OCLC symbol] (OCLC)
APA	Alabama Pawnbrokers Association (SRA)
APA	Alabama Pharmacy Association (SRA)
APA	Alabama Press Association (SRA)
APA	Alan Pascoe Associates [British]
APA	Alaska Power Administration [Department of Energy]
APA	Albanian People's Army
APA	Alberta Psychiatric Association (AC)
APA	Aldosterone-Producing Adenoma [Clinical chemistry]
APA	Alkaline Phosphatase Activity [Marine science] (OSRA)
APA	Alkaline Phosphatase Activity (USDC)

APA	Alliance of Poles of America (EA)
APA	Allied Pilots Association (EA)
APA	Allowance for Project Adjustment
APA	All Party Alliance [British]
APA	All Points Addressable [Computer science]
APA	Amalgamated Printers' Association (EA)
APA	Amapa [Brazil] [Airport symbol] (AD)
APA	Amateur Press Alliance [Defunct] (EA)
APA	Amateur Press Association [Generic term]
APA	Amateur Printers' Association (DGA)
APA	Amateur Publishers' Association
APA	Ambulatory Pediatric Association (EA)
APA	American Pancreatic Association (EA)
APA	American Paralysis Association (EA)
APA	American Parquet Association [Defunct] (EA)
APA	American Patients Association (EA)
APA	American Pawnbrokers Association (EA)
APA	American Pax Association [Later, PC-USA] (EA)
APA	American Payroll Association (EA)
APA	American Pedestrian Association (EA)
APA	American Petanque Association USA (EA)
APA	American Pharmaceutical Association
APA	American Philological Association (EA)
APA	American Philosophical Association (EA)
APA	American Photoplatemakers Association [Later, IAP]
APA	American Physiotherapy Association [Later, APTA]
APA	American Piedmontese Association (EA)
APA	American Pilots' Association (EA)
APA	American Pinzgauer Association (EA)
APA	American Planning Association (EAIO)
APA	American Plywood Association (EA)
APA	American Podiatry Association [Later, APMA]
APA	American Poetry [A publication]
APA	American Poetry Association (EA)
APA	American Police Academy (EA)
APA	American Polygraph Association (EA)
APA	American Poolplayers Association (EA)
APA	American Poultry Association (EA)
APA	American Produce Association (EA)
APA	American Protective Association [Late-19th-century organization opposed to so-called encroachments of the Catholic Church in the US]
APA	American Protestant Association
APA	American Psychiatric Association (EA)
APA	American Psychoanalytic Association (EA)
APA	American Psychological Association (EA)
APA	[Division of Child and Youth Services] American Psychological Association (PAZ)
APA	American Psychopathological Association
APA	American Psychotherapy Association [Inactive] (EA)
APA	American Puffer Alliance [An association] (EA)
APA	American Pulpwood Association (EA)
APA	American Pyrotechnics Association (EA)
APA	Americans for Peace in the Americas (EA)
APA	Aminopenicillanic Acid [Biochemistry]
APA	Aminophenylacetylene [Organic chemistry]
APA	Amorphous Polyamide [Organic chemistry]
APA	Animal Protective Association (EA)
APA	Animal Transport [Navy ship symbol] [Obsolete]
APA	Animation Producers' Association [Defunct] (EA)
APA	Annual Print Awards (DGA)
APA	Annual Procurement Agreement (MCD)
APA	Antenna Pattern Analyzer
APA	Antiparietal Antibody
APA	Antipernicious Anemia Factor [Also, APAF, EF, LLD] [Hematology] (AAMN)
apa	Apache [MARC language code Library of Congress] (LCCP)
APA	Apache Corp. [NYSE symbol] (SPSG)
APA	[The] Apache Railway Co. [AAR code]
APA	Apachito [Race of maize]
APA	APA Optics, Inc. [Associated Press] (SAG)
APA	Apatity [Former USSR Seismograph station code, US Geological Survey] (SEIS)
APA	Apple Processors Association (EA)
APA	Appropriation Purchases Account
APA	Archconfraternity of Perpetual Adoration [Defunct] (EA)
APA	Architectural Photographers Association [Defunct] (EA)
APA	Architectural Precast Association (EA)
APA	Arizona Pharmacy Association (SRA)
APA	Arizona Planning Association (SRA)
APA	Arkansas Pharmacists Association (SRA)
APA	Arkansas Press Association (SRA)
APA	Army Parachute Association [British military] (DMA)
APA	Army Procurement Appropriation
APA	Ashton-Potter America [Printer of U.S. postage stamps] (BARN)
APA	Asian/Pacific American
APA	Assistance Payments Administration [Later, Office of Family Assistance] [Social Security Administration]
APA	Associate in Practical Arts
APA	Associate in Public Administration
APA	Associate Member of Institute of Accredited Public Accountants
APA	Association du Patrimoine d'Aylmer (AC)
APA	Association for Parents of Addicts [British] (BI)
APA	Association for People with Arthritis [Defunct] (EA)
APA	Association for the Protection of the Adirondacks (EA)

APA	Association of Paediatric Anaesthetists of Great Britain and Ireland [*Birmingham, England*] (EAIO)
APA	Association of Paroling Authorities International (EA)
APA	Association of Port Authorities
APA	Association of Practicing Accountants
APA	Association of Practising Accountants [*British*] (DBA)
APA	Association of Producing Artists
APA	Association of Public Analysts [*British*]
APA	Association pour la Protection des Automobilistes [*Canada*]
APA	Associative Principle for Addition [*Mathematics*]
APA	Atlantic Pilotage Authority
APA	Atlantic Publishers Association (AC)
APA	Attack Transport [*Later, LPA*] [*Navy symbol*]
APA	Audio Publishers Association [*Defunct*] (EA)
APA	Augmented Predictive Analyzer [*Computer science*] (DIT)
APA	Australian Perendale Association
APA	Australian Podiatry Association
APA	Australian Population Association
APA	Austria Presse Agentur [*Press agency*] [*Austria*]
APA	Automatic Photographic Analysis
APA	Automatic Pulse-Analyzer (DNAB)
APA	Automobile Protection Association [*Canada*]
APA	Automotive Press Association
APA	Auxiliary Personnel, Attack [*Navy designation for combat landing craft*] [*World War II*]
APA	Available Phosphoric Acid
APA	Aviation Procurement Authorization [*Army*]
APA	Axial Pressure Angle [*Gears*]
APA	Denver, CO [*Location identifier FAA*] (FAAL)
APA	International Airline Passengers Association
APA	Member of the Institute of Accredited Public Accountants [*Canada*] (DD)
APAA	Adelaide [*Australia ICAO location identifier*] (ICLI)
APAA	American Physicians Art Association (EA)
APAA	American Podiatry Association Auxiliary [*Later, APMAA*] (EA)
APAA	Art Patrons Association of America (EA)
APAA	ASEAN [*Association of South East Asian Nations*] Port Authorities Association (DS)
APAA	Asian Patent Attorneys Association (EA)
APAA	Automotive Parts and Accessories Association (EA)
APAAE	Asia-Pacific Association for Agricultural Education
APAAP	Alkaline Phosphatase:Antialkaline Phosphatase [*Immunochemistry*]
APAAP	Association de la Presse Anglo-Americaine de Paris [*Anglo-American Press Association of Paris*] (EAIO)
APAB	Antiphospholipid Antibody [*Medicine*] (DMAA)
APABA	Australian Pig Artificial Breeding Association
APABC	Adlerian Psychological Association of British Columbia (AC)
APAC	Administrator's Pesticide Advisory Committee [*Terminated, 1985*] [*Environmental Protection Agency*]
APAC	Aerial Photographic Analysis Center
APAC	Airborne Parabolic Arc Computer
APAC	Alkaline Permanganate Ammonium Citrate (OA)
APAC	American Puppet Arts Council [*Defunct*]
APAC	Antenna Pointing Angle Change
APAC	APAC TeleServices [*NASDAQ symbol*] (TTSB)
APAC	APAC TeleServices, Inc. [*NASDAQ symbol*] (SAG)
APAC	Appointment and Promotion Advisory Committee [*UN Food and Agriculture Organization*]
APAC	Area Planning-Action Councils
APAC	Asphalt-Plastic-Asphalt-Chip (PDAA)
APAC	Association of Patternmakers and Allied Craftsmen [*A union*] [*British*] (DCTA)
APAC	Australian Pesticides Analytical Committee
APAC	Automotive Parts Association of the Carolinas (SRA)
APAC	Auto Parts Advisory Committee [*US Committee designed to combat the trade deficit with Japan*] (ECON)
APACA	Australian Preservation and Conservation Abroad Group
APacBk	American Pacific Bank [*Associated Press*] (SAG)
APACE	Aldermaston Project for the Application of Computers to Engineering [*United Kingdom Atomic Energy Authority*] (NITA)
APACE	Asian Pacific Alliance for Creative Equality
APACHE	Accelerated Project to Automate Critical Hardware Hardcore Systems
APACHE	Accelerator for Physics and Chemistry of Heavy Metals
APACHE	Active Thermal Protection for Avionics Crew and Heat-Sensitive Equipment [*Air Force*] (MCD)
APACHE	Acute Physiology and Chronic Health Evaluation
APACHE	Analog Programming and Checking [*Computer science*]
APACHE	Analog Programming and Checking [*Computer science*]
APACHE	Analysis of Pacific Area Communications for Hardening to Electromagnetic Pulse
Apache	Apache Corp. [*Associated Press*] (SAG)
APACHE	Application Package for Chemical Engineers
APACHE	Aviation Performance Assessment in a Chemical Environment (PDAA)
APACHES	Automated Personnel Accounting, Cost, Historical Estimating System [*Army*]
APACI	Association for the Promotion of African Community Initiatives (EAIO)
APACL	Asian Peoples' Anti-Communist League
APACM	American Physicians Association of Computer Medicine (EA)
APACM	Atmospheric Physical and Chemical Monitor
APacMin	American Pacific Minerals Ltd. [*Associated Press*] (SAG)
APACS	Adaptive Planning and Control Sequence [*Marketing*]
APACS	Airborne Position and Altitude Camera System (OA)
APACS	Association of Payment Clearing Services [*British*] (DBA)
APACT	APAC TeleServices, Inc. [*Associated Press*] (SAG)

APACVS	Association of Physician's Assistants in Cardio-Vascular Surgery (EA)
APAD	Acetylpyridineadenine Dinucleotide [*Biochemistry*]
APAD	Adelaide [*Australia ICAO location identifier*] (ICLI)
APADAS	Automatic Phase and Amplitude Data System (MCD)
APADE	Automation of Procurement and Accounting Data Entry [*Navy*] (GFGA)
APadP	American Pad & Paper [*Associated Press*] (SAG)
APADS	Air-conditioning Protection and Diagnostic System [*Automotive electronics*]
APADS	Automatic Programmer and Data System [*Air Force*]
APAE	Association of Public Address Engineers [*British*] (BI)
APAE	Attached Payload Accommodations Equipment (SSD)
APAETP	(Aminopropylamino)ethylthiophosphate [*Biochemistry*]
APAF	Antipernicious Anemia Factor [*Also, APA, EF, LLD*] [*Hematology*]
APAG	American Photographic Artisans Guild (EA)
APAG	Apco Argentina [*NASDAQ symbol*] (SAG)
APAG	Association Europeenne des Producteurs d'Acides Gras [*European Association of Fatty Acid Producing Companies*] (EAIO)
APAG	Atlantic Political Advisory Group [*NATO*]
APAGA	Atlantic Provinces Art Gallery Association [*Canada*]
APAGF	Apco Argentina [*NASDAQ symbol*] (TTSB)
APAH	Amino Polycyclic Aromatic Hydrocarbon [*Environmental chemistry*]
AP/AHC	Accreditation Program / Ambulatory Health Care (MEDA)
APAHC	Asian Pacific American Heritage Council (EA)
APAI	Advanced Planning Acquisition Information (AAGC)
APAI	Asphalt Pavement Association of Indiana (SRA)
APAI	Asphalt Paving Association of Iowa (SRA)
APAIF	Association de Prevention des Accidents dans l'Industrie Forestiere [*Forest Products Accident Prevention Association*] [*Canada*]
APAJ	Asia Pacific Association of Japan
A-PAL	Activists for Protective Animal Legislation (EA)
APAL	Albany [*Australia ICAO location identifier*] (ICLI)
APAL	American Puerto-Rican Action League
APAL	Array Processor Assembly Language [*Computer science*]
APALA	Asian/Pacific American Librarians Association (EA)
APALA	Atlantic Provinces Association of Landscape Architects (AC)
APalmer	Arnold Palmer Golf Co. (The) [*Associated Press*] (SAG)
APALMER	Atlantic Provinces Association of Learning Materials and Education Representatives [*Canada*]
APALS	Autonomous Precision Approach and Landing System [*Lockheed-Martin's radical landing-guidance system*]
APAM	Alternating Pressure Air Mattress [*for prevention of pressure sores*]
APAM	Antipersonnel Antimaterial [*Weaponry*] (MCD)
APAM	Array Processor Access Method [*Computer science*] (BUR)
APAM	Association for the Preservation of the Auction Market [*Defunct*] (EA)
APAMS	Automated Pilot Aptitude Measurement System (MCD)
APAN	Alberta Pesticide Action Network (AC)
APANA	Airline Passengers Association of North America (EA)
APANA	Asian and Pacific Americans for Nuclear Awareness (EA)
AP/A/N/AF	Aircraft Procurement (Appropriations), Army/Navy/Air Force (AAGC)
AP & AE	Attached Payload and Associated Equipment (SSD)
AP & D	Advanced Planning and Design [*NASA*] (KSC)
AP&EA	Alabama Poultry and Egg Association (SRA)
AP & L	Anteroposterior and Lateral [*X-ray views*] (AAMN)
A-P & Lat	Anterior-Posterior and Lateral [*Chest x-ray*] (CPH)
AP & Lat	Anteroposterior and Lateral [*X-ray views*] (AAMN)
AP & PO	Advance Programming and Proposal Operations (MCD)
AP & SC	Army Port and Service Command
AP & WS	American Pheasant and Waterfowl Society (EA)
APANY	Association of Personnel Agencies of New York
APAO	Aggregate Producers Association of Ontario (AC)
APAO	Amorphous Polyalphaolefin [*Plastics technology*]
APAO	Asia-Pacific Academy of Ophthalmology [*Tokyo, Japan*] (EAIO)
APAP	Acetaminophen [*Medicine*] (DMAA)
APAP	Acetyl-para-aminophenol [*Pharmacology*]
APAP	American People for American Prisoners (EA)
APAP	Apollo Propulsion Analysis Program [*NASA*]
APAP	Approach Path Alignment Panel [*Aviation*] (FAAC)
APAP	Army Pollution Abatement Program (MCD)
APAP	Association of Performing Arts Presenters (EA)
APAP	Association of Physician Assistant Programs (EA)
APAPA	Association for the Preservation of Anti-Psychiatric Artifacts [*Defunct*] (EA)
APAPI	Abbreviated Precision Approach Path Indicator [*Aviation*] (DA)
APAPI	Association Professionnelle des Aides Pedagogiques Individuels [*Professional Association of Individual Educational Assistants*] [*Canada*]
APAQ	Association des Proprietaires d'Autobus du Quebec (AC)
APAR	Adaptive Phase Array RADAR
APAR	Adelaide [*Australia ICAO location identifier*] (ICLI)
APAR	Apparatus (MUGU)
APAR	Authorized Program Analysis Report [*Computer science*] (IBMDP)
APAR	Automatic Processing and Recording (NITA)
APAR	Automatic Program Analysis Report [*Computer science*] (BUR)
APAR	Automatic Programming and Recording [*Computer science*]
APARE	East Asian-North Pacific Regional Experiment (USDC)
APARS	Army Procurement Appropriation Reporting System
APART	Adelphi Parent Administered Readiness Test [*Educational development test*]
APART	Alliance of Pan American Round Tables
A-PART	Alpha Particle (ADA)
APART	Apartment [*Classified advertising*] (ADA)
APAS	Academy of Psychic Arts and Sciences (EA)

APAS	Adaptable-Programmable Assembly System [*Computer science*] (PDAA)
APAS	Advanced Passive Array Sonobuoy [*Navy*] (CAAL)
APAS	Alternative Performance Appraisal System (DOMA)
APAS	Annular Phased-Array System [*Cardiology*] (DAVI)
APAS	Association of Personal Assistants and Secretaries [*Leamington Spa, Warwickshire, England*] [*Defunct*] (EAIO)
APAS	Association of Public Authority Surveyors [*Australia*]
APAS	Automated Program for Aerospace-Vehicle Synthesis
APAS	Automated Programmable Assembly System [*Computer science*]
APAS	Automatic Performance Analysis System
APASE	Association for the Promotion & Advancement of Science Education (AC)
APASTO	ADCC [*Air Defense Command Computer*] Programming and System Training Office (SAA)
APAT	APA Optics [*NASDAQ symbol*] (TTSB)
APAT	APA Optics, Inc. [*Blaine, MN*] [*NASDAQ symbol*] (NQ)
APAT	Atmospheric Pressure and Ambient Temperature
APAT	Australasian Porcelain Art Teachers [*An association*]
APAT	Auxiliary Propelled Anti-Tank [*Military*] (PDAA)
APATS	Acquisition Planning and Tracking System
APATS	Antenna Pattern Test System [*Army*] (AABC)
APATS	ARIA [*Advanced Range Instrumentation Aircraft*] Phased Array Telemetry System [*Air Force*]
APATS	Automatic Programmer and Test System [*Army*]
APAUC	Association des Professeurs d'Allemand des Universites Canadiennes [*Canadian Association of University Teachers of German - CAUTG*]
APAUC	Association des Professeurs d'Anglais des Universites Canadiennes [*Association of Canadian University Teachers of English - ACUTE*]
APAVIT	Asociacion Panamena de Agencias de Viajes y Turismo (EY)
APAW	Asphalt Paving Association of Washington (SRA)
APAW	Association of Philippine-American Women (EA)
APAX	Adelaide [*Australia ICAO location identifier*] (ICLI)
APAZINE	Amateur Publishers' Association Magazine [*Generic term for one-person science-fiction fan magazine*]
APB	Abductor Pollicis Brevis [*Muscle*] [*Anatomy*] (DAVI)
APB	Aboriginal Protection Board [*Australia*]
APB	Accounting Principles Board [*Later, Financial Accounting Standards Board*] [*American Institute of Certified Public Accountants*]
APB	Acquisition Program Baseline (DOMA)
APB	Acute Pernicious Beriberi [*Medicine*] (PDAA)
AP/B	Additional Pension/Benefit
APB	Adorers of the Precious Blood (TOCD)
APB	Advanced Planning Briefing [*Program*] [*DoD*] (RDA)
APB	Aim Point Bias [*Military*]
APB	Air Atlantique Air Publicite [*France ICAO designator*] (FAAC)
APB	Air Portable Bridge (PDAA)
APB	Allied Publications Board [*World War II*]
APB	All Points Bulletin [*Police call*]
APB	All Points Bulletin [*Law enforcement*] (WDMC)
APB	Amalgamate Paper Books [*British*]
APB	American Pacific Bank [*Vancouver Stock Exchange symbol*]
APB	American Part-Blooded Horse Registry (EA)
APB	American Program Bureau [*Lectures*]
APB	Aminophosphonobutyric Acid [*Organic chemistry*]
APB	Anoxygenic Phototrophic Bacteria
APB	Antipersonnel Bomb
APB	Antiphase Boundaries [*Mineralogy*]
APB	Apollo Problem Bulletin [*NASA*]
APB	Applied Physics Branch [*Air Proving Ground Center*]
APB	[*The*] Archaeology of Palestine and the Bible [*A publication*] (BJA)
APB	Army Packaging Board (AABC)
APB	Arterial Premature Beat [*Cardiology*]
APB	Artillery Barge [*Navy symbol Obsolete*]
APB	Ashurst's Paper Books, Lincoln's Inn Library [*A publication*] (DLA)
APB	Asia Pacific Fund [*NYSE symbol*] (SPSG)
APB	Associated Press Broadcasters (EA)
APB	Association for Public Broadcasting (EA)
APB	Atrial [*or Auricular*] Premature Beat [*Cardiology*] (DAVI)
APB	Atrial Premature Beats [*Cardiology*]
APB	Auditing Practices Board [*British*] (ECON)
APB	Auricular Premature Beat [*Medicine*] (MAE)
APB	Australian Publishers' Bureau
APB	Auxiliary Barracks Ship (Self-Propelled) (DNAB)
APB	Picture Butte Public Library, Alberta [*Library symbol National Library of Canada*] (NLC)
APB	Religiosae Adoratrices Pretiosissimo Sanguinis [*Sisters Adorers of the Precious Blood*] [*Roman Catholic religious order*]
APB	Self-Propelled Barracks Ship [*Navy symbol*]
APB	United States Army FORSCOM, Fort Bragg Command Reference Center and Main Post, Fort Bragg, NC [*OCLC symbol*] (OCLC)
APBA	Aboriginal People's Business Association (AC)
APBA	American Pet Boarding Association (EA)
APBA	American Power Boat Association (EA)
APBA	American Professional Basketball Association [*Game*] [*Pronounced "ap-bah"*]
APBA	Amino(phenyl)butanoic Acid [*Organic chemistry*]
APBA	Asia Pacific Business Association
APBA	Associated Press Broadcasters Association [*Later, APB*] (EA)
APBA	Atlantic Professional Boatman's Association [*Defunct*] (EA)
APBA	Australian Pig Breeders' Association
APBC	Association of Professional Boardsailing Centres [*British*] (DBA)
APBE	Anti-Phase Boundary Energy (PDAA)

APBE	Association for Professional Broadcasting Education [*Later, Broadcast EducationAssociation*] (EA)
APBH	After Peak Bulkhead [*Shipping*] (DS)
APBH	Broken Hill [*Australia ICAO location identifier*] (ICLI)
APBI	Advanced Planning Briefs [*or Briefings*] for Industry (MCD)
APBI	Applied Bioscience [*NASDAQ symbol*] (TTSB)
APBI	Applied Bioscience International, Inc. [*NASDAQ symbol*] (NQ)
APBIC	Action for Prevention of Burn Injuries to Children [*Later, AAB*] (EA)
ApBiomet	Applied Biometrics, Inc. [*Associated Press*] (SAG)
Ap Bon	Apud Bonifacium [*Latin*] (DSA)
APB Op	Accounting Principles Board Opinions [*A publication*] (DLA)
APBP	Association of Professional Baseball Physicians (EA)
APBP	Association of Professional Bridge Players (EA)
APBPA	Association of Professional Ball Players of America (EA)
APBPA	Australian PaintBall Players' Association
APBR	Broome [*Australia ICAO location identifier*] (ICLI)
Ap Bre	Appendix to Breese's Reports [*Illinois*] [*A publication*] (DLA)
APBS	Advanced Post Boost System [*Military*]
APBS	Australian Pig Breeders' Society
APBS	Automated PEMA [*Procurement of Equipment and Munition Appropriations*] Bud get System [*Military*] (AABC)
APBSNY	Association of Public Broadcasting Stations of New York (SRA)
APBT	Aminopyrine Breath Test [*Clinical chemistry*]
APBV	Advanced Post Boost Vehicle (MCD)
APC	Abacus Programming Corp.
APC	Abbreviated Performance Characteristics [*Army*]
APC	Abingdon Pottery Club (EA)
APC	Absolute Pressure Control
APC	Academic Potential Coding [*Military*] (DNAB)
APC	Academic Profile Code [*Military*] (DNAB)
APC	Academy of Parish Clergy (EA)
APC	Accelerated Pacification Campaign [*South Vietnam*]
APC	Accelerometer Pulse Converter
APC	Accounting Processing Code (AABC)
APC	Acetylsalicylic Acid [*Aspirin*], Phenacetin, and Caffeine Compound [*Slang translation is, "All Purpose Capsules"*] [*Pharmacy*]
APC	Acoustical Phase Constant
APC	Acoustical Plaster Ceiling [*Technical drawings*]
APC	Acoustical Propagation Constant
APC	Activated Protein C
APC	Activity Processing Code
APC	Acute Pharyngoconjunctival Fever [*Medicine*] (MEDA)
APC	Adaptive Predictive Coding [*Telecommunications*] (TEL)
APC	Additional Planning Capability (SAA)
APC	Address Plate Cabinet
APC	Adelaide Potters' Club [*Australia*]
APC	Adenoidal-Pharyngeal-Conjunctival [*Virus*] [*Obsolete usage*]
APC	Adenomatous Polyposis Coli [*Genetics*]
APC	Adjustable Pressure Conveyor
APC	Advanced Performance Computer
APC	Advanced Personal Computer (NITA)
APC	Advanced Piston Coring [*Drilling technology*]
APC	Advanced Polymer Composite [*Materials science*]
APC	Advanced Procurement Change [*or Check*] (MCD)
APC	Advanced Professional Certificate (PGP)
APC	Advanced Professional Computer (HGAA)
APC	Advanced Programming Course [*Computer science*]
APC	Advanced Propulsion Comparison Study [*NASA*] (NASA)
APC	Advanced Propulsion Cooling
APC	Advanced Protocol Controller [*Adax, Inc.*]
APC	Advertising-Press Club [*Republic of Ireland*] (BI)
APC	Advertising Production Club of New York (EA)
APC	Aerobic Plate Count [*Microbiology*]
APC	Aeronautical Passenger Communication [*A class of communication which supports passenger communication*] (GAVI)
APC	Aeronautical Planning Chart [*Military*]
APC	Aeronautical Public Correspondence (DA)
APC	Aerospace Primus Club
APC	African Peanut (Groundnut) Council
APC	Aft Power Controller (MCD)
APC	Aimpoint Correlator [*Weaponry*] (MCD)
APC	Airpac Airlines, Inc. [*ICAO designator*] (FAAC)
APC	Air Pollution Control
APC	Air Project Coordinator [*Military*] (DNAB)
APC	Alabama Petroleum Council (SRA)
APC	Alcohol Policy Council (EA)
APC	Alianza Popular Conservadora [*Nicaragua*] [*Political party*] (EY)
APC	Alien Property Custodian [*World War II*]
APC	Alliance des Pays Producteurs de Cacao [*Cocoa Producers' Alliance*] [*Use COPAL*] (AF)
APC	Alliance for Philippine Concerns (EA)
APC	Alliance Property and Construction [*Commercial firm British*]
APC	Allied Purchasing Co. (EA)
APC	Allophycocyanin [*Also, AP*] [*Biochemistry*]
APC	All-People's Congress [*Sierra Leone*] [*Political party*] (PPW)
APC	All-Peoples Congress [*An association*] (EA)
APC	All Purpose Carrier (SSD)
APC	Alternative Press Center (EA)
APC	AMARC [*Automatic Message Accounting Recording Center*] Protocol Converter (TEL)
APC	AMCEL Propulsion Co. [*Later, Northrup Caroline Co.*] (KSC)
APC	American Palestine Committee [*Defunct*] (EA)
APC	American Parents Committee (EA)
APC	American Philatelic Congress (EA)
APC	American Pointer Club (EA)

APC	American Pomeranian Club (EA)
APC	American Power Committee [*Defunct*] (EA)
APC	American Power Conversion Co. (PCM)
APC	American President Companies Ltd.
APC	American Productivity Center [*Houston, TX*] (EA)
APC	Ammonium Perchlorate [*Inorganic chemistry*]
APC	Amplitude Phase Conversion [*Telecommunications*] (OA)
APC	AMSA, [*Acridinylamine Methanesulphon-M-Aniside*] Prednisone, and Chlorambucil [*Antineoplastic drug regimen*]
APC	Amyloid Pack Core [*Pathology*]
APC	Anadarko Petroleum [*NYSE symbol*] (SPSG)
APC	Analog to Pressure Converter
APC	Analytic Plotter Coordinagraph [*Geoscience*]
APC	Anaphase-Promoting Complex [*Cytology*]
ApC	Andronicus Publishing Co., Inc., New York, NY [*Library symbol Library of Congress*] (LCLS)
APC	Angular Position Counter (SAA)
APC	Anno post Christum Natum [*In the Year after Christ Was Born*] [*Latin*] (ROG)
APC	Annotated Predicate Calculus (MCD)
APC	Annular Primary Combustor
APC	Antenna Pattern Correction [*for spacecraft data*]
APC	Antigen-Presenting Cell [*Immunology*]
APC	Antiphlogistic-Corticoid [*Medicine*] (MAE)
APC	Aperture Current [*Medicine*] (DMAA)
APC	Apneustic Center [*Brain anatomy*]
APC	Appalachian Power Co.
APC	Applied Psychology Corp. (KSC)
APC	Applied to Previous Charge [*Business term*]
Apc	Appreciate
apc	Appreciate [*Wire service abbreviation*] (WDMC)
APC	Appreciate [*Wire service abbreviation*] (WDMC)
APC	Approach Control [*Aviation*]
APC	Approach Positive Control
APC	Approach Power Compensator [*NASA*]
APCAC	Apricot Producers of California (EA)
APC	Archives Publiques du Canada [*Public Archives of Canada - PAC*]
APC	Area of Positive Control [*FAA*]
APC	Area Planning Council [*Department of Education*] (OICC)
APC	Argon Purge Cart [*Nuclear energy*] (NRCH)
APC	Arizona Pork Council (SRA)
APC	Arkansas Petroleum Council (SRA)
APC	Arkansas Polytechnic College [*Later, Arkansas Technical University*]
APC	Armament Practice Camp [*British military*] (DMA)
APC	Armored Personnel Carrier [*Military*]
APC	Armor-Piercing Capped [*Ammunition*]
APC	Army Aspirin (VNW)
APC	Army Pay Corps [*Later, RAPC*] [*British*]
APC	Army Petroleum Center
APC	Army Pictorial Center
APC	Army Policy Council
APC	Army Postal Clerk (AABC)
APC	Arterial Premature Contraction [*Cardiology*]
APC	Arunachal People's Conference [*India*] [*Political party*] (PPW)
APC	Aseptic Packaging Council (EA)
APC	Aspirin Compound [*Pharmacology*] (DAVI)
APC	Aspirin, Phenacetin, Caffeine [*Medicine*] (DHSM)
APC	Assemblee Populaire Communale [*People's Communal Assembly*] [*Algeria*] (AF)
APC	Assessment Policy Committee [*National Assessment of Educational Progress*] (EDAC)
APC	Assistant Principal Chaplain [*British*] (ADA)
APC	Assisted Places Committee [*Education*] [*British*]
APC	Associated Pennsylvania Constructors (SRA)
APC	Associated Pimiento Canners [*Defunct*] (EA)
APC	Associated Porcupine Mines Ltd. [*Toronto Stock Exchange symbol*]
APC	Association des Parlementaires du Commonwealth [*Commonwealth Parliamentary Association*] [*Canada*]
APC	Association des Professionnels du Chauffage (AC)
APC	Association des Psychiatres du Canada [*Canadian Psychiatric Association*] (EAIO)
APC	Association for Progressive Communications
APC	Association of Pathology Chairmen (EA)
APC	Association of Principals of Colleges [*British*]
APC	Association of Private Camps [*Later, AIC*] (EA)
APC	Association of Professional Collectors
APC	Association of Professional Composers [*British*] (DBA)
APC	Association of Professors of Cardiology (EA)
APC	Association of Profiles Consultants (EA)
APC	Association of Public Corporations [*Miami, FL*] (EA)
APC	Association of Pulp Consumers, Inc. [*Later, American Paper Institute*] (EA)
APC	Associative Processor Control [*Computer science*]
APC	Associu di Patrioti Corsi [*Association of Corsican Patriots*] [*France Political party*] (PPE)
APC	Atelier de Production et Creation [*French fashion label*]
APC	Atomic Power Construction Ltd.
APC	Atrial Premature Contraction [*Cardiology*]
APC	Attitude and Pointing Control System [*NASA*] (MHDW)
APC	Auditing Practices Committee [*British*]
APC	Australian Pioneers' Club
APC	Australian Podiatry Council
APC	Australian Polo Council
APC	Autographed Presentation Copy
APC	Automated Packaging Code [*Army*] (MCD)

APC	Automated Production and Control [*Industrial engineering*]
APC	Automatic Page Composition (DGA)
APC	Automatic Passenger Counter [*FTA*] (TAG)
APC	Automatic Passenger Counting
APC	Automatic Performance Control
APC	Automatic Phase Control [*Telecommunications*] (TEL)
APC	Automatic Picture Control (IDOE)
APC	Automatic Pitch Control
APC	Automatic Potential Control (MHDI)
APC	Automatic Power Control (NTCM)
APC	Automatic Pressure Conveyor
APC	Automotive Presidents Council (EA)
A/PC	Autopilot Capsule
APC	Autoplot Controller (IEEE)
APC	Average Power Control [*Telecommunications*] (TEL)
APC	Average Propensity to Consume [*Economics*]
APC	Awaiting Plant Clearance (AAGC)
APC	Cavalry Transport [*Navy ship symbol*] [*Obsolete*]
APc	Compound Action Potential [*Biology*]
APC	Napa, CA [*Location identifier FAA*] (FAAL)
APC	Pincher Creek Public Library, Alberta [*Library symbol National Library of Canada*] (NLC)
APC	Small Coastal Transport [*Navy symbol Obsolete*]
APCA	Abandoned Property Collection Act [*1863*]
APCA	Aft Power Controller Assembly [*NASA*] (MCD)
APCA	Air Pollution Control Association (EA)
APCA	American Petroleum Credit Association [*Minneapolis, MN*] (EA)
APCA	American Planning Civic Association [*Later, NUC*] (EA)
APCA	Arizona Pest Control Association (SRA)
APCA	Association pour la Prevention de la Contamination Atmospherique (AC)
APCA	Audio Peak Clipping Amplifier
APCA	Australian Payments Clearing Association
APCA	Automatic Phono-Cardiac Analyzer (SAA)
APCA	National Association of Aeronautical Production Controllers
APCAC	Asia-Pacific Council of American Chambers of Commerce (EA)
APCAE	Association of Principals of Colleges for Adult Education [*British*]
APCAPS	Automated Payroll, Cost, and Personnel System [*Defense Supply Agency*]
APCAS	Asia and the Pacific Commission on Agricultural Statistics [*Formerly, Asia and theFar East Commission on Agricultural Statistics*] (EA)
APCBC	Armor-Piercing-Capped, Ballistic-Capped [*Ammunition*] (MSA)
APCBC	Armor-Piercing, Carbide, Ballistic Cap [*Ammunition*] (NATG)
APCC	Air Pollution Control Code (SAA)
APCC	American-Paraguayan Cultural Center [*Paraguay*] (EAIO)
APCC	American Power Conversion [*NASDAQ symbol*] (SAG)
APCC	American Public Communications Council (EA)
APCC	Antique Phonograph Collectors Club (EA)
APCC	Apollo Program Control Center [*NASA*] (KSC)
APCC	Asian and Pacific Coconut Community [*Jakarta, Indonesia*] (EAIO)
APC-C	Aspirin, Phenacetin, Caffeine with Codeine [*Medicine*] (MAE)
APCC	Association of Professional Computer Consultants [*Canada*] (EAIO)
APCC	Atmospheric Pressure and Composition Control (NASA)
APCC	Australian Pony Club Council
APCC	Cocos Islands [*Australia ICAO location identifier*] (ICLI)
APCCA	American Protestant Correctional Chaplains Association (EA)
APCChE	Asian Pacific Confederation of Chemical Engineering (EAIO)
APCCLA	Aviation Petroleum Coordinating Committee, Latin American
APCD	Adult Polycystic Disease [*Nephrology*] (DAVI)
APCD	Air Pollution Control District
APCD	Association of Philippine Coconut Desiccators
APCD	Ceduna [*Australia ICAO location identifier*] (ICLI)
APCE	Association Petroliere pour la Conservation de l'Environnement Canadien [*Petroleum Association for Conservation of the Canadian Environment*]
APCE	Automated Product Control Environment (SSD)
APCEC	Army Precommission Extension Course (AABC)
APCEF	Advanced Power Conversion Experimental Facility
APCEMA	Air Pollution Control Equipment Manufacturers' Association
APCF	Acute Pharyngo-Conjunctival Fever [*Medicine*]
APCF	Atlas Pacific Ltd. [*NASDAQ symbol*] (SAG)
APCG	Aperture Plate Character Generator
APCG	Apex Cardiogram [*Medicine*]
APCGF	Advanced Protein Crystal Growth Facility (SSD)
APCH	Approach
APCHE	Automatic Programmed Checkout Equipment
ApcheM	Apache Medical Systems, Inc. [*Associated Press*] (SAG)
APCHG	Approaching
APCHQ	Association Provinciale des Constructeurs d'Habitations du Quebec Inc. [*Provincial Home Builders Association of Quebec Inc.*] (AC)
APCI	Amusement Park Club International [*Defunct*] (EA)
APCI	Armor-Piercing-Capped Incendiary [*Ammunition*]
APCI	Association of Pulp Consumers, Inc.
APCI	Atmospheric Pressure Chemical Ionization
APCIMS	Association of Private Client Investment Managers and Stockbrokers (ODBW)
APCISS	Alumni Presidents' Council of Independent Secondary Schools (EA)
APCIT	Armor-Piercing-Capped Incendiary with Tracer [*Ammunition*]
APCK	Association for Promoting Christian Knowledge [*Church of Ireland*]
APCKD	Adult-Onset Polycystic Kidney Disease [*Medicine*]
APCL	American Postal Chess League [*Defunct*] (EA)
APCL	Association of Professional Color Laboratories (EA)
APCL	Atomic Power Construction Ltd.
APCM	Adaptive Pulse Code Modulation [*Telecommunications*] (TEL)
APCM	American Presbyterian Congo Mission

APCM	Asia Pacific Christian Mission
APCM	Asiatic-Pacific Campaign Medal [*Military decoration*]
APCM	Associated Portland Cement Manufacturers of Great Britain
APCM	Association of Plastic Cable Makers [*British*] (BI)
APCM	Association of Professional Conservatories of Music (EA)
APCM	Authorized Protective Connecting Module (MHDB)
APCMI	Association of Pastoral Care of the Mentally Ill [*British*] (DBA)
APCN	Active Pulse Compression Network
APCN	Advanced Product Change Notice
APCN	Anno post Christum Natum [*In the Year after Christ Was Born*] [*Latin*]
APCN	Assembly Page Change Notice (SAA)
APCNY	Analytical Psychology Club of New York (EA)
APCO	Air Pollution Control Office [*Obsolete Environmental Protection Agency*]
APCO	Alamo Personal Computer Organization (PCM)
Apco	Apco Argentina, Inc. [*Associated Press*] (SAG)
APCO	Appomattox Court House National Historic Park
APCO	Arab Political and Cultural Organization [*Iran*] (PD)
APCO	Asian Parasite Control Organization [*Japan*] (EAIO)
APCO	Associated Public-Safety Communications Officers (EA)
APCO	Association of Pleasure Craft Operators [*British*] (BI)
APCO	Automobile Protection-APCO [*NASDAQ symbol*] (TTSB)
APCO	Automobile Protection Corp. [*NASDAQ symbol*] (NQ)
APCOD	Applicability Code
APCOM	International Symposium on the Application of Computers and Operations Research in the Mineral Industries
APCON	Approach Control [*FAA*]
APCOPPLSRF	Analysis and Program for Calculation of Optimum Propellant Performance for Liquid and Solid Rocket Fuels
APCOR	Atomic Physics Consortium at Oak Ridge
APCP	Activation Project Control Plan
APCP	Advance Prediction Computer Program
APCP	Association of Paid Circulation Publications (EA)
APCPA	Association of Practicing Certified Public Accountants (SRA)
APCQ	Association des Parents Catholiques du Quebec (AC)
APCQ	Association Professionnelle des Criminologues du Quebec (AC)
APC/QC	Armored Personnel Carrier/Qualification Course [*Army*]
APCQI	Association de la Paralysie Cerebrale du Quebec [*Quebec Cerebral Palsy Association*] (AC)
APCR	Air Pollution Control Regulation (MCD)
A-PCR	Anchored Polymerase Chain Reaction [*Genetics*]
Apcr	Apocrypha (BJA)
APCR	Apollo Program Control Room [*NASA*] (KSC)
APCR	Armor-Piercing Reduced (Caliber) [*Ammunition*]
APCR	Armour-Piercing Composite Rigid [*British military*] (DMA)
APCR	Carnarvon [*Australia ICAO location identifier*] (ICLI)
APCRIQ	Association des Proprietaires de Camions-Remorques Independants du Quebec Inc. (AC)
APCRP	Aquatic Plant Control Research Program [*Army Corps of Engineers Waterways Experiment Station*] (MSC)
APCS	Accredited Pet Cemetary Society
APCS	Aeronautical Production Control System
APCS	Air Photographic and Charting Service
APCS	American Pencil Collectors Society (EA)
APCS	American Podiatric Circulatory Society (EA)
APCS	American Portuguese Cultural Society [*Later, APS*] (EA)
APCS	Approach Path Control System [*NASA*] (MCD)
APCS	Approach Power Compensator System [*NASA*]
APCS	Approach Power Control Set (NG)
APCS	Associative Processor Computer System
APCS	Atlantic Provinces Council on the Sciences (AC)
APCS	Attitude and Pointing Control System [*NASA*] (KSC)
APCT	American Postal Chess Tournaments (EA)
APCT	Armor-Piercing-Capped with Tracer [*Ammunition*]
APCT	Association of Painting Craft Teachers [*British*]
APCT	Association of Piano Class Teachers [*British*] (BI)
APCT	Association of Psychological Counselling and Training [*British*] (DBA)
A/P CTL	Autopilot Control (AAG)
APCTP	Asian Pacific Center for Theoretical Physics [*Institute, based in Seoul, Korea*]
APCTT	Asian and Pacific Centre for Transfer of Technology [*India*] (EAIO)
APCU	Association of Presbyterian Colleges and Universities (EA)
APCUG	Association of Personal Computer User Groups (PCM)
APCUG	Association of Private Colleges and Universities in Georgia (SRA)
APCV	Air-Piloted Control Valve
APCV	Association Professionnelle Catholique des Voyageurs de Commerce du Canada [*Catholic Professional Association of Commercial Representatives of Canada*]
APCVD	Atmospheric Pressure Chemical Vapor Deposition [*Photovoltaic energy systems*]
APCYA	[*A*] Presidential Classroom for Young Americans (EA)
apcys	Apocalypse (VRA)
APD	Ablative Photo Decomposition [*Physics*]
APD	Action Potential Duration [*Electrophysiology*]
APD	Active Personnel Dosimeter
APD	Adjustable Pitch Device
APD	Admiralty Press Division [*British military*] (DMA)
APD	Adult Polycystic Disease [*Medicine*]
APD	Advanced Planning Document [*DoD*] (AABC)
APD	Advanced Program Development
APD	Aerial Port Detachment
APD	Aeronautical Propulsion Division [*NASA*]
APD	Aerospace Power Division [*Air Force*]
APD	Afferent Pupillary Defect [*Ophthalmology*] (DAVI)

APD	Agricultural Pipe Drain
APD	Aiming Point Determination
APD	Air Particulate Detector (IEEE)
APD	Airport Directory [*FAA*]
APD	Air Procurement Directive (MCD)
APD	Air Procurement District [*Air Force*]
APD	Air Products & Chem [*NYSE symbol*] (TTSB)
APD	Air Products & Chemicals, Inc. [*NYSE symbol*] (SPSG)
APD	Air to Pneumatic Distribution [*Aerospace*]
APD	Albany Port District [*AAR code*]
APD	Alien Property Division [*Department of Justice*] (DLA)
APD	Alloy Phase Diagram
APD	All-Purpose Decontaminant (MCD)
APD	Ambulatory Peritoneal Dialysis [*Medicine*] (CPH)
APD	Amino(hydroxy)propylidine [*Organic chemistry*]
APD	Amplitude Probability Distribution [*Telecommunications*]
APD	Analog-to-Pulse Duration
APD	Angiotensin Pressor Dose [*Medicine*]
APD	Angular Position Digitizer
A-PD	Anteroposterior [*or Anterior-posterior*] Diameter [*Pelvic measurement*] [*Medicine*]
APD	Antiphase Domains [*Mineralogy*]
APD	Antipsychotic Drug
APD	Antisocial Personality Disorder [*Psychology*] (WDAA)
APD	Apollo Program Directive [*NASA*] (KSC)
APD	Archives de Philosophie du Droit [*A publication*] (ILCA)
APD	Area Passive Dosimeter (MCD)
APD	Area Postal Directory [*Army*] (AFIT)
APD	Army Pay Department [*British*]
APD	Army Pictorial Division
APD	Army Procurement District
APD	Asia Pacific Distribution [*Australia ICAO designator*] (FAAC)
Apd	Assessment Paid
APD	Association for Prevention of Disabilities (EAIO)
APD	Association of Paper Distributors (DGA)
APD	Atrial Premature Depolarization [*Cardiology*]
APD	Authors' and Printers' Dictionary [*A publication*] (DGA)
APD	Autoimmune Progesterone Dermatitis [*Medicine*] (DMAA)
APD	Automated Payment and Deposit [*Banking*]
APD	Automated Percutaneous Discectomy [*Spinal surgery*]
APD	Automated Peritoneal Dialysis [*Medicine*]
APD	Automated Powder Diffractometer
APD	Automated Program Debugging System (MCD)
APD	Automobile Physical Damage [*Insurance*]
APD	Auxiliary Personnel, Destroyer [*British military*] (DMA)
APD	Auxiliary Power Distribution (KSC)
APD	Avalanche Photodiode [*Solid state physics*]
APD	Avalanche Photodiode Detector
APD	Average Particle Diameter
APD	Average Percentage Damage [*Meteorology*]
APD	Average Percentage Difference [*Mathematics*]
APD	Average Pore Diameter [*Filtration*]
APD	Average Power Dissipation
APD	High-Speed Transport [*Navy symbol Obsolete*]
APD	Pennsylvania State's Agricultural Progress Days (TSPED)
APDA	Acidified Potato-Dextrose Agar [*Microbiology*]
APDA	American Parkinson Disease Association (EA)
APDA	American Power Drinkers Association
APDA	Apple Programmers and Developers Association (DOM)
APDA	Appliance Parts Distributors Association (EA)
APDA	Army Physical Disability Activity (MCD)
APDA	Atomic Power Development Associates, Inc.
APDA	Australian Poll Dorset Association
APDA	Australian Porcelain Decorators' Association
APDA	Auxiliary Pump-Drive Assembly
APDAB	Army Physical Disability Appeal Board
APDB	Derby [*Australia ICAO location identifier*] (ICLI)
APDC	Air Procurement District Commander [*Air Force*]
APDC	Ammonium Pyrrolidinedithiocarbamate [*Also, APDTC*] [*Organic chemistry*]
APDC	Asian and Pacific Development Centre (EAIO)
ApdCmp	Applied Computer Technology, Inc. [*Associated Press*] (SAG)
ApdCptr	Applied Computer Technology, Inc. [*Associated Press*] (SAG)
ApdDgtl	Applied Digital Access [*Associated Press*] (SAG)
APDEA	Aminopropyldiethanolamine [*Organic chemistry*]
APDER	Anterior-Posterior Dual Energy Radiography [*Medicine*] (DMAA)
ApdExtr	Applied Extrusion Technologies [*Associated Press*] (SAG)
APDF	Africa Project Development Facility [*United Nations*] (EY)
APDF	Aircraft Program Data File
APDF	Association of Professional Design Firms (EA)
APDF/APRO	Asian Pacific Dental Federation/Asian Pacific Regional Organisation (EAIO)
APDH	Asociacion pro Derechos Humanos de Espana [*Spanish Human Rights Association*]
APDHE	Asociacion pro Derechos Humanos de Espana [*Spanish Human Rights Association*] (EAIO)
APDI	Adult Personal Data Inventory [*Medicine*] (DMAA)
APDIM	Association of Program Directors in Internal Medicine (EA)
ApdImu	Applied Immune Sciences, Inc. [*Associated Press*] (SAG)
APDL	Aids Production and Distribution List (SAA)
APDL	Algorithmic Processor Description Language [*Computer science*] (MHDI)
APDL	American Protestant Defense League (EA)
APDM	Amended Program Decision Memorandum [*Navy*] (NVT)
ApdM	Applied Microbiology, Inc. [*Associated Press*] (SAG)

APDM .... Associative Push Down Memory [*Computer science*] (MHDB)
APDME .... Americans for Peace and Democracy in the Middle East (EA)
ApdMicr .... Applied Microbiology, Inc. [*Associated Press*] (SAG)
APDMS .... Advanced Point Defense Missile System [*Navy*]
APDMS .... Axial Power Distribution Monitoring Systems [*Nuclear energy*]
          (NRCH)
APDP .... Acquisition Professional Development Program [*DoD*]
APDP .... Aminohydroxypropane Diphosphonate
APDP .... Apollo Program Definition Phase [*NASA*] (KSC)
APDP .... Automatic Payroll Deposit Plan (DNAB)
APDS .... Advanced Personnel Data System (MCD)
APDS .... Advanced Planning Data Sheet
APDS .... Aminophenyl Disulfide [*Biochemistry*]
APDS .... Armor-Piercing Discarding Sabot [*Ammunition*] (NATG)
APDS .... Automated Procurement Documentation System [*Environmental
          Protection Agency*] (GFGA)
APDSA .... Asian Pacific Dental Students' Association [*Singapore, Singapore*]
          (EAIO)
ApdSci .... Applied Science & Technology, Inc. [*Associated Press*] (SAG)
APDSFS ...... Armor-Piercing Discarding Sabot, Fin-Stabilized [*Ammunition*] (MCD)
APDSMS ...... Advanced Point Defense Surface Missile System [*Navy*]
APDS-T .... Armor-Piercing Discarding Sabot with Tracer [*Ammunition*] (AABC)
APDTC .... Ammonium Pyrrolidinedithiocarbamate [*Also, APDC*] [*Organic
          chemistry*]
APDU .... Application Protocol Data Unit [*Telecommunications*] (OSI)
APDU .... Association of Public Data Users (EA)
Apdusa .... African People's Democratic Union of South Africa (PD)
APDV .... Air Pump Diverter Valve [*Automotive engineering*]
APDVE .... Aide aux Personnes Deplacees et Ses Villages Europeens [*Aid to
          Displaced Persons and Its European Villages*] (EAIO)
ApdVoice ..... Applied Voice Technology, Inc. [*Associated Press*] (SAG)
APDW .... Advanced Personal Defense Weapon [*Army*] (INF)
APDW .... Advance Procurement Data Worksheets [*Air Force*] (AFIT)
APDW .... Apple and Pear Disease Workers (EA)
APDY .... Appropriate Duty [*Air Force*] (AFM)
APE .... Acetone Powder Extract (MAE)
APE .... Acute Psychotic Episode
APE .... Acute Pulmonary Edema (DAVI)
APE .... Adaptation to Premises and Equipment Scheme [*Education*] (AIE)
APE .... Adenomatous Polyposis Coli [*Medicine*]
APE .... Advanced Procurement Engineering (MCD)
APE .... Advanced Production Engineering
APE .... Aerial Port of Embarkation [*Military*]
APE .... Agency to Prevent Evil [*Organization in TV series "Lancelot Link"*]
APE .... Air Parcel Express [*ICAO designator*] (FAAC)
APE .... Alfven Propulsion Engine [*Aerospace*]
APE .... Alkylphenol Ethoxylate [*Organic chemistry*]
APE .... Amalgamated Power Engineering (ODBW)
APE .... American Puritan Ethic
APE .... American Pyramid Resources, Inc. [*Vancouver Stock Exchange
          symbol*]
APE .... Aminopentanoic Acid [*An amino acid*]
APE .... Aminophylline, Phenobarbital, Ephedrine [*Medicine*] (MAE)
APE .... Ammunition Peculiar Equipment (AABC)
APE .... Amphibious Pionier Erkundungsfahrzeug [*Amphibious Engineer
          Reconnaissance Vehicle*] [*German*] (MCD)
APE .... Anchor Placement Equipment
APE .... Annual Planning Estimate [*Navy*] (NVT)
APE .... Anomalous Photovoltaic Effect (MCD)
APE .... Anterior Pituitary Extract [*Endocrinology*]
APE .... Apeiranthos Of Naxos [*Greece*] [*Seismograph station code, US
          Geological Survey*] (SEIS)
APE .... Aperient [*Pharmacy*] (ROG)
APE .... Appleton, OH [*Location identifier FAA*] (FAAL)
APE .... Aramaeische Papyri aus Elephantine [*A publication*] (BJA)
APE .... Arecaidine Propargyl Ester [*Biochemistry*]
APE .... Army Preliminary Evaluation
APE .... Assemblee Parlementaire Europeenne
APE .... Assistant Project Engineer
APE .... Association for the Protection of Evolution [*British*]
APE .... Associative Processing Element (MCD)
APE .... Athinaikon Praktoreion Eidiseon [*Athens News Agency*] [*Greece*]
APE .... Atomic Photoelectric Effect
APE .... Automatic Positioning Equipment
APE .... Available Potential Energy [*Geophysics*]
APE .... Available Power Efficiency
APE .... [*A*] Programmable Emulator [*Hi-Q International*] [*Computer
          science*] (PCM)
APEA .... Agri-Products Exporters Association (EA)
APEA .... American Photo-Engravers Association (DGA)
APEA .... Antenna Pattern Error Analysis
APEA .... Association de la Presse Eurafricaine [*Eurafrican Press Association*]
          [*Belgium*]
APEA .... Association des Producteurs Europeens d'Azote [*European
          Association of Nitrogen Manufacturers*] (EAIO)
APEA .... Association for Petroleum and Explosives Administration [*British*]
APEA .... Association for Professional Environmental Auditing in Nova Scotia
          [*Formerly, Association for Professional Environmental Auditors*]
          (AC)
APEA .... Association Parlementaire Europe-Afrique [*Eur-African Parliamentary
          Association*]
APEA JI .... APEA [*Australian Petroleum Exploration Association*] Journal
          [*A publication*]
APEAL .... Automotive Performance Execution and Layout
APEAR .... Appearance [*In urinalysis*] [*Biochemistry*] (DAVI)

APEB .... Army Physical Evaluation Board
APEC .... Acquisition Planning Executive Council (AAGC)
APEC .... Alliance for the Preservation of English in Canada
APEC .... All-Purpose Electronic Computer (IEEE)
APEC .... American Paper Exchange Club [*Later, PIR*] (EA)
APEC .... Asia Pacific Economic Cooperation [*Forum*]
APEC .... Association Professionnelle des Enseignants et Enseignantes en
          Commerce (AC)
APEC .... Atlantic Provinces Economic Council
APEC .... Automated Procedures for Engineering Consultants, Inc.
APEC .... Automotive Products Emissions Committee (EA)
APEC .... Automotive Products Export Council [*Defunct*] (EA)
APECA .... American Package Express Carriers Association (EA)
APECC .... Asia Pacific Economic Council
APECM .... Adaptive Polarization Electronic Countermeasure (MCD)
APECO .... American Photograph Equipment Co.
AP Ed .... Associate in Physical Education
APED .... Atomic Power Equipment Department (SAA)
APED .... Edinburgh [*Australia ICAO location identifier*] (ICLI)
APEE .... Association for Pediatric Education in Europe (PDAA)
APEE .... Association of Private Enterprise Education (EA)
APEF .... Advance-Purchase Excursion Fare [*Airline fare code*] (ADA)
APEF .... Association des Pays Exportateurs de Mineral de Fer [*Association of
          Iron Ore Exporting Countries*] [*Switzerland*] (EAIO)
APEG .... Aquatic Processes and Effects Group [*Army*]
APEG .... Asia Pacific Economic Group
APEG BC ..... Association of Professional Engineers & Geoscientists of British
          Columbia (AC)
APEGGA ...... Association of Professional Engineers, Geologists & Geophysicists of
          Alberta (AC)
APEGGA ...... Association of Professional Engineers, Geologists, and Geophysicists
          of Alberta [*Canada*] (DD)
APEGN .... Association of Professional Engineers & Geoscientists of
          Newfoundland [*Formerly, Association of Professional Engineers
          of Newfoundland*] (AC)
APEHC .... Alternator-Powered Electrically Heated Catalyst [*Automotive
          engineering*]
APEI .... Associated Poultry and Egg Industries [*Defunct*] (EA)
APEID .... Asian Program for Education Innovation for Development
APEIQ .... Association pour l'Education Interculturelle du Quebec [*Quebec
          Association for Intercultural Education*] (AC)
APEL .... Advanced Product Evaluation Laboratory
APEL .... Aeronautical Photographic Experimental Laboratory [*Johnsville, PA*]
          [*Navy*]
APELS .... Airborne Precision Emitter Location System (MCD)
APELSCOR ... Architects, Professional Engineers, Land Surveyors Council on
          Registration
APEM .... Association for Professional Education for Ministry [*Later, APT*] (EA)
APEM .... Association of Professional Energy Managers (EA)
APEM .... Association of Professional Engineers of Manitoba (AC)
APENAC ...... Association du Personnel Navigant des Lignes Aeriennes
          Canadiennes [*Canadian Air Line Flight Attendants' Association -
          CALFA*]
APENB .... Association of Professional Engineers of New Brunswick (AC)
APENPLAN ... Asian and Pacific Energy Planning Network [*of the Asian and Pacific
          Development Centre*] (EAIO)
APENS .... Association of Professional Engineers of Nova Scotia (AC)
APEO .... Advance Process Engineering Order [*Manufacturing*] (MCD)
APEO .... Alkylphenol Polyethoxylate [*Organic chemistry*]
APEO .... Professional Engineers Ontario [*Canada*] (DD)
APEP .... Academic Program Evaluation Project (EDAC)
APEPEI .... Association of Professional Engineers of Prince Edward Island (AC)
APEQ .... Association des Professionnels en Exposition du Quebec (AC)
APEQS .... Airborne Photography of the Eclipse of the Quiet Sun
APER .... Air Pollutant Emissions Report [*Environmental Protection Agency*]
APER .... Antipersonnel [*Projectile*]
APER .... Aperient [*Pharmacy*] (ROG)
APER .... Aperture
APER .... Association of Publishers' Educational Representatives [*British*]
APERS .... Antipersonnel [*Projectile*] (AABC)
A PERS .... [*The*] Era of Persia [*Beginning 632AD*] (ROG)
APERT .... Aperture (MSA)
Apertus .... Apertus Technologies, Inc. [*Associated Press*] (SAG)
APES .... Association des Pharmaciens des Etablissements de Sante du
          Quebec (AC)
APES .... Association of Professional Engineers of Saskatchewan (AC)
APESMA ..... Association of Professional Engineers, Scientists, and Managers,
          Australia
APET .... Application Program Evaluator Tool [*Computer science*] (MHDB)
APETQ .... Association Professionnelle des Enseignants de Technologie du
          Quebec (AC)
APeVE .... Valley Elementary School, Pelham, AL [*Library symbol*] [*Library of
          Congress*] (LCLS)
APEX .... Acid Precipitation Experiment
APEX .... Additive System of Photographic Exposure (DICI)
APEX .... Advance-Purchase Excursion [*Airline fare code*]
APEX .... Advance Purchase Excursion Fare [*Aviation*] (DA)
APEX .... Air Pollution Exercise
Apex .... Apex Municipal Fund, Inc. [*Associated Press*] (SAG)
APEX .... Apparatus for Pore Examination [*Geophysics*]
APEX .... Application Executive [*Software interface for Integrated Modular
          Avionics*] [*Computer science*]
APEX .... ARCAS [*Atlantic Research Corporation Atmospheric Sounding
          Missile*] Piggyback Emulsion Experiment (MUGU)
APEX .... Arctic Polynya Experiment [*Marine science*] (OSRA)

APEX.......... Arctic Polynya Experiment (USDC)
APEX.......... Association of Professional and Executive Staff [British]
APEX.......... Association of Professional, Executive, Clerical, and Computer Staff (AIE)
APEX.......... Atlantische Passatwind Experiment [Atlantic Tradewind Experiment] [US, England, Germany] (MSC)
APEX.......... Automated Procurement Planning, Execution, and Control
APEX.......... Awards for Publication Excellence
APEX.......... Institute for Astrophysics and Planetary Exploration [University of Florida] [Research center] (RCD)
APExC........ All Purpose Electronic x Computer [Early computer] [Birkbeck College] [British]
APEXER...... Approach Indexer
APF............. Accurate Position Finder
APF............. Acidproof Floor [Technical drawings]
APF............. Acidulated Phosphofluoride
APF............. Adjustable Pawl Fastener
APF............. Administrative Flagship [Navy symbol Obsolete]
APF............. Advanced Procurement Funding (MCD)
APF............. Aerial Port Flight [Air Force]
APF............. Afloat Prepositioning Force (DOMA)
APF............. After Puparium Formation [Entomology]
APF............. Aircraft Parachute Flare (SAA)
APF............. American Pathology Foundation (EA)
APF............. American Physicians Fellowship for Medicine in Israel (EA)
APF............. American Porphyria Foundation (EA)
APF............. American Progress Foundation
APF............. American Psychological Foundation
APF............. Anabolism-Promoting Factor (MAE)
APF............. Anglican Pacifist Fellowship [Oxford, England] (EAIO)
APF............. Animal Protein Factor
APF............. Antarctic Polar Front [Meteorology]
APF............. Apple Preferred Format [Computer science]
APF............. Approach Control Function [Aviation] (AIA)
APF............. Appropriated Funds (AABC)
APF............. Arkansas Poultry Federation (SRA)
A-P-F.......... Ashbrooke-Pembleton-Ffrench [Mythical British family appearing in "Announcements" column of Times of London]
APF............. Asia-Pacific Fellowship
APF............. Association of Pacific Fisheries [Later, PSPA] (EA)
APF............. Association of Professional Foresters (EAIO)
APF............. Atomic Packing Factor (IEEE)
APF............. Atrial Pore Field [Botany]
APF............. Australian Petanque Federation
APF............. Australian Powerlifting Federation
APF............. Australian Products First [An association]
APF............. Authorized Program Facility [Computer science] (BUR)
APF............. Authorized Program File [Computer science] (PCM)
APF............. Automatic Press Feed
APF............. Automatic Program Finding [Electronics]
APF............. Morgan Stanley Asia-Pac Fund [NYSE symbol] (TTSB)
APF............. Morgan Stanley Asia Pacific Fund [NYSE symbol] (SAG)
APF............. Naples [Florida] [Airport symbol] (OAG)
APF............. Transporte de Carga Aeropacifico SA de CV [Mexico ICAO designator] (FAAC)
APFA.......... Accelerator Pulsed Fast Assembly
APFA.......... American Pipe Fittings Association (EA)
APFA.......... American Professional Faceters Association [Defunct] (EA)
APFA.......... Appalachian Finance Association [Later, Eastern Finance Association] (EA)
APFA.......... Association des Professeurs de Francais en Afrique [Association of French Teachers in Africa - AFTA] [Khartoum, Sudan] (EAIO)
APFA.......... Association des Professeurs Franco-Americains [Defunct] (EA)
APFA.......... Association for Protection of Fur-Bearing Animals [Canada]
APFA.......... Australian Picture Framers' Association
APFBA........ Association for the Protection of Fur-Bearing Animals (EAIO)
APFC.......... American Pacific Corp. [NASDAQ symbol] (NQ)
APFC.......... American Printed Fabrics Council (EA)
APFC.......... Amer Pacific [NASDAQ symbol] (TTSB)
APFC.......... Asia-Pacific Forestry Commission [UN Food and Agriculture Organization]
APFC.......... Asia Pacific Foundation of Canada [Fondation Asie Pacifique du Canada] (AC)
APFC.......... Assembly Process Flow Chart (IAA)
APFC.......... Association of Physical Fitness Centers (EA)
APFCB........ Association des Parents Francophones de la Colombie-Britannique (AC)
APFCS........ Automatic Power-Factor-Control Systems (IEEE)
APFD.......... Autopilot Flight Director
APFF.......... Association de Planification Fiscale et Financiere (AC)
APFHA........ American Paso Fino Horse Association (EA)
APFIM........ Atom-Probe Field-Ion Microscopy
APFL.......... Aero-Propulsion Fuels Laboratory [Air Force]
APFO......... Aerial Photography Field Office [Department of Agriculture] (GFGA)
APFO......... Association of Playing Fields' Officers [British] (BI)
APFO......... Association on Programs for Female Offenders (EA)
APFO......... Automated Planning Fabrication Outline (MCD)
APFO & LM... Association of Playing Fields Officers and Landscape Managers [British] (DBA)
APFP.......... Army Physical Fitness Program
APFRI........ American Physical Fitness Research Institute [Defunct] (EA)
APFS.......... Association of Podiatrists in Federal Service [Later, FSPMA] (EA)
APFSDS...... Armor-Piercing Fin Stabilized Discarding Sabot [Ammunition] (MCD)
APFSDS-T.... Armor-Piercing Fin Stabilized Discarding Sabot with Tracer [Ammunition] (INF)

APFT........... Advanced Physical Fitness Test (INF)
APFT........... Army Physical Fitness Test (INF)
APFT........... Army Physical Fitness Training (ADDR)
APFT........... Forrest [Australia ICAO location identifier] (ICLI)
APFTQ........ Association des Producteurs de Films et Television du Quebec (AC)
APFTU........ Amalgamated Picture Frame Trade Union [British]
APFUC....... Association des Professeurs de Francais des Universites Canadiennes [Association of Canadian University Teachers of French]
APFUCC...... Association des Professeurs de Francais des Universites et Colleges Canadiens [Association of Canadian University and College Teachers of French - ACUCTF]
APFX........... Apply Fixture (AAG)
APG .... Aberdeen, MD [Location identifier FAA] (FAAL)
APG .... Aberdeen Proving Ground [Maryland] [Army]
APG .... Accessory Pedal Ganglia
APG .... Acid-Precipitable Globulin [Clinical chemistry]
APG .... ACLANT [Allied Command, Atlantic] Planning Guidance [NATO]
APG .... Advanced Pay Grade (DNAB)
APG .... Aerial Port Group [Air Force] (AFM)
APG .... Aerotaxis Pegaso SA de CV [Mexico ICAO designator] (FAAC)
APG .... Airplane, General (MCD)
APG .... Air Proving Ground
APG .... Alkyl Polyglycoside [Organic chemistry]
APG .... American Pewter Guild (EA)
APG .... American Programmers Guild
APG .... American Publicists Guild [Defunct] (EA)
APG .... Antenna Power Gain
APG .... Apex Energy Corp. [Vancouver Stock Exchange symbol]
APG .... Apogee
APG .... Application Program Generator [Computer science]
APG .... Aprogenex, Inc. [AMEX symbol] (SPSG)
APG .... Argus Press Group [British]
APG .... Army Planning Group
APG .... Army Proving Grounds
APG .... Association for Precision Graphics [Defunct] (EA)
APG .... Association of Professional Genealogists (EA)
APG .... Astronomiae Professor Greshamii [Professor of Astronomy at Gresham College, London]
APG .... Atomic Power Group [Nuclear energy] (NUCP)
APG .... Automatic Precipitation Gauge (NOAA)
APG .... Automatic Priority Group [Fujitsu Ltd.] [Japan] (MCD)
APG .... Azidophenylglyoxal [Organic chemistry]
APG .... Azimuth Pulse Generator
APG .... Sisters of Perpetual Adoration (TOCD)
APG .... Supporting Gunnery Ship [Navy symbol Obsolete]
APGA........ Alabama Propane Gas Association (SRA)
APGA........ American Personnel and Guidance Association [Later, AACD] (EA)
APGA........ American Public Gas Association (EA)
APGA........ Aminopteroylglutamic Acid [Organic chemistry]
APGA........ Arkansas Propane Gas Association (SRA)
APGA........ Australian Pistacio Growers' Association
APGA........ Australian Protea Growers' Association
APGAR........ Adaptability, Partnership, Growth, Affection, and Resolve [Family Therapy Questionnaire]
APGAR........ American Pediatric Gross Assessment Record
APGASA...... Apple and Pear Growers' Association of South Australia
APGBRL...... Aberdeen Proving Ground/Ballistics Research Laboratory [Army]
APGC........ Air Proving Ground Center [or Command] [Eglin Air Force Base, FL]
APGC........ Arnold Palmer Golf Co. (The) [NASDAQ symbol] (SAG)
APGCE........ Air Proving Ground Center - Eglin Air Force Base
APGCU........ Autopilot Ground Control Unit
APGF.......... Perth [Australia ICAO location identifier] (ICLI)
APGG .... Apogee, Inc. [NASDAQ symbol] (SAG)
APG/HEL...... Aberdeen Proving Ground/Human Engineering Laboratory [Army]
APGI.......... Green(A.P.)Indus [NASDAQ symbol] (TTSB)
APGI .... Green [A. P.] Industries, Inc. [NASDAQ symbol] (NQ)
APGL.......... Alkaline Phosphatase Activity, Granular Leukocytes [Immunochemistry] (MAE)
APGM .... Association des Peres Gais de Montreal Inc. [Gay Fathers of Montreal Inc.] (AC)
APGM .... Autonomous Precision-Guided Munition [NATO]
APG/MT ...... Aberdeen Ground/Materiel Testing Directorate [Maryland] [Army]
APGN.......... Geraldton [Australia ICAO location identifier] (ICLI)
APGO.......... Association of Professors of Gynecology and Obstetrics (EA)
APG/OBDC ... Aberdeen Proving Ground/Ordnance Bomb Disposal Center [Army] (KSC)
APGOMS...... Association du Personnel de Geneve OMS [Geneva Staff Association World Health Organization] [Switzerland] (EAIO)
APG/OTC..... Aberdeen Proving Ground/Ordnance Training Command [Army] (KSC)
APGp.......... Aerial Port Group [Air Force]
APGQ.......... Association Professionnelle des Geographes du Quebec (AC)
APGR........ Arch Communications Group [NASDAQ symbol] (SPSG)
APGRA........ American Pediatric Gastroesophageal Reflux Association (EA)
Ap Greg...... Apud Gregorium [Latin] (DSA)
APGS.......... Apollo Propellant Gauging System [NASA] (KSC)
APGS.......... Association of Professional Geological Scientists [Later, AIPG] (EA)
APGTC........ Administration du Petrole et du Gaz des Terres du Canada [Canada Oil and Gas Lands Administration]
APH .... Access Permit Holder
APH .... Actual Production History Program
APH .... Airport Hangar [New York] [Seismograph station code, US Geological Survey] (SEIS)
APH .... Air Power History [A publication]

APH	Alberta Hospital, Ponoka, Alberta [*Library symbol National Library of Canada*] (NLC)
APH	Alpha Aviation, Inc. [*ICAO designator*] (FAAC)
APH	American Printing House for the Blind (EA)
APH	Amino(phosphono)heptanoic Acid [*Organic chemistry*]
APH	Amphenol Corp. [*NYSE symbol*] (SAG)
APH	Amphenol Corp'A' [*NYSE symbol*] (TTSB)
APH	Antepartum Hemorrhage [*Medicine*]
APH	Anterior Pituitary Hormone [*Endocrinology*]
Aph	Aphasia [*Medicine*] (DMAA)
APH	Aphetic (BARN)
aph	Aphorism
APH	Approach Resources, Inc. [*Vancouver Stock Exchange symbol*]
A Ph.	Associate in Philosophy
APH	Association of Private Hospitals (EA)
APH	Automatic Parts Handler
APH	Automotive Planner's Handbook
APH	Aviator's Protective Helmet (NG)
APH	Bowling Green, VA [*Location identifier FAA*] (FAAL)
APH	Fort Hood Post Library, Library Service Center, Fort Hood, TX [*OCLC symbol*] (OCLC)
a-ph--	Philippines [*MARC geographic area code Library of Congress*] (LCCP)
APH	Transport [*Fitted to evacuate wounded*] [*Navy ship symbol*] [*Obsolete*]
APHA	Aged Persons Homes Act [*Australia*]
APhA	Alberta Pharmaceutical Association (AC)
APHA	Alberta Public Health Association (AC)
APHA	American Paint Horse Association (EA)
APHA	American Performance Horse Association (EA)
APhA	American Pharmaceutical Association (EA)
APHA	American Pinto Horse Association (EA)
APHA	American Polled Hereford Association (EA)
APHA	American Printing History Association (EA)
APHA	American Protestant Health Association (EA)
APHA	American Protestant Hospital Association (DAVI)
APHA	American Public Health Association (EA)
APHA	Associate of Public Health Association
APHA	Australian Poll Hereford Association
APHA	Australian Psychology and Hypnotherapy Association
APHAZ	Aircraft Proximity Hazard (DA)
APHB	American Printing House for the Blind
APHB	Army Pearl Harbor Board [*World War II*]
AP/HC	Accreditation Program / Hospice (MEDA)
ApHC	Appaloosa Horse Club (EA)
AP-HC	Armour Piercing - Hard Core (PDAA)
APhC	Association Pharmaceutique Canadienne [*Canadian Pharmaceutical Association*] (EAIO)
APHC	Halls Creek [*Australia ICAO location identifier*] (ICLI)
APHCA	Alabama Primary Health Care Association (SRA)
APHCA	Animal Production and Health Commission for Asia [*Australia*]
APH-CARL	American Printing House for the Blind Central Automated Resource List [*Information service or system*] (CRD)
ApHCC	Appaloosa Horse Club of Canada (AC)
APHE	Armor-Piercing High Explosive [*Ammunition*]
APHE	Armor-Piercing High Explosive Weaponry [*Army*] (VNW)
Aphe	Audiophile [*Record label*]
APHEX	Aural Perception Heterodyne Exciter [*Inter-Technology Exchange Ltd.*] [*Psychoacoustics*]
APHF	American Poultry and Hatchery Federation [*Later, PEIA*] (EA)
APHFFF	Ames Prototype Hypersonic Free Flight Facility (KSC)
APHH	Port Hedland [*Australia ICAO location identifier*] (ICLI)
AP/HHC	Accreditation Program / Home Health Care (MEDA)
APHI	Animal and Plant Health Inspection Service
APHI	Association of Public Health Inspectors
APHIA	Association for the Promotion of Humor in International Affairs (EA)
APHIS	Animal and Plant Health Inspection Service [*Department of Agriculture*] [*Also, an information service or system*] (IID)
APHLC	All-Party Hill Leaders' Conference [*India*] [*Political party*] (PPW)
APhoe	American Phoenix Group, Inc. [*Associated Press*] (SAG)
APHP	Anti-Pseudomonas Human Plasma [*Immunology*] (MAE)
APHRO	Aphrodisiac [*Medicine*] (ROG)
APHS	American Photographic Historical Society (EA)
APHS	American Poultry Historical Society (EA)
APHS	Antique Powercraft Historical Society [*Defunct*] (EA)
APHT	Aphton Corp. [*NASDAQ symbol*] (SPSG)
Aphton	Aphton Corp. [*Associated Press*] (SAG)
APHX	American Phoenix Group, Inc. [*NASDAQ symbol*] (SAG)
APhyG	American Physicians Service Group, Inc. [*Associated Press*] (SAG)
API	Absolute Position Indication [*Nuclear energy*] (NRCH)
API	Academic Press, Inc. [*Publishers*] (MCD)
API	Accelerator Pedal with Idler [*Automotive engineering*]
API	Accel International Corp. Productivity Interface [*Computer science*] (BYTE)
API	Acceptable Periodic Inspection
API	Accountants for the Public Interest [*Washington, DC*]
API	Accurate Position Indicator
API	Activity Performing Inspection (SAA)
API	Advanced Performance Interceptor
API	Advanced Photonix'A' [*AMEX symbol*] (TTSB)
API	Advanced Photonix, Inc. [*AMEX symbol*] (SPSG)
API	Advanced Procurement Information (MCD)
API	Affective Perception Inventory [*Student personality test*]
API	Agence Angolaise de Presse et d'Information [*Angolan Press and Information Agency*]

API	Agence de Presse Ivoirienne [*Ivorian Press Agency*]
API	Air Panama Internacional [*ICAO designator*] (FAAC)
API	Air Position Indicator [*Air Force*]
API	Alabama Polytechnic Institute (MCD)
API	Alignment Progress Indicator (KSC)
API	All-Purpose Interface [*Computer science*] (HGAA)
API	Amalgamated Publishers, Inc.
API	American Paper Institute (EA)
API	American Paramedical Institute [*Hawaii*]
API	American Petroleum Institute (EA)
API	American Photonics, Inc. [*Brookfield Center, CT*] (TSSD)
API	American Pistol Institute (EA)
API	American Potash Institute [*Later, PPI*] (EA)
API	American Poultry International (EA)
API	American Prepaid Legal Services Institute (EA)
API	American Press Institute (EA)
API	American Psychical Institute
API	Americans for Progressive Israel (EA)
API	AMP Exploration & Mining Co. Ltd. [*Vancouver Stock Exchange symbol*]
API	Amyloplast Pressure Index [*Botany*]
API	Analytical Profile Index [*Microbiology*]
API	Angle Position Indicator
API	Animal Protection Institute of America (EA)
API	Antecedent Precipitation Index
API	Antenna Position Indicator
API	Anthocyanin Pigmented Juices [*Food technology*]
API	Apia [*Samoa Islands*] [*Seismograph station code, US Geological Survey*] (SEIS)
API	Application Process Invocation [*Telecommunications*] (OSI)
API	Application Program Interface [*Telecommunications*] (OSI)
API	Application Program Interface
API	Application Programming Interface [*Telecommunications*] (ACRL)
API	Appreciation of Capital, Protection, Income [*Finance*]
API	Archconfraternity of Prayer for Israel (EA)
API	Architectural Periodicals Index [*Royal Institute of British Architects*] [*Information service or system*] (IID)
API	Area of Possible Incompatibility [*Military*] (DNAB)
API	Armor-Piercing Incendiary [*Ammunition*]
API	Associated Paper Industries [*British*]
API	Associated Photographers International (EA)
API	Associate of the Plastics Institute [*British*]
API	Association des Producteurs d'Isoglucose de la CE [*Association of the Producers of Isoglucose of the European Community*] [*Common Market*]
API	Association of Pharmaceutical Importers [*British*] (DBA)
API	Association of Private Investors [*British*] (DBA)
API	Association Phonetique Internationale [*International Phonetic Association*]
API	Astro-Psychology Institute (EA)
API	Atmospheric Pressure Ionization [*Physics*]
API	Auerbach Power Index (NITA)
API	Australian Petroleum Institute
API	Automated Pronunciation Instructor
API	Automatic Priority Interrupt [*Computer science*]
API	Automatic Programming Instruction [*Computer science*]
API	Aviation Professionals International [*New Orleans*]
APIA	Antitrust Procedural Improvements Act of 1980
APIA	Application Program Interface Association (BTTJ)
APIA	Association pour la Promotion Industrie - Agriculture [*Association for the Promotion of Industry - Agriculture*] (EAIO)
APIB	Applications Program Integration Board [*NASA*]
APIBQ	Association des Physiciens et Ingenieurs Biomedicaux du Quebec (AC)
APIC	Advanced Programmable Interrupt Controller [*Computer science*]
APIC	Alliance des Patriotes Independants du Congo [*Alliance of Independent Patriots of the Congo*]
APIC	Alliance des Proletaires Independants du Congo [*Alliance of Independent Proletarians of the Congo*]
APIC	Allied Press Information Center [*NATO*] (NATG)
APIC	American Political Items Collectors (EA)
APIC	Analytical Processing for Improved Composite (MCD)
APIC	Apiculture
APIC	Apollo Parts Information Center [*NASA*] (MCD)
APIC	Army Photo Interpretation Center
APIC	Association for Practitioners in Infection Control (EA)
APIC	Association of Psychology Internship Centers (EA)
APIC	Association pour la Protection des Interets des Consommateurs [*Association for the Protection of Consumer Interests*] [*Canada*]
APIC	Australian Potato Industry Council
APIC	Automatic Power Input Controller
APIC	Automatic Programming Information Centre [*British*]
APICA	Association pour la Promotion des Initiatives Communautaires Africaines [*Association for the Promotion of African Community Initiatives - APACI*] (EAIO)
APICE	Asociacion Panamericana de Instituciones de Credito Educativo [*Pan American Association of Educational Credit Institutions - PAAECI*] (EAIO)
APICM	Antipersonnel Improved Conventional Munitions [*Army*] (ADDR)
APICON	Aircraft Position Information Converter [*Air Force*]
APICORP	Arab Petroleum Investments Corp. (ECON)
APICP	Association for the Promotion of the International Circulation of the Press [*Distipress*]
APICS	Air Pollution Information and Computation System
APICS	American Production and Inventory Control Society (EA)

APID .... Army Photo Interpretation Detachment
APID .... Association of Photographic Importers and Distributors (EA)
APIE .... Antioch Program for Interracial Education [*Antioch College*] (EA)
APIE .... Assessment, Plan, Implementation, and Evaluation [*Medicine*] (DMAA)
APIE .... Atmospheric Pressure Ion Evaporation
APIF .... Aerodynamic Propulsive Interactive Force [*Air Force*]
APIF .... Automated Process Information File [*Library of Congress*]
APIGQ .... Association Professionnelle des Ingenieurs du Gouvernement du Quebec [*Association of Professional Engineers of the Government of Quebec*] (AC)
API-HH .... Americans for Progressive Israel - Hashomer Hatzair (EA)
APII .... Action Products International, Inc. [*NASDAQ symbol*] (NQ)
APII .... Action Products Intl. [*NASDAQ symbol*] (TTSB)
APIICQ .... Association Professionnelle des Infirmieres et Infirmiers Cadres du Quebec (AC)
APIJAC .... Australian Pet Industry Joint Advisory Council
APIL .... Axial Power Imbalance Limit (IEEE)
APILAS .... Armor-Piercing Infantry Light-Arm System [*Ammunition*]
APILIT .... API [*American Petroleum Institute*] Literature [*New York, NY*] [*Bibliographic database*]
APIM .... Associated Petroleum Industries of Michigan (SRA)
APIM .... Association Professionnelle Internationale des Medicins [*International Professional Association of Physicians*]
APIN .... Alianza Popular de Integracion Nacional [*Bolivia*] [*Political party*] (PPW)
APIN .... System of Computerized Processing of Scientific Information [*Technical University of Wroclaw*] [*Information service or system*] (IID)
APINESS ...... Asia-Pacific Information Network in Social Sciences
APINMAP ..... Asian and Pacific Information Network on Medicinal and Aromatic Plants [*UNESCO*] [*United Nations*] (DUND)
APIO .... Association of Pensioners & Injured Workmen of Ontario (AC)
APIP .... Additional Personal Injury Protection [*Insurance*]
APIP .... AMDF [*Army Master Data File*] Positive Improvement Program (MCD)
APIP .... Annual Permanent Improvement Program (AAGC)
APIP .... Apollo Personnel Identification [*or Investigation*] Program [*NASA*] (KSC)
APIP .... Associations' Publications in Print [*Database*] [*R. R. Bowker Co.*] [*Information service or system*] (CRD)
APIP .... Australian Periodicals in Print [*A publication*] (APTA)
API-PA .... Associated Petroleum Industries of Pennsylvania (SRA)
APIPAT .... American Petroleum Institute Patents (NITA)
APIPOCC ..... Appropriating Property in Possession of Common Carrier [*FBI standardized term*]
APIR .... American Petroleum Institute Research (MCD)
APIRA .... Australian Petroleum Industry Research Association
APIRD .... Authorized Procurement Information Requirements Description [*NASA*] (NASA)
APIRL .... Authorized Procurement Information Requirements List [*NASA*] (NASA)
APIRP .... American Petroleum Institute Research Project
APIS .... Advanced Papyrological Information System
APIS .... Air Position Indicating Station [*Air Force*] (IAA)
APIS .... Apogee-Perigee Injection System (PDAA)
APIS .... Approved Production Inspection System [*Manufacturing*] (MCD)
APIS .... Army Photographic Interpretation Section [*British*]
APIS .... Array Processing Instruction Set [*Computer science*] (MSA)
APIS .... Austrian Press and Information Service (EA)
APIT .... Armor-Piercing Incendiary Tracer [*Ammunition*]
APITCA .... American Producers of Italian Type Cheese Association (EA)
APIU .... Army Photo Interpretation Unit (NATG)
APIVR .... Artificial Pacemaker-Induced Ventricular Rhythm [*Medicine*] (DMAA)
APIW .... Association of Professional Insurance Women [*Acronym is now organization's official name*] (EA)
APIX .... Automated Personnel Information Exchange (DNAB)
APJ .... American Power Jet Co.
APJ .... Angle Panel Jack
APJ .... Appalachian Power Co. [*NYSE symbol*] (SAG)
APJ .... Association for Public Justice (EA)
APJ .... Auspex Gold Ltd. [*Vancouver Stock Exchange symbol*]
APJ .... Public Library of Pine Bluff and Jefferson County, Pine Bluff, AR [*OCLC symbol*] (OCLC)
APJA .... Appliance Parts Jobbers Association [*Later, APDA*]
AP JC .... Apres Jesus-Christ [*After Christ*] [*French*]
APJE .... Association of Philosophy Journal Editors (EA)
APJEF .... Association for Public Justice Education Fund [*Later, CPJ*] (EA)
APJI .... Assistant Parachute Jump Instructor [*British military*] (DMA)
APJT .... Perth/Jandakot [*Australia ICAO location identifier*] (ICLI)
Ap Just .... Apud Justinianum [*Latin*] (DLA)
Ap Justin ..... Apud Justinianum [*Latin*] (DLA)
APK .... Accelerometer Package (KSC)
APK .... Amplitude Phase Keyed [*Telecommunications*] (NITA)
APK .... Amplitude Phase Shift Keying (MCD)
APK .... Angel's Peak [*Nevada*] [*Seismograph station code, US Geological Survey*] (SEIS)
APK .... Antiparkinsonian [*Medicine*] (MEDA)
APK .... Apataki [*French Polynesia*] [*Airport symbol*] (OAG)
APK .... Arbetarpartiet Kommunisterna [*Communist Workers' Party*] [*Sweden*] (PPE)
APK .... Asia Pacific Air Cargo PTE Ltd. [*Singapore*] [*ICAO designator*] (FAAC)
APK .... Astronaut Preference Kit [*NASA*]

APK .... Fort Campbell Post Library, Fort Campbell, KY [*OCLC symbol*] (OCLC)
a-pk-- .... Pakistan [*MARC geographic area code Library of Congress*] (LCCP)
APKA .... Karratha [*Australia ICAO location identifier*] (ICLI)
APKCA .... Associated Pot and Kettle Clubs of America [*Later, IPKC*] (EA)
APKD .... Adult-Onset Polycystic Kidney Disease [*Medicine*]
APKG .... Kalgoorlie [*Australia ICAO location identifier*] (ICLI)
APKK .... An Party Kenethlegek Kernow (EA)
APKU .... Kununurra [*Australia ICAO location identifier*] (ICLI)
APL .... Abductor Pollicis Longus [*Medicine*] (DMAA)
APL .... Accelerated Painless Labor (MAE)
APL .... Acceptable Process Level
APL .... Acceptable Productivity Level [*Quality control*]
APL .... Accreditation of Prior Learning (AIE)
APL .... Acute Progranulocytic [*or Promyelocytic*] Leukemia [*Hematology*]
APL .... Acute Promyelocytic Leukemia [*Medicine*]
APL .... Additional Programming Language (IAA)
APL .... Aden Protectorate Levies [*British military*] (DMA)
APL .... Adjustment Payment Level [*Social Security Administration*]
APL .... Adult Performance Level Project [*Defunct*] (EA)
APL .... Advanced Parts List (SAA)
APL .... Advanced Product Line (IAA)
APL .... Advanced Programming Language [*Computer science*]
APL .... Advance Procurement List (MCD)
APL .... Aero-Propulsion Laboratory [*Air Force*]
APL .... Airplane (KSC)
APL .... Airport Lights [*FAA*] (TAG)
APL .... Airport Lights (FAAC)
APL .... Akron-Summit County Public Library, Akron, OH [*OCLC symbol*] (OCLC)
APL .... Algorithmic Procedural Language [*Computer science*] (IAA)
APL .... Algorithm Programming Language [*Computer science*] (HGAA)
APL .... Allowance Parts List
APL .... All-Purpose Linotype (DGA)
APL .... American Poetry League
APL .... American President Lines
APL .... Amygdala Pars Lateralis [*Neuroanatomy*]
APL .... Analog Private Line [*Telecommunications*] (ACRL)
APL .... Angleplied Laminate
APL .... Annular Pressure Loss [*Well drilling technology*]
APL .... Anterior Pituitary-Like [*Endocrinology*]
APL .... Antigen-Presenting Liposome [*Immunochemistry*]
APL .... Aperture Lip
APL .... Appalachian Flying Service, Inc. [*ICAO designator*] (FAAC)
APL .... Applied Physics Laboratory [*Johns Hopkins University*]
APL .... Approved Parts List
APL .... April
A/PL .... Armor Plate (MUGU)
APL .... Army Personnel Letter (AABC)
APL .... Army Promotion List (AABC)
APL .... As per List
APL .... Assembly Page Listing (SAA)
APL .... Assembly Part List
APL .... Assembly Programming Language [*Computer science*]
APL .... Assessment of Prior Learning
APL .... Assignment of (Construction) Permit and License [*FCC*] (NTCM)
APL .... Assistant Patrol Leader (DI)
APL .... Association of Pension Lawyers [*British*] (DBA)
APL .... Association of Photographic Laboratories [*British*] (DBA)
APL .... Association of Private Libraries (EA)
APL .... Association of Programmed Learning [*London, England*] (MCD)
APL .... Associative Programming Language [*Computer science*] (BUR)
APL .... Authorized Possession Limits [*Nuclear energy*] (NRCH)
APL .... Authorized Price List
APL .... Automatic Personnel Locator
APL .... Automatic Phase Lock
APL .... Automatic Premium Loan [*Insurance*]
APL .... Automatic Production Line
APL .... Automatic Programming Language [*Computer science*] (CMD)
APL .... Automotive Pigeon Loft
APL .... Average Picture Level
AP$_L$ .... Average Product of Labor
APL .... Aviation Psychology Laboratory [*Ohio State University*] [*Research center*] (RCD)
APL .... Barracks Craft [*Non-self-propelled*] [*Navy symbol*]
APL .... Chorionic Gonadotropin [*Endocrinology*] (DAVI)
APL .... Minneapolis, MN [*Location identifier FAA*] (FAAL)
APL .... Nampula [*Mozambique*] [*Airport symbol*] (OAG)
APL .... Plamondon Public Library, Alberta [*Library symbol National Library of Canada*] (NLC)
APL .... [*A*] Programming Language [*1960*] [*Computer science*] (CSR)
APLA .... American Patent Law Association [*Later, AIPLA*] (EA)
APLA .... Armenian Progressive League of America (EA)
APLA .... Arrowhead Professional Libraries Association [*Library network*]
APLA .... Asociacion Petroquimica Latinoamericana [*Argentina*] (EAIO)
APLA .... Association of Parliamentary Librarians of Australasia
APLA .... Atlantic Provinces Library Association (AC)
APLA .... Atlantic Provinces Linguistic Association [*Canada*]
APLA .... Australian Product Liability Association
APLA .... Authors' and Publishers' Lending Right Association Committee
APLA .... Aviation Pilot, Airship [*Navy*]
APLA Bull .... Bulletin. American Patent Law Association [*A publication*] (DLA)
APLAC .... Analysis Program Linear Active Circuits (NASA)
APLB .... Australian Property Law Bulletin [*A publication*]
APLC .... American Pro Life Council (EA)

APLC	Army Propulsion Laboratory and Center (KSC)
APLC	Assistant Poor Law Commissioner [British] (ROG)
APLC	Automated Parking Lot Control (MCD)
APLC	Leigh Creek [Australia ICAO location identifier] (ICLI)
APL Cas	Archbold's Poor Law Cases [1842-58] [A publication] (DLA)
APL/CAT	A Public Library/Community Access Tool [Acronym used by Community Information Database Dallas Public Library Texas] [Information service or system] (IID)
AplCell	Applied Cellular Technology [Associated Press] (SAG)
APL/CID	Allowance Parts List/Component Identification Number
APLCN	Appalachian (FAAC)
APLD	Applied (MSA)
APLD	Aspiration Percutaneus Lumber Dickectomy [Medicine]
APLD	Association of Professional Landscape Designers (EA)
ApldIndIT	Applied Industrial Technology [Associated Press] (SAG)
ApldMat	Applied Materials [Associated Press] (SAG)
ApldPw	Applied Power, Inc. [Associated Press] (SAG)
ApldSig	Applied Signal Technology, Inc. [Associated Press] (SAG)
APLE	Airportable Lifting Equipment [British military] (PDAA)
APLE	Association of Public Lighting Engineers [British] (BI)
APLET	Association for Programmed Learning and Educational Technology
Aplewds	Applewoods, Inc. [Associated Press] (SAG)
APLF	Alliance of Progressive and Left-Wing Forces [Greek] (PPE)
APLHGR	Average Planar Heat Generation Rate [Nuclear energy] (NRCH)
APLI	AUI Peace Language International
APLIC	Alaska Public Lands Information Center
APLIC	Association for Population/Family Planning Libraries and Information Centers - International [Also, an information service or system] (IID)
APLIC	Association of Parliamentary Librarians in Canada
APLIC-Intl	Association for Population/Family Planning Libraries and Information Centers, International (EA)
AplInov	Applied Innovation, Inc. [Associated Press] (SAG)
apliq	Applique (VRA)
APLIS	Australasian Public Libraries and Information Services [A publication]
APL/JHU	Applied Physics Laboratory/Johns Hopkins University
APLL	Analog Phased-Locked Loop (PDAA)
APLL	Automatic Phased-Locked Loop (PDAA)
APLL	Automatic Phase-Locked Loop [Electronics] (IAA)
APLM	Asynchronous Pulse Length Modulation [Electronics] (IAA)
APLM	Learmonth [Australia ICAO location identifier] (ICLI)
APLMI	Allowance Parts List Master Index (MCD)
APLN	Apollo Program Logic Network [NASA] (KSC)
APLNB	Association of Professional Librarians of New Brunswick (AC)
APLO	Aerial Port Liaison Office [or Officer] [Air Force] (AFM)
APLO	Aerial Port Logistics Office [Air Force]
APLO	Alaska Apollo Gold Mines [NASDAQ symbol] (SAG)
APLOF	Alaska Apollo Res Ltd [NASDAQ symbol] (TTSB)
APLP	Amyloid Precursor-Like Protein [Medicine] (DMAA)
APLPV	American Plum Line Pattern Virus [Plant pathology]
APLQ	Agence de Presse Libre du Quebec [Free Press Agency of Quebec] [Canada]
APLQ	Applique (MSA)
APLR	Australian Product Liability Reporter [A publication]
AplRecy	Appliance Recycling Centers of America [Associated Press] (SAG)
APLS	Administrator Professional Leadership Scale
APLS	American Plant Life Society (EA)
APLS	American Private Line Services, Inc. [Newton, MA] [Telecommunications] (TSSD)
AP-LS	American Psychology-Law Society (EA)
APLS	Apparel Performance Level Standards [Pronounced "apples"]
APLS	Association for Politics and the Life Sciences (EA)
APL/S	[A] Programming Language/Structured [Computer science] (CSR)
APLSTATPACK	Advanced Programming Language Statistical Package (MCD)
APLSV	[A] Programming Language Shared Variables [Computer science]
AP/LTC	Accreditation Program / Long Term Care [Medicine] (MEDA)
APLTR	Asian Pacific Law and Tax Review [A publication]
APLU	Automatic Program Loading Unit [Computer science]
APLUM	[A] Programming Language/University of Massachusetts [Computer science] (CSR)
A Plus	A Plus Network, Inc. [Associated Press] (SAG)
APL/UW	Applied Physics Laboratory/University of Washington
APLV	Andean Potato Latent Virus [Plant pathology]
APLWR	Advanced Passive Light Water Reactor [Nuclear energy]
APLX	Applix, Inc. [NASDAQ symbol] (SAG)
APM	Absolute Plate Motion [Geophysics]
APM	Academy of Parapsychology and Medicine [Defunct] (EA)
APM	Academy of Psychosomatic Medicine (EA)
APM	Acid-Precipitable Material [Antiviral agent]
APM	Acid-Prepared Mesostructure [Inorganic chemistry]
APM	Acoustic Performance Monitor
APM	Acquisition Project Manager
APM	Adelaide Produce Market [Australia]
APM	Admission Pattern Monitoring [Medicine] (HCT)
APM	Advanced Penetration Model (MCD)
APM	Advanced Power Management [Computer science] (PCM)
APM	Advanced Progressive Matrices [Intelligence test]
APM	Affected Pair Method [Statistics]
APM	Affected-Pedigree-Member [Technique for genetic study]
APM	African People's Movement [British]
APM	Agricultural Production and Management
APM	Aim-Point-Miss
APM	Air Pacific Airlines [ICAO designator] (FAAC)
APM	Air Particulate Matter [Environmental science]
APM	Air Particulate Monitor [Nuclear energy] (NRCH)
APM	Air Permeability Meter
APM	Air Pollution Meteorologist (NOAA)
APM	Air Provost Marshal
APM	Alarm Panel Monitor (AFM)
APM	Alfalfa Pest Management
APM	Alliance for a Paving Moratorium (EA)
APM	All Pilots Meeting [Military] (DNAB)
APM	Aluminum Powder Metallurgy
APM	American People's Mobilization [Formerly, American Peace Mobilization] [World War II]
APM	American Prison Ministry [An association] (EA)
APM	Aminopimelic Acid [An amino acid]
APM	Aminopropylmorpholine [Organic chemistry]
APM	Amiprophos Methyl [Organic chemistry]
APM	Amygdala Pars Medialis [Neuroanatomy]
APM	Analog Panel Meter (IEEE)
APM	Antenna Positioning Mechanism
APM	Anterior Papillary Muscle [Cardiology] (DAVI)
APM	Antipersonnel Missile
apm	Apomict [Biology] (BARN)
APM	Applied Magnetics [NYSE symbol] (SAG)
APM	Armenian Pan-National Movement [Political party] (EY)
APM	Army Program Memorandum (AABC)
APM	Army Projects Management Department (SAA)
APM	Aspartame [Sweetening agent]
APM	Assembly Page Maintenance (SAA)
APM	Assistant Paymaster [Marine Corps]
APM	Assistant Project Manager [NASA] (NASA)
APM	Assistant Provost Marshal [Facetious translation: "A Permanent Malingerer"]
APM	Association for Psychoanalytic Medicine (EA)
APM	Association of Professors of Medicine (EA)
APM	Association of Professors of Mission (EA)
APM	Associative Principle for Multiplication [Mathematics]
APM	Attached Pressurized Module [European Space Agency]
APM	Automated People Mover [MOCD] [TXDOT] (TAG)
APM	Automated Performance Measurement (MCD)
APM	Automated Plate Measuring [for Spectrography]
APM	Automatic Plugging Meter (PDAA)
APM	Automatic Predictive Maintenance (MHDI)
APM	Automatic Programming Machine [Computer science]
APM	Auxiliary Pastoral Ministry [Church of England]
APM	Mechanized Artillery Transport [Navy symbol Obsolete]
APM	Pro Musica [Record label]
APMA	Absorbent Paper Manufacturers Association [Defunct]
APMA	Advance Payment of Mileage Authorized [Army]
APMA	American Paper Machinery Association (EA)
APMA	American Podiatric Medical Association (EA)
APMA	American Podiatric Medical Students Association (EA)
APMA	American Productivity Management Association [Skokie, IL] (EA)
APMA	Aminophenylmercuric Acid [Organic chemistry]
APMA	Asia/Pacific Market Analysis [MMS International] [Information service or system] (CRD)
APMA	Australian Plastic Modellers' Association
APMA	Automatic Phonograph Manufacturers Association
APMA	Automotive Parts Manufacturers' Association [Association des Fabricants de Pieces d'Automobile] (AC)
APMAA	American Podiatric Medical Association Auxiliary (EA)
APMALTA	Advance Payment of Monetary Allowance in Lieu of Transportation Is Authorized [Army]
APMAST	Analysis of Packing Methods for Ammunition Storage and Transportation (MCD)
APMBA	Assistant Project Manager for Business Administration
APMC	Academy of Psychologists in Marital Counseling [Later, APMSFT]
APMC	Allied Political and Military Commission [World War II]
APMC	Applied Microsystems [NASDAQ symbol] (TTSB)
APMC	Applied Microsystems Corp. [NASDAQ symbol] (SAG)
APMC	Automatic Permanent Magnetic-Field Compensator (PDAA)
APMCA	Asian Pacific Materials and Corrosion Association
APMCSOG	Australian Police Ministers' Council, Senior Officers' Group
A/P MCU	Autopilot Monitor and Control Unit
APME	Area Precipitation Measurement Equipment
APME	Associated Press Managing Editors (EA)
APME	Association of Plastics Manufacturers in Europe (EA)
APME	Association Professionelle de Mesure en Education [Professional Association of Educational Measures] [Canada]
APME	Associative Processor Microelectronic Element
APMEA	Associated Press Managing Editors Association (DGA)
APMG	Assistant Postmaster-General [British]
APMH	Association of Professions for the Mentally Handicapped [British]
APMHC	Association of Professional Material Handling Consultants (EA)
APMI	American Powder Metallurgy Institute (EA)
APMI	Area Precipitation Measurement Indicator (IEEE)
APMI	Associate Member of the Pensions Management Institute [British] (DBQ)
APMI	Association of Printing Machinery Importers (DGA)
ApMicro	Applied Microsystems Corp. [Associated Press] (SAG)
APMIS	Aboriginal Programs Management Information System [Australia]
APMIS	Automated Project Management Information System [Computer science]
APML	American Pacific Minerals Ltd. [NASDAQ symbol] (SAG)
APML	Applied Physics and Materials Laboratory [Princeton University]
APML	Assistant Project Manager for Logistics
APMLQ	Association des Proprietaires de Machinerie Lourde du Quebec Inc. (AC)

APMLTU ...... Association of Professors of Modern Languages in Technological Universities (AIE)
APMMA .... Australasian Presentation and Multi-Media Association
APMM-EEC ... Association of Preserved Milk Manufacturers of the EEC [*European Economic Community*] [*France*] (EAIO)
APMMRI .... Automatic Point Marking, Measuring, and Recording Instrument
A/P MON ...... Autopilot Monitor (AAG)
APMP .... Aluminum Powder Metallurgy Product
APMP .... Association of Proposal Management Professionals
APMPPE ...... Acute Posterior Multifocal Placoid Pigment Epitheliopathy [*Ophthalmology*]
APMQ .... Association Professionnelle des Meuniers du Quebec [*Quebec Feed Manufacturer's Association*] (AC)
APMR .... Ancient Philosophies for Modern Readers [*A publication*]
APMR .... Association for Physical and Mental Rehabilitation [*Later, ACTA*] (EA)
APMR .... Meekatharra [*Australia ICAO location identifier*] (ICLI)
APMS .... Advanced Power Management System [*Jammer*] (MCD)
APMS .... Airborne Particle Monitoring System (MCD)
APMS .... Aquatic Plant Management Society (EA)
APMS .... Assistant Professor of Military S cience (INF)
APMS .... Automated Performance Measurement System [*FAA*] (TAG)
APMS .... Automated Performance Measurement System (GAVI)
APMS .... Automated Publications Maintenance System (DNAB)
APMSFT .... Academy of Psychologists in Marital Sex and Family Therapy (EA)
APMT .... Advanced Planetary Mission Technology [*NASA*]
APMT .... Antenna Pattern Measurement Test [*Army*] (AABC)
APMT .... Associated Professional Massage Therapists and Bodyworkers [*Later, ABMP*] (EA)
APMT .... Association of Professional Music Therapists [*British*] (DBA)
APMV .... Andean Potato Mottle Virus [*Plant pathology*]
ApMV .... Apple Mosaic Virus
APMWA .... American Podiatric Medical Writers Association (EA)
APN .... Acute Pyelonephritis [*Medicine*] (MAE)
APN .... Aerovia del Altiplano SA de CV [*Mexico ICAO designator*] (FAAC)
APN .... Agentstvo Pechati Novosti [*News agency*] [*Former USSR*]
APN .... Aircraft Procurement, Navy (NVT)
APN .... Aircraft Pulse Navigation
APN .... All Pass Network
APN .... Alpena [*Michigan*] [*Airport symbol*] (OAG)
APN .... Apron [*Aviation*]
APN .... Armee Populaire Nationale [*National People's Army*] [*Congo*] (AF)
APN .... Armenian Express Canada [*Vancouver Stock Exchange symbol*]
APN .... Army Part Number (MCD)
APN .... Artificial Pneumothorax [*Medicine*]
APN .... Aspen Airways [*Air carrier designation symbol*]
APN .... Assemblee des Premieres Nations (AC)
APN .... Assemblee Populaire Nationale [*Haiti*] [*Political party*] (EY)
APN .... Assyrian Personal Names [*A publication*] (BJA)
APN .... Australian Property News [*A publication*] (ADA)
APN .... Authorized Part Number
APN .... Average Peak Noise (MAE)
APN .... Aviation Procurement, Navy (MCD)
APn .... Die Aegyptischen Personnennamen [*A publication*] (BJA)
APN .... Nonmechanized Artillery Transport [*Navy symbol Obsolete*]
APNA .... American Power Net Association [*Later, EFMCNTA*] (EA)
APNA .... American Psychiatric Nurses Association (EA)
APNA .... Atlantic Provinces Numismatic Association [*Canada*]
APNA .... Australian Product Number Association
APNB .... Association Professionnelle des Nettoyeurs et Buandiers du Quebec (AC)
APNC .... Administration du Pipeline du Nord Canada [*Northern Pipeline Agency Canada - NPAC*]
APNEU .... Auxiliary Pneumatic (AAG)
APNG .... Australia - Papua New Guinea [*Submarine cable*] [*Telecommunications*]
APNGFA .... Australia-Papua New Guinea Friendship Association
APNI .... Alliance Party of Northern Ireland [*Political party*] (EAIO)
APNIC .... Asia Pacific Network Information Center
APNIC .... Automatic Programming National Information Center
APNIC .... Azidophenyl Norisocarbacyclin [*Organic chemistry*]
APNM .... Amorite Personal Names in the Mari Texts [*A publication*] (BJA)
ApNPM .... Apel. Notation of Polyphonic Music [*A publication*]
APNPS .... Acetyl(p-nitrophenyl)sulfanilamide [*Pharmacology*]
APNR .... American Professional Needlework Retailers (EA)
APNRP .... American-Polish National Relief for Poland (EA)
APNSS .... American Plate Number Single Society (EA)
APNT .... Appoint (FAAC)
APO .... Accountable Property Officer [*Military*]
APO .... Accounting Property Officer
APO .... Acquisition Program Office [*DoD*]
APO .... Acting Pilot Officer [*British*]
APO .... Action Print Only [*Cinematography*] (WDMC)
APO .... Adriamycin, Prednisone, Oncovin [*Vincristine*] [*Antineoplastic drug regimen*]
APO .... Advanced Post Office [*Military*]
APO .... Adverse Patient Occurence [*Medicine*] (HCT)
APO .... Adverse Patient Occurrences [*Medicine*] (MEDA)
APO .... Advisory Panel for Oceanography [*National Science Foundation*] (MSC)
APO .... Aeropro [*Canada ICAO designator*] (FAAC)
APO .... African People's Organization (WDAA)
APO .... Air Force Post Office
APO .... Air Force Procurement Officer (AAGC)

APO .... Air Post Office (MCD)
APO .... Air Procurement Office
APO .... Air Programs Office [*Environmental Protection Agency*]
APO .... Amorphous Polyolefin [*Organic chemistry*]
APO .... Andean Pact Organization [*Chile, Peru, Bolivia, Ecuador, Colombia*]
APO .... Animal Procurement Office [*Military*]
APO .... Annual Program Objectives [*Navy*] (NG)
APO .... Answer Print, Optical (DOAD)
APO .... Aphoxide [*Also, TEPA*] [*Mutagen*]
APO .... Apochromatic [*Photography*]
APO .... Apogee
Apo .... Apolipoprotein [*Biochemistry*]
Apo .... Apollo [*A publication*] (BRI)
APO .... Apollo Program Office [*NASA*] (KSC)
APO .... Apomorphine [*Neurochemistry, pharmacology*]
Apo .... Apoprotein [*Biochemistry*]
APO .... Area Petroleum Office [*or Officer*]
APO .... Areawide Planning Organization [*Department of Housing and Urban Development*] (GFGA)
APO .... Army/Air Force Post Office (AAGC)
APO .... Army Post Office
APO .... Asian Productivity Organization [*Japan*] (EAIO)
APO .... Asociacion Panamericana de Oftalmologia [*Panamerican Association of Ophthalmology*] [*Washington, DC*]
APO .... Assembly Production Order [*Manufacturing*] (AAG)
APO .... Assistant Project Officer
APO .... Astrophysical Observatory [*Smithsonian Museum*]
APO .... Asymptotically Pointwise Optimal (DNAB)
APO .... Attach Points Only (MCD)
APO .... AWIPS [*Advanced Weather Interactive Processing System*] Program Office [*Marine science*] (OSRA)
APO .... AWIPS [*Advanced Weather Interactive Processing System*] Program Office (USDC)
APO .... Office of Aviation Policy and Plans [*FAA*] (TAG)
APO .... Ponoka Public Library, Alberta [*Library symbol National Library of Canada*] (NLC)
APO .... Tris(aziridinyl)phosphine Oxide [*Organic chemistry*]
APOA .... Alabama Peace Officers Association (SRA)
ApoA .... Apolipoprotein A [*Biochemistry*]
APOA .... Arctic Petroleum Operators' Association [*Canada*]
APOAF .... All Present or Accounted For
APOAM .... Acting Petty Officer Air Mechanic [*British military*] (DMA)
APOB .... Actual Projected on Board [*Allowance*] (DNAB)
APOB .... Apolipoprotein-B [*Biochemistry*] (ECON)
APOBA .... Associated Pipe Organ Builders of America (EA)
APOBS .... Antipersonnel Obstacle Breaching System [*Marine Corps*] (INF)
APOC .... Advance Post Office Check [*Bureau of the Census*] (GFGA)
APOC .... Aerial Port Operations Center
APOC .... Anglia and Prefect Owners' Club [*British*] (BI)
Apoc .... Apocalypse
Apoc .... Apocalyptic (BJA)
Apoc .... Apocrypha (BJA)
ApoC .... Apolipoprotein C [*Biochemistry*]
APOC .... Army Point of Contact (AABC)
APOC .... Army Post Office Corps [*British military*] (DMA)
APOC .... Association of Postal Officials of Canada
ApocAbr .... Apocalypse of Abraham (BJA)
APOC BAR ... Apocalypse of Baruch [*Apocalyptic book*]
ApocElij .... Apocalypse of Elijah (BJA)
ApocGen ...... [*The*] Genesis Apocryphon from Qumran. Cave One (BJA)
APOCH .... Apocrypha (ROG)
ApocMos ...... Apocalypse of Moses (BJA)
Apocol .... Apocolocyntosis [*of Seneca the Younger*] [*Classical studies*] (OCD)
ApocPet .... Apocalypse of Peter (BJA)
apocph .... Apocrypha (VRA)
APOCR .... Apocrypha
Apocr .... [*The*] Genesis Apocryphon from Qumran. Cave One (BJA)
APOD .... Aerial Port of Debarkation [*Military*]
APOD .... [*A*] Pea in the Pod, Inc. [*NASDAQ symbol*] (SAG)
APOE .... Aerial Port of Embarkation [*Military*]
ApoE .... Apolipoprotein E [*Biochemistry*]
APOFDF .... Application of Filters to Demand Forecasting (MCD)
APOG .... Aerial Port Group [*Air Force*] (AFM)
APOG .... Apogee
APOG .... Apogee Enterprises [*NASDAQ symbol*] (TTSB)
APOG .... Apogee Enterprises, Inc. [*NASDAQ symbol*] (NQ)
Apogee .... Apogee, Inc. [*Associated Press*] (SAG)
ApogEn .... Apogee Enterprises, Inc. [*Associated Press*] (SAG)
APOGI .... Advanced Polaris Guidance Information
APOI .... Association of Palm Oil Importers [*British*] (DBA)
APOJI .... Automatic Processing of Jezebel [*Sonobuoy System*] Information
APOL .... Aerospace Program-Oriented Language [*Computer science*] (PDAA)
APOL .... Apollo Group 'A' [*NASDAQ symbol*] (TTSB)
APOL .... Apollo Group, Inc. [*NASDAQ symbol*] (SAG)
Apol .... Apologeticus [*of Tertullian*] [*Classical studies*] (OCD)
Apol .... Apologia [*of Apuleius*] [*Classical studies*] (OCD)
APOL .... Australian Political Register [*Australian Consolidated Press*] [*Database*]
A Pol J .... Australian Police Journal [*A publication*]
APOLLO ...... Article Procurement with Online Local Ordering [*Document delivery system*] [*Telecommunications*]
Apollod .... Apollodorus [*Second century BC*] [*Classical studies*] (OCD)
ApolloG .... Apollo Group, Inc. [*Associated Press*] (SAG)
APOMA .... American Precision Optics Manufacturers Association (EA)
APOMS .... Automated Propeller Optical Measurement System

APON	Association of Pediatric Oncology Nurses (EA)
APOP	Apollo Preflight Operations Procedures [*NASA*] (KSC)
APOPA	Association of Private Office Personnel Agencies
APOPEC	Agence de Presse de l'OPEC [*OPEC News Agency - OPECNA*] [*Vienna, Austria*] (EAIO)
Apophth	Apophthegmata [*of Julian*] [*Classical studies*] (OCD)
APOR	Advisory Panel for Operations Research
APORF	Acute Postoperative Renal Failure [*Medicine*] (AAMN)
APORS	Army Performance-Oriented Review and Standards Program
APORS	Army Performance-Oriented Reviews and Standards
APORTS	Aerial Ports [*And Air Operating Base File*] [*Military*] (DOMA)
APOS	Advanced Polar Orbiting Satellite
APOS	Advanced Polymer Sys [*NASDAQ symbol*] (TTSB)
APOS	Advanced Polymer Systems, Inc. [*NASDAQ symbol*] (NQ)
APOS	Apostrophe
APOS	Cocos Islands [*Australia ICAO location identifier*] (ICLI)
APOSS	Automatic Point of Sale System (IAA)
apost	Apostolic (BJA)
APOSW	Association of Pediatric Oncology Social Workers (EA)
APOT	[*The*] Apocrypha and Pseudepigrapha of the Old Testament [*A publication*] (BJA)
APOTA	Automatic Positioning Telemetering Antenna
APOTH	Apothecary
APOTV	All Propulsive Orbited Transfer Vehicle [*NASA*]
APP	Abandoned Private Property
APP	Academy of Pharmacy Practice (EA)
APP	Accelerated Pacification Program [*Vietnam, 1968*] (VNW)
APP	Access Point Pace (KSC)
APP	Accident Prevention Plan
APP	Accion Politica Progresista [*Progressive Political Action*] [*Ecuador*] [*Political party*] (PPW)
APP	Acid-Precipitated Protein [*Food analysis*]
APP	Acoustic Performance Prediction [*Navy*] (MSC)
APP	Acquisition Plan (Procurement)
APP	Adjusted Performance Percentile (DNAB)
APP	Advanced Parts Procurement (MCD)
APP	Advanced Placement Program
APP	Advanced Planetary Probe
APP	Advanced Procurement Package (MCD)
APP	Advanced Procurement Plan [*Navy British*]
APP	Advanced Project Planning
APP	Advance Port Purchase [*Investment term*] (ECON)
APP	Advance Procurement Plan [*Navy*]
APP	Aerolineas Pacifico Atlantico SA [*Spain ICAO designator*] (FAAC)
APP	African People's Party [*Kenya*] (AF)
APP	Agence Parisienne de Presse [*Parisian Press Agency*] [*French*] (AF)
APP	Aggregate Production Planning (PDAA)
APP	Air Parcel Post [*Shipping*] (AABC)
APP	Air Pollution Potential
APP	Allied Procedures Publications (NATG)
APP	Allopurinol Phosphate [*Biochemistry*]
APP	All Purpose Paper [*Euphemism for toilet paper*]
APP	Alum-Precipitated Protein [*Biochemistry*] (DAVI)
APP	Alum Precipitated Pyridine [*Medicine*] (MAE)
APP	American Paging, Inc. [*AMEX symbol*] (SAG)
APP	Amer Paging [*AMEX symbol*] (TTSB)
APP	Aminopyrazolopyrimidine [*Biochemistry*]
APP	Ammonium Polyphosphate [*Fertilizer*]
APP	Ammunition Post Processor [*Computer science Military*]
APP	Amorphous Polypropylene [*Organic chemistry*]
APP	Amortization and Partial Prepayment [*Business term*]
APP	Amyloid Protein Precursor [*Biochemistry*]
APP	Analysis Production Persistency [*LIMRA*]
APP	Anguilla People's Party [*Later, ADP*] [*Political party*] (PPW)
APP	Antenna Position Programmer [*Manned Space Flight Network*]
APP	Antipersonnel Projectile
APP	Antipodal Propagation Phenomena
APP	A Posteriori Probability (MCD)
APP	Apostles
APP	Apparatus (KSC)
APP	Apparently
APP	Appeal (ADA)
App	Appeal Cases [*A publication*] (DLA)
App	Appeals (AAGC)
APP	Appearance (MSA)
APP	Appelbo [*Sweden*] [*Seismograph station code, US Geological Survey*] (SEIS)
APP,	Appellate [*Legal term*] (DLA)
App	Appellate (AAGC)
APP	Append [*or Appendix*] (AFM)
App	Appendix (AAGC)
App	Appian [*Second century AD*] [*Classical studies*] (OCD)
App	Appleton's Reports [*19, 20 Maine*]
APP	Application
app	Application [*Computer science*]
APP	Application Date [*Bell System*] (TEL)
APP	Applications Portability Profile [*Computer science*] (BARN)
APP	Applied
APP	Applied Psychology Panel [*of NDRC*] [*World War II*]
APP	Appointed
APP	Appraised (WGA)
APP	Apprehend (AABC)
APP	Apprentice
APP	Approach
APP	Approach Astrophysics Payload [*NASA*] (MCD)

APP	Approach Control Office [*Aviation code*]
APP	Appropriated (ROG)
APP	Approval (ADA)
APP	Approximate
APP	Army Procurement Procedure
APP	Ashford Press Publishing [*British*]
APP	Asia Pacific Capital Corp. [*Vancouver Stock Exchange symbol*]
APP	Associated Press of Pakistan
APP	Associated Purchasing Publications
APP	Association of Pakistani Physicians (EA)
APP	Association of Professional Photogrammetrists (EA)
APP	Associative Parallel Processor [*Computer science*]
APP	Astrophysics Payload [*NASA*] (MCD)
APP	Atactic Polypropylene [*Organic chemistry*]
APP	Atmospheric Physics Programme [*International Council of Scientific Unions*]
APP	Australian Psychologists Press [*A publication*]
APP	Automatic Plate Processor
APP	Automatic Position Planning
APP	Auxiliary Pneumatics Panel
APP	Auxiliary Power Package (MCD)
APP	Auxiliary Power Plant
APP	Avian Pancreatic Polypeptide
APP	Axactic Polypropylene
APP	Fort McPherson Library System, Fort McPherson, GA [*OCLC symbol*] (OCLC)
App	Illinois Appellate Court Reports [*A publication*] (DLA)
App	Office of Airport Planning and Programming [*FAA*] (TAG)
App	Ohio Appellate Reports [*A publication*] (DLA)
a-pp--	Papua New Guinea [*MARC geographic area code Library of Congress*] (LCCP)
App	Texas Court of Appeals Reports [*A publication*] (DLA)
APP	Troop Barge, Class A [*Navy symbol Obsolete*]
APPA	Advise Present Position and Altitude [*Aviation*] (FAAC)
APPA	Alabama Peanut Producers Association (SRA)
APPA	American Paper and Pulp Association [*Later, API*]
APPA	American Physicians Poetry Association (EA)
APPA	American Probation and Parole Association (EA)
APPA	American Professional Practice Association (EA)
APPA	American Psychological Practitioners Association (EA)
APPA	American Psychopathological Association (EA)
APPA	American Public Power Association (EA)
APPA	Arizona Professional Photographers Association (SRA)
APPA	Arkansas Pork Producers Association (SRA)
APPA	Association for the Preservation and Presentation of the Arts
APPA	Association for the Preservation of Political Americana (EA)
APPA	Association of Philippine Physicians in America (EA)
APPA	Association of Physical Plant Administrators of Universities and Colleges (EA)
APPA	Port Hedland [*Australia ICAO location identifier*] (ICLI)
APPAC	Association of Professional Placement Agencies & Consultants [*Association de Placement en Personnel Agences et Conseillers*] (AC)
APPAC	Aviation Petroleum Products Allocation Committee
APPAC-L	Aviation Petroleum Products Allocation Committee, London
APPALLING	Acronym Production Particularly at Lavish Level Is No Good [*Term coined by Theodore M. Bernstein*]
Appal St U	Appalachian State University (GAGS)
APPAM	Association for Public Policy Analysis and Management (EA)
AppAnl	Applied Analytical Industries, Inc. [*Associated Press*] (SAG)
APPANT	Appellant [*Legal shorthand*] (LWAP)
APPAR	Apparatus (AFM)
APPAR	Apparent
APPARAT	Archive Preservation Programme and Retrieval by Automated Techniques [*Computer science*]
APPATS	Automated Program to Project AIT [*Advanced Individual Training*] Training Spaces [*DoD*]
APPAUC	Association of Physical Plant Administrators of Universities and Colleges (EA)
APPB	Airborne Provisioning Parts Breakdown
APPB	Applebee's International, Inc. [*NASDAQ symbol*] (NQ)
APPB	Applebee's Intl. [*NASDAQ symbol*] (TTSB)
App Bd OCS	Office of Contract Settlement, Appeal Board Decisions [*A publication*] (DLA)
APPC	Advanced Program-to-Program Communication [*Computer science*]
APPC	Advance Planning Procedure Change (SAA)
APPC	Advance Procurement Planning Council [*DoD*] (PDAA)
APPC	Army Provisioning Process Course [*DoD*] (RDA)
APPC	Automatic Power Plant Checker
App Ca	Buchanan. Cape Colony Court of Appeal Reports [*South Africa*] [*A publication*] (DLA)
App Cas	Appeal Cases, District of Columbia [*1-74*] [*A publication*] (DLA)
App Cas	Appeal Cases, English Law Reports [*1875-90*] [*A publication*] (DLA)
App Cas	Appeal Cases in the United States [*A publication*] (DLA)
App Cas	Appeal Cases of the Different States [*A publication*] (DLA)
App Cas	Law Reports, Appeal Cases [*England*] [*A publication*] (DLA)
App Cas 2d	Appeal Cases, English Law Reports, Second Series [*A publication*] (DLA)
App Cas Beng	Sevestre and Marshall's Bengal Reports [*A publication*] (DLA)
App Cas (DC)	Appeal Cases, District of Columbia [*1-74*] [*A publication*] (DLA)
App CC	Texas Civil Cases [*A publication*] (DLA)
App CC (White & W)	Texas Civil Cases [*A publication*] (DLA)
App CC (Willson)	Texas Civil Cases [*A publication*] (DLA)
APPCE	Appearance (ROG)
App Civ Cases	Texas Civil Cases [*A publication*] (DLA)

APPCo .... Association of Post Production Companies [*British*] (DBA)
app code ..... Application Code (CDE)
APPCON ...... Approach Control [*Aviation*] (AFM)
APPC/PC ...... Advanced Program-to-Program Communication/Personal Computer [*IBM Corp.*] (BYTE)
APPCR .... Arbitrarily Primed Polymerase Chain Reaction [*Genetics*]
APPCS .... Association of Parents Paying Child Support (EA)
App Ct .... Appellate Court (BARN)
App Ct Rep... Appeal Court Reports, New Zealand [*A publication*] (DLA)
App Ct Rep... Bradwell's Illinois Appellate Reports [*A publication*] (DLA)
APPD .... Appeared (ROG)
APPD .... Approved (KSC)
APPD .... Aviation Personnel Planning Data [*Navy*] (NG)
APPD .... Port Hedland [*Australia ICAO location identifier*] (ICLI)
App D .... South Africa Law Reports, Appellate Division [*A publication*] (DLA)
APPDA .... Atlantic Provinces Power Development Act [*Canada*]
App DC .... Appeal Cases, District of Columbia [*A publication*] (DLA)
app den ...... Appeal Denied (DLA)
APP/DEP ..... Approach/Departure [*Aviation*] (DNAB)
App Dep't .... Appellate Department (DLA)
App Dept Super Ct... Appellate Department of the Superior Court, California (ILCA)
APPDI .... American Professional Pet Distributors, Inc. [*An association*] (EA)
app dism ..... Appeal Dismissed (DLA)
App Div....... Appellate Division (DLA)
App Div....... New York Supreme Court, Appellate Division Reports [*A publication*] (DLA)
App Div 2d... New York Supreme Court, Appellate Division Reports, Second Series [*A publication*] (DLA)
App Div (NY)... New York Supreme Court, Appellate Division Reports [*A publication*] (DLA)
App Div NY Sup Ct... New York Supreme Court, Appellate Division Reports [*A publication*] (DLA)
App Div R.... New York Supreme Court, Appellate Division Reports [*A publication*] (DLA)
App Div Rep... Massachusetts Appellate Division Reports [*A publication*] (DLA)
APPE.......... Association for Practical and Professional Ethics (EA)
APPE.......... Association of Petrochemical Producers in Europe (ECON)
APPE.......... Average per Pupil Expenditure [*Education*] (GFGA)
APPE.......... Pearce [*Australia ICAO location identifier*] (ICLI)
APPEC .... Asia-Pacific Petroleum Conference
APPECS ...... Adaptive Pattern-Perceiving Electronic Computer System
APPEM........ Anovulatory Persistent Proliferative Endometrium [*Medicine*]
APPEN .... Appendage
APPEN .... Asia-Pacific People's Environment Network [*Penang, Malaysia*] (EAIO)
Append .... Appendix (DLA)
App Ev .... Appleton's Rules of Evidence [*A publication*] (DLA)
App Exam .... Appeal [*or Appeals*] Examiner (DLA)
AP/PF.......... Accreditation Program / Psychiatric Facilities (MEDA)
APPF.......... Adelaide/Parafield [*Australia ICAO location identifier*] (ICLI)
APPF.......... Association Provinciale des Parents Fransaskois [*Fransaskois Parents Association*] (AC)
APPF.......... Automated Payload Processing Facility [*NASA*] (NASA)
App Fish Com... Appeals from Fisheries Commission [*1861-93*] [*Ireland*] [*A publication*] (DLA)
APPG .... Adjacent Phase Pulse Generator [*Electronics*] (OA)
APPG .... Aqueous Procaine Penicillin G [*Antibiotic*]
APPGM .... Army Planning and Programming Guidance Memorandum (MCD)
AppGrp .... Applied Intelligence Group, Inc. [*Associated Press*] (SAG)
AppGrph ...... Appied Graphics Technologies, Inc. [*Associated Press*] (SAG)
APPH .... Perth/International [*Australia ICAO location identifier*] (ICLI)
APPHR .... American Peruvian Paso Horse Registry (EA)
APPI........... Advance Planning Procurement Information [*Army*] (MCD)
APPI........... Association of Professional Police Investigators (EA)
APPI........... Australian Pulp and Paper Institute [*Monash University*] [*Australia*]
APPI........... International Association for the Promotion and Protection of Private Foreign Investments
ApplGrp ...... Applied Intelligence Group, Inc. [*Associated Press*] (SAG)
AppImg .... Applied Imaging Corp. [*Associated Press*] (SAG)
App Jur Act 1876... Appellate Jurisdiction Act of 1876 [*39, 40 Victoria, c. 59*] (DLA)
APPL .... Aircraft Precision Position Location Equipment (DA)
APPL........... Appeal
APPL........... Appellant (WDAA)
APPL.......... Appliance
APPL.......... Applicable (AFM)
APPL.......... Applicant [*or Application*] (DNAB)
APPL.......... Applied
appl .... Applied (VRA)
APPL.......... As Planned Parts List (MCD)
AP Plan ...... Advance Procurement Plan (AAGC)
APPLAN ...... Applanation [*Ophthalmology*]
applan .... Applantus [*Flattened*] [*Latin*] (MAE)
APPLAUSE... Appeal, Plain Facts, Personalities, Local Angle, Action, Uniqueness [*or Universality*], Significance, Energy
APPLCTN ..... Application
APPLCTR ..... Applicator
APPLD .... Applied
APPLD .... Applied
APPLE......... Advanced Pioneering Performance by Leading Engineering
APPLE......... Advanced Propulsion Payload Effects [*NASA*] (NASA)
APPLE......... Aerotherm Prediction Procedure for LASER Effects (MCD)
APPLE.......... AIDS [*Acquired Immune Deficiency Syndrome*] Prevention League (EA)
APPLE.......... Analog Phased Processing Loop Equipment [*Computer science*] (MHDB)

APPLE........ Apollo Payload Exploration [*NASA*]
APPLE........ Applied Parallel Programming Language Experiment [*Computer science*] (MCD)
APPLE........ ARIANE [*Artificial Satellite*] Passenger Payload Experiment (PDAA)
APPLE.......... Association of Public and Private Labor Employees
APPLE.......... Associative Processor Programming Language Evaluation
Applebee..... Applebee's International, Inc. [*Associated Press*] (SAG)
AppleC........ Apple Computer, Inc. [*Associated Press*] (SAG)
APPLEE....... Appellee [*Legal shorthand*] (LWAP)
APPLE-MD ... Age; Prior Service; Physical, Legal, Educational, and Marital Status; and Dependents [*Army recruiting questionnaire*]
Apple PIE.... Parental Involvement in Education
APPLES....... Asian and Pacific Professional Language and Education Services [*Defunct*] (EA)
Appleton...... Appleton's Reports [*19, 20 Maine*] [*A publication*] (DLA)
APPLIC .... Applicatur [*Let It Be Applied*] [*Pharmacy*] (ROG)
APPLICAND... Applicandus [*To Be Applied*] [*Pharmacy*]
APPLICAT ... Applicatur [*Let It Be Applied*] [*Pharmacy*]
Applix........ Applix, Inc. [*Associated Press*] (SAG)
ApplMg....... Applied Magnetics Corp. [*Associated Press*] (SAG)
APPLN........ Application
APPLNC...... Appliance
APPLON...... Application
APPLQ .... Applique
ApplSou...... Apple South, Inc. [*Associated Press*] (SAG)
Appltree...... Appletree Companies [*Associated Press*] (SAG)
APPM........ Alliance des Professeures et Professeurs de Montreal (AC)
APPM........ Associated Pulp and Paper Mills (DGA)
APPM........ Association of Publication Production Managers (EA)
APPM........ Atom Parts per Million (MCD)
APPMA........ American Pet Products Manufacturers Association (EA)
APPME........ American Professors for Peace in the Middle East [*Defunct*] (EA)
App ME........ Applied Mechanics Engineer [*Academic degree*]
App ME........ Applied Mechanics Engineer (PGP)
APPMI........ American Peanut Product Manufacturers, Inc. (EA)
AppMinSci ... Applied Mineral Sciences (DD)
APPMSA ..... American Paper and Pulp Mills Superintendents' Association (DGA)
APPMT........ Appointment
APPN........ Advanced Peer-to-Peer Networking [*Computer science*]
APPN........ Appropriation
APPNET ...... MicroBilt Applications Network [*MicroBuilt Corp.*] [*Telecommunications service*] (TSSD)
APPNT........ Appointment (WGA)
APPNTD...... Appointed
App NZ .... Appeal Reports, New Zealand [*A publication*] (DLA)
App NZ 2d... Appeal Reports, New Zealand, Second Series [*A publication*] (DLA)
APPO......... Advanced Product Planning Operation (MUGU)
APPO......... Army Power Procurement Office
A/P POI ...... Autopilot Positioning Indicator
APPOR....... Army Power Procurement Officer Representative (MCD)
APPOS....... Appositive (WDAA)
APPPP........ Advanced Procurement Planning Program
APPP........ Association of Planned Parenthood Professionals [*Later, ARHP*] (EA)
APPP........ Perth [*Australia ICAO location identifier*] (ICLI)
APPPA........ Association of Philippine Practicing Physicians in America [*Later, APPA*] (EA)
APPPC........ Asia and Pacific Plant Protection Commission [*Formerly, Plant Protection Committeefor the Southeast Asia and Pacific Region*] (EA)
APPQ .... Association des Policiers Provinciaux du Quebec [*Quebec Provincial Police Association*] (AC)
APPR .... Allopurinol Phosphate Ribonucleotide [*Biochemistry*]
APPR .... Aminopyrazolopyrimidine Ribonucleoside [*Biochemistry*]
APPR .... Appear (FAAC)
APPR .... Apprehend (AFM)
APPR .... Apprenticeship (AABC)
APPR .... Approach/Approach Mode (GAVI)
APP-R .... Approach Control RADAR (DA)
APPR .... Approaching Lactate Dehydrogenase [*LD*] 1:2 Flip [*Cardiology*] (DAVI)
APPR .... Approval (AFM)
APPR .... Approximate (ADA)
APPR .... Army Package Power Reactor
APPR .... Perth [*Australia ICAO location identifier*] (ICLI)
APPRAIST... Appraisement (ROG)
APPRC....... American Partridge Plymouth Rock Club (EA)
APPRCE...... Apprentice (ROG)
APPRCHR ... Approacher
App Ref ...... Appeal Referee (DLA)
APPRENT..... Apprentice
Apprent News... Apprenticeship News [*A publication*]
App Rep ...... Ontario Appeal Reports [*A publication*] (DLA)
App Rep Ont... Ontario Appeal Reports [*A publication*] (DLA)
APPRES...... Applied Research
APPRL....... Apparel
APPRNTC.... Apprentice
App RNZ ..... Appeal Reports, New Zealand [*A publication*] (DLA)
APPRO........ Approbation
APPRO........ Approval
approp .... Appropriate (DMAA)
APPROP...... Appropriation
APPROV...... Approved (DAVI)
APPROX...... Approximate (EY)
APPROX...... Approximation (DAVI)
Apprs........ Approaches [*Maps and charts*]

APPRSER..... Appraiser
APPRSL..... Appraisal
APPRSOR..... Appraisor
APPRTS...... Apparatus
APPRV........ Approve
apprvd........ Approved (ILCA)
APPRX........ Approximate
APPS .... Adenosine Phosphate Phosphosulfate [*Also, PAPS*] [*Biochemistry*]
APPS .... Advanced Planning Program Scheduling
APPS .... Advanced Protein Purification System
APPS .... Aerosol Physical Properties of the Stratosphere [*NASA*] (MCD)
APPS .... Amyloid Precursor Protein Secretase [*Medicine*] (DMAA)
APPS .... Analytical Photogrammetric Positioning System (MCD)
APPS .... Analytical Photogrammetric Processing System (MCD)
apps........... Appendixes (DLA)
APPS .... Applications Server [*Computer science*]
APPS .... Application Support System (IAA)
APPS .... Arylated Poly(phenylene Sulfide) [*Organic chemistry*]
APPS .... Association of Private Postal Systems [*Later, AAPS*] (EA)
APPS .... Atmospheric Pressure Plasma Sprayed [*Thermal barrier coating*]
APPS .... Autologic Paginating and Photoimaging System [*Typography*] (DGA)
APPS .... Automated Packaging Planning System (MCD)
APPS .... Automated Photogrammetric Positioning System (DNAB)
APPS .... Automated Publication Preparation System [*Army*] (MCD)
APPS .... Automated Purchase and Payment System [*United Nations*] (DUND)
APPS .... Automatic Point Positioning System (MCD)
APPS .... Auxiliary Payload Power System (MCD)
App Sc........ Applied Scientist (PGP)
APPS II....... Analytical Photogrammetric Positioning System - II
APPSMS...... Automated Procurement and Production Scheduling and Management System [*Army*]
APPSQ........ Association Professionnelle des Pharmaciens Salaries du Quebec (AC)
APPSSA...... Advanced Procurement Planning System for Security Assistance
APPT.......... Appointment (AFM)
appt........... Appointment [*Medicine*] (DMAA)
APPT.......... Assessment of the Provision of Part Time Training [*Education*] (AIE)
App T......... Supreme Court Appellate Term (DLA)
App Tax Serv... Appeals Relating to Tax on Servants [*1781*] [*England*] [*A publication*] (DLA)
APPTD .... Appointed
APPTNT ...... Appointment (ROG)
App Trib ..... Appeal Tribunal (DLA)
APPTS .... Appellants (ROG)
APPTT......... Appointment (ROG)
APPU .... Air Photo Production Unit [*Canada*]
APPU .... Application Program Preparation Utility (MHDI)
APPU .... Asian-Pacific Parliamentary Union
APPU .... Asian-Pacific Postal Union [*Manila, Philippines*] (EAIO)
APPURTS..... Appurtenances (ROG)
APPV .... Approve (MSA)
APPVAL ...... Approval (ROG)
APPVL .... Approval (MSA)
ApPw .... Appalachian Power Co. [*Associated Press*] (SAG)
APPWP .... Association of Private Pension and Welfare Plans (EA)
APPX .... Appendix (KSC)
appx........... Appendix [*Medicine*] (DMAA)
appx........... Approximate (VRA)
Appx Bre..... Appendix to Breese's Reports [*Illinois*] [*A publication*] (DLA)
APPY .... Appendectomy [*Medicine*] (AAMN)
appy........... Appendectomy [*Medicine*] (DMAA)
APQ .... Air Philippines Corporation, Inc. [*ICAO designator*] (FAAC)
APQ .... Arithmetic Processor Queue (IAA)
APQ .... Asia-Pacific Resources [*Vancouver Stock Exchange symbol*]
APQ .... Association des Proprietaires du Quebec (AC)
APQ .... Association des Prospecteurs du Quebec [*Quebec Prospectors Association*] (AC)
APQ .... Association des Psychologues du Quebec [*Quebec Psychological Association*] (AC)
APQ .... Autonomic Perception Questionnaire [*Psychology*] (EDAC)
APQC .... Asia Pacific Resources Ltd. [*NASDAQ symbol*] (SAG)
APQCF .... Asia Pacific Resources Ltd [*NASDAQ symbol*] (TTSB)
APR .... Abdominoperineal Resection [*Medicine*]
APR .... Absolute Proximal Reabsorption [*Medicine*] (DMAA)
APR .... Academy for Peace Research (EA)
APR .... Accredited in Public Relations
APR .... Accredited in Public Relations [*Canadian Public Relations Society, Inc.*] (DD)
APR .... Acoustic Paramagnetic Resonance [*Physics*]
APR .... Active Page Register [*Computer science*] (MHDI)
APR .... Acute Phase Reactant [*Medicine*]
APR .... Acute Phase Response [*Medicine*]
APR .... Advanced Parts Release (NASA)
APR .... Advance Production Release (NRCH)
APR .... Aerial Photographic Reconnaissance
APR .... Agency Procurement Request
APR .... Agency Progress Report
APR .... Airborne Profile Recorder
APR .... Airman Performance Report
APR .... Airports Program Report (FAAC)
APR .... Air Priority Rating
APR .... Air-Purifying Respirator (FFDE)
APR .... Alien Priory
APR .... All-Purpose Room
APR .... Alteration and Project Report (DNAB)

APR .... Alternate Path Reentry [*Fujitsu Ltd.*] [*Computer science*] (MCD)
APR .... Amebic Prevalence Rate (MAE)
APR .... American Poetry Review [*A publication*] (BRI)
APR .... American Precision Industries, Inc. [*NYSE symbol*] (SPSG)
APR .... American Public Radio
APR .... Amer Precision Indus [*NYSE symbol*] (TTSB)
APR .... Ammunition Performance Report [*Military*] (NVT)
APR .... Analog Parameter Record (IAA)
APR .... Anatomic Porous Replacement [*Orthopedics*] (DAVI)
APR .... Annual Percentage Rate
APR .... Annual Planning Report
APR .... Annual Progress Report
APR .... Anonymous Peer Refereeing
APR .... Antenna Position Recorder
APR .... Anterior Pituitary Reaction [*Endocrinology*] (AAMN)
APR .... Anterior Pituitary Resection [*Medicine*] (MAE)
APR .... Antiplugging Relay
APR .... Apollo Program Requirements [*NASA*] (KSC)
APR .... Applied Property Research [*British*]
APR .... Apprentice (AFM)
APR .... April (AFM)
APR .... Area Planning Report
APR .... Arecibo [*Puerto Rico*] [*Seismograph station code, US Geological Survey*] (SEIS)
APR .... Army Procurement Regulation [*or Requirement*]
APR .... Asian Profiles [*Database*] [*SRG International Ltd.*] [*Information service or system*] (CRD)
APR .... Assigned Procurement Responsibility (AAG)
APR .... Associated Press Radio
APR .... Association for Promoting Retreats [*British*] (BI)
APR .... Association of Petroleum Re-Refiners (EA)
APR .... Association of Publishers Representatives [*Later, NAPR*] (EA)
APR .... Auburn-Placer County Library, Auburn, CA [*OCLC symbol*] (OCLC)
APR .... Auropalpebral Reflex [*Response to sound*]
APR .... Automatic Paralleling Relay (MCD)
APR .... Automatic Passbook Reader (BUR)
APR .... Automatic Pattern Recognition
APR .... Automatic Performance Reserve
APR .... Automatic Performance Review [*Aerospace*]
APR .... Automatic Power Reserve [*Aeronautics*]
APR .... Automatic Pressure Relief [*Nuclear energy*] (NRCH)
APR .... Automatic Production Recording
APR .... Automatic Programming and Recording [*Computer science*] (MCD)
APR .... Available Power Response
APR .... Awaiting Price Redetermination (AAGC)
APR .... Provost Public Library, Alberta [*Library symbol National Library of Canada*] (NLC)
APR .... Rescue Transport [*Navy symbol*]
APR .... Societe Nouvelle d'Exploitation Air Provence [*France ICAO designator*] (FAAC)
APRA .... Aircraft Production Resources Agency
APRA .... Air Public Relations Association [*British*] (BI)
APRA .... Alberta Plastics Recycling Association (AC)
APRA .... Alianza Popular Revolucionaria Americana [*American Popular Revolutionary Alliance*] [*Peru*] [*Political party*] (PPW)
APRA .... American Park Rangers Association (EA)
APRA .... American Petroleum Refiners Association [*Later, AIRA*] (EA)
APRA .... American Pigeon Racing Association (EA)
APRA .... American Pistol and Revolver Association [*Defunct*] (EA)
APRA .... American Popular Revolutionary Alliance [*Peru*] [*Political party*]
APRA .... American Prospect Research Association (EA)
APRA .... American Public Relations Association [*Later, PRSA*]
APRA .... Apria Healthcare Group, Inc. [*NASDAQ symbol*] (SAG)
APRA .... Arizona Parks and Recreation Association (SRA)
APRA .... Armed Forces Production Resources Agency (MUGU)
APRA .... Army Pulsed Experimental Research Assembly
APRA .... Association for the Protection of Rural Australia
APRA .... Association of Political Risk Analysts [*Later, CIBRM*] (EA)
APRA .... Australasian Performing Right Association (EAIO)
APRA .... Australian Professional Rodeo Association
APRA .... Automotive Parts Rebuilders Association (EA)
APRAC .... Air Pollution Research Advisory Committee
APRACA ...... Asian and Pacific Regional Agricultural Credit Association (EA)
APRAPS...... Active/Passive Reliable Acoustic Path SONAR (MCD)
aprax .... Apraxia [*Neurology*] (DAVI)
APRB .... Acquisition Plan Review Board [*Army*]
APRC .... Alliance for Patriotic Re-Orientation and Construction [*Gambia*] [*Political party*]
APRC .... Anno post Roman Conditam [*In the Year after the Building of Rome*] [*753 BC*] [*Latin*]
APRC .... Army Personnel Research Committee (MCD)
APRC .... Army Physical Review Council
APRC .... Association for Promoting the Reform of Convocation [*British*]
APRC .... Automotive Public Relations Council (EA)
APRC .... Awaiting Patent and Royalty Clearance (AAGC)
APRCAS...... All-Purpose Rocket for Collecting Atmospheric Soundings [*Navy*] (IAA)
APRCG........ Asia-Pacific Railway Cooperation Group (MHDB)
APRCH........ Approach (MSA)
APRD .... Army Pulse Radiation Directorate (PDAA)
APRD .... Atmosphere Particulate Radioactivity Detector (IEEE)
APRE .... Acute-Phase Response Element [*Biochemistry*]
APRE .... Aerospace Photographic Reconnaissance Equipment
APRE .... Air Procurement Region, Europe (AFM)

APRE .... Alianza Popular Revolucionaria Ecuatoriana [*Ecuadorean Popular Revolutionary Alliance*] [*Political party*] (PPW)
APRE .... Army Personnel Research Establishment [*British*]
APREA .... American Peanut Research and Education Association [*Later, APRES*] (EA)
APrec .... American Precision Industries, Inc. [*Associated Press*] (SAG)
APREF .... A. Philip Randolph Educational Fund (EA)
APREN .... Alberta Environment, Peace River, Alberta [*Library symbol National Library of Canada*] (NLC)
APREQ .... Approval Request [*Military*] (DNAB)
APREQS ...... Approval Requests [*Military*] (AABC)
APRES .... American Peanut Research and Education Society (EA)
APresid........ American President Companies Ltd. [*Associated Press*] (SAG)
APRF .... Aberdeen Pulsed Reactor Facility
APRF .... Active Purchase Request File [*DoD*]
APRF .... Acute-Phase Response Factor [*Biochemistry*]
APRF .... Advanced Photon Research Facility [*Proposed, 1986, for high-energy physics*]
APRF .... American Parapsychological Research Foundation [*Later, AAP*] (EA)
APRF .... Army Pulse Radiation Facility [*Aberdeen Proving Ground, MD*]
APRF .... Perth [*Australia ICAO location identifier*] (ICLI)
APRFE .... Air Procurement Region, Far East (AFM)
APRFP .... Americans for President Reagan's Foreign Policy [*Defunct*] (EA)
APRFR .... Army Pulse Radiation Facility Reactor [*Nuclear energy*] (OA)
APRHC .... Association for Puerto Rican-Hispanic Culture (EA)
Ap Rhod ...... Apollonius Rhodius [*Third century BC*] [*Classical studies*] (OCD)
APRI .... Air Priority
APRI .... American Prosecutors Research Institute (EA)
APRI .... A. Philip Randolph Institute (EA)
APRI .... Associate of the Plastics and Rubber Institute (ODBW)
APRI .... Australian Particleboard Research Institute
Apria .... Apria Healthcare Group, Inc. [*Associated Press*] (SAG)
APRICOT ...... Antithrombotics in the Prevention of Reocclusion in Coronary Thrombolysis [*Cardiology study*]
APRICOT ...... Automatic Printed Circuit Board Routing with Intermediate Control of the Tracking (MHDB)
APRIL .... Aquaplaning Risk Indicator for Landings
APRIL .... Automatically Programmed Remote Indication Logged
APRIMA ...... Australian Public Risk Insurance Management Association
APRINT .... Army's Program for Individual Training (MCD)
APRIS .... Alcoa Picturephone Remote Information System [*AT&T Co.*] (NITA)
APRK .... Air Park
APRL .... Alliance for the Preservation of Religious Liberties (DICI)
APRL .... American Philatelic Research Library (EA)
APRL .... American Prosthetic Research Laboratory (DAVI)
APRL .... Architecture and Planning Research Laboratory [*University of Michigan*] [*Research center*] (RCD)
APRL .... Army Prosthetics Research Laboratory
APRL .... Association for the Preservation of Rural Life [*British*] (BI)
APRM .... Adelaide [*Australia ICAO location identifier*] (ICLI)
APRM .... Automatic Position Reference Monitor (IEEE)
APRM .... Average Power Range Monitor [*Nuclear energy*] (NRCH)
APRM .... Peace River Municipal Library, Alberta [*Library symbol National Library of Canada*] (NLC)
APRMD .... Appointment Recommended (NOAA)
APRMD .... Association of Plastic Raw Material Distributors [*Defunct*] (EA)
APRN .... Alaska Public Radio Network
APRN .... Associated Press Radio Network (NTCM)
APRNT .... Apparent (MSA)
APRO .... Aerial Phenomena Research Organization [*Defunct*] (EA)
APRO .... Airline Public Relations Organization [*British*] (DBA)
APRO .... America First Apartment Investors LP [*NASDAQ symbol*] (SAG)
APRO .... American Professional Racquetball Organization (EA)
APRO .... Aprobarbital (DAVI)
APRO .... Army Personnel Research Office [*Washington, DC*]
APRO .... Army Plant Representative's Offices
APRO .... Army Procurement Research Office
APRO .... Association of Progressive Rental Organizations (EA)
APROC .... Adaptive Statistical Processor [*Computer science*] (MHDI)
Aprognx ...... Aprogenex, Inc. [*Associated Press*] (SAG)
APROH........ Asociacion para el Progreso de Honduras [*Association for the Progress of Honduras*] [*Political party*]
AProL.......... Acute Progranulocytic Leukemia [*Hematology*] (DAVI)
AProL.......... Acute Promyelocytic Leukemia [*Hematology*] (MAE)
APROP .... Appropriate (AABC)
APROSOMA... Association pour la Promotion Sociale de la Masse [*Association for the Social Betterment of the Masses*] [*Burundi and Rwanda*] (AF)
APRP .... Acidic Proline-Rich Protein [*Medicine*] (DMAA)
APRP .... Acute Phase Reactant Protein [*Medicine*] (DMAA)
APRP .... Aged Persons' Residential Program [*Australia*]
APRP .... All Peoples' Republican Party [*Ghana*] (AF)
APRPLS ...... Peace Library System, Peace River, Alberta [*Library symbol National Library of Canada*] (NLC)
APRRB........ Airman Performance Report Review Board (AFM)
APRRE .... Active Participation Rental Real Estate [*IRS*]
APRRE .... Association of Professors and Researchers in Religious Education (EA)
APRRN .... Advance Personnel Requirements Research Note
APRS .... Affirmative Poll Response State (IAA)
APRS .... Alliance for Perinatal Research and Services (EA)
APRS .... American Park and Recreation Society (EA)
APRS .... American Performing-Rights Society
APRS .... Applied Physics Research Section
APRS .... Army Personnel Research Service

APRS .... Ascension Poetry Reading Series (EA)
APRS .... Association for the Preservation of Rural Scotland (BI)
APRS .... Association for the Protection of Rural Scotland [*British*]
APRS .... Association of Professional Recording Studios Ltd. [*British*] (BI)
APRS .... Association of Public Radio Stations [*Later, NPR*] (EA)
APRS .... Automatic Position Reference System
APRS .... Automatic Pressure Relief System [*Military*] (CAAL)
APRS .... Automatic Production Record System
APRST .... Averaged Probability Ratio Sequential Test (MHDI)
APRT .... Adenine Phosphoribosyltransferase [*An enzyme*]
APRT .... Adenine Phosphoribosyltransferase [*An enzyme*]
APRT .... Advanced Productivity Research and Technology (MCD)
APRT .... Airport (AFM)
APRT .... Army Physical Readiness Test (INF)
APRT .... Association for Past-Life Research and Therapy (EA)
APRTA .... Associated Press Radio-Television Association [*Later, APB*]
APRU .... Applied Psychology Research Unit (SAA)
APRU .... Australian Population Research Institute
APRV .... Approve (KSC)
APRVL .... Approval (KSC)
APRX .... Approximate (AFM)
APRXLY ...... Approximately (DEN)
APS............. Aborigines Protection Society [*Later, Anti-Slavery Society for the Protection of Human Rights*]
APS............. Absolute Pressure Sensor [*Automotive engineering*]
APS............. Academy of Pharmaceutical Sciences (EA)
APS............. Academy of Political Science (EA)
APS............. Accelerated Photosynthetic System [*Sewage purification*]
APS............. Accelerated Propagation System [*Gardening*]
APS............. Acceleration Position Sensor [*Diesel engines*]
APS............. Accelerator Pedal Position Sensor [*Automotive engineering*]
APS............. Accelerometer Parameter Shift
APS............. Accessory Power Supply (AABC)
APS............. Accion Politica Socialista [*Socialist Political Action*] [*Peru*] [*Political party*] (PPW)
APS............. Acoustic Playback System [*Army*]
APS............. Active Protection System [*Military*] (INF)
APS............. Acts of the Parliaments of Scotland
APS............. Acute Physiology Score [*In evaluating impact of intensive care*]
APS............. Adaptive Processor, SONAR (CAAL)
APS............. Adenosine Phosphosulfate [*Biochemistry*]
APS............. Administration for Public Services [*Office of Human Development Services*]
APS............. Adult Protective Services
APS............. Advanced Personnel System
APS............. Advanced Photon Source [*Particle accelerator*] [*Argonne National Laboratory*]
APS............. Advanced Photosynthetic System
APS............. Advanced Photo System
APS............. Advanced Photo System
APS............. Advanced Photo System [*Camera and film system introduced in 1996*] [*Eastman Kodak Co.*]
APS............. Advanced Power System
APS............. Advanced Propellant System
APS............. Advanced Proton Source [*Physics*]
APS............. Aerial Port Squadron [*Air Force*]
APS............. Aerotransporte Peruanos Internacionales SA [*Peru*] [*ICAO designator*] (FAAC)
APS............. Afloat Planning System [*Navy*] (DOMA)
APS............. Afloat Prepositioned Ship [*Navy*] (DOMA)
APS............. Aft Propulsion System [*or Subsystem*] [*NASA*] (NASA)
APS............. Agathon Publication Services, Inc. [*Later, APS Publications*]
APS............. Agence de Presse Senegalaise [*Senegalese Press Agency*]
APS............. Airborne Power Supply (KSC)
APS............. Airborne Power System (IAA)
APS............. Airborne Pulse Search RADAR after Passing [*Aviation*] (FAAC)
APS............. Air-Breathing Propulsion System [*or Subsystem*] [*NASA*] (NASA)
APS............. Aircraft Position Sensor (PDAA)
APS............. Aircraft Prepared for Service
APS............. Air Pictorial Service
APS............. Air Pollution Syndrome
APS............. Air Pressure Switch
APS............. Airway Planning Standard [*FAA*] (TAG)
APS............. Algerie Presse Service [*Algerian Press Service*] (AF)
APS............. Allegheny Power System, Inc.
APS............. Allied Provincial Securities [*British*] (ECON)
APS............. Allotment-of-Probability Shares (PDAA)
APS............. Alphanumeric Photocomposer System (IEEE)
APS............. Alternative Press Syndicate [*Defunct*] (EA)
APS............. Altitude Proximity Sensor (MCD)
APS............. American Pain Society (EA)
APS............. American Paraplegia Society (EA)
APS............. American Peace Society (EA)
APS............. American Pediatric Society (EA)
APS............. American Penstemon Society (EA)
APS............. American Peony Society (EA)
APS............. American Pet Society (EA)
APS............. American Pheasant Society [*Later, AP & WS*] (EA)
APS............. American Philatelic Society (EA)
APS............. American Philosophical Society (EA)
APS............. American Physical Society (EA)
APS............. American Physiological Society (EA)
APS............. American Phytopathological Society (EA)
APS............. American Plant Selections [*An association Defunct*] (EA)
APS............. American Poinsettia Society [*Defunct*] (EA)

APS............ American Point System [*Typography*] (DGA)
APS............ American Polar Society (EA)
APS............ American Pomological Society (EA)
APS............ American Portrait Society (EA)
APS............ American Portuguese Society (EA)
APS............ American President Companies Ltd. [*NYSE symbol*] (SPSG)
APS............ American Primrose Society (EA)
APS............ American Proctologic Society [*Later, ASCRS*] (EA)
APS............ American Prosthodontic Society (EA)
APS............ American Protestant Society
APS............ American Psychological Society (DAVI)
APS............ American Psychosomatic Society (EA)
APS............ American Purchasing Society (EA)
APS............ Amer President Cos. [*NYSE symbol*] (TTSB)
APS............ Ammonium Persulfate [*Inorganic chemistry*]
APS............ Ammonium Polysulfide [*Fertilizer*]
APS............ Amplifier Power Supply
APS............ Analytical Procedures Subsystem (MCD)
APS............ Anapolis [*Brazil*] [*Airport symbol*] (AD)
APS............ Angstrom Pyrheliometric Scale
APS............ Angular Position Sensor
APS............ Animal Parasitic Systems
APS............ Antenna Pointing Subsystem
APS............ Antiprostaglandin Antiserum [*Immunology*]
APS............ Apollo Program Specifications [*NASA*] (KSC)
APS............ Appearance Potential Spectroscopy [*Physics*]
APS............ Appearance Station (SAA)
AP(S)......... Application Process [*or Program*] (Structure) [*Telecommunications*] (TEL)
APS............ Application Process Subsystem [*Telecommunications*] (TEL)
APS............ Applied Peripheral System (IAA)
APS............ Applied Physics Staff (SAA)
APS............ Applied Psychological Services (KSC)
APS............ Approved Prescription Services Ltd. [*British*]
Aps............ Apus [*Constellation*]
APS............ Aqueous Powder Suspension [*For coating plastics*]
APS............ Arc-Plasma Spraying [*Magnetic film*]
APS............ Arizona Psychiatric Society (SRA)
APS............ Armament Practice Station [*British military*] (DMA)
APS............ Armor-Piercing Sabot [*Ammunition*] (SAA)
APS............ Army Pictorial Service
APS............ Army Pilot School
APS............ Army Postal Service
APS............ Array Processor Software [*Computer science*] (IEEE)
APS............ Ascending Pharyngeal System [*Anatomy*]
APS............ Ascent Propulsion System [*NASA*]
APS............ Assembly Programming System [*Computer science*] (IEEE)
APS............ Assimilations per Second
APS............ Assisted Places Scheme (AIE)
APS............ Associated Patternmakers of Scotland [*A union*]
APS............ Associated Press Service
APS............ Associate of the Pharmaceutical Society [*British*]
APS............ Association of Photo Sensitizers (EA)
APS............ Association of Productivity Specialists (EA)
APS............ Atmospheric Pollution Sensor
APS............ Atmospheric Pressure Sensor
APS............ Atomic Power Station (NRCH)
APS............ Atropine-Like Psycho-Chemical Substance (PDAA)
APS............ Attached Processor for Speech [*IBM Corp.*] (NITA)
APS............ Attached Processor System [*Telecommunications*] (TEL)
APS............ Attended Pay Station [*Attended Public Telephone*] (TEL)
APS............ Attending Physician's Statement
APS............ Attitude and Pointing Control System [*NASA*]
APS............ Attitude Propulsion Subsystem
APS............ Auction Preferred Stock [*Investment term*] (DFIT)
APS............ Augustan Prose Sample [*Machine readable selection of English prose*] (NITA)
APS............ Austin Public Schools Media, Austin, MN [*OCLC symbol*] (OCLC)
APS............ Australian Prosthodontic Society
APS............ Australian Psychoanalytical Society
APS............ Autocorrelator Photon Spectroscopy
APS............ Autograph Poem Signed [*Manuscript descriptions*] (ADA)
APS............ Autograph Postcard Signed [*Manuscript descriptions*]
APS............ Automated Parking System
APS............ Automated Patent Searching [*Computer science*]
APS............ Automated Productivity Services (MCD)
APS............ Automatic Page Search [*Imtec Co.*] [*Information retrieval*] (NITA)
APS............ Automatic Patching System (IEEE)
APS............ Automatic Phase Shifter
APS............ Automatic Phase Synchronization
APS............ Automatic Pilot System
APS............ Automatic Planetary Station [*Astronomy*]
APS............ Automatic Processing System (MCD)
APS............ Automatic Program Selection [*Automobile accessory*]
APS............ Automatic Program System [*Computer science*]
APS............ Automatic Propulsion Control System (DNAB)
APS............ Automatic Protection Switching [*Telecommunications*] (ACRL)
APS............ Automatic Provisioning System [*Military*] (CAAL)
APS............ Auxiliary Power Subsystem (MCD)
APS............ Auxiliary Power Supply
APS............ Auxiliary Power System (NRCH)
APS............ Auxiliary Program Storage [*Computer science*] (BUR)
APS............ Auxiliary Propulsion System [*or Subsystem*] [*Apollo*] [*NASA*]
APS............ Average Propensity to Save [*Economics*]
APS............ Avionics Processing System

APS............ IEEE Antennas and Propagation Society (EA)
APS............ Minelaying Submarine [*Navy symbol*]
APS............ Transport, Submarine [*Later, SSP*] [*Navy symbol*]
APSA.......... Aerolineas Peruanas Sociedad Anonima [*Peruvian Air Lines*]
APSA.......... American Pediatric Surgical Association (EA)
APSA.......... American Political Science Association (EA)
APSA.......... American Polypay Sheep Association (EA)
APSA.......... American Professional Surfing Association (EA)
APSA.......... American Psychologists for Social Action [*Later, PSA*]
APSA.......... Ammunition Procurement and Supply Agency [*Army*]
APSA.......... Association for the Psychiatric Study of Adolescents [*British*]
APSA.......... Association of Point-of-Sale-Advertising [*British*]
APSA.......... Australian Peak Shippers' Association
APSA.......... Automatic Particle Size Analyzer (OA)
APSA.......... Axisymmetrical and Planar Structural Analysis (MCD)
APsaA........ American Psychoanalytic Association (EA)
APSAC........ Acylated Plasminogen-Streptokinase Activator Complex [*Anticlotting agent*]
Apsac.......... American Professional Society on the Abuse of Children
APSAC........ Anisoylated-Plasminogen-Streptokinase Activator Complex [*Thrombolytic*]
APSAM........ Association Paritaire pour la Sante et la Securite du Travail - Affaires Municipales (AC)
APSAP........ Auxiliary Propulsion System Aft POP (MCD)
APSAS........ Association of Public Service Administrative Staff [*British*] (DBA)
APSB.......... Aid to the Potentially Self-Supporting Blind (IIA)
APSBSI........ Australian Public Service Benevolent Society Inc.
APSBU........ Australian Public Sector and Broadcasting Union
APSC.......... Adelaide Pistol Shooting Club [*Australia*]
APSC.......... Advanced Processing Science Center [*Oak Ridge National Laboratory*]
APSC.......... Alabama Public Service Commission Decisions [*A publication*] (DLA)
APSC.......... Andorran Philately Study Circle [*Defunct*] (EA)
APSC.......... Army Personnel System Committee
APSC.......... Asian-Pacific Society of Cardiology (EA)
APSC.......... Austin Peay State College [*Later, Austin Peay State University*] [*Tennessee*]
APSCUF....... Association of Pennsylvania State College and University Faculties (SRA)
APSD.......... American Professional Society of the Deaf (EA)
APSD.......... Aorticopulmonary Septal Defect [*Medicine*] (DMAA)
APSDIN....... APSDEP Information Network [*Islamabad, Pakistan*] [*Information service or system*] (IID)
APSDIN....... Asian and Pacific Skill Development Information Network [*ILO*] [*United Nations*] (DUND)
APSE.......... Abstracts of Photographic Science and Engineering Literature [*A publication*]
APSE.......... Ada Programming Support Environments [*Computer science*] (RDA)
APSE.......... Armour-Piercing Secondary Effects [*British military*] (DMA)
APSE.......... Associated Press Sports Editors [*Defunct*] (EA)
Ap Sed........ Apostolica Sedes [*Apostolic See*] [*Latin*] [*Reference to the papacy*] (BARN)
APSEDC....... Association for Pre-School Education of Deaf Children
APSET........ Aviation Personnel and Survival Equipment Team [*Navy*] (NG)
APSF.......... Armed Public Security Force (CINC)
APSFA........ Association of Public Service Financial Administrators [*Association des Gestionnaires Financiers de la Fonction Publique*] (AC)
APSFSL....... Assistant Private Secretary to the First Sea Lord [*Navy British*]
APSG.......... After Passing [*ICAO*] (FAAC)
APSG.......... Applied Signal Technology [*NASDAQ symbol*] (TTSB)
APSG.......... Applied Signal Technology, Inc. [*NASDAQ symbol*] (SAG)
APSG.......... Association pour le Socialisme au Gabon [*Political party*] (EY)
APSGB........ Association of Police Surgeons of Great Britain
APSGD........ Army Procurement - Sharpe General Depot
APSGN........ Acute Poststreptococcal Glomerulonephritis [*Immunology*]
APSGUSA.... Asian Political Scientists Group in USA (EA)
ApSHA........ Appaloosa Sport Horse Association (EA)
APS Hld....... APS Holding Corp. [*Associated Press*] (SAG)
APSI.......... Academy for the Psychology of Sports International [*Later, ASPI*] (EA)
APSI.......... Advanced Propulsion Subsystem Integration [*Air Force*]
APSI.......... Aircraft Propulsion Subsystem Integration
APSI.......... Allstates-Programming & Systems, Inc.
APSI.......... Amperes per Square Inch
APSI.......... APS Holding 'A' [*NASDAQ symbol*] (TTSB)
APSI.......... APS Holding Corp. [*NASDAQ symbol*] (SAG)
APSIA........ Association of Professional Schools of International Affairs (EA)
APSIG........ Asia and Pacific Special Interest Group [*Australian Library and Information Association*]
APS-IPRS.... Asian-Pacific Section - IPRS [*International Confederation for Plastic and Reconstructive Surgery*] [*Singapore*] (EAIO)
APSL.......... Acting Paymaster Sub-Lieutenant [*Navy British*]
APSL.......... Army Primary Standards Laboratory
APSL.......... Authorized Parts Substitution List
APSLF........ Association de Psychologie Scientifique de Langue Francaise [*French-Language Association of Scientific Psychology*] (EAIO)
APSM.......... Academy of Product Safety Management [*Defunct*] (EA)
APSM.......... Association for Physical and System Mathematics (EA)
APSM.......... Association Paritaire pour le Sante et le Securite du Travail - Mines (AC)
APSN.......... Architects and Planners in Support of Nicaragua (EA)
APSN.......... Association Package Sequence Number (MCD)
APSNY........ Austria Philatelic Society of New York (EA)
APSO.......... Allied Petroleum Service Organization
APSO.......... Apple South [*NASDAQ symbol*] (SPSG)

APSO	Asia-Pacific Socialist Organization [*Political party Tokyo, Japan*] (EAIO)
APSO	Assistant Polaris Systems Officer [*British military*] (DMA)
APSO	Association of Poultry Slaughterhouse Operators (EA)
APSO	Audio Precision Series One Analyzer [*CD-sound quality test*] (PCM)
APSP	Array Processor Subroutine Package [*Computer science*] (BUR)
APSQ	Abbreviated Parent Symptom Questionnaire [*Medicine*] (DMAA)
APSQ	Advance Payment of Subsistence and Quarters
APSq	Aerial Port Squadron [*Air Force*] (AFM)
APSQ	Association de la Presse Sportive du Quebec (AC)
APSQ	Association des Professeurs de Sciences du Quebec (AC)
APSR	Airport Surveillance RADAR (MSA)
APSR	American Political Science Review [*A publication*] (BRI)
APSR	Available Pay Survey Reports [*Information service or system*] (IID)
APSR	Axial Power Shaping Rods [*Nuclear energy*] (NRCH)
APSRA	Axial Power Shaping Rods Assembly [*Nuclear energy*] (NRCH)
APSS	Advanced Planetary Spacecraft System
APSS	American Polled Shorthorn Society (EA)
APSS	Area/Point Search System (CAAL)
APSS	Army Printing and Stationery Services [*British*]
APSS	Associated Public School Systems
APSS	Association for the Psychophysiological Study of Sleep [*Later, Sleep Research Society - SRS*]
APSS	Association of Professional Sleep Societies (EA)
APSS	Atmospheric Pressure Supply System [*or Subsystem*] [*NASA*] (NASA)
APSS	Automated Program Support System [*Computer science*]
APSS	Transport, Submarine [*Later, LPSS*] [*Navy symbol Obsolete*]
APSSEAR	Association of Pediatric Societies of the Southeast Asian Region (EA)
APsSI	Associate of the Psychological Society of Ireland
APSSNM	Advisory Panel on Safeguarding Special Nuclear Material
APSSP	Association of Professional Student Services Personnel [*Association du Personnel Professionnel des Services aux Etudiants*] (AC)
APST	Associate in Public Service Technology
APSTLC	Apostolic
APSTLT	Apostolate
APSTRAT	Aptitude Strategies (PDAA)
APSU	Amateur Pistol Shooting Union of Australia
APSU	Austin Peay State University [*Tennessee*]
APSU	Auxiliary Power Supply Unit (MCD)
APSW	Association of Psychiatric Social Workers [*British*] (BI)
APSWU	American Philatelic Society Writers Unit (EA)
APsyOI	Association des Psychologues de l'Ocean Indien (EAIO)
APT	Academic Promise Test [*Psychology*] (AEBS)
APT	Accelerated Pavement Testing [*FHWA*] (TAG)
APT	Accelerator Production of Tritium [*Physics*]
APT	Adaptive Programming Technology
APT	Advanced Passenger Train [*British*]
APT	Advanced Passenger Transport (OA)
APT	Advanced Patent Technique
APT	Advanced Photoscale Technology (PCM)
APT	Advanced Pilot Training (PDAA)
APT	Advanced Pointing Tracking (MCD)
APT	Advanced Power Technology [*Army*]
APT	Advanced Propulsion Test (SSD)
APT	Aerial Profiling of Terrain [*System*] [*Department of the Interior*]
APT	Africa Publications Trust [*British*]
APT	Aft Peak Tank [*Shipping*]
APT	Age Progression Technique [*Criminology*] (LAIN)
APT	Airborne Pointer and Tracker
APT	Airmen Proficiency Test
APT	Airport (AFIT)
APT	Airportable [*British military*] (DMA)
APT	Allarcom Pay Television Ltd. [*Canada*]
APT	All-Purpose Terminal [*Computer technology*]
APT	All-Purpose Tween [*Microorganism growth medium*]
APT	Alum Precipitated Toxoid [*Medicine*]
APT	Amberhill Petroleum Ltd. [*Vancouver Stock Exchange symbol*]
APT	American Peace Test (EA)
APT	American Place Theatre (EA)
APT	American Playwrights Theatre [*Defunct*]
APT	American Printing Technologies (DGA)
APT	Ammonium Paratungstate [*Metallurgy*]
APT	Analog Pressure Transducer
APT	Analog Program Tape [*Computer science*]
APT	Angeles Participating Mortgage Trust [*AMEX symbol*] (SPSG)
APT	Angeles Ptc Mtge'A'SBI [*AMEX symbol*] (TTSB)
APT	Animation Photo Transfer [*Animation technique developed by Disney Studio*]
APT	Antiphosphotyrosine [*Biochemistry*]
APT	Apartamento
APT	Apartment
apt	Apartment (VRA)
APT	Apartment
APT	Apollo Pad Test [*NASA*] (KSC)
APT	Applied Potential Tomography [*Medicine*]
APT	Appoint (AABC)
APT	Aptitude (AABC)
APT	Arbitrage Pricing Theory [*Finance*]
APT	Arizona Photopolarimeter Telescope
APT	Armed Propaganda Team [*Military*]
APT	Armor-Piercing with Tracer [*Ammunition*]
APT	Army Parachute Team
APT	Asia-Pacific Telecommunity [*Thailand*] [*Telecommunications*]
APT	Asset Protection Trust
APT	Associated Pharmacologists and Toxicologists (EPA)
APT	Association for Poetry Therapy [*Later, NAPT*] (EA)
APT	Association for Practical Theology (EA)
APT	Association for Preservation Technology [*Later, APTI*] (EA)
APT	Association for Productive Teaching (AEBS)
APT	Association for Psychological Type (EA)
APT	Association of Pensioneer Trustees [*British*] (DBA)
APT	Association of Polysomnographic Technologists (EA)
APT	Association of Polytechnic Teachers [*British*]
APT	Association of Printing Technologists [*Later, IOP*] (DGA)
APT	Association of Private Traders [*British*] (BI)
APT	Astronaut Preference Test [*NASA*] (NASA)
APT	AT & T Philips Telecommunications
APT	Augmented Programming Training [*Computer science*] (IEEE)
APT	Automated Pit Trading [*Developed by London International Financial Futures Exchange*] [*Stock exchange term*]
APT	Automatically Programmed Tool [*Computer software*] [*Computer science*]
APT	Automatic Parts Testing (IAA)
APT	Automatic Picture Taking (IEEE)
APT	Automatic Picture Transmission [*NASA*]
APT	Automatic Position Telemetering
APT	Automatic Programming Tool [*Computer science*] (NITA)
APT	Automatic Progression Testing (TEL)
APT	Automation Planning and Technology
APT	Avery Point [*Connecticut*] [*Seismograph station code, US Geological Survey Closed*] (SEIS)
APT	Fort Stewart/Hunter AAF Library System, Fort Stewart, GA [*OCLC symbol*] (OCLC)
APT	Jasper, TN [*Location identifier FAA*] (FAAL)
APT	Lineas Aereas Petroleras [*Colombia*] [*ICAO designator*] (FAAC)
APT	North Carolina State Agency for Public Telecommunications [*Raleigh*] (TSSD)
a-pt--	Portuguese Timor [*a-io (Indonesia) used in records cataloged after April 1980*] [*MARC geographic area code Library of Congress*] (LCCP)
APT	Troop Barge, Class B [*Navy symbol Obsolete*]
APTA	Advanced Pork Technology Association (AC)
APTA	American Physical Therapy Association (EA)
APTA	American Pioneer Trails Association (EA)
APTA	American Platform Tennis Association (EA)
APTA	American Public Transit Association (EA)
APTA	Aptitude Area
APTA	Atlantic Provinces Trucking Association [*Canada*]
APTA	Australian Professional Triathletes Association
APTA	Automotive Products Trade Act of 1965
APT-AC	Automatically Programmed Tool - Advanced Contouring [*IBM Corp.*]
APT&C	Administrative, Professional, Technical, and Clerical Grades [*Education*] (AIE)
Aptar	Aptargroup, Inc. [*Associated Press*] (SAG)
APTC	Airport Traffic Controller (IAA)
APTC	Allied Printing Trades Council (DGA)
APTC	Aperture Card (MSA)
APTC	Army Physical Training Corps [*British*]
APTC	Association of Publicly Traded Companies (EA)
APTD	Aid to the Permanently and Totally Disabled [*HEW*]
APTD	Air Pollution Technical Data [*Series*] [*A publication*]
APTDEPM	Association Professionnelle des Technologues Diplomes en Electrophysiologie Medicale (AC)
APTDQ	Association Professionnelle des Techniciens en Documentation du Quebec (AC)
APTE	Abrams Power Train Evolution
APTE	Automatic Production Test Equipment (DNAB)
APTE	Avalanche Punch-Through Erase (MCD)
APTEC	Advanced Power Train Electronic Controller [*Automotive engineering*]
APTEC	Appropriate Technology Ltd. [*British*] (IRUK)
APTEM	Association of Passenger Transport Executives and Managers [*British*] (DCTA)
APTES	Administrative Professional and Technical Evaluation System (DNAB)
APTES	(Aminopropyl)triethoxysilane [*Organic chemistry*]
APTEU	Amalgamated Printing Trades Employees' Union [*Australia*] (DGA)
APTF	American Physical Therapy Foundation (DMAA)
APTF	Automated Program Testing Facility (MHDI)
APTGS	Automatic Picture Transmission Ground System (NOAA)
APTI	Actions per Time Interval
APTI	Air Pollution Training Institute [*Environmental Protection Agency*] (GFGA)
APTI	American Protestants for Truth about Ireland (EA)
APTI	Amer Portable Telecom [*NASDAQ symbol*] (TTSB)
APTI	Arab Petroleum Training Institute [*Defunct*] (EA)
APTI	Association of Principals of Technical Institutions [*British*]
APTI	Automatic Point Transfer Instrument (MCD)
APTI	Automatic Programmed Test Input (NASA)
APTIC	Air Pollution Technical Information Center [*Also, NAPTIC*] [*Bibliographic database*] [*Environmental Protection Agency*]
APT-IC	Automatically Programmed Tool - Intermediate Contouring [*IBM Corp.*]
APTIF	Association of Publicly Traded Investment Funds [*Defunct*] (EA)
AptInv	Apartment Investment & Management Co. [*Associated Press*] (SAG)
APTIRC	Asian-Pacific Tax and Investment Research Centre [*Singapore*]
APTIS	All-Purpose Ticket Issuing System (PDAA)
APTIS	Asia-Pacific Technology Information System [*ESCAP*] [*United Nations*] (DUND)

APTLF......... Association de Psychologie du Travail de Langue Francaise [*French-Language Association of Work Psychology*] (EAIO)
APTMD .... Air, Pesticides, and Toxics Management Division [*Environmental Protection Agency*] (GFGA)
APTMS........ Aminopropyltrimethoxysilane [*Organic chemistry*]
APTO .... Association for the Professional Treatment of Offenders [*Defunct*] (EA)
APTP........... Arithmetic Proficiency Training Program [*Computer-assisted training program*]
APTP........... Association des Producteurs de Theatre Professionnel (AC)
AP-TP .... Association of Part-Time Professionals (EA)
APTP........... (Azidophenylthio)phthalimide [*Organic chemistry*]
APTPDA ...... Advance Payment of Travel per Diem Authorized [*Army*]
APTR .... Advanced Pressure Tube Reactor [*Nuclear energy*]
APTRA .... Air Operational Training
APTS........... Activity Providing Telephone Service (DNAB)
APTS........... Advanced Public Transportation Systems
APTS........... Air Traffic Control Proficiency Training System [*Navy*]
APTS........... Aminopropyltrimethoxysilane [*Organic chemistry*]
APTS........... Aminopyrene-trisulfonate [*Organic chemistry*]
APTS........... Apartments
APTS........... Apertus Technologies [*NASDAQ symbol*] (TTSB)
APTS........... Apertus Technologies, Inc. [*NASDAQ symbol*] (SPSG)
APTS........... Army Physical Training Staff [*British military*] (DMA)
APTS........... Association for the Prevention of Thefts in Shops [*British*]
APTS........... Automatic Picture Transmission System [*or Subsystem*] [*NASA*]
APTS........... Automatic Programmer and Test System [*Army*] (MCD)
A/P TSTMN.. Autopilot Test Monitor (AAG)
A/P TSTPG... Autopilot Test Programmer (AAG)
APTT .... Activated Partial Thromboplastin Time [*Hematology*]
APTT .... Aircrew Part Task Trainer (MCD)
APTT .... Apollo Part Task Trainer [*NASA*] (KSC)
APTT .... Association of Package Tour Travellers [*British*] (DBA)
APTU .... Aerodynamic and Propulsion Test Unit
APTUS .... Apparatus
APTV .... Advanced Promotion Technology [*NASDAQ symbol*] (SPSG)
APTV .... Associated Press Television
APTW.......... Asiatic-Pacific Theater of War
APU .... Accessory Power Unit (MUGU)
APU .... Acoustics Propellant Utilization
APU .... Aeropuma SA [*El Salvador*] [*ICAO designator*] (FAAC)
APU .... Airborne Power Unit (IAA)
APU .... Airborne Processing Unit
APU .... Aircraft Propulsion Unit
APU .... Alianca Popular Unida/Alianca Povo Unido [*United People's Alliance*] [*Portugal Political party*] (PPW)
APU .... Amerigas Partners LP [*NYSE symbol*] (SAG)
APU .... AmeriGas Partners L.P. [*NYSE symbol*] (TTSB)
APU .... Analog Processing Unit [*Computer science*] (NITA)
APU .... Analytic Processing Unit
APU .... Angkatan Perpaduan Ummah [*Muslim Unity Movement*] [*Malaysia*] [*Political party*] (EY)
APU .... Anti-Poaching Unit (BARN)
APU .... Applied Psychology Unit
APU .... Arab Postal Union
APU .... Arithmetic Processing Unit [*Computer science*]
APU .... Army Postal Unit
APU .... Asian Parliamentarians' Union
APU .... Assessment of Performance Unit [*Education*] [*British*]
APU .... Association for Philosophy of the Unconscious (EA)
APU .... Asynchronous Processing Unit [*Computer science*] (NITA)
APU .... Audio Playback Unit
APU .... Authorized Pick-Up [*Trucking terminology*]
APU .... Auxiliary Power [*or Propulsion*] Unit [*Military*]
APU .... Auxiliary Processing Unit
APU .... Avian Philately Unit [*Defunct*] (EA)
APUA .... Alliance for the Prudent Use of Antibiotics (EA)
APUA .... Association du Peuple pour l'Unite et l'Action [*Algeria*] [*Political party*] (EY)
APUC .... Area Production Urgency Committee
APUC .... Association de Placement Universitaire et Collegial [*University and College Placement Association*] [*Canada*]
APUC .... Association des Presses Universitaires Canadiennes [*Association of Canadian University Presses - ACUP*]
APUC .... Association for Promoting Unity of Christendom
APUD .... Amine Precursor Uptake and Decarboxylation [*Cytology*]
APUD-Oma... Amine Precursor Uptake and Decarboxylation Tumor [*Endocrinology*] (DAVI)
APUG......... AutoPrep 5000 Users Group (EA)
APUHS........ Automatic Program Unit, High-Speed [*Component of ADIS*]
Apul............ Apuleius [*Second century AD*] [*Classical studies*] (OCD)
APULS .... Automatic Program Unit, Low-Speed [*Component of ADIS*]
APUPA........ Alien, Penumbral, Umbral, Penumbral, Alien
APUR .... Atelier Parisien d'Urbanisme [*Paris Office of Urbanization*] [*France*] [*Information service or system*] (IID)
APUS .... Auxiliary Power Unit Subsystem (MCD)
AP/USA....... Airline Passengers of America [*Defunct*] (EA)
APUSM .... Auxiliary Power Unit System Module (MCD)
A-Put.......... Associate Pulmonary Technologist [*Academic degree*]
APUT .... Auxiliary Power Unit Test (MCD)
APV .... Abnormal Posterior Vector [*Medicine*] (DMAA)
APV .... Adaptive Phase Velocimeter
APV .... Agence Presse Voltaique [*Upper Voltan Press Agency*] (AF)
APV .... Air-Piloted Valve
APV .... Air Plan International [*Zaire*] [*FAA designator*] (FAAC)

APV .... All-Purpose Vehicle [*Automotive engineering*]
APV .... Amino(phosphono)valerate [*Organic chemistry*]
APV .... Amino(phosphono)valeric Acid [*An amino acid*]
APV .... Anomalous Photovoltaic Effect (MCD)
APV .... Apple Valley [*California*] [*Airport symbol Obsolete*] (OAG)
APV .... Approve
APV .... Armored Personnel Vehicle [*Military*] (IAA)
APV .... Autopiloted Vehicle
APV .... Paradise Valley Public Library, Alberta [*Library symbol National Library of Canada*] (NLC)
APV .... Transport and Aircraft Ferry [*Navy symbol Obsolete*]
APV .... Van Deusen Post Library, Fort Monmouth, Fort Monmouth, NJ [*OCLC symbol*] (OCLC)
APVA .... Association for the Preservation of Virginia Antiquities (EA)
APVAST ...... Airborne Platform Versus Airbreathing Strategic Threats (MCD)
APVD .... Anomalous Pulmonary Venous Drainage [*Medicine*] (DAVI)
APVD .... Approved (MSA)
APVD .... Association of Professional Video Distributors [*British*] (DBA)
APVDC .... Association of Parents of Vaccine Damaged Children [*British*]
APVE........... Association of Professional Vocal Ensembles [*Later, Chorus America*] (EA)
APVL.......... Approval
APVM........ Analog Process Variable Measurement [*Process control*]
APVO......... Soviet Air Defense Aviation (MCD)
APVOI........ Advanced PVO [*Protivo-Vozdushnaia Oborona*] Intercepter [*Military*] (MCD)
APVT........... Ammons Picture Vocabulary Test [*Speech and language therapy*] (DAVI)
APW .... Accelerated Public Works [*Program*] [*Department of the Interior*]
APW .... Action Program for Women
APW .... Alkaline Peptone Water (DMAA)
APW .... American Prisoner of War (AABC)
A/PW .... Analog-to-Pulse Width Converter
APW .... Apia [*Samoa Islands*] [*Airport symbol*] (OAG)
APW .... Apparent Polar Wander [*Paleomagnetism*]
APW .... Applied Power A [*NYSE symbol*] (SAG)
APW .... Applied Power CI'A' [*NYSE symbol*] (TTSB)
APW .... Applied Power, Inc. [*NYSE symbol*] (SPSG)
APW .... Architectural Projected Window [*Technical drawings*]
APW .... Armistice and Post-War Committee [*British World War II*]
APW .... Arrow Airways, Inc. [*ICAO designator*] (FAAC)
APW .... Association of Petroleum Writers (EA)
APW .... Augmented Phase Wave [*Thermodynamics*]
APW .... Augmented Plane Wave
APWA .... American Public Welfare Association (EA)
APWA .... American Public Works Association (EA)
APWA .... Association of Principals, Wardens, and Advisers of University Women Students [*British*] (AIE)
APWA .... Australian Plaiters and Whipmakers' Association
APWC .... Association of Professional Writing Consultants (EA)
APWCS .... Advanced Program Weight Control System
APWD .... Aircraft Proximity Warning Device
APWD .... Applewoods, Inc. [*NASDAQ symbol*] (SAG)
APWD .... Applewoods Inc. [*NASDAQ symbol*] (TTSB)
APWI .... Airborne Proximity Warning Indicator (DA)
APWI .... Air Prisoner of War Interrogation
APWIB .... American Prisoner of War Information Bureau (AABC)
APWL .... Automatically Processed WIR [*Weapons Inspection Report*] List (CET)
APWO .... Assistant Public Works Officer
APWP .... Accelerated Public Works Program [*Department of the Interior*]
APWP .... Apparent Polar Wander Path [*Paleomagnetism*]
APWR .... Advanced Pressurized-Water Reactor [*Nuclear energy*]
APWR .... American Polish War Relief [*Post-World War II*]
APWR .... Woomera [*Australia ICAO location identifier*] (ICLI)
APWRC .... Association of Private Weather Related Companies (EA)
APwrCnv..... American Power Conversion [*Associated Press*] (SAG)
APWS .... Aircraft Proximity Warning System
APWS .... Attending Physician Work Station (DMAA)
APWSS .... Asian Pacific Weed Science Society (EA)
ap wt.......... Apothecaries' Weight (BARN)
APWT......... Arterial Pulse Wave Transducer
APWU......... American Postal Workers Union (EA)
APWUS....... Association of Polish Women in the United States (EA)
APX............ Ad-Page Exposure (NTCM)
APX............ Advance Payment Plan [*Airlines*]
APX............ Apex Air Cargo [*ICAO designator*] (FAAC)
APX............ Apex Municipal Fund, Inc. [*NYSE symbol*] (SPSG)
APX............ Apex Muni Fund [*NYSE symbol*] (TTSB)
APX............ Appendix (WGA)
apx............ Approximately (WDMC)
APX............ Automatic Programming System Extended [*Computer science*] (IAA)
apx............ Average Page Exposure [*Advertising*] (WDMC)
APX............ Fort Sam Houston Morale Support Library, Fort Sam Houston, TX [*OCLC symbol*] (OCLC)
APXM......... Christmas Island [*Australia ICAO location identifier*] (ICLI)
APXS......... Alpha Proton X-Ray Spectrometer
APY............ Allmerica Prop & Cas Cos. [*NYSE symbol*] (TTSB)
APY............ Allmerica Property & Casualty [*NYSE symbol*] (SAG)
APY............ Alto Parnaiba [*Brazil*] [*Airport symbol*] (AD)
APY............ Annual Percentage Yield
APY............ APA Internacional [*Dominican Republic*] [*ICAO designator*] (FAAC)
APY............ Apoyeque [*Nicaragua*] [*Seismograph station code, US Geological Survey*] (SEIS)
APY............ Australian Payroll Tax Manual [*A publication*]

APY............ Giant "Y" Boat [Navy symbol Obsolete]
APYF.......... Asian Pacific Youth Forum (EA)
APYFL........ Asian Pacific Youth Freedom League [Tokyo, Japan] (EAIO)
APZ............ Air Patrol Zone (NVT)
APZ............ Applied Industrial Technology [NYSE symbol] (SAG)
APZ............ Hydro-Quebec [Canada] [FAA designator] (FAAC)
APZ............ Zapala [Argentina] [Airport symbol] (OAG)
APZA.......... Asociacion pro Zarzuela en America (EA)
AQ............. Accomplishment Quotient
AQ............. Achievement Quotient
AQ............. Acquisicorp Capital [Vancouver Stock Exchange symbol]
AQ............. Acquisition Message
AQ............. Adversity Quotient [Psychology]
AQ............. Air Anglia [ICAO designator] (AD)
AQ............. Aircraft Quality (AAG)
AQ............. Air Queensland [Australia]
AQ............. Air Quenched (IAA)
AQ............. Alcohol Quotient
AQ............. Aloha Airlines [ICAO designator] (AD)
A/Q............ Amendment /Query [Computer science] (NITA)
AQ............. Aminoquinoline [Biochemistry] (OA)
AQ............. Annual Questionnaire
AQ............. Antarctica [ANSI two-letter standard code] (CNC)
AQ............. Anthraquinone [Organic chemistry]
aq............. Antigua [MARC country of publication code Library of Congress] (LCCP)
AQ............. Any Quantity
AQ............. Apollo Qualification [NASA] (KSC)
AQ............. Aqua [Water] [Pharmacy]
AQ............. Aqueous
Aq............. Aquila's Greek Translation of the Bible [A publication] (BJA)
AQ............. As Quoted [Business term]
AQ............. Assimulatory Quotient
AQ............. Attainment Quotient
AQ............. Autoquote [Computer science] (TEL)
AQ............. Aviation Fire Control Technician [Navy rating]
Aq............. De Aquae Ductu Urbis Romae [of Frontinus] [Classical studies] (OCD)
AQ............. Syria [License plate code assigned to foreign diplomats in the US]
AQ............. Westminster Aquarium [British music hall popular in the 1870s-80s] (DSUE)
AQ1........... Aviation Fire Control Technician, First Class [Navy rating]
AQ2........... Aviation Fire Control Technician, Second Class [Navy rating]
AQ3........... Aviation Fire Control Technician, Third Class [Navy rating]
AQA .... Accredited Quality Assurance
AQA .... Air Quality Act
AQA .... Application Quality Assurance [Automotive engineering] [3M Co.]
AQA .... Approved Quality Assurance
AQA .... Araraquara [Brazil] [Airport symbol Obsolete] (OAG)
AQA .... Australian Quilters' Association
a-qa-- .... Qatar [MARC geographic area code Library of Congress] (LCCP)
AQAA......... Airman Apprentice, Aviation Fire Control Technician, Striker [Navy rating]
AQAB......... Air Quality Advisory Board
AQAD......... Aeronautical Quality Assurance Directorate [British] (PDAA)
AQAD......... Association Quebecoise des Auteurs Dramatiques (AC)
AQA EMS .... AST/Quadram/Ashton-Tate Enhanced Memory Specification [Quadram] [Norcross, GA] [Computer science]
AQAM .... Air Quality Assessment Model [Air Force]
AQAM .... Association Quebecoise des Archivistes Medicales (AC)
AQ AMMON... Aqua Ammoniae [Ammoniated Water] [Pharmacy] (ROG)
AQAN .... Airman, Aviation Fire Control Technician, Striker [Navy rating]
AQAN .... Any Quantity
AQ ANETH ... Aqua Anethi [Dill Water] [Pharmacy] (ROG)
AQ ANIS ...... Aqua Anisi [Anise Water] [Pharmacy] (ROG)
AQAP .... Allied Quality Assurance Provision [NATO] (MCD)
AQAP .... Allied Quality Assurance Publication [NATO] (NATG)
Aqar........... Aquarius [Constellation]
AQ ASTR...... Aqua Astricta [Frozen Water] [Pharmacy] (ROG)
AQB .... Alberta Attorney General, Queen's Bench Libraries [UTLAS symbol]
AQB .... Aqua 1 Beverage [Vancouver Stock Exchange symbol]
AQB .... Army Qualification Battery [of tests]
AQB .... Aviation Fire Control Technician, Bomb Direction [Navy rating]
AQBBA........ Australian Queen Bee Breeders' Association
AQ BULL...... Aqua Bulliens [Boiling Water] [Pharmacy]
AQ BULLIENS... Aqua Bulliens [Boiling Water] [Pharmacy] (ROG)
AQC........... Alaska Quaternary Center [University of Alaska, Fairbanks] [Research center] (RCD)
AQC........... Associate of Queen's College [London]
AQC........... Automatic Quench Calibration [or Correction]
AQC........... Automatic Quench Compensation [Beckman Instruments, Inc.] [Instrumentation]
AQC........... Aviation Fire Control Technician, Chief [Navy rating]
AQC........... Queensland Conveyancing Law and Practice [A publication]
AQ CAL....... Aqua Calida [Hot Water] [Pharmacy]
AQ CALID..... Aqua Calida [Hot Water] [Pharmacy] (ROG)
AQCC......... Association Quebecoise des Critiques de Cinema (AC)
AQCCT .... Air Quality Criteria and Control Techniques [Environmental Protection Agency] (GFGA)
AQCESS...... Automated Quality of Care Evaluation Support System [Military]
AQCH......... Association of Qualified Curative Hypnotherapists [British] (DBA)
AQCIE .... Association Quebecoise des Consommateurs Industriels d'Electricite (AC)
AQ CINNAM... Aqua Cinnamoni [Cinnamon Water] [Pharmacy] (ROG)
AQCKV .... Association Quebecoise de Canoe-Kayak de Vitesse (AC)

AQCL .... Analytical Quality Control Laboratory (IID)
AQCM .... Aviation Fire Control Technician, Master Chief [Navy rating]
AQ COM ...... Aqua Communis [Tap Water] [Pharmacy]
aq comm ..... Aqua Communis [Tap water] [Pharmacology] (DAVI)
AQCR .... Air Quality Control Region [Environmental Protection Agency]
AQCR .... Aqua Care Systems [NASDAQ symbol] (SAG)
AQCRW ...... Aqua Care Sys Wrrt'A' [NASDAQ symbol] (TTSB)
AQCS .... Aviation Fire Control Technician, Senior Chief [Navy rating]
AQCT .... Association Quebecoise des Critiques de Theatre (AC)
AQD .... Additional Qualification Designator (NVT)
AQD .... Aeronautical Quality Assurance Directorate [British]
AQD .... Alleged Quarter [of the year] Disability Began [Social Security Administration] (OICC)
AQD .... Average Quarterly Demand
AQD .... Hartford, CT [Location identifier FAA] (FAAL)
AQ DEST..... Aqua Destillata [Distilled Water] [Pharmacy]
AQDHS........ Air Quality Data Handling System [or Subsystem] [Environmental Protection Agency]
Aq Dist .... Distilled Water [Pharmacology] (DAVI)
AQDLM .... Association Quebecoise des Directeurs et Directrices du Loisir Municipal (AC)
AQDM .... Air Quality Display Model
AQDR......... Association Quebecoise pour la Defense des Droits des Retraites et des Pre-Retraites (AC)
AQDS .... Anthraquinone Disulfonate [Organic chemistry]
aqdt .... Aqueduct (VRA)
AQD/U........ Additional Qualification Designation/Utilization (DNAB)
AQE........... Air Aquitaine [France ICAO designator] (FAAC)
AQE........... Airman Qualifying Examination
AQE........... Greenville, NC [Location identifier FAA] (FAAL)
AQEA .... Association Quebecoise des Enterprises Adaptees (AC)
AQEA .... Association Quebecoise d'Etudes Americaines (AC)
AQEFT........ Association Quebecoise des Ecoles de Francais (AC)
AQEM .... Association Quebecoise des Editeurs de Magazines (AC)
AQEP .... Association Quebecoise des Educateurs du Primaire (AC)
AQEPA .... Association du Quebec pour Enfants avec Problemes Auditifs (AC)
AQETA .... Association Quebecoise pour les Troubles d'Apprentissage (AC)
AQF........... Advanced Quickfix [Military]
AQF........... Air Quality Forecast
AQF........... Association Quebec-France (AC)
AQF........... Aviation Fire Control Technician, Fire Control [Navy rating]
AQ FERV ..... Aqua Fervens [Warm Water] [Pharmacy]
AQFIM........ Association Quebecoise des Fabricants de l'Industrie Medicale (AC)
AQ FLUV ..... Aqua Fluviatilis [River Water] [Pharmacy] (ROG)
AQ FONT..... Aqua Fontis [Spring Water] [Pharmacy] (ROG)
AQ FORT..... Aqua Fortis [Sulphuric Acid] [Pharmacy] (ROG)
AQ FRIG ..... Aqua Frigida [Cold Water] [Pharmacy]
AQ FRIGID.... Aqua Frigida [Cold Water] [Pharmacy] (ROG)
AQ GEL....... Aqua Gelida [Cold Water] [Pharmacy]
Aqgnx........ Aquagenix, Inc. [Associated Press] (SAG)
AQGV........ Air Quality Guideline Values [World Health Organization]
AQGV........ Azimuth Quantized Gated Video [Air Force]
AQH.......... Average Quarter Hour (WDMC)
AQH.......... Average Quarter Hour Rating [Television] [Radio] (WDMC)
AQHA......... American Quarter Horse Association (EA)
AQHRC........ American Quarter Horse Racing Council (EA)
AQI........... Air Quality Index
AQI........... American Quicksilver Institute [Defunct] (EA)
AQI........... Qaisumah [Saudi Arabia] [Airport symbol] (OAG)
AQIC......... Anima Quiescat in Christo [May His, or Her, Soul Repose in Christ] [Latin]
Aqil .... Aquila [Constellation]
AQIN .... Association Quebecoise de l'Industrie du Nautisme [Quebec Marine Trades Association] (AC)
AQIP .... Association Quebecoise de l'Industrie de la Peche [Quebec Fish Processor Association] (AC)
AQIP .... Association Quebecoise de l'Industrie de la Peinture (AC)
AQIP .... Association Quebecoise d'Interpretation du Patrimoine (AC)
AQIRP .... Air Quality Improvement Research Program [Automotive industry, research consortium]
AQIS .... Association du Quebec pour l'Integration Sociale [Quebec Association for Community Living] (AC)
AQISEP ...... Association Quebecoise d'Information Scolaire et Professionnelle (AC)
AQJ........... Aqaba [Jordan] [Airport symbol] (OAG)
AQL........... Acceptable Quality Level [Quality control]
AQL........... Advanced Quick Look [Army]
AQL........... Airworthiness Qualification Program
Aql .... Aquila [Constellation]
AQL........... Aquila Air Ltd. [Canada ICAO designator] (FAAC)
AQL........... Average Quality Limit
AQL........... Average Quality of the Lot (IAA)
AQLA......... Aquila Biopharmaceuticals, Inc. [NASDAQ symbol] (SAG)
AQLPA .... Association Quebecoise de Lutte Contre la Pollution Atmospherique (AC)
AQLPH....... Association Quebecoise de Loisir pour Personnes Handicapees [Quebec Leisure Association for Handicapped Persons] (AC)
AQM.......... Air Quality Management
AQM.......... American Antiquarian Society, Worcester, MA [OCLC symbol] (OCLC)
AQM.......... Assistant Quartermaster
AQM.......... Association Quebecoise des Marionnettistes (AC)
AQM.......... Atmospheric Quality and Modification [National Center for Atmospheric Research]
AQM.......... Drone Target [Navy symbol British]

AQM.............	QMS, Inc. [*NYSE symbol*] (SPSG)
AQMA.........	Air Quality Maintenance Area [*Environmental Protection Agency*] (GFGA)
AQ MAR......	Aqua Marina [*Sea Water*] [*Pharmacy*] (ROG)
AQMC.........	Army Quartermaster Corps [*Merged with Supply and Maintenance Command*]
AQMC.........	Association of Quality Management Consultants [*British*] (DBA)
AQMD.........	Air Quality Management District
AQME.........	Association Quebecoise pour la Maitrise de l'Energie (AC)
AQ MENTH...	Aqua Mentha [*Mint Water*] [*Pharmacy*] (ROG)
AQ MENTH PIP...	Aqua Mentha Piperitae [*Peppermint Water*] [*Pharmacy*] (ROG)
AQMG.........	Assistant Quartermaster-General [*Military*]
AQMP.........	Air Quality Maintenance Plan [*Environmental Protection Agency*] (GFGA)
AQMS........	Armourer Quartermaster Sergeant [*British*]
AQMS.........	Artificer Quartermaster Sergeant [*British*]
AQMS.........	Artisan Quartermaster Sergeant [*British*]
AQN.............	Acton, TX [*Location identifier FAA*] (FAAL)
AQN............	Air Queensland [*Australia ICAO designator*] (FAAC)
AQN.............	Azimuthal Quantum Number
AQ NIV.......	Aqua Nivalis [*Snow Water*] [*Pharmacy*] (ROG)
AQO............	Aminoquinoline Oxide [*Biochemistry*] (OA)
AQOCI.........	Association Quebecoise des Organismes de Co-operation Internationale [*Canada*] (CROSS)
AQP............	Advanced Qualification Program [*FAA*] (TAG)
AQP............	Advanced Qualification Program (GAVI)
AQP............	Airworthiness Qualification Plan
AQP............	Airworthiness Qualification Program (MCD)
AQP............	Aquila Gas Pipeline [*NYSE symbol*] (SPSG)
AQP............	Arequipa [*Peru*] [*Airport symbol*] (OAG)
AQP............	Association for Quality and Participation (EA)
AQP............	Association Quebecoise du Propane (AC)
AQPA.........	American Quarter Pony Association (EA)
AQPA.........	American Quick Printing Association [*Defunct*] (EA)
AQPC.........	Association Quebecoise de Pedagogie Collegiale (AC)
AQPDE.......	Association Quebecoise du Personnel de Direction des Ecoles (AC)
AQPF.........	Association Quebecoise des Professeurs de Francais (AC)
AQPI..........	Association Quebecoise pour le Patrimoine Industriel (AC)
AQ PIMENT..	Aqua Pimentae [*Allspice Water*] [*Pharmacy*] (ROG)
AQ PLUV.....	Aqua Pluvialis [*or Pluviatilis*] [*Rain Water*] [*Pharmacy*] (ROG)
AQPP.........	Association Quebecoise des Professionnels de la Philatelie (AC)
AQPPT.......	Association Quebecoise des Personnes de Petite Taille (AC)
AQPPT........	Association Quebecoise du Personnes de Direction des Ecoles (AC)
AQPU.........	Association Quebecoise des Presses Universitaires (AC)
AQ PUR......	Aqua Pura [*Pure Water*] [*Pharmacy*] (ROG)
AQQ............	Annual Qualifications Questionnaire [*Navy*] (NVT)
AQQ............	Apalachicola, FL [*Location identifier FAA*] (FAAL)
AQQ............	Association Quebecoise de la Qualite (AC)
AQQA.........	Aquanatural Co. [*NASDAQ symbol*] (TTSB)
AQQPRI.......	Advanced Qualitative and Quantitative Personnel Requirements Information [*Army*]
AQR............	Acceptable Quality Rate [*Quality control*]
AQR............	Afterloaded Quick Release [*Physiology*]
AQR............	Air Quality Region
AQR............	Alenquer [*Brazil*] [*Airport symbol*] (AD)
Aqr.............	Aquarius [*Constellation*]
AQR............	Aquarius Resources Ltd. [*Vancouver Stock Exchange symbol*]
AQR............	Assembly Quality Record
AQR............	Assessment Quality Report (MCD)
AQR............	Average Quarter-Hour Rating [*Of radio and television programming*] (WDMC)
A Qr D........	After Quarter Day [*Freemasonry*] (ROG)
AQREC........	Army Quartermaster Research and Engineering Command (MCD)
AQRM.........	Average Quantity Repaired Monthly
AQ ROS......	Aqua Rosa [*Rose Water*] [*Pharmacy*] (ROG)
AQRRCT......	Association Quebecoise des Realisateurs et Realisatrices de Cinema et de Television (AC)
AQ RUT......	Aqua Ruta [*Rue Water*] [*Pharmacy*] (ROG)
AQRV.........	Air Quality Related Values/Visibility Test [*Environmental Protection Agency*]
AQS............	Additional Qualifying Symptom [*Medicine*] (MAE)
AQS............	Air Quality Standard
AQS............	Airworthiness Qualification Specification
AQS............	Ambient Quality Standard [*Environmental science*] (FFDE)
AQS............	American Quilter's Society (EA)
AQS............	AmeriQuest Technol [*NYSE symbol*] (TTSB)
AQS............	Ameriquest Technology Co. [*Formerly, CMS Enhancements*] [*NYSE symbol*] (SAG)
AQS............	Approximate Quadratic Search [*Mathematics*]
AQS............	Aquarius Seafarms [*Vancouver Stock Exchange symbol*]
AQS............	Association Quebec Solaire (AC)
AQS............	Automated Quotation System (IAA)
AQS............	Saqani [*Fiji*] [*Airport symbol*] (OAG)
AQSFR........	Association Quebecoise des Sports en Fauteuil Roulants (AC)
AQSG.........	American Quilt Study Group (EA)
AQSM.........	Air Quality Simulation Model [*Environmental Protection Agency*]
AQ SOD......	Aqua Soda [*Soda Water*] [*Pharmacy*] (ROG)
AQSP.........	Association Quebecoise des Soins Palliatifs (AC)
AQT.............	Acceptable Quality Test [*Quality control*] (MSA)
AQT.............	Acquisitor Mines Ltd. [*Vancouver Stock Exchange symbol*]
AQT.............	Applicant Qualification Test [*Navy*]
AQT.............	Aviation Qualification Test
AQT.............	Aviones de Renta de Quintana Roo, SA de CV [*Mexico*] [*FAA designator*] (FAAC)
AQTA..........	Association Quebecoise des Transporteurs Aeriens (AC)

AQTA	Association Quebecoise du Theatre Amateur Inc. (AC)
AQTAD........	Air Quality Technical Assistance Demonstration [*Environmental Protection Agency*] (GFGA)
AQTD.........	Airworthiness Qualification Test Directorate [*Military*] (RDA)
AQTE...........	Association Quebecoise des Techniques de l'Eau [*Canada*] (ASF)
AQ TEP.......	Aqua Tepida [*Lukewarm Water*] [*Pharmacy*]
AQ TEPID....	Aqua Tepida [*Lukewarm Water*] [*Pharmacy*] (ROG)
AQTESOLV..	Aquifer Test Solver
AQTN.........	Aequitron Medical [*NASDAQ symbol*] (TTSB)
AQTN.........	Aequitron Medical, Inc. [*Minneapolis, MN*] [*NASDAQ symbol*] (NQ)
AQTR.........	Association Quebecoise du Transport et des Routes Inc. (AC)
AQTX..........	Aquatic Toxicity
AQTY	Allowance Quality (DNAB)
AQU............	Acqualin Resources Ltd. [*Vancouver Stock Exchange symbol*]
AQU............	Aquair Luftfahrt GmbH [*Germany ICAO designator*] (FAAC)
AQU............	Aquarius [*Constellation*]
AQU............	Aqueous (AAMN)
AQU............	Aquidauana [*Brazil*] [*Airport symbol*] (AD)
AQU............	Aquila [*Italy*] [*Seismograph station code, US Geological Survey*] (SEIS)
AQU............	Aquila Airways Ltd.
Aqua..........	Aquamarine [*Philately*]
AQUA..........	Aquatic
AquaC........	Aqua Care Systems [*Commercial firm Associated Press*] (SAG)
AquaCre.....	Aqua Care Systems [*Commercial firm Associated Press*] (SAG)
Aquagnx.....	Aquagenix, Inc. [*Associated Press*] (SAG)
AQUAID.......	Acquisition Aid
AQUARIUS ...	[*A*] Query and Retrieval Interactive Utility System [*Computer science*] (ADA)
Aquarn........	Aquarion Co. [*Associated Press*] (SAG)
AquC...........	Aqua Care Systems [*Commercial firm Associated Press*] (SAG)
AQUEFLS	Association Quebecoise des Enseignants de Francais Langue Seconde [*Quebec Association of Teachers of French as a Second Language*] (AC)
AquilaB.......	Aquila Biopharmaceuticals, Inc. [*Associated Press*] (SAG)
AquilaG.......	Aquila Gas Pipeline Corp. [*Associated Press*] (SAG)
AQUIRE.......	Aquatic Information Retrieval Database [*Chemical Information Systems, Inc.*] [*Information service or system*]
AQUIS........	Acquisition (KSC)
AQUOPS	Association Quebecoise des Utilisateurs de l'Ordinateur au Primaire et au Secondaire (AC)
aqut	Aquatint (VRA)
AQUX..........	Aquagenix, Inc. [*NASDAQ symbol*] (SAG)
AQUXW.......	Aquagenix Inc. Wrrt [*NASDAQ symbol*] (TTSB)
AQY	Girdwood, AK [*Location identifier FAA*] (FAAL)
AQZ	Aerodyne Charter [*ICAO designator*] (FAAC)
AR...............	Aberdeen & Rockfish Railroad Co. [*AAR code*]
AR...............	Academic Ranking (EDAC)
AR...............	Acceptance Readiness (NASA)
AR...............	Acceptance Requirement
AR...............	Acceptance Review (NASA)
AR...............	Accept-Reject Rule [*Statistics*]
AR...............	Accomplishment Ratio (ADA)
AR...............	Accounting Review [*A publication*] (BRI)
AR...............	Accounts Receivable [*Accounting*]
AR...............	Accounts Register [*Computer science*]
AR...............	Accumulator Register [*Computer science*]
A/R...............	Accumulator/Reservoir (MCD)
AR...............	Achievement Ratio
AR...............	Acid Resisting [*Technical drawings*]
AR...............	Acknowledgment of Receipt [*Message handling*] [*Telecommunications*]
AR...............	Acoustic Reflex
AR...............	Acquisition RADAR
AR...............	Actinic Reticuloid Syndrome [*Medicine*] (DMAA)
A/R...............	Action and/or Reply [*Control system*]
AR...............	Action Register
AR...............	Active Range (MCD)
AR...............	Active Resistance [*Occupational therapy*]
AR...............	Activity Report (MCD)
AR...............	Actual Range (IAA)
AR...............	Additional Requirements (DLA)
AR...............	Address Register (CMD)
AR...............	Adherence Ratio [*Medicine*] (DMAA)
AR...............	Administrative Ruling [*US*]
AR...............	Adrenergic Receptor [*Physiology*]
AR...............	Advanced Reactor (KSC)
AR...............	Advanced Readiness (MCD)
AR...............	Advice of Receipt
AR...............	Aerial [*In-Flight*] Refueling
AR...............	Aerodynamic Report
AR...............	Aeronautical Radio (IAA)
AR...............	Aeronautical [*or Aircraft*] Requirement [*Military*] (MCD)
AR...............	Aeronautical Research (IAA)
AR...............	Aeronca Manufacturing [*ICAO aircraft manufacturer identifier*] (ICAO)
AR...............	Aero Repair (MCD)
AR...............	Aft Right (MCD)
AR...............	Agencja Robotricza [*Press agency*] [*Poland*]
AR...............	Agent Report (MCD)
AR...............	Age Replacement
AR...............	Agricultural Research
AR...............	Air and Radiation Division [*Environmental Protection Agency*] (GFGA)
AR...............	Airborne Receiver
AR...............	Air Conditioning and Refrigeration Program [*Association of Independent Colleges and Schools specialization code*]

AR	Aircraft Ready (AFIT)
AR	Aircraft Rocket (NVT)
AR	Airman Records [*Air Force*] (AFM)
AR	Airman Recruit
AR	Air Radio [*Special duties officer*] [*British*]
AR	Air Receive
AR	Air Reconnaissance (IAA)
AR	Air Refueling
AR	Air Register [*Combustion emission control*]
AR	Air Regulator
AR	Air Rescue
AR	Air Reserve
AR	Air Resistance
AR	Airship Rigger
AR	Alarm Reaction [*Psychology*]
AR	Allard Register (EA)
AR	Allegheny Region
AR	Allergic Reaction [*Immunology*]
AR	Allergic Rhinitis [*Medicine*]
AR	Allocated Reserve
AR	Alloy Restoration [*Medicine*] (DMAA)
AR	All Rail [*Railroad*]
A/R	All Returned (DGA)
AR	All Risks [*Insurance*]
A/R	All Round [*Price*] (ROG)
A/R	Alternate Route [*Telecommunications*] (TEL)
AR	Altesse Royale [*Royal Highness*] [*French*]
A/R	Altitude Reporting (DA)
AR	Amateur (Radio) Station [*ITU designation*] (CET)
AR	Amendment Request [*Navy*]
AR	American Reports [*A publication*] (DLA)
AR	American Rivers (EA)
AR	American Smelting & Refining Co. (IIA)
AR	America Remembers (EA)
AR	Amilcar Register (EA)
AR	Amphibian Reconnaissance [*Military*]
AR	Amphiregulin [*Biochemistry*]
AR	Amplification Ratio (MCD)
AR	Amplifier (IAA)
AR	Amrinone [*Cardiotonic*]
AR	Analytical Reagent [*Chemistry*]
AR	Analytic Reaction (AAMN)
AR	Anaphylactoid Reaction [*Immunology*]
AR	Androgen Receptors [*Endocrinology*]
AR	Angle Resolved [*Physics*]
AR	Animal Rights [*An association Australia*]
AR	Anna Regina [*Queen Anne*]
AR	Anno Regni [*In the Year of the Reign*] [*Latin*]
AR	Annual Rate
AR	Annual Register [*A publication*]
AR	Annual Report
AR	Annual Return
AR	Annual Review (NATG)
AR	Annual Reviews (EA)
AR	Anode Reaction
AR	Anomaly Report (MCD)
AR	Anterior Resection [*Medicine*]
AR	Antiphonale Sacrosanctae Romanae Ecclesiae
AR	Antiracketeering
AR	AntiRADAR (NATG)
AR	Antireflection
AR	Antireversionary [*Method of exhaust control*] [*Automotive engineering*]
AR	Aortic Regurgitation [*Medicine*]
AR	Aortic Root [*Cardiology*]
A/R	Apical/Radial [*Pulse*] [*Medicine*]
AR	Apical Rate [*Medicine*]
AR	Appeal Reports, Upper Canada [*1846-66*] [*A publication*] (DLA)
AR	Application Review (IAA)
AR	Applied Research [*of ASRA*] [*National Science Foundation*]
AR	Appointments Register
AR	Approved for Release
ar-----	Arabian Peninsula [*MARC geographic area code Library of Congress*] (LCCP)
AR	Arabic
Ar	Arabinoside
Ar	Arakhin [*or Arakin*] (BJA)
AR	Aramaic [*Language, etc.*] (ROG)
Ar	Archidiaconus [*Authority cited in pre-1607 legal work*] (DSA)
AR	Architecture
AR	Arcuate [*Brain anatomy*]
AR	Area
AR	Area Altitude Requirement (SAA)
AR	Area of Resolution
AR	Area Redesignation [*Environmental Protection Agency*]
AR	Area Weapon Right (MCD)
AR	Argentina [*ANSI two-letter standard code*] (CNC)
AR	Argentum [*Silver*] [*Numismatics*]
Ar	Argon [*Preferred form, but also see A*] [*Chemical element*]
AR	Argus Corp. Ltd. [*Toronto Stock Exchange symbol*]
AR	Argyll Robertson Pupil [*Ophthalmology*] (MAE)
Ar	Ariprandus [*Flourished, 12th century*] [*Authority cited in pre-1607 legal work*] (DSA)
Ar	Aristophanes [*Greek playwright, c. 445-380BC*] [*Classical studies*] (OCD)

AR	Arithmetic Register
AR	Arkansas [*Postal code*]
Ar	Arkansas Library Commission, Little Rock, AR [*Library symbol Library of Congress*] (LCLS)
AR	Armagh [*County in Ireland*] (ROG)
AR	Armament (SAA)
AR	Armed RECCE [*Reconnaissance*] [*Military*] (VNW)
A/R	Armed Reconnaissance (MUGU)
AR	Armored Reconnaissance
AR	Army
AR	Army Receiving-Valve (IAA)
AR	Army Regulation
AR	Army Reserve [*Formerly, ERC, ORC*]
ar	Aromatic [*Chemistry*]
AR	Arrested Relaxation [*Molecular dynamics*]
AR	Arrester [*Electricity*] (IAA)
AR	Arrete [*Decision, Ordinance, By-law*] [*French*]
AR	Arrival
AR	Arrival and Return [*Shipping*]
Ar	Arsendinus de Forlivio [*Authority cited in pre-1607 legal work*] (DSA)
AR	Arsphenamine [*Antisyphilitic compound*] (MAE)
AR	Articulare [*Craniometric point*]
AR	Artificial Respiration [*Medicine*]
Ar	Aryl [*Chemistry*]
AR	ASARCO, Inc. [*Formerly, American Smelting & Refining Co.*] [*NYSE symbol*] (SPSG)
ar	Ascensio Recta [*Right Ascension*] [*Latin*]
AR	Aspect Ratio
AR	As Required (AFM)
AR	As Rolled [*Technical drawings*] (DAC)
AR	Assigned Rating [*Sailing*]
AR	Assistant Registrar (ROG)
AR	Assisted Resonance (NTCM)
AR	Associated Rediffusion [*Television*]
AR	Associate in Retailing
AR	Associative Register [*Computer science*]
AR	Asthma Rhinitis [*Immunology*]
AR	Astrodynamical Report (SAA)
AR	Atlantic Reporter [*A publication*] (DLA)
AR	Atlantic Route [*Aviation*] (FAAC)
AR	Atmospheric Revitalization (MCD)
AR	Atrial Rate [*Cardiology*]
AR	At Risk (MAE)
AR	Atrophic Rhinitis [*Medicine*] (DMAA)
AR	Attenuation Reaction
A/R	At the Rate Of (MUGU)
AR	Attrition Reserve
AR	Audience Research (NTCM)
AR	Audio Response
AR	Auditor of Receipts
AR	Auditor of Revenue
AR	Aufsichtsrat [*Supervisory Board*] [*German*]
AR	Augmentation Reliability (MCD)
AR	Augmented Roman (ADA)
AR	Augustinian Recollect Sisters [*An association Australia*]
AR	Austin Rover [*British-built automobile*]
AR	Authority Record [*Database terminology*] (NITA)
A/R	AUTOLAND [*Automatic Landing*] Rollout [*NASA*] (MCD)
AR	Automated Radioimmunoassay
AR	Automated Reagin [*Serology*]
AR	Automatic Radio Manufacturing Co., Inc.
AR	Automatic Resupply (NVT)
AR	Automatic Rifle [*or Rifleman*] [*DoD*]
AR	Autonomous Republic
AR	Autoradiographic
AR	Autoradiography [*Medicine*] (DAVI)
AR	Autoregressive [*Mathematical bioscience*]
AR	Autosomal Recessive [*Genetics*]
AR	Auxiliary Routine (IAA)
AR	Availability Rate
AR	Average Rating
AR	Average Revenue
AR	Aviation Radionavigation, Land [*FCC*] (IEEE)
AR	Avionics Requirements (MCD)
AR	Avis de Reception [*Return Receipt*] [*French*]
AR	Awaiting Reply [*Telecommunications*] (TEL)
A/R	Azimuth/Range (RDA)
AR	Bomber [*Russian aircraft symbol*]
AR	Egypt [*IYRU nationality code*] (IYR)
AR	Handmaids of the Sacred Heart of Jesus for Reparation (TOCD)
AR	Ontario Appeal Reports [*A publication*] (DLA)
AR	Ralston Public Library, Alberta [*Library symbol National Library of Canada*] (NLC)
AR	Repair Ship [*Navy symbol*]
AR	Stanlabs, Inc. [*Research code symbol*]
AR1	Volcano Arenal [*Costa Rica*] [*Seismograph station code, US Geological Survey*] (SEIS)
AR2	Lago De Cote [*Costa Rica*] [*Seismograph station code, US Geological Survey*] (SEIS)
AR3	Automatic Reserve Ripcord Release [*for a parachute*] (RDA)
AR3	Tierras Morenas [*Costa Rica*] [*Seismograph station code, US Geological Survey*] (SEIS)
AR4	Solania [*Costa Rica*] [*Seismograph station code, US Geological Survey*] (SEIS)

AR5............ Santa Elena [*Costa Rica*] [*Seismograph station code, US Geological Survey*] (SEIS)

AR6............ Chripa [*Costa Rica*] [*Seismograph station code, US Geological Survey*] (SEIS)

AR7............ Cabo Frio [*Costa Rica*] [*Seismograph station code, US Geological Survey*] (SEIS)

AR8............ Nicoya [*Costa Rica*] [*Seismograph station code, US Geological Survey*] (SEIS)

AR9............ Volcan Norte [*Costa Rica*] [*Seismograph station code, US Geological Survey*] (SEIS)

AR 55-80 .... Highways for National Defense [*MTMC*] (TAG)

ARA .... Abbreviated Registered Address

ARA .... Academy of Rehabilitative Audiology (EA)

ARA .... Accelerated Readiness Analysis (NG)

ARA .... Accredited Rural Appraiser [*American Society of Farm Man agers and Rural Appraisers*] [*Designation awarded by*]

ARA .... Acetylene Reduction Assay [*Botany*]

ARA .... Active Retrodirective Array (MCD)

ARA .... Actual Range Angle (IAA)

ARA .... Adapter, Right Angle

ARA .... Address Register Area [*Bureau of the Census*] (GFGA)

ARA .... Aerial Refueling Area

ARA .... Aerial Rocket Artillery

ARA .... Aerial Ropeways Association [*British*] (BI)

ARA .... Aerobeira, Sociedade de Transportes Aeros [*Portugal ICAO designator*] (FAAC)

ARA .... Aerospace Research Association (MCD)

ARA .... Agricultural Research Administration [*Superseded by ARS, 1953*] [*Department of Agriculture*]

ARA .... Airborne RADAR Approach (AFM)

ARA .... Airborne Receiving Antenna

ARA .... Airborne Research Australia

ARA .... Aircraft Recovery Association (EA)

ARA .... Aircraft Replaceable Assemblies

ARA .... Aircraft Research Association (EAIO)

ARA .... Air Reserve Association [*Later, Air Force Association*]

ARA .... Alabama Restaurant Association (SRA)

ARA .... Alabama Retail Association (SRA)

ARA .... Allied Research Associates, Inc. (MCD)

ARA .... Aluminum Recycling Association (EA)

ARA .... Amateur Riders Association [*British*] (DBA)

ARA .... Amateur Rocketeers of America

ARA .... Amateur Rowing Association [*British*]

ARA .... American Archives Association (EA)

ARA .... American Radio Association (EA)

ARA .... American Rafting Association [*Defunct*] (EA)

ARA .... American Railway Association [*Later, AAR*]

ARA .... American Recovery Association (EA)

ARA .... American Recreational Activities

ARA .... American Relief Administration Association

ARA .... American Reloaders Association (EA)

ARA .... American Remount Association (EA)

ARA .... American Rental Association (EA)

ARA .... American Republics Area [*Department of State*]

ARA .... American Restitution Association (EA)

ARA .... American Retiree Association [*An association*]

ARA .... American Retreaders Association (EA)

ARA .... American Revenue Association (EA)

ARA .... American Rheumatism Association [*Later, ACR*] (EA)

ARA .... American Romagnola Association (EA)

ARA .... American Romanian Academy of Arts and Sciences (EA)

ARA .... American Rowing Association (EA)

ARA .... American Royal Association (EA)

ARA .... Amsterdam, Rotterdam, Antwerp

ARA .... Analog RADAR Absorber

ARA .... Ancient Records of Assyria [*A publication*] (BJA)

ARA .... Antireceptor Antibody [*Immunology*]

ARA .... Apple Remote Access [*Apple Computer, Inc.*] (PCM)

ARA .... Appletalk Remote Access [*Apple Computer Inc.*]

ARA .... Arabesque [*Embossed*] [*Bookbinding*] (ROG)

ara .... Arabic [*MARC language code Library of Congress*] (LCCP)

ARA .... Arabic [*Language, etc.*]

Ara .... Arabinose [*Also, a*] [*A sugar*]

ara .... Arabinose (DMAA)

ARA .... Arab Relief Agency

ARA .... Arab Roads Association [*Cairo, Egypt*] (EAIO)

ARA .... Aracruz Celulose SA [*NYSE symbol*] (SPSG)

ARA .... Aracruz Celulose S.A. ADS [*NYSE symbol*] (TTSB)

ARA .... Arapuni [*New Zealand*] [*Seismograph station code, US Geological Survey Closed*] (SEIS)

ARA .... Arcade & Attica Railroad Corp. [*AAR code*]

ARA .... Area Redevelopment Act

ARA .... Area Redevelopment Administration [*Terminated, 1965; functions transferred to Economic Development Administration*] [*Department of Commerce*]

Ar A .... Arithmetic Age [*Education*] (BARN)

ARA .... Arizona Restaurant Association (SRA)

ARA .... Arizona Retailers Association (SRA)

ARA .... Arkansas Railroad Association (SRA)

ARA .... Arkansas Realtors Association (SRA)

ARA .... Army Reactor Area (SAA)

ARA .... Army Reserve Association

ARA .... Army Rifle Association [*British military*] (DMA)

ARA .... Artists' Representatives Association [*Defunct*] (EA)

ARA .... Artists Rights Association [*Defunct*]

ARA .... Asian Recycling Association (EAIO)

ARA .... Asphalt Roads Association [*British*] (BI)

ARA .... Assigned Responsible Agency [*DoD*]

ARA .... Assistant Regional Administrator [*Environmental Protection Agency*] (GFGA)

ARA .... Associate in Religious Arts

ARA .... Associate of the Royal Academy [*British*]

ARA .... Associate Regional Administrator

ARA .... Associates for Radio Astronomy

ARA .... Association of Relocation Agents [*British*] (DBA)

ARA .... Association of Retired Americans (EA)

ARA .... Association of River Authorities [*British*] (BI)

ARA .... Attitude Reference Assembly (MCD)

ARA .... Augmented Roman Alphabet (DGA)

ARA .... Australian Renderers' Association

ARA .... Australian Romney Association

ARA .... Automatic Retailers of America (MCD)

ARA .... Automatic Route Advancement (MCD)

ARA .... Automotive Recyclers Association [*Salvage yards*]

ARA .... Automotive Retailers Association [*Canada*]

ARA .... Auto-Resonant Accelerator [*For atomic particles*]

ARA .... Auxiliary Reactor Area

ARA .... Auxiliary Recovery Antenna [*NASA*] (KSC)

ARA .... Average Response Amplitude

ARA .... Avionics Repairable Assemblies (AFIT)

ARA .... Avionics Research Aircraft (MCD)

ARA .... AVVI [*Altimeter Vertical Velocity Indicator*] RADAR Altitude (GFGA)

ARA .... New Iberia, LA [*Location identifier FAA*] (FAAL)

ARA .... Society of American Registered Architects (EA)

ARA-A .... Adenine Arabinoside [*Also called vidarabine*] [*Antineoplastic drug*] (DAVI)

ARAA .... Aerodrome RADAR/Radio Approach Aid

ARAA .... American Registry of Architectural Antiquities (EA)

ARAA .... American Russian Aid Association (EA)

ara-A .... Arabinofuranosyladenine [*or Adenine Arabinoside*] [*Also, Vira-A Antiviral compound*]

ara-AMP ..... Adenine Arabinoside Monophosphate [*Biochemistry*]

ARAAS .... Annual Reports on Analytical Atomic Spectroscopy [*Later, JAAS*] [*A publication*]

ara-ATP ...... Adenine Arabinoside Triphosphate [*Biochemistry*]

ARAAV .... Armored Reconnaissance Airborne Assault Vehicle (AABC)

ARAB .... American Riding Association of Berlin [*Post-World War II*]

ARAB .... Ancient Records of Assyria and Babylonia [*A publication*] (BJA)

Arab .... Arabia (VRA)

ARAB .... Army Research and Development Bulletin [*A publication*] (RDA)

ARABHA ...... Arab Historians Association (EAIO)

ARABIC .... Ar-Rajhi Banking & Investment Co. [*Saudi Arabia*] (EY)

Arabin .... Decision of Sergeant Arabin [*A publication*] (DLA)

ARABS .... Active RADAR Augmentor Beacon System (MCD)

ARABS .... Association of Religion and Applied Behavioral Science [*Later, ACC*] (EA)

ARABSAT ..... Arab Satellite Communications Organization [*Saudi Arabia*] [*Telecommunications*]

ArabSh .... Arabian Shield Development Co. [*Associated Press*] (SAG)

ARAC .... Academie Royale des Arts du Canada [*Royal Canadian Academy of Arts - RCA*]

ARAC .... Accredited Review Appraisers Council (EA)

ARAC .... Aerospace Research Applications Center [*Indiana University*] [*NASA*]

ARAC .... Afghan Refugee Aid Committee (AC)

ARAC .... AIDS Research Advisory Committee [*National Institutes of Health*] (EGAO)

ARAC .... Airborne RADAR Approach Control (DNAB)

ARAC .... Alcoma Community Library, Rainier, Alberta [*Library symbol National Library of Canada*] (NLC)

ARAC .... Antarctic Research Advisory Council

ara-C .... Aracytidine [*Cytarabine*] [*Also, CA, CAR*] [*Antineoplastic drug*]

ARAC .... Area Airports Checked (FAAC)

ARAC .... Army RADAR Approach Control Facility (FAAC)

ARAC .... Array Reduction Analysis Circuit (MHDB)

ARAC .... Associate of the Royal Agricultural College [*British*] (BARN)

ARAC .... Association of Rain Apparel Contractors (EA)

ARAC .... Atmospheric Release Advisory Capability [*Energy Research and Development Administration*]

ARAC .... Australasian Register of Agricultural Consultants

ARAC .... Aviation Regulatory Advisory Committee [*FAA*] (TAG)

ARAC .... Aviation Rulemaking Advisory Committee (GAVI)

ARAC .... Avis Rent a Car

ara-C .... Cytosine Arabinoside [*Antineoplastic drug*] (MAE)

ARACH .... Arachnology

ara-C-HU ..... Aracytidine, Hydroxyurea [*Antineoplastic drug regimen*]

ara-CMP ..... Cytosine Arabinoside Monophosphate [*Biochemistry*]

Aracruz .... Aracruz Celulose SA [*Associated Press*] (SAG)

Aracrz .... Aracruz Celulose SA [*Associated Press*] (SAG)

ara-CTP ...... Cytosine Arabinoside Triphosphate [*Biochemistry*]

ARAD .... Airborne RADAR and Doppler

ARAD .... Alpha Research and Development (KSC)

ARAD .... Altitude Radial (FAAC)

ARAD .... Associate of the Royal Academy of Dancing [*British*]

ARAD .... Automated Requirements Allocation Data (MCD)

ARAD .... Average Response Amplitude Data

ARAD .... Radway Public Library, Alberta [*Library symbol National Library of Canada*] (NLC)

ARADCOM ... Army Air Defense Command [*or Commander*] [*Later, AADCOM*]

Aradigm ...... Aradigm Corp. [*Associated Press*] (SAG)

ARadio .... American Radio Systems Corp. [*Associated Press*] (SAG)

ARADMAC.... Army Aeronautical Depot Maintenance Center [*AMC-ASMC*]
ARADS......... Army Recruiting and Accession Data System (GFGA)
ARADS......... Artillery Registration/Adjustment System [*ARRADCOM*] (MCD)
ARADSCH .... Army Air Defense School
ARAE.......... Advanced Radio Astronomy Explorer (PDAA)
ARAE.......... American Retail Association Executives [*Defunct*] (EA)
ARAeS........ Associate of the Royal Aeronautical Society [*British*]
ARAF.......... Associated Regional Accounting Firms [*Atlanta, GA*] (EA)
ara-FC........ Arabinofuranosylfluorocytosine [*Also, FCA*] [*Antineoplastic drug*]
ARAG......... Antireflective, Antiglare [*Cathode ray tube treatment*] (PCM)
ara-H......... Arabinosylhypoxanthine [*Biochemistry*]
Arakis........ Arakis Energy Corp. [*Associated Press*] (SAG)
ARAL......... Adjustment Reaction to Adult Life [*Medicine*] (DMAA)
ARAL......... Association to Repeal Abortion Laws (EA)
ARAL......... Automatic Record Analysis Language [*Computer science*]
ARALL........ Aramid Reinforced Aluminum Laminate (MCD)
ARAM........ Analog Random Access Memory [*Computer science*] (HGAA)
ARAM........ Antigen Recognition Activation Motif [*Immunology*]
ARAM........ Aramaic [*Language, etc.*]
ARAM........ Aramed, Inc. Gensia Pharmaceuticals [*NASDAQ symbol*] (SAG)
ARAM........ Army Achievement Medal [*Military decoration*]
ARAM........ Associate of the Royal Academy of Music [*British*]
ARAM........ Association of Railroad Advertising and Marketing (EA)
ARAMCO..... Arabian-American Oil Co.
Aramed....... Aramed Incorporated Gensia Pharmaceuticals [*Associated Press*] (SAG)
ARAMIS...... Agencement en Rames Automatisees de Modules Independants dans les Stations [*Arrangement in automated trains of independent modules in stations*] [*A satirical novel by Bruno Latour*] [*Based on an actual Personal Rapid Transit program pursued by the French government*]
ARAMIS...... American Rheumatism Association Medical Information System [*Information service or system*] (IID)
ARAMIS...... Automation Robotics and Machine Intelligence System (PDAA)
ARAMMIS.... Aramis en Rames Automatisees de Modules Independants dans les Stations [*Arrangement in Automated Trains of Independent Modules in Stations*] [*France*]
ara-MP....... Arabinosylmercaptopurine [*Antineoplastic drug*]
ARAN......... Aran Energy Ltd. [*NASDAQ symbol*] (SAG)
ARAN......... Association for the Reduction of Aircraft Noise (EA)
ARAN......... Automatic Road Analyzer [*FHWA*] (TAG)
ARAND........ Analysis of Random Data [*System documentation*] [*Oregon State University*]
AR & D....... Advanced Research and Development
AR & D....... Air Research and Development
AR & D....... Atkins Research & Development [*W.S. Atkins Group Ltd.*] [*Research center British*]
AR & FA..... American Running and Fitness Association (EA)
AR & RSq.... Aerospace Rescue and Recovery Squadron [*Air Force*]
AR & T....... Advanced Research and Technology (MUGU)
AR & TD...... Advanced Research and Technology Development Program [*Department of Energy*]
AranEgy...... Aran Energy Ltd. [*Associated Press*] (SAG)
ArAO.......... Ouachita Baptist University, Arkadelphia, AR [*Library symbol Library of Congress*] (LCLS)
ARAOLA...... Association of Romanian-American Orthodox Ladies Auxiliaries (EA)
ARAP......... Administration du Retablissement Agricole des Prairies [*Prairie Farm Rehabilitation Administration - PFRA*]
ARAP......... Aeronautical Research Associates of Princeton (MCD)
ARAP......... Alternative Resource Allocation Priorities [*Military*]
ARAP......... Appletalk Remote Access Protocol [*Apple Computer Inc.*]
ARAP......... Army Research Associates Program (DOMA)
ARAP......... Astronaut Rescue Air Pack [*NASA*] (KSC)
ARAP......... Automated Reliability Assessment Program [*FAA*]
ARAP......... Average Revenue/Average Physical Product [*Economics*]
ARAPCS...... Association for Research, Administration, Professional Councils, and Societies (EA)
ARAPH........ Automated Reading Aid for the Physically Handicapped
ARAPS........ Area Requirements and Product Status [*Military*] (DNAB)
ARAPT........ Advanced Research Agency Project Tempo (MCD)
ARAQ......... Association des Residences d'Accueil du Quebec (AC)
ARAR......... Applicable or Relevant and Appropriate Requirement [*Environmental science*]
ARARA....... American Rock Art Research Association (EA)
ar/arm........ Arms & Armor (VRA)
ARAS......... Agricultural Research and Advisory Station [*New South Wales, Australia*]
ARAS.......... Antireflective, Antistatic [*Cathode ray tube treatment*] (PCM)
ARAS.......... Artillery Registration/Adjustment System [*ARRADCOM*] (MCD)
ARAS.......... Ascending Reticular Activating [*or Activation*] System
ARAS.......... Associate of the Royal Astronomical Society [*British*]
ARAS.......... Association of Regular Army Sergeants (EA)
ARAS.......... Atomic Resonance Absorption Spectroscopy [*Physics*]
ARaS.......... Redstone Scientific Information Center, United States Army Missile Command, Redstone Arsenal, AL [*Library symbol Library of Congress*] (LCLS)
ARASEM...... Artificially Random Self-Motivated (MHDI)
ARASUSA... Association of Russian-American Scholars in the United States of America (EA)
ARAT......... Acyl Coenzyme A: Retinal Acyltransferase [*An enzyme*]
ARAT......... Advise [*names of*] Representatives, Accommodations, and Transportation [*desired*] [*Army*] (AABC)
ARAT......... Aerial Rocket Antitank Program (MCD)
ara-T......... Arabinofuranosylthymine [*Biochemistry*]
Arat.......... Aratea [*of Germanicus*] [*Classical studies*] (OCD)

Arat.......... Aratus [*of Plutarch*] [*Classical studies*] (OCD)
ARAT .... Atmospheric Research and Remote Sensing Plane [*Marine science*] (OSRA)
ARAT .... Automatic Random Access Transport
ArAT.......... Henderson State University, Arkadelphia, AR [*Library symbol Library of Congress*] (LCLS)
ARATDL....... Air Resources Atmospheric Turbulence and Diffusion Laboratory [*National Oceanic and Atmospheric Administration*] (NOAA)
A/RATLR..... Antirattler [*Automotive engineering*]
ara-U......... Uracil Arabinoside [*Biochemistry*]
AR Austrl..... Industrial Arbitration Reports, New South Wales (Australia) [*A publication*] (ILCA)
ARAV......... Army Aviator (AABC)
AR Av Bad... Army Aviator Badge [*Military decoration*]
AR Av MO Bad... Army Aviation Medical Officer's Badge [*Military decoration*]
ARAVS......... Auxiliary and RADWASTE Area Ventilation System [*Nuclear energy*] (NRCH)
ARAWA....... Amateur Rowing Association of Western Australia
ARAY.......... Raymond Public Library, Alberta [*Library symbol National Library of Canada*] (NLC)
ARAZP........ Australasian Regional Association of Zoological Parks and Aquaria
ARB .... Accounting Research Board Opinion [*A publication*] (DLA)
ARB .... Accounting Research Bulletin [*A publication*]
ARB .... Acquisition Review Board [*Military*] (CAAL)
ARB .... Administrative Research Bulletin
ARB .... Adrenergic Receptor Binder [*Physiology*] (DMAA)
ARB .... Africa Research Bulletin [*A publication*]
ARB .... Agricultural Requirements Board [*Queensland, Australia*]
ARB .... Aircraft Reactors Branch
ARB .... Aircraft Recovery Bulletin (MCD)
ARB .... Air Refueling Boom (MCD)
ARB .... Air Registration Board [*British*]
ARB .... Air Research Bureau
ARB .... Air Reserve Base
ARB .... Air Resources Board [*California*]
ARB .... Airworthiness Requirements Board [*British*] (AIA)
ARB .... Alianza Revolucionaria Barrientista [*Bolivia*] [*Political party*] (PPW)
ARB .... All Routes Busy [*Telecommunications*] (TEL)
ARB .... Alternate Reproductive Behavior [*Zoology*]
ARB .... American Realty Trust SBI [*NYSE symbol*] (SPSG)
ARB .... American Research Bureau
ARB .... Amer Realty Tr SBI [*NYSE symbol*] (TTSB)
ARB .... Amnesty Review Board [*Terminated, 1976*]
ARB .... Ann Arbor, MI [*Location identifier FAA*] (FAAL)
ARB .... Any Reliable Brand [*Pharmacology*]
ARB .... APCHE [*Automatic Program Checkout Equipment*] Relay Box
ARB .... Appeals Review Board [*Formerly, BAR*] [*Civil Service Commission*]
ARB .... Arbiter (ADA)
Arb .... Arbitrageur [*Stock exchange term*]
ARB .... Arbitrageur [*Stock exchange term*] (ODBW)
ARB .... Arbitrary (MSA)
Arb .... Arbitration (DLA)
ARB .... Arbitration (AAGC)
Arb .... Arbitrator (DLA)
ARB .... Arbitron Radio Summary Data [*Arbitron Ratings Co.*] [*Information service or system*]
ARB .... Armored Rifle Battalion
ARB .... Army Reactors Branch (SAA)
ARB .... Army Rearming Base
ARB .... Army Retiring Board
ARB .... Arubair [*Aruba*] [*ICAO designator*] (FAAC)
ARB .... Association of Radio Broadcasters (BARN)
ARB .... ASTIA [*Armed Services Technical Information Agency*] Report Bibliography (MCD)
ARB .... Audience Research Bureau (IIA)
ARB .... Automatic RADAR Beacon
ARB .... Auxiliary Repair Battle Damage [*British military*] (DMA)
ARB .... Battle Damage Repair Ship [*Navy symbol*]
ARB .... Concise Australian Reference Book [*A publication*] (ADA)
ARB .... Labor Arbitration Awards [*Commerce Clearing House*] [*A publication*] (DLA)
ARBA .... Alabama Road Builders Association (SRA)
ARBA .... Amateur Rose Breeders Association [*British*] (DBA)
ARBA .... American Rabbit Breeders Association (EA)
ARBA .... American Red Brangus Association (EA)
ARBA .... American Reference Books Annual [*A publication*] (BRI)
ARBA .... American Revolution Bicentennial Administration [*Formerly, ARBC*] [*Disbanded, 1977*]
ARBA .... American Road Builders' Association [*Later, ARTBA*]
ARBA .... American Romney Breeders' Association (EA)
ARBA .... Associated Retail Bakers of America [*Later, Retail Bakers of America*] (EA)
ARBA .... Associate of the Royal Society of British Artists
ArBaA .... Arkansas College, Batesville, AR [*Library symbol Library of Congress*] (LCLS)
ARBAC........ American Revolution Bicentennial Advisory Council [*American Revolution Bicentennial Administration*]
ARB & A..... Arbitration and Award [*Legal term*] (DLA)
ARBAT........ Application of RADAR to Ballistic Acceptance Testing [*of ammunition*] (MCD)
Arb Ausgl G... Gesetz u. d. Ausgleichs und Schiedsverfahren Arbeitsstreitigkeiten [*Law on Labor Arbitration*] [*German*] (ILCA)
ArBaWR....... White River Regional Library, Batesville, AR [*Library symbol*] [*Library of Congress*] (LCLS)

ARBB .... American Revolution Bicentennial Board [*American Revolution Bicentennial Administration*]
ARBBA .... American Railway Bridge and Building Association (EA)
ARBC .... American Reperatory Ballet Company [*Formerly, Princeton Ballet*]
ARBC .... American Revolution Bicentennial Commission [*Later, ARBA*]
ARBC .... Associate of the Royal British Colonial Society of Artists
ARBC .... Attitude Reference Bombing Computer (MCD)
ARBCS .... Attitude Reference Bombing Computer Set [*or System*] (MCD)
Arbeitg........ Arbeitgeber [*Employer*] [*German*]
Arbeitsgem... Arbeitsgemeinschaft [*Study Group*] [*German*]
ArBerC .... Carroll County Heritage Center, Berryville, AR [*Library symbol Library of Congress*] (LCLS)
Arb G .... Arbeitsgericht [*Labor Court*] [*German*] (DLA)
Arb GG .... Arbeitsgerichtsgesetz [*Law on labor courts*] [*German*] (ILCA)
ARBHC........ Association of Registered Bank Holding Companies [*Later, ABHC*] (EA)
ARBI .... Association for the Rehabilitation of the Brain Injured (AC)
ARBITER ...... Access Refusal and Barrier Interface Terminal [*Hardware-based security device from Computer Security Systems*]
Arbitr .... Arbitration (DLA)
ARBITRN...... Arbitration (ADA)
ARBITS .... Army Base Information Transfer System (MCD)
Arb J .... Arbitration Journal (AAGC)
ARBL .... Assets Repriced Before Liabilities [*Business term*] (MHDB)
Arb L Dig.... Arbitration Law: A Digest of Court Decisions [*A publication*] (DLA)
ArBIM .... Mississippi County Library System, Blytheville, AR [*Library symbol Library of Congress*] (LCLS)
ARBN .... Arabian
ARBNE........ Associated Rare Breeds of New England [*Defunct*] (EA)
ARBO .... Arthropod-Borne [*Also, ARBOR*] [*Virology*]
ARBOR........ Arboriculture
ARBOR........ Argonne Boiling Water Reactor (NRCH)
ARBOR........ Arthropod-Borne [*Also, ARBO*] [*Virology*]
ArborD .... Arbor Drugs [*Associated Press*] (SAG)
ArborHI .... Arbor Health Care Co. [*Associated Press*] (SAG)
ArborPT ...... Arbor Property Trust Co. [*Formerly, EQK Green Acres Trust*] [*Associated Press*] (SAG)
ArborSft ...... Arbor Software Corp. [*Associated Press*] (SAG)
ARBP .... Associated Reinforcing Bar Producers (EA)
ARBR .... Arbitrator (ROG)
ARBR .... Arbor Drugs [*NASDAQ symbol*] (TTSB)
ARBR .... Arbor Drugs, Inc. [*NASDAQ symbol*] (NQ)
ARBRL .... Army Armament Research Ballistic Research Laboratory [*Aberdeen Proving Ground, MD*] (MCD)
ARBRON ...... Arbitration (ROG)
ARBROR ...... Arbitrator (ROG)
ARBRY........ Arbitrary
ARBS .... Angle Rate Bombing Set (DWSG)
ARBS .... Angular Rate Bombing System (MCD)
ARBS .... Associate of the Royal Society of British Sculptors
ARBS .... Association of Recognition Business Schools [*British*] (DBA)
ARBS .... Automatic RADAR Beacon Sequencer
ARBSA .... Associate of the Royal Birmingham Society of Artists [*British*] (DI)
arbsq .... Arabesque (VRA)
ARBTRN...... Arbitration (WGA)
Arbuth......... Arbuthnot's Select Criminal Cases [*Madras*] [*A publication*] (DLA)
ARC .... Abnormal [*or Anomalous*] Retinal Correspondence [*Ophthalmology*]
ARC .... Aboriginal Research Club (EA)
ARC .... Aboriginal Rights Coalition [*Coalition pour les Droits des Autochtones*] [*Project North*] (AC)
ARC .... Academy of Roofing Contractors [*Defunct*] (EA)
ARC .... Accelerated Remittance Cycle [*Business term*] (EMRF)
ARC .... Accelerating Rate Calorimeter [*Instrumentation*]
ARC .... Acceleration Restraint Curve [*Automotive engineering*]
ARC .... Accessory Record Card (DNAB)
ARC .... Accounting Requirements Code [*Military*] (AABC)
ARC .... Accounting Research and Education Centre [*McMaster University*] [*Canada Research center*] (RCD)
ARC .... Accounting Research Centre [*University of Sydney*] [*Australia*]
ARC .... Acid Resistant Cement
ARC .... Acoustic Research Center (MCD)
ARC .... Acquisition Review Committee [*Navy*] (CAAL)
ARC .... Action pour la Renaissance de Corse [*Action for the Rebirth of Corsica*] [*French*]
ARC .... Action Resource Centre [*British*] (CB)
ARC .... Action Revolutionnaire Corse [*Corsican Revolutionary Action*] (PD)
ARC .... Active Reduction of Contrast (MCD)
ARC .... Activity Readiness Code (DNAB)
ARC .... Adaptive Residual Coding (MCD)
ARC .... Addiction Research Center [*Baltimore, MD*] [*Department of Health and Human Services*]
ARC .... Addict Rehabilitation Counselor
ARC .... Ad Hoc Requirements Committee [*Later, COMOR*]
ARC .... Administrative Radio Conference [*International Telecommunications Union*]
ARC .... Adult Rehabilitation Centre [*Canada*]
ARC .... Advanced Reentry Concepts [*Aerospace*]
ARC .... Advanced Research Center [*Aerospace*]
ARC .... Advanced RISC [*Reduced Instruction Set Computer*] Computing (CDE)
ARC .... Advance Reading Copy [*Publishing*] (WDMC)
ARC .... Aerial Reconnaissance Camera [*Military*] (PDAA)
ARC .... Aerial Resupply and Communications [*Air Force*] (LAIN)
ARC .... Aeronautical Research Council [*British*]
ARC .... Aerophysics Research Corp.

ARC .... Aerospace Remote Calculator (MCD)
ARC .... Aerospace Research Chamber
ARC .... Afghanistan Relief Committee (EA)
ARC .... Agency Ranking Committee [*Environmental Protection Agency*] (GFGA)
ARC .... Aggregation of Red Blood Cells [*Hematology*]
ARC .... Agreements for Recreation and Conservation [*Canada*]
ARC .... Agricultural Relations Council (EA)
ARC .... Agricultural Research Center [*of ARS, Department of Agriculture*]
ARC .... Agricultural Research Council [*Research center British*] (IRC)
ARC .... Agronomy Research Center [*Southern Illinois University at Carbondale*] [*Research center*] (RCD)
ARC .... AIDS [*Acquired Immune Deficiency Syndrome*]-Related Complex [*Medicine*]
ARC .... Aiken Relay Calculator
ARC .... Airborne Radio Communicating
ARC .... Airborne Radio Control
ARC .... Airborne Research Capsule
ARC .... Aircrew Reception Centre [*British military*] (DMA)
ARC .... Air Reduction Center [*NASA*] (KSC)
ARC .... Air Release Capacity [*Aviation*]
ARC .... Air Reporting Control (NVT)
ARC .... Air Reserve Center
ARC .... Air Reserve Components [*Military*]
ARC .... Air Routing International Corp. [*ICAO designator*] (FAAC)
ARC .... Airworthiness Requirements Committee
ARC .... Ajstra Resources Corp. [*Vancouver Stock Exchange symbol*]
ARC .... Alcohol Rehabilitation Center (NVT)
ARC .... Alexander Railroad Co. [*AAR code*]
ARC .... All-Breeds Rescue Conservancy (EA)
ARC .... Alliance for Rail Commuter Progress [*Later, ARCP*] (EA)
ARC .... Alliance Research Center [*Nuclear energy*] (NRCH)
ARC .... Alliance Revolutionnaire Caraibe [*Guadeloupe*] [*Political party*] (EY)
ARC .... Alternate Route Cancel [*Telecommunications*] (TEL)
ARC .... Alternatively Refined Carrageenan [*Food grade*]
ARC .... Alternative Resource Center
ARC .... Altitude Rate Command
ARC .... Amateur Radio Club (LAIN)
ARC .... American Radio Co. of the Air [*Radio program*]
ARC .... American Radio Council [*Later, PRO-IF*] (EA)
ARC .... American Railway Cases [*Legal*]
ARC .... American Reading Council [*Defunct*] (EA)
ARC .... American Recreation Coalition (EA)
ARC .... American Red Cross (EA)
ARC .... American Refugee Committee (EA)
ARC .... American Rehabilitation Committee [*FEGS*] [*Absorbed by*] (EA)
ARC .... American Rose Council [*Defunct*] (EA)
ARC .... American Rottweiler Club (EA)
ARC .... Ames Research Center [*Moffett Field, CA*] [*NASA*]
ARC .... Ammunition Readiness Concept (MCD)
ARC .... Amphibious Research Craft
ARC .... Amplitude and Rise Time Compensation (IEEE)
ARC .... Amplitude Ratio Characteristic (PDAA)
ARC .... Analog Recursive Computer (IAA)
ARC .... Analog Response Conditioner (MCD)
ARC .... Analyzer-Recorder-Controller
ARC .... Anarchist Red Cross
ARC .... Ancestry Research Club (EA)
ARC .... Andrulis Research Corp.
ARC .... Animal Research Centre [*Canada*] (ARC)
ARC .... Animal Research Committee
ARC .... Animal Resources Center [*University of Texas at Austin*] [*Research center*] (RCD)
ARC .... Animal Rights Coalition (EA)
ARC .... Annual Report Council (EA)
ARC .... Annual Research Conference [*Bureau of the Census*] (GFGA)
ARC .... Annual Review Committee [*NATO*] (NATG)
ARC .... Anomalous Retinal Correspondence [*Ophthalmology*]
ARC .... Anthropological Research Center [*Memphis State University*] [*Research center*] (RCD)
ARC .... Anthropological Research Council [*British*]
ARC .... Anthropology Resource Center [*Defunct*] (EA)
ARC .... Antigen-Reactive Cell [*Immunology*]
ARC .... Appalachian Regional Commission [*Washington, DC*]
ARC .... Applications Research Corp.
ARC .... Applied Research Corp.
ARC .... Applied Research of Cambridge [*British*] (NITA)
ARC .... Aquaculture Research Center [*Texas A & M University*] [*Research center*] (RCD)
ARC .... Arab Research Centre [*British*] (CB)
arc .... Aramaic [*MARC language code Library of Congress*] (LCCP)
ARC .... Arcade (MCD)
ARC .... Arcade [*Commonly used*] (OPSA)
ARC .... Arcade
ARC .... Arcata [*California*] [*Seismograph station code, US Geological Survey*] (SEIS)
ARC .... Arcato [*With the Bow*] [*Music*]
ARC .... ARC Capital [*Associated Press*] (SAG)
ARC .... Architects' Registration Council [*British*]
ARC .... Archival Research Catalog
ARC .... Archival Research Catalog [*A publication*]
ARC .... Archive and Records Centre [*Geneva, Switzerland*] [*United Nations*] (ECON)
arc .... Archiving Utility [*Computer science*]
ARC .... ARC International Corp. [*Associated Press*] (SAG)

ARC	Arctic (WDAA)
ARC	Arctic Ocean
ARC	Arctic Village [*Alaska*] [*Airport symbol*] (OAG)
ARC	Arcuate Nucleus [*Neuroanatomy*]
ARC	Area of Responsibility Centre [*Aviation*]
ARC	Area Resource Center [*Library network*]
ARC	Argonne Reactor Computation (IEEE)
ARC	Armored Reconnaissance Carrier (MCD)
ARC	Army Radio Code
ARC	Army Research Consortium (RDA)
ARC	Army Reserve Components (MCD)
ARC	Art and Requirements of Command (MCD)
ARC	Arthritis and Rheumatism Council for Research [*British*] (IRUK)
ARC	Arthritis Rehabilitation Center
ARC	Art Resources in Collaboration (EA)
ARC	Asbestosis Research Council [*British*]
ARC	Asian Racing Conference
ARC	Asia Resource Center (EA)
ARC	Assistant Regional Commissioner [*IRS*]
ARC	Associated Retail Confectioners of North America [*Later, RCI*] (EA)
ARC	Association des Restauratrices-Cuisinieres (EA)
ARC	Association for Research in Cosmecology (EA)
ARC	Association for Residential Care [*British*] (EAIO)
ARC	Association for Retarded Children (DAVI)
ARC	Association for Retarded Citizens (EA)
ARC	Association of Railway Communicators (EA)
ARC	Association of Rehabilitation Centers [*Later, NARF*] (EA)
ARC	Association of Residential Communities [*British*] (DBA)
ARC	Association of Rover Clubs (EAIO)
ARC	Associaton for Responsible Communication (AC)
ARC	Asthma Research Council [*British*]
ARCA	Astrophysical Research Consortium
ARC	Astro Research Corp. (KSC)
ARC	Asymmetric Resonant Cavity [*Physics*]
ARC	Atlantic Research Center (KSC)
ARC	Atlantic Research Corp. (MCD)
ARC	Atlantic Richfield Co. [*NYSE symbol*] (SPSG)
ARC	Atlantis Research Centre (EA)
ARC	Atomedic Research Center (EA)
ARC	Attached Resource Computer (MHDB)
ARC	Attended Resource Computer [*Datapoint Corp.*] (NITA)
ARC	Audio Response Control (BUR)
ARC	Augmentation Research Center [*Stanford Research Institute*]
ARC	Australian Capital Territory Recycling Campaign
ARC	Australian Registrars Committee
ARCC	Australian Research Council
ARC	Australian Review Council
ARC	Australian Rowing Council
ARC	Austra Resources Corp. [*Vancouver Stock Exchange symbol*]
ARC	Automated Radiotheodolite [*Marine science*] (OSRA)
ARC	Automated Radiotheodolite (USDC)
ARC	Automated Rent Collections
ARC	Automatic Radio Control
ARC	Automatic Radio Control (ECII)
ARC	Automatic Ram Control (CAAL)
ARC	Automatic Range Compensating [*Firearms*]
ARC	Automatic Range Control
ARC	Automatic Rate Changer
ARC	Automatic Rate Control
ARC	Automatic Recirculation Valve [*Engineering*]
ARC	Automatic Relay Calculator [*Early computer*] [*Birkbeck College*] [*British*] (MCD)
ARC	Automatic Relay Computer (IAA)
ARC	Automatic Remote Control (DEN)
ARC	Automatic Reset Counter
ARC	Automatic Responsivity Control (MCD)
ARC	Automatic Ride Control Suspension [*Automotive engineering*]
ARC	Autopilot Rate Control
ARC	Auxiliary Roll Control
ARC	Average Response Computer
ARC	Cable Repairing Ship [*Navy symbol*]
ARC	L'Association pour la Recherche contre le Cancer [*Association for Research Against Can cer*] [*France*]
ARC	Rainbow Group [*Party group in the European Parliament*] (ECED)
ARC	Society for the Arts, Religion, and Contemporary Culture (EA)
ARCA	Acquired Red Cell Aplasia [*Hematology*]
ARCA	Acquired Red Cell Aplasia [*Medicine*] (DMAA)
ARCA	Adult Residential Colleges Association [*British*] (DBA)
ARCA	Air Conditioning and Refrigeration Contractors Association of New Jersey (SRA)
ARCA	Alberta Roofing Contractors Association Ltd. (AC)
ARCA	American Arts and Crafts Alliance (EA)
ARCA	American Rehabilitation Counseling Association (EA)
ARCA	American Retail Coal Association (EA)
ARCA	Antique Radio Club of America (EA)
ARCA	Appliance Recycling Centers of America (PS)
ARCA	Arizona Roofing Contractors Association (SRA)
ARCA	Asbestos Removal Contractors Association (EAIO)
ARCA	Associate of the Royal Cambrian Academy [*British*]
ARCA	Associate of the Royal Canadian Academy
ARCA	Associate of the Royal Canadian Academy of Arts (NGC)
ARCA	Associate of the Royal College of Art [*British*] (EY)
ARCA	Association of Romanian Catholics of America (EA)
ARCA	Automobile Racing Club of America
ARCAC	Annapolis Region Community Arts Council (AC)
ARCAD	Association for Recreation and Cultural Activities with People in Detention [*Canada*]
ARCADE	Arcade [*Commonly used*] (OPSA)
ARCADE	Argonne Computer-Aided Diffraction Equipment
ARCADE	Automatic RADAR Control and Data Equipment
Arcadn	Arcadian Partners Ltd. [*Associated Press*] (SAG)
ARCADS	Armament Control and Delivery System (MCD)
ARCAIC	Archives and Record Cataloging and Indexing by Computer (MHDB)
ARCAIDS	Army Cost Analysis Information and Data System (MCD)
ARCAM	Army Reserve Components Achievement Medal [*Military decoration*] (AABC)
ARCamA	Associate of the Royal Cambrian Academy [*British*]
ARCAN	Aeronautical Radio of Canada
ARCAN	Atlantic Richfield Canada Ltd.
ARCAR	American Romanian Committee for Assistance to Refugees (EA)
ARCAS	All-Purpose Rocket for Collecting Atmospheric Soundings [*Navy*]
ARCAS	Atlantic Research Corporation Atmospheric Sounding [*Missile*] (MUGU)
ARCAS	Automatic RADAR Chain Acquisition System [*Air Force*]
ARCASP	Army Reserve Civilian Acquired Skills Program (MCD)
ARCAT	Army Radio Code Aptitude Test (IAA)
ARCAVEX	Army Cavalry Scout Experiment (MCD)
ARCB	Association of Reserve City Bankers (EA)
ARCC	Alfa Romeo Club of Canada (AC)
ARCC	American Restaurant China Council (EA)
ARCC	American Rivers Conservation Council [*Later, AR*] (EA)
ARCC	ARC Capital [*NASDAQ symbol*] (SAG)
ARCC	ARTADS Requirements Coordinating Committee
ARCC	ARTINS [*Army Terrain Information System*] Requirements Coordination Committee (RDA)
ARCC	Association for the Rights of Catholics in the Church (EA)
ARCCA	ARC Capital CI'A' [*NASDAQ symbol*] (TTSB)
ArCCA	University of Central Arkansas, Conway, AR [*Library symbol Library of Congress*] (LCLS)
ARCCap	ARC Capital [*Associated Press*] (SAG)
ARCCCWA	Association of Registered Child Care Centers of Western Australia
ARCCEC	Al-Rajhi Co. for Currency Exchange and Commerce [*Saudi Arabia*]
ARCCF	American Red Cross Children's Fund
ARCCLMA	Aromatic Red Cedar Closet Lining Manufacturers Association (EA)
ARCcMD	Abnormal Record Compatible with Myocardial Disease [*Lower-case c in acronym means "with"*] [*Cardiology*]
ARCcMDE	Abnormal Record Compatible with Myocardial Drug Effect [*Lowercase c in acronym means "with"*] [*Cardiology*]
ARCCNET	Army Command and Control Communications Network (MCD)
ARCCO	Associate of the Royal Canadian College of Organists
ARCCOS	Inverse Cosine [*Mathematics*]
ARCCOT	Inverse Cotangent [*Mathematics*]
ARCCSE	Inverse Cosecant [*Mathematics*]
ARCCW	ARC Cap Wrrt'A' [*NASDAQ symbol*] (TTSB)
ARCCZ	ARC Cap Wrrt'B' [*NASDAQ symbol*] (TTSB)
ARCD	Associate of the Royal College of Dancing [*British*]
ARCDI	Assistant Regional Commissioner Disability Insurance [*Social Security Administration*] (OICC)
ARCE	Academical Rank of Civil Engineers
ARCE	Amphibious River Crossing Equipment [*Military*]
ARCEA	American Railway Car Export Association (EA)
ARCEDEM	African Regional Centre for Engineering Design and Manufacturing (EA)
ARCENT	Army [*Forces US*] Central [*Command*] (DOMA)
ARCFCP	Alliance for Responsible CFC [*Chlorofluorocarbon*] Policy (EA)
ARCFOD	Asian Religio-Cultural Forum on Development
ARCGSC	Army Command and General Staff College
ARCH	Advocacy Resource Centre for the Handicapped [*Canada*]
ARCH	Archaic
ARCH	Archaism
Arch	Archbishop (ADA)
ARCH	Archdeacon (ROG)
ARCH	Archduke (WDAA)
Arch	Archeology (BJA)
ARCH	Archery
ARCH	Arches National Monument
Arch	Archidiaconus [*Authority cited in pre-1607 legal work*] (DSA)
ARCH	Archipelago [*Maps and charts*]
ARCH	Architect [*or Architecture*]
ARCH	Architects Renewal Committee in Harlem [*Defunct*]
arch	Architecture (VRA)
ARCH	Architecture
ARCH	Archive (MSA)
ARCH	Arch Petroleum, Inc. [*NASDAQ symbol*] (NQ)
ARCH	Articulated Computing Hierarchy [*British*]
ARCH	Association of Residential Care Homes of New Jersey (SRA)
ARCH	Automated Reports Control Handling (MCD)
ARCH	Automatic Remote Cassette Handler (NTCM)
ARCH	Autoregressive Conditional Heteroscedastic [*Electronics*] (PCM)
Arch	Court of Arches [*England*] (DLA)
ArCH	Hendrix College, Conway, AR [*Library symbol Library of Congress*] (LCLS)
Arch	Pro Archia [*of Cicero*] [*Classical studies*] (OCD)
ARCHAE	Archaeology [*or Archaeologist*]
Arch Ael	Archaeologia Aeliana [*A publication*] (OCD)
ARCHAEOL	Archaeology
Arch Anz	Archaeologischer Anzeiger in Jahrbuch des [*Kaiserlichen*] Deutschen Archaeologischen Instituts [*A publication*] (OCD)
Arch Arb	Archbold's Law of Arbitration and Award [*A publication*] (DLA)

Arch Baines' Act... Archbold on Baines' Acts on Criminal Justice [*A publication*] (DLA)
Arch Bank.... Archbold on Bankruptcy [*1825-56*] [*A publication*] (DLA)
Archb Civil Pl... Archbold's Civil Pleading [*A publication*] (DLA)
Archb Civ Pl... Archbold's Civil Pleading and Evidence [*A publication*] (ILCA)
Archb Crim Pl... Archbold's Criminal Pleading [*A publication*] (DLA)
Arch Cr Prac & Pl... Archbold's Pleading and Evidence in Criminal Cases [*A publication*] (DLA)
Arch BL........ Archbold's Bankrupt Law [*A publication*] (DLA)
Arch Black... Archbold's Edition of Blackstone's Commentaries [*A publication*] (DLA)
Archb Landl & Ten... Archbold's Landlord and Tenant [*A publication*] (DLA)
Archb New Pr... Archbold's New Practice [*A publication*] (DLA)
Archb NP..... Archbold's Law of Nisi Prius [*A publication*] (DLA)
Archb N Prac... Archbold's New Practice [*A publication*] (DLA)
ARCHBP...... Archbishop
Archb Pr..... Archbold's Practice [*A publication*] (DLA)
Archb Pr KB... Archbold's Practice in the King's Bench [*A publication*] (DLA)
Arch Civ Pl... Archbold's Civil Pleading and Evidence [*A publication*] (DLA)
Arch CL Pr... Archbold's New Common Law Practice [*A publication*] (DLA)
ArchCm...... Arch Communications Group, Inc. [*Associated Press*] (SAG)
Arch CP ...... Archbold's Practice in the Common Pleas [*A publication*] (DLA)
Arch Cr....... Archbold's Pleading and Evidence in Criminal Cases [*A publication*] (DLA)
Arch Cr L..... Archbold's Criminal Law [*A publication*] (DLA)
Arch Cr Law... Archbold's Pleading and Evidence in Criminal Cases [*A publication*] (DLA)
Arch Cr Pl... Archbold's Criminal Pleading [*A publication*] (DLA)
Arch Cr Prac... Archbold's Criminal Practice [*A publication*] (DLA)
Arch Cr Proc... Archbold's Criminal Procedure [*A publication*] (DLA)
Arch CS Pr... Archibald. Country Solicitor's Practice in the Queen's Bench [*1881*] [*A publication*] (DLA)
ARCHD...... Archdeacon [*or Archdeaconry*]
ARCHD........ Archduke
ArchDan...... Archer Daniels Midland [*Associated Press*] (SAG)
ARCHDIOC... Archdiocese (ADA)
ArchDn...... Archer-Daniels-Midland Co. [*Associated Press*] (SAG)
Arch E........ Architectural Engineer
ARCHEDDA... Architectures for Heterogeneous European Distributed Databases
archeo........ Archaeology (VRA)
ARCHEOL..... Archeological
Archer.......... Archer's Reports [*2 Florida*] [*A publication*] (DLA)
Archer & H... Archer and Hogue. Reports [*2 Florida*] [*A publication*] (DLA)
Arch Forms... Archbold. Indictments, with Forms [*1916*] [*A publication*] (DLA)
Arch Forms Ind... Archbold's Forms of Indictment [*A publication*] (DLA)
Archi.......... Archidiaconus [*Authority cited in pre-1607 legal work*] (DSA)
Archid........ Archidiaconus [*Authority cited in pre-1607 legal work*] (DSA)
Archidi....... Archidiaconus [*Authority cited in pre-1607 legal work*] (DSA)
ARCHIDIAC... Archidiaconal [*Ecclesiastical*] (ROG)
Archil.......... Archilochus [*Seventh century BC*] [*Classical studies*] (OCD)
ARCHIT....... Architecture
Architects' LR... Architects' Law Reports [*British A publication*] (DLA)
Archiv......... Archivaria [*A publication*] (BRI)
Arch JC Pr... Archibald on Practice of Judges' Chambers [*A publication*] (DLA)
Arch Journ... Archaeological Journal [*A publication*] (OCD)
Arch JP....... Archbold. Justice of the Peace [*7th ed.*] [*1859*] [*A publication*] (DLA)
Arch KB Forms... Archbold's Forms in King's Bench and Common Pleas [*A publication*] (DLA)
Arch KB Pr... Archbold's King's Bench Practice [*A publication*] (DLA)
ARCHL......... Architectural
Arch L & T... Archbold. Law of Landlord and Tenant [*3rd ed.*] [*1864*] [*A publication*] (DLA)
ARCHLR...... Architects' Law Reports [*British*]
Arch Lun..... Archbold. Lunacy Laws [*5th ed.*] [*1915*] [*A publication*] (DLA)
Arch Ms....... Archives and Manuscripts [*A publication*]
Arch Mun Corp... Archbold. Municipal Corporations Act [*1836*] [*A publication*] (DLA)
Arch NP...... Archbold's Law of Nisi Prius [*A publication*] (DLA)
Arch Off R ... Archiv des Oeffentlichen Rechts [*A publication*] (ILCA)
ARCHOLOGY... Archeology and Ecology [*Coined by Paolo Soleri, Italian-born architect*]
Arch Pap...... Archiv fuer Papyrusforschung [*A publication*] (OCD)
Arch Part..... Archbold's Law of Partnership [*A publication*] (DLA)
Arch PC ...... Archbold's Pleas of the Crown [*A publication*] (DLA)
Arch P Ch... Archbold's Practice by Chitty [*A publication*] (DLA)
Arch PCP .... Archbold. Practice of the Court of Common Pleas [*1829*] [*A publication*] (DLA)
ArchPet...... Arch Petroleum [*Associated Press*] (SAG)
Arch PKB..... Archbold's Practice in the King's Bench [*A publication*] (DLA)
Arch PL ..... Archbold's Poor Law [*1840-1930*] [*A publication*] (DLA)
Arch PLC .... Archbold's Poor Law Cases [*1842-58*] [*A publication*] (DLA)
Arch PL Cas... Archbold's Abridgment of Poor Law Cases [*1842-58*] [*A publication*] (DLA)
Arch PL Pr... Archbold's New Practice in Poor Law Removals and Appeals [*A publication*] (DLA)
Arch Pr Ch... Archbold's Practice, by Cholty [*A publication*] (DLA)
Arch Pr CP... Archbold's Practice in the Common Pleas [*A publication*] (DLA)
Arch Pr JC... Archbold's Practice in Judges Chambers [*A publication*] (DLA)
Arch Pr QS... Archbold's Practice in Quarter Sessions [*A publication*] (DLA)
Arch QB .... Archbold's Practice in the Queen's Bench [*A publication*] (DLA)
Arch Rep .... Archaeological Reports [*A publication*] (OCD)
Arch R Soz Phil... Archiv fuer Rechts und Sozialphilosophie [*A publication*] (ILCA)
ARCHRY .... Archery
ARCHS........ Army Reactor Systems Health and Safety Review Committee (AABC)
Archs Man... Archives and Manuscripts [*A publication*]

Arch Sum..... Archbold's Summary of Laws of England [*A publication*] (DLA)
ARCHT........ Architect
archt.......... Architect (VRA)
ARCHT........ Architect
archtr.......... Architrave (VRA)
archv .... Archive (VRA)
ARCHV........ Archive
Arch Ziv Pr... Archiv fuer die Zivilistische Praxis [*A publication*] (ILCA)
ARCI .... Addiction Research Center Inventory [*Psychology*]
ARCI .... Aid Refugee Chinese Intellectuals [*Defunct*] (EA)
ARCI .... Alkali and Radiochemical Inspectorate [*British*] (NUCP)
ARCI .... American Railway Car Institute (EA)
ARCI .... Appliance Recycling Centers of America [*NASDAQ symbol*] (SAG)
ARCI .... Associate of the Royal Colonial Institute [*British*]
ARCI .... Association of Racing Commissioners International (EA)
ARCI .... Association Regionale Caraibeenne des Infirmieres [*Martinique*] (EAIO)
ARCIC-II..... Anglican-Roman Catholic International Commission
ARCIP........ Army Commanders Initiatives Program (RDA)
ARCIXS........ Area Command Information Exchange System (MCD)
ARCK........ Advanced Research Craft Hydrokeel (MCD)
ArCIC .... College of the Ozarks, Clarksville, AR [*Library symbol Library of Congress*] (LCLS)
ARCLUB...... Archonist Club (EA)
ArcM .... Archival Micrographics, Midland Park, NJ [*Library symbol Library of Congress*] (LCLS)
ARCM .... Army Commendation Medal [*Military decoration*]
ARCM .... Associate of the Royal College of Music [*British*] (EY)
ARCMR........ Atlantic Research Centre for Mental Retardation [*Dalhousie University*] [*Canada Research center*] (RCD)
ARCNET....... Army Command and Control Network (MCD)
ARCnet....... Attached Resource Computer Network
ARCNET....... Attached Resources Computer Network [*Microcomputer LAN*] [*Datapoint Corp.*] (NITA)
ARCO .... Aerolineas Colonia SA [*Airline*] [*Uruguay*]
ARCO .... Agricultural Research Center Operations [*of ARS, Department of Agriculture*]
ARCO .... Airborne Remote Control Operator (DNAB)
ARCO .... Aircraft Resources Control Office
ARCO .... Arcato [*With the Bow*] [*Music*] (ROG)
ARCO .... ARC Capital [*NASDAQ symbol*] (SAG)
ARCO .... Army Requirements Control Office (AABC)
ARCO .... Associate of the Royal College of Organists [*British*] (EY)
ARCO .... Atlantic Richfield Co.
ARCO .... Automatic Reservation and Communication (IAA)
ARCO .... Auxiliary Resources Control Office
ARCOA........ American Red Cross Overseas Association (EA)
ARCOB........ Verdi Arcobaleno [*Italy*] [*Political party*] (ECED)
ARCOCh....... ARCO Chemical Co. [*Associated Press*] (SAG)
ARCO(CHM)... Associate of the Royal College of Organists (Choir-Training Diploma) [*British*]
ARCOM........ Arctic Communication Satellite (IAA)
ARCOM........ Army Commendation Medal [*Military decoration*]
ARCOM........ Army Reserve Command
ARCOM........ Associated Roofing Contractors of Maryland (SRA)
ARCOMET.... Area Commanders' Meeting [*NATO*] (NATG)
ARCOMS...... Armor Combat Operations Model Support [*TCATA*] (RDA)
ARCOMSAT.. Arabian Communication Satellite
ARCON........ Advanced Research Consultants (MCD)
ARCON........ Automatic Rudder Control (MUGU)
ARCONA...... Austin Rover Cars of North America, Inc.
ARCONET..... Army Command and Control Communications Network (MCD)
ARCOPS....... Arctic Operations [*Military*] (NVT)
ARCOS........ All-Russian Cooperative Society [*English equivalent of AMTORG*]
ARCOS........ Architects Job Costing [*ICS*] [*Software package*] (NCC)
ARCOST....... Army Cohesion and Stability Program
ARCOST...... Army Cohesion Study (MCD)
ARCOTR....... Army Reserve Components Overseas Training Ribbon [*Military decoration*] (GFGA)
ARCOV........ Army Combat Operations Vietnam (AABC)
ARCP .... Aerodrome Reference Code Panel [*ICAO*] (DA)
ARCP .... Agricultural Resources Conservation Program [*Department of Agriculture*]
ARCP .... Air Refueling Control Point (AFM)
ARCP .... Alliance of Rail Citizens for Progress (EA)
ARCP .... Army [*Forces*] Command Post
ARC-PA....... Accreditation Review Committee on Education for Physicians Assistants (EA)
ARCPACS..... American Registry of Certified Professionals in Agronomy, Crops, and Soils (EA)
ARCPrA....... Atlantic Rich $3 Cv Pref [*NYSE symbol*] (TTSB)
ARCPrC....... Atlantic Rich$2.80 Cv Pref [*NYSE symbol*] (TTSB)
ARCPsych..... Associate of the Royal College of Psychiatrists [*British*] (DI)
ARCQ .... Association de la Recherche en Communication du Quebec (AC)
ARCQ .... Association des Radiodiffuseurs Communautaires du Quebec (AC)
ARCRFT....... Aircraft
ARCRL........ Agricultural Research Council Radiological Laboratory [*British*]
ARCRT........ American Registry of Clinical Radiography Technologists (EA)
ARCS .... Accrediting and Recording Centralized System (MCD)
ARCS .... Achievement Rewards for College Scientists [*Foundation*]
ARCS .... Acoustic Optical RADAR Classification System (CAAL)
ARCS Sum... Acquisition RADAR and Control System
ARCS .... Adaptive Reliability Control System [*Electronics*] (IAA)
ARCS .... Advanced Reconfigurable Computer System
ARCS .... Aerial Rocket Control System [*or Subsystem*] (MCD)

ARCS .... Aft Reaction Control System [*or Subsystem*] [*NASA*] (NASA)
ARCS .... Airborne Advanced Reconfigurable Computer System (PDAA)
ARCS .... Aircraft Requirements Computer System
ARCS .... Airline Request Communication System (DA)
ARCS .... Air Resupply and Communication Service
ARCS .... Alternative Remedial Contracting Strategy (AAGC)
ARCS .... Alternative Remedial Contracting Systems [*Environmental Protection Agency*]
ARCS .... Altitude Rate Command System (MCD)
ARCS .... AMSAA [*Army Materiel Systems Analysis Agency*]/RARDE Combat Simulation [*Royal Armament Research and Development Establishment*] (MCD)
ARCS .... ArcSys, Inc. [*NASDAQ symbol*] (SAG)
ARCS .... Army Ration Credit System (AABC)
ARCS .... Assessment and Remediation of Contaminated Sediments [*Environmental science*]
ARCS .... Associate of the Royal College of Science [*British*] (EY)
ARCS .... Associate of the Royal College of Surgeons [*British*] (ROG)
ARCS .... Association of Regulatory and Clinical Scientists
ARCS .... Association of Retail Candy Shops
ARCS .... Automated Records Control System
ARCS .... Automated Reproduction and Collating System (MCD)
ARCS .... Automated Revenue Collection System [*Business term*] (MHDW)
ARCS .... Automated Ring Code Search (DIT)
ARCS .... Automatic Recogniton of Continuous Speech (PDAA)
ARCS .... Automatic Route Control System [*Truck-delivery computer system*]
ARCS .... Autonomous Remotely Controlled Submersible [*Autonomous underwater vehicle*]
ARCSA .... Aviation Requirements for the Combat Structure of the Army (AABC)
ARCSc .... Associate of the Royal College of Science [*British*]
ARCSEC ...... Arcseconds
ARCSEC ...... Inverse Secant [*Mathematics*]
ARCSF .... Active Requisition Control and Status File [*DoD*]
ARCSIN .... Inverse Sine [*Mathematics*]
ARCSIP .... Automated Requirement Computation System Initial Provisioning [*Army*]
ARCSL .... Army Armament Research and Development Command Chemical Systems Laboratory
ARCSS .... Arctic System Science [*Program*] [*Marine science*] (OSRA)
ARCSS .... Arctic System Science [*Program*] (USDC)
ARCSS .... Center for Social Science Research and Documentation for the Arab Region [*UNESCO*] [*Information service or system*] (IID)
ARC-ST .... Accreditation Review Council for Educational Programs in Surgical Technology (HCT)
ARCST .... Associate of the Royal College of Science and Technology, Glasgow [*Later, ARTC*] [*Scotland*]
ARCSTAR .... Area Recruiting Concept Special Test Army Reserve
ArcSys .... ArcSys, Inc. [*Associated Press*] (SAG)
ARCT .... African Regional Centre for Technology [*See also CRAT*] (EA)
ARCT .... Air Refueling Control Time (AFM)
Arct .... Arctic
ARCT .... Army Radio Code Aptitude Test
ARCT .... Associate of the Royal Conservatory of Music of Toronto
ArCT .... State College of Arkansas, Conway, AR [*Library symbol Library of Congress*] (LCLS)
ARCTAN ...... Inverse Tangent [*Mathematics*]
Arctco .... Arctco, Inc. [*Associated Press*] (SAG)
ARCUK .... Architects' Registration Council of the UK (DI)
ARCUS .... Agricultural Research Council Unit of Statistics [*British*] (ARC)
ARCUS .... Arctic Research Consortium of the United States
ARCUS .... Associated Retail Confectioners of the United States [*Later, RCI*]
ARCVS .... Associate of the Royal College of Veterinary Surgeons [*British*]
ARC/W .... Arc Weld (KSC)
ARCWRO ..... Agricultural Research Council Weed Research Organization [*British*]
ARCWU .... Australian Rope and Cordage Workers' Union
ARD .... Absolute Reaction of Degeneration
ARD .... Accelerated Rural Development
ARD .... Acid Rock Draining [*Mining technology*]
ARD .... Active Range of the Day (MCD)
ARD .... Acute Respiratory Disease [*Medicine*]
ARD .... Adenovirus Respiratory Disease [*Medicine*] (PDAA)
ARD .... Adult Respiratory Distress [*Medicine*]
ARD .... Advanced Reactors Division [*of the Nuclear Regulatory Commission*] (NRCH)
ARD .... Advanced Research Division
ARD .... Aeronautical Research Division [*NASA*]
ARD .... Air and Radiation Division [*Environmental Protection Agency*] (GFGA)
ARD .... Air-Raid Defence [*British World War II*]
ARD .... Air Reserve District
ARD .... Alcohol Recovery [*or Rehabilitation*] Drydock (DNAB)
ARD .... Alor [*Indonesia*] [*Airport symbol*] (OAG)
ARD .... Ammunition Reliability Division [*Military*]
ARD .... Andradina [*Brazil*] [*Airport symbol*] (AD)
ARD .... Anorectal Dressing (MAE)
ARD .... Answering, Recording, and Dialing
ARD .... Antibiotic Removal Device [*Pharmacology*] (DAVI)
ARD .... Antimicrobial Removal Device
ARD .... Application for Review Decisions [*A publication*] (DLA)
ARD .... Aquatic Resource Division [*Environmental Protection Agency*] (GFGA)
ARD .... Arbeits Gemeinschaft der Offentlichrechtlichen Rundfunk Anstalten der Bundesrepublik Deutschland [*Broadcasting organization*]
Ard .... Archidiaconus [*Authority cited in pre-1607 legal work*] (DSA)
ARD .... Ardent [*Music*] (DSUE)
ARD .... Ardito [*Ardently*] [*Music*] (ROG)

ARD .... Arida [*Japan*] [*Seismograph station code, US Geological Survey*] (SEIS)
ARD .... Armament Research Development [*British*] (MCD)
ARD .... Armaments Research Department [*Ministry of Supply*] [*British*]
ARD .... Armored Training Devices [*Army*] (RDA)
ARD .... Army Renegotiation Division [*of ASRB*]
ARD .... Army Research and Development [*Later, R, D & A*] [*A publication*] (SAA)
ARD .... Arthritis and Rheumatic Disease [*Medicine*] (DAVI)
ARD .... Arthritis and Rheumatic Diseases Abstracts [*A publication*]
ARD .... Association for Responsible Dissent (EA)
ARD .... Association of Research Directors (EA)
ARD .... Astromechanics Research Division (SAA)
ARD .... Ata-Aerocondor Transportes Aereos Ltda. [*Portugal ICAO designator*] (FAAC)
ARD .... Automatic Release Data (AAGC)
ARD .... Automatic Release Date [*Military*] (AABC)
ARD .... Auxiliary Repair Dry Dock [*Non-self-propelled*] [*Navy ship symbol*]
ARD .... Average Response Data
ARD .... Red Deer Public Library, Alberta [*Library symbol National Library of Canada*] (NLC)
ARD .... Research and Development Service [*FAA*] (TAG)
ARD .... Yardley, PA [*Location identifier FAA*] (FAAL)
ARDA .... Advanced Reactor Development Associates
ARDA .... Advanced Reseach and Development Agency
ARDA .... Agricultural and Rural Development Act [*Canada*]
ARDA .... Alberta Registered Dietitians Association (AC)
ARDA .... American Railway Development Association (EA)
ARDA .... American Rescue Dog Association (EA)
ARDA .... Analog Recording Dynamic Analyzer [*Computer science*]
ARDA .... Appalachian Regional Development Act of 1965
ARDA .... Astronautical Research and Development Agency (SAA)
ARDA .... Atomic Research and Development Authority [*Nuclear Regulatory Commission*] (GFGA)
ARDAA .... Army Research, Development, and Acquisition
ARDAC .... Army Research, Development, and Acquisition
ArDar .... Arkansas River Valley Regional Library, Dardanelle, AR [*Library symbol Library of Congress*] (LCLS)
ARDAR .... Regional Office, Alberta Agriculture, Red Deer, Alberta [*Library symbol National Library of Canada*] (NLC)
ARDB .... Analytical Results Database
ARDBC .... American Rubberband Duckpin Bowling Congress (EA)
ARDC .... Aberdeen Research and Development Center (MCD)
ARDC .... Air Research and Development Center [*Later, Air Force Systems Command*]
ARDC .... Air Research and Development Command [*Washington, DC Air Force*]
ARDC .... Air Research and Development Council [*NATO*] (NATG)
ARDC .... American Racing Driver's Club (EA)
ARDC .... Applied Research and Design Center [*Research center*] (RCD)
ARDC .... Arctic Research Directors Committee [*Canada*]
ARDC .... Armament Research and Development Center [*Army*] (RDA)
ARDC .... Army Research and Development Command
ARDC .... Association des Redacteurs de Devis du Canada [*Specification Writers Association of Canada*]
ARDC .... Auxiliary Repair Dry Dock, Concrete [*Later, AFDL*] [*Navy symbol Obsolete*]
ARDC .... Red Deer College, Alberta [*Library symbol National Library of Canada*] (NLC)
ARDCA .... Air Research and Development Command - Andrews Air Force Base
ARDCF .... Air Research and Development Command Forms
ARDCM .... Air Research and Development Command Manual [*Air Force*]
ARDCOM ...... Armament Research and Development Command (MCD)
ARDCR .... Air Research and Development Command Regulations
ARDCS .... Association of Rural District Council Surveyors [*British*] (BI)
ARDE .... Aircraft and Rocket Design Engineers
ARDE .... Alianza Revolucionaria Democratica [*Democratic Revolutionary Alliance*] [*Nicaragua*] [*Political party*] (PD)
ARDE .... Armament Research and Development Establishment [*British*] (MCD)
ARDE .... Aspect Ratio Dependent Etching [*Microlithography*]
ARDEC .... Armament Research, Development, and Engineering Center [*Picatinny Arsenal*] [*Dover, NJ*] [*Army*] (RDA)
Ar de For .... Arsendinus de Forlivio [*Authority cited in pre-1607 legal work*] (DSA)
ARDEMS ...... Airborne-Delivered Multipurpose Submunition (MCD)
ARDEMS ...... Artillery-Delivered Multipurpose Submunition (AABC)
Arden .... Arden Group, Inc. [*Associated Press*] (SAG)
ArdenPd ...... Arden Industrial Products [*Associated Press*] (SAG)
ArdenRlt ...... Arden Realty, Inc. [*Associated Press*] (SAG)
ARDF .... Airborne Radiation Detection and Fixing [*Military*]
ARDF .... Airborne Radio Direction Finding (AFM)
ARDF .... Air Reconnaissance Detection Force (CINC)
ARDF .... Amateur Radio Direction Finding
ARDF .... Applications Research and Defense Fund (DNAB)
ARDF .... Association Reunion Departement Francais [*Association for Reunion as a French Department*] [*Political party*] (PPW)
ARDG .... Army Research and Development Group (MCD)
ARDG(E) ...... Army Research and Development Group (Europe)
ARDG(FE) .... Army Research and Development Group (Far East)
ARDI .... Analysis, Requirements Determination, Design and Development, and Implementationand Evaluation (MHDB)
ARDI .... Association of Registered Driving Instructors [*British*] (BI)
ARDIC .... Association pour la Recherche et le Developpement en Informatique Chimique [*Association for Research and Development of Chemical Informatics*] [*Information service or system*] (IID)

Ardis	Advanced National Radio Data Service [*Joint venture of IBM and Motorola*] (CDE)
ARDIS	Advanced Radio Data Information Service [*IBM Corp., Motorola, Inc.*]
ARDIS	Army Research and Development Test and Evaluation Information Systems
ARDISC	Argonne Dispersion Code (MCD)
ARDISO	Army Research and Development Information Systems Office (RDA)
ARDL	Ardleigh [*England*]
ARDL	Small Auxiliary Floating Drydock, Non-Self-Propelled [*Navy symbol*] (DNAB)
ARDM	Aradigm Corp. [*NASDAQ symbol*] (SAG)
ARDM	Association of Refrigerant and Desuperheating Manufacturing (EA)
ARDM	Asynchronous Time-Division Multiplexing [*Computer science*] (IAA)
ARDM	Medium Auxiliary Repair Dry Dock [*Navy symbol*]
ARDMA	Asset Requirements Depot Maintenance Data (MCD)
ARDMA	Auto-Refresh Direct Memory Access [*Computer science*] (PDAA)
ARDMC	Michener Centre Library, Red Deer, Alberta [*Library symbol National Library of Canada*] (NLC)
ARDMD	Autosomal Recessive Distal Muscular Dystrophy [*Medicine*]
ARDME	Automatic RADAR Data Measuring Equipment
ARDME	Automatic RADAR Distance Measuring Equipment (MSA)
ARDME	Automatic Range Detection and Measuring Equipment
ARDMS	American Registry of Diagnostic Medical Sonographers (EA)
ARDN	Arden Group, Inc. [*NASDAQ symbol*] (NQ)
ARDNA	Arden Group Cl'A' [*NASDAQ symbol*] (TTSB)
Ardo	Ardito [*Ardently*] [*Music*]
ARDONA	Alfa-Romeo Distributors of North America
ARDP	Army Requirements Development Plan (AABC)
ARDP	Association pour la Reduction des Depenses Publiques [*Association for the Reduction of Public Spending*] (AC)
ARDRH	Red Deer Regional Hospital Center, Red Deer, Alberta [*Library symbol National Library of Canada*] (NLC)
ARDS	Aboriginal Resource and Development Services [*Australia*]
ARDS	Acute Respiratory Distress Syndrome [*Medicine*]
ARDS	Adult Respiratory Distress Syndrome [*Medicine*]
ARDS	Advanced Range Data System [*Air Force*]
ARDS	Advanced Remote Display Station (IAA)
ARDS	Advance Remote Display System [*Computer science*] (PDAA)
ARDS	Associate of the Royal Drawing Society [*British*]
ARDS	Atmospheric Resid Desulfurization [*Petroleum technology*]
ARDS	Automated Requirements Development System (MCD)
ARDS	Aviation Research and Development Service [*FAA*]
ARDSA	Agriculture and Rural Development Subsidiary Agreement [*Canada*]
ARDT	Automatic Remote Data Terminal (IAA)
ARDU	Aircraft Research and Development Unit [*Australia*]
ARDU	Analytical Research and Development Unit [*British*]
ARE	Acoustic Radiation Element
ARE	Activated Reactive Evaporation [*Coating technology*]
ARE	Active Resistive Exercise
ARE	Activin Responsive Element [*Biochemistry*]
ARE	Admiralty Research Establishment [*British*] (IRUK)
ARE	Adoption Resource Exchange [*British*] (DI)
ARE	Advanced Real-Time Executive (BUR)
ARE	Advanced Research Engine (MCD)
ARE	Aerothermal Re-Entry Experiment (MCD)
ARE	Aircraft Reactor Equipment
ARE	Aircraft Reactor Experiment (NUCP)
ARE	Aircraft Recovery Equipment
ARE	Aires, Aerovias de Integracion Regional SA [*Colombia*] [*ICAO designator*] (FAAC)
ARE	Airline Revenue (DA)
ARE	Air Mobile Refueling Equipment
ARE	Air Reactor Experiment
ARE	All Routes Explorer [*Source route bridging*] (ACRL)
ARE	Ancient Records of Egypt [*A publication*] (BJA)
ARE	Anion-Responsive Electrode
ARE	Antenna Range Equipment
ARE	Apollo Reliability Engineering [*NASA*] (KSC)
ARE	Arab Republic of Egypt
Ar E	Architectural Engineer
ARE	Arecibo [*Diocesan abbreviation*] [*Puerto Rico*] (TOCD)
ARE	Arequipa [*Peru*] [*Seismograph station code, US Geological Survey*] (SEIS)
ARE	Arid Lands Ecology
ARE	Armbro Enterprises, Inc. [*Toronto Stock Exchange symbol*]
ARE	Aspect Ratio Enhancement (MCD)
ARE	Assemblee des Regions d'Europe [*Later, AER*] (EAIO)
ARE	Assembly of European Regions [*Later, AER*] (EAIO)
ARE	Associate in Religious Education
ARE	Associate of the Royal Society of Painter-Etchers and Engravers [*British*]
ARE	Association for Recurrent Education [*British*]
ARE	Association for Religious Education
ARE	Association for Research and Enlightenment (EA)
ARE	Association of Railroad Editors [*Formerly, ARMEA*] (EA)
ARE	Asymptotic Relative Efficiency [*Statistics*]
ARE	Atmospheric Research Equipment
ARE	Attack Response Evaluation (MCD)
ARE	Attack Response Exercise (MCD)
ARE	Automated Responsive Environment (BUR)
ARE	Automatic Record Evaluation
ARE	Auxiliary Rocket Engine
ARE	Aviation Readiness Evaluation (NVT)
ARE	Axiomatic Requirements Engineering (MCD)

ARE	Characato [*Formerly, Arequipa*] [*Peru Later, FRD*] [*Geomagnetic observatory code*]
ARE	Redcliff Public Library, Alberta [*Library symbol National Library of Canada*] (NLC)
ARE	United Arab Emirates [*ANSI three-letter standard code*] (CNC)
AREA	Academic Research Enhancement Award [*NIH*]
AREA	Aerovias Ecuatoriana SA
AREA	Alberta Real Estate Association (AC)
AREA	American Railway Engineering Association (EA)
AREA	American Recreational Equipment Association (EA)
AREA	Arctic Research in Environmental Acoustics [*Navy*] (MSC)
AREA	Area Bancshares [*NASDAQ symbol*] (TTSB)
AREA	Area Bancshares Corp. [*NASDAQ symbol*] (SAG)
AREA	Army Reactor Experimental Area
AREA	Association for Rational Environmental Alternatives [*Defunct*] (EA)
AREA	Association of Records Executives and Administrators [*Later, ARMA*] (EA)
AreaBnc	Area Bancshares Corp. [*Associated Press*] (SAG)
AREAC	Alabama Rural Electric Association of Cooperatives (SRA)
AREACORD	Area Coordination to Command Designated in Appropriate Instructions (MCD)
AREAL	Atmospheric Research and Exposure Assessment Laboratory [*Environmental Protection Agency*]
AREAOPREP	Area Commanders Operations Report
AREBA	Accelerated Reeducation of Emotions, Behavior, and Attitudes [*Rehabilitation program*]
AREC	Agricultural Research and Educational Center [*American University of Beirut*]
AREC	Agricultural Research and Education Center, Belle Glade [*University of Florida*] [*Research center*] (RCD)
AREC	Agricultural Research and Education Center, Fort Lauderdale [*University of Florida*] [*Research center*] (RCD)
AREC	Air Element Coordinator [*Military*] (CAAL)
AREC	Amateur Radio Emergency Corps [*of ARPSC*]
ARECA	Alaska Rural Electric Cooperative Association (SRA)
ARecr	American Recreation Centers, Inc. [*Associated Press*] (SAG)
ARED	Acoustic Reflex Ear Defender
ARED	Aperture Relay Experiment Definition (MCD)
ARED	Redwater Public Library, Alberta [*Library symbol National Library of Canada*] (NLC)
AREDS	Acoustic Reflex Ear Defender System (RDA)
AREDS	Aged-Related Eye Disease Study [*National Eye Institute*]
AREDYLD	Acrorenal Field Defect, Ectodermal Dysplasia, Lipoatrophic Diabetes [*Medicine*] (DMAA)
AREE	Admiralty Regional Electrical Engineer [*British*] (IAA)
AREE	American Resources Corp, Inc. [*NASDAQ symbol*] (SAG)
AREE	Amer Resource [*NASDAQ symbol*] (TTSB)
AREE	Apollo Reliability Engineering Electronics [*NASA*] (KSC)
AREE	Association of Radio and Electrical Engineers [*A union*] [*British*]
AREELS	Angle-Resolved Electron Energy Loss Spectroscopy
AREF	Awaiting Removal of Excess Funds (AAGC)
AREFS	Air Refueling Squadron
AREFSQ	Air Refueling Squadron
AREFW	Air Refueling Wing
AREG	Accumulator Register [*Computer science*] (IAA)
AREG	Apparatus Repair - Strategy Evaluation Guidelines [*Telecommunications*] (TEL)
AREG	[*A*] Register (IAA)
AREIAC	Association of Inspectors, Advisers, and Consultants for Religious Education (AIE)
AREInv	American Real Estate Investment Corp. [*Associated Press*] (SAG)
AREIS	Army Education Information System (MCD)
AREL	Air Resources Environmental Research Laboratory [*National Oceanic and Atmospheric Administration*] (NOAA)
AREL	Alpharel, Inc. [*NASDAQ symbol*] (SAG)
A Rel	Associate in Religion
Arel C	Arel Communications & Software Ltd. [*Associated Press*] (SAG)
ArelCom	Arel Communications & Software Ltd. [*Associated Press*] (SAG)
ARELEM	Arithmetic Element Program
ARELS	Association of Recognised English Language Schools [*British*]
AREMA	Antoky ny Revolosiona Malagasy [*Vanguard of the Malagasy Revolution*] (PPW)
AREMA	Avantgarde de la Revolution Malgache [*Vanguard of the Malagasy Revolution*] [*Political party*] (PPW)
AREN	American Rehabilitation Educational Network [*Pittsburgh, PA*] [*Telecommunications service*] (TSSD)
ARENA	Adoption Resource Exchange of North America [*Later, NAIES*] (EA)
ARENA	Alianca Renovadora Nacional [*Alliance for National Renewal*] [*Brazil Political party*] (PPW)
ARENA	Alianza Republicana Nacionalista [*Nationalist Republican Alliance*] [*El Salvador*] [*Political party*] (PPW)
ARENA	Applied Research Ethics National Association (EA)
Arena	Arena Magazine [*A publication*] (BRI)
ARENBD	Armor and Engineer Board [*Army*] (PDAA)
ARENTO	Arab Republic of National Telephone Organization (ACRL)
ARENTS	ARPA [*Advanced Research Projects Agency*] Environmental Test Satellite
ARENUM	Analysis, Refinement, and Extension of Nuclear Methodology [*Military*]
AREO	Area Real Estate Office
AREP	Air Refueling Egress Point [*Aviation*] (FAAC)
A Rep	American Reports [*A publication*] (DLA)
AREP	Ammunition Reliability Evaluation Program (SAA)
A Rep	Atlantic Reporter [*A publication*] (DLA)

AREP .... Atmospheric Research and Environment Program [*Marine science*] (OSRA)
AREP .... Automatic Regulation and Electronic Protection
AREP .... Auxiliary Regulation Excitation Principle [*Industrial engines*]
AREP .... Office of Applied Research, Evaluation, and Planning [*West Virginia University*] [*Research center*] (RCD)
AREPA .... Acetazolamide-Responsive Familial Paroxysmal Ataxia [*Medicine*] (DMAA)
AREPG .... Army Electronic Proving Ground (IIA)
AREPS .... Advanced Reconnaissance Electrically-Propelled Spacecraft [*Military*] (PDAA)
AREPT .... Agent Report [*Army*] (AABC)
AREQ .... Association des Religieuses Enseignantes du Quebec (AC)
ARES .... Advanced Radiation Effects Simulation
ARES .... Advanced Railroad Electronics System [*A space guidance system made by Collins Air Transport*]
ARES .... Advanced Research EMP [*Electromagnetic Pulse*] Simulator
ARES .... Advanced Rocket Engine Storable (MCD)
ARES .... Aeroelastic Rotor Experimental System (MCD)
ARES .... AGILE [*Autonetics General Information Learning Equipment*] Responsive Effective Support [*Army/Air Force*]
ARES .... Airplane Responsive Engine Selection (MCD)
ARES .... Amateur Radio Emergency Service
ARES .... American Real Estate Society (EA)
ARES .... Antireticulo-Endothelial Serum [*Medicine*] (DMAA)
ARES .... Army Executives for Software Program [*Army Materiel Command*] (RDA)
ARES .... Army Readiness Evaluation System (MCD)
ARES .... Artillery Engagement Simulation System (MCD)
ARES .... Association of Real Estate Syndicators (EA)
ARES .... Automatic Record Evaluation System
ARES .... Automatic Requirements Engineering Systems (MCD)
AResA .... Army Reserve Association
AResidS .... American Residential Services, Inc. [*Associated Press*] (SAG)
ARESLD .... Alcohol-Related End-Stage Liver Disease [*Medicine*]
AREST .... Advanced RADAR Experimental Systems Technology [*Army*]
AREst .... American Real Estate Partners Ltd. [*Associated Press*] (SAG)
ARESTEM .... [*A*] Recording Stray Energy Monitor
ARestr .... American Restaurant Partners Ltd. [*Associated Press*] (SAG)
Arethusa ...... Arethusa Off-Shore Ltd. [*Associated Press*] (SAG)
ARETL .... Associate for Religious Education for Teachers and Lecturers [*British*]
ARETS .... Arizona Regional Ecological Test Site [*Department of the Interior*]
ARETS .... Armor Remoted Target System (RDA)
AREUEA .... American Real Estate and Urban Economics Association (EA)
AREX .... Air Refueling Exit [*Aviation*] (FAAC)
ARF .... Accretion-Induced Rotational Fragmentation [*Astrophysics*]
ARF .... Acoustic Range-Finder (MCD)
ARF .... Active Responsive Factor [*Biochemistry*]
ARF .... Acute Renal Failure [*Medicine*]
ARF .... Acute Respiratory Failure [*Medicine*]
ARF .... Acute Rheumatic Fever [*Medicine*]
ARF .... Addiction Research Foundation [*Fondation de la Recherche sur la Toxicomanie*] [*Formerly, Alcoholism & Drug Addiction Research Foundation*] (AC)
ARF .... Addiction Research Foundation of Ontario Library [*UTLAS symbol*]
ARF .... ADP [*Adenosine Diphosphate*]-Ribosylation Factor [*Biochemistry*]
ARF .... Adventitious Root Formation [*Botany*]
ARF .... Advertising Research Foundation (EA)
ARF .... Aerofer, SL [*Spain ICAO designator*] (FAAC)
ARF .... Aeronautical Research Foundation
ARF .... Aerospace Recovery Facility (MCD)
ARF .... Aesthetic Realism Foundation (EA)
ARF .... Afghan Refugee Fund (EA)
ARF .... African Research Foundation (EA)
ARF .... Agricultural Research Foundation [*Oregon State University*] [*Research center*] (RCD)
ARF .... Airborne Relay Facility (MCD)
ARF .... Airport Reservation Function [*FAA*] (TAG)
ARF .... Air Refueling Facility [*Military*] (DOMA)
ARF .... Air Reserve Forces
ARF .... Albertville, AL [*Location identifier FAA*] (FAAL)
ARF .... Alliance of Reform Forces [*Macedonia*] [*Political party*]
ARF .... Almost Ready to Fly [*Remote-control plane*]
ARF .... American Railroad Foundation [*Defunct*] (EA)
ARF .... American Rationalist Federation (EA)
ARF .... American Rehabilitation Foundation [*Later, SKI*] (EA)
ARF .... American Retail Federation [*Later, NRF*] (EA)
ARF .... American Rose Foundation (EA)
ARF .... Animal Research Facilities
ARF .... Apparel Research Foundation [*Defunct*]
ARF .... Application Replacement Factor
ARF .... Aquarian Research Foundation (EA)
ARF .... Area Resource File [*Public Health Service*] [*Information service or system*] (IID)
ARF .... Arfendazam [*Biochemistry*]
ARF .... Armenian Revolutionary Federation [*Political party*] (EY)
ARF .... Armour Research Foundation [*Later, IITRI*]
ARF .... Arthritis and Rheumatism Foundation [*Later, Arthritis Foundation*]
ARF .... ASEAN [*Association of Southeast Asian Nations*] Regional Forum (ECON)
ARF .... Auburn Research Foundation (KSC)
ARF .... Automatic Reporting Feature (MCD)
ARF .... Automatic Return Fire [*ARPA*]
ARF .... Auto-Regressive Random Field (PDAA)

ARF .... Auxin Response Factor [*Biochemistry*]
ARF .... Aviation Route Forecast (MCD)
ARF .... Awareness Research Foundation (EA)
ARF .... Axial Rotating Filtration
ARFA .... Alberta Restaurant & Foodservices Association (AC)
ARFA .... Allied Radio Frequency Agency [*Formerly, ERFA*] [*Brussels, Belgium*] [*NATO*]
ARFA .... Antirecession Fiscal Assistance
ARFA .... Armenian Revolutionary Federation of America [*Later, ARF*] (EA)
ARFC .... AIDS Resource Foundation for Children (EA)
ARFC .... Air Reserve Flying Center [*Air Force*]
ARFC .... Aldo Ray Fan Club (EA)
ARFC .... Autologous Rosette-Forming Cell [s] [*Immunology*]
ARFC .... Average Rectified Forward Current [*Electronics*] (IAA)
ARFCOS ...... Armed Forces Courier Service
ARFCOSTA .. Armed Forces Courier Station (AFM)
ARF/CRF ..... Acute Renal Failure and Chronic Renal Failure [*Nephrology*] (DAVI)
ARFCW .... Athletic and Recreation Federation of College Women (EA)
ARFDS .... Automatic Reentry Flight Dynamics Simulator [*NASA*] (NASA)
ARFF .... Aircraft Rescue and Fire Fighting [*Air Traffic Control*] (FAAC)
ARFF .... Aircraft Rescue and Fire Fighting
ARFF .... Air Reserve Forces Facility [*Military*]
ARFF .... Angry Revengeful Frequent Fliers [*Aeronautics*]
ARFFOK ...... Airport Rescue and Fire Fighting Alarm Checked (FAAC)
ARFFV .... Aircraft Rescue and Fire Fighting Vehicle
ARFI .... Association for Research into the Folklore of Imagination [*French*] (ECON)
ARFL .... Addiction Research Foundation Library [*Canada*] (DI)
ARFL .... Artificial
ARFLS .... Australian Rules Football League of Sydney
ARFMS .... Air Reserve Forces Meritorious Service Medal [*Military decoration*] (GFGA)
ARFMSA ..... Air Reserve Forces Meritorious Service Award [*Military decoration*]
ARFMSR ..... Air Reserve Forces Meritorious Service Ribbon [*Military decoration*] (AFM)
ArFO .... Ozarks Regional Library, Fayetteville, AR [*Library symbol Library of Congress*] (LCLS)
AR/FOR ...... Active Records/Fiche-Oriented Retrieval (DNAB)
ARFOR .... Area Forecast [*Aviation*]
ARFOR .... Army Forces [*Element of a joint task force*]
ARFOR .... Army Forces [*Element of a joint task force*]
ARFORA ...... Asociatiunea Reuniunilor Femeilor Ortodoxe Romane-Americane [*Association of Romanian-American Orthodox Ladies Auxiliaries*]
ARFORM ...... Atomic Resonance Filter Optical Receiver Module (MCD)
ARFORSTAT... Army Force Status Reporting System (AABC)
ARFPC .... Air Reserve Forces Policy Committee
ARFPC .... Army Reserve Forces Policy Council (MCD)
ARFPDS ...... Air Reserve Forces Personnel Data System (AFM)
ARFS .... Area Resource File System [*Department of Health and Human Services*] (GFGA)
ArFs .... Fort Smith Carnegie City Library, Fort Smith, AR [*Library symbol Library of Congress*] (LCLS)
ArFsD .... Donrey Media Group, Fort Smith, AR [*Library symbol Library of Congress*] (LCLS)
ArFsW .... Westark Community College, Fort Smith, AR [*Library symbol*] [*Library of Congress*] (LCLS)
ARG .... Accident Response Group [*Department of Energy*]
ARG .... Aerolineas Argentinas [*Argentina ICAO designator*] (FAAC)
ARG .... African Rhino Group (EA)
ARG .... Airgas, Inc. [*NYSE symbol*] (SPSG)
ARG .... Air Refueling Group [*Air Force*] (DOMA)
ARG .... Alcohol Research Group [*Research center*] (RCD)
ARG .... American Resources Group (EA)
ARG .... Americans for Responsible Government [*Defunct*] (EA)
ARG .... Amphibious Ready Group
ARG .... Archangelos [*Greece*] [*Seismograph station code, US Geological Survey*] (SEIS)
ARG .... Argent [*Heraldry*]
ARG .... Argentina [*ANSI three-letter standard code*] (CNC)
Arg .... Argentina (VRA)
ARG .... Argentum [*Silver*]
Arg .... Arginine [*Also, R*] [*An amino acid*]
arg .... Arginine [*Also, R*] [*An amino acid*] (DOG)
ARG .... Argo [*Constellation*]
ARG .... Argo Development Corp. [*Vancouver Stock Exchange symbol*]
ARG .... Argosy [*A publication*] (ROG)
ARG .... Argument (OCD)
ARG .... Argumento [*By an argument drawn from such a law*] [*Latin*]
ARG .... Argyll [*County in Scotland*]
ARG .... Armoured Replacement Group [*British and Canadian*] [*World War II*]
ARG .... Arresting
ARG .... Atlantic Fleet Amphibious Ready Group (MCD)
ARG .... Atlantis Research Group (EA)
ARG .... Atlas Reliability Group
ARG .... Austin Rover Group Ltd.
ARG .... Automation Resource Group [*Wellesley, MA*]
ARG .... Autoradiography
ARG .... Internal Combustion Engine Repair Ship [*Navy symbol*]
ARG .... Walnut Ridge, AR [*Location identifier FAA*] (FAAL)
ARGA .... American Recreational Golf Association (EA)
ARGA .... Antique Radio Guild of America
ARGA .... Appliance, Range, Adjust [*Computer science*]
ArgA .... Argentine Angel [*Record label*]
ARGADS ...... Army Gun Air Defense Systems (RDA)
Arg Bills Ex... Argles' French Law of Bills of Exchange [*A publication*] (DLA)

ArgC............ Argentine Columbia [Record label]
ARGC .... Graham Community Library, Ralston, Alberta [Library symbol National Library of Canada] (NLC)
ARGCA........ American Rice Growers Cooperative Association [Defunct] (EA)
ArgD .... Argentine Decca [Record label]
ARGE .... Arbeitsgemeinschaft der Verbande der Europaischen Schloss- und Beschlagindustrie [European Federation of Associations of Lock and Builders' Hardware Manufacturers] (EAIO)
ARGE ALP.... Arbeitsgemeinschaft Alpenlaender [Working Group of Alpine Regions] (EAIO)
Argent.......... Argentinien [Argentina] [German]
Argentar........ Corporacion Bancaria de Espana [Associated Press] (SAG)
ArgentB........ Argent Bank [Associated Press] (SAG)
ArgentFd...... Argentina Fund [Associated Press] (SAG)
ArGeO .... Ozark Academy, Gentry, AR [Library symbol Library of Congress] (LCLS)
ARGH.......... Adult Rat Growth Hormone [Endocrinology]
argil............ Argillite (VRA)
ARGL .... Argyle Television 'A' [NASDAQ symbol] (TTSB)
ARGL .... Argyle Television, Inc. [NASDAQ symbol] (SAG)
ArgLon......... Argentine London [Record label]
ARGM .... Advanced Rifle Grenade Munition [Army] (INF)
ARGMA........ Army Rocket and Guided Missile Agency [Redstone Arsenal, AL]
Arg Mo .... Moore's English King's Bench Reports (Arguments of Moore) [A publication] (DLA)
ARGN .... Amerigon, Inc. [NASDAQ symbol] (SAG)
ARGNA........ Amerigon Inc.'A' [NASDAQ symbol] (TTSB)
ARGO .... Advanced Research Geophysical Observatory (IAA)
ArgOd .... Argentine Odeon [Record label]
ArgoGp........ Argonaut Group, Inc. [Associated Press] (SAG)
Argon.......... Argonautica [of Apollonius Rhodius] [Classical studies] (OCD)
ARGONAUT... Argonne Nuclear Assembly for University Training
Argosy .... Argosy Gaming Co. [Associated Press] (SAG)
ARGP .... Aeronautical Radionavigation Glide Path (IAA)
ArgP .... Argentine Parlophone [Record label]
ArgPat......... Argentine Pathe [Record label]
ARGR .... Association for Research in Growth Relationships [Defunct] (EA)
ARGS .... Advanced Raster-Graphics System (MHDB)
ARGS .... American Rock Garden Society (EA)
ARGS .... Antiradiation Guidance Sensor
ARG-SLF...... Amphibious Ready Group-Special Landing Force (DNAB)
ARGT .... Argent Bank [NASDAQ symbol] (SAG)
ARGT .... ArgentBank [NASDAQ symbol] (TTSB)
ARGUS........ Analytical Reports Gathering and Updating System [Navy] (NG)
ARGUS........ Associative Registers for Generalized User Switching [Computer typesetting system]
ARGUS........ Automatic Routine Generating and Updating System [Compiler] [Computer science]
Argus ONE... Argus Open Numerical Environments [Computer science]
ArgV........... Argentine Victor [Record label]
ARGY .... Argosy Gaming [NASDAQ symbol] (TTSB)
ARGY .... Argosy Gaming Co. [NASDAQ symbol] (SAG)
ARGYL .... Argyllshire [County in Scotland]
ArgyleT........ Argyle Television, Inc. [Associated Press] (SAG)
ARGYLLS..... Argyllshire [County in Scotland] (ROG)
ARH .... Advanced Reconnaissance Helicopter
ARH .... Aerial Reconnaissance Helicopter [Army]
ARH .... Ammunition Railhead
a Rh............ Am Rhein [on the River Rhine] [German] (ODBW)
ARH .... Antenna RADOME [RADAR Dome] Heater
ARH .... Antigenreceptor Homology [Immunochemistry]
ARH .... Antiradiation Homer
arh .... Arch (VRA)
ARH .... Archignac [France] [Seismograph station code, US Geological Survey] (SEIS)
ARH .... Arrowhead Airways [ICAO designator] (FAAC)
ARH .... Asia Pacific Resources International Holdings Ltd. [NYSE symbol] (SAG)
ARH .... Asia Pac Resources Intl'A' [NYSE symbol] (TTSB)
ARH .... Atharan Hazari [Pakistan] [Airport symbol] (AD)
ARH .... Atlantic Richfield Hanford Co. (MCD)
ARH .... Audit Reports Handbook [IRS]
ARH .... Heavy-Hull Repair Ship [Navy symbol Obsolete]
ARH .... Rolling Hills Public Library, Alberta [Library symbol National Library of Canada] (NLC)
ARHA .... American Rural Health Association (EA)
ArHA........... Arizona Hospital Association (SRA)
ARHA .... Associate of the Royal Hibernian Academy [British]
ARHAG........ African Refugee Housing Action Group [British]
ARHAWS..... Anti-Radiation Homing and Warning System [Military] (DNAB)
ARHCO........ Atlantic Richfield Hanford Co.
ARHDS........ Atmospheric Residue Hydrodesulfurization [Petroleum technology]
Ar-Hi........... Arkansas History Commission, Department of Archives and History, Little Rock, AR [Library symbol Library of Congress] (LCLS)
ARH/IR........ Anti-Radiation Homing / Infrared [Military] (PDAA)
ArHN........... North Arkansas Regional Library, Harrison, AR [Library symbol Library of Congress] (LCLS)
ArHo........... Southwest Arkansas Regional Library, Hope, AR [Library symbol] [Library of Congress] (LCLS)
ARHOC........ Army Housing Committee (AABC)
ARHP.......... Association of Reproductive Health Professionals (EA)
ARHRF........ Australian Rotary Health Research Fund
AR(HS) .... Airman Recruit (High School) (DNAB)
ARHS .... Anthracite Railroads Historical Society (EA)

ArHsT.......... Tri-Lake Regional Library, Hot Springs, AR [Library symbol] [Library of Congress] (LCLS)
Arhyth......... Arrhythmia Research Technology, Inc. [Associated Press] (SAG)
ARI .... Accruing Return Investments [Business term]
ARI .... Acne Research Institute (EA)
ARI .... Active Retirees in Israel [An association]
ARI .... Activity Routing Indicator (MCD)
ARI .... Actuarial Removal Interval (AFIT)
ARI .... Acupuncture Research Institute (EA)
ARI .... Acute Respiratory Illness [Medicine] (DMAA)
ARI .... Aerial RADIAC Instrument
ARI .... Aerodyne Research, Inc.
ARI .... Aeronautical Radio, Inc. (KSC)
ARI .... Aero Vics SA de CV [Mexico ICAO designator] (FAAC)
ARI .... African Research Institute [La Trobe University] [Australia]
ARI .... Aging Research Institute [Defunct] (EA)
ARI .... Agricultural Research Institute (EA)
ARI .... Aileron Rudder Interconnect (MCD)
ARI .... Airborne Radio Installation [RADAR]
ARI .... Airborne Radio Instrument
ARI .... Air-Conditioning and Refrigeration Institute (EA)
ARI .... Airpower Research Institute [Air University] [Research center] (RCD)
ARI .... Airway Reactivity Index [Physiology]
ARI .... Aldose Reductase Inhibitor [Organic chemistry] (DAVI)
ARI .... Allied Research Institute [Later, Aluminum Recycling Association] (EA)
ARI .... Alternate Rod Insertion [Nuclear energy] (NRCH)
ARI .... Aluminum Research Institute
ARI .... Amaryllis Research Institute (EA)
ARI .... American Rayon Institute [Defunct]
ARI .... Animal Rights International (EA)
ARI .... Approved Research Institute
ARI .... Aquatic Research Institute (EA)
ARI .... Archaeology and the Religion of Israel [A publication] (BJA)
ARI .... Arden Realty, Inc. [NYSE symbol] (SAG)
ARI .... Arica [Chile] [Airport symbol] (OAG)
ARI .... Arica [Chile] [Seismograph station code, US Geological Survey] (SEIS)
Ari .... Aries [Constellation]
Ari .... Ariprandus [Flourished, 12th century] [Authority cited in pre-1607 legal work] (DSA)
ARI .... Arithmetic (DNAB)
ARI .... Arizona
ARI .... Army Research Institute (RDA)
ARI .... Army Research Institute for the Behavioral and Social Sciences [Alexandria, VA]
ARI .... Asbestos Related Illness
ARI .... Association Resource Institute [Commercial firm] (EA)
ARI .... Attribute Requirement Inventory
ARI .... ATWS [Anticipated Transient without Scram] Rod Injection System [Nuclear energy] (NRCH)
ARI .... Audience Reaction Indicator (IIA)
ARI .... Audience Research Institute [Also, AIPO] (NTCM)
ARI .... Australasian Religion Index [A publication] (APTA)
ARi .... Australian Road Index [Australian Road Research Board] (NITA)
ARI .... Authority Is Requested to Inter [the remains of] [Army] (AABC)
ARI .... Automated Readability Index (MCD)
ARI .... Automatic Radio Information [System which relays traffic information through car radios]
ARi .... Automatic Return Items (AABC)
ARi .... Automobile Drivers Radio Information [System for turning on car radio automatically, e.g. important messages] (NITA)
ARI .... Automobile Road Information [Traffic management]
ARI .... Automotive Recyclers of Indiana (SRA)
ARI .... Average Recurrent Interval
ARI .... Average Relationship Index
ARI .... Ayn Rand Institute (EA)
ARI .... Rimbey Public Library, Alberta [Library symbol National Library of Canada] (NLC)
ARIA .... Accounting Researchers International Association [Defunct] (EA)
ARIA .... Acetylcholine Receptor-Inducing Activity [Biochemistry]
ARIA .... Administration, Ryukyu Islands, Army (AABC)
ARIA .... Adult Reading Improvement Association
ARIA .... Advanced Range Instrumentation Aircraft
ARIA .... Air Conditioning & Refrigeration Industry Association of British Columbia (AC)
ARIA .... Alberta Recording Industry Association (AC)
ARIA .... American Radio Importers Association (EA)
ARIA .... American Risk and Insurance Association [Orlando, FL] (EA)
ARIA .... Apollo Range Instrumentation Aircraft [NASA]
ARIA .... Ariad Pharmaceutical, Inc. [NASDAQ symbol] (SAG)
ARIA .... ARIAD Pharmaceuticals [NASDAQ symbol] (TTSB)
ARIA .... Automated Radioimmunoassay [Immunology] (DAVI)
ARIA .... Autoradiographic Immunoassay (MCD)
Ariad.......... Ariad Pharmaceuticals, Inc. [Associated Press] (SAG)
AriadP........ Ariad Pharmaceuticals, Inc. [Associated Press] (SAG)
ARIAS .... Associate of the Royal Incorporation of Architects in Scotland
ARIAW .... ARIAD Pharmaceuticals Wrrt [NASDAQ symbol] (TTSB)
ARIB .... Aspen Imaging International [NASDAQ symbol] (NQ)
ARIB .... Aspen Imaging Intl. [NASDAQ symbol] (TTSB)
ARIB .... Asphalt Roofing Industry Bureau [Later, ARMA] (EA)
ARIBA .... Associate of the Royal Institute of British Architects
ARIC .... Acid Rain Information Clearinghouse (GNE)
ARIC .... Admission Referral and Information Center [Commission on Independent Colleges and Universities]

ARIC .... Agricultural Research Information Centre [*Indian Council of Agricultural Research*] (IID)
ARIC .... Air Resources Information Clearinghouse [*Also, an information service or system*] (EA)
ARIC .... Arizona Research Information Center [*Information service or system*] (EA)
ARIC .... Associate of the Royal Institute of Chemistry [*Formerly, AIC*] [*British*]
ARIC .... Atherosclerosis Risk in Communities Study [*Department of Health and Human Services*] (GFGA)
ARIC .... Australian Railways Industry Commission
ARICD .... American Research Institute for Community Development (EA)
ARICS .... Associate of the Royal Institution of Chartered Surveyors [*Formerly, PASI*] [*British*]
ARICS .... Professional Associate of the Royal Institution of Chartered Surveyors [*Canada*] (DD)
ARIDO .... Association of Registered Interior Designers of Ontario [*Formerly, Interior Designers of Ontario*] (AC)
Arie .... Aries [*Constellation*]
Ariel .... Ariel Corp. [*Associated Press*] (SAG)
ARIEL .... Automated Real-Time Investments Exchange [*NASDAQ trading computer*]
ArielCp .... Ariel Corp. [*Associated Press*] (SAG)
Ariely .... Ariely Advertising Ltd. [*Associated Press*] (SAG)
ARIEM .... Army Research Institute for Environmental Medicine
ARIES .... Advanced RADAR Information Evaluation System
ARIES .... Airborne Reconnaissance Integrated Electronic System (MCD)
ARIES .... Airborne Research Integration Engineering Support (MCD)
ARIES .... Aircraft Reply and Interference Environment Simulator (MCD)
ARIES .... Alvey Research for Insurance Expert Systems (NITA)
ARIES .... Ammunition Reliability Information Evolution System (MCD)
ARIES .... Animal Rights Information and Education Service (EA)
ARIES .... Astronomical Radio Interferometric Earth Survey [*or Surveying*] [*NASA*]
ARIES .... Authentic Reproduction of an Independent Earth Satellite
ARIES .... Automated Registration, Indexing, and Enquiries System [*Computer science*]
ARIES .... Automated Reliability Estimation Program [*Computer science*]
ARIF .... Association pour le Retablissement des Institutions et Oeuvres Israelites en France (EA)
ARIHSL .... Association of Rhode Island Health Sciences Librarians [*Library network*]
AR II .... American Revolution II Committee (EA)
ARIL .... Associates for Religion and Intellectual Life (EA)
ARIL .... Automatic Return Item List (MCD)
ARIM .... Accelerator and Reactor Improvement and Modification
ARIMA .... Autoregressive-Integrated-Moving-Average [*Statistics*]
ARIMO .... Association of Russian Imperial Medical Officers [*Defunct*] (EA)
ARIMS .... Airborne RADAR Inflight Monitoring System
ARIMS-LOG ... Armor Information Management System-Logistics
ARIN .... Afghan Refugee Information Network [*British Defunct*]
ARIN .... Arista Investors Corp. [*NASDAQ symbol*] (NQ)
ARIN .... Automotive Recycling Industry of Nebraska (SRA)
ARIN .... National Aeronautics and Space Administration Library Network [*Information service or system*] (IID)
ARINA .... Arista Invs Corp. [*NASDAQ symbol*] (TTSB)
ARINA .... Associate of the Royal Institution of Naval Architects [*British*] (DI)
ARINC .... Aeronautical Radio, Inc.
ARINC .... Aeronautical Research, Inc. (MCD)
ARINC .... Aircraft Radio, Inc. (MCD)
ARINCO .... Aeronautical Radio, Inc.
ARI Net .... ARI Network Services, Inc. [*Associated Press*] (SAG)
ARINOA .... Association of Russian Imperial Naval Officers in America (EA)
ARIP .... Air Refueling Initial Point [*Air Force*] (AFM)
ARIP .... APACHE [*Active Thermal Protection for Avionics Crew and Heat-Sensitive Equipment*] Readiness Improvement Program [*Army*]
Arip .... Ariprandus [*Flourished, 12th century*] [*Authority cited in pre-1607 legal work*] (DSA)
AriP .... Arizona Public Service [*Associated Press*] (SAG)
ARIP .... Automatic Rocket Impact Predictor
ARIPES .... Angle-Resolved Inverse Photoelectron Spectroscopy
ARIPHH .... Associate of the Royal Institute of Public Health and Hygiene [*British*]
Aripnd .... Ariprandus [*Flourished, 12th century*] [*Authority cited in pre-1607 legal work*] (DSA)
ARIPPS .... Australian Region of the International Plant Propagators' Society
ARIS .... Aboriginal and Torres Strait Islander Commission Regional Information Syste
ARIS .... Activity Reporting Information System (PDAA)
ARIS .... Adult Basic Education Resource and Information Service [*Australia*]
ARIS .... Advanced Range Instrumentation Ship [*Navy symbol*]
ARIS .... Advanced Range Instrumentation Systems (MCD)
ARIS .... Advanced Research Instrument System, Inc.
ARIS .... Aerial RADIAC Instrument System
ARIS .... Aeronautical Research Institute of Sweden (MCD)
ARIS .... Agricultural Information System (NITA)
ARIS .... Airborne Range Instrumentation Station
ARIS .... Aircraft Recording Instrumentation System [*British*]
ARIS .... Aircraft Research Instrumentation System
ARIS .... Alabama Resources Information System [*Auburn University*] [*Information service or system*] (IID)
ARIS .... Alcohol Research Information Service (EA)
ARIS .... Altitude and Rate-Indicating System (DNAB)
ARIS .... Apoenzyme Reactivation Immunoassay System [*Clinical chemistry*]
ARIS .... ARI Network Services [*NASDAQ symbol*] (SPSG)
ARIS .... Association Referral Information Service
ARIS .... Atlantic Range Instrumentation Ship

ARIS .... Atomic Reactor in Space (MUGU)
ARIS .... Attitude and Rate Indicating System
ARIS .... Audio Response Interface System (PDAA)
ARIS .... Automated Reactor Inspection System [*Nuclear energy*] (NRCH)
ARIS .... Automated Real-Time Imaging System
ARIS .... Automatic Recording Infrared Spectrometer
ARIS .... Auto-Regulated Inspiratory Support [*Medicine*] (DMAA)
ARISC .... Association pour la Recherche dans l'Industrie Siderurgique Canadienne (AC)
ARISE .... Association of Reserves for Improving Social Economics (AC)
ARISF .... Association of the IOC Recognized International Sports Federations [*Seoul, Republic of Korea*] (EAIO)
ARIST .... Annual Review of Information Science and Technology [*A publication*]
ARIST .... Aristophanes [*Greek playwright, c. 445-380BC*] [*Classical studies*] (ROG)
ARIST .... Aristotle [*Greek philosopher, 384-322BC*] [*Classical studies*] (ROG)
Arist .... Letter of Aristeas (Pseudepigrapha) (BJA)
AristIn .... Arista Investors Corp. [*Associated Press*] (SAG)
ARISTO .... Aristocrat (DSUE)
AristoIn .... Aristo International Corp. [*Associated Press*] (SAG)
ARISTOTE .... Association de Reseaux Informatique en Systeme Totalement et Tres Elabore [*Association of Information Networks in a Completely Open and Very Elaborate System*] [*France*] [*Computer science*] (TNIG)
ARISTOTLE... Annual Review and Information Symposium on the Technology of Training, Learning,and Education [*DoD*]
Aristotle ...... Aristotle Corp. [*Associated Press*] (SAG)
Aristox .... Aristoxenus [*Fourth century BC*] [*Classical studies*] (OCD)
ARIT .... American Registered Inhalation Therapist [*Academic degree*]
ARIT .... American Registry of Inhalation Therapists [*Later, NBRT*] (EA)
ARIT .... American Research Institute of Turkey [*University of Pennsylvania*] [*Research center*] (RCD)
ARITH .... Arithmetic [*Flowchart*]
ARITHMETIC... A Rat in the House May Eat the Ice Cream [*Mnemonic guide for spelling "arithmetic"*]
ARITHU .... Arithmetic Unit [*Computer science*]
ARIZ .... Arizona (AFM)
Ariz Admin Code... Arizona Administrative Code [*A publication*] (AAGC)
Ariz Admin Comp... Arizona Official Compilation of Administrative Rules and Regulations [*A publication*] (DLA)
Ariz Admin Comp R... Arizona Official Compilation of Administrative Rules and Regulations [*A publication*] (DLA)
Ariz Admin Dig... Arizona Administrative Digest [*A publication*] (DLA)
Ariz Admin Reg... Arizona Administrative Register [*A publication*] (AAGC)
Ariz App... Arizona Appeals Reports [*A publication*] (DLA)
Ariz Const.... Arizona Constitution [*A publication*] (DLA)
ArizInst .... Arizona Instrument Corp. [*Associated Press*] (SAG)
ArizLd .... Arizona Land Income Corp. [*Associated Press*] (SAG)
Ariz Rev Stat... Arizona Revised Statutes [*A publication*] (DLA)
Ariz Rev Stat Ann... Arizona Revised Statutes, Annotated [*A publication*] (DLA)
Ariz Rev State... Arizona Revised Statutes [*A publication*] (DLA)
Ariz Sess Laws... Arizona Session Laws [*A publication*] (DLA)
Ariz State LJ... Arizona State Law Journal [*A publication*] (DLA)
Ariz St U...... Arizona State University (GAGS)
ARJ.............. Acquisition RADAR Jamming
ARJ.............. Aerojet de Costa Rica SA [*ICAO designator*] (FAAC)
ARJ.............. Austin Rover Japan
ARJ.............. Providence, RI [*Location identifier FAA*] (FAAL)
ARJCC .... Andrew R. Jennings Computing Center [*Case Western Reserve University*] [*Research center*] (RCD)
ArJCR .... Crowley Ridge Regional Library, Jonesboro, AR [*Library symbol*] [*Library of Congress*] (LCLS)
ARJS .... Airborne RADAR Jamming System (MCD)
ARK .... Air Corse [*France ICAO designator*] (FAAC)
ARK .... Arkansas (AFM)
Ark .... Arkansas Supreme Court Reports [*A publication*] (DLA)
ARK .... Ark Energy Ltd. [*Vancouver Stock Exchange symbol*]
ARK .... Arkhangelsk [*Former USSR Geomagnetic observatory code*]
Ark .... Arkley's Justiciary Reports [*Scotland*] [*A publication*] (DLA)
ARK .... Arrick, Douglas B., Denver CO [*STAC*]
ARK .... Author's Resource Kit [*Asymetrix Co.*] [*Computer software*] (PCM)
ARK .... Reconnaissance Seaplane [*Russian symbol*]
ARK .... Senior High Income Portfolio [*NYSE symbol*] (SPSG)
Ark Acts ...... General Acts of Arkansas [*A publication*] (DLA)
Ark Admin Reg... Arkansas Register [*A publication*] (DLA)
Ark App........ Arkansas Appellate Reports [*A publication*] (DLA)
Ark App Rep... Arkansas Appellate Reports [*A publication*] (DLA)
Ark BA .... Arkansas Bar Association. Proceedings [*A publication*] (DLA)
ArkBest........ Arkansas Best Corp. [*Associated Press*] (SAG)
ArkBst.......... Arkansas Best Corp. [*Associated Press*] (SAG)
Ark CC .... Arkansas Corporation Commission Report [*A publication*] (DLA)
Ark Code Ann... Arkansas Code Annotated [*A publication*] (AAGC)
Ark Const..... Arkansas Constitution [*A publication*] (DLA)
Ark Just .... Arkley's Justiciary Reports [*Scotland*] [*A publication*] (DLA)
Arkl .... Arkley's Justiciary Reports [*Scotland*] [*A publication*] (DLA)
ARKLA .... Arkansas Louisiana Gas Co.
Arkley.......... Arkley's Justiciary Reports [*Scotland*] [*A publication*] (DLA)
Ark LJ .... Arkansas Law Journal [*A publication*] (DLA)
ArkPL.......... Arkansas Power & Light Co. [*Associated Press*] (SAG)
Ark PU .... Arkansas Department of Public Utilities Report [*A publication*] (DLA)
Ark R .... Arkansas Reports [*A publication*] (DLA)
ARKR .... Ark Restaurants [*NASDAQ symbol*] (SAG)
Ark Reg ...... Arkansas Register [*A publication*] (AAGC)
Ark Rep ...... Arkansas Reports [*A publication*] (DLA)

ArkRst......... Ark Restaurants [*Associated Press*] (SAG)
Ark's......... Arkansas Reports [*A publication*] (DLA)
Ark Stat Ann... Arkansas Statutes, Annotated [*A publication*] (DLA)
Ark Stats...... Arkansas Statutes [*A publication*] (DLA)
Ark St U...... Arkansas State University (GAGS)
ARL............. Acceptable Reliability Level [*Quality control*]
ARL............. Admiralty Research Laboratory [*British*]
ARL............. Aerial
ARL............. Aerial Reconnaissance Laboratory
ARL............. Aeromedical Research Laboratory [*Army*] (KSC)
ARL............. Aerospace Research Laboratory [*Wright-Patterson Air Force Base, OH*] (AFM)
ARL............. Age Run Length
ARL............. Airborne Recce Low (DOMA)
ARL's......... Aircraft Radio Laboratory
ARL............. Airlec [*France ICAO designator*] (FAAC)
ARL............. Air Reconnaissance Low [*Army*] (RDA)
ARL............. Air Resources Laboratory [*Silver Spring, MD*] [*National Oceanic and Atmospheric Administration*]
ARL............. Amateur Radio League (SAA)
ARL............. American Leduc Petroleums Ltd. [*Toronto Stock Exchange symbol*]
ARL............. American Roque League (EA)
ARL............. Americans for Religious Liberty (EA)
ARL............. Antiriot Laws
ARL............. Applied Research Laboratories [*Commercial firm*]
ARL............. Applied Research Laboratory [*Johns Hopkins University, University of Texas at Austin, Pennsylvania State University*] [*Research center*]
ARL............. Archeological Research Laboratory [*Texas A & M University*] [*Research center*] (RCD)
ARL............. Arctic Research Laboratory [*Point Barrow, AK*] [*Army*]
ARL............. Arlington [*Diocesan abbreviation*] [*Virginia*] (TOCD)
ARL............. Army Radiation Laboratory
ARL............. Army Research Laboratory (RDA)
ARL............. Associate in Recreation Leadership
ARL............. Association of Research Libraries (EA)
ARL............. Astronautical Research Laboratory (SAA)
ARL............. Atlantic Research Laboratories [*National Research Council of Canada*] (MCD)
ARL............. Authorized Retention Level [*Military*] (AABC)
ARL............. Automatic Record Level (IAA)
ARL............. Average Remaining Lifetime (MAE)
ARL............. Average Response Latency [*Biochemistry*]
ARL............. Average Run Length [*Statistics*]
ARL............. Aviation Research Laboratory [*University of Illinois*] (MCD)
ARL............. Aviator Readiness Level (MCD)
ARL............. Landing Craft, Repair Ship [*Navy symbol*]
ArL............. Little Rock Public Library, Little Rock, AR [*Library symbol Library of Congress*] (LCLS)
ARL's......... United States Army Library, Washington, DC [*OCLC symbol*] (OCLC)
ArLA............ Arkansas Arts Center, Little Rock, AR [*Library symbol Library of Congress*] (LCLS)
ARLA .... Association of Residential Letting Agents [*British*] (DBA)
ARLABANK... Arab Latin American Bank
ArLAD.......... Arkansas Democrat, Little Rock, AR [*Library symbol Library of Congress*] (LCLS)
ARLAN .... Arlington Annex [*Navy*] (DNAB)
ARLANT....... Army Forces Atlantic (MCD)
ARLB .... Automatic Radio Location Beacon (PDAA)
ARLC .... Arel Communications & Software Ltd. [*NASDAQ symbol*] (SAG)
ARLCAP ...... Association of Research Libraries Collection Analysis Project
ARLCF .... Arel Comm & Software [*NASDAQ symbol*] (TTSB)
ARLD .... Alcohol-Related Liver Disease [*Medicine*]
ARLE .... Admiralty Research Laboratory Extension [*British*]
ARLEA .... Army Logistics Evaluation Agency (MCD)
ARLEX .... Arlington Annex [*Navy*] (DNAB)
ARL-FRO...... Air Resources Laboratory - Field Research Office [*National Oceanic and Atmospheric Administration*] (NOAA)
ARLFT......... Airlift
ARLIS .... Arctic Research Laboratory Island [*A floating ice island in the Arctic Ocean*] [*Navy*]
ARLIS .... Art Libraries Society [*British*] (BI)
ARLIS/NA.... Art Libraries Society/North America (EA)
ARLL .... Advanced Run Length Limited [*Computer science*]
ARLL .... Audible Rumble Loudness Level [*Stereo*]
ARLLUC ...... Alpha Roster Locator List (United States Army Reserve) Colonels
ARLM.......... Rainbow Lake Municipal Library, Alberta [*Library symbol National Library of Canada*] (NLC)
ARLN .... Airline
ARLO .... Air Reconnaissance Liaison Officer
ARLO .... Alkali-Refined Linseed Oil [*Organic chemistry*]
ARLO .... Art Research Libraries of Ohio [*Library network*]
ARLP .... Alliance Republicaine pour les Libertes et le Progres [*Republican Alliance for Liberties and Progress*] [*France Political party*] (PPE)
ARLS .... Association for Recognizing the Life of Stillborns (EA)
ARLS .... Automated Runbook/Library System
ARLS .... Automatic Resupply Logistics System (AFM)
ARLSEA ...... Active-Retired Lighthouse Service Employees' Association (EA)
ArLSJ......... Saint John's Seminary, Little Rock, AR [*Library symbol Library of Congress*] (LCLS)
ARLT.......... Associate for Reform of Latin Teaching [*British*]
ArLUA......... University of Arkansas at Little Rock, Little Rock, AR [*Library symbol Library of Congress*] (LCLS)
ArLUA-L...... University of Arkansas at Little Rock, Law Library, Little Rock, AR [*Library symbol Library of Congress*] (LCLS)

ArLVA .... United States Veterans Administration Hospital, Little Rock, AR [*Library symbol Library of Congress*] (LCLS)
arl vw .... Aerial View (VRA)
ARLW .... Arel Communications & Software Ltd. [*NASDAQ symbol*] (SAG)
ARLWF .... Arel Comm & Software Wrrt'A' [*NASDAQ symbol*] (TTSB)
ARM............. Accelerated Relaxation Method (PDAA)
ARM............. Account Resources Manager
ARM............. Accredited Resident Manager [*Institute of Real Estate Management of the N ational Association of Realtors*] [*Designation awarded by*]
ARM............. Accumulator Read-In Module (OA)
ARM............. Acorn RISC Machine [*Acorn Computers*] [*Reduced instruction set computer*] (NITA)
ARM............. Action Research Model [*Program of Keep America Beautiful, Inc.*]
ARM............. Adjustable Rate Mortgage
ARM............. Administrative Rules of Montana [*A publication*] (AAGC)
ARM............. Adrenergic Receptor Material [*Physiology*] (DMAA)
ARM............. Advanced Recovery Mode [*Computer science*]
ARM............. Advanced Rifle Marksmanship [*Military*] (INF)
ARM............. Advanced RISC [*Reduced Instruction-Set Computerizing*] Machine (ECON)
ARM............. Aeromarket Express [*Spain ICAO designator*] (FAAC)
ARM............. African Resistance Movement [*South Africa*] (PD)
ARM............. Agent Reference Material [*Used by airline agents*]
ARM............. Aggregate Ready-Mix of Minnesota (SRA)
ARM............. Aircraft Regression Model (MCD)
ARM............. Air Resources Management [*Environmental Protection Agency*] (GFGA)
ARM............. Algorithmic Remote Manipulation [*Programming language*]
ARM............. Allergy Relief Medicine [*Pharmacology*] (DAVI)
ARM............. Alliance Reformee Mondiale [*World Alliance of Reformed Churches - WARC*] [*Geneva, Switzerland*] (EAIO)
ARM............. All Risk Management [*Insurance*]
ARM............. All Roads Ministry [*An association*] (EA)
ARM............. Alternating Rate of Motion [*Neurophysiology*] (DAVI)
ARM............. Amateur Radio Monitor
ARM............. Ambulatory Renal Monitoring [*Medicine*]
ARM............. AMPEX [*Alexander M. Poniatoff, Excellence*] Replacement Memory (IAA)
ARM............. Anhysteretic Remanent Magnetization
ARM .... Animal Rights Mobilization (EA)
ARM............. Anisotropic Remanent Magnetism (PDAA)
ARM............. AntiRADAR Missile
ARM............. Antiradiation Missile
ARM............. Apollo Requirements Manual [*NASA*] (KSC)
ARM............. Application Reference Manual (IAA)
ARM............. Applied Research Management
ARM............. Area Radiation Monitor (NRCH)
ARM............. Arginine Rich Motif [*Biochemistry*]
ARM............. Armada Gold & Mining [*Vancouver Stock Exchange symbol*]
ARM............. Armagh [*County in Ireland*] (WGA)
ARM............. Armament
ARM............. Armature (KSC)
ARM............. Armed Resistance Movement (EA)
ARM............. Armed Revolutionary Movement [*Puerto Rico*]
ARM............. Armenia
Arm............. Armenia (VRA)
arm............. Armenian [*MARC language code Library of Congress*] (LCCP)
ARM............. Armenian Catholic Exarchate [*Diocesan abbreviation*] [*Pennsylvania*] (TOCD)
ARM............. ARM Financial Group [*AMEX symbol*] (SPSG)
ARM............. Armidale [*Australia Airport symbol*] (OAG)
ARM............. Arming (MSA)
ARM............. Armored (CINC)
ARM............. Armorican
ARM............. Army Ready Materiel
ARM............. Arteriovenous Malformation [*Medicine*] (CPH)
ARM............. Artificial Rupture of Membranes [*Medicine*]
ARM............. Assistant Regional Manager
ARM............. Associate in Risk Management [*Canada*] (DD)
ARM............. Association of Radical Midwives [*British*] (DBA)
ARM............. Association of Railway Museums (EA)
ARM............. Association of Recovering Motorcyclists (EA)
ARM............. Association of Rooflight Manufacturers [*British*] (DBA)
ARM............. Association of Rotational Molders (EA)
ARM............. Asynchronous Response Mode [*Computer science*]
ARM............. Atmosphere Radiation Monitor (IEEE)
ARM............. Atmospheric Radiation Measurement [*Program*]
ARM............. Atmospheric Radiation Measurement Program [*Department of Energy*] (ECON)
ARM............. Atomic Resolution Microscope
ARM............. Attenuated RADAR Monitor
ARM............. Australian Rights Movement
ARM............. Automated RADAR Monitor System
ARM............. Automated Route Management (DEN)
ARM............. Automatic Reel Mounting
ARM............. Availability, Reliability, and Maintainability [*Computer performance*]
ARM............. Aviation Radioman [*Navy*]
ARM............. Heavy Machinery Repair Ship [*Navy symbol*]
ARM............. Internal Revenue Bureau Committee on Appeals and Review, Memorandum [*United States*] [*A publication*] (DLA)
ARM............. Rockyford Municipal Library, Alberta [*Library symbol National Library of Canada*] (NLC)
ARM............. Wharton, TX [*Location identifier FAA*] (FAAL)
ARMA .... Accumulator Reservoir Manifold Assembly

ARMA .... Aluminium Radiator Manufacturers Association [*British*] (DBA)
ARMA .... American Bosch Arma Corp. (AAG)
ARMA .... American Records Management Association (NITA)
ARMA .... American Registry of Medical Assistants (EA)
ArMA .... Arizona Medical Association (SRA)
ARMA .... Armature
ARMA .... Army Attache
ARMA .... Asphalt Roofing Manufacturers Association (EA)
ARMA .... Association of Records Managers and Administrators (EA)
ARMA .... Australian Records Management Association
ARMA .... Autoregressive Moving Average [*Statistics*]
ARMAAP ..... Army Resource Management Advisory and Assessment Program
ARMAC .... Aviation Radioman, Combat Aircrewman [*Navy*]
ARMACCEL... Armature Acceleration (IAA)
ARMACS ..... Aviation Resources Management and Control System
ARMAD .... Armored and Mechanized Unit Air Defense [*Army*]
ARMADA ..... Aircraft Reliability, Maintainability, Availability Design Analysis (PDAA)
ARMADA ..... American Record Merchandisers and Distributors Association [*Defunct*] (EA)
ArMag .... Columbia-Lafayette-Ouachita-Calhoun Regional Library, Magnolia, AR [*Library symbol*] [*Library of Congress*] (LCLS)
ArMagS .... Southern State College, Magnolia, AR [*Library symbol Library of Congress*] (LCLS)
ARMALCOLITE... Armstrong Aldren Collins [*Lunar mineral named after three astronauts*]
ArMalM .... Mid-Arkansas Regional Library, Malvern, AR [*Library symbol*] [*Library of Congress*] (LCLS)
Arman .... Armanino Foods of Distinction, Inc. [*Associated Press*] (SAG)
ARMAN .... Artificial Methods Analyst (MCD)
Arm & O ...... Armstrong, Macartney, and Ogle's Irish Nisi Prius Reports [*A publication*] (DLA)
ARMATSC ... Army Materiel Status Committees (AABC)
ARMB .... Army Requirements and Management Board
Armc .... Armco, Inc. [*Formerly, Armco Steel Corp.*] [*Associated Press*] (SAG)
ARMC .... Automatic Repeat Request Mode Counter [*Computer science*] (IAA)
ARMCA .... Arkansas Ready Mixed Concrete Association (SRA)
ARMCANZ .... Agriculture and Resource Management Council of Australia and New Zealand
ARMCM .... Associate, Royal Manchester College of Music [*British*] (ROG)
Armco .... Armco, Inc. [*Formerly, Armco Steel Corp.*] [*Associated Press*] (SAG)
ARMCOM ..... Armament Command [*Army*] (AABC)
ARMD .... Age-Related Macular Degeneration [*Ophthalmology*] (CPH)
ARMD .... American Red Magen David for Israel [*An association*]
ARMD .... Armed (CINC)
ARMD .... Armed
ARMD .... Armored (AFM)
ARMD .... Armored Division [*Army*]
ARMDAS ...... Army Damage Assessment System (AABC)
Arm Det ...... Armchair Detective [*A publication*] (BRI)
ARMDEV ...... Arming Device
ARMDI .... American Red Magen David for Israel (EA)
ARMDLL ...... Armadillo
ARME .... Automatic Reseau Measuring Equipment (MCD)
ARMEA .... American Railway Magazine Editors Association [*Later, Association of Railroad Editors*] (EA)
ARMED .... Army Medical Department
ARMEDASH... Armed Advanced Scout Helicopter (AABC)
ARMEL .... Armament and Electronics [*Air Force*] (IAA)
Armen .... Armenian (BJA)
ARMET .... Area Forecast in Metric Unit [*Meteorology*] (BARN)
ARMF .... Advanced Reactivity Measurement Facility [*Idaho Falls, ID*] [*Department of Energy*]
ARMF .... All-Russian Monarchist Front [*Defunct*] (EA)
ARMF .... Armanino Foods Distinction [*NASDAQ symbol*] (TTSB)
ARMF .... Armanino Foods of Distinction, Inc. [*NASDAQ symbol*] (SAG)
ARM F .... ARM Financial Group [*Associated Press*] (SAG)
Arm F & S ... Armed Forces and Society [*A publication*] (BRI)
ARMGRD ..... Armed Guard (MUGU)
ARMH .... Academy of Religion and Mental Health [*Later, Institutes of Religion and Health*]
ARMH .... Association for Rural Mental Health [*Later, NARMH*] (EA)
ARMH .... Rocky Mountain House Public Library, Alberta [*Library symbol National Library of Canada*] (NLC)
Arm Hist Soc J... Armidale Historical Society. Journal [*A publication*]
ARMHS .... American Rat, Mouse, and Hamster Society (EA)
ARMI .... American Research Merchandising Institute [*Later, NASM*] (EA)
ARMI .... Associated Risk Managers International [*Austin, TX*] (EA)
ARMIA .... Associate of the Retail Management Institute of Australia
ARMINGF ..... Armingford [*England*]
ARMIP .... Accounting and Reporting Management Improvement Program [*Army*] (AABC)
ARMIS .... Arsenal Management Information System
ARMIS .... Automated Reporting and Management Information System [*Federal Communications Commission*] (GFGA)
ARMISH .... United States Military Mission with the Iranian Army
ARMIS-LOG... Armor Management Information System - Logistics
ARML .... Airmail (FAAC)
ARMLA .... Ayn Rand Memorial Library Association [*Defunct*] (EA)
ARMLO .... Army Liaison Officer (MUGU)
ARMM .... Accelerated Refuge Maintenance Management [*Department of the Interior*]
ARMM .... Analysis and Research of Methods for Management
ARMM .... Association of Reproduction Materials Manufacturers (EA)
ARMM .... Automatic Reliability Mathematical Model (DNAB)
ARMMA .... American Railway Master Mechanics' Association

Arm Mac & Og... Armstrong, Macartney, and Ogle's Irish Nisi Prius Reports [*A publication*] (DLA)
Arm M & O... Armstrong, Macartney, and Ogle's Irish Nisi Prius Reports [*A publication*] (DLA)
ARMMS .... Automated Reliability and Maintenance Management [*or Measurement*] System [*Navy*] (NG)
ARMMS .... Automatically Reconfigurable Modular Multiprocessor [*or Multiprocessing*] System [*Computer science*]
ARMM/TTC... Auxiliary Removable Memory Media/Tape-Transport Cartridge (MCD)
ARMN .... Airman [*British military*] (DMA)
ARMN .... Airman
ARMNY .... Associated Risk Managers of New York State (SRA)
ARMO .... Automotive Restoration Market Organization
ARMO .... Automotive Restoration Market Organization
ARM/OH...... Associated Risk Managers of Ohio (SRA)
ArMonD .... Southeast Arkansas Regional Library, Monticello, AR [*Library symbol Library of Congress*] (LCLS)
ARMOP .... Army Mortar Program (RDA)
Armor .... Armor All Products Corp. [*Associated Press*] (SAG)
ArmorH .... Armor Holdings, Inc. [*Associated Press*] (SAG)
Armour .... Manitoba Queen's Bench Tempore Wood, by Armour [*A publication*] (DLA)
ArMoW .... Winrock International Library, Petit Jean Mountain, Morrilton, AR [*Library symbol*] [*Library of Congress*] (LCLS)
ARMP .... Allied Reliability and Maintainability Publication (MCD)
ARMP .... Average Revenue/Marginal Physical Product [*Economics*]
ARM-PL .... Armor Plate (KSC)
ARMPr .... ARM Fin'l 9.50% Pfd [*AMEX symbol*] (TTSB)
ARMR .... Armor All Products [*NASDAQ symbol*] (TTSB)
ARMR .... Armor All Products Corp. [*NASDAQ symbol*] (NQ)
ARMR .... Armorer (AABC)
ARMR .... Army Readiness and Mobilization Regions (MCD)
ARMRD .... Armored
ARMRY .... Armory
ARMS .... Acid Rain Mitigation Strategies
ARMS .... Action Research into Multiple Sclerosis [*See also Arms of America - AA*] [*British*]
ARMS .... ADPE [*Automatic Data Processing Equipment*] Resources Management System (AFM)
ARMS .... Advanced Receiver Model System
ARMS .... Adverse Reaction Monitoring System [*Food and Drug Administration*] (PAZ)
ARMS .... Aerial Radiological Measurement and Survey [*Program*]
ARMS .... Aerial Radiological Measurements System [*Nuclear energy*] (NRCH)
ARMS .... Aircraft Readiness Maintainability Simulator (MCD)
ARMS .... Aircraft Reliability and Maintainability Simulation
ARMS .... Aircraft Resources Management System [*Military*]
ARMS .... All Radio Marketing Study [*Business term*] (DOAD)
ARMS .... All-Radio Methodology Study [*Audience ratings*] (NTCM)
ARMS .... AMDF [*Army Master Data File*] Reader Microfilm System [*Formerly, AMDFRMS*] (AABC)
ARMS .... Ammunition Reporting Management System [*Air Force*] (AFM)
ARMS .... Amplification Refractory Mutation System [*Biochemistry*]
ARMS .... Application of Remote Manipulators in Space [*Robot*] [*NASA*]
ARMS .... Archaeological Resources Management Service [*Ball State Univesity*] [*Research center*] (RCD)
ARMS .... Area Radiological Monitoring System (NRCH)
ARMS .... Armament Retooling and Manufacturing Support Initiative [*1993*]
ARMS .... Army Master Data File Retrieval Microform System
ARMS .... Army Readiness Management [*or Measurement*] System (MCD)
ARMS .... Associate of the Royal Society of Miniature Painters [*British*]
ARMS .... Association of Racquetsports Manufacturers and Suppliers [*Inactive*] (EA)
ARMS .... Association of Researchers in Medical Sciences [*British*]
ARMS .... Atmospheric or Remote Manipulator System [*Deep-sea diving*]
ARMS .... Atmospheric Roving Manipulator System (PDAA)
ARMS .... Automated RADAR Measurement System (MCD)
ARMS .... Automated Range Management System (MCD)
ARMS .... Automated Real-time Mapping System [*Navigation systems*]
ARMS .... Automated Records Management System [*Computer science*] (HGAA)
ARMS .... Automated Resource Management System (MCD)
ARMS .... Automatic Radiation Monitoring System (MCD)
ARMS .... Automatic Radio Meteorological Measurements and Survey (IAA)
ARMS .... Automatic Receiving and Measuring System (MCD)
ARMS .... Automatic Remote Manned System (MCD)
ARMS .... Automatic Reporting Maintenance System (MCD)
ARMS .... Automotive Repair Management Systems [*3M Co.*]
ARMS .... Automotive Research and Marketing Services
Arms Br P Cas... Armstrong's Breach of Privilege Cases, New York [*A publication*] (DLA)
Arms Con El... Armstrong. Contested Election Cases [*New York*] [*A publication*] (DLA)
Arms Con Elec... Armstrong's New York Contested Elections [*A publication*] (DLA)
ARMSEF ...... Atmospheric Reentry Materials and Structural Evaluation Facility (MCD)
Arms Elect Cas... Armstrong's Cases of Contested Elections, New York [*A publication*] (DLA)
ARMSH .... Armature Shunt [*Electromagnetism*] (IAA)
ARMSHT ...... Armature Shunt [*Electromagnetism*]
ARMSI .... Alaska Resources for the Moderately/Severely Impaired (EDAC)
ARMSLC ...... Army Missile Command (MUGU)
Arms Mac & Og... Armstrong, Macartney, and Ogle's Irish Nisi Prius Reports [*A publication*] (DLA)

Arms M & O... Armstrong, Macartney, and Ogle's Irish Nisi Prius Reports [*A publication*] (DLA)
ARMSPAC.... Aircraft Resources Management System, Pacific [*Military*] (NVT)
ArmSSR...... Armenian Soviet Socialist Republic
Arms Tr ...... Armstrong's Limerick Trials [*Ireland*] [*A publication*] (DLA)
Armstrong M & O (Ir)... Armstrong, Macartney, and Ogle's Irish Nisi Prius Reports [*A publication*] (DLA)
Armstrong St C... Armstrong State College (GAGS)
Armstrong U... Armstrong University (GAGS)
ARMT.......... Armament (AFM)
armt.......... Armature (VRA)
ARMTA .... Alberta Registered Music Teachers' Association (AC)
ARMTE........ Army Materiel Test and Evaluation Directorate [*White Sands Missile Range, NM*]
ARMTE........ Army Missile Test and Evaluation
armtr .... Armature
ARMTR .... Armature
Armtrn .... Armatron International, Inc. [*Associated Press*] (SAG)
ARMTS .... Advance RADAR Maintenance Target Set (DWSG)
ARMU .... Addressable Remote Multiplexer Unit (MCD)
ARMU .... Associated Rocky Mountain Universities [*AEC*]
ARMV .... Arabis Mosaic Virus [*Plant pathology*]
ARMVAL ..... Advanced Antiarmor Vehicle Evaluation Test (RDA)
ArmWI .... Armstrong World Industries, Inc. [*Formerly, Armstrong Cork Co.*] [*Associated Press*] (SAG)
ARMX .... Aramex International Ltd. [*NASDAQ symbol*] (SAG)
ArmxIntl...... Aramex International Ltd. [*Associated Press*] (SAG)
Army Law ... Army Lawyer [*A publication*] (AAGC)
ARN .... Aboth [*or Avot*] d'Rabbi Nathan (BJA)
ARN .... Acorn Resources Ltd. [*Vancouver Stock Exchange symbol*]
ARN .... Action and Reply Notice (SAA)
ARN .... Additional Reference Number [*NASA*] (NASA)
ARN .... Advanced Remote Node [*Bay Networks*] [*Computer science*]
ARN .... Airborne RADAR Navigational Aid (MCD)
ARN .... Airborne Radio Navigation
ARN .... Air Nova, Inc. [*Canada ICAO designator*] (FAAC)
ARN .... Air Reporting Net (NATG)
ARN .... Alteration Request Number
ARN .... American Realty Corp. [*NYSE symbol*] (SPSG)
ARN .... American Re Corp. Capital [*NYSE symbol*] (SAG)
ARN .... Amer Re Corp. [*NYSE symbol*] (TTSB)
ARN .... Animal Rights Network (EA)
arn .... Araucanian [*MARC language code Library of Congress*] (LCCP)
ARN .... Arena
ARN .... Armata Revoluzione Nucleare [*Armed Revolutionary Nucleus*] [*Italy*]
ARN .... Arnold Ranch [*California*] [*Seismograph station code, US Geological Survey*] (SEIS)
Arn.............. Arnold's English Common Pleas Reports [*1838-39*] [*A publication*] (DLA)
Arn.............. Arnot's Criminal Trials [*1536-1784*] [*Scotland*] [*A publication*] (DLA)
Arn.............. Arnould on Marine Insurance [*A publication*] (DLA)
ARN .... Association of Rehabilitation Nurses (EA)
ARN .... Atmospheric Radio Noise
ARN .... Stockholm [*Sweden*] Arlanda Airport [*Airport symbol*] (OAG)
ARNA......... Alfa Romeo Nissan Autoveicoli [*Italian-Japanese alliance for the joint manufacture of automobiles with Alfa engines and Nissan bodies*]
ARNA......... American Radiological Nurses Association (EA)
ARNA......... Arab Revolution News Agency
ArNA......... Arkansas Nurses Association (SRA)
ARNA......... Army with Navy [*Personnel*]
ARNA......... Association of Radio News Analysts [*Later, ARTNA*]
Arn & H ...... Arnold and Hodges' English Queen's Bench Reports [*1840-41*] [*A publication*] (DLA)
Arn & HBC... Arnold and Hodges' English Bail Court Reports [*A publication*] (DLA)
Arn & Hod ... Arnold and Hodges' English Queen's Bench Reports [*1840-41*] [*A publication*] (DLA)
Arn & Hod BC... Arnold and Hodges' English Bail Court Reports [*A publication*] (DLA)
Arn & Hod PC... Arnold and Hodges' English Practice Cases [*A publication*] (DLA)
Arn & Hod Pr Cas... Arnold and Hodges' English Practice Cases [*A publication*] (DLA)
ARND.......... Around (FAAC)
ARNE .... Accion Revolucionaria Nacional Ecuatoriana [*National Revolutionary Action*] [*Ecuador*] [*Political party*]
ARNE .... Accountant's Resource Network [*Information service or system*] (IID)
ArNeJM........ James Logan Morgan, Jr., Newport, AR [*Library symbol Library of Congress*] (LCLS)
Arn El Cas ... Arnold's Election Cases [*England*] [*A publication*] (DLA)
ARnet.......... Alberta Research Network [*Computer science*] [*Canada*] (TNIG)
ARNEWS..... Army News Service
ARNG.......... Arcing (MSA)
ARNG.......... Army National Guard
ARNG.......... Arrange (AABC)
ARNGMIS ... Army National Guard Management Information System (GFGA)
ARNG-TSP ... Army National Guard Troop Structure Program
ARNGUS ..... Army National Guard of the United States
ARNI .... Adenine Ribose Naphthaline Imide [*Genetics*]
ARNI .... Association of Rhodesian and Nyasaland Industries
Arn Ins........ Arnould on Marine Insurance [*A publication*] (DLA)
ArNIr .... William F. Laman Public Library, North Little Rock, AR [*Library symbol*] [*Library of Congress*] (LCLS)
ARNMD....... Association for Research in Nervous and Mental Disease (EA)
Arn Mun Cor... Arnold's Municipal Corporations [*A publication*] (DLA)
ARNN.......... Analog Recurrent Neural Network [*Computer science*]
ARNN.......... Association of Registered Nurses of Newfoundland (AC)

ARNO.......... Association of Retired Naval Officers [*British military*] (DMA)
Arnold........ Arnold Industries, Inc. [*Associated Press*] (SAG)
Arnold........ Arnold's English Common Pleas Reports [*1838-39*] [*A publication*] (DLA)
Arnold & H... Arnold and Hodges' English Queen's Bench Reports [*1840-41*] [*A publication*] (DLA)
ARNOON ..... Afternoon (ROG)
ARNOT........ Area Notice (FAAC)
Arnot Cr C ... Arnot's Criminal Cases [*1536-1784*] [*Scotland*] [*A publication*] (DLA)
ARNOVA ..... Association for Research on Nonprofit Organizations and Voluntary Action (EA)
ARNP.......... Advanced Registered Nurse Practitioner
ARNPrA....... Amer Re Capital 8.50% 'QUIPS' [*NYSE symbol*] (TTSB)
Arn Pub M ... Arnold. Public Meetings and Political Societies [*1833*] [*A publication*] (DLA)
Arn Pub Meet... Arnold. Public Meetings and Political Societies [*1833*] [*A publication*] (DLA)
ARNS.......... Airborne Reference Noise Source (MCD)
ARNT.......... Arylhydrocarbon-Receptor Nuclear Translocator [*Genetics*]
ARNTCL ...... Aeronautical
ARNX.......... Aronex Pharmaceuticals [*NASDAQ symbol*] (TTSB)
ARNX.......... Aronex Pharmaceuticals, Inc. [*NASDAQ symbol*] (SAG)
ARO .... Adaptec RAIDport Option [*Computer science*]
ARO .... Advanced Research Objective (MCD)
ARO .... Aerial Refueling Operator (MCD)
ARO .... After Receipt of Order
ARO .... Airborne Range Only [*RADAR ranging set for use with various gun computers*]
ARO .... Airport Reservation Office [*FAA*] (TAG)
ARO .... Airport Reservations Office (FAAC)
ARO .... Air Radio Officer
ARO .... Air Research Organization (SAA)
ARO .... Air Traffic Services Reporting Office [*Aviation*]
ARO .... Algonquin Radio Observatory [*Research center*] (RCD)
ARO .... Alignment Requirements Outline (MCD)
ARO .... All Rods Out [*Nuclear energy*] (NRCH)
ARO .... Alternative Regulatory Option [*Environmental Protection Agency*] (GFGA)
ARO .... Applied Research Objective
ARO .... Arboletas [*Colombia*] [*Airport symbol*] (OAG)
ARO .... Area Records Officer (MCD)
ARO .... Armeno Resources, Inc. [*Vancouver Stock Exchange symbol*]
ARO .... Army Research Office [*Research Triangle Park, NC*]
ARO .... Army Routine Order
Aro .... Aromatics [*Organic chemistry*]
ARO .... Arrow Aviation Ltd. [*Canada ICAO designator*] (FAAC)
ARO .... Arta Observatory [*Djibouti*] (SEIS)
ARO .... Asian Regional Organization
ARO .... Assembly and Rework Operation
ARO .... Assistant Research Officer [*Ministry of Agriculture, Fisheries, and Food*] [*British*]
ARO .... Associate for Research in Ophthalmology (DMAA)
ARO .... Association for Research in Ophthalmology [*Later, ARVO*] (EA)
ARO .... Audio Receive Only (NTCM)
ARO .... Authorized Review Officer
ARO .... Automatic Range Only
ARO .... Automatic Recovery Option [*NCR Corp.*] (NITA)
ARO .... Auxiliary Readout (CAAL)
ARO .... Rosemary Public Library, Alberta [*Library symbol National Library of Canada*] (NLC)
AROC .... Air Rescue Operations Center [*Air Force*]
AROC .... Alfa Romeo Owners Club (EA)
AROC .... American River Oil [*NASDAQ symbol*] (TTSB)
AROC .... American River Oil Co. [*NASDAQ symbol*] (SAG)
AROC .... Rochester Public Library, Alberta [*Library symbol National Library of Canada*] (NLC)
AROCA........ Alfa Romeo Owners' Club of Australi
AROCC........ Association for Research of Childhood Cancer (EA)
AROD.......... Airborne Ranging and Orbit Determination System
AROD.......... Airborne Remotely Operated Device [*Marine Corps*]
ARO-D .... Army Research Office - Durham
ARODS........ Airborne RADAR Orbital Determination System
ARODYN ..... Aerodynamics
ARO-E .... Army Research Office - Europe
AROF .... Atomic Resonance Optical Filter (MCD)
ARO-FE .... Army Research Office - Far East (AABC)
AROI .... Annual Return of Investment [*Business term*]
AROICC........ Area Resident Officer-in-Charge of Construction (DNAB)
ARO-ICFTU... Asian Regional Organization - International Confederation of Free Trade Unions
ARO-J .... Army Research Office - Japan
AROM .... Active Range of Motion [*Medicine*]
AROM .... Alterable Read-Only Memory [*Computer science*]
AROM .... Aromatic (MSA)
AROM .... Artificial Rupture of Membrane [*Medicine*] (CPH)
AROM .... Associative Read-Only Memory [*Computer science*] (IAA)
AROMAT ...... Aromatica [*Essence*] [*Chemistry*] (ROG)
ARON .... Aaron Rents [*NASDAQ symbol*] (TTSB)
ARON .... Aaron Rents, Inc. [*NASDAQ symbol*] (NQ)
ARONA .... Aaron Rents Cl'A' [*NASDAQ symbol*] (TTSB)
AronexPh...... Aronex Pharmaceuticals, Inc. [*Associated Press*] (SAG)
AR (Ont) ...... Ontario Appeal Reports [*A publication*] (DLA)
AronxPh........ Aronex Pharmaceuticals, Inc. [*Associated Press*] (SAG)
AROP .... Activity Reorder Point [*Military*] (AFIT)
AROP .... Association pour le Rayonnement de l'Opera de Paris [*France*]

AROPS	Association of Representatives of Old Pupils' Societies [*British*]
AROPS	Association of Representatives of Old Pupils' Societies (AIE)
AROS	Advance Ross Corp. [*NASDAQ symbol*] (NQ)
AROS	Alterable Read-Only Operating System [*Computer science*]
A/ROS	American Indian Radio on Satellite
AROTC	Air Reserve Officers' Training Corps [*Air Force*]
AROTC	Army Reserve Officers Training Corps (AEE)
AROU	Aviation Repair and Overhaul Unit
ARO/URI	Army Research Office/University Research Initiative (RDA)
AROUSPHS	Association of Reserve Officers of the US Public Health Service [*Defunct*] (EA)
AROW	Apprenticeship, Referral, and Outreach for Women [*An association Defunct*] (EA)
AROW	Arrow Bank Corp. [*NASDAQ symbol*] (NQ)
AROW	Arrow Financial [*NASDAQ symbol*] (TTSB)
AROWA	Applied Research: Operation Weather Analysis [*Navy*]
ArowE	Arrow Electronics, Inc. [*Associated Press*] (SAG)
AROWF	Association of Retailer-Owned Wholesalers in Foodstuffs [*Later, ACROWE*] (EAIO)
ArowFn	Arrow Bank Corp. [*Associated Press*] (SAG)
ArowInt	Arrow International, Inc. [*Associated Press*] (SAG)
AROY	American Romanian Orthodox Youth (EA)
ARP	Abrasion-Resistant Print Coating [*for plastic laminates*] [*Nevamar*]
ARP	Absolute Refractory Period
ARP	Accept Response (IAA)
ARP	Account Reconciliation Plan
ARP	Acreage Reduction Program [*Department of Agriculture*] (GFGA)
ARP	Acres, Roods, Perches [*Land measurement*] [*British*] (ROG)
ARP	Active Recording Program (SAA)
ARP	Active Rest Point (IAA)
ARP	Address Resolution Protocol [*Telecommunications*] (BYTE)
ARP	Adiabatic Rapid Passage [*Physics*]
ARP	Adjustable-Rate Preferred Stock (MHDB)
ARP	Adjustable Rear Plate [*Air conditioning systems*] [*Automotive engineering*]
ARP	Adult Retraining Program
ARP	Advanced Reentry Program [*Aerospace*]
ARP	Advanced Research Projects
ARP	Aeronautical [*or Aerospace*] Recommended Practice
ARP	Aero Rifle Platoon [*Military*] (VNW)
ARP	Aerospace Recommended Practice (MCD)
ARP	Aerospace Reference Project [*Formerly, ATP*] [*Library of Congress*]
ARP	After Receipt of Proposal
ARP	Age Replacement Policy (PDAA)
ARP	Agree en Relations Publiques [*Canada*] (DD)
ARP	Airborne RADAR Platform [*Air Force*]
ARP	Aircraft Recommended Practice (DNAB)
ARP	Aircraft Reference Point
ARP	Aircrew Respiratory Protection
ARP	Airport Reference Point
ARP	Airports [*Public-performance tariff class*] [*British*]
ARP	Air Raid Precautions [*British World War II*]
ARP	Air Raid Protection (NATG)
ARP	Air Refueling Probe
ARP	Air Report [*Aviation*]
ARP	Albanian Republican Party [*Partia Republikane Shqiptare*] [*Political party*] (EY)
ARP	Alternativa Revolucionaria del Pueblo [*Bolivia*] [*Political party*] (EY)
ARP	Alternative Release Procedures (MCD)
ARP	Alternator Research Package
ARP	Altitude Reconnaissance Probe (MUGU)
ARP	American Registry of Pathologists
ARP	American Registry of Pathology (EA)
ARP	American Relief for Poland [*Defunct*] (EA)
ARP	Ammunition Refilling Point
ARP	Ammunition Resupply Projectile [*Military*] (RDA)
ARP	Analogous Random Process (PDAA)
ARP	Analytical Rework Program [*Navy*] (NG)
ARP	Angle-Resolved Photoemission (MCD)
ARP	Animal Resources Program [*Bethesda, MD*] [*Department of Health and Human Services*] (GRD)
ARP	Annunciator Response Procedure [*Nuclear energy*] (NRCH)
ARP	Antenna Radiation Pattern
ARP	Antilles Research Program [*Yale University*]
ARP	Antiradiation Projectile
ARP	Anti-Revolutionaire Partij - Evangelische Volkspartij [*Antirevolutionary Party*] [*Netherlands Political party*] (PPW)
ARP	Aragip [*Papua New Guinea*] [*Airport symbol*] (OAG)
arp	Arapaho [*MARC language code Library of Congress*] (LCCP)
ARP	Archaeology Research Program [*Southern Methodist University*] [*Research center*] (RCD)
ARP	Arctic Red Resources [*Vancouver Stock Exchange symbol*]
ARP	Area Redevelopment Program
ARP	Argonne Reactor Physics [*AEC*] (PDAA)
Arp	Ariprandus [*Flourished, 12th century*] [*Authority cited in pre-1607 legal work*] (DSA)
ARP	Arizona Public Services [*NYSE symbol*] (SPSG)
ARP	Armament Recording Program [*Military*]
ARP	Armament Release Panel (DNAB)
ARP	Army Research Plan
ARP	Arpeggio [*Music*]
Arp	Arpeggio [*Record label*] [*Italy*]
ARP	As-Run Procedure [*Military*] (MCD)
ARP	Assimilation Regulatory Protein [*Medicine*] (DMAA)
ARP	Assisted Rental Program [*Canada*]
ARP	Associated Reformed Presbyterian
ARP	Association for Realistic Philosophy [*Defunct*] (EA)
ARP	Association of Retired Persons International [*Later, IARP*]
ARP	At Risk Period (MAE)
ARP	At Risk Provision (DICI)
ARP	Attack Reference Point
ARP	Autofocus RADAR Projector
ARP	Automatic Recovery Process (MCD)
ARP	Automatic Relative Plotter (IAA)
ARP	Automatic Reporting Post [*Air defense*] [*NATO*] (NATG)
ARP	Automation and Robotics Panel
ARP	Azimuth Reset Pulse
ARP	Societe d'Exploitation Aeropostale [*France ICAO designator*] (FAAC)
ARPA	Advanced Research Projects Agency [*Later, DARPA*] [*DoD*]
ARPA	Alabama Recreation and Parks Association (SRA)
ARPA	American Rape Prevention Association (EA)
ARPA	American Red Poll Association (EA)
ARPA	Archaeological Resources Protection Act
ARPA	Archeological Resources Protection Act [*1979*]
ARPA	Arctic Research and Policy Act of 1984
ARPA	Area RADAR Prediction Analysis (PDAA)
ARPA	Arizona Rock Products Association (SRA)
ARPA	Association of Representatives of Professional Athletes (EA)
ARPA	Association pour les Recherches sur les Parodontopathies [*International Association for Research in Paradentosis*]
ARPA	Australian Retinitis Pigmentosa Association
ARPA	Australian Rural Publishers' Association
ARPA	Automatic RADAR Plotting Aids
ARPAC	Agricultural Research Policy Advisory Committee [*Terminated, 1977*] [*Department of Agriculture*]
ARPAC	Army Pacific (CINC)
ARPAD	Army Armament Research and Development Command Product Assurance Directorate
ARPANET	Advanced Research Projects Agency Network [*DoD*]
ARPARSCHCEN	Advanced Research Projects Agency Research Center [*DoD*] (DNAB)
ARPAS	Air Reserve Pay and Allowance System
ARPAS	Automated Resource Planning and Analysis System (MCD)
ARPAT	Advanced Research Projects Agency Terminal [*DoD*]
ArPb	Pine Bluff and Jefferson County Public Library, Pine Bluff, AR [*Library symbol Library of Congress*] (LCLS)
ArPbUA	University of Arkansas at Pine Bluff, Pine Bluff, AR [*Library symbol Library of Congress*] (LCLS)
ARPC	Air Raid Precautions Controller [*British World War II*]
ARPC	Air Reserve Personnel Center [*Air Force*]
ARPC	Annual Report Producers Council
ARPC	Association de Recyclage du Polystyrene du Canada (AC)
ARPCBA	Australian Red Poll Cattle Breeders' Association
ARPCFT	Automated Reiter Protein Complement - Fixation Test (PDAA)
ARPC Ionospheric Bull	Australia. Radio Propagation Committee. Ionospheric Bulletin [*A publication*]
ARPCS	Atmospheric Revitalization Pressure Control System (MCD)
ARPD	Advanced Research Planning Document
ARPD	Advanced Research Program Directive (MCD)
ARPD	Automatic Radar Plotting Disc [*Navy*]
ARPD	Autosomal Recessive Polycystic Disease [*Medicine*] (DMAA)
ARPDP	Association of Rehabilitation Programs in Data Processing (EA)
ARPE	American Registry of Professional Entomologists (EA)
ARPE	Army Physiological Research Establishment [*British*]
ARPEFS	Angle-Resolved Photoemission Extended Fine Structure [*Analytical technique*]
ARPEL	Asistencia Reciproca Petrolera Estatal Latinoamericana [*Mutual Assistance of the Latin American Government Oil Companies*] (EAIO)
ARPERCEN	Army Reserve Personnel Center [*St. Louis, MO*] (INF)
ARPES	Angle-Resolved Photoelectron Spectroscopy
ARPESH	Accurate and Reliable Prototype Earth Sensor Head [*NASA*]
ARPFA	Alberta Registered Professional Foresters Association (AC)
ARPFNB	Association of Registered Professional Foresters of New Brunswick [*Association des Forestiers Agrees du Nouveau-Brunswick*] (AC)
ARPG	Asphalt Rubber Producers Group (EA)
ARPI	Absolute Rod Position Indication [*Nuclear energy*] (NRCH)
ARPI	Analog Rod Position Indicator [*Electronics*] (IAA)
ARPI	Automotive Refrigeration Products Institute (EA)
ARPIC	Aerospace Radioisotope Power Information Center (KSC)
ARPKD	Autosomal Recessive Polycystic Kidney Disease [*Medicine*]
ARPM	Average Revenue per Message
ARPMA	Advanced Remotely Piloted Modular Aircraft (MCD)
ARPMA	Aluminium Rolled Products Manufacturers Association [*British*] (DBA)
ARPMV	Advanced Road Profile Measurement Vehicle [*Suspension design and testing*] [*Automotive engineering*]
ARPN	Aircraft and Related Procurement, Navy
Arpn	Ariprandus [*Flourished, 12th century*] [*Authority cited in pre-1607 legal work*] (DSA)
ARPNET	Advance Research Projects Agency Network [*Australia*]
ARPO	Acid Rain Policy Office [*Environmental Protection Agency*] (GFGA)
ARPO	Air Raid Precautions Officer [*British World War II*]
ARPO	Applied Research Program
ARPO	Arkansas Post National Monument
ARPO	Arpeggio [*Music*]
ARPO	Association of Resort Publicity Officers [*British*] (BI)
ARPP	Africa Research and Publications Project
ARPPRN	Adenine-D-ribose-phosphate-phosphate-D-ribose-nicotinamide [*Also, NAD, DPN*] [*Biochemistry*]
ARPPrQ	Arizona Pub SvAdj Rt Q Pfd [*NYSE symbol*] (TTSB)

ARPPrW...... Arizona Pub Svc $1.8125 Pfd [*NYSE symbol*] (TTSB)
ARPR.......... Academy of Religion and Psychical Research (EA)
ARPR.......... Advanced RADAR Pattern Recognition
ARPR.......... Automatic RADAR Pattern Recognition (MCD)
ArPreC........ Nevada County Library, Prescott, AR [*Library symbol Library of Congress*] (LCLS)
ARPRINT...... Army Program for Individual Training
ARPRO........ Army Plant Representative Office (AAGC)
ARPROIMREP... Arrival Further Proceed Immediately and Report [*Navy*]
ARPROPORICH... Arrival Further Proceed Port in which Activity Designated May Be [*Navy*]
ARPRT........ Airport
ARPRT........ Airport
ARPS.......... Adjustable Rate Preferred Stock
ARPS.......... Advanced RADAR Processing System
ARPS.......... Advanced Real-Time Processing System (PDAA)
ARPS.......... Advanced Regional Prediction System [*Marine science*] (OSRA)
ARPS.......... Advanced Regional Prediction System (USDC)
ARPS.......... Aerospace Research Pilot School [*Air Force*]
ARPS.......... Air Reserve Pay System (AFM)
ARPS.......... Associate of the Royal Photographic Society [*British*]
ARPS.......... Association of Railway Preservation Societies Ltd. [*British*]
ARPS.......... Atmospheric Research Program Staff [*Environmental Protection Agency*] (GFGA)
ARPS.......... Australian Red Poll Society
ARPS.......... Automatic RADAR Plotting System [*Collision avoidance aid*]
ARPSA........ Army Postal Service Agency (AFM)
ARPSC........ Amateur Radio Public Service Corps
ARPSE........ Aerospace Research Pilot School - Edwards Air Force Base [*Air Force*]
ARPSIM....... Antiradiation Projectile Simulation (MCD)
ARPT.......... Airport
ARPT.......... American Registry of Physical Therapists [*Defunct*] (EA)
ARPT.......... Army Registry of Physical Therapists
ArPTA........ American Physical Therapy Association, Arkansas Chapter (SRA)
ARPTT........ Air Refueling Part Task Trainer
ARPU.......... American Racing Pigeon Union (EA)
ARPV.......... Advanced Remotely Piloted Vehicle [*Aviation*] (AIA)
ARQ............ Accept Request (IAA)
ARQ............ Acquisition Review Quarterly [*A publication*] (AAGC)
ARQ............ Andoraq Resources Corp. [*Vancouver Stock Exchange symbol*]
ARQ............ Annual Review Questionnaire [*Military*] (AABC)
ARQ............ Answer-Return Query
Ar Q........... Arithmetic Quotient (BARN)
ARQ............ Armstrong Air, Inc. [*Canada ICAO designator*] (FAAC)
ARQ............ Association des Restaurateurs du Quebec [*Quebec Restaurant Association*] (AC)
ARQ............ Asterriquinone [*Antineoplastic drug*]
ARQ............ Australian Resources Quarterly [*A publication*]
ARQ............ Automated Response to Query
ARQ............ Automatic Error Request Equipment [*Aviation*]
ARQ............ Automatic Repeat Request [*Computer science*] (MCD)
ARQ............ Automatic Request (IAA)
ARQ............ Automatic Request [*Computer science*] (DOM)
ARQ............ Automatic Request for Correction (NITA)
ARQ............ Automatic Retransmission Queue [*Computer science*] (HGAA)
ARQ............ Automatic Retransmission Request for Correction [*Computer science*] (NTCM)
ARQL.......... ArQule, Inc. [*NASDAQ symbol*] (SAG)
ArQule........ ArQule, Inc. [*Associated Press*] (SAG)
ARR............ Academically-Related Research
ARR............ Accounting Rate of Return (ADA)
ARR............ Advanced Restricted Report
ARR............ Advanced Robotics Research
ARR............ Advanced Rocket Ramjet (MCD)
ARR............ Advance Release Record (AAG)
ARR............ Aerial Refueling Receptacle (MCD)
ARR............ Aeronautical Radionavigation RADAR
ARR............ Aerora SA [*Mexico ICAO designator*] (FAAC)
ARR............ Aerospace Rescue and Recovery
ARR............ AFOS [*Automation of Field Operations and Services*] Regional Representative [*National Weather Service*] (NOAA)
ARR............ Airborne Radio Receiver
ARR............ Airborne Reference RADAR (PDAA)
ARR............ Aircraft Radio Regulations
ARR............ Air Regional Representative
ARR............ [*The*] Alaska Railroad [*AAR code*]
ARR............ Allowance Requirement Register (MCD)
ARR............ Altitude Referenced Radiometer
ARR............ Alto Rio Senguerr [*Argentina*] [*Airport symbol*] (OAG)
ARR............ American Railway Reports [*A publication*] (DLA)
ARR............ American Right to Read [*Defunct*] (EA)
ARR............ Anno Regni Regis [*or Reginae*] [*In the Year of the King's, or Queen's, Reign*] [*Latin*]
ARR............ Antenna Radiation Resistance
ARR............ Antenna Rotation Rate (NVT)
ARR............ Antirepeat Relay
ARR............ Aortic Root Replacement [*Medicine*] (DMAA)
ARR............ Arab Report & Record [*A publication*]
ARR............ Arges [*Romania*] [*Seismograph station code, US Geological Survey*] (SEIS)
ARR............ Armour Research Foundation Reactor
ARR............ Army Readiness Region (AABC)
ARR............ Army Retail Requirements
ARR............ Arranged

ARR............ Arrangement [*Music*]
arr............. Arranger [*MARC relator code*] [*Library of Congress*] (LCCP)
ARR............ Array (NASA)
ARR............ Arrester [*Electricity*] (KSC)
Arr............ Arrete [*Decision, Order*] [*French*] (ILCA)
Arr............ Arrian [*Second century AD*] [*Classical studies*] (OCD)
ARR............ Arrington [*England*]
ARR............ Arrival [*or Arrive*]
ARR............ Arrival Message [*Aviation code*]
Ar R........... Arthmetic Ratio (BARN)
ARR............ Asset Report Request
ARR............ Associate for Radiation Research [*British*]
ARR............ Association for Radiation Research [*British*] (NRCH)
ARR............ Association for Regulatory Reform (EA)
ARR............ Aurora, IL [*Location identifier FAA*] (FAAL)
ARR............ Australian Rainfall and Runoff [*Meteorology*]
ARR............ Automatic Rerouting [*Telecommunications*] (TEL)
ARR............ Internal Revenue Bureau Committee on Appeals and Review, Recommendation [*United States*] [*A publication*] (DLA)
ARRA.......... American Road Racing Association (EA)
ARRA.......... Asphalt Recycling and Reclaiming Association (EA)
ARRA.......... Association of Road Racing Athletes (EA)
ARRADCOM... Army Armament Research and Development Command [*Dover, NJ*] (MCD)
Arrang........ Arrangement (DLA)
ARRANGT..... Arrangement
ARRC.......... Aeronautical RADAR Research Complex
ARRC.......... Aerospace Rescue and Recovery Center [*Air Force*] (AFM)
ARRC.......... Air Reserve Records Center
ARRC.......... American Road Race of Champions
ARRC.......... Area Reference Resource Center [*Library network*]
ARRC.......... Army Reserve Review Committee
ARRC.......... Associate of the Royal Red Cross [*British*]
ARRC.......... Association of Regional Religious Communicators (EA)
ARRC.......... Association of Road Racing Clubs [*British*] (DBA)
ARRC.......... Audio Recording Rights Coalition [*Defunct*] (EA)
ARRCOM...... Army Armament Materiel Readiness Command
ARRCOM...... Army Reserve Command (MCD)
ARRCS........ Air Raid Reporting Control Ship [*Navy*] (NVT)
ARRD.......... Arranged
ARRD.......... Arrived
ARRDA........ American Resort and Residential Development Association (EA)
ARRDATE..... Arrival Date (DOMA)
ARRE.......... Alarm Receiving and Reporting Equipment [*Telecommunications*] (TEL)
ARRE.......... Antigen Receptor Response Element [*Immunology*]
ARRE.......... Arrange (ROG)
ARRE.......... Assault Regiment Royal Engineers [*British military*] (DMA)
ARRE.......... Auto Read Reallocation [*Computer science*]
ARRE.......... Average Relative Representation Error (IAA)
ARRED........ Army Forces Readiness Command (MCD)
ARRED........ Army Readiness Region
ARREP........ Arrival Report [*Navy*]
ARREPCOVES... Arrival Report Commanding Officer that Vessel Duty [*Navy*]
ARREPISIC... Arrival Report Immediate Superior in Command [*Navy*]
ARRES........ Automatic RADAR Reconnaissance Exploitation System
ARREST....... Acoustic Response of Reusable Shuttle Tiles (MCD)
AR-RET-ST... Arm Retracting Strut [*Nuclear energy*] (AAG)
ARRF.......... Automatic Recording and Reduction Facility
ARRG.......... Aerospace Rescue and Recovery Group [*Air Force*]
ARRG.......... Association for Research into Restricted Growth [*British*]
ARRGp........ Aerospace Rescue and Recovery Group [*Air Force*] (AFM)
ARRGT........ Arrangement (ROG)
ARRHA........ American RSROA [*Roller Skating Rink Operators Association of America*] Roller Hockey Association (EA)
ARRI.......... Alligator Rivers Research Institute [*Australia*]
ARRI.......... Arriflex [*Camera*] [*Named for manufacturers Arnold and Richter*]
ARRI.......... Automation and Robotics Research Institute [*University of Texas at Arlington*] [*Research center*] (RCD)
arric........... Arricaccato (VRA)
ARRIP........ Australian Rural Research in Progress [*Database*]
ArrisPh....... Arris Pharmaceutical Corp. [*Associated Press*] (SAG)
ARRIVEDREP... Arrival Report [*Navy*] (NVT)
ARRJ.......... Advanced Rocket Ramjet
ARRL.......... Aeronautical Radio and RADAR Laboratory [*Navy*]
ARRL.......... Air Resources Solar Radiation Laboratory [*National Oceanic and Atmospheric Administration*] (NOAA)
ARRL.......... American Radio Relay League (EA)
ARRLF........ ARRL [*American Radio Relay League*] Foundation (EA)
ARRM.......... Association of Residential Resources in Minnesota (SRA)
ARRO.......... Afro-Asian Rural Reconstruction Organization (EAIO)
ARRO.......... All Rock-and-Roll Oldies [*Radio station format*] (WDMC)
ARRO.......... Archery Range and Retailers Organization (EA)
ARRO.......... Arrow International [*NASDAQ symbol*] (TTSB)
ARRO.......... Arrow International, Inc. [*NASDAQ symbol*] (SAG)
ARROTCA.... Army Reserve and Reserve Officers Training Corps Affairs
ARROW....... Army's Requirement to Own and Operate Watercraft (MCD)
ARROW....... Associated Roller Rink Operators of Wisconsin (SRA)
ArrowA........ Arrow Automotive Industries, Inc. [*Associated Press*] (SAG)
ArrowM....... Arrow-Magnolia International, Inc. [*Associated Press*] (SAG)
ArrowTrn..... Arrow Transportation Co. [*Associated Press*] (SAG)
ARRP.......... Acid Rain Research Program [*Environmental Protection Agency*] (GFGA)
ARRPA........ Air Resources Regional Pollution Assessment Model [*Environmental Protection Agency*] (GFGA)

ARRR	American Railway Reports [*A publication*] (DLA)
ARRS	Advanced Rescue and Recovery System [*Proposed VTOL aircraft*] [*Also, ARS*] (MCD)
ARRS	Adverse Reactions Reporting System [*FDA*]
ARRS	Aerospace Rescue and Recovery Service [*Scott Air Force Base, IL*] (MCD)
ARRS	Airborne Radioactivity Removal System (NRCH)
ARRS	Aircraft Refuel/Rearm Study (MCD)
ARRS	Air Recovery and Rescue Service (NASA)
ARRS	Air Rescue and Recovery Squadron
ARRS	American Roentgen Ray Society (EA)
ARRS	Arris Pharmaceutical [*NASDAQ symbol*] (TTSB)
ARRS	Arris Pharmaceutical Corp. [*NASDAQ symbol*] (SAG)
ARRS	Association of Radio Reading Services (EA)
ARRS	Attitude-Referenced Radiometer Study [*NASA*]
ARRSA	American Recreational Racket Sports Association (EA)
ARRSq	Aerospace Rescue and Recovery Squadron [*Air Force*] (AFM)
ARRT	Absolute Reaction Rate Theory [*Physical chemistry*]
ARRT	American Registered Respiratory Therapist
ARRT	American Registry of Radiologic [*or Radiology*] Technologists (EA)
ARRT	American Revolution Round Table
ARRT	Anti-Repression Resource Team (EA)
ARRTC	Aerospace Rescue and Recovery Training Center [*Air Force*] (AFM)
ARRTC	Army Reserve Readiness Training Center [*Fort McCoy, WI*] (INF)
ARRTL	Arranged Total Loss [*Insurance*]
ARRTS	Automated Remote Recognition and Tracking System
ARRTVC	Association for Restriction of Radio and Television Commercials [*Defunct*] (EA)
ARRU	Army Reserve Recruiting Unit
ArRu	Pope County Library, Russellville, AR [*Library symbol*] [*Library of Congress*] (LCLS)
ArRuA	Arkansas Polytechnic College [*Later, Arkansas Technical University*], Russellville, AR [*Library symbol Library of Congress*] (LCLS)
ARRUS	Arrived Within Continental Limits of US [*Navy*]
ARRW	Aerospace Rescue and Recovery Wing [*Air Force*] (MCD)
ARRW	Arrow Transportation [*NASDAQ symbol*] (TTSB)
ARRW	Arrow Transportation Co. [*NASDAQ symbol*] (SAG)
ARRWg	Aerospace Rescue and Recovery Wing [*Air Force*] (AFM)
Arry	Arrhythmia [*Cardiology*] (DAVI)
ARS	Absolute Radiation Scale (PDAA)
ARS	Accelerated Random Search (MCD)
ARS	Accidents and Road Safety [*British*]
ARS	Accion Revolucionaria Socialista [*Socialist Revolutionary Action*] [*Peru*] [*Political party*] (PPW)
ARS	Accounting Research Study
ARS	Accumulator Right Shift (SAA)
ARS	Acid-Rinsing Solution [*Clinical chemistry*]
ARS	Acoustic Rate Sensor (PDAA)
ARS	Action Republicaine et Sociale [*Republican and Social Action*] [*France Political party*] (PPE)
ARS	Active RADAR Seeker
ARS	Active Repeater Satellite [*Air Force*]
ARS	Active Roll Stabilization [*Automotive suspension*]
ARS	Acute Radiation Syndrome [*Medicine*]
ARS	Admiralty Recruiting Service [*British*]
ARS	Adult Recovery Services [*Chemical dependency and rehabilitation*] (DAVI)
ARS	Advanced Reconnaissance Satellite
ARS	Advanced Reconnaissance System (MUGU)
ARS	Advanced Record System [*Air Force*]
ARS	Advanced Recovery Sequencer (DWSG)
ARS	Advanced Reentry System [*Aerospace*]
ARS	Advanced Regulating Station [*British military*] (DMA)
ARS	Advanced Rescue System [*Proposed VTOL aircraft*] [*Also, ARRS*]
ARS	Advanced Rocket System [*Military*] (DOMA)
ARS	Aerial Reconnaissance and Security
ARS	Aerial Reconnaissance Surveillance (MCD)
ARS	Aerial Refueling Squadron (SAA)
ARS	Aeronautical Research Scientist
ARS	Aerospace Research Satellite
ARS	Agricultural Research Service [*Washington, DC Department of Agriculture Also, an information service or system*]
ARS	Agricultural Research Station (ADA)
ARS	Airborne Ranging System
ARS	Airborne Rapid-Scan Spectrometer
ARS	Airborne Refrigeration System
ARS	Airborne Relay Stations (MCD)
ARS	Aircraft Radio Sight (IAA)
ARS	Aircraft Repair Ship [*Navy*]
ARS	Aircraft Report, Special (ADA)
ARS	Aircraft Rocket Subsystem [*Army/Air Force*]
ARSAG	Airline Reservation System [*Aviation*] (ECII)
ARS	Air Regulating Squadron
ARS	Air Rescue Science (NASA)
ARS	Air Rescue Service [*Air Force*]
ARS	Air Rescue Ship
ARS	Air Reserve Squadron [*Air Force*]
ARS	Air Revitalization System (MCD)
ARS	Air Sardinia International [*ICAO designator*] (FAAC)
ARS	Alcohol Recovery Service (DNAB)
ARS	Alizarin Red S [*An indicator*] [*Chemistry*]
ARS	All Red Series [*A publication*]
ARS	Almazy Rossii-Sakha
ARS	Alpha Ray Spectrometer
ARS	Amateur Radio Service (ECII)
ARS	Amateur Radio Station (IDOE)
ARS	American Racing Series
ARS	American Radium Society (EA)
ARS	American Recorder Society (EA)
ARS	American Recreation Society [*Later, APRS*] (EA)
ARS	American Repair Service
ARS	American Residential Services, Inc. [*NYSE symbol*] (SAG)
ARS	American Rhinologic Society (EA)
ARS	American Rhododendron Society (EA)
ARS	American Robot Society (EA)
ARS	American Rocket Society [*Later, AIAA*]
ARS	American Rose Society (EA)
ARS	Amplified Response Spectrum [*Nuclear energy*] (NRCH)
ARS	Anaesthetic Research Society (EAIO)
ARS	Analog Recording System
ARS	Anchored Radiosight
ARS	Anglo-Rhodesian Society (EA)
ARS	Angular Rate Sensor
ARS	Anno Reparatae Salutis [*In the Year of Our Redemption*] [*Latin*]
ARS	Annual Refrigerated Machinery Survey [*of a vessel*] (DS)
ARS	Annual Report to Shareholders [*Securities and Exchange Commission*] (IID)
ARS	Antigen Recognition Site [*Genetics*]
ARS	Antirabies Serum [*Medicine*]
ARS	Apollo Reentry Ship [*NASA*]
ARS	Aragarcas [*Brazil*] [*Airport symbol*] (OAG)
ARS	Area Resupply
ARS	Arizona Revised Statutes [*A publication*] (DLA)
ARS	Armenian Relief Society [*Later, ARSNA*] (EA)
ARS	Armenian Rugs Society (EA)
ARS	Army Radio School [*British military*] (DMA)
ARS	Army Radio Station (IAA)
ARS	Army Records Society (EAIO)
ARS	Army Regulations Supplement [*A publication*] (AAGC)
ARS	Army Relief Society [*AER*] [*Absorbed by*] (EA)
ARS	Arsanilic Acid [*Organic chemistry*]
ARS	Arsenal (AABC)
ARS	Arshan [*Former USSR Seismograph station code, US Geological Survey*] (SEIS)
ARS	Arsine [*Inorganic chemistry*]
ARS	Arson [*Criminology*] (LAIN)
ARS	Arsphenamine [*Antisyphilitic compound*]
ARS	Artina Resources Ltd. [*Vancouver Stock Exchange symbol*]
ARS	Asbestos Roof Shingles [*Technical drawings*]
ARS	Atmosphere Revitalization Section [*or System*] [*NASA*]
ARS	At Reactor Storage [*Nuclear energy*] (NUCP)
ARS	Attitude Reference System (KSC)
ARS	Audio Response System
ARS	Augustan Reprint Society (EA)
ARS	Automated Reference Service [*Ohio State University Libraries*] (OLDSS)
ARS	Automatic Recording Spectrometer
ARS	Automatic Recovery System
ARS	Automatic Reference System (MCD)
ARS	Automatic Route Selection [*Also, MERS*] [*Bell System*] [*Telecommunications*]
ARS	Autonomously Replicating Sequence [*Genetics*]
ARS	Autonomous Replication Sequence [*Genetics*]
ARS	Average Rectified Slope [*FHWA*] (TAG)
ARS	Awaiting Report of Survey (AAGC)
ARS	Ayr Research Station [*Queensland, Australia*]
ARS	Azimuth Reference System (MCD)
ARS	Azobenzenearsonate [*Also, ABA*] [*Organic chemistry*]
ARS	Defence Research Establishment Suffield, Canada Department of National Defence [*Centre de Recherches pour la Defense Suffield, Ministere de la Defense Nationale*] Ralston, Alberta [*Library symbol National Library of Canada*] (NLC)
ARS	Salvage Ship [*Navy symbol*]
Ar S	Sister of Arts
ARS	Special Air-Report [*Aviation code*]
ARS	Sverdlovsk (Arti) [*Former USSR Geomagnetic observatory code*]
ARSA	Aeronautical Repair Station Association (EA)
ARSA	Airport RADAR Service Area [*Aeronautics*]
ARSA	Allied Railway Supply Association [*Later, RSA*]
ARSA	American Reye's Syndrome Association [*Defunct*] (EA)
ARSA	Annual Reevaluation of Safe Areas (MCD)
ARSA	Arylsulfatase A (DMAA)
ARSA	Associate of the Royal Scottish Academy
ARSA	Associate of the Royal Society of Antiquaries [*British*]
ARSA	Associate of the Royal Society of Arts [*British*] (EY)
ARSAG	Austrian RADAR Site Analysis
ARSAG	Aerial Refueling Systems Advisory Group [*Military*] (CAAL)
Ars Am	Ars Amatoria [*of Ovid*] [*Classical studies*] (OCD)
ARSANI	Associate of the Royal Sanitary Institute [*British*] (ROG)
ARSAP	Army Small Arms Program
ARSB	Aircraft Repair and Supply Base (AFIT)
ARSB	Air Reconnaissance Support Battalion
ARSB	Anchored Radio Sonobuoy
ARSB	Automated Repair Service Bureau (TEL)
ARSBA	American Rambouillet Sheep Breeders Association (EA)
ARSC	Aircraft Repair and Supply Center
ARSC	Analog Rotation Speed Control
Ar-SC	Arkansas Supreme Court Library, Little Rock, AR [*Library symbol Library of Congress*] (LCLS)
ARSC	Arylsulfatase C (DMAA)

ARSC	Associate of the Royal Society of Chemistry [British] (DAVI)
ARSC	Association for Recorded Sound Collections (EA)
ARSC	Automatic Resolution Selection Control (NITA)
ARSCM	Associate Member of the Royal School of Church Music [British]
ARSD	Administrative Rules of South Dakota [A publication] (AAGC)
ARSD	Arabian Shield Dev [NASDAQ symbol] (TTSB)
ARSD	Arabian Shield Development Co. [NASDAQ symbol] (NQ)
ARSD	Association of Road Surface Dressing Contractors [British] (BI)
ARSD	Aviation Repair Supply Depot
ARSD	Salvage Lifting Ship [Navy symbol]
ARSDA	Advanced Radiation Space Defense Application (MCD)
ARSE	Alpha Ray Spectrometric Equipment
ArSeH	Harding College, Searcy, AR [Library symbol Library of Congress] (LCLS)
ARSEM	Army Registry of Special Educational Materials (AABC)
ARSEN	Arsenic [Chemical element] (DAVI)
ARSF	Artistic Roller Skating Federation (EA)
ARSH	Associate of the Royal Society of Health [Later, AMRSH] [British]
ARSI	Associate of the Royal Sanitary Institute [British]
ARSI	Automated Roadside Safety Inspection [FHWA] (TAG)
ARSIP	Arrears in Pay [Military]
ARSL	Arsenal (MCD)
ARSL	Associate of the Royal Society of Literature [British]
ARSL	Atmospheric Rendezvous Space Logistics [NASA] (MCD)
ARSLOE	Atlantic Remote Sensing Land Ocean Experiment (MCD)
ARSM	Acute Respiratory System Malfunction [Medicine]
ARSM	Associate of the Royal School of Mines [British] (EY)
ARSM	Associate of the Royal Society of Musicians [British]
ARSM-HACCA...	Alabama Roofing, Sheet Metal, Heating and Air Conditioning Contractors Association (SRA)
ARSN	Air Sensors, Inc. [NASDAQ symbol] (SAG)
ARSN	AirSensors, Inc. [NASDAQ symbol] (NQ)
ARSNA	Armenian Relief Society of North America (EA)
ARSNL	Arsenal
ARSNW	AirSensors Wrrt [NASDAQ symbol] (TTSB)
ARSO	African Regional Organization for Standardization [Kenya]
ARSO	Armament Supply Officer [British Navy slang] [World War II] (DSUE)
ARSOC	Army Special Operations Command (DOMA)
ARSOF	Army Special Operations Forces (GFGA)
ARSOF C4I PYSOP and CA...	Army Special Operation Forces Command, Control, Communications, Computers, Intelligences, Psychological Operations, and Civil Affairs System (RDA)
ARSOFTF	Army Special Operations Forces Task Force (DOMA)
ARSOP	Airborne Remote Sensing Oceanography Project
ARSOTF	Army Special Operation Task Force
ARSP	Aerospace Research Support Program [Air Force]
ARSP	Analog RADAR Signal Processor (MCD)
ARSP	Applied Remote Sensing Program (MCD)
Ars P	Ars Poetica [of Horace] [Classical studies] (OCD)
ARSPA	Aerial Reconnaissance and Surveillance Penetration Analysis [Army]
ARSPAC	Army Space [Command]
ARSPC	Aerospace
ARSPH	Associate of the Royal Society for the Promotion of Health [British] (DAVI)
ARSPOC	Army Space Operations Center
ARSPT	Air Reconnaissance Support (AABC)
ARSR	Air Route Surveillance RADAR
ARSR	Air Route Surveillance RADAR (FAAC)
ARSR	Arrester [Electricity]
ARSR	Australian Religion Studies Review [A publication] (APTA)
ARSS	Active Relaxed Static Stability (MCD)
ARSS	Airborne Remote Sensing System [Coast Guard] (MCD)
ARSS	American Radiator & Standard Sanitary Corp. [Later, American Standard, Inc.]
ARSS	Antiquariorum Regiae Societatis Socius [Fellow of the Royal Society of Antiquaries] [Latin]
ARSS	Atmosphere Reactants Supply Subsystem
ARSSA	Aerial Reconnaissance and Surveillance Survivability Analysis [Army]
ARSSC	Associate of the Royal Society of Sciences [British] (ROG)
ARSSG	Atmosphere Reactants Supply Subsystem Group (MCD)
ArSsJ	John Brown University, Siloam Springs, AR [Library symbol Library of Congress] (LCLS)
ARS/SLA	Automatic Reference System/Sequential Launch Adapter
ARSSS	Automated Ready-Supply Stores System (DNAB)
ARST	Aerial Reconnaissance and Security Troop
ARST	All-Reflecting Schmidt Telescope (PDAA)
ARST	Army Requirements for Space Technologies (MCD)
ARST	Arrest (FAAC)
ARST	Salvage Craft Tender [Navy ship symbol]
ARSTADS	Army Staff Automated Administrative Support System (MCD)
ARSTAF	[The] Army Staff (AABC)
ArStC	Arkansas State University, State University, AR [Library symbol Library of Congress] (LCLS)
ARSTCRT	Aristocrat
ARSTEC	Adaptive Random Search Technique [Computer science] (MHDI)
ARSTN	Airway Radio Station (IAA)
ARSTS	Air Reserve Specialist Training Squadron
ARSTT	Aerostat
ArSuL	Public Library, Sulphur Springs, AR [Library symbol Library of Congress] (LCLS)
ArSuN	New Subiaco Abbey, Subiaco, AR [Library symbol Library of Congress] (LCLS)
ARSUP	Area Supervisor (FAAC)
ARSV	Armored Reconnaissance Scout Vehicle [Army] (AABC)
ARSV-TF	Armored Reconnaissance Scout Vehicle - Task Force (MCD)

ARSW	Arbor Software [NASDAQ symbol] (TTSB)
ARSW	Arbor Software Corp. [NASDAQ symbol] (SAG)
ARSW	Associate of the Royal Scottish Society of [Painting] in Water Colours (BARN)
ART	Absolute Rate Theory [Statistics]
ART	Absolute Retention Time (MAE)
ART	Academic Remedial Training [Navy]
ART	Accelerated Research Initiative [Marine science] (OSRA)
ART	Accredited Record Technician [American Medical Record Association]
ART	Achilles Tendon Reflex Test [Neurology and orthopedics] (DAVI)
ART	ACNielsen Corp. [NYSE symbol] (SAG)
ART	Acoustic Reflex Test [Audiology]
ART	Active Reference Table (HGAA)
ART	Adaptive Recognition Technology [Calera Recognition Systems, Inc.] [Computer science] (PCM)
ART	Adaptive Resonance Theory [Computer science]
ART	Additional Reference Carrier Transmission [Telecommunications] (TEL)
ART	Adenine Ribose Thymine [Genetics]
ART	Adjustable Ranging Telescope [Army] (MCD)
ART	Admissible Rank Test [Statistics]
ART	Advanced Reactor Technology (IEEE)
ART	Advanced Reproductive Technology [Medicine]
ART	Advanced Research and Technology
ART	Aerodynamically Regenerated Trap
ART	Aerosol Release and Transport [Nuclear energy] (NRCH)
ART	Aerotal Aerolineas Territoriales de Colombia Ltd. [ICAO designator] (FAAC)
ART	Africa Resources Trust
ART	Airborne Radiation Thermometer
ART	Aircraft Reactor Test (IAA)
ART	Air Reserve Technician [Air Force]
ART	Airwolf Recovery Team [An association Defunct] (EA)
ART	Alarm Reporting Telephone [Telecommunications] (TEL)
ART	Alarm Response Team [Military]
ART	Alert Reaction Time
ART	Algebraic Reconstruction Technique
ART	Almine Resources [Vancouver Stock Exchange symbol]
ART	Ambiguity Reference Tone
ART	American Radiography Technologists (EA)
ART	American Refrigeration Transit Co. [AAR code]
ART	American Repertory Theatre
ART	Angst, Revolution, Titillation [Art films]
ART	Animated Reconstruction of Telemetry
ART	Annual Renewable Term [Insurance]
ART	Antenna-Receiver-Transmitter (IAA)
ART	Anticipatory Reactor Trips (NRCH)
ART	Approximate Ray Tracing [Of seismic waves]
ART	Arc Resistance Tester
ART	Area Responsibilities Transfer (SAA)
ART	Arithmetic Reading Test [Military]
ART	Arithmetic Reasoning Test
ART	Armatron International, Inc. [AMEX symbol] (SPSG)
ART	Army Regional Threat
ART	Army Reserve Technician
ART	Army Resident Training (MCD)
ART	Arta [Djibouti] [Seismograph station code, US Geological Survey Closed] (SEIS)
ART	Artery [or Arterial]
ART	Article (AFM)
ART	Articulated [or Articulation] (ADA)
ART	Artificer
ART	Artificial (TEL)
ART	Artificial Resynthesis Technology [Mechanical mouth used in dental research]
ART	Artillery
ART	Artillery Repair Truck [British]
art	Artist [MARC relator code] [Library of Congress] (LCCP)
ART	Artist
ART	Artist
art	Art Leather [Abbreviation of artificial] [Visual material] (WDMC)
art	Art Velum [Abbreviation of artificial] [Visual material] (WDMC)
art	Artwork (WDMC)
ART	Asphalt Residual Treatment [Petroleum refining]
ART	Association pour la Recherche en Tourisme [Travel Research Association] [Canada]
ART	Audio Renaissance Tapes [Los Angeles, CA]
ART	Augmented Reentry Test (IAA)
ART	Automated Reagin Test [Serology]
ART	Automated Reasoning Tool (MCD)
ART	Automated Request Transmission (MHDB)
ART	Automatic Radiating Tester
ART	Automatic Radiotheodolite [Meteorology]
ART	Automatic Range Tracker [or Tracking]
ART	Automatic Ranging Telescope [Weaponry] (INF)
ART	Automatic Reasoning Tool (MCD)
ART	Automatic Reporting Telephone [Telecommunications] (TEL)
ART	Average Response Time
ART	Average Retrieval Time (OA)
ART	Aviation Radio Technician
ART	Watertown [New York] [Airport symbol] (OAG)
ARTA	Amateur Radio Technical Abstracts
ARTA	American Reuseable Textile Association (EA)
ARTA	American River Touring Association

ARTA .... Association of Retail Travel Agents (EA)
ARTA .... Aviation Research and Technology Activity [*Moffett Field, CA*] [*Army*] (RDA)
ARTAC .... Advanced Reconnaissance and Target Acquisition Capabilities
ARTACOM .. Army Requirements for Tactical Communications (AABC)
ARTADS ...... Army Tactical Data Systems (AABC)
Art Am .... Art in America [*A publication*] (BRI)
Art & Law ... Art and the Law [*A publication*] (DLA)
Art & T .... Art and Text [*A publication*]
Art Asiae ..... Artibus Asiae [*A publication*]
Art Aust ...... Art and Australia [*A publication*]
ARTB .... Advanced Radar Test-Bed [*Military*] (DOMA)
ARTB .... American Road and Transportation Builders Association
ARTBA .... American Road and Transportation Builders Association (EA)
ARTBASS ..... Army Training Battle Simulation System (MCD)
ARTBSS .... Army Training Battle Simulation System
Art Bull .... Art Bulletin [*A publication*] (BRI)
ARTC .... Addiction Research and Treatment Corp. (EA)
ARTC .... Aerospace Research and Testing Committee (SAA)
ARTC .... Aircraft Research and Testing Committee (MCD)
ARTC .... Air Research and Testing Committee (MUGU)
ARTC .... Air Route Traffic Control [*Aviation*]
ARTC .... ArthroCare Corp. [*NASDAQ symbol*] (SAG)
ARTC .... ArthroCare Corp. [*NASDAQ symbol*] (TTSB)
ARTC .... Articulation Control Subsystem [*NASA*]
ARTC .... Associate of the Royal Technical College, Glasgow [*Formerly, ARCST*]
ARTC .... Association de Recherches Theatrales au Canada (AC)
ARTC .... Association des Routes et Transports du Canada [*Roads and Transportation Association of Canada*]
ARTC .... Auxiliary Rescue Team Chief [*Air Force*]
ARTCA .... Asbestos Removal and Treatment Contractors' Association [*Australia*]
ARTCA .... Association of Round Tables in Central Africa
ARTCC .... Air Route Traffic Control Center [*Aviation*]
ARTCLD ...... Articulated
ARTCS .... Advanced RADAR Traffic Control System [*Air Force*] (AFM)
ARTC(S) ...... Associate of the Royal Technical College (Salford) [*British*]
Art D .... Doctor of Arts
Art Dir .... Art Direction [*A publication*] (BRI)
ARTDO .... Asian Regional Training and Development Organization
ARTE .... Admiralty Reactor Test Establishment (MCD)
ARTEC .... Association of Radio and Television Employees of Canada
ARTEMIS ..... Administrative Real Time Express Mortgage and Investment System (MHDB)
ARTEMIS ..... Automated Reporting, Tracking, and Evaluation Management Information System (SSD)
ARTEMIS ..... Automatic Retrieval of Text from Europe's Multinational Information Service
ARTEMIS ..... Automatic Retrieval of Text through European Multipurpose Information (NITA)
ARTEN .... Anti Racist Teacher Education Network (AIE)
ARTEP .... Army Training and Evaluation Program (AABC)
ArtesRes..... Artesian Resources Corp. [*Associated Press*] (SAG)
ARTF.......... Artificial (MSA)
ARTFL.......... American and French Research on the Treasury of the French Language [*University of Chicago*] [*Research center*] (RCD)
ARTG .... Artistic Greetings [*NASDAQ symbol*] (TTSB)
ARTG .... Artistic Greetings, Inc. [*NASDAQ symbol*] (NQ)
ARTG .... Australian Register of Therapeutic Goods
ARTG .... Azimuth Range and Timing Group (KSC)
ARTH .... Arethusa Off-Shore Ltd. [*NASDAQ symbol*] (SAG)
arth............. Arthritis (DMAA)
arthr........... Athrotomy [*Orthopedics*] (DAVI)
arthro.......... Arthroscopy [*Orthopedics*] (DAVI)
ArthroC ...... ArthroCare Corp. [*Associated Press*] (SAG)
ARTI........... Acoustic Ray Trace Indicator (PDAA)
ARTI........... Acute Respiratory Tract Illness
ARTI........... Advanced Rotorcraft Technology Integration (MCD)
ARTIC .... Articulation
ARTIC .... Associometrics Remote Terminal Inquiry Control System (IEEE)
ARTIC .... [*A*] Real-Time Interface Coprocessor (BTTJ)
Artic Cl....... Articled Clerk [*1867-68*] [*A publication*] (DLA)
Artic Cl Deb.. Articled Clerk and Debater [*1866*] [*A publication*] (DLA)
Artic Cleri .... Articuli Cleri [*Articles of the Clergy*] [*Latin*] (DLA)
Artic Cl J Exam... Articled Clerks' Journal and Examiner [*1879-81*] [*A publication*] (DLA)
Artic Sup Chart... Articuli Super Chartas [*Articles upon the Charters*] [*Latin*] (DLA)
ARTIF......... Artificer (ADA)
ARTIF......... Artificial
artif............. Artificial (VRA)
ARTIFCL ...... Artificial
ARTIL......... Artillery
ARTILL........ Artillery
ARTINS........ Army Terrain Information [*or Intelligence*] System (MCD)
ARTINS........ Automated Terrain Information System
art insem..... Artificial Insemination [*Medicine*] (HGAA)
Art Inst Chicago... [*The*] School of the Art Institute of Chicago (GAGS)
ARTIS .... African Regional Trade Information System [*ECA*] [*United Nations*] (DUND)
ARTIS .... Airborne Real-Time Instrumentation System (MCD)
ARTIS .... ALPHA [*AMC Logistics Program - Hardcore Automated*] Remote Terminal Interactive System
ARTIS .... Automatic Remote Terminal Information System

ARTISS .... Advanced Requirements Tasking Information and Support System (MCD)
ARTISS .... Agricultural Real Time Imaging Satellite System (PDAA)
artist coll .... Artist's Collection (VRA)
ArtistG .... Artistic Greetings, Inc. [*Associated Press*] (SAG)
Art J........... Art Journal [*A publication*] (BRI)
ARTL.......... Aristotle Corp. [*NASDAQ symbol*] (SPSG)
Artl............. Artillerie [*Artillery*] [*German*]
ARTL.......... Awaiting Results of Trial [*Military*]
ARTLF......... Association of Railway Trainmen and Locomotive Firemen (EA)
ARTLY .... Artillery
ARTN .... Artesian Resources Corp. [*NASDAQ symbol*] (SAG)
Art N .... ARTnews [*A publication*] (BRI)
ARTNA .... Artesian Resources'A' [*NASDAQ symbol*] (TTSB)
ARTNA .... Association of Radio-Television News Analysts [*Defunct*] (EA)
ART/NY .... Alliance of Resident Theatres/New York (EA)
ARTO .... Advanced Radiation Technology Office [*Military*]
ARTO .... Area Railway Transport Officer [*British military*] (DMA)
ARTOC .... Army Tactical Operations Central
ARTOS .... Alternative Route to Ordained Service (DICI)
ARTP .... Advanced Resident Training Plan [*Military*] (AABC)
ARTP .... Air Reserve Technician Program [*Air Force*]
ARTP .... Army Rocket Transportation System (MCD)
ARTP .... Association of Reclaimed Textile Processors [*British*] (DBA)
ART PF .... Artist's Proof (ADA)
ART/R .... Airframe Repair Technician-Repairman (AAG)
Artra .... Artra Group, Inc. [*Associated Press*] (SAG)
ARTRAC ...... Advanced Range Testing, Reporting, and Control
ARTRAC ...... Advanced Real-Time Range Control (IEEE)
ARTRIS .... Automated Real-Time Radiography Inspection System
ARTRON ...... Artificial Neuron
ARTRY .... Artery
ARTS .... Acquisition Requirements Tracking System (MCD)
ARTS .... Active RADAR Test System (MCD)
ARTS .... Advanced RADAR Terminal System (IEEE)
ARTS .... Advanced RADAR Traffic Control System [*Air Force*]
ARTS .... Advanced Real-Time Simulation (MCD)
ARTS .... Advanced Real-Time System (MCD)
ARTS .... Advanced Remote Tracking Station (MCD)
ARTS .... Advanced Resource Tracking Spreadsheet [*Scitor Corp.*] [*Computer science*] (PCM)
ARTS .... Advanced Rural Transportation Systems [*FHWA*] (TAG)
ARTS .... Adventist Radio Television Services [*Canada*]
ARTS .... Aerial Relay Transportation System
ARTS .... Airborne RADAR Target Simulator
ARTS .... All-Altitude Air-Bearing Research and Training Simulator
ARTS .... Alpha Repertory Television Service [*Cable-television system*]
ARTS .... American Radio Telephone System (TEL)
ARTS .... Annual Report on Transport Statistics
ARTS .... Annual Research Task Summary
ARTS .... Arkansas Research Test Station
ARTS .... Army Research Task Summary
ARTS .... Army Training Study
ARTS .... Articulated Requirements Transaction System [*NASA*]
ARTS .... Arts Documentation Service [*Australian Council Library*] [*Information service or system*]
ARTS .... Arts Recognition and Talent Search [*National Foundation for Advancement in the Arts*]
ARTS .... Audio Response Time-Shared System [*Computer science*] (MHDB)
ARTS .... Automated Radar Terminal System [*FAA*] (TAG)
ARTS .... Automated Radar Terminal System (GAVI)
ARTS .... Automated RADAR Tracking System (MCD)
ARTS .... Automated Remote Tracking Station (MCD)
ARTS .... Automated Requirements Traceability System (SSD)
ARTS .... Automatic Resistance Test Set
ARTS .... Media Arts Group [*NASDAQ symbol*] (TTSB)
ARTS .... Media Arts Group, Inc. [*NASDAQ symbol*] (SAG)
ARTSD .... Army Armament Research and Development Center [*or Command*] Technical Support Directorate [*Dover, NJ*]
Arts D .... Doctor of Arts
ARTS/DB..... Analysis of Real-Time Systems / Data Base Oriented Systems (MHDI)
ARTSEM ...... Artificial Insemination [*From George Orwell's novel, "1984"*]
Artsft........... Artisoft, Inc. [*Associated Press*] (SAG)
ARTSM .... Association of Road Traffic Sign Makers [*British*] (EAIO)
ARTSN .... Artisan
ARTSq .... Aerospace Reconnaissance Technical Squadron [*Air Force*]
ARTSTC ...... Artistic
ARTSTRY .... Artistry
ARTT.......... Advanced Radio Telecom Corp. [*NASDAQ symbol*] (SAG)
ARTT.......... Annual Review Traveling Team [*NATO*] (NATG)
artt.............. Artikelen [*Articles*] [*Dutch*] (ILCA)
ARTT.......... Automatic Rubber Tensile Tester (PDAA)
ARTTC........ Alaska Rural Teacher Training Corps (EDAC)
ARTTel........ Automated Request Transmission by Telephone (PDAA)
ARTU .... Automatic Range Tracking Unit [*Military*]
ArtVasc....... Arterial Vascular Engineering, Inc. [*Associated Press*] (SAG)
ARTVC .... Association for Restriction of TV Commercials [*Later, ARRTVC*] (EA)
ARTW .... Aerospace Reconnaissance Technical Wing (MCD)
ARTW .... Art's Way Manufacturing Co., Inc. [*NASDAQ symbol*] (NQ)
ARTW .... Art's Way Mfg [*NASDAQ symbol*] (TTSB)
ArtWay........ Art's Way Manufacturing Co. [*Associated Press*] (SAG)
art wks coy... Artisan Works Co. [*British and Canadian*] [*World War II*]
ARTY .... Artillery (AFM)
ARTYLO .... Artillery Liaison Office [*or Officer*] (DNAB)

ARTYMET	Artillery Meteorological Team [*Army*] (ADDR)
arty R	Artillery Reconnaissance [*British and Canadian*] [*World War II*]
ARU	Aboriginal Reconciliation Unit [*Australia*]
ARU	Aboriginal Resource Unit [*University of New England*] [*Australia*]
ARU	Acoustic Resistance Unit
ARU	Address Recognition Unit
ARU	Administrative Reform Unit
ARU	Aeromedical Research Unit [*Army*] (MCD)
ARU	Air Aruba [*ICAO designator*] (FAAC)
ARU	Airborne RADAR Unit [*Aviation*] (FAAC)
ARU	Air Reserve Unit
ARU	Airspace Reservation Unit [*Canada*] (FAAC)
ARU	Alcohol Rehabilitation Unit (DNAB)
ARU	Allure Industries Corp. [*Vancouver Stock Exchange symbol*]
ARU	Alturas, CA [*Location identifier FAA*] (FAAL)
ARU	Alure Resource Corp. [*Vancouver Stock Exchange symbol*]
ARU	American Railway Union
ARU	Analog Remote Unit (MCD)
ARU	Analog Response Unit
ARU	Aracatuba [*Brazil*] [*Airport symbol*] (OAG)
ARU	Arithmetical Unit [*Computer science*] (NITA)
aru	Arkansas [*MARC country of publication code Library of Congress*] (LCCP)
ARU	Armed Resistance Unit (EA)
ARU	Arti [*Former USSR Seismograph station code, US Geological Survey*] (SEIS)
ARu	Assyrische Rechtsurkunden [*A publication*] (BJA)
ARU	Attitude Reference Unit
ARU	Audio Response Unit
ARU	Automatic Range Unit
ARU	Auxiliary Read-Out Unit [*Computer science*] (MHDB)
ArU	University of Arkansas, Fayetteville, AR [*Library symbol Library of Congress*] (LCLS)
ARUB	Authorized Repair Unaccomplished at Base [*Military*] (AFIT)
ARUCC	Association des Registraires d'Universites et de Colleges du Canada [*Association of Registrars of the Universities and Colleges of Canada*]
ARUCC	Association of Registrars of the Universities and Colleges of Canada
ARUG	Air Reserve Unit (General Training)
ArU-H	University of Arkansas, Area Health Education Center, Jonesboro, AR [*Library symbol*] [*Library of Congress*] (LCLS)
ARUM	Rumsey Municipal Library, Alberta [*Library symbol National Library of Canada*] (NLC)
ArU-M	University of Arkansas Medical Center, Little Rock, AR [*Library symbol Library of Congress*] (LCLS)
ArU-Mon	University of Arkansas at Monticello, Monticello, AR [*Library symbol Library of Congress*] (LCLS)
ARUNK	Arrival Unknown [*Aviation*]
Arun Mines...	Arundell on the Law of Mines [*A publication*] (DLA)
ARUPS	Angle-Resolved Ultraviolet Photoelectron Spectroscopy
ARUSA	Abarth Register, USA (EA)
ARUSNP	Air Reserve Unit (General Training, Nonpay)
ARUSP	Air Reserve Unit (General Training, Pay)
ARV	Aeroballistic Reentry Vehicle
ARV	Aerospace Research Vehicle
ARV	AIDS [*Acquired Immune Deficiency Syndrome*]-Associated Retrovirus
ARV	AIDS [*Acquired Immune Deficiency Syndrome*] Related Virus [*Immunology*] (DAVI)
ARV	Airborne Relay Vehicle
ARV	Aircraft Repair Ship [*Navy symbol*]
ARV	Aircraft Rescue Vessel [*Navy*] (MCD)
ARV	Air Recreational Vehicle
ARV	Air Research Vehicle (MCD)
ARV	Alternate Record-Voice
ARV	Alternative Reproduction Vehicle [*Medicine*]
ARV	American Revised Version [*of the Bible*]
ARV	Anterior Right Ventricular Wall [*Cardiology*] (DAVI)
ARV	Aravco Ltd. [*British ICAO designator*] (FAAC)
ARV	Arch Development Corp. [*Vancouver Stock Exchange symbol*]
ARV	Arctic Research Vessel
ARV	Armored Reconnaissance Vehicle (MCD)
ARV	Armored Recovery Vehicle
ARV	Army Vietnam
ARV	Arrive (WGA)
ARV	Arvin Indus [*NYSE symbol*] (TTSB)
ARV	Arvin Industries [*NYSE symbol*] (SAG)
ARV	Avian Retrovirus
ARV	Minocqua/Woodruff, WI [*Location identifier FAA*] (FAAL)
ARV	Rich Valley Public Library, Alberta [*Library symbol National Library of Canada*] (NLC)
ARVA	Aircraft Repair Ship (Aircraft) [*Navy symbol*]
ArVA	Arkansas Vocational Association (SRA)
ARVA	Associate of the Rating and Valuation Association [*British*] (DBQ)
ARVAC	Association of Researchers in Voluntary Action and Community Involvement [*British*]
ARVC	Agricultural Research and Veterinary Centre [*New South Wales, Australia*]
ARVD	Arteriosclerotic Renal Vascular Disease [*Medicine*]
ARVE	Aircraft Repair Ship (Engine) [*Navy symbol*]
ARVEE	Recreational Vehicle [*Formed by phonetic spelling of initials R and V*]
ARVH	Aircraft Repair Ship (Helicopter) [*Navy symbol*]
ARVI	Arrhythmogenic Right Ventricular Dysplasia [*Cardiology*] (DMAA)
ARVI R	ARV Assisted Living [*NASDAQ symbol*] (TTSB)
ARVI	ARV Assisted Living, Inc. [*NASDAQ symbol*] (SAG)
ARVIA	Associate of the Royal Victoria Institute of Architects [*British*]

ARVIC	Association for Religious and Value Issues in Counseling (EA)
ARVIDA	Arthur Vining Davis Corp.
ARVIN	Army of the Republic of Vietnam [*Also, ARVN*] [*South Vietnam*]
Arvin	Arvin Industries, Inc. [*Associated Press*] (SAG)
ARVLA	American Recreational Vehicle Living Association [*Defunct*] (EA)
ARVLiv	ARV Assisted Living, Inc. [*Associated Press*] (SAG)
arvlt	Archivolt (VRA)
ARVm	American Revised Version [*of the Bible*], Margin
ARVN	Army of the Republic of Vietnam [*Also, ARVIN*] [*South Vietnam*] [*Defunct*]
ARVN SEAL..	Army of the Republic of Vietnam Sea, Air, and Land Team (VNW)
ARVO	Association for Research in Vision and Ophthalmology (EA)
ARVP	Accelerated Retirement of Vehicles Program [*Air quality implementation plans*]
ARVP	Arginine-Vasopressin (DMAA)
ARVR 22.....	Anno Regni Victoriae Regina Vicesimo Secundo (DLA)
ARVSG	Air Reserve Volunteer Support Group
ARVX	Aerovox, Inc. [*NASDAQ symbol*] (SAG)
ARW	Advanced Recoilless Weapon (MCD)
ARW	Advanced Research Workshop
ARW	Aerial Refueling Wing [*Aeronautics*]
ARW	Aeroelastic Research Wing (MCD)
ARW	Air-Conditioning and Refrigeration Wholesalers (EA)
ARW	Air Raid Warden
ARW	Air Raid Warning [*Air Force*]
ARW	Air Reserve Wing [*Canada*] (DD)
ARW	American Rescue Workers (EA)
ARW	Ammunition Repair Workshop (NATG)
ARW	Arad [*Romania*] [*Airport symbol*] (OAG)
arw	Arawak [*MARC language code Library of Congress*] (LCCP)
ARW	[*The*] Arkansas Western Railway Co. [*AAR code*]
ARW	Arrow
ARW	Arrow Electronics [*NYSE symbol*] (TTSB)
ARW	Arrow Electronics, Inc. [*NYSE symbol*] (SPSG)
ARW	Arrowfield Resources [*Vancouver Stock Exchange symbol*]
ARW	Arrows Ltd. [*British ICAO designator*] (FAAC)
ARW	Atmospheric Radio Wave
ARW	Attitude Reaction Wheel
ARWA	Alabama Rural Water Association (SRA)
ARWA	American Right of Way Association [*Later, IRWA*] (EA)
ARWA	Associate of the Royal West of England Academy
ARWAB	Army Rotary Wing Aptitude Battery (AABC)
ARWAF	Army Personnel Attached to the Air Force for Duty
ARWARCOL...	Army War College (MCD)
ARWC	Army War College
ARWDS	Afterwards (ROG)
ARWG	Acquisition Reform Working Group [*Coalition of nine industry groups*] (AAGC)
ARWI	Association of Russian War Invalids of World War II (EA)
ARWM	Arrow-Magnolia International, Inc. [*NASDAQ symbol*] (SAG)
ARWM	Arrow-Magnolia Intl. [*NASDAQ symbol*] (TTSB)
ARWR	Advanced RADAR Warning Receiver (MCD)
ARWS	Advanced RADAR Warning System (MCD)
ARWS	Aircraft Response to Wind Spectrum (MCD)
ARWS	Antiradiation Weapon System (NVT)
ARWS	Associate of the Royal Society of Painters in Water Colours [*British*]
ARWS	Associate of the Royal Water-Colour Society [*British*] (ROG)
ARWY	Airway
ARX	Aeroflex, Inc. [*NYSE symbol*] (SAG)
ARX	Air Express, Inc. [*ICAO designator*] (FAAC)
ARX	Air Regenerative Exhaust
ARX	Asbury Park/Monmouth County [*New Jersey*] [*Airport symbol*] (OAG)
ARX	Aurex Resources, Inc. [*Vancouver Stock Exchange symbol*]
ARX	Automatic Retransmission Exchange [*ITT World Communications, Inc.*] [*Secaucus, NJ*] (TSSD)
ARY	Antilles Resources Ltd. [*Vancouver Stock Exchange symbol*]
ARY	Ararat [*Australia Airport symbol Obsolete*] (OAG)
ARY	Argosy Airways [*Canada ICAO designator*] (FAAC)
ARY	Artillery Resources Ltd. [*Vancouver Stock Exchange symbol*]
ARY	Arusha [*Tanzania*] [*Airport symbol*] (AD)
ARY	Australian Rural Youth
ArY	Marion County Library, Yellville, AR [*Library symbol Library of Congress*] (LCLS)
ARY	Ryley Public Library, Alberta [*Library symbol National Library of Canada*] (NLC)
ARYM	Rycroft Municipal Library, Alberta [*Library symbol National Library of Canada*] (NLC)
ARYT	Aryt Optronics Industries Ltd. [*NASDAQ symbol*]
ARYTF	Aryt Inds Ltd [*NASDAQ symbol*] (TTSB)
ArytInd	Aryt Industries Ltd. [*Associated Press*] (SAG)
ARZ	Active Reconnaissance Zone
ARZ	Air Resorts [*ICAO designator*] (FAAC)
ARZ	Arizona Silver Corp. [*Vancouver Stock Exchange symbol*]
ARZ	Aurizon Mines Ltd. [*Toronto Stock Exchange symbol Vancouver Stock Exchange symbol*]
ARZ	Auto-Restricted Zone [*Environmental Protection Agency*] (GFGA)
ARZ	N'Zeto [*Angola*] [*Airport symbol*] (OAG)
ARZA	Association of Reform Zionists of America (EA)
ArzanInt	Arzan International Ltd. [*Associated Press*] (SAG)
Arzi	Hed-Arzi [*Israel*] [*Record label*]
ARZN	Arzan International Ltd. [*NASDAQ symbol*] (SAG)
ARZNF	Arzan Intl(1991) Ltd [*NASDAQ symbol*] (TTSB)
ARZW	Arzan International Ltd. [*NASDAQ symbol*] (SAG)
ARZWF	Arzan Intl(1991) Wrrt [*NASDAQ symbol*] (TTSB)
AS..............	Abilene & Southern Railway Co. [*AAR code*]

AS	Abortion Sydney [*An association Australia*]
AS	Above Scale [*Laboratory*] (DAVI)
aS	Absiemens [*Unit of conductance*]
AS	Abstract Syntax [*Data structure*] [*Computer science*] (TNIG)
AS	Academy of Sciences
AS	Account Sales
AS	Accumulated Surplus [*Profit margin*]
AS	Acetosyringone [*Organic chemistry*]
AS	Acetylstrophanthidin [*Organic chemistry*] (MAE)
AS	Acquisitions Section [*Resources and Technical Services Division of ALA*]
AS	Acquisition Strategy [*Army*] (RDA)
AS	Acrylic Styrene [*Plastics technology*]
AS	Action Socialiste [*Socialist Action*] [*Congo*]
AS	Active Security [*Investment term*]
AS	Active Sleep [*Physiology*]
AS	Act of Sederunt (DLA)
AS	Acton Society [*British*] (EAIO)
AS	Actors Studio (EA)
AS	Acute Salpingitis [*Medicine*] (MEDA)
A-S	Adams-Stokes [*Cardiology*]
AS	Adapter Section [*NASA*] (KSC)
AS	Adapter, Straight
AS	Additional Sources
AS	Address Strobe [*Signal*] [*Computer science*]
AS	Address Syllable (IAA)
AS	Add-Subtract
AS	Adhesion Society (EA)
AS	Administrative Support
AS	Admiral Superintendent [*Obsolete British*]
AS	Advanced Supplementary [*Education level*] [*British*]
AS	Advanced System [*NAS*]
A/S	Advertising/Sales Ratio (WDMC)
AS	Aerial Sensor
AS	Aerial Surveillance (MCD)
AS	Aeronautical Specifications
AS	Aeronautical Standards
AS	Aeronaut Society (EA)
AS	Aerospace (IEEE)
AS	Aerospace Standards
AS	Aerospace Studies [*AFROTC*] (AFM)
AS	Aerospray [*Ionization*] [*Physics*]
AS	Aetherius Society (EA)
As	Aethestan [*King of England, 895-940*] (ILCA)
AS	Affective System
AS	Affirmist Society [*Defunct*] (EA)
AS	African Star [*Decoration*] [*British*]
AS	Afrolit Society [*Defunct*] (EAIO)
AS	Aftersight [*Billing*]
AS	Aged Spouse [*Social Security Administration*] (OICC)
AS	Agency State [*Database Terminology*] (NITA)
AS	Aggregate Supply
AS	Aggressor Squadron [*Air Force*]
AS	Aileron Station (MCD)
AS	Aiming Symbol (DNAB)
AS	Ain Shems (BJA)
AS	Aircraft Standards
AS	Airports Service [*of FAA*]
AS	Air Sacculitis [*Avian pathology*]
AS	Airscoop
AS	Air Screw
AS	Air Seasoned (IAA)
AS	Air Section
AS	Air Service
A-S	Air Shuttle (CDAI)
AS	Airspace (IAA)
AS	Air Specification (NG)
AS	Airspeed
AS	Air Staff [*Air Force*]
AS	Air Station
AS	Air Steward [*British military*] (DMA)
A/S	Air Strike
AS	Air Superiority (MCD)
AS	Air Supply (NRCH)
AS	Air Support
AS	Air Surveillance [*Air Force*]
AS	Air-to-Surface [*Missiles*] (NATG)
as	Akciova Spolecnost [*Joint-Stock Company*]
A/S	Aksjeselskap [*Joint-Stock Company*] [*Norway*] (GPO)
A/S	Aktieselskab [*Joint-Stock Company*] [*Sweden*]
AS	Alaska Airlines, Inc. [*ICAO designator*] (OAG)
AS	Albanian Society (EAIO)
AS	Alcuin Society (EA)
AS	Alimentary Sleep [*Medicine*] (BABM)
AS	Alimentary System [*Medicine*]
AS	Alkan Society [*Surrey, England*] (EAIO)
AS	Alkyl Sulfate [*Surfactant*] [*Organic chemistry*]
AS	Alloter Switch (IAA)
AS	Alloy Steel (IAA)
AS	All-Season
AS	Alongside
AS	Alport Syndrome [*Medicine*]
AS	Al Segno [*At the Sign*] [*Music*] (ROG)
AS	Alternative Society [*British*]
AS	Altostratus [*Also, ALST*] [*Meteorology*]

AS	Aluminium Suisse, SA [*Commercial firm*]
AS	Aluminum and Steel [*Freight*]
AS	Alveolar Sac (MAE)
AS	American Samoa [*Postal code*] [*ANSI two-letter standard code*] (CNC)
as	American Samoa [*MARC country of publication code Library of Congress*] (LCCP)
AS	American Scholar [*A publication*] (BRI)
AS	American Songbag [*A publication*]
AS	American Standard
AS	American Statesmen [*A publication*]
AS	Americas Society (EA)
AS	Amertool Services
AS	Ammeter Switch (MSA)
AS	Ammonia Service [*Military*] (DNAB)
AS	Ammunition Specialist [*Military*] (GFGA)
AS	Amorphous Semiconductor (PDAA)
As	Ampere Second
A's	Amphetamine Sulfate [*Also callde Benzedrine*] [*Pharmacology*] (DAVI)
AS	Amyloid Substance [*Medicine*]
AS	Anal Sphincter [*Anatomy*]
AS	Analytical Stereoplotter (DNAB)
AS	Androsterone Sulfate [*Biochemistry*] (AAMN)
AS	Angelman Syndrome [*Genetics*]
AS	Angled Single [*Outdoor advertising*] (NTCM)
AS	Angle of Sight (IAA)
AS	Angle Shot [*Cinematography*] (NTCM)
AS	Anglican Society (EA)
A-S	Anglo-Saxon [*Language, etc.*]
AS	Ankylosing Spondylitis [*Medicine*]
AS	Annals of Science [*A publication*] (BARN)
AS	Anno Salvatoris [*or Salutis*] [*In the Year of Salvation*] [*Latin*]
AS	Annual Survey (DNAB)
AS	Anomalous Scattering [*Crystallography*]
AS	Anonim Sirketi [*Corporation, Joint-Stock Company*]
AS	Anovulatory Syndrome [*Medicine*] (DMAA)
AS	Answering Service (LAIN)
AS	Antarctican Society (EA)
AS	Antenna Assembly (IAA)
AS	Antennas, Complex [*JETDS nomenclature*] [*Military*] (CET)
AS	Anthologie Sonore [*Record label*] [*France*]
AS	Anthranilate Synthase [*An enzyme*]
AS	(Anthroyloxy)stearic Acid [*Organic chemistry*]
AS	Antisense Orientation
AS	Antiserum [*Immunology*]
A-S	Anti-Spoofing [*Jamming resistance feature on global positioning satellites*] (SSD)
AS	Antistreptolysin [*Immunology*] (MAE)
AS	Antisubmarine
A/S	Antisurface [*Military*] (NVT)
AS	Anxiety Score [*Psychology*]
AS	Anxiety State [*Psychology*]
AS	Aortic Sac [*Cardiology*] (DAVI)
AS	Aortic Stenosis [*Medicine*]
AS	Apollo-Saturn [*NASA*] (MCD)
AS	Application System (ADA)
AS	Applied Science
AS	Apprentice Seaman
AS	Aqueous Solution
AS	Aqueous Suspension
AS	Arator Society [*Defunct*] (EA)
AS	Arba Sicula [*Sicilian Dawn*] (EA)
AS	Arbeit und Sitte in Palaestina [*A publication*] (BJA)
AS	Archeology Section (EA)
AS	Area Source [*Environmental Protection Agency*] (GFGA)
AS	Area Specialized Division [*Army*] (MCD)
AS	Area Supervisor [*Bureau of Apprenticeship and Training*] [*Department of Labor*]
AS	Area Surveillance
AS	Arginase [*An enzyme*]
AS	Argininosuccinate Synthetase [*An enzyme*]
AS	Aristotelian Society [*British*] (EAIO)
AS	Armature Shunt [*Electromagnetism*] (IAA)
AS	Armco, Inc. [*Formerly, Armco Steel Corp.*] [*NYSE symbol*] (SPSG)
AS	Armed Services
AS	Armor School [*Army*] (MCD)
A/S	Arm/Safe (SAA)
AS	Army Security
AS	Army Service [*British*] (ROG)
AS	Army Staff
As	Arsenic [*Chemical element*]
AS	Arteriosclerosis [*Medicine*]
AS	Articulation Score [*Percentage of words correctly understood over a radio channel perturbed by interference*] [*Telecommunications*]
AS	Artificial Satellite
AS	Artificial Sweetener
AS	Artists Space (EA)
AS	Ascendance-Submission [*Psychology*]
AS	Ascent
A/S	Ascent Stage
AS	Ascent Stage [*NASA*] (MCD)
AS	Ashoka Society [*Later, Ashoka: Innovators for the Public*] (EA)
AS	Asia
As	Asia (VRA)

AS	Asia Society (EA)
as----	Asia, Southeastern [*MARC geographic area code Library of Congress*] (LCCP)
AS	Asmonean (BJA)
AS	Assault Squadron [*British military*] (DMA)
AS	Assembler [*Computer science*] (IAA)
AS	Assembly System
AS	Assented Security [*Investment term*]
AS	Assessable Stock [*Investment term*]
AS	Assistant Secretary
AS	Assistant Surgeon (DAS)
AS	Associate in Science
AS	Association for Singles (EA)
AS	Association of Surgeons of Great Britain and Ireland (BI)
AS	Association-Sensation [*Psychology*] (BARN)
AS	As Stated
As	Astigmatism [*Also, Ast*] [*Ophthalmology*]
AS	Astronomy (ROG)
as	Asymmetric [*Chemistry*]
AS	Atherosclerosis [*Medicine*] (MAE)
AS	Atlantic Semiconductor (IAA)
AS	Atmosphere and Space
AS	Atrial Stenosis [*Cardiology*] (AAMN)
AS	At Sight
AS	Attitude Set [*Aerospace*] (MCD)
AS	Audiogenic Seizure [*Neurophysiology*]
AS	Audio Sensitivity
AS	Augmentation System
AS	Augmented Surveyor [*NASA*] (MCD)
AS	Augustan Society (EA)
AS	Auris Sinistra [*Left Ear*] [*Latin*]
AS	Australasian Sketcher [*A publication*]
AS	Australia
AS	Australiana Society
AS	Australian Society [*A publication*] (ADA)
AS	Australian Swimming [*An association*]
AS	Austrian Schilling [*Monetary unit*]
AS	Authorizations Subsystem [*Military*]
AS	Automated System (ACRL)
AS	Automatic Skin [*NASA*] (KSC)
AS	Automatic Sprinkler [*Technical drawings*]
AS	Automatic Switching [*Telecommunications*] (OA)
AS	Automatic Synchronizer
AS	Automation Society (EA)
AS	Autosampler
AS	Auto Sequential (NRCH)
A/S	Auxiliary Stage [*NASA*] (NASA)
AS	Auxiliary Steam [*Nuclear energy*] (NRCH)
AS	Auxiliary Storage [*Computer science*]
A/S	Aux Soins De [*Care Of, c/o*] [*French*]
AS	Availability, Steady
AS	Aviaeskadra [*Russian term for an air squadron*]
AS	Aviation Support Equipment Technician [*Navy rating*]
AS	[*The*] Avicultural Society [*British*]
AS	Axis Select (IAA)
AS	Das Akkadische Syllabar [*A publication*] (BJA)
AS	Dr. Madaus & Co. [*Germany*] [*Research code symbol*]
AS	Hawker Siddeley Aviation Ltd. [*British ICAO aircraft manufacturer identifier*] (ICAO)
As	Oesterreichische Nationalbibliothek, Vienna, Austria [*Library symbol Library of Congress*] (LCLS)
AS	Sister of Arts
AS	Standard Atmosphere
AS	Start of Answer [*Telecommunications*] (TEL)
AS	Submarine Tender [*Navy symbol*]
AS1	Aviation Support Equipment Technician, First Class [*Navy rating*]
AS2	Angel, Second Class [*Classification of angel Clarence Oddbody in 1947 film, "It's a Wonderful Life"*]
AS2	Aviation Support Equipment Technician, Second Class [*Navy rating*]
AS²WRE	American Society of Senior Wire Rope Engineers (EA)
AS3	Aviation Support Equipment Technician, Third Class [*Navy rating*]
AS3AP	Standard Scalable and Portable [*Standard High-Level Query Language*] [*Benchmark test for relational database systems*] (PCM)
AS/400	Application System/400 [*IBM minicomputer series*] (CDE)
ASA	Abort Sensor Assembly [*Apollo*] [*NASA*]
ASA	Accelerated Storage Adapter (IAA)
ASA	Accommodation Sales Authorization (MCD)
ASA	Acetylsalicylic Acid [*Aspirin*]
ASA	Acoustical Society of America (EA)
ASA	Acrylic-Styrene-Acrylonitrile [*Organic chemistry*]
ASA	Acrylonitrile Styrene Acrylate [*Plastics*] [*Organic chemistry*]
ASA	Acrylonitrile-Styrene-Acrylate
ASA	Active Surface Area (MCD)
ASA	Actuarial Society of America [*Later, SA*]
ASA	Adams-Stokes Attack [*Cardiology*] (MAE)
ASA	Adapter Service Area (MCD)
ASA	Adastral Resources Ltd. [*Vancouver Stock Exchange symbol*]
ASA	Adjustable Shock Absorber
ASA	Administrative Support Airlift (MCD)
ASA	Advanced Surveillance Aircraft (MCD)
ASA	Advanced System Avionics [*Air Force*]
ASA	Advertising Standards Authority [*British*]
ASA	Advice Services Alliance [*British*] (DBA)
ASA	Aerospace Amplifier (MCD)

ASA	Aerosurface Amplifier (NASA)
ASA	Aerosurface Servo Amplifier [*NASA*] (NASA)
ASA	Afghanistan Studies Association (EA)
ASA	African Studies Association (EA)
ASA	Aged Services Association [*Australia*]
ASA	Airline Services Association [*ARSA*] [*Absorbed by*] (EA)
ASA	Air Security Agency (MCD)
ASA	Air Services Agreement (DA)
ASA	Air Stagnation Advisories [*National Weather Service*]
ASA	Air Starline AG [*Switzerland ICAO designator*] (FAAC)
ASA	Alabama Sheriff's Association (SRA)
ASA	Alan Stratford and Associates [*Aviation consultants*] [*British*] (ECON)
ASA	Alaska Airlines, Inc. [*ICAO designator*] (FAAC)
ASA	Alberta Simmental Association (AC)
ASA	Alberta Snowmobile Association (AC)
ASA	Alberta Society of Artists [*1931*] [*Canada*] (NGC)
ASA	Alkenyl Succinic Anhydride [*Organic chemistry*]
ASA	Alkylsuccinic Anhydride [*Organic chemistry*]
ASA	Aluminium Stockholders' Association [*British*]
ASA	Aluminum Siding Association [*Later, AAMA*] (EA)
ASA	Amateur Softball Association of America (EA)
ASA	Amateur Swimming Association
ASA	Amegroid Society of America (EA)
ASA	American Sailing Association (EA)
ASA	American Salers Association (EA)
ASA	American Saluki Association (EA)
ASA	American Schizophrenia Association (EA)
ASA	American Schools Association (EA)
ASA	American Schooner Association (EA)
ASA	American Scientific Affiliation (EA)
ASA	American Sentic Association
ASA	American Shark Association (EA)
ASA	American Shellfisheries Association
ASA	American Shiatsu Association (EA)
ASA	American Shorthorn Association (EA)
ASA	American Shrimpboat Association [*Defunct*] (EA)
ASA	American Sightseeing Association [*Later, ASI*]
ASA	American Simmental Association (EA)
ASA	American Ski Association (EA)
ASA	American Snowmobile Association [*Defunct*]
ASA	American Snowplowing Association [*Defunct*] (EA)
ASA	American Society for Abrasives [*Superseded by AES*] (EA)
ASA	American Society for Aesthetics (EA)
ASA	American Society of Agronomy (EA)
ASA	American Society of Anesthesiologists (EA)
ASA	American Society of Appraisers [*Acronym also used as designation awarded to group's senior members*] [*Washington, DC*] (EA)
ASA	American Society of Artists (EA)
ASA	American Society of Auctioneers [*Defunct*] (EA)
ASA	American Society on Aging (EA)
ASA	American Sociological Association (EA)
ASA	American Sociometric Association [*Defunct*] (EA)
ASA	American Soybean Association (EA)
ASA	American Speed Association
ASA	American Sportfishing Association
ASA	American Sportscasters Association (EA)
ASA	American Standards Association [*Later, USASI, ANSI*]
ASA	American Statistical Association (EA)
ASA	American Sternwheel Association (EA)
ASA	American Stomatological Association (DAVI)
ASA	American Student Association (EA)
ASA	American Studies Association (EA)
ASA	American Subcontractors Association (EA)
ASA	American Sugar Alliance (EA)
ASA	American Sunbathing Association (EA)
ASA	American Supply Association (EA)
ASA	American Surety Association (EA)
ASA	American Surfing Association (EA)
ASA	American Surgical Association (EA)
ASA	American Survival Association [*Defunct*] (EA)
ASA	American-Swiss Association (EA)
ASA	Aminosalicyclic Acid [*Biochemistry*]
ASA	Amplifier and Switch Assembly (MCD)
ASA	Amputee Sports Association [*Defunct*] (EA)
ASA	Angle Side Angle [*Geometry*] (BARN)
ASA	Angus Society of Australia
ASA	Ankylosing Spondylitis Association (EA)
ASA	Anterior Septal Artery [*Anatomy*]
ASA	Anterior Sorting Area
ASA	Anthropogenic Sulfate Aerosol [*Meteorology*]
ASA	Anthroposophical Society in America (EA)
ASA	Antistatic Additive
ASA	Applied Science Associates
ASA	Appropriate Superior Authority [*British military*] (DMA)
ASA	Archaeological Society of Alberta (AC)
ASA	Architectural Secretaries Association [*Later, SAA*] (EA)
ASA	Area Scanning Alarm
ASA	Argininosuccinate [*Biochemistry*] (DAVI)
ASA	Argininosuccinic Acid (MAE)
ASA	Arizona School Administrators Association (SRA)
ASA	Arizona Sign Association (SRA)
ASA	Arizona Software Association (SRA)
ASA	Arkansas Sheriffs' Association (SRA)
ASA	Armenian Students Association of America (EA)
ASA	Army Seal of Approval

ASA............ Army Security Agency [*Later, INSCOM*] [*Arlington, VA*]
ASA............ Army Ski Association [*British military*] (DMA)
ASA............ Army Strategic Appraisal
ASA............ Articulation Screening Assessment [*Speech development test*]
ASA............ Arylsulfatase-A (MAE)
ASA............ Asahikawa [*Japan*] [*Seismograph station code, US Geological Survey*] (SEIS)
ASA............ ASA Ltd. [*Formerly, American-South African Investment Co. Ltd.*] [*NYSE symbol*] (SPSG)
ASA............ Asian Students' Association [*Kowloon, Hong Kong*] (EAIO)
ASA............ Asian Surgical Association (EAIO)
ASA............ Assab [*Ethiopia*] [*Airport symbol*] (OAG)
ASA............ Assistant Secretary of the Army
ASA............ Assistant Stores Accountant [*British military*] (DMA)
ASA............ Associated Stenotypists of America [*Later, NSRA*] (EA)
ASA............ Associate in Secretarial Administration
ASA............ Associate of the Society of Actuaries [*Society of Actuaries*] [*Designation awarded by*]
ASA............ Association des Statisticiens de l'Athletisme [*Association of Track and Field Statisticians*] (EAIO)
ASA............ Association for the Study of Abortion [*Later, NAF*]
ASA............ Association of Sealant Applicators [*British*] (DBA)
ASA............ Association of Social Anthropologists of the Commonwealth [*British*] (EAIO)
ASA............ Association of Subscription Agents [*British*] (DBA)
ASA............ Atlantic Salmon Association (EA)
ASA............ Atlantic Southeast Airlines, Inc.
ASA............ Atomic Scientists' Association [*Great Britain*]
ASA............ Atomic Security Agency [*Army*]
ASA............ Audiological Society of Australia
ASA............ Auditory Sensation Area
ASA............ Australian Salvadorian Association
ASA............ Australian Shipbuilders' Association
ASA............ Australian Society of Accountants (ODBW)
ASA............ Australian Sociological Association
ASA............ Australian Songwriters' Association
ASA............ Australian Steel Association
ASA............ Australian Studies Association
ASA............ Australian Sunflower Association
ASA............ Australian Surfers' Association
ASA............ Australian Surfriders' Association
ASA............ Autism Society of America (EA)
ASA............ Autocostruzioni Societa per Azione [*Automobile manufacturing company*] [*Italy*]
ASA............ Automatic Slack Adjuster [*Truck brakes*]
ASA............ Automatic Spectrum Analyzer (MHDB)
ASA............ Automatic Steering Antenna
ASA............ Automatic Stop Announcement
ASA............ Automatic Systems Analysis (KSC)
ASA............ Automotive Service Association (EA)
ASA............ Aviation Supply Annex
ASA............ Avicultural Society of America (EA)
ASA............ Azalea Society of America (EA)
ASA............ Azimuth Servo Assembly
ASA............ Die Aramaeische Sprache unter den Achaimeniden [*A publication*] (BJA)
ASA............ Southern Arkansas University, Magnolia, AR [*OCLC symbol*] (OCLC)
ASA............ St. Albert Public Library, Alberta [*Library symbol National Library of Canada*] (NLC)
ASAA .... Acquired Severe Aplastic Anemia [*Hematology*] (DAVI)
ASAA .... Airman Apprentice, Aviation Support Equipment Technician, Striker [*Navy rating*]
ASAA .... Alberta Schools Athletic Association (AC)
ASAA .... American Society of Aviation Artists [*An association*]
ASAA .... Amputee Sports Association of Australia
ASAA .... Armenian Students Association of America (EA)
ASAA .... Army Special Award for Accomplishment (RDA)
ASAA .... ASA International Ltd. [*NASDAQ symbol*] (NQ)
ASAA .... ASA Intl Ltd [*NASDAQ symbol*] (TTSB)
ASAA .... Asian Studies Association of Australia
ASA(A)........ Assistant Secretary of the Army (Acquisition)
ASAA .... Associate of the Society of Incorporated Accountants and Auditors [*British*]
ASAA .... Australian Ski Areas Association
ASAAA .... Alliance of State Aftermarket Associations
ASAAD .... American Society for Advancement of Anesthesia in Dentistry (EA)
ASAA-I........ Aviation Security Association of America - International [*Defunct*] (EA)
ASAA Rev .... Asian Studies Association of Australia. Review [*A publication*]
ASAAS .... Association of Suppliers to Airlines, Airports, and Shipping [*British*] (DBA)
ASAAS .... Asymmetric Stress Analysis of Axisymmetric Solids [*Computer program*]
ASAAT .... Austrian Society of Acupuncture and Auricular Therapy [*Multinational organization*] (EAIO)
ASAAWE ..... Association of South Asian Archaeologists in Western Europe (EAIO)
ASAB .... Association for the Study of Animal Behavior
ASAB .... Atlanta & Saint Andrews Bay Railway Co. [*AAR code*]
ASAC .... Active Satellite Attitude Control
ASAC .... Administrative Sciences Association of Canada [*Association des Sciences Administratives du Canada*]
ASAC .... Aerodynamic Surface Assembly and Checkout [*NASA*] (NASA)
ASAC .... Air Service Area Command
ASAC .... Air Surveillance and Airspace Control (MCD)
ASAC .... All Source Analysis Center (MCD)

ASAC .... Altostratus and Altocumulus [*Meteorology*]
ASAC .... American Samoa Administrative Code [*A publication*] (DLA)
ASAC .... American Society of Agricultural Consultants (EA)
ASAC .... American Society of Arms Collectors (EA)
ASAC .... American-Southern Africa Council [*Defunct*]
ASAC .... Antisubmarine Air Control [*Navy*] (MCD)
ASAC .... Army Study Advisory Committee
ASAC .... Asian Securities Analysts Council [*See also CAAF*] [*Japan*] (EAIO)
ASAC .... Association of Surf Angling Clubs (EA)
ASAC .... Australian Science Advisory Committee
ASAC .... Australian Sport Aviation Confederation
ASAC .... Automated Systems Army Commissaries (AABC)
ASACG .... Automatic Selection of Any Channel (IAA)
ASACG .... Army Security Assistance Coordinating Group
ASACOT ...... American-Southern Africa Chamber of Trade and Industry (EA)
ASACS .... Airborne Surveillance and Control System [*ASD*]
ASACT .... Advanced Strategic Aerodynamic Configuration Technology (MCD)
ASACUT ...... Academic Staff Association of Curtin University of Technology [*Australia*]
ASA(CW)..... Assistant Secretary of the Army (Civil Works)
ASAD .... Advanced Strategic Air Defense
ASAD .... Alpha Solar Array Drive (SSD)
ASAD .... Assembly Aid [*Tool*] (AAG)
ASAD .... Authorized Shortages and Discrepancies (KSC)
ASADA .... American Space and Development Agency (NUCP)
ASADA .... Atomic Space and Development Authority [*Nuclear energy*] (NRCH)
ASAE .... American Society for Aerospace Education (EA)
ASAE .... American Society of Aeronautical Engineers [*Later, SAE*] (KSC)
ASAE .... American Society of Agricultural Engineers (EA)
ASAE .... American Society of Association Executives (EA)
ASAE .... Arkansas Society of Association Executives (SRA)
ASAE .... Associate of Society of Association Executives
ASAE-HI ...... Aloha Society of Association Executives - Hawaii (SRA)
ASAF .... Assistant Secretary of the Air Force (MCD)
ASAF .... Australian Sports Acrobatic Federation
ASAF(A) ...... Assistant Secretary of the Air Force (Acquisition) (DOMA)
ASAF(FM)..... Assistant Secretary of the Air Force (Financial Management)
ASA (FM).... Assistant Secretary of the Army (Financial Management)
ASAFMA ...... Assistant Secretary of the Air Force (Materiel)
ASAF (MRA & 1L)... Assistant Secretary of the Air Force (Manpower, Reserve Affairs and Installations Logistics)
ASAF(RD & A)... Assistant Secretary of the Air Force (Research, Development, and Acquisition) (MCD)
ASAF(RDL)... Assistant Secretary of the Air Force (Research, Development, and Logistics) (MCD)
ASAFS .... Automated Single Area Field Scanner [*Department of Agricultural Meteorology, University of Nebraska*]
ASAG .... Aegis Surface Action Group [*Military*] (DOMA)
ASAG .... Automotive Service Association of Georgia (SRA)
ASAGAD...... American Society for Advancement of General Anesthesia in Dentistry [*Later, ASAAD*] (EA)
ASAH .... American Squadron of Aviation Historians (EA)
ASAHC .... American Society of Architectural Hardware Consultants [*Later, DHI*] (EA)
AsahiAm ...... Asahi/America, Inc. [*Associated Press*] (SAG)
ASA Hold .... ASA Holdings, Inc. [*Associated Press*] (SAG)
ASAHP .... American Society of Allied Health Professions (EA)
ASAI........... Adjunct/Switch Applications Interface [*Tekelec*]
ASAI........... American Society of Ancient Instruments [*Defunct*] (EA)
ASAI........... Aortic Stenosis and Aortic Insufficiency ·Murmurs [*Cardiology*] (MAE)
ASAI........... ASA Holdings, Inc. [*NASDAQ symbol*] (SAG)
ASAI........... Atlantic So'east Air [*NASDAQ symbol*] (TTSB)
ASAI........... Atlantic Southeast Airlines, Inc. [*NASDAQ symbol*] (NQ)
ASA (I & L).. Assistant Secretary of the Army (Installations and Logistics)
ASAIC .... Assistant Special Agent in Charge
ASAIHL .... Association of Southeast Asian Institutions of Higher Learning [*Bangkok, Thailand*]
ASA(IL & FM)... Assistant Secretary of the Army (Installations, Logistics, and Financial Management) (AABC)
ASAI Mech E... Associate of the South African Institute of Mechanical Engineers
ASA Int .... ASA International Ltd. [*Associated Press*] (SAG)
ASAIO .... American Society for Artificial Internal Organs (EA)
ASAJEQ....... Association des Services d'Aide aux Jeunes Entrepreneurs du Quebec (AC)
ASAL .... Annual Survey of Australian Law [*A publication*]
ASAL .... Arginosuccinic Acid Lyase (DMAA)
ASALA .... Armenian Secret Army for the Liberation of Armenia [*Turkey*] (PD)
ASALH .... Association for the Study of Afro-American Life and History (EA)
ASALM........ Advanced Strategic Air-Launched Missile (MCD)
ASALT......... Assessment of Survivability Against LASER Threat (MCD)
ASA Ltd ...... ASA Ltd. [*Formerly, American-South African Investment Co. Ltd.*] [*Associated Press*] (SAG)
ASALU .... Arkansas State Association of Life Underwriters (SRA)
ASAM......... American Society for Abrasive Methods [*Later, AES*] (EA)
ASAM......... American Society of Addiction Medicine (EA)
ASAM......... American Society of Asset Managers (EA)
ASAM......... Annals. South Africa Museum [*A publication*]
ASAM......... ASAHI/AMERICA [*NASDAQ symbol*] (TTSB)
ASAM......... Asahi/America, inc. [*NASDAQ symbol*] (SAG)
ASAM......... Assistant Secretary for Administration and Management [*Department of Labor*]
ASAM......... Associate of the Society of Art Masters [*British*]
ASAM......... Association of Sales Administration Managers (EA)
ASA (M & RA)... Assistant Secretary of the Army (Manpower and Reserve Affairs) (AABC)

ASAMAT ...... Assistant Secretary of the Army, Materiel (SAA)
ASAMLM ...... MLM Groundwater Engineering, St. Albert, Alberta [Library symbol National Library of Canada] (NLC)
ASAMN .... American Society of Anthropometric Medicine and Nutrition [Defunct] (EA)
ASAMP .... Airplane Sizing and Mission Performance [Computer program]
ASAMPE ...... Allied States Association of Motion Picture Exhibitors [Later, NATO]
ASAMS .... Austere Surface-to-Air Missile System
ASAMS .... Automatic Structure Analysis of Mass Spectra
ASAN .... Airman, Aviation Support Equipment Technician, Striker [Navy rating]
AS & A .... Anthony, Smallhorn & Associates [British]
AS & B .... Aloin, Strychnine, and Belladonna [Pharmacy]
AS & C .... Aerospace Surveillance and Control [Air Force] (AFM)
AS & EWD .. Air, Surface, and Electronic Warfare Division [Navy] (MCD)
AS & I .... Arming, Safing, and Initiating (SAA)
AS & L .... Administrative Support and Logistic Company [Military]
AS & SB ...... Automated Systems and Services Branch [NTIS]
AS & SL ...... All Ships and Stations Letters
AS & T .... Administrative, Staff, and Technical [Budget term]
AS & T .... Advanced Systems and Technology (MCD)
AS & TA ..... Airborne Surveillance and Target Acquisition (SAA)
AS & W .... American Steel and Wire Gauge
ASA Newsl ... Association for the Study of Abortion. Newsletter [A publication] (DLA)
ASANS .... Sangudo Public and School Library, Alberta [Library symbol National Library of Canada] (NLC)
Asante .... Asante Technologies, Inc. [Associated Press] (SAG)
ASAO .... Association for Social Anthropology in Oceania (EA)
ASAO .... Association of Show and Agricultural Organisations [British]
ASAP .... Academic and Social Anxiety Program [Cornell University]
ASAP .... Academic Strategic Alliances Program
ASAP .... Academic Strategic Alliances Program
ASAP .... Accelerated Solicitation to Award Process [National Institutes of Health]
ASAP .... Advanced Space Applications Program [Military]
ASAP .... Advanced Supersonic All-Purpose Dispenser (MCD)
ASAP .... Advanced Survival Avionics Program (MCD)
ASAP .... Advanced Symbolic Artwork Preparation (MCD)
ASAP .... Advanced System Architecture for Postscript [Printer technology] [QMS, Inc.] [Computer science] (PCM)
ASAP .... [The] Aerospace Safety Advisory Panel [NASA/Air Force] (NASA)
ASAP .... After Sale Assurance Program
ASAP .... AIDS Services and Prevention Coalition (EA)
ASAP .... Aircraft Synthesis Analysis Program
ASAP .... Aircraft Systems Activation Program [Military]
ASAP .... Aircrew Systems Advisory Panel [NASA, Air Force] (MCD)
ASAP .... Alcohol Safety Action Project [Department of Transportation]
ASAP .... Alliance for South Asian AIDS Prevention (AC)
ASAP .... Americans for a Sound AIDS [Acquired Immune Deficiency Syndrome] Policy (EA)
ASAP .... American Society for Adolescent Psychiatry (EA)
ASAP .... American Society for Adolescent Psychology (DAVI)
ASAP .... American Society for Association Publishing (EA)
ASAP .... American Society for Automation in Pharmacy (EA)
ASAP .... American Society of Access Professionals (EA)
ASAP .... American Society of Adlerian Psychology (AEBS)
ASAP .... American Society of Adults with Pseudo-Obstruction
ASAP .... American Society of Advertising and Promotion, Inc. (NTCM)
ASAP .... American Society of Aerospace Pilots [Defunct] (EA)
ASAP .... American Society of Animal Production [Later, ASAS]
ASAP .... American Syringomyelia Alliance Project (EA)
AS/AP .... Amplified Substrate/Alkaline Phosphatase
ASAP .... Analog System Assembly Pack
ASAP .... Annular Suspension and Pointing System (MCD)
ASAP .... Antisubmarine Attack Plotter [Navy]
ASAP .... Applied Systems and Personnel (BUR)
ASAP .... Army Scientific Advisory Panel [Later, ASB]
ASAP .... Army Scientific Assistance Program (RDA)
ASAP .... Army Streamlined Acquisition Process [or Program] (RDA)
ASAP .... Army (Wives) Senior Assistance Program
ASAP .... As Soon as Possible
asap .... As Soon As Possible (ODBW)
asap .... As Soon As Possible [Pronounced a-sap] (WDMC)
ASAP .... As Soon As Possible [Internet language] [Computer science]
ASAP .... Automated Statistical Analysis Program
ASAP .... Automatic Spooling with Asynchronous Processing [Computer science] (PDAA)
ASAP .... Automatic Switching and Processing [Command Communications, Inc.] [Telecommunications] (PCM)
ASAP .... Auto-Trace Steam Analysis Program [Computer software]
ASAP .... Auxiliary Storage and Playback [Assembly] [Apollo Telescope Mount] [NASA]
ASAP .... North American Society of Adlerian Psychology [Later, NASAP] (EA)
ASAPAC ...... Army Security Agency, Pacific (CINC)
ASAPHA ...... Association of Sea and Air Ports Health Authority [British]
ASAPR .... Accelerated Strike Aircraft Program Requirement [DoD] (MCD)
ASAPS .... American Society for Aesthetic Plastic Surgery (EA)
ASAPSS ...... American Society for Amusement Park Security and Safety (EA)
ASAPT .... Americans for Substance Abuse Prevention and Treatment (EA)
ASAQ .... Ambulance Superintendents' Association of Queensland [Australia]
ASAR .... Advanced Surface-to-Air Ramjet [Navy]
ASAR .... Advanced Synthetic Aperture RADER [Marine science] (OSRA)
ASAR .... Air Search Acquisition RADAR (CAAL)
ASAR .... All Source Analysis System [Military] (DOMA)
ASAR .... All South Africa Law Reports [A publication] (DLA)

ASAR .... Army Selective Aerial Rocket (MCD)
ASARA .... Australian Small-Bore and Air Rifle Association
ASA (R & D) ... Assistant Secretary of the Army (Research and Development)
ASARB .... Association of Statisticians of American Religious Bodies (EA)
ASARC .... Army Systems Acquisition Review Council
ASARC .... Army Systems Acquisition Review Council (DOMA)
ASARC IET ... Army Systems Acquisition Review Council Independent Evaluation Team (MCD)
Asarco .... ASARCO, Inc. [Formerly, American Smelting & Refining Co.] [Associated Press] (SAG)
ASA(RDA) .... Assistant Secretary of the Army (Research, Development, and Acquisition)
ASAR-ER ..... Advanced Surface-to-Air Ramjet, Extended Range (MCD)
Asarh .... Asarhaddon (BJA)
ASAR-MR .... Advanced Surface-to-Air Ramjet, Medium Range (MCD)
ASARR .... Advanced Surface-to-Air Rocket Ramjet (MCD)
ASARS .... Advanced Sensor Analog Relay System [Army] (MCD)
ASARS .... Advanced Strategic Airborne RADAR System
ASARS .... Advance Synthetic Aperture RADAR System (MCD)
ASARS .... Army Small Arms Requirements Simulation [Battle model] (MCD)
ASARS .... Army Small Arms Requirements Studies (MCD)
ASAS .... Active Scattering Aerosol Spectrometer [Aerosol measurement device]
ASAS .... Aerodynamic Stability Augmentation System [or Subsystem] [NASA] (NASA)
ASAS .... Agostiniani Secolari Agustinos Seculares [Order Secular of St. Augustine - OSSA] [Rome, Italy] (EAIO)
ASAS .... All Source Analysis System [DoD]
ASAS .... American Society of Abdominal Surgery (EA)
ASAS .... American Society of Animal Science (EA)
ASAS .... Amorphous Sodium Aluminosilicate [Inorganic chemistry]
ASAS .... Argininosuccinate Synthetase [An enzyme] (AAMN)
ASAS .... Army Security Agency School [Merged with Defense Security Agency School]
ASAS .... Association of South-East Asian States
ASAS .... Atkins Stress Analysis System [Atkins Research & Development] [Software package] (NCC)
ASAS .... Atkins Structural Analysis System (MCD)
ASAS .... Australian Special Air Services (VNW)
ASAS .... Aviation Safety Analysis System [FAA] (GFGA)
ASASP .... Active Scattering Aerosol Spectrometer Probe (MCD)
ASAS/SFT ... All Source Analysis System/Software [Military] (RDA)
ASASTSM ... Amalgamated Society of Anchorsmiths, Ship Tackle, and Shackle Makers [A union] [British]
ASASV .... Association for the Study and Advancement of Supportive Values (EA)
ASAT .... Acoustic Surface Analysis Technology
ASAT .... Advanced Satellite
ASA/T .... Airframe and System Assembly/Test (MCD)
ASAT .... Air Search Attack Team [Military]
ASAT .... American School Achievement Test [Education] (AEBS)
ASAT .... Antisatellite
ASAT .... Antisatellite Satellite
ASAT .... Antisubmarine Attack Teacher
ASAT .... Aspartate Aminotransferase [Also, AAT, AST, GOT] [An enzyme]
ASAT .... Automated Statistical Analysis Technique (DNAB)
ASAT .... Automatic Spares Analysis Technique
ASATT .... Advanced Small Axial Turbine Technology (RDA)
ASATTU .... Antisubmarine Attack Teacher Training Unit
ASAU .... Air Search Attack Unit [Military]
ASAUCUNSW ... Academic Staff Association of University College, University of New South Wales [Australia]
ASAUK .... African Studies Association United Kingdom
ASA(VB) ...... Anthroposophical Society in Australia, Victorian Branch
ASAW .... American Society of Aviation Writers [Later, IATJ] (EA)
ASAW .... Association of Southern Agricultural Workers [Later, SAAS]
ASAW .... Automatic Submerged Arc Welding Process (NUCP)
ASAWS .... Advance Surface-to-Air Weapons System
ASAXP .... Average Sorties per Aircraft Actually Possessed [Air Force] (AFIT)
ASB............. Accounting Standards Board [British] (ECON)
ASB............. Acoustical Standards Board (MUGU)
ASB............. Administration and Storage Building
ASB............. Advanced Systems Buying
ASB............. Aerated Stabilization Basin [For water purification]
ASB............. Aggregated School Budget (AIE)
ASB............. Agricultural Statistics Board [Department of Agriculture] [Information service or system] (IID)
ASB............. Airborne Special Bombing
ASB............. Aircraft Safety Beacon
ASB............. Aircraft Services Base
ASB............. Airlock Stowage Bag [NASA] (MCD)
ASB............. Air Safety Board
ASB............. Air-Spray 1967 Ltd. [Canada ICAO designator] (FAAC)
ASB............. Air Staff Board [Air Force] (AFM)
ASB............. Air Supply Board [Ministry of Aircraft Production] [British]
ASB............. Air Surveillance Broadcast (MCD)
ASB............. Alabama State Bar (SRA)
ASB............. Albania Society of Britain [British] (EAIO)
ASB............. Allied Staff, Berlin [Post-World War II]
ASB............. Alternative Book Service [Reference to an edition of the Anglican Book of Common Prayer] (BARN)
ASB............. Altitude Sensor Bypass (MCD)
ASB............. Amchitka [Alaska] [Seismograph station code, US Geological Survey Closed] (SEIS)
ASB............. American Society of Bacteriologists (BARN)

ASB............ American Society of Bacteriology (DAVI)
ASB............ American Society of Bariatrics [*Later, ASBP*]
ASB............ Amphibious Support Battalion [*Military*]
ASB............ Anesthesia Standby [*Medicine*]
ASB............ Antishock Body
ASB............ Antisurface Boat
ASB............ Anxiety Scale for the Blind [*Psychology*]
Asb .... Apostilb [*Unit of luminance*]
ASB............ Aptitude Test for School Beginners [*Child development test*]
ASB............ Arctic Survey Boat [*Coast Guard*] (DNAB)
ASB............ Armed Services Bulletin
ASB............ Armor Support Battalion (MCD)
ASB............ Army Science Board [*Formerly, ASAP*] (RDA)
ASB............ Artists' Service Bureau (NTCM)
ASB............ Asbestos (KSC)
asb .... Asbestos (VRA)
ASB............ Asbestos
ASB............ Ashburton Oil Ltd. [*Vancouver Stock Exchange symbol*]
ASB............ Ashkhabad [*Former USSR Airport symbol*] (OAG)
ASB............ Associated Services for the Blind (EA)
ASB............ Associate in Science in Business
ASB............ Associate in Specialized Business
ASB............ Association of Shell Boilermakers [*British*] (DBA)
ASB............ Association of Software Brokers (EA)
ASB............ Asymmetrical Sideband
ASB............ Asymptomatic Bacteriuria [*Medicine*] (PDAA)
ASB............ Auditing Standards Board
ASB............ Automated Status Board
ASB............ Seba Beach Public Library, Alberta [*Library symbol National Library of Canada*] (NLC)
ASBA .... Alberta School Boards Association [*Formerly, Alberta School Trustees' Association*] (AC)
ASBA .... Alberta Sheep Breeders Association (AC)
ASBA .... Alberta Swine Breeders' Association (AC)
ASBA .... American Shore and Beach Preservation Association (NOAA)
ASBA .... American Shorthorn Breeders Association [*Later, ASA*]
ASBA .... American Skibob Association [*Later, USSBF*] (EA)
ASBA .... American Small Businesses Association (EA)
ASBA .... American Southdown Breeders' Association (EA)
ASBA .... American Standardbred Breeders Association (EA)
ASBA .... Arizona School Boards Association (SRA)
ASBA .... Arizona Small Business Association (SRA)
ASBA .... Arkansas School Boards Association (SRA)
ASBA .... Association for Small Business Advancement [*Defunct*] (EA)
ASBA .... Association of Ship Brokers and Agents - USA (EA)
ASBA .... Australian Sheep Breeders' Association
ASBA .... Australian Small Business Awards
ASBAH .... Association for Spina Bifida and Hydrocephalus [*Australia British*] (IRUK)
ASBAL .... [*A*] Stack Based Abstraction Language [*1978*] [*Computer science*] (CSR)
ASB & I .... Aloin, Strychnine, Belladonna, and Ipecac [*Pharmacy*]
ASBC .... Advanced Standard Buried Collector (IAA)
ASBC .... American Seat Belt Council [*Later, AORC*] (EA)
ASBC .... American Silkie Bantam Club (EA)
ASBC .... American Society of Biological Chemists [*Later, ASBMB*] (EA)
ASBC .... American Society of Brewing Chemists (EA)
ASBC .... American Standard Building Code (IEEE)
ASBC .... Archaeological Society of British Columbia (AC)
ASBC .... Associated Banc-Corp [*NASDAQ symbol*] (NQ)
ASBCA .... Armed Services Board of Contract Appeals
ASBC & D ..... American Society of Bookplate Collectors and Designers (EA)
ASBCM .... Association of Southern Baptist Campus Ministers (EA)
ASBCS .... Association of Southern Baptist Colleges and Schools (EA)
ASBD .... Active Service Base Date (DNAB)
ASBD .... Advanced Sea-Based Deterrent [*Navy*]
ASBD .... American Society of Bank Directors [*Arlington, VA*] (EA)
ASBDA .... American School Band Directors' Association (EA)
ASBDC .... Association of Small Business Development Centers [*Washington, DC*] (EA)
ASBE .... American Society of Bakery Engineers (EA)
ASBE .... American Society of Body Engineers (EA)
ASBE .... Associate in Science in Basic Engineering
ASB Fn .... ASB Financial Corp. [*Associated Press*] (SAG)
ASBHCA .... Average Season Busy Hour Call Attempts [*Telecommunications*] (TEL)
ASBHCC .... Average Season Busy Hour Call Completions [*Telecommunications*] (TEL)
ASBHQ .... L'Association de Spina-Bifida et d'Hydrocephalie du Quebec (AC)
ASBI .... Ameriana Bancorp [*NASDAQ symbol*] (SAG)
ASBIPC .... American Sugar Beet Industry Policy Committee [*Defunct*] (EA)
ASBK .... Aspen Bancshares [*NASDAQ symbol*] (TTSB)
ASBK .... Aspen Bankshares, Inc. [*NASDAQ symbol*] (SAG)
ASBK .... Sydney/Bankstown [*Australia ICAO location identifier*] (ICLI)
ASBL .... Assemble (AABC)
ASBLY .... Assembly (AFM)
ASBM .... Air-to-Surface Ballistic Missile
ASBM .... Associate in Business Management
ASBMB .... American Society for Biochemistry and Molecular Biology (EA)
ASBMR .... American Society for Bone and Mineral Research (EA)
ASBMT .... American Society for Blood and Marrow Transplantation
ASBO .... Asbestos and Small Business Ombudsman [*Environmental Protection Agency*]
ASBO .... Association of School Business Officials International (EA)
ASBP .... American Society of Bariatric Physicians (EA)

ASBP .... ASB Financial Corp. [*NASDAQ symbol*] (SAG)
ASBPA .... American Shore and Beach Preservation Association (EA)
ASBPAC .... America's Small Business Political Action Committee [*Defunct*] (EA)
ASBPE .... American Society of Business Press Editors
ASBPO .... Armed Services Blood Program Office (DOMA)
ASBR .... Academically-Separated Budgeted Research
ASBR .... ASB Financial [*NASDAQ symbol*] (TTSB)
ASBREM ...... Armed Services Biomedical Research and Evaluation Management Committee
ASBREM ...... Armed Services Biomedical Research Evaluation and Management (RDA)
ASBS .... American Society for Bariatric Obesity Surgery (HCT)
ASBS .... American Striped Bass Society (EA)
ASBS .... Arteriosclerotic Brain Syndrome [*Cardiology and neurology*] (DAVI)
ASBS .... Association of Social and Behavioral Scientists (EA)
ASBSBSW ..... Amalgamated Society of Boilermakers, Shipwrights, Blacksmiths, and Structural Workers [*A union*] [*British*] (DCTA)
ASBSD .... Associated School Boards of South Dakota (SRA)
ASBSTS .... Asbestos
ASBTh......... Associate of the Society of Health and Beauty Therapists [*British*] (DBQ)
ASBU .... Arab States Broadcasting Union
ASBUG........ Australian Synchrotron Beam Users' Group
ASBV .... Avocado-Sunblotch Viroid
ASBVd .... Avocado-Sunblotch Viroid [*Plant pathology*]
ASBW .... Amalgamated Society of Brass Workers [*A union*] [*British*]
ASBWMMA..... Amalgamated Scale, Beam, and Weighing Machine Makers Association [*A union*] [*British*]
ASBYP .... Appraisal: Science Books for Young People [*A publication*] (BRI)
ASC............ Abbe Sine Condition
ASC............ Above Suspended Ceiling [*Technical drawings*]
ASC............ Accelerometer Signal Conditioner (KSC)
ASC............ Accounting Standards Committee [*British*]
ASC............ Accredited Standards Committee (AAGC)
ASC............ Acetylsulfanilyl Chloride [*Organic chemistry*]
ASC............ Acid-Soluble Collagen [*Biochemistry*]
ASC............ Action Socialiste Congolaise [*Congolese Socialist Action*]
ASC............ Active Signal Correction [*Video technology*]
ASC............ Activity Sections Council [*Association of College and Research Libraries*]
ASC............ Adams State College [*Alamosa, CO*]
ASC............ Adaptive Signal Correction (IAA)
ASC............ Adaptive Speed Control (PDAA)
ASC............ Adelaide Steamship Co. (MHDB)
ASC............ Adhesive and Sealant Council (EA)
ASC............ Administrative Sciences Corp.
ASC............ Administrative Service Centers (AABC)
ASC............ Administrative Services Contract [*Health insurance*] (GHCT)
ASC............ Administrative Staff College [*British*] (DI)
ASC............ Administrative Support Center [*Marine science*] (OSRA)
ASC............ Adorers of the Blood of Christ [*Roman Catholic women's religious order*]
ASC............ Advanced Scientific Computer [*Texas Instruments, Inc.*]
ASC............ Advanced Ship Concepts
ASC............ Advanced Simulation Center [*Army*] (MCD)
ASC............ Advanced Sonobuoy Communications Link [*Navy*] (MCD)
ASC............ Advanced Surgical Centre [*British and Canadian*] [*World War II*]
ASC............ Advanced System Concept (MCD)
ASC............ Advertising Standards Council [*Canada Australia*]
ASC............ Aerodynamics Surface Control (MCD)
ASC............ Aerojet Services Co.
ASC............ Aeronautical Systems Center [*Air Force*]
ASC............ Aeronca Sedan Club (EA)
ASC............ Aerosol Scattering Coefficient [*Climatology factor*]
ASC............ Aerospace Control [*Air Force*] (MCD)
ASC............ Aerospace Planning Charts
ASC............ Aerospace Static Converter
ASC............ Aerospace Systems Center [*Dayton, OH*] [*Air Force*] (MCD)
ASC............ Aerosurface Control [*NASA*] (NASA)
ASC............ African Studies Center [*Michigan State University*] [*Research center*] (RCD)
ASC............ Agnes Scott College [*Decatur, GA*]
ASC............ Agreed Syllabus Conference [*Education*] (AIE)
ASC............ Agricultural Stabilization and Conservation
ASC............ Airborne Software Change (MCD)
ASC............ Aircraft Service Change [*Navy*]
ASC............ Aircraft Supply Council [*Ministry of Aircraft Production*] [*British*]
ASC............ Aircrew Systems Change (MCD)
ASC............ Airport Security Council (EA)
ASC............ Air Service Command
ASC............ Air Situation Coordinator (SAA)
ASC............ Air Star Corp. [*Canada ICAO designator*] (FAAC)
ASC............ Air Support Command (SAG)
ASC............ Air Support Control
ASC............ Air Support Coordinator (MCD)
ASC............ Air Systems Command [*Navy*]
A-SC .... Alabama State Supreme Court Library, Montgomery, AL [*Library symbol Library of Congress*] (LCLS)
ASC............ Albany State College [*Georgia*]
ASC............ Alcohol Studies Centre [*British*] (CB)
ASC............ Allied Staff Chiefs [*World War II*]
ASC............ Allied Supreme Council [*World War II*]
ASC............ Allowance Source Code [*Military*] (AFM)
ASC............ Allowance Summary Code
ASC............ All Savers Certificate [*Banking*]

ASC............	All-Sky Camera
ASC............	Altered State of Consciousness [*Parapsychology*]
ASC............	Alternate Source Council (MCD)
ASC............	Alternate Squadron Commander [*Air Force*]
ASC............	Alzheimer Society of Canada [*Societe Alzheimer du Canada*] (AC)
ASC............	Amalgamated Society of Casters [*A union*] [*British*]
ASC............	Ambulatory Surgical Center [*Medicine*]
ASC............	Amchitka [*Alaska*] [*Seismograph station code, US Geological Survey Closed*] (SEIS)
ASC............	American Safety Council (EA)
ASC............	American Sailing Council [*of the National Marine Manufacturers Association*] [*Chicago, IL*]
ASC............	American Satellite Corp. (TSSD)
ASC............	American Security Council (EA)
ASC............	American Shuffleboard Co. (EA)
ASC............	American Silk Council [*Defunct*] (EA)
ASC............	American Singers Club (EA)
ASC............	American Society for Cybernetics (EA)
ASC............	American Society of Cartographers [*Defunct*] (EA)
ASC............	American Society of Cinematographers (EA)
ASC............	American Society of Criminology (EA)
ASC............	American Society of Cytology (EA)
ASC............	American Spaniel Club (EA)
ASC............	American Spanish Committee (EA)
ASC............	American Spoon Collectors (EA)
ASC............	American Sportsman's Club [*Commercial firm*] (EA)
ASC............	American Standard Code (OA)
ASC............	American Stores Co. [*NYSE symbol*] (SPSG)
ASC............	American Studebaker Club
ASC............	American Studies Centre [*University of Sydney*] [*Australia*]
ASC............	American Sunroof Corp., Inc.
ASC............	Amer Stores [*NYSE symbol*] (TTSB)
ASC............	Amicable Society of Coachmakers [*A union*] [*British*]
ASC............	Amperes per Square Centimeter (IAA)
ASC............	Analog Signal Converter
ASC............	Analog Signal Correlator
ASC............	Analog Strip Chart
ASC............	Analog-to-Stochastic Converter (IAA)
ASC............	Anglo-Saxon Chronicle
ASC............	Annapolis Science Center
ASC............	Annual Support Cost (MCD)
ASC............	Annual Survey of Colleges [*The College Board*] [*Information service or system*] (CRD)
ASC............	Anterior Subcapsular Cataract [*Ophthalmology*] (DAVI)
ASC............	Antibody-Secreting Cells [*Immunology*]
ASC............	Antique Studebaker Club (EA)
ASC............	Antistatic Compound
ASC............	Apple Sound Chip [*Apple Computer, Inc.*] (BYTE)
ASC............	Applied Science Corp. (MCD)
ASC............	Applied Superconductivity Conference, Inc. (MCD)
ASC............	Applied Superconductivity Research Center [*University of Wisconsin - Madison*] [*Research center*] (RCD)
ASC............	Approvisionnements et Services Canada [*Supply and Services Canada - SSC*]
ASC............	Arab Sports Confederation [*Saudi Arabia*] (EAIO)
ASC............	Area Signal Conditioner (MCD)
ASC............	Area Source Category [*Environmental Protection Agency*] (GFGA)
ASC............	Arizona Silver Corp. [*Vancouver Stock Exchange symbol*]
ASC............	Arizona State College
ASC............	Arkansas State College [*Later, ASU*]
ASC............	Arlington State College [*Texas*]
ASC............	Armed Services Committee [*US Senate*] (AAG)
ASC............	Army Selection Centre [*British*]
ASC............	Army Service Corps [*Initialism also facetiously translated during World War I as "Ally Sloper's Cavalry," Ally Sloper being a comic-paper buffoon*] [*Later, RASC*] [*British*]
ASC............	Army Signal Corps [*Later, CEC*]
ASC............	Army Specialist Corps [*Functions transferred to Officer Procurement Service*]
ASC............	Army Staff College (DOMA)
ASC............	Army Staff Council
ASC............	Army Staff Counsel (AAGC)
ASC............	Army Subsistence Center
ASC............	Arteriosclerosis [*or Arteriosclerotic*] [*Medicine*]
ASC............	Ascending
ASC............	Ascension [*Bolivia*] [*Airport symbol Obsolete*] (OAG)
ASC............	Ascent (MCD)
ASC............	Ascorbic Acid [*Also called vitamin C*] (DAVI)
ASC............	Ashland College, Ashland, OH [*OCLC symbol*] (OCLC)
ASC............	Asian Socialist Conference
ASC............	Asian Studies Centre [*St. Antony's College*] [*British*] (CB)
ASC............	Asian Studies Council [*Australia*]
ASC............	Asphalt Surface Course (DAC)
ASC............	Assembly of State Conferences [*American Association of University Professors*] (EDAC)
ASC............	Assembly Shortage Control (MCD)
ASC............	Assessment of Skills in Computation [*Mathematics test*]
ASC............	Asset Status Cards
ASC............	Assigned Service Contractor
AS(C).........	Assistant Secretary, Controller [*Admiralty*] [*British*]
ASC............	Assistant Sector Controller [*Aviation*] (DA)
ASC............	Associated Sandblasting Contractors (EA)
ASC............	Associated Schools of Construction (EA)
ASC............	Associated Specialty Contractors (EA)
ASc............	Associate in Science

ASC............	Associate in Science in Commerce
ASC............	Association for Student Counsellors (AIE)
ASC............	Association for Systematics Collections [*Taxonomy*]
ASC............	Association of Speakers Clubs [*British*] (DBA)
ASC............	Association of Student Counselling [*British*] (DBA)
ASC............	Association of Study Curriculum [*British*] (DBA)
ASC............	Associative Structure Computer (BUR)
ASC............	Asthma Society of Canada [*Societe Canadienne de l'Asthme*] (AC)
ASC............	Astronautical Society of Canada
ASC............	Astronautics Support Center
ASC............	Asynchronous Communication Procedure (BUR)
ASC............	Atlantic Seaboard Circuit [*Horse racing*]
ASC............	Atlantic Systems Conference [*Navy/NATO*] (MCD)
ASC............	Aughey Spark Chamber
ASC............	Australian Seismological Center
ASC............	Australian Shiatsu College
ASC............	Australian Society of Calligraphers
ASC............	Authorization Source Code (SAA)
ASC............	Authorized Signature Card (MCD)
ASC............	Autism Services Center (EA)
ASC............	Autism Society Canada
ASC............	AUTODIN Switching Center
ASC............	Automated Service Center
ASC............	Automated System Charter (IAA)
ASC............	Automatic Scan Counter
ASC............	Automatic Selectivity Control (DEN)
ASC............	Automatic Sensitivity Control [*Aviation*]
ASC............	Automatic Sequence Control [*Computer science*] (EECA)
ASC............	Automatic Stability Control System [*Bavarian Motor Works*] [*Automotive engineering*]
ASC............	Automatic Submarine Control [*Navy*] (MCD)
ASC............	Automatic Switching Center
ASC............	Automatic Synchronized Control (DEN)
ASC............	Automatic System Control
ASC............	Automation Security Committee [*Military*] (GFGA)
ASC............	Automotive Sales Council (EA)
ASC............	Automotive Service Councils [*Later, ASA*] (EA)
ASC............	Auxiliary Switch [*Breaker*] Normally Closed [*Electricity*]
ASC............	Average Standing Crop
ASC............	Aviation Service Code (AFM)
ASC............	Aviation Support Equipment Technician, Chief [*Navy rating*]
ASC............	Aviation Systems Command [*Army*] (RDA)
ASC............	Axial Summit Caldera [*Volcanology*]
ASC............	Movimiento de Accion Social Cristiana [*Christian Social Action Movement*] [*Dominican Republic*] [*Political party*] (PPW)
ASC............	Office of System Capacity and Requirements [*FAA*] (TAG)
ASCA	Advanced Satellite for Cosmology and Astrophysics [*Japanese spacecraft*]
ASCA	Airlines Sports and Cultural Association (EA)
ASCA	Alabama Chiropractic Association (SRA)
ASCA	American School Counselor Association (EA)
ASCA	American Senior Citizens Association (EA)
ASCA	American-Serbian Cultural Association (EA)
ASCA	American Shrimp Canners Association [*Later, ASPA*]
ASCA	American Society for Church Architecture [*Later, IFRAA*] (EA)
ASCA	American Society for Conservation Archaeology (EA)
ASCA	American Society of Consulting Arborists (EA)
ASCA	American Society of Contemporary Artists (EA)
ASCA	American Sprint Car Association [*Auto racing*]
ASCA	American Standard Chinchilla Association [*Later, ASCRA*]
ASCA	American Subacute Care Association
ASCA	American Swimming Coaches Association (EA)
ASCA	Ameristar Casinos [*NASDAQ symbol*] (TTSB)
ASCA	Ameristar Casinos, Inc. [*NASDAQ symbol*] (SAG)
ASCA	AMF Apollo Sailing Class Association (EA)
ASCA	Architectural Spray Coaters Association (EA)
ASCA	Associate of the Society of Company and Commercial Accountants [*British*] (DCTA)
ASCA	Association for Sickle Cell Anemia [*Defunct*]
ASCA	Association of State Correctional Administrators (EA)
ASCA	Atlantic Salmon Convention Act of 1982
ASCA	Automatic Science Citation Alerting (IEEE)
ASCA	Canberra [*Australia ICAO location identifier*] (ICLI)
ASCAA	Automobile Seat Cover Association of America (EA)
ASC/ABT	Ascent/Abort (MCD)
ASCAC	Acoustical Signal Classification and Analysis Center [*Navy*] (CAAL)
ASCAC	Antisubmarine Classification and Analysis Center [*Navy*]
ASCAC	Antisubmarine Combat Activity Center (DNAB)
ASCAC	Association for the Study of Classical African Civilizations (EA)
ASCAC/TSC...	Antisubmarine Classification and Analysis Center/Tactical Support Center (DNAB)
ASCAD	Arteriosclerotic Coronary Artery Disease [*Cardiology*] (MAE)
ASC/AIA	Association of Student Chapters, American Institute of Architects
ASCAM	Aerospace Catalog Automated Microfilm, Inc. (MCD)
ASCAM	Anti-Shipping Campaign Model (MCD)
ASCAP	Aeronautical Satellite Communications Processor (DA)
ASCAP	American Society of Composers, Authors, and Publishers (EA)
ASCAP	At-Sea Calibration Procedure
ASCAP Sympos...	Copyright Law Symposium. American Society of Composers, Authors, and Publishers (DLA)
ASCAS	All-Service Close Air Support [*Military*]
ASCAS	Automated System for the Control of Atmospheric Sampling [*Marine science*] (MSC)
ASCAT	Air Service Command Advisory Team
ASCAT	Analog Self-Checking Automatic Tester

ASCAT .... Antisubmarine Classification Analysis Test
ASCAT .... Association Internationale des Editeurs de Catalogues de Timbres-Poste [*International Association of Publishers of Postage Stamp Catalogues*] (EA)
ASCATS ...... Apollo Simulation Checkout and Training System [*NASA*]
ASCB .... Address Space Control Block [*Computer science*] (MHDI)
ASCB .... American Society for Cell Biology (EA)
ASCB .... Army Sports Control Board [*British*]
ASCB .... Avionics Standard Communications Bus (DA)
ASCB .... Canberra [*Australia ICAO location identifier*] (ICLI)
ASCC .... Aeronautical Satellite Communications Center (NITA)
ASCC .... Aeronautical Services Communication Center [*Great Britain*]
ASCC .... Airborne Sonobuoy Communications Center
ASCC .... Air Standardization Coordinating Committee
ASCC .... Air Support Coordination and Control (MCD)
ASCC .... Alaska State Chamber of Commerce (SRA)
ASCC .... American Social Communications Conference (EA)
ASCC .... American Society for Concrete Construction (EA)
ASCC .... American Society of Camera Collectors (EA)
ASCC .... American Society of Check Collectors (EA)
ASCC .... Area Security Coordination Center
ASCC .... Area Support and Coordination Committee [*Military*] (VNW)
ASCC .... Arkansas State Chamber of Commerce (SRA)
ASCC .... Armstrong Siddeley Car Club [*Australia*]
ASCC .... Army Strategic Communications Command
ASCC .... Association des Syndicats de Cheminots Canadiens [*Canadian Railway Labour Association - CRLA*]
ASCC .... Association of Scottish Climbing Clubs (BI)
ASCC .... Australian Schools' Cricket Council
ASCC .... Automatic Sequence Controlled Calculator [*First all-automatic calculating machine*]
ASCC .... Aviation Supply Control Center (NVT)
ASCCC .... Academic Senate for California Community Colleges (EDAC)
ASCCI .... American Society for Crippled Children in Israel (EA)
ASCCP .... American Society for Colposcopy and Cervical Pathology (EA)
ASCCS .... Advanced Shipboard Command Communications System (SAA)
ASCCSS ...... Army Signal Corps, Communications Security Service (MUGU)
ASCD .... Academy of Stress and Chronic Disease (EA)
ASCD .... Advanced Ship Concept Development
ASCD .... Aircraft Sensor Correlation Device (MCD)
ASCD .... American Society of Computer Dealers (EA)
ASCD .... Association for Supervision and Curriculum Development (EA)
ASCD .... Automatic Speed Control Device
AscdGp ...... Associated Group, Inc. (The) [*Associated Press*] (SAG)
ASCE .... Abrupt Space Charge Edge [*Algorithm*]
ASCE .... Airlock Signal Conditioning Electronics (MCD)
ASCE .... American Society of Childbirth Educators [*Inactive*] (EA)
ASCE .... American Society of Christian Ethics [*Later, SCE*]
ASCE .... American Society of Civil Engineers (EA)
ASCE .... Annual Schedule of Circuit Estimates [*Telecommunications*] (NITA)
ASCE .... Application Control Service Element (ACII)
ASCE .... Association of Safety Council Executives (EA)
ASCEA .... American Society of Civil Engineers and Architects (WDAA)
ASCEND ...... Advanced System for Communications and Education in National Development (MCD)
Ascend .... Ascend Communications, Inc. [*Associated Press*] (SAG)
ASCENT ...... Assembly System for Central Processor [*Computer science*]
AscentEnt .... Ascent Entertainment Group, Inc. [*Associated Press*] (SAG)
ASCEP .... American Society for Clinical Evoked Potentials (EA)
ASCES .... Antisubmarine Contact Evaluation System [*Navy*] (MCD)
ASCET .... American Society of Certified Engineering Technicians (EA)
ASCF .... American Security Council Foundation (EA)
ASCF .... Application Specific Coding Flag (NTCM)
ASCF .... Australian Sport Climbing Federation
AscFCap ..... Associates First Capital Corp. [*Associated Press*] (SAG)
ASCG .... Automatic Solution Crystal Growth [*Materials processing*]
ASCGB .... American Stamp Club of Great Britain (EA)
ASCGBI .... Amalgamated Society of Coremakers of Great Britain and Ireland [*A union*]
ASCGD .... American Society of Clinical Genetics and Dysmorphology [*Later, BDCGS*] (EA)
ASCGW .... Action-Study Center for a Governed World [*Defunct*] (EA)
ASCH .... American Society of Church History (EA)
ASCH .... American Society of Clinical Hypnosis (EA)
ASCH .... Association of Supportive Care Homes
ASCH .... Coffs Harbour [*Australia ICAO location identifier*] (ICLI)
ASCHB .... Association for Studies in the Conservation of Historic Buildings [*British*]
ASChE .... American Society of Chemical Engineers (BARN)
ASCH-ERF.... American Society of Clinical Hypnosis - Education and Research Foundation (EA)
ASCI .... Acute Spinal Cord Injury (DMAA)
ASCI .... American Society for Clinical Investigation (EA)
ASCI .... American Society of Construction Inspectors (EA)
ASCI .... Art Self-Concept Inventory (EDAC)
ASCID .... Altered State of Consciousness Induction Device [*Parapsychology*]
ASciE .... American Science & Engineering, Inc. [*Associated Press*] (SAG)
ASCII .... American Standard Code for Information Interchange [*Pronounced "ask-ee"*] [*American National Standards Institute*] [*Computer science*]
ASCIM .... Association of Casing Importers Ltd. [*British*] (BI)
ASCIS .... Australian School Catalogue Information Service (ADA)
Ascit Fl .... Ascitic Fluid (MAE)
ASCJ .... Apostles of the Sacred Heart of Jesus [*Roman Catholic women's religious order*]

ASCL .... Advanced Sonobuoy Communications Link [*Navy*] (MCD)
ASCL .... Advanced System Concepts Laboratory [*Army*]
ASCL .... Airborne Sonobuoy Communications Link
ASCL .... American Sugar Cane League of the USA (EA)
ASCL .... Arteriosclerosis [*Cardiology*] (DAVI)
ASCLA .... Association of Specialized and Cooperative Library Agencies (EA)
ASCLA LSSPS... ASCLA [*Association of Specialized and Cooperative Library Agencies*] Libraries Serving Special Populations Section
ASCLA LSSPS ALAD... ASCLA LSSPS [*Association of Specialized and Cooperative Library Agencies - Libraries Serving Special Populations Section*] Academic Librarians Assisting the Disabled Discussion Group
ASCLA LSSPS BF... ASCLA LSSPS [*Association of Specialized and Cooperative Library Agencies - Libraries Serving Special Populations Section*] Bibliotherapy Forum
ASCLA LSSPS HCLF... ASCLA LSSPS [*Association of Specialized and Cooperative Library Agencies - Libraries Serving Special Populations Section*] Health Care Libraries Forum
ASCLA LSSPS LSBPHF... ASCLA LSSPS [*Association of Specialized and Cooperative Library Agencies - Libraries Serving Special Populations Section*] Library Service to the Blind andPhysically Handicapped Forum
ASCLA LSSPS LSDDP MAG... ASCLA LSSPS [*Association of Specialized and Cooperative Library Agencies - Libraries Serving Special Populations Section*] Library Service to Developmentally Disabled Persons Membership Activity Group
ASCLA LSSPS LSDF... ASCLA LSSPS [*Association of Specialized and Cooperative Library Agencies - Libraries Serving Special Populations Section*] Library Service to the Deaf Forum
ASCLA LSSPS LSIEF... ASCLA LSSPS [*Association of Specialized and Cooperative Library Agencies - Libraries Serving Special Populations Section*] Library Service to the Impaired Elderly Forum
ASCLA LSSPS LSPF... ASCLA LSSPS [*Association of Specialized and Cooperative Library Agencies - Libraries Serving Special Populations Section*] Library Service to Prisoners Forum
ASCLA Multi-LINCS... ASCLA [*Association of Specialized and Cooperative Library Agencies*] Multitype Library Networks and Cooperatives Section
ASCLA SLAS... ASCLA [*Association of Specialized and Cooperative Library Agencies*] State Library Agency Section
ASCLD .... American Society of Crime Laboratory Directors (EA)
Asclep .... Asclepius [*of Apuleius*] [*Classical studies*] (OCD)
ASCLIC .... Association of South Carolina Life Insurance Companies (SRA)
Ascls .... Ascension of Isaiah (BJA)
ASCLT .... American Society of Clinical Laboratory Technicians [*Later, ASMT*]
ASCLU .... American Society of Chartered Life Underwriters [*Later, ASCLU, ChFC*] (EA)
ASCLU & ChFC... American Society of CLU [*Chartered Life Underwriters*] and ChFC [*Chartered Financial Consultants*] [*Bryn Mawr, PA*] (EA)
ASCM .... Acquisition Strategy Comparison Model (MCD)
ASCM .... Aluminum, Silicon, Calcium, Magnesium [*Geology*]
ASCM .... American Society of Chinese Medicine [*Inactive*]
ASCM .... American Society of Country Music (EA)
ASCM .... Antiship Capable Missile (NVT)
ASCM .... Antiship Cruise Missile
ASCM .... Association of Ships' Compositions Manufacturers [*British*] (BI)
ASCM .... Association of Sprocket Chain Manufacturers [*Defunct*]
ASCM .... Aviation Support Equipment Technician, Master Chief [*Navy rating*]
ASCM .... Cooma [*Australia ICAO location identifier*] (ICLI)
ASCMA .... American Sprocket Chain Manufacturers Association [*Later, American Chain Association*]
ASCMP .... Association of Second Class Mail Publishers (EA)
ASCMS .... American Society of Contemporary Medicine and Surgery (EA)
ASCN .... American Society for Clinical Nutrition (EA)
ASCN .... Camden [*Australia ICAO location identifier*] (ICLI)
ASCNSW ...... Agricultural Societies Council of New South Wales [*Australia*]
ASCO .... Abort Sensing Control Unit
ASCO .... Advanced Systems Concepts Office [*Army*] (RDA)
ASCO .... Air Service Coordination Office [*Military*] (DNAB)
ASCO .... Alpha Solarco [*NASDAQ symbol*] (TTSB)
ASCO .... Alpha Solarco, Inc. [*NASDAQ symbol*] (NQ)
ASCO .... American Society of Clinical Oncology (EA)
ASCO .... American Society of Contemporary Ophthalmology (EA)
ASCO .... Arab Satellite Communications Organization [*League of Arab States*] [*Riyadh, Saudi Arabia*] (EAIO)
ASCO .... Asian Science Communicators' Organization [*International Council of Scientific Unions*]
ASCO .... Associated Spring Corp.
ASCO .... Association of Schools and Colleges of Optometry (EA)
ASCO .... ATMDC [*Apollo Telescope Mount Digital Computer*] Software Control Officer [*NASA*]
ASCO .... Automatic Sustainer Cutoff (MUGU)
ASCO .... Canberra [*Australia ICAO location identifier*] (ICLI)
ASCOA .... American Supercharger Club and Owner's Association (EA)
ASCOA .... Antique Snowmobile Club of America (EA)
AsCoal .... Ashland Coal, Inc. [*Associated Press*] (SAG)
ASCOB .... Any Solid Color Other than Black [*Refers to cocker spaniels*] (IIA)
ASCOD .... Army Systems Coordinating Documents
AS Code ..... American Samoa Code [*A publication*] (DLA)
ASCOFAM... Association Mondiale de Lutte Contre la Faim [*World Association for the Struggle Against Hunger*]
ASCOM .... Army Service Command
ASCOMACE... Association des Constructeurs de Machines a Coudre de la CEE [*Association of Sewing Machine Manufacturers of the EEC*]
ASCOMED... Air Service Coordination Office, Mediterranean [*Military*] (DNAB)
ASCOMM..... Antisubmarine Warfare Communications (DNAB)
ASCOMMDET... Antisubmarine Warfare Communications Detachment (DNAB)

ASCON........ Automated Switched Communications Network (MCD)
A-SCOOR..... Air-Scooping Orbital Rocket (PDAA)
ASCOP........ Advanced Submarine Control Program (MCD)
ASCOP........ Applied Science Corp. of Princeton (MCD)
ASCOP........ [A] Statistical Computing Procedure
ASCOPE...... ASEAN [Association of South East Asian Nations] Council on
                Petroleum [Indonesia]
ASCORE...... Automatic Shipboard Checkout and Readiness Equipment (MCD)
ASCOT........ Adaptive Signal Control Optimization Techniques
ASCOT........ Analogue Simulation of Competitive Operational Tactics [Game]
ASCOT........ A Severity Characterization of Trauma [Medicine] (DMAA)
ASCOT........ Asphalt Coking Technology
ASCOT........ Association of Soil Conservation Officer Trainees
ASCOT........ Atmospheric Studies in Complex Terrain (PDAA)
ASCOTA...... American Student Committee of the Occupational Therapy
                Association [American Occupational Therapy Association]
ASCP .... Aboriginal Staff Cadetship Program [Australia]
ASCP .... African Safari Club of Philadelphia (EA)
ASCP .... Air Standardization Coordination Program [NATO]
ASCP .... American Society of Clinical Pathologists (EA)
ASCP .... American Society of Clinical Pathologists (DMAA)
ASCP .... American Society of Consultant Pharmacists (EA)
ASCP .... American Society of Consulting Pharmacists (DMAA)
ASCP .... American Society of Consulting Planners (EA)
ASCP .... Anglo-Saxon Christian Patriot (EA)
ASCP .... Army Small Computers Program
ASCP .... Army Strategic Capabilities Plan
ASCP .... Attitude Set Control Panel [Aerospace] (NASA)
ASCP .... Automatic System Checkout Program
ASCP .... Aviation System Capacity Plan [FAA] (TAG)
ASCPA .... American Shrimp Canners and Processors Association [Later,
                ASPA] (EA)
ASCPC .... American Society of Clinical Pharmacology and Chemotherapy
                (DAVI)
ASCR .... Advanced Sodium-Cooled Reactor
ASCR .... American Society of Chiropodical Roentgenology
ASCR .... American Society of Clinic Radiologists (EA)
ASCR .... Analog Strip Chart Recorder
ascr .... Ascriptum [Ascribed To] [Latin] (MAE)
ASCR .... Association of Specialists in Cleaning and Restoration (EA)
ASCR .... Asymmetric Silicon Controlled Rectifier [Electronics] (TEL)
ASCRA .... American Standard Chinchilla Rabbit Association (EA)
ASCRE .... Assistant Secretary for Conservation and Renewable Energy
ASCRO........ Active Service Career for Reserve Officers
ASCRS .... American Society of Cataract and Refractive Surgery (EA)
ASCRS .... American Society of Colon and Rectal Surgeons (EA)
ASCRT .... Association for the Study of Canadian Radio and Television
                [Pronounced "Askrat"] [See also AERTC]
ASCRT .... Association for the Study of Canadian Radio & Television
                [Association pour les Etudes sur la Radio-Television
                Canadienne] (AC)
ASCS .... Academic Self-Concept Scale (EDAC)
ASCS .... Admission Scheduling and Control System [Hospital management]
ASCS .... Advanced Stirling Conversion System [Mechanical engineering]
ASCS .... Aerospace Surveillance and Control Squadron [Air Force]
ASCS .... Agricultural Stabilization and Conservation Service [Department of
                Agriculture]
ASCS .... American Society of Corporate Secretaries [New York, NY] (EA)
ASCS .... American Society of Cosmetic Surgeons [Later, AACS] (EA)
ASCS .... Area Surveillance Control System (IEEE)
ASCS .... Association des Conseils Sub-Aquatiques Canadiens [Association of
                Canadian Underwater Councils]
ASCS .... Atmospheric Storage and Control Section [Spacelab] [NASA]
ASCS .... Attitude and Spin Control Subsystem [NASA]
ASCS .... Attitude Stabilization and Control System (MCD)
ASCS .... Australian Society for Classical Studies
ASCS .... Automated Ship Classification System (MCD)
ASCS .... Automated Storage Control System (MCD)
ASCS .... Automatic Scan Counter System
ASCS .... Automatic Stabilization and Control System
ASCS .... Aviation Support Equipment Technician, Senior Chief [Navy rating]
ASCSA .... American School and Community Safety Association [Later, The
                Safety Society]
ASCSR .... Armed Services Commissary Store Regulations (DNAB)
ASCSRA...... Alberta Senior Citizens Sport & Recreation Association (AC)
ASCT.......... Address Space Control Task [Fujitsu] (NITA)
ASCT.......... Agricultural Show Council of Tasmania [Australia]
ASCT.......... Americans for Safe and Competitive Trucking (EA)
ASCT.......... American Society for Cytotechnology (EA)
ASCT.......... Associate Member of the Society of Cardiological Technicians
                [British] (DBQ)
ASCT.......... Associate Member of the Society of Commercial Teachers [British]
                (DBQ)
ASCT.......... Association of String Class Teachers [British] (BI)
ASCT.......... Australasian Smaller Companies Trust
ASCTLA...... Armed Services Court Lawyers Association [Now BCALA] (AAGC)
ASCTRLA..... Alliance of State Car and Truck Renting and Leasing Associations
                [Defunct] (EA)
ASCU .... Air Support Control Units
ASCU .... Alarm System Control Unit
ASCU .... Armament Station Control Unit
ASCU .... Armament Systems Control Unit (MCD)
ASCU .... Association of Small Computer Users [Later, ACU] (EA)
ASCU .... Association of State Colleges and Universities [Later, AASCU]
ASCU .... Automatic Scanning Control Unit

ASCUE .... Association of Small Computer Users [Later, ACU] (CSR)
ASCUE .... Association of Small Computer Users in Education (NITA)
ASCUFRO .... Association of State Colleges and Universities Forestry Research
                Organizations
ASCUS .... Association for School, College, and University Staffing (EA)
ASCUS .... Atypical Squamous Cells of Undetermined Significance [Medicine]
ASCVD .... Arteriosclerotic Cardiovascular Disease [Cardiology]
ASCVD .... Atherosclerotic Cardiovascular Disease [Medicine] (MAE)
ASCVIS .... Armed Services - Civilian Interest Survey [Test]
ASCVRD....... Arteriosclerotic Cardiovascular Renal Disease [Medicine] (DAVI)
AScW .... Association of Scientific Workers [British]
ASD .... Academy for Sports Dentistry (EA)
ASD .... Accao Social Democratica [Social Democratic Action] [Portugal
                Political party] (PPE)
ASD .... Acceleration Spectral Density (PDAA)
ASD .... Adaptive Seating Device [Occupational therapy]
ASD .... Adaptive Solution Domain
ASD .... Adjustable Speed Drive
ASD .... Administrative Services Department [Queensland, Australia]
ASD .... Administrative Services Division [Census] (OICC)
ASD .... Administrative Survey Detachment [Army] (LAIN)
ASD .... Admiralty Salvage Department [British military] (DMA)
ASD .... Adult Services Division [American Library Association] [Later,
                RASD] (EA)
ASD .... Advanced Ship Development
ASD .... Advanced Submarine Detection (MCD)
ASD .... Advanced Surveillance Drone (MCD)
ASD .... Advanced Systems and Design
ASD .... Advanced Systems Division [IBM Corp.]
ASD .... Aeronautical System Development (NG)
ASD .... Aeronautical Systems Division [Wright-Patterson Air Force Base, OH]
                [Air Force]
ASD .... Aerospace Services Division [NASA] (KSC)
ASD .... Affective Spectrum Disorder [Psychiatry] (ECON)
ASD .... Aircraft Situation Display [FAA] (TAG)
ASD .... Aircraft Statistical Data
ASD .... Air Sinai [Egypt] [ICAO designator] (FAAC)
ASD .... Air Situation Display (SAA)
ASD .... Air Support Director [Military] (NVT)
ASD .... Airworthiness Substantiation Document [Army] (RDA)
ASD .... Aldosterone Secretion Defect [Endocrinology] (MAE)
ASD .... Alliance pour la Social-Democratie [Benin] [Political party] (EY)
ASD .... All Saints' Day
ASD .... Alternate Source Development
ASD .... Amchitka [Alaska] [Seismograph station code, US Geological Survey
                Closed] (SEIS)
ASD .... American Society of Dermatopathology (EA)
ASD .... American Society of Dowsers (EA)
ASD .... American Standard Companies, Inc. [NYSE symbol] (SAG)
ASD .... Amer Standard [NYSE symbol] (TTSB)
ASD .... (Amino)selenadiazole [Antiviral compound]
ASD .... Ammunition Subdepot [United Kingdom] (NATG)
ASD .... Ammunition Supply Depot
ASD .... Ammunition Supply Dump [British World War II]
ASD .... Amplitude Spectral Density [Physics]
ASD .... Analysis and Support Division [Environmental Protection Agency]
                (GFGA)
ASD .... Andros Town [Bahamas] [Airport symbol] (OAG)
ASD .... Anterior Sagittal Diameter [Medicine] (MEDA)
ASD .... Anthracene Scintillation Dosimeter
ASD .... Antislack Device
ASD .... Anti-Slip Differential [Automotive engineering]
ASD .... Anti-Submarine Division [British military] (DMA)
ASD .... Apollo Standard Detonator [NASA]
ASD .... Apollo Support Department [NASA] (KSC)
ASD .... Application Systems Developer [Army]
ASD .... Applied Science Division [GAO] (AAGC)
ASD .... Armament Supply Department [Navy British]
ASD .... Army Schools Department [British military] (DMA)
ASD .... Army Shipping Document
ASD .... Artillery Spotting Division [Air Force]
ASD .... Assented [Investment term]
ASD .... Assignment Selection Date [Military] (AFM)
ASD .... Assign Symbolic Device (IAA)
ASD .... Assistant Secretary of Defense
ASD .... Assistant State Director
ASD .... Associated Surplus Dealers (EA)
ASD .... Association for Social Design [Later, BRI] (EA)
ASD .... Association for the Study of Dreams (EA)
ASD .... Association of Steel Distributors (EA)
ASD .... Assumed
ASD .... Atomic Solution Diffusion
ASD .... Atrial Septal Defect [Cardiology]
ASD .... Australian Sentencing Digest [A publication]
ASD .... Automated Structural Design [NASA]
ASD .... Automatic Shutdown [Automotive engineering]
ASD .... Automatic Synchronized Discriminator (DEN)
ASD .... Average Sorties per Day [Air Force] (AFIT)
ASD .... Aviation Service Date (AFM)
ASD .... Aviation Supply Depot
ASDA .... Accelerate-Stop Distance Available [FAA] (TAG)
ASDA .... Accelerate-Stop Distance Available [Aviation] (FAAC)
ASDA .... Accountable Supply Distribution Activity (MCD)
ASDA .... Alabama Soft Drink Association (SRA)
ASDA .... All Star Dairy Association (EA)

ASDA .... American Seafood Distributors Association (EA)
ASDA .... American Society for Dental Aesthetics (EA)
ASDA .... American Stamp Dealers Association (EA)
ASDA .... American Student Dental Association (EA)
ASDA .... Arizona State Dental Association (SRA)
ASDA .... Arkansas Soft Drink Association (SRA)
ASDA .... Arkansas State Dental Association (SRA)
ASDA .... Asbestos & Danville [AAR code]
ASD (A) ...... Assistant Secretary of Defense (Administration) (AABC)
ASDA .... Associated Dairies [Commercial firm British]
ASDA .... Associate of Speech and Drama, Australia
ASDA .... Association for the Support and Diffusion of Art (EA)
ASDA .... Association of Structural Draftsmen of America (EA)
ASDA .... Atomic Space and Development Authority [Nuclear energy]
ASDA .... Australian Screen Directors' Association
ASD/A-10-SPO... Aeronautical Systems Division A-10 System Program Office [Wright-Patterson Air Force Base, OH]
ASD(A & L)... Assistant Secretary of Defense for Acquisition and Logistics
ASDACS...... Acoustic Signal Data Analysis and Conversion System [Navy]
ASDAE .... Association of Seventh-Day Adventist Educators (EA)
ASDAL .... Association of Seventh-Day Adventist Librarians (EA)
ASD/AMD..... Associated Surplus Dealers and Associated Merchandise Dealers Trade Show (ITD)
ASD & SVN... Army Switched Data and Secure Voice Network
ASDAP........ Army Systems Development and Acquisition Priorities (MCD)
ASDAR........ Aircraft-to-Satellite Data Relay [Meteorology]
AsDB .... Asian Development Bank (EY)
AsdBnc .... Associated Banc-Corp. [Associated Press] (SAG)
ASDC .... Aeronomy and Space Data Center [Later, NGSDC] [National Oceanic and Atmospheric Administration]
ASDC .... Alaska State Data Center [Alaska State Department of Labor] [Information service or system] (IID)
ASDC .... Alberta Scuba Divers Council (AC)
ASDC .... Alternative System Design Concept
ASDC .... American Society for Deaf Children [Defunct] (EA)
ASDC .... American Society of Dentistry for Children (EA)
ASDC .... Army Strategic Defense Command [Huntsville, AL]
ASD (C) ...... Assistant Secretary of Defense (Comptroller)
ASDC .... Associate of the Society of Dyers and Colourists [British] (DBQ)
ASDC .... Association of Sleep Disorders Centers (EA)
ASDC .... Association of State Democratic Chairs (EA)
ASDC .... Association Social-Democrate du Cameroun [Political party] (EY)
ASD(C3I)... Assistant Secretary of Defense (Communications, Command-Control, and Intelligence) (AABC)
ASD (CD).... Assistant Secretary of Defense (Civil Defense)
ASDCL .... Alaska State District Council of Laborers (SRA)
ASDD .... Antisubmarine Development Detachment [Atlantic Fleet] [Norfolk, VA]
ASDD .... Apollo Signal Definition Document [NASA] (KSC)
ASDE .... Aerospace Driver (GFGA)
ASDE .... Airport Surface Detection Equipment [RADAR]
ASDE .... American Society of Danish Engineers (EA)
ASDE .... American Society of Design Engineers (EA)
ASDE .... Antenna Slave Data Equipment (IAA)
ASDE .... Asbestos and Danville [Railroad] (MHDB)
A/S DE........ Aux Soins De [Care Of, c/o] [French]
ASDEC........ Applied Systems Development and Evaluation Center
ASDEC........ Automatic Selection of Digital Electronic Computers
ASDEFORLANT... Antisubmarine Defense Forces, Atlantic [Obsolete Navy]
ASDEFORPAC... Antisubmarine Defense Forces, Pacific [Obsolete Navy]
ASDEM .... Association of Sterilizer and Disinfector Equipment Manufacturers [British] (EAIO)
ASD(ES)...... Assistant Secretary of Defense for Economic Security (RDA)
AsdEst .... Associated Estates Realty [Associated Press] (SAG)
AsdEstat ...... Associated Estates Realty [Associated Press] (SAG)
ASDEVDET... Antisubmarine Development Detachment [Navy] (DNAB)
ASDEVLANT... Antisubmarine Development Detachment, Atlantic Fleet [Navy]
ASDF .... Aeronautical Systems Division Form
ASDF .... Air Self-Defense Force [Japan] (CINC)
ASDF .... Air Staff Defense Force (CINC)
ASD(FM & P)... Assistant Secretary of Defense (Force Management and Personnel) (DOMA)
ASDG .... Aircraft Storage and Disposition Group [Air Force]
ASDG .... Antisubmarine Defense Group
ASDH .... Acute Subdural Hematoma [Medicine]
ASD(HA)...... Assistant Secretary of Defense (Health Affairs) (AABC)
ASD (H & E)... Assistant Secretary of Defense (Health and Environment)
ASD/H & M... Assistant Secretary of Defense (Health and Medical)
ASDI .... All Source Document Index [Army]
ASD (I) .... Assistant Secretary of Defense (Intelligence)
ASDI .... Associacao Social Democrata Independente [Independent Social Democrat Association] [Portugal Political party] (PPE)
ASDI .... Automatic Selective Dissemination of Information
ASD (I & L)... Assistant Secretary of Defense (Installations and Logistics)
ASDIC .... Antisubmarine Detection Investigation Committee [A group in World War I that gave rise to the device that bore its name in World War II]
ASDIC .... Armed Services Documents Intelligence Center [DoD]
ASDIC .... Association of Information and Dissemination Centers (MHDB)
ASDIC .... British term for sonar (DOMA)
ASDIRS........ Army Study Documentation and Information Retrieval System [Later, ALAS]
ASD/ISA...... Assistant Secretary of Defense (International Security Affairs)
ASDJ.......... American Society of Disk Jockeys [Defunct] (EA)
ASDL .... Advanced STANO [Surveillance, Target Acquisition, and Night Observation] Data Link [Military] (MCD)

ASDL .... Aeronautical Satellite Datalink System [Mitre Corp.] (NITA)
ASDL .... Automated Ship Data Library (IEEE)
ASD(LA)....... Assistant Secretary of Defense (Legislative Affairs) (DOMA)
ASDM .... Aeronautical Systems Division Manual
ASDM .... Aerosurface Driver/Monitor [NASA] (MCD)
ASDM .... Air Bag System Diagnostic Module [Automotive engineering]
ASDM .... America's Society of Separated and Divorced Men (EA)
ASDM .... Apollo-Soyuz Docking Module [NASA]
ASD (M) ...... Assistant Secretary of Defense (Manpower)
ASDM .... Association of Steel Drum Manufacturers [British] (BI)
ASD (M & RA)... Assistant Secretary of Defense (Manpower and Reserve Affairs) [Later, ASD (MRA & L)] (AABC)
ASD/MP & R... Assistant Secretary of Defense (Manpower, Personnel, and Reserves)
ASD (MRA & L)... Assistant Secretary of Defense (Manpower, Reserve Affairs, and Logistics) [Formerly, ASD (M & RA)]
ASD-NSC .... Aviation Supply Depot - Naval Supply Center (MCD)
ASDO .... Assistant Staff Duty Officer (CINC)
ASDO .... Aviation Safety District Office
ASDP .... Advance Sensor Development Program [Military] (MCD)
ASDP .... Assistant Secretary for Defense Programs
ASDP .... Automatic Shot Dispensing Pump
ASD (PA) .... Assistant Secretary of Defense (Public Affairs)
ASDPA........ Association of Seventh Day Pentecostal Assemblies (EA)
ASD (PA & E)... Assistant Secretary of Defense (Program Analysis and Evaluation) (AABC)
ASD/P & I.... Assistant Secretary of Defense (Properties and Installations)
ASD(P & L)... ASD (Production and Logistics) (DOMA)
ASDPSIM.... Advanced System Data Processing Simulation (AABC)
ASDR .... Aeronautical Systems Division Regulation
ASDR .... Airport Surface Detection RADAR
ASDR .... American Society of Dental Radiographers
ASDR .... American Society of Dermatological Retailers (EA)
ASDR .... Avionic Systems Demonstrator Rig (PDAA)
ASD(RA)...... Assistant Secretary of Defense (Reserve Affairs) [DoD] (GFGA)
ASD/R & D... Assistant Secretary of Defense (Research and Development)
ASD/R & E... Assistant Secretary of Defense (Research and Engineering)
ASDS .... Advanced Seal Delivery System [Formerly, Advanced Swimmer Delivery System] [Navy] (DOMA)
ASDS .... Aircraft Sound Description System [FAA]
ASDS .... American Society for Dermatologic Surgery (EA)
ASDS .... Association for the Study of Dada and Surrealism (EA)
ASD (SA).... Assistant Secretary of Defense (Systems Analysis) (AABC)
ASD/S & L... Assistant Secretary of Defense (Supply and Logistics)
ASDSO .... Association of State Dam Safety Officials (EA)
ASDSRS...... Automatic Spectrum Display and Signal Recognition System (IEEE)
ASDSVN....... Army Switched Data and Secure Voice Network
ASDT .... American Spanish Dance Theatre
ASD (T) ...... Assistant Secretary of Defense (Telecommunications)
ASDTIC .... Analog Signal to Discrete Time Interval Converter [NASA]
ASDTP .... Apollo Spacecraft Development Test Plan [NASA] (KSC)
ASDU .... Dubbo [Australia ICAO location identifier] (ICLI)
ASDV .... Aspect Development [NASDAQ symbol] (SAG)
ASDV .... Aspect Development [NASDAQ symbol] (TTSB)
ASDV .... Swimmer Delivery Vehicle Support Craft (DNAB)
ASDVS........ American Society of Directors of Volunteer Services (EA)
ASDW .... Admiralty Sailing Directions for the World (BARN)
ASDWA........ Association of State Drinking Water Administrators (EA)
ASE .... Active Seismic Experiment [NASA] (MCD)
ASE .... Acute Stress Erosion [Gastroenterology] (DAVI)
ASE .... Administration Support Equipment (MCD)
ASE .... Admiralty Signal Establishment [British]
ASE .... Advanced Space Engine (NASA)
ASE .... Advanced Systems Engineering
ASE .... Aerial Survival Equipment
ASE .... Aerospace Support Equipment
ASE .... Agence Spatiale Europeenne [European Space Agency] (EAIO)
ASE .... Airborne Search Equipment
ASE .... Airborne Support Equipment (MCD)
ASE .... Aircraft Stabilization Equipment [Aviation] (PDAA)
ASE .... Aircraft Stores Establishment [Navy]
ASE .... Aircraft Survivability Equipment
ASE .... Aircraft Survivability Equipment (DOMA)
ASE .... Airport Surface Detection Equipment [RADAR] (IAA)
ASE .... Air Standard Efficiency
ASE .... Air Surveillance Evaluation (SAA)
ASE .... Alberta Stock Exchange (HGAA)
ASE .... Alliance to Save Energy (EA)
ASE .... Allied Supply Executive [World War II]
ASE .... Allowable Steering Error
ASE .... All-Steel Equipment, Inc.
ASE .... Alternative Sources of Energy (EA)
ASE .... Alternative System Exploration (MCD)
ASE .... Altimetry System Error [Aviation] (DA)
ASE .... Amalgamated Society of Engineers [A union] [British]
ASE .... American Science & Engineering, Inc. [AMEX symbol] (SPSG)
ASE .... American Scientific Engineering (KSC)
ASe .... American Sephardi (BJA)
ASE .... American Society for Ethnohistory (EA)
ASE .... American Society of Echocardiography (EA)
ASE .... American Society of Educators [Later, AAMSL] (EA)
ASE .... American Society of Employers (SRA)
ASE .... American Society of Engineers
ASE .... American Society of Enologists (EA)
ASE .... American Stock Exchange (EA)

ASE	Amer Science & Engr [*AMEX symbol*] (TTSB)
ASE	Amplified Spontaneous Emission (MCD)
ASE	Amplified Stimulated Emission (PDAA)
ASE	Anisotropic Stress Effect (PDAA)
ASE	Anomolous Skin Effect (PDAA)
ASE	Antisubmarine Establishment [*Navy British*]
ASE	Application Service Element [*Telecommunications*] (OSI)
ASE	Application Swapping Extensions [*Computer science*] (PCM)
ASE	Arizona State University, College of Educational Technology and Library Science, Tempe, AZ [*OCLC symbol*] (OCLC)
ASE	Armed Services Edition [*Publishing*] [*World War II*]
ASE	Army School of Education [*British*]
ASE	Aserradero [*Nicaragua*] [*Seismograph station code, US Geological Survey*] (SEIS)
ASE	Aspen [*Colorado*] [*Airport symbol*] (OAG)
ASE	Associate in Engineering
ASE	Associate in Science in Engineering
ASE	Association for Science Education [*British*] (DEN)
ASE	Association for Social Economics (EA)
ASE	Association for Special Education [*British*] (BI)
ASE	Association for Stamp Exhibitions [*Defunct*]
ASE	Association for Surgical Education (EA)
ASE	Association of Scientists and Engineers of the Naval Sea Systems Command (EA)
ASE	Association of Senior Engineers [*NAVSHIPS*]
ASE	Association of Space Explorers [*Later, ASE-USA*] (EA)
ASE	Asymptotic Standard Error [*Statistics*]
ASE	Atlantic Southeast Airlines, Inc. [*ICAO designator*] (FAAC)
ASE	Audio Support Equipment
ASE	Augmentation Stabilization Equipment
ASE	Australasian Society of Engineers
ASE	Australian Stock Exchange Indices [*Database*] [*Sydney Stock Exchange*] [*Information service or system*] (CRD)
ASE	AutoCAD [*Computer-Aided Design*] Sequel Extension [*Computer science*]
ASE	AutoCAD [*Computer-Aided Design*] SQL Extension [*Structured Query Language*] (PCM)
ASE	Automated Speed Enforcement
ASE	Automatic Sequence Enable
ASE	Automatic Stabilization Equipment
ASE	Automatic Support Equipment [*Military*]
ASE	Automotive Service Excellence
ASE	Aviation Support, Electrical [*Navy rating*]
ASE	Aviation Support Equipment (CAAL)
ASE	Axilla, Shoulder, Elbow [*Bandage*]
ASE	NAS System Engineering Service [*FAA*] (TAG)
ASE	National Institute for Automotive Service Excellence (EA)
ASE	Sedgewick Public Library, Alberta [*Library symbol National Library of Canada*] (NLC)
ASE2	Aviation Support Equipment Technician, Electrical, Second Class [*Navy rating*] (DNAB)
ASE3	Aviation Support Equipment Technician, Electrical, Third Class [*Navy rating*] (DNAB)
ASEA	Agricultural Show Exhibitors' Association [*British*] (BI)
ASEA	Alabama State Employees Association (SRA)
ASEA	American Society for Eastern Arts
ASEA	American Society of Engineers and Architects
ASEA	American Solar Energy Association (EA)
ASEA	Arizona State Electronics Association (SRA)
ASEA	Arkansas State Employees Association (SRA)
ASEA	ASEA AB [*NASDAQ symbol*] (NQ)
ASEA	Augustinian Secondary Educational Association (EA)
ASEAA	Aviation Support Equipment Technician, Electrical, Airman Apprentice [*Navy rating*] (DNAB)
ASEAMS	Association of South-East Asian Marine Scientists [*Marine science*] (OSRA)
ASEAN	Association of Southeast Asian Nations (ECON)
ASEAN	Association of Southeast Asian Nations (DOMA)
ASEAN-ABC	ASEAN [*Association of South East Asian Nations*] - Australia Business Council
ASEANAM	ASEAN [*Association of South East Asian Nations*] Association of Museums (EAIO)
ASEANIS	Association of South East Asian Nations: Indonesia-Singapore [*Submarine cable*] [*Telecommunications*]
ASEANPS	Association of South East Asian Nations: Philippines-Singapore [*Submarine cable*] [*Telecommunications*] (TEL)
ASEAQ	Association of Special Education Administrators in Queensland [*Australia*]
ASEAS(UK)	Association of Southeast Asian Studies in the (United Kingdom)
ASEAUS	Association of Southeast Asian University Students
ASEB	Aeronautics and Space Engineering Board [*National Academy of Engineering*]
ASEBS	Association of Senior Engineers of the Bureau of Ships [*Later, ASE*] (EA)
ASEC	Action Sports Entertainment Cable [*Cable TV programming service*]
ASEC	Airworthiness Standards Evaluation Committee [*FAA*]
ASEC	Allied Secretariat [*Allied German Occupation Forces*]
ASE(C)	Allied Supply Executive, China [*World War II*]
ASEC	American Standard Elevator Code
ASEC	Aseco Corp. [*NASDAQ symbol*] (SAG)
ASECA	Association for Education and Cultural Advancement [*South Africa*]
ASECA	Association of Securities and Exchange Commission Alumni (EA)
ASECC	American Stock Exchange Clearing Corp.

ASECNA	Agence pour la Securite de la Navigation Aerienne en Afrique et Madagascar [*Agency for Air Navigation Safety in Africa and Madagascar*] (AF)
ASECNA	Agency for the Security of Air Navigation (AFM)
Aseco	Aseco Corp. [*Associated Press*] (SAG)
ASECS	American Society for Eighteenth-Century Studies (EA)
ASECT	American Society of Extra-Corporeal Technology [*Medicine*] (DAVI)
ASECUC	Association des Services aux Etudiants des Colleges et Universites du Canada [*Canadian Association of College and University Student Services*]
ASED	Ammoniaque Synthetique et Derives [*Belgium*]
ASED	Army School of Education and Depot [*British*] (BI)
ASED	Assessment Statute Expiration Date [*IRS*]
ASEd	Associate in Science Education
ASED	Automated Speed Enforcement Device
ASED	Aviation and Surface Effects Department [*David W. Taylor Naval Ship Research and Development Center*]
ASED	Aviation Service Entry Data (AABC)
ASED	Avionics Systems Engineering Division [*Johnson Space Center*] [*NASA*] (NASA)
ASEdCert	Advanced Specialist in Education Certificate (GAGS)
ASEDO	Association of Self Employment Developers of Ontario (AC)
ASEDP	Army Space Exploitation Demonstration Program [*Army*]
ASEE	Advanced Semiconductor Equipment Exposition (TSPED)
ASEE	American Society for Engineering Education (EA)
ASEE	American Society for Environmental Education (EA)
ASEE	American Society of Electrical Engineers (NTCM)
A/SEE	Antisubmarine Experimental Establishment
ASEE	Associate in Science in Electronic Engineering (IAA)
ASEE	Association of Supervisory and Executive Engineers [*A union*] [*British*]
ASEET	Associate in Science in Electronic Engineering Technology
ASEF	Association of Stock Exchange Firms [*Later, SIA*] (EA)
ASEFNS	Association of South East Field Naturalists Societies
ASEG	All-Services Evaluation Group [*Military*]
ASEH	American Society for Environmental History (EA)
ASEI	American Sports Education Institute (EA)
ASEI	Australian Sports and Economics Institute
ASEIB	American Sanitary Engineering Intersociety Board [*Later, AAEE*] (EA)
ASEINDEX	Australian Stock Exchange Indices [*Database*] [*Sydney Stock Exchange*] [*Information service or system*]
ASEIP	Army Command and Control System Engineering Implementation Plan
ASEL	Airplane Single-Engine Land [*Aviation rating*]
ASeLC	Alabama Lutheran College, Selma, AL [*Library symbol Library of Congress*] (LCLS)
ASelPort	American Select Portfolios, Inc. [*Associated Press*] (SAG)
ASELT	Association Europeenne pour l'Echange de la Litterature Technique dans le Domaine de la Siderurgie [*European Association for the Exchange of Technical Literature in the Field of Ferrous Metallurgy - EAETLFFM*] (EAIO)
ASEM	American Society for Engineering Management (EA)
ASEM	Analytical Scanning Electron Microscope
ASEM	Anti-Satellite Engagement Model [*Military*]
ASEM	Anti-Surface Euromissile Consortium (PDAA)
ASEM	Association of State Employees in Management (SRA)
ASEMC	Autobody Supply and Equipment Manufacturers Council [*Defunct*] (EA)
ASE(ME)	Allied Supply Executive, Middle East [*World War II*]
ASEMSMP	Amalagmated Society of Engineers, Machinists, Smiths, Millwrights, and Pattern Makers [*A union*] [*British*]
ASensrs	American Sensors, Inc. [*Associated Press*] (SAG)
ASEO	Army System Engineering Office (RDA)
ASE(OA)	Allied Supply Executive, Other Allies [*World War II*]
ASE(OC)	Allied Supply Executive, Chinese Oil Supplies [*World War II*]
ASEODCG	Armed Services Explosive Ordnance Disposal Coordinating Group
ASEP	Accident Sequence Evaluation Program [*Nuclear energy*] (NRCH)
ASEP	Advanced Science Education Program [*National Science Foundation*]
ASEP	Advanced Skills Education Program [*Army*]
ASEP	American Society for Experimental Pathology [*Later, AAP*] (EA)
ASEP	American Society of Electroplated Plastics (EA)
ASEP	Array Structure Experiment Package [*Computer science*] (IAA)
ASEP	Association of Special Events Professionals (SRA)
ASEP	Automated Signal Excess Prediction (MCD)
ASEP	Automatic Sequence Execution and Processor (MCD)
ASEP	Automotive Service Education Program [*General Motors*] (EDAC)
ASEPELT	Association Scientifique Europeenne pour la Prevision Economique a Moyen et LongTerme [*European Scientific Association for Medium and Long-Term Economic Forecasts*]
ASE(PG)	Allied Supply Executive, Persian Gulf [*World War II*]
ASE-PM	Aircraft Survivability Equipment - Product Manager
ASEPS	Astronomical Studies of Extrasolar Planetary Systems [*NASA*]
ASEPS	Automatic Signal Excess Prediction System (CAAL)
ASE(R)	Allied Supply Executive, Russia and Persian Gulf [*World War II*]
ASER	Amplification by Stimulated Emission of Radiation
ASER	Armed Services Exchange Regulation [*DoD*]
ASERCA	Aeroservicios Carabobo CA [*Venezuela*] [*ICAO designator*] (FAAC)
ASERCA	Association for Strengthening Agricultural Research in Eastern and Central Africa (ECON)
ASERL	Association of Southeastern Research Libraries [*Library network*]
ASERTT	Alliance for Simple, Equitable, and Rational Truck Taxation (EA)
ASES	Aircraft Single Engine Sea [*Pilot rating*] (AIA)
ASES	American Shoulder and Elbow Surgeons (EA)
ASES	American Solar Energy Society (EA)

ASES........... Assistant Secretary for Employment Standards [*Department of Labor*]
A Se S .... Associate in Secretarial Science
ASES........... Automated Software Evaluation System
ASESA .... Armed Services Electro-Standards Agency [*Later, DESC*]
ASESB .... Armed Services Explosives Safety Board [*Army*]
ASESBD ...... Armed Services Explosives Safety Board [*Army*] (AABC)
A Se Sc .... Associate in Secretarial Science
ASESH .... Assistant Secretary for Environment, Safety, and Health
ASESS .... Aerospace Environment Simulation System
ASET .... Academy of Security Educators and Trainees (EA)
ASET .... ADA and Software Engineering Technology [*British*] (NITA)
ASET .... Adaptive Subbands Excited Transform [*Computer science*]
ASET .... Advanced Sensor Evaluation and Test [*NASA*]
ASET .... Advanced Surface Engineering Technologies
ASET .... Aeronautical Services Earth Terminal (OA)
ASET .... Aircrew Standardization and Evaluation Team [*Military*]
ASET .... Alberta Society of Engineering Technologists (AC)
ASE(T) .... Allied Supply Executive, Transportation [*World War II*]
ASET .... American Society of Electroencephalographic Technologists (EA)
ASET .... American Society of Electro-Neurodiagnostic Technologists (EA)
ASET .... Assistant Secretary for Employment and Training [*Department of Labor*]
ASET .... Associate in Engineering Technology (WGA)
ASET .... Association for Special Education Technology
ASET .... Automated Security Enhancement Tool
ASETA .... Asociacion de Empresas Estatales de Telecomunicaciones del Acuerdo Subregional Andino [*Association of State Telecommunication Undertakings of the Andean Sub regional Agreement*] [*Ecuador*] (EAIO)
ASETC........ Armed Services Electron Tube Committee
ASETDS ...... Aeronautical Support Equipment Type Designation System
AsetInv .... Asset Investors Corp. [*Associated Press*] (SAG)
ASETS........ Advanced System Environment and Threat Simulation
ASETS........ Airborne Seeker Evaluation Test System [*Air Force*]
ASE Tst .... ASE Test Ltd. [*Associated Press*] (SAG)
ASE-USA ..... Association of Space Explorers - USA (EAIO)
ASEV.......... American Society for Enology and Viticulture (EA)
ASEV.......... Arctic Surface Effects Vehicle [*Navy*]
ASEW.......... Airborne and Surface Early Warning
ASEX.......... Atlantic Southeast Airlines, Inc. [*Air carrier designation symbol*]
ASF............. Activation Sequence Factor [*Genetics*]
ASF............. Active Segment Field [*Computer science*] (MHDI)
ASF............. Active Streaming Format [*Computer science*]
ASF............. Activity Support File (DNAB)
ASF............. Additional Selection Factor
ASF............. Advanced Simulation Facility [*Army*] (MCD)
ASF............. Advisory Support Force [*Military*]
ASF............. Aeromedical Staging Facility
ASF............. Aeromedical Staging Flight [*Air Force*]
ASF............. Aeronautical Staging Flight (DNAB)
ASF............. Aerospace Security Force (AFM)
ASF............. African Swine Fever [*Veterinary medicine*]
ASF............. Agricultural Special Fund [*Asian Development Bank*] [*United Nations*] (EY)
ASF............. Aim Safety Co. [*Vancouver Stock Exchange symbol*]
ASF............. Aircraft Services Facility
ASF............. Air Schefferville, Inc. [*Canada ICAO designator*] (FAAC)
ASF............. Air Service Force (IIA)
ASF............. Air Superiority Fighter
ASF............. Alaskan Sea Frontier [*Navy*]
ASF............. Alaska Synthetic Aperture RADAR Facility [*NASA*] (GRD)
ASF............. Albert Schweitzer Fellowship (EA)
ASF............. Alinine, Sulphur, and Formaldehyde [*Medicine*] (BABM)
ASF............. Alternative Salient Future (PDAA)
ASF............. Alternative Splicing Factor [*Genetics*]
ASF............. Ambulatory Surgery Facility [*Health insurance*] (GHCT)
ASF............. American Sailing Foundation (EA)
ASF............. American-Scandinavian Foundation (EA)
ASF............. American Scottish Foundation (EA)
ASF............. American Sephardi Federation (EA)
ASF............. Americans for Safe Food (GNE)
ASF............. American Ski Federation (EA)
ASF............. American Space Foundation [*Defunct*] (EA)
ASF............. American Suicide Fund [*An association*]
ASF............. Amerisafe, Inc. [*NYSE symbol*] (SAG)
ASF............. Ammunition Storage Facility [*Military*]
ASF............. Amperes per Square Foot
ASF............. Aniline, Sulfur, and Formaldehyde [*Resin*] (AAMN)
ASF............. Antistreptolysin Factor (PDAA)
ASF............. Arab Sugar Federation [*Khartoum, Sudan*] (EAIO)
ASF............. Area Sampling Frames
ASF............. Area Spatial Filtering (MCD)
ASF............. Arithmetic Statement Function
ASF............. Army Service Forces [*Formerly, SOS*]
ASF............. Army Stock Fund
ASF............. Assignable Square Feet
ASF............. Assist Ship's Force Funds [*Navy*] (NVT)
ASF............. Associate of the Institute of Shipping and Forwarding Agents (ODBW)
ASF............. Association of State Foresters [*Later, NASF*]
ASF............. Atlantic Salmon Federation (EA)
ASF............. Atmospheric Science Facility [*NASA*] (NASA)
ASF............. Atmospheric Simulation Facility (MCD)
ASF............. Atomic Scattering Factor
ASF............. Audi Space Frame [*Concept car*] [*Automotive engineering*]
ASF............. Automated Submarine Frame [*Navy*]

ASF............. Automatic Sheet Feeder
ASF............. Automatic Signal Filtration [*Electronics*] (IAA)
ASF............. Automatic Store and Forward
ASF............. Automotive Safety Foundation (EA)
ASF............. Auxiliary Stabilizing Support - "A" Frame
ASF............. Auxiliary Supporting Feature (IEEE)
ASFA.......... Agricultural Subterminal Facilities Act of 1980
ASFA.......... American Science Fiction Association (EA)
ASFA.......... American Science Film Association (EA)
ASFA.......... American Sighthound Field Association (EA)
ASFA.......... American Society for Apheresis (EA)
ASFA.......... American Steel Foundrymen's Association
ASFA.......... Aquatic Sciences and Fisheries Abstracts [*Database producer*] (NITA)
ASFA.......... Association pour la Solidarite Franco-Algerienne [*Association for Franco-Algerian Solidarity*] [*French*] (AF)
ASFALEC..... Association des Fabricants de Laits de Conserve des Pays de la CEE [*Association of Powdered Milk Manufacturers of the EEC*]
ASFAP .... AIDS Society for Asia and the Pacific
ASFAR........ Active SONAR Frequency Analysis and Recording
AS(FBM)..... Submarine Tender (Fleet Ballistic Missile) [*Navy symbol*]
ASFC.......... Aircraft Specification Forum Committee
ASFC.......... Air Supply Fan Club (EA)
ASFC.......... Allison Smith Fan Club (EA)
ASFC.......... American Space Frontier Committee [*Defunct*] (EA)
ASFC.......... Andrews Sisters Fan Club (EA)
ASFC.......... Association of Sea Fisheries Committees of England and Wales (DCTA)
ASFC.......... Astoria Financial [*NASDAQ symbol*] (SAG)
ASFD.......... American Society of Furniture Designers (EA)
A/SFDO....... Antisubmarine Fixed Defenses Officer [*Navy*]
ASFE.......... Accelerometer Scale Factor Error
ASFE.......... Assistant Secretary for Fossil Energy
ASFE.......... Association of Soil and Foundation Engineers [*Later, ASFE/The Association of Engineering Firms Practicing in the Geosciences*] (EA)
ASFE.......... Association of Specialized Film Exhibitors [*Defunct*] (EA)
ASFEAEFPG... ASFE [*Association of Soil and Foundation Engineers*]/Association of Engineering Firms Practicing in the Geosciences (EA)
ASFETM...... Association Sectorielle, Fabrication d'Equipement de Transport et de Machines (AC)
ASFFHF....... Academy of Science Fiction, Fantasy, and Horror Films (EA)
ASFG.......... Atmospheric Sound-Focusing Gain
ASFI........... Association of Suppliers to the Furniture Industry [*British*] (EAIO)
ASFI........... Asta Funding, Inc. [*NASDAQ symbol*] (SAG)
ASFI........... Astqa Funding [*NASDAQ symbol*] (TTSB)
ASFIP......... Accelerometer Scale Factor Input Panel
ASFIR......... Active Swept-Frequency Interferometer RADAR [*RADC*]
ASFIS......... Aquatic Sciences and Fisheries Information System [*Food and Agriculture Organization*] [*United Nations*] (IID)
ASFISS .... Advance Simulation Facility Interconnection and Setup System [*or Subsystem*] [*Air Force*]
ASFIT......... Anisotropic Source Flux Iteration Technique (PDAA)
ASFL.......... Australian State Family Law Legislation [*A publication*]
ASFLH........ American Society of the French Legion of Honor (EA)
AS-FLUGZEUG... Luftuberlegenheits Flugzeug (Air Superiority) [*German*] (MCD)
ASFM.......... Association of State Floodplain Managers
ASFMRA ..... American Society of Farm Managers and Rural Appraisers (EA)
ASFMV....... Attempt to Steal from Motor Vehicle [*Criminology*]
ASFN.......... Allstate Financial [*NASDAQ symbol*] (TTSB)
ASFN.......... Allstate Financial Corp. [*NASDAQ symbol*] (NQ)
ASF/NSF ..... Army Stock Fund/Non-Stock Fund
ASFO.......... American Society of Forensic Odontology (EA)
ASFP.......... Association of Smoked Fish Processors (EA)
ASFP.......... Association of Specialised Film Producers [*British*] (BI)
ASFPCM ..... Association of Structural Fire Protection Contractors and Manufacturers Ltd. [*British*] (DBA)
ASFPM....... Association of State Floodplain Managers (EA)
ASFR.......... Age-Specific Fertility Rate
ASFS........... American Seamen's Friend Society [*Defunct*] (EA)
ASFS........... American Society for Friendship with Switzerland [*Later, ASA*] (EA)
ASFS........... Association for the Study of Food and Society (EA)
ASFS........... Automated Shipboard Forecasting System
ASFSA .... American School Food Service Association (EA)
ASFSE........ American Swiss Foundation for Scientific Exchange (EA)
ASFT.......... Artisoft, Inc. [*NASDAQ symbol*] (SPSG)
ASFTC........ Army Service Forces Training Center
ASFTCU ...... Army Service Forces Training Center Unit
ASFTRNTRARONPAC... Auxiliary Service Force, Transition Training Squadron, Pacific
ASFTS........ Airborne Systems Functional Test Stand (IAA)
ASFTS........ Auxiliary Systems Function Test Stand [*NASA*] (KSC)
ASFX.......... Assembly Fixture [*Tool*] (AAG)
ASG........... Administrative Support Group [*Army*]
ASG........... Advanced Studies Group [*Air Force*]
ASG........... Advance Strike Gully [*Mining engineering*]
ASG .... Advocates for Self-Government (EA)
ASG........... Aeronautical Standards Group [*Military*]
ASG........... Aircraft Supply Group
ASG .... Air Safety Group [*British*]
ASG .... Air Service Group [*Air Force*]
ASG .... Air Surveillance Group (SAA)

ASG .... Aktion Soziale Gemeinschaft, die Partei der Sozialversicherten Arbeitnehmer und Rentner [*Social Community Action (Party of Socially Insured Employees and Pensioners)*] [*Germany Political party*] (PPW)
ASG .... American Sewing Guild (EA)
ASG .... American Society for Genetics (DAVI)
ASG .... American Society of Genealogists (EA)
ASG .... American Society of Geolinguistics (EA)
ASG .... Antenna Steering Group
ASG .... Application System Generator
ASG .... Area Support Group [*Military*] (AABC)
ASG .... Army Surgeon General
ASG .... Art Services Grants [*British*]
ASG .... ASG Industries, Inc. [*Formerly, American St. Gobain*]
ASG .... Asialoglycoprotein [*Biochemistry*]
ASG .... Assessment Subgroup [*NATO*] (NATG)
ASG .... Assign (AABC)
asg............. Assignee [*MARC relator code*] [*Library of Congress*] (LCCP)
ASG .... Assistant Secretary General (NATG)
ASG .... Assistant Solicitor-General (DAS)
ASG .... Assistant Surgeon General (DAS)
ASG .... Association of Student Governments
ASG .... Australasian Seabird Group (EA)
ASG .... Automatiches Schaltgetriebe
ASG .... Automatic Spray Gun
ASG .... Auxiliary Steam Generator [*Nuclear energy*] (NRCH)
ASG .... Avionics Subsystem Group [*NASA*] (NASA)
ASG .... Liberty All Star Growth [*NYSE symbol*] (SAG)
ASG .... Liberty ALL-STAR Growth Fd [*NYSE symbol*] (TTSB)
ASG .... Spruce Grove Public Library, Alberta [*Library symbol National Library of Canada*] (NLC)
ASG .... Ukraine Air Service [*FAA designator*] (FAAC)
ASGA .... Advertising Specialty Guild of America
ASGA .... American Sugarbeet Growers Association (EA)
ASGA .... Association des Services Geologiques Africains [*Association of African Geological Surveys - AAGS*] [*ICSU*] (EAIO)
ASGA .... Australian Sporting Goods Association
ASGAN ...... Assistant Secretary General for Air Navigation [*ICAO*]
ASGAP .... Association of Societies for Growing Australian Plants
ASGB .... Adlerian Society of Great Britain (BI)
ASGB .... Aeronautical Society of Great Britain (BI)
ASGB .... Anatomical Society of Great Britain and Ireland (DAVI)
ASGB .... Anthroposophical Society in Great Britain (EAIO)
ASGBI .... Anatomical Society of Great Britain and Ireland
ASGCA .... American Society of Golf Course Architects (EA)
ASGD .... American Society for Geriatric Dentistry
ASGD .... Assigned (AABC)
ASGE .... Acoustic Signal Generator System
ASGE .... American Society for Gastrointestinal Endoscopy (EA)
ASGE .... American Society of Gas Engineers (EA)
ASGE .... Amputee Shoe and Glove Exchange (EA)
ASGE .... Association for the Study of the Grants Economy (EA)
ASGED .... Assigned
ASGEE .... Assignee [*Legal shorthand*] (LWAP)
ASGEN ...... As Generated (MCD)
ASGF .... Association of Scottish Games and Festivals (EA)
ASG ILCO... Assistant Secretary General for Infrastructure, Logistics, and Council Operations [*NATO*]
ASGLS .... Advanced Space Ground Link Subsystem (MCD)
ASGLSSC.... American Society for German Literature of the 16th and 17th Centuries (EA)
ASGM .... American Scripture Gift Mission [*Later, SGM/USA*] (EA)
ASGMT ...... Assignment
asgmt .... Assignment (WDMC)
ASGN .... Assign (AFM)
ASGN .... On Assignment [*NASDAQ symbol*] (TTSB)
ASGN .... On Assignment, Inc. [*NASDAQ symbol*] (SAG)
ASGOBS...... Army Standard Group Order of Battle System (MCD)
ASGOR........ Assignor [*Legal shorthand*] (LWAP)
ASGOSDZ ... American Society of the Greek Order of Saint Dennis of Zante (EA)
ASGP .... Aeronautical Standards Group [*Military*] (AFIT)
ASGP .... Association of Secretaries General of Parliaments (EA)
AS/GPD...... Attitude Set and Gimbal Position Display [*NASA*] (KSC)
ASGPI .... Association of Sea Grant Program Institutes [*Marine science*] (OSRA)
ASGPI .... Association of Sea Grant Program Institutes (USDC)
AS/GPI .... Attitude Set and Gimbal Position Indicator [*NASA*]
ASGPP .... American Society of Group Psychotherapy and Psychodrama (EA)
ASGPR .... Asialoglycoprotein Receptor [*Biochemistry*]
ASGR .... America Service Group, Inc. [*NASDAQ symbol*] (SAG)
ASGR .... Amer Service Group [*NASDAQ symbol*] (TTSB)
ASGRO....... Armed Services Graves Registration Office [*Later, AFIRB*]
ASGS .... Advanced Space Guidance System (IIA)
ASGS .... American Scientific Glassblowers Society (EA)
ASGS .... Assistant Secretary of the General Staff
ASGTMEM ... Amalgamated Society of General Tool Makers, Engineers, and Machinists [*A union*] [*British*]
AsGTU .... Technische Universitat Graz, Graz, Austria [*Library symbol Library of Congress*] (LCLS)
ASGV .... Apple Stem Grooving Virus [*Plant pathology*]
ASGW .... Association for Specialists in Group Work (EA)
ASGY .... Yellowhead Regional Library, Spruce Grove, Alberta [*Library symbol National Library of Canada*] (NLC)
ASH .... Academy of Scientific Hypno Therapy (EA)
ASH .... Achaete-Scute Homologue [*Genetics*]
ASH .... Action on Smoking and Health (EA)

ASH .... Advanced Scout Helicopter [*Military*]
ASH .... Aerial Scout Helicopter (MCD)
ASH .... Aldosterone-Stimulating Hormone [*Also, AGTr*] [*Endocrinology*]
ASH .... American Society of Hematology (EA)
ASH .... American Society of Hypertension (EA)
ASH .... American-Soviet Homestays (EA)
ASH .... Antiself Homing [*System*] [*Torpedo safety device*] [*Navy*]
ASH .... Antistreptococcal Hyaluronidase [*Medicine*] (DMAA)
ASH .... Armature Shunt [*Electromagnetism*]
ASH .... Ashendon [*England*]
ASH .... Ashkhabad [*Former USSR Seismograph station code, US Geological Survey*] (SEIS)
ASH .... Ashland, Inc. [*NYSE symbol*] (SAG)
ASH .... Ashland Inc. [*NYSE symbol*] (TTSB)
Ash .... Ashmead's Pennsylvania Reports [*1808-41*] [*A publication*] (DLA)
ASH .... Assault Support Helicopter [*Military*]
ASH .... Assistant Secretary for Health [*HEW*]
ASH .... Association for the Sexually Harassed (EA)
AsH .... Astigmatism, Hypermetropic [*Also, AH*] [*Ophthalmology*]
ASH .... Asymmetric [*or Asymmetrical*] Septal Hypertrophy [*Medicine*]
ASH .... Australian Industrial Safety, Health, and Welfare [*A publication*]
ASH .... Australian School of Hypnotherapy
ASH .... Author of "Southern Harmony" [*Initials singer Billy Walker put after his name*]
ASH .... Average Student Hours [*Education*] (AIE)
ASH .... Aviation Support, Hydraulic [*Navy rating*]
ASH .... Mesa Airlines, Inc. [*ICAO designator*] (FAAC)
ASH .... Nashua, NH [*Location identifier FAA*] (FAAL)
ASH .... Spring Hill College, Mobile, AL [*OCLC symbol*] (OCLC)
ASH .... Submarine-Exhaust Detector [*Navy British*]
ASH .... Swan Hills Public Library, Alberta [*Library symbol National Library of Canada*] (NLC)
ASH2 .... Aviation Support Equipment Technician, Hydraulics and Structures, Second Class [*Navy rating*] (DNAB)
ASH3 .... Aviation Support Equipment Technician, Hydraulics and Structures, Third Class [*Navy rating*] (DNAB)
ASHA .... Amalgamated Shipyard Helpers Association [*A union*] [*British*]
ASHA .... American Saddlebred Horse Association (EA)
ASHA .... American School Health Association (EA)
ASHA .... American Schools and Hospitals Abroad [*Program*] [*Agency for International Development*]
ASHA .... American Seafood Harvesters Association
ASHA .... American Shire Horse Association (EA)
ASHA .... American Social Health [*formerly, Hygiene*] Association (EA)
ASHA .... American Society of Hospital Attorneys (EA)
ASHA .... American Speech and Hearing Association (DAVI)
ASHA .... American Speech-Language-Hearing Association (EA)
ASHA .... American Spelean Historical Association (EA)
ASHA .... American Suffolk Horse Association (EA)
ASHA .... Arabian Sport Horse Association (EA)
ASHA .... Aviation Safety and Health Association (EA)
ASHAA .... Asbestos School Hazard Abatement Act (GFGA)
ASHAA .... Aviation Support Equipment Technician, Hydraulics and Structures, Airman Apprentice [*Navy rating*] (DNAB)
ASHAC........ Acquired Immunodeficiency Syndrome Self-Help and Care [*Medicine*] (DMAA)
ASHACE....... American Society of Heating and Air-Conditioning Engineers [*Later, ASHRAE*]
ASHAE .... American Society of Heating and Air-Conditioning Engineers [*Later, ASHRAE*]
ASHAN........ Aviation Support Equipment Technician, Hydraulics and Structures, Airman [*Navy rating*] (DNAB)
Ashanti .... Ashanti Goldfields Co. Ltd. [*Associated Press*] (SAG)
ASHAP .... Adriamycin, Cisplatin, Arabinosylcytosine, Adrenocorticoid [*Antineoplastic drug*] (CDI)
ASHAY .... Aeronomic South Hemisphere and Antarctic Year (PDAA)
Ashb .... Ashburner. Principles of Equity [*2nd ed.*] [*1933*] [*A publication*] (DLA)
ASHB .... Australian School of Health and Beauty
ASHBA .... Alaska State Homebuilders Association (SRA)
ASHBA .... American Saddle Horse Breeders Association [*Later, ASHA*] (EA)
ASHBA .... American Scotch Highland Breeders' Association (EA)
ASHBEAMS... American Society of Hospital-Based Emergency Air Medical Services (EA)
ASHBM .... Associate Scottish Hospital Bureau of Management (DAVI)
ASHC .... Aeronautics and Space Historical Center (EA)
ASHC .... All States Hobby Club [*Later, NASHC*]
ASHC .... American Society of Hospice Care [*Defunct*] (EA)
ASHC .... AmeriSource Health Corp. [*NASDAQ symbol*] (SAG)
ASHC .... Assault Support Helicopter Company [*Army*] (VNW)
AShC........... Spring Hill College, Spring Hill, AL [*Library symbol Library of Congress*] (LCLS)
ASHCMPR.... American Society for Health Care Marketing and Public Relations (EA)
ASHCSP....... American Society for Healthcare Central Service Personnel [*American Hospital Association*] (EA)
ASHD .... Arteriosclerotic Heart Disease [*Cardiology*]
ASHD .... Atrioseptal Heart Disease [*Cardiology*] (DMAA)
ASHE .... Aasche Transportation [*NASDAQ symbol*] (TTSB)
ASHE .... Aasche Transportation Services [*NASDAQ symbol*] (SAG)
ASHE .... Aircraft Salvage-Handling Equipment (DNAB)
ASHE .... American Society for Hospital Engineering - of the American Hospital Association (EA)
Ashe .... Ashe's Tables to the Year Books, Coke's Reports, or Dyer's Reports [*A publication*] (DLA)
ASHE .... Association for the Study of Higher Education (EA)

ASheR	Reynolds Metals, Reduction Research Division, Sheffield, AL [*Library symbol Library of Congress*] (LCLS)
ASHES	American Society for Healthcare Environmental Services of the American Hospital Association (EA)
ASHES	Axial Seamount Hydrothermal Emissions Study [*Marine science*] (OSRA)
ASHES	Axial Seamount Hydrothermal Emissions Study (USDC)
ASHET	American Society for Healthcare Education and Training - of the American Hospital Association (EA)
ASHEW	Aasche Transport Svcs Wrrt [*NASDAQ symbol*] (TTSB)
ASHF	American Swedish Historical Foundation and Museum (EA)
ASHFSA	American Society for Hospital Food Service Administrators (EA)
ASHG	American Society of Human Genetics (EA)
ASHHRA	American Society for Healthcare Human Resources Administration (EA)
ASHI	American Society for Histocompatibility and Immunogenetics (EA)
ASHI	American Society of Home Inspectors (EA)
ASHI	Association for the Study of Human Infertility (DAVI)
Ashken	Ashkenazic [*Jews from Central or Eastern Europe*] (BJA)
Ashland	Ashland, Inc. [*Formerly, Ashland Oil*] [*Associated Press*] (SAG)
AshInd	Ashland, Inc. [*Associated Press*] (SAG)
Ashm	Ashmead's Pennsylvania Reports [*1808-41*] [*A publication*] (DLA)
ASHM	Australasian Society for HIV [*Human Immunodeficiency Virus*] Medicine
Ashmead	Ashmead's Pennsylvania Reports [*1808-41*] [*A publication*] (DLA)
Ashmead (PA)	Ashmead's Pennsylvania Reports [*1808-41*] [*A publication*] (DLA)
Ashmead's Penn Rep	Ashmead's Pennsylvania Reports [*1808-41*] [*A publication*] (DLA)
ASHMM	American Society for Hospital Materials Management (EA)
Ashm (PA)	Ashmead's Pennsylvania Reports [*1808-41*] [*A publication*] (DLA)
ASHMPR	American Society for Hospital Marketing and Public Relations [*Later, ASHCMPR*] (EA)
ASHMS	Automatic Ship's Heading Measurement System (DNAB)
ASHN	Acute Sclerosing Hyaline Necrosis [*Medicine*] (MAE)
ASHNHA	Alaska State Hospital and Nursing Home Association (SRA)
ASH-NI	Action on Smoking and Health - Northern Ireland (EAIO)
ASHNS	American Society for Head and Neck Surgery (EA)
AS/Ho	Antiserum/Horse [*Medicine*] (DMAA)
ASHOE	Airborne Southern Hemisphere Ozone Expedition [*Marine science*] (OSRA)
ASHOE	Airborne Southern Hemisphere Ozone Expedition (USDC)
ASHOF	Air Shutoff
ASHORAD	Advanced Short-Range Air Defense System (MCD)
ASHP	Airship
ASHP	American Society for Hospital Planning
ASHP	American Society for Hospital Planning (DMAA)
ASHP	American Society of Handicapped Physicians (EA)
ASHP	American Society of Health-System Pharmacists [*Formerly, American Society of Hospital Pharmacists*]
ASHP	American Society of Hospital Pharmacists (EA)
ASHPA	American Society for Hospital Personnel Administration [*Later, ASHHRA*] (EA)
ASHPMM	American Society for Hospital Purchasing and Materials Management [*Later, ASHMM*] (EA)
ASHPr	Ashland Inc. $3.125 Cv Pfd [*NYSE symbol*] (TTSB)
ASHPREF	American Society of Hospital Pharmacists Research and Education Foundation (EA)
ASHPS	American Scenic and Historic Preservation Society [*Defunct*] (EA)
ASHR	African Society for Human Rights [*Defunct*] (EA)
ASHR	American Sport Horse Registry [*Defunct*] (EA)
ASHRA	American Spa and Health Resort Association (EA)
ASHRACE	American Society of Heating, Refrigerating and Air-Conditioning Engineers (MHDB)
ASHRAE	American Society of Heating, Refrigerating, and Air-Conditioning Engineers (EA)
ASHRF	African Starvation and Hunger Relief Fund (EA)
ASHRM	American Society for Healthcare Risk Management (EA)
ASH-S	Action on Smoking and Health - Scotland (EAIO)
ASHS	American Society for Horticultural Science (EA)
ASHS	Association of Sacred Heart Schools [*Australia*]
ASHS	Australian Society of Horticultural Science
ASHS	Australian Stock Horse Society
ASHT	American Society of Hand Therapists (EA)
ASH-TF	Advanced Scout Helicopter Task Force [*Army*] (RDA)
AshtnT	Ashton Technology Group, Inc. (The) [*Associated Press*] (SAG)
Ashton	Ashton's Reports [*9-12 Opinions of the United States Attorneys General*] [*A publication*] (DLA)
ASHUR	Apollo Spacecraft Hardware Utilization Request [*NASA*]
Ashurst	Ashurst's Manuscript Reports, Printed in Volume 2, Chitty [*A publication*] (DLA)
Ashurst	Ashurst's Paper Books, Lincoln's Inn Library [*A publication*] (DLA)
Ashurst MS	Ashurst's Manuscript Reports, Printed in Volume 2, Chitty [*A publication*] (DLA)
Ashurst MS	Ashurst's Paper Books, Lincoln's Inn Library [*A publication*] (DLA)
ASHVE	American Society of Heating and Ventilating Engineers
ASHW	Action on Smoking and Health in Wales (EAIO)
ASHW	Ashworth, Inc. [*NASDAQ symbol*] (SAG)
ASHW	Holsworthy [*Australia ICAO location identifier*] (ICLI)
Ashwrth	Ashworth, Inc. [*Associated Press*] (SAG)
ASHY	Agudath Shofte ha-Hakhra'ah ha-Yehudit (BJA)
ASHYC	American Saddle Horse Youth Club (EA)
ASI	Accounting Systems International World Group [*Consortium of resellers*] (PCM)
ASI	AccuStaff, Inc. [*NYSE symbol*] (SAG)
ASI	Action Surveys, Inc. [*Information service or system*] (IID)

ASI	Actuator Sensor Interface (ACII)
ASI	Adam Smith Institute (EA)
ASI	Additional Skill Identifier [*Army*] (INF)
ASI	Addressing Systems International (NITA)
ASI	Admiralty Supply Item
ASI	Adoption Search Institute [*Inactive*] (EA)
ASI	Advanced Sales Index [*LIMRA*]
ASI	Advanced Scientific Instruments [*AMR, Inc.*]
ASI	Advanced Study Institutes (NATG)
ASI	Advance Sciences, Inc. (GAAI)
ASI	Advertising Specialty Institute (WDMC)
ASI	Aerospace Static Inverter
ASI	Aerospace Studies Institute [*Air Force*] (MCD)
ASI	Aerospace Systems, Inc.
ASI	AeroSun International, Inc. [*ICAO designator*] (FAAC)
ASI	African Scientific Institute
ASI	Africa Service Institute of New York [*Defunct*]
ASI	Agri-Silviculture Institute (EA)
ASI	Aircraft Sampling Inspection (MCD)
ASI	Air Sea International [*British*]
ASI	Air Society, International (EA)
ASI	Airspeed Indicator
ASI	Allied Stone Industries (EA)
ASI	Alphabetic Subject Index [*A publication*]
ASI	Alternate Space Inversion (ACRL)
ASI	Althydusamband Islands [*Icelandic Federation of Labor*]
ASI	Altimeter Setting Indicator [*Aviation*] (FAAC)
ASI	Ambulance Service Institute [*British*] (DBA)
ASI	Ambulatory Surgery Initiative [*Health insurance*] (GHCT)
ASI	Amended Shipping Instruction [*Military*]
ASI	Amended Shipping Instrument (MCD)
ASI	American Scientific Institute
ASI	American Sightseeing International (EA)
ASI	American Society of Indexers (EA)
ASI	American Society of Interpreters (EA)
ASI	American Society of Inventors (EA)
ASI	American Soybean Institute [*Defunct*] (EA)
ASI	American Specification Institute [*Defunct*]
ASI	American Standards Institute (IAA)
ASI	American Statistics Index [*Congressional Information Service, Inc.*] [*Bibliographic database*] [*A publication*]
ASI	American Supplier Institute (EA)
ASI	American Swedish Institute (EA)
ASI	Ammunition Supply Installation [*Army*] (INF)
ASI	Amperes per Square Inch [*Electrochemistry*]
ASI	Andrei Sakharov Institute [*Later, FUWPH*] (EA)
ASI	Annual Supply Inspection [*Military*] (NVT)
ASI	Answer Search Interface (MCD)
ASI	Antisaturation Inverter
ASI	Anti-Slavery International [*England*] (EAIO)
ASI	Anxiety Status Inventory [*Medicine Medicine*] (DMAA)
ASI	Apollo Standard Initiator [*NASA*]
ASI	Architects and Surveyors Institute (EAIO)
ASI	Arctic Survival Instructor [*British military*] (DMA)
ASI	ARGO Systems, Inc., Sunnyvale, CA [*OCLC symbol*] (OCLC)
ASI	Aril Society International (EA)
ASI	Arion Systems, Inc.
ASI	Armaments Standardization and Interoperability [*NATO*] (NATG)
ASI	Armored Systems Integration [*Army*] (RDA)
ASI	Army School on Instructional Technology [*British*]
ASI	Arnold Schoenberg Institute [*University of Southern California*] [*Research center*] (RCD)
ASI	Articulated Subject Index (NITA)
ASI	Asian Statistical Institute
ASI	Association of Privately Owned Seventh-Day Adventist Services and Industries (EA)
ASI	Association of Seafood Importers (EA)
ASI	Association Stomatologique Internationale [*International Stomatological Association*]
ASI	Associative Surface Ionization [*Organic chemistry*]
ASI	Asynchronous Serial Interface [*Telecommunications*] (NITA)
ASI	ATV [*All-Terrian Vehicle*] Safety Institute (EA)
ASI	Audience Studies, Inc. [*Television program testing system*]
ASI	Augmented Spark Igniter [*NASA*]
ASI	Augmented System Ignition [*NASA*] (KSC)
ASI	Augustana Swedish Institute [*Later, AHS*]
ASI	Australian Skeptics, Inc. [*An association*]
ASI	Automated Security Holdings ADS [*NYSE symbol*] (SPSG)
ASI	Automatic Sampling Injector
ASI	Aviation Safety Institute (EA)
ASI	Aviation Services, Inc.
ASI	Aviation Status Indicator (DNAB)
ASI	Axial Shape Index (NRCH)
ASI	Azimuth Speed Indicator
a-si--	Singapore [*MARC geographic area code Library of Congress*] (LCCP)
ASIA	Airlines Staff International Association (EAIO)
ASIA	American Sheep Industry Association (EA)
ASIA	American Society of Industrial Auctioneers (EA)
ASIA	American Spinal Injury Association (EA)
ASIA	American Stone Importers Association (EA)
ASIA	Arizona Self-Insurers Association (SRA)
ASIA	Army Signal Intelligence Agency
ASIA	Associate of the Society of Investment Analysts [*British*] (DBQ)
ASIA	Association of Sri-Lankans in America (EA)

ASIA Australian Security Industry Association
ASIA Automotive Service Industry Association (EA)
ASIA Aviation Security Improvement Act [*FAA*] (TAG)
ASIA Avionics System Integration and Acquisition (MCD)
ASIA Sunbase Asia [*NASDAQ symbol*] (TTSB)
ASIAC Aerospace Structures Information and Analysis Center [*Wright-Patterson Ai r Force Base, OH*] [*Air Force*] (MCD)
ASIAC Australian Seed Industry Advisory Council
ASIAC Australian Society for Intercountry Aid (Children)
ASIA(Ed) Associate of the Society of Industrial Artists (Education) [*British*]
ASIAEE Assistant Secretary for International Affairs and Energy Emergencies
ASIAM [*The*] Asian American Magazine [*A publication*]
Asian Comp L Rev Asian Comparative Law Review [*A publication*] (DLA)
AsiaPac Asia Pacific Resources Ltd. [*Associated Press*] (SAG)
ASIAPACK South East Asia International Exhibition of Packaging Machinery and Materials and Food Processing Machinery
AsiaPc Asia Pacific Fund [*Associated Press*] (SAG)
AsiaPlp Asia Pulp and Paper Co. Ltd. [*Associated Press*] (SAG)
AsiaPR Asia Pacific Resources International Holdings Ltd. [*Associated Press*] (SAG)
AsiaPWi Asia Pacific Wire & Cable Corp. Ltd. [*Associated Press*] (SAG)
ASIAS Airline Schedules and Interline Availability Study [*IATA*] (DS)
AsiaSat Asia Satellite Telecommunications Holdings Ltd. [*Associated Press*] (SAG)
ASIATEX South East Asia's International Exhibition of Textile and Garment Machinery and Fabrics Trade
AsiaTigr Asia Tigers Fund [*Associated Press*] (SAG)
ASIB American Society of Independent Business [*Defunct*] (EA)
ASIC Access Solutions International, Inc. [*NASDAQ symbol*] (SAG)
ASIC Air Service Information Circular
ASIC All Source Intelligence Center (MCD)
ASIC American Society of Irrigation Consultants (EA)
ASIC Antique Stove Information Clearinghouse (EA)
ASIC Application-Specific Integrated Circuit [*Electronics*]
ASIC Area Security Information Center
ASIC Associated States of Indochina (NATG)
ASIC Association de la Securite Industrielle du Canada [*Industrial Security Association of Canada*]
ASIC Association Scientifique Internationale du Cafe [*International Scientific Association of Coffee*] (EAIO)
ASIC Avionics Subsystems Interface Contractor [*Air Force*]
ASIC St. Isidore Community Library [*Bibliotheque de St-Isidore*] Alberta [*Library symbol National Library of Canada*] (NLC)
ASICA Association Internationale pour le Calcul Analogique [*International Association for Analogue Computation*] [*Later, IMACS*]
ASID Address Space Identifier (BUR)
ASID Advanced System Integration Demonstration [*Military*]
ASID American Society of Industrial Designers [*Later, IDSA*] (EA)
ASID American Society of Interior Designers (EA)
ASID Association for the Study of International Development [*See also AEDI*] [*Canada*]
ASID Association of Sports Information Directors (EA)
ASID Australian Society of Infectious Diseases
ASID Automatic Station Identification Device
ASIDIC Association of Information and Dissemination Centers (EA)
ASIDIC Association of Scientific Information Dissemination Centers (NITA)
ASIDS Airborne Surveillance and Intercept Defense System
ASIDS Aircraft Stores Interface Data Systems
ASIDSI American Sudden Infant Death Syndrome Institute (EA)
ASIE American Society of International Executives [*Blue Bell, PA*] (EA)
ASIEP Autism Screening Instrument for Educational Planning
ASIF Airlift Service Industrial Fund [*Military*]
ASIF Aldosterone Secretion Inhibitory Factor [*Endocrinology*]
ASIF Association for Study of Internal Fixation (DMAA)
ASIFA Association Internationale du Film d'Animation [*International Animated Film Association*] (EAIO)
ASIG Absurd Special Interest Group (EA)
ASIG Alarm System Improvement Guide (MCD)
ASIG Ansaldo Signal [*NASDAQ symbol*] (SAG)
ASIGCEN Area Signal Center [*Army*] (AABC)
ASIGSCH Army Signal School (MCD)
ASIH Absent Sick in Hospital (DAVI)
ASIH American Society of Ichthyologists and Herpetologists (EA)
ASII Airport Systems [*NASDAQ symbol*] (SAG)
ASII Airport Systems Intl [*NASDAQ symbol*] (TTSB)
ASII American Science Information Institute
ASIL Alcohol Sensors International Ltd. [*NASDAQ symbol*] (SAG)
ASIL American Society of International Law (EA)
ASILS Association of Student International Law Societies (EA)
ASILU Alcohol Sensors Intl Unit [*NASDAQ symbol*] (TTSB)
ASIM Aircraft Stores Interface Manual (MCD)
ASIM Alpha-Comp Simulation Package [*Alpha-Comp Ltd.*] [*Software package*] (NCC)
ASIM American Society of Insurance Management [*Later, RIMS*] (EA)
ASIM American Society of Internal Medicine (EA)
ASIM Associate in Industrial Management
ASIMIS Aircraft Structural Integrity Management Information System [*Air Force*] (AFIT)
ASIMS Army Standard Information Management System
ASIN Agricultural Sciences Information Network [*National Agricultural Library*] [*Beltsville, MD*]
ASIN Agricultural Service Information Network [*Database producer*] (NITA)
Asin Asinaria [*of Plautus*] [*Classical studies*] (OCD)
ASInt American Studies International [*A publication*] (BRI)
ASIO Australian Secret Intelligence Organization (LAIN)
ASIOE Associated Support Items of Equipment (MCD)
ASIP Acquisition System Integration Program (DWSG)
ASIP Aircraft Structural Integrity Program
ASIP Airspace Flight Inspection Pilot (FAAC)
ASIP All-Sky Imaging Photometer
ASIP Anangel American Shipholdings Ltd. [*NASDAQ symbol*] (SAG)
ASIP Army Stationing and Installation Plan (AABC)
ASIP Australian Serials in Print [*A publication*]
ASIP Avionic System Integration Plan (MCD)
ASIP Joint Air-Sea Interaction Panel [*Federal Council for Science and Technology*] (NOAA)
ASIPI Asociacion Interamericana de la Propiedad Industrial [*Inter-American Association of Industrial Property - IAAIP*] (EAIO)
ASIPRE Army Snow, Ice, and Permafrost Research Establishment
ASIPY Anangel-Amer Shiphldgs ADS [*NASDAQ symbol*] (TTSB)
ASIR Aeronautical Shipboard Installation Representative (NVT)
ASIR Air Safety Incident Reporting
ASIR Airspeed Indicator Reading
ASIRC Aquatic Sciences Information Retrieval Center [*University of Rhode Island*]
ASIRC Armed Services Industrial Readiness Council
ASIS Abort Sensing and Implementation System
ASIS Advanced Scientific Instrument (IAA)
ASIS Alcohol Safety Interlock System
ASIS American Society for Industrial Security (EA)
ASIS American Society for Information Science [*Formerly, ADI*] (EA)
ASIS American Society for Information Science, Washington, DC [*Library symbol*] [*Library of Congress*] (LCLS)
ASIS American Student Information Service
ASIS Ammunition Stores Issue Ship
ASIS Amphibious Support Information System (NVT)
ASIS Anterior Superior Iliac Spine [*Anatomy*]
ASIS Arbeitsschutzinformationssystem [*Information System for Occupational Safety and Health*] [*West Germany*] (IID)
ASIS Armament Stores Issuing Ship [*Navy*]
ASIS Army Space Initiatives Study
ASIS Aromatic Solvent-Induced Shift [*Physical chemistry*]
ASIS Assateague Island National Seashore [*National Park Service designation*]
ASIS Automated Schedule Information System
ASIS Automotive Sensor Instrumentation System Van [*Automotive engineering*]
ASIS Auxiliary Ship Information System [*Navy*] (CAAL)
ASISS Alpine Science Information Service [*Information service or system*] (IID)
ASIST Accelerated Specialized Inspection Sites [*Customs inspection at airports*]
ASIST Advanced Scientific Instruments Symbolic Translator [*Assembly program*] (DEN)
ASIST Alberta Statistical Information System [*Alberta Treasury, Bureau of Statistics*] [*Database*]
ASIT Adaptable Surface Interface Terminal (MCD)
ASIT American School Intelligence Test [*Education*] (AEBS)
ASIT Army School on Instructional Technology [*British*]
ASIT Association of Surgeons in Training [*British*] (DBA)
ASITC Association des Scientifiques, Ingenieurs, et Techniciens du Canada [*Association of the Scientific, Engineering, and Technological Community of Canada*]
AsIU Leopold-Franzens Universitat Insbruck, Insbruck, Austria [*Library symbol Library of Congress*] (LCLS)
ASIWPCA Association of State and Interstate Water Pollution Control Administrators (EA)
ASJ AAA Stamp & Coin [*Vancouver Stock Exchange symbol*]
ASJ Action for Soviet Jewry (EA)
ASJ Ahoskie, NC [*Location identifier FAA*] (FAAL)
ASJ AIDS Saint John (AC)
ASJ Air Satellite, Inc. [*Canada ICAO designator*] (FAAC)
ASJ Alianca Socialista de Juventude [*Socialist Youth Alliance*] [*Portugal Political party*] (PPE)
ASJ Amami O Shima [*Japan*] [*Airport symbol*] (OAG)
ASJ Asosan [*Japan*] [*Seismograph station code, US Geological Survey*] (SEIS)
ASJ Association for Scientific Journals (EA)
ASJA American Salers Junior Association (EA)
ASJA American Society of Journalists and Authors (EA)
ASJA Assistant Staff Judge Advocate [*Air Force*]
ASJB Australian Sentencing Judgements Bulletin [*A publication*]
ASJFHAW Amalgamated Society of Journeymen Felt Hatters and Allied Workers [*A union*] [*British*] (DCTA)
ASJG Albanian Society Jusuf Gervalla (EA)
ASJJA Association of State Juvenile Justice Administrators [*NAJCA*] [*Absorbed by*] (EA)
ASJL Association for the Study of Jewish Languages [*Haifa, Israel*] (EAIO)
ASJM American Society for Jewish Music (EA)
ASJMC Association of Schools of Journalism and Mass Communication (EA)
ASJR Army Summary Jurisdiction Regulations [*British military*] (DMA)
ASJSA American Society of Journalism School Administrators (EA)
ASK Actively Shared Knowledge [*Data processing system*]
ASK Adjustable Stroke Kit
ASK Aeolian-Skinner Organ Co. [*Record label*]
ASK Agent Selection Kit [*LIMRA*]
ASK Aircraft Station Keeper (MCD)
ASK Alaska Apollo Gold Mines Ltd. [*Vancouver Stock Exchange symbol*]
ASK Alerting Search Service from Kinokuniya [*Kinokuniya Co. Ltd.*] [*Japan Information service or system*] (IID)

ASK............	American Simplified Keyboard [*Typewriter*]
ASK............	Amplitude Shift Keying
ASK............	Analog Select Keyboard [*Computer science*] (KSC)
ASK............	Anomalous State of Knowledge [*Term used in artificial intelligence and concept experimentally used information systems*] (NITA)
ASK............	Antistreptokinase [*Immunology*]
ASK............	Applied Systems Knowledge Ltd. [*British*] (NITA)
ASK............	Askania Theodolite Camera (MUGU)
ASK............	Association for Study of Karma (EA)
ASK............	Astronaut Survival Kit [*NASA*]
ASK............	Automatic Shift Keying (HGAA)
ASK............	Available Seat-Kilometres [*Air travel*]
a-sk--..........	Sikkim [*MARC geographic area code Library of Congress*] (LCCP)
ASK............	Sudania Aviation Co. [*Sudan*] [*ICAO designator*] (FAAC)
ASK............	Yamoussoukro [*Ivory Coast*] [*Airport symbol*] (OAG)
ASKA..........	Automatic Systems for Kinematic Analysis [*NASA*] (NASA)
ASKARS.....	Automated Storage, Kitting, and Retrieval Systems [*Tandem Computers*] [*Navy*]
ASKNG........	Asking [*Automotive advertising*]
ASKS	Automatic Station Keeping System
ASKS	Sydney [*Australia ICAO location identifier*] (ICLI)
ASKT..........	Akkadische Keilschrifttexte [*A publication*] (BJA)
ASKT..........	American Society of Knitting Technologists (EA)
ASkyB	America Sky Broadcasting
ASL............	Abbe's Sine Law
ASL............	Above Sea Level
ASL............	Acceptable Supplier List
ASL............	Acting Sub-Lieutenant [*Navy British*]
ASL............	Activity Safety Level (AFIT)
ASL............	Actuator Selection Logic (SAA)
ASL............	Advanced Student in Law [*British*] (ROG)
ASL............	Advanced Systems Laboratory
ASL............	Aeronautical Structures Laboratory [*Navy*]
ASL............	Aircraft Specialties Lines
ASL............	Aircraft Summary List
ASL............	Alabama Public Library Service, Montgomery, AL [*OCLC symbol*] (OCLC)
ASL............	Allowable Supply List [*Military*] (DOMA)
ASL............	American Association of State Libraries [*Later, ASCLA*] (EA)
ASL............	American School in London
ASL............	American Scientific Laboratories (AEBS)
ASL............	American Shuffleboard Leagues (EA)
ASL............	American Sign Language [*for the deaf*]
ASL............	American Soccer League
ASL............	Antenna Systems Laboratory [*University of New Hampshire*] (PDAA)
ASL............	Antistreptolysin [*Immunology*]
ASL............	Applied Science Laboratory
ASL............	Approved Source List (SAA)
ASL............	Approved Suppliers' List (DNAB)
ASL............	Arctic Submarine Laboratory [*Navy*] (MSC)
ASL............	Argininosuccinate Lyase [*Also, AL*] [*An enzyme*]
ASL............	Arithmetic Shift Left [*Computer science*]
ASL............	Army Standards Laboratory
ASL............	Ashanti Goldfields Co. Ltd. [*NYSE symbol*] (SAG)
ASL............	Ashanti Goldfields Ltd GDS [*NYSE symbol*] (TTSB)
ASL............	Association for Symbolic Logic (EA)
ASL............	Association of Standards Laboratories
ASL............	Astigmatic Spectral Line
ASL............	A-Strain Spontaneous Leukemia [*Type of cell line*]
ASL............	Astro-Space Lab, Inc. (MCD)
ASL............	Astrosurveillance Science Laboratory
ASL............	Atmospheric Sciences Laboratory [*Army Laboratory Command*] [*White Sands Missile Range, NM*]
ASL............	Atmospheric Surface Layer [*Marine science*] (OSRA)
ASL............	Atmospheric Surface Layer (USDC)
ASL............	Atomic Safety Line (IAA)
ASL............	Australian Special Libraries [*A publication*]
ASL............	Authorized Stockage List [*Army*]
ASL............	Authorized Stock Level (CINC)
ASL............	Automated Soft Lander [*Aerospace*] (MCD)
ASL............	Available Space List [*Computer science*]
ASL............	Average Service Life
ASL............	Average Staffing Level
ASL............	Aviation Systems Laboratory (MCD)
ASL............	Azimuth Steering Line (MCD)
ASL............	Marshall, TX [*Location identifier FAA*] (FAAL)
ASL............	Salvage Tug [*Navy symbol*] (DNAB)
ASL............	Smoky Lake Public Library, Alberta [*Library symbol Library of Canada*] (NLC)
ASL............	Spurling Aviation [*ICAO designator*] (FAAC)
ASL............	Submarine Tender (Small) [*Navy ship symbol*] (NATG)
ASLA..........	American Savings and Loan Association (EA)
ASLA..........	American Society of Landscape Architects (EA)
ASLA..........	Armenian Secret Liberation Army
ASLA..........	Association for the Study of Literature and Alchemy (EA)
ASLA..........	Association of State Library Agencies [*Formerly, Association of State Libraries*] [*Later, ASCLA*]
ASLAB	Atomic Safety and Licensing Appeal Board (NRCH)
ASLADS.......	Automatic Shipboard Launch Aircraft Data System
ASLAMS......	Automated Ship Location and Attitude Measuring System
ASLAP	American Society of Laboratory Animal Practitioners (EA)
ASLAP	Atomic Safety and Licensing Appeal Panel [*Nuclear Regulatory Commission*]
ASLAR	Aircraft Surge Launch and Recovery [*FAA*] (TAG)
ASLB...........	Atomic Safety and Licensing Board [*Nuclear Regulatory Commission*]

ASLBM........	Air-to-Ship Launched Ballistic Missile [*Navy*] (IAA)
ASLBM........	Antisubmarine Launched Ballistic Missile
ASLBP	Atomic Safety and Licensing Board Panel [*Nuclear Regulatory Commission*]
ASLC..........	Adaptive Side-Lobe Canceller [*RADAR*] (MCD)
ASLC..........	Advanced Secretarial Language Certificate [*British*] (DI)
ASLC..........	Association of Street Lighting Contractors [*British*] (DBA)
ASLCM........	Advanced Sea-Launched Cruise Missile (MCD)
ASLE..........	Account Sales
ASLE..........	American Society of Lubrication Engineers (EA)
ASLEC.........	Association of Street Lighting Erection Contractors [*British*] (BI)
ASLEEP	Automated Scanning Low-Energy Electron Probe (IEEE)
ASLEF.........	Associated Society of Locomotive Engineers and Firemen [*A union*] [*British*] (DCTA)
Aslef	Associated Society of Locomotive Engineers and Firemen [*British*] (ODBW)
ASLET.........	American Society of Law Enforcement Trainers (EA)
ASLG	Academy for State and Local Government (EA)
ASLG	Aviation Signal Light Gun [*Military*] (PDAA)
ASLH	American Society for Legal History (EA)
ASLH	Lord Howe Island [*Australia ICAO location identifier*] (ICLI)
ASLHC	Association of Scottish Local Health Councils [*British*]
ASLI...........	American Savings and Loan Institute [*Later, IFE*] (EA)
Aslib	Association of Special Libraries and Information Bureaux [*Acronym is now organization's official name*]
ASLIB..........	Association of Special Libraries and Information Bureaux [*Association for Information Management*] [*British*] (AIE)
ASLK-CGER...	Algemene Spaar- en Lijfrentekas/Caisse Generale d'Espargne et de Retraite [*Commercial bank*] [*Belgium*] (EY)
ASLL...........	American Savings and Loan League [*Later, ALFI*] (EA)
ASLM	American Society of Law and Medicine (EA)
ASLM	Apple Shared Library Manager [*Computer science*]
ASLM	Slave Lake Municipal Library, Alberta [*Library symbol National Library of Canada*] (NLC)
ASLMR	Assistant Secretary for Labor-Management Relations [*Department of Labor*]
ASLMS........	American Society for Laser Medicine and Surgery (EA)
ASLNY	Art Students' League of New York (EA)
ASLO	American Society of Limnology and Oceanography (EA)
ASLO	American Society of Local Officials [*Defunct*] (EA)
ASLO	Antistreptolysin-O [*Also, ASO*] [*Clinical chemistry*]
ASLO	Assembly Layout [*Computer science*] (MHDB)
ASLO	Associated Scottish Life Offices (EAIO)
ASLP..........	Amalgamated Society of Lithographic Printers (DGA)
ASLP..........	Association of Special Libraries of the Philippines
ASLR	American Short Line Railroads
ASLRA	American Short Line Railroad Association (EA)
ASLRA	Association of State Labor Relations Agencies (EA)
ASLS	Advocates to Save Legal Services [*Inactive Defunct*] (EA)
ASLS	Association for Scottish Literary Studies [*Aberdeen, Scotland*] (EAIO)
ASLSPCTWA...	American Society of Learned Societies on the Protection of Cultural Treasures inWar Areas [*World War II*]
ASLT..........	Acting Sub-Lieutenant [*Canadian*]
ASLT..........	Advanced Solid Logic Technology [*Computer science*]
ASLT..........	Aerial Stores Lift Truck (MCD)
ASLT..........	Antistreptolysin Test [*Medicine*] (DMAA)
ASLT..........	Assault (AFM)
ASLTG	Assault Gun (AABC)
ASLTPHIBBN...	Assault Amphibious Battalion (DNAB)
ASLU	Antenna Select Logic Unit [*NASA*] (NASA)
ASLV	Advanced Small Launch Vehicle
ASLV	Assurance sur la Vie [*Life Insurance*] [*French*]
ASLV	Augmented Satellite Launch Vehicle [*India*]
ASLV	Avian Sarcoma-Leukosis Virus
ASM	Acquisition Strategy Meeting (AAGC)
ASM	Acting Sergeant-Major [*Military*] (WDAA)
ASM	Adaptive System (IAA)
ASM	Address Space Manager [*Computer software*] (NITA)
ASM	Ad Hoc Schedule Message (DA)
ASM	Administrative Support Manual (DNAB)
ASM	Advanced Scatterable Mine [*Air Force*] (MCD)
ASM	Advanced Semiconductor Materials
ASM	Advanced Servomanipulator
ASM	Advanced Strategic Missile System [*DoD*]
ASM	Advanced Surface Missile
ASM	Aerospace Structural Material
ASM	After Sales Manager (DCTA)
ASM	Agency Sales Magazine [*Manufacturers' Agents National Association*] [*A publication*]
ASM	Aircraft Survival Measures Programme [*NATO*]
ASM	Airfield Surface Movement Indicator [*RADAR*] [*Aviation*] (IAA)
ASM	Airlift Simulation Model
ASM	Airspace Management (DA)
ASM	Air Stagnation Model
ASM	Air-to-Surface Missile
ASM	Alarm and Status Module
ASM	Algebraic Stress Model (MCD)
ASM	Algorithmic State Machine [*Computer science*] (ODBW)
Asm	All India Reporter, Assam Series [*A publication*] (DLA)
ASM	Allocation Strategy Module (IAA)
ASM	All-Sky Monitor [*Optics*]
ASM	American Samoa [*ANSI three-letter standard code*] (CNC)
ASM	American Society for Metals [*Later, ASMI*] (EA)
ASM	American Society for Microbiology (EA)
ASM	American Society of Mammalogists (EA)

ASM............ American Society of Missiology (EA)
ASM............ American Solidarity Movement [*Defunct*] (EA)
ASM............ American Street Machines [*Defunct*] (EA)
ASM............ Angular Second Moment
ASM............ Anhydrous Sodium Metasilicate [*Inorganic chemistry*]
ASM............ Annual Survey of Manufactures [*Department of Commerce Information service or system*]
ASM............ Antarctica Service Medal [*Military decoration*]
ASM............ Antenna Switching Matrix
ASM............ Antiship Missile (NVT)
ASM............ Apollo Service Module [*NASA*] (MCD)
ASM............ Apollo Systems Manual [*A publication*] (MCD)
ASM............ Application Software Module (MCD)
ASM............ Area Sales Manager (DS)
ASM............ Area Stores Module (NITA)
ASM............ Arizona State Museum [*University of Arizona*] [*Research center*] (RCD)
ASM............ Armament Sergeant Major [*British*]
ASM............ Armed Scout Mission [*Military*] (DOMA)
ASM............ Armored Systems Modernization [*Formerly, Heavy Forces Modernization Program*] [*Army*] (RDA)
ASM............ Army System Management
ASM............ Artificer Sergeant Major [*British*]
ASM............ Asama [*Japan*] [*Seismograph station code, US Geological Survey*] (SEIS)
ASM............ Asmara [*Ethiopia*] [*Airport symbol*] (OAG)
ASM............ Asmara [*Ethiopia*] [*Airport symbol*] (AD)
asm............ Assamese [*MARC language code Library of Congress*] (LCCP)
ASM............ Assembler [*Computer science*]
ASM............ Assembler (NITA)
ASM............ Assembly (WGA)
ASM............ Assistant Service Manager [*Automobile sales*]
ASM............ Assistant Staff Meteorologist [*NASA*] (KSC)
ASM............ Assistant Stage Manager
ASM............ Assistant Station Master [*British*] (ADA)
ASM............ Associated Society of Moulders [*A union*] [*British*]
ASM............ Associated Subcontractors of Massachusetts (SRA)
ASM............ Association for Systems Management (EA)
ASM............ Association of Spectacle Makers [*Australia*]
AsM............ Astigmatism, Myopic [*Also, AM*] [*Ophthalmology*]
ASM............ Asynchronous State Machine (IEEE)
ASM............ Attache Support Message (MCD)
ASM............ Audiosonometry (IAA)
ASM............ Authentic Fitness [*NYSE symbol*] (TTSB)
ASM............ Authentic Fitness Corp. [*NYSE symbol*] (SPSG)
ASM............ Automatic Safety Monitor [*PUR*] (PS)
ASM............ Automatic Scheduling Message (GFGA)
ASM............ Automatic Space Management
ASM............ Autonomous Spacecraft Maintenance (MCD)
ASM............ Auxiliary Storage Manager [*Computer science*]
ASM............ Available Seat Miles [*Airlines term*]
ASM............ Aviation School of Medicine
ASM............ Aviation Support, Mechanical [*Navy rating*]
ASM............ Avionics Shop Maintenance
ASM............ SCTA Air St. Martin [*ICAO designator*] (FAAC)
ASM............ Strathmore Municipal Library, Alberta [*Library symbol National Library of Canada*] (NLC)
ASM2.......... Aviation Support Equipment Technician, Mechanical, Second Class [*Navy rating*] (DNAB)
ASM3.......... Aviation Support Equipment Technician, Mechanical, Third Class [*Navy rating*] (DNAB)
AsMA.......... Aerospace Medical Association (EA)
ASMA.......... Alaska State Medical Association (SRA)
ASMA.......... American Ski Manufacturers' Association (EA)
ASMA.......... American Society of Marine Artists (EA)
ASMA.......... American Society of Music Arrangers (EA)
ASMA.......... American Sports Medicine Association Board of Certification
ASMA.......... American Squid Marketing Association [*Defunct*] (EA)
ASMA.......... American Student Media Association (EA)
ASMA.......... Antismooth Muscle Antibody [*Immunology*]
ASMA.......... Association of State Mediation Agencies [*Later, ALRA*]
ASMA.......... Australian Speedway Media Association
ASMA.......... Automotive Services Marketing Association [*Canada*]
ASMAA........ Aviation Support Equipment Technician, Mechanical, Airman Apprentice [*Navy rating*] (DNAB)
ASMAN........ Aviation Support Equipment Technician, Mechanical, Airman [*Navy rating*] (DNAB)
ASMB.......... Acoustical Standards Management Board
ASMB.......... Assembling [*FBI standardized term*]
ASMBD........ Assembled
ASMBL........ Assemble (IAA)
asmblg........ Assemblage (VRA)
asmblr........ Assembler (MHDB)
ASMBLY...... Assembly
ASMC.......... Adaptive Static Margin Controller (MCD)
ASMC.......... American Society of Mature Catholics [*Defunct Defunct*] (EA)
ASMC.......... American Society of Military Comptrollers (EA)
ASMC.......... American Society of Music Copyists (EA)
ASMC.......... Army Supply and Maintenance Command
ASMC.......... ASEAN [*Association of South-East Asian Nations*] Specialized Meteorological Centre [*Marine science*] (OSRA)
ASMC.......... AUTODIN Station Maintenance Console (AABC)
ASMC.......... Automatic Systems Management and Control [*Aviation*] (OA)
ASMC.......... Aviation Surface Material Command (MCD)

ASMCHCCD... Association of State Maternal and Child Health and Crippled Children's Directors [*Later, AMCHCCP*] (EA)
ASMCOM ..... Army Supply and Maintenance Command (MUGU)
ASMCTMA ... Amalgamated Sewing Machine, Cycle, and Tool Makers Association [*A union*] [*British*]
ASMD .... Air-to-Surface Missile Development (MCD)
ASMD .... Antiship Missile Defense
ASMD .... Association of Science Museum Directors (EA)
ASMD .... Assumed (FAAC)
ASMD .... Atmospheric Sciences Modeling Division [*Air Resources Laboratory*] (USDC)
ASMD .... Atmospheric Sciences Modeling Division [*Marine science*] (OSRA)
ASMD/EW .... Anti-Ship Missile Defense / Electronic Warfare (PDAA)
ASMDHS..... Airshed Model Data-Handling System [*Environmental Protection Agency*] (GFGA)
ASMDMS..... Antiship Missile Defense Missile System (MCD)
ASMDT .... American Society of Master Dental Technologists (EA)
ASME .... Agricultural Soil Moisture Estimation (MCD)
ASME .... Airport Surface Movement Equipment
ASME .... American Society of Magazine Editors (EA)
ASME .... American Society of Mechanical Engineers (EA)
ASME .... Association des Specialistes de la Mesure en Education [*Association of Specialists in Educational Measures*] [*Canada*]
ASME .... Association for the Study of Medical Education
ASMEA........ Aviation Support Material and Equipment (MCD)
ASMEA........ American Society of Mechanical Engineers Auxiliary (EA)
ASMEIGTI ... ASME [*American Society of Mechanical Engineers*] International Gas Turbine Institute (EA)
ASMER .... Association for the Study of Man-Environment Relations (EA)
ASMET........ Accelerated Simulated Mission Endurance Test (MCD)
ASMF .... Area Supply and Maintenance Facility (MCD)
ASM-F .... Armored Systems Modernization - Future [*Formerly, Heavy Forces Modernization Program*] [*Army*] (RDA)
ASMF .... Australian Street Machine Federation
ASMFC........ Atlantic States Marine Fisheries Commission (EA)
ASMFER ...... ASM [*American Society for Metals*] Foundation for Education and Research [*ASM International*]
ASMHBA..... American Society of Mental Hospital Business Administrators [*Later, AMHA*] (EA)
ASMHF .... Association of Sports Museums and Halls of Fame [*Later, IASMHF*] (EA)
ASMI........... Advanced Semiconductor Materials International NV [*NASDAQ symbol*] (NQ)
ASMI........... Aerodrome Surface Movement Indicator (SAA)
ASMI........... Airfield Surface Movement Indicator [*RADAR*] [*Aviation*]
ASMI........... Anteroseptal Myocardial Infarct [*or Infarction*] [*Cardiology*] (MAE)
ASMI........... ASM [*American Society for Metals*] International (EA)
ASMI........... Association for Services Management International (EA)
ASMIC......... American Society of Military Insignia Collectors (EA)
ASMIF......... Advanced Semiconductor Materials International (MHDW)
ASMIF......... Advanced Semi Mat's [*NASDAQ symbol*] (TTSB)
ASMILF....... ASM Litography Hldg NV [*NASDAQ symbol*] (TTSB)
As Min........ Asia Minor (VRA)
ASM Intl ...... ASM International NV [*Associated Press*] (SAG)
ASMIS......... Army Safety Management Information System (MCD)
ASMIS......... Army Subordinate Command Management Information System [*Formerly, CARMOCS*] (AABC)
ASML.......... Annual Survey of Massachusetts Law [*A publication*] (ILCA)
ASML.......... ASM Lithography Holding NV [*NASDAQ symbol*] (SAG)
ASML.......... [*The*] Atlanta, Stone Mountain & Lithonia Railway Co. [*AAR code*]
ASM Lit ...... ASM Lithography Holding NV [*Associated Press*] (SAG)
ASM Litho ... ASM Lithography Holding NV [*Associated Press*] (SAG)
ASMLS........ Marigold Library System, Strathmore, Alberta [*Library symbol National Library of Canada*] (NLC)
ASMM.......... American Society of Medical Missionaries
ASMMA........ American Supply and Machinery Manufacturers Association (EA)
ASMMCC .... Armed Services Medical Material Coordination Committee (CINC)
ASMNT .... Assessment
ASMO .... Arab Organization for Standardization and Metrology (EAIO)
ASMO .... Association of State Medical Officers [*Western Australia*]
ASMO .... Automatic Standard Magnetic Observatory
ASMO .... Canberra [*Australia ICAO location identifier*] (ICLI)
ASMOLV ..... Afford Service Member Opportunity to Apply for Ordinary Leave [*Army*] (AABC)
ASMOR .... Automatic Standard Magnetic Observatory - Remote
ASMP .... American Society of Magazine Photographers (EA)
ASMP .... Army Survival Measures Plan (AABC)
ASMP .... Association of Screen Magazine Publishers [*Defunct*]
ASMP.......... Asymmetric Multiprocessing (CDE)
ASMP .... Australasian Species Management Plan
ASMPA .... Armed Services Medical Procurement Agency [*Later, Medical Material Directorate*]
ASMPE........ American Society of Motion Picture Engineers [*Later, ASMPTE*]
ASMP M ...... Assumption of Moses [*Apocalyptic book*]
ASMPS ...... Automated Staff Message Processing System
ASMPTE...... American Society of Motion Picture and Television Engineers [*Formerly, ASMPE*]
ASMR .... Advanced Short-to-Medium Range
ASMR .... Age-Specific Mortality Rate
ASMR .... Age Standardized Mortality Ratio
ASMRA .... Adjustment of Scheduled Maintenance Requirements through Analysis (MCD)
ASMRCC ..... Associated Sheet Metal/Roofing Contractors, Connecticut Chapter (SRA)
ASMRO .... Armed Services Medical Regulating Office

ASMRO........ Armed Services Medical Regulating Office (DOMA)
ASMS.......... Advanced Strategic Missile System [*DoD*] (MCD)
ASMS.......... Advanced Strategic Missile Systems [*Air Force*] (DOMA)
ASMS.......... Advanced Surface Missile System
ASMS.......... Advanced Synchronous Meteorological Satellite
ASMS.......... American Society for Mass Spectrometry (EA)
ASMS.......... American Society of Maxillofacial Surgeons (EA)
ASMS.......... Associate in Science in Medical Secretarial
ASMS.......... Atmosphere Sensing and Maintenance System [*NASA*] (KSC)
ASMS.......... Automated Systems Management System (MCD)
ASMSA........ Army Signal Material [*or Missile*] Support Agency
ASMSC........ Army Spectrum Management Steering Committee (MCD)
ASMT.......... Airspace Management (DA)
ASMT.......... Air-Space Multiple-Twin (IAA)
ASMT.......... American Society for Medical Technology (EA)
ASMT.......... Antiship Missile Target (MCD)
ASMT.......... Assessment
ASMT.......... Association of Sexual and Marital Therapists [*British*] (DBA)
ASMT.......... Assortment
ASMU.......... Automatically Stabilized Maneuvering Unit [*NASA*]
ASMW........ Amalgamated Society of Metal Workers [*A union*] [*British*]
ASN .... Abstract Syntax Notation [*Computer science*]
ASN .... Abstract Syntax Notation (CDE)
ASN .... Advanced Shipment Notification [*Inventory control*] [*Automotive manufacturing*]
ASN .... Airborne Special-Type Navigational Aid (MCD)
ASN .... Air Services Nantes [*France ICAO designator*] (FAAC)
ASN .... Air Straubing Luftfahrtgesellschaft MbH, Atting [*Germany*] [*FAA designator*] (FAAC)
ASN .... Alco Standard [*NYSE symbol*] (TTSB)
ASN .... Alco Standard Corp. [*NYSE symbol*] (SPSG)
ASN .... Alkali-Soluble Nitrogen (MAE)
ASN .... Allotment Serial Number (AFM)
ASN .... American Society for Neurochemistry (EA)
ASN .... American Society of Naturalists (EA)
ASN .... American Society of Nephrology (EA)
ASN .... American Society of Neuroimaging (EA)
ASN .... American Society of Notaries (EA)
ASN .... Ammonium Sulfate-Nitrate [*Fertilizer*]
ASN .... Arizona Sports Network [*Cable TV programming service*]
ASN .... Army Serial Number
ASN .... Army Service Number
ASN .... Arteriosclerotic Nephritis [*Medicine*] (DMAA)
Asn .... Asparagine [*Also, Asp(NH$_2$), N*] [*An amino acid*]
asn .... Asparagine [*Also, N*] [*An amino acid*] (DOG)
ASN .... Assistant Secretary of the Navy
asn .... Associated Name [*MARC relator code*] [*Library of Congress*] (LCCP)
ASN .... Associate in Nursing
ASN .... Associate in Nursing Science
ASN .... Association for the Study of the Nationalities (USSR and East Europe) (EA)
ASN .... Atlantic Satellite Network [*Cable-television system*]
ASN .... Atlantic Steam Navigation (MHDW)
ASN .... Atomic Strike Net (AABC)
ASN .... Australian Scholarly Newsletter [*A publication*]
ASN .... Authority Sequence Number [*Online bibliographies*]
ASN .... Average Sample Number [*Quality control*]
ASN .... Axially Symmetric Nozzle
ASN .... Talladega, AL [*Location identifier FAA*] (FAAL)
ASNA.......... Alabama State Nurses Association (SRA)
ASNA.......... American SMR [*Special Mobile Radio*] Network Association (EA)
ASNA.......... Arctic Slope Native Association
ASNAP........ Automatic Steerable Null Antenna Processor
ASNAUT....... Astronautical (MSA)
ASNC .... Association de Ski Nautique du Canada [*Canadian Water Ski Association*]
ASND .... Ascend Communications [*NASDAQ symbol*] (TTSB)
ASND .... Ascend Communications, Inc. [*NASDAQ symbol*] (SAG)
ASNE .... American Society of Naval Engineers (EA)
ASNE .... American Society of Newspaper Editors (EA)
ASNE .... Assistant Secretary for Nuclear Energy
ASNEMGE.... Association des Societes Nationales, Europeennes, et Mediterraneennes de Gastroenterologie [*Association of National, European, and Mediterranean Societies of Gastroenterology*] (EAIO)
ASNF .... Norfolk Island [*Australia ICAO location identifier*] (ICLI)
ASN (FM)..... Assistant Secretary of the Navy (Financial Management)
ASNHS........ American Society for Neo-Hellenic Studies (EA)
ASNHS........ Association of School Natural History Societies [*British*]
ASN(I & L).. Assistant Secretary of the Navy (Installation and Logistics)
ASNLH........ Association for the Study of Negro Life and History [*Later, Association for theStudy of Afro-American Life and History*] (EA)
ASN(M & RA)... Assistant Secretary of the Navy (Manpower and Reserve Affairs) (MCD)
ASNOL........ Assistant Senior Naval Officer Landing [*British and Canadian*] [*World War II*]
ASNP .... Agricultural Society of Nigeria. Proceedings [*A publication*]
ASNP .... American Society for Netherlands Philately (EA)
ASNP .... Army Student Nurse Program (AABC)
ASNPIDBAD... Army Student Nurse Program Identification Badge (GFGA)
ASNPIdentBad... Army Student Nurse Program Identification Badge (AABC)
ASNPrB....... Alco Std $5.04 Cv Dep Pfd [*NYSE symbol*] (TTSB)
ASNR .... American Society of Neuroradiology (EA)
ASN(R & D)... Assistant Secretary of the Navy (Research and Development)

ASN(RD & A)... Assistant Secretary of the Navy (Research, Development, and Acquisition) (DOMA)
ASN(RE & S)... Assistant Secretary of the Navy (Research, Engineering, and Systems) (DNAB)
ASN(RES) .... Assistant Secretary of the Navy (Research and Development) (DNAB)
ASNS .... Autism Society Nova Scotia [*Formerly, Nova Scotia Society for Autistic Children*] (AC)
ASNSA........ American Society for Nursing Service Administrators [*Later, AONE*] (EA)
ASN(S & L)... Assistant Secretary of the Navy (Shipbuilding and Logistics) (MCD)
ASNT .... American Society for Nondestructive Testing (EA)
ASNT .... Asante Technologies, Inc. [*NASDAQ symbol*] (SAG)
ASNT .... Asantle Technologies [*NASDAQ symbol*] (TTSB)
ASNW .... Nowra [*Australia ICAO location identifier*] (ICLI)
ASO .... Accessory Sex Organ [*Anatomy*]
ASO .... Accommodation Sales Order
ASO .... Acid-Soluble Oil [*Petroleum refining*]
ASO .... Acoustic Sensor Operator
ASO .... Administrative Service Office
ASO .... Administrative Service Only
ASO .... Advanced Solar Observatory (DEN)
ASO .... Aeronautics Supply Officer (MUGU)
ASO .... Aero Slovakia [*FAA designator*] (FAAC)
ASO .... Air Sarthe Organisation - Societe [*France ICAO designator*] (FAAC)
ASO .... Air Signal Officer
ASO .... Air Staff Officer
ASO .... Air Staff Orientation (AFM)
ASO .... Air Support Officer [*Military*]
ASO .... Air Support Operations (CAAL)
ASO .... Air Surveillance Officer [*Air Force*]
ASO .... Alarm System Operation
ASO .... Allele-Specific Oligonucleotide [*Genetics*]
ASO .... American Indian Community House [*An association*]
ASO .... American Society for Oceanography [*Later, MTS*] (EA)
ASO .... American Society of Onomatologists [*Defunct*] (EA)
ASO .... American Society of Orthodontists [*Later, AAO*] (EA)
ASO .... American Sokol Educational and Physical Culture Organization (EA)
ASO .... American Symphony Orchestra
ASO .... Ammonia System Operations [*NASA*] (NASA)
ASO .... Ammunition Supply Officer (AFM)
ASO .... AmSouth Bancorp. [*NYSE symbol*] (SPSG)
ASO .... Anisotropic Spin-Orbit (PDAA)
ASO .... Antistreptolysin-O [*Also, ASLO*] [*Clinical chemistry*]
ASO .... Area of Safe Operation
ASO .... Area Safety Officer
ASO .... Area Supply Officer [*Army*]
ASO .... Armament Supply Officer [*Navy British*] (DMA)
ASO .... Arteriosclerosis Obliterans [*Medicine*]
ASO .... Ashland Chemical Co., Research Library, Columbus, OH [*OCLC symbol*] (OCLC)
ASO .... Aso [*Japan*] [*Seismograph station code, US Geological Survey Closed*] (SEIS)
ASO .... Asosa [*Ethiopia*] [*Airport symbol*] (OAG)
ASO .... Assistant Secretary's Office [*Navy*]
ASO .... Assistant Section Officer [*Air Force British*]
ASO .... Association for the Study of Obesity (EAIO)
ASO .... Atomic Spin Orbital (IAA)
ASO .... Automated Safety Officer
ASO .... Auxiliary Switch [*Breaker*] Normally Open [*Electricity*]
ASO .... Aviation Safety Office [*or Officer*] [*Military*] (MCD)
ASO .... Aviation Supply Office [*Philadelphia, PA*] [*Navy*]
ASO .... Aviation Supply Officer (DOMA)
ASO .... Washington, DC [*Location identifier FAA*] (FAAL)
ASOA .... American Society of Ophthalmic Administrators (EA)
ASOA .... Avicultural Society of America (EA)
ASOAP........ Army Spectrometric Oil Analysis Program (AABC)
ASOAS........ Air Staff Office Automation System [*Air Force*] (GFGA)
ASOBAN...... Asociacion de Bancos e Instituciones Financieras de Bolivia (EY)
ASOblit .... Arteriosclerosis Obliterans [*Cardiology*] (DAVI)
ASOC .... Administrative Service Officer Class
ASOC .... Air Support Operations Center [*Air Force*]
ASOC .... Alzheimer Society of Oxford County (AC)
ASOC .... Antarctica and Southern Oceans Coalition (EA)
ASOC .... Armstrong Siddeley Owners Club (EA)
ASOC .... Asociacion [*Association*] [*Spanish*]
ASOC .... ASTRO Satellite Operations Center (MCD)
AsOCOA...... Asia-Oceania Clinical Oncology Association
ASOCS........ Air Support Operations Center Squadron [*Air Force*]
ASOD .... Anterior Segmental Ocular Dysgenesis [*Medicine*] (DMAA)
ASODAS...... Augmented Synoptic Oceanographic Data Acquisition System [*Navy*] (MSC)
ASODDS ...... ASWEPS [*Antisubmarine Warfare Environmental Prediction Service*] Submarine Oceanographic Digital Data System
ASOE .... Amalgamated Society of Operative Engineers [*A union*] [*British*]
ASOE .... Australian Society of Engineers
ASOF .... Army Special Operations Force [*Army*]
AS of A .... Assistant Secretary of the Army
AS of AC..... American Society of Arms Collectors
AS of AF..... Assistant Secretary of the Air Force
ASOFAF...... Assistant Secretary of the Air Force
AS of ISES... American Section of the International Solar Energy Society (EA)
AsOFNM ..... Asia-Oceania Federation of Nuclear Medicine
AS of NY..... Australian Society of New York [*Later, Australia-New Zealand Society of New York*] (EA)

ASoft.......... American Software, Inc. [*Associated Press*] (SAG)
ASOG......... Air Support Operations Group [*Air Force*]
ASOG......... Analytical Solution of Groups [*Thermodynamics*]
ASOGUA..... Association in Solidarity with Guatemala (EA)
ASO/ICP...... Aviation Supply Office/Inventory Control Point
ASOJ.......... Anti-Standoff Jammer [*Defense system*] (MCD)
ASOL......... American Symphony Orchestra League (EA)
A-SOL........ Antisolar (KSC)
ASOOA........ American Society of Ophthalmologic and Otolaryngologic Allergy
                [*Later, AAOA*] (EA)
ASOP......... Analytical Satellite Orbit Predictor (MCD)
ASOP......... Army Strategic Objectives Plan
ASOP......... Atomic Standing Operating Procedures (NATG)
ASOP......... Automated Structural Optimization Program [*Air Force*]
ASOP......... Automatic Scheduling and Operating Program (BUR)
ASOP......... Aviation Supply Office Philadelphia [*Navy*]
ASOPD........ Army Special Operations Pictorial Detachment
ASOR......... American Schools of Oriental Research (EA)
ASOr......... Asialo-Orosomucoid [*Liver metabolism*]
ASORF........ Apollo Ship's Operational Readiness Force [*NASA*]
ASORN........ American Society of Ophthalmic Registered Nurses (EA)
ASOS......... Administrative Service Officer Structure
ASOS......... American Society of Oral Surgeons [*Later, AAOMS*] (EA)
ASOS......... American Society of Outpatient Surgeons (EA)
ASOS......... Antimony Trisulfide Oxysulfide
ASOS......... Army Secure Operating System
ASOS......... Assistant Supervisor of Shipbuilding [*Navy*]
ASOS......... Automated Seismological Observation System [*Marine science*]
                (OSRA)
ASOS......... Automated Surface Observing System [*Meteorology*] (FAAC)
ASOS......... Automatic Storm Observation Service [*AFCRL*]
ASOS......... [*A*] Study of Schooling (EDAC)
ASOSH........ Assistant Secretary for Occupational Safety and Health [*Department
                of Labor*]
ASOSS........ American Society of Sephardic Studies (EA)
ASOT......... Annual System Operating Time (CAAL)
ASOT......... Antistreptolysin-O Titer [*Clinical chemistry*] (AAMN)
ASOTS........ Africa South of the Sahara [*Military*] (EA)
ASOTS........ Automatic Sparrow Operational Test Systems (MCD)
AS-OUR...... Anti-Saccade Oculomotor Delayed Response [*Neurobiology*]
ASP............ Abstract Service Primitive [*Telecommunications*] (OSI)
ASP............ Accao Socialista Portugues [*Portuguese Socialist Action*] (PPE)
ASP............ Accelerated Surface Post [*British*] (DCTA)
ASP............ Accident Sequence Precursor Study [*Nuclear Regulatory
                Commission*]
ASP............ Acoustic Signal Processor (MHDB)
AS/P........... Acquisition Strategy/Plan [*Military*] (CAAL)
ASP............ Activated Sludge Process
ASP............ Active Server Page [*Computer science*]
ASP............ Active Server Page [*Microsoft Corp.*]
ASP............ Active Site Peptide [*Immunochemistry*]
ASP............ Active SONAR Processor
ASP............ Activity Scheduling Processor [*NASA*]
ASP............ Activity Scheduling Program [*NASA*]
ASP............ Actual Ship Position
ASP............ Acute Suppurative Parotitis [*Otorhinolaryngology*] (DAVI)
ASP............ Additional Secondary Phase [*Navigation*]
ASP............ Administrative Site Procedures [*Nuclear energy*] (NRCH)
ASP............ Advanced Self-Protection [*Jammer*] (MCD)
ASP............ Advanced Signal Processor [*Computer science*]
ASP............ Advanced Speech Processor (ACRL)
ASP............ Advanced Study Program
ASP............ Advanced Support Processor [*Computer science*] (IAA)
ASP............ Advanced System Planning [*Air Force*] (MCD)
ASP............ Aero Scout Platoon [*Military*] (VNW)
ASP............ Aerospace Plane
ASP............ Aerosurface Position (NASA)
ASP............ African Swine Pox [*Medicine*] (DMAA)
ASP............ Afro-Shirazi Party [*Tanzania*] (AF)
ASP............ Afro-Shirazi Party [*Zanzibar*]
ASP............ After Sale Price
ASP............ Aggregated Switch Procurement Program [*General Services
                Administration*] (GFGA)
ASP............ Airborne Science Program [*NASA*] (NASA)
ASP............ Airborne Sensor Platform (MCD)
ASP............ Airborne Support Platform [*Army*]
ASP............ Aircraft Servicing Platform [*DA*]
ASP............ Aircraft Standard Parts (NATG)
ASP............ Airspace Subcommittee [*ACC*]
ASP............ Airspeed
ASP............ Air Stores Park [*British military*] (DMA)
ASP............ Air Superiority Program
ASP............ ALCOA Smelting Process
ASP............ Alcohol Soluble Propionate [*Press coating*] (DGA)
ASP............ Alice Springs [*Australia Seismograph station code, US Geological
                Survey*] (SEIS)
ASP............ All-Altitude Spin Projected [*Munition*]
ASP............ Alliance of Small Firms and Self Employed People [*British*] (DBA)
ASP............ Allied Standing Procedure [*NATO*] (NATG)
ASP............ All-Season Performance
ASP............ All-Source Production [*Army*] (ADDR)
ASP............ All South Pole (IAA)
ASP............ Altitude Sounding Projectile (MUGU)
ASP............ Aluminum Silicate Pigment
ASP............ American Self-Protection Association

ASP............ American Selling Price
ASP............ American Society for Photobiology (EA)
ASP............ American Society for Plasticulture (EA)
ASP............ American Society of Papyrologists (EA)
ASP............ American Society of Parasitologists (EA)
ASP............ American Society of Perfumers [*Defunct*] (EA)
ASP............ American Society of Periodontists [*Later, AAP*]
ASP............ American Society of Pharmacognosy (EA)
ASP............ American Society of Photogrammetry [*Later, ASPRS*] (EA)
ASP............ American Society of Photographers (EA)
ASP............ American Society of Primatologists (EA)
ASP............ American Strategic Income Portfolio [*NYSE symbol*] (SAG)
ASP............ Amer Strategic Inc. Portfolio [*NYSE symbol*] (TTSB)
ASP............ Ammunition Sub-Park [*British military*] (DMA)
ASP............ Ammunition Supply Plan [*Army*]
ASP............ Ammunition Supply Point
ASP............ Amnesic Shellfish Poisoning [*Medicine*]
ASP............ Amphibious Supply Platform [*Army*]
ASP............ Analytical Services Progam
ASP............ Anglo-Saxon Protestant
ASP............ Anglo-Soviet Pact (DAS)
ASP............ Ankylosing Spondylitis [*Medicine*] (DMAA)
ASP............ Annual Service Practice [*Firings*] [*Military*]
ASP............ Annual System Practice (MCD)
ASP............ Antiship Phoenix
ASP............ Antisocial Personality [*Psychology*]
ASP............ Antisubmarine Patrol
ASP............ Apollo Simple Penetrometer [*NASA*]
ASP............ Apollo Spacecraft Project [*NASA*] (IAA)
ASP............ AppleTalk Session Protocol [*Apple Computer, Inc.*] (BYTE)
ASP............ Approval to Start Production [*Automotive project management*]
ASP............ Arab Socialist Party [*Egypt*] [*Political party*] (PPW)
ASP............ Arab Socialist Party [*Syria*] [*Political party*] (PPW)
ASP............ Archival Security Program [*An association Defunct*] (EA)
ASP............ Arc Spraying [*Welding*]
ASP............ Area Search Program
ASP............ Area Specialist Program [*Air Force training program*]
ASP............ Areas Source Program [*Environmental Protection Agency*]
ASP............ Area Systolic Pressure (MAE)
ASP............ Armed Services Papers
ASP............ Army Standardization Program
ASP............ Army Strategic Plan [*A document*]
ASP............ Army Supply Program
ASP............ Array Signal Processing (MCD)
ASP............ Arrival Sequencing Program [*FAA*] (TAG)
ASP............ Asocial Personality
ASP............ Asparaginase [*An enzyme*] (AAMN)
ASP............ Asparaginase [*Antineoplastic drug*] (CDI)
asp............ aspartate (DOG)
asp............ Aspartic Acid [*Also, D*] [*An amino acid*] (DOG)
Asp............ Aspartic Acid [*Also, D*] [*An amino acid*]
ASP............ Aspect (ROG)
ASP............ Aspen Exploration Corp. [*Vancouver Stock Exchange symbol*]
ASP............ Asphalt
Asp............ Aspinall's Maritime Law Cases [*1871-1940*] [*England*]
                [*A publication*] (DLA)
ASP............ Aspirator (NASA)
ASP............ Assault Support Patrol Boat (DNAB)
ASP............ Associate Safety Professional [*Board of Certified Safety
                Professionals*] [*Designation awarded by*]
ASP............ Association for Software Protection (EA)
ASP............ Association of Shareware Professionals [*Canada*]
ASP............ Association of Shareware Professionals
ASP............ Association of Surfing Professionals (EA)
ASP............ Association-Storing Processor [*Computer science*]
ASP............ Associative String Processor (MCD)
ASP............ Associative Structures Package (BUR)
ASP............ As Soon as Possible
ASP............ Astronautics Standard Practice (AAG)
ASP............ Astronomical Society of the Pacific (EA)
ASP............ Astronomy Spacelab Payloads [*NASA*] (MCD)
ASP............ Asymmetric Multiprocessing System [*Electronics*] (ECII)
ASP............ Atmosphere Sounding Projectile
ASP............ Atomic Solvation Parameter [*Physical chemistry*]
ASP............ Atomic Strike Plan (AFM)
ASP............ Attached Support Processor [*Computer science*]
ASP............ Augmented Support Period [*or Plan*]
ASP............ Australian Shooters Party [*Political party*]
ASP............ Automated Schedule Procedures
ASP............ Automated Seismic Processor [*Earthquake analyzer*]
ASP............ Automated Spooling Priority [*Computer science*]
ASP............ Automatic Sample Processor (KSC)
ASP............ Automatic Schedule Procedure
ASP............ Automatic Self-Powered Cannon (MCD)
ASP............ Automatic Services and Products
ASP............ Automatic Servo Plotter
ASP............ Automatic Specimen Positioning
ASP............ Automatic Switching Panel
ASP............ Automatic Synthesis Program
ASP............ Auxiliary Spacecraft Power [*NASA*] (MCD)
ASP............ Average Speech Power
ASP............ Aviation Safety Program [*FAA*] (TAG)
ASP............ Avionics Status Panel (MCD)
ASP............ Empresa de Servicios Maritima y Aerea SA [*Peru*] [*FAA
                designator*] (FAAC)

ASP............. Oscoda, MI [*Location identifier FAA*] (FAAL)
ASP............. Stony Plain Public Libary, Alberta [*Library symbol National Library of Canada*] (NLC)
ASP............. [*A*] System for Programmers
ASP90........ Australia's Strategic Planning in the Nineties [*An association*]
ASPA.......... Acoustic Ship Positioning - Advanced (MCD)
ASPA.......... Advanced Strategic Penetrator Aircraft (MCD)
ASPA.......... Aircraft Service Period Adjustments [*Air Force*] (DOMA)
ASPA.......... Air Space
ASPA.......... Aluminosilicate Polyacrylate [*Type of dental cement*]
ASPA.......... American Salvage Pool Association (EA)
ASPA.......... American Self-Protection Association (EA)
ASPA.......... American Shrimp Processors Association (EA)
ASPA.......... American Society for Personnel Administration [*Later, SHRM*] (EA)
ASPA.......... American Society for Public Administration (EA)
ASPA.......... American Society of Pension Actuaries (EA)
ASPA.......... American Society of Physician Analysts (EA)
ASPA.......... American Society of Podiatric Assistants [*Later, ASPMA*] (EA)
ASPA.......... American Society of Practicing Architects
ASPA.......... American Society of Professional Appraisers (EA)
ASPA.......... American Sod Producers' Association (EA)
ASPA.......... Arizona Society of Practicing Accountants (SRA)
ASPA.......... Arkansas State Police Association (SRA)
ASPA.......... Armed Services Petroleum Agency
ASPA.......... Armed Services Procurement Act
ASPA.......... Association of South Pacific Airlines
ASPA.......... Australian Scrabble Players' Association
ASPA.......... Automatic Systems Pressure Alarm (PDAA)
ASPA.......... Auxiliary Storage and Playback Assembly [*Apollo Telescope Mount*] [*NASA*] (KSC)
ASPAB........ Armed Services Patent Advisory Board [*DoD*]
ASPAC........ Asian and Pacific Council
ASPAC........ Asian-Pacific Section [*International Union of Local Authorities*] [*Australia*]
ASPAC........ [*Annual*] Asia-Pacific Conference
ASPAC........ Australian Soil and Plant Analysis Council
ASPA/I........ American Society for Personnel Administration International (EA)
AsPALMS.... Asian-Pacific Association of LASER Medical Surgery
ASPAN........ American Society of Post-Anesthesia Nurses (EA)
ASPAR........ American Society of Professional Automobile Racing
ASPAS........ Acoustic Sensor Pattern Assessment System (MCD)
AsPASL....... Asian-Pacific Association for the Study of the Liver
ASPAT........ Antistreptococcal Polysaccharide Test [*Medicine*] (DMAA)
ASPAU........ African Scholarship Program of American Universities [*Joint undertaking, headquartered in Cambridge, MA, to provide aid to African applicants for admission to American universities*]
AsPAvMA..... Asia-Pacific Aviation Medicine Association
ASPB.......... Alberta Society of Professional Biologists (AC)
ASPB.......... American Society of Professional Biologists [*Later, AIBS*] (EA)
ASPB.......... Armed Services Petroleum Board
ASPB.......... Armored Support Patrol Boat [*Military*]
ASPB.......... Assault Support Patrol Boat [*Navy symbol*]
ASPC.......... Accepte sous Protet pour Compte [*Accepted under Protest for Account*] [*French*]
ASPC.......... Aerojet Solid Propulsion Co.
ASPC.......... Air Space Paper Core
ASPC.......... American Sheep Producers Council [*Later, ASIA*] (EA)
ASPC.......... American Shetland Pony Club (EA)
ASPC.......... American Society for the Prevention of Crime [*Defunct*] (EA)
ASPC.......... Analysis of Spare Parts Change (MCD)
ASPC.......... Association of Strategic Planning Consultants (EA)
ASPC.......... Association of Swimming Pool Contractors [*British*] (BI)
ASPC.......... Australian Softwood Producers' Council
ASPCA........ American Society for the Prevention of Cruelty to Animals (EA)
Asp Cas...... Aspinall's Maritime Law Cases [*1871-1940*] [*England*] [*A publication*] (DLA)
ASPCC........ All Service Postal Chess Club (EA)
AsPCDE....... Asian-Pacific Society for Digestive Endoscopy
ASPCGA...... Atomic Strike Plan Control Group Alternate (AABC)
AspctDv...... Aspect Development [*Associated Press*] (SAG)
AspctTl....... Aspect Telecommunications Corp. [*Associated Press*] (SAG)
ASPD.......... Advanced Space Propellant Demonstration (MCD)
ASPD.......... American Society for Preventive Dentistry [*Defunct*]
ASPD.......... American Society of Podiatric Dermatology (EA)
ASPD.......... Aviation Ships Planning Document (MCD)
ASPDA........ American Society of Professional Draftsmen and Artists (EA)
ASPDA........ Association of State Planning and Development Agencies [*Later, NASDA*] (EA)
ASPDE........ Automatic Shaft-Position Data Encoder
ASPDM........ American Society of Psychosomatic Dentistry and Medicine [*IPI*] [*Absorbed by*] (EA)
ASPE.......... Alabama Society of Professional Engineers (SRA)
ASPE.......... American Society of Plumbing Engineers (EA)
ASPE.......... American Society of Professional Ecologists (EA)
ASPE.......... American Society of Professional Estimators (EA)
ASPE.......... American Society of Psychopathology of Expression (EA)
ASPE.......... Arizona Society of Professional Engineers (SRA)
ASPE.......... Arkansas Society of Professional Engineers (SRA)
ASPE.......... Assistant Secretary for Planning and Evaluation [*Department of Health and Human Services*]
ASPE.......... Association for Special Education [*British*]
ASPE.......... Association for the Study of Primary Education (AIE)
ASPEC........ Association of Sorbitol Producers in the European Community (EAIO)
ASPEC........ Automatic Sample Preparation Extraction Column [*Chromatography*]
A SPEC........ System Specification (AAGC)

ASPECT....... Acoustic Short-Pulse Echo Classification Technique (NVT)
ASPECT....... American Study Program for Educational and Cultural Training (EA)
ASPECT....... Anticoagulants in the Secondary Prevention of Events in Coronary Thrombosis
ASPECT....... Automatic Speckle Cancellation Techniques (PDAA)
AspectTel..... Aspect Telecommunications [*Associated Press*] (SAG)
ASPEI......... Association of South Pacific Environmental Institutions
ASPEICP...... Associated Schools Project in Education for International Cooperation and Peace [*UNESCO*] [*Paris, France*] (EAIO)
ASPEMRCM... CANMET [*Canada Centre for Mineral and Energy Technology*] Library, Western Research Laboratory, Energy, Mines, and Resources Canada , Sherwood Park, Alberta [*Bibliotheque CANMET, Laboratoire de Recherche de l'Ouest, Energie, Mines, et Ressources Canada*] [*Library symbol National Library of Canada*] (NLC)
ASPEN........ Advanced System for Process Engineering
ASPEN........ American Society for Parenteral and Enteral Nutrition (EA)
ASPEN........ Automated Space Production Experimenters Network [*Robotics*]
ASPEN........ Automatic Speech Exchange System [*Voice messaging*]
AspenB........ Aspen Bankshares, Inc. [*Associated Press*] (SAG)
AspenTc....... Aspen Technology, Inc. [*Associated Press*] (SAG)
ASPEP........ Association of Scientists and Professional Engineering Personnel
ASPER........ Aspergillosis [*A fungal disease*] (DAVI)
ASPER........ Assembly System for Peripheral Processors [*Computer science*]
ASPER........ Assistant Secretary for Policy Evaluation and Research [*Department of Labor*]
ASPERA....... Automatic Space Plasma Experiment with a Rotating Analyser [*Instrumentation*]
ASPERS....... Armed Services Procurement Regulations
ASPET........ American Society for Pharmacology and Experimental Therapeutics (EA)
ASPEW........ American Society of Professional and Executive Women [*Defunct*] (EA)
ASPEX........ Automated Surface Perspective (MHDI)
ASPG.......... Antispleen Globulin [*Medicine*] (DMAA)
ASPG.......... Australasian Study of Parliament Group
ASPH.......... Asphalt (KSC)
ASPH.......... Association of Schools of Public Health (EA)
ASPH.......... Association of Schools of Public Health (EA)
ASPHA........ American Saddlebred Pleasure Horse Association [*Later, ASHA*] (EA)
ASPHER....... Association of Schools of Public Health in the European Region (EAIO)
ASPHIO....... Association of Supervisory Public Health Inspectors (Ontario) (AC)
ASPHLT....... Asphalt
ASPHO........ American Society of Pediatric Hematology/Oncology (EA)
ASPHPF....... Asphalt-Plank Floor (MSA)
ASPHRS....... Asphalt Roof Shingles [*Technical drawings*]
ASPHV........ Association of State Public Health Veterinarians [*Later, NASPHV*] (EA)
ASPI........... Academy of Sports Psychology International (EA)
ASPI........... Advanced SCSI [*Small Computer System Interface*] Programming Interface (PCM)
ASPI........... Aerosurface Position Indicator (MCD)
ASPI........... American Society for Performance Improvement [*Defunct*] (EA)
ASPI........... Apollo Supplemental Procedural Information [*NASA*] (KSC)
ASPI........... Appalachia Science in the Public Interest [*An association*]
ASPI........... Association of Student and Professional Italian-Americans (EA)
ASPI........... Asynchronous Synchronous Programmable Interface [*Computer science*]
ASPI........... Automatic Sample Processor and Injector
ASPIC......... Armed Services Personnel Interrogation Center (AFM)
ASPIC......... Author's Standard Pre-Press Interface Code [*Mark-up code for word processing/typesetter interface*] (NITA)
ASPIC......... Authors' Symbolic Pre-Press Interfacing Codes (DGA)
ASPIL......... American Standard Practice for Industrial Lighting (IAA)
Aspin.......... Aspinall's Maritime Law Cases [*1871-1940*] [*England*] [*A publication*] (DLA)
ASPIRE....... Achieve Successful Performance, Intensify Reliability Effort
ASPIRE....... Advanced Special Projects in Radiation Effects
ASPIRE....... Associated Students Promoting Individual Rights for Everyone
ASPIS......... Advanced Self-Protection Integrated Suite [*Military*] (DOMA)
ASPJ.......... Advanced Self-Protection Jammer
ASPJ.......... Airborne Self-Protection Jammer (MCD)
ASPJRA....... Airborne Self-Protection Jammer Rack Assembly (DWSG)
ASPK.......... Accompanying Spare Parts Kit [*Navy*]
ASPL.......... American Society for Pharmacy Law (EA)
ASPL.......... Approved Spare Parts List (MCD)
ASPL.......... Army Standard Program Languages
ASPL.......... Assistant Sector Programming Leader (SAA)
ASPLO........ Association of Small Public Libraries of Ontario (AC)
ASPLP........ American Society for Political and Legal Philosophy (EA)
ASPLS........ Alabama Society of Professional Land Surveyors (SRA)
ASPM.......... Air Scatterable Antipersonnel Mine (MCD)
ASPM.......... American Society of Paramedics (EA)
ASPM.......... American Society of Podiatric Medicine (EA)
ASPM.......... Armed Services Pricing Manual [*A publication*] (AAGC)
ASPM.......... Armed Services Procurement Manual (MCD)
ASPM.......... Armed Services Procurement Medal
ASPM.......... Association of Sanitary Protection Manufacturers [*British*] (DBA)
ASPM.......... Automated System for Production Management (IAA)
ASPMA........ American Smoking Pipe Manufacturers Association [*Defunct*] (EA)
ASPMA........ American Society of Podiatric Medical Assistants (EA)
Asp Mar Law Cas... Aspinall's Maritime Law Cases [*1871-1940*] [*England*] [*A publication*] (DLA)

Asp Mar L Cas (Eng)... Aspinall's Maritime Law Cases [1871-1940] [England] [A publication] (DLA)

ASP/MC .... Aspencade Motorcyclists Convention (EA)

Asp MC .... Aspinall's Maritime Law Cases [1871-1940] [England] [A publication] (DLA)

Asp MCL ...... Aspinall's Maritime Law Cases [1871-1940] [A publication] (DLA)

ASPMIS .... Apollo Spacecraft Parts and Materials Information Services [NASA] (KSC)

Asp MLC ...... Aspinall's Maritime Law Cases [1871-1940] [England] [A publication] (DLA)

ASPMM .... Amalgamated Society of Plate and Machine Moulders [A union] [British]

ASPMS .... Aircraft Space Position Measurement System (MCD)

ASPN .... American Society for Pediatric Neurosurgery (EA)

ASPN .... American Society for Portuguese Numismatics [Defunct] (EA)

ASPN .... American Society of Precision Nailmakers [Defunct]

Asp N .... Asparagine (BARN)

Asp(NH₂) ..... Asparagine [Also, Asn, N] [An amino acid]

ASPNI .... American Society for the Protection of Nature in Israel (EA)

AspnIm .... Aspen Imaging International, Inc. [Associated Press] (SAG)

ASPO .... Acquisition Sponsor Project Officer [USMC] (AAGC)

ASPO .... Acquisition Systems Protection Office [DoD] (RDA)

ASPO .... Advanced Systems Project Office

ASPO .... AGORA-SPORTS [Agence France-Presse] [Information service or system] (CRD)

ASPO .... American Society for Psychoprophylaxis in Obstetrics (EA)

ASPO .... American Society of Planning Officials [Later, American Planning Association] (EA)

ASPO .... American Society of Preventive Oncology (EA)

ASPO .... Antisubmarine Systems Project Office [Navy]

ASPO .... Apollo Spacecraft Project Office [NASA]

ASPO .... Army Space Program Office (MCD)

ASPO .... Avionics System Project Officer

ASPOC .... Active Spacecraft Potential Control [Instrumentation]

ASPOE .... American Society of Petroleum Operations Engineers (EA)

A spol .... A Spolecnost [and Company] [Czech] (BARN)

ASPOL .... [A] Simulation Process Oriented Language [1972] [Computer science] (CSR)

ASPO/Lamaze... American Society for Prophylaxis in Obstetrics (PAZ)

AS/POT .... Agena Systems/Power-On Test [NASA] (KSC)

ASPP .... Advanced Satellite Products Project [Madison, WI] [NOAA/NESDIS] (GRD)

ASPP .... Aeronautical Fixed Systems Planning for Data Interchange Panel [ICAO] (DA)

ASPP .... Alloy-Steel Protective Plating

ASPP .... American Society of Picture Professionals (EA)

ASPP .... American Society of Plant Physiologists (EA)

ASPP .... American Society of Polar Philatelists (EA)

ASPP .... Antenna Solar Panel Positioner

ASPP .... Association for Sane Psychiatric Practices (EA)

ASPP .... Association of SIDS [Sudden Infant Death Syndrome] Program Professionals (EA)

ASPP .... Atmospheric and Space Plasma Physics [NASA] (NASA)

ASPPA .... Auto Steel Partnership Program [Industry manufacturing standards]

ASPPA .... Armed Services Petroleum Purchasing Agency

ASPPF .... Association of Seminary Professors in the Practical Fields [Later, APT] (EA)

ASPPI .... Azimuth-Stabilized Plan Position Indicator (DEN)

ASPPO .... Armed Services Procurement Planning Officer

ASPPO .... Armed Services Production Planning Officer (MCD)

ASPPP .... American Society for Philatelic Pages and Panels (EA)

ASPPR .... Association of Sugar Producers of Puerto Rico [Defunct] (EA)

ASPQ .... Association pour la Sante Publique du Quebec [Quebec Public Health Association] (AC)

ASPR .... Aircraft Structural Integrity Program Recorder

ASPR .... American Society for Psychical Research (EA)

ASPr .... Armco Inc,$2.10 Cv Pfd [NYSE symbol] (TTSB)

ASPR .... Armed Services Procurement Regulation [Later, DAR]

ASPR .... Armor Systems Program Review (MCD)

ASPR .... Average Specific Polymerization Rate (OA)

ASPR .... Aviation Systems Program Review (MCD)

ASPrA .... Armco $4.50 Cv B Pfd [NYSE symbol] (TTSB)

ASPrB .... Armco $3.625 Cv A Pfd [NYSE symbol] (TTSB)

ASPRC .... Academy of the Street of Puerto Rican Congress (EA)

ASPRDEC .... Advanced Systems Planning, Research, Development, and Engineering Course [Army]

Asp Rep ...... Aspinall's Maritime Law Cases [1871-1940] [A publication] (DLA)

ASPRL .... Armament Systems Personnel Research Laboratory [Lowry Air Force Base, CO]

ASPRM .... Armed Services Procurement Regulation Manual (AABC)

Aspro .... Associate Professor (ADA)

ASPRO .... Associative Processor [Computer science] (MCD)

ASPRS .... American Society for Photogrammetry and Remote Sensing (EA)

ASPRS .... American Society of Plastic and Reconstructive Surgeons (EA)

ASPRS .... Armed Services Procurement Regulation Supplement (AABC)

ASPRSN ...... American Society of Plastic and Reconstructive Surgical Nurses (EA)

ASPRT .... Adjusted Sequential Probability Ratio Test [Statistics]

AS-PRT .... Anthranilate Synthase - Phosphoribosyl Transferase [Enzyme complex]

ASPRTR .... Aspirator (MSA)

ASPS .... Acoustic Ship Positioning System

ASPS .... Adaptable Space Propulsion System [Military]

ASPS .... Advanced Sleep Phase Syndrome [Medicine] (DMAA)

ASPS .... African Succulent Plant Society [Defunct] (EA)

ASPS .... All-Source Production Section [Army] (ADDR)

ASPS .... Alveolar Soft Part Sarcoma [Oncology]

ASPS .... American Selling Price System

ASPS .... American Society of Pre-Dental Students (EA)

ASPS .... American Society of Professional Salesmen (EA)

ASPS .... Annular Suspension and Pointing System (SSD)

ASPS .... Armed Services Procurement Regulation Supplement

ASPS .... Association of Supervisors in Purchasing and Supply [British] (DBQ)

ASPS .... Automated Small Purchase System [DoD]

ASPS .... Automatic Specimen Positioning System

ASPS .... County of Strathcona Library, Sherwood Park, Alberta [Library symbol National Library of Canada] (NLC)

AsPSC .... Asian-Pacific Society of Cardiology

ASPSC .... Association of State and Provincial Safety Coordinators [Later, ASPSO] (EA)

AsPSIR .... Asia-Pacific Society for Impotence Research

ASPSL .... ASPP [Atmospheric and Space Plasma Physics] Sortie Laboratory [NASA] (NASA)

AsPSN .... Asian-Pacific Society of Nephrology

ASPSO .... Association of State and Provincial Safety Officials [Formerly, ASPSC] (EA)

AsPSPGN .... Asian-Pacific Society of Paediatric Gastroenterology and Nutrition

ASPSPOM .... American Society for the Preservation of Sacred, Patriotic, and Operatic Music (EA)

ASPSU .... Attitude Sensor Parachute Staging Unit (MCD)

ASPT .... Academy of Screen Printing Technology (EA)

ASPT .... Advanced Simulator for Pilot Training (MCD)

ASPT .... American Society of Plant Taxonomists (EA)

ASPT .... Army School of Physical Training [British]

ASPT .... Aspect Telecommunications [NASDAQ symbol] (TTSB)

ASPT .... Aspect Telecommunications Corp. [NASDAQ symbol] (SAG)

ASPTC .... Army Support Center (AABC)

ASPU .... Abrupt Symmetrical Pull Up (MCD)

ASPU .... Automatic Signal Processing Unit (MCD)

ASPVD .... Arteriosclerotic Peripheral Vascular Disease [Medicine] (MEDA)

ASPX .... Auspex Systems [NASDAQ symbol] (TTSB)

ASPX .... Auspex Systems, Inc. [NASDAQ symbol] (SAG)

ASQ .... Abbreviated Symptom Questionnaire [Medicine] (AAMN)

ASQ .... Active Singles Quest [Technique] [In book title]

ASQ .... Air Service [Poland ICAO designator] (FAAC)

ASQ .... Algebraic Solution for Queues

ASQ .... Analytic Solution to Queues (MHDI)

ASQ .... Anxiety Scale Questionnaire [Psychology]

ASQ .... Asia Service Airlines [Kazakhstan] [FAA designator] (FAAC)

ASQ .... Association des Sculpteurs du Quebec [1961, CSQ from 1978] [Canada] (NGC)

ASQ .... Association des Sexologues du Quebec (AC)

ASQ .... Attitude toward School Questionnaire [Test]

ASQ .... Austin [Nevada] [Airport symbol Obsolete] (OAG)

ASQA .... Automatic Sky Quality Assessment (MCD)

ASQC .... American Society for Quality Control (EA)

ASQDE .... American Society of Questioned Document Examiners (EA)

A/SQK .... Antisqueak [Automotive engineering]

ASQL .... Apogee Structured Query Language [Computer science]

ASQP .... Airline Service Quality Performance [FAA] (TAG)

ASR .... Absolute Specular Reflectance [Spectroscopy]

ASR .... Acceleration Slip Regulation [Automotive engineering]

ASR .... Acceptance Summary Report

ASR .... Accion Socialista Revolucionaria [Peru] [Political party] (EY)

ASR .... Accommodation Sales Requisition

ASR .... Accounting Series Release [Securities and Exchange Commission]

ASR .... Accounting Series Releases (TDOB)

ASR .... Accumulators Shift Right [Computer science] (BUR)

ASR .... Acoustic Stapedius Reflex [Medicine]

ASR .... Acquisition Strategy Report [Military] (DOMA)

ASR .... Active Status Register

ASR .... Ada Software Repository

ASR .... Address Shift Register [Computer science] (NITA)

ASR .... Address Start Register [Computer science] (IAA)

ASR .... Advanced Salvo Rifle (MCD)

ASR .... Advanced Surveillance RADAR

ASR .... Advanced Systems Requirements

ASR .... Age/Sex Rate

ASR .... Agricultural Science Review [A publication]

ASR .... Airborne Scanning Radiometer

ASR .... Airborne Surveillance RADAR (IEEE)

ASR .... Airport Surveillance RADAR

ASR .... Air Search RADAR

ASR .... Air-Sea Rescue

ASR .... Air Staff Requirement

ASR .... Air Surveillance RADAR (AFM)

ASR .... Aldosterone Secretion Rate [Endocrinology]

ASR .... Alkalisilica Reaction [Chemistry]

ASR .... All Star Airlines, Inc. [ICAO designator] (FAAC)

ASR .... All Star Resources [Vancouver Stock Exchange symbol]

ASR .... Alternate Supply Rate (MCD)

ASR .... Alternate Supply Route

ASR .... Altimeter Setting Region [Aviation] (AIA)

ASR .... American Iron and Steel Institute. Statistical Report [A publication] (EAAP)

ASR .... American River College, Sacramento, CA [OCLC symbol] (OCLC)

ASR .... American Saudi Roundtable (EA)

ASR .... American Service Radio [English-language broadcasting] (VNW)

ASR .... American Society of Rocketry

ASR .... American State Reports [A publication] (DLA)

ASR .... Analog Shift Register [Computer science]

ASR	Anisotropic Saturation Recovery [*NMR imaging*]
ASR	Annual Summary Report
ASR	Answer Send and Receive [*Telecommunications*] (DGA)
ASR	Anti-Slip Regulation [*Automotive engineering*]
ASR	Anti-Streptolysin Reaction [*Medicine*] (DMAA)
ASR	Aperiodic Stochastic Resonance [*Model of neurophysiological reactions*]
ASR	Approved System Requirement
ASR	Aquifer Storage and Recovery [*Water supply technology*]
ASR	Architects for Social Responsibility (EA)
ASR	Area Surveillance RADAR
ASR	Arithmetic Shift Right [*Computer science*]
ASR	Armed Strike Reconnaissance (AABC)
ASR	Armed Surface Reconnaissance [*Navy*] (DOMA)
ASR	Army Scripture Reader [*British military*] (DMA)
ASR	Army Service Reserve [*British*] (ROG)
ASR	Army Service Ribbon [*Military decoration*]
ASR	Army Status Report (AABC)
ASR	As Required (MCD)
ASR	ASR Investments [*AMEX symbol*] (TTSB)
ASR	ASR Investments Corp. [*Formerly, American Southwest Mortgage Investment Co.*] [*Associated Press*] (SAG)
ASR	Asset Support Request
ASR	Assigned Slot Release (MHDI)
ASR	Association for the Sociology of Religion (EA)
ASR	Astronomy Space and Radio Board [*Science and Engineering Research Council*] (PDAA)
ASR	Atmospheric Sound Refraction
ASR	Atomic Strike Recording [*Air Force*]
ASR	Attack, Sustain, Release [*Electronic musical instruments*]
ASR	Australian Society of Rheology
ASR	Authorized Selling Representative [*Marketing*] (WDMC)
AS/R	Automated Storage/Retrieval [*Computer science*]
AS/R	Automatic Send/Receive Teletypewriter [*or Terminal*] [*Communications equipment*]
ASR	Automatic Sequence Register (NTCM)
ASR	Automatic SONAR Readout
ASR	Automatic Speech Recognition
ASR	Automatic Sprinkler Riser [*Technical drawings*]
ASR	Automatic Stability Regulation [*Automotive engineering*]
ASR	Automatic Step Regulator
ASR	Automatic Strength Regulation (IAA)
ASR	Automatic Surveillance Receiver (MCD)
ASR	Automobile Shredder Residue
ASR	Automotive Service Reports [*A publication*] (EAAP)
ASR	Auxiliary Submarine Rescue Ship [*Navy symbol*]
ASR	Available Supply Rate
ASR	Aviation Safety Regulation
ASR	Avionics System Review (NASA)
ASR	Kayseri [*Turkey*] [*Airport symbol*] (OAG)
ASR	Submarine Rescue Ship [*Navy symbol*]
ASRA	ADP [*Automatic Data Processing*] Systems Resources Analysis
ASRA	American Seafood Retailers Association (EA)
ASRA	American Shropshire Registry Association (EA)
ASRA	American Society of Regional Anesthesia (EA)
ASRA	Applied Science and Research Applications [*Program*] [*Supersedes RANN*] [*National Science Foundation*]
ASRA	Athwartships Reference Axis
ASRA	Automatic Stereo Recording Amplifier
ASRAA	Advanced Short-Range Air-to-Air Missile (MCD)
ASRAAM	Advanced Short-Range Air-to-Air Missile (RDA)
ASRAB	Alberta Sports & Recreation Association for the Blind (AC)
ASRADI	Adaptive Surface-Signal Recognition and Direction Indicator [*Navy*]
ASRAO	Advanced Systems Research and Analysis Office [*Army and NASA joint operation*] (RDA)
ASRAP	Acoustic Sensor [*or SONAR*] Range Prediction (NVT)
ASRAPS	Acoustic Sensor [*or SONAR*] Range Prediction System (NVT)
ASRB	Armed Services Renegotiation Board [*Later, RB*]
ASRB	Army Security Review Board
ASRBA	American Satin Rabbit Breeders' Association (EA)
ASRC	Air-Sea Rescue Craft
ASRC	American Synthetic Rubber Corp.
ASRC	Atmospheric Sciences Research Center [*State University of New York*] [*Research center*]
ASRC	Australian Standard Research Classification
ASRD	Advanced Systems Research Department
ASRD	Aircraft Shipment Readiness Date [*Army*] (AABC)
ASRD	American Society of Retired Dentists (EA)
ASRD	Avionic Subsystem Requirement Document (MCD)
ASRDI	Aerospace Safety Research and Data Institute [*Lewis Research Center*] [*NASA*]
ASRDL	Army Signal Research and Development Laboratory
ASRE	Admiralty Signal and RADAR Establishment [*British*]
ASRE	American Society of Refrigerating Engineers [*Later, ASHRAE*]
ASREAV	Australian Society of Real Estate Agents and Valuers
ASREC	American Society of Real Estate Counselors (EA)
ASREFO	Anthony Sharp and Rachael Ellison Family Organization. (EA)
ASRF	Advanced Size Reduction Facility (MCD)
ASRF	Air-Sea Rescue Flight [*British military*] (DMA)
ASRF	American Seed Research Foundation (EA)
ASRF	Sydney [*Australia ICAO location identifier*] (ICLI)
ASRFU	Australian Schools' Rugby Football Union
ASRG	Advanced Sciences Research Group (SAA)
ASRGN	Altimeter Setting Region [*Aviation*]
ASRHA	American Small and Rural Hospital Association (EA)

ASRI	Agricultural Systems Research Institute [*Beltsville, MD*] [*Department of Agriculture*] (GRD)
ASRI	Aluminum Smelters Research Institute [*Later, ARA*] (EA)
ASRI	Richmond [*Australia ICAO location identifier*] (ICLI)
ASR Inv	ASR Investments Corp. [*Associated Press*] (SAG)
ASRK	Air Sea Rescue Kit [*Military*]
ASRL	Aeroelastic and Structures Research Laboratory [*Massachusetts Institute of Technology*]
ASRL	Aerolastic and Structures Research Laboratory (SAA)
ASRL	Alberta Sulphur Research Ltd. (AC)
ASRL	Associate in Science in Recreation Leadership
ASRL	Astro Systems Research Laboratory (SAA)
ASRL	Atmospheric Sciences Research Laboratory [*Research Triangle Park, NC*] [*Environmental Protection Agency*] (GRD)
ASRL	Australian Scientific Research Liaison [*British*]
ASRL	Average Sample Run Length [*Statistics*] (PDAA)
ASRM	Abort Solid Rocket Motor [*NASA*] (NASA)
ASRM	Advanced Solid Rocket Motor [*Proposed*] [*NASA*]
ASRM	American Society for Reproductive Medicine (PAZ)
ASRM	American Society of Range Management [*Later, SRM*] (EA)
ASRM	Antenna System Readiness Monitor (MCD)
ASRm	Spirit River Municipal Library, Alberta [*Library symbol National Library of Canada*] (NLC)
asRNA	Antisense RNA [*Ribonucleic Acid*] [*Genetics*] (DOG)
ASRNH	American Society for Russian Naval History (EA)
ASRO	Amateur Scientist Research Organization (EA)
ASRO	Assistant Superintendent, Range Operations [*NASA*] (KSC)
ASRO	Association of Social Research Organisations [*British*]
ASROC	Antisubmarine Rocket [*Navy*]
ASROC	Antisubmarine Rocket Computer [*Navy*] (IAA)
ASROC(ERA)...	Antisubmarine Rocket (Extended Range) (DNAB)
ASR/OPS	Air Surveillance RADAR/Operations Center System
ASRP	African Studies and Research Program [*Howard University*] [*Research center*] (RCD)
ASRP	Airborne SIGINT Reconnaissance Program (MCD)
ASRP	Ammunition Stockpile Reliability Program (MCD)
ASRP	Ancillary Services Review Program [*Health insurance*] (GHCT)
ASRP	Arab Socialist Renaissance Party [*Syria*]
ASRPA	Army Signal Radio Propagation Agency
ASRPB	Aviation Selected Reserve Programs Branch [*BUPERS*]
ASRR	American Society for Reformation Research
ASRS	Adjusted Service Rating Score [*Military*]
ASRS	Advanced Assembly Sequence Record Sheet (MCD)
ASRS	Advanced Strategic Reconnaissance System [*Air Force*]
ASRS	Airborne Satellite Receiving Station
ASRS	Air Safety Reporting System [*NASA*]
ASRS	Air-Sea Rescue Service [*British military*] (DMA)
ASRS	American Sable Rabbit Society (EA)
ASRS	American Society of Roommate Services (EA)
ASRS	Ammunition Stock Recording System
ASRS	Anglo-Soviet Recognition Signals
ASRS	Anti-Stoke Stimulated Raman Scattering [*Spectrometry*] (MCD)
ASRS	Apollo Simulated Remote Site [*NASA*] (KSC)
ASRS	Assembly Sequence Record Sheet
ASRS	Automated Seat Reservation System [*Aviation*]
ASRS	Automated Shareholder Records System (MCD)
AS/RS	Automated Storage/Retrieval Systems (EA)
ASRS	Auxiliary Support Reaction System
ASRS	Aviation Safety Reporting System (MCD)
ASRSC	Armed Services Research Specialists Committee
ASRSC	Atlantic Sea Run Salmon Commission (EA)
ASRSD	Ammunition Systems Reliability and Safety Division [*Picatinny Arsenal*] [*Army*]
ASRSOW	Associated Society of Range Stove and Ornamental Workers [*A union*] [*British*]
ASRSQ	Association des Services de Rehabilitation Sociale du Quebec Inc. [*Association of Social Rehabilitation Agencies of Quebec Inc.*] (AC)
ASRSWS	Assembly Sequence Record Sheet - Work Sheet
ASRT	Adaptive Source Routing Transparent [*Computer science*] (PCM)
ASRT	Air Support RADAR Team [*Marine Corps*]
ASRT	American Society of Radiologic Technologists (EA)
ASRT	Assort (MSA)
ASRU	Automatic Signal Recognition Unit (IAA)
ASRV	Armoured Scout Reconnaissance Vehicle [*Military*] (PDAA)
ASRWPM	Association of Semi-Rotary Wing Pump Manufacturers (MHDB)
ASS	Accessory Supply System
ASS	Acoustical Society of Scandinavia [*Formerly, Nordic Acoustics Society*] (EA)
ASS	Acquisition Sun Sensor (MCD)
ASS	Acta Sanctorum [*Acts of the Saints*] [*Latin*]
ASS	Acute Serum Sickness [*Medicine*] (DMAA)
ASS	Admiralty Standard Stockless [*Anchor*] (PDAA)
ASS	Advanced Space Station
ASS	Aerosol Sampling System
ASS	Aerospace Support Systems (MCD)
ASS	Aerospace Surveillance System
ASS	Affective Sensitivity Scale
ASS	Airborne Surveillance Set
ASS	Aircraft Security System (MCD)
ASS	Airlock Support Subsystem [*NASA*] (NASA)
ASS	Air Sampling System
ASS	Airspace Surveillance Station
ASS	Air Surveillance System
ASS	Alberta Speleological Society (AC)

ASS............ Altitude Sensing System
ASS............ Amalgamated Society of Shuttlemakers [*A union*] [*British*]
ASS............ Analog Simulation System
ASS............ Analog Switching Subsystem [*Telecommunications*] (NITA)
ASS............ Anterior Superior Spine [*Anatomy*]
ASS............ Approved Study Structure
ASS............ Argininosuccinate Synthetase [*An enzyme*]
ASS............ Armament Systems Section [*Air Force*]
ASS............ Army Signal School [*British*]
ASS............ Army Signal Squadron (IAA)
ASS............ Army Special Staff
ASS............ Assassination (ROG)
Ass............ Assemblee Generale du Contentieux, Conseil d'Etat [*France*] (ILCA)
ASS............ Assembler (NITA)
ASS............ Assembler Language [*Computer science*] (CMD)
ASS............ Assembly
Ass............ Assessor [*Assistant, Assessor*] [*German*]
ASS............ Assigns (ROG)
ASS............ Assistant
ASS............ Assistant Secretary of State (DAS)
ASS............ Assize Rolls [*British*]
ASS............ Associate in Secretarial Science
ASS............ Associate in Secretarial Studies
ASS............ Association
Ass............ Assurance [*Insurance*] [*French*] (ILCA)
ASS............ Assyria
ASS............ Atmospheric Structure Satellite (SAA)
ASS............ Australian Sahiwal Society
ASS............ Australian Social Security Guide [*A publication*]
ASS............ Australian Synchronised Swimming
ASS............ Automatic Stabilization System
ASS............ Automatic Start-Up System [*Reactor*]
ASS............ Autopilot Surface Servo
AS(S).......... Auxiliary Steam (System) [*Nuclear energy*] (NRCH)
ASS............ Axisymmetric Spiral [*Astronomy*]
Ass............ Liber Assisarum [*Book of Assizes, or pleas of the crown*] [*Pt. 5 of Year Books*] [*A publication*] (DLA)
ASSA.......... Advanced Strategic Standoff Aircraft (MCD)
ASSA.......... Allied Social Science Associations (EA)
ASSA.......... American Shetland Sheepdog Association (EA)
ASSA.......... American Society for the Study of Arteriosclerosis [*Later, CAAHA*]
ASSA.......... Area Supply Support Activity [*Army*] (AFIT)
ASSA.......... [*The*] Army Signal Supply Agency (MCD)
ASSA.......... Army Signal Support Agency
ASSA.......... Assembly Area (IAA)
ASSA.......... Australian Society of Sport Administrators
ASSA.......... Australian Stevedoring Supervisors' Association
ASSA.......... Cargo Submarine [*Navy symbol Obsolete*]
ASSAB....... Australasian Society for the Study of Animal Behaviour
ASSAFOET... Assafoetida [*Pharmacy*] (ROG)
ASSAM....... Advanced Strategic Standoff Attack Missile (MCD)
ASSAP....... Association for the Scientific Study of Anomalous Phenomena
ASSAS........ Assassination (ROG)
ASSASSIN... Agricultural System for Storage and Subsequent Selection of Information [*British*] [*Information service or system*] (NITA)
ASSASSIN... Automated System for Storing and Subsequently Selecting Information [*Developed by ICI, Inc.*]
ASSAULT..... Automated Support System for Army Unit Logistics Training
ASSAW....... Aerospace Surveillance and Warning
ASSB......... Anonymous Society of Second Bananas (EA)
ASSB......... Apollo Site Selection Board [*NASA*] (KSC)
ASSB......... Asynchronous Single Sideband [*Electronics*] (IAA)
ASSB......... Avionics Subsystem for Strategic Bombers
ASSBA....... Association of Stud Sheep Breeders of Australia
ASSB & OM... American Society to Save Biharis and Other Minorities
ASSBT........ American Society of Sugar Beet Technologists (EA)
ASSBWMM... Amalgamated Society of Scale Beam and Weighing Machine Makers [*A union*] [*British*]
ASSBY....... Assembly (AAMN)
ASSC......... Accounting Standards Steering Committee (ODBW)
ASSC......... Acute Splenic Sequestration Crisis [*Medicine*] (DMAA)
ASSC......... Advanced Shipboard Satellite Communications (DNAB)
ASSC......... Airborne Systems Support Center
ASSC......... Air, Sea, and Space Club (EA)
ASSC......... Air Service Signal Corps
ASSC......... American Shooting Sports Council
ASSC......... Army Subsistence Supply Center [*Merged with Defense Subsistence Supply Center*]
ASSC......... Association of Search and Selection Consultants [*British*] (DBA)
ASSC......... Australian Schools Sports Council
ASSC......... Australian Social Security Cases [*A publication*]
ASSC......... Australian Sports Science Council
ASSC......... Savanna Community Library, Silver Valley, Alberta [*Library symbol National Library of Canada*] (NLC)
ASSCAS...... Advanced Spacecraft Subsystem Cost Analysis Structure (MCD)
Assce......... Assurance [*Insurance*] [*French*]
ASSCI........ American Section of the Societe de Chimie Industrielle (EA)
ASSCM....... Avionics Software Support Cost Model (MCD)
ASSCN....... Association (EY)
Ass Com Gen... Assistant-Commissary-General [*British*]
AS-SCORE... Assessing Severity: Age of Patient, Systems Involved, State of Disease, Complications, Response to Therapy [*Medicine*] (MEDA)
AssCPHO's... Association of County Public Health Officers [*British*]
ASSD.......... Assessed (WGA)

Assd............ Assigned (DLA)
ASSD.......... Associated
ASSD.......... Assorted (ROG)
ASSD.......... Assured (ROG)
ASSDD........ Association of Summer Session Deans and Directors [*Later, AUSS*] (EA)
AssDipFor.... Associate Diploma in Forestry
ASSDR....... Alliance for Social Security and Disability Recipients (EA)
ASSE......... American Society of Safety Engineers (EA)
ASSE......... American Society of Sanitary Engineering (EA)
ASSE......... American Society of Swedish Engineers (EA)
ASSE......... Automation System for Scientific Experiments
ASSEA........ Association of Surgeons of South East Asia (EAIO)
ASSEM....... Assemble (MSA)
Assem .... Assembly (DLA)
ASSER....... Assessor of Archdeaconry [*Ecclesiastical*] (ROG)
ASSERON.... Army Service Squadron [*Corresponds to Navy's CASU*]
ASSES .... Analytical Studies of Surface Effects of Submerged Submarines [*Navy*] (DNAB)
ASSESMT ... Assessment (KSC)
ASSESS ...... Airborne Science Shuttle Experiments System Simulation [*NASA*] (NASA)
ASSESS ...... Airborne Science Shuttle [*or Spacelab*] Experiment System Simulation [*NASA*] (MCD)
ASSESS ...... Analytical Studies of Surface Effects of Submerged Submarines [*Navy*]
ASSET......... Advanced Skewed Sensory Electronic Triad [*Navy*]
ASSET......... Advanced System Synthesis and Evaluation Technique [*Lockheed Aircraft*]
ASSET......... Aerothermodynamic Structural Systems Environmental Test [*Military*]
ASSET......... Aircraft Support and Service Equipment Tug (PDAA)
ASSET......... Air Surveillance Subsystem Evaluation and Training [*Air Force*] (IAA)
ASSET......... American Society of Scientific and Engineering Translators
ASSET......... American-South African Study and Educational Trust
ASSET......... Anglo-Scandinavian Study of Early Thrombolysis
ASSET......... Assessment of Safety Significant Events Team [*IAEA*] (NUCP)
ASSET......... Asset Source for Software Engineering Technology
ASSET......... Association of Supervisory Staffs, Executives, and Technicians (KSC)
ASSET......... ASW [*Antisubmarine Warfare*] Submarine System Evaluation Technique
ASSET......... Automated Spares Simulation Estimating Technique [*The Boeing Co.*]
ASSET......... Automated System for Sequential Extraction and Tabulation (NVT)
ASSET......... Automated Systems and Software Engineering Technology (MCD)
ASSET......... Automotive Student Service Educational Training
ASSETS....... Acquisition Streamlining and Standardization Electronic Transfer System (AAGC)
ASSETS....... [*A*] Survey of Students' Educational Talents and Skills [*Educational test*]
ASSF.......... Arbetarnas och Smabrukarnas Socialdemokratiska Foerbund [*Social Democratic League of Workers and Smallholders*] [*Finland Political party*] (PPE)
ASSFJ....... Aleksandr Solzhenitsyn Society for Freedom and Justice (EA)
ASSFN .... American Society for Stereotactic and Functional Neurosurgery (EA)
ASSG .... Assignment (IAA)
ASSGB........ Association of Ski Schools in Great Britain
ASSGN....... Assignee
ASSGT .... Assignment (ROG)
ASSH .... Advance Space System Hardening (MCD)
ASSH .... American Society for Surgery of the Hand (EA)
ASSH .... Australian Society for Sports History
ASSI.......... Accurate Surgical and Scientific Instruments Corp. (DAVI)
ASSIA .... Applied Social Sciences Index and Abstracts [*Information service or system*] (IID)
ASSIBS .... American Society for the Study of Ideological Belief Systems (EA)
ASSIFONTE... Association de l'Industrie de la Fonte de Fromage de la CEE [*Association of the Processed Cheese Industry of the European Economic Community*]
ASSIFQ .... Association de Sante et Securite des Industries de la Foret du Quebec [*Quebec Logging Health & Safety Association Inc.*] (AC)
ASSIG .... Assignation (DSUE)
AS-SIGNAL... Austast-Synchron-Signal (MCD)
Assign for Crs... Assignments for Benefits of Creditors [*A publication*] (DLA)
ASSIGT .... Assignment
ASSILEC ...... Association de l'Industrie Laitiere de la CE [*European Community Dairy Trade Association*] [*Belgium*] (EAIO)
ASSIM .... Assimilated
Ass Ind .... Assam, India (ILCA)
ASSINSEL .... Association Internationale des Selectionneurs pour la Protection des Obtentions Vegetales [*International Association of Plant Breeders for the Protection of Plant Varieties - IAPBPPV*] (EAIO)
ASSIST .... Acquisition Streamlining and Standardization Information System (AAGC)
ASSIST .... Afloat Supply Systems Improvement and Support Team (MCD)
ASSIST .... Alliance of States Supporting Indians in Science and Technology [*Montana State Universty*]
ASSIST .... American Stop Smoking Intervention Study [*National Institutes of Health*] (EGAO)
ASSIST .... Army System for Standardized Intelligence Support Terminals (MCD)
ASSIST .... Assistant
ASSIST .... Assistant
Assist.......... Assistent [*Assistant*] [*German*]
ASSIST .... Automation Services - System Improvement - Solution and Tracking (MCD)

ASSIST .... Award Scheme for Science, Industry and School-Teaching [*Science Research Council*] (PDAA)
ASSIST .... [*A*] Simple Systematic Integration of Statistical Techniques (BUR)
Assist.......... Writ of Assistance [*Legal term*] (DLA)
ASSITEJ....... Association Internationale du Theatre pour l'Enfance et de la Jeunesse [*International Association of Theatre for Children and Youth*] (EAIO)
ASSITEJ Canada...... Cente Francophone ASSITEJ Canada (AC)
ASSIU .... Avionics Subsystem Interface Unit (MCD)
ASSJ........... Association for the Sociological Study of Jewry (EA)
Ass Jerus..... Assizes of Jerusalem [*A publication*] (DLA)
ASSL........... Abnormal Steady State Limits (MCD)
ASSLT & B... Assault and Battery [*Legal term*] (DLA)
ASSM.......... Aligned Short Fiber Sheet Molding Compound (MCD)
ASSM.......... Antisurface Ship Missile [*NATO*] (MCD)
ASSM.......... Assembler [*Computer science*]
AssM .... Associated Microfilming Service, Inc., Mountain Lakes, NJ [*Library symbol Library of Congress*] (LCLS)
ASSM.......... Association of Shopfront Section Manufacturers [*British*] (BI)
ASSM.......... Association of State Supervisors of Mathematics (EA)
ASSM.......... Authorization for Sale of Salvage Material
ASSM.......... Shannon Municipal Library, Sexsmith, Alberta [*Library symbol National Library of Canada*] (NLC)
ASSMBL ..... Assemble
ASSMBLR .... Assembler
AssMos....... Assumption of Moses (Pseudepigrapha) (BJA)
ASSMPTN.... Assumption
ASSMR .... American Society for Surface Mining and Reclamation (EA)
ASSMT........ Assessment [*Business term*]
ASSMT........ Assignment (ROG)
ASSMT........ Assortment [*Business term*]
ASSN .... Assign
ASSN .... Association
ASSN .... Association
assn........... Association (ODBW)
Assn........... Association (AAGC)
Assn........... Association (DD)
ASSNCE ...... Assurance
assnd........ Assigned (BARN)
ASSNS .... Assigns (ROG)
Ass'n Trial Law Am Newsl... Association of Trial Lawyers of America. Newsletter [*A publication*] (DLA)
ASSO .... American Society for the Study of Orthodontics (EA)
ASSO .... Associate
Asso & Man... Asso and Manuel's Institutes of Spanish Civil Law [*A publication*] (DLA)
ASSOC......... Associate [*or Association*] (AFM)
Assoc.......... Associate (AAGC)
ASSOC......... Associate
assoc.......... Associates (VRA)
Assoc.......... Association (ODBW)
Assoc.......... Association (AAGC)
Assoc Brit IRE... Associate of the British Institution of Radio Engineers
ASSOCD....... Associated (EY)
ASSOCD....... Associated
AssocDip ..... Associate Diploma
AssocDipAbComMgt & Dev... Associate Diploma in Aboriginal Community Management and Development
AssocDipAbHlth... Associate Diploma in Aboriginal Health
AssocDipAbStudies... Associate Diploma in Aboriginal Studies
AssocDipAcctg... Associate Diploma in Accounting
AssocDipAdmin... Associate Diploma in Administration
AssocDipAdvrt... Associate Diploma in Advertising
AssocDipAg... Associate Diploma in Agriculture
AssocDipAgProd... Associate Diploma in Agricultural Production
AssocDipAgr... Associate Diploma in Agriculture
AssocDipAgServs... Associate Diploma in Agricultural Services
AssocDipAHCD... Associate Diploma in Aboriginal Health and Community Development
AssocDipAppBiol... Associate Diploma in Applied Biology
AssocDipAppSc... Associate Diploma in Applied Science
AssocDipAppSci(Ag)... Associate Diploma in Applied Science (Agriculture)
AssocDipAppSci(AnimalSc)... Associate Diploma in Applied Science (Animal Science)
AssocDipAppSci(AnimalTech)... Associate Diploma in Applied Science (Animal Technology)
AssocDipAppSci(GrainMgmt)... Associate Diploma in Applied Science (Grain Management)
AssocDipArchDraft... Associate Diploma in Architectural Drafting
AssocDipArchTech... Associate Diploma in Architectural Technology
AssocDipArts... Associate Diploma in Arts
AssocDipArts(AppPhotog)... Associate Diploma in Arts (Applied Photography)
AssocDipArts(ComArt)... Associate Diploma in Arts (Commercial Art)
AssocDipAsianSt... Associate Diploma in Asian Studies
AssocDipBiolSc(AnimalTech)... Associate Diploma in Biological Science (Animal Technology)
AssocDipBltEnvir... Associate Diploma Built Environment Technician
AssocDipBuildCons... Associate Diploma in Building Construction
AssocDipBus... Associate Diploma in Business
AssocDipCart... Associate Diploma in Cartography (ADA)
AssocDipCHN... Associate Diploma in Community Health Nursing
AssocDipCivEng... Associate Diploma in Civil Engineering
AssocDipClinLabTech... Associate Diploma in Clinical Laboratory Techniques
AssocDipClinNursStud(Gerontol)... Associate Diploma in Clinical Nursing Studies (Gerontology)

AssocDipCompAppl... Associate Diploma in Computer Applications
AssocDipDT... Associate Diploma in Diversional Therapy
AssocDipEd... Associate Diploma in Education
AssocDipElecEng... Associate Diploma in Electrical Engineering
AssocDipFor... Associate Diploma in Forestry
AssocDipFurnTechnology... Associate Diploma in Furniture Technology
AssocDipHorseMgmt... Associate Diploma in Horse Management
AssocDipHort... Associate Diploma in Horticulture
AssocDipHumanSt... Associate Diploma in Human Studies
AssocDipIntTrade... Associate Diploma in International Trade
AssocDipLegPrac... Associate Diploma in Legal Practice
AssocDipLoc&AppHist... Associate Diploma in Local and Applied History
AssocDipMechEng... Associate Diploma in Mechanical Engineering
AssocDipMedLabTech... Associate Diploma in Medical Laboratory Technology
AssocDipMktg... Associate Diploma in Marketing
AssocDipMktgJap... Associate Diploma in Marketing and Japanese
AssocDipMMT... Associate Diploma of Mining and Mineral Technology
AssocDipModLang... Associate Diploma of Modern Languages
AssocDipMus... Associate Diploma in Music
AssocDipNursEd... Associate Diploma in Nurse Education
AssocDipNursStudies... Associate Diploma in Nursing Studies
AssocDipOccHlth&Saft... Associate Diploma in Occupational Health and Safety
AssocDipOffAdmin... Associate Diploma in Office Administration
AssocDipPolSt... Associate Diploma in Political Studies
AssocDipRc... Associate Diploma in Rehabilitation Counselling
AssocDipRec... Associate Diploma in Recreation
AssocDipSc... Associate Diploma in Science
AssocDipSc(AnimalScience)... Associate Diploma in Science (Animal Science)
AssocDipSc(SystemsAg)... Associate Diploma in Science (Systems Agriculture)
AssocDipSecMgt... Associate Diploma in Security Management
AssocDipSmallBusMgt... Associate Diploma in Small Business Management
AssocDipSocSc... Associate Diploma of Social Science
AssocDipSptSc... Associate Diploma in Sports Science
AssocDipSurv... Associate Diploma of Surveying
AssocDipSurvMap... Associate Diploma in Surveying and Mapping
AssocDipTrainDev... Associate Diploma in Training and Development
AssociateIElecIE... Associate of the Institution of Electrical and Electronics Incorporated Engineers [*British*] (DBQ)
Assoc IEE... Associate of the Institution of Electrical Engineers [*British*]
Assoc I Min E... Associate of the Institution of Mechanical Engineers [*British*]
Assoc INA... Associate of the Institution of Naval Architects [*British*]
AssocInstAEA... Associate of the Institute of Automotive Engineer Assessors [*British*] (DBQ)
AssocInstAEA (Body Dvn)... Associate of the Institute of Automotive Engineer Assessors (Body Division) [*British*] (DBQ)
Assoc Inst MM... Associate of the Institute of Mining and Metallurgy [*British*]
ASSOC IOP... Associate of the Institute of Printing (DGA)
AssocIPHE... Associate of the Institution of Public Health Engineers [*British*] (DBQ)
AssocISI... Associate of the Iron and Steel Institute [*British*]
AssocMCT... Associateship of the Manchester College of Technology [*British*]
AssocMIAeE... Associate Member of the Institution of Aeronautical Engineers [*British*]
Assoc (M) Inst CE... Associate (Member) of the Institution of Civil Engineers [*British*]
ASSOCN....... Association
Assoc RCATS... Associate of the Royal College of Advanced Technology [*British*]
AssocRINA... Associate of the Royal Institution of Naval Architects [*British*]
Assoc Sc...... Associate in Science
AssocSLAET... Associate of the Society of Licensed Aircraft Engineers and Technologists [*British*] (DBQ)
ASSOGLACE... Association des Artisans Glaciers et des Fabricants de Mix pour Glace des Pays de la CEE [*Association of Home-Made Ice-Cream and Ice-Mix Manufacturers in the European Economic Community*]
ASSOPOMAC... Association des Obtenteurs de Pommes de Terre du Marche Commun [*Association of Certified Seed Potato Suppliers of the Common Market*]
ASSORECO... Association des Ressortissants du Haut et du Moyen Congo [*Association of Natives of the Upper and Middle Congo*]
ASSORT....... Automatic System for Selection of Receiver and Transmitter [*Computer science*] (MHDB)
ASSOTW...... Airfield and Seaplane Stations of the World (MUGU)
ASSP .... Acoustics, Speech, and Signal Processing (MCD)
ASSP .... Aerosol Scattering Spectrometer Probe [*Marine science*] (OSRA)
ASSP .... Aerosol Scattering Spectrometer Probe (USDC)
ASSP .... Aerospace Systems Security Program (AFM)
ASSP .... African Social and Environmental Studies Programme [*Formerly, African Social Studies Programme*] [*Kenya*] (EAIO)
ASSP .... African Social Studies Programme (EA)
ASSP .... Agence de Surveillance du Secteur Petrolier [*Petroleum Monitoring Agency, Energy, Mines & Resources, Canada*]
ASSP .... Aircrew Station Standardization Panel
ASSP .... Application Specific Standard Part (CDE)
ASSP .... Approved Species - Specfic Protocol [*Marine science*] (OSRA)
ASSP .... Approved Species-Specific Protocol (USDC)
ASSP .... Area Supply Support Plan [*Military*] (DNAB)
ASSP .... Argininosuccinate Synthetase Pseudogene (DMAA)
ASSP .... Australian Studies Schools Project
ASSP .... Automated Seavan Shipment Planning System [*MTMC*] (TAG)
ASSP .... Auxiliary Surface Simulator Platform [*Navy*] (CAAL)
ASSP .... Axially Scattering Spectrometer Probe (MCD)
ASSP .... Transport, Submarine [*Later, LPSS*] [*Navy symbol Obsolete*]
ASSPA .... Aboriginal Sacred Sites Protection Authority [*Northern Territory, Australia*]
ASSPC .... IEEE Acoustics, Speech, and Signal Processing Society (EA)

ASSPHR......	Anti-Slavery Society for the Protection of Human Rights (EA)
ASSPPQ.......	Association de Sante et Securite des Pates et Papiers du Quebec Inc. [Quebec Pulp & Paper Health & Safety Association Inc.] (AC)
ASSPT	Assumpsit [Legal shorthand] (LWAP)
ASSR	Adult Situation Stress Reaction [Psychology] (DAVI)
ASSR	Airborne Sea/Swell Recorder [Oceanography] (MSC)
ASSR	Airport Surface Surveillance RADAR (DA)
ASSR	American Society for the Study of Religion (EA)
ASSR	Autonomous Soviet Socialist Republic
ASSR	Sydney [Australia ICAO location identifier] (ICLI)
ASSRA	American Single Shot Rifle Association (EA)
ASSRC........	Aviation Section Signal Reserve Corps
Ass Reg Da...	Assia Regis David [A publication] (DLA)
ASSRM	Air Supplemented Solid Rocket Motor (MCD)
ASSRON	Air Service Support Squadron [Army]
ASSRS	Adaptive Step-Size Random Search [Computer science] (IAA)
ASSS	Aerospace Systems Safety Society (MCD)
ASSS	American Society for the Study of Sterility [Later, AFS] (EA)
ASSS	American Suffolk Sheep Society (EA)
ASSS	Area Security Surveillance System (SAA)
ASSS	Assigns (ROG)
ASSS	Associate in Science in Secretarial Studies
ASSS	Sydney [Australia ICAO location identifier] (ICLI)
ASST...........	Advanced Supersonic Transport
ASST...........	American Society for Steel Treaters [Later, ASM]
ASST...........	Antiship Surveillance and Targeting [Navy] (NVT)
ASST...........	Antisurface Ship Surveillance and Targeting (MCD)
ASST...........	Assented [Securities]
ASST...........	Assessment
ASST...........	Asset
ASST..........	Assignment (ROG)
ASST..........	Assistance [or Assist] (DAVI)
ASST..........	Assistant (EY)
asst.............	Assistant (WDMC)
asst.............	Assistant (DD)
ASST..........	Association of Social Science Teachers [Later, ASBS] (EA)
ASST..........	Assort
ASST..........	Automatic System Self-Test [Aviation] (MCD)
Ass Tax.......	Assessed Taxes (Decisions of Judges) [A publication] (DLA)
Asst Cash	Assistant Cashier (MHDB)
ASSTD	Assented (WGA)
ASSTD	Associated
ASSTD	Assorted
ASSTG	Assisting
ASSTL..........	Assistant Sector System Training Leader (SAA)
ASSTN	Assistance (MSA)
ASSTNCE	Assistance
ASSTSAS	Association pour la Sante et la Securite du Travail, Secteur Affaires Sociales [Association for the Health and Safety of Labour, Social Affairs Sector] [Canada]
ASSTSECDEF...	Assistant Secretary of Defense (DNAB)
ASSTSECDEF(COMPT)...	Assistant Secretary of Defense (Comptroller) (DNAB)
ASSTSECDEF(HELAFF)...	Assistant Secretary of Defense (Health Affairs) (DNAB)
ASSTSECDEF(INTEL)...	Assistant Secretary of Defense (Intelligence) (DNAB)
ASSTSECDEF(INTSECAFF)...	Assistant Secretary of Defense (International Security Affairs) (DNAB)
ASSTSECDEF(MPRRESAFFLOG)...	Assistant Secretary of Defense (Manpower, Reserve Affairs, and Logistics) (DNAB)
ASSTSECDEF(PUBAFF)...	Assistant Secretary of Defense (Public Affairs) (DNAB)
ASSTSECNAVFINMGMT...	Assistant Secretary of the Navy (Financial Management) (DNAB)
ASSTSECNAVINSTLOG...	Assistant Secretary of the Navy (Installation and Logistics) (DNAB)
ASSTSECNAVMPRESAFF...	Assistant Secretary of the Navy (Manpower and Reserve Affairs) (DNAB)
ASSTSECNAVRES...	Assistant Secretary of the Navy (Research and Development) (DNAB)
ASSTSECNAVRESENGSYS...	Assistant Secretary of the Navy (Research, Engineering, and Systems) (DNAB)
ASSTSECNAVSHIPLOG...	Assistant Secretary of the Navy (Shipbuilding and Logistics) (DNAB)
Asst Surg.....	Assistant Surgeon [Department of Health and Human Services] (GFGA)
ASSU	Air Support Signal Unit (NATG)
ASSU	American Sunday School Union [Later, AMF]
ASSUC........	Association des Organisations Professionnelles du Commerce des Sucres pour les Pays de la Communaute Economique Europeenne [Association of Sugar Trade Organizations for the European Economic Community Countries] [Belgium]
Assump C	Assumption College (GAGS)
Assur	Assurance
ASSUR........	Assure
Assurb	Assurbanipal [King of ancient Assyria] (BJA)
ASSURE.......	A Selective Strategy for Utilization Review Effectiveness [Health insurance] (GHCT)
ASSURE.......	Automated Software System Used for Reliability Evaluation
ASSURNC.....	Assurance
ASSVd	Apple Scar Skin Viroid [Plant pathology]
ASSW..........	Antisurface Ship Warfare (MCD)
ASSX	Sydney [Australia ICAO location identifier] (ICLI)
ASSY	Assembly
ASSY	Sydney/Kingsford Smith International [Australia ICAO location identifier] (ICLI)
ASSYR	Assyria

AST.............	Abort-Scan Table [NASA]
AST.............	Above Ground Storage Tank
AST.............	Absolute Sensation Threshold
AST.............	Absolute Space-Time
AST.............	Accelerated Service Test (MCD)
AST.............	Action Sociale Tchadienne [Chadian Social Action]
AST.............	Action Speed Tactical
AST.............	Active Segment Table (HGAA)
AST.............	Additional Specialty Training [Military]
AST.............	Add-Subtract Time
AST.............	Adiabatic Storage Test [For hazardous chemicals]
AST.............	Administrative Service Test
AST.............	Administrative-Supply Technician [Army] (AABC)
AST.............	Advanced Simulation Technology [DoD] (IEEE)
AST.............	Advanced Supersonic Technology
AST.............	Advanced Supersonic Transport
AST.............	Advanced System Technology
AST.............	Aerial Survey Team (AFM)
AST.............	Aerolineas del Oeste SA de CV [Mexico ICAO designator] (FAAC)
AST.............	Aerospace Technologist [or Technology] [NASA]
AST.............	AIM Strategic Income Fd [AMEX symbol] (TTSB)
AST.............	AIM Strategic Income Fund [AMEX symbol] (SPSG)
AST.............	Airborne Surveillance Testbed [Army]
AST.............	Aircraft Systems Trainer (MCD)
AST.............	Airlock Systems Test [NASA] (MCD)
AST.............	Air Staff Target [Royal Air Force] [British]
AST.............	Air-Supported Threat [Army]
AST.............	Air Support Tactics
AST.............	Air Surveillance Technician [Air Force]
AST.............	Alaskan Standard Time [Aviation] (SAA)
AST.............	Allowable Ship Turn
AST.............	All-Season Touring
AST.............	All Systems Test [NASA] (KSC)
ASt.............	Altostratus [Cloud] [Meteorology] (AIA)
AST.............	Aminosultopride [Biochemistry]
AST.............	Angiotensin Sensitivity Test [Medicine]
AST.............	Antisidetone [Telecommunications] (TEL)
AST.............	Antisyphilitic Treatment [Medicine]
AST.............	Apollo Systems Test [NASA] (IAA)
AST.............	Apparent Sidereal Time (PDAA)
AST.............	Apparent Solar Time (PDAA)
AST.............	Archery Society of Tasmania [Australia]
AST.............	Area Specialist Team [Army]
AST.............	Arkansas State Library, Little Rock, AR [OCLC symbol] (OCLC)
AST.............	Arming System Tester (MCD)
AST.............	Army Satellite Tracking Center
AST.............	Army Specialized Training
AST.............	Artificial Site Tuff [Geology]
AST.............	Artillery Supply Truck [British]
AST.............	Aspartate Aminotransferase [Also, AAT, ASAT, GOT] [An enzyme]
AST.............	Assembly and Structure Test
AST.............	Assented [Economics]
AST.............	Assertive Sentence Title [Report writing]
AST.............	Assessment
AST.............	Assistant [Navy]
AST.............	Association for Student Teaching [Later, ATE] (EA)
AST.............	Association of Surgical Technologists (EA)
AST.............	Association of Swimming Therapy [British]
Ast.............	Astemizole [Pharmacology]
Ast.............	Astigmatism [Also, As] [Ophthalmology]
AST.............	Astoria [Oregon] [Airport symbol Obsolete] (OAG)
AST.............	AST Research, Inc. [Associated Press] (SAG)
AST.............	Astrida [Rwanda] [Seismograph station code, US Geological Survey Closed] (SEIS)
AST.............	Astrology
AST.............	Astronomy (NASA)
A ST............	Atlanta Street Railroad
AST.............	Atlantic School of Theology [Canada]
AST.............	Atlantic Standard Time
AST.............	Atmospheric Surveillance Technology (MCD)
AST.............	Atomized Suspension Technique
AST.............	Atrial Overdrive Stimulation Rate [Cardiology] (DMAA)
AST.............	At Same Time
AST.............	Audiometry Sweep Test
AST.............	Augustus Resources Ltd. [Vancouver Stock Exchange symbol]
AST.............	Automated Screen Trading [Business term]
AST.............	Automated Speech Technology (MCD)
AST.............	Automatic Scan Tracking [Videotape head] (NTCM)
ASt.............	Automatic Shop Tester (OA)
AST.............	Automatic Starter
AST.............	Auxiliary Segment Table [Electronics] (OA)
AST.............	Average Sampling Time [Statistics]
AST.............	Ayres Space Test [Psychology]
AST.............	Stettler Public Library, Alberta [Library symbol National Library of Canada] (NLC)
ASTA...........	Advanced Strategic Transport Aircraft
ASTA...........	Advertiser Syndicated Television Association (NTCM)
ASTA...........	Aerial Survey and Target Acquisition [Military]
ASTA...........	Airport Surface Traffic Automation [FAA] (TAG)
ASTA...........	American Sail Training Association (EA)
ASTA...........	American Satellite Television Alliance (EA)
ASTA...........	American Scouting Traders Association (EA)
ASTA...........	American Seed Trade Association (EA)
ASTA...........	American Society of Travel Agents (EA)
ASTA...........	American Spasmodic Torticollis Association (EA)

ASTA........... American Spice Trade Association (EA)
ASTA........... American String Teachers Association (EA)
ASTA........... American Surgical Trade Association (EA)
ASTA........... Anti-alpha-staphylolysin [Immunology]
ASTA........... Associate of the Swimming Teachers' Association [British] (DBQ)
ASTA........... Association of Short-Circuit Testing Authorities, Inc. [British] (BI)
ASTA........... AST Research [NASDAQ symbol] (TTSB)
ASTA........... AST Research, Inc. [NASDAQ symbol] (NQ)
ASTA........... Australian Sogetsu Teachers' Association
ASTA........... Australian String Teachers' Association
ASTA........... Automatic System Trouble Analysis [Computer science] (MHDB)
ASTA........... Aviation Systems Test Activity [Later, AEFA] (MCD)
ASTA........... Stavely Public Library, Alberta [Library symbol National Library of Canada] (NLC)
ASTAA........ Airborne Special-Type Auxiliary Assembly (MCD)
ASTAB .... Automated Status Board (DNAB)
ASTABS ...... Automatic Status Board Subsystem (MCD)
ASTACC ...... Advanced Ship Types and Combatant Craft (MCD)
ASTACS .... ASW [Antisubmarine Warfare] Tactical Center Systems [Data or Support] (MCD)
ASTADIS ..... Advise Status and/or Disposition [Army] (DNAB)
AstaFd .... Asta Funding, Inc. [Associated Press] (SAG)
ASTAMIDS ... Airborne Standoff Minefield Detection System [Military] (RDA)
ASTAN .... American Ski Teachers Association of Natur Teknik (EA)
AST&L .... American Society of Transportation and Logistics [MTMC] (TAG)
ASTAP .... Acoustic Sensor Training Aids Program [Navy] (CAAL)
ASTAP .... Advanced Statistical Analysis Program [Computer science] (MCD)
ASTAPA .... Armed Services Textile and Apparel Procurement Agency (DNAB)
ASTAR .... Advanced Surveillance and Target Acquisition RADAR
ASTAR .... Airborne Search Target Attack RADAR (MCD)
ASTAS .... AntiRADAR Surveillance and Target Acquisition System
ASTB........... Advanced Survivability Test Bed [Military] (INF)
ASTB........... And So To Bed [Commercial firm British]
ASTB........... Astable (MSA)
AST.BA .... ASTRA Compania Argentina [BA Symbol] (TTSB)
AStbC........... St. Bernard College, St. Bernard, AL [Library symbol Library of Congress] (LCLS)
ASTC........... Administrative Section for Technical Cooperation [United Nations]
ASTC........... Advanced Satellite Tracking Center
ASTC........... Airport Surface Traffic Control (OA)
ASTC........... Allied Signal Training Center [NATO] (IAA)
ASTC........... American Sealyham Terrier Club (EA)
ASTC........... American Shih Tzu Club (EA)
ASTC........... American Society of Theater Consultants (EA)
ASTC........... American Society of Trial Consultants (EA)
ASTC........... Appalachian State Teachers College [Later, ASU] [North Carolina]
ASTC........... Arkansas State Teachers College [Later, University of Central Arkansas]
ASTC........... Army Satellite Tracking Center (IAA)
ASTC........... Aroostook State Teachers College [Merged with University of Maine]
ASTC........... Association of Science-Technology Centers (EA)
ASTC........... Australian Sales Tax Cases [Australia]
ASTC........... Australian Silky Terrier Club
ASTC........... Automatic Steam-Temperature Control
ASTCC .... American Sabbath Tract and Communications Council (EA)
ASTCDPD..... Association of State and Territorial Chronic Disease Program Directors (EA)
ASTCON .... Australian Science and Technology Counsellor Network
ASTD .... Advanced Space Technology Division [NASA] (NASA)
ASTD .... Advanced Structures Technology Demonstration
ASTD .... Air-Supported Threat Defense [Army] (AABC)
ASTD .... American Society for Testing and Development (AAGC)
ASTD .... American Society for Training and Development (EA)
ASTD .... American Society of Teachers of Dancing (EA)
ASTD .... Antiship Torpedo Defense [or Device] (MCD)
ASTD .... Area Scale Temperature Display
ASTD .... Army Specialized Training Division
ASTD .... Assented [Investment term]
ASTD .... Assistant Steward [British military] (DMA)
ASTD .... Associate of the Society of Typographic Designers (DGA)
ASTDD .... Association of State and Territorial Dental Directors (EA)
ASTDLHS...... Association of State and Territorial Directors of Local Health Services [Defunct] (EA)
ASTDM .... Advanced Smokeless Technology Demonstration Motor (MCD)
ASTDN .... Association of State and Territorial Directors of Nursing (EA)
ASTDP .... Academic Staff Training and Development Programme [British] (AIE)
ASTDPHN .... Association of State and Territorial Directors of Public Health Nursing [Later, ASTDN] (EA)
ASTDS .... Air-Supported Threat Defense System [Army]
ASTDS .... Antisubmarine Tactical Data System (DNAB)
ASTE .... Aeronautical System Training Equipment (SAA)
ASTE .... Aerospace Systems Test Environment
ASTE .... Amalgamated Society of Telephone Employees [A union] [British]
ASTE .... American Society of Test Engineers (EA)
ASTE .... American Society of Tool Engineers [Later, SME]
ASTE .... Armament System Test Environment (MCD)
ASTE .... Association for Software Testing and Evaluation [Defunct] (EA)
ASTE .... Association for the Study of Soviet-Type Economies [Later, ACES] (EA)
ASTE .... Astec Industries [NASDAQ symbol] (TTSB)
ASTE .... Astec Industries, Inc. [NASDAQ symbol] (NQ)
Astea .... Astea International, Inc. [Associated Press] (SAG)
ASTEC......... Advanced Solar Turbo-Electric Conversion
ASTEC......... Advanced Systems Technology (IEEE)
ASTEC......... Aerospace System Test and Evaluation Complex (KSC)

ASTEC........ American Steamship Traffic Executives Committee
ASTEC........ Antisubmarine Technical Evaluation Center [Navy]
ASTEC........ Applied Software Technology [Computer science] (HGAA)
ASTEC........ Association of Science-Technology Centers
Astec .... Astec Industries, Inc. [Associated Press] (SAG)
ASTEC........ Avionics System Test Equipment Comparator (MCD)
ASTED .... Association pour l'Avancement des Sciences et des Techniques de la Documentation [Acronym is now organization's official name]
ASTED .... Automated Sequential Trace Enrichment of Dialysate
ASTEG .... All Systems Test Equipment Group
A Sten .... Aortic Stenosis [Cardiology] (DAVI)
A sten .... Aortic Stenosis [Medicine] (BABM)
Ast Ent........ Aston's Entries [1673] [A publication] (DLA)
ASTEP .... Algorithm Simulation Test and Evaluation Program [NASA]
ASTER .... Antisubmarine Terrier Missile [Navy]
ASTER .... Atmosphere/Surface Turbulent Exchange Research
ASTERIX ...... All Purpose Structure Eurocontrol RADAR Information Exchange (DA)
ASTEX .... Atlantic Stratocumulus Transition Experiment [Meteorology]
ASTF .... AccuStaff, Inc. [NASDAQ symbol] (SAG)
ASTF .... Aeropropulsion Systems Test Facility [Arnold Air Force Station, TN] [Air Force] (MCD)
ASTF .... Aerospace Structures Test Facility [Air Force]
ASTF .... American Sovereignty Task Force (EA)
ASTG .... Advanced Status Threat Generator (DWSG)
ASTG .... Aerospace Test Group (NASA)
ASTGO .... Authorization of Special Types General Order [British] (DCTA)
ASTH .... Asthenopia [Ophthalmology] [Medicine]
ASTHE .... Average Straight Time Hourly Earnings [Accounting]
ASTHMA ...... Aerotherm Axisymmetric Transient Heating and Material Ablation [Program]
ASTHO .... Association of State and Territorial Health Officials (EA)
ASTHTC ...... Aesthetic
ASTI .... Active Sodium Transport Inhibitor [Biochemistry]
ASTI .... Antispasticity Index [Neurology] (DAVI)
ASTI .... Anti-Submarine Training Indicator [Military] (PDAA)
ASTI .... Applied Statistics Training Institute
ASTI .... Association for Science, Technology, and Innovation (EA)
ASTI .... Association of Secondary Teachers, Ireland (BI)
ASTI .... Automated System for Transportation Intelligence [Army] (RDA)
ASTI .... Stirling Public Library, Alberta [Library symbol National Library of Canada] (NLC)
ASTIA .... Armed Services Technical Information Agency [Later, Defense Documentation Center]
ASTIAB .... Armed Services Technical Information Agency Bulletin [A publication] (DNAB)
ASTIC.......... Algonquian Syllabic Texts in Canadian Repositories [Bibliographic project]
ASTIG .... Astigmatism [Electronics]
Astigm .... Astigmatism [Ophthalmology] (DAVI)
ASTIIT......... American Society for Technion-Israel Institute of Technology (EA)
ASTIN .... Actuarial Studies in Non-Life Insurance [of the International Actuarial Association] [Brussels, Belgium] (EA)
ASTINDMAN... Assistant Industrial Manager [of Naval District] (MUGU)
ASTINFO ...... Asian Scientific and Technological Information Network (EAIO)
ASTIO .... Advanced Systems Technology and Integration Office [Army]
ASTIP .... Army Scientific and Technical Information Program (DIT)
ASTIS.......... Arctic Science and Technology Information System [Arctic Institute of North America] [University of Calgary] [Information service or system] (IID)
ASTIS.......... Astronomy Information Service [Space Telescope Science Institute] [Information service or system] (IID)
ASTL .... American Society of Transportation and Logistics (EA)
ASTL........... Approved Supplier Tab List
AstLiving ..... Assisted Living Concepts, Inc. [Associated Press] (SAG)
ASTM .... Advance STOL [Short Takeoff and Landing] Transport (Medium) [Aviation] (MCD)
ASTM .... Amalgamated Society of Tobacco Manufacturers [A union] [British]
ASTM .... American Society for Testing and Materials [Acronym is now organization's official name] (EAIO)
ASTM .... American Standard of Testing Materials
ASTM .... American Standards Test Manual
ASTM .... Asterism (DGA)
ASTM .... Australian Stamp Duties [A publication]
ASTM .... Standard Municipal Library, Alberta [Library symbol National Library of Canada] (NLC)
ASTMC........ ARS [American Rocket Society] Structures and Materials Committee
ASTME........ American Society of Tool and Manufacturing Engineers [Later, SME] (EA)
ASTMH .... American Society of Tropical Medicine and Hygiene (EA)
ASTMO .... Association des Secretaires et Tresoriers Municipaux de l'Ontario (AC)
ASTMP......... Army Science and Technology Master Plan (RDA)
ASTMS........ Association of Scientific, Technical, and Managerial Staffs [British]
ASTN .... Air Station [Air Force]
ASTN .... Ashton Tech Group [NASDAQ symbol] (TTSB)
ASTN .... Ashton Technology Group, Inc. (The) [NASDAQ symbol] (SAG)
ASTN .... Astern
ASTN .... Astronomic (AABC)
ASTN .... Automotive Satellite Television Network [Automotive engineering]
ASTND .... Association of State and Territorial Nutrition Directors
ASTNW .... Ashton Tech Group Wrrt [NASDAQ symbol] (TTSB)
ASTO .... Antistreptolysin [Immunology] (DHSM)
ASTO .... Assembly Tool (AAG)
ASTO .... Association of Sea Training Organisations [British] (DBA)

ASTO	Association of Sun Tanning Organisations [*British*] (DBA)
as tol	As Tolerated [*Medicine*] (CPH)
ASTOR	Antiship Torpedo (IEEE)
ASTOR	Antisubmarine Torpedo (MSA)
ASTOR	Antisubmarine Torpedo Ordnance Rocket (MCD)
AstoriaF	Astoria Financial [*Associated Press*] (SAG)
ASTOVL	Advanced Short Takeoff and Vertical Landing [*Military*]
ASTP..........	Accelerated Service Test Program (SAA)
ASTP..........	Advanced Space Technology Program [*Military*] (DOMA)
ASTP..........	Advanced Systems and Technology Programme [*European Space Agency*]
ASTP..........	American Society of Tax Professionals (EA)
ASTP..........	Apollo-Soyuz Test Project [*NASA/USSR*]
ASTP..........	Army Specialized Training Program [*World War II*]
ASTP..........	Association for Short Term Psychotherapy (EA)
ASTP..........	St. Paul Public Library, Alberta [*Library symbol National Library of Canada*] (NLC)
ASTPHLD	Association of State and Territorial Public Health Laboratory Directors (EA)
ASTPHND	Association of State and Territorial Public Health Nutrition Directors [*Defunct*] (EA)
ASTPO	Accident Source Term Program Office [*Nuclear energy*] (NRCH)
ASTR	Addition, Subtraction, Timing, and Ratio
ASTR	Aerospace Systems Test Reactor [*Formerly, Aircraft Shield Test Reactor*]
ASTR	Aircraft Shield Test Reactor (SAA)
ASTR	American Society for Theatre Research (EA)
ASTR	American Society of Therapeutic Radiologists [*Later, ASTRO*] (EA)
ASTR	Astronomy
ASTR	Astrosystems, Inc. [*NASDAQ symbol*] (NQ)
ASTR	Asynchronous Synchronous Transmitter Receiver [*Electronics*] (IAA)
ASTR	Automated Software Trouble Report
ASTRA	Adapted Swimming-Pool Tank Reactor, Austria
ASTRA	Advanced Static Test Recording Apparatus
ASTRA	Advanced Structural Analyser (IAA)
ASTRA	Air Space Transportation
ASTRA	Air Staff Trainee [*or Training*] [*Air Force*]
ASTRA	American Sport Touring Rider's Association (EA)
ASTRA	Analysis and Simulation Tool for Resource Allocation (MCD)
ASTRA	Application of Science and Technology to Rural Areas [*An association*]
ASTRA	Application of Space Techniques Relating to Aviation [*International Civil Aviation Organization*]
ASTRA	Applications of Space Technology Panel to Requirements of Civil Aviation [*ICAO*] (DA)
ASTRA	Applied Space Technology Regional Advancement (KSC)
ASTRA	Association in Scotland to Research into Astronautics (EAIO)
ASTRA	Astronomical and Space Techniques for Research on the Atmosphere [*National Science Foundation project*]
ASTRA	Astronomical Space Telescope Research Assembly (MCD)
ASTRA	Automatic Scheduling with Time-Integrated Resource Allocation
ASTRA	Automatic Sorting, Testing, Recording Analysis
ASTRA	Automatic Strobe Tracking (CET)
AstraA........	Astra AB [*Associated Press*] (SAG)
AstraB........	Astra AB [*Associated Press*] (SAG)
ASTRAC	Arizona Statistical Repetitive Analog Computer
ASTRACCS...	Army Strategic Command and Control Systems (MCD)
ASTRAIL	Analog Schematic Translator to Algebraic Language [*Computer science*] (MHDB)
ASTRAIL	Assurance and Stabilization Trends for Reliability by Analysis of Lots (MHDI)
ASTRAL	Analog Schematic Translator to Algebraic Language [*Computer science*] (IEEE)
ASTRE	Airport Surface Traffic RADAR Equipment (MCD)
ASTRE	Applied Science through Research and Engineering
ASTREC	Atomic Strike Evaluation Center
ASTREC	Atomic Strike Recording System [*Air Force*]
ASTREX	Advanced Space Structure Technology Research Experiments (MCD)
ASTRG	Air Starting
ASTRID	Association Scientifique et Technique pour la Recherche en Informatique Documentaire [*Scientific and Technical Association for Research in Documentary Information*] [*Belgium*] [*Information service or system*]
ASTRNTC	Astronautic
ASTRO	Advanced Spacecraft Trainer [*or Transport or Truck*] Reusable Orbiter [*NASA*] (MCD)
ASTRO	Aerodynamic Spacecraft Two-Stage Reusable Orbiter [*NASA*]
ASTRO	Air Space Travel Research Organization
ASTRO	Amalgamated Slaters, Tilers and Roofing Operatives Society [*British*] (BI)
ASTRO	American Society for Therapeutic Radiology and Oncology (EA)
ASTRO	America's Sound Transportation Review Organization [*AAR*] [*Defunct*]
ASTRO	Antarctic Submillimeter Telescope and Remote Observatory Project [*AT & T Bell Labs, Boston University, University of Illinois*]
ASTRO	Antisubmarine Test Requirement Outline
ASTRO	Army Space Technology and Research Office (RDA)
ASTRO	Army Strategic and Tactical Reorganization Objective
ASTRO	Artificial Satellite Time and Radio Orbit (MCD)
ASTRO	Astronautical
Astro	Astronautics (DD)
Astro	Astronomical
ASTRO	International Association of State Trading Organizations of Developing Countries [*Ljubljana, Yugoslavia*] (EAIO)
ASTROC	Automatic Stellar Tracking, Recognition, and Orientation Computer

ASTROCOM....	Astronaut Communications (MCD)
ASTROL	Astrology [*or Astrologer*]
AstroM........	Astro-Med, Inc. [*Associated Press*] (SAG)
Astron	Astronics Corp. [*Associated Press*] (SAG)
ASTRON	Astronomer [*or Astronomy*]
Astron	Astronomy [*A publication*] (BRI)
ASTROS	Advanced Star/Target Reference Optical Sensor (SSD)
ASTROS	Advanced Systematic Techniques for Reliable Operational Software [*Computer science*] (MHDI)
ASTROS	Artillery Saturation Rocket System [*Army*]
ASTROS	Automated Shell Theory for Rotating Structures [*NASA*]
AstroSci	Astro Sciences Corp. [*Associated Press*] (SAG)
ASTROSPACE...	Astronautics and Space (KSC)
Astrosy	Astrosystems, Inc. [*Associated Press*] (SAG)
Astrotc	Astrotech International Corp. [*Associated Press*] (SAG)
ASTRP	Army Specialized Training Reserve Program
Astrux	Astruxius [*Authority cited in pre-1607 legal work*] (DSA)
ASTS	Administrative Systems Testing Section [*Social Security Administration*]
ASTS	Advanced SAGE [*Semiautomatic Ground Environment*] Tracking Study [*Military*] (IAA)
ASTS	Airport Surface Traffic Simulator
ASTS	American Sabbath Tract Society [*Later, ASTCC*] (EA)
ASTS	American Society of Transplant Surgeons (EA)
ASTS	Armament System Test Set (MCD)
ASTS	ASE Test Ltd. [*NASDAQ symbol*] (SAG)
ASTS	ASROC [*Antisubmarine Rocket*] Splashpoint Telemetry System [*Navy*]
ASTS	Automated Stock Transfer System (MCD)
ASTS	Avionics System Test Specification (MCD)
ASTSECAF....	Assistant Secretary of the Air Force
ASTSECNAV...	Assistant Secretary of the Navy
ASTSECNAVAIR...	Assistant Secretary of the Navy for Air
ASTSECNAVFIN...	Assistant Secretary of the Navy (Financial Management)
ASTSECNAVINSLOG...	Assistant Secretary of the Navy (Installation and Logistics)
ASTSECNAVRESDEV...	Assistant Secretary of the Navy (Research and Development)
ASTSP	American-Soviet Textbook Study Project [*An association Defunct*] (EA)
ASTSWMO...	Association of State and Territorial Solid Waste Management Officials (EA)
ASTT..........	Action Speed Tactical Trainer (SAA)
ASTT..........	American Society of Traffic and Transportation (EA)
ASTT..........	Apollo Special Task Team [*NASA*]
ASTt..........	Arctic Small Tool Tradition [*Archeology*]
ASTT..........	Associate in Science in Teacher Training
ASTTBC......	Applied Science Technologists & Technicians of British Columbia [*Formerly, Society of Engineering Technologists of BC*] (AC)
ASTTCM......	Amalgamated Society of Telegraph and Telephone Construction Men [*A union*] [*British*]
ASTTE........	Artillery Siege Train Traction Engine [*British*]
ASTU	Air Support Test Unit
ASTU	Air Support Training Units
ASTU	Army Specialized Training Unit
ASTU	Automatic Systems Test Unit
AStudio.......	American Studios, Inc. [*Associated Press*] (SAG)
ASTUTE.......	A Search Tree Underlying the Experiment [*University of Michigan's experimental online catalog*]
ASTUTE.......	Association of System 2000 Users for Technical Exchange
ASTVC	American Society of TV Cameramen (EA)
AST/VCE	Acoustic Shield Thermal/Variable Cycle Engine (MCD)
ASTW.........	Aerospace Test Wing [*Air Force*]
ASTW.........	Australian Society of Travel Writers
ASTW.........	Tamworth [*Australia ICAO location identifier*] (ICLI)
ASTWg........	Aerospace Test Wing [*Air Force*] (AFM)
ASTWKT......	Amalgamated Society of Textile Workers and Kindred Trades [*A union*] [*British*] (DCTA)
ASTX..........	Applied Science & Tech [*NASDAQ symbol*] (TTSB)
ASTX..........	Applied Science & Technology, Inc. [*NASDAQ symbol*] (SAG)
ASTXW........	Applied Science & Tech Wrrt [*NASDAQ symbol*] (TTSB)
Asty	Artistry [*Record label*]
ASTZ..........	Antistreptozyme (DMAA)
ASTZ..........	Antistreptozyme Test [*Clinical chemistry*]
ASU	Acknowledgement Signal Unit [*Telecommunications*] (TEL)
ASU	Acoustic Sensor Unit [*Navy*] (CAAL)
ASU	Acquisition and Synchronization Unit (LAIN)
ASU	Active Service Unit [*Irish Republican Army*] [*Northern Ireland*]
ASU	Acute Stroke Unit [*Medicine*] (DAVI)
ASU	Administrative Service Unit
ASU	Administrative Support Unit
ASU	Aeromedical Staging Unit (AFM)
ASU	Airborne Self-Propelled Gun
ASU	Aircraft Scheduling Unit
ASU	Aircraft Starting Unit
ASU	Aircraft Storage Unit [*Military British*]
ASU	Air Separation Unit [*For oxygen production*]
ASU	Altitude Sensing Unit [*Aviation*] (AIA)
ASU	American Servicemen's Union (EA)
ASU	American Snowshoers Union (EA)
ASU	American Student Union
ASU	Analog Stimulus Unit
ASU	Antisurface Ship Warfare [*Navy*] (CAAL)
ASU	Appalachian State University [*Boone, NC*]
ASU	Apparatus Slide-In Unit [*Computer science*] (NITA)
ASU	Approval for Service Use [*Military*] (NVT)

ASU .... Arab Socialist Union [*Syria*] [*Political party*] (PPW)
ASU .... Area of Substantial Unemployment [*CETA*] [*Department of Labor*]
ASU .... Area Service Unit
ASU .... Arizona State University [*Arizona*] [*Seismograph station code, US Geological Survey*] (SEIS)
ASU .... Arkansas State University [*Beebe*]
ASU .... Arkansas State University Library, State University, AR [*OCLC symbol*] (OCLC)
ASU .... Aston Resources Ltd. [*Vancouver Stock Exchange symbol*]
ASU .... Astronomy Study Unit [*American Topical Association*] (EA)
ASU .... Asuncion [*Paraguay*] [*Airport symbol*] (OAG)
ASU .... Automatic Switching Unit [*Telecommunications*]
ASU .... Automotive Study Unit [*American Topical Association*] (EA)
ASU .... Autonomous Switch Unit [*Telecommunications*] (NITA)
ASU .... Auxiliary Sensor Unit (MCD)
ASU .... Auxiliary Storage Unit [*Computer science*] (IAA)
ASU .... Compania Aerea del Sur SA [*Uruguay*] [*ICAO designator*] (FAAC)
a-su-- .... Saudi Arabia [*MARC geographic area code Library of Congress*] (LCCP)
ASUA .... Arizona Small Utilities Association (SRA)
ASUBJSCD... Army Subject Schedule (AABC)
ASUC .... American Society of University Composers (EA)
ASUC .... Associated Students of the University of California
ASUD .... Aerovia Sud Americana
ASUG .... American Software Users Group (EA)
ASUI .... American Society of Utility Investors (EA)
ASULGC ...... Association of State Universities and Land-Grant Colleges (EA)
ASUN .... Sundre Public Library, Alberta [*Library symbol National Library of Canada*] (NLC)
ASUNW .... Sunwapta Shores Public Library, Alberta [*Library symbol National Library of Canada*] (NLC)
ASUP .... Air Supply
ASUP .... AUTODIN Switch Upgrade Project (MCD)
ASUPS .... Ammunition Supply Squadron [*Air Force*]
ASUPT .... Advanced Simulator for Undergraduate Pilot Training [*Air Force*]
A/SUPT .... Assistant Superintendent (DCTA)
ASUR .... Advanced Surgical, Inc. [*NASDAQ symbol*] (SAG)
ASURS .... Advanced Surveillance and Reconnaissance Systems
ASUS .... Apostleship of the Sea in the United States (EA)
A/SUSP .... Air Suspension [*Automotive engineering*]
ASUSSR ...... Academy of Science (Union of Soviet Socialist Republics)
ASUT .... Adapter Subunit Tester
ASUT .... Association Suisse d'Usagers de Telecommunications [*Swiss Association of Telecommunications Users*] [*Zurich*] (TSSD)
ASUTS .... American Society of Ultrasound Technical Specialists [*Later, SDMS*] (EA)
ASUUS .... Amateur Skating Union of the United States (WGA)
ASU-USA ..... Amateur Skating Union of the United States of America (EA)
ASUVCW ..... Auxiliary to Sons of Union Veterans of the Civil War (EA)
ASUW .... Antiship Underwater Warfare (MCD)
ASUW .... Antisurface Warfare [*Navy*]
ASUWC .... Antisurface Warfare Commander [*Navy*]
ASV .... Acceleration Switching Valve
ASV .... Adaptive Sensing Vehicle [*Robot*]
ASV .... Advanced Safety Vehicle [*Automotive engineering*]
ASV .... Advocates for a Safe Vaccine (EA)
ASV .... Aerospace Vehicle (KSC)
ASV .... Aerothermodynamic Structural Vehicle [*Air Force*]
ASV .... Ag Services of America, Inc. [*NYSE symbol*] (SAG)
ASV .... Airborne Surface Vessel Detection [*RADAR device*]
ASV .... Aircraft-to-Surface Vessel [*Navy*]
ASV .... Air Savoie [*France ICAO designator*] (FAAC)
ASV .... Air Shutoff Valve
ASV .... Air Solenoid Valve
ASV .... Air Suction Valve [*Automotive engineering*]
ASV .... All Systems Vehicle
ASV .... Alpine Silver Ltd. [*Vancouver Stock Exchange symbol*]
ASV .... Aluminum Structured Vehicle [*Automotive engineering*]
ASV .... American Standard Version [*of the Bible, 1901*]
ASV .... Ampere-Seconds per Volt (IAA)
ASV .... Angle Stop Valve [*Technical drawings*]
ASV .... Anode Supply Voltage
ASV .... Anodic Stripping Voltammetry [*Chemical analysis*]
ASV .... Antisnake Venom [*Medicine*]
ASV .... Antisurface Vessel [*Navy*]
ASV .... Area of Strategic Value [*Military*]
ASV .... Arithmetic Simple Variable
ASV .... Armored Security Vehicle [*Army*]
ASV .... Armored Support Vehicle (MCD)
A/SV .... Arterio/Superficial Venous [*Medicine*] (MAE)
ASV .... Asparagus Stunt Virus [*Plant pathology*]
ASV .... Asset Share Value [*Insurance*]
ASV .... Authorized Standard Version [*of the Bible*] [*A publication*]
ASV .... Autogenous Saphenous Vein (Graft) [*Surgery*]
ASV .... Automatic Self-Verification
ASV .... Automatic Shuttle Valve
ASV .... Auxiliary Survey Vessel [*Oceanography*] (MSC)
ASV .... Avian Sarcoma Virus [*Same as RSV*]
ASV .... RADAR [*Navy symbol Obsolete British*]
ASVA .... Acupuncture Society of Virginia (SRA)
ASVA .... Associate of the Incorporated Society of Valuers and Auctioneers [*British*] (DBQ)
ASVA .... Association of Summer Villages of Alberta (AC)
ASVAB .... Armed Services Vocational Aptitude Battery [*Tests*]
A/Svc .... Air Service

ASVC .... Automatic Secure Voice Communications (CAAL)
ASVD .... Arteriosclerotic Vascular [*or Vessel*] Disease [*Cardiology*] (DAVI)
ASVE .... American Society of Veterinary Ethology (EA)
ASVI .... Alien Status Verification Index [*Immigration and Naturalization Service*] (GFGA)
ASVI .... American Society for Value Inquiry (EA)
ASVI .... ASV, Inc. [*NASDAQ symbol*] (SAG)
ASVI .... A S V Inc. [*NASDAQ symbol*] (TTSB)
ASV Inc. ..... ASV, Inc. [*Associated Press*] (SAG)
ASVIP .... American Standard Vocabulary for Information Processing (BUR)
ASVIP .... Atrial Synchronous Ventricular Inhibited Pacemaker [*Cardiology*]
ASVO .... American Society of Veterinary Ophthalmology (EA)
ASVOL .... Assign Volume (IAA)
ASVPP .... American Society of Veterinary Physiologists and Pharmacologists (EA)
ASVS .... Airborne Stabilized Viewing System
ASVS .... Automatic Signature Verification System
ASVT-- .... Aluminum Structured Vehicle Technology [*Automotive engineering*]
ASVT .... Applications Systems Verification and Transfer (MCD)
ASVT .... Applications Systems Verification Test [*NASA*]
ASW .... Absatzwirtschaft Data Bank [*Dusseldorf, Federal Republic of Germany*] [*Database producer Information service or system*] (IID)
ASW .... Acoustic Surface Wave
ASW .... Air Southwest [*Canada ICAO designator*] (FAAC)
ASW .... Air-to-Surface Weapon
ASW .... Allied Steel and Wire, Ltd. [*British*]
ASW .... Amalgamated Society of Woodworkers [*British*] (BI)
ASW .... Amorphous Solid Water [*Materials science*]
ASW .... Anti-Satellite Weapon (IAA)
ASW .... Antisubmarine Warfare
ASW .... Antisubmarine Warfare Force [*Atlantic Fleet*] [*Norfolk, VA*]
ASW .... Antisubmarine Weapon (NATG)
ASW .... Applications Software [*Computer science*]
asw .... Artificially Sweetened (HGAA)
ASW .... Artificial Seawater
AsW .... Asia Watch Committee (EA)
ASW .... Assistant Secretary of War
ASW .... Association of Social Workers [*British*] (BI)
ASW .... Aswan [*Egypt*] [*Airport symbol*] (OAG)
ASW .... Audits & Surveys Worldwide [*AMEX symbol*] (TTSB)
ASW .... Audits & Surveys Worldwide, Inc. [*AMEX symbol*] (SAG)
ASW .... Australian Standard White [*Wheat*] (ADA)
ASW .... Australia Standard White [*Variety of wheat*]
ASW .... Automotive Specialty Warehouse
ASW .... Auxiliary Switch [*Electricity*]
ASW .... Warsaw, IN [*Location identifier FAA*] (FAAL)
ASWA .... American Society of Women Accountants (EA)
ASWA .... American Steel Warehouse Association [*Later, SSCI*]
ASWA .... Antiskywave Antenna (NTCM)
ASWA .... Assistant Secretary of War for Air [*World War II*]
ASWA .... Audio Switch Assembly [*Ground Communications Facility, NASA*]
A/SWA .... Aviation/Space Writers Association
ASWAAF ..... Arms and Services with the Army Air Forces
ASW/AAW ... Antisubmarine Warfare and Antiair Warfare
ASWAC .... Aerospace Warning and Control (MCD)
ASWAC .... Antisubmarine Warfare Advisory Committee
ASWACS ..... Antisubmarine Warfare Air Control Ship (NVT)
ASWAF .... Arms and Services on Duty with Air Force
ASWAS .... Antisubmarine Warfare Area System [*Italy*]
ASWASP ..... Antisubmarine Warfare Airborne Simulation Program [*Navy*] (CAAL)
ASWB .... Antisubmarine Warfare Barriers [*Military*]
ASWB .... Association of Solid Woven Belting Manufacturers [*British*] (BI)
ASWBPL ..... Armed Services Whole Blood Processing Laboratory (AABC)
ASWC .... Antisubmarine Warfare Center [*NATO*] (NATG)
ASWC .... Antisubmarine Warfare Commander [*Navy*] (NVT)
ASWC .... Army Special Warfare Center
ASWC .... ASW [*Antisubmarine Warfare*] Coordinator (MCD)
ASWCCCS ... Antisubmarine Warfare Centers Command and Control System [*Navy*] (CAAL)
ASWCCS ..... Antisubmarine Warfare Command and Control Centers System (MCD)
ASWCR .... Airborne Surveillance Warning and Control RADAR [*ASD/ADC*]
ASWCRL ..... Appalachian Soil and Water Conservation Research Laboratory [*Beckley, WV*] [*Department of Agriculture*] (GRD)
ASWCS .... Antisubmarine Warfare Control System [*Navy*] (CAAL)
ASWCSI ...... Antisubmarine Warfare Combat System Integration [*Navy*] (CAAL)
A/SWD .... Antisubmarine War Division [*British*]
ASWD .... Army Special Weapons Depot
ASWDKW .... Amalgamated Society of Wire Drawers and Kindred Workers [*A union*] [*British*] (DCTA)
ASWE .... Admiralty Surface Weapons Establishment [*British Ministry of Defense*] [*Research center*]
ASWEA .... Association for Social Work Education in Africa [*See also AESA*] (EAIO)
ASWEC .... Antisubmarine Warfare Electronic Countermeasures System (MCD)
ASWEPS ..... Antisubmarine Warfare Program System [*Navy*] (GFGA)
ASWEPS ..... Antisubmarine Weapons Environmental Prediction Service [*Navy*]
ASWEX .... Antisubmarine Warfare Exercise (NVT)
ASWF......... Arithmetic Series Weight Function (PDAA)
ASWF......... [*A*] Special Wish Foundation (EA)
ASWFCO ..... Antisubmarine Warfare Fire Control Officer [*Navy*] (CAAL)
ASWFITRON... Antisubmarine Warfare Fighter Squadron (DNAB)
ASWFORSIXTHF... Antisubmarine Warfare Force, Sixth Fleet [*Navy*]
ASWG .... American Steel and Wire Gauge

ASWG	Wagga Wagga [Australia ICAO location identifier] (ICLI)
ASWGA	Australian Superfine Wool Growers' Association
ASWGRU	Antisubmarine Warfare Group
ASWGW	Anti-Submarine Wire-Guided Weapon [British military] (DMA)
ASWH	Advise Soldier Write Home
ASWHS	Advanced Submarine Weapon Handling System (MCD)
ASWI	Antisubmarine Warfare Installations [NATO] (NATG)
ASWICS	Antisubmarine Warfare Integrated Combat System [Navy] (MCD)
ASWILS	Antisubmarine Warfare Improved Localization System (NVT)
ASWIPT	Antisubmarine Warfare Training in Port [Navy] (NVT)
ASWIS	Australian Sheep and Wool Information Service [Database]
ASWIXS	Antisubmarine Warfare Information Exchange System [or Subsystem] [Navy] (NVT)
ASWL	Antisubmarine Warfare Laboratory [Military]
ASWLC	American Shortwave Listeners Club (EA)
ASW-LR	Antisubmarine Warning - Long Range (NATG)
ASWM	Amalgamated Society of Woodcutting Machinists [British] (BI)
ASWM	Antisubmarine Warfare Missile [Navy] (CAAL)
ASWM	Association of State Wetland Managers (EA)
ASWM	ASW [Antisubmarine Warfare] Module [Navy]
ASWM	Williamtown [Australia ICAO location identifier] (ICLI)
ASWO	Air Stations Weekly Orders [Navy]
ASWO	Antisubmarine Warfare Officer [Navy] (CAAL)
ASWOC	Antisubmarine Warfare Operations Centers [Navy] (NVT)
ASWOC	Antisubmarine Warfare Operations Controller [Navy] (CAAL)
ASWORG	Antisubmarine Warfare Operational Research Group [World War II]
ASWP	American Society of Wedding Professionals (EA)
ASWPO	Antisubmarine Warfare Project Office [Navy]
ASWPTL	Antisubmarine Warfare Operations Patrol (NVT)
ASWR	Antisubmarine Warfare RADAR (IIA)
ASWR	Antisubmarine Warfare Systems Project Office [Washington, DC Navy]
ASWRC	Antisubmarine Warfare Research Center [NATO] (NATG)
ASWRECEN	Antisubmarine Warfare Research Center [NATO]
ASWS	Advanced Strike Weapon System (MCD)
ASWS	Aerospace Surveillance Warning System (MCD)
ASWS	Antisubmarine Warfare Systems [Navy]
ASWSAG	Antisubmarine Warfare Systems Analysis Group [Navy]
ASWSCCS	Antisubmarine Warfare Ship Command and Control System (NVT)
ASW/SOW	Antisubmarine Warfare Standoff Weapon
ASWSPO	Antisubmarine Warfare Systems Project Office [Navy]
ASW-SR	Antisubmarine Warning - Short Range (NATG)
ASWSS	Antisubmarine Warfare Schoolship [Navy] (NVT)
ASWSYSPROJOFC	Antisubmarine Warfare Systems Project Office [Navy] (DNAB)
ASWTACSCOL	Antisubmarine Warfare Tactical School
ASWTC	Antisubmarine Warfare Training Center [Navy]
ASWTDS	Antisubmarine Warfare Tactical Data System [Navy] (NVT)
ASWTNS	Antisubmarine Warfare Tactical Navigation System [Navy] (NG)
ASWTRACEN	Antisubmarine Warfare Training Center [Navy]
ASWTRO	Antisubmarine Warfare Test Requirement Outline (MCD)
ASWTU	Antisubmarine Warfare Training Unit
ASWTV	Antisubmarine Warfare Target Vehicle (MCD)
ASWU	Antisubmarine Warfare Unit [Navy]
ASW/UW	Antisubmarine Warfare/Underwater Warfare
ASWW	Amalgamated Society of Wood Workers [British]
ASX	Air Special [Czechoslovakia] [ICAO designator] (FAAC)
ASX	American States Financial Corp. [NYSE symbol] (SAG)
ASX	Amer States Financial [NYSE symbol] (TTSB)
ASX	Ashland [Wisconsin] [Airport symbol Obsolete] (OAG)
Asx	Aspartic Acid [or Asparagine] [Also, B An amino acid]
Asx	Asymptomatic [Medicine] (MEDA)
ASX	Australian Stock Exchange
ASXT	American Society of X-Ray Technicians [Later, ASRT]
ASY	Ashley, ND [Location identifier FAA] (FAAL)
ASY	Asylum
ASY	Royal Australian Air Force [ICAO designator] (FAAC)
a-sy--	Syria [MARC geographic area code Library of Congress] (LCCP)
ASYA	American Stock Yards Association (EA)
ASYG	Assistant Secretary General (NATG)
ASYL	Afro-Shirazi Youth League [Tanzania] (AF)
ASYL	Asylum
ASYL	Sylvan Lake Public Library, Alberta [Library symbol National Library of Canada] (NLC)
ASYM	Association of Synthetic Yarn Manufacturers (EA)
ASYM	Asymmetric (MSA)
ASYMCA	Armed Services Young Men's Christian Association [Military]
ASYMCA	Association of Secretaries Young Men's Christian Associations [Later, YMCA]
ASYMP	Asymptote [Mathematics]
ASYN	Asynchronous (MSA)
ASYNC	Asynchronous
ASYNCH	Asynchronous
ASYS	Amtech Systems [NASDAQ symbol] (TTSB)
ASYS	Amtech Systems, Inc. [NASDAQ symbol] (NQ)
ASYSTD	Advanced System Time Domain
AsystTch	Asyst Technologies [Commercial firm Associated Press] (SAG)
ASYSW	Amtech Sys Wrrt [NASDAQ symbol] (TTSB)
ASYT	Asyst Technologies [NASDAQ symbol] (SAG)
ASZ	Air Sardinia SpA [Italy ICAO designator] (FAAC)
ASZ	American Society of Zoologists (EA)
ASZ	AMSCO International [NYSE symbol] (SPSG)
ASZ	Ashizuri [Japan] [Seismograph station code, US Geological Survey] (SEIS)
ASZ	Astrakhan [Former USSR] [FAA designator] (FAAC)

ASZD	American Society for Zero Defects [Later, American Society for Performance Improvement]
AT	Abdominal Tympany [Medicine] (AAMN)
AT	Absolute Term (IAA)
AT	Absolute Threshold
AT	Absolute Title [Business term]
AT	Academically Talented (DAVI)
AT	Accelerometer-Timer (SAA)
AT	Acceptance Tag (NRCH)
AT	Acceptance Test (NRCH)
AT	Acceptance Trials [Shipbuilding]
AT	Access Tandem
AT	Access Time
AT	Accounting Tabulating [Card] (AAG)
AT	Achievement Test
AT	Achilles Tendon [Anatomy]
AT	Across Tape [Curve]
AT	Action Taken
A/T	Action Time [Air Force]
AT	Active Training [Army]
AT	Activity Test
AT	Act Together [Defunct] (EA)
AT	Acyltransferase [An enzyme]
AT	Adapter, Tee
AT	Address Translator [Computer science]
AT	Adenine and Thymine [Genetics] (DAVI)
AT	Adjacent Tone (IAA)
AT	Adjunctive Therapy [Medicine]
AT	Adjuvant Therapy [Antineoplastic drug regimen] (DAVI)
AT	Administrative Trainee [Civil Service] [British]
AT	Advanced Technology [In PC AT, model name of a computer] [IBM Corp.]
AT	Advanced Trainer [Air Force]
AT	Advanced Treatment (GNE)
AT	Aerial Tape Armor [Telecommunications] (TEL)
AT	Aerial Target
AT	Aerial Torpedo
AT	Airport Traffic [ICAO] [Information service or system United Nations] (DUND)
AT	Air Technician [Air National Guard] (AFM)
AT	Air Temperature
AT	Airtight [Technical drawings]
A/T	Air Tracker (DNAB)
AT	Air Traffic [FAA] (TAG)
AT	Air Transmit
AT	Air Transport [Military]
AT	[The] Alalakh Tablets (BJA)
AT	Alcadd Test [Psychology]
AT	Alcohol and Tobacco Tax Division [Internal Revenue Service] [United States] (DLA)
AT	Allergen Tachyphylaxis [Immunology]
A/T	Allowance Type [Military] (AFIT)
AT	ALLTEL Corp. [Formerly, Allied Telephone Co.] [NYSE symbol] (SPSG)
AT	All Together (EA)
AT	Alpha Track (GNE)
AT	Alternative Technology
AT	Altes Testament [Old Testament] [German]
AT	Alt Tuberculin [Old Tuberculin] [German]
AT	Amateur Station [ITU designation]
AT	Ambient Temperature
AT	American Terms [Business term]
AT	American Translation [of the Bible]
AT	American Turners (EA)
AT	Aminotransferase [An enzyme]
AT	Aminotriazole [Herbicide] (MAE)
AT	Amis de la Terre [Friends of the Earth] [Canada] (EAIO)
AT	Amitriptyline [Also, AMI] [Antidepressant compound]
AT	Ammunition Technician [British military] (DMA)
A/T	Ammunition Torque (SAA)
AT	Amount Tendered
A/T	Amperes per Terminal
A-T	Ampere-Turn [Technical drawings]
AT	Anaerobic Threshold
A/T	Analog to Time (MCD)
AT	Analysis Time
AT	Analytical Tree [Method used to analyze and design physical security for facilities] [Military] (RDA)
AT	Anaphylatoxin [Immunology]
AT	Ancien Testament [Old Testament] [French]
AT	Angiotensin [Biochemistry]
AT	Angle of Train
AT	Angle Template
A/T	Angle Tracker (MUGU)
AT	Animal Transport [British and Canadian] [World War II]
AT	Anistropy Telescope [Instrumentation]
AT	Annual Tour
AT	Annual Training [Military] (AFM)
AT	Antennas, Simple [JETDS nomenclature] [Military] (CET)
AT	Anterior Tibial (Muscle) [Anatomy]
AT	Antitank [Also, ATk]
AT	Antiterrorism [Measure] [DoD]
AT	Antithrombin [Hematology]
AT	Antitorpedo [Navy]
AT	Anti-Trust (LAIN)

AT .... Antitrypsin [*Biochemistry*]
AT .... Antur Teifi [*Teifi Valley Business Centre*] [*British*]
AT .... Appalachian Trail
AT .... Apparent Time   (ADA)
AT .... Appeal Tribunal   (DLA)
AT .... Applanation Tonometry [*Ophthalmology*]
AT .... Apply Template   (MCD)
AT .... Appropriate Technology
AT .... Aptitude Test
AT .... Aquatic Toxicity [*Environmental science*]
AT .... Arch-Treasurer
AT .... Arizona Territory [*Obsolete*]   (ROG)
AT .... Armament Test
AT .... Armoured Tractor [*British*]
AT .... Armoured Train [*British*]
AT .... Army of Tennessee, CSA [*An association*]   (EA)
AT .... Army Telegraph [*Stamp surcharge*] [*British*]   (ROG)
AT .... Army Transport [*British military*]   (DMA)
AT .... Arrival Time   (AABC)
AT .... Article Type [*Database terminology*]   (NITA)
AT .... Artillery   (CINC)
AT .... Artillery Tractor [*British*]
AT .... Aspartocin [*Endocrinology*]
AT .... Asphalt Tile [*Technical drawings*]
AT .... Assay Ton
A/T .... Assembly and Test [*Aerospace*]   (AAG)
AT .... Assembly Telling   (SAA)
AT .... Assertiveness Training   (WGA)
AT .... Asset Type [*Database terminology*]   (NITA)
AT .... Associate in Technology
AT .... Assortment
At .... Astatine [*Chemical element*]
AT .... Astern Flag [*Navy British*]
AT .... Astronomical Time
AT .... At [*An altitude*]   (GAVI)
AT .... Ataxia Telangiectasia [*Genetic disease*]
AT .... A Tempo [*In Strict Time*] [*Music*]
AT .... Athlone Resources Ltd. [*Vancouver Stock Exchange symbol*]
AT .... Atlantic Ocean
At .... Atlantic Reporter [*A publication*]   (DLA)
AT .... Atlantic Standard Time
AT .... Atlas Chemical Industries, Inc. [*Research code symbol*]
at .... Atmosphere, Technical [*Unit of pressure*]
AT .... Atomic
AT .... Atomic Time
AT .... Atopic Dermatitis [*Medicine*]
AT .... Atraumatic [*Medicine*]   (DAVI)
AT .... Atrial [*Cardiology*]   (DAVI)
A/T .... Attack Teacher
AT .... Attainment Target   (AIE)
AT .... Attention [*Electronics*]
AT .... Attenuation   (DEN)
AT .... Attorney   (WGA)
AT .... Audit Trail
AT .... Auroral Time [*Geophysics*]
at .... Australia [*MARC country of publication code Library of Congress*]   (LCCP)
AT .... Austria [*ANSI two-letter standard code*]   (CNC)
AT .... Author's Time [*Publishing*]
AT .... Autogenic Training [*Influencing the body through autosuggestion*]
AT .... Automated [*or Automatic*] Teller Machine   (ADA)
AT .... Automatic TAEM [*Terminal Area Energy Management*] [*NASA*]   (NASA)
AT .... Automatic Telephone   (IAA)
AT .... Automatic Test
AT .... Automatic Ticketing
AT .... Automatic Tracking   (IAA)
AT .... Automatic Translation
A/T .... Automatic Transmission [*Automotive engineering*]
AT .... Automatic Transmitter
AT .... Automatic Typewriter   (IAA)
A/T .... Autothrottle [*Aerospace*]
AT .... Auxiliary Timer
AT .... Available Time
AT .... Aviation Electronics Technician [*Navy rating*]
AT .... Awaiting Transportation   (AFM)
AT .... [*The*] Bible - An American Translation (1935) [*A publication*]   (BJA)
AT .... Cytosine Arabinoside and Thioguanine [*Antineoplastic drug regimen*]   (DAVI)
AT .... Royal Air Maroc [*ICAO designator*]   (AD)
AT .... Simple Antenna   (MCD)
at---- .... Tienshan Mountain Region [*MARC geographic area code Library of Congress*]   (LCCP)
AT .... Tug, Ocean-Going [*Navy symbol*]
AT1 .... Aviation Electronics Technician, First Class [*Navy rating*]
AT1 .... West Kanaga [*Alaska*] [*Seismograph station code, US Geological Survey Closed*]   (SEIS)
AT2 .... Aviation Electronics Technician, Second Class [*Navy rating*]
AT2 .... South Tanaga [*Alaska*] [*Seismograph station code, US Geological Survey Closed*]   (SEIS)
AT³ .... Advanced Technology Tactical Transport [*Proposed low-altitude long-range airlifter*] [*Military*]
AT3 .... Appropriate Technology in the Third World [*G. V. Olsen Associates*] [*Information service or system*]   (CRD)
AT3 .... Aviation Electronics Technician, Third Class [*Navy rating*]

AT3 .... North Tanaga [*Alaska*] [*Seismograph station code, US Geological Survey Closed*]   (SEIS)
AT-10 .... Anti-Tetany Substance 10 [*Same as DHT, Dihydrotachysterol*] [*Pharmacology*]
AT40 .... America's Top 40 [*Radio program*]
AT123D .... Analytical Transient One-, Two-, and Three-Dimensional Model
ATA .... Aboriginal Teaching Assistant [*Australia*]
ATA .... Abort Time Assembly [*NASA*]   (NASA)
ATA .... Academic Travel Abroad   (EA)
ATA .... Actoma Resources Ltd. [*Vancouver Stock Exchange symbol*]
ATA .... Actual Time of Arrival
ATA .... Additional Training Assemblies
ATA .... Administrative Telecommunications Agency [*Canada*]
ATA .... Advanced Tactical Aircraft [*Army*]
ATA .... Advanced Technology Attachment [*Hard disk interface*] [*Computer science*]
ATA .... Advanced Test Accelerator [*Lawrence Livermore National Laboratory*]
ATA .... Advanced Transport Aircraft   (MCD)
ATA .... Advertising Typographers Association   (EA)
ATA .... Africa Travel Association   (EA)
ATA .... Agence des Telecommunications Administratives [*Administrative Telecommunications Agency*] [*Canada*]
ATA .... Aid to Artisans   (EA)
ATA .... Airborne Target Augmenter
ATA .... Aircraft Development Test Activity [*Army*]   (MCD)
ATA .... Air Force Training Auxiliary [*British*]
ATA .... Airline Tariff Analysis   (DA)
ATA .... Airport Traffic Area   (MCD)
ATA .... Air-to-Air
ATA .... Air Training Advisor   (NATG)
ATA .... Air Training Association [*British*]   (DA)
ATA .... Air Transport Association
ATA .... Air Transport Association of America   (EA)
ATA .... Air Transportation Association   (AAGC)
ATA .... Air Transport Auxiliary [*British World War II*]
ATA .... Air Turbine Alternator
ATA .... Alabama Trucking Association   (SRA)
ATA .... Alaska Telephone Association   (SRA)
ATA .... Alaska Trucking Association   (SRA)
ATA .... Albanian Telegraphic Agency [*News agency*]   (EY)
ATA .... Alberta Teachers' Association [*Association des Enseignants de l'Alberta*]   (AC)
ATA .... Alimentary Toxic Aleukia
ATA .... Alliance for Technology Access
ATA .... Aloe Technology Association   (EA)
ATA .... Alpha Tau Alpha   (EA)
ATA .... Alternate Training Assemby [*Army*]   (ADDR)
ATA .... Alternative Technologies and Approaches [*Military*]   (RDA)
ATA .... Alternative Technology Association [*Australia*]
ATA .... Alternative to Amniocentesis [*Medicine*]
ATA .... Alternative Type Acceptance [*Model for interference measurement*]   (NITA)
ATA .... Amateur Television Association   (EA)
ATA .... Amateur Trapshooting Association   (EA)
ATA .... American Tarentaise Association   (EA)
ATA .... American Taxation Association   (EA)
ATA .... American Taxicab Association [*Later, ITA*]   (EA)
ATA .... American Taxpayers Association   (EA)
ATA .... American Teachers Association [*Later, NEA*]   (EA)
ATA .... American Teilhard Association   (EA)
ATA .... American Telemarketing Association [*Deerfield, IL*]   (EA)
ATA .... American Tennis Association   (EA)
ATA .... American Theatre Annual [*A publication*]
ATA .... American Theatre Association [*Defunct*]   (EA)
ATA .... American Thyroid Association   (EA)
ATA .... American Tinnitus Association   (EA)
ATA .... American Title Association [*Later, ALTA*]
ATA .... American Topical Association   (EA)
ATA .... American Traffic Association
ATA .... American Trainers Association   (EA)
ATA .... American Trakehner Association   (EA)
ATA .... American Transit Association [*Later, APTA*]   (EA)
ATA .... American Translators Association   (EA)
ATA .... American Transplant Association   (EA)
ATA .... American Travel Association [*Later, ATI*]
ATA .... American Tree Association
ATA .... American Trucking Associations   (EA)
ATA .... American Tube Association/FMA   (EA)
ATA .... American Tunaboat Association   (EA)
ATA .... Aminotriazole [*Herbicide*]
ATA .... Amusement Trades Association [*British*]   (BI)
ATA .... Angling Trade Association   (EAIO)
ATA .... Anta [*Peru*] [*Airport symbol*]   (OAG)
ATA .... Antarctica [*ANSI three-letter standard code*]   (CNC)
ATA .... Anthranilamide [*Organic chemistry*]
ATA .... Antithyroglobulin Antibody [*Immunochemistry*]
ATA .... Anti-Toxoplasma Antibody [*Immunology*]   (MAE)
ATA .... Appropriation Transfer Account   (AFM)
ATA .... ARCNET Trade Association   (EA)
ATA .... Arkansas Telephone Association   (SRA)
ATA .... Arkansas Transit Association   (SRA)
ATA .... Army Technical Architecture [*Military*]
ATA .... Army Transportation Association
ATA .... Arta Group [*NYSE symbol*]   (TTSB)

ATA	Artra Group, Inc. [*NYSE symbol*] (SPSG)
ATA	Assembly and Test Area [*NASA*] (KSC)
ATA	Associate in Technical Arts
ATA	Associate Technical Aide
ATA	Association Algerienne des Transports Automobiles [*Algerian Automobile Transport Association*] [*Algeria*]
ATA	Association des Technologistes Agricoles [*Association of Agricultural Technologists*] [*Canada*]
ATA	Association des Technologistes Agro-Alimentaires [*Association of Subsistence Agriculture Technologists*] [*Canada*]
ATA	Association des Tremblay d'Amerique [*Tremblay (Family) Association of America*] [*Canada*]
ATA	Association du Traite Atlantique [*Atlantic Treaty Association*] (EAIO)
ATA	Association for Academic Travel Abroad (EA)
ATA	Association of Talent Agents (EA)
ATA	Association of Technical Artists [*Later, IG*]
ATA	Asynchronous Terminal Adapter [*Telecommunications*]
ATA	Atar [*Djibouti*] [*Seismograph station code, US Geological Survey*] (SEIS)
ATA	Atlanta, TX [*Location identifier FAA*] (FAAL)
ATA	Atlantic Treaty Association (EA)
ATA	Atmosphere, Absolute
ATA	Auction Transfer Authority
ATA	Auditor of Traffic Accounts
ATA	Aurintricarboxylic Acid (MAE)
ATA	Australian Touch Association
ATA	Australian Toy Association
ATA	Australian Transcontinental Airways
ATA	Australia-Thailand Association
ATA	Authorization for Temporary Admission [*Customs*]
ATA	Authorized Training Associate Program [*Novell, Inc.*]
ATA	Automated Testing Analyzer [*Computer science*]
ATA	Automatic Target Acquisition (MCD)
ATA	Automatic Terrain Avoidance [*Air Force*]
ATA	Automatic Track Acquisition
ATA	Automatic Tracking Antenna
ATA	Automatic Trouble Analysis (TEL)
ATA	Automotive Technicians Association International (EA)
ATA	Automotive Trades Association Inc. (AC)
ATA	Auto-Throttle Actuator (MCD)
ATA	Auxiliary Ocean Tug [*Navy symbol*]
ATA	Auxiliary Timer Assembly
ATA	Average T-Matrix Approximation (MCD)
ATA	Average Turnaround [*Computer science*]
ATA	Aviation Training Aids
ATA	Avionics Test Article (NASA)
ATA	Azimuth Torquer Amplifier
ATA	Taber Public Library, Alberta [*Library symbol National Library of Canada*] (NLC)
ATAA	Advertising Typographers Association of America (DGA)
ATAA	Air Transport Association of America
ATAA	Air Transport Auxiliary Association (DA)
ATAA	Aminothiazolineacetic Acid [*Biochemistry*]
ATAA	Army Theatre Arts Association [*Defunct*] (EA)
ATAA	Assembly of Turkish American Associations (EA)
ATAA	Auto-Throttle Actuator Assembly (MCD)
ATAAC	Air-to-Air Aftercooling System [*Pronounced "attack"*]
ATAACT	Agricultural Teachers' Association of the Australian Capital Territory
ATAAD	Antitank Assault Air Defense (MCD)
ATAADS	Antitank/Assault/Air Defense System (MCD)
ATAAM	Advanced Tactical Air-to-Air Missile (MCD)
ATAB	Aviation Training Aids Branch [*Military*] (DNAB)
ATABCS	Airborne Tactical Air Battle Control System
ATABE	Automatic Target and Battery Evaluation [*Military*]
ATABW	American Trade Association for British Woolens (EA)
ATAC	Abbreviated Transportation Accounting Classification [*Army*]
ATAC	Active Thermo-Atmosphere Combustion (PDAA)
ATAC	Active Thermo-Atmosphere Combustion
ATAC	Advanced Tactical
ATAC	Advanced Tank Cannon (DOMA)
ATAC	Advanced Tanker Cargo [*Aircraft*] (MCD)
ATAC	Aftermarket Technology Corp. [*NASDAQ symbol*] (SAG)
ATAC	Airborne Tactical Air Coordinator [*Navy*] (NVT)
ATAC	Airborne Two-Way Acoustic and Control System (MCD)
ATAC	Air Transportable Acoustic Communications (CAAL)
ATAC	Air Transport Advisory Council [*British*]
ATAC	Air Transport Association of Canada
ATAC	All Tariffs Computerized [*Project*]
ATAC	All-Terrain All-Purpose Cart [*Military*] (INF)
ATAC	American Transportation Advisory Council
ATAC	Analytical Technology Applications Corp.
ATAC	Anti-Terrorist Alert Center [*Navy*] (LAIN)
ATAC	Applied Technology Advanced Computer
ATAC	Armored Tank Cannon [*Army*]
ATAC	Army Tank-Automotive Center [*or Command*] [*Warren, MI*]
ATACAP	Antenna to Antenna Compatibility Analysis Program (MCD)
ATACC	Absolute Total and Complete Camouflage [*Hunting*]
ATACC	Advanced Tactical Air Command Center [*Marine Corps*] (DOMA)
ATACC	Advanced Tactical Air Command Central (AAGC)
ATACC	Advanced Tactical Air Control Central
ATACC	Advanced Tactical Air Control Capability [*Air Force*] (AFM)
ATACC	Automatic Tactical Air Control Center (MCD)
ATACCIS	Army Tactical Command and Control/Information System (MCD)
ATACCO	Aviation Tactical Coordinator [*Navy*] (NVT)
ATACCS	Advanced Tactical Air Command and Control System (MCD)

ATACM	Army Tactical Missile System (MCD)
ATACMS	Advanced Tactical Air Command Missile Systems (AAGC)
ATACMS	Army Tactical Missile System (RDA)
ATACMS-BAT	Army Tactical Missile System-Brilliant Anti-Armor Submunition (RDA)
ATACMS BLK II	Army Tactical Missile System Block II (RDA)
ATACNET	Analysis of Tactical Single Channel Net Radios (MCD)
ATACO	Air Tactical Control Officer (NVT)
ATACO	Air Tactical Control Operator
ATACO	Assistant Tactical Officer [*Navy*] (CAAL)
ATACS	Advanced Tactical Air Combat Simulation
ATACS	Advanced Tank Cannon System [*Army*]
ATACS	Airborne Target Acquisition Control System (MCD)
ATACS	Analyst-to-Analyst Communications Service (MCD)
ATACS	Army Tactical Area Communications System
ATAD	Absent on Temporary Additional Duty [*Navy*]
ATAD	Air Technical Analysis Division (SAA)
ATAD	Atlanta Army Depot [*Georgia*] (AABC)
ATAD	Atmospheric Transport and Dispersion [*Model*] [*Marine science*] (OSRA)
ATAD	Atmospheric Transport and Dispersion [*Model*] (USDC)
ATAD	Automatic Target Acquisition, Detection (MCD)
ATAD	Automatic Target Designation
ATADS	Antitank Air Defense System
ATADS	FAA Air Traffic Activity Data Base [*BTS*] (TAG)
ATADSIA	Allied Tactical Data Systems Interoperability Agency [*NATO*] (NATG)
ATAE	American Trade Association Executives [*Later, ASAE*]
ATAE	Associated Telephone Answering Exchanges [*Formerly, ATE*] (EA)
ATAE	Association of Tutors in Adult Education [*British*]
ATAE	Automotive Trade Association Executives (EA)
ATAF	Advanced Technology Applications Facility [*UNCHS*] [*United Nations*] (DUND)
ATAF	Agricultural Technical Assistance Foundation [*Defunct*] (EA)
ATAF	Allied Tactical Air Force [*NATO*]
ATAF	Association des Transporteurs Aeriens de la Zone Franc [*Association of Air Transporters of the Franc Zone*] (AF)
ATAFCS	Airborne Target Acquisition and Fire Control System (MCD)
ATAFG	African Region Traffic Analysis Forecasting Group [*ICAO*] (DA)
ATAFM	American Teilhard Association for the Future of Man [*Later, ATA*] (EA)
ATAG	Air Training Advisory Group
ATAGAS	Air-to-Air Gunnery Assessment (MCD)
ATAH	Automatic Target Handoff System (DOMA)
ATAIRS	Army Tactical Requirements for Infrared Systems (MCD)
ATAK	Attack (DNAB)
ATALARS	Advanced Tactical Aircraft Launch and Recovery System (MCD)
AtalSos	Atalanta Sosnoff Capital Corp. [*Associated Press*] (SAG)
ATAM	Air-to-Air Missile (RDA)
ATAM	At and Maintain [*Aviation*] (FAAC)
ATAM	Automotive Trade Association Managers [*Later, ATAE*]
ATAMS	Advanced Tactical Attacks/Manned System (IEEE)
ATAMS	Automated Tracking and Monitoring System
ATAN	Airman, Aviation Electronics Technician [*Navy rating*]
AT&CDA	Alabama Tobacco and Candy Distributors Association (SRA)
AT & SF	[*The*] Atchison, Topeka & Santa Fe Railway Co. [*Also known as Santa Fe*]
AT & SFR	[*The*] Atchison, Topeka & Santa Fe Railway Co. [*Also known as Sante Fe*]
AT & SS	Assembly, Test, and System Support
AT&T	American Telephone & Telegraph Co. (ACRL)
AT & T Co Com L	American Telephone & Telegraph Co. Commission. Leaflets [*A publication*] (DLA)
AT & T Co TC	American Telephone & Telegraph Co. Commission Telephone Cases [*A publication*] (DLA)
AT&T GIS	AT&T Global Information Solutions [*Computer science*]
AT&T GIS	AT&T Global Information Solutions [*Dayton, OH*] [*Formerly, NCR Corp.*] (CDE)
ATANSW	Airedale Terrier Association of New South Wales [*Australia*]
ATAO	Das Alte Testament im Lichte des Alten Orients [*A publication*] (BJA)
ATAP	Active Tuition Assistance Plan [*UAW-General Motors Corp.*]
ATAP	Anti-Terrorism Assistance Program [*FAA*] (TAG)
ATAP	Apollo Telemetry Aircraft Project [*NASA*]
ATAP	Automated Time and Attendance Procedures (MHDB)
ATAPI	AT [*Advanced Technology*] Attachment Packet Interface (CDE)
ATAPS	Advanced Tactical Aircraft Program System
ATAQ	Association des Traducteurs Anglophones du Quebec [*Association of Anglophone Translators of Quebec*]
ATAR	Above Transmitted as Received (FAAC)
ATAR	Acquisition Tracking and Recognition [*Aviation*]
ATAR	Advanced Tactical Avionics RADAR
ATAR	Airborne Tracking, Acquisition, and Recognition
ATAR	Air-to-Air Recovery [*Air Force*] (AFM)
ATAR	Air-to-Air Visual Recognition [*Aviation*]
ATAR	Antitank Aircraft Rocket
ATAR	Automated Travel Agents Reservation
Atari	Atari Corp. [*Associated Press*] (SAG)
ATARRS	[*The*] Army Training Requirements and Resource System
ATARS	Advanced Tactical Aerial Reconnaissance System [*Cancelled 1993*] [*Air Force*] (DOMA)
ATARS	Advanced Tactical Airborne Reconnaissance System [*Air Force*] (MCD)
ATARS	Advanced Tactical Air Reconnaissance System (AAGC)
ATARS	Aircraft Traffic Advisory Resolution System
ATARS	Antiterrain Avoidance RADAR System (MCD)
ATARS	Army Tactical Airspace Regulation System (MCD)

ATARS .... Automated Traffic Advisory and Resolution Service [*Collision-avoidance system*] [*Aviation*]
ATARS .... Automated Travel Agents Reservation Systems (PDAA)
ATAS .... Academy of Television Arts and Sciences (EA)
ATAS .... Advanced Tactical Attack System (MCD)
ATAS .... Advanced Target Acquisition Sensor [*Air Force*] (MCD)
ATAS .... Advanced Target Acquisition System [*Air Force*]
ATAS .... Advance Technology Alert System [*United Nations*] (DUND)
ATAS .... Air-to-Air Stinger (MCD)
ATAS .... Air Transport Auxiliary Service [*British World War II*]
ATAS .... Association of Telephone Answering Services (EA)
ATAS .... Automatic Terminal Approach System (MCD)
ATAS .... Automatic Terrain Avoidance System [*Military*]
ATAS .... Automatic Test Analysis System
ATAS .... Automatic Three-Axis Stabilization
ATAS .... Automatic Tracking Antenna System
ATASCII .... Atari-Version American Standard Code for Information Interchange [*Character code*]
ATASMA ...... Advanced Tactical Attack System Mission Analysis (MCD)
ATAT .... Advanced Technology Airfoil Tests (MCD)
ATaT .... Talladega College, Talladega, AL [*Library symbol Library of Congress*] (LCLS)
ATATS .... Air [*Defense*] Anti-Tank System (DOMA)
AT/AV .... Antitank/Antivehicle (MCD)
ATAW .... Advanced Tactical Assault Weapon
ATAW .... Antitank Assault Weapon [*Army*]
ATAWDS ..... Advanced Terminal Aerial Weapon Delivery Simulation (MCD)
ATAWS .... Autonomous Tactical All-Weather Strike (MCD)
ATAWT .... Aerodynamics-Thermodynamics-Acoustic Wind Tunnel [*Automotive research*]
ATAX .... America First Tax Exempt Mortgage Fund [*NASDAQ symbol*] (NQ)
ATAXZ .... Amer First Tax Exempt Mtg 2 [*NASDAQ symbol*] (TTSB)
ATB .... Access Type BIT [*Binary Digit*] [*Computer science*]
ATB .... Acetylene-Terminated Bisphel [*Organic chemistry*]
ATB .... Across the Board
ATB .... Added Thermal Barrier (CAAL)
ATB .... Address Translation Buffer [*Telecommunications*] (TEL)
AT(B) .... Administration of Territories Committee (Balkans) [*World War II*]
ATB .... Advanced Technology Bomber [*Air Force*]
ATB .... Advanced Test Battery [*Aptitude and skills test*]
ATB .... Advanced Torsion Bar (MCD)
ATB .... Aeration Test Burner [*Heating*]
ATB .... Age at Time of Bomb [*Of survivors at Hiroshima*]
ATB .... Airborne Test Bed
ATB .... Aircraft Technical Bulletin
ATB .... Air Technical Battalion (MCD)
ATB .... Air-to-Boil Temperature [*Mechanical engineering*]
ATB .... Air Transportation Board
ATB .... Air Transport Bureau [*ICAO*]
ATB .... All-Terrain Bike
ATB .... All Trunks Busy [*Telecommunications*]
ATB .... Alternate-Top-Bevel Teeth [*Saw blades*]
ATB .... Amphibious Training Base [*Navy*]
ATB .... Anterior Tibialis [*Anatomy*]
ATB .... Antibiotic [*Pharmacology*] (DAVI)
ATB .... Antitactical Ballistic Missile (MCD)
ATB .... Antitank Battery [*Military*]
ATB .... Apollo Test Box [*NASA*] (SAA)
ATB .... Aptitude Test Battery [*Educational test*]
ATB .... Arab Tunisian Bank
ATB .... Arctic Test Branch [*Army*] (MCD)
ATB .... Army Training Board
ATB .... Army Transportation Board (MCD)
ATB .... Articulated Total Body (MCD)
ATB .... Articulated Total Body
ATB .... Artillery Test Board [*Army*]
ATB .... Asphalt-Tile Base [*Technical drawings*]
ATB .... Asphalt Treated Base [*FHWA*] (TAG)
ATB .... Association for Tropical Biology (EA)
ATB .... Atbara [*Sudan*] [*Airport symbol*] (OAG)
ATB .... ATCCS [*Army Tactical Command and Control System*] Test Bed
ATB .... Atlantair Ltd. [*Canada ICAO designator*] (FAAC)
ATB .... Atrial Tachycardia with Block [*Cardiology*] (AAMN)
ATB .... At the Time of Bombing [*Radiation Effects Research Foundation, Japan*]
ATB .... Automated Ticket and Boarding Pass [*Travel industry*]
ATB .... Automobile Transporters Tariff Bureau, Inc., Southfield MI [*STAC*]
ATB .... Average Time of Burning
ATBA .... American Transportation Bowling Association (EA)
ATBA .... American Truckers Benevolent Association [*Defunct*] (EA)
ATBA .... Arizona Thoroughbred Breeders Association (SRA)
ATBA .... Association of Theatre Benefit Agents [*Defunct*] (EA)
ATBA .... Automatic Test Break and Access [*Telecommunications*] (TEL)
ATBAN .... Atomic Bargain Analysis Report (CINC)
ATBC .... Acetyl Tributylcitrate [*Organic chemistry*]
ATBC .... Architectural and Transportation Barriers Compliance [*Board*] (AAGC)
ATBC .... Association of Trial Behavior Consultants [*Later, ASTC*] (EA)
ATBC .... Australia-Taiwan Business Council
ATBC .... Australia-Thailand Business Council
ATBCB .... Architectural and Transportation Barriers Compliance Board [*Office of Human Development Services*] [*Washington, DC*]
ATBD .... Automatic Torque Biasing Differential [*Automotive engineering*]
ATBE .... Absolute Time Base Error [*Computer science*] (IAA)
ATBI .... Allied Trades of the Baking Industry (EA)

ATBI .... All Taxa Biodiversity Inventory [*Proposed*] [*National Science Foundation*]
ATBL .... Air Transportable Buffet Lab (DWSG)
ATBM .... Advanced Tactical Ballistic Missile [*AMC - Missile*]
ATBM .... Antitactical Ballistic Missile
ATBM .... Average Time between Maintenance
ATBMC .... Airborne Test Bed Mode Control
ATBMP .... Army Technology Base Master Plan (RDA)
ATBN .... Antitank Battalion [*Marine Corps*]
ATBOA .... Australian Tuna Boat Owners' Association
ATBQ .... Attitudes Toward Blindness Questionnaire [*Psychology*] (EDAC)
ATBT .... Acoustic Telemetry Bathythermometer
ATBT .... Airborne Test Bed Turret
ATC .... Ablative Thrust Chamber [*NASA*]
ATC .... Ablative Thrust Control (MCD)
ATC .... Ablative Toroidal Compressor
ATC .... Accredited Training Centre [*Education*] [*British*] (AIE)
ATC .... Achilles Track Club (EA)
ATC .... Acoustical Test Chamber
ATC .... Acoustical Tile Ceiling [*Technical drawings*]
ATC .... Action Taken Code (MCD)
ATC .... Action Training Coalition [*Defunct*] (EA)
ATC .... Activated Thymus Cell [*s*] [*Immunochemistry*]
ATC .... Active Thermal Control
ATC .... Active Transfer Command
ATC .... Activity Therapy center
ATC .... Adaptive Traffic Control [*Automotive engineering*]
ATC .... Adaptive Transform Coding (PDAA)
ATC .... Address Translation Cache [*Motorola, Inc.*] [*Computer science*]
ATC .... Address Translation Chip
ATC .... Adiabatic Toroidal Compressor [*Nuclear energy*]
ATC .... Advanced Technology Center [*Aerospace*]
ATC .... Advanced Technology Components [*Program*] [*Army, Navy*] (RDA)
ATC .... Advanced Telecommunications Corp. [*Atlanta, GA*] (TSSD)
ATC .... Advanced Training Command (MCD)
ATC .... Advertising Training Center [*New York, NY*]
ATC .... Aerial Tuning Condenser
ATC .... Aetna Telecommunications Consultants [*Centerville, MA*] [*Telecommunications*] (TSSD)
ATC .... After Top Center [*Valve position*]
ATC .... Agence Transcongolaise des Communications [*Trans-Congolese Communications Agency*] (AF)
ATC .... Agricultural Trade Council (EA)
ATC .... Airborne Test Conductor (MUGU)
ATC .... Aircraft Technical Committee [*Aerospace Industries Association*] (MCD)
ATC .... Airline Travel Clubs (EA)
ATC .... Airport [*or Airway*] Traffic Control
ATC .... Air Tactical Communications [*FAA*] (TAG)
ATC .... Air Tanzania [*ICAO designator*] (FAAC)
ATC .... Air Target Chart (CINC)
ATC .... Air Temperature Control (IEEE)
AT C .... Airtight Containers [*Freight*]
ATC .... Air Traffic Conference of America [*Defunct*] (EA)
ATC .... Air Traffic Control [*or Controller*]
ATC .... Air Training Command [*Randolph Air Force Base, TX*]
ATC .... Air Training Corps [*RAF*] [*British*]
ATC .... Air Transportable Clinic (MCD)
ATC .... Air Transport Command [*Air Force*]
ATC .... Air Transport Committee [*ICAO*]
ATC .... Air Transport Council [*New South Wales, Australia*]
ATC .... Air Travel Card [*Airline notation*]
ATC .... Alabama Travel Council (SRA)
ATC .... Alert Transmit Console (SAA)
ATC .... Allergic to Combat [*A play on the initialism for the Air Transport Command*]
ATC .... Allied Telecommunications Committee [*Allied Control Commission for Italy*]
ATC .... Allied Textiles Companies [*British*]
ATC .... All-Terrain Carrier [*Roscoe Brown Corp.*]
ATC .... All-Terrain Cycle
ATC .... All Things Considered [*Radio program*]
ATC .... Alpine Tourist Commission [*See also TGA*] [*Switzerland*] (EAIO)
ATC .... American Television & Communications Corp. [*Cable TV operator*]
ATC .... American Textbook Council (EA)
ATC .... American Trade Consortium
ATC .... Analog Technology Co.
ATC .... Annotated Tax Cases [*A publication*]
ATC .... Annular Turbojet Combustor
ATC .... Antenna Tuning Capacitor (IAA)
ATC .... Anterior Trabeculae Carneae [*Heart anatomy*]
ATC .... Antigen-Transporting Cell [*Immunology*]
ATC .... Antiseparation Tailored Contour (MCD)
ATC .... Anti-Torpedo Craft [*British military*] (DMA)
ATC .... Any-to-Come [*Type of wager where any cash forthcoming from earlier bets finances further bets*] [*British*]
ATC .... Apollo Time Conditioner [*NASA*]
ATC .... Appalachian Trail Conference (EA)
ATC .... Applied Technology Council (EA)
ATC .... Apprenticeship and Training Conference [*Bureau of Apprenticeship and Training*] [*Department of Labor*]
ATC .... Approved Type Certificate [*Governmental airworthiness certification for planes*]
ATC .... Architectural Terra-Cotta [*Technical drawings*] (DAC)

ATC	Architecture Technology Corp. [*Minneapolis, MN*] [*Information service or system Telecommunications*] (TSSD)
ATC	Arctic Test Center [*Army*]
ATC	Area Training Center [*Environmental Protection Agency*] (GFGA)
ATC	Armament Test Center [*Military*]
ATC	Armament Training Camp [*Military*] (OA)
ATC	Armored Troop Carrier [*Army*]
ATC	Army Tactical Command (NVT)
ATC	Army Terminal Command
ATC	Army Topographic Command [*Formerly, Army Map Service*]
ATC	Army Training Center
ATC	Army Transportation Corps
ATC	Arnold Transit Co. [*Later, ATCO*] [*AAR code*]
ATC	Around the Clock [*Medicine*]
ATCS	Arthur's Town [*Bahamas*] [*Airport symbol*] (OAG)
ATC	Artificial Top Component [*Virology*]
ATC	Art Teacher's Certificate [*British*]
ATC	Aspartate Transcarbamylase [*Also, ATCase*] [*An enzyme*]
ATC	Assembly Text Chip [*Computer science*]
ATC	Assessed Tax Case (DLA)
ATC	Assistant Test Chief
ATC	Assistant Test Conductor
ATC	Assistant Town Clerk [*British*]
ATC	Assistant Transmission Controller
ATC	Assistant Trial Counsel
ATC	Associated Technology Co. [*Information service or system*] (IID)
ATC	Associated Traffic Clubs of America [*Later, TCI*] (EA)
ATC	Association des Transports du Canada [*Transportation Association of Canada*] (EAIO)
ATC	Association of Tax Consultants (EA)
ATC	Association of Translation Companies [*British*] (DBA)
ATC	Asynchronous Terminal Concentrator [*Telecommunications*] (TSSD)
ATC	Atari Corp. [*AMEX symbol*] (SPSG)
ATC	ATE Computer (MCD)
ATC	Atlantic Coast Copper Corp. Ltd. [*Toronto Stock Exchange symbol*]
ATC	Atlantic Richfield Co., R and D Library, Dallas, TX [*OCLC symbol*] (OCLC)
ATC	Attachie [*British Columbia*] [*Seismograph station code, US Geological Survey Closed*] (SEIS)
ATC	Australian Tibet Council
ATC	Australian Trade Commission (EA)
ATC	Austrian Trade Commission (EA)
ATC	Authorization to Copy [*Computer science*] (ODBW)
ATC	Automated Technical Control [*System*] [*Honeywell, Inc.*] [*Army*] (RDA)
ATC	Automated Telecommunications Center (MCD)
ATC	Automatic Tap Changing
ATC	Automatic Target Counting
ATC	Automatic Telephone Call (IAA)
ATC	Automatic Temperature Compensation
ATC	Automatic Temperature Control
ATC	Automatic Test Equipment Compute [*or Computer*]
ATC	Automatic Testing Committee (AAGC)
ATC	Automatic Threshold Circuit (MCD)
ATC	Automatic Throttle Control (SAA)
ATC	Automatic through Center [*Telecommunications*] (OA)
ATC	Automatic Timing Corrector
ATC	Automatic Tint Control [*Electronics*] (IAA)
ATC	Automatic Tone Control
ATC	Automatic Tone Correction
ATC	Automatic Tool Changer
ATC	Automatic Tracking Control (MSA)
ATC	Automatic Traction Control [*Automotive engineering*]
ATC	Automatic Traffic Control
ATC	Automatic Train Control
ATC	Automatic Tuning Control
ATC	Automatic Turbidity Compensation Hemoglobin Test
ATC	Automation Technology Center [*Vicksburg, MS*] [*Army*]
ATCHD	Automation Training Center (MCD)
ATC	Automotive Transportation Center [*Purdue University*] [*Research center*] (RCD)
ATC	Average Total Cost
ATC	Aviation Electronics Technician, Chief [*Navy rating*]
ATC	Aviation Training Center
ATC	Certified Athletic Trainer (DAVI)
ATC	Mini Armored Troop Carrier [*Navy symbol*]
ATC	National Council of Athletic Training [*Athletic Training Council*] [*Acronym is based on former name,*] (EA)
ATC	Project ASTIC [*UTLAS symbol*]
ATCA	Advanced Tanker Cargo Aircraft
ATCA	Airedale Terrier Club of America (EA)
ATCA	Air Traffic Conference of America [*Defunct*] (EA)
ATCA	Air Traffic Control Advises (FAAC)
ATCA	Air Traffic Control Assistant (DA)
ATCA	Air Traffic Control Association (EA)
ATCA	Air Training Corps of America
ATCA	Allied Tactical Communications Agency [*Brussels, Belgium*] [*NATO*] (NATG)
ATCA	American Teilhard de Chardin Association [*Later, ATAFM*]
ATCA	American Theatre Critics Association (EA)
ATCA	American Transit Collectors' Association (EA)
ATCA	Antique Telephone Collectors Association [*Later, TCI*] (EA)
ATCA	Antique Toy Collectors of America (EA)
ATCA	Antique Truck Club of America (EA)
ATCA	Atlantic Tuna Convention Act of 1975

ATCA	Attitude and Translation Control Assembly [*Aviation*] (MCD)
ATCA	Australian Terrier Club of America (EA)
ATCA	Australia Telescope Compact Array
ATCA	Automatic Tuned Circuit Adjustment [*Telecommunications*] (OA)
ATCAA	Air Traffic Control Assigned Airspace [*FAA*] (TAG)
ATCAA	Automatic Tuned Circuit Adjustment Amplitude [*Telecommunications*] (OA)
ATCAC	Air Traffic Control Advisory Committee [*Department of Transportation*]
ATCALS	Air Traffic Control and Landing System [*DoD*]
ATCAP	Air Traffic Control Automation Panel [*International Civil Aviation Organization*]
ATCAP	Army Telecommunications Center Automatic Programming (MCD)
ATCAR	Active Transfer and Conversion, Army
ATCAS	Air Traffic Control Automatic System [*Sweden*]
ATCase	Aspartate Transcarbamylase [*Also, ATC*] [*An enzyme*]
ATCBGS	Air Traffic Control Beacon Ground Station
ATCBI	Air Traffic Control Beacon Interrogator
ATCC	Aerial Target Control Central (NG)
ATCC	Aerospace Traffic Control Center
ATCC	Air Traffic Control Center [*Air Force*]
ATCC	Air Traffic Control Clears (FAAC)
ATCC	Air Traffic Control Communication
ATCC	Air Training Corps Cadet [*British*]
ATCC	AirTran Corp. [*NASDAQ symbol*] (SPSG)
ATCC	American Type Culture Collection (EA)
ATCC	Anti-Terrorism Coordinating Committee (DOMA)
ATCC	Army Type Classification Code
ATCC	Association of Transport Coordinating Officers (DCTA)
ATCC	Atlantic Division Transport Control Center [*Military*]
ATCC	Automated Telecommunications Center
ATCCC	Advanced Tactical Command and Control Capabilities
ATCCC	Air Traffic Control Command Center [*FAA*] (TAG)
ATCCC	Air Traffic Control Coordination Center (IAA)
ATCC (L)	Allied Tanker Coordinating Committee in London
ATC Com	ATC Communications, Inc. [*Associated Press*] (SAG)
ATCCS	Army Tactical Command and Control System
ATCC (W)	Allied Tanker Coordinating Committee in Washington
ATCD	Advanced Concept Technology Demonstration [*DoD*]
ATCD	Air Training Communications Division [*Air Force*]
ATCDE	Association of Teachers in Colleges and Departments of Education [*British*]
ATCE	Ablative Thrust Chamber Engine [*NASA*]
ATCE	Air Threat to Central Europe
ATCE	Association de Textiles des Cantons de l'Est (AC)
ATCE	ATC Environmental [*NASDAQ symbol*] (TTSB)
ATCE	ATC Environmental, Inc. [*NASDAQ symbol*] (NQ)
ATCE	Attitude and Translation Control Electronics
ATCE	Automatic Test and Checkout Equipment (AFM)
ATCEI	Angiotensin Converting Enzyme Inhibitor [*Biochemistry*]
ATCEL	ATC Environmental Wrrt 'C' [*NASDAQ symbol*] (TTSB)
ATC EnC	ATC Environmental, Inc. [*Associated Press*] (SAG)
ATC Env	ATC Environmental, Inc. [*Associated Press*] (SAG)
ATCEU	Air Traffic Control Evaluation Unit [*British*]
ATCF	After Tax Cash Flow
ATCF	Air Traffic Control Facility
ATCF	Air Traffic Control Flight
ATCFAS	Air Traffic Control Flight Advisory Service (MCD)
ATCFITC	Australian Textile, Clothing, and Footwear Industry Training Council
ATC Grp	ATC Group Services, Inc. [*Associated Press*] (SAG)
ATC GrpC	ATC Group Srvices, Inc. [*Associated Press*] (SAG)
ATC (H)	Armored Troop Carrier (Helicopter) [*Army*] (SAA)
ATCH	ASW [*Antisubmarine Warfare*] Torpedo-Carrying Helicopter (MCD)
Atch	Atchison. English Navigation and Trade Reports [*A publication*] (DLA)
ATCH	Attach [*or Attachment*] (AFM)
ATCH	Autochrome (VRA)
AtchCst	Atchison Casting Corp. [*Associated Press*] (SAG)
ATCHD	Attached
Atch EC	Atcheson's Election Cases [*England*] [*A publication*] (DLA)
ATCHEMPI	Attach on Morning Report the Following Named EM [*Enlisted Man*] Who Has Been Authorized to Report to Your Station upon Expiration of Leave. Retain Him/Her Pending Further Instructions (AABC)
ATCHMT	Attachment (MUGU)
ATCI	Adult T-Cell Leukemia [*Medicine*] (DMAA)
ATCI	Autonomous Tech [*NASDAQ symbol*] (TTSB)
ATCI	Autonomous Technologies Corp. [*NASDAQ symbol*] (SAG)
ATCK	Attack (MSA)
ATCL	Acceleration-Type Control Law
ATCL	Air Traffic Control Line (AFM)
ATCL	Associate of Trinity College of Music, London [*British*]
ATCLO	Amphibious Training Command Liaison Officer [*Navy*]
ATCM	Advanced Technology Cruise Missile (MCD)
ATCM	Airborne Toxic Control Measure
ATCM	Air Training Command Manual [*Air Force*]
ATCM	Associate of the Toronto Conservatory of Music
ATCM	Associate, Trinity College of Music [*Canadian*]
ATCM	Aviation Electronics Technician, Master Chief [*Navy rating*]
ATCMD	Advance Transportation Control and Movement Document
ATCMD	Atlantic Contract Management District (SAA)
ATCMU	Associated Third Class Mail Users [*Later, TCMA*] (EA)
ATCNB	Air Traffic Control and Navigation Board
ATCO	Active Token Collectors Organization (EA)
ATCO	Air Taxi-Commercial Operator

ATCO	Air Traffic Control Office [or Operations] [Air Force]
ATCO	Air Traffic Coordinating Officer
ATCO	Air Transportation Coordination Office (CINC)
ATCO	Arnold Transit Co. [Formerly, ATC] [AAR code]
ATCO	Association of Transport Co-ordinating Officers [British] (DBA)
ATCO	Australian Tourism Commission
ATCODE	Association of Teachers in Colleges and Departments of Education (AIE)
ATCOGS	Army Telecommunications Combat Theater and General Support [5 Year Plan] (MCD)
ATCOM	Air Traffic Communications (MCD)
ATCOM	Atoll Commander [In Pacific operations] [World War II]
ATCOM	Aviation and Troop Command [Army]
ATCOM	Aviation and Troop Support Command [Army] (RDA)
ATCOPS	Atlantis Commodities Purchasing Service
ATC OPSCEN	ATC [Air Training Command] Operations Center
ATCOR	Air Traffic Coordinator
ATCOREU	Air Traffic Coordinator Europe
ATCORUS	Air Transport Coordinator for the United States
ATCOS	Atmospheric Composition Satellite [NASA]
ATCP	Advanced Technology Crew Protection (MCD)
ATCP	Air Traffic Control Procedures
ATCP	Air Traffic Control Product [Army]
ATCP	Air Training Command Pamphlet [Air Force]
ATCP	Antarctic Treaty Consultative Parties
ATCPA	Air Taxi and Commercial Pilots Association [Defunct] (EA)
ATCPROSAT	Air Traffic Control Project for Satellite (DA)
ATCPS	Audio Tape Cassette Player Set
ATCQ	Air Travel Card of High Credit [Airline notation]
ATCR	Air Traffic Control Request (FAAC)
ATCR	Air Training Command Regulation [Air Force]
ATCRB	Air Traffic Control RADAR Beacon
ATCRBS	Air Traffic Control RADAR Beacon System
ATCRS	Air Traffic Control RADAR System
ATCRU	Air Traffic Control RADAR Unit (AFM)
ATCS	Active Thermal Control Subsystem [NASA] (MCD)
ATCS	Advanced Tactical Control System
ATCS	Advanced Train Control System [Union Pacific Railroad Co.]
ATCS	Airborne Tactical Command System [Formerly, ATDS] (MCD)
ATCS	Aircraft Tactical Control System
ATCS	Air Traffic Communications Service (MCD)
ATCS	Air Traffic Communications Station
ATCS	Air Traffic Communication System [NASA] (KSC)
ATCS	Air Traffic Control Satellite (IIA)
ATCS	Air Traffic Control Service (OA)
ATCS	Anterior Tibial Compartment Syndrome [Medicine] (DMAA)
ATCS	ATC Group Services, Inc. [NASDAQ symbol] (SAG)
ATCS	Attitude and Translation Control System (MCD)
ATCS	Automatic Test Control System [Air Force]
ATCS	Aviation Electronics Technician, Senior Chief [Navy rating]
ATCSCC	Air Traffic Control System Command Center (GAVI)
ATCSCC	ATC [Air Traffic Control] Systems Command Center [Marine science] (OSRA)
ATCSCO	ATC [Air Traffic Control] Systems Command Center (USDC)
ATCSF	Air Traffic Control Simulation Facility
ATCSS	Air Traffic Control Signaling System
ATCSS	Army Tactical Communication System Simulator (MCD)
ATCT	Air [or Airport] Traffic Control Tower
ATCT	Air Traffic Control Transponder
ATCT	Association des Techniciens Congolais des Telecommunications [Association of Congolese Telecommunications Technicians] [Zaire]
ATCT	ATC Communications [NASDAQ symbol] (TTSB)
ATCT	ATC Communications, Inc. [NASDAQ symbol] (SAG)
ATCT	NRP, Inc [NASDAQ symbol] (SAG)
ATCU	Air Transportable Communications Unit (NVT)
ATCU	Association of Texas Colleges and Universities (SRA)
ATCU	Attitude and Translation Control Unit
ATCU	Automatic Transmission Control Unit [Automotive engineering]
ATCW	Air Traffic Control and Warning (IAA)
ATD	Absent on Temporary Duty [Navy]
ATD	Absolutely to Die [Slang]
ATD	Academic Training Division [Military] (DNAB)
ATD	Acceptance and Takeover Date [Telecommunications] (TEL)
ATD	Accession Treaty and Decision Concerning the European Coal and Steel Community [A publication] (DLA)
ATD	Actual Time of Departure
ATD	Advanced Technology Demonstration
ATD	Advanced Technology Developments (MCD)
ATD	Advanced Technology Directorate [Army Strategic Defense Command] [Huntsville, AL]
ATD	Advanced Torpedo Decoy (CAAL)
ATD	Aerospace Technology Division [Formerly, Aerospace Information Division; later, ARP] [Library of Congress]
ATD	Aerotours Dominican, C por A [Dominican Republic] [ICAO designator] (FAAC)
ATD	Aid to the Totally Disabled (IIA)
ATD	Air and Toxics Division [Environmental Protection Agency] (GFGA)
ATD	Aircrew Training Device (MCD)
ATD	Airlift and Training Division [Air Force] (MCD)
ATD	Air Traffic Delay
ATD	Air Traffic Division [Air Traffic Control] (FAAC)
ATD	Air Transportable Dispensary (AFM)
ATD	Air Turbine Drive (NG)
ATD	Alzheimer Type Dementia [Medicine]

ATD	American Truck Dealers (EA)
ATD	Ammunition Technology Division [Lake City Army Ammunition Plant] [Independence, MO]
ATD	Analog to Time to Digital [Computer science]
ATD	Androstatrienedione [Organic chemistry]
ATD	Annual Training Deployment (MCD)
ATD	Annual Training Duty [Marine Corps]
ATD	Anthropometric Test Device [Automotive safety]
ATD	Anthropomorphic Test Device [MM] (TAG)
ATD	Anthropomorphic Test Dummy
ATD	Antithyroid Drug (AAMN)
ATD	Armor Training Devices (RDA)
ATD	Armoured Tank Destroyer [Military] (PDAA)
ATD	Arrival Time Distribution [Chemical physics]
ATD	Articulotrochanteric Distance (PDAA)
ATD	Art Teacher's Diploma [British]
ATD	Asphyxiating Thoracic Dystrophy [Medicine]
ATD	Assistant Test Director
ATD	Association for Theatre and Disability (EA)
ATD	Association of Tongue Depressors (EA)
ATD	Asynchronous Time Division [Telecommunications]
ATD	Audio-Tactile Display (PDAA)
ATD	Audio Tone Decoder
ATD	Autoimmune Thyroid Disease (DAVI)
ATD	Automated Ticket Dispenser
ATD	Automatic Tape Degausser
ATD	Automatic Target Designation
ATD	Automatic Target Detection (MCD)
ATD	Automatic Teaching Device
ATD	Automatic Threat Detection System [Aviation] (DA)
ATD	Automatic Timing Device [Diesel engines]
ATD	Automatic Tuning Device
ATD	Dayton, OH [Location identifier FAA] (FAAL)
ATD	[A] Touch of Days [An association] (EA)
ATDA	Advanced Technology Demonstration Aircraft
ATDA	Alternate Target Docking Adapter [NASA] (MCD)
ATDA	American Train Dispatchers Association (EA)
ATDA	Army Training Device Agency [Orlando, FL] (AABC)
ATDA	Augmented Target Docking Adapter [Gemini] [NASA]
ATDA	Australian Tyre Dealers' Association
ATDB	ACE Target Data Base (MCD)
ATDB	Aerothermodynamic Data Book [NASA] (NASA)
ATDBMS	Automated Test Data Base Management System [Army]
ATDC	After Top Dead Center [Valve position]
ATD/C	Aided Target Detection / Classification [Military]
ATDC	Association of Thalidomide-Damaged Children
ATDC	Austin Ten Drivers Club [High Wycombe, Buckinghamshire, England] (EAIO)
ATDD	Asynchronous Time Diversity Device (MCD)
ATDD	Atmospheric Turbulence and Diffusion Division [Marine science] (OSRA)
ATDD	Atmospheric Turbulence and Diffusion Division [Air Resources Laboratory] (USDC)
ATDD	Average Total Diametrical Displacement (IAA)
ATDDL	Apollo Technical Documentation Distribution List [NASA] (KSC)
ATDE	Advanced Technology Demonstrator Engine
ATDES	Adaptive Threshold Detection with Estimated Sequence (LAIN)
ATDESA	Automatic Three-Dimensional Electronics Scanning Array (IAA)
ATDE/T	Associate Technical Director for Engineering and Test [Army] (RDA)
ATDG	Automated Test Data Generator [Computer science]
ATDI	Advanced Terminal Defense Interceptor (MCD)
ATDip	Art Teacher's Diploma [British]
ATDL	Army Tactical Data Link
ATDL	Atmospheric Turbulence and Diffusion Laboratory [Oak Ridge, Tennessee]
ATD/LC	Aerospace Technology Division [Formerly, Aerospace Information Division; later, ARP]/Library of Congress (AFM)
ATDLG	Advanced Technology Demonstration LASER Gyro (MCD)
ATDLP	Apollo Trajectory Decision Logic Prototype [NASA]
ATDLP	Army-Wide Training and Doctrinal Literature Program
ATDM	Asynchronous Time Division Multiplexing [Telecommunications]
ATDMA	Advanced Time-Division Multiple Access (IEEE)
ATDNet	Advanced Technology Demonstration Network [Telecommunications]
ATDNT	Attendant (MUGU)
ATDO	Airways Technical District Office [FAA]
ATDP	Air Traffic Data Processor
ATDP	Attitudes toward Disabled Persons [Psychology]
ATDPS	Airborne Tactical Data Processing System
ATDR	Aeronautical Technical Directive Requirement [Obsolete]
ATDS	Airborne Tactical Data System [Later, ATCS]
ATDS	Air Tactical Data System (MCD)
ATDS	Airways Technical District Supervisor [FAA]
ATDS	Association of Teachers of Domestic Science [British] (BI)
ATDS	Association of Teachers of Dramatic Science [British]
ATDS	Automatic Telemetry Decommutation System
ATDS	Automatic Transient Detection System (MCD)
ATDS	Aviation Tactical Data System
ATDT	Attendant
ATDT	Attention Dial Tone [Computer science] (DOM)
ATDU	Aircraft Torpedo Development Unit [British]
ATDU	Air Transport Development Unit [British]
ATE	Above Target Elevation (MCD)
ATE	Acceptance Test Equipment (MCD)
ATE	Achilles Tectonic Exhibit
ATE	Acquisition and Tracking Electronics (MCD)

ATE............ Adipose Tissue Extract [Biochemistry] (MAE)
AT(E) .... Administration of Territories Committee (Europe) [World War II]
ATE............ Advanced Technology Engine (MCD)
ATE............ Advanced Turbofan Engine
ATE............ Aerospace Test Equipment
ATE............ Airborne Teletypewriter Equipment
ATE............ Airborne Test Equipment (MCD)
ATE............ Air Traffic Engineer [British] (DA)
ATE............ Air Turbo Exchanger
ATE............ Altitude Transmitting Equipment [FAA]
ATE............ Aluminum Triethyl [Organic chemistry]
ATE............ Anti-Terrorismo ETA [Anti-ETA Terrorism] [Spanish] (PPE)
ATE............ Approximation to English
ATE............ Area Test Equipment
ATE............ Artificial Traffic Equipment [Telecommunications] (NITA)
ATE............ Assessment and Training for Employment (AIE)
ATE............ Associated Telephone Exchanges [Later, ATAE]
ATE............ Associate in Technical Education
ATE............ Association for the Therapeutic Education [British]
ATE............ Association of Teacher Educators (EA)
ATE............ ATE Management Service Co., Inc., Cincinnati, OH [OCLC symbol]
              (OCLC)
ATE............ Atlantic Capital I [NYSE symbol] (SAG)
ATE............ Atlantic Energy [NYSE symbol] (SPSG)
ATE............ Atlantis Enterprise [Vancouver Stock Exchange symbol]
ATE............ Atlantis Transportation Services Ltd. [Canada ICAO designator]
              (FAAC)
ATE............ Australian Tourism Exchange
ATE............ Autographic Theme Extraction [System]
ATE............ Automated Test Equipment
ATE............ Automatic Telephone Exchange (NITA)
ATE............ Automatic Test and Evaluation
ATE............ Automatic [or Automated] Test Equipment [or Testing] (NASA)
ATE............ Automatic Test Equipment (AAGC)
ATE............ Mobile, AL [Location identifier FAA] (FAAL)
ATEA.......... American Technical Education Association (EA)
ATEA.......... American Toy Export Association (EA)
ATEA.......... Amphibian Tank Escape Apparatus
ATEA.......... Astea International, Inc. [NASDAQ symbol] (SAG)
ATEA.......... Astea Intl. [NASDAQ symbol] (TTSB)
A-TEAM....... Acquisition Team [Army] (RDA)
ATEC.......... Agence Transequatoriale des Communications [Trans-Equatorial
              Communications Agency] [Africa] (AF)
ATEC.......... Agency for Tele-Education in Canada
ATEC.......... Allison Transmission Electronic Control [Detroit Diesel Allison]
ATEC.......... Army Test and Evaluation Command [AMC]
ATEC.......... Association for Tele-Education in Canada (AC)
ATEC.......... ATEC Group [NASDAQ symbol] (TTSB)
ATEC.......... ATEC Group, Inc. [NASDAQ symbol] (SAG)
ATEC.......... ATEC Group, Inc. [Associated Press] (SAG)
ATEC.......... Atlantic Treaty Education Committee [NATO] (NATG)
ATEC.......... Australian Technology Export Committee
ATEC.......... Automated Technical Control [System] [Honeywell, Inc.] [Army]
ATEC.......... Automatic Test Equipment Complex (MCD)
ATEC.......... Average Total Episode Cost [Medicine]
ATEC.......... Aviation Technician Education Council (EA)
ATEC.......... Hillside Bedding Corp. [NASDAQ symbol] (SAG)
ATEC Gp .... ATEC Group, Inc. [Associated Press] (SAG)
ATECH........ Associate in Technology (NADA)
ATechC ...... American Technical Ceramics [Associated Press] (SAG)
ATECO .... Automatic Telegram Transmission with Computers
              [Telecommunications] (TEL)
ATECOM ..... Army Test and Evaluation Command [AMC] (MUGU)
ATECP........ Army Training Extension Course Program
AT-ECT....... Atrial Ectopy [Cardiology]
ATECW....... ATEC Group Wrrt [NASDAQ symbol] (TTSB)
ATEE......... Acetyltyrosine Ethyl Ester [Biochemistry]
ATEE......... Association for Teacher Education in Europe [Belgium] (EAIO)
ATEE......... Association of Teachers of Electrical Engineering [British]
ATEED........ Advanced Technology Energy Efficient Demonstrator (MCD)
ATEGG .... Advanced Turbine Engine Gas Generator [Air Force]
ATEI.......... Amusement Trades Exhibition International [British] (ITD)
ATE/ICE...... Automatic Test Equipment for Internal Combustion Engines (MCD)
ATEL......... American Telecasting, Inc. [NASDAQ symbol] (SAG)
ATEL......... Amer Telecasting [NASDAQ symbol] (TTSB)
ATEL......... Audio Techniques and Evaluation Laboratory [NASA]
ATEL......... Aviation Traders Engineering Ltd. [British]
ATEM......... Advanced Technical Engagement Model (MCD)
ATEM......... Aircraft Test Equipment Modification
ATEM......... Air Traffic Flow Management [ICAO designator] (FAAC)
ATEM......... Analytical Transmission Electron Microscope
A Tem........ A Tempo [In Strict Time] [Music]
ATEM......... Automatic Test Equipment, Missile (MCD)
ATEMIS....... Automatic Traffic Engineering and Management Information System
              (MHDI)
ATEMM....... Automatic Test Equipment Materiel Manager
A TEMP....... A Tempo [In Strict Time] [Music]
ATENE....... Association for Theological Education in the Near East [Later,
              ATIME]
Ateneo LJ .... Ateneo Law Journal [A publication] (DLA)
ATEOS........ Airborne Toxic Elements and Organic Species
ATEP.......... Advanced Technical Education Program
ATEP.......... AEGIS [Airborne Early Warning Ground Environment Integrated
              Segment] Tactical Executive Program
ATEP.......... Annual Training Equipment Pools (AABC)

ATEP.......... Association of Training and Employment Professionals (EA)
ATEP.......... Augmented Thermally Electric Propulsion
ATEPS........ Advanced Techniques for Electrical Power Management, Control, and
              Distribution Systems [Army] (RDA)
ATEQ.......... Association of Teachers of English in Quebec (AC)
ATER.......... Association of Theaters of Emilia and Romagna [Ballet company]
ATER.......... Automatic Testing, Evaluation, and Reporting
ATERIS....... Air Toxics Exposure & Risk Information System (ACII)
ATERIS....... Air Toxics Exposure and Risk Information System (GNE)
ATERM....... Air Terminal
ATERS .... Attitudes Toward Educational Research Scale [Psychology] (EDAC)
ATES......... Advanced Techniques Integration into Efficient Scientific Application
              Software [ESPRIT project] (NITA)
ATES......... Air Transportable Earth Station (IAA)
ATES......... Aquifer Thermal Energy Storage
ATES......... Army Test and Evaluation Seminar
ATES......... Association for Technical Education in Schools [British] (BI)
ATES......... Automated Tactical Environmental System
ATESC........ Automatic Test Equipment Support Center [Army]
ATESEA...... Association for Theological Education in South East Asia (EAIO)
ATESL........ Association of Teachers of English as a Second Language (EA)
ATESS........ Automated Tactical Environmental System (MCD)
ATESSE...... Automatic Test Equipment Software Support Environment [Computer
              science]
ATESSEA.... Air Traffic Service System Error Analysis (SAA)
AT(E)SSS.... Administration of Territories Committee (Europe), Shipping and
              Supply Subcommittee [World War II]
ATET.......... Advanced Technical Experimental Transportation (MCD)
Atetra P ..... Adenosine Tetraphosphate [Biochemistry]
ATEV.......... Alfalfa Temperate Virus [Plant pathology]
ATEV.......... Approximate Theoretical Error Variance (MHDB)
ATEWA........ Automatic Target Evaluator and Weapon Assignor
ATEWS....... Advanced Tactical Electronic Warfare System (AFM)
ATEX.......... Atlantic Tradewind [or Tropical] Experiment [National Science
              Foundation]
ATF........... Acceptance Test Facility [Nuclear energy]
ATF........... Accounting Tabulating Form (AAG)
ATF........... Across the Fence [Real estate] (DICI)
ATF........... Activating Transcription Factors [Genetics]
ATF........... Active Thermal Feedback (PCM)
ATF........... Actual Time of Fall
ATF........... Actuating Transfer Function (SAA)
ATF........... Advanced Tactical Fighter [Air Force] (MCD)
ATF........... Advanced Technology Fighter
ATF........... Advanced Toroidal Facility [Oak Ridge National Laboratory]
ATF........... Advanced Traffic Management [FAA] (GFGA)
ATF........... After the Fact (MCD)
ATF........... Air Task Force
ATF........... Air Torpedo-Firing (DNAB)
ATF........... Air Traffic Flow [Later, ATIF] (MCD)
ATF........... Air Transport Force
ATF........... Algebraic Technological Function [Computer science]
ATF........... American Tennis Federation (EA)
ATF........... American Trails Foundation [Defunct] (EA)
ATF........... American Typecasting Fellowship (EA)
ATF........... American Type Founders (DGA)
ATF........... Amorphous Thin Film (PDAA)
ATF........... Amphibious Task Force [Navy] (NVT)
ATF........... Angiotensin-II-Ferritin [Biochemistry]
ATF........... Antarctic Task Force
ATF........... Antelope Resources [Vancouver Stock Exchange symbol]
ATF........... Antenna Test Facility
ATF........... Armed Tactical Fighter [General Dynamics Corp.] (ECON)
ATF........... Army Training Film
ATF........... Asphalt-Tile Floor [Technical drawings]
ATF........... Association of Teachers of French (AIE)
ATF........... Astrometric Telescope Facility (SSD)
ATF........... As Trustee For [Banking]
ATF........... AT & T Stock Fund [Equity Income Fund] [AMEX symbol] (SPSG)
ATF........... Atico Financial Corp. (IIA)
ATF........... Auditorium and Training Facility [NASA] (NASA)
ATF........... Australian Turkey Federation
ATF........... Automatic Target Finder (IAA)
ATF........... Automatic Target Follow
ATF........... Automatic Terrain Following [Military] (MCD)
ATF........... Automatic Test Formatter (NITA)
ATF........... Automatic Text Formatter
ATF........... Automatic Track Finding [System] [Video technology]
ATF........... Automatic Tracking Feature (NVT)
ATF........... Automatic Transmission Fluid
ATF........... Autotumorolytic Factor [Oncology]
ATF........... Aviation Turbine Fuel
ATF........... Bureau of Alcohol, Tobacco, and Firearms [Department of the
              Treasury]
ATF........... Bureau of Alcohol, Tobacco, and Firearms Laboratory, Washington,
              DC [OCLC symbol] (OCLC)
ATF........... Compania Aerotecnicas Fotograficas [Spain ICAO designator]
              (FAAC)
ATF........... Equity Income Fund [AMEX symbol] (TTSB)
ATF........... Fleet Ocean Tug [Navy symbol]
ATF........... French Southern and Antarctic Lands [ANSI three-letter standard
              code] (CNC)
ATFA.......... American Telephone Fundraisers Association (NFD)
ATFA.......... Atomic-Type Field Army (SAA)
ATFAC......... American Turpentine Farmers Association Cooperative (EA)

ATFAP.........	Arson Task Force Assistance Program
ATFAR	Adjusted Total Financial Assistance Requirement
ATF/ATA......	Automatic Terrain Following/Automatic Terrain Avoidance [Military]
ATFB...........	Alcohol, Tobacco, Firearms Bureau [Department of the Treasury] (PDAA)
ATFC..........	Aboriginal Trappers Federation of Canada (AC)
ATFC..........	Account Traffic [Aviation] (FAAC)
ATFC..........	Air Task Force Commander (MUGU)
ATFC..........	Alan Thicke Fan Club (EA)
ATFC..........	American-Turkish Friendship Council
ATFC..........	Association of Tasmanian Forum Clubs [Australia]
ATFC..........	Automatic Traffic-Flow Control (MHDB)
ATFC..........	Automatic Traffic-Flow Control (MHDB)
ATFCA.........	Asian Track and Field Coaches Association [India] (EAIO)
ATFCB.........	Alcohol, Tobacco, and Firearms Cumulative Bulletin [A publication] (DLA)
ATFCNN	Allied Task Force Commander, North Norway [NATO] (NATG)
ATFCV.........	Australian Trust for Conservation Volunteers
ATFD..........	Automated Tactical Fusion Division
ATFE..........	Advanced Thermal Flight Experiment (MCD)
ATFEF.........	Advertising, Typesetting and Foundry Employers Federation (DGA)
ATFERO	Atlantic Ferry Organization [Based in Canada under Ministry of Aircraft Production] [British World War II]
ATFES.........	Army Tactical Frequency Engineering System
ATFGF........	Association of Toy and Fancy Goods Factors [British] (BI)
ATFI...........	Attitudes Toward Feminist Issues Scales [Psychology] (EDAC)
ATFI...........	Automated Tariff Filing and Information System [Washington, DC] (EGAO)
AT FIB	Atrial Fibrillation [Cardiology]
ATFM..........	Air Traffic Flow Management (DA)
ATFMA.........	Advanced Tactical Fighter Mission Analysis (MCD)
ATFM & S....	Acquisition Task Force on Modeling and Simulation [Army]
ATFMG........	Alliance Telecommunications Frequency Management Group [Telecommunications service] (TSSD)
ATFMU........	Air Traffic Flow Management Unit (DA)
ATFO..........	Airways Technical Field Office [FAA]
ATFOS	Alignment and Test Facility for Optical Systems [Navy]
ATFP..........	Alliance of Television Film Producers [Later, Association of Motion Picture andTelevision Producers] (EA)
ATFR..........	Arlin Test of Formal Reasoning [Intelligence test]
ATFR..........	Automatic Terrain-Following RADAR [Military]
ATFRAM	Airborne Time/Frequency Range/Altitude Monitor (MCD)
ATFS...........	Association of Track and Field Statisticians [British] (EAIO)
ATFX..........	Fleet Tug [Navy symbol] (MCD)
ATG...........	Accordion Teachers' Guild (EA)
ATG...........	Acoustic Target Generator
ATG...........	Adaptive Threshold Gate (PDAA)
ATG...........	Adenine, Thymine, Guanine [Genetics] (DAVI)
ATG...........	Adenin, Thymine, Guanine [Medicine] (BABM)
ATG...........	Advanced Technology Group [Navy]
ATG...........	Agence des Telecommunications Gouvernementales [Government Telecommunications Agency] [Canada]
ATG...........	AGL Resources [NYSE symbol] (TTSB)
ATG...........	AGL Resources, Inc. [NYSE symbol] (SAG)
ATG...........	Air-to-Ground [Photos, missiles, etc.]
ATG...........	Air Turbine Generator
ATG...........	Alaskan Territorial Guard
ATG...........	Alcatel Thomson Gigadisc [Optical disk]
ATG...........	All Test Go (MCD)
ATG...........	American Traders Group (EA)
ATG...........	Ammonium Thioglycolate
ATG...........	Angiotensinogen [Biochemistry]
ATG...........	Antenna Test Group [Army] (AABC)
ATG...........	Antigua-Barbuda [ANSI three-letter standard code] (CNC)
ATG...........	Antihuman Thymocyte Globulin [Medicine] (DAVI)
ATG...........	Antitank Gun [Military]
ATG...........	Antithrombocyte Globulin [Immunology] (MAE)
ATG...........	Antithymocyte Globulin [Immunochemistry]
ATG...........	Antithyroglobulin [Immunochemistry] (MAE)
ATG...........	Association of Teachers of Geology [British]
ATG...........	Association of Teachers of German [British]
ATG...........	Atlanta Gas & Light Co. [NYSE symbol] (SPSG)
ATG...........	Atlant-SV [Ukraine] [FAA designator] (FAAC)
ATG...........	Automated Test-Case Guidance [Computer science]
ATG...........	Automatic Test Generator
ATG...........	Automatic Test Grading
ATG...........	Automatic Test Guide
ATGA	American Toy Goat Association (EA)
ATGAF	Advanced Technology Ground Attack Fighter [Air Force]
ATGAM	Antimocyte Gamma-Globulin [Immunology]
ATGAR	Antitank Guided Air Rocket
ATGAS	Applied Technology Gasification [Coal]
ATGER	Association of Teachers of German [British]
ATGF..........	Automatic Test Generation Facility (MHDI)
ATGGA	Australian Table Grape Growers' Association
ATGI...........	Alpha Technologies Grp [NASDAQ symbol] (TTSB)
ATGI...........	Alpha Technology Group, Inc. [NASDAQ symbol] (SAG)
ATGIN.........	Atomic Ground Intercept (MCD)
ATGL..........	Antitank Grenade Launcher (AABC)
ATGM..........	Antitank Guided Missile
ATG/MAB......	Amphibious Task Group/Marine Amphibious Brigade (DNAB)
ATGPr.........	Atlanta Gas Lt 7.70% Dep Pfd [NYSE symbol] (TTSB)
ATGS	Advanced Terminal Guidance System
ATGS	Association of Texas Graduate Schools (SRA)
ATGSB	Admission Test for Graduate Study in Business

ATGW..........	Antitank Guided Weapon (MCD)
ATH..............	Above the Horizon
ATH..............	Acetyltyrosine Hydrazide (MAE)
ATH..............	Advanced Therapeutic Sys [AMEX symbol] (TTSB)
ATH..............	Advanced Therapeutic Systems Ltd. [AMEX symbol] (SAG)
ATH..............	Air Transportable Hospital (AFM)
ATH..............	Air Travel Corp. [ICAO designator] (FAAC)
ATH..............	Alumina Trihydrate [Inorganic chemistry]
ATH..............	Aluminum Trihydrate
ATH..............	Antitank Helicopter (MCD)
ATH..............	Apostolate to Hungarians [Diocesan abbreviation] [District of Columbia] (TOCD)
ATH..............	Arapahoe Mining [Vancouver Stock Exchange symbol]
ATH..............	Artificial Time History [Nuclear energy] (NRCH)
A Th.............	Associate in Theology
ATh..............	Associate in Therapy
ath	Athapascan [MARC language code Library of Congress] (LCCP)
Ath..............	Athenaeus [First century AD] [Classical studies] (OCD)
ATH..............	Athens [Greece] [Airport symbol] (OAG)
ATH..............	Athens Observatory [Greece] [Seismograph station code, US Geological Survey] (SEIS)
ATH..............	Athletic (MUGU)
ATH..............	Athwartships
ATH..............	Automatic Tape Handler (IAA)
ATH..............	Autonomous Terminal Homing [Air Force]
a-th--...........	Thailand [MARC geographic area code Library of Congress] (LCCP)
ATHA	American Turkey Hunters Association [Defunct] (EA)
ATHAS	Advanced Thermal Analysis (MCD)
AthBE	Athletes for a Better Education
ATHC..........	Allotetrahydrocortisol [Organic chemistry] (DAVI)
ATHC..........	Association of Thrift Holding Companies [Washington, DC] (EA)
ATHE..........	Association for Theatre in Higher Education (EA)
ATHELO	Attack Helicopter Organization [Military]
Athena	Athena Neurosciences, Inc. [Associated Press] (SAG)
ATHENA	Award to Honor Excellent Newspaper Advertising (DGA)
ATHESA	Automatic Three-Dimensional Electronics Scanning Array (MUGU)
Athey..........	Athey Products Corp. [Associated Press] (SAG)
ATHI...........	Attitudes Toward Handicapped Individuals Scale [Psychology] (EDAC)
ATHI...........	Two Hills Public Library, Alberta [Library symbol National Library of Canada] (NLC)
ATHL...........	Athletic
ATHL...........	Athletic
Athlr...........	Aethelred [King of England] (ILCA)
ATHM..........	Three Hills Municipal Library, Alberta [Library symbol National Library of Canada] (NLC)
Ath Mar Set...	Atherley on Marriage Settlements [A publication] (DLA)
ATHN..........	Athena Neurosciences [NASDAQ symbol] (SPSG)
ATHOC.........	Automatic Target Handoff Computer (MCD)
ATHODYD ...	Aerothermodynamic Duct
ATHOM	Thorhild Municipal Library, Alberta [Library symbol National Library of Canada] (NLC)
ATHP	American Industrial Heritage Project
ATHP	Autonomous Terminal Homing Program (MCD)
ATHR	Angina Threshold Heart Rate [Cardiology] (DAVI)
ATHR	Autothrust System (GAVI)
ATHRS	Air Transportation Hydrant Refueling System (AFIT)
ATHRTY	Authority
ATHS	Airborne Target Handover System [Military] (DOMA)
ATHS	American Truck Historical Society (EA)
ATHS	Automatic Target Handover System [Army]
ATHS/AI	Automatic Target Handover System/Avionics Integration
ATHSC	Atherosclerosis [Medicine]
ATI.............	Abdominal Trauma Index [Medicine] (DMAA)
ATI.............	Above-Threshold Ionization (MCD)
ATI.............	Acetylene-Terminated Imide [Polymer technology]
ATI.............	Acoustic Telephone Interface [Telecommunications]
ATI.............	Actual Time of Interception
ATI.............	Advanced Technology Innovation [Computer science]
ATI.............	Advanced Terminal Interceptor
ATI.............	Advanced Turbocharged Intercooled [Truck engineering]
ATI.............	Aerial Tuning Inductance
ATI.............	Aerosol Techniques, Inc.
ATI.............	Aero Transporti Italiani SpA [Italy ICAO designator] (FAAC)
ATI.............	Airborne Track Illuminator [Military] (DOMA)
ATI.............	Air Target Indicator
ATI.............	Air Technical Index [Air Force]
ATI.............	Air Technical Information [Used by Armed Services Technical Information Agency - later, Defense Documentation Center - to accession and identify documents]
ATI.............	Air Technical Intelligence [Air Force]
ATI--..........	AirTouch Communications [NYSE symbol] (TTSB)
ATI.............	Airtouch Communications Co. [Formerly, PacTel Corp.] [NYSE symbol] (SAG)
ATI.............	American Technology & Information, Inc. [Vancouver Stock Exchange symbol]
ATI.............	American Telco, Inc. [Telecommunications service] (TSSD)
ATI.............	American Travel Inns (EA)
ATI.............	Antenna Tuning Inductance (IAA)
ATI.............	Apprentice Training Incentive
ATI.............	Appropriate Technology International (EA)
ATI.............	Aptitude-Treatment Interactions [Education]
ATI.............	Armored Transportation Institute (EA)
ATI.............	Army Training Instruction
ATI.............	Artigas [Uruguay] [Airport symbol] (OAG)

ATI	Artillery Target Intelligence (MCD)	
ATI	Asbestos Textile Institute (EA)	
ATI	Associated Telemanagement, Inc. [*Newburyport, MA*] [*Telecommunications*] (TSSD)	
ATI	Associate of the Textile Institute [*British*]	
ATI	Association of Teachers of Italian [*British*]	
ATI	Association of Technical Institutions (EY)	
ATI	Atico [*Peru*] [*Seismograph station code, US Geological Survey*] (SEIS)	
ATI	AtLANta Technologies, Inc. [*Atlanta, GA*] [*Telecommunications service*] (TSSD)	
ATI	A-Track Initiator (SAA)	
ATI	Attitudes toward Industrialization [*Psychology*]	
ATI	Audiometer Telephone Interface [*for the hearing-impaired*]	
ATI	Automated Technical Information (MCD)	
ATI	Automatic Target Identification	
ATI	Automatic Track Initiation	
ATI	Automation Techniques, Inc.	
ATI	Average Total Inspection [*QCR*]	
ATI	Tilley Public Library, Alberta [*Library symbol National Library of Canada*] (NLC)	
ATIA	Arizona Travel Industry Association (SRA)	
ATIA	Australian Tourism Industry Association	
ATIB	Army Tactical Intelligence Agency Blueprint (MCD)	
ATIBT	Association Technique Internationale des Bois Tropicaux [*International Technical Tropical Timber Association*] (EAIO)	
ATIC	Adaptable Terminal Interface Configuration [*Military*] (MCD)	
ATIC	Aerospace Technical Intelligence Center	
ATIC	Air Technical Intelligence Center	
ATIC	Air Terminal Identifier Code	
ATIC	Army Tactical Intelligence Committee (MCD)	
ATIC	Army Tactical Intelligence Concept (MCD)	
ATIC	Association des Transitaires Internationaux Canadiens, inc. (AC)	
ATIC	Association Technique de l'Importation Charbonniere (EA)	
ATID	American Trade and Industrial Development	
ATIEP	Association of Telephone Information and Entertainment Providers [*British*]	
ATIF	Alpha Trans-Inducing Factor [*Genetics*]	
ATIF	American Tennis Industry Federation (EA)	
ATIF	Australian Timber Importers' Federation	
ATIF	Australian Turkish Islamic Federation	
ATIG	Alternative Technology Information Group (EAIO)	
ATIGS	Advanced Tactical Inertial Guidance System [*Navy*]	
ATII	Advanced Techniques for Imagery Interpretation (AABC)	
ATII	Associate of the Institute of Taxation [*British*] (DBQ)	
ATIL	Air Target Intelligence Liaison Program [*Air Force*]	
ATILH	Association Technique de l'Industrie des Liants Hydrauliques [*Technical Association for the Hydraulic Binders Industry*] (IID)	
ATIME	Association of Theological Institutes in the Middle East (EAIO)	
ATIMS	Automatic Time Interval Measurement System [*Air Force*]	
ATIN	Adoption Taxpayer Identification Number	
ATIN	AIDS [*Acquired Immune Deficiency Syndrome*] Targeted Information Newsletter [*Williams & Wilkins*] [*A publication*]	
ATIO	Anguilla Tourist Information Office [*Later, ATIRO*] (EA)	
ATIO	Association of Translators & Interpreters of Ontario [*Association des Traducteurs et Interpretes de l'Ontario*] (AC)	
ATIP	Analog Tune in Progress (IAA)	
ATIR	Absolute Terminal Innervation Ratio [*Psychiatry*]	
ATIRCM	Advanced Threat Infrared Countermeasures Program (DWSG)	
ATIRO	Anguilla Tourist Information and Reservation Office (EA)	
ATIS	Adirondack Trail Improvement Society (EA)	
ATIS	Advanced Thermal Imaging Scanner [*or System*]	
ATIS	Advanced Tissue Sci [*NASDAQ symbol*] (TTSB)	
ATIS	Advanced Tissue Sciences, Inc. [*NASDAQ symbol*] (SAG)	
ATIS	Advanced Travel Information Systems [*Formerly, ADI*] [*Highway safety research*]	
ATIS	Airborne Test Instrumentation System [*Air Force*] (MCD)	
ATIS	Air Technical Intelligence Study [*Air Force*]	
ATIS	Air Traffic Information Service (DA)	
ATIS	Allied Translator and Interpreter Service	
ATIS	Antenna and Transmitter Improvement Study	
ATIS	Appropriate Technology Information Service [*International Council of Scientific Unions*]	
ATIS	Association of Teachers in Independent Schools in New York City and Vicinity (EA)	
ATIS	Association of Translators & Interpreters of Saskatchewan [*Association des Traducteurs et Interpretes de la Saskatchewan*] (AC)	
ATIS	AT & T Information Systems [*Telecommunications*]	
ATIS	Automated Technical Information Support	
ATIS	Automatic Terminal Information Service [*Aviation*] (AFM)	
ATIS	Automatic Transmitter Identification System [*Citizens band radio*]	
ATISC	Air Technical Intelligence Services Command [*Air Force*]	
ATISNYCV	Association of Teachers in Independent Schools in New York City and Vicinity (EA)	
ATISS	Advanced Traffic Information Supply System [*Highway traffic management*]	
ATIT	Advanced Terminal Interceptor Technology	
ATITA	Air Transport Industry Training Association (DA)	
ATITP	Advanced Terminal Interceptor Technology Program	
ATIWG	Apollo Test Integration Working Groups [*NASA*] (KSC)	
ATIX	Airlantic Transport [*Air carrier designation symbol*]	
ATJ	Air Traffic GmbH [*Germany ICAO designator*] (FAAC)	
ATJ	Association of Teachers of Japanese (EA)	
ATJ	AT Plastics [*AMEX symbol*] (TTSB)	

ATJ	AT Plastics, Inc. [*AMEX symbol*] (SAG)	
ATJ	Australasian Typographical Journal [*A publication*]	
ATJ	Automatic through Junction [*Telecommunications*] (OA)	
ATJ	Aviation Training Jacket (DNAB)	
ATJC	Annular Turbojet Combustor	
ATJS	Advanced Tactical Jamming System [*Aircraft*]	
ATJS	Airborne Tactical Jamming System [*Air Force*]	
ATK	Aerotaxi Casanare Ltda. [*Colombia*] [*ICAO designator*] (FAAC)	
ATK	Alliant Techsystems [*NYSE symbol*] (SPSG)	
ATK	Alliant Techsystems [*NYSE symbol*] (TTSB)	
ATK	AMTRAK Library, Washington, DC [*OCLC symbol*] (OCLC)	
ATK	Antitank [*Also, AT*] (NATG)	
ATK	Asitka Resources Corp. [*Vancouver Stock Exchange symbol*]	
ATK	Atkasuk Village, AK [*Location identifier FAA*] (FAAL)	
Atk	Atkinson's Quarter Sessions Records [*Yorkshire, England*] [*A publication*] (DLA)	
Atk	Atkyn's English Chancery Reports [*1736-55*] [*A publication*] (DLA)	
ATK	Atqasuk [*Alaska*] [*Airport symbol*] (OAG)	
ATK	Attack (AABC)	
ATK	Available Tonne-Kilometer (ADA)	
ATK	Aviation Turbine Kerosine (IAA)	
ATKCARAIRWING	Attack Carrier Air Wing [*Navy*]	
Atk Ch Pr	Atkinson's Chancery Practice [*A publication*] (DLA)	
Atk Con	Atkinson on Conveyancing [*A publication*] (DLA)	
ATKHB	Attack Helicopter Battalion [*Army*] (ADDR)	
ATKHC	Attack Helicopter Company [*Military*] (AABC)	
ATK HEL	Attack Helicopter [*MTMC*] (TAG)	
Atkinsn	Atkinson [*Guy F.*] Co. of California [*Associated Press*] (SAG)	
Atkinson	Atkinson's Law of Solicitors' Liens [*1905*] [*A publication*] (DLA)	
ATKN	Atkinson (Guy F.) Co. of California [*NASDAQ symbol*] (NQ)	
ATKN	Atkinson (Guy F.)Calif [*NASDAQ symbol*] (TTSB)	
Atk PT	Atkyn's Parliamentary Tracts [*A publication*] (DLA)	
ATKRON	Attack Squadron [*Navy*] (MUGU)	
ATKRONDET	Attack Squadron Detachment [*Navy*] (DNAB)	
ATKSC	Attack Surveillance Committee [*Army*] (AABC)	
ATKSC	Attack Surveillance Coverage [*Army*] (AABC)	
Atk Sher	Atkinson on Sheriffs [*A publication*] (DLA)	
Atk Titles	Atkinson on Marketable Titles [*A publication*] (DLA)	
ATL	Achilles Tendon Lengthening [*Medicine*]	
ATL	Acoustic Test Laboratory	
ATL	Active Task List [*Computer science*] (MHDI)	
ATL	Active Time List [*Computer science*]	
ATL	Actual Total Loss	
ATL	Adult T-Cell Leukemia [*Medicine*]	
ATL	Advanced Technology Laboratory [*Navy*] (MCD)	
ATL	Advanced Technology Labortories, Inc. (DAVI)	
AT/L	Advanced Technology/Libraries [*Information service*]	
ATL	Aeronautical Turbine Laboratory [*Navy*]	
ATL	Air Atlantic [*Canada ICAO designator*] (FAAC)	
ATL	Air Transport Liaison [*Military British*]	
ATL	Albuquerque Testing Laboratory (AAGC)	
ATL	American Tariff League [*Later, TRC*]	
ATL	American Theological Library Association, Princeton, NJ [*OCLC symbol*] (OCLC)	
ATL	Analog Threshold Logic	
ATL	Antitension Line (MAE)	
ATL	Antitrust Law	
ATL	Applications Terminal Language [*Computer science*] (MHDB)	
ATL	Applied Technology Laboratory [*Army*] (GRD)	
ATL	Armament Technology Division [*Air Force*] (MCD)	
ATL	Armament Technology Laboratory [*Air Force*]	
ATL	Armywide Training Literature	
ATL	Arranged Total Loss [*Insurance*] (AIA)	
ATL	Artificial Transmission Line	
ATL	Association des Traducteurs Litteraires [*Literary Translators' Association*] [*Canada*]	
ATL	Association of Teachers and Lecturers (AIE)	
ATL	Atalanta Sosnoff Capital Corp. [*NYSE symbol*] (SPSG)	
ATL	[*The*] Athenian Tribute Lists [*A publication*] (OCD)	
ATL	Atlanta [*Georgia*] [*Seismograph station code, US Geological Survey*] (SEIS)	
ATL	Atlanta/Sosnoff [*NYSE symbol*] (TTSB)	
Atl	Atlantic [*Record label*]	
ATL	Atlantic (AFM)	
ATL	Atlantic	
Atl	Atlantic Monthly [*A publication*] (BRI)	
Atl	Atlantic Reporter [*A publication*] (BARN)	
ATL	Atlantis Tank Landing Craft	
ATL	Atlas (ROG)	
ATL	Atlas Basic Language [*Computer science*] (ECII)	
ATL	Attempt to Locate	
ATL	Atypical Lymphocytes (DAVI)	
ATL	Auspuff-Turbolaeder [*Exhaust turbocharger*] [*German Automotive engineering*]	
ATL	Australian Income Tax Legislation [*A publication*]	
ATL	Automated Tape Library	
ATL	Automatic Telling [*Banking*] (IAA)	
ATL	Automatic Test Line	
ATL	Automatic Turret Lathe	
ATL	Awaiting Trial	
ATL	Tank Landing Craft [*Navy symbol Obsolete*]	
ATL 1	Atlantic Site 1 (GAAI)	
ATL 2	Atlantic Site 2 (GAAI)	
Atl 2d	Atlantic Reporter, Second Series (West) [*A publication*] (DLA)	
ATLA	Adult T-Cell Leukemia Antigen [*Medicine*]	

ATLA...........	Air Transport Licensing Authority [*British*]
ATLA...........	Alabama Trial Lawyers Association (SRA)
ATLA...........	American Theological Library Association (EA)
ATLA...........	American Theological Library Association, Yale University Divinity School, New Haven, CT [*Library symbol Library of Congress*] (LCLS)
ATLA...........	Antiquarian Trade List Annual [*A publication*]
ATLA...........	Arkansas Trial Lawyers Association (SRA)
ATLA...........	Association of Teachers of Lipreading to Adults [*British*] (DBA)
ATLA...........	Association of Trial Lawyers of America (EA)
ATLA...........	Atlantis Group, Inc. [*NASDAQ symbol*] (SAG)
ATLA...........	Australian Toy Library Association
ATLAI..........	American Theological Library Association. Indexes
ATLAM........	Antiterritorial Land Mine (MCD)
AtlAm.........	Atlantic American Corp. [*Associated Press*] (SAG)
Atlantis.......	Atlantis Plastics, Inc. [*Associated Press*] (SAG)
AtlantisG.....	Atlantis Group, Inc. [*Associated Press*] (SAG)
ATLAS........	Abbreviated Test Language for Avionics Systems
ATLAS........	Advanced Tactical Lightweight Air Superiority [*RADAR*] [*Air Force*] (MCD)
ATLAS........	Advanced Tactical Lightweight Avionics System
ATLAS........	Advanced Target Location and Strike
ATLAS........	Advanced Technology Large Aircraft System [*Air Force*] (MCD)
ATLAS........	ALITALIA, Lufthansa, Air France, Sabena [*Consortium of airlines*] (MCD)
ATLAS........	All Terrain Lifter Articulated System [*MTMC*] (TAG)
ATLAS........	All-Terrain Lightweight Articulating Suspension
ATLAS........	Antitank LASER-Assisted System [*British*]
ATLAS........	Argonne Tandem/LINAC Accelerator System [*Department of Energy*]
ATLAS........	Army Tactical, Logistical, and Air Simulation (MCD)
ATLAS........	Artillery Towing Light Auxiliary System [*Army*] (MCD)
ATLAS........	Association of Teachers of Latin American Studies (EA)
Atlas..........	Atlas Corp. [*Associated Press*] (SAG)
ATLAS........	Atmospheric Laboratory for Applications and Science [*NASA*] (OSRA)
ATLAS........	Attendance and Labor System (MCD)
ATLAS........	Automated Tape Label Assignment System (MCD)
ATLAS........	Automatic Tabulating, Listing, and Sorting System [*Software*]
ATLAS........	Automatic Tape Load Audit System
ATLAS........	Automatic Test Equipment Language Standardization (MCD)
ATLAS........	Automatic Test Language for All Systems [*DoD*]
ATLAS........	Automatic Thin-Layer Analytical System
ATLAS........	Autonomous Temperature Line Acquisition System [*Moorings*] [*Marine science*] (OSRA)
ATLAS........	Autonomous Temperature Line Acquisition System [*Moorings*] (USDC)
ATLAS........	[*A*] Tactical, Logistical, and Air Simulation [*NATO*] (NATG)
ATLAS........	[*A*] Total Library Automation System
AtlasAir.......	Atlas Air, Inc. [*Associated Press*] (SAG)
AtlasPac.....	Atlas Pacific Ltd. [*Associated Press*] (SAG)
ATLASS........	Advanced Technology for Large Structural Systems [*National Science Foundation*]
ATLB..........	Air Transport Licensing Board
ATLB..........	Atlantic Bank & Trust [*NASDAQ symbol*] (TTSB)
ATLB..........	Atlantic Bank and Trust Co. [*NASDAQ symbol*] (SAG)
AtlBev.........	Atlantic Beverage Corp. [*Associated Press*] (SAG)
AtlBkTC......	Atlantic Bank and Trust Co. [*Associated Press*] (SAG)
Atl BT	Atlantic Books Today [*A publication*] (BRI)
ATLC..........	Atlantic Pharmaceuticals [*NASDAQ symbol*] (TTSB)
ATLC..........	Atlantic Pharmaceuticals,Inc. [*NASDAQ symbol*] (SAG)
AtlCap........	Atlantic Capital I [*Associated Press*] (SAG)
Atl Comm Q...	Atlantic Community Quarterly [*A publication*] (DLA)
AtlCstAir......	Atlantic Coast Airlines, Inc. [*Associated Press*] (SAG)
ATLCU........	Atlantic Pharma'l Units 2000 [*NASDAQ symbol*] (TTSB)
ATLCW.......	Atlantic Pharm'l Wrrt 2000 [*NASDAQ symbol*] (TTSB)
ATLD..........	Air Transportable Loading Dock (AFM)
AtlEnrg........	Atlantic Energy, Inc. [*Associated Press*] (SAG)
AtlGas........	Atlanta Gas & Light Co. [*Associated Press*] (SAG)
AtlGs..........	Atlanta Gas & Light Co. [*Associated Press*] (SAG)
AtlGulf........	Atlantic Gulf Communities Corp. [*Associated Press*] (SAG)
ATLI...........	Advanced Technology Laboratories, Inc. [*Formerly, Westmark International, Inc.*] [*NASDAQ symbol*] (SPSG)
ATLI...........	Advanced Technology Labs [*NASDAQ symbol*] (TTSB)
ATLID.........	Atmospheric LIDAR [*LASER Infrared RADAR*] (SSD)
ATLIS.........	Airborne Tracking LASER Identification System
ATLIS.........	Army Technical Library Improvement Studies
ATLIS.........	Automatic Tracking LASER Illumination System (MCD)
ATLIT.........	Advanced Technology Light Twin Engine Aircraft (MCD)
ATLIT.........	Advanced Technology Light Twin Engine Research Aircraft [*Air Force*] (MCD)
ATLJ..........	American Trial Lawyers Association. Journal [*A publication*] (DLA)
ATLL..........	Adult T-Cell Leukemia-Lymphoma [*Medicine*]
ATLO..........	Acceptance Test and Launch Operations [*NASA*] (MCD)
ATLO..........	Air Transport Liaison Officer [*British*]
AtlO...........	Atlantic Ocean
ATLP..........	Army-Wide Training Literature Program (AABC)
AtlPharm	Atlantic Pharmaceuticals, Inc. [*Associated Press*] (SAG)
AtlPhr........	Atlantic Pharmaceuticals, Inc. [*Associated Press*] (SAG)
Atl PR	Atlantic Province Reports [*Information service or system A publication*] (DLA)
Atl Prov	Atlantic Province Reports [*Information service or system A publication*] (DLA)
AT/LR........	Air Tracker/Long-Range (DNAB)
atlr...........	Antler (VRA)
ATLR..........	Atlantic Realty Trust SBI [*NASDAQ symbol*] (SAG)
Atl R	Atlantic Reporter [*A publication*] (DLA)

AtlRc..........	Atlantic Richfield Co. [*Associated Press*] (SAG)
AtlReal	Atlantic Realty Trust SBI [*Associated Press*] (SAG)
Atl Rep	Atlantic Reporter [*A publication*] (DLA)
Atl Repr	Atlantic Reporter [*A publication*] (DLA)
AtlRich........	Atlantic Richfield Co. [*Associated Press*] (SAG)
AtlRich97.....	Atlantic Richfield Co. [*Associated Press*] (SAG)
ATLRS	Aircraft Tube-Launched Recoilless System (MCD)
ATLRS	Atlantic Realty Trust [*NASDAQ symbol*] (TTSB)
ATLS..........	Advanced Trauma Life Support System
ATLS..........	Atlas
ATLS..........	Atlas Air [*NASDAQ symbol*] (TTSB)
ATLS..........	Atlas Air, Inc. [*NASDAQ symbol*] (SAG)
ATLS..........	Australian Transport Literature Informatin System [*Database on AUSINET*] (NITA)
AtlsAir........	Atlas Air, Inc. [*Associated Press*] (SAG)
AtlSeAir......	Atlantic Southeast Airlines [*Associated Press*] (SAG)
ATLSS.........	Center for Advanced Technology for Large Structural Systems [*Lehigh University*] [*Research center*] (RCD)
AtlTele........	Atlantic Tele-Network, Inc. [*Associated Press*] (SAG)
ATLV..........	Adult T-Cell Leukemia Virus
ATM	Abstract Test Method [*Telecommunications*] (OSI)
ATM	Access ATM Network, Inc. [*Toronto Stock Exchange symbol*]
ATM	Actuation Test Mode [*Automotive service*]
ATM	Acute Transverse Myelopathy [*Medicine*] (DMAA)
ATM	Address Translation Memory [*Computer science*] (IAA)
ATM	Adobe Type Manager [*Computer software*] [*Adobe Systems, Inc.*] (PCM)
ATM	Adoption Triangle Ministries [*Later, AFRC*] (EA)
ATM	Advanced Technology Maintenance [*British*] (NITA)
ATM	Advanced Telescope Mission [*Skylab*] [*NASA*]
ATM	Air Atlas/Air Maroc
ATM	Aircraft Thermal Management (MCD)
ATM	Aircrew Training Manual [*A publication*] (MCD)
ATM	Airlines of Tasmania [*Australia ICAO designator*] (FAAC)
ATM	Airspace and Traffic Management [*ICAO*] (DA)
ATM	Air Target Materials [*Military*]
ATM	Air Target Mosaic (MCD)
ATM	Air Traffic Management
ATM	Air Transportation Management (GAVI)
ATM	Air Turbine Motor
ATM	Altamira [*Brazil*] [*Airport symbol*] (OAG)
ATM	Altimeter Transmitter Multiplier (DNAB)
ATM	Aluminum Trimethyl [*Organic chemistry*]
ATM	Amici Thomae Mori [*Angers, France*] [*An association*] (EA)
AT/M	Ampere-Turn per Meter (MCD)
ATM	Ampere Turns per Motor (IAA)
ATM	Antarctic Treaty Meeting
ATM	Antenna Test Model
ATM	Antenna Turning Motor (IAA)
ATM	Antitactical Missile
ATM	Antitank Missile [*Army*]
ATM	Apollo Telescope Mount [*NASA*]
ATM	Arc Tangent Mechanism
ATM	Armament Technical Manual (SAA)
ATM	Armor Target Mechanism [*Army*]
ATM	Army TMDE Modernization (RDA)
ATM	Army Training Memorandum [*British*]
ATM	Assistant Traffic Manager
ATM	Associated Tobacco Manufacturers [*Defunct*] (EA)
ATM	Association of Teachers of Management [*British*]
ATM	Association of Teachers of Mathematics [*Derby, England*] (EAIO)
ATM	Association of Trailer Manufacturers [*British*] (DBA)
ATM	Asynchronous Time Multiplexing (IAA)
ATM	Asynchronous Traction Motor (PDAA)
ATM	Asynchronous Transfer Mode [*Computer science*]
ATM	Ataxia Telangiectasia Mutated
ATM	Ataxia Telangiectasia Mutated [*Medicine*]
ATM	Atmosphere
atm	Atmosphere, Standard [*Unit of pressure*]
ATM	Atomic Energy of Canada Ltd. Library [*UTLAS symbol*]
ATM	Atomic Mass (IIA)
ATM	At the Market [*Market order*] [*Stock exchange term*]
ATM	Augmented Telemetry
ATM	Australian Tax Monitor [*A publication*]
ATM	Australian Teachers of Media [*An association*]
ATM	Authentication Maneuver [*Aviation*] (FAAC)
ATM	Automated [*or Automatic*] Teller Machine [*Banking*]
ATM	Automatic Toning Machine [*Color printing technology*]
ATM	Auxiliary Tape Memory [*Spacecraft guidance*]
ATM	Axial Thrust Misalignment
ATM	Axial Turbo Machine
ATM	Thorsby Municipal Library, Alberta [*Library symbol National Library of Canada*] (NLC)
ATMA..........	Adhesive Tape Manufacturers Association (EAIO)
ATMA..........	Alabama Textile Manufacturers Association (SRA)
ATMA..........	American Textile Machinery Association (EA)
ATMA..........	American Tour Managers Association [*Defunct*] (EA)
ATMA..........	Antithyroid Plasma Membrane Antibody [*Medicine*] (DMAA)
ATMA..........	Associated Tie Manufacturers of Australia
ATMA..........	Australian Tire Manufacturers' Association
ATMAC........	Advanced Technology Microelectronic Array Computer (MCD)
ATMAC........	Air Traffic Management Automated Center (AABC)
ATMAT........	Atmospheric Attenuation of Sound (MCD)
ATMC..........	Advanced Technology Multimedia Communications (MCD)
ATMC..........	Airspace and Traffic Management Center (DA)

ATMC	Air Transport Movement Control Center
ATMC	Atomic
ATMC	Automotive Training Managers Council (EA)
ATMCC	Air Transport Movement Control Center [Military]
ATMCH	Association of Teachers of Maternal and Child Health (EA)
ATMCHG	Atmospheric Change (IAA)
ATMC(O)	Apollo Telescope Mount Console [NASA]
ATMCS	Army Tactical Multichannel Communications System (MCD)
AtMcS	Atlas Microfilming Service, Pennsauken, NJ [Library symbol] [Library of Congress] (LCLS)
ATM-D	Apollo Telescope Mount - Deployed [NASA] (MCD)
ATMDA	Apollo Telescope Mount Deployment Assembly [NASA]
ATMDC	Apollo Telescope Mount Digital Computer [NASA]
ATMDE	Army Theater Missile [Air] Defense Element [Army]
ATMDS	Antitank Mine Dispensing System (MCD)
ATME	Aluminum Tube Multi-Effect (PDAA)
ATME	American Textile Machinery Exhibition - Yarn, Fiber, and Non-Woven ManufacturingProcesses (ITD)
ATME	Association of Travel Marketing Executives (EA)
ATME	Atmospheric Transmission Measurement Equipment
ATME	Automatic Transmission Measuring Equipment [Telecommunications] (TEL)
Atmel	Atmel Corp. [Associated Press] (SAG)
ATMES	Atmosphere Transport Model Evaluation Study (OSRA)
ATMG	Angus Telemanagement Group, Inc. [Pickering, ON] [Information service or system Telecommunications] (TSSD)
ATMG	Arms Transfer Management Group
ATMG	Atomizing
ATMH	Automatic Test Message Handling (MCD)
ATMI	Advanced Technology Materials [NASDAQ symbol] (SAG)
ATMI	Advanced Technology Matr'l [NASDAQ symbol] (TTSB)
ATMI	American Textile Manufacturers Institute (EA)
ATMI	Association for Technology in Music Instruction (EA)
ATML	Atmel Corp. [NASDAQ symbol] (SPSG)
ATMN	Amalgamated Tin Mines of Nigeria
ATMO	Atmospheric
ATMOS	Atmos Energy Corp. [Associated Press] (SAG)
ATMOS	Atmosphere (KSC)
atmos	Atmosphere (VRA)
ATMOS	Atmospheric Trace Molecules Observed by Spectroscopy
ATMOS	Automatic Testing Multiple Operating System (MCD)
ATMP	Air Target Materials Program [Military] (AFM)
ATMP	All-Terrain Mobile Platform
ATMPR	Atmospheric Pressure (IAA)
ATMR	Advanced-Technology Medium-Range Transport
ATMS	Administrative Terminal Management System [Computer science] (HGAA)
ATMS	Administrative Transport Management Survey (MCD)
ATMS	Advanced Text Management System [IBM Corp.]
ATMS	Advanced Traffic Management System
ATMS	Air Traffic Management System [Army] (AABC)
ATM-S	Apollo Telescope Mount - Stowed [NASA] (MCD)
ATMS	Assembly Tracking and Management System (MCD)
ATMS	Association of Telephone Messaging Suppliers [Defunct] (EA)
ATMS	Assumption-Based Truth Maintenance System [Philosophy]
ATMS	Atmospheric Turbulence Measuring Set (MCD)
ATMS	Attitudes Toward Mainstreaming Scale [Psychology] (EDAC)
ATMS	Automatic Transmission Measuring System [Terminated]
ATMS	Automatic Trunk Measuring System [Bell System]
ATMSS	Automatic Telegraph Message Switching System (PDAA)
ATMT	Antitank Missile Test (MCD)
ATMT	Attempt (FAAC)
ATMTC	Attempt to Contact (FAAC)
ATMU	Aircraft Torpedo Maintenance Unit [Navy]
ATN	Actual Test Number [NASA]
ATN	Acute Tubular Necrosis [Nephrology]
ATN	Adaptive Tactical Navigation (MCD)
ATN	Aeronautical Telecommunications Network
ATN	Air Transport International [ICAO designator] (FAAC)
ATN	Alabama, Tennessee & Northern R. R. [AAR code]
ATN	Amateur Traffic Net [Radio]
ATN	Arts Training New South Wales [An association Australia]
ATN	Astrogeophysical Transmission Network [Air Force's Air Weather Service Teletypewriter circuit]
ATN	Atna Resources Ltd. [Vancouver Stock Exchange symbol]
ATN	Attention
ATN	Audio Teleconference Network [Acadia University] [Wolfville, NS] (TSSD)
ATN	Augmented Transition Network [Language analysis]
ATN	Australian Television Network
ATN	Autonomously Functioning Thyroid Nodule [Endocrinology]
ATN	Aviation Technician, Navigation
ATN	Avionics Technical Note
ATN	Helena/Fort Harrison, MT [Location identifier FAA] (FAAL)
ATN	Namatanai [Papua New Guinea] [Airport symbol] (OAG)
ATNAV	Acoustic Transponder Navigation (PDAA)
ATNC	Apparent Total Nitroso Compound [Organic chemistry]
ATNC	Atraumatic Normocephalic [Medicine]
ATNF	Australia Telescope National Facility
ATNG	AlaTenn Resources, Inc. [NASDAQ symbol] (NQ)
ATNI	Atlantic Tele-Network [NASDAQ symbol] (SPSG)
ATNM	Antitank, Nonmetallic
ATNO	Atomic Number
ATNR	Asymmetrical Tonic Neck Reflex
ATNSW	Adoptive Triangle New South Wales [Australia An association]

ATO	Abort-to-Orbit [NASA] (NASA)
ATO	Academy of Teachers of Occupations [Defunct] (EA)
ATO	Accelerated Take-Off [British military] (DMA)
ATO	Action Technical Order
ATO	Actual Time Over (MCD)
ATO	Aeronautical Telecommunications Officers (ADA)
ATO	Aeronautical Telecommunications Operator
ATO	Afghan Tourist Organization (MENA)
ATO	African Timber Organization (EAIO)
ATO	Agricultural Trade Office [Foreign Agricultural Service]
ATO	Aircraft Technical Order
ATO	Aircraft Transfer Order
ATO	Aircraft Transportation Officer [Navy] (DOMA)
ATO	Air Tactics Officer [Air Force]
ATO	Air Targets Officer
ATO	Air Tasking Order
ATO	Air Terminal Officer [Air Force]
ATO	Air Tonga [ICAO designator] (FAAC)
ATO	Air Traffic Operations Service [FAA] (TAG)
ATO	Air Training Officer [Air Force]
ATO	Air Transfer Order
ATO	Allied Travel Office (NATG)
ATO	Alpha Tau Omega [Fraternity]
ATO	Ammunition Technical Officer [Ireland]
ATO	Antarctic Treaty Organization (ASF)
ATO	Antimony Tin Oxide (IAA)
ATO	Apollo Test Operations [NASA] (KSC)
ATO	Approved Test Officer
ATO	Approved Training Organisation [Manpower Services Commission] (AIE)
ATO	Arab Towns Organization [Safat, Kuwait] (EAIO)
ATO	Area Traffic Officer
ATO	Army Tank Office (RDA)
ATO	Assisted Takeoff [British aviation and rocket term]
ATO	Athenaeum of Ohio, Norwood, OH [OCLC symbol] (OCLC)
ATO	Atlantic Ocean (SAA)
ATO	Atmos Energy Corp. [NYSE symbol] (SPSG)
ATO	At the Opening [Investment term]
ATO	Automatic Train Operation (BARN)
ATO	Automatic Trunk Office [Telecommunications] (OA)
ATO	Auto Transport de l'Ouest [Western Auto Transport] [Madagascar]
ATO	Aviation Test Office [Edwards Air Force Base, CA] [Army]
ATO	Ocean Tug, Old [Navy symbol]
ATO	Tomahawk Public Library, Alberta [Library symbol National Library of Canada] (NLC)
ATOA	Air Transport Operators Association (EAIO)
ATOA	American Truck Owners Association [New York, NY] (EA)
ATOA	American Tung Oil Association [Defunct]
AtoBond	AutoBond Acceptance Corp. [Associated Press] (SAG)
ATOC	Acoustic Thermometry of Ocean Climate [International oceanographic project]
ATOC	Acoustic Thermometry of Ocean Climate
ATOC	Acoustic Thermometry of Ocean Climate
ATOC	Air Tactical Operations Center [Military]
ATOC	Air Transport Operation Centre [Military British]
ATOC	Allied Tactical Operations Center [Military]
ATOC	Average Total Operating Cost (KSC)
A-to-D	Analog-to-Digital [Converter] [Computer science]
ATOE	American Theatre Organ Enthusiasts [Later, ATOS]
ATOF	Tofield Public Library, Alberta [Library symbol National Library of Canada] (NLC)
ATOFMS	Aerosol Time-of-Flight Mass Spectrometer
ATOG	Abnormal Transient Operational Guidelines [Nuclear energy] (NRCH)
ATOG	Air-to-Ground Gunnery (MCD)
ATOG	Allowable Takeoff Gross [Weight] [for an aircraft]
ATOG	Andover Togs, Inc. [NASDAQ symbol] (NQ)
ATOG	Anticipated Transient Operating Guideline [Nuclear energy] (NRCH)
ATOIC	Antiterrorism Operations and Intelligence Cell [Army]
A to K	Assault to Kill [FBI standardized term]
ATOL	Air Travel Organisers Licence [British]
ATOLL	Acceptance Test of Launch Language [NASA]
ATOLL	Atlantic Tropical Oceanic Lower Layer [National Oceanic and Atmospheric Administration]
ATOLS	Advanced Takeoff and Landing System (MCD)
ATOM	Advanced Technology of Management (SAA)
ATOM	Advisory, Training, and Operaions Mission (VNW)
ATOM	Against Testing on Mururoa [An association Australia]
ATOM	Analog Tree-Organized Multiplexer
ATOM	Antimony Trisisooctyl Mercaptoacetate (GNE)
ATOM	Apollo Telescope Orientation Mount Program [NASA] (MCD)
ATOM	Arizona Trade-Off Model [State of Arizona and Department of Commerce project to resolve conflicts between economic and environmental goals]
ATOM	Astronomical Telescope Orientation Mount [NASA]
ATOM	Automatic Topographic Mapper
ATOM	Automatic Transmission of Mail [Early electronic mail system]
ATOMDEF	Atomic Defense
ATOMDEV	Atomic Device [Military]
Atom Energy LJ	Atomic Energy Law Journal [A publication] (DLA)
Atom Energy LJ	Atomic Energy Law Journal [A publication] (AAGC)
Atom En L Rep CCH	Atomic Energy Law Reporter (Commerce Clearing House) [A publication] (DLA)
ATOMIC	Automated Train Operation by Minicomputer [Computer science] (PDAA)
ATOMS	Air Traffic Operations Management System [FAA] (TAG)

ATOMS .... Automated Technical Order Maintenance Sequences [*or Systems*] [*The Boeing Co.*] (MCD)
ATOMSTATSREP... Atomic Status Report (NATG)
ATON .... Aids to Navigation
A to N.......... Aids to Navigation
Aton.......... Atonement
ATONU........ Assistance Technique de l'Organisation des Nations Unies
A to OC........ Attached to Other Correspondence [*Business term*]
ATOP .... Ambient Temperature Observer/Predictor (MCD)
ATOP .... Australian Taxation Office Practice [*A publication*]
A to P .... Authority to Prospect (ADA)
ATOP .... Automated Traffic Overload Protection (DNAB)
ATOPS .... Advanced Transport Operating System (MCD)
ATOR .... Australian Torts Reporter [*A publication*]
ATORP .... Antitorpedo (MSA)
ATORP .... Atomic Torpedo [*Military*]
ATOS .... American Theatre Organ Society (EA)
ATOS .... Assisted Takeoff System
ATOS .... Association of Temporary Office Services
ATOS .... Automated Technical Order System [*Air Force*] (MCD)
ATOT.......... Actual Time over Target (AFM)
ATOT.......... Angle Track on Target [*Military*]
ATOVS .... Advanced TIROS [*Television Infrared Observation Satellite*] Operational Vertical Sounder
ATOWA .... Australian Tug-of-War Association
ATOWG .... Advanced Technical Objective Working Group
ATOY .... American Toys, Inc. [*NASDAQ symbol*] (SAG)
ATOY .... Amer Toys [*NASDAQ symbol*] (TTSB)
AToys.......... American Toys, Inc. [*Associated Press*] (SAG)
ATOYW .... American Toys Wrrt [*NASDAQ symbol*] (TTSB)
ATOYZ .... American Toys Non-Red Wrrt [*NASDAQ symbol*] (TTSB)
ATP.......... Accelerator-Tritium Producer [*Nuclear physics*]
ATP.......... Acceptance Test Plan [*or Procedure*]
ATP.......... Accord Transports Permissables [*European agreement on the transport of perishable foodstuffs*]
ATP.......... Acquisition, Tracking, and Pointing [*Military*] (SDI)
ATP.......... Action Table Print (SAA)
ATP.......... Activation Test Program (MCD)
ATP.......... Actual Time of Penetration [*Aviation*] (FAAC)
ATP.......... Adenosine Triphosphate [*Biochemistry*]
ATP.......... Admissions Testing Program
ATP.......... Adult Employment Training Programme [*British*] (AIE)
ATP.......... Advanced Tactical Processor
ATP.......... Advanced Tactical Prototype (DOMA)
ATP.......... Advanced Technical Payload (SAA)
ATP.......... Advanced Technology Park
ATP.......... Advanced Technology Program [*Department of Commerce*]
ATP.......... Advanced Technology Pultrusion
ATP.......... Advanced Telescopes Project [*University of Colorado*] [*Research center*] (RCD)
ATP.......... Advanced Test in Psychology
ATP.......... Advanced Tracking Program (MCD)
ATP.......... Advanced Turboprop [*Aeronautics*]
ATP.......... Advance Test Plant (AAG)
ATP.......... Aerotransportes Especiales Ltda. [*Colombia*] [*ICAO designator*] (FAAC)
ATP.......... Affiliation Testing Program [*for Catholic secondary schools*] (AEBS)
ATP.......... Agence Tchadienne de Presse [*Chadian Press Agency*] (AF)
ATP.......... Agence Transcontinentale de Presse [*Transcontinental Press Agency*] [*France*] (AF)
ATP.......... Agreement for the International Transport of Perishable Products
ATP.......... Aid and Trade Provision [*Shipping*] (DS)
ATP.......... Aircraft Technical Publishers [*Information service or system*] (IID)
ATP.......... Airline Tariff Publishing Co.
ATP.......... Airline Transport Pilot [*Certificate*] [*British*] (IEEE)
ATP.......... Air Tactical Publication
ATP.......... Air Traffic Procedures
ATP.......... Air Travel Plan (IIA)
ATP.......... Aitape [*Papua New Guinea*] [*Airport symbol*] (OAG)
ATP.......... Alcohol Treatment Program
ATP.......... Alert Transmit Panel (SAA)
ATP.......... Allied Tactical Publication [*Army NATO*]
ATP.......... Allied Technical Publication [*Navy NATO*]
ATP.......... Alternate Target Point
ATP.......... Alternate Test Procedure [*for aviation jet fuels*] [*Navy*]
ATP.......... Alternative Term Plan (IIA)
ATP.......... American Telephone & Telegraph Co., Technical Process, Piscataway, NJ [*OCLC symbol*] (OCLC)
ATP.......... American Theater Productions, Inc.
ATP.......... Ammunition Transfer Point [*or Pack*] (MCD)
ATP.......... Anode Tapping Point (IAA)
ATP.......... Antitorque Pedal
ATP.......... AppleTalk Transaction Protocol [*Apple Computer, Inc.*]
ATP.......... Application Transaction Program (ACRL)
ATP.......... Appropriate Technology Project [*Maintained by the Volunteers in Asia*]
ATP.......... Army Tank Plant
ATP.......... Army Tank Program (MCD)
ATP.......... Army Training Plan (MCD)
ATP.......... Army Training Program
ATP.......... Array Transform Processor
ATP.......... Assembly Test Program (IAA)
ATP.......... Association for the Teaching of Psychology [*British*]
ATP.......... Association for Transpersonal Psychology (EA)
ATP.......... Association of Technical Professionals [*Defunct*] (EA)

ATP.......... Association of Tennis Professionals [*Defunct*] (EA)
ATP.......... Association of Tequila Producers (EA)
ATP.......... Association of Transportation Practitioners (EA)
ATP.......... Astronautics Test Procedures (AAG)
ATP.......... Atlas Pacific Limited [*All Symbol*] (TTSB)
AtP.......... Attending Physician (DMAA)
ATP.......... Augmented Thrust Propulsion
ATP.......... Authority to Participate Card
ATP.......... Authority to Proceed (MCD)
ATP.......... Authorization to Purchase [*Food stamp card*] [*Department of Agriculture*]
ATP.......... Automated Test Plan (BUR)
ATP.......... Automatic Train Protection [*TRB*] (TAG)
ATP.......... Auxiliary Tool Production (MCD)
ATP.......... Power Control Technologies [*NYSE symbol*] (TTSB)
ATP.......... Power Control Technologies, Inc. [*NYSE symbol*] (SAG)
ATPA.......... Alpha Temperature Probe Assembly [*NASA*] (MCD)
ATPA.......... Andean Trade Preference Act
ATPA.......... Arizona Travel Parks Association (SRA)
ATPA.......... Australian Tin Producers' Association
ATPA.......... Australian Tomato Processors' Association
ATPA.......... Auto Theft Prevention Authority
ATPA.......... Auxiliary Turbopump Assembly
ATPAC.......... Air Traffic Procedures Advisory Committee [*FAA*] (TAG)
ATPAM.......... Association of Theatrical Press Agents and Managers (EA)
ATPAS.......... Association of Teachers of Printing and Allied Subjects [*British*]
ATP-ASCP.... Army Transportation Plan in Support of the Army Strategic Capabilities Plan (AABC)
ATPase .... Adenosine Triphosphatase [*An enzyme*]
ATPC.......... Assist for Telecommunications Program and Control (IAA)
ATPC.......... Association of Temporary Personnel Contractors
ATPC.......... Association of Tin Producing Countries [*Australia*]
ATPC.......... Athey Products [*NASDAQ symbol*] (TTSB)
ATPC.......... Athey Products Corp. [*NASDAQ symbol*] (NQ)
ATPC.......... Australian Tin Producers' Council
ATPCC .... Attitudes toward Parental Control of Children [*Psychology*]
ATPCO .... Airline Tariff Publishing Co. (IID)
ATPD.......... Aid to the Totally and Permanently Disabled [*Social Security Administration*] (OICC)
ATPD .... Ambient Temperature and Pressure, Dry [*Medicine*]
ATPDC .... Atomic Transition Probabilities Data Center
ATPE.......... Association of Teachers in Penal Establishments [*British*]
ATPE.......... Association of Texas Professional Educators (SRA)
ATPF.......... Armament Test Preparation Facility
ATP-FC ...... Acquisition, Tracking, Pointing, and Fire Control [*Military*] (SDI)
ATPFS.......... Air Transportable Pantograph Fueling System (MCD)
ATPG.......... Automatic Test Pattern [*or Program*] Generation (MCD)
ATPI.......... American Tax Policy Institute (EA)
ATPI.......... American Textbook Publishers Institute [*Later, AAP*] (EA)
ATPI.......... American Transfer Printing Institute [*Later, ITPI*] (EA)
ATPL.......... Airline Transport Pilot's Licence [*British*] (DBQ)
AT Plas .... AT Plastics, Inc. [*Associated Press*] (SAG)
ATPLO .... Army of Tripura People's Liberation Organization [*India*] (PD)
ATPM.......... Association of Teachers of Preventive Medicine (EA)
ATPM.......... Association of Toilet Paper Manufacturers [*British*] (BI)
ATPM.......... Association of Touring and Production Managers [*British*] (BI)
ATPO .... Associate Technical Project Officer
ATPOS .... Atomic Post-Strike Analysis Report
ATPQ.......... Acetylene-Terminated Phenylquinoxaline [*Polymer technology*]
ATPR.......... Advanced Triga Prototype Reactor
ATPr.......... ALLTEL Corp. $2.06 Cv Pfd [*NYSE symbol*] (TTSB)
ATPR.......... Annual Technical Progress Report
ATPR (Com)... Australian Trade Practices Reporter. Commission Decisions [*A publication*]
ATPR (Digest)... Australian Trade Practices Reporter. Cases and Decisions Digest [*A publication*]
ATPS.......... Alternate Thermal Protection System (MCD)
ATPS.......... Ambient Temperature and Pressure, Saturated [*Medicine*]
ATPS.......... AppleTalk Print Service [*Apple Computer, Inc.*] (PCM)
A Tps .... Army Troops [*British and Canadian*] [*World War II*]
ATPS.......... Automatic Type Placement System
ATPSK .... Adjacent Tone-Reference Phase-Shift Keying [*Computer science*] (IAA)
ATPsych....... Association for Teaching of Psychology [*British*] (DBA)
ATPU .... Air Transport Pressurizing Unit
ATQ.......... Air Transport Schiphol [*Netherlands ICAO designator*] (FAAC)
ATQ.......... Amritsar [*India*] [*Airport symbol*] (OAG)
ATQMRA...... American Three-Quarter Midget Racing Association [*Auto racing*]
ATR.......... Acceptance Test Report (MCD)
ATR.......... Achates Resources Ltd. [*Vancouver Stock Exchange symbol*]
ATR.......... Achilles Tendon Reflex [*Neurology*]
ATR.......... Actual Time of Refueling (SAA)
ATR.......... Advanced Tactical RADAR [*Army*] (MCD)
ATR.......... Advanced Technical Requirements [*DoD*]
ATR.......... Advanced Telecommunication Research
ATR.......... Advanced Test Reactor [*Nuclear energy*]
ATR.......... Advanced Thermal Reactor
ATR.......... Advance Tax Rulings [*Also, Tax Advance Rulings*] [*Database*] (IID)
ATR.......... Advance Technical Requirements (MCD)
ATR.......... Aided Target Recognition [*Army*]
ATR.......... Airborne Test Reactor (SAA)
ATR.......... Aircraft Transmitter-Receiver (IAA)
ATR.......... Aircraft Trouble Report
ATR.......... Air-Launched Trainer Rocket (AFM)
ATR.......... Airline Transport Rating (IIA)

ATR	Air Traffic Regulations
ATR	Air Transportation Rack [*NASA*] (NASA)
ATR	Air Transport of Radiation
ATR	Air Transport Radio [*NASA*] (NASA)
ATR	Air Turbo Rocket
ATR	All Transistor (IAA)
ATR	Ambient Temperature Range
ATR	Americans for Tax Reform (EA)
ATR	Analog Tape Recorder
ATR	Angle, Time, Range [*Computer science*]
ATR	Answering Time Recorder [*Telecommunications*] (TEL)
ATR	Antenna Transmit Receive (IAA)
ATR	Antitank Regiment [*Military*]
ATR	Anti-Torture Research [*Copenhagen, Denmark*] [*An association*] (EAIO)
ATR	Anti-Transmit-Receive
ATR	Apollo Test Requirements [*NASA*] (KSC)
ATR	Apprenticeship and Training Representative [*Bureau of Apprenticeship and Training*] [*Department of Labor*]
ATR	Aptargroup, Inc. [*NYSE symbol*] (SAG)
ATR	AptarGroup Inc. [*NYSE symbol*] (TTSB)
ATR	Art Therapist, Registered
ATR	Assembly Test Record (IAA)
ATR	Association of Teachers of Russian [*British*]
ATR	Atar [*Mauritania*] [*Airport symbol*] (OAG)
ATR	Atlantic Richfield Co., Geoscience Library, Dallas, TX [*OCLC symbol*] (OCLC)
ATR	Atlantic Tracking Range [*NASA*]
ATR	Atlas Airlines [*ICAO designator*] (FAAC)
ATR	Atresia [*Medicine*]
atr	Atrial [*Cardiology*] (DAVI)
atr	Atrophy (MAE)
ATR	Attenuated Total Reflectance [*Instrumentation*]
ATR	Attribute
ATR	Audiotape Recorder (WDMC)
ATR	Audio Tape Recording
ATR	Austin Trumbull Radio [*Air transport radio prior to April 15, 1967*] (MCD)
ATR	Automated Target Recognition [*Military*]
ATR	Automatic Tape Reader (DNAB)
ATR	Automatic Target Recognition
ATR	Automatic Traffic Recorder [*Telecommunications*] (NITA)
ATR	Automatic Trunk Routiner (MCD)
ATR	Automotive Test Rig [*Military*] (RDA)
ATR	Aviation Technician, RADAR
ATR	Aviation Training Record
ATR	Rescue Ocean Tug [*Navy symbol*]
ATR	Star [*Mauritania*] [*Airport symbol*] (AD)
ATR	Waterloo, DE [*Location identifier FAA*] (FAAL)
ATRA	Advanced Transit Association (EA)
A-TRA	Akhal-Teke Registry of America (EA)
ATRA	Alberta Therapeutic Riding Association (AC)
ATRA	All-Terrain Racing Association (EA)
ATRA	All-Trans-Retinoc Acid [*Medicine*]
ATRA	American Therapeutic Recreation Association (EA)
ATRA	American Tort Reform Association (EA)
ATRA	American Toy Retailers Association (EA)
ATRA	Automatic Tracking Razor Action [*The Gillette Co.*]
ATRA	Automatic Transmission Rebuilders Association (EA)
ATRAC	Angle Tracking Computer (MHDI)
ATRAN	Automatic Terrain Recognition and Navigation Guidance System
ATRANH	Auto and Truck Recyclers Association of New Hampshire (SRA)
A/TRANS	Automatic Transmission [*Automotive engineering*]
ATRAP	Automatic Technical Reliability Assessment of PATRIOT [*Phased Array Tracking to Intercept of Target*]
ATRAQ	Associations Touristiques Regionales Associees du Quebec [*Quebec Regional Tourist Associations Inc.*] (AC)
ATravel	American Travellers Corp. [*Associated Press*] (SAG)
ATRAX	Air Transportable Communications Complex
ATRC	Advanced Television Research Consortium (PS)
ATRC	Advanced Test Reactor Critical Facility [*Nuclear energy*]
ATRC	Air Traffic Regulation Center (AFM)
ATRC	Air Training Command [*Air Force*]
ATRC	Antitracking Control
ATRC	Arizona Transportation Research Center [*Arizona State University*] [*Research center*] (RCD)
ATRC	Army Transportation Research Command
ATRC	Atria Communities, Inc. [*NASDAQ symbol*] (SAG)
ATRCE	Advanced Test Reactor Critical Experiment [*Nuclear energy*]
ATRCF	Advanced Test Reactor Critical Facility [*Nuclear energy*] (GFGA)
ATRCH	Association to Resource Co-Operative Housing [*Australia*]
ATRCV	All-Terrain Remote Control Vehicle (MCD)
ATRD	Automatic Target Recognition Device
ATRDB	Army Terrain Requirements Data Base
ATRE	Animal Tumor Research Facility [*Rochester University*] (PDAA)
ATRE	Appletree Companies [*NASDAQ symbol*] (SAG)
ATREP	Air Traffic Representative (FAAC)
At Rep	Atlantic Reporter [*A publication*] (DLA)
ATREX	Astrophysics Transient Explorer
atr fib	Atrial Fibrillation [*Cardiology*] (MAE)
ATRHTRBAA	Association to Remind Husbands to Remember Birthdays and Anniversaries [*Probably mythical*]
ATRI	Air Transportable Radio Installations
ATRI	Artists Technical Research Institute (EA)
ATRI	Atrion Corp. [*NASDAQ symbol*] (SAG)

ATRI	Atrion Corp. [*NASDAQ symbol*] (TTSB)
ATRI	Australian Timber Research Institute
ATRI	Australian Tourism Research Institute
ATRI	Auto and Truck Recyclers of Illinois (SRA)
AtriaCo	Atria Communities, Inc. [*Associated Press*] (SAG)
AtriaSft	Atria Software, Inc. [*Associated Press*] (SAG)
ATRIB	Average Transfer Rate of Information BITS [*Binary Digits*] [*Computer science*] (IEEE)
ATRID	Automatic Target Recognition, Identification, and Detection
ATRID	Automatic Terrain Recognition and Identification Device (PDAA)
ATRIF	Air Transportation Research International Forum (MCD)
ATRIMA	As Their Respective Interests May Appear [*Legal term*] (ADA)
Atrion	Atrion Corp. [*Associated Press*] (SAG)
ATRIP	Asociacion Internacional para el Progreso de la Ensenanza y de la Investigacion de la Propiedad Intelectual [*International Association for the Advancement of Teaching and Research in Intellectual Property*] (EAIO)
ATRIP	International Association for the Advancement of Teaching and Research in Intellectual Property (EA)
ATRIS	Air Traffic Regulation Identification System [*Army*]
ATRIS	Air Transportation Research Information Service [*National Academy of Sciences*] [*Information service or system*]
AtrixInt	Atrix International, Inc. [*Associated Press*] (SAG)
AtrixL	Atrix Laboratories, Inc. [*Associated Press*] (SAG)
ATRJ	Advanced Threat Radar Jammer [*DoD*]
ATRL	Antitank Rocket Launcher Imagery Interpretation (AABC)
ATRLS	Actual Time of Release [*Aviation*]
ATRM	Acute Transient Radiation Myelopathy [*Oncology*]
ATRM	Aetrium, Inc. [*NASDAQ symbol*] (SAG)
ATRM	After Torpedo Room
ATRM	American Tax Reduction Movement (EA)
ATRM	Association Touristique Regionale de la Monteregie (AC)
ATRM	Trochu Municipal Library, Alberta [*Library symbol National Library of Canada*] (NLC)
ATRMRD	Air Toxics and Radiation Monitoring Research Division [*Environmental Protection Agency*] (EPA)
ATRN	Army Tactical Requirements for National Reconnaissance (MCD)
ATrnz	AmerTranz Worldwide Holding Corp. [*Associated Press*] (SAG)
ATRO	Acting Transportation Officer
ATRO	Actual Time of Return to Operation (AFM)
ATRO	Astronics Corp. [*NASDAQ symbol*] (NQ)
ATRON	Atlantic Squadron
ATRP	Air Transport Regulation Panel [*ICAO*] (DA)
ATrP	Allied Training Publications [*NATO*] (NATG)
ATRP	American Tax Reform Project (EA)
ATRP	Atom Transfer Radical Polymerization [*Chemistry*]
ATRR	Allocated Transfer Risk Reserve [*Banking*]
ATRRS	Army Training Requirements and Resources System
ATRS	Advanced Tactical Reconnaissance System (MCD)
ATRS	Advanced Technology Rotor System (MCD)
ATRS	Air, Toxics, and Radiation Staff [*Environmental Protection Agency*] (GFGA)
ATRS	Assembly Test Recording System
ATRS	Automatic Temporary Roof Support [*Mining industry*]
ATRSC	American Tan Rabbit Specialty Club (EA)
ATRSO	Accepts Transfer as Offered (NOAA)
ATRT	Anti-Transmit-Receive Tube
ATrT	Troy State University, Troy, AL [*Library symbol Library of Congress*] (LCLS)
ATrT-N	Troy State University, School of Nursing, Montgomery, AL [*Library symbol Library of Congress*] (LCLS)
ATRU	Australian Income Tax Rulings [*A publication*]
ATRVAL	Attribute Value (MHDI)
ATRX	Atrix Laboratories [*NASDAQ symbol*] (TTSB)
ATRX	Atrix Laboratories, Inc. [*NASDAQ symbol*] (SAG)
ATS	Absolute Temperature Scale
ATS	Abstract Test Suite [*Telecommunications*] (OSI)
ATS	Academically Talented Student
ATS	Accelerometer-Timer Switch (IAA)
ATS	Acceptance Test Specification [*DoD*]
ATS	Acetylene-Terminated Sulfone [*Organic chemistry*]
ATS	Achard-Thiers Syndrome [*Medicine*] (DMAA)
ATS	Acoustic Target Sensor
ATS	Acoustic Telemetry Subsystem (MCD)
ATS	Acoustic Transmission System
ATS	Acquisition and Tracking System
ATS	Acquisition Target and Search
ATS	Action Tracking System [*Environmental Protection Agency*] (GFGA)
ATS	Active Television System (MCD)
ATS	Adjustable Thigh Antiembolism Stockings [*Cardiology*] (DAVI)
ATS	Administrative Terminal System [*IBM Corp.*]
ATS	Administrator's Tracking System [*Environmental Protection Agency*] (GFGA)
ATS	Adult Training Strategy (AIE)
ATS	Advanced Tactical Strike (MCD)
ATS	Advanced Tactical Support [*Aircraft*] [*Navy*] (DOMA)
ATS	Advanced Technology Satellite
ATS	Advanced Technology Spacecraft [*NASA*] (MCD)
ATS	Advanced Technology Systems, Inc. [*Arlington, VA*] [*Telecommunications*] (TSSD)
ATS	Advanced Teleprocessing System (IAA)
ATS	Advanced Television Services [*FCC*] (NTCM)
ATS	Advanced Training System [*Air Force*]
ATS	Advanced Turbo Systems [*Automotive industry supplier*]
ATS	Aeronautical Training Society

ATS............. Aerospace Test System (MCD)
ATS............. Agence Telegraphique Suisse [*Swiss News Agency*] [*Berne, Switzerland*]
ATS............. Aided Tracking System (IAA)
ATS............. Aircraft Trouble-Shooting System (MCD)
ATS............. Aircrew Training System (MCD)
ATS............. Air-Cure Technologies, Inc. [*AMEX symbol*] (SAG)
ATS............. Airmanship Training Squadron [*Air Force*]
ATS............. Air Tactical School [*Air Force*]
ATS............. Air Technical Service (IAA)
ATS............. Air Temperature Sensor [*Automotive engineering*]
ATS............. Air-to-Ship (DNAB)
ATS............. Air-to-Surface [*Missiles*] (MCD)
ATS............. Air Traffic Section (AFM)
ATS............. Air Traffic Service [*of FAA*] [*Also known as AAT, AT*]
ATS............. Air Transportable SONAR
ATS............. Air Transport Service [*Zaire*] [*ICAO designator*] (FAAC)
ATS............. Air Transport Service [*Navy*]
ATS............. Air Transport Squadron [*Air Force*] (MCD)
ATS............. Air Transport Statistics
ATS............. Air Turbine Starter (NG)
ATS............. Alarm Termination Subsystem [*Telecommunications*] (TEL)
ATS............. Alexis De Tocqueville Society (EA)
ATS............. Alkali-Tin-Silicate [*Glass for possible nuclear waste storage*]
ATS............. Alkali-Treated Straw (PDAA)
ATS............. Alliance for Traffic Safety (EA)
ATS............. Alliance of Transylvanian Saxons [*Cleveland, OH*] (EA)
ATS............. American Tarantula Society [*Defunct*] (EA)
ATS............. American Teachers' Series [*A publication*]
ATS............. American Technical Society
ATS............. American Television Society (NTCM)
ATS............. American Temperance Society [*Later, AHTS*] (EA)
ATS............. American Tentative Society
ATS............. American Theatre Society [*Commercial firm*] (EA)
ATS............. American Theological Society - Midwest Division (EA)
ATS............. American Therapeutic Society [*Later, American Society for Clinical Pharmacologyand Therapeutics*] (EA)
ATS............. American Thermographic Society [*Later, American Academy of Thermology*] (EA)
ATS............. American Thesaurus of Slang
ATS............. American Thoracic Society (EA)
ATS............. American Tolkien Society (EA)
ATS............. American Tract Society (EA)
ATS............. American Trauma Society (EA)
ATS............. American Travel Survey [*BTS*] (TAG)
ATS............. American Trudeau Society [*Later, American Thoracic Society*]
ATS............. American-Turkish Society (EA)
ATS............. Ammonium Thiosulfate [*Fertilizer*]
ATS............. Analog Tone Signal (MCD)
ATS............. Analytic Trouble Shooting (MHDB)
ATS............. Angle Tracking System [*NASA*]
ATS............. Animal-Tub-Sized [*Paper*]
ATS............. Antarctic Treaty System
ATS............. Antirat Thymocyte Serum [*Medicine*] (DMAA)
ATS............. Antitetanus Serum [*Medicine*]
ATS............. Antithymocyte Serum [*Immunochemistry*]
ATS............. Anxiety Tension State [*Psychology*]
ATS............. Apparent Time at Ship (DS)
ATS............. Applicant Tracking System [*Human resources*] (WYGK)
ATS............. Applications Technology Satellite [*Communications satellite*] [*NASA*]
ATS............. Application Transfer Study [*IBM problem solving process*]
ATS............. APT Satellite Holdings Ltd. [*NYSE symbol*] (SAG)
ATS............. Armament Training Station [*Military*] (OA)
ATS............. Army Technical School [*British military*] (DMA)
ATS............. Army Telecommunications System (GFGA)
ATS............. Army Topographic Station (AABC)
ATS............. Army Transport Service [*Later, Military Sea Transportation Service, then Military Sealift Command*] [*Obsolete*]
ATS............. Arteriosclerosis [*Medicine*] (MAE)
ATS............. Artesia, NM [*Location identifier FAA*] (FAAL)
ATS............. Arturo Toscanini Society (EA)
ATS............. Assembly Truss and Structure (SSD)
ATS............. Assistant Traffic Supervisor (DCTA)
ATS............. Associated Technical Services, Inc. [*Glen Ridge, NJ*] [*Information service or system*]
ATS............. Associated Training Specialist (SAA)
ATS............. Associate of Theological Study [*British*]
ATS............. Association for Transarmament Studies [*Later, CBDA*] (EA)
ATS............. Association of Theological Schools (EA)
ATS............. Association of Theological Schools in the United States and Canada (PGP)
ATS............. Astronomical Time Switch
ATS............. Asymptotic Threshold Shift [*Hearing*]
ATS............. Asynchronous Task Storage [*NASA*] (NASA)
ATS............. AT & T Transfer System [*Telecommunications*]
ATS............. Atherosclerosis [*Cardiology*] (DAVI)
ATS............. Atlantic Shopping Centres Ltd. [*Toronto Stock Exchange symbol*]
ATS............. Atlantic Test Site (SAA)
ATS............. Atlantic Tracking Ship [*NASA*] (KSC)
ATS............. Atlantic Trade Study
ATS............. At the Suit Of
ATS............. Attitude Thrustor System
ATS............. Attitude Transfer System (MCD)
ATS............. Audio Test Set (NITA)
ATS............. Authorized Terminal Strength

ATS............. Automated Telecommunications System [*Army*] (ADDR)
ATS............. Automated Time Standards (MCD)
ATS............. Automated Trading System [*NYSE computer*]
ATS............. Automatic Tally and Sort (PDAA)
ATS............. Automatic Telemetry System
ATS............. Automatic Telephone Set
ATS............. Automatic Terminal System [*NASA*] (NASA)
ATS............. Automatic Test Scoring
ATS............. Automatic Test System
ATS............. Automatic Throttle/Speed Control System (MCD)
ATS............. Automatic Train Stop (SAA)
ATS............. Automatic Train Supervision (BARN)
ATS............. Automatic Transfer of Savings [*Banking*]
ATS............. Automatic Transfer Service [*Banking*]
ATS............. Automatic Transfer Switch
ATS............. Automatic Transfer Switches [*Standby electrical power systems*]
ATS............. Automatic Transmission System [*Telecommunications*] (NTCM)
ATS............. Automatic Trim System (PDAA)
ATS............. Automatic Trunk Synchronizer [*Telecommunications*] (TEL)
ATS............. Automatic Tuning System
ATS............. Automobili Turismo Sport [*Auto manufacturing company*] [*Italy*]
ATS............. Auxiliary Territorial Service [*Later, WRAC*] [*British women's service*] [*World War II*]
ATS............. Auxiliary Tug Service (PDAA)
ATS............. Aviation Transport Services [*Italy ICAO designator*] (FAAC)
ATS............. Avionics Test Station (MCD)
ATS............. Avionic Test Set (MCD)
ATS-- .... Salvage and Rescue Ship [*Navy symbol*]
a-ts-- .... Trucial States [*United Arab Emirates*] [*MARC geographic area code Library of Congress*] (LCCP)
ATS............. [*A*] Tutorial System [*1971*] [*Computer science*] (CSR)
ATS............. United States Army Troop Support and Aviation Material Readiness Command, St. Louis, MO [*OCLC symbol*] (OCLC)
ATSA.......... Advanced Tactical Support Aircraft [*Navy*] (DOMA)
ATSA.......... Aero Transportes Sociedad Anonima [*Mexican airline*]
ATSA.......... American Tarpan Studbook Association (EA)
ATSA.......... American Traffic Services Association [*Later, ATSSA*] (EA)
ATSA.......... American Tramp Shipowners Association (EA)
ATSA.......... Association of Technical Studies Advisers [*British*]
ATSA.......... Australian Transplant Sports Association
ATSAC .... Association of Theatre Screen Advertising Companies [*Defunct*]
ATSAC .... Automated Traffic Surveillance and Control [*Automotive engineering*]
ATS/AD ...... Air Turbine Starter/Accessory Drive (MCD)
ATSAQ .... Association des Techniciens en Sante Animal du Quebec (AC)
ATSB .... Advanced Tactical Support Base [*Navy*] (NVT)
ATSB .... Airborne Test Safety Board (MCD)
ATSB .... AmTrust Capital [*NASDAQ symbol*] (TTSB)
ATSB .... AmTrust Capital Corp. [*NASDAQ symbol*] (SAG)
ATSC .... Advanced Television Systems Committee [*FCC*] (NTCM)
ATSC .... Advanced TV Systems Committee (EA)
ATSC .... Air Technical Service Command [*Air Force*]
ATSC .... Air Traffic Service Communications [*Communications related to air traffic services.*] (GAVI)
ATSC .... Air Turbine Starter, Cartridge (MCD)
ATSC .... American Torah Shelemah Committee (EA)
ATSC .... Army Technical Service Corps
ATSC .... Army Training Support Center [*Fort Eustis, VA*]
ATSC .... Associate in the Technology of Surface Coatings [*British*] (DBQ)
ATSC .... Atlanta Service Center [*IRS*]
ATSC .... Australian Telecommunication Standardization Committee (ACRL)
ATSCCP ..... Air Traffic Service Contingency Command Post (FAAC)
ATSCV .... Air Turbine Starter Control Value (MCD)
ATSD .... Airborne Traffic Situation Display [*FAA*]
ATSD .... Arctic Tent Stake Driver (MCD)
ATSD .... Assembly Type Supply Directive [*Military*] (AFIT)
ATSD .... Assistant to the Secretary of Defense (DOMA)
ATSDA .... American Tang Soo Do Association [*Defunct*] (EA)
ATSDA .... Arizona Tire and Service Dealers Association (SRA)
ATSD (AE) ... Assistant to the Secretary of Defense (Atomic Energy)
ATSD(IO) .... Assistant to the Secretary of Defense (Intelligence Oversight) (DOMA)
ATSD(IP)..... Assistant to the Secretary of Defense (Intelligence Policy) (DOMA)
ATSDR .... Agency for Toxic Substances and Disease Registry [*Atlanta, GA*] [*Department of Health and Human Services*]
ATSDR .... Attente [*Leave on*] [*Knitting term*] [*French*] (BARN)
ATSD(R & O)... Assistant to the Secretary of Defense (Review and Oversight)
ATSE .... Advanced Throttling Slurry Engine (KSC)
ATSE .... Automatic Test Set [*Support*] [*Military*] (DOMA)
ATSER .... Agency for Toxic Substances and Emergency Response
ATSES .... Assembly Time Standard Estimating Sheet (MCD)
AtSetBib ..... Atti della Settimana Biblica [*A publication*] (BJA)
ATSF .... American Truck Stop Foundation (EA)
ATSF .... [*The*] Atchison, Topeka & Santa Fe Railway Co. [*Also known as Santa Fe*] [*AAR code*]
ATSF .... Automatic Target Selection File (CINC)
ATSFSD ...... Air Traffic Service Flight Services Division [*of FAA*]
ATSG .... Acoustic Test Signal Generator (CAAL)
ATSI .... Association of Telemessaging Services International (EA)
ATSI .... ATS Medical [*NASDAQ symbol*] (TTSB)
ATSI .... ATS Medical, Inc. [*NASDAQ symbol*] (SAG)
ATSILRN ...... Aboriginal and Torres Strait Islander Library and Resource Network [*Australia*]
ATSILS .... Aboriginal and Torres Strait Islander Legal Service [*Australia*]
ATSIT .... Automatic Techniques for Selection and Identification of Targets [*Army/Air Force*] (MCD)

ATSIW .... ATS Med Inc. Wrrt [*NASDAQ symbol*] (TTSB)
ATSJEA ...... Automatic Test System Jet Engine Accessories
ATSM .... Advanced Tactical Stand-Off Missile (MCD)
ATS(M) .... Air Transportation Squadron (Medium)
ATS M .... ATS Medical, Inc. [*Associated Press*] (SAG)
ATSM .... Automated Technique for Spacecraft Monitoring [*NASA*]
ATS Med ..... ATS Medical, Inc. [*Associated Press*] (SAG)
ATSO .... Advanced Telecommunications Sciences Office [*STRATCOM*] [*Army*] (RDA)
ATSO .... Air Traffic Services Organization [*Military*] (DOMA)
ATSOA .... Association of Trading Standards Officers [*British*] (DBA)
ATSOA .... American Truck Stop Operators Association (EA)
ATSOCC ...... Applications Technology Satellite Operations Control Center [*NASA*]
ATSORA ...... Air Traffic Services Outside Regulated Airspace [*British*] (DA)
ATSP .... Air Transport Statistical Programme [*International Civil Aviation Authority*] [*Canada*] (NITA)
ATSP .... Aristo International [*NASDAQ symbol*] (TTSB)
ATSP .... Aristo International Corp. [*NASDAQ symbol*] (SAG)
ATSP .... Association of Teachers of Spanish and Portuguese [*British*]
ATSP .... Association of Technical and Supervisory Professionals (EA)
ATSPM .... Air Traffic Services Planning Manual (DA)
ATSq .... Air Transport Squadron [*Air Force*]
ATSQMC ..... Army Transport Service Quartermaster Corps [*Obsolete*]
ATSR .... Activity Time Status Report (MCD)
AT/SR .... Air Tracker/Short-Range (DNAB)
ATSR .... Along-Track Scanning Radiometer
ATSR .... Argonne Thermal Source Reactor
ATSR .... Attitudes Toward Sex Roles Instrument [*Psychology*] (EDAC)
ATSS .... Acquisition and Tracking Subsystem (MUGU)
ATSS .... Advanced Tactical Support System (DOMA)
ATSS .... Advanced Traffic Signal System
ATSS .... Air-Cure Technologies [*NASDAQ symbol*] (TTSB)
ATSS .... Air-Cure Technologies, Inc. [*NASDAQ symbol*] (SAG)
ATSS .... Association of Teachers of Social Studies [*British*]
ATSS .... Association of Track and Structure Suppliers [*Later, REMSA*] (EA)
ATSS .... As The Subject Says [*Internet language*] [*Computer science*]
ATSS .... Augmented Target Screening Subsystem (MCD)
ATSS .... Automatic Target Scoring Systems (MCD)
ATSS .... Automatic Telecommunications Switching System
ATSS .... Automatic Telegraph Subsystem [*Navy British*] (MCD)
ATSS .... Automatic Telephone Switching System (NITA)
ATSS .... Automatic Test Support Systems (RDA)
ATSS .... Auto Tracking Scan System [*for television video quality*] [*Sony Corp.*]
ATSS .... Auxiliary Training Submarine [*Navy symbol*]
ATSS .... Aviation Training Support System [*Navy*] (GFGA)
ATSSA .... American Traffic Safety Services Association (EA)
ATSS-D .... Automatic Telecommunications Switching System - Data Services [*Computer science*] (MHDI)
ATSSM .... Automatic Telecommunications System Security Manager [*Military*] (GFGA)
ATSSS .... Air Transportable SONAR Surveillance System
Atst .... Artist [*Record label*]
ATST .... Atlantic Standard Time
ATSU .... Air Traffic Service Unit (OA)
ATSU .... Air Travel Security Unit
ATSU .... Association of Time-Sharing Users [*Later, ACU*] (EA)
ATSW .... Atria Software [*NASDAQ symbol*] (TTSB)
ATSW .... Atria Software, Inc. [*NASDAQ symbol*] (SAG)
ATSWCD ...... Association of Texas Soil and Water Conservation Districts (SRA)
ATT .... Accelerated Test Technology
ATT .... Acceptance Thermal Test [*or Testing*] [*NASA*] (NASA)
ATT .... Advanced Technician's Test (MCD)
ATT .... Advanced Technology Training [*Army*] (VNW)
ATT .... Advanced Technology Transport
ATT .... Advanced Transonic Technology (MCD)
ATT .... Advanced Transport Telematics [*Traffic management*] (ECON)
ATT .... Aer Turas Teoranta [*Republic of Ireland*] [*ICAO designator*] (FAAC)
ATT .... Air Terminal Team
ATT .... Air Traffic Transponder
ATT .... Air Training Team (NATG)
ATT .... All Thrust Termination (MUGU)
ATT .... American Telephone & Telegraph Co. [*New York, NY*]
ATT .... American Telephone & Telegraph Co., Long Lines, Bedminister, NJ [*OCLC symbol*] (OCLC)
ATT .... Amphibian Technology Tested
ATT .... Application Transfer Teams [*IBM Corp.*]
ATT .... Aquifer Test Toolbox [*Computer science*]
ATT .... Aquifer Test Toolbox
ATT .... Arginine Tolerance Test [*Endocrinology*]
ATT .... Army Training Test
ATT .... Artillery Tactical Terminal
ATT .... Aspirin Tolerance Time [*Medicine*] (DMAA)
ATT .... Associated Talmud Torahs [*A publication*] (BJA)
ATT .... Association Technique du Tourisme [*Tourism Technique Association*] [*Canada*]
ATT .... Atmautluak [*Alaska*] [*Airport symbol*] (OAG)
ATT .... Attach (KSC)
ATT .... Attache
ATT .... Attaché
att .... Attached (WDMC)
ATT .... Attachment [*Telecommunications*] (TEL)
ATT .... Attempted [*FBI standardized term*]
ATT .... Attempts
ATT .... Attendant (MSA)
ATT .... Attended Public Telephone [*Telecommunications*] (TEL)

ATT .... Attending
ATT .... Attention
att .... Attention (WDMC)
ATT .... Attenuation [*Instrumentation*]
ATT .... Attic [*Greek dialect*] (ROG)
ATT .... Attica [*New York*] [*Seismograph station code, US Geological Survey Closed*] (SEIS)
Att .... Atticus [*of Nepos*] [*Classical studies*] (OCD)
ATT .... Attitude
ATT .... Attorney
ATT .... Augmented Transition Tree (MCD)
ATT .... Automatic Target Tracking (MCD)
ATT .... Automatic Toll Ticketing (TEL)
ATT .... Automatic Turbine Tester (NRCH)
ATT .... Avalanche Transit Time
ATT .... Average Task Time
Att .... Epistulae ad Atticum [*of Cicero*] [*Classical studies*] (OCD)
ATT .... Tuskegee Institute, Tuskegee, AL [*Library symbol Library of Congress*] (LCLS)
ATTA .... Advanced Training Technology Associates [*Commercial firm British*]
ATTA .... Alberta Table Tennis Association (AC)
ATTA .... American Tin Trade Association (EA)
ATTA .... Australian Table Tennis Association
ATTAC .... Advanced Technologies for Tactical Aircraft (MCD)
ATTACHT ..... Attachment
ATTAS .... Advanced Technologies Testing Aircraft System [*NASA*]
Att Ber .... Die Attische Beredsamkeit [*A publication*] (OCD)
ATTC .... Advanced Technical Training Center [*Military*] (MUGU)
ATTC .... Advanced Television Test Center [*Telecommunications*] (TSSD)
ATTC .... Army Tropic Test Center (MCD)
ATTC .... Atlantic Transportation Terminal Command [*Army*]
ATTC .... Attic
ATTC .... Automatic Transmission Test and Control [*Telecommunications*] (TEL)
ATTC .... Auto-trol Technology [*NASDAQ symbol*] (TTSB)
ATTC .... Auto-Trol Technology Corp. [*NASDAQ symbol*] (NQ)
ATTC .... Aviation Technical Test Center [*Army*] (RDA)
ATTC .... Aviation Technical Training Center
ATT Cap ...... AT & T Capital Corp. [*Associated Press*] (SAG)
ATTCDE .... Association of Teacher Training Colleges and Departments of Education [*British*] (DI)
ATTCE .... Attendance (ROG)
ATTCOM ...... AT & T Communications [*Telecommunications*] (TSSD)
ATTCS .... Automatic Takeoff Thrust Control System (IEEE)
ATTD .... Advanced Technology Transition Demonstration [*Army*] (INF)
ATTD .... Alcohol and Tobacco Tax Division [*Internal Revenue Service*]
ATTD .... Attend (ROG)
ATTD .... Attitude (KSC)
ATTD .... Avalanche Transit Time Diode
ATTD .... Aviation Technical Training Division [*Military*] (DNAB)
ATTE .... Automatic Transistor Test Equipment
ATTEN .... Attention
ATTEN .... Attenuator (KSC)
ATTESA .... Advanced Total Traction Engineering System for All-Terrain [*Automotive engineering*]
ATTESTG ..... Attesting (ROG)
ATTESTN ..... Attestation
ATTF .... Advanced Technical Training Facility [*Military*]
ATTF .... Air Toxics Task Force [*Environmental Protection Agency*] (GFGA)
ATTF .... Air Transportation Training Flight [*Military*]
ATTF .... Amphibious Tanker Terminal Facility [*Navy*]
ATT Fd .... AT & T Stock Fund (Equity Income Fund) [*Associated Press*] (SAG)
ATTG .... Adversary Threat Training Group [*Military*]
ATTG .... Attending
ATTG .... Automated Tactical Target Graphic
ATTGEN ...... Attorney General (ADA)
ATTI .... American Telephone & Telegraph Co. International (TEL)
ATTI .... Association of Teachers in Technical Institutions [*British*]
Atti Parl ...... Atti Parlamentari [*Parliamentary Acts*] [*Italian*] (ILCA)
ATTIS .... American Telephone & Telegraph Co. Information Systems (TEL)
ATTIS .... AT & T Information Systems [*Telecommunications*] (TSSD)
ATTITB .... Air Transport and Travel Industry Training Board [*British*] (AIA)
ATTIX .... American Telephone & Telegraph Co. Interexchange Carrier (TEL)
ATTK .... Attack
ATTLA .... Air Transportability Test Loading Agency
ATTLC .... Association des Traducteurs et Traductrices Litteraires du Canada [*Literary Translators Association of Canada*] (EAIO)
ATTM .... At This Time
ATTM .... Authorization to Transfer Material
ATTMA .... Advanced Transport Technology Mission Analysis (MCD)
ATTMCA ...... Association of Tile, Terrazzo, Marble Contractors and Affiliates [*Later, NTCA*] (EA)
ATTN .... Attain (ROG)
ATTN .... Attention (AFM)
ATTN .... Attention
attn .... Attention (ODBW)
ATTN .... Attenuator
Attn .... Austroton [*Austria, Germany, etc.*] [*Record label*]
ATTND .... Attendant (AABC)
ATTNDIR ...... Attention Director (MCD)
ATTNDNT .... Attendant
ATTNG .... Attending
ATTNINV ..... Attention Invited (MCD)
ATTO .... Army Test Technology Office
ATTO .... Avalanche Transit Time Oscillator (IAA)

ATTP	Advanced Transport Technology Program [*NASA*] (OA)
ATTPO	Advanced Transport Technology Program Office [*NASA*]
ATTR	All Thrust Terminate Relay (MUGU)
attr	Attributed (VRA)
ATTR	Audit Technical Time Report [*IRS*]
ATTR	Average Time to Repair (MCD)
ATTRA	Appropriate Technology Transfer for Rural Areas [*National Center for Appropriate Technology*] (GNE)
ATTRA	Automatic Telemetry Tracking Receiving Antenna
ATTRAS	Automatic Telemetry Tracking Antenna System (MCD)
ATTREF	Attitude Reference Program [*NASA*]
ATTRIB	Attribute
ATTRIB	Attributed
ATTRS	Automatic Tracking Telemetry Receiving System (DNAB)
ATTS	Active Torque Transfer System
ATTS	Amalgamated Typefounders Trade Society (DGA)
ATTS	American Tax Token Society (EA)
ATTS	American Time Travel Society [*Defunct*] (EA)
ATTS	Antitank Target System [*Military*] (INF)
ATTS	Army Training Target System (MCD)
ATTS	Asymptotic Temporary Threshold Shift (PDAA)
ATTS	Automatic Tank Target System [*Military*] (INF)
ATTS	Automatic Telemetry Tracking System [*NASA*]
ATTSq	Aircrew Training and Test Squadron [*Air Force*]
ATTT	Advanced Technology Tactical Transport [*Proposed low-altitude long-range airlifter*] [*Military*] (MCD)
ATTT	American Telephone & Telegraph Co. Technologies (TEL)
ATTTD	Attitude
ATTU	Air Transportable Telecommunications Unit
ATTU	Atlantic to the Urals [*Conventional forces in Europe treaty zone*]
ATTUN	Automatic Tuning (IAA)
ATTW	Aircrew Training Test Wing [*Air Force*]
ATTW	Association of Teachers of Technical Writing (EA)
ATTY	Attorney (AFM)
ATTY	Attorney
Atty Gen	Attorney General (WGA)
Att'y Gen Ann Rep	Attorney General's Annual Report [*A publication*] (DLA)
Att'y Gen LJ	Attorney General's Law Journal [*A publication*] (DLA)
Atty Gen Op	Attorney General's Opinions [*A publication*] (DLA)
Atty Gen Op NY	Attorney General's Opinions [*A publication*] (DLA)
Att'y Gen Rep	United States Attorneys-General Reports [*A publication*] (DLA)
ATU	Address Translation Unit (NITA)
ATU	Advanced Training Unit
ATU	Aerial Tuning Unit [*Telecommunications*] (OA)
ATU	Air Toulon [*France ICAO designator*] (FAAC)
ATU	Alcohol Tax Unit [*Department of the Treasury*]
ATU	Alliance of Independent Telephone Unions [*Later, TIU*]
ATU	Amalgamated Transit Union (EA)
ATU	American Technological University (MCD)
ATU	Amphibious Task Unit [*Military*] (DNAB)
ATU	Antenna Tuning Unit (MSA)
ATU	Application Terminal Unit [*Telecommunications*] (TEL)
ATU	Arab Telecommunications Union (EA)
ATU	Arthurian Resources Ltd. [*Vancouver Stock Exchange symbol*]
ATU	Athens University [*Greece*] [*Seismograph station code, US Geological Survey*] (SEIS)
ATU	Atomic Time Unit
ATU	Attu, AK [*Location identifier FAA*] (FAAL)
ATU	Audio Terminal Unit (NASA)
ATU	Audio Thermal Unit (MCD)
ATU	Augsburg Transmission Upgrade (MCD)
ATU	Automatic Tracking Unit
ATU	Autonome Transfer Unit [*Computer science*] (DIT)
ATU	Auxiliary Test Unit
ATu	Friedman Library (Hugo Friedman Memorial), Tuscaloosa, AL [*Library symbol Library of Congress*] (LCLS)
a-tu--	Turkey [*MARC geographic area code Library of Congress*] (LCCP)
ATUA	Air Transport Users' Association [*British*] (DA)
ATUC	Aden Trade Union Congress
ATUC	African Trade Union Confederation [*Later, OATUU*]
ATUC	Average Total Unit Cost
ATUCH	American Trade Union Council for Histadrut (EA)
ATUC(SR)	African Trades Union Congress of Southern Rhodesia
ATUF	Austrian Trade Union Federation
ATuGS	Geological Survey of Alabama, Tuscaloosa, AL [*Library symbol*] [*Library of Congress*] (LCLS)
AT-UK	Appropriate Technology - United Kingdom Unit [*ITDG*] [*British*]
ATUR	Apollo Test Unsatisfactory Report [*NASA*] (IAA)
ATUR	Automatic Telephone Using Radio [*Telecommunications service*] (TEL)
ATURF	Airborne TOW [*Tube-Launched, Optically Tracked, Wire-Guided Weapon*] USAREUR Repair Facility [*United States Army, Europe*] (MCD)
ATURM	Amphibious Training Unit, Royal Marines [*British*]
ATURS	Automatic Traffic Usage Recording System (TEL)
ATUS	Advanced Technology Upper Stage (MCD)
ATuS	Stillman College, Tuscaloosa, AL [*Library symbol Library of Congress*] (LCLS)
ATuSC	Shelton State Community College, Tuscalossa, AL [*Library symbol*] [*Library of Congress*] (LCLS)
ATuV	United States Veterans Administration Hospital, Tuscaloosa, AL [*Library symbol Library of Congress*] (LCLS)
ATV	Abelson Virus Transformed [*Medicine*] (DMAA)
ATV	Accurate Traffic Volume [*BTS*] (TAG)
ATV	Activin [*Biochemistry*]

ATV	Advanced Technology Vehicle
ATV	Advanced Television [*See also HDTV*]
ATV	Advanced Test Vehicle (MCD)
ATV	Advanced Tethered Vehicle [*Navy*]
ATV	Aerodynamic Test Vehicle (MCD)
ATV	Agena Target Vehicle [*NASA*] (KSC)
ATV	Aircraft Trailing Vortices
ATV	Air Test Vehicle
ATV	Air-to-Vessel (IAA)
ATV	Akademiet for de Tekniska Videnskaber [*Academy of Technical Sciences*] [*Denmark*]
ATV	All-Terrain Vehicle
ATV	Amateur Television (MSA)
ATV	ARC International Corp. [*AMEX symbol*] (SPSG)
ATV	ARC Intl. [*AMEX symbol*] (TTSB)
ATV	Armored Transport Vehicle (NATG)
ATV	Associated Television Ltd. [*British independent, commercial television company*]
ATV	Ati [*Chad*] [*Airport symbol*] (AD)
ATV	Attached Training Vessel [*Navy*]
ATV	Automated Test Validation
ATV	Automated Transfer Vehicle [*Space technology*]
ATV	Automatic Threshold Variation
ATV	Automatic Ticket Vendors (ADA)
ATV	Avanti Air [*Austria ICAO designator*] (FAAC)
ATV	Avian Tumor Virus [*Medicine*] (DMAA)
ATV	Turner Valley Public Library, Alberta [*Library symbol National Library of Canada*] (NLC)
ATV	United States Veterans Administration Hospital, Tuskegee, AL [*Library symbol Library of Congress*] (LCLS)
ATVA	Tennessee Valley Authority, Technical Library, Muscle Shoals, AL [*Library symbol Library of Congress*] (LCLS)
ATVC	American Travellers Corp. [*NASDAQ symbol*] (NQ)
ATVC	Amer Travellers [*NASDAQ symbol*] (TTSB)
ATVC	Ascent Thrust Vector Control [*or Controller*] [*NASA*] (MCD)
ATVC	Automatic Thrust Vector Control [*NASA*]
ATVCD	Ascent Thrust Vector Control Driver [*NASA*] (MCD)
ATVI	Activision, Inc. [*NASDAQ symbol*] (SAG)
ATVI	Australia Television International
ATVIC	Association of Teachers in Sixth Form and Tertiary Colleges [*British*] (AIE)
ATVM	Attenuator-Thermoelement Voltmeter
AT VOL	Atomic Volume (DNAB)
ATVS	Advanced Television Seeker (MCD)
ATVSC	Advanced TV Systems Committee (EA)
ATVW	Attached Trailer Towed Vehicle Weight [*Automotive engineering*]
ATVWS	Airport Trailing Vortex Warning System
ATW	Accelerator Transmutation of Waste [*Nuclear waste*]
ATW	Advanced Technology Workstation [*Computer system*]
ATW	Aerospace Test Wing [*Air Force*]
ATW	Aero Trades (Western) Ltd. [*Canada ICAO designator*] (FAAC)
ATW	Ahead-Throwing Weapon [*Antisubmarine*]
ATW	Aircraft Tail Warning
ATW	Air Transport Wing [*Air Force*]
ATW	American Theatre Wing (EA)
ATW	Antitank Weapon (NATG)
ATW	Appleton [*Wisconsin*] [*Airport symbol*] (OAG)
ATW	Approved Tank Wagon
ATW	Atlantic & Western Railway Co. [*AAR code*]
ATW	Atmospheric Tactical Warning (MCD)
AT/W	Atomic Hydrogen Weld
ATW	Atwater Library of the Mechanics' Institute of Montreal [*UTLAS symbol*]
Atw	Atwater's Reports [*1 Minnesota*] [*A publication*] (DLA)
ATW	Automatic Tape Winder (IAA)
ATW	Aviation Electronics Technician Airborne CIC [*Combat Information Center*] Equipment
ATWA	Association of Third World Affairs (EA)
ATWAR	Assessment of Theater Warfare [*Model*] (MCD)
Atwater	Atwater's Reports [*1 Minnesota*] [*A publication*] (DLA)
ATWC	Alaska Tsunami Warning Center [*Army*] (OSRA)
ATWC	Alaska Tsunami Warning Center (USDC)
ATWD	Atwood Oceanics [*NASDAQ symbol*] (TTSB)
ATWD	Atwood Oceanics, Inc. [*NASDAQ symbol*] (NQ)
ATWDDS	Automated Terminal Weather Dissemination Display System (MCD)
AtwdOc	Atwood Oceanics, Inc. [*Associated Press*] (SAG)
ATWESS	Antitank Weapons Effect Signature Simulator [*Army*] (INF)
ATWg	Air Transport Wing [*Air Force*] (AFM)
ATWL	Acoustic Traveling Wave Lens
ATWS	Adjustable Thermal Wire Stripper
ATWS	Alaska Tsunami Warning System [*National Oceanic and Atmospheric Administration*] (GFGA)
ATWS	Anticipated Transient without Scram [*Physics*]
ATWS	Association of Third World Studies (EA)
ATWS	Automatic Track-while-Scan [*Radar*]
ATWT	As the World Turns [*A television program*]
ATWT	Atmospheric Thermonuclear Weapons Testing
ATWT	Atomic Weight
ATWTFC	As the World Turns Fan Club (EA)
ATWU	Amalgamated Textile Workers' Union [*British*] (DCTA)
ATX	Abingdon, VA [*Location identifier FAA*] (FAAL)
ATX	Ameritex Resources Ltd. [*Vancouver Stock Exchange symbol*]
ATX	Automatic TELEX Exchange [*Telecommunications*] (TEL)
ATX	Automatic Transaxle
ATX	Birmingham Aviation Ltd. [*British ICAO designator*] (FAAC)

ATX............ Cross [A. T.] Co. [AMEX symbol] (SPSG)
ATX............ Warwickshire Aerocentre Ltd. [British] [FAA designator] (FAAC)
ATXI.......... Atrix International [NASDAQ symbol] (TTSB)
ATXI.......... Atrix International, Inc. [NASDAQ symbol] (SAG)
ATXPL........ Atomic Explosion
ATY........... Grupo Casa Autrey [NYSE symbol] (SPSG)
ATY........... Grupo Casa Autrey ADS [NYSE symbol] (TTSB)
ATY........... International Airports Authority of India [ICAO designator] (FAAC)
ATY........... Watertown [South Dakota] [Airport symbol] (OAG)
ATYP......... Ambrotype (VRA)
ATYPI......... Association Typographique Internationale [International Typographic
                  Association]
ATZ........... Acquisition Trigger at Zero Beat
ATZ........... Aerodrome Traffic Zone
ATZ........... Air Service Training Ltd. [British ICAO designator] (FAAC)
ATZ........... Assiut [Egypt] [Airport symbol] (AD)
ATZ........... Atypical Transformation Zone [Gynecology] (DAVI)
AU............ Absorbance Unit [Physical chemistry]
AU............ Access Unit [Computer science] (TNIG)
AU............ Accounting Unit (NATG)
AU............ Address Unit [Computer science]
AU............ Ad Usum [According to Custom] [Pharmacy]
AU............ Airborne Unit
AU............ Air to Underwater (SAA)
AU............ Air University [Maxwell Air Force Base, AL]
AU............ Alignment Unit
AU............ Allergenic Unit [Medicine] (DAVI)
AU............ All Up (ADA)
AU............ Alma Urbis [Beloved City] [Rome]
AU............ Almost Uncirculated [Condition of coins] [Numismatics]
AU............ Alternate Uses [Personality research] [Psychology]
AU............ Amax Gold, Inc. [NYSE symbol] (SPSG)
AU............ Americana Unit [American Topical Association] (EA)
AU............ American University [Washington, DC]
AU............ Amplifier Unit (OA)
AU............ Analytical Ultracentrifugation [Separation science]
AU............ Analyzer Unit (CAAL)
AU............ Angstrom Unit [Also, A]
AU............ Anno Urbis [In the Year of the City of Rome] [Latin]
AU............ Anson Unit [Of hydrolytic enzyme activity]
AU............ Answer Unit (IAA)
AU............ Antitoxin Unit [Immunology]
AU............ Anti-U-Boat Warfare [British World War II]
AU............ Apprentices Union [British]
au----........ Arabian Sea and Area [MARC geographic area code Library of
                  Congress] (LCCP)
AU............ Arbitrary Unit
AU............ Ariel Resources [TS Symbol] (TTSB)
AU............ Arithmetic Unit [Computer science]
AU............ Army Unit
AU............ Assembler Unit [Computer science] (IAA)
AU............ Astronomical Unit [Equal to average distance from earth to sun]
AU............ Astronomy Unit [Later, ASU] [American Topical Association] (EA)
AU............ Atheists United (EA)
AU............ Atlantic Union (DAS)
AU............ Atomic Units (MCD)
AU............ Attachment Unit (MCD)
Au............ Auberger [Blood group]
AU............ Auburn University [Alabama]
AU............ Audio and Electroacoustics [IEEE]
AU............ Audit
AU............ Augmitto Explorations Ltd. [Toronto Stock Exchange symbol]
AU............ August
AU............ Aunes [French Ells]
AU............ Aures Unitas [Both Ears] [Latin]
AU............ Auris Uterque [Each Ear] [Latin]
Au............ Aurum [Gold] [Chemical element]
AU............ Australia [ANSI two-letter standard code] (CNC)
Au............ Australia Antigen [Immunology]
AU............ Austral Lineas Aereas [ICAO designator] (AD)
AU............ Austria
au .... Austria [MARC country of publication code Library of Congress]
                  (LCCP)
AU............ Author [Online database field identifier] [Computer science]
au .... Author [Editing notation] (WDMC)
Au............ Author [Editing notation] (WDMC)
AU............ Authorized User (DCTA)
AU............ Automatic (IAA)
AU............ Automobile
AU............ Autopsy [Also, AUT] [Medicine]
Au............ Autumn
AU............ Auxiliary Unit
AU............ Azauridine (MAE)
Au............ Gold [Chemical Element] (DOG)
Au............ National Library of Australia, Canberra, Australia [Library symbol
                  Library of Congress] (LCLS)
AU............ University of Alabama, University, AL [Library symbol Library of
                  Congress] (LCLS)
au .... Unix Sound File [Computer science]
AUA........... Alkylation Unit Acid [Petroleum refining]
AUA........... Allied Underwear Association (EA)
AUA........... American Underground-Space Association (EA)
AUA........... American Unitarian Association
AUA........... American Urological Association (EA)
AUA........... Argonne Universities Association

AUA........... Arithmetic Underachievers [Education]
AUA........... Aruba [Netherlands Antilles] [Airport symbol]
AUA........... Asamera Minerals Ltd. [Toronto Stock Exchange symbol]
AUA........... Associated Unions of America [Later, OPEIU] (EA)
AUA........... Association des Universites Africaines [Association of African
                  Universities - AAU] (EAIO)
AUA........... Association of University Anesthetists (EA)
AUA........... Association of University Architects (EA)
AUA........... Atari Users Association (EA)
AUA........... Austrian Airlines [ICAO designator] (FAAC)
AUA........... Austrian Airways [Oesterreichische Luftverkehrs AG]
AUA........... Automated Universal Array (MCD)
AUAA.......... American Urological Association Allied (EA)
AUAA.......... Artists United Against Apartheid (EA)
AUAA.......... Atlantic Universities Athletic Association [Association Sportive
                  Interuniversitaire de l'Atlantique] (AC)
AUAF.......... Association of University Affiliated Facilities [Later, AAUAP] (EA)
Au Ag......... Australia Antigen [Immunology] (MAE)
AUAIP......... Aeronautics Upper Atmosphere Impact Program [NASA]
AuAP.......... Parliamentary Library, Parliament House, Adelaide, SA, Australia
                  [Library symbol Library of Congress] (LCLS)
AuAr.......... Armidale City and Dumarasq Shire War Memorial Library, Armidale,
                  NSW, Australia [Library symbol Library of Congress] (LCLS)
AuArA .... Armidale Newspaper Co. Ltd., Armidale, NSW, Australia [Library
                  symbol Library of Congress] (LCLS)
AU-ARI........ Air University-Airpower Research Institute [Maxwell Air Force Base,
                  AL]
AuArU .... University of New England, Armidale, NSW, Australia [Library symbol
                  Library of Congress] (LCLS)
AUAS.......... Academy of Underwater Arts and Sciences [Defunct] (EA)
AuASA .... Public Library of South Australia, Adelaide, SA, Australia [Library
                  symbol Library of Congress] (LCLS)
AUASAM ..... Automatic Aimpoint Selection and Maintenance (MCD)
AUASM .... Automatic Aimpoint Selection and Maintenance (DNAB)
AuAU .... University of Adelaide, Adelaide, SA, Australia [Library symbol Library
                  of Congress] (LCLS)
AuAU-AR..... University of Adelaide, Mawson Institute for Antartic Research,
                  Adelaide, SA, Australia [Library symbol] [Library of Congress]
                  (LCLS)
AUAW .... Amalgamated Union of Asphalt Workers [British] (DCTA)
AUB .... Abnormal Uterine Bleeding [Gynecology] (DMAA)
AUB .... Aft Utility Bridge (NASA)
AUB .... American University of Beirut [Lebanon]
AUBBER...... Associated University Bureaus of Business and Economic Research
                  [Later, AUBER]
AUBC.......... Association of Universities of the British Commonwealth
AUBER........ Association for University Business and Economic Research
                  [University, AL] (EA)
AuBh.......... Broken Hill Municipal Library, Broken Hill, NSW, Australia [Library
                  symbol Library of Congress] (LCLS)
AUBL.......... LaTrobe University, Bundoora, V, Australia [Library symbol Library of
                  Congress] (LCLS)
AUBN.......... Auburn National [NASDAQ symbol] (SAG)
AUBN.......... Auburn Natl Bancorp [NASDAQ symbol] (TTSB)
AubNB .... Auburn National [Associated Press] (SAG)
AuBon........ Au Bon Pain, Inc. [Associated Press] (SAG)
AuBpF......... Flinders University of South Australia, Bedford Park, SA, Australia
                  [Library symbol Library of Congress] (LCLS)
AuBrP .... Queensland Parliamentary Library, Parliament House, Brisbane,
                  QLD, Australia [Library symbol Library of Congress] (LCLS)
AuBrS .... State Library of Queensland, Brisbane, QLD, Australia [Library
                  symbol Library of Congress] (LCLS)
AuBrS-O....... State Library of Queensland, Oxley Memorial Library, Brisbane, QLD,
                  Australia [Library symbol Library of Congress] (LCLS)
AuBrU .... University of Queensland, St. Lucia, Brisbane, QLD, Australia [Library
                  symbol Library of Congress] (LCLS)
Auburn U ..... Auburn University (GAGS)
Auburn U (Montgomery)... Auburn University at Montgomery (GAGS)
AuBut......... Butterworths Proprietary Ltd., Chatswood, NSW, Australia [Library
                  symbol Library of Congress] (LCLS)
AUBV .... Air University Board of Visitors
AUC .... Ab Urbe Condite [From the Year of the Founding] [Latin]
AUC .... ADT Aviation Ltd. [British ICAO designator] (FAAC)
AUC .... Airline Users' Committee [British] (DI)
AUC .... Air Users' Committee [British]
AUC .... American University of Cairo
AUC .... American University of the Caribbean
AUC .... Ammonium Uranyl Carbonate [Inorganic chemistry]
AUC .... Anno Urbis Conditae [In the Year from the Building of the City
                  (Rome)] [753 BC] [Latin]
AUC .... Apple University Consortium
AUC .... Arauca [Colombia] [Airport symbol] (OAG)
AUC .... Area under Plasma Concentration Curve [Hematology]
AUC .... Area Under the Curve [Medicine] (DMAA)
AUC .... Asociacion de Universidades del Caribe [Association of Caribbean
                  Universities and Research Institutes] (EAIO)
AUC .... Associated Underground Contractors (SRA)
AUC .... Association of Unity Churches (EA)
AUC .... Association of Uptown Converters (EA)
AUC .... Atlantic Union College [South Lancaster, MA]
AUC .... Auckland [New Zealand] [Seismograph station code, US Geological
                  Survey] (SEIS)
AUC .... Authentication Center
AUC .... Average Unit Cost
AUC .... Coeur D'Alene, ID [Location identifier FAA] (FAAL)

AUCA .... American Unitarian Christian Association (EA)

AUCANUKUS... Australia, Canada, United Kingdom, United States (ADA)

AUCAS .... Association of University Clinical Academic Staff [British]

AUCBE .... Advisory Unit for Computer Based Education [Hatfield, England] [Information service or system Telecommunications] (TSSD)

AUCBM .... Arab Union for Cement and Building Materials [See also UACMC] (EAIO)

AUCC .... Association of Universities and Colleges of Canada [Association des Universites et Colleges du Canada]

AUCCCD ...... Association of University and College Counseling Center Directors (EA)

AUCCTU .... All Union Central Council of Trade Unions [Former USSR]

AUCE .... Association of University and College Employees [See also AEUC] [Canada]

AUCEN .... Association Universitaire Canadienne d'Etudes Nordiques [Association of Canadian Universities for Northern Studies]

AUCF .... Americans United to Combat Fluoridation [Later, AUDF] (EA)

AUCF .... Average Unit of Council Funding [Higher Education Funding Council] (AIE)

AuCF .... Federal Capital Press of Australia, Canberra, ACT, Australia [Library symbol Library of Congress] (LCLS)

Auch .... Auchinleck's Manuscript Cases, Scotch Court of Session [A publication] (DLA)

AUCL .... Allowable Utilities Consumption Level [Department of Housing and Urban Development] (GFGA)

AuCIM .... Monash University, Clayton, V, Australia [Library symbol Library of Congress] (LCLS)

AUCM .... Associated Utility Contractors of Maryland (SRA)

AUCM .... Automated Urease-Chromous Method [Analytical chemistry]

AUCN .... Auction (ROG)

AuCNL .... Commonwealth National Library, Parliament House, Canberra, ACT, Australia [Library symbol Library of Congress] (LCLS)

AUCOA .... Association of United Contractors of America [Defunct] (EA)

AUCPD .... Air University Center for Professional Development [Military]

AUCS .... Advanced UHF Communication System (MCD)

AUCT .... Auction

auct .... Auctoris [One that Gives Increase; an Originator] [Latin]

auct .... Auctorum [Of Authors] [Biology, taxonomy]

AuCT .... Auxiliary Current Transformer

AUCTA .... Australian Underground Construction and Tunnelling Association

AUCTNR ...... Auctioneer

AUCTNR ...... Auctioneer

AUCTNRG ...... Auctioneering

Auct Reg & L Chron... Auction Register and Law Chronicle [A publication] (DLA)

AuCU .... Australian National University, Canberra, ACT, Australia [Library symbol Library of Congress] (LCLS)

AUD .... Agree-Undecided-Disagree [Multiple choice test] (BARN)

AUD .... Aktionsgemeinschaft Unabhaengiger Deutscher [Action Group of Independent Germans] [Germany Political party] (PPE)

AUD .... Association for Union Democracy (EA)

AUD .... Association to Unite the Democracies (EA)

AUD .... Asynchronous Unit Delay [Computer science] (IAA)

AUD .... Audi Air, Inc. [ICAO designator] (FAAC)

AUD .... Audible (WGA)

AUD .... Audio [or Audible or Audiology] (MSA)

AUD .... Audio

aud .... Audit (ODBW)

AUD .... Audit [or Auditor] (AFM)

AUD .... Auditorium (DAC)

aud .... Auditory (DAVI)

Aud .... Audubon [A publication] (BRI)

AUD .... Augustus Downs [Australia Airport symbol Obsolete] (OAG)

AUD .... Augustus Downs [Queensland] [Airport symbol] (AD)

AUD .... Australian Dollar [Monetary unit]

AUD .... Automatic Data Proc [NYSE symbol] (TTSB)

AUD .... Automatic Data Processing, Inc. [NYSE symbol] (SPSG)

AuD .... Doctorate in audiology

AudA .... Audio Archives [Record label]

AUDACIOUS... Automatic Direct Access to Information with the On-Line UDC [Universal Decimal Classification] System [American Institute of Physics] [Information retrieval]

AUDAR .... Autodyne Detection and Ranging

AUDB .... Arming Unit Distribution Box [Army] (MCD)

AudC .... Audio Collectors [Record label]

AuDDa .... Department of Aboriginal Affairs, Darwin, NT, Australia [Library symbol Library of Congress] (LCLS)

AUDDIT .... Automatic Dynamic Digital Test System (MHDB)

AUDECAM ...... Association Universitaire pour le Developpement de l'Enseignement et de la Culture en Afrique et a Madagascar [University Association for the Development of Teaching and Culture in Africa and Madagascar] [Paris, France] (AF)

AUDELCO .... Audience Development Committee (EA)

AUDEQUIP ... Audio Equipment (IAA)

AUDGENAV... Auditor General of the Navy

AUDGENNAV... Auditor General of the Navy (DNAB)

AUDI .... Arab Urban Development Institute (EA)

AUDI .... Societe Internationale d'Audiologie

AUDINET ...... American Electric Power Co., Inc. Unified Dial Network (TEL)

AUDIOPR ...... Audioprothesis

AUDIT .... Aircraft Unitized Diagnostic Inspection and Test [Boeing]

AUDIT .... Alcohol Use Disorders Identification Test

AUDIT .... Army Uniform Data Inquiry Technique

audit .... Auditorium (VRA)

AUDIT .... Auditory Input Task [Computer science]

AUDIT .... Automatic Unattended Detection Inspection Transmitter [Raytheon Co.]

AUDITRPT .... Audit Trail Report [Military]

AUDK .... Audio King [NASDAQ symbol] (TTSB)

AUDK .... Audio King, Inc. [NASDAQ symbol] (SAG)

AudKng .... Audio King, Inc. [Associated Press] (SAG)

AUDLGST.... Audiologist

AUDLGY ...... Audiology

AuDpAr .... Queensland State Archives, Dutton Park, QLD, Australia [Library symbol Library of Congress] (LCLS)

AUDPC .... Area under the Disease Progress Curve [Botany]

Aud Q .... Audita Querela [A publication] (DLA)

AudR .... Audio Rarities [Record label]

AUDREY ...... Audio Reply (IEEE)

AUDREY ...... Automatic Digit Recognition

AUDRI .... Automated Drug Identification

auds............ Audiences (WDMC)

auds............ Auditoriums (WDMC)

AUDSNL ...... Audio Signal (IAA)

AudSurv ...... Audits & Surveys Worldwide, Inc. [Associated Press] (SAG)

AUDT .... Audit

AUDTR .... Auditor

AUDTR .... Auditor (MSA)

Audvox........ Audiovox Corp. [Associated Press] (SAG)

AUE............ Akron University College of Engineering [Ohio]

AUE............ Army User Equipment (MCD)

AUE............ Association des Universitaires d'Europe

AUE............ Au Resources Ltd. [Vancouver Stock Exchange symbol]

AUE............ Aurora High School PRECIS Project [UTLAS symbol]

AUE............ Sebring, FL [Location identifier FAA] (FAAL)

AUEA .... Auxiliary Utility Equipment Area (NRCH)

AUEBF .... All-Ukrainian Evangelical Baptist Fellowship (EA)

AUEC .... Association of University Evening Colleges [Later, ACHE] (EA)

AUEFW ...... Amalgamated Union of Engineering and Foundry Workers [British]

AUEHSC...... Association of University Environmental Health/Sciences Centers (EA)

AUEL .... Automated Unit Equipment List

AUET .... Armored, Universal Engineer Tractor

AUEW .... Amalgamated Union of Engineering Workers [British] (DCTA)

AUEW(C)...... Amalgamated Union of Engineering Workers - Constructional [British] (DCTA)

AUEW(E)...... Amalgamated Union of Engineering Workers - Engineering [British] (DCTA)

AUEW(F)...... Amalgamated Union of Engineering Workers - Foundry [British] (DCTA)

AUEW-TASS... Amalgamated Union of Engineering Workers - Technical and Supervisory [British] (DCTA)

AUF............ Augustine Island [Alaska] [Seismograph station code, US Geological Survey] (SEIS)

AUF............ Average Utilization Factor

Auff............ Auffuehrung [Performance] [German]

AUFFVA ...... Australian United Fresh Fruit and Vegetable Association

Aufg............ Aufgabe [Task] [German]

AuFirGS ...... Church of Jesus Christ of Latter-Day Saints, Genealogical Society Library, Adelaide Stake Branch, Firle, SA, Australia [Library symbol Library of Congress] (LCLS)

AUFL.......... Auflage [Edition] [German]

AUFM.......... Asociacion Universal de Federalistas Mundiales [World Association of World Federalists]

AUFS .... Absorbance Units Full Scale [Physical chemistry]

AUFS .... American Universities Field Staff [Later, UFSI-IWA] (EA)

AUFS .... American Universities Field Staff. Reports Series [A publication]

Aufs............ Aufsatz [Essay] [German]

AUFSC .... Association of University Forestry Schools of Canada [Association des Ecoles Forestieres Universitaires du Canada] (AC)

AUFS-IWA.... American Universities Field Staff - Institute of World Affairs [Later, UFSI-IWA] (EA)

Auftr............ Auftrag [Order] [German]

AUFW .... Amalgamated Union of Foundry Workers [British]

AUFWPA...... Association of University Fisheries and Wildlife Program Administrators (EA)

Aufz............ Aufzeichnung [Note] [German]

AUG............ Adenine, Uracil, Guanine [Biochemistry]

AUG............ Amdahl Users Group (EA)

AUG............ Augat, Inc. [NYSE symbol] (SPSG)

AUG............ Augdome Corp. [Vancouver Stock Exchange symbol]

AUG............ Augere [Increase] [Pharmacy]

AUG............ Augment (AABC)

Aug............ Augmentation [Music]

AUG............ August (EY)

AUG............ Augusta [Maine] [Airport symbol] (OAG)

AUG............ Augusta Railroad Co. [AAR code]

AUG............ CPA Cesar Augusto de la Cruze Lepe [Mexico ICAO designator] (FAAC)

Aug............ Divus Augustus [of Suetonius] [Classical studies] (OCD)

AUG .... University of Maine at Augusta, Augusta, ME [OCLC symbol] (OCLC)

Augat............ Augat, Inc. [Associated Press] (SAG)

AUGB.......... Association of Ukrainians in Great Britain Ltd. (BI)

Aug Bero .... Augustinus Berous [Deceased, 1554] [Authority cited in pre-1607 legal work] (DSA)

AUGC .... Americans United for God and Country (EA)

AUGI .... American United Global, Inc. [NASDAQ symbol] (SAG)

AUGI .... Amer United Global [NASDAQ symbol] (TTSB)

AUGIW........ American United Global Wrrt [NASDAQ symbol] (TTSB)

Augm.......... Augmentation [Music]

AUGM .... Augmentative
AUGRA .... Authority Granted (NOAA)
AUGT .... August (ROG)
AUGU .... Augmenting Unit [*Navy*]
Augu .... Augustinus Berous [*Deceased, 1554*] [*Authority cited in pre-1607 legal work*] (DSA)
August .... Augustine [*354-430AD*] [*Classical studies*] (OCD)
Augusta C .... Augusta College (GAGS)
Augustana C ... Augustana College (GAGS)
AUH .... Abu Dhabi [*United Arab Emirates*] [*Airport symbol*] (OAG)
AUH .... American University Hospital [*Lebanon*]
AUH .... Aurora, NE [*Location identifier FAA*] (FAAL)
AuH_2O .... Goldwater, Barry [*Chemical symbols for gold and water; used to refer to the 1964 Republican presidential candidate*]
AUHA .... Australian Underwater Hockey Association
AUHAA .... Australia Hepatitis-Associated Antigen [*Immunology*] (MAE)
AuHaA .... Australian Council for Educational Research, Hawthorn, V, Australia [*Library symbol Library of Congress*] (LCLS)
AUHC .... Adelaide University Hockey Club [*Australia*]
AuHP .... Parliamentary Library, Parliament House, Hobart, TAS, Australia [*Library symbol Library of Congress*] (LCLS)
AUHS .... Adapted Uzgiris-Hunt Scales (EDAC)
AuHS .... State Library of Tasmania, Hobart, TAS, Australia [*Library symbol Library of Congress*] (LCLS)
AU-HS .... University of Alabama Health Sciences Library, University, AL [*Library symbol*] [*Library of Congress*] (LCLS)
AuHU .... University of Tasmania, Hobart, TAS, Australia [*Library symbol Library of Congress*] (LCLS)
AUI .... Action d'Urgence Internationale [*International Emergency Action - IEA*] [*Paris, France*] (EAIO)
AUI .... Air Ukraine International [*ICAO designator*] (FAAC)
AUI .... Al Akhawayn University, Ifrane [*Morocco*]
AUI .... Alcohol Use Inventory [*Medicine*] (DMAA)
AUI .... Applied Urbanetics, Inc. [*Information service or system*] (IID)
AUI .... Asociacion Universitaria Interamericana [*Interamerican University Association*] [*Spanish*]
AUI .... Associacao Universitaria Interamericana [*Interamerican University Association*] [*Portuguese*]
AUI .... Associated Universities, Inc. (EA)
AUI .... Association Universitaire Interamericaine [*Interamerican University Association*] [*France*]
AUI .... Attachment Unit Interface [*Computer science*] (PCM)
AUI .... Aua [*Papua New Guinea*] [*Airport symbol*] (OAG)
AUI .... Augustine Island [*Alaska*] [*Seismograph station code, US Geological Survey*] (SEIS)
AUI .... Las Vegas, NV [*Location identifier FAA*] (FAAL)
AUIB .... Aircrew Uniform, Integrated Battlefield [*Army*]
AUID .... Association of University Interior Designers (EA)
AuIpQT .... Queensland Times Proprietory Ltd., Ipswich, QLD, Australia [*Library symbol Library of Congress*] (LCLS)
AUIUSA .... Americans for Undivided Israel USA (EA)
AUJ .... Active Universal Joints
AUJ .... Air-to-Umbilical Junction Box
AUJ .... Ambunti [*Papua New Guinea*] [*Airport symbol*] (OAG)
AUJ .... Atigaru Point, AK [*Location identifier FAA*] (FAAL)
AUJ .... Aujourd'hui [*Today*] [*French*]
AUJS .... Advanced Universal Jamming System
AUJW .... Allgemeine Unabhaengige Juedische Wochenzeitung (BJA)
AUK .... Alakanuk [*Alaska*] [*Airport symbol*] (OAG)
AUK .... Auckland Explorations Ltd. [*Vancouver Stock Exchange symbol*]
AUK .... Auki [*Solomon Islands*] [*Seismograph station code, US Geological Survey*] (SEIS)
AuKirGS .... Church of Jesus Christ of Latter-Day Saints, Genealogical Society Library, Sydney South Branch, Sutherland Ward Chapel, Kirrawee, NSW, Australia [*Library symbol Library of Congress*] (LCLS)
AUKML .... Association of United Kingdom Media Librarians (DBA)
AUKOI .... Association of United Kingdom Oil Independents
AuKU .... University of New South Wales, Kensington, NSW, Australia [*Library symbol Library of Congress*] (LCLS)
AUL .... Above Upper Limit (MHDB)
AUL .... Acute Undifferentiated Leukemia [*Hematology*]
AUL .... Air University Library
AUL .... Americans United for Life (EA)
AUL .... Archangelsk Airlines [*Former USSR*] [*FAA designator*] (FAAC)
AUL .... Athabasca University Library [*UTLAS symbol*]
AUL .... Aur [*Marshall Islands*] [*Airport symbol*] (OAG)
Au(I) .... Australia Antigen [*Medicine*] (MAH)
AUL .... Average Useful Life
AU-L .... University of Alabama, Law Library, University, AL [*Library symbol Library of Congress*] (LCLS)
AULLA .... Australasian Universities Language and Literature Association (EAIO)
AULLDF .... Americans United for Life Legal Defense Fund (EA)
AULR .... Attrition, Utilization, and Loss Rate (AFM)
AU-LS .... University of Alabama, Library Sciences School, University, AL [*Library symbol Library of Congress*] (LCLS)
AULT .... Ault, Inc. [*NASDAQ symbol*] (NQ)
Ault .... Court Rolls of Ramsey Abbey [*1928*] [*England*] [*A publication*] (DLA)
AUM .... Advanced Underwater Missile
AUM .... Air Atlantic Uruguay [*ICAO designator*] (FAAC)
AUM .... Air-to-Underwater Missile [*Air Force*]
AUM .... American Union of Men (EA)
AUM .... Animal-Unit Month
AUM .... Association for the Understanding of Man (EA)
AUM .... Association of Umbrella Manufacturers and Suppliers [*Defunct*] (EA)
AUM .... Augustine Island [*Alaska*] [*Seismograph station code, US Geological Survey*] (SEIS)
aum .... Aumentado [*Enlarged*] [*Spanish*] (BARN)
AUM .... Austin [*Minnesota*] [*Airport symbol*] (AD)
AUM .... Austin, MN [*Location identifier FAA*] (FAAL)
AUM .... Auto Marine Electric Ltd. [*Vancouver Stock Exchange symbol*]
AU-M .... University of Alabama, Medical Center, Birmingham, AL [*Library symbol Library of Congress*] (LCLS)
AUM .... University of Massachusetts-Amherst, Amherst, MA [*OCLC symbol*] (OCLC)
AUMA .... Alberta Urban Municipalities Association (AC)
AuMacD .... Daily Mercury, Mackay, QLD, Australia [*Library symbol Library of Congress*] (LCLS)
AuMDS .... David Syme & Co. Ltd., Melbourne, V, Australia [*Library symbol Library of Congress*] (LCLS)
AUME .... Association pour l'Union Monetaire de l'Europe [*Association for the Monetary Union of Europe*] [*France*] (EAIO)
AUMIST .... Associateship of the University of Manchester Institute of Science and Technology [*British*] (DI)
AUMLGC .... Affirmation: United Methodists for Lesbian/Gay Concerns (EA)
AUMN .... Air-to-Underwater Missile - Nuclear [*Air Force*] (IAA)
AuMP .... Parliamentary Library of Victoria, Parliament House, Melbourne, V, Australia [*Library symbol Library of Congress*] (LCLS)
AuMS .... State Library of Victoria, Melbourne, V, Australia [*Library symbol Library of Congress*] (LCLS)
AuMU .... University of Melbourne, Melbourne, V, Australia [*Library symbol Library of Congress*] (LCLS)
AuMuU .... Murdoch University, Murdoch, WA, Australia [*Library symbol Library of Congress*] (LCLS)
AUN .... Absque Ulla Nota [*Without Any Marking or Note*] [*Latin*]
AUN .... Auburn, CA [*Location identifier FAA*] (FAAL)
AUN .... Aviones Unidos SA de CV [*Mexico ICAO designator*] (FAAC)
AuNaG .... Griffith University, Nathan, QLD, Australia [*Library symbol Library of Congress*] (LCLS)
AuNc .... Newcastle Public Library, Civic Center, Newcastle, NSW, Australia [*Library symbol Library of Congress*] (LCLS)
AuNcU .... University of Newcastle, Newcastle, NSW, Australia [*Library symbol Library of Congress*] (LCLS)
AuNeU .... University of Western Australia, Nedlands, WA, Australia [*Library symbol Library of Congress*] (LCLS)
AuNL .... National Library of Australia, Canberra, ACT, Australia [*Library symbol*] [*Library of Congress*] (LCLS)
AuNocGS .... Church of Jesus Christ of Latter-Day Saints, Genealogical Society Library, Melbourne Branch, Northcote, V, Australia [*Library symbol Library of Congress*] (LCLS)
AuNqIT .... Queensland Institute of Technology, North Quay, QLD, Australia [*Library symbol Library of Congress*] (LCLS)
AuNrM .... Macquarie University, North Ryde, NSW, Australia [*Library symbol Library of Congress*] (LCLS)
AUNT .... Alliance for Undesirable but Necessary Tasks [*From book title, "The Woman from AUNT"*]
AUNT .... Automatic Universal Translator
AUNTIE .... Automatic Unit for National Taxation and Insurance (MHDB)
AUO .... Administratively Uncontrollable Overtime
AUO .... Amulet Resources Corp. [*Vancouver Stock Exchange symbol*]
AUO .... Amyloid of Unknown Origin [*Medicine*]
AUO .... Area Utilization Office [*GSA*]
AUO .... Auburn/Opelika [*Alabama*] [*Airport symbol*] (OAG)
AUO .... Empresa Aero Uruguay SA [*ICAO designator*] (FAAC)
AUOD .... Alliance Universelle des Ouvriers Diamantaires [*Universal Alliance of Diamond Workers - UADW*] [*Antwerp, Belgium*] (EAIO)
AUOF .... Americans United to Outlaw Fluoridation (EA)
AUP .... Acceptable Use Policy
AUP .... Actual Unit Price [*Billing*] (MCD)
AUP .... Adult Unemployed Project [*Department of Education and Science*] [*British*] (AIE)
AUP .... African Union of Physics [*See also UAP*] (EAIO)
AUP .... Aguan [*Papua New Guinea*] [*Airport symbol*] (OAG)
AUP .... Air University Press
AUP .... American University of Paris
AUP .... Ames Unitary Plan (SAA)
AUP .... Athletes United for Peace (EA)
AUP .... Australian United Press
AUP .... AUTODIN Upgrade Program (MCD)
AUPA .... Association of Unclaimed Property Administrators [*Later, NAUPA*]
AuPaE .... Economic Society of Australia and New Zealand, Melbourne University, Parkville, V, Australia [*Library symbol Library of Congress*] (LCLS)
AuPaU .... University of Melbourne, Baillieu Library, Parkville, V, Australia [*Library symbol Library of Congress*] (LCLS)
AUPC .... Average Unit Procurement Cost [*Military*] (DOMA)
AUPE .... Alberta Union of Provincial Employees [*Canada*] (BARN)
AUPE .... Amalgamated Union of Public Employees [*Singapore*]
AUPELF .... Association des Universites Partiellement ou Entierement de Langue Francaise [*Association of Wholly or Partially French Language Universities*] [*Montreal, PQ*] (EA)
AUP(Fr) .... Association of University Professors (French) [*British*]
AUPG .... American University Publishers Group Ltd.
AUPHA .... Association of University Programs in Health Administration (EA)
AuPL .... Library Board of Western Australia, State Bibliographical Centre, Perth, WA, Australia [*Library symbol Library of Congress*] (LCLS)
AUPM .... Automated Unit Placement Model
AUPO .... Association of University Professors of Ophthalmology (EA)
AUPOHS .... Association of University Programs in Occupational Health and Safety (EA)

AUPrB .... Amax Gold $3.75 SrB'Cv Pfd [*NYSE symbol*] (TTSB)
AUPS .... American University Press Services, Inc. [*Information service or system*] (IID)
AuPT .... Auxiliary Potential Transformer
AUQ .... Atuona [*Marquesas Islands*] [*Airport symbol*] (OAG)
AUQ .... Aurogin Resources [*Vancouver Stock Exchange symbol*]
AUR .... Accomplishment Utilization Report
AUR .... Active Unattached Reserve [*Royal Australian Navy*]
AUR .... Aircraft Utilization Report
AUR .... All Up Round (MCD)
AUR .... Ambulatory Utilization Review
AUR .... Association of University Radiologists (EA)
AUR .... Aurakhmat [*Former USSR Seismograph station code, US Geological Survey Closed*] (SEIS)
AUR .... Aural
AUR .... Auricular [*or Auricle*] [*Also, A*] [*Medicine*]
Aur .... Auriga [*Constellation*]
AUR .... Aurigny Air Services Ltd. [*British ICAO designator*] (FAAC)
AUR .... Aurillac [*France*] [*Airport symbol Obsolete*] (OAG)
AUR .... Auris [*Ear*] [*Latin*]
AUR .... Aurora Electronics [*AMEX symbol*] (TTSB)
AUR .... Aurora Electronics Co., Inc. [*Formerly, BSN Corp.*] [*AMEX symbol*] (SPSG)
AUR .... Aurora High School PRECIS Project [*UTLAS symbol*]
AUR .... Aurora, NC [*Location identifier FAA*] (FAAL)
AUR .... AUR Resources, Inc. [*Toronto Stock Exchange symbol*]
AUR .... Aurum [*Gold*] [*Latin*]
AUR .... York Region Board of Education [*UTLAS symbol*]
AURA .... Adventure Unlimited Retail Association [*Commercial firm*] (EA)
AURA .... American University Institute for Research in Risk Analysis [*American University*] [*Research center*] (RCD)
AURA .... Army Unit Resiliancy Analysis [*Computer science*] (RDA)
AURA .... Association of Universities for Research in Astronomy (EA)
AURA .... Association of Users of Research Agencies [*British*] (DBA)
AURA .... Audience Reaction Assessment [*Television ratings*] [*British*]
AURA .... Aura Systems, Inc. [*NASDAQ symbol*] (NQ)
AURA .... Automated Reasoning Assistant (IAA)
AURANT .... Auranteum [*Orange (Rind)*] [*Pharmacy*] (ROG)
AuraSy .... Aura Systems, Inc. [*Associated Press*] (SAG)
AURBO .... Aurora Borealis
Aurd .... Auris Dextra [*Right Ear*] [*Otorhinolaryngology*] (DAVI)
AURE .... Aurora Environmental, Inc. [*NASDAQ symbol*] (NQ)
Aurel .... Aurelian [*of Scriptores Historiae Augustae*] [*Classical studies*] (OCD)
Aurel Corbul... Aurelius Corbulus [*Flourished, 16th century*] [*Authority cited in pre-1607 legal work*] (DSA)
AUREQ .... Authority Is Requested (NOAA)
AURF .... Americans United Research Foundation (EA)
aur fib .... Auricular Fibrillation [*Medicine*] (MAE)
AURI .... Ankatan Udara Republik Indonesia
Auri .... Auriga [*Constellation*]
auric .... Auricular [*Cardiology*] (DAVI)
Aurig .... Aurignacian (VRA)
AURIN .... Aurinarium [*Ear Cone*] [*Medicine*]
AURIS .... Aberdeen University Research and Industrial Services (AIE)
AURIS .... Aberdeen University Research & Industrial Services Ltd. [*British Research center*] (IRUK)
AURIST .... Auristillae [*Ear Drops*] [*Pharmacy*]
AURISTILL... Auristillae [*Ear Drops*] [*Pharmacy*]
AURM .... Aurum Software, Inc. [*NASDAQ symbol*] (SAG)
AurmSft ...... Aurum Software, Inc. [*Associated Press*] (SAG)
AurorEl .... Aurora Electronics Co., Inc. [*Formerly, BSN Corp.*] [*Associated Press*] (SAG)
AURP .... Apple-Talk Update-Based Routing Protocol [*Computer science*]
AURPO .... Association of University Radiation Protection Officers [*British*]
AURRP .... Association of University Related Research Parks (EA)
Aurs .... Auris Sinistra [*Left Ear*] [*Otorhinolaryngology*] (DAVI)
AURS .... Automated Unit Reference Sheets (MCD)
AURT .... Aurtex, Inc. [*NASDAQ symbol*] (SAG)
Aurtex .... Aurtex, Inc. [*Associated Press*] (SAG)
AUS .... Actum ut Supra [*Done as Above*] [*Latin*]
AUS .... Advanced Underwriting Service [*Database*] [*R & R Newkirk*] [*Information service or system*] (CRD)
AUS .... Ambassador of the United States
AUS .... American Union of Students (EA)
AuS .... Arbeit und Sitte in Palaestina [*A publication*] (BJA)
AUS .... Army of the United States
AUS .... Assistant Under-Secretary (ADA)
AUS .... Augusta & Summerville Railroad Co. [*AAR code*]
AUS .... Auscultation [*Medicine*] (AAMN)
AUS .... Austin [*Texas*] [*Seismograph station code, US Geological Survey Closed*] (SEIS)
AUS .... Austin Resources, Inc. [*Vancouver Stock Exchange symbol*]
AUS .... Australia [*ANSI three-letter standard code*] (CNC)
AUS .... Australian Airlines [*ICAO designator*] (FAAC)
AuS .... Australia Serum Hepatitis [*Medicine*] (DMAA)
AUS .... Austria
AUS .... Automated Ultrasonic Scanner (MCD)
AuS .... Auxiliary Switch [*Electricity*]
AuS .... City of Sydney Public Library, Sydney, NSW, Australia [*Library symbol Library of Congress*] (LCLS)
AUS .... Robert Mueller Municipal Airport [*FAA*] (TAG)
AUSA .... American Underground-Space Association (EA)
AUSA .... Assistant United States Attorney (EPA)
AUSA .... Association of the United States Army (EA)
AUSA .... Athabasca University Students' Association (AC)

Aus Ab St ... Australian Aboriginal Studies [*A publication*]
AuSAJ .... Department of the Attorney General and of Justice, Sydney, NSW, Australia [*Library symbol Library of Congress*] (LCLS)
Ausb .... Ausbildung [*Education*] [*German*]
AUSBC .... ASEAN [*Association of South East Asian Nations*] - United States Business Council [*Bangkok, Thailand*] (EAIO)
AUSBCM ..... Apollo Unified S-Band Circuit Margin [*Program*] [*NASA*]
AuSbW .... West Australian Institute of Technology, South Bentley, WA, Australia [*Library symbol Library of Congress*] (LCLS)
AUSC .... Auscultation [*Medicine*] (AAMN)
AUSC .... Austin Service Center [*IRS*]
AUSCANUKUS... Australia, Canada, United Kingdom, United States (MCD)
AUSCJ .... Association of US Chess Journalists [*Later, CJA*] (EA)
AUSC-NA .... Association of Ukrainian Sports Clubs in North America (EA)
AUSCOR ...... Automatic Scanning Correlator
AUSCS .... Americans United for Separation of Church and State (EA)
AUSCUL....... Auscultation [*Medicine*] (AAMN)
Aus Drama St... Australasian Drama Studies
AUSEAnet..... Australasia and South East Asia Network [*Computer science*] (TNIG)
AUSED .... Australian Ethnic Democrats [*An association*]
Aus Ed Res... Australian Education Researcher [*A publication*]
AUSEX .... Acoustic Underwater Sound Experiment (MCD)
AUSF .... Australian Universities Sports Federation
AUSFS .... Americans United for a Smoke Free Society [*Defunct*] (EA)
AUS(G) .... Assistant Under-Secretary, General [*Air Ministry*] [*British*]
AUSG........... Ausgabe [*Edition*] [*German*]
Aus Geo ...... Australian Geographer [*A publication*]
AuSGS .... Church of Jesus Christ of Latter-Day Saints, Genealogical Society Library, Sydney Branch, Sydney, NSW, Australia [*Library symbol Library of Congress*] (LCLS)
Aus G Stud... Australian Geographical Studies [*A publication*]
AuSH .... Australia Serum Hepatitis [*Antigen*] [*Immunology*] (MAE)
AUSHEP...... Australian Institute of Higher Energy Physics
AUSINET...... Australian Information Network (NITA)
Aus J Lin .... Australian Journal of Linguistics [*A publication*]
Aus J Phil.... Australasian Journal of Philosophy [*A publication*]
Aus L Rev... Australian Left Review [*A publication*]
AUSM .... Advanced Upper Stage Motor (MCD)
AUSM .... Advanced Utility Simulation Model [*Environmental Protection Agency*] (GFGA)
AUSMARC.... Australian MARC [*Machine readable catalogue*] (NITA)
AUSMEAT .... Authority for Uniform Specification of Meat and Livestock [*Australia*]
AUSMIISL.... Association of US Members of the International Institute of Space Law (EA)
AUSMIN...... Australian-United States Ministerial Talks [*Conference*]
AuSN .... Library of New South Wales, Sydney, NSW, Australia [*Library symbol Library of Congress*] (LCLS)
AuSN-M .... Library of New South Wales, Mitchell Library, Sydney, NSW, Astralia [*Library symbol Library of Congress*] (LCLS)
AUSNVM..... Association of United States Night Vision Manufacturers (EA)
AusNZ.......... Australia & New Zealand Banking Group [*Associated Press*] (SAG)
Auson .... Ausonius [*Fourth century AD*] [*Classical studies*] (OCD)
Aus Outl ...... Australian Outlook [*A publication*]
AuSP........... Parliamentary Library, Parliament House, Sydney, NSW, Australia [*Library symbol Library of Congress*] (LCLS)
AUSPE .... Audiology and Speech Pathology (DAVI)
Aus Peay St U... Austin Peay State University (GAGS)
Auspex .... Auspex Systems, Inc. [*Associated Press*] (SAG)
AUSPORT .... Australian Sport Index [*Database*]
Aus Psych.... Australian Psychologist [*A publication*]
AUSQS .... Australian Unlisted Securities Quotation System
Aus Rep....... Austin's Appeal Reports [*Ceylon*] [*A publication*] (ILCA)
AUSS .... Advanced Underwater Search System (MCD)
AUSS .... American Union of Swedish Singers (EA)
AUSS .... Assistant Under-Secretary of State (DAS)
AUSS .... Association of University Summer Sessions (EA)
AUSSAT ...... Australian Satellite [*Telecommunications*] (NITA)
ausserd....... Ausserdem [*Furthermore*] [*German*]
Aus Soc ...... Australian Society [*A publication*]
Aus Soc W... Australian Social Work [*A publication*]
Ausst .... Ausstellung [*Exhibition*] [*German*]
AUSSTATS... Australian Statistics [*Database*]
Aust .... Austin's English County Court Cases [*1867-69*] [*A publication*] (DLA)
AUST .... Austins International [*NASDAQ symbol*] (SAG)
AUST .... Austin's International [*NASDAQ symbol*] (TTSB)
AUST .... Australian
AUST .... Austria
Aust .... Austria (VRA)
AusT .... Austrian Telefunken [*Record label*]
Aust Acad Res Libs... Australian Academic and Research Libraries [*A publication*]
Aust Account Student... Australian Accountancy Student [*A publication*]
Aust Acctnt... Australian Accountant [*A publication*]
Aust & NZJ Crim... Australian and New Zealand Journal of Criminology [*A publication*]
Aust & NZ Phys... Australian and New Zealand Physicist [*A publication*]
Aust Bar Rev... Australian Bar Review [*A publication*]
Aust Bk R... Australian Book Review [*A publication*] (BRI)
Aust BL.... Australian Bulletin of Labour [*A publication*]
Aust Build.... Australian Builder [*A publication*]
Aust Bus Brief... Australian Business Brief [*A publication*]
Aust Bus Cond Bull... Australasian Business Conditions Bulletin [*A publication*]
Aust Bus Law Rev... Australian Business Law Review [*A publication*]
Aust Bus Lawyer... Australian Business Lawyer [*A publication*]
Aust Bus Rev... Australian Business Law Review [*A publication*]
Aust Child Family Welf... Australian Child and Family Welfare [*A publication*]

Aust Children TV Com Newsl... Australian Children's Television Committee. Newsletter [*A publication*]
Aust Civil Engng Constr... Australian Civil Engineering and Construction [*A publication*]
AUSTCIVPOL.... Australian Civil Police
AUSTCOM.... Australian Commodities [*Database*]
Aust Con LR... Australian Construction Law Reporter [*A publication*]
Aust Council Aeronautics Rept... Australian Council for Aeronautics. Report [*A publication*]
AustCP......... Australian Country Party [*Political party*]
Aust Credit Unions Mag... Australian Credit Unions Magazine [*A publication*]
Aust D 2d... Australian Digest, Second Edition [*A publication*] (DLA)
Aust DFA Treaty Series... Australia. Department of Foreign Affairs. Treaty Series [*A publication*]
Aust Econ P... Australian Economic Papers [*A publication*]
Aust Econ R... Australian Economic Review [*A publication*]
Aust Ed Res... Australian Education Researcher [*A publication*]
Aust Ed Rev... Australian Education Review [*A publication*]
Aust Elec Times... Australasian Electrical Times [*A publication*]
Aust Eng... Australasian Engineer [*A publication*]
Aust Fed Police... Australian Federal Police [*A publication*]
Aust Fisheries... Australian Fisheries [*A publication*]
Aust For Aff Rec... Australian Foreign Affairs Record [*A publication*]
Aust Forest Grower... Australian Forest Grower [*A publication*]
Aust Her...... Australia's Heritage [*A publication*]
Aust Hist Bibl... Australian Historical Bibliography [*A publication*]
Aust Hist Stud... Australian Historical Studies [*A publication*]
Austin.......... Austin's Reports [*Ceylon*] [*A publication*] (DLA)
Austin CC..... Austin's English County Court Reports [*A publication*] (DLA)
Austin (Ceylon)... Austin's Ceylon Reports [*A publication*] (DLA)
Austins........ Austins Steak & Saloon, Inc. [*Associated Press*] (SAG)
AustInt......... Austin's International, Inc. [*Associated Press*] (SAG)
AUSTIS........ Australian Timber Industry Stabilization Conference
Aust'J Adv Ed... Australian Journal of Advanced Education [*A publication*]
Aust J Exper Biol & Med Sci... Australian Journal of Experimental Biology and Medical Science [*A publication*]
Aust J Foren Sci... Australian Journal of Forensic Sciences [*A publication*]
Aust J Hlth Phys Ed Rec... Australian Journal of Health, Physical Education, and Recreation [*A publication*]
Aust J Inst Transp... Australian Journal. Institute of Transport [*A publication*]
Aust JLS...... Australian Journal of Law and Society [*A publication*]
Aust JM...... Australian Journal of Management [*A publication*]
Aust J Mgmt... Australian Journal of Management [*A publication*]
Aust Jnl of Social Issues... Australian Journal of Social Issues [*A publication*]
Aust J Psych & Phil... Australian Journal of Psychology and Philosophy [*A publication*]
Aust J Publ Admin... Australian Journal of Public Administration [*A publication*]
Aust Jr........ Austin's Lectures on Jurisprudence [*A publication*] (DLA)
Aust J Soc Is... Australian Journal of Social Issues [*A publication*]
Aust J Spec Ed... Australian Journal of Special Education [*A publication*]
Aust J Teach Ed... Australian Journal of Teacher Education [*A publication*]
Aust Jur...... Austin's Lectures on Jurisprudence [*A publication*] (ILCA)
Aust Jur Abr... Austin's Lectures on Jurisprudence, Abridged [*A publication*] (DLA)
Aust Jur R ... Australian Jurist Reports [*A publication*] (ILCA)
Aust KA....... Austin's Kandran Appeals [*Ceylon*] [*A publication*] (DLA)
AUSTL......... Australasia (BARN)
AUSTL .... Australia
Austl Acts .... Acts of the Australian Parliament [*A publication*] (DLA)
Austl AD ...... Australian Annual Digest [*A publication*] (DLA)
Austl C Acts... Commonwealth Acts (Australia) [*A publication*] (DLA)
Austl Cap Terr Subs Leg... Subsidiary Legislation of the Australian Capital Territory [*A publication*] (DLA)
Austl Convey & Sol J... Australian Conveyancer and Solicitors' Journal [*A publication*] (DLA)
Austl Current L Rev... Australian Current Law Review [*A publication*] (DLA)
Austl D .... Australian Digest [*A publication*] (DLA)
Aust Left R... Australian Left Review [*A publication*]
Aust Left Rev... Australian Left Review [*A publication*]
Aust Libr News... Australian Library News [*A publication*]
Austl JL Soc'y... Australian Journal of Law and Society [*A publication*] (DLA)
Austl Jr........ Australian Jurist [*A publication*] (DLA)
Austl Law .... Australian Lawyer [*A publication*] (DLA)
Austl LMD .... Australian Legal Monthly Digest [*A publication*] (DLA)
Austl LR ...... Australian Law Reports [*A publication*] (DLA)
Austl L Times... Australian Law Times [*A publication*] (DLA)
Aust Mger.... Australian Manager [*A publication*]
Aust Mining Stand... Australian Mining Standard [*A publication*]
Aust Mon Mag... Australian Monthly Magazine [*A publication*]
Aust National Rev... Australian National Review [*A publication*]
Aust Natn Rev... Australian National Review [*A publication*]
AustNZ....... Australia & New Zealand Banking Group [*Associated Press*] (SAG)
Aust NZ Jl Criminol... Australian and New Zealand Journal of Criminology [*A publication*]
Aust NZ Jl Sociol... Australian and New Zealand Journal of Sociology [*A publication*]
Aust NZ Jl Surgery... Australian and New Zealand Journal of Surgery [*A publication*]
AUSTOCK..... Australian Stock Exchanges Share Prices [*Database*]
AUSTPAC..... Australian Packet Switching Service [*Telecommunications*] (NITA)
Aust Parl Paper... Australian Parliamentary Paper [*A publication*]
Aust Photo Rev... Australasian Photo Review [*A publication*]
Aust Pol J... Australian Police Journal [*A publication*]
Aust Presb Life... Australian Presbyterian Life [*A publication*]
Aust Presch Q... Australian Pre-School Quarterly [*A publication*]
Aust Prod Action... Australian Productivity Action [*A publication*]

Aust Publ Libr Issues... Australian Public Library Issues [*A publication*]
AUSTR....... Australia
Austr............ Australia (VRA)
Aust R .... Australian Review [*A publication*]
Austr............ Austria Fund [*Associated Press*] (SAG)
AUSTRADE.... Australian Trade Commission
AUSTRAL..... Australasian (ROG)
AUSTRAL..... Australia
Australas Cath Rec... Australasian Catholic Record [*A publication*]
Australas Insur Banking Rec... Australasian Insurance and Banking Record [*A publication*]
Australas Insur J... Australasian Insurance Journal [*A publication*]
Australas Schoolmaster... Australasian Schoolmaster and Literary Review [*A publication*]
AUSTROADS... National Association of Australian Road Authorities
AUSTROP ... Australian Tropical Research Foundation
Austr Tax... Australian Tax Decisions [*A publication*] (DLA)
Aust Saf N... Australian Safety News [*A publication*]
Aust School Libn... Australian School Librarian [*A publication*]
AUSTSIA...... Australasia (ADA)
AUSTSN...... Australasian (ADA)
Aust Soc...... Australian Society [*A publication*] (APTA)
Aust Soc Welf... Australian Social Welfare [*A publication*]
Aust Soc Welf Impact... Australian Social Welfare Impact [*A publication*]
Aust Soc Work... Australian Social Work [*A publication*]
AustStk .... Austria [*Republic of*] Stock Index Growth Notes [*Associated Press*] (SAG)
AUST STUDY... Australian Studies Resources [*Database*]
Aust Teacher... Australian Teacher [*A publication*]
Aust Torts Reports... Australian Torts Reports [*A publication*]
Aust Y Int L... Australian Yearbook of International Law [*A publication*] (DLA)
AuSU........ University of Sydney, Sydney, NSW, Australia [*Library symbol Library of Congress*] (LCLS)
AUSUDIAP ... Association of US University Directors of International Agricultural Programs [*Later, AIARD*] (EA)
AUSVETPLAN... Australian Veterinary Emergency Plan
Ausw........... Auswaertiges [*Nonresident*] [*German*]
Auswasch .... Auswaschung [*Erosion*] [*German*]
AUT............ Access Upsizing Tools [*Microsoft Corp.*] (PCM)
AUT............ Advanced Unit Training [*Army*]
AUT............ Advanced User Terminal [*Navy*] (MCD)
AUT............ American Union Transport [*Steamship*] (MHDW)
AUT............ American United Telecom (NITA)
AUT............ Ammonium Uranyl Tricarbonate [*Inorganic chemistry*]
AUT............ Asian University [*EDUCATSS*] [*UTLAS symbol*]
AUT............ Association of Ukrainians in Tasmania [*Australia*]
AUT............ Association of University Teachers [*A union*] [*British*]
AUT............ Austral Lineas Aereas [*Argentina ICAO designator*] (FAAC)
AUT............ Austria [*ANSI three-letter standard code*] (CNC)
AUT............ Au Tau [*Hong Kong*] [*Later, HKO*] [*Geomagnetic observatory code*]
Aut............ Authenticum [*A publication*] (DSA)
AUT............ Author [*Online database field identifier*] [*Computer science*]
AUT............ Authority
AUT............ Autograph
AUT............ Automatic
AUT............ Autonomous
AUT............ Autopsy [*Also, AU*] [*Medicine*]
aut............ Autoroute (DD)
AUT............ Autrex, Inc. [*Toronto Stock Exchange symbol*]
AUT............ Autumn
AUTA .... Association of University Teachers in Accounting [*British*]
AUT-ATFM ... Automation on Air Traffic Flow Management (DA)
AUTDEX ...... Author Index
AUtdG .... American United Global, Inc. [*Associated Press*] (SAG)
AUtdGlb .... American United Global, Inc. [*Associated Press*] (SAG)
AUTEC .... Atlantic Undersea Test and Evaluation Center [*Acronym also used to refer to device for detection, amplification, and transmission of undersea noise*] [*Navy*]
AUT/GMBH... Automation GMBH [*McDonnell Douglas Corp.*] [*Germany*]
AUTH .... Authentic
auth .... Authentic (WDMC)
auth .... Author (WDMC)
AUTH .... Author
auth .... Author (VRA)
AUTH .... Authority (AFM)
AUTH .... Authorization [*or Authorized*] (EY)
auth .... Authorized (WDMC)
AUTH .... Authorized Version [*or King James Version of the Bible, 1611*] (ROG)
AUTHAB...... Authorized Abbreviation (MCD)
AUTHAB...... Authorized About
AUTHBUPERSMAN... Authorized in Bureau of Naval Personnel Manual
AUTHD........ Authorized (ROG)
AUTHEN...... Authentic (AABC)
Authen........ Authenticum [*A publication*] (DSA)
AUTHEXANDO... Authority Granted to Execute Acceptance and Oath of Office for
AuthFit......... Authentic Fitness Corp. [*Associated Press*] (SAG)
AUTHGR ...... Authority Granted [*Army*]
AUTHGRA ..... Authority Granted [*Military*] (NVT)
authn .... Authentic (VRA)
AUTHN........ Authentication (AFM)
AUTHPROBOUT... Authorized to Proceed On or About [*Date*] [*Military*]
AUTHR........ Authorization Response
AUTHTRAV.... Authorized to Travel [*Military*] (DNAB)
AUTHY .... Authority

AuTJC .... James Cook University of North Queensland, Townsville, QLD, Australia [*Library symbol Library of Congress*] (LCLS)
AUT/KY .... Automation Co. of Kentucky [*McDonnell Douglas Corp.*]
AUTM .... Association of Unit Trust Managers [*British*] (BI)
AUTM .... Association of University Technology Managers (AAGC)
AUTM .... Association of Used Tyre Merchants [*British*] (BI)
AUTM .... Automatic
AUTMV .... Automotive (MUGU)
AUTM WTR CK... Automatic Water Check [*Freight*]
AuTNQ .... North Queensland Newspaper Co. Ltd., Townsville, QLD, Australia [*Library symbol Library of Congress*] (LCLS)
AUTO .... AutoInfo, Inc. [*NASDAQ symbol*] (SPSG)
AUTO .... Automatic (AFM)
Auto .... Automatic Coupling [*Music*]
AUTO .... Automobile
AUTO .... Automobile
AUTOAB ...... Autoantibody [*Panel*] [*Biochemistry*] (DAVI)
AUTOBILL .... Automotive Billing Module [*GSA*] (TAG)
AUTOBUS .... Automated Budget System
Auto C .... Automobile Cases [*Commerce Clearing House*] [*A publication*] (DLA)
Autocam ...... Autocam Corp. [*Associated Press*] (SAG)
AUTOCAP .... Automated Continuous Acceptance of Propellants (MCD)
AUTOCAP .... Automotive Consumer Action Program (EA)
Auto Cas ..... Automobile Cases [*Commerce Clearing House*] [*A publication*] (DLA)
Auto Cas 2d.. Automobile Cases, Second Series [*Commerce Clearing House*] [*A publication*] (DLA)
AUTOCAT .... Automatic Communication Relay (NVT)
AUTOCAT .... Automatic Control of Air Transmissions (NATG)
AUTOCOM.... Automated Combustor [*Computer code*]
AUTO CV ..... Automatic Check Valve (MSA)
Autodesk ..... Autodesk, Inc. [*Associated Press*] (SAG)
AUTODIN ..... Automatic Digital Network [*DoD*]
AUTODIN EMOD... Automatic Digital Network - Evolutionary Modernization [*Military*] (DNAB)
AUTODIN ICCDP... Automatic Digital Network - Integrated Circuits Communications Data Processor [*Military*] (DNAB)
AUTODOC .... Automated Documentation (IAA)
AutoDt .... Automatic Data Processing [*Associated Press*] (SAG)
AutoDta .... Automatic Data Processing, Inc. [*Associated Press*] (SAG)
AUTOEXEC BAT... Automatic Execute Batch (CDE)
AUTOFAC .... AUTODIN Facility (MCD)
AUTO-FETS... Automated Field Evaluation and Test System (MCD)
AUTOFLOW... Automatic Flowcharting
AUTOG .... Autograph
AUTO-GOSS... Automated Ground Operations Scheduling System [*Also, AGOSS*] (MCD)
AUTOGRP .... Automatic Grouping System [*Hospital records*] (DHSM)
AutoICS .... Automated Immunochemistry System
Auto ID .... Automatic Identification [*Computer science*]
Autoimu .... Autoimmune, Inc. [*Associated Press*] (SAG)
AutoInd .... Automatic Industries Holdings [*Associated Press*] (SAG)
AutoInf .... AutoInfo, Inc. [*Associated Press*] (SAG)
Auto Ins Cas... Automobile Insurance Cases [*Commerce Clearing House*] [*A publication*] (DLA)
AutoKo .... Automatic Corps [*Communications System*] [*General Electric Co.*]
Autoko .... Automatische Korpsstamunetz [*Tactical Communications System*] [*Germany*]
AutoL .... AutoLend Group, Inc. [*Associated Press*] (SAG)
AUTOLABS... Automatic Low-Altitude Bombing System (MCD)
AUTOLAND... Automatic Landing [*NASA*] (NASA)
AutoLend ..... AutoLend Group, Inc. [*Associated Press*] (SAG)
AUTOLING ... Automated Linguistic Fieldworker [*Computer science*] (DIT)
Autolog .... Autologic Information International, Inc. [*Associated Press*] (SAG)
Auto L Rep... Automobile Law Reporter [*Commerce Clearing House*] [*A publication*] (DLA)
AUTOM ...... Automated
AUTOM ...... Automotive (MSA)
AUTOMAD.... Automatic Adaptation Data (DNAB)
AUTOMAN... European Automated Manufacturing Exhibition and Conference [*British Robot Association*]
AUTOMAP.... Automatic Machining Program
AUTOMASIA... South East Asian International Automated Manufacturing Technology and Robotics Show and Conference
AUTOMAST... Automatic Mathematical Analysis and Symbolic Translation [*Computer science*]
AUTOMAT.... Automated Material System (MCD)
AUTOMET .... Automatic Meteorological Correction [*A missile guidance technique*]
AUTOMEX.... Automatic Message Exchange Service
AUTOMN...... Automation (MSA)
AUTOMTC ... Automatic
AUTOMTN ... Automation
AUTOMTV ... Automotive
AUTOMV ..... Automotive (AABC)
AUTON .... Automation (AFM)
AUTONEST... Automatic Nesting Program [*Kongsberg Vaapenfabrikk*] [*Software package*] (NCC)
AUTONET .... Automatic Network Display
AutonoT ...... Autonomous Technologies Corp. [*Associated Press*] (SAG)
AuTooT .... Toowoomba Newspapers Publishers Ltd., Toowoomba, QLD, Australia [*Library symbol Library of Congress*] (LCLS)
AUTOOVLD... Automatic Overload (IAA)
AUTOP .... Automatic Pistol
Auto PA ...... Automatic Personal Accident [*Insurance*] (AIA)
AUTOPARTAC... International Automotive Parts and Accessories Trade Show [*British*] (ITD)

AUTOPASS... Automated Parking Support System [*Vehicle storage*]
AUTOPAY..... Automotive Payment Module [*GSA*] (TAG)
AUTOPIC...... Automatic Personal Identification Code [*IBM Corp.*]
AUTOPLOT... Automatic Plotting Routine (ADA)
AUTOPOD .... Automatic Proof of Delivery
AUTOPOL .... Automatic Programming of Lathes (PDAA)
AUTOPOLL... Automatic Polling [*Computer science*] (EECA)
AUTOPROBE... Automated Programming, Budgeting, and Operational Evaluation [*Army*]
AUTOPROC... Automatic Procurement Capability System
AUTOPROD... Automated Projective Drawing [*GMW Computers Ltd.*] [*Software package*] (NCC)
AUTO PROG... Automatic Programming [*Computer science*]
AUTOPROMT... Automatic Programming of Machine Tools [*IBM Corp.*]
AUTOPROPS... Automatic Programming for Positioning System (DNAB)
AUTOPROS... Automated Process Planning System (PDAA)
AUTOPSY..... Automatic Operating System [*IBM Corp.*]
AUTO PTS... Automobile Parts [*Freight*]
AUTOQEST... Automatic Generation of Requests [*Computer science*] (DIT)
AUTORECL... Automatic Reclosing (IAA)
AUTOROS ... Automated Retail Outlet System (MCD)
AutoSACE ... Automatic Shorebased Acceptance Checkout Equipment (PDAA)
AUTOSAG ... Ad Universiterrarum Orbis Summi Architecti Gloriam [*To the Glory of the GrandArchitect of the Universe*] [*Freemasonry*] [*Latin*]
AUTO S & CV... Automatic Stop and Check Valve (AAG)
AUTOSATE... Automated System Analysis Technique
AUTOSCAN... Automatic Satellite / Computer Aid to Navigation [*Computer science*] (PDAA)
AUTOSCAN... Automatic Stereo Broadcast Scanner (IAA)
AUTOSCRIPT... Automated System for Composing, Revising, Illustrating, and Phototypesetting
AUTOSD....... Automatic SDI [*Selective Dissemination of Information*] [*British Library Automated Information Service*] (NITA)
AUTOSERVCEN... Automated Service Center
AUTOSEVCOM... Automatic Secure Voice Communications
AUTOSEVOCOM... Automatic Secure Voice Communications (NVT)
AUTOSEVOCON... Automatic Secure Voice Communications Network
AUTOSPEC... Automated Specifications [*Computer science*] (DIT)
AUTOSPOT... Automatic System for Positioning Tools
AUTOSTIF... Automatic Stiffening (MSA)
AUTOSTRAD... Automated System for Transportation Data [*Military*]
AUTOSTRT... Automatic Starter
AUTOSTRTG... Automatic Starting
AUTOSYN ... Automatically Synchronous [*Remote-indicating system*] [*Trade name Western Electric Co.*]
Autotote ...... Autotote Corp. [*Associated Press*] (SAG)
AUTOTR...... Autotransformer
AUTOTRAN... Automatic Translation
AUTO-TRIP... Automatic Transportation Research Investigation Program (PDAA)
AUTOVON .... Automatic Voice Network [*DoD*]
AUTOWEAP... Automatic Weapon (DNAB)
AutoZone ..... Autozone, Inc. [*Associated Press*] (SAG)
Aut Pand...... Authenticis Pandectis [*Latin*] (DSA)
AUTPOL....... Automatic Polarity Indication (IAA)
AutProt .... Automobile Protection Corp. [*Associated Press*] (SAG)
AUTRA .... Automobile Utility Trailer Rental Association (EA)
AUTRAN...... Automatic Target Recognition Analysis
AUTRAN...... Automatic Utility Translator (IEEE)
AUTRANAV... Automated Transponder Navigation System (PDAA)
AUTRAX...... Automatic Traffic Recording and Analysis Complex (IAA)
AUTRE .... Associated Universities for Toxicology Research and Education [*Research center*] (RCD)
AUTS .... Adult Use of Tobacco Survey [*1986*]
AUTS .... Automatic Update Transaction System [*DoD*]
AutSec .... Automated Security Holdings Ltd. [*Associated Press*] (SAG)
AUT/TEX ..... Automation Co. of Texas [*McDonnell Douglas Corp.*]
AutTrT........ Auto Trol Technology Corp. [*Associated Press*] (SAG)
AUTTUN...... Automatic Tuning (IAA)
AUU .... Americans for the Universality of UNESCO (EA)
AUU .... Association of Urban Universities [*Defunct*] (EA)
AUU .... Atlanta University Center, Atlanta, GA [*OCLC symbol*] (OCLC)
AUU .... Aurukun Mission [*Australia Airport symbol*] (OAG)
AuU........... Australian National University, Canberra, ACT, Australia [*Library symbol Library of Congress*] (LCLS)
AUUA.......... Americas UNIVAC [*Universal Automatic Computer*] Users Association [*Formerly, USE, UUA*] (EA)
AUUC......... Association of United Ukrainian Canadians (AC)
AuUqP .... University of Queensland Press, Microform Division, St. Lucia, Brisbane, QLD, Australia [*Library symbol Library of Congress*] (LCLS)
AUV .... Administrative Use Vehicle [*Military*] (AABC)
AUV .... Aerial Unmanned Vehicle [*Military*]
AUV .... Anterior Urethral Valve [*Medicine*] (DMAA)
AUV .... Ardmore, OK [*Location identifier FAA*] (FAAL)
AUV .... Armored Utility Vehicle
AUV .... Atruvera [*Former USSR*] [*FAA designator*] (FAAC)
AUV .... Autonomous Underwater Vehicle [*Navy*]
AUVIS .... Authorised Unregistered Vehicle Inspection Station [*Australia*]
AUVL .... Airborne Ultraviolet LASER
AUVMIS ...... Administrative Use Vehicle Management Information System [*Military*] (MCD)
AUVS .... Association for Unmanned Vehicle Systems (EA)
AUW .... Advanced Underseas Weapons [*Army*]
AUW .... Advanced Underwater Warfare [*Navy*]
AUW .... Airframe Unit Weight

AUW	All Up Weight (DOMA)
AUW	Antiunderwater Warfare [*Navy*] (CINC)
AUW	Automatic Winder (IAA)
AUW	Wausau [*Wisconsin*] [*Airport symbol*] (OAG)
AUWC	Advanced Underseas Weapons Circuitry
AuWol	Wollongong Public Library, Wollongong, NSW, Australia [*Library symbol Library of Congress*] (LCLS)
AUWS	Automatic Unmanned Weather Station
AUWT	Ames Unitary Wind Tunnel (SAA)
AUX	Apple UNIX [*Computer science*] (ACRL)
AUX	Araguaina [*Brazil*] [*Airport symbol*] (OAG)
AUX	Auxiliary (AFM)
aux	Auxiliary (WDMC)
AUX	Auxiliary
Aux	Auxiliary Light [*Navigation signal*]
AUX COMMO	Auxiliary Communications
AUXCP	Auxiliary Airborne Command Post (MCD)
AUXGCS	Auxiliary Ground Control Station [*NASA*] (KSC)
AUXIL	Auxiliary
AUXOPS	Auxiliary Operational Members [*Coast Guard*]
AUXOSC	Auxiliary Oscillator
AUXR	Auxiliary Register
AUXRC	Auxiliary Recording Control [*Circuit*] [*Bell System*]
AUXTRAC	Auxiliary Track (MUGU)
AUY	Aerolinas Uruguayas SA [*Uruguay*] [*ICAO designator*] (FAAC)
AUY	Aneityum [*Vanuatu*] [*Airport symbol*] (OAG)
AUY	Audrey Resources, Inc. [*Toronto Stock Exchange symbol*]
AUZ	Aus-Air [*Australia ICAO designator*] (FAAC)
AV	Abbreviated Visual Approach Slope Indicator System [*Aviation*] (DA)
AV	Abnormal Voltage
aV	Abvolt [*Unit of electromotive force*]
AV	Acid Value [*Chemistry*]
AV	Actual Value
AV	Actual Velocity
AV	Adriamycin, Vincristine [*Antineoplastic drug regimen*]
AV	Ad Valorem [*According to the Value*] [*Latin Business term*]
AV	Advanced Voyager
AV	Aerospace Vehicle (AFM)
AV	Aerovironment, Inc.
AV	Air-Cushion Vehicle built by Air Vehicles [*England*] [*Usually used in combination with numerals*]
AV	Air Vent
AV	Allgemeine Verwaltungsvorschrift [*or Vorschrift*] [*General Administrative Regulation*] [*German*] (ILCA)
AV	Allport-Vernon [*Psychology*] (BARN)
AV	Almost Verbatim (AAGC)
AV	Alternative Vote
AV	Alveolar Duct (MAE)
AV	American Vegetarian (EA)
AV	American Viewpoint [*Later, ERC*]
AV	Anglo-Vernacular
AV	Angular Velocity (MCD)
AV	Animal-Vues (EA)
AV	Anion Vacancy (IAA)
AV	Anno Vixit [*He Lived (a given number of) Years*] [*Latin*]
AV	Annual Value (ADA)
AV	[*The*] Answering Voice [*A publication*]
AV	Anterior Ventral Neuron [*Neurophysiology*]
AV	Anteversion [*Medicine*]
AV	Anticipated Vacancy [*Civil Service*]
AV	Antivehicle [*Munitions*]
A/V	Anti-Vermin [*Battle dress*] [*British and Canadian*] [*World War II*]
AV	Antivirus [*Computer science*]
AV	Anti-Vivisection Party [*British*]
AV	Aonde Vamos (BJA)
AV	Aortic Valve [*Cardiology*]
AV	Aperture Value [*Photography*]
AV	Arbeitsverwendungsfaehig [*Fit for labor duty only*] [*German military - World War II*]
AV	Area Weapon Verify (MCD)
AV	Armored Vehicle (MCD)
A:V	Arterial/Venous [*Ratio in fundi*] [*Ophthalmology*] (DAVI)
AV	Arteriovenous [*Medicine*]
AV	Artificial Vagina [*Veterinary science*] (OA)
AV	Artillery Volunteers
AV	Asparagus Virus
AV	Asset Value (WDAA)
AV	Association Value [*Psychometrics*]
AV	Atomic Value (ADA)
AV	Atrioventricular [*Cardiology*]
AV	Audio Video (WDMC)
A/V	Audio/Video (WDMC)
A/V	Audio/Visual (WDMC)
AV	Audiovisual
a/v	Audio-Visual (IDOE)
AV	Auditory-Visual (DAVI)
AV	Auriculoventricular [*Medicine*]
AV	Aurum [*Gold*] [*Numismatics*]
AV	Austere Version (MCD)
AV	Authorized Version [*or King James Version of the Bible, 1611*]
AV	Automatic Volume [*Electronics*] (ECII)
AV	Autophagic Vacuole [*Botany*]
AV	AUTOVON (MCD)
AV	Auxiliary Vessel (NOAA)
AV	Availability (NITA)
AV	Available [*or Availability*] [*Online database field identifier*] [*Computer science*]
AV	Avenue [*Correspondence*] (EY)
av	Avenue (DD)
AV	Average
AV	Average Value (NASA)
AV	Average Variability
Av	Aves [*Birds*] [*of Aristophanes*] [*Classical studies*] (OCD)
Av	Avesta [*Language, etc.*]
Av	Avestan (BARN)
AV	Avianca (GAVI)
AV	Avianca [*ICAO designator*] (AD)
AV	Aviation [*Special duties officer*] [*British*]
AV	AVIC Group International, Inc. [*AMEX symbol*] (SAG)
AV	Avionics (NASA)
AV	Avoir [*Credit*] [*French*]
AV	Avoirdupois
AV	Hawker Siddeley Aviation Ltd. [*British ICAO aircraft manufacturer identifier*] (ICAO)
AV	Seaplane Tender [*Navy symbol*]
AV	Vimy Public Library, Alberta [*Library symbol National Library of Canada*] (NLC)
AV 3V	Anteroventral Portion of the Third Ventricle [*Neuroanatomy*]
AVA	Absolute Virtual Address [*Computer science*]
AVA	Academy of Veterinary Allergy (EA)
AVA	Action Volunteers for Animals (AC)
AVA	Activity Vector Analysis [*Psychology*]
AVA	Administration of Veterans Affairs [*Army*]
AVA	Adult Video Association (EA)
AVA	Alabama Vending Association (SRA)
AVA	Alabama Vocational Association (SRA)
AVA	Alaska Visitors Association (SRA)
AVA	Alberta Volleyball Association (AC)
AVA	Amateur Volleyball Association [*British*] (BI)
AVA	American Vaulting Association (EA)
AVA	American Vecturist Association (EA)
AVA	American Ventilation Association [*Defunct*] (EA)
AVA	American Veterans Alliance (EA)
AVA	American Veterans Association - National Headquarters
AVA	American Victims of Abortion (EA)
AVA	American Video Association (EA)
AVA	American Vocational Association (EA)
AVA	American Volkssport Association (EA)
AVA	American Voyager Association (EA)
AVA	Apovincaminic Acid [*Biochemistry*]
AVA	Arracacha Virus A [*Plant pathology*]
AVA	Arteriovenous Anastomosis [*Medicine*]
AVA	Asbestos Victims of America (EA)
AVA	ASEAN [*Association of South East Asian Nations*] Valuers Association [*Kuala Lumpur, Malaysia*] (EAIO)
AVA	Association for Volunteer Administration
AVA	Association of Veterinary Anaesthetists [*British*]
AVA	Audiovisual Annunciator
AVA	Audio Visual Association [*British*] (DBA)
AVA	Audio Visual Authoring [*Computer programming language*] (PCM)
AVA	Australian Volleyball Association
AVA	Authorized Validating Agency (AIE)
AVA	Automated Vision Association [*Later, AIA*] (EA)
AVA	Automatic Voice Answering [*Computer-generated recording unit for telephone directory assistance*]
AVA	Avance International, Inc. [*Vancouver Stock Exchange symbol*]
ava	Avaric [*MARC language code Library of Congress*] (LCCP)
AVA	Average Alarm
AVA	Avianca, Aerovias Nacionales de Colombia SA [*ICAO designator*] (FAAC)
AVA	Azimuth Versus Amplitude
AVA	Grand Forks, ND [*Location identifier FAA*] (FAAL)
AVA	Vauxhall Public Library, Alberta [*Library symbol National Library of Canada*] (NLC)
AVAA	African Violet Association of Australia
AVAA	American Viticultural Area Association (EA)
AVAB	Automatic Vending Association of Britain (EAIO)
AVAC	Aids Vaccine Advocacy Coalition
AVAC	Audio-Visual Aids Committee [*British*]
AVAC	Automated Vacuum
AVAC	Automated Vacuum-Assisted Collection System [*Disney World trash disposal system*]
AVACOM-ETARP	Availability Computation - Element Transient and Asymptotic Repair Process (PDAA)
AVAD	Automatic Voice Alerting Device (DA)
'Avad	'Avadim (BJA)
Av Adj Assoc Dig	Digest of Reports of the Average Adjusters Association [*1895*] [*A publication*] (DLA)
AVADS	Advanced Vulcan Air Defense System (MCD)
AVADS	Autotrack Vulcan Air Defense System
AVADSC	Australian Veterans and Defense Services Council [*Also, AVDSC*]
AVAE	Association for Voluntary Action in Europe [*See also AVE*] (EAIO)
AV/AF	Anteverted, Anteflexed [*Medicine*] (MAE)
AVAIL	Available [*or Availability*] (KSC)
AVAL	Available [*or Availability*] (AFM)
AvaIn	Avalon Properties [*Associated Press*] (SAG)
Avalon	Avalon Community Services, Inc. [*Associated Press*] (SAG)
AvalonC	Avalon Capital, Inc. [*Associated Press*] (SAG)
AvalonPr	Avalon Properties [*Associated Press*] (SAG)
AVAM	American Visionary Art Museum

AVANA	Altitude Reservation Void for Aircraft Not Airborne By [*Aviation*] (FAAC)
Av & HBL	Avery and Hobb's Bankrupt Law [*A publication*] (DLA)
AVang	American Vanguard Corp. [*Associated Press*] (SAG)
AVANT	Association of Voluntary Agencies on Narcotics Treatment
Avanti	Avant Corp. [*Associated Press*] (SAG)
AVAP	Airport Vicinity Air Pollution
AVAR	Asymptomatic Variance
AVAR	Regional Office, Alberta Agriculture, Vermilion, Alberta [*Library symbol National Library of Canada*] (NLC)
AVAS	Association of Voluntary Action Scholars [*Later, ARNOVA*] (EA)
AVAS	Automated Voice Annunciator Systems [*FTA*] (TAG)
AVAS	Automatic VFR [*Visual Flight Rules*] Advisory Service [*Aviation*] (OA)
AVASI	Abbreviated Visual Approach Slope Indicator [*Aviation*]
AVASIS	Abbreviated Visual Approach Slope Indicator System [*Aviation*]
AVASS	Association of Voluntary Aided Secondary Schools [*British*]
Avatar	Avatar Holdings, Inc. [*Associated Press*] (SAG)
AVATI	Asphalt and Vinyl Asbestos Tile Institute [*Later, RFCI*] (EA)
AVAWA	Auctioneers and Valuers' Association of Western Australia
AV-AWOS	Aviation Automated Weather Observation System (NOAA)
AV-AWOS-T	Aviation-Automatic/Weather Observing System Developmental Model (T) (MCD)
AVB	Advanced Aviation Base Ship [*Navy symbol Obsolete*]
AVB	Allgemeine Versicherungsbedingungen [*General conditions of insurance*] [*German*] (ILCA)
AVB	Analog Video Bandwidth
AVB	Arracacha Virus B [*Plant pathology*]
AVB	Association of Volunteer Bureaus [*Later, NVC*] (EA)
AVB	Atrioventricular Block [*Cardiology*] (DMAA)
AVB	Aviation Baseship
AVB	Aviation Beauport Ltd. [*British ICAO designator*] (FAAC)
AVBA	Avionics Bulletin (MCD)
AVBA	Australian/Victorian Biathlon Association
AVBAD	Army Aviator Badge [*Military decoration*]
AVBAT	Aviation Battalion [*Army*]
AVBAY	Avionics Bay (MCD)
AVBL	Armoured Vehicle Bridge Launcher [*Military*] (PDAA)
AVBL	Available [*or Availability*]
AVBLE	Available (ECII)
AVBLTY	Availability
AVBS	Absolute Value BIT [*Binary Digit*] Synchronizer
AVBV	Artichoke Vein Banding Virus [*Plant pathology*]
AVC	Abdominal Vena Cava [*Medicine*]
AVC	Academy of Veterinary Cardiology (EA)
AVC	Acceleration Vector Control
AVC	Acute Vertebral Collapse [*Medicine*]
AVC	Additional Voluntary Contribution [*Employee's wage contribution toward a company pension plan*]
AVC	AddValue Communications [*Telecommunications service*] (TSSD)
AVC	Adriamycin, Vincristine, Cyclophosphamide [*Antineoplastic drug regimen*]
AVC	Advocat, Inc. [*NYSE symbol*] (SAG)
AVC	Aeronautical Video Charts (MCD)
AVC	Aeronautica Venezolana, CA [*Venezuela*] [*ICAO designator*] (FAAC)
AVC	Agricultural and Veterinary Chemical
AVC	Aireworth Volunteer Corps [*British military*] (DMA)
AVC	Allantoin Vaginal Cream [*Gynecology*] (MAE)
AVC	Altitude Velocity Chart
AVC	Amateur Volume Control
AVC	American Values Center (EA)
AVC	American Veterans Committee (EA)
AVC	American Video Channels, Inc. [*New York, NY*] [*Telecommunications*] (TSSD)
AVC	American Viewcard Club (EA)
AVC	Annular Vortex Combustor [*Coal technology*] (PS)
AVC	Appraisal & Valuation Consultants Ltd. [*British*]
AVC	Arc Vacuum Cast
AVC	Arivaca Silver Mines Ltd. [*Vancouver Stock Exchange symbol*]
AVC	Army Veterinary Corps [*Facetious translation during World War I "All Very Cushy"*] [*Later, RAVC*] [*British*]
AVC	Army Volunteers Corps [*British*]
AVC	Artillery Volunteer Corps [*British*]
AVC	Association of Visual Communicators (EA)
AVC	Association of Vitamin Chemists (EA)
AVC	Associative Visual Cortex [*Anatomy*]
AVC	Atrioventricular Canal [*Cardiology*]
AVC	Audio-Visual Connection (PCM)
AVC	Automatic Valve Control (IEEE)
AVC	Automatic Vehicle Classification [*Automotive engineering*]
AVC	Automatic Vent Control (IEEE)
AVC	Automatic Vibration Control
AVC	Automatic Voltage Control (NATG)
AVC	Automatic Volume Control [*Telecommunications*]
AVC	Avco-Everett Research Laboratory, Everett, MA [*OCLC symbol*] (OCLC)
AvC	Aventi Cristo [*Before Christ*] [*Italian*]
AVC	Average Variable Cost [*Of production*]
AVC	Average Variable Costs
AvC	Aviation Cadet
AVC	Avionics Change (MCD)
AVC	Lakeland College, Vermilion, Alberta [*Library symbol National Library of Canada*] (NLC)
AVC	Large Catapult Lighter [*Navy symbol Obsolete*]
AVCA	American Volleyball Coaches Association (EA)
AVCAA	Agricultural and Veterinary Chemicals Association of Australia

AVCAD	Aviation Cadet [*Navy*]
AVCAL	Aviation Calibration Equipment (MCD)
AVCAL	Aviation Consolidated Allowance List [*Military*] (NVT)
AVCARS	Augmented Visual Carrier Aircraft Recovery System (MCD)
Av Cas	Aviation Cases [*Commerce Clearing House*] [*A publication*] (DLA)
AVCAT	Aviation Carrier Turbine Fuel
AVCAT	Aviation Fuel, High-Flash Point [*NATO*]
AVCATT	Aviation Combined Arms Tactical Trainer [*Army*]
AVCC	Acorn Venture Cap [*NASDAQ symbol*] (TTSB)
AVCC	Acorn Venture Capital Corp. [*NASDAQ symbol*] (NQ)
AVCC	Association of Venture Capital Clubs [*Defunct*] (EA)
AVCC	Automatic Variable Character Compensation (DGA)
AVCC	Average Carbonaceous Chondrite [*Meteorology*]
AVCCOA	Audiovisual, Computer, and Communication Office Automation
AVCD	Atrioventricular Canal Defect [*Also called endocardial cushion defect*] [*Cardiology*] (DAVI)
AVCG	Attitude Vapor Crystal Growth (SSD)
AVCG	Automatic Vapor Crystal Growth [*Materials processing*]
AVCH	Assistant Vice Chancellor (DLA)
AVCI	Audio-Visual Credit Interchange [*Defunct*] (EA)
AVCM	Master Chief Avionics Technician [*Navy rating*]
AVCM	Valhalla Centre Municipal Library, Alberta [*Library symbol National Library of Canada*] (NLC)
AVCN	Anteroventral Cochlear Nucleus
AVCO	Average Cost [*Accounting term*]
AVC of SA	Assistant Vice Chief of Staff, Army [*Later, AVCSA*] (AABC)
AVCOM	Aviation Materiel Command [*St. Louis, MO*] [*Army*]
AVCP	Victoria Civil Procedure Updater [*Australia A publication*]
AVCRAD	Aviation Classification Repair Activity Depot [*Army*] (RDA)
AVCS	Advanced Vehicle Control System [*Automotive engineering*]
AVCS	Advanced Vidicon Camera System
AVCS	Assistant Vice Chief of Staff
AVCS	Atrioventricular Conduction System [*Cardiology*]
AVCS	Australian Visual Copyright Society
AVCSA	Assistant Vice Chief of Staff, Army [*Formerly, AVC of SA*] (AABC)
AVCU	Agricultural and Veterinary Chemicals Unit
AVD	Aerospace Vehicle Detection
AVD	Air Vehicle Detection (MCD)
AVD	Air Velocity Detector
AVD	Air Vendee [*France ICAO designator*] (FAAC)
AVD	Alternate Voice Data
AVD	Anode Voltage Drop
AVD	Antivehicle Device [*Air Force*] (MCD)
AVD	Aortic Valve Disease [*Cardiology*]
AVD	Apparent Volume of Distribution [*Clinical chemistry*]
AVD	Army Veterinary Department [*British*]
AVD	Army Victualling Department [*British*]
AVD	Atmospheric Vehicle Detection
AVD	Audio-Visual Division [*Environmental Protection Agency*] (GFGA)
AVD	Automatic Voice Data (MCD)
AVD	Automatic Voltage Digitizer
AVD	Aviation Training Devices (Provisional) [*Army*] (RDA)
AVD	Avondale Resources, Inc. [*Vancouver Stock Exchange symbol*]
AVD	Axial Vapor Deposition [*Coating technology*]
AVD	Seaplane Tender, Destroyer [*Navy symbol Obsolete*]
AVDA	American Venereal Disease Association (EA)
AVDA	American Veterinary Distributors Association (EA)
AVDA	Associated Video Dealers of America [*Defunct*] (EA)
AVDA	Avenida [*Avenue*] (EY)
AVDAC	Aviation Data Analysis Center (MCD)
AVDC	Acoustics and Vibration Data Center (MCD)
AVDD	Advanced Vehicle Design Department
AVDL	Avondale Industries [*NASDAQ symbol*] (TTSB)
AVDL	Avondale Industries, Inc. [*NASDAQ symbol*] (NQ)
AVDLRS	Aviation Depot Level Repairables (MCD)
AVDM	Axial Vector Dominance Model
AVDO	Aerospace Vehicle Distribution Office [*or Officer*] [*Air Force*] (AFM)
AVDO	Arteriovenous Oxygen Saturation Difference [*Medicine*] (DMAA)
AV DO₂	Arteriovenous Oxygen Differnce [*Biochemistry*] (DAVI)
AVDP	Aided Visual Development Program
AVDP	Alaska Village Demonstration Project [*Environmental Protection Agency*]
AVDP	Asparaginase, Vincristine, Doxorubicin, Prednisone [*Antineoplastic drug*] (CDI)
AVDP	Avoirdupois [*Unit of measurement*] (KSC)
AVDPS	Avoirdupois [*Unit of measurement*]
AV drive	Audio Visual Drive (CDE)
AVDS	American Veterinary Dental Society (EA)
AVDS	Articulated Vehicle Dynamic Simulator (PDAA)
AVDS	Audiovisual Distribution System (MCD)
AVDS	Automatic Vacuum Deposition System (IAA)
AVDSC	Aviation Depot Squadron [*Air Force*]
AVDSC	Australian Veterans and Defence Services Council [*Also, AVADSC*]
AVDTH	Average Depth (NOAA)
AVDU	Audiovisual Display Unit
AVE	Ad Valorem [*According to the Value*] Equivalent
AVE	Advanced Visual Extension (PCM)
AVE	Aerospace Vehicle Electronics (MCD)
AVE	Aerospace [*or Airborne*] Vehicle Equipment
AVE	Airborne Vehicle Equipment (MCD)
AVE	Alta Velocidad Espanola [*Spain*] [*High speed train*]
AVE	Aontas Vaimheolochta na hEireann [*Speleological Union of Ireland*] (EAIO)
AVE	Aortic Valve Echophonocardiogram [*Cardiology*]
AVE	Association of Vermiculite Exfoliators Ltd. [*British*] (BI)

AVE.............	Association pour le Volontariat a l'Acte Gratuit en Europe [*Association for Voluntary Action in Europe - AVAE*] (EAIO)
AVE.............	Atmospheric Variability Experiment [*NASA*]
AVE.............	Automated Voltammetric Electrode [*Electrochemistry*]
AVE.............	Automatic Volume Expansion
AVE.............	AVEMCO Corp. [*NYSE symbol*] (SPSG)
AVE.............	Avenal, CA [*Tactical Air Navigation Station*] [*Air Force*]
AVE.............	Avensa Aerovias Venezolanas SA [*Venezuela*] [*ICAO designator*] (FAAC)
AVE.............	Avenue [*Correspondence*] (AFM)
ave.............	Avenue (VRA)
Ave.............	Avenue (DD)
AVE.............	Avenue
AVE.............	Avenue [*Postal Service standard*] (OPSA)
AVE.............	Avenue Resources, Inc. [*Vancouver Stock Exchange symbol*]
AVE.............	Average
AVE.............	Averroes [*Morocco*] [*Seismograph station code, US Geological Survey*] (SEIS)
ave.............	Avesta [*MARC language code Library of Congress*] (LCCP)
AVE.............	Vegreville Public Library, Alberta [*Library symbol National Library of Canada*] (NLC)
AVEA.............	American Veterinary Exhibitors' Association (EA)
AVEA.............	National Adult Vocational Education Association (EA)
AVEBD.............	Average Blank Data [*Computer science*]
AVEC.............	Allen Video-Enhanced Contrast [*Microscopy*]
AVEC.............	Amplitude Vibration Exciter Control (PDAA)
AVEC.............	Association of Poultry Processors and Poultry Import- and Export-Trade in the EEC Countries (EAIO)
AVEC.............	Automatic Vibration Exciter Control
AVEC.............	Avecor Cardiovascular [*NASDAQ symbol*] (TTSB)
AVEC.............	Avecor, Inc. [*NASDAQ symbol*] (SAG)
AVEC DIC....	Allen Video-Enhanced Differential Interference Contrast [*Microscopy*]
Avecor.........	Avecor, Inc. [*Associated Press*] (SAG)
AVED.............	Avionics Engineering Division [*Air Force*]
AVEE.............	Alberta Environment Centre, Vegreville, Alberta [*Library symbol National Library of Canada*] (NLC)
AVEFF.............	Average Efficiency (IAA)
AVEI.............	Arterial Vascular Engineering [*NASDAQ symbol*] (TTSB)
AVEI.............	Arterial Vascular Engineering, Inc. [*NASDAQ symbol*] (SAG)
AVEL.............	Aircraft Velocity (MCD)
AVEM.............	Association of Vacuum Equipment Manufacturers (EA)
AVEMCO......	AVEMCO Corp. [*Associated Press*] (SAG)
AVEN	Avenue [*Commonly used*] (OPSA)
AVENS.........	Audiovisual Education in Neurosurgery
AVENSA.......	Aerovias Venezolanas Sociedad Anonima [*Airline*] [*Venezuela*]
AVENU.........	Avenue [*Commonly used*] (OPSA)
AVENUE......	Avenue [*Commonly used*] (OPSA)
AVEOS	Advanced Visual [*Near Visual*] Electro-Optic Sensor [*Simulator*] (MCD)
AVEP.............	Average Visual Evoked Potential [*Neurophysiology*]
AVEPDA.......	American Vocational Education Personnel Development Association (EA)
AVER	Assistant Veterans Employment Representative [*Department of Labor*]
AVER	Average
AVER	Vermilion Public Library, Alberta [*Library symbol National Library of Canada*] (NLC)
AVERA	American Vocational Education Research Association (EA)
AVERAGE.....	Adrian Van Reypen Egerton [*Near-acronym used as shortened first name of detective-story character Average Jones, in stories by Samuel Hopkins Adams*]
Averbach Acci Cas...	Averbach on Handling Accident Cases [*A publication*] (DLA)
AVERDISROP...	Avert Disruption of Operation
AVERE	Association Europeenne des Vehicules Electriques Routiers [*European Electric Road Vehicle Association*] (EAIO)
AVERT	AIDS Virus Education and Research Trust [*British*]
AVERT	Anti-Virus Emergency Response Team [*McAfee*] [*Computer science*]
AVERT	Anti-Virus Emergency Response Team [*Computer security system*]
AVERT	Association of Volunteer Emergency Radio Teams
AVERT	Automatic Verification, Evaluation, and Readiness Tester
Avert.............	Avert, Inc. [*Associated Press*] (SAG)
AveryD.........	Avery Dennison Corp. [*Associated Press*] (SAG)
AVES.............	Air Vane Erection System
AVES.............	Automatic Vertical Electrophoresis System [*Instrumentation*]
AVESCA	Aerovias Especiales de Carga Ltda. [*Colombia*] [*ICAO designator*] (FAAC)
AVEXS	Aviation Electronic Equipment Information Exchange System (MCD)
AVF.............	Advanced Financial [*AMEX symbol*] (TTSB)
AVF.............	Advanced Financial, Inc. [*AMEX symbol*] (SPSG)
AVF.............	Afrikaner Volkfront [*An association*]
AVF.............	All-Volunteer Force [*Army*]
AVF.............	American Vineyard Foundation (EA)
AVF.............	America's Victory Force [*An association*] (EA)
AVF.............	America Victory Force (EA)
AVF.............	Antiviral Factor
AVF.............	Arteriovenous Fistula [*Medicine*]
AVF.............	Association of Venture Founders [*Defunct*] (EA)
AVF.............	Augmented V Lead, Left Leg [*Electrocardiogram*] [*Medicine*]
AVF.............	Availability Factor
AVF.............	Aviair Aviation Ltd. [*Canada ICAO designator*] (FAAC)
AVF.............	Avril Sur Loire [*France*] [*Seismograph station code, US Geological Survey*] (SEIS)
AVF.............	Azimuthally Varying Field
AVFG.............	Air Vehicle Functional Group [*Military*]
AVFI.............	Advanced Financial, Inc. [*NASDAQ symbol*] (SAG)
AVFIP.............	Advanced Finl 10.50% Cv'B' Pfd [*NASDAQ symbol*] (TTSB)
AVFMER	Air Vehicle Field Maintenance Evaluation Requirement (MCD)
AVF/PAR	All-Volunteer Force Program Action Request [*Military*] (DNAB)
AVFR	Available for Reassignment
AVFUEL........	Aviation Fuel (MSA)
AVG.............	Advanced Growth Systems, Inc. [*Vancouver Stock Exchange symbol*]
AVG	Aircraft Escort Vessel [*Navy symbol Obsolete*]
AVG	Air Ventilation Garment [*NASA*]
AVG	Ambulatory Visit Group [*Patient classification*] [*Medicine*] (DAVI)
AVG	American Volunteer Group [*Flying Tigers*] [*World War II*]
AVG	Aminoethoxyvinylglycine [*Organic chemistry*]
AVG	Association of Voluntary Groups [*Republic of Ireland*] (BI)
AVG	Average (AFM)
AVG	Avialgarve, Taxis Aereos do Algarve Ltd. [*Portugal ICAO designator*] (FAAC)
AVG	Goals-Against Average [*Hockey*]
AVGAS	Aviation Gasoline
AVGC	Association of Victorian Greyhound Clubs [*Australia*]
av-gd	Avant-Garde (VRA)
AVGE	Average (ADA)
Av Gen........	Avocat General [*District Attorney*] [*French*] (ILCA)
AVGF	Australian Vegetable Growers' Federation
AVGH	Average Grid Heading (SAA)
AVGN	Avigen, Inc. [*NASDAQ symbol*] (SAG)
AVGN	Avigen Inc. [*NASDAQ symbol*] (TTSB)
AVGP	Armored Vehicle General Purpose [*General Motors armored car*] [*Canada*]
AVGS	Adaptive Video Guidance System (MCD)
AVGSAP......	Automated Viscoelastic Grain Structural Analysis Program (MCD)
AVH	Acute Variceal Haemorrhage [*Medicine*] (PDAA)
AVH	Acute Viral Hepatitis [*Medicine*]
AVH	Adventure Vehicle [*Vancouver Stock Exchange symbol*]
AVH	Aircraft Rescue Boat [*Navy symbol*]
AVH	Allamvedelmi Hivatal [*Hungarian secret police*]
AVH	Average Heading
AVH	Aviser SA [*Spain ICAO designator*] (FAAC)
AVHB	Atrioventricular Heart Block [*Cardiology*] (DAVI)
AVHMA	American Veterinary Holistic Medical Association [*Later, AHVMA*] (EA)
AVHOM........	Aided Visual Homing Missile (MCD)
AVHRR.........	Advanced Very-High-Resolution Radiometer [*NASA*]
AVHS	Advanced Vehicle Highway System [*Automotive engineering*]
AVI	Active Vibration Isolator (MCD)
AVI	Acuvision Systems, Inc. [*Vancouver Stock Exchange symbol*]
AVI	Adjustable Voltage Inverter (PDAA)
AVI	Advanced Vehicle Identification
AVI	Advanced Video Imaging [*Zenith Electronics Corp.*]
AVI	AIDS Vancouver Island [*Also Vancouver Island AIDS Society*] (AC)
AVI	Airborne Vehicle Identification
AVI	Air Velocity Index
AVI	American Veterans of Israel (EA)
AVI	American Video Institute [*Rochester Institute of Technology*] [*Research center*] (RCD)
AVI	Appalachian Volunteers, Inc. (EA)
AVI	Association of Veterinary Inspectors
AVI	Association Universelle d'Aviculture Scientifique [*World's Poultry Science Association - WPSA*] (EAIO)
AVI	Audio-Video Interactive
AVI	Audio Video Interleave [*Computer science*]
AVI	Audio-Video Interleaved [*Computer science*]
AVI	Audio Visual Innovations [*Computer science*]
avi	Audio/Visual Interleave [*Windows*] [*Computer science*]
AVI	Audio Visual Interleaved [*Computer science*] (PCM)
AVI	Automatic Vehicle Identification [*Automotive engineering*]
AVI	Aviation (DLA)
AVI	Aviorrenta SA [*Mexico ICAO designator*] (FAAC)
AVI	Avoid Verbal Instructions [*DoD*] (MCD)
AVI	Vilna Public Library, Alberta [*Library symbol National Library of Canada*] (NLC)
AVI.............	Waterville, ME [*Location identifier FAA*] (FAAL)
AVIA.............	Aviation Pay [*Navy*]
AVIAC..........	Aviation Industry Advisory Council (ADA)
AVIACO........	Aviacion y Comercio SA [*Aviation and Trade Corporation*] [*Airline*] [*Spain*]
Aviall.............	Aviall, Inc. [*Associated Press*] (SAG)
AVIANCA......	Aerovias Nacionales de Colombia [*Colombian National Airways*]
AVIATECA ...	Empresa Guatemalteca de Aviacion [*Airline*] [*Guatemala*]
Aviation	Aviation Sales Co. [*Associated Press*] (SAG)
Aviation Q ...	United States Aviation Quarterly [*A publication*] (DLA)
AVIC.............	Association of Vermont Independent Colleges (SRA)
AVIC.............	Aviation Industries of China (ECON)
AVIC Gp......	AVIC Group International, Inc. [*Associated Press*] (SAG)
AVID	Advanced Visual Information Display
AVID	Aerospace Vehicle Interactive Design (MCD)
AVID	Airborne Vehicle Identification (AABC)
AVID	Automated Vibration Diagnostic System (MCD)
AVID	Avid Technology [*NASDAQ symbol*] (TTSB)
AVID	Avid Technology, Inc. [*NASDAQ symbol*] (SAG)
AviDist........	Aviation Distributors, Inc. [*Associated Press*] (SAG)
AvidTch........	Avid Technology, Inc. [*Associated Press*] (SAG)
AVIEN.........	Aviation Engineering Corp. (MCD)
AVIG.............	Antivaccinial Immunoglobulin [*Medicine*] (PDAA)
Avigen	Avigen, Inc. [*Associated Press*] (SAG)
AVII.............	Asparagus Virus II [*Plant pathology*]

AVIK............ Viking Public Library, Alberta [Library symbol National Library of Canada] (NLC)
AVIM............ Aviation Intermediate Maintenance [Army] (MCD)
A-V IMA........ Arteriovenous Internal Mammary [Fistula] [Cardiology] (DAVI)
AVIOB.......... Aviation Observation (NOAA)
AVIONICS .... Aviation Electronics
AVIOS.......... American Voice Input/Output Society (EA)
AVIP............ Association of Viewdata Information Providers (EA)
AVIR............ Aviron [NASDAQ symbol] (SAG)
AVIRA.......... Awareness Vision Imagination Responsibility Action
AVIRIS......... Airborne Visible-Infrared Imaging Spectrometer
Aviron.......... Aviron [Associated Press] (SAG)
AVIS............ Active Vibration Isolation System
AVIS............ Association of Voluntary/Independent Schools [British] (DBA)
AVIS............ Audiovisual Information System
AVIS............ Automatic Visual Inspection System [NASA]
AVISAM........ Average Index Sequential Access Method [Computer science] (MHDI)
AVISNET ...... Avionics Integrated Support Networks (PDAA)
AVISPA........ Aerovias Interamericanas de Panama SA
AVISURS....... Aerospace Vehicle Inventory, Status, and Utilization Reporting System
AVIT............ Audiovisual Instructional Technology [Military] (AABC)
AVIT............ Audio-Visual Integrated Trainer (PDAA)
AVIT............ Avitar, Inc. [NASDAQ symbol] (SAG)
Avitar.......... Avitar, Inc. [Associated Press] (SAG)
AVITW......... Avitar Inc. Wrrt [NASDAQ symbol] (TTSB)
AvivaPet....... Aviva Petroleum, Inc. [Associated Press] (SAG)
AVJ............. Aeroviajes Ejecuitvos SA de CV [Mexico ICAO designator] (FAAC)
AVJ............. Antivibration Joint
AVJ............. Atrioventricular Junction [Medicine] (DMAA)
AVJC........... Antelope Valley Junior College [Later, Antelope Valley College] [Lancaster, CA]
AV J-C......... Avant Jesus-Christ [Before Christ] [French]
AV/JV.......... Air Vehicle/Jet Vane
AVK............ Alva, OK [Location identifier FAA] (FAAL)
AVK............ Audiovisual Kit [Army]
AVK............ Avia Kargo Sisitem, AS [Turkey] [FAA designator] (FAAC)
AVKO .... Audio, Visual, Kinesthetic, and Oral [Teaching techniques] (EA)
AVKOERF..... AVKO Educational Research Foundation (EA)
AVL............ Address Validity (MCD)
AVL............ Adelson-Velskii and Landis Trees [Computer science]
AVL............ Aerovial [Chile] [ICAO designator] (FAAC)
AVL............ Aerovias Las Amricas, SA [Panama] [FAA designator] (FAAC)
AVL............ Allegheny College, Meadville, PA [OCLC symbol] (OCLC)
AVL............ Allport-Vernon-Lindzey [Study of values]
AVL............ Angle Versus Length [Computer science]
AVL............ Approved Vendors List
AVL............ Armored Vehicle Launched [Military] (MCD)
AVL............ Aroostook Valley Railroad Co. [AAR code]
AVL............ Asheville [North Carolina] [Airport symbol] (OAG)
AVL............ Asheville-Henderson [North Carolina] [Airport symbol] (AD)
AVL............ Associated Veterinary Laboratories [Defunct] (EA)
AVL............ Audio Visual Library, University of Toronto [UTLAS symbol]
AVL............ Augmented V Lead, Left Arm [Electrocardiogram] [Medicine]
aVL............ Automated Volt Left [Medicine] (DMAA)
AVL............ Automatic Vehicle Location (IEEE)
AVL............ Aviall, Inc. [NYSE symbol] (SPSG)
AVL............ Avionics Verification Laboratory (MCD)
AVLA.......... Audio-Visual Language Association [British]
AVLABS........ Aviation Laboratories [Army]
AVLB.......... Armored Vehicle Launched Bridge [Military] (INF)
AVLBL......... Available [or Availability] (MSA)
AVLBLTY...... Availability
AVLC........... Aesthetics and Visual Literacy Council [Australia]
AVLD .... Acoustic Valve Leak Detector (DNAB)
AVLD .... Aviation LASER Device
AVLDS .... American Veterinary Lyme Disease Society
AVLF.......... Airborne Very-Low-Frequency (NG)
AVLF........... Alberta Fire Training School, Alberta Labour, Vermilion, Alberta [Library symbol National Library of Canada] (NLC)
AVLH .... Assam Valley Light Horse [British military] (DMA)
AVLINE .... Audiovisuals On-Line [National Library of Medicine] [Rockville Pike, MD Database]
AVLIS.......... Atomic Vapor LASER Isotope Separation
AV/LM......... Air Vehicle/Launch Module
AVLM......... Antivehicle Land Mine
AVLO .... Audiovisual Liaison Officer [Army]
AVLOC .... Airborne Visible-LASER Optical-Communications
AVLOC .... Aviation Logistics Officer Course [Army] (INF)
AVLP........... Association of Valuers of Licensed Property [British] (DBA)
Av L Rep ..... Aviation Law Reporter [Commerce Clearing House] [A publication] (DLA)
AVLS .... Automatic Vehicle Location System (DA)
AVLSI.......... Advanced Very-Large-Scale Integration [Electronics]
AVLUB .... Aviation Lubricant (MUGU)
AVM........... Acoustic Velocity Meter (NOAA)
AVM........... Acute Viral Meningitis [Medicine]
AVM........... Adriamycin, Vinblastine, Methotrexate [Antineoplastic drug regimen] (DAVI)
AVM........... Advanced Magnetics [AMEX symbol] (SAG)
AVM........... Advanced Virtual Machine (IAA)
AVM........... Airborne Vibration Monitor (NG)
AVM........... Air Velocity Meter
AVM........... Air Vice-Marshal [British]

AVM............ AlertVIEW [Virtual Interface Environment Workstation] Manager [Shany, Inc.] (PCM)
AVM............ Anterior Ventral Microtubule [Anatomy]
AVM............ Antivehicle Mine
AVM............ Arteriovenous Malformation [Medicine]
AVM............ Audiovisual Modulator
AVM............ Automatic Vehicle Monitoring [Antihijack device]
AVM............ Automatic Voting Machine
AVM............ Ave Maria
AVM............ Aviacion Ejecutiva Mexicana SA [Mexico ICAO designator] (FAAC)
AVM............ Aviation Medical
AVM............ Guided Missile Ship [Navy symbol]
AVM............ Veteran Municipal Library, Alberta [Library symbol National Library of Canada] (NLC)
AVMA.......... Action for Victims of Medical Accidents [British] [An association] (DBA)
AVMA.......... Alabama Veterinary Medical Association (SRA)
AVMA.......... Alberta Veterinary Medical Association (AC)
AVMA.......... American Veterinary Medical Association (EA)
AVMA.......... Arkansas Veterinary Medical Association (SRA)
AVMA.......... Audio-Visual Management Association (EA)
AVMA.......... Automatic Vending Machine Association [British] (BI)
AVMAINTECH... Aviation Maintenance Technician [Military] (DNAB)
AVMARC....... Audiovisual Machine Readable Catalogue [A database] [British Library Automated Dissemination of Information] (NITA)
AVMC.......... Association for Vertical Market Computing [Defunct] (EA)
AVMCS........ Ambient Air Ventilation Microclimate System [Army] (RDA)
AVMDA........ Amusement and Vending Machine Distributors Association (EA)
AVMF.......... Aviatsiya Voenno Morskogo Flota [Aviation - Naval Fleet] [Former USSR]
AVMH.......... Available Manhours (AFM)
AVMI.......... Automated Video Maintenance Information (MCD)
AVMP.......... Audio Video Market Place [A publication]
AVMR.......... Association of Visual Merchandise Representatives (EA)
AVMRI .... Arctic Vessel and Marine Research Institute [National Research Council of Canada] [Later, Institute of Marine Dynamics] [Research center] (RCD)
AVMS.......... Administration de la Voie Maritime du Saint-Laurent [St. Lawrence Seaway Authority - SLSA] [Canada]
AVMS.......... Annulus Vacuum Maintenance System [Nuclear energy] (NRCH)
AVMS.......... Automatic Vehicle Monitoring System [Army] (MCD)
AVMS.......... Naval Aviation [USSR designation]
AVN .... Acute Vasomotor Nephropathy [Medicine] (DAVI)
AVN .... Air Vanuatu [ICAO designator] (FAAC)
AVN .... Atrioventricular Node [Cardiology]
AVN .... Avalon Properties [NYSE symbol] (SPSG)
AVN .... Avanti Productions, Inc. [Vancouver Stock Exchange symbol]
AVN .... Avenue [Commonly used] (OPSA)
AVN .... AVIANCA [Aerovias Nacionales de Colombia SA] [Colombian airline]
AVN .... Aviation (AFM)
AVN .... Aviation
AVN .... Aviation Company [Military] (VNW)
AVN .... Avignon [France] [Airport symbol] (OAG)
AVN .... Rochester, NY [Location identifier FAA] (FAAL)
a-vn--.......... Vietnam, North [MARC geographic area code Library of Congress] (LCCP)
AVNA.......... American Veterinary Neurology Association [Defunct] (EA)
AVNB.......... Avascular Necrosis of Bone [Medicine]
AVNC.......... Aviation Center [Army]
AVNC.......... Avionic
AVN(CM)..... Aviation Pay (Crewmember) [Navy]
AVND.......... Atrioventricular Node Dysfunction [Medicine] (DMAA)
AVND.......... Avondale Financial [NASDAQ symbol] (TTSB)
AVND.......... Avondale Financial Corp. [NASDAQ symbol] (SAG)
Avndle .... Avondale Industries, Inc. [Associated Press] (SAG)
AVNDTA....... Aviation Development Test Activity [Test and Evaluation Command] [Army] (RDA)
AVNEC .... Army Aviation Employment Conference
AVNENGRBN... Aviation Engineer Battalion [Marine Corps]
AVNET .... Aviation Network (IAA)
Avnet .... Avnet, Inc. [Associated Press] (SAG)
AVNFH........ Avascular Necrosis of the Femoral Head [Medicine] (DMAA)
AVNIR .... Advanced Visible and Near-Infrared Radiometer [Instrumentation]
AVNL.......... Automatic Video Noise Leveling [or Limiting]
AVNMATOLANT... Aviation Material Office, Atlantic [Military] (DNAB)
AVNMATORES... Aviation Material Office, Reserve [Military] (DNAB)
AVNMED....... Aviation Medicine [Military] (AABC)
AVN(NCM) ... Aviation Pay (Non-Crewmember) [Navy]
AVNPrA........ Avalon Prop 9% Sr'A'Pfd [NYSE symbol] (TTSB)
AVNR.......... Air Vehicle Nuclear Radiation
AVNR.......... Atrioventricular Nodal Reentry [Cardiology]
AVNS .... Aviation School [Army]
AVNSAFCEN... Naval Aviation Safety Center
AVNSCOLCOM... Naval Aviation School Command
AVNT.......... Avant Corp. [NASDAQ symbol] (SAG)
AVNT.......... Avant Corp. [NASDAQ symbol] (TTSB)
AVNU.......... Aviation Unit [Marine Corps]
AVNUE........ Avenue [Commonly used] (OPSA)
AVO .... Administrative Veterinary Officer [British military] (DMA)
AVO .... Aerovias Oaxaquenas SA [Mexico ICAO designator] (FAAC)
AVO .... Ampere, Volt, Ohm (IAA)
AVO .... Apprehended Violence Order [A publication]
AVO .... Automatic Variable Orifice [Steam trap of Agontz Corp.]
AVO .... Available Vehicle Occupancy [VDOT] (TAG)
AVO .... Avino Mines & Resources Ltd. [Vancouver Stock Exchange symbol]

AVO .... Avoid Verbal Orders [*Military*]
AVO .... Avon [*Australia Seismograph station code, US Geological Survey*] (SEIS)
AVO .... Avon Park, FL [*Location identifier FAA*] (FAAL)
A-VO₂ .... Arteriovenous Oxygen Difference [*Medicine*] (MAE)
AVOCON ...... Automated Vocabulary Control [*Subsystem of PLIS*] [*Computer science*]
AVOID .... Accelerated View of Input Data
AVOID .... Airfield Vehicle Obstacle Indication Device
AVOIDS .... Avionic Observation of Intruder Danger Systems [*Army*]
AVOIL .... Aviation Oil [*Military*]
AVOIR .... Avoirdupois
AVOLO .... Automatic Voice Link Observation
Avon .... Avon Products, Inc. [*Associated Press*] (SAG)
AvondF .... Avondale Financial Corp. [*Associated Press*] (SAG)
AVOPTECH... Aviation Operations Technician (DNAB)
AVORDTECH... Aviation Ordnance Technician (DNAB)
AVOS .... Acoustic Valve Operating System (PDAA)
AVOS .... Advisor Virtual Memory Operating System [*Computer science*] (MHDI)
AVP.............. Acoustic Video Processor (DWSG)
AVP.............. Actinomycin D, Vincristine, Platinol [*Cisplatin*] [*Antineoplastic drug regimen*]
AVP.............. Adaptive Video Processor
AVP.............. Address Verification Pulse (KSC)
AVP.............. Administrative Vice President (HGAA)
AVP.............. Adriamycin, Vincristine, Procarbazine [*Antineoplastic drug regimen*] (DAVI)
AVP.............. Aeronautical Video Plates (MCD)
AVP.............. Aktionsgemeinschaft Vierte Partei [*Fourth Party Action Group*] [*Germany Political party*]
AVP.............. Alvin W. Vogtle, Jr. Plant [*Nuclear energy*] (NRCH)
AVP.............. Antiviral Protein [*Immunology*]
AVP.............. Arginine Vasopressin [*Antidiuretic hormone*]
AVP.............. Army Validation Program
AVP.............. Arubaanse Volks Partij [*Aruban People's Party*] [*Netherlands Antilles*] [*Political party*] (PPW)
AVP.............. Assistant Vice President
AVP.............. Association of Volleyball Professionals (EA)
AVP.............. Attached Virtual Processor [*Computer science*] (NITA)
AVP.............. Automatic Variable Perforating
AVP.............. Avcorp Industries, Inc. [*Toronto Stock Exchange symbol*]
AVP.............. Aviation Enterprises [*Denmark ICAO designator*] (FAAC)
AVP.............. Aviation Publication (MCD)
AVP.............. Avoirdupois (ADA)
AVP.............. Avon Products [*NYSE symbol*] (TTSB)
AVP.............. Avon Products, Inc. [*NYSE symbol*] (SPSG)
AVP.............. Scranton-Wilkes-Barre [*Pennsylvania*] [*Airport symbol*] (AD)
AVP.............. Small Seaplane Tender [*Navy symbol Obsolete*]
AVP.............. Wilkes-Barre/Scranton [*Pennsylvania*] [*Derived from location of airport: Avoca, Pennsylvania*] [*Airport symbol*]
AVPA .... American Veneer Package Association (EA)
AVPAC .... Aviation VHF [*Very High Frequency*] Packet Communications [*Computer science*] (TNIG)
AVPC .... Association of Vice-Principals in Colleges [*British*]
AVPI .... Agricultural and Veterinary Products Index [*A publication*]
AVPIDS .... Acoustic Video Processor Integrated Display Station
AVP-II .... Actinomycin D, Vincristine, Cisplatin [*Antineoplastic drug regimen*] (DAVI)
AVPL .... Average Picture Level (MSA)
AVPO .... Axial Vapor-Phase Oxidation Process [*Optical fibre technology*] (EECA)
AVPOOL....... Available Labor Pool Model (MCD)
AVPU .... Alert, Verbal, Painful, Unresponsive [*Neurologic test*] [*Medicine*] (DMAA)
AVPUG .... AV [*Audiovisual*] Pansophic Users Group [*Defunct*] (EA)
AVQ .... Aviation Services, Inc. [*ICAO designator*] (FAAC)
AVR .... Accelerated Ventricular Rhythm [*Cardiology*] (DMAA)
AVR .... Adjustable Voltage Rectifier (IAA)
AVR .... Advanced VLF/LF [*Very Low Frequency/Low Frequency*] Receiver (DWSG)
AVR .... Advance Murgor [*Vancouver Stock Exchange symbol*]
AVR .... Agent's Vehicle Record (DS)
AVR .... Airborne Video Recorder [*Automotive engineering*]
AVR .... Aircraft [*or Aviation*] Rescue Vessel [*Navy symbol Obsolete*]
AVR .... American Ventures [*Vancouver Stock Exchange symbol*]
AVR .... Aortic Valve Replacement [*Cardiology*]
AVR .... Arkansas River Valley Regional Library, Dardanelle, AR [*OCLC symbol*] (OCLC)
AVR .... Armoured Vehicle, Reconnaissance [*British military*] (DMA)
AVR .... Army Veterinary and Remount Services [*British*]
AVR .... Army Volunteer Reserve [*British*]
AVR .... Assembly and Verification Review (SSD)
AVR .... Augmented V Lead, Right Arm [*Electrocardiogram*] [*Medicine*]
AVR .... Automatic Voice Recognition (NITA)
AVR .... Automatic Voice Relay
AVR .... Automatic Voice Response [*Telephone*] (WDMC)
AVR .... Automatic Voltage Regulator
AVR .... Automatic Volume Recognition (MCD)
AVR .... Avenor Inc. [*TS Symbol*] (TTSB)
AVR .... Avery [*Printer of U.S. postage stamps*] (BARN)
AVR .... Aviator (AABC)
AVR .... Avior Pty Ltd. [*Australia ICAO designator*] (FAAC)
AVR .... Avirulence
AVR .... Axial Velocity Ratio

AVRAD......... Altitude Variation Rate and Displacement
AVRADA....... Avionics Research and Development Activity [*Fort Monmouth, NJ*] [*Army*] (GRD)
AVRADCOM... Army Aviation Research and Development Command [*Fort Monmouth, NJ*] (MCD)
AVRD .... Audio Video Review Digest [*A publication*]
AVRDC .... Asian Vegetable Research and Development Center (EA)
AVRDEC....... Aviation Research Development and Engineering Center [*Army*] (RDA)
AVRE .... Armoured Vehicle, Royal Engineers [*British and Canadian*] [*World War II*]
AVRE .... Assault Vehicle, Royal Engineers [*British*]
AVRHS......... Association for Vital Records and Health Statistics (EA)
AVRI .... Acute Viral Respiratory Infection [*Medicine*] (DMAA)
AVRI .... Animal Virus Research Institute [*British*] (ARC)
AVRLSS .... Arkansas Valley Regional Library Service System [*Library network*]
AVRO .... Association of Vehicle Recovery Operators [*British*] (DBA)
AVRO .... A. V. Roe & Co. Ltd. [*Acronym used as designation for a British aircraft and is formed from the name of the aircraft's manufacturer*]
AVROC .... Aviation Reserve Officers Candidate Program
AVRP .... Atrioventricular Refractory Period [*Cardiology*] (MAE)
AVRS .... American Veterinary Radiology Society [*Defunct*] (EA)
AVRS .... Army Veterinary and Remount Services [*British military*] (DMA)
AVRS .... Atrial Vascular Relaxant Substance [*Biochemistry*]
AVRS .... Audio-Video Recording System [*Air Force*]
AVRS .... Automated Voice Response System [*DoD*]
AVRT .... Atrioventricular Reentrant Tachycardia [*Cardiology*] (DMAA)
AVRT .... Avert, Inc. [*NASDAQ symbol*] (SAG)
AVRTW .... Avert Inc. Wrrt [*NASDAQ symbol*] (TTSB)
AVRV .... Avian Retrovirus
AVS.............. Aboriginal Visitors' Scheme [*Australia*]
AVS.............. Acid-Volatile Sulfide [*Chemistry*]
AVS+.......... Address Verification System Plus [*Information Design, Inc.*] [*Information service or system*] (IID)
AVS.............. Adjustable Voltage Screwdown
AVS.............. Advanced Vehicle System [*Automotive engineering*]
AVS.............. Advanced Vertical Strike Fighter (MCD)
AVS.............. Advanced Visual System
AVS.............. Advanced Vortex System (MCD)
AVS.............. Advanced V/STOL [*Vertical/Short Takeoff and Landing*] Weapon System (MCD)
AVS.............. Advance in Schedule (KSC)
AVS.............. Aerospace Vehicle Simulation (PDAA)
AVS.............. Aerospace Vehicle System (MCD)
AVS.............. Aided Visual System
AVS.............. Airborne Viewing System
AVS.............. Airborne V/STOL [*Vertical/Short Takeoff and Landing*] Simulator (MCD)
AVS.............. Air Valve Silencer
AVS.............. Air Vehicle Specification (MCD)
AVS.............. AlertVIEW [*Virtual Interface Environment Workstation*] Station [*Shany, Inc.*] [*Computer science*] (PCM)
AVS.............. Altitude-Vertical Scale
AVS.............. American Vacuum Society (EA)
AVS.............. American Vegan Society (EA)
AVS.............. American Videotext Services, Inc. [*Peekskill, NY*] [*Telecommunications*] (TSSD)
AVS.............. American Viola Society (EA)
AVS.............. Anti-Vivisection Society [*VIL*] [*Absorbed by*] (EA)
AVS.............. Aortic Valve Stenosis [*Cardiology*] (DMAA)
AVS.............. Application Visualization System [*Computer science*] (BTTJ)
AVS.............. Applied Videotex Systems, Inc. [*Telecommunications service*] (TSSD)
AVS.............. Army Veterinary Service [*British*] (DAS)
AVS.............. Artac [*Spain*] [*FAA designator*] (FAAC)
AVS.............. Arteriovenous Shunt [*Cardiology*]
AVS.............. Association for Voluntary Sterilization, Inc. [*New York, NY Research center*]
AVS.............. Association of Veterinary Students of Great Britain and Ireland (BI)
AVS.............. Audio-Visual Squadron [*Air Force*]
AVS.............. Auditory Vocal Sequencing [*Medicine*] (DMAA)
AVS.............. Australian Vegetarian Society
AVS.............. Automated Verification System [*Computer science*] (MCD)
AVS.............. Aviation Sales Co. [*NYSE symbol*] (SAG)
AVS.............. Aviation Seychelles Ltd. [*ICAO designator*] (FAAC)
AVS.............. Aviation Standards [*FAA*] (TAG)
AVS.............. Aviation Supply Ship [*Navy symbol*]
AVS.............. Aviva Resources, Inc. [*Vancouver Stock Exchange symbol*]
a-vs-- .... Vietnam, South [*MARC geographic area code Library of Congress*] (LCCP)
AVSA .... African Violet Society of America (EA)
A/VSA .... Altimeter/Velocity Sensor Antenna
AVSAB .... American Veterinary Society of Animal Behavior (EA)
AVSAT .... Aviation Satellite (DNAB)
AVSC .... Aortic Valve Cusp Separation [*On echocardiogram*] [*Cardiology*] (DAVI)
AVSC .... Association for Voluntary Surgical Contraception (EA)
AVSC .... Audiovisual Support Center [*Army*] (AABC)
AVSCM .... American Veterinary Society for Computer Medicine (EA)
AVSCOM ..... Aviation and Surface Material Command [*Air Force*]
AVSCOM ..... Aviation Support Command [*Military*] (DOMA)
AVSCOM ..... Aviation Systems Command [*St. Louis, MO*] [*Army*]
AVSD .... Atrioventricular Septal Defect [*Cardiology*] (DMAA)
AVSD .... Avco Systems Development (MCD)
AVSEC .... Aviation Security Panel [*ICAO*] (DA)

AVSECOM	Aviation Security Command [*Philippines*]
AVSEP	Audiovisual Superimposed Electrocardiogram Presentation
AVSER	Aviation Safety Engineering and Research (KSC)
AVSF............	Advanced Vertical Strike Fighter
AVSI.............	Advanced Vertical Speed Indicator
AVSIM	Avionic System Simulation (MCD)
AVSL............	Association of Visual Science Librarians (EA)
AVSL............	Available Space List [*Computer science*] (IAA)
AVSM	Auxiliary Video Switching Matrix
AV/SN	Air Vehicle / Swivel Nozzle [*Military*]
AVSN	Automatic Voice Switching Network (AFIT)
AVSq............	Audiovisual Squadron [*Air Force*]
AVSR	Avionics Verification Status Room [*NASA*] (NASA)
AVSS	Afebrile, Vital Signs Stable [*Medicine*] (DAVI)
AVSS	Aided Visual Sensor System
AVSS	Apollo Vehicle Systems Section [*NASA*] (KSC)
AVSS	Automated Vendor Selection System (NRCH)
AVSS	Automatic Video Scoring System [*Army*] (INF)
AVST............	Advanced Vehicle Simulation Technique
AVST............	Australian Investment Planning Guide [*A publication*]
AVST............	Automated Visual Sensitivity Tester
AVSV............	Aortic Valve Stroke Volume [*Cardiology*]
AVSYCOM	Aviation Systems Command [*Army*] (MCD)
AVSYN	Air Vehicle Synthesis [*Program*]
AVT..............	Acceptance Vibration Testing [*NASA*] (NASA)
AVT..............	Active Valve Train [*Automotive engineering*]
AVT..............	Adult Vocational Training [*HEW*]
AVT..............	Ad Valorem Tax [*Added Value Tax*]
AVT..............	Advanced Vehicle Technologies [*Military*] (RDA)
AVT..............	Advanced Video Terminal
AVT..............	Air Velocity Transducer
AVT..............	Air Vibrating Table
AVT..............	Air Volume Totalizer [*Navy*]
AVT..............	Allen Vision Test [*Ophthalmology*] (DAVI)
AVT..............	All Vehicle Test
AVT..............	All Volatile Treatment [*Nuclear energy*] (NRCH)
AVT..............	Apollo Validation Test [*NASA*] (KSC)
AVT..............	Applications Vertical Test Program [*Communication Satellite program*]
AVT..............	Applied Voice Technology [*Telecommunications service*] (TSSD)
AVT..............	Area Ventralis of Tsai [*Of the brain*] [*Neurology*] (DAVI)
AVT..............	Arginine Vasotocin [*Endocrinology*]
AVT..............	ATS Aircharter Ltd. [*British ICAO designator*] (FAAC)
AVT..............	Atypical Ventricular Tachycardia [*Cardiology*] (DAVI)
AVT..............	Audiovisual-Tutorial [*Instruction*] [*Media System Corp.*]
AVT..............	Austin Area Vocational-Technology Institute, Austin, MN [*OCLC symbol*] (OCLC)
AVT..............	Automatic Video Tracker
AVT..............	Automatic Vision Testing (NITA)
AVT..............	Autovend Technology Corp. [*Vancouver Stock Exchange symbol*]
AVT..............	Auxiliary Aircraft Training Ship
AVT..............	Auxiliary Aircraft Transport [*Navy symbol Obsolete*]
AVT..............	Available Time (AFM)
AVT..............	Aviation Medicine Technician [*Navy*]
AVT..............	Avnet, Inc. [*NYSE symbol*] (SPSG)
AVT..............	Spokane, WA [*Location identifier FAA*] (FAAL)
AVT..............	Training Carrier
a-vt--	Vietnam [*MARC geographic area code Library of Congress*] (LCCP)
AVTA............	Armored Vehicle Technology Associates [*Army*] (RDA)
AVTA............	Automatic Vocal Transaction Analysis (IAA)
AVTAG	Aviation Fuel [*Gasoline/Kerosene*] [*NATO*]
AVTAS	Advanced Visual Target Acquisition System (MCD)
AVTC............	American Video Teleconferencing Corp. [*Farmingdale, NY*] [*Telecommunications*] (TSSD)
AVTC............	Applied Voice Technology [*NASDAQ symbol*] (TTSB)
AVTC............	Applied Voice Technology, Inc. [*NASDAQ symbol*] (SAG)
AVTE............	Adult, Vocational, and Technical Education
AVTK............	Anti-Virus Toolkit for Windows [*Dr. Solomon's Software, Inc.*]
AVTM............	AVTEAM, Inc. [*NASDAQ symbol*] (SAG)
AVTMP.........	Average Temperature (NOAA)
AVTP............	Adult Vocational Training Program [*HEW*]
AVTP............	Allied Vehicle Testing Publication [*Army*] (RDA)
AVTR	Advanced Video Tape Recorder
AVTR	Airborne Video Tape Recorder (MCD)
AVTR	Analog Video Tape Recorder (MCD)
AVTR	Avatar Hldgs [*NASDAQ symbol*] (TTSB)
AVTR	Avatar Holdings, Inc. [*NASDAQ symbol*] (NQ)
AVTRW	Association of Veterinary Teachers and Research Workers [*British*]
AVTS............	Advanced Visual Technology System [*NASA*]
AVTS............	Australian Vocational Training System
AVTSS	Automated Video Target Scoring System
AVTUR	Aviation Turbine Fuel (ADA)
AVU	Adventura Energy [*Vancouver Stock Exchange symbol*]
AVU	American Vegetarian Union [*Defunct*] (EA)
AVU	Avia Sud [*France ICAO designator*] (FAAC)
AVU	Avu Avu [*Solomon Islands*] [*Airport symbol*] (OAG)
AVU	Vulcan Public Library, Alberta [*Library symbol National Library of Canada*] (NLC)
AVUM	Aviation Unit Maintenance [*Army*] (MCD)
AVUM	Avionics Unit Maintenance (MCD)
AVUS	Automobil Versuchs- und Untersuchungs Strecke [*Automobile Test Track*] [*Department of Energy*]
AVV.............	AirVantage, Inc. [*ICAO designator*] (FAAC)
AVV.............	Algemeen Vrijzinning Vakverbond in Nederland [*General Liberal Labor Federation*] [*Netherlands*]
AVV	Avinda Video, Inc. [*Toronto Stock Exchange symbol*]
AVV	Aviva Petroleum Dep [*AMEX symbol*] (TTSB)
AVV	Aviva Petroleum, Inc. [*AMEX symbol*] (SAG)
AVV	Avvocato [*Solicitor*] [*Italian*] (EY)
AVVI............	Altimeter Vertical Velocity Indicator [*NASA*] (MCD)
AVVI............	Altitude-Vertical Velocity Indicator [*NASA*] (AFM)
AVVM...........	Valleyview Municipal Library, Alberta [*Library symbol National Library of Canada*] (NLC)
AVVOS	Oscar Adolphson Primary School, Valleyview, Alberta [*Library symbol National Library of Canada*] (BIB)
AVVTS	Twilight Colony School, Valleyview, Alberta [*Library symbol National Library of Canada*] (BIB)
AVW............	Average Width
AVW............	Aviator SA [*Greece*] [*ICAO designator*] (FAAC)
AVW............	Victorian Accident Compensation Practice Guide [*Australia A publication*]
AVWA	Auctioneers and Valuers of Western Australia [*An association*]
AVWVT	Australian Vietnam War Veterans' Trust
AVX.............	Audio Voice Exchange
AVX.............	Avalon Bay [*Santa Catalina, California*] [*Airport symbol*] (AD)
AVX.............	Avalon, CA [*Location identifier FAA*] (FAAL)
AVX.............	Avcon AG [*Switzerland ICAO designator*] (FAAC)
AVX.............	Aviapaslauga [*Lithuania*] [*FAA designator*] (FAAC)
AVX.............	AVX Corp. [*NYSE symbol*] (SAG)
AVX.............	Catalina Island [*California*] [*Airport symbol*] (OAG)
AVX Cp	AVX Corp. [*Associated Press*] (SAG)
AVY.............	Aerovaradero SA [*Cuba*] [*FAA designator*] (FAAC)
AVY.............	Angavokely [*Madagascar*] [*Seismograph station code, US Geological Survey*] (SEIS)
AVY.............	Avery Dennison Corp. [*NYSE symbol*] (SPSG)
AVZ.............	Aeroservice [*Kazakhstan*] [*FAA designator*] (FAAC)
AVZ.............	Avascular Zone [*Medicine*] (DMAA)
AVZ.............	Avocet Ventures, Inc. [*Vancouver Stock Exchange symbol*]
'AvZar.........	'Avodah Zarah (BJA)
AW..............	A. A. Weinman [*Designer's mark, when appearing on US coins*]
AW..............	Above Waist [*Medicine*]
AW..............	Above Water
A/W.............	Accordance With (MSA)
AW..............	Acid Waste
AW..............	Acoustic Warfare (NVT)
AW..............	Acoustic Wave
AW..............	Actual Weight [*Business term*]
aw..............	Actual Weight [*Business term*] (ODBW)
A-W.............	Addison-Wesley [*Publisher*]
AW..............	Advanced WESTAR (MCD)
AW..............	Aerodrome Warning (DA)
AW..............	Aeroquetzal [*ICAO designator*] (AD)
AW..............	Africa Watch [*An association*] (EA)
AW..............	[*The*] Ahnapee & Western Railway Co. [*Later, AHW*] [*AAR code*]
AW..............	Aircraft Warning (IAA)
AW..............	Airlock Wall (MCD)
AW..............	Airspace Warning (DNAB)
AW..............	Air-to-Water
AW..............	Air Warning
aw..............	Airways [*Medicine*] (DAVI)
AW..............	Airways
AW..............	Air Weapon [*British military*] (DMA)
AW..............	Airwork Ltd. [*British*]
AW..............	Air-World Co.
A/W.............	Airworthy (ADA)
AW..............	Aisin Warner [*Automotive industry supplier*] [*Japan*]
AW..............	Alignment Window
AW..............	All Water
AW..............	All-Weather [*As applied to fighter aircraft, etc.*]
AW..............	All Widths [*Lumber*]
AW..............	Alternate Weapon
A/W.............	Alternate Weeks [*Advertising term*] (WDMC)
AW..............	Altertumswissenschaft (BJA)
AW..............	American Waste Services [*NYSE symbol*] (SPSG)
AW..............	American Wildlands (EA)
AW..............	Americas Watch (EA)
AW..............	Amer Waste Svcs'A' [*NYSE symbol*] (TTSB)
AW..............	Amit Women (EA)
AW..............	Amphibious Warfare [*British military*] (DMA)
AW..............	Anglian Water Services Ltd. [*Commercial firm British*] (ECON)
AW..............	Anterior Wall [*Anatomy*]
AW..............	Antiwear
AW..............	Apparent Watt [*Electricity*] (IAA)
AW..............	Arcana Workshops [*Teaches philosophy of Alice A. Bailey toward human relations*] (EA)
AW..............	Arc Welding
AW..............	[*The*] Arkansas Western Railway Co. (IIA)
AW..............	Armature Winding [*Wiring*] (DNAB)
AW..............	Arming Wire [*Bombs*]
AW..............	Arm Width
AW..............	Army-Wide
AW..............	Articles of War
A/W.............	Artwork (WDMC)
AW..............	Aruba [*ANSI two-letter standard code*] (CNC)
aw----	Asia, Southwestern [*MARC geographic area code Library of Congress*] (LCCP)
AW..............	Assembly Week (MCD)
AW..............	Assembly Workstand [*NASA*] (NASA)
AW..............	Atomic Warfare
AW..............	Atomic Weight

AW............. Augmentor-Wing [*Aviation*]
AW............. Australian White [*Cattle*]
AW............. Australian Worker [*A publication*]
AW............. Australian Workman [*A publication*]
AW............. Automatic Weapons
AW............. Automatic Welding
AW............. Automatic Word (SAA)
AW............. Auxiliary Winding
AW............. Average Wage
AW............. Aviation ASW [*Antisubmarine Warfare*] Operator [*Navy rating*]
AW............. Awardee [*Database terminology*] (NITA)
AW............. AW Computer Systems [*Associated Press*] (SAG)
AW............. Axial Width
AW............. Azure Wove [*Paper*] (DGA)
AW............. Distilling Ship [*Navy symbol*]
AW............. Wander AG [*Research code symbol*] [*Switzerland*]
AW............. Wetaskiwin Public Library, Alberta [*Library symbol National Library of Canada*] (NLC)
AW1............ Aircraftwoman, First Class [*Canadian*]
AW1............ Aviation ASW [*Antisubmarine Warfare*] Operator, First Class [*Navy rating*]
AW2......... Aircraftwoman, Second Class [*Canadian*]
AW2......... Aviation ASW [*Antisubmarine Warfare*] Operator, Second Class [*Navy rating*]
AW3............ Aviation ASW [*Antisubmarine Warfare*] Operator, Third Class [*Navy rating*]
AWA............. Acoustic Wave Analysis
AWA............. Advise When Able [*Aviation*] (FAAC)
AWA............. Aerobic Way Association [*Defunct*] (EA)
AWA............. African West Air [*Senegal*] [*ICAO designator*] (FAAC)
AWA............. Air Warfare Analysis Section [*British*]
AWA............. Air Weather Association (EA)
AWA............. Alberta Wilderness Association (AC)
AWA............. Albinism World Alliance
AWA............. Alliance of Women in Architecture (EA)
AWA............. All Wave Antenna
AWA............. All-Weather Attack
AWA............. Aluminium Window Association [*British*] (DBA)
AWA............. Aluminum Wares Association [*Later, CMA*]
AWA............. Amalgamated Wireless Australasia Ltd. [*Telecommunications service*]
AWA............. Ambulate with Assistance [*Medicine*]
AWA............. Amchitka [*Alaska*] [*Seismograph station code, US Geological Survey Closed*] (SEIS)
AWA............. American Warehousemen's Association (EA)
AWA............. American Watch Association (EA)
AWA............. American Waterfowl Association
AWA............. American Welders Association (EA)
AWA............. American Whitewater Affiliation (EA)
AWA............. American Wilderness Alliance [*Later, AW*] (EA)
AWA............. American Wine Association (EA)
AWA............. American Woman's Association [*Defunct*] (EA)
AWA............. American Wrestling Association (DAVI)
AWA............. America West Airlines 'B' [*NYSE symbol*] (TTSB)
AWA............. America West Airlines, Inc. [*NYSE symbol*] (SAG)
AWA............. Anglian Water Authority [*British*] (DCTA)
AWA............. Antique Wireless Association (EA)
AWA............. Assist Work Authorization
AWA............. Association of Women in Architecture [*Defunct*] (EA)
AWA............. Atlantic Airline Ltd. [*Gambia*] [*FAA designator*] (FAAC)
AWA............. Atmospheric Winds Aloft
AWA............. Audio Warning Amplifier (AAG)
AWA............. Audio Wave Analyzer
AWA............. Australian Waterbird Association
AWA............. Australian Wheelchair Athletes [*An association*]
AWA............. Australian Wide Array of Geomagnetic Stations
AWA............. Australian Windscreen Association
AWA............. Aviation/Space Writers Association (EA)
awa............. Awadhi [*MARC language code Library of Congress*] (LCCP)
AWA............. Away without Authorization
AWA............. Warburg Public Library, Alberta [*Library symbol National Library of Canada*] (NLC)
AWAA .... Airman Apprentice, Aviation ASW [*Antisubmarine Warfare*] Operator, Striker [*Navy rating*]
AWAAG .... Automotive Wholesalers Association of Alabama and Georgia (SRA)
AWAAM .... All-Weather Air-to-Air Missile (MCD)
AWAAPM ..... Advanced Wide-Area Antipersonnel Mine (MCD)
AWAAS .... All-Weather Attack Avionics System (MCD)
AWAC .... Airborne Weapon and Control
AWAC .... Auto Workers Action Caucus (EA)
AWACG .... Airborne Warning and Control Group [*Air Force*]
AWACS .... Advanced Warning Airborne Command System
AWACS .... Advanced Warning and Control System (IEEE)
AWACS .... Airborne Warning and Control Squadron [*Air Force*]
AWACS .... Airborne [*or Aircraft*] Warning and Control System [*Air Force*]
AWACS .... Amalgamated Wireless Australasia Computers Division Services (NITA)
AWACS .... Chipewyan Lake School, Wabasca, Alberta [*Library symbol National Library of Canada*] (BIB)
AWACS/CAP... Advanced Warning and Control System/Combat Air Patrol [*Air Force*]
AWACTS ...... Airborne Warning and Control Training Squadron [*Air Force*]
AWACW .... Airborne Warning and Control Wing [*Air Force*]
AWAD .... Dairy Division, Alberta Agriculture, Wetaskiwin, Alberta [*Library symbol National Library of Canada*] (NLC)
AWADM .... Advanced Wide Area Defense Missile (MCD)

AWADS .... Adverse Weather [*or All-Weather*] Aerial Delivery System [*Ordnance delivery method*]
AWADS .... All-Weather Air Delivery System (SAA)
AWADS .... Army Wartime Asset Distribution Study
AWAE .... Automotive Wholesalers Association Executives (EA)
AWAF .... All Weather Flying Division [*Air Force*]
AWAFC .... American West African Freight Conference (EA)
AWAG .... Actors Working for an Actors Guild (EA)
AWAG .... All-Weather Aircraft Guided Missile (MCD)
AWAG .... American Wit and Gags [*Book title*]
AWAG .... American Woman above Ground [*Lifestyle classification*]
AWAGS .... Australian Wide Array of Geomagnetic Stations
AWAHF .... Adjustment With a Human Face [*UNICEF phrase to describe African adjustment programs*]
AWAIC .... Abused Women's Aid in Crisis (EA)
AWAIC .... Wainwright Community Library, Alberta [*Library symbol National Library of Canada*] (NLC)
AWAIR .... Arab World and Islamic Resources and School Services (EA)
AWAM .... Advanced Wide-Area Missile (MCD)
AWAN .... Airman, Aviation ASW [*Antisubmarine Warfare*] Operator, Striker [*Navy rating*]
AW & P .... Authority, Worldliness, and Power
AW & SHG... American Warmblood and Sport Horse Guild (EA)
AWANE .... Automotive Wholesalers of New England (SRA)
AWANS .... Aviation Weather and Notice to Airmen System (MCD)
AWANS .... Wanham School, Alberta [*Library symbol National Library of Canada*] (BIB)
AWAPA .... Academy of Wind and Percussion Arts (EA)
AWAR .... Anterior Wall of Aortic Root [*Cardiology*] (DMAA)
AWAR .... Area Weighted Average Resolution [*Photography*]
AWAR .... Warner Public Library, Alberta [*Library symbol National Library of Canada*] (NLC)
AWARDS..... Aircraft Wide-Angle Reflective Display System [*Singer Co., Link Division*]
AWARDS..... Automated Weather Acquisition and Retrieval Data System [*Marine science*] (OSRA)
AWARDS..... Automated Weather Acquisition and Retrieval Data System (USDC)
AWARE .... Adirondack World Affairs Resources for Education
AWARE .... Advanced Weapon/Aircraft Requirements Evaluation (MCD)
AWARE .... Airborne Warning and Recording Equipment
AWARE .... All Women's Archaeological Research Expedition
AWARE .... American Women's Association for Renewable Energy (EA)
AWARE .... Assisting Women to Advance through Resources and Encouragement Project (EDAC)
AWARE .... Association for Women's Active Return to Education [*Defunct*]
AWARE .... Association for Women's AIDS [*Acquired Immune Deficiency Syndrome*] Research and Education
Aware .... Aware, Inc. [*Associated Press*] (SAG)
AWARS .... Airborne Weather and Reconnaissance System (MCD)
AWAS .... Acoustic Wave Analysis System
AWAS .... Airborne Wind-Shear Alert Sensor (PDAA)
AWAS .... Air Warfare Analysis Section [*British*]
AWAS .... American Waldensian Aid Society [*Later, AWS*] (EA)
AWAS .... American Women's Association of Saigon (VNW)
AWAS .... Ansett Worldwide Aviation Services [*Australia*]
AWAS .... Automated Weather Advisory Station (GAVI)
AWAS .... Automated Work Authorization System (MCD)
AWAS .... Waskatenau Public Library, Alberta [*Library symbol National Library of Canada*] (NLC)
AWASP .... Advance Weapon Ammunition Support Point
AWASTS ...... St. Theresa School, Wabasca, Alberta [*Library symbol National Library of Canada*] (BIB)
AWat........... American Water Works [*Associated Press*] (SAG)
AWAT.......... Area Weighted Average T-Number (IEEE)
AWAT.......... Automotive Wholesalers Association of Tennessee (SRA)
AWAVS .... Aviation Wide-Angle Visual System (MCD)
AWA.WS..... America West Airlines Wrrt [*NYSE symbol*] (TTSB)
AWB........... Aboriginal Welfare Board [*New South Wales, Australia*]
AWB........... Adelaide Wool Brokers' Association [*Australia*]
AWB........... Afrikaner Weerstandsbeweging [*Afrikaner Resistance Movement*] [*South Africa*] [*Political party*] (ECON)
AWB........... Agricultural Wages Board [*British*]
AWB........... Air Waybill [*Shipping*]
AWB........... Airways International, Inc. [*ICAO designator*] (FAAC)
AWB........... Alliance of Women Bikers (EA)
AWB........... Amphibious Warfare Branch [*Navy*] (DNAB)
AWB........... Association of Washington Business (SRA)
AWB........... Association of Women Broadcasters
AWB........... Average White Back [*Football*]
AWB........... [*The*] Average White Band [*Rock music group*]
AWBA .... American Wheelchair Bowling Association (EA)
AWBA .... American Wholesale Booksellers Association (EA)
AWBA .... American World's Boxing Association (BARN)
AWBC .... American Women Buyers Club (EA)
AWBC .... Australian Women's Bowling Council
AWBE .... Automatic Weather Broadcast Equipment (FAAC)
AWBER .... Awaiting Berth [*Military*] (DNAB)
AWBLA .... Arizona Wholesale Beer and Liquor Association (SRA)
AWBMS ...... Amalgamated Welded Boiler Makers Society [*A union*] [*British*]
AWBPA....... Australian Wine and Brandy Producers' Association
AWBR .... Australian Women's Book Review [*A publication*]
AWBWA ...... Alabama Wholesale Beer and Wine Association (SRA)
AWC........... Absolute Worst Case
AWC........... Acting Wing-Commander [*British*]
AWC........... Aerial Weapons Company [*Military*] (VNW)

AWC............	Affiliated Warehouse Companies (EA)
AWC............	Agricultural Wages Committee [*British*] (DAS)
AWC............	Airborne Weapons Control
AWC............	Air War College [*Maxwell Air Force Base, AL*]
AWC............	Air Warfare Center [*Air Force*] (DOMA)
AWC............	Air Warfare Control (MCD)
AWC............	Air Warfare Co-Ordination [*British military*] (DMA)
AWC............	Air Weapons Controller
AWC............	Air Wing Commander
AWC............	Allied Works Council [*World War II*]
AWC............	All-Wheel Control [*Mitsubishi*] [*Transmisssion systems*]
AWC............	Alma White College [*New Jersey*]
AWC............	American Watershed Council (EA)
AWC............	American Whippet Club (EA)
AWC............	American Women Composers (EA)
AWC............	American Wood Council (EA)
AWC............	American Wool Council (EA)
AWC............	Amphibians and Watercraft [*Army*] (RDA)
AWC............	Amphibious and Watercraft (MCD)
AWC............	Amphibious Warfare Communications [*Navy*] (MCD)
AWC............	Angelic Warfare Confraternity [*Defunct*] (EA)
AWC............	Arab Women's Council (EA)
AWC............	Army War College
AWC............	Army Weapons Command [*AMC*]
AWC............	Asia Pacific Wire & Cable Corp. Ltd. [*NYSE symbol*] (SAG)
AWC............	Assisting Work Center
AWC............	Association for Women in Computing (EA)
AWC............	Association of Washington Cities (SRA)
AWC............	Association of World Citizens (EA)
AWC............	Astronauts' Wives Club
AWC............	Atlantic Waterfowl Council (EA)
AWC............	Available Water-Holding Capacity [*Soil science*]
AWC............	Titan Airways Ltd. [*British ICAO designator*] (FAAC)
AWC............	United States Army War College, Carlisle Barracks, PA [*OCLC symbol*] (OCLC)
AWC............	Wanham Community Library, Alberta [*Library symbol National Library of Canada*] (NLC)
AWCA.........	American Women's Clergy Association (EA)
AWCA.........	Wetaskiwin City Archives, Alberta [*Library symbol National Library of Canada*] (BIB)
AWCAP.......	Airborne Weapons Corrective Action Program (MCD)
AWCAP.......	Air War College Associate Program (AFM)
AWCAS........	Adverse Weather Close Air Support [*Military*] (MCD)
AWCC........	Active Well Coincidence Counter [*Nuclear energy*] (NRCH)
AWCC........	Association of Wisconsin Cleaning Contractors (SRA)
AWCCD.......	Australian Worker's Compensation Case Digests [*A publication*]
AWCCQ.......	Association of Wall and Ceiling Contractors of Queensland [*Australia*]
AWCCS.......	Army War College Correspondence Studies (MCD)
AWCCSC.....	Army War College Corresponding Studies Course (INF)
AWCCV.......	Advanced Weapons Carriage Configured Vehicle (MCD)
AWCCV.......	Association of Wall and Ceiling Contractors of Victoria [*Australia*]
AWCCWA....	Association of Wall and Ceiling Contractors of Western Australia
AWCD........	All-Weather Chassis Dynamometer (PDAA)
AWCEA.......	American Wood Chip Export Association (EA)
AWCI..........	Affective Work Competencies Inventory (EDAC)
AWCI..........	Aircraft and Weapons Control Interceptor
AWCI..........	American White Cross [*NASDAQ symbol*] (SAG)
AWCI..........	American Wire Cloth Institute (EA)
AWCI..........	Association of the Wall and Ceiling Industries - International (EA)
AWCI..........	[*A*] Wellness Center, Inc. (EA)
AWCIS........	Aircraft and Weapons Control Interceptor System
AWCIT........	Advanced Weapon Carriage Integration Technology (MCD)
AWCLS........	All-Weather Carrier Landing System [*Navy*]
AWCM........	Aviation ASW [*Antisubmarine Warfare*] Operator, Master Chief [*Navy rating*]
AWCMA.......	American Window Covering Manufacturers Association (EA)
AWCo.........	Aircraft Warning Company [*Army*]
AWCO.........	Air Warfare Control Officer
AWCO.........	Area Wage and Classification Office
AWCO.........	Assistant Weapons Control Officer
AWCOA.......	American Wrestling Coaches and Officials Association [*Later, NWCA*] (EA)
AWCP.........	Associated Water Colour Painters, Toronto [*1912*] [*Canada*] (NGC)
AWC-PM.....	Amphibians and Watercraft Product Manager [*Army*] (RDA)
AWCRC........	Adam Walsh Child Resource Center (EA)
AWCS.........	Agency-Wide Coding Structure [*Military*]
AWCS.........	Airborne Weapon Control System (MCD)
AWCS.........	Air Weapons Control System [*Air Force*]
AWCS.........	American Water Color Society, New York [*1878, founded 1866 as American Society of Painters in Water Colors*] (NGC)
AWCS.........	Automatic Warning and Control System
AWCS.........	Automatic Weapons Control System
AWCS.........	Automatic Work Control System [*Military*] (MCD)
AWCS.........	Aviation ASW [*Antisubmarine Warfare*] Operator, Senior Chief [*Navy rating*]
AWCS.........	AW Computer Systems, Inc. [*NASDAQ symbol*] (NQ)
AWCSA.......	AW Computer Systems'A' [*NASDAQ symbol*] (TTSB)
AWCSq.......	Airborne Warning and Control Squadron [*Air Force*]
AWCU.........	Association of World Colleges and Universities [*Later, AWE*]
AWD...........	Abbey Woods Development [*Vancouver Stock Exchange symbol*]
AWD...........	Advanced Workshop Detachment [*British and Canadian*] [*World War II*]
AWD...........	Air Warfare Division [*Navy*]
AWD...........	Air World Ltd. [*British*] [*FAA designator*] (FAAC)
AWD...........	Alive with Disease [*Medicine*]

AWD	All-Wheel Drive [*Automotive engineering*]
AWD	American War Dads (EA)
AWD	Association for Women in Development (EA)
AWD	Association for Workplace Democracy [*Defunct*] (EA)
AWD	Association of Welding Distributors [*British*] (DBA)
AWD	Astrogeodetic World Datum
AWD	Average Working Depth
AWD	Award (AABC)
AWD	Awning Deck [*of a ship*] (DS)
AWD	Worsley and District Library Society, Alberta [*Library symbol National Library of Canada*] (BIB)
AWDA.........	Automotive Warehouse Distributors Association (EA)
AWDATS.....	Artillery Weapons Data Transmission System (MCD)
AWDD.........	American Wholesalers and Distributors Directory [*Pronounced "awed"*] [*A publication*]
AWDEA........	Admiralty Works Department Employees Association [*A union*] [*British*]
AWDI	Automated Worthless Document Index
AWDISCH ...	Awaiting Discharge [*Military*] (DNAB)
AWDISCOM...	Awaiting Disciplinary Action This Command [*Army*]
AWDL	Aviation Weather Development Laboratory [*FAA*] (TAG)
AWDN.........	Automated Weather Data Network [*National Climate Program Office*]
AWDO.........	Air Wing Duty Officer (DNAB)
AWDR.........	Advanced Weapon Delivery RADAR
AWDREY.....	Atomic Weapon Detection, Recognition and Yield (PDAA)
AWDS.........	Automated Weather Distribution System (MCD)
AWDS.........	Automated Wire Data System
AWDS.........	Automatic Waveform Digitizing System (MCD)
AWDS.........	Automatic Wire Data System (MCD)
AWDT.........	Average Weekday Daily Traffic [*TXDOT*] (TAG)
AWE...........	Accepted Weight/Estimate [*Ships*]
AWE...........	Advanced Warfighter [*or Warfighting*] Experiment [*Military*] (RDA)
AWE...........	Advanced Warfighting Experiment [*Military*] (INF)
AWE...........	Advanced Warfighting Experiment
AWE...........	Advanced Wave Effects [*Sound synthesis*] (DOM)
AWE...........	Advise When Established [*Aviation*] (FAAC)
AWE...........	Alliance of Women for Equality
AWE...........	All-Weather Electronics
AWE...........	America West Airlines [*ICAO designator*] (FAAC)
AWE...........	Association for World Education (EA)
AWE...........	Association for World Evangelism (EA)
AWE...........	Association of Women Executives [*Canada*]
AWE...........	Automobil-Werke Eisenach [*Automobile manufacturer*] [*Germany*]
AWE...........	Average Weekly Earnings
AWE...........	Awesome Resources Ltd. [*Vancouver Stock Exchange symbol*]
AWE...........	Tazewell, TN [*Location identifier FAA*] (FAAL)
AWEA.........	American Wind Energy Association (EA)
AWEA.........	Awaiting Weather [*Military*] (DNAB)
AWEASVC...	Air Weather Service [*Scott Air Force Base, IL*] (IAA)
AWEBB........	Association of Wholesale Electrical Bulk Buyers [*British*] (DBA)
AWEC........	Albury-Wodonga Environment Center [*Australia*]
AWECOM	Army Weapons Command [*AMC*] (MCD)
AWECS	Advanced Wind Energy Conversion System (MCD)
AWED	American Woman's Economic Development Corp. (EA)
AWEG	Australian Writers and Editors' Guide [*A publication*]
AWeldI........	Associate of the Welding Institute [*British*] (DBQ)
AWEMS........	Wembley Elementary School, Alberta [*Library symbol National Library of Canada*] (BIB)
AWEP..........	Aboriginal Work Experience Program [*Australia*]
AWES..........	Association of West European Shipbuilders [*London, England*] (EAIO)
AWES..........	Westlock Public Library, Alberta [*Library symbol National Library of Canada*] (NLC)
AWESS	Automatic Weapons Effect Signature Simulator (MCD)
AWest.........	America West Holdings Corp. [*Associated Press*] (SAG)
AWF...........	Acceptable Workload Factor [*Management*]
AWF...........	Adjoint Wave Function
AWF...........	Adrenal Weight Factor [*Endocrinology*]
AWF...........	African Wildlife Foundation (EA)
AWF...........	African Workers Federation [*Kenya*] (AF)
AWF...........	Air Weather Flight [*Military*]
AWF...........	Alliance of Warehouses and Federations [*Defunct*] (EA)
AWF...........	Alliance World Dollar Government Fund [*NYSE symbol*] (SPSG)
AWF...........	Alliance World Dollar Gvt Fd II [*NYSE symbol*] (TTSB)
AWF...........	Alliance World Fellowship (EA)
AWF...........	All-Weather Flare
AWF...........	Arab Air Cargo [*Jordan*] [*ICAO designator*] (FAAC)
AWF...........	Art for World Friendship (AEBS)
AWF...........	Australian Weightlifting Federation
AWF...........	Australian Wine Foundation
AWF...........	Australian Winemakers' Forum
AWF...........	Aviation Weather Facility
AWFC.........	Andy Williams Fan Club (EA)
AWFCA	Association of Women's Forum Clubs of Australia
AWFI..........	American Wood Fabric Institute
AWFSR........	Automation of Wartime Functional Supply Requirements (MCD)
AWG	Activation Working Group [*Military*] (MCD)
AWG	Agriculture Working Group
AWG	Airtaxi Wings AG [*Switzerland ICAO designator*] (FAAC)
AWG	Alliance World Dollar Government Fund [*NYSE symbol*] (SPSG)
AWG	Alliance World Dollar Gvt Fd [*NYSE symbol*] (TTSB)
AWG	All-Weather Guidance (MCD)
AWG	American Wire Gauge [*Standard*]
AWG	Arbitrary Waveform Generator [*Electronics*]

AWG	Arctic Working Group [*University of Toronto*] [*Research center*] (RCD)
AWG	Art Workers Guild (EAIO)
AWG	Association for Women Geoscientists (EA)
AWG	Association of Waterloo Groups [*British*] (DI)
AWG	Association of Women Gemologists [*Defunct*] (EA)
AWG	Attack Working Group [*Military*]
AWG	Washington, IA [*Location identifier FAA*] (FAAL)
AWGIC	Arctic Winter Games International Committee [*Formerly, Arctic Winter Games Corporation*] (AC)
AWGN	Additive Voice Gaussian Noise [*Telecommunications*] (NITA)
AWGN	Additive White Gaussian Noise [*Telecommunications*] (TEL)
awgz--	Gaza Strip [*MARC geographic area code Library of Congress*] (LCCP)
AWH	American Women's Hospitals [*Later, AWHS*]
AWH	Association of Western Hospitals [*Later, HCF*]
AWH	Whitecourt Public Library, Alberta [*Library symbol National Library of Canada*] (NLC)
AWHA	American Walking Horse Association (EA)
AWHC	Available Water-Holding Capacity [*Soil science*] (OA)
AWHDA	American Wholesale Horticultural Dealers Association [*Later, HDA*] (EA)
AWHE	American Women's Himalayan Expeditions
AWHMT	Association of Waste Hazardous Materials Transporters
AWHRC	American Women's Hospital Reserve Corps [*British*] (DAS)
AWHS	American Women's Hospitals Service [*Formerly, AWH*] [*Later, AWHS/AMWA*] (EA)
AWHS	Whitelaw School, Alberta [*Library symbol National Library of Canada*] (BIB)
AWHS/AMWA...	American Women's Hospitals Service Committee of AMWA [*American Medical Women's Association*] (EA)
AWHSL	Association of Women Highway Safety Leaders
AWHT	Helen E. Taylor School, Wembley, Alberta [*Library symbol National Library of Canada*] (BIB)
AWHV	Aircraft Weapons Handling Vehicle
AWI.............	Accommodation Weight Investigation (KSC)
AWI.............	Air Warfare Instructor [*Navy British*]
AWI.............	Air Wisconsin [*ICAO designator*] (FAAC)
AWI.............	Alberta Women's Institutes (AC)
AWI.............	All-Weather Interceptor
AWI.............	America and West Indies [*Obsolete British*]
AWI.............	American Watchmakers Institute (EA)
AWI.............	American Welding Institute (EA)
AWI.............	Animal Welfare Institute (EA)
AWI.............	Anterior Wall Infarction [*Cardiology*] (MAE)
AWI.............	Antigua [*Antigua*] [*Seismograph station code, US Geological Survey Closed*] (SEIS)
AWI.............	Architectural Woodwork Institute (EA)
AWI.............	Arm Width Index
AWI.............	Authorized Walk-In [*Patient*] [*Medicine*] (DAVI)
AWI.............	Winfield Public Library, Alberta [*Library symbol National Library of Canada*] (NLC)
AWIA	American Wood Inspection Agency
AWIA	Association of Wyoming Insurance Agents (SRA)
AWIAV	Aluminium Window Industry Association of Victoria [*Australia*]
AWIC	Aircraft Wireless Intercom (DWSG)
AWIC	Animal Welfare Information Center [*Department of Agriculture Information service or system*] (IID)
AWID	Association for Women in Development (EA)
AWII............	Ameriwood Indus Intl. [*NASDAQ symbol*] (TTSB)
AWII............	Ameriwood Industries International Corp. [*NASDAQ symbol*] (SAG)
AWIL...........	Willingdon Public Library, Alberta [*Library symbol National Library of Canada*] (NLC)
AWILD	Wildwood Public Library, Alberta [*Library symbol National Library of Canada*] (NLC)
AWIN	Allied Waste Ind [*NASDAQ symbol*] (TTSB)
AWIN	Allied Waste Industries [*NASDAQ symbol*] (SPSG)
AWIN	Association of Women in Natural Foods (EA)
AWIPS	Advanced Weather Interactive Processing System [*National Oceanic and Atmospheric Administration*]
AWIPS	Automated Weather Information Processing System
AWIPS-90	Advanced Weather Interactive Processing System of the 1990's [*National Oceanic and Atmospheric Administration*]
AWIR	ADCOM Weekly Intelligence Review Support (MCD)
AWIR	Ankole-Watusi International Registry (EA)
AWIR	Annual Worldwide Industry Review (IMH)
AWIRA	American Wax Importers and Refiners Association
AWIS	All-Weather Identification Sensor
AWIS	Army WWMCCS [*Worldwide Military Command and Control System*] Information System (GFGA)
AWIS	Association for Women in Science (EA)
AWIU	Aluminum Workers International Union [*Later, ABCWIU*] (EA)
awiu--	Israel-Syria Demilitarized Zones [*MARC geographic area code Library of Congress*] (LCCP)
AWIU(I).......	Allied Workers International Union (Independent)
awiw--	Israel-Jordan Demilitarized Zones [*MARC geographic area code Library of Congress*] (LCCP)
awiy--	Iraq-Saudi Arabia Neutral Zone [*MARC geographic area code Library of Congress*] (LCCP)
AWJM	Abrasive Water Jet Machining [*Factory automation*] (BTTJ)
AWJSRA	Augmenter Wing Jet STOL [*Short Takeoff and Landing*] Research Aircraft
awk.............	Aho Weinberger Kernighan (CDE)
AWK............	Airwork Service Training [*British ICAO designator*] (FAAC)
AWK............	Americans Want to Know [*Defunct*] (EA)

AWK............	American Water Works Co., Inc. [*NYSE symbol*] (SPSG)
AWK............	Amer Water Works [*NYSE symbol*] (TTSB)
AWK............	Arwick International Resources Ltd. [*Vancouver Stock Exchange symbol*]
AWK............	Australian Workers' Compensation Guide [*A publication*]
AWK............	Awkward Expression or Construction [*Used in correcting manuscripts, etc.*]
AWK............	Wake [*Wake Island, Pacific Ocean*] [*Airport symbol*] (AD)
AWK............	Water Tankers [*Navy symbol*] (MUGU)
AWKPrA	Amer Water Wks 5%Pref [*NYSE symbol*] (TTSB)
AWKPrB	Amer Water Wks,5% Pfd [*NYSE symbol*] (TTSB)
AWL............	Absent With Leave [*Military*]
AWL............	Absent Without Leave [*Military British*]
AWL............	Administrative Weight Limitation [*Military*] (AABC)
AWL............	Agarwal Resources Ltd. [*Vancouver Stock Exchange symbol*]
AWL............	All-Weather Landing
AWL............	American Wildlands Alliance (GNE)
AWL............	Artificial White Light
AWL............	Association for a World Language (EA)
AWL............	Association of Women Launderers [*British*] (BI)
AWL............	Automated Wire List [*NASA*] (NASA)
AWL............	Average Work Load
AWLA	American Weight Lifting Association (EA)
AWLF	African Wildlife Leadership Foundation
AWLLA........	All Wales Ladies Lacrosse Association (BI)
AWLOG	Army Wholesale Logistic System (AABC)
AWLREM	Association of Webbing Load Restraint Equipment Manufacturers [*British*] (DBA)
AWLRF	All-Weather Long-Range Fighter
AWLS	All-Weather Landing System [*Also, ALS*]
AWLSA	Animal Welfare League of South Australia
AWLTNI	Association of the Wholesale Licensed Trade of Northern Ireland (BI)
AWLU	Aural Warning Logic Unit (MCD)
AWM	Abnormal Wall Motion [*Medicine*] (DMAA)
AWM	Air and Waste Management (OICC)
AWM	American War Mothers (EA)
AWM	Appliance Wiring Material
AWM	Arc Welding Machine
AWM	Armed White Male (ECON)
AWM	Association for Women in Mathematics (EA)
AWM	Automatic Writing Machine
AWM	Awaiting Maintenance (AFM)
AWM	West Memphis, AR [*Location identifier FAA*] (FAAL)
AWMA	Air and Waste Management Association (FFDE)
AWMA	Aluminum Window Manufacturers Association [*Later, Architectural Aluminum Manufacturers Association*]
AWMA	American Walnut Manufacturers Association [*Later, FHAWA*] (EA)
AWMA	Australian Waste Management Association
AWMA	Automatic Welding Machinery Association [*Defunct*] (EA)
AWMAC	Architectural Woodwork Manufacturers Association of Canada (AC)
AWMC	Army Weapons and Mobility Command
AWMC	Association of Workers for Maladjusted Children [*British*]
AWMCS	Aviation Weapons Movement Control System (MCD)
AWMD	Air and Waste Management Division [*Environmental Protection Agency*] (GFGA)
AWMG	American Wooden Money Guild (EA)
AWMI	Anterior Wall Myocardial Infarction [*Cardiology*] (MAE)
Awmn	Airwoman
AWMV	Amplitude-Weighted Mean Velocity (DMAA)
AWN	Activation Work Notice
AWN	Air Niger [*ICAO designator*] (FAAC)
AWN	Air Weather Network
AWN	Allahabad Weekly Notes [*India*] [*A publication*] (DLA)
AWN	Alton Downs [*Australia Airport symbol Obsolete*] (OAG)
AWN	Aston Whole Number [*Chemistry*]
AWN	Automated Weather Network [*Air Force*]
AWN	Awning (MSA)
AWN	Awning
AWNA	Alberta Weekly Newspapers Association (AC)
AWNCS	Automated Weather Network Coordinating Station [*Air Force*]
AWNDLS.....	Anchor Windlass
AWNMC	Automated Weather Network Management Center [*Military*]
AWNY	Advertising Women of New York [*New York, NY*] (EA)
AWO	Accounting Work Order
AWO	Administrative Watch Officer (DNAB)
AWO	Admiralty Weekly Order [*British military*] (DMA)
AWO	Agricultural Workers' Organization
AWO	All Weather Operations (DA)
AWO	Alterio Resources Ltd. [*Toronto Stock Exchange symbol*]
AWO	American Waterways Operators (EA)
AWO	Arlington, WA [*Location identifier FAA*] (FAAL)
AWO	Army Welfare Officer [*British*]
AWO	Army Wireless Officer [*Obsolete*] (IAA)
AWO	Association of Water Officers [*British*] (DBA)
AWO	Association of Waterworks Officers [*British*] (BI)
AWO	Automotive Wholesalers of Oklahoma (SRA)
AWO	Awood Air Ltd. [*Canada ICAO designator*] (FAAC)
AWOA	American West Overseas Association (EA)
AWOA	Automotive Wholesalers of Arizona (SRA)
AWOC.........	Agricultural Workers Organizing Committee [*Later, UFWA*] [*AFL-CIO*]
AWOC.........	All-Weather Operations Committee [*ATA*]
AWOD.........	All-Weather Operations Division [*ICAO*] (MCD)
AWOI	Automotive Wholesalers of Illinois (SRA)

AWOIS......... Automated Wreck and Obstruction Information System [*National Oceanic and Atmospheric Administration Information service or system*] (IID)
AWOL......... Absent without Official Leave [*Military*]
AWOL......... After Women or Liquor [*Slang*]
AWOL......... [*A*] Wolf on the Loose [*Slang*]
AWood........ American Woodmark Corp. [*Associated Press*] (SAG)
AWOP......... Absent without Pay (MCD)
AWOP......... All-Weather Operations Panel [*International Civil Aviation Organization*]
AWORD....... Awaiting Orders [*Military*] (DNAB)
AWORS....... Worsley School, Alberta [*Library symbol National Library of Canada*] (BIB)
AWOS......... Automated Weather Observing Station [*FAA*] (TAG)
AWOS......... Automatic Weather Observing/Reporting System (FAAC)
AWOS......... Woking School, Alberta [*Library symbol National Library of Canada*] (BIB)
AWOT......... Adsorption Wall Open Tubular Column [*Chromatography*]
AWOT......... Automotive Wholesalers of Texas (SRA)
AWP........... Actual Working Pressure
AWP........... Advanced Workstation Products [*El Segundo, CA*] (ECON)
AWP........... Aero Weapons Platoon (VNW)
AWP........... Airway Pressure [*Pulmonary ventilation*]
AWP........... Albania Workers' Party [*Political party*]
AWP........... ALCAN [*Aluminum Co. of Canada Ltd.*] World Price [*Obsolete*] (FEA)
AWP........... Allied Weather Publications [*NATO*] (NATG)
AWP........... Amusement with Prizes [*Pinball machines*] [*British*]
AWP........... Annual Work Plan
AWP........... Anthology of World Poetry [*A publication*]
AWP........... Antisubmarine Warfare Programs [*Navy*] (MCD)
AWP........... Army Warranty Program
AWP........... Associated Writing Programs (EA)
AWP........... Association for Women in Psychology (EA)
AWP........... Association for World Peace [*Founded in 1951*] [*Defunct British*]
AWP........... Atlanta & West Point Rail Road Co. [*AAR code*]
AWP........... Automatic Wage Payments (MCD)
AWP........... Automatic Withdrawal Prohibit [*Nuclear energy*] (NRCH)
AWP........... Average Wholesale Price
AWP........... Aviation Weather Processor [*ICAO designator*] (FAAC)
AWP........... Awaiting Parts (AFM)
AWPA .... Alberta Water Polo Association (AC)
AWPA .... American Walking Pony Association (EA)
AWPA .... American Wire Producers Association (EA)
AWPA .... American Women Playwrights Association (EA)
AWPA .... American Wood Preservers' Association (EA)
AWPA .... American Word Processing Association (EA)
AWPA .... Arizona Wool Producers Association (SRA)
AWPA .... Australian Wood Panels Association
AWPB .... American Wood Preservers Bureau [*Defunct*] (EA)
AWPC .... Australian Wildlife Protection Council
AWPC .... Australian Wool Processors' Council
AWPDS....... Attack Warning Processing and Display System (MCD)
AWPE.......... Abstracts of Working Papers in Economics [*Cambridge University Press*] [*Information service or system*] (IID)
AWPG .... Aviation Weather Products Generator [*FAA*] (TAG)
AWPGM....... Adverse Weather Precision Guided Munition [*Air Force*] (DOMA)
AWPI .... American Wood Preservers Institute (EA)
AWPPW....... Association of Western Pulp and Paper Workers (EA)
A/WPR .... Air/Water Pollution Report [*Business Publishers, Inc.*] [*Information service or system*] (CRD)
AWPR .... Association of Women in Public Relations [*British*] (DBA)
AWPS .... American Welara Pony Society (EA)
AWPU .... Age Weighted Pupil Unit [*Education*] (AIE)
AWQA .... Arizona Warfare Quality Association (SRA)
AWQPP........ Agricultural Water Quality Protection Program [*Department of Agriculture*]
AWR .... Actual Weight Report
AWR .... Adaptive Waveform Recognition
AWR .... Advanced Weather RADAR (MCD)
AWR .... Adventist World Radio (NTCM)
AWR .... Allahabad Weekly Reporter [*India*] [*A publication*] (DLA)
AWR .... All-Weather Radial Tire [*Automotive accessory*]
AWR .... American Warmblood Registry (EA)
AWR .... Ammunition War Reserve (CINC)
AWR .... Annual Wage Reporting [*Social Security Administration*]
AWR .... Arctic Wings and Rotors Ltd. [*Canada*] [*FAA designator*] (FAAC)
AWR .... Army War Room (AABC)
AWR .... Aromatic Weathering Ratio [*Ecology*] (DAVI)
AWR .... Arrowhead Resources Ltd. [*Vancouver Stock Exchange symbol*]
AWR .... Association for the Study of the World Refugee Problem [*Vaduz, Liechtenstein*] (EAIO)
AWR .... Association of Western Railways [*Later, WRA*]
AWR .... Automated Work Request (NVT)
AWR .... Wandering River Public Library, Alberta [*Library symbol National Library of Canada*] (NLC)
AWR .... Window Rock, AZ [*Location identifier FAA*] (FAAL)
AWRA .... American Water Resources Association (EA)
AWRA .... Augmentor Wing Research Aircraft [*Aviation*] (MCD)
AWRAM ...... Reynolds Alberta Museum, Wetaskiwin, Alberta [*Library symbol National Library of Canada*] (BIB)
AWRD......... Air Warfare Research Department [*Navy*] (MCD)
AWRD......... Award
AWRD......... Award Software International, Inc. [*NASDAQ symbol*] (SAG)
AwrdSft........ Award Software International, Inc. [*Associated Press*] (SAG)

AWRE .... Atomic Weapons Research Establishment [*British Ministry of Defense*] [*Research center*]
AWRE .... Aware, Inc. [*NASDAQ symbol*] (SAG)
AWRF .... Associated Wire Rope Fabricators (EA)
AWRIS .... Army War Room Information System
AWRL .... Ammo War Reserve Level (CINC)
AWRN .... Awareness (KSC)
AWRNCO .... Aircraft Warning Company [*Marine Corps*]
AWRO .... Atomic Weapon Retrofit Order
AWRRA....... Alliance of Women Road Riders and Associates (EA)
AWRRC....... Arkansas Water Resources Research Center [*University of Arkansas*] [*Research center*] (RCD)
AWRS .... Airborne Weather and Reconnaissance System (MCD)
AWRS .... Airborne Weather RADAR System
AWRS .... Aircraft Weapons Release Set [*or System*] (NG)
AWRS .... All-Weather Reconnaissance System
AWRS .... Anti-Whole Rabbit Serum [*Immunology*]
AWRS .... Automatic Weapons Release System (DNAB)
AWRS .... Aviation Weather Reporting Station
AWRSA....... Australian Window Roller Shutter Association
AWRT .... American Women in Radio and Television (EA)
AWRU .... Aircraft Weapons Release Unit [*DoD*] (MCD)
AWS........... Abundant Wildlife Society of North America (EA)
AWS........... Acoustic Warfare System [*Navy*] (MCD)
AWS........... Active Work Space [*Computer science*] (NITA)
AWS........... Adjustable Wire Stripper
AWS........... Advanced Warning System
AWS........... Advanced Weapons System (MCD)
AWS........... African Writers Series [*A publication*]
AWS........... Aircraft Warning Service [*Military*]
AWS........... Air Warning Squadron [*Marine Corps*]
AWS........... Air Warning System
AWS........... Air Weapon Systems [*Air Force*]
AWS........... Air Weather Service [*Scott Air Force Base, IL*]
AWS........... Air Weather Service [*AEC*] (DOMA)
AWS........... Air Wing Staff [*Air Force*]
AWS........... Alba-Waldensian [*AMEX symbol*] (TTSB)
AWS........... Alba-Waldensian, Inc. [*AMEX symbol*] (SPSG)
AWS........... All-Weather System (MCD)
AWS........... All Wood Screw (DAC)
AWS........... Alston Wilkes Society (EA)
AWS........... Alternative Work Schedule (GFGA)
AWS........... Altitude Warning System (MCD)
AWS........... American Waldensian Society (EA)
AWS........... American Warmblood Society (EA)
AWS........... American War Standards [*DoD*]
AWS........... American Watercolor Society (EA)
AWS........... American Welding Society (EA)
AWS........... American Wine Society (EA)
AWS........... Amphibious Warfare School (DNAB)
AWS........... Annual Wage Survey (OICC)
AWS........... Annual Work Schedule
AWS........... Arab Wings Co. [*Jordan*] [*ICAO designator*] (FAAC)
AWS........... Area Wage Survey (OICC)
AWS........... Area Working Standards
AWS........... Army Weather Service (NATG)
AWS........... Army Welfare Services [*British*]
AWS........... Association of Winery Suppliers (EA)
AWS........... Association of Women Surgeons (EA)
AWS........... Astronaut Work Station [*NASA*]
AWS........... Attack Warning System [*Civil Defense*]
AWS........... Automated Wiring System (MCD)
AWS........... Automatic Weather Station
AWS........... Automatic Welding System
AWS........... Aviation Weather Specialist (DNAB)
AWS........... Aviation Weather Service [*of National Weather Service*]
AWS........... Awaiting Sentence [*of court-martial*]
AWS........... Columbus, GA [*Location identifier FAA*] (FAAL)
AWSA .... Airborne Waveguide Slotted Array
AWSA .... Air Warfare Systems Analysis
AWSA .... American Water Ski Association (EA)
AWSA .... Association of Wisconsin School Administrators (SRA)
AWSAA ...... Airborne Waveguide Slotted Array Antenna
AWSACS...... All-Weather Standoff Attack Control System (MCD)
AWSBEF ...... Australian Wool Selling Brokers Employers' Federation
AWSC .... Agricultural Weather Service Center [*National Oceanic and Atmospheric Administration*]
AWSC .... Air Warfare Simulation Complex (MCD)
AWSC .... American Waterways Shipyard Conference (EA)
AWSCOM ..... Advanced Weapons Support Command [*Army*] (AABC)
AWSCPA ..... American Woman's Society of Certified Public Accountants [*Chicago, IL*] (EA)
AWSD .... Air Warfare Systems Development (DNAB)
AWSEF....... American Water Ski Educational Foundation (EA)
AWSF.......... Alpha Waste Storage Facility [*Nuclear energy*]
AWSF.......... Australian Wheelchair Sports Federation
AWSG .... Armstrong-Whitworth Sperry Gyroscope (IAA)
AWSG .... Army Work Study Group
AW-SHORADS... All-Weather Short-Range Air Defense Missile System (MCD)
AWSI .... Adaptive Wafer Scale Integration (MCD)
AWSI .... American Friends of the Association for Welfare of Soldiers in Israel (EA)
AWSKA .... Australian Water Ski Association
AWSM .... Acoustic Warfare Support Measures (NVT)
AWSM .... Air Weapons Systems Management

AWSM .... Air Weather Service Manual
AWSM .... Association for Women in Sports Media (EA)
AWSMV ...... American Wheat Striate Mosaic Virus [*Plant pathology*]
AWSNA .... Association of Waldorf Schools of North America (EA)
AWSO .... All-Weather Sleepout (ADA)
AWSO .... All-Weather Surface Observations [*NASA*] (PDAA)
AWSO .... Assembly Work Schedule Order
AWSOS .... Army Women's Services Officers School [*British military*] (DMA)
AWSP .... Air Weapons Systems Plan
AWSP .... Army-Wide Signature Program (MCD)
AWSP .... Association of Washington School Principals (SRA)
AWSP .... Automatic Weapons (Self-Propelled) [*Military*]
AWSPA .... Australian Wheat Starch Producers' Association
AWSS .... Altitude Warning Signal System (PDAA)
AWSS .... Association of Women Soil Scientists (EA)
AWST .... Atomic Weapons Special Transport (DNAB)
AWSTA .... All-Weather Station
AWSTAS ..... All-Weather Sea Target Acquisition System [*Navy*] (MCD)
AWste .... American Waste Services [*Associated Press*] (SAG)
AWSTG .... Air Weather Service Training Guide
AWSTL......... Air Weather Service Technical Library [*Air Force Information service or system*] (IID)
AWSV .... Alligatorweed Stunting Virus [*Plant pathology*]
AWSVC .... Air Warning Service (IAA)
AWSWA ...... Alaska Wine and Spirits Wholesalers Association (SRA)
AWSWO ...... Air Weather Service Office
AWT .... Abstract Windowing Toolkit [*Computer science*]
AWT .... Abstract Windowing Toolkit [*Computer science*]
AWT .... Abstract Window Toolkit [*Computer science*]
AWT .... Actual Work Time [*Bell System*]
AWT .... Advanced Waste Treatment [*of water*]
AWT .... Advanced Windowing Toolkit (PCM)
AWT .... Aeroelastic Wind Tunnel
AWT .... Air & Water Tech'A' [*AMEX symbol*] (TTSB)
AWT .... Air & Water Technologies Corp. [*AMEX symbol*] (SPSG)
AWT .... Air West [*Canada ICAO designator*] (FAAC)
AWT .... Altitude Wind Tunnel
AWT .... Anechoic Water Tank
AWT .... Anterior Wall Thickness [*Anatomy*]
AWT .... Arc-Jet Wind Tunnel
AWT .... Arctic Warfare Training [*British military*] (DMA)
AWT .... Associate in Wildlife Technology
AWT .... Association of Wind Teachers [*British*]
AWT .... Atomic Weight (IAA)
AWT .... Average Work Time
AWT .... Await
AWT .... Awaiting Trial [*by court-martial*]
AWTA .... Alabama World Trade Association (SRA)
AWTA .... American Working Terrier Association (EA)
AWTA .... Australian Women's Tennis Association
AWTAO .... Association of Water Transportation Accounting Officers [*New York, NY*] (EA)
AWTAS .... Automated Weapons Test Analysis System
AWTB .... All-Weather Test Bed (MCD)
AWTBS .... All-Weather Tactical Bombing System
AWTC .... Airway Traffic Controller (IAA)
AWTC .... Amman World Trade Center [*Jordan*] (EAIO)
AWTC .... Association of Women Tax Clerks [*A union*] [*British*]
AWTCE .... Association of World Trade Chamber Executives (EA)
AWTD .... Air Warfare Training Division [*Navy British*]
AWTE .... Association for World Travel Exchange (EA)
AWTF .... American Writers Theatre Foundation (EA)
AWTG .... Atomic Weapons Training Group [*DASA*]
AWTI .... Air Weapons Training Installation (NATG)
AWTL .... Advanced Waste Treatment Laboratory [*National Environmental Research Center*]
AWTMS .... All-Weather Topographic Mapping System [*Army*]
AWTR .... Advanced Waste Treatment Processes (PDAA)
AWTR .... Assistant Writer [*British military*] (DMA)
AWTS .... Army-Wide Training Support (AABC)
AWTSS .... All-Weather Tactical Strike System [*Air Force*] (MCD)
AWTSS .... Army-Wide Training Support System
AWTT .... Above Water Thrown Torpedo [*Navy*] (CAAL)
AWTT .... Above Water Torpedo Tube [*Navy*] (NVT)
AWTTP......... Apollo Wind-Tunnel Testing Program [*NASA*]
AWU .... Agricultural Workers' Union (DAS)
AWU .... Aluminum Workers International Union [*Later, ABCWIU*]
AWU .... Associated Western Universities [*Salt Lake City, UT*] [*Department of Energy*]
AWU .... Associated Workers' Union [*Philippines*]
AWU .... Association for the World University (EA)
AWU .... Atomic Weight Unit
AWU .... Australian Wrestling Union
AWV .... Airwave Transport, Inc. [*Canada ICAO designator*] (FAAC)
AWV .... American Lightwave [*Vancouver Stock Exchange symbol*]
AWV .... Association for Women Veterinarians (EA)
AWV .... Atmospheric Wind Velocity
AWV .... Water Valley Public Library, Alberta [*Library symbol National Library of Canada*] (NLC)
AWVA .... Another World Viewer Alliance (EA)
AWVA .... Australian Women's Vigoro Association
AWVS .... American Women's Voluntary Services [*World War II*] (EA)
AWW .... Above Water Warfare [*Navy*] (NVT)
AWW .... Advanced Wild Weasel [*RADAR warning system*]
AWW .... Alert Weather Watch [*Meteorology*] (DA)

AWW .... Algers, Winslow & Western Railway Co. [*AAR code*]
AWW .... All's Well That Ends Well [*Shakespearean work*]
AWW .... American Westwater Technology Group Ltd. [*Vancouver Stock Exchange symbol*]
AWW .... Association of Women Welders [*A union*] [*British*]
AWW .... Winchester, IN [*Location identifier FAA*] (FAAL)
AWWA .... American Water Works Association (EA)
AWWA .... Armenian Women's Welfare Association (EA)
AWWARF ...... American Water Works Association Research Foundation (EPA)
AWWBT .... Association of Women Workers in the Bedstead Trade [*A union*] [*British*]
AWWC .... Association of Workshop Way Consultants (EA)
AWWDA ...... Alberta Water Well Drilling Association (AC)
AWWI .... American Wash and Wear Institute
AWWI .... American Wood Window Institute (DAC)
AWWM .... Association of Wholesale Woollen Merchants Ltd. [*British*] (BI)
AWWM .... Automatic Wire Wrap Machine
AWWMCCS... Army Worldwide Military Command and Control Information Systems (RDA)
AWWP .... Amphibious Warfare Working Party (NATG)
AWWPA ...... American Wire Weavers Protective Association
AWWS .... Automated Want and Warrant System [*Data processing system used in police work*]
AWWU .... American Watch Workers Union
AWX........... All-Weather Aircraft [*Air Force*] (NATG)
AWX........... Andaurex Resources, Inc. [*Vancouver Stock Exchange symbol*]
AWX(F)........ All-Weather Fighter
AWX(I)........ All-Weather Intruder
AWY........... Airway
AWY........... Erie, PA [*Location identifier FAA*] (FAAL)
AWYDC .... All-Weather Yaw Damper Computer
AWZ........... Ahwaz [*Iran*] [*Airport symbol Obsolete*] (OAG)
AWZ........... Merced, CA [*Location identifier FAA*] (FAAL)
AX............. Abnormal Xylem Elements [*Botany*]
AX............. Aged, Adrenalectomized Animals [*Endocrinology*]
AX............. Agility Excellent
AX............. Altex Resources Ltd. [*Toronto Stock Exchange symbol*]
AX............. Amer Exploration(New) [*AMEX symbol*] (TTSB)
AX............. American Exploration Co. [*AMEX symbol*] (SPSG)
AX............. American Express Co. (ADA)
A/X............ Armani Exchange (ECON)
AX............. Armpit [*Medicine*] (DHSM)
AX............. Attack Experimental [*Air Force*] (MCD)
AX............. Aviation ASW [*Antisubmarine Warfare*] Technician [*Navy rating*]
ax .... Axial (DAVI)
ax .... Axilla (DAVI)
AX............. Axillary [*Medicine*]
AX............. Axiom
AX............. Axis (AAG)
AX............. Axle Housing Cover Gasket [*Automotive engineering*]
AX............. Connectair [*ICAO designator*] (AD)
AX............. Quarterdeck [*i.e., "after castle," by analogy with FX - forecastle*] [*Navy British*]
AX1 .... Aviation ASW [*Antisubmarine Warfare*] Technician, First Class [*Navy rating*]
AX2 .... Aviation ASW [*Antisubmarine Warfare*] Technician, Second Class [*Navy rating*]
AX3 .... Aviation ASW [*Antisubmarine Warfare*] Technician, Third Class [*Navy rating*]
AXA............ Alexa Ventures, Inc. [*Vancouver Stock Exchange symbol*]
AXA............ Algona, IA [*Location identifier FAA*] (FAAL)
AXA............ Anguilla [*West Indies*] [*Airport symbol*] (OAG)
AXA............ Anguilla [*Leeward Islands*] [*Airport symbol*] (AD)
AXA............ AXA ADS [*NYSE symbol*] (SAG)
AXA............ Kiev AAR Airlines [*Ukraine*] [*FAA designator*] (FAAC)
AXAA.......... Airman Apprentice, Aviation ASW [*Antisubmarine Warfare*] Technician, Striker [*Navy rating*]
AXAF.......... Advanced X-Ray Astrophysics Facility [*Great Observatory Program*] [*NASA*]
AXAN .... Airman, Aviation ASW [*Antisubmarine Warfare*] Technician, Striker [*Navy rating*]
AXAS .... Abraxas Petroleum [*NASDAQ symbol*] (TTSB)
AXAS .... Abraxas Petroleum Corp. [*NASDAQ symbol*] (SAG)
AXB........... Auxiliary Boiler [*of a ship*] (DS)
AXBS.......... Auxiliary Boiler Survey [*of a ship*] (DS)
AXBT.......... Airborne Expendable Bathythermograph
AXBT.......... Airborne XBT [*Expendable Bathythermograph*] (USDC)
AXC........... Alpine Exploration [*Vancouver Stock Exchange symbol*]
AXC........... Ampex Corp. [*AMEX symbol*] (SAG)
AXC........... Ampex Corp.'A' [*AMEX symbol*] (TTSB)
AXC........... Aramac [*Australia Airport symbol*] (OAG)
AXC........... Aviation ASW [*Antisubmarine Warfare*] Technician, Chief [*Navy rating*]
AXCM.......... Aviation ASW [*Antisubmarine Warfare*] Technician, Master Chief [*Navy rating*]
AXCP .... Airborne Expendable Current Profiler [*Marine science*] (OSRA)
AXCP .... Airborne Expendable Current Profiler (USDC)
AXCS .... Aviation ASW [*Antisubmarine Warfare*] Technician, Senior Chief [*Navy rating*]
AXD .... Alexandroupolis [*Greece*] [*Airport symbol*] (OAG)
AXD .... Alpha Xi Delta [*Sorority*]
AXD .... Amer Exp 6.25% 'DECS' '96 [*NYSE symbol*] (TTSB)
AXD .... American Express Co. [*NYSE symbol*] (SAG)
AXD .... Auxiliary Drum (CET)
AXD .... Axillary Dissection [*Medicine*] (DMAA)

AXE............. Acetyl Xylan Esterase [An enzyme]
AXE............. American Resource [Vancouver Stock Exchange symbol]
AXE............. Anixter International, Inc. [NYSE symbol] (SAG)
AXE............. Anixter Intl. [NYSE symbol] (TTSB)
AXE............. Executive Air [Zimbabwe] [ICAO designator] (FAAC)
AxentT......... Axent Technologies, Inc. [Associated Press] (SAG)
AXF............. AABBAX International Financial [Vancouver Stock Exchange symbol]
AXF............. Advanced X-Ray Facility
AXFBS .... Auxiliary Fire Tube Boiler Survey [of a ship] (DS)
AXFL............ Axial Flow
AXFMR .... Automatic Transformer (IEEE)
AXFTB .... Auxiliary Fire Tube Boiler [of a ship] (DS)
AXFTBS .... Auxiliary Fire Tube Boiler Survey [of a ship] (DS)
AXG............. Adult Xanthogranuloma [Medicine] (DMAA)
AXG............. Amax Gold, Inc. [Toronto Stock Exchange symbol]
AXG............. Axogen Ltd. [AMEX symbol] (SAG)
ax grad........ Axial Gradient (MAE)
AXH............. Arcola, TX [Location identifier FAA] (FAAL)
AXI............. Aeron International Airlines, Inc. [ICAO designator] (FAAC)
AXI............. American Express Interactive [Corporate travel computer site]
AXI............. Argonex International Ltd. [Vancouver Stock Exchange symbol]
AXI............. Mount Airy, NC [Location identifier FAA] (FAAL)
AXICS .... Apollo XI Collector Society [Defunct] (EA)
AXIS........... Atmospheric X-Ray Imaging Spectrometer (MCD)
AXIS........... Automatic X-Ray Inspection (MCD)
AXIS........... Auxiliary System for Interactive Statistics [Sweden Information service or system] (IID)
AXL............. Air Exel Netherlands BV [ICAO designator] (FAAC)
AXL............. Anderson Exploration Ltd. [Toronto Stock Exchange symbol]
AXL............. Arc Xenon Lamp
AXLE.......... TJT, Inc. [NASDAQ symbol] (SAG)
AXLE.......... T.J.T. Inc. [NASDAQ symbol] (TTSB)
AXLEW........ T.J.T. Inc. Wrrt [NASDAQ symbol] (TTSB)
AXM............. Acetoxycycloheximide [Biochemistry]
AXM............. Armenia [Colombia] [Airport symbol] (OAG)
AXM............. United States Army Materiel Command, Alexandria, VA [OCLC symbol] (OCLC)
AXMIN .... Axminster [England]
AXN............. Alexandria [Minnesota] [Airport symbol Obsolete] (OAG)
AXN............. Alexis Nihon Finance, Inc. [Toronto Stock Exchange symbol]
AXNT .... AXENT Technologies [NASDAQ symbol] (TTSB)
AXNT .... Axent Technologies, Inc. [NASDAQ symbol] (SAG)
AXO............. Aaxico Air Lines
AXO............. Alamco, Inc. [AMEX symbol] (SPSG)
AXO............. Alberta Exploration [Vancouver Stock Exchange symbol]
AXO............. Assistant Experimental Officer [Ministry of Agriculture, Fisheries, and Food] [Also, AEO, AExO] [British]
AXOD .... Automatic Overdrive Transaxle [Automotive engineering]
Axogen .... Axogen Ltd. [Associated Press] (SAG)
axon........... Axonometric (VRA)
AXP............. Air Express AS [Norway ICAO designator] (FAAC)
AXP............. Allied Exercise Publications [NATO]
AXP............. Ambulance Exchange Point [Army] (INF)
AXP............. Amer Express [NYSE symbol] (TTSB)
AXP............. American Express Co. [NYSE symbol Toronto Stock Exchange symbol] (SPSG)
AXP............. Associative Crosspoint Processor (MHDI)
AXP............. Axial Pitch (IEEE)
AXP............. Spring Point [Bahamas] [Airport symbol] (OAG)
AXpC........... American Exploration Co. [AMEX symbol] (SAG)
AXPrC......... Amer Explor Cv Dep'C'Pfd [AMEX symbol] (TTSB)
AXPS.......... Air Express
AXQ .... JIB, Inc. [ICAO designator] (FAAC)
AXR............. Abdominal X-Ray [Medicine]
AXR............. AMREP Corp. [NYSE symbol] (SPSG)
AXR............. Argentex Resource Exploration Corp. [Vancouver Stock Exchange symbol]
AXR............. Automatic X-Ray Radiograph
AXR............. Axel Rent SA [Mexico ICAO designator] (FAAC)
AXrEM .... Association of X-Ray Equipment Manufacturers [British] (DBA)
AXROS........ Automated X-Ray Orientation System (MCD)
AXS............. Access
AXS............. Advanced X-Ray System (DWSG)
AXS............. Altus [Oklahoma] [Airport symbol] (OAG)
AXS............. Altus Airlines [ICAO designator] (FAAC)
AXS............. Altus, OK [Location identifier FAA] (FAAL)
AxS............. Anxiety Sign [Psychology]
AXSIGCOMM... Axis [or Axes] of Signal Communication [Army]
AxsysTch ..... Axsys Technologies, Inc. [Associated Press] (SAG)
AXT............. Address to Index, True
AXT............. Akita [Japan] [Airport symbol] (OAG)
AXT............. Alternating Exotropia [Ophthalmology]
AXT............. American Municipal Term Trust [NYSE symbol] (SPSG)
AXT............. Amer Muni Term Trust [NYSE symbol] (TTSB)
AXU .... Axum [Ethiopia] [Airport symbol] (OAG)
AXV............. Alexis Nihon Finance, Inc. [Vancouver Stock Exchange symbol]
AXV............. Wapakoneta, OH [Location identifier FAA] (FAAL)
AXV-V .... Advanced Experimental Vehicle - 5th Generation [Toyota]
AXWHB .... Auxiliary Waste Heat Boiler [of a ship] (DS)
AXWHBS........ Auxiliary Waste Heater Boiler Survey [of a ship] (DS)
AXWTB .... Auxiliary Water Tube Boiler [of a ship] (DS)
AXWTBS .... Auxiliary Waste Tube Boiler Survey [of a ship] (DS)
AXX............. Avioimpex [Yugoslavia] [ICAO designator] (FAAC)
AXX............. Axiom International Development Corp. [Formerly, Axiom Explorations, Inc.] [Vancouver Stock Exchange symbol]

AXYS .... Axsys Technologies, Inc. [NASDAQ symbol] (SAG)
AY............... Abundantly Yours (EA)
AY............... Academic Year (MCD)
AY............... Aeritalia SpA [Italy ICAO aircraft manufacturer identifier] (ICAO)
AY............... Agency
AY............... Ahoy [Slang] (DNAB)
AY............... Airway (IAA)
AY............... Allied Youth [Later, AYFCC]
AY............... Alsatian Yiddish (BJA)
AY............... Annual Yield [Business term]
ay............... Antarctica [MARC country of publication code Library of Congress] (LCCP)
AY............... Anyone (IAA)
AY............... Assembly (DNAB)
AY............... Aster Yellows [A plant disease]
AY............... Atlas Yellowknife Resources Ltd. [Toronto Stock Exchange symbol]
AY............... Ayerst Laboratories [Research code symbol]
AY............... Ayrshire Yeomanry [British military] (DMA)
AY............... Finnair [ICAO designator] (AD)
AY............... Finnair [Airline flight code] (ODBW)
ay---- .... Yellow Sea and Area [MARC geographic area code Library of Congress] (LCCP)
AYA........... Acute Yellow Atrophy [Medicine] (DMAA)
AYA........... American Yachtsmen's Association [Later, BOAT/US] (EA)
AYA........... American Yankee Association (EA)
AYA........... American Yoga Association (EA)
AYA........... Awana Youth Association (EA)
AYA........... Ayagualo [El Salvador] [Seismograph station code, US Geological Survey Closed] (SEIS)
AYA........... Federal Aviation Administration [ICAO designator] (FAAC)
AYB........... Accessory Bulletin (MCD)
AYB........... Force Terrestre Belge [Belgium] [FAA designator] (FAAC)
AYC........... Accessory Change (MCD)
AYC........... Aerodynamic Yaw Coupling
AYC........... American Yorkshire Club (EA)
AYC........... American Youth Congress
AYC........... Association of Yukon Communities [Formerly, Association of Yukon Municipalities] (AC)
AYC........... Automatic Yaw Control
AYC........... Aviacion y Comercio SA [Spain ICAO designator] (FAAC)
AYCA .... Afghan Youth Council in America (EA)
AYCC .... American Yugoslav Claims Committee (EA)
AYCF .... Association of Young Computer Enthusiasts (AIE)
Ayck Ch F .... Ayckbourn's Chancery Forms [A publication] (DLA)
Ayck Ch Pr... Ayckbourn's Chancery Practice [A publication] (DLA)
Ayck Jur ..... Ayckbourn's Jurisdiction of the Supreme Court of Judicature [A publication] (DLA)
AYCP .... Aerodynamic Yaw Coupling Parameters
AYD .... Alleged Year Disability Began [Social Security Administration] (OICC)
AYD .... American Youth for Democracy
AYD .... Associate of Youth Development [British] (DBQ)
AYD .... Association of Yarn Distributors (EA)
AYD .... Average Yarding Distance [Forestry]
AYD .... Average Yearly Demands
AYD .... Aydin Corp. [NYSE symbol] (SPSG)
Aydin .... Aydin Corp. [Associated Press] (SAG)
AYE .... Alcohol Education for Youth [An association]
AYE .... Argyll Energy Corp. [Toronto Stock Exchange symbol]
AYE .... Ayenquera [Peru] [Seismograph station code, US Geological Survey] (SEIS)
AYE .... Fort Devens (Ayer), MA [Location identifier FAA] (FAAL)
a-ye-- .... Yemen (Sanaa) [MARC geographic area code Library of Congress] (LCCP)
AYF .... American Youth Foundation (EA)
AYF .... Antiyeast Factor [Medicine]
AYF .... Armenian Youth Federation of America - Youth Organization of the ARF [Armenian Revolutionary Federation of America] (EA)
AYFCC .... Allied Youth and Family Counseling Center (EA)
AYFYRA .... American Y-Flyer Yacht Racing Association (EA)
AYG .... Yuguara [Colombia] [Airport symbol] (OAG)
AYGA .... Goroka [Papua New Guinea] [ICAO location identifier] (ICLI)
AYH .... American Youth Hostels (EA)
AYI .... Academic Year Institute [National Science Foundation]
AYI .... Angle of Yaw Indicator
AYI .... Antony Resources [Vancouver Stock Exchange symbol]
AYI .... Kiln, MS [Location identifier FAA] (FAAL)
AYI .... Yari [Colombia] [Airport symbol] (OAG)
AYIG .... Australian Youth Initiatives Grant
AYJUSA .... Association of Yugoslav Jews in the USA (EA)
AYK .... Ayerok Petroleum [Vancouver Stock Exchange symbol]
AYL .... As You Like It [Shakespearean work]
AYLA .... Lae [Papua New Guinea] [ICAO location identifier] (ICLI)
AYLB .... Aylesbeare [England]
AYLB .... Aylesbury [England]
Ayl Char ..... Ayliffe's Calendar of Ancient Charters [1774] [A publication] (DLA)
AYLI........... As You Like It [Shakespearean drama] (BARN)
Ayliffe .... Ayliffe's Pandects [A publication] (DLA)
Ayliffe .... Ayliffe's Parergon Juris Canonici Anglicani [A publication] (DLA)
Ayl Int........ Ayliffe's Introduction to the Calendar of Ancient Charters [A publication] (DLA)
Ayl Pan ...... Ayliffe's Pandect of the Roman Civil Law [A publication] (DLA)
Ayl Pand ..... Ayliffe's Pandect of the Roman Civil Law [A publication] (DLA)
Ayl Par ...... Ayliffe's Parergon Juris Canonici Anglicani [A publication] (DLA)
AYM............. Ancient York Mason [Freemasonry]
AYM............. Anglican Youth Movement [Canada]

AYM............ Angry Young Man (BARN)
AYM............ Assistant Yard Master [Railroads] [British]
aym .... Aymara [MARC language code Library of Congress] (LCCP)
Aym .... Aymo Cravetta [Deceased, 1569] [Authority cited in pre-1607 legal work] (DSA)
AYM............ Youngstown Municipal Library, Alberta [Library symbol National Library of Canada] (NLC)
AYMD .... Madang [Papua New Guinea] [ICAO location identifier] (ICLI)
AYMH .... Mount Hagen [Papua New Guinea] [ICAO location identifier] (ICLI)
AYN .... Abercynon [Cardiff] [Welsh depot code]
AYN .... Lehman Br Amgen'YEELD "97 [AMEX symbol] (TTSB)
AYN .... Lehman Brothers, Inc. [AMEX symbol] (SAG)
AYN .... Watsonville, CA [Location identifier FAA] (FAAL)
AYNZ .... Nadzab [Papua New Guinea] [ICAO location identifier] (ICLI)
AYO .... Albany Corp. [Toronto Stock Exchange symbol]
AYO .... Area Youth Office [British]
AYP............ Alaska Yukon Pioneers (EA)
AYP............ Allegheny Power Sys [NYSE symbol] (TTSB)
AYP............ Allegheny Power System, Inc. [NYSE symbol] (SPSG)
AYP............ Allentown Public Library, Allentown, PA [OCLC symbol] (OCLC)
AYP............ Autolysed Yeast Protein [Biochemistry] (DAVI)
AYP............ Ayacucho [Peru] [Airport symbol] (OAG)
AYPA .... Anglican Young People's Association [British]
AYPY .... Port Moresby [Papua New Guinea] [ICAO location identifier] (ICLI)
AYQ .... Ayers Rock [Australia Airport symbol] (OAG)
AYQ .... Ponca City, OK [Location identifier FAA] (FAAL)
AYR .... Ayrshire [County in Scotland] (WGA)
Ayr............. Ayr's Registration Cases [Scotland] [A publication] (DLA)
AYR .... British Aerospace Flying College Ltd. [ICAO designator] (FAAC)
Ayr & Wig ... Ayr and Wigton's Registration Cases [Scotland] [A publication] (DLA)
AYRB .... Rabaul [Papua New Guinea] [ICAO location identifier] (ICLI)
AYRCGA....... All Year Round Chrysanthemum Growers' Association (EAIO)
Ayr Land Tr... Ayrton's Land Transfer Act [A publication] (DLA)
AYRS .... Amateur Yacht Research Society [Turnchapel, Plymouth, England] (EAIO)
AYRS .... Ayrshire [County in Scotland]
AYRV .... Artichoke Yellow Ringspot Virus [Plant pathology]
AYS............ Agni Yoga Society (EA)
AYS............ At Your Service
a-ys--.......... Southern Yemen (Aden) [MARC geographic area code Library of Congress] (LCCP)
AYS............ Waycross [Georgia] [Airport symbol] (OAG)
AYS............ Waycross, GA [Location identifier FAA] (FAAL)
AYSA .... American Yarn Spinners Association (EA)
AYSO .... American Youth Soccer Organization (EA)
AYSS .... Allegheny & South Side [AAR code]
AYT............ Antalya [Turkey] [Airport symbol] (OAG)
AYT............ Army Youth Team [British]
AYT............ Ayeet Aviation & Tourism [Israel] [FAA designator] (FAAC)
AYU............ Aiyura [Papua New Guinea] [Airport symbol Obsolete] (OAG)
AYW............ Archives of Yad Washem [A publication] (BJA)
AYWC .... American Youth Work Center (EA)
AYWK .... Wewak [Papua New Guinea] [ICAO location identifier] (ICLI)
AYWS .... Australian Yugoslav Welfare Society
AYY............ Air Economy [Ukraine] [FAA designator] (FAAC)
AYZ............ Atlant-Soyuz [Former USSR] [FAA designator] (FAAC)
AZ .... Aboda Zara (BJA)
AZ .... Abscission Zone [Botany]
AZ .... Academy of Zoology [Uttar Pradesh, India] (EA)
AZ .... Active Zone
AZ .... Airship Tender [Navy symbol Obsolete]
AZ .... Air Zero
AZ .... ALITALIA [Aerolinee Italiane Internazionali] [Italian airline] [ICAO designator]
AZ .... Alpha Zeta (EA)
AZ .... Aluminium-Zentrale eV
AZ .... Arizona [Postal code]
AZ .... Aschheim-Zondek [Pregnancy] Test [Medicine] (AAMN)
AZ .... Atlas Corp. [NYSE symbol] (SPSG)
AZ .... Atlas Corp. [NYSE symbol] (TTSB)
AZ .... Aviation Maintenance Administrationman [Navy rating]
AZ .... Azathioprine [Also, AZA, AZT] [Immunosuppressive drug]
AZ .... Azimuth (AFM)
AZ .... Azores Islands
AZ .... Azote [Nitrogen] [French]
AZ .... Azure [Heraldry] [Philately]
AZ1............ Aviation Maintenance Administrationman, First Class [Navy rating]
AZ2............ Aviation Maintenance Administrationman, Second Class [Navy rating]
AZ3............ Aviation Maintenance Administrationman, Third Class [Navy rating]
AZA............ Ahavah, Zedakah, Ahdut (BJA)
AZA............ Aleph Zadik Aleph [Society]
AZA............ Alitalia-Linee Aeree Italiane SpA [Italy ICAO designator] (FAAC)
AZA............ Alza Corp. [NYSE symbol] (SAG)
AZA .... ALZA Corp. [NYSE symbol] (TTSB)
AZA............ American Zinc Association (EA)
AZA............ American Zombie Association [Defunct] (EA)
AZ A........... Arizona Court of Appeals Reports [A publication] (DLA)
AZA............ Arizona Golden Pacific [Vancouver Stock Exchange symbol]
AZA............ Australian Zebu Association
AZA............ Azacytidine [or Azacitidine] [Also, AC, Aza-C] [Antineoplastic drug]
AZA............ Azathioprine [Also, AZ, AZT] [Immunosuppressive drug]
AZA............ Azidodideoxyadenosine [Antiviral]
AZA............ University of Arizona, Health Sciences Center Library, Tucson, AZ [OCLC symbol] (OCLC)

AZAA........... Airman Apprentice, Aviation Maintenance Administrationman, Striker [Navy rating]
Aza-C .... Azacytidine [or Azacitidine] [Also, AC, AZA] [Antineoplastic drug]
AZACCO ...... Azanian Co-Ordinating Committee [South Africa Political party] (EY)
AzAFP .... Arizona Academy of Family Physicians (SRA)
AzAHA .... Arizona Association of Homes and Housing for the Aging (SRA)
AzAHU .... Arizona Association of Health Underwriters (SRA)
AZAN .... Airman, Aviation Maintenance Administrationman, Striker [Navy rating]
AZAP.......... Agence Zaire-Presse [Zaire Press Agency]
AZAPO......... Azanian People's Organization [South Africa] (PPW)
AZAR .... Adjustable Zero, Adjustable Range
AZAS .... Adjustable Zero, Adjustable Span (IAA)
AzAUTO........ Arizona Automotive Trade Organization (SRA)
AzAv........... Avondale Public Library, Avondale, AZ [Library symbol] [Library of Congress] (LCLS)
AZB .... Amazon Bay [Papua New Guinea] [Airport symbol] (OAG)
AZB .... Arizona Motor Tariff Bureau, Inc., Phoenix AZ [STAC]
AZB .... Azamat [Kazakhstan] [ICAO designator] (FAAC)
AzB .... Copper Queen Library, Bisbee, AZ [Library symbol Library of Congress] (LCLS)
AzBC .... Cochise County Library District, Bisbee, AZ [Library symbol] [Library of Congress] (LCLS)
AzBe .... Benson Public Library, Benson, AZ [Library symbol Library of Congress] (LCLS)
Az-BPH .... Arizona Regional Library for the Blind and Physically Handicapped, Phoenix, AZ [Library symbol Library of Congress] (LCLS)
AzBu .... Buckeye Public Library, Buckeye, AZ [Library symbol Library of Congress] (LCLS)
AZC .... American Zionist Council [Later, AZF] (EA)
AZC .... Arizona State University, College of Law Library, Tempe, AZ [OCLC symbol] (OCLC)
AZC .... Aviation Maintenance Administrationman, Chief [Navy rating]
AZC .... Azco Mining [AMEX symbol] (TTSB)
AZC .... Azco Mining, Inc. [AMEX symbol] (SAG)
AzCc .... Cave Creek Public Library, Cave Creek, AZ [Library symbol Library of Congress] (LCLS)
AZCC .... Zama City Community Library, Alberta [Library symbol National Library of Canada] (NLC)
AzCg .... Casa Grande Public Library, Casa Grande, AZ [Library symbol Library of Congress] (LCLS)
AzCh .... Chandler Public Library, Chandler, AZ [Library symbol Library of Congress] (LCLS)
AzCH .... Chinle High School Library, Chinle, AZ [Library symbol Library of Congress] (LCLS)
AZCM.......... Aviation Maintenance Administrationman, Master Chief [Navy rating]
AzCN.......... Navajo Community College, Chinle, AZ [Library symbol Library of Congress] (LCLS)
Azco........... Azco Mining, Inc. [Associated Press] (SAG)
AzCo .... Coolidge Public Library, Coolidge, AZ [Library symbol Library of Congress] (LCLS)
AzCoC .... Central Arizona College, Instructional Materials Center, Coolidge, AZ [Library symbol Library of Congress] (LCLS)
AzCot .... Cottonwood Public Library, Cottonwood, AZ [Library symbol Library of Congress] (LCLS)
AZCS .... Aviation Maintenance Administrationman, Senior Chief [Navy rating]
AZD............ Aral [Kazakhstan] [FAA designator] (FAAC)
AZD............ Arizona Public Services Co. [NYSE symbol] (SAG)
AZD............ Arizona Pub Svc 10%'MIDS' [NYSE symbol] (TTSB)
AzD .... Douglas Public Library, Douglas, AZ [Library symbol] [Library of Congress] (LCLS)
AZD............ Scottsdale Public Library, Scottsdale, AZ [OCLC symbol] (OCLC)
AZD............ Yazd [Iran] [Airport symbol] (OAG)
AZDA .... Arizona Dietetics Association (SRA)
AzDC .... Cochise College, Douglas, AZ [Library symbol Library of Congress] (LCLS)
AZDDU .... Azidodideoxyuridine [Antiviral]
AZDU .... Azidodideoxyuridine [Antiviral]
AZE .... Arcus-Air-Logistic GmbH [Germany ICAO designator] (FAAC)
aze............. Azerbaijani [MARC language code Library of Congress] (LCCP)
AZE .... Hazlehurst, GA [Location identifier FAA] (FAAL)
AZEL .... Azimuth and Elevation (MSA)
AZ-EL.......... Azimuth-Elevation (IDOE)
Azerb .... Azerbaijani (BARN)
AzerSSR ...... Azerbaydzhani Soviet Socialist Republic
AZEU .... Azido(ethyl)dideoxyuridine [Antiviral]
AZF .... American Zionist Federation (EA)
AZF............. Azoospermia Factor [Genetics]
AzF .... Flagstaff City-Coconino County Public Library, Flagstaff, AZ [Library symbol Library of Congress] (LCLS)
AZFC .... Alexander Zonjic Fan Club (EA)
AzFGM .... W.L. Gore Associates, Medical Products Division, Flagstaff, AZ [Library symbol] [Library of Congress] (LCLS)
AzFGS .... Church of Jesus Christ of Latter-Day Saints, Genealogical Society Library, Flagstaff Branch, Flagstaff, AZ [Library symbol Library of Congress] (LCLS)
AzFhA .... United States Army, Technical Reference Division Library, Fort Huachuca, AZ [Library symbol Library of Congress] (LCLS)
AzFlCo .... Pinal County Public Library, Florence, AZ [Library symbol Library of Congress] (LCLS)
AzFlP .... Arizona State Prison Library, Florence, AZ [Library symbol Library of Congress] (LCLS)
AzFM .... Museum of Northern Arizona, Flagstaff, AZ [Library symbol Library of Congress] (LCLS)

AzFU .... Northern Arizona University, Flagstaff, AZ [*Library symbol Library of Congress*] (LCLS)
AZG .... Air Zero Gas
AZG .... Australian Gold [*Vancouver Stock Exchange symbol*]
azg .... Azaguanine (MAE)
AZG .... Azidodideoxyguanosine [*Antiviral*]
AZG .... Karadeniz Hava Yollari, AS [*Turkey*] [*FAA designator*] (FAAC)
AzG .... Velma Teague Library, Glendale, AZ [*Library symbol Library of Congress*] (LCLS)
AzGAF .... United States Air Force, Luke Air Force Base Library, Glendale, AZ [*Library symbol Library of Congress*] (LCLS)
AzGAGS ...... American Graduate School of International Management, Glendale, AZ [*Library symbol*] [*Library of Congress*] (LCLS)
AzGaH .... Ganado High School Library, Ganado, AZ [*Library symbol Library of Congress*] (LCLS)
AzGC .... Glendale Community College, Glendale, AZ [*Library symbol Library of Congress*] (LCLS)
AzGi .... Gilbert Public Library, Gilbert, AZ [*Library symbol Library of Congress*] (LCLS)
AzGoU .... UMC Industries, Unidynamics Phoenix, Inc. Library, Goodyear, AZ [*Library symbol Library of Congress*] (LCLS)
AzGrcN .... United States National Park Service, Grand Canyon National Park Library, Grand Canyon, AZ [*Library symbol Library of Congress*] (LCLS)
AZGS .... Azusa Ground Station
AzHA .... Hayden Public Library, Hayden, AZ [*Library symbol Library of Congress*] (LCLS)
AzHGS .... Church of Jesus Christ of Latter-Day Saints, Genealogical Society Library, Holbrook Branch, Holbrook, AZ [*Library symbol Library of Congress*] (LCLS)
AzHH .... Holbrook High School Library, Holbrook, AZ [*Library symbol Library of Congress*] (LCLS)
AzHMA .... Arizona Hotel and Motel Association (SRA)
AzHP .... Petrified Forest National Park, Painted Desert Library, Holbrook, AZ [*Library symbol Library of Congress*] (LCLS)
AzHUC .... Arizona Highway Users Conference (SRA)
AZI .... American Zellter, Inc.
AZI .... American Zinc Institute [*Later, ZI*] (EA)
AZi .... American Zionist (BJA)
AZI .... Association Zen Internationale [*International Zen Association - IZA*] (EAIO)
AZI .... Azidothymidine [*Later, ZDV*] [*Antiviral*]
AZIC .... Arizona Instrument [*NASDAQ symbol*] (TTSB)
AZIC .... Arizona Instrument Corp. [*NASDAQ symbol*] (SAG)
AZII .... American Zinc Institute, Inc. [*Later, ZI*] (MCD)
AZK .... Arizako Mines Ltd. [*Vancouver Stock Exchange symbol*]
AzKaH .... Monument Valley High School Library, Kayenta, AZ [*Library symbol Library of Congress*] (LCLS)
AzKiM .... Kingman City-Mohave County Library, Kingman, AZ [*Library symbol Library of Congress*] (LCLS)
AzKiMC .... Mohave Community College, Resource Center, Kingman, AZ [*Library symbol Library of Congress*] (LCLS)
AZL .... Air Zanzibar [*Tanzania*] [*ICAO designator*] (FAAC)
AZL .... Arizona Land Income 'A' [*AMEX symbol*] (TTSB)
AZL .... Arizona Land Income Corp. [*AMEX symbol*] (SPSG)
AZL .... University of Arizona College of Law, Library, Tucson, AZ [*OCLC symbol*] (OCLC)
AzLA .... Arizona Library Association (SRA)
AzLa .... Lakeside Public Library, Lakeside, AZ [*Library symbol Library of Congress*] (LCLS)
AZLD .... Azure Laid (ADA)
AzLhc .... Lake Havasu City Public Library, Lake Havasu City, AZ [*Library symbol Library of Congress*] (LCLS)
AZLK .... Avtomobilei Zavod Lenin Komsomol [*Lenin Collective Automobile Works*] [*Former USSR*]
AzLp .... Litchfield Park Public Library, Litchfield Park, AZ [*Library symbol Library of Congress*] (LCLS)
AZM .... Aerocozumel SA [*Mexico ICAO designator*] (FAAC)
AZM .... Assumption College, Worcester, MA [*OCLC symbol*] (OCLC)
AZM .... Azimuth
AZM .... Azora Minerals [*Vancouver Stock Exchange symbol*]
AZM .... Azoxymethane [*A carcinogen*]
AzM .... Mesa Public Library, Mesa, AZ [*Library symbol Library of Congress*] (LCLS)
AzMa .... Mammoth Public Library, Mammoth, AZ [*Library symbol Library of Congress*] (LCLS)
Az Mar Law... Azuni's Maritime Law [*A publication*] (DLA)
AzMC .... Mesa Community College, Mesa, AZ [*Library symbol Library of Congress*] (LCLS)
AzMGS .... Church of Jesus Christ of Latter-Day Saints, Genealogical Society Library, Mesa Branch, Mesa, AZ [*Library symbol Library of Congress*] (LCLS)
AzMi .... Miami Memorial-Gila County Library, Miami, AZ [*Library symbol Library of Congress*] (LCLS)
AzML .... Latter-Day Saints Genealogical Library, Mesa, AZ [*Library symbol Library of Congress*] (LCLS)
AzMo .... Morenci Public Library, Morenci, AZ [*Library symbol Library of Congress*] (LCLS)
AzN .... Nogales Public Library, Nogales, AZ [*Library symbol Library of Congress*] (LCLS)
AZN .... Northern Arizona University, Flagstaff, AZ [*OCLC symbol*] (OCLC)
AZN .... Servicios Aereos Amazonicos [*Peru*] [*FAA designator*] (FAAC)
AZN .... St. Joseph, MO [*Location identifier FAA*] (FAAL)
AzNA .... Arizona Nurses Association (SRA)

AzNPHi .... Pimeria Alta Historical Society Museum, Nogales, AZ [*Library symbol Library of Congress*] (LCLS)
AZO .... Alpha Zeta Omega [*Fraternity*]
AZO .... Arzaero [*Azerbaijan*] [*FAA designator*] (FAAC)
AZO .... AutoZone Inc. [*NYSE symbol*] (TTSB)
AZO .... AutoZone, Inc. [*NYSE symbol*] (SPSG)
Azo .... Azores (VRA)
AZO .... Kalamazoo [*Michigan*] [*Airport symbol*] (OAG)
AzO .... Oracle Public Library, Oracle, AZ [*Library symbol Library of Congress*] (LCLS)
AzOA .... Arizona Optometric Association (SRA)
AZON .... Azimuth Only
AZOV .... Aufschlagzuender ohne Verzoegerung [*Nondelay fuze*] [*German military - World War II*]
AZP .... Archiv fuer die Zivilistische Praxis [*A publication*] (ILCA)
AZP .... Arizona Department of Library Archives, Tempe, AZ [*OCLC symbol*] (OCLC)
AZP .... Arizona Pacific Airways [*Arizona Flight School, Inc.*] [*ICAO designator*] (FAAC)
AzP .... Page Public Library, Page, AZ [*Library symbol Library of Congress*] (LCLS)
AzPa .... Colorado River Indian Tribes Public Library, Parker, AZ [*Library symbol Library of Congress*] (LCLS)
AzPe .... Peoria Public Library, Peoria, AZ [*Library symbol*] [*Library of Congress*] (LCLS)
AzPh .... Phoenix Public Library, Phoenix, AZ [*Library symbol Library of Congress*] (LCLS)
AzPhC .... Phoenix College, Phoenix, AZ [*Library symbol*] [*Library of Congress*] (LCLS)
AzPhDA .... United States Department of Agriculture, Water Conservation Laboratory Library, Phoenix, AZ [*Library symbol Library of Congress*] (LCLS)
AzPhE .... Evans, Kitchel, Jenckes P.C. Library, Phoenix, AZ [*Library symbol*] [*Library of Congress*] (LCLS)
AzPhF .... First National Bank Library, Phoenix, AZ [*Library symbol Library of Congress*] (LCLS)
AzPhFC .... Fennimore, Craig, von Ammom, Udall & Powers, Phoenix, AZ [*Library symbol*] [*Library of Congress*] (LCLS)
AzPhGK .... Gallagher & Kennedy, P.A., Phoenix, AZ [*Library symbol*] [*Library of Congress*] (LCLS)
AzPhGS .... Church of Jesus Christ of Latter-Day Saints, Genealogical Society Library, Phoenix Arizona North Branch, Phoenix, AZ [*Library symbol Library of Congress*] (LCLS)
AzPhH .... Honeywell Information Systems, Phoenix, AZ [*Library symbol Library of Congress*] (LCLS)
AzPhJ .... Jennings, Strouss, Salmon, Phoenix, AZ [*Library symbol*] [*Library of Congress*] (LCLS)
AzPhL .... Lewis & Roca, Phoenix, AZ [*Library symbol*] [*Library of Congress*] (LCLS)
AzPhM .... Maricopa County Free Library, Phoenix, AZ [*Library symbol Library of Congress*] (LCLS)
AzPhMC .... Maricopa County Community College, Phoenix, AZ [*Library symbol Library of Congress*] (LCLS)
AzPhMH ...... Meyer, Hendricks, Victor, Osborn & Maledon, P.A., Phoenix, AZ [*Library symbol*] [*Library of Congress*] (LCLS)
AzPhML ...... Maricopa County Law Library, Phoenix, AZ [*Library symbol Library of Congress*] (LCLS)
AzPhMM ..... Maricopa County Medical Society, Phoenix, AZ [*Library symbol Library of Congress*] (LCLS)
AzPhMo ...... Motorola, Inc., Semiconductor Products Division Library, Phoenix, AZ [*Library symbol Library of Congress*] (LCLS)
AzPhOC ...... O'Connor, Cavanagh, Anderson, Westover, Killingsworth & Beshears, Law Library, Phoenix, AZ [*Library symbol*] [*Library of Congress*] (LCLS)
AzPhS .... Streich, Lang, Weeks & Cardon, Phoenix, AZ [*Library symbol*] [*Library of Congress*] (LCLS)
AzPhSW ...... Snell & Wilmer, Phoenix, AZ [*Library symbol*] [*Library of Congress*] (LCLS)
AzPhWGS .... Church of Jesus Christ of Latter-Day Saints, Genealogical Society Library, Phoenix Arizona West Branch, Phoenix, AZ [*Library symbol Library of Congress*] (LCLS)
AZPN .... Aspen Technology [*NASDAQ symbol*] (TTSB)
AZPN .... Aspen Technology, Inc. [*NASDAQ symbol*] (SAG)
AZPPA .... Arizona Promotional Products Association (SRA)
AzPr .... Prescott City-Yavapai County Library, Prescott, AZ [*Library symbol Library of Congress*] (LCLS)
AzPrER .... Embry-Riddle Aeronautical University, Prescott Campus, Prescott, AZ [*Library symbol*] [*Library of Congress*] (LCLS)
AzPrGS .... Church of Jesus Christ of Latter-Day Saints, Genealogical Society Library, Prescott Branch, Prescott, AZ [*Library symbol Library of Congress*] (LCLS)
AzPrP .... Prescott College, Prescott, AZ [*Library symbol Library of Congress*] (LCLS)
AzPrSH .... Sharlott Hall Museum, Prescott Historical Society, Prescott, AZ [*Library symbol Library of Congress*] (LCLS)
AzPrV .... United States Veterans Administration Center, Prescott, AZ [*Library symbol Library of Congress*] (LCLS)
AzPrY .... Yavapai College, Prescott, AZ [*Library symbol Library of Congress*] (LCLS)
AzPrYC .... Yavapai County Free Library District, Prescott, AZ [*Library symbol*] [*Library of Congress*] (LCLS)
AzPrY-V .... Yavapai College, Verde Campus, Clarkdale, AZ [*Library symbol Library of Congress*] (LCLS)
AzPTA .... Arizona Physical Therapy Association (SRA)
AZQ .... Aziridinyl Benzoquinone [*Organic chemistry*]

AZQ............. Diaziquone [*Antineoplastic drug*] (DAVI)
AZR............. Adrar [*Algeria*] [*Airport symbol*] (OAG)
AZR............. Air Zaire, Societe [*ICAO designator*] (FAAC)
AZR............. Alizarin (DMAA)
AZR............. Armour Research Center, Scottsdale, AZ [*OCLC symbol*] (OCLC)
AZR............. Aztar Corp. [*NYSE symbol*] (SPSG)
AZR............. Azure Resources [*Vancouver Stock Exchange symbol*]
AZRAN........ Azimuth and Range
AZRD .... Arizona Road Dust [*Environmental chemistry*]
AZRNG........ Azimuth and Range (MSA)
AzRou .... Rough Rock Public Library, Rough Rock, AZ [*Library symbol Library of Congress*] (LCLS)
AZRU .... Aztec Ruins National Monument
AZS............. Alloyed Zinc Sheet
AZS............. Alumina-Zirconia-Silica [*Inorganic chemistry*]
AZS............. Arizona Star Resource Corp. [*Vancouver Stock Exchange symbol*]
AZS............. Arizona State University, Tempe, AZ [*OCLC symbol*] (OCLC)
AZS............. Automatic Zero Set [*Military*]
AZS............. Charlottesville, VA [*Location identifier FAA*] (FAAL)
AzS............. Scottsdale Public Library, Scottsdale, AZ [*Library symbol Library of Congress*] (LCLS)
AzSAE .... Arizona Society of Association Executives (SRA)
AzSaf .... Safford City-Graham County Public Library, Safford, AZ [*Library symbol Library of Congress*] (LCLS)
AzSafGS...... Church of Jesus Christ of Latter-Day Saints, Genealogical Society Library, Safford Branch, Safford, AZ [*Library symbol Library of Congress*] (LCLS)
AzSArm....... Armour Research Center Library, Scottsdale, AZ [*Library symbol Library of Congress*] (LCLS)
AzSe .... Sedona Public Library, Sedona, AZ [*Library symbol Library of Congress*] (LCLS)
AzSh .... Show Low Public Library, Show Low, AZ [*Library symbol Library of Congress*] (LCLS)
AzShGS....... Church of Jesus Christ of Latter-Day Saints, Genealogical Society Library, Show Low Branch, Show Low, AZ [*Library symbol Library of Congress*] (LCLS)
AzSHP......... Arizona Society of Health System Pharmicists (SRA)
AZSITE........ Archaeological Sites Data Base [*Tucson*] [*Information service or system*] (IID)
AzSj .... Saint Johns Public Library, Saint Johns, AZ [*Library symbol Library of Congress*] (LCLS)
AzSjGS........ Church of Jesus Christ of Latter-Day Saints, Genealogical Society Library, St. Johns Branch, Stake Center, St. Johns, AZ [*Library symbol Library of Congress*] (LCLS)
AzSnGS....... Church of Jesus Christ of Latter-Day Saints, Genealogical Society Library, Snowflake Branch, Snowflake, AZ [*Library symbol Library of Congress*] (LCLS)
AzSo .... Somerton Public Library, Somerton, AZ [*Library symbol Library of Congress*] (LCLS)
AzSp .... Springerville Public Library, Springerville, AZ [*Library symbol Library of Congress*] (LCLS)
AzStdGS...... Church of Jesus Christ of Latter-Day Saints, Genealogical Society Library, St. David Arizona Stake Branch, St. David, AZ [*Library symbol Library of Congress*] (LCLS)
AzSu .... Sun City Public Library, Sun City, AZ [*Library symbol Library of Congress*] (LCLS)
AzSv........... Sierra Vista Public Library, Sierra Vista, AZ [*Library symbol*] [*Library of Congress*] (LCLS)
AZT .... Ascheim-Zondek Test [*Medicine*]
AZT .... Azathioprine [*Also, AZ, AZA*] [*Immunosuppressive drug*]
AZT .... Azidodeoxythymidine [*Biochemistry*]
AZT .... Azidothymidine [*Later, ZDV*] [*Antiviral*]
AZT .... Azimut SA [*Spain ICAO designator*] (FAAC)
AZT .... Azusa Transponder
AzT............. Tucson Public Library, Tucson, AZ [*Library symbol Library of Congress*] (LCLS)
AZT .... Tucson Public Library, Tucson, AZ [*OCLC symbol*] (OCLC)
AzTAM .... Arizona Medical Center, University of Arizona, Tucson, AZ [*Library symbol Library of Congress*] (LCLS)
AzTAP .... Aerial Phenomena Research Organization, Inc., Information Services Division, Tucson, AZ [*Library symbol Library of Congress*] (LCLS)
Aztar .... Aztar Corp. [*Associated Press*] (SAG)
AZTC .... Aztec Manufacturing Co. [*NASDAQ symbol*] (NQ)
AZTC .... Aztec Mfg Co. [*NASDAQ symbol*] (TTSB)
AZTC .... Azusa Transponder Coherent
AztcM.......... Aztec Manufacturing Co. [*Associated Press*] (SAG)
AzTCM .... Walter Chiles Cox Memorial Foundation, Tucson, AZ [*Library symbol Library of Congress*] (LCLS)
AzTDP .... City of Tucson, Department of Planning, Tucson, AZ [*Library symbol*] [*Library of Congress*] (LCLS)

AzTe........... Tempe Public Library, Tempe, AZ [*Library symbol Library of Congress*] (LCLS)
AzTeS .... Arizona State University, Tempe, AZ [*Library symbol Library of Congress*] (LCLS)
AzTeS-Hi...... Arizona Historical Foundation, Arizona State University, Tempe, AZ [*Library symbol Library of Congress*] (LCLS)
AzTeS-L ...... Arizona State University, College of Law, Tempe, AZ [*Library symbol Library of Congress*] (LCLS)
AzTGS......... Church of Jesus Christ of Latter-Day Saints, Genealogical Society Library, Tucson Branch, Tucson, AZ [*Library symbol Library of Congress*] (LCLS)
AzThE......... Eastern Arizona College, Thatcher, AZ [*Library symbol Library of Congress*] (LCLS)
AzTK .... Kitt Peak National Observatory, Tucson, AZ [*Library symbol Library of Congress*] (LCLS)
AzTLA .... Arizona Trial Lawyers Association (SRA)
AzTo........... Tombstone-Cochise County Library, Tombstone, AZ [*Library symbol Library of Congress*] (LCLS)
AzTol .... Tolleson Public Library, Tolleson, AZ [*Library symbol Library of Congress*] (LCLS)
AzTP .... Arizona Historical Society, Tucson, AZ [*Library symbol Library of Congress*] (LCLS)
AzTPC .... Pima College, Tucson, AZ [*Library symbol Library of Congress*] (LCLS)
AzTS .... Tucson Unified School District, Tucson, AZ [*Library symbol*] [*Library of Congress*] (LCLS)
AZT-TP........ Azidothymidine-Triphosphate [*Biochemistry*]
AzTu........... Tuba City Public Library, Tuba City, AZ [*Library symbol Library of Congress*] (LCLS)
AzTV .... United States Veterans Administration Hospital, Tucson, AZ [*Library symbol Library of Congress*] (LCLS)
AZU .... Air Star Zanzibar [*Tanzania*] [*ICAO designator*] (FAAC)
azu.............. Arizona [*MARC country of publication code Library of Congress*] (LCCP)
AZU............. Azauracil [*Antineoplastic drug*] (DAVI)
AZU............. Azul [*Race of maize*]
AZU............. Azurin
AzU .... University of Arizona, Tucson, AZ [*Library symbol Library of Congress OCLC symbol*] (OCLC)
AzU-A.......... University of Arizona, Arid Lands Information Center, Tucson, AZ [*Library symbol*] [*Library of Congress*] (LCLS)
AzU-L.......... University of Arizona, College of Law, Tucson, AZ [*Library symbol Library of Congress*] (LCLS)
AzU-M......... University of Arizona, Health Sciences Center, Tucson, AZ [*Library symbol Library of Congress*] (LCLS)
Azuni Mar Law... Azuni's Maritime Law [*A publication*] (DLA)
AZUR .... Azauridine [*Antineoplastic drug*] (DAVI)
AZUSA .... Azimuth, Speed, Altitude
Azusa Pac U... Azusa Pacific University (GAGS)
AZV .... Zodiac Air [*Bulgaria*] [*ICAO designator*] (FAAC)
AzVA .... Arizona Vocational Association (SRA)
AzVMA .... Arizona Veterinary Medical Association (SRA)
AZW .... Air Zimbabwe [*ICAO designator*] (FAAC)
AzWhr.......... Whiteriver Public Library, Whiteriver, AZ [*Library symbol Library of Congress*] (LCLS)
AzWi .... Williams Public Library, Williams, AZ [*Library symbol Library of Congress*] (LCLS)
AzWic .... Wickenburg Public Library, Wickenburg, AZ [*Library symbol Library of Congress*] (LCLS)
AzWin .... Roxanne Whipple Memorial Library, Winslow, AZ [*Library symbol Library of Congress*] (LCLS)
AZWO .... Azure Wove (ADA)
AzWr........... Window Rock Public Library, Window Rock, AZ [*Library symbol Library of Congress*] (LCLS)
AZ.WS .... Atlas Corp. Wrrt [*AMEX symbol*] (TTSB)
AzWWA....... Arizona Water Well Association (SRA)
AZX............. Air Bristol, Ltd. [*British*] [*FAA designator*] (FAAC)
AZX............. Arizona Stock Exchange
AZY............. Arizona Airways, Inc. [*ICAO designator*] (FAAC)
AZY............. Arizona Western College, Yuma, AZ [*OCLC symbol*] (OCLC)
AzY .... Yuma City-County Public Library, Yuma, AZ [*Library symbol Library of Congress*] (LCLS)
AzYAW........ Arizona Western College, Yuma, AZ [*Library symbol Library of Congress*] (LCLS)
AZYC .... American Zionist Youth Council (EA)
AZYF........... American Zionist Youth Foundation (EA)
AzYGS......... Church of Jesus Christ of Latter-Day Saints, Genealogical Society Library, Yuma Branch, Yuma, AZ [*Library symbol Library of Congress*] (LCLS)
AzYo .... Youngtown Public Library, Youngtown, AZ [*Library symbol Library of Congress*] (LCLS)
AZZ .... Azza Transport Co. Ltd. [*Sudan*] [*FAA designator*] (FAAC)

B
By Acronym

B .... Air Force Training Category [24 inactive duty training periods and 15 days active duty training per year]
B .... All India Reporter, Bombay Series [A publication] (DLA)
B .... Annual Rate Plus Stock Dividend [Investment term] (DFIT)
B .... Aspartic Acid [or Asparagine] [Also, Asx An amino acid Symbol]
B .... At or Below [Constrained Altitude] (GAVI)
B .... Baccalaureate
B .... Bachelor
B .... Bacillus [Bacteriology]
B .... Back
B .... Backward Edge [Skating]
B .... Bag [Shipping]
B .... Bagarottus dei Corradi da Bologna [Flourished, 1200-42] [Authority cited in pre-1607 legal work] (DSA)
B .... Baht [Monetary unit] [Thailand]
B .... Bailie [British] (ROG)
B .... Bajocian [Geology]
B .... Baker [Phonetic alphabet] [World War II] (DSUE)
B .... Balanced
B .... Balanced Fund [Investment term]
B .... Balantidium [Biochemistry] (DAVI)
B .... Balboa [Monetary unit] [Panama]
B .... Baldus de Ubaldis [Deceased, 1400] [Authority cited in pre-1607 legal work] (DSA)
B .... Bale [Shipping]
B .... Ball
B .... Ballast (IAA)
B .... Ballinger Publishing Co.
B .... Ballistic
B .... Balneum [Bath] [Medicine]
B .... Ban (WGA)
B .... Bancus [Common Bench] [Legal] [British] (ROG)
B .... Band
B .... Bands (Civilian and Military) [Public-performance tariff class] [British]
B .... Bandwidth [Frequency range]
B .... Bani [Monetary unit] [Romania]
B .... Bank
B .... Baptist
B .... Bar
B .... Barber [Charles E.] [Designer's mark, when appearing on US coins]
B .... Barber's Gold Law [South Africa] [A publication] (DLA)
B .... Barbour's New York Reports [A publication] (DLA)
B .... Barge
B .... Baritone [Music]
b .... Barn [Area of nuclear cross-section]
B .... Barnes Group [NYSE symbol] (TTSB)
B .... Barnes Group, Inc. [NYSE symbol] (SPSG)
B .... Barometric [Medicine] (DAVI)
B .... Barometric Pressure Correction [Symbol]
B .... Baron
B .... Baroness Publications Ltd., Inc. [Publisher]
B .... Barrel [Shipping]
B .... Bartholomaeus Brixiensis [Deceased circa 1258] [Authority cited in pre-1607 legal work] (DSA)
B .... Bartholomaeus de Capua [Deceased, 1328] [Authority cited in pre-1607 legal work] (DSA)
B .... Bartolus de Sassoferrato [Deceased, 1357] [Authority cited in pre-1607 legal work] (DSA)
B .... Baryon Scale (WDAA)
B .... Base
B .... Basin [of a river] [Geology]
B .... Basophil [Hematology]
B .... Bass [or Basso] [Music]
b .... Bass (IDOE)
B .... Bassoon [Music] (ROG)
b .... Bass Transistor [Music]
B .... Bastard [Slang] (DSUE)
B .... Bat
B .... Batch [Computer science]
B .... Bath
B .... Batsman (ADA)
B .... Battery
B .... Battle
B .... Baud [Unit of data transmission speed] (MCD)
B .... Baume [Scale] [Measurement] (GPO)
b .... Bavli [or Babylonian Talmud] (BJA)

B .... Bay [Maps and charts]
B .... Bay [Thoroughbred racing]
B .... Bayou [Maps and charts]
B .... Bazianus [Deceased, 1197] [Authority cited in pre-1607 legal work] (DSA)
B .... BCE, Inc. [Formerly, Bell Canada Enterprises] [Toronto Stock Exchange symbol]
B .... BCE, Inc. [Formerly, Bell Canada Enterprises] [Vancouver Stock Exchange symbol]
B .... Beacon [Aviation]
B .... Beak
B .... Beam [of a ship]
B .... Bearing [Angle]
b .... Beauty [or Bottom] (Quark) [Atomic physics]
B .... Beavan's English Rolls Court Reports [A publication] (DLA)
B .... Beaver [On lead tokens used as payment in the Canadian fur trade during the 1700's]
b .... Bed [Medicine]
B .... Beda [Deceased, 735] [Authority cited in pre-1607 legal work] (DSA)
B .... Bedroom (ROG)
B .... Beer [Phonetic alphabet] [Pre-World War II] (DSUE)
B .... Before
B .... Behavior (WGA)
B .... Bei [At, With] [German]
B .... Bel [Ten decibels]
B .... Belga [Monetary unit] [Belgium]
B .... Belgium [IYRU nationality code]
B .... Bell (NFPA)
B .... Bell Canada Enterprises, Inc. [Toronto Stock Exchange symbol Vancouver Stock Exchange symbol]
b .... Ben (BJA)
B .... Benediction
B .... Benedictus de Isernia [Flourished, 1221-52] [Authority cited in pre-1607 legal work] (DSA)
B .... Benoist Scale (MAE)
B .... Benzedrine
B .... Benzoate (MAE)
B .... Bernardus Compostellanus, Junior [Deceased, 1267] [Authority cited in pre-1607 legal work] (DSA)
B .... Bernardus Compostellanus, Senior [Flourished, 1198-1216] [Authority cited in pre-1607 legal work] (DSA)
B .... Bernardus de Bottone de Parma [Deceased, 1266] [Authority cited in pre-1607 legal work] (DSA)
B .... Bernardus de Pavia [Deceased, 1213] [Authority cited in pre-1607 legal work] (DSA)
B .... Bernoulli Number [Mathematics]
B .... Bertrandus de Montefaventino [Deceased, 1342] [Authority cited in pre-1607 legal work] (DSA)
B .... Best (IAA)
B .... Beta
B .... Beva [A prefix meaning multiplied by one billion; same as "giga"]
B .... Bias [Telecommunications]
B .... Bible
b .... Bible (WDMC)
B .... Biblical (ROG)
B .... Bicuspid [Dentistry]
B .... Bid [Stock exchange term] (SPSG)
B .... Biennial
B .... Bight
B .... Bilateral [Anatomy] (DAVI)
B .... Bilateral School [British]
B .... Billion (MCD)
B .... Bills (ROG)
b .... Bi-Monthly
B .... Binary (BUR)
B .... Binding Chain [Toxin]
B .... Bin-Tainer [Shipping] (DCTA)
B .... Bioactive
B .... Biology [Secondary school course] [British]
B .... Biomass [Biology]
B .... Biopsy [Medicine]
B .... Biosedra [France] [Research code symbol]
B .... Biotin
B .... Biplane
B .... Birth
b .... Birthdate (DD)

B	Bis [*Twice*] [*Pharmacy*]
B	Bishop [*Chess*]
B	Bishop [*Ecclesiastical*]
B	BIT [*Binary Digit*] [*Data transmission speed*] [*Computer science*] (DIT)
B	Bitch
B	Black [*Philately*]
B	Black [*Pencils*]
B	Black [*Buoy*]
b	Black (VRA)
b	Black (WDMC)
B	Black and White [*Photography, television, etc.*]
B	Blank (BUR)
B	Blend
B	Bleomycin [*Also, Bl, Bleo, BLM*] [*Antineoplastic drug*]
B	Blessed
B	Blinkers [*Horse racing*]
b	Block (Copolymerized) [*Organic chemistry*]
B	Blood (AAMN)
B	Bloody [*Slang British*] (DSUE)
B	Blower (IAA)
B	Blue [*Philately*]
B	Blue Return [*Round trip fare*] [*British*]
B	Blue Sky (ROG)
B	Board
B	Boarding [*Schools or pupils*]
B	Boat
B	Boatswain
B	Boatyard [*British Waterways Board sign*]
B	Body
B	[*The*] Boeing Co. [*ICAO aircraft manufacturer identifier*] (ICAO)
B	Boiler
B	Boilermaker [*Navy*]
B	Boils At
B	Boise [*Diocesan abbreviation*] [*Idaho*] (TOCD)
B	Bolivar [*Monetary unit*] [*Venezuela*]
B	Boliviano [*Monetary unit*] [*Bolivia*]
B	Bolton Point [*Medicine*] (DMAA)
B	Bomb (NG)
B	Bombardier
B	Bomber [*Designation for US military aircraft*]
B	Bomber Field
B	Bombing [*JETDS nomenclature*]
B	Bond [*Investment term*]
B	Bonded
B	Bone-Marrow Derived [*Hematology*]
B	Book
b	Book (WDMC)
B	Boolean [*Mathematics*]
B	Booster
b	Booster Pump [*Liquid gas carriers*]
B	Bordetella [*Biochemistry*] (DAVI)
B	Born
b	Born (VRA)
b	Born (WDMC)
B	Boron [*Chemical element*]
B	Borrelia [*Biochemistry*] (DAVI)
B	Boston Stock Exchange
B	Both (DAVI)
B	Bottom
B	Bound (ADA)
B	Bowels [*Medicine*] (BARN)
B	Bowled [*Cricket*]
B	Bowled Out
B	Box Van [*Shipping*] (DCTA)
B	Boys School [*British*]
B	Brace [*Medicine*]
B	Braid (IAA)
B	Brake Horsepower
B	Branch (IAA)
B	Brass (WGA)
B	Bravo [*International phonetic alphabet*] (DSUE)
B	Brazing
B	Breadth
B	Break [*Electronics*]
B	Breakfast (CDAI)
B	Breaking [*FBI standardized term*]
B	Breezing [*Horse racing*]
B	Brewster [*Unit*] [*Physics*]
B	Brick (WGA)
B	Bridge [*Shipping*]
B	Brightness
B	Bristol [*Board/paper*]
B	Bristol [*France*] [*Research code symbol*]
B	British
b-----	British Commonwealth [*MARC geographic area code Library of Congress*] (LCCP)
B	Broad [*Also, BR*] [*Spectral*]
B	Broadcast [*FCC*] (NTCM)
B	Broadcasting
B	Broke [*Rough finish of paper*]
B	Broken
B	Broken Sea [*Navigation*]
B	Broker [*London Stock Exchange*]
B	Bromouridine [*One-letter symbol; see BrUrd*]
B³E	Bronchodilator [*Medicine*]
B	Brooke's Abridgment [*England*] [*A publication*] (DSA)
B	Brother [*or Brotherhood*]
B	Brought Down [*Horse racing*]
B	Brucella [*Bacteriology*]
B	Bruder [*Brother*] [*Freemasonry*] [*German*] (ROG)
B	Brunei (BARN)
B	Brunswick [*Record label*] [*Great Britain*]
B	Buccal [*Pertaining to the cheek*]
B	Buchanan's Supreme Court Reports, Cape Of Good Hope [*1868-79*] [*South Africa*] [*A publication*] (DLA)
B	Buckingham [*Electrostatic measure*]
B	Bucky [*Cassette film in Potter-Bucky Diaphragm*] [*Radiology*] (DAVI)
B	Budget (DLA)
B	Buffer [*Computer science*] (TEL)
B	Bug (DSUE)
B	Bugler [*British military*] (DMA)
B	Building (ADA)
B	Built for British [*As suffix to plane designation*]
B	Bulb
B	Bulgarus de Bulgarinis [*Deceased, 1166*] [*Authority cited in pre-1607 legal work*] (DSA)
B	Bulletin
b	Bunt [*Baseball*] (BARN)
B	Buoyancy
B	Burchardus Wormatiensis [*Deceased, 1025*] [*Authority cited in pre-1607 legal work*] (DSA)
B	Burgerlijk Wetboek [*Civil Code*] [*Netherlands*] (DLA)
B	Buried (ROG)
B	Burned [*Ecology*]
B	Bursa Cells [*Of thymus or lymph nodes*]
B	Bursitis [*Medicine*]
B	Bus [*Computer science*]
B	Bust (ADA)
B	Butcher [*Navy*]
B	Butter [*Phonetic alphabet*] [*Royal Navy World War I*] (DSUE)
B	Butut [*Monetary unit*] [*Gambia*]
B	Buyer
B	By (ROG)
B	Bye [*Cricket*]
B	Byte [*Usually 8 BITS*] [*Computer science*]
B	Called to the Bar [*British*] (ROG)
B	Class "B" Preferred or Common Stock [*Investment term*]
B	Codex Vaticanus (BJA)
B	Common Bench [*Legal term*] (DLA)
B	Degrees Baume
B	Excursion [*Also, BE*] [*Airline fare code*]
B	Farbenfabriken Bayer [*Germany*] [*Research code symbol*]
B	Flammable Liquids [*Fire classification*]
b	Galactic Latitude [*Astronomy*] (BARN)
B	Gauss [*Physics*] (DAVI)
B	Human Being Detail [*Rorschach*] [*Psychology*]
B	Hydrogen Burning (IEEE)
B	Indian Law Reports, Bombay Series [*A publication*] (DLA)
B	Kelco Co. [*Research code symbol*]
B	Laake Oy [*Finland*] [*Research code symbol*]
B	Lack Characteristics of Desirable Investment [*Moody's bond rating*] [*Investment term*]
b	Magnetic Flux [*or Flow*] Density
B	Magnetic Induction (DAS)
B	Mean Barometric Pressure [*Symbol*]
B	Medium [*Women's shoe width*]
B	Multiple [*Missile launch environment symbol*]
B	Narrow [*Men's shoe width*]
B	Negative Feedback (BARN)
B	Polar Radius of Earth [*Symbol*]
b	Regression Coefficient [*Statistics*] (BARN)
B	Second Layer of Soil Next Below the Surface Layer (BARN)
B	Series "B" Bonds or Debentures [*Investment term*]
B	Shoe Width Greater than A and Less than C (BARN)
B	Speculative [*Standard & Poor's bond rating*] [*Investment term*]
B	Susceptance [*Symbol*] [*IUPAC*]
B	Takeda Pharm. Industries [*Japan*] [*Research code symbol*]
B	Tomogram with Oscillating Bucky [*Radiology*] (DAVI)
B	Usually Reliable Source of Intelligence Information [*Military*]
B	Weekly Law Bulletin [*Ohio*] [*A publication*] (DLA)
B₁-C	Thiamine Hydrochloride [*Pharmacology*] (DAVI)
B-1-C	Beta-1-C [*Also called complement C₃*] [*Biochemistry*] (DAVI)
B1S	Beaded [*or Banded*] One Side [*Lumber*]
B2	Biosphere [*Self-contained scientific experimental community*]
B²	Brooks Brothers [*Clothing store*]
B₂	Riboflavin [*Pharmacology*] (DAVI)
B2C2	Battalion and Below Command and Control [*Army*]
B2C2	Brigade and Below Command and Control [*Military*] (RDA)
B2H2	Ball-Burton-Hill-Hatch Plan [*Senate resolution calling for international cooperation during wartime, named after four senators who introduced plan*]
B2S	Beaded [*or Banded*] Two Sides [*Lumber*]
B2S	Bright Two Sides [*Lumber*] (DAC)
B2S1E	Banded Two Sides and One End [*Lumber*] (DAC)
B3C	Beverage Container Control Coalition [*Later, WCFR*] (EA)
B³E	Balancing the Budget on the Backs of the Elderly [*Political charge*]
B3E	Beveled on Three Edges [*Lumber*] (DAC)
B³P	Balancing the Budget on the Backs of the Poor [*Political charge*]
B4	Before [*Slang*] (DAVI)

b4	Before [Internet language] [Computer science]
B4	Block of Four [Philately]
B4E	Beveled on Four Edges [Lumber] (DAC)
B₆	Pyridoxine Hydrochloride [Pharmacology] (DAVI)
B₇	Biotin [Pharmacology] (DAVI)
B7D	Buyer Has Seven Days to Take Up [Securities brokerage] [Investment term]
B₈	Adenosine Phosphate [Pharmacology] (DAVI)
B8ZS	Bipolar with Eight-Zero Substitution [Coding] [Telecommunications]
B₁₂	Cyanocobalamin [Pharmacology] (DAVI)
B₁₂b	Hydroxocobalamin [Pharmacology] (DAVI)
B 26	Bulk Carrier of 26,000 Deadweight Tons [Shipping] (DS)
B 30	Bulk Carrier of 30,000 Deadweight Tons [Shipping] (DS)
B-52	Stratofortress strategic bomber [Boeing Co.]
BA	Baccalaureus Artium [Bachelor of Arts] [Latin]
BA	Bachelor of Agriculture
B/A	Bachelor of Applied Arts
BA	Bachelor of Arts
BA	Bacillary Angiomatosis [Medicine]
BA	Backache [Medicine]
BA	Backlash Allowance (MSA)
BA	Backup Aerospace Vehicle [or Aircraft]
BA	Bacterial Agglutination (MAE)
Ba	Bagarottus dei Corradi da Bologna [Flourished, 1200-42] [Authority cited in pre-1607 legal work] (DSA)
BA	Bahamas [IYRU nationality code] (IYR)
ba	Bahrain [MARC country of publication code Library of Congress] (LCCP)
BA	Balanced Asynchronous (ACRL)
BA	Ball
BA	Balneum Arenae [Sand Bath] [Medicine]
BA	Banco Amazonas [Amazon Bank] [Ecuador]
Ba	Bandinus Familiatus de Pisa [Deceased, 1218] [Authority cited in pre-1607 legal work] (DSA)
BA	Bands of America (EA)
BA	Bank Acceptance
BA	Bank Administration [Bank Administration Institute] [A publication]
BA	BankAmericard [Later, Visa] [Credit card]
BA	Bank Angle
BA	Bank of America
BA	Baptized
BA	Bar [Freight]
Ba	Barium [Chemical element]
Ba	Barium Enema [Medicine] (DMAA)
BA	Barometric Altimeter (MCD)
BA	Baron (ROG)
BA	Barremian-Aptian [Paleontology]
Ba	Baruch [Book of the Bible] (BJA)
BA	Base Activation
BA	Base Assembly
BA	Basic Agreement
BA	Basic Assembler [Computer science] (IAA)
BA	Basic Authorization
BA	Basilar Artery [Anatomy]
BA	Basion [Craniometric point]
BA	Basketball Australia [An association]
BA	Bastard Amber [Stage-lighting filter] (WDMC)
BA	Bath (WGA)
BA	Bathroom [Classified advertising]
BA	Batterers Anonymous (EA)
BA	Battery (IAA)
BA	Battery Adjust (AABC)
BA	Batting Average [Baseball]
BA	Battle of Atlantic [World War II]
BA	Baume
BA	Beach Abort
B/A	Beam Approach (DEN)
BA	Bedstead Alliance [A union] [British]
BA	Bell Aerosystems Co. (KSC)
BA	Bell Alarm (IAA)
BA	Bell Atlantic
BA	Belt Association (EA)
BA	Bending Allowance [Engineering] (IAA)
BA	Bentonite Agglutination (OA)
BA	Benzanthracene [Also, BzAnth] [Organic chemistry]
BA	Benzyladenine [Biochemistry]
BA	Berkeley Association (EA)
BA	Best Available (WDMC)
ba	Best Available (WDMC)
BA	Beta Activity [Measure of radioactivity]
BA	Beta Anneal (PDAA)
BA	Betamethasone Acetate [Medicine] (DMAA)
BA	Biblical Aramaic (BJA)
BA	Bicycle Australia [An association]
BA	Bifidus Acidophilus Live [Health-food product]
BA	Bikes for Africa (EA)
BA	Bilateral Asymmetrical [Medicine] (DMAA)
BA	Bile Acid [Gastroenterology] (AAMN)
BA	Biliary Atresia [Medicine] (DMAA)
B/A	Billed At [Commerce]
BA	Billiards Association [British] (BI)
BA	Binary Add [Computer science]
BA	Biography Almanac [Later, Almanac of Famous People] [A publication]
BA	Biological Activity

BA	Blanket Agreement
BA	Blanking Amplifier (IAA)
BA	Blasting Agent (MCD)
BA	Blind Approach [Aviation]
BA	Blocking Antibody [Immunology] (MAE)
BA	Blood Agar [Growth medium]
BA	Blood Alcohol (WGA)
BA	Blue Anchor, Inc. [Formerly, CFE] [Later, BAI] [An association]
BA	Bnei Akiva (BJA)
BA	[The] Boeing Co. [NYSE symbol] (SPSG)
BA	Bolshoi Ballet Academy [Former USSR]
BA	Bolt Action [British military] (DMA)
B/A	Bomb-Aimer [British military] (DMA)
BA	Bone Age [Medicine]
B + A	Bone Greater Than Air [Conduction]
BA	Booksellers Association of Great Britain and Ireland (EAIO)
BA	Boolean Algebra [Mathematics]
BA	Boric Acid [Inorganic chemistry]
BA	Boston & Albany Railroad [AAR code]
BA	Bourns Assist [Medicine] (DAVI)
BA	Bovine Albumin [Physiology] (MAE)
BA	Brachial Artery [Pressure] [Cardiology] (DAVI)
BA	Braniff Airways, Inc. [of Braniff International Corp.]
B/A	Breaking Action (DNAB)
BA	Breaks Above
BA	Breathing Air (MCD)
BA	Breathing Apparatus
BA	Brewmeisters Anonymous (EA)
BA	Bridge Amplifier
B/A	Bridle Arrester (MCD)
BA	Bright Annealed (DAC)
BA	Brith Abraham (BJA)
BA	British Academy
BA	British Admiralty
BA	British Aerospace Ltd.
BA	British Aircraft Corp. Ltd. [ICAO aircraft manufacturer identifier] (ICAO)
BA	British Airtours Ltd. [Airline]
BA	British Airways [British ICAO designator] (ICDA)
BA	British Aluminium Co. Ltd.
BA	British America
BA	British Army
BA	British Artists [A publication]
BA	British Association for the Advancement of Science (BI)
BA	British Association Screw Thread
BA	Brodmann's Areas [Brain anatomy]
BA	Bromoacetone [War gas]
BA	Bromoacetyl [Organic chemistry]
BA	Bronchial Asthma [Medicine]
BA	Bronsted Acid [Biochemistry]
BA	Bronze Age
BA	Brucellus Abortus [Bacteriology]
BA	Brymon Airways [British]
BA	Buccoaxial [Dentistry]
BA	Budget Activity [Navy]
BA	Budget Authority [Office of Management and Budget]
BA	Budget Authorization [Air Force] (AFM)
BA	Buenos Aires [Argentina]
BA	Buffer Amplifier [Computer science]
BA	Buffoons of America (EA)
BA	Bugger All [Slang British] (DSUE)
BA	Building Advisor [Red Cross Disaster Services]
BA	Buisson Ardent [The Burning Bush] [Freemasonry]
BA	Bulb Angle [Shipfitting]
BA	Bulletin des Assurances [A publication] (ILCA)
BA	Bundesanwalt [Public Prosecutor or Attorney General] [German] (ILCA)
BA	Bundesanwaltschaft [The Office of Public Prosecutor] [German] (ILCA)
BA	Bundle Assembly (SAA)
BA	Bureau of Accounts [Department of the Treasury]
B/A	Bureau of Aeronautics [Later, Naval Air Systems Command]
BA	Burglar Alarm
BA	Burmese Army (CINC)
BA	Burned Area [Ecology]
BA	Burns Federation [Scotland] (EAIO)
BA	Bus Automation [Computer science] (ODBW)
BA	Bus Available [Computer science]
BA	Business Acronyms [A publication]
BA	Busted Aristocrat [A cadet officer reduced to the ranks] [Military slang]
BA	Butyl Acrylate [Organic chemistry]
Ba	Ciba-Geigy AG [Switzerland] [Research code symbol]
BA	Graduate in Arts
BA	Primary Type Battery [JETDS nomenclature] [Military] (CET)
Ba	Siegfried AG [Switzerland] [Research code symbol]
Ba	Speculative Elements [Moody's bond rating] [Investment term]
BAA	Baccalaureat en Administration des Affaires [Canada] (DD)
BAA	Bachelor of Applied Arts
BAA	Bachelor of Art and Architecture (ADA)
BAA	Backup Aerospace Vehicle [or Aircraft] Authorization
BAA	Bank of America Australia
BAA	Barber, Albert P., Kenosha WI [STAC]
BAA	Battlefield Automation Appraisal (MCD)
BAA	Benzoylarginine Amide [Biochemistry]

BAA............. Bialla [*Papua New Guinea*] [*Airport symbol*] (OAG)
BAA............. Billeting and Accommodations Advisory [*Military communications*]
BAA............. Blindmakers' Association of Australia
BAA............. Board of Assistance Appeals [*Environmental Protection Agency*] (GFGA)
BAA............. Booking Agents Association of Great Britain Ltd. (BI)
BAA............. Boomerang Association of Australia
BAA............. Bordeaux Agents Association [*British*] (BI)
BAA............. Bosnaair [*Yugoslavia*] [*ICAO designator*] (FAAC)
BAA............. Branched Amino Acid (DMAA)
BAA............. Branched-Chain Amino Acid [*Biochemistry*]
BAA............. Breed Age Average [*Dairy science*] (OA)
BAA............. Brewers Association of America (EA)
BAA............. Brigade Administrative Area [*Military British*]
BAA............. British Accounting Association (DBA)
BAA............. British Acetylene Association (BI)
BAA............. British Acupuncture Association and Register (DBA)
BAA............. British Agrochemicals Association
BAA............. British Airports Authority
BAA............. British Alsatian Association (BI)
BAA............. British Anodising Association
BAA............. British Archaeological Association
BAA............. British Association of Accountants and Auditors (BI)
BAA............. British Astronomical Association
BAA............. Broad Agency Announcement [*National automotive center*] (RDA)
BAA............. Broad Area Announcement
BAA............. Broadband Active Analyzer
BAA............. Budget Activity Account [*Army*] (AABC)
BAA............. Buenos Aires [*Argentina*] [*Seismograph station code, US Geological Survey*] (SEIS)
BAA............. Buffer Address Array [*Computer science*] (IAA)
BAA............. Bureau of African Affairs [*Department of State*]
BAA............. Butylacetanilide [*Organic chemistry*]
BAA............. Buy American Act (AAGC)
Baa............. Lower Medium [*Moody's bond rating*]
BAA............. Vardar Air [*Republic of Macedonia*] [*FAA designator*] (FAAC)
BAAA............. British-American Arts Association (EA)
BAAB............. British Amateur Athletic Board
BAAC............. Basic Army Administrative Course
BAAC............. British Aviation Archaeological Council (DBA)
BAACMIR..... British Aerospace Air Combat Maneuvering Instrumentation Range (DA)
BAADS......... Bangor Air Defense Sector (SAA)
BAAE........... Bachelor of Aeronautical and Astronautical Engineering (WGA)
BAAEMS...... British Association of Airport Equipment Manufacturers and Services (DA)
BAAF........... Brigade Airborne Alert Force [*Military*]
BAAF........... British Agencies for Adoption and Fostering (DI)
BAAF........... Butts Army Airfield [*Fort Carson, CO*]
BAAG.......... British Army Aid Group [*China*] [*World War II*]
BAAL.......... Black Academy of Arts and Letters [*Defunct*] (EA)
BAAL.......... British Association of Applied Linguists [*British*]
BAALPE....... British Association of Advisers and Lecturers in Physical Education
BAAM.......... Basic Administration and Management
BAAN.......... Baan Co. NV [*NASDAQ symbol*] (SAG)
BAAN.......... Budget Authorization Account Number [*Air Force*] (AFM)
Ba & B........ Ball and Beatty's Irish Chancery Reports [*1807-14*] [*A publication*] (ILCA)
Ba & Be....... Ball and Beatty's Irish Chancery Reports [*1807-14*] [*A publication*] (DLA)
BA & F........ Budget, Accounting, and Finance (AFM)
BAANF........ Baan Co.NV [*NASDAQ symbol*] (TTSB)
BAAP.......... Badger Army Ammunition Plant (AABC)
BAAP.......... British Association of Academic Phoneticians (DBA)
BAAPS........ British Association of Aesthetic Plastic Surgeons (EAIO)
BAAR.......... Board for Aviation Accident Research [*Army*]
BAAR.......... British Acupuncture Association and Register (EA)
BAARINC...... Booz-Allen Applied Research, Inc.
BAAS.......... British Association for American Studies (EA)
BAAS.......... British Association for the Advancement of Science
BAAS.......... Broadband Acoustic Array Section
BA(AsianStudies)... Bachelor of Arts (Asian Studies)
BAAT.......... British Association of Art Therapists Ltd.
BAAT.......... Bromoacetylmono(azobenzenearsonic Acid)-L-tyrosine [*Biochemistry*]
BAATC........ Bay Area Army Terminal Center
BAB............. Babbing [*Fishing for eels*]
BAB............. Babbitt [*Metallurgy*]
BAB............. Babinski [*Reflex*] [*Medicine*]
BAB............. Babson College, Babson Park, MA [*OCLC symbol*] (OCLC)
Bab............. Babylonia (BJA)
Bab............. Babylonian Talmud (BJA)
BAB............. Beni-Abbes [*Algeria*] [*Seismograph station code, US Geological Survey*] (SEIS)
BAB............. Black Americans for Bush [*Defunct*] (EA)
BAB............. Blood Agar Base [*Growth medium*]
BAB............. Booster Assembly Building [*NASA*]
BAB............. Branch and Bound [*Algorithm*]
BAB............. Branched Alkylbenzene [*Organic chemistry*]
BAB............. British Airways ADS [*NYSE symbol Toronto Stock Exchange symbol*] (SPSG)
BAB............. British Airways Board (AIA)
BAB............. Budget Advisory Board (SAA)
BAB............. Marysville, CA [*Location identifier FAA*] (FAAL)
BABA.......... Boys' Apparel Buyers Association (EA)
BABA.......... British-American Business Association (EAIO)

BABA........... British Anaerobic and Biomass Association (PDAA)
BABA........... Burma-America Buddhist Association (EA)
BABA LTD.... British Anaerobic & Biomass Association Ltd.
Bab Auc...... Babington's Law of Auctions [*A publication*] (DLA)
BABB.......... Back-Arc-Basin Basalt [*Geology*]
BABC.......... Barrington Bancorp [*NASDAQ symbol*] (TTSB)
BABC.......... Barrington Bancorp, Inc. [*NASDAQ symbol*] (SAG)
BABC.......... Black American Baptist Churchmen [*An association*] (EA)
BABEL......... Baltic and Bothnian Echoes from the Lithosphere [*Collaborative seismic project*] [*Britain, Denmark, Finland, Germany, and Sweden*]
BABF.......... British Amateur Baseball Federation
BABF.......... Fraser Valley Regional Library, Abbotsford, British Columbia [*Library symbol National Library of Canada*] (NLC)
BABFO......... British Association of Bio-Fuel and Oil
BABFVL....... Library Technician Program, Fraser Valley College, Abbotsford, British Columbia, [*Library symbol National Library of Canada*] (NLC)
BABHId....... BAB Holdings, Inc. [*Associated Press*] (SAG)
BABI.......... Basaltic Achondrite Best Initial (DICI)
BABI.......... Blastomere Analysis before Implantation
BABIM........ Bis(amidino-benzimidazolyl)methane [*Biochemistry*]
BabK.......... Baboon Kidney (DMAA)
BABM.......... Alert Bay Public Library and Museum, British Columbia [*Library symbol National Library of Canada*] (NLC)
BA/BMgmt ... Bachelor of Arts/Bachelor of Management Combines (DD)
BAB MTL .... Babbitt Metal [*Freight*]
BaBo.......... [*The*] Ballad Book [*A publication*]
BABO.......... Boolean Approach for Bivalent Optimization [*Computer science*] (PDAA)
BABP.......... British Association of Behavioural Psychotherapy (DI)
BABP.......... British Association of Behavioural Psychotherapy (DBA)
BAbPr........ Beitraege zum Altbabylonischen Privatrecht [*A publication*] (BJA)
BABS.......... [*The*] Babbage Society (EA)
BA/BS........ Bachelor of Arts/Bachelor of Science Combined (DD)
BABS.......... Batch Automated Balancing System [*Computer science*] (MHDI)
BABS.......... Beam Approach Beacon System [*Aviation*] (KSC)
BABS.......... Biosynthetic Antibody Binding Site [*Biochemistry*]
BABS.......... Blind Approach Beacon System [*Aviation*]
BABS.......... Book Acquisition and Bibliographic Service [*National Book Centre*] [*Canada*]
BABS.......... British Aluminium Building Service (BI)
BABS.......... British Association for Brazing and Soldering
BABS.......... British Association of Barbershop Singers (EAIO)
Bab Set-Off... Babington's Law of Set-Off [*A publication*] (DLA)
Babson C.... Babson College (GAGS)
BABT.......... British Approvals Board for Telecommunications
BABT.......... Brotherhood of Associated Book Travelers (EA)
BABTAC...... British Association of Beauty Therapy and Cosmetology (DBA)
BA Bull LA... Bar Association Bulletin, Los Angeles [*A publication*] (DLA)
BABYL........ Babylonia [*or Babylonian*]
BabySst...... Baby Superstore, Inc. [*Associated Press*] (SAG)
Babyst....... Babystar, Inc. [*Associated Press*] (SAG)
Babystr...... Babystar, Inc. [*Associated Press*] (SAG)
BAC............. Bacau [*Romania*] [*Seismograph station code, US Geological Survey*] (SEIS)
BAC............. Baccalaureate Exam [*France*]
BAC............. Baccalaureus
B Ac............ Bachelor of Accounts
BAc............. Bachelor of Acupuncture [*British*] (DBQ)
BAC............. Bacillus [*or Bacilli*] [*Bacteriology*] (WDAA)
BAC............. Back Association of Canada
BAC............. BAC Leasing Ltd. [*British*] [*FAA designator*] (FAAC)
BAC............. Bacteria (DAVI)
BAC............. Bacterial Adherent Colonies
BAC............. Bacterial Antigen Complex [*Immunochemistry*]
BAC............. Bacterial Artificial Chromosome [*Genetics*]
BAC............. Bacterial Artificial Chromosome [*Genetics*]
BAC............. Bacterial Artificial Chromosome [*Genetics*]
BAC............. Bacteriological
BAC............. Banister Continental Ltd. [*Toronto Stock Exchange symbol*]
BAC............. BankAmerica Corp. [*Formerly, Security Pacific Corp.*] [*NYSE symbol*] (SPSG)
BAC............. BankAmericard [*Later, Visa*] [*Credit card*]
BAC............. BAPTA [*Bearing and Power Transfer Assembly*] Accelerometer and Conditioner [*Aerospace*]
BAC............. Barometric Altitude Control
BAC............. Base Area Commandant
BAC............. Bateria Artifical Chromosome [*Genetics*]
BAC............. Beech Aircraft Corp. (KSC)
BAC............. Bell Aerospace Co.
BAC............. Bell Aircraft Corp. (MCD)
BAC............. Belmont Abbey College [*North Carolina*]
BAC............. Below All Clouds [*Aviation*]
BAC............. Bendix Aviation Corp. [*Later, Bendix Corp.*]
BAC............. Benzalkonium Chloride [*Organic chemistry*]
BAC............. Bile Acid Concentration [*Gastroenterology*]
BAC............. Billing Advice Code
BAC............. Binary-Analog Conversion [*Computer science*] (DIT)
BAC............. Binary Asymmetric Channel
BAC............. Biological Activated Carbon [*Water treatment*]
BAC............. Biospecific Affinity Chromatography
BAC............. Biotechnology Advisory Committee [*Environmental Protection Agency*] (GFGA)
BAC............. Bipolar Active-Plastic Cell

BAC	Bird Airplane Club (EA)
BAC	Bird Association of California (EA)
BAC	Bis(acryloyl)cystamine [*Organic chemistry*]
BAC	Bis(aminomethyl)cyclohexane [*Organic chemistry*]
BAC	Black Affairs Center [*Later, BACTOD*] (EA)
BAC	Blood Alcohol Concentration [*or Content*] [*Sobriety test*]
BAC	Blower Access Cover
BAC	Board of the Army Council
BAC	Boating Anti-Pollution Council (EA)
BAC	Boeing Aerospace [*or Aircraft*] Corp. (MCD)
BAC	Bollettino di Archeologia Cristiana [*A publication*] (BJA)
BAC	Booster Assembly Contractor [*NASA*] (NASA)
BAC	Boric Acid Concentrator (NRCH)
BAC	Born-Again Christian
BAC	Breath Alcohol Concentration
BAC	Bristol Aeroplane Co. (MCD)
BAC	British Action for Children's Television (AIE)
BAC	British Air Commission [*Washington*]
BAC	British Aircraft Corp. Ltd.
BAC	British Archives Council (DIT)
BAC	British Association for Counselling
BAC	British Association of Chemists
BAC	British Atlantic Committee (EAIO)
BAC	British Atomic Committee
BAC	Bromacetylcellulose [*or Bromoacetycellulose*] [*Organic chemistry*]
BAC	Bromoacetylcholine [*Biochemistry*]
BAC	Bronchial Allergen Challenge [*Immunology*]
BAC	Bronchoalveolar Cells [*Medicine*]
BAC	Brotherhood of Anglican Churchmen [*Canada*]
BAC	Buccoaxiocervical [*Dentistry*]
BAC	Buchanan's Appeal Court Reports, Cape Of Good Hope [*A publication*] (DLA)
BAC	Budget Advisory Committee [*Army*]
BAC	Budget at Completion (MCD)
BAC	Budgeted Actual Cost
BAC	Budgeted Cost at Completion (AAGC)
BAC	Buffer Access Card [*Computer science*] (NASA)
BAC	Building Access Card [*Issued to Senate staff members to ensure security in the Capitol*]
BAC	Building Advisory Committee
BAC	Burdekin Agricultural College [*Australia*]
BAC	Bureau of Air Commerce [*Later, Civil Aeronautics Authority*]
BAC	Burlington Autosport Club (AC)
BAC	Burma Airways Corp. [*Rangoon*] (EY)
BAC	Business Advisory Council [*Later, Business Council*]
BAC	Business Archives Council [*British*]
BAC	Buy a Car [*Slogan during automobile sales slump of 1974-75*]
BAC	International Union of Bricklayers and Allied Craftsmen (EA)
BACA	Bar Association for Commerce, Finance, and Industry [*British*] (DBA)
BACA	British Advisory Committee for Aeronautics
BACA	British Association of Clinical Anatomists
BACA	British Association of Concert Agents
BACA	Business and Consumer Affairs (WDAA)
Bac Ab	Bacon's Abridgment [*1736-1832*] [*A publication*] (DLA)
Bac Abr	Bacon's Abridgment [*1736-1832*] [*A publication*] (DLA)
BACAH	British Association of Consultants in Agriculture and Horticulture (BI)
BACAIC	Boeing Airplane Co. [*later, The Boeing Co.*] Algebraic Interpretive Computing System
BACAN	British Association for the Control of Airport Noise
BACAS	Biological Agent Casualty Assessment System (MCD)
BACAT	Barge Aboard Catamaran
Bac Ben Soc	Bacon on Benefit Societies and Life Insurance [*A publication*] (DLA)
BACC	Baccalaureate
B Acc	Bachelor of Accountancy
BACC	Brazilian-American Chamber of Commerce (EA)
BACC	British-American Chamber of Commerce (EA)
BACC	British-American Collectors' Club (EA)
BACC	British-American Coordinating Committee [*Turkey*]
Bac Ca	Bacon's Case of Treason [*1641*] [*A publication*] (DLA)
BACCC	Base Activation Central Control Committee
Bacch	Bacchae [*of Euripides*] [*Classical studies*] (OCD)
Bacch	Bacchides [*of Plautus*] [*Classical studies*] (OCD)
Bac Chanc	Bacon's Chancery Cases [*England*] [*A publication*] (DLA)
BACCHUS	Boost Alcohol Consciousness Concerning the Health of University Students [*In association name BACCHUS of the US*] (EA)
BACCHUS	British Aircraft Corp. Ltd. Commercial Habitat under the Sea
Bacchyl	Bacchylides [*Fifth century BC*] [*Classical studies*] (OCD)
Bac Comp Arb	Bacon's Complete Arbitrator [*A publication*] (DLA)
B Acc's	Bachelor of Accounts
BACD	Ballet America Concert Dancers
BACD	Basic Alteration Class Drawing [*Navy*] (CAAL)
Bac Dec	Bacon's Decisions (Ritchie) [*England*] [*A publication*] (DLA)
Bac Dig	Bacon's Georgia Digest [*A publication*] (DLA)
BACE	Bachelor of Air Conditioning Engineering
BACE	Basic Aircraft Check-Out Equipment (PDAA)
BACE	Basic Automatic Checkout Equipment
BACE	British Association of Consulting Engineers
Bac El	Bacon's Elements of the Common Law [*A publication*] (DLA)
BAC Eng	Bachelor of Air Conditioning Engineering
BACER	Biological and Climatic Effects Research
BACFID	British Association of Canned and Preserved Food Importers and Distributors (DBA)
BACG	British Association of Crystal Growth
Bac Gov	Bacon on Government [*A publication*] (DLA)

BACH	Bachelor
BACH	Bachman Information Sys [*NASDAQ symbol*] (TTSB)
BACH	Bachman Information Systems [*NASDAQ symbol*] (SPSG)
Bach	Bach's Reports [*19-21 Montana*] [*A publication*] (DLA)
BACH	Backscatler / Absorption Chamber (PDAA)
BACH	British Association for Construction Heads (AIE)
BACHAD	Brit Chalutzim Datiyim (BJA)
BA Chem	Bachelor of Applied Chemistry
BA CHEM	Bachelor of Arts in Chemistry (WDAA)
Bache Pa Just	Bache's Pennsylvania Justice's Manual [*A publication*] (DLA)
BachInf	Bachman Information Systems, Inc. [*Associated Press*] (SAG)
BACHR	Bachelor
BACI	Brazilian-American Cultural Institute (EA)
BACIE	British Association for Commercial and Industrial Education (DCTA)
Bac Ins	Bacon on Benefit Societies and Life Insurance [*A publication*] (DLA)
BACIS	Budget Accounting Information System [*IBM Corp.*]
back	Backing [*Publishing*] (WDMC)
back	Backstage [*Theater*] (WDMC)
back	Backstrip [*Book-binding*] (WDMC)
BACK	Backwardation [*Commodity futures trading*] (ROG)
BACK	Boublik, Alder, Chen, Kreglewski Equation [*Physical chemistry*]
BackBay	Back Bay Restaurant Group, Inc. [*Associated Press*] (SAG)
Back Sher	Backus on Sheriffs [*A publication*] (DLA)
BackYrd	Back Yard Burgers, Inc. [*Associated Press*] (SAG)
BA Class	Bachelor of Arts - Classical
Bac Lease	Bacon on Leases and Terms of Years [*A publication*] (DLA)
Bac Lib Reg	Bacon's Liber Regis, vel Thesaurus Rerum Ecclesiasticarum [*A publication*] (DLA)
BACLIN	Baroclinic Prognosis [*NWS*] (FAAC)
BACM	BACM Industries Ltd. [*Formerly, British-American Construction & Materials Ltd.*]
BACM	British Association of Colliery Management (DCTA)
BACMA	British Aromatic Compounds Manufacturers' Association (BI)
BACMA	British Artists' Colour Manufacturers' Association (BI)
BACMC	British Anti-Common Market Campaign [*An association*] (DBA)
BACMI	British Aggregate Construction Materials Industry
BACMM	British Association of Clothing Machinery Manufacturers (PDAA)
BAC MUS	Bachelor of Music (BARN)
BACO	Base Activation Change Order
BACO	Bleomycin, Adriamycin, CCNU [*Lomustine*], Oncovin [*Vincristine*] [*Antineoplastic drug regimen*] (DAVI)
BACO	British Aluminium Co. Ltd. (ODBW)
BACOD	Bleomycin, Adriamycin, Cyclophosphamide, Oncovin [*Vincristine*], Dexamethasone [*Antineoplastic drug regimen*]
BACODINE	Batse Coordinates Distribution Network
BACON	Backfile Conversion Project [*European Patent Office*]
Bacon	Bacon. Arguments in Law [*A publication*] (DLA)
Bacon	Bacon on Government [*A publication*] (DLA)
Bacon	Bacon on Leases and Terms of Years [*A publication*] (DLA)
Bacon	Bacon's Abridgment [*1736-1832*] [*A publication*] (DLA)
Bacon	Bacon's Complete Arbitrator [*A publication*] (DLA)
Bacon	Bacon's Elements of the Common Law [*A publication*] (DLA)
Bacon	Bacon's Essay on Uses [*A publication*] (DLA)
Bacon	Bacon's Liber Regis [*A publication*] (DLA)
BACON	, Nitrogen Mustard [*Vincristine*] [*Antineoplastic drug regimen*]
BACOP	Bleomycin, Adriamycin, Cyclophosphamide, Oncovin [*Vincristine*], Prednisone [*Antineoplastic drug regimen*]
BACP	Bandwidth Allocation Control Protocol [*Telecommunications*] (ACRL)
BACP	Bandwidth Allocation Control Protocol [*Computer science*] (PCM)
BACP	Bandwidth Allocation Control Protocol (PCM)
BACP	British Association of Community Physicians (DBA)
BACP	Business Advisory Committee on Procurement [*DoD*]
BACPrA	BankAmer Adj cm A Pfd [*NYSE symbol*] (TTSB)
BACPrB	BankAmer Adj cm B Pfd [*NYSE symbol*] (TTSB)
BACPrH	BankAmer 9% cm Ser'H'Pfd [*NYSE symbol*] (TTSB)
BACPrK	BankAmer 8.375% cm Ser'K'Pfd [*NYSE symbol*] (TTSB)
BACPrL	BankAmer 8.16% cm Ser'L'Pfd [*NYSE symbol*] (TTSB)
BACPrM	BankAmer 7.875% cm Ser'M'Pfd [*NYSE symbol*] (TTSB)
BACPrN	BankAmer 8.50% cm Ser'N'Pfd [*NYSE symbol*] (TTSB)
BACR	British Association for Cancer Research
BA(Creative)	Bachelor of Creative Arts
Bac Rep	Bacon's Decisions (Ritchie) [*England*] [*A publication*] (DLA)
BACS	Backup Acquisition System
BACS	Bankers' Automated Clearing Services [*British*] (DCTA)
BACS	Banks Automated Clearing System [*British*] (NITA)
BACS	Bay Area Cryonics Society [*Later, American Cryonics Society*] (EA)
BACS	Beacon Collision Avoidance System [*Aviation*] (DA)
BACS	Bibliographic Access and Control System [*Washington University*] [*Information service or system*] (IID)
BACS	Black American Cinema Society (EA)
BACS	Bloomington Academic Computer Services [*Indiana University*] [*Research center*] (RCD)
BACS	Body Axis Coordinate System (MCD)
BACS	Boeing Applied Computing Service (SAA)
BACS	British Association for Canadian Studies
BACS	British Association for Chemical Specialities
BACS	British Association of Chinese Studies (DBA)
BACS	British Association of Cosmetic Surgeons
BACSA	British Association for Cemeteries in South Asia
BACSEB	BUWEPS [*Bureau of Naval Weapons, now obsolete*] Aviation Clothing and Survival Equipment Bulletin (MCD)
bact	Bacteriology [*Biochemistry*] (DAVI)
BACT	Bacterium [*Bacteria*] [*Latin*]
BACT	BCNU [*Carmustine*], ara-C, Cyclophosphamide, Thioguanine [*Antineoplastic drug regimen*]

B Act............ Bellum Actiacum [of Ausonius] [Classical studies] (OCD)
BACT........... Best Available Control Technology [Environmental Protection Agency]
BACT........... Bleomycin, Adriamycin, Cytoxan, Tamoxifen [Antineoplastic drug regimen] (DAVI)
BACT........... British Association of Canoe Traders (DBA)
BACT........... British Association of Conference Towns
BACTA.......... British Amusement Catering Trades Association (DBA)
Bac TE........ Bacon's Liber Regis, vel Thesaurus Rerum Ecclesiasticarum [A publication] (DLA)
BACTER........ Bacteriology
Bacti Lab..... Bacteriology Laboratory (DAVI)
BACTLGY...... Bacteriology
BACTM......... Bifurcation Analysis and Catastrophy Theory Methodology (MCD)
BACTOD....... Black Affairs Center for Training and Organizational Development (EA)
Bactr........... Bactrian (VRA)
BActSci....... Bachelor of Actuarial Sciences (DD)
BACU.......... Bacou USA [NASDAQ symbol] (TTSB)
BACU.......... Battle Area Control Unit [Military]
BACU.......... Black American Colleges and Universities [A publication]
BACUP........ British Association of Cancer United Patients
BACUS........ Booz, Allen & Hamilton Inc. Computer Utilization System (IAA)
Bac Uses..... Bacon's Essay on Uses [A publication] (DLA)
BACV.......... Barrel Cactus Virus [Plant pathology]
BACV.......... Budget at Completion Variance (MCD)
BACVSR....... British Air Cushion Vehicle Safety Requirements (PDAA)
BAD .... Bank Account Debits Tax (ADA)
BAD .... Banque Africaine de Developpement [African Development Bank] [Use ADB] (AF)
BAD .... Base Ammunition Depot (NATG)
BAD .... Behind Armor Debris [Army] (RDA)
BAD .... Berlin Airlift Device [Military decoration]
BAD .... Biological Aerosol Detection [Army] (MCD)
BAD .... Bipolar Affective Disorder [Psychology] (DAVI)
BAD .... British Admiralty Delegation [to Washington]
BAD .... British Association of Dermatologists [or Dermatology] (EAIO)
BAD .... Broken as Designed [Computer hacker terminology] (NHD)
BAD .... Buck-a-Day (PDAA)
BAD .... Buzz Attenuation Device (CAAL)
BAD .... Department of Bantu Administration and Development [An agency of South African government]
BAD .... Shreveport, LA [Location identifier FAA] (FAAL)
BADA.......... Base Air Depot Area [Air Force]
BADA.......... British Antique Dealers' Association
BADA.......... British Audio Dealers Association (DBA)
BADADUQ .... Banque de Donnees a acces direct de l'Universite du Quebec [Database of the holdings of the University of Quebec] [Canada] (NITA)
BADAS........ Binary Automatic Data Annotation System
BADB.......... Badbury [England]
BADB.......... Boating Accident Data Base [Database] [Coast Guard]
BADB.......... Bromoacetyl-DNP-Diamino-L-Butyric Acid [Biochemistry]
BADC.......... Bar Association of the District of Columbia (SRA)
BADC.......... Binary Asymmetric Dependent Channel
BADCT........ Best Available Demonstrated Control Technology [Environmental Protection Agency]
BADD.......... BIT [Binary Digit] Attention Deficit Disorder [Computer science]
BADD.......... Bothered about Dungeons & Dragons [Video game]
BADE.......... Bromoacetyl-DNP-Ethylenediamine [Biochemistry]
BADEA........ Bromoacetaldehyde Diethyl Acetal [Organic chemistry]
Ba de Ca ..... Bartholomaeus de Capua [Deceased, 1328] [Authority cited in pre-1607 legal work] (DSA)
BADESP...... Banco de Desenvolvimento do Estado de Sao Paulo SA [Brazil] (EY)
BADF.......... Bile Acid-Dependent Fraction [Medicine]
BADGE........ Base Air Defense Ground Environment [Air Force]
BADGE........ Bekesy Ascending Descending Gap Evaluation
BadgrM........ Badger Meter, Inc. [Associated Press] (SAG)
BadgrP........ Badger Paper Mills, Inc. [Associated Press] (SAG)
BADIC......... Biological Analysis Detection Instrumentation and Control
BADL.......... Badlands National Monument [South Dakota]
BADL.......... Bromoacetyl-DNP-L-Lysine [Biochemistry]
BADLG........ British Archaeologists and Developers Liaison Group
B Adm .... Bachelor of Administration
B Adm Eng... Bachelor of Administrative Engineering
BADMEP...... Burlington Atmospheric Density Model Evaluation Program [IBM Corp.]
BAdmin........ Bachelor of Administration
BADO.......... Bromoacetyl-DNP-L-Ornithine [Biochemistry]
BADOPA...... Best Average Definition Over the Picture Area (SAA)
BADS .... Biological Agent Decontamination Simulant (MCD)
BADSA........ Backup Air Data Sensor Assembly (MCD)
BADT .... Bank Account Debits Tax (ADA)
BADT .... Best Available Demonstrated Technology [Environmental Protection Agency] (FFDE)
BAE............ Bachelor of Aeronautical Engineering
B Ae............ Bachelor of Aeronautics
BAE............ Bachelor of Agricultural Economics (IIA)
BAE............ Bachelor of Agricultural Engineering
BAE............ Bachelor of Architectural Engineering
BAE............ Bachelor of Art Education
BAE............ Bachelor of Arts in Education
BAE............ Back-Action Evasion [Physics]
BAE............ Badminton Association of England (EAIO)
BaE............ Barium Enema [Medicine]

BAE............ Barrier Tech [Vancouver Stock Exchange symbol]
BAE............ Beacon Antenna Equipment
BAE............ Belfast Association of Engineers [Northern Ireland] (BARN)
BAE............ Board of Architectural Education [British] (BI)
BAE............ Bovine Aortic Endothelium
BAE............ Brasilia [Brazil] [Seismograph station code, US Geological Survey] (SEIS)
BAE............ British Academy of Experts (DBA)
BAE............ British Admiralty Establishment
BAe............ British Aerospace Ltd.
BAE............ British Aerospace PLC [ICAO designator] (FAAC)
BAE............ British Antarctic Expedition
BAE............ British Association of Electrolysists
BAE............ British Association of Electrolysists (DBA)
BAE............ Bronchial Artery Embolization [Cardiology] (DAVI)
BAE............ Buenos Aires Embotell'a [NYSE symbol] (SPSG)
BAE............ Buenos Aires Embotell'a ADS [NYSE symbol] (TTSB)
BAE............ Bureau for Africa and Europe [AID]
BAE............ Bureau of Agricultural Economics [Functions dispersed, 1953] [Department of Agriculture]
BAE............ Bureau of American Ethnology [of the Smithsonian Institution]
BAE............ Milwaukee, WI [Location identifier FAA] (FAAL)
BAEA.......... British Actors' Equity Association [A union] (DCTA)
BAeA.......... British Aerobatic Association (PDAA)
BAeA.......... British Aerospace Australia
BAEA.......... British Atomic Energy Authority
BAEB.......... Bituminous and Aggregate Equipment Bureau (EA)
BAEC.......... Bovine Artery Endothelial Cell [Cytology]
BAEC.......... British Agricultural Export Council
BAEC.......... British Amateur Electronics Club (PDAA)
BAECE......... [The] British Association for Early Childhood Education
BA (Econ).... Bachelor of Arts (Economics)
BA Ed......... Bachelor of Art Education
BA Ed......... Bachelor of Arts in Education
BAEDS .... Best Alternative Equally Effective Data System
BA(Educ).... Bachelor of Arts (Education)
B Ae E .... Bachelor of Aeronautical Engineering
BAEE.......... Bachelor of Arts in Elementary Education (WGA)
BAEE.......... Benzoylarginine Ethyl Ester [Biochemistry]
BAEE.......... British Army Equipment Exhibition (MCD)
B Ae Eng ..... Bachelor of Aeronautical Engineering
BAEF.......... Belgian American Educational Foundation (EA)
BAeF.......... British Aerophilatelic Federation (DBA)
BAEF.......... British American Educational Foundation (EA)
B Aegypt..... Carmen de Bello Aegyptiaco sive Actiaco [of Ausonius] [Classical studies] (OCD)
BAEmb........ Buenos Aires Embotelladora [Commercial firm Associated Press] (SAG)
BaEn .... Barium Enema [Medicine] (MEDA)
Ba Enem...... Barium Enema [Medicine] (DAVI)
Ba enem...... Barium Enema [Medicine] (BABM)
BAEP.......... Brainstem Auditory Evoked Potential [Neurophysiology]
BAER .... Brainstem Auditory Evoked Response [Neurophysiology]
B/AERE .... British Atomic Energy Research Establishment
B Aero E ...... Bachelor of Aeronautical Engineering
B Ae S .... Bachelor of Aeronautical Science
B Ae Sc ...... Bachelor of Aeronautical Science
BaEV.......... Baboon Endogenous Virus
BAF............ Backup Alert Force
BAF............ Baffle [Regulating device] (KSC)
BAF............ Balance Fixture (MCD)
BAF............ Barrier Reef Resources [Vancouver Stock Exchange symbol]
BAF............ B-Cell Activating Factor [Immunology]
BAF............ Belacker [France] [Seismograph station code, US Geological Survey] (SEIS)
BAF............ Belgian Air Force
BAF............ Bioaccumulation Factor [Nuclear energy] (NRCH)
BAF............ Bottom of Active Fuel [Nuclear energy] (GFGA)
BAF............ Brith Abraham Foundation [Later, BZ] (EA)
BAF............ British Abrasive Federation (EAIO)
BAF............ British Air Ferries Ltd. [ICAO designator] (FAAC)
BAF............ British Air Force
BAF............ British Aqueous Fusion Process (MCD)
BAF............ Bunker Adjustment Factor [Business term]
BAF............ Burmese Air Force
BAF............ Westfield, MA [Location identifier FAA] (FAAL)
BAFA.......... British Accounting and Finance Association (PDAA)
BAFA.......... British Arts Festivals Association (DBA)
BAFA.......... Bul Bul Academy of Fine Arts [Dacca, Pakistan]
BAFATT....... British Association for Autogenic Training and Therapy (DBA)
BAFC.......... Bryan Adams Fan Club (EA)
BAFCOM ..... Basic Armed Forces Communication Plan
BAFE.......... British Approvals for Fire Equipment
BAFF.......... British Air Forces in France [World War II]
BAFFI......... British Association of Fitted Furniture Installers (DBA)
BAFG.......... British Air Forces in Greece [British military] (DMA)
BAFL.......... Baltic American Freedom League (EA)
BAFM.......... British Association in Forensic Medicine
BAFM.......... British Association of Friends of Museums
BAFMA........ British and Foreign Maritime Agencies (BARN)
BAFO.......... Base Accounting and Finance Office [Air Force] (AFM)
BAFO.......... Best and Final Offer [DoD] (MCD)
BAFO.......... British Air Forces of Occupation [Military]
BAFO.......... British Army Forces Overseas

BAFPE	Bay Area Functional Performance Evaluation [*Personality research*] [*Psychology*]
B Afr	Bellum Africum [*of Ausonius*] [*Classical studies*] (OCD)
BAFRA	British Aluminium Foil Rollers Association (BI)
BAFS	[*The*] British Academy of Forensic Sciences
BAFSM	Basic Artillery Force Simulation Model (MCD)
BAFSM	British Association of Feed Supplement Manufacturers (DBA)
BAFSV	British Armed Forces Special Vouchers [*British military*] (DMA)
BAFT	Bankers Association for Foreign Trade [*Washington, DC*] (EA)
BAFTA	British Academy of Film and Television Arts
BAFV	British Armed Forces Voucher [*Pronounced "baff"*] [*Paper money used on military bases*] (DSUE)
BAFVC	Bids Accepted for the Following Vacancies (FAAC)
B Ag	Bachelor of Agriculture
BAG	Bag All Garbage
Bag	Bagarottus dei Corradi da Bologna [*Flourished, 1200-42*] [*Authority cited in pre-1607 legal work*] (DSA)
BAG	Baggage (AFM)
BAG	Baguio [*Philippines*] [*Seismograph station code, US Geological Survey*] (SEIS)
BAG	Ballistic Attack Game
bag	Basque [*MARC language code Library of Congress*] (LCCP)
BAG	Battalion Artillery Group (MCD)
BAG	Behavioral Assessment Grid
BAG	Beta Absorption Gauge
BAG	Bibliographic and Grouping System [*A software program for iconography*] (NITA)
BAG	Bloc Africain de Guinee [*African Bloc of Guinea*]
BAG	Bonneville Power Acquisition Guide [*A publication*] (AAGC)
BAG	Book Arts Guild (EA)
BAG	British Artists in Glass
BAG	Broad Audit Guidelines
BAG	Buccoaxiogingival [*Dentistry*]
BAG	Bundesarbeitsgericht [*Federal Supreme Labour Court*] [*German*] (DLA)
BAG	Deutsche Ba Luftfahrtgesellschaft MBH [*Germany ICAO designator*] (FAAC)
BAGA	British Amateur Gymnastics Association
BAGAG	Research Station, Agriculture Canada [*Station de Recherches, Agriculture Canada*] Agassiz, British Columbia [*Library symbol National Library of Canada*] (NLC)
BAGB	Bicycle Association of Great Britain (EAIO)
BAGC	Business Alliance on Government Competition [*Defunct*] (EA)
BAGCA	British Association of Golf Course Architects (DBA)
BAGCD	British Association of Green Crop Driers (DBA)
Bag Ch Pr	Bagley's Practice at Chambers [*1834*] [*A publication*] (DLA)
BAGDA	British Advertising Gift Distributors' Association (DI)
B Ag E	Bachelor of Agricultural Engineering
BAgEc	Bachelor of Agricultural Economics (ADA)
B AG ECO	Bachelor of Agricultural Economics (WDAA)
Bag Eng Const	Bagehot. English Constitution [*8th ed.*] [*1904*] [*A publication*] (DLA)
Bag Engl Const	Bagehot. English Constitution [*8th ed.*] [*1904*] [*A publication*] (DLA)
BA(GenStud)	Bachelor of Arts in General Studies [*British*] (DBQ)
BAGG	Buffered Azide Glucose Glycerol [*Broth*] [*Microbiology*]
BAGI	Backscatter/Absorption Gas Imaging (MCD)
BAGL	BAB Holdings [*NASDAQ symbol*] (TTSB)
BAGL	BAB Holdings, Inc. [*NASDAQ symbol*] (SAG)
Bagl	Bagley's Reports [*16 California*] [*A publication*] (DLA)
Bagl & H	Bagley and Harman's Reports [*17-19 California*] [*A publication*] (DLA)
Bagl & Har	Bagley and Harman's Reports [*17-19 California*] [*A publication*] (DLA)
Bagl & Har (Cal)	Bagley and Harman's Reports [*17-19 California*] [*A publication*] (DLA)
Bagl (Cal)	Bagley's Reports [*16-19 California*] [*A publication*] (DLA)
BAGMA	British Agricultural and Garden Machinery Association
BAGNet	Bay Area Gigabit Network [*Computer science*] (TNIG)
BAGO	Bloque Antiguerrillero del Oriente [*Eastern Anti-Guerrilla Bloc*] [*El Salvador*] (PD)
BAgoEco	Bachelor of Agricultural Economics (NADA)
B Agr	Bachelor of Agriculture
BAGR	Bureau of Aeronautics General Representative [*Obsolete Navy*]
B Agr E	Bachelor of Agricultural Engineering
BAgrEcon	Bachelor of Agricultural Economics
BAGRED	Bureau of Aeronautics General Representative, Eastern District [*Obsolete Navy*]
BAgResEcon	Bachelor of Agricultural Research and Economics
BAgri	Bachelor of Agriculture
BAgric	Bachelor of Agriculture [*British*]
B Agr S	Bachelor of Agricultural Science
B Agr Sc	Bachelor of Agricultural Science
BAGRWD	Bureau of Aeronautics General Representative, Western District [*Obsolete Navy*]
BAGS	Bachelor of Arts in General Studies
BAGS	Bombing and Gunnery School [*British*] (DMA)
BAGS	Bullpup All-Weather Guidance System [*Naval Ordnance Systems Command*]
BAgSc	Bachelor of Agricultural Science (ADA)
BAgSci	Bachelor of Agricultural Science (BARN)
BAH	Amiri Flight-Bahrain [*ICAO designator*] (FAAC)
BAH	Bahamas (ROG)
BAH	Baha Resources Ltd. [*Vancouver Stock Exchange symbol*]
BAH	Bahrain Islands [*Airport symbol*] (OAG)

BAH	Barrette [*Hawaii*] [*Seismograph station code, US Geological Survey Closed*] (SEIS)
BAH	Basic Adaptive Hardware
Baha	Bahamas (VRA)
BAHA	British Activity Holiday Association (DBA)
BAHA	British Association of Hotel Accountants (DBA)
BAHC	Baptist Association of Hospital Chaplains (EA)
BAHC	Biospheric Aspects of the Hydrological Cycle [*Marine science*] (OSRA)
Bah LR	Bahamas Law Reports [*A publication*] (DLA)
BAHO	British Association of Helicopter Operators (PDAA)
BAHOH	British Association of the Hard of Hearing
BAHP	British Association of Homoeopathic Pharmacists
BAHPA	British Agricultural and Horticultural Plastics Association (PDAA)
BAHR	Bahrain
Bahr	Bahrain (VRA)
BAH Re	Bachelor of Arts in Human Relations
BAHRGNY	Bar Association for Human Rights of Greater New York (EA)
BAHS	British Agricultural History Society
BAHS	British-Australian Heritage Society
BAHT	Basic Attack Helicopter Team [*Army*] (RDA)
BAHVS	British Association of Homoeopathic Veterinary Surgeons
BAI	Baccalaureus in Arte Ingeniaria [*Bachelor of Engineering*] (EY)
BAI	Backup Aerospace Vehicle [*or Aircraft*] Inventory
BA I	Bahama Islands (WDAA)
BAI	Baika Women's College [*EDUCATSS*] [*UTLAS symbol*]
BAI	Baikonur [*Satellite launch complex*] [*Former USSR*]
Bai	Bailey's Law Reports [*South Carolina*] [*A publication*] (DLA)
BAI	Baird-Associates, Inc. (MCD)
BAI	Balch Institute Library, Philadelphia, PA [*OCLC symbol*] (OCLC)
BAI	Bank Administration Institute (EA)
BAI	Barair SA [*Spain ICAO designator*] (FAAC)
BAI	Bari [*Italy*] [*Seismograph station code, US Geological Survey Closed*] (SEIS)
BAI	Barometric Altitude Indicator (NASA)
BAI	Basal Area Increment [*Forestry*]
BAI	Base Activation Instruction
BAI	Basic Area of Interest [*Army*] (ADDR)
BAI	Battlefield Air Interdiction (MCD)
BAI	Bearing Altitude Indicator [*Aerospace*]
BAI	Behavior Analysis in Ireland (EAIO)
BAI	Bell Adjustment Inventory (EDAC)
BAI	Bentonite Agglutination Inhibition (OA)
BAI	Blue Anchor, Inc. [*An association*] (EA)
BAI	Bnos Agudath Israel (EA)
BAI	Boeing Airborne Instrumentation Equipment (SAA)
BAI	Book Association of Ireland (BARN)
BAI	Bureau of Animal Industry [*Department of Agriculture*]
BAIB	Bailey Corp. [*NASDAQ symbol*] (CTT)
BAIB	Beta-Aminoisobutyric Acid (MAE)
BAIC	Binary Asymmetric Independent Channel
BAIC	British Aviation Insurance Co. (AIA)
BAIC	Bureau of Agricultural and Industrial Chemistry [*Department of Agriculture*]
BAICF	Bile Acid-Independent Canalicular Fraction [*Medicine*]
BAICO	Bendix Atlantic Inflator Co. [*Automotive industry supplier*]
BAID	Black Americans Information Directory [*A publication*]
BAID	Boolean Array Identifier [*Mathematics*]
BAIE	British Association of Industrial Editors (EAIO)
Bai Eq	Bailey's Equity Reports [*South Carolina*] [*A publication*] (DLA)
BAIF	Bile Acid-Independent Fraction [*Medicine*]
BAII	Banque Arabe et Internationale d'Investissement [*France*]
BAIID	Breath Alcohol Ignition Interlock Device [*Automotive safety*]
Bail	Bailey's Law Reports [*South Carolina*] [*A publication*] (DLA)
BAIL	Boundary and Interior Layer (MCD)
Bail CC	Bail Court Cases [*A publication*]
Bail CC	Lowndes and Maxwell's English Bail Court Cases [*1852-54*] [*A publication*] (DLA)
Bail Cr Rep	Lowndes and Maxwell's English Bail Court Cases [*1852-54*] [*A publication*] (DLA)
Bail Ct Cas	Lowndes and Maxwell's English Bail Court Cases [*1852-54*] [*A publication*] (DLA)
Bail Ct R	Bail Court Reports (Saunders and Cole) [*England*] [*A publication*] (DLA)
Bail Ct Rep	Lowndes and Maxwell's English Bail Court Cases [*1852-54*] [*A publication*] (DLA)
Bail Ct Rep	Saunders and Cole's English Bail Court Reports [*1846-48*] [*A publication*] (DLA)
Baild	Baildon's Select Cases in Chancery [*Selden Society Publication, Vol. 10*] [*A publication*] (DLA)
Bail Dig	Bailey's North Carolina Digest [*A publication*] (DLA)
Bail Eq	Bailey's Equity Reports [*South Carolina*] [*A publication*] (DLA)
Bail Eq (SC)	Bailey's Equity Reports [*South Carolina*] [*A publication*] (DLA)
Bailey	Bailey Corp. [*Associated Press*] (SAG)
Bailey	Bailey's Equity Reports [*South Carolina*] [*A publication*] (DLA)
Bailey	Bailey's Law Reports [*South Carolina*] [*A publication*] (DLA)
Bailey Ch	Bailey's Chancery Reports [*South Carolina*] [*A publication*] (DLA)
Bailey Dict	Nathan Bailey's English Dictionary [*A publication*] (DLA)
Bailey Eq	Bailey's Equity Reports, South Carolina Court of Appeals [*A publication*] (DLA)
Bailey Mast Liab	Bailey's Law of Master's Liability for Injuries to Servant [*A publication*] (DLA)
Bail L	Bailey's Law Reports [*South Carolina*] [*A publication*] (DLA)
Baill Dig	Baillie's Digest of Mohammedan Law [*A publication*] (DLA)
Baill Inher	Baillie's Mohammedan Law of Inheritance [*A publication*] (DLA)

Bail L (SC)... Bailey's Law Reports [*South Carolina*] [*A publication*] (DLA)
Bailm......... Bailment [*Legal term*] (DLA)
BAIMR........ United States Bureau of Animal Industry. Monthly Record [*A publication*] (DLA)
BA in A & Sci... Bachelor of Arts in Arts and Sciences
BA in BA...... Bachelor of Arts in Business Administration
BA in B & E... Bachelor of Arts in Business and Economics
Bainb M & M... Bainbridge on Mines and Minerals [*A publication*] (DLA)
Bainb Mines... Bainbridge on Mines and Minerals [*A publication*] (DLA)
BA in Cer A... Bachelor of Arts in Ceramic Art
BA in E & B... Bachelor of Arts in Economics and Business
BA in E Ed... Bachelor of Arts in Elementary Education
BA(InfoMan)... Bachelor of Arts (Information Management)
BA in J....... Bachelor of Arts in Journalism
BA in M Ed... Bachelor of Arts in Music Education
BA in Rel Ed... Bachelor of Arts in Religious Education
BAINS......... Basic Advanced Integrated Navigation System
BA in Sp..... Bachelor of Arts in Speech
BA in Text... Bachelor of Science in Textiles
BAIO........... Brigade Artillery Intelligence Officer [*Military British*]
BAIR........... Breathing Air (NASA)
BAIR........... British Airports Information Retrieval [*System*]
BAIR........... Bureau for the Advancement of Independent Retailing (EA)
BAIR........... Bureau of Aeronautics Industrial Reserve [*Obsolete Navy*]
Bairnco...... Bairnco Corp. [*Associated Press*] (SAG)
BAIS........... Bachelor of Arts in Information Systems
Ba Is........ Bahama Islands (BARN)
BAIS........... Battlefield Airborne Illumination System (CINC)
BAIS........... British Association for Irish Studies
BAIS........... Bulletin Articles Information Subsystem [*Computer science*]
BAISEMP..... Battlefield Automation Interoperability System Engineering Management Plan [*Army*]
BAIT........... Bacterial Automated Identification Technique
BAIT........... Black Awareness in Television (EA)
BAIX........... Buckeye Airways International [*Air carrier designation symbol*]
BAJ........... Bachelor of Arts in Journalism
BAJ........... Baker Aviation, Inc. [*ICAO designator*] (FAAC)
BAJ........... Bali [*Papua New Guinea*] [*Airport symbol*] (OAG)
BAJ........... Sterling, CO [*Location identifier FAA*] (FAAL)
BAJI........... Basic Approved Jury Instructions (HGAA)
B A Jour... Bachelor of Arts in Journalism (BARN)
BAJSR........ Board of Australian Journals of Scientific Research
BAK........... Backer Resources [*Vancouver Stock Exchange symbol*]
BAK........... Backup File [*Computer science*]
BAK........... Baker [*Diocesan abbreviation*] [*Oregon*] (TOCD)
BAK........... Bakery
BAK........... Baku [*Former USSR Seismograph station code, US Geological Survey*] (SEIS)
BAK........... Barrier Arresting Kit (PDAA)
bak........... Bashkir [*MARC language code Library of Congress*] (LCCP)
BAK........... Binary Adaptation Kit [*Computer science*] (PCM)
BAK........... Blackhawk Airways, Inc. [*ICAO designator*] (FAAC)
BAK........... British Cargo Ship
BAK........... Broadband Antenna Kit
BAK........... Bundesaufsichtsamt fur das Kreditwesen [*Federal Supervisory Office for Credit*] [*Germany*]
BAK........... Clinicorp, Inc. [*AMEX symbol*] (SPSG)
BAK........... Columbus, IN [*Location identifier FAA*] (FAAL)
Bak Bur... Baker on the Law Relating to Burials [*A publication*] (DLA)
Bak Corp... Baker's New York Corporation Laws [*A publication*] (DLA)
BAKE........... Greenberg(William Jr)Desserts [*NASDAQ symbol*] (TTSB)
Baker........... Baker [*Michael*] Corp. [*Associated Press*] (SAG)
BakerJ........ Baker [*J.*], Inc. [*Associated Press*] (SAG)
Baker Quar... Baker's Law of Quarantine [*A publication*] (DLA)
BAK file... Backup File (CDE)
Bak Health L... Baker's Health Laws [*A publication*] (DLA)
Bak Highw... Baker's Law of Highways [*A publication*] (DLA)
BakrF........ Baker, Fentress & Co. [*Associated Press*] (SAG)
BakrHu..... Baker Hughes, Inc. [*Associated Press*] (SAG)
BAKS........... Barracks
BAKUP........ Banking Users' Group [*British*]
bal........... Balance [*Medicine*] (DAVI)
BAL........... Balance [*Accounting*] (AFM)
bal........... Balance [*Bookkeeping*] (ODBW)
BAL........... Balance
Bal........... Balasingham's Reports [*Ceylon*] [*A publication*] (DLA)
BAL........... Balcony (WDAA)
BAL........... Balcor Resources Corp. [*Vancouver Stock Exchange symbol*]
Bal........... Baldus de Ubaldis [*Deceased, 1400*] [*Authority cited in pre-1607 legal work*] (DSA)
BAL........... Ballistic [*or Ballistics*] (MSA)
Bal........... Balmoral Shoe [*Orthosis*]
BAL........... Balsamic [*Mild, Healing*] [*Medicine*] (ROG)
BAL........... Baltimore [*Diocesan abbreviation*] [*Maryland*] (TOCD)
bal........... Baluchi [*MARC language code Library of Congress*] (LCCP)
BAL........... Base Allowance List (MUGU)
BAL........... Base Authorization List
BAL........... Basic Assembly Language [*Programming language*] [*Sperry UNIVAC*] [*Computer science*]
BAL........... Benzaldehyde [*Organic chemistry*]
BAL........... Berul Associates Ltd. [*Information service or system*] (IID)
BAL L (SC)... Bibliography of American Literature [*A publication*]
BAL........... Bioartificial Liver
BAL........... Biological Assessment Laboratory
BAL........... Blood Alcohol Level [*Medicine*]

BAL........... Boat Allowance List [*Navy*] (CAAL)
BAL........... Bohn's Artist's Library [*A publication*]
BAL........... Bonanza Airlines (MHDB)
BAL........... Branch and Link (CDE)
BAL........... Britannia Airways Ltd. [*British ICAO designator*] (FAAC)
BAL........... British Anti-Lewisite [*Also, DMP: Dimercapto, propanol*] [*Detoxicant*]
BAL........... British Architectural Library [*Royal Institute of British Architects*] [*Information service or system*] (IID)
BAL........... Broad Absorption Line [*Quasar*] [*Astrophysics*]
BAL........... Bronchoalveolar Lavage [*Medicine*]
BAL........... Business Application Language
BAL........... Butler Area Librarians [*Library network*]
BAL........... University of Baltimore, Baltimore, MD [*OCLC symbol*] (OCLC)
BALAD........ Bleachable Absorber LASER Amplifier and Detector
BA(Lan)..... Bachelor of Languages [*British*] (DBQ)
BALANCE.... Basic and Logically Applied Norms - Civil Engineering (AFM)
Bal Ann Codes... Ballinger's Annotated Codes and Statutes [*Washington*] [*A publication*] (DLA)
BALARE...... Buoyancy-Actuated Launch and Retrieval Elevator (PDAA)
BAL ARENAE... Balneum Arenae [*Sand Bath*] [*Medicine*]
Balas........... Balasingham's Supreme Court Reports [*Ceylon*] [*A publication*] (DLA)
BALAS........ Business Association of Latin American Studies (EA)
Balasingham Rep... Balasingham's Reports of Cases [*Ceylon*] [*A publication*] (ILCA)
Balas NC.... Balasingham's Notes of Cases [*Ceylon*] [*A publication*] (DLA)
Balas RC.... Balasingham's Reports of Cases [*1904-09*] [*Ceylon*] [*A publication*] (DLA)
BALAST...... Balloon Astronomy
BA(Law)..... Bachelor of Arts in Law
BALB........... Binaural Alternate Loudness Balance Test (MAE)
Balb........... Pro Balbo [*of Cicero*] [*Classical studies*] (OCD)
BALC........... Balcony [*Classified advertising*] (ADA)
BALC........... Brotherhood of the American Lutheran Church [*Later, American Lutheran Church Men*] (EA)
BALCE........ Balance [*Accounting*] (ROG)
Balchem..... Balchem Corp. [*Associated Press*] (SAG)
Bald........... Baldasseroni on Maritime Law [*A publication*] (DLA)
Bald........... Baldus (Commentator on the Code) [*A publication*] (DLA)
Bald........... Baldwin's United States Circuit Court Reports [*A publication*] (DLA)
Bald App..... Appendix to 11 Peters, United States Reports [*A publication*] (DLA)
Bald App 11 Pet... Baldwin. Appendix to 11 Peters [*A publication*] (DLA)
BALDAS...... Ballistic Data Acquisition System (MCD)
Bald Bank... Baldwin. Law of Bankruptcy [*11th ed.*] [*1915*] [*A publication*] (DLA)
baldc........... Baldachino (VRA)
Bald CC...... Baldasseroni on Maritime Law [*A publication*] (DLA)
Bald CC...... Baldus (Commentator on the Code) [*A publication*] (DLA)
Bald CC...... Baldwin's United States Circuit Court Reports [*A publication*] (DLA)
Bald Cir C.... Baldwin's United States Circuit Court Reports [*A publication*] (DLA)
Bald Conn Dig... Baldwin's Connecticut Digest [*A publication*] (DLA)
Bald Const... Baldwin's View of the United States Constitution with Opinions [*A publication*] (DLA)
Baldev PC.... Baldeva Ram Dave. Privy Council Judgment [*India*] [*A publication*] (DLA)
BALDICER... Balanced Diet Certificates [*Economics simulation game*]
BaldLy........ Baldwin & Lyons, Inc. [*Associated Press*] (SAG)
BaldLyB..... Baldwin & Lyons, Inc. [*Associated Press*] (SAG)
Bald Novell... Baldus Bartolinus Novellus [*Deceased, 1490*] [*Authority cited in pre-1607 legal work*] (DSA)
BALDNY...... Ballistic Density
Bald Op...... Baldwin's View of the United States Constitution with Opinions [*A publication*] (DLA)
Baldor......... Baldor Electric Co. [*Associated Press*] (SAG)
Bald Pat Cas... Baldwin's Patent, Copyright, Trade-Mark Cases [*A publication*] (DLA)
Bald Pat Etc Cas... Baldwin's Patent, Copyright, Trade-Mark Cases [*A publication*] (DLA)
BaldPia....... Baldwin Piano & Organ Co. [*Associated Press*] (SAG)
Bald Rep..... Baldwin's United States Circuit Court Reports [*A publication*] (DLA)
Bald US Sup Ct Rep... United States Supreme Court Reports, Photo Reproduction Set by Baldwin [*A publication*] (DLA)
Baldw......... Baldwin's United States Circuit Court Reports [*A publication*] (DLA)
Baldw......... Baldwin Technology Corp. [*Associated Press*] (SAG)
Baldw Dig.... Baldwin's Connecticut Digest [*A publication*] (DLA)
Baldwin..... Baldwin on Bankruptcy [*A publication*] (DLA)
Baldwin's CC US Rep... Baldwin's United States Circuit Court Reports [*A publication*] (DLA)
Baldwin's Rep... Baldwin's United States Circuit Court Reports [*A publication*] (DLA)
BaldwLy..... Baldwin & Lyons, Inc. [*Associated Press*] (SAG)
BALEAP........ British Association of Lecturers in English for Academic Purposes (AIE)
BA(LeisureStud)... Bachelor of Arts (Leisure Studies)
B Alex........ Bellum Alexandrinum [*of Ausonius*] [*Classical studies*] (OCD)
Balf............. Balfour's Practice Laws of Scotland [*A publication*] (DLA)
BALF........... Blue Army of Our Lady of Fatima [*Later, World Apostolate of Fatima - WAF*] (EA)
BALF........... Bronchoalveolar Lavage Fluid [*Medicine*]
BALF........... Bronchoalveolar Lavage Fluid
Balf Pr....... Balfour's Practice Laws of Scotland [*A publication*] (DLA)
BALFRAN..... Balanced Force Requirements Analysis (MCD)
BALGOL....... Burroughs Algebraic Compiler (IEEE)
BALH........... British Association for Local History
BALI........... British Association of Landscape Industries
BALIA........... Biotin-Avidin-Linked Immunoassay [*Immunochemistry*]

BALIB.......... Banque Arabe-Libyenne-Burkinabe pour le Commerce et le Developpement (EY)
BA(LibSc) .... Bachelor of Arts (Library Science)
BALIC......... Board of Action on Letter of Intent Conversion [Navy]
BAL IS .... Balearic Islands
BALIS.......... Bay Area Library and Information System [Library network]
BALIS.......... Bayerisches Landwirtschaftliches Informationssystem [Bavarian Agricultural Information System] [Databank] [Germany] (IID)
Bal Isls....... Balearic Islands
BALITAC ...... Basic Literal Automatic Coding
Ball............ Ballard's Somerton Court Rolls [Oxford Archaeological Society, No. 50] [England] [A publication] (DLA)
BALL.......... Ballast (KSC)
Ball........... Ball Corp. [Associated Press] (SAG)
Ball........... Balliol College [Oxford, England] (BARN)
BALL.......... Ballistic (AFM)
B-ALL......... B-Cell Acute Lymphoblastic Leukemia [Medicine]
BALLAD .... Ballistic LORAN Assist Device
Ball & B ..... Ball and Beatty's Irish Chancery Reports [1807-14] [A publication] (DLA)
Ball & Beatty... Ball and Beatty's Irish Chancery Reports [1807-14] [A publication] (DLA)
Ball & B (Ir)... Ball and Beatty's Irish Chancery Reports [1807-14] [A publication] (DLA)
Ballard........ Ballard Medical Products [Associated Press] (SAG)
Ballard........ Ballard Power Systems, Inc. [Associated Press] (SAG)
BA/LLB........ Bachelor of Arts/Bachelor of Laws (ADA)
Ball Banks ... Ball on National Banks [A publication] (DLA)
Ball Conv..... Ball's Popular Conveyancer [A publication] (DLA)
Ball Dig ...... Ball's Digest of the Common Law [A publication] (DLA)
Ballentine.... Ballentine's Law Dictionary [A publication] (DLA)
Ballentine's Law Dict... Ballentine's Self Pronouncing Law Dictionary [A publication] (DLA)
Ball Ind....... Ball's Index to Irish Statutes [A publication] (DLA)
Ballinger's Ann Codes & St... Ballinger's Annotated Codes and Statutes [Washington] [A publication] (DLA)
Ball Lim ...... Ballantine. Statute of Limitations [1810] [A publication] (DLA)
Ballntyn...... Ballantyne of Omaha, Inc. [Associated Press] (SAG)
BALLOTS ...... Bibliographic Automation of Large Library Operations Using a Time-Sharing System [Later, RLIN] [Stanford University]
Ball St Guide... Ball's Student Guide to the Bar [A publication] (DLA)
Ball St U ..... Ball State University (GAGS)
BALLT......... Ballast Tube (IAA)
BALLUTE...... Balloon Parachute
BALLWIN ..... Ballistic Wind
BallyEnt...... Bally Entertainment Corp. [Formerly, Bally Manufacturing] [Associated Press] (SAG)
Ballys .... Ballys Grand, Inc. [Associated Press] (SAG)
BallysGr...... Ballys Grand, Inc. [Associated Press] (SAG)
BallyTot...... Bally Total Fitness Holding Corp. [Associated Press] (SAG)
BALM......... Block and List Manipulator [Computer science] (CSR)
BAL MAR..... Balneum Mariae [Salt-Water Bath] [Medicine]
BALMI........ Ballistic Missile (MUGU)
BALN .... Balneum [Bath] [Medicine] (ROG)
BALN CAL .... Balneum Calidum [Warm Bath] [Medicine] (ROG)
BALNCNG .... Balancing
BALNET....... Balancing Network (IAA)
Bal Notes..... Balasingham's Notes of Cases [Ceylon] [A publication] (ILCA)
Bal Novel.... Baldus Bartolinus Novellus [Deceased, 1490] [Authority cited in pre-1607 legal work] (DSA)
BALOC .... Balance Location
BALOE .... British-American Light Opera Exchange
BALOG........ Base Logistical Command
BALOP .... Balopticon (IEEE)
balop .... Balopticon [An opaque projector] (WDMC)
B Alp .... Basses-Alpes [Lower Alps] [French] (BARN)
BALPA .... Balance of Payments [Accounting]
BALPA .... British Airline Pilots Association
Bal Pak....... Baluchistan, Pakistan (ILCA)
BALPAY ...... International Balance of Payments [Economics simulation game]
Bal Pay't Rep... Balance of Payments Report [A publication] (DLA)
BALPM........ British Association of Lithographic Plate Manufacturers (DBA)
BALPPA .... British Association of Leisure Parks, Piers, and Attractions (DBA)
BALPRO....... Balance of Payments Program (AAGC)
Bal RD........ Baldeva Ram Dave. Privy Council Judgment [India] [A publication] (DLA)
Bal Rep ...... Balasingham's Reports of Cases [Ceylon] [A publication] (ILCA)
BALRHEO..... Balancing Rheostat
BALS.......... Bachelor of Arts in Library Science (WDAA)
BALS.......... Balancing Set (IEEE)
BALS.......... Balsamum [Balsam] [Pharmacy]
BALS.......... Blind Approach Landing System [Aviation]
BALSA .... Black American Law Students Association (EA)
BALSA .... Brown Algorithm Simulator and Animator [Framework for software construction] [Brown University] (NITA)
BALSPACON... Balance of Space to Space Control Agencies
balstr.......... Balustrade (VRA)
BALT.......... Baltimore [Maryland]
BALT.......... Barometric Altitude (MCD)
BALT.......... British Association for Language Teaching
BALT.......... Bronchus Associated Lymphoid Tissue
BALTAP........ Allied Forces Baltic Approaches [NATO]
Balt C Rep... Baltimore City Reports [A publication] (DLA)
Baltek .... Baltek Corp. [Associated Press] (SAG)
BaltGE .... Baltimore Gas & Electric Co. [Associated Press] (SAG)

BALTHUM .... Balloon Temperature and Humidity [Sonde] [Meteorology]
Baltic .... Baltic International USA, Inc. [Associated Press] (SAG)
BalticInt....... Baltic International USA, Inc. [Associated Press] (SAG)
Balt LT...... Baltimore Law Transcript [A publication] (DLA)
Balt L Tr ..... Baltimore Law Transcript [A publication] (DLA)
BALTO......... Baltimore [Maryland]
BALTR .... Balancing Transformer (IAA)
BALTRAC ..... Ballastable Tractor
BALUN .... Balanced-to-Unbalanced Line Transformer [Telecommunications] (TEL)
BALUN .... Balance-to-Unbalance Network [Telecommunications]
BALUN .... Balancing Unit [Radio]
BAL VAP ..... Balneum Vaporis [Vapor Bath] [Medicine]
bal wd .... Balsa Wood (VRA)
BALWND ...... Ballistic Wind
BalyGm....... Bally Gaming International Corp. [Associated Press] (SAG)
BAM .... Bachelor of Applied Mathematics
BAM .... Bachelor of Arts in Music
BAM .... Bachelor of Ayurvedic Medicine
BAM .... Bacteriological Analytical Manual [A publication]
BAM .... Baikal-Amur Mainline [USSR railroad in Siberia]
BAM .... Ballistic Advanced Missile (MCD)
bam .... Bambara [MARC language code Library of Congress] (LCCP)
BAM .... Band Approximation Method (MCD)
BaM .... Barium Meal [Medicine]
BAM .... Base Automotive Maintenance
BAM .... Basic Access Method [Computer science]
BAM .... Basic and Applied Myology [A publication]
BAM .... Battlefield Automation Management (MCD)
BAM .... Battle Mountain [Nevada] [Airport symbol Obsolete] (OAG)
BAM .... Belize Action Movement (PD)
Bam .... Benzamide (DMAA)
BAM .... Bidirectional Associative Memory [Computer science]
BAM .... Bikers Against Manslaughter (EA)
BAM .... Binary Angular Measurement [Military] (CAAL)
BAM .... Bituminous Aggregate Mixture (OA)
BAM .... Black Action Movement
BAM .... Block Access Method [Computer science]
BAM .... Block Allocation Map (IAA)
BAM .... Block Availability Map (IAA)
BaM .... Boite-a-Musique, Paris [Record label] [France]
BaM .... Book About Me [Psychological testing]
BAM .... Booker Aircraft Museum [Wycombe Air Park, Booker, Buckinghamshire, England]
BAM .... Bowling Apparel Manufacturers of America (EA)
BAM .... Bradley Aberration Method
BAM .... Brewster Angle Microscopy
BAM .... British Air Ministry
BAM .... British Association of Myasthenics (DBA)
BAM .... Broad Anatomy Marine [See also HAM] [Slang term for female marines] [Bowdlerized version]
BAM .... Broadcasting Amplitude Modulation
BAM .... Brooklyn Academy of Music
BAM .... Brothers to All Men [An association]
BAM .... Builders Association of Minnesota (SRA)
BAM .... Builders Association of Missouri (SRA)
BAM .... Bulk Airmail
BAM .... Bundesanstalt fuer Materialforschung und -Pruefung [Federal Institute for Materials Research and Testing] [Database producer] [Germany Information retrieval] (IID)
BAM .... Bundesanstalt fuer Materialprufung Unter den Eichen [International Association for Structural Mechanics in Reactor Technology] (EAIO)
BAM .... Bureau of Aviation Medicine (KSC)
BAM .... Bus Access Module
BAM .... Bus Arbitration Module [Motorola, Inc.]
BAM .... Business Air Services (Toronto) Ltd. [Canada ICAO designator] (FAAC)
BAM .... Canadian Bureau for the Advancement of Music (AC)
BAM .... Matsqui-Sumas-Abbotsford Museum, Abbotsford, British Columbia [Library symbol National Library of Canada] (NLC)
BAm .... Mean Brachial Artery [Pressure] [Cardiology] (DAVI)
BAMA.......... Boys and Young Men's Apparel Manufacturers Association [Defunct] (EA)
BAMA .... British Aerosol Manufacturers Association
BAMA .... British Army Motoring Association [British military] (DMA)
BAMA .... British Automobile Manufacturers Association (EA)
BAMA .... Brotherhood Association of Military Airmen
BAMAC .... British Automobile Manufacturers Association in Canada (PDAA)
BAMAGAT..... Block-a-Matic, Block-a-Gram, and Block-a-Text (SAA)
BAMB.......... Bureau of Administrative Management and Budget [United Nations Development Program]
BAMBAM ..... Bookline Alert: Missing Books and Manuscripts [Information service or system A publication]
Bamber........ Report of Mining Cases Decided by the Railway and Canal Commission [A publication] (DLA)
BAMBI .... Ballistic Missile Bombardment [or Boost] Interceptor [Military]
BAMBI .... Bayesian Analysis Modified by Inspection [Computer science]
BAMBY .... Bran and Multiple Vitamins and Minerals, B-Complex Vitamins, and Yogurt [A nutritional plan]
BAMC.......... Brooke Army Medical Center
BAMCO .... British Air Ministry Control Office
BAMD.......... Bis(acetatomercurimethyl)dioxane [Organic chemistry]
BAME.......... Benzoylarginine Methyl Ester [Biochemistry]

BAMEO .... Base Aircraft Maintenance and Engineering Organization [*Canadian Navy*]
BAMES........ Banque Malgache d'Escompte et de Credit [*Malagasy Discount and Credit Bank*] (AF)
BAMF.......... Bundesamt fuer Militarflugplatze [*Switzerland ICAO designator*] (FAAC)
BAMG .... Browning Aircraft Machine Gun
BAMH.......... [*The*] Burnaby Association for the Mentally Handicapped
BAMI........... Brothers to All Men International (EA)
BAMIRAC..... Ballistic Missile Radiation Analysis Center
BAMIS .... Banque al-Baraka Mauritanienne Islamique (EY)
BAMM......... Balloon Altitude Mosaic Measurements (MCD)
BAMM......... Basic Acrylic Monomer Manufacturers Association (EA)
BAMM......... Books-A-Million [*NASDAQ symbol*] (TTSB)
BAMM......... Books A Million, Inc. [*NASDAQ symbol*] (SAG)
BAMM......... British Association of Manipulative Medicine
BAMN .... By Any Means Necessary
BAMO .... Bureau of Aeronautics Material Officer [*Obsolete Navy*]
BAMON .... Bleomycin, Adriamycin, Methotrexate, Oncovin [*Vincristine*], Nitrogen mustard [*Antineoplastic drug regimen*]
BAMOS .... Batch Processing Multilanguage Operating System [*Computer science*] (IAA)
BAMP.......... Bampton [*England*]
BAMP.......... Basic Analysis and Mapping Program (DNAB)
BAMP.......... Battlefield Automation Management Plan [*or Program*] (MCD)
BAMP.......... Build Ada Main Program [*Computer science*]
BAMPA .... British Aeromedical Practitioners Association (DBA)
BAMR .... Bureau of Aeronautics Maintenance Representative [*Obsolete Navy*]
BA Mrch ..... BA Merchant Services, Inc. [*Associated Press*] (SAG)
BAMRG .... British Agricultural Marketing Research Group
BAMRO .... Bureau of Aeronautics Maintenance Repair Officer [*Obsolete Navy*]
BAMRRO...... Bureau of Aeronautics Maintenance Resident Representative Office [*Obsolete Navy*]
BAMS .... Band Archive Management Service (IAA)
BAMS.......... Base Automated Mobility System (MCD)
BAMS.......... Bell Atlantic Mobile Systems [*Telecommunications*]
BAMS.......... British Air Mail Society (BI)
BAMS.......... British American Minesweeper [*British military*] (DMA)
BAMS.......... British Art Medal Society (DBA)
BAMS.......... Broadcast to Allied Merchant Ships
BAMSL......... Bar Association of Metropolitan St. Louis. Bankruptcy Reporter [*A publication*] (DLA)
BAMSR .... British Admiralty Maintenance and Supply Representative
BAMT.......... Boric Acid Mix Tank [*Nuclear energy*] (NRCH)
BAMTM....... British Association of Machine Tool Merchants, Inc. (BI)
BA (Mus).... Bachelor of Arts (Music)
BAMusEd.... Bachelor of Arts in Music Education (BARN)
BAMV.......... Bamboo Mosaic Virus [*Plant pathology*]
BAMW .... British Association of Meat Wholesalers Ltd. (BI)
BAN .... Air Ban Ltd. [*Bulgaria*] [*FAA designator*] (FAAC)
BAN .... Andover Newton Theological School, Newton Center, MA [*OCLC symbol*] (OCLC)
BAN .... Banbury [*British depot code*]
Ban .... Bandinus Familiatus de Pisa [*Deceased, 1218*] [*Authority cited in pre-1607 legal work*] (DSA)
BAN .... Banff [*Alberta*] [*Seismograph station code, US Geological Survey Closed*] (SEIS)
BAN .... Bangor [*City in Wales*] (ROG)
BAN .... Banished (ROG)
BAN .... Banister Foundation [*Formerly, Banister, Inc.*] [*AMEX symbol*] (SPSG)
Ban .... Banner [*Record label*]
BAN .... Base Activation Notice
BAN .... Best Asymptotically Normal [*Estimates*] [*Econometrics*]
BAN .... Bionics Adaptive Network
BAN .... Black Audio Network, Inc. (NTCM)
BAN .... Blacks Against Nukes (EA)
BAN .... Bond Anticipation Note [*Banking*]
BAN .... British American Bank Note, Inc. [*Toronto Stock Exchange symbol Vancouver Stock Exchange symbol*]
BAN .... British Approved Name
BAN .... British Association of Neurologists (DI)
BAN .... Budget Allocation Notice (MCD)
BANA .... Benzoylargininenaphthylamide
BANA .... Braille Authority of North America (EA)
BANAIM ...... Bureau d'Amenagement du Nouvel Aeroport International de Montreal [*New Montreal International Airport Project Office - NMIAPO*] [*Canada*]
Banamex ..... Banco Nacional de Mexico [*National Bank of Mexico*]
BANANA....... Build Absolutely Nothing Anywhere Near Anything [*Facetious successor to NIMBY*]
BANANAS .... Benevolent Association for Naming All Nonentities After Schools
Ban & A...... Banning and Arden's Patent Cases [*United States*] [*A publication*] (DLA)
Banaras LJ... Banaras Law Journal [*India*] [*A publication*] (DLA)
BANAVAVNOFFSCOL... Basic Naval Aviation Officers School (DNAB)
Banbury (Eng)... Banbury. English Exchequer Reports [*145 English Reprint*] [*A publication*] (DLA)
BANC .... BankAtlantic Bancorp'B' [*NASDAQ symbol*] (TTSB)
BANC .... BankAtlantic Bancorp, Inc. [*NASDAQ symbol*] (SAG)
BANC .... BankcAtlantic Bancorp, Inc. [*NASDAQ symbol*] (SAG)
BANC .... Brick Association of North Carolina (SRA)
BANC .... British Association of Nature Conservationists
BANCA .... BankAtlantic Bancorp'A' [*NASDAQ symbol*] (TTSB)
BANCA .... Bank Atlantic Bancorp, Inc. [*NASDAQ symbol*] (SAG)

Banca Borsa Tit Cred... Banca, Borsa, e Titoli di Credito [*A publication*] (ILCA)
Bancins........ Bancinsurance Corp. [*Associated Press*] (SAG)
BANCOBU ... Banque Commerciale du Burundi (EY)
BANCOLAT.. Banco de Latinoamerica, SA [*Panama*] (EY)
BancOne ...... Banc One Corp. [*Associated Press*] (SAG)
BANCS .... Bell Administrative Network Communications System [*Telecommunications*] (ACRL)
BANCS .... Bell Administrative Network Communication System [*Telecommunications*] (TEL)
BANC SUP .. Bancus Superior [*King's Bench*] [*British Legal term*] (ROG)
Banctec....... Banctec, Inc. [*Associated Press*] (SAG)
BAND .... Bandelier National Monument
Band .... Bandinus Familiatus de Pisa [*Deceased, 1218*] [*Authority cited in pre-1607 legal work*] (DSA)
BAND .... Bandolier
BAND .... Book Action for Nuclear Disarmament [*British*]
BAND .... Burlington Association for Nuclear Disarmament (AC)
B & A......... Baltimore & Annapolis Railroad Co. (IIA)
B & A......... Bangor & Aroostook Railroad Co. (IIA)
B & A......... Banning and Arden's Patent Reports [*United States*] [*A publication*] (DLA)
B & A.......... Barnewall and Adolphus' English King's Bench Reports [*109-110 English Reprint*] [*1830-34*] [*A publication*] (DLA)
B & A.......... Barnewall and Alderson's English King's Bench Reports [*1817-22*] [*A publication*] (DLA)
B & A.......... Barron and Arnold's English Election Cases [*1843-46*] [*A publication*] (DLA)
B & A.......... Barron and Austin's English Election Cases [*1842*] [*A publication*] (DLA)
B & A.......... Barros & Associates Ltd. [*Information service or system*] (IID)
B&A.......... Bernstein & Associates [*Computer science*]
B & A.......... Bid and Asked [*Investment term*]
B & A.......... Boat and Aircraft (CAAL)
B & A.......... Bond and Allotment (DNAB)
B & A.......... Boston & Albany Railroad
B & Ad........ Barnewall and Adolphus' English King's Bench Reports [*109-110 English Reprint*] [*1830-34*] [*A publication*] (DLA)
Bandag........ Bandag, Inc. [*Associated Press Associated Press*] (SAG)
B & Ald....... Barnewall and Alderson's English King's Bench Reports [*A publication*] (DLA)
B & AO........ Body and Assembly Operation [*Ford Motor Co.*]
B & AR........ Bangor & Aroostook Railroad Co.
B & Arn .... Barron and Arnold's English Election Cases [*1843-46*] [*A publication*] (DLA)
B & ARR...... Boston & Albany Railroad
B & Aust...... Barron and Austin's English Election Cases [*1842*] [*A publication*] (DLA)
B & Aust Cases (Eng)... Barron and Austin's English Election Cases [*1842*] [*A publication*] (DLA)
B & B.......... Ball and Beatty's Irish Chancery Reports [*1807-14*] [*A publication*] (DLA)
B & B.......... Balled and Burlapped [*Plant industry*]
B & B.......... B & B Productions [*New Jersey*] [*Record label*]
B & B.......... Banks & Barns [*Commercial firm British*]
B & B.......... Bath and Basin [*Classified advertising*] (ADA)
B & B.......... Bed and Board (WDAA)
B & B.......... Bed and Breakfast [*Tourist accommodations*]
B & B.......... Bell and Bell [*Technical drawings*]
B & B.......... Benedictine and Brandy
B & B.......... Benton & Bowles [*Advertising agency*]
B & B.......... Biculturalism and Bilingualism [*Canada*]
b & b.......... Blood and Bone (ADA)
B & B.......... Bowler and Bowers' United States Comptroller's Decisions [*2, 3*] [*A publication*] (DLA)
B & B.......... Brandy and Benedictine (CDAI)
B & B.......... Broderip and Bingham's English Common Pleas Reports [*A publication*] (DLA)
B & B.......... Brown & Bigelow
B & B.......... Buffet and Bull [*Slang for a political dinner*]
B & B.......... Buttons and Bows [*Magazine in Judith Krantz's novel "I'll Take Manhattan"*]
B & B.......... National Block and Bridle Club (EA)
B & BR .... Bristol and Birmingham Railway (ROG)
B&BRSWW... Bed & Breakfast Reservation Services World-Wide [*An association*]
B & BU .... Bond and Burglary
B & C.......... Ball and Chain [*Slang for a wife*]
B & C.......... Banking and Currency Committee [*US Senate*]
B & C.......... Barnewall and Cresswell's English King's Bench Reports [*107-109 English Reprint*] [*A publication*] (DLA)
B & C.......... Barre & Chelsea Railroad (IIA)
B & C.......... Bed and Chair [*Rest*] [*Medicine*]
B & C.......... Bennettsville & Cheraw Railroad (IIA)
B & C.......... Biopsy and Curettage [*Gynecology*]
B & C.......... Board and Care [*Medicine*] (DAVI)
B & C.......... British & Commonwealth [*Company*]
B & C.......... British & Commonwealth Holdings [*Commercial firm*] (ECON)
B & C.......... Building and Contents [*Insurance*]
B & C Comp... Bellinger and Cotton's Annotated Codes and Statutes [*Oregon*] [*A publication*] (DLA)
B & CD .... Barrier and Countersurveillance Division [*Army*] (RDA)
B & CE........ Building and Civil Engineer [*British*]
B & Cie....... Bordier & Compagnie [*Bank*] [*Switzerland*]
B & CMA .... Biscuit and Cracker Manufacturers' Association (EA)
B & C Pr Cas... British and Colonial Prize Cases [*A publication*] (DLA)

B & CR	Reports of Bankruptcy and Companies Winding-Up Cases [*1918-41*] [*England*] [*A publication*] (DLA)
B & D	Bad and Doubtful Debt (DCTA)
B & D	Barker & Dobson [*British*]
B & D	Benloe and Dalison's English Common Pleas Reports [*A publication*] (DLA)
B & D	Black & Decker Manufacturing Co.
B & D	Bondage and Discipline [*or Domination*]
b & d	Brandy and Dry Ginger (ADA)
B & E	Beginning and Ending (ADA)
B & E	Breaking and Entering
B&E	Brisk and Equal [*Medicine*] (DMAA)
B & E	Building and Engineering [*British*]
B & ENT & PL...	Breaking and Entering in Nighttime and Petty Larceny
B & ERS	Boat and Engine Repair Shop [*Coast Guard*]
BANDES	National Bank for Social and Economical Development [*Cuba*]
B & F	Bell and Flange [*Technical drawings*]
B & F	Boston & Fitchburg Railroad
B & F	Breslich & Foss [*British*]
B & F	Broderick and Freemantle's English Ecclesiastical Reports [*1840-64*] [*A publication*] (DLA)
B & F	Business and Farm [*IRS*]
Bandg	Bandag, Inc. [*Associated Press*] (SAG)
B & G	Barton & Guestier [*Wine*]
B & G	Brownlow and Goldesborough's Nisi Prius Reports [*1569-1624*] [*England*] [*A publication*] (DLA)
B & GF	Bombing and Gunnery Flight [*British military*] (DMA)
B & H	Becker & Hayes, Inc. [*Information service or system*] (IID)
B & H	Benson & Hedges (ADA)
B & H	Blatchford and Howland's United States District Court Reports [*A publication*] (DLA)
B & H	Boosey & Hawkes [*Record label*] [*Great Britain, USA*] (ADA)
B & H	Breitkopf & Haertel [*Music*]
B & H Black...	Broom and Hadley's Blackstone [*A publication*] (DLA)
B & H Cr Cas...	Bennett and Heard's Leading Criminal Cases [*England*] [*A publication*] (DLA)
B & H Crim Cas...	Bennett and Heard's Leading Criminal Cases [*England*] [*A publication*] (DLA)
B & H Dig....	Bennett and Heard's Massachusetts Digest [*A publication*] (DLA)
B & H Lead Ca...	Bennett and Heard's Leading Criminal Cases [*England*] [*A publication*] (DLA)
B & H Lead Cas...	Bennett and Heard's Leading Criminal Cases [*England*] [*A publication*] (DLA)
B & H Mr.....	B & H Maritime Carriers Ltd. [*Associated Press*] (SAG)
B & H HO	B & H Ocean Carriers Ltd. [*Associated Press*] (SAG)
B & I	Bankruptcy and Insolvency Cases [*Legal*] [*British*]
B & I	Bankruptcy and Insolvency Reports [*1853-55*] [*England*] [*A publication*] (DLA)
B & I	Base and Increment [*Technical drawings*]
B & I	Billeting and Inventory [*Military*]
B & I	Brilliant and Ivory [*Jewelry*] (ROG)
B & IB	Billing and Instruction Book
B & ICO	British and Irish Communist Organization [*Irish*]
B & I SPC....	British & Irish Steam Packet Co. (MHDB)
B & J	Barrie & Jenkins [*Publisher's imprint*]
B & J	Bone and Joint [*Medicine*]
B & L	Bellar & Lichtenberg [*Device*]
B & L	Browning and Lushington's English Admiralty Reports [*1863-65*] [*A publication*] (DLA)
B & L	Building and Loan
B & L	Building and Loan Association (DLA)
B & L	Bullen and Leake's Precedents of Pleading [*A publication*] (ILCA)
B & L	Burns & Laird Line [*Steamship*] (MHDW)
B & LE	Bessemer & Lake Erie Railroad Co.
B & L Pr	Bullen and Leake's Precedents of Pleading [*A publication*] (DLA)
B & M	Boiler and Machinery
B & M	Boston & Maine Corp.
B and M	Brown Ale and Mild Bitters [*British*] (DSUE)
B & M	Browne and MacNamara's Railway Cases [*A publication*] (DLA)
B & Mac	Browne and MacNamara's Railway Cases [*A publication*] (DLA)
B & Macn	Browne and MacNamara. Railway Cases [*A publication*] (DLA)
B & MD	Boat & Motor Dealer [*A publication*]
BANDMR....	Bandmaster [*Military British*] (ROG)
B & MRR	Boston & Maine Railroad [*Later, Boston & Maine Corp.*]
B & N	Bills and Notes [*Legal term*] (DLA)
B & NCR.....	Belfast and North Counties Railway [*British*] (ROG)
B & NW RY BN...	Bengal & North-Western Railway Battalion [*British military*] (DMA)
B & O	[*The*] Baltimore & Ohio Railroad Co. [*Chessie System, Inc.*]
B & O	Band and Orchestra [*Musical slang*]
Bando	Bando McGlocklin Capital Corp. [*Associated Press*] (SAG)
B & O	Belladonna and Opium [*Toxicology*]
B and O	Bulletins and Orders (NUCP)
B & O Bd of Rev...	Selected Decisions of the Board of Revenue, Bihar and Orissa [*A publication*] (DLA)
B & O CT.....	[*The*] Baltimore & Ohio Chicago Terminal Railroad Co.
BandoM.....	Bando McGlocklin Capital Corp. [*Associated Press*] (SAG)
B & ORHS	Baltimore & Ohio Railroad Historical Society
B & O RR	[*The*] Baltimore & Ohio Railroad Co. [*Chessie System, Inc.*]
B & OTF.....	Bulletins and Orders Task Force [*Nuclear Regulatory Commission*] (NRCH)
b & p	Bare and Painted (BARN)
B & P	Bid and Proposal
B & P	Blueprints and Plans (MCD)
B & P	Bosanquet and Puller's English Common Pleas, Exchequer, and House of Lords Rep orts [*1796-1804*] [*A publication*] (DLA)
B and P	Bread and Puppet Theater [*Vermont*]
B & P	Budgetary and Planning (NASA)
B & PNR.....	Bosanquet and Puller's New Reports, English Common Pleas [*1804-07*] [*A publication*] (DLA)
B & Q	Barracks and Quarters [*Army*]
BANDR.	Bandmaster [*Military British*] (ROG)
B & R	Bread and Roses (EA)
B & R	Budget and Reporting (NRCH)
B and R	Building and Repair [*Red Cross Disaster Services*]
B & RD	Department of Business and Regional Development [*New South Wales, Australia*]
B & S	Bachelors' and Spinsters' Dance (ADA)
B & S	Bartholin and Skene [*Glands*] [*Medicine*]
B & S	Beams and Stringers [*Technical drawings*]
B & S	Bell and Spigot [*Technical drawings*]
B & S	Best and Smith's English Queen's Bench Reports [*A publication*] (DLA)
B & S	Beven and Siebel's Reports [*Ceylon*] [*A publication*] (DLA)
B & S	Bevier and Southern [*Railroad*] (MHDB)
B & S	Booster and Sustainer
B and S	Brandy and Soda
B & S	Briggs & Stratton Corp.
B & S	Brown and Sharpe [*Wire gauge*]
B & SG	Brown and Sharpe Gauge
B & SI	Building and Service Industry
B & SV	Barkston Ashe and Skyrac Volunteers [*British military*] (DMA)
B & T	Baker & Taylor Co.
B & T	Ball and Tube [*Photography*]
B & T	Bank and Trust
B and T	Bridges and Tunnels Crowd [*Derogatory reference to people who reach Manhattan via these routes*]
B & T	Brief and Time [*Photography*]
B & T	Bulb and Time [*Photography*]
B & TBL	Braille and Talking Book Library (ADA)
B & V	Beling and Vanderstraaten's Ceylon Reports [*A publication*] (DLA)
B & W	Babcock & Wilcox Co.
B & W	Black and White [*Photography, television, etc.*]
B & W	Black and White [*Milk of magnesia and aromatic cascara fluid extract*] [*Pharmacy*]
b&w	Black & White (VRA)
b&w	Black and White (IDOE)
B&W	Black and White (IDOE)
B & W	Bread and Water
B & W	Brocklebank & Well Lines [*Steamship*] (MHDB)
B & W	Brown & Williamson Tobacco Corp.
B & W Dgns...	Berkshire and Westminster Dragoons [*British military*] (DMA)
B&W-NES	Babcock and Wilcox Nuclear Environmental Services (GAAI)
BANEC	Balanced Nuclear Economy Code (IAA)
BANERJ	Banco do Estado do Rio de Janiero SA [*Brazil*] (EY)
BANESTO	Banco Espanol de Credito [*Spain*] (ECON)
BANEWS	British Army News Service [*British military*] (DMA)
BANEXI	Banque pour l'Expansion Industrielle [*Industrial Development Bank*] [*France*] (EY)
BANF	BancFirst Corp. [*NASDAQ symbol*] (TTSB)
BANF	BancFirst Corp. Oklahoma [*NASDAQ symbol*] (SAG)
BANF	Bilateral Acoustic Neurofibromatosis [*Medicine*]
B-ANF	Biological Receptors - Atrial Natriuretic Factor
BANF	Business Account Number File [*IRS*]
BanFd	Bancroft Convertible Fund, Inc. [*Associated Press*] (SAG)
BANG	Angle at Leaf Base [*Botany*]
Bang	Bangladesh (ILCA)
BangH	Bangor Hydro-Electric Co. [*Associated Press*] (SAG)
BangI	Bangladesh [*E. Pakistan*] (VRA)
BANGLA	Bangladash
BANGLE	Angle at Leaf Base [*Botany*]
Bang LR	Bangala Law Reporter [*India*] [*A publication*] (DLA)
BANHC	Bengal Army Native Hospital Corps [*British military*] (DMA)
BANHICO	Banco Hipotecario de la Construccion SA [*The Dominican Republic*] (EY)
BANI	Benzoylargininenitroanilide [*Organic chemistry*]
BAnimSc	Bachelor of Animal Science
BANIR	Bombing and Navigation Inertial Reference
Bank	Bankruptcy [*Legal term*] (DLA)
Bank	Bankruptcy Court [*Legal term*] (DLA)
BankAm	BankAmerica Corp. [*Associated Press*] (SAG)
BANKANAL...	Bank Analysis System [*Robinson-Humphrey Co.*] [*Defunct Information service or system*] (CRD)
Bank & Ins...	Bankruptcy and Insolvency Reports [*1853-55*] [*England*] [*A publication*] (DLA)
Bank & Insol Rep...	Bankruptcy and Insolvency Reports [*1853-55*] [*England*] [*A publication*] (DLA)
Bank & Ins R...	Bankruptcy and Insolvency Reports [*1853-55*] [*England*] [*A publication*] (DLA)
BankAtl	BankAtlantic, a Federal Savings Bank [*Associated Press*] (SAG)
Bank C	Banking Code [*A publication*] (DLA)
Bank Cas	Banking Cases [*A publication*] (DLA)
Bank Ct Rep...	American Law Times, Bankruptcy Reports [*A publication*] (DLA)
Bank Ct Rep...	Bankrupt Court Reporter [*New York*] [*A publication*] (DLA)
BANKCY	Bankruptcy
Banker's LJ...	Banker's Law Journal [*A publication*] (DLA)
Bank Gaz	Bankruptcy Gazette [*A publication*] (DLA)
Bank I	Bankter's Institutes of Scottish Law [*A publication*] (DLA)

Bank Insol Rep... Bankruptcy and Insolvency Reports [*1853-55*] [*England*] [*A publication*] (DLA)

Bank Inst ..... Bankter's Institutes of Scottish Law [*A publication*] (DLA)

BankLA .... Bank of Los Angeles [*Associated Press*] (SAG)

Bank NSW Circular... Bank of New South Wales. Circular [*A publication*]

Bank NY ..... Bank of New York [*Associated Press*] (SAG)

BANKPAC..... Banking Profession Political Action Committee [*Acronym now used as official name of organization*] (EA)

Bankr .... Bankruptcy [*Legal term*] (DLA)

Bankr Act.... Bankruptcy Act [*Legal term*] (DLA)

Bankr B Bull... Bankruptcy Bar Bulletin [*A publication*] (DLA)

Bankr Ct Dec.. Bankruptcy Court Decisions [*A publication*] (DLA)

Bank Reg..... Bankruptcy Register [*A publication*] (DLA)

Bankr Rep... American Law Times, Bankruptcy Reports [*A publication*] (DLA)

Bankr Form.. Bankruptcy Forms [*A publication*] (DLA)

Bankr Ins R... Bankruptcy and Insolvency Reports [*1853-55*] [*England*] [*A publication*] (DLA)

Bankr L Rep.. Bankruptcy Law Reports [*CCH*] [*A publication*] (AAGC)

Bankr R ...... Rules of Bankruptcy and Official Forms [*A publication*] (DLA)

Bankr Reg .. National Bankruptcy Register [*New York*] [*A publication*] (DLA)

Bankr Rule... Rules of Bankruptcy and Official Forms [*A publication*] (DLA)

Bankrs Cp ... Bankers Corp. [*Associated Press*] (SAG)

Banks......... Banks' Reports [*1-5 Kansas*] [*A publication*] (DLA)

BankSC .... Bank of South Carolina (The) Charleston [*Associated Press*] (SAG)

Bank St C ... Bank Street College of Education (GAGS)

Bankt .... Macdowall's Institute of Laws of Scotland [*3 vols.*] [*1751-53*] [*A publication*] (DLA)

Bankt I........ Bankter's Institutes of Scottish Law [*A publication*] (DLA)

BankTr .... Bankers Trust New York Corp. [*Associated Press*] (SAG)

Ban LJ .... Banaras Law Journal [*India*] [*A publication*] (DLA)

Bann .... Bannister's Reports, English Common Pleas [*A publication*] (DLA)

Bann & A .... Banning and Arden's Patent Cases [*United States*] [*A publication*] (DLA)

Bann & A Pat Cas... Banning and Arden's Patent Cases [*United States*] [*A publication*] (DLA)

Bann & Ard... Banning and Arden's Patent Cases [*United States*] [*A publication*] (DLA)

Bann Br ...... Bannister's Edition of Orlando Bridgman's English Common Pleas Reports [*A publication*] (DLA)

Bann Lim..... Banning. Limitations of Actions [*3rd ed.*] [*1906*] [*A publication*] (DLA)

BA Non-Class... Bachelor of Arts - Non-Classical

BANP .... [*The*] Book of American Negro Poetry [*A publication*]

BanPn .... BanPonce Corp. [*Associated Press*] (SAG)

BanPonc ...... BanPonce Corp. [*Associated Press*] (SAG)

BanrAer ...... Banner Aerospace [*Associated Press*] (SAG)

BANS .... Back, Arm, Neck, Scalp [*Medicine*]

BANS .... Basic Air Navigation School [*Military*] (OA)

BANS .... Bright Alphanumeric Sub-System (PDAA)

BANS .... British Association of Numismatic Societies

BANSDOC .... Bangladesh National Scientific and Technical Documentation Centre [*Information service or system*] (IID)

BANSHEE ..... Balloon and Nike Scaled High Explosive Experiment (KSC)

Banstr......... Banister, Foundation [*Associated Press*] (SAG)

BANSW .... Blindmakers' Association of New South Wales [*Australia*]

BANSW .... Board of Architects of New South Wales [*Australia*]

BANSW .... Boxing Authority of New South Wales [*Australia*]

BANSW .... Brewers' Association of New South Wales [*Australia*]

Banta .... Banta Corp. [*Associated Press*] (SAG)

BanTex .... Banc Texas Group [*Associated Press*] (SAG)

BANTSA ...... Bank of American National Trust and Savings Association (MHDW)

BA NURS ..... Bachelor of Arts in Nursing (WDAA)

BANW .... Business Alert to Nuclear War (EA)

BANWYS...... Black and Non-White YMCA Staffs [*An association Defunct*] (EA)

BANY .... Bus Association of New York State (SRA)

BanyHI......... Banyan Hotel Investment Fund (SAG)

BanyMF .... Banyan Mortgage Investment Fund [*Associated Press*] (SAG)

BanynSh ...... Banyan Short Term Income Trust [*Associated Press*] (SAG)

BanynSy ..... Banyan Systems, Inc. [*Associated Press*] (SAG)

BanyRT .... Banyan Strategic Realty Trust [*Associated Press*] (SAG)

BanySL .... Banyan Strategic Land Fund [*Associated Press*] (SAG)

BanySL2 ...... Banyan Strategic Land Fund II [*Associated Press*] (SAG)

BANZARE .... British-Australian-New Zealand Antarctic Research Expedition [*1929-31*]

BAO .... Bachelor of Art of Oratory

BAO .... Bachelor of the Art of Obstetrics

BAO .... Bankruptcy Annulment Order [*Legal term*] (DLA)

BAO .... Banque d'Afrique Occidentale [*Bank of French West Africa*]

BAO .... Bardine Oils Ltd. [*Vancouver Stock Exchange symbol*]

BAO .... Basal Acid Output [*Medicine*]

BAO .... Base of Air Operations

BAO .... Basic Attack Option (MCD)

BAO .... Batavia Area Office [*Energy Research and Development Administration*]

BAO .... Battalion Administration Officer (MCD)

BAO .... Bay Air Cargo, SA [*Brazil*] [*FAA designator*] (FAAC)

BAO .... Bisaminophenyloxadiazole [*Organic chemistry*]

BAO .... Body and Assembly Operations

BAO .... Boulder Atmospheric Observatory [*Army*] (OSRA)

BAO .... Boulder Atmospheric Observatory (USDC)

BAO .... Brasilia Array [*Brazil*] [*Seismograph station code, US Geological Survey*] (SEIS)

BAO .... British Army of Occupation [*World War II*]

BAO .... British Association of Orthodontists

BAO .... British Association of Otolaryngologists

BAO .... Brookhaven Area Office [*Energy Research and Development Administration*]

BAO .... Budget and Accounting Officer [*Military*]

BAO .... Burlington Area Office [*Energy Research and Development Administration*]

BAODA...... British Association of Operating Department Assistants (DBA)

BA of E ...... Badminton Association of England (DBA)

BA of NA.... Bnei Akiva of North America (EA)

BAOFR....... British Association of Overseas Furniture Removers (BI)

Baol .... British Association for Open Learning

BAOL .... British Association of Otolaryngologists (DBA)

BAO-MAO ... Basal Acid Output to Maximal Acid Output [*Ratio*] [*Medicine*] (AAMN)

BAOMS .... British Association of Oral and Maxillofacial Surgeons (DBA)

BAOPS .... Base Operations

BAOR .... British Army of the Rhine [*NATO/NORTHAG*]

BAOS .... British Association of Oral and Maxillo-Facial Surgeons

BAOT .... British Association of Occupational Therapists

BA(OU) .... Bachelor of Arts (Open University) [*British*] (DI)

BAP .... 6-Benzylaminopurine (DOG)

BAP .... Bacillary Angiomatosis-Bacillary Peliosis

BAP .... Bacterial Alkaline Phosphatase [*or Bacterial Alkaline Phosphomonoesterase*] [*An enzyme*]

BAP .... Baibara [*Papua New Guinea*] [*Airport symbol*] (OAG)

BAP .... Ballistic Aimpoint [*Military*] (CAAL)

BAP .... Band Amplitude Product

BAP .... Bandwidth Allocation Protocol [*Telecommunications*] (ACRL)

BAP .... Baptist

BAP .... Baptized

BAP .... BA Resources [*Vancouver Stock Exchange symbol*]

BAP .... Barometric Absolute Pressure [*Automotive engineering*]

BAP .... Basaltic Achondrite Parent [*Planetary body*]

BAP .... Base Auxiliary Power (KSC)

BAP .... Basic Assembler Program [*Computer science*]

BAP .... Beacon Aircraft Position (MUGU)

BAP .... Benefits Analysis Program [*Environmental Protection Agency*] (GFGA)

BaP .... Benzo(a)pyrene

BAP .... Benzyl-Aminophenol [*Organic chemistry*]

BAP .... Benzylaminopurine [*Biochemistry*]

BAP .... Best Adaptive Path [*NASA*]

BAP .... Beta Alpha Psi (EA)

BAP .... Beta-Anyloid Protein Bi-Anyloid Protein

BAP .... Billet a Payer [*Bill Payable*] [*French Business term*]

BAP .... Bleed Air Precooler

BAP .... Bleomycin, Adriamycin, Prednisone [*Antineoplastic drug regimen*] (DAVI)

BAP .... Blood Agar Plate [*Microbiology*]

BAP .... Boeing Associated Products (MCD)

BAP .... [*The*] Book of American Poetry [*A publication*]

BAP .... Born Again Pagans (EA)

BAP .... Bovine Albumin in Phosphate Buffer [*Medicine*] (DMAA)

BAP .... Brachial Artery Pressure [*Medicine*]

BAP .... Branch Arm Piping [*Nuclear energy*] (NRCH)

BAP .... Brief Adaptive Psychotherapy [*Psychology*]

BAP .... British Association for Psychopharmacology

BAP .... British Association of Psychotherapists (DBA)

BAP .... Bromoform-Triallyl Phosphate [*Flame retardant*]

BAP .... Bulgarian Agrarian Party [*Political party*] (PPW)

BAP .... Business Automobile Policy [*Insurance*]

BAP .... Butte, Anaconda & Pacific Railway Co. [*AAR code*]

BAP .... Oredicorp Ltd. [*NYSE symbol*] (SAG)

BAPA .... Benzoylarginine p-Nitroanilide [*Also, BAPNA*] [*Biochemistry*]

BAPA .... British Aeromedical Practitioners Association (DA)

BAPA .... British Amateur Press Association (BI)

BAPC .... British Aircraft Preservation Council

BAPC .... Business Applications Performance Corp. (CDE)

BAPCT .... Bachelor of Arts in Practical Christian Training

BAPE .... Bachelor of Arts in Physical Education (NADA)

BAPE .... Balloon Atmospheric Propagation Experiment [*NASA*]

BAPE .... Baseplate [*Technical drawings*]

BAPE .... Branch Arm Piping Enclosure [*Nuclear energy*] (NRCH)

BAPed .... Bachelor of Arts in Pedagogy (DD)

BAPERS ...... Battalion Automated Personnel System

BAPEX .... British Association of Paper Exporters (PDAA)

BAPG .... Business Applications Programming Guide (MCD)

BAPHE....... British Association of Professional Hairdressing Employers (DBA)

BAPHR........ Bay Area Physicians for Human Rights (EA)

BAPhysMed... British Association of Physical Medicine (BABM)

BAPI......... Barcelona, Spain - Pisa, Italy [*Submarine cable*] [*Telecommunications*]

BAPI......... Barley Alkaline Protease Inhibitor [*Medicine*] (DMAA)

BAPIP .... British Association of Palestine-Israel Philatelists (BI)

BAPL .... Base Assembly Parts List (IAA)

BAPL .... Bettis Atomic Power Laboratory [*AEC*] (MCD)

BAPL .... British Association of Parascending Clubs (DBA)

BAPLA .... British Association of Picture Libraries and Agencies (DBA)

BAPM .... British Association of Physical Medicine (BI)

BAPMoN ..... Background Air Pollution Monitoring Network (GNE)

BAPN .... Beta-Aminopropionitrile [*Organic chemistry*]

BAPNA .... Benzoylarginine p-Nitroanilide [*Also, BAPA*] [*Biochemistry*]

BAPO .... British Army Post Office [*British military*] (DMA)

BAPP .... Beta-Amyloid Precursor Protein

BAPP .... Bis(aminopropyl)piperazine [*Organic chemistry*]

BAPP .... British Association for Perinatal Paediatrics (PDAA)

BAPP .... British Association of Pig Producers (BI)

BAPP .... Bulgarian Agrarian People's Party [*Political party*] (PPW)
BAPP .... Bureau Arabe de Presse et de Publications [*Paris*] (BJA)
BAppArts...... Bachelor of Applied Arts (NADA)
BAppEc .... Bachelor of Applied Economics (ADA)
B Applied Sc... Bachelor of Applied Science
BAppSc .... Bachelor of Applied Science (ADA)
BAppSc-BltEnvir... Bachelor of Applied Science - Built Environment
BAppSc-Comptg... Bachelor of Applied Science - Computing
BAppSc-ConstMgmt... Bachelor of Applied Science - Construction Management
BAppSc-ElectSysComptg... Bachelor of Applied Science - Electronic Systems and Computing
B APP SCI ... Bachelor of Applied Science (WDAA)
BAppScInfo... Bachelor of Applied Science - Information
BAppSci(Nsg)... Bachelor of Applied Science (Nursing) (ADA)
BAppSci(Optom)... Bachelor of Applied Science (Optometry)
BAppSci(SocEcol)... Bachelor of Applied Science (Social Ecology)
BAppSc-Optom... Bachelor of Applied Science - Optometry
BAppSc-QuantSurv... Bachelor of Applied Science - Quantity Surveying
BAppSc-Surv... Bachelor of Applied Science - Surveying
BAPREPT ..... Beds and Patients Report
BAPRR .... Budget and Program Resources Review [*Army*]
BAPS .... Beam and Plate System (PDAA)
BAPS .... Bovine Albumin Phosphate Saline [*Physiology*]
BAPS .... Branch Arm Piping Shielding [*Nuclear energy*] (NRCH)
BApS .... British Appaloosa Society (DBA)
BAPS .... British Association of Paediatric Surgeons (EAIO)
BAPS .... British Association of Plastic Surgeons
BAPS .... Bureau of Air Pollution Sciences
BAPSA .... Broadcast Advertising Producers Society of America (NTCM)
BAPT .... Baptist
bapt .... Baptist (VRA)
BAPT .... Baptist
BAPT .... Baptized
BAPT........... Basic Avionics Procedure Trainer [*British military*] (DMA)
BAPTA .... Bearing and Power Transfer Assembly [*Aerospace*]
BAPTA .... Bis(aminophenoxy)ethanetetraacetic Acid [*Organic chemistry*]
BAPTO .... British Association of Pool Table Operators (DBA)
BAPU .... Bulgarian Agrarian People's Union-United [*Political party*] (EY)
BAPU-NP ..... Bulgarian Agrarian People's Union - Nikola Petkov [*Political party*]
BAPV .... Bovine Alimentary Papilloma Virus [*Medicine*] (DMAA)
BAQ .... Bachelor Airmen's Quarters [*Air Force*]
BAQ .... Bar Association of Queensland [*Australia*]
BAQ .... Barranquilla [*Colombia*] [*Airport symbol*] (OAG)
BAQ .... Basic Allowance for Quarters [*Military*]
BAQ .... Bibliotheque Administrative du Quebec [*UTLAS symbol*]
BAQ .... Board of Architects of Queensland [*Australia*]
BAQ .... Brain-Age Quotient [*Medicine*] (DMAA)
BAQ(AC) ...... Basic Allowance for Quarters for Adopted Child [*Military*]
BAQ(DIS RET)... Basic Allowance for Quarters Pending Disability Retirement [*Military*]
BAQ(F) .... Basic Allowance for Quarters for Father [*Military*]
BAQ(H) .... Basic Allowance for Quarters for Husband [*Military*]
BAQ(LC)...... Basic Allowance for Quarters for Legitimate Children [*Military*]
BAQ(M)........ Basic Allowance for Quarters for Mother [*Military*]
BAQ(SC)....... Basic Allowance for Quarters for Stepchildren [*Military*]
BAQ(W)....... Basic Allowance for Quarters for Wife [*Military*]
BAR .... Babinet Absorption Rule
B Ar .... Bachelor of Architecture
BAR .... Bacille Acido-Resistant [*Acid-Fast Bacillus*] [*Medicine*]
BAR .... Bailed Aircraft Repairables (MCD)
BAR .... Baker Analyzed Reagent [*Chemistry*]
BAR .... Banco Resources Ltd. [*Vancouver Stock Exchange symbol*]
BAR .... Bangor & Aroostook Railroad Co. [*AAR code*]
BAR .... Banner Aerospace [*NYSE symbol*] (SPSG)
BAR .... Banner Elk, NC [*Location identifier FAA*] (FAAL)
BAR .... Bar Address Register [*Computer science*] (NITA)
Bar............ Barber's Reports [*14-42 Arkansas*] [*A publication*] (DLA)
BAR .... Baritone [*Music*]
BAR .... Bark (WGA)
BAR .... Barleycorn [*Unit of weight*] [*Obsolete British*] (ROG)
Bar............ Barnardiston's English King's Bench Reports [*A publication*] (DLA)
BAR .... Barometer [*or Barometric*]
BAR .... Barque [*Bark, Boat*] [*French*] (ROG)
BAR .... Barrel [*Shipping*]
Bar............ Bar Reports in All Courts [*England*] [*A publication*] (DLA)
BAR .... Barrett [*California*] [*Seismograph station code, US Geological Survey*] (SEIS)
BAR .... Barrier (NVT)
bar............. Barrister (ADA)
Bar............ Barrows' Reports [*18 Rhode Island*] [*A publication*] (DLA)
Bar............ Bartholomaeus Brixiensis [*Deceased circa 1258*] [*Authority cited in pre-1607 legal work*] (DSA)
Bar............ Bartholomaeus de Saliceto [*Deceased, 1411*] [*Authority cited in pre-1607 legal work*] (DSA)
Bar.............. Bartolus de Sassoferrato [*Deceased, 1357*] [*Authority cited in pre-1607 legal work*] (DSA)
Bar............ Baruch [*Book of the Bible*]
BAR .... Base Address Register [*Computer science*] (BUR)
BAR .... Base Register [*Computer science*] (IAA)
BAR .... Battery Acquisition RADAR
BAR .... Biblical Archaeologist Reader [*A publication*] (BJA)
BAR .... Billet a Recevoir [*Bill Receivable*] [*French Business term*]
BAR .... Blade Area Ratio
BAR .... Bleach-Accelerator-Releasing Couplers [*Photography*]
BAR .... Blueprint Analysis Report (MCD)

BAR .... Board of Appeals and Review [*Later, ARB*] [*Civil Service Commission*] (AFM)
BAR .... Bone Apposition Rate [*Physiology*]
BAR .... Bonneville Power Administration Acquisition [*A publication*] (AAGC)
BAR .... Book Auction Records [*A publication British*]
BAR .... Bradley Air (Charter) Services Ltd. [*Canada ICAO designator*] (FAAC)
BAR .... Brigade Aeroportee Renforcee [*Reinforced Airborne Brigade*] [*Zaire*] (AF)
BAR .... British Army Review [*A publication*]
BAR .... British Association for the Retarded
BAR .... British Association of Removers (DBA)
BAR .... Broadcast Advertisers Reports [*Information service or system Defunct*]
BAR .... Browning Automatic Rifle
BAR .... Budget Adjustment Request
BAR .... Buffer Address Register [*Computer science*]
BAR .... Bureau of Aeronautics [*Later, Naval Air Systems Command*]
BAR .... Bureau of Aeronautics Representative [*Obsolete Navy*]
BAR .... Bureau of Automotive Regulation
BARAC .... Black American Response to the African Crisis (EA)
Bar Anc Stat... Barrington's Observations upon the Statutes from Magna Charta to 21 James I [*A publication*] (DLA)
Bar & Ad .... Barnewall and Adolphus' English King's Bench Reports [*109-110 English Reprint*] [*1830-34*] [*A publication*] (DLA)
Bar & Al ..... Barnewall and Alderson's English King's Bench Reports [*A publication*] (DLA)
Bar & Arn .... Barron and Arnold's English Election Cases [*1843-46*] [*A publication*] (DLA)
Bar & Au ..... Barron and Austin's English Election Cases [*1842*] [*A publication*] (DLA)
Bar & Aust... Barron and Austin's English Election Cases [*1842*] [*A publication*] (DLA)
Bar & Cr ..... Barnewall and Cresswell's English King's Bench Reports [*A publication*] (DLA)
Bar & Leg W... Bar and Legal World [*England*] [*A publication*] (DLA)
Bar Ar......... Bartholomaeus Archamonus [*Authority cited in pre-1607 legal work*] (DSA)
Bar Archa .... Bartholomaeus Archamonus [*Authority cited in pre-1607 legal work*] (DSA)
BARB .... Ballast Aerating Retrieval Boom (MCD)
BARB .... Barbados (ROG)
Barb........... Barbados (VRA)
BARB .... Barber
Barb........... Barber's Gold Law [*South Africa*] [*A publication*] (DLA)
Barb........... Barber's Reports [*14-42 Arkansas*] [*A publication*] (DLA)
BARB .... Barbette [*Military*]
barb........... Barbiturate [*Pharmacology*]
BARB .... Barbiturate Screen [*Biochemistry*] (DAVI)
Barb........... Barbour's Supreme Court Reports [*New York*] [*A publication*] (DLA)
BarB........... Barclays Bank [*Associated Press*] (SAG)
BARB .... British Angular Rate Bombsight
BARB .... British Association of Rose Breeders
BARB .... Broadcasters Audience Research Board [*British Information service or system*]
BARB .... Button at Right Bottom [*Telephone touch-tone dial*]
Barb Abs..... Barbour's Abstracts of Chancellor's Decisions [*New York*] [*A publication*] (DLA)
Barb & C KY St... Barbour and Carroll's Kentucky Statutes [*A publication*] (DLA)
Barb App Dig... Barber's Digest [*New York*] [*A publication*] (DLA)
Barb Ark ..... Barber's Reports [*14-42 Arkansas*] [*A publication*] (DLA)
Barb Ch .... Barbour's Chancery Reports [*New York*] [*A publication*] (DLA)
Barb Chancery Rep... Barbour's Chancery Reports [*New York*] [*A publication*] (DLA)
Barb Ch (NY)... Barbour's Chancery Reports [*New York*] [*A publication*] (DLA)
Barb Ch Pr... Barbour's Chancery Practice [*New York*] [*A publication*] (DLA)
Barb Ch Rep... Barbour's Chancery Reports [*New York*] [*A publication*] (DLA)
Barb Cr L.... Barbour's Criminal Law [*A publication*] (DLA)
Barb Cr Law... Barbour's Criminal Law [*A publication*] (DLA)
Barb Cr P..... Barbour's Criminal Pleadings [*A publication*] (DLA)
Barb Cr P..... Barbour's Criminal Practice [*A publication*] (DLA)
Barb Dig .... Barber's Digest of Kentucky [*A publication*] (DLA)
Barbe.......... Barber's Reports [*14-42 Arkansas*] [*A publication*] (DLA)
Barber .... Barber's Gold Law [*South Africa*] [*A publication*] (DLA)
Barber .... Barber's Reports [*14-42 Arkansas*] [*A publication*] (DLA)
BArbG .... Bundesarbeitsgericht [*Federal Labor Court*] [*German*] (ILCA)
Barb Gro...... Barbeyrac's Edition of Grotius on War and Peace [*A publication*] (DLA)
BARBI .... Baseband RADAR Bag Initiator (PDAA)
Barb Ins...... Barber on Insurance [*A publication*] (DLA)
Barb LR .... Barbados Law Reports [*A publication*] (DLA)
Barb (NY) SCR... Barbour's Supreme Court Reports [*New York*] [*A publication*] (DLA)
Barbour........ Barbour's Supreme Court Reports [*New York*] [*A publication*] (DLA)
Barbour (NY)... Barbour's Supreme Court Reports [*New York*] [*A publication*] (DLA)
Barbour's Ch R... Barbour's Chancery Reports [*New York*] [*A publication*] (DLA)
Barbour's Sup Court Rep... Barbour's Supreme Court Reports [*New York*] [*A publication*] (DLA)
Barb Par ...... Barbour on Parties in Law and Equity [*A publication*] (DLA)
Barb Puf ...... Barbeyrac's Edition of Puffendorf's Law of Nature and Nations [*A publication*] (DLA)
Barb R .... Barbour's Supreme Court Reports [*New York*] [*A publication*] (DLA)
Bar Brix .... Bartholomaeus Brixiensis [*Deceased circa 1258*] [*Authority cited in pre-1607 legal work*] (DSA)

Bar Brixi...... Bartholomaeus Brixiensis [*Deceased circa 1258*] [*Authority cited in pre-1607 legal work*] (DSA)

Bar Brixien.. Bartholomaeus Brixiensis [*Deceased circa 1258*] [*Authority cited in pre-1607 legal work*] (DSA)

Barb SC...... Barbour's Supreme Court Reports [*New York*] [*A publication*] (DLA)

Barb SCR..... Barbour's Supreme Court Reports [*New York*] [*A publication*] (DLA)

Barb Set-Off... Barbour on the Law of Set-Off [*A publication*] (DLA)

Barb Sup Ct.. Barbour's Supreme Court Reports [*New York*] [*A publication*] (DLA)

Barb Sup Ct Reports... Barbour's Supreme Court Reports [*New York*] [*A publication*] (DLA)

BarBu........... University of the West Indies, Cave Hill Campus, Bridgetown, Barbados [*Library symbol Library of Congress*] (LCLS)

BarBU-L...... University of the West Indies, Law Library, St. Michael, Barbados [*Library symbol Library of Congress*] (LCLS)

Bar Bull (NY County La)... Bar Bulletin, New York County Lawyers' [*A publication*] (DLA)

BARC.......... Barge, Amphibious, Resupply, Cargo

BARC.......... Barge, Amphibious, Resupply Craft [*Navy*] (VNW)

BARC.......... Bay Area Reference Center [*San Francisco Public Library*] [*San Francisco, CA*] [*Library network*]

BARC.......... Bay Area Religious Channel [*Cable TV programming service*]

BARC.......... Beltsville Agricultural Research Center [*Maryland*] [*Department of Agriculture*]

BARC.......... Bhabba Atomic Research Centre [*India*]

BARC.......... Bikini Atoll Rehabilitation Committee [*Federal government*]

BARC.......... Block Adaptive Rate Controlled [*Computer science*]

BARC......... British Aeronautical Research Committee

BARC......... British American Repertory Company

BARC......... British Automobile Racing Club

BARC......... Budget Analysis and Review Committee [*American Library Association*]

BARCAP...... Barrier Combat Air Patrol [*Navy*]

Barc Dig...... Barclay's Missouri Digest [*A publication*] (DLA)

Barc Dig Law Sc... Barclay's Digest of the Law of Scotland [*A publication*] (DLA)

B Arc E........ Bachelor of Architectural Engineering

BARCEP....... Barclays Australia Investment Services Consensus Earnings Profile

B Arch......... Bachelor of Architecture

BArch.......... Bachelor of Architecture (NADA)

Bar Ch......... Barnardiston's English Chancery Reports [*A publication*] (DLA)

BArch & TP... Bachelor of Architecture and Town Planning (ADA)

B Arch (Arch)... Bachelor of Architecture in Architecture

B Arch (ArchE)... Bachelor of Architecture in Architectural Engineering

B Arch Des.... Bachelor of Architectural Design

BArchE........ Bachelor of Architectural Engineering (NADA)

B Arch Eng... Bachelor of Architectural Engineering

BArchHist..... Bachelor of Architectural History

Barc High.... Barclay's Law of Highways [*A publication*] (DLA)

B Arch in City Pl... Bachelor of Architecture in City Planning

BArchSt........ Bachelor of Architectural Studies

BArchStudies... Bachelor of Architectural Studies

BArchTech.... Bachelor of Architectural Technology

Bar Chy........ Barnardiston's English Chancery Reports [*A publication*] (DLA)

BARCIS........ British Airport Rapid Control and Indication Systems (PDAA)

Barclay........ Barclays Ltd. [*Associated Press*] (SAG)

Barclay........ Barclays PLC [*Associated Press*] (SAG)

Barc Mo Dig... Barclay's Missouri Digest [*A publication*] (DLA)

BARCS......... Battlefield Area Reconnaissance System [*RADAR*] [*Army*]

Bard............. Bard [*C.R.*], Inc. [*Associated Press*] (SAG)

BARD........... Binational Agricultural Research and Development Fund [*US-Israeli*] [*Research center*] (IRC)

BARD........... British Association of Rally Doctors (DBA)

Bar de C...... Bartholomaeus de Capua [*Deceased, 1328*] [*Authority cited in pre-1607 legal work*] (DSA)

Bar de Ca.... Bartholomaeus de Capua [*Deceased, 1328*] [*Authority cited in pre-1607 legal work*] (DSA)

Bar de Cap... Bartholomaeus de Capua [*Deceased, 1328*] [*Authority cited in pre-1607 legal work*] (DSA)

Bar de Sa.... Bartholomaeus de Saliceto [*Deceased, 1411*] [*Authority cited in pre-1607 legal work*] (DSA)

Bar de Sal... Bartholomaeus de Saliceto [*Deceased, 1411*] [*Authority cited in pre-1607 legal work*] (DSA)

Bar de Sali... Bartholomaeus de Saliceto [*Deceased, 1411*] [*Authority cited in pre-1607 legal work*] (DSA)

Bar Dig........ Barclay's Digest of the Law of Scotland [*A publication*] (DLA)

BARDOC....... Barrier Doctrine [*Military*] (NVT)

B Ar E.......... Bachelor of Architectural Engineering

BARE........... Barefoot, Inc. [*NASDAQ symbol*] (SPSG)

BARE........... Base Area Refueling Equipment

BAREA......... Basal Leaf Area [*Botany*]

Barefoot....... Barefoot, Inc. [*Associated Press*] (SAG)

BAREMA....... British Anaesthetic and Respiratory Equipment Manufacturers Association (DBA)

Bar Eq.......... Barton's Suit in Equity [*A publication*] (DLA)

BaretRs........ Barrett Resources [*Associated Press*] (SAG)

Bar Ex Ann... Bar Examination Annual [*1893-94*] [*A publication*] (DLA)

Bar Ex Guide... Bar Examination Guide [*1895-99*] [*A publication*] (DLA)

Bar Ex J....... Bar Examination Journal [*A publication*] (DLA)

Bar Ex Jour... Bar Examination Journal [*A publication*] (DLA)

BARF........... Best Available Retrofit Facility [*Environmental Protection Agency*] (GFGA)

BARF........... British Auto Racing Funatics [*An association*]

BARF......... Burning Anomaly Rate Factor (MCD)

BARFO......... Best and Revised Final Offer [*DoD*]

BARG........... Bargain (ADA)

BARGN......... Bargain (ROG)

BarHair........ Barber Hairstyling for Men and Women [*Associated Press*] (SAG)

Barh Pre Ex... Barham's Student's Guide to the Preliminary Examinations [*A publication*] (DLA)

Bar Int Pr R... Bar. Das Internationale Privat-und-Strafrecht [*A publication*] (DLA)

Baristr......... Barrister Information Systems Corp. [*Associated Press*] (SAG)

barit............ Baritone [*Music*] (ADA)

BARITT........ Barrier Injection Transit Time [*Physics*]

BARK.......... Barking [*Borough in England*]

B-ARK.......... Beta-Androgenic Receptor Kinase [*An enzyme*]

BARKTH........ Bark Thickness [*Botany*]

BARLA.......... British Amateur Rugby League Association (DBA)

BARLAB....... Behavioral Alcohol Research Laboratory (DICI)

BARLANT...... Atlantic Barrier Patrol [*Eastern seaward extension of the DEW Line*] [*Obsolete*]

barlf............ Bas Relief (VRA)

Barl Just...... Barlow. Justice of Peace [*1745*] [*A publication*] (DLA)

BARM.......... British Admiralty Repair Mission

Bar Mag...... Barrington's Magna Charta [*A publication*] (DLA)

Barn........... Barnabites [*Also, CRSP*] [*Roman Catholic men's religious order*]

Barn........... Barnard [*Star second closest to the sun*] (BARN)

Barn........... Barnardiston's English King's Bench Reports [*A publication*] (DLA)

Barn........... Barnes' English Common Pleas Reports [*A publication*] (DLA)

Bar N.......... Barnes' Notes of Cases of Practice in Common Pleas [*94 English Reprint*] [*A publication*] (DLA)

Barn........... Barnfield's Reports [*19-20 Rhode Island*] [*A publication*] (DLA)

BARN.......... Barnwell, SC [*Commercial waste site*] (GAAI)

BARN.......... Biological Agricultural Reactor of the Netherlands

BARN.......... Body Awareness Resource Network

BARN.......... Bombing and Reconnaissance Navigation

Barn & A..... Barnewall and Adolphus' English King's Bench Reports [*109-110 English Reprint*] [*1830-34*] [*A publication*] (DLA)

Barn & A..... Barnewall and Alderson's English King's Bench Reports [*A publication*] (DLA)

Barn & Ad... Barnewall and Adolphus' English King's Bench Reports [*109-110 English Reprint*] [*A publication*] (DLA)

Barn & Ad (Eng)... Barnewall and Adolphus' English King's Bench Reports [*109-110 English Reprint*] [*A publication*] (DLA)

Barn & Adol... Barnewall and Adolphus' English King's Bench Reports [*109-110 English Reprint*] [*1830-34*] [*A publication*] (DLA)

Barn & Ald... Barnewall and Alderson's English King's Bench Reports [*A publication*] (DLA)

Barn & Ald (Eng)... Barnewall and Alderson's English King's Bench Reports [*A publication*] (DLA)

Barn & C..... Barnewall and Cresswell's English King's Bench Reports [*107-109 English Reprint*] [*A publication*] (DLA)

Barn & C (Eng)... Barnewall and Cresswell's English King's Bench Reports [*107-109 English Reprint*] [*A publication*] (DLA)

Barn & Cr.... Barnewall and Cresswell's English King's Bench Reports [*107-109 English Reprint*] [*A publication*] (DLA)

Barn & Cress... Barnewall and Cresswell's English King's Bench Reports [*107-109 English Reprint*] [*A publication*] (DLA)

Barnard....... Barnardiston's English King's Bench Reports [*A publication*] (DLA)

Barnard....... Barnardiston's Tempore Hardwicke Reports, Chancery [*1740-41*] [*England*] [*A publication*] (DLA)

Barnard Ch... Barnardiston's English Chancery Reports [*1740-41*] [*A publication*] (DLA)

Barnard Ch (Eng)... Barnardiston's English Chancery Reports [*1740-41*] [*A publication*] (DLA)

Barnard Ch Rep... Barnardiston's English Chancery Reports [*1740-41*] [*A publication*] (DLA)

Barnardiston CC... Barnardiston's English Chancery Cases [*1740-41*] [*A publication*] (DLA)

Barnard KB... Barnardiston's English King's Bench Reports [*A publication*] (DLA)

BarNbl........ Barnes & Noble, Inc. [*Associated Press*] (SAG)

Barn C........ Barnardiston's English Chancery Reports [*1740-41*] [*A publication*] (DLA)

Barn Ch....... Barnardiston's English Chancery Reports [*1740-41*] [*A publication*] (DLA)

Barn Eq Pr... Barnes' Equity Practice [*A publication*] (DLA)

Barnes........ Barnes' Notes of Cases of Practice in Common Pleas [*94 English Reprint*] [*A publication*] (DLA)

Barnes NC... Barnes' Notes of Cases of Practice in Common Pleas [*94 English Reprint*] [*A publication*] (DLA)

Barnes Notes... Barnes' Notes of Cases of Practice in Common Pleas [*94 English Reprint*] [*A publication*] (DLA)

Barnes Notes (Eng)... Barnes' Notes of Cases of Practice in Common Pleas [*94 English Reprint*] [*A publication*] (DLA)

Barnes's Fed Code... Barnes's Federal Code [*A publication*] (DLA)

Barnet......... Barnet's English Central Criminal Courts Reports [*27-92*] [*A publication*] (DLA)

Barnett........ Barnett Banks, Inc. [*Associated Press*] (SAG)

Barnett........ Barnett, Inc. [*Associated Press*] (SAG)

Barnf & S.... Barnfield and Stiness' Reports [*20 Rhode Island*] [*A publication*] (DLA)

BarnGp........ Barnes Group, Inc. [*Associated Press*] (SAG)

Barn KB....... Barnardiston's English King's Bench Reports [*A publication*] (DLA)

Barn No....... Barnes' Notes of Cases of Practice in Common Pleas [*94 English Reprint*] [*A publication*] (DLA)

Barn Pr M.... Barnstaple's Printed Minutes and Proceedings [*A publication*] (DLA)

Barn Sh....... Barnes' Exposition of the Law Respecting Sheriff [*1816*] [*A publication*] (DLA)

BARNST....... Barnstaple [*Municipal borough in England*]

Barnt........... Barnett Banks, Inc. [*Associated Press*] (SAG)

Barnw Dig.... Barnwall's Digest of the Year Books [*A publication*] (DLA)

Barnwl......... Barnwell Industries, Inc. [*Associated Press*] (SAG)

BARO .... Barometer (AABC)

BARO .... Barostat (KSC)

Bar Obs St ... Barrington's Observations upon the Statutes from Magna Charta to 21 James I [*A publication*] (DLA)

Bar Ob Stat ... Barrington's Observations upon the Statutes from Magna Charta to 21 James I [*A publication*] (DLA)

Baroda LR ... Baroda Law Reports [*India*] [*A publication*] (DLA)

Baron .... Barony of Urie Court Records [*1604-1747*] [*Scotland*] [*A publication*] (DLA)

BARON .... Business/Accounts Reporting Operating Network [*Computer science*] (PDAA)

Baron Ch Mort ... Baron on Chattel Mortgages [*A publication*] (DLA)

BAROPS .... Barrier Operations [*Military*] (NVT)

BARP .... British Association of Rehabilitated Psychotherapy (DI)

BARP .... British Association of Retired Persons (DI)

BARPAC .... Pacific Barrier Patrol [*Western seaward extension of the DEW Line*] [*Obsolete*]

Bar Prec Conv ... Barton's Modern Precedents in Conveyancing [*A publication*] (DLA)

Barq .... Baroque (VRA)

BARR .... Barratry [*FBI standardized term*]

BARR .... Barrier (MSA)

BARR .... Barringer Resources, Inc. [*NASDAQ symbol*] (NQ)

BARR .... Barringer Technologies Inc. [*NASDAQ symbol*] (TTSB)

BARR .... Barrister

Barr .... Barrows' Reports [*18 Rhode Island*] [*A publication*] (DLA)

Barr .... Barr's Reports [*1-10 Pennsylvania*] [*A publication*] (DLA)

BARR .... British Association for Rheumatology and Rehabilitation

BARR .... Bureau of Aeronautics Resident Representative [*Obsolete Navy*]

BARR .... Bureau on Agriculture and Renewable Resources

Barra .... Barra, Inc. [*Associated Press*] (SAG)

Barr & Arn ... Barron and Arnold's English Election Cases [*1843-46*] [*A publication*] (DLA)

Barr & Aus ... Barron and Austin's English Election Cases [*1842*] [*A publication*] (DLA)

Barr Ch Pr ... Barroll. Chancery Practice [*Maryland*] [*A publication*] (DLA)

Bar Re .... Bar Reports in All Courts [*England*] [*A publication*] (DLA)

Bar Rep .... Bar Reports [*1865-71*] [*A publication*] (DLA)

BarrettB ...... Barrett Business Services [*Associated Press*] (SAG)

BarrettB ...... Barrett Business Services [*Associated Press*] (SAG)

BarrickG ...... Barrick Gold Corp. [*Associated Press*] (SAG)

Barring Obs St ... Barrington's Observations upon the Statutes from Magna Charta to 21 James I [*A publication*] (DLA)

Barring St .... Barrington's Observations upon the Statutes from Magna Charta to 21 James I [*A publication*] (DLA)

BarrLb .... Barr Laboratories, Inc. [*Associated Press*] (SAG)

Barr M .... Barradall. Manuscript Reports [*Virginia*] [*A publication*] (DLA)

Barr MSS ..... Barradall. Manuscript Reports [*Virginia*] [*A publication*] (DLA)

BARRnet ...... Bay Area Regional Research Network [*Acquired from Stanford University by Bolt Beranek and Newman*] [*Internet service*] [*Also, an information service or system*]

BarrngTch .... Barringer Resources [*Associated Press*] (SAG)

Barrngtn ...... Barrington Bancorp, Inc. [*Associated Press*] (SAG)

Barr Ob .... Barrington's Observations upon the Statutes from Magna Charta to 21 James [*A publication*] (DLA)

Barr Obs St ... Barrington's Observations upon the Statutes from Magna Charta to 21 James I [*A publication*] (DLA)

Barron & H Fed Pr & Proc ... Barron and Holtzoff's Federal Practice and Procedure [*A publication*] (DLA)

Barron Mir ... Barron's Mirror of Parliament [*A publication*] (DLA)

Barrows ...... Barrows' Reports [*18 Rhode Island*] [*A publication*] (DLA)

Barrows (RI) ... Barrows' Reports [*18 Rhode Island*] [*A publication*] (DLA)

Barr (PA) ..... Barr's Reports [*1-10 Pennsylvania*] [*A publication*] (DLA)

Barr St .... Barrington's Observations upon the Statutes from Magna Charta to 21 James I [*A publication*] (DLA)

Barr Ten ...... Barry on Tenures [*A publication*] (DLA)

Barry Build Soc ... Barry on Building Societies [*A publication*] (DLA)

Barry Ch Jur ... Barry. Statutory Jurisdiction of Chancery [*1861*] [*A publication*] (DLA)

Barry Ch Pr ... Barry. Statutory Jurisdiction of Chancery [*1861*] [*A publication*] (DLA)

Barry Conv ... Barry. Practice of Conveyancing [*1865*] [*A publication*] (DLA)

Barry Forms Conv ... Barry on Forms and Precedents in Conveyancing [*A publication*] (DLA)

BarryJwl ...... Barrys Jewelers [*Associated Press*] (SAG)

BarryR .... Barry [*R.G.*] Corp. [*Associated Press*] (SAG)

Barry Ten ..... Barry on Tenures [*A publication*] (DLA)

Barry U .... Barry University (GAGS)

BARS .... Armstrong-Spallumcheen Museum and Archives Society, Armstrong, British Columbia [*Library symbol National Library of Canada*] (NLC)

BARS .... Backup Attitude Reference System

BARS .... Ballistic Analysis Research System

BARS .... Baryon-Isobar Rest System

BARS .... Baseband RADAR Sensor Technology (PDAA)

BARS .... Baseline Accounting and Reporting System (NASA)

BARS .... Behaviorally Anchored Rating Scale

BARS .... Bell Audit Relate System [*Bell Laboratories*]

BARS .... Bid Analysis and Reporting System (AAGC)

BARS .... Boating Accident Reports System [*Coast Guard Information service or system*] (IID)

B-ARS .... British-American Rhykenological Society [*Defunct*] (EA)

BARS .... British Association for Romanian Studies (EAIO)

BARS .... British Association of Residential Settlements (BI)

BARS .... Budget Analysis Reporting System (MCD)

BARSA .... Billing, Accounts Receivable, Sales Analysis (IBMDP)

B Ar Sc .... Bachelor of Arts and Sciences

Bar SC Rep ... Barbour's Supreme Court Reports [*New York*] [*A publication*] (DLA)

BARS-F .... Bomber Air Relay System - Fly Along (MCD)

BARSTUR .... Barking Sands Tactical Underwater Range [*Naval Oceanographic Office*]

BARS-X .... Bomber Air Relay System - Extension (MCD)

BART .... Baronet [*British*]

Bart .... Bartolus de Sassoferrato [*Deceased, 1357*] [*Authority cited in pre-1607 legal work*] (DSA)

BART .... Baseline Armor Reliability Test [*Army*] (MCD)

BART .... Basic Armor Reliability Test (MCD)

BART .... Bay Area Rapid Transit [*San Francisco area, California*]

BART .... Best Available Retrofit Technology [*Environmental Protection Agency*]

BART .... Bio-Automated Roving Target [*Gun-like toy*]

BART .... Blood-Activated Recalcification [*Medicine*] (DMAA)

BART .... Brooklyn Army Terminal

BARTAP ...... Barge Transportation Appraisal Program [*Military*] (MCD)

Bart Bri .... Bartholomaeus Brixiensis [*Deceased circa 1258*] [*Authority cited in pre-1607 legal work*] (DSA)

BarTc .... Barringer Resources, Inc. [*Associated Press*] (SAG)

Bart Cepol ... Bartholomaeus Cepolla [*Deceased, 1477*] [*Authority cited in pre-1607 legal work*] (DSA)

BarTch .... Barringer Resources, Inc. [*Associated Press*] (SAG)

Bart Cong Election Cases ... Bartlett's Congressional Election Cases [*A publication*] (DLA)

Bart Conv .... Barton's Science of Conveyancing [*2nd ed.*] [*1810-22*] [*A publication*] (DLA)

Bart de Cap ... Bartholomaeus de Capua [*Deceased, 1328*] [*Authority cited in pre-1607 legal work*] (DSA)

BArtEd .... Bachelor of Art Education

Bart El Cas ... Bartlett's Congressional Election Cases [*A publication*] (DLA)

Bart Elec Cas ... Bartlett's Congressional Election Cases [*A publication*] (DLA)

Bart Eq .... Barton's Suit in Equity [*A publication*] (DLA)

BARTG .... British Amateur Radio Teleprinter Group (BI)

Barth .... Bartholomaeus Brixiensis [*Deceased circa 1258*] [*Authority cited in pre-1607 legal work*] (DSA)

Barth Belenz ... Bartholomaeus Belenzinus de Modena [*Deceased, 1478*] [*Authority cited in pre-1607 legal work*] (DSA)

Barth Brix .... Bartholomaeus Brixiensis [*Deceased circa 1258*] [*Authority cited in pre-1607 legal work*] (DSA)

Bartho Belenz ... Bartholomaeus Belenzinus de Modena [*Deceased, 1478*] [*Authority cited in pre-1607 legal work*] (DSA)

Bartho de Sali ... Bartholomaeus de Saliceto [*Deceased, 1411*] [*Authority cited in pre-1607 legal work*] (DSA)

Barthol .... Bartholomaeus de Exeter [*Flourished, 12th century*] [*Authority cited in pre-1607 legal work*] (DSA)

Bartholoman ... Bartholoman's Reports, Yorkshire Lent Assize [*March 9, 1911*] [*England*] [*A publication*] (DLA)

Bartho Mutinen ... Bartholomaeus Belenzinus (Mutinensis) [*Deceased, 1478*] [*Authority cited in pre-1607 legal work*] (DSA)

Bart Ind ...... Bartlett's Index of the Laws of Rhode Island [*A publication*] (DLA)

Bart L Pr ...... Barton's Law Practice [*A publication*] (DLA)

Bart Max ...... Barton's Maxims in Conveyancing [*A publication*] (DLA)

Bart Mines ... Bartlett's Law of Mining [*1850*] [*A publication*] (DLA)

Barto .... Bartholomaeus [*Authority cited in pre-1607 legal work*] (DSA)

Barto .... Bartolus de Sassoferrato [*Deceased, 1357*] [*Authority cited in pre-1607 legal work*] (DSA)

Bartol Camer ... Bartholomaeus Camerarius [*Deceased, 1564*] [*Authority cited in pre-1607 legal work*] (DSA)

Bart Prec Conv ... Barton's Modern Precedents in Conveyancing [*3rd ed.*] [*1826*] [*A publication*] (DLA)

BART REG .... Barton Regis [*England*]

BARTS .... St. Bartholomew's Hospital [*London*]

Bart Socin ... Bartholomaeus Socinus [*Deceased, 1507*] [*Authority cited in pre-1607 legal work*] (DSA)

BArtTh .... Bachelor of Art Theory

BARTU .... Bureau of Aeronautics Training Unit [*Obsolete Navy*]

BARU .... Barometric Altitude Reference Unit

Baruch C (CUNY) ... Bernard M. Baruch College of the City University of New York (GAGS)

BARUK .... Board of Airline Representatives in the United Kingdom

BARV .... Beach Armored Recovery Vehicle

bar vlt .... Barrel Vault (VRA)

BARY .... Barry's Jewelers [*NASDAQ symbol*] (TTSB)

BARY .... Barry's Jewelers, Inc. [*NASDAQ symbol*] (NQ)

BaryJ .... Barry's Jewelers, Inc. [*Associated Press*] (SAG)

BaryJw .... Barry's Jewelers, Inc. [*Associated Press*] (SAG)

BARYW .... Barry's Jewelers Wrrt [*NASDAQ symbol*] (TTSB)

BARZ .... BARRA, Inc. [*NASDAQ symbol*] (SPSG)

BARZREX ..... Bartok Archives Z-Symbol Rhythm Extraction [*Computer science*]

BAS .... Aero Services [*Barbados*] [*ICAO designator*] (FAAC)

BAS .... Baccalaureat en Sciences Administratives [*Canada*] (DD)

BAS .... Bachelor of Agricultural Science

BAS .... Bachelor of Applied Science

BAS .... Bachelor of Architectural Science

BAS .... Bachelor of Arts and Sciences

BAS .... Bachelor of Arts in Speech

BAS .... Bachelor of Science in Agriculture (DD)

BAS .... Balalae [*Solomon Islands*] [*Airport symbol*] (OAG)

BAS .... Balloon Atrial Septostomy [*Cardiology*] (DMAA)

BAS .... Base (DCTA)

BAS .... Basel [*Bale*] [*Switzerland*] [*Seismograph station code, US Geological Survey*]

BAS............ Basic [*Rate*] [*Value of the English pound*]
BAS............ Basic Activity Subset [*Telecommunications*] (OSI)
BAS............ Basic Airspeed [*Aviation*]
BAS............ Basic Allowance for Subsistence [*Military*]
BAS............ Basic Allowance for Subsistence (DOMA)
BAS............ Basic Angle System
BAS............ BASIC [*Beginner's All-Purpose Symbolic Instruction Code*] Program File [*Computer science*]
Bas............. Basophil [*Hematology*]
BAS............ Bass ADS [*NYSE symbol*] (SPSG)
BAS............ Basso [*Music*]
BAS............ Bass PLC [*NYSE symbol*] (SAG)
BAS............ Bastard [*Slang*] (DSUE)
Bas............. Basutoland (BARN)
BAS............ Battalion Aid Station [*Army*]
BAS............ Battlefield Automated Systems [*Computer science Military*] (RDA)
BAS............ Bay Area Library and Information System, Hayward, CA [*OCLC symbol*] (OCLC)
Bas............. Bazianus [*Deceased, 1197*] [*Authority cited in pre-1607 legal work*] (DSA)
BAS............ Beacon Airborne S-Band (IAA)
BAS............ Behavioral Approach Scale [*Psychology*]
BAS............ Bell Audit System [*Bell Laboratories*]
BAS............ Bendix Antiskid System [*Automotive engineering*]
BAS............ Benzyl Analogue of Serotonin [*Medicine*] (DAVI)
BAS............ Benzylantiserotonin [*Pharmacology*]
BAS............ Bibliographic Access System (EDAC)
BAS............ Bibliotheks Automatisierung-System [*Online Cataloguing System*] [*Federal Republic of Germany*] (NITA)
BAS............ Binaural Analysis System [*Noise testing*] [*Automotive engineering*]
BAS............ Bioactive Aortic Substance [*Biochemistry*]
BAS............ Bioanalytical Systems
BAS............ Biological Agent Simulant (MCD)
BAS............ Biological Anthropological Section (EA)
BAS............ Bleed Air System
BAS............ Blind Approach System [*Aviation*] (MCD)
BAS............ Block Automation System [*NYSE trading computer*]
BAS............ Bomb Alarm System [*Air Force*]
BAS............ Bomb Assembly Spares (NG)
BAS............ Book of Alternative Services [*Ecclesiastical*]
BAS............ Books-Across-the-Sea [*Project*]
BAS............ Boolean Assignment Statement [*Mathematics*]
BAS............ Boresight Adjustment System (PDAA)
BAS............ Boundary and Annexation Survey [*Bureau of the Census*] (GFGA)
BAS............ Brazilian-American Society [*Defunct*] (EA)
BAS............ Brazilian American Survey [*A publication*]
B-AS........... Britain-Australia Society (DBA)
BAS............ British Ability Scales (EDAC)
BAS............ British Acoustical Society
BAS............ British Allergy Society
BAS............ British Antarctic Survey [*Research center*] (IRC)
BAS............ British Army Staff
BAS............ British Association of Settlements and Social Action Centres
BAS............ British Association Standard (IAA)
BAS............ Budget Allocation Sheets (MCD)
BAS............ Budget Allocation Summary (MCD)
BAS............ Building Advisory Service [*British*] (BI)
BAS............ Bulletin of the Atomic Scientists [*A publication*] (BRI)
BAS............ Bureau of Analyzed Samples [*British*]
BAS............ Business Air Service Ltd. [*Airline*] [*Canada*]
BASA .... Babysitting Association of South Australia
BASA .... Behavioral Assessment of Speech Anxiety (EDAC)
BASA .... Boston Assesment of Severe Aphasia [*Medicine*] (DMAA)
BASA .... British Adhesive and Sealants Association
BASA .... British Air Survey Association (DBA)
BASA .... British Amputee Sports Association (DBA)
BASA .... British Architectural Students' Association (BI)
BASA .... British Association of Seed Analysts
BASA .... British-Australian Studies Association
BASA .... British Automatic Sprinkler Association (DBA)
BASA .... Buckeye Association of School Administrators [*Ohio*] (SRA)
Bas Adv Tra... Basic Advance Training
BASAF .... British and South African Forum
BASAM .... British Association of Grain, Seed Feed and Agricultural Merchants (PDAA)
BASA Mag ... BASA [*British Australian Studies Association*] Magazine [*A publication*]
BASAR .... Breathing Apparatus Self-Contained Compressed Air Search and Rescue (PDAA)
BASATA ...... British and South Asian Trade Association [*British Overseas Trade Board*] (DS)
BASBWE ..... British Association of Symphonic Bands and Wind Ensembles (EAIO)
BA Sc.......... Bachelor of Agricultural Science
BA Sc.......... Bachelor of Applied Science
BASC.......... Base Activation Statistical Control
BASC.......... Basic Assessment System for Children
BASC.......... Berlin Air Safety Center
BASC .... Booth American Shipping Corp. (MHDB)
BASC .... Brick Association of South Carolina (SRA)
BASC .... British Association for Shooting and Conservation
BASC .... British Association of Skin Camouflage (DBA)
BASC .... British Association of Sound Collections (DBA)
BASCA .... British Academy of Songwriters, Composers, and Authors
BASCD .... British Association for the Study of Community Dentistry

BASCELT..... British Association of State Colleges in English Language Teaching (DBA)
BAS CON .... Basso Continuo [*Continued Bass*] [*Music*] (ROG)
BASCOP....... Base Communications Plan [*United States Army Communications Command*] (MCD)
BASD .... Basic Active Service Date (AABC)
BASE.......... BankAmericard Service Exchange
BASE.......... Base Ten Systems, Inc. [*NASDAQ symbol*] (NQ)
BASE.......... Basic Army Strategic Estimate [*A document*]
BASE.......... Basic Automation Systems Elements
BASE.......... Basic Semantic Element [*Computer science*] (DIT)
BASE.......... Battlefield Surveillance [*RADAR*] Electronics (MCD)
BASE.......... Behavioral Academic Self-Esteem [*Student personality test*] [*Psychology*]
BASE.......... Beta-Alumina Solid Electrolyte
BASE.......... British Association for Service to the Elderly (DBA)
BASE.......... Brokerage Accounting System Elements [*IBM computer program*]
BASE.......... Buildings, Antennas, Spans, and Earth Formations [*Fixed-object parachuting*]
BASE.......... Business Assessment Study and Evaluation (PDAA)
BASE.......... Buyer Attitudes and Sales Experiences [*LIMRA*]
BASEA .... Base Ten Sys CI'A' [*NASDAQ symbol*] (TTSB)
BASEB .... Base Ten Sys CI'B' [*NASDAQ symbol*] (TTSB)
BASEC .... Base Section [*Military*]
BASEC .... British Approvals Service for Electric Cables (PDAA)
BASecStud.. Bachelor of Arts in Secretarial Studies (ADA)
BASEDEV .... Base Development Report
BASEEFA..... British Approvals Service for Electrical Equipment in Flammable Atmospheres [*General Council of British Shipping*] [*Research center*] (DS)
BASEFOR..... Base Force
BASEMAG ... Base de Datos Geomagneticos [*Instituto Geografico Nacional*] [*Database*]
BASEOPS..... Base Operations
BASES .... Battlefield Automated System Engineering Support [*Army*]
BASES .... Beam Approach Seeker Evaluation System [*Air Force*] (MCD)
BASES .... British Anti-Smoking Education Society
BASESERVUNIT... Base Service Unit [*Navy*]
BASEX .... Basic Experimental Language [*Computer science*] (IAA)
BASEX .... Basic-Extension (IAA)
BasExpl........ Basin Exploration, Inc. [*Associated Press*] (SAG)
BASF.......... Badische Anilin und Soda-Fabrik [*Automotive industry supplier*]
BASG .... Blacktown Agoraphobia Support Group [*Australia*]
BASH .... Baroque All Style High [*Acronym is title of silk screen by sculptor Eduardo Paolozzi*]
BASH .... Bird Aircraft Strike Hazard
BASH .... Body Acceleration Synchronous with the Heartbeat [*Cardiology*]
BASH .... Booksellers' Association Service House [*British*]
BASH .... Bulimia, Anorexia Self-Help
BashSSR..... Bashkir Soviet Socialist Republic
BASI.......... British Association of Ski Instructors (DI)
BAsianStudies... Bachelor of Asian Studies
BASIC .... Banking and Securities Industry Committee [*Inactive*]
BASIC .... Bank of Small Industries and Commerce [*Bangladesh*] (EY)
BASIC .... Basic Algebraic Symbolic Interpretive Compiler (IEEE)
BASIC .... Basic Appraisal System for Incoming Components
BASIC .... Basic Automatic Stored Instruction Computer (BUR)
BASIC .... Basic Aviation Sub-System Integration Concept (PDAA)
BASIC .... Battle Area Surveillance and Integrated Communications System [*Marine Corps*]
BASIC .... Bedell Advertising Selling Improvement Corp.
BASIC .... Beginners Algebraic Symbolic Interpretive Compiler [*Computer science*] (NITA)
BASIC .... Beginner's All-Purpose Symbolic Instruction Code [*Programming language invented by T. E. Kurtz and J. G. Kemeny at Dartmouth College in 1963-64*]
BASIC .... Biological Abstracts' Subjects in Context [*A publication*]
BASIC .... Body Armor System Individual Countermine Armor [*Army*] (INF)
BASIC .... Bridge and Structures Information Center [*University of Pittsburgh Department of Civil Engineering*] [*Information service or system*] (IID)
BASIC .... Brothers and Sisters in Christ [*An association*] (EA)
BASIC (English)... British-American Scientific International Commercial English
BASICPAC.... BASIC [*Beginner's All-Purpose Symbolic Instruction Code*] Processor and Computer
BASICPAC... Battle Area Surveillance and Integrated Communications System Processor and Computer [*Marine Corps*]
BASICS .... Battle Area Surveillance and Integrated Communications System [*Marine Corps*] (IEEE)
BASICS .... British Association of Immediate Care Schemes (PDAA)
BASICTNG... Basic Training [*Military*] (NVT)
BASIS .... Bank Automated Service Information System (BUR)
BASIS .... Bases and Stations Information System [*Navy*] (GFGA)
BASIS .... Base-Stored Image Sensor
BASIS .... Basic Achievement Skills Individual Screener [*Educational test*]
BASIS .... Battelle Automated Search Information System [*Database management system*] [*Battelle Memorial Institute*] [*Information service or system*]
BASIS .... Bay Area Spatial Information System [*Geogroup Corp.*] [*Information service or system*] (IID)
BASIS .... Biological and Agricultural Sciences Information Service [*University of Minnesota, St. Paul*] [*Information service or system*] (IID)
BASIS .... Booking and Sampling for Indirect Standards [*British*]
BASIS .... British Airways Safety Information System (GAVI)
BASIS .... Budgetary and Scheduling Information System (MCD)

BASIS	Bureau of Accreditation and School Improvement Studies [*University of Michigan*] [*Research center*] (RCD)
BASIS	Burroughs Advanced Statistical Inquiry System [*Computer science*] (BUR)
BASIS	Burroughs and Sperry Information Systems [*Suggested name for the corporation formed by the Burroughs/Sperry merger*]
BASIS-E	Bibliothekarisch-Analytisches System zur Informations Speicherung-Erschleissung [*Library analytical system for information storage/retrieval*] [*Federal Republic of Germany*] (NITA)
BASIX	Bay Area Seismic Imaging Experiment [*Geology*]
BASJE	Bolivian Air-Shower Joint Experiment
basl	Basilica (VRA)
BASLC	British Association of Sports Ground and Landscape Contractors Ltd. (BI)
BASLP	Bulletin. Australian Society of Legal Philosophy [*A publication*]
BASM	Ashcroft Museum, British Columbia [*Library symbol National Library of Canada*] (NLC)
BASM	Bachelor of Arts in Sacred Music (BJA)
BASM	Bachelor of Arts, Master of Science
BASM	British Association of Sport Medicine
BASMA	Boot and Shoe Manufacturers' Association and Leather Trades Protection Society [*British*] (BI)
BASMM	British Association of Sewing Machine Manufacturers (PDAA)
BASMON	British Association Sovereign and Military Order of Malta (BI)
BASNET	Basic Network (IAA)
BASO	Base Accountable Supply Officer [*Air Force*]
BASO	Basophil [*Hematology*] (DHSM)
BASO	Brigade Air Support Officer [*Military British*]
BASO	British Association of Surgical Oncology
BASO	Bureau of Aeronautics Shipment Order [*Obsolete Navy*]
BASOC	Brigade Air Support Operations Centre [*Military British*]
BASOPS	Base Operating Information System [*Formerly, COCOAS*]
BASOPS	Base Operations Office
BASOPS (SMS)	Base Operating Information System (Supply Management System)
BASP	Biomedical Analog Signal Processor (IAA)
BASP	British Association of Social Psychiatry
BASPA	British Amateur Strand Pulling Association
BASPCAN	British Association for the Study and Prevention of Child Abuse and Neglect (DI)
BasPetr	Basic Petroleum International Ltd. [*Associated Press*] (SAG)
BASPM	Basic Planning Memorandum (NATG)
BAS-R	Basic Research
BASR	Bureau of Applied Social Research [*Columbia University*] (IID)
BASRA	British American Scientific Research Association
B/ASRE	British Admiralty Signal RADAR Establishment
BASRM	British Association of Synthetic Rubber Manufacturers (PDAA)
BASS	Bachelor of Arts in Social Science (WDAA)
B As S	Bachelor of Association Science
BASS	Backup Avionics Subsystem Software (MCD)
BASS	Ballistic Armor Subsystem [*Military*] (DOMA)
BASS	Base Augmentation Support Set (MCD)
BASS	Basic Analog Simulation System (PDAA)
BASS	Bass Anglers Sportsman Society (EA)
Bass	Bass Public Ltd. [*Associated Press*] (SAG)
BASS	Battlefield Area Surveillance System (MCD)
BASS	Behavioral and Social Sciences
BASS	Belgian Archives for the Social Sciences [*Information service or system*] (IID)
BASS	Bendigo Agricultural Show Society [*Australia*]
BASS	Benthic Acoustic Stress Sensor [*Oceanographic instrument*]
BASS	Best Available Shelter Survey [*of fallout shelters*] [*Civil Defense*]
BASS	Bond and Share Society [*British*] (DBA)
BASS	British Airways Shuttle Services
BASS	British Association of Ship Suppliers (DBA)
BASS	British Australian Settlers Society
BASS	Broadband Analysis SONAR Surveillance (MCD)
BASSA	Bangladesh-Australia Society of South Australia
BASSAC	British Association of Settlements and Social Action Centres
B As Sc	Bachelor of Association Science
BASS CON	Basso Continuo [*Continued Bass*] [*Music*]
BASS CONT	Basso Continuo [*Continued Bass*] [*Music*]
Bass Crim Pl	Bassett's Illinois Criminal Pleading and Practice [*A publication*] (DLA)
BASSEES	British Association for Soviet, Slavonic, and East European Studies (DBA)
BassettF	Bassett Furniture [*Associated Press*] (SAG)
BAST	Bastard (DLA)
BAST	Bastardy [*FBI standardized term*]
BAST	Best Available and Safest Technology
BAST	Board on Army Science and Technology [*National Research Council, Academies of Science and Engineering, and Institute of Medicine*]
BAST	Boric Acid Storage Tank (IEEE)
BASTUR	Baking Sands Tactical Underwater Range [*Oahu, HI*]
BASW	Bell Alarm Switch (AAG)
BASW	British Army Staff, Washington (MCD)
BASW	British Association of Social Workers
baswd	Basswood (VRA)
BASX	Basler Airlines, Inc. [*Air carrier designation symbol*]
BASYC	Benefit Assessment for System Change (MHDB)
BASYS	Basic System (IEEE)
BAT	Bachelor of Arts in Teaching
BAT	Backup Auxiliary Transformer [*Nuclear energy*] (GFGA)
bat	Baltic [*MARC language code Library of Congress*] (LCCP)
BAT	Banat Air Service Ltd. [*Romania*] [*FAA designator*] (FAAC)
BAT	Base Address and Transfer [*Military*]
BAT	Basic Air Temperature
BAT	Basic Armor Training (MCD)
BAT	Batch [*Computer science*] (CDE)
BAT	Batch File [*Computer science*]
BAT	Batean [*Ship's rigging*]
BAT	Bathurst Paper Ltd. [*Toronto Stock Exchange symbol*]
BAT	BAT Industries Ltd. [*Associated Press*] (SAG)
BAT	Battalion
BAT	Battalion Antitank Recoilless Rifle
BAT	Batter
BAT	Battery (AAG)
BAT	Battle (AABC)
BAT	Battleship (MUGU)
BAT	Bayram-Ali [*Former USSR Seismograph station code, US Geological Survey Closed*] (SEIS)
BAT	Beam Approach Training [*Military*]
BAT	Behavioral Avoidance Test [*Psychometrics*]
BAT	Behaviroal Assertiveness Test [*Psychometrics*] (EDAC)
BAT	Bell Advanced Tilt Rotor (MCD)
BAT	Bell Aerospace Textron
BAT	Benzilic Acid Tropine Ester [*Also, BETE, BTE*] [*Pharmacology*]
BAT	Best Available Technology
BAT	Best Available Treatment (MCD)
BAT	Beta, Atla, and Themis [*Regions on planet Venus*]
BAT	Bioassay Tank [*Spacecraft*] [*NASA*]
BAT	Biological Abstracts on Tape [*Biosciences Information Service*] [*Information service or system*]
BAT	Biological Antiseptic Tampon (IIA)
BAT	Biomedical Application Teams [*NASA*]
BAT	Blackrock Advantage Term [*NYSE symbol*] (TTSB)
BAT	Blackrock Advantage Term Trust [*NYSE symbol*] (SPSG)
BAT	Blind Approach Training [*Air Force*]
BAT	Block Address Translation [*Computer science*] (PCM)
BAT	Bloom Analogies Test [*Intelligence test*]
BAT	Boeing Air Transport
BAT	Bolshoi Alt-Azimuth Telescope [*Former USSR*]
BAT	Bore Autonomic Tester
BAT	Boric Acid Tank [*Nuclear energy*] (NRCH)
BAT	Boric Acid Transfer [*Nuclear energy*] (NRCH)
BAT	Boston Athenaeum, Boston, MA [*OCLC symbol*] (OCLC)
BAT	Branch Assistance Team [*Military*] (AABC)
BAT	Break-Away Torque [*Automotive engineering*]
BAT	Brilliant Anti-Armor Submunition [*Army*] (RDA)
BAT	Brilliant Anti-Armor [*Submunition*] Technology
BAT	Brilliant Anti-Tank System [*Army*]
BAT	British Aerial Transport Ltd.
BAT	British-American Tobacco Co.
BAT	British Antarctic Territory
BAT	Bromoacetamidothymidine [*Antineoplastic drug*]
BAT	Brown Adipose Tissue [*Physiology*]
BAT	Bureau de l'Assistance Technique [*Technical Assistance Bureau*]
BAT	Bureau of Apprenticeship and Training [*Department of Labor*]
BAT	Buses and Trucks
BAT	Bushwaster Armored Turret (MCD)
BAT	Butler Air Transport Ltd.
BATA	Bakery and Allied Trades Association Ltd. [*British*] (BI)
BATA	Black American Travel Association [*Defunct*]
BATA	British Air Transport Association (DA)
BATAB	Baker and Taylor Automated Buying [*A teleordering system*] (NITA)
BATAB	Baker and Taylor's Automated Buying System [*Teleordering system*] [*Baker & Taylor Companies*] [*Information service or system*] (IID)
BaTaSYSTEMS	Baker & Taylor Electronic Book Ordering Service [*Baker & Taylor Companies*] [*Trademark*]
BATBAMS	British Antitank Bar Mine System (MCD)
BAT-C	Behavioral Assertiveness Test for Children
BATC	Big Apple Triathlon Club (EA)
BATC	Boeing Atlantic Test Center (KSC)
BATC	British Amateur Television Club
BATC	British-American Tobacco Co.
BATC	British Arabian Technical Cooperation (PDAA)
BATC	Burnside-Ott Aviation Training Center [*Florida*]
BAT CHG	Battery Charger [*Military*] (MSA)
Batch Mfg Cor	Batchelder's Law of Massachusetts Manufacturing Corporations [*A publication*] (DLA)
BATCLM	British Association of Trade Computer Label Manufacturers (DBA)
BATCO	Battery Cutoff [*Telecommunications*] (IAA)
BATCRULANT	Battleships and Cruisers, Atlantic Fleet
BATCRUPAC	Battleships and Cruisers, Pacific Fleet
BATD	British Association of Teachers of the Deaf (AIE)
BAT-D	Deception Battalion [*Army*] (ADDR)
Bat Dig	Battle's Digest [*North Carolina*] [*A publication*] (DLA)
BATDIV	Battleship Division
BATE	Base Activation Test Equipment
BATE	Base Assembly and Test Equipment (SAA)
BATEA	Best Available Technology Economically Achievable [*Wastewater treatment*]
Bate Ag	Bateman on Agency [*A publication*] (DLA)
BATEAM	Biomedical Technology Transfer Team
Bate Auct	Bateman. Law of Auctions [*11th ed.*] [*1953*] [*A publication*] (DLA)
Bate Com L	Bateman's Commercial Law [*A publication*] (DLA)
Bate Const	Bateman's United States Constitutional Law [*A publication*] (DLA)
Bate Exc	Bateman. General Laws of Excise [*2nd ed.*] [*1840*] [*A publication*] (DLA)

BATELCO ..... Bahamas Telecommunications Corp. [*Telecommunications service*] (TSSD)
BATELCO ..... Bahrain Telecommunications Co.
BATES .... Ballistic Test and Evaluation Systems (KSC)
Bates .... Bates' Delaware Chancery Reports [*A publication*] (DLA)
BATES .... Battlefield Artillery Target Engagement System (MCD)
Bates' Ann St... Bates' Annotated Revised Statutes [*Ohio*] [*A publication*] (DLA)
Bates Ch ...... Bates' Delaware Chancery Reports [*A publication*] (DLA)
Bates' Dig ..... Bates' Digest [*Ohio*] [*A publication*] (DLA)
Bateson ...... Leicester Records [*Municipal Courts, 1103-1603*] [*England*] [*A publication*] (DLA)
Bates Part ... Bates' Law of Partnership [*A publication*] (DLA)
BATEX .... Batch Executive (IAA)
BATF .... Beam Approach Training Flight [*British military*] (DMA)
BATF .... Biological Aerosol Test Facility [*Army*]
BATF .... Bureau of Alcohol, Tobacco, and Firearms [*Department of the Treasury*]
BATFOR ...... Battle Force
BATFU .... Battery Fuse (IAA)
BATH .... Back Again to Hoover [*Slogan during 1974 economic downturn*]
BATH .... Bacterial Adhesion to Hydrocarbons
BATH .... Best Available True Heading (MCD)
BA Theo ...... Bachelor of Arts in Theology
B A Theol .... Bachelor of Arts in Theology (BARN)
BATHRM ..... Bathroom [*Classified advertising*] (ADA)
bathrm .... Bathroom (VRA)
BATHY .... Bathythermograph [*Oceanography*] (MSC)
BATI .... Battalion Tactical Initialization [*Military*]
BATLANT ..... Battleships, Atlantic Fleet
BatlMt .... Battle Mountain Gold Co. [*Associated Press*] (SAG)
BATLSK .... British Army Training Liaison Staff, Kenya
BATM .... Atlin Historical Museum, British Columbia [*Library symbol National Library of Canada*] (NLC)
BATM .... British Admiralty Technical Mission [*World War II*]
BATM .... Bureau of Air Traffic Management
BATMA .... Bookbinding and Allied Trades Management Association (DGA)
BATN .... Battalion (ROG)
BATNEEC .... Best Available Technology Not Entailing Excessive Costs [*British*]
BATO .... Balloon-Assisted Takeoff [*Air Force*]
BATO .... British Association of Tourism Officers (EAIO)
BATOD .... British Association of Teachers of the Deaf
BATP .... Boric Acid Transfer Pump (IEEE)
BATP .... Bridge Across the Pond Tom Jones Fan Club (EA)
BATPAC ...... Battleships, Pacific Fleet
BATR .... Beginning Assessment Test of Reading (EDAC)
BATRAM ...... Battery Random Access Memory [*External storage system*] [*Computer science*]
BATREADCOM... Battle Readiness and Competition Instructions (NVT)
BATREADCOMP... Battle Readiness and Competition Instructions (NVT)
BATRECON... Battle Reconnaissance (MCD)
Bat Rev St ... Battle's Revised Statutes of North Carolina [*1873*] [*A publication*] (DLA)
BATRON ...... Battleship Squadron
BATROP ...... Barotropic Prognosis (FAAC)
BATRS .... British Amateur Tape Recording Society
BATRY .... Battery
BATS .... Bakers' and Allied Traders' Golfing Society [*British*] (BI)
BATS .... Ballistic Aerial Target System
BATS .... Basic Additional Teleprocessing Support [*Computer science*] (BUR)
BATS .... Batteries Batteries [*NASDAQ symbol*] (TTSB)
BATS .... Batteries Batteries, Inc. [*NASDAQ symbol*] (SAG)
BATS .... Bermuda Atlantic Time Series [*Oceanographic Station*]
BATS .... Beta Alternating Transmission System (MCD)
BATS .... Biosphere-Atmosphere Transfer Scheme [*Meteorology*]
BATS .... Bradford Action on Teacher Shortages (AIE)
BATS .... British Association of Trauma in Sport (DBA)
BATS .... British Association of Traumatology in Sport (DI)
BATS .... Bulk Filtering Acquisition and Tracking System (MCD)
BATS .... Business Air Transport Service
BATSE .... Burst and Transient Source Experiment [*Gamma Ray Observatory satellite data collection*]
BATSHIP ...... Battleship
BATSHIPSBATFORPAC... Battleships, Battle Force, Pacific Fleet
BATSHIPSLANT... Battleships, Atlantic Fleet
BATSHIPSPAC... Battleships, Pacific Fleet
Bat Sp Perf... Batten. Specific Performance on Contracts [*1849*] [*A publication*] (DLA)
BATSS .... Battlefield Automated Tactical Support System (MCD)
Bat Stan ..... Batten on the Stannaries Act [*A publication*] (DLA)
Bat Stat ...... Battle's Revised Statutes of North Carolina [*1873*] [*A publication*] (DLA)
BATSUP ...... Battery Supply (IAA)
BATSW .... Batteries Batteries Wrrt [*NASDAQ symbol*] (TTSB)
BATT .... Barry All the Time (EA)
BATT .... Battalion
BATT .... Batten (KSC)
BATT .... Battery [*FBI standardized term*]
BATT .... Battery
BATT .... Battle (WGA)
Batt .... Batty's Irish King's Bench Reports [*A publication*] (DLA)
BATT .... British Army Training Team
BatTech ...... Battery Tech, Inc. [*Associated Press*] (SAG)
Batter .... Batteries Batteries, Inc. [*Associated Press*] (SAG)
Batteries...... Batteries Batteries, Inc. [*Associated Press*] (SAG)

BATTLE .... Battalion Analyzer and Tactical Trainer for Local Engagements (MCD)
Battle's Revisal... Battle's Revised Statutes of North Carolina [*1873*] [*A publication*] (DLA)
BATTN .... Battalion (ADA)
BATTOPER ... Battery Operated (IAA)
Batts' Ann St... Batts' Annotated Revised Civil Statutes [*Texas*] [*A publication*] (DLA)
Batts' Rev St... Batts' Annotated Revised Civil Statutes [*Texas*] [*A publication*] (DLA)
BATTY .... Battery
Batty (Ir)..... Batty's Irish King's Bench Reports [*A publication*] (DLA)
BATUS .... British Army Training Unit, Suffield [*British military*] (DMA)
BATV .... Boilerplates Aerodynamic Test Vehicle (MCD)
BATV .... Bureau for Adult Thalidomide Victims [*West Germany*]
BAU .... Baseband Assembly Unit
BAU .... Basic Assembly Unit (WDAA)
BAU .... Bauru [*Brazil*] [*Airport symbol*] (OAG)
BAU .... Bay Resources [*Vancouver Stock Exchange symbol*]
BAU .... Beau Canada Exploration Ltd. [*Toronto Stock Exchange symbol*]
BAU .... Bombing Analysis Unit [*Supreme Headquarters, Allied Expeditionary Force*] [*World War II*]
BAU .... British Absolute Unit
BAU .... British Association Unit (IAA)
BAU .... Bulgarian Agrarian Union [*Political party*]
BAU .... Business as Usual
BAUA .... Business Aircraft Users' Association [*British*]
BAUD .... Baudot (IAA)
BAUD .... Baudot Code
B Au E .... Bachelor of Automobile Engineering
B Au Eng .... Bachelor of Automobile Engineering
BAUF .... Budget Authorization and Updating Form (MCD)
BAUFO .... Bauforschungsprojekte [*Building Research Projects*] [*Fraunhofer Society*] [*Information service or system*] (IID)
BAUP .... Bovie-Assisted Uvulopalatoplasty (DMAA)
BAUS .... British Association of Urological Surgeons
BauschL ...... Bausch & Lomb, Inc. [*Associated Press*] (SAG)
BAV .... Air Varna Co. [*Bulgaria*] [*ICAO designator*] (FAAC)
BAV .... Bachelier en Arts Visuels [*Bachelor of Visual Arts*] [*French*]
BAV .... Baotou [*China*] [*Airport symbol*] (OAG)
BAV .... Bavaria [*State in West Germany*] (ROG)
BAV .... Bavarian Lion Industries Ltd. [*Vancouver Stock Exchange symbol*]
BAV .... Bicuspid Aortic Valve [*Cardiology*] (DMAA)
BAV .... Blacksburg [*Virginia*] [*Seismograph station code, US Geological Survey*] (SEIS)
BAV .... Bolivar, TN [*Location identifier FAA*] (FAAL)
BAV .... [*A*] Book of American Verse [*A publication*]
BA(VA) .... Bachelor of Arts (Visual Arts)
BAVA .... Byelorussian-American Veteran Association (EA)
BAVF .... Blinded American Veterans Foundation (EA)
BAVFO .... Bradycardia after Arteriovenous Fistula Occlusion [*Cardiology*] (DMAA)
BAVIP .... Bleomycin, Adriamycin, Vinblastine, Imidazole carboxamide [*Dacarbazine*], Prednisone [*Antineoplastic drug regimen*]
BAVIP .... Bleomycin, Dacarbazine [*DTIC*], Vincristine, Adriamycin, Prednisone [*Antineoplastic drug regimen*] (DAVI)
BAVIP .... British Association of Viewdata Information Providers
BAVisCom... Bachelor of Arts in Visual Communication
BAVP .... Balloon Aortic Valvuloplasty [*Cardiology*] (DAVI)
BAVTE .... Bureau of Adult, Vocational, and Technical Education (OICC)
BAW .... Bare Aluminum Wire
BAW .... Baywest Capital [*Vancouver Stock Exchange symbol*]
BAW .... Beet Armyworm Larvae [*Entomology*]
BAW .... British Airways [*ICAO designator*] (FAAC)
BAW .... Bronchoalveolar Wash Fluids [*Medicine*]
BAW .... Bulk Acoustic Wave [*Physics*]
BAW .... Bureau of Animal Welfare [*Victoria, Australia*]
BAW .... Butanol/Acetic Acid/Water [*Solvent system*]
BAWA .... Badminton Association of Western Australia
BAWA .... British Amateur Wrestling Association (BI)
BAWA .... British-American Wrestling Association (DI)
BAWA .... Burley Auction Warehouse Association (EA)
BAWA .... Byelorussian-American Women Association (EA)
BAWA .... Unitarian Universalists for Black and White Action (EA)
BaWb .... Beitraege zum Assyrischen Woerterbuch [*A publication*] (BJA)
BAWB .... Bomber Activity Weekly Brief (MCD)
BAWC .... Brisbane Amateur Winemakers' Club [*Australia*]
BAWD .... British Association of Wheelchair Distributors (DBA)
BAWE .... British Association of Women Entrepreneurs (DBA)
BAWE .... British Association of Women Executives (DI)
BAWHA .... Bide-a-Wee Home Association (EA)
BAWLA .... British Amateur Weight Lifters' Association
BAWPE .... Biased Antiworld Paw Entry [*Testing of left and right laterality in mice*]
BAWRA .... British Australian Wool Realization Association
BAWS .... Basic Acoustic Warfare System (MCD)
BAWTR .... Babcock & Wilcox Test Reactor
BAX .... Bad Axe, MI [*Location identifier FAA*] (FAAL)
BAX .... Baxter International [*NYSE symbol*] (SPSG)
BAX .... Baxter Laboratories, Inc. [*of Baxter Travenol Laboratories, Inc.*] [*Research code symbol*]
Bax .... Baxter's Reports [*60-68 Tennessee*] [*A publication*] (DLA)
BAX .... Beacon Airborne X-Band (IAA)
BAX .... Burlington Air Express [*ICAO designator*] (AD)

BAX	Travenol Laboratories [of Baxter Travenol Laboratories, Inc.] [Research code symbol]
Bax Jud Acts	Baxter on Judicature Acts and Rules [A publication] (DLA)
Baxt	Baxter's Reports [60-68 Tennessee] [A publication] (DLA)
Baxter	Baxter International, Inc. [Associated Press] (SAG)
Baxter	Baxter's Reports [60-68 Tennessee] [A publication] (DLA)
Baxt (Tenn)	Baxter's Reports [60-68 Tennessee] [A publication] (DLA)
BAY	Baia Mare [Romania] [Airport symbol] (OAG)
BAY	Bay Air Aviation [New Zealand] [ICAO designator] (FAAC)
BAY	Bayandai [Former USSR Seismograph station code, US Geological Survey Closed] (SEIS)
BAY	Bay Mills Ltd. [Toronto Stock Exchange symbol]
BAY	Bay Networks [NYSE symbol] (TTSB)
BAY	Bay Networks, Inc. [NYSE symbol] (SAG)
BAY	Bayonet (MSA)
Bay	Bay's Reports [1-3, 5-8 Missouri] [A publication] (DLA)
Bay	Bay's South Carolina Reports [1783-1804] [A publication] (DLA)
BAY	Coos Bay Public Library, Coos Bay, OR [OCLC symbol] (OCLC)
BAY	Farbenfabriken Bayer [Germany] [Research code symbol]
Bayan	Bagong Alyansang Makabayan [Philippines] [Political party] (EY)
BayApt	Bay Apartment Communities [Associated Press] (SAG)
Bay Bills	Bayley on Bills and Notes [A publication] (DLA)
BayBks	Baybanks, Inc. [Associated Press] (SAG)
BAYC	Bayonet Candelabra
BAYCANDDC	Bayonet Candelabra Double Contact
BAYCANDSC	Bayonet Candelabra Single Contact
Bay Cons	Bayard on the Constitution of the United States [A publication] (DLA)
Bay Dig Ind	Baylies' Digested Index of English and American Reports [A publication] (DLA)
Bay Dom Serv	Baylies on Domestic Servants [A publication] (DLA)
Bay Ev	Bayard on Evidence [A publication] (DLA)
Bayl B	Bayley on Bills [A publication] (DLA)
Bayl Ch Pr	Bayley's Commentaries on the Laws of England [A publication] (DLA)
Bayl F & R	Bayley on Fines and Recoveries [A publication] (DLA)
Baylles Sur	Baylles on Sureties and Guarantors [A publication] (DLA)
Baylor U	Baylor University (GAGS)
Bayl Q & A	Bayley's Questions and Answers for Students [A publication] (DLA)
BayMea	Bay Meadows Operating Co. [Associated Press] (SAG)
BAYMV	Barley Yellow Mosaic Virus [Plant pathology]
BayNtwk	Bay Networks, Inc. [Associated Press] (SAG)
BAYO	Byelorussian-American Youth Organization (EA)
BAYOO	Bayoo [Commonly used] (OPSA)
Bayou	Bayou Steel Corp. of La Place [Associated Press] (SAG)
Bayport	Bayport Restaurant Group, Inc. [Associated Press] (SAG)
BayRidge	Bay Ridge Bancorp [Associated Press] (SAG)
BAYS	British Association of Young Scientists (BI)
BaySGs	Bay State Gas Co. [Associated Press] (SAG)
BAYSK	Bayonet Skirted
BayVw	Bay View Capital Corp. [Associated Press] (SAG)
Baz	Bazianus [Deceased, 1197] [Authority cited in pre-1607 legal work] (DSA)
Baz	Bazianus de Baldone de Vaude [Flourished, 13th century] [Authority cited in pre-1607 legal work] (DSA)
BAZ	Bazil [Red sheep] [Bookbinding] (ROG)
BAZ	New Braunfels, TX [Location identifier FAA] (FAAL)
Baza	Bazianus [Deceased, 1197] [Authority cited in pre-1607 legal work] (DSA)
Bazan	Bazianus [Deceased, 1197] [Authority cited in pre-1607 legal work] (DSA)
BAZE	Bayesian Zero-Failure [Computer science] (MCD)
BAZO-PS	British Anti-Zionist Organisation - Palestine Solidarity
BB	Air Great Lakes [ICAO designator] (AD)
BB	Baba Bathra [or Bava Batra] (BJA)
Bb	Babbitt [Metallurgy]
BB	Baby Bond [Investment term]
B/B	Baby Incendiary Bomb
BB	Babylonische Briefe aus der Zeit der Hammurapi Dynastie [A publication] (BJA)
BB	Babylonische Bussspalmen [A publication] (BJA)
BB	Bachelor of Bacteriology
BB	Bachelor of Business
BB	Backboard [Telecommunications] (TEL)
BB	Backbord [Portside] [German military]
BB	Bad Breath
BB	Bail Bond (DLA)
BB	Balanced Budget
BB	Ball Bearing [Technical drawings]
BB	Ball on National Banks [A publication] (DLA)
BB	Balloon Barrage
BB	Banca Brignone [Italy]
BB	Banco BHIF [NYSE symbol] (SAG)
BB	Banco de Bilbao [Italian]
BB	Banco de Bilbao [Spain]
BB	B and Better [Lumber]
BB	Bandblock (IAA)
BB	Bangkok Bank [Thailand]
BB	Bank Book
BB	Bank Burglary
BB	Bankim Barotra [Commerce Bank] [Malagasy] (AF)
BB	Barbadensis [Pharmacy] (ROG)
bb	Barbados [MARC country of publication code Library of Congress] (LCCP)
BB	Barbados [ANSI two-letter standard code] (CNC)
BB	Bare Base [Air Force] (AFM)
BB	Barrel Bulk [Shipping] (ROG)
BB	Barrels [or Boxes] [Freight]
BB	Barry's Babes [Later, BGR] (EA)
BB	Baseband (AAG)
BB	Base Burning (MCD)
BB	Bases on Balls [Baseball]
BB	Basketball (ADA)
BB	Bath Blanket [Medicine] (MEDA)
BB	Bats Both Right-Handed and Left-Handed [Baseball]
BB	Battleship [Navy symbol]
BB	Bayley on Bills [A publication] (DLA)
BB	Bayonet Base [Lens mount] (NTCM)
BB	Beacon Buoy (IAA)
BB	Bearer Bond [Investment term] (ADA)
BB	Beautiful Books [A publication]
BB	Bed Bath [Medicine]
BB	Bedspread Blanket
BB	Beer Barrel (WDAA)
BB	Begin Bracket [Indicator] [Computer science] (IBMDP)
BB	Below Bridges [Navigation]
BB	Bennington Bunch [An association] (EA)
BB	Beobachtung [Observation] [German]
BB	Berlin Brigade
BB	Berlinetta Boxer [Ferrari sports car]
BB	Bernard Berenson [American art critic, 1865-1959]
BB	Best Black [Pencil leads] (ROG)
BB	Best of Breed
BB	Beta-Blocker [Pharmacology] (DAVI)
BB	Bible
Bb	Biblica [A publication] (BJA)
BB	Biceps Brachii [A muscle]
BB	Big Band [Music] (WDMC)
BB	Big Bear Stores Co. (IIA)
BB	Big Block [Series of Chevrolet V-8 engines]
BB	Big Board [The New York Stock Exchange, Inc.] [Slang]
BB	Big Brother [From George Orwell's novel, "1984"]
BB	Bill Blass [Couturier]
BB	Bill Book [Shipping]
BB	Billion Barrels [Shipping]
BB	Birmingham Belt R. R. [AAR code]
BB	Bishops (ADA)
BB	BIT [Binary Digit]/Byte Conversion [Telecommunications] (TEL)
BB	Bitter and Burton [British] (DSUE)
BB	Black-Bordered [Stationery]
BB	Blanket Bath [Medicine]
BB	Block Brazing
BB	Blocking Back [Football]
BB	Blood Bank
BB	Blood Buffer Base [Biochemistry] (DAVI)
BB	Bloody Bastard [British slang]
BB	Blowback
BB	Blow Bottle [Medicine] (DAVI)
BB	Bluebird [Division of Victor] [Record label]
BB	Blue-Black
BB	Blue Bloaters [Emphysema] [Slang Medicine] (MAE)
BB	Blue Bomber [Valium tablet] [Slang]
BB	Blue Book [Directory of proprietaries]
BB	B'nai B'rith [Later, BBI] (EA)
B/B	Body Belts [Medicine] (DAVI)
BB	Body Burden [of radiation]
BB	Bomb (MUGU)
BB	Bomb Bay [of an aircraft]
BB	Bomber [Russian aircraft symbol]
BB	Bombesin [Biochemistry]
BB	Bonner-Bibel (BJA)
BB	Books (WDAA)
BB	Booster Battery
BB	Borg & Beck [Automotive industry supplier]
BB	Both Bones [With reference to fractures] [Medicine]
B/B	Both-to-Blame [Shipping]
B/B	Bottled in Bond [Wines and spirits]
BB	Bottom Bounce [SONAR propagation mode] [Navy] (NG)
BB	Bought Book [Tea trade] (ROG)
BB	Bowel or Bladder [Medicine] (DAVI)
BB	Boys' Brigade [British]
BB	Branch Bill
BB	Breadboard [NASA] (KSC)
BB	Break Bulk [Shipping]
BB	Breaker Block
BB	Breaks Below
BB	Breakthrough Bleeding [Medicine]
BB	Breast Biopsy [Medicine]
BB	Brigitte Bardot [French actress]
BB	Brisbane Basketball
BB	Brisbane Biennial
BB	British Blue [A British sailor]
BB	Broadband [Communications channel description] (IEEE)
BB	Broadcast Bureau [of FCC]
BB	Bronsted Base [Biochemistry]
BB	Brownish-Black
BB	Brown Sedge Growth with Brown Sedge [Ecology]
BB	Brush Border [of intestinal epithelial cell] [Cell physiology]
BB	Buffer Base (MAE)
BB	Building Block (KSC)
BB	Bulk Burning (IEEE)

BB	Bulletin Board [*Computer online message system*]
BB	Bulletin Board (PCM)
BB	Bum Boy [*Slang British*] (DSUE)
BB	Bunching Block (MSA)
BB	Bundle-Branch [*Cardiology*] (DAVI)
BB	Bureau of Biologics [*Also, BOB*] [*FDA*]
BB	Bureau of the Budget [*Later, OMB*]
BB	Burgan Bank [*Kuwait*]
BB	Burnaby Public Library, British Columbia [*Library symbol National Library of Canada*] (NLC)
BB	Burning Bush [*Freemasonry*]
BB	Burroughs Bibliophiles (EA)
BB	Burton and Bitter [*Drink served in British public houses*]
BB	Bus-Bar Layout Drawing [*Computer science*] (TEL)
B-B	Business-to-Business [*Advertising*] (WDMC)
BB	Bust Bodice [*Early name for brassiere*]
BB	Busy BIT [*Binary Digit*] [*Computer science*] (IAA)
B-B	Butane-Butene Fraction
BB	Buy Back [*Investment term*]
BB	Double Black [*Pencil*]
BB	Drawing Paper Having a Medium Rough Surface (BARN)
BB	Hawker Siddeley Aviation Ltd. [*British ICAO aircraft manufacturer identifier*] (ICAO)
BB	Lower Medium [*Standard & Poor's bond rating*] [*Investment term*]
BB	Secondary Type Battery [*JETDS nomenclature*] [*Military*] (CET)
BBA	Bachelor of Business Administration
BBA	Balanced Budget Amendment
BBA	Balmaceda [*Chile*] [*Airport symbol*] (OAG)
BBA	Barclays Bank Australia
BBA	Beclobrinic Acid [*Biochemistry*]
BBA	Benzoylbenzoic Acid [*Organic chemistry*]
BBA	Bermuda Benevolent Association
BBA	Big Brothers of America [*Later, BB/BSA*] (EA)
BBA	Bishop Baraga Association (EA)
BBA	Black Business Alliance (EA)
BBA	Blind Book Auxiliary (DGA)
BBA	Bluetick Breeders of America (EA)
BBA	Bogart-Brociner Associates [*Information service or system*] (IID)
BBA	Bolshoi Ballet Academy [*Moscow*]
BBA	Bolt and Bond Assembly
BBA	Bombay Co. [*NYSE symbol*] (SPSG)
BBA	Bombay Company [*NYSE symbol*] (TTSB)
BBA	Born before Arrival [*of mother at hospital*] [*Medicine*]
BBA	British Bankers' Association
BBA	British Bloodstock Agency
BBA	British Board of Agreement [*Department of the Environment*] [*Research center*] (IRUK)
BBA	British Bobsleigh [*or Bobsled*] Association (EAIO)
BBA	British Bonsai Association (DBA)
BBA	British Burn Association (DBA)
BBA	British Business Association [*Singapore*] (DS)
BBA	British Businessmen's Associaton (DBA)
BBA	Broadband Antenna
BBA	Bureau of the Budget Approval [*Obsolete*]
BBA	Burnaby Art Gallery, British Columbia [*Library symbol National Library of Canada*] (NLC)
BBAA	Barzona Breeders Association of America (EA)
BBAA	Big Band Academy of America (EA)
BBAA	Bridal and Bridesmaids Apparel Association (EA)
B Bac	Bachelor of Bacteriology
BBAC	British Balloon and Airship Club
BBAC	Bus-to-Bus Access Circuit [*Bell System*]
BB Ad	Bachelor of Business Administration
BB Adm	Bachelor of Business Administration
BBAM	Bamfield Marine Station, Bamfield, British Columbia [*Library symbol National Library of Canada*] (BIB)
BB & CIRly	Bombay, Baroda, and Central India Railway
BB & EA	British Building and Engineering Appliances
BB & EM	Bed, Breakfast, and Evening Meal [*Tourist accommodations*]
BB & PA	British Box and Packaging Association (DBA)
BB & T	Blocking, Bracing, and Tie-Down [*Military*] (DOMA)
BBAR	Bass Baritone [*Music*]
BBAS	Balloon-Borne Astronomical Studies (MCD)
BBB	Back to the Bible Broadcast (NTCM)
BBB	Bad Black Brother
BBB	Bags, Barrels, or Boxes [*Freight*]
BBB	Balair AG [*Switzerland ICAO designator*] (FAAC)
BBB	Bankers' Blanket Bond [*Investment term*]
BBB	Baseband Breadboard
BBB	Basic Boxed Base
BBB	Bed, Breakfast, and Bath [*Tourist accommodations*]
BBB	Beecham Bovril Brands [*Commercial firm British*]
BBB	Benson, MN [*Location identifier FAA*] (FAAL)
BBB	Best Berlin Broadcast [*Radio program broadcast from Berlin by Robert H. Best, former South Carolina journalist*] [*World War II*]
BBB	Better Business Bureau
BBB	Blanke Bevrydingsbeweging [*White Protection Movement*] [*South Africa Political party*] (EY)
BBB	Blood Brain Barrier [*Neurology*]
BBB	B'nai B'rith Bulletin [*A publication*] (ADA)
BBB	Body Bound Bolts (MSA)
BBB	Building Better Boards for Community Organizations Project [*American Association of Community and Junior Colleges*] (EDAC)
BBB	Bundle Branch Block [*Cardiology*]

B-B-B	Burn-Bash-Bury [*Australian trash disposal policy in Vietnam*] (VNW)
BBB	Medium [*Standard & Poor's bond rating*] [*Investment term*]
BBB	Treble Black [*Pencil*]
BBBA	British Bird Breeders' Association (BI)
BBBB	Bilateral Bundle Branch Block [*Cardiology*]
BBBC	British Boxing Board of Control
BBBCM	British Columbia Microelectronics, Burnaby, British Columbia [*Library symbol National Library of Canada*] (NLC)
BBBG	Battleship Battle Group [*Usually BBG*] [*Navy*] (DOMA)
BBBM	British Columbia Museum of Mining, Britannia Beach, British Columbia [*Library symbol National Library of Canada*] (NLC)
BBBS	Bang-Bang-Bang Surfaces (PDAA)
BB/BSA	Big Brothers/Big Sisters of America (EA)
BBBT	Bisbutoxybenzylidenebitoluidine [*Organic chemistry*]
BBBY	Bed Bath & Beyond [*NASDAQ symbol*] (TTSB)
BBBY	Bed Bath & Beyond, Inc. [*NASDAQ symbol*] (SAG)
BBC	Bachelor of Beauty Culture
BBC	Bachelor of Building Construction
BBC	Backup Bus Controller [*Computer science*]
BBC	Bangladesh Biman [*ICAO designator*] (FAAC)
BBC	Bank of British Columbia [*Toronto Stock Exchange symbol Vancouver Stock Exchange symbol*]
BBC	Bareboat Charter (DNAB)
BBC	Barrels, Boxes, or Crates [*Freight*]
BBC	Baseball Club
BBC	Basic Building Code
BBC	Battery Booster Cable
BBC	BC [*British Columbia*] Bancorp [*Toronto Stock Exchange symbol Vancouver Stock Exchange symbol*]
BBC	Beam-to-Beam Correlation (NVT)
BBC	Before Bottom Center [*Valve position*]
BBC	Before Business Clearance (NASA)
BBC	Belfast Banking Co. [*Ireland*]
BBC	Bergen Brunswig 'A' [*NYSE symbol*] (TTSB)
BBC	Bergen Brunswig Corp. [*NYSE symbol*] (SPSG)
BBC	Bermuda Base Command [*World War II*]
BBC	Big Bear [*California*] [*Seismograph station code, US Geological Survey Closed*] (SEIS)
BBC	Billionaire Boys Club (EA)
BBC	Biplabi Bangla Congress [*India*] [*Political party*] (PPW)
BBC	Black Body Cavity (PDAA)
BBC	Blade-Brake Clutch [*on lawn mowers*]
BBC	Blockhouse Battery Charger [*NASA*]
BBC	B'nai Birth Canada [*Also, Children of the Convenant*] (AC)
BBC	Boiler Blower Control (DNAB)
BBC	Breeding Bird Census (BARN)
BBC	Brisbane Bushwalkers Club
BBC	British Bathroom Council (DBA)
BBC	British Broadcasting Corp. [*State-operated radio and television*]
BBC	Broadband Conducted (IEEE)
BBC	Bromobenzyl Cyanide [*Tear gas*]
BBC	Brooks Bird Club (EA)
BBC	Brown, Boveri & Co. Ltd. [*Switzerland*]
BBC	Browne, Bortz & Coddington, Inc. [*Denver, CO*] [*Telecommunications*] (TSSD)
BBC	Brush Beryllium Co. (MCD)
BBC	Buffered Block Channel (MCD)
BBC	Building Block Concept [*Army-ROAD concept*]
BBC	Bumper to Back of Cab [*Automotive engineering*]
BBC	Davenport, IA [*Location identifier FAA*] (FAAL)
BBCAU	Big Borneo Civil Affairs Unit [*World War II*]
BBCC	Big Bands Collectors' Club (EA)
BBCF	British Bacon Curers' Federation (BI)
BBCJC	Genealogical Society Library, Church of Jesus Christ of Latter-Day Saints, Burnaby, British Columbia [*Library symbol National Library of Canada*] (NLC)
BBCM	Bella Coola Museum, British Columbia [*Library symbol National Library of Canada*] (NLC)
BBCMA	British Baby Carriage Manufacturers' Association (BI)
BBCP	(Benzyl)benzylidenecyclopentanone [*Organic chemistry*]
BBCRN	West Kootenay District Nursing Archives, Registered Nurses Association of British Columbia, Blueberry Creek, British Columbia [*Library symbol National Library of Canada*] (NLC)
BB-CS	British Beer-Mat Collectors' Society (EA)
BBCS	British Butterfly Conservation Society
BBCS-DIAG	Bracken Basic Concept Scale - Diagnostic Scale [*Educational development test*]
BBCSO	British Broadcasting Corp. Symphony Orchestra
BBCSSO	British Broadcasting Corp. Scottish Symphony Orchestra
BBCT	Broad-Based Consumption Tax (ADA)
BBCW	Bare Beryllium Copper Wire
BBD	Baby Born Dead [*Medicine*]
BBD	Benign Breast Disease [*Medicine*] (DMAA)
BBD	Blackboard
BBD	Bombardier, Inc. [*Toronto Stock Exchange symbol*]
BBD	Brady, TX [*Location identifier FAA*] (FAAL)
BBD	Bubble Bath Detector (OA)
BBD	Bucket-Brigade Device [*Electronics*]
BBD	Bulletin Board [*Technical drawings*]
BBD & O	Batten, Barton, Durstine & Osborn [*Advertising agency*]
BBD.B	Bombardier Inc.Cl'B' [*TS Symbol*] (TTSB)
BBDC	Before Bottom Dead Center [*Valve position*]
BBDC	Brantley Capital Corp. [*NASDAQ symbol*] (SAG)
BBDE	Berlin Brigade
BB DL	Baby or Doll [*Freight*]

BBDO .... Batten, Barton, Durstine, and Osborn [*An advertising agency*] [*New York, NY*] (WDMC)
Bbds .... Barbadensis [*Pharmacy*] (ROG)
BBE .... Bacteroids Bile Esculin [*Agar*] [*Microbiology*]
BBE .... Bradbury International Equity [*Vancouver Stock Exchange symbol*]
BBE .... Eastind Airlines, Inc. [*FAA designator*] (FAAC)
BBEA .... Brewery and Bottling Engineers Association (PDAA)
BB Ed .... Bachelor of Business Education
BBEDCRA..... Balanced Budget and Emergency Deficit Control Reaffirmation Act [*1987*]
BBehavSci ... Bachelor of Behavioral Sciences
BBEIUWWA... Breweries and Bottleyard Employees' Industrial Union of Workers of Western Australia
BBEP.......... Brush Border Endopeptidase [*Medicine*] (DMAA)
BBER .... Bureau of Business and Economic Research [*Old Dominion University*] [*Norfolk, VA*] [*Research center*] (RCD)
BBES.......... Bang-Bang Erection System [*Electronics*] (IAA)
BBEU .... Breweries and Bottleyards Employees' Union [*Australia*]
BBEUMCS ... Bureau of the Budget in Exile Unrequited Marching and Chowder Society (EA)
BBF .... Bacus/B'Gosh Families [*An association Defunct*] (EA)
BBF .... Balloon-Borne Filter
BBF .... Better Boys Foundation (EA)
BBF .... Beyond Baroque Foundation (EA)
BBF .... Boron-Based Fuel
BBF .... Breathable Barrier Film [*Organic chemistry*]
BBF .... Brilliant Buff Finishing [*Metal finishing*]
BBF .... British Baseball Federation (DBA)
BBF .... Broadbed and Furrow System (GNE)
BBF .... Bronchial Blood Flow [*Medicine*] (DMAA)
BBF .... Brother's Brother Foundation (EA)
BBF .... International Brotherhood of Boilermakers, Iron Shipbuilders, Blacksmiths, Forgers, and Helpers
BBFA .... British Binders and Finishers Association (DBA)
BBFC .... Bama Band Fan Club (EA)
BBFC .... Barry Bostwick Fan Club (EA)
BBFC .... Bellamy Brothers Fan Club (EA)
BBFC .... Bibi Besch Fan Club (EA)
BBFC .... Billy Blanton Fan Club (EA)
BBFC .... Bobby Bare Fan Club (EA)
BBFC .... Bobby Blue Fan Club [*Defunct*] (EA)
BBFC .... Boris Becker Fan Club (EA)
BBFC .... British Board of Film Censors (BI)
BBFC .... British Board of Film Classification
BBFC .... Bruce Boxleitner Fan Club (EA)
BBFC .... Buford's Boosters Fan Club (EA)
BBFC .... Slim and Steve: the Bogart and Bacall Fan Club (EA)
BBFFL .... Barbara Bush Foundation for Family Literacy (EA)
BBFI .... Baptist Bible Fellowship International (EA)
BBFLP .... Billy Barty Foundation for Little People (EA)
BBFO .... Bardsey Bird and Field Observatory [*British*] (BI)
BBFR .... Balloon-Borne Filter Radiometer
BBFS .... British Bulgarian Friendship Society (DBA)
BBFU .... Beach Boys Freaks United (EA)
BBG .... Banbury Gold Mines [*Vancouver Stock Exchange symbol*]
BBG .... Battleship Battle Group [*Sometimes the more awkward BBBG*] [*Navy*] (DOMA)
BBG .... Benziger, Bruce & Glencoe, Inc.
BBG .... Berlin Border Guard [*East Germany*]
BBG .... Big Big Gastrin [*Endocrinology*]
BBG .... Board of Broadcast Governors [*Later, Canadian Radio-Television Commission*]
BBG .... Bouncing-Ball Generator
BBG .... Brooklyn Botanic Garden [*Brooklyn, NY*]
BBG .... Bull & Bear US Government Securities Fund [*AMEX symbol*] (SAG)
BBG .... Butaritari [*Kiribati*] [*Airport symbol*] (OAG)
BBG .... Guided Missile Capital Ship [*Navy symbol Obsolete*]
BBGA .... Belgian Begonia Growers Association [*Defunct*] (EA)
BBGA .... British Broiler Growers' Association (BI)
BBGKY .... Bogoliubov-Born-Green-Kirkwood-Yvon [*Plasma kinetic theory hierarchy*]
B BGS .... Barrels or Bags [*Freight*]
BBGS .... British Business Graduates Society (DBA)
BBGV .... Greater Vancouver Regional District, Burnaby, British Columbia [*Library symbol National Library of Canada*] (BIB)
BBGVL .... Greater Vancouver Library Federation, Burnaby, British Columbia [*Library symbol National Library of Canada*] (NLC)
BBH .... Al-Baha [*Saudi Arabia*] [*Airport symbol*] (OAG)
BBH .... Bartle Bogle Hegarty [*Commercial firm British*]
BBH .... Battalion Beachhead [*Army*]
BBH .... Bowdoin College, Brunswick, ME [*OCLC symbol*] (OCLC)
BBH .... Brown Brothers Harriman (ECON)
BBH .... Paris, ID [*Location identifier FAA*] (FAAL)
BBHB .... Bundle-Branch Heart Block [*Cardiology*] (DAVI)
BBHC .... Buffalo Bill Historical Center (EA)
BBHF .... Barber Hairstyling for Men and Women [*NASDAQ symbol*] (SAG)
BBHF .... Barbers,Hairstyling Men&Women [*NASDAQ symbol*] (TTSB)
BBHF .... B'nai B'rith Hillel Foundations (EA)
BBHFC .... Boston Bruins Hockey Fan Club (EA)
BBHG .... British Branded Hosiery Group [*An association*] (DBA)
BBHOAM...... Board of Brethren Homes and Older Adult Ministries [*Later, BHOAM*] (EA)
BBHP .... Barkerville Historic Park, British Columbia [*Library symbol National Library of Canada*] (NLC)

BBHS .... Australian Business Brief and Hansard Service [*Australian Chamber of Commerce*] [*Information service or system Defunct*] (IID)
BBHS .... British Buddy Holly Society (EAIO)
BBHW .... Baseboard Hot Water [*Heating system*] [*Classified advertising*]
BBI .... Barbara Bain International
BBI .... Barbecue Briquet Institute [*Later, BIA*]
BBI .... Barnett Banks, Inc. [*NYSE symbol*] (SPSG)
BBI .... Beauty and the Beast International [*An association Defunct*] (EA)
BBI .... Behavioral Books Institute [*Book club*]
BBI .... Bhubaneswar [*India*] [*Airport symbol*] (OAG)
BBI .... Big Bend [*Idaho*] [*Seismograph station code, US Geological Survey*] (SEIS)
BBI .... Bis(benzimidazole) [*Organic chemistry*]
BBI .... Biscuit Bakers Institute [*B & CMA*] [*Absorbed by*] (EA)
BBI .... Blue Blazes Irregulars (EA)
BBI .... B'nai B'rith International (EA)
BBI .... Boring But Important Information [*Journalism*] (WDMC)
BBI .... Bowen Island Public Library, British Columbia [*Library symbol National Library of Canada*] (BIB)
BBI .... Bowman-Birk Soybean Inhibitor [*Medicine*] (DMAA)
BBI .... Brandeis - Bardin Institute (EA)
BBI .... British Bottlers' Institute (DBA)
BBI .... Broadband Interneuron [*Neuroanatomy*]
BBI .... Brother to Brother International (EA)
BBI .... Brown Bag Institute (EA)
BBI .... Builders' Benevolent Institution [*British*] (BI)
BBI .... Buxom Belles, International (EA)
BBIA .... Billiard and Bowling Institute of America (EA)
B Bib Arts .... Bachelor of Biblical Arts
BBIC .... Behavior-Based Incentive Compensation [*Human resources*] (WYGK)
BBICAJE...... B'nai B'rith International Commission on Adult Jewish Education [*Later, BBICCJE*] (EA)
BBICCJE...... B'nai B'rith International Commission on Continuing Jewish Education (EA)
B Bi Ch .... Bachelor of Biological Chemistry
B Bi Chem ... Bachelor of Biological Chemistry
B Bi E .... Bachelor of Biological Engineering
B Bi Eng ..... Bachelor of Biological Engineering
BBII........... Boston Biomedica, Inc. [*NASDAQ symbol*] (SAG)
BBII........... Brass and Bronze Ingot Institute (EA)
BBIM .... Buoyant Ballistic Inertial Missile (MCD)
BBIO .... British Bio-Technologies, Inc. [*NASDAQ symbol*] (SAG)
BBiomed ..... Bachelor of Biomedical Sciences
BBIOY .... British Biotech plc ADS [*NASDAQ symbol*] (TTSB)
BBIP.......... British Books in Print [*Whitaker & Sons, Ltd.*] [*Information service or system*] (IID)
B Bi Phy ..... Bachelor of Biological Physics
BBIRA .... British Baking Industries Research Association (PDAA)
B Bi S .... Bachelor of Biological Sciences
B Bi Sc .... Bachelor of Biological Sciences
BBISCHC..... B'nai B'rith International Senior Citizens Housing Committee (EA)
BBIT .... British Columbia Institute of Technology, Burnaby, British Columbia [*Library symbol National Library of Canada*] (NLC)
BBJ .... Aircorp Airlines, Inc. [*Canada ICAO designator*] (FAAC)
BBJ .... Ball Bearing Joint
BBK .... Bargmann Bowen and Kemp, Inc. [*Telecommunications service*] (TSSD)
BBK .... Berliner Beitraege zur Keilschriftforschung [*A publication*] (BJA)
BBK .... Bibliotechno-Bibliograficheskaya Klassifikatsiya [*Library Bibliographical Classification*] [*Russian Federation*] (NITA)
BBK............ Big Bar Gold Corp. [*Vancouver Stock Exchange symbol*]
BBK............ Breadboard Kit [*NASA*]
BBK............ Kingsway Branch, Burnaby Public Library, British Columbia [*Library symbol National Library of Canada*] (NLC)
BBKA .... British Bee Keepers Association (BI)
BBKC .... Boycott Burger King Coalition [*Defunct*] (EA)
BB/KR .... Brown, Boveri-Krupp Reaktorbau [*Germany*]
BBKS .... Bobbie Brooks [*NASDAQ symbol*] (TTSB)
BBKS .... Bobbie Brooks, Inc. [*NASDAQ symbol*] (NQ)
BBL .... Baltic Bankers Ltd. [*Finland*]
BBL .... Baltimore Biological Laboratory
BBL .... Banque Bruxelles Lambert [*Belgium*] (ECON)
BBL .... Barrel (AFM)
BBL .... Basic Business Language [*Computer science*] (IEEE)
BBL .... Beacons and Blind Landing (IAA)
BBL .... Be Back Later [*Computer hacker terminology*] (NHD)
bbl .... Be Back Later [*Internet language*] [*Computer science*]
BBL .... Bed and Breakfast League (EA)
BBL .... Benthic Boundary Layer [*Oceanography*]
BBL .... Brampton Brick Ltd. [*Toronto Stock Exchange symbol*]
BBL .... Branch Back and Load [*Computer science*]
BBL .... British Bio-Technology Ltd. (IRC)
BBL .... Brooklyn Business Library
BBL .... Buried-BIT [*Binary Digit*] Line [*Computer science*] (IAA)
BBL .... Buys Ballot Law
BBL .... IBM, Euroflight-Operations [*Switzerland ICAO designator*] (FAAC)
BBL .... Lenkurt Electric Co., Burnaby, British Columbia [*Library symbol National Library of Canada*] (NLC)
BBLA........... Audiobook Service to the Handicapped, British Columbia Library Services Branch, Burnaby [*Library symbol National Library of Canada*] (NLC)
BBLC .... Boston Biomedical Library Consortium [*Library network*]
bbl/d .... Barrels per Day (IMH)
BBldg .... Bachelor of Building (ADA)
BBldgSc .... Bachelor of Building Science

BBIdSc......... Bachelor of Building Science (ADA)
BBLG.......... Bovine Beta-Lactoglobulin [Biochemistry]
BBLIP.......... Base Burning/Lateral Injection Propulsion (MCD)
BBLL.......... Banner Blade Length [Botany]
BBLL.......... Blackbody Limited Line (PDAA)
BBLM.......... Lakes District Museum, Burns Lake, British Columbia [Library symbol National Library of Canada] (NLC)
BBLMV.......... Blueberry Leaf Mottle Virus
BBLS.......... Barrels [Shipping]
BBLT.......... Bus Block Transfer
BBM.......... Bachelor of Business Management
BBM.......... Banked Breast Milk [Neonatology] (DAVI)
BBM.......... Basic Brazeau Medium [Culture media]
BBM.......... Big Bend [Montana] [Seismograph station code, US Geological Survey Closed] (SEIS)
BBM.......... Binary BIT [Binary Digit] Mapped [Computer science]
BBM.......... Books by Mail
BBM.......... Bread, Butter, and Marmalade [Slang]
BBM.......... Break-Before-Make
BBM.......... Broadcast Bureau of Measurement [FCC] (NTCM)
BBM.......... Brush Border Membrane [Medicine] (DMAA)
BBM.......... Building Block Monochromator
BBM.......... Bulk Biomass Model [Pisciculture]
BBM.......... Bulk Rate Business Mail
BBM.......... Bull & Bear Municipal Income Fund, Inc. [AMEX symbol] (SAG)
BBM.......... Bureau of Broadcast Measurement [Canada] (NTCM)
BBM.......... Mandela Bush Negro Liberation Movement [Suriname] [Political party] (EY)
BBMA.......... British Bath Manufacturers' Association Ltd. (BI)
BBMA.......... British Battery Manufacturers Association (DBA)
BBMA.......... British Brush Manufacturers Association (PDAA)
BBMA.......... British Button Manufacturers Association (BI)
BBMA.......... Building Board Manufacturers Association (PDAA)
BBMB.......... Bank Bumiputra Malaysia Berhad (FEA)
BBME.......... British Bank of the Middle East
BBMI.......... Brush Border Myosin [Biology]
BBMIP.......... Branch-Bound Mixed Integer Programming [Computer science]
BBML.......... Bottle-Baby Meal [Airline notation]
BBMLC.......... Bring Back Mark Lindsay Campaign (EA)
BBMO.......... Bis(bromomethyl)oxetane [Organic chemistry]
BBMRA.......... British Brush Manufacturers Research Association (IRUK)
BBMS.......... Brace Bit Makers Society [A union] [British]
BBMS.......... British Battery Makers' Society (BI)
BBMT.......... Technical Library, Microtel Pacific Research Ltd., Burnaby, British Columbia [Library symbol National Library of Canada] (NLC)
BBMV.......... Blueberry Mottle Virus
BBMV.......... Broad Bean Mottle Virus [Plant pathology]
BBN.......... Babylon, NY [Location identifier FAA] (FAAL)
BBN.......... Balloon-Borne Nephelometer
BBN.......... Bario [Malaysia] [Airport symbol] (OAG)
BBN.......... BBN Corp. [NYSE symbol] (SAG)
BBN.......... BBN Corp. [NYSE symbol] (TTSB)
BBN.......... Belize Broadcasting Network (EY)
BBN.......... Big Brand Names [i.e., well-established writers] [Publishing slang]
BBN.......... Black Butte [New Mexico] [Seismograph station code, US Geological Survey Closed] (SEIS)
BBN.......... Bolt, Beranek & Newman, Inc. [NYSE symbol] (SPSG)
BBN.......... Borabicyclononane [Organic chemistry]
BBN.......... Broad Band Noise (DMAA)
BBN.......... Bromobenzylnitrile [Toxic compound]
BBN.......... Scampton BAE [British ICAO designator] (FAAC)
BBNA.......... Black Bolt and Nut Association [British] (DBA)
BBnd.......... Big Band [Radio station format] (WDMC)
BBNHA.......... Big Bend Natural History Association (EA)
BBNK.......... BayBanks, Inc. [NASDAQ symbol] (NQ)
BBNM.......... Bulletin Board Note Manager [Prodigy offline reader]
BBNP.......... Botany Bay National Park [Australia]
BBNV.......... Broad Bean Necrosis Virus [Plant pathology]
BBO.......... Barium Boron Oxide [Inorganic chemistry]
BBO.......... Berbera [Somalia] [Airport symbol] (OAG)
BBO.......... Billion Barrels of Oil
BBO.......... Bis(biphenylyl)oxazole [Organic chemistry]
BBO.......... Booster Burn-Out (IAA)
BBO.......... British Ballet Organization
BBO.......... Buy-Build-Operate (AAGC)
BBO.......... Morgantown, WV [Location identifier FAA] (FAAL)
BBOD.......... Bis(biphenyl)oxadiazole [Organic chemistry]
BB/ODT.......... Bottom Bounce/Omnidirectional Transmission [Navy]
BBOE.......... Billions of Barrels of Oil Equivalent (MCD)
BBOL.......... Building Block Oriented Language [Computer science] (PDAA)
B-BOP.......... Bristol Bay Oceanographic Processes
BBOT.......... Bis(tert-butylbenzoxazolyl)thiophene [Organic chemistry]
BBOX.......... Black Box Corp. [NASDAQ symbol] (SAG)
BBP.......... Bavarian Border Police [Germany]
BBP.......... Bennettsville, SC [Location identifier FAA] (FAAL)
BBP.......... Benzyl Butyl Phthalate [Organic chemistry]
BBP.......... Bilin-Binding Protein [Biochemistry]
BBP.......... Boletim de Bibliografia Portuguesa [A bibliographic publication] [Portugal]
BBP.......... Border Boundary Police [Thailand] (CINC)
BBP.......... Boxes, Barrels, or Packages [Freight]
BBP.......... Break Bulk Point [Transportation]
BBP.......... Building Block Principle
BBP.......... Butyl Benzyl Phthalate [Organic chemistry]
BBPA.......... Black Business & Professional Association (AC)

BBPA.......... British Bedding Plant Association (DBA)
BBPCT.......... Blocking, Bracing, Packing, Crating, and Tiedown Materials [Military] (INF)
BBPM.......... Bralorne Pioneer Museum, British Columbia [Library symbol National Library of Canada] (NLC)
BBPN.......... Balloon-Borne Polar Nephelometer
BBPS.......... Behavior-Based Personnel Systems
BBPS.......... Build and Blood Pressure Study [Society of Actuaries]
BBQ.......... Barbecue (ADA)
BBQ.......... Barbuda [West Indies] [Airport symbol] (OAG)
BBQ.......... Brooklyn, Bronx, and Queens [New York City slang for nightclub or restaurant that has fallen out of favor with the pacesetters]
BBQC.......... British Board of Quality Control
BBR.......... Bafour, Blanchard, and Raymond [Computer typesetting] (DGA)
BBR.......... Balloon-Borne Radio
BBR.......... Basse-Terre [Guadeloupe] [Airport symbol] (OAG)
BBR.......... Beebe Ranch [California] [Seismograph station code, US Geological Survey] (SEIS)
BBR.......... Black Body Radiator
BBR.......... Broadband Radiated (IEEE)
BBR.......... Bureau of Biological Research [Rutgers University] [Research center] (RCD)
BBR.......... Bureau of Business Research [University of Texas, Austin] [Information service or system] (IID)
BBR.......... Butler Manufacturing [NYSE symbol] (SAG)
BBRC.......... Ball Brothers Research Corp.
BBRC.......... Burr-Brown Corp. [NASDAQ symbol] (NQ)
BBRG.......... Ball Bearing
B Bri.......... Bartholomaeus Brixiensis [Deceased circa 1258] [Authority cited in pre-1607 legal work] (DSA)
BBRI.......... Boston Biomedical Research Institute [Research center] (RCD)
B Brix.......... Bartholomaeus Brixiensis [Deceased circa 1258] [Authority cited in pre-1607 legal work] (DSA)
B/BRK.......... Booster Brake [Automotive engineering]
BBRM.......... British Bombing Research Mission [World War II]
BBRO.......... Bomb Bay Ring Out (SAA)
BBRPDC.......... Botany Bay Regional Planning and Development Committee [Australia]
BBRR.......... Brookhaven Beam Research Reactor
BBRS.......... Balloon-Borne Radio System
BBRS.......... Blair Bell Research Society [British]
BBRS.......... Burks' Behavior Rating Scale [Psychology] (DAVI)
BBS.......... Bachelor of Business Science
BBS.......... Bachelor of Business Studies
BBS.......... Barber Suggestibility Scale [Psychology]
BBS.......... Bardet-Beidl Syndrome [Medicine]
BBS.......... Bare Base Set [Air Force]
BBS.......... Battalion Battle Simulation [Army]
BBS.......... Below Bridges [Transportation]
BBS.......... Berean Bible Society (EA)
BBS.......... Best of a Bad Situation
BBS.......... Betriebsberufsschule [Factory Training School] [Germany]
BBS.......... Bhutan Broadcasting Service (EY)
BBS.......... Bilateral Breath Sounds [Medicine] (DAVI)
BBS.......... Biological, Behavioral, and Social Sciences [Directorate]
BBS.......... Blind Bronchial Sampling [Clinical chemistry]
BBS.......... Bombesin [Biochemistry]
BBS.......... Books for Bible Students [A publication]
BBS.......... Box Bark Strips [Construction] (BARN)
BBS.......... Breeding Bird Survey [Department of the Interior]
BBS.......... Brigade/Battalion Simulation [Army] (DOMA)
BBS.......... Brigade/Battalion Simulations [Army] (INF)
BBS.......... Brigade Battle Simulation [Army]
BBS.......... Britannia Building Society [British]
BBS.......... British Biophysical Society
BBS.......... British Bone Society
BBS.......... British Bryological Society
BBS.......... British Button Society (DBA)
BBS.......... Brittany Base Section [World War II]
BBS.......... Brittle Bone Society [British]
BBS.......... Brunei Broadcasting Service
BBS.......... Building Block System
BBS.......... Bulletin Board Service
BBS.......... Bulletin Board Systems [Personal computer message network system]
BBSA.......... Bridge and Building Supply Association [Defunct]
BBSA.......... British Blind and Shutter Association (DBA)
BBSATRA.......... British Boot, Shoe and Allied Trades Research Association (BI)
BBSc.......... Bachelor of Behavioural Science
BB Sc.......... Bachelor of Business Science
bbscrc.......... Biotechnology and Biological Sciences Research Council [British]
BBSFC.......... Beach Boys Stomp Fan Club (EAIO)
BBSI.......... Barrett Business Services, Inc. [NASDAQ symbol] (SAG)
BBSI.......... Beauty and Barber Supply Institute (EA)
BBSJ.......... Ball Bearing Swivel Joint
BBSL.......... Bee Biology and Systematics Laboratory [Department of Agriculture] [Research center] (RCD)
BBSO.......... Big Bear Solar Observatory [California Institute of Technology] [Research center] (RCD)
BBSOC.......... Battalion/Brigade Signal Officer Course [Military] (INF)
BBSP.......... Balloon-Borne Solar Pointer
BBSP.......... Bare Base Support Package (MCD)
BBSP.......... Building Block Signal Processor [Computer science] (MHDI)
BBSRC.......... Biotechnology and Biological Sciences Research Council [British]
BBSSV.......... Blueberry Shoestring Virus

BBST	Barrett Business Svcs [*NASDAQ symbol*] (TTSB)
BBSU	Bid Bond Service Undertaking
BBSU	British Bombing Survey Units [*World War II*]
BBSV	Broad Bean Stain Virus [*Plant pathology*]
BBT	Backlight Burtek Trainer
BBT	Ball Bearing Torque
BBT	Barbados Board of Tourism (EA)
BBT	Basal Body Temperature [*Medicine*]
BBT	BBC Realty Investors [*Toronto Stock Exchange symbol Vancouver Stock Exchange symbol*]
BBT	Betar Brith Trumpeldor (EA)
BBT	Black Ball Transport, Inc. [*AAR code*]
BBT	Blackrock 1998 Term Tr [*NYSE symbol*] (TTSB)
BBT	Blackrock 1998 Term Trust [*NYSE symbol*] (SPSG)
BBT	Blood Bank Technologist (DAVI)
BBT	Bombardment (KSC)
BB/T	Bottom Bounce/Track [*Navy*]
BBT	Brotherhood of Book Travelers [*Later, ABT*] (EA)
BBT	Buck-Boost Transformer
BBTA	British Bureau of Television Advertising
BBTC	Balloon Barrage Training Center [*Army*]
BBTK	BroadBand Technologies [*NASDAQ symbol*] (TTSB)
BBTK	BroadBand Technologies, Inc. [*NASDAQ symbol*] (SAG)
BBTL	Baby Brother Tender Love [*Doll manufactured by Mattel, Inc.*]
BBTMV	Broad Bean True Mosaic Virus [*Plant pathology*]
BB to MM	Belly Button to Medial Malleolus [*Measurement*] [*Anatomy*] (DAVI)
BBTR	Battle Bridge Tier [*Shipping*] (ROG)
BBTU	Barge Builders Trade Union [*British*]
BBU	Beefmaster Breeders Universal (EA)
BBU	BIT [*Binary Digit*] Buffer Unit [*Computer science*] (CET)
BBU	Bucharest [*Romania*] Banesa Airport [*Airport symbol*] (OAG)
BBUC	British Columbia Union Catalogue, Burnaby, British Columbia [*Library symbol National Library of Canada*] (NLC)
BBUC	Michigan Brewery, Inc. [*NASDAQ symbol*] (SAG)
BBUGVACT	Black Box Under Glass Variable Angle Controlled Temperature [*Automotive paint durability testing*]
BBuild	Bachelor of Building (ADA)
BBuilding	Bachelor of Building
BBUL	Burns Lake Public Library, British Columbia [*Library symbol National Library of Canada*] (NLC)
B Bull	Bar Bulletin [*A publication*] (DLA)
BBus	Bachelor of Business (ADA)
BBus-Accy	Bachelor of Business - Accountancy
BBusAd	Bachelor of Business Administration (ADA)
BBusAdmin	Bachelor of Business Administration
BBus-Comn	Bachelor of Business - Communication
BBus-Comptg	Bachelor of Business - Computing
BBusHA	Bachelor of Business - Health Administration
BBus-HealthAdmin	Bachelor of Business - Health Administration
BBusMgmt	Bachelor of Business Management
BBus-Mgt	Bachelor of Business - Management
BBus-PubAdmin	Bachelor of Business - Public Administration
BBV	Banco Bilbao Vizcaya (ECON)
BBV	Banco Bilbao Vizcaya ADS [*NYSE symbol*] (TTSB)
BBV	Banco Bilbao Vizcaya SA [*NYSE symbol*] (CTT)
BBV	Black Beetle Virus
BBV	[*The*] Boy's Book of Verse [*A publication*]
BBVM	Burnaby Village Museum, British Columbia [*Library symbol National Library of Canada*] (NLC)
BBVS	B'nai B'rith Vocational Service [*Later, B'nai B'rith Career and Counseling Services*] (EA)
BBW	Bare Brass Wire
BBW	Bath & Body Works
BB/W	Biobreeding/Worcester [*Rat variety*]
BBW	B'nai B'rith Women (EA)
BBW	Broken Bow, NE [*Location identifier FAA*] (FAAL)
BBWA	Bright Belt Warehouse Association (EA)
BBWAA	Baseball Writers Association of America (EA)
BBWC	Broadband Waveguide Circulator
BBWI	Black Business Women - International [*French*] (EAIO)
BBWR	Bezpartyjny Blok Wspolpracy z Rzadem [*Non-Party Bloc of Cooperation with the Government*] [*Poland Political party*] (PPE)
BBWV	Broad Bean Wilt Virus [*Plant pathology*]
B Bx	Bartholomaeus Brixiensis [*Deceased circa 1258*] [*Authority cited in pre-1607 legal work*] (DSA)
BBX	Blue Bell [*Pennsylvania*] [*Airport symbol*] (OAG)
B Bx	Breast Biopsy [*Medicine*]
BBXRT	Broadband X-Ray Telescope
BBY	Best Buy Capital LP [*NYSE symbol*] (SAG)
BBY	Best Buy Co. [*Bloomington, MN*] [*NYSE symbol*] (SPSG)
BBYCY	Bow Buoyancy
BBYO	B'nai B'rith Youth Organization (EA)
BBYPrM	Best Buy Cap 6.50%'MIPS' [*NYSE symbol*] (TTSB)
BBz	Bearing Bronze [*Metallurgy*]
BBZ	Zambezi [*Zambia*] [*Airport symbol*] (OAG)
BC	Baccalaureus Chirurgiae [*Bachelor of Surgery*]
BC	Bach Choir [*Record label*]
BC	Bachelor of Chemistry
BC	Bachelor of Classics
BC	Bachelor of Commerce
BC	Back-Connected [*Technical drawings*]
BC	Back Course (FAAC)
BC	Back Cover [*Publishing*] (WDMC)
BC	Backpackers Club [*Reading, Berkshire, England*] (EAIO)
BC	Back to the City [*An association Defunct*] (EA)

BC	Backward Chaining [*Psychology*]
BC	Bactericidal Concentration (MAE)
BC	Bad Character
BC	Bad Check [*Banking*]
BC	Bad Conduct [*British military*] (DMA)
BC	Baha'i Community [*Australia*]
BC	Bail Court [*Legal term*] (DLA)
BC	Baja California [*Mexico*]
BC	Balanced Current [*Electronics*] (IAA)
B/C	Bales of Cotton [*Shipping*]
BC	Ball Change [*Dance terminology*]
BC	Ballistic Camera
BC	Ballistic Coefficient
BC	Balloon Command (DAS)
BC	Banc Cymru [*Bank of Wales*]
BC	Band Corporal
BC	Bankcard
BC	Bank Clearing [*Business term*] (ADA)
BC	Bankers Committee (EA)
BC	Bank for Cooperatives
BC	Bank of Canada [*Banque du Canada*]
BC	Bankruptcy Cases [*A publication*] (DLA)
BC	Bankruptcy Court [*Legal term*] (DAS)
BC	Bareboat Charter (DNAB)
BC	Bare Copper
BC	Barge Cargo (AAG)
BC	Bar (Handle) Control [*Early automobiles*] (ROG)
BC	Barium Crown
BC	Barleycorn [*Unit of weight*] [*Obsolete British*] (ROG)
BC	Barrel Coating
BC	Barrick-Culalton Gold Trust Units [*Toronto Stock Exchange symbol*]
BC	Barrier Coat (MSA)
BC	Barter Clubs (EA)
BC	Base Collector
BC	Base Command
BC	Base Connection [*Engineering*] (IAA)
BC	Base Count (IAA)
BC	Basel Club (EAIO)
BC	Basic Control [*Mode*] [*Computer science*]
BC	Basic Copy [*Genetics*]
BC	Bass Clarinet
BC	Basso Continuo [*Continued Bass*] [*Music*]
BC	Bathyconductograph
BC	Battalion Commander (MCD)
BC	Battered Child (CPH)
BC	Battery Capability
BC	Battery Charger [*Military*]
BC	Battery Commander [*Army*]
BC	Battle Casualty (MAE)
BC	Battle Cruiser [*Navy*]
BC	Battle Cruiser Flag [*Navy British*]
BC	Bayonet Cap
BC	BC (VRA)
BC	Beacon College [*Defunct*] (EA)
BC	Beam Collimator
BC	Beatles Connection [*An association*] (EA)
BC	Become (DA)
BC	Before Calculators
BC	Before Casinos
BC	Before Christ
BC	Before Cloning [*Cytology*]
BC	Before Commercialism
BC	Before Competition [*Term associated with the divestiture of AT & T*]
BC	Before Computer
BC	Before Cook [*Era preceding discovery of Australia by British explorer, James Cook*] (ECON)
BC	Before Credit Cards [*Slang*]
BC	Before Croonery [*Musical slang*]
BC	Before the Crash [*i.e., before the 1929 stock market collapse*] [*Slang*]
BC	Beginning Climb [*Aviation*] (FAAC)
BC	Behavior Cards [*Psychological testing*]
BC	Bellanca Contact (EA)
BC	Bell Canada [*Toronto Stock Exchange symbol*]
BC	Bell Cord [*Technical drawings*]
BC	Bell's Commentaries on the Laws of Scotland [*A publication*] (DLA)
B/C	Bench Check (NASA)
B-C	Benefit-Cost [*Ratio*]
BC	Bengal Cavalry [*British military*] (DMA)
BC	Bereavement Center (EA)
BC	Berlin Command [*Allied German Occupation Forces*]
BC	Beta-Carotene [*Biochemistry*]
BC	Between Centers [*Technical drawings*]
BC	Biblical Colloquium [*Defunct*] (EA)
BC	Bibliographic Classification [*System of library classification devised by Henry Evelyn Bliss*]
BC	Bicomponent [*Laboratory tubing*]
BC	Bicycle Club [*Generic term*] (WGA)
BC	Bile Canaliculi [*Anatomy*]
BC	Biliary Colic [*Medicine*] (DMAA)
BC	Bilingual Counsellor
B/C	Bill for Collection
BC	Billing Cease Date (TEL)
BC	Binary Code
BC	Binary Counter

BC	Binding Capacity
BC	Biogenic Carbon [Chemistry]
BC	Biological and Chemical
BC	Biological and Chemical Warfare (NATG)
BC	Biosystematic Code [Databank terminology] (NITA)
BC	Bipolar Cell [Biochemistry]
BC	Birth Certificate
BC	Birth Control
BC	Bisexual Center [Defunct] (EA)
BC	BIT [Binary Digit] Control
BC	Black-Capped Chickadee [Ornithology]
BC	Black Code [Law passed after the Civil War limiting the rights of Negroes in the South]
BC	Black Colt (ROG)
BC	Blastodermal Cell [Insect embryology]
BC	Blind Child [Social Security Administration] (OICC)
BC	Blind Copy (DNAB)
BC	Bliss Classification
BC	Block Count [Computer science]
BC	Blood Culture [Medicine]
BC	Bloomsday Club (EA)
BC	Blue Card (EA)
BC	Blue Chip [Investment term]
BC	Blue Crescent [Later, BCI] [An association] (EAIO)
BC	Blue Cross [Health insurance plan]
BC	Board Certified [Physician] (BARN)
BC	Board of Control [British] (ROG)
BC	Boat Club
BC	Body-Centered [Crystallography]
BC	Body Count [Military] (CINC)
BC	Bogus Check [Banking]
BC	Bohemian Club (EA)
BC	Bolometric Correction
BC	Bolt Circle [Technical drawings]
BC	Bombay Cavalry [British military] (DMA)
BC	Bomber Command
BC	Bonded Single Cotton [Wire insulation] (MSA)
BC	Bone Conduction [Medicine]
BC	Bookcase (MSA)
BC	Book Collector [A publication] (BRI)
BC	Boom Controller (MCD)
BC	Boresight Camera
BC	Born in Colony [British] (ADA)
BC	Borocarbon
BC	Borough Constituency
BC	Borough Council
BC	Boston College [Chestnut Hill, MA]
BC	Bottom Center [Valve position]
BC	Bottom Chord
BC	Bottom Contour [Navy British]
BC	Boundary-Condition
BC	Bowling Club [Generic term] (WGA)
BC	Bowman's Capsule (MAE)
BC	Box Core [Marine geology]
BC	Boxes or Crates [Freight]
BC	Boyle-Conway Solution [Neurophysiology]
BC	Brachium [Neurology]
BC	Brachium Conjunctivum [Neuroanatomy]
BC	Brachycardia [Cardiology]
BC	Bradford College [Formerly, BJC] [Massachusetts]
BC	Bradley Commander [Army] (INF)
BC	Branch City [Databank terminology] (NITA)
BC	Branch Conditional (IAA)
BC	Breaking Capacity (IAA)
BC	Breguet Cruise [SST]
BC	Brightness Contrast
BC	Bristol Channel [British]
BC	British Columbia [Canadian province] [Postal code]
BC	British Columbia Law Reports [Canada] [A publication] (DLA)
BC	British Columbia Teachers' Federation [Canada] (AEBS)
BC	British Commissioner [Salvation Army]
BC	British Commonwealth
BC	British Corp.
BC	British Council
BC	Brixton College [London, England]
B/C	Broadcast (NATG)
BC	Broadcast (IDOE)
BC	Broadcast Control
BC	Broadcasting (MCD)
BC	Broadcasting Council [Australia]
BC	Broadcasting Program [Association of Independent Colleges and Schools specialization code]
BC	Broadcasting Station [ITU designation] (CET)
BC	Bronchial Carcinoid
BC	Bronchial Carcinoma [Medicine] (DAVI)
BC	Bronchiectatic Cyst [Pulmonary medicine]
BC	Bronchogenic Cyst
BC	Brotherhood Commission (EA)
BC	Brunswick Corp. [NYSE symbol] (SPSG)
BC	Brymon Airways [ICAO designator] (AD)
BC	Brymon Airways [Airline flight code] (ODBW)
BC	Bubble Chamber
BC	Bubble Column [Engineering]
BC	Bubble Curtain [Pisciculture]
BC	Buccal Cartilage [Dentistry]

BC	Buccal Commissure [Dentistry]
BC	Buccocervical [Dentistry]
BC	Budgetary Control (DCTA)
BC	Budget Center (MCD)
BC	Budget Code [Air Force] (AFIT)
BC	Budgeted Cost (ADA)
BC	Buecker Flugzeugbau GmbH & Hagglund-Soner [Germany ICAO aircraft manufacturer identifier] (ICAO)
BC	Buffer Cell (IAA)
BC	Buffer Cycle (IAA)
BC	Building Code (DAC)
BC	Bulbocavernosus [Muscle group]
BC	Bulbus Chordae [Cardiology] (DAVI)
BC	Bulk Core (MHDI)
BC	Bulkhead Connector
BC	Buoyancy Compensators
BC	Buoyant Capsule (MCD)
BC	Burden Center
BC	Bureau of Consultation [Federal Trade Commission]
BC	Bureau of Customs [Later, US Customs Service] [Department of the Treasury]
BC	Bureau of the Census [Department of Commerce] (MCD)
BC	Burro Club [Democratic political organization] [Defunct] (EA)
BC	Burroughs Corp.
BC	Bursting Charge [Military]
BC	Bus Compatible (IAA)
BC	Bus Controller (MCD)
BC	Bus Coupler [Computer science] (MCD)
BC	Business Census
BC	Business Computer (IAA)
BC	Business Council (EA)
BC	Butacaine [Topical anesthetic]
BC	Bythotrephes Cederstroemi [Zoology]
Bc	Conjugated Bilirubin [Chemistry]
BC	Coquitlam Public Library, British Columbia [Library symbol National Library of Canada] (NLC)
BC	Notre Dame du BonConseil (Quebec) (TOCD)
BC	Sandoz AG [Switzerland] [Research code symbol]
BC	Y Blaengwyr Cenedlaethol [The National Resurgence Party of the Peoples of Britain]
BCA	Bachelor of Commerce and Administration (BARN)
BCA	Bachelor of Commercial Arts
BCA	Bachelor of Creative Arts
BCA	Badgery's Creek Airport [Australia]
BCA	Balloon Catheter Angioplasty
BCA	Bangladesh Cultural Association (EA)
BCA	Banknote Corp of America [Printer of U.S. postage stamps] (BARN)
BCA	Baracoa [Cuba] [Airport symbol] (OAG)
BCA	Barca [Ship's rigging] (ROG)
BCA	Barium Chloranilate [Organic chemistry]
BCA	Basal Cell Atypia [Medicine] (DAVI)
BCA	Base Closure Action (MCD)
BCA	Basenji Club of America (EA)
BCA	Bataillon de Commandement et d'Appui [Headquarters and Support Battalion] [Algeria] (AF)
BCA	Battery Control Area [Army]
BCA	Battlefield Commanders' Aid [Army]
BCA	BCA Credit Information [Later, Broadcast Credit Association] (EA)
BCA	Beale Cypher Association (EA)
BCA	Benefit Cost Analysis [Accounting]
BCA	Benzenecarboxylic Acid [Organic chemistry]
BCA	Benzylcyclopropylamine [Organic chemistry]
BCA	Best Copy Available
BCA	Best Cruise Altitude
BCA	Bicinchoninic Acid [Organic chemistry]
BCA	Bicycle Club of America (EA)
BCA	Bilderberg Continuum Atmosphere
BCA	Billiard Congress of America (EA)
BCA	Biological Control Agent [Agriculture]
BCA	BIT [Binary Digit] Count Appendage [Computer science] (MHDI)
BCA	Black Coaches Association (EA)
BCA	Bliss Classification Association [London, England]
BCA	Bloated Clay Aggregate [Engineering]
BCA	Blood Color Analyzer [Medicine]
BCA	Blue Cross Association [Later, BCBSA] (EA)
BCA	Board of Certification in Anesthesiology (EA)
BCA	Board of Contract Appeals [Energy Research and Development Administration]
BCA	Board of Contract Appeals Decisions [CCH] [A publication] (AAGC)
BCA	Book Club Associates [British]
BCA	Booster Change Assembly (MCD)
BCA	Bovine Carbonic Anhydrase [An enzyme]
BCA	Box Culvert Association [British] (DBA)
BCA	Boy Clerks Association [A union] [British]
BCA	Boys' Clubs of America (EA)
BCA	Brachiocephalic Artery [Cardiology] (DAVI)
BCA	Brascade Resources, Inc. [Toronto Stock Exchange symbol]
BCA	Briard Club of America (EA)
BCA	British Caledonian Airways Ltd.
BCA	British Car Auctions
BCA	British Carton Association (BI)
BCA	British Casino Association (DBA)
BCA	British Cement Association [Also, an information service or system] (IID)
BCA	British Central Africa [Pre-World War II]

BCA............ British Chicken Association Ltd. (BI)
BCA............ British Chief Administrator
BCA............ British Chiropractors' Association
BCA............ British College of Accountancy, Ltd.
BCA............ British College of Acupuncture (DI)
BCA............ British Colonial Airlines, Inc.
BCA............ British Colostomy Association (DBA)
BCA............ British Commonwealth Alliance (ADA)
BCA............ British Confectioners' Association (BI)
BCA............ British Council in Australia
BCA............ Broadcast Control Authority (NVT)
BCA............ Broadcast Credit Association (EA)
BCA............ Broadcasting Co. of America (NTCM)
BCA............ Buddhists Concerned for Animals [Defunct] (EA)
BCA............ Buffered Communications Adapter [Computer science] (IAA)
BCA............ Buick Club of America (EA)
BCA............ Bulbocavernosus Activity [Physiology]
BCA............ Bulgarian Air Cargo [ICAO designator] (FAAC)
BCA............ Bulldog Club of America (EA)
BCA............ Bullseye Class Association (EA)
BCA............ Bureau of Co-Ordination of Arabization (EA)
BCA............ Bush Church Aid Society [Australia]
BCA............ Business Committee for the Arts (EA)
BCAA .... Branched-Chain Amino Acid [Biochemistry]
BCAA .... Bristol Centre for the Advancement of Architecture [British] (CB)
BCAA .... British Columbia Automobile Association (AC)
BCAA .... Building Control Accreditation Authority [Victoria, Australia]
BCAB .... Birth Control Advisory Bureau [British] (BI)
BCAB .... British Columbia Association of Broadcasters (AC)
BCAB .... British Computer Associated for the Blind (PDAA)
BCABA .... Board of Contract Appeals Bar Association (AAGC)
BCABP .... British Campaign Against Book Piracy
BCABP .... Bureau of Competitive Assessment and Business Policy [Department of Commerce]
BCAC .... Battalion Command and Coordination [Military]
BCAC .... Biology Classroom Activity Checklist (EDAC)
BCAC .... Breast Cancer Advisory Center (EA)
BCAC .... British Conference on Automation and Computation
BCACC .... British Columbia Association of Community Care (AC)
BCACL .... British Columbia Association for Community Living [Formerly, British Columbians for Mentally Handicapped People] (AC)
BCACL .... British Columbia Association for Community Living
BCAD .... Banque de Credit Agricole et de Developpement [Central African Republic] (EY)
BCAF........... Bowling Centers Association of Florida (SRA)
BCAFBWA .... Buddhist Churches of America Federation of Buddhist Women's Associations (EA)
BCAHA .... British Columbia Association of Health Care Auxiliaries (AC)
BCAIQ .... Blackrock California Investment Quality Municipal Trust [Associated Press] (SAG)
BCAJA......... Board of Contract Appeals Judges Association (AAGC)
B Cal .... British Caledonian Airways (DCTA)
BCAL........... British Caledonian Airways [ICAO designator] (AD)
BCALA .... Black Caucus of the American Library Association (EA)
BCALA .... Black Librarians Caucus (EA)
BCALA .... Board of Contract Appeals Lawyers Association [Formerly ASCTLA] (AAGC)
BCAM........... Basic Communication Access Method [Computer science] (IAA)
BCAM........... BCAM International, Inc. [Associated Press] (SAG)
BCAM........... Biomechanics Corp. of America [NASDAQ symbol] (SAG)
BCAM........... Bowling Centers Association of Michigan (SRA)
BCAM Int .... BCAM International, Inc. [Associated Press] (SAG)
BCAML........ BCAM Intl Wrrt'B' [NASDAQ symbol] (TTSB)
BCAMPL ...... Broadcast Amplifier (IAA)
BCAMRT ...... British Columbia Association of Medical Radiation Technologists (AC)
BCAMZ........ BCAM Intl Wrrt'E' [NASDAQ symbol] (TTSB)
BCAN .... Bureau Control Activity Number
BCANJ .... Building Contractors Association of New Jersey (SRA)
B Can L ...... Bachelor of Canon Law
BCANSW...... Bus and Coach Association of New South Wales
BCAO .... Branch Cultural Affairs Officer [United States Information Service]
BCAO .... British Columbia Association of Optometrists (AC)
BCAP .... Bipartite Civil Aviation Panel [Post-World War II, Germany]
BCAP .... British Code of Advertising Practice (ODBW)
BCAP .... British Columbia Association of Podiatrists (AC)
BCAP .... Budget/Cost Account Plan (MCD)
BCAPT .... Braverman-Chevigny Auditory Projective Test [Psychology]
BCAR .... British Civil Airworthiness Requirements
BCAR .... British Civil Aviation Regulations (MCD)
BCAR .... British Council for Aid to Refugees
BCARS .... Base Closure and Realignment Commission [DoD]
BCAS .... Barclay Classroom Assessment System [Student personality test]
BCAS .... Base Contracting Automated System [Computer science]
BCAS .... Beacon Collision Avoidance System [Aviation]
BCAS .... British Compressed Air Society
BCASA .... Bush Church Aid Society of Australia
BCASW .... British Columbia Association of Social Workers [Association des Travailleurs Sociaux de la Colombie-Britannique] (AC)
BCATA .... British Columbia Art Therapy Association (AC)
BCATP .... British Commonwealth Air Training Plan [World War II]
B-CAVe .... Bleomycin, CCNU, Adriamycin, and Velban [Antineoplastic drug regimen] (DAVI)
BCAVE .... Bleomycin, CCNU [Lomustine], Adriamycin, Vinblastine [Antineoplastic drug regimen]
BCAVM .... British Catalogue of Audiovisual Materials [British Library] (NITA)

BC-B .... Bacteriochlorophyll-B [Biochemistry]
BCB............. Ballet Contemporani de Barcelona
BCB............. Banque du Congo Belge [Bank of the Belgian Congo]
BCB............. Barclays Bank [NYSE symbol] (SPSG)
BCB............. Battery Control Building [Army]
BCB............. Benzocyclobutene [Organic chemistry]
BCB............. Big Creek Baldy [Montana] [Seismograph station code, US Geological Survey Closed] (SEIS)
BCB............. Binary Code Box
BCB............. BIT [Binary Digit] Control Block [Computer science] (IBMDP)
BCB............. Blacksburg, VA [Location identifier FAA] (FAAL)
BCB............. Brilliant Cresyl Blue [Biological stain]
BCB............. British Consultants Bureau (CB)
BCB............. Broadcast Band
BCB............. Broadcasting Corp. of the Bahamas
BCB............. Business Corporation Board
BCB............. Button Cell Battery
BCB............. Carib Express [Barbados] [FAA designator] (FAAC)
BCB............. Cott Beverages Ltd. [Toronto Stock Exchange symbol]
BCBA .... BC Biotechnology Alliance (AC)
BCBC .... Being for Carter before the Convention [One of the Carter Administration's criteria for appointment of federal judges]
BCBC .... British Citizens' Band Council (DBA)
BCBC .... Brooklyn Center for the Performing Arts at Brooklyn College
BCBEC .... British Columbia Building Envelope Council [Formerly, Building Envelope Council of British Columbia] (AC)
BCBF .... BCB Financial Services Corp. [NASDAQ symbol] (SAG)
BCBF .... BCB Financial Svcs [NASDAQ symbol] (TTSB)
BCB Fin ...... BCB Financial Services Corp. [Associated Press] (SAG)
BCBG .... Bon Chic, Bon Genre [Good Style, Good Family] [Initialism used to denote French Yuppies] [Lifestyle classification]
BcBilV......... Banco Bilbao Vizcaya SA [Associated Press] (SAG)
BCBL .... Battle Command Battle Laboratory [Army]
BCBPr......... Barclays Bk E1/E2 UnitADS [NYSE symbol] (TTSB)
BCBPrC....... Barclays Bk C1/C2Unit ADS [NYSE symbol] (TTSB)
BCBPrD....... Barclays Bk D1/D2Unit ADS [NYSE symbol] (TTSB)
BCBR .... Bilateral Cartoid Body Resection [Medicine] (DMAA)
BC Branch Lectures... British Columbia Branch Lectures [A publication] (DLA)
BC/BS .... Blue Cross/Blue Shield [Health insurance plan]
BCBSA .... Blue Cross and Blue Shield Association [Chicago, IL] (EA)
BCC............. Badge Collectors Circle [British] [An association] (DBA)
BCC............. Bail Court Cases [Legal] [British]
BCC............. Bail Court Reports (Saunders and Cole) [England] [A publication] (DLA)
BCC............. Balanced Colorimeter Chamber (MCD)
BCC............. Ballistic Camera Control (KSC)
BCC............. Baltimore College of Commerce [Maryland]
BCC............. Basal Cell Carcinoma [Medicine]
BCC............. Basic Cryptanalysis Course
BCC............. Basis Computer Center (IAA)
BCC............. Battery Control Central [Army]
BCC............. Baylor Computing Center [Baylor College of Medicine] [Research center] (RCD)
BCC............. Beacon Control Console (IAA)
BCC............. Beam Coupling Coefficient
BCC............. Bear Creek, AK [Location identifier FAA] (FAAL)
BCC............. Behavior Classification Checklist [Psychology]
BCC............. Belleville & District Chamber of Commerce (AC)
BCC............. Benard Convection Cell
BCC............. Bentall Capital Corp. [Toronto Stock Exchange symbol]
BCC............. Berkshire Community College [Pittsfield, MA]
BCC............. Best Candidate Committee (EA)
BCC............. Bethune-Cookman College [Daytona Beach, FL]
BCC............. Binary Convolutional Code (IAA)
BCC............. Birth Control Clinic
BCC............. Blank Carbon Copy
BCC............. Blind Carbon Copy
bcc............. Blind Carbon Copy (WDMC)
bcc............. Blind Carbon Copy (ODBW)
BCC............. Block Calls Cleared [Telecommunications] (ACRL)
BCC............. Block Check [or Control] Character [Computer science]
BCC............. Block Check Character [Computer science] (TNIG)
BCC............. Block Check Code [Telecommunications] (OSI)
BCC............. Blocked Calls Cleared [Telecommunications]
BCC............. Body-Centered Cubic [Also, BCCUB] [Crystallography]
BCC............. Boise Cascade [NYSE symbol] (SAG)
BCC............. Boone and Crockett Club (EA)
BCC............. Branch Conditionally [Computer science]
BCC............. Brevard Community College [Florida] (KSC)
BCC............. Briar Cliff College [Sioux City, IA]
BCC............. British Caravanners Club (DBA)
BCC............. British Ceramic Confederation (DBA)
BCC............. British Chamber of Commerce (DS)
BCC............. British Clothing Industry Productivity and Technology Centre (CB)
BCC............. British Colour Council
bcc............. British Columbia [MARC country of publication code Library of Congress] (LCCP)
BCC............. British Columbia Reports [A publication] (DLA)
BCC............. British Copyright Council (ILCA)
BCC............. British Council of Churches
BCC............. British Crafts Centre (CB)
BCC............. British Crown Colony
BCC............. British Cryogenics Council (DBA)
BCC............. Broadcast Control Center
BCC............. Broadcasting Complaints Commission [British]

BCC............ Broadcasting Corp. of China
BCC............ Bronx Community College [*New York*]
BCC............ Brookdale Community College, Lincroft, NJ [*OCLC symbol*] (OCLC)
BCC............ Brown's Chancery Cases [*England*] [*A publication*] (DLA)
BCC............ Budget Classification Code (NVT)
BCC............ Buick Compact Club [*Defunct*] (EA)
BCC............ Bureau Central de Compensation [*Central Bureau of Compensation - CBC*] (EAIO)
BCC............ Bureau of Community Corrections (OICC)
BCC............ Bus and Coach Council [*British*]
BCC............ Bus Control Card [*Electronics*] (ACRL)
BCC............ Business Communications Co., Inc. [*Norwalk, CT*] [*Information service or system Telecommunications*] (TSSD)
BCC............ Business Cooperation Center [*EC*] (ECED)
BCC............ Colson Canyon [*California*] [*Seismograph station code, US Geological Survey*] (SEIS)
BCC............ Family History Library, Church of Jesus Christ of Latter-Day Saints, Cranbrook, British Columbia [*Library symbol National Library of Canada*] (BIB)
BCC-52 .... BASIC-52 Computer/Controller
BCCA .... Bank of Credit and Commerce Australia
BCCA .... Basal Cell Carcinoma [*Medicine*] (DAVI)
BCCA .... Bearded Collie Club of America
BCCA .... Beer Can Collectors of America (EA)
BCCA .... Belgian Chamber of Commerce for Australia
BCCA .... British Correspondence Chess Association (BI)
BCCA .... British Cyclo-Cross Association (DBA)
BCCA .... Buick Collector's Club of America [*Defunct*]
BCCA .... Buick Compact Club of America [*Later, BCC*] (EA)
BCCA .... Byelorussian Congress Committee of America (EA)
BCCAA .... British Columbia Colleges Athletic Association (AC)
BCCB .... British Chamber of Commerce, Bangkok (DS)
BCCB .... British Coordinating Committee for Biotechnology
BCCB .... Columbia Bible College, Clearbrook, British Columbia [*Library symbol National Library of Canada*] (BIB)
BCCBRU...... Banque Centrale du Congo Belge et du Ruanda-Urundi [*Central Bank of the Belgian Congo and Rwanda-Urandi*]
BCCC .... Ballistic Compressor Computer Code
BC/CC .... Base Coat/Clear Coat [*Automotive body and refinishing*]
BCCC .... Black Community Crusade for Children [*Children's Defense Fund (CDF)*] (PAZ)
BCCC .... British Chilean Chamber of Commerce (DBA)
BCCC .... Bullseye Cancel Collectors Club
BCCCA .... Biscuit, Cake, Chocolate, and Confectionery Alliance (EAIO)
BCCD .... Bulk-Channel Charge-Coupled Device [*Electronics*] (TEL)
BCCE .... British Cleaning Council Exhibition (ITD)
BCCF .... BC Council for the Family (AC)
BCCF .... British Calcium Carbonates Federation (DBA)
BCCFC .... Billy "Crash" Craddock Fan Club (EA)
BCCFSUA...... Barn Cleaner, Cattle Feeder, and Silo Unloader Association [*Later, FEA*] (EA)
BCCG .... British Chamber of Commerce in Germany (DBA)
BCCG .... British Co-Operative Clinical Group (BABM)
BCCI........... Bank of Credit & Commerce International [*Facetious Translation: Bank of Crooks and Criminals International*] (ECON)
BCCI........... Base Case Coordinating Instructions (DOMA)
BCCI........... Business Card Collectors International (EA)
BCCJ.......... British Chamber of Commerce in Japan (DBA)
BCCL .... Birkbeck College Computation Laboratory [*British*]
BCCLPN .... British Columbia Council of Licensed Practical Nurses (AC)
BCCN .... Bank of Credit and Commerce Niger (EY)
BCCNR........ Buccaneer
BCCNSW...... Building and Construction Council, New South Wales [*Australia*]
BCCO .... Base Consolidation Control Office (AFM)
BCCP .... Biotin Carboxyl Carrier Protein [*Biochemistry*]
BCCPD .... British Columbia Coalition of People with Disabilities (AC)
BCCPrF........ Boise Cascade 9.40% Dep Pfd [*NYSE symbol*] (TTSB)
BCCPrG....... Boise Cascade 7.48% Dep Pfd [*NYSE symbol*] (TTSB)
BCCQ .... Border Collie Club of Queensland [*Australia*]
BCCS .... Barber Coin Collector Society (EA)
BCCS .... Body-Centered Cubic System [*Crystallography*] (IAA)
BC/CS .... Bottle Cleaning/Charging Station
BCCS .... British Carpet Classification Scheme (PDAA)
BCCS .... British Cheque Collectors Society (DBA)
BCCT........... [*The*] Bible in Current Catholic Thought [*A publication*]
BCCT........... Break Control Command Transducers (NASA)
BCCT........... British Chamber of Commerce in Turkey (DBA)
BCCT........... British Columbia Coast Terminals [*Canada*]
BCCT........... British Columbia College of Teachers (AC)
BCCUB .... Body-Centered Cubic [*Also, BCC*] [*Crystallography*]
BCCUS........ Belgian Chamber of Commerce in the United States [*Later, Belgian American Chamber of Commerce in the United States*]
BCCW .... Bare Copper-Clad Wire
BCD .... Bacolod [*Philippines*] [*Airport symbol*] (OAG)
BCD .... Bacterial Carbon Demand [*Marine biology*]
BCD .... Bad Conduct Discharge [*Military*]
BCD .... Barrels per Calendar Day (IAA)
BCD .... Basal Cell Dysplasia [*Medicine*] (DAVI)
BCD .... Base-Catalysed Dechlorination
BCD .... Base-Catalyzed Destination [*Environmental science*]
BCD .... Base Circle Diameter (IAA)
BCD .... Baseline Configuration Document (SSD)
BCD .... Battle Correlator Display
BCD .... Behind Completion Date
BCD .... Beta-Cyclodextrin [*Organic chemistry*]

BCD .... Between Comfort and Discomfort
BCD .... Binary-Coded Data [*or Decimal*] [*Computer science*]
BCD .... Binary Coded Decimal (NITA)
BCD .... Biological/Chemical Detector (DOMA)
BCD .... Bleomycin, Cyclophosphamide, Dactinomycin [*Antineoplastic drug regimen*]
BCD .... Blocked Calls Delayed [*Telecommunications*]
BCd............. Blood Cadmium Level
BCD .... Bramalea Ltd. [*Toronto Stock Exchange symbol*]
BCD .... Brill, C. D., Washington DC [*STAC*]
BCD .... Budget Change Document [*Accounting*] (SSD)
BCD .... Buoyancy Compensator Device
BCD .... Burst Cartridge Detection
BCD .... Burst Cladding Detection System [*Nuclear energy*] (NUCP)
BCD .... Business Cycle Developments [*Bureau of the Census*] [*A publication*]
BCD .... Casitas Dam [*California*] [*Seismograph station code, US Geological Survey*] (SEIS)
BCD .... Castlegar and District Public Library, Castlegar, British Columbia [*Library symbol National Library of Canada*] (NLC)
BCDA .... Barge and Canal Development Association [*British*]
BCDA .... Biscuit and Cracker Distributors Association (EA)
BCD/B .... Binary-Coded Decimal/Binary (DEN)
BCDC .... Benzylcinchonidinium Chloride [*Organic chemistry*]
BCDC .... Binary-Coded Decimal Counter
BCDC .... Black Country Development Corp. [*Department of Environment*] [*British*]
BCDC .... Breast Cancer Detection Center [*University of Michigan*] [*Research center*] (RCD)
BCDD .... Base Construction Depot Detachment [*Navy*]
BCDD .... Binary Coded Decimal Digit (IAA)
BCDD .... Boost-Controlled Decelerating Device
BCDDP........ Breast Cancer Detection Demonstration Project [*NCI/ACS cosponsored project*]
BCDE .... Bulk-Cohesion-Dipolarity-Elasticity [*Factor analysis of physical property data of liquid compounds*]
BCDF .... B-Cell Differentiation Factor [*Immunology*]
BCDI .... Black Child Development Institute [*Later, NBCDI*] (EA)
BCDI .... Bureau de la Cooperation et du Developpement International [*Office for International Cooperation & Development*] (AC)
BCDIC .... Binary-Coded Decimal Interchange Code (IEEE)
B-CDMA ...... Broadband Code Division Multiple Access [*Telecommunications*] (ACRL)
BCDMOS...... Bipolar-CMOS-DMOS (MCD)
BCDMV .... Bean Curly Dwarf Mosaic Virus [*Plant pathology*]
BCDNA........ British Columbia Dietitians' & Nutritionists' Association (AC)
BCDNAF....... Binary-Coded Decimal Nonadjacent Form [*Computer science*] (MHDI)
BCDP .... Base-Catalyzed Decomposition Process
BCDP .... Battery Control Data Processor [*Army*]
BCD/Q......... Binary-Coded Decimal/Quaternary (DEN)
BCDR .... Beta-Cedrene
BCDRS........ Brief Carroll Depression Rating Scale [*Psychology*] (DMAA)
BCDS .... Bulimia Cognitive Distortions Scale [*Psychology*] (DMAA)
BCDSF .... BC Deaf Sports Federation (AC)
BCDTA .... British Chemical and Dyestuffs Traders' Association (BI)
BCDTA .... British Chemical Distributors and Traders Association (DBA)
BCDVM .... Doukhobor Village Museum, Castelgar, British Columbia [*Library symbol National Library of Canada*] (NLC)
BCE .... Bachelor of Chemical Engineering
BCE .... Bachelor of Christian Education
BCE .... Bachelor of Civil Engineering
BCE .... Backup Control Electronics (MCD)
BCE .... Baikal Commodity Exchange [*Russian Federation*] (EY)
BCE .... Barium Cloud Experiment [*NASA*]
BCE .... Barium Contrast Enema [*Medicine*] (CPH)
BCE .... Basal Cell Epithelioma [*Obsolete Medicine*]
BCE .... Base Civil Engineer [*Military*] (AFM)
BCE .... Base Level Commercial Equipment [*DoD*]
BCE .... Baseline Cost Estimate (AABC)
BCE .... Basic Comparison Element (MHDI)
BCE .... Battle Coordination Element [*Army*] (MCD)
BCE............. BCE, Inc. [*Formerly, Bell Canada Enterprises*] [*NYSE symbol*] (SPSG)
BCE............. Beam Collimation Error (MUGU)
BCE............. Before Christian Era
BCE............. Before the Common Era [*Jewish equivalent of BC*]
BCE............. Bench Checkout Equipment
BCE............. Bilingual Community Educator
BCE............. Bishops' Committee for Education [*Australia*]
BCE............. Board of Customs and Excise [*British*]
BCE............. Boston Computer Exchange
BCE............. Bovine Capillary Endothelial [*Cytology*]
BCE............. Brace Resources Ltd. [*Vancouver Stock Exchange symbol*]
BCE............. Bradley Crew Evaluator [*Army*] (INF)
BCE............. British Coal Enterprise
BCE............. British Columbia Hydro and Power Authority [*Formerly, British Columbia Electric Co. Ltd.*] [*AAR code*]
BCE............. British Commonwealth and Empire
BCE............. Bryce Canyon, UT [*Location identifier FAA*] (FAAL)
BCE............. Bubble Chamber Experiment
BCE............. Bus Control Electronics (MCD)
BCE............. Bus Control Element (MCD)
BCEADS....... British Columbia Educational Association of Disabled Students (AC)
BCEAEC....... Banque Centrale des Etats de l'Afrique Equatoriale et de Cameroun [*Central Bank of the States of Equatorial Africa and Cameroon*] (AF)

BCEAO.......... Banque Centrale des Etats de l'Afrique de l'Ouest [*Central Bank of the West African States*] [*Dakar, Senegal*] (AF)
BCEC............ Blue-Collar Ethnic Catholic [*Political demography*]
BCECA .... British Chemical Engineering Contractors Association (PDAA)
BCECC .... British-Central-European Chamber of Commerce (DAS)
BCECEC....... British Conference and Exhibition Centres Export Council (DBA)
BCECF.......... Bis(carboxyethyl)carboxyfluorescein [*Organic chemistry*]
BCECRS .... Base Civil Engineering Course [*Air Force*]
BC Ed........... Bachelor of Commercial Education
BCED .... Bibliography of the Computer in Environmental Design [*A publication*]
B Ce Eng ..... Bachelor of Cement Engineering
BCEFCU .... Bankers Committee to Eliminate Favoritism to Credit Unions (EA)
BCEI............ Base Closing Economic Injury [*Loan*]
BCEI............ Breast Cancer Estrogen-Inducible [*Medicine*] (DMAA)
BCEI............ Bureau Canadien de l'Education Internationale [*Canadian Bureau for International Education - CBIE*]
BCEIA.......... Bishops' Committee for Ecumenical and Interreligious Affairs (EA)
BCEL............ British Commonwealth Ex-Services League [*Formerly, British Empire Services League*] [*British*]
BCEL............ Business Council for Effective Literacy [*Defunct*] (EA)
BCelts.......... Boston Celtics Ltd. [*Associated Press*] (SAG)
BCEM........... Bureau of Community Environmental Management [*Terminated, 1973*] [*HEW*]
BCEMA........ British Combustion Equipment Manufacturers Associaton (DBA)
BCE MC ...... BCE Mobile Communications, Inc. [*Associated Press*] (SAG)
BCEN .... BC Environmental Network (AC)
BCEN .... Black College Educational Network (TSSD)
BCent........... Bible du Centenaire [*A publication*] (BJA)
BCEP........... Book of Classic English Poetry [*A publication*]
BCEPS .... Butoxycarbonylethyl Polysulfide [*Organic chemistry*]
BCER .... Block Check Error [*Electronics*] (ECII)
BCeramRA... British Ceramic Research Association (PDAA)
B Cer E .... Bachelor of Ceramic Engineering
B Cer Eng .... Bachelor of Ceramic Engineering
BCERPO .... Base Civil Engineer Real Property Office (SAA)
BCES........... Bis(chloroethyl)sulfide [*Biochemistry*]
BCES........... British Comparative Education Society (AIE)
BCESCH .... Base Civil Engineering School [*Air Force*]
BCEX........... Bundle Controlled Expansion
BCF............. Bachelor of City Forestry
BCF............. Bandpass Crystal Filter
BCF............. Basic Control Frequency
BCF............. Basophil Chemotactic Factor [*Hematology*]
BCF............. Battle Cruiser Force [*British military*] (DMA)
BCF............. Beam Correction Factor
BCF............. Before Columbus Foundation (EA)
BCF............. Billion Conductor Feet [*Telecommunications*] (TEL)
BCF............. Billion Cubic Feet
BCF............. Bioconcentration Factor [*of chemicals by living organisms*]
BCF............. Blood Cancer Foundation [*Defunct*] (EA)
BCF............. Body/Caudal Fin [*Ichthyology*]
BCF............. British Chess Federation (BI)
BCF............. British Commonwealth Forces
BCF............. British Cycling Federation
BCF............. Bromochlorodifluoromethane [*Fire extinguishing agent*] [*Organic chemistry*] (ADA)
BCF............. Budgetaire, Comptable, et Financier [*Budget, Accounting, and Finance - BA & F*]
BCF............. Bulk Continuous Filament [*Textile science*]
BCF............. Bulked Continuous Fiber [*or Filament*] [*Textile*]
BCF............. Bureau of Commercial Fisheries [*Later, National Marine Fisheries Service*]
BCF............. Burlington Coat Factory [*NYSE symbol*] (TTSB)
BCF............. Burlington Coat Factory Warehouse Corp. [*NYSE symbol*] (SPSG)
BCF............. FM Broadcasting Station [*ITU designation*] (CET)
BCFA........... Britain-China Friendship Association (BI)
BCFA........... British Columbia Federation of Agriculture (AC)
BCFA........... British Columbia Forestry Association [*Formerly, Canadian Forestry Association of BC*] (AC)
BCFA........... British Contract Furnishing Association (PDAA)
BCFAG .... Bouguer Corrected Free-Air Gradient [*Geophysics*]
B-CFC .... B-Colony Forming Cells
BCFC........... Billy Cate Fan Club (EA)
BCFC........... Bobby "C" Fan Club [*Defunct*] (EA)
BCFC........... Brandon Call Fan Club (EA)
BCFC........... Buddy Clark Fan Club [*Defunct*] (EA)
BCFC........... Business Coalition for Fair Competition (EA)
BCFCA .... British Columbia Floor Covering Association (AC)
BCFD .... Billions of Cubic Feet per Day [*of gas*]
BCFESR .... British Commonwealth Far East Strategic Reserve
BCFFPA .... British Columbia Federation of Foster Parent Associations (AC)
BCFG .... British Camp Fire Girls (BI)
BCFK .... British Commonwealth Forces, Korea [*British military*] (DMA)
BCFL .... British Columbia Federation of Labour [*Federation du travail de la Colombie-Britannique*] (AC)
BCFLS.......... Best Commercial Flight Line Test Set (MCD)
BCFM........... Black Citizens for a Fair Media (EA)
BCFM........... Broken Corn and Foreign Material [*Quality measure for grain*]
BCFMA........ Broadcast Cable Financial Management Association (EA)
BCFMWU...... British Columbia Ferry & Marine Workers' Union [*Syndicat des Travailleurs Marins et de Bacs de la Colombie-Britannique*] (AC)
BCFP........... Breast-Cyst Fluid Protein [*Immunochemistry*]
BCF/PCF ...... Bridging and Routing Packet Control Facility [*Network Systems Corp.*] (PCM)
BCFSK .... Binary Code Frequency Shift Keying [*SAGE*]

BCFT........... Business Council for Fair Trade (AC)
BCFTE......... British Commonwealth Forest Translation Exchange
BCFVA .... Fraser Valley Antique Farm Machinery Association, Clearbrook, British Columbia [*Library symbol National Library of Canada*] (NLC)
BCG........... Bacillus Calmette-Guerin [*TB vaccine*] (GPO)
BCG........... Ballistocardiogram [*Medicine*]
BCG........... Battalion Control Group [*Army*]
BCG... BC Gas [*TS Symbol*] (TTSB)
BCG........... Bemichi [*Guyana*] [*Airport symbol*] (OAG)
BCG........... Bicolor Guaiac [*Test*] [*Medicine*]
BCG........... Bidirectional Categorical Grammar
BCG........... Bilateral Cystogram [*Radiography*] (DAVI)
BCG........... Block-Connected Graph [*Mathematics*] [*Used in GPRS*]
BCG........... Blue-Collar Guy [*Lifestyle classification*]
BCG........... Blue Compact Galaxy [*Astronomy*]
BCG........... Board for Certification of Genealogists (EA)
BCG........... Body-Cooling Garment [*NASA*] (MCD)
BCG........... Boston Consulting Group (ECON)
BCG........... British Columbia Government [*Canada ICAO designator*] (FAAC)
BCG........... Bromcresol Green [*An indicator*] [*Chemistry*]
BCG........... Bucking Current Generator
BCGA .... Bank Corp. (GA) [*NASDAQ symbol*] (TTSB)
BCGA .... Bank Corp. of Georgia [*NASDAQ symbol*] (SAG)
BCGA .... BC Gymnastics Association (AC)
BCGA .... British Compressed Gases Association (DBA)
BCGA .... British Cotton Growing Association (BI)
BCGBA .... British Crown Green Bowling Association (DBA)
BCGC .... Bradley Commander/Gunner Certification Test [*Army*] (INF)
BCGD .... Background
BCGeolEng... Bachelor of Science in Geological Engineering (NADA)
BCGF .... B-Cell Growth Factor [*Biochemistry*]
BCGI .... Boston Communications Group, Inc. [*NASDAQ symbol*] (SAG)
BCGLO .... British Commonwealth Geographical Liaison Office (PDAA)
BCGMA .... British Commerical Glasshouse Manufacturers Association (DBA)
BCGTMA ...... British Ceramic Gift and Tableware Manufacturers' Association (DBA)
B Ch........... Baccalaureus Chirurgiae [*Bachelor of Surgery*]
BCh........... Bachelor in Surgery (DD)
B Ch........... Bachelor of Chemistry
BCH........... Banco Cent Hispanoamer ADS [*NYSE symbol*] (TTSB)
BCH........... Banco Central Hispanoamericano [*NYSE symbol*] (SAG)
BCH........... Bankers Clearing House [*California*] (SRA)
B Ch........... Barbour's Chancery Reports [*New York*] [*A publication*] (DLA)
BCH........... Basal Cell Hyperplasia [*Medicine*]
BCH .... Basic Decision Height [*Aviation*] (DA)
BCH .... Beach (MCD)
BCH .... Beach
BCh........... Ben Chajim (BJA)
BCH .... Bids per Circuit per Hour [*Telecommunications*]
BCH .... Binary-Coded Hexadecimal (MCD)
BCH .... Binary-Coded Hollerith
BCH .... BIT [*Binary Digit*] per Circuit per Hour [*Computer science*] (IAA)
BCH .... Block Control Header [*Computer science*] (IBMDP)
BCH .... Blocked Calls Held [*Telecommunications*]
BCH .... Bomber Command Headquarters [*British military*] (DMA)
BCH .... Booksellers Clearing House [*Commercial firm British*]
BCH .... Bose-Chaudhuri-Hocquenghem [*Cyclic codes*] [*Telecommunications*] (MCD)
BCH .... Branch (ADA)
B/CH .... Bristol Channel [*British*]
BCH .... British Columbia Power and Hydro Authority [*Canada ICAO designator*] (FAAC)
BCH .... Bunch (WGA)
BCH .... Chilliwack Public Library, British Columbia [*Library symbol National Library of Canada*] (NLC)
BChA.......... British Chiropody Association (DBA)
BCHA .... British Columbia Health Association (AC)
BCHA .... [*The*] British Columbia Humanist Association [*Also, Humanist Association of BC*] [*Formerly, Humanist Association of Greater Vancouver*] (AC)
B-channel ... Bearer Channel [*A component of ISDN interfaces*] (PCM)
BCHCM .... Board of Certified Hazard Control Management (EA)
B Ch D .... Baccalaureus Chirurgiae Dentium [*Bachelor of Dental Surgery*]
B Ch E .... Bachelor of Chemical Engineering
BCHE .... Chetwynd Public Library, British Columbia [*Library symbol National Library of Canada*] (NLC)
B Chem........ Bachelor of Chemistry
B Chem E .... Bachelor of Chemical Engineering
BChemEng... Bachelor of Chemical Engineering (DD)
B Ch Eng ..... Bachelor of Chemical Engineering
BCHF.......... Fraser Valley College, Chilliwack, British Columbia [*Library symbol National Library of Canada*] (NLC)
BCHFA .... British-Canadian Holstein-Friesian Association (BI)
BCHG .... Bunching (MSA)
BCHG .... Test a BIT [*Binary Digit*] and Change [*Computer science*]
B Chir .... Baccalaureus Chirurgiae [*Bachelor of Surgery*]
BChir .... Bachelor in Surgery (DD)
BChl .... Bacteriochlorophyll [*Biochemistry*]
BCHLR .... Bachelor
BCHM .... Chilliwack Museum, British Columbia [*Library symbol National Library of Canada*] (NLC)
B-CHOP....... Bleomycin, Cyclophosphamide, Hydroxydaunomycin [*Adriamycin*], Oncovin , Prednisone [*Vincristine*] [*Antineoplastic drug regimen*]
BCHP .... Blue Chip Computerware, Inc. [*NASDAQ symbol*] (SAG)
BCHPE......... Blue Chip Computerware [*NASDAQ symbol*] (TTSB)

B Chr Ed ...... Bachelor of Christian Education
BChrom .... Bachelor of Chromatics
BCHS .... Bing Crosby Historical Society (EA)
BCHS .... Bureau of Community Health Services [*Health Services Administration*]
BCHW .... Black Caucus of Health Workers (EA)
BCHX .... Biochem Pharma, Inc. [*NASDAQ symbol*] (SAG)
BCHXF .... BioChem Pharma [*NASDAQ symbol*] (TTSB)
BCI .... Banca Commerciale Italiana [*Italy*]
BCI .... Barcaldine [*Australia Airport symbol*] (OAG)
BCI .... Barro Colorado Island [*Canal Zone*] [*Site of Smithsonian Tropical Research Institute*]
BCI .... Base Line Configuration Identification (SAA)
BCI .... Basic Concepts Inventory [*Psychology*]
BCI .... Basic Cost Information (AFIT)
BCI .... Bat Conservation International (EA)
BCI .... Battalion Command Inspection [*Army*] (INF)
BCI .... Battery Condition Indicator (MCD)
BCI .... Battery Council International (EA)
BCI .... Bell Canada International, Inc. [*Ottawa, ON*] [*Telecommunications*] (TSSD)
BCI .... Beverage Canners International Corp.
BCI .... Bidirectional Computer Interface Program
BCI .... Binary-Coded Information
BCI .... Biomedical Communications Inventory [*National Library of Medicine*]
BCI .... BIT [*Binary Digit*] Count Integrity [*Telecommunications*] (TEL)
BCI .... Bituminous Coal Institute [*Absorbed by NCA*]
BCI .... Blue Circle Industries [*British*]
BCI .... Blue Crescent International (EAIO)
BCI .... Bluff Creek Industries R. R. [*AAR code*]
BCI .... Bonsai Clubs International (EA)
BCI .... Brain-Computer Interface (DMAA)
BCI .... Brazilian Coffee Institute (EA)
BCI .... British Columbia Institute of Technology Library [*UTLAS symbol*]
BCI .... British Columbia Resources Investment Corp. [*Toronto Stock Exchange symbol Vancouver Stock Exchange symbol*]
BCI .... Broadcast Interference [*Telecommunications*]
BCI .... Budgetary Cost Information [*Accounting*]
BCI .... Bulk Current Injection [*Electronics*]
BCI .... Bureau of Contract Information [*Defunct*] (EA)
BCI .... Bureau of Criminal Investigation (BARN)
BCI .... Business Competitive Intelligence
BCI .... International Broadcasting Station [*ITU designation*] (DEN)
BCIA .... Bishops' Committee for Industrial Affairs [*Australia*]
BCIA .... Bounded Carry Inspection Adder (PDAA)
BCIA .... British Clothing Industry Association (DBA)
BCIA .... British Cooking Industry Association (BI)
BCIC .... Birth Control Investigation Committee (BABM)
BCIC .... Breast Cancer Information Clearinghouse
BCIC .... Building and Construction Industry Council [*Australia*]
BCICA .... British Columbia Insulation Contractors Association (AC)
BCICA .... British Columbia Interior Curling Association (AC)
BCID .... Battlefield Combat Identification [*Army*] (RDA)
BCIE .... Banco Centroamericano de Integracion Economica [*Central American Bank for Economic Integration*] [*Spanish*] (BARN)
BCIE .... British Channel Island Ferries
BCIF .... British Channel Island Ferries
BCII .... Bone Care International, Inc. [*NASDAQ symbol*] (SAG)
BCII .... Bone Care Intl. [*NASDAQ symbol*] (TTSB)
BCIL .... Bulk/Common Items List (MCD)
BCILSB .... Building and Construction Industry Long Service Leave Board [*Australia*]
BCIM .... Beyond Capacity of Intermediate Maintenance [*Army*] (MCD)
BCIM .... Bureau of Catholic Indian Missions (EA)
BCINA .... British Commonwealth International News Agency
BC Indus & Com L Rev ... Boston College Industrial and Commercial Law Review [*A publication*] (AAGC)
BCIP .... Belgian Centre for Information Processing
BCIP .... Bromo(chloro)indolylphosphate [*Organic chemistry*]
BCIPPA .... British Cast Iron Pressure Pipe Association (PDAA)
BCIR .... Bomber Command Intelligence Report
BCIRA .... British Cast Iron Research Association
BCIRA .... British Cotton Industry Research Association (DI)
BCIRL .... Biological Control of Insects Research Laboratory [*Department of Agriculture*] (GRD)
BCIS .... Bancinsurance Corp. [*NASDAQ symbol*] (SAG)
BCIS .... Battlefield Combat Identification System [*Army*] (RDA)
BCIS .... Binary Constitution Information Service (MCD)
BCIS .... Bomber Command Intelligence Summary
BCIS .... Building Cost Information Service [*Royal Institute of Chartered Surveyors*] [*Information service or system*] (IID)
BCIT .... British Columbia Institute of Technology [*Canada*] (ASF)
BCITP .... Business Council for Improved Transport Policies (EA)
BCITSS .... British Columbia Institute of Technology Staff Society [*Societe du Personnel de l'Institut de la Technolgie de la Colombie-Britannique*] (AC)
BCIU .... Bus Control Interface Unit (MCD)
BCIU .... Business Council for International Understanding (EA)
BCiv .... Bellum Civile [*of Caesar*] [*Classical studies*] (OCD)
BCJ .... Bicer Medical Systems [*Vancouver Stock Exchange symbol*]
BCJC .... Bay City Junior College [*Michigan*]
BCJS .... Buffer Control Junction Switch [*Computer science*]
BCJS .... Bureau for Careers in Jewish Service [*Defunct*] (EA)
BCK .... Back
BCK .... Black River Falls, WI [*Location identifier FAA*] (FAAL)
BCK .... Bolworra [*Australia Airport symbol Obsolete*] (OAG)
BCK .... British Columbia Packers Ltd. [*Toronto Stock Exchange symbol*]
BCK .... Brock University Library [*UTLAS symbol*]
BCK .... Bucak [*Turkey*] [*Seismograph station code, US Geological Survey*] (SEIS)
BCK .... [*The*] Buffalo Creek Railroad Co. [*Absorbed into Consolidated Rail Corp.*] [*AAR code*]
BCK .... Compagnie de Chemin de Fer Bas-Congo-Katanga [*Lower Congo-Katanga Railway*] [*Zaire*]
BCK .... Priority Aviation Co., Inc. [*ICAO designator*] (FAAC)
BCKA .... Branched-Chain Ketoacid [*Biochemistry*]
BCKB .... British Commonwealth Korean Base [*British military*] (DMA)
BCKD .... Branched-Chain Ketoacid Dehydrogenase [*Biochemistry*]
BCKEYE .... Buckeye
BCKG .... Backing (FAAC)
BCKHOE .... Backhoe
BckIns .... Beckman Instruments, Inc. [*Associated Press*] (SAG)
bcksk .... Buckskin (VRA)
BCKT .... Becket [*Bracket*]
BCKT .... Bucket
BCL .... Bachelor of Canon Law
BCL .... Bachelor of Civil Law
BCL .... Bachelor of Commercial Law
BCL .... Bar Coded Label (NITA)
BCL .... Barra Colorado [*Costa Rica*] [*Airport symbol*] (OAG)
BCL .... Base-Coupled Logic [*Computer science*] (PDAA)
BCL .... Basic Contour Line
BCL .... Basic Cycle Length [*Medicine*] (DAVI)
BCL .... Battelle-Columbus Laboratories
BCL .... B-Cell Line [*Cytology*]
BCL .... BC [*British Columbia*] Rail Ltd. [*Toronto Stock Exchange symbol Vancouver Stock Exchange symbol*]
BCL .... Bechtel Client Letter (IEEE)
BCL .... Behavioral Checklist [*Psychology*]
BCL .... Bicycle (MSA)
BCL .... Binary Compatibility Layer [*Computer science*] (PCM)
BCL .... Biocraft Laboratories, Inc. [*NYSE symbol*] (SPSG)
BCL .... Biocraft Labs [*NYSE symbol*] (TTSB)
BCL .... Bishops' Committee on the Liturgy (EA)
BCL .... Books for College Libraries [*A publication of ALA*]
BCL .... Bootstap Confidence Level [*Mathematics*]
BCL .... Bougainville Copper Ltd. [*Australia*]
BCL .... Bristol City Line [*Steamship*] (MHDW)
BCL .... British Caribbean Airways Ltd. [*ICAO designator*] (FAAC)
BCL .... Broadcast Listener [*Amateur radio*]
BCL .... Broadcast Listening (IDOE)
BCL .... Broom Closet
BCL .... Building and Construction Law [*Australia A publication*]
BCL .... Burroughs Common Language [*Computer science*] (BUR)
BCL .... Business Comptuer Systems Ltd. [*Later, Business Computer Systems PLC*] [*British*] (NITA)
BCL .... Business Computers Ltd. [*British*] (NITA)
BCL .... Business Corp. Law [*A publication*]
BCL .... Casitas Lake [*California*] [*Seismograph station code, US Geological Survey Closed*] (SEIS)
BCL .... Media Reference and Referral Center [*Library network*]
BCLA .... BC Lung Association (AC)
BCLA .... British Columbia Library Association [*Canada*] (AEBS)
BCLA .... British Contact Lens Association
BCLAR .... Bass Clarinet [*Music*]
BcLatn .... Banco Latinamericano de Exportaciones [*Associated Press*] (SAG)
BCLB .... Broadband Connectionless Bearer Service [*Telecommunications*] (ACRL)
BCLB .... Butterworth's Co. Law Bulletin [*Australia A publication*]
BCLCA .... British Colombia Ladies Curling Association (AC)
BCLDI .... British Clayware Land Drain Industry [*An association*] (DBA)
BCLDP .... Battelle Columbus Laboratories Decommissioning Project (DOGT)
BCLDP .... Battelle Columbus Laboratories Decommissioning Project [*Department of Energy*] (GAAI)
BCLDP .... Battelle Columbus Laboratories Decommissioning Project
BCLF .... Fraser Valley College, Abbotsford, British Columbia [*Library symbol National Library of Canada*] (NLC)
BCLL .... Banner Claw Length [*Botany*]
B-CLL .... B-Cell Chronic Lymphocytic Leukemia [*Medicine*]
BCL Lectures ... British Columbia Annual Law Lectures [*Canada*] [*A publication*] (DLA)
BCLM .... Clinton Museum, British Columbia [*Library symbol National Library of Canada*] (NLC)
BCLMA .... British Columbia Lumber Manufacturers' Association [*Canada*] (BI)
BCLN .... British Columbia Library Network [*Canada*] (NITA)
BCL Notes ... British Columbia Law Notes [*A publication*] (DLA)
BCLO .... Bomber Command Liaison Officer (NATG)
BCLP .... Bilateral Cleft of Lip and Palate [*Medicine*] (DMAA)
BCLR .... British Columbia Law Reports [*Canada A publication*] (DLA)
BCLR .... Test a BIT [*Binary Digit*] and Clear [*Computer science*]
BCLRBD .... British Columbia Labour Relations Board Decisions [*Database*] [*Western Legal Publications Ltd.*] [*Information service or system*] (CRD)
BCLS .... Basic Cardiac Life Support [*System*] [*Medicine*]
BCLS .... Corporation of Land Surveyors of the Province of British Columbia [*Also, BC Land Surveyors*] [*Formerly, Provincial Land Surveyors*] (AC)
BCLT .... Books for College Libraries [*UTLAS symbol*]
BCLTA .... British Columbia Library Trustees Association (AC)
BCLU .... Base Construction Liaison Unit (SAA)

BCLYM......... Yellowhead Museum, Clearwater, British Columbia [*Library symbol National Library of Canada*] (NLC)
BCM............. Bacau [*Romania*] [*Airport symbol*] (OAG)
BCM............. Bachelor of Church Music
BCM............. Bachelor of Computer and Mathematical Sciences
BCM............. Bachelor of Computer Management (DD)
BCM............. Back Course Marker (FAAC)
BCM............. Backer Petroleum Corp. [*Vancouver Stock Exchange symbol*]
BCM............. Balance Calibration Machine
BCM............. Balanced Crystal Mixer (IAA)
BCM............. Ballistic Correction of the Moment
BCM............. Banco Comercial de Mocambique
BCM............. Base Correlation Matrix [*Air Force*] (DOMA)
BCM............. Baseline Correlation Matrix [*Air Force*] (AAGC)
BCM............. Basic Combat Maneuver (MCD)
BCM............. Basic Control Monitor (BUR)
BCM............. Battery Control and Monitor [*Army*]
BCM............. Become (FAAC)
BCM............. Below Center of Mass [*Command report*] [*Army*] (INF)
BCM............. Best Cruise Mach Number [*Aviation*]
BCM............. Beyond Capacity of Maintenance (MCD)
BCM............. Bible Club Movement (EA)
BCM............. Bile Canalicular Membrane
BCM............. Billion Cubic Meters
BCM............. Binary Coded Matrix [*Telecommunications*] (TEL)
BCM............. Birth Control Medication
BCM............. Blunt Conical Model
BCM............. Body Cell Mass
BCM............. Body Computer Module [*General Motors' computer system*]
BCM............. Body Control Module [*Automotive engineering*]
BCM............. Boots Contract Manufacturing
BCM............. Boston Conservatory of Music
BCM............. Bowie State College Library, Bowie, MD [*OCLC symbol*] (OCLC)
BCM............. Brassboard Configuration Model (MCD)
BCM............. British Catalogue of Music [*British National Bibliography*]
BCM............. British Chess Magazine
BCM............. Broken Cubic Meter (DAC)
BCM............. Buried Coarctate Mesa [*LASER diode technology*] (NITA)
BCM............. Business Clearance Memorandum (AAGC)
BCM............. Courier-Mail (Brisbane) [*A publication*]
BCMA.......... Bank Capital Markets Association [*Washington, DC*] (EA)
BCMA.......... Breast Care and Mastectomy Association (DBA)
BCMA.......... British Caramel Manufacturers Association (DBA)
BCMA.......... British Carpet Manufacturers Association (PDAA)
BCMA.......... British Chain Manufacturers Association (DBA)
BCMA.......... British Chip Board Manufacturers' Association (BI)
BCMA.......... British Colour Makers' Association (DI)
BCMA.......... British Columbia Medical Association (AC)
BCMA.......... British Cookware Manufacturers Association (DBA)
BCMA.......... British Country Music Association
BCMA.......... British Crayfish Marketing Association (DBA)
BCMC.......... British Cable Makers Confederation (DBA)
BCmCA .... Bank of Commerce (California) [*Associated Press*] (SAG)
B Cmd .... Bomber Command [*British military*] (DMA)
BCMD .... Brush Creek Mining & Development Co., Inc. [*NASDAQ symbol*] (NQ)
BCMD .... Brush Creek Mining/Dvlp [*NASDAQ symbol*] (TTSB)
BCME.......... Bis(chloromethyl) Ether [*Organic chemistry*]
BCME.......... Building Construction Materials and Equipment [*A publication*] (ADA)
BCMES........ BC Multicultural Education Society (AC)
BCMET........ Bud Collins' Modern Encyclopedia of Tennis [*A publication*]
BCMF.......... Bleomycin, Cyclophosphamide, Methotrexate, Fluorouracil [*Antineoplastic drug regimen*]
BCMF.......... British Ceramic Manufacturers' Federation (DBA)
BCMG .... Birmingham Contemporary Music Group [*British*]
BCMI........... Boston College Mathematics Institute [*Boston College*] [*Research center*] (RCD)
BCML........... Burroughs Current Mode Logic
BCMO .... Bis(chloromethyl)oxetane [*Organic chemistry*]
BCMOS........ Bipolar Complementary Metal-Oxide Semiconductor (IAA)
BCMP......... Bell Cablemedia Ltd. [*NASDAQ symbol*] (SAG)
BCMP.......... Biomedical Measurement and Control Panel (ACII)
BCMP.......... Bleached Chemimechanical Pulping Process [*Pulp and paper technology*]
BCMPA .... British Columbia Motion Picture Association (AC)
BCMPY .... Bell Cablemedia [*NASDAQ symbol*] (TTSB)
BCMR .... Board for Correction of Military Records
BCMS.......... Bible Churchmen's Missionary Society [*Church of England*]
BCMS.......... Bioethic Citation Maintenance System (DMAA)
BCMS.......... Bismorpholinecarbamylsulfenamide [*Organic chemistry*]
BCMV.......... Bean Common Mosaic Virus
BCN .... Backbone Concentrator Node [*Routing device*] [*Telecommunications*] (PCM)
BCN .... Ballistic Correction to Normal
BCN .... Banco de Credito Nacional SA [*Private bank*] [*Brazil*] (EY)
BCN .... Banque Canadienne Nationale
BCN .... Barcelona [*Spain*] [*Airport symbol*] (OAG)
BCN .... Beacon [*Aviation*] (AFM)
BCN .... Beacon Properties [*NYSE symbol*] (TTSB)
BCN .... Beacon Properties Corp. [*NYSE symbol*] (SAG)
BCN .... Beauty Counselors International, Inc. [*Toronto Stock Exchange symbol*]
BCN .... Bilateral Cortical Necrosis [*Medicine*]
BCN .... Biomedical Communications Network [*Proposed*] [*National Library of Medicine*]

BCN .... Boulder City [*Nevada*] [*Seismograph station code, US Geological Survey Closed*] (SEIS)
BCN .... Breakdown Control Number (MCD)
BCN .... Brecon [*Welsh depot code*]
BCN .... British Commonwealth of Nations
BCN .... Broadband Communication Network (BUR)
BCN .... Bureau Control Number
BCN .... Business Computer Network, Inc. [*San Antonio, TX*] [*Telecommunications*] (TSSD)
BCNC .... Benzylcinchoninium Chloride [*Organic chemistry*]
BCNC .... Black Christian Nationalist Church
BCNET .... [*The*] British Columbia Regional Network [*Computer science*] [*Canada*] (TNIG)
BCNF .... British Columbia Neurofibromatosis Foundation (AC)
BCNI .... Business Council on National Issues [*Canadian research and lobbying organization*] (CROSS)
BCNO .... British College of Naturopathy and Osteopathy
BCNR .... Board for Correction of Naval Records
BCNS .... Basal Cell Nevus Syndrome [*Medicine*] (DMAA)
BCNT .... Bushfires Council of the Northern Territory [*Australia*]
BCNU .... Be Seein' You [*Computer science*] (DOM)
BCNU .... Bis(chloroethyl)nitrosourea [*Carmustine*] [*Also, BiCNU*] [*Antineoplastic drug regimen*]
BCNU .... British Columbia Nurses' Union [*Syndicat des Infirmieres de la Colombie-Britannique*] (AC)
BCNWS........ British Columbia Native Women's Society (AC)
BCNY .... Bond Club of New York [*New York, NY*] (EA)
BCNY .... Brazilian Center of New York (EA)
BCNZ .... Broadcasting Corp. of New Zealand
BCO .... Base Contracting Officer [*Military*]
BCO .... Battery Control Officer [*Army*] (AABC)
BCO .... Battery Cutoff [*Telecommunications*] (TEL)
BCO .... Bill in Care Of [*Telecommunications*] (TEL)
BCO .... Binary-Coded Octal [*Computer science*]
BCO .... Blessings Corp. [*AMEX symbol*] (SPSG)
BCO .... Booster Engine Cutoff [*Rocketry*]
BCO .... Bridge Cutoff (IEEE)
BCO .... British College of Optometrists (DBA)
BCOA .... Basenji Club of America (EA)
BCOA .... Bituminous Coal Operators' Association (EA)
BCOA .... Borzoi Club of America (EA)
BcoAEd .... Bancode A Edwards [*Associated Press*] (SAG)
BcoAEdw..... Banco de A. Edwards [*Associated Press*] (SAG)
BCOB .... Booster Cutoff Backup
BCOB .... Broadband Connection-Oriented Bearer Service [*Telecommunications*] (ACRL)
BCOB .... Broken Clouds or Better (MUGU)
BcoBHIF...... Banco BHIF [*Associated Press*] (SAG)
BCOC .... Bowel Care of Choice [*Medicine*] (DMAA)
BCODH........ Branched-Chain Oxoacid Dehydrogenase [*An enzyme*]
BCOE .... Bench Checkout Equipment
BCOF .... British Commonwealth Occupation Force [*Military*]
B/C of A ...... British College of Aeronautics
BcOHig .... Banco OHiggins [*Associated Press*] (SAG)
BCOI .... British Central Office of Information
BcoIndl .... Banco Industrial Columbiano SA [*Associated Press*] (SAG)
BCOL .... British Columbia Railway Co. [*AAR code*]
B Com .... Bachelor of Commerce
BCOM .... Balance of Commitments
BCOM .... Bank of Commerce (California) [*NASDAQ symbol*] (SAG)
BCOM .... Burroughs Computer Output to Microfilm (IEEE)
BCOM .... Courtenay and District Museum, Courtenay, British Columbia [*Library symbol National Library of Canada*] (NLC)
BCom(Acc)... Bachelor of Commerce (Accounting)
B Com Adm... Bachelor of Commercial Administration
BCombStuds... Bachelor of Combined Studies [*British*] (DBQ)
BCom-LLB ... Bachelor of Commerce-Bachelor of Laws
B Comm ...... Bachelor of Commerce
BCommSc .... Bachelor of Commercial Science
BCOMN........ North Island College, Courtenay, British Columbia [*Library symbol National Library of Canada*] (NLC)
BComp......... Bachelor of Computing
B Compos.... Bernardus Compostellanus [*Authority cited in pre-1607 legal work*] (DSA)
BCompSc..... Bachelor of Computer Science
BCompScEng... Bachelor of Computer Science and Engineering
BComSc....... Bachelor of Commercial Science
BComStuds... Bachelor of Combined Studies [*British*] (DI)
BComSysEng... Bachelor of Computer Systems Engineering
BcOne......... Banc One Corp. [*Associated Press*] (SAG)
B/CONF....... Bearing/Confidence
BConstrucEc... Bachelor of Construction Economics
BCOO .... Bomber Command Operational Order
BCOO .... British College of Ophthalmic Opticians (DBQ)
BCOP .... BCNU [*Carmustine*], Cyclophosphamide, Oncovin , Prednisone [*Vincristine*] [*Antineoplastic drug regimen*]
BCOP .... Broken Clouds or Better [*Meteorology*] (DA)
BCOQ .... Baptist Convention of Ontario & Quebec (AC)
BCOR .... Biacore International AB [*NASDAQ symbol*] (SAG)
BCORP........ Business Council on the Reduction of Paperwork (EA)
BCOS .... British Chiefs of Staff
BcoSanti ...... Banco De Santiago [*Associated Press*] (SAG)
BcOsorno..... Banco Osorno y La Union [*Associated Press*] (SAG)
BcoWiese .... Banco Wiese Limitado [*Associated Press*] (SAG)
BCP............. Bachelor of City Planning

BCP .... Bag Cell Peptide [Biochemistry]
BCP .... Balchem Corp. [AMEX symbol] (SAG)
BCP .... Ballast Control Panel
BCP .... Banco Comercial Portugues [Portuguese Commercial Bank] (ECON)
BCP .... Barker Code Processing
BCP .... Barrincorp Industries, Inc. [Toronto Stock Exchange symbol]
BCP .... Base Condemnation Percent (NASA)
BCP .... Basic Calcium Phosphate [Biochemistry] (DAVI)
BCP .... Basic Control Program (DNAB)
BCP .... Basotho Congress Party [Lesotho] [Political party] (PPW)
BCP .... Battery Command Post [Army]
BCP .... B-Cell Precursor [Biochemistry]
BCP .... BCNU [Carmustine], Cyclophosphamide, Prednisone [Antineoplastic drug regimen]
BCP .... Beam Candlepower
BCP .... Behavioral Characteristics Progression [Scale]
BCP .... Bench Mark Control Point (NASA)
BCP .... Bereaved Children's Program [Later, BC] (EA)
BCP .... Bing Crosby Productions
BCP .... Biochemical Profile (DAVI)
BCP .... Biology, Chemistry, Physics (DD)
BCP .... Birth Control Pill [Medicine]
BCP .... Bisynchronous Communications Processor (NITA)
BCP .... BIT [Binary Digit] Control Panel [Computer science] (MCD)
BCP .... Blanket Crime Policy [Insurance]
BCP .... Blended Credit Program [Federal government]
BCP .... Block Copolymer [Organic chemistry]
BCP .... Blood Pressure Cuff [Cardiology] (DAVI)
BCP .... Blue Cross Plan [Health insurance]
BCP .... Board of Certification in Pedorthics (EA)
BCP .... Boise Cascade Office Products [NYSE symbol] (SAG)
BCP .... Book of Common Prayer [Episcopalian]
BCP .... Bootstrap Commissioning Program [Air Force]
BCP .... Brilliant Computer Products Co. (PCM)
BCP .... British Commonwealth Pacific Airlines Ltd. (ADA)
BCP .... Broken-Case Price [Marketing] (DOAD)
BCP .... Bromcresol Purple [An indicator] [Chemistry]
BCP .... Bruccoli-Clark Publishers
BCP .... Budget Change Proposal [Accounting]
BCP .... Built-Up Cast Iron Propeller [of a ship] (DS)
BCP .... Bulgarian Communist Party [Bulgarska Komunisticheska Partiia] [Political party] (PPW)
BCP .... Bulk Copy Program [Computer science] (PCM)
BCP .... Bund-Communist Party [Political party] (BJA)
BCP .... Burma Communist Party ["White Flag" party] [Political party] (PD)
BCP .... Butyl Carbitol Piperonylate [Organic chemistry]
BCP .... Byte Control Protocol [Computer science]
BCPA .... Boys Club Professional Association [Later, ABGCP] (EA)
BCPA .... British Columbia Paraplegic Association (AC)
BCPA .... British Commonwealth Pacific Airlines Ltd.
BCPA .... British Concrete Pumping Association (PDAA)
BCPA .... British Copyright Protection Association (PDAA)
BCPA .... British Council of Productivity Association (PDAA)
BCPAA .... British China and Porcelain Artists Association (DBA)
BCPB .... Bromochlorophenol Blue [Organic chemistry]
BCP Bk ...... BCP International Bank Ltd. [Associated Press] (SAG)
BCPC .... Bradley Commander Proficiency Course [Army] (INF)
BCPC .... British Crop Protection Council
BCPC .... Butyl (Chlorophenyl)carbamate [Organic chemistry]
BCPD .... Branch Circuit Protection Device
BCP-D .... Bromocresol Purple Desoxycholate [Agar] [Chemistry] (DAVI)
BCPDA .... Bis(chlorosulfophenyl)phenanthrolinedicarboxylic Acid [Organic chemistry]
BCPDA .... British Columbia Parkinson's Disease Association (AC)
BCPF .... Bishops' Committee on Priestly Formation (EA)
BcPh .... Benzo(c)phenanthrene [Organic chemistry]
BcpHaw ..... Bancorp Hawaii, Inc. [Associated Press] (SAG)
BcpHw .... Bancorp Hawaii, Inc. [Associated Press] (SAG)
BCPI .... Beef Cattle Price Index
BCPIA .... British Columbia Printing Industries Association (AC)
BCPIC .... BC Parents in Crisis Society (AC)
BCPIT .... British Council for the Promotion of International Trade (BI)
BCPL .... Basic Combined Programming Language
BCPL .... Binary Code Procedural Language [Computer science]
BCPL .... Bootstrap Combined Programming Language [Computer science] (CSR)
BCPMA ...... British Chemical Plant Manufacturers' Association (BI)
BCPMA ...... British Columbia Paint Manufacturers' Association (AC)
BCPMMA .... British Ceramic Plant and Machinery Manufacturers Association (PDAA)
BCPO .... British Commonwealth Producers' Organization
BCPS .... Basic Call Processing System [Telecommunications] (NITA)
BCPS .... Beam Candlepower Seconds
BCPSG .... British Caribbean Philatelic Study Group (EA)
BCPSM ...... Board of Certified Product Safety Management (EA)
BcpSou ...... Bancorp South, Inc. [Associated Press] (SAG)
BCPV .... Bovine Cutaneous Papilloma Virus [Medicine] (DMAA)
BCQ .... Dibromoquinonechlorimide [Solution] [Organic chemistry] (DAVI)
BCQB .... Building Control Qualifications Board [Victoria, Australia]
B Cr .... Bachelor of Criminology
BCR .... Badge Card Reader (MHDI)
BCR .... Bail Court Cases (Lowndes and Maxwell) [England] [A publication] (DLA)
BCR .... Bail Court Reports [Legal] [British]

BCR .... Bail Court Reports (Saunders and Cole) [England] [A publication] (DLA)
BCR .... Bank Cash Ratio (ADA)
BCR .... Bank Cash Reserve (ADA)
BCR .... Banque Commerciale du Rwanda [Commercial Bank of Rwanda] (AF)
BCR .... Bar Chart Report (MCD)
BCR .... Bard (C.R.) [NYSE symbol] (TTSB)
BCR .... Bard [C. R.], Inc. [NYSE symbol] (SPSG)
BCR .... Battery Charge Regulator
BCR .... Battery Control RADAR [Army]
BCR .... Battlefield Communications Review
BCR .... B-Cell Antigen Receptor [Immunology]
BCR .... Bearing Capacity Ratio [Materials technology]
BCR .... Benefit-Cost Ratio [Finance]
BCR .... Best Critical Region (IAA)
BCR .... Bibliographical Center for Research, Denver, CO [OCLC symbol] (OCLC)
BCR .... Bibliographical Center for Research, Rocky Mountain Region [Library network]
BCR .... Billing-Collecting-Remitting [Accounting] (TEL)
BCR .... Bituminous Coal Research (EA)
BCR .... Blocked Calls Released [Telecommunications]
BCR .... Borocarbon Resistor (CET)
BCR .... Bragg Cell Receiver (MCD)
BCR .... Breakpoint Cluster Region [Genetics]
BCR .... British Charter [ICAO designator] (FAAC)
BCR .... British Circus Ring (BI)
BCR .... British Columbia Reports [A publication] (DLA)
BCR .... Brown's Chancery Cases [England] [A publication] (DLA)
BCR .... Bucaramanga [Colombia] [Seismograph station code, US Geological Survey] (SEIS)
BCR .... Budget Change Request [Accounting] (MCD)
BCR .... Buffer Control Register (NITA)
BCR .... Bulbocavernosus Reflex [Medicine] (DAVI)
BCR .... Byte Count Register [Computer science] (MHDI)
BCR .... Cranbrook Public Library, British Columbia [Library symbol National Library of Canada] (NLC)
BCR .... European Community Bureau of Reference (ACII)
BCRA .... Base Closure and Realignment Act [Military]
BCRA .... Bosnian Canadian Relief Association (AC)
BCRA .... British Car Rental Association (BI)
BCRA .... British Cave Research Association
BCRA .... British Ceramic Research Association (PDAA)
BCRA .... British Coke Research Association (PDAA)
BCRA .... Bureau Central des Renseignements et d'Action [French Resistance organization]
BCRA .... Business Clearance Reviewing Authority (AAGC)
BCR & M ..... Burlington, Cedar Rapids & Minnesota Railroad
BCR & N ..... Burlington, Cedar Rapids & Northern Railway
BCRC .... Beef Cattle Research Center [Michigan State University] [Research center] (RCD)
BCRC .... Blissymbolics Communication Resource Centre [British] (CB)
BCRD .... Basic Consolidated Requirements Document (NASA)
BCRD .... British Council for Rehabilitation of the Disabled (BI)
BCRE .... Creston Public Library, British Columbia [Library symbol National Library of Canada] (NLC)
BCREA .... British Columbia Real Estate Association (AC)
BCreativeArts... Bachelor of Creative Arts
BCREK .... East Kootenay Community College, Cranbrook, British Columbia [Library symbol National Library of Canada] (NLC)
BC Rep .... Bail Court Cases (Lowndes and Maxwell) [England] [A publication] (DLA)
BC Rep .... Bail Court Reports (Saunders and Cole) [England] [A publication] (DLA)
BC Rep .... British Columbia Reports [A publication] (DLA)
BC Rep .... Brown's Chancery Cases [England] [A publication] (DLA)
BCREQ .... Broadcast Requested (FAAC)
BC Rev Stat... British Columbia Revised Statutes [Canada] [A publication] (DLA)
BCRG .... Banque Centrale de la Republique de Guinee [Central Bank of the Republic of Guinea] (AF)
BCRHA .... British Columbia Railway Historical Association (AC)
B/CRK .... Bell Crank [Automotive engineering]
BCRLSB ...... Library Services Branch, Ministry of Provincial Secretary and Government Services, Cranbrook, British Columbia [Library symbol National Library of Canada] (NLC)
BCRM .... Campbell River Museum and Archives, British Columbia [Library symbol National Library of Canada] (NLC)
BCRNL .... BCR [Bituminous Coal Research] National Laboratory [Defunct] (EA)
BCROS .... Black Crossover Vote [Political science]
BCRPA .... British Columbia Recreation & Parks Association (AC)
BCRR .... Boyne City Railroad Co. [AAR code]
BCRR .... Bureau du Coordonnateur, Reforme de la Reglementation [Office of the Coordinator, Regulatory Reform] [Canada]
BCRR .... Railway Museum, Cranbrook, British Columbia [Library symbol National Library of Canada] (NLC)
BCRRR .... Buddhist Council for Refugee Rescue and Resettlement (EA)
BCRS .... Bar-Code Reader/Sorter [Marketing] (PDAA)
BCRS .... Brief Cognitive Rating Scale [Medicine] (DMAA)
BCRST .... Bibliography on Cold Regions Science and Technology [A publication]
BCRT .... Binary-Coded Range Time (MUGU)
BCRT .... Bright Cathode-Ray Tube (DEN)
BCRTS .... Binary-Coded Range Time Signal (MUGU)
BCRV .... Blunt Conical Reentry Vehicle

BCRX	Biocryst Pharmaceuticals, Inc. [*NASDAQ symbol*] (SAG)
BCRX	BioCryst Pharm'l [*NASDAQ symbol*] (TTSB)
BCS	Bachelor of Chemical Science
BCS	Bachelor of College Studies
BCS	Bachelor of Commercial Science
BCS	Bachelor of Computer Science
BCS	Bachelor of Criminal Science (NADA)
BCS	Backup Control System
BCS	Ballistic Computer Systems (AAGC)
BCS	Banking Communication System (IAA)
BCS	Banque Centrale de Syrie [*Central Bank of Syria*] (BJA)
BCS	Banque Commerciale du Senegal (EY)
BCS	Baptist Community Service [*Australia*]
BCS	Baptist Counselling Service [*Australia*]
BCS	Barclays Ltd. [*NYSE symbol*] (SPSG)
BCS	Barclays PLC [*NYSE symbol*] (SAG)
BCS	Barclays plc ADS [*NYSE symbol*] (TTSB)
BCS	Bardeen-Cooper-Schrieffer Theory [*Theoretical physics*]
BCS	Baseline Comparison System [*Army*]
BCS	Basic Carriage Service [*Telecommunications*]
BCS	Basic Combined Subset [*Telecommunications*] (OSI)
BCS	Basic Contract Specification
BCS	Basic Control System [*For satellites*] (MDG)
BCS	Basic Court System (PDAA)
BCS	Battered Child Syndrome
BCS	Battery Computer System (MCD)
BCS	Battle Cruiser Squadron [*Navy*]
BCS	Battlefield Computer System
BCS	BC [*British Columbia*] Sugar Refinery Ltd. [*Toronto Stock Exchange symbol*]
BCS	Beam Communications Set
BCS	Beam Control Subsystem (MCD)
BCS	Belleek Collector's Society [*Commercial firm*] (EA)
BCS	Benefits Control System [*Insurance*]
BCS	Bengal Civil Service [*British*]
BCS	Biblical Creation Society [*British*]
BCS	Bibliographic Control System (ADA)
BCS	Bidirectional Category System
BCS	Binary Communications: Synchronous [*Computer science*] (NITA)
BCS	Binary Compatibility Specification [*Computer science*] (PCM)
BCS	Binary Compatibility Standard (CDE)
BCS	Biomedical Computing Society [*Later, SIGBIO*] (BUR)
BCS	Black Country Society [*British*]
BCS	Blip Counter System
BCS	Block Check Sequence [*Computer science*] (IAA)
BCS	Block Control Sheet [*Computer science*]
BCS	Block Control Signal [*Telecommunications*] (TEL)
BCS	Blood Cell Separator [*Medicine*]
BCS	Board of Certification in Surgery (EA)
BCS	Boeing Computer Services Co. [*Information service or system*] (IID)
BCS	Bombing Computer Set
BCS	Bookbinders' Charitable Society (DGA)
BCS	Book Communications System [*Information service*]
BCS	Border Cargo Selectivity [*USTTA*] (TAG)
BCS	Boston Computer Society (EA)
BCS	Bounded Cellular Space (PDAA)
BCS	Branch if Carry Set
BCS	Bridge Control System (IAA)
BCS	British Cable Services (NITA)
BCS	British Calibration Service [*Research center*] (IRC)
BCS	British Cardiac Society (DBA)
BCS	British Cartographic Society
BCS	British Ceramic Society
BCS	British Chiefs of Staff
BCS	British Computer Society [*London*]
BCS	British Crime Survey (ECON)
BCS	Broadcast Communications System
BCS	Brothers of Charity of Spokane [*Roman Catholic religious order*]
BCS	Brothers of Christian Service (TOCD)
BCS	Bucknell Computer Services [*Bucknell University*] [*Research center*] (RCD)
BCS	Budd-Chiari Syndrome [*Medicine*]
BCS	Buildings and Community Systems (EG)
BCS	Bureau of Criminal Statistics (BARN)
BCS	Burst Communications Systems (MCD)
BCS	Business Communications Service [*British Telecommunications International*] [*London*] (TSSD)
BCS	Business Communications Systems [*Telecommunications*] (TEL)
BCS	Business Control System
BCS	Business Customer Services [*Telecommunications*] (TEL)
BCS	European Air Transport [*ICAO designator*] (FAAC)
BCS	Office of Buildings and Community Systems [*Department of Energy*]
BCS	Selkirk College, Castlegar, British Columbia [*Library symbol National Library of Canada*] (NLC)
BCSA	Book Collectors' Society of Australia
BCSA	British Colleges Sports Association
BCSA	British Columbia Society of Artists [*1949-68, founded 1908 as BCSFA*] [*Canada*] (NGC)
BCSA	British Commonwealth Sugar Agreement
BCSA	British Constructional Steelwork Association (PDAA)
BCSA	British Cutlery and Silverware Association (EAIO)
BcSantCh	Banco Santander Chile [*Associated Press*] (SAG)
BCSBANSW ..	Black and Coloured Sheep Breeders' Association of New South Wales [*Australia*]
BC Sc	Bachelor of Commercial Science

BCSC	Bat Conservation Society of Canada (AC)
BCSC	British Council of Shopping Centres
BCSD	Blank Corrected Sample Data [*Computer science*]
BC Se	Bachelor of Commercial Service
BCSE	Board of US Civil Service Examiners
BCSF	BC Snowmobile Federation (AC)
BCSFA	BC Salmon Farmers Association (AC)
BCSFA	British Columbia Society of Fine Arts [*1908, BCSA from 1949*] [*Canada*] (NGC)
BCSGA	BC Shellfish Growers Association (AC)
BCSH	Barat College of the Sacred Heart [*Later, Barat College*] [*Lake Forest, IL*]
BCSH	British Committee for Standards in Haematology
BCSI	Biometric Computer Service, Inc.
BCSI	Breast Cancer Screening Indicator
BCSI	Built-In Cleaning Systems Institute [*Defunct*] (EA)
BCSLA	British Columbia Society of Landscape Architects (AC)
BCSM	British Control Supply Mission [*World War II*]
BCSMC	British Columbia Sports Medicine Clinic [*University of British Columbia*] [*Research center*] (RCD)
BCSO	British Columbia Special Olympics (AC)
BCSO	British Commonwealth Scientific Office
BCSOC	Binary Convolutional Self-Orthogonal Code [*Computer science*] (PDAA)
BCSO(NA)	British Commonwealth Scientific Office (North America) [*Washington, DC*]
BCSP	Board of Certified Safety Professionals (EA)
BCSP	Built-Up Cast Steel Propeller [*of a ship*] (DS)
BCSR	Bubble Column Slurry Reactor [*Chemical engineering*]
BCSR	Bureau of Crime Statistics and Research [*New South Wales, Australia*]
BCSS	Bishops' Committee for the Spanish Speaking [*Later, SHA*]
BCSS	British Cactus and Succulent Society (DBA)
BCSS	British Charollais Sheep Society (DBA)
BCSS	British Columbia Surgical Society (AC)
BCSSC	British Computer Society Schools Committee (AIE)
BCSSE	Best Controlled Similar Source Emission [*Environmental Protection Agency*]
bcst	Broadcast
BCST	Broadcast [*Information transmission*] (AFM)
BC Stat	British Columbia Statutes [*Canada*] [*A publication*] (DLA)
BCSTG	Broadcasting
BCSTN	Broadcast Station (FAAC)
BCSTR	Broadcaster
BCSWS	Battalion Close Support Weapon System (MCD)
BCT	Bachelor of Christian Training
BCT	Bandwidth Compression Technique
BCT	Bank Credit Transfer (DI)
BCT	Banque Centrale de Tunisie [*Central Bank of Tunisia*] (AF)
BCT	Banque des Connaissances et des Techniques [*Knowledge and Technique Bank*] [*National Agency for the Promotion of Research*] [*Information service or system*] (IID)
BCT	Basic Combat Training [*Later, BT*] [*Army*]
BCT	Bat Conservation Trust [*British*] (EAIO)
BCT	Battalion Combat Team
BCT	Battery Control Trailer (NATG)
BCT	Bell. Competing Titles [*Scotland*] [*A publication*] (DLA)
BCT	Best Control Technology [*Environmental Protection Agency*] (ERG)
BCT	Best Conventional Pollutant Control Technology (GNE)
BCT	Best Conventional Technology [*Environmental Protection Agency*]
BCT	Between Commands Testing [*Computer science*]
BCT	Blackrock Broad Investment Grade 2009 Term Trust [*AMEX symbol*] (SPSG)
BCT	Blackrock Broad Inv Gr 2009 [*AMEX symbol*] (TTSB)
BCT	Block-Cutpoint-Tree [*Mathematics*] [*Used in ASAMS*]
BCT	Boca Raton, FL [*Location identifier FAA*] (FAAL)
BCT	Body-Centered Tetragonal [*Crystallography*]
BCT	Bomber Control Team [*Air Force*] (DOMA)
BCT	Booklet Category Test [*Brain dysfunction test*]
BCT	Boulangerie, Confiserie, Tabac [*Bakery, Confectionary, and Tobacco*] [*Canadian Union*]
BCT	Branch on Count (IAA)
BCT	Briefcase Terminal [*Army*] (INF)
BCT	Brigade Combat Team [*Army*] (INF)
BCT	British Caribbean Territory
BCT	British Caspian Trust
BCT	British Columbia Telephone Co. [*Toronto Stock Exchange symbol Vancouver Stock Exchange symbol*]
BCT	British Columbia Telephone Ltd. [*Canada ICAO designator*] (FAAC)
BCT	Brookfield [*Connecticut*] [*Seismograph station code, US Geological Survey*] (SEIS)
BCT	Building Center Trust (PDAA)
BCT	Building Conservation Trust [*An association*] (DBA)
BCT	Bus Configuration Table (MCD)
BCT	Bushing Current Transformer (KSC)
BCT	Gordon-Conwell Theological Seminary, South Hamilton, MA [*OCLC symbol*] (OCLC)
BCT	Television Broadcasting Station [*ITU designation*] (CET)
BCTA	British Canadian Trade Association (BI)
BCTA	British Children's Theatre Association
BCTA	British Columbia Trucking Association (AC)
BCTAC	Building Control Technical Advisory Council [*Victoria, Australia*]
BC Tax Rep (CCH)...	British Columbia Tax Reporter (Commerce Clearing House) [*A publication*] (DLA)
BCTC	British Carpet Technical Centre (CB)

BCTC.............	British Ceramic Tile Council Ltd. (BI)
BCTCD.........	Building and Construction Trades Council of Delaware (SRA)
BCTC-ND......	Building and Construction Trades Council - North Dakota (SRA)
BCTD...........	Building and Construction Trades Department [AFL-CIO]
BCTE.............	Bankers Committee for Tax Equality [of the National Tax Equality Association] (EA)
BCTF.............	Breast Cancer Task Force [National Cancer Institute]
BCTF.............	British Columbia Teachers' Federation [Federation des Enseignants de la Colombie-Britannique] (AC)
BCTGA.........	British Christmas Tree Growers Association (DBA)
BC Third World LJ...	Boston College. Third World Law Journal [A publication] (DLA)
BCTI..............	BCT International [NASDAQ symbol] (SAG)
BCTIC...........	Biomedical Computing Technology Information Center [Oak Ridge National Laboratory] [Department of Energy] (IID)
BCT Int	BCT International, Inc. [Associated Press] (SAG)
BCTLA..........	British Columbia Teacher-Librarians' Association (AC)
BCTMP.........	Bleached Chemi-Thermomechanical Pulp
BCTN	Baja California - Territorio Norte
BCTOS	Bicentennial Council of the Thirteen Original States [Later, CTOS] [Defunct] (EA)
BCTP...........	Battle Command Training Program [Army]
BCTPC	Bomber Command Tactical Planning Committee
BCtr	Bovine Chymotrypsin (DMAA)
BCTRA	BC Therapeutic Riding Association (AC)
BCTS	Baja California - Territorio Sur
BCTS	Brine Chiller Test Stand (DWSG)
BCTV...........	Beet Curly Top Virus [Plant pathology]
BCTV...........	Berks Community Television [Reading, PA] [Telecommunications] (TSSD)
BCTV...........	Bibliography on Cable Television [A publication] (TSSD)
BCTWIU	Bakery, Confectionery, and Tobacco Workers' International Union (EA)
BCU	Ballistics Computer Unit
BCU	Basic Computer Unit
BCU	Battery/Coolant Unit (RDA)
BCU	Bayamon Central University, Bayamon, PR [OCLC symbol] (OCLC)
BCU	Bay Cabinet Unit
BCU	BCU Industries, Inc. [Toronto Stock Exchange symbol]
BCU	Bear Canyon [Utah] [Seismograph station code, US Geological Survey Closed] (SEIS)
BCU	Bible Christian Union (EA)
BCU	Big Close-Up [A photograph or motion picture sequence taken from a short distance]
BCU	Binary Counting Unit (IEEE)
BCU	Blender Control Unit (ECII)
BCU	Block Control Unit [Computer science] (IBMDP)
BCU	Bombardment Control Unit
BCU	Boom Control Unit (MCD)
BCU	Borden Chemical & Plastics Ltd. [NYSE symbol] (SAG)
BCU	Borden Chem/Plastics L.P. [NYSE symbol] (TTSB)
BCU	B'rith Christian Union [Later, FSJ] (EA)
BCU	British Canoe Union
BCU	British Commonwealth Union (ADA)
BCU	Buffer Control Unit [Computer science] (CET)
BCU	Bus Control Unit (KSC)
BCU	Hyannis, MA [Location identifier FAA] (FAAL)
BCUA	Business Computers Users Association (MHDB)
BCUICE	British Canoe Union International Canoeing Exhibition [British]
BCUL	Buildings for College and University Libraries Committee [Library Administration and Management Association] [American Library Association]
BCUM	Cumberland Museum, British Columbia [Library symbol National Library of Canada] (NLC)
BCUN	Business Council for the United Nations (EA)
BCUPO	British Civil Uranium Procurement Directorate (NUCP)
BCUPP	BCNU [Carmustine], Vinblastine, Procarbazine, and Prednisone [Antineoplastic drug regimen] (DAVI)
BCURA.........	British Coal Utilisation Research Association
B Current L...	Butterworth's Current Law [A publication] (DLA)
BCUSA	Buddhist Center of the United States of America (EA)
BCV.............	Ball Check Valve
BCV.............	Baltic Council of Victoria [Australia]
BCV.............	Banco de Cabo Verde [Bank of Cape Verde] (EY)
BCV.............	Bancroft Convertible Fd [AMEX symbol] (TTSB)
BCV.............	Bancroft Convertible Fund, Inc. [AMEX symbol] (SPSG)
BCV.............	Barge Carrying Vessel
BCV.............	Barrel Cactus Virus
BCV.............	Basal Cell Vigilance (DAVI)
BCV.............	Basal Cerebral Vigilance [Sleep]
BCV.............	Battery Control Van (NATG)
BCV.............	Battle Casualty Vietnam
BCV.............	Beet Cryptic Virus [Plant pathology]
BCV.............	Belgian Circle in Victoria [An association Australia]
BCV.............	Bishop's Committee on Vocations (EA)
BCV.............	Bovine Coronavirus [Biochemistry]
BCV.............	Brightness Contrast Value
BCVA	British Cattle Veterinary Association (DBA)
BCVM..........	Creston Valley Museum, Creston, British Columbia [Library symbol National Library of Canada] (NLC)
BCVMA........	British Columbia Veterinary Medical Association (AC)
BCVP	BCNU [Carmustine], Cyclophosphamide, Vincristine, Prednisone [Antineoplastic drug regimen]
BCVPP	BCNU [Carmustine], Cyclophosphamide, Vinblastine, Procarbazine, Prednisone [Antineoplastic drug regimen]

BCVTP	Buciclovir Triphosphate [Antiviral]
BCVX	Biconvex
BCW.............	Bachelor of Community Welfare
BCW.............	Bachelor of Community Work
BCW.............	Bakery and Confectionery Workers' International Union of America [Later, BCTWIU]
BCW.............	Bare Copper Wire
BCW.............	Binary Chemical Warhead System (DWSG)
BCW.............	Biological and Chemical Warfare
BCW.............	Bobbin Coil Winder
BCW.............	Buffer Control Word [Computer science]
BCW.............	Bureau of Child Welfare (BARN)
BCW.............	Bury Cooper Whitehead Ltd. [British] (IRUK)
BCWA	British Car Wash Association (DBA)
BCWD	Biological and Chemical Warfare Division [DoD]
BCWIU of A...	Bakery and Confectionery Workers' International Union of America [Later, BCTWIU] (EA)
BCWL	Basic Carbonate White Lead [Paint technology]
BCWMA	British Clock and Watch Manufacturers Association (PDAA)
BCWP	Beam Candle Watt Power (MCD)
BCWP	Budgeted Cost for Work Performed
BCWPA	British Columbia Water Polo Association (AC)
BCWPA	British Columbia Watershed Protection Alliance (AC)
BCWr	Base Course Wear Rate [Tire testing]
BCWS	Beam Candle Watt Seconds (MCD)
BCWS	Budgeted Cost for Work Scheduled
BCWWA	British Colombia Water & Wastewater Association (AC)
BCX.............	BCE Mobile Communications, Inc. [Toronto Stock Exchange symbol]
BCY.............	Banco Central [Toronto Stock Exchange symbol]
Bcy.............	Bankruptcy [Legal term] (DLA)
BCY.............	Boise City, OK [Location identifier FAA] (FAAL)
BCY.............	Broken Cubic Yard (DAC)
BCY.............	City Jet [Ireland] (FAAC)
BCYC	British Corinthian Yacht Club (DI)
BCYR	Bucyrus-Erie Co. [NASDAQ symbol] (SAG)
BCYR	Bucyrus Intl. [NASDAQ symbol] (TTSB)
BCZ.............	Barracuda Resources Ltd. [Vancouver Stock Exchange symbol]
BCZ.............	Berlin Control Zone [Allied German Occupation Forces]
BCZ.............	Butler, AL [Location identifier FAA] (FAAL)
BD.............	Bachelor of Divinity
BD.............	Back Dividends
BD.............	Backward Diode
BD.............	Bad Delivery [Investment term]
BD.............	Bahrain Dinar [Monetary unit] (BJA)
BD.............	Balfour Declaration [1917] [For protection of the Jewish settlement of Palestine] (BJA)
BD.............	Balloon Destroyer [British]
BD.............	Band [Volume] [German]
BD.............	Band (KSC)
BD.............	Bande Dessinee [Comic strip] [French]
BD.............	Bangladesh [ANSI two-letter standard code] (CNC)
BD.............	Bank Dividend (IIA)
BD.............	Bank Draft
BD.............	Barbital-Dependent [Medicine] (DMAA)
BD.............	Barbiturate Dependence [Medicine] (DMAA)
BD.............	Bar Draft [Depth of water over a bar]
BD.............	Bark Dieback [Plant pathology]
BD.............	Barkley Dam [TVA]
BD.............	Barrack Department [British military] (DMA)
BD.............	Barrels per Day
BD.............	Base Deficit
BD.............	Base Detonating
BD.............	Base Diameter
BD.............	Base-Down (Prism) [Ophthalmology]
BD.............	Base of Prism Down [Medicine] (DMAA)
BD.............	Basic Democrats [Pakistan]
BD.............	Basophilic Degeneration [Hematology]
BD.............	Batten's Disease [Medicine]
BD.............	Battle Dress [Military]
Bd.............	Baud [Unit of data transmission speed] (CET)
BD.............	Baudot Code (IAA)
BD.............	Bead (IAA)
BD.............	Beam Degrader
BD.............	Beaver Defenders (EA)
BD.............	Becton-Dickinson [Spinal needle] [Medicine] (DAVI)
B-D.............	Becton, Dickinson & Co. [Initialism used in titles of a series of technical publications]
BD.............	Before Divestiture [AT & T] (IT)
BD.............	Behavioral Differential
BD.............	Behavior Disorder
BD.............	Behcet's Disease [Medicine]
BD.............	Belladonna [Deadly Nightshade (or its medicinal extract)]
BD.............	Below Deck [of a ship] (DS)
BD.............	Below Diaphragm [Medicine] (DAVI)
BD.............	Benday [Type of dye] (WDMC)
BD.............	Bend Down
BD.............	Benzoylated DEAE [Diethylaminoethyl] [Organic chemistry]
BD.............	Berger's Disease [Medicine]
BD.............	Berlin District [Allied German Occupation Forces]
BD.............	Bernoulli Disk
BD.............	Best Delay [Audiometry]
BD.............	Bible Dictionary [A publication] (BJA)
BD.............	Big Deal [An association] (EA)
BD.............	Bile Driver (DWSG)
BD.............	Bile Duct [Medicine]

BD............	Billing Day (DCTA)
BD............	Bills Discounted
BD............	Binary Decoder [Computer science]
BD............	Binary Digit [Computer science] (MCD)
BD............	Binary Discrete (MCD)
BD............	Binary Divide
B/D...........	Binary to Decimal [Computer science]
BD............	Binocular Deprivation [Optics]
BD............	Biographical Dictionaries and Related Works [A publication]
BD............	Birth Defect [Neonatology] (DAVI)
BD............	Bis in Die [Twice a Day] [Pharmacy]
BD............	BIT [Binary Digit] Density [Computer science]
BD............	Bite Detector
BD............	Black Death [1348-49]
BD............	Blank Display (MHDI)
BD............	Block Delete (IAA)
BD............	Block Design [Psychometrics]
BD............	Block Diagram (IAA)
BD............	Block Downconverter [Satellite communications]
BD............	Blocker Deflector [Aviation] (OA)
BD............	Blocking Device [Nuclear energy] (OA)
BD............	Bloedel-Donovan Railroad (IIA)
BD............	Blowdown [Nuclear energy] (NRCH)
BD............	Blowing Dust (BARN)
BD............	Blue Diaper Syndrome [Medicine] (DMAA)
B/D...........	Blur Diameter [Optics]
BD............	Board
bd............	Board (VRA)
bd............	Board (WDMC)
BD............	Board
BD............	Bodansky Unit [Clinical chemistry]
BD............	Bold (ADA)
BD............	Bomb Disposal
BD............	Bond [Investment term]
B/D...........	Bondage/Domination (WGA)
BD............	Bone Dry
BD............	Bonner Durchmusterung [Star chart]
BD............	Boom Defence [Navy British]
BD............	Booster Development
BD............	Borderline Dull [Medicine]
BD............	Borna Disease [Medicine] (PDAA)
BD............	Bottle Drainage
BD............	Bottom Down (OA)
BD............	Boulevard (EY)
BD............	Bound
bd............	Bound (WDMC)
BD............	Boundary (WGA)
BD............	Box Diffusion [Oceanography]
BD............	Brain Dead [Medicine] (DAVI)
BD............	Brand Development [Marketing] (DOAD)
BD............	Brindled (WGA)
BD............	British Midland Airways [ICAO designator] (AD)
BD............	Broad (ADA)
BD............	Broadband Distributive Services [Telecommunications]
B/D...........	Broker-Dealer
BD............	Broker-Dealer (DFIT)
BD............	Bronchial Drainage [Medicine] (DAVI)
BD............	Brought Down [Accounting]
BD............	Buccodistal [Dentistry]
BD............	Budget Division [Environmental Protection Agency] (GFGA)
BD............	Building Density (SAA)
BD............	Built-Down [Military] (INF)
BD............	Bulk Density (IAA)
BD............	Bundle (MCD)
bd............	Bundle (WDMC)
BD............	Bureau of Drugs [Later, Center for Drugs and Biologics] [FDA]
BD............	Buried (ROG)
BD............	Bursal Dependent [Cells] [Immunology]
bd............	Burundi [MARC country of publication code Library of Congress] (LCCP)
BD............	Bus Driver [Electronics] (IAA)
BD............	Bus Duct [Electronics] (IAA)
BD............	Buydown (TDOB)
BD............	Buydown Mortgage [Business term] (EMRF)
BD............	[The] Egyptian Book of the Dead (BJA)
BDA...........	Bachelor of Domestic Arts
BDA...........	Bachelor of Dramatic Art
BDA...........	Backup Drive Amplifier (MCD)
BDA...........	Balloon Dilation Angioplasty [Cardiology] (DMAA)
BDA...........	Barriada
BDA...........	Basotho Democratic Alliance [Lesotho] [Political party] (EY)
BDA...........	Battle Damage Assessment
BDA...........	Beer Drinkers of America (EA)
BDA...........	Belt Driven Type A [Cosworth racing engines] [Automotive engineering]
BDA...........	Bermuda [Airport symbol] (OAG)
BDA...........	Bermuda Island
BDA...........	Bermuda Resources Ltd. [Vancouver Stock Exchange symbol]
BDA...........	Bermuda Tracking Station [NASA] (KSC)
BDA...........	Beth Din of America (EA)
BDA...........	Binary Discriminant Analysis [Statistics]
BDA...........	Blast Danger Area (NASA)
BDA...........	Bleed Door Actuator
BDA...........	Block Decoder Assembly [Space Flight Operations Facility, NASA]
BDA...........	Bomb Damage Assessment

BDA...........	Boomerangs Disabled Association [Australia]
BDA...........	Booster-Distribution Amplifier
BDA...........	Border Airways [South Africa ICAO designator] (FAAC)
BDA...........	Boulder Dam [Arizona] [Seismograph station code, US Geological Survey Closed] (SEIS)
BDA...........	Brick Development Association [British] (DBA)
BDA...........	British Deaf Association (DI)
BDA...........	British Decorators Association (DBA)
BDA...........	British Deming Association (DBA)
BDA...........	British Dental Association
BDA...........	British Diabetic Association (IRUK)
BDA...........	[The] British Dietetic Association
BDA...........	British Doll Artists Association (DBA)
BDA...........	British Drilling Association (DBA)
BDA...........	British Dyslexia Association
BDA...........	Broadcast Designers Association (EA)
BDA...........	Broker-Dealer-Investment Advisor Directory [Securities and Exchange Commission] (GFGA)
BDA...........	Bulb Distributors' Association [British] (DBA)
BDA...........	Burma Defense Army [Later, BNA] [World War II]
BDA...........	Hamilton [Bermuda] [Airport symbol]
BDAA.........	Balalaika and Domra Association of America (EA)
BDAA.........	Bio-Dynamic Agricultural Association [British]
BDABS.......	Blonde d'Aquitaine Breeders Society [British] (DBA)
BDAC.........	Biological Diversity Advisory Committee [Australia]
BDAC.........	Bureau of Drug Abuse Control [Absorbed by Bureau of Narcotics and Dangerous Drugs of Department of Justice]
BDAE.........	Banque de Developpement de l'Afrique de l'Est [East African Development Bank - EADB] (EAIO)
BDAE.........	Boston Diagnostic Aphasia Examination
BDAFSA......	British Defence and Aid Fund for Southern Africa (EAIO)
BDAI.........	Bird Dog Association, International (EA)
BDAL.........	Biographical Dictionary of Australian Librarians [A publication]
BDAM........	Basic Data Access Method [Computer science] (EECA)
BDAM........	Basic Direct Access Method [IBM Corp.] [Computer science] (BUR)
BDAM........	Basic Disk Access Method (MCD)
Bd & C.......	Board and Care [Medicine] (DAVI)
BD & O.......	Blackham, Dundas, and Osborne's Irish Nisi Prius Reports [1846-48] [A publication] (DLA)
BDAR.........	Battle Damage and Assessment Review [Military]
BDAR.........	Battlefield Damage Assessment and Repair [Technical manual] [Army] (RDA)
BDART.......	Battle Damage Assessment and Reporting Team
BDAS.........	Buddy DeFranco Appreciation Society (EA)
BDASA.......	Building Design Association of South Australia
BDAT.........	Battle Damage Assessment Team [Navy] (DOMA)
BDAT.........	Beacon Data [Aviation] (FAAC)
BDAT.........	Best Demonstrated Available Technology
BDAT.........	Best Developed Alternate [Environmental Protection Agency]
BDATS.......	Biological Detection and Alarm Training Simulant (MCD)
BDB...........	Bagneres De Bigorre [France] [Seismograph station code, US Geological Survey] (SEIS)
BDB...........	Bahrain Development Bank (EY)
BDB...........	Base Development Board [Military] (AABC)
BDB...........	Bibliographic Database
BDB...........	Big Dumb Booster Rocket
BDB...........	Bis-diazotized Benzidine [Hematology]
BDB...........	Bjerrum Double Band [Physics]
BDB...........	Broadcasters Database [Houston, TX] [Information service or system] (IID)
BDB...........	Bundaberg [Australia Airport symbol] (OAG)
BDB...........	Byelorussian Democratic Bloc [Political party]
BDB...........	[A] Hebrew and English Lexicon of the Old Testament (Brown, Driver, and Briggs) [A publication] (BJA)
BDBD.........	Bureau of Domestic Business Development [Department of Commerce]
BDBE.........	Basic Data Base Environment [Computer science] (MHDI)
BDBJ.........	Board of Deputies of British Jews
BDC...........	Bachelier en Droit Canonique [Bachelor of Canon Law] [French]
BDC...........	Backup Digital Computer
BDC...........	Batch Data Class [Telecommunications]
BDC...........	Before Dead Center [Valve position]
BDC...........	Benedict College, Columbia, SC [OCLC symbol] (OCLC)
BDC...........	Beneficiary Developing Country [Trade status]
BDC...........	Bentley Drivers Club (EA)
BDC...........	Benzenediazonium Chloride [Organic chemistry]
BDC...........	Berlin Document Center [Allied German Occupation Forces]
BDC...........	Bi-Directional Converter (NASA)
BDC...........	Binary Decimal Counter [Computer science]
BDC...........	Block Downconverter [Satellite communications]
BDC...........	Bomb Data Center [International Association of Chiefs of Police]
BDC...........	Bonded Double Cotton [Wire insulation] (KSC)
BDC...........	Book Development Council [British]
BDC...........	Bottom Dead Center [Engineering]
BDC...........	Bridge Display Console
BDC...........	Brigade Data Center [Military] (AABC)
BDC...........	Bullet Drop Compensator (DICI)
BDC...........	Bureau International de Documentation des Chemins de Fer [International Office of Railway Documentation]
BDC...........	Bureau of Domestic Commerce [Formerly, Business and Defense Services Administration and Office of Field Services] [Department of Commerce Terminated, 1977, functions transferred to Domestic and International Business Administration]
BDC...........	Burn-Dressing Change [Medicine]
BDC...........	Business Development Consultants International, Ltd. [British]

BDC .... Dawson Creek Public Library, British Columbia [*Library symbol National Library of Canada*] (NLC)
BDCAA .... Booster Dynamic Condition at Abort (SAA)
BDCB .... Buffered Data and Control Bus
BDCC/ME ...... British Defence Coordination Committee, Middle East (NATG)
BDCF .... Baseline Data Collection Facility (MCD)
BDCGS .... Birth Defect and Clinical Genetic Society [*Defunct*] (EA)
BDCL .... Library Advisory Council, Dawson Creek, British Columbia [*Library symbol National Library of Canada*] (NLC)
BDCLSB ...... Library Services Branch, Ministry of Provincial Secretary and Government Services, Dawson Creek, British Columbia [*Library symbol National Library of Canada*] (NLC)
BDCNL .... Northern Lights College, Dawson Creek, British Columbia [*Library symbol National Library of Canada*] (NLC)
BDCO .... Blue Dolphin Energy [*NASDAQ symbol*] (TTSB)
BDCO .... Blue Dolphin Energy Co. [*NASDAQ symbol*] (SAG)
Bd Cont App Dec ... Board of Contract Appeals Decisions [*Commerce Clearing House*] [*A publication*] (DLA)
Bd/Cpl .... Band Corporal [*British military*] (DMA)
BDCR .... Baseline Document Change Request (MCD)
BDCS .... Below Deck Communications System [*Navy*] (LAIN)
Bd/CSgt .... Band Colour Sergeant [*British military*] (DMA)
BDCT .... Bradford Durfee College of Technology [*Later, Southeastern Massachusetts Technical Institute*]
BDCWW .... Walter Wright Pioneer Village, Dawson Creek, British Columbia [*Library symbol National Library of Canada*] (NLC)
BDD .... Balanced-Deficit Diet
BDD .... Balzac Deflection Door
BDD .... Banque Dahomeenne de Developpement [*Dahomean Development Bank*]
BDD .... Bantam, Doubleday, Dell Publishing Group
BDD .... Baseline Definition Document (NASA)
BDD .... Binary Digital Data [*Computer science*]
BDD .... Binary-to-Decimal Decoder [*Computer science*]
bdd .... Binding Designer [*MARC relator code*] [*Library of Congress*] (LCCP)
BDD .... Blanket Delivery Date [*Military*] (AABC)
BDD .... Body Dysmorphic Disorder [*Medicine*]
BDD .... Boom Defence Depot [*Navy British*]
BDD .... British Defence Directory [*Brassey's Defence Publishers Ltd.*] [*Information service or system*] (IID)
BDD .... Brodsky, David, New York NY [*STAC*]
BDD .... Brookport, IL [*Location identifier FAA*] (FAAL)
BDD .... Bureau of Dangerous Drugs [*Canada*]
BDD .... Business Dateline Database [*Information service or system*] (IT)
BDDA .... British Deaf and Dumb Association (BI)
BDDA .... Butanediol Diacetate [*Organic chemistry*]
BD D & M ..... Board of Decorations and Medals [*Navy*]
BDDB .... Baseline Design Data Book (MCD)
BDDC .... Battelle Defense Document Center [*Battelle Memorial Institute*] (SAA)
BD/DET .... Board/Detached [*Bookselling*] (DGA)
BDDI .... Beading Die
BDDT .... Bench Detergency Dispersancy Test (PDAA)
BDDV .... Beading Device [*Tool*] (AAG)
BDDV .... Biocular Display Driver's Viewer
BDDY .... Buddy
BDE .... Baende [*Volumes*] [*German*]
BDE .... Barnhart Dictionary of Etymology [*A publication*]
BDE .... Basic Design Engineering (MCD)
BDE .... Baudette, MN [*Location identifier FAA*] (FAAL)
BDE .... Beta Disintegration Energy
BDE .... Bevelled Deckle Edges [*Cards*] (DGA)
BDE .... Bile Duct Examination [*Medicine*]
BDE .... Bile Duct Exploration [*Gastroenterology*] (DAVI)
BDE .... Bond Dissociation Energy [*Chemistry*]
BDE .... Borland Database Engine [*Borland International, Inc.*] [*Computer science*]
BDE .... Brigade (AABC)
BDE .... Bright Display Equipment
BDE .... Brilliant Digital Entertainment, Inc. [*AMEX symbol*] (SAG)
BDE .... British Destroyer Escort
BDE .... British Document Exchange
BDE .... Brown, Durbin, and Evans [*Statisticians*]
BDE .... Buyer Designated Equipment (MCD)
BDEA .... Butyldiethanolamine [*Organic chemistry*]
BDEAF .... British Columbia Chapter, American Foundrymen's Society Archives and Museum, Delta, British Columbia [*Library symbol National Library of Canada*] (NLC)
B de C .... Bartholomaeus de Capua [*Deceased, 1328*] [*Authority cited in pre-1607 legal work*] (DSA)
B de Ca .... Bartholomaeus de Capua [*Deceased, 1328*] [*Authority cited in pre-1607 legal work*] (DSA)
BD/ECC .... Blowdown/Emergency Core Cooling [*Nuclear energy*] (NRCH)
BDECW .... Pacific & Yukon Region, Canadian Wildlife Service, Environment Canada [*Service Canadien de la Faune de la Region du Pacifique et du Yukon, Environnement Canada*] Delta, British Columbia [*Library symbol National Library of Canada*] (NLC)
BDEF .... Base Detonating Fuze (MCD)
BDEGL .... Banque de Developpement des Etats du Grand Lac [*Development Bank of the Great Lakes States*] (EAIO)
BDELT .... Brigade Landing Team [*Army*] (AABC)
BDEM .... Delta Museum and Archives, British Columbia [*Library symbol National Library of Canada*] (NLC)
Bde Maj ...... Brigade Major [*Military*]
B de Monfa ... Bertrandus de Montefaventino [*Deceased, 1342*] [*Authority cited in pre-1607 legal work*] (DSA)

BDentistry .... Bachelor of Dentistry
BDentSc .... Bachelor in Dental Science [*British*]
BDentSci ...... Bachelor of Dental Science [*British*] (BABM)
BDEOA .... British Columbia Orchard Archives Society, Delta, British Columbia [*Library symbol National Library of Canada*] (NLC)
B Des .... Bachelor of Design
BDES .... Boeing Data Entry System [*Boeing Computer Services*] (NITA)
B des A .... Bachelier des Arts [*Bachelor of Arts*] [*French*]
B de Sa .... Bartholomaeus de Saliceto [*Deceased, 1411*] [*Authority cited in pre-1607 legal work*] (DSA)
B Des A Ed ... Bachelor of Design in Art Education
BDesign .... Bachelor of Design
B des L .... Bachelier des Lettres [*Bachelor of Letters*] [*French*]
B des S .... Bachelier des Sciences [*Bachelor of Science*] [*French*]
BDF .... 1838 Bond-Deb Trad'g [*NYSE symbol*] (TTSB)
BDF .... Backwards Differentiation Formula (MHDI)
BDF .... Ballroom Dancers Federation [*British*] (DBA)
BDF .... Barclay's Development Fund [*Barclay's Bank*] [*British*]
BDF .... Base Defense Force [*Military*] (NVT)
BDF .... Base Detonating Fuse
BDF .... BCE Place Finance Corp. [*Toronto Stock Exchange symbol Vancouver Stock Exchange symbol*]
BDF .... Belize Defense Forces [*Military*]
BDF .... Black Development Foundation
BDF .... Blocked Data Format (MCD)
BDF .... Boxcar Doppler Filter (PDAA)
BDF .... Bradford, IL [*Location identifier FAA*] (FAAL)
BDF .... Brasilia [*Brazil*] [*Seismograph station code, US Geological Survey*] (SEIS)
BDF .... British Digestive Foundation (IRUK)
BDF .... Building Distribution Frame [*Telecommunications*] (NITA)
BDF .... Bus Differential [*Electronics*] (IAA)
BDF .... Eighteen Thirty Eight Bond Fund [*NYSE symbol*] (SAG)
BDFA .... Basic Daily Food Allowance (AABC)
BDFA .... British Deer Farmers Association (DBA)
BDFC .... Bobby Darin Fan Club (EA)
BDFC .... Bob Dylan Fan Club (EA)
BDFGA .... Bio-Dynamic Farming and Gardening Association (EA)
BDFJ .... Biographical Dictionary of Federal Judiciary [*A publication*]
BDFS .... Bachelor Degrees for Soldiers [*Program*]
BDFS .... Base Development Feasibility Study [*Navy*]
B/DFT .... Bank Draft (DS)
BD-FT .... Board-Foot (MUGU)
BDG .... Badger Mountain [*Washington*] [*Seismograph station code, US Geological Survey*] (SEIS)
BDG .... Bandag, Inc. [*NYSE symbol*] (SPSG)
BDG .... Beacon Data Generation (SAA)
BDG .... Bilirubin Diglucuronide [*Biochemistry*]
BDG .... Binding (MSA)
BDG .... Blanding [*Utah*] [*Airport symbol*] (OAG)
BDG .... Blanding, UT [*Location identifier FAA*] (FAAL)
BDG .... Bloc Democratique Gabonais [*Gabonese Democratic Bloc*] [*Later, PDG*]
BDG .... Blue Diamond Growers [*An association*] (EA)
BDG .... Bridge [*Board on Geographic Names*] (KSC)
BDG .... Bridger Resources, Inc. [*Vancouver Stock Exchange symbol*]
BDG .... Bridging [*Graphics*]
BDG .... Buffered Deoxycholate Glucose [*Broth*] [*Microbiology*]
BDG .... Buffered Desoxycholate Glucose [*Agar or broth*] [*Biochemistry*] (DAVI)
BDG .... Building (ADA)
BdG .... Bundesgesetz [*Federal Act or Statute*] [*German*] (ILCA)
BDG .... Business Development Group
BDG A .... Bandag Inc.'A' [*NYSE symbol*] (TTSB)
BDGA .... British Dahlia Growers Association (DBA)
BDGC .... Bad Conduct Discharge, General Court-Martial, after Confinement in Prison [*Navy*]
BDG CL .... Bookbinding Cloth (DGA)
BDGE .... Bridge (ADA)
BDGE .... Butanediol Diglycidyl Ether [*Organic chemistry*]
BdGes .... Bundesgesetz [*Federal Act or Statute*] [*German*] (ILCA)
BDGF .... Bile Duct Growth Factor [*Biochemistry*]
BDGF .... Bone-Derived Growth Factor [*Genetics*]
BDGF .... Bovine Derived Growth Factor [*Biochemistry*]
BDGF .... Brain Derived Growth Factor [*Biochemistry*]
BDGH .... Binding Head
BDGI .... Bad Conduct Discharge, General Court-Martial, Immediate [*Navy*]
BDGNA .... Bavarian Dance Group of North America (EA)
BDGP .... Bad Conduct Discharge, General Court-Martial, after Violation of Probation [*Navy*]
BDH .... Bandar Lengh [*Iran*] [*Airport symbol*] (OAG)
BDH .... Bearing, Distance, and Heading
BDH .... Binding Head (IAA)
BDH .... British Drug Houses Ltd. [*Research code symbol*]
BDHA .... British Dental Hygienists Association
BDHCA .... Belgian Draft Horse Corp. of America (EA)
BDHF .... British Dental Health Foundation (DI)
BDHI .... Bearing, Distance, and Heading Indicator
BDHI .... Buss Durkee Hostility Inventory (EDAC)
BDHO .... British Dental Health Organisation (DI)
BDHSA .... Bomb Director High-Speed Aircraft
BDHT .... Blowdown Heat Transfer [*Nuclear energy*]
BDi .... Bachelor of Didactics
BDI .... Bank Descriptor Index [*Computer science*]
BDI .... Base Diffusion Isolation

BDI.............. Bearing Deviation Indicator [*Aerospace*]
BDI.............. Beck Depression Inventory [*Psychology*]
BDI.............. Becton Dickinson Diagnostics [*Commercial firm*] (DAVI)
BDI.............. Beijing Dance Institute [*China*]
BDI.............. Biological Damage Indicator
BDI.............. Bird Island [*Seychelles Islands*] [*Airport symbol*] (OAG)
BDI.............. Both Dates Inclusive [*Business term*]
BDI.............. Brand Development Index (WDMC)
BDI.............. British Dental Institute (DI)
BDI.............. Buffered Direct Injection (IAA)
BDI.............. Bullet Dispersion Indicator
BDI.............. Bundesverband der Deutschen Industrie [*Federation of German Industries*]
BDI.............. Bureau of Dairy Industry [*Department of Agriculture*] [*Functions transferred to ARS, 1953*]
BDI.............. Bureau of Disability Insurance [*Social Security Administration*]
BDI.............. Burn Depth Indicator [*A video camera*] [*Medicine*] (DAVI)
BDI.............. Burundi [*ANSI three-letter standard code*] (CNC)
BDI.............. Business Directory International (ACII)
BDIA............ Base Diameter
BDIAC.......... Battelle - Defense Information Analysis Center [*Battelle Memorial Institute*]
BDIBS......... Boston Diagnostic Inventory of Basic Skills [*Speech and language therapy*] (DAVI)
BDIC .... Battelle - Defense Information Center [*Battelle Memorial Institute*] (MCD)
BDIC .... Binary-Coded Decimal Interchange Code
B Did .... Bachelor of Didactics
BDID........... Bystander Dominates Initial Dominant [*Sociology*]
B Di E .... Bachelor of Diesel Engineering
B Di Eng..... Bachelor of Diesel Engineering
BD in E....... Bachelor of Divinity in Education
B Dipl......... Bachelor of Diplomacy
BDIR........... Bus Direction [*Computer science*] (TEL)
BDIS........... Battle Damage Information Script (SAA)
BDIS .... Birth Defects Information System [*Center for Birth Defects Information Services, Inc.*] [*Information service or system*] (IID)
BDIS .... Bis((dimethylaminoethyl)indole)sulfide [*Biochemistry*]
BDI SF........ Beck's Depression Index-Short Form [*Psychiatry*] (DAVI)
BDJ............. Banjarmasin [*Indonesia*] [*Airport symbol*] (OAG)
BDJ............. Boulder Junction, WI [*Location identifier FAA*] (FAAL)
BDJ............. Brans-Dicke-Jordan [*Scalar-tensor theory*]
BDJI............ First Fed Bancorp(MN) [*NASDAQ symbol*] (TTSB)
BDJI............ First Federal Bancorporation MN [*NASDAQ symbol*] (SAG)
BDK .... Bedrock Resources Ltd. [*Vancouver Stock Exchange symbol*]
BDK .... Black & Decker Corp. [*NYSE symbol*] (SPSG)
BDK .... Bondoukou [*Ivory Coast*] [*Airport symbol*] (OAG)
BDL............. Bachelor of Divine Literature
BDL............. Bad Data Lister
BDL............. Banque de Developpement Local [*Algeria*] (EY)
BDL............. Banque de Donnees Locales [*Local Area Data Bank*] [*National Institute of Statistics and Economic Studies*] [*Information service or system*] (IID)
BDL............. Baseline Demonstration LASER (MCD)
BDL............. Base of Dorsal Lip
BDL............. Basic Dead Load [*Construction*] (DICI)
BDL............. Battery Data Link [*Air Force*]
BDL............. Beach Discharge Lighter
BDL............. Below the Detectable Limit
BDL............. Bennett, D. L., Wheeling WV [*STAC*]
BDL............. Best Dressed List
BDL............. Bradley International Airport [*FAA*] (TAG)
BDL............. British Drama League (DI)
BDL............. Building Description Language
BDL............. Bundle
BDL............. Burndale Resources Ltd. [*Vancouver Stock Exchange symbol*]
BDL............. Business Definition Language [*Computer science*] (IAA)
BDL............. Flanigan's Enterprises [*AMEX symbol*] (TTSB)
BDL............. Flanigan's Enterprises, Inc. [*Formerly, Big Daddy's Lounges, Inc.*] [*AMEX symbol*] (SPSG)
BDL............. Hartford [*Connecticut*]/Springfield [*Massachusetts*] [*Derived from name of airport: Bradley Field*] [*Airport symbol*]
BDL............. Windsor Locks, CT [*Location identifier FAA*] (FAAL)
BDLC........... Bissync Data Link Control (LAIN)
BDLC .... Burroughs Data Link Control [*Computer science*] (BUR)
BDLE........... Bundle
BDLR .... Bandolier (MSA)
BDLS .... Battery Data Link System [*Air Force*]
BDLS .... Brachmann-De Lange Syndrome [*Medicine*] (DMAA)
BDLS .... Bundles
BDLT........... Bow Designation Light (IAA)
BDLTEA....... Burley and Dark Leaf Tobacco Export Association (EA)
BDM............ Ballistic Defense Missile
BDM............ Banque de Donnees Macroeconomiques [*Macroeconomic Data Bank*] [*National Institute of Statistics and Economic Studies*] [*Information service or system*]
BDM............ Baryonic Dark Matter [*Galactic science*]
BDM............ BDM Federal, Inc. (GAAI)
BDM............ BDM Intl. [*NASDAQ symbol*] (TTSB)
BDM............ Becker's Muscular Dystrophy [*Medicine*] (DMAA)
BDM............ Binary Delta Modulation
BDM............ Binary Digital Multiplier [*Computer science*]
BDM............ Births, Deaths, and Marriages
BDM............ Blackdome Mining Corp. [*Toronto Stock Exchange symbol Vancouver Stock Exchange symbol*]

BDM............ Bomber Defense Missile [*Air Force*]
BDM............ Border Detection Method [*Radiology*] (DAVI)
BDM............ Brazil Democratic Movement [*Political party*]
BDM............ Bubble Domain Memory
BDM............ Bunker Defeat Munition [*Army*] (INF)
BDMA .... Benzyldimethylamine [*Organic chemistry*]
BDMA .... British Defence Manufacturers Association (PDAA)
BDMA .... British Direct Marketing Association
BDMA .... British Disinfectant Manufacturers' Association (BI)
BDMA .... Butylene Dimethacrylate [*Organic chemistry*]
BDMAA ...... British Direct Mail Advertising Association (DI)
BDMG.......... Banco de Desenvolvimento de Minas Gerais SA [*Brazil*] (EY)
BDMHL .... Bachelor of Divinity and Master of Hebrew Literature (BJA)
BDMI .... BDM International, Inc. [*NASDAQ symbol*] (SAG)
BDMI .... Biographical Dictionaries Master Index [*A publication*]
BDMInt .... BDM International, Inc. [*Associated Press*] (SAG)
BDMS .... Bactometer Data Management System
BDMS .... Bulk Direct Mail Service (ADA)
BDMS .... Bureau of Data Management and Strategy [*Department of Health and Human Services*] (GFGA)
BDMSC .... BDM Service Co. (MCD)
BDMSG....... British Dental Migraine Study Group [*An association*] (DBA)
BDN .... Badana [*Saudi Arabia*] [*Airport symbol Obsolete*] (OAG)
BDN .... Banco di Napoli [*Italy*]
BDN .... Bank Draft Number (TEL)
BDN .... Bell Data Network [*Telecommunications*]
BDN .... Bend Down
BDN .... Bodon [*Former USSR Seismograph station code, US Geological Survey*] (SEIS)
BDN .... Boscombe Down MOD/PE [*British ICAO designator*] (FAAC)
BDN .... Brandywine Realty Trust [*Formerly, Linpro Specified Properties*] [*AMEX symbol*] (SPSG)
BDN .... Brandywine Rlty Trust SBI [*AMEX symbol*] (TTSB)
B DNA .... Deoxyribonucleic Acid, Traditional Form [*DNA with right-handed helix*] [*Biochemistry, genetics*]
BDNF .... Brain-Derived Neurotrophic Factor [*Neurochemistry*]
BDNG.......... Bedding (MSA)
BDNG.......... Binding
BDNMSSS.... Board of Directors NATO Maintenance Supply Service System (NATG)
BDO .... Ballett der Deutschen Oper [*Berlin*]
BDO .... Bandung [*Indonesia*] [*Airport symbol*] (OAG)
BDO .... Base de Donnees des Obligations Francaises [*DAFSA*] [*Database*]
BDO .... Battle Dress Overgarment [*Military*] (INF)
BDO .... Bile Duct Obstruction [*Medicine*]
BDO .... Blanket Delivery Order (MCD)
BDO .... Boom Defense Officer
BDO .... Bottom Dropped Out [*Investment term*]
BDO .... Bow Door
BDO .... British Darts Organization (DBA)
BDO .... Budoia [*Papua New Guinea*] [*Seismograph station code, US Geological Survey*] (SEIS)
BDO .... Bus for Data Output (IAA)
BDO .... Butanediol [*Organic chemistry*]
B/DOE .... Barrels per Day Oil Equivalent
B-DOPA....... Bleomycin, Dacarbazine, Oncovin [*Vincristine*], Prednisone, Adriamycin [*Antineoplastic drug regimen*]
BDOS .... Basic Disk Operating System
BDOS .... Batch Disk Operating System
BDOT .... British Department of Transport
BDOZER....... Bulldozer [*Freight*]
BDP .... Bahamian Democratic Party [*Political party*] (PPW)
BDP .... Base Development Plan (AABC)
BDP .... Battlefield Development Plan (RDA)
BDP .... BCED Capital Investment Corp. [*Toronto Stock Exchange symbol Vancouver Stock Exchange symbol*]
BDP .... Beach Discharge Point (MCD)
BDP .... Beclomethasone Dipropionate [*Pharmacology*]
BDP .... Bhadrapur [*Nepal*] [*Airport symbol*] (OAG)
BDP .... Bonded Double Paper [*Wire insulation*] (KSC)
BDP .... Boogie Down Productions [*Rap recording group*]
BDP .... Bophuthatswana Democratic Party [*Political party*] (PPW)
BDP .... Botswana Democratic Party [*Political party*] (PPW)
BDP .... Bottom Dead Point
BDP .... Bridge Display Panel [*Navy*] (CAAL)
BDP .... Brine Disposal Program [*Environmental Data and Information Service*] (MSC)
BDP .... British Democratic Party [*Political party*]
BDP .... Broad Pass [*Alaska*] [*Seismograph station code, US Geological Survey Closed*] (SEIS)
BDP .... Brookes Deflection Potentiometer
BDP .... Bulk Data Processing (IAA)
BDP .... Bundle Drawing Process [*Metal fiber technology*]
BDP .... Business Data Processing
BDPA .... Black Data Processing Associates (EA)
BDPA .... British Disposable Products Association (PDAA)
BDPA .... Bureau of Data Processing and Accounts [*Social Security Administration*]
BDPE .... Bromodiphenyl(ethylphenyl)ethylene [*Endocrinology*]
BDPEC .... Bureau of Disease Prevention and Environmental Control
BDPI .... Base Data Processing Installation
BDPN .... Bedpan (MSA)
BDPO .... Business Data Processing Operation
BDPS .... Brigade Data Processing System
BDPS .... British Deer Producers' Association (DBA)

BDPSK........... Binary Differential Phase-Shift Keying [*Telecommunications*] (TEL)
BDQ............ Biet-Dong-Quan [*South Vietnamese Rangers*] (VNW)
BDQ............ Vadodara [*India*] [*Airport symbol*] (OAG)
BDR............ Background Diabetic Retinopathy [*Endocrinology and ophthalmology*] (DAVI)
BDR............ Bad Demographic Risk [*Television*]
BDR............ Bandmaster [*Military British*] (ROG)
BDR............ Bank Descriptor Registers [*Computer science*]
BDR............ Battle Damage Repair [*Army*] (RDA)
BDR............ Beardmore Resources [*Vancouver Stock Exchange symbol*]
BDR............ Bearer Depositary Receipt [*Investment term*]
BDR............ Bell Doesn't Ring [*Telecommunications*] (TEL)
BDR............ Belt Driven Retrofit [*Cosworth racing engines*] [*Automotive engineering*]
BDR............ Best Depth Range [*Military*] (NVT)
BDR............ Bi-Duplexed Redundancy [*Telecommunications*]
BDR............ Binary Dump Routine
BDR............ Binder (MSA)
BDR............ Binder
BDR............ Blonder Tongue Laboratories, Inc. [*AMEX symbol*] (SAG)
BDR............ Blonder Tongue Labs [*AMEX symbol*] (TTSB)
BDR............ Bombardier
BDR............ Bomb Damage Repair
BDR............ Border (FAAC)
BDR............ Bridgeport [*Connecticut*] [*Airport symbol*] (OAG)
BDR............ Bridgewater State College, Bridgewater, MA [*OCLC symbol*] (OCLC)
BDR............ Brigadier
BDR............ Business Development Report [*Department of Commerce*] (GFGA)
BDRA........... British Drag Racing Association (BI)
B Dr Art....... Bachelor of Dramatic Art
BDRC........... Becton, Dickinson & Co. Research Center
B/DR/F/I....... Ballantine/Del Rey/Fawcett/Ivy [*Publishing group*]
BDRI........... Brick Development Research Institute [*Australia*]
BDRI........... Bright Display RADAR Indicator
BDRL........... Biological Defense Research Laboratory
BDRM.......... Bedroom
bdrm........... Board Room (VRA)
BDRN.......... Banque de Developpement de la Republique du Niger [*Development Bank of the Republic of Niger*] (AF)
BDRP........... Biological Defense Research Program [*DoD*]
BDRP........... Biological Defense Research Program [*Military*] (DOMA)
BDRP........... Business Directory of Registered Plumbers [*A publication*]
BDRS........... Business Development Report System [*Department of Commerce*] [*Database*]
BDRT........... Baud Rate [*Data transmission speed*] [*Computer science*]
BDRY........... Bindery
BDRY........... Boundary (AABC)
BDS .... Bachelor of Dental Surgery
BDS .... Bachelor of Dental Surgery (NADA)
BDS .... Ballistics Dispensing System (MCD)
BdS .... Banco di Sicilia [*Italy*]
BDS .... Barbados [*Seismograph station code, US Geological Survey*] (SEIS)
BDS .... Bard Silver & Gold [*Vancouver Stock Exchange symbol*]
BDS .... Base Data System (AFM)
BDS .... Base Design Section [*Military*] (IAA)
BDS .... Base Development Survey (MCD)
BDS .... Base Distribution System [*Air Force*] (AFM)
BDS .... Base Divider Strip (AAG)
BDS .... Battle Dressing Station [*Military*] (NVT)
BDS .... Battlefield Data System
BDS .... Beitraege zur Danziger Statistik [*Danzig*]
BDS .... Bibliographic Database Search Service [*University of Wyoming Libraries*] (OLDSS)
BDS .... Binary Decode Scaler [*Computer science*]
BDS .... Bindings [*Publishing*]
BDS .... Biographical Dictionaries and Related Works. Supplement [*A publication*]
BDS .... Biological Defense System
BDS .... Biological Detection System
BDS .... Bis in Die Sumendus [*To Be Taken Twice a Day*] [*Pharmacy*]
BDS .... Bloc Democratique Senegalais [*Senegal*] [*Political party*] (PPW)
BDS .... Blood Derived Serum
BDS .... Boards
BDS .... Bomb Damage Survey
BDS .... Bomb Director Set [*or System*] [*Army*]
BDS .... Bomb-Disposal Squad
BDS .... Bonded Double Silk [*Wire insulation*]
BDS .... Bound in Boards
bds. .... Bound in Boards [*Book production*] (WDMC)
BDS .... Brass Divider Strip [*Technical drawings*]
BDS .... Brindisi [*Italy*] [*Airport symbol*] (OAG)
BDS .... British Deer Society
BDS .... British Defence Staff
BDS .... British Display Society (BI)
BDS .... British Driving Society (BI)
BDS .... Broker's Daily Statement
BDS .... Building Design System [*Applied Research of Cambridge Ltd.*] [*Software package*] (NCC)
BDS .... Bulk Data Switching
BDS .... Business Definition System (MHDI)
BDS........... Business Development Specialist (DOMA)
BDS .... Butanediol Succinate [*Organic chemistry*]
BDSA.......... Bis(dimethylsilyl)acetamide [*Organic chemistry*]
BDSA.......... British Dental Students' Association (BI)

BDSA .... Business and Defense Services Administration [*Later, BDC*] [*Department of Commerce*]
BDSANZ....... Blonde D'Aquitaine Society of Australia and New Zealand
BD Sc .... Bachelor of Dental Science
BDSC .... Black Diamond Steamship Corp. (MHDW)
BDSC .... British Deaf Sports Council (DBA)
BDSD .... Base Detonating, Self-Destroying
BDS-D......... Battlefield Distributed Simulation-Developmental [*Army*] (RDA)
BDS-D......... Battlefield Distributed Simulation - Developmental Program [*Army*] (RDA)
BDSF .... Bone-Marrow-Derived Suppressor Factor [*Immunology*]
Bd/Sgt.......... Band Sergeant [*British military*] (DMA)
BDSI .... Bad Conduct Discharge, Sentence of Summary Court-Martial, Immediate [*Navy*]
BDSI .... Basic Direct Shipping Instructions
BDSLD .... Bids Solicited (FAAC)
BDSM .... Bandsman [*Military British*]
BDSMN....... Bandsman [*Military British*]
BDSOFI....... Base Design Section - Operational Facility Installation [*Military*] (IAA)
BDSP .... Bad Conduct Discharge, Summary Court-Martial, after Violation of Probation [*Navy*]
BDSP .... Basic Data Set Project [*National Science Foundation*]
BDSRA........ Batten's Disease Support and Research Association (EA)
BDSSFI....... Base Design Section - Support Facility Installation [*Military*] (IAA)
BDST .... Bed Depth Service Time [*Wastewater treatment*]
BDST .... British Double Summer Time
BDSW .... British Defence Staff, Washington, DC [*Also, BDSWASHDC*] (NATG)
BDSWASHDC... British Defence Staff, Washington, DC [*Also, BDSW*] (NATG)
BDT............ Back Door Trot [*i.e., a call of nature*] [*Obsolete slang*]
BDT............ Bado Lite [*Zaire*] [*Airport symbol*] (OAG)
BDT............ Balletto di Toscana [*Florence, Italy*]
BDT............ Ballistic Damage Tolerance (MCD)
BDT............ Banque de Developpement du Tchad [*Development Bank of Chad*] (AF)
BDT............ Beam Deflection Tube
BDT............ Belt Driven Turbocharged [*Cosworth racing engines*] [*Automotive engineering*]
BDT............ Best Demonstrated Technology (GFGA)
BDT............ Bhumibol Dam [*Thailand*] [*Seismograph station code, US Geological Survey*] (SEIS)
BDT............ Binary Deck-to-Tape [*Computer science*]
BDT............ Binary-to-Decimal Transmitter [*Computer science*] (NOAA)
BDT............ Block Data Transfer (MCD)
BDT............ Bone-Dried Ton
BDT............ Bradley Desktop Trainer [*Military*]
BDT............ Breed Technologies [*NYSE symbol*] (SPSG)
BDT............ Building Disputes Tribunal [*Australia*]
BDT............ Burdett Resources Ltd. [*Vancouver Stock Exchange symbol*]
BDT............ Burst Delay Timer (MCD)
BDT............ Telecommunications Development Bureau [*United Nations*] (DUND)
BDTA .... British Dental Trade Association (DBA)
BDTC .... Bio-Dental Technologies [*NASDAQ symbol*] (TTSB)
BDTC .... BioDental Technologies Corp. [*NASDAQ symbol*] (SAG)
BDTD .... Balanced Digital Transmission Device [*Army*]
BDTF .... Bomber Defence Training Flight [*British military*] (DMA)
BDTN .... Beam-Driven Thermonuclear (MCD)
BDTR .... Basic Data Transmission Routine (IAA)
BDTS .... Batch Data Transmission System
BDTS .... Boost Discrimination and Track System
BDTS .... Brass Dressers Trade Society [*A union*] [*British*]
BDTS .... Buffered Data Transmission Simulator
BDTS .... Bulk Data Transfer Subsystem [*Telecommunications*] (TEL)
BDTVMI .... Beery Development Test of Visual-Motor Integration [*Psychiatry*] (DAVI)
BDU .... Banque de Donnees Urbaines de Paris et de la Region d'Ile-De-France [*Urban Data Bank of Paris and the Paris Region*] [*Paris Office of Urbanization France*] [*Information service or system*] (IID)
BDU .... Bardufoss [*Norway*] [*Airport symbol*] (OAG)
BDU .... Barograph Display Unit
BDU .... Baseband Distribution Unit
BDU .... Basic Device Unit [*Computer science*] (IBMDP)
BDU .... Basic Display Unit [*Computer science*]
BDU .... Battery Display Unit [*Army*]
BDU .... Battle Damage Umpire (SAA)
BDU .... Battle Dress Uniform [*Military*]
BDU .... Big Dutch Hollow [*Utah*] [*Seismograph station code, US Geological Survey*] (SEIS)
BDU .... Biomedical Display Unit (KSC)
BDU .... Bomb-Disposal Unit
BDU .... Bomb, Dummy Unit (AFM)
BDU .... Bombing Development Unit
BDU .... Bradsue Resources [*Vancouver Stock Exchange symbol*]
BDU .... Bromodeoxyuridine [*Also, BDUR, BrDU*] [*Biochemistry*]
BDUCVM...... Cowichan Valley Museum, Duncan, British Columbia [*Library symbol National Library of Canada*] (NLC)
BDUFM .... British Columbia Forest Museum, Duncan, British Columbia [*Library symbol National Library of Canada*] (NLC)
BDUR .... Bromodeoxyuridine [*Also, BDU, BrDU*] [*Biochemistry*]
BDV .... Bend-Down Virginia [*A picked-up stub of a cigarette*]
BDV .... Best Dark Virginia [*Tobacco*] [*British*] (ROG)
BDV .... Binary Divide (MSA)
BDV .... Blow-Down Valve [*Railroad term*]
BDV .... Boom Defence Vessel [*Navy British*]
BDV .... Borna Disease Virus [*Veterinary medicine*]

BDV	Breakdown Voltage [Telecommunications] (TEL)
BDV	Bremen Demokratische Volkspartei [Bremen Democratic People's Party] [Germany Political party] (PPE)
BDV	Budkov [Czechoslovakia] [Geomagnetic observatory code]
BDVG	Bow Diving
BDW	Bank Descriptor Word [Computer science]
BDW	Beach, Dewey W., Denver CO [STAC]
BDW	Blunted Delta Wing
BDW	Boulder [Wyoming] [Seismograph station code, US Geological Survey] (SEIS)
BDW	Buffered Distilled Water [Chemistry]
BDW	Buried Distribution Wire [Telecommunications] (TEL)
Bdway	Broadway Stores [Associated Press] (SAG)
BDWB	Bone Dry-Weight Basis (IAA)
BDWPHGS	Beauty, Divinity, Wisdom, Power, Honor, Glory, Strength [Freemasonry] (ROG)
BDWTU	British Diamond Workers Trade Union
BDWY	Broadway [A street name]
BdwySey	Broadway & Seymour, Inc. [Associated Press] (SAG)
BDX	Becton, Dickinson [NYSE symbol] (TTSB)
BDX	Becton, Dickinson & Co. [NYSE symbol] (SPSG)
BDX	Bendix Aviation Corp. [Later, Bendix Corp.] (MCD)
BDX	Bourdeaux Resources Ltd. [Vancouver Stock Exchange symbol]
BDX	Broadus, MT [Location identifier FAA] (FAAL)
BDXR	Block Demultiplexer [Ground Communications Facility, NASA]
BDY	Betty Lake, AK [Location identifier FAA] (FAAL)
BDY	Bindley Western Indus [NYSE symbol] (TTSB)
BDY	Bindley Western Industries [NYSE symbol] (SAG)
BDY	Body
BDY	Bookbindery (DGA)
BDY	Boundary (KSC)
BDY	Broadway [A street name] [British]
bdyco	Bodycolor (VRA)
BDYFLP	Body Flap (NASA)
Bdy Mon	Boundary Monument [Control point] [Nautical charts]
BDYN	Biodynamics International [NASDAQ symbol] (SAG)
BDYN	Biodynamics Intl. [NASDAQ symbol] (TTSB)
BDY or RF	Body or Roof [Freight]
BDZR	Bulldozer (MSA)
BE	Bachelor of Education
BE	Bachelor of Elocution
BE	Bachelor of Engineering
BE	Bachelor of Engineering Science (DD)
BE	Bachelor of English
BE	Bachelor of Expression
BE	Bachelor of Science in Engineering (DD)
BE	Bachelor of the Elements
BE	Bacillary Emulsion [Tuberculin] [Medicine] (MAE)
BE	Bacillen Emulsion [Clinical chemistry] (AAMN)
BE	Back End (MSA)
BE	Backscattered Electron (MCD)
BE	Bacterial Endocarditis [Medicine]
BE	Bale
BE	Baltimore & Eastern Railroad Co. [Absorbed into Consolidated Rail Corp.] [AAR code]
BE	Band Elimination
BE	Bank Error
BE	Barium Enema [Medicine]
BE	Baron of Exchequer [British] (ROG)
BE	Barrett's Esophagus [Medicine]
BE	Base Ejection
BE	Base-Emitter (DNAB)
BE	Base Excess [Medicine]
BE	Basic Encyclopedia [Army] (AABC)
BE	Basic English
BE	Battlefield Environment (MCD)
Be	Baume [Hydrometer scale or specific gravity] [Organic chemistry] (DAVI)
BE	Bazillenemulsion [Bacillary emulsion] [Immunology]
BE	Beacon Explorer [Satellite] [NASA]
BE	Bearing Error [Military] (CAAL)
Be	Becker [Blood group]
Be	Beda [Deceased, 735] [Authority cited in pre-1607 legal work] (DSA)
BE	Beech Aircraft Corp. [ICAO aircraft manufacturer identifier] (ICAO)
BE	Beginning Event (DNAB)
BE	Belgium [ANSI two-letter standard code] (CNC)
be	Belgium [MARC country of publication code Library of Congress] (LCCP)
BE	Bell End
BE	Below Elbow [Medicine]
Be	Benedictus de Isernia [Flourished, 1221-52] [Authority cited in pre-1607 legal work] (DSA)
BE	Benguet Corp. [NYSE symbol] (SPSG)
BE	Benzoylecgonine [Cocaine metabolite]
BE	Berkeley Exchange (EA)
Be	Beryllium [Chemical element]
BE	Best Estimate Model (NRCH)
BE	Bevelled Edges [Printing] (DGA)
BE	Biblical Essays [A publication] (BJA)
BE	Biblical Evangelism (EA)
Be	Bibliotheque Royale d'Albert 1er, Bruxelles, Belgium [Library symbol Library of Congress] (LCLS)
BE	Biennial
BE	Bile Esculin [Medicine]
BE	Bilingual Education (EDAC)

B/E	Bill of Entry [Shipping]
BE	Bill of Exchange [Accounting]
BE	Binding Edge (ADA)
BE	Binding Energy
BE	Biplane Experimental [Aircraft] [World War I]
BE	Black Enamelled
BE	Black English [Dialect]
BE	Black Enterprise [A publication]
BE	Bleriot Experimental [British military] (DMA)
BE	Bluie East [US air bases in Greenland] [World War II]
BE	Board Eligible (MEDA)
BE	Board Examined [of a physician] (BARN)
BE	Board of Education
BE	Bombing Encyclopedia (CINC)
BE	Bond Equivalent (TDOB)
BE	Booster Engine [Rocketry]
BE	Bose-Einstein [Statistics] (IAA)
BE	Bovine Enteritis [Medicine] (MAE)
B/E	Boy Entrant [British military] (DMA)
BE	Brain Edema [Medicine] (DMAA)
BE	Bread Equivalent [Medicine] (DMAA)
BE	Breaker End (MSA)
B/E	Break-Even Point [Accounting]
BE	Breast Examination (DAVI)
BE	Brief Entry
BE	Brilliant Eyes
BE	British Eagle Airlines (IIA)
BE	British Element
B/E	British Embassy (DS)
BE	British Empire
BE	Bronchoesophagology [Medicine]
BE	Bucyrus-Erie Co.
BE	Buddhist Era
BE	Bull Elephants (EA)
BE	Bureau of Economics [Federal Trade Commission]
BE	Bureau of Explosives [Later, HMS (BOE)]
BE	Business Equipment
b/e	By-Election [Politics]
BE	Enterprise Airlines [ICAO designator] (AD)
BE	Excursion [Also, B] [Airline fare code]
Be2	Beriev [Russian aircraft designation] (DOMA)
BEA	Background Equivalent Activity
BEA	Banque Exterieure d'Algerie [Algerian Foreign Bank] (AF)
BEA	Barbados Environmental Association (EAIO)
BEA	Barn Equipment Association [Later, FEA] (EA)
BEA	Basic Electric Arc (PDAA)
BE-A	Beacon Explorer A [Satellite] [NASA]
bea	Beads (VRA)
BEA	Beatty [Nevada] [Seismograph station code, US Geological Survey Closed] (SEIS)
BEA	Beaumont [Diocesan abbreviation] [Texas] (TOCD)
Bea	Beaver [Record label] [Canada]
BEA	Beaver College, Glenside, PA [OCLC symbol] (OCLC)
BEA	Beeville, TX [Location identifier FAA] (FAAL)
BEA	Beginning Education Assessment [Educational development test]
BEA	Bereina [Papua New Guinea] [Airport symbol] (OAG)
BEA	BEST [Beneficial Employees Security Trust] Employers Association (EA)
BEA	Bilingual Education Act of 1968 (EDAC)
BEA	Bills of Exchange Act [1882] [British]
BEA	Binary Encounter Approximation [Nuclear physics]
BEA	Blue Etch-Anodize (PDAA)
BEA	Board of Ethnic Affairs [Queensland, Australia]
BEA	Break Even Analysis [Accounting]
BEA	British East Africa
BEA	British Egg Association (BI)
BEA	British Electricity Authority
BEA	British Engineers Association
BEA	British Epilepsy Association
BEA	British Esperanto Association, Inc. (BI)
BEA	British European Airways Corp. [Later, British Airways]
BEA	British Exhibitors' Association (BI)
BEA	Broadcast Education Association (EA)
BEA	Budget Enforcement Act [1990]
BEA	Budget Enhancement Act (AAGC)
BEA	Building Economic Alternatives [Co-Op America] [A publication]
BEA	Bureau of Economic Affairs [Later, Bureau of Economic and Business Affairs] [Department of State]
BEA	Bureau of Economic Analysis [Department of Commerce] [Washington, DC] (IID)
BEA	Bureau of European Affairs [Department of State]
BEAA	Business Education Adminstrators Association [Defunct] (EA)
BEAB	British Electrical Approvals Board
BEAB	British Electrotechnical Approvals Board (NITA)
Bea Bank	Beames' Commitments in Bankruptcy [A publication] (DLA)
BEAC	Banque des Etats de l'Afrique Centrale [Bank of Central African States] (AF)
BEAC	Beaconsfield [Urban district in England]
BEAC	Boeing Engineering Analog Computer (IEEE)
BEAC	British European Airways Corp. [Later, British Airways]
BEAC	Broadcast Educators Association of Canada (AC)
Bea CE	Beames' Costs in Equity [A publication] (DLA)
BEACH	Beach [Commonly used] (OPSA)
BEACH	[The] Beaches Environmental Assessment, Closure, and Health Act 1993

Beach Contrib Neg... Beach on Contributory Negligence [*A publication*] (DLA)
Beach Eq Prac... Beach's Modern Practice in Equity [*A publication*] (DLA)
Beach Inj..... Beach on Injunctions [*A publication*] (DLA)
Beach Mod Eq Jur... Beach's Commentaries on Modern Equity Jurisprudence [*A publication*] (DLA)
Beach Priv Corp... Beach on Private Corporations [*A publication*] (DLA)
Beach Pub Corp... Beach on Public Corporations [*A publication*] (DLA)
Beach Rec... Beach on the Law of Receivers [*A publication*] (DLA)
BeacnP........ Beacon Properties Corp. [*Associated Press*] (SAG)
BeacnPr....... Beacon Properties Corp. [*Associated Press*] (SAG)
BEACON....... Boston Exchange Automated Communication Order-Routing Network (DFIT)
BEACON....... British European Airways Corp. [*later, British Airways*] Computerized Office Network
Bea Costs.... Beames' Costs in Equity [*A publication*] (DLA)
BEACOTRON... Beam Coupling Tube (NATG)
Bea Eq Pl.... Beames' Equity Pleading [*A publication*] (DLA)
BE Aero....... BE Aerospace, Inc. [*Associated Press*] (SAG)
BEAFA.......... Biomass Energy and Alcohol Fuels Act of 1980
BE(Ag)......... Bachelor of Engineering (Agriculture)
BEAG........... Bateria de Examenes de Aptitud General [*General Aptitude Test Battery*] [*Spanish*]
BEA Inco...... BEA Income Fund [*Associated Press*] (SAG)
BEAIRA........ British Electrical and Allied Industries Research Association (MCD)
BEAL............ Banco Europeu para a America Latina [*Bank*] [*Portuguese*] (EY)
BEAL............ Banque Europeenne pour l'Amerique Latine [*Bank*] [*French*] (EY)
BEAM........... Beaminster [*England*]
Be-Am......... Bibliotheque Royale d'Albert 1er, American Studies Center, Bruxelles, Belgium [*Library symbol Library of Congress*] (LCLS)
BEAM........... Bidders Early Alert Message (PDAA)
BEAM........... Biology, Electronics, Aesthetics, Mechanics [*Robotics competition*]
BEAM........... Brain Electrical Activity Mapping
BEAM........... Broiler and Egg Association of Minnesota (SRA)
BEAM........... Building Equipment Accessories and Materials [*Program*] [*Canada*]
BEAM........... Burroughs Electronic Accounting Machine (BUR)
BEAM........... Summit Technology [*NASDAQ symbol*] (TTSB)
BEAM........... Summit Technology, Inc. [*NASDAQ symbol*] (NQ)
BEAMA......... British Electrical and Allied Manufacturers Association
Beames Glanv... Beames' Glanville [*A publication*] (DLA)
BEAMOS...... Beam Accessed Metal Oxide Semiconductor [*Memory technology*] (NITA)
BEAMOS...... Beam Addressed Metal Oxide Semiconductor [*Memory technology*]
BEAMS......... Base Engineering Automated Management System (AFM)
BEAMS......... Basic Education Assistance Material Service [*National Multimedia Center for Adult Basic Education*] (IID)
BEAMS......... British Emergency Air Medical Service (DA)
BEAMS......... Budget Execution Appropriation Maintenance System [*Military*]
BEAN........... Bloc d'Esquerra d'Alliberament Nacional [*Left Bloc for National Liberation*] [*Spain*] (PPW)
BEAN........... Body Electronics Area Network
BEAN........... Brothers Gourmet Coffees [*NASDAQ symbol*] (SAG)
BE & C......... British Empire and Commonwealth
BE & CWLC... British Empire and Commonwealth Weight-Lifting Council
BE & E.......... Basic Electricity and Electronics
BE & S.......... Break, Enter, and Steal (ADA)
Bea Ne Ex... Beames on the Writ of Ne Exeat Regno [*A publication*] (DLA)
Bea Ord....... Beames' Orders in Chancery [*England*] [*A publication*] (DLA)
BEAP........... British East Africa Protectorate [*British government*]
BEAP........... Bronchiectasis, Eosinophilia, Asthma, Pneumonia [*Medicine*] (DMAA)
BEAPA......... Bureau of East Asian and Pacific Affairs [*Formerly, Bureau of Far Eastern Affairs*] [*Department of State*]
Bea Pl Eq.... Beames' Pleas in Equity [*A publication*] (DLA)
BEAR........... Beacon Experiment and Auroral Research
BEAR........... Beam Experiment Aboard Rocket (MCD)
BEAR........... Berkeley Elites Automated Retrieval [*University of California at Berkeley*] [*Information service or system*] (NITA)
BEAR........... Biological Effects of Atomic Radiation
BEAR........... Bonus, Extension, and Reenlistment [*Army*] (INF)
BeAR........... Rijksuniversitaire Centrum te Antwerpen [*State University Center of Antwerp*], Antwerpen, Belgium [*Library symbol Library of Congress*] (LCLS)
BEAR........... Vermont Teddy Bear [*NASDAQ symbol*] (TTSB)
BEAR........... Vermont Teddy Bear Co. [*NASDAQ symbol*] (SAG)
BEARA......... British Electronic and Applied Research Association (MCD)
Bearb........... Bearbeiter [*Editor*] [*German*] (BARN)
bearb........... Bearbeitet [*Revised*] [*German*] (BARN)
BeardCo....... Beard Co. [*Associated Press*] (SAG)
Bearng......... Bearings, Inc. [*Associated Press*] (SAG)
BearS........... Bear Stearns Companies, Inc. [*Associated Press*] (SAG)
BEARS......... Bond Enabling Annual Retirement Savings (DFIT)
BEARS......... Breadboard of an Electrochemical Air Revitalization System [*NASA*]
BearSt......... Bear Stearns Companies, Inc. [*Associated Press*] (SAG)
BEART......... Beaver Army Terminal [*Oregon*]
Bear Tithes... Bearblock. Treatise upon Tithes [*6th ed.*] [*1832*] [*A publication*] (DLA)
Beas............ Beasley's New Jersey Chancery Reports [*A publication*] (DLA)
Beas............ Beasley's New Jersey Equity Reports [*12-13*] [*A publication*] (DLA)
BEAS............ British Executive Air Services
Beasl........... Beasley's New Jersey Equity Reports [*A publication*] (DLA)
BEAST.......... Basic Experimental Automatic Syntactic Translator [*Bunker Ramo Corp.*] (NITA)
BEAST.......... Brookings Economics and Statistical Translator [*Computer science*]
BEAST.......... Business, Engineering, Appropriate Technology, and Skilled Trades [*Peace Corps program*]
BEA Strat..... BEA Strategic Income Fund [*Associated Press*] (SAG)
BEASY......... Boundary Element Analysis System [*Computational Mechanics Ltd.*] [*Software package*] (NCC)
Beat............. Beatty's Irish Chancery Reports [*1814-36*] [*A publication*] (DLA)
BEAT............ Best Execution Analysis Tabulation [*Computer science*]
BEAT............ Breaking and Entering and Auto Theft [*Police crime computer*]
BEATS.......... Both Ends, All Time Saved [*Shipping*]
Beatt............ Beatty's Irish Chancery Reports [*1814-36*] [*A publication*] (DLA)
Beatty.......... Beatty's Irish Chancery Reports [*1814-36*] [*A publication*] (DLA)
Beatty Ir Ch... Beatty's Irish Chancery Reports [*1814-36*] [*A publication*] (DLA)
Beau & Fl.... [*Francis*] Beaumont and [*John*]Fletcher [*17th century English dramatists*] (BARN)
Beau Bills.... Beaumont. Bills of Sale [*1855*] [*A publication*] (DLA)
BeauCtl........ Beauti Control Cosmetics, Inc. [*Associated Press*] (SAG)
Beau Ins...... Beaumont. Life and Fire Insurance [*2nd ed.*] [*1846*] [*A publication*] (DLA)
Beaur Org.... Beauregard. Organisation de la Famille [*A publication*] (DLA)
BeAUSI........ Universitaire Faculteiten Sint-Ignatius te Antwerpen, Antwerp, Belgium [*Library symbol Library of Congress*] (LCLS)
BEAV............ BE Aerospace [*NASDAQ symbol*] (TTSB)
BEAV............ BE Aerospace, Inc. [*NASDAQ symbol*] (SPSG)
Beav............ Beavan's English Rolls Court Reports [*A publication*] (DLA)
Beav............ Beaver [*A publication*] (BRI)
Beavan Ch... Beavan's English Rolls Court Reports [*A publication*] (DLA)
Beav & W.... Beavan and Walford's Railway and Canal Cases [*England*] [*A publication*] (DLA)
Beav & Wal... Beavan and Walford's Railway and Canal Cases [*England*] [*A publication*] (DLA)
Beav & Wal Ry Cas... Beavan and Walford's Railway and Canal Cases [*England*] [*A publication*] (DLA)
Beav & W Ry Cas... Beavan and Walford's Railway and Canal Cases [*England*] [*A publication*] (DLA)
Beav (Eng)... Beavan's English Rolls Court Reports [*A publication*] (DLA)
BEAVER....... Be Ever Alert, Vigilant/Error Removal [*United States Air Force Security System's acronym for the Zero Defects Program*]
Beav OC...... Beavan's Ordines Cancellariae [*A publication*] (DLA)
Beav R & C... Beavan. Railway and Canal Cases [*England*] [*A publication*] (DLA)
Beav R & C Cas... English Railway and Canal Cases, by Beavan and Others [*A publication*] (DLA)
Beaw........... Beawes' Lex Mercatoria [*England*] [*A publication*] (DLA)
Beawes' Lex Merc... Beawes' Lex Mercatoria [*England*] [*A publication*] (DLA)
beawk......... Beadwork (VRA)
Beaw Lex Mer... Beawes' Lex Mercatoria [*England*] [*A publication*] (DLA)
BeazHm....... Beazer Homes USA [*Associated Press*] (SAG)
Beazr.......... Beazer Homes USA [*Associated Press*] (SAG)
BeazrHm...... Beazer Homes USA [*Associated Press*] (SAG)
BEB............. Beach Erosion Board [*Army*]
BE-B............ Beacon Explorer B [*Satellite*] [*NASA*]
BEB............. Benbecula [*Hebrides Islands*] [*Airport symbol*] (OAG)
BEB............. Benign Essential Blepharospasm [*Medicine*] (EA)
BEB............. Best Ever Bottled [*Wines and spirits*]
BEB............. Binary Exponential Backoff [*Telecommunications*] (OSI)
BEB............. Bridge Erection Boat
BEB............. British Export Board (PDAA)
BEBA........... Beebas [*NASDAQ symbol*] (SAG)
BEBA........... Bilingual Education Bibliographic Abstracts [*National Clearinghouse for Bilingual Education*] [*Rosslyn, VA Database*]
BEBA........... Breeze Electron Ballistic Accelerometer (SAA)
BEBA........... Bring 'Em Back Alive [*AAA Holiday News Service*]
BEBA........... Bureau of Economic and Business Affairs [*Formerly, Bureau of Economic Affairs*] [*Department of State*]
BEBC........... Big European Bubble Chamber [*Nuclear particle detector*]
BEBI............ Breast Examination Bras, Inc.
BEBIM......... Bulletin of Experimental Biology and Medicine [*A publication*]
BEBO........... Bond-Energy Bond-Order [*Chemical kinetics*]
BEBR........... Bureau of Economic and Business Research [*University of Florida*] [*Gainesville*] [*Information service or system*] (IID)
BEBR........... Bureau of Economic and Business Research [*University of Delaware*] [*Research center*] (RCD)
BEBRF......... Benign Essential Blepharospasm Research Foundation (EA)
B Ec............ Bachelor of Economics
BEC............. Bachelor of Engineering Construction
BEC............. Background Equivalent Concentration [*Computer science*]
BEC............. Bacterial Endocarditis
BEC............. Banque Europeenne de Credit [*Belgium*]
BEC............. Barbecon, Inc. [*Toronto Stock Exchange symbol*]
BEC............. Barnes Engineering Co. (KSC)
BEC............. Base Equipment Container
BEC............. Base Extension Course
BEC............. Because (ADA)
BEC............. Beckman Instruments [*NYSE symbol*] (TTSB)
BEC............. Beckman Instruments, Inc. [*NYSE symbol*] (CTT)
BEC............. Beech Aircraft Corp. [*ICAO designator*] (FAAC)
Bec............. Beechcraft [*Airplane code*]
BEC............. Beginning of Equilibrium Cycle [*Nuclear energy*] (NRCH)
BEC............. Behavioral Emergency Committee [*Medicine*] (HCT)
BEC............. Berkeley Enthusiasts Club [*Woking, Surrey, England*] (EAIO)
BEC............. Bermuda-Columbia [*Bermuda*] [*Seismograph station code, US Geological Survey*] (SEIS)
BEC............. Best Estimate Constrained
BEC............. Big East Conference (EA)
BEC............. Big Eight Conference (EA)
BEC............. Binary-Erasure Channel (IAA)
BEC............. Bioelectrochemistry
BEC............. Bio-Energy Council [*Defunct*] (EA)
BEC............. Blood Ethanol Concentration [*Medicine*]

BEC............ Boeing Engineering Co. (MCD)
BEC............ Books on Egypt and Chaldea [*A publication*]
BEC............ Bose-Einstein Condensation [*Cryogenius*] [*Physics*]
BEC............ Bowles Engineering Corp.
BEC............ Brevard Engineering College [*Florida*] (KSC)
BEC............ British Employers' Confederation
BEC............ British Engineers Club
BEC............ Broad Economic Category
BEC............ Bromoergocryptine [*Organic chemistry*]
BEC............ Brown Engineering Co. (KSC)
BEC............ Budget Execution Code
BEC............ Building Employers' Confederation [*A union*] [*British*]
BEC............ Bureau Europeen de Coordination des Organisations Internationales
de Jeunesse [*European Coordination Bureau for International
Youth Organizations - ECB*] (EAIO)
BEC............ Bureau of Employees' Compensation [*Later, OWCP*] [*Department of
Labor*]
BEC............ Burst-Error Channel (IAA)
BEC............ Burst Error Correction [*Encoder/decoder*] (MCD)
BEC............ Business Education Connection (OICC)
BEC............ Business Education Council
BEC............ Business Electronics Computer [*Used in training*]
BEC............ Business Enterprise Center [*Australia*]
BEC............ Riverview Hospital, Port Coquitlam, British Columbia [*Library symbol
Library network*] (NLC)
BEC............ Wichita, KS [*Location identifier FAA*] (FAAL)
BECA.......... Beam Calibrator (PDAA)
BECA.......... British Electrostatic Control Association (EAIO)
BECA.......... British Exhibition Contractors Association (EAIO)
BECA.......... Bureau of Educational and Cultural Affairs [*Later Known as USIA,
then as ICA or USICA, then again as USIA*]
BECAIT........ Bezafibrate Coronary Atherosclerosis Intervention Trial
BECAMP ...... Ballistic Environmental Characteristics and Measurement Program
[*Army*] (AABC)
BECAN .... Biomedical Engineering Current Awareness Notification [*Database,
publication*] [*Brunel University*] [*Information service or system*]
(CRD)
BECBSG .... Big Eight Council on Black Student Government (EA)
BECC.......... Biomass Energy Coordinating Committee [*Department of Energy*]
BECC.......... British Empire Cancer Council
BECCA .... Business Espionage Controls and Countermeasures Association
(EA)
BECCE......... Basic Engineering Casualty Control Exercise [*Military*] (NVT)
B Ecc L........ Burn's Ecclesiastical Law [*A publication*] (DLA)
Bec Cr .... Beccaria on Crimes and Punishments [*A publication*] (DLA)
BECCR .... British Empire Cancer Campaign for Research [*Later, Cancer
Research Campaign*] (PDAA)
BECE.......... Bachelor of Electro-Chemical Engineering
BECEG .... Bureau Europeen de Controle et d'Etudes Generales
Be (Ceylon)... Beven's Ceylon Reports [*A publication*] (DLA)
BECF.......... Blood Extracellular Fluid [*Medicine*] (DMAA)
BECG.......... Bipartite Economics Control Group [*Post-World War II, Germany*]
BECG .... British Educational Contractors Group (AIE)
BECGF .... British Empire and Commonwealth Games Federation
BEC Gp .... BEC Group, Inc. [*Associated Press*] (SAG)
BEChem....... Bachelor of Chemical Engineering (ADA)
Bech Hist..... Bechard. Histoire du Droit Municipal [*A publication*] (DLA)
BECI.......... Bibliografia Espanola de Ciencias de la Informacion [*Database*]
[*Universidad Complutense de Madrid*] [*Spanish*] [*Information
service or system*] (CRD)
BECIP.......... Battlefords Early Childhood Intervention Home-Based Program Inc.
(AC)
Beck............ Beck's Colorado Reports [*12-16 Colorado and 1 Colorado Court of
Appeals*] [*A publication*] (DLA)
Beck (Colo)... Beck's Colorado Reports [*12-16 Colorado and 1 Colorado Court of
Appeals*] [*A publication*] (DLA)
Beck Med Jur... Beck's Medical Jurisprudence [*A publication*] (DLA)
BECKTRAN... Beckman Translation [*Programming language*] [*Beckman
Instruments, Inc.*]
BE CLEAR.... Bradford Community Learning and Education Resource (AIE)
BEc/LLB ...... Bachelor of Economics/Bachelor of Laws (ADA)
BECM.......... British Electrical Conduit Manufacturers
BECMA......... British Electro-Ceramic Manufacturers' Association (BI)
BECMG .... Becoming [*ICAO*] (FAAC)
BECN .... Backward-Explicit Congestion Notification [*Computer science*]
BECO .... Booster Engine Cutoff [*Rocketry*]
BECO .... Brown Engineering Co. (KSC)
BEcon .... Bachelor of Economics
BECOR .... Building Envelope Council of Ottawa Region (AC)
BECS.......... Basic Error Control System
BECS.......... Battlefield Electronic Communications System (DWSG)
BECS.......... Bulk Electronic Clearance System
BECSAS ...... Barclay Early Childhood Skill Assessment Center (EDAC)
BECSM......... British Electric Conduit Systems Manufacturers [*Later, British
Electrical Systems Association*] (PDAA)
BEc(SocSc)... Bachelor of Economics (Social Sciences)
BectDk .... Becton, Dickinson & Co. [*Associated Press*] (SAG)
BECTIS........ Bell College Technical Information Service, Hamilton [*British*] (NITA)
BECTO .... British Electric Cable Testing Organisation (MCD)
BECTU .... Broadcasting Entertainment Cinematograph and Theatre Union
[*British*] (EAIO)
BECUN .... Battelle's Educational Computer User's Network [*Battelle Memorial
Institute*] [*Information service or system*] (IID)
becwd.......... Beech (VRA)
B Ed............ Bachelor of Education

BED............ Bachelor of English Divinity
BED............ Bald Eagle [*District of Columbia*] [*Seismograph station code, US
Geological Survey Closed*] (SEIS)
BED............ Basic Engineering Development
BED............ Bedford [*Massachusetts*] [*Airport symbol*] (OAG)
BED............ Bedford, MA [*Location identifier FAA*] (FAAL)
BED............ Bedford Property Investors, Inc. [*NYSE symbol*] (SPSG)
BED............ Bedford Prop Investors(New) [*NYSE symbol*] (TTSB)
BED............ Block Error Detector (MCD)
BED............ Blue Diamond Energy [*Vancouver Stock Exchange symbol*]
BEd............ Board of Education
BED............ Board of Educational Development [*University of California, Berkeley*]
BED............ Box External Data
BED............ Bridge-Element Delay (IEEE)
BED............ Bureau of Export Development [*Department of Commerce*]
BED............ Business Equipment Digest [*British*] [*A publication*] (NITA)
BEDA .... British Electrical Development Association (DI)
BEDA .... British Entertainment and Dancing Association (DBA)
BEDA .... Bureau of European Designers Associations (EA)
BEDAC .... Burst Error Detection and Correlation
BedBath....... Bed Bath & Beyond, Inc. [*Associated Press*] (SAG)
BEDCE......... Basic Engineering Damage Control Exercise [*Military*] (NVT)
Bed Dr Comm... Bedarride. Droit Commercial [*A publication*] (DLA)
Bedell.......... Bedell's Reports [*163-191 New York*] [*A publication*] (DLA)
BEDFD .... Bedford [*Borough and county in England*]
Bedford........ Bedfordshire [*England*] (BARN)
BedfrdBc...... Bedford Bancshares, Inc. [*Associated Press*] (SAG)
BedfrdP....... Bedford Property Investors [*Associated Press*] (SAG)
BedfrdPr...... Bedford Property Investors, Inc. [*Associated Press*] (SAG)
BEDG .... Bedding
BEd(IndArts)... Bachelor of Education (Industrial Arts)
BEDIT.......... Boxed Edit [*Control*] [*Computer science*] (PCM)
BEDM.......... Builders Exchange of Detroit and Michigan (EA)
BEDO .... Burst EDO [*Extended Data Out*] [*Computer science*]
BEDOC......... Beds Occupied
BEd(Prelim)... Bachelor of Education (Preliminary Studies)
BEDR .... [*The*] Bureau for Excellence in Durham Region (AC)
BEDRM .... Bedroom [*Classified advertising*] (ADA)
bedrm.......... Bedroom (VRA)
BEDS .... Basic Education Development System (OICC)
BEDS .... Bedfordshire [*County in England*]
Beds .... Bedfordshire [*County in England*] (ODBW)
BEdSc .... Bachelor of Educational Science (ADA)
BEDSD .... Hillside Bedding [*NASDAQ symbol*] (TTSB)
BEdSt.......... Bachelor of Educational Studies (ADA)
BEdStud....... Bachelor of Educational Studies
BEDT........... Brooklyn Eastern District Terminal [*AAR code*]
BEd(TAFE) ... Bachelor of Education (Technical and Further Education)
BEd(TAS) .... Bachelor of Education (Technological and Applied Studies)
BEDT-TTF ... Bis(ethylenedithiolo)tetrathiafulvalene [*Organic chemistry*]
BEE .... Bachelor of Electrical Engineering
BEE .... Band Edge Energy
BEE .... Basal Energy Expenditure [*Nutrition*] (DMAA)
BEE .... Beecham Products-Western Hemisphere Research, Parsippany, NJ
[*OCLC symbol*] (OCLC)
Bee .... Bee's United States District Court Reports [*A publication*] (DLA)
BEE .... Benton, IL [*Location identifier FAA*] (FAAL)
BEE .... Bombardment Enhanced Etch Rate (IAA)
BEE .... Books for Equal Education [*An association Defunct*]
BEE .... Bureau of Educational Evaluation [*Research center*] (RCD)
BEE .... Business Efficiency Exhibition [*British*] (DIT)
BEE .... Busy Bee of Norway AS [*ICAO designator*] (FAAC)
BEEA .... British Educational Equipment Association (DS)
Bee Adm...... Bee's Admiralty. An Appendix to Bee's District Court Reports
[*A publication*] (DLA)
Bee Anal...... Beebee's Analysis of Common Law Practice [*A publication*] (DLA)
Beebas .... Beeba's Creations, Inc. [*Associated Press*] (SAG)
Beebe Cit..... Beebe's Ohio Citations [*A publication*] (DLA)
BEEC.......... Binary Erasure Channel (IEEE)
Bee CCR...... Bee's English Crown Cases Reserved [*A publication*] (DLA)
BEEF.......... Base Engineer Emergency Force [*Air Force*] (AFM)
BEEF.......... Business and Engineering Enriched FORTRAN [*Programming
language*] [*Sperry UNIVAC*]
BEEF.......... Western Beef, Inc. [*NASDAQ symbol*] (SPSG)
BEEFS......... Bypass Electronic Emergency Fuel System
BE/E INLS.... Basic Electricity and Electronics Individualized Learning System
[*Military*] (DNAB)
Beeler......... Beeler's Reports [*Tennessee*] [*A publication*] (DLA)
BEEM......... Beech Mountain Railroad Co. [*AAR code*]
BEEM......... Bureau Electronics Equipment Model [*Navy*] (MCD)
BEEO.......... Battlefield Electromagnetic Environment Office [*Fort Huachuca, AZ*]
[*United States Electronic Proving Ground*] (GRD)
BEEP.......... Battalion Equipment Evaluation Program [*DoD*]
BEEP.......... Black Executive Exchange Program [*of The National Urban
League*] (EA)
BEEP.......... Bureau Europeen de l'Education Populaire [*European Bureau of
Adult Education - EBAE*] (EAIO)
BEER.......... Battery Exhaust Emergency Recirculation (DNAB)
BEER.......... Big Rock Brewery [*NASDAQ symbol*] (SAG)
BEER.......... Binary-Element Error Ratio (IAA)
BEER.......... Biological Effects [*of Nonionizing*] Electromagnetic Radiation (MCD)
BEER.......... Bombardment Enhanced Etch Rate
BEER.......... Brief Easy Editing Routine (ADA)
BEERF......... Big Rock Brewery [*NASDAQ symbol*] (TTSB)
BEES.......... Basic Electricity and Electronics School [*Military*] (DNAB)

BEES	Battlefield Environmental Effects Software [*Army*]
BEET	Best-Estimated Evaluation Trajectory [*NASA*] (KSC)
BEF	Band Elimination Filter
BEF	Battalion Expeditionary Force (CINC)
BEF	Baughan, E. F., Baltimore MD [*STAC*]
BEF	Before
bef	Before (VRA)
BEF	Best Excitatory Frequency [*Neurophysiology*]
BEF	Blunt End Forward (KSC)
BEF	Bonus Expeditionary Force
BEF	Brazilian Expeditionary Force
BEF	British Empire Forces
BEF	British Equestrian Federation (DBA)
BEF	British Expeditionary Force
BEF	Bromine Efficiency Factor
BEF	Buffered Emitter Follower
BEFAP	Bell Laboratories FORTRAN Assembly Program [*Computer science*] (IEEE)
BEFC	Bob Everhart Fan Club (EA)
BEFE	Before
BEFEMENTD...	Before Mentioned [*Legal*] [*British*] (ROG)
BEFLIX	Bell FLICKS [*Programming language*] [*1973*] (CSR)
BEFM	Bending Form [*Tool*] (AAG)
BEFMC	British Educational Furniture Manufacturers Council (AIE)
BEFOURRA...	Belgian Fourragere [*Military decoration*]
BEFourragere...	Belgian Fourragere [*Military decoration*]
BEFS	Beta Environmental Fine Structure [*Physics*]
BEFT	Bureau of Education for Fair Trade
BEG	Beginning
beg	Beginning (VRA)
BEG	Being (ROG)
BEG	Belgrade [*Former Yugoslavia*] [*Airport symbol*] (OAG)
BEG	Brigade Engineer Group [*Marine Corps*] (CINC)
BEG	Budget Estimate Guidance [*Military*]
Begg Code...	Begg. Conveyancing Code [*Scotland*] [*A publication*] (DLA)
Begg L Ag ...	Begg. Law Agents [*Scotland*] [*A publication*] (DLA)
BEGL	Begleitung [*Accompaniment*] [*Music*]
BEGR	Bore Erosion Gauge Reading
BEGS	British and European Geranium Society (EAIO)
BEGTS	Book Edge Guilders' Trade Society (DGA)
BEH	Behavior (AAMN)
beh	Behaviorism [*Psychology*] (DAVI)
BEH	Beheaded (ROG)
BEH	Benign Exertional Headache [*Medicine*] (DMAA)
BEH	Benton Harbor [*Michigan*] [*Airport symbol*] (OAG)
BEH	Bibliografia General Espanola e Hispanoamericana [*A bibliographic publication*] [*Spain*]
BEH	Bureau of Education for the Handicapped [*Office of Education*] [*Later, SEP*]
BEHA	British Export Houses' Association (DS)
Behari	Revenue Reports of Upper Provinces [*India*] [*A publication*] (DLA)
BEHAV	Behavioral
Behav Sci & L...	Behavior Sciences and the Law [*A publication*] (DLA)
BEHD	Behind (ROG)
BEHEMOTH...	Big Electronic Human-Energized Machine, Only Too Heavy [*High technology*]
BEHF	Behalf (ROG)
BEHP	Bis(ethylhexyl) Phthalate [*Organic chemistry*]
BEHSTU	Behavioral Skills Training Unit [*Navy*] (DNAB)
BEHVL	Behavioral (AFM)
BEI	Banca Europea degli Investimenti [*European Investment Bank - EIB*] [*Italian*]
BEI	Banco Europeo de Inversion [*European Investment Bank - EIB*] [*Spanish*]
BEI	Banque d'Expansion Industrielle [*Industrial Development Bank*] [*Canada*]
BEI	Banque Europeenne d'Investissement [*European Investment Bank - EIB*] [*French*]
BEI	Bear River Range [*Idaho*] [*Seismograph station code, US Geological Survey*] (SEIS)
BEI	Beica [*Ethiopia*] [*Airport symbol*] (OAG)
BEI	Benair [*Italy ICAO designator*] (FAAC)
BEI	Benefit Eligibility Interview [*Unemployment insurance*] (OICC)
BEI	Berg Electronics [*NYSE symbol*] (TTSB)
BEI	Berg Electronics Corp. [*NYSE symbol*] (SAG)
BEI	Biological Exposure Index
BEI	Breakerless Electronic Ignition (DICI)
BEI	Bridgeport Engineering Institute [*Connecticut*]
BEI	Budget Enactment Instruction
BEI	Budget Executives Institute [*Later, PEI*] (EA)
BEI	Butanol-Extractable Iodine [*Clinical chemistry*]
BEIA	Bureau d'Education Ibero-Americain
BEIB	Biomedical Engineering and Instrumentation Branch [*National Institutes of Health*]
BEICIP	Bureau d'Etudes Industrielles et de Cooperation, Institut Francais du Petrole [*Office of Industrial Studies and Cooperation, French Institute of Petroleum*] [*Canada*]
BEID	Behavioral Effects of Infectious Diseases [*Army*]
BEI EI	BEI Electronics, Inc. [*Associated Press*] (SAG)
BEIF	Beifolgend [*Herewith*] [*German*]
BEIFC	Barbara Eden International Fan Club (EA)
beigeb	Beigebunden [*Bound With*] [*German*] (BARN)
BEII	BEI Electronics [*NASDAQ symbol*] (TTSB)
BEII	BEI Electronics, Inc. [*NASDAQ symbol*] (NQ)
BEIR	Biological Effects of Ionizing Radiation

BEIS	British Egg Information Service (DI)
BEISP	Beispiel [*Example*] [*Music*] [*German*]
BEITA	Business Equipment and Information Technology Association [*British*]
BEITC	Business Energy Investment Tax Credit [*IRS*]
Beitr	Beitraeg [*or Beitraege*] [*Contribution, Share*] [*German*] (OCD)
BEJ	Bannon, E. J., Buffalo NY [*STAC*]
bej	Beja [*MARC language code Library of Congress*] (LCCP)
BEJ	Berau [*Indonesia*] [*Airport symbol*] (OAG)
BEJ	Best Engineering Judgement [*Environmental Protection Agency*] (FFDE)
BEJ	Best Expert Judgment [*Environmental Protection Agency*] (ERG)
BEJE	Bureau Europeen de la Jeunesse et de l'Enfance
BEK	Becker Milk Co. Ltd. [*Toronto Stock Exchange symbol*]
Bek	Beechcraft Kingair [*Airplane code*]
BEK	Belbek-5P [*Ukraine*] [*FAA designator*] (FAAC)
BEK	Beli, AK [*Location identifier FAA*] (FAAL)
BEK	Bleached Eucalypt Kraft
BEK	Bovine Embryonic Kidney Cells [*Medicine*] (DMAA)
BEK	Butyl Ethyl Ketene [*Organic chemistry*]
BEKM	Bleached Eucalypt Kraft Mill
B El	Bachelor of Elocution
BEL	Bachelor of English Literature
BEL	Bahaa Esperanto-Ligo (EA)
BEL	Basic Equipment List (MCD)
BEL	Beleaguered (AABC)
BEL	Belem [*Brazil*] [*Airport symbol*] (OAG)
Bel	Belgian (ODBW)
BEL	Belgic [*Language*] (BARN)
BEL	Belgium [*ANSI three-letter standard code*] (CNC)
Bel	Belgium (ODBW)
Bel	Beling's Ceylon Reports [*A publication*] (DLA)
Bel	Belize (BARN)
BEL	Bell [*Computer science*] (DOM)
BEL	Bell-Air Executive Air Travel Ltd. [*New Zealand*] [*ICAO designator*] (FAAC)
Bel	Bellasis. Bombay Reports [*A publication*] (DLA)
BEL	Bell Atlantic Corp. [*NYSE symbol*] (SPSG)
BEL	Bell Character [*Keyboard*]
BEL	Belleville [*Diocesan abbreviation*] [*Illinois*] (TOCD)
Bel	Bellewe's English King's Bench Reports Tempore Richard II [*1378-1400*] [*A publication*] (DLA)
Bel	Bellinger's Reports [*4-8 Oregon*] [*A publication*] (DLA)
bel	Belorussian [*MARC language code Library of Congress*] (LCCP)
BEL	Below [*Technical drawings*]
BEL	Belsk [*Poland*] [*Seismograph station code, US Geological Survey Closed*] (SEIS)
BEL	Blood Ethanol Level [*Medicine*] (DMAA)
BEL	Book of English Literature [*A publication*]
BEL	Bovine Embryonic Lung [*Medicine*] (DMAA)
BEL	British Electrotechnical Committee (BARN)
BEL	British Empire League
BEL	Broad Emission Line [*Spectra*]
BEL	Bureau Equipment List (MCD)
BEL	Bus-Earth Tracking Station Link [*NASA*]
BEL	United States Army, TRADOC, Fort Belvoir, Van Noy Post Library, Fort Belvoir, V A [*OCLC symbol*] (OCLC)
BELA	Black Entertainment Lawyers Association [*Later, BESLA*] (EA)
BELAIR	Belgian Air Staff [*NATO*] (NATG)
Bel and Dr...	Bel and the Dragon [*Old Testament book*] [*Apocrypha*]
BEL AND DRAGON...	[*The*] History of the Destruction of Bel and the Dragon [*Apocrypha*]
BELB	Below Elbow [*Orthopedics*] (DAVI)
BelBcp	Belmont Bancorp [*Associated Press*] (SAG)
BELC	Black Employees of the Library of Congress (EA)
Bel Cas T R II...	Bellewe's Cases Tempore Richard II [*1378-1400*] [*A publication*] (ILCA)
BELCH	Belchamp [*England*]
Belco	Belco Oil & Gas Corp. [*Associated Press*] (SAG)
BELCRK	Bell Crank [*Automotive engineering*]
BELD	Battlefield Environment LASER Designator [*MIRADCOM*] (MCD)
BELD	Belden & Blake Corp. [*NASDAQ symbol*] (TTSB)
BELD	Belden & Blake Energy Co. [*NASDAQ symbol*] (SAG)
BeldBlk	Belden & Blake Energy Co. [*Associated Press*] (SAG)
Belden	Belden, Inc. [*Associated Press*] (SAG)
BeldHem	Belding Heminway Co., Inc. [*Associated Press*] (SAG)
BELDWSS	Battlefield Environment LASER Designator/Weapon System Simulation [*MIRADCOM*] (RDA)
B Ele	Bachelor of Elements
BElec&TelEng...	Bachelor of Electronics and Telecomunications Engineering (NADA)
BEL EX	Bel Exemplaire [*Typography*] (DGA)
Bel Ex	Bell on Excise [*A publication*] (DLA)
BELF	Belfast [*City in Northern Ireland*] (ROG)
BELF	Bel Fuse, Inc. [*NASDAQ symbol*] (NQ)
BELF	Bicyclists Educational and Legal Foundation (EA)
BELF	Break-Even Load Factor (IIA)
BELFOX	Belgian Futures and Options Exchange [*Stock exchange*] [*Belgium*] (EY)
BelFuse	Bel Fuse, Inc. [*Associated Press*] (SAG)
BELG	Belgium
Belg	Belgium (VRA)
BelgAE	Belgian Antarctic Expedition [*1897-99, 1957-58*]
Belg Jud	Belgique Judiciaire [*A publication*] (ILCA)
Belg P	Belgium Pharmacopoeia [*A publication*]
Belg Rev Int'l L...	Belgian Review of International Law [*A publication*] (DLA)

BELINDIS..... Belgian Information and Dissemination Service [*European host database system*] [*Ministry of Economic Affairs*] (IID)

Beling......... Beling's Ceylon Reports [*A publication*] (DLA)

Beling & Van... Beling and Vanderstraaten's Ceylon Reports [*A publication*] (DLA)

BelJud .... Bellum Judaicum [*Josephus*] [*Classical studies*] (BJA)

BELK........... Elkford Public Library, British Columbia [*Library symbol National Library of Canada*] (NLC)

Bell............ Bellasis. Bombay Reports [*A publication*] (DLA)

BELL........... Bell Bancorp [*NASDAQ symbol*] (TTSB)

BELL........... Bell Bancorp, Inc. [*NASDAQ symbol*] (SAG)

Bell............ Bell. Calcutta Reports [*A publication*] (DLA)

Bell............ Bellewe's English King's Bench Reports [*A publication*] (DLA)

Bell............ Bellinger's Reports [*4-8 Oregon*] [*A publication*] (DLA)

Bell............ Bell's Cases in the Scotch Court of Session [*A publication*] (DLA)

Bell............ Bell's English Crown Cases Reserved [*169 English Reprint*] [*A publication*] (DLA)

Bell............ Bell's Scotch Appeal Cases [*A publication*] (DLA)

BELL........... Binary Envelope Locked Loop (MCD)

Bell............ Brooke's New Cases (Collected by Bellewe) [*A publication*] (DLA)

Bell 8vo ...... Bell's Octavo Reports, Scotch Court of Sessions [*1790-92*] [*A publication*] (DLA)

BELLAD........ Belladonna [*Deadly Nightshade (or its medicinal extract)*] (ROG)

BELLADON... Belladonna [*Deadly Nightshade (or its medicinal extract)*] (ROG)

Bell Ap Ca ... Bell's Scotch Appeal Cases [*A publication*] (DLA)

Bell App ...... Bell's House of Lords Scotch Appeal Cases [*1842-50*] [*A publication*] (DLA)

Bell App Bell (SC)... Bell's House of Lords Scotch Appeal Cases [*1842-50*] [*A publication*] (DLA)

Bell App Cas... Bell's House of Lords Scotch Appeal Cases [*1842-50*] [*A publication*] (DLA)

Bell Arb ...... Bell's Law of Arbitration in Scotland [*A publication*] (DLA)

Bellas .... Bellasis. Civil Cases [*Bombay*] [*A publication*] (DLA)

Bellas .... Bellasis. Criminal Cases [*Bombay*] [*A publication*] (DLA)

Bellasis ...... Bombay Sadr Diwani Adalat Reports [*A publication*] (DLA)

BellAtl........ Bell Atlantic Corp. [*Associated Press*] (SAG)

Bell Aw....... Bell's Law of Awards [*A publication*] (DLA)

BellBcp....... Bell Bancorp, Inc. [*Associated Press*] (SAG)

Bell C .... Bell's Reports, Court of Session [*1790-92*] [*Scotland*] [*A publication*] (DLA)

BellCabl....... Bell Cablemedia Ltd. [*Associated Press*] (SAG)

Bell Cas....... Bell's Cases in the Scotch Court of Session [*A publication*] (DLA)

Bell Cas T Hen VIII... Brooke's New Cases, English King's Bench [*1515-58*] [*A publication*] (DLA)

Bell Cas T H VIII... Brooke's New Cases (Collected by Bellewe) [*A publication*] (DLA)

Bell Cas T Rich II... Bellewe's English King's Bench Reports Tempore Richard II [*1378-1400*] [*A publication*] (DLA)

Bell Cas T R II... Bellewe's English King's Bench Reports Tempore Richard II [*1378-1400*] [*A publication*] (DLA)

Bell CC .... Bellasis. Civil Cases [*Bombay*] [*A publication*] (DLA)

Bell CC .... Bellasis. Criminal Cases [*Bombay*] [*A publication*] (DLA)

Bell CC .... Bell's English Crown Cases Reserved [*169 English Reprint*] [*A publication*] (DLA)

Bell CC (Eng)... Bell's English Crown Cases Reserved [*169 English Reprint*] [*A publication*] (DLA)

Bell CHC..... Bell's Reports, High Court of Calcutta [*India*] [*A publication*] (DLA)

Bell Comm... Bell's Commentaries on the Laws of Scotland [*A publication*] (DLA)

Bell Convey... Bell. Lecture on Conveyancing [*Scotland*] [*A publication*] (DLA)

Bellcore....... Bell Communications Research, Inc. (TSSD)

Bell Cr C ..... Beller's Criminal Cases [*Bombay*] [*A publication*] (DLA)

Bell Cr C...... Bell's English Crown Cases [*A publication*] (DLA)

Bell Cr Ca.... Beller's Criminal Cases [*Bombay*] [*A publication*] (DLA)

Bell Cr Ca.... Bell's English Crown Cases [*A publication*] (DLA)

Bell Cr Cas... Beller's Criminal Cases [*Bombay*] [*A publication*] (DLA)

Bell Cr Cas... Bell's English Crown Cases [*A publication*] (DLA)

Bell CT .... Bell. Competing Titles [*Scotland*] [*A publication*] (DLA)

Bell Ct of Sess Fol R... Bell's Decisions, Scotch Court of Session [*A publication*] (DLA)

Bell Deeds... Bell. System of the Forms of Deeds [*Scotland*] [*A publication*] (DLA)

Bell Del ...... Beller's Delineations of Universal Law [*A publication*] (DLA)

Bell Dict ...... Bell's Dictionary and Digest of the Laws of Scotland [*A publication*] (DLA)

Bell Dict Dec... Bell's Dictionary of Decisions, Scotch Court of Session [*A publication*] (DLA)

Bell Elec..... Bell. Election Law of Scotland [*A publication*] (DLA)

Beller.......... Bellerophon [*of Euripides*] [*Classical studies*] (OCD)

Belles Let.... Belles Lettres [*A publication*] (BRI)

Bellewe .... Bellewe's English King's Bench Reports [*A publication*] (DLA)

Bellewe (Eng)... Bellewe's English King's Bench Reports [*A publication*] (DLA)

Bellewe's Ca Temp Hen VIII... Brooke's New Cases, English King's Bench [*1515-58*] [*A publication*] (DLA)

Bellewe's Ca Temp R II... Bellewe's Cases Tempore Richard II [*1378-1400*] [*A publication*] (DLA)

Bellewe T H VIII... Brooke's New Cases (Collected by Bellewe) [*A publication*] (DLA)

Bell Exp Test... Bell on Expert Testimony [*A publication*] (DLA)

Bell Fol....... Bell's Folio Reports, Scotch Court of Session [*1794-95*] [*A publication*] (DLA)

Bell HC .... Bell's Reports, High Court of Calcutta [*India*] [*A publication*] (DLA)

Bell HL .... Bell's House of Lords Scotch Appeal Cases [*1842-50*] (DLA)

Bell HL Sc... Bell's House of Lords Scotch Appeal Cases [*1842-50*] [*A publication*] (DLA)

Bell HW....... Bell. Property as Arising from the Relation of Husband and Wife [*1849*] [*A publication*] (DLA)

BellHwl....... Bell & Howell Holdings Co. [*Associated Press*] (SAG)

Bell Illus...... Bell's Illustrations of Principles [*A publication*] (DLA)

Bell (In)....... Bell's Reports, High Court of Calcutta [*India*] [*A publication*] (DLA)

BellInd........ Bell Industries, Inc. [*Associated Press*] (SAG)

Bellinger...... Bellinger's Reports [*4-8 Oregon*] [*A publication*] (DLA)

Bellingh Tr... Report of Bellingham's Trial [*A publication*] (DLA)

Belli's Mod Trials... Belli's Modern Trials [*A publication*] (DLA)

BellJud .... De Bello Judaico [*Josephus*] (BJA)

Bell L & T ... Bell on Landlord and Tenant [*Bengal*] [*A publication*] (DLA)

Bell Leas .... Bell on Leases [*Scotland*] [*A publication*] (DLA)

BELLMATIC... Bell Laboratories Machine-Aided Technical Information Center (DIT)

Bell Med LJ... Bell's Medico-Legal Journal [*A publication*] (DLA)

BellMic....... Bell Microproducts, Inc. [*Associated Press*] (SAG)

Bell No .... Bell's Supplemented Notes to Hume on Crimes [*A publication*] (DLA)

Bell Oct ...... Bell's Octavo Reports, Scotch Court of Sessions [*1790-92*] [*A publication*] (DLA)

Bell (Or) ..... Bellinger's Reports [*4-8 Oregon*] [*A publication*] (DLA)

Bell PC .... Bell's Cases in Parliament: Scotch Appeals [*A publication*] (DLA)

Bell Prin ..... Bell's Principles of the Law of Scotland [*10 eds.*] [*1829-99*] [*A publication*] (DLA)

Bell Put Mar... Bell's Putative Marriage Case [*Scotland*] [*A publication*] (DLA)

BELLREL...... Bell Laboratories Library Real-Time Loan System

Bell S .... Bell. Sale of Food and Drugs [*14th ed.*] [*1968*] [*A publication*] (DLA)

Bell Sale .... Bell. Sale of Food and Drugs [*14th ed.*] [*1968*] [*A publication*] (DLA)

Bell's App... Bell's House of Lords Scotch Appeal Cases [*1842-50*] [*A publication*] (DLA)

Bell Sc App... Bell's Appeals to House of Lords from Scotland [*A publication*] (DLA)

Bell Sc App Cas... Bell's Scotch Appeal Cases [*A publication*] (DLA)

Bell Sc Cas... Bell's Cases in the Scotch Court of Session [*A publication*] (DLA)

Bell Sc Dig... Bell's Scottish Digest [*A publication*] (DLA)

Bell's Comm Bell's... Commentaries on Laws of Scotland [*7 eds.*] [*1800-70*] [*A publication*] (DLA)

Bell Scot Dig... Bell's Scottish Digest [*A publication*] (DLA)

Bell's Dict ... Bell's Dictionary of Decisions, Scotch Court of Session [*A publication*] (DLA)

Bell Ses Cas... Bell's Cases in the Scotch Court of Session [*A publication*] (DLA)

BellSo........ BellSouth Corp. [*Associated Press*] (SAG)

BellSpt........ Bell Sports Corp. [*Associated Press*] (SAG)

Bell Sty ...... Bell. System of the Forms of Deeds (Styles) [*Scotland*] [*A publication*] (DLA)

BellTch....... Bell Technology Group Ltd. [*Associated Press*] (SAG)

Bell TD .... Bell. Testing of Deeds [*Scotland*] [*A publication*] (DLA)

BellTech...... Bell Technology Group Ltd. [*Associated Press*] (SAG)

BELLTEL...... Bell Telephone

Bell UL .... Beller's Delineation of Universal Law [*A publication*] (DLA)

Bellweth ..... Bellwether Expl Co. [*Associated Press*] (SAG)

Bellweth ..... Bellwether Exploration Co. [*Associated Press*] (SAG)

BELM.......... Bell Microproducts [*NASDAQ symbol*] (TTSB)

BELM.......... Bell Microproducts, Inc. [*NASDAQ symbol*] (SAG)

Belmac....... Belmac Corp. [*Associated Press*] (SAG)

BelmH........ Belmont Homes [*Associated Press*] (SAG)

BELNAV...... Belgian Naval Staff [*NATO*] (NATG)

BeloAH....... Belo [*A.H.*] Corp. [*Associated Press*] (SAG)

Bel Prob ..... Belknap's Probate Law of California [*A publication*] (DLA)

BELRA........ British Empire Leprosy Relief Association

BelS........... [*The*] Best Love Story Poems [*A publication*]

BelSSR .... Byelorussian Soviet Socialist Republic

BELT.......... Bell Tech Group Ltd [*NASDAQ symbol*] (TTSB)

BELT.......... Bell Technology Group Ltd. [*NASDAQ symbol*] (SAG)

Belt Bro ...... Belt's Edition of Brown's Chancery Reports [*1778-94*] [*A publication*] (DLA)

Belt's Supp (Eng)... Belt's Supplement to Vesey, Senior's, English Chancery Reports [*1746-56*] [*A publication*] (DLA)

Belt Sup ..... Belt's Supplement to Vesey, Senior's, English Chancery Reports [*1746-56*] [*A publication*] (DLA)

Belt Supp.... Belt's Supplement to Vesey, Senior's, English Chancery Reports [*1746-56*] [*A publication*] (DLA)

Belt Sup Ves... Belt's Supplement to Vesey, Senior's, English Chancery Reports [*1746-56*] [*A publication*] (DLA)

BELTUG ...... Belgian Telecommunications User Group (ACRL)

Belt Ves Sen... Belt's Edition of Vesey, Senior's, English Chancery Reports [*A publication*] (DLA)

BELTW....... Bell Technology Wrrt [*NASDAQ symbol*] (TTSB)

BeLU.......... Universite de Liege, Liege, Belgium [*Library symbol Library of Congress*] (LCLS)

BELW......... Bellwether Exploration [*NASDAQ symbol*] (TTSB)

BELW......... Bellwether Exploration Co. [*NASDAQ symbol*] (NQ)

BEM........... Bachelor of Engineering of Mines

BEM........... Bachelor of Mining Engineering

BEM........... Back Emergency Speed (DNAB)

BEM........... Ballistic Evaluation Motor (MCD)

BEM........... Basic Editor Monitor [*Computer science*] (MHDI)

BEM........... Behavior Engineering Model (EDAC)

bem........... Bemba [*MARC language code Library of Congress*] (LCCP)

BEM........... Bergstrom Capital [*AMEX symbol*] (SPSG)

BEM........... Big Emerging Markets (ACII)

BEM........... Biological Effect Monitoring [*Toxicology*]

BEM........... Boundary Element Method (IAA)

BEM........... British Empire Medal

BEM........... Bug-Eyed Monster [*Science fiction or fantastic literature which makes great use of monsters in its storyline or illustrations*]

BEM........... Bureau of Executive Manpower [*Civil Service Commission*]

BEM........... Business Executives Move for New National Priorities [*An association*] (EA)

BEM .... Business Executives Move for Peace [*An association*] (VNW)
BEM .... Buthylethylmagnesium [*Organic chemistry*]
BEM .... Enderby and District Museum, Enderby, British Columbia [*Library symbol National Library of Canada*] (NLC)
BEM .... Montreal City & District Savings Bank [*Toronto Stock Exchange symbol*]
BEMA .... Bakery Equipment Manufacturers Association (EA)
BEMA .... British Essence Manufacturers' Association (BI)
BEMA .... Business Equipment Manufacturers Association [*Later, CBEMA*]
BEMAC .... British Exports Marketing Advisory Committee [*Defunct*]
BemaGold... Bema Gold Corp. [*Associated Press*] (SAG)
BEMAR .... Backlog of Essential Maintenance and Repair (AFM)
BEMAS .... British Education Management and Administration Society (DBA)
BEMB .... Bituminous Equipment Manufacturers Bureau [*Later, BAEB*] (EA)
BEMB .... British Egg Marketing Board (DI)
BE-ME .... Bachelor of Engineering in Mechanical Engineering
BEME .... Brigade Electrical and Mechanical Engineer [*Military British*]
BEMF .... Back Electromotive Force (DEN)
BEMI .... Biciklista Esperantista Movado Internacia [*International Movement of Esperantist Bicyclists - IMEB*] (EAIO)
BEMI .... Bio-Electro-Magnetics Institute (EA)
Bemidji St U... Bemidji State University (GAGS)
Bemis .... Bemis Co., Inc. [*Associated Press*] (SAG)
BeMMR........ Besseler. Musik des Mittelalters und der Renaissance [*A publication*]
BEMO........... Bare Equipment Modernization Officer [*Military*] (DNAB)
BEMO........... Base Equipment Management Office [*Air Force*] (AFM)
BEMP .... Bubble Electromagnetic Pulse
BEMPEX ...... Barotropic Electromagnetic and Pressure Experiment [*North Pacific, 1986-87*] [*Marine science*] (OSRA)
BEMS .... Bakery Equipment Manufacturers Society (PDAA)
BEMS .... Bioelectromagnetics Society (EA)
BEMS .... British Energy Management Systems
BEMS .... Building-Energy Management System
BEMSA .... British Eastern Merchant Shippers' Association (BI)
BEMSEE...... British Motor Cycle Racing Club (DBA)
BEM SIG ..... Bioelectromagnetics Special Interest Group (EA)
BEMT .... Basic Electronics Maintenance Trainer
BEMT .... Bureau of Health Professions Education and Manpower Training [*HEW*]
BEMV........... Belladonna Mottle Virus [*Plant pathology*]
BEn .... Bachelor of Engineering
B En .... Bachelor of English
BEN .... Bene [*Well*] [*Pharmacy*]
BEN .... Benedictio [*Blessing*] [*Latin*] (ADA)
Ben .... Benedict's United States District Court Reports [*A publication*] (DLA)
BEN .... Beneficiary [*Legal shorthand*] (LWAP)
ben .... Benefit Performance [*Theater*] [*Slang*] (WDMC)
ben .... Bengali [*MARC language code Library of Congress*] (LCCP)
Ben .... Bengal Law Reports [*India*] [*A publication*] (DLA)
BEN .... Benghazi [*Libya*] [*Airport symbol*] (OAG)
BEN .... Benin [*ANSI three-letter standard code*] (CNC)
Ben .... Benloe's English King's Bench and Common Pleas Reports [*A publication*] (DLA)
BEN .... Bennett College, Greensboro, NC [*OCLC symbol*] (OCLC)
BEN .... Bennington Aviation, Inc. [*ICAO designator*] (FAAC)
BEN .... Bermuda - Navy [*Bermuda*] [*Seismograph station code, US Geological Survey Closed*] (SEIS)
BEN .... Bus Enable [*Computer science*] (MHDI)
Ben .... De Beneficiis [*of Seneca the Younger*] [*Classical studies*] (OCD)
BEN .... Franklin Resources [*NYSE symbol*] (TTSB)
BEN .... Franklin Resources, Inc. [*NYSE symbol*] (SPSG)
BENA .... Belgian Engineers in North America [*Defunct*] (EA)
BENA .... British Empire Naturalist Association
Ben Adm...... Benedict's American Admiralty Practice [*A publication*] (DLA)
Ben Adm Prac... Benedict's American Admiralty Practice [*A publication*] (DLA)
Ben & D ...... Benloe and Dalison's English Common Pleas Reports [*A publication*] (DLA)
Ben & Dal ... Benloe and Dalison's English Common Pleas Reports [*A publication*] (DLA)
Ben & HLC... Bennett and Heard's Leading Criminal Cases [*England*] [*A publication*] (DLA)
Ben & S Dig... Benjamin and Slidell's Louisiana Digest [*A publication*] (DLA)
Ben Av .... Stephen and Benecke on Average [*A publication*] (DLA)
BenchE .... Benchmark Electronics, Inc. [*Associated Press*] (SAG)
BENCOM ...... Beneficial Communications [*Computer system*] [*Beneficial Management Corp.*]
BEN CS .... Bengal Civil Service [*British*] (ROG)
BEND .... Bend [*Commonly used*] (OPSA)
B-END......... Beta-Endorphin [*Biochemistry*]
BENDEX .... Beneficiary Data Exchange System [*between state welfare agencies and the Social Security Administration*]
Bendl .... Bendloe's [*or Benloe's*] English Common Pleas [*1531-1628*] [*A publication*] (DLA)
Bendloe .... Bendloe's [*or Benloe's*] Reports, English Common Pleas [*Edition of 1661*] [*A publication*] (DLA)
B en Dr........ Bachelier en Droit [*Bachelor of Laws*] [*French*]
BENDS .... Both Ends
Bene .... Benedict's United States District Court Reports [*A publication*] (DLA)
Bene .... Benedictus de Isernia [*Flourished, 1221-52*] [*Authority cited in pre-1607 legal work*] (DSA)
BENE........... Beneficiary
BENECHAN... BENELUX [*Belgium, Netherlands, Luxembourg*] Subarea Channel [*NATO*] (NATG)
BENED .... Benedictine
Bened .... Benedict's United States District Court Reports [*A publication*] (DLA)

Benedict ...... Benedict's United States District Court Reports [*A publication*] (DLA)
Benef .... Beneficial Corp. [*Associated Press*] (SAG)
BENEF......... Beneficiary (AFM)
BenefCp....... Beneficial Corp. [*Wall Street slang name: "Big Nose Louie"*] [*Associated Press*] (SAG)
Benefit Series UCIS... United States Social Security Board Unemployment Compensation Interpretation Service. Benefit Series [*A publication*] (DLA)
BENEFL........ Beneficial (ROG)
BENEFY........ Beneficiary (ROG)
BENELUX ..... Belgium, Netherlands, Luxembourg [*Economic union*]
Benet Ct-M... Benet on Military Law and Courts-Martial [*A publication*] (DLA)
Beneton .... Benetton Group SpA [*Associated Press*] (SAG)
BENEV .... Benevolent (ROG)
BenEye .... Benson Eyecare Corp. [*Associated Press*] (SAG)
Ben FB........ Full Bench Rulings, High Court [*Fort William, Bengal*] [*A publication*] (DLA)
Ben FI Cas... Bennett's Fire Insurance Cases [*A publication*] (DLA)
B Eng .... Bachelor of Engineering
BENG .... Basic Engineering (DNAB)
BENG .... Bengal
BENG .... Bengali [*Language, etc.*] (ROG)
Beng .... Bengal Law Reports [*India*] [*A publication*] (DLA)
B Eng A ...... Bachelor of Agricultural Engineering
BEng and Man... Bachelor of Mechanical Engineering, Manufacture, and Management [*British*] (DBQ)
BEng/BBus... Bachelor of Engineering/Bachelor of Business
BEng-Civil... Bachelor of Engineering - Civil
BEngE .... Bachelor of Electrical Engineering
BEng-Elec... Bachelor of Engineering - Electrical
BEng-Elect... Bachelor of Engineering - Electrical
Beng LR ...... Bengal Law Reports [*India*] [*A publication*] (DLA)
Beng LR App Cas... Bengal Law Reports, Appeal Cases [*India*] [*A publication*] (DLA)
Beng LRPC... Bengal Law Reports, Privy Council [*India*] [*A publication*] (DLA)
Beng LR Supp... Bengal Law Reports, Supplement [*India*] [*A publication*] (DLA)
BEng-Mech... Bachelor of Engineering - Mechanical
B Engr .... Bachelor of Engineering (WGA)
B Eng S ...... Bachelor of Engineering Science (WGA)
BEngSc .... Bachelor of Engineering Science (ADA)
BEngSci ...... Bachelor of Engineering Science (NADA)
Beng SDA.... Bengal Sadr Diwani Adalat Cases [*India*] [*A publication*] (DLA)
BengtB......... Benguet Corp. [*Associated Press*] (SAG)
B Eng (Tech).. Bachelor of Engineering (Technology)
Beng Zillah... Decisions of the Zillah Courts, Lower Provinces [*India*] [*A publication*] (DLA)
Benhn .... Benihana National Corp. [*Associated Press*] (SAG)
BENHS .... British Entomological and Natural History Society
Benihan .... Benihana National Corp. [*Associated Press*] (SAG)
Ben in Keil... Benloe's English King's Bench Reports [*73 English Reprint*] [*1531-1628*] [*A publication*] (DLA)
Ben Ins........ Benecke on Marine Insurance [*A publication*] (DLA)
Ben Ins Cas... Bennett's Insurance Cases [*A publication*] (DLA)
Benj .... Benjamin on Sales of Personal Property [*1868-1955*] [*A publication*] (DLA)
Benj .... Benjamin's New York Annotated Cases [*A publication*] (DLA)
Benj Chalm Bills & N... Benjamin's Chalmer's Bills and Notes [*A publication*] (DLA)
BenJerry...... Ben & Jerry's Homemade, Inc. [*Associated Press*] (SAG)
Benj Sa........ Benjamin on Sales of Personal Property [*1868-1955*] [*A publication*] (DLA)
Benj Sales... Benjamin on Sales of Personal Property [*1868-1955*] [*A publication*] (DLA)
Ben Just ...... Benedict's New York Civil and Criminal Justice [*A publication*] (DLA)
Benl .... Benloe and Dalison's English Common Pleas Reports [*A publication*] (DLA)
Benl .... Benloe's English King's Bench Reports [*73 English Reprint*] [*1531-1628*] [*A publication*] (DLA)
Benl & D ..... Benloe and Dalison's English Common Pleas Reports [*A publication*] (DLA)
Benl & Dal... Benloe and Dalison's English Common Pleas Reports [*A publication*] (DLA)
Benl & D (Eng)... Benloe and Dalison's English Common Pleas Reports [*A publication*] (DLA)
Benl (Eng) ... Benloe's English King's Bench Reports [*73 English Reprint*] [*1531-1628*] [*A publication*] (DLA)
Benl in Ashe... Benloe at the End of Ashe's Tables [*A publication*] (DLA)
Benl in Keil... Benloe in Keilway's Reports [*A publication*] (DLA)
Benl KB .... Benloe's English King's Bench Reports [*73 English Reprint*] [*1531-1628*] [*A publication*] (DLA)
Benl New..... Benloe's English King's Bench and Common Pleas Reports [*A publication*] (DLA)
Benloe .... Benloe's English King's Bench Reports [*73 English Reprint*] [*1531-1628*] [*A publication*] (DLA)
Benl Old ...... Benloe and Dalison's English Common Pleas Reports [*A publication*] (DLA)
BenM........... Benediktinische Monatsschrift [*A publication*] (BJA)
Ben Monroe... Ben Monroe's Kentucky Reports [*A publication*] (DLA)
Benn .... Bennett's Reports [*1 Dakota*] [*A publication*] (DLA)
Benn .... Bennett's Reports [*1 California*] [*A publication*] (DLA)
Benn .... Bennett's Reports [*16-21 Missouri*] [*A publication*] (DLA)
Benn & H Cr Cas... Bennett and Heard's Leading Criminal Cases [*England*] [*A publication*] (DLA)
Benn & H Dig... Bennett and Heard's Massachusetts Digest [*A publication*] (DLA)

Benn & H Lead Crim Cas... Bennett and Heard's Leading Criminal Cases [*England*] [*A publication*] (DLA)
Benn Cal...... Bennett's Reports [*1 California*] [*A publication*] (DLA)
Benn (Dak)... Bennett's Dakota Cases [*A publication*] (DLA)
Benne...... Reporter of Vol. 7, Modern Reports [*England*] [*A publication*] (DLA)
Benn Farm... Bennett's Rights and Liabilities of Farmers [*A publication*] (DLA)
Benn Fl Cas... Bennett's Fire Insurance Cases [*A publication*] (DLA)
BEN NI...... Bengal Native Infantry [*Military British*] (ROG)
Bennington C... Bennington College (GAGS)
Benn (MO)... Bennett's Missouri Cases [*A publication*] (DLA)
Benn Pr MC... Bennett's Dissertation on Practice of Masters in Chancery [*A publication*] (DLA)
Benn Rec..... Bennett on Receivers [*A publication*] (DLA)
BENNY SUGG... Beneficial Suggestions [*Program*]
BENNY SUGGS... Beneficial Suggestions [*Program*] (DNAB)
Ben Ord...... Benevolent Orders (DLA)
BENREP....... Big Ben Report [*World War II*]
BENS......... Bounded Error Navigation System (MCD)
BENS......... Business Executives for National Security (EA)
BEN SC...... Bengal Staff Corps [*Military British*] (ROG)
BENS/ED.... Business Executives for National Security Education Fund (EA)
BensonF...... Benson Financial Corp. [*Associated Press*] (SAG)
BEN SUG... Beneficial Suggestions [*Program*] (DNAB)
B Ent.......... Bachelor of Entomology
BENT........ Beginning Evening Nautical Twilight
Bent........... Bentley's Irish Chancery Reports [*A publication*] (DLA)
B Ent......... Black Enterprise [*A publication*] (BRI)
BENT.......... Breast Exposure National Trends [*Study*] [*FDA*]
Bent Abr ..... Benton's Abridgement of the Debates of Congress [*A publication*] (DLA)
Bent Cod..... Bentham's Codification [*A publication*] (DLA)
Bent Const Code... Bentham's Constitutional Code for All Nations [*A publication*] (DLA)
Bent Ev....... Bentham's Judicial Evidence [*A publication*] (DLA)
Benth Ev...... Bentham on Rationale of Judicial Evidence [*A publication*] (DLA)
Benth Jud Ev... Bentham on Rationale of Judicial Evidence [*A publication*] (DLA)
Bent Jud Ev... Bentham's Judicial Evidence [*A publication*] (DLA)
Bent Jud Ev... Bentham's Judicial Evidence [*A publication*] (DLA)
Bentl Atty-Gen... Bentley's Reports [*13-19 Attorneys-General's Opinions*] [*A publication*] (DLA)
Bent Mor Leg... Bentham's Principles of Morals and Legislation [*A publication*] (DLA)
BentOG .... Benton Oil & Gas Co. [*Associated Press*] (SAG)
Bent Pack Jur... Bentham's Act of Packing as Applied to Special Juries [*1821*] [*A publication*] (DLA)
BentPh........ Bentley Pharmaceutical [*Associated Press*] (SAG)
Bent Pun...... Bentham's Rationale of Punishment [*A publication*] (DLA)
Bent The Leg... Bentham's Theory of Legislation [*A publication*] (DLA)
BEnvSc .... Bachelor of Environmental Science
BEnvSci ...... Bachelor of Environmental Science
BENZ........... Benzidine [*Carcinogen*]
BEO......... Banquet Event Order [*Food service industry*]
BEO........... Basque Educational Organization (EA)
BEO........... Belmont [*Australia Airport symbol*]
BEO........... Belmont Resources [*Vancouver Stock Exchange symbol*]
BEO........... Beograd [*Belgrade*] [*Yugoslavia*] [*Seismograph station code, US Geological Survey*] (SEIS)
beO........... Beryllium Oxide (IDOE)
BEO........... Black Elected Official
BEO........... Body Engineering Office
BEO........... Broadcast Engineering Officer (ADA)
BEOA .... British and European Osteopathic Association [*Sutton, Surrey, England*] (EAIO)
BEOC .... Battery Echelon Operating Control (AFM)
BEOG .... Basic Educational Opportunity Grants [*Office of Education*]
BEOL .... Bent's Old Fort National Historic Site
BEOP .... Best Estimate of Orbital Parameters
BEP............ Bachelor of Engineering Physics
BEP............ Back-End Processor [*Computer*] (TSSD)
BEP............ Basic Education Program (EDAC)
BEP............ Basic Element of Performance [*Medicine*] (DMAA)
BEP............ Battalion Etranger de Parachutistes [*Foreign Battalion of Parachutists*] [*French Foreign Legion*]
Bep............ Bepaling [*Provision in statute or contract*] [*Netherlands*] (ILCA)
BEP............ Beppu [*Japan*] [*Seismograph station code, US Geological Survey Closed*] (SEIS)
BEP............ Best Efficiency Point (KSC)
BEP............ Bet Ltd. ADS [*NYSE symbol Toronto Stock Exchange symbol*] (SPSG)
BEP............ BET Public Ltd ADS [*NYSE symbol*] (TTSB)
BEP............ Biological Effects Program [*IDOE project*] [*Terminated, 1978*] (MSC)
BEP............ Biomolecular Engineering Program [*EC*] (ECED)
BEP............ BIT [*Binary Digit*] Error Probability [*Computer science*] (KSC)
BEP............ Black Employment Program (EPA)
BEP............ Bleomycin, Etoposide, Platinol [*Cisplatin*] [*Antineoplastic drug regimen*]
BEP............ Border Ecology Project [*Staff consists of Americans and Mexicans concerned with environmental issues*] (CROSS)
BEP............ Brain Evoked Potential [*Neurophysiology*]
BEP............ Brain Stem Evoked Potential [*Neurology*] (DAVI)
BEP............ British Equestrian Promotions, Inc.
BEP............ Budget Execution Plan [*Army*]
BEP............ Bureau of Engraving and Printing [*Department of the Treasury*]
BEP............ Business Emergency Plan
BEP............ Perry, GA [*Location identifier FAA*] (FAAL)

BEPA......... Bald Eagle Protection Act [*1940*]
BEPA......... Basic Engineering Product Assumption
BEPA......... Binding Energy per Atom (IAA)
BEPA......... British Egg Products Association (DI)
BEPC......... Beijing Electron-Positron Collider [*High-energy physics*] [*China*]
BEpc......... Blood Erythrocytes Particle Counter [*Medicine*]
BEPC......... British Electrical Power Convention (MCD)
BEPD......... Basic Entry Pay Date
BEPD......... Bureau of Educational Personnel Development [*HEW*]
BEPD......... Butyl-ethyl-propanediol [*Organic chemistry*]
BEPE......... Body Engineering Product Engineering
BEPEO........ Body Engineering Product Engineering Office
BE Phy........ Bachelor of Engineering Physics
BePI.......... Benzo(e)pyridoindole [*Organic chemistry*]
BEPI......... Budget Estimates Presentation Instructions (AFM)
BEPI......... Bureau of Elec Pub [*NASDAQ symbol*] (TTSB)
BEPI......... Bureau of Electronic Publishing, Inc. [*NASDAQ symbol*] (SAG)
BEPIW .... Bureau Electr Pubg Wrrt [*NASDAQ symbol*] (TTSB)
BePJ.......... Beautiful Poems on Jesus [*A publication*]
BEPN......... Defence Research Establishment Pacific, Canada Department of National Defence [*Centre de Recherches pour la Defense Pacifique, Ministere de la Defense Nationale*] Esquimalt, British Columbia [*Library symbol National Library of Canada*] (NLC)
BEPO......... British Experimental Pile Operation [*Nuclear reactor*] (DEN)
BEPOC .... Burroughs Electrographic Printer-Plotter for Ordnance Computing
BEPP......... Binding Energy per Particle (IAA)
BEPP........... Biometry and Epidemiology Program [*Department of Health and Human Services*] (GFGA)
BEPQ .... Bureau of Entomology and Plant Quarantine [*Department of Agriculture*] [*Functions transferred to ARS, 1953*]
BEPS......... Building Energy Performance Standards
BEPTI.......... Bionomics, Environment, Plasmodium, Treatment, Immunity [*Malaria epidemiology*] (AAMN)
BEQ.......... Bachelor Enlisted Quarters
BEQ.......... Bequeath [*Legal term*] (WDAA)
BEQ.......... Bessemer, AL [*Location identifier FAA*] (FAAL)
BEQ.......... Best Estimated Quantity (AAGC)
BEQ.......... Binary Encoded Quaternary (MCD)
BEQD......... Bequeathed [*Legal term*]
BEQT.......... Bequest
BEQTH........ Bequeath [*Legal term*] (ROG)
BEQTHD ...... Bequeathed [*Legal term*]
BER.......... Air Berlin, USA [*Germany ICAO designator*] (FAAC)
BER.......... Basal Energy Requirement [*Nutrition*]
BER.......... Base-Excision Repair [*Genetics*]
BER.......... Basic Electrical Rhythm [*Neurophysiology*]
BER.......... Basic Encoding Rule [*Telecommunications*] (OSI)
BER.......... Bearings, Inc. [*NYSE symbol*] (SPSG)
BeR.......... Before the Romantics [*A publication*]
Ber.......... Berakhot [*or Berakot*] (BJA)
ber.......... Berber [*MARC language code Library of Congress*] (LCCP)
BER.......... Bergen [*Norway*] [*Seismograph station code, US Geological Survey*] (SEIS)
BER.......... Bergen Community College, Paramus, NJ [*OCLC symbol*] (OCLC)
BER.......... Berlin [*Germany*] [*Airport symbol*] (OAG)
Ber.......... Bernardus Compostellanus, Senior [*Flourished, 1198-1216*] [*Authority cited in pre-1607 legal work*] (DSA)
Ber.......... Bernardus de Bottone de Parma [*Deceased, 1266*] [*Authority cited in pre-1607 legal work*] (DSA)
BER.......... Bern Resources Ltd. [*Vancouver Stock Exchange symbol*]
Ber.......... Berton's New Brunswick Reports [*A publication*] (DLA)
BER.......... Best Evidence Rule [*Legal shorthand*] (LWAP)
BER.......... Beyond Economical Repair (MCD)
BER.......... Biological and Environmental Research Program [*Department of Energy*]
BER.......... Biological Energy Research [*Department of Energy*]
BER.......... BIT [*Binary Digit*] Effectiveness Report (CAAL)
BER.......... BIT [*Binary Digit*] Error Rate [*Computer science*]
BER.......... Blue Emerald Resources [*Vancouver Stock Exchange symbol*]
BER.......... Board for Engineers' Registration (ACII)
BER.......... Bremerton, WA [*Location identifier FAA*] (FAAL)
BER.......... Budget Execution Review [*Army*] (AABC)
BER.......... Built-In Bit Error Rate [*Computer science*]
BER.......... Bureau of Economic Regulation [*of CAB*]
BER.......... Bureau of Equipment and Recruiting [*Abolished, 1914*] [*Navy*]
BERA......... Biomass Energy Research Association (EA)
BERA .... Brain Stem Evoked Response Audiometry [*Neurology and otorhinolaryngology*] (DAVI)
BERA .... British Educational Research Association
BERA .... Business Education Research of America [*Hato Rey, PR*] (EA)
BerADev...... Berlin Airlift Device [*Military decoration*] (AABC)
Berar......... Berar Law Journal [*India*] [*A publication*]
BERBOH....... British Examining and Registration Board in Occupational Hygiene
BERC......... Bartlesville Energy Research Center [*Department of Energy*]
BERC......... Biomedical Engineering Research Corp. [*Illinois*]
BERC......... Black Economic Research Center (EA)
BERC......... Black Educational Resources Center [*Later, BMCERC*] (EA)
BERC......... Business and Economic Research Center [*Middle Tennessee State University*] [*Research center*] (RCD)
BERCO........ British Electric Resistance Co. (IAA)
BERCOMB... Berlin Commission British [*Post-World War II*]
Ber Compos... Bernardus Compostellanus [*Authority cited in pre-1607 legal work*] (DSA)
BERCON....... Berlin Contingency [*NATO*] (NATG)

BERD .... Bureau of Economic Research and Development [*Virginia State University*] [*Research center*] (RCD)

BERD .... Business Expenditure Research and Development

BERD .... East European Development Bank [*Acronym is based on foreign phrase*]

BERD .... Office of Buildings Energy Research and Development [*Department of Energy*]

BERDEV ...... Berlin Airlift Device [*Military decoration*]

BERE .... Bureau of Educational Research and Evaluation [*Mississippi State University*] [*Research center*] (RCD)

BERF .... Business Education Research Foundation (EA)

berg .... Iceberg (ODBW)

BergBr .... Bergen Brunswig [*Associated Press*] (SAG)

BergCa .... Bergstrom Capital Corp. [*Associated Press*] (SAG)

BergElc .... Berg Electronics Corp. [*Associated Press*] (SAG)

BergHld .... Berger Holdings, Inc. [*Associated Press*] (SAG)

BERH .... Board of Engineers for Rivers and Harbors [*Army*]

BerHald .... Bernard Haldane [*Commercial firm Associated Press*] (SAG)

BERH-RSP ... Board of Engineers for Rivers and Harbors Resident Scholar Program [*Fort Belvoir, VA*] [*Army*]

BERI .... Bernadia [*Italy*] [*Seismograph station code, US Geological Survey*] (SEIS)

BERI .... Biomolecular Engineering Research Institute [*Formerly, PERI*] [*Japan*]

BERI .... Business Environment Risk Information [*Information service or system*] (IID)

Ber Is .... Bermuda Islands (BARN)

BERJAYA ..... Bersatu Rakyat Jelata Sabah [*Sabah People's Union*] [*Malaysia*] [*Political party*] (PPW)

BERK .... Berkeley [*England*]

Berk .... Berkeley [*California*] (BARN)

BerkGs........ Berkshire Gas Co. [*Associated Press*] (SAG)

BerkH.......... Berkshire Hathaway [*Associated Press*] (SAG)

BerkHa........ Berkshire Hathaway, Inc. [*Associated Press*] (SAG)

Berkley .... Berkley [*W.R.*] Corp. [*Associated Press*] (SAG)

Berkly .... Berkely [*W.R.*] Corp. [*Associated Press*] (SAG)

BerkR.......... Berkshire Realty Co., Inc. [*Associated Press*] (SAG)

BerkRty........ Berkshire Realty Company, Inc. [*Associated Press*] (SAG)

BERKS .... Berkshire [*County in England*]

Berks .... Berkshire [*County in England*] (ODBW)

BERL .... Berlin (ROG)

BERL .... Beryl [*Jewelry*] (ROG)

Berl Abh ...... Abhandlungen der Preussische Akademie der Wissenschaften zu Berlin [*A publication*] (OCD)

Berlitz.......... Berlitz International [*Associated Press*] (SAG)

BERM .... Basic Encyclopedic Redundancy Media (IEEE)

BERM.......... Bermuda (DLA)

BERM.......... Binary Entity-Relationship Model [*Computer science*] (HGAA)

BERM.......... Biological and Environmental Reference Materials

BERM.......... BIT [*Binary Digit*] Error Rate Monitor

Ber May ...... Bernardus Maynardi [*Authority cited in pre-1607 legal work*] (DSA)

Bern .... Bernard's Church Cases [*Ireland*] [*A publication*] (DLA)

Bern .... Bernardus de Bottone de Parma [*Deceased, 1266*] [*Authority cited in pre-1607 legal work*] (DSA)

Bernar .... Bernardus de Bottone de Parma [*Deceased, 1266*] [*Authority cited in pre-1607 legal work*] (DSA)

Bern Ch Cas... Bernard's Church Cases [*Ireland*] [*A publication*] (DLA)

BERP .... British Experimental Rotor Program

BERPM .... Basic Exchange Rate Planning Model [*Telecommunications*] (TEL)

BerRabb ...... Bereshit Rabba (BJA)

Berry .... Berry's Reports [*1-28 Missouri Appeals*] [*A publication*] (DLA)

Berry C .... Berry College (GAGS)

BERRY F V... Berry, Fruit, or Vegetable [*Freight*]

BerryP .... Berry Petroleum Co. [*Associated Press*] (SAG)

BERS .... Bureau of Educational Research and Service [*Memphis State University*] [*Research center*] (RCD)

BERS .... Bureau of Educational Research and Service [*University of Tennessee at Knoxville*] [*Research center*] (RCD)

Ber Sachs Ges Wiss... Berichte. Verhandlungen der Saechsischen Gesellschaft der Wissenschaf ten zu Leipzig [*A publication*] (OCD)

BERSEAPAT... Bering Sea Patrol [*Navy*]

BERT.......... Basic Energy Reduction Technology (IEEE)

Bert........... Berton's New Brunswick Reports [*A publication*] (DLA)

Bert........... Bertrandus [*Authority cited in pre-1607 legal work*] (DSA)

BERT.......... Bertucci's, Inc. [*NASDAQ symbol*] (SPSG)

BERT.......... BIT [*Binary Digit*] Error Rate Test [*Computer science*]

BERTH .... Berthing

Bertr .... Bertrandus de Montefaventino [*Deceased, 1342*] [*Authority cited in pre-1607 legal work*] (DSA)

Bertran .... Bertrandus [*Authority cited in pre-1607 legal work*] (DSA)

Bertuci........ Bertuccis, Inc. [*Associated Press*] (SAG)

BERW .... Berwick [*Former county in Scotland*] (WGA)

Berwicks...... Berwickshire [*County in England*]

BES .... Aero Services Executive [*France ICAO designator*] (FAAC)

BES .... Bachelor of Engineering Sciences

BES .... Bachelor of Environmental Studies

BES .... Bachelor of Science in Engineering

BES .... Balanced Electrolyte Solution [*Physiology*]

BES .... Bank Education Service [*British*] (BI)

BES .... Basic Energy Sciences Program [*Department of Energy*] [*Washington, DC*]

BES .... Basic Executive System [*Honeywell, Inc.*]

BES .... Batch Execution System [*Computer science*] [*Engineering*]

BES .... Behavior Evaluation Scale [*Educational testing*]

BES .... Bennettsville, SC [*Location identifier FAA*] (FAAL)

Bes .... Besah (BJA)

BES .... Besancon [*France*] [*Seismograph station code, US Geological Survey*] (SEIS)

BES .... Bessel Function [*Mathematics*] (IAA)

BES .... Bet 'Eked Sefarim (BJA)

BES .... Binocular Earth Sensor (MCD)

BES .... Bioelectrochemical Society (EA)

BES .... Biological Engineering Society [*British*]

BES .... Biomass Energy Systems Program [*Department of Energy*]

BES .... Bis(hydroxyethyl)aminoethanesulfonic Acid [*A buffer*] [*Organic chemistry*]

BES .... Black Enamel Slate (MSA)

BES .... Block Error Status (IAA)

BES .... Booster Exhaust Stream

BES .... Bose-Einstein Statistics

BES .... Brest [*France*] [*Airport symbol*] (OAG)

BES .... British Ecological Society

BES .... British Empire Series [*A publication*]

BES .... British Endodontic Society

BES .... Broadcast Executives Society (AC)

BES .... Bromoethanesulfonic Acid [*Organic chemistry*]

BES .... Budget Estimate Submission [*DoD*]

BES .... Buildings and Equipment Section [*Library Administration and Management Association*]

BES .... Bulletin d'Epigraphie Semitique [*A publication*] (BJA)

BES .... Bureau of Employment Security [*Later, US Employment Service*] [*Department of Labor*]

BES .... Business Expansion Scheme [*British*]

BES .... Saskatoon Board of Education [*UTLAS symbol*]

BESA .... Bank Export Services Act [*1982*]

BESA .... British Earth Sheltering Association (DBA)

BESA .... British Educational Suppliers Association (AIE)

BESA .... British Electrical Systems Association (DBA)

BESA .... British Engineering Standards Association

BESA .... British Ex-Services Association [*Australia*]

BESA .... Building Energy Systems Analysis Project [*Public Works Canada*]

BESAC .... Basic Energy Sciences Committee [*Department of Energy Washington, DC*] (EGAO)

BESc .... Bachelor of Engineering Science

BESC .... Binary Electronics Sequence Computer (BARN)

BESD .... Bank Economic and Social Database [*World Bank*] [*United Nations*] (DUND)

BESD .... Basic Enlisted Service Date (AABC)

BESE .... Bureau of Elementary and Secondary Education [*Office of Education*]

BESEP.......... Base Electronics System Engineering Plan (NG)

BESERL........ Behavior and Systems Research Laboratory [*Army*]

BESEX.......... Bering Sea Expedition [*or Experiment*]

BESFA.......... Bakery Employees and Salesmen's Federation of Australia

BESI .... BioProcess Engineering Society International (EA)

BESI .... Black Educational Services, Inc.

Besicp .... Besicorp Group [*Associated Press*] (SAG)

BESIF .... BE Semiconductor Indus [*NASDAQ symbol*] (TTSB)

BESL .... British Empire Service League

BESLA .... Black Entertainment and Sports Lawyers Association (EA)

BESM .... Bovine Embryo Skeletal Muscle

BESMA........ British Electrostatic Manufacturers Association (DBA)

BESMEX...... Bering Sea Marine Mammal Experiment [*National Oceanic and Atmospheric Administration*] (MSC)

BESO .... Bank of England Staff Organisation

BESO .... British Executive Service Overseas [*Overseas Development Administration*] (DS)

BESOM .... Brookhaven Energy System Optimization Model (MCD)

BESP .... Basic Energy Sciences Program [*Department of Energy*] [*Washington, DC*]

BESP .... Bovine Embryonic Spleen Cells [*Medicine*] (DMAA)

BESRL .... Behavior and Systems Research Laboratory [*Arlington, VA*] [*Army*] (IEEE)

BESS .... Basic Enlisted Submarine School [*Navy*] (DOMA)

BESS .... Battery Energy Storage System (DWSG)

BESS .... Beneficiary Evaluation Survey Service [*LIMRA*]

BESS .... Bessemer [*Metallurgy*]

BESS .... Binary Electromagnetic Signal Signature

BESS .... Biomedical Experiment Scientific [*or Support*] Satellite [*NASA*] (NASA)

BESS .... Bolton Environmental Sensing System (NOAA)

BESS .... Bottom Environmental Sensing System

B es SC ...... Bachelier es Sciences [*Bachelor of Science*] [*French*] (ROG)

Bess Prec ... Besson's New Jersey Precedents [*A publication*] (DLA)

BESSY .... Berlin Electron Storage Ring for Synchrotron Radiation

BEST .... Ballastable Earthmoving Sectionalized Tractor [*Formerly, UET*] [*Army*]

BEST .... Ballistic Evaluation Static Test (MCD)

BEST .... Bare Essentials of Surface Transfer

BEST .... Basic Educational Skills Test

BEST .... Basic Educational Skills through Technology Project [*U.S. Department of Education*] (EDAC)

BEST .... Basic Essential Skills Testing

BEST .... Basic Executive Scheduler and Timekeeper (PDAA)

BEST .... Basic Extraction Sludge Treatment

BEST .... Battery Energy Storage Test

BEST .... Beginning Entrepreneurial Support Team

BEST .... Behavioral Skills Training [*Navy*]

BEST .... Best Building Economic Solutions Together [*Committee redesigning the defunct Charleston Navy Base and Shipyard*] (ECON)

BEST .... Best Educational Systems for Teaching

BEST............ Best Products [*NASDAQ symbol*] (TTSB)
BEST............ Best Products Co., Inc. [*NASDAQ symbol*] (SAG)
BEST............ Better Electronic Service Technicians
BEST............ Black Efforts for Soul in Television
BEST............ Blockhouse Equipment Switching Test (SAA)
BEST............ Board of Environmental Studies and Toxicology [*NRC*]
BEST............ Booster Exhaust Study Test [*NASA*] (NASA)
BEST............ Breast Examination through Simultaneous Temperature Evaluation
BEST............ British Expertise in Science and Technology [*Longman Cartermill Ltd.*] [*Scotland*] [*Information service or system*] (IID)
BEST............ Broad-Based Enhanced Savings Tax
BEST............ Bureau of Evaluative Studies and Testing [*Indiana University*] [*Research center*] (RCD)
BEST............ Business EDP [*Electronic Data Processing*] Systems Technique [*NCR Corp.*] (IEEE)
BEST............ Business Equipment Software Techniques [*Computer science*]
Best & S...... Best and Smith's English Queen's Bench Reports [*A publication*] (DLA)
Best & S (Eng)... Best and Smith's English Queen's Bench Reports [*A publication*] (DLA)
Best & Sm... Best and Smith's English Queen's Bench Reports [*A publication*] (DLA)
BestB.......... Best Buy Capital Ltd. [*Associated Press*] (SAG)
Best Beg & Rep... Best on the Right to Begin and Reply [*A publication*] (DLA)
BestBuy....... Best Buy Co. [*Associated Press*] (SAG)
Best Ev....... Best on Evidence [*A publication*] (DLA)
Best Jur Tr... Best on Trial by Jury [*A publication*] (DLA)
Best Law Dic... Best's Law Dictionary [*A publication*] (DLA)
BestPd......... Best Products Company, Inc. [*Associated Press*] (SAG)
Best Pres... Best on Presumptions of Law and Fact [*A publication*] (DLA)
Best Presumptions... Best on Presumptions of Law and Fact [*A publication*] (DLA)
BESTS.......... Belgian Educational Student Travel Service
BESW(UK)A... British Ex-Services Womens (United Kingdom) Association
BET............. Bachelor of Engineering Technology
BET............. Background Elimination Technique (MCD)
BET............. Balanced-Emitter Technology (IAA)
BET............. Balanced Expansion Technique (MCD)
BET............. Basic Economics Test [*Educational test*]
BET............. Beltec Enterprises Ltd. [*Vancouver Stock Exchange symbol*]
BET............. Bennett's Transport [*Commercial firm British*]
BET............. Bentley College, Waltham, MA [*OCLC symbol*] (OCLC)
BET............. Best Estimate of Trajectory [*Apollo*] [*NASA*]
BET............. Bethel [*Alaska*] [*Seismograph station code, US Geological Survey Closed*] (SEIS)
BET............. Bethlehem Corp. [*AMEX symbol*] (SPSG)
BET............. Between (KSC)
bet............. Between (VRA)
BET............. Billet [*Bill*] [*French Business term*] (ROG)
BET............. Binary Encoded Ternary (MCD)
BET............. Black Entertainment Television [*Cable-television system*]
BET............. Blow-Out Emergency Team [*British government*]
BET............. Boundary Element Tape [*Computational Mechanics Ltd.*] [*Software package*] (NCC)
BET............. Bridge Educational Trust Ltd. [*British*]
BET............. [*The*] British Electric Traction Co. Ltd.
BET............. Brunauer-Emmett-Teller [*Adsorption equation*]
BET............. Business English Test [*Vocational guidance test*]
BET............. Business Experience Training (BARN)
BETA.......... Babcock Easy Terminal Access System (MCD)
BETA.......... Balanced Extravehicular Training Aircraft [*NASA*]
BETA.......... Basic English for Testing Applications (PDAA)
BETA.......... Basic Extension to Alpha [*Alaska long period array*]
BETA.......... Battlefield Exploitation and Target Acquisition (MCD)
Beta.......... Betamax [*First home VCR (Video Cassette Recorder) format*] (CDE)
BETA.......... Bilingual Evaluation Technical Assistance Project (EDAC)
BETA.......... Billion Channel Extraterrestrial Assay [*Search for intelligent life*]
BETA.......... Birth Education, Training, and Acceptance
BETA.......... Boeing Engineering Thermal Analyzer (MCD)
BETA.......... British Equestrian Trade Association (IAA)
BETA.......... Broadcasting and Entertainment Trades Alliance [*A union*] [*British*] (EAIO)
BETA.......... Business Equipment Trade Association [*London, England*]
BETAP........ Bell Laboratories Formula Translation Assembly Program (IAA)
BETC.......... Bartlesville Energy Technology Center [*Later, NIPER*] [*Department of Energy Bartlesville, OK*] [*Information service or system*] (GRD)
BETC.......... Broadcast, Execute This Command [*Telecommunications*] [*Electronics*] (ECII)
BETE.......... Benzilic Acid Tropine Ester [*Also, BAT, BTE*] [*Pharmacology*]
BETFOR....... Headquarters British Element Trieste Forces
BethCp........ Bethlehem Corp. [*Associated Press*] (SAG)
BethI.......... Bethlemita, Daughters of the Sacred Heart of Jesus (TOCD)
BethIBc....... Bethel Bancorp [*Associated Press*] (SAG)
BethId........ Bet Holdings, Inc. [*Associated Press*] (SAG)
BethStl....... Bethlehem Steel Corp. [*Associated Press*] (SAG)
BET Isotherm... Brunauer-Emmett-Teller Isotherm [*Adsorption isotherm equation*]
BETM.......... American Wagering, Inc. [*NASDAQ symbol*] (SAG)
BETM.......... Amer Wagering [*NASDAQ symbol*] (TTSB)
BETN.......... Between (ROG)
BETNET....... Bilingual Education Telecommunications Network [*National Clearinghouse for Bilingual Education*] [*Wheaton, MD*] (TSSD)
BET Plc....... BET PLC [*Associated Press*] (SAG)
BETR.......... Basic Exchange Telephone Radio [*Telecommunications*] (TNIG)
BETR.......... Betreffend [*Referring To*] [*German*]
BETR.......... Better
BETRO........ British Export Trade Research Organisation

BetrRG........ Betriebsrategesetz [*Law on Works Councils*] [*German*] (ILCA)
BetrVG........ Betriebsverfassungsgesetz [*Law on the Representation of Workers and Works Councils*] [*German*] (ILCA)
BETS.......... Benign Epileptiform Transients of Sleep [*Neurology*] (DAVI)
BETS.......... Black Elderly Twin Study [*National Institute on Aging*]
BETS.......... Bullseye Engineering and Technical Services (DNAB)
BETS.......... Florida Gaming [*NASDAQ symbol*] (TTSB)
BETS.......... Florida Gaming Corp. [*NASDAQ symbol*] (SAG)
BEtSS......... Better Education thru Simplified Spelling (EA)
BETT.......... Bettis Corp. [*NASDAQ symbol*] (SAG)
BETT.......... Bolt Extrusion Thrust Termination (MCD)
BETT.......... British Education and Training Technology Exhibition (ITD)
BETT.......... Buildings Energy Technology Transfer Program [*Canada*]
Bettis........ Bettis Corp. [*Associated Press*] (SAG)
Betts' Adm Pr... Betts' Admiralty Practice [*A publication*] (DLA)
Betts' Dec.... Blatchford and Howland's United States District Court Reports [*A publication*] (DLA)
Bett's Dec.... Olcott's United States District Court Reports [*A publication*] (DLA)
BETV.......... Bald Eagle Total Value
BETW.......... Between (ROG)
BETY.......... BEATTY, NV [*Commercial waste site*] (GAAI)
BetzDearb.... BetzDearborn, Inc. [*Associated Press*] (SAG)
BetzLb........ Betz Laboratories, Inc. [*Associated Press*] (SAG)
BEU........... Basic Encoding Unit
BEU........... Bedourie [*Australia Airport symbol Obsolete*] (OAG)
BEU........... Bellevue Oil & Minerals [*Vancouver Stock Exchange symbol*]
BEU........... BENELUX Economische Union [*Belgium, Netherlands, and Luxembourg Economic Union*] (EAIO)
BEU........... Best Estimate Unconstrained
BEU........... British Empire Union
BEU........... Independent Bakery Employees Union
BEUC.......... Bureau Europeen des Unions de Consommateurs [*European Bureau of Consumers' Unions*] (EAIO)
BEUL.......... Building Energy Utilization Laboratory [*Iowa State University*] [*Research center*] (RCD)
BEV........... Baboon Endogenous Virus
BEV........... Baculovirus Expression Vector [*Biochemistry*]
BEV........... Barrier-Equivalent Velocity [*Automotive safety*]
BEV........... Beersheba [*Israel*] [*Airport symbol Obsolete*] (OAG)
BEV........... Bevatron
BEV........... Bevel
bev........... Bevel (VRA)
bev........... Beverage (DMAA)
BEV........... Beverage
BEV........... Beverage
BEV........... Beverley [*Jamaica*] [*Seismograph station code, US Geological Survey Closed*] (SEIS)
BEV........... Beverly Enterprises [*NYSE symbol*] (SPSG)
BeV........... Billion Electron Volts
BEV........... Bird's-Eye-View
BEV........... Black English Vernacular [*Dialect*]
BEV........... Bovine Enterovirus
BEV........... Broadway Beverages [*Vancouver Stock Exchange symbol*]
BEVA.......... British Equine Veterinary Association (DBA)
BEVA.......... British Exhibition Venues Association
BEVALAC.... Bevatron/Super-HILAC [*Combination of accelerators*]
Bev & M...... Bevin and Mill's Reports [*Ceylon*] [*A publication*] (DLA)
Bev & Sieb... Beven and Siebel's Reports [*Ceylon*] [*A publication*] (DLA)
BEVB.......... Beverly Bancorporation, Inc. [*NASDAQ symbol*] (SAG)
BevBanc...... Beverly Bancorporation, Inc. [*Associated Press*] (SAG)
Bev Ceylon... Beven's Ceylon Reports [*A publication*] (ILCA)
Bev Emp L... Bevin on Employer's Liability for Negligence of Servants [*A publication*] (DLA)
Beven........ Beven on Negligence in Law [*1889-1928*] [*A publication*] (DLA)
Beven........ Beven's Ceylon Reports [*A publication*] (DLA)
Bev Hills BAJ... Beverly Hills Bar Association. Journal [*A publication*] (DLA)
Bev Hom...... Bevil on Homicide [*A publication*] (DLA)
Bev Pat....... Bevill's Patent Cases [*England*] [*A publication*] (DLA)
BEVR.......... Broadcast Electronic Video Recording (IAA)
Bevrly........ Beverly Enterprises [*Associated Press*] (SAG)
BevT.......... Bev-Tyme, Inc. [*Associated Press*] (SAG)
BEVT.......... Bev-Tyme, Inc. [*NASDAQ symbol*] (SAG)
BEVTC........ Bev-Tyme Inc. [*NASDAQ symbol*] (TTSB)
BEVTP........ Bev Tyme 10% Cv'C' Pfd [*NASDAQ symbol*] (TTSB)
BevTym....... Bev-Tyme, Inc. [*Associated Press*] (SAG)
BEVTZ........ Bev-Tyme Inc.Wrrt'C' [*NASDAQ symbol*] (TTSB)
BEW........... Beira [*Mozambique*] [*Airport symbol*] (OAG)
BEW........... Board of Economic Warfare [*World War II*]
BEW........... British Electronics Week [*Trade show*] (ITD)
BEW........... Butanol/Ethanol/Water [*Solvent system*]
BEWA.......... British Effluent and Water Association [*Trade association*]
Bew & N Pr... Bewley and Naish on Common Law Procedure [*A publication*] (DLA)
BeWiU......... Universitaire Instelling Antwerpen, Wilrijk, Belgium [*Library symbol Library of Congress*] (LCLS)
BEWT.......... Bureau of East-West Trade [*Department of Commerce*]
B Ex.......... Bachelor of Expression
BEX........... Baden Explorations [*Vancouver Stock Exchange symbol*]
Bex........... Base Excess [*Biochemistry*] (DAVI)
BEX........... Benin Air Express [*ICAO designator*] (FAAC)
BEX........... Bexhill Museum [*British*]
BEX........... Bloomfield, IA [*Location identifier FAA*] (FAAL)
BEX........... Board of Examiners for the Foreign Service [*Department of State*]
BEX........... Broadband Exchange [*Western Union communication system*]
BEX........... Broadcast Exchange (IAA)
BEX........... Extecapital Ltd. [*NYSE symbol*] (SPSG)

BExA	British Exporters Association (DBA)
BEXA	Business Efficiency Exhibition [*Business Equipment Association of South Africa*]
B Exam J	Bar Examination Journal [*A publication*] (DLA)
BEXEC	Budget Execution [*Army*] (AABC)
BEXPr	Extecapital Ltd'A'Pref [*NYSE symbol*] (TTSB)
BEY	Beirut [*Lebanon*] [*Airport symbol*] (OAG)
BEY	Bond Equivalent Yield [*Business term*] (EMRF)
BEY	Butte, MT [*Location identifier FAA*] (FAAL)
BEYN	Beynhurst [*England*]
BEZ	Baldor Electric [*NYSE symbol*] (SAG)
BEZ	Baldor Electric [*NYSE symbol*] (TTSB)
B/EZ	Beautiful Music/Easy Listening [*Radio station format*] (WDMC)
BEZ	Beru [*Kiribati*] [*Airport symbol*] (OAG)
Bez.	Bezah (BJA)
BEZ	Bezueglich [*Concerning*] [*German*]
BEZ G	Loris, SC [*Location identifier FAA*] (FAAL)
Bez G	Bezirksgericht [*District Court*] [*German*] (DLA)
Bez Ger	Bezirksgericht [*District Court*] [*German*] (DLA)
BEZW	Beziehungsweise [*Respectively*] [*German*]
BF	Bachelor of Finance
BF	Bachelor of Forestry
BF	Backdoor Financing [*Public debt transactions*] [*Investment term*]
BF	Backface (MSA)
BF	Back Face (SAA)
BF	Back Fat [*Animal husbandry*]
BF	Back-Feed
BF	Back Focal
BF	Back Folded [*Freight*]
BF	Back Full Speed (DNAB)
BF	Backup Force
BF	Baha'i Faith
bf	Bahamas [*MARC country of publication code Library of Congress*] (LCCP)
BF	Bandpass Filter
BF	Bankruptcy Fee (ADA)
BF	Banque de France [*Bank of France*]
BF	Banqueting/Catered Functions [*Public-performance tariff class*] [*British*]
BF	Bark Forager [*Ornithology*]
BF	Barren Foundation [*Defunct*] (EA)
BF	Barrier Filter [*Medicine*]
BF	Basal Fold
BF	Base File
BF	Base Frequency (ADA)
BF	Base Funded (AFM)
BF	Base Fuze
BF	Batch Fabrication
BF	Battle Fatigue (INF)
BF	Battleship Firing (SAA)
BF	Bayonet Fighting
BF	Beam-Foil (PDAA)
BF	Beam Forming
BF	Bearing Factor [*Mechanical engineering*]
BF	Beaten Favourite [*Horse racing*] [*British*]
BF	Beat-Frequency
BF	Beef (ROG)
BF	Beer Firkin
BF	Before Flight (MCD)
BF	Belgian Fourragere [*Military decoration*]
BF	Bellerive Foundation (EAIO)
BF	Bengal Fusiliers [*British military*] (DMA)
BF	Bentonite Flocculation [*Test*]
B/F	Best and Final Offer
BF	Best Fit Algorithm [*Mathematics*] (IAA)
BF	Best Friend [*Initialism used by author E. B. White to describe his wife*]
BF	Beverly Foundation (EA)
BF	Bibelforskaren (BJA)
BF	Bibliotherapy Forum [*Association of Specialized and Cooperative Library Agencies*]
BF	Biceps Femoris [*A muscle*] [*Anatomy*]
BF	Bile Flow [*Physiology*]
BF	Black Female
BF	Black Filly [*Horse racing*] (ROG)
BF	Black Firsts [*A publication*]
BF	Blank Flange
BF	Blast Furnace [*Ironmaking*]
BF	Blastogenic Factor [*Immunochemistry*]
BF	Bleeding Frequency [*Medicine*]
B/F	Blip/Frame (CET)
BF	Blocking Factor
BF	Blood Flow [*Medicine*]
BF	Bloody Fool [*British slang*]
BF	Blue Affirmative Flag [*Navy British*]
BF	Blues Foundation (EA)
BF	Board-Foot
BF	Boat Foreman (DNAB)
BF	Boiler Feed [*Technical drawings*]
BF	Bold Face [*Printing term*]
bf	Boldface [*Typography*] (WDMC)
BF	Bonae Feminae [*To the Good Woman*] [*Latin*]
BF	Bona Fide [*In Good Faith*] [*Latin*]
BF	Bond Fund [*Finance*]
BF	Bone Formation
BF	Bone Fragment [*Orthopedics*] (DAVI)
BF	Bonum Factum [*A Good or Proper Act, Deed, or Decree*] [*Latin Legal term*] (DLA)
BF	Boring Fixture (MCD)
BF	Born Fool (DAS)
BF	Borough Fiscal [*British*] (ROG)
BF	Both Faces [*Technical drawings*]
BF	Bottom Face [*Technical drawings*]
BF	Bouillon Filtre [*Bouillon Filtrate*]
B/F	Bound/Free [*Ratio*] [*Biochemistry*]
BF	Boyfriend [*Slang*]
BF	Branching Filter [*Telecommunications*] (TEL)
BF	Brandon Films, Inc.
BF	Brazed Joint-Face Fed (DNAB)
BF	Breadalbane Fencibles [*British military*] (DMA)
BF	Breaker Failure (IAA)
BF	Breakfast Fed (MAE)
BF	Breakthrough Foundation (EA)
BF	Breast Fed [*Medicine*]
BF	Bridge/Forecastle [*of a ship*] (DS)
BF	Brief
BF	Bring Forward
BF	Bristol Fighter [*Aircraft*] [*World War I*]
BF	British Forces (DMA)
BF	Broadband Frequency
BF	Bronze Floors [*On ships*]
BF	Broth Filtrate [*Microbiology*]
BF	Brought Forward [*Business term*]
BF	Brown-Forman [*NYSE symbol*] (SPSG)
BF	Brown Forman, Inc. [*NYSE symbol*] (SAG)
BF	Buffered [*Medicine*]
BF	Burkina Faso [*ANSI two-letter standard code*] (CNC)
BF	Burning Feet Syndrome [*Medicine*] (DMAA)
BF	Burnup Fraction [*of fuel in plasma*] (MCD)
BF	Butter Fat (MAE)
BF	Deny's Tuberculin [*Medicine*] (DAVI)
BF	Disputation between Bird and Fish (BJA)
BF	Fernie Public Library, British Columbia [*Library symbol National Library of Canada*] (NLC)
BF	Franc [*Monetary unit*] [*Belgium*]
BF	Iowa Airlines and Horizon Airways [*ICAO designator*] (AD)
BF	MarkAir (GAVI)
BF1	Virus Isolated from Bovine Feces [*Medicine*]
BFA	Bachelor of Financial Administration
BFA	Bachelor of Fine Arts
BFA	Bacon Families Association [*Defunct*] (EA)
BFA	Balloon Federation of America (EA)
BFA	Barrel Futurities of America (EA)
BFA	Battlefield Functional Area [*Army*]
BFA	Before Flight Abort [*NASA*] (MCD)
BFA	Benzylfurylmethyl Alcohol [*Organic chemistry*]
BFA	Bilingual Foundation of the Arts (EA)
BFA	Biological Farmers of Australia
BFA	Blackburn Family Association (EA)
BFA	Blank Firing Adaptor [*Army*] (MCD)
BFA	Blank Firing Attachment (MCD)
BFA	Board, Family, and Associates [*Company stockholders*]
BFA	Bocce Federation of Australia
BFA	Boyne Falls, MI [*Location identifier FAA*] (FAAL)
BFA	Bream Fishermen Association
BFA	Brefeldin A [*Antibiotic*]
BFA	British Fabric Association (DBA)
BFA	British First Army
BFA	British Foundry Association (DBA)
BFA	British Franchise Association (DBA)
BFA	Broadcasting Foundation of America [*Defunct*] (EA)
BFA	Brown-Forman'A' [*NYSE symbol*] (TTSB)
BFA	Budget-Funded Agency
BFA	Bureau of Finance and Administration [*US Postal Service*] (MCD)
BFA	Burkina Faso [*ANSI three-letter standard code*] (CNC)
BFA	Business Flights Ltd. [*Canada ICAO designator*] (FAAC)
BFA	Category B Flying Accident [*British military*] (DMA)
BFAA	Biblical Fine Arts Association (EA)
BFAC	British Federation of Aesthetics and Cosmetology (BI)
B-FACT	Booster Flight-Acceptance Composite Test [*NASA*]
BFAD	British First Airborne Division
BFAG	British Foods Action Group (DI)
BfAi	Bundesstelle fuer Aussenhandelsinformation [*Federal Office of Foreign Trade Information*] [*German Ministry of Economics*] (IID)
BFA in DA	Bachelor of Fine Arts in Dramatic Art
BFA in Ed	Bachelor of Fine Arts in Education
BFA in Mus	Bachelor of Fine Arts in Music
BFA in PS	Bachelor of Fine Arts in Painting and Sculpture
BFA in Sp	Bachelor of Fine Arts in Speech
BFALA	Bachelor of Fine Arts in Landscape Architecture
BFAM	Budget Formulation and Appropriation Model (MCD)
BF & VCA	British Fruit and Vegetable Canners Association (DBA)
BFAP	Binary Fault Analysis Program [*Computer science*] (MHDB)
BFAP	British Forces, Arabian Peninsula [*British military*] (DMA)
BFAR	British Foundation for Age Research (IRUK)
BFAR	Bureau of Fisheries and Aquatic Resources [*Phillippines*] [*Marine science*] (OSRA)
BFAS	Basic File Access System
B'FAST	Breakfast [*Classified advertising*] (ADA)
BFAWU	Bakers' Food and Allied Workers' Union [*British*] (DCTA)

BFB............ Banco Fonsecas & Burnay [*Fonsecas & Burnay Bank*] [*Portugal*]
BFB............ Bang for the Buck
BFB............ Bifascicular Block [*Electrocardiogram*] (CPH)
BFB............ Biofeedback
BFB............ Bowater Faculty of Business [*Deakin University*] [*Australia*]
BFB............ British Flight Battalion
BFB............ Broad-Flanged Beam
BFB............ Brown-Forman CI'B' [*NYSE symbol*] (TTSB)
BFB............ Bulgarian Flying Cargo [*FAA designator*] (FAAC)
BFB............ Bush Fires Board [*Western Australia*]
BFBB......... British Federation of Brass Bands (DBA)
BFBC......... Bubbling Fluidized Bed Combustion
BFBG......... British Francophone Business Group [*An association*] (DBA)
BFBPW...... British Federation of Business and Professional Women (ODBW)
BFBS......... British and Foreign Bible Society
BFBS......... British Forces Broadcasting Service [*or Station*]
BFBU......... British Forces Broadcasting Unit (IAA)
BFBV......... Beaver Valley Public Library, Fruitvale, British Columbia [*Library symbol National Library of Canada*] (NLC)
BFBWA .... Bush Fire Board of Western Australia
BFC............ Backup Flight Control (MCD)
BFC............ Badfinger Fan Club (EA)
BFC............ Bangles Fan Club [*Later, Bangles n' Mash International*] [*Defunct*] (EA)
BFC............ Banque Francaise pour le Commerce [*French Commercial Bank*] (AF)
BFC............ Base des Forces Canadiennes [*Canadian Forces Base - CFB*]
BFC............ Basler Flight Service, Inc. [*ICAO designator*] (FAAC)
BFC............ Battle Force Combatant [*Navy*]
BFc............ Belgian Franc [*Monetary unit*]
BFC............ Bellefonte Central Railroad Co. [*AAR code*]
BFC............ Bending Feedback Control
BFC............ Benign Febrile Convulsion [*Medicine*] (MAE)
BFC............ Berlin Fan Club [*Defunct*] (EA)
BFC............ Blackrock CA Ins Muni 2008 Tr [*NYSE symbol*] (TTSB)
BFC............ Blackrock California Insurance Municipal 2008 Trade [*NYSE symbol*] (SPSG)
BFC............ Body-Fitted Coordinates [*Computer science*]
BFC............ Body Flap Control (MCD)
BFC............ Bogie Fan Club [*Canada*] (EAIO)
BFC............ Bohr Frequency Condition
BFC............ Bold Face Capitals [*Printing term*]
BFC............ Braking Force Coefficient (PDAA)
BFC............ British Free Corps [*Corps formed by Germans among POW's and civil internees*] [*World War II*]
BFC............ Broadcasting and Film Commission [*Later, CC*] (EA)
BFC............ Budget and Forecast Calendarization [*Accounting*]
BFC............ Bureau International du Film des Chemins de Fer [*International Railway Film Bureau*]
BFC............ Bureau of Foreign Commerce [*Abolished, 1961*] [*Department of Commerce*]
BFCA......... Benzylfurancarboxylic Acid [*Organic chemistry*]
BFCA......... Bichon Frise Club of America (EA)
BFCA......... British Federation of Commodity Associations (ODBW)
BFCC......... British Foreign and Colonial Corp. [*Finance*]
BFCE......... Banque Francaise du Commerce Exterieur [*French state-owned bank*]
BFCF......... Bremerton Freight Car Ferry [*AAR code*]
BFCHP........ British Federation of Care Home Proprietors (DBA)
BFCI.......... Braun's Fashions [*NASDAQ symbol*] (TTSB)
BFCI.......... Brauns Fashions Corp. [*NASDAQ symbol*] (SAG)
BFCIB......... Banque pour le Financement du Commerce et des Investissements du Burkina (EY)
BFCLD .... Union Canadienne des Travailleurs Unis des Brasseries, Farines, Cereales, Liqueurs Douces, et Distilleries [*International Union of United Brewery, Flour, Cereal, Soft Drink, and Distillery Workers of America - BFCSD*]
BFCMA........ British Flue and Chimney Manufacturers Association (DBA)
BFC/NCC.... Broadcasting and Film Commission/National Council of the Churches of Christ in the USA (NTCM)
BFCNSW...... Board of Fire Commissioners, New South Wales [*Australia*]
BFCNT .... Bush Fire Council of the Northern Territory [*Australia*]
BFCO .... Band Filter Cutoff (MSA)
BFCO .... Bank/Fund Conferences Office [*World Bank, IMF*]
BFCOI .... Banque Francaise Commerciale Ocean Indian [*Reunion*] (EY)
BFCS......... Backup Flight Control System [*NASA*] (NASA)
BFCS......... Bing's Friends and Collectibles Society (EA)
BFCS......... British Friesian Cattle Society of Great Britain and Ireland
BFCSD .... International Union of United Brewery, Flour, Cereal, Soft Drink, and Distillery Workers of America [*Later, Brewery and Soft Drink Workers Conference - USA and Canada*]
BFCT.......... Boiler Feed Compound Tank [*Technical drawings*]
BFCU .... Bureau of Federal Credit Unions [*Later, NCUA*] [*Social Security Administration*]
BFCX.......... Benson Financial [*NASDAQ symbol*] (TTSB)
BFCX.......... Benson Financial Corp. [*NASDAQ symbol*] (SAG)
BFCY.......... Beneficiary
BFCY-P .... Best-Fit Central Y-Plane
BFD............ Back Focal Distance (MSA)
BFD............ Banque Federale de Developpement [*Federal Business Development Bank - FBDB*] [*Canada*]
BFD............ BASIC [*Bank Automated Service Information System*] File Directory (HGAA)
BFD............ Basic Floppy Disk
BFD............ Battery Firing Device (MCD)

BFD............ Battlefield Day (RDA)
BFD............ Beat-Frequency Detection (IAA)
BFD............ Beaufield Resources, Inc. [*Toronto Stock Exchange symbol*]
BFD............ Bellfield [*Australia Seismograph station code, US Geological Survey*] (SEIS)
BFD............ Big Fatal Disease [*Slang*] (DNAB)
BFD............ Big Fine Deal
BFD............ Binary-Floating-Decimal [*Computer science*]
BFD............ Blank Film Door
BFD............ Blind Fire Director (NATG)
BFD............ Bookform Drawing (MSA)
BFD............ Boolean Function Designator [*Mathematics*]
BFD............ BostonFed Bancorp [*AMEX symbol*] (TTSB)
BFD............ Bostonfed Bancorp, Inc. [*AMEX symbol*] (SAG)
BFD............ Bradford [*Pennsylvania*] [*Airport symbol*] (OAG)
BFD............ Brake Force Distributor [*Automotive engineering*]
BFD............ Budget Formulation Directive [*Military*] (AABC)
BFDA......... Brisbane Funeral Directors' Association [*Australia*]
BFDC......... Battalion Fire Distribution Center (AABC)
BFDC......... Bureau of Foreign and Domestic Commerce [*Functions later dispersed*] [*Department of Commerce*]
BFDG......... British Film Designers Guild (DBA)
BFDI.......... Bronchodilation Following Deep Inspiration [*Medicine*] (DMAA)
BFDK .... Before Dark (FAAC)
BFDL .... Blue Force Data Link [*Military*] (CAAL)
BFDS......... Board of Faculty of Dental Surgery [*British*]
BFE............ Bachelor of Forest Engineering
BFE............ Battlefield Estimate
BFE............ Battlefield Exercise (DNAB)
BFE............ Beam-Forming Electrode
BFE............ Biofilm Electrode
BFE............ Blood Flow Energy [*Medicine*] (DMAA)
BFE............ Board for Fundamental Education (EA)
BFE............ Bromotrifluoroethylene [*Organic chemistry*]
BFE............ Brownfield, TX [*Location identifier FAA*] (FAAL)
BFE............ Browning Ferris [*NYSE symbol*] (SAG)
BFE............ Browning-Ferris 7.25% 'ACES' [*NYSE symbol*] (TTSB)
BFE............ BTL [*Bell Telephone Laboratories*] Furnished Equipment (MCD)
BFE............ Buyer Furnished Equipment (MCD)
BFEA......... Bureau of Far Eastern Affairs [*Department of State*]
BFEC......... Banking Federation of the European Economic Community [*Belgium*] (EAIO)
BFEC......... Bendix Field Engineering Corp. [*of Bendix Corp.*]
BFEC......... Benign Focal Epilepsy of Childhood [*Medicine*] (DMAA)
BFEC......... British Food Export Council (DS)
BFEE......... Boron Fluoride-Ethyl Ether [*Organic chemistry*]
BFEEC........ Banking Federation of the European Economic Community [*Belgium*] (EAIO)
BFEEE .... Bureau Federal d'Examen des Evaluations Environnementales [*Federal Environmental Assessment Review Office*] [*Canada*]
BFEL.......... Buffelsfontein Gold Mining Co. Ltd. [*NASDAQ symbol*] (NQ)
BFEN.......... BF Enterprises [*NASDAQ symbol*] (TTSB)
BFEN.......... BF Enterprises, Inc. [*NASDAQ symbol*] (NQ)
BF Eng........ Bachelor of Forest Engineering
BF Ent........ BF Enterprises, Inc. [*Associated Press*] (SAG)
BFER......... Base Field Effect Register [*Electronics*] (OA)
BFES......... British Families Education Service
BFF............ Black Filmmaker Foundation (EA)
BFF............ Bovine Follicular Fluid
BFF............ Budget Furniture Forum [*Later, ROFF*] (EA)
BFF............ Buffalo - Larkin [*New York*] [*Seismograph station code, US Geological Survey Closed*] (SEIS)
BFF............ Buffered Flip-Flop [*Computer science*]
BFF............ Bundesforschungsanstalt fuer Fischerei [*Database producer*] [*Germany*]
BFF............ Bureau of Flora and Fauna [*Australia*]
BFF............ Burma Frontier Force [*British military*] (DMA)
BFF............ Scottsbluff [*Nebraska*] [*Airport symbol*] (OAG)
BFFA......... British Film Fund Agency
BFFC......... Big Foot Financial Corp. [*NASDAQ symbol*] (SAG)
BFFC......... Bill Farrar Fan Club (EA)
BFFEIFC...... Bobby Fuller Four-Ever International Fan Club [*Defunct*] (EA)
BFFF......... British Frozen Food Federation (DBA)
BFFS......... British Federation of Film Societies
BfG............ Bank fuer Gemeinwirtschaft [*Germany*]
BFG............ B. F. Goodrich Co.
BFG............ Big Friendly Giant [*In the children's bestseller "The BFG" by Roald Dahl*]
BFG............ Binary Frequency Generator (IEEE)
BFG............ Briefing (AABC)
BFG............ British Forces Germany [*NATO*]
BFG............ Brute Force Gyro
BFG............ Buffing (MSA)
BFGA......... Biodynamic Farming and Gardening Association [*Australia*]
BFGA......... Blue Flame Gas Association [*Nebraska*] (SRA)
BFGF......... Basic Fibroblast Growth Factor [*Biochemistry*]
BFH............ Benign Familial Hematuria [*Medicine*] (DMAA)
BFH............ British Field Hospital [*British military*] (DMA)
BFH............ Bundesfinanzhof [*Federal Supreme Fiscal Court*] [*German*] (DLA)
BFHFI......... Black Filmmakers Hall of Fame, Inc. (EA)
BFHGH & SC... British Federation of Hotel, Guest House, and Self-Catering Associations (DBA)
BFHP .... Base Fuze Hole Plug
BFI............. Baltic Freight Index [*of spot market rates*] [*Shipping*] (DS)
BFI............. Batch Freeform Input [*Computer science*] (MHDI)

BFI............. Battlefield Interdiction (MCD)
BFI............. Beam-Forming Interfact (PDAA)
BFI............. Bearing Frequency Indicator (NVT)
BFI............. Beat-Frequency Interferometer (PDAA)
BFI............. Betriebsforschungsinstitut [*Institute for Industrial Research*] [*German Iron and Steel Engineers Association Dusseldorf*] [*Information service or system*] (IID)
BFI............. British Film Institute
BFI............. Broadcaster's Foundation, Inc. (NTCM)
BFI............. Browning Ferris [*NYSE symbol*] (SAG)
BFI............. Browning-Ferris Indus [*NYSE symbol*] (TTSB)
BFI............. Browning-Ferris Industries, Inc. [*NYSE symbol*] (SPSG)
BFI............. Brute Force and Ignorance [*Computer science Slang*] (WDMC)
BFI............. Buckminster Fuller Institute (EA)
BFI............. Business Forms Institute [*Defunct*]
BFI............. Seattle, WA [*Location identifier FAA*] (FAAL)
BFIA........... British Flower Industry Association (PDAA)
BFIA........... British Forging Industry Association (EAIO)
BFIAS.......... Ballistics Force Integrator and Analyzer System (MCD)
BFIC........... Binary Fault Isolation Chart [*Computer science*] (MHDB)
BFICC......... British Facsimile Industry Consultative Committee (NITA)
BFID........... Boolean Function Identifier [*Mathematics*]
BFIFC.......... Bureau of Foods Irradiated Foods Committee [*Food and Drug Administration*]
BFin........... Bachelor of Finance
BFinAdmin.. Bachelor of Financial Administration (ADA)
BFISS......... British Federation of Iron and Steel Stockholders (BI)
BFIT........... Bally Total Fitness Holding [*NASDAQ symbol*] (TTSB)
BFIT........... Bally Total Fitness Holding Corp. [*NASDAQ symbol*] (SAG)
BFIT........... Battle Force Inport Training [*Navy*] (DOMA)
BFJ............. Ba [*Fiji*] [*Airport symbol*] (OAG)
BFJ............. B. F. Jones Memorial Library, Aliquippa, PA [*OCLC symbol*] (OCLC)
BFJ............. Booster Fuel Jacket
BFJSC......... Benjamin Franklin Junior Stamp Club [*Later, BFSC*] (EA)
BFK............. Buffalo, OK [*Location identifier FAA*] (FAAL)
BFL............. Bachelor of Family Life
BFL............. Back Focal Length [*Optics*]
BFL............. Bakersfield [*California*] [*Airport symbol*] (OAG)
BFL............. Bakersfield, CA [*TACAN station*] (NASA)
BFL............. Baptists for Life (EA)
BFL............. Bird-Fanciers Lung [*Medicine*]
BFL............. Bomb Fall Line [*Military*] (NVT)
BFL............. Books for Libraries [*Program*]
BFL............. Books for Libraries Micropublications, Freeport, NY [*Library symbol Library of Congress*] (LCLS)
BFL............. Brackenridge Field Laboratory [*University of Texas at Austin*] [*Research center*] (RCD)
BFL............. British Foreign Legion [*British military*] (DMA)
BFL............. Buffalo Airways Ltd. [*Canada ICAO designator*] (FAAC)
BFL............. Buffered FET [*Field Effect Transistor*] Logic [*Integrated circuitry*]
BFL............. Bunzl Flexpack Ltd. [*British*]
BFL............. Busy Flash [*Telecommunications*] (NITA)
BFL............. United States Food and Drug Administration, Bureau of Food, Washington, DC [*OCLC symbol*] (OCLC)
BFLC.......... Billings Family Life Center [*Australia*]
BFLCM........ Langley Centennial Museum and National Exhibition Centre, Fort Langley, British Columbia [*Library symbol National Library of Canada*] (NLC)
BFLFMM...... British Columbia Farm Machinery Museum, Fort Langley, British Columbia [*Library symbol National Library of Canada*] (NLC)
BFLIQ.......... Blackrock Florida Investment Quality Municipal Trust [*Associated Press*] (SAG)
BFLMS........ Benjamin Franklin Literary and Medical Society (EA)
BFLOPS....... Billion Floating-Point Operations per Second [*Computer science*]
BFLPC......... Fort Langley National Historic Park, Parks Canada [*Parc Historique National de Fort Langley, Parcs Canada*] British Columbia [*Library symbol National Library of Canada*] (NLC)
BFLRF......... Belvoir Fuels and Lubricants Research Facility [*Southwest Research Institute*] [*San Antonio, TX*]
BFLS........... Borjeson-Forssman-Lehmann Syndrome [*Medicine*] (DMAA)
BFM............ Balance Forward Master
BFM............ Barium Ferrite Magnet
BFM............ Basic Field Manual [*Military*]
BFM............ Basic Fighter Maneuver [*Air Force*] (MCD)
BFM............ Basic Flight Maneuvering [*Navy*] (DOMA)
BFM............ Before Full Moon [*Freemasonry*] (ROG)
BFM............ Bendroflumethiazide [*Organic chemistry*] (MEDA)
BFM............ Bessel Function Model (MCD)
BFM............ Bethany Fellowship Missions (EA)
BFM............ Branch of Full Minus (SAA)
BFM............ British Food Mission [*World War II*]
BFM............ British Furniture Manufacturers' Federated Associations (BI)
BFM............ Broadcast Financial Management Association [*Later, BCFMA*] (EA)
BFM............ Bureau of Facilities and Material (AAGC)
BFM............ Business and Financial Manager [*Military*] (DOMA)
BFM............ Fernie Museum, British Columbia [*Library symbol National Library of Canada*] (NLC)
BFM............ Mobile, AL [*Location identifier FAA*] (FAAL)
BFMA.......... British Floorcovering Manufacturers Association (DBA)
BFMA.......... Business Forms Management Association (EA)
BFMC.......... British Friction Materials Council (BI)
BFMDS........ Base Flight Management Data System (AFM)
BFMF.......... British Federation of Musical Festivals
BFMF.......... British Footwear Manufacturers' Federation
BFMI.......... Business Firms Master Index [*A publication*]

BFMIRA....... British Food Manufacturing Industries Research Association (ARC)
BFMO.......... Base Fuels Management Officer [*Air Force*] (AFM)
BFMP.......... British Federation of Master Printers [*A union*]
BFN............. Beam-Forming Network
BFN............. Bloemfontein [*South Africa*] [*Airport symbol*] (OAG)
BFN............. British Forces Network
BFN............. Compagnie Nationale Naganagani [*Burkina Faso*] [*ICAO designator*] (FAAC)
BFN............. Fort Nelson Public Library, British Columbia [*Library symbol National Library of Canada*] (NLC)
BFNC.......... Benign Familial Neonatal Convulsions [*Medicine*]
BFNP.......... Browns Ferry Nuclear Plant (NRCH)
BFNPP........ Browns Ferry Nuclear Power Plant (NRCH)
BFNS.......... Black Fox Nuclear Station (NRCH)
BFO............. Balanced Forearm Orthosis [*Medicine*]
BFO............. Beat-Frequency Oscillator
BFO............. Buffalo (WDAA)
BFO............. Buffalo Range [*Zimbabwe*] [*Airport symbol*] (OAG)
BFO............. Bunker Fuel Oil (DS)
BFO............. Buyer's Fashion Outlet [*Retailing*]
BF of A....... Bicycle Federation of America (EA)
BFOH.......... Bancfirst Ohio Corp. [*NASDAQ symbol*] (SAG)
BFOODAB ... Budget Formulation Office, Office of the Director of the Army Budget
BFOQ......... Bona Fide Occupational Qualification
B For .... Bachelor of Forestry (ADA)
BFORM........ Budget Formulation [*Army*] (AABC)
BForSc........ Bachelor of Forestry Science (ADA)
BForSci....... Bachelor of Forestry Science (NADA)
BFOV.......... Broad Field of View (MCD)
BFOZ-P ...... Best-Fit Optic Z-Plane
BFP............. Balco Industries [*Toronto Stock Exchange symbol Vancouver Stock Exchange symbol*]
BFP............. Batters Faced by Pitcher [*Baseball*]
BFP............. Battery Fuse Panel (IAA)
BFP............. Battlefield Period (MCD)
BFP............. Bayes Fixed Sample-Size Procedure [*Statistics*]
BFP............. Beaver Falls [*Pennsylvania*] [*Airport symbol*] (OAG)
BFP............. Biological False Positive [*Clinical chemistry*]
BFP............. Boiler Feed Pump [*Technical drawings*]
BFP............. Bona Fide Purchaser [*Legal term*] (DLA)
BFP............. Bottom Finding Pinger
BFP............. Bundle-Forming Pili [*Microbiology*]
BFP............. Bureau of Freelance Photographers [*British*] (CB)
BFP............. UCLA Business Forecasting Project [*Information service or system*] (IID)
BFPA.......... Brisbane Forest Park Administration [*Australia*]
BFPA.......... British Fibreboard Packaging Association (DBA)
BFPA.......... British Fluid Power Association (EAIO)
BFPC.......... British Farm Produce Council (BI)
BFPDA........ British Fluid Power Distributors Association (DBA)
BFPDDA...... Binary Floating-Point Digital Differential Analyzer (IEEE)
BFPEA........ British Fireboard Packaging Employers' Association
BFPHC........ Basic Filter Power Handling Capacity (IAA)
BFP/MAP .... Books for Professionals/Miller Accounting Publications [*Harcourt, Brace, Jovanovich, Inc.*]
BFPMS........ British Federation of Printing Machinery and Supplies
BFPO .... British Field Post Office [*World War II*]
BFPO .... British Forces Post Office
BFPPS .... Bureau of Foods, Pesticides, and Product Safety [*FDA*]
BFPQ .... Block Floating Point Quantizer (MCD)
BFPR .... Basic Fluid Power Research Program (IAA)
BFPR .... Binary Floating Point Resistor [*Computer science*] (MHDB)
BFPr........... Brown-Forman Inc. 4% Pfd [*NYSE symbol*] (TTSB)
BFPSA .... British Fire Protection Systems Association (PDAA)
BFPT .... Brooks Fiber Properties [*NASDAQ symbol*] (TTSB)
BFPT .... Brooks Fiber Properties, Inc. [*NASDAQ symbol*] (SAG)
BFPV.......... Bona Fide Purchaser for Value [*of a security, or other negotiable instrument*] [*Legal term*]
BFR............. Banco Frances del Rio ADS [*NYSE symbol*] (TTSB)
BFR............. Banco Frances del Rio La Plata [*NYSE symbol*] (SAG)
BFR............. Barrier Film Rectifier
BFR............. Beauford Resources Ltd. [*Vancouver Stock Exchange symbol*]
BFR............. Bedford, IN [*Location identifier FAA*] (FAAL)
BFR............. Before (MSA)
BFR............. Before Flight Reliability (MCD)
BFR............. BF Realty Holdings Ltd. [*Toronto Stock Exchange symbol*] (SPSG)
BFR............. Biennial Flight Review [*Aviation*] (DA)
BFR............. Bile Flow Rate [*Physiology*]
BFR............. Biologic False-Positive Reactor (MAE)
BFR............. Black, Female Republican
BFR............. Blast Furnace Research, Inc. [*Defunct*] (EA)
BFR............. Bleach Filtrate Recycle [*Pulp and paper technology*]
BFR............. Blip-Frame Ratio (MSA)
BFR............. Block Format Recording
BFR............. Blood Flow Rate [*Medicine*]
BFR............. Bone Formation Rate [*Medicine*]
BFR............. Bridged Frequency Ringing [*Telecommunications*] (TEL)
BFR............. Briefer
BFR............. Buffer [*Computer science*] (MSA)
BFR............. Buffered Ringer's Solution [*Medicine*]
BFrankR....... Ben Franklin Retail Stores, Inc. [*Associated Press*] (SAG)
BFRC.......... British Flat Roofing Council (DBA)
BFRL.......... Basic Facility Requirements List [*Navy*]
BFRL.......... Fraser Lake Public Library, British Columbia [*Library symbol National Library of Canada*] (NLC)

BFRO	Black Family Research Organization (EA)
BFRP	Boron Fiber Reinforced Plastics (NASA)
BFRS	Ben Franklin Retail Stores, Inc. [*NASDAQ symbol*] (SAG)
BFRS	Bio-Feedback Research Society [*Later, BSA*] (EA)
BFR Sol	Buffered Ringer's Solution [*Medicine*] (CPH)
BFS	Bachelor of Foreign Service
BFS	Backup Flight System (MCD)
BFS	Balanced File Organization Scheme (MHDI)
BFS	Band Filter Set
BFS	Base Facilities for SACLANT [*NATO*] (NATG)
BFS	BASIC [*Bank Automated Service Information System*] File System [*Computer science*] (HGAA)
BFS	Battlefield Functional System (MCD)
BFS	Beam-Foil Spectroscopy
BFS	Bedford Software Ltd. [*Toronto Stock Exchange symbol*]
BFS	Beef Friesian Society (EA)
BFS	Belfast [*Northern Ireland*] [*Airport symbol*] (OAG)
BFS	Benelux Falcon Service [*Belgium ICAO designator*] (FAAC)
BFS	Ben Franklin Society [*Defunct*] (EA)
BFS	Best Fit Sphere (MCD)
BFS	Bird Friends Society [*Defunct*] (EA)
BFS	Black Fox Station [*Nuclear energy*] (NRCH)
BFS	Blast Furnace Slag
BFS	Blood Fasting Sugar [*Medicine*] (DMAA)
BFS	Board of Foreign Scholarships [*Department of State*] [*Washington, DC*]
BFS	Bonney-Fessenden Sociograph [*Psychology*]
BFS	Border-Fault System [*Geology*]
BFS	Branded Furniture Society [*British*] (BI)
BFS	British Fantasy Society (DBA)
BFS	British Frontier Service (BARN)
BFS	British Fuchsia Society (BI)
BFS	Brute Force [*Unregulated*] Supply (IEEE)
BFS	Bundesamt fur Statistik [*Federal Statistical Office*] [*Information service or system*] (IID)
BFS	Bureau of Family Services [*of SSA*]
BFS	Bureau of Federal Supply (AAGC)
BFS	Bureau of Flight Standards (KSC)
BFS	Business Funding Scheme
BFS	Saul Centers [*NYSE symbol*] (TTSB)
BFS	Saul [*B. F.*] Real Estate Investment Trust [*NYSE symbol*] (SPSG)
BFSA	Behaviorists for Social Action (EA)
BFSA	British Fire Services Association (PDAA)
BFSA	British Fulbright Scholars Association (PDAA)
BFSB	Bedford Bancshares [*NASDAQ symbol*] (TTSB)
BFSB	Bedford Bancshares, Inc. [*NASDAQ symbol*] (SAG)
BFSc	Bachelor of Fisheries Science
BFSC	Battlefield Functional System Concept (MCD)
BFSC	Benjamin Franklin Stamp Club (EA)
BFSC	Building Fire Safety Committee [*South Australia*]
BF Set	British Field [*Wireless*] Set [*British military*] (DMA)
BFSH	Bovine Follicle-Stimulating Hormone [*Biochemistry*]
BFSI	BFS Bankorp [*NASDAQ symbol*] (TTSB)
BFSI	BFS Bankorp, Inc. [*NASDAQ symbol*] (NQ)
BFSJ	Fort St. John Public Library, British Columbia [*Library symbol National Library of Canada*] (NLC)
BFSJA	Fort St. James Public Library, British Columbia [*Library symbol National Library of Canada*] (NLC)
BFSJHS	Fort St. James National Historic Site [*Parc Historique National Fort St.-James*], British Columbia [*Library symbol National Library of Canada*] (NLC)
BFSLYC	British Federation of Sand and Land Yacht Clubs
BFS NY	BFS Bancorp, Inc. [*Associated Press*] (SAG)
BFSO	Base Fuels Supply Officer [*Air Force*] (AFM)
BFSP	Best Fixed-Sample Procedure [*Statistics*]
BFSP	British Foreign and State Papers [*A publication*] (DLA)
BFSPHP	Fort Steele Provincial Historic Park, British Columbia [*Library symbol National Library of Canada*] (NLC)
BFSS	British and Foreign Schools Society (AIE)
BFSS	British Field Sports Society
BFSV	Bradley Fire Support Vehicle [*Army*] (INF)
BFSVEA	British Fishing and Small Vessel Equipment Association [*Later, BSSEA*] (PDAA)
BFSW	Buffered Filtered Seawater
BFT	Bachelor of Foreign Trade
BFT	Bank for Foreign Trade of the USSR
BFT	Basic Fighter Transition [*Air Force*] (DOMA)
BFT	Basic Fitness Test [*British military*] (DMA)
BFT	Batch Fabrication Technique
BFT	Beaufort [*South Carolina*] [*Airport symbol*] (OAG)
BFT	Bentonite Flocculation Test (AAMN)
BFT	Binary File Transfer (CDE)
BFT	Biofeedback Training [*Physiology*]
BFT	Bulk Function Transfer (PDAA)
BFT	Cleveland, OH [*Location identifier FAA*] (FAAL)
BFTA	British Fur Trade Association (DBA)
BFTA	Bulk Fuel Tank Assembly (MCD)
BFTB	Better Fabrics Test Bureau
BFTC	Ben Franklin Technology Center [*Research center*] (RCD)
BFTC	Boeing Flight Test Center [*NASA*] (IAA)
BFTD	Battalion Field Training Days (MCD)
BFTM	Ballistic Flight Test Missile (MCD)
BFT-NSF	Binary-File Transfer - Non-Standard Facilities Frame [*Microsoft Corp.*] (PCM)
BFTP	Bailment Flight Test Program

BFTPA	British Film and Television Producers' Association
BFTS	Bomber Fighter Training System (MCD)
BFTSC	Brassboard Fault Tolerant Spaceborne Computer (MCD)
BFTSS	Bohemian Free Thinking School Society (EA)
BFTT	Battle Field Tactical Trainer
BFTT	British Federation of Textile Technicians (DCTA)
BFTU	Boeing Field Test Unit [*NASA*] (IAA)
BFTV	Bachelor of Film and Television
BFU	Benjamin Franklin University [*Washington, DC*]
BFU	Burst-Forming Unit
BFU	Franc [*Monetary unit*] [*Burundi*]
BFUA	Banking, Finance, and Urban Affairs (DLA)
BFUe	Burst-Forming Unit erythroid [*Hematology*]
BFUP	Board of Fire Underwriters of the Pacific [*Later, ISO*]
BFUSA	Basketball Federation of the United States of America [*Defunct*]
BFUSA	Beach Front USA [*An association*] (EA)
BFUW	British Federation of University Women
BFV	Ballast Flood Valve
BFV	Bovine Feces Virus [*Veterinary medicine*] (DAVI)
BFV	Bradley Fighting Vehicle [*Army*]
BFV	Buddhist Foundation of Victoria [*Australia*]
BfV	Bundesamt fuer Verfassungsschutz [*Federal Office for the Protection of the Constitution*] [*West German counterintelligence agency*]
BFV	Clinton, OK [*Location identifier FAA*] (FAAL)
BFVA	Bradley Fighting Vehicle Armament [*Army*] (RDA)
BFVMTL	Baseline Flight Vehicle Mission Time Line
BFVN	Black Film & Video Network (AC)
BFVS	Bradley Fighting Vehicle Systems [*Army*] (RDA)
BFVS-C2V ...	Bradley Fighting Vehicle Systems Command and Control Vehicle [*Army*] (RDA)
BFW	Baw Faw Mountain [*Washington*] [*Seismograph station code, US Geological Survey*] (SEIS)
BFW	Bayerische Flugzeug Werke [*Bavarian Airplane Works*] [*German*]
BFW	Bibles for the World (EA)
BFW	Boiler Feed Water [*Technical drawings*]
BFW	Bread for the World (EA)
BFWS	Big Fat Wide Shot [*Photography*] (WDMC)
BFWTT	Boilerwater/Feedwater Test and Treatment
BFX	Bafoussam [*Cameroon*] [*Airport symbol*] (OAG)
BFX	Buffton Corp. [*AMEX symbol*] (SPSG)
BFY	Budget Fiscal Year
BFY	Library and Resource Collection, Yoho National Park, Field, British Columbia [*Library symbol National Library of Canada*] (NLC)
BFYC	Books for Your Children [*A publication*] (BRI)
BFYC	British Federation of Young Choirs (DBA)
BFZ	Branch of Fall Zero
BFZ	Huntsville, AL [*Location identifier FAA*] (FAAL)
BG	[*The*] Babylonian Genesis [*A publication*] (BJA)
BG	Bacillus globigii [*Biological warfare with bacteria*]
BG	Back Gear [*Technical drawings*]
BG	Background [*Low-priority processing*] [*Computer science*]
bg	Background (WDMC)
BG	Bag
BG	Banca del Gottardo [*Gotthard Bank*] [*Switzerland*]
bg	Bangladesh [*MARC country of publication code Library of Congress*] (LCCP)
BG	Bangladesh Biman [*ICAO designator*] (AD)
BG	Barge
BG	Basal Ganglion [*Medicine*] (DMAA)
BG	Basal Groove
BG	Basic Gastrin [*Medicine*] (DMAA)
BG	Battle Group
BG	Bay Gelding [*Horse*]
BG	Beach Group
BG	Bearing
BG	Bearing Pennant [*Navy British*]
BG	Before Girls [*i.e., before women became part of armed forces*] [*Military*]
BG	Before Goetz [*A reference to "vigilante" Bernhard Goetz, who shot four youths on a New York subway in 1984 after allegedly being threatened by them*] [*See also AG*]
BG	Beige (WGA)
BG	Being
B-G	Bender-Gestalt Test [*Psychology*]
BG	Bengal [*or Bengalese*] (WDAA)
BG	Benny Goodman [*Clarinetist*]
BG	Benzylideneglucose [*Biochemistry*]
BG	Berufungsgericht [*Court of Appeal*] [*German*] (ILCA)
BG	Best Game [*Billiards*] (BARN)
BG	Beta-Gamma
BG	Bevel Gear
BG	Bicolor Guaiac [*Test*] [*Medicine*]
BG	Big
BG	Billing Group [*Telecommunications*] (TEL)
BG	Billion Gallons (EPA)
BG	Binders' Guild (EA)
BG	Birmingham Gauge
BG	Birmingham Wire Gauge (IDOE)
BG	Black Gelding [*Horse racing*] (ROG)
BG	Black Giant Mines Ltd. [*Vancouver Stock Exchange symbol*]
BG	Blanket Gas (SAA)
BG	Blast Gauge (MUGU)
BG	Blasting Gelatine (IAA)
BG	Block Group [*Bureau of the Census*] (GFGA)

BG .... Blood and Guts [*Code name used to refer to Oliver North, National Security Council aide during Reagan administration*]
B/G .... Blood/Gas [*Clinical chemistry*]
BG .... Blood Glucose [*Medicine*]
BG .... Blood Group (ADA)
BG .... Bluegill [*Ichthyology*]
BG .... Bluegrass (WGA)
BG .... Bluish Green
BG .... Board of Governors
BG .... Board of Guardians [*British*] (ROG)
BG .... Body Guard [*Special Air Service*] [*British*]
Bg .... Bogen [*Bow*] [*Music*]
B/G .... Bonded Goods [*International trade*]
BG .... Bond International Gold, Inc. [*Toronto Stock Exchange symbol*]
BG .... Bone Graft [*Orthopedics*]
BG .... [*The*] Book Guild Ltd. [*British*] (ECON)
BG .... Bordet-Gengou [*Bacillus*] [*Microbiology*]
BG .... Botanic Garden
BG .... Bottom Grille (OA)
BG .... Breeding Gain
BG .... Breguet-Dassault [*Societe Anonyme des Ateliers d'Aviation Louis Breguet*] [*France ICAO aircraft manufacturer identifier*] (ICAO)
BG .... Bren Gun [*or Gunner*] [*British military*] (DMA)
BG .... Brig [*Ship*] (ROG)
BG .... Brigade of Gurkhas [*British military*] (DMA)
BG .... Brigadier General
BG .... Brilliant Green [*An indicator*] [*Chemistry*]
BG .... British Gas (ECON)
BG .... British Gauge [*Metal industry*]
BG .... British Grenadiers
BG .... British Guiana
BG .... British Guiana Law Reports [*A publication*] (DLA)
BG .... Broad Gage (IAA)
BG .... Brown Group [*NYSE symbol*] (TTSB)
BG .... Brown Group, Inc. [*NYSE symbol*] (SPSG)
BG .... Buccogingival [*Dentistry*]
BG .... Bulgaria [*ANSI two-letter standard code*] (CNC)
BG .... Bundesgericht [*Federal Supreme Court*] [*German*] (DLA)
BG .... Bundesgesetz [*Federal Act or Statute*] [*German*] (ILCA)
BG .... Burg
BG .... Burg
BG .... Bus Grant (IAA)
BG .... Butylene Glycol [*Organic chemistry*]
BG .... Buying [*Rate*] [*Value of the English pound*]
BGA .... American Belted Galloway Cattle Breeders' Association [*Later, BGS*] (EA)
BGA .... Banco Ganadero [*NYSE symbol*] (SAG)
BGA .... Banco Ganadero ADS [*NYSE symbol*] (TTSB)
BGA .... Barre Granite Association (EA)
BGA .... Behavior Genetics Association (EA)
BGA .... Bernard Geis Associates [*Publisher*] [*Obsolete*]
BGA .... Better Government Association (EA)
BGA .... Block Grant Authority
BGA .... Blood Gas Analyzer [*Physiology*]
BGA .... Blue-Green Algae [*Water purification*]
BGA .... Brigade Resources, Inc. [*Vancouver Stock Exchange symbol*]
BGA .... Brilliant Green Agar (OA)
BGA .... British Gaming Association (BARN)
BGA .... British Gliding Association (MCD)
BGA .... British Go Association (DBA)
BGA .... Bucaramanga [*Colombia*] [*Airport symbol*] (OAG)
BGA .... Bundesgesundheitsamt [*Database producer*]
BGAAWC .... Battle Group Anti-Air Warfare Coordinator [*No longer used*] [*Navy*] (DOMA)
BGAD .... Bluegrass Army Depot
BGAL .... Banco de Galicia y Buenos Aires [*NASDAQ symbol*] (SAG)
BGal .... Betagalactoside
BGAL .... British Guiana Airways Ltd. [*A national airline*]
BGall .... Bellum Gallicum [*of Caesar*] [*Classical studies*] (OCD)
BGALY .... Banco de Galicia-Buenos Aires [*NASDAQ symbol*] (TTSB)
BGAM .... Angmagssalik [*Greenland*] [*ICAO location identifier*] (ICLI)
BGAM .... Basic Graphic Access Method (IAA)
BGanadro .... Banco Ganadero [*Associated Press*] (SAG)
BGandro .... Banco Ganadero [*Associated Press*] (SAG)
BGAPr .... Banco Ganadero 'C'Pref ADS [*NYSE symbol*] (TTSB)
BGAS .... Angissoq [*Greenland*] [*ICAO location identifier*] (ICLI)
BGAS .... Berkshire Gas [*NASDAQ symbol*] (TTSB)
BGASH .... Berkshire Gas Co. [*NASDAQ symbol*] (NQ)
BGASH .... Botanic Gardens of Adelaide and State Herbarium [*Australia*]
BGAT .... Aputiteq [*Greenland*] [*ICAO location identifier*] (ICLI)
BGAV .... Blue-Green Algal Virus (OA)
BGB .... Bankgesellschaft Berlin [*Germany*] (ECON)
BGB .... Bat Groups of Britain (EAIO)
BGB .... Big Ben Resources, Inc. [*Vancouver Stock Exchange symbol*]
BGB .... Booksellers of Great Britain
BGB .... Booue [*Gabon*] [*Airport symbol*] (OAG)
BGB .... Brilliant Green Bile [*Microorganism growth medium*]
BGB .... Bubble-Gum Brigade [*Preteens*]
BGB .... Builders of Greater Britain [*A publication*]
BGBA .... Boys' and Girls' Brigades of America (EA)
BGBW .... Narssarssuaq [*Greenland*] [*ICAO location identifier*] (ICLI)
BGC .... Bailiff Grand Cross
BGC .... Bank Giro Credit [*British*] (DCTA)
BGC .... Baptist General Conference of Canada (AC)
BGC .... Basal-Ganglion Calcification [*Neurology*] (DAVI)

BGC .... Bay State Gas [*NYSE symbol*] (SAG)
BGC .... Bay State Gas [*NYSE symbol*] (TTSB)
BGC .... Berkeley Geochronology Center
BGC .... Black Gold Cooperative Library System, Ventura, CA [*OCLC symbol*] (OCLC)
BGC .... Blood Group Class
BGC .... Board of Green Cloth (ROG)
BGC .... Boat Group Commander [*Navy*] (NVT)
BGC .... Bolinger Road [*California*] [*Seismograph station code, US Geological Survey*] (SEIS)
BGC .... Braganca [*Portugal*] [*Airport symbol*] (OAG)
BGC .... Bren Gun Carrier [*British military*] (DMA)
BGC .... British Gas Corp.
BGCA .... Bean Growers Cooperative Association [*Australia*]
BGCA .... Bronchogenic Carcinoma [*Medicine*] (DMAA)
BGCC .... Bowling Green College of Commerce [*Later, a division of Western Kentucky State College*]
BG/CDR .... Battle Group Commander (MCD)
BGCE .... Banque Guineenne du Commerce Exterieur [*Guinean Bank of Foreign Commerce*] (AF)
BGCG .... Battery Guidance Command Group
BGCH .... Christianshab [*Greenland*] [*ICAO location identifier*] (ICLI)
BGCO .... Constable Point [*Greenland*] [*ICAO location identifier*] (ICLI)
BGCOB .... Background Compiler COBOL [*Common Business-Oriented Language*] (IAA)
BGCPS .... British Gas Corporation Pension Scheme
BGCS .... Botanical Gardens Conservation Secretariat (GNE)
BGCTT .... Battle Group Commanders Team Training (DOMA)
BgCtyB .... Big City Bagels, Inc. [*Associated Press*] (SAG)
BGD .... Bachelor of Graphic Design
BGD .... Bangladesh [*ANSI three-letter standard code*] (CNC)
BGD .... Banque Gabonaise de Developpement [*Gabonese Development Bank*] (AF)
BGD .... BGM Diversified Energy, Inc. [*Vancouver Stock Exchange symbol*]
BGD .... Billion Gallons per Day
BGD .... Blood Group-Degrading [*Medicine*] (MAE)
BGD .... Bogdanovka [*Former USSR Seismograph station code, US Geological Survey Closed*] (SEIS)
BGD .... Booksellers of Great Britain and Ireland (DGA)
BGD .... Borger, TX [*Location identifier FAA*] (FAAL)
BGD .... Golden and District Museum, Golden, British Columbia [*Library symbol National Library of Canada*] (NLC)
BGDA .... Bluegrass Depot Activity [*Army*] (AABC)
BGDB .... Daneborg [*Greenland*] [*ICAO location identifier*] (ICLI)
BGDE .... Brigade
BGDH .... Danmarkshavn [*Greenland*] [*ICAO location identifier*] (ICLI)
BGDN .... Butylene Glycol Dinitrate [*Organic chemistry*]
BGDU .... Dundas [*Greenland*] [*ICAO location identifier*] (ICLI)
BGE .... Bachelor of Geological Engineering
BGE .... Bainbridge, GA [*Location identifier FAA*] (FAAL)
BGE .... Baltimore Gas & El [*NYSE symbol*] (TTSB)
BGE .... Baltimore Gas & Electric Co. [*NYSE symbol*] (SPSG)
BGE .... Barge (ROG)
BGE .... Battle Group Exercise [*Navy*] (DOMA)
BGE .... Booker Gold Explorations [*Vancouver Stock Exchange symbol*]
BGE .... Bord Gais Eirecann [*Irish Gas Board*] (EY)
BGE .... Bull General Electric
BGE .... Butyl Glycidyl Ether [*Organic chemistry*]
BGEA .... Bill Glass Evangelistic Association (EA)
BGEA .... Billy Graham Evangelistic Association (EA)
B Ge E .... Bachelor of Geological Engineering
B Ge Eng .... Bachelor of Geological Engineering
BGEI .... Background Emission Index [*Automotive engineering*]
BGEM .... Egedesminde [*Greenland*] [*ICAO location identifier*] (ICLI)
BGEN .... Biogen, Inc. [*NASDAQ symbol*] (NQ)
BGEN .... Brigadier General
BGen .... Business Education Council General Award (AIE)
B Gen Ed .... Bachelor of General Education
BGF .... Bangui [*Central African Republic*] [*Airport symbol*] (OAG)
BGF .... Big Flower Holdings, Inc. [*NYSE symbol*] (SAG)
BGF .... Big Flower Press Hldgs [*NYSE symbol*] (TTSB)
BGF .... Grand Forks Public Library, British Columbia [*Library symbol National Library of Canada*] (NLC)
BGF .... Winchester, TN [*Location identifier FAA*] (FAAL)
BGFBM .... Boundary Museum, Grand Forks, British Columbia [*Library symbol National Library of Canada*] (NLC)
BGFC .... Banana Growers' Federation Cooperative [*Australia*]
BGFC .... Bobby Goldsboro Fan Club (EA)
BGFD .... Frederiksdal [*Greenland*] [*ICAO location identifier*] (ICLI)
BGFE .... Boston Grain and Flour Exchange (EA)
BGFH .... Frederikshab [*Greenland*] [*ICAO location identifier*] (ICLI)
BGFMA .... Bridge Grid Flooring Manufacturers Association (EA)
BGFO .... Bureau of Government Financial Operations [*Department of Treasury*]
BGFRS .... Board of Governors, Federal Reserve System
BGFS .... British Ground Freezing Society (PDAA)
BGG .... Black Granite Gauge
BGG .... Booster Gas Generator
BGG .... Bovine Gamma Globulin [*Immunology*]
BGG .... Briggs & Stratton [*NYSE symbol*] (TTSB)
BGG .... Briggs & Stratton Corp. [*NYSE symbol*] (SPSG)
BGG .... Burg Eltz [*Federal Republic of Germany*] [*Seismograph station code, US Geological Survey*] (SEIS)
BGGA .... British Golf Greenkeepers' Association (BI)
BGGD .... Gronnedal [*Greenland*] [*ICAO location identifier*] (ICLI)

BGGH .... Godthab [*Greenland*] [*ICAO location identifier*] (ICLI)
BGGL .... Sondrestrom [*Greenland*] [*ICAO location identifier*] (ICLI)
BGGN .... Godhavn [*Greenland*] [*ICAO location identifier*] (ICLI)
BGGRA .... British Gelatine and Glue Research Association (DAVI)
BGH .... Bear Gulch [*California*] [*Seismograph station code, US Geological Survey*] (SEIS)
BGH .... Borough (ROG)
BGH .... Bovine Growth Hormone [*Endocrinology*]
BGH .... British General Hospital
BGH .... Bundesgerichtshof [*Federal Supreme Court*] [*German*] (DLA)
BGHB .... Holsteinsborg [*Greenland*] [*ICAO location identifier*] (ICLI)
BGHS .... Squamish Valley Museum, Garibaldi Highlands, British Columbia [*Library symbol National Library of Canada*] (NLC)
BGHT .... Bought (WGA)
BGI .... Barbados [*Airport symbol*] (OAG)
BGI .... Beaver Resources, Inc. [*Toronto Stock Exchange symbol Vancouver Stock Exchange symbol*]
BGI .... Besicorp Group [*AMEX symbol*] (SAG)
BGI .... Borland Graphics Interface [*Borland International*] (BYTE)
BGI .... British Gas International
BGI .... Gibsons Public Library, British Columbia [*Library symbol National Library of Canada*] (NLC)
BGI .... International Gravimetric Bureau [*Marine science*] (OSRA)
BGIEC .... Besicorp Group [*ECM Symbol*] (TTSB)
BGIFH .... Boys and Girls International Floor Hockey (EA)
BGII .... Bally Gaming International [*NASDAQ symbol*] (SPSG)
BGII .... Bally Gaming Intl. [*NASDAQ symbol*] (TTSB)
BGIPM .... Ephinstone Pioneer Museum, Gibsons, British Columbia [*Library symbol National Library of Canada*] (NLC)
BGIRA .... British Glass Industry Research Association [*Research center*] (IRC)
BGIS .... Isortoq [*Greenland*] [*ICAO location identifier*] (ICLI)
BGIT............ Ivigtut [*Greenland*] [*ICAO location identifier*] (ICLI)
BGJ .... Borgarfjordur [*Iceland*] [*Airport symbol*] (OAG)
BGJH .... Julianehab [*Greenland*] [*ICAO location identifier*] (ICLI)
BGJN .... Jakobshavn [*Greenland*] [*ICAO location identifier*] (ICLI)
BGK .... Bangkok [*Thailand*] (WDAA)
BGK .... Bhatnagar-Gross-Krook [*Equation*]
BGKD .... Kap Dan [*Greenland*] [*ICAO location identifier*] (ICLI)
BGKK .... Kulusuk [*Greenland*] [*ICAO location identifier*] (ICLI)
BGKM .... Kungmiut [*Greenland*] [*ICAO location identifier*] (ICLI)
BGKT .... Kap Tobin [*Greenland*] [*ICAO location identifier*] (ICLI)
BGL............. Bachelor of General Laws (DLA)
BGL............. Baglung [*Nepal*] [*Airport symbol*] (OAG)
BGL............. Below Ground Level (WDAA)
BGL............. Betriebsgewerkschaftsleitung [*Factory Union Headquarters*] [*Germany*]
BGL............. Brooke Group Ltd. [*NYSE symbol*] (SPSG)
BGLA .... British Growers' Look Ahead International Exhibition (ITD)
BGLA .... Business Group for Latin America [*Later, COA*]
BGLB .... Brilliant Green Lactose Broth (MAE)
BGLE .... British Graham Land Expedition [*1934-37*]
BGLR .... British Guiana Law Reports (Old and New Series) [*A publication*] (DLA)
BGLR .... Bugler
BGLS .... Manhattan Bagel [*NASDAQ symbol*] (TTSB)
BGLS .... Manhattan Bagel Company, Inc. [*NASDAQ symbol*] (SAG)
BGLT........... Battle Group Landing Team
BGlu........... Blood Glucose [*Medicine*] (MAE)
BGLV .... Bally's Grand [*NASDAQ symbol*] (TTSB)
BGLV .... Ballys Grand, Inc. [*NASDAQ symbol*] (SAG)
BGLVW .... Ballys Grand Wrrt [*NASDAQ symbol*] (TTSB)
BGM............ Background Music (WDAA)
BGM............ Basegram [*Navy*]
BGM............ Bedside Glucose Monitoring [*Medicine*] (DMAA)
BGM............ BENELUX Group on Mortality (EAIO)
BGM............ Biennial General Meeting
BGM............ Binghamton [*New York*] [*Airport symbol*] (OAG)
BGM............ British Gallantry Medal
BGM............ Buglemaster [*Navy*]
BGM............ Greenwood Museum, British Columbia [*Library symbol National Library of Canada*] (NLC)
BGMA .... British Gear Manufacturers Association (MCD)
BGMA .... British Guiana Militia Artillery [*British military*] (DMA)
BGMC .... BOCES [*Boards of Cooperative Educational Services*] Geneseo Migrant Center (EA)
BGMC .... British Glass Manufacturers Confederation (DBA)
BGMI .... Biography and Genealogy Master Index [*A publication*]
BGMM .... Marmorilik [*Greenland*] [*ICAO location identifier*] (ICLI)
BGMRAO..... Balance General Mobilization Reserve Acquisition Objective [*DoD*]
BGMSTR...... Buglemaster
BGMTS .... Bradley Gunnery and Missile Target System [*Army*] (INF)
BGMV .... Bean Golden Mosaic Virus
BGMV .... Mesters Vig [*Greenland*] [*ICAO location identifier*] (ICLI)
BGN .... Berglynn Resources [*Vancouver Stock Exchange symbol*]
BGN .... Big Creek [*Nevada*] [*Seismograph station code, US Geological Survey Closed*] (SEIS)
BGN .... Board of Geographic Names
BGN .... Board on Geographic Names [*Defense Mapping Agency*] [*Washington, DC*]
BGN .... Bogen Communications International [*AMEX symbol*] (SAG)
BGN .... Bogen Communic Intl. [*AMEX symbol*] (TTSB)
BGN .... Branchioganglionic Neuron [*Neurology*]
BGN .... Brigantine [*Ship*]
BGN .... Busch Grand National [*Auto racing*]
BGN .... North Platte, NE [*Location identifier FAA*] (FAAL)

BGND .... Beginning Descent [*Aviation*] (FAAC)
BGndo .... Banco Ganadero [*Associated Press*] (SAG)
BGN.E .... Bogen Communic Intl Unit [*AMEX symbol*] (TTSB)
BGNG .... Beginning
BGNN .... Nanortalik [*Greenland*] [*ICAO location identifier*] (ICLI)
BGNS .... Background Natural Sound
BGNS .... Narssaq [*Greenland*] [*ICAO location identifier*] (ICLI)
BGN.WS ...... Bogen Communic Intl Wrrt [*AMEX symbol*] (TTSB)
BGO .... Bema Gold [*AMEX symbol*] (TTSB)
BGO .... Bema Gold Corp. [*AMEX symbol*] (SAG)
BGO .... Bema Gold Ltd. [*Toronto Stock Exchange symbol Vancouver Stock Exchange symbol*]
BGO .... Bergen [*Norway*] [*Airport symbol*] (OAG)
BGO .... Bismuth Germanate [*Inorganic chemistry*]
BGO .... Bismuth, Germanium, and Oxygen [*Inorganic chemistry*]
BGO .... Bowling Green [*Ohio*] [*Seismograph station code, US Geological Survey*] (SEIS)
BGORS .... Battle Group Operational Readiness System (DOMA)
BGOS .... Orssuiorssuaq [*Greenland*] [*ICAO location identifier*] (ICLI)
BGP .... Background Perfume
BGP .... Bagra [*Pakistan*] [*Seismograph station code, US Geological Survey*] (SEIS)
BGP .... Barrier, Grease Proof (MSA)
BGP .... Barrington Properties Ltd. [*Toronto Stock Exchange symbol Vancouver Stock Exchange symbol*]
BGP .... Beta-Glycerophosphatase (MAE)
BGP .... Border Gateway Protocol [*Computer science*] (PCM)
BGP .... Borders Group [*NYSE symbol*] (TTSB)
BGP .... Borders Group, Inc. [*NYSE symbol*] (SAG)
BGP .... Bridgeport [*Diocesan abbreviation*] [*Connecticut*] (TOCD)
BGPA .... Bateria General de Preubas de Aptitud [*General Aptitude Test Battery*] [*Spanish*]
BGPA .... British Goose Producers Association (DBA)
BGPC .... Prins Christian Sund [*Greenland*] [*ICAO location identifier*] (ICLI)
BGPDC........ Brouwer General Perturbations Differential Correction Program (MCD)
BGPHES....... Battle Group Passive Horizon Extension System [*Reconnaissance*]
BGPHES-ST... Battle Group Passive Horizon Extension System - Surface Terminal [*Reconnaissance*] (DWSG)
BGPP .... Beneficiary Government Production Program
BGPW .... Bare Gold-Plated Wire
BGQ .... Big Lake, AK [*Location identifier FAA*] (FAAL)
BGQ .... Bulk Grains Queensland [*An association Australia*]
BGQS .... Qutdligssat [*Greenland*] [*ICAO location identifier*] (ICLI)
BGR .... Bailey, G. R., Escanaba MI [*STAC*]
BGR .... Bangor [*Maine*] [*Airport symbol*] (OAG)
BGR .... Bangor Hydro Electric [*NYSE symbol*] (TTSB)
BGR .... Bangor Hydro Electric Co. [*NYSE symbol*] (SPSG)
BGR .... Barry Gibb Record (EA)
BGR .... Basal Granule
BGR .... Bombing and Gunnery Range
BGR .... British Gas Region
BGR .... Bulgaria [*ANSI three-letter standard code*] (CNC)
BGR .... Bureau of Governmental Research [*University of California*] [*Research Center*] (AEBS)
BGR .... Burger
BGR .... Granisle Public Library, British Columbia [*Library symbol National Library of Canada*] (NLC)
BGR .... Sigi Air [*Bulgaria*] [*ICAO designator*] (FAAC)
BGRE .... Greenwood Public Library, British Columbia [*Library symbol National Library of Canada*] (NLC)
BGRG .... British Geomorphological Research Group
BGRH .... Berger Hldgs Ltd [*NASDAQ symbol*] (TTSB)
BGRH .... Berger Holdings, Inc. [*NASDAQ symbol*] (SAG)
BGRM .... Groundbirch Museum, British Columbia [*Library symbol National Library of Canada*] (NLC)
BGRNS........ Nootka Sound Historical Society, Gold River, British Columbia [*Library symbol National Library of Canada*] (NLC)
BGRR .... Brookhaven Graphite Research Reactor
BGRS .... Blood Glucose Reagent Strip [*Endocrinology*] (DAVI)
BGRS .... Bureau of Governmental Research and Service [*University of Oregon*] [*Research center*] (RCD)
BGRS .... Ravns Storo [*Greenland*] [*ICAO location identifier*] (ICLI)
BGRV .... Boost Glide Reentry Vehicle [*Air Force*]
BGS .... Bachelor of General Studies
BGS .... Backup Gimbal Servo
BGS .... Backup Guidance System [*NASA*]
BGS .... Bags
BGS .... Bailly Generating Station [*Nuclear energy*] (NRCH)
BGS .... Below Ground Surface
BGS .... Belted Galloway Society (EA)
BGS .... Beta Gamma Sigma
BGS .... BGS Systems, Inc. [*Associated Press*] (SAG)
BGS .... Big Spring, TX [*Location identifier FAA*] (FAAL)
BGS .... Blood Group Substances [*Hematology*]
BGS .... Bluegrass Petroleum, Inc. [*Vancouver Stock Exchange symbol*]
BGS .... Boeing Ground Support (KSC)
BGS .... Bombing and Gunnery School [*British*]
BGS .... Brigadier, General Staff [*Army British*]
BGS .... British Gas Corp. [*Toronto Stock Exchange symbol*]
BGS .... British Geological Survey
BGS .... British Geotechnical Society
BGS .... British Geriatrics Society
BGS .... British Glaciological Society (NOAA)
BGS .... British Gladiolus Society (BI)

BGS	British Goat Society
BGS	British Grassland Society
BGS	Brothers of the Good Shepherd [*Roman Catholic religious order*]
BGS	Bundesgrenzschutz [*Germany ICAO designator*] (FAAC)
BGS	Bundesgrenzschutz [*West Germany*] [*Military*] (NATG)
BGS	Burgs
BGS	Burgs [*Postal Service standard*] (OPSA)
BGS	Business and Government Services (ACRL)
BGS	Business Grant Services [*Information service or system*]
BGS	Gulf Islands Secondary School, Ganges, British Columbia [*Library symbol Library network*] (NLC)
bgs	Little Brothers of the Good Shepherd (TOCD)
BGS	Little Brothers of the Good Shepherd (TOCD)
BGSA	Blood Granulocyte-Specific Activity [*Hematology*] (MAE)
BGSA	British Gas Staff Association [*A union*]
BGSC	Scoresbysund [*Greenland*] [*ICAO location identifier*] (ICLI)
BGSCA	Buick GS [*Gran Sport*] Club of America (EA)
BGSDA	Brilliant Green Suphadiazine-Deoxycholate Agar (PDAA)
BGSF	Sondre Stromfjord [*Greenland*] [*ICAO location identifier*] (ICLI)
BGSG	Sermiligaq [*Greenland*] [*ICAO location identifier*] (ICLI)
BGSI	Mary Hawkins Memorial Library, Saltspring Island Public Library, Ganges, BritishColumbia [*Library symbol National Library of Canada*] (NLC)
BGSIA	Beginning Standard Instrument Approach [*Aviation*] (IAA)
BGSPS	British Gas Staff Pension Scheme
BGSR	British Gas Ltd. American Depository Receipts [*Toronto Stock Exchange symbol*]
BGSS	Battalion Ground Surveillance Section [*Army*] (AABC)
BGSS	BGS Systems [*NASDAQ symbol*] (TTSB)
BGSS	BGS Systems, Inc. [*NASDAQ symbol*] (NQ)
BGST	Bradley Gunnery Skills Test [*Army*] (INF)
BGST	Sukkertoppen [*Greenland*] [*ICAO location identifier*] (ICLI)
BGSTA	Beginning Straight-In Approach [*Aviation*] (IAA)
BGSU	Bowling Green State University [*Ohio*]
BGT	Bender-Gestalt Test [*Psychology*]
BGT	Bight (ROG)
BGT	Blackrock Strategic Term [*NYSE symbol*] (TTSB)
BGT	Blackrock Strategic Term Trust [*NYSE symbol*] (SPSG)
BGT	Bought (ROG)
BGT	Budget
BGT	Bungarotoxin [*Also, BTX, BuTx*] [*Biochemistry*]
BGTB	Brazilian Government Trade Bureau (EA)
BGTD	Beigetretene Teile Deutschlands [*Newly Adhered Parts of Germany*] [*Name given to former East German territory after unification*]
BGTL	Thule Air Base [*Greenland*] [*ICAO location identifier*] (ICLI)
BGTM	Tingmiarmiut [*Greenland*] [*ICAO location identifier*] (ICLI)
BGTN	Tiniteqilaq [*Greenland*] [*ICAO location identifier*] (ICLI)
BGTO	Bonaire Government Tourist Office (EA)
BGTS	Boeing Gulf Test Section (SAA)
BGTS	British Geotechnical Society
BGTT	Battle Group Tactical Training [*Navy*] (DOMA)
BGTT	Borderline Glucose Tolerance Test [*Medicine*] (MAE)
BGTTL	Bagatelle
BGU	Ben-Gurion University (BJA)
BGU	Berliner Griechische Urkunden [*A publication*] (OCD)
BGU	Bowling Green State University, Bowling Green, OH [*OCLC symbol*] (OCLC)
BGU	Bridge Resources Ltd. [*Vancouver Stock Exchange symbol*]
BGU	British Guiana
BGUM	Unanak [*Greenland*] [*ICAO location identifier*] (ICLI)
BGUP	Upernavik [*Greenland*] [*ICAO location identifier*] (ICLI)
BGV	Bac-Giang [*Vietnam*] [*Seismograph station code, US Geological Survey*] (SEIS)
BGVF	British Guiana Volunteer Force [*British military*] (DMA)
BGW	Baghdad [*Iraq*] [*Airport symbol*] (OAG)
BGW	Battlefield Guided Weapon (MCD)
BGWF	British Granite and Whinstone Federation (PDAA)
BGX	Bage [*Brazil*] [*Airport symbol*] (OAG)
BGX	Biologix (BC) Ltd. [*Vancouver Stock Exchange symbol*]
BGY	Bergamo [*Italy*] [*Airport symbol*] (OAG)
BGY	Bright Greenish Yellow [*Fluorescence*] [*A fungal metabolite property*] (OA)
BGYF	Bright Greenish Yellow Fluorescence [*A fungal metabolite property*]
BGZ	Brasil Gold Resources [*Vancouver Stock Exchange symbol*]
BGZ	Kansas City, KS [*Location identifier FAA*] (FAAL)
BH	Augusta Airways [*ICAO designator*] (AD)
BH	Bachelor of Hamburgerology [*McDonald's Corp. Hamburger University*]
BH	Bachelor of Hebrew
BH	Bachelor of Humanics
Bh	Bachelor's Degree (Honours) [*British*]
BH	Bahrain [*IYRU nationality code*] [*ANSI two-letter standard code*] (CNC)
BH	Bank Holiday
BH	Barker-Henderson [*Theory*] [*Chemical physics*]
BH	Barnes-Hind/Hydrocurve [*Commercial firm*] (DAVI)
B-H	Barnes-Hind Pharmaceutical (DAVI)
B/H	Base-Height Ratio
BH	Base Hospital [*Military*]
BH	Basic Heterostructure (IAA)
BH	Baskets or Hampers [*Freight*]
BH	Bath & Hammondsport Railroad Co. [*AAR code*]
b h	Bay Horse (BARN)
BH	Beach (ADA)
BH	Beer House (ROG)

BH.	Bell & Howell Co.
BH.	Beni Hasan [*Egyptology*] (ROG)
BH.	Benjamin Harrison [*US president, 1833-1901*]
BH.	Benzalkonium and Heparin (MAE)
bh	Benzhydryl [*As substituent on nucleoside*] [*Biochemistry*]
BH.	Beverly Hills (IIA)
BH.	Biblia Hebraica (BJA)
BH.	Biblical Hebrew (BJA)
BH.	Bibliographia Huntiana [*Computer-based bibliography*]
BH.	Bill of Health
BH.	Binary to Hexadecimal (BUR)
BH.	Birthday Honours [*Titles conferred on the sovereign's birthday*] [*British*]
BH.	Black Hawk [*Military*] (MCD)
BH.	Blasthole
BH.	Bleomycin Hydrolase [*An enzyme*]
BH.	Block Handler [*Computer science*]
BH.	Blockhouse [*NASA*] (KSC)
BH.	Bloody Hell [*British slang*]
BH.	Blue Hills Power Plant [*Nuclear energy*] (NRCH)
BH.	Boiler House [*Technical drawings*]
BH.	Books for the Heart [*A publication*]
BH.	Boosey & Hawkes [*Record label*] [*Great Britain, USA*]
B/H	Bordeaux-Hamburg Inclusive [*Shipping*]
BH.	Borehole
BH.	Both Hands [*Psychometrics*]
BH.	Boys Hope (EA)
BH.	Brain Hormone [*Endocrinology*]
BH.	Brake Horsepower (IAA)
BH.	Branch Head
BH.	Breath-Hold Diving
BH.	Brigade Headquarters [*Army*]
BH.	Brinell Hardness Number [*Also, BHN, BHNo, HB*]
BH.	Bristol Hotel [*NYSE symbol*] (TTSB)
BH.	Bristol Hotel Co. [*NYSE symbol*] (SAG)
BH.	British Honduras
bh	British Honduras [*MARC country of publication code Library of Congress*] (LCCP)
BH.	British Hovercraft
BH.	Brookhaven Office [*AEC*]
BH.	Buestenhalter [*Brassiere*] [*German slang*]
BH.	Bulk Head
BH.	Bunch (DNAB)
BH.	Bundle of His [*Cardiology*] (DAVI)
BH.	Bung-Hole [*i.e., cheese*] [*British slang*]
BH.	Buried Heterostructure (IAA)
BH.	Buried History: Quarterly Journal of the Australian Institute of Archaeology [*A publication*] (APTA)
BH.	Business Hours
BH.	Busy Hour (IAA)
BH.	Flux Density Versus Magnetizing Force [*Symbol*] (MCD)
BH.	Houston Public Library, British Columbia [*Library symbol National Library of Canada*] (NLC)
BH.	Turks & Caicos Airways Ltd. [*ICAO designator Obsolete*] (OAG)
BH₄	Tetrahydrobiopterin [*Biochemistry*]
BHA	Bachelor of Hospital Administration
BHA	Bahama Resources Ltd. [*Vancouver Stock Exchange symbol*]
BHA	Bankcard Holders of America (EA)
BHA	Baptist Hospital Association (EA)
BHA	Base Helix Angle [*NASA*]
BHA	Bengal Horse Artillery [*British military*] (DMA)
BHA	Better Hearing Australia [*An association*] (EAIO)
BHA	BHA Group, Inc. [*Associated Press*] (SAG)
BHA	Bioinstrumentation Harness Assembly
BHA	Biscayne Apparel [*AMEX symbol*] (TTSB)
BHA	Biscayne Apparel, Inc. [*Formerly, Biscayne Holdings, Inc.*] [*AMEX symbol*] (SPSG)
BHA	Blazer Horse Association (EA)
BHA	Bleed Hose Assembly
BHA	Bombay Horse Artillery [*British military*] (DMA)
BHA	Bottom Hole Assembly [*Well drilling technology*]
BHA	Bound Hepatitis Antibody [*Medicine*] (DMAA)
BHA	Breeders and Hatchermen's Association [*Australia*]
BHA	British Handball Association (DBA)
BHA	British Hardmetal Association (DBA)
BHA	British Homeopathic Association
BHA	British Hotels Association (BARN)
BHA	British Humanist Association
BHA	British Hypnotherapy Association
BHA	Broken Hill [*Kabwe*] [*Zambia*] [*Seismograph station code, US Geological Survey*] (SEIS)
BHA	Bureau of Hearings and Appeals [*Social Security Administration*]
BHA	Bus History Association (EA)
BHA	Butylated Hydroxyanisole [*Antioxidant*]
BHA	Harvard Divinity School, Cambridge, MA [*OCLC symbol*] (OCLC)
BHA	Hazelton Public Library, British Columbia [*Library symbol National Library of Canada*] (NLC)
BHAB	British Helicopter Advisory Board (AIA)
BHAD	Beachhead Air Defense (MCD)
BHAD	Black Hills Army Depot
BHAD	Broach Adapter
BH Adm	Bachelor of Hospital Administration
BHAG	BHA Group 'A' [*NASDAQ symbol*] (TTSB)
BHAG	BHA Group, Inc. [*NASDAQ symbol*] (NQ)
BHAL	Bernard Haldane [*NASDAQ symbol*] (SAG)

BHAL	Bernard Haldane Assoc Inc. [*NASDAQ symbol*] (TTSB)
BHAM	Birmingham [*City, county borough, and university in England*]
BH & G	Better Homes and Gardens [*Information service or system A publication*] (IID)
BH & HPA	British Holiday and Home Parks Association (DBA)
BH & SM	Better Hearing and Speech Month
BH & T	Ballistic Hull and Turret Vehicle (MCD)
BHAP	Business Health Assessment Program
BHARC	Battelle Human Affairs Research Center [*Seattle, WA*]
BHAS	Burroughs Hospital Administrative System [*Computer science*] (BUR)
BHAT	Beta-Blocker Heart Attack Trial [*Cardiology*]
BHB	Bachelor of Human Biology
BHB	Bar Harbor [*Maine*] [*Airport symbol*] (OAG)
BHB	Bipod Heavy Barrel [*Weaponry*] [*Military*] (INF)
BHB	Blue Horizontal Branch
BHB	Butropium Bromide [*Pharmacology*]
BHBA	Beta-Hydroxybutyric Acid (MAE)
BHBFC	Bangladesh House Building Finance Corp. (EY)
BHBMA	British Hacksaw and Bandsaw Manufacturers' Association (DBA)
BHBN	Butyl(hydroxybutyl)nitrosamine [*Organic chemistry*]
BHBR	Boat Harbor
BHC	Ballistic Height Correction
BHC	Baltimore Hebrew College (BJA)
BHC	Bank Holding Company
BHC	Beam-Heated Cathode
BHC	Bell Helicopter Co. (MCD)
BHC	Benedictine Heights College [*Oklahoma*]
BHC	Benzene Hexachloride [*Also, GBH, HCH*] [*Insecticide*]
BHC	Better Heating-Cooling Council [*Later, HI*] (EA)
BHC	BHC Communications [*Associated Press*] (SAG)
BHC	BHC Communications 'A' [*AMEX symbol*] (TTSB)
BHC	BHC Communications, Inc. [*AMEX symbol*] (SPSG)
BHC	Blockhouse Computer [*NASA*] (KSC)
BHC	Body Heat Content
BHC	Bombay High Court Reports [*1862-75*] [*India*] [*A publication*] (DLA)
BHC	Borehole Capsule
BHC	Borehole Compensated [*Sonic log*]
BHC	Born-Haber Cycle [*Physics*]
BHC	Boston Hebrew College (BJA)
BHC	British Herdsmen's Club (BI)
BHC	British High Commissioner
BHC	British Hovercraft Corp.
BHC	Brotherhood of the Holy Cross [*Anglican religious community*]
BHC	Bullhead City [*Arizona*]/Laughlin [*Nevada*] [*Airport symbol*] (OAG)
BHC	Burst Height Compensator [*Military*] (CAAL)
BHC	Business History Conference (EA)
BHC	Busy Hour Call [*Telecommunications*] (TEL)
BHC	Holy Cross Greek Orthodox School of Theology, Brookline, MA [*OCLC symbol*] (OCLC)
BHC	Journeymen Barbers, Hairdressers, Cosmetologists and Proprietors' International Union of America
BHCA	Bank Holding Company Act [*of 1956*] (TDOB)
BHCA	Basset Hound Club of America (EA)
BHCA	British Health Care Association (DBA)
BHCA	Busy Hour Call Attempts [*Telecommunications*]
BHCAG	Buyers Health Care Action Group [*Minnesota*]
BHCC	British Hellenic Chamber of Commerce (DBA)
BHCC	Broken Hill Chamber of Commerce [*Australia*]
BHCC	Busy Hour Call Completions [*Telecommunications*] (ACRL)
BHCDA	Bureau of Health Care Delivery and Assistance [*Department of Health and Human Services*]
BHCEC	British Health-Care Export Council (DS)
BHCF	BHC Financial [*NASDAQ symbol*] (TTSB)
BHCF	BHC Financial, Inc. [*NASDAQ symbol*] (SAG)
BHCF	British Hire Cruiser Federation (DBA)
BHCFC	Buddy Holly and the Crickets Fan Club (EAIO)
BHC Fncl	BHC Financial, Inc. [*Associated Press*] (SAG)
B-HCG	Beta Human Chorionic Gonadotropin [*Endocrinology*] (DAVI)
BHCNU	Bis(hydroxycyclohexyl)nitrosourea [*Antineoplastic drug*]
BHCPJ	Bombay High Court Printed Judgments [*1869-1900*] [*India*] [*A publication*] (DLA)
BHCR	Bombay High Court Reports [*1862-75*] [*India*] [*A publication*] (DLA)
BHCSA	British Hospitals Contributory Schemes Association (PDAA)
BHCT	Bottom Hole Circulating Temperature [*Oil well borehole*]
BHD	BCNU [*Carmustine*], Hydroxyurea, Dacarbazine [*Antineoplastic drug regimen*]
BHD	Beachhead (AFM)
BHD	Belfast [*Northern Ireland*] Harbour [*Airport symbol*] (OAG)
BHD	Berhad [*Public Limited Company*] [*Malaysia*] (FEA)
BHD	Beta-Hydroxysteroid Dehydrogenase [*An enzyme*]
BHD	Bighorn Development Corp. [*Vancouver Stock Exchange symbol*]
BHD	Binary Homing Device
BHD	Birkenhead [*British depot code*]
Bhd	Brotherhood (ILCA)
BHD	Bulkhead (AAG)
BHDP	Baltimore Huntington's Disease Project [*Johns Hopkins University*] [*Research center*] (RCD)
BHDV	BCNU [*Carmustine*], Hydroxyurea, Dacarbazine, Vincristine [*Antineoplastic drug regimen*]
BHE	Bachelor of Home Economics (NADA)
BHE	Bachelor of Household Economics
BHE	Benchmark Electronics [*AMEX symbol*] (TTSB)
BHE	Benchmark Electronics, Inc. [*AMEX symbol*] (SAG)
BHE	Biggin Executive Aviation Ltd. [*British ICAO designator*] (FAAC)
BHE	Biharmonic Equation

BHE	Blenheim [*New Zealand*] [*Airport symbol*] (OAG)
BHE	Bolton-Hunter Reagent-Labeled Eledoisin [*Analytical biochemistry*]
BHE	Bureau of Higher Education [*Later, Bureau of Higher and Continuing Education*] [*Office of Education*]
BH Ec	Bachelor of Home Economics
BHEC	British Health-Care Export Council (EAIO)
BHEC	British Hospitals Export Council [*Later, BHCEC*] (DS)
BHED	Bis(hydroxyethyl)dimerate [*Organic chemistry*]
BHEDC	British Hospital Equipment Display Centre (CB)
B-HEF	Business-Higher Education Forum [*Washington, DC*] (EA)
BHEL	Bharat Heavy Electricals Ltd. [*India*]
BHEP	Bis(hydroxyethyl)piperazine [*Organic chemistry*]
BHERT	Business/Higher Education Round Table
BHET	(Beta-Hydroxyethyl)theophylline [*Biochemistry*]
BHET	Bis(hydroxyethyl)terephthalate [*Organic chemistry*]
BHF	Background Heat Flux
BHF	Berliner Handels- & Frankfurter Bank [*Berlin & Frankfurt Bank*]
BHF	Blues Heaven Foundation (EA)
BHF	Bolivian Hemorrhagic Fever [*Medicine*] (DMAA)
BHF	British Hardware Federation (DBA)
BHF	British Heart Foundation (EAIO)
BHF	British Holiday Fellowship Ltd. (BI)
BHF	Business History Foundation [*Defunct*] (EA)
BHFB	British Home Furnishings Bureau (DBA)
BHFC	Bob Hastings Fan Club [*Inactive*] (EA)
BHFC	Bob Homan Fan Club (EA)
BHFC	Bonnie Hartle Fan Club (EA)
BHFC	Boyce and Hart Fan Club (EA)
BHFC	Brice Henderson Fan Club (EA)
BHFCBV	Baseball Hall of Fame Committee on Baseball Veterans (EA)
BHFT	Basic Human Factor Technology (SSD)
BHFTA	British Health Food Trade Association (DBA)
BHFX	Broach Fixture
BHG	Bad Reichenhall [*Federal Republic of Germany*] [*Seismograph station code, US Geological Survey*] (SEIS)
BHG	Blackwood Hodge (Canada) Ltd. [*Toronto Stock Exchange symbol*]
BHG	Booth-Henry-Gorin [*Equations for calculation of net charge and valence of molecule*]
BHG	British Hat Guild (DBA)
BHG	Sulphur Springs, TX [*Location identifier FAA*] (FAAL)
BHGA	British Hang Gliding Association
BHGMF	British Hang Glider Manufacturers Federation (PDAA)
BHH	Barkston-Heath FTU [*British*] [*Military*] [*FAA designator*] (FAAC)
BHH	Biblisch-Historisches Handwoerterbuch [*A publication*] (BJA)
BHH	Bisha [*Saudi Arabia*] [*Airport symbol*] (OAG)
BHH	Hudson Hope Public Library, British Columbia [*Library symbol National Library of Canada*] (NLC)
BHHCNH	Better Home Heat Council of New Hampshire (SRA)
BHHI	British Home and Hospital for Incurables
BHHM	Hudson Hope Museum, British Columbia [*Library symbol National Library of Canada*] (NLC)
BHHMA	British Hardware and Housewares Manufacturers Association (DBA)
BHHMC	Board of Hospitals and Homes of the Methodist Church [*Later, National Association of Health and Welfare Ministries of the United Methodist Church*] (EA)
BHHS	British Hosta and Hemerocallis Society (EAIO)
BHHW	Biblisch-Historisches Handwoerterbuch [*A publication*] (BJA)
BHI	Bahia Blanca [*Argentina*] [*Airport symbol*] (OAG)
BHI	Baker Hughes, Inc. [*NYSE symbol*] (SPSG)
BHI	Bertha Hill [*Idaho*] [*Seismograph station code, US Geological Survey Closed*] (SEIS)
BHI	Better Hearing Institute (EA)
BHI	Binaural Hearing Impairment
BHI	Biosynthetic Human Insulin [*Medicine*]
BHI	Brain-Heart Infusion [*Growth medium*]
BHI	British Horological Institute
BHI	Bullet Hit Indicator (MCD)
BHI	Bureau Hydrographique International [*International Hydrographic Organization*] (EAIO)
BHI	Bureau of Health Insurance [*Social Security Administration*]
BHI	Burst-Height Indicator
BHIA	Brain-Heart Infusion Agar [*Growth medium*] (OA)
BHI-Ac	Brain-Heart Infusion [*Broth*] with Acetone [*Growth medium*]
BHIB	Beef Heart Infusion Broth [*Microbiology*]
BHIBA	Brain-Heart Infusion Blood Agar [*Growth medium*]
BHIC	British Heritage Institute (Canada) Inc. (AC)
BHI Cp	BHI Corp. [*Associated Press*] (SAG)
BHIF	Better Highways Information Foundation [*Later, ARTBA*]
BHIF	British Headwear Industries Federation (DBA)
BHIK	BHI Corp. [*NASDAQ symbol*] (SAG)
BHIKF	BHI Corp. [*NASDAQ symbol*] (TTSB)
BHIPA	British Honey Importers and Packers Association (DBA)
BHIS	Beef Heart Infusion Supplement [*Broth or agar*] [*Growth medium*] (DAVI)
BHIS	Brain-Heart Infusion Supplemented [*Broth or agar*] [*Growth medium*]
BHIX	Belmont Homes [*NASDAQ symbol*] (SAG)
BHJ	Bhuj [*India*] [*Airport symbol*] (OAG)
BHJ	Bulkhead Jack
BHJL	Jack Lynn Memorial Museum, Horsefly, British Columbia [*Library symbol National Library of Canada*] (NLC)
BHK	Baby Hamster Kidney
BHK	Bhakra [*India*] [*Seismograph station code, US Geological Survey*] (SEIS)
BHK	Biblia Hebraica (R. Kittel) [*A publication*] (BJA)
BHK	Black Hawk Mining, Inc. [*Toronto Stock Exchange symbol*]

BHK .... Bukhara [*Former USSR Airport symbol*] (OAG)
BHKIM .... Ksan Indian Village and Museum, Haselton, British Columbia [*Library symbol National Library of Canada*] (NLC)
BHL............. Bachelor of Hebrew Letters
BHL............. Bachelor of Hebrew Literature
BHL............. Bachelor of Humane Letters
BHL............. Bernard-Henri Levy [*French writer and philosopher*]
BHL............. Better Humanity League [*Commercial firm*] (EA)
BHL............. Biblical History and Literature (BJA)
BHL............. Bilateral Hilar Lymphadenopathy [*Medicine*] (DMAA)
BHL............. Biological Half-Life
BHL............. Bristow Helicopters Group Ltd. [*British ICAO designator*] (FAAC)
BHL............. British Housewives' League (DI)
BHLA .... Busy Hour Load [*Telecommunications*] (TEL)
BHLA .... Ben Hur Life Association [*Crawfordsville, IN*] (EA)
BHLF........... Blair House Library Foundation [*Defunct*] (EA)
BHLH .... Agassiz-Harrison Historical Society, Agassiz, British Columbia [*Library symbol National Library of Canada*] (BIB)
BHLH .... Basic Helix-Loop-Helix [*Genetics*]
BHLS .... Below/Hook Lifters Section of the Material Handling Institute (EA)
BHIthSc....... Bachelor of Health Science
BHM............ B&H Maritime Carriers [*AMEX symbol*] (TTSB)
BHM............ B & H Maritime Carriers Ltd. [*AMEX symbol*] (CTT)
BHM............ Bible Holiness Movement (EA)
BHM............ Birmingham [*Alabama*] [*Airport symbol*]
BHM............ Bureau of Health Manpower [*Later, Health Resources Administration*] [*HEW*]
BHM............ Busy Hour Model [*Computer science*]
BHM............ Hope Museum, British Columbia [*Library symbol National Library of Canada*] (NLC)
BHMA .... Bald-Headed Men of America (EA)
BHMA .... British Hard Metal Association
BHMA .... British Herbal Medicine Association
BHMA .... British Holistic Medical Association [*British*]
BHMA .... Builders' Hardware Manufacturers Association (EA)
BHMA .... Builders Hardware Manufacturers Association, Inc. (AAGC)
BHMAC .... Builders Hardware Manufacturers Association of Canada [*Association Canadienne des Fabricants de Quincaillerie de Batiment*] (AC)
BHMC .... Bell & Howell/Mamiya Co.
BHME .... Bureau of Health Manpower Education [*National Institutes of Health*]
BHMF........... Bis(hydroxymethyl)ferrocene [*Organic chemistry*]
BHMF........... Bis(hydroxymethyl)furan [*Organic chemistry*]
BHMH .... Butylazo(hydroxy)(methyl)hexane [*Organic chemistry*]
BHMHFC ...... Bret "Hit Man" Hart Fan Club (EA)
BHMK .... Kilby Provincial Historic Park, Harrison Mills, British Columbia [*Library symbol National Library of Canada*] (NLC)
BHMNAFWB... Board of Home Missions of the National Association of Free Will Baptists (EA)
BHMO .... Blue Hill Meteorological Observatory [*Harvard University*] (MCD)
BHMP .... Bis(hydroxymethyl)peroxide [*Organic chemistry*]
BH/MP .... Breather Hose/Mouthpiece (MCD)
BHMR .... Barclays Home Mortgage Rate [*British*] (DCTA)
BHMRB .... Black History Month Resource Book [*A publication*]
BHMS .... Bachelor of Human Movement Studies
BHMS .... British Holistic Medical Society
BHMS .... Buddy Holly Memorial Society (EA)
BHMT.......... Bis(hexamethylene)triamine [*Organic chemistry*]
BHN .... Basic Human Needs
BHN .... Bephenium Hydroxynaphthoate (MAE)
BHN .... Bridging Hepatic Necrosis [*Gastroenterology*] (DAVI)
BHN .... Brinell Hardness Number [*Also, BH, BHNo, HB*]
BHN .... Brotherhood of the Holy Name
BHN .... Fort Leonard Wood, MO [*Location identifier FAA*] (FAAL)
BHND.......... Behind (FAAC)
BHNHE........ Bureau of Human Nutrition and Home Economics [*Department of Agriculture*] [*Functions transferred to ARS, 1953*]
BHNo .... Brinell Hardness Number [*Also, BH, BHN, HB*]
BHNRC........ Beltsville Human Nutrition Research Center [*Department of Agriculture*]
BHO .... B&H Ocean Carriers [*AMEX symbol*] (TTSB)
BHO .... B & H Ocean Carriers Ltd. [*AMEX symbol*] (CTT)
BHO .... Barkhor Resources, Inc. [*Vancouver Stock Exchange symbol*]
BHO .... Bartley Herbarium, Ohio University [*Athens, OH*]
BHO .... Bhoja Airlines [*Pakistan*] [*ICAO designator*] (FAAC)
bho .... Bhojpuri [*MARC language code Library of Congress*] (LCCP)
BHO .... Bhopal [*India*] [*Airport symbol*] (OAG)
BHO .... Black Hole Ocarina (MCD)
BHO .... Branch Hydrographic Office [*Navy*]
BHOAM .... Brethren Homes and Older Adult Ministries [*An association*] (EA)
B Ho Ec ...... Bachelor of Household Economy
Bhop .... All India Reporter, Bhopal Series [*A publication*] (DLA)
B Hor.......... Bachelor of Horticulture
BHort .... Bachelor of Horticulture
BHortSc ...... Bachelor of Horticultural Science
BHortSci ..... Bachelor of Horticultural Science
BHortSci ..... Bachelor of Horticultural Science (NADA)
B Ho Sc ...... Bachelor of Household Science
BHospitality... Bachelor of Hospitality
BHP .... Balboa Heights [*Canal Zone*] [*Seismograph station code, US Geological Survey*] (SEIS)
BHP .... Basic Health Profile
BHP .... Beverly Hills Public Library, Beverly Hills, CA [*OCLC symbol*] (OCLC)
BHP .... Bhojpur [*Nepal*] [*Airport symbol*] (OAG)
BHP .... Biological Hazard Potential [*Atomic energy*]
BHP .... Bishop

BHP .... Bishop's University Library [*UTLAS symbol*]
BHP .... Boiler Horsepower
BHP .... Bottom Hole Pressure [*Oil well borehole*]
BHP .... Brake Horsepower
BHP .... Brashear-Hastings Prism
BHP .... British Horsepower
BHP .... Broken Hill Prop ADR [*NYSE symbol*] (TTSB)
BHP .... Broken Hill Proprietary ADR [*NYSE symbol*] (SPSG)
BHP .... Broken Hill Proprietary Co. Ltd. [*Associated Press*] (SAG)
BHP .... Butyl Hydroperoxide [*Organic chemistry*]
BHPC .... British Hardware Promotion Council Ltd. (BI)
BHPH .... Buy Here - Pay Here [*Used car sales*]
BHP-HR .... Brake Horsepower-Hour (AAG)
BHP JI .... BHP [*Broken Hill Proprietary Ltd.*] Journal [*A publication*]
BHPr .... Bureau of Health Professions [*Department of Health and Human Services*] (DAVI)
BHPRD........ Bureau of Health Planning and Resource Development [*Later, Bureau of Health Planning*] [*HEW*]
BHPRIC....... Bishopric
BHPT .... (Beta-Hydroxypropyl)theophylline [*Biochemistry*]
BHQ .... Battalion Headquarters [*British military*] (DMA)
BHQ .... Brigade Headquarters [*Army*]
BHQ .... Broken Hill [*Australia Airport symbol*] (OAG)
BHQU .... Brake Headquarters USA, Inc. [*NASDAQ symbol*] (SAG)
BHR .... Bahrain [*ANSI three-letter standard code*] (CNC)
BHR .... Basal Heart Rate [*Medicine*]
BHR .... Bharatpur [*Nepal*] [*Airport symbol Obsolete*] (OAG)
BHR .... Bighorn Airways, Inc. [*ICAO designator*] (FAAC)
BHR .... Biotechnology and Human Research
BHR .... Black Hill Resources Ltd. [*Vancouver Stock Exchange symbol*]
BHR .... Block Handler Routine [*Computer science*] (BUR)
BHR .... Block Header Record [*Computer science*]
BHR .... Brandl, H. R., Chicago IL [*STAC*]
BHR .... Broad Host Range [*Biochemistry*]
BHR .... Bulkhead Receptacle
BHR .... Business History Review [*A publication*] (BRI)
BHRA .... British Hotels and Restaurants Association (BI)
BHRA .... British Hydromechanics Research Association [*Later, BHRA Ltd.*]
BHRA .... British Hypnosis Research Association
BHRB .... British Humanities Research Board (AIE)
BHRC.......... Beverly Hills Racquets Club [*Book title*]
BHRC.......... British Harness Racing Club (DBA)
BHRCA .... British Hotels, Restaurants, and Caterers Association
BHRE .... British Hypnosis Research [*An association*] (DBA)
BHRI .... Brewers Hop Research Institute [*Later, USBA*]
BHRN .... Black Human Resources Network [*An association*] (EA)
BHS .... Bachelor of Health Science
BHS .... Bachelor of Home Science
BHS .... Bahamas [*ANSI three-letter standard code*] (CNC)
BHS .... Bahamasair Holdings Ltd. [*Bahamas*] [*ICAO designator*] (FAAC)
BHS .... [*The*] Baptist Historical Society [*British*]
BHS .... Baseball Hall of Shame [*Defunct*] (EA)
BHS .... Base Heat Shield
BHS .... Basic Hole System
BHS .... Bathurst [*Australia Airport symbol*] (OAG)
BHS .... Bernard Herrmann Society (EA)
BHS .... Beta-Hemolytic Streptococcus [*Medicine*]
BHS .... Biblia Hebraica Stuttgartensia [*A publication*] (BJA)
BHS .... Bimetal Heat Sensor [*Automotive engineering*]
BHS .... Binding Head Steel (IAA)
BHS .... Black Hills State College, Spearfish, SD [*OCLC symbol*] (OCLC)
BHS .... Blue Hills Station [*Nuclear energy*] (NRCH)
BHS .... Bonhomie & Hattiesburg Southern R. R. [*AAR code*]
BHS .... Borehole Seismometer
BHS .... British Heritage Society (EA)
BHS .... British Herpetological Society
BHS .... British Holstein Society (DBA)
BHS .... British Home Stores [*Retail chain*]
BHS .... British Horse Society (DI)
BHS .... Bureau of Health Services [*Public Health Service*]
BHS .... Burlesque Historical Society (EA)
BHSA .... British Heavy Steel Association (BI)
BHSc........... Bachelor of Health Science
BHSc........... Bachelor of Household Science
BHSci.......... Bachelor of Household Science (NADA)
BHSCS .... Bone Haft and Scale Cutters Society [*A union*] [*British*]
BHSDO........ Been Here Since Day One [*Group of Reagan administration staffers*]
BHSI .... Bicycle Helmet Safety Institute (EA)
BHSK .... Bolton-Hunter Reagent-Labeled Substance K [*Analytical biochemistry*]
BHSL .... Basic Hytran Simulation Language [*Computer science*] (PDAA)
BHSMA .... British Hay and Straw Merchants' Association (DBA)
BHSNSW...... Baptist Historical Society of New South Wales [*Australia*]
BHSR .... Balanced Half-Sample Replication [*Statistics*]
BHST .... Bottom Hole Static Temperature [*Oil well borehole*]
BHT............. Babylonian Historical Texts Relating to the Capture and Downfall of Babylon [*A publication*] (BJA)
BHT............. Backhoe Trench [*Archaeology*]
BHT............. Baht [*Monetary unit*] [*Thailand*]
BHT............. Bell Helicopter Textron, Inc.
BHT............. Beta-Hydroxytheophylline [*Medicine*] (DMAA)
BHT............. Blowdown Heat Transfer [*Nuclear energy*] (OA)
BHT............. Bob Hope Theatre [*British*]
BHT............. Bogazici Hava Tasimacilik AS [*Turkey*] [*ICAO designator*] (FAAC)
BHT............. Bottom Hole Temperature [*Oil well borehole*]

BHT	Branch History Table [Computer science]
BHT	Breath-Hold Time
BHT	Breath Hydrogen Test
BHT	Brotherhood of the Holy Trinity
BHT	Butylated Hydroxytoluene [Also, DBPC] [Antioxidant]
BHTA	British Herb Trade Association (DBA)
BHTC	Black Hills Teachers College [Later, Black Hills State College] [South Dakota]
BHTC	Book House Training Centre [British]
BHTD	Bureau of Hygiene and Tropical Diseases [Database producer]
BHthSc	Bachelor of Health Science
BH(T)P	Bottom Hole (Treating) Pressure [Oil well borehole]
BHTPA	Best Holiday Trav-L-Park Association (EA)
BHTV	Borehole Televiewer [Drilling technology]
B Hu	Bachelor of Humanities
BHU	Banco Holandes Unido [Dutch Union Bank] [Ecuador]
BHU	Basic Health Unit (DMAA)
BHU	Bhavnagar [India] [Airport symbol] (OAG)
Bhu	Bhutan
BHU	Latrobe, PA [Location identifier FAA] (FAAL)
BHUA	Banking, Housing, and Urban Affairs (DLA)
BHUMMVT	Bachelor of Human Movement
BHUT	Bhutan
BHV	Book of Heroic Verse [A publication]
BH/VH	Body Hematocrit-Venous Hematocrit Ratio (MAE)
BHVRL	Behavioral
BHW	Bell & Howell [NYSE symbol] (TTSB)
BHW	Bell & Howell Holdings Co. [NYSE symbol] (SAG)
BHW	Bombardment (Heavy) Wing [Air Force]
BHW	West Branch, MI [Location identifier FAA] (FAAL)
BHWK	Black Hawk Gaming & Development Co., Inc. [NASDAQ symbol] (SAG)
BHWK	Black Hawk Gaming & Dvlp [NASDAQ symbol] (TTSB)
BHWKW	Black Hawk Gaming Wrrt 'A' [NASDAQ symbol] (TTSB)
BHWKZ	Black Hawk Gaming Wrrt 'B' [NASDAQ symbol] (TTSB)
BHWR	Boiling Heavy Water Reactor
BHX	Birmingham [England] [Airport symbol] (OAG)
BHXU	Brayton Heat Exchanger Unit
B Hy	Bachelor of Hygiene
BHY	Belding Heminway [NYSE symbol] (TTSB)
BHY	Belding Heminway Co., Inc. [NYSE symbol] (SPSG)
BHY	Birgenair [Turkey] [ICAO designator] (FAAC)
B HYG	Bachelor of Hygiene
BHZ	Belo Horizonte [Brazil] [Airport symbol] (OAG)
BI	Background Information (MCD)
BI	Background Investigation
BI	Backward Indicator [Telecommunications] (TEL)
BI	Bacteriologic Index [Clinical microbiology]
BI	Balch Institute [Philadelphia, PA]
BI	Balearic Islands
BI	Banco Internacional [International Bank] [Ecuador]
BI	Baptist Independent Church [Also, BIC]
BI	Base Composite Price Index (MCD)
BI	Base Ignition
BI	Base Injection (IAA)
BI	Base-In (Prism) [Ophthalmology]
BI	Basic Index (NITA)
BI	Basic Infantry
BI	Batch Input (NITA)
BI	Battalion Infantry (CINC)
BI	Batted In [Short form for RBI, Runs Batted In] [Baseball]
BI	Battery Inverter (AAG)
BI	Battlefield Illumination (AABC)
BI	Battlefield Interdiction (MCD)
BI	Bearing Indicator (MCD)
BI	Beer Institute (EA)
BI	Befrienders International [Later, BISW] (EAIO)
BI	Behavioral Inventory
BI	Bell Industries [NYSE symbol] (TTSB)
BI	Bell Industries, Inc. [NYSE symbol] (SPSG)
BI	Bermuda Islands
BI	Beta-Ionone [Biochemistry]
BI	Beth Israel (BJA)
BI	Bibliographic Instruction [Library science]
Bi	Bicolor
Bi	Bile [Blood group]
BI	Billing Instructions [Telecommunications] (TEL)
BI	Biological Indicator [Microbiology]
BI	Biological Inventory
Bi	Biology (DSUE)
Bi	Biot [Also, aA] [Unit of electric current]
Bi	Bipolar Cell [In the retina]
Bi	Bisexual (DSUE)
Bi	Bismuth [Chemical element]
BI	Bismuth Institute [Brussels, Belgium] (EAIO)
BI	Black Information [Banking] [British]
BI	Black Iron
BI	Blanking Input (IEEE)
BI	Blind Individual [Social Security Administration] (OICC)
BI	Block-In (MCD)
BI	Bnai Israel (BJA)
BI	Bobov in Israel [An association] (EA)
BI	Bobs International [An association] (EAIO)
BI	Bodily Injury [Insurance]
BI	Boehringer Ingelheim Pharmaceuticals, Inc. [Commercial firm] (DAVI)

B(I)	Bomber (Intruder) [British military] (DMA)
BI	Bone Injury [Medicine]
BI	Boring Institute (EA)
BI	Boston Irish
BI	Bowel Impaction [Gastroenterology] (DAVI)
BI	Bowel Injection
BI	Braille Institute (EA)
BI	Brain Injured (EDAC)
BI	Branch Immaterial
BI	Braniff International Airways (IIA)
BI	Break-In Cycle (SAA)
BI	Bricklin International (EA)
BI	Brief Introduction
BI	British India
bi	British Indian Ocean Territory [MARC country of publication code Library of Congress] (LCCP)
BI	British India Steam Navigation Co. (IIA)
BI	British Industry [Vancouver Stock Exchange symbol]
BI	British Institution (ROG)
BI	British-Israel World Federation
BI	Broadcast Intercept (MCD)
BI	Broca Index [Medicine]
BI	Brookings Institution (EA)
BI	Browning Institute (EA)
BI	Bubble-Up Initiation [Automotive project management]
BI	Buffer Index [Computer science]
BI	Building Industry Association (ECON)
B/I	Built-In [Classified advertising] (ADA)
BI	Bulk Issue (ADA)
BI	Bureau Inlichtingen [Netherlands Information Office] [World War II]
BI	Bureau of Investigation [Federal Trade Commission]
BI	Burn Index [Medicine]
BI	Burundi [ANSI two-letter standard code] (CNC)
BI	Business Intelligence
BI	Business International Corp.
BI	Business Interruption [Insurance]
B/I	Bus Interface [Computer science]
BI	Input Blocking Factor [Computer science] (IBMDP)
BI	Royal Brunei Airlines [ICAO designator] (AD)
BI1	Barter Island [Alaska] [Seismograph station code, US Geological Survey] (SEIS)
BI2	Barter Island [Alaska] [Seismograph station code, US Geological Survey] (SEIS)
BI3	Barter Island [Alaska] [Seismograph station code, US Geological Survey] (SEIS)
BI4	Barter Island [Alaska] [Seismograph station code, US Geological Survey] (SEIS)
bi7d	Bis in Septem Diebus [Twice a Week] [Pharmacy]
BIA	Administrative Decisions under Immigration and Nationality Laws of the United States [A publication] (DLA)
BIA	Bachelor of Industrial Administration (WGA)
BIA	Bachelor of Industrial Arts
BIA	Baltic International Airlines [Latvia] [ICAO designator] (FAAC)
BIA	Bangor International Airport
BIA	Barbecue Industry Association (EA)
BIA	Bastia [Corsica] [Airport symbol] (OAG)
BIA	Bee Industries Association [Defunct] (EA)
BIA	Bicycle Institute of America [Defunct] (EA)
BIA	Binding Industries of America (EA)
BIA	Biogenic Institutes of America [Later, AHMI] (EA)
BIA	Bioindustry Association [Great Britain]
BIA	Block Improved Abrams [Battle tank] [Army]
BIA	Board of Immigration Appeals [Department of Justice]
BIA	Boating Industry Association [Later, NMMA]
BIA	Booster Interstage Assembly [Aerospace]
BIA	Boost, Insertion, and Abort [Aerospace]
BIA	Bouraq Indonesia Airlines (FEA)
BIA	Braille Institute of America [Later, BI] (EA)
BIA	Brazilian International Airlines
BIA	Bread Industry Authority [Queensland, Australia]
BIA	Briana Resources Ltd. [Vancouver Stock Exchange symbol]
BIA	Brick Institute of America (EA)
BIA	Bridal Industry Association (EA)
BIA	British and International Addressing Post [A publication]
BIA	British Insurance Association
BIA	British Ironfounders Association (BI)
BIA	British Island Airways Ltd.
BIA	Broadcasting in Australia [A publication]
BIA	Building Industry Association (SRA)
BIA	Bureau d'Investissement en Afrique [Office of Investments in Africa] [France] (AF)
BIA	Bureau International Afghanistan (EA)
BIA	Bureau Issues Association (EA)
BIA	Bureau of Indian Affairs [Department of the Interior]
BIA	Bureau of Insular Affairs [Originally, part of War Department; functions transferred to Department of Interior, 1939]
BIA	Bureau of Internal Affairs
BIA	Bureau of International Affairs (MCD)
BIA	Burma Independence Army [Fighting on the side of the Japanese] [World War II]
BIA	Buses International Association (EA)
BIA	Business and Industry Association of New Hampshire (SRA)
BIA	Business Improvement Area
BIA	Bus Interface Adapter (SSD)
BIA	Real-Aerovias Brasil [Brazilian international airline]

BIAA............ Beef Improvement Association of Australia
BIAA............ British Industrial Advertising Association (PDAA)
BIAA............ Bureau of Inter-American Affairs [Department of State]
BIAB............ Brief Index of Adaptive Behavior [Educational development test]
BIAC............ Beth Israel Ambulatory Center (DAVI)
BIAC............ BI, Inc. [NASDAQ symbol] (NQ)
BIAC............ Bioinstrumentation Advisory Council [Defunct]
BIAC............ British Institute of Agricultural Consultants (DBA)
BIAC............ Building Industry Advisory Council [Australia]
BIACC........... Business and Industry Advisory Committee [NATO] (NATG)
BIACC........... Basic Integrated Aircraft Command and Control [Navy]
Biacore......... Biacore International AB [Associated Press] (SAG)
BIAD............ Bureau International d'Anthropologie Differentielle [International Bureau of Differential Anthropology]
BIAE............ Bunbury Institute of Advanced Education [Australia]
BIAG............ Banque Internationale pour l'Afrique en Guinee (EY)
BIA-HI.......... Building Industry Association of Hawaii (SRA)
BIALL........... British and Irish Association of Law Librarians (DLA)
BIAM............ Bank of Ireland Asset Management
BIAM............ Banque d'Informations Automatisees sur les Medicaments [Data Bank for Medicaments] [Information service or system] (IID)
Biamp........... Biamperometric [Electromagnetics]
BIAM PA....... Banque d'Information Automatisee sur les Medicaments Principes Actifs [Databank on active ingredients of drugs] [French] (NITA)
BI & BI........ Biculturalism and Bilingualism [Canada]
BI & I.......... Boiler Inspection and Insurance
BIANSW......... Baking Industry Association of New South Wales [Australia]
BIANSW......... Boating Industry Association of New South Wales [Australia]
BIAO............ Banque Internationale pour l'Afrique Occidentale [International Bank for West Africa] [France] (AF)
BIAO-CI........ Banque Internationale pour l'Afrique Occidentale - Cote d'Ivoire (EY)
BIAP............ Bureau International d'Audiophonologie [International Office for Audiophonology - IOA] [Brussels, Belgium] (EA)
BIAPR.......... Bureau of Indian Affairs Procurement Regulation [A publication] (AAGC)
BIAPS.......... Battery Inverter Accessory Power Supply
BIAQ............ Boating Industry Association of Queensland [Australia]
BIAR............ Akureyri [Iceland] [ICAO location identifier] (ICLI)
BIAR............ Base Installation Action Requirements
BIAR............ Base Interrupt Address Register (IAA)
BI(A)R.......... Board of Inquiry (Army) Rules [British military] (DMA)
BI Arch........ Bachelor of Interior Architecture
BI Arch E...... Bachelor of Interior Architectural Engineering
BI Arch Eng... Bachelor of Interior Architectural Engineering
BIAS............ Battlefield Illumination Airborne System (AFM)
BIAS............ Bibliotheks Ausleihverwaltungssystem [Library circulation system] [Federal Republic of Germany] (NITA)
BIAS............ Biomedical Instrumentation Advisory Service [Clinical Research Centre] [British] (NITA)
BIAS............ Broadcast Industry Automation System [Data Communications Corp.] [Information service or system] (IID)
BIAS............ Brooklyn Institute of Arts and Sciences
BIAS............ Buoy Integrated Antenna Submarine [or System] (MCD)
BIAS............ Byelorussian Institute of Arts and Science (EA)
BIASA.......... Boating Industry Association of South Australia
BIASILL........ Basic Iron Aluminum Silicate [Du Pont trademark]
BIAT............ British Institute of Architectural Technicians (EAIO)
BIAT............ Burn-In/Aging Tester
BIAT............ Business Information Analysis and Integration Technique [Computer science]
BIATA.......... British Independent Air Transport Association
BIAW........... Building Industry Association of Washington (SRA)
BIAWA.......... Boating Industry Association of Western Australia
BIAX............ Biaxial (IAA)
BIB............. Baby Incendiary Bomb
BIB............. Backward Indicator BIT [Binary Digit] [Telecommunications] (TEL)
BIB............. Bag in Box [Packaging]
BIB............. Balanced Incomplete Block [Statistical design]
BIB............. Banque Internationale du Burkina [Burkina Faso] (EY)
BIB............. Bibe [Drink] [Pharmacy]
BIB............. Bible
BIB............. Bible Grove, IL [Location identifier FAA] (FAAL)
Bib............. Bibletone [Record label]
BIB............. Biblical (ROG)
BIB............. Bibliography (ROG)
BIB............. Biographical Information Blank
BIB............. Bipartite Board [Post-World War II, Germany]
BIB............. Board for International Broadcasting [Independent government agency]
BIB............. Boat Information Book [Navy] (CAAL)
BIB............. Bottled in Bond [Wines and spirits]
BIB............. British Interactive Broadcasting
BIB............. Broadcast Information Bureau, Inc.
BIB............. Brought-in-By (HGAA)
BIB............. Brunel Institute for Bioengineering [Brunel University] [Information service or system] (IID)
BIBA............ Babson Institute of Business Administration [Massachusetts]
BIBA............ British Insurance Brokers' Association (DLA)
BIBAM.......... Bibliography of Australian Medicine and Health Services [A publication]
Bibb............ Bibb's Kentucky Reports [4-7 Kentucky] [1808-17] [A publication] (DLA)
BIBBA.......... British Isles Bee Breeders Association (DBA)
Bibb (KY)..... Bibb's Kentucky Reports [4-7 Kentucky] [1808-17] [A publication] (DLA)

BIBCO.......... Bibliographic Cooperative Program [American Library Association]
BIBCON......... Bilbilographic Records Conversion (EDAC)
BIBD........... Balanced Incomplete Block Design [Mathematics]
BIBDATA........ Bibliographic Data (ADA)
BIBDES......... Bibliographic Data Entry System [Computer science] (PDAA)
BIBE........... Big Bend National Park
BIBE........... International Bulletin of Bibliography on Education [A publication] (AIE)
BIBF........... British and Irish Basketball Federation (DBA)
BIBIC.......... British Institute for Brain Injured Children
BIBL........... Biblical
BIBL........... Bibliografia Espanola [Ministerio de Cultura] [Spain Information service or system] (CRD)
BIBL........... Bibliography
BIBL........... Bibliotheca [Library] [Latin]
Bibl........... Bibliotheca [of Photius] [Classical studies] (OCD)
Bibl........... Bibliotheca [of Apollodorus] [Classical studies] (OCD)
bibl........... Bibliotheque (VRA)
BIBL........... Blonduos [Iceland] [ICAO location identifier] (ICLI)
Bibl Ec Franc... Bibliotheque des Ecoles Francaises d'Athenes et de Rome [A publication] (OCD)
bibl-f......... Bibliographical Footnotes
BIBLIO......... Bibliografia (Nazionale Italiano) (NITA)
BIBLIO......... Bibliographical Note (DSUE)
BIBLIODATA..... National Bibliographic Data Base [Deutsche Bibliothek] [Germany]
BIBLIOG........ Bibliography
BIBLIOS........ Book Inventory Building and Library Oriented System (EDAC)
BIBLIOS........ Book Inventory Building Library Information Oriented System [Orange County Public Library, California] (NITA)
BiblOr......... Bibliotheca Orientalis [A publication] (BJA)
Bibl Topogr... Bibliographie Topographique des Principales Cites Grecques de l'Italie Meridionale et de la Sicile dans l'Antiquite [A publication] (OCD)
BIBM........... Bureau International du Beton Manufacture [International Bureau for Precast Concrete] (EAIO)
BIBNET......... Bibliographic Network [OCLC retrieval system] [Computer science]
BibO........... Bibbia e Oriente Fossano, Cuneo (BJA)
BIBO........... Bounded-Input Bounded-Output [Computer science] (MHDB)
BIBO........... Bureau of International Business Operations [Department of Commerce] [Abolished, 1963]
BIBOM.......... Binary Input - Binary Output Machine (IAA)
BIBOMM......... Binary Input - Binary Output Moore Machine (IAA)
BIBPD.......... Brought in by Police Department [Emergency medicine] (DAVI)
BIBRA.......... British Industrial Biological Research Association (ARC)
BIBS........... Built-In Breathing System
BIC............ Baha'i International Community
BIC............ Balkan Information Centre [British World War II]
BIC............ Banana Industry Committee [New South Wales, Australia]
BIC............ Bank Investment Contract
BIC............ Banque Internationale des Comores (EY)
BIC............ Baptist Independent Church [Also, BI]
BIC............ Barium Ion Cloud [NASA]
BIC............ Battery Interconnecting Cables (NATG)
BIC............ Battlefield Information Center [Army] (AABC)
BIC............ Battlefield Intelligence Coordinator [Army] (DOMA)
BIC............ Bayes Information Criterion
BIC............ Beatles Information Center [Sweden] (EAIO)
BIC............ Beef Industry Council (EA)
BIC............ Belgian International Air Carriers [ICAO designator] (FAAC)
BIC............ Bibas in Christo [May You Live in Christ] [Latin]
BIC............ Bic Corp. [NYSE symbol] (SAG)
BIC............ Bicuculline [Organic chemistry]
BIC............ Biodeterioration Information Centre [British]
BIC............ Biographical Inventory Creativity
BIC............ Biomedical Instrumentation Consultant
BIC............ Bipolar Integrated Circuit [Electronics] (EECA)
BIC............ Blood Isotope Clearance [Medicine] (DMAA)
BIC............ Bombardment-Induced Conductivity
BIC............ Book Industry Communication [British An association]
BIC............ Books in Canada [A publication] (BRI)
BIC............ Braduskill Intercept Concept
BIC............ Braniff International Council [Club for frequent flyers] (EA)
BIC............ British Importers' Confederation (DS)
BIC............ British Insulated Cables
BIC............ Broadband Interface Controller [Motorola, Inc.]
BIC............ Building Information Centre [Cauldon College of Further and Higher Education] [British] (CB)
BIC............ Bureau International de la Chaussure et du Cuir
BIC............ Bureau International des Containers [International Container Bureau] [Paris, France] (EAIO)
BIC............ Bureau International du Cinema [International Cinematograph Bureau]
BIC............ Bureau of International Commerce [Department of Commerce] [Functions transferred to Domestic and International Business Administration]
BIC............ Business and Investments Centre [British]
B-I-C.......... Business Intelligence Center [SRI International] [Information service or system] (IID)
BIC............ Business in the Community [British]
BIC............ Bus Interface Circuit [Computer science] (MDG)
BIC............ Bus Interface Controller [Computer science] (NITA)
BIC............ Butec International Chemical Corp. [Formerly, Tay River Petroleum Ltd.] [Vancouver Stock Exchange symbol]
BIC............ Butter Information Council [British]
BIC............ Butyl Isocyanate [Organic chemistry]

BIC..............	Byte Input Control [Computer science]
BICA............	Bighorn Canyon National Recreation Area
BICA............	Reykjavik [Iceland] [ICAO location identifier] (ICLI)
BICARB........	Bicarbonate
BICARSA......	Billing, Inventory Control, Accounts Receivable, Sales Analysis (IBMDP)
BI/CAS	Business International Country Assessment Service [Business International Corp.] [Defunct Information service or system] (CRD)
BICC............	Battlefield Information Communications Center (MCD)
BICC............	Battlefield Information Control Center [Army] (AABC)
BICC............	Battlefield Integration Coordination Center
BICC............	Boston International Choreography Competition
BICC............	British Insulated Callender's Cable
B-ICC...........	British-Israel Chamber of Commerce (DBA)
BICC............	Bureau d'Interventions Cliniques et Communautaires [Office of Clinical and Communal Operations] [Canada]
BICC............	Reykjavik [Iceland] [ICAO location identifier] (ICLI)
BICCC..........	Business Industry Community College Coalition (EDAC)
BicCp...........	Bic Corp. [Associated Press] (SAG)
BICE............	Bureau International Catholique de l'Enfance [International Catholic Child Bureau - ICCB] [Geneva, Switzerland] (EA)
BICEMA........	British Internal Combustion Engine Manufacturers' Association
BICENT.........	Bicentenary [or Bicentennial]
BICEP..........	British Industrial Collaborative Exponential Program
BICEPS........	Basic Industrial Control Engineering Programming System (IAA)
BICEPT.........	Book Indexing with Context and Entry Points from Text [Indexing method] [Computer science] (DIT)
BICERI.........	British Internal Combustion Engine Research Institute Ltd. [Research center] (IRUK)
BICES..........	Battlefield Information Collection and Exploitation System
BICFET.........	Bipolar Inversion Channel Field Effect Transistor (MCD)
BICH	Bichromate (VRA)
Bich Crim Proc...	Bishop on Criminal Procedure [A publication] (DLA)
BICI.............	Broadband Inter-Carrier Interface [Telecommunications]
BICINE.........	Bis(hydroxyethyl)glycine [A buffer] [Organic chemistry]
BICIV..........	Bipartite Civil Service Advisors [Post-World War II, Germany]
Bick............	Bicknell and Hawley's Reports [10-20 Nevada] [A publication] (DLA)
Bick & H.......	Bicknell and Hawley's Reports [10-20 Nevada] [A publication] (DLA)
Bick & Hawl...	Bicknell and Hawley's Reports [10-20 Nevada] [A publication] (DLA)
Bick Civ Pr...	Bicknell's Indiana Civil Practice [A publication] (DLA)
Bick Cr Pr...	Bicknell's Indiana Criminal Practice [A publication] (DLA)
Bick (In)	Bicknell's Reports [India] [A publication] (DLA)
BICMA	British Industrial Ceramic Manufacturers Association (DBA)
BICMOS........	Bipolar Complementary Metal Oxide Semiconductor [Electronics] (BARN)
BICMV	Blackeye Cowpea Mosaic Virus [Plant pathology]
BiCNU	Bis(chloroethyl)nitrosourea [Carmustine] [Also, BCNU] [Antineoplastic drug regimen]
BICO	Biocontrol Technology [NASDAQ symbol] (TTSB)
BICO	Biocontrol Technology, Inc. [NASDAQ symbol] (NQ)
BICO	Bipartite Control Office [Post-World War II, Germany]
BICOM	Bipartite Communications Panel [Post-World War II, Germany]
BICOM	Brunel Institute of Computational Mathematics [Research center British] (IRUK)
BICOND.......	Biconditional
BICORD.......	Bistatic Coherent RADAR Display (MCD)
BICP............	Biomedical Interdisciplinary Curriculum Project [National Science Foundation]
BICP............	Bureau of Industrial Costs and Prices [India] (ECON)
BICRAM	Beijer Institute Centre for Resource Assessment and Management [British] (IRUK)
BICS............	Basic Interpersonal Communicative Skills (EDAC)
BICS............	[The] British Institute of Cleaning Science
BICS............	Building Industry Consulting Service [Telecommunications] (TEL)
BICS............	Burroughs Inventory Control System [Computer science] (BUR)
BICSA	British Industry Committee on South Africa
BICSC	British Institute of Cleaning Science
BICSI	Building Industry Consulting Service International [Tampa, FL] [Telecommunications service]
BIC/SVP	Business Information Centre/SVP [Information service or system] (IID)
BICTA..........	British Investment Casting Trade Association
BICWM........	Brethren in Christ World Missions (EA)
BID..............	Bachelor of Industrial Design
BID..............	Background Information Document [Environmental Protection Agency]
BID..............	Bacterial Identification
BID..............	Banco Interamericano de Desarrollo [Inter-American Development Bank] [Spanish]
BID..............	Banque Interamericaine de Developpement [Inter-American Development Bank] [French]
BID..............	Base Installation Department (SAA)
BID..............	Bellevue Index of Depression
BID..............	Bibliografia di Informatica e Diritto [Bibliography of Legal/Rights Information] [CSC-Corte Suprema di Cassazione] [Italy] (NITA)
Bid..............	Bidder's Court of Referees Reports [England] [A publication] (DLA)
Bid..............	Bidder's Locus Standi Reports [England] [A publication] (DLA)
BID..............	Biddy [Slang] (DSUE)
BID..............	Bidston [England] [Seismograph station code, US Geological Survey Closed] (SEIS)
BID..............	Big I Development Ltd. [Vancouver Stock Exchange symbol]
BID..............	Bis in Die [Twice a Day] [Pharmacy]
BID..............	Blast-Induced Distortion (MCD)
BID............	Blockade Intelligence Department [Ministry of Economic Warfare] [British World War II]
BID............	Block Island [Rhode Island] [Airport symbol] (OAG)
BID...........	Blow in Door
BID...........	Brazilian Infantry Division [World War II]
BID...........	British Investors Database
BID...........	Brought in Dead [Medicine]
BID...........	Bumper Impulse Detector
BID...........	Buoyancy Induced Dispersion (GFGA)
BID...........	Bureau, Institute, and Division [National Institutes of Health]
BID...........	Bureau of Institutional Development [Office of Education]
BID...........	Inter-American Development Bank, Washington, DC [OCLC symbol] (OCLC)
BID...........	Sotheby's Hldgs CI'A' [NYSE symbol] (TTSB)
BID...........	Sotheby's Holdings, Inc. Class A [NYSE symbol] (SPSG)
BIDAP	Bibliographic Data Processing Program [For keyword indexing] [Information retrieval software]
BIDC	Bureau Interafricain de Developpement et de Cooperation [Inter-African Development and Cooperation Office] (AF)
BIDC	Business/Industry Data Center [Bureau of the Census] (GFGA)
BIDCO.........	Business and Industrial Development Corporation [Generic term for a for-profit investment company]
Bidd	Bidder's Locus Standi Reports, I [1820-36] [A publication] (DLA)
Biddies	Baby Boomers in Debt [Lifestyle Classification]
BIDE............	Built-In Diagnostic Equipment [Analytical chemistry]
BIDEC..........	Binary-to-Decimal Converter [Computer science]
BIDEC..........	Bipartite Decartelization Commission [Berlin] [Post-World War II, Germany]
BIDEF..........	Bideford [Municipal borough in England]
BIDESC	Bipartite Decartelization Sub-Commission [Minden] [Post-World War II, Germany]
BIDGE	Building Engineer (HGAA)
BIDI	Banque Ivoirienne de Developpement Industriel [Ivorian Bank for Industrial Development] (AF)
BIDI	Business and Industrial Development Institute [Saginaw Valley State College] [Database search service] (OLDSS)
BIDICS	Bond Index to the Determination of Inorganic Crystal Structures [McMaster University, Canada]
Bid Ins.........	Biddle on Insurance [A publication] (DLA)
BIDLB	Block in Posteroinferior Division of Left Branch [Medicine] (DMAA)
BIDO	British Industrial Development Office [Through foreign branches, encourages investments in Britain from abroad]
BIDOPS........	Bi-Doppler Scoring System (MCD)
BIDP	Basic Institutional Development Program [Under Title III of the Higher Education Act]
BIDR	Business Information Desk Reference [A publication]
Bid Retr Leg...	Biddle on Retrospective Legislation [A publication] (DLA)
BIDS	Base Intrusion Detection System (MCD)
BIDS	Bath Information and Data Services [Computer science] [British] (TNIG)
BIDS	Battlefield Information Distribution System (MCD)
BIDS	Bedtime Insulin, Daytime Sulfonylurea [Therapy] [Pharmacology] (DAVI)
BIDS	Bendix Integrated Data System
BIDS	Biological Integrated Detection System [Army]
BIDS	Biological Integrated Detection System [US Army]
BIDS	Boiler Information Data System [Southwest Research Institute]
BIDS	British Institute of Dealers in Securities [Defunct]
BIDS	Building Industry Development Services
BIDS	Burroughs Input and Display Terminal (IAA)
BIDS	Moody's Bond Information Database Service [Moody's Investors Service, Inc.] [Information service or system] (CRD)
Bid Tab Stat...	Biddle's Table of Statutes [A publication] (DLA)
BIDV	Djupivogur [Iceland] [ICAO location identifier] (ICLI)
Bid War Sale Chat...	Biddle on Warranties in Sale of Chattels [A publication] (DLA)
BIE..............	Bachelor of Industrial Engineering
BIE..............	Beatrice, NE [Location identifier FAA] (FAAL)
BIE..............	Binaural Intensity Effect
BIE..............	Biotinoyl (Iodoacetyl) Ethylenediamine [An enzyme]
BIE..............	Blackout Restrictions in Industrial Establishments [British World War II]
BIE..............	Books in English (AIE)
BIE..............	Boundary Integral Equation (MCD)
BIE..............	British Institute of Embalmers
BIE..............	British Institute of Engineers (MCD)
BIE..............	Bureau International d'Education [International Bureau of Education - IBE] (EAIO)
BIE..............	Bureau International des Expositions [International Bureau of Exhibitions] (EAIO)
BIE..............	Bureau of Industrial Economics [Department of Commerce]
BIE..............	Business-Industry-Education [Days] [Usually sponsored by chambers of commerce]
BIEANSW	Bakery Industry Employees' Association of New South Wales [Australia]
BIEAP..........	Burrard Inlet Environmental Action Program (AC)
BIECO	Bipartite Economic Panel [Post-World War II, Germany]
BIECO/RAIL...	Bipartite Economic Panel Railway Supplies Committee [Post-World War II, Germany]
BIEE............	British Institute of Electrical Engineers
BIEE............	British Institute of Energy Economics (DBA)
BIEG............	Egilsstadir [Iceland] [ICAO location identifier] (ICLI)
BIEM............	Bureau International de l'Edition Mecanique
bien............	Biennial [Botany]
BIEN............	Business Information Exchange Network [Databank] [Canada]
BI Eng..........	Bachelor of Industrial Engineering

BIENN .... Biennial
Biennial Rep & Op W Va Att'y Gen... Biennial Report and Official Opinions of the Attorney General of the State of West Virginia [*A publication*] (DLA)
Biennial Rep Iowa Att'y Gen... Biennial Report of the Attorney General of the State of Iowa [*A publication*] (DLA)
Biennial Rep SD Att'y Gen... Biennial Report of the Attorney General of the State of South Dakota [*A publication*] (DLA)
Biennial Rep VT Att'y Gen... Biennial Report of the Attorney General of the State of Vermont [*A publication*] (DLA)
BIENYS .... Building Industry Employers of New York State (SRA)
BieOr .... Bibbia e Oriente Fossano, Cuneo (BJA)
BIEPR .... Bureau of International Economic Policy and Research [*Department of Commerce*]
BIESANSW... Bread Industry Employees and Salespersons' Association of New South Wales [*Australia*]
BIET .... Basic Initial Entry Test (MCD)
BIET .... Basic Initial Entry Training (MCD)
BIET .... Board of Incorporated Engineers and Technicians [*British*] (EAIO)
BIET .... British Institute of Engineering Technology (DI)
BietOr .... Biblica et Orientalia. Sacra Scriptura Antiquitatibus Orientalibus Illustrata [*Rome*] [*A publication*] (BJA)
BIF .... Balanced Income & Growth Fund Trust Units [*Toronto Stock Exchange symbol*]
BIF .... Banded Iron Formation [*Geology*]
BIF .... Bank Insurance Fund
BIF .... Basic Imagery File (MCD)
BIF .... Basic in Flow (NRCH)
BIF .... Beef Improvement Federation (EA)
BIF .... Beer Industry of Florida (SRA)
BIF .... Benchmark Interface Format [*Computer science*] (BTTJ)
BIF .... Best Inhibitory Frequency [*Neurophysiology*]
BIF .... Boiler and Industrial Furnace [*Environmental Protection Agency*]
BIF .... Bombardier's Information File
BIF .... British Industries Fair
BIF .... British Industries Federation
BIF .... Budget Information Form (OICC)
BIF .... El Paso, TX [*Location identifier FAA*] (FAAL)
BIFA .... British Independent Factors Association (DBA)
BIFA .... British International Freight Association (EAIO)
BIFAD .... Board for International Food and Agricultural Development [*Agency for International Development*] [*Washington, DC*]
BIF & A .... Bipartite Food and Agriculture Panel [*Post-World War II, Germany*]
BIFCA .... British Industrial Furnace Construction Association (DBA)
BIFET .... Bipolar Field Effect Transistor (IAA)
BIFF .... Battlefield Identification Friend or Foe (MCD)
BIFF .... Binary Interchange File Format (CDE)
BIFF .... Bistatic Identification, Friend or Foe (MCD)
BIFF .... British Industrial Fasteners Federation (DBA)
BIFFEX .... Baltic International Freight Futures Exchange [*London, England*]
BIFI .... Block Island - Fisher Island Range [*Navy*] (GFGA)
BIFIN .... Bipartite Finance Panel [*Post-World War II, Germany*]
BIFM .... Fagurholsmyri [*Iceland*] [*ICAO location identifier*] (ICLI)
BIFMA .... Business and Institutional Furniture Manufacturers Association (EA)
BIFORE .... Binary Fourier Representation (PDAA)
BIFU .... Banking, Insurance, and Finance Union [*British*] (DBA)
BIFU .... British Insurance and Finance Union (DI)
BIFV .... Bradley Infantry Fighting Vehicle [*Army*] (INF)
BIG .... BCS [*Boeing Computer Services*] Interactive Graphics
BIG .... Best in Group
BIG .... Bicycle-Motocross Industrial Guild (EA)
BIG .... Bigamy [*or Bigamist*] (WDAA)
BIG .... Big, Intrusive Government
BIG .... Big Island Air, Inc. [*ICAO designator*] (FAAC)
BIG .... Big Mountain [*Alaska*] [*Seismograph station code, US Geological Survey*] (SEIS)
Big .... Bignell's Reports [*India*] [*A publication*] (DLA)
BIG .... Bigstone Minerals [*Vancouver Stock Exchange symbol*]
BIG .... Biological Isolation Garment [*NASA*]
BIG .... Blacks in Government (EA)
BIG .... British Institute of Graphologists (DBA)
BIG .... Business Information Group [*Information service or system*] (IID)
BIG .... Business Investment Game
BIG .... Delta Junction/Fort Greely, AK [*Location identifier FAA*] (FAAL)
BIG .... Melbourne Business Information Guide [*A publication*] (APTA)
BIGA .... British Independent Garages Association (DBA)
BIGA .... British Independent Grocers' Association (DBA)
BIGB .... Big B, Inc. [*NASDAQ symbol*] (NQ)
Big B .... Big B, Inc. [*Associated Press*] (SAG)
Big B & B .... Bigelow's Bench and Bar of New York [*A publication*] (DLA)
Big B & N .... Bigelow's Cases on Bills and Notes [*A publication*] (DLA)
BIGC .... Big City Bagels [*NASDAQ symbol*] (TTSB)
BIGC .... Big City Bagels, Inc. [*NASDAQ symbol*] (SAG)
Big Cas .... Bigelow's Cases, William I to Richard I [*A publication*] (DLA)
Big Cas B & N... Bigelow's Cases on Bills and Notes [*A publication*] (DLA)
Big Cas Torts... Bigelow's Leading Cases on Torts [*A publication*] (DLA)
BigCityB .... Big City Bagels, Inc. [*Associated Press*] (SAG)
BIGCW .... Big City Bagels Wrrt [*NASDAQ symbol*] (TTSB)
BIGE .... Big Entertainment'A' [*NASDAQ symbol*] (TTSB)
BIGE .... Big Entertainment, Inc. [*NASDAQ symbol*] (SAG)
Bigelow Estop... Bigelow on Estoppel [*A publication*] (DLA)
Bigelow Lead Cas... Bigelow's Leading Cases on Bills and Notes, Torts, or Wills [*A publication*] (DLA)
Big Eng Proc... Bigelow's English Procedure [*A publication*] (DLA)
BigEnt .... Big Entertainment, Inc. [*Associated Press*] (SAG)
Big Eq .... Bigelow on Equity [*A publication*] (DLA)
Big Est .... Bigelow on Estoppel [*A publication*] (DLA)
BIGFET .... Bipolar Insulated Gate Field-Effect Transistor [*Bell Laboratories*]
BigFlower .... Big Flower Holdings, Inc. [*Associated Press*] (SAG)
BigFlwr .... Big Flower Holdings, Inc. [*Associated Press*] (SAG)
BIGFON .... Broadband Integrated Glass Fibre Optical Network [*Project*] [*Federal Republic of Germany*] (NITA)
BigFoot .... Big Foot Financial Corp. [*Associated Press*] (SAG)
Big Fr .... Bigelow on Frauds [*A publication*] (DLA)
Bigg Cr L ..... Bigg's Criminal Law [*A publication*] (DLA)
BIGGL .... Biggleswade [*Urban district in England*]
Bigg RR Acts... Biggs on Acts Relating to Railways [*A publication*] (DLA)
BIGGY .... Bismuth Glycine Glucose Yeast [*Medicine*] (DMAA)
BIGI .... Bond Investors Guaranty Insurance
BIGIT .... Binary Digit (IAA)
Big Jarm Wills... Bigelow's Edition of Jarman on Wills [*A publication*] (DLA)
Big L & A Ins Cas... Bigelow's Life and Accident Insurance Cases [*A publication*] (DLA)
Big L & A Ins Rep... Bigelow's Life and Accident Insurance Reports [*A publication*] (DLA)
Big Lead Cas... Bigelow's Leading Cases on Bills and Notes, Torts, or Wills [*A publication*] (DLA)
Big Ll Cas ... Bigelow's Life and Accident Insurance Cases [*A publication*] (DLA)
Bign .... Bignell's Reports [*India*] [*A publication*] (DLA)
BIGO .... Big O Tires, Inc. [*NASDAQ symbol*] (NQ)
BigOTir .... Big O Tires, Inc. [*Associated Press*] (SAG)
Big Ov Cas... Bigelow's Overruled Cases [*United States, England, Ireland*] [*A publication*] (DLA)
Big Plac .... Bigelow's Placita Anglo-Normanica [*A publication*] (DLA)
Big Proc ...... Bigelow's English Procedure [*A publication*] (DLA)
BIGR .... Grimsey [*Iceland*] [*ICAO location identifier*] (ICLI)
BigRck .... Big Rock Brewery [*Associated Press*] (SAG)
BIGS .... Booster Inertial Guidance System [*Aerospace*]
Big Torts ...... Bigelow on Torts [*A publication*] (DLA)
BIH .... Benign Intracranial Hypertension [*Medicine*]
BIH .... Bilateral Inguinal Herniae [*Gastroenterology*] (DAVI)
BIH .... Bishop [*California*] [*Airport symbol*] (OAG)
BIH .... British International Helicopters Ltd. [*ICAO designator*] (FAAC)
BIH .... Built-In Hold [*of countdown*] [*NASA*] (KSC)
BIH .... Bureau International de l'Heure [*International Time Bureau*] (EAIO)
BIHA .... Black, Indian, Hispanic, and Asian Women in Action [*An association*] (EA)
BIHA .... British Ice Hockey Association (DI)
BIHC .... Boat Inlet/High-Capacity [*Analytical combustion system*]
BIHFS .... British Institute of Hardwood Flooring Specialists (BI)
Bih LJ Rep... Bihar Law Journal Reports [*India*] [*A publication*] (DLA)
BIHN .... Hofn/Hornafjordur [*Iceland*] [*ICAO location identifier*] (ICLI)
BIHO .... Big Hole National Battlefield
BIHOR .... Bihorium [*During Two Hours*] [*Pharmacy*]
BIHR .... British Institute of Human Rights (DLA)
Bih Rep .... Bihar Reports [*India*] [*A publication*] (DLA)
BI-HTGR .... Binary Cycle High-Temperature Gas-Cooled Reactor [*Nuclear energy*] (NUCP)
BIHU .... Husavik [*Iceland*] [*ICAO location identifier*] (ICLI)
BII .... Background Illumination Intensity
BII .... Ballen Booksellers International, Inc. [*UTLAS symbol*]
BII .... Banca Internationala de Investitii [*International Investment Bank*]
BII .... Banque d'Information Industrielle [*Industrial Information Data Base*] [*Industrial Research Center of Quebec*] [*Information service or system*] (IID)
BII .... Basic Issue Items [*Army*] (AABC)
BII .... Battery Information Index [*Battelle Memorial Institute*] (IID)
BII .... Beckman Instruments Inc. (IAA)
BII .... BII Enterprises, Inc. [*Toronto Stock Exchange symbol*]
BII .... Bilingual Information Instructor
BII .... Biosophical Institute, Inc. [*Defunct*]
BII .... Biotechnica International, Inc.
BII .... British Institute of Innkeeping
BII .... Business Interruption Insurance
BIIA .... British Institute of Industrial Art
BIIB .... Basic Imagery Interpretation Brief (MCD)
BIIBA .... British Insurance and Investment Brokers' Association
BIIC .... Battlefield Integrated Information Center (MCD)
BIICC .... Bureau International d'Information des Chambres de Commerce
BIICL .... British Institute of International and Comparative Law
BIIL .... Basic Issue Items List [*Army*] (AABC)
BI Inc .... BI, Inc. [*Associated Press*] (SAG)
BIINVD .... Battlefield Illumination Integrated Night Vision Devices (MCD)
BIIPAM-CTIF... Banque d'Information Industrielle de Pont-A-Mousson et du CTIF [*Centre Technique des Industries de la Fonderie*] [*French Information service or system*] (CRD)
BIIPS .... Battery Inverter Instrument Power Supply (IAA)
BIIR .... Basic Imagery Interpretation Report (MCD)
BIIR .... Bromoisobutene Isoprene Rubber [*Organic chemistry*]
BIIS .... Isafjordur [*Iceland*] [*ICAO location identifier*] (ICLI)
Bi Isch .... Between Ischial Tuberosities [*Gynecology*] (BABM)
Bi Isch .... Between Ischial Turberosities [*Medicine*] (MEDA)
BIIT .... British Institute of Industrial Therapy
BIJ .... Bijou
BIJ .... Born in Japan
BIJS .... British Institute of Jazz Studies (BI)
BIJTR .... Bijouterie
BIK .... Biak [*Indonesia*] [*Airport symbol*] (OAG)
BIK .... Bikitaite [*A zeolite*]
BIKA .... British Institute of Kitchen Architecture (DBA)

BIKE............	Bicycle (ROG)
BIKE............	Bicycle
BIKE............	Cannondale Corp. [NASDAQ symbol] (SAG)
BIKF............	Keflavik [Iceland] [ICAO location identifier] (ICLI)
BIKP............	Kopasker [Iceland] [ICAO location identifier] (ICLI)
BIKR............	Saudarkrokur [Iceland] [ICAO location identifier] (ICLI)
BIL............	Bank in Liechtenstein
BIL............	Banque Internationale a Luxembourg SA (ECON)
BIL............	Basal Insulin Level [Medicine] (DMAA)
BIL............	Base Isolation Level (IAA)
BIL............	Basic Impulse Insulation Level [Electronics]
BIL............	Bilateral
bil............	Bilingual [Texts] (BJA)
BIL............	Bilirubin [Biochemistry] (AAMN)
BIL............	Bilirubin [Medicine] (DMAA)
BIL............	Billet (AABC)
BIL............	Billikin Resources, Inc. [Vancouver Stock Exchange symbol]
BIL............	Billings [Montana] [Airport symbol] (OAG)
BIL............	Billion
BIL............	Bill of Lading
BIL............	Block Input Length [Computer science] (BUR)
BIL............	Blue Indicator Light
BIL............	Brother-in-Law (ADA)
BIL............	Bulk Items List
BIL............	Buried Injector Logic (IAA)
BILA............	Battelle Institute Learning Automation [Battelle Memorial Institute] (IEEE)
BILA............	Bible Institute of Los Angeles
BILA............	British Insurance Law Association (DLA)
BILA............	Bureau of International Labor Affairs [Department of Labor]
BILA Bull.....	British Insurance Law Association. Bulletin [A publication] (DLA)
Bilas............	All India Reporter, Bilaspur Series [A publication] (DLA)
BILAT............	Bilateral
bilat............	bilateral (DMAA)
BILAT SLC...	Bilateral Short-Leg Casts [Orthopedics] (DAVI)
BILAT SXO...	Bilateral Salpingo-Oophorectomy [Gynecology] (DAVI)
Bil Aw..........	Billing. Law of Awards and Arbitration [1845] [A publication] (DLA)
BILB............	Built-In Light Beacon
bilbd............	Billboard (VRA)
BILBO............	Built-In Logic Block Observer [Computer science] (MHDB)
Bilb Ord.......	Ordinances of Bilboa [A publication] (DLA)
BILC............	British International Law Cases [A publication] (DLA)
BILCO.........	Bidder's List Control (SAA)
BILD............	Bibliographic Index of Library Documents [Helsinki School of Economics] [Database]
BILDG..........	Bill of Lading [Shipping] (NOAA)
BILE............	Balanced Inductor Logical Element
BILI............	Basic Issue List Items [Army]
bili............	Bilirubin [Clinical chemistry]
BILI-C........	Conjugated Bilirubin [Gastroenterology and neonatology] (DAVI)
Bili D/I.......	Bilirubin, Direct and Indirect [Clinical chemistry] (CPH)
BILIR.........	Bilirubin [Gastroenterology and neonatology] (DAVI)
bilirub........	Bilirubin [Gastroenterology and neonatology] (DAVI)
Bili T..........	Bilirubin, Total [Clinical chemistry] (CPH)
BILL............	Beer Industry League of Louisiana (SRA)
BILL............	Before Infantry Light and Lethal [Antitank] (MCD)
BILL............	Billericay [England]
BILL............	Billiards
BILL............	Billing Information Concepts [NASDAQ symbol] (SAG)
Bill & Pr Pat...	Billing and Prince's Law and Practice of Patents [A publication] (DLA)
BILLD..........	Billiard [Freight]
BILLD..........	Billiard
BILLI............	Billion (EECA)
Bill Info.......	Billing Information Concepts [Associated Press] (SAG)
Bill of Rights J...	Bill of Rights Journal [A publication] (DLA)
Billot Extrad...	Billot. Traite de l'Extradition [A publication] (DLA)
Bill Rights Rev...	Bill of Rights Review [A publication] (DLA)
Bill Rts J.....	Bill of Rights Journal [A publication] (DLA)
bills...........	Handbills (WDMC)
Bil Pews......	Billing. Law Relating to Pews [1845] [A publication] (DLA)
BILS............	British International Law Society (DLA)
BILU............	Bet Ya'akov Lekhu ve-Nelkhah (BJA)
BIM............	Bachelor of Indian Medicine (NADA)
BIM............	Bachelor of Industrial Management
BIM............	Ballet Intensive from Moscow
BIM............	Banco Industrial del Mediterraneo [Industrial Bank of the Mediterranean] [Spain]
BIM............	Basic Industrial Materials [Program] [Navy]
BIM............	Beacon Identification Method (DNAB)
BIM............	Beginning of Information Marker [Computer science]
BIM............	Best in Match
BIM............	Big M Petroleum, Inc. [Vancouver Stock Exchange symbol]
BIM............	Bimini [Bahamas] [Airport symbol] (OAG)
BI-M............	Bimonthly
BIM............	Binter-Mediterraneo [Spain ICAO designator] (FAAC)
BIM............	Biographical Inventory for Medicine
BIM............	Biologically Induced Mineralization [Microbial metabolism]
BIM............	BIT [Binary Digit] Image Memory [Computer science]
BIM............	Blade Inspection Method
BIM............	Blade Integrity Monitor [Aviation] (DA)
BIM............	Board of International Ministries (EA)
BIM............	Branch If Multiplexer
BIM............	British Institute of Management
BIM............	Bubble Interfacial Microlayer Sampler [Oceanography] (MSC)
BIM............	Business Inventory Management System (HGAA)
BIM............	Bus Interface Module
BIM............	Bus Interrupter Module [Motorola, Inc.]
BIMA............	Berkeley-Illinois-Maryland Association [Consortium for astronomical study]
BIMA............	Bilateral Internal Mammary Arteries [Anatomy] (DAVI)
BIMA............	British Interlining Manufacturers Association (DBA)
BIMA............	British International Motorcycle Association (EA)
BIMA............	Business and Industry Management Abstracts [A publication]
BIMAC........	Bistable Magnetic Core [Computer science]
BIMAG........	Bistable Magnetic Core [Computer science]
BIMAP........	Bill of Material Processor (IAA)
BIMBO.........	Blacks in Media Broadcasting Organization
BIMC...........	[The] Baltic and International Maritime Conference
BIMCAM........	British Industrial Measuring and Control Apparatus Manufacturers' Association
BIMCO........	Baltic and International Maritime Conference [or Council] [Copenhagen, Denmark] (EAIO)
BIME...........	Bath Institute of Medical Engineering [University of Bath] [British] (IRUK)
BIME...........	Biomune Systems [NASDAQ symbol] (TTSB)
BIME...........	Biomune Systems, Inc. [NASDAQ symbol] (SAG)
BIMH...........	British Institute of Mental Handicap
BIMM..........	Base Installation - Minuteman [Military] (IAA)
bimo...........	Bimodular [Journalism] (WDMC)
Bi-Mo L Rev...	Bi-Monthly Law Review. University of Detroit [A publication] (DLA)
BiMOS.........	Bipolar Metal-Oxide Semiconductor (IEEE)
BIMP...........	Beijing Institute of Modern Physics [China]
BIMP...........	Brunei, Indonesia, Malaysia, Philippines [International trade]
BIMP-EAGA...	Brunei, Indonesia, Malaysia, Philippines East Asian Growth Area [International trade]
BIMRAB........	BUWEPS [Bureau of Naval Weapons, now obsolete] - Industry Material Reliability Advisory Board
BIMS...........	Battlefield Integration Management System [Army]
BIMS...........	Blade Inspection Method System (MCD)
BIMS...........	Bubble Interfacial Microlayer Sampler [Oceanography]
BIMS...........	Bus Ion Mass Spectrometer [Space science instrumentation]
BIMSOC........	British Institute of Management Secretariat for Overseas Countries (PDAA)
BIMV...........	Bearded Iris Mosaic Virus [Plant pathology]
BIMV...........	Bidens Mottle Virus [Plant pathology]
BIN............	Babylonian Inscriptions in the Collection of James B. Nies (BJA)
BIn............	Bachelor of Informatics
BIN............	Bamian [Afghanistan] [Airport symbol Obsolete] (OAG)
BIN............	Banco Inmobilario [Nicaragua] (EY)
BIN............	Bank Identification Number
BIN............	Basic Identification Number (EECA)
BIN............	Bell Information Network
BIN............	Benign Intradermal Nevus [Dermatology] (DAVI)
BIN............	Billboard Information Network [Billboard Publications, Inc.] [Information service or system] (IID)
BIN............	Billion Instructions [Power measurement] [Computer science] (IAA)
BIN............	Binary (AFM)
BIN............	Binks Manufacturing Co. [AMEX symbol] (SPSG)
BIN............	Binks Mfg. [AMEX symbol] (TTSB)
Bin............	Binney's Pennsylvania Reports [1799-1814] [A publication] (DLA)
BIN............	Binza [Leopoldville] [Zaire] [Seismograph station code, US Geological Survey] (SEIS)
BIN............	Bis in Noctus [Twice a Night] [Pharmacy]
BIN............	BOMARC [Boeing-Michigan Aeronautical Research Center] Interceptor
BIN............	Bullion Range Exploration [Vancouver Stock Exchange symbol]
BIN............	Business Information Network [Billboard Publications, Inc.] [New York, NY Telecommunications] (TEL)
BIN............	Butylisonitrile (DMAA)
BIN............	Invermere Public Library, British Columbia [Library symbol National Library of Canada] (NLC)
BINA............	Broadcast Institute of North America (NTCM)
BINAC.........	Binary Automatic Computer [Eckert-Maudely Computer Corp.]
BINAC.........	Binary Northrop Automatic Computer [Computer science] (HGAA)
BINAGRI......	Biblioteca Nacional de Agricultura [National Library of Agriculture] [Brazil] [Information service or system] (IID)
BINC	Biospherics [NASDAQ symbol] (TTSB)
BINC	Biospherics, Inc. [NASDAQ symbol] (NQ)
BINC	Black Incumbent
BINCOS........	Binder Control Subsystem
B Ind	Bachelor of Industry
BIND...........	Bacterial Ice Nucleation Diagnosis [DNA Plant Technology Corp. test]
BIND...........	Binding (ROG)
BIND...........	Building Item Name Directory [A publication]
BIND...........	The Berkeley Internet Name Domain
BIndDes......	Bachelor of Industrial Design
B Ind E	Bachelor of Industrial Engineering
B Ind Ed	Bachelor of Industrial Education
BINDEX.......	Book Indexing
Bin Dig	Binmore's Index-Digest of Michigan Reports [A publication] (DLA)
BINDIS........	Binomial Probability Distributions (MCD)
Bindly.........	Bindley Western Industries [Associated Press] (SAG)
B Ind Mgt ...	Bachelor of Industrial Management
BINDT.........	British Institute of Non-Destructive Testing (PDAA)
BIndTech......	Bachelor of Industrial Technology
BINET.........	Bicentennial Information Network [American Revolution Bicentennial Administration]
BINF...........	Nordfjordur [Iceland] [ICAO location identifier] (ICLI)
BInfoSc........	Bachelor of Information Science

BInfoSys	Bachelor of Information Systems
BInfoTech	Bachelor of Information Technology and Communication
Bing	Baccalaureat en Ingenierie [*Canada*] (DD)
Bing	Bingham's English Common Pleas Reports [*130-131 English Reprint*] [*A publication*] (DLA)
BING	Federation of European Rigid Polyurethane Foam Associations (EAIO)
Bing Act & Def	Bingham's Actions and Defences in Real Property [*A publication*] (DLA)
Bing & Colv Rents	Bingham and Colvin on Rents [*A publication*] (DLA)
Bing Des	Bingham on the Laws of Descent [*A publication*] (DLA)
Bing (Eng)	Bingham's English Common Pleas Reports [*130-131 English Reprint*] [*A publication*] (DLA)
Bing Ex	Bingham. Judgments and Executions [*1815*] [*A publication*] (DLA)
Bing Ex Cont	Bingham's Executory Contracts, Etc. [*A publication*] (DLA)
Bing Inf	Bingham. Infancy and Coveture [*1826*] [*A publication*] (DLA)
Bing Judg	Bingham. Judgments and Executions [*1815*] [*A publication*] (DLA)
Bing L & T	Bingham. Landlord and Tenant [*1820*] [*A publication*] (DLA)
Bing NC	Bingham. New Cases, English Common Pleas [*131-133 English Reprint*] [*A publication*] (DLA)
Bing N Cas	Bingham. New Cases, English Common Pleas [*131-133 English Reprint*] [*A publication*] (DLA)
Bing NC (Eng)	Bingham. New Cases, English Common Pleas [*131-133 English Reprint*] [*A publication*] (DLA)
BINGO	Beacon Instrumented Guided Ordnance (MCD)
BINGO	Bearing Indicator and Navigator to Grounded Operator (MCD)
BI/NGO	Bilateral/Non-Governmental Organization (ADA)
BINGO	Business and Industry Nongovernment Organization
BINGO	Business International Non-Governmental Organization (MHDB)
Bing RP	Bingham on the Law of Real Property [*A publication*] (DLA)
BinkMf	Binks Manufacturing Co. [*Associated Press*] (SAG)
BINL	Basic Inventory of Natural Language [*Test*]
Binm Ind	Binmore's Index-Digest of Michigan Reports [*A publication*] (DLA)
BIN MUN	Binary Munitions
Binn	Binney's Pennsylvania Supreme Court Reports [*1799-1814*] [*A publication*] (DLA)
Binn Jus	Binns' Pennsylvania Justice [*A publication*] (DLA)
Binn (PA)	Binney's Pennsylvania Reports [*1799-1814*] [*A publication*] (DLA)
Binns' Just	Binns' Pennsylvania Justice [*A publication*] (DLA)
BINOCS	Binoculars [*Slang British*] (DSUE)
BINOMEXP	Binomial Expansion [*Mathematics*]
BINO(S)	Binoculars (VNW)
BINOVC	Break in Overcast [*Meteorology*]
BINR	Basic Intrinsic Noise Ratio (CET)
BINSS	Binary to Seven Segment [*Computer science*]
BInst NDT	British Institute of Non-Destructive Testing (EAIO)
BINSUM	Brief Intelligence Summary (NATG)
BIntArch	Bachelor in Interior Architecture
BIntDesign	Bachelor in Interior Design
B Int L	Bachelor of International Law
BIO	Base Installation Officer
BIO	Basic Input-Output Support Program Package (IAA)
bio	Basic Input/Output System [*Computer science*] (WDMC)
BIO	Bedford Institute of Oceanography [*Canada*] (MSC)
BIO	Bilbao [*Spain*] [*Airport symbol*] (OAG)
BIO	Bilingual Information Officer
BIO	Biographics (AABC)
BIO	Biography (DSUE)
bio	Biography (WDMC)
BIO	Biological Information-Processing Organization [*Later, SIGBIO*]
BIO	Biological Research Module [*NASA*] (NASA)
BIO	Biology [*or Biological*] (KSC)
Bio	Biology (DD)
BIO	Biology
BIO	Biophysics (ADA)
BIO	Bio-Rad Laboratories, Inc. [*AMEX symbol*] (SPSG)
BIO	Bio-Research Module (MCD)
BIO	Biorka [*Alaska*] [*Seismograph station code, US Geological Survey Closed*] (SEIS)
BIO	Bioscope [*The cinema*] [*Obsolete British*] (DSUE)
BIO	Biotechnology Industry Organization
BIO	Biotechnology Investment Opportunities [*Database*] [*High Tech Publishing Co.*] [*Information service or system*] (CRD)
BIO	Branch Intelligence Officer [*Military British*]
BIO	Brit Ivrit Olamit [*World Association for Hebrew Language and Culture*] (EAIO)
BIO	Buffered Input/Output [*Computer science*] (NITA)
BIO.A	Bio-Rad Labs CI'A' [*AMEX symbol*] (TTSB)
BIOA	Bureau of International Organization Affairs [*Department of State*]
BIOALRT	Bioastronautics Laboratory Research Tool (IEEE)
BIO.B	Bio-Rad Labs CI'B' [*AMEX symbol*] (TTSB)
BIOBUND	Computerized Biology Data and Program Bank at the University of Notre Dame [*Information service or system Defunct*] (IID)
BIOC	Biocircuits Corp. [*NASDAQ symbol*] (SAG)
BIOCAS	BIOSIS/CAS [*BioSciences Information Service/Chemical Abstracts Service*] Registry Number Concordance [*American Chemical Society*] [*Information service or system*] (CRD)
BIOCC	Branch Immaterial Officer Candidate Course
Biocft	Biocraft Laboratories, Inc. [*Associated Press*] (SAG)
BIOCHEM	Biochemical [*or Biochemistry*]
BIOCHEM	Biochemistry
Biochem	Biochemistry (DD)
BIO-CHEM	Biological-Chemical
Biocirc	Biocircuits Corp. [*Associated Press*] (SAG)
BIOCORE	Biological Cosmic Ray Experiment (MCD)
Biocryst	Biocryst Pharmaceuticals, Inc. [*Associated Press*] (SAG)
Bioctrl	Biocontrol Technology, Inc. [*Associated Press*] (SAG)
BIOD	Battalion Input/Output Device (MCD)
BIOD	Bell Integrated Optical Device [*Electronics*] (EECA)
BIOD	Bony Intraorbital Distance [*Medicine*] (DMAA)
BIODEF	Biological Defense [*Military*]
BIODEG	Biodegrade [*or Biodegradable*] (WDAA)
BioDent	BioDental Technologies Corp. [*Associated Press*] (SAG)
BiodyInt	Biodynamics International [*Associated Press*] (SAG)
Bio-Dyn	Bio-Dyne Corp. [*Associated Press*] (SAG)
BIOENG	Bioengineering
BIOENVMT	Bioenvironmental
BIOETHICSLINE	Bioethics Online [*Database*]
Biofield	Biofield Corp. [*Associated Press*] (SAG)
BIOG	Biografias [*Database*] [*Ministerio de Cultura*] [*Spanish*] [*Information service or system*] (CRD)
BIOG	Biographer (ROG)
BIOG	Biography
Biogen	Biogen, Inc. [*Associated Press*] (SAG)
BIOGEOG	Biogeography (ADA)
Biography	Biography: An Interdisciplinary Quarterly [*A publication*] (BRI)
BIOGST	Biologist
BIOI	BioSource International [*NASDAQ symbol*] (SAG)
BIOI	BioSource Intl. [*NASDAQ symbol*] (TTSB)
BioIm	Bio-Imaging Technologies, Inc. [*Associated Press*] (SAG)
BioImag	Bio-Imaging Technologies, Inc. [*Associated Press*] (SAG)
Bioject	Bioject Medical Technologies, Inc. [*Associated Press*] (SAG)
BIOL	Biological (ROG)
BIOL	Biological
BIOL	Biology (EY)
biol	Biology (DMAA)
BioLase	BioLase Technology, Inc. [*Associated Press*] (SAG)
BIOLDEF	Biological Defense [*Military*] (AABC)
bioLH	Bioassay of Luteinizing Hormone (DMAA)
BioLogic	Bio-Logic Systems Corp. [*Associated Press*] (SAG)
BIOLOPS	Biological Operations [*Military*] (GFGA)
BIOLREPT	Biological Report (AABC)
BIOLRSCH	Biological Research (AABC)
BIOLWPN	Biological Weapons [*Military*] (AABC)
BIOLWPNSYS	Biological Weapons System [*Military*] (AABC)
BIOM	Biomira, Inc. [*NASDAQ symbol*] (SAG)
BIO-M	Bi-Phase Mark (MHDI)
BIOM	Buffer Input-Output Memory [*Computer science*]
Biomag	Biomagnetic Technology [*Commercial firm Associated Press*] (SAG)
BIOMASS	Biological Investigation of Marine Antarctic Systems and Stocks Program [*Texas A & M University*] [*Research center*] (RCD)
Biomatr	Biomatrix, Inc. [*Associated Press*] (SAG)
BIOMDCL	Biomedical
BIOMED	Biological Medicine
BiomedEng	Biomedical Engineering (DD)
Biomer	Biomerica, Inc. [*Associated Press*] (SAG)
Biomerica	Biomerica, Inc. [*Associated Press*] (SAG)
Biomet	Biomet, Inc. [*Associated Press*] (SAG)
BIOMET	Biometry
BIOMF	Biomira Inc. [*NASDAQ symbol*] (TTSB)
Biomira	Biomira, Inc. [*Associated Press*] (SAG)
Biomne	Biomune Systems, Inc. [*Associated Press*] (SAG)
BIOMOD	Biochemical Modeling [*Computer science*]
BION	Believe It or Not
BIONIC	Biological and Electronic (NITA)
BIONICS	Biological Electronics (IEEE)
BIONMC	Bionomic
BIONUCL	Bionucleonics
BIOO	Block Input-Output Output [*Computer science*] (MHDI)
BIOP	Biosys Medical [*NASDAQ symbol*] (TTSB)
BIOP	Buffer Input/Output Processor [*Computer science*] (NITA)
BIOPAC	Biological Packs (DNAB)
BIOPACK	Biological Packs (NG)
BioPhar	Biochem Pharma, Inc. [*Associated Press*] (SAG)
Biophys	Biophysics (DAVI)
BioPlex	Bio-Plexus, Inc. [*Associated Press*] (SAG)
Biopool	Biopool International, Inc. [*Associated Press*] (SAG)
BIOQUIP	Biotechnology Equipment Suppliers [*Deutsche Gesellschaft fuer Chemisches Apparatewesen, Chemische Technik, und Biotechnologie eV*] [*Germany*] (IID)
BioR	Bio-Rad Laboratories, Inc. [*Associated Press*] (SAG)
BIOR	Business Input/Output Rerun [*UNIVAC compiling system*] [*Computer science*]
Bior & D Laws	Bioren and Duane's United States Laws [*A publication*] (DLA)
BioRef	Bio-Reference Laboratories, Inc. [*Associated Press*] (SAG)
BIOREP	Biological Report
BIOREP	Biotechnical Research Project [*EC*] (ECED)
BIOREP/CHEMREP	Biological/Chemical Attack Report
BioRf	Bio-Reference Laboratories, Inc. [*Associated Press*] (SAG)
BIOS	Basic Input-Output System [*IBM Corp.*]
BIOS	Biological Investigation of Space [*NASA*]
BIOS	Biological Orbiting Satellite (MCD)
BIOS	Biological Satellite
BIOS	Biosys, Inc. [*NASDAQ symbol*] (NQ)
BIOS	biosys Inc. [*NASDAQ symbol*] (TTSB)
BIOS	British Institute of Organ Studies (DBA)
BIOS	British Intelligence Objectives Subcommittee
BioSafe	BioSafe International, Inc. [*Associated Press*] (SAG)
BioSafety	Biosafety Systems, Inc. [*Associated Press*] (SAG)
BIOSAT	Biological Satellite (KSC)

BioSci......... BioScience [*A publication*] (BRI)
Biosepra...... Biosepra, Inc. [*Associated Press*] (SAG)
BioSf.......... BioSafe International, Inc. [*Associated Press*] (SAG)
BIOSID........ Biomechanically Faithful Side Impact Dummy [*Automotive engineering*]
BIOSIS........ BioSciences Information Service [*Database producer*] [*Philadelphia, PA*]
BIOSOMA...... Biological, Social, Machine [*Combination*]
BioSpecif..... BioSpecifics Technologies, Inc. [*Associated Press*] (SAG)
BIOSPEX...... Biological Space Experiments (MCD)
Biosph......... Biospherics, Inc. [*Associated Press*] (SAG)
BioSrce....... BioSource International [*Associated Press*] (SAG)
BIOSTAT...... Biostatistics
Biosys......... Biosys [*Associated Press*] (SAG)
BIOT........... Bio Technica Intl. [*NASDAQ symbol*] (TTSB)
BIOT........... Biotechnics International, Inc. [*NASDAQ symbol*] (NQ)
BIOT........... British Indian Ocean Territory
BIOTA......... Biological Institute of Tropical America (EA)
BioTcG........ Biotechnology Gen Corp. [*Associated Press*] (SAG)
BIOTEC....... Biotechnology
BIOTECH..... Biotechnology
BIOTECH..... Biotechnology
BIOTEX....... Bio-Technology Exhibition (TSPED)
BioTG......... Biotechnology Gen Corp. [*Associated Press*] (SAG)
BIOT GR SCH... Biotite Granite Schist [*Geology*]
Biotime....... BioTime, Inc. [*Associated Press*] (SAG)
BioTInt....... Biotechnics International, Inc. [*Associated Press*] (SAG)
BioTrans...... BioTransplant, Inc. [*Associated Press*] (SAG)
BIOTROP...... Regional Center for Tropical Biology [*SEAMEO*] [*Indonesia*] [*Research center*] (IRC)
Biovail........ Biovail Corp. International [*Associated Press*] (SAG)
BioVasc....... Bio-Vascular, Inc. [*Associated Press*] (SAG)
BIOWAR....... Biological Warfare
Biowht........ BioWhittaker, Inc. [*Associated Press*] (SAG)
BIOX .... Biomatrix, Inc. [*NASDAQ symbol*] (SPSG)
BIP........... Background-Limited Infrared Photoconductor (IAA)
BIP........... Bacterial Intravenous Protein (MAE)
BIP........... Baggage Improvement Program [*IATA*] (DS)
BIP........... Bakersfield Individualized Process (EDAC)
BIP........... Balanced Indigenous Population
BIP........... Balanced in Plane (IEEE)
BIP........... Balloon Interrogation Package
BIP........... Banque International de Placement
BIP........... Basic Information Package
BIP........... BASIC Interpreter Package [*Computer science*]
BIP........... Binary Image Processor [*Computer science*]
BIP........... Biparietal Diameter [*Gynecology*] (MAE)
BIP........... Bi-Petro Resources [*Vancouver Stock Exchange symbol*]
BIP........... Bipropellant (KSC)
BIP........... Bismuth Iodoform Paraffin [*Medicine*]
BIP........... Bit Interleaved Parity [*Electronics*] (ACRL)
BIP........... Block Improvement Program [*for M1A1 tank*] [*Army*]
BIP........... Blow in Place
BIP........... Blue Cross Interim Payment [*Insurance*]
BIP........... Books in Print [*Bibliographic database*] [*R. R. Bowker Co.*] [*A publication*]
BIP........... Botswana Independence Party [*Political party*] (PPW)
BIP........... British Industrial Plastics (ODBW)
BIP........... Budget Increment Package [*DoD*]
BIP........... Buergerinitiative Parlament [*Citizens' Parliamentary Initiative*] [*Austria Political party*] (EY)
BIP........... Bulimba [*Australia Airport symbol Obsolete*] (OAG)
BIP........... Bureau d'Information et de Presse [*Circulated Allied propaganda in France and informed Allies of resistance activities*] [*World War II*]
BIP........... Bureau of International Programs [*Department of Commerce*]
BIP........... Business Information Processing
B-I-P .... Business Intelligence Program Research Catalog [*SRI International*] [*Information service or system*] (IID)
BIPA........... Banque d'Informations Politiques et d'Actualite [*Political and Current Events Information Bank*] [*Database Telesystems - Questel*] [*Information service or system*] (IID)
BIPA........... Patreksfjordur [*Iceland*] [*ICAO location identifier*] (ICLI)
BIPAC .... Britian Israel Public Affairs Centre
BIPAC .... Business-Industry Political Action Committee (EA)
BIPAD .... Binary Pattern Detector
BIPAD .... Bureau of Independent Publishers and Distributors (EA)
BIPAP .... Bilevel Positive Airway Pressure [*Medicine*] (DMAA)
BIPAR .... Bureau International des Producteurs d'Assurances et de Reassurances [*International Association of Insurance and Reinsurance Intermediaries - IAIRI*] [*Paris, France*] (EAIO)
bipart.......... Bipartisan [*Politics*] (WDMC)
BIPASS .... Burroughs Inventory Planning Analysis and Simulation System [*Computer science*] (BUR)
BIPB.......... Banana Industry Protection Board [*Australia*]
BIPCA .... Bureau International Permanent de Chimie Analytique pour les Matieres Destinees a l'Alimentation de l'Homme et des Animaux [*Permanent International Bureau of Analytical Chemistry of Human and Animal Food*]
BIPCO .... Built-in-Place Component [*Electronics*]
BiPD .... Biparietal Diameter [*Obstetrics*] (DAVI)
BIPD .... Biparting Door
BI/PD .... Bodily Injury and Property Damage [*Insurance*]
BIPE.......... Bureau d'Informations et de Previsions Economiques [*Office of Economic Information and Forecasting*] [*Information service or system*] (IID)

BIPEA........ British Independent Plastic Extruders Association (DBA)
BIPEX........ British International Postcard Exhibition
BIPL.......... Biopool International, Inc. [*NASDAQ symbol*] (NQ)
BIPL.......... Biopool Intl. [*NASDAQ symbol*] (TTSB)
BIPLED .... Bilateral, Independent, Periodic, Lateralized Epileptiform Discharge [*Medicine*] (DMAA)
BIPM.......... Benzimidazolylphenylmaleimide [*Organic chemistry*]
BIPM.......... Bureau International des Poids et Mesures [*International Bureau of Weights and Measures*] [*Sevres, France*] (EA)
BIPM.......... International Bureau of Weights and Measures (IDOE)
BIPO.......... British Institute of Public Opinion
BIPOLT .... Bulk Inland Petroleum, Oil, and Lubrication Transport (NATG)
BIPP.......... Bismuth Iodoform and Paraffin Paste [*Medicine*]
BIPP.......... Bismuth Iodoform Petrolatum Paste [*Biochemistry*] (DAVI)
BIPP.......... Briefings/Issues/Projects/Programs (DNAB)
BIPP.......... British Institute of Practical Psychology Ltd. (BI)
BIPP.......... British Institute of Professional Photography (AIE)
BIPP.......... Bureau of Intergovernmental Personnel Programs
BIPS.......... Banking Information Processing System [*Computer science*] (BUR)
BIPS.......... Billion Instructions per Second [*Computing power measurement*] [*Computer science*]
BIPS.......... Branch Information Processing System [*Computer science*]
BIPS.......... Brayton Isotope Power System
BIPS.......... British Institute of Persian Studies (DBA)
BIPY.......... Bipyridine [*Also, BPY*] [*Organic chemistry*]
BIQ........... Base Inspection Questionnaire [*Air Force*]
BIQ........... Biarritz [*France*] [*Airport symbol*] (OAG)
BIQ........... Flint, MI [*Location identifier FAA*] (FAAL)
BIR........... Bachelor of Industrial Relations (DD)
BIR........... Backward Internal Rotation [*Orthopedics*] (DAVI)
BIR........... Banque d'Information sur les Recherches [*INSERM Research Information Bank*] [*National Institute for Health and Medical Research*] [*Information service or system*] (IID)
BIR........... Basic Incidence Rate [*Medicine*]
BIR........... Before Initial Release [*Information system*] (MCD)
B-IR.......... Bell-Independent Relations [*Telecommunications*] (TEL)
BIR........... Bibliography on Incineration of Refuse and Waste [*Air Pollution Control Association*] [*A publication*]
BIR........... Biratnagar [*Nepal*] [*Airport symbol*] (OAG)
bir........... Birch (VRA)
BIR........... Bird Leasing, Inc. [*ICAO designator*] (FAAC)
BIR........... Birmingham [*Diocesan abbreviation*] [*Alabama*] (TOCD)
BIR........... Birmingham Steel [*NYSE symbol*] (TTSB)
BIR........... Birmingham Steel Corp. [*NYSE symbol*] (SPSG)
BIR........... Board of Inland Revenue [*British*]
BIR........... Break-In Relay
BIR........... British Institute of Radiology (DEN)
BIR........... Bureau International de la Recuperation [*International Bureau of Recuperation*] [*Brussels, Belgium*] (EA)
BIR........... Bureau of Intelligence and Research [*Department of State*]
BIR........... Bureau of Internal Revenue [*Department of the Treasury*] [*Later, Internal Revenue Service*]
BIRA.......... British Institute of Regulatory Affairs (DBA)
BIRAC........ Bureau of Immigration Research Advisory Committee [*Australia*]
BIRAG........ Big Island Rainforest Action Group (EA)
BIRAP .... Balloon Infrared Astronomy Platform
BIRC.......... Bio-Integral Resource Center (EA)
BIRD.......... Banque d'Information Robert Debre [*Centre International de l'Enfance*] [*Database*]
BIRD .... Banque Internationale pour la Reconstruction et le Developpement [*International Bank for Reconstruction and Development; also known as the World Bank*] [*French*]
BIRD .... Base d'Information Robert Debre [*Robert Debre Information Base*] [*International Children's Center*] [*Information service or system*] (IID)
BIRD.......... Bird Corp. [*NASDAQ symbol*] (NQ)
BIRD.......... Bird Investigation, Review, and Deterrent [*NASA*]
BIRD.......... Centre for Brain Injury Rehabilitation and Development [*British*] (CB)
BIRD.......... Reykjavik [*Iceland*] [*ICAO location identifier*] (ICLI)
BirdC .... Bird Corp. [*Associated Press*] (SAG)
Bird Conv.... Bird. New Pocket Conveyancer [*5th ed.*] [*1830*] [*A publication*] (DLA)
BirdCp........ Bird Corp. [*Associated Press*] (SAG)
BIRDIE .... Battery Integration and RADAR Display Equipment [*Air defense system*]
BIRDIE .... Battery Integration Routing Display Equipment (MCD)
Bird L & T... Bird. Laws Respecting Landlords, Tenants, and Lodgers [*11th ed.*] [*1833*] [*A publication*] (DLA)
BIRDP .... Bird Corp. $1.85 Cv Pref [*NASDAQ symbol*] (TTSB)
Bird Sol Pr... Bird. Solution of Precedents of Settlements [*1800*] [*A publication*] (DLA)
Birds St ...... Birdseye's Statutes [*New York*] [*A publication*] (DLA)
Bird Supp ... Bird's Supplement to Barton's Conveyancing [*A publication*] (DLA)
Birdw......... Birdwood's Printed Judgments [*India*] [*A publication*] (DLA)
B Ir E .... Bachelor of Irrigation Engineering
BIRE.......... British Institute of Radio Engineers
B Ir Eng ..... Bachelor of Irrigation Engineering
BIRES .... Broadband Isotropic Real-Time Electric Field Sensor (MCD)
BIRF.......... Banco Internacional de Reconstruccion y Fomento [*International Bank for Reconstruction and Development; also known as World Bank*] [*Spanish*]
BIRF.......... Brewing Industry Research Foundation [*British*]
BIRG.......... Raufarhofn [*Iceland*] [*ICAO location identifier*] (ICLI)
BIRI........... Brainerd International, Inc. [*NASDAQ symbol*] (NQ)
BIRI........... Brewing Industries Research Institute [*Defunct*] (EA)

BIRISPT .... Bureau International de Recherche sur les Implications Sociales du Progres Technique

BIRK .... Reykjavik Airport [*Iceland*] [*ICAO location identifier*] (ICLI)

Birk J .... Birkenhead's Judgments, House of Lords [*1919-22*] [*England*] [*A publication*] (DLA)

BIRL .... Basic Industry Research Laboratory

BIRL .... Beneficial Insects Research Laboratory [*Department of Agriculture*] [*Newark, DE*] (GRD)

BIRLS .... Beneficiary Identification Records Location Subsystem (MCD)

BIRM .... Birmingham [*City, county borough, and university in England*]

BIRM .... Birmingham Utilities, Inc. [*NASDAQ symbol*] (SAG)

BIRM .... Birmingham Utils [*NASDAQ symbol*] (TTSB)

BIRMAS .... Boeing Infrared Missile Attack Simulation (MCD)

BIRMO .... British Infrared Manufacturers Organization (PDAA)

BirmUtl .... Birmingham Utilities, Inc. [*Associated Press*] (SAG)

BIRO .... Base Industrial Relations Office [*or Officer*] [*Military*]

BIRPI .... Bureaux Internationaux Reunis pour la Protection de la Propriete Intellectuelle [*United International Bureau for the Protection of Intellectual Property*] [*Later, WIPO*]

BIRPS .... British Institutions Reflection Profiling Syndicate [*Seismic profiling*]

BIRS .... Baptist Information Retrieval System [*Southern Baptist Convention*] [*Nashville, TN*] [*Library network*] [*Defunct*]

BIRS .... Basic Indexing and Retrieval System [*Computer science*] (DIT)

BIRS .... Basic Information Retrieval System (NITA)

BIRS .... Biology Information Retrieval System [*Marine science*] (MSC)

BIRS .... British Institute of Recorded Sound

BirStl .... Birmingham Steel Corp. [*Associated Press*] (SAG)

BIRT .... Bird Impact Resistant Transparency (PDAA)

BIRT .... Bolt Installation and Removal Tool

BIS .... Bachelor of Interdisciplinary Studies

BIS .... Bank for International Settlements [*Basel, Switzerland*] (AF)

BIS .... Banking Information Service [*British*]

BIS .... Barrister Information Systems Corp. [*AMEX symbol*] (SPSG)

BIS .... Barrister Info Sys [*AMEX symbol*] (TTSB)

BIS .... Baseline Intelligence Summary Supplement (MCD)

BIS .... Battlefield Illumination System

BIS .... Battlefield Information System [*Army*] (RDA)

BIS .... Bechtel Information Services (IID)

BIS .... Beet Invert Syrup [*Food sweetener*]

BIS .... Best in Show [*Dog show term*]

BIS .... Bibliographic Instruction Section [*Association of College and Research Libraries*]

BIS .... Bibliotheks- und Informationssystem [*Library and Information System*] [*German*]

BIS .... Biocide Injection System (MCD)

BIS .... Biographical Inventory for Students [*Psychology*]

BIS .... Biomedical Information Service [*University of Minnesota, Minneapolis*] [*Information service or system*] (IID)

BIS .... Bishop College, Dallas, TX [*Inactive*] [*OCLC symbol*] (OCLC)

BIS .... Bishop Resources Development Ltd. [*Vancouver Stock Exchange symbol*]

BIS .... Bismarck [*North Dakota*] [*Airport symbol*] (OAG)

BIS .... Bismuth [*Chemical element*] (ROG)

Bis .... Bissell's United States Circuit Court Reports [*A publication*] (DLA)

BIS .... Bissextile Year [*Leap Year*] (ROG)

BIS .... Bistre [*Yellowish Brown*] (ROG)

BIS .... Blood Information Service (NITA)

BIS .... Board of Inspection and Survey [*Navy*]

BIS .... Books in Series [*A publication*]

BIS .... Boundary Intermediate System [*Computer science*] (TNIG)

BIS .... Bounty Information Service (EA)

BIS .... Bowne Information Systems (NITA)

BIS .... Brain Information Service (EA)

BIS .... Breakerless Ignition System [*Automotive engineering*]

BIS .... Bremsstrahlung Isochromat Spectroscopy (MCD)

BIS .... British and Irish Skeptic (EAIO)

BIS .... British Ichthyological Society

BIS .... British Imperial System

BIS .... British Information Services

BIS .... British Interplanetary Society

BIS .... British Iris Society (EAIO)

BIS .... Brought into Service [*Telecommunications*] (TEL)

BIS .... Brucellosis Information System [*Department of Agriculture*] (GFGA)

BIS .... Budget Information for the States [*Office of Management and Budget*] (GFGA)

BI's .... Buergerinitiativen [*Citizens' action groups*] [*Germany*]

BIS .... Bureau Interafricain des Sols [*Inter-African Soils Office*] (AF)

BIS .... Bureau Interafricain des Sols et de l'Economie Rurale [*Inter-African Bureau of Soils and Rural Economy*]

BIS .... Bureau International du Scoutisme

BIS .... Bureau of Inspection and Survey

BIS .... Burn-In Screening

BIS .... Business Improvement Services (AIE)

BIS .... Business Information Service [*Financial Times Business Information Ltd.*] [*British Information service or system*] (IID)

BIS .... Business Information Services [*Control Data Corp.*] [*Information service or system*] (IID)

BIS .... Business Information Systems [*Bell System*]

BIS .... Business Instruction Set [*Computer science*] (IAA)

BIS .... Business Intelligence Services Ltd. [*British*]

BIS .... Bypass Isolation Switch

BISA .... Baltic International USA, Inc. [*NASDAQ symbol*] (SAG)

BISA .... Baltic Intl. USA [*NASDAQ symbol*] (TTSB)

BISA .... Bibliographic Information on Southeast Asia [*University of Sydney Library*] [*Database*] [*Information service or system*] (IID)

BISA .... Biographical Index of South Australians [*A publication*] (APTA)

BISA .... British International Studies Association (DBA)

BISAC .... Book Industry Systems Advisory Committee [*Book Industry Study Group*] [*New York, NY*]

BISAD .... Business Information Systems Analysis and Design [*Bell System*] (DIT)

BISAHR .... Bistatic Synthetic Aperture Harmonic RADAR (MCD)

BISAKTA ..... British Iron, Steel and Kindred Trades Association (BI)

BI-SAL .... Bi-State Academic Libraries [*Library network*]

BISAM .... Basic Indexed Sequential Access Method [*IBM Corp.*] [*Computer science*]

BISAW .... Baltic Intl USA Wrrt [*NASDAQ symbol*] (TTSB)

BISC .... Biblical Institute for Social Change (EA)

BISC .... Biscayan

BISC .... British Institute of Sports Coaches (DBA)

BISC .... British Iron and Steel Corp.

BISC .... Bulletin. International Seismological Centre [*A publication*]

BiscApp .... Biscayne Apparel, Inc. [*Associated Press*] (SAG)

BISCLANT ... Bay of Biscay Subarea [*NATO*]

BISCOM ...... Business Information Systems Communications [*Bell System*]

BISCUS .... Business Information Systems Customer Service [*Bell System*]

BISCUS/FACS... Business Information Systems Customer Service/Facilities Assignment and Control System [*Bell System*] (MCD)

BISD .... Basic Instruments and Selected Documents of the GATT (AAGC)

BISD .... Bowker's International Serials Database [*R. R. Bowker Co.*] [*Information service or system*] (IID)

BISDN .... Broadband Integrated Services Digital Network [*Telecommunications*]

B-ISDN .... Broadband Integrated Services Digital Network (ACRL)

BISEC .... Bipartite Secretariat [*Post-World War II, Germany*]

BISER .... Bureau Interafricain des Sols et de l'Economie Rurale [*Inter-African Soils and Rural Economy Office*] (AF)

BISF .... Bolton Institute for a Sustainable Future (EA)

BISF .... British Iron and Steel Federation

BISFA .... British Industrial and Scientific Film Association

BISFA .... Bureau International pour la Standardisation de la Rayonne et des Fibres Synthetiques [*International Bureau for the Standardisation of Manmade Fibres*] (EAIO)

BISG .... Bockus International Society of Gastroenterology (EA)

BISG .... Book Industry Study Group (EA)

BIS-GMA ...... Bisphenol A-Glycidyl Methacrylate [*Organic chemistry*]

BISH .... Bishop (DSUE)

Bish Burr ..... Bishop's Edition of Burrill on Assignments [*A publication*] (DLA)

Bish Con ...... Bishop on Contracts [*A publication*] (DLA)

Bish Cont ..... Bishop on Contracts [*A publication*] (DLA)

Bish Cr Law... Bishop on Criminal Law [*A publication*] (DLA)

Bish Cr Proc... Bishop on Criminal Procedure [*A publication*] (DLA)

Bish First Bk... Bishop. First Book of the Law [*A publication*] (DLA)

Bish Ins .... Bishop on Insolvent Debtors [*A publication*] (DLA)

Bish Mar & Div... Bishop on Marriage and Divorce [*A publication*] (DLA)

Bish Mar Div & Sep... Bishop on Marriage, Divorce, and Separation [*A publication*] (DLA)

Bish Mar Wom... Bishop on Married Women [*A publication*] (DLA)

Bish New Cr Law... Bishop's New Criminal Law [*A publication*] (DLA)

Bish New Cr Proc... Bishop's New Criminal Procedure [*A publication*] (DLA)

Bish Noll Pros... Bishop's Law of Nolle Prosequi [*A publication*] (DLA)

Bish Non-Cont Law... Bishop on Non-Contract Law, Rights, and Torts [*A publication*] (DLA)

Bishop Dig... Bishop's Digest [*Montana*] [*A publication*] (DLA)

BIS HOR ...... Bis Horis [*Every Two Hours*] [*Pharmacy*] (ROG)

Bish Stat Cr... Bishop on Statutory Crimes [*A publication*] (DLA)

Bish St Crimes... Bishop on Statutory Crimes [*A publication*] (DLA)

Bish Wr L .... Bishop on Written Law [*A publication*] (DLA)

BISI .... Siglufjordur [*Iceland*] [*ICAO location identifier*] (ICLI)

BIS in 7 D ... Bis in Septem Dies [*Twice in Seven Days*] [*Pharmacy*] (ROG)

BIS in D ...... Bis in Die [*Twice a Day*] [*Pharmacy*] (ROG)

BISITS .... British Iron and Steel Industry Translation Service

BISITS .... British Iron and Steel Institute Translation Service (NITA)

BISL .... British Informatics Society Ltd. (NITA)

BISL .... British Institute of Securities Laws (DBA)

BISM .... Business Information Systems Management [*Mountain View, CA*] [*Telecommunications service*] (TSSD)

BISMAC .... Business Machine Computer

BISMAPS ..... Business Information Systems Modeling and Planning System [*Bell System*]

BISMPL .... BITs [*Binary Digits*] per Sample (MCD)

BISMRA ...... Bureau of Inter-Industrial Statistics and Multiple Regression Analysis (MCD)

BISN .... British India Steam Navigation Co.

BISNC .... British India Steam Navigation Co. (ROG)

BISNET .... Bank Information System Network

BISON .... Belo Information Systems Online Network [*A. H. Belo Corp.*] [*Discontinued service*] [*Information service or system*] (IID)

BISON .... Birmingham Solar Oscillations Network

BISp .... Between Ischial Spines [*Pelvic measurement*] [*Gynecology*]

bisp .... Bispinous [*or Interspinous*] [*Gynecology*]

Bisp .... Bispinous [*or Interspinous*] Diameter [*Orthopedics*] (DAVI)

BISP .... British Institute of Sewage Purification

BISp .... Bundesinstitut fuer Sportwissenschaft [*Federal Institute for Sports Science*] [*Germany*] (IID)

BISP .... Business Information Systems Programs [*Bell System*]

BISPA .... British Independent Steel Producers Association (PDAA)

Bisp Diam ... Bispinous Diameter [*Pelvic measurement*] (CPH)

BISPE .... Board of Inspection and Survey, Preliminary Evaluation [*Navy*]

Bisp Eq .... Bispham's Principles of Equity [*A publication*] (DLA)

Bisph Eq ..... Bispham's Principles of Equity [*A publication*] (DLA)

BISQ .... Bank for International Settlements, Quarterly [Database] [I. P. Sharp Associates] [Information service or system] (CRD)
BISRA .... Belize Institute of Social Research and Action
BISRA .... British Iron and Steel Research Association
BISS .... Bank for International Settlements, Semi-Annual [Database] [I. P. Sharp Associates] [Information service or system] (CRD)
BISS .... Base and Installation Security System [Military]
BISS .... Base Intrusion Surveillance System (MCD)
BISS .... Battlefield Identification System Study [NATO] (NATG)
BISS .... Bioisolator Suit System [NASA] (MCD)
BISS .... Biological Isolator Suit System (MCD)
Biss .... Bissell's United States Circuit Court Reports [A publication] (DLA)
BISS .... Sandskeid [Iceland] [ICAO location identifier] (ICLI)
Biss & Sm.... Bissett and Smith's Digest [South Africa] [A publication] (DLA)
BISSC .... Baking Industry Sanitation Standards Committee (EA)
Bissell .... Bissell's United States Circuit Court Reports, Seventh Circuit [A publication] (DLA)
Biss Est ...... Bissett on Estates for Life [A publication] (DLA)
Bissett Est ... Bissett on Estates for Life [A publication] (DLA)
Biss Part..... Bisset's Partnership and Joint Stock Companies [1847] [A publication] (DLA)
Biss Stat..... Bissell's Minnesota Statutes [A publication] (DLA)
Biss (US).... Bissell's United States Circuit Court Reports, Seventh Circuit [A publication] (DLA)
bist .... Bistre (VRA)
BIST............ British Institute of Surgical Technologists
BIST............ Built-In Self-Test
BIST............ Stykkisholmur [Iceland] [ICAO location identifier] (ICLI)
BISTA.......... Bureau of International Scientific and Technological Affairs [Department of State]
BISTAR .... Bistatic Thinned Array RADAR (MCD)
BISTSS .... Business Information System/Trunks and Special Services [Telecommunications] (TEL)
BISU .... Base Interface Surveillance Unit (IAA)
BISU .... Boeing Interface Surveillance Unit (KSC)
B-ISUP....... Broadband ISDN [Integrated Services Digital Network] User Part [Telecommunications] (ACRL)
BISVOT....... Bibliographic Information Service for Vocational Training [ILO] [United Nations] (DUND)
BISW.......... Befrienders International Samaritans Worldwide (EA)
BISYNC....... Binary Synchronous Communications protocol [IBM Co.] (ACRL)
BISYNC....... Binary Synchronous Transmission [or Communication] [Computer science]
BISYNC....... Bisynchronous (NITA)
BISYS .... BISYS Group, Inc. [Associated Press] (SAG)
BIT.............. Bachelor of Industrial Technology
BIT.............. Backscatter Imaging Tomography [Factory automation] (BTTJ)
BIT.............. Baitadi [Nepal] [Airport symbol] (OAG)
BIT.............. Band Ignitor Tube
BIT.............. Beijing Institute of Technology [China]
BiT.............. Between Great Trochanters [Orthopedics] (DAVI)
BIT.............. Binary Digit [Computer science]
bit.............. Binary Digit (IDOE)
BIT.............. Biotechnica International, Inc.
BIT.............. Bituminous [Technical drawings]
BIT.............. Board Information Terminal [Automotive electronic displays]
BIT.............. Boric Acid Injection Tank (IEEE)
BIT.............. Born-Infeld Theory [Physics]
BIT.............. Boron Injection Tank [Nuclear energy] (NRCH)
Bit.............. Borrowed Light (DAC)
Bit.............. Built (DAC)
BIT.............. Built-In Test [or Testing] [Computer science]
BIT.............. Bureau International du Travail [International Labour Office] [French]
BIT.............. Business Information Technology
BIT.............. Business Information Terminal [Computer science] (HGAA)
BIT.............. Business Insurance Trust (DLA)
BITA............ British Impact Treatment Association (DBA)
BITA............ British Industrial Truck Association
BITA............ Reykjavik [Iceland] [ICAO location identifier] (ICLI)
Bit & Wise... Bittleston and Wise. New Magistrates' Cases [England] [A publication] (DLA)
BIT/BITE...... Built-In Test/Built-In Test Equipment [Military] (RDA)
BITBLT........ BIT [Binary Digit]-Block Transfer
BITC............ Base Information Transfer Center [Military]
BITCH .... Black Intelligence Test of Cultural Homogeneity [Sometimes facetiously translated "Black Intelligence Test to Counter Honkeyism"]
BITDOC....... BITNET [Because It's Time Network] Development and Operations Center
BITE .... Backward Interworking Telephony Event [Telecommunications] (TEL)
BITE .... Base Installation Test Equipment [Military] (IAA)
BITE .... Benthic Inflatable Toolstore Enclosure (PDAA)
BITE .... Built-In Test Equipment
BITE .... Bulimic Investigatory Test [Psychology] (DMAA)
BITE .... Thingeyri [Iceland] [ICAO location identifier] (ICLI)
BITEJ .... Bureau International pour le Tourisme et les Echanges de la Jeunesse [International Bureau for Youth Tourism and Exchanges] (EAIO)
BITER.......... British Institute of Traffic Education Research (DBA)
BITEST........ Binomial Proportion Test (MCD)
BITG .... Bureau International Technique des Gelatines (EAIO)
BITH........... Thorshofn [Iceland] [ICAO location identifier] (ICLI)
BITI............. Bio-Imaging Technologies [NASDAQ symbol] (SAG)
BITI............. Bio Imaging Technologies Inc. [NASDAQ symbol] (TTSB)

BITIFP......... Bureau International Technique des "Inorganic Feed Phosphates" [Inorganic Feed Phosphates International Technical Bureau - IFPITB] (EAIO)
BITIW.......... Bio Imaging Technol Wrrt'G' [NASDAQ symbol] (TTSB)
BITL............ Bureau International Technique de l'ABS [Acronitrile-Butadiene-Styrene] [of the European Council of Chemical Manufacturers' Federations] (EAIO)
BITLC.......... Baking Industry and Teamster Labor Conference (EA)
BITM........... Bureau International Technique du Methanol [European Council of Chemical Manufacturers' Federations] [Belgium] (EAIO)
BITN........... Bilateral Iterative Network
BITN........... Bitumen
BITNET........ Because It's There Network [Electronic mail system] (TNIG)
BITNET........ Because It's Time Network [Interuniversity communications network]
BITNSC....... BITNET [Because It's Time Network] Network Support Center
BITO........... British Institution of Training Officers (PDAA)
BITO........... Burnishing Tool
BITOA......... British Incoming Tour Operators Association (DBA)
BITP........... Bureau International Technique des Polyesters (EAIO)
BITPI.......... Bureau International Technique des Polyesters Insatures [of the European Council of Chemical Manufacturers' Federations] (EAIO)
Bit Prac Cas... Bittleston's Practice Cases under Judicature Acts [England] [A publication] (DLA)
BITS............ Base Information Transfer System [Navy] (GFGA)
BITS............ Battlefield Information Transmission System [Army]
BITS............ Binary Information Transfer System (IAA)
BITS............ Binary Intersystem Transmission Standard
BITS............ BIOSIS [BioSciences Information Service] Information Transfer Service
BIT/s.......... BITS [Binary Digits] per second (NITA)
BITS............ Bitstream, Inc. [NASDAQ symbol] (SAG)
BITS............ Boeing Intelligent Terminal System [Boeing Computer Services Co.] [Information service or system] (IID)
BITS............ Building Integrated Timing Supply (ACRL)
BITS............ Built-In Test System [Military] (CAAL)
BITS............ Bureau International du Tourisme Social [International Bureau of Social Tourism - IBST] (EAIO)
BITS............ Bypass Isolation Transfer Switch
BIT/SEC....... Binary Digits per Second [Computer science] (HGAA)
Bitstrm....... Bitstream, Inc. [Associated Press] (SAG)
Bitt.............. Bittleston's Reports in Chambers, Queen's Bench Division [England] [A publication] (DLA)
Bitt Ch .... Bittleston's Reports in Chambers, Queen's Bench Division [England] [A publication] (DLA)
Bitt Cha Cas... Bittleston's Chamber Cases [1883-84] [A publication] (DLA)
Bitt Chamb Rep... Bittleston's Reports in Chambers, Queen's Bench Division [England] [A publication] (DLA)
Bitt Ch Cas... Bittleston's Reports in Chambers, Queen's Bench Division [England] [A publication] (DLA)
Bitt PC .... Bittleston's Practice Cases under Judicature Acts [England] [A publication] (DLA)
Bitt Prac Cas... Bittleston's Practice Cases [A publication] (ILCA)
Bitt Pr Cas... Bittleston's Practice Cases under Judicature Acts [England] [A publication] (DLA)
Bitt Pr Case... Bittleston's Practice Cases under Judicature Acts [England] [A publication] (DLA)
Bitt Rep in Ch... Bittleston's Reports in Chambers, Queen's Bench Division [England] [A publication] (DLA)
Bitt W & P... Bittleston, Wise, and Parnell's Reports [2, 3 New Practice Cases] [England] [A publication] (DLA)
BITU........... Benzyl-Iso-Thiourea [Organic chemistry]
BITUM .... Bituminous (MSA)
BITUMD .... Bituminized [Freight]
Bitwse .... Bitwise Designs [Associated Press] (SAG)
BIU............. Bar-Ilan University (BJA)
BIU............. Basic Income Unit (WDAA)
BIU............. Basic Information Unit (BUR)
BIU............. Battery Interface Unit (MCD)
BIU............. Bildudalur [Iceland] [Airport symbol] (OAG)
BIU............. Biological Indicator Unit [Food testing]
BIU............. British Import Union (DBA)
BIU............. Broadcasting for International Understanding (AC)
BIU............. Buffer Interface Unit [Computer science] (NASA)
BIU............. Built-In Unit (SSD)
BIU............. Bureau International des Universites
BIU............. Bus Interface Unit [Computer science]
BIV............. Bivouac (AABC)
BIV............. Bovine Immunodeficiency-Like Virus [Immunology] (DAVI)
BIV............. Bovine Immunodeficiency Virus
BIV............. Built-In Variance (MCD)
BIVA............ British Interactive Video Association [Information service or system] (IID)
BIVAR .... Bivariant Function Generator (DEN)
BIVM........... Vestmannaeyjar [Iceland] [ICAO location identifier] (ICLI)
BIVO........... Vopnafjordur [Iceland] [ICAO location identifier] (ICLI)
BIW............ Bath Iron Works [Maine] (DOMA)
BIW............ Battle Injury or Wound
BI-W .... Biweekly
BIW............ Body in White [Automotive manufacturing]
BIW............ Body in White
BIW............ Business Information Wire [Database] [The Canadian Press] [Information service or system] (CRD)
BIWF........... British-Israel World Federation
BiWM........... Bisexual White Male

BIWS	Bureau of International Whaling Statistics (BARN)
BIX	Biloxi, MS [*Location identifier FAA*] (FAAL)
BIX	Binary Information Exchange
BIX	BYTE Information Exchange [*Electronic conferencing system provided by McGraw-Hill's Byte magazine*]
BIY	Bedfordshire Imperial Yeomanry [*British military*] (DMA)
BIY	Buy-It-Yourself
BIZ	Bank fuer Internationalen Zahlungsausgleich [*Bank for International Settlements*] [*German*]
BIZ	Bicaz [*Romania*] [*Seismograph station code, US Geological Survey*] (SEIS)
BIZ	Bizarre (DAVI)
BIZ	Business [*Slang*] (DSUE)
biz	Business [*As in show biz*] (WDMC)
BIZFORC	Business Forecasting (MCD)
BIZMAC	Business Machine Computer (MHDI)
BIZNET	American Business Network [*US Chamber of Commerce*] [*Washington, DC Cable-television system*] [*Telecommunications*] (TSSD)
BJ	Bachelor of Journalism
BJ	Bachelor of Jurisprudence
B-J	Bach Jahrbuch [*A publication*]
BJ	Back Judge [*Football*]
BJ	Bakhtar Afghan Airlines [*ICAO designator*] (AD)
bj	Ball-Jointed [*Body*] [*Doll collecting*]
BJ	Bar Joist [*Building construction*] (OA)
BJ	Bar Journal [*A publication*]
BJ	Barrage Jammers [*RADAR*]
BJ	Bellum Judaicum [*Josephus*] [*Classical studies*] (OCD)
BJ	Bence Jones [*As in Bence Jones protein, Bence Jones reaction, etc.*] [*Named for Henry Bence Jones, 19th century London physician*]
BJ	Benin [*ANSI two-letter standard code*] (CNC)
BJ	Bharatiya Janata Party [*Indian People's Party*] [*Political party*]
BJ	Bibliotheca Judaica [*A publication*] (BJA)
BJ	Biceps Jerk [*Neurology*]
BJ	Bielschowsky-Jansky Syndrome [*Medicine*] (DMAA)
BJ	Black Jumbo [*Diplomatic codes*] [*World War II*]
BJ	Bonding Jig (MCD)
BJ	Bone and Joint [*Medicine*]
BJ	Break Jaw (MSA)
BJ	Bulkhead Jack
BJA	Ball Joint Actuator
BJA	Basic Journal Abstracts [*A publication*]
BJA	Bejaia [*Algeria*] [*Airport symbol*] (OAG)
BJA	British Jewellers Association (PDAA)
BJA	British Judo Association
BJA	Bureau of Justice Assistance
BJA	Burlap and Jute Association (EA)
BJA	Unifily [*Italy ICAO designator*] (FAAC)
BJAL	British Journal of Administrative Law [*A publication*] (DLA)
BJB	Burnham, J. B., Chicago IL [*STAC*]
BjBI	Balkan-ji-Bari International [*Children's Own Garden International - COGI*] (EAIO)
BJC	Babinet Jamin Compensator
BJC	Baltimore Junior College [*Maryland*]
BJC	Bear Stearns Companies, Inc. [*AMEX symbol*] (SAG)
BJC	Bennett Junior College [*New York*]
BJC	Bismarck Junior College [*North Dakota*]
BJC	Boise Junior College [*Idaho*]
BJC	Boone Junior College [*Iowa*]
BJC	Bradford Junior College [*Later, BC*] [*Massachusetts*]
BJC	Brisbane Jazz Club [*Australia*]
BJC	British Jewish Cockney
BJC	British Junior Chamber [*An association*] (DBA)
BJC	Brotherhood of the Jungle Cock (EA)
BJC	Denver, CO [*Location identifier FAA*] (FAAL)
BJCB	British Joint Communications Board [*British military*] (DMA)
BJCC	Bicentennial Junior Committees of Correspondence [*American Revolution Bicentennial Administration, US Postal Service, and National Association of Elementary School Principals*]
BJCC	British Junior Chambers of Commerce (BI)
BJCE	Bibliography of Jewish Communities in Europe [*Catalog at General Archives for the History of the Jewish People, Jerusalem*] [*A publication*] (BJA)
BJCEB	British Joint Communications-Electronics Board [*Military*]
BJCO	British Joint Communications Office (NATG)
BJCPA	Baptist Joint Committee on Public Affairs (EA)
BJCT	Bioject Medical Technologies [*NASDAQ symbol*] (NQ)
BJCT	Bioject Medl Technologies [*NASDAQ symbol*] (TTSB)
BJD	Bakkafjordur [*Iceland*] [*Airport symbol*] (OAG)
bjd	Bookjacket Designer [*MARC relator code*] [*Library of Congress*] (LCCP)
BJE	Bachelor of Jewish Education (BJA)
BJE	Bones, Joints, and Examination [*Medicine*] (DAVI)
BJE	Books-on-Japan-in-English [*A publication*]
BJE	Britannica Junior Encyclopedia [*A publication*]
BJE	Bureau of Jewish Education
BJ Ed	Bachelor of Jewish Education
BJEP	Bureau on Jewish Employment Problems (EA)
BJer	Bible de Jerusalem [*A publication*] (BJA)
BJF	Ball Joint Fitting
BJF	Batch Job Foreground [*Computer science*]
BJF	Batsfjord [*Norway*] [*Airport symbol*] (OAG)
BJF	Black, James F., Baltimore MD [*STAC*]

BJG	Bestand Juedischer Gemeinden in Staatsarchiv Hamburg [*A publication*] (BJA)
BJG	[*The*] Book of Joshua in Greek [*A publication*] (BJA)
BJGF	British Jewellery and Giftware Federation (DBA)
BJH	Bajhang [*Nepal*] [*Airport symbol*] (OAG)
BJH	Brown, James H., Atlanta GA [*STAC*]
BJI	Bemidji [*Minnesota*] [*Airport symbol*] (OAG)
BJI2	Peking [*Republic of China*] [*Seismograph station code, US Geological Survey*] (SEIS)
BJIC	Ben & Jerry's Homemade, Inc. [*NASDAQ symbol*] (NQ)
BJIC	Black-Jewish Information Center [*Defunct*] (EA)
BJICA	Ben & Jerry's CI'A' [*NASDAQ symbol*] (TTSB)
BJJ	Wooster, OH [*Location identifier FAA*] (FAAL)
BJK	Atlantic World Airways, Inc. [*ICAO designator*] (FAAC)
BJK & E	Bozell, Jacobs, Kenyon & Eckhardt [*Advertising agency*] [*New York, NY*]
BJL	Bachelor of Jewish Literature (BJA)
BJL	Banjul [*Gambia*] [*Airport symbol*] (OAG)
BJL	Beeler, J. L., Los Angeles CA [*STAC*]
BJ Lea	Lea's Tennessee Reports [*A publication*] (DLA)
BJM	Between Job Monitor [*Computer science*]
BJM	Bioject Medical Systems Ltd. [*Vancouver Stock Exchange symbol*]
BJM	Bluejacket's Manual [*Navy*]
BJM	Bones, Joints, Muscles [*Medicine*]
BJM	Bujumbura [*Burundi*] [*Airport symbol*] (OAG)
BJN	Basic Jet Navigation (DNAB)
BJN	Bear Island [*Formerly, Bjornoya*] [*Norway*] [*Geomagnetic observatory code*]
B/JNT	Ball Joint [*Automotive engineering*]
BJO	Banjo
BJO	Saint John's Seminary, Brighton, MA [*OCLC symbol*] (OCLC)
BJOH	Bureau des Jeux Olympiques d'Hiver de 1988, Gouvernement du Canada [*Office of the 1988 Winter Olympic Games, Government of Canada*]
BJP	Bachelor of Jewish Pedagogy
BJP	Bear Stearns Companies, Inc. [*AMEX symbol*] (SAG)
BJP	Bence Jones Protein [*Named for Henry Bence Jones, 19th century London physician*] (MAE)
BJP	Bharatiya Janata Party [*Indian People's Party*] [*Political party*] (PPW)
BJP	Indianapolis, IN [*Location identifier FAA*] (FAAL)
BJPL	British Jigsaw Puzzle Library [*An association*] (DBA)
B J PR	Bence Jones Protein [*Named for Henry Bence Jones, 19th century London physician*] (DAVI)
BJPS	British Journal for the Philosophy of Science [*A publication*]
BJR	Bahar Dar [*Ethiopia*] [*Airport symbol*] (OAG)
BJR	Barch, John R., New York NY [*STAC*]
BJR	Battaillon des Jeunes Ruraux [*Rural Youth Battalion*] [*Zaire*]
BJS	Bell Jar System
BJS	BJ Services [*NYSE symbol*] (TTSB)
BJS	BJ Services Co. [*NYSE symbol*] (SPSG)
BJS	British Joint Services
BJS	Bureau of Justice Statistics [*Department of Justice*] [*Also, an information service or system*] (IID)
BJSFC	Billie Jo Spears Fan Club (EA)
BJSM	British Joint Services Mission [*Later, SUKLO*]
BJSM	British Joint Staff Mission [*World War II*]
BJS.WS	BJ Services Wrrt [*NYSE symbol*] (TTSB)
BJT	Bed Joint [*Technical drawings*]
BJT	Bipolar Junction Transistor [*Electronics*]
BJTFC	B. J. Thomas Fan Club (EA)
BJTRA	British Jute Trade Research Association (PDAA)
BJU	Beach Jumper Unit
BJU	Beatrice, NE [*Location identifier FAA*] (FAAL)
BJU	Bob Jones University [*South Carolina*]
B Jur	Baccalaureus Juris [*Bachelor of Law*] (DLA)
B Jur & Soc S	Bachelor of Juridical and Social Sciences (DLA)
BJuris	Bachelor of Jurisprudence
B Just	Burn's Justice of the Peace [*England*] [*A publication*] (DLA)
BJV	Braswell, J. V., Dallas TX [*STAC*]
BJVN	Dokumentationszentrum des Bundes Judischer Verfolger des Naziregimes [*Jewish Documentation Centre - JDC*] (EAIO)
BJW	Bajawa [*Indonesia*] [*Airport symbol*] (OAG)
BJZ	Badajoz [*Spain*] [*Airport symbol*] (OAG)
BK	Baba Kama [*or Bava Kamma*] (BJA)
BK	Back [*Dance terminology*]
BK	Backwardation [*Commodity futures trading*]
BK	Balks [*Baseball*]
BK	Bank
BK	Bank
BK	Bank Book
BK	Bankers' [*Rate*] [*Value of the English pound*]
BK	Bank of New York [*NYSE symbol*] (TTSB)
BK	Bank of New York Co., Inc. [*NYSE symbol*] (SPSG)
BK	Barge, Knockdown (MSA)
BK	Bark [*or Barque*] (ROG)
BK	Bar Keel [*Shipping*] (DS)
BK	Barque
BK	Bart Resources Ltd. [*Vancouver Stock Exchange symbol*]
BK	Beekeeper
BK	Behavioral Kinesiology [*Book title*]
BK	Below Knee [*Medicine*]
BK	Bent Knees [*Doll collecting*]
Bk	Berkelium [*Chemical element*]
BK	Berliner Konferenz Europaischer Katholiken [*Berlin Conference of European Catholics*] [*Germany*] (EAIO)

BK	Berlin Kommandatura
BK	Biblischer Kommentar zum Alten Testament [*A publication*] (BJA)
BK	Black
BK	Black Knight [*Missile*]
Bk	Black's United States Supreme Court Reports [*66-67 United States Reports*] [*A publication*] (DLA)
BK	Blendkoerper [*Frangible-glass smoke grenade*] [*German military - World War II*]
BK	Block (WGA)
bk	Block (WDMC)
BK	Blue Knights International Law Enforcement Motorcycle Club (EA)
BK	Book (AAG)
bk	Book (VRA)
bk	Book (WDMC)
BK	Bookcase [*s*] [*Freight*]
BK	Book-Keeper (ADA)
BK	Bradykinin [*Biochemistry*]
BK	Brake (KSC)
BK	Break (IDOE)
BK	Break-In (IDOE)
BK	Break-In Keying (IAA)
BK	Brick [*Classified advertising*] (ADA)
BK	British Knights [*Brand name of athletic shoe*]
BK	Brook (WGA)
BK	Bulk Containers [*Shipping*] (DCTA)
Bk	Bulk Tainers [*Shipping*] (DS)
BK	Bundeskanzler [*Federal Chancellor*] [*German*] (ILCA)
BK	Bundeskanzleramt [*Federal Chancery*] [*German*] (ILCA)
BK	Burger King Corp.
BK	Chalk's International Airline [*ICAO designator*] (AD)
BK	Kamloops Public Library, British Columbia [*Library symbol National Library of Canada*] (NLC)
BKA	Bankair, Inc. [*ICAO designator*] (FAAC)
BkA	BankAmerica Corp. [*Associated Press*] (SAG)
BKA	Bank fuer Kredit und Aussenhandel AG [*Bank for Credit and Export Trade*] [*German*]
BKA	Bee Keepers Association
BKA	Below Knee Amputation [*Medicine*]
BKA	Blackmist Resources, Inc. [*Vancouver Stock Exchange symbol*]
BKA	Bradykinin Antagonist [*Medicine*]
BKA	British Kodaly Academy (DBA)
BKA	British Korfball Association (EAIO)
BKA	Broadband Klystron Amplifier
BKA	Bundeskartellamt [*Federal Cartel Office*] [*German*] (ILCA)
BKA	Bundeskriminalamt [*Federal Criminal Police Bureau*] [*Germany*]
BKA	Sitka, AK [*Location identifier FAA*] (FAAL)
BKAG	Research Station, Agriculture Canada [*Station de Recherches, Agriculture Canada*] Kamloops, British Columbia [*Library symbol National Library of Canada*] (NLC)
BkAm	BankAmerica Corp. [*Associated Press*] (SAG)
BK & S	Basic Knowledge and Skills [*Training*] [*Military*]
BKAS	Technical Library, Alcan Smelters Chemicals Ltd., Kitimat, British Columbia [*Library symbol National Library of Canada*] (NLC)
BKASL	Kaslo Public Library, British Columbia [*Library symbol National Library of Canada*] (NLC)
BkAtlB	Bank Atlantic Bancorp, Inc. [*Associated Press*] (SAG)
BKB	Bangladesh Krishi Bank (EY)
BKB	Bank of Boston [*NYS*] (TTSB)
BKB	Bank of Boston Corp. [*NYSE symbol*] (SPSG)
BKB	British Karate Board (DI)
BKB	Kirbyville, TX [*Location identifier FAA*] (FAAL)
Bkbird	Bookbird [*A publication*] (BRI)
BKBK	Britton & Koontz Capital Corp. [*NASDAQ symbol*] (SAG)
BKBNDG	Bookbinding (DGA)
BKBNDNG	Bookbinding
BKBNDR	Bookbinder
BKBNDR	Bookbinder (DGA)
BkBost	Bank of Boston Corp. [*Associated Press*] (SAG)
BKBPrA	Bank of Boston Adj Rt A Pfd [*NYSE symbol*] (TTSB)
BKBPrB	Bank of Boston Adj Rt B Ptd [*NYSE symbol*] (TTSB)
BKBPrC	Bank of Boston Adj Rt C Pfd [*NYSE symbol*] (TTSB)
BKBPrE	Bank of Boston 8.60% Dep Pfd [*NYSE symbol*] (TTSB)
BKBPrF	Bank of Boston 7.875%DepPfd [*NYSE symbol*] (TTSB)
BKBPT	Brotherhood of Knights of the Black Pudding Tasters (EA)
BKC	Amer Bank, Conn [*AMEX symbol*] (TTSB)
BKC	American Bank of Connecticut [*AMEX symbol*] (SPSG)
BKC	Black Cliff Mines Ltd. [*Toronto Stock Exchange symbol*]
BKC	Brookwood Reservoir [*California*] [*Seismograph station code, US Geological Survey*] (SEIS)
BKC	Buckland [*Alaska*] [*Airport symbol*] (OAG)
BKCA	Bank Cable (IAA)
BKCC	Cariboo College, Kamloops, British Columbia [*Library symbol National Library of Canada*] (NLC)
BKCEC	British Knitting and Clothing Export Council (DBA)
BKCM	Kitimat Centennial Museum, British Columbia [*Library symbol National Library of Canada*] (NLC)
BKCO	Bankers Corp. [*NASDAQ symbol*] (SAG)
BkCpGa	Bank Corp. of Georgia [*Associated Press*] (SAG)
BKCS	BKC Semiconductors [*NASDAQ symbol*] (TTSB)
BKCS	BKC Semiconductors, Inc. [*NASDAQ symbol*] (SAG)
BKC Sem	BKC Semiconductors, Inc. [*Associated Press*] (SAG)
BKCT	Bancorp Connecticut [*NASDAQ symbol*] (TTSB)
BKCT	Bancorp Connecticut, Inc. [*NASDAQ symbol*] (SAG)
BKCT	Cariboo-Thompson Nicola Library System, Kamloops, British Columbia [*Library symbol National Library of Canada*] (NLC)
BKCY	Bankruptcy
bkcy	Bankruptcy (ODBW)
BKD	Backward (WDAA)
BKD	Bacterial Kidney Disease [*Ichthyology*]
BKD	Baked
BKD	Blackboard (MSA)
bkd	Book Designer [*MARC relator code*] [*Library of Congress*] (LCCP)
BKD	Breckenridge, TX [*Location identifier FAA*] (FAAL)
BKDI	Brake Die
BKDN	Breakdown (MSA)
BKDNDIO	Breakdown Diode [*Electronics*]
BKE	Baker, OR [*Location identifier FAA*] (FAAL)
BKE	Bankeno Resources Ltd. [*Toronto Stock Exchange symbol*]
BKE	Brock Exploration Corp. [*AMEX symbol*] (SPSG)
BKEM	Keremeos Museum, British Columbia [*Library symbol National Library of Canada*] (NLC)
BK ENG	Break Engage (CAAL)
BKEP	Boosted Kinetic Energy Penetrator [*Proposed submunition*]
BKER	Block Error Rate [*Computer science*] (MHDI)
BKESVM	Similkameen Valley Museum, Keremeos, British Columbia [*Library symbol National Library of Canada*] (NLC)
BKF	Baker, Fentress & Co. [*NYSE symbol*] (CTT)
BKF	Blocking Factor (CMD)
bkf	Breakfast (DAVI)
BKF	Denver, CO [*Location identifier FAA*] (FAAL)
BKFS	British-Kurdish Friendship Society
bkfst	Breakfast
bkft	Breakfast
BKG	Background (NTCM)
BKG	Baker Gold Ltd. [*Vancouver Stock Exchange symbol*]
BKG	Baking
bkg	Banking (ODBW)
BKG	Banking
BKG	Booking (WDAA)
BKG	Bookkeeping
BKG	Breakage (WGA)
BKG	Lehman Brothers, Inc. [*AMEX symbol*] (SAG)
BKG	Lehman Br Reg'l Bk'SUNS' 1996 [*AMEX symbol*] (TTSB)
BKG	Utica, NY [*Location identifier FAA*] (FAAL)
BKGD	Background
bkgr	Background (VRA)
BkGranit	Bank of Granite [*Associated Press*] (SAG)
BKGRD	Background [*Low-priority processing*] [*Computer science*]
BKH	Black Hills Corp. [*NYSE symbol*] (SPSG)
BKH	[*The*] Book House [*ACCORD*] [*UTLAS symbol*]
BKH	Kekaha, HI [*Location identifier FAA*] (FAAL)
Bkhd	Bulkhead
BKHS	Blockhouse [*NASA*] (AAG)
BKI	Bering [*Komandorsky Islands*] [*Former USSR Seismograph station code, US Geological Survey*] (SEIS)
BKI	Better Kitchens Institute (EA)
BKI	Break-In [*Telecommunications*] (TEL)
BKI	Buckeye Cellulose [*NYSE symbol*] (TTSB)
BKI	Buckeye Cellulose Corp. [*NYSE symbol*] (SAG)
BKI	Kimberley Public Library, British Columbia [*Library symbol National Library of Canada*] (NLC)
BKI	Kota Kinabalu [*Malaysia*] [*Airport symbol*] (OAG)
BKIF	Business Name and Address Key Index File [*IRS*]
BKIHM	Kimberley and District Heritage Museum, Kimberley, British Columbia [*Library symbol National Library of Canada*] (NLC)
BkIreInd	Governor & Co. of the Bank of Ireland [*Associated Press*] (SAG)
BKIT	Kitimat Public Library, British Columbia [*Library symbol National Library of Canada*] (NLC)
BKJ	Barken International, Inc. [*ICAO designator*] (FAAC)
BK JUB	Book of Jubilees [*Apocalyptic book*]
Bk Judg	Book of Judgments, by Townshend [*A publication*] (DLA)
BKK	Bangkok [*Thailand*] [*Airport symbol*] (OAG)
BKKA	Diocese of Kootenay Archives, Kelowna, British Columbia [*Library symbol National Library of Canada*] (NLC)
BKL	Baikal [*Russian Federation*] [*ICAO designator*] (FAAC)
BKL	Bakel [*Senegal*] [*Seismograph station code, US Geological Survey*] (SEIS)
B KI	Bass Klarinette [*Bass Clarinet*] [*Music*]
BK L	Break Line [*Printing*] (DGA)
BKL	Cleveland [*Ohio*] Burke Lakefront [*Airport symbol*] (OAG)
BKLA	Bank of Los Angeles [*NASDAQ symbol*] (SAG)
BKLE	Buckle (ROG)
BKLE	Buckle, Inc. [*NASDAQ symbol*] (SAG)
BKLKTNG	Break-Lock ECM [*Electronic Countermeasures*] Training [*Navy*] (ANA)
BKLN	Brooklyn
BKLR	Black Letter [*Printing*]
BKLT	Booklet (AFM)
BKLY	Berkley [*W. R.*] Corp. [*NASDAQ symbol*] (NQ)
Bklyn	Brooklyn [*New York*] (BARN)
BklynBc	Brooklyn Bancorp, Inc. [*Associated Press*] (SAG)
BklyUG	Brooklyn Union Gas Co. [*Associated Press*] (SAG)
BKLYZ	Berkley(W.R.)7.375% Dep'A'Pfd [*NASDAQ symbol*] (TTSB)
BKM	Bakalalan [*Malaysia*] [*Airport symbol*] (OAG)
BKM	Battelle Memorial Institute, Columbus, OH [*OCLC symbol*] (OCLC)
BKM	Buckram (ADA)
BKM	Kamloops Museum, British Columbia [*Library symbol National Library of Canada*] (NLC)
BKME	Bank of Kuwait & the Middle East (ECON)
BKME	Bleached Kraft Mill Effluent [*Pulp and paper processing*]

BkMont	Bank of Montreal [*Associated Press*] (SAG)
BKN	Barquentine [*Ship*]
BKN	Belkin, Inc. [*Toronto Stock Exchange symbol*]
BKN	Blackrock Investment Quality Municipal Trust [*NYSE symbol*] (SPSG)
BKN	Blackrock Inv Qual Muni Tr [*NYSE symbol*] (TTSB)
BKN	Broken
BkNash	Bank of Nashville [*Associated Press*] (SAG)
BKNG	Banknorth Group [*NASDAQ symbol*] (TTSB)
BKNG	Banknorth Group, Inc. [*NASDAQ symbol*] (NQ)
BKNO₃	Boron Potassium Nitrate
BkNsh	Bank of Nashville [*Associated Press*] (SAG)
Bknth	Banknorth Group, Inc. [*Associated Press*] (SAG)
BKNW	British Columbia Native Women's Society, Kamloops, British Columbia [*Library symbol National Library of Canada*] (NLC)
BkNY	Bank of New York Co., Inc. [*Associated Press*] (SAG)
BKO	Bamako [*Mali*] [*Airport symbol*] (OAG)
BKO	Barkhausen-Kurz Oscillator
BKO	Below-Knee Orthosis [*Orthopedics*] (DAVI)
BKO	Okanagan Regional Library, Kelowna, British Columbia [*Library symbol National Library of Canada*] (NLC)
BKOC	Okanagan College, Kelowna, British Columbia [*Library symbol National Library of Canada*] (NLC)
BKOCH	Ocelot Chemicals, Kitimat, British Columbia [*Library symbol National Library of Canada*] (NLC)
BKOM	Kelowna Centennial Museum and Archives, British Columbia [*Library symbol National Library of Canada*] (NLC)
BKP	Bangkok Airways [*Thailand*] [*ICAO designator*] (FAAC)
BKP	Bayerische Koenigpartei [*Bavarian Royalist Party*] [*Pre-World War II*]
BKP	Black Pearl Resources Ltd. [*Vancouver Stock Exchange symbol*]
BKP	Bookplate (WGA)
BkP	Brookhaven Press, Washington, DC [*Library symbol Library of Congress*] (LCLS)
BKP	Bulgarska Komunisticheska Partiia [*Bulgarian Communist Party*] [*Political party*] (PPE)
BKPA	British Kidney Patient Association (DI)
BKPG	Bookkeeping (MUGU)
BKPG	Bookkeeping
BKPR	Bookkeeper
BKPR	Bookkeeper (WGA)
BKPrB	Bk of N.Y.8.60% Dep Pfd [*NYSE symbol*] (TTSB)
BKPT	Bankrupt (ROG)
BKPTCY	Bankruptcy [*Legal shorthand*] (LWAP)
BKQ	Bakra Resources Ltd. [*Vancouver Stock Exchange symbol*]
BKQ	Blackall [*Australia Airport symbol*] (OAG)
BKR	Baker
BKR	Baker [*Michael*] Corp. [*AMEX symbol*] (SPSG)
BKR	Bakuriani [*Former USSR Seismograph station code, US Geological Survey*] (SEIS)
BKR	Bankit Resource Corp. [*Vancouver Stock Exchange symbol*]
BKR	Breaker (KSC)
BKR	Broker [*Business term*]
BKR	Circuit Breaker (NTCM)
BKR	South Carolina Wing, Civil Air Patrol [*FAA designator*] (FAAC)
Bkr-Dir	Directory of Bankruptcy Attorneys [*Information service or system*] (IID)
Bk Reg	National Bankruptcy Register Reports [*A publication*] (DLA)
BKRM	Kettle Valley Railway Museum, Kelowna, British Columbia [*Library symbol National Library of Canada*] (NLC)
BKRP	Bankruptcy File [*Canada Systems Group*] [*Ottawa, ON*] [*Information service or system*] (IID)
BKRPCY	Bankruptcy (ADA)
BKRPT	Bankrupt
BKRPTCY	Bankruptcy
BkrsLH	Bankers Life Holding Corp. [*Associated Press*] (SAG)
BKRUPT	Bankrupt (ROG)
BKRY	Bakery (AABC)
BKRY	Bakery
BKS	Backstrip (WGA)
BKS	Barnes & Noble [*NYSE symbol*] (TTSB)
BKS	Barnes & Noble, Inc. [*NYSE symbol*] (SPSG)
BKS	Barracks (AABC)
BKS	Beekeeper Serum [*Medicine*] (DMAA)
BKS	Bengkulu [*Indonesia*] [*Airport symbol*] (OAG)
BKS	Berkeley-Byerly [*California*] [*Seismograph station code, US Geological Survey*] (SEIS)
BKS	Berkley Resources, Inc. [*Vancouver Stock Exchange symbol*]
BKS	Blutkorpersenkung [*Blood Sedimentation Rate*] [*German Medicine*]
BKS	Bohr-Kramers-Slater [*Quantum theory*]
bks	Books (DLA)
BKS	Broadcast Keying Station (NVT)
BKS	Falfurrias, TX [*Location identifier FAA*] (FAAL)
Bks & Cult	Books & Culture [*A publication*] (BRI)
BKSC	[*The*] Bank of South Carolina [*NASDAQ symbol*] (NQ)
BkSClara	Bank of Santa Clara [*Associated Press*] (SAG)
BK SH	Book Shelf [*Technical drawings*] (DAC)
BKSHLF	Bookshelf
Bks Keeps	Books for Keeps [*A publication*] (BRI)
BKSLF	Back Shelf
BKSLLR	Bookseller
BKSO	Bank South Corp. [*NASDAQ symbol*] (NQ)
BkSouth	Bank South Corp. [*Associated Press*] (SAG)
BKSP	Backspace Character [*Keyboard*] [*Computer science*] (BUR)
BKSSM	S. S. Moyie Museum, Kaslo, British Columbia [*Library symbol National Library of Canada*] (NLC)
BKST	Backstamp

BKST	Brookstone, Inc. [*NASDAQ symbol*] (SAG)
BkSthg	Bank of Southington [*Associated Press*] (SAG)
BKSTR	Bookstore
BKSTS	British Kinematography, Sound, and Television Society
BKT	Bakertalc, Inc. [*Toronto Stock Exchange symbol*]
BKT	Basket
BKT	Berliner Klassikertexte [*A publication*] (OCD)
BKT	Blackrock Income Trust [*NYSE symbol*] (SPSG)
BKT	Blackstone, VA [*Location identifier FAA*] (FAAL)
BKT	Blinker Tube
BKT	Bracket
BKT	British Trades Union Congress [*TUC*]
BKT	Bucket
BKTCY	Bankruptcy
BKTL	Blessed Kateri Tekakwitha League (EA)
BkTokyo	Bank of Mitsubishi Ltd. [*Associated Press*] (SAG)
BKTT	Below Knee to Toe [*Medicine*] (MAE)
BKU	Baker, MT [*Location identifier FAA*] (FAAL)
BKU	Bank United of Texas FSB [*NYSE symbol*] (SPSG)
BKU	Betioky [*Madagascar*] [*Airport symbol*] (OAG)
BKUN	BankUnited Financial Corp. [*NASDAQ symbol*] (NQ)
BKUNA	BankUnited Financial'A' [*NASDAQ symbol*] (TTSB)
BKUNO	BankUnited Finl 9% Perp Pfd [*NASDAQ symbol*] (TTSB)
BKUNP	BankUnited Finl 8% Cv Pfd [*NASDAQ symbol*] (TTSB)
BKUP	Backup (KSC)
BKUPrA	Bank Utd Texas FSB Pfd [*NYSE symbol*] (TTSB)
BKUPrB	Bank Utd Texas 9.60% 'B' Pfd [*NYSE symbol*] (TTSB)
BkUtd	Bank United of Texas FSB [*Associated Press*] (SAG)
BkUtF	BankUnited Financial Corp. [*Associated Press*] (SAG)
BKV	Brookmere Ventures [*Vancouver Stock Exchange symbol*]
BKV	Brooksville, FL [*Location identifier FAA*] (FAAL)
BKV	Brotherhood of the Knights of the Vine (EA)
BKW	Beckley [*West Virginia*] [*Airport symbol*] (OAG)
BKW	Bible Key Words [*London, 1949-1965*] [*A publication*] (BJA)
BKW	Breakwater
BKWA	Branded Knitting-Wool Association Ltd. [*British*] (BI)
BKWC	Below Knee Walking Cast (MEDA)
BKWD	Backward (KSC)
Bk West	Bank West Financial Corp. [*Associated Press*] (SAG)
BKWP	Below Knee Walking Plaster [*Medicine*] (MAE)
BKX	Brookings [*South Dakota*] [*Airport symbol*] (OAG)
BKY	Bankruptcy
BKY	Bluesky Oil & Gas [*Toronto Stock Exchange symbol Vancouver Stock Exchange symbol*]
BKY	Bukavu [*Zaire*] [*Airport symbol*] (OAG)
BKY	St. Louis, MO [*Location identifier FAA*] (FAAL)
BKZ	Brinkley, AR [*Location identifier FAA*] (FAAL)
BKZ	Bukoba [*Tanzania*] [*Airport symbol*] (OAG)
BL	Air BVI [*ICAO designator*] (AD)
BL	Baccalaureat en Loisirs [*Canada*] (DD)
BL	Bachelor in Law (DD)
BL	Bachelor of Laws
BL	Bachelor of Letters
BL	Bachelor of Literature
BL	Background Listening [*Music*]
BL	Backlash (MSA)
BL	Badminton Library [*A publication*]
BL	Bale
BL	Ball Lightning
BL	Bank Larceny
BL	Barrel (MCD)
BL	Barrister-at-Law
BL	Basal Lamina [*Neuroanatomy*]
BL	Baseline
BL	Basic Load [*Ammunition*] (AABC)
BL	Basolateral [*Anatomy*]
BL	Basutoland
BL	Bath Road [*Bristol*] [*British depot code*]
BL	Bats Left-Handed [*Baseball*]
BL	Beak Line
BL	Bell (IEEE)
BL	Bellanca Aircraft Corp. [*ICAO aircraft manufacturer identifier*] (ICAO)
BL	Bell on Leases [*A publication*] (DLA)
BL	Bend Line (MSA)
BL	Bengal Lancers [*British military*] (DMA)
BL	Bessey-Lowry Unit [*Medicine*] (MAE)
BL	Bibel-Lexikon [*A publication*] (BJA)
BL	Bibel und Liturgie [*A publication*] (BJA)
BL	Bible League (EA)
BL	Bilevel (MCD)
BL	Billet (MSA)
BL	Bill Lodged [*British*] (ADA)
BL	Bill of Lading [*Shipping*]
B/L	Bill of Lading [*MARAD*] (TAG)
BL	Biological Laboratory [*Army*] (MCD)
BL	Bioluminescence
BL	Black
bl	Black (WDMC)
Bl	Blackford's Indiana Reports [*1817-47*] [*A publication*] (DLA)
BL	Black Leghorn [*Poultry*]
BL	Black Letter [*Printing*]
BL	Black Light
BL	Black Liquor [*Pulp and paper technology*]
BL	Black Lung [*Social Security Administration*] (OICC)

Bl	Blackstone's Commentaries on the Laws of England [A publication] (DLA)
Bl	Black's United States Supreme Court Reports [66-67 United States Reports] [A publication] (DLA)
BL	Blade (MSA)
BL	Blair Corp. [AMEX symbol] (SPSG)
BL	BLAISE [British Library Automated Information Service] number [Database terminology] (NITA)
BL	Blank [Microtiter plate]
BL	Blanking (DEN)
BL	Blank Line [Computer science]
BL	Blaser [Blower] [Wind instrument player]
Bl	Blasinstrumente [Wind Instruments] [Music]
BL	Blast
Bl	Blatchford's United States Circuit Court Reports [A publication] (DLA)
Bl	Blatt [Newspaper, Sheet] [German] (BJA)
Bl	Bleed (MSA)
Bl	Bleomycin [Also, B, Bleo, BLM] [Antineoplastic drug]
BL	Blessed
BL	Bloch & Co., Cleveland, OH [Library symbol Library of Congress] (LCLS)
BL	Block
BL	Block Label [Computer science] (IAA)
BL	Block Length
BL	Blood
BL	Blood Loss [Medicine] (AAMN)
BL	Bloom [or Blossom] (ROG)
BL	Bloque
Bl	Blount's Law Dictionary [A publication] (DLA)
BL	Blower
BL	Blowing [ICAO] (FAAC)
BL	Blowline
BL	Blue (KSC)
bl	Blue (VRA)
BL	Blue Laid [Paper] (DGA)
BL	Blue Line (MCD)
BL	Blue Pennant [Navy British]
BL	Boat Lanes
BL	Bodleian Library (DAS)
BL	Body Line [Typography] (WDMC)
BL	Bombline
BL	Bomb Line (DNAB)
BL	Bone-Marrow-Derived Lymphocyte [Hematology]
BL	Booklist [A publication] (BRI)
BL	Border Leicester [Sheep]
BL	Border Line
BL	Borderline Lepromatous [Medicine]
BL	Bottom Layer [Technical drawings]
BL	Bottom Level
BL	Boundary Layer
BL	Brascan Ltd. [Toronto Stock Exchange symbol]
bl	Brazil [IYRU nationality code] [MARC country of publication code Library of Congress] (LCCP)
BL	Breadth-Length
BL	Breech-Loading [Weapon]
B/L	Bridgelayer [British military] (DMA)
BL	Bristol Laboratories
BL	British Legion
BL	British Leyland [Later, BL Ltd., then Rover Group] [Auto manufacturing company]
BL	British Library [Formerly, The British Museum Reading Room]
BL	British Lion [Motion picture company]
BL	Buccolingual [Dentistry]
BL	Building Line [Technical drawings]
BL	Bullock Ridge Splitting [Agriculture]
BL	Bundelkund Legion [British military] (DMA)
BL	Bureau of Litigation [Federal Trade Commission]
BL	Burkitt's Lymphoma [Medicine]
B-L	Bursa Equivalent Lymphocyte (MAE)
BL	Business Licence [British] (ADA)
BL	Bus Link (IAA)
BL	Butt Line [Technical drawings]
BL	Buttock Line [Engineering]
BL	By-Line [Publishing]
BL	Graduate in Letters
BL	South Africa [Formerly, FY] [License plate code assigned to foreign diplomats in the US]
BLA	All Charter Ltd. [British ICAO designator] (FAAC)
BLA	Bachelor of Landscape Architecture
BLA	Bachelor of Law and Administration
BLA	Bachelor of Liberal Arts
BLA	Bagala [Ship's rigging] (ROG)
BLA	[The] Baltimore & Annapolis Railroad Co. [AAR code]
BLA	Baptist Life Association [Buffalo, NY] (EA)
BLA	Barcelona [Venezuela] [Airport symbol] (OAG)
BLA	Base Loaded Antenna
BLA	Bear Lake Resources Ltd. [Vancouver Stock Exchange symbol]
BLA	Belarussian Literary Association [Canada] (EAIO)
BLA	Belgian Linen Association [Later, ILPC] (EA)
BLA	Bilateral Agreements
BLA	Bills of Lading Act
BLA	Binary Logical Association
BLA	Bird Lovers Anthology [A publication]
bla	Blackfoot [MARC language code Library of Congress] (LCCP)
BLA	Black Liberation Army (EA)

BLA	Black Lung Association (EA)
BLA	Blacksburg [Virginia] [Seismograph station code, US Geological Survey] (SEIS)
BLA	Blocking Acknowledgement Signal [Telecommunications] (NITA)
BLA	Blocking Acknowledgment [Telecommunications] (TEL)
BLA	Bracket and Linkage Assembly
BLA	British Legal Association (DLA)
BLA	British Liberation Army [Later, British Army of the Rhine]
BLA	British Library Association (BARN)
BLA	British Lift Association (DBA)
BLA	Brown Lung Association (EA)
BLA	Bureau de Liaison des Syndicats Europeens (CEE) des Produits Aromatiques [Liaison Bureau of the European and EEC Unions of Aromatic Products] (EAIO)
BLA	Bureau for Latin America [Agency for International Development]
BLA	Byelorussian Literary Association (EA)
BLA	Graduate in Liberal Arts
BLA	Grammatik des Biblische-Aramaeischen [H. Bauer and P. Leander] [A publication] (BJA)
BLAC	Bladder Urine [Urology] (DAVI)
BLAC	British Light Aviation Center (MCD)
Bla Ch	Bland's Maryland Chancery Reports [A publication] (DLA)
Black	Blackerby's Magistrates' Reports [1327-1716] [England] [A publication] (DLA)
Black	Blackford's Indiana Reports [1817-47] [A publication] (DLA)
Black	Black's Reports [30-53 Indiana] [A publication] (DLA)
Black	Black's United States Supreme Court Reports [66-67 United States Reports] [A publication] (DLA)
Black Abr	Blackstone's Commentaries on the Laws of England, Abridged [A publication] (DLA)
Black Anal	Blackstone's Analysis of the Laws of England [A publication] (DLA)
Blackb	Blackburn on Sales [A publication] (DLA)
Black Bk Adm	Twiss. Black Book of the Admiralty [A publication] (DLA)
Blackb Sales	Blackburn on Sales [A publication] (DLA)
BlackBx	Black Box Corp. [Associated Press] (SAG)
Black Com	Blackstone's Commentaries on the Laws of England [A publication] (DLA)
Black Cond	Blackwell's Condensed Illinois Reports [A publication] (DLA)
Black Cond Rep	Blackwell's Condensed Illinois Reports [A publication] (DLA)
Black Const Law	Black on Constitutional Law [A publication] (DLA)
Black Const Prohib	Black's Constitutional Prohibitions [A publication] (DLA)
BlackD	Black & Decker Corp. [Associated Press] (SAG)
Black D & O	Blackham, Dundas, and Osborne's Irish Nisi Prius Reports [1846-48] [A publication] (DLA)
Black Dict	Black's Law Dictionary [A publication] (DLA)
Black Emp Li	Black on Employer's Liability [A publication] (DLA)
Blackf	Blackford's Indiana Reports [1817-47] [A publication] (DLA)
Blackf (Ind)	Blackford's Indiana Reports [1817-47] [A publication] (DLA)
Blackford's Ia R	Blackford's Indiana Reports [1817-47] [A publication] (DLA)
Black Hills St C	Black Hills State College (GAGS)
Black Interp Laws	Black on Construction and Interpretation of Laws [A publication] (DLA)
Black Intox Liq	Black on the Laws Regulating the Manufacture and Sale of Intoxicating Liquors [A publication] (DLA)
Black Judg	Black on Judgments [A publication] (DLA)
Black Judgm	Black on Judgments [A publication] (DLA)
Black Jus	Blackerby's Justices' Cases [England] [A publication] (DLA)
Black Just	Blackerby's Justices' Cases [England] [A publication] (DLA)
Black Law Dict	Black's Law Dictionary [A publication] (DLA)
Black LD	Black's Law Dictionary [A publication] (DLA)
Black L Tr	Blackstone's Law Tracts [A publication] (DLA)
BLACKM	Blackmore [England]
Black Mag Ch	Blackstone on Magna Charta [A publication] (DLA)
Black R	Blackford's Indiana Reports [1817-47] [A publication] (DLA)
Black R	Black's United States Supreme Court Reports [66-67 United States Reports] [A publication] (DLA)
Black Rep	Black's United States Supreme Court Reports [66-67 United States Reports] [A publication] (DLA)
Black Sal	Blackburn on Sales [A publication] (DLA)
Black Ship Ca	Black's Decisions in Shipping Cases [A publication] (DLA)
Black's Law Dict	Black's Law Dictionary [A publication] (DLA)
Black St Const	Black on Construction and Interpretation of Laws [A publication] (DLA)
Blackstone's Commen	Blackstone's Commentaries on the Laws of England [A publication] (DLA)
Black Tax Tit	Blackwell's Tax Titles [A publication] (ILCA)
Blackw Cond	Blackwell's Condensed Illinois Reports [A publication] (DLA)
Blackw Sc Act	Blackwell's Scotch Acts [A publication] (DLA)
Blackw Tax Titles	Blackwell's Tax Titles [A publication] (DLA)
Blackw TT	Blackwell's Tax Titles [A publication] (DLA)
Bla Com	Blackstone's Commentaries on the Laws of England [A publication] (DLA)
Bla Comm	Blackstone's Commentaries on the Laws of England [A publication] (ILCA)
BLAD	Borderline Left-Axis Deviation [Cardiology]
BLADE	Basic Level Automation of Data through Electronics
BLADE	Bell Laboratories Automatic Device
BLADES	Bell Laboratories Automatic Design System [Computer program]
BLADING	Bill of Lading [Shipping]
BLAdmin	Bachelor of Law Administration
BLADS	Bell Laboratories Automatic Design System [Computer program]
BLAG	Benign Lymphocytic Angiitis and Granulomatosis [Medicine]
Blair	Blair. Manual for Scotch Justices of the Peace [A publication] (DLA)
Blair Co	Blair County Law Reports [Pennsylvania] [A publication] (DLA)
Blair Co LR	Blair County Law Reports [Pennsylvania] [A publication] (DLA)

Blair Co LR (PA)... Blair County Law Reports [*Pennsylvania*] [*A publication*] (DLA)
BlairCp .... Blair Corp. [*Associated Press*] (SAG)
BLAIS .... Battlefield Location and Information System [*Army*] (RDA)
BLAISE .... British Library Automated Information Service [*European host database system*] (IID)
Blake .... Blake's Reports [*1-3 Montana*] [*A publication*] (DLA)
Blake & H ..... Blake and Hedges' Reports [*2-3 Montana*] [*A publication*] (DLA)
B La L .... Bachelor of Latin Letters
Bla Life Ass ... Blayney. Life Assurance [*1837*] [*A publication*] (DLA)
BLAM .... Ballistically Launched Aerodynamic Missile
BLAM .... Barrel-Launched Adaptive Munitions
BLAM .... Boundary Layer Acoustic Monitor (MCD)
Blan & W Lead Cas ... Blanchard and Weeks' Leading Cases on Mines [*A publication*] (DLA)
Blanc & WLC ... Blanchard and Weeks' Leading Cases on Mines [*A publication*] (DLA)
Blanch .... Blanch [*E.W.*] Holdings, Inc. [*Associated Press*] (SAG)
Bland .... Bland's Maryland Chancery Reports [*A publication*] (DLA)
BLandArch .... Bachelor in Landscape Architecture
Bland Ch (MD) ... Bland's Maryland Chancery Reports [*A publication*] (DLA)
Bland Ch R .... Bland's Maryland Chancery Reports [*A publication*] (DLA)
BLANDF .... Blandford [*England*]
Bl & H .... Blake and Hedges' Reports [*2-3 Montana*] [*A publication*] (DLA)
Bl & H .... Blatchford and Howland's United States District Court Reports [*A publication*] (DLA)
Bl & How ..... Blatchford and Howland's United States District Court Reports [*A publication*] (DLA)
BLandInfo .... Bachelor of Land Information
BL & P .... Blind Loaded and Plugged [*Projectile*]
BLandResSc .. Bachelor of Land Resource Science
Bland's Ch ... Bland's Maryland Chancery Reports [*A publication*] (DLA)
Bland's Ch R ... Bland's Maryland Chancery Reports [*A publication*] (DLA)
Bland's Chy Rep ... Bland's Maryland Chancery Reports [*A publication*] (DLA)
BL & SP .... Butter, Lard, and Salt Provisions
BL & T .... Blind Loaded and Traced [*Projectile*]
Bl & W Mines ... Blanchard and Weeks' Leading Cases on Mines [*A publication*] (DLA)
Blan Lim ..... Blanshard. Statutes of Limitations [*A publication*] (DLA)
Blansh Lim ... Blanshard. Statutes of Limitations [*A publication*] (DLA)
BLAPL .... Belgian and Luxembourg Association of Penal Law (EAIO)
BL Arch .... Bachelor of Landscape Architecture
BLARD .... Boat Launching and Recovery Device (PDAA)
BLAS .... Basic Linear Algebra Subroutines (MCD)
BLAS .... Blasphemy (DLA)
BLASA .... Belgian-Luxembourg American Studies Association [*Belgium*] (EAIO)
Blash Juries ... Blashfield. Instructions to Juries [*A publication*] (DLA)
BLAST .... Black Legal Action for Soul in Television [*Student legal action organization*]
BLAST .... Blocked Asynchronous Transmission [*Message protocol*] [*Computer science*] (PCM)
BLAST .... Boolean Logic And State Transfer (EECA)
BLAST .... Building Loads Analysis and System Thermodynamics [*Computer program*]
BLASTO .... Blastomyces [*A fungus*] [*Biochemistry*] (DAVI)
BLAT .... Blind Learning Aptitude Test [*Education*]
BLAT .... Boundary Layer Aerodynamic Technology [*Auto racing*]
BLAT .... British Life Assurance Trust
Blat CCR ..... Blatchford's United States Circuit Court Reports [*A publication*] (DLA)
Blatch .... Blatchford's United States Circuit Court Reports [*A publication*] (DLA)
Blatch & H ... Blatchford and Howland's United States District Court Reports [*A publication*] (DLA)
Blatchf .... Blatchford's United States Circuit Court Reports [*A publication*] (DLA)
Blatchf & H ... Blatchford and Howland's United States District Court Reports [*A publication*] (DLA)
Blatchf CC ... Blatchford's United States Circuit Court Reports [*A publication*] (DLA)
Blatchf CC Rep ... Blatchford's United States Circuit Court Reports [*A publication*] (DLA)
Blatchford & H ... Blatchford and Howland's Reports [*United States*] [*A publication*] (DLA)
Blatchf Pr Cas ... Blatchford's Prize Cases [*United States*] [*A publication*] (DLA)
Blatchf Prize Cas ... Blatchford's Prize Cases [*United States*] [*A publication*] (DLA)
Blatch (US Circ Ct) ... Blatchford's United States Circuit Court Reports [*A publication*] (DLA)
Blatch (US Cir Ct) ... Blatchford's United States Circuit Court Reports [*A publication*] (DLA)
BLATS .... Built-Up Low-Cost Advanced Titanium Structures (MCD)
B-LAV .... B-Cell-Lymphadenopathy Associated Virus
BLAV .... British Latin America Volunteers [*British military*] (DMA)
BLAVA .... British Laboratory Animals Veterinary Association (DBA)
Blax Eng Co ... Blaxland's Codex Legum Anglicanum [*A publication*] (DLA)
Blay Ann ..... Blayney. Life Annuities [*1817*] [*A publication*] (DLA)
Blay Life Ins ... Blayney. Life Assurance [*1837*] [*A publication*] (DLA)
BLB .... Atlantic Air BVI Ltd. [*British ICAO designator*] (FAAC)
BLB .... Banking Law Bulletin [*Australia A publication*]
BLB .... Bed and Light Breakfast [*Hotel accomodations*]
BLB .... Bessey-Lowry-Brock Unit [*Medicine*] (MAE)
BLB .... Big Little Book [*of comic strips*]
BLB .... Black Label Resources, Inc. [*Vancouver Stock Exchange symbol*]
BLB .... Black Light Blue [*Source for near ultraviolet radiation*]
BLB .... Blood Banking [*Medical specialty*] (DHSM)
BLB .... Bookmakers' Licensing Board [*South Australia*]
BLB .... Boothby, Lovelace, Bulbulian [*Of Mayo Clinic*] Unit (DAVI)
BLB .... Boy's Life Brigade
BLB .... British Linen Bank
BLBA .... Black Lung Benefits Act [*1972*]

BLBA .... British List Brokers Association (DBA)
Bl B Adm ..... Twiss. Black Book of the Admiralty [*A publication*] (DLA)
BLBCCA .... Big Little Book Collector's Club of America (EA)
BLBD .... Babylonian Legal and Business Documents [*A publication*] (BJA)
BLBD .... Binary Light Beam Deflector
BLBFC .... Bonnie Lou Bishop Fan Club (EA)
BLBG .... Biological Laboratory, Brunswick, Georgia [*US Bureau of Commercial Fisheries; later, National Marine Fisheries Service*]
BLBP .... Blind Loaded and Blind Plugged [*Projectile*] (MCD)
BLBS .... British Library Bibliographic Services [*London, England*]
BLBSB .... Better Light Better Sight Bureau [*Defunct*] (EA)
BLBSD .... [*The*] British Library Bibliographic Services Division (NITA)
BLC .... Backlight Compensation [*Photography*]
BLC .... Baker Lake [*Northwest Territories*] [*Seismograph station code, US Geological Survey*] (SEIS)
BLC .... Balance (WGA)
BLC .... Bali [*Cameroon*] [*Airport symbol*] (OAG)
BLC .... Barrier Layer Cell
BLC .... Baseband Level Control (MCD)
BLC .... Baseline Configuration
BLC .... Battery Level Computer (MCD)
BLC .... Beef Liver Catalase [*An enzyme*] (OA)
BLC .... Belo (A.H.)CI'A' [*NYSE symbol*] (TTSB)
BLC .... Belo [*A. H.*] Corp. [*NYSE symbol*] (SPSG)
BLC .... Bengal Light Cavalry [*British military*] (DMA)
BLC .... Blackberry Gold Resources, Inc. [*Vancouver Stock Exchange symbol*]
BLC .... Black Literature Criticism [*A publication*]
Bl C .... Blood Culture [*Medicine*]
BlC .... Blood Culture [*Medicine*] (DMAA)
BLC .... Blue Line Copy
BLC .... Bluffton College, Bluffton, OH [*OCLC symbol*] (OCLC)
BLC .... Board Level Computer (MHDI)
BLC .... Bollettino di Legislazione Comparata [*A publication*] (ILCA)
BLC .... Bombay Light Cavalry [*British military*] (DMA)
BLC .... Boundary Layer Control
BLC .... Brasil-Central Linhas Areas Regional SA [*Brazil*] [*ICAO designator*] (FAAC)
BLC .... Brisbane Latvian Club [*Australia*]
BLC .... British Leather Confederation (IRUK)
BLC .... British Library General Catalogue of Printed Books [*A publication*]
BLC .... British Lighting Council [*Defunct*]
BLC .... Broadband Latching Circulator
BLC .... Burlington Liars Club (EA)
BLCA .... Black Canyon of the Gunnison National Monument
B-LCC .... Belgium-Luxembourg Chamber of Commerce [*Australia*]
BLCC .... Belo-Luxembourg Chamber of Commerce (DS)
Bl CC .... Blatchford's United States Circuit Court Reports [*A publication*] (DLA)
Bl CCR .... Blatchford's United States Circuit Court Reports [*A publication*] (DLA)
BLCE .... Balance (ADA)
BLCE .... Baseline Calibration Equipment
BLCHD .... Bleached [*Freight*]
BLCHG .... Bleaching [*Freight*]
BlChip .... Blue Chip Computerware, Inc. [*Associated Press*] (SAG)
Bl Chr R .... Bland's Chancery Reports [*A publication*] (DLA)
Bl Chy Pr ..... Blake. Chancery Practice [*A publication*] (DLA)
BLCK .... Black
BLCK .... Block (BUR)
BLCK .... Kaatza Historical Museum, Lake Cowichan, British Columbia [*Library symbol National Library of Canada*] (NLC)
BlckD .... Block Drug Co. [*Associated Press*] (SAG)
BlckHR .... Block [*H. & R.*], Inc. [*Associated Press*] (SAG)
BLCL .... B-Lymphoblastoid Cell Line [*Biochemistry*]
BLCMP .... Birmingham Libraries Cooperative Mechanisation Project [*Later, Library Services Ltd.*] (NITA)
BLCO .... Boundary Layer Control Outlet [*Mitsubishi*] [*Aerodynamics*] [*Automotive engineering*]
Bl Com .... Blackstone's Commentaries on the Laws of England [*A publication*] (DLA)
Bl Comm ..... Blackstone's Commentaries on the Laws of England [*A publication*] (DLA)
BLCS .... Boundary Layer Control System [*Fluid mechanics*] (IAA)
BLCS .... British Limousin Cattle Society (DBA)
BLCT .... Basic Language Concepts Test [*Child development test*]
BL CULT .... Blood Culture [*Medicine*] (AAMN)
BLCV .... Beet Leaf Curl Virus [*Plant pathology*]
BLD .... Bachelor of Landscape Design [*British*] (DBQ)
BLD .... Balanced Line Driver (MSA)
BLD .... Balance Resources Ltd. [*Vancouver Stock Exchange symbol*]
BLD .... Baldwin Technology'A' [*AMEX symbol*] (TTSB)
BLD .... Baldwin Technology Corp. [*AMEX symbol*] (SPSG)
BLD .... Balled [*Freight*]
BLD .... Baseline Documentation (MCD)
BLD .... Beam-Lead Device (IEEE)
BLD .... Below Limit of Detection
BLD .... Bharatiya Lok Dal [*India*] [*Political party*] (PPW)
BLD .... Billion Liters per Day
BLD .... Binary Load Dump [*Computer science*] (MHDI)
BLD .... Blinder (MSA)
BLD .... Blond (WGA)
bld .... Blood [*Philately*]
Bl D .... Blount's Law Dictionary [*A publication*] (DLA)
BLD .... Blue-Laid [*Paper*]
BLD .... Blue-Line Drawing
BLD .... Bold (ADA)

Bld............	Boulder [Maps and charts]
BLD............	Boulder City, NV [Location identifier FAA] (FAAL)
BLD............	Boulevard (EY)
BLD............	Build (DNAB)
BLD............	Building (NATG)
BLD............	Bulletin Legislatif Dalloz [A publication] (ILCA)
BI D & O	Blackham, Dundas, and Osborne's Irish Nisi Prius Reports [1846-48] [A publication] (DLA)
BI D & Osb..	Blackham, Dundas, and Osborne's Irish Nisi Prius Reports [1846-48] [A publication] (DLA)
Bld Bk.........	Blood Bank (DAVI)
BLD BKG.....	Blind Blocking [Bookbinding] (DGA)
Bld Chem.....	Blood Chemistry (DAVI)
BLDCS	Bureau of Laundry and Dry Cleaning Standards (EA)
BL Des.........	Bachelor of Landscape Design
BLDG	Building (AFM)
BLDG	Building
bldg............	Building (DD)
BLDG	NCI Building Systems [NASDAQ symbol] (SAG)
Bldg Contr ...	Building and Construction Contracts [A publication] (DLA)
Bldg E.........	Building Engineer
BLDG WDWRK...	Building Woodwork [Freight]
BLDI............	Blank Die
BI Dict	Black's Law Dictionary [A publication] (DLA)
BLDIS	Blood Information Service [Information service or system] (IID)
BLDN	Blowdown (NASA)
BLDP	Ballard Power Systems, Inc. [NASDAQ symbol] (SAG)
BLDPF	Ballard Power Systems [NASDAQ symbol] (TTSB)
BLDR	Bleeder (MSA)
BLDR	Builder
bldr............	Builder (VRA)
BLDR	Builder
BldrWr	Builders Warehouse Association, Inc. [Associated Press] (SAG)
BLDS	Blinds [Classified advertising] (ADA)
Blds	Boulders [Quality of the bottom] [Maps and charts]
BLDSC	British Library Document Supply Centre (CB)
bldst............	Bloodstone (VRA)
BLDT...........	Balloon-Launched Decelerator Test [Air Force]
BLD TLG	Blind Tooling [Bookbinding] (DGA)
BLDU	Blowing Dust [ICAO] (FAAC)
BLDUP.........	Buildup (FAAC)
BLDY	Grossly Bloody [Biochemistry] (DAVI)
BLE	Bachelor of Library Economics
BLE	Ballatar Explorations [Vancouver Stock Exchange symbol]
BLE	Basal Level Element [Genetics]
BLE	Basal Level Enhancer [Genetics]
BLE	Bessemer & Lake Erie Railroad Co. [AAR code]
BLE	Binary Logic Element [Computer science] (BUR)
BLE	Blacks in Law Enforcement [An association] (EA)
BLE	Blake Resources Ltd. [Toronto Stock Exchange symbol]
BLE	Block Length Error [Computer science] (IAA)
BLE	Blunt Leading Edge
BLE	Bombardment-Induced Light Emission [Physics]
BLE	Borlange [Sweden] [Airport symbol] (OAG)
BLE	Both Lower Extremities [Medicine]
BLE	Bradlees, Inc. [NYSE symbol] (SPSG)
B-LE............	Broadband Local Exchange [Telecommunications] (ACRL)
BLE	Budhana Ligo Esperantista [Buddhist League of Esperantists - BLE] [Germany] (EAIO)
BLE	Collingwood Air Services Ltd. [Canada ICAO designator] (FAAC)
BLe	Grammatik des Biblische-Aramaeischen [H. Bauer and P. Leander] [A publication] (BJA)
BLE	Lake Providence, LA [Location identifier FAA] (FAAL)
BLEACH	Babel Language Editing and Checking (PDAA)
B Leader......	Bar Leader [A publication] (DLA)
BLEAP........	Bought Ledger and Expenditure Analysis Package (PDAA)
BL Ec	Bachelor of Library Economics
Bleck	Bleckley's Reports [34, 35 Georgia] [A publication] (DLA)
Bleckley......	Bleckley's Reports [34, 35 Georgia] [A publication] (DLA)
BLED..........	Bledisloe [England]
BLEDCO	Brooklyn Local Economic Development Corp.
BLEDE.........	Backscattered LASER Energy Digitizing Equipment (MCD)
BLEED.........	Bleeding Time [Hematology] (DAVI)
BLegS.........	Bachelor of Legal Studies (ADA)
BLegSt........	Bachelor of Legal Studies
BLeisureStud...	Bachelor of Leisure Studies
BI Emp L	Black on Employer's Liability [A publication] (DLA)
BLEN..........	Blend
BLEND	Birmingham Loughborough Electronic Network Development [British] (NITA)
BL Eng........	Bachelor of Landscape Engineering
Bleo............	Bleomycin [Also, B, Bl, BLM] [Antineoplastic drug]
BLEO...........	Bleomycin Sulfate [Antineoplastic drug] (DAVI)
BLEO...........	British Leyland Europe and Overseas [Commercial firm]
BLEO-COMF...	Bleomycin, Cyclophosphamide, Oncovin [Vincristine], Methotrexate, Fluorouracil [Antineoplastic drug regimen]
BLEO-MOPP...	Bleomycin, Nitrogen Mustard, Oncovin [Vincristine], Procarbazine, and Prednisone [Antineoplastic drug regimen] (DAVI)
bleph	Blepharoplasty [Ophthalmology and plastic surgery] (DAVI)
BLEPS.........	Ballistic and LASER Eye Protection Spectacles [Army] (INF)
BLEPS.........	Ballistic LASER Protection System [Army] (INF)
BLERT.........	Block Error Rate Test [Telecommunications]
BLE's	Both Lower Extremities [Neurology and orthopedics] (DAVI)
BLESLB-IL ...	Brotherhood of Locomotive Engineers State Legislative Board, Illinois (SRA)
BLESMA......	British Limbless Ex-Service Men's Association
BLESS.........	Bath, Laxative, Enema, Shampoo, and Shower [Medicine] (AAMN)
BLESSED	Bell Little Electrodata Symbolic System for the Electrodata [Symbolic assembly program]
Blessings.....	Blessings Co. [Associated Press] (SAG)
BLESTO-VIII...	Bears, Lions, Eagles, Steelers, Vikings, Colts, Dolphins, and Bills [Computerized scouting combine for professional football teams; name comprises membership teams]
BLET	Bletsoe [England]
BLET	Bureau of Libraries and Educational Technology [Later, BLLR] [HEW]
BLEU..........	Belgium-Luxembourg Economic Union [Political party] (PPE)
BLEU..........	Blind Landing Experimental Unit [Aviation]
BLEVE........	Boiling Liquid Expanding Vapor Explosion [Chemical engineering]
BLEWS........	Baseline Electronic Warfare System (MCD)
BLF............	Ballast Lumen Factor (PDAA)
BLF............	Baluchistan Liberation Front [Pakistan] [Political party] (PD)
BLF............	Band Limiting Filter [Electronics] (OA)
BLF............	Baryta Light Fling (MSA)
BLF............	Blocking Factor [Computer science] (IAA)
BLF............	Bloemfontein [South Africa] [Seismograph station code, US Geological Survey] (SEIS)
BLF............	Bluefield [West Virginia] [Airport symbol] (OAG)
BLF............	Bluff
BLF............	Bluff
BLF............	Bluff [Commonly used] (OPSA)
BLF............	Boundary Layer Flow
BLF............	British Leather Federation (BI)
BLF............	British Lubricants Federation (DBA)
BLF............	Bubble Lattice File [Computer science] (HGAA)
BLF............	Bulgarian Lucky Flight [ICAO designator] (FAAC)
BLF............	Busy Lamp Field [Phone console] [Bell System]
BLF............	Byelorussian Liberation Front [Defunct] (EA)
BLFC...........	Brenda Lee Fan Club (EA)
BLFC...........	British Leather Fashion Council (DBA)
BLFE...........	Brotherhood of Locomotive Firemen and Enginemen [Later, United Transportation Union] [AFL-CIO]
BLFG...........	Bilateral Firm (Hand) Grips (MEDA)
BLFS...........	Bluffs [Postal Service standard] (OPSA)
BLFS...........	Bluffs
BLFST.........	Belfast [City in Northern Ireland]
BL-FST........	Blood-Fasting [Glucose tolerance test] [Endocrinology] (DAVI)
BLG............	Bachelor Lake Gold Mines, Inc. [Toronto Stock Exchange symbol]
BLG............	Bailing
BLG............	Belaga [Malaysia] [Airport symbol] (OAG)
BLG............	Belgavia (Societe de Handling) [Belgium ICAO designator] (FAAC)
BLG............	Beluga, AK [Location identifier FAA] (FAAL)
BLG............	Beta-Lactoglobulin [Biochemistry]
BLG............	Blooming Gate (IAA)
BIG............	[The] Blue and the Gray [A publication]
BLG............	Breech Loading Gun
BLG............	Building
BLG............	Business Leader Group [Washington, DC] (EA)
BLG............	Laguna Peak [California] [Seismograph station code, US Geological Survey] (SEIS)
BLGM..........	Buffelsfontein Gold Mines Ltd. [NASDAQ symbol] (SAG)
BLH............	Band-Limited Hiss [NASA]
BLH............	Bankers Life Holding Corp. [NYSE symbol] (SPSG)
BLH............	Bankers Life Holdings [NYSE symbol] (TTSB)
BLH............	Bihar Light Horse [British military] (DMA)
BLH............	Blade Loading Harmonics [Helicopter]
BLH............	Blue Horizon Travel Club [ICAO designator] (FAAC)
BLH............	Blythe [California] [Airport symbol] (OAG)
BL-H...........	Bristol Laboratories [Research code symbol]
BLH............	British Legion Headquarters
BLH............	Historische Grammatik der Hebraeischen Sprache [H. Bauer and P. Leander] [A publication] (BJA)
BLHA	British Linen Hire Association (PDAA)
BLHS	Ballistic LASER Holographic System (MCD)
BLI.............	Bachelor of Literary Interpretation
BLI.............	Banking Law Institute (EA)
BLI.............	Banking Literature Index [A publication]
BLI.............	Basic Learning Institute
BLI.............	Belair [Belarus] [ICAO designator] (FAAC)
BLI.............	Bellingham [Washington] [Airport symbol] (OAG)
BLI.............	Bible Literature International (EA)
Bli.............	Bligh's English House of Lords Reports [A publication] (DLA)
BLI.............	Bondell Industries, Inc. [Vancouver Stock Exchange symbol]
BLI.............	Bowling League of Ireland (EAIO)
BLI.............	Brazil Labor Information and Resource Center (EA)
BLI.............	Butterfly Lovers International (EA)
BLI.............	Buyers Laboratory, Inc.
BLib...........	Bachelor of Library Science (ADA)
BLibS.........	Bachelor of Library Science (NADA)
BLibSc........	Bachelor in Library Science (ADA)
BLibSci.......	Bachelor of Library Science (NADA)
BLibSt........	Bachelor of Liberal Studies
BLibStudies...	Bachelor of Liberal Studies
BLIC...........	Beam-Lead Individual Carrier (PDAA)
BLIC...........	Bureau de Liaison des Industries du Caoutchouc de la CEE [Rubber Industries Liaison Bureau of the EEC] [Belgium]
Blick Rev	Blickenaderfer. Law Student's Review [A publication] (DLA)
Bligh..........	Bligh's English House of Lords Reports, Old Series [1819-21] [A publication] (DLA)

Bligh NS (Eng)... Bligh's English House of Lords Reports, New Series [1827-37] [*A publication*] (DLA)

BLIHS .... Hawkshaw Ranch, Lasqueti Island Historical Society, British Columbia [*Library symbol National Library of Canada*] (NLC)

BLIJ .... Burma Law Institute. Journal [*A publication*] (DLA)

BLIM .... Berthing Latch Interface Mechanism (SSD)

BLIM .... Lillooet Museum, British Columbia [*Library symbol National Library of Canada*] (NLC)

BLIMP .... Boundary Layer Integral Matrix Procedure (KSC)

Blimpie .... Blimpie International, Inc. [*Associated Press*] (SAG)

BLIMPRON... Blimp Squadron [*Navy*]

BLIN .... BIT [*Binary Digit*] Light Inspection (DNAB)

BLIN .... Budget Line Item Number (MCD)

BLing .... Bachelor of Linguistics, University of Manchester [*British*] (DBQ)

BLING .... Bladed Ring [*Turbine component*]

B-LINK .... Birmingham Library and Information Network [*British*] (NITA)

Bli NS .... Bligh's English House of Lords Reports, New Series [1827-37] [*A publication*] (DLA)

Bli (OS) ...... Bligh's English House of Lords Reports, Old Series [1819-21] [*A publication*] (DLA)

BLIP .... Background-Limited Infrared Photography

BLIP .... Beta-Lactamase Inhibitory Protein [*Biochemistry*]

BLIP .... Boundary Layer Instrumentation Package [*Meteorology*]

BLIP .... Brookhaven Linac Isotope Producer [*Nuclear energy*]

BLIPS .... Benthic Layer Interactive Profiling System [*Marine science*] (OSRA)

BLIPS .... Benthic Layer Interactive Profiling System (USDC)

BLIROI .... Bureau de Liaison de l'Information Religieuse dans l'Ocean Indien [*Indian Ocean Religious Information Liaison Office*] (AF)

BLIS .... Baffle/Liner Interface Seal [*Nuclear energy*] (NRCH)

BLIS .... Base Level Inquiry System

BLIS .... Bell Laboratories Interpretive System [*Computer program*]

BLIS .... Biblio-Techniques Library and Information System [*Washington Library Network*] (NITA)

BLIS .... Bliss & Laughlin Industries, Inc. [*NASDAQ symbol*] (CTT)

BLIS .... Boundary Layer Instrumentation System [*Meteorology*]

BLIS .... British Library Information Skills (AIE)

BLIS .... Buried Line Intrusion Sensor [*Military*] (LAIN)

BLIS .... Business Lead Identification System [*Timeplace, Inc.*] [*Database*]

BLIS .... Business License Information Service

BLISK .... Bladed Disc [*Turbine component*]

BlisLau .... Bliss & Laughlin Industries, Inc. [*Associated Press*] (SAG)

BLISS .... Baby Life Support System (DI)

BLISS .... Balloon-Borne LASER In-Situ Sensor [*Spectrometer*]

BLISS .... Basic Language for the Implementation of System Software [*Computer science*]

BLISS .... Basic Library Inquiry Subsystem [*Computer science*]

BLISS .... Betriebswirtschaftliches Literatursuchsystem [*Business Literature Search System*] [*Society for Business Information*] [*Information service or system*] (IID)

BLISS .... Bibliographic and Library Information Search Service [*Louisiana State University*]

BLISS .... Bibliographic and Library Instruction for Secondary Schools

BLISS .... Boundary Layer Induction Stack Suppressor (CAAL)

BLISS .... British Library Information Sciences Service

Bliss .... Delaware County Reports [*Pennsylvania*] [*A publication*] (DLA)

Bliss Co Pl.. Bliss on Code Pleading [*A publication*] (DLA)

Bliss Ins ...... Bliss on Life Insurance [*A publication*] (DLA)

Bliss NY Co... Bliss' New York Code [*A publication*] (DLA)

Bliss NY Code... Bliss' New York Code, Annotated [*A publication*] (DLA)

B Lit .... Bachelor of Letters

B Lit. .... Bachelor of Literature

BLITS .... Bureau Local d'Intervention Traitant du Sida (AC)

B Litt .... Bachelor of Letters

BLitt .... Bachelor of Letters (ODBW)

B Litt .... Bachelor of Literature

BLittComm... Bachelor of Literature and Communication

BLIX .... Bleach-Fix [*Photography*]

BLJ .... Bachelor of Letters in Journalism

BLJ .... Bel-Air Ltd. [*Slovakia*] [*FAA designator*] (FAAC)

BLJ .... Bellabon Resources [*Vancouver Stock Exchange symbol*]

BLJ .... Bihar Law Journal Reports [*India*] [*A publication*] (DLA)

BLJ .... Bumper Lift Jack

BLJ .... Burma Law Journal [*A publication*] (DLA)

Bl Judgm... Black on Judgments [*A publication*] (DLA)

BLK .... Benign Lichenoid Keratosis [*Medicine*]

BLK .... Black (KSC)

BLK .... Black [*Thoroughbred racing*]

BLK .... Black Butte [*Montana*] [*Seismograph station code, US Geological Survey Closed*] (SEIS)

BLK .... Black Diamond Resources [*Vancouver Stock Exchange symbol*]

BLK .... Blackpool [*England*] [*Airport symbol*] (OAG)

BLK .... Blackrock 2001 Term Trust [*NYSE symbol*] (TTSB)

BLK .... Blackrock 2001 Term Trust Inc. [*NYSE symbol*] (SPSG)

BLK .... Blank (MSA)

BLK .... Block [*Unit of data*]

blk .... Block (VRA)

BLK .... Block

BLK .... Bulk

BLK .... Bulk Carriers Conference, Arlington VA [*STAC*]

BLK .... Burrell-Lawrence-Kennedy [*Vacuum milking device*]

BLK .... Westcoast Energy [*Canada*] [*FAA designator*] (FAAC)

Blk1998 ...... Blackrock 1998 Term Trust, Inc. [*Associated Press*] (SAG)

Blk1999 ...... Blackrock 1999 Term Trust [*Associated Press*] (SAG)

Blk2001 ...... Blackrock 2001 Term Trust [*Associated Press*] (SAG)

Blk2008 ...... Blackrock Insured Municipal 2008 Term Trust [*Associated Press*] (SAG)

BlkAdv .... Blackrock Advantage Term Trust [*Associated Press*] (SAG)

BLK B .... Bulk in Barrels [*Freight*]

BlkBI09 .... Blackrock Broad Investment Grade 2009Term Trust [*Associated Press*] (SAG)

BlkCA08 ...... Blackrock California Insured Municipal 2008 Term Trust [*Associated Press*] (SAG)

BLK CAR..... Bulk Carrier [*Shipping*] (DS)

BLKD .... Blocked

BLKD .... Bulkhead (MUGU)

BlkFL08 .... Blackrock Florida Insured Municipal 2008 Term Trust [*Associated Press*] (SAG)

BLKG .... Blanking (MSA)

BLKG .... Blocking (MSA)

BLKGD .... Blanking Die

BLKHD .... Bulkhead (KSC)

BlkHG .... Black Hawk Gaming & Development [*Associated Press*] (SAG)

BlkHICp....... Black Hills Corp. [*Associated Press*] (SAG)

BLKHLS ...... Black Hills (FAAC)

BlkHwkG ..... Black Hawk Gaming & Development Co. [*Associated Press*] (SAG)

BlkIMT .... Blacrock Insured Municipal Term Trust [*Associated Press*] (SAG)

BlkIQM......... Blackrock Investment Quality Municipal Trust [*Associated Press*] (SAG)

BlkIQT .... Blackrock Investment Quality Term Trust [*Associated Press*] (SAG)

BlkIT .... Blackrock Income Trust [*Associated Press*] (SAG)

BLKM .... Black Mesa & Lake Powell [*AAR code*]

BlkMTar....... Blackrock Municipal Target Term Trust [*Associated Press*] (SAG)

BLKN .... Blacken

BlkNA .... Blackrock North American Government Income Trust [*Associated Press*] (SAG)

BLKNG .... Blackening

BlkNY08....... Blackrock New York Insured Municipal 2008 Term Trust [*Associated Press*] (SAG)

BLKP .... Blanking Pulse

blkpr .... Block Print (VRA)

BLKS .... Blocks [*Freight*]

BLKSTP .... Blackstrap [*Freight*]

BlkStr .... Blackrock Strategic Term Trust [*Associated Press*] (SAG)

BLKT .... Blanket (MSA)

BlkTT .... Blackrock Target Term Trust [*Associated Press*] (SAG)

BLL .... Baccalaureus Legum [*Bachelor of Laws*]

BLL .... Bachelor of Latin Letters

BLL .... Ball Corp. [*NYSE symbol*] (SPSG)

BLL .... Barrels (ROG)

BLL .... Base Locator Linkage (MHDI)

BLL .... Base of Lateral Lip

BLL .... Bellevue Public Library, Bellevue, NE [*OCLC symbol*] (OCLC)

BLL .... Bellingham [*Washington*] [*Seismograph station code, US Geological Survey Closed*] (SEIS)

BLL .... Below Lower Limit (IEEE)

BLL .... Bibliographie Linguistischer Literatur [*Bibliography of Linguistic Literature*] [*Stadt- und Universitatbibliothek Frankfurt*] [*Information service or system*] [*Information service or system*] (CRD)

BLL .... Billund [*Denmark*] [*Airport symbol*] (OAG)

BLL .... Blood Lead Level [*Medicine*]

BLL .... Boch & Limoges [*Vancouver Stock Exchange symbol*]

BLL .... Bovine Lung Lipids [*Biochemistry*]

BLL .... British Library Lending Division

BLL .... Brows, Lids, and Lashes [*Anatomy*] (DAVI)

Bl Law Tracts... Blackstone's Law Tracts [*A publication*] (DLA)

Bl LD .... Black's Law Dictionary [*A publication*] (DLA)

Bl LD .... Blount's Law Dictionary [*A publication*] (DLA)

BLLD .... British Library Lending Division

BLLDZG .... Bulldozing

BLLE .... Balanced Line Logical Element

BLLKNG .... Billing

BLLN .... Bullion (ROG)

BLLR .... Baller

BLLR .... Bureau of Libraries and Learning Resources [*Formerly, BLET*] [*HEW*]

BLLRM .... Ballroom

BL-LS .... Biosafety Level - Large Scale [*For laboratories utilizing biological agents*]

BLLS .... Boundary Layer LIDAR System (MCD)

Bl LT .... Blackstone's Law Tracts [*A publication*] (DLA)

BLLT .... Bullet

BLLTN .... Bulletin

BLLTNG .... Billeting

BLM .... Bachelor of Land Management (NADA)

BLM .... Bachelor of Landscape Management

BLM .... Background Luminance Monitor [*Aviation*] (DA)

BLM .... Basic Language Machine [*Computer*] (BUR)

BLM .... Belmac Corp. [*AMEX symbol*] (SPSG)

BLM .... Belmar/Farmingdale, NJ [*Location identifier FAA*] (FAAL)

BLM .... Best Loiter Mach Number [*Aviation*]

BLM .... Bilayer Lipid Membrane [*Physical chemistry*]

BLM .... Bimolecular Lipid Membrane

BLM .... Bimolecular Liquid Membrane [*Biochemistry*] (DAVI)

BLM .... Black Magic Project Ltd. [*British ICAO designator*] (FAAC)

BLM .... Bleomycin [*Sulfate*] [*Also, B, Bl, Bleo*] [*Antineoplastic drug*]

BLM .... Blinking Light Monitor

BLM .... Blue Mountain [*Alaska*] [*Seismograph station code, US Geological Survey*] (SEIS)

BLM .... Book-Library-Management [*System*]

BLM............	Boundary Layer Model (MCD)
BLM............	Branch on Left Minus (SAA)
BLM............	Bureau of Land Management [Department of the Interior]
BLMA.........	British Leathergoods Manufacturers Association (DBA)
BLMAS........	Bible Lands' Missions Aid Society [British] (BI)
BLMB.........	Benzoyl Leuco Methylene Blue [Organic chemistry]
BLMC.........	British League of Male Chauvinists (EAIO)
BLMC.........	British Leyland Motor Corp. [Auto manufacturing company]
BLMCS........	Base Level Maintenance Cost System (AFIT)
BLMH.........	British Leyland Motor Holdings [Auto manufacturing company]
Blm Neg.....	Bloomfield's Manumission (or Negro) Cases [New Jersey] [A publication] (DLA)
BLMPS........	Base Level Military Personnel System
BLMPX........	Block Multiplexer Channel (MHDI)
BLMR.........	Bureau of Labor - Management Reports [Department of Labor]
BLMRA........	British Lawn Mower Racing Association (DBA)
BLMRA	British Leather Manufacturers Research Association
BLMRCP	Bureau of Labor - Management Relations and Cooperative Programs [Department of Labor]
BLMT.........	Bailment (AAGC)
BLMT.........	Belmont Bancorp [NASDAQ symbol] (SAG)
BLMTH........	Bellmouth [Design engineering]
BLMUX........	Block Multiplexer Channel (IAA)
BLN...........	Bali International Air Service [Indonesia] [ICAO designator] (FAAC)
BLN...........	Balloon (AFM)
BLN...........	Balloon
BLN...........	Blackrock New York Insurance Municipal 2008 Trade [NYSE symbol] (SPSG)
BLN...........	Blackrock NY Ins Muni 2008 Tr [NYSE symbol] (TTSB)
BLN...........	Blend (MSA)
BLN...........	Blyn Mountain [Washington] [Seismograph station code, US Geological Survey] (SEIS)
BLN...........	Bronchial Lymph Node [Medicine] (MAE)
BLN...........	Bullion (ROG)
BLND..........	Blind
BLND..........	Reading Material for the Blind and Physically Handicapped [Library of Congress Information service or system] (CRD)
BLNDMSA....	Black Top and National Delaine Merino Sheep Association (EA)
BLNG.........	Belling
Blnk..........	Blank (HGAA)
BLNKT........	Blanket (AAG)
Bl NS..........	Bligh's English House of Lords Reports, New Series [A publication] (DLA)
BLO...........	Aerotransportes Barlovento SA de CV [Mexico ICAO designator] (FAAC)
BLO...........	Backtell Lateraltell Output (SAA)
BLO...........	Base Level Operations
BLO...........	Bellco Energy Corp. [Vancouver Stock Exchange symbol]
BLO...........	Below
BLO...........	Below Clouds [Aviation code]
BLO...........	Black Liquor Oxidation [For pollution control in paper mills]
BLO...........	Blocking [Telecommunications] (TEL)
BLO...........	Blocking Signal [Telecommunications] (NITA)
BLO...........	Blonduos [Iceland] [Airport symbol] (OAG)
BLO...........	Bloomfield College, Bloomfield, NJ [OCLC symbol] (OCLC)
BLO...........	Bloomington [Indiana] [Seismograph station code, US Geological Survey] (SEIS)
BLO...........	Blower (KSC)
BLO...........	Bombardment Liaison Officer [Navy]
BLO...........	British Liaison Officer
BLO...........	Building Liaison Officer (ADA)
BLO...........	Butyrolactone [Organic chemistry]
BLO...........	Laconia, NH [Location identifier FAA] (FAAL)
BLOB	Binary Large Object [Computer science]
bl obs	Bladder Observation [Medicine] (CPH)
BLOBS........	Bladder Obstruction [Medicine]
BLOC	Battalion Logistical Operations Center [Military] (INF)
BLOC	Blockade (AABC)
BLOC	Blockage
BLOC	Block Drug Co., Inc. [NASDAQ symbol] (NQ)
BLOC	Block-Oriented Compiler
BLOC	Booth Library On-Line Circulation [Data processing system] [Eastern Illinois University Charleston, IL]
BLOCA	Block Drug A'non-vtg [NASDAQ symbol] (TTSB)
BLODI	Block Diagram Compiler
BLODIB	Block Diagram Compiler B (IEEE)
BLODIC	Block Diagram Compiler [Engineering program] (IAA)
BLODI-G	Block Diagram - Graphics (PDAA)
BLOEMF.......	Bloemfontein [South Africa] (ROG)
BLOKOPS......	Blockade Operations [Military] (NVT)
BLOM.........	Booster Lift-Off Mass [NASA] (KSC)
BlondT	Blonder Tongue Laboratories, Inc. [Associated Press] (SAG)
Bloom Man...	Bloomfield's Manumission (or Negro) Cases [New Jersey] [A publication] (DLA)
Bloom Man Neg Cas...	Bloomfield's Manumission (or Negro) Cases [New Jersey] [A publication] (DLA)
Bloom Rev...	Bloomsbury Review [A publication] (BRI)
Bloomsburg U...	Bloomsburg University of Pennsylvania (GAGS)
BLOOP	Benevolent and Loyal Order of Pessimists (EA)
BLOS..........	Beyond Line of Sight
BLOSSOM.....	Basic Liberation of Smokers and Sympathizers of Marijuana
BLOT..........	British Library of Tape
Blount.........	Blount International [Associated Press] (SAG)
Blount.........	Blount's Law Dictionary [A publication] (DLA)
Blount Frag Ant...	Blount. Fragmenta Antiquitatis [A publication] (DLA)

Blount LD ...	Blount's Law Dictionary [A publication] (DLA)
Blount Ten...	Blount on Tenures [A publication] (DLA)
Blount Tr	Blount's Impeachment Trial [A publication] (DLA)
BLOW	Booster Lift-Off Weight [NASA] (KSC)
BLOWS	British Library of Wildlife Sound
BLOX	Block Order Exposure System [Business term]
BLP............	Back Loading Point [Military British]
BLP............	Ball Lock Pin
BLP............	Barbados Labor Party
BLP............	Basic Launch Plan [NASA] (KSC)
BLP............	Basket Loading Pool [Nuclear energy] (NRCH)
BLP............	Bela Lyons Pratt [Designer's mark, when appearing on US coins]
BLP............	Beta-Lipoprotein [Medicine] (DMAA)
BLP............	Bilevel Pulse (MCD)
BLP............	Blaettchenpulver [Flake powder] [German military - World War II]
BLP............	Blood Pressure [Medicine]
BIP............	Blood Pressure [Medicine] (DMAA)
BLP............	Blue Line Print
BLP............	Bombesin-Like Peptide [Biochemistry]
BLP............	Bombing Landplane
BLP............	Bonded Laminates Profiled Ltd. [British]
BLP............	Book of Living Poems [A publication]
BLP............	Botswana Liberal Party [Political party] (PPW)
BLP............	Boundary Layer Profile [Meteorology]
BLP............	Bromine-Loading Potential [Atmospheric science]
BLP............	Bulgarian Liberal Party [Political party]
BLP............	Buoyant Line and Point Source Model [Environmental Protection Agency] (GFGA)
BLP............	Bypass Label Processing [Computer science]
BLP............	Compania Boliviana De Energia [NYSE symbol] (TTSB)
BLP............	Compania Boliviana de Energia Electrica SA [NYSE symbol] (SPSG)
BLP............	Lompoc [California] [Seismograph station code, US Geological Survey] (SEIS)
BLPA..........	Barley Leaf Piece Agar [Microbiology]
BLPA..........	Best Loved Poems of the American People [A publication]
BLPC..........	Backward Limit Photocell
Blpc..........	Blood Lymphocytes Particle Counter [Instrumentation] [Medicine]
BLPES.........	British Library of Political and Economic Science [London School of Economics]
BLP L & M Cas...	Brainard's Legal Precedents in Land and Mining Cases [United States] [A publication] (DLA)
BL/PP.........	Bumper Limiter/Protective Plates (MCD)
bl pr..........	Blood Pressure [Medicine] (MAE)
Bl Pr Cas....	Blatchford's Prize Cases [United States] [A publication] (DLA)
Bl Prize......	Blatchford's Prize Cases [United States] [A publication] (DLA)
BLPS..........	Ballistic and LASER Protective Spectacles [Military] (RDA)
BLPS..........	Base Level Personnel System [Air Force] (GFGA)
BLPS..........	British Landrace Pig Society (BI)
BLPZZ.........	Bent Logarithmically Periodic Zig-Zags
BLQ...........	Blue Gold Resources [Vancouver Stock Exchange symbol]
BLQ...........	Bologna [Italy] [Airport symbol] (OAG)
BLR...........	Atlantic Coast Airlines [Westair Airlines, Inc.] [ICAO designator] (FAAC)
BLR...........	Bahamas Law Reports [A publication] (DLA)
BLR...........	Bangalore [India] [Airport symbol] (OAG)
BLR...........	Barbados Law Reports [A publication] (DLA)
BLR...........	Barrier Layer Rectifier
BLR...........	Baseline Restorer (IEEE)
BLR...........	Basic and Long-term Research
BLR...........	Below Layer Range (NVT)
BLR...........	Bengal Law Reports, High Courts [India] [A publication] (DLA)
BLR...........	Bermuda Law Reports [A publication] (DLA)
BLR...........	Beyond Local Repair [Weaponry] [British]
BLR...........	Black Rapids [Alaska] [Seismograph station code, US Geological Survey] (SEIS)
BLR...........	Block Load Request [Military]
BLR...........	Blower (NVT)
BLR...........	Boiler (AAG)
BLR...........	Bombay Law Reporter [India] [A publication] (DLA)
BLR...........	Breech-Loading Rifle
BLR...........	Broad-Line Region [Spectra]
BLR...........	Business and Law Review [Corporate Agents, Inc.] [Information service or system] (CRD)
BLRA	British Launderers Research Association (PDAA)
BLRA	British Leprosy Relief Association (BI)
BLRAC........	Bengal Law Reports, Appeal Cases [India] [A publication] (DLA)
BLR & DD ...	[The] British Library Research and Development Department (NITA)
BLRD	[The] British Library Reference Division (NITA)
BLRDD........	British Library Research and Development Division (AIE)
BL REQ	Blue Line Requisition
BLRG	Breech-Loading Rifled Guns
BLRG	Broad-Line Radio Galaxy [Astrophysics]
BLRI..........	Barrett-Lennard Relationship Inventory (EDAC)
BLRI..........	Blue Ridge Parkway [National Park Service designation]
BLROA........	British Laryngological, Rhinological, and Otological Association (MAE)
BLRP	Best Loved Religious Poems [A publication]
BLRPC........	Bengal Law Reports, Privy Council [India] [A publication] (DLA)
BLR Suppl Vol...	Bengal Law Reports, Supplemental Volume, Full Bench Rulings [India] [A publication] (DLA)
BLR Sup Vol...	Bengal Law Reports, Supplemental Volume, Full Bench Rulings [India] [A publication] (ILCA)
BLRT..........	Brotherly Love, Relief, and Truth [Freemasonry]
BLS...........	Bachelor of Liberal Studies
BLS...........	Bachelor of Library and Information Studies
BLS...........	Bachelor of Library Science

BLS............ Bachelor of Library Service (NADA)
BLS............ Balanced Line System
BLS............ Balloon Launching Station
BLS............ Band-Limited Signal
BLS............ Bare Lymphocytes Syndrome [Medicine]
BLS............ Barrels [Shipping]
BLS............ Base Loading System (DNAB)
BLS............ Basic Life Support [System]
BLS............ Beach Landing Site [Military] (DOMA)
BLS............ Bearskin Lake Air Service Ltd. [Canada ICAO designator] (FAAC)
BLS............ Bel-Air Resources [Vancouver Stock Exchange symbol]
BLS............ Bela Lugosi Society [Defunct] (EA)
BLS............ Bell Log System
BLS............ BellSouth Corp. [NYSE symbol] (SPSG)
BLS............ Benevolenti Lectori Salutem [Greeting to the Well-Wishing Reader]
                [Latin]
BLS............ Ben Line Steamers (MHDB)
BLS............ Big Liver and Spleen Disease [Poultry]
BLS............ Black Liquor Solids [Pulp and paper technology]
Bl S........... Black Scholar [A publication] (BRI)
BLS............ Blind Loop Syndrome [Medicine] (DMAA)
BLS............ Blood and Lymphatic System [Medicine]
Bl S........... Blood Sugar [Medicine]
BlS............ Blood Sugar [Medicine] (DMAA)
BLS............ Bloom Syndrome [Medicine] (DMAA)
BLS............ Botswana, Lesotho, Swaziland
BLS............ Bottom Left Side (MCD)
BLS............ Boundary Layer Separation
BLS............ Brake Light Switch [Automotive engineering]
BLS............ Branch Line Society [British]
BLS............ British Lichen Society (EAIO)
BLS............ Broadband Latching Switch
BLS............ Brooklyn Law School [New York, NY]
BLS............ Bureau of Labor Standards [Absorbed by OSHA] [Department of
                Labor] [Washington, DC]
BLS............ Bureau of Labor Statistics [Department of Labor] [Washington, DC]
BLS............ Burst Limit Switch (MCD)
BLSA.......... Baltimore Longitudinal Study of Aging [Department of Health and
                Human Services] (GFGA)
BLSA.......... Basic Load Storage Area [Military]
BLSA.......... Black Law Student Association (EA)
BLSA.......... Blowing Sand [ICAO] (FAAC)
BLSA.......... Border Leicester Sheepbreeders' Association [Australia]
BLSA.......... British Legal Services Agency (DLA)
BLSANSW.... Border Leicester Sheepbreeders' Association of New South Wales
                [Australia]
BLSB.......... Ball-Lock Separation Bolt
BLS Bull ..... Bureau of Labor Statistics. Bulletin [A publication] (DLA)
BL Sc......... Bachelor of Library Science
BLSC.......... Bio-Logic Systems [NASDAQ symbol] (TTSB)
BLSC.......... Bio-Logic Systems Corp. [NASDAQ symbol] (NQ)
BLSD.......... Bovine Lumpy Skin Disease [Medicine] (DMAA)
BLSG .... Brigade Logistic Support Group [Marine Corps] (CINC)
BLSGMA ...... British Lamp Blown Scientific Glassware Manufacturers' Association
                Ltd. (BI)
BLSI........... Boston Life Sciences [NASDAQ symbol] (TTSB)
BLSI........... Boston Life Sciences, Inc. [NASDAQ symbol] (SAG)
BLSIW........ Boston Life Sciences Wrrt [NASDAQ symbol] (TTSB)
BLSJ.......... Beam Lead Sealed Junction [Electronics] (IAA)
BLSJICP...... Beam Lead Sealed Junction Integrated Circuit Package (AABC)
BLSL.......... British Leyland Systems Ltd. (NITA)
BLSN.......... Blowing Snow [Meteorology] (DA)
BLSR .... Bidirectional Line Switched Ring [Telecommunications] (ACRL)
BLSR .... Bi-Directional Line-Switched Rings
BLSS.......... Base Level Self-Sufficiency [Air Force]
BLSSD........ Blessed
BLSSS .... Base-Level Self-Sufficiency Spare [Air Force] (DOMA)
BLST.......... Ballast (MSA)
BLST.......... Bankson Language Screening Test [Child development test]
BL/ST......... Bluestone [Inferior gin or whiskey] [Slang] (ADA)
BLSTL......... Billet Steel (MSA)
B Lt........... Bachelor of Literature
BLT............ Bacon, Lettuce, and Tomato Sandwich
BLT............ Baltic Aviation, Inc. [ICAO designator] (FAAC)
BLT............ Baltimore Law Transcript [A publication] (DLA)
BLT............ Base Level of Treatment (DICI)
BLT............ BASIC [Beginner's All-Purpose Symbolic Instruction Code] Language
                Translator [Computer science] (MCD)
BLT............ Battalion Landing Team [Military]
BLT............ Battalion Landing Team [Marine Corps] (DOMA)
BLT............ Battery of Leukocyte Tests [Clinical medicine]
BLT............ Bert Leston Taylor [American columnist, 1866-1921] [Initials used as
                pseudonym]
BLT............ Bilateral Tubal Ligation [Gynecology] (DAVI)
BLT............ Biltrite Nightingale, Inc. [Toronto Stock Exchange symbol]
BLT............ Blackwater [Australia Airport symbol] (OAG)
BLT............ Bladder Tumor [Oncology and urology] (DAVI)
BLT............ Blit [Computer science] (NHD)
BLT............ Block Transfer [Computer science]
BLT............ Blood-Clot Lysis Time [Medicine]
Bl T........... Blood Type [Medicine]
BLT............ Bloomer Learning Test [Intelligence test]
BLT............ Blount International [NYSE symbol] (SAG)
BLT............ Boat Landing Team
BLT............ Bolt (MSA)

BLT............ Borrowed Light (KSC)
BLT............ Branch if Less Than [Computer science] (NHD)
BLT............ Branch Liaison Team [US Army Chemical School] [Fort McClellan,
                AL] (RDA)
BLT............ Break-Loose Torque [Automotive engineering]
blt............. Built (BARN)
BLT............ Built
BLT............ Burma Law Times [A publication] (DLA)
BLT............ But Less Than
BLT.A......... Blount Intl Cl'A' [NYSE symbol] (TTSB)
BLT.B......... Blount Intl Cv'B' [NYSE symbol] (TTSB)
BLTC.......... Bottom-Loading Transfer Cask [Nuclear energy] (NRCH)
BLTDA........ Burley Leaf Tobacco Dealers Association (EA)
BLTG.......... Belting [Freight]
BltGE......... Baltimore Gas & Electric Co. [Associated Press] (SAG)
BLTI.......... Better Lawn and Turf Institute (EA)
BLTI.......... BIOLASE Technology [NASDAQ symbol] (TTSB)
BLTI.......... BioLase Technology, Inc. [NASDAQ symbol] (SAG)
Bl Ti......... Block on Tithes [A publication] (DLA)
BLTIN........ Built-In
BLTLEX....... Battalion Landing Exercise [Military] (NVT)
BLTM.......... Battalion Level Training Model [DoD]
blts........... Bit-Block Transfers [Computer science]
Bl TT......... Blackwell's Tax Titles [A publication] (DLA)
BLTVC........ Boundary Layer Thrust Vector Control (MCD)
BLTW.......... Trinity Western College, Langley, British Columbia [Library symbol
                National Library of Canada] (NLC)
BLU........... Basic Link Unit [Computer science] (BUR)
BLU........... Basic Logic Unit (IEEE)
BLU........... Bessey-Lowry Unit (MAE)
BLU........... Bipolar Line Unit [Electronics] (IAA)
BLU........... Blue (KSC)
BLU........... Blue Chip Value Fund [NYSE symbol] (SPSG)
Blu........... Bluett's Advocate's Note Book, Isle Of Man [1720-1846]
                [A publication] (DLA)
BLU........... Bomb Line Unit (MCD)
BLU........... Bomb, Live Unit (AFM)
BLU........... Emigrant Gap, CA [Location identifier FAA] (FAAL)
BLU........... IMP Aviation Services Ltd. [Canada ICAO designator] (FAAC)
BLUD......... Immucor, Inc. [NASDAQ symbol] (NQ)
BluDolp....... Blue Dolphin Energy Co. [Associated Press] (SAG)
BLUE......... Best Linear Unbiased Estimator [Statistics]
BLUE......... Frederick Brewing [NASDAQ symbol] (TTSB)
BLUE......... Frederick Brewing Co. [NASDAQ symbol] (SAG)
BlueChp...... Blue Chip Fund [Associated Press] (SAG)
Bluegreen.... Bluegreen Corp. [Associated Press] (SAG)
Blue Sky L Rep... Blue Sky Law Reporter [Commerce Clearing House]
                [A publication] (DLA)
BlueSq........ Blue Square Israel Ltd. [Associated Press] (SAG)
Bluett........ Bluett's Isle Of Man Cases [A publication] (DLA)
BLUF......... Bluff [Commonly used] (OPSA)
BLUFF........ Bluff [Commonly used] (OPSA)
BLUFFS....... Bluffs [Commonly used] (OPSA)
BLUFOR....... Blue Force (DOMA)
Blum B'k'cy... Blumenstiel on Bankruptcy [A publication] (DLA)
BLUP......... Best Linear Unbiased Prediction [Genetics]
BLUPRNT..... Blueprint
BLV........... Bailadores [Venezuela] [Seismograph station code, US Geological
                Survey] (SEIS)
BLV........... Belleville, IL [Location identifier FAA] (FAAL)
BLV........... Bell-View Airlines Ltd. [Nigeria] [ICAO designator] (FAAC)
BLV........... Bleed Valve (MCD)
BlV........... Blood Viscosity [Medicine] (DMAA)
BLV........... [The] Book of Living Verse [A publication]
BLV........... Bovine Leukemia Virus
BLV........... British Legion Village
BLV........... Scott Air Force Base Library, Scott AFB, IL [OCLC symbol] (OCLC)
BLVD.......... Boulevard (EY)
blvd.......... Boulevard (VRA)
BLVD.......... Boulevard
Blvd.......... Boulevard (DD)
BLVD.......... Boulevard [Postal Service standard] (OPSA)
BLW........... Back Lay Welding (NUCP)
BLW........... Bellwether Resources [Vancouver Stock Exchange symbol]
BLW........... Below (MSA)
BLW........... Boiling Light Water [Nuclear energy]
BLW........... Waimanalo, HI [Location identifier FAA] (FAAL)
BLWA......... British Laboratory Ware Association Ltd. (BI)
BLWC......... Bread Loaf Writers Conference (EA)
BLWDN....... Blowdown [Chemical engineering]
BLWI......... Belgisch-Luxembourg Wissel Instituut [Benelux]
B/LWL........ Beam to Waterline Length
BLW (PB).... Boiling Light Water Cooled Plutonium Burner [Nuclear energy]
                (NUCP)
BLWR......... Blower (KSC)
BLWS......... Bellows (MSA)
BLWT......... Blowout
BLWT......... Blowtorch
BLX........... Banco Latinoamer de Export'E' [NYSE symbol] (TTSB)
BLX........... Banco Latinoamericano de Export 'E' [NYSE symbol] (SPSG)
BLX........... Biloxi [Diocesan abbreviation] [Mississippi] (TOCD)
bl x.......... Bleeding Time [Clinical chemistry]
BLX........... Block (FAAC)
BLY........... Bally Entertainment [NYSE symbol] (TTSB)

BLY	Bally Entertainment Corp. [Formerly, Bally Manufacturing] [NYSE symbol] (SAG)
BLY	Banja Luka [Yugoslavia] [Seismograph station code, US Geological Survey] (SEIS)
BLY	Bell Molybdenum Mines [Vancouver Stock Exchange symbol]
BLY	Milwaukee, WI [Location identifier FAA] (FAAL)
BLYD	Blyvooruitzicht Gold [NASDAQ symbol] (SAG)
BLYH	Blyth Holdings [NASDAQ symbol] (TTSB)
BLYH	Blyth Holdings, Inc. [NASDAQ symbol] (NQ)
BLYM	Bursal Lymphomas [Oncology]
BLYP	Bernstein, Lee, Yang, Primakoff [Physicists]
BLYPrP	Bally Entertain't 8.00% 'PRIDES' [NYSE symbol] (TTSB)
Blyth	Blyth Holdings, Inc. [Associated Press] (SAG)
BlythInd	Blyth Industries, Inc. [Associated Press] (SAG)
Bly Us	Blydenburgh. Law of Usury [1844] [A publication] (DLA)
BLYV	Blyvooruitzicht Gold Mining Co. Ltd. [NASDAQ symbol] (NQ)
Blyvoor	Blyvooruitzicht Gold Mining Co. Ltd. [Associated Press] (SAG)
BLYVY	BlyvoorGold Mng ADR [NASDAQ symbol] (TTSB)
BLZ	Aero Barloz SA de CV [Mexico ICAO designator] (FAAC)
BLZ	Belize [ANSI three-letter standard code] (CNC)
blz	Bladzijde [Page] [Netherlands] (ILCA)
BLZ	Blantyre [Malawi] [Airport symbol] (OAG)
BLZ	Bolzano [Italy] [Seismograph station code, US Geological Survey] (SEIS)
BLZ	Boundary Layer Zone
BLZD	Blizzard [NWS] (FAAC)
BLZN	Blazon
BM	Aero Transporti Italiani [ICAO designator] (AD)
BM	Baba Mezi'a [or Bava Mezi'a] (BJA)
BM	Bachelor of Mathematics
BM	Bachelor of Medicine
BM	Bachelor of Music
BM	Bachelor of Physic
BM	Back Marker [Aviation]
BM	Backmixing [Chemical engineering]
BM	Balance of Material (MCD)
BM	Ballistic Missile (AFM)
BM	Balneum Marinum [Sea-Water Bath] [Medicine]
BM	Banca Mondiale [World Bank] [Italian]
BM	Banco Mundial [World Bank] [Spanish]
BM	Bandmaster (ROG)
BM	Bar Mitzvah (BJA)
BM	Barrels per Month (IAA)
BM	Basal Medium [Microbiology]
BM	Basal Metabolism [Medicine]
BM	Base Maintenance [Air Force] (AFM)
BM	Basement Membrane [Medicine]
BM	Basilar Membrane [Ear anatomy]
BM	Battle Management [Military] (SDI)
BM	Battle Manning (DNAB)
BM	Beachmaster
BM	Beam (KSC)
BM	Beam Monitor
BM	Bearing Magnetic [Navigation] (IAA)
BM	Bear Market [Investment term]
BM	Beatae Memoriae [Of Blessed Memory] [Latin]
BM	Beata Maria [The Blessed Virgin] [Latin]
BM1	Beautiful Music (NTCM)
BM	Be-'eravon Mugbal (BJA)
BM	Before Marriage
BM	Before Midnight (ROG)
BM	Beit Mikra (BJA)
BM	Bench Maintenance [NASA] (KSC)
BM	Benchmark [Computer system evaluation]
BM	Bench Mark Control Point [Nautical charts]
BM	Bending Magnet
BM	Bending Moment [Aerospace]
BM	Bene Merenti [To the Well-Deserving] [Latin]
BM	Ben Marcato [Well Marked] [Music] (ROG)
BM	Ben Monroe's Kentucky Reports [A publication] (DLA)
bm	Bermuda [MARC country of publication code Library of Congress] (LCCP)
BM	Bermuda [ANSI two-letter standard code] (CNC)
BM	Billet Master [Military British] (ROG)
BM	Bill of Materials [Manufacturing] (MUGU)
BM	Bimonthly
BM	Binary Multiply
BM	Binding Margin [Bookbinding] (ADA)
BM	Biomatrix
BM	Bishop and Martyr [Church calendars]
BM	Bistable Multivibrator [Electronics] (IAA)
BM	Black Male
BM	Black Mountain [California]
BM	Black Muslim
BM	Blasius de Morcono [Flourished, 14th century] [Authority cited in pre-1607 legal work] (DSA)
BM	Blessed Mary [or Mother] (BARN)
BM	Blessed Memory (BARN)
BM	Blind Matching [Parapsychology]
BM	Blow Molding [Bottle manufacturing]
BM	Blume [Germany ICAO aircraft manufacturer identifier] (ICAO)
BM	Board Measure [Lumber]
BM	Board's Minute [Custom house] [British] (ROG)
BM	Boatswain's Mate [Navy rating]
BM	Body Mass [Medicine]
BM	Body Mounted (MCD)
BM	Bohr Magneton [Atomic physics]
BM	Boilermaker [Military British]
BM	Bolted Manhole Cover Plate [Shipfitting]
BM	Bonae Memoriae [Of Happy Memory] [Latin]
BM	Bond Maturity [Investment term]
BM	Bone Marker [Aviation]
BM	Bone Marrow
BM	Boom (DS)
BM	Bordmechaniker [Flight engineer] [German military - World War II]
BM	Boston & Maine Corp. [AAR code]
BM	Boundary Marker (MCD)
BM	Bowel Movement [Medicine]
BM	Brake Electromagnet
BM	Branch Manager (MCD)
BM	Branch Material [Military] (AABC)
BM	Branch Memorandum
BM	Branch on Minus
BM	Bravery Medal (ADA)
BM	Breakdown Maintenance
BM	Breast Milk [Neonatology and obstetrics] (DAVI)
BM	Brecon and Merthyr Railway [Wales]
BM	Breech Mechanism [of a weapon]
BM	Brigade Major
BM	Brightness Merit
B-M	Bristol-Myers Co.
BM	British Medal (DI)
BM	British Midland Airways Ltd.
BM	British Movement [Political party]
BM	British Museum [London]
BM	Broad Measure (ADA)
BM	Bronze Medal
BM	Bubble Memory [Data storage device] [Computer science] (BUR)
BM	Buccal Mass [Dentistry]
BM	Buccomesial [Dentistry]
BM	Buffer Mark [Computer science] (IAA)
BM	Buffer Memory
BM	Buffer Module [Computer science]
B/M	Buffer/Multiplexer [Computer science] (CET)
BM	Bulk Mail
BM	Bulky Mechanical [Paper] (DGA)
BM	Bureau of Medicine [of FDA]
BM	Bureau of Mines [Department of the Interior]
BM	Bureau of the Mint [Department of the Treasury]
BM	Burgomaster
BM	Burlington Magazine [A publication] (BRI)
BM	Burrow's Reports Tempore Mansfield [England] [A publication] (DLA)
BM	Business Machine
BM	Business Manager (MCD)
BM	Bus Multiplexer
BM	Butts Master [British and Canadian] [World War II]
BM	Buyers' Market [Investment term]
BM	Byte Machine [Computer science] (IAA)
BM	Byte Multiplexer Mode [Computer science] (IAA)
BM	Monitor [Ship] [Navy] (MCD)
BM	Moore's Reports [England] [A publication] (DLA)
BM	Societa Aero Trasporti Italiani SpA [Italy ICAO designator] (ICDA)
BM1	Boatswain's Mate, First Class [Navy rating]
BM2	Boatswain's Mate, Second Class [Navy rating]
BM3	Boatswain's Mate, Third Class [Navy rating]
BMA	Bachelor of Management Arts (DD)
BMA	Bachelor of Municipal Administration
BMA	Backup Maintenance Activity (MCD)
BMA	Bahrain Monetary Agency (IMH)
BMA	Balanced Magnetic Amplifier
BMA	Bangladesh Medical Association of North America (EA)
BMA	Bank Marketing Association [Chicago, IL] (EA)
BMA	Basic Maintenance Allowance
BMA	Beach Maintenance Area [British and Canadian] [World War II]
BMA	Besson [Frank S.] Memorial Award [American Defense Preparedness Association] (RDA)
BMA	Bible Memory Association, International (EA)
BMA	Bicycle Manufacturers Association of America (EA)
BMA	Biomedical Marketing Association (EA)
BMA	Black Music Association [Defunct] (EA)
BMA	Boat Manufacturers Association [Later, NMMA] (EA)
BMA	Body-Mounted Accelerometer
BMA	Bone Marrow Arrest [Medicine] (DMAA)
BMA	Bone Marrow Aspirate [Hematology] (DAVI)
BMA	Brahma Resources, Inc. [Vancouver Stock Exchange symbol]
BMA	Brigade Maintenance Area [British military] (DMA)
BMA	British Majorettes' Association (DI)
BMA	British Manufacturers' Association Ltd. (BI)
BMA	British Medical Association
BMA	British Midland Airways Ltd. [ICAO designator] (FAAC)
BMA	British Military Administration
BMA	British Military Authority
BMA	(Bromobenzoyl)methyladamantylamine [Biochemistry]
BMA	Butyl Methacrylate [Organic chemistry]
BMA	Stockholm [Sweden] Bromma Airport [Airport symbol] (OAG)
BMAA	Barracks Master-at-Arms
BMAA	Beta-Methylamino-alanine [An amino acid]
BMAA	Beverage Manufacturers' Agents Association (EA)
BMAA	Boat Manufacturers' Association of Australia
BMAA	British Marine Aquarist Association

BMAA........... British Medical Acupuncture Association (PDAA)
BMAA........... British Microlight Aircraft Association (PDAA)
BMAA........... Brushware Manufacturers' Association of Australia
BMAB........... Butyl(methoxy)azobenzene [*Organic chemistry*]
BMA(BB)...... British Military Administration, British Borneo
BMAC........... Basic Memory Access Controller [*Memory management unit*]
        [*Computer science*]
BMAC........... Black Music Association of Canada (AC)
BMAC........... Boeing Military Airplane Co.
B-MAC........ Multiplexed Analogue Component, Type B [*Satellite television*]
BMADO........ Boeing Military Airplane Development Organization
B Ma E .... Bachelor of Marine Engineering
B Ma Eng ... Bachelor of Marine Engineering
BMAG........... Body-Mounted Attitude Gyro (KSC)
BMAGNY...... Box Manufacturers Association of Greater New York [*Defunct*] (EA)
B Maj........... Brigade Major (DAS)
BM & O ...... Baltimore, Maryland, and Ohio
BM & SIAL.. Bureau of Medicine and Supply Integrated Allowance List
BMANSW..... Bread Manufacturers' Association of New South Wales [*Australia*]
BMANT .... Boom Antenna (IAA)
BManufTech... Bachelor of Manufacturing Technology
BMAP........... Barometric and Manifold Absolute Pressure [*Automotive engineering*]
BMAP........... BITmap Images
BMAP........... BMA [*British Medical Association*] Press Cuttings Database
        [*Information service or system*] (IID)
BMAP........... Boost Measurement and Analysis Program (MCD)
BMAP........... [*The*] Brooklyn Museum Aramaic Papyri [*A publication*] (BJA)
BMAP........... Buffer Map [*Computer science*] (NASA)
BMAPS .... Bexley-Maudsley Automated Psychological Screening [*Test*]
BMAR .... Backlog of Maintenance and Repair (MCD)
BMAR .... Ballistic Missile Acquisition RADAR
BMAR .... Base Maintenance and Repair
B Mar E ...... Bachelor of Marine Engineering
BMarEng..... Bachelor of Marine Engineering (NADA)
BMAS........... Barium-Magnesia-Alumina-Silicate [*Inorganic chemistry*]
BMAS........... British Medical Acupuncture Society
BMASA .... Bread Manufacturers' Association of South Australia
BMASR........ Bureau of Military Application of Scientific Research (NATG)
BMAT........... Basic Motor Ability Test [*Education*]
BMAT........... Beginning Morning Astronomical Twilight [*Navigation*] (MCD)
BMAT........... Bill of Materials (DNAB)
BMAT........... Blind Manufacturers' Association of Tasmania [*Australia*]
BMath........... Bachelor of Mathematics
BMaths......... Bachelor of Mathematics
BMAT/S........ Ballistic Missile Analyst Technician-Specialist
BMAV .... Bread Manufacturers' Association of Tasmania [*Australia*]
BMAW .... Bare Metal Arc Welding
BMAWA .... Bread Manufacturers' Association of Western Australia
BMAWA .... Building Management Authority of Western Australia
BMAX........... Maximum Beam [*IOR*]
B May.......... Bernardus Maynardi [*Authority cited in pre-1607 legal work*] (DSA)
BMB............. Bahrain Middle East Bank
BMB............. Ballistic Missile Branch
BMB............. Barclays Merchant Bank [*British*]
BMB............. Barry Melton Band [*Pop music group*]
BMB............. Base Maintenance Building (MCD)
BMB............. Biomedical Belt [*NASA*]
BMB............. BMB Compuscience Canada Ltd. [*Toronto Stock Exchange symbol*]
BMB............. Boehringer Mannheim Biochemicals
BMB............. Bomber [*Military*]
BMB............. British Metrication Board
BMB............. Broadcast Measurement Bureau (NTCM)
BMB............. Bumba [*Zaire*] [*Airport symbol*] (OAG)
BMB............. Butter Marketing Board [*Queensland, Australia*] ·
BMB............. McBride Public Library, British Columbia [*Library symbol National Library of Canada*] (NLC)
BMBA........... British Merchant Banking and Securities Houses Association (EAIO)
BMBA........... British Moth Boat Association (BI)
BMBCh........ Bachelor of Medicine, Bachelor of Surgery
BMBDR........ Bombardier (AFM)
BMBL........... Benign Monoclonal B-Cell Lymphocytosis [*Medicine*] (DMAA)
BMBNSW.... Barley Marketing Board of New South Wales [*Australia*]
BMBR .... Bomber [*Air Force*] (AFM)
BMBR .... Bomber
BMBRI........ Brewing & Malting Barley Research Institute [*Institut de Recherche-Brassage et Orge de Maltage*] (AC)
BMBS........... Bachelor of Medicine and Bachelor of Surgery
BMBSq......... Bombardment Squadron [*Air Force*]
BMBT........... Bis(methyloxybenzylidene)bitoluidine [*Organic chemistry*]
BMC............. Ballistic Missile Center [*Air Materiel Command*] [*Obsolete*]
BMC............. Banque de Madagascar et des Comores [*Bank of Madagascar and of the Comoro Islands*] (AF)
BMC............. Base Metal Catalyst [*Automotive engineering*]
BMC............. Basic Machine Cycle (IAA)
BMC............. Basic Military Compensation (MCD)
BMC............. Basic Missile Checker (NATG)
BMC............. Battelle Monte Carlo [*Computer science*]
BMC............. Bearing Mounted Clutch
BMC............. Biel's Microfilm Co., West Seneca, NY [*Library symbol Library of Congress*] (LCLS)
BMC............. Billing Memo Charge [*Business term*]
BMC............. Binary Magnetic Core
BMC............. Biomedical Chromatography [*A publication*]
BMC............. Biomedical Computer
BMC............. Biomimetic Affinity Chromatography

BMC............. Black Mountain College [*1933-1956*]
BMC............. Blind Mating Connector (MCD)
BMC............. Block Multiplexer Channel
BMC............. Blue Mountain College [*Mississippi*]
BMC............. BMC Industries [*NYSE symbol*] (TTSB)
BMC............. BMC Industries, Inc. [*NYSE symbol*] (SPSG)
BMC............. Boatswain's Mate, Chief [*Navy rating*]
BMC............. Boehringer Mannheim Corp. [*Chemical industry supplier*]
BMC............. Bone Marrow Cell [*Cytology*]
BMC............. Bone Mineral Content [*Medicine*]
BMC............. Book Marketing Council [*British*]
BMC............. Boycott McDonald's Coalition (EA)
BMC............. Brethren/Mennonite Council for Lesbian and Gay Concerns (EA)
BMC............. Brigham City, UT [*Location identifier FAA*] (FAAL)
BMC............. British Medical Council
BMC............. British Motor Corp. Ltd.
BMC............. British Mountaineering Council
BMC............. British Museum Catalogue
BMC............. Brittle Matrix Composite [*Materials science*]
BMC............. Broker Management Council (EA)
BMC............. Bromo-Methoxychalcone [*Organic chemistry*]
BMC............. Bryn Mawr College [*Pennsylvania*]
BMC............. Bryn Mawr College, Bryn Mawr, PA [*OCLC symbol*] (OCLC)
BMC............. Bubble Memory Controller [*Computer science*]
BMC............. Bulk Mail Center [*Postal Service*]
BMC............. Bulk Media Conversion
BMC............. Bulk Molding Compound
BMC............. Bullnose Morris Club (EA)
BMC............. Bureau of Motor Carriers [*ICC*]
BMC............. Burnout Missile Configuration [*Military*]
BMC............. Burst Multiplexer Channel [*Telecommunications*]
BMC............. Joint Brazil-United States Military Commission
BM/C3........ Battle Management/Command, Control, Communications (MCD)
BM/C3I .... Battle Management/Command, Control, Communications, and Intelligence [*Military*]
BMC/AMC ... Ballistic Missile Center, Air Materiel Command [*Obsolete*]
BMCBB .... Boatswain's Mate, Construction Battalion, Boatswain [*Navy rating*]
BMCBS .... Boatswain's Mate, Construction Battalion, Stevedore [*Navy rating*]
BMCC........... Bando McGlocklin Capital [*NASDAQ symbol*] (TTSB)
BMCC........... Bando McGlocklin Capital Corp. [*NASDAQ symbol*] (NQ)
BMCC........... British Metal Castings Council (DBA)
BMCCC .... Bishop Method of Clothing Construction Council (EA)
BMCCP .... Bando McGlocklin Adj Rt'A'Pfd [*NASDAQ symbol*] (TTSB)
BMCD .... Banque Malienne de Credits et de Depots [*Malian Credit and Deposits Bank*] (AF)
BMCE .... Banque Marocaine pour le Commerce Exterieur [*Moroccan Foreign Trade Bank*] (AF)
BMCERC ..... Black and Multiethnic Christian Education Resources Center (EA)
BMCET/S..... Ballistic Missile Checkout Equipment Technician-Specialist
BMCM.......... Boatswain's Mate, Master Chief [*Navy rating*]
BMCMC....... Bone-Marrow-Derived Cultured Mast Cell
BMCO.......... Ballistic Missile Construction Office
BMCO .... Biomechanical Combined Oxidation [*Water treatment*]
B M Coins Rom Emp... British Museum Catalogue of Coins of the Roman Empire [*A publication*] (OCD)
BMCR .... Black Methodists for Church Renewal (EA)
BMCS........... BMC Software [*NASDAQ symbol*] (TTSB)
BMCS........... BMC Software, Inc. [*NASDAQ symbol*] (NQ)
BMCS........... Boatswain's Mate, Senior Chief [*Navy rating*]
BMCS........... Bureau of Motor Carrier Safety [*Department of Transportation*]
BMCS........... Business Management Control System [*Computer science*] (IAA)
BMC Sf .... BMC Softwear, Inc. [*Associated Press*] (SAG)
BMC Soft .... BMC Softwear [*Associated Press*] (SAG)
BMCSRP...... Business Management Control System Research Project (IAA)
BMCT.......... Beginning Morning Civil Twilight [*Navigation*]
BMCT.......... Bennett Mechanical Comprehension Test [*Mechanical ability test*]
BMCW .... BMC West [*NASDAQ symbol*] (SPSG)
BMC/W........ Bone Mineral Content/Width [*Medicine*]
BMC Wst .... BMC West Corp. [*Associated Press*] (SAG)
BMD............. AL Laboratories, Inc. [*NYSE symbol*] (SPSG)
BMD............. Bacitracin Methylene Disalicylate [*Animal antibiotic*]
BMD............. Ballistic Missile Defense
BMD............. Ballistic Missile Defense Systems Command [*Huntsville, AL*]
BMD............. Ballistic Missile Division [*Ballistic Research Laboratory*]
BMD............. Banque Mauritanienne de Developpement [*Mauritanian Development Bank*] (AF)
BMD............. Baseband Modulator-Demodulator (IAA)
BMD............. Base Maintenance Division [*Navy*]
BMD............. Basic Manufacturing Technology
BMD............. Becker Muscular Dystrophy [*Medicine*]
BMD............. Belo [*Madagascar*] [*Airport symbol*] (OAG)
BMD............. Benchmark Monitor Display System [*Sperry UNIVAC*]
BMD............. Bengal Medical Department [*British military*] (DMA)
BMD............. Big Mahogany Desk
BMD............. Biomedical
BMD............. Births, Marriage and Deaths (WDAA)
BMD............. Bone Marrow Depression [*Hematology*] (AAMN)
BMD............. Bone Mineral Densitrometry [*Medicine*]
BMD............. Bone Mineral Density [*Medicine*]
BMD............. British Medical [*Vancouver Stock Exchange symbol*]
BMD............. British Medical Charter [*ICAO designator*] (FAAC)
BMD............. Brittle Materials Design (MCD)
BMD............. Broadcasting Maintenance District
BMD............. Bronevaya Mashina Destany [*Soviet airborne combat vehicle*] (INF)
BMD............. Bubble Memory Device [*Computer science*]

BMD............ Buick Motor Division [General Motors Corp.]
BMD............ Bureau of Medical Devices [Food and Drug Administration]
BMD............ United States Food and Drug Administration, Bureau of Medical Devices Library, Silver Spring, MD [OCLC symbol]   (OCLC)
BMDA .... Blue Military Damage Assessment
BMDADS...... Biomedical Data Analysis and Display System [NASA]
BMDATC...... Ballistic Missile Defense Advanced Technology Center   (AABC)
BMDC .... Ballistic Missile Defense Center   (MCD)
BMDC .... Ballistic Missile Defense Command
BMDC .... Ballistic Missile Defense Committee
BMDCA........ Bernese Mountain Dog Club of America   (EA)
BMDCP........ Ballistic Missile Defense Command Post   (AABC)
BMDCP........ Battalion Mortar and Davy Crockett Platoon [Army]   (AABC)
BMDDP........ Bureau of Medical Devices and Diagnostic Products [FDA]
BMDEAR...... Ballistic Missile Defense Emergency Action Report   (AABC)
BMDES........ Ballistic Missile Defense Engagement Simulator
BMDF.......... Black Mesa Defense Fund   (EA)
BMD-FO....... Ballistic Missile Division - Field Office [Ballistic Research Laboratory]   (SAA)
BMDH .... Basic Minimum Descent Height [Aviation]   (DA)
BMDITP .... Ballistic Missile Defense Integrated Training Plan   (AABC)
BMDMB .... Ballistic Missile Defense Missile Battalion   (AABC)
BMDMCS .... (Bromomethyl)dimethyl Chlorosilane [Organic chemistry]
BMDMP .... Ballistic Missile Defense Master Plan   (AABC)
BMDMPO...... Ballistic Missile Defense Materials Program Office   (MCD)
BMD-NEAT... Ballistic Missile Defense - Nuclear Effects and Threat Committee   (AABC)
BMDNS .... Basic Mission, Design Number, and Series [Aircraft]   (AFM)
BMDO .... Ballistic Missile Defense Operations [or Organization] [or Office]   (AABC)
BMDO .... Ballistic Missile Defense Organization
BMDO .... Bomb and Mine Disposal Officer [British military]   (DMA)
BMDOA .... Ballistic Missile Defense Operations Activity   (AABC)
BMDPM .... Ballistic Missile Defense Program Manager   (AABC)
BMDPO .... Ballistic Missile Defense Program Office   (AABC)
BMDR .... Bombardier
BMDS .... Ballistic Missile Defense System
BMDS .... Base Mail Distribution Scheme [Air Force]   (AFM)
BMDS .... Base Manager Data System
BMDS .... Base Manpower Data System [Air Force]   (OAG)
BMDS .... British Medical Data Systems   (NITA)
BMDSB .... Ballistic Missile Defense Surveillance Battalion   (AABC)
BMDSCOM... Ballistic Missile Defense Systems Command   (AABC)
BME............ Bachelor of Mechanical Engineering
BME............ Bachelor of Mining Engineering
BME............ Bachelor of Music Education
BME............ Barrage Mansour Eddahbi [Morocco] [Seismograph station code, US Geological Survey]   (SEIS)
BME............ Basal Medium, Eagle's [Diploid cell cultures]   (MAE)
BME............ Battalion Maintenance Equipment [Military]
BME............ Beaver, Meade & Englewood [AAR code]
BME............ Belmoral Mines Ltd. [Toronto Stock Exchange symbol]
BME............ Bench Maintenance Equipment [NASA]   (KSC)
BME............ Beta-Mercaptoethanol [Organic chemistry]
BME............ Biomedical Electronics   (MCD)
BME............ Biomedical Engineering Program [Carnegie-Mellon University] [Research center]   (RCD)
BME............ Born-Mayer Equation [Physics]
BME............ Brief Maximal Effort [Orthopedics and physical therapy]   (DAVI)
BME............ British Museum Expeditions to Middle Egypt [London] [A publication]   (BJA)
BME............ Broome [Australia Airport symbol]   (OAG)
BME............ Brotherhood of Marine Engineers [Later merged with MEBA]
BME............ Buck Memory Element   (MCD)
BME............ Division of Biomedical Engineering [University of Virginia] [Research center]   (RCD)
BMEA.......... British Marine Equipment Association   (DBA)
BMEA.......... Building Maintenance Employers Association [Later, SEA]   (EA)
BMEA.......... Building Material Exhibitors Association [Defunct]   (EA)
BME (Aero Option)...   Bachelor of Mechanical Engineering (Aeronautical Option)
BMEC.......... Ball Manufacturers Engineers Committee   (EA)
BMEC.......... British Marine Equipment Council   (DS)
B Mech .... Bachelor of Mechanics
B Mech E..... Bachelor of Mechanical Engineering
B Med.......... Bachelor of Medicine
BM Ed.......... Bachelor of Music Education
B Med Biol... Bachelor of Medical Biology
BMedLabSc.. Bachelor of Medical Laboratory Science
BMEDS........ Base Management Engineering Data System
B Med Sc..... Bachelor of Medical Sciences
B Med Sci ... Bachelor of Medical Sciences
BMEF.......... British Mechanical Engineering Federation   (DI)
BMEG.......... Building Materials Export Group [British]   (DS)
BM Eng .... Bachelor of Mechanical Engineering
BMEO.......... British Middle East Office
BMEP.......... [The] Book of Modern English Poetry [A publication]
BMEP.......... Brake Mean Effective Pressure
BMES.......... Biomedical Engineering Society   (EA)
B Met.......... Bachelor of Metallurgy
BMET.......... Basal Metabolic Rate   (CPH)
BMET.......... Biomedical Equipment Technology
BMET.......... Biomet, Inc. [NASDAQ symbol]   (NQ)
B Metal E ... Bachelor of Metallurgical Engineering
B Met E ...... Bachelor of Metallurgical Engineering
B Met Eng ... Bachelor of Metallurgical Engineering

BMETO........ Ballistic Missiles European Task Organization [Military]
BMEU.......... Biomedical Engineering Unit [McGill University] [Canada Research center]   (RCD)
BMEW......... Ballistic Missile Early Warning [System]
BMEWS....... Ballistic Missile Early Warning System
BMF............ Basic Main Frame   (NATG)
BMF............ Basic Mobile Facility   (MCD)
BMF............ B-Cell Maturation Factor [Immunology]
BMF............ Beautiful Music Friends   (EA)
BMF............ Bending Mode Filters
BMF............ Bene Merenti Fecit [He Erected This to the Well-Deserving] [Latin]
BMF............ Bimodal Filter   (PDAA)
BMF............ BIT [Binary Digit] Map Font [Computer science]   (PCM)
BMF............ BIT [Binary Digit] Matched Filter
BMF............ BMO II Financial Corp. [Toronto Stock Exchange symbol]
BMF............ Board Measurement Feet
BMF............ Bone Marrow Failure [Medicine]   (DMAA)
BMF............ Boron Metal Fiber
BMF............ Building Merchants' Federation [British]
BMF............ Business Mail Foundation [Later, DMMA]   (EA)
BMF............ Business Master File [OMB]
BMFA.......... Boston Museum of Fine Arts
BMFC.......... Barry Morse Fan Club   (EA)
BMFC.......... Big Man's Fan Club   (EA)
BMFC.......... Buddy Max Fan Club   (EA)
BMFC.......... Bunnie Mills Fan Club   (EA)
BMFF.......... British Man-Made Fibres Federation   (BI)
BMfgMgt..... Bachelor of Manufacturing Management
BMFL.......... Bidders Master File Listing [DoD]
BMFPRA...... BMO II Financial Pr [Toronto Stock Exchange symbol]
BMFT.......... Bundesministerium fuer Forschung und Technologie [Ministry for Research and Technology] [Information service or system Germany]   (IID)
BMG........... Baader-Meinhof Group [Revolutionary group] [Germany]
BMG........... Battery Maintenance Group [Military]
BMG........... Battle Mountain Gold Co. [Toronto Stock Exchange symbol NYSE symbol]
BMG........... Battle Mtn Gold [NYSE symbol]   (TTSB)
BMG........... Benign Monoclonal Gammopathy [Immunochemistry]
BMG........... Bertelsmann Music Group [Record company]   (ECON)
BMG........... Bilirubin Monoglucuronide [Biochemistry]
BMG........... Bloomington [Indiana] [Airport symbol]   (OAG)
BMG........... Body-Mounted [Altitude] Gyroscope   (SAA)
BMG........... British Measures Group
BMG........... British Menswear Guild Ltd.   (BI)
BMG........... British Military Government
BMG........... Browning Machine Gun
BMG........... Budget and Manpower Guidance [Military]   (AABC)
BMG........... Business Machines Group [Burroughs Corp.]
BMG........... Business Management Game
BMGA .... British Machine Guarding Authority
BMgmt....... Bachelor of Management   (DD)
BMGPr........ Battle Mtn Gold $3.25 Cv Pfd [NYSE symbol]   (TTSB)
BMGR........ Bone Marrow Granulocyte Reserve [Physiology]
B Mgt E ..... Bachelor of Management Engineering
BMgtEng...... Bachelor of Management Engineering   (NADA)
BMH.......... Bank Mees & Hope NV
BMH.......... Beaufort & Morehead Railroad Co. [AAR code]
BMH.......... Benign Monoclonal Hypergammaglobulinemia [Medicine]
BMH.......... Bis(maleimido)hexane [Organic chemistry]
BMH.......... Bomai [Papua New Guinea] [Airport symbol]   (OAG)
BMH.......... Bristow Masayu Helicopter PT [Indonesia] [ICAO designator]   (FAAC)
BMH.......... British Military Hospital
BMH.......... British Motor Heritage
BMH.......... British Motor Holdings
BMHA .... Black Mental Health Alliance   (EA)
BMHDA....... Beta-Methylheptadecanoic Acid [Organic chemistry]
BMHF........ British Materials Handling Federation   (DBA)
BMHIA....... Black Military History Institute of America   (EA)
BMHP........ Biomedicine and Health Program
BMHP .... Bromomercurihydroxypropane [Clinical chemistry]
BMHS........ British Morgan Horse Society
BMHS .... British Morgan Horse Society   (DBA)
BMHS .... British Music Hall Society   (BI)
BMI........... Badger Meter [AMEX symbol]   (TTSB)
BMI........... Badger Meter, Inc. [AMEX symbol]   (SPSG)
BMI........... Ballistic Missile Interceptor
BMI........... Bangles n' Mash International [Defunct]   (EA)
BMI........... Bank Melli Iran
BMI........... Barley and Malt Institute [Defunct]   (EA)
BMI........... Battelle Memorial Institute   (EA)
BMI........... Bay Microfilm, Incorporated, Palo Alto, CA [Library symbol Library of Congress]   (LCLS)
BMI........... Bemoair [Czechoslovakia] [FAA designator]   (FAAC)
BMI........... Bibliography Master Index [A database] [Gale Research]   (NITA)
BMI........... Biography Master Index [Gale Research, Inc.] [Information service or system A publication]   (IID)
BMI........... Bismaleimide [Organic chemistry]
BMI........... Bismaleimide [Plastics]
BMI........... Bloomington [Illinois] [Airport symbol]   (OAG)
BMI........... Body Mass Index [Medicine]
BMI........... Book Manufacturers Institute   (EA)
BMI........... Bravais-Miller Indices [Physics]
BMI........... British Ministry of Information   (DAS)
BMI........... Broadcast Music, Inc.   (EA)

BMI	Building Maintenance Information Ltd. (DBA)
BMIAA	Bread Manufacturers' Industrial Association of Australia
BMIB	Bank Markazi Iran. Bulletin [*A publication*]
B Mic	Bachelor of Microbiology
BMIC	Basic Metals Industry Council [*Australia*]
BMIC	British Music Information Centre (CB)
BMIC	Bureau of Mines. Information Circular [*Department of the Interior A publication*]
BMIC	Bus Master Interface Controller [*Computer science*] (PCM)
B Mi E	Bachelor of Mining Engineering
B Mi Eng	Bachelor of Mining Engineering
BMIF	British Marine Industries Federation (EAIO)
BMIGT	Ballistic Missile Inertial Guidance Technician (IAA)
BMIGT/M	Ballistic Missile Inertial Guidance Technician-Mechanic
BMILS	Bottom-Mounted Impact Locations System [*Missile technology*]
BMIM	Mayne Island Museum, British Columbia [*Library symbol National Library of Canada*] (NLC)
BMin	Bachelor of Ministry
BMinE	Bachelor of Mining Engineering
BMiningE	Bachelor of Mining Engineering
BMIP	Basic Medical Insurance Plan [*UN Food and Agriculture Organization*]
BMIR	Below Market Interest Rate (GFGA)
BMIS	Bank Management Information System
BMIS	Beet Medium Invert Syrup [*Food sweetener*]
BMIS	British Medical Informatics Society (ACII)
BMIT	Behaviour Modification Information Test (AIE)
BMIT	Biomedical Informatics Today (ACII)
BMITA	British Malaysian Industry and Trade Association (DS)
BMIU	Bricklayers, Masons Independent Union of Canada
BMJ	Baramita [*Guyana*] [*Airport symbol*] (OAG)
BMJ	Basic Military Journalist [*Department of Defense Information School course*] (DNAB)
BMJ	Bemidji Aviation Services, Inc. [*ICAO designator*] (FAAC)
BMJ	BMJ Financial Corp. [*Associated Press*] (SAG)
BMJ	Bones, Muscles, Joints [*Medicine*] (DMAA)
BMJ	British Medical Journal [*A publication*]
BMJ	Bundesminister der Justiz [*Federal Minister of Justice*] [*German*] (ILCA)
BMJF	B M J Financial [*NASDAQ symbol*] (TTSB)
BMJF	BMJ Financial Corp. [*NASDAQ symbol*] (NQ)
BMK	Baby Mouse Kidney Cells
BMK	Birthmark [*Dermatology*] (DAVI)
BMK	Borkum [*Germany Airport symbol*] (OAG)
BMK	Mackenzie Public Library, British Columbia [*Library symbol National Library of Canada*] (NLC)
BMKR	Boilermaker (MSA)
BMKRM	Kettle River Museum, Midway, British Columbia [*Library symbol National Library of Canada*] (NLC)
BML	Bachelor of Modern Languages
BML	Bank of Maldives Ltd. (FEA)
BML	Belfast & Moosehead Lake Railroad Co. [*AAR code*]
BML	Ben May Laboratory for Cancer Research [*University of Chicago*] [*Research center*] (RCD)
BML	Benthic Mixed Layer [*Nuclear energy*] (NUCP)
BML	Berlin, NH [*Location identifier FAA*] (FAAL)
BML	Bible Meditation League [*Later, BLI*] (EA)
BML	Bidders Mailing List (AAGC)
BML	BIT [*Binary Digit*] Manipulate Load
BML	Blue Mountain Lake [*New York*] [*Seismograph station code, US Geological Survey Closed*] (SEIS)
BML	Bodega Marine Laboratory [*University of California*] [*Research center*] (RCD)
BML	Bone-Marrow Leucocyte [*Physiology*]
BML	Bone Marrow Lymphocytosis [*Medicine*] (DMAA)
BML	Bovine Milk Lysozyme [*Biochemistry*] (OA)
BML	Bren-Mar Resources [*Vancouver Stock Exchange symbol*]
BML	British Museum Library [*London*]
BML	Bulk Material Length (NRCH)
BML	Business Modeling Language (MCD)
BMLA	British Maritime Law Association
BMLA	British Medical LASER Association
BML-BS	British Matchbox Label and Booklet Society
BMLC	Ballarat Music Lovers' Club [*Australia*]
BMLC	Basic Multiline Controller [*Computer science*] (MHDI)
BMLD	Binaural Masking Level Difference (PDAA)
BMLET/R	Ballistic Missile Launch Equipment Technician-Repairman
BMLO	Ballistic Missile Logistics Office
BMLS	Balloon-Borne Microwave Limb Sounder [*Atmospheric research*]
BMLS	Burke Mills [*NASDAQ symbol*] (TTSB)
BMLS	Burke Mills, Inc. [*NASDAQ symbol*] (NQ)
BMLUS	Business Men's League of the United States (EA)
BMM	Bachelor of Mining and Metallurgy
BMM	Ballistic Missile Manager
BMM	Baptist Mid-Missions (EA)
BMM	Basement Membrane Matrix [*Biochemistry*]
BMM	Basic Multi-Minutes (PDAA)
BMM	Belfast, Mersey and Manchester [*Steamship*] (MHDB)
BMM	Benthic Metabolism Measurement
BMM	Big Maria Mountains [*California*] [*Seismograph station code, US Geological Survey*] (SEIS)
BMM	Bitam [*Gabon*] [*Airport symbol*] (OAG)
BMM	Bohr and Mottleson Model [*of nuclear structure*]
BMM	Bone-Marrow-Derived Macrophage [*Biochemistry*]
BMM	Borrowed Military Manpower

BMM	British Military Mission
BMM	Burman Aviation (Charter) Ltd. [*British*] [*FAA designator*] (FAAC)
BMM	Butler Mountain Minerals [*Vancouver Stock Exchange symbol*]
BMM	Mission Museum and Archives, British Columbia [*Library symbol National Library of Canada*] (NLC)
BMMA	Bacon and Meat Manufacturers' Association [*British*]
BMMA	Beverage Machinery Manufacturers Association (EA)
BMMA	British Mantle Manufacturers' Association (BI)
BMMA	British Micrographic Manufacturers Association (DBA)
BMMC	Basic Monthly Maintenance Charge (NITA)
BMMC	Bone-Marrow-Derived Mast Cells [*Cytology*]
BMMC	Bulk Molding Compound [*Plastics technology*]
BMMCDC	Binary Metal and Metalloid Constitution Data Center [*Illinois Institute of Technology*]
BMMD	Birmingham & Midland Motor Omnibus Co. Ltd. [*British*] (DCTA)
BMMD	Body Mass Measurements Device (KSC)
BMMF	Beatrice M. Murphy Foundation (EA)
BMMF	Bible and Medical Missionary Fellowship [*Later, BMMFI/USA*] (EA)
BMMFF	British Man-Made Fibres Federation
BMMFI	BMMF [*Bible and Medical Missionary Fellowship*] International [*Later, IUSA*] (EA)
BMMFI/USA	BMMF [*Bible and Medical Missionary Fellowship*] International/USA [*Later, IUSA*] (EA)
BMMG	British Microcomputer Manufacturers' Group (NITA)
BMMG	British Micro Manufacturer Group
BMMMA	British Mat and Matting Manufacturers Association (BI)
BMMP	Barge-Mounted Methanol Plant [*Chemical industry*]
BMMP	Benign Mucous Membrane Pemphigus [*Medicine*] (MAE)
BMMPIC	Basic Metals and Minerals Processing Industry Council [*Australia*]
BMMT	Basic Morse Mission Trainer [*Military*]
BMMV	Bean Mild Mosaic Virus [*Plant pathology*]
BMN	Base Manager's Notice
BMN	Battle Management Node
BMN	Battle Mountain [*Nevada*] [*Seismograph station code, US Geological Survey*] (SEIS)
BMN	Benzylidenemalononitrile [*Organic chemistry*]
BMN	Blackrock Municipal Target Term Trust [*NYSE symbol*] (SPSG)
BMN	Blackrock Muni Target Term [*NYSE symbol*] (TTSB)
BMN	BMO NT Financial Corp. [*Toronto Stock Exchange symbol*]
BMN	Bowman Aviation, Inc. [*ICAO designator*] (FAAC)
BMN	British Merchant Navy
BMN	Bulky Mechanical Newsprint (DGA)
BMNA	Baptist Mission of North America [*Defunct*] (EA)
BMNH	British Museum (Natural History) [*London*]
BMNLF	Bangsa Moro National Liberation Front [*Philippines*] [*Political party*] (FEA)
BmNPV	Bombyx mori Nuclear Polyhedrosis Virus
BMNSW	Bread Manufacturers of New South Wales [*Australia*]
BMNT	Beginning Morning Nautical Twilight [*Navigation*]
BMNV	Nicola Valley Museum-Archives, Merritt, British Columbia [*Library symbol National Library of Canada*] (NLC)
BMO	Ballistic Missile Office [*Norton Air Force Base, CA*] [*United States Air Force Systems Command*] (GRD)
BMO	Bank of Montreal [*Toronto Stock Exchange symbol Vancouver Stock Exchange symbol*]
BMO	Base Maintenance Operation (MCD)
BMO	Battalion Maintenance Officer [*Army*] (INF)
BMO	Battalion Motor Officer [*Military*] (INF)
BMO	Beach Modulator Oscillator
BMO	Bhamo [*Myanmar*] [*Airport symbol*] (OAG)
BMO	Blue Mountains Array [*Oregon*] [*Seismograph station code, US Geological Survey Closed*] (SEIS)
BMO	Bond Molecular Orbitals
BMO	Book Marketing Opportunities Database [*Ad-Lib Publications*] [*Information service or system*] (CRD)
BMO	British Meteorological Office (MCD)
BMO	Brotherhood of Marine Officers (EA)
BMOC	Ballistic Missile Orientation Course
BMOC	Big Machine on Campus [*Computer*]
BMOC	Big Man on Campus [*Slang*]
BMOC	British Mail Order Corp. (DGA)
B-MOD	Behavior Modification [*Psychology*]
B-Mode	Brightness Modulation [*Ultrasound scanning*] [*Medicine*] (DAVI)
BMOI	Banque Malgache de l'Ocean Indien [*Indian Ocean Malagasy Bank*] [*Madagascar*] (EY)
BMOM	Base Maintenance and Operations Model
B Mon	Ben Monroe's Kentucky Supreme Court Reports [*A publication*] (DLA)
B Mon (KY)	Ben Monroe's Kentucky Reports [*A publication*] (DLA)
B Monr	Ben Monroe's Kentucky Reports [*A publication*] (DLA)
B Monr	Burrow's Reports Tempore Mansfield [*England*] [*A publication*] (DLA)
B Monr	Moore's Reports [*England*] [*A publication*] (DLA)
B Moore	Bayly Moore. English Common Pleas Reports [*A publication*] (DLA)
B-MOPP	Bleomycin, Mustargen, Oncovin [*Vincristine*], Procarbazine, Prednisone [*Antineoplastic drug regimen*]
BMOS	Back-Gate Metal-Oxide Semiconductor (IAA)
B/MOS	British Ministry of Supply (AAG)
BMOSFET	Back-Gate Metal-Oxide Semiconductor Field-Effect Transistor (IAA)
BMOTR	Ballistic Missile Operational Training Readiness
BMOV	Blackgram Mottle Virus [*Plant pathology*]
BMOW	Boatswain's Mate-of-the-Watch (DNAB)
BMP	Background Measurements Program (MCD)
BMP	Ballard Medical Prod [*NYSE symbol*] (TTSB)
BMP	Ballard Medical Products [*NYSE symbol*] (SPSG)

BMP............ BCNU [Carmustine], Methotrexate, Procarbazine [Antineoplastic drug regimen]
BMP............ Best Management Practice [Environmental Protection Agency]
BMP............ Binary Mobile Phase [Chromatography]
BMP............ Biomass Protein
BMP............ BIT [Binary Digit] Map [Computer science] (PCM)
bmp............ BitMap Image [Computer science]
BMP............ Bit-Mapped Graphics [Computer science]
BMP............ Blind-Made Products
BMP............ BMP Technologies Ltd. [Vancouver Stock Exchange symbol]
BMP............ Boevaya Mashina Pekhota [Infantry Fighting Vehicle] [Russian]
BMP............ Bone Marrow Pressure [Orthopedics and radiology] (DAVI)
BMP............ Bone Morphogenetic Protein
BMP............ Boron Metals Plant (SAA)
BMP............ Brake Mean Power
BMP............ Brampton Island [Australia Airport symbol] (OAG)
BMP............ Bricklayers, Masons, and Plasterers' International of America [Later, BAC]
BMP............ Bumped [Bookselling] (DGA)
BMP............ Bureau of Mines, Pittsburg (MCD)
BMP............ Burma Military Police [British military] (DMA)
BMP............ National Council of Building Material Producers [A union] [British]
BMPA.......... Broadband Microwave Power Amplifier
BMPAP .... Bone Marrow Prostatic Acid Phosphatase
BMPC.......... Bone Marrow Plasmacytosis [Oncology]
BMPCA .... British Metallurgical Plant Constructors Association (DBA)
BMPE .... Blimpie International, Inc. [NASDAQ symbol] (SAG)
BMPE.......... Blimpie Int'l [NASDAQ symbol] (TTSB)
BMPP.......... Benign Mucous Membrane Pemphigus [Dermatology] (DAVI)
BMPR .... Bimonthly Progress Report
BMPR .... Bumper [Automotive engineering]
BMPS.......... British Musicians' Pensions Society (BI)
BMQ............ Bamburi [Kenya] [Airport symbol Obsolete] (OAG)
BMQ............ Basic Mission Qualified [NASA]
BMQ............ Burnet, TX [Location identifier FAA] (FAAL)
BMQA.......... Board of Medical Quality Assurance (DAVI)
BMQT.......... Brigade Major of the Queen's Troops [British] (ROG)
BMQUE .... Bread Manufacturers of Queensland Union of Employers [Australia]
BMR............ Basal Metabolic Rate [Medicine]
BMR............ Baseline Monitoring Report [Environmental Protection Agency] (GFGA)
BMR............ Basic Metabolic Rate [Biochemistry] (DAVI)
BMR............ Basic Military Requirement
BMR............ Beachmaster
BMR............ Bearingless Main Rotor (RDA)
BMR............ Bihar Mounted Rifles [British military] (DMA)
BMR............ Bipolar Magnetic Region (OA)
BMR............ Body-Mounted Radiator (SSD)
BMR............ Bomber (AABC)
BMR............ Border Mounted Rifles [British military] (DMA)
BMR............ Boulder Mountain Resources [Vancouver Stock Exchange symbol]
BMR............ British Marine RADAR (IAA)
BMR............ Brookhaven Medical Reactor
BMR............ Bureau of Municipal Research [Canada] (IRC)
BMR............ River Monitor [Navy symbol] (DNAB)
BMRA .... Basic Multi-Role Avionics (PDAA)
BMRA .... Biomerica, Inc. [NASDAQ symbol] (NQ)
BMRA .... Brigade Major, Royal Artillery [British and Canadian]
BMRA .... British Medical Representatives Association (BI)
BMR & ECG... Basic Metabolism Rate and Electrocardiogram [Medicine]
BMRB .... British Market Research Bureau Ltd. [Information service or system] (IID)
BMRC .... British Medical Research Council
BMRC .... Brookhaven Medical Research Center
BMRC .... Bureau of Meteorology Research Center [Marine science] (OSRA)
BMRC .... Bureau of Meteorology Research Center (USDC)
BMRC .... Bureau of Meteorology Research Centre
BMRG .... British Micropalaeontological Research Group
BMRI .... Base Maintenance Removal Interval [Air Force] (AFIT)
BMRL.......... Small River Monitor [Navy symbol] (DNAB)
BMRM .... Maple Ridge Museum, British Columbia [Library symbol National Library of Canada] (NLC)
BMRMC ...... British Motor Racing Marshals Club (DBA)
BMRMO ...... Balance Mobilization Reserve Materiel Objective [Army] (AABC)
BMRP .... Pacific Vocational Institute, Maple Ridge, British Columbia [Library symbol Obsolete National Library of Canada] (NLC)
BMRQ .... BENCHMARQ Microelectronics [NASDAQ symbol] (TTSB)
BMRR .... Beech Mountain Railroad (MHDB)
BMRR .... Brookhaven Medical Research Reactor (NRCH)
BMRRT .... British Motor Racing Research Trust
BMRS .... Ballistic Missile Reentry System
BMRSYS ..... Ballistic Missile Reentry System (AABC)
BMRU .... Blind Mobility Research Unit [University of Nottingham] [British] (IRC)
BMS............ Bachelor of Marine Science
BMS............ Bachelor of Mechanical Science
BMS............ Bachelor of Medical Science
BMS............ Background Mapping Sensor
BMS............ Background Measurement Satellite (NASA)
BMS............ Ballistic Missile Ship [Navy]
BMS............ Ballistic Missile Specification (IAA)
BMS............ Baptist Mission Society
BMS............ Basic Mapping Support [Computer science]
BMS............ Basic Meteorological Services (FAAC)
BMS............ Battalion Maintenance Sergeant [Military] (INF)
BMS............ Battalion Mortar System [Army]

BMS............ Battlefield Management System [Military] (INF)
BMS............ Behavior Monitor System
BMS............ Below Minimum Standards [TV ratings]
BMS............ Bemis Co. [NYSE symbol] (TTSB)
BMS............ Bemis Co., Inc. [NYSE symbol] (SPSG)
BMS............ Berlin Mills [AAR code]
BMS............ Bill of Material System (MCD)
BMS............ Biomedical Monitoring System
BMS............ Biomedical Studies Section [Oak Ridge National Laboratory] (IID)
BMS............ Biowaste Monitoring System (MCD)
BMS............ BIT [Binary Digit] Manipulate Store
BMS............ BIT [Binary Digit] Mark Sequencing [Computer science] (IAA)
BMS............ Bleomycin Sulphate [Antineoplastic drug] (DAVI)
BMS............ Bloc des Masses Senegalaises [Bloc of the Senegalese Masses] (AF)
BMS............ Blow Molding System
BMS............ Boeing Materials Specification
BMS............ Bombardment Squadron [Air Force]
BMS............ Bomb Maintenance Spares
BMS............ Bondi-Metzner-Sachs [Physics]
BMS............ Borane Methyl Sulfide [Organic chemistry]
BMS............ Boron Management System [Nuclear energy] (NRCH)
BM(S)......... Boron Measurement (System) [Nuclear energy] (NRCH)
BMS............ Breathing Metabolic Simulator [IBM Corp.]
BMS............ Bristol-Myers Squibb's
BMS............ British Magical Society (DBA)
BMS............ British Malaysian Society (DBA)
BMS............ British Manufacture and Research
BMS............ British Meteor Society (EAIO)
BMS............ British Mexican Society (DBA)
BMS............ British Microcirculation Society (EAIO)
BMS............ British Ministry of Supply
BMS............ British Music Society
BMS............ British Mycological Society
BMS............ Brumado [Brazil] [Airport symbol] (OAG)
BMS............ Brunswick Mining & Smelting Corp. Ltd. [Toronto Stock Exchange symbol]
BMS............ Budget Management System
BMS............ Building Management System (ACII)
BMS............ Building Management Systems (NITA)
BMS............ Building Materials and Structures (SAA)
BMS............ Building Material Series [National Institute of Standards and Technology]
BMS............ Building Monitoring System (ADA)
BMS............ Bureau Militaire de Standardisation [Military Agency for Standardization] [NATO]
BMS............ Bureau of Medical Services [Public Health Service]
BMS............ Bureau of Medicine and Surgery [Later, Naval Medical Command] [Navy]
BMS............ Burst Measuring System
BMS............ Business Management System (BUR)
BMS............ Bypass Monochrome Signal
BMSA.......... British Medical Students Association (BI)
BMSA.......... Seaman Apprentice, Boatswain's, Mate, Striker [Navy rating]
BMSB.......... Bis(methylstyryl)benzene [Organic chemistry]
BM Sc .... Bachelor of Mechanical Science
BMSc.......... Bachelor of Medical Science, University of Dundee [British] (DBQ)
BMSC.......... Ballistic Missile Systems Command [Army] (RDA)
BMSC.......... Bone Marrow Stem Cell [Hematology]
BMSD .... Bendix Missile Systems Division (MCD)
BMSF.......... Ballistic Missile Surface Force
BMSGMA .... British Maize Starch and Glucose Manufacturers Association (BI)
BMSL.......... Boomsail [Ship's rigging] (ROG)
BMSM.......... British Merchant Shipping Mission
BMSM.......... British Military Supply Mission [World War II]
BMSN.......... Seaman, Boatswain's Mate, Striker [Navy rating]
BMSO .... Base Medical Supply Office [or Officer] [Air Force] (AFM)
BMSO .... Blue Mountain Seismological Observatory
BMSOA........ British Motor Ship Owners Association (DBA)
BMSP.......... Biomedical Sciences Program (DMAA)
BMSR .... Bench Model Solar Receiver (MCD)
BMSRC........ Boatswain's Mate, Ship Repair, Crane Operator [Navy rating]
BMSRDE...... British Ministry of Supply Research and Development Establishment
BMSRR .... Boatswain's Mate, Ship Repair, Rigger [Navy rating]
BMSRS .... Boatswain's Mate, Ship Repair, Canvasman [Navy rating]
BMSS.......... British Model Soldier Society
BMSS.......... Buoy Messenger
BMSS.......... Butterfly and Moth Stamp Society (EA)
B Ms Sc...... Bachelor of Mechanical Sciences
BMST.......... Bruce Maximum Stress Test [Medicine] (DMAA)
BMST.......... Business Management System Team [Air Force] (MCD)
BMSTR .... Bandmaster
BMSTRG ..... Beamsteering (MSA)
BMT............ Bachelor of Medical Technology
BMT............ Bailliere's Medical Transparencies [A publication] (DAVI)
BMT............ Basic Military Training
BMT............ Basic Motion-Time Study
BMT............ Battalion Maintenance Technician [Military] (INF)
BMT............ Beaumont, TX [Location identifier FAA] (FAAL)
BMT............ Before Morning Twilight (SAA)
BMT............ Beginning Morning Nautical Twilight [Navigation] (CINC)
BMT............ Beginning of Magnetic Tape [Computer science] (MDG)
BMT............ Bene Merenti [To the Well-Deserving] [Latin]
BMT............ Bet Midrash le Torah (BJA)
BMT............ Bibliography of Medical Translations [A publication]

BMT............ Bilateral Myringotomy Tubes [*Otorhinolaryngology*] (DAVI)
BMT............ Blackrock Ins Muni Term [*NYSE symbol*] (TTSB)
BMT............ Blackrock Insurance Municipal Term Trust [*NYSE symbol*] (SPSG)
BMT............ Bone Marrow Transplant [*Medicine*]
BMT............ Brisbane Market Trust [*Australia*]
BMT............ British Maritime Technology Ltd. [*Research center*] (IRC)
BMT............ British Mean Time (DAS)
BMT............ Brooklyn-Manhattan Transit Corp. [*A New York City subway line*]
BMT............ Buschke Memory Test [*Psychology*] (DAVI)
BM/TA......... Battlefield Mobility / Target Acquistion [*Military*]
BMTA......... Blue Mountains Tourism Authority [*Australia*]
BMTA......... British Measurement and Testing Association (ACII)
BMTA......... British Motor Trade Association (BI)
BMTC......... British Mass Transit Consultants [*Commercial firm*]
BMTC......... Bryn Mawr Bank [*NASDAQ symbol*] (TTSB)
BMTC......... Bryn Mawr Bank Corp. [*NASDAQ symbol*] (NQ)
BMTC......... Bureau of Meteorology Training Centre
BMTD......... Ballistic Missile Terminal Defense
BMTD......... Birlesmis Milletler Turk Dernegi [*United Nations Association of Turkey*] (EAIO)
BMTF......... Bench Mark Test Files (MCD)
BMTFA....... British Malleable Tube Fittings Association (BI)
BMTI......... Block Mode Terminal Interface [*Computer science*]
BMTLC....... Bimetallic
BMTN......... Boomtown, Inc. [*NASDAQ symbol*] (SAG)
BMTP......... Blagden Management Training Programme [*British*] (AIE)
BMTP......... Bureau of Mines Technical Paper
BMTR......... Bonded Motors [*NASDAQ symbol*] (TTSB)
BMTR......... Bonded Motors, Inc. [*NASDAQ symbol*] (SAG)
BMTS......... Ballistic Missile Target System (MCD)
BMTS......... Ballistic Missile Test System (IEEE)
BMTS......... Basic Military Training School
BMTS......... Basic Military Training Squadron [*Air Force*]
BMTS......... Bench Maintenance Test Set (SAA)
BMTS USAF... Basic Military Training School, United States Air Force
BMTT......... Buffered Magnetic Tape Transfer [*Computer science*] (NITA)
BMTT......... Buffered Magnetic Tape Transport [*Computer science*] (OA)
BMTU......... Bone Marrow Transplant Unit [*Hematology*] (DAVI)
BMTV......... Ballistic Missile Test Vessel
BMTV......... British Medical Television
B Mu.......... Bachelor of Music
BMU.......... Basic Metabolic Unit [*Medicine*] (DMAA)
BMU.......... Basic Multicellular Unit [*Medicine*] (DMAA)
BMU.......... Beach Master Unit [*Navy*]
BMU.......... Bermuda [*ANSI three-letter standard code*] (CNC)
BMU.......... Bima [*Indonesia*] [*Airport symbol*] (OAG)
BMU.......... Board for Mission and Unity [*Church of England*]
BMU.......... Bureau of Manpower Utilization [*World War II*]
BMU.......... Bus Monitor Unit (MCD)
BMU.......... University of Massachusetts, Boston, Boston, MA [*OCLC symbol*] (OCLC)
BMUG........ Berkeley Macintosh Users' Group (IID)
BmuHB....... Bermuda Library, Hamilton, Bermudas [*Library symbol Library of Congress*] (LCLS)
B Mus......... Bachelor of Music
B Mus......... Bachelor of Music (ODBW)
BMUS........ British Medical Ultrasound Society (EAIO)
BMusA....... Bachelor of Applied Music
B Mus E...... Bachelor of Music Education
BMusEd...... Bachelor of Music Education
BMusPerf..... Bachelor of Music (Performance)
B Mus (PSM)... Bachelor of Music in Public School Music
BMusT........ Bachelor of Music Teaching
BMV.......... Base Mount Valve
BMV.......... Basic Minute Value (PDAA)
BMV.......... Beata Maria Virgo [*Blessed Mary the Virgin*] [*Latin*]
BMV.......... Bistable Multivibrator
BMV.......... Blessed Mary the Virgin (DAS)
BMV.......... Bromegrass Mosaic Virus
BMVA........ British Machine Vision Association
BMVA........ Sorores Franciscanae Beatae Mariae Virginis Angelorum [*Franciscan Sisters of Our Lady of the Holy Angels*] [*Roman Catholic religious order*]
BMvD......... Bureau Marcel van Dijk, SA [*Information service or system*] (IID)
BMVP......... Barrier, Moisture Vapor Proof (MSA)
BMW.......... Bare Molybdenum Wire
BMW.......... Bayerische Motoren Werke [*Bavarian Motor Works*] [*German automobile manufacturer; initialism used as name of its cars and motorcycles*]
BMW.......... Beamwidth (MSA)
BMW.......... Beat Matsushita Whatsoever [*Facetious translation of BMW - Bavarian Motor Works, Originated by Sony Corp.*] (ECON)
BMW.......... Biomedical Waste
BMW.......... Boilermaker/Welder
BMW.......... Bombardment (Medium) Wing [*Air Force*]
BMW.......... Brain Missile Wound [*Medicine*]
BMW-ACA.... BMW [*Bavarian Motor Works*] Automobile Club of America (EA)
BMWAS...... Building and Monument Workers Association of Scotland [*A union*]
BMWCCA.... BMW [*Bavarian Motor Works*] Car Club of America (EA)
BMW-CCC.... BMW [*Bavarian Motor Works*] Car Club of Canada (EAIO)
BMWE........ Brotherhood of Maintenance of Way Employes (EA)
BMWI........ Biomedical Waste Incinerator [*or Incineration*]
BMWNA...... Bayerische Motoren Werke [*Bavarian Motor Works*] North America
BMWRA...... BMW [*Bavarian Motor Works*] Riders Association (EA)
BMWS........ Ballistic Missiles Weapon System

BMWT....... British Ministry of War Transport [*World War II*]
BMWVCA..... BMW [*Bavarian Motor Works*] Vintage Club of America (EA)
BMX.......... Banco de Mexico [*ICAO designator*] (FAAC)
BMX.......... Bicycle Motocross
BMXR........ Batch Mixer
BMXR........ Block Multiplexer [*Ground Communications Facility, NASA*]
BMY.......... Belep [*New Caledonia*] [*Airport symbol*] (OAG)
BMY.......... Black Marlin Energy [*Vancouver Stock Exchange symbol*]
BMY.......... Bristol Myers Squibb [*NYSE symbol*] (SAG)
BMY.......... Bristol-Myers Squibb [*NYSE symbol*] (TTSB)
BMY.......... Bristol-Myers Squibb Co. [*NYSE symbol*] (SPSG)
BMYPr........ Bris-Myr Squibb,$2 Cv Pfd [*NYSE symbol*] (TTSB)
BMYV........ Beet Mild Yellowing Virus [*Plant pathology*]
BMZ.......... Balance Magnetometric Zero (NOAA)
BMZ.......... Bamu [*Papua New Guinea*] [*Airport symbol*] (OAG)
BMZ.......... Basement Membrane Zones [*Anatomy*]
BN............ Bachelor of Nursing
BN............ Balancing Network
BN............ Ballistic Number (MCD)
BN............ Banco de la Nacion [*National Bank*] [*Peru*]
BN............ Banknote
BN............ Barisan Nasional [*Malaysia*] [*Political party*] (EY)
BN............ Barn
BN............ Baron
BN............ Barons Oil Ltd. [*Toronto Stock Exchange symbol*]
BN............ Bassoon [*Music*]
BN............ Battalion (AFM)
BN............ Bauxite & Northern Railway Co. [*Later, BXN*] [*AAR code*]
BN............ Beacon
BN............ Becklin-Neugebauer [*Astronomy*]
BN............ Been
Bn............ Benedictus de Isernia [*Flourished, 1221-52*] [*Authority cited in pre-1607 legal work*] (DSA)
BN............ Ben Naphtali (BJA)
BN............ Benzonitrile [*Organic chemistry*]
Bn............ Benzyl [*Organic chemistry*]
BN............ Beta-Naphthol [*Organic chemistry*]
BN............ Bet Nahrain (EA)
BN............ Beverage Network [*An association*] (EA)
BN............ Bicycle Network (EA)
BN............ Billion
BN............ Bills and Notes
BN............ Binary Number [*Computer science*]
BN............ Blind Navigation
BN............ Bloody Nuisance [*British slang*]
Bn............ Blue Nose Minnow [*Ichthyology*]
BN............ Bolt and Nut
BN............ Bombardier-Navigator (MUGU)
Bn............ Bombesin [*Biochemistry*]
B/N............ Bombing/Navigation (NG)
BN............ Bond Number [*Chemistry*]
BN............ Born (ADA)
BN............ Boron Nitride [*Inorganic fiber*]
BN............ Brachial Neuritis [*Medicine*] (MAE)
BN............ Branch on Nonzero
BN............ Braniff Airways, Inc. [*of Braniff International Corp.*] [*ICAO designator*] (OAG)
BN............ Brazilian Navy
BN............ Brigantine [*Ship*] (ROG)
BN............ Britten Norman (Bembridge) Ltd. [*British ICAO aircraft manufacturer identifier*] (ICAO)
BN............ Brown Norway [*Rat variety*]
B'n............ Bruedern [*Brethren*] [*Freemasonry*] [*German*]
BN............ Brunei Darussalam [*ANSI two-letter standard code*] (CNC)
BN............ Brussels Nomenclature [*Standard customs nomenclature published by the Customs Cooperation Council*]
BN............ Bulimia Nervosa [*Medicine*]
B/N............ Bulletin with Newsweek [*A publication*] (APTA)
BN............ Bull Nose
BN............ Bureau Number [*Database terminology*] (NITA)
BN............ Bureau of Narcotics [*Department of the Treasury*] [*Absorbed by BNDD of Department of Justice*]
BN............ Burlington Northern, Inc. [*AAR code*]
BN............ Burmese Navy (CINC)
BN............ But Not
B Na.......... Bachelor of Navigation
BNA........... Banca Nazionale dell'Agricoltura [*National Bank of Agriculture*] [*Italy*] (ECON)
BNA........... Banco de la Nacion Argentina [*National Bank of Argentina*]
BNA........... Banco Nacional de Angola [*National Bank of Angola*]
BNA........... Bangladesh News Agency
BNA........... Banque Nationale Agricole [*National Agricultural Bank*] [*Tunisia*] (AF)
BNA........... Baromedical Nurses Association (EA)
BNA........... Basle Nomina Anatomica [*Basel Anatomical Nomenclature*] [*Medicine*]
BNA........... Beta-Naphthylamine [*Organic chemistry*]
BNA........... Billing Name and Address
BNA........... Blackrock No Amer Gvt Inc. [*NYSE symbol*] (TTSB)
BNA........... Blackrock North American Government, Inc. [*NYSE symbol*] (SPSG)
B/NA......... Blackwell North America, Inc. [*Information service or system*] (IID)
BNA........... Blackwell North America, Inc. [*New Jersey*] [*ACCORD*] [*UTLAS symbol*]
BNAVCA..... Block Numbering Area [*Bureau of the Census*] (GFGA)
BNA........... Boeing Network Architecture [*Telecommunications*] (TSSD)
BNA........... Botswana National Airways

BNA .... Brazil Nut Association
BNA .... Brisbane Netball Association [*Australia*]
BNA .... British Naturalists' Association (BARN)
BNA .... British Naval Attache (NATG)
BNA .... British North America
BNA .... British North Atlantic (DS)
BNA .... British Nursing Association (BI)
BNA .... Bunia-Ruampara [*Zaire*] [*Geomagnetic observatory code*]
BNA .... Bureau of National Affairs (EA)
BNA .... Burma National Army [*Formerly, BDA*]
BNA .... Nakusp Public Library, British Columbia [*Library symbol National Library of Canada*] (NLC)
BNA .... Nashville [*Tennessee*] [*Derived from Berry Field-Nashville*] [*Airport symbol*]
BNAA .... British North American Act
BNAC .... British-North American Committee (EA)
BNAF .... Brazil Nut Advertising Fund [*Defunct*] (EA)
BNAF .... British North Africa Force
BNAF .... Business Name and Address File [*IRS*]
BNAKM .... Nakusp Museum, British Columbia [*Library symbol National Library of Canada*] (NLC)
BNAM .... Naramata Museum, British Columbia [*Library symbol National Library of Canada*] (NLC)
BNAO .... Basic Naval Aviation Officers School (DNAB)
BNAPM .... British National Association of Perry Makers
BNAPS .... British North America Philatelic Society (EA)
BN Arch ...... Bachelor of Naval Architecture
BNAS .... British Naval Air Service
BNAS .... British Naval Air Staff
BNASEES ..... British National Association for Soviet and East European Studies (PDAA)
BNASS .... Biennial National Atomic Spectroscopy Symposium
BNatRes ...... Bachelor of Natural Resources (ADA)
BNav .... Bachelor of Navigation (NADA)
BNB .... Banque Nationale de Belgique [*National Bank of Belgium*]
BNB .... Baton Broadcasting, Inc. [*Toronto Stock Exchange symbol*]
BNB .... Bikes Not Bombs (EA)
BNB .... Blue Nile Bank Ltd. [*Sudan*]
BNB .... Boende [*Zaire*] [*Airport symbol*] (OAG)
BNB .... Bracton's Note Book Tempore Henry III [*A publication*] (DLA)
BNB .... Brazilian News Briefs [*A publication*] (EAAP)
BNB .... British North Borneo
BNB .... Butylnitrosobenzene [*Organic chemistry*]
BNBC .... British National Book Centre
BNBC .... Broad National Bancorp [*NASDAQ symbol*] (NQ)
BNBC .... Broad Natl Bancorp [*NASDAQ symbol*] (TTSB)
BNBD .... Bovine Neutrophil Beta-Defensin [*Biochemistry*]
BNBE .... Bibliografia Extranjera Depositada en la Biblioteca Nacional [*Ministerio de Cultura*] [*Spain Information service or system*] (CRD)
BNBG .... Bull & Bear Group, Inc. [*NASDAQ symbol*] (NQ)
BNBGA .... Bull & Bear Group'A' [*NASDAQ symbol*] (TTSB)
BNBM .... British Nuclear Ballistic Missile
BNBRF .... British National Bibliography Research Fund
BNBSA .... British National Bibliographical Staff Association
BNC .... Baby "N" Connector (IEEE)
BNC .... Banque de Nouvelle - Caledonie (EY)
BNC .... Banque Nationale du Congo [*National Bank of the Congo*]
BNC .... Barcan Communications, Inc. [*Vancouver Stock Exchange symbol*]
BNC .... Base Neutralizing Capacity [*Chemistry*]
BNC .... Bayonet Coaxial Connector [*Telecommunications*] (ECII)
BNC .... Bayonet Naval Connector [*Electronics*] (NTCM)
BNC .... Bayonet Neil Councilman [*Telecommunications*] (ACRL)
BNC .... Bayonet Nut Coupling [*Telecommunications*] (EECA)
BNC .... Bayonette Connector, for Coaxial Cable [*Electronics*] (NITA)
BNC .... Benzoylated-Naphthoylated (DEAE)[*Diethylaminoethyl*]-Cellulose [*Analytical biochemistry*]
BNC .... Bethany Nazarene College [*Oklahoma*]
BNC .... Bibliotheque Nationale du Canada [*National Library of Canada - NLC*]
BNC .... Bingham. New Cases, English Common Pleas [*A publication*] (DLA)
BNC .... Bladder Neck Contracture [*Medicine*] (MAE)
BNC .... Blimped Noiseless Reflex Camera (NTCM)
BNC .... BNCCORP, Inc. [*Associated Press*] (SAG)
BNC .... Board of Navy Commissioners [*1815-1842*]
BNC .... Brand Name Contract (AABC)
BNC .... Brasenose College [*Oxford*]
BNC .... British National Committee on Surface Active Agents
BNC .... British Naval Connector (CDE)
BNC .... British Needlecrafts Council (DBA)
BNC .... Brooke's New Cases, English King's Bench [*1515-58*] [*A publication*] (DLA)
BNC .... Bulgarian National Committee (EA)
BNC .... Bulk Negative Conductance [*Electronics*] (IAA)
BNC .... Busbee's North Carolina Law Reports [*A publication*] (DLA)
BNC .... Sundance Air Operations, Inc. [*FAA designator*] (FAAC)
BNCA .... Buccaneer National Class Association (EA)
BNCA .... Bureau of National Capital Airports [*of FAA*]
BNCAR .... British National Committee on Antarctic Research
BncBil .... Banco Bilbao Vizcaya International [*Associated Press*] (SAG)
BncBI .... Banco Bilbao Vizcaya International [*Associated Press*] (SAG)
BNCC .... BNCCORP, Inc. [*NASDAQ symbol*] (SAG)
BNCC .... BUIC [*Backup Interceptor Control*] NOPAD Control Center
BncCtrl .... Banco Central Hispanoamericano SA [*Associated Press*]

BNCDST ...... British National Committee on Data for Science and Technology (DIT)
BNCE .... British National Committee for Electroheat (PDAA)
BNCF .... Biblioteca Nazionale Centrale, Florence [*Italy*]
BncfstOH ...... Bancfirst Ohio Corp. [*Associated Press*] (SAG)
BncFstOK ..... BancFirst Corp. Oklahoma [*Associated Press*] (SAG)
BncGalic ...... Banco de Galicia y Buenos Aires [*Commercial firm Associated Press*] (SAG)
BNCH .... Bench (MSA)
BNCHBD ...... Benchboard (KSC)
BNCI .... Banque Nationale pour le Commerce et l'Industrie [*National Bank for Commerce and Industry*] [*Togo*] [*French*]
BNC/ICC ..... British National Committee of the International Chamber of Commerce (DS)
BNCIEA .... British National Committee for International Engineering Affairs (PDAA)
BNCL .... Binnacle (MSA)
BNCLR .... Binocular (MSA)
BNCM .... British National Committee on Materials
BNCM .... Nanaimo Centennial Museum, British Columbia [*Library symbol National Library of Canada*] (NLC)
BNCNDT...... British National Committee for Non-Destructive Testing (ACII)
BNCO .... British Non-Commissioned Officer [*British military*] (DMA)
BNCOC........ Basic Noncommissioned Officer Course [*Army*] (INF)
BNCOD .... British National Conference on Databases (NITA)
BNCOE .... British National Committee on Ocean Engineering
BncoFrn ...... Banco Frances del Rio La Plata [*Associated Press*] (SAG)
BNCOQ .... Bachelor Noncommissioned Officers' Quarters [*Air Force*] (AFM)
BNCOR .... British National Committee on Research
BN-CP .... Battalion Command Post (DNAB)
Bncp CT ...... Bancorp Connecticut, Inc. [*Associated Press*] (SAG)
BnCPort ...... Banco Comercial Portugues SA [*Associated Press*] (SAG)
BncQuad ..... Banca Quadrum SA [*Associated Press*] (SAG)
BNCR .... Banque Nationale de Credit Rural [*Gabon*] (EY)
BNCRC .... Bethesda National Christian Resource Center (EA)
BNCS .... British National Carnation Society (BI)
BNCS .... British Numerical Control Society (MCD)
BNCSAA ..... British National Committee on Surface Active Agents (BI)
BNCSR .... British National Committee on Space Research
BNCT .... Boron Neutron Capture Therapy
BNCW .... Bare Nickel Chrome Wire
BND .... Bachelor of Nutrition and Dietetics
BND .... Banco Nacional de Desarrollo [*National Development Bank*] [*Argentina*]
BND .... Band (KSC)
BND .... Bandar Abbas [*Iran*] [*Airport symbol*] (OAG)
BND .... Bandung [*Indonesia*] [*Seismograph station code, US Geological Survey Closed*] (SEIS)
BND .... Bankers Tr6.125%CapSec [*AMEX symbol*] (TTSB)
BND .... Bankers Trust New York Corp. [*AMEX symbol*] (SPSG)
BND .... Bend
BND .... Benzoylated-Naphthoylated DEAE [*Diethylaminoethyl*]
bnd .... Binder [*MARC relator code*] [*Library of Congress*] (LCCP)
B/ND .... Binding/No Date [*Publishing*] (DGA)
BND .... Bond (ROG)
BND .... Bonded (MSA)
BND .... Bond Helicopters Ltd. [*British ICAO designator*] (FAAC)
Bnd .... Bonus Delivery [*Shares*]
BND .... Brenda Mines Ltd. [*Toronto Stock Exchange symbol Vancouver Stock Exchange symbol*]
BND .... Bundesnachrichtendienst [*Federal Intelligence Service*] [*Germany*]
BNDA .... Banque Nationale pour le Developpement Agricole [*National Agricultural Development Bank*] [*Ivory Coast*] (AF)
BNDB .... Banque Nationale de Devellopement du Burkina (EY)
BNDC .... Banque Nationale de Developpement du Congo [*National Development Bank of the Congo*] (AF)
BNDC .... British Nuclear Design and Construction
BNDC .... Bulk Negative Differential Conductivity [*Electronics*] (IAA)
BNDD .... Bureau of Narcotics and Dangerous Drugs [*Formerly, Bureau of Narcotics and Bureau of Drug Abuse Control; later, Drug Enforcement Administration*] [*Department of Justice*]
BNDDIS........ Band Display
BNDE .... Banco Nacional do Desenvolvimento Economico [*National Economic Development Bank*] [*Brazil*]
BNDE .... Banque Nationale de Developpement Economique [*National Economic Development Bank*] [*France*] (AF)
BNDE .... Banque Nationale pour le Developpement Economique [*National Bank for Economic Development*] [*Morocco*] (IMH)
BNDG .... Bonding
BNDHV........ Banque Nationale de Developpement de la Haute-Volta [*National Development Bank of Upper Volta*] (AF)
BNDL .... Bundle
BNDO .... Bureau National des Donnees Oceaniques [*National Bureau for Ocean Data*] [*European host database system*] [*France*] [*Information service or system*] (IID)
BNDP .... Bet-Nahrain Democratic Party [*Political party*] (BJA)
BNDP .... Brunei National Democratic Party [*Political party*] (FEA)
Bndr........... Bandmaster [*Military British*] (DMA)
BNDR.......... Binder
bndr........... Binder (VRA)
BNDRY........ Boundary (AFM)
BNDS .... Silvery Slocan Historical Museum, New Denver, British Columbia [*Library symbol National Library of Canada*] (NLC)
BNDSMN...... Bondsman
BNDY.......... Boundary (DNAB)

BNDZ .... Bonderize
BNE .... Bachelor of Naval Engineering
Bne .... Bartone [*Record label*]
BNE .... Bathymetric Navigation Equipment
BNE .... Board of National Estimates [*Terminated*] [*CIA*]
BNE .... Board of Nurse Examiners
BNE .... Bowne & Co. [*AMEX symbol*] (TTSB)
BNE .... Bowne & Co., Inc. [*AMEX symbol*] (SPSG)
BNE .... Brisbane [*Australia Airport symbol*] (OAG)
BNE .... Burnie High School [*Tasmania*] [*Seismograph station code, US Geological Survey*] (SEIS)
BNE .... But Not Exceeding
BNE .... Nelson Public Library, British Columbia [*Library symbol National Library of Canada*] (BIB)
BNE .... Richmond, VA [*Location identifier FAA*] (FAAL)
BNEA .... British Naval Equipment Association (PDAA)
BNEC .... British National Export Council
BNEC .... British Nuclear Energy Conference
BN Ed .... Bachelor of Nursing Education
BNEG .... B negative [*Blood type*] (DAVI)
BNEM .... Nelson Museum, British Columbia [*Library symbol National Library of Canada*] (NLC)
BNEMRL ...... Battelle New England Marine Research Laboratory [*Battelle Memorial Institute*] [*Research center*] (RCD)
BN Eng .... Bachelor of Naval Engineering
BNEP .... Basic Naval Establishment Plan
BNES .... British Nuclear Energy Society
BNESAA .... Bureau of Near Eastern and South Asian Affairs [*Department of State*]
BNET .... Bay Networks, Inc. [*NASDAQ symbol*] (SAG)
BNF .... Backus Naur [*or Normal*] Form [*ALGOL*] [*Computer science*] (BUR)
BNF .... Baranof, AK [*Location identifier FAA*] (FAAL)
BNF .... Belarusky Narodny Front [*Belarussian Popular Front*] [*Political party*] (EY)
BNF .... Best Noise Figure (IAA)
BNF .... Beta-Naphthoflavone [*Organic chemistry*]
BNF .... Big Name Fan [*of science fiction or fantastic literature*] [*See also LNF*]
BNF .... Biological Nitrogen Fixation [*Agriculture*]
BNF .... Bomb Nose Fuze
BNF .... Boolean Normal Form [*Mathematics*]
BNF .... Boron Nitride Fiber [*Inorganic fiber*]
BNF .... Botswana National Front [*Political party*] (PPW)
BNF .... Brand Names Foundation (EA)
BNF .... Braniff International Corp. [*ICAO designator*]
BNF .... British National Formulary [*A publication*]
BNF .... British Non-Ferrous Metals Abstracts [*BNF Metals Technology Centre*] [*Information service or system*] (CRD)
BNF .... British Nuclear Forum
BNF .... British Nuclear Fuels Ltd.
BNF .... British Nutrition Foundation
BNF .... Bulgarian National Front (EA)
BNFA .... British Narrow Fabrics Association (DBA)
BNF ABS .... British Non-Ferrous Abstracts [*A database*] [*British Non-Ferrous Metals Technology Centre*] (NITA)
BNFC .... Benefice
BNFC .... British National Film Catalogue (DIT)
BNFCL .... Beneficial
BNFEX .... Battalion Field Exercise [*Military*] (NVT)
BNFL .... British Nuclear Fuels Ltd.
BNFMF .... British Non-Ferrous Metals Federation (BI)
BNFMRA ..... British Non-Ferrous Metals Research Association
BNFMS .... British Bureau of Non-Ferrous Metal Statistics (BI)
BNFMTC ..... British Non-Ferrous Metals Technology Centre (EAIO)
BNFP .... Barnwell Nuclear Fuel Plant (NRCH)
BNFT .... Benefit
bnfts .... Benefits (BARN)
BNG .... Bangui [*Central African Republic*] [*Seismograph station code, US Geological Survey*] (SEIS)
BNG .... Banning, CA [*Location identifier FAA*] (FAAL)
BNG .... Bending (MSA)
BNG .... Benetton Group ADS [*NYSE symbol*] (TTSB)
BNG .... Benetton Group SpA [*NYSE symbol*] (SPSG)
BNG .... Bingo
BNG .... Bloque Nacionalista Galego [*Galician Nationalist Block*] [*Spain Political party*] (EY)
BNG .... Branch No Group [*Computer science*] (MDG)
BNG .... British New Guinea (ADA)
BNG .... Broadland Noise Generator
BNG .... Bromo-Naphthyl-Beta-Galactoside (MAE)
BNG .... Bureau of Natural Gas [*of FPC*]
BNG .... State University of New York at Binghamton, Binghamton, NY [*OCLC symbol*] (OCLC)
BNGA .... British Nursery Goods Association (BI)
BNGase .... Bromo-Naphthyl-Beta-Galactosidase [*An enzyme*] (MAE)
BNGL .... Bangladesh (WDAA)
BNGM .... British Naval Gunnery Mission [*British military*] (DMA)
BNGO .... AMER BINGO & GAMING [*NASDAQ symbol*] (TTSB)
BNGO .... American Bingo & Gambing Corp. [*NASDAQ symbol*] (SAG)
BNGOW .... Amer Bingo & Gaming Wrrt [*NASDAQ symbol*] (TTSB)
BNGS .... Bomb Navigation Guidance System
BNH .... Berlin [*New Hampshire*] [*Seismograph station code, US Geological Survey*] (SEIS)
BNH .... BNH Bancshares, Inc. [*Associated Press*] (SAG)
BNH .... Brenham, TX [*Location identifier FAA*] (FAAL)

BNH .... Bunker Hill Mining [*Vancouver Stock Exchange symbol*]
BNH .... Burnish (KSC)
BNHB .... BNH Bancshares [*NASDAQ symbol*] (TTSB)
BNHB .... BNH Bancshares, Inc. [*NASDAQ symbol*] (NQ)
BNHC .... Bank of New Hampshire Corp. [*NASDAQ symbol*] (NQ)
BNHN .... Benihana Inc. [*NASDAQ symbol*] (TTSB)
BNHN .... Benihana National Corp. [*NASDAQ symbol*] (NQ)
BNHNA .... Benihana Inc.'A' [*NASDAQ symbol*] (TTSB)
BNHQ .... Battalion Headquarters [*Marine Corps*]
BNHS .... British Natural Hygiene Society
BNHSC .... Boston National Historic Sites Commission [*Government agency, discontinued, 1960*]
BNI .... Alberni Airway [*Canada ICAO designator*] (FAAC)
BNI .... Bechtel National, Inc. (GAAI)
BNI .... Bengal Native Infantry [*Military British*]
BNI .... Benin City [*Nigeria*] [*Airport symbol*] (OAG)
BNI .... Borkin Industries Corp. [*Vancouver Stock Exchange symbol*]
BNI .... Burlington Northern, Inc. [*NYSE symbol*] (SPSG)
BNI .... Burlington Northern Santa Fe [*NYSE symbol*] (TTSB)
BNIG .... Boron Nitride Image Guide (PDAA)
BNIO .... British National Institute of Oceanography
BNIP .... Bridge Needs and Investment Process [*FHWA*] (TAG)
BNIST .... Bureau National de l'Information Scientifique et Technique [*National Scientific and Technical Information Bureau*] [*France Information service or system*] (IID)
BNITA .... British Nautical Instrument Trade Association (DBA)
BNJ .... Bonn [*Germany Airport symbol*] (OAG)
BNJIQ .... Blackrock New Jersey Investment Quality Municipal Trust [*Associated Press*] (SAG)
BNK .... Ballina [*Australia Airport symbol*]
BNK .... Bank (ROG)
BNK .... CNB Bancshares [*NYSE symbol*] (TTSB)
BNK .... CNB Bancshares, Inc. [*NYSE symbol*] (SAG)
BnkAtla .... BankAtlantic Bancorp, Inc. [*Associated Press*] (SAG)
BNKF .... Bankers First Corp. [*NASDAQ symbol*] (NQ)
BnkFst .... Bankers First Corp. [*Associated Press*] (SAG)
BNKG .... Banking (ADA)
BnkLA .... Bank of Los Angeles [*Associated Press*] (SAG)
BNKM .... Marine Bank [*Board on Geographic Names*]
BNKNG .... Banking
BnkNH .... Bank of New Hampshire Corp. [*Associated Press*] (SAG)
BnkPlus ...... Bank Plus Corp. [*Associated Press*] (SAG)
BNKR .... Banker
BnkrN .... Banker's Note [*Associated Press*] (SAG)
BnkT .... Bankers Trust New York Corp. [*Associated Press*] (SAG)
BNKU .... Bank United Corp. [*NASDAQ symbol*] (SAG)
BnkUntd ...... Bank United Corp. [*Associated Press*] (SAG)
BnkUt .... BankUnited Financial Corp. [*Associated Press*] (SAG)
BnkUtd .... BankUnited Financial Corp. [*Associated Press*] (SAG)
BNL .... Background Noise Level (CAAL)
BNL .... Banca Nazionale del Lavoro [*National Bank of Labor*] [*Italy*] (ECON)
BNL .... Barnwell, SC [*Location identifier FAA*] (FAAL)
BNL .... Battelle Northwest Laboratories
BNL .... Beneficial Corp. [*NYSE symbol*] (SAG)
BNL .... Benthic Nepheloid Layer [*Oceanography*]
BNL .... Berkeley Nuclear Laboratories [*England*]
BNL .... Breast Needle Location [*Radiology*] (DAVI)
BNL .... Broadcast News Ltd. (NTCM)
BNL .... Brookhaven National Laboratory [*Department of Energy*] [*Upton, NY*]
BNLO .... British Naval Liaison Officer
BNLPrA .... Beneficial Corp.,$4.50 Pfd [*NYSE symbol*] (TTSB)
BNLPrB .... Beneficial Corp.,$4.30 Pfd [*NYSE symbol*] (TTSB)
BNLPrC .... Beneficial Corp.,$5.50 Cv Pfd [*NYSE symbol*] (TTSB)
BNLPrV .... Beneficial Corp.,5% Pfd [*NYSE symbol*] (TTSB)
BNLUS .... British Naval Liaison [*Office*] US Navy [*London*]
BNM .... Banque Nationale de Mauritanie (EY)
BNM .... Banque Nationale Malgache de Developpement [*Malagasy National Development Bank*] (AF)
BNM .... Before New Moon [*Freemasonry*] (ROG)
BNM .... Board of National Ministries (EA)
BNM .... Bodinumu [*Papua New Guinea*] [*Airport symbol*] (OAG)
BNM .... Malaspina College, Nanaimo, British Columbia [*Library symbol National Library of Canada*] (NLC)
BNMA .... British Nonwovens Manufacturers Association (DBA)
BNMBL .... MacMillan Bloedel Ltd., Nanaimo, British Columbia [*Library symbol National Library of Canada*] (NLC)
BNML .... Bitter National Magnet Laboratory
BNML .... Burlington Northern (Manitoba) Limited [*AAR code*]
BNMRA .... British Non-Ferrous Metals Research Association
BNMS .... Bus Neutral Mass Spectrometer [*Space science instrumentation*]
BNMSE .... Brief Neuropsychological Mental Status Examination
BNN .... Banner Entertainment [*Vancouver Stock Exchange symbol*]
BNN .... Blackrock 1999 Term Tr [*NYSE symbol*] (TTSB)
BNN .... Blackrock 1999 Term Trust [*NYSE symbol*] (SAG)
BNN .... Bronnoysund [*Norway*] [*Airport symbol*] (OAG)
BNND .... Learning Resources Centre, David Thompson Library, Nelson, British Columbia [*Library symbol National Library of Canada*] (BIB)
BNNT .... Barnes' Notes on the New Testament [*A publication*]
BN Nursing Studies... Bachelor of Nursing, Nursing Studies, University of Southampton [*British*] (DBQ)
BNO .... Backus Normal [*or Naur*] Form [*ALGOL*] [*Computer science*]
BNO .... Barrels of New Oil (MHDB)
BNO .... Bipartite News Office [*Post-World War II, Germany*]
BNO .... Bladder Neck Obstruction [*Medicine*]
BNO .... Bowels Not Open [*Medicine*]

BNO .... Burns, OR [*Location identifier FAA*] (FAAL)
BNOA .... Beta-Naphthoxyacetic Acid [*Plant growth compound*]
BNOA .... British Naturopathic and Osteopathic Association
BNOC .... Basic Noncommissioned Officer Course [*Army*]
BNOC .... British National Oil Corp. [*Pronounced "bee-knock"*] [*Nationalized industry*] [*British*]
BNOC .... British National Opera Company
BNOM .... Background Natural Organic Matter [*Environmental chemistry*]
BNOS .... Broadband Network Operating System
BNOV .... But Not Over
BNP .... Background Noise Power
BNP .... Bangladesh Nationalist Party [*Political party*]
BNP .... Bangladesh National Party [*Bangladesh Jatiyabadi Dal*] (PPW)
BNP .... Bannu [*Pakistan*] [*Airport symbol*] (OAG)
BNP .... Banque Nationale de Paris [*National Bank of Paris*] [*France*]
BNP .... Basotho National Party [*Lesotho*] [*Political party*] (PPW)
BNP .... Bellefonte Nuclear Plant (NRCH)
BNP .... Boddie-Noell Properties [*AMEX symbol*] (TTSB)
BNP .... Boddie-Noell Properties, Inc. [*AMEX symbol*] (SPSG)
BNP .... Brain Natriuretic Peptide [*Biochemistry*]
BNP .... British National Party (PPW)
BNP .... Buller's Law of Nisi Prius [*England*] [*A publication*] (DLA)
BNP .... Bureau of Naval Personnel [*Also, BUPERS, NAVPERS*]
BNP .... Pacific Biological Station, Fisheries and Oceans Canada [*Station Biologique du Pacifique, Peches et Oceans Canada*] Nanaimo, British Columbia [*Library symbol National Library of Canada*] (NLC)
BNPA .... Beta-Nitropropionic Acid [*Organic chemistry*]
BNPA .... Binasal Pharyngeal Airway [*Anatomy*] (MAE)
BNPC .... Botswana National Productivity Centre
BNPCL .... Bureau of Naval Personnel Circular Letters
BNPE .... Bis(nitrophenyl)ethyl [*Organic radical*]
BNPEOC ...... Bis(nitrophenyl)ethyloxycarbonyl [*Organic radical*]
BNPF .... Beginning, Negative, Positive, Finish [*ASCII subset*]
BNPG-PSG ... Bloque Nacional Popular de Galicia - Partido Socialista Gallego [*Popular National Bloc of Galicia - Galician Socialist Party*] [*Political party*] (PPW)
BNPM .... Bureau of Naval Personnel Manual
BNPP .... Barisan Nasional Penbebasan Pattani [*Thailand*] [*Political party*]
BNQ .... Bibliotheque Nationale du Quebec [*UTLAS symbol*]
BNR .... Bell Northern Research [*Telecommunications*] (TEL)
BNR .... Billed but Not Received (AFIT)
BNR .... Bladder Neck Resection [*Medicine*]
BNR .... Bladder Neck Retraction [*Urology*] (DAVI)
BNR .... Bonair Aviation Ltd. [*Canada ICAO designator*] (FAAC)
BNR .... Bond Negative Resistor
BNR .... Botswana Notes and Records [*A publication*]
BNR .... Brand Name Resale (AABC)
BNR .... Brassey's Naval Record [*Brassey's Defence Publishers Ltd.*] [*No longer maintained*] [*Information service or system*] (IID)
BNR .... Broulan Resources, Inc. [*Toronto Stock Exchange symbol*]
BNR .... Burner (MSA)
BNR .... Findlay, OH [*Location identifier FAA*] (FAAL)
BNRC .... Bulletin of the National Research Council [*A publication*] (BARN)
BNRID .... Basic Net Radio Interface Device (MCD)
BNRMAS...... Bolt, Nut, and Rivet Makers Association of Scotland [*A union*]
BNRVR........ Bengal-Nagpore Railway Volunteer Rifles [*British military*] (DMA)
BNRY .... Bonray Drilling [*NASDAQ symbol*] (TTSB)
BNRY .... Bonray Drilling Corp. [*NASDAQ symbol*] (NQ)
BNS .... Bachelor of Natural Science (BARN)
BNS .... Bachelor of Natural Science
BNS .... Bachelor of Nursing Science
BNS .... Balanced Nutrient Solution
BNS .... Bangong-Nujiang Suture [*Paleogeography*]
BNS .... Bank of Nova Scotia [*Toronto Stock Exchange symbol Vancouver Stock Exchange symbol*]
BNS .... Barinas [*Venezuela*] [*Airport symbol*] (OAG)
BNS .... Bell Number Screening [*Telecommunications*] (TEL)
BNS .... Benign Nephrosclerosis [*Medicine*] (MAE)
BNS .... Bensberg [*Federal Republic of Germany*] [*Seismograph station code, US Geological Survey*] (SEIS)
BNS .... Biblical Numismatic Society [*Defunct*] (EA)
BNS .... Binary Number System [*Computer science*]
BNS .... Biological Nuclear Solvent [*Physiology*]
BNS .... Board of Nursing Studies [*Queensland, Australia*]
BNS .... Bombing-Navigation System (AFM)
BNS .... Bonus (ADA)
BNS .... Boston Naval Shipyard
BNS .... British Naval Staff
BNS .... British Neuropathological Society
BNS .... British Numismatic Society
BNS .... Broadband Network Service [*Telecommunications*] (ACRL)
BNS .... Broadcasters Nonprofit Satellite Service [*Ford Foundation*]
BNS .... Broadcast News Service (NTCM)
BNS .... Brown & Sharpe Manufacturing Co. [*NYSE symbol*] (SPSG)
BNS .... Brown & Sharpe Mfg'A' [*NYSE symbol*] (TTSB)
BNS .... Bureau of Naval Ships [*Obsolete*] (MCD)
BNS .... Sheridan, WY [*Location identifier FAA*] (FAAL)
BNSA .... Background Noise Suppression Amplifier (DICI)
BNSA .... Baha'i National Spiritual Assembly [*Australia*]
BnSant........ Banco de Santander Sociedad Anonima de Credito [*Associated Press*]
BN Sc .... Bachelor of Nursing Science
BNSC .... Bank of Santa Clara [*NASDAQ symbol*] (SAG)
BNSC .... British National Space Centre

BNSF .... Burlington Northern Santa Fe Corp. [*Associated Press*] (SAG)
BNSFCP ...... Battalion Shore Fire Control Party
BNSH .... Burnish (MSA)
BNSIFCO...... Brian Nolan Spradlin International Fan Club Organization (EA)
BNSIG .... Behavioral Neuropsychology Special Interest Group (EA)
BNSO .... Bonso Electronics International, Inc. [*NASDAQ symbol*] (NQ)
BNSOF .... Bonso Electronics Intl. [*NASDAQ symbol*] (TTSB)
BNSP .... Basic National Security Police (MCD)
BNSS .... Baroness (ROG)
BNST .... Bed Nucleus of the Stria Terminalis [*Brain anatomy*]
BNSV .... Vocational Division, Selkirk College, Nelson, British Columbia [*Library symbol National Library of Canada*] (NLC)
BNSW .... Bonso Electronics International, Inc. [*NASDAQ symbol*] (SAG)
BNSWF .... Bonso Electrs Intl. Wrrt [*NASDAQ symbol*] (TTSB)
BNSY .... Boston Naval Shipyard
BNT............ Banco Nacional de Trabajadores [*Paraguay*] (EY)
BNT............ Bank of Alberta [*Toronto Stock Exchange symbol*]
BNT............ Basketball Northern Territory [*Australia An association*]
BNT............ Bennington College, Bennington, VT [*OCLC symbol*] (OCLC)
BNT............ Bent
BNT............ Bentley Pharmaceutical [*AMEX symbol*] (SAG)
BNT............ Bentley Pharmaceuticals [*AMEX symbol*] (TTSB)
BNT............ Bonnet (MSA)
BNT............ Boreal Northern Titles [*Database*] [*Boreal Institute for Northern Studies*] [*Information service or system*] (CRD)
BNT............ Boston Naming Test [*Analysis of lexical processing disorders*]
BNT............ Broadband Network Termination [*Telecommunications*]
BNT............ Brussels Tariff Nomenclature (ILCA)
BNT............ Bundi [*Papua New Guinea*] [*Airport symbol*] (OAG)
BNT............ Burnt (ROG)
BNT............ Salt Lake City, UT [*Location identifier FAA*] (FAAL)
BNTA .... Banta Corp. [*NASDAQ symbol*] (NQ)
BNTA .... Brisbane Night Tennis Association [*Australia*]
BNTA .... British Numismatic Trade Association
BNTF .... Battalion Task Force (MCD)
BNTH .... Beneath (FAAC)
BNTN .... Benton Oil & Gas [*NASDAQ symbol*] (TTSB)
BNTN .... Benton Oil & Gas Co. [*NASDAQ symbol*] (SAG)
BNTNW .... Benton Oil & Gas Wrrt [*NASDAQ symbol*] (TTSB)
BNTO .... Bonding Tool (AAG)
BntOG .... Benton Oil & Gas Co. [*Associated Press*] (SAG)
BNTT .... Barnett, Inc. [*NASDAQ symbol*] (SAG)
BNTT .... Barnett Inc. [*NASDAQ symbol*] (TTSB)
BNTVA .... British Nuclear Test Veterans Association (DBA)
bntwd.......... Bentwood (VRA)
BNU .... Basic Networking Utilities
BNU .... Basic Notch Unit
BNU .... Benson Needham Univas [*International advertising network*]
BNUP .... Brunei National United Party [*Political party*] (EY)
BNurs.......... Bachelor of Nursing, University of Manchester [*British*] (DBQ)
BNursing...... Bachelor of Nursing
BNV .... Benevento [*Italy*] [*Seismograph station code, US Geological Survey Closed*] (SEIS)
BNV .... North Vancouver City Library, British Columbia [*Library symbol National Library of Canada*] (NLC)
BNVBR........ Ballard Research, Inc., North Vancouver, British Columbia [*Library symbol National Library of Canada*] (NLC)
BNVD .... District of North Vancouver Library, British Columbia [*Library symbol National Library of Canada*] (NLC)
BNVHRTVG... Bedside Network of the Veterans Hospital Radio and TV Guild [*Later, VBN*] (EA)
BNVI .... Vancouver Island Regional Library, Nanaimo, British Columbia [*Library symbol National Library of Canada*] (NLC)
BNVIC .... Insurance Corp. of British Columbia, North Vancouver [*Library symbol National Library of Canada*] (BIB)
BNVLNT .... Benevolent
BNVPM .... Pacific Marine Training Institute, North Vancouver, British Columbia [*Library symbol National Library of Canada*] (NLC)
BNVSL .... Special Libraries Cataloguing, Inc., North Vancouver, British Columbia [*Library symbol National Library of Canada*] (NLC)
BNVTW .... Western Regional Library, Transport Canada [*Bibliotheque Regionale de l'Ouest, Transports Canada*], North Vancouver, British Columbia [*Library symbol National Library of Canada*] (NLC)
BNW .... Barnwell Industries, Inc. [*Toronto Stock Exchange symbol*]
BNW .... Battlefield Nuclear Warfare [*Army*]
BNW .... Blackwell North America, Inc. [*Oregon*] [*ACCORD*] [*UTLAS symbol*]
BNW .... Boone, IA [*Location identifier FAA*] (FAAL)
BNW .... Bureau of Naval Weapons [*Obsolete*]
BNW .... New Westminster Public Library, British Columbia [*Library symbol National Library of Canada*] (NLC)
BNWAG........ Agricultural Development Branch, Agriculture Canada [*Direction Generale du Developpement Agricole, Agriculture Canada*], New Westminster, British Columbia [*Library symbol National Library of Canada Obsolete*] (BIB)
BNWB .... British Columbian, New Westminster, British Columbia [*Library symbol National Library of Canada*] (NLC)
BNWCR........ CanOcean Resources Ltd., New Westminster, British Columbia [*Library symbol National Library of Canada*] (NLC)
BNWD .... Douglas College, New Westminster, British Columbia [*Library symbol National Library of Canada*] (NLC)
BNWHC........ New Westminster Historic Centre and Museum, British Columbia [*Library symbol National Library of Canada*] (NLC)
BNWL .... Battelle Northwest Laboratories (KSC)
BNWL .... British Nuclear Waste Ltd. (NUCP)

BNWL .... Lower Mainland Regional Planning Board, New Westminster, British Columbia [*Library symbol National Library of Canada*] (NLC)
BNWLH .... Canadian Lacrosse Hall of Fame, New Westminster, British Columbia [*Library symbol National Library of Canada*] (NLC)
BNWLP .... Lockheed Petroleum Services Ltd., New Westminster, British Columbia [*Library symbol National Library of Canada*] (NLC)
BNWRC .... Royal Columbian Hospital, New Westminster, British Columbia [*Library symbol National Library of Canada*] (NLC)
BNWSP .... Stuart Plastics Ltd., New Westminster, British Columbia [*Library symbol National Library of Canada*] (NLC)
BNX .... Brenair Ltd. [*British ICAO designator*] (FAAC)
BNX .... British Nuclear Export Executives [*Group to promote export of nuclear power stations of British design*]
BNX .... Falmouth, MA [*Location identifier FAA*] (FAAL)
BNX .... Welsh Dragon Aviation Ltd. [*British*] [*FAA designator*] (FAAC)
BNY .... Bellona Island [*Solomon Islands*] [*Airport symbol*] (OAG)
BNY .... Binghamton [*New York*] [*Seismograph station code, US Geological Survey*] (SEIS)
BNY .... Burney, CA [*Location identifier FAA*] (FAAL)
BNYD .... Boston Navy Yard [*Later, Boston Naval Shipyard*]
BNYD .... Bureau of Navy Yards and Docks [*Later, NFEC*]
BNYIQ .... Blackrock New York Investment Quality Municipal Trust [*Associated Press*] (SAG)
BNYN .... Banyan Systems [*NASDAQ symbol*] (TTSB)
BNYN .... Banyan Systems, Inc. [*NASDAQ symbol*] (SAG)
BNYV .... Broccoli Necrotic Yellows Virus [*Plant pathology*]
BNYVV .... Beet Necrotic Yellow Vein Virus
BNZ .... BANZ [*British-Australian-New Zealand*] [*Papua New Guinea*] [*Airport symbol*] [*Obsolete*] (OAG)
BNZ .... Bonanza Resources Ltd. [*Toronto Stock Exchange symbol*]
BNZS .... Bipolar with N Zeros Substitution [*Electronics*] (NITA)
BNZS .... Bulgarski Naroden Zemedelski Suiuz [*Bulgarian National Agrarian Union*] (PPE)
B-NZTC .... British New Zealand Trade Council, Inc. (DBA)
BO .... Bachelor of Oratory
BO .... Bachelor of Osteopathy
BO .... Back Order
BO .... Bad Order [*i.e., requiring repair*]
BO .... Bail Out
BO .... Banker's Order
BO .... Barkhausen-Kurz Oscillator
BO .... Base Order
BO .... Base-Out (Prism) [*Ophthalmology*]
BO .... Basioccipital [*Anatomy*]
BO .... Battalion Orders [*British military*] (DMA)
BO .... Beat Oscillator
BO .... Behavioral Objective
BO .... Bench Order
BO .... Beneficial Occupancy
BO .... Benzoyloxime [*Organic chemistry*]
BO .... Best Offer [*Classified advertising*]
BO .... Bibbia e Oriente [*A publication*] (BJA)
BO .... Binary to Octal [*Computer science*] (BUR)
BO .... Bingo Clubs and Halls [*Public-performance tariff class*] [*British*]
BO .... Biological Origin
BO .... Blackout
BO .... Blanking Oscillator (MCD)
BO .... Blockhouse Operation [*NASA*]
BO .... Blocking Oscillator
BO .... Blockout
BO .... Blowoff
BO .... Blowout (IAA)
BO .... Board of Ordnance
BO .... Board's Order [*British*] (ROG)
BO .... Bob Oscar Plenty [*Character in "Dick Tracy" comic strip*]
Bo .... Bodenstein Number
BO .... Body Odor [*Slang*]
Bo .... Boghazkoi-Sammlung des Berliner Museum (BJA)
Bo .... Boghazkoy [*Museum of the Ancient Orient, Istanbul*] (BJA)
Bo .... Bohemium [*Chemical element*] (MAE)
BO .... Boiled [*Linseed*] Oil
BO .... Boiler Manufacturer (DS)
B-O .... Boil-Off
BO .... Bolivia [*ANSI two-letter standard code*] (CNC)
bo .... Bolivia [*MARC country of publication code Library of Congress*] (LCCP)
BO .... Bolt
BO .... Bolton [*Craniometric point*]
Bo .... Bonaguida de Aretio [*Flourished, 1251-58*] [*Authority cited in pre-1607 legal work*] (DSA)
BO .... Bonding
Bo .... Bond Number
BO .... Booking Office [*British*] (ROG)
BO .... Book Order
B/O .... Booster Orbiter (MCD)
BO .... Born
BO .... Born-Oppenheimer Method [*Physical chemistry*]
BO .... Borough
BO .... Boston [*Diocesan abbreviation*] [*Massachusetts*] (TOCD)
Bo .... Boston Records [*Record label*]
BO .... Botanical Origin
BO .... Bottom
BO .... Bottu [*France*] [*Research code symbol*]
BO .... Bought
BO .... Bought Off (MCD)

BO .... Boundary Lights [*Aviation*] (DA)
BO .... Bouraq Indonesia Airlines [*ICAO designator*] (AD)
BO .... Bowel [*Medicine*]
BO .... Bowel Obstruction [*Medicine*]
BO .... Bowels Opened [*Medicine*]
BO .... Box Office [*Theatrical slang*]
bo .... Box Office [*Theater*] (WDMC)
BO .... Branch Office
B/O .... Breakout (NASA)
BO .... Breakout Box [*Computer service industry*] (MCD)
BO .... Breakover [*Electronics*]
BO .... British Officer [*British military*] (DMA)
BO .... Broker's Order [*Finance*]
B/O .... Brought Over [*Business term*]
BO .... Bucco-Occlusal [*Dentistry*]
B/O .... Budget Obligation [*or Overlay*] (NRCH)
BO .... Bug Off [*Slang*]
BO .... Bureau of Ordnance [*Functions transferred to Bureau of Naval Weapons, 1960, and later to Naval Ordnance Systems Command*] [*Navy*]
BO .... Burnout (KSC)
BO .... Buyer's Option [*Business term*]
B-O .... Buy-Off
BO .... Buy Order [*Investment term*]
BO .... MBB-UV [*Messerschmitt-Boelkow-Blohm*] [*Germany ICAO aircraft manufacturer identifier*] (ICAO)
BO .... Output Blocking Factor [*Computer science*] (IBMDP)
BO1 .... Boulder [*Colorado*] [*Seismograph station code, US Geological Survey Closed*] (SEIS)
B-O$_2$S ...... Blood Oxygen Saturation [*On blood gas determinations*] [*Medicine*] (DAVI)
BOA .... Bank of Africa [*Mali*] (EY)
BOA .... Basic Ordering Agreement
BOA .... Basis of Allocation
BOA .... Benzoic Acid [*Organic chemistry*]
BOA .... Big Optical Array [*Proposed, 1992*]
BOA .... Bipolar Operational Amplifier
BOA .... Boaco [*Nicaragua*] [*Seismograph station code, US Geological Survey*] (SEIS)
Boa .... Boatinus de Mantua [*Deceased, 1300*] [*Authority cited in pre-1607 legal work*] (DSA)
BOA .... Bonsai and Orchid Association (EAIO)
BOA .... Borcan Resources [*Vancouver Stock Exchange symbol*]
BOA .... Born on Arrival [*of mother at hospital*] [*Medicine*]
BOA .... Born Out of Asepsis [*Neonatology and obstetrics*] (DAVI)
BOA .... Boulder Valley School District, Boulder, CO [*OCLC symbol*] (OCLC)
BOA .... Break-Off Altitude [*Aviation*] (AFM)
BOA .... British Olympic Association
BOA .... British Oncological Association (DBA)
BOA .... British Optical Association
BOA .... British Orthopaedic Association
BOA .... British Osteopathic Association
BOA .... British Overseas Airways Corp. [*Later, British Airways*]
BOA .... Broad Ocean Area
BOA .... Brush Owner's Association [*Defunct*] (EA)
BOA .... Bush Boake Allen [*NYSE symbol*] (TTSB)
BOA .... Bush, Boake Allen, Inc. [*NYSE symbol*] (SAG)
BOA .... Butoxyacetanilide [*Pharmacology*]
BOAA .... Beta-Oxalylamino-alanine [*An amino acid*]
BOAC .... Bang on a Can Festival
BOAC .... Billed Office Account Code [*Army*] (AFIT)
BOAC .... British Overseas Airways Corp. [*Humorously interpreted as "Better on a Cam el"*] [*Later, British Airways*]
BOAD .... Banque Ouest Africaine de Developpement [*West African Development Bank - WADB*] (EAIO)
BOAD .... Business Organizations and Agencies Directory [*Later, BOAPD*] [*A publication*]
BOADICEA .. British Overseas Airways Corp. [*later, British Airways*] Digital Information Computer for Electronic Automation
BOA(Disp) .... British Optical Association (Dispenser) (DI)
BOAE .... Bureau of Occupational and Adult Education [*Office of Education*]
BOAFG .... British Order of Ancient Free Gardeners
BOAG .... British Overseas Aid Group (DS)
BOAM .... Bell Owned and Maintained [*Telecommunications*] (TEL)
BOA-MILS ... Broad Ocean Area - Missile Impact Locating System [*Navy*] (NG)
BOAMP .... Bulletin Officiel des Annonces des Marches Publics [*Direction des Journaux Officiels*] [*Database*]
BO & SW .... Baltimore, Ohio & Southwestern Railway
BOAP .... Bleomycin, Oncovin [*Vincristine*], Adriamycin, Prednisone [*Antineoplastic drug regimen*]
BOAPD .... Business Organizations, Agencies, and Publications Directory [*Formerly, BOAD*] [*A publication*]
BOAR .... Board of Action on Redetermination [*Navy*]
BoardC .... Boardwalk Casino [*Associated Press*] (SAG)
BoardCas .... Boardwalk Casino [*Associated Press*] (SAG)
BOAS .... British Quality Awards Scheme (AIE)
BOASI .... Bureau of Old-Age and Survivors Insurance [*Social Security Administration*]
BOAT .... Basics of Adult Teaching (OICC)
Boat .... Boatinus de Mantua [*Deceased, 1300*] [*Authority cited in pre-1607 legal work*] (DSA)
BOAT .... Boatmen's Bancshares [*NASDAQ symbol*] (TTSB)
BOAT .... Boatmen's Bankshares, Inc. [*NASDAQ symbol*] (NQ)
BoatBnc ...... Boatmen's Bankshares, Inc. [*Associated Press*] (SAG)

BOATS .... BMT [*British Maritime Technology Ltd.*] Abstracts Online [*Wallsend, Tyne, and Wear, England*] [*Information service or system*] (IID)

BOATS .... Boat Owners Association of the United States

BOAT/US ...... Boat Owners Association of the United States (EA)

BOB .... Back of Book

BOB .... Ball on Back (DAVI)

BOB .... Barges on Board [*Shipping*]

BOB .... Beginning of Business

BOB .... Berner Oberland-Bahnen [*Bernese Overland Railways*]

BOB .... Best of Breed

BOB .... Best on Best (MCD)

BOB .... Bibliography of Bioethics [*A publication*]

BOB .... Bobbin (KSC)

BOB .... Bora-Bora [*French Polynesia*] [*Airport symbol*] (OAG)

BOB .... Bora-Bora [*Society Islands*] [*Airport symbol*] (AD)

BOB .... Brains on Board [*Robot*] [*Androbot, Inc.*]

BOB .... Branch Office, Boston [*Office of Naval Research*] (DNAB)

BOB .... Breakout Box [*Computer service industry*]

BOB .... Brick of Bytes [*Computer software*] [*Army High-Performance Computing Research Center*] (RDA)

BOB .... Bureau of Biologics [*Also, BB*] [*FDA*]

BOB .... Bureau of the Budget [*Later, OMB*]

BOB .... Business Opportunity Bank [*Institute for New Enterprise Development*]

BOBA .... Beta-Oxybutyric Acid [*Organic chemistry*] (MAE)

BobBrk .... Bobbie Brooks, Inc. [*Associated Press*] (SAG)

BOBE .... Bob Evans Farms [*NASDAQ symbol*] (TTSB)

BOBE .... Bob Evans Farms, Inc. [*NASDAQ symbol*] (NQ)

BOBELE .... Boris Becker of Leimen [*Acronym also refers to pretzel produced by German bakers in recognition of this tennis player*]

BobEvn .... Bob Evans Farms, Inc. [*Associated Press*] (SAG)

BOBJ .... Business Objects SA [*NASDAQ symbol*] (SAG)

BOBJY .... Business Objects ADS [*NASDAQ symbol*] (TTSB)

BOBMA .... British Oat and Barley Millers Association (DBA)

BOBMA .... British Oil Burner Manufacturers' Association (BI)

BOBO .... Big Oil Bail Out [*Reference by Rep. James H. Scheuer (NY) to a particular toxic waste clean-up bill*]

BOBO .... Burnt Out But Opulent

BOBR .... Boring Bar

BOBS .... Beacon Only Bombing System

BOB's.......... Blitter Objects [*Amiga computer hardware*]

BO/BS .... Bolted-on-Base

BOBS .... Brazil Fast Food [*NASDAQ symbol*] (TTSB)

BOBS .... Brazil Fast Food Corp. [*NASDAQ symbol*] (SAG)

BOBS .... Bruininks-Oseretsky Balance Subtest [*Occupational therapy*]

BOBSW .... Brazil Fast Food Wrrt'A' [*NASDAQ symbol*] (TTSB)

BOBSZ .... Brazil Fast Food Wrrt'B' [*NASDAQ symbol*] (TTSB)

Bob W .... Best of Both Worlds [*Apple Computer's Macintosh Due System's nickname*] [*Pronounced as a proper name: Bob W.*]

BOC .... Back of Cab [*TII*] (TAG)

BOC .... Back Office Crunch [*Business term*]

BOC .... Bacterial Organic Carbon [*Water chemistry*]

BOC .... Bank of Communications [*China*]

BOC .... Base Operations Contract (SSD)

BOC .... Basic Operational Capability (SSD)

BOC .... Battalion Operations Center (AABC)

BOC .... Battalion Orderly Corporal [*British and Canadian*]

BOC .... Battery Operations Center [*Air Force*]

BOC .... Bayes Operating Characteristic

BOC .... Beard Co. [*AMEX symbol*] (SPSG)

BOC .... Beginning of Cycle (NRCH)

BOC .... Bell Operating Co. [*Also, BSOC*] [*Post-divestiture division of American Telepho ne & Telegraph Co.*]

BOC .... Best Operational Capability

BOC .... Best Output and Color [*Computer science*] (IAA)

BOC .... Bevitron Orbit Code

BOC .... Billet Occupational Code [*Military*] (CAAL)

BOC .... Bingham Oceanographic Collection

BOC .... Block-Oriented Computer

BOC .... Blood Oxygen Capacity [*Medicine*] (DMAA)

BOC .... Blowout Coil

BOC .... Blue Oyster Cult [*Rock music group*]

BOC .... Board of Customs [*British*] (DAS)

BOC .... Bocas Del Toro [*Panama*] [*Airport symbol*] (OAG)

BOC .... Bochum [*Federal Republic of Germany*] [*Seismograph station code, US Geological Survey*] (SEIS)

BOC .... Body-on-Chassis [*Technical drawings*]

BOC .... Borgward Owners' Club (EA)

BOC .... Bottom of Conduit (NRCH)

BOC .... Branch Office, Chicago [*Office of Naval Research*] (DNAB)

BOC .... Breach of Contract [*Legal term*]

BOC .... Bristol Owners' Club (EA)

BOC .... Bristol Owners Club, US Branch (EA)

BOC .... British Ornithologists' Club

BOC .... British Overseas Citizenship

BOC .... British Oxygen Co. [*Later, BOC Group*]

BOC .... Brittany Oceanological Center

BOC .... Brought on Charge (MCD)

BOC .... Buick-Oldsmobile-Cadillac Group [*General Motors Corp.*]

BOC .... Build Out Capacitor [*Telecommunications*] (TEL)

BOC .... Bureau of Customs [*Later, US Customs Service*] [*Department of the Treasury*]

BOC .... Butoxycarbonyl [*Also, Boc*] [*Organic chemistry*]

BOC .... Byte Output Control [*Computer science*]

BOCA .... Benelli Owner's Club of America (EA)

BOCA .... Boat Owners Council of America [*Defunct*]

BOCA .... Borland Object Component Architecture [*Borland International, Inc.*] (PCM)

BOCA .... Building Officials and Code Administrators International (EA)

BOCA .... Building Officials Conference of America, Inc.

BOC ADS ..... BOC Group [*Associated Press*] (SAG)

BoCaPo........ [*The*] Book of Canadian Poetry [*A publication*]

BocaRs .... Boca Research, Inc. [*Associated Press*] (SAG)

BOCB .... Buffets, Inc. [*NASDAQ symbol*] (NQ)

BOCBA........ British Overseas and Commonwealth Banks Association (DBA)

BOCC .... Boccaccio [*Italian author, 1313-1375*] (ROG)

BOCC .... Branch Officer Candidate Course [*DoD*]

BOCCA .... Board for Coordination of Civil Aviation [*NATO*]

BOccThy ...... Bachelor of Occupational Therapy (ADA)

BOCE .... Board of Customs and Excise [*British*] (ODBW)

BOCES .... Boards of Cooperative Educational Services

BOCF .... Bureau of Commercial Fisheries [*Later, National Marine Fisheries Service*] (MCD)

BOCG .... Brudzinski, Oppenheim, Chaddock, and Gullaird [*Reflexes and signs*] [*Neurology*] (DAVI)

BoChLi........ [*A*] Book of Children's Literature [*A publication*]

BOCI .... Boca Research [*NASDAQ symbol*] (TTSB)

BOCI .... Boca Research, Inc. [*NASDAQ symbol*] (SAG)

BOCI .... Business Organization Climate Index (MHDB)

BOCLE .... Ball-on-Cylinder Lubricity Evaluator

BOCLE .... Ball On Cylinder Lubricity Evaluator [*Fuels and lubricants testing*]

BOCM .... Bailey Oil Content Monitor [*Ship ballast discharge*]

BOCM .... British Oil and Cake Mills

BOCO .... Bogota [*Colombia*] [*Seismograph station code, US Geological Survey*] (SEIS)

BOCOEX....... Boston Computer Exchange (CDE)

BOCOL........ Basic Operating Consumer-Oriented Language [*Computer science*]

BoCom........ Bank of Communications [*China*]

BOCP .... Broadcast Operator's Certificate of Proficiency

BOCS .... Bendix Optimum Configuration Satellite (IEEE)

BOCS .... Box-Office Computer System

BOCT .... [*The*] Baltimore & Ohio Chicago Terminal Railroad Co. [*AAR code*]

BOCTC .... Bank of China Trust and Consultancy Co.

BOD .... Bacteriological Oxygen Demand [*Water pollution*]

BOD .... Base Only Density (DGA)

BOD .... Base Operations Division [*NASA*] (KSC)

BOD .... Base Ordnance Depot

BOD .... Basic Operational Data

BOD .... Battery Operated Device

BOD .... Beneficial Occupancy Date

BOD .... Bid Opening Date

BOD .... Biochemical Oxygen Demand

BOD .... Biological Oxygen Demand

BOD .... Bistable Optical Device

BOD .... Blackout Door [*Military*]

BOD .... Board of Directors (NATG)

BOD .... Bodansky Unit [*Clinical chemistry*]

BOD .... Bodaybo [*Former USSR Seismograph station code, US Geological Survey*] (SEIS)

BOD .... Bodleian Library [*British*] (DGA)

BOD .... Bodoni [*Printing*] (DGA)

BOD .... Body [*Slang*] (DSUE)

BOD .... Boeing on Dock

BOD .... Bond Air Services Ltd. [*Uganda*] [*ICAO designator*] (FAAC)

BOD .... Booksellers Order Distribution [*British*]

BOD .... Bordeaux [*France*] [*Airport symbol*] (OAG)

BOD .... Borderline [*Biochemistry*] (DAVI)

BOD .... Boston Ordnance District [*Military*] (AAG)

BOD .... Bowman, ND [*Location identifier FAA*] (FAAL)

BOD .... Break Over Diode [*Electronics*] (EECA)

BOD .... Broad Ocean Deployment

BOD .... Broad Ocean Development (MCD)

BOD .... Buyer's Option to Double (ROG)

BOD .... Buy-Off Date

BOD5 .... Biochemical Oxygen Demand Over Five Days [*Biological*] (GNE)

BODA .... Bistable Optical Differential Amplifier (MCD)

BoDaBa........ [*A*] Book of Danish Ballads [*A publication*]

BODAS......... Brigade Operations Display and After Action Review System [*Army*] (RDA)

BODC .... British Oceanographic Data Centre [*Marine science*] (OSRA)

Boddie .... Boddie-Noell Properties, Inc. [*Associated Press*] (SAG)

BODEPE .... Boiler Design and Performance

bodh .... Bodhisattva (VRA)

BodI .... Bodleian Library [*Oxford University*] [*British*] (BARN)

BODL LIB..... Bodleian Library (DGA)

BODM .... Bodmin [*Municipal borough in England*]

BODMA........ British Oncology Data Managers (DBA)

BODN .... Bowdon Railway Co. [*AAR code*]

BODO .... Bauobjektdokumentation [*Buildings Documentation*] [*Fraunhofer Society*] [*Germany*] [*Information service or system*] (IID)

BODS .... British Oceanographic Data Service

BoDS .... [*A*] Second Book of Danish Verse [*A publication*]

BODU .... Bureau of Ordnance Design Unit [*Obsolete Navy*]

BODY .... Bio-Dyne Corp. [*NASDAQ symbol*] (SPSG)

BODY .... British Organ Donor Society (PDAA)

BOE............ Bachelor of Oral English

BOE............ Barrels of Oil Equivalent

BOE............ Basis of Estimate (AAGC)

BOE............ Benign Occipital Epilepsy [*Medicine*] (DMAA)

BOE............ Bilateral Otitis Externa [*Otorhinolaryngology*] (DAVI)

BOE............ Blackout Exit Time
BOE............ Blanket Open End [Contract] [Business term] (MCD)
BOE............ Board of Education (AIE)
BOE............ Board of Education
BOE............ Boeing Commericial Airplane Group [ICAO designator] (FAAC)
BOE............ Bottom of Edge
BOE............ Boundji [Congo] [Airport symbol] (OAG)
BOE............ Break of Entry (NASA)
BOE............ Bureau of Enforcement
BOE............ Bureau of Explosives [A publication] (EAAP)
BOEA......... British Offshore Equipment Association (DS)
BOEA......... Ethyl Biscoumacetate [Organic chemistry] (DAVI)
BOEC......... Beginning of Equilibrium Cycle [Nuclear energy] (NRCH)
BOEC......... British Oil Equipment Credits Ltd.
BOED......... Barrels of Oil Equivalent per Day
BOEEOWLA... Board of Examiners of Engineers and Overseers of Works to Local
                    Authorities [Australia]
Boeing......... [The] Boeing Co. [Associated Press] (SAG)
BoekOT....... Boeken van het Oude Testament [Roermond/Maaseik]
                    [A publication] (BJA)
BOEL.......... Beginning of Equilibrium Life (NUCP)
BOE(S)........ Board of Examiners (Scaffolding) [Victoria, Australia]
BOESEDBA... Board of Examiners for Steam Engine Drivers and Boiler Attendants
                    [Victoria, Australia]
BOE(WBPV)... Board of Examiners (Welders of Boilers and Pressure Vessels)
                    [Victoria, Australia]
BOF............ Barium Oxide Ferrite
BOF............ Basic Oxygen Furnace [Steelmaking]
BOF............ Beginning of File (NASA)
BOF............ Beurre, Oeufs, Fromages [Butter, Eggs, Cheese] [French]
BOF............ Bias Oscillator Frequency
BOF............ Billing and Ordering Forum [Exchange Carriers Standards
                    Association] [Telecommunications]
BOF............ Binary Oxide Film [Memory]
BOF............ Bio-Feed Industries Ltd. [Vancouver Stock Exchange symbol]
BOF............ Body-over-Frame [Automotive engineering]
BOF............ Bordaire Ltd. [Canada ICAO designator] (FAAC)
BOF............ Boring Old Fart [Slang] (DSUE)
BOF............ British Organic Farmers
BOF............ British Orienteering Federation (DBA)
BOF............ Building Owners Federation of Mutual Insurance Companies
                    [Defunct] (EA)
BOF........... Washington, DC [Location identifier FAA] (FAAL)
B of A........ Bank of America
B of A........ Bibliography of Agriculture [Oryx Press] [Phoenix, AZ] [A publication]
B of A........ Bureau of Advertising [American Newspaper Publishers
                    Association] (NTCM)
B of AA....... Bachelor of Aeronautical Administration
BOFADS....... Business Office Force Administration Data System [Bell System]
B of Adv Art & Des... Bachelor of Advertising Arts and Design
B of AE....... Bachelor of Aeronautical Engineering
B of B........ Back of Board (MSA)
B of BC....... Bachelor of Building Construction
B of BK....... Baronet of British Kingdom [Initials used by Arthur Orton in his
                    diary] (ROG)
BOFC.......... Buck Owens Fan Club [Defunct] (EA)
B of E........ Bank of England
B of E........ Board of Education
B of EE (Com Opt)... Bachelor of Electrical Engineering, Communication Option
B of EE (Power Opt)... Bachelor of Electrical Engineering, Power Option
B of EP....... Bachelor of Engineering Physics
B of G........ Bank of Ghana
BofG.......... Bank of Ghana
B of GP....... Board of General Purposes [Freemasonry]
B of H........ Band of Hope [British]
B of H........ Board of Health
B of ID....... Bachelor of Interior Design
B of IM....... Bachelor of Industrial Management
B of LE....... Brotherhood of Locomotive Engineers
B of M........ Bureau of Mines [Department of the Interior]
B-of-P........ Balance of Payments [International trade]
B of P........ Breach of Peace [FBI standardized term]
B of P........ Breach of Promise [Legal term]
B of PDPH of A... Brotherhood of Painters, Decorators, and Paperhangers of
                    America [Later, IBPAT] (EA)
BoFr.......... [The] Book of Friendship [A publication]
B of RS....... Brotherhood of Railroad Signalmen (EA)
BOFS.......... Biogeochemical Ocean Flux Study [Oceanography]
BOFS.......... Black Oil Finish Slate (MSA)
B of S........ Bureau of Standards
BOFSA........ Bureau of Oceans, Fisheries, and Scientific Affairs [Department of
                    State]
B-of-T........ Balance of Trade [International trade]
B of T........ Board of Trade [Shipping]
B of TC....... Bachelor of Textile Chemistry
B of TCC..... Board of Trade of the City of Chicago
B of TE....... Bachelor of Textile Engineering
B of TE....... Bureau of Ordnance Fleet Test Equipment [Obsolete Navy]
B of TKC..... Board of Trade of Kansas City [Missouri]
B of TM...... Bachelor of Textile Management
BOFX.......... Boring Fixture (AAG)
BOG.......... Belco Oil & Gas [NYSE symbol] (TTSB)
BOG.......... Belco Oil & Gas Corp. [NYSE symbol] (SAG)
BOG.......... Board of Governors [Federal Reserve System]

BOG............ Bogota [Colombia] [Seismograph station code, US Geological
                    Survey] (SEIS)
BOG............ Boiling
BOG............ Boil-Off Gas [Petroleum product transportation]
BOG............ Brigade of Guards
BOGA.......... British Onion Growers' Association (BI)
Bogen......... Bogen Communications International [Associated Press] (SAG)
BogenC........ Bogen Communications International [Associated Press] (SAG)
Bogert Trusts... Bogert on Trusts and Trustees [A publication] (DLA)
BOGF.......... Burden of Going Forward [Legal shorthand] (LWAP)
BOGSAAT..... [A] Bunch of Guys Sitting around a Table Method [Facetious
                    description of a decision-making process]
BOGSAT....... [A] Bunch of Guys Seated around a Table Method [Facetious
                    description of a decision-making process]
BogSmot....... Bogoslovska Smotra [Zagreb] [A publication] (BJA)
BogVest........ Bogoslovni Vestnik [Ljubljana] [A publication] (BJA)
BOH............ Bancorp Hawaii [NYSE symbol] (TTSB)
BOH............ Bancorp Hawaii, Inc. [NYSE symbol] (SPSG)
BOH............ Band of Hope [British] (DAS)
BOH............ Beautiful Old House
BOH............ Beta-Hydroxyethylhydrazine [Plant growth compound]
BOH............ Board of Health (DAVI)
Boh............ Bohairic Version of the Bible (BJA)
BOH............ Bohemia
BOH............ Bohemian [Language, etc.] (ROG)
BOH............ Bottom of Hole [Geology]
BOH............ Bournemouth [England] [Airport symbol] (OAG)
BOH............ Bureau of Ordnance and Hydrography [Obsolete Navy]
BOH............ Oliver Heritage Society Museum and Archives, British Columbia
                    [Library symbol National Library of Canada] (NLC)
Boh Att .... Bohun. Practising Attorney [A publication] (DLA)
BOHC.......... Boron-Oxygen Hole Centre (PDAA)
Boh Curs Can... Bohun's Cursus Cancellariae (ILCA)
Boh Dec...... Bohun's Declarations and Pleadings [A publication] (DLA)
Boh Eccl Jur... Bohun. Ecclesiastical Jurisdiction [A publication] (DLA)
BOHEM........ Bohemian [Language, etc.] (ROG)
Boh Eng L.... Bohun. English Lawyer [A publication] (DLA)
BOHICA....... Bend Over, Here It Comes Again [Business term]
Boh Inst Leg... Bohun's Institutio Legalis (ILCA)
BOHO.......... Big Office Head Office [Business term] (PCM)
BOHP.......... Boiler Horsepower (IAA)
Boh Priv Lond... Bohun. Privilegia Londini [A publication] (DLA)
BoHrPo........ [A] Book of Historical Poems [A publication]
BOHS.......... British Occupational Hygiene Society (EAIO)
Boh Ti......... Bohun. Titles [A publication] (DLA)
Bohun .... Bohun's Election Cases [England] [A publication] (DLA)
Bohun Curs Canc... Bohun's Cursus Cancellariae [A publication] (DLA)
Bohun Inst Leg... Bohun's Institutio Legalis [A publication] (DLA)
BOHUNK ...... Bohemian-Hungarian [Slang]
BoHV .... [The] Book of Humorous Verse [A publication]
BOI............ Aboitiz Air Transport Corp. [Philippines] [ICAO designator] (FAAC)
BOI............ Basis of Issue [Army]
BOI............ Bay of Islands Complex [Newfoundland] [Geology]
BOI............ Beginning of Information [Computer science] (NITA)
BOI............ Blackout Initiation Time
BOI............ Board of Investments [Generic term]
BOI............ Boiler (DNAB)
BOI............ Boise [Idaho] [Airport symbol] (OAG)
BOI............ Bolt-On Intelligence [Proposed use for the biochip]
BOI............ Branch Operating Instruction [Air Force]
BOI............ Branch Output Interrupt [Computer science] (MDG)
BOI............ Break of Inspection
BOI............ Break of Integrity (NASA)
BOI............ Bulletins of Ordnance Information
BOIA .... Bureau of Indian Affairs [Better known as BIA] [Department of the
                    Interior] (MCD)
BOIMARS..... Basis of Issue Monitoring and Recording System [Army] (AABC)
BOIP.......... Basis of Issue Plan [Army]
BOIP-C........ Basis of Issue Plan - Complete [Army]
BOIPFD....... BOIP [Basis of Issue Plan] Feeder Data [DoD]
BOIP II........ Basis of Issue Plan II [Army] (AABC)
BOIP-T .... Basis of Issue Plan - Tentative [Army]
BOIS.......... Basis of Issue System [Army]
BoisC.......... Boise Cascade Corp. [Associated Press] (SAG)
BoisCOff...... Boise Cascade Office Products [Associated Press] (SAG)
BoiseC........ Boise Cascade Corp. [Associated Press] (SAG)
Boise St U ... Boise State University (GAGS)
BOJ............ Bank of Japan
BoJ............ Bank of Japan (ODBW)
BOJ............ Booster Jettison
BOJ............ Bourgas [Bulgaria] [Airport symbol] (OAG)
BOJ............ Burgas [Bulgaria] [Airport symbol] (AD)
BOK............ Bokaro [India] [Seismograph station code, US Geological Survey]
                    (SEIS)
BOK .... BOK Financial Corp. [Associated Press] (SAG)
BOK .... Brookings, OR [Location identifier FAA] (FAAL)
BOKF.......... BOK Financial [NASDAQ symbol] (TTSB)
BOKF.......... BOK Financial Corp. [NASDAQ symbol] (SAG)
Bokh .... Bokhara (VRA)
BOL............ Bachelor of Oriental Language
BOL............ Basics of Language [Method]
BOL............ Bausch & Lomb [NYSE symbol] (TTSB)
BOL............ Bausch & Lomb, Inc. [NYSE symbol] (SAG)
BOL............ Bearing-Only Launch [Navy] (CAAL)
BOL............ Beginning of Life

BOL............	Be On the Lookout [Police term]
BoL.............	Bill of Lading [Shipping]
BOL............	Bingham Oceanographic Laboratory (NOAA)
BOL............	Biotechnology Orbital Laboratory (KSC)
BOL............	Bolito [Race of maize]
BOL............	Bolivia [ANSI three-letter standard code] (CNC)
Bol..............	Bolivia (VRA)
Bol.............	Bollard [Shipping] [British]
BOL............	Bologna [Italy] [Seismograph station code, US Geological Survey] (SEIS)
BOL............	Bolus [Large Pill] [Pharmacy]
BoL.............	[A] Book of Lullabies [A publication]
BOL............	Boundary Light (IAA)
BOL............	Branch Office London [ONR]
BOL............	Build Out Lattice [Telecommunications] (TEL)
BOL............	Transportes Aeros Boliviands [Bolivia] [ICAO designator] (FAAC)
BOLA..........	Bank Official Loan Act [1933]
BOLA..........	Betting Office Licensees Association [British] (DBA)
BOLD..........	Bibliographic On-Line Display [Document storage and retrieval system] [Computer science]
BOLD..........	Bibliographic Online Library Display [Scientific Documentation Centre] [British] (NITA)
BOLD..........	Bleomycin, Oncovin [Vincristine], Lomustine, Dacarbazine [Antineoplastic drug regimen]
BOLD..........	Blind Outdoor Leisure Development (EA)
BOLD..........	Blood Oxygenation Level-Dependent [Physiology]
BOLD..........	Bolder Tech [NASDAQ symbol] (TTSB)
BOLD..........	Bomb LASER Directed (MCD)
BOLDS........	Burroughs Optical Lens Docking System (MCD)
BOLF..........	Barge Off Loading Facility
BOLiVe........	[The] Book of Living Verse [A publication]
Bolland........	Select Bills in Eyre [Selden Society Publication No. 30] [England] [A publication] (DLA)
Boll Com Arch...	Bollettino. Commissione Archeologica Comunale in Roma [A publication] (OCD)
Boll Fil Class...	Bollettino di Filologia Classica [A publication] (OCD)
Boll Ist Dir Rom...	Bollettino. Istituto di Diritto Romano [A publication] (OCD)
BOLM..........	Bureau of Land Management [Department of the Interior] (MCD)
BOLMADA....	British Ophthalmic Lens Manufacturers and Distributors Association (DBA)
Bol Min Justica...	Boletim. Ministerio de Justica [Portugal] [A publication] (DLA)
BOLMM........	Brothers of Our Lady, Mother of Mercy [Netherlands] (EAIO)
BOLO..........	Be On the Lookout [Police term]
BOLO..........	Bilingual Obstetric Liaison Officer
BOLOVAC.....	Bolometric Voltage and Current [Voltage measurement] [National Institute of Standards and Technology]
BOLS..........	Bolster (KSC)
BOLS..........	Bur Oak Library System [Library network]
BOLSA........	Bank of London and South America
BOLT..........	Bahia Oral Language Test (EDAC)
BOLT..........	Basic Occupational Language Training
BOLT..........	Basic Occupational Literacy Test
BOLT..........	Beam of Light Transistor (MSA)
BOLT..........	Beam of Light Transmitter
BOLT..........	Bomb LASER Tracking (MCD)
BoltBer........	Bolt, Beranek & Newman, Inc. [Associated Press] (SAG)
BOLTOP.......	Better on Lips than on Paper [Put at the end of a letter with kisses] [British]
BoltTch........	Bolt Technology Corp. [Associated Press] (SAG)
BOM..........	Bank of Melbourne [Australia]
BOM..........	Base Operation Manager
BOM..........	Basic Operating Monitor
BOM..........	Basic Operation Memory [Computer science] (IAA)
BOM..........	Beginning of Message (IAA)
BOM..........	Beginning of Month [Accounting] (NASA)
BOM..........	Benzyloxymethyl [Organic chemistry]
BOM..........	Bilateral Otitis Media [Medicine] (MAE)
BOM..........	Billings Ovulation Method Association of the United States (EA)
BOM..........	Bill of Materials [Digital Dynamics Ltd.] [Software package]
bom..........	Bill of Materials [Manufacturing] (ODBW)
BOM..........	Binary Order of Magnitude [Computer science]
BOM..........	BIT [Binary Digit]-Oriented Message (RDA)
BOM..........	Board on Medicine [of the National Academy of Sciences] [Later, IOM] (EA)
BOM..........	Bomb (DNAB)
BOM..........	Bombardier
BOM..........	Bombay [India] [Seismograph station code, US Geological Survey] (SEIS)
BOM..........	Bombay [India] [Later, ABG] [Geomagnetic observatory code]
Bom..........	Bombay High Court Reports [1862-75] [India] [A publication] (DLA)
BOM..........	Bombing (AABC)
BOM..........	Book-of-the-Month Club (WDMC)
BOM..........	Born-Oppenheimer Method [Physical chemistry]
BOM..........	Bottom Ocean Monitor [Marine science] (MSC)
BOM..........	Bowmar Instrument [AMEX symbol] (TTSB)
BOM..........	Bowmar Instrument Corp. [AMEX symbol] (SPSG)
BOM..........	British Oil and Mineral
BOM..........	Builders Old Measurement
BOM..........	Built on Mask [Microlithography]
BOM..........	Bureau of Meteorology
BOM..........	Bureau of Mines [Department of the Interior]
BOM..........	Business Office Must [Copy that must be printed] [Publishing]
BOM..........	Butyl(octyl)magnesium [Organic chemistry]
BOM..........	Buying on Margin [Investment term]
BOM..........	By Other Means (NVT)

BOM............	Osoyoos Museum, British Columbia [Library symbol National Library of Canada] (NLC)
BOM............	Service Aerien Gouvernmental Ministere des Transports Gouvernment du Quebec [Canada ICAO designator] (FAAC)
BOMA.........	British Overseas Mining Association (BI)
BOMA.........	Building Owners and Managers Association International (EA)
BOMAA.......	Building Owners and Managers' Association of Australia
Bom AC.......	Bombay Reports, Appellate Juris [India] [A publication] (DLA)
BOMAI........	Building Owners and Managers Association International
BOMAP.......	Barbados Oceanographic and Meteorological Analysis Project
BOMAP.......	BOMEX [Barbados Oceanographic and Meteorological Experiment] Analysis Program (NOAA)
BOMARC.....	Boeing-Michigan Aeronautical Research Center
BOMB.........	Bombardier [British] (ROG)
BOMB.........	Bombardment
BOMB.........	Bombardon [Musical instrument]
BOMB.........	British Overseas Media Bureau
Bomb.........	Indian Law Reports, Bombay Series [A publication] (DLA)
BOMB.........	Vincristine, Adriamycin, 6-Mercaptopurine, and Prednisone [Antineoplastic drug regimen] (DAVI)
Bombay.......	Bombay Co. [Associated Press] (SAG)
Bombay LJ....	Bombay Law Journal [India] [A publication] (DLA)
Bomb Cr Cas...	Bombay Reports, Crown Cases [India] [A publication] (DLA)
Bomb Cr Rul...	Bombay High Court Criminal Rulings [India] [A publication] (DLA)
BOMBDR.....	Bombardier
BOMBEX......	Bombing Exercise [Military] (NVT)
Bomb HC.....	Bombay High Court Reports [1862-75] [India] [A publication] (DLA)
Bomb H Ct...	Bombay High Court Reports [1862-75] [India] [A publication] (DLA)
Bomb Hg Ct...	Bombay High Court Reports [1862-75] [India] [A publication] (DLA)
Bomb LR.....	Bombay Law Reporter [India] [A publication] (DLA)
BOMB/NAV...	Bombardier/Navigator (DOMA)
BOMB/NAV...	Bombing/Navigation (DOMA)
Bomb SC.....	Bombay Staff Corps [British military] (DMA)
Bomb Sel Cas...	Bombay Select Cases, Sadr Diwani Adalat [India] [A publication] (DLA)
Bomb Ser	Indian Law Reports, Bombay Series [A publication] (DLA)
BOMC.........	Baronial Order of Magna Charta (EA)
BOMC.........	Book-of-the-Month Club, Inc.
BOMCOM.....	Bomber Command [Army]
Bom Cr Cas...	Bombay Reports, Crown Cases [India] [A publication] (ILCA)
BOMEX	Barbados Oceanographic and Meteorological Experiment [National Oceanic and Atmospheric Administration]
BOMFOG......	[The] Brotherhood of Man under the Fatherhood of God [Journalistic slang for political platitudes; said to be taken from a speech by Hubert H. Humphrey]
Bom HCR....	Bombay High Court Reports [1862-75] [India] [A publication] (DLA)
BOMI.........	Box Office Management International [An association] (EA)
BOMID........	Branch Office, Military Intelligence Division [Army]
BOMINE.......	Bomb Mine (MCD)
BOMIS........	Bottom-Mounted Instrumentation System (MCD)
Bom LJ.......	Bombay Law Journal [India] [A publication] (DLA)
Bom LR.......	Bombay Law Reporter [India] [A publication] (DLA)
Bom L Rep...	Bombay Law Reports [India] [A publication] (DLA)
Bom LRJ.....	Bombay Law Reporter [India] [A publication] (DLA)
BOMMA.......	British Ophthalmic Mass Manufacturers Association (DBA)
BOMO.........	Bomb or Missile Optics (MCD)
Bom OC......	Bombay Reports, Oudh Cases [India] [A publication] (DLA)
BOMOS.......	Buried-Oxide Metal-Oxide Semiconductor (IAA)
BOMP.........	Base Organization and Maintenance Processor (IEEE)
BOMP.........	Bill of Material Processor
BOMPr........	Bowmar Instr $3.00 Cv Pfd [AMEX symbol] (TTSB)
BOMREP......	Bombing Report [Military]
BOMREPT....	Bombing Report (NATG)
BOMROC.....	Bombardment Rocket (KSC)
BOMRON	Bombing Squadron
BOMS	BancorpSouth [NASDAQ symbol] (TTSB)
BOMS	Bancorp South, Inc. [NASDAQ symbol] (SAG)
BOMS	Base Operations Maintenance Simulator (MHDI)
BOMS	Bill of Material Status (MCD)
BOMS	Bureau for Overseas Medical Service [British] (CB)
BOMST	Bombsight (AABC)
Bom Unrep Cr C...	Bombay Unreported Criminal Cases [1862-98] [India] [A publication] (DLA)
Bon	Apud Bonifacium [Latin] (DSA)
BON	Balance of Need Campaign [Red Cross fund-raising]
BON	Bank of Nauru
BON	Baron (ROG)
BON	Beta-Oxynaphthoic Acid [Also, BONA] [Organic chemistry]
BON	Bibliography of Newfoundland, Memorial University [UTLAS symbol]
BON	Blending Octane Number [Petroleum technology]
BON	Bon Accord Airways [British ICAO designator] (FAAC)
BON	Bonaire [Netherland Antilles] [Airport symbol] (OAG)
BON	Bonar, Inc. [Toronto Stock Exchange symbol]
BoN	[The] Book of Nonsense [A publication]
BON	Bristol, TN [Location identifier FAA] (FAAL)
BON	British Organisation of Non-Parents (DBA)
BONA	Bachad Organization of North America (EA)
BONA	Beta-Oxynaphthoic Acid [Also, BON] [Organic chemistry]
Bona	Bonaguida de Aretio [Flourished, 1251-58] [Authority cited in pre-1607 legal work] (DSA)
Bonag	Bonaguida de Aretio [Flourished, 1251-58] [Authority cited in pre-1607 legal work] (DSA)
BONC	Broadcasting Organizations of Non-Aligned Countries [Belgrade, Yugoslavia] (EAIO)
BOND	Bandwidth on Demand (PCM)

BOND	[The] Board on Natural Disasters [National Research Council]
Bond	Bond's United States Circuit Reports [A publication] (DLA)
BONDING	Bandwidth on Demand Interoperability Working Group [Telecommunications] (ACRL)
Bond LR	Bond Law Review [A publication]
Bond MD App	Proceedings of Court of Appeal of Maryland [In American Legal Records, 1] [A publication] (DLA)
BondMot	Bonded Motors, Inc. [Associated Press] (SAG)
BONE	Banc One Corp. [NASDAQ symbol] (SAG)
BoneCre	Bone Care International, Inc. [Associated Press] (SAG)
BONENT	Board of Nephrology Examiners for Nursing and Technology
BONEO	Banc One $3.50 Cv Pfd [NASDAQ symbol] (TTSB)
Bone Prec	Bone. Precedents in Conveyancing [1838-40] [A publication] (DLA)
BONES	Block-Oriented Network Simulator [Computer science]
Bon Ins	Bonney on Insurance [A publication] (DLA)
BONIS	Bibliography of Old Norse-Icelandic Studies [A publication]
Bon Mem	Bonae Memoriae [of Happy Memory] [Reference to a deceased person] [Latin] (BARN)
BONMOT	Sinnspruche, Aphorismen, und Lebensweisheiten [Mottos, Aphorisms, and Witticisms] [Society for Business Information] [Information service or system] (IID)
Bonn Car	Bonney's Railway Carriers [A publication] (DLA)
Bonner Jahrb	Bonner Jahrbuecher [A publication] (OCD)
Bonnet	Baronne [Baroness] [French] (BARN)
Bonnetti Ital Dict	Bonnetti's Italian Dictionary [A publication] (DLA)
Bonn Ins	Bonney on Insurance [A publication] (DLA)
BONP	Bleomycin, Oncovin [Vincristine], Natulan , Prednisolone [Procarbazine hydrochloride] [Antineoplastic drug regimen]
BON-P	British Organisation of Non-Parents (DI)
Bonray	Bonray Drilling Corp. [Associated Press] (SAG)
Bon RR Car	Bonney's Railway Carriers [A publication] (DLA)
Bonso	Bonso Electronics [Associated Press] (SAG)
BONT	Bon-Ton Stores [NASDAQ symbol] (SPSG)
BONT	Bon-Ton Stores [NASDAQ symbol] (TTSB)
BoNT	Botulinum Neurotoxin
BonTon	Bon-Ton Stores, Inc. [Associated Press] (SAG)
BONUS	Boiling Nuclear Superheat Reactor
BONUS	Borrower's Option for Notes and Underwritten Standby [Finance]
BONUS-CX	Boiling Nuclear Superheat Critical Experiment (NRCH)
BONZ	Interpore International [NASDAQ symbol] (SAG)
BONZ	Interpore Intl. [NASDAQ symbol] (TTSB)
BOO	Bladder Outlet Obstruction [Urology] (DAVI)
BOO	Bodo [Norway] [Airport symbol] (OAG)
Boo	Bootes [Constellation]
BOO	Brake On/Off Sensor [Automotive engineering]
BOO	Brigade Ordnance Officer [British]
BOO	Build, Own, Operate [Property development]
BOOB	Block out of Balance [Computer science]
BOOB	Bolt Out of the Blue [Surprise nuclear attack]
BOOBOISIE	Boob and Bourgeoisie [H. L. Mencken's portmanteau for the American middle class]
BOOC	Barcelona Olympic Organizing Committee [Spain] (EAIO)
BOOG	British Osborne Owners Group [A user group] (NITA)
BOOGIE	BOOG [British Osborne Owners Group] Information Exchange (NITA)
BOOK	Bibliographic On-Line Organized Knowledge [Computer science] (KSC)
Book	Book Records [Record label]
BOOK	Built-In Orderly Organized Knowledge [Learning device]
BOOK	Village Green Bookstore [NASDAQ symbol] (TTSB)
BOOKB	[The] Village Green Bookstore, Inc. [NASDAQ symbol] (NQ)
BOOKB	Bookbinding (ROG)
BOOKK	Bookkeeping (ROG)
BookMill	Books A Million, Inc. [Associated Press] (SAG)
Book of Judg	Book of Judgments [England] [A publication] (DLA)
BOOKS	Bookselling (ROG)
Books	Books Magazine [A publication] (BRI)
Books S	Books of Sederunt [A publication] (DLA)
Books Sed	Books of Sederunt [A publication] (DLA)
BOOKW	Village Green Bookstore Wrrt [NASDAQ symbol] (TTSB)
BOOL	Boolean [Mathematics]
BOOL	Boole & Babbage [NASDAQ symbol] (TTSB)
BOOL	Boole & Babbage, Inc. [NASDAQ symbol] (NQ)
BooleB	Boole & Babbage, Inc. [Associated Press] (SAG)
BOOM	Becoming One's Own Man [Psychology]
BOOM	Dynamic Materials [NASDAQ symbol] (TTSB)
BOOM	Dynamic Materials Corp. [NASDAQ symbol] (SAG)
Boomtwn	Boomtown, Inc. [Associated Press] (SAG)
Boone Corp	Boone on Corporations [A publication] (DLA)
BOOP	Bronchiolitis Obliterans-Organizing Pneumonia [Medicine] (DMAA)
Boor	Booraem's Reports [6-8 California] [A publication] (DLA)
BOOR	Bureau of Outdoor Recreation [Terminated, 1978, functions transferred to Heritage Conservation and Recreation Service] [Department of the Interior] (MCD)
Boo R Act	Booth on Real Actions [A publication] (DLA)
Booraem	Booraem's Reports [6-8 California] [A publication] (DLA)
BOOS	Burners Out of Service [Combustion emission control]
BOOST	Bettering Oregon's Opportunity for Saving Talent [Educational project] (EA)
BOOST	Broadened Opportunities for Officer Selection and Training [Navy] (NVT)
Boot	Bootes [Constellation]
BOOT	Bootstrap [Computer science]
BOOT	Build, Own, Operate, Transfer [Property development]
BOOT	LaCrosse Footwear [NASDAQ symbol] (TTSB)
BOOT	La Crosse Footwear, Inc. [NASDAQ symbol] (SAG)

BOOT	LaCrosse Footwear, Inc. [NASDAQ symbol] (SAG)
Boote	Boote's Suit at Law [A publication] (DLA)
Boote Act	Boote. Action at Law [A publication] (ILCA)
Boote Ch Pr	Boote. Chancery Practice [A publication] (DLA)
Boote SL	Boote's Suit at Law [A publication] (DLA)
Booth	Chester Palatine Courts [1811] [England] [A publication] (DLA)
Booth In Of	Booth. Indictable Offences [A publication] (DLA)
Booth R Act	Booth on Real Actions [A publication] (DLA)
Booth Real Act	Booth on Real Actions [A publication] (DLA)
Booth Wills	Booth's Law of Wills [A publication] (DLA)
BOOTP	Bootstrap Protocol [Telecommunications] (ACRL)
BOOTS	Basic Organizing/Optimizing Training Schedules (MCD)
BOOW	Battalion Officer-of-the-Watch (DNAB)
BOP	Association for Balance of Political Power (EA)
BOP	Balance of Payments [International trade]
BOP	Balance of Plant [Nuclear energy] (NRCH)
BOP	Balance of Power (IEEE)
BOP	Bands-of-Performance (MCD)
BOP	Baseline Operations Plan (MCD)
BOP	Base of Preference Program [for reenlisting airmen]
BOP	Basic Occupational Preparation
BOP	Basic Operating Program [Computer science] (NITA)
BOP	Basic Operation Plan [Army]
BOP	Basic Overall Polarity (IAA)
BOP	Basic Oxygen Process [Steelmaking]
BOP	Bathyscaphe Oceanographic Program
BOP	Beginning of Period
BOP	Bend-Over Point (PDAA)
BOP	Binary Output Program
BOP	Biocompatible Orthopedic Polymer [Medicine]
BOP	Bipolar Operational Power
BOP	BIT [Binary Digit]-Oriented Protocol
BOP	Bleomycin, Oncovin [Vincristine], Prednisone [Antineoplastic drug regimen] (DAVI)
BOP	Blowout Preventer [or Prevention]
BOP	Boise Cascade Office Products [NYSE symbol] (SAG)
BOP	Boise Cascade Office Products [NYSE symbol] (TTSB)
BOP	Book-on-Payment [Travel industry]
BOP	Bop Air (Pty) Ltd. [South Africa ICAO designator] (FAAC)
BOP	Bouar [Central African Republic] [Airport symbol] (AD)
BOP	[The] Boy's Own Paper [Late nineteenth- and early twentieth-century periodical] [British]
BOP	Branch Office, Pasadena [Office of Naval Research] (DNAB)
BOP	Breach of Peace
BOP	Broken Orange Pekoe [Tea]
BOP	Bronco Petroleum Ltd. [Vancouver Stock Exchange symbol]
BOP	Buffalo Orphan Prototype [Medicine] (MAE)
BOP	Buick-Oldsmobile-Pontiac [General Motors Corp.]
BOP	Building Optimization Program [Computer science]
BOP	Burden of Proof [Legal shorthand] (LWAP)
BOP	Bureau of Operations and Programming [United Nations Development Program]
BOP	Burnout Proof
BOP	Businessowners Policy [Insurance]
BOP	, Prednisone [Vincristine] [Antineoplastic drug regimen]
BOPA	Balance of Payments Act [International trade] (AABC)
BOPACE	Boeing Plastic Analysis Capability for Engines [Computer science NASA]
BOPAM	Bleomycin, Oncovin [Vincristine], Prednisone, Adriamycin, Mustargen , Methotrexate [Nitrogen mustard] [Antineoplastic drug regimen]
BOPAT	Border Patrol
BOPD	Barrels of Oil per Day (WGA)
BOPD	Bataan Ocean Petroleum Depot (CINC)
BO PEEP	Bangor [Wales] Orange Position Estimating Equipment for Pastures [Electronic beeper to be attached to sheep]
BOPF	Basic Oxygen Process Furnace [Steelmaking] (EG)
BOPF	Broken Orange Pekoe Fannings [Tea]
BOPO	Browned-Off Passed-Over (SAA)
BOPP	Balance of Payments Programmed [International trade] (AABC)
BOPP	Biaxially-Oriented Polypropylene [Plastics technology]
BOPP	Boronated Protoporphyrin [Organic chemistry]
BOPP	, Procarbazine, Prednisone [Vincristine] [Antineoplastic drug regimen]
BOPRESS	Boiler Pressure
BOPS	Banking On-Line Package System (BUR)
BOPS	Billions of Operations per Second (DOMA)
BOPS	Bomber Operations [Air Ministry] [British World War II]
BOPSSAR	Balance of Plant Standard Safety Analysis Report [Nuclear energy] (NRCH)
B Opt	Bachelor of Optometry
BOptom	Bachelor of Optometry (ADA)
BOptometry	Bachelor of Optometry
BOPTT	Boom Operator Part Task Trainer (MCD)
BOPTTS	Boom Operator Part Task Training Simulator
BOPWG	Backorder Problem Working Group [DoD]
BOQ	Bachelor Officers' Quarters [Army]
BOQ	Bank of Queensland Ltd.
BOQ	Beginning of Quarter [Accounting]
BOQ	Boku [Papua New Guinea] [Airport symbol Obsolete] (OAG)
B Or	Bachelor of Oratory
BOR	Battalion Orderly Room [British]
BOR	Beginning of Record [Computer science] (IAA)
BOR	Belady Optimum Replacement [Algorithm] [Computer science]
BOR	Belfort [France] [Airport symbol] (OAG)
BOr	Bibbia e Oriente [A publication] (BJA)
BOR	Board of Optical Registration [South Australia and Tasmania]

BOR .... Board of Optometrical Registration [*New South Wales, Australia*]
BOR .... Board of Review [*Army*]
BOR .... Bolero Resources, Inc. [*Vancouver Stock Exchange symbol*]
BoR .... [*A*] Book of Russian Verse [*A publication*]
BOR .... Borg-Warner Corp. [*NYSE symbol*] (SPSG)
BOR .... Borg-Warner Security [*NYSE symbol*] (TTSB)
BOR .... Borg Warner Security Corp. [*NYSE symbol*] (SAG)
Bor .... Borneo
BOR .... Boron [*Symbol is B*] [*Chemical element*] (ROG)
BOR .... Borough
BOR .... Borrowings [*Banking*]
BOR .... Borzhomi [*Former USSR Seismograph station code, US Geological Survey Closed*] (SEIS)
BOR .... Bowels Opened Regularly [*Medicine*] (MAE)
BOR .... Branch Officer Roster [*Army*]
BOR .... British Other Ranks
BOR .... Broadcast Officer
BOR .... Bureau of Operating Rights [*ICC*]
BOR .... Bureau of Outdoor Recreation [*Terminated, 1978, functions transferred to Heritage Conservation and Recreation Service*] [*Department of the Interior*]
BOR .... Bureau of Reclamation [*Later, WPRS*] [*Department of the Interior*] (MCD)
BOR .... Bus Out Register [*Computer science*]
BOR .... Orion Air [*Bulgaria*] [*ICAO designator*] (FAAC)
BORA .... Boray Ltd. [*NASDAQ symbol*] (SAG)
BORACS .... Bureau of Research and Community Services [*Duquesne University*] [*Research center*] (RCD)
BORAL .... Borate and Aluminum (IIA)
Boral .... Boray Ltd. [*Associated Press*] (SAG)
BORAL .... Boron-Aluminum
BORAM .... Block-Oriented Random-Access Memory [*Computer science*]
BORAX .... Boiling Reactor Experiments [*Nuclear energy*]
BORAY .... Boral Ltd ADS [*NASDAQ symbol*] (TTSB)
B or B .... Brass or Bronze [*Top*] [*Freight*]
BORD .... Book Order and Record Document (PDAA)
BORD .... Bordereau [*Statement*] [*French Business term*]
BORD .... Borderline [*Biochemistry*] (DAVI)
BordCh .... Borden Chemicals & Plastics Ltd. [*Associated Press*] (SAG)
Borden .... Borden, Inc. [*Wall Street slang name: "Moo Moo"*] [*Associated Press*] (SAG)
Borders .... Borders Group, Inc. [*Associated Press*] (SAG)
BORE .... Beryllium Oxide Reactor Experiment [*Formerly, EBOR*] [*Nuclear energy*]
Borealis .... Borealis Technology Corp. [*Associated Press*] (SAG)
BOREAS ...... Borea Ecosystem-Atmosphere Study [*Marine science*] (OSRA)
BOREAS ...... Boreal Ecosystem-Atmosphere Study (USDC)
BO REL .... Back Order Release (DNAB)
BORF .... Bill of Rights Foundation (EA)
BORG .... Basic Operational Requirements and Planning Criteria Group [*ICAO*] (DA)
Borgnin Cavalcan... Borginus Cavalcanus [*Flourished, 16th century*] [*Authority cited in pre-1607 legal work*] (DSA)
BorgWAu ..... Borg-Warner Automotive [*Associated Press*] (SAG)
BORI .... Bordano [*Italy*] [*Seismograph station code, US Geological Survey*] (SEIS)
B or I .... Brass or Iron [*Freight*]
B Orient .... Bachelor of Oriental Studies
BORIS .... Bankruptcy Official Receivers' Information System
BORIS .... Board of Realty Information Systems [*Professional Guidance Systems, Inc.*] [*Information service or system*] (IID)
BORIS .... Book Ordering, Registering and Inventory System (PDAA)
BORIS .... Book Order Register and Invoicing System [*British*] (NITA)
BORIS .... Box-Office Reservation and Information Service
BORIS .... Breathe on Recirculation Ignition System (PDAA)
BORIS .... Broadcasting Operations Recording and Information System
BORL .... Borland International, Inc. [*NASDAQ symbol*] (SAG)
BORL .... Borland Intl. [*NASDAQ symbol*] (TTSB)
BorlInd .... Borland International, Inc. [*Associated Press*] (SAG)
BORM .... Bureau of Raw Materials for American Vegetable Oils and Fats Industries (EA)
BORN FREE... Build Options, Renew Norms, Free Roles through Educational Equity [*National project to help students choose appropriate future careers*]
Boro .... Borobudur (VRA)
BORO .... Borough (ROG)
BORO .... Borough
BORON .... Borax and Carbon (IIA)
B or R .... Bales or Rolls [*Freight*]
Borr .... Borradaile's Civil Cases, Bombay [*1800-24*] [*India*] [*A publication*] (DLA)
BORR .... Borror Corp. [*NASDAQ symbol*] (SAG)
Borror .... Borror Corp. [*Associated Press*] (SAG)
BoRS .... [*A*] Second Book of Russian Verse [*A publication*]
B Or Sc .... Bachelor of the Science of Oratory
BORSCHT .... Battery, Overvoltage Protection, Ringing, Supervision, Coding, Hybrids, Testing [*Seven basic functions performed by line circuits*] [*Telecommunications*]
Borth .... Borthwick. Modes of Prosecuting for Libel [*1830*] [*A publication*] (DLA)
BORU .... Boat Operating and Repair Unit [*Navy*]
BorWSc .... Borg-Warner Security Corp. [*Associated Press*] (SAG)
BOS .... Background Operating System (IEEE)
BOS .... Back-Off System
BOS .... Back Order and Selection

BOS .... Backup Operating System (NASA)
BOS .... Balance of State [*Department of Labor*]
BOS .... Balance-of-System [*Power plant efficiency*]
BOS .... Bank of Singapore
BOS .... Base Operating Service [*Contract*] [*DoD*]
BOS .... Base Operating Supplies
BOS .... Base Operating Support (AFM)
BOS .... Basic Oblate Spheroid
BOS .... Basic Operating System [*IBM Corp.*] [*Computer science*]
BOS .... Basic Oxygen Steel [*Steelmaking*]
BOS .... Batch Operating System [*Computer science*]
BOS .... Battalion Orderly Sergeant [*British and Canadian*]
BOS .... Battlefield Operating System [*Military*] (RDA)
BOS .... Bell Operating System [*Telecommunications*] (TEL)
BOS .... Best Opposite Sex (to Best of Breed) [*Dog show term*]
BOS .... Bicycles on Stamps [*Study unit*] [*American Topical Association*] (EA)
BOS .... Blended Old Scotch [*Whiskey*] (ROG)
BOS .... Boise Creek Resources [*Vancouver Stock Exchange symbol*]
BOS .... Book Order and Selection [*Computer science*]
BOS .... Book Order System [*Computer science*] (NITA)
BOS .... Bookseller's Order Service [*For-profit subsidiary of American Booksellers Association*] [*Defunct*]
BOS .... Bosal International Management NV [*Belgium ICAO designator*] (FAAC)
BOS .... Bosque Alegre [*Argentina*] [*Seismograph station code, US Geological Survey Closed*] (SEIS)
BOS .... Boston [*Massachusetts*] [*Airport symbol*]
BOS .... Boston Celtics [*NYSE symbol*] (SPSG)
BOS .... Boston Celtics L.P. [*NYSE symbol*] (TTSB)
BOS .... Boston University, Boston, MA [*OCLC symbol*] (OCLC)
Bos .... Bosworth's New York Superior Court Reports [*A publication*] (DLA)
BOS .... Breed of Sire
BOS .... Bright Object Sensor (MCD)
BOS .... British Origami Society
BOS .... British Orthoptic Society
BOS .... Building Out Section
BOS .... Business Office Supervisor [*Telecommunications*] (TEL)
BOS .... General Edward Lawrence Logan International Airport [*FAA*] (TAG)
BOSA .... Board on Ocean Science Affairs [*National Academy of Science*] (MSC)
BoSA .... [*A*] Book of South African Verse [*A publication*]
BOSA .... Boston Acoustics [*NASDAQ symbol*] (TTSB)
BOSA .... Boston Acoustics, Inc. [*NASDAQ symbol*] (NQ)
BOSAC .... Bofors Spent Acid Concentration [*Chemical industry*]
Bos & D Lim... Bosanquet and Darby's Limitations [*A publication*] (DLA)
Bos & P .... Bosanquet and Puller's English Common Pleas Reports [*126, 127 English Reprint*] [*A publication*] (DLA)
Bos & P (Eng)... Bosanquet and Puller's English Common Pleas Reports [*126, 127 English Reprint*] [*A publication*] (DLA)
Bos & PNR... Bosanquet and Puller's New Reports, English Common Pleas [*1804-07*] [*A publication*] (DLA)
Bos & PNR (Eng)... Bosanquet and Puller's New Reports, English Common Pleas [*1804-07*] [*A publication*] (DLA)
Bos & Pu .... Bosanquet and Puller's English Common Pleas Reports [*126, 127 English Reprint*] [*A publication*] (DLA)
Bos & Pul .... Bosanquet and Puller's English Common Pleas Reports [*126, 127 English Reprint*] [*A publication*] (DLA)
Bos & Pul NR... Bosanquet and Puller's New Reports, English Common Pleas [*1804-07*] [*A publication*] (DLA)
BOSC .... BOS Better Online Solutions Ltd. [*NASDAQ symbol*] (SAG)
BOSCA .... British Oil Spill Control Association (ASF)
Bosc Con ..... Boscawen on Convictions [*A publication*] (DLA)
BOSCF .... B.O.S. Better Online Solutions [*NASDAQ symbol*] (TTSB)
BOSCO .... BOMARC [*Boeing-Michigan Aeronautical Research Center*] SAGE Compatibility [*Semiautomatic Ground Environment*] (IAA)
BOSDET .... Boating Safety Detachment [*Coast Guard*]
BosE .... Boston Edison Co. [*Associated Press*] (SAG)
BOSEX .... Baltic Open Sea Experiment (GNE)
BOSEY .... Board of Supply, Executive Yuan [*Responsible for removing surplus US war material to China from Guam*]
BOSF .... Burnout Safety Factor (SAA)
BOSFET....... Bidirectional Output Switch Field Effect Transistor [*Electronics*] (NITA)
BOSFW .... Bureau of Sport Fisheries and Wildlife [*Superseded by US Fish and Wildlife Service*] [*Department of the Interior*] (MCD)
BOSH .... Bottom-Oriented Shrimp Harvester
BOSLtd .... BOS Better Online Solutions Ltd. [*Associated Press*] (SAG)
BOSN .... Boatswain (KSC)
Bos N R .... Bosanquet and Puller's New Reports, English Common Pleas [*1804-07*] [*A publication*] (ILCA)
BOSNYWASH... Boston, New York, Washington [*Proposed name for possible "super-city" formed by growth and mergers of other cities*]
BOSO .... Bureau of Ordnance Shipment Order [*Obsolete Navy*]
BOSOR........ Buckling of Shells of Revolution [*Computer program*] [*NASA*] (MCD)
BOSOX........ Boston Red Sox [*Baseball team*]
BOSP .... Bioastronautics Orbital Space Program [*Air Force*]
Bos Pl .... Bosanquet's Rules of Pleading [*A publication*] (DLA)
Bos Pol Rep... Boston Police Court. Reports [*A publication*] (DLA)
BOSS .... Backup Optical Storage System [*Aquidneck Data Corp.*] (NITA)
BOSS .... Ballistic Offense Suppressive System [*Military*]
BOSS .... Base Operating Supply System
BOSS .... Basic Operating System [*Computer science*] (NITA)
BOSS .... Basic Operating System Software [*Toshiba Corp.*] [*Japan*]
BOSS .... Basics of Supervisory Skills
BOSS .... Basis of Standard System (IAA)

BOSS	Batch Operating Software System
BOSS	Battalion Operated Surveillance System [*Army*] (INF)
BOSS	Behavior of Offshore Structures [*Conference*]
BOSS	Berkeley-Oakland Service System [*Library network*]
BOSS	Better Opportunities for Single Soldiers [*Army*]
BOSS	Biased Optimal Steering Selector (PDAA)
BOSS	Bioastronautic Orbiting Space Station [*or System*] (MUGU)
BOSS	Biological Orbiting Space Station (IAA)
BOSS	Bistable Optically Controlled Semiconductor Switch (IAA)
BOSS	BLCMP [*Birmingham Libraries Cooperative Mechanisation Project*] Online Support Services (NITA)
BOSS	Block-Oriented Systems Simulator [*Computer software*]
BOSS	BMEWS [*Ballistic Missile Early Warning System*] Operational Simulation System (IAA)
BOSS	Boeing Operational Supervisory System
BOSS	Bomb Orbital Strategic System
BOSS	Book of the Season Scheme [*British*]
BOSS	Broad Ocean Scoring System [*Missiles*]
BOSS	Bureau of State Security [*Later, Department of National Security*] [*South Africa*]
BOSS	Business Opportunities Sourcing System [*Information service or system Canada*]
BOSS	Business Organizer Scheduling System
BOSS	Business-Oriented Search Service [*Information service or system*] (IID)
BOSS	Business-Oriented Software System [*Digital Equipment Corp.*] [*Computer science*] (BUR)
BOSS	Buy Our Spares Smart [*Program*] (AAGC)
BOSSCO	Boeing Shaped Scan Correlator (MCD)
BOSSF	British Office Systems and Stationery Federation (DBA)
BOSS-WEDGE	Bomb Orbital Strategic System - Weapon Development Glide Entry
BoSt	Boghazkoi-Studien [*Leipzig, 1916-1924*] [*A publication*] (BJA)
BOST	Boston [*Massachusetts*]
BOST	Boston Chicken [*NASDAQ symbol*] (TTSB)
BOST	Boston Chicken, Inc. [*NASDAQ symbol*] (SAG)
BostAc	Boston Acoustics, Inc. [*Associated Press*] (SAG)
BostBc	Boston Bancorp. [*Associated Press*] (SAG)
BostBeer	Boston Beer Co. [*Associated Press*] (SAG)
BostChk	Boston Chicken, Inc. [*Associated Press*] (SAG)
BostEd	Boston Edison Co. [*Associated Press*] (SAG)
BOSTI	Buffalo Organization for Social and Technological Innovation (EA)
BOSTID	Board on Science and Technology for International Development [*National Academy of Sciences*]
Bost Law Rep	Boston Law Reporter [*A publication*] (DLA)
BostLfSci	Boston Life Sciences, Inc. [*Associated Press*] (SAG)
Bost LR	Boston Law Reporter [*A publication*] (DLA)
BostnBio	Boston Biomedica, Inc. [*Associated Press*] (SAG)
BostnCm	Boston Communications Group, Inc. [*Associated Press*] (SAG)
Bostnfd	Bostonfed Bancorp, Inc. [*Associated Press*] (SAG)
Boston C	Boston College (GAGS)
Boston College L Rev	Boston College. Law Review [*A publication*] (DLA)
Boston R	Boston Review [*A publication*] (BRI)
Boston U	Boston University (GAGS)
Bost Pol Rep	Boston Police Court. Reports [*A publication*] (DLA)
BostPrv	Boston Private Bancorp [*Associated Press*] (SAG)
BostRest	Boston Restaurant Associates [*Associated Press*] (SAG)
BostRs	Boston Restaurant Associates [*Associated Press*] (SAG)
BostSc	Boston Scientific Corp. [*Associated Press*] (SAG)
BostTc	Boston Technology, Inc. [*Associated Press*] (SAG)
BostTech	Boston Technology [*Associated Press*] (SAG)
BOSU	Bioastronautics Operational Support Unit (MCD)
BOSUN	Boatswain
BOSVA	British Offshore Support Vessels Association (DS)
BOSW	BOS Better Online Solutions Ltd. [*NASDAQ symbol*] (SAG)
Bosw	Boswell's Reports, Scotch Court of Sessions [*A publication*] (DLA)
Bosw	Bosworth's New York Superior Court Reports [*A publication*] (DLA)
BOSWASH	Boston to Washington [*Proposed name for possible "super-city" formed by growth and mergers between these two*]
BOSWF	B.O.S. Better Online Sol Wrrt [*NASDAQ symbol*] (TTSB)
BOSX	BO-S-AIRE Corp. [*Air carrier designation symbol*]
BOT	Air Botswana (Pty) Ltd. [*ICAO designator*] (FAAC)
BOT	Bachelor of Occupational Therapy
BOT	Balance of Trade [*International trade*]
BOT	Bank of Thailand (IMH)
BOT	Bank of Tokyo
BOT	Base of Tongue [*Anatomy and otorhinolaryngology*] (DAVI)
BOT	Beginning of Tape [*Computer science*]
BOT	Black on Tone [*Printing*] (DGA)
BOT	Board of Trade [*Shipping*]
BOT	Board of Transport [*NATO*] (NATG)
BOT	Board of Trustees
BOT	Books on Tape
BOT	Boom Operator Trainer
BOT	Botany [*or Botanist*]
BOT	Botswana [*Spaceflight Tracking and Data Network*] [*NASA*]
BOT	Bottle
BOT	Bottom (KSC)
bot	Bottom (VRA)
BOT	Bottom [*Commonly used*] (OPSA)
BOT	Botulinum Toxin
BOT	Bought
BOT	Bright Old Thing [*A member of established society in Washington, DC*]
BOT	Build, Operate, Transfer [*Business term*]

BOT	Build, Own, Transfer [*Property development*]
BOT	Bulk Oil Temperature (PDAA)
BOT	Burst-on-Target (MCD)
BOT	De Boeken van het Oude Testament [*Roermond/Maaseik*] [*A publication*] (BJA)
bot	Knowbot [*Computer program*] (WDMC)
BOTA	Bank of Tokyo Australia Ltd.
BOTAC	British Overseas Trade Advisory Committee
BOTAN	Botanical
BOTB	Basic Officers Training Battalion [*Army*] (INF)
BOTB	British Overseas Trade Board
BOTD	Ball On Three Disk
BOTEX	British Office for Training Exchange
BOTGI	British Overseas Trade Group for Israel (DS)
BOTH	Bombing over the Horizon
BOT Jo	Board of Trade Journal [*A publication*] (DLA)
BOTLD	Bottled
BOTMA	British Office Technology Manufacturers Alliance (NITA)
BOTMG	Bottoming (MSA)
BOTMP	Bruininks-Oseretsky Test of Motor Proficiency [*Occupational therapy*]
BOTOSS	Bottom Topography Survey System [*Naval Oceanographic Office*]
BOTP	Base Operacional de Tropas Paraquedistas [*Paratroopers Operational Base*] [*Air Force Portugal*]
BoTP	[*The*] Book of a Thousand Poems [*A publication*]
BOTP	Both of This Parish
BOTS	Botswana
Botsw	Botswana (VRA)
Bott	Bott's Poor Law Settlement Cases [*A publication*] (DLA)
BOTTM	Bottom [*Commonly used*] (OPSA)
BOTTOM	Bottom [*Commonly used*] (OPSA)
Bott PL	Bott's Poor Laws [*A publication*] (DLA)
Bott PL Cas	Bott's Poor Law Cases [*1560-1833*] [*England*] [*A publication*] (DLA)
Bott PL Const	Const's Edition of Bott's Poor Law Cases [*A publication*] (DLA)
Bott Poor Law Cas	Bott's Poor Law Settlement Cases [*A publication*] (DLA)
BOTTS	Busy Tone Trunks [*Telecommunications*] (TEL)
Bott Set Cas	Bott's Poor Law Settlement Cases [*A publication*] (DLA)
Bott's PL	Bott's Poor Law Cases [*1560-1833*] [*England*] [*A publication*] (DLA)
BOTU	Board of Trade Unit [*British and Canadian*] [*Military*]
BoTU	Die Boghazkoi-Texte im Umschrift [*A publication*] (BJA)
BOTU(FW)	Basic Operational Training Unit (Fixed Wing)
BOTU(RW)	Basic Operational Training Unit (Rotary Wing)
BOTVAL	Bottom Value
BOTX	Georgia Bonded Fibers [*NASDAQ symbol*] (TTSB)
BOTX	Georgia Bonded Fibers, Inc. [*NASDAQ symbol*] (SAG)
BOU	Banco Osorno y La UnionADS [*NYSE symbol*] (TTSB)
BoU	Bank of Uganda
BOU	Basic Ordering Unit
BOU	Boat Operating Unit [*Navy*]
BOU	Bonus Petroleum Corp. [*Vancouver Stock Exchange symbol*]
BOU	Boulder [*Colorado*] [*Seismograph station code, US Geological Survey Closed*] (SEIS)
BOU	Bouraq Indonesia Airlines PT [*ICAO designator*] (FAAC)
BOU	Branchio-Oto-Ureteral [*Syndrome*] [*Medicine*] (DMAA)
BOU	British Ornithologists' Union
Bouch Ins Dr Mar	Boucher's Instituts au Droit Maritime [*A publication*] (DLA)
Bou Dic	Bouvier's Law Dictionary [*A publication*] (DLA)
Bou Inst	Bouvier's Institutes of American Law [*A publication*] (DLA)
BOUL	Boulevard
boul	Boulevard (DD)
Bould	Bouldin's Reports [*119 Alabama*] [*A publication*] (DLA)
BOULEVARD	Boulevard [*Commonly used*] (OPSA)
Bouln	Boulnois' Reports [*Bengal*] [*A publication*] (DLA)
Boulnois	Boulnois' Reports [*Bengal*] [*A publication*] (DLA)
Boul P Dr Com	Boulay-Paty. Droit Commun [*A publication*] (DLA)
BOULV	Boulevard [*Commonly used*] (OPSA)
BOUMAC	Boulder Laboratory Macrosystem [*National Institute of Standards and Technology*]
Bourd LT	Bourdin on the Land Tax [*A publication*] (DLA)
BOURG	Bourgeois [*Typography*] (DGA)
Bourke	Bourke's Reports, Calcutta High Court [*India*] [*A publication*] (DLA)
Bourke Lim	Bourke on the Indian Law of Limitations [*A publication*] (DLA)
Bourke PP	Bourke's Parliamentary Precedents [*1842-56*] [*England*] [*A publication*] (DLA)
BOuT	De Boeken van het Oude Testament [*Roermond/Maaseik*] [*A publication*] (BJA)
Bout Man	Boutwell's Manual of the United States Tax System [*A publication*]
Bouv	Bouvier's Law Dictionary [*A publication*] (DLA)
Bouvier	Bouvier's Law Dictionary [*A publication*] (DLA)
Bouv Inst	Bouvier's Institutes of American Law [*A publication*] (DLA)
Bouv Law Dict	Bouvier's Law Dictionary [*A publication*] (DLA)
Bouv L Dict	Bouvier's Law Dictionary [*A publication*] (DLA)
Bouygs	Bouygues Offshore SA [*Associated Press*] (SAG)
BOV	Best of Variety (WDAA)
BOV	Blending Octane Value
BOV	Boang [*Papua New Guinea*] [*Airport symbol*] (OAG)
BOV	Board of Visitors (DOMA)
BOV	Bogong [*Victoria*] [*Australia*] [*Seismograph station code, US Geological Survey*] [*Closed*] (SEIS)
BOV	Boletus Virus [*Plant pathology*]
BOV	Boolarra Virus
BOV	Brown Oil of Vitriol
BOV	Burnout Velocity
BOVC	Base of Overcast [*Meteorology*]
Bov Pat Ca	Bovill's Patent Cases [*A publication*] (DLA)

BOW	Bag of Waters [Medicine]
BOW	Bartow, FL [Location identifier FAA] (FAAL)
BOW	Base Ordnance Workshop [British and Canadian]
BOW	Beryllium Oxide Washer
BOW	Bill of Work (NASA)
BOW	Blackout Window [Military]
BoW	Book of the Winter [A publication]
BOW	Bowater, Inc. [NYSE symbol] (SPSG)
Bow	Bowler and Bowers' United States Comptroller's Decisions [2, 3] [A publication] (DLA)
Bow	Bowler's London Session Records [1605-85] [A publication] (DLA)
BOW	Bowman [South Carolina] [Seismograph station code, US Geological Survey] (SEIS)
BOW	Bow Valley Resource Services Ltd. [Toronto Stock Exchange symbol]
BOW	Breach of Warranty [Insurance] (AIA)
BOWA	Booker T. Washington National Monument
BOWA	Brisbane Overseas Wharfowners' Association [Australia]
BOWASH	Boston-to-Washington Corridor
Bowat	Bowater, Inc. [Associated Press] (SAG)
Bowatr	Bowater, Inc. [Associated Press] (SAG)
BOWC	Brethren of the White Cross [Book written by James De Mille (1873)]
Bow Civ Law	Bowyer's Modern Civil Law [A publication] (DLA)
Bow Com	Bowyer. Commentaries on Universal Public Law [1854] [A publication] (DLA)
Bow Cons Law	Bowyer. Commentaries on the Constitutional Law of England [2nd ed.] [1846] [A publication] (DLA)
BOWD	Budget Office, War Department [World War II]
Bowen Pol Econ	Bowen's Political Economy [A publication] (DLA)
BOWI	Bibliographie zur Offentlichen Unternehmung und Verwaltung [Bibliography of Public Management and Administration] [NOMOS Datapool] [Information service or system]
Bowie St U	Bowie State University (GAGS)
Bow Int	Bowyer. Introduction to the Study and Use of the Civil Law [1874] [A publication] (DLA)
BOWL	Bowling
BowlA	Bowl America, Inc. [Associated Press] (SAG)
Bowler's First Comp Dec	Decisions of the First Comptroller of the United States Treasury [A publication] (DLA)
Bowl Gr St U	Bowling Green State University (GAGS)
Bowl Lib	Bowles on Libel [A publication] (DLA)
Bowmr	Bowmar Instrument Corp. [Associated Press] (SAG)
Bowne	Bowne & Co., Inc. [Associated Press] (SAG)
BOWO	Brigade Ordnance Warrant Officer [British]
BOWP	Black Ordinary Working People
BOWPrB	Bowater Inc. Dep'B'7%'PRIDES' [NYSE symbol] (TTSB)
BOWPrC	Bowater Inc.'C'8.40% Dep Pfd [NYSE symbol] (TTSB)
Bow Pub Law	Bowyer. Commentaries on Universal Public Law [1854] [A publication] (DLA)
BOWR	Boiler Water
BOWS	[The] Barretts of Wimpole Street [A play by Rudolf Besier]
Bowstead	Bowstead on Agency [1896-1951] [A publication] (DLA)
Bowyer Mod Civil Law	Bowyer's Modern Civil Law [A publication] (DLA)
BOX	Bilirubin Oxidase [An enzyme]
BOX	BOC Group [NYSE symbol] (SAG)
BOX	Borok [Former USSR Geomagnetic observatory code]
BOX	Borroloola [Airport symbol]
BOX	Houston, TX [Location identifier FAA] (FAAL)
BOX	Tiphook PCL [British ICAO designator] (FAAC)
BoxEn	Box Energy Corp. [Associated Press] (SAG)
BOXX	Box Energy Corp. [NASDAQ symbol] (SAG)
BOXXA	Box Energy'A' [NASDAQ symbol] (TTSB)
BOXXB	Box Energy 'B' [NASDAQ symbol] (TTSB)
BOY	Beginning of Year [Accounting]
BOY	Bobo Dioulass [Volta] [Airport symbol] (AD)
BOY	Bobo-Dioulasso [Burkina Faso] [Airport symbol] (OAG)
BOY	Boycott [Legal shorthand] (LWAP)
BOY	Boykin Lodging Co. [NYSE symbol] (SAG)
BOY	Boysen Reservoir, WY [Location identifier FAA] (FAAL)
Boyce	Boyce's Delaware Supreme Court Reports [1909-19] [A publication] (DLA)
Boyce US Pr	Boyce's Practice in the United States Courts [A publication] (DLA)
Boy Char	Boyle. Charities [1837] [A publication] (DLA)
BOYD	Boyd Bros.Transport'n [NASDAQ symbol] (TTSB)
BOYD	Boyd Brothers Transportation, Inc. [NASDAQ symbol] (SAG)
Boyd Adm	Boyd's Admiralty Law [Ireland] [A publication] (DLA)
BoydBros	Boyd Brothers Transportation, Inc. [Associated Press] (SAG)
BoydGm	Boyd Gaming Corp. [Associated Press] (SAG)
Boyd Jus	Boyd. Justice of the Peace [A publication] (DLA)
Boyd Sh	Boyd. Merchant Shipping Laws [1876] [A publication] (DLA)
BoykinL	Boykin Lodging Co. [Associated Press] (SAG)
BOYL	Bank of Yorba Linda [NASDAQ symbol] (SAG)
Boyle Act	Boyle's Precis of an Action at Common Law [A publication] (DLA)
Boyle Char	Boyle. Charities [1837] [A publication] (DLA)
Boys Cor	Boys on Coroners [A publication] (DLA)
BOYSNC	Beginning of Year Significant Non-Complier [Environmental Protection Agency] (ERG)
BOYSNC	Beginning of Year Significant NonCompliers [Environment] (GNE)
BoZ	Bote aus Zion (BJA)
BOZ	Bozeman [Montana] [Seismograph station code, US Geological Survey Closed] (SEIS)
boz	Bozzetto (VRA)
BOZ	Sterling Rockfalls, IL [Location identifier FAA] (FAAL)
BP	Air Botswana [ICAO designator] (AD)
BP	Bachelor of Painting

BP	Bachelor of Pedagogy
BP	Bachelor of Pharmacy
BP	Bachelor of Philosophy
Bp	Bachelor's Degree (Pass) [British]
BP	Bacillus Pumilis [Bacteriology]
BP	Background Paper
BP	Backpack
BP	Back Plane (MCD)
BP	Back Plaster [Technical drawings]
BP	Back Pressure
BP	Back Projection (DEN)
BP	Baghdad Pact (CINC)
B/P	Baking Powder (WDAA)
BP	Balance of Payments [International trade]
BP	Ballistic Processor [Military] (CAAL)
BP	Bandpass
bp	Bandpass (IDOE)
BP	Baptized
BP	Barber Pole (KSC)
BP	Barometric Pressure
BP	Barrier Preparation (MCD)
BP	Basal Period
bp	Base Pairs [Genetics] (DOG)
BP	Base Pairs in DNA [Genetics]
BP	Base Pay [Military]
BP	Base Percussion
BP	Base Pioneer [Cell neuron]
BP	Base Pitch (MSA)
BP	Baseplate [Technical drawings]
BP	Base Point
BP	Base Pointer [Computer science]
BP	Base Position [Phylogenetic analysis]
BP	Base Procured (AFM)
BP	Base Protein
BP	Basic Pay
BP	Basic Process (ECII)
BP	Basic Protein [Immunology]
BP	Basilar Papilla [Anatomy]
BP	Basis Point [Finance] (ODBW)
BP	Basse Pression [Low Pressure] [French]
BP	Bassposaune [Bass Trombone] [Music]
BP	Batch Processing
BP	Bathophenanthroline [Organic chemistry]
BP	Bathroom Privileges [Medicine]
BP	Battery Package
BP	Battery-Powered (ADA)
BP	Batting Practice [Baseball]
BP	Battle Position (AABC)
BP	Bayernpartei [Bavarian Party] [Germany Political party] (PPE)
BP	BCNU [Carmustine], Prednisone [Antineoplastic drug regimen]
BP	Beach Party
BP	Beacon Point
BP	Beacon Press [Publisher]
BP	Bearing Pile [Technical drawings] (DAC)
BP	Beatissime Pater [Most Holy Father] [Latin]
BP	Beautiful People [Slang for the wealthy, world-traveling, partying set]
BP	Bedpan
BP	Before the Present
BP	Beginning Period (AABC)
BP	Behavior Pattern (ADA)
BP	Bell's Palsy [Medicine] (DMAA)
BP	Below Proof
BP	Benedictines for Peace (EA)
BP	Benefit Principles (DLA)
BP	Benzopyrene [or Benzpyrene] [Also, BZ Carcinogen]
BP	Benzoyl Peroxide [Also, BPO] [Organic chemistry]
BP	Bermuda Plan [Travel accomodations]
BP	Between Perpendiculars [Technical drawings]
BP	Bibliotheque du Parlement [Library of Parliament] [Canada]
BP	Bill of Parcels
BP	Bills Payable [Business term]
BP	Binding Post (KSC)
BP	Binding Protein [Biochemistry]
BP	Bioassay Program
BP	Biological Processing (SSD)
BP	Biopack [NASA] (KSC)
BP	Biophysical Society
BP	Bioregional Project (EA)
BP	Bioscience Program [NASA]
BP	Biotic Potential
BP	Biparietal Diameter [Gynecology]
Bp	Bipost [Lamp base] (NTCM)
BP	Birthplace
BP	Bishop
BP	Bishop
BP	Bit Processor (NITA)
BP	Bizarre People [Extension of BP - Beautiful People] [Slang]
BP	Blackout Preparedness
BP	Black Powder
BP	Blacky Pictures [Psychological testing]
BP	Blast Propagation (AAG)
BP	Blind Purchase
BP	Blister Pack
BP	Block Parity [Error checking method] [Telecommunications] (TEL)
B/P	Blood Precautions [Isolation] [Medicine]

BP...............	Blood Pressure [*Medicine*]
B/P.............	Blood Pressure [*Medicine*] (DMAA)
BP...............	Blood Program [*Red Cross*]
BP...............	Blueprint
BP...............	Board of Parole [*Abolished, 1976, functions transferred to United States Parole Commission*] [*Department of Justice*]
B/P.............	Board President
BP...............	Body Part [*Anatomy*] (DAVI)
BP...............	Boeren Partij [*Farmers' Party*] [*Netherlands Political party*] (PPE)
BP...............	Boiler Plate
BP...............	Boiler Pressure
BP...............	Boiling Point
BP...............	Boite Postale [*Post Office Box*] [*French*]
BP...............	Bollard Pull [*Shipping*] [*British*]
BP...............	Bolted Plate [*Technical drawings*]
BP...............	Bolton Point [*Medicine*] (DMAA)
BP...............	Bond and Preferred [*Business term*]
BP...............	Bonded Part [*Wire insulation*] (IAA)
BP...............	Bonded Single Paper [*Wire insulation*] (IAA)
BP...............	Bonum Publicum [*The Public Good*] [*Latin*]
BP...............	Bonus Points
BP...............	Booklet Pane [*Philately*]
BP...............	Bookplates [*A publication*]
BP...............	Book Profit [*Investment term*]
BP...............	Book Publishing
BP...............	Boost Pump (MCD)
BP...............	Border Patrol
BP...............	Boring Party (EA)
BP...............	Bornier Programmable (IAA)
BP...............	Boron Plastic
BP...............	Bottom Plane (MSA)
BP...............	Box Project (EA)
BP...............	Brazed Joint-Preinserted Ring (DNAB)
BP...............	Breakpoint [*Telecommunications*] (TEL)
bp...............	Brick Piers (BARN)
BP...............	Brick Protected [*Insurance classification*]
BP...............	Briefing Papers (AAGC)
BP...............	Brilliant Pebbles
BP...............	Bristol Polytechnic [*Bristol, England*]
BP...............	British Patent
BP...............	British Petrol ADS [*NYSE symbol*] (TTSB)
BP...............	British Petroleum Co. [*NYSE symbol Toronto Stock Exchange symbol*] (SPSG)
BP...............	British Pharmacopoeia [*A publication in pharmacy*]
BP...............	British Pound [*Monetary unit*]
BP...............	British Public [*Slang*]
bp...............	British Solomon Islands [*MARC country of publication code Library of Congress*] (LCCP)
BP...............	Broadcast Pioneers (EA)
BP...............	Bronchopleural [*Medicine*]
BP...............	Bronchopulmonary [*Medicine*] (DAVI)
BP...............	Bubble Pulse (IAA)
BP...............	Buccopulpal [*Dentistry*]
BP...............	Buckingham Palace [*British*]
BP...............	Budgetary Policy
BP...............	Budget Program [*DoD*] (GFGA)
BP...............	Budget Project [*Navy*] (CAAL)
BP...............	Buergerpartei [*Citizens' Party*] [*Germany Political party*] (PPE)
BP...............	Buffered Printing
BP...............	Buff Polish [*Optics*]
BP...............	Bullet Path [*Ballistics*]
BP...............	Bullous Pemphigoid [*Medicine*]
B/P.............	Bureau of Power [*of FPC*]
BP...............	Bureau of Prisons [*Department of Justice*]
BP...............	Burry Port [*Welsh depot code*]
BP...............	Butt Plane
BP...............	Bypass
BP...............	By Procuration [*In power of attorney*] [*Legal term*]
BP...............	La Bible et les Peres [*A publication*] (BJA)
Bp...............	Magnetic Induction Field [*Radiology*] (DAVI)
BP...............	Penticton Public Library, British Columbia [*Library symbol National Library of Canada*] (NLC)
BP7.............	Borland Pascal 7 [*Borland International, Inc.*] [*Computer programming*] (PCM)
BP 120/80 Lar...	in the Left Arm While Reclining [*Diastolic*] [*or Recumbent*] [*Cardiology*] (DAVI)
BP 120/80 Rar...	in the Right Arm While Reclining [*Diastolic*] [*or recumbent*] [*Cardiology*] (DAVI)
B Pa............	Bachelor of Painting
BPA.............	Bachelor of Professional Arts
BPA.............	Bachelor of Public Administration
BPA.............	Back Pain Association [*British Research center*] (EAIO)
BPA.............	Bahn Post Amt [*Railway Post Office*] [*German*]
BPA.............	Balanced Parametric Amplifier
BPA.............	Balloon Platoon of America [*Later, HBC*] (EA)
BPA.............	Baltimore Publishers Association (EA)
BPA.............	Banco Portugues do Atlantico [*Portuguese Bank of the Atlantic*] (ECON)
BPA.............	Basic Pressure Altitude
BPA.............	Basic Purchase Agreement (MCD)
BPA.............	Beam Plasma Amplification (MCD)
B Pa............	Bernardus Papiensis [*Deceased, 1213*] [*Authority cited in pre-1607 legal work*] (DSA)
BPA.............	Bethpage, NY [*Location identifier FAA*] (FAAL)
BPA.............	Billiard Players Association of America

BPA.............	Biological Photographic Association (EA)
BPA.............	Bioprocessing Aid
BPA.............	Bioshield Power Assembly [*NASA*]
BPA.............	Biphenylamine [*Organic chemistry*]
BPA.............	Black Psychiatrists of America (EA)
BPA.............	Blanket Purchase Agreement (KSC)
BPA.............	Blanket Purchase Authority
BPA.............	Blocked Precedence Announcement (DNAB)
BPA.............	Blood Pressure Assembly (KSC)
BPA.............	Board on Personnel Administration (AEBS)
BPA.............	Bonneville Power Administration [*Department of Energy*] [*Portland, OR*]
BPA.............	Bookmakers' Protection Association Ltd. (BI)
BPA.............	Book Packagers Association [*British*] (DBA)
BPA.............	Book Publisher's Association (NTCM)
BPA.............	Border Patrol Academy
BPA.............	Boronophenylalanine [*Organic chemistry*]
BPA.............	Bottom Pumparound [*Drilling technology*]
BPA.............	Bovine Plasma Albumin
BPA.............	Brazil Philatelic Association (EA)
BPA.............	Breakpoint Address Register (IAA)
BPA.............	British Paediatric Association
BPA.............	British Pantomime Association
BPA.............	British Parachute Association
BPA.............	British Parking Association
BPA.............	British Peace Assembly
BPA.............	British Pediatric Association (BARN)
BPA.............	British Philatelic Association Ltd. (BI)
BPA.............	British Photographic Association (DBA)
BPA.............	British Pilots Association [*A union*]
BPA.............	British Ploughing Association (BI)
BPA.............	British Ports Association (DS)
BPA.............	British Professional Association (DBA)
BPA.............	British Psychodrama Association (DBA)
BPA.............	British Pyrotechnists' Association (BI)
BPA.............	Broadcasters' Promotion Association [*Later, BPME*] (EA)
BPA.............	Budget Project Account [*Military*] (AABC)
BPa.............	Buergerpartei [*Citizens' Party*] [*Germany Political party*] (PPW)
BPA.............	Buffered Pyrophosphatase Activity [*Chemistry*]
BPA.............	Bullous Pemphigoid Antigen [*Immunology*]
BPA.............	Bureau of Pension Advocates [*Canada*]
BPA.............	Bureau of Public Administration [*University of Tennessee at Knoxville*] [*Research center*] (RCD)
BPA.............	Bureau of Public Assistance [*Later, BFS*] [*Social Security Administration*]
BPA.............	Burst-Promoting Activity [*Cytology*]
BPA.............	Bush Pilots Airways Ltd. [*Australia*] (ADA)
BPA.............	Business Process Analysis
BPA.............	Business Publications Audit of Circulation (EA)
BPA.............	Major League Baseball Players Association
BPAA...........	Bowling Proprietors' Association of America (EA)
BPAA...........	British Poster Advertising Association (DGA)
B/PAA.........	Business/Professional Advertising Association [*New York, NY*] (EA)
BPAA-DAD ...	Bowling Proprietors' Association of America - Duckpin Activities Department [*Defunct*] (EA)
BPAB..........	Biotinyl-para-aminobenzoate [*Biochemistry*]
BPAC..........	Better Packaging Advisory Council (EA)
BPAC..........	Book Promoters' Association of Canada (AC)
BPAC..........	Book Publishers' Association of Canada
BPAC	Budget Program Activity Code
BPAC/MPC ..	Budget Program Activity Code Material Program Code (MCD)
BPAD..........	Bipolar Affective Disorder [*Genetics*]
BPAD	BISYNC Packet Assembler/Disassembler [*Telecommunications*] (ACRL)
BPAD	Bowker's Publisher Authority Database [*R. R. Bowker Co.*] [*Information service or system*] (CRD)
BPADA........	Alberni District Archives, Port Alberni, British Columbia [*Library symbol National Library of Canada*] (BIB)
BP Adm	Bachelor of Public Administration
BPaed.........	Bachelor of Paediatrics (ADA)
BPaed.........	Bachelor of Pedagogy
BPAG.........	Bullous Pemphigoid Antigen [*Medicine*] (DMAA)
BPAM.........	Alberni Valley Museum, Port Alberni, British Columbia [*Library symbol National Library of Canada*] (NLC)
BPAM.........	Basic Partitioned Access Method [*IBM Corp.*] [*Computer science*]
BP & CO	Burns, Philip, & Co. [*Steamship*] (MHDW)
BPAO.........	Baldwin Piano [*NASDAQ symbol*] (SAG)
BPAO	Baldwin Piano & Organ [*NASDAQ symbol*] (TTSB)
BPAO	Branch Public Affairs Officer [*United States Information Service*]
BPAP.........	Benzoyl(Phenylalanyl)Proline [*Biochemistry*]
BPAR.........	Bureau of Prisons Acquisition Regulation [*A publications*] (AAGC)
BPAS.........	Benzoyl-para-aminosalicylate [*Pharmacology*]
BPA-SDI......	Bonneville Power Administration Selective Dissemination of Information [*Department of the Interior*]
BPAT..........	Bakers and Pastrycooks' Association of Tasmania [*Australia*]
BPATSS......	Bias Power and Temperature Step Stress (PDAA)
BPAV.........	Bus Proprietors' Association, Victoria [*Australia*]
BPB............	Bachelor of Physical Biology
BP-B...........	Bacteriopheophytin-B [*Biochemistry*]
BPB............	Baltimore Photo & Blue Print Co., Baltimore, MD [*Library symbol Library of Congress*] (LCLS)
BPB............	Bankers Tr N.Y.7.50% Dep Pfd [*AMEX symbol*] (TTSB)
BPB............	Bankers Trust New York Corp. [*AMEX symbol*] (SAG)
BPB............	Bank Pass Book (ROG)
BPB............	Bank Post Bill [*Business term*]

BPB............. Base Planning Board [*Military*] (DNAB)
BPB............. BIOS [*Basic Input-Output System*] Parameter Block [*Computer science*] (PCM)
BPB............. Black Pigmented Bacteria [*Microbiology*]
BPB............. Blanket Position Bond [*Insurance*]
BPB............. Boom Patrol Boat [*British Marines' Special Forces*] [*World War II*]
BPB............. Bromophenacyl Bromide [*Organic chemistry*]
BPB............. Bromophenol Blue [*A pH indicator*] [*Organic chemistry*] (DAVI)
BPB............. Bromphenol [*or Bromophenol*] Blue [*A dye*]
BPB............. Business Planning Board [*Later, BTPB*] (EA)
BPBC........... Boston Private Bancorp [*NASDAQ symbol*] (SAG)
BPBD........... International Alliance of Bill Posters, Billers, and Distributors of US and Canada [*Defunct*] (EA)
BPBF........... British Paper Box Federation (DGA)
BPBG........... Butyl Phthalyl Butyl Glycolate [*Organic chemistry*]
BPBHA........ British Poultry Breeders and Hatcheries Association (DBA)
BPBIF.......... British Paper and Board Industry Federation (DGA)
BPBIRA....... British Paper and Board Industry Research Association
BPBMA....... British Paper and Board Makers' Association (DGA)
BPBMF....... British Paper Box Manufacturers' Federation (DGA)
BPBW .... Bare Phosphor Bronze Wire
BPC............. Back-Pressure Control
BPC............. Banco Comercial Portugues [*NYSE symbol*] (SPSG)
BPC............. Banco Coml Portugues ADS [*NYSE symbol*] (TTSB)
BPC............. Bandpass Crystal
BPC............. Base Point Configuration (AAG)
BPC............. Basic Peripheral Channel
BPC............. Battery Park City [*New York City*]
BPC............. BCP International Bank Ltd. [*NYSE symbol*] (SAG)
BPC............. Beach Patrol Craft [*British military*] (DMA)
BPC............. Beagle Pup Club [*British*]
BPC............. Behavior Problem Checklist (EDAC)
BPC............. Binding Post Chamber [*Telecommunications*] (TEL)
BPC............. Biomaterials Profiling Center [*University of Utah*] [*Research center*] (RCD)
BPC............. Black People's Convention [*South Africa*] (PD)
BPC............. Blast-Furnace Portland Cement (PDAA)
BPC............. Bonded Phase Chromatography
BPC............. Book and Periodical Circulation (DGA)
BPC............. Book & Periodical Council (AC)
BPC............. Book Prices Current [*1887-1956*] [*A publication British*]
BPC............. Boost Protective Cover [*Apollo*] [*NASA*]
BPC............. BP Canada, Inc. [*Toronto Stock Exchange symbol Vancouver Stock Exchange symbol*]
BPC............. [*The*] Briefing Papers Collection [*A publication*] (AAGC)
BPC............. British Pharmaceutical Code
BPC............. British Pharmaceutical Codex [*A publication in pharmacy*]
BPC............. British Phosphate Commission (FEA)
BPC............. British Printing Corp. [*Later, BPCC*]
BPC............. British Productivity Council
BPC............. British Purchasing Commission
BPC............. Brown's Cases in Parliament [*A publication*] (DLA)
BPC............. Bulk Petrol Co. [*British and Canadian*] [*Military*]
BPC............. Bulk Pharmaceutical Chemical [*Manufacturing Plant*]
BPC............. Bulk Pharmaceutical Chemical [*Manufacturing*]
BPC............. Bureau of Provisions and Clothing [*See also BSA*] [*Navy*]
BPC............. Business Publications Audit (DGA)
BPC............. Butylpyridinium Chloride [*Organic chemistry*]
BPC............. Port Coquitlam Public Library, British Columbia [*Library symbol National Library of Canada*] (NLC)
BPCA .... Bioshield Pyrotechnic Control Assembly [*for Mariner Venus-Mercury Project spacecraft*] [*NASA*]
BPCA .... British Pest Control Association (EAIO)
BPCC .... Balloon Post Collectors Club (EA)
BPCC .... Better Postcard Collectors' Club [*Later, D of A*] (EA)
BPCC .... Bipyridinium Chlorochromate [*Organic chemistry*]
BPCC .... British Printing & Communication Corporations [*Later, MCC*]
BPCD .... Barrels per Calendar Day
BPCDI .... Brookhaven Portable Cesium Developmental Irradiator Unit [*Nuclear energy*]
BPCF........... Bandpass Crystal Filter
BPCF........... British Postal Chess Federation (BI)
BPCF........... British Precast Concrete Federation (EAIO)
BPCH .... Craig Heritage Park, Parksville, British Columbia [*Library symbol National Library of Canada*] (NLC)
BPCI........... Bulk Packaging and Containerization Institute [*Later, CII*] (EA)
BPCI........... ISI Infosearch, Port Coquitlam, British Columbia [*Library symbol National Library of Canada*] (NLC)
BPCM.......... Best Practical Control Method [*Wastewater treatment*] (DICI)
B-PCO₂ .... Blood Partial Pressure of Carbon Dioxide [*On blood gas determinations*] (DAVI)
BP/CP .... Base Procured/Central Procured (AFM)
BPCR .... Breakout Procurement Center Representative (AAGC)
BPCS .... Back Pain Classification Scale [*Medicine*] (DMAA)
BPCS .... Business Periodicals Circulation Services [*Harcourt Brace Jovanovich*]
BPCT .... Best Practicable Control Technology [*Wastewater treatment*]
BPCTCA...... Best Practicable Control Technology Currently Available (MCD)
B Pd............ Bachelor of Pedagogy [*or Pedagogics*]
BPD .... Bachelor of Planning and Design
BPD .... Banco Popular de Desenvolvimento
BPD .... Barrels per Day
BPD .... Baseline Program Document (NASA)
BPD .... Base Period Density
BPD .... Basic Planning Document [*Military*] (AABC)

BPD .... Basic Point Defense [*Military*] (NVT)
BPD .... Battlefield Plan Development (MCD)
BPD .... Beach Party Division [*Navy*] (NVT)
BPD .... Beam Positioning Drive (OA)
BPD .... Beaupre Explorations [*Vancouver Stock Exchange symbol*]
BPD .... Biparietal Diameter [*Gynecology*]
BPD .... Blood Pressure Decreased [*Medicine*] (MAE)
BPD .... Blood Program Directives [*Red Cross*]
BPD .... Board of Contract Appeals Bid Protest Decisions 1985-96 [*A publication*] (AAGC)
bpd .... Bookplate Designer [*MARC relator code*] [*Library of Congress*] (LCCP)
BPD .... Book Publisher's Directory [*Later, PD*] [*A publication*]
BPD .... Borderline Personality Disorder [*Psychology*]
BPD .... British Society of Poster Designers
BPD .... Bronchopulmonary Dysplasia [*Medicine*]
BPD .... Bureau of the Public Debt [*Department of the Treasury*]
BPD .... Bushing Potential Device (MSA)
BPD .... Business Periodicals Directory [*A publication*]
BPD .... Buy per Drawing (SAA)
BPD .... Doctor of Bio-Psychology
BPDA .... Bibliographic Pattern Discovery Algorithm (PDAA)
BPDA .... Biphenyl Dianhydride [*Organic chemistry*]
BPDC .... Berkeley Particle Data Center
BPDE .... Benzopyrenedihydrodiolepoxide [*Organic chemistry*]
BPDG .... Berkeley Particle Data Group [*Lawrence Radiation Laboratory*]
BPDLS .... Base Point Defense Launching System (DNAB)
BPDMS .... Basic Point Defense Missile System (MCD)
BPDP. .... Book Publishing Development Program [*Canada*]
BPDP. .... Brotherhood of Painters, Decorators, and Paperhangers of America [*Later, IBPAT*]
BPDS .... Basic Point Defense System (MCD)
BPDS .... Bathophenanthroline Disulphonate [*Organic chemistry*]
BPDSMS ..... Basic Point Defense Surface Missile System (NVT)
BPDU .... Bridge Protocol Data Unit [*Telecommunications*] (ACRL)
B Pe .... Bachelor of Pedagogy
BPE............. Bachelor of Petroleum Engineering (WGA)
BPE............. Bachelor of Physical Education
BPE............. Back Porch Effect
BPE............. Bacterial Phosphatidylethanolamine [*Physiological chemistry*]
BPE............. Beauchamp Exploration, Inc. [*Vancouver Stock Exchange symbol*]
BPE............. Best Preliminary Estimate (AFM)
BPE............. Binaural Phase Effect
BPE............. BIT [*Binary Digit*]-Plane Encoding [*Computer science*]
BPE............. Boiling Point Elevation
BPE............. Bovine Pituitary Extract
BPE............. Bremen Port of Embarkation [*West Germany*]
BPE............. Budget Program Estimate (MCD)
BPE............. Bureau of Postsecondary Education [*Later, Bureau of Higher and Continuing Education*] [*Office of Education*]
BPE............. Butyl Phenyl Ether [*Organic chemistry*]
BPEAOA .... Bureau of Professional Education of the American Osteopathic Association (EA)
BPEC........... Bovine Pulmonary Artery Endothelium Cell [*Cell line*]
BPEC........... Building Products Executives Conference
B Ped.......... Bachelor of Pedagogy [*or Pedagogics*]
BP Ed.......... Bachelor of Physical Education
BPED .... Basic Pay Entry Date
B Pe E .... Bachelor of Petroleum Engineering
B Pe Eng .... Bachelor of Petroleum Engineering
BPEF........... Broadcast Pioneers Educational Fund, Inc. (NTCM)
BPEG .... British Photographic Export Group (DBA)
BPEHC .... Battery-Powered Electrically Heated Catalyst [*Automotive exhaust emissions*]
BPEI............ Blepharophimosis, Ptosis, Epicanthus Inversus [*Medicine*] (DMAA)
BPE-LCA ...... Board of Parish Education, Lutheran Church in America (EA)
BPEM.......... Peachland Museum, British Columbia [*Library symbol National Library of Canada*] (NLC)
BPEMM........ Pemberton Museum, British Columbia [*Library symbol National Library of Canada*] (NLC)
BPEO .... Best Practicable Environmental Option (ECON)
BPEQ .... Board of Professional Engineers of Queensland [*Australia*]
BPerfArts ..... Bachelor of Performing Arts
BPES........... Blepharophimosis-Ptosis-Epicanthus Inversus Syndrome [*Medicine*] (DMAA)
B Pet E .... Bachelor of Petroleum Engineering
BPEX .... Business Passenger's Extra Option [*Proposed*] [*Travel industry*]
BPF............. Bandpass Filter
BPF............. Baptist Peace Fellowship (EA)
BPF............. Base Productivity Factor (MCD)
BPF............. Bicycling Parking Foundation (EA)
BPF............. Biliary Protein Fraction
BPF............. Blade-Passing Frequency (PDAA)
BPF............. Blue Print Files (NRCH)
BPF............. Bon pour Francs [*Value in Francs*] [*French*]
BPF............. Books for the People Fund (EA)
BPF............. Bottom Pressure Fluctuation
BPF............. Bradykinin-Potentiating Factor [*Biochemistry Medicine*] (DMAA)
BPF............. Brethren Peace Fellowship [*Inactive*] (EA)
BPF............. British Pacific Fleet [*Obsolete*]
BPF............. British Philatelic Federation (DBA)
BPF............. British Plastics Federation
BPF............. British Plastics Federation
BPF............. British Polio Fellowship [*British*]
BPF............. British Ports Federation (DBA)

BPF .... British Poultry Federation (EAIO)
BPF .... British Property Federation (DBA)
BPF .... Bromine Pentafluoride [*Corrosive compound*]
BPF .... Bronchopleural Fistula [*Anatomy*]
BPF .... Buddhist Peace Fellowship (EA)
BPF .... Burst-Promoting Factor [*Endocrinology; hematology*]
BPF .... Byelorussian Popular Front [*Political party*]
BPF(I) .... Ball-Pass Frequency, Inner Race [*Machinery*]
BPFILO .... British Pacific Fleet Intelligence Liaison Officer
BPFLO .... British Pacific Fleet Liaison Officer
BPFM .... Bypass Flow Module [*Nuclear energy*] (NRCH)
BPFMA .... British Plumbing Fittings Manufacturers Association (DBA)
BPFNA .... Baptist Peace Fellowship of North America (EAIO)
BPF(O) .... Ball-Pass Frequency, Outer Race [*Machinery*]
BPFP .... Botswana Protectorate Federal Party
BPFS .... Bulk Petroleum Facilities and Systems
BPFT .... Basic Physical Fitness Test (MCD)
BPG .... Beach Party Group [*Navy*] (NVT)
BPG .... Beach Party Guard [*Navy*] (NVT)
BPG .... Benzathine Penicillin G [*Antibacterial*]
BPG .... Beveled Plate Glass (DAC)
BPG .... Biased Proportional Guidance
BPG .... Big Plasma Glucagon [*Endocrinology*]
BPG .... Bisphosphoglycerate [*Biochemistry*]
BPG .... Blood Pressure Gauge [*Medicine*]
BPG .... Boron Pyrolytic Graphite
BPG .... Break Pulse Generator (CET)
BPG .... Prince George Public Library, British Columbia [*Library symbol National Library of Canada*] (NLC)
BPGAG .... Experimental Farm, Agriculture Canada [*Ferme Experimentale, Agriculture Canada*], Prince George, British Columbia [*Library symbol National Library of Canada*] (BIB)
BPGC .... Bearing per Gyro Compass [*Navigation*]
BPGC .... Bricks, Pottery, Glass, Cement [*Department of Employment*] [*British*]
BPGC .... College of New Caledonia, Prince George, British Columbia [*Library symbol National Library of Canada*] (NLC)
BPGLSB ...... Library Services Branch, Ministry of Provincial Secretary and Government Services, Prince George, British Columbia [*Library symbol National Library of Canada*] (NLC)
BPGMA .... British Pressure Gauge Manufacturers Association (BI)
BPGRG .... British Plant Growth Regulator Group (EAIO)
BPGRM .... Fraser - Fort George Regional Museum, Prince George, British Columbia [*Library symbol National Library of Canada*] (NLC)
BPGV .... Burry Port & Gwendraeth Valley Railway [*Wales*]
BPh .... Bachelor of Pharmacy (DD)
B Ph .... Bachelor of Philosophy
BPH .... Bachelor of Public Health
BPH .... Barrels per Hour
BPH .... Benign Prostatic Hyperplasia [*Medicine*]
BPH .... Benign Prostatic Hyperplasia [*Medicine*] (CDI)
BPH .... Benign Prostatic Hypertrophy [*Medicine*]
BPH .... Bislig [*Philippines*] [*Airport symbol*] (OAG)
B-P-H .... Botanico-Periodicum-Huntianum [*Book title*]
BPh .... British Pharmacopoeia [*A publication*] (MAE)
BPH .... Brown Planthopper [*Entomology*]
BPH .... Bump Protection Hat
BPH .... Bypass Graft (DAVI)
BPHA .... Benzoylphenylhydroxylamine (NRCH)
B Pharm ..... Bachelor of Pharmacy
B Ph C .... Bachelor of Pharmaceutical Chemistry
BPHC .... Bangladesh Population and Health Consortium/NGO Project
BPHE .... Bachelor of Physical and Health Education
BPHE .... Bachelor of Public Health Engineering
Bphe .... Bacteriopheophytin [*Biochemistry*]
BPH Ed .... Bachelor of Public Health Education
BPH Eng ..... Bachelor of Public Health Engineering
BPheo .... Bacteriopheophytin [*Biochemistry*]
BPHI .... Boost Phase Intercept (AABC)
B Phil .... Bachelor of Philosophy
BPhil(Ed) ..... Bachelor of Philosophy (Education), University of Birmingham [*British*] (DBQ)
B Phil Woch... Berliner Philologische Wochenschrift [*A publication*] (OCD)
BPHN .... Bachelor of Public Health Nursing
B Pho .... Bachelor of Photography
B Ph S .... Bachelor of Physical Science
BPHS .... British Percheron Horse Society (BI)
BPHS .... British Polled Hereford Society Ltd. (BI)
BPhty .... Bachelor of Physiotherapy (ADA)
B Phy .... Bachelor of Physics
BPhys .... Bachelor of Physics (NADA)
BPhysEd ..... Bachelor of Physical Education
BPhysHlthEd... Bachelor of Physical Health Education
BPhysio ...... Bachelor of Physiotherapy
B PHYS THY... Bachelor of Physical Therapy (WDAA)
BPI .... Bachelor of Planning, University of Manchester [*British*]
BPI .... Bactericidal/Permeability Increasing [*Protein*] [*Immunology*]
BPI .... BA Merchant Services, Inc. [*NYSE symbol*] (SAG)
BPI .... Banco Portugues do Investimento [*Portuguese Investment Bank*]
BPI .... Bangladesh Press International
BPI .... Big Piney, WY [*Location identifier FAA*] (FAAL)
BPI .... Billboard Publications, Inc.
BPI .... Biochemical Process Industry
BPI .... Bio-Degradable Plastics, Inc.
BPI .... Bipolar Illness [*Psychiatry*] (CPH)

BPI .... Bipolar Psychological Inventory [*Personality development test*] [*Psychology*]
BPI .... BITs [*Binary Digits*] per Inch [*Data density measurement*] [*Computer science*]
bpi .... Bits per Inch (IDOE)
BPI .... Bituminous Pipe Institute [*Defunct*] (EA)
BPI .... Blood Pressure Increased [*Medicine*] (MAE)
BPI .... Board of Patent Interferences [*of Patent Office*]
BPI .... Bookman's Price Index [*A reference publication listing rare books and their list prices*]
BPI .... Booksellers' Provident Institution [*British*] (DGA)
BPI .... Boost Phase Intercept
BPI .... BPI ...A Growers Organization (EA)
BPI .... BPI Packaging Technologies, Inc. [*Associated Press*] (SAG)
BPI .... Brand Potential Index [*Marketing*] (DOAD)
BPI .... Break-Point Instruction
BPI .... British Phonographic Industry
BPI .... Bureau of Plant Industry [*Later, BPISAE*] [*Department of Agriculture*]
BPI .... Bureau of Public Inquiries
BPI .... Business People, Inc. [*Minneapolis, MN*] [*Telecommunications service*] (TSSD)
BPI .... Business Press International (DGA)
BPI .... Business Process Improvement (AAGC)
BPI .... Business Publishers, Inc. [*Silver Spring, MD*] [*Information service or system*] (IID)
BPI .... Buying Power Index
BPI .... Bytes per Inch [*Computer science*]
BPIA .... British Photographic Importers Association (DBA)
BPIA .... Business Publications Index and Abstracts [*A publication*]
BPICA .... Bureau Permanent International des Constructeurs d'Automobiles [*International Permanent Bureau of Motor Manufacturers*] (EAIO)
BPICM .... Bureau Permanent International des Constructeurs de Motocycles [*Permanent International Bureau of Motorcycle Manufacturers*] (EAIO)
BPICS .... British Production and Inventory Control Society (DBQ)
B-PID .... Book-Physical Inventory Difference [*AEC*]
BPIE .... BPI Packaging Tech [*NASDAQ symbol*] (TTSB)
BPIE .... BPI Packaging Technologies, Inc. [*NASDAQ symbol*] (SAG)
BPIEC .... Beijing Publications Import & Export Corp.
BPIEP .... BPI Pkg Tech 8.50%'A'Pfd [*NASDAQ symbol*] (TTSB)
BPIEZ .... BPI Pkg Technologies Wrrt'B' [*NASDAQ symbol*] (TTSB)
BPIF .... British Printing Industries' Federation (DCTA)
BPIF .... Brunei People's Independence Front [*Political party*] (FEA)
BPIL .... Basic Petroleum International Ltd. [*NASDAQ symbol*] (NQ)
BPILE .... Bored Insitu Piles [*Camutek*] [*Software package*] (NCC)
BPILF .... Basic Petroleum Intl. [*NASDAQ symbol*] (TTSB)
BPIM .... British Printing Ink Manufacturers (DGA)
BPI Pkg ...... BPI Packaging Technologies, Inc. [*Associated Press*] (SAG)
BPIR .... Booksellers' Provident Institution and Retreat [*British*] (DGA)
BPIS .... British Printing Ink Society (DGA)
BPISAE .... Bureau of Plant Industry, Soils, and Agricultural Engineering [*Formerly, BPI*] [*Functions transferred to ARS, 1953 Department of Agriculture*]
BPIT .... Basic Parameter Input Tape [*Computer science*] (IAA)
BPITT .... Bureau Permanent Interafricain de la Tse-Tse et de la Trypanosomiase
BPJ .... Balanced Pressure Joint
BPJ .... Best Professional Judgment [*Environmental Protection Agency*]
BPJC .... Bay Path Junior College [*Longmeadow, MA*]
BPK .... Black Peak [*Arizona*] [*Seismograph station code, US Geological Survey Closed*] (SEIS)
BPK .... Black Photo Corp. Ltd. [*Toronto Stock Exchange symbol*]
bPKC .... Bovine Protein Kinase C [*An enzyme*]
BPKT .... Basic Programming Knowledge Test (MCD)
BPL .... Bachelor of Patent Law
BPL .... Bandpass Limiter (IAA)
BPL .... Band Pressure Level
BPL .... Barrington Petroleum Ltd. [*Formerly, Barrington Properties Ltd.*] [*Toronto Stock Exchange symbol*]
BPL .... Baseplate [*Technical drawings*]
BPL .... Basic Parts List
BPL .... Beam Packing Loss (IAA)
BPL .... Bearing Plate [*Technical drawings*]
BPL .... Bell Propulsion Laboratory (IAA)
BPL .... Benign Proliferative Lesion [*Medicine*] (DMAA)
BPL .... Benzylpenicilloyl Polylysine [*Organic chemistry*]
BPL .... Beta-Propriolactone [*Organic chemistry*]
BPL .... Binary Program Loader
BPL .... Bio-Products Laboratory [*Central Blood Laboratories Authority*] [*British*] (IRC)
BPL .... Birmingham Public Library [*Alabama*]
BPL .... Birthplace
BPL .... Block Proof List [*Computer science*]
BPL .... Blood-Products Laboratory [*British*]
BPL .... Bohn's Philosophical Library [*A publication*]
BPL .... Bone Phosphate of Lime
B/PL .... Bookplate [*Bibliography*]
BPL .... Bott's Poor Law Cases [*1560-1833*] [*England*] [*A publication*] (DLA)
BPL .... Brass Pounders League [*Unit of American Radio Relay League*]
BPL .... British Physical Laboratories Ltd. (NUCP)
BPL .... Broadcast Pioneer's Library (NTCM)
BPL .... Brooklyn Public Library [*New York, NY*]
BPL .... Buckeye Partnership [*NYSE symbol*] (SPSG)
BPL .... Buckeye Ptnrs L.P. [*NYSE symbol*] (TTSB)
BPL .... Burroughs Programming Language (IAA)

BPL............	Burst Position Locator
BPL............	Business Planning Language [*Computer science*] (MHDI)
BPI............	La Bible. Bibliotheque de la Pleiade [*A publication*] (BJA)
BPL............	Veterans Memorial Public Library, Bismarck, ND [*OCLC symbol*] (OCLC)
BPLA...........	Bow Plane
BPL Cas.......	Bott's Poor Law Cases [*1560-1833*] [*England*] [*A publication*] (DLA)
BPL Cases...	Bott's Poor Law Cases [*1560-1833*] [*England*] [*A publication*] (DLA)
B-PLL..........	B-Cell Prolymphocytic Leukemia
BPLN	Bilateral Pelvic Lymph Node [*Medicine*] (DAVI)
BPLND.........	Bilateral Pelvic Lymph Node Dissection [*Medicine*] (DAVI)
BPLS...........	Bank Plus Corp. [*NASDAQ symbol*] (SAG)
BPLS...........	Bank Plus Corp. [*NASDAQ symbol*] (TTSB)
BPLSA	Bird Protection League of South Australia
BPLX...........	Bio-Plexus, Inc. [*NASDAQ symbol*] (SAG)
BPM............	Balanced Processing Monitor [*Mitsubishi*] (NITA)
BPM............	Balanced Property Management (ADA)
BPM............	Ballistic Particle Manufacturing [*Desktop manufacturing*]
BPM............	Barbuda People's Movement [*Antigua*] [*Political party*] (PD)
BPM............	Barrels per Minute
BPM............	Barrels per Month (IAA)
BPM............	Batch Processing Monitor [*Xerox Corp.*] [*Computer science*] (MCD)
BPM............	Beam Positioning Magnet
BPM............	Beam Position Monitor
BPM............	Beats per Minute [*Cardiology*]
bpm............	Beats per Minute [*Medicine*] (DMAA)
BPM............	Best Practicable Means
BPM............	Best Practical Means [*Business term*] (DCTA)
BPM............	Bible Protestant Missions (EA)
BPM............	Biological Production Module (SSD)
BPM............	Bi-Phase Modulation (IAA)
BPM............	Bipiperidyl Mustard [*Pharmacology*]
BPM............	BITs [*Binary Digits*] per Minute [*Data transmission speed*] [*Computer science*]
BPM............	Boiling Point Margin [*Engineering*]
BPM............	Bottles per Minute (WGA)
BPM............	Breaths per Minute
BPM............	Brompheniramine Maleate [*Antihistamine*]
BPM............	Penticton Museum and Archives, British Columbia [*Library symbol National Library of Canada*] (NLC)
BPMA.........	Barrier Paper Manufacturers Association [*Defunct*] (EA)
BPMA.........	Bio-Technology Purchasing Management Association [*Defunct*] (EA)
BPMA.........	Blotting Paper Manufacturers' Association (DGA)
BPMA.........	Book Paper Manufacturers' Association (DGA)
BPMA.........	Brisbane Produce Merchants' Association [*Australia*]
BPMA.........	British Payroll Managers Association (DBA)
BPMA.........	British Photographic Manufacturers Association (DGA)
BPMA.........	British Pottery Managers Association (DBA)
BPMA.........	British Printing Machinery Association (DGA)
BPMA.........	British Promotional Merchandise Association (DBA)
BPMA.........	British Pump Manufacturers Association (EAIO)
BPMC.........	Bertelsmann Printing & Manufacturing Corp.
BPME.........	Broadcast Promotion and Marketing Executives (EA)
BPMEL........	Base Precision Measurement Equipment Laboratories (AFM)
BPMF.........	British Postgraduate Medical Federation
BPMF.........	British Poultry Meat Federation (EAIO)
BPMF.........	British Powder Metal Federation (DBA)
BPMH	Brompton Park Military Hospital [*British military*] (DMA)
BPMI	Badger Paper Mills [*NASDAQ symbol*] (TTSB)
BPMI	Badger Paper Mills, Inc. [*NASDAQ symbol*] (NQ)
BPMM........	BITs [*Binary Digits*] per Millimeter [*Data density measurement*] [*Computer science*]
BPMM........	Port Moody Station Museum, British Columbia [*Library symbol National Library of Canada*] (NLC)
BPMMA......	British Paper Machinery Makers Association (DBA)
BPMP........	Port Moody Public Library, British Columbia [*Library symbol National Library of Canada*] (NLC)
BPMS.........	Blood Plasma Measuring System [*Medicine*]
BPMS.........	Bulk Petroleum Management System
BPMS.........	Buy per Manufacturing Specification (SAA)
BPMTG	[*The*] British Puppet and Model Theatre Guild
BPMV........	Bean Pod Mottle Virus [*Plant pathology*]
BPN	Bacitracin, Polymyxin B, Neomycin Sulfate [*Medicine*] (DMAA)
BPN	Balikpapan [*Indonesia*] [*Airport symbol*] (OAG)
BPN	Balloon-Borne Polar Nephelometer
BPN	Bandpass Network
BPN	Bloody Public Nuisance [*British slang*]
BPN	Boiling Point Number [*Chemical engineering*]
BPN	Brachial Plexus Neuropathy [*Medicine*] (DMAA)
BPN	Breakdown Pulse Noise (KSC)
BPN	British Poets of the Nineteenth Century [*A publication*]
BPN	Budget Project Number [*Navy*] (NG)
BPN	Bureau Politique National [*National Political Bureau*] (AF)
BPNA.........	British Petroleum North America
BPNL	Battelle Pacific Northwest Laboratories [*Nuclear energy*] (NRCH)
BPNR.........	Bosanquet and Puller's New Reports, English Common Pleas [*1804-07*] [*A publication*] (DLA)
BPO	Barracks Petty Officer (DNAB)
BPO	Bartlesville Project Office [*Bartlesville, OK*] [*Department of Energy*] (GRD)
BPO	Basal Pepsin Output [*Medicine*] (DMAA)
BPO	Base Post Office
BPO	Base Procurement Office [*Air Force*] (AFM)
BPO	Basic Postflight (MCD)
BPO	Benzoyl Peroxide [*Also, BP*] [*Organic chemistry*]

BPO	Benzylpenicilloyl [*Organic chemistry*]
BPO	Berlin Philharmonic Orchestra
BPO	Bicycling Promotion Organization [*Later, BIA*] (EA)
BPO	(Biphenylyl)phenyloxazole [*Organic chemistry*]
BPO	Blood Program Office (DNAB)
BPO	BOMARC [*Boeing-Michigan Aeronautical Research Center*] Prelaunch Output (IAA)
BPO	BP Flight Operations Ltd. [*British ICAO designator*] (FAAC)
BPO	Branch Processing Unit [*Computer science*]
BPO	British Post Office
BPO	Broadcast Production Officer
BPO	Bromoperoxidase [*An enzyme*]
BPO	Budget Project Officer [*Navy*] (DNAB)
BPO	Business Periodicals Ondisc [*UMI/Data Courier*] [*Information service or system*] (CRD)
BPO	Oneida, TN [*Location identifier FAA*] (FAAL)
B-PO2........	Blood Partial Pressure of Oxygen [*On blood gas determinations*] (DAVI)
BPOA	Business Professionals of America
BPOC	Before Proceeding on Course [*Aviation*]
BPOC	Pouce Coupe Public Library, British Columbia [*Library symbol National Library of Canada*] (NLC)
BPOE	Benevolent and Protective Order of Elks (EA)
BPOF	Binary Phase-Only Filter [*Optics*]
B Pol Sc	Bachelor of Political Science
BPOP	BanPonce Corp. [*NASDAQ symbol*] (NQ)
BPOP	Bulk Packed on Pallets [*Paper*] (DGA)
BPOPP........	BanPonce 8.35%.Mthly Inc. Pfd [*NASDAQ symbol*] (TTSB)
BPORH........	Powell River Historical Museum, British Columbia [*Library symbol National Library of Canada*] (NLC)
BPOS	Batch Processing Operating System (IAA)
BPOS	British Pipe Organ Society (DBA)
BPP	Beach Protection Program [*Australia*]
BPP	Beacon Portable Packset
BPP	Belize Popular Party [*Political party*] (EY)
BPP	Bhutan People's Party [*Political party*]
BPP	Black Panther Party [*Defunct Political party*]
BPP	Black People's Party [*South Africa*] [*Political party*] (PPW)
BPP	[*A*] Book of Personal Poems [*A publication*]
BPP	Borge Prien Prove [*Danish intelligence test*]
BPP	Botswana People's Party [*Political party*] (PPW)
BPP	Boundary Phase Plasticity (PDAA)
BPP	Bovine Pancreatic Polypeptide
BPP	Bubble Pulse Period
BPP	Bulk Packed on Pallets [*Paper*] (DGA)
BPP	Bulk Petroleum Products
BPP	Bulk Polymerization Process [*Plastics technology*]
BPP	Burnham Pacific Prop [*NYSE symbol*] (TTSB)
BPP	Burnham Pacific Properties [*NYSE symbol*] (SPSG)
BPP	Bursting Pacemaker Potential [*Electrophysiology*]
BPP	Business Partnership for Peace (EA)
BPP	Buyer Protection Plan [*Sales*]
BPPA	British Pasta Products Association (DBA)
BPPA	British Precision Pilots Association (DA)
BPPF	Base Program Preparation Facility [*Computer science*] (MHDI)
BPPG	Biased Predictive Proportional Guidance
BPPG	Bureau Planned Procurement Guide [*Navy*]
BPPM	Princeton and District Museum and Archives, Princeton, British Columbia [*Library symbol National Library of Canada*] (NLC)
BPPMA	British Power Press Manufacturers Association (MCD)
BPPN	Benign Paroxysmal Positioning Nystagmus [*Medicine*] (DMAA)
BPPO	Buckingham Palace Press Office [*British*]
BPPRM	BOIP [*Basis of Issue Plan*] Retrieval Program [*DoD*]
BPPRT	Blood Pressure, Pulse, Respiration, and Temperature [*On examination*] [*Medicine*] (DAVI)
BP Pru	BP Prudhoe Bay Royalty Trust [*Associated Press*] (SAG)
BPPS	Bulleid Pacific Preservation Society [*British*] (BI)
BPPS	Bureau for Policy and Program Support [*United Nations*] (ECON)
BPPSJ	Balanced Pressure Plane Swivel Joint
BPPSP	Block Point Plan Scheduling Procedure (SAA)
BPPV	Begign Paroxysmal Positional Vertigo [*Medicine*]
BPPV	Benign Paroxysmal Positioning Vertigo
BPPV	Bovine Paragenital Papilloma Virus [*Medicine*] (DMAA)
BPQ	British Columbia Packers Ltd. [*Vancouver Stock Exchange symbol*]
BPQ	Budgetary and Planning Quotations (MCD)
BPQP	Boise Peace Quilt Project (EA)
BPR	Back Pressure Regulator
BPR	Banana Plug Resistor
BPR	Bankers Tr N.Y. 7.625%Dep Pfd [*AMEX symbol*] (TTSB)
BPR	Bankers Trust New York Corp. [*AMEX symbol*] (SAG)
BPR	Bar-Pattern Response [*Computer science*] (IAA)
BPR	Battery Plotting Room
BPR	Battery-Powered Recorder
BPR	Berry Pseudorotation
BPR	Beryllium Physics Reactor (NRCH)
BPR	Bimonthly Progress Report
BPR	Block Proof Record [*Computer science*]
BPR	Blood Pressure Recorder [*Medicine*]
BPR	Bloque Popular Revolucionario [*Popular Revolutionary Bloc*] [*El Salvador*] (PD)
BPR	Boiling Point Rise
BPR	Book Publishing Record (DIT)
BPR	Bottom Pressure Recorder [*Marine science*] (OSRA)
BPR	Bottom Pressure Recorder (USDC)
BPR	Bramalea Properties, Inc. [*Toronto Stock Exchange symbol*]

BPR .... Bridge Plotting Room [*Navy*]
BPR .... Bridgeport, TX [*Location identifier FAA*] (FAAL)
BPR .... Bromopyrogallol Red [*An indicator*] [*Chemistry*]
BPR .... Brown's Parliamentary Reports [*England*] [*A publication*] (DLA)
BPR .... Bubble Position Register [*Computer science*] (IAA)
BPR .... Building Products Register [*American Institute of Architects*]
BPR .... Bureau of Public Relations [*War Department*] [*World War II*]
BPR .... Bureau of Public Roads [*Department of Transportation*]
BPR .... Burnable Poison Rod [*Nuclear energy*] (NRCH)
BPR .... Business Process Readiness [*GSA*] (AAGC)
BPR .... Business Process Re-Engineering (ECON)
BPR .... Bypass Ratio
BPR .... Prince Rupert Public Library, British Columbia [*Library symbol National Library of Canada*] (NLC)
BPRA .... Baptist Public Relations Association (EA)
BPRA .... Book Publishers Representatives' Association [*British*] (BI)
BPRA .... British Pattern Recognition Association (ACII)
BPRA .... British Pattern Recognition Association (NITA)
BPRA .... Burnable Poison Assembly [*Nuclear energy*] (NRCH)
BPRA .... Prince Rupert Regional Archives, Prince Rupert, British Columbia [*Library symbol National Library of Canada*] (NLC)
BPRACS ...... Synod Office, Diocese of Caledonia, Anglican Church of Canada, Prince Rupert, British Columbia [*Library symbol National Library of Canada*] (NLC)
BPRB .... Beef Promotion and Research Board (EA)
BPRC .... Battery Protection and Reconditioning Circuit (MCD)
BPRC .... Biomedical Primate Research Centre [*The Netherlands*]
BPRC .... Byrd Polar Research Center [*Ohio State University*] [*Information service or system*] (IID)
BPRD .... Powell River District Libraries, British Columbia [*Library symbol National Library of Canada*] (NLC)
BPRDP .... Powell River District Public Library Association, British Columbia [*Library symbol National Library of Canada*] (NLC)
BPreis .... Preiss (Byron) Multimedia Co., Inc. [*Associated Press*] (SAG)
BPRF .... Birds of Prey Rehabilitation Foundation (EA)
BPRF .... Bulletproof [*Army*] (AABC)
BPRFA .... Britannia Petite Rabbit Fanciers Association [*Defunct*] (EA)
BPRG .... Bomb Pulsed Release Generator (DWSG)
BPRI .... British Polarographic Research Institute
BPRM .... Museum of Northern British Columbia, Prince Rupert, British Columbia [*Library symbol National Library of Canada*] (NLC)
BPRMA .... Bank Public Relations and Marketing Association [*Later, BMA*]
BPRO .... Blind Persons Resettlement Officer [*Department of Employment*] [*British*]
BPRO .... Branch Public Relations Office
B Proc .... Baccalaureus Procurationis (DLA)
BPRS .... Brief Psychiatric Rate Scale (DAVI)
BPRS .... Brief Psychiatric Rating Scale
BPRS .... Brief Psychiatric Reacting Scale (DAVI)
BPRS .... British Polarological Research Society (DBA)
BPRS .... National Black Public Relations Society (EA)
BPRT .... Biostructures Participating Research Team [*Biostructures Institute*] (RCD)
BPR-THM .... Bureau of Public Roads Transport Highway Mobilization [*Federal emergency order*]
BPRX .... Bradley Pharmaceuticals, Inc. [*NASDAQ symbol*] (SAG)
BPRXA .... Bradley Pharmaceuticals'A' [*NASDAQ symbol*] (TTSB)
BPRXL .... Bradley Pharm Wrrt 'D' [*NASDAQ symbol*] (TTSB)
BPRXW .... Bradley Pharm Wrrt'A' [*NASDAQ symbol*] (TTSB)
BPRXZ .... Bradley Pharm Wrrt 'B' [*NASDAQ symbol*] (TTSB)
BPRZ .... Bipolar Return to Zero [*Electronics*] (ACRL)
BPS .... Bachelor of Professional Studies
B Ps .... Bachelor of Psychology
BPS .... Ballistic Protected Shelter (MCD)
BPS .... Base Postal Section [*Air Force*] (AFM)
BPS .... Basic Programming Support [*IBM Corp.*] (BUR)
BPS .... Basic Programming System
BPS .... Basic Psychological Study (MCD)
BPS .... Batch Processing System
BPS .... Baud Programming System [*Computer science*] (IAA)
BPS .... Beacon Processing System
BPS .... Bearing Procurement Specification (MSA)
BPS .... Beats per Second [*Cardiology*]
BPS .... Beginning Professional Salary
BPS .... Behavioral Pharmacology Society (EA)
BPS .... Beijing Proton Synchrotron [*China*]
BPS .... Belgium Philatelic Society (EA)
BPS .... Benchmark Portability System (PDAA)
BPS .... Benelux Phlebology Society (EA)
BPS .... Bhutan Philatelic Society (EA)
BPS .... Binary Program Space [*Computer science*]
BPS .... Biophysical Society (EA)
BPS .... Bipolar Power Supply (DWSG)
BPS .... BITs [*Binary Digits*] per Second [*Data transmission speed*] [*Computer science*]
bps .... Bits Per Second [*Computer science*] (WDMC)
BPS .... Blanked Picture Signal
BPS .... Bloc Populaire Senegalais [*Senegal*] (PPW)
BPS .... Blowout Pipe System
BPS .... Booklet Pane Society [*Defunct*] (EA)
BPS .... Book Promotion Society [*Canada*]
BPS .... Boost Pump Start (MCD)
BPS .... Boundary Plasma Sheet
BPS .... Brain Protein Solvent [*Biochemistry*]
BPS .... Branch Point Sequence [*Genetics*]

BPS .... Breaths per Second
BPS .... British Pharmacological Society
BPS .... British Photobiology Society
BPS .... British Phycological Society
BPS .... British Plain Spirits
BPS .... British Postmark Society (EA)
BPS .... British Printing Society (DGA)
BPS .... British Psychoanalytical Society (EAIO)
BPS .... British Psychological Society (EAIO)
BPS .... British Pteridological Society (DBA)
BPS .... Buddhist Publication Society [*Multinational association based in Sri Lanka*] (EAIO)
BPS .... Budget Preparation System Master File [*Office of Management and Budget*] (GFGA)
BPS .... Buoy Power Supply
BPS .... Bureau of Product Safety [*FDA*]
BPS .... Business and Professional Software [*Software publisher*]
BPS .... Business Plan System
BPS .... Bytes per Second [*Computer science*] (BUR)
BPS .... Episcopal Divinity School, Cambridge, MA [*OCLC symbol*] (OCLC)
BPS .... Porto Seguro [*Brazil*] [*Airport symbol*] (OAG)
BPSA .... Bachelor of Public School Art
BPSA .... British Pharmaceutical Students' Association (BI)
BPSA .... British Polytechnics Sports Association (DBA)
BPSA .... Bronchopulmonary Segmental Artery [*Medicine*] (DMAA)
BPSA .... Business Products Standards Association (NITA)
BPSANSW .... British Public Schools Association of New South Wales [*Australia*]
BPSC .... Bearing per Standard Compass [*Navigation*]
BPSD .... Barrels per Stream Day [*Also, BSD*]
BPSD .... Bronchopulmonary Segmental Drainage [*Medicine*] (DAVI)
BPSH .... Border Patrol Sector Headquarters
BPSI .... Bank Personnel Selection Inventory [*Test*]
BPSI .... BITs [*Binary Digits*] per Square Inch [*Data density measurement*] [*Computer science*]
BPSJ .... Balanced Pressure Swivel Joint
BPSK .... Binary Phase Shifting Key [*Computer science*] (ACRL)
BPSK .... Binary Phase-Shift Keying [*Computer science*] (IEEE)
BPSM .... Bachelor of Public School Music
BPSM .... Bulk Presorted Mail (ADA)
BPSN .... Budget Project Symbol Number (AFM)
BPSO .... Base Personnel Staff Officer [*Air Force British*]
BPSS .... Barge-Mounted Production and Storage System (DS)
BPSS .... Base Perimeter Security System
BPSS .... Base Procurement Service Stores [*Air Force*] (AFM)
BPSS .... Basic Production Scheduling System (IAA)
BPSS .... Biopack Subsystem [*NASA*] (KSC)
BPSS .... British Paraplegic Sports Society (DBA)
B Ps Sc ...... Bachelor of Psychic Sciences
BPSTGC ...... Bearing per Steering Gyro Compass [*Navigation*]
B Ps Th .... Bachelor of Psychotherapy
Bp Suff .... Bishop Suffrogan [*or Suffrogan Bishop*] (BARN)
BPSW .... Bulletin of the Philosophical Society of Washington [*A publication*] (BARN)
BPsy .... Bachelor of Psychology
BPsych .... Bachelor of Psychology
BPsys .... Blood Pressure, Systolic
BPT .... Bachelor of Physical Therapy
BPT .... Bachelor of Physiotherapy (NADA)
BPT .... Back Pressure Transducer [*Automotive engineering*]
BPT .... Balanced Property Trust (ADA)
BPT .... Bandpass Transformer
BPT .... Base Point
BPT .... Bathophenanthroline [*Analytical chemistry*]
BPT .... Battle Practice Target [*Obsolete Navy British*]
BPT .... Beach Party Team [*Navy*] (NVT)
BPT .... Beaumont/Port Arthur [*Texas*] [*Airport symbol*] (OAG)
BPT .... Beginning Procedure Turn (FAAC)
BPT .... Benign Paroxysmal Torticollis [*Medicine*] (DMAA)
BPT .... Best Practicable Technology [*Environmental Protection Agency*]
BPT .... Best Practicable Treatment (GNE)
BPT .... BGR Precious Metals, Inc. [*Toronto Stock Exchange symbol*]
BPT .... Bicentennial Park Trust [*Australia*]
BPT .... Bipost
BPT .... Bis(pyridiniumtrimethylene) [*Dichloride*] [*Biochemistry*]
BPT .... Black Panel Temperature [*Automotive paint durability testing*]
BPT .... Blade Passage Tone [*Aviation*]
BPT .... Body Point (MCD)
BPT .... Boiling Point
BPT .... Bonus Aviation [*British*] [*FAA designator*] (FAAC)
BPT .... Borderline Pumping Temperature [*Automotive engineering*]
BPT .... Bound Plasma Tryptophan (PDAA)
BPT .... BP Prudhoe Bay Royalty [*NYSE symbol*] (SPSG)
BPT .... Breakpoint
BPT .... Break Pressure Tank (PDAA)
BPT .... Bridgeport [*Connecticut*] [*Seismograph station code, US Geological Survey Closed*] (SEIS)
BPT .... Bridgeport Public Library, Bridgeport, CT [*OCLC symbol*] (OCLC)
BPT .... British Petroleum Co. (IIA)
BPT .... British Philatelic Trust (DI)
BPT .... Bronchial Provocation Test [*Medicine*]
BPTA .... Briar Pipe Trade Association [*British*] (DBA)
BPTCA .... Best Practicable Control Technology Currently Available [*Clean Water Act*] (ERG)
BPTEU .... Bombay Port Trust Employees' Union [*India*]
bPTH .... Bovine Parathyroid Hormone [*Endocrinology*]

BPTI............ Bovine Pancreatic Trypsin Inhibitor [Biochemistry]
BPTM........... Bridgeport Machines [NASDAQ symbol] (TTSB)
BPTM........... Bridgeport Machines, Inc. [NASDAQ symbol] (SAG)
BptMach....... Bridgeport Machines, Inc. [Associated Press] (SAG)
BPTO........... Blind Persons Technical Officer [British] (AIE)
BPTO .... BMEWS [Ballistic Missile Early Warning System] Performance Test Outline
BPTS............ Boost Phase Track System
BPU............. Base Production Unit [Army] (AABC)
BPU............. Basic Pole Unit
BPU............. Basic Processing Unit (CET)
BPU............. Beijing Polytechnic University [China]
BPU............. BITBLT [Binary Digit-Block Transfer] Processing Unit
BPU............. Botswana Progressive Union
BPU............. Bountiful Peak [Utah] [Seismograph station code, US Geological Survey Closed] (SEIS)
BPU .... Branch Prediction Unit [Computer science] (PCM)
BPubAdmin... Bachelor of Public Administration
BPubPol....... Bachelor of Public Policy
BPV............. Benign Paroxysmal Vertigo [Medicine] (DMAA)
BPV............. Benign Positional Vertigo [Neurology] (DAVI)
BPV............. Bipropellant Valve (MCD)
B + PV .... Boiler and Pressure Vessel [Nuclear energy] (NRCH)
BPV............. Bordetella Pertussis Vaccine
BPV............. Bovine Papillomavirus [Veterinary medicine]
BPV............. Bovine Papillomavirus Vaccine [Veterinary medicine]
BPV............. Bypass Valve (NRCH)
BPVA .... Bay of Pigs Veterans Association (EA)
BPVC .... Boiler and Pressure Vessel Committee [Nuclear Regulatory Commission] (GFGA)
BP(Vet)........ British Pharmacopoeia (Veterinary)
BPVMAA ...... Boiler and Pressure Vessel Manufacturers' Association of Australia
BPW............ Bare Platinum Wire
BPW............ Board of Public Works
BPW............ Business and Professional Women's Foundation
BPWA .... British Public Works Association (EAIO)
BPWC .... Black Political Women's Caucus
BPWC .... Business and Professional Women's Club [Australia]
BPWCP........ Business and Professional Women's Club of Perth [Australia]
BPWF........... Business and Professional Women's Foundation (EA)
BPWG .... British Plastics Windows Group [An association] (DBA)
BPWMA .... Buff and Polishing Wheel Manufacturers Association [Defunct]
BPWR .... Burnable Poison Water Reactor (IEEE)
BPWS .... Banked Position Withdrawal Sequence (IEEE)
BPWTT........ Best Practicable Waste Treatment Technology (EG)
BPW/USA..... National Federation of Business and Professional Women's Clubs (EA)
BPX............. British Petroleum Exploration [Columbia] [FAA designator] (FAAC)
BPX............. Broadband Packet Exchange [Telecommunications] (ACRL)
B Py .... Bachelor of Pedagogy
BPY............. Besalampy [Madagascar] [Airport symbol] (OAG)
BPY............. Bipyridine [Also, BIPY] [Organic chemistry]
BPY............. BPI Resources Ltd. [Vancouver Stock Exchange symbol]
BQ............... Baba Qama [or Bava Qamma] (BJA)
BQ............... Back-Up Quantity
BQ............... Barque [Bark, Boat] [French]
BQ............... Base Quota
BQ............... Basis Quote [Investment term]
Bq............... Becquerel [Symbol] [SI unit of activity of ionizing radiation source]
BQ............... Before Queues [Referring to pre-World War II period] [Slang British]
BQ............... Bene Quiescat [May He, or She, Rest Well] [Latin]
BQ............... Bioquant
BQ............... Bloc Quebecois [Canada Political party] (ECON)
BQ............... Briquet
BQ............... Business Jets [ICAO designator] (AD)
BQ............... Quesnel Library, British Columbia [Library symbol National Library of Canada] (BIB)
BQA .... Bilateral Quarantine Agreement
BQA .... British Quality Association (DBA)
BQA .... Bureau of Quality Assurance [HEW]
BQAP .... Bilevel Quality Assurance Program [NASA] (KSC)
BQC .... Basic Qualification Course (DNAB)
BQC .... Bureau of Quality Control [Department of Health and Human Services] (GFGA)
BQC .... Charlotte, NC [Location identifier FAA] (FAAL)
BQCM .... Queen Charlotte Islands Museum, Queen Charlotte, British Columbia [Library symbol National Library of Canada] (NLC)
BQC Sol ...... Dibromoquinonechlorimide Solution [Organic chemistry] (DAVI)
BQE............. Toledo, OH [Location identifier FAA] (FAAL)
BQG .... Woodbridge, VA [Location identifier FAA] (FAAL)
BQHA .... British Quarter Horse Association (DBA)
BQK .... Brunswick [Georgia] [Airport symbol] (OAG)
BQK .... Brunswick, GA [Location identifier FAA] (FAAL)
BQL............. Bank of Queensland Ltd. [Australia]
BQL............. Basic Query Language [Computer science] (BUR)
BQL............. Batch Query Language [Programming language]
BQL............. Boulia [Australia Airport symbol] (OAG)
BQLI............ Brooklyn, Queens, Long Island [Section of New York Times]
BQM............ Airborne Drone Missile Target [DOD missile designation] (MCD)
BQM............ Base Quartermaster [Marine Corps]
BQM............ Becker Junior College, Worcester, MA [Inactive] [OCLC symbol] (OCLC)
BQM............ Louisville, KY [Location identifier FAA] (FAAL)
BQM............ Quesnel and District Museum, Quesnel, British Columbia [Library symbol National Library of Canada] (NLC)

BQMS .... Battery Quartermaster-Sergeant [British]
BQN .... Aguadilla [Puerto Rico] [Airport symbol] (OAG)
BQO .... Bouna [Ivory Coast] [Airport symbol] (OAG)
BQP .... Bastrop, LA [Location identifier FAA] (FAAL)
BQQ .... Barra [Brazil] [Airport symbol] (OAG)
BQR .... Butare [Rwanda] [Airport symbol] (AD)
BQR .... Quick & Reilly Group [NASDAQ symbol] (TTSB)
BQR .... Quick & Reilly Group, Inc. [NYSE symbol] (SPSG)
BQS .... Bright QUASAR Survey [Astronomy]
BQSI .... Brooklyn-Queens-Staten Island Health Sciences Group [Library network]
BQT .... Blackrock Investment Quality Term Trust [NYSE symbol] (SPSG)
BQT .... Blackrock Inv Qual Term Tr [NYSE symbol] (TTSB)
BQUE .... Barque [Bark, Boat] [French]
BQV .... Bartlett Cove, AK [Location identifier FAA] (FAAL)
BQVSA .... British Quality Vegetable Salad Association (DBA)
BR.............. Background Radiation (SAA)
BR.............. Back Reflection (DNAB)
bR.............. Bacteriorhodopsin [Biochemistry]
BR.............. Bahama Route [Aviation] (FAAC)
BR.............. Ballast Rack (MCD)
BR.............. Baltimore City Reports [A publication] (DLA)
BR.............. Banco Regis [or Reginae] [The King's (or Queen's) Bench] [Latin]
BR.............. Band Reject (IAA)
BR.............. Bank Rate [Banking]
BR.............. Bank Robbery
BR.............. Bankroll [Slang]
BR.............. Bankruptcy Register [A publication] (DLA)
BR.............. Bankruptcy Reporter [West] [A publication] (AAGC)
BR.............. Bankruptcy Reports [A publication] (DLA)
BR.............. Bar
BR.............. Baron (ROG)
BR.............. Barrage Rocket (NATG)
BR.............. Barrel Roll (CINC)
BR.............. Barry Railway [Wales]
BR.............. Base Reclamation [of critical materials] (AAG)
BR.............. Base Register (CMD)
BR.............. Basic Research
BR.............. Batch Reactor [Chemical engineering]
BR.............. Bathroom
BR.............. Baton Rouge [Diocesan abbreviation] [Louisiana] (TOCD)
BR.............. Bats Right-Handed [Baseball]
BR.............. Bayerische Rundfunk [Radio network] [West Germany]
BR.............. Beam Ride (AAG)
BR.............. Bearing (WDAA)
BR.............. Bed Rest [Medicine]
BR.............. Bedroom
BR.............. Bedroom Steward [In the first class aboard an ocean liner]
BR.............. Beevers-Ross [Beta-alumina crystallography]
BR.............. Belgian Reactor
BR.............. Bend Radius (MCD)
BR.............. Benzing Retrograde (DAVI)
BR.............. Bereshit Rabba (BJA)
BR.............. Biblia Rabbinica [A publication] (BJA)
Br............... Biblioteca Nacional, Rio De Janeiro, Brazil [Library symbol Library of Congress] (LCLS)
BRMS .... Biblisches Reallexikon [A publication] (BJA)
BR.............. Bilateral Impedance Rheograph [Instrumentation]
BR.............. Bilirubin [Biochemistry]
BR.............. Bill of Rights
BR.............. Bills Receivable [Business term]
BR.............. Binder
BR.............. Bioassay Reagent
bR............... Biological Reagent [Peptide grade]
BR.............. Biological Research (NVT)
BR.............. Bioresmethrin [Biochemistry]
BR.............. Biosphere Reserve (GNE)
BR.............. Bird Resistant [Sorghum variety]
BR.............. Birmingham Repair [British military] (DMA)
BR.............. Birmingham Revision [of BNA] [Medicine British]
BR.............. Birthrate
B/R............. Bistatic RADAR (LAIN)
BR.............. BIT [Binary Digit] Rate [Data transmission speed] [Computer science] (MCD)
BR.............. Blackout Restrictions [British World War II]
BR.............. Blade Rate (NVT)
BR.............. Block Replacement
BR.............. Blue Ridge Railroad (IIA)
BR.............. Board of Rabbis
BR.............. Board of Review [Army]
BR.............. Body Rot of Papaya [Plant pathology]
BR.............. Boilermaker [Navy rating]
BR.............. Boiler Room
BR.............. Boiling Range
BR.............. Bombardier [British] (ADA)
BR.............. Bomber Reconnaissance Aircraft
BR.............. Bond Rating [Investment term]
BR.............. Bone Resorption
BR.............. Book of Reference
BR.............. Book Rack (MSA)
BR.............. Book Review
BRMS .... Booster-Regulator [NASA]
B/R............. Bordeaux or Rouen [Shipping] (ROG)
BR.............. Border Regiment [British]
BR.............. Bottom Reflection [Navy] (NVT)

BR.............. Bottom Register (OA)
BR.............. Boundary Router [Computer science] (TNIG)
BR.............. Braced and Racked [Freight]
BR.............. Brake Relay
BR.............. Bralorne Resources Ltd. [Toronto Stock Exchange symbol]
BR.............. Branch (EY)
BR.............. Branch
BR.............. Branch [Postal Service standard] (OPSA)
BR.............. Branch Report
BR.............. Brass
BR.............. Bratschen [Viola]
BR.............. Brazil [ANSI two-letter standard code] (CNC)
BR.............. Breach [Legal shorthand] (LWAP)
BR.............. Breakdown [Electronics]
BR.............. Break Request [Computer science] (MDG)
BR.............. Breath [Medicine]
BR.............. Breathing Reserve (ADA)
Br.............. Breech [Obstetrics] (DAVI)
BR.............. Breeder Reactor
BR.............. Breeding Ratio [Nuclear energy] (NRCH)
BR.............. Brick Construction
BR.............. Bridge [Dentistry] (DAVI)
BR.............. Bridge [Interconnects computer networks]
B/R.............. Bridge/Router [Telecommunications] (ACRL)
BR.............. Bridging Key [on Dial Assistance Switchboard] (CET)
br.............. Brief
BR.............. Briefing Room [Navy]
BR.............. Brig
BR.............. Brigadas Revolucionarias [Revolutionary Brigades] [Portugal Political party] (PPE)
BR.............. Brigade (WGA)
Br.............. Brigadier [British military] (DMA)
BR.............. Brigate Rosse [Red Brigades] [Italy] (PD)
BR.............. Britain (ROG)
BR.............. British
BR.............. British Aircraft Corp. Ltd. [ICAO aircraft manufacturer identifier] (ICAO)
BR.............. British Caledonian Airways Ltd. [ICAO designator] (OAG)
BR.............. British Railways
BR.............. British Revision [of BNA] [Medicine]
BR.............. Broad [Also, B] [Spectral]
BR.............. Broadcasting Reports [Australia A publication]
Br.............. Bromine [Chemical element]
br.............. Bromo [As substituent on nucleoside] [Biochemistry]
Br.............. Bromocriptine [Pharmacology]
BR.............. Bronchitis [Medicine]
BR.............. Bronze
Br.............. Brooke's Abridgment [England] [A publication] (DSA)
BR.............. Brother
BR.............. Brown
BR.............. Brown [Thoroughbred racing]
BR.............. Brucella [Bacteriology] (AAMN)
Br.............. Bruce's Scotch Court of Session Reports [1714-15] [A publication] (DLA)
BR.............. Brush (MSA)
BR.............. Brymon Airways [British]
BR.............. Buffer Register [Computer science]
BRCH.............. Bugler
BR.............. Builder's Risk [Insurance]
BR.............. Bulkhead Receptacle
BR.............. Bulk Resistance (IAA)
BR.............. Bureau of Reclamation [Later, WPRS] [Department of the Interior]
br.............. Burl (VRA)
BR.............. Burlington Resources [NYSE symbol] (TTSB)
BRACS.............. Burlington Resources, Inc. [NYSE symbol] (SPSG)
br.............. Burma [IYRU nationality code] [MARC country of publication code Library of Congress] (LCCP)
BR.............. Burn Rate
BR.............. Business Roundtable (EA)
BR.............. Bus Request [Computer science] (IAA)
BR.............. Butadiene Rubber
Br.............. Quebec Official Reports, Queen's Bench [1892-1900] [Canada] [A publication] (DLA)
BR.............. Rossland Public Library, British Columbia [Library symbol National Library of Canada] (BIB)
BR.............. United States Bankruptcy Court (DLA)
BR.............. West's Bankruptcy Reporter [A publication] (DLA)
BR1.............. Boilermaker, First Class [Navy rating]
BR2.............. Boilermaker, Second Class [Navy rating]
BR3.............. Boilermaker, Third Class [Navy rating]
BRA.............. Asheville, NC [Location identifier FAA] (FAAL)
BRA.............. Bacterial Releasing Agent [Microbiology]
BRA.............. Bankruptcy Reform Act [1978]
BRA.............. Barreiras [Brazil] [Airport symbol] (OAG)
BRA.............. Base Rate Area [Telecommunications] (TEL)
BRA.............. Beam Ride Actuator
BRA.............. Beef Recording Association [British] (BI)
BRA.............. Bee Research Association [Later, IBRA]
BRA.............. Bench Replaceable Assembly (MCD)
BRA.............. Bennett, Richard A., Stockton CA [STAC]
BRA.............. Beta-Resorcylic Acid [Organic chemistry]
BRA.............. Bilateral Renal Agenesis [Medicine] (DMAA)
BRA.............. Biomira, Inc. [Toronto Stock Exchange symbol]
BRA.............. Bomber Replenishment Area [Military]
BRA.............. Bombing Restriction Area [British military] (DMA)

BRA .... Booster Release Actuator (MCD)
BRA .... Boston Redevelopment Authority
BRA .... Bougainville Revolutionary Army [Papua New Guinea] [Political party] (EY)
BRA .... Braathens South American & Far East Airtransport AS [Norway] [ICAO designator] (FAAC)
BRA .... Bracciera [Ship's rigging] (ROG)
BRA .... Brachial Artery [Anatomy]
Bra .... Bracton. De Legibus Angliae [A publication] (DLA)
Bra .... Brady's English History [1648] [A publication] (DLA)
BRA .... Brain [Neurology] (DAVI)
BRA .... Brain Research Association [British]
bra .... Braj [MARC language code Library of Congress] (LCCP)
BRA .... Branch Address
BRA .... Branch Always [Computer science]
BRA .... Brandon Systems [AMEX symbol] (SPSG)
BRA .... Brassiere (DSUE)
BRA .... Bratislava [Czechoslovakia] [Seismograph station code, US Geological Survey Closed] (SEIS)
BRA .... Brazil [ANSI three-letter standard code] (CNC)
BRA .... Brigadier, Royal Artillery [British]
BRA .... British Racketball Association (DBA)
BRA .... British Radiesthesia Association (BI)
BRA .... British Records Association
BRA .... British Refrigeration Association (DBA)
BRA .... British Resorts Association
BRA .... British Rheumatism and Arthritis Association (BI)
BRA .... British Robot Association Ltd.
Br-A .... Bromoamiloride [Biochemistry]
BRA .... Building Renovating Association
BRA .... Burden Rate Adjustment (MCD)
BRA .... Business Rankings Annual [A publication]
BRA .... Butterworth's Rating Appeals [1913-31] [England] [A publication] (DLA)
BRA(AA) ...... Brigadier, Royal Artillery (Antiaircraft Artillery) [British and Canadian]
BRAAT .... Base Recovery After Attack (MCD)
BRAB .... Brabazon Aircraft [British] (DSUE)
BRAB .... Building Research Advisory Board [Later, ABBE] [National Academy of Sciences]
Br Abr .... Brooke's Abridgment [England] [A publication] (DLA)
BRAC .... Bangladesh Rural Advancement Committee [Development program]
BRAC .... Base Realignment Aid Closure [Military]
BRAC .... Base Realignment and Closure [DoD] (RDA)
BRAC .... Base Realignment and Closure (AAGC)
BRAC .... Basic Rest-Activity Cycle [Medicine] (DMAA)
BRAC .... Bomb Release Angle Computer (MCD)
BRAC .... Bonneville Regional Advisory Council [Terminated, 1978] [Department of Energy] (EGAO)
Brac .... Bracton. De Legibus et Consuetudinibus Angliae [England] [A publication] (DLA)
Brac .... Bracton's Note Book, King's Bench [1217-40] [A publication] (DLA)
BrAC .... Breath-Alcohol Concentration [Sobriety test]
BRAC .... Britannica Reading Achievement Center
BRAC .... Brotherhood of Railway, Airline, and Steamship Clerks; Freight Handlers; Expressand Station Employes (EA)
BRAC .... Building Regulations Advisory Committee [British]
Brach .... Brachial [Medicine] (DMAA)
BRACH .... Brachio [To the Arm] [Pharmacy]
BRACHS....... Institute for Bronx Regional and Community History Studies [Lehman College of City University of New York] [Research center] (RCD)
Bra Cit .... Brady's Historical Treatise on Cities [A publication] (DLA)
Brack Misc.... Brackenridge's Miscellanies [A publication] (DLA)
Brack Tr....... Brackenridge on the Law of Trusts [A publication] (DLA)
BRACOB...... Blast Response and Collapse of Buildings (MCD)
BRACS........ Blast Resistant Artillery Camouflage Screen (MCD)
BR Act .... Booth on Real Actions [A publication] (DLA)
Bract .... Bracton. De Legibus et Consuetudinibus Angliae [England] [A publication] (DLA)
Bract .... Digest of Maxims, by James S. Bracton [A publication] (DLA)
Bracton .... Bracton. De Legibus et Consuetudinibus Angliae [England] [A publication] (DLA)
Brad .... Bradford's New York Surrogate's Court Reports [A publication] (DLA)
Brad .... Bradford's Reports [1838-41] [Iowa] [A publication] (DLA)
Brad .... Bradford's Somerset Star Chamber [A publication] (DLA)
Brad .... Bradwell's Illinois Appellate Reports [A publication] (DLA)
Brad .... Brady's History of the Succession of the Crown of England [A publication] (DLA)
BRAD .... British Rate and Data
BRAD .... Bureau of Research and Development (KSC)
Bradb .... Bradbury's Pleading and Practice Reports [New York] [A publication] (DLA)
Brad Dis ...... Bradby on Distresses [A publication] (DLA)
BRADF .... Bradfield [England]
Bradf........... Bradford's New York Surrogate's Court Reports [A publication] (DLA)
Bradf........... Bradford's Proceedings in the Court of Star Chamber [Somerset Record Society Publications, Vol. 27] [A publication] (DLA)
Bradf........... Bradford's Reports [1838-41] [Iowa] [A publication] (DLA)
Bradford ...... Bradford's Iowa Supreme Court Reports [1839-41] [A publication] (DLA)
Bradford's R... Bradford's New York Surrogate's Court Reports [A publication] (DLA)
Bradford's Sur R... Bradford's New York Surrogate's Court Reports [A publication] (DLA)
Bradf Rep .... Bradford's New York Surrogate's Court Reports [A publication] (DLA)
Bradf Sur..... Bradford's New York Surrogate's Court Reports [A publication] (DLA)

Bradf Sur R... Bradford's New York Surrogate's Court Reports [*A publication*] (DLA)

Bradl.......... Bradley's Rhode Island Reports [*A publication*] (DLA)

Bradlee........ Bradlees, Inc. [*Associated Press*] (SAG)

Bradley U.... Bradley University (GAGS)

Bradl PB...... Bradley's Point Book [*A publication*] (DLA)

Bradl (RI).... Bradley's Rhode Island Reports [*A publication*] (DLA)

BradP.......... Bradley Pharmaceuticals, Inc. [*Associated Press*] (SAG)

BRadPA...... British Radiation Protection Association (DBA)

BradPhm...... Bradley Pharmaceuticals, Inc. [*Associated Press*] (SAG)

Brad R........ Bradford's New York Surrogate's Court Reports [*A publication*] (DLA)

BradRE....... Bradley Real Estate [*Formerly, Bradley Real Estate Trust*] [*Associated Press*] (SAG)

Brad Sur...... Bradford's New York Surrogate's Court Reports [*A publication*] (DLA)

Bradw.......... Bradwell's Illinois Appellate Reports [*A publication*] (DLA)

brady.......... Bradycardia [*Cardiology*] (DAVI)

Brady Ind..... Brady's Index, Arkansas Reports [*A publication*] (DLA)

Brady's Tr.... Brady's Treatise upon Cities and Boroughs [*A publication*] (DLA)

BradyW........ Brady [*W. T.*] Co. [*Associated Press*] (SAG)

B Ra E........ Bachelor of Radio Engineering

BrAE........... British Antarctic Expedition [*1898-1900, 1907-09, 1910-13*]

B Ra Eng..... Bachelor of Radio Engineering

BRAF.......... Braking Action Fair [*Aviation*] (FAAC)

BRAG.......... Black Radical Action Group

BRAG.......... Braking Action Good [*Aviation*] (FAAC)

BRAGS........ Bioelectrical Repair and Growth Society (EA)

BRAH.......... Bioengineering and Research to Aid the Handicapped Program [*Washington, DC National Science Foundation*] (GRD)

BRAI........... Boston Restaurant Assoc [*NASDAQ symbol*] (TTSB)

BRAI........... Boston Restaurant Associates [*NASDAQ symbol*] (SAG)

BRAID......... Bidirectional Reference Array, Internally Derived [*Computer science*] (DIT)

BRAID......... Buying, Receiving, and Accounts Payable Integrated Data (MCD)

BRAILLE..... Balanced Resource Allocation Information for Logical Lucid Evaluation (PDAA)

BRAIN......... Baruch Retrieval of Automated Information for Negotiations [*City University of New York*] [*Information service or system*] (IID)

BRAIN......... Basic Research in Adaptive Intelligence [*EEC*]

BRAIN......... Bay-Area Random Access Information Network [*Defunct*] (TSSD)

Bra Ind Soc... Brabrook. Industrial and Provident Societies [*1869*] [*A publication*] (DLA)

Brainerd....... Brainerd International [*Associated Press*] (SAG)

Brain LP...... Brainard's Legal Precedents in Land and Mining Cases [*United States*] [*A publication*] (DLA)

BRAINS....... Behavior Replication by Analog Instruction of the Nervous System [*Electrical stimulation of the brain*]

BRAINS....... Brokerage Accounting Information System (SAA)

BRAINT....... Braintree [*Urban district in England*]

Braith......... Jamaica Law Reports (Braithwaite) [*A publication*] (DLA)

Braith Chy... Braithwaite. Times of Procedure in Chancery [*1864*] [*A publication*] (DLA)

Braith Oaths... Braithwaite. Oaths in Chancery [*2nd ed.*] [*1864*] [*A publication*] (DLA)

Braith Oaths... Braithwaite. Oaths in the Supreme Court [*4th ed.*] [*1881*] [*A publication*] (DLA)

Braith Pr...... Braithwaite. Record and Writ Practice of the Court of Chancery [*1858*] [*A publication*] (DLA)

BRAIW........ Boston Restaurant Assoc Wrrt [*NASDAQ symbol*] (TTSB)

BRALUP...... Bureau of Resource Assessment and Land Use Planning

BRAM......... Blocked Random Access Method (MCD)

BR AM........ British America (BARN)

BRAMATEC... Brain Mapping Technique

Brame......... Brame's Reports [*66-72 Mississippi*] [*A publication*] (DLA)

BRAMS........ British Trans-Atlantic Air Mail Service (IAA)

BRAMS....... Broome Regional Aboriginal Medical Service [*Australia*]

BRAN......... Braking Action Nil [*Aviation*] (FAAC)

BRANA........ Bumper Recycling Association of North America (EA)

BRANCH...... Branch [*Commonly used*] (OPSA)

Branch........ Branch's Reports [*1 Florida*] [*A publication*] (DLA)

Branch Max... Branch's Maxims [*A publication*] (DLA)

Branch Pr.... Branch's Principia Legis et Equitatis [*Maxims*] [*A publication*] (DLA)

Branch Princ... Branch's Principia Legis et Equitatis [*Maxims*] [*A publication*] (DLA)

BRANCHYDRO... Branch Hydrographic Office [*Navy*]

Brand.......... Brandenburg's Reports [*21 Opinions Attorneys-General*] [*A publication*] (DLA)

Br & B........ Broderip and Bingham's English Common Pleas Reports [*A publication*] (DLA)

BR & CL...... Branch and Class (DNAB)

Br & Col...... British and Colonial Prize Cases [*A publication*] (DLA)

Br & Col Pr Cas... British and Colonial Prize Cases [*A publication*] (DLA)

Brande........ Brande's Dictionary of Science, Etc. [*A publication*] (DLA)

BR & EA...... Banking Research and Economic Analysis [*Unit*] [*Department of the Treasury*] (GRD)

Brandeis U... Brandeis University (GAGS)

Brandenburg Bankr... Brandenburg's Bankruptcy Digest [*A publication*] (DLA)

Brandenburg Dig... Brandenburg's Bankruptcy Digest [*A publication*] (DLA)

Brand F Attachm... Brandon on Foreign Attachment [*A publication*] (DLA)

Br & F Ecc... Broderick and Freemantle's Ecclesiastical Cases [*1840-64*] [*A publication*] (DLA)

Brand For Att... Brandon on Foreign Attachment [*A publication*] (ILCA)

Brand For Attachm... Brandon on Foreign Attachment [*A publication*] (DLA)

Br & Fr........ Broderick and Freemantle's Ecclesiastical Cases [*1840-64*] [*A publication*] (DLA)

Br & G......... Brownlow and Goldesborough's English Common Pleas Reports [*A publication*] (DLA)

Br & Gold.... Brownlow and Goldesborough's English Common Pleas Reports [*A publication*] (DLA)

Br & Had..... Broom and Hadley's Commentaries on the Laws of England [*A publication*] (DLA)

Br & L........ Browning and Lushington's English Admiralty Reports [*1863-65*] [*A publication*] (DLA)

Br & Lush.... Browning and Lushington's English Admiralty Reports [*1863-65*] [*A publication*] (DLA)

Brand May Ct... Brandon. Practice of the Mayor's Court [*1864*] [*A publication*] (DLA)

Brandn........ Brandon Systems Corp. [*Associated Press*] (SAG)

BR & P........ Buffalo, Rochester & Pittsburgh Railroad

BR & PRY..... Buffalo, Rochester & Pittsburg Railway [*Terminated*]

Br & R........ Brown and Rader's Reports [*137 Missouri*] [*A publication*] (DLA)

BRANDS....... Bright Alphanumeric Display System (CAAL)

BR & T........ Bowdon Railway & Transportation (IIA)

BR & TC...... Better Roads and Transportation Council (EA)

Brandt Sur... Brandt on Suretyship and Guaranty [*A publication*] (DLA)

Brandyw....... Brandywine Realty Trust [*Associated Press*] (SAG)

BRANE........ Bombing RADAR Navigation Equipment

BranfdSv...... Branford Savings Bank [*Associated Press*] (SAG)

Brans Dig.... Branson's Digest [*Bombay*] [*A publication*] (DLA)

Brant.......... Brantly's Reports [*80-90 Maryland*] [*A publication*] (DLA)

BrantCp....... Brantley Capital Corp. [*Associated Press*] (SAG)

Brantly........ Brantly's Reports [*80-90 Maryland*] [*A publication*] (DLA)

Brantre........ Braintree Savings Bank [*Associated Press*] (SAG)

BRAO.......... Branch Retinal Artery Occlusion [*Ophthalmology*] (DAVI)

BRAP.......... Biometry and Risk Assessment Program (GNE)

BRAP.......... Braking Action Poor [*Aviation*] (FAAC)

BRAS.......... Ballistic Rocket Air Suppression

BRAS.......... Brassiere (DSUE)

BRAS.......... Building Research Advisory Service [*Building Research Establishment*] [*Department of Industry*] [*British*] (DS)

BRAS.......... Bureau Regional d'Action Sida (AC)

BRASA........ Brazilian Studies Association

BRASC........ Brotherhood of Railway, Airline, and Steamship Clerks; Freight Handlers; Expressand Station Employees

BRASCAN..... Brasil [*Portuguese spelling*] and Canada [*In company name "Brascan Ltd."*]

BRASH........ Behavioral Research Aspects of Safety and Health Working Group [*University of Kentucky*] [*Research center*] (RCD)

BRASO........ Branch Aviation Supply Office [*Navy*]

BRASS........ Ballistic Range for Aircraft Survivability Studies (DNAB)

BRASS........ BEEF [*Base Engineer Emergency Forces*] Reporting, Analysis, and Status System [*Air Force*] (AFM)

BRASS........ Bistatic RADAR System (MCD)

BRASS........ Bottom Reflection Active SONAR System

BRASS........ Bridge Rating and Analysis Structural System (MCD)

BRASS........ Business Reference and Services Section [*American Library Association*]

BrassieG...... Brassie Golf Corp. [*Associated Press*] (SAG)

BRASTACS.... Bradford Science Technology and Commercial Services [*Information service or system*] (NITA)

BRAT.......... Banana, Rice Cereal, Apple Sauce, and Tea [*Diet*] (DAVI)

BRAT.......... Bananas, Rice Cereal, Applesauce, and Toast [*Bland diet*] [*Medicine*]

BRAT.......... Baylor Rapid Autologous Transfusion [*System*] [*Medicine*] (DMAA)

BRAT.......... Bi-Drive Recreational All-Terrain Transporter [*Subaru automobile*]

Bra Tr Un.... Brabrook's Law of Trade Unions [*A publication*] (DLA)

BRATS........ Bottom Refraction Acoustic Telemetry System (MCD)

BRATT........ Bananas, Rice, Apple Sauce, Tea, and Toast [*Diet*] (DAVI)

BRAUN........ Braunton [*England*]

Brauns........ Braun's Fashions Corp. [*Associated Press*] (SAG)

BRAVC........ Baker River Audiovisual Center [*Library network*]

BRAVE........ Boeing Robotic Air Vehicles

BRAVO........ Best Range of Aging Verified Oscillator (MUGU)

BRAVO........ Business Risk and Value of Operation in Space [*NASA*] (NASA)

Bray........... Brayton's Reports [*Vermont*] [*A publication*] (DLA)

Bray R........ Brayton's Reports [*Vermont*] [*A publication*] (DLA)

Brayt.......... Brayton's Reports [*Vermont*] [*A publication*] (ILCA)

Brayton's Rep... Brayton's Reports [*Vermont*] [*A publication*] (DLA)

Brayton (VT)... Brayton's Reports [*Vermont*] [*A publication*] (DLA)

Brayt Rep.... Brayton's Reports [*Vermont*] [*A publication*] (DLA)

braz........... Brazed (VRA)

BRAZ.......... Brazier (MSA)

BRAZ.......... Brazil

Braz........... Brazil (VRA)

BRAZH........ Brazier Head

Brazil.......... Brazil Fast Food Corp. [*Associated Press*] (SAG)

Brazil.......... Brazil Fund, Inc. [*Associated Press*] (SAG)

BrazilEF....... Brazilian Equity Fund [*Associated Press*] (SAG)

BrazlFst....... Brazil Fast Food Corp. [*Associated Press*] (SAG)

BRB............ Babe Ruth Baseball (EA)

BRB............ Ballistic Recoverable Booster (MCD)

BRB............ Ballistic Reentry Body

BRB............ Barbados [*Seismograph station code, US Geological Survey Closed*] (SEIS)

BRB............ Barbados [*ANSI three-letter standard code*] (CNC)

BRB............ Base Rate Boundary [*Telecommunications*] (TEL)

BRB............ Benefits Review Board [*Department of Labor*] (OICC)

BRB............ Be Right Back [*Computer hacker terminology*] (NHD)

brb............ Be Right Back [*Internet language*] [*Computer science*]

BRB............ Biopharmaceutics Research Branch [*Washington, DC Department of Health and Human Services*] (GRD)

BRB............ Blood-Retinal Barrier [*Ophthalmology*] (DAVI)

BRB .... Brick Brewing Co. Ltd. [*Toronto Stock Exchange symbol*]
BRB .... Bright Red Blood [*Medicine*]
BRB .... British Railways Board
BRB .... Bryant College, Smithfield, RI [*OCLC symbol*] (OCLC)
BRB .... Building Research Board (EA)
BRBA .... Brucella, Vitamin K Blood Agar [*Bacteriology*] (DAVI)
BRBC .... Bay Ridge Bancorp [*NASDAQ symbol*] (SAG)
BRBC .... Bovine Red Blood Cell [*Hematology*] (MAE)
BRBC .... Burro Red Blood Cells
BrBEV .... [*The*] Broadway Book of English Verse [*A publication*]
BRBF .... Babe Ruth Birthplace Foundation (EA)
BRBK .... Brenton Banks [*NASDAQ symbol*] (TTSB)
BRBK .... Brenton Banks, Inc. [*NASDAQ symbol*] (NQ)
BRBNS........ Blue Rubber Bleb Nevus Syndrome [*Medicine*] (DMAA)
BRBPR........ Bright Red Blood per Rectum [*Medicine*]
BRBQ .... Building Registration Board of Queensland [*Australia*]
BRBR......... Big Red Bike Ride [*Fundraising event*] [*British*]
Br Brev Jud... Brownlow's Brevia Judicialia, Etc. [*1662*] [*A publication*] (DLA)
Br Brev Jud & Ent... Brownlow's Brevia Judicialia, Etc. [*1662*] [*A publication*] (DLA)
BRBS .... Benefits Review Board Service (Matthew Bender) [*A publication*] (DLA)
BR BUR ...... British Burma
BRBWA....... Builders' Registration Board of Western Australia [*Australia*]
br bx .... Breast Biopsy [*Gynecology*] (DAVI)
BRBY .... Bribery [*FBI standardized term*]
BRBZC........ Brass, Bronze, or Copper [*Freight*]
BRC .... Bannister Research & Consulting
BRC .... Bantam Reconnaissance-Command [*Jeep prototype*]
BRC .... Barley Canyon [*New Mexico*] [*Seismograph station code, US Geological Survey*] (SEIS)
BRC .... Barley Research Council [*Australia*]
BRC .... Barrick Resources Corp. [*Toronto Stock Exchange symbol*]
BRC .... Base Recovery Course [*Military*] (NVT)
BRC .... Base Repair Cycle (MCD)
BRC .... Base Residence Course
BRC .... BCA Charter [*British ICAO designator*] (FAAC)
BRC .... Before Rotary Cutting [*Quilting*]
BRC .... Behavioral Research Council (EA)
BRC .... Below Regulatory Concern [*Nuclear Regulatory Commission classification*]
BRC .... [*The*] Belt Railway Co. of Chicago [*AAR code*]
BRC .... Beveren Rabbit Club [*Defunct*] (EA)
BRC .... Biological Radio Communications
BRC .... Biological Records Centre [*Institute of Terrestrial Ecology*] [*Information service or system*] (IID)
BRC .... Biological Research Center [*Philippines*]
BRC .... Biomass Research Center [*University of Arkansas*]
BRC .... Biomedical Recovery Capsule (MUGU)
BRC .... BIT [*Binary Digit*] Reversion Circuit [*Computer science*] (MHDI)
BRC .... Black Rock Coalition (EA)
BRC .... Blue Ribbon Coalition [*An association*] (EA)
BRC .... Boilermaker, Chief [*Navy rating*]
BRC .... Bookmakers' Revision Committee [*New South Wales, Australia*]
BRC .... Boonton Radio Corp. (IAA)
BRC .... Bounded Right Context (MHDI)
BRC .... Brace (MSA)
BRC .... Branch Conditional
BRC .... Breeder Reactor Corp.
BRC .... Brief Record Cataloging
BRC .... Bristol Community College, Fall River, MA [*OCLC symbol*] (OCLC)
BRC .... British Rabbit Council (BI)
BRC .... British Radio Communication (IAA)
BRC .... British Retail Consortium (EAIO)
BRC .... British Ruling Cases [*A publication*] (DLA)
BRC .... Broadcast Rating Council [*Later, EMRC*]
BRC .... Brooks Resources Corp. [*Vancouver Stock Exchange symbol*]
BRC .... Brotherhood of Railway Carmen of America [*Later, BRC of US & C*] [*AFL-CIO*]
BRC .... Brownstone Revival Committee (EA)
BRC .... Budget Review Committee
BRC .... Burlingame Research Center (MCD)
BRC .... Burroughs Corp. (AAG)
BRC .... Business Reply Card [*Advertising*]
BRC .... Business Research Corp. [*Boston, MA*] [*Information service or system*] (IID)
BRC .... Royal Roads Military College, Victoria, British Columbia [*Library symbol National Library of Canada*] (NLC)
BRC .... San Carlos De Bariloche [*Argentina*] [*Airport symbol*] (OAG)
BRCA .... British Roller Canary Association (BI)
BRCA .... Bryce Canyon National Park
BRCC .... Bovine Research Center at Cornell [*Cornell University*] [*Research center*] (RCD)
Br CC .... British [*or English*] Crown Cases [*A publication*] (DLA)
BRCC .... British Roller Canary Club (BI)
Br CC .... Brown's Chancery Cases [*England*] [*A publication*] (DLA)
BRCD .... Bob Rumball Centre for the Deaf (AC)
BRCD .... Braced
BRCD .... Breast Cancer, Ductal [*Medicine*] (DMAA)
brcd .... Brocade (VRA)
BRCE .... Bureau de Recherche et de Consultation en Education [*Bureau of Research and Consultation in Education*] [*Canada*]
Brcg........... Bracing (DAC)
BRCH .... Branch (ADA)
BRCH .... Broach (MSA)
BRC Hld....... BRC Holdings, Inc. [*Associated Press*] (SAG)

BRCK .... Brick
BrckwSt ...... Brockway Standard Holdings, Inc. [*Associated Press*] (SAG)
BRCM .... Below Right Costal Margin [*Anatomy*] (DAVI)
BRCM .... Boilermaker, Master Chief [*Navy rating*]
BRCMA .... British Radio Cabinet Manufacturers' Association (IAA)
BRCN .... [*An*] Elizabeth Barrett Browning Concordance [*A publication*]
BRCNSW..... Barley Research Committee, New South Wales [*Australia*]
BRCO .... Brady [*W.H.*] Co. [*NASDAQ symbol*] (NQ)
BRCOA........ Brady(W.H.)'A'non-vtg [*NASDAQ symbol*] (TTSB)
BRC of A..... Brotherhood of Railway Carmen of America [*Later, BRC of US & C*] [*AFL-CIO*] (EA)
BRC of US & C... Brotherhood of Railway Carmen of the United States and Canada [*AFL-CIO*] (EA)
Br Col .... British Columbia (ILCA)
Br Com........ Broom. Common Law [*9th ed.*] [*1896*] [*A publication*] (DLA)
Br Cons Law... Broom. Constitutional Law [*3rd ed.*] [*1885*] [*A publication*] (DLA)
Br Coy .... Bearer Company [*British military*] (DMA)
BRCP .... BRC Holdings [*NASDAQ symbol*] (TTSB)
BRCP .... BRC Holdings, Inc. [*NASDAQ symbol*] (SAG)
BRCP .... Business Records Holding Corp. [*NASDAQ symbol*] (SPSG)
BRCQ .... Barley Research Committee for Queensland [*Australia*]
BRCR .... Brices Crossroads National Battlefield Site
Br Cr Ca ..... British [*or English*] Crown Cases [*A publication*] (DLA)
Br Cr Cas.... British [*or English*] Crown Cases [*A publication*] (DLA)
BRCS .... Bahamas Red Cross Society (EAIO)
BRCS .... Basic Reference Coordinate System (MCD)
BRCS .... BMEWS [*Ballistic Missile Early Warning System*] Rearward Communications System (AFM)
BRCS .... Boilermaker, Senior Chief [*Navy rating*]
BRCS .... British Red Cross Society
BRCS .... British Romagnola Cattle Society (DBA)
BRCS .... Business and Residence Centrex Services [*Telecommunications*] (ACRL)
BRCSA........ Barley Research Committee for South Australia
BRCT .... Broadband Rectangular-to-Circular Transition [*Telecommunications*] (IAA)
BRCT .... Burlington Randomized Controlled Trial [*Criterion for medical evaluation*]
BRCWA....... Barley Research Committee for Western Australia
BRD .... Ball Reduction Drive
BRD .... Base Remount Depot [*British military*] (DMA)
BRD .... Base [*or Basic*] Retirement Date [*Air Force*]
BRD .... Bellofram Rolling Diaphragm
BRD .... Binary Rate Divider
BRD .... Binary Read [*Computer science*] (HGAA)
BRD .... Blank Recording Disc
BRD .... Board
BRD .... Bomb Release Distance [*Army*] (AABC)
BRD .... Booster Requirements Document
BRD .... Borderline
BRD .... Bradner Resources Ltd. [*Vancouver Stock Exchange symbol*]
BRD .... Braid (KSC)
BRD .... Brainerd [*Minnesota*] [*Airport symbol*] (OAG)
BRD .... Brake Die (MCD)
Brd.............. Bread [*Dietetics*]
BRD .... Bridge (ROG)
BRD .... Broadband Subsystem
BRD .... Brock Air Services Ltd. [*Canada ICAO designator*] (FAAC)
BRD .... Brodart Co. [*ACCORD*] [*UTLAS symbol*]
BRD .... Brooder [*s*] [*Freight*]
BRD .... Bundesrepublik Deutschland [*Federal Republic of Germany*]
BRD .... Bycatch Reduction Device [*Fishing technology*]
BRD .... Ragan (Brad) [*AMEX symbol*] (TTSB)
BRD .... Ragan [*Brad*], Inc. [*AMEX symbol*] (SPSG)
BRDA .... Boxboard Research and Development Association (EA)
BRDAA .... Bicycle Ride Directors Association of America (EA)
BrdbdTc ...... BroadBand Technologies, Inc. [*Associated Press*] (SAG)
BRDC .... Bare Refractory, Double Containment [*Boiler*] [*NASA*]
BRDC .... British Racing Drivers Club
BRDC .... British Research and Development Corp. (NUCP)
BRDC .... Bureau of Research and Development Center [*FAA*] (AAG)
BRDCST...... Broadcast
BRDCSTR ... Broadcaster
BRDEC .... Belvoir Research, Development, and Engineering Center [*Fort Belvoir, VA*] [*Army*] (RDA)
Brd Ex........ Bread Exchange [*Dietetics*]
BRDF .... Bidirectional Reflectance-Distribution Function
BRDF .... Biomedical Research Defense Fund [*Defunct*] (EA)
BRD FO....... Broad Folio [*Typography*] (DGA)
BRDG .... Biomedical Research Development Grants
BRDG .... Breeding
BRDG .... Bridge (KSC)
BrdgF......... Brigford Foods Corp. [*Associated Press*] (SAG)
BrdgF......... Brigford Foods Corp. [*Associated Press*] (SAG)
BRDGSCIT ... Bridge Excitation
BrdgVw....... Bridge View Bancorp [*Associated Press*] (SAG)
BRDL .... Biomedical Research and Development Laboratory [*Army*] (RDA)
BRDL .... Brendle's, Inc. [*NASDAQ symbol*] (NQ)
BRDL .... Bridal
BRDM .... Soviet Amphibious Armored Reconnaissance Vehicle (MCD)
BRDNG .... Boarding
BRDP .... Blue Ribbon Defense Panel
BrdP St....... Bradley Pharmaceuticals, Inc. [*Associated Press*] (SAG)
BRDR......... Breeder
BRDR......... Breeder

BRDSCT.......	Broadcast
BRDSCTG	Broadcasting
BRDT	Bayesian Reliability Demonstration Test [*Computer science*]
BRDTH	Breadth
Brdu...........	5-Bromodeoxyuridine (DOG)
BrDU	Bromodeoxyuridine [*Also, BDU, BDUR*] [*Biochemistry*]
BrdUrd	Bromodeoxyuridine [*Also, BDU, BDUR*] [*Antineoplastic drug*] (DAVI)
BRDWY	Broadway
BrdwyF	Broadway Financial Corp. [*Associated Press*] (SAG)
BrdyW	Brady, W.T. Co. Class A [*Associated Press*] (SAG)
BRE............	Bachelor of Recreation Education (DD)
B Re	Bachelor of Religion
BRE	Bachelor of Religious Education
BRE	Beam Ride Error
BRE	Berridale [*Airport symbol*]
BRe	Biblia Revuo [*A publication*] (BJA)
BRe	Biblical Research [*A publication*] (BJA)
BRE	Bore [*Freight*]
BRE	Bremen [*Germany Airport symbol*] (OAG)
BRE	Brencham Air Charter Ltd. [*British ICAO designator*] (FAAC)
BRE	BRE Properties Cl A [*NYSE symbol*] (SPSG)
BRE	BRE Properties, Inc. [*Associated Press*] (SAG)
BRE	Breslau [*Wroclaw*] [*Poland*] [*Seismograph station code, US Geological Survey*] [*Closed*] (SEIS)
bre	Breton [*MARC language code Library of Congress*] (LCCP)
BRE	Brewsterite [*A zeolite*]
BRE	Bridge Relay Element [*Electronics*] (ACRL)
BrE	British English [*Language*] (WGA)
BRE	British Rail Engineering
BRE	Brower Exploration, Inc. [*Vancouver Stock Exchange symbol*]
BRE	Building Research Establishment [*Research center British*] (IRC)
BRE	Building Research Establishment
BRE	Bureau of Railway Economics [*Later, AAR*]
BRE	Bureau of Recruiting and Examining [*Civil Service Commission*]
BRE	Bureau of Research and Engineering [*US Postal Service*]
BRE	Business Reply Envelope [*Advertising*]
BREACH	Battlefield Related Evaluation of Countermeasure Hardware [*Model*] (MCD)
BREATHE	Breathers for the Reduction of Atmospheric Hazards to the Environment [*Student legal action organization*]
BREB	Association of Battlefords Realtors (AC)
b rec...........	Bills Receivable [*Business term*] (ODBW)
BREC	Bills Recoverable [*Business term*] (ADA)
Brec	Brecknockshire [*Wales*] (BARN)
BREC	Bridgeville Savings Bank FSB [*Pennsylvania*] [*NASDAQ symbol*] (SAG)
BRECH PROM...	Breach of Promise [*Legal term*] (DLA)
BRECK	Brecknockshire [*County in Wales*] (ROG)
BRECOM	Broadcast Radio Emergency Communication [*Air Force*]
BRECONS	Brecknockshire [*County in Wales*] (ROG)
BRECSU	Building Research Energy Conservation Support Unit [*British*]
BR Ed	Bachelor of Religious Education
BredTch	Breed Technologies [*Associated Press*] (SAG)
B Re E	Bachelor of Refrigeration Engineering
BREED	Project Breed Rescue Efforts and Education [*An association*] (EA)
BREEMA	British Radio and Electronic Equipment Manufacturers Association (DS)
B Re Eng	Bachelor of Refrigeration Engineering
Breese........	Breese's Illinois Reports [*1 Illinois*] [*A publication*] (DLA)
Breese........	Breese's Illinois Supreme Court Reports [*1 Illinois*] [*1819-31*] [*A publication*] (DLA)
BREF...........	Book Review Editors File [*University Press of New England*] [*Information service or system*] (IID)
B Reg	Bankrupt Register [*A publication*] (DLA)
BREG	British Rivet Export Group (BI)
BREL...........	Boeing Radiation Effect Laboratory
BREMA	British Radio and Electronic Equipment Manufacturers Association [*Formerly, British Radio Equipment Manufacturers Association*]
BREN	Bare Reactor Experiment at Nevada
BREN	Brenco, Inc. [*NASDAQ symbol*] (NQ)
BREN	Brno-Enfield [*Machine gun*]
Brenco	Brenco, Inc. [*Associated Press*] (SAG)
Brendle........	Brendle's, Inc. [*Associated Press*] (SAG)
Br Ent	Brownlow's Entries [*A publication*] (DLA)
BrentBk.......	Brenton Banks, Inc. [*Associated Press*] (SAG)
BRENTW	Brentwood [*Urban district in England*]
BREPAIR......	Bolted Repair [*Composite structures*] (MCD)
BRER	Basic Radiation Effects Reactor
BRESCU	Building Research Energy Conservation Support Unit (AIE)
Bresl Phil Abh...	Breslauer Philologische Abhandlungen [*A publication*] (OCD)
BResMA.......	British Resin Manufacturers Association (DBA)
BRESS	Behavioral Risk Factor Surveillance System
BRESTCHAN...	Brest Subarea, Channel [*NATO*]
BRET...........	Beilstein Registry Connection Tables [*Chemistry*]
BRET...........	Bistatic Reflected Energy Target (MCD)
BRET...........	Botswana Renewable Energy Technology Project [*Ministry of Mineral Resources and Water Affairs in cooperation with United States Agency for International Development*] [*Research center*]
BRET...........	Breton [*Language, etc.*] (ROG)
BRET...........	Burning Rate Extraction Technique (MCD)
Brett Ca Eq...	Brett's Cases in Modern Equity [*A publication*] (DLA)
Brev	Brevard's South Carolina Reports [*1793-1816*] [*A publication*] (DLA)
BREV	Brevet [*Military*]
BREV	Brevete [*Patent*] [*French*]
BREV	Breveted [*Military British*] (ROG)

brev	Breviary (VRA)
BREV	Brevier
Brev Dig	Brevard's Digest of the Public Statute Law, South Carolina [*A publication*] (DLA)
Brev Ju	Brevia Judicialia [*Judicial Writs*] [*Latin Legal term*] (DLA)
Brev Sel	Brevia Selecta [*Choice Writs*] [*Latin Legal term*] (DLA)
Brew	Brewer's Reports [*19-26 Maryland*] [*A publication*] (DLA)
BREW	Brewing (ROG)
BREW	Rock Bottom Restaurants [*NASDAQ symbol*] (TTSB)
BREW	Rock Bottom Restaurants, Inc. [*NASDAQ symbol*] (SAG)
Brewer........	Brewer's Reports [*19-26 Maryland*] [*A publication*] (DLA)
Brew (MD)...	Brewer's Reports [*19-26 Maryland*] [*A publication*] (DLA)
BREWS	Battlefield Related Electronic Warfare Simulator (MCD)
Brews	Brewster's Pennsylvania Reports [*A publication*] (DLA)
Brews (PA)...	Brewster's Pennsylvania Reports [*A publication*] (DLA)
Brewst........	Brewster's Pennsylvania Reports [*A publication*] (DLA)
Brewster......	Brewster's Pennsylvania Reports [*A publication*] (DLA)
Brewst PA Dig...	Brewster's Pennsylvania Digest [*A publication*] (DLA)
BREX	Banner Reflex [*Botany*]
BreXMn........	Bre-X Minerals Ltd. [*Associated Press*] (SAG)
BRF	Air Bravo [*Uganda*] [*ICAO designator*] (FAAC)
BRF	Baltic Research Foundation [*Australia*] (EAIO)
BRF	Bandrejection Filter (IAA)
BRF	Baptist Revival Fellowship [*British*]
BRF	Bass Research Foundation (EA)
BRF	Bell Rings Faintly [*Telecommunications*] (TEL)
BRF	Best Replacement Factor (CAAL)
BRF	Bible Reading Fellowship [*British*]
BRF	Bioprocessing Research Facility [*Oak Ridge, TN*] [*Oak Ridge National Laboratory*] [*Department of Energy*] (GRD)
BRF	Bioresources Research Facility [*University of Arizona*] [*Research center*] (RCD)
BRF	Blackrock Fl Ins Muni 2008 Tr [*NYSE symbol*] (TTSB)
BRF	Blackrock Florida Insurance Municipal 2008 Trade [*NYSE symbol*] (SPSG)
BRF	Blood Research Foundation (EA)
BRF	Bone-Resorbing Factor [*Medicine*] (DMAA)
BRF	Bradford [*England*] [*Airport symbol*] (AD)
BRF	Brain Research Foundation (EA)
BRF	Branchial Filament
BRF	Brewing Research Foundation [*British*]
BRF	Brief (FAAC)
BRF	Brief
BRF	Brigades Revolutionnaires Francaises [*Revolutionary French Brigades*] [*French*] (PD)
BRF	British Road Federation Ltd. (BI)
BRF	Broach Fixture (MCD)
BRFA	British Retail Florist's Association (DBA)
BRFA	British Romanian Friendship Association (DBA)
BRFA	Fireman Apprentice, Boilermaker, Striker [*Navy rating*]
BRFC	Bridgeville Savings Bank FSB PA [*NASDAQ symbol*] (SAG)
BRFC	Bridgeville Savings Bk [*NASDAQ symbol*] (TTSB)
BRFC	Buddy Rich Fan Club (EA)
BRFC	Burt Reynolds Fan Club (EA)
BRFD	Branford Steam Railroad [*AAR code*]
Br Fed Dig...	Brightly's Federal Digest [*A publication*] (DLA)
BRFG	Briefing (KSC)
BRFM	British Retail Footwear Market
BRFN	Fireman, Boilermaker, Striker [*Navy rating*]
BRFP	Baseline Reference Flight Plan (KSC)
BRFSS	Behavioral Risk Factor Surveillance System [*Health survey*]
BRG	Baud Rate Generator [*Computer science*]
BRG	Beacon Reply Group [*Aviation*] (OA)
BRG	Bearing (AFM)
BRG	Berggiesshubel [*German Democratic Republic*] [*Seismograph station code, US Geological Survey*] (SEIS)
BRG	Bering Air, Inc. [*ICAO designator*] (FAAC)
BRG	Blackwell Retail Group [*British*]
BRG	Blue Ridge Resources Ltd. [*Vancouver Stock Exchange symbol*]
BRG	Bridge [*or Bridging*] [*Telecommunications*] (TEL)
BRG	Bridge
BRG	Bridge [*Postal Service standard*] (OPSA)
BRG	Brig [*Shipping*] (ROG)
BRG	British Gas ADS [*NYSE symbol*] (SPSG)
BRG	British Racing Green (ADA)
BRG	Budget Review Group (IAA)
BRG	Whitesburg, KY [*Location identifier FAA*] (FAAL)
BRGBLN.......	Barrage Balloon
BRGHD........	Bridgehead (MSA)
BRGM	Bureau de Recherches Geologiques et Minieres [*Bureau of Geological and MiningResearch*] [*Burkina Faso*] [*Information service or system*] (IID)
BRGN..........	Bargain
BRGP..........	Business Resource Group [*NASDAQ symbol*] (SAG)
BRGS..........	Birthparent & Relative Group Society (AC)
BRGT..........	Bright (FAAC)
BRGW.........	Brake Release Gross Weight
BRH	Berry, R. H., San Leandro CA [*STAC*]
BRH	Birch Hill [*Alaska*] [*Seismograph station code, US Geological Survey Closed*] (SEIS)
BRH	Braathens Helicopter AS [*Norway ICAO designator*] (FAAC)
BRH	Bridgehead (AABC)
BRH	British Rail Hovercraft (PDAA)
BRH	Brohm Resources, Inc. [*Toronto Stock Exchange symbol Vancouver Stock Exchange symbol*]

BRH .... Brush Holder
BRH .... Bureau of Radiological Health [*FDA*]
BRH .... Bureau of Radiological Health, Rockville, MD [*OCLC symbol*] (OCLC)
BRH .... Cases in King's Bench Tempore Hardwicke [*1733-38*] [*England*] [*A publication*] (DLA)
BRH/DEP ..... Bureau of Radiological Health / Division of Electronics Products [*FDA*] (PDAA)
BRH/DER ..... Bureau of Radiological Health / Division of Environmental Radiation [*FDA*] (PDAA)
BRH/DMRE ... Bureau of Radiological Health / Division of Medical Radiation Exposure [*FDA*] (PDAA)
BRHG .... Breaching (MSA)
BRHLR .... Brush Holder (IAA)
BRH/NERHL ... Bureau of Radiological Health / Northeastern Radiological Health Laboratory [*FDA*] (PDAA)
bRHOD .... Bovine Rhodopsin [*Physiology*]
BRH/ORO ..... Bureau of Radiological Health / Office of Regional Operations [*FDA*] (PDAA)
BRHP .... Brake Rating Horsepower [*Automotive engineering*]
Brhp .... Bronchophony [*Medicine*] (DAVI)
BRH/SERHL ... Bureau of Radiological Health / Southeastern Radiological Health Laboratory [*FDA*] (PDAA)
BRH/SWRHL ... Bureau of Radiological Health / Southwestern Radiological Health Laboratory [*FDA*] (PDAA)
BRI .... Babson's Reports, Inc. (IIA)
BRI .... Banque des Reglements Internationaux [*Bank for International Settlements*]
BRI .... Bari [*Italy*] [*Airport symbol*] (OAG)
BRI .... Base Recirculation Insulation (IAA)
BRI .... Basic Rate Interface [*Telecommunications*] (PCM)
BRI .... Basic Reading Inventory (EDAC)
BRI .... Bearing and Range Indicator
BRIGH .... Behavior Research Institute (EA)
BRI .... Bellairs Research Institute [*Canada*] (MSC)
BRI .... Benefit Rights Interview [*Unemployment insurance*]
BRI .... Berkshire Realty [*NYSE symbol*] (TTSB)
BRI .... Berkshire Realty, Inc. [*NYSE symbol*] (SPSG)
BRI .... Biomedical Research Institute [*American Foundation for Biological Research*] [*Research center*] (RCD)
BRI .... Bionetics Research Institute [*Rockville, MD*]
BRI .... Biosystematics Research Institute [*Canada*] (ARC)
BRI .... Biotechnology Research Institute [*Montreal, PQ*] [*Canada*]
BRI .... Bombesin-Releasing Immunoreactivity
BRI .... Bomb Run Insert (SAA)
BRI .... Book Review Index [*Gale Research, Inc.*] [*Detroit, MI*] [*Information service or system*] [*A publication*]
BRI .... Brain Research Institute [*UCLA*] [*Research center*]
BRI .... Brand Rating Index Corp.
BRI .... Breakdown of Recoverable Items (MCD)
BRI .... Brican Resources [*Vancouver Stock Exchange symbol*]
bri .... Brick (VRA)
BRI .... Bridge
BRI .... Brig [*Switzerland*] [*Seismograph station code, US Geological Survey Closed*] (SEIS)
BRI .... Brightness (KSC)
BRI .... British Library, London, England [*OCLC symbol*] (OCLC)
BRI .... Brown & Root International (ECON)
BRI .... Building Related Illness
BRI .... Building Research Institute [*Later, BRAB, ABBE*] (EA)
BRI .... Bureau of Retirement and Insurance [*Civil Service Commission*]
B-RI .... Burlington-Rock Island Railroad Co.
BRI .... Business Risks International, Inc. [*Database producer*] (IID)
BRI .... Richmond Public Library, British Columbia [*Library symbol National Library of Canada*] (NLC)
BRIA .... Beef Research and Information Act [*1976*]
BRIA .... Bioradioimmunoassay
BRIA .... Bread Research Institute of Australia
BRIAAC .... Behavior Rating Instrument for Autistic and Other Atypical Children [*Child development test*] [*Psychology*]
BRIAAC .... Burdekin River Irrigation Area Advisory Committee [*Queensland, Australia*]
BRIAG .... Animal Pathology Laboratory, Food Production and Inspection Branch, Agriculture Canada [*Laboratoire de Pathologie Veterinaire, Direction Generale de la Production et de l'Inspection des Aliments, Agriculture Canada*], Richmond, BritishColumbia [*Library symbol National Library of Canada*] (BIB)
BRIATAC ...... Burdekin River Irrigation Area Technical Advisory Committee [*Queensland, Australia*]
BRIB .... Bribery (DLA)
BRIC .... Benign Recurrent Intrahepatic Cholestasis [*Medicine*] (DMAA)
BRIC .... Black Resources and Information Centre [*Canada*]
BRIC .... Brick Institute of California (SRA)
Brice Ult V... Brice's Ultra Vires [*A publication*] (DLA)
Brick Ala Dig... Brickell's Digest [*Alabama*] [*A publication*] (DLA)
Brick Dig .... Brickell's Digest [*Alabama*] [*A publication*] (DLA)
BRICLAW ..... British Institute of International and Comparative Law (EA)
BRICMICS ... British Committee for Map Information and Catalogue Systems (NITA)
BRICS .... Black Resources Information Coordinating Services [*Information service or system*] (IID)
BRI-Cum ...... Book Review Index Annual Cumulation [*A publication*]
BRID .... Bridgford Foods [*NASDAQ symbol*] (TTSB)
BRID .... Bridgford Foods Corp. [*NASDAQ symbol*] (NQ)
BRID .... Bridlington [*Yorkshire resort town*] [*England*] (DSUE)
BRIDG .... Bridgettines [*Roman Catholic religious order*]

Bridg Conv ... Bridgman on Conveyancing [*A publication*] (DLA)
Bridg Dig Ind... Bridgman's Digested Index [*A publication*] (DLA)
BRIDGE .... Biotechnology Research for Innovation, Development, and Growth in Europe [*EC*] (ECED)
BRIDGE .... Bridge [*Commonly used*] (OPSA)
Bridg Eq Ind... Bridgman. Index to Equity Cases [*A publication*] (DLA)
Bridgewater St C... Bridgewater State College (GAGS)
BRIDGEX ...... Bridge Construction Exercise [*Military*] (NVT)
Bridg Leg Bib... Bridgman. Legal Bibliography [*1801*] [*A publication*] (DLA)
Bridg O .... Orlando Bridgman's English Common Pleas Reports [*A publication*] (DLA)
Bridg Ref ..... Bridgman. Reflections on the Study of the Law [*1804*] [*A publication*] (DLA)
Bridg Thes ... Bridgman's Thesaurus Juridicus [*A publication*] (DLA)
BridgvSv ..... Bridgeville Savings Bank FSB [*Pennsylvania*] [*Associated Press*] (SAG)
BRIDP .... Bridport [*Municipal borough in England*]
BRIE .... Berkeley Roundtable on the International Economy [*University of California*]
Brief .... Brief of the Phi Delta Phi [*Menasha, Wisconsin*] [*A publication*] (DLA)
BRIEX .... British Railway Industry Export Group
BRIG .... BMEWS [*Ballistic Missile Early Warning System*] Raid Input Generator (IAA)
BRIG .... Brigade
BRIG .... Brigadier (EY)
BRIG .... Brigadier
Brig .... Brigadier (ODBW)
BRIGAND ..... Bistatic RADAR Intelligence Generation and Analysis System (NVT)
BRIGARTY .... Brigade Artillery [*Army*] (INF)
BRIGEN .... Brigadier General
BRIG GEN .... Brigadier General (AFM)
Briggs Ry Acts... Brigg's General Railway Acts [*A publication*] (DLA)
BRIGH .... Brighton [*County borough in England*]
BRIGHED ...... Brigade Headquarters [*Army*]
Bright .... Brightly's Pennsylvania Nisi Prius Reports [*A publication*] (DLA)
Bright Bank Law... Brightly's Annotated Bankrupt Law [*A publication*] (DLA)
Bright Costs... Brightly on the Law of Costs in Pennsylvania [*A publication*] (DLA)
Bright Dig .... Brightly's Analytical Digest of the Laws of the United States [*A publication*] (DLA)
Bright Dig .... Brightly's Digest [*Pennsylvania*] [*A publication*] (DLA)
Bright Dig .... Brightly's Digest [*New York*] [*A publication*] (DLA)
Bright EC ..... Brightly's Leading Election Cases [*Pennsylvania*] [*A publication*] (DLA)
Bright Elec Cas... Brightly's Leading Election Cases [*Pennsylvania*] [*A publication*] (DLA)
Bright Eq Jur... Brightly's Equitable Jurisdiction [*Pennsylvania*] [*A publication*] (DLA)
Bright Fed Dig... Brightly's Federal Digest [*A publication*] (DLA)
Bright H & W... Bright. Husband and Wife [*3rd ed.*] [*1849*] [*A publication*] (DLA)
Brightly .... Brightly's Pennsylvania Nisi Prius Reports [*A publication*] (DLA)
Brightly Dig... Brightly's Analytical Digest of the Laws of the United States [*A publication*] (DLA)
Brightly Dig... Brightly's Digest [*New York*] [*A publication*] (DLA)
Brightly Dig... Brightly's Digest [*Pennsylvania*] [*A publication*] (DLA)
Brightly El ... Brightly's Leading Election Cases [*Pennsylvania*] [*A publication*] (DLA)
Brightly El Cas... Brightly's Leading Election Cases [*Pennsylvania*] [*A publication*] (DLA)
Brightly Elect Cas... Brightly's Leading Election Cases [*Pennsylvania*] [*A publication*] (DLA)
Brightly Election Cas (PA)... Brightly's Leading Election Cases [*Pennsylvania*] [*A publication*] (DLA)
Brightly NP... Brightly's Pennsylvania Nisi Prius Reports [*A publication*] (DLA)
Brightly's Elec Cas... Brightly's Leading Election Cases [*Pennsylvania*] [*A publication*] (DLA)
Brightly's Rep... Brightly's Pennsylvania Nisi Prius Reports [*A publication*] (DLA)
Bright NP ..... Brightly's Pennsylvania Nisi Prius Reports [*A publication*] (DLA)
Bright NY Dig... Brightly's New York Digest [*A publication*] (DLA)
Bright (PA)... Brightly's Pennsylvania Nisi Prius Reports [*A publication*] (DLA)
Bright PA Dig... Brightly's Pennsylvania Digest [*A publication*] (DLA)
Brightpt .... Brightpoint, Inc. [*Associated Press*] (SAG)
Bright Purd... Brightly's Edition of Purdon's Digest of Pennsylvania Laws [*A publication*] (DLA)
Bright Pur Dig... Brightly's Edition of Purdon's Digest of Pennsylvania Laws [*A publication*] (DLA)
Bright Tr & H Pr... Brightly's Edition of Troubat and Haly's Practice [*A publication*] (DLA)
Bright US Dig... Brightly's Analytical Digest of the Laws of the United States [*A publication*] (DLA)
BRIGHTW BAR... Brightwells Barrow [*England*]
BRIGLEX ...... Brigade Landing Exercise [*Military*] (NVT)
BrigSt .... Briggs & Stratton Corp. [*Associated Press*] (SAG)
BrigStrat ...... Briggs & Stratton Corp. [*Associated Press*] (SAG)
BRIHT .... Bistatic RADAR Identification of Hostile Target
BRIL .... Brilliance (KSC)
bril .... Brilliant [*Philately*]
BRILAB .... Bribery-Labor [*FBI undercover investigation*]
BRILL .... Brillante [*Brilliantly*] [*Music*]
BRILL .... Brilliant [*British Slang*]
BrilIChA .... Brilliance China Automotive Holding Ltd. [*Associated Press*] (SAG)
BrilIDig .... Brilliant Digital Entertainment, Inc. [*Associated Press*] (SAG)
BRIM .... Brimm Energy Corp. [*NASDAQ symbol*] (SAG)
BRIMAFEX ... British Manufacturers of Malleable Tube Fittings Export Group
BRIMARC ..... Brighton MARC [*Machine-Readable Catalogue*] Project [*British*] (NITA)

BRI-MC....... Book Review Index Master Cumulations [*A publication*]
BRIME........ Brief Repetitive Isometric Maximal Exercise (DMAA)
BRIMF........ Brimm Energy Corp. [*NASDAQ symbol*] (TTSB)
Brimm........ Brimm Energy Corp. [*Associated Press*] (SAG)
BRINC........ Basic Research, Inc. (EA)
BRINDEX..... Association of British Independent Oil Exploration Companies
Brinker........ Brinker International [*Formerly, Chili's, Inc.*] [*Associated Press*]
    (SAG)
BRINSMAT... Branch Officer, Inspector of Naval Material (DNAB)
BRIO.......... Brio Industries [*NASDAQ symbol*] (TTSB)
BRIOF......... Brio Industries [*NASDAQ symbol*] (TTSB)
BrioInd........ Brio Industries [*Associated Press*] (SAG)
BRIP .... Biomedical Research in Progress (ECII)
BRI-PR........ Book Review Index: Periodical Reviews, 1976-1984 [*A publication*]
Bri Pub Wor... Brice. Law Relating to Public Worship [*1875*] [*A publication*] (DLA)
BRIQ .... Briquette (ADA)
briq............. Briquettes (VRA)
BRI-RB........ Book Review Index: Reference Books, 1965-1984 [*A publication*]
Bris............. Brisbane [*Australia*]
BRIS .... Bristol [*City and county borough in England*] (ROG)
Brisbin........ Brisbin's Reports [*1 Minnesota*] [*A publication*] (DLA)
Brisb Minn.. Brisbin's Reports [*1 Minnesota*] [*A publication*] (DLA)
BRISC......... Brighton Reading and Individualized Skills Continuum (EDAC)
BRISC......... Buffered Remote Interactive Search Console (PDAA)
BRISCC....... British Iron and Steel Consumers' Council
BRISFIT ...... Bristol Fighter [*British aircraft*] (DSUE)
BristHtl....... Bristol Hotel Co. [*Associated Press*] (SAG)
BristIT........ Bristol Technology Systems, Inc. [*Associated Press*] (SAG)
BRIT.......... Britain [*or British*]
Brit............. Britain (VRA)
BRIT.......... Britannia
BRIT.......... Britannica
Brit............. Briticism (BARN)
BRIT........... British (DLA)
Brit............. Briton
Brit............. Britton's Ancient Pleas of the Crown [*A publication*] (DLA)
BritAir........ British Airways [*Associated Press*] (SAG)
BRITAIR...... Brittany Air International [*Airline*] [*France*]
Brit & Col Pr Cas... British and Colonial Prize Cases [*A publication*] (DLA)
BritBio........ British Bio-Technology Group [*Associated Press*] (SAG)
Brit Burm..... British Burma (ILCA)
BRIT COL..... British Columbia (DLA)
Brit Col (Can)... British Columbia, Canada (ILCA)
BritColl .... Britannia Royal Naval College
Brit Cr Cas... British [*or English*] Crown Cases [*A publication*] (DLA)
BRITDOC...... British Document Exchange
BRITE......... Basic Rate Interface Transmission Equipment
    [*Telecommunications*] (ACRL)
BRITE.......... Basic Research in Industrial Technology for Europe
BRITE.......... Bright RADAR Indicator-Tower Equipment
BRITEC .... British Information Technology Exhibition and Conference on
    Engineering Software [*Computational Mechanics Institute*]
BriteV .... Brite Voice Systems, Inc. [*Associated Press*] (SAG)
BritGas........ British Gas Ltd. [*Associated Press*] (SAG)
BritGFO........ British Guild of Flight Operations Officers (DA)
Brit Gui....... British Guiana (ILCA)
Brit Hond..... British Honduras (ILCA)
BRITIRE....... British Institute of Radio Engineers (IAA)
Brit J Admin Law... British Journal of Administrative Law [*A publication*] (DLA)
Brit J Adm L... British Journal of Administrative Law [*A publication*] (DLA)
Brit J Int'l L... British Journal of International Law [*A publication*] (DLA)
BRITPAT ...... British Patent (IAA)
Brit Prac Int'l L... British Practice in International Law [*A publication*] (DLA)
BritPt .... British Petroleum Co. Ltd. [*Associated Press*] (SAG)
Brit Rul Cas... British Ruling Cases [*A publication*] (DLA)
Brit Ship L... British Shipping Laws [*A publication*] (DLA)
BRITSHIPS... British Shipbuilding Integrated Production System (PDAA)
BritSky........ British Sky Broadcasting Ltd. [*Associated Press*] (SAG)
BritStl......... British Steel Ltd. [*Associated Press*] (SAG)
BRITT.......... Bandwidth Reduction and Intelligence Target Tracking (MCD)
BRITT.......... Britannarium [*Of All the Britains*] [*Coin inscription*] (ROG)
Britt............. Britton's Ancient Pleas of the Crown [*A publication*] (DLA)
BritTel .... British Telecommunications Ltd. [*Associated Press*] (SAG)
Brit TS .... British Treaty Series [*A publication*] (DLA)
Bri Ult V ..... Brice's Ultra Vires [*A publication*] (DLA)
BRJ............. Barco Rotary Joint
BRJ............. Beijing Royal Jelly [*Biochemistry*]
BRJ............. Bill of Rights Journal [*A publication*] (DLA)
BRJ............. Black River [*Jamaica*] [*Seismograph station code, US Geological
    Survey Closed*] (SEIS)
BRJ............. Blind Riveted Joint
BRJ............. Brachioradialis Jerk [*Neurology and orthopedics*] (DAVI)
BRJ............. Braner Resources [*Vancouver Stock Exchange symbol*]
BRJ............. Martinsville, VA [*Location identifier FAA*] (FAAL)
BR-JC (Army)... Board of Review and Judicial Council of the Army (DLA)
BRK .... Baby Rat Kidney [*Immunology*]
brk............. Bark (VRA)
BRK .... Berkeley-Haviland [*California*] [*Seismograph station code, US
    Geological Survey*] (SEIS)
BRK .... Berkshire Hathaway, Inc. [*NYSE symbol*] (CTT)
BRK .... Bourke [*Australia Airport symbol*] (OAG)
BRK .... Bracknell Resources Ltd. [*Toronto Stock Exchange symbol*]
BRK .... Brake [*Automotive engineering*]
BRK .... Brake
BRK .... Break (KSC)

BRK .... Brecknockshire [*County in Wales*] (ROG)
BRK .... Brick (MSA)
brk .... Broken [*Quality of the bottom*] [*Nautical charts*]
BRK .... Brook (MCD)
BRK .... Brook
BRK .... Brooklyn [*Diocesan abbreviation*] [*New York*] (TOCD)
BRKB .... Brooklyn Bancorp, Inc. [*NASDAQ symbol*] (SAG)
BRKBD .... Brakeband (MSA)
brkcth .... Barkcloth (VRA)
BrkeHd........ Brake Headquarters USA, Inc. [*Associated Press*] (SAG)
BRKF .... Breakfast
BRKG .... Braking [*Aviation*] (FAAC)
BRKG .... Breaking
BRKHIC....... Breaks in Higher Overcast [*NWS*] (FAAC)
BRKKV .... Algemene Bond van Rooms Katholieke Kiesverenigingen [*General
    League of Roman Catholic Election Societies*] [*Netherlands*]
    (PPE)
BRKN .... Broken
BRKR .... Breaker
BRKR .... Broker
BRKRGE .... Brokerage
BRKS .... Breakers [*Freight*]
BRKS .... Brecknockshire [*County in Wales*]
BRKS .... Brooks
BRKS .... Brooks [*Postal Service standard*] (OPSA)
BRKS .... Brooks Automation [*NASDAQ symbol*] (TTSB)
BRKS .... Brooks Automation, Inc. [*NASDAQ symbol*] (SAG)
BRKSHR ...... Berkshire (FAAC)
BRKT .... Bracket (KSC)
brkt............. Breakfast (CPH)
BRKT .... Brooktrout Technologies, Inc. [*NASDAQ symbol*] (SAG)
BRKT .... Brooktrout Technology [*NASDAQ symbol*] (TTSB)
Brktree........ Brooktree Corp. [*Associated Press*] (SAG)
BRKWTR...... Breakwater (WDAA)
BRL............. Air Bras d'Or [*Canada ICAO designator*] (FAAC)
BRL............. Babe Ruth League (EA)
BRL............. Balance Return Loss [*Telecommunications*] (TEL)
BRL............. Ballistic Research Laboratory [*Aberdeen Proving Ground, MD*]
    [*Army*]
BRL............. Barrel
BRL............. Barrel
BRL............. Barr Laboratories [*AMEX symbol*] (TTSB)
BRL............. Barr Laboratories, Inc. [*AMEX symbol*] (SPSG)
BRL............. Beecham Research Laboratories Ltd. [*Great Britain*] [*Research code
    symbol*]
BRL............. Behavioral Research Laboratories
BRL............. Berle Resources Ltd. [*Vancouver Stock Exchange symbol*]
BRL............. Berlin - Free University [*West Germany*] [*Seismograph station code,
    US Geological Survey*] (SEIS)
BRL............. Bethesda Research Laboratories [*Life Technologies, Inc.*]
    [*Gaithersburg, MD*]
BRL............. Biological Research Laboratories [*Syracuse University*] [*Research
    center*] (RCD)
BRL............. Biometrics Research Laboratory (DAVI)
BRL............. BIT [*Binary Digit*] Rate Low [*Computer science*] (IAA)
BRL............. Bomb Release Line
BRL............. Boresight Reference Line (DNAB)
BRL............. Braille Revival League (EA)
BRL............. Branch and Link (IAA)
BR/L............ Brown Line Positive
BRL............. Buffalo Rat Liver [*Cytology*]
BRL............. Building Research Laboratory [*Ohio State University*] [*Research
    center*] (RCD)
BRL............. Building Restriction Line [*FAA*] (TAG)
BRL............. Burlington [*Iowa*] [*Airport symbol*] (OAG)
Br Leg Max... Broom's Legal Maxims [*A publication*] (DLA)
BRLESC ...... Ballistic Research Laboratories Electronic Scientific Computer
BRLG .... Bomb, Radio, Longitudinal, Generator-Powered
BRLI............ Bio-Reference Laboratories, Inc. [*NASDAQ symbol*] (NQ)
BRLI............ Bio-Reference Labs [*NASDAQ symbol*] (TTSB)
BRLIW .... Bio-Reference Labs Wrrt'A' [*NASDAQ symbol*] (TTSB)
BRLIZ .... Bio-Reference Labs Wrrt'B' [*NASDAQ symbol*] (TTSB)
BRLO .... British Routing Liaison Officer [*World War II*]
BRLP .... Burlap
BrlRsc......... Burlington Resources, Inc. [*Associated Press*] (SAG)
BRLS .... Barrier Ready Light System (MSA)
BRLS .... Borealis Technology Corp. [*NASDAQ symbol*] (SAG)
BRLSYS .... Barrier Ready Light System (IAA)
BRLT .... Basic Reference Lottery Ticket (PDAA)
BRLU .... Broadband Remote Line Unit [*Telecommunications*] (ACRL)
BRLV .... Black Raspberry Latent Virus [*Plant pathology*]
BRM........... Air 500 Ltd. [*Canada ICAO designator*] (FAAC)
BRM........... Babylonian Records in the Library of J. Pierpont Morgan (BJA)
BRM........... Barandium Resources [*Vancouver Stock Exchange symbol*]
BRM........... Barometer (FAAC)
BRM........... Barquisimeto [*Venezuela*] [*Airport symbol*] (OAG)
BRM........... Baseline Reference Mission (MCD)
BRM........... Basic Rifle Maintenance
BRM........... Basic Rifle Marksmanship [*Program of instruction*] [*Army*] (INF)
B'RM .... Bedroom [*Classified advertising*] (ADA)
BRM........... Bernie [*Missouri*] [*Seismograph station code, US Geological Survey
    Closed*] (SEIS)
BRM........... Binary Rate Multiplier (IAA)
BRM........... Binary Relationship Model [*Computer science*] (NITA)
BRM........... Biological Reference Materials

BRM............	Biological Research Module [*NASA*] (NASA)
BRM............	Biological Response Modifier Technology [*Biotechnology*]
BRM............	Biuret-Reactive Material [*Biochemistry*] (MAE)
BRM............	Blackrock Ins Muni 2008 Tr [*NYSE symbol*] (TTSB)
BRM............	Blackrock Insurance Municipal 2008 Trade [*NYSE symbol*] (SPSG)
BRM............	Branch on Right Minus (SAA)
BRM............	Bras D'Or Mines [*Vancouver Stock Exchange symbol*]
BrM............	Breast Milk [*Neonatology and obstetrics*] (DAVI)
BRM............	Brimstone R. R. [*AAR code*]
BRM............	British Racing Motors
BRM............	Business Reply Mail [*Advertising*]
BRM............	Rossland Historical Museum, British Columbia [*Library symbol National Library of Canada*] (NLC)
BRMA.........	Board of Registration of Medical Auxiliaries [*British*]
BRMA.........	Braided Rug Manufacturers Association [*Defunct*] (EA)
BRMA.........	British Reinforcement Manufacturers Association (DBA)
BRMA.........	British Rubber Manufacturers' Association (EAIO)
BRMA.........	Business Records Manufacturers Association [*Later, ABPM*] (EA)
BRMA.........	Richmond Museum and Archives, British Columbia [*Library symbol National Library of Canada*] (NLC)
BRMAS........	Business Reply Mail Accounting System [*US Postal Service*]
Br Max........	Broom's Legal Maxims [*A publication*] (DLA)
BRMC.........	Barometric (WGA)
BRMC.........	British Royal Marine Corps (CINC)
BRMC.........	Business Research Management Center [*Wright-Patterson Air Force Base, OH*]
BRMCA.......	British Ready Mixed Concrete Association (BI)
BRMD.........	MacDonald, Dettwiler & Associates Ltd., Richmond, British Columbia [*Library symbol National Library of Canada*] (NLC)
BRMF.........	British Rainwear Manufacturers Federation (BI)
BRMM.........	British Raw Materials Mission [*World War II*]
BRMNA........	British Railway Modellers of North America [*Canada*]
BRMP.........	Biological Response Modifiers Program [*National Cancer Institute*]
BrMSq........	Bristol Myers Squibb [*Associated Press*] (SAG)
BrMSq........	Bristol-Myers Squibb Co. [*Associated Press*] (SAG)
BRMV.........	Bean Rugose Mosaic Virus [*Plant pathology*]
BrMySq.......	Bristol Myers Squibb [*Associated Press*] (SAG)
BrMySq.......	Bristol-Myers Squibb Co. [*Associated Press*] (SAG)
BRN...........	Barisan Revolusi Nasional [*Thailand*] [*Political party*]
BRN...........	Barnwell Indus [*AMEX symbol*] (TTSB)
BRN...........	Barnwell Industries, Inc. [*AMEX symbol*] (SPSG)
BRN...........	Basal Retinal Neuron [*Neurology*]
BRN...........	Berlin [*West Germany*] [*Seismograph station code, US Geological Survey*] (SEIS)
BRN...........	Berne [*Switzerland*] [*Airport symbol*] (OAG)
BRN...........	Board of Registered Nursing
BRN...........	Book Registration Number
BRN...........	Brain
BRN...........	Brinco Ltd. [*Toronto Stock Exchange symbol*]
BRN...........	Broadcast Net (NATG)
BRN...........	Brown (KSC)
brn.............	Brown (VRA)
BRN...........	Brown & Root-Northrop
BRN...........	Brunei Darussalam [*ANSI three-letter standard code*] (CNC)
BRN...........	Eclipse Airlines, Inc. [*ICAO designator*] (FAAC)
BRN...........	Mountain Home, ID [*Location identifier FAA*] (FAAL)
bRNA..........	Branched Ribonucleic Acid [*Genetics*]
BrNAE........	British National Antarctic Expedition [*1901-04*]
BRNAVCOMMSTO...	Branch Navy Commissary Store (DNAB)
Br NB........	Bracton's Note Book, King's Bench [*1217-40*] [*A publication*] (DLA)
BRNC.........	Britannia Royal Naval College
Br NC........	Brooke's New Cases, English King's Bench [*1515-58*] [*A publication*] (DLA)
Br N Cas......	Brooke's New Cases, English King's Bench [*1515-58*] [*A publication*] (DLA)
BRNCH........	Branch [*Commonly used*] (OPSA)
BrnF..........	Brown-Forman, Inc. [*Associated Press*] (SAG)
BrnF..........	Brown Forman, Inc. [*Associated Press*] (SAG)
BrnFAC.......	Browning Ferris [*Associated Press*] (SAG)
BRNG.........	Bearing
BRNG.........	Burning
BRNNG........	Burning
BRNO.........	Bruno's, Inc. [*NASDAQ symbol*] (NQ)
Br Not........	Brooke's Office and Practice of a Notary [*A publication*] (DLA)
BRNR.........	Burner
brnsh..........	Brownish [*Philately*]
BRNSHR.....	Burnisher (MSA)
brnt............	Burnt [*Philately*]
Brnwk........	Brunswick Corp. [*Associated Press*] (SAG)
brnz............	Bronze [*Philately*]
BRO............	Base Requirements Overseas (CINC)
BRO............	Brigade Routine Order [*British*]
BRO............	British Routing Office
BRO............	Broach (KSC)
BRO............	Broadband Remote Oculometer (KSC)
BRO............	Bronchoscopy [*Medicine*] (DAVI)
BRO............	Bronze (WGA)
BRO............	BRO Resources Ltd. [*Vancouver Stock Exchange symbol*]
BRO............	Brother
bro.............	Brother (DMAA)
BRO............	Brother
Bro.............	Browne's Reports [*Pennsylvania*] [*A publication*] (DLA)
Bro.............	Browne's Reports [*Sri Lanka*] [*A publication*] (DLA)
Bro.............	Brown's English Chancery Reports [*28, 29 English Reprint*] [*A publication*] (DLA)

Bro.............	Brown's Michigan Nisi Prius Reports [*A publication*] (DLA)
Bro.............	Brown's Parliamentary Cases [*England*] [*A publication*] (DLA)
Bro.............	Brown's Reports [*53-65, 80-136 Missouri*] [*A publication*] (DLA)
BRO............	Brownsville [*Texas*] [*Airport symbol*] (OAG)
BRO............	Brush-Off [*Slang*]
BRO............	Revelstoke Branch, Okanagan Regional Library, British Columbia [*Library symbol National Library of Canada*] (BIB)
Bro A & R...	Brown's United States District Court Reports (Admiralty and Revenue Cases) [*A publication*] (DLA)
Bro Ab........	Brooke's Abridgment [*England*] [*A publication*] (DLA)
Bro Abr.......	Brooke's Abridgment [*England*] [*A publication*] (DLA)
Bro Abr in Eq...	Browne's New Abridgment of Cases in Equity [*A publication*] (DLA)
Bro Ac........	Browne. Actions at Law [*1843*] [*A publication*] (DLA)
Bro (A) CL...	Arthur Brown's Compendious View of the Civil Law [*A publication*] (DLA)
Bro Act.......	Browne. Actions at Law [*1843*] [*A publication*] (DLA)
BROADCAP...	Broadcast Capital Fund, Inc. (NTCM)
Bro Adm......	Brown's United States Admiralty Reports [*A publication*] (DLA)
BroadN........	Broad National Bancorp [*Associated Press*] (SAG)
BroadVis......	BroadVision, Inc. [*Associated Press*] (SAG)
BROADWOODW...	Broadwoodwidger [*England*]
Bro Ag........	Brown. Agency and Trusts [*1868*] [*A publication*] (ILCA)
Bro Ag........	Brown on Agency and Trust [*A publication*] (DLA)
Bro & F.......	Broderick and Freemantle's Ecclesiastical Cases [*1840-64*] [*A publication*] (DLA)
Bro & Fr......	Broderick and Freemantle's Ecclesiastical Cases [*1840-64*] [*A publication*] (DLA)
Bro & G.......	Brownlow and Goldesborough's English Common Pleas Reports [*A publication*] (DLA)
Bro & H.......	Brown and Hemingway's Reports [*53-58 Mississippi*] [*A publication*] (DLA)
Bro & L.......	Browning and Lushington's English Admiralty Reports [*1863-65*] [*A publication*] (DLA)
Bro & Lush...	Browning and Lushington's English Admiralty Reports [*1863-65*] [*A publication*] (DLA)
Bro & Lush M & D...	Browning and Lushington on Marriage and Divorce [*A publication*] (DLA)
Bro & M......	Brown and McCall's Yorkshire Star Chamber [*Yorkshire Archaeological Society Record, Series 44, 45, 51, 70*] [*A publication*] (DLA)
Bro & M......	Browne and MacNamara's Railway Cases [*A publication*] (DLA)
Bro & Mac...	Browne and MacNamara's Railway Cases [*A publication*] (DLA)
BROC..........	Brigade Rouge d'Occitanie [*Red Brigade of Occitania*] [*France*] (PD)
BROC..........	Brock Control Systems, Inc. [*NASDAQ symbol*] (SAG)
BROC..........	Brock Intl Inc. [*NASDAQ symbol*] (TTSB)
Bro C & AL...	Browne's Civil and Admiralty Law [*A publication*] (DLA)
Bro Car.......	Browne. Law of Carriers [*1873*] [*A publication*] (DLA)
Bro CC........	Brown's English Chancery Cases [*or Reports*] [*A publication*] (DLA)
Bro Ch........	Brown's English Chancery Reports [*28, 29 English Reprint*] [*A publication*] (DLA)
Bro Ch Cas...	Brown's English Chancery Reports [*28, 29 English Reprint*] [*A publication*] (DLA)
Bro Ch Pr.....	Browne's Practice of the High Court of Chancery [*A publication*] (DLA)
Bro Ch R......	Brown's English Chancery Reports [*28, 29 English Reprint*] [*A publication*] (DLA)
Bro Civ Law...	Browne's Civil and Admiralty Law [*A publication*] (DLA)
Bro Civ Proc...	Broughton's Indian Civil Procedure [*A publication*] (DLA)
Brock..........	Brockenbrough's Marshall's Decisions, United States Circuit Court [*A publication*] (DLA)
Brock & H....	Brockenbrough and Holmes. Virginia Cases [*A publication*] (DLA)
Brock & Ho...	Brockenbrough and Holmes. Virginia Cases [*A publication*] (DLA)
Brock & Hol...	Brockenbrough and Holmes. Virginia Cases [*A publication*] (DLA)
Brock & Hol Cas...	Brockenbrough and Holmes. Virginia Cases [*A publication*] (DLA)
Brock Cas....	Brockenbrough. Virginia Cases [*A publication*] (DLA)
Brock CC......	Brockenbrough's Marshall's Decisions, United States Circuit Court [*A publication*] (DLA)
BrockCp.......	Brock Exploration Corp. [*Associated Press*] (SAG)
BrockCS.......	Brock Control Systems, Inc. [*Associated Press*] (SAG)
Brock Marsh...	Brockenbrough's Marshall's Decisions, United States Circuit Court [*A publication*] (DLA)
Bro Co Act...	Browne on the Companies' Acts [*A publication*] (DLA)
Bro Com......	Broom's Commentaries on the Common Law [*A publication*] (DLA)
BROD..........	Broderbund Software [*NASDAQ symbol*] (TTSB)
BROD..........	Broderbund Software, Inc. [*NASDAQ symbol*] (SPSG)
Brod............	Broderick and Freemantle's Ecclesiastical Cases [*1840-64*] [*A publication*] (DLA)
Brod & B.....	Broderip and Bingham's English Common Pleas Reports [*A publication*] (DLA)
Brod & Bing...	Broderip and Bingham's English Common Pleas Reports [*129 English Reprint*] [*A publication*] (DLA)
Brod & F.....	Broderick and Freemantle's Ecclesiastical Cases [*1840-64*] [*A publication*] (DLA)
Brod & F Ecc Cas...	Broderick and Freemantle's Ecclesiastical Cases [*1840-64*] [*A publication*] (DLA)
Brod & Fr....	Broderick and Freemantle's Ecclesiastical Cases [*1840-64*] [*A publication*] (DLA)
Brod & Fr Ecc Cas...	Broderick and Freemantle's Ecclesiastical Cases [*1840-64*] [*A publication*] (DLA)
Brod & Frem...	Broderick and Freemantle's Ecclesiastical Cases [*1840-64*] [*A publication*] (DLA)
Bro Dig Div...	Browne's Digest of Decisions on Divorce and Alimony [*A publication*] (DLA)

Bro Div Pr ... Browne's Divorce Court Practice [*A publication*] (DLA)
Brodix Am & Eng Pat Cas... Brodix's American and English Patent Cases [*A publication*] (DLA)
Brodix Am & E Pat Cas... Brodix's American and English Patent Cases [*A publication*] (DLA)
BrodSft .... Broderbund Software, Inc. [*Associated Press*] (SAG)
Brod Stair .... Brodie's Notes and Supplement to Stair's Institutions [*Scotland*] [*A publication*] (DLA)
Bro Ecc .... Brooke's Six Ecclesiastical Judgments [*A publication*] (DLA)
Bro Ent .... Brownlow's Latine Redivivus [*or Entries*] [*A publication*] (DLA)
Bro Ent .... Brown's Entries [*A publication*] (DLA)
BR of C .... [*The*] Belt Railway Co. of Chicago
BROFICON ... Broadcast Fighter Control [*Military*]
Bro Fix .... Brown on Fixtures [*A publication*] (DLA)
Bro For .... Brown on Forestalling, Regrating, and Monopolizing, with Cases [*A publication*] (DLA)
Bro For .... Brown's Forum [*A publication*] (DLA)
Bro Form ..... Brown's Formulae Bene Placitandi [*A publication*] (DLA)
Bro Fr .... Browne on the Statute of Frauds [*A publication*] (DLA)
BroGour .... Brothers Gourmet Coffees [*Associated Press*] (SAG)
Bro Hered .... Browne. Law of Rating of Hereditaments [*2nd ed.*] [*1886*] [*A publication*] (DLA)
BROI .... Branch Operating Instruction [*Air Force*] (AFM)
Bro Ins........ Browne's Medical Jurisprudence of Insanity [*A publication*] (DLA)
Bro Just....... Broun's Reports, Scotch Justiciary Court [*1842-45*] [*A publication*] (DLA)
BROK .... Broker (WDAA)
BROK .... Brokerage (ROG)
BROK .... Tube Broke [*Organic chemistry*] (DAVI)
Broktrt .... Brooktrout Technology, Inc. [*Associated Press*] (SAG)
Bro Law Dic... Brown's Law Dictionary [*A publication*] (DLA)
Bro Leg Max.. Broom's Legal Maxims [*A publication*] (DLA)
Bro Lim .... Brown. Limitations as to Real Property [*1869*] [*A publication*] (DLA)
BROM .... Bipolar Read Only Memory [*Computer science*] (MHDI)
BROM .... Bromide [*Chemistry*] (ADA)
Bro M & D..... Browning on Marriage and Divorce [*A publication*] (DLA)
Bro Max....... Broom's Legal Maxims [*A publication*] (DLA)
BRON.......... Bronchial
BRON.......... Bronchoscopy [*Medicine*]
Bro NB Cas... Browne's National Bank Cases [*A publication*] (DLA)
Bro NC........ Brooke's New Cases, English King's Bench [*1515-58*] [*A publication*] (DLA)
bronch .... Bronchoscopist [*Medicine*] (DAVI)
BRONCH ...... Bronchoscopy [*Medicine*]
broncho .... Bronchoscopy [*Medicine*] (DAVI)
Bro Not .... Brooke on the Office of a Notary in England [*A publication*] (DLA)
Bro NP .... Brown's English Nisi Prius Cases [*A publication*] (DLA)
Bro NP .... Brown's Michigan Nisi Prius Reports [*A publication*] (DLA)
BROOK........ Brook [*Commonly used*] (OPSA)
Brook Abr .... Brooke's Abridgment [*England*] [*A publication*] (DLA)
Brooke .... Brooke Group Ltd. [*Associated Press*] (SAG)
Brooke .... Brooke's Ecclesiastical Cases [*1850-72*] [*England*] [*A publication*] (DLA)
Brooke .... Brooke's New Cases, English King's Bench [*1515-58*] [*A publication*] (DLA)
Brooke Abr... Brooke's Abridgment [*England*] [*A publication*] (DLA)
Brooke Bib Leg... Brooke's Bibliotheca Legum Angliae [*A publication*] (DLA)
Brooke Ch W... Brooke's Churchwarden's Guide [*A publication*] (DLA)
Brooke Eccl... Brooke's Six Ecclesiastical Judgments [*A publication*] (DLA)
Brooke Eccl Judg... Brooke's Ecclesiastical Judgments [*A publication*] (DLA)
Brooke Lim... Brooke's Reading on the Statute of Limitations [*A publication*] (DLA)
Brooke NC ... Brooke's New Cases, English King's Bench [*1515-58*] [*A publication*] (DLA)
Brooke Not... Brooke's Office and Practice of a Notary [*A publication*] (DLA)
Brooke (Petit)... Brooke's New Cases, English King's Bench [*1515-58*] [*A publication*] (DLA)
Brooke Six Judg... Brooke's Six Ecclesiastical Judgments [*A publication*] (DLA)
Brookl Rec ... Brooklyn Daily Record [*A publication*] (DLA)
Brooklyn C (CUNY)... Brooklyn College of the City University of New York (GAGS)
Brooklyn Daily Rec... Brooklyn Daily Record [*A publication*] (DLA)
Brooklyn Law... Brooklyn Law School (GAGS)
Brook N Cas... Brooke's New Cases, English King's Bench [*1515-58*] [*A publication*] (DLA)
BROOKS ...... Brooks [*Commonly used*] (OPSA)
Brooks .... Brooks' Reports [*106-119 Michigan*] [*A publication*] (DLA)
BrooksA .... Brooks Automation, Inc. [*Associated Press*] (SAG)
BrooksAu ..... Brooks Automation, Inc. [*Associated Press*] (SAG)
BrooksF .... Brooks Fiber Properties, Inc. [*Associated Press*] (SAG)
Brookstn ...... Brookstone, Inc. [*Associated Press*] (SAG)
BROOM........ Ballistic Recovery of Orbiting Man (KSC)
Broom......... Broom's Legal Maxims [*A publication*] (DLA)
Broom & H Com... Broom and Hadley's Commentaries on the Laws of England [*A publication*] (DLA)
Broom & H Comm... Broom and Hadley's Commentaries on the Laws of England [*A publication*] (DLA)
Broom CL .... Broom's Commentaries on the Common Law [*A publication*] (DLA)
Broom Com Law... Broom's Commentaries on the Common Law [*A publication*] (DLA)
Broom Const L... Broom. Constitutional Law [*3rd ed.*] [*1885*] [*A publication*] (DLA)
Broom Leg Max... Broom's Legal Maxims [*A publication*] (DLA)
Broom Max... Broom's Legal Maxims [*A publication*] (DLA)
Broom Part... Broom on Parties to Actions [*A publication*] (DLA)
Broom Ph Law... Broom. Philosophy of Law [*3rd ed.*] [*1883*] [*A publication*] (DLA)
Bro PA .... Browne's Pennsylvania Reports [*1801-14*] [*A publication*] (DLA)
Bro Parl Cas... Brown's Cases in Parliament [*A publication*] (DLA)

Bro Pat Pr ... Browne's Patent Office Practice [*A publication*] (DLA)
Bro PC .... Brown's English Parliamentary Cases [*A publication*] (DLA)
Bro Prac ..... Brown's Practice (Praxis) [*or Precedents*] in Chancery [*A publication*] (DLA)
Bro Prob Pr... Browne's Probate Practice [*A publication*] (DLA)
BROR.......... Brother (ROG)
Bro Read ..... Brooke's Reading on the Statute of Limitations [*A publication*] (DLA)
Bro Reg Act... Browne's Parliamentary and Municipal Registration Act [*A publication*] (DLA)
Bro RPL....... Brown. Limitations as to Real Property [*1869*] [*A publication*] (DLA)
BROS.......... Brothers
Bros .... Brothers (ODBW)
Bro Sal .... Brown. Treatise on Law of Sale [*Scotland*] [*A publication*] (DLA)
Bro St .... Brodie's Notes and Supplement to Stair's Institutions [*Scotland*] [*A publication*] (DLA)
Bro Stair...... Brodie's Notes and Supplement to Stair's Institutions [*Scotland*] [*A publication*] (DLA)
Bro St Fr ..... Browne on the Statute of Frauds [*A publication*] (DLA)
Bro Supp ..... Brown's Supplement to Morison's Dictionary, Scotch Court of Sessions [*A publication*] (DLA)
Bro Sup to Mor... Brown's Supplement to Morison's Dictionary of Decisions, Scotch Court of Sessions [*A publication*] (DLA)
Bro Syn........ Brown's Synopsis of Decisions, Scotch Court of Sessions [*1540-1827*] [*A publication*] (DLA)
Bro Synop.... Brown's Synopsis of Decisions, Scotch Court of Sessions [*1540-1827*] [*A publication*] (DLA)
BROT .... Brought (ADA)
Bro Tr M...... Browne on Trade Markets [*A publication*] (DLA)
BROTS .... Beneficial Rays of the Sun [*In reference to suntanning, supposedly occuring between 10am and 2pm*] [*See also SROTS*]
Brough Civ Pro... Broughton's Indian Civil Procedure [*A publication*] (DLA)
Brough Elec... Brough's Law of Elections [*A publication*] (DLA)
Broun.......... Broun's Reports, Scotch Justiciary Court [*1842-45*] [*A publication*] (DLA)
Broun Just ... Broun's Reports, Scotch Justiciary Court [*1842-45*] [*A publication*] (DLA)
Bro Us & Cus... Browne's Law of Usages and Customs [*A publication*] (DLA)
Bro VM .... Brown's Vade Mecum [*A publication*] (DLA)
Brow Brev.... Brownlow's Brevia Judicialia, Etc. [*1662*] [*A publication*] (DLA)
Brown .... Brownlow and Goldesborough's English Common Pleas Reports [*A publication*] (DLA)
Brown .... Brown's English Chancery Reports [*28, 29 English Reprint*] [*A publication*] (DLA)
Brown .... Brown's English Parliamentary Cases [*A publication*] (DLA)
Brown .... Brown's Law Dictionary [*A publication*] (DLA)
Brown .... Brown's Law Dictionary and Institute [*1874*] [*A publication*] (DLA)
Brown .... Brown's Michigan Nisi Prius Reports [*A publication*] (DLA)
Brown .... Brown's Reports [*53-65 Mississippi*] [*A publication*] (DLA)
Brown .... Brown's Reports [*80-137 Missouri*] [*A publication*] (DLA)
Brown .... Brown's Reports [*4-25 Nebraska*] [*A publication*] (DLA)
Brown .... Brown's Scotch Reports [*A publication*] (DLA)
Brown .... Brown's United States Admiralty Reports [*A publication*] (DLA)
Brown .... Brown's United States District Court Reports [*A publication*] (DLA)
Brown A & R... Brown's United States District Court Reports (Admiralty and Revenue Cases) [*A publication*] (DLA)
Brown Adm... Brown's United States Admiralty Reports [*A publication*] (DLA)
Brown & G (Eng)... Brownlow and Goldesborough's English Common Pleas Reports [*A publication*] (DLA)
Brown & Gold... Brownlow and Goldesborough's English Common Pleas Reports [*A publication*] (DLA)
Brown & H... Brown and Hemingway's Reports [*53-58 Mississippi*] [*A publication*] (DLA)
Brown & Hemingway... Brown and Hemingway's Reports [*53-58 Mississippi*] [*A publication*] (DLA)
Brown & L... Browning and Lushington's English Admiralty Reports [*1863-65*] [*A publication*] (DLA)
Brown & L (Eng)... Browning and Lushington's English Admiralty Reports [*1863-65*] [*A publication*] (DLA)
Brown & Lush... Browning and Lushington's English Admiralty Reports [*1863-65*] [*A publication*] (DLA)
Brown & Lush M & D... Browning and Lushington on Marriage and Divorce [*A publication*] (DLA)
Brown & MacN... Browne and MacNamara's Railway Cases [*A publication*] (DLA)
Brown & R... Brown and Rader's Reports [*137 Missouri*] [*A publication*] (DLA)
Brown C...... Brown's English Chancery Cases [*or Reports*] [*A publication*] (DLA)
Brown CC..... Brown's English Chancery Cases [*or Reports*] [*A publication*] (DLA)
Brown Ch..... Brown's Chancery Cases Tempore Lord Thurlow [*England*] [*A publication*] (DLA)
Brown Ch C... Brown's Chancery Cases Tempore Lord Thurlow [*England*] [*A publication*] (DLA)
Brown Dict... Brown's Law Dictionary [*A publication*] (DLA)
Brown Div Pr... Browning's Divorce Court Practice [*A publication*] (DLA)
Browne .... Browne's Civil Procedure Reports [*New York*] [*A publication*] (DLA)
Browne .... Browne's Reports [*Sri Lanka*] [*A publication*] (DLA)
Browne .... Browne's Reports [*Massachusetts*] [*A publication*] (DLA)
Browne .... Browne's Reports [*Pennsylvania*] [*A publication*] (DLA)
Browne Act... Browne. Actions at Law [*1843*] [*A publication*] (DLA)
Browne & G... Browne and Gray's Reports [*A publication*] (DLA)
Browne & Gray... Browne and Gray's Reports [*A publication*] (DLA)
Browne & MacN... Browne and MacNamara's English Railway and Canal Cases [*A publication*] (DLA)
Browne & Th Railw... Browne and Theobald. Railways [*4th ed.*] [*1911*] [*A publication*] (DLA)
Browne Bank Cas... Browne's National Bank Cases [*A publication*] (DLA)
Browne Car... Browne on Carriers [*A publication*] (DLA)

Brown Ecc ... Brown's English Ecclesiastical Reports [*A publication*] (DLA)
Browne Civ L... Browne's Civil and Admiralty Law [*A publication*] (DLA)
Browne Civ Law... Browne's Civil and Admiralty Law [*A publication*] (DLA)
Browne Div... Browne's Divorce Court Practice [*A publication*] (DLA)
Browne Div Pr... Browne. Practice in Divorce and Matrimonial Causes [*11th ed.*] [*1931*] [*A publication*] (DLA)
Browne Fr... Browne on the Statute of Frauds [*A publication*] (DLA)
Browne Jud Interp... Browne's Judicial Interpretation of Common Words and Phrases [*A publication*] (DLA)
Browne NBC... Browne's National Bank Cases [*A publication*] (DLA)
Brown Ent... Brownlow's Entries [*A publication*] (DLA)
Browne (PA)... Browne's Reports [*Pennsylvania*] [*A publication*] (DLA)
Browne PA R... Browne's Reports [*Pennsylvania*] [*A publication*] (DLA)
Browne Prob... Browne's Probate Practice [*A publication*] (ILCA)
Browne Prob Pr... Browne's Probate Practice [*A publication*] (DLA)
Browne's Rep... Browne's Reports [*Pennsylvania*] [*A publication*] (DLA)
Browne St Frauds... Browne on the Statute of Frauds [*A publication*] (DLA)
Browne Tr M... Browne on Trade Markets [*A publication*] (DLA)
Browne Us... Browne on Usages and Customs [*A publication*] (DLA)
Brown GA Pl & Pr Anno... Browne. Georgia Pleading and Practice and Legal Forms, Annotated [*A publication*] (DLA)
Brownl........ Brownlow and Goldesborough's English Common Pleas Reports [*A publication*] (DLA)
Brownl & G... Brownlow and Goldesborough's English Common Pleas Reports [*A publication*] (DLA)
Brownl & Gold... Brownlow and Goldesborough's English Common Pleas Reports [*A publication*] (DLA)
Brownl Brev... Brownlow's Brevia Judicialia, Etc. [*1662*] [*A publication*] (DLA)
Brownl Ent... Brownlow's Entries [*A publication*] (DLA)
Brownl Redv... Brownlow's Latine Redivivus [*or Entries*] [*A publication*] (DLA)
Brown M & D... Browning on Marriage and Divorce [*A publication*] (DLA)
Brown NP .... Brown's Michigan Nisi Prius Reports [*A publication*] (DLA)
Brown NP Cas... Brown's English Nisi Prius Cases [*A publication*] (DLA)
Brown NP (Mich)... Brown's Michigan Nisi Prius Reports [*A publication*] (DLA)
Brown Parl... Brown's House of Lords Cases [*England*] [*A publication*] (DLA)
Brown Parl Cas... Brown's House of Lords Cases [*England*] [*A publication*] (DLA)
Brown PC... Brown's House of Lords Cases [*England*] [*A publication*] (DLA)
BROWNS ..... Brownshall [*England*]
Brown's Adm App... Brown's United States Admiralty Reports (Appendix) [*A publication*] (DLA)
Brown's (Penn)... Browne's Reports [*Pennsylvania*] [*A publication*] (DLA)
Brown's Penn Rep... Browne's Reports [*Pennsylvania*] [*A publication*] (DLA)
Brown's Roman Law... Brown's Epitome and Analysis of Savigny's Treatise on Obligations in Roman Law [*A publication*] (DLA)
Brown Sup ... Brown's Supplement to Morison's Dictionary, Scotch Court of Sessions [*A publication*] (DLA)
Brown Sup Dec... Brown's Supplement to Morison's Dictionary, Scotch Court of Sessions [*A publication*] (DLA)
Brown Syn ... Brown's Synopsis of Decisions, Scotch Court of Sessions [*1540-1827*] [*A publication*] (DLA)
Brown U ...... Brown University (GAGS)
BROWRO ..... Brouwer-Lyddane Orbit Generation Routine
BROWSER ... Browsing On-Line with Selective Retrieval
BRP .... Barrier Pressure [*Medicine*]
BRP .... Bathroom Privileges [*Medicine*]
BRP .... Beacon Ranging Pulse
BRP .... Behavior Rating Profile [*Educational testing*]
BRP .... Biaru [*Papua New Guinea*] [*Airport symbol*] (OAG)
BRP .... Bilirubin Production [*Biochemistry*] (MAE)
BRP .... Brain Retraction Pressure [*Neurophysiology*]
BRP .... Brakes Release Point (ADA)
BRP .... British Patent
BRP .... Budget Related Papers
BRP .... Bulgarska Rabotnicheska Partiia [*Bulgarian Workers Party*] [*Political party*] (PPE)
BRP .... Bureau of Radiation Protection (NRCH)
BRP .... Business Reply Post [*British*] (ADA)
BRPA .... British Radiological Protection Association (DEN)
Br Par .... Brown's Parties to Actions [*A publication*] (DLA)
BRPB .... British Rail Property Board
Br PC .... Brown's Chancery Cases [*England*] [*A publication*] (DLA)
BRPC .... Parks Canada [*Parcs Canada*] Revelstoke, British Columbia [*Library symbol National Library of Canada*] (NLC)
BRPF .... Bertrand Russell Peace Foundation (EA)
Br Phil Law... Broom. Philosophy of Law [*3rd ed.*] [*1883*] [*A publication*] (DLA)
BrPI .... Instituto Zimotecnico, Piracicaba, Brazil [*Library symbol Library of Congress*] (LCLS)
BRPM .... Breath Rate per Minute (MCD)
BRPNP......... Big Rock Point Nuclear Plant (NRCH)
BRPRA....... British Rubber Products Research Association (MCD)
BRPS .... British Retinitis Pigmentosa Society
BRPT .... Behavioral Role-Playing Test (EDAC)
B Rpt .... Book Report [*A publication*] (BRI)
BRPT .... Bromoil Print (VRA)
BRQ .... Baroque Resources Ltd. [*Vancouver Stock Exchange symbol*]
BRQ .... Brno [*Former Czechoslovakia*] [*Airport symbol*] (OAG)
BRQM .... Brigade Quartermaster [*Marine Corps*]
BRQTT .... Briquette
BRR .... Balanced Repeated Replication [*Statistics*]
BRR .... Barra [*Hebrides Islands*] [*Airport symbol*] (OAG)
BRR .... Barrett Resources [*NYSE symbol*] (SAG)
BRR .... Barrett Resources [*NYSE symbol*] (TTSB)
BRR .... Basic Recommended Reading (ADA)
BRR .... Battelle Research Reactor
BRR .... Bearer

BRR .... Belton Railroad Co. [*AAR code*]
BRR .... Berryman [*Missouri*] [*Seismograph station code, US Geological Survey Closed*] (SEIS)
BRR .... Biological Research Resources
BRR .... Bridge Receiving Room [*Navy*]
BrR .... Bridled with Rainbows [*A publication*]
BRR .... Brigade Receiving Room
BRR .... Brookhaven Research Reactor
Br R .... Browne's Reports [*Ceylon*] [*A publication*] (DLA)
BRR .... Bruncor, Inc. [*Toronto Stock Exchange symbol*]
BRR .... Lake Jackson, TX [*Location identifier FAA*] (FAAL)
BRR .... Mountain Air Service, Inc. [*ICAO designator*] (FAAC)
BRRA .... BMW [*Bavarian Motor Works*] Rolls-Royce AeroEngines [*Commercial firm*] (ECON)
BRRAMA ...... British Rubber and Resin Adhesive Manufacturers' Association (BI)
BRRD .... Barred
Br Reg .... Braithwaite's Register [*A publication*] (DLA)
BrRF .... Fundacao Casa de Rui Barbosa, Rio De Janeiro, Brazil [*Library symbol Library of Congress*] (LCLS)
BRRG .... Barring
BR/RL .... Bomb Rack/Rocket Launcher (NG)
BRRL .... British Road Research Laboratory
BRRPC .... Rogers Pass Centre, Revelstoke, British Columbia [*Library symbol National Library of Canada*] (NLC)
BRRS .... Banana River Repeater Station [*NASA*] (KSC)
BRRSTR...... Barrister
BRRTF .... Building Regulation Review Task Force
Br Rul Cas... British Ruling Cases [*A publication*] (DLA)
BRRV .... Blueberry Red Ringspot Virus [*Plant pathology*]
BrRvo.......... Branch Retinal Vein Occlusion [*Ophthalmology*] (DAVI)
BRS .... Bachelor of Religious Studies
BRS .... Ballistic Recording System
BRS .... Balloon Radio System
BRS .... Barometric Read Solenoid [*Automotive engineering*]
BRS .... Bartok Recording Studio [*Record label*]
BRS .... Beacon-Radio Set
BRS .... Bertrand Russell Society (EA)
BRS .... Bible Research Systems [*Information service or system*] (IID)
BRS .... Bibliographic Retrieval Services, Inc. [*Database host system*] [*Scotia, NY*]
BRS .... Big Red Switch [*Computer science*] (NHD)
BRS .... Binary Ring Sequence
BRS .... Biofeedback Research Society [*Later, BSA*] (EA)
BRS .... Biomedical Research Support Program [*Bethesda, MD*] [*National Institutes of Health*] (GRD)
BRS .... Birch, Raymond Sr., Southampton PA [*STAC*]
BRS .... Block Received Signal [*Telecommunications*] (TEL)
BRS .... Blower Ramp Sensor [*Automotive air conditioning*]
BRS .... B-Mode Receiving Station [*Telecommunications*] (TEL)
BRS .... Body Restraint System
BRS .... Bohemia Ragtime Society (EA)
BRS .... Boron Recycle System [*Nuclear energy*] (NRCH)
BRS .... Bottom Right Side (MCD)
BRS .... Brascan Ltd. [*AMEX symbol*] (SPSG)
BRS .... Brass (KSC)
BRS .... Brass Ring Society (EA)
BRS .... Brazilian Air Force [*ICAO designator*] (FAAC)
BRS .... Brazos Petroleum [*Vancouver Stock Exchange symbol*]
BRS .... Break Request Signal [*Computer science*]
BrS............ Breath Sounds [*Medicine*]
BRS .... Brisbane [*Australia Seismograph station code, US Geological Survey*] (SEIS)
BRS .... Bristol [*England*] [*Airport symbol*] (OAG)
BRS .... British Receiving Station (IAA)
BRS .... British Record Society
BRS .... British Research Station
BRS .... British Road Services
BRS .... British Roentgen Society (MAE)
BRS .... Broadcasting Squadron [*Air Force*]
BRS .... Brotherhood of Railroad Signalmen (EA)
BRS .... Building Research Station [*British*]
BRS .... Building Research Station News [*A publication*]
BRS .... Bureau of Railroad Safety [*Department of Transportation*]
BRS .... Business Radio Service
BRS .... Business Recovery Service (ACRL)
BRSAC .... Biomedical Research Support Advisory Committee [*National Institutes of Health*] (EGAO)
BRSc.......... Bachelor of Religious Sciences
BRSC .... Brotherhood of Railway and Steamship Clerks, Freight Handlers, Express and Station Employees [*Later, BRAC*] (EA)
BRSCC .... British Racing and Sport Car Club
Brscn.......... Brascan Ltd. [*Associated Press*] (SAG)
BRSE .... Bibliography of Research Studies in Education, 1926-1940 [*A publication*]
BRSF .... Biafra Relief Services Foundation (EA)
BRSG .... Biomedical Research Support Grants
BrshWI.......... Brush Wellman, Inc. [*Associated Press*] (SAG)
BRSI .... Bureau of Retirement Survivors Insurance [*Social Security Administration*]
BRSIT .... Boresight (MSA)
BRSKT .... Brisket (ABBR)
BRSKY .... Briskly (ABBR)
BRSL .... Bristle (ABBR)
BRSL .... British Robotics Systems Ltd. (NITA)
BRSLD .... Bristled (ABBR)

BRSLG .... Bristling (ABBR)
BRSM .... Steveston Museum, Richmond, British Columbia [Library symbol National Library of Canada] (NLC)
BRSNLW ...... Brothers-in-Law (ABBR)
BRSNS .... Brassiness (ABBR)
BRSO .... Bermuda Range Safety Officer [NASA] (KSC)
BRSQ .... Brusque (ABBR)
BRSQNS ...... Brusqueness (ABBR)
BRSQY .... Brusquely (ABBR)
BRSR .... Bursar (ABBR)
BRSR .... Bursar
BRSRY .... Bursary (ABBR)
BRSS .... Breema Rug Study Society [Later, CRSS] (EA)
BRSSIR .... Brassiere (ABBR)
BRSSR .... Brasserie
BRSSY .... Brassy (ABBR)
BRST .... Breast (ABBR)
BRST .... Broadcast (MUGU)
BRST .... Burst
BRSTBN ...... Breastbone (ABBR)
BRSTD .... British Standard (IAA)
BRSTG .... Bursting (ABBR)
BRSTL .... Bristol [City and county borough in England]
BRSTPLT ..... Breastplate (ABBR)
BRSTR .... Barrister (ABBR)
BRSTR .... Burster
BRSTRM ...... Brainstorm (ABBR)
BRSTRMG.... Brainstorming (ABBR)
BRSTS .... Bursitis (ABBR)
BrSU .... Universidade de Sao Paulo, Sao Paulo, Brazil [Library symbol Library of Congress] (LCLS)
BrSU-H .... Universidade de Sao Paulo, Faculdade de Higiene e Saude Publica, Sao Paulo, Brazil [Library symbol Library of Congress] (LCLS)
BrSU-MV...... Universidade de Sao Paulo, Faculdade de Medicina Veterinaria, Sao Paulo, Brazil [Library symbol Library of Congress] (LCLS)
Br Sup .... Brown's Supplement to Morison's Dictionary, Scotch Court of Sessions [A publication] (DLA)
BrSU-P........ Universidade de Sao Paulo, Escola Politecnica, Sao Paulo, Brazil [Library symbol Library of Congress] (LCLS)
BrSU-Q .... Universidade de Sao Paulo, Conjunto das Quimicas, Sao Paulo, Brazil [Library symbol Library of Congress] (LCLS)
BRSY .... Brassy (ABBR)
Br Syn .... Brown's Synopsis of Decisions, Scotch Court of Sessions [1540-1827] [A publication] (DLA)
BRT............. Base Resistance Transistor
BRT............. Bathurst Island [Australia Airport symbol] (OAG)
BRT............. Bayrak Radyo-Televisyon [Bayrak Radio-Television]
BRT............. Belgische Radio en Televisie [Belgian Radio and Television - Dutch Service]
BRT............. Bend Radius Template (MCD)
BRT............. Bilateration Ranging Transponder (MCD)
BRT............. Binary Run Tape [Computer science] (BUR)
BRT............. BioResearch Titles (DIT)
BRT............. Biotechnical Research Technology [NIH]
BRT............. Bolt Removal Tool
BRT............. Bomber Recovery Team [Air Force] (DOMA)
BRT............. Bright (MSA)
BRT............. Bright [T. G.] & Co. Ltd. [Toronto Stock Exchange symbol]
BRT............. Brightness (GAVI)
BRT............. British (ROG)
BRT............. British Time (IAA)
BRT............. Brooklyn Rapid Transit Co. [A New York City subway line] [Became BMT]
BRT............. Brook Reaction Test [Medicine] (DMAA)
BRT............. Brotherhood of Railroad Trainmen [Later, United Transportation Union] (EA)
BRT............. Brought
BRT............. BRT Realty Trust [Associated Press] (SAG)
BRT............. BRT Realty Trust SBI [NYSE symbol] (SPSG)
BRT............. BRT Realty Trust SBI [NYSE symbol] (TTSB)
BRT............. Brucella Ring Test [Dairy science] (OA)
BRT............. Brute (ABBR)
BRT............. Bruttoregistertonne [Gross Registered Ton] [German]
BRT............. Business Roundtable
BRTA .... British Racing Tobaggan Association (BI)
BRTA .... British Regional Television Association (BI)
BRTA .... British Road Tar Association (BI)
BRTA .... Bureau of Resources and Trade Assistance [Department of Commerce]
Brt&Ktz ...... Britton & Koontz Capital Corp. [Associated Press] (SAG)
BRTC .... British Railwaymen's Touring Club (BI)
BRTD .... Bright RADAR Tube Display (AAG)
BRTDY........ Birthday (ABBR)
BRTE.......... Bachelor of Radio and Television Engineering
BRT Eng ...... Bachelor of Radio and Television Engineering
BRTG .... Bomb, Radio, Transverse, Generator-Powered (IAA)
BRTH .... Breath [or Breathe] (ABBR)
BRTH .... Breathe (MSA)
BRTHD........ Breathed (ABBR)
BRTHD........ Brotherhood
BRTHDY....... Birthday (ABBR)
BRTHE .... Breathe (ABBR)
BRTHG........ Breathing (ABBR)
BRTHL .... Brothel (ABBR)
BRTHMK..... Birthmark (ABBR)

BRTHPL ...... Birthplace (ABBR)
BRTHR........ Breather (MSA)
BRTHRGT ... Birthright (ABBR)
BRTHRN....... Brethren (ABBR)
BRTHSTN.... Birthstone (ABBR)
BRTHTKG.... Breathtaking (ABBR)
BRTK .... Bayrak Radio & TV Corp. [Turkish Cyprus] (EY)
BRTL .... Brittle (ABBR)
BRTL .... Brutal (ABBR)
BRTLT .... Brutality (ABBR)
BRTLY .... Brutally (ABBR)
BRTLZ .... Brutalize (ABBR)
BRTLZD ...... Brutalized (ABBR)
BRTLZG ...... Brutalizing (ABBR)
BRTMK .... Birthmark (ABBR)
BRTNDR ..... Bartender (ABBR)
BrTom .... Brown [Tom], Inc. [Associated Press] (SAG)
BRTP .... Bachelor of Regional and Town Planning (ADA)
BRTP .... Biomedical Research Technology Program [Bethesda, MD] [National Institutes of Health] (GRD)
BRTPLC .... Birthplace (ABBR)
BRTR .... Barter (ABBR)
BRTRA........ Regional Air Traffic Services School, Transport Canada [Ecole Regionale des Services de la Circulation Aerienne, Transports Canada], Richmond, British Columbia [Library symbol National Library of Canada] (NLC)
BRTRT .... Birthright (ABBR)
BRTS .... Bilateration Ranging Transponder System (MCD)
BRTS .... Bioradiotelemetric System
BRTSH .... British
BRTSH .... Brutish (ABBR)
BRTSHNS .... Brutishness (ABBR)
BRTSHY ...... Brutishly (ABBR)
BRTST .... Birthstone (ABBR)
BRTT........... British Reports, Translations, and Theses [A publication]
BRTTS .... British Roll Tuners Trade Society [A union] (DCTA)
BRTVIA .... Vancouver International Airport, Transport Canada [Aeroport International de Vancouver, Transports Canada], Richmond, British Columbia [Library symbol National Library of Canada] (NLC)
BRU .... Atlanta, GA [Location identifier FAA] (FAAL)
BRU .... Babylonische Rechtsurkunden aus der Regierungzeit Artaxerxes I und Darius II [A publication] (BJA)
BRU .... Base Records Unit (SAA)
BRU .... Basic Resolution Unit [Computer science]
BRU .... Battery Replacement Unit (MCD)
BRU .... Bearing Repeater Unit (IAA)
BRU .... Belavia [Belarus] [ICAO designator] (FAAC)
BRU .... Bilevel Response Unit
BRU .... Boat Repair Unit [Navy]
BRU .... Bomb Rack Unit
BRU .... Boresight Reticle Unit (MCD)
BRU .... Branch Unconditionally
BRU .... Brayton Rotating Unit
Bru............. Bruce's Scotch Court of Session Reports [1714-15] [A publication] (DLA)
BRU .... Brunei [International vehicle registration] (ODBW)
bru............. Brush (VRA)
BRU .... Brussels [Belgium] [Airport symbol] (OAG)
BRU .... Burlington Res CoalSeamGasRty [NYSE symbol] (TTSB)
BRU .... Burlington Resources Coal Seam Gas Royalty Trust [NYSE symbol] (SAG)
Bru & Wil Adm... Bruce and Williams. Admiralty Jurisdiction [A publication] (DLA)
Bruce.......... Bruce's Scotch Court of Session Reports [1714-15] [A publication] (DLA)
BRUCE........ Buffer Register Under Computer Edict [Computer science] (PDAA)
BRUCL .... Brucella Agglutinins [Bacteriology] (DAVI)
B Ru E .... Bachelor of Rural Engineering
B Ru Eng ..... Bachelor of Rural Engineering
BRUFMA ..... British Rigid Urethane Foam Manufacturers Association
BRUFS........ British Council Undergraduate Fellowship Scheme (AIE)
BRuG .... Bundesrueckerstattungsgesetz [A publication] (BJA)
BRUIN......... Brown University Interpreter [Computer science]
Br Ult V .... Brice's Ultra Vires [A publication] (ILCA)
Bru ML .... Bruce's Military Law [A publication] (DLA)
BRUN .... Brunei
BRUNCH ..... Breakfast and Lunch [Refers to a late morning or early afternoon meal]
Brun Col Cas... Brunner's Collected Cases [United States] [A publication] (DLA)
Brunk Ir Dig... Brunker's Irish Common Law Digest [A publication] (DLA)
Brunn Col Cas (F)... Brunner's Collected Cases [United States] [A publication] (DLA)
Brunn Coll Cas... Brunner's Collected Cases [United States] [A publication] (DLA)
BRUNNEL..... Bridge-Tunnel [Proposed English Channel link between Britain and France]
Brunner Col Cas... Brunner's Collected Cases [United States] [A publication] (DLA)
Brunner Sel Cas... Brunner's Selected Cases, United States Circuit Courts [A publication] (DLA)
Brunn Sel Cas... Brunner's Selected Cases [United States] [A publication] (DLA)
Brun Sel Cas... Brunner's Selected Cases [United States] [A publication] (DLA)
Brunskill...... Brunskill's Land Cases [Ireland] [A publication] (DLA)
Bruns LC...... Brunskill's Land Cases [Ireland] [A publication] (DLA)
Bru Princip... Bruce, Principia Juris Feudalis [A publication] (DLA)
BRUPT........ Bankrupt [or Bankruptcy] (DCTA)
BrUrd .... Bromouridine [Also, B] [A nucleoside]

BRurSc	Bachelor of Rural Science (ADA)
BRurScEd	Bachelor of Rural Science Education
BRUS	Bruise (ABBR)
BRUSA	British-United States Agreement [*Signed May 17, 1943; formalized cooperation between the communications intelligence agencies of Great Britain and the United States*]
BRuSci	Bachelor of Rural Science (NADA)
BRUSD	Bruised (ABBR)
BRUSG	Bruising (ABBR)
BrushCrk	Brush Creek Mining & Development [*Associated Press*] (SAG)
BRUSR	Bruiser (ABBR)
BRUSTA	Bureau Regional de l'UNESCO pour la Science et la Technologie en Afrique [*UNESCO Regional Office for Science and Technology in Africa - UNESCO-ROSTA*] [*Nairobi, Kenya*] (EAIO)
BRUT	Brunet (ABBR)
Brut.............	Brutus [*of Plutarch*] [*Classical studies*] (OCD)
Brut.............	Brutus or De Claris Oratoribus [*of Cicero*] [*Classical studies*] (OCD)
BRUTH	Brutish (ABBR)
BRUX	Bruxelles [*Belgium*] [*City in Belgium*] (ROG)
Bruzard	Mauritius Reports, by Bruzard [*1842-45*] [*A publication*] (DLA)
BRV	Ballistic Reentry Vehicle
BRV	Basic Research Vehicle [*Automotive engineering*]
BRV	Bill of Rights of Virginia [*A publication*] (DLA)
BRV	Brave (ABBR)
BRV	Bremerhaven [*Germany Airport symbol*] (OAG)
BRV	Brooke, VA [*Location identifier FAA*] (FAAL)
BRVD	Braved (ABBR)
BRVDO	Bravado (ABBR)
BRVE	Bereave (ABBR)
BRVED	Bereaved (ABBR)
BRVG	Braving (ABBR)
BRVMA	British Radio Valve Manufacturers' Association
BRVNS	Braveness (ABBR)
BRVO	Branch Retinal Vein Occlusion [*Ophthalmology*] (CPH)
BRVT	Brevity (ABBR)
BRVY	Bravely (ABBR)
BRW	Barrow [*Alaska*] [*Seismograph station code, US Geological Survey Closed*] (SEIS)
BRW	Barrow [*Alaska*] [*Airport symbol*] (OAG)
BRW	Biased Random Walk [*Mathematics*]
BRW	Black River & Western Corp. [*AAR code*]
BRW	Brown-Roberts-Wells [*Computerized tomographic stereotaxic guide*] [*Radiology*] (DAVI)
BRWBT	Browbeat (ABBR)
BRWBTG	Browbeating (ABBR)
BRWBTN	Browbeaten (ABBR)
BRWLD	Brawled (ABBR)
BRWLG	Brawling (ABBR)
BRWM	Board on Radioactive Waste Management (EA)
BRWN	Brown
BrwnFA	Brown Forman, Inc. [*Associated Press*] (SAG)
BrwnFB	Brown Forman, Inc. [*Associated Press*] (SAG)
BrwnFr	Browning Ferris [*Associated Press*] (SAG)
BrwnFr	Browning-Ferris Industries, Inc. [*Associated Press*] (SAG)
BRWNG	Brewing
BrwnGp	Brown Group, Inc. [*Associated Press*] (SAG)
BRWPF	Black Revolutionary War Patriots Foundation (EA)
BRWR	Brewer (ABBR)
BRWRY	Brewery
BRWS	Browse (ABBR)
BRWSD	Browsed (ABBR)
BRWSG	Browsing (ABBR)
BRX	Barahona [*Dominican Republic*] [*Airport symbol*] (OAG)
BRX	Benton Resources Ltd. [*Vancouver Stock Exchange symbol*]
BRX	Buffalo Express Airlines, Inc. [*ICAO designator*] (FAAC)
BRY	Bardstown, KY [*Location identifier FAA*] (FAAL)
BRY	Barry [*Cardiff*] [*Welsh depot code*]
BrY.............	Belorussian Yiddish (BJA)
BRY	Berry (ABBR)
BRY	Berry
BRY	Berry Petroleum'A' [*NYSE symbol*] (TTSB)
BRY	Berry Petroleum Co. Class A [*NYSE symbol*] (SPSG)
BRY	Brotherly (ABBR)
BRY	Brymon European Airway [*British ICAO designator*] (FAAC)
BRY	Bryology
Bry & Str Com L...	Bryant and Stratton. Commercial Law [*A publication*] (DLA)
Bryant C	Bryant College (GAGS)
Bryce Civ L...	Bryce's Study of the Civil Law [*A publication*] (DLA)
Bryce Tr M...	Bryce. Registration of Trade Marks [*A publication*] (DLA)
BRYG	Berrying (ABBR)
BRYG	Burying (ABBR)
Bryn Mawr C...	Bryn Mawr College (GAGS)
BrynMw	Bryn Mawr Bank Corp. [*Associated Press*] (SAG)
BRYOL	Bryology (ROG)
BRZ	Better Resources Ltd. [*Vancouver Stock Exchange symbol*]
BRZ.............	Braze
BRZ.............	Breeze (ABBR)
BRZ.............	Bronze (KSC)
BRZ.............	Bruzual [*Venezuela*] [*Airport symbol*] (AD)
BRZ.............	Wittman, AZ [*Location identifier FAA*] (FAAL)
BrzA.............	Brazilian Angel [*Record label*]
BrzC.............	Brazilian Columbia [*Record label*]
BrzCont.......	Brazilian Continental [*Record label*]
BRZD	Brazed (ABBR)
BrzEli..........	Brazilian Elite [*Record label*]

BRZG	Brazing (KSC)
BRZIR	Brazier (ABBR)
BRZIR	Breezier (ABBR)
BrzMGM	Brazilian MGM [*Record label*]
BRZN	Bravo Zone (SAA)
BRZN	Brazen (ABBR)
BRZND	Brazened (ABBR)
BRZNG	Brazening (ABBR)
BRZNS	Breeziness (ABBR)
BrzOd.........	Brazilian Odeon [*Record label*]
BRZST	Breeziest (ABBR)
BrzV...........	Brazilian Victor [*Record label*]
BRZWY	Breezeway (ABBR)
BRZY	Breezy (ABBR)
BS.............	Auxaire-Bretagne [*ICAO designator*] (AD)
BS.............	Bachelor of Science
BS.............	Bachelor of Science in Pure Science
BS.............	Bachelor of Surgery
BS.............	Backscattering Spectroscopy [*Surface analysis*]
BS.............	Backsight (DNAB)
BS.............	Backspace [*ASCII format effector*] [*Computer science*] (NITA)
BS.............	Backspace Character [*Keyboard*] [*Computer science*]
BS.............	Back Spread [*Investment term*]
BS.............	Backstage (ADA)
BS.............	Backstairs [*Gossip*]
BS.............	Backward Signaling [*Telecommunications*] (TEL)
BS.............	Bahamas [*ANSI two-letter standard code*] (CNC)
BS.............	Balance Sheet [*Accounting*]
BS.............	Ballistic Shell
BS.............	Bancus Superior [*King's Bench*] [*British Legal term*] (DLA)
BS.............	Band Setting (IAA)
BS.............	Bandstop [*Electronics*] (IAA)
BS.............	Band System (IAA)
BS.............	Bank-Switching [*Computer technology*]
BS.............	Bantock Society (EA)
BS.............	Baroswitch
BS.............	Base (IAA)
BS.............	Base Salvage (AAG)
BS.............	Base Section [*Military*]
BS.............	Base Shell
BS.............	Base Shield (IAA)
BS.............	Base Skirt
BS.............	Base Supply (KSC)
BS.............	Basic Sediment [*Petroleum*]
BS.............	Basic Size [*Printing*] (WDMC)
BS.............	Basilian Salvatorian Fathers [*Roman Catholic religious order*]
BS.............	Basisphenoid [*Anatomy*]
Bs.............	Bass [*or Basso*] [*Music*]
BS.............	Bathymetric Swath [*Survey System*] [*National Ocean Survey*] (PDAA)
BS.............	Battery Simulator
BS.............	Battlefield Surveillance (MCD)
BS.............	Battleship
BS.............	Battleship Flag [*Navy British*]
BS.............	Battleship Squadron
BS.............	Battle Star
BS.............	Bead Society (EA)
BS.............	Beam Spacer (DAC)
BS.............	Beam Splitter [*Instrumentation*]
BS.............	Beam Steering
BS.............	Beam Stop
BS.............	Bedside [*Medicine*]
BS.............	Beef Shorthorn [*Cattle*]
BS.............	Before Sleep [*Pharmacy*] (DAVI)
BS.............	Behcet Syndrome [*Medicine*] (DMAA)
B/S.............	Behind Schedule
BS.............	Belinfante-Swihart [*Theory*]
BS.............	Bellwether Stock [*Investment term*]
BS.............	Below Slab (OA)
B/S.............	Bench Stock [*Air Force*] (AFIT)
Bs.............	Benedictus [*Blessed*] [*Latin*]
BS.............	Beneficial Suggestion (MCD)
BS.............	Berlin Sector [*Allied German Occupation Forces*]
BS.............	Be Specific
BS.............	Beta Spectrometer
BS.............	Bethe-Salpeter Equation [*Physics*] (OA)
BS.............	Bethlehem Steel (TTSB)
BS.............	Bethlehem Steel Corp. [*Wall Street slang name: "Bessie"*] [*NYSE symbol*] (SPSG)
BS.............	Bibliographical Society [*British*] (DIT)
BS.............	Bile Salts [*Biochemistry*]
BS.............	Bill of Sale
BS.............	Bill of Sight [*Customs*]
BS.............	Bill of Store
BS.............	Binary Scale (AAG)
BS.............	Binary Subtract
BS.............	Binder Aviatik, Scheibe-Bruns, Schleicher-Bruns [*Germany ICAO aircraft manufacturer identifier*] (ICAO)
BS.............	Binet-Simon [*Test*] [*Psychology*] (DAVI)
BS.............	Biochemical Society [*London, England*] (EAIO)
BS.............	Biometric Society
BS.............	Biophysical Society (MCD)
BS.............	Biosystematic Code [*Online database field identifier*]
BS.............	Birmingham Southern Railroad Co. [*AAR code*]
BS.............	Birmingham Standard [*Wire gauge*]
BS.............	Bishop Suffragan

BS..............	Bismuth Subsalicylate [*Antidiarrhea agent*]
BS..............	Bismuth Sulfite [*Agar*] [*Bacteriology*]
B/S..............	Bistable (NRCH)
BS..............	BIT [*Binary Digit*] Space [*Computer science*] (IAA)
B/S..............	BITs [*Binary Digits*] per Second [*Data transmission speed*] [*Computer science*] (CET)
BS..............	BIT [*Binary Digit*] Sync [*Computer science*]
BS..............	Black Scale (MSA)
BS..............	Blank Spike
BS..............	Blatant Self-Promotion
BS..............	Blessed Sacrament
BS..............	Blind Sports [*Later, LBSF*] (EA)
BS..............	Blind Spouse [*Title XVI*] [*Social Security Administration*] (OICC)
B/S..............	Blip/Scan (MUGU)
BS..............	Block Sale [*Investment term*]
BS..............	Block Specification (MCD)
BS..............	Blood Sugar [*Medicine*]
BS..............	Bloom Syndrome [*Medicine*]
BS..............	Blowing Sand [*Meteorology*] (DNAB)
BS..............	Blowing Snow [*Meteorology*] (BARN)
BS..............	Blue Shade [*Paper*]
BS..............	Blue Shield [*Health insurance plan*]
BS..............	Blue Steel [*Guns*]
BS..............	Bluestone (ABBR)
BS..............	Blue Straggler [*Star*] [*Astronomy*]
BS..............	Blue Streak [*Military*] (SAA)
B/S..............	Board of Inspection and Survey [*Navy*]
BS..............	Board Secretary
BS..............	Body Shell
BS..............	Body Station (MCD)
BS..............	Boiler Survey
BS..............	Bomber Support
BS..............	Bomb Service
BS..............	Bomb Sight
BS..............	Bonded Single Silk [*Wire insulation*] (MSA)
BS..............	Bonifay Sand [*A soil type*]
BS..............	Bookplate Society [*London, England*] (EAIO)
BS..............	Border Surveillance [*Military*]
BS..............	Borescope (MSA)
BS..............	Boresight (KSC)
BS..............	Bostonian Society (EA)
BS..............	Both Sides [*Technical drawings*]
bs	Botswana [*MARC country of publication code Library of Congress*] (LCCP)
BS..............	Bottom Sediment [*Maps and charts*]
BS..............	Bottom Settlings [*of crude oil in storage*]
BS..............	Boundary Stimulus [*To light*]
BS..............	Bound Seam (DNAB)
BS..............	Bow and Stern Thruster [*of a ship*] (DS)
BS..............	Bowel Sounds [*Medicine*]
BS..............	Bow Shock [*Astrophysics*]
BS..............	Boy Scouts
BS..............	Brada-Svejda [*Tumor*] [*Medicine*]
BS..............	Braidwood Station [*Nuclear energy*] (NRCH)
BS..............	Branch Stack
BS..............	Branch State [*Database terminology*] (NITA)
bs	Brass (VRA)
BS..............	Breaking Strain [*Of fishing lines or casts*]
BS..............	Breaking Strength (MAE)
BS..............	Breath Sounds [*Medicine*]
BS..............	Brewster Society (EA)
BS..............	Brickmakers Society [*A union*] [*British*]
BS..............	Brillouin Scattering (PDAA)
BS..............	Brith Sholom (EA)
BS..............	British Shipbuilders
BS..............	British Size (IAA)
BS..............	British Standard
BS..............	Broadcasting Station
BS..............	Broadcast Satellite [*Japan*]
BS..............	Broadside [*Paper*] (DGA)
BS..............	Brocades-Stheeman [*Netherlands*] [*Research code symbol*]
BS..............	Bromeliad Society (EA)
BS..............	Bronte Society (EA)
BS..............	Brown's Supplement to Morison's Dictionary of Decisions, Scotch Court of Sessions [*A publication*] (DLA)
BS..............	Brush Style [*Computer science*] (PCM)
BS..............	Bucking Signal
BS..............	Budgerigar Society [*British*] (DBA)
BS..............	Building Society (ODBW)
BS..............	Bull Session [*Slang for a random conversation*]
BS..............	Bullsling [*or Bullslinger*] [*Bowdlerized version*]
BS..............	Bureaucratic Syndrome [*In book title "B.S.: The Bureaucratic Syndrome"*]
BS..............	Bureau of Ships [*Later, Naval Sea Systems Command*]
BS..............	Bureau of Standards
BS..............	Burned, Shaded [*Ecology*]
BS..............	Burns and Schreiber Comedy Hour [*Television program*] [*Obsolete*]
BS..............	Bur-Sin (BJA)
BS..............	Business Administration, Management, and/or Marketing Programs [*Association of Independent Colleges and Schools specialization code*]
BS..............	Butterfly Spread [*Investment term*]
BS..............	Button Switch
BS..............	Byron Society (EA)
BS..............	Byron Station (NRCH)

BS..............	Graduate in Science
BS..............	Nederlandse Binnenlandse Strijdkrachten [*Netherlands Forces of the Interior, 1944*]
BS..............	Smithers Public Library, British Columbia [*Library symbol National Library of Canada*] (NLC)
BS3B..........	British Standard Three-Color Blue [*Ink*] (DGA)
BS4B..........	British Standard Four-Color Blue [*Ink*] (DGA)
BSA..............	Baccalaureat en Sciences Administratives [*Canada*] (DD)
BSA..............	Bachelier en Sciences Administratives [*Bachelor in Administrative Sciences*] [*French*]
BSA..............	Bachelor of Agricultural Science (NADA)
BSA..............	Bachelor of Science in Agriculture
BSA..............	Bachelor of Scientific Agriculture
BSA..............	Bank Secrecy Act (TDOB)
BSA..............	Bank Stationers Association [*Later, FSA*] (EA)
BSA..............	Base Support Area [*Military*]
BSA..............	Basic Service Arrangement (ACRL)
BSA..............	Basic Standardization Agreement [*Military*]
BSA..............	Basic Stock Allowance [*Military*]
BSA..............	Battlefield System Architecture (MCD)
BSA..............	Beach Support Area (CINC)
BSA..............	Bearing Specialists Association (EA)
BSA..............	Beef Serum Albumin [*Medicine*] (MEDA)
BSA..............	Benzenesulfonic Acid [*Organic chemistry*]
BSA..............	Betonvereniging van Suidelike Africa [*Concrete Society of South Africa*] (EAIO)
BSA..............	Bible Sabbath Association (EA)
BSA..............	Bible-Science Association (EA)
BSA..............	Bibliographical Society of America (EA)
BSA..............	Bimetal Steel-Aluminum (OA)
BSA..............	Biofeedback Society of America [*Later, AAPB*] (EA)
BSA..............	Birmingham Small Arms, Inc. (MCD)
BSA..............	Bismuth-Sulfite Agar [*Medicine*] (MAE)
BSA..............	Bis(trimethylsilyl)acetamide [*Organic chemistry*]
BSA..............	BIT [*Binary Digit*] Sync Acquisition [*Computer science*]
BSA..............	Black Stuntmen's Association (EA)
BSA..............	Blind Service Association (EA)
BSA..............	Blue Shield Association [*Later, BCBSA*] (EA)
BSA..............	Boarding School Allowance [*Government scholarship*] [*British*]
BSA..............	Boarding Schools Association (AIE)
BSA..............	Board of Scientific Affairs
BSA..............	Body Sensor Assembly [*Military*]
BSA..............	Body Surface Area
BSA..............	Bohr-Sommerfeld Atom
BSA..............	Bonsai Society of Australia
BSA..............	Boresight Axis
BSA..............	Borrows, S. A., Detroit, MI [*STAC*]
BSA..............	Bosaso [*Somalia*] [*Airport symbol*] (OAG)
BSA..............	Boston Shipping Association (EA)
BSA..............	Botanical Society of America (EA)
BSA..............	Boundary-Spanning Activity (PDAA)
BSA..............	Bovine Serum Albumin [*Immunology*]
BSA..............	Boy Scouts of America (EA)
BSA..............	Brecht Society of America [*Defunct*] (EA)
BSA..............	Brief Stop for Ammunition Lift [*Military*] (NVT)
BSA..............	Brigade Support Area [*Military*] (AABC)
BSA..............	Brisa International [*Toronto Stock Exchange symbol*]
BSA..............	British School of Archaeology in Jerusalem
BSA..............	British Shipbreakers' Association (BI)
BSA..............	British Sign Association (DBA)
BSA..............	British Social Attitudes [*Survey*]
BSA..............	British Society of Aesthetics
BSA..............	British Society of Audiology
BSA..............	[*The*] British Sociological Association
BSA..............	British South Africa
BSA..............	British Speleological Association (BI)
BSA..............	British Standards Association
BSA..............	British Surfing Association
BSA..............	Brotherhood of Saint Andrew (EA)
BSA..............	Bruckner Society of America (EA)
BSA..............	Budgerigar Society of Australia
BSA..............	Building Services Authority [*Queensland, Australia*]
BSA..............	Building Societies Act [*British*]
BSA..............	Building Societies Association [*British*]
BSA..............	Bureau of Supplies and Accounts [*Later, NSUPSC*] [*Navy*]
BSA..............	Business Software Alliance [*Formerly, Business Software Association*] (EA)
BSA..............	Byrd [*Antarctica*] [*Seismograph station code, US Geological Survey Closed*] (SEIS)
BSA..............	Ecole d'Aviation Civile [*Belgium ICAO designator*] (FAAC)
BSA..............	Salmo Public Library, British Columbia [*Library symbol National Library of Canada*] (NLC)
BSAA	Bachelor of Science in Applied Arts (WGA)
BSAA	British School of Archeology at Athens (BARN)
BSAA	British South American Airways Corp.
BSAAC........	British South American Airways Corp. [*Later absorbed by BOAC*]
BSA Adm	Bachelor of Science in Agricultural Administration
BSAAF	Boy Scouts of America Alumni Family [*Defunct*] (EA)
BSAAM	Salmon Arm Museum and Heritage Association, British Columbia [*Library symbol National Library of Canada*] (NLC)
BSAB	Balthazar Scales of Adaptive Behavior [*Psychology*]
BSABACT.....	Barristers and Solicitors' Admission Board of the Australian Capital Territory
BSABNSW....	Barristers and Solicitors Admission Board of New South Wales [*Australia*]

BSAC	British Society for Antimicrobial Chemotherapy
BSAC	British South Africa Co. (ROG)
BSAC	British South Africa Corps
BSAC	British Sub-Aqua Club (BI)
BSAC	Brotherhood of Shoe and Allied Craftsmen (EA)
BS (Acc)	Bachelor of Science in Accounting
BSACI	British Society for Allergy and Clinical Immunology
BSAD	Beta Solar Array Drive (SSD)
BSAD	British Sports Association for the Disabled
BS Adv	Bachelor of Science in Advertising
BSAE	Bachelor of Science in Aeronautical Engineering
BSAE	Bachelor of Science in Agricultural Engineering (WGA)
BSAE	Bachelor of Science in Architectural Engineering
BS Ae E	Bachelor of Science in Aeronautical Engineering
BSAE-E	Bachelor of Science in Aeronautical Engineering - Electronics Major
BS (Ae Elec)	Bachelor of Science with Aeronautical Engineering Electives
BSAEM	British Society of Allergy and Environmental Medicine (DBA)
BSAER	Brain Stem Auditory Evoked Response [Neurology and otorhinolaryngology] (DAVI)
BS (Aero E)	Bachelor of Science in Aeronautical Engineering
BSAF	Bids Solicited as Follows
BSAF	British Sulphate of Ammonia Federation Ltd. (BI)
BS Ag	Bachelor of Science in Agriculture
BSAG	Bristol Social Adjustment Guides [Psychology]
BSAG	Research Station, Agriculture Canada [Station de Recherches, Agriculture Canada] Sidney, British Columbia [Library symbol National Library of Canada] (NLC)
BS Ag E	Bachelor of Science in Agricultural Engineering
BS Agr	Bachelor of Science in Agriculture
BSAIF	British Sports and Allied Industries Federation (DBA)
BSAL	Base Spares Allowance List (MCD)
BSAL	Basic Stock Allowance List [Military] (NVT)
BSAL	Block Structured Assembly Language
BSAL	Block Structured Assembly Language [Computer science] (NITA)
BSALS	British Society for Agricultural Labour Science
BSAM	Basic Sequential Access Method [IBM Corp.] [Computer science]
BSAM	Basic Sequential Access Method [Electronics] [Computer science] (ECII)
BS (A Math)	Bachelor of Science in Applied Mathematics
BSAME	Bachelor of Science in Aircraft Maintenance Engineering
BS & T	Blood, Sweat, and Tears [Rock music group]
BS & W	Basic Sediment and Water [in crude oil]
BSANSW	Blind Sporting Association of New South Wales [Australia]
BSAO	Big Sisters Association of Ontario (AC)
BSAO	Bovine Serum Amine Oxidase [An enzyme]
BSAP	Basic Skills Assessment Program [Academic achievement and aptitude test]
BSA-P	Bibliographical Society of America Papers [A publication] (BRI)
BSAP	Brief Short-Action Potential (MAE)
BSAP	Brief, Small, Abundant Potential (MAE)
BSAP	British Society of Animal Production
BSAP	British Society of Australian Philately
BSAP	British South Africa Police
B Sapo	Bernardus Saporis [Flourished, 1327-36] [Authority cited in pre-1607 legal work] (DSA)
B Sapor	Bernardus Saporis [Flourished, 1327-36] [Authority cited in pre-1607 legal work] (DSA)
BSArch	Bachelor of Science in Architecture (NADA)
BS Arch (Arch)	Bachelor of Science in Architecture in Architecture
BS Arch (Arch E)	Bachelor of Science in Architecture in Architectural Engineering
BS Arch E	Bachelor of Science in Architectural Engineering
BSArchEng	Bachelor of Science in Architectural Engineering (NADA)
BS Art Ed	Bachelor of Science in Art Education
BSAS	Bakery Students Association of Scotland (BI)
BSAS	Battlefield Surveillance Airship System (PDAA)
BSAS	British Ship Adoption Society
B Sa Sc	Bachelor of Sacred Sciences
BSAT	Bachelor of Science in Air Transportation
BSAUD	British Society of Audiology
BSAV	Blind Soldiers Association of Victoria [Australia]
BSAVA	British Small Animal Veterinary Association (EAIO)
BSAWA	Billiards and Snooker Association of Western Australia
BSA-WV	Builders Supply Association of West Virginia (SRA)
BSB	Bachelor of Science in Business
BSB	Bahraini Saudi Bank (EY)
BSB	Banco Santander Chile [NYSE symbol] (SAG)
BSB	Bangladesh Shilpa Bank [Industrial Development Bank] (EY)
BSB	Baseband (MUGU)
BSB	Body Surface Burned [Medicine]
BSB	Both Sideband
BSB	Brasilia [Brazil] [Airport symbol] (OAG)
BSB	British Satellite Beam (BARN)
BSB	British Satellite Broadcasting [Telecommunications]
BSB	British Savings Bond
BSB	British Standard Beam [Engineering]
BSB	British Supply Board [Ottawa] [World War II]
BSBA	Bachelor of Science in Business Administration
BSBA	British Shingon Buddhist Association (EAIO)
BSB Ad	Bachelor of Science in Business Administration
BSBB	Baryon Symmetric Big Band (PDAA)
BSB Bcp	BSB Bancorp [Associated Press] (SAG)
BSBC	Branford Savings Bank [NASDAQ symbol] (NQ)
BSBC	Branford Savings Bank(CT) [NASDAQ symbol] (TTSB)
BSBC	British Social Biology Council
BSBC	Buffalo Sabres Booster Club (EA)

BSBD	Baseboard (ABBR)
BSB Ed	Bachelor of Science in Business Education
BSBG	Burst and Synchronous BIT [Binary Digit] Generator [Computer science] (IAA)
BSBH	Busy Season Busy Hour [Telecommunications] (ACRL)
BSBI	Big Smith Brands [NASDAQ symbol] (TTSB)
BSBI	Big Smith Brands, Inc. [NASDAQ symbol] (SAG)
BSBI	Botanical Society of the British Isles
BS Biol	Bachelor of Science in Biology
BSBIW	Big Smith Brands Wrrt [NASDAQ symbol] (TTSB)
BSBL	Bangladesh Samabaya Bank Ltd. (EY)
BSBL	Baseball (ABBR)
BSBL	Score Board [NASDAQ symbol] (TTSB)
BSBL	[The] Score Board, Inc. [NASDAQ symbol] (NQ)
BS BLK	British Standard Black [Ink] (DGA)
BSBLL	Baseball
BSBMA	British Structural Bearings Manufacturers Association (DBA)
BSBN	BSB Bancorp [NASDAQ symbol] (TTSB)
BSBN	BSB Bancorp, Inc. [NASDAQ symbol] (NQ)
BS BSF	Boot or Shoes, or Boot or Shoe Findings [Freight]
BSBSPA	British Sugar Beet Seed Producers Association (DBA)
BS Bus	Bachelor of Science in Business
BS Bus Ad	Bachelor of Science in Business Administration
BSBusEd	Bachelor of Science in Business Education
BS (Bus-MR)	Bachelor of Science in Business - Medical Records
BSBW	Backer Spielvogel Bates Worldwide [Commercial firm British] (ECON)
BSBY	Busboy (ABBR)
B Sc	Baccalaureus Scientiae [Bachelor of Science] [Latin]
B Sc	Bachelor of Christian Science
B Sc	Bachelor of Science
BSc	Bachelor of Science [Academic degree] (AIE)
BSC	Bachelor of Science in Commerce
BSC	Backspace Contact
BSC	Bahia Solano [Colombia] [Airport symbol] (OAG)
BSC	Balkan Supply Center [Navy]
BSC	Baltic Steamship Co. (MHDB)
BSC	Baptist Students Concerned [Defunct] (EA)
BSC	Barber-Scotia College [Concord, NC]
BSC	Base Security Council [Air Force] (AFM)
BSC	Base Statistical Control (AAG)
BSC	Basic (MUGU)
BSC	Basic
BSC	Basic Configuration
BSC	Basic Message Switching Center [Computer science]
BSC	Basic Synchronous Communication [Computer science] (IAA)
BSC	Battle Simulation Center (MCD)
BSC	Beam Steering Computer
BSC	Bear Stearns Companies, Inc. [NYSE symbol] (SPSG)
BSC	Bear Stearns Cos. [NYSE symbol] (TTSB)
BSC	Bedside Commode (CPH)
BSC	Beltsville Space Center [Later, Goddard Space Flight Center] [NASA]
BSC	Bemidji State College [Later, Bemidji State University] [Minnesota]
BSC	Bench Scale Calorimeter
BSC	Benevolent Society of Coachmakers [British]
BSC	Bengal Staff Corps [British Military]
BSC	Benzylselenocyanate [Antineoplastic drug]
BSC	Better Sleep Council [National Association of Bedding Manufacturers] (EA)
BSC	Bibliographical Society of Canada (DGA)
BSC	Bibliographic Systems Center [Case Western Reserve University] (IID)
BSC	Bicycle Stamps Club (EA)
BSC	Billet Sequence Code
BSC	Binary Symmetric Channel [Computer science]
BSC	Binary Synchronous [Telecommunications] (NITA)
BSC	Binary Synchronous Communication [IBM Corp.] [Computer science]
BSC	Binary Synchronous Communications [Protocol] [IBM Co.] (ACRL)
BSC	Binary Synchronous Control
BSC	Biological Safety Cabinet [Pharmaceutical processing]
BSC	Biological Species Concept [Theory of E. Mayr-1942]
BSC	Biological Stain Commission (EA)
BSC	Biomedical Sciences Corps [Air Force] (AFM)
BSC	Biomedical Signal Conditioner
BSC	Biophysical Society of Canada [La Societe de Biophysique du Canada] (AC)
BSC	Bird Sweep Completed [Aviation] (FAAC)
BSC	Birmingham Southern College [Alabama]
BSC	Bis(trimethylsilyl)carbamate [Organic chemistry]
BSC	Bisync [Protocol] (PCM)
BSC	BIT [Binary Digit] Scan Command [Computer science]
BSC	Blip-Scan Counter
BSC	Bluefield State College [West Virginia]
BSC	Blue Sky Carrier Co. Ltd. [Poland ICAO designator] (FAAC)
BSC	Boating Safety Circular [USCG] (TAG)
BSC	Body Support Cradle
BSC	Boeing Systems Coordinator (MUGU)
BSC	Bolted Separable Connector
BSC	Boresight Camera (MUGU)
BSC	Borosilicate Crown (MSA)
B/SC	Brake Skid Control [or Controller] (NASA)
BSC	Bram Stoker Club [Ireland] (EAIO)
BSC	Brethren Service Commission [Later, World Ministries Commission] (EA)
BSC	Brief Stop for Cargo Lift [or Delivery] [Military] (NVT)
BSC	Brighton & South Coast Railway [British] (ROG)

BSC............. British Safety Council
BSC............. British Samoyed Club (BI)
BSC............. British Security Coordination [*World War II*]
BSC............. British Seeds Council (DBA)
BSC............. British Shippers Council (DS)
BSC............. British Shoe Corp.
BSC............. British Society of Cinematographers (DBA)
BSC............. British Society of Commerce (BI)
BSC............. British Standard Channel (IAA)
BSC............. British Standard Cycle (IAA)
BSC............. British Stationery Council (DGA)
BSC............. British Steel Corp.
BSC............. British Sugar Corp.
BSC............. British Supply Council
BSC............. Broadcast Specialist Course [*Department of Defense Information School*] (DNAB)
BSC............. Bronfman Science Center [*Williams College*] [*Research center*] (RCD)
BSC............. Brookhaven Service Center [*IRS*]
BSC............. Building Services Calculations [*Amazon Computers*] [*Software package*] (NCC)
BSC............. Building Societies' Commission [*British*]
BSC............. Burley Stabilization Corp. (EA)
BSC............. Business Service Center
BSC............. Business Service Center (USGC)
BSC............. Cincinnati Bible Seminary, Cincinnati, OH [*OCLC symbol*] (OCLC)
BSC............. Coqualeetza Archives, Sardis, British Columbia [*Library symbol National Library of Canada*] (NLC)
B Sc............. Graduate in Science
B Sc............. Mistress of Science
BSC............. Santa Cruz Island [*California*] [*Seismograph station code, US Geological Survey*] (SEIS)
BScA............. Bachelier es Sciences Appliquees [*Bachelor of Applied Science*] [*French*]
BScA............. Bachelor of Science in Agriculture
BSCA............. Belgian Sheepdog Club of America (EA)
BSCA............. Best Support Concept Approach
BSCA............. Binary Synchronous Communications Adapter [*Computer science*]
BSCA............. British Stock Car Association
BSCA............. British Sulphate of Copper Association (Export) Ltd. (BI)
BSCA............. Building Service Contractors Association International (EA)
BSCAA........ Basal Starch Cycloheximide Antibiotic Agar [*Microbiology*]
B SC ACC.... Bachelor of Science in Accounting (WDAA)
BScAg........... Bachelor of Science in Agriculture
BScAg&AH... Bachelor of Science in Agriculture and Animal Husbandry (NADA)
B Sc Agr...... Bachelor of Science in Agriculture
BScAgrBio.... Bachelor of Science in Agricultural Biology (NADA)
BScAgrEco.... Bachelor of Science in Agricultural Economics (NADA)
BScAgrEng... Bachelor of Science in Agricultural Engineering (NADA)
BScAgri........ Bachelor of Science in Agriculture
BScAgric....... Bachelor of Science in Agriculture
BSc(AgricEng)... Bachelor of Science in Agricultural Engineering
BSc(AH)....... Bachelor of Science (Animal Husbandry) (ADA)
BSCAI........... Building Service Contractors Association International (EAIO)
BScApp........ Bachelor of Applied Science (ADA)
BSc(Arch) .... Bachelor of Science (Architecture)
BScArch....... Bachelor of Science in Architecture (NADA)
BSCB........... British Society for Cell Biology
BScBA......... Bachelor of Science in Business Administration (NADA)
BSCBA........ Brown Swiss Cattle Breeders Association of the USA (EA)
BSCC .... Billiards and Snooker Control Council [*An association*] (EAIO)
BSCC .... Binary Synchronous Communications Controller [*Computer science*] (MHDI)
BSCC .... Biotechnology Science Coordinating Committee [*An interagency governmental group*] [*Washington, DC*]
BSCC .... Boston Sickle Cell Center [*Boston City Hospital*] [*Research center*] (RCD)
BSCC .... Brisbane Sporting Car Club [*Australia*]
BSCC .... British Shell Collectors Club
BSCC .... British Society for Clinical Cytology
BSCC .... British-Soviet Chamber of Commerce (DS)
BScCE......... Bachelor of Science in Civil Engineering (NADA)
BScChemE.. Bachelor of Science in Chemical Engineering (NADA)
BSc(ChemEng)... Bachelor of Science (Chemical Engineering) (ADA)
BSCCO........ Bismuth, Strontium, Calcium, Copper, Oxide [*Inorganic chemistry*]
BScCom....... Bachelor of Commercial Science
BScComm.... Bachelor of Commercial Science (DD)
BSCD .... Bradley Subcaliber Device [*Army training device*] (INF)
BSCD .... British Ski Club for the Disabled (DBA)
BSc (Dent).. Bachelor of Science (Dentistry)
BSc(DesStud)... Bachelor of Science (Design Studies)
B Sc (Dn)..... Bachelor of Science in Dianoetics
B Sc (Dom Sc)... Bachelor of Science (Domestic Science)
BSCE.......... Bachelor of Science (Civil Engineering)
BScE........... Bachelor of Science, Engineering (DD)
BSCE.......... Bird Strike Committee Europe [*Denmark*] (EAIO)
B Sc Econ.... Bachelor of Science in Economics
BScEd......... Bachelor of Science in Education
BSc(Educ).... Bachelor of Science (Education)
BScElEd....... Bachelor of Science in Elementary Education (ADA)
BSc(Eng)..... Bachelor of Science (Engineering) (EY)
BSc(Eng)...... Bachelor of Science in Engineering (DD)
BSc(Engg).... Bachelor of Science (Engineering)
BSc(Engin).. Bachelor of Science (Engineering)
BS (Cer E).. Bachelor of Science in Ceramic Engineering

B Sc (Est Man)... Bachelor of Science (Estate Management)
B Sc F ...... Bachelor of Science in Forestry
BSCFL.......... Bisynchronous Frame Level [*Telecommunications*] (NITA)
B Sc For ..... Bachelor of Science in Forestry
BSc(Forestry).... Bachelor of Science (Forestry)
BSc(GenSc)... Bachelor of Science (General Science) (ADA)
BSCh........... Bachelor of Science in Chemistry
BSCH.......... Beseech (ABBR)
B-SCH......... Bomber [*Russian aircraft symbol*]
BSCHD........ Beseeched (ABBR)
BS Ch E ..... Bachelor of Science in Chemical Engineering
BSc(HEc).... Bachelor of Science in Home Economics
BS (Ch E Elect)... Bachelor of Science with Chemical Engineering Electives
BS Chem E.. Bachelor of Science in Chemical Engineering
BS Ch Eng ... Bachelor of Science in Chemical Engineering
BSCHG........ Beseeching (ABBR)
BSChm......... Bachelor of Science in Chemistry (NADA)
B Sch Mus... Bachelor of School Music
BSc(HomeSc)... Bachelor of Science (Home Science)
BSc(HomeSci)... Bachelor of Science (Home Science)
BSc(HomeScience)... Bachelor of Science in Home Science
B (School)... Business School
BSc(Hort)..... Bachelor of Science in Horticulture
B Sc in Agr Engr... Bachelor of Science in Agricultural Engineering
B Sc in Bact... Bachelor of Science in Bacteriology
B Sc in CE... Bachelor of Science in Civil Engineering
BSc(IndArts)... Bachelor of Science (Industrial Arts)
B Sc in EE ... Bachelor of Science in Electrical Engineering
B Sc in HE... Bachelor of Science in Home Economics
B Sc in ME... Bachelor of Science in Mechanical Engineering
B Sc in Med... Bachelor of Science in Medicine
B Sc in Med Tech... Bachelor of Science in Medical Technology
B Sc in Nurs... Bachelor of Science in Nursing
B Sc in Occ Ther... Bachelor of Science in Occupational Therapy
B Sc in Opt... Bachelor of Science in Optometry
B Sc in Phar... Bachelor of Science in Pharmacy
B Sc in Phys... Bachelor of Science in Physics
B Sc in Phys Ther... Bachelor of Science in Physical Therapy
B Sc in Rest Mgt... Bachelor of Science in Restaurant Management
B Sc in Soc Adm... Bachelor of Science in Social Administration
BSCJ........... Bachelor of Science in Criminal Justice
B Sc L .... Bachelor of the Science of Law
BSCL........... Bell System Common Language [*Telecommunications*] (TEL)
BSCL........... Biological Standards Control Laboratory [*Medical Research Council*] (PDAA)
BSCM.......... Binary Synchronous Communications Macro
BSCM.......... Bisynchronous Communications Macro (NITA)
BSCMA........ British Soluble Coffee Manufacturers Association (DBA)
BScME........ Bachelor of Science in Mining Engineering (CAS)
BSc(MechEng)... Bachelor of Science (Mechanical Engineering)
BSc(Med).... Bachelor of Science (Medical)
B Sc (Med Sci)... Bachelor of Science (Medical Science)
B Sc Met ..... Bachelor of Science in Metallurgy
BScMin........ Bachelor of Science in Mining (ADA)
BSc(MLS).... Bachelor of Science in Medical Laboratory Science (ADA)
BScN.......... Bachelor of Science in Nursing
B Scn.......... Bachelor of Scientology
BSCN.......... BIT [*Binary Digit*] Scan [*Computer science*] (BUR)
BScNurs....... Bachelor of Science in Nursing (NADA)
BSc(Nursing)... Bachelor of Science (Nursing)
BSc(Nutr).... Bachelor of Science (Nutrition)
BSCNY......... Burns Society of the City of New York (EA)
B Sc O .... Bachelor of the Science of Oratory
BSCO .... Brake Specific Carbon Monoxide [*Automotive engineering*]
BSc(Oen).... Bachelor of Science (Oenology)
BS Com .... Bachelor of Science in Communications
BSCompSci... Bachelor of Science in Computer Science
BSc(OT)...... Bachelor of Science (Occupational Therapy)
BScP.......... Bachelor of Science in Pharmacy (DAS)
BSCP .... Biological Sciences Communication Project [*American Institute of Biological Sciences*]
BSCP .... Bleached Semichemical Pulping Process [*Pulp and paper technolgy*]
BSCP .... Bovine Spinal Cord Protein [*Medicine*] (DMAA)
BSCP .... British Standard Code of Practice
BSCP .... Brotherhood of Sleeping Car Porters (IIA)
BSc (P & OT)... Bachelor of Science in Physical and Occupational Therapy
BSc(PE)..... Bachelor of Science in Physical Education
BSc(PEd) .... Bachelor of Science in Physical Education (ADA)
BSc(Pharm)... Bachelor of Science in Pharmacy
BSCPrA....... Bear Stearns Adj Rt Pfd [*NYSE symbol*] (TTSB)
BSCPrB....... Bear Stearns 7.88%'B'Dep Pfd [*NYSE symbol*] (TTSB)
BSCPrC....... Bear Stearns 7.60%'C'Dep Pfd [*NYSE symbol*] (TTSB)
BSCPrZ....... Bear Stearns Fin LLC'EPICS' [*NYSE symbol*] (TTSB)
BSc(PT)...... Bachelor of Science (Physical Therapy)
BSc(QS)...... Bachelor of Science in Quantity Surveying (ADA)
BSCR .... Brighton & South Coast Railway [*British*] (ROG)
BSCRA......... British Slot Car Racing Association (DBA)
BSCRA......... British Steel Castings Research Association [*Later, SCRATA*] (EA)
BS Cr E ...... Bachelor of Science in Ceramic Engineering
BSc(RS)...... Bachelor of Science (Rural Science) (ADA)
BScRT......... Bachelor of Science in Radiologic Technology (ADA)
BSCS .... Binary Synchronous Communication System (MHDB)
BSCS .... Biological Sciences Curriculum Study [*Colorado College*] [*Research center National Science Foundation*]
BSCS .... Blip-Scan Counter System

BSCS .... British Soil Classification System (NUCP)
B Sc (Soc)... Bachelor of Science (Sociology)
BScSoc .... Bachelor of Science of Social Science
BSc(Social Science)... Bachelor of Science (Social Science), University of Edinburgh [British]
BSc(Social Sciences)... Bachelor of Science in the Social Sciences, University of Southampton [British]
BSc(SocSc)... Bachelor of Science (Social Sciences)
BScSS .... Bachelor of Science in Secretarial Studies (ADA)
BSC/SS .... Binary Synchronous Communications/Start-Stop
BScSur .... Bachelor of Science in Land Surveying (ADA)
BSc(Surg) .... Bachelor of Science (Surgery)
BSCT .... Biscuit
B Sc Tchg .... Bachelor of Science in Teaching (ADA)
BSc(TE) .... Bachelor of Science in Textile Engineering (ADA)
BSCTE .... Bell System Center for Technical Education
B Sc (Tech)... Bachelor of Science (Technology)
B Sc Tech .... Bachelor of Technical Science
BSc(Text) .... Bachelor of Science in Textiles (ADA)
BSc(Town & Regional Planning)... Bachelor of Science (Town and Regional Planning), University of Dundee [British] (DBQ)
BSCTS .... Boresight Collimator Test Set (DWSG)
BSCU .... Background Storage and Control Unit
BSCUB .... Bear Stearns Companies, Inc. [Associated Press] (SAG)
BSCUT .... Biscuit (ABBR)
BSc(Vet) ...... Bachelor of Science (Veterinary)
BScVetSc ..... Bachelor of Science in Veterinary Science (NADA)
BSCW .... Buddhist Society of Compassionate Wisdom [Canada] (EAIO)
BSCWA .... Badger State Car Wash Association [Wisconsin] (SRA)
BSCY .... Basically (ABBR)
BSD .... Baccalaureus Scientiae Didacticae [Bachelor of Didactic Science]
BSD .... Bachelor of Science in Dentistry (ADA)
BSD .... Bachelor of Science in Design
BSD .... Ballistic Systems Division [Norton Air Force Base, CA]
BSD .... Bangladesh Samajtantrik Dal [Bangladesh Socialist Party] (PPW)
BSD .... Baoshan [China] [Airport symbol] (OAG)
BSD .... Barrels per Stream Day [Also, BPSD]
BSD .... Barsand Resources, Inc. [Vancouver Stock Exchange symbol]
BSD .... Based (ABBR)
BSD .... Base Supply Depot
BSD .... Battlefield Situation Display [DoD]
BSD .... Battlefield Surveillance Devices (MCD)
BSD .... Beam Steering Device
BSD .... Bedside Drainage [Medicine]
BSD .... Bedside Drainage [Medicine] (DMAA)
BSD .... Berkeley Software Distribution [University of California] [Computer science] (TNIG)
BSD .... Berkeley Standard Distribution [Computer science] (BYTE)
BSD .... Beside (ABBR)
BSD .... Besonders [Particularly] [German]
BSD .... Bibliographic Services Division [The British Library] (NITA)
BSD .... Biological Sciences Division [Office of Naval Research] (DNAB)
BSD .... BIT [Binary Digit] Storage Density [Computer science]
BSD .... Blank Spike Duplicate
BSD .... Blast Suppression Device
BSD .... Bloc pour la Social-Democratie [Benin] [Political party] (EY)
BSD .... British Society for Dermatopathology (EAIO)
BSD .... [The] British Society of Dowsers
BSD .... British Standard Dimension
BSD .... Building Societies Database [British]
BSD .... Building Systems Division [Washington, DC Department of Energy] (GRD)
BSD .... Bulk Storage Device (IEEE)
BSD .... Burst Slug Detection
BSD .... Business Software Database [Information Sources, Inc.] [Information service or system] (CRD)
BSD .... Buyer has Seven Days to Take Up [Investment term] (MHDW)
BSDA .... British Sheep Dairying Association (DBA)
BSDA .... British Soft Drinks Association (DBA)
BSDA .... British Spinners and Doublers Association (PDAA)
BSDA .... Business Services and Defense Administration [Department of Commerce] (BARN)
BSDB .... British Society for Developmental Biology
BSDC .... Binary Symmetric Dependent Channel [Computer science]
BSDC .... Boundary-Layer Sub-Programme Data Centre [GARP Atlantic Tropical Experiment] (MSC)
BSDC .... British Space Development Co.
BSDC .... British Standard Data Code (BUR)
BSDE .... British Society for Digestive Endoscopy
BSDent .... Bachelor of Science in Dentistry (NADA)
BS Des .... Bachelor of Science in Design
BS Des (Dec Des)... Bachelor of Science in Design in Decorative Design
BSDF .... Beet Sugar Development Foundation (EA)
BSDG .... Basic Structural Design Gross Weight (MCD)
BSDH .... Bachelor of Science in Dental Hygiene (NADA)
BSDH .... British Society of Dentistry for the Handicapped (DBA)
BSD Hyg ...... Bachelor of Science in Dental Hygiene
BS Di .... Bachelor of Scientific Didactics
BSDI .... Berkeley Software Design, Inc.
BSDI .... Berkeley Software Design, Inc.
BSDL .... Boresight Datum Line [Military]
BSDLB .... Block in the Anterosuperior Division of the Left Branch [Cardiology] (DAVI)
BSDN .... Block-Switching Digital Network

BSDP .... Bibliographic Service Development Program [Council on Library Resources] (NITA)
BSDP .... Boost Stage Discharge Pressure (MCD)
BSDP .... Bulgarska Socialdemokraticheska Partiia [Bulgarian Social Democratic Party] [Political party] (PPE)
BSDR .... British Society for Dental Research (DBA)
BSDS .... Bartholomew Sales & Distribution Services [British]
BSDU .... Bomber Support Development Unit
BSD UNIX ... Berkeley Software Distribution UNIX (CDE)
BSDV .... Bean Summer Death Virus [Plant pathology]
BSE .... Bachelor of Sanitary Engineering
BSE .... Bachelor of Science Education (NADA)
BSE .... Bachelor of Science in Education
BSE .... Bachelor of Science in Engineering
BSE .... Back-Scattered Electron [Microscopic imaging]
BSE .... Backscatter Electron
BSE .... Basaba Enterprises, Inc. [Vancouver Stock Exchange symbol]
BSE .... Base Support Equipment [Military]
BSE .... Basic Service Element [Computer science] (TNIG)
BSE .... Basis Set Extension [Physical chemistry]
BSE .... Bethe-Salpeter Equation [Physics]
BSE .... Bilateral Sphenoethmoidectomy [Medicine]
BSE .... Bilateral, Symmetrical, and Equal (MAE)
BSE .... Birmingham & Southeastern R. R. [AAR code]
BSE .... Black Sea Expedition [1969] [Turkey, US] (MSC)
BSE .... Boise [Idaho] [Seismograph station code, US Geological Survey] (SEIS)
BSE .... Bombay Stock Exchange [India]
BSE .... Booster Systems Engineer [NASA] (KSC)
BSE .... Boresight Error
BSE .... Boston Edison [NYSE symbol] (TTSB)
BSE .... Boston Edison Co. [NYSE symbol] (SPSG)
BSE .... Boston Stock Exchange [Massachusetts]
BSE .... Bovine Spongiform Encephalopathy [Veterinary medicine]
BSE .... Breast Self Exam [Gynecology] (DAVI)
BSE .... Breast Self-Examination [for cancer] [Medicine]
BSE .... British Shipbuilding Exports (BI)
BSE .... Broadband Switching Element [Telecommunications]
BSE .... Broadcasting Satellite Experimental [Japan] (MCD)
BSE .... Building and Safety Engineering
BSE .... Building Service Employees' International Union [Later, SEIU] (EA)
BSE .... Building Services Estimating [Tipdata Ltd.] [Software package] (NCC)
BSE .... Bulk Silicate Earth [Biology]
BSE .... Bureau of Steam Engineering [Navy]
BSE .... Sechelt Public Library, British Columbia [Library symbol National Library of Canada] (NLC)
BSE .... Sematan [Sarawak, Malaysia] [Airport symbol] (AD)
BSE .... Sodium Barbital-Sucrose EDTA Buffer
B Se A .... Bachelor of Secretarial Arts
BSEA .... British School of Egyptian Archaeology
BSEA .... British Steel Export Association (BI)
BSE (Ae E)... Bachelor of Science in Engineering in Aeronautical Engineering
BSE & E ...... Bachelor of Science in Engineering and Economics
BS Ec .... Bachelor of Science in Economics
B/sec .... BITs [Binary Digits] per Second [Data transmission speed] [Computer science] (NASA)
BSE (CE) ..... Bachelor of Science in Engineering and Civil Engineering
BSECH .... Beseech (ABBR)
BSECH .... British Society for Experimental and Clinical Hypnosis (DBA)
BSECHD .... Beseeched (ABBR)
BSE (Ch E) ... Bachelor of Science in Engineering in Chemical Engineering
BS Econ ...... Bachelor of Science in Economics (WGA)
BSECS .... British Society for Eighteenth Century Studies
B Sec Sc .... Bachelor of Secretarial Science
BS Ed .... Bachelor of Science in Education
BSED .... Ballistic Systems Education Division [Air University] [Air Force]
BSEE .... Bachelor of Science in Electrical Engineering
BSEE .... Bachelor of Science in Elementary Education
BSE (EE) ..... Bachelor of Science in Engineering in Electrical Engineering
BSE (EM) .... Bachelor of Science in Engineering in Engineering Mechanics
BSEE-ME .... Bachelor of Science in Electrical and Mechanical Engineering
BSEG .... Besiege (ABBR)
BSEG .... British Surgical Export Group (DBA)
BSEG .... Broadband Service Expert Group
BSEGD .... Besieged (ABBR)
BSE (Geod & Surv)... Bachelor of Science in Engineering in Geodesy and Surveying
BSEGG .... Besieging (ABBR)
BSE (Ind E).. Bachelor of Science in Engineering in Industrial Engineering
BSEL .... Bachelor of Science and English Literature
BSELCH ...... Buffered Selector Channel
BS El E .... Bachelor of Science in Electronic Engineering
BS El Ed ..... Bachelor of Science in Elementary Education
BS Elem ...... Bachelor of Science in Elementary Education
BSEM .... Bachelor of Science in Engineering of Mines
BSEM .... Backscattered Electron Microscopy
BSEM .... British Society for Electronic Music
BSE (M & Ind E)... Bachelor of Science in Engineering in Mechanical and Industrial Engineering
BSE (Mat E)... Bachelor of Science in Engineering in Materials Engineering
BSE (ME).... Bachelor of Science in Engineering in Mechanical Engineering
BSE (Met E)... Bachelor of Science in Engineering in Metallurgical Engineering
BSE (Nav Arch & Mar E)... Bachelor of Science in Engineering in Naval Architecture and Marine Engineering
BS Eng .... Bachelor of Sanitary Engineering

BSEng.........	Bachelor of Science in Engineering (NADA)
BS Engr Ad...	Bachelor of Science in Engineering Administration
BS Engr Phys...	Bachelor of Science in Engineering Physics
BS Engr Sci...	Bachelor of Science in Engineering Science
BS Eng Sci...	Bachelor of Science in Engineering Sciences
BSEP...........	Bachelor of Science in Engineering Physics
BSEP...........	Basic Skills Education Program [Army]
BSEP...........	Biosepra, Inc. [NASDAQ symbol] (SAG)
BSEP...........	BioSepra Inc. [NASDAQ symbol] (TTSB)
BSEP...........	Brain Stem Evoked Potential [Neurophysiology] (DMAA)
BSEP...........	Brunswick Steam Electric Plant (NRCH)
BSE Phys....	Bachelor of Science in Engineering Physics
BSEPrA.......	Boston Edison 8.25% Dep Pfd [NYSE symbol] (TTSB)
BSEPrB.......	Boston Edison 7.75% Dep Ptd [NYSE symbol] (TTSB)
BSER..........	Brainstem-Evoked Response [Neurophysiology]
BSERBN......	Base Service Battalion [Marine Corps]
BSerSoc....	Bachelier en Service Social [Bachelor of Social Work] [French]
BSES..........	Bachelor of Science in Engineering Sciences
BSES..........	Boresight Error Slope
BSES..........	British Schools Exploration Society
BSE Sc....	Bachelor of Science in Engineering Sciences
B Se St.......	Bachelor of Secretarial Studies
BSET..........	Bachelor of Science in Engineering Technology (IEEE)
BSET..........	Bassett Furniture [NASDAQ symbol] (TTSB)
BSET..........	Bassett Furniture Industries, Inc. [NASDAQ symbol] (NQ)
BSET..........	Test a BIT [Binary Digit] and Set [Computer science]
BSF...........	Bachelor of Science in Forestry
BSF...........	Back Scatter Factor [Medicine] (MAE)
BSF...........	Backspace File (BUR)
BSF...........	Back Surface Field [Photovoltaic energy systems]
BSF...........	Ballon De Servance [France] [Seismograph station code, US Geological Survey] (SEIS)
BSF...........	Ball Spin Frequency [Machinery]
BSF...........	Ball Spinning Friction
BSF...........	Baltic Student Federation
BSF...........	Bandstop Filter (PDAA)
BSF...........	Bandwidth Shape Factor
BSF...........	B-Cell Stimulatory Factor [Biochemistry]
BSF...........	Benign Senescent Forgetfulness [Medicine]
BSF...........	Binational Science Foundation [U.S.-Israel] [Research center]
BSF...........	Bis(trimethylsilyl)formamide [Organic chemistry]
BSF...........	Blade Slap Factor [Helicopter]
BSF...........	Boresight Fixture (MCD)
BSF...........	Brief Stop for Fuel [Military] (NVT)
BSF...........	British Salonica Force
BSF...........	British Scrap Federation (DBA)
BSF...........	British Shipping Federation (DS)
BSF...........	British Ski Federation (EAIO)
BSF...........	British Slag Federation [A union]
BSF...........	British Society of Flavourists
BSF...........	British Software Factory (NITA)
BSF...........	British Spas Federation (DBA)
BSF...........	British Standard Fine Thread
BSF...........	British Stone Federation (BI)
BSF...........	Bulk Shielding Facility [ORNL]
BSF...........	Bureau of Commerical Fisheries [Now National Marine Fisheries Service] (USDC)
BSF...........	Business Flight Service [Denmark ICAO designator] (FAAC)
BSF...........	Busulfan [Also, BUS] [Antineoplastic drug]
BSF...........	Camp Pohakuloa, HI [Location identifier FAA] (FAAL)
BSF...........	Santander Financial [NYSE symbol] (SPSG)
BSF...........	US-Israel Binational Science Foundation (EA)
BSFA..........	British Sanitary Fireclay Association (BI)
BSFA..........	British Science Fiction Association Ltd.
BSFA..........	British Snail Farmers Association (DBA)
BSFC..........	Brake Specific Fuel Consumption
BSFE..........	BioSafe International, Inc. [NASDAQ symbol] (SAG)
BSFE..........	BioSafe Intl. [NASDAQ symbol] (TTSB)
BSFEL........	BioSafe Intl. Wrrt'E' [NASDAQ symbol] (TTSB)
BSFEW........	BioSafe Intl. Wrrt'C' [NASDAQ symbol] (TTSB)
BSFF..........	Buffer Stock Financing Facility [International Monetary Fund]
BS (Fin)......	Bachelor of Science in Finance
BSFL..........	Bandstop Filter (MSA)
BSFM..........	Bachelor of Science in Forest Management
BSFMA........	British Spectacle Frame Makers Association (DBA)
BSF Mgt.......	Bachelor of Science in Fisheries Management
BS FOCI.......	Bering Sea Fisheries-Oceanography Cooperation Investigations [Marine science] (OSRA)
BS FOCI.......	Bering Sea FOCI [Fisheries-Oceanography Cooperative Investigations] (USDC)
BS For........	Bachelor of Science in Forestry
BSFPrA.......	Santander Fin Pref'A' [NYSE symbol] (TTSB)
BSFPrB.......	Santander Fin Pref'B' [NYSE symbol] (TTSB)
BSFPrC.......	Santander Fin Pref'C' [NYSE symbol] (TTSB)
BSFS..........	Bachelor of Science in Foreign Service
BSFS..........	British Soviet Friendship Society (BI)
BS Fsty.......	Bachelor of Science in Forestry
BSFT..........	Bachelor of Science in Fuel Technology
BSFV-E........	BRADLEY-STINGER Fighting Vehicle-Enhanced [Army]
BSFW..........	Bureau of Sport Fisheries and Wildlife [Superseded by US Fish and Wildlife Service] [Department of the Interior]
BSG...........	Base Spares Group
BSG...........	Basing (ABBR)
BSG...........	Bata [Spanish Guinea] [Airport symbol] (AD)
BSG...........	Bay St. George Community College [UTLAS symbol]

BSG...........	Beam Steering Group
BSG...........	Besiege (ABBR)
BSG...........	BIT [Binary Digit] Sync Generator [Computer science]
BSG...........	Blue Supergiant [Astronomy]
BSG...........	Bootstrap Gyroscope (IAA)
BSG...........	Boro-Silicate Glass (PDAA)
BSG...........	Brass Ring Resources [Vancouver Stock Exchange symbol]
BSG...........	Brewer's Spent Grain
BSG...........	British Society of Gastroenterology
BSG...........	British Society of Gerontology (DBA)
BSG...........	British Standard Gauge [Telecommunications] (TEL)
BSG...........	British Stickmakers Guild (DBA)
BSG...........	Buffered-Saline/Glucose [Clinical chemistry]
BSG...........	Bundessozialgericht [Federal Court of Social Security] [German] (ILCA)
BSG...........	Business Strategy Group [of ABT Associates, Inc.] [Cambridge, MA] [Telecommunications service] (TSSD)
BSG...........	Buyers Screening Guide
BSGA.........	Beta-Streptococcus Group A [Bacteriology] (DAVI)
BSGB.........	Brewer's Spent Grain Bran
BSGD.........	Besieged (ABBR)
BSGDG........	Brevete sans Garantie du Gouvernement [Patent without Government Guarantee] [French]
BSGE	Bachelor of Science in General Engineering
BS Gen Ed...	Bachelor of Science in General Education
BSGenNur...	Bachelor of Science in General Nursing (NADA)
BS (Geog)....	Bachelor of Science in Geography
BS (Geol)....	Bachelor of Science in Geology
BS Geol E....	Bachelor of Science in Geological Engineering
BSGG.........	Besieging (ABBR)
BS Ggr........	Bachelor of Science in Geography
BS Gl.........	Bachelor of Science in Geology
BSGL.........	Branch System General License [Information technology]
BS Gl E........	Bachelor of Science in Geological Engineering
BSG Mgt.....	Bachelor of Science in Game Management
BSGP.........	Bachelor of Science in Geology and Physics
BSGP.........	Base Support Group [Air Force]
BSGPA........	Brisbane Sand and Gravel Producers' Association [Australia]
BS Gph........	Bachelor of Science in Geophysics
BSGS.........	Base Support Group System [Air Force]
BSH	Benign Sexual Headache [Medicine] (DMAA)
BSH	Benzenesulfonohydrazide [Organic chemistry]
BSH	Brighton [England] [Airport symbol] (AD)
BSH	British Columbia Hydro and Power Authority, Surrey, British Columbia [Library symbol National Library of Canada] (NLC)
BSH	British Pacific [Vancouver Stock Exchange symbol]
BSH	British Shipbuilding Hydrodynamics
BSH	British Society for Haematology
BSH	British Society of Hypnotherapists
BSH	British Standard Handful [Slang] (DSUE)
BSH	Bushel (ROG)
BSH	Bush Indus CI'A' [NYSE symbol] (TTSB)
BSH	Bush Industries [NYSE symbol] (SAG)
BSHA	Bachelor of Science in Hospital Administration
BSHA	British Social Hygiene Association
BSHAP........	Shape of Base of Leaf [Botany]
BSHC.........	Brake Specific Hydrocarbons [Automotive engineering]
BSHD.........	Bushed (ABBR)
BSHE.........	Bachelor of Science in Health Education
BSHE.........	Bachelor of Science in Hebrew Education (BJA)
BSHE.........	Bachelor of Science in Home Economics
BS H Ec	Bachelor of Science in Home Economics
BSHEco........	Bachelor of Science in Home Economics (NADA)
BSHEd	Bachelor of Science in Health Education (NADA)
BSHF	Building and Social Housing Foundation [British]
BSHFL.........	Bashful (ABBR)
BSHFLNS.....	Bashfulness (ABBR)
BSHFLY.......	Bashfully (ABBR)
BSHG.........	Bushing (MSA)
BSHK	Bear Stearns Companies, Inc. [Associated Press] (SAG)
BSHL	Bushel (ABBR)
BSHM	British Society for the History of Mathematics (DBA)
BSHMA	Basket, Skip, and Hamper Makers Association [A union] [British]
BSHNS........	Bushiness (ABBR)
BSHP.........	Beginning Standard Holding Procedure [Aviation] (FAAC)
BSHP	Bishop
BSHP	British Society for the History of Pharmacy
BSHR.........	Bushier (ABBR)
BSHS	[The] British Society for the History of Science
BSHST........	Bushiest (ABBR)
BSHWHK.....	Bushwhack (ABBR)
BSHWHKR ..	Bushwhacker (ABBR)
B/S/Hz.........	BITS [Binary Digit] per Second per Hertz [Telecommunications] (NITA)
BSI.............	Baker Street Irregulars (EA)
BSI.............	Banca della Svizzera Italiana [Swiss-Italian Bank] [Switzerland]
BSI.............	Basic Shipping Instructions (NASA)
BSI.............	Basketball Saskatchewan Inc. [Formerly, Saskatchewan Basketball] (AC)
BSI.............	Battery Status Indicator (NATG)
BSI.............	Battlefield Systems Integration (MCD)
BSI.............	Behavior Status Inventory [Personality development test] [Psychology]
BSI.............	Biogenic Silica [In water sediments]
BSI.............	Blairsville, PA [Location identifier FAA] (FAAL)

BSI............. Blue Square Israel Ltd. [*NYSE symbol*] (SAG)
BSI............. Boeing Services International, Inc. (MCD)
BSI............. Book Services International [*ACCORD*] [*UTLAS symbol*]
BSI............. Booster Situation Indicator
BSI............. Bound Serum Iron [*Serology*]
BSI............. Branch and Store Instruction [*Computer science*] (MDG)
BSI............. Brasair Transportes Aereos [*Brazil*] [*FAA designator*] (FAAC)
BSI............. Brief Symptom Inventory [*Personality development test*] [*Psychology*]
BSI............. British Societies Institute (BI)
BSI............. [*The*] British Society for Immunology
BSI............. British Solomon Islands
BSI............. British Standards Institution (ARC)
BSI............. British Studies Intelligencer (EA)
BSI............. British Suzuki Institute (EAIO)
BSI............. Broadax Systems, Inc. (PCM)
BSI............. Broadcast Satellite International, Inc. [*Dallas, TX*]
　　　　　 [*Telecommunications service*] (TSSD)
BSI............. Broker Services, Inc. [*Englewood, CO*] [*Information service or*
　　　　　 system] (IID)
BSI............. Building Societies' Institute (BARN)
BSI............. Building Stone Institute (EA)
BSI............. Building Systems Institute (EA)
BSI............. Bureau Socialiste International [*Brussels*]
BSIA........... Bead and Stone Importers Association (EA)
BSIA........... British Security Industry Association (EAIO)
BSIA........... British Starch Industry Association (DBA)
BSIAP .... Beginning Straight-In Approach [*Aviation*] (FAAC)
BSIB........... Boy Scouts International Bureau
BSIB........... British Society for International Bibliography [*Later, Aslib*]
BSIC........... Binary Symmetric Independent Channel [*Computer science*]
BSICEN .... Battlefield System Integration Center (MCD)
BSID .... Bayley Scales of Infant Development
BSID .... Beside (ABBR)
BSID .... British Standards Institution (DAVI)
BSIE........... Bachelor of Science in Industrial Education
BSIE........... Bachelor of Science in Industrial Engineering
BSIE........... Banking Systems Information Exchange
BSIE........... Bio-Sciences Information Exchange [*Smithsonian Institution*]
BSIF........... Bile Salt Independent Fraction [*Medicine*] (DMAA)
BSIHE......... British Society for International Health Education (AEBS)
BSIL .... Basic Switching Impulse Insulation Level (IAA)
BSIM.......... Bachelor of Science in Industrial Management
BSIM.......... Broadband Service Integration Multiplexer [*Telecommunications*]
BSIM.......... Bulletin Francais. Societe Internationale de Musique [*A publication*]
BS in Acc... Bachelor of Science in Accounting
BS in AD..... Bachelor of Science in Agricultural Education
BS in AE..... Bachelor of Science in Administrative Engineering
BS in AE..... Bachelor of Science in Aeronautical Engineering
BS in AE..... Bachelor of Science in Architectural Engineering
BS in Ae E... Bachelor of Science in Aeronautical Engineering
BS in Aero Adm... Bachelor of Science in Aeronautical Administration
BS in Aero E... Bachelor of Science in Aeronautical Engineering
BS in Ag..... Bachelor of Science in Agriculture
BS in Ag & Ed... Bachelor of Science in Agriculture and Education
BS in Ag (DM)... Bachelor of Science in Agriculture in Dairy Manufacturing
BS in Ag E... Bachelor of Science in Agricultural Engineering
BS in Agr & Chem... Bachelor of Science in Agriculture and Chemistry
BS in Agr E... Bachelor of Science in Agricultural Engineering
BS in Agr Ed... Bachelor of Science in Agricultural Education
BS in Agr Eng... Bachelor of Science in Agricultural Engineering
BS in AM..... Bachelor of Science in Agricultural Administration
BS in AN..... Bachelor of Science in Agricultural Engineering
BS in Arch... Bachelor of Science in Architecture
BS in BA..... Bachelor of Science in Business Administration
BS in B Ad... Bachelor of Science in Business Administration
BS in B Ed... Bachelor of Science in Business Education
BS in Biomed Eng... Bachelor of Science in Biomedical Engineering
BS in BMS... Bachelor of Science in Basic Medical Sciences
BS in Bus.... Bachelor of Science in Business
BS in Bus Ad... Bachelor of Science in Business Administration
BS in Bus Ed... Bachelor of Science in Business Education
BS in C....... Bachelor of Science in Chemistry
BS in C....... Bachelor of Science in Commerce
BS in C & BA... Bachelor of Science in Commercial and Business Administration
BS in C & Ec... Bachelor of Science in Commerce and Economics
BS in Cart... Bachelor of Science in Cartography
BS in CE..... Bachelor of Science in Chemical Engineering
BS in CE..... Bachelor of Science in Civil Engineering
BS in CE - Music... Bachelor of Science in Christian Education - Music
BS in Cer..... Bachelor of Science in Ceramics
BS in Cer E... Bachelor of Science in Ceramic Engineering
BS in Cer Tech... Bachelor of Science in Ceramic Technology
BS in Ch..... Bachelor of Science in Chemistry
BS in Ch E... Bachelor of Science in Chemical Engineering
BS in Chem E... Bachelor of Science in Chemical Engineering
BS in Chem Tech... Bachelor of Science in Chemical Technology
BS in Ch Eng... Bachelor of Science in Chemical Engineering
BS in Chm... Bachelor of Science in Chemistry
BS in Chm E... Bachelor of Science in Chemical Engineering
BS in CN..... Bachelor of Science in Chemical Engineering
BS in Com... Bachelor of Science in Commerce
BS in Com & Bus... Bachelor of Science in Commerce and Business
BS in Com Ed... Bachelor of Science in Commercial Education
BS in Comm... Bachelor of Science in Commerce
BS in Comm Rec... Bachelor of Science in Community Recreation

BSIndArt ...... Bachelor of Science in Industrial Art (NADA)
BSIndChem... Bachelor of Science in Industrial Chemistry (NADA)
BSIndEd....... Bachelor of Science in Industrial Education
BS Ind Eng... Bachelor of Science in Industrial Engineering
BS in Dent... Bachelor of Science in Dentistry
BS in DH .... Bachelor of Science in Dental Hygiene
BS Ind Mgt... Bachelor of Science in Industrial Management
BSIndTech .. Bachelor of Science in Industrial Technology
BS in E....... Bachelor of Science in Education
BS in E....... Bachelor of Science in Engineering
BS in Ec..... Bachelor of Science in Economics
BS in Ed..... Bachelor of Science in Education
BS in EE..... Bachelor of Science in Electrical Engineering
BS in Elect Eng... Bachelor of Science in Electronic Engineering
BS in Elem Ed... Bachelor of Science in Elementary Education
BS in EM.... Bachelor of Science in Engineering of Mines
BS in E Math... Bachelor of Science in Engineering Mathematics
BS in Eng... Bachelor of Science in Engineering
BS in EP..... Bachelor of Science in Engineering Physics
BS in E Phys... Bachelor of Science in Engineering Physics
BS in ES..... Bachelor of Science in Engineering Sciences
BS in Fin.... Bachelor of Science in Finance
BS in For..... Bachelor of Science in Forestry
BS in FS..... Bachelor of Science in Foreign Service
BS in Fy..... Bachelor of Science in Forestry
BS in GE.... Bachelor of Science in General Engineering
BS in Ge E... Bachelor of Science in Geological Engineering
BS in Gen Bus... Bachelor of Science in General Business
BS in Gen Eng... Bachelor of Science in General Engineering
BS in Gen Nurs... Bachelor of Science in General Nursing
BS in Gen Sci... Bachelor of Science in General Science
BS in Gen Std... Bachelor of Science in General Studies
BS in Geod & Surv... Bachelor of Science in Geodesy and Surveying
BS in Geol E... Bachelor of Science in Geological Engineering
BS in Gph E... Bachelor of Science in Geophysical Engineering
BS in GS.... Bachelor of Science in General Studies
BS in GSM... Bachelor of Science in General Science and Mathematics
BS in GWE... Bachelor of Science in Group Work Education
BS in H & PE... Bachelor of Science in Health and Physical Education
BS in H & RA... Bachelor of Science in Hotel and Restaurant Administration
BS in HD.... Bachelor of Science in Home Economics Education
BS in HE..... Bachelor of Science in Home Economics
BS in H Ec... Bachelor of Science in Home Economics
BS in H Econ... Bachelor of Science in Home Economics
BS in H Ed... Bachelor of Science in Health Education
BS in HPE... Bachelor of Science in Health and Physical Education
BS in IA..... Bachelor of Science in Industrial Arts
BS in IE...... Bachelor of Science in Industrial Engineering
BS in IE & M... Bachelor of Science in Industrial Engineering and Management
BS in IM.... Bachelor of Science in Industrial Management
BS in Ind Art... Bachelor of Science in Industrial Art
BS in Ind Ch... Bachelor of Science in Industrial Chemistry
BS in Ind E... Bachelor of Science in Industrial Engineering
BS in Ind Ed... Bachelor of Science in Industrial Education
BS in J....... Bachelor of Science in Journalism
BS in L & S... Bachelor of Science in Letters and Science
BS in Lat.... Bachelor of Science in Latin
BS in LP..... Bachelor of Science in Land Planning
BS in LS..... Bachelor of Science in Library Service
BS in LT..... Bachelor of Science in Laboratory Technology
BS in MA.... Bachelor of Science in Mechanical Arts
BS in Math... Bachelor of Science in Applied Mathematics
BS in Math Stat... Bachelor of Science in Mathematical Statistics
BS in Md.... Bachelor of Science in Medical Technology
BS in ME.... Bachelor of Science in Mechanical Engineering
BS in Mech... Bachelor of Science in Engineering Mechanics
BS in Mech... Bachelor of Science in Mechanics
BS in Mech Eng... Bachelor of Science in Mechanical Engineering
BS in Mech Ind... Bachelor of Science in Mechanical Industries
BS in Med... Bachelor of Science in Medicine
BS in Med Rec... Bachelor of Science in Medical Records
BS in Med Rec Lib... Bachelor of Science in Medical Records Librarianship
BS in Med S... Bachelor of Science in Basic Medical Science
BS in Med Sc... Bachelor of Science in Medical Secretarial Science
BS in Med Tech... Bachelor of Science in Medical Technology
BS in M Educ... Bachelor of Science in Music Education
BS in M Engr... Bachelor of Science in Mechanical Engineering
BS in Met.... Bachelor of Science in Metallurgy
BS in Met.... Bachelor of Science in Meteorology
BS in Met E... Bachelor of Science in Metallurgical Engineering
BS in Met Engin... Bachelor of Science in Metallurgical Engineering
BS in Mgt Engr... Bachelor of Science in Management Engineering
BS in Mgt Sc... Bachelor of Science in Management Science
BS in Min... Bachelor of Science in Mining
BS in Min E... Bachelor of Science in Mining Engineering
BS in Min Eng... Bachelor of Science in Mining Engineering
BS in MRL... Bachelor of Science in Medical Record Library Science
BS in MS.... Bachelor of Science in Military Science
BS in MT .... Bachelor of Science in Medical Technology
BS in Mu Ed... Bachelor of Science in Music Education
BS in Mus Ed... Bachelor of Science in Musical Education
BS in N....... Bachelor of Science in Nursing
BS in Nat G Engin... Bachelor of Science in Natural-Gas Engineering
BS in Nat Hist... Bachelor of Science in Natural History
BS in NE..... Bachelor of Science in Nursing Education

BS in N Ed...	Bachelor of Science in Nursing Education
BS in Nr.....	Bachelor of Science in Nursing
BS in NS.....	Bachelor of Science in Natural Science
BS in N Sc...	Bachelor of Science in Natural Science
BS in Nurs...	Bachelor of Science in Nursing
BS in Nurs Ed...	Bachelor of Science in Nursing Education
BS in Occ Ther...	Bachelor of Science in Occupational Therapy
BS in Ocean...	Bachelor of Science in Oceanography
BS in OH.....	Bachelor of Science in Ornamental Horticulture
BS in Opt.....	Bachelor of Science in Optics
BS in Opt.....	Bachelor of Science in Optometry
BS in Ortho...	Bachelor of Science in Orthoptics
BS in OT.....	Bachelor of Science in Occupational Therapy
BS in PA.....	Bachelor of Science in Practical Arts
BS in PA.....	Bachelor of Science in Public Administration
BS in PAL...	Bachelor of Science in Practical Arts and Letters
BS in PE.....	Bachelor of Science in Petroleum Engineering
BS in PE.....	Bachelor of Science in Physical Education
BS in P Ed...	Bachelor of Science in Physical Education
BS in Pet.....	Bachelor of Science in Petroleum
BS in Pet Engin...	Bachelor of Science in Petroleum Engineering
BS in Petr E...	Bachelor of Science in Petroleum Engineering
BS in Ph.....	Bachelor of Science in Pharmacy
BS in Phar...	Bachelor of Science in Pharmacy
BS in PHN...	Bachelor of Science in Public Health Nursing
BS in PHPM...	Bachelor of Science in Public Health and Preventative Medicine
BS in Phy Ed...	Bachelor of Science in Physical Education
BS in Phys Ed...	Bachelor of Science in Physical Education
BS in Phys Th...	Bachelor of Science in Physical Therapy
BS in Phys Ther...	Bachelor of Science in Physical Therapy
BS in Prac Arts...	Bachelor of Science in Practical Arts
BS in Pr Ge...	Bachelor of Science in Professional Geology
BS in Pr Met...	Bachelor of Science in Professional Meteorology
BS in PSM...	Bachelor of Science in Public School Music
BS in PT.....	Bachelor of Science in Physical Therapy
BS in RAH ..	Bachelor of Science in Range Animal Husbandry
BSinRE	Bachelor of Science in Religious Education (BJA)
BS in Rec	Bachelor of Science in Recreation
BS in Rec Lead...	Bachelor of Science in Recreation Leadership
BS in RT.....	Bachelor of Science in Radiological Technology
BS in Ry ME...	Bachelor of Science in Railway and Mechanical Engineering
BS in San E...	Bachelor of Science in Sanitary Engineering
BS in San Sci...	Bachelor of Science in Sanitary Science
BS in Sec Ed...	Bachelor of Science in Secondary Education
BS in Sec Sc...	Bachelor of Science in Secretarial Science
BS in Sec Sci...	Bachelor of Science in Secretarial Science
BS in Soc Serv...	Bachelor of Science in Social Service
BS in Soc St...	Bachelor of Science in Social Studies
BS in Spec Flds...	Bachelor of Science in Special Fields
BS in SS.....	Bachelor of Science in Social Science
BS in S Sc...	Bachelor of Science in Social Science
BS in Stat....	Bachelor of Science in Statistics
BS in Struc E...	Bachelor of Science in Structural Engineering
BS in TE	Bachelor of Science in Textile Engineering
BS in Th	Bachelor of Science in Physical and Occupational Therapy
BS in Voc Ag...	Bachelor of Science in Vocational Agriculture
BS in Voc Ed...	Bachelor of Science in Vocational Education
BS in ZS	Bachelor of Science in Zoological Sciences
BSIP............	British Solomon Islands Protectorate (ADA)
BSIR	Bachelor of Science in Industrial Relations
BSIRA	British Scientific Instrument Research Association
BSIS	Broadway & Seymour [NASDAQ symbol] (SAG)
BSIS	Broadway & Seymour Inc. [NASDAQ symbol] (TTSB)
BSIT	Bachelor of Science in Industrial Technology
BSIT	Bipolar-Mode Static Induction Transistor (MCD)
BSIT	Building Supply Institute of Technology [Canada]
BSIU	British Society for International Understanding (BI)
BSJ	Bachelor of Science in Journalism
BSJ	Bairnsdale [Australia Airport symbol Obsolete] (OAG)
BSJ	Balanced Swivel Joint
BSJ	Ball and Socket Joint
BSJ	Bureau of Ships Journal [Obsolete Navy]
BSJA	British Show Jumping Association (DI)
BSJC	British Seafarers' Joint Council (DS)
BSJE	Bachelor of Science in Jewish Education (BJA)
BSJpn	Bear Stearns Companies, Inc. [Associated Press] (SAG)
BS Jr	Bachelor of Science in Journalism
BSJS	Bachelor of Science in Judaic Studies (BJA)
BSK	Backpack Survival Kit (MCD)
BSK	Back Shunt Keying
BSK	Banque Senegalo-Koweitienne [Senegal-Kuwait Bank]
BSK	Basket
BSK	Basket
BSK	Biskra [Algeria] [Airport symbol] (OAG)
bSK	Bovine Substance K
BSK	British Silbak Premier Mines [Vancouver Stock Exchange symbol]
BSK	Miami Air International, Inc. [ICAO designator] (FAAC)
BSKBL	Basketball (ABBR)
BSKC	Kwantlen College, Surrey, British Columbia [Library symbol National Library of Canada] (NLC)
BSKD	Basked (ABBR)
BSKG	Basking (ABBR)
BSKN	Buskin (ABBR)
BSKT	Basket (KSC)
bskt............	Basket (VRA)

BSKTBLL......	Basketball
BSKTY	Basketry (ABBR)
BSkyB	British Sky Broadcasting [Satellite-television consortium] (ECON)
BSL	Bachelor of Sacred Literature
BSL	Bachelor of Science in Languages
BSL	Bachelor of Science in Law
BSL	Bachelor of Science in Linguistics
BSL	Back Stage Left [A stage direction]
BSL	Barber Steamship Lines (MHDW)
BSL	Bar Resources Ltd. [Vancouver Stock Exchange symbol]
BSL	Baselined Software Library (MCD)
BSL	Basel/Mulhouse [Switzerland] [Airport symbol] (OAG)
BSL	Basic Switching-Surge Level (IAA)
BSL	Beam Shape Loss (IAA)
BSL	Behavioral Sciences Laboratory [University of Cincinnati] [Information service or system] (IID)
BSL	Benign Symmetric Lipomatosis [Medicine]
BSL	Bermuda Star Lines, Inc. (MHDW)
BSL	Best Straight Line [Mathematics]
BSL	Bile-Salt Limited Lipase [An enzyme]
BSL	Billet Split Lens
Bs/L	Bills of Lading (ODBW)
BSL	Biologic Safety Level
BSL	Biot-Savart Law [Physics]
BSL	BIT [Binary Digit] Serial Link
BSL	Black Star Line [Steamship] (MHDB)
BSL	Blood Sugar Level [Clinical chemistry]
BSL	Blue Sky Laws
BSL	Bohn's Standard Library [A publication]
bsl	Bookseller [MARC relator code] [Library of Congress] (LCCP)
BSL	Botanical Society, London
BSL	British Sign Language (DI)
BSL	BSL Airlines [Ukraine] [FAA designator] (FAAC)
BSL	Bucknall Steamship Lines Ltd. (ROG)
BSL	Building Service League [Later, SEA] (EA)
BSL	Bulk Semiconductor Limiter
BSLA	Bachelor of Science in Landscape Architecture
BSLA	Bible Study League of America [Defunct] (EA)
BSL Lab Rel...	Bachelor of Science in Labor Relations
BSL & W	Beaumont, Sour Lake & Western Railway Co.
BSL Arch	Bachelor of Science in Landscape Architecture
BSLF..........	Bulgarian Socialist Labor Federation [Defunct] (EA)
BSLHS	Shawinigan Lake Historical Society, British Columbia [Library symbol National Library of Canada] (NLC)
BSLM..........	Bachelor of Science in Landscape Management
BSLR	Bus Selector [Computer science]
BSLS..........	Bachelor of Science in Library Science
BSLS..........	Baseless (ABBR)
BSLS..........	Basic Skills Learning System (EDAC)
BSLSS........	Buddy Secondary Life Support System [Aerospace]
BSLY..........	Busily (ABBR)
BSM............	Austin, TX [Location identifier FAA] (FAAL)
BSM............	Bachelor of Sacred Music
BSM............	Bachelor of School Music
BSM............	Bachelor of Science in Medicine
BSM............	Bachelor of Science in Music
BSM............	Balsam Resources, Inc. [Vancouver Stock Exchange symbol]
BSM............	Basic Storage Module (MCD)
BSM............	Basic Stripping Method (DICI)
BSM............	Basic Subsystem Module
BSM............	Basic Sustainment Materiel [Army]
BSM............	Basic System Memory [Computer science] (BUR)
BSM............	Battery Sergeant-Major
BSM............	Battery Shop Maintenance [NASA] (KSC)
BSM............	Bilingual Syntax Measure [English and Spanish test]
BSM............	Bistable Multivibrator
BSM............	Blue Star Mothers of America (EA)
BSM............	Body Side Molding
BSM............	Booster Separation Motors [NASA] (NASA)
BSM............	Bottom SONAR Marker
BSM............	Braked Servomotor
BSM............	British School of Motoring (DI)
BSM............	British Society for Mycopathology (DBA)
BSM............	British Supply Mission [World War II]
BSM............	Bronze Star Medal [Military decoration]
BSM............	San Miguel Island [California] [Seismograph station code, US Geological Survey] (SEIS)
BSMA..........	Bram Stoker Memorial Association (EA)
BSMA..........	British Secondary Metals Association (DBA)
BSMA..........	British Skate Makers' Association (BI)
BSMA..........	Building Societies Members Association [British] (DBA)
bsman	Businessman
BSMarEng.....	Bachelor of Science in Marine Engineering (NADA)
BSMAS........	Bond Strength Model of Active Sites
BSMC..........	Bachelor of Science in Mathematics and Chemistry
BSMC..........	Black Silent Majority Committee of the USA (EA)
BSMC..........	Bronchial Smooth Muscle Cell [Medicine] (DMAA)
BSMCP........	Blue Shield Medical Care Plans [Later, BSA] [An association]
BSMD	Bulk Store Memory Device (MCD)
BSMDH	British Society for Medical and Dental Hypnosis (DBA)
BSME..........	Bachelor of Science in Mechanical Engineering
BSME..........	Bachelor of Science in Mining Engineering
BSME..........	Bachelor of Science in Music Education
BSME..........	Battalion Supply and Maintenance Equipment [Military]
BSMed	Bachelor of Science in Medicine (NADA)

BSM Ed.......	Bachelor of Science in Music Education
BSMedRec...	Bachelor of Science in Medical Records (NADA)
BSMedRecLib...	Bachelor of Science in Medical Records Libarianship (NADA)
BS Med T....	Bachelor of Science in Medical Technology
BS Med Tech...	Bachelor of Science in Medical Technology
BS (ME Elect)...	Bachelor of Science with Mechanical Engineering Electives
BSMER........	Besmear (ABBR)
BSMet........	Bachelor of Science in Metallurgy (NADA)
BS Met........	Bachelor of Science in Meteorology
BS Met E....	Bachelor of Science in Metallurgical Engineering
BS Met Eng...	Bachelor of Science in Metallurgical Engineering
BSMF.........	Bata Shoe Museum Foundation (AC)
BSMF.........	BIT [Binary Digit] Sync Matched Filter [Computer science]
BS Mg E.....	Bachelor of Science in Mining Engineering
BSMGP......	British Society of Master Glass Painters (BI)
BSMgtSci...	Bachelor of Science in Management Science (NADA)
BS Min.......	Bachelor of Science in Mineralogy
BSMIN........	Bachelor of Science in Mining (NADA)
BS Min E....	Bachelor of Science in Mining Engineering
BSMinEng...	Bachelor of Science in Mining Engineering (NADA)
BSmith........	Big Smith Brands, Inc. [Associated Press] (SAG)
BSMITH.......	Blacksmith
BSMITH.......	Blacksmith
BSMMA.......	British Sugar Machinery Manufacturers Association (PDAA)
BS Mng E....	Bachelor of Science in Mining Engineering
BSMNT.......	Basement
BSMO.........	Base Supply Management Office [Air Force] (AFM)
BSMP.........	Brussels Sprouts Marketing Program (EA)
B/SMPL.......	BITs [Binary Digits] per Sample (NASA)
BSMR.........	Besmear (ABBR)
BSMRCH......	Besmirch (ABBR)
BSMRD........	Besmeared (ABBR)
BSMRG........	Besmearing (ABBR)
BS MRK.......	Bear Stearns Companies, Inc. [Associated Press] (SAG)
BSMS.........	Bus Service Management System [FTA] (TAG)
BSMSP........	Bernoulli Society for Mathematical Statistics and Probability [Voorburg, Netherlands] (EA)
BSMT.........	Bachelor of Science in Medical Technology
BSMT.........	Basement (MSA)
BSMT.........	Basement
BSMT.........	Board of Schools of Medical Technology [Later, NAACLS] (EA)
BSMT.........	British Society for Music Therapy
BSMT.........	Filene's Basement [NASDAQ symbol] (TTSB)
BSMT.........	Filene's Basement Corp. [NASDAQ symbol] (SPSG)
BS/MTAR.....	Battlefield Surveillance/Moving Target Acquisition Plan (MCD)
BS Mt E.......	Bachelor of Science in Metallurgical Engineering
BS Mu........	Bachelor of Sacred Music
BS Mus.......	Bachelor of Sacred Music
BS Mus.......	Bachelor of School Music
BS Mus.......	Bachelor of Science in Music
BS Mus Ed...	Bachelor of Science in Music Education
BSMV.........	Barley Stripe Mosaic Virus
BSMV.........	Bistable Multivibrator (MUGU)
BSN............	Bachelor of Science in Nursing
BSN............	Back-end Storage Network [Computer science] (EECA)
BSN............	Backward Sequence Number [Telecommunications] (TEL)
BSN............	Barium Sodium Niobate [Crystal]
BSN............	Basin [Board on Geographic Names]
BSN............	Basin Petroleum Resources Ltd. [Vancouver Stock Exchange symbol]
Bsn............	Bassoon [Music]
BSN............	Bibliotheque Scientifique Nationale [National Science Library] [Canada]
BSN............	Bisegmental Neuron [Neurology]
BSN............	Bison (ABBR)
BSN............	Bossangoa [Central African Republic] [Airport symbol] (AD)
BSN............	Boston Technology [NYSE symbol] (SAG)
BSN............	Bowel Sounds Normal [Medicine]
BSN............	Brine Shrimp Nauplii [Ichthyology]
BSN............	British Standard Number
BSN............	Broadband Switching Network [Telecommunications]
BSN............	Business Services on the Net
BSN............	Connectair Charters Ltd. [Canada ICAO designator] (FAAC)
BSN............	Novotech Services Ltd., Sidney, British Columbia [Library symbol National Library of Canada] (NLC)
BSN............	San Nicolas Island [California] [Seismograph station code, US Geological Survey] (SEIS)
BSNA.........	Bachelor of Science in Nursing Administration
BSNA.........	Bowel Sounds Normal and Active [Medicine] (AAMN)
BSNA.........	Bureau of Salesmen's National Associations (EA)
BSNatHist....	Bachelor of Science in Natural History (NADA)
BSNC.........	Bristol Steam Navigation Co. (MHDB)
BSNCOC......	Battle Staff Noncommissioned Officer Course [Army] (INF)
BSNDT........	British Society for Non-Destructive Testing (MCD)
BSNE.........	Bachelor of Science in Nursing Education
BSN Ed.......	Bachelor of Science in Nursing Education
BSNIT........	Bachelor of Science in Nautical Industrial Technology (NADA)
BSNk.........	Bear Stearns Companies, Inc. [Associated Press] (SAG)
BSNM.........	British Society of Nutritional Medicines
BSNO.........	Brake Specific Oxides of Nitrogen [Exhaust emissions] [Automotive engineering]
BSNOX........	Brake Specific Oxides of Nitrogen [Automotive engineering]
BSNS..........	Business (ABBR)
BSNSLK.......	Businesslike (ABBR)
BSNSMN......	Businessman (ABBR)

BSNSW.......	Benevolent Society of New South Wales [Australia]
BSNSW.......	Bromeliad Society of New South Wales [Australia]
BSNSW.......	Buddhist Society of New South Wales [Australia]
BSNSWMEN..	Businesswomen (ABBR)
BSNSWMN..	Businesswoman (ABBR)
BS Nurs.......	Bachelor of Science in Nursing
BS Nurs Ed...	Bachelor of Science in Nursing Education
BSNX..........	Basin Exploration [NASDAQ symbol] (SAG)
BSNY..........	Bible Seminary in New York
B So............	Bachelor of Sociology
BSO............	Bachelor of the Science of Oratory
BSO............	Baluchi Students' Organization [Pakistan] (PD)
BSO............	[The] Bank of Southington [AMEX symbol] (SPSG)
BSO............	Bank of Southington [AMEX symbol] (TTSB)
BSO............	Bank Standing Order (DI)
BSO............	Basco [Philippines] [Airport symbol] (OAG)
BSO............	Base Salvage Officer (MCD)
BSO............	Base Signal Officer [Military] (IAA)
BSO............	Base Supply Officer [Navy]
BSO............	Basilian Salvatorian Fathers (TOCD)
bso............	Basisian Salvatorian Fathers (TOCD)
BSO............	Battalion Signal Officer (INF)
BSO............	Battle Simulation Officer (SAA)
BSO............	Beach Signal Office [Military] (IAA)
BSO............	Benzene-Soluble Organics [Pollutant]
BSO............	Bilateral Sagittal Osteotomy [Medicine] (MAE)
BSO............	Bilateral Salpingo-Oophorectomy [Gynecology]
BSO............	Bilateral Serous Otitis [Otorhinolaryngology] (DAVI)
BSO............	Biological Safety Officer [National Institutes of Health]
BSO............	Bismuth Silicon Oxide [LASER Crystal] (NITA)
BSO............	Black September Organization [Israel]
BSO............	Blue Stellar Object [Astronomy]
BSO............	Boating Service Officer
BSO............	Bomb Safety Officer [Navy]
BSO............	Boston Symphony Orchestra
BSO............	British School of Osteopathy
BSO............	British Statistics Office
BSO............	British Supply Office
BSO............	Broad System of Ordering (MCD)
BSO............	Business Statistics Office [Department of Trade and Industry] [Information service or system] (IID)
BSO............	Buthionine Sulfoximine [Biochemistry]
BSO............	Buy Support Objective (AFIT)
BSO............	National Security Organization [Royal Thai Government]
BSO............	RAF Benson, FTU [British] [FAA designator] (FAAC)
BSO............	Squamish Public Library, British Columbia [Library symbol National Library of Canada] (NLC)
BSOAL........	Bank-Share Owners Advisory League [Inactive]
BSOC..........	Bell System Operating Co. [Also, BOC] [Post-divestiture division of American Telephone & Telegraph Co.]
BSOCA........	British Sociological Associates
BSocAdmin...	Bachelor of Social Administration
BSOccTher...	Bachelor of Science in Occupational Therapy (NADA)
BSocSc........	Bachelor of Social Sciences
BSocSci.......	Bachelor of Social Science (NADA)
BSocSt.........	Bachelor of Social Studies (ADA)
BSocStud.....	Bachelor of Social Studies (ADA)
BSocW.........	Bachelor of Social Work
BSocWk.......	Bachelor of Social Work
BSOEA.........	British Stationery and Office Equipment Association (BI)
BSOIW........	International Association of Bridge, Structural, and Ornamental Iron Workers
BSOM..........	Bilateral Serous Otitis Media [Otorhinolaryngology] (DAVI)
BSOM..........	British Society of Oral Medicine (DBA)
BSOM..........	Sointula Museum, British Columbia [Library symbol National Library of Canada] (NLC)
BSOO..........	Berlin State Opera Orchestra
BS (Opt).......	Bachelor of Science in Optometry
BSORM........	Sooke Region Museum, Sooke, British Columbia [Library symbol National Library of Canada] (NLC)
BS Orn Hort...	Bachelor of Science in Ornamental Horticulture
BSOS..........	Building Societies Ombudsman Scheme [British]
B So Sc.......	Bachelor of Social Science
B So Se.......	Bachelor of Social Service
BSOT..........	Bachelor of Science in Occupational Therapy
BSOT..........	Boston School of Occupational Therapy [Tufts University]
BSOTH........	Bilateral Salpingo-Oophorectomy with Hysterectomy [Medicine]
BSoUP........	British Society of Underwater Photographers (DBA)
B So W.......	Bachelor of Social Work
B Soz G.......	Bundessozialgericht [Federal Supreme Social Security Court] [German] (DLA)
BSP............	American Strategic Income Portfolio II [NYSE symbol] (SAG)
BSP............	Amer Strategic Inc. Portfolio II [NYSE symbol] (TTSB)
BSP............	Bachelor of Science in Pharmacy
B Sp............	Bachelor of Speech
BSP............	Bacterial Secondary Production [Water chemistry]
BSP............	Bahujan Samaj Party [Political party Italy] (ECON)
BSP............	Bahujan Samaj Party [India]
BSP............	Ballstop (MSA)
BSP............	Baltimore Steam Packet Co. [AAR code]
BSP............	Bank Settlement Plan (ADA)
BSP............	Baseline Schedule Plan (MCD)
BSP............	Battalion Supply Point [Army] (INF)
BSP............	Bayerische Staatspartei [Bavarian State Party] [Germany] (PPW)
BSP............	Bayes Sequential Procedure [Statistics]

BSP............ Beam Steering Processor [Military]
BSP............ Belgian Socialist Party
BSP............ Belgische Socialistische Partij [Belgian Socialist Party] (PPW)
BSP............ Bell System Practices
BSP............ Benchmark Soils Project [University of Hawaii, University of Puerto Rico]
BSP............ Bensbach [Papua New Guinea] [Airport symbol] (OAG)
BSP............ Billet Selection Program [Military] (DNAB)
BSP............ Bills Payable [Business term]
BSP............ Binary Space Partition [Computer science] (PCM)
BSP............ Bison Petroleum & Minerals [Vancouver Stock Exchange symbol]
BSP............ Blip-Scan RADAR (IAA)
BSP............ BMEWS [Ballistic Missile Early Warning System] Specification (AFM)
BSP............ Border Security Police [NATO] (NATG)
BSP............ Bosphorus Hava Yollari Turizm Ve Ticaret AS [Turkey] [ICAO designator] (FAAC)
BSP............ Brief Stop for Embarking or Debarking Personnel [Military] (NVT)
BSP............ Bright Source Protection [Optics]
BSP............ British Socialist Party
BSP............ British Society for Parasitology (EAIO)
BSP............ [The] British Society for Phenomenology
BSP............ British Society of Perfumers (DBA)
BSP............ British Society of Periodontology
BSP............ British Standard Pipe Thread
BSP............ Broad Street Pneumonia [Center for Disease Control]
BSP............ Bromosulfophthalein [Clinical chemistry]
BSp............ Bronchospasm [Medicine]
BSP............ Building Services Programs [Amazon Computers] [Software package] (NCC)
BSP............ Bulgarian Socialist Party [Political party] (EY)
BSP............ Burroughs Scientific Processor [Computer science] (BUR)
BSP............ Business Strategy Panel [Military]
BSP............ Business System Planning
BSP............ Byte Stream Protocol [Telecommunications] (OSI)
BSPA .... Bachelor of Science in Public Administration
BSPA .... Black Students Psychological Association
BSPA .... British Speedway Promoters Association (BI)
BSPA .... Brushmakers of Scotland Protection Association [A union]
BSPA .... Sparwood Public Library, British Columbia [Library symbol National Library of Canada] (NLC)
BSPB .... British Society of Plant Breeders (DBA)
BSPE.......... Bachelor of Science in Physical Education
B SPEC .... Development Specification (AAGC)
BSpecEd ..... Bachelor of Special Education
BSpEd......... Bachelor of Special Education
BSpeechTherapy... Bachelor of Speech Therapy
BS (Per & Ind Rel)... Bachelor of Science in Personnel and Industrial Relations
BSPer&PubRel... Bachelor of Science in Personnel and Public Relations (NADA)
BSPet.......... Bachelor of Science in Petroleum (NADA)
BSPetEng.... Bachelor of Science in Petroleum Engineering (NADA)
BSPGR .... British Society for Plant Growth Regulation (EAIO)
BS Ph .... Bachelor of Science in Pharmacy
BSPH .... Bachelor of Science in Public Health
BS Phar ...... Bachelor of Science in Pharmacy
BSPharm .... Bachelor of Science in Pharmacy
BSPHN........ Bachelor of Science in Public Health Nursing
BS Ph Th .... Bachelor of Science in Physical Therapy
BS Phys...... Bachelor of Science in Physics
BSPhysEd .... Bachelor of Science in Physical Education (NADA)
BSPhysEdu... Bachelor of Science in Physical Education (NADA)
BSPhysTher... Bachelor of Science in Physical Therapy (NADA)
BSPI............ Birth Support Providers, International [Affiliated with National Association of Childbirth Assistants (NACA)] (PAZ)
BSPL.......... Behavioral Science Programming Language [Computer science]
BS/PL.......... Bile Salts/Phospholipid [Ratio]
B-spline ...... Basic Spline (DOM)
BSPM.......... Battlefield Systems Project Management
BSPM.......... Body Surface Potential Mapping [Dermatology] (DAVI)
BSPMA .... British Sewage Plant Manufacturers Association (PDAA)
BSPMC .... Brake System Parts Manufacturers Council (EA)
BSPO .... BMEWS [Ballistic Missile Early Warning System] System Program Office (AFM)
BSPOGA....... British Society of Psychosomatic Obstetrics and Gynecology and Andrology (DBA)
BSPP .... British Society for Plant Pathology
BSPP .... Burma Socialist Programme Party [Political party] (PPW)
BSpPS .... British Spotted Pony Society (DBA)
BSPr .... Bethlehem Steel $5 cm Cv Pfd [NYSE symbol] (TTSB)
BSPRA .... Builder's and Sponsor's Profit and Risk Allowance [Department of Housing and Urban Development] (GFGA)
BSPrB .... Bethlehem Steel $2.50 cm Cv Pfd [NYSE symbol] (TTSB)
BSPS .... British Show Pony Society (DBA)
BSPS .... British Society for the Philosophy of Science
BSPSM .... Saanich Pioneer Society Museum, Saanichton, British Columbia [Library symbol National Library of Canada] (NLC)
BSPT.......... Bachelor of Science in Physical Therapy
BSPT.......... Bell Sports [NASDAQ symbol] (TTSB)
BSPT.......... Bell Sports Corp. [NASDAQ symbol] (SAG)
BSpThy .... Bachelor of Speech Therapy (ADA)
BSPUP .... Beam Steering Programmer Microprocessor [Military]
BSPW .... Bare Silver-Plated Wire
BSQ .... Bachelor Sergeant Quarters [Air Force]
BSQ .... Bachelor Staff Quarters [Military] (DNAB)
BSQ .... Bach Society of Queensland [Australia]
BSQ .... Basque (ABBR)

BSQ .... Behavior Style Questionnaire [Medicine] (DMAA)
BSQ .... Bisbee [Arizona] [Airport symbol] (OAG)
BSQ .... Buddhist Society of Queensland [Australia]
BSQ .... Myrtle Beach, SC [Location identifier FAA] (FAAL)
BSQI .... Basic Schedule of Quantified Items (MHDI)
BSR .... Bachelor of Science in Recreation
BSR .... Bachelor of Science in Rehabilitation (NADA)
BSR .... Backspace Recorder
BSR .... Back Stage Right [A stage direction]
BSR .... Back Surface Reflectance [Photovoltaic energy systems]
BSR .... Bacterial Sulfate Reduction
BSR .... Ballistic Simulated Round (MCD)
BSR .... Balloon Supported Rocket
BSR .... Basair AB [Sweden ICAO designator] (FAAC)
BSR .... Basal [or Baseline] Skin Resistance [Medicine]
BSR .... Basic System Release (MCD)
BSR .... Basra [Iraq] [Airport symbol] (AD)
BSR .... Battlefield Surveillance RADAR (MCD)
BSR .... Battle Short Relay
BSR .... Best Speed Rating [of a horse]
BSR .... Better Sound Reproduction (IAA)
BSR .... Big Sur, CA [Location identifier FAA] (FAAL)
BSR .... BITE [Built-In Test Equipment] Status Register (MCD)
BSR .... BIT [Binary Digit] Slippage Rate [Computer science]
BSR .... Blip-Scan Ratio
BSR .... Blood Sedimentation Rate [Medicine]
BSR .... Blue Streak Request [Military]
BSR .... Board of Standards Review [American National Standards Institute]
BSR .... Boilermaker, Ship Repair [Navy rating]
BSR .... Bottom Simulating Reflector [Oceanography]
BSR .... Brain Stimulation Reinforcement [Electrophysiology]
BSR .... Branch to Subroutine [Computer science]
BSR .... Bresea Resources Ltd. [Vancouver Stock Exchange symbol]
BSR .... Bristol Simplified Reheat [Aircraft] (NATG)
BSR .... British School at Rome [Italy]
BSR .... British Society for Rheology (DBA)
BSR .... British Society for Rheumatology (EAIO)
BSR .... British [formerly, Birmingham] Sound Reproduction [Initialism is now name of company and brand name of its products]
BSR .... British Standard Red [Ink] (DGA)
BSR .... Brown Stem Rot [Plant pathology]
BSR .... Buffered Send/Receive
BSR .... Building Space Requirement (DAC)
BSR .... Bulk Shielding Reactor
BSR .... Bump, Squeak, and Rattle [Automotive characterization]
BSR .... Bureau of Safety Regulations (SAA)
BSR .... Business for Social Responsibility
BSR .... Butane Secondary Refrigerant
BSRA .... British Shipbuilding Research Association
BSRA .... British Ship Research Association [Research center] (IRC)
BSRA .... British Society for Research on Ageing (EAIO)
BSRh .... British Sound Recording Association (BI)
BSRAE .... British Society for Research in Agricultural Engineering (BI)
BSRAP .... Beginning Standard Range Approach [Aviation] (FAAC)
BSRC .... Biological Sciences Research Center [University of North Carolina at Chapel Hill] [Research center] (RCD)
BSRC .... British Ship Research Council
BSRC .... British Shoe Repair Council (DBA)
BSRC .... British Sporting Rifle Club (PDAA)
BSRD .... British Society of Restorative Dentistry
BS Rec .... Bachelor of Science in Recreation
BS Ret .... Bachelor of Science in Retailing
BSRF .... Basic System Reference Frequency (ACRL)
BSRF .... Borderland Sciences Research Foundation (EA)
BSRFS .... Bell System Reference Frequency Standard [Telecommunications] (TEL)
BSRI .... Bem Sex-Role Inventory [Research test] [Psychology]
BSRIA .... Building Services Research and Information Association [Information service or system] (IID)
BSRK .... Berserk (ABBR)
BSRL .... Boeing Scientific Research Laboratories
BSRM .... Boeing Small Research Module [NASA]
BSRM .... Booster Solid Rocket Motor [NASA] (NASA)
BSRN .... Baseline Surface Radiation Network [Marine science] (OSRA)
BSRN .... Baseline Surface Radiation Network [World Meteorlogical Organization] (USDC)
BSRO .... Begin Standard Refuel Orbit [Aviation] (FAAC)
BSRO .... Beitraege zur Statistik der Republik Oesterreich [Austria]
BSRS .... Bell System Repair Specification [Telecommunications] (TEL)
BSRT .... Bachelor of Science in Radiological Technology
BSS............. Bachelor of Sanitary Science
BSS............. Bachelor of Science in Science
BSS............. Bachelor of Secretarial Science
BSS............. Bachelor of Social Science
BSS............. Bachelor of Special Studies
BSS............. Backup System Services [NASA] (NASA)
BSS............. Backup System Services
BSS............. Balanced Salt Solution [Cell incubation medium]
BSS............. Balsas [Brazil] [Airport symbol] (AD)
BSS............. Bangladesh Sanwad Sanstha [News agency]
BSS............. Baroness (ROG)
BSS............. Base Service Store [Air Force] (AFIT)
BSS............. Basic Shaft System
BSS............. Basic Synchronized Subset [Telecommunications] (OSI)
BSS............. Beam Steering System

BSS............. Before Stephen Sondheim [*A reference to simpler, less sophisticated, and more sentimental musicals*]
BSS............. Behavioral and Social Sciences
BSS............. Beitraege zur Semitischen Sprachwissenschaft [*A publication*] (BJA)
BSS............. Bell's Science Series [*A publication*]
BSS............. Bernard Shaw Society (EA)
BSS............. Bernard-Soulier Syndrome [*Hematology*]
BSS............. Bessie Smith Society (EA)
BSS............. Bibliographical Services Section [*of a library*]
BSS............. Bibliographic Search Services [*University of Minnesota*] (OLDSS)
BSS............. Bibliography of Soil Science [*A publication*]
BSS............. Bistatic SONAR (CAAL)
BSS............. Bisymmetric Spiral [*Astronomy*]
BSS............. BIT [*Binary Digit*] Storage and Sense [*Computer science*] (IAA)
BSS............. Black Silk Suture [*Medicine*]
BSS............. Board of Secondary Studies
BSS............. BOMARC [*Boeing-Michigan Aeronautical Research Center*] Squadron Simulator
BSS............. Bond and Share Society (EA)
BSS............. Brain Stimulation Reinforcement [*Neurology*] (DAVI)
BSS............. Bram Stoker Society (EA)
BSS............. British Sailors Society (BI)
BSS............. British Standard Size [*Typography*] (DGA)
BSS............. British Standard Specification
BSS............. British Standards Society (DBA)
BSS............. Broadband Switching System [*Telecommunications*] (ACRL)
BSS............. Broadcasting Support Services (AIE)
BSS............. Broadcast Satellite Service
BSS............. Bronze Service Star [*Military decoration*] (AFM)
BSS............. Buffered Saline Solution (AAMN)
BSS............. Building Science Series [*National Institute of Standards and Technology*]
BSS............. Bulk Storage System
BSS............. Bureau of School Systems [*Office of Education*]
BSS............. Bureau of State Services [*of Public Health Service*]
BSS............. Bureau of Student Support [*Office of Education*]
BSS............. Business Start-Up Scheme [*British*]
BSS............. Business Systems Services (MCD)
BSS............. School District 88, Skeena-Terrace, British Columbia [*Library symbol National Library of Canada*] (NLC)
BSSA.......... Bachelor of Science in Secretarial Administration
BSSA.......... Beef Shorthorn Society of Australia
BSSA.......... British Shops and Stores Association (DBA)
BSSA.......... British Sjogren's Syndrome Association (DBA)
BSSanE....... Bachelor of Science in Sanitary Engineering
BSSAR........ Babcock & Wilcox Standard Safety Analysis Report [*Nuclear energy*] (NRCH)
BSSBG........ British Society of Social and Behavioural Gerontology
BS Sc.......... Bachelor of Sanitary Science
BS Sc.......... Bachelor of Social Science
BSSC.......... Battle Staff Support Center [*Air Force*]
BSSC.......... BIT [*Binary Digit*] Synchronizer / Signal Conditioner (PDAA)
BSSC.......... British Shooting Sports Council (DBA)
BS Sc E....... Bachelor of Science in Science Engineering
BSScEng...... Bachelor of Science in Science Engineering (NADA)
BSSE.......... Bachelor of Science in Secondary Education
BSSE.......... Basis Set Superposition Error [*Physical chemistry*]
BSSE.......... Beliefs about Science and Science Education Scale (EDAC)
BSSEA........ British Special Ship Equipment Association (PDAA)
BS Sec........ Bachelor of Science in Secondary Education
BS (Sec Adm)... Bachelor of Science in Secretarial Administration
BS Sec Ed ... Bachelor of Science in Secondary Education
BSSecSci..... Bachelor of Science in Secretarial Science (NADA)
BSSF.......... British Students Sports Federation (DBA)
BSSG.......... British Society of Scientific Glassblowers
BSSG.......... Sitogluside [*Organic chemistry*] (DAVI)
BSSH.......... British Society of Sports History (DBA)
BSSH.......... British Society of Surgery of the Hand (DBA)
BSSI........... Basic School Skills Inventory [*Education*]
BSSI........... Biosafety Systems [*NASDAQ symbol*] (SAG)
BSSI-D........ Basic School Skills Inventory - Diagnostic
BSSI-S........ Basic School Skills Inventory - Screen
BSSJ.......... British Society of Stamp Journalists (BI)
BSSM.......... British Society for Strain Measurement
BSSMA .... Business Systems and Security Marketing Association (EA)
BSSMS .... British Society for the Study of Mental Subnormality
BSSO .... British Society for the Study of Orthodontics (BI)
BSSocServ... Bachelor of Science in Social Service (NADA)
BSSocSt...... Bachelor of Science in Social Studies (NADA)
BS (Soc Wk)... Bachelor of Science in Social Work
BS Sp .... Bachelor of Science in Speech
BSSP .... Benevolent Society of St. Patrick
BSSP .... Broadband Solid-State Preamplifier
BSSPD .... British Society for the Study of Prosthetic Dentistry
BSSR .... Beam Steering Shift Register [*Military*]
BSSR .... Bureau of Social Sciences Research, Inc. (MCD)
BSSR .... Byelorussian Soviet Socialist Republic
BSSRS .... British Society for Social Responsibility in Science
BSSRS .... Bureau of Safety and Supply Radio Services
BSSS .... Bachelor of Science in Secretarial Studies
BSSS .... Bachelor of Science in Social Science
BSSS .... Bathymetric Swath Survey System [*National Ocean Survey*] (MSC)
BSSS .... British Society of Soil Science
BSSSA .... British Surgical Support Suppliers Association (BI)
BSSSc .... Bachelor of Science in Social Science (NADA)

BSSSC .... Behavioral and Social Sciences Survey Committee (EA)
BSS Sci ...... Bachelor of Science in Secretarial Science
BSST.......... Baby Superstore [*NASDAQ symbol*] (TTSB)
BSST.......... Baby Superstore, Inc. [*NASDAQ symbol*] (SAG)
BSStrucEng.. Bachelor of Science in Structural Engineering (NADA)
BSSU .... Bench Stock Support Unit [*Military*]
BSSUI .... Benefit Service Series, Unemployment Insurance [*Department of Labor*] [*A publication A publication*] (DLA)
BSSV .... Blueberry Shoestring Virus [*Plant pathology*]
BSSW .... Bare Stainless-Steel Wire
BST............. Bachelor of Sacred Theology
BST............. Bachelor of Science in Teaching
B St .... Bachelor of Statistics
BST............. Baker-Schmidt Telescope (PDAA)
BST............. Ballets de San Juan [*Puerto Rico*]
BST............. Banque Senegalo-Tunisienne (EY)
bst .... Basalt (VRA)
BST............. Base Shop Tester
BST............. Basic Skills Trainer [*Army*] (INF)
BST............. Basic Storage Unit [*Computer science*] (IAA)
BST............. Baste (ABBR)
BST............. Battle Staff Team
BST............. Beam Steering Transducer
BST............. Beam-Switching Tube
BST............. Belfast, ME [*Location identifier FAA*] (FAAL)
BST............. Beobachtungsstelle [*Observation post*] [*German military - World War II*]
BST............. Bereitschaftsstellung [*Line of support*] [*German military - World War II*]
BST............. Bering Standard Time (HGAA)
BST............. Best (ROG)
BST............. Best Resources, Inc. [*Vancouver Stock Exchange symbol*]
BST............. Beth Simchat Torah (BJA)
B/ST .... Bill of Sight [*Customs*]
B/St............ Bill of Sight (ODBW)
BST............. Binary Search Tree (IAA)
BST............. Biochemical Systems Theory
BST............. Biocontrol Science and Technology [*A publication*]
BST............. Blast Saturation Temperature (PDAA)
BST............. Bleed Storage Tank [*Nuclear energy*] (NRCH)
BST............. Blood Serological Test [*Medicine*]
BST............. Blowdown Suppression Tank [*Nuclear energy*] (NRCH)
BST............. Bonded Spoon Type (DNAB)
BST............. Booster (MUGU)
BST............. Booster Test Department [*NASA*] (KSC)
BST............. Boresight
BST............. Boresight Tower (MUGU)
BST............. Boron Storage Tank [*Nuclear energy*] (NRCH)
BST............. Boston State College Library, Boston, MA [*OCLC symbol*] (OCLC)
BST............. Boundary-Scan Test [*John Fluke Manufacturing Co., Inc.*]
BST............. Bovine Somatotropin [*Endocrinology*]
BST............. Brief Stimulus Therapy [*Psychology*]
BST............. Brief Systems Test [*NASA*] (KSC)
BST............. British School Technology (NITA)
BST............. British Standard Time (NATG)
BST............. British Steel ADS [*NYSE symbol*] (TTSB)
BST............. British Steel Ltd. [*NYSE symbol*] (CTT)
BST............. British Summer Time
BST............. Bulk Supply Tariff (MHDB)
BST............. Burst (IAA)
BST............. Business Systems Technology, Inc.
BST............. Societa' Besit SRL [*Italy*] [*FAA designator*] (FAAC)
BST............. Stamp Behaviour Study Technique [*Psychology*]
BSTA.......... Boston Star Trek Association (EA)
BSTA.......... British Surgical Trades Association (BI)
BST & IE ..... Bachelor of Science in Trade and Industrial Engineering
BSTANY ...... Boot and Shoe Travelers Association of New York (EA)
BSTANY ...... Boot and Shoe Travelers Association of New York (SRA)
BSTAR........ Battlefield Surveillance and Target Acquisition RADAR (MCD)
BSTB.......... Blackie's Science Text Books [*A publication*]
BSTBA........ Benzoyl(sulfamoyl)(thenyloxy)benzoic Acid [*Biochemistry*]
BstBeer........ Boston Beer Co. [*Associated Press*] (SAG)
BSTC.......... Ball State Teachers College [*Later, Ball State University*] [*Indiana*]
BSTC.......... BioSpecifics Technologies [*NASDAQ symbol*] (TTSB)
BSTC.......... BioSpecifics Technologies, Inc. [*NASDAQ symbol*] (SAG)
BSTD .... Bastard [*Size or material*]
BSTD .... Basted (ABBR)
B St E .... Bachelor of Structural Engineering
BSTech........ Bachelor of Science in Technology
B St Eng ..... Bachelor of Structural Engineering
BSText........ Bachelor of Science in Textiles (NADA)
BSTF.......... Base Shop Test Facility [*Military*]
BSTF.......... British Science and Technology in Education (AIE)
BSTF.......... British Student Tuberculosis Foundation (BI)
BSTFA......... Bis(trimethylsilyl)trifluoroacetamide [*Organic chemistry*]
BSTG .... Basting (ABBR)
BSTHM .... Stewart Historical Museum, British Columbia [*Library symbol National Library of Canada*] (NLC)
BSTING .... Ballistic Sight Technology Improving Night/(Day) Gunnery [*Project*] [*Military*]
BSTL.......... Bestial (ABBR)
BSTL.......... Bistaple
BSTL.......... Bustle (ABBR)
BSTLD .... Bustled (ABBR)
BSTLG .... Bustling (ABBR)

BSTLT.........	Bestiality (ABBR)
BSTLY.........	Bestially (ABBR)
BSTM.........	Biaxial Shock Test Machine [CERL] [Army] (RDA)
BsTn.........	Base Ten Systems [Associated Press] (SAG)
BSTN	Boston Technology [NASDAQ symbol] (SAG)
BSTO	Bestow (ABBR)
BSTP	British Society of Toxicological Pathologists (DBA)
BSTR	Batch, Stirred-Tank Reactor (PDAA)
BSTR	Bistro
BSTR	Booster [Military] (AFM)
BS Trans.....	Bachelor of Science in Transportation
BSTRD........	Bastard (ABBR)
BSTRDY......	Bastardly (ABBR)
BSTRDZ......	Bastardize (ABBR)
BSTRDZD....	Bastardized (ABBR)
BSTRDZG....	Bastardizing (ABBR)
BSTRK	Bomb Service Truck (MUGU)
BSTRU	Boisterous (ABBR)
BSTRUS.......	Boisterous (ABBR)
BSTRUSNS..	Boisterousness (ABBR)
BSTRUSY....	Boisterously (ABBR)
BSTS...........	Base Shop Test Station [Military]
BSTS...........	Benefit Systems Testing Section [Social Security Administration]
BSTS...........	Boost Surveillance and Tracking System [Satellite] [Military]
BSTSA	British Surface Treatment Suppliers Association (DBA)
BSTW..........	Bestow (ABBR)
BSTW..........	Bestway Inc. [NASDAQ symbol] (TTSB)
BSTWB	Bestowable (ABBR)
BSTWD	Bestowed (ABBR)
BSTWG	Bestowing (ABBR)
BSTWL	Bestowal (ABBR)
BSTWT	Bestowment (ABBR)
BSU	Baptist Student Union (IIA)
BSU	Bartholin's Skene's, and Urethral [Glands] [Gynecology] (DAVI)
BSU	Basankusu [Zaire] [Airport symbol] (OAG)
BSU	Baseband Separation Unit (MCD)
BSU	Base Service Unit [Navy]
BSU	Basic Selection Unit [Computer science] (IAA)
BSU	Basic Sounding Unit [Telecommunications] (TEL)
BSU	Basic Structural Unit
BSU	Beach Support Unit [Military] (DNAB)
BSU	Beam Steering Unit (DA)
BSU	Bicycle Study Unit [American Topical Association] (EA)
BSU	Bilevel Stimulus Unit
BSU	Bis(trimethylsilyl)urea [Organic chemistry]
BSU	Black Students Union
BSU	Blood Supply Unit [Military British]
BSU	Boat Support Unit (CINC)
BSU	Book Stacks Unlimited [Networked bookseller]
BSU	British Seafarers' Union
BSU	Broadband Switching Unit [Telecommunications]
BSU	Business Service Unit [Telecommunications] (TEL)
BSUAG........	Research Station, Agriculture Canada [Station de Recherches, Agriculture Canada] Summerland, British Columbia [Library symbol National Library of Canada] (NLC)
BSUB	Ball and Socket Upper Bearing
BSUCNY......	British Schools and Universities Club of New York (EA)
BSUF	British Schools and Universities Foundation (EA)
BSUG..........	Bedford Systems Users Group (EA)
BSUI	Benefit Service Series, Unemployment Insurance [Department of Labor] [A publication]
BSUM	Summerland Museum, British Columbia [Library symbol National Library of Canada] (NLC)
B Sup Airfld...	Base Supply Airfield [British and Canadian]
B Sur	Bachelor of Surgery
BSUR	Surrey Public Library, British Columbia [Library symbol National Library of Canada] (NLC)
BSURCM......	Surrey Centennial Museum, British Columbia [Library symbol National Library of Canada] (NLC)
BSURCW......	Canada West Gold Rush Museum, Surrey, British Columbia [Library symbol National Library of Canada] (NLC)
BSURE	Barking Sands Underwater Range Expansion [Naval Oceanographic Office] (MCD)
BSurv..........	Bachelor of Surveying
BSurvSc.......	Bachelor of Surveying Science
BSUS	Bolivarian Society of the United States (EA)
BSUT	Beam Steering Ultrasonic Transducer
BSUV	Bibliographical Society of the University of Virginia (EA)
BSV............	Backfire Suppressor Valve [Automotive engineering]
BSV............	Batten-Spielmyer-Vogt [Syndrome] [Medicine] (AAMN)
BSV............	Beach Support Vehicle [Navy] (CAAL)
BSV............	Binocular Single Vision [Ophthalmology]
BSV............	Black Sheep Ventures, Inc. [Vancouver Stock Exchange symbol]
BSV............	[A] Book of Scottish Verse [A publication]
BSV............	Boolean Simple Variable [Mathematics]
BSV............	Briggs, OH [Location identifier FAA] (FAAL)
BSV............	Bromeliad Society of Victoria [Australia]
BSVocEd......	Bachelor of Science in Vocational Education (NADA)
BS VPt........	Bear Stearns [Associated Press] (SAG)
BSW...........	Bachelor of Social Work
BSW...........	Bank Street Writer [A computer program manufactured by Bank Street and Intentional Educations, Inc.]
BSW...........	Bare Steel Wire
BSW...........	Barrel Switch (IAA)
BSW...........	Black Swan Gold Mines Ltd. [Vancouver Stock Exchange symbol]

BSW............	Boot and Shoe Workers' Union [Later, UFCWIU]
BSW............	Bottom Sediment and Water [in crude oil]
BSW............	British Standard Whitworth (MCD)
BSW............	Broadcast Services for Windows (PCM)
BSW............	Brown Stock Washer [Pulp and paper technology]
BSWA...........	Bonsai Society of Western Australia
BSWB	Boy Scouts World Bureau [Later, WSB]
BSWC	British Subject without Citizenship
BSWG	British Standard Wire Gauge
BSWM	Bureau of Soils and Water Management [Department of Agriculture]
BSWM	Bureau of Solid Waste Management [Environmental Protection Agency]
BSWU	Boot and Shoe Workers' Union [Later, UFCWIA] (IIA)
BSWX	Beeswax (ABBR)
BSX	Bassein [Myanmar] [Airport symbol] (OAG)
BSX	Boston Scientific [NYSE symbol] (TTSB)
BSX	Boston Scientific Corp. [NYSE symbol] (SPSG)
BSY	Big Sky Airline [ICAO designator] (FAAC)
BSY	Biscayne Bay, FL [Location identifier FAA] (FAAL)
BSY	British Sky Broadcasting Ltd. [NYSE symbol] (SAG)
BSY	British Sky Broadcsting Gp ADS [NYSE symbol] (TTSB)
BSY	British Standard Yellow [Ink] (DGA)
BSY	Busy
BSYBDY......	Busybody (ABBR)
BSYG..........	Busying (ABBR)
BSYM..........	Boy Savior Youth Movement [Defunct] (EA)
BSYn..........	Bear Stearns Companies, Inc. [Associated Press] (SAG)
BSYS..........	BISYS Group [NASDAQ symbol] (TTSB)
BSYS..........	BISYS Group, Inc. [NASDAQ symbol] (SAG)
B Sy Th	Bachelor of Systematic Theology
BSZ	Ballistic Systems Zeus [Aerospace]
BSZ	Battlesight Zero (MCD)
BSZ	Block Store Zero [Computer science] (IAA)
BT	Air Martinique (Satair) [ICAO designator] (AD)
BT	American Association of Behavioral Therapists (EA)
BT	Babylonian Talmud (BJA)
BT	Babylonische Texte [A publication] (BJA)
BT	Bachelor of Teaching
BT	Bachelor of Technology
BT	Bachelor of Theatre
BT	Bachelor of Theology
BT	Bacillus thuringiensis [Also, Bt] [Bacteriology]
BT	Back Taxiing [Aviation] (FAAC)
BT	Back, Training [Parachute]
BT	Balanced, Total [Business term]
BT	Ballistic Trajectory (DNAB)
BT	Bankers Trust New York Corp. [NYSE symbol] (SPSG)
BT	Bankers Trust NY [NYSE symbol] (TTSB)
BT	Bank of Tonga
BT	Barge, Training (MSA)
BT	Baronet (EY)
BT	Barred Trunk [Telecommunications] (NITA)
BT	Base Target (MCD)
BT	Basic Technique [Parapsychology]
BT	Basic Trainer [Air Force]
BT	Basic Training [Military]
BT	Basse Tension [Low Tension] [French]
BT	Bateau Torpilleur [Torpedo Boat] [French]
BT	Bathtub (ABBR)
BT	Bathythermal Traces
BT	Bathythermograph [Oceanography]
BT	Battery Target [British and Canadian] [Military]
BT	BCNU [Carmustine] and Triazinate [Antineoplastic drug] (DAVI)
BT	Beam-Rider Tail Control
BT	Beam-Rider Terrier [Missile] (MCD)
BT	Bearing Technology
BT	Beat
BT	Bedtime
BT	Before Touching [Parapsychology]
BT	Beginning of Tape [Computer science] (IAA)
BT	Begin Transmission, Break
BT	Behavior Therapy [Psychology]
BT	Bellini-Tose System
Bt...............	Benedict's United States District Court Reports [A publication] (DLA)
BT	Benefit (ADA)
BT	Bent (MSA)
BT	Benzothiophene [Organic chemistry]
BT	Benzoyltyrosine [Biochemistry]
BT	Berth Terms [Shipping]
BT	Bhutan [ANSI two-letter standard code] (CNC)
bt...............	Bhutan [MARC country of publication code Library of Congress] (LCCP)
BT	Bias Temperature
BT	Biblical Theologians (EA)
BT	Biceps Tendon [Anatomy]
BT	Bill Tomorrow [Business term]
BT	Biologist's Toolbox
BT	Bioprocessing Technology [Technical Insights, Inc.] [Information service or system] (CRD)
BT	Biotechnology
BT	Biotechnology Thrust
BT	Bishop's Transcript [British] (ROG)
BT	BIT [Binary Digit] (IAA)
BT	Bitemporal (ROG)
BT	Bituberous [Anatomy] (DAVI)

BT .... Blacky Test [*Psychology*] (DAVI)
BT .... Bladder Tremor [*Urology*] (DAVI)
BT .... Bladder Tumor [*Medicine*]
BT .... Blalock-Taussig [*Cardiology*]
BT .... Blanchi-Backlund Transformation [*Engineering*]
BT .... Blast Test
BT .... Bleaching Treatment [*Dentistry*]
BT .... Bleeding Time [*Clinical chemistry*]
BT .... Blind Toss
BT .... Block Template
BT .... Block Terminal [*Telecommunications*] (NITA)
BT .... Blood Transfusion [*Hematology*] (DAVI)
BT .... Blue Tetrazolium [*A dye*]
BT .... Blue-Tongue [*Medicine*] (DMAA)
BT .... Board of Trade [*Shipping*]
BT .... Boat (AABC)
BT .... Boat-Tail [*Bullet*] (DICI)
BT .... Body Temperature [*Medicine*]
BT .... Boilerman [*Navy rating*]
BT .... Boiling Transition [*Nuclear energy*] (NRCH)
BT .... Bolt (ABBR)
BT .... Bomber Transport [*Air Force*]
BT .... Borderline Tuberculoid [*Medicine*]
BT .... Bottle (MCD)
BT .... Bought
BT .... Boundary Trap
BT .... Bow Thruster [*of a ship*] (DS)
BT .... Bradley Table [*Army*] (INF)
BT .... Brain Tumor [*Medicine*]
BT .... Breakdown Truck [*British*]
BT .... Breakfast Time [*Early morning television program*] [*BBC*]
BT .... Breakthrough
BT .... Break Transmission (NVT)
BT .... Breast Tumor [*Medicine*]
BT .... Breath Test
BT .... Brevet [*Military*]
BT .... Brick and Tile (ADA)
BT .... Bridging Truck [*British*]
BT .... British Telecom [*or Telecommunications*] [*Common carrier*]
BT .... British Tissues, Ltd.
BT .... Broadcasting Station, Television [*ITU designation*]
BT .... Broader Term [*Cross-reference*] [*Indexing*]
BT .... Builder's Trials [*Shipbuilding*]
BT .... Built (ROG)
BT .... Buried Tape Armor [*Telecommunications*] (TEL)
BT .... Burnt (ROG)
BT .... Burnthrough (NVT)
BT .... Burn Time [*NASA*]
BT .... Burst Tolerance [*Telecommunications*] (ACRL)
BT .... Burst Trapping (MHDI)
BT .... Business Traveler Magazine [*National Association of Business Travel Agents*] [*A publication*]
BT .... Bus Tie [*Technical drawings*]
BT .... Busy Tone [*Telecommunications*] (TEL)
BT .... Byte [*Computer science*] (IAA)
BT .... Scottish Aviation Ltd. [*ICAO aircraft manufacturer identifier*] (ICAO)
BT .... Trail Public Library, British Columbia [*Library symbol National Library of Canada*] (NLC)
BT1 .... Boilerman, First Class [*Navy rating*]
BT2 .... Boilerman, Second Class [*Navy rating*]
BT3 .... Boilerman, Third Class [*Navy rating*]
BTA .... Balkan Turks of America [*Later, BTAA*] (EA)
BTA .... Ballistic Track Assignor (AAG)
BTA .... Basic Trading Area (ACRL)
BTA .... [*Rand McNally*] Basic Trading Areas
BTA .... Basic Travel Allowance
BTA .... Beam Transfer Area [*LASER technology*]
BTA .... Been to America [*Slang British*]
BTA .... Behavioral Task Analysis (MCD)
BTA .... Benzotriazole [*Organic chemistry*]
BTA .... Benzotriazole [*Lubricants*]
BTA .... Benzoyltrifluoroacetone [*Organic chemistry*]
BTA .... Bertoua [*Cameroon*] [*Airport symbol*] (OAG)
BTA .... Best Technical Approach [*Military*] (AABC)
BTA .... Best Times Available [*Television*]
BTA .... Better than Average
BTA .... Bicycle Transportation Action (EA)
BTA .... Big Thicket Association (EA)
BTA .... Billiards Trade Association [*British*] (BI)
BTA .... Black Theater Alliance (EA)
BTA .... Blood Transfusion Association (EA)
BTA .... Board of Tax Appeals
BTA .... Border Trade Alliance [*Mexico/US relations*] (CROSS)
BTA .... Boston Transportation Authority (BARN)
BTA .... Brith Trumpeldor of America (EA)
BTA .... British Theatre Association [*Defunct*]
BTA .... British Throwsters Association (DBA)
BTA .... British Tinnitus Association
BTA .... British Tourist Authority (EA)
BTA .... British Transport Advertising
BTA .... British Travel Association (BI)
BTA .... British Triathlon Association (DBA)
BTA .... British Troops, Austria [*World War II*]
BTA .... British Trout Association (DBA)
BTA .... British Tugowners Association (BI)

BTA .... Britt Airways, Inc. [*ICAO designator*] (FAAC)
B-TA .... Broadband Terminal Adapter [*Telecommunications*] (ACRL)
BTA .... Bruce Trail Association (EA)
BTA .... Bulgarian Telegraph Agency [*News agency*]
BTA .... Bulgarska Telegrafna Agentsiya [*Bulgarian News Agency*]
BTA .... Burlington, WA [*Location identifier FAA*] (FAAL)
BTA .... Business Technology Association [*Kansas City, MO*] [*An association*] (CDE)
BTA .... Business Travel Accident [*Insurance*]
BTA .... Business Trend Analysts, Inc. [*Commack, NY*] [*Information service or system*] (IID)
BTA .... Bute Resources [*Vancouver Stock Exchange symbol*]
BTA .... Butylated Hydroxyanisole [*Antioxidant*] (WGA)
BTA .... Totta & Acores Financing Ltd. [*NYSE symbol*] (SAG)
BTA .... United States Board of Tax Appeals Reports [*A publication*] (DLA)
BTAA .... Balkan Turks of America Association (EA)
BTAA .... Bulgarian Turkish Association of Australia
BTAC .... Branch-Target Address Cache [*Computer science*]
BTAC .... Burrows Trail Arts Council (AC)
BTAC .... Quality Loss Factor [*Manufacturing*]
BTACCH ...... Board of Tax Appeals Decisions (Commerce Clearing House) [*A publication*] (DLA)
BTAD .... Benzophenone Tetracarboxylic Acid Dianhydride (PDAA)
BTADC .... British Telecom Action for Disabled Customers (NITA)
BTAF .... British Tactical Air Force
BTAF .... British Tattoo Artists Federation (DBA)
BTAM .... Basic Tape Access Method [*Computer science*]
BTAM .... Basic Telecommunications Access Method [*IBM Corp.*] [*Computer science*]
BTAM .... Basic Teleprocessing Access Method
BTAM .... Basic Terminal Access Method [*Computer science*]
BTAM (P-H)... Board of Tax Appeals Memorandum Decisions (Prentice-Hall, Inc.) [*A publication*] (DLA)
BTAMS .... British Trans-Atlantic Air Mail Service
BT & RP ..... Bachelor of Town and Regional Planning (ADA)
BTAO .... Bureau of Technical Assistance Operations [*UN*]
BTAP .... Bond Trade Analysis Program [*IBM Corp.*]
BTAPH .... Board of Tax Appeals Decisions (Prentice-Hall, Inc.) [*A publication*] (DLA)
BTAS .... Band Training and Advisory Services Branch [*Canada, Indian and Inuit Affairs Program*] [*Canada*]
BTASA .... Bicycle Traders' Association of South Australia
BTAT .... Boating Trades Association of Texas (SRA)
BTB .... Bankers Tr6% Cap Sec [*AMEX symbol*] (TTSB)
BTB .... Bankers Trust New York Corp. [*AMEX symbol*] (SPSG)
BTB .... Basic Test Battery [*Navy*]
BTB .... Biblical Theology Bulletin [*A publication*] (BRI)
BTB .... Bituminous Treated Base (DAC)
BTB .... Blind Transmission Broadcast [*Army*] (ADDR)
BTB .... Bomb Thermal Battery (DNAB)
BTB .... Bone-Patellar Tendon-Tubercle Bone [*Graft*]
BTB .... Braided Tube Bundle
BTB .... Branch Target Buffer [*Computer science*] (PCM)
BTB .... Breakthrough Bleeding [*Medicine*]
BTB .... Bromthymol [*or Bromothymol*] Blue [*A dye*]
BTB .... Bumper to Bumper
BTB .... Bus Tie Breaker
BTBA .... British Tenpin Bowling Association, Ltd.
BTBA .... British Twinning and Bilingual Association (BI)
BTBC .... Boehm Test of Basic Concepts [*Psychology*]
BTBL .... Bromothymol Blue Lactose [*Medicine*] (DMAA)
BTBMF .... British Tin Box Manufacturers Federation (PDAA)
BTBPE .... Bis(tribromophenoxy)ethane [*Flame retardant*] [*Organic chemistry*]
BTBS .... Book Trade Benevolent Society [*British*]
BTBS .... British Telecom Business Systems (NITA)
BTBT .... BT Shipping Ltd. [*NASDAQ symbol*] (NQ)
BTBTY .... BT Shipping Ltd ADR [*NASDAQ symbol*] (TTSB)
BTC .... Bachelor of Textile Chemistry
BTC .... Bahrain Tourism Co. (EY)
BTC .... Banctec, Inc. [*NYSE symbol*] (SAG)
BTC .... BancTec, Inc. [*NYSE symbol*] (TTSB)
BTC .... Bankers Trust Co. (MHDW)
BTC .... Bashkirian Airlines [*Former USSR*] [*International*] (FAAC)
BTC .... Basic Technical Course [*Military*]
BTC .... Basic Training Center [*Military*]
BTC .... Batch Terminal Controller [*Computer science*] (IAA)
BTC .... Battery Training Corps [*British*]
BTC .... Batticaloa [*Ceylon*] [*Airport symbol*] (AD)
BTC .... Baxter Technologies Corp. [*Toronto Stock Exchange symbol*]
BTC .... Before Top Center [*Valve position*]
BTC .... Begin Telemetry Cycle
BTC .... Believe the Children [*An association*] (EA)
BTC .... Bell Telephone Co. of Canada (IIA)
BTC .... Below Threshold Change [*Air Force*]
BTC .... Bench Test Console
BTC .... Benzenetricarboxylate [*Organic chemistry*]
BTC .... Beryllium Thrust Chamber
BTC .... Bethlehem Transportation Corp. [*Steamship*] (MHDW)
BTC .... Bhutan Tourism Corp. (EY)
BTC .... Bicycle Touring Club [*British*]
BTC .... Binary Time Code (MCD)
BTC .... BIT [*Binary Digit*] Time Counter [*Computer science*]
BTC .... Block Terminating Character [*Computer science*] (IAA)
BTC .... Block Transfer Controller [*Computer science*]
BTC .... Blood Transfusion Centre [*British*]

BTC	Boilerman, Chief [*Navy rating*]
BTC	Boys Town Center for the Study of Youth Development, Omaha, NE [*OCLC symbol*] (OCLC)
BTC	Brands and Their Companies [*Formerly, TND*] [*A publication*]
BTC	British Technical Council [*of the Motor and Petroleum Industries*]
BTC	British Textile Confederation (DCTA)
BTC	British Transport Commission
BTC	Brown Trout Club (EA)
BTC	Business and Technology Center [*Control Data Corp.*] [*British*]
BTC	Business Telecommunications Corp. [*Chicago, IL*] (TSSD)
BTC	Business Training College
BTC	Bus Tie Contractor (MCD)
BTC	Butembo [*Zaire*] [*Seismograph station code, US Geological Survey*] (SEIS)
BTC	Butt-Treated Cedar (IAA)
BTC	Central Technical Library, Cominco Ltd., Trail, British Columbia [*Library symbol National Library of Canada*] (NLC)
BTC	Organon Laboratories Ltd. [*Great Britain*] [*Research code symbol*]
BTCA	Basic Tables of Commissioning Allowances [*Navy*]
BTCA	Bedlington Terrier Club of America (EA)
BTCA	Big Thicket Conservation Association (EA)
BTCA	Border Terrier Club of America (EA)
BTCA	Boston Terrier Club of America (EA)
BTCA	Bull Terrier Club of America (EA)
BTCA	Butanetetracarboxylic Acid [*Organic chemistry*]
BTCA	Trail City Archives, British Columbia [*Library symbol National Library of Canada*] (NLC)
BTCC	Basic Traffic Control Center (IAA)
BTCC	Big Thicket Coordinating Committee [*Defunct*] (EA)
BTCC	Broome Technical Community College [*New York*]
BTCD	Banque Tchadienne de Credit et de Depots [*Chad*] (EY)
BTCE	Bureau of Transport and Communications Economics [*Austria Also, an information service or system*] (IID)
BTCG	Bipartite Transport Control Group [*Post-World War II, Germany*]
BT Ch	Bachelor of Textile Chemistry
BTCHD	Batched (ABBR)
BTCHG	Batching (ABBR)
BTCHR	Butcher (ABBR)
BTCHR	Butcher
BTCHRY	Butchery (ABBR)
BTCM	Boilerman, Master Chief [*Navy rating*]
BTCMPI	British Technical Council of Motor and Petroleum Industries
BTCN	Beautician (ABBR)
BTCN	Beautician
BTCO	Boston Terminal Co. [*AAR code*]
BTCP	British Transport Commission Police
BTCR	Butcher (MSA)
BTCS	Benzyltrichlorosilane [*Organic chemistry*]
BTCS	Boilerman, Senior Chief [*Navy rating*]
BTCV	British Trust for Conservation Volunteers
BTD	Bachelor of Textile Dyeing
BTD	Balanced Tape Drive
BTD	Bathythermal Data (MCD)
BTD	Bell. Testing of Deeds [*Scotland*] [*A publication*] (DLA)
BTD	Best Time of the Day [*Automotive racing*]
BTD	Bias Telegraph Distortion
BTD	Biliary Tract Disease [*Medicine*] (DMAA)
BTD	Binary to Decimal [*Computer science*] (BUR)
BTD	Bitec Development Corp. [*Vancouver Stock Exchange symbol*]
BTD	Bomb Testing Device
BTD	Bond Test Device (MCD)
BTD	Brief Task Description (AAG)
BTD	Brunett Downs [*Northern Territory, Australia*] [*Airport symbol*] (AD)
BTD	Bulk Tape Degausser
BTD	Burn to Depletion [*NASA*] (KSC)
BTDA	Benzophenonetetracarboxylic Dianhydride [*Organic chemistry*]
BTDB	British Transport Docks Board
BTDC	Before Top Dead Center [*Valve position*]
BTDCPF	Bathythermographic Data Collection and Processing Facility [*Oceanography*]
BTDE	Benzophenonetetracarboxylic Diethylester [*Organic chemistry*]
BT Des	Bachelor of Textile Design
BTDL	Basic Transient Diode Logic [*Computer science*] (BUR)
BTDMSBA	Black-Top Delaine Merino Sheep Breeders' Association (EA)
BTDO	British Trade Development Office [*Later, BTIO*] (EA)
BTDPAF	Bathythermographic Data Processing and Analysis Facility [*Oceanography*]
BTE	Bachelor of Textile Engineering
BTE	Baker & Taylor Co. [*ACCORD*] [*UTLAS symbol*]
BTE	Battery Terminal Equipment
BTE	Battery Timing Equipment (AAG)
BTE	Battle Energy Corp. [*Vancouver Stock Exchange symbol*]
BTE	Behind the Ear [*Hearing aid*] [*Audiology*]
Bte	Benedicite [*Bless You*] [*Latin*]
BTE	Benzilic Acid Tropine Ester [*Also, BAT, BETE*] [*Pharmacology*]
BTE	Better than Expected [*Politics*]
BTE	Bidirectional Transceiver Element [*Telecommunications*]
BTE	Blunt Trailing Edge
BTE	Boltzmann Transport Equation [*Physics*]
BTE	Bonthe [*Sierra Leone*] [*Airport symbol*] (OAG)
BTE	Bord Telecom Eireann [*Nationalized industry*] [*Ireland*] (EY)
BTE	Bourdon Tube Element
BTE	Brake Thermal Efficiency [*Automotive engineering*]
BTE	Brayton Turboelectric Engine
BTE	Brevete [*Patent*] [*French*]

BTE	British Telecom Enterprises (NITA)
BTE	British Troops in Egypt [*World War II*]
B-TE	Broadband Terminal Equipment [*Telecommunications*] (ACRL)
BTE	Bulk Tape Eraser
BTE	Business Telecommunications Equipment [*Canada*]
BTE	Business Terminal Equipment [*Telecommunications*] (TEL)
BTE	Terrace Public Library, British Columbia [*Library symbol National Library of Canada*] (NLC)
BTEA	Boston Test for Examining Aphasia [*Speech and language therapy*] (DAVI)
BTEA	British Textile Employers' Association (EAIO)
BTEA	Building Trades Employers Association (SRA)
BTeach	Bachelor of Teaching
BTE & S	Bureau of Transport Economics and Statistics [*ICC*]
BTEC	BancTec, Inc. [*NASDAQ symbol*] (NQ)
BTEC	Blanket Tool Expenditure Control (MCD)
BTEC	Bristol Technology Systems, Inc. [*NASDAQ symbol*] (SAG)
BTEC	Business and Technician Education Council [*British*]
B Tech	Bachelor of Technology
BTECH	Business and Technician Education Council (ACII)
BTechEd	Bachelor of Technology Education
BTechInfSys	Bachelor of Technology in Information Systems
BTechSc	Bachelor of Technical Science
BTECNC	Business and Technology Education Council National Certificate (AIE)
BTEE	Benzoyltyrosine Ethyl Ester [*Biochemistry*]
BTEE	Brayton Turboelectric Engine
BTEF	Book Trade Employers' Federation (DGA)
BTEK	Baltek Corp. [*NASDAQ symbol*] (NQ)
BTelE	Bachelor of Telecommunications Engineering (ADA)
B-TELL	Back Telling (SAA)
BTEMA	British Tanning Extract Manufacturers' Association (BI)
BT Eng	Bachelor of Textile Engineering
BTENW	North West College, Terrace, British Columbia [*Library symbol National Library of Canada*] (NLC)
BTES	Beginning Teacher Evaluation Study (EDAC)
BTESM	Building Thermal Envelope Systems and Materials
B (Test)	Breath Test [*For determining whether or not an auto driver is legally drunk*] [*British*]
BTEUNSW	Baking Trades Employees' Union of New South Wales [*Australia*]
BTEV	Beet Temperate Virus [*Plant pathology*]
BTE/Vass	British Telecom Enterprises' Value Added Systems and Services (NITA)
BTEX	Bezene, Toluene, Ethylbenzene, and Xylene [*Organic mixture*]
BText	Bachelor of Textiles
BTF	Balance to Follow (WDAA)
B/TF	Balance/Transferred [*Banking*] (WDAA)
BTF	Ballet Theatre Foundation (EA)
BTF	Ballistic Test Facility [*Air Research and Development Command*] (AAG)
BTF	Basic Transcription Factor [*Genetics*]
BTF	Beam Rider Tail Control Fragmentation [*Missile*] (MCD)
BTF	Bench Test Fixture
BTF	Benzotrifuroxan [*Organic chemistry*]
BTF	Bidirectional Test Fixture (MCD)
BTF	Binary Transversal Filter (IAA)
BTF	Biotechnology Facility (SSD)
BTF	Bomb Tail Fuse
BTF	Bountiful, UT [*Location identifier FAA*] (FAAL)
BTF	Brazilian Tourism Foundation (EA)
BTF	Breakthrough Foundation (EA)
BTF	British Pacific Financial, Inc. [*Formerly, British Pacific Resources, Inc.*] [*Vancouver Stock Exchange symbol*]
BTF	British Tarpaviors Federation Ltd. (BI)
BTF	British Trampoline Federation (DBA)
BTF	British Trawler Federation
BTF	British Turkey Federation Ltd. (BI)
BTF	BT Office Prod Intl. [*NYSE symbol*] (TTSB)
BTF	BT Office Products International, Inc. [*NYSE symbol*] (SAG)
BTF	Bulk Transfer Facility
BTFA	Basic and Traditional Food Association [*Inactive*] (EA)
BTFA	Benzoyltrifluoroacetone [*Organic chemistry*] (NRCH)
BTFA	Bilinear Target Factor Analysis [*Mathematics*]
BTFA	Bistrifluoroacetamide [*Organic chemistry*]
BTFA	Fireman Apprentice, Boilerman, Striker [*Navy rating*]
BTFC	Billy Troy Fan Club [*Defunct*] (EA)
BTFC	BT Financial [*NASDAQ symbol*] (TTSB)
BTFC	BT Financial Corp. [*NASDAQ symbol*] (NQ)
BTFCN	Beautification (ABBR)
BTFHA	British Touch for Health Association
BT Fin	BT Financial Corp. [*Associated Press*] (SAG)
BTFL	Beautiful (ABBR)
BTFL	Butterfly (MSA)
BTFLNS	Beautifulness (ABBR)
BTFLY	Beautifully (ABBR)
BTFN	Fireman, Boilerman, Striker [*Navy rating*]
BT font	Bitstream font [*Bitstream Inc.*] (CDE)
BTFS	Breast Tumor Frozen Section [*Medicine*] (DMAA)
BTFY	Beautify (ABBR)
BTFYG	Beautifying (ABBR)
BTG	Ball Tooth Gear
BTG	Battery Timing Group
BTG	Beacon Trigger Generator
BTG	Beating [*FBI standardized term*]
BTG	Beating the Gun [*Investment term*]

BTG............ Becoming the Gift [*Religious education test*]
BTG............ Beta Thickness Gauge (DEN)
BTG............ Beta-Thromboglobulin [*Hematology*]
BTG............ Biting (ABBR)
BTG............ Blood Triacylglycerol [*Hematology*]
BTG............ Boiler Turbine Generator (IAA)
BTG............ Brent Resources Group Ltd. [*Vancouver Stock Exchange symbol*]
BTG............ British Technology Group [*Research center*]
BTG............ British Toymakers' Guild (BI)
BTG............ British Troops in Germany (DMA)
BTG............ Burst Transmission Group
BTG............ Butterworths Tax Guide [*A publication*]
BTGA.......... Best Technology Generally Available [*Environmental Protection Agency*]
btga .... Bottega (VRA)
BTGC.......... Bio-Technology General Corp. [*NASDAQ symbol*] (SP86)
BTGC.......... Bio-Technology Genl [*NASDAQ symbol*] (TTSB)
BTGCA........ Burley Tobacco Growers Cooperative Association (EA)
BTGCL........ Bio Technology Gen Wrrt'A' [*NASDAQ symbol*] (TTSB)
BTGI........... BTG Inc. [*NASDAQ symbol*] (TTSB)
BTGI........... BTG, Inc. [*NASDAQ symbol*] (SAG)
BTG Inc..... BTG, Inc. [*Associated Press*] (SAG)
BTGJ........... Ball Tooth Gear Joint
B Th........... Bachelor of Theology
BTH............ Barth's Aviation [*France ICAO designator*] (FAAC)
BTH............ Basic Transmission Header [*Computer science*] (IBMDP)
BTH............ Bath (ADA)
BTH............ Bathroom (ADA)
BTH............ Bathurst [*Gambia*] [*Airport symbol*] (AD)
BTH............ Batu Besar [*Indonesia*] [*Airport symbol*] (OAG)
BTH............ Berth (MSA)
BTH............ Bethlehem Resources Corp. [*Toronto Stock Exchange symbol Vancouver Stock Exchange symbol*]
BTH............ Beyond the Horizon (MCD)
BTH............ Birth (ADA)
BTH............ Bis(benzylidene)thiocarbohydrazone [*Organic chemistry*]
BTH............ Blyth Industries [*NYSE symbol*] (TTSB)
BTH............ Blyth Industries, Inc. [*NYSE symbol*] (SAG)
BTH............ British Thomson-Houston Co.
BTH............ British Transport Hotels [*Commercial firm*]
BTH............ Bulk Transfer Hose
BTH............ Butylated Hydroxytolulene [*Antioxidant*] (BABM)
BTHA.......... British Toy and Hobby Association (EAIO)
BTHA.......... British Travel and Holidays Association [*Later, British Travel Association*]
BThE.......... Brake Thermal Efficiency
BTheol........ Bachelor of Theology
BTHG.......... Business Traveler Hotel Guide [*National Association of Business Travel Agents*] [*A publication*]
BTHL.......... Bethel Bancorp [*NASDAQ symbol*] (NQ)
Bthol.......... Bartholomaeus Brixiensis [*Deceased circa 1258*] [*Authority cited in pre-1607 legal work*] (DSA)
BTHR.......... Bother (ABBR)
BTHRD........ Bothered (ABBR)
BTHRG........ Bothering (ABBR)
BTHRM....... Bathroom [*Classified advertising*] (ADA)
BTHRSM..... Bothersome (ABBR)
BthS........... Bethlehem Steel Corp. [*Wall Street slang name: "Bessie"*] [*Associated Press*] (SAG)
BthSt.......... Bethlehem Steel Corp. [*Wall Street slang name: "Bessie"*] [*Associated Press*] (SAG)
BTHU.......... British Thermal Unit
BTHW......... Biblisch-Theologisches Handwoerterbuch [*A publication*] (BJA)
BTI............. Bacillus Thuringiensis Israelensis [*Bacteriology*]
BTI............. Balanced Technology Initiative [*DoD*] (RDA)
BTI............. Balanced Technology Institute (AAGC)
BTI............. Bank and Turn Indicator [*Aviation*]
BTI............. Barter Island [*Alaska*] [*Airport symbol*] (OAG)
BTI............. Basic Timesharing, Inc. [*Later,*] (NITA)
BTI............. B.A.T.Idus Ord ADR [*AMEX symbol*] (TTSB)
BTI............. BAT Industries Ltd. [*AMEX symbol*] (SPSG)
BTI............. Bilateral Tubal Interruption [*Gynecology*]
BTI............. Biotechnica International, Inc.
BTI............. Boston Theological Institute (EA)
BTI............. Boston Theological Institute, Cambridge, MA [*OCLC symbol*] (OCLC)
BTI............. Boston Theological Institute Library [*Library network*]
BTI............. Boys' Towns of Italy (EA)
BTI............. Bridged Tap Isolator (IEEE)
BTI............. British Technology Index (AIE)
BTI............. British Telecom International (NITA)
BTI............. British Theatre Institute (EA)
BTI............. British Tobacco Industry
BTI............. British Troops in Iraq (DMA)
BTI............. British Tutorial Institute
BTI............. BTI Computer Systems [*Formerly, Basic Timesharing, Inc.*]
BTI............. B-Track Initiator (SAA)
BTI............. Bureau of Technical Information (SAA)
BTI............. Burst Time Indicator (MCD)
BTIA........... British Turf Irrigation Association (DBA)
BTIC........... Bomb Targets Information Committee [*Air Ministry*] [*British World War II*]
BTID........... Bis Terve in Die [*Two or Three Times a Day*] [*Pharmacy*]
BTIF........... Business Taxpayer Information File [*IRS*]
BTIM.......... Biotime, Inc. [*NASDAQ symbol*] (SAG)
B'TINE .... Brigantine [*Ship*] (ADA)

BTIO........... Battery Tech, Inc. [*NASDAQ symbol*] (SAG)
BTIO........... British Trade and Investment Office (EA)
BTIOF......... Battery Technologies [*NASDAQ symbol*] (TTSB)
BTIS........... Bankers Trust Information Service [*Database producer*]
BTIS........... Bureau of Transportation and International Services [*US Postal Service*]
BTIX........... Biomagnetic Tech [*NASDAQ symbol*] (TTSB)
BTIX........... Biomagnetic Technology [*NASDAQ symbol*] (SAG)
BTJ............. American Friends of Boys Town of Jerusalem [*BTJFA*] [*Superseded by*] (EA)
BTJ............. Ball Tooth Joint
BTJ............. Banda Aceh [*Indonesia*] [*Airport symbol*] (OAG)
BTJ............. Banda Atjeh [*Indonesia*] [*Airport symbol*] (AD)
BTJ............. Bibliotekstjanst AB [*Library Service Ltd.*] [*Sweden Information service or system*] (IID)
BTJ............. Bolt Technology Corp. [*AMEX symbol*] (SAG)
BTJ............. British Trade Journal [*A publication*] (ROG)
BTJ............. Brotherhood of Traveling Jewelers (EA)
BTJE........... Bypass Turbojet Engine Noise
BTJFA......... Boys Town Jerusalem Foundation of America (EA)
BTK............ Batik (ABBR)
btk............. Batik (VRA)
BTK............ Big Strike Resources [*Vancouver Stock Exchange symbol*]
BTK............ Bratsk [*Former USSR Airport symbol*] (OAG)
Btk............. Bruton's Tyrosine Kinase [*An enzyme*]
BTK............ Buttock [*Shipfitting*]
BTKN.......... Betoken (ABBR)
BTL............ Backtell (IAA)
BTL............ Balanced Transformer (IAA)
BTL............ Baltia Air Lines, Inc. [*ICAO designator*] (FAAC)
BTL............ Battle (ABBR)
BTL............ Battle Creek [*Michigan*] [*Airport symbol*] (OAG)
BTL............ Beacon Tracking Level (KSC)
BTL............ Beginning of Tape Level (NITA)
BTL............ Beginning Tape Label [*Computer science*] (BUR)
BTL............ Behind the Lens (NTCM)
BTL............ Behind the Line [*Air Force*]
BTL............ Bell Telephone Laboratories, Inc. [*Murray Hill, NJ*]
BTL............ Bell Telephone Laboratories, Inc., Holmdel, NJ [*OCLC symbol*] (OCLC)
BTL............ Below the Line [*Budget*]
BTL............ Bend Tangency Line (MCD)
BTL............ Between Layers [*ICAO*] (FAAC)
BTL............ BetzDearborn, Inc. [*NYSE symbol*] (SAG)
BTL............ Betz Laboratories [*NYSE symbol*] (SPSG)
BTL............ Bilateral Tubal Ligation [*Gynecology*]
BTL............ Birmingham Technology Ltd. at Aston Science Park [*Research center British*] (IRUK)
BTL............ Bitolterol [*Pharmacology*]
BTL............ Board Test Language (PDAA)
BTL............ Bottle
BTL............ BTL Corp. [*Formerly, Butler Brothers*]
BTLB.......... Block Translation Lookaside Buffer [*Computer science*] (PCM)
BTLD.......... Battled (ABBR)
BTLD.......... Bottled (ABBR)
BTLEX........ Battalion Landing Team Landing Exercise [*Military*] (NVT)
BTLFLD....... Battlefield (ABBR)
BTLG.......... Battling (ABBR)
BTLG.......... Bottling (ABBR)
BTLG.......... Bottling
BTL ILUM-L... Battlefield Illumination L System (MCD)
BTLL.......... Bottom Lead Left (MSA)
BTLM.......... Botulism [*Medicine*] (ABBR)
BTLMT........ Battlement (ABBR)
BTLN.......... Battalion (ABBR)
BTLP.......... Butt-Treated Lodgepole Pine (IAA)
BTLR.......... Bottom Lead Right (MSA)
BTLR.......... Butler (ABBR)
BTLR.......... Butler
BTLR.......... Butler Manufacturing Co. [*NASDAQ symbol*] (NQ)
BTLR.......... Butler Mfg [*NASDAQ symbol*] (TTSB)
BTLS.......... Basic Trauma Life Support [*Medicine*] (DMAA)
BTLSP........ Breadboard Terminal Landing System [*NASA*] (KSC)
BTLSP........ Battleship (ABBR)
BTLV.......... Biological Threshold Limit Value (PDAA)
BTLZ.......... British Telecom Lempel Ziv (CDE)
BTM........... Ballast Tank Meter
BTM........... Bantam (ABBR)
BTM........... Batch Time-Sharing Monitor [*Xerox Corp.*] [*Computer science*] (MCD)
BTM........... Battalion Training Model [*Military*]
BTM........... Bellows Tankage Module
BTM........... Bell Telephone Manufacturing Co. [*Telecommunications*]
BTM........... Benign Tertian Malaria [*Medicine*] (DMAA)
Btm........... Benzylthiomethyl [*Biochemistry*]
BTM........... Benzyltrimethylammonium Chloride [*Also, TMBAC*] [*Organic chemistry*]
BTM........... Biochemical Test Monitor
BTM........... Blast Test Missile (NG)
BTM........... Blast Test Motor (MCD)
BTM........... Bottom
BTM........... Bottom
BTM........... British Theatre Museum (BI)
BTM........... British Trade Mission
BTM........... Broadband Trunk Module [*Telecommunications*]

BTM	Bromotrifluoromethane [*Fire extinguishing agent*] [*Organic chemistry*] (ADA)
BTM	Brushless Torque Motor
BTM	Buffered Terminal Multiplexer [*Computer science*] (IAA)
BTM	Bulling the Market [*Investment term*]
BTM	Butte [*Montana*] [*Airport symbol*] (OAG)
BTM	Trail Museum, British Columbia [*Library symbol National Library of Canada*] (NLC)
BTMA	Basic Telecommunication (MCD)
BTMA	Boat Trailer Manufacturers Association [*Later, TMA*] (EA)
BTMA	Bow Tie Manufacturers Association (EA)
BTMA	Braided Trimming Manufacturers Association [*Later, EFMCNTA*] (EA)
BTMA	British Textile Machinery Association (DS)
BTMA	British Timber Merchants Association (DBA)
BTMA	British Turned-Parts Manufacturers Association (DBA)
BTMA	British Typewriter Manufacturers Association (PDAA)
BTMA	Busy Tone Multiple-Access [*Telecommunications*] (MHDB)
BTMC	British Tabulating Machinery Co.
BTMC	British Telecom Mobile Communications
BTMD	Batten-Turner Muscular Dystrophy [*Syndrome*] [*Medicine*]
BTMD	Bottomed (ABBR)
BTME	Babcock Test of Mental Efficiency [*Psychology*]
BTMF	Block Type Manipulation Facility
BTMG	Bottoming (ABBR)
BTMLS	Bottomless (ABBR)
BTMS	Battalion Training Management System [*Army*] (INF)
BTMS	Body Temperature Measuring System
BTMS	Brake Temperature Monitoring System (MCD)
BTMS	Brisbane Tramway Museum Society [*Australia*]
BTMSA	Bis(trimethylsilyl)acetylene [*Organic chemistry*]
BTMV	Beet Mosaic Virus [*Plant pathology*]
BTMWT	Bantamweight (ABBR)
BTN	Ballantyne of Omaha [*AMEX symbol*] (TTSB)
BTN	Ballantyne of Omaha, Inc. [*AMEX symbol*] (SAG)
BTN	Baptist Telecommunications Network [*Nashville, TN*] [*Cable-television system*]
BTN	Baton (WDAA)
BTN	Battalion
BTN	Beam-Riding Tail-Controlled Nuclear Missile
BTN	Beam Tracking Nuclear [*Military*] (CAAL)
BTN	Between
BTN	Bhutan [*ANSI three-letter standard code*] (CNC)
BTN	Billing Telephone Number [*Telecommunications*] (TEL)
BTN	Britton, SD [*Location identifier FAA*] (FAAL)
BTN	Brunei Town [*Brunei*] [*Airport symbol*] (AD)
BTN	Brussels Tariff Nomenclature [*See also CCCN*] [*EEC Belgium*]
BTN	Button (AAG)
BTN	Butuan [*Philippines*] [*Seismograph station code, US Geological Survey Closed*] (SEIS)
BTNA	British Troops in North Africa [*World War II*]
BTNEC	Bis(trinitroethyl)carbonate [*An explosive*]
BTNEN	Bis(trinitroethyl)nitramine [*An explosive*]
BTNHD	Button Head
BTO	Bachman-Turner Overdrive [*Rock music group*]
Bto	Bartolus de Sassoferrato [*Deceased, 1357*] [*Authority cited in pre-1607 legal work*] (DSA)
BTO	Battalion Transport Officer [*British military*] (DMA)
BTO	Belgian Tourist Office (EA)
BTO	Big-Time Operator [*Slang*]
BTO	Blanket Tool Order
BTO	Blanket Travel Order (MCD)
BTO	Blocking-Tube Oscillator
BTO	Bombing through Overcast [*By means of RADAR equipment*]
BTO	Botopasie [*Surinam*] [*Airport symbol*] (OAG)
BTO	Branch Transportation Office [*or Officer*] [*Army*]
BTO	Brazil Tourism Office (EA)
BTO	Brief Task Outline (AAG)
BTO	Brigade Transport Officer [*British*]
BTO	Britcol Resource Development [*Vancouver Stock Exchange symbol*]
BTO	British Trust for Ornithology
BTO	Brussels Treaty Organization [*Later, Western European Union*]
BTO	Build-to-Order [*Compaq Computer Corp.*] [*Computer science*]
BTO	Hancock [*John*] Bank & Thrift Opportunity Fund [*NYSE symbol*] (SAG)
BTO	John Hancock Bk/Thrift Opp [*NYSE symbol*] (TTSB)
BTO	St. Barthelemy [*Leeward Islands, West Indies*] [*Airport symbol*] (AD)
BTO	Translation Bureau Library, Secretary of State [*UTLAS symbol*]
B to B	Back to Back [*Technical drawings*]
B-to-B	Business-to-Business [*Advertising*] (WDMC)
BTOC	Battalion Tactical Operations Center [*Military*]
BTOC	Brigade Tactical Operations Center
BTOF	British Trawler Officers Federation [*A union*]
BT Off	BT Office Products International, Inc. [*Associated Press*] (SAG)
BTOG	British Transport Officers Guild (DBA)
BTOGW	Basic Takeoff Gross Weight [*Aviation*] (MCD)
BTOMM	West Coast Maritime Museum, Tofino, British Columbia [*Library symbol National Library of Canada*] (NLC)
BTON	Benetton Group S.p.A [*ML, exchange symbol*] (TTSB)
BTON	Brighton (ROG)
BTP	Bachelor of Town Planning
BTP	Batch Transfer Program
BTP	Beam Tape Packaging [*Computer science*]
BTP	Bis Tris Propane [*Biological buffer*]
BTP	Black Thunder Petroleum [*Vancouver Stock Exchange symbol*]

BTP	BMEWS [*Ballistic Missile Early Warning System*] Test Procedure (AFM)
BTP	Body Temperature and Pressure [*Medicine*] (WDAA)
BTP	[*A*] Book of Treasured Poems [*A publication*]
BTP	Bovine Trophoblast Protein [*Biochemistry*]
BTP	Braille Technical Press [*Defunct*] (EA)
BTP	Branch Technical Position [*Nuclear energy*] (NRCH)
BTP	British Telecom Phonecards [*Prepaid cards for use in noncoin pay telephones*]
BTP	Broken Time Payment [*US Olympic Committee*]
BTP	Buoni del Tesoro Poliennali [*Italy*] (ECON)
BTP	Burst Time Plan (LAIN)
BTP	Butler, PA [*Location identifier FAA*] (FAAL)
BTPA	British Tractor Pullers Association (DBA)
BT PABA	Benzoyl-Tyrosyl Para-Aminobenzoic Acid [*Organic chemistry*]
BTPC	Brussels Treaty Permanent Commission (NATG)
BTPD	Body Temperature, [*Ambient*] Pressure, Dry [*Medicine*]
BTPD	Busy Tax Practitioner's Digest [*Australia A publication*]
BTPI	Benzothiopyranoindazole [*Organic chemistry*]
BTPII	Boston Tea Party II [*An association*] (EA)
BTPrI	Bankers Tr N.Y.8.55% Sr'l'Pfd [*NYSE symbol*] (TTSB)
BTPrQ	Bankers Tr N.Y. Adj Dep'Q'Pfd [*NYSE symbol*] (TTSB)
BTPrR	Bankers Tr N.Y. Adj Dep'R'Pfd [*NYSE symbol*] (TTSB)
BTPrS	Bankers Tr N.Y.7.75% Dep'S'Pfd [*NYSE symbol*] (TTSB)
BTPS	Ballarat Tramway Preservation Society [*Australia*]
BTPS	Body Temperature, Pressure [*Prevailing atmospheric*], and Saturation [*With water vapor*] (DAVI)
BTPS	Body Temperature, [*Ambient*] Pressure, Saturated [*with water*] [*Medicine*]
BTQ	Ballet Theatre of Queensland [*Australia*]
BTQ	Banque de Terminologie du Quebec [*Terminology Bank of Quebec*] [*French Language Board*] [*Information service or system*] (IID)
BTQ	Boutique
BTR	Back Tape Reader
BTR	Ballast Tube Resistor
BTR	Barrel-Tile Roof [*Technical drawings*]
BTR	Baton Rouge [*Louisiana*] [*Airport symbol*] (OAG)
BTR	Bearing Time Recorder
BTR	Behind Tape Reader (MCD)
BTR	Belize Transair [*ICAO designator*] (FAAC)
BTR	Betrust Investments [*Vancouver Stock Exchange symbol*]
BTR	Better (BARN)
BTR	Bezold-Type Reflex [*Medicine*] (MAE)
BTR	Biceps Tendon Reflex [*Medicine*] (DMAA)
B Tr	Bishop's Trial [*A publication*] (DLA)
BTR	Bladder Tumor Recheck [*Urology*] (DAVI)
BTR	Blanket Tritium Recovery [*Subsystem*] (MCD)
BTR	Block Tape Recorder
BTR	BMEWS [*Ballistic Missile Early Warning System*] Test Report (AFM)
BTR	Board of Teacher Registration
BTR	Boom Time Remaining (NASA)
BTR	Bradley Real Estate [*Formerly, Bradley Real Estate Trust*] [*NYSE symbol*] (SAG)
BTR	Brewing Trade Review Licensing Law Reports [*England*] [*A publication*] (DLA)
BTR	British Tire & Rubber Co.
BTR	Broadcast and Television Receivers (MCD)
BTR	Broneje Transporter [*Soviet Armored Personnel Carrier*]
BTR	Bureau of Trade Regulation [*Department of Commerce*]
BTR	Burn Time Remaining (MCD)
BTR	Business Technology Research, Inc. [*Telecommunications service*] (TSSD)
BTR	Bus Transfer (AAG)
BTR	Butare [*Astrida*] [*Rwanda*] [*Seismograph station code, US Geological Survey*] [*Closed*] (SEIS)
BTR	Tumbler Ridge Public Library, British Columbia [*Library symbol National Library of Canada*] (BIB)
BTRA	British Truck Racing Association (DBA)
Btran	Bertrandus [*Authority cited in pre-1607 legal work*] (DSA)
BTRC	Brain Tumor Research Center [*University of California, San Francisco*] [*Research center*] (RCD)
BTRDA	British Trials and Rally Drivers Association
BTRE	Broadcast-Television Recording Engineers [*An association*] (NTCM)
BTRE	Brooktree Corp. [*NASDAQ symbol*] (SPSG)
B-tree	Balanced-Tree [*Technique for organizing indexes*] (CDE)
BTRG	Bullet-Trap Rifle Grenade [*Army*] (INF)
BTRL	British Telecom Research Laboratories
BTRLR	Brewing Trade Review Law Reports [*A publication*] (DLA)
BTRMLK	Buttermilk [*Freight*]
BTRN	BioTransplant, Inc. [*NASDAQ symbol*] (SAG)
BTRN	Bio Transplant Inc. [*NASDAQ symbol*] (TTSB)
B TRON	Business The Real-Time Operating System Nucleus [*Computer science*] (NITA)
BTRP	Bachelor of Town and Regional Planning (ADA)
BTRS	Behavior Therapy and Research Society (EA)
BTRS	Boron Thermal Regeneration System [*Nuclear energy*] (NRCH)
BTRY	Battery (AFM)
BTRY	Buttrey Food & Drug Stores [*NASDAQ symbol*] (TTSB)
BTRY	Buttrey Food & Drug Stores Co. [*NASDAQ symbol*] (SAG)
BTRY CP	Battery Command Post [*Army*]
BTS	Bachelor of Technological Science
BTS	Back to School (WDAA)
BTS	Balloon Transport System
BTS	Barrier Terminal Strip
BTS	Base of Terminal Service [*for airmen*]

BTS .... Base Transceiver Station
BTS .... Basic Training School
BTS .... Batch Terminal Simulator [*Computer science*]
BTS .... Bates College, Lewiston, ME [*OCLC symbol*] (OCLC)
BTS .... Battalion Targeting System (DOMA)
BTS .... Battery Test Set
BTS .... Beacon Tracking System
BTS .... Beam Transport System
BTS .... Behind The Scenes [*Film*] [*Television*] (WDMC)
BTS .... Bellini-Tose System
BTS .... Bench Test Specification
BT's .... Benoctol [*French illicit drug available in Vietnam*] (VNW)
BTS .... Betsy-Tacy Society (EA)
BTS .... Bible et Terre Sainte [*A publication*] (BJA)
BTS .... Biomet Tech, Inc. [*Vancouver Stock Exchange symbol*]
BTS .... Biotelemetry System
BTS .... Bithionol Sulfoxide [*Pharmacology*]
BTS .... Black Turtle Soup
BTS .... Blessed Trinity Society [*Defunct*]
BTS .... Blood Transfusion Service [*Medicine*]
BTS .... Blue Tool Steel (MSA)
BTS .... Board of Thoracic Surgery [*Later, American Board of Thoracic Surgery*] (EA)
BTS .... Boeing Test Support [*NASA*] (KSC)
BTS .... Boolean Time Sequence [*Mathematics*]
BTS .... Boys Technical School [*British military*] (DMA)
BTS .... Bratislava [*Former Czechoslovakia*] [*Airport symbol*] (OAG)
BTS .... Brazilian Thorium Sludge
BTS .... Brisbane Theosophical Society [*Australia*]
BTS .... British Tarantula Society (DBA)
BTS .... British Telecommunications Systems Ltd. (TEL)
BTS .... British Temperance Society (BI)
BTS .... [*The*] British Thoracic Society
BTS .... British Toxicology Society (DBA)
BTS .... British Transplantation Society
BTS .... British Travel Survey (ECON)
BTS .... British Trolleybus Society (DCTA)
BTS .... Broadcast Transmission Systems (MCD)
BTS .... Budget Tracking System
BTS .... Bureau of Transportation Statistics [*BTS*] [*OFR*] (TAG)
BTS .... Bureau of Transportation Statistics (USGC)
BTS .... Burster-Trimmer-Stacker [*Printing*] (DGA)
BTS .... Business Telecommunications Services (ADA)
BTS .... Bus Tie Relay (MCD)
BTS .... IEEE Broadcast Technology Society (EA)
BTSA .... British Tensional Strapping Association (PDAA)
BTSB .... Bound to Stay Bound Books, Inc.
BTSB .... [*The*] Braintree Savings Bank [*NASDAQ symbol*] (NQ)
BTSC .... Ban the Soviets Coalition (EA)
BTSC .... British Transport Staff College (BI)
BTSC .... Broadcast Television Systems Committee Recommendation [*FCC*] (NTCM)
BTSF .... Black Tennis and Sports Foundation (EA)
BTSG .... Brain Tumor Study Group [*National Cancer Institute*]
BTSH .... Beef Thyroid-Stimulating Hormone [*Endocrinology*] (MAE)
BTSH .... Bovine Thyroid-Stimulating Hormone [*Endocrinology*]
BTSH .... Bovine Thyrotropin [*Endocrinology*] (DAVI)
BT Shp .... BT Shipping Ltd. [*Associated Press*] (SAG)
BTSI .... Brake-Transmission Shift Interlock [*Automotive engineering*]
BTSI .... Brake-Transmission Shift Interlock
BTSM .... Ballistic Test Submodule (RDA)
BTSN .... Book Trade Systems Network [*Publishers' Association*] [*British*]
BTSP .... Bootstrap [*Computer science*] (HGAA)
BTSS .... Basic Time-Sharing System (BUR)
BTSS .... Braille Time-Sharing System
BTST .... Ballistic Test Site Terminal (MCD)
BTST .... BIT [*Binary Digit*] Test [*Computer science*]
BTST .... Bootstrap (MSA)
BTST .... Busy-Tone Start Lead
BTSU .... Biblical Topics Study Unit [*American Topical Association*] (EA)
BTSWN .... Boatswain (AABC)
BTT .... Bachelor of Textile Technology
BTT .... Bank to Turn [*Aviation*] (MCD)
BTT .... Beginning to Tape Test
BTT .... Bettles [*Alaska*] [*Airport symbol*] (OAG)
BTT .... Bitterroot Resources Ltd. [*Vancouver Stock Exchange symbol*]
BTT .... Blackrock Target Term [*NYSE symbol*] (TTSB)
BTT .... Blackrock Target Term Trust [*NYSE symbol*] (SAG)
BTT .... Brainstem Transmission Time [*Neurophysiology*]
BTT .... Branch Training Team [*Army*]
BTT .... British Tea Table Co. (ROG)
BTT .... Business Transfer Tax [*Proposed*] [*Canada*]
BTT .... Business Turnover Tax (IMH)
BTT .... Busy Tone Trunk [*Telecommunications*]
BTTA .... British Thoracic and Tuberculosis Association
BTTFFC .... Back to the Future Fan Club
BTTG .... British Textile Technology Group (ECON)
BTTLR .... Bottler
BTTN .... Butanetriol Trinitrate [*An explosive*]
BTTP .... British Towing Tank Panel (MCD)
BTTS .... Buddhist Text Translation Society (EA)
BTU .... Bankers Trust New York Corp. [*NYSE symbol*] (SAG)
BTU .... Basic Transmission Unit [*Computer science*]
BTU .... Bateaux Resources, Inc. [*Vancouver Stock Exchange symbol*]
BTU .... Bintulu [*Malaysia*] [*Airport symbol*] (OAG)

BTU .... Block Transfer Unit [*Computer science*] (IAA)
BTU .... Board of Trade Unit [*British*]
BTU .... British Thermal Unit
BTU .... Bus Terminal Unit (MCD)
BTU .... Rolls Royce Ltd. (Bristol Engine Division) [*British ICAO designator*] (FAAC)
BTUC .... British Telecom Unions Committee
BTUC .... Burma Trade Union Congress
BTU/h .... British Thermal Units per Hour (MCD)
BTU/HR .... British Thermal Units per Hour (DNAB)
BTUI .... BTU International [*NASDAQ symbol*] (TTSB)
BTUI .... BTU International, Inc. [*NASDAQ symbol*] (CTT)
BTU Int .... BTU International, Inc. [*Associated Press*] (SAG)
BTURN .... Black Turnout [*Political science*]
BTUSA .... Baking Trade Union of South Australia
BTUSQFTMIN... Basic Transmission Unit per Square Foot per Minute (IAA)
BTV .... Basic Transportation Vehicle
BTV .... Batavia [*Indonesia*] [*Later, TNG*] [*Geomagnetic observatory code*]
BTV .... Beance Tubaire Volontaire [*Voluntary opening of eustachian tubes*] [*Deep-sea diving*] [*French*]
BTV .... BET Holdings [*NYSE symbol*] (SPSG)
BTV .... BET Holdings'A' [*NYSE symbol*] (TTSB)
BTV .... Blast Test Vehicle (NG)
BTV .... Blue Tongue Virus [*Medicine*] (DMAA)
BTV .... Buoyancy Transport Vehicle (MCD)
BTV .... Burlington [*Vermont*] [*Airport symbol*] (OAG)
BTV .... Business Television (WDMC)
BTVP .... British Tertiary Volcanic Province [*Geology*]
BTW .... Backward Traveling Wave
BTW .... Bare Tungsten Wire
BTW .... Between
BTW .... Bimetal Turbine Wheel
BTW .... Bitterwater Creek [*California*] [*Seismograph station code, US Geological Survey*] (SEIS)
BTW .... Boat Wave
BTW .... By the Way [*Internet language*] [*Computer science*]
btw .... By The Way [*Internet language*] [*Computer science*]
BTWF .... Booker T. Washington Foundation (EA)
BTWLD .... Butt Welded
BTWN .... Between (AABC)
BTWS .... Bitwise Designs [*NASDAQ symbol*] (SAG)
BTWS .... Buried Trench Weapons System (MCD)
BTWSM .... Board of Trade of the Wholesale Seafood Merchants (EA)
BTX .... Banctexas Group, Inc. [*NYSE symbol*] (SPSG)
BTX .... Barytex Resources Corp. [*Vancouver Stock Exchange symbol*]
BTX .... Batrachotoxin [*Biochemistry*]
BTX .... Benzene, Toluene, and Xylene
BTX .... Betoota [*Queensland*] [*Airport symbol*] (AD)
BTX .... Bildschirmtext [*Viewdata system*] [*Federal Ministry of Posts and Telecommunications*] [*Germany*]
BTX .... Bungarotoxin [*Also, BGT, BuTx*] [*Biochemistry*]
BTX .... Butadiene Extraction [*Chemical engineering*]
BTX-B .... Brevetoxin-B [*Biochemistry*]
BTY .... Battery
BTY .... Beatty [*Nevada*] [*Seismograph station code, US Geological Survey Closed*] (SEIS)
BTY .... Beatty, NV [*Location identifier FAA*] (FAAL)
BTY .... Beauty
BTY .... British Telecommn ADR [*NYSE symbol*] (TTSB)
BTY .... British Telecommunications Ltd. [*NYSE symbol Toronto Stock Exchange symbol*] (SPSG)
BTZ .... Below the Treatment Zone (GNE)
BTZ .... Berlitz International [*NYSE symbol*] (SPSG)
BTZ .... Bursa [*Turkey*] [*Airport symbol Obsolete*] (OAG)
BTZ .... Butazolidin [*Pharmacology*] (DAVI)
BU .... Backup (KSC)
BU .... Bakers' Union [*British*] (DI)
BU .... Baptist Union
BU .... Bargaining Unit (GFGA)
BU .... Base Unit
BU .... Base-Up (Prism) [*Ophthalmology*]
BU .... Bath Unit [*British and Canadian*] [*Military*]
BU .... Beatles Unlimited (EA)
BU .... Bend Up
BU .... Biblische Untersuchungen [*A publication*] (BJA)
BU .... Binding Unit (IEEE)
BU .... Biology Unit [*American Topical Association*] (EA)
Bu .... Blue
BU .... Boatowners Unlimited [*An association*] (EA)
BU .... Bodansky Unit [*Also, BD, BOD*] [*Clinical chemistry*] (AAMN)
BU .... Boston University [*Massachusetts*]
BU .... Bottom Up
BU .... Braathens SAFE Airtransport [*ICAO designator*] (AD)
BU .... Branch Unit [*Computer science*] (PCM)
BU .... Brandeis University [*Waltham, MA*] (BJA)
B/U .... Breaking Up (ADA)
BU .... Breath Units
BU .... Brick Unprotected [*Insurance classification*]
BU .... Brilliant Uncirculated [*Condition of coins*] [*Numismatics*]
BU .... Bromouracil [*Biochemistry*]
BU .... Brooklyn Union Gas [*NYSE symbol*] (TTSB)
BU .... Brooklyn Union Gas Co. [*Wall Street slang name: "Bug"*] [*NYSE symbol*] (SPSG)
BU .... Brown University [*Rhode Island*]
BU .... Builder [*Navy rating*]

BU............ Buildup (KSC)
bu .... Bulgaria [*MARC country of publication*] [*Library of Congress*] (LCCP)
BU............ Bulgaria [*IYRU nationality code*]
Bu .... Bulgarus de Bulgarinis [*Deceased, 1166*] [*Authority cited in pre-1607 legal work*] (DSA)
BU............... Bulk [*Substrate*] [*Electron device*] (MSA)
BU............... Bulk Freight Containers [*Shipping*] (DCTA)
BU ..... Bulletin (WGA)
BU............... Buoy Boat
BU............... Bureau (AABC)
BU............... Burglary
BU............... Buried (ROG)
BU............... Burma [*ANSI two-letter standard code*] (CNC)
BU............... Burn Unit [*Medicine*]
BU............... Burnup
BU............... Bushel
BU............... Bushmaster Aircraft Corp. [*ICAO aircraft manufacturer identifier*] (ICAO)
BU............... Busulfan [*Antineoplastic drug*] (CDI)
BU............... Bus Unit [*Computer science*]
Bu .... Butyl [*Organic chemistry*]
BU............... Buzzer (IEEE)
BU............... USAF [*United States Air Force*] Specification Bulletin (MCD)
BU1............ Builder, First Class [*Navy rating*]
BU2............ Builder, Second Class [*Navy rating*]
BU3............ Builder, Third Class [*Navy rating*]
BUA............ Air Busol [*Ukraine*] [*FAA designator*] (FAAC)
BuA............. Babylonien und Assyrien [*A publication*] (BJA)
BUA .... Baptist Union of Australia
BUA .... Blood Uric Acid [*Clinical chemistry*] (CPH)
BUA .... Booster Umbilical Assembly
BUA .... British United Airways
BUA .... Buffalo, SD [*Location identifier FAA*] (FAAL)
BUA .... Buka Island [*Papua New Guinea*] [*Airport symbol*] (OAG)
BUA .... Business Aviation AS [*Denmark ICAO designator*] (FAAC)
BUAC .... British Universities Accommodation Consortium
BUAER .... Bureau of Aeronautics [*Later, Naval Air Systems Command*] [*Obsolete*]
BUAS .... Border Union Agricultural Society [*British*]
BUAS .... British Universities Association of Slavists
BUAV .... British Union for the Abolition of Vivisection
BUB .... Backup Block (MCD)
BUB .... Bubble (KSC)
BUB .... Buchberg [*Switzerland*] [*Seismograph station code, US Geological Survey*] (SEIS)
BUB .... Budding Uninhibited by Benzimidazole [*Cytology*]
BuB .... Bureau of the Budget [*Later, OMB*]
BUB .... Burwell, NE [*Location identifier FAA*] (FAAL)
BUBGRO ...... Bubble Growth (PDAA)
BUBL .... Bulletin Board for Libraries [*British*]
BUBMEM ..... Bubble Memory [*Data storage device*] [*Computer science*] (MSA)
BUBUD .... Bureau of the Budget [*Later, OMB*]
BUC .... Backup Computer (CET)
BUC .... Backup Controller (MCD)
Buc .... Buccal [*Dentistry*] (DAVI)
BUC .... Bucharest [*Romania*] [*Seismograph station code, US Geological Survey*] (SEIS)
BUC .... Buckhorn, California [*Spaceflight Tracking and Data Network*] [*NASA*]
BUC .... Bucks County Community College, Newtown, PA [*OCLC symbol*] (OCLC)
BUC .... Buffalo, Union-Carolina Railroad (IIA)
BUC .... Burketown [*Australia Airport symbol*] (OAG)
BUC .... Chief Builder [*Navy rating*]
BUC .... MK Burundi Air Cargo [*ICAO designator*] (FAAC)
BUC1 .... Bucharest [*Romania*] [*Seismograph station code, US Geological Survey*] (SEIS)
BUC2 .... Bucharest [*Romania*] [*Seismograph station code, US Geological Survey*] (SEIS)
BUCA .... Baseball Umpires Council of Australia
BUCA .... Constructionman Apprentice, Builder, Striker [*Navy rating*]
BUCAIN .... Dibucaine Number [*Organic chemistry*] (DAVI)
BUC & R....... Bureau of Construction and Repair [*Until 1940*] [*Navy*]
BUCC .... Buccaneer Aircraft [*"Banana Bomber"*] [*British*] (DSUE)
Buch .... Buchanan's Cape Of Good Hope Reports [*A publication*] (DLA)
Buch .... Buchanan's Court of Session [*1800-13*] [*Scotland*] [*A publication*] (DLA)
Buch .... Buchanan's New Jersey Equity Reports [*A publication*] (DLA)
Buch .... Buchanan's Supreme Court Reports [*Cape Colony*] [*A publication*] (DLA)
Buch AC....... Buchanan's Appeal Court Reports, Cape Of Good Hope [*A publication*] (DLA)
Buchan .... Buchanan's New Jersey Equity Reports [*A publication*] (DLA)
Buchanan ..... Buchanan's Reports, Court of Session and Justiciary [*Scotland*] [*A publication*] (DLA)
Buch App Cas... Buchanan's Appeal Court Reports, Cape Of Good Hope [*A publication*] (DLA)
Buch Cas ..... Buchanan's Remarkable Criminal Cases [*Scotland*] [*A publication*] (DLA)
Buch Ct Ap Cape GH... Buchanan's Appeal Court Reports, Cape Of Good Hope [*A publication*] (DLA)
Buch Ct App Cape G H... Buchanan's Appeal Court Reports, Cape Of Good Hope [*A publication*] (ILCA)
BuChE......... Butyrylcholinesterase [*An enzyme*]
Buch E Cape GH... Buchanan's Cape Of Good Hope Reports [*A publication*] (DLA)

Buch Eq (NJ)... Buchanan's New Jersey Equity Reports [*A publication*] (DLA)
Buch J Cape GH... Buchanan's Reports, Cape Of Good Hope [*A publication*] (DLA)
Buch Lien Law... Buchan's California Lien Laws [*A publication*] (DLA)
Buch Pr Pl ... Buchanan's Precedents of Pleading [*A publication*] (DLA)
Buch Rep..... Buchanan's Cape Of Good Hope Reports [*A publication*] (DLA)
Buch SC Rep... Buchanan's Supreme Court Reports, Cape Of Good Hope [*1868-79*] [*South Africa*] [*A publication*] (DLA)
Buch Tr........ Buchanan's Remarkable Criminal Cases [*Scotland*] [*A publication*] (DLA)
BUCK .... Buckhead America [*NASDAQ symbol*] (TTSB)
BUCK .... Buckhead America Corp. [*NASDAQ symbol*] (SAG)
BUCK .... Buckingham [*Municipal borough in England*]
BUCK .... Buckland [*England*]
BUCK .... Buckram [*Fabric*]
Buck........... Buck's English Cases in Bankruptcy [*1816-20*] [*A publication*] (DLA)
Buck........... Buck's Reports [*7-8 Montana*] [*A publication*] (DLA)
BuckAm ...... Buckhead America Corp. [*Associated Press*] (SAG)
Buck Bankr (Eng)... Buck's English Cases in Bankruptcy [*1816-20*] [*A publication*] (DLA)
Buck Cas ..... Buck's English Cases in Bankruptcy [*1816-20*] [*A publication*] (DLA)
BuckCel ...... Buckeye Cellulose Corp. [*Associated Press*] (SAG)
Buck Comp Act... Buckley on the Companies Acts [*1873-1949*] [*A publication*] (DLA)
Buck Cooke... Bucknill's Cooke's Cases of Practice, Common Pleas [*England*] [*A publication*] (DLA)
Buck Dec ..... Buckner's Decisions [*in Freeman's Mississippi Chancery Reports, 1839-43*] [*A publication*] (DLA)
Buck Eccl Law... Buck's Massachusetts Ecclesiastical Law [*A publication*] (DLA)
Buckeye ...... Buckeye Partners Ltd. [*Associated Press*] (SAG)
Buck Ins ..... Bucknill. Care of the Insane [*1880*] [*A publication*] (DLA)
Buckl .... Buckley on the Companies Acts [*1873-1949*] [*A publication*] (DLA)
Buckle .... Buckle, Inc. [*Associated Press*] (SAG)
Buck Lun ..... Bucknill on Lunacy [*A publication*] (DLA)
Bucknell U ... Bucknell University (GAGS)
BUCKS .... Buckinghamshire [*County in England*]
Bucks.......... Buckinghamshire [*County in England*] (ODBW)
Bucks.......... Bucks County Law Reporter [*Pennsylvania*] [*A publication*] (DLA)
Bucks Co L Rep... Bucks County Law Reporter [*Pennsylvania*] [*A publication*] (DLA)
Bucks Co LR (PA)... Bucks County Law Reporter [*Pennsylvania*] [*A publication*] (DLA)
BUCM .... Master Chief Builder [*Navy rating*]
BUCN .... Builder, Constructionman (DNAB)
BUCO .... Buildings Control Officer
BUCO .... Build-Up Control Organization [*Established to supervise flow of personnel and equipment to the Continent, immediately following Normandy invasion*] [*British World War II*]
BUCON........ Bureau of Construction and Repair [*Until 1940*] [*Navy*]
BUCOP........ British Union Catalogue of Periodicals [*A publication*]
BUCS .... Backup Control System (MCD)
BUCS .... Bath University Computing Services [*British*] (AIE)
BUCS .... Senior Chief Builder [*Navy rating*]
BUCS/ST...... BUCS [*Backup Control System*] Self Test (MCD)
BUCT .... Beijing University of Chemical Technology
BUCU .... Burring Cutter
BucyEr........ Bucyrus-Erie Co. [*Associated Press*] (SAG)
BUD .... Air Budapest Club Ltd. [*Hungary ICAO designator*] (FAAC)
BUD .... Anheuser Busch [*NYSE symbol*] (SAG)
BUD .... Anheuser-Busch Cos. [*NYSE symbol*] (TTSB)
BUD .... Basic Underwater Demolition Team [*Marine Corps*]
BUD .... Beneficial Use Date
BUD .... Benefits and Use Division [*Environmental Protection Agency*] (GFGA)
BUD .... Big Ugly Dish [*Traditional satellite dish antenna*]
BUD .... British Urban Development
BUD .... Budapest [*Hungary*] [*Airport symbol*] (OAG)
BUD .... Budapest [*Hungary*] [*Seismograph station code, US Geological Survey*] (SEIS)
BUD2 .... Budd Canada, Inc. [*Toronto Stock Exchange symbol*]
BUD .... Budget (AFM)
bud .... Budget (ODBW)
BUD .... Budget Office [*Army*]
BUD .... Budget Office, Department of the Army (AAGC)
BUD .... Marion, OH [*Location identifier FAA*] (FAAL)
BUDC .... Backup Digital Computer
BUDD.......... Buddhism
BUDFIN....... Budget and Finance Division [*NATO*] (NATG)
budgie .... Budgerigar (ODBW)
BUDL .... Budleigh [*England*]
BUDO .... Ballistic Missile Defense Organization (AAGC)
BUDOCKS..... Bureau of Yards and Docks [*Later, NFEC*] [*Washington, DC*] [*Navy*]
Budpst .... Budapest (BARN)
BUDR.......... 5-Bromodeoxyuridine (DOG)
BUdR .... BromouraciIdeoxyriboside [*Antineoplastic drug*]
BUDS .... Backup Digital System
BUD/S......... Basic Underwater Demolition/SEAL [*Sea, Air, and Land Capability*] Training Department [*Navy*]
BUDS .... Bilateral Upper Dorsal Sympathectomy [*Medicine*] (DMAA)
BUDS .... Building Utility Design System (MHDI)
BUDSU........ British Urban Development Services Unit [*Department of Environment*] (DI)
BUDU .... Bromodeoxyuridine [*Antineoplastic drug*] (DAVI)
BUDWSR ..... Brown University Display for Working Set References
BUE............ Banque de l'Union Europeenne [*European Union Bank*] [*France*]
BUE............ Bilateral Upper Extremity [*Occupational therapy*]
BUE............ Both Upper Extremities [*Medicine*] (DMAA)

BUE............ Buddhist Union of Europe (EAIO)
BUE............ Buenos Aires [*Argentina*] [*Airport symbol*] (OAG)
BUE............ Built-Up Edge (MCD)
BUEC .... Backup Emergency Communications
BUENG........ Bureau of Engineering [*Obsolete Navy*]
BUE's......... Both Upper Extremities [*Neurology and orthopedics*] (DAVI)
BUF............ Backup Facility [*Nuclear war games*]
BUF............ Big Ugly Fellow [*Slang for B-52 bomber or other large aircraft*] [*Bowdlerized version*] (DOMA)
BUF............ Black United Front [*South Africa*] (PD)
BUF............ British Ultimate Federation (DBA)
BUF............ British Union of Fascists
BUF............ Buffalo [*New York*] [*Seismograph station code, US Geological Survey Closed*] (SEIS)
BUF............ Buffalo [*Rat variety*]
BUF............ Buffalo [*New York*] [*Airport symbol*]
BUF............ Buffalo Resources [*Vancouver Stock Exchange symbol*]
BUF............ Buffer [*Computer science*]
BUF............ State University of New York at Buffalo, Buffalo, NY [*OCLC symbol*] (OCLC)
BUFCA .... British Urethane Foam Contractors Association (DBA)
BUFCS .... Backup Flight Control System (MCD)
Bufete......... Bufete Industrial [*Associated Press*] (SAG)
BUFF.......... Big Ugly Fat Fellow [*Nickname for B-52 bomber*]
BUFF.......... Brothers United for Future Foreskins (EA)
BUFF.......... Buffalo
BUFF.......... Buffer (NASA)
Buff ADR..... Buffelsfontein Gold Mines Ltd. [*Associated Press*] (SAG)
Buffels........ Buffelsfontein Gold Mining Co. [*Associated Press*] (SAG)
Buffets........ Buffets, Inc. [*Associated Press*] (SAG)
Buff Super Ct... Sheldon's Superior Court Reports [*Buffalo, New York*] [*A publication*] (DLA)
Buff Super Ct (NY)... Sheldon's Superior Court Reports [*Buffalo, New York*] [*A publication*] (DLA)
Buffton......... Buffton Corp. [*Associated Press*] (SAG)
BUFLY .... Butterfly [*Stroke*] [*Swimming*]
BUFORA...... British UFO Research Association (EAIO)
BUFORA...... British Unidentified Flying Objects Research Association
BUFR.......... Binary Universal for Representation [*Computer science*]
BUFVC .... British Universities Film and Video Council [*Information service or system*] (IID)
BUG .... Basic Update Generator (MHDB)
BUG .... Benguela [*Angola*] [*Airport symbol*] (OAG)
BUG .... Bochum - University [*Federal Republic of Germany*] [*Seismograph station code, US Geological Survey*] (SEIS)
BUG .... BOMARC [*Boeing-Michigan Aeronautical Research Center*] Unintegrated Guidance (IAA)
BUG .... Bottom-Up Greedy
BUG .... Brooklyn Union Gas Co.
BUG .... Buccal Ganglion [*Dentistry*]
BUG .... Bugatti [*Automobile*]
BUG .... Bugler [*Navy*]
BUG .... Business User Group [*Computer science*]
BugCreek..... Bugaboo Creek Steak House [*Associated Press*] (SAG)
BUGINAR .... Buginarium [*Nasal Bougie*] [*Pharmacy*]
BUGS .... Backup Guidance System [*NASA*]
BUGS .... Brown University Graphic System
BUH .... Bucharest [*Romania*] [*Airport symbol*] (OAG)
BUH .... Buehlerhoehe [*Federal Republic of Germany*] [*Seismograph station code, US Geological Survey*] (SEIS)
BUH .... Builder, Heavy [*Navy rating*]
BUI.............. Badminton Union of Ireland (EAIO)
BUI.............. Bokoudini [*Indonesia*] [*Airport symbol*] (OAG)
BUI.............. Brain Uptake Index [*Physiology*]
BUI.............. Knoxville, TN [*Location identifier FAA*] (FAAL)
BUIA .... British United Island Airways
BUIC .... Backup Interceptor Control [*System*] [*Air Force*]
BUIC .... Bureau [*of Naval Personnel*] Unit Identification Code
BUICS .... Backup Interceptor Control System [*Air Force*]
BUII .... Buia [*Italy*] [*Seismograph station code, US Geological Survey*] (SEIS)
BUILD .... Base for Uniform Language Definition [*Computer science*] (IEEE)
BUILD .... Bi-University Institutional Liaison for Development (SAA)
BUILD .... BOI [*Board of Investments*] Unit for Industrial Linkage Development (ECON)
BUILD .... Building (ROG)
Building & Eng J... Building and Engineering Journal [*A publication*]
BuildT......... Builders Transport, Inc. [*Associated Press*] (SAG)
BUILT.......... Birmingham University Industrial Liaison for Technology [*Research center British*]
BU Int'l LJ... Boston University. International Law Journal [*A publication*] (DLA)
BUIRA......... British Universities Industrial Relations Association
BUIS .... Barrier Up Indicator System (MSA)
BUIS .... Buck Island Reef National Monument
BUISYS....... Barrier Up Indicator System
BUJ............. Baccalaureus Utriusque Juris [*Bachelor of Both Laws; i.e., Canon and Civil Laws*]
BUJ............. Blue Ridge, TX [*Location identifier FAA*] (FAAL)
BUK .... Albuq [*Yemen*] [*Airport symbol*] (OAG)
BUK .... Aspen, CO [*Location identifier FAA*] (FAAL)
BUKS .... Butler National Corp. [*NASDAQ symbol*] (SAG)
BUKS .... Butler Natl [*NASDAQ symbol*] (TTSB)
BUL............. Blue Airlines [*Zaire*] [*ICAO designator*] (FAAC)
BUL............. Brandon University Library [*UTLAS symbol*]
BUL............. Builder, Light [*Navy rating*]

BUL............ Bulawayo [*Zimbabwe*] [*Seismograph station code, US Geological Survey*] (SEIS)
BUL............ Bulgaria (WDAA)
bul .... Bulgarian [*MARC language code Library of Congress*] (LCCP)
Bul............ Bulgarus de Bulgarinis [*Deceased, 1166*] [*Authority cited in pre-1607 legal work*] (DSA)
BUL............ Bullet Group, Inc. [*Formerly, Bullet Energy Ltd.*] [*Vancouver Stock Exchange symbol*]
BUL............ Bulletin (AFM)
BUL............ Bulolo [*Papua New Guinea*] [*Airport symbol*] (OAG)
BUL............ Bulolo [*New Guinea*] [*Airport symbol*] (AD)
BUL............ Miami, FL [*Location identifier FAA*] (FAAL)
BULG .... Bulgaria
Bulg............ Bulgaria (VRA)
Bulg............ Bulgarus de Bulgarinis [*Deceased, 1166*] [*Authority cited in pre-1607 legal work*] (DSA)
Bulg............ Radioprom & Orfei (Bulgaria) [*Record label*]
BULIT.......... Bulimia Test [*Personality development test*] [*Psychology*]
BULL.......... Bulletin
bull........... Bulletin [*News*] [*Advertising*] (WDMC)
BULL.......... Bulliat [*Let It Boil*] [*Pharmacy*]
BULL.......... Bull Run Corp. [*NASDAQ symbol*] (NQ)
Bull Am Acad Psych & L... Bulletin. American Academy of Psychiatry and the Law [*A publication*] (DLA)
Bull & B Bank... Buller and Bund's Manual of Bankruptcy [*A publication*] (DLA)
Bull & C Dig... Bullard and Curry's Louisiana Digest [*A publication*] (DLA)
Bull & Cur Dig... Bullard and Curry's Louisiana Digest [*A publication*] (DLA)
Bull & L...... Bullen and Leake's Pleadings on Actions in King's Bench Decisions [*A publication*] (DLA)
Bull & L Pr... Bullen and Leake's Precedents of Pleading [*A publication*] (DLA)
Bull Anglo-Sov LA... Bulletin. Anglo-Soviet Law Association [*A publication*] (DLA)
Bull Aust Ind Devt Ass... Australian Industries Development Association. Bulletin [*A publication*]
BullBear ...... Bull & Bear Group, Inc. [*Associated Press*] (SAG)
Bull Can Welfare Law... Bulletin of Canadian Welfare Law [*A publication*] (DLA)
Bull Coll Wm & Mary... William and Mary College. Bulletin [*A publication*] (DLA)
Bull Comp L... American Bar Association. Comparative Law Bureau. Bulletin [*A publication*] (DLA)
Bull Comp Lab Rel... Bulletin of Comparative Labour Relations [*A publication*] (DLA)
Bull Crim..... Bulletin des Arrets de la Chambre Criminelle de la Cour de Cassation [*A publication*] (ILCA)
Bull Czech L... Bulletin of Czechoslovak Law [*A publication*] (DLA)
Bull Dis ...... Buller's Law of Distress for Rent [*A publication*] (DLA)
Bull Eccl ..... Bullingbroke's Ecclesiastical Law [*A publication*] (DLA)
Buller NP..... Buller's Law of Nisi Prius [*England*] [*A publication*] (DLA)
Bulletin Comp L... Bulletin. Comparative Law Bureau [*A publication*] (DLA)
BulletSp....... Bullet Sports International, Inc. [*Associated Press*] (SAG)
Bull Geol Survey Sth Aust... Bulletin. Geological Survey of South Australia [*A publication*]
Bull HN....... Bull HN [*Honeywell and NEC*] Information Systems Inc. [*Billerica, MA*] (CDE)
Bull IBA ...... Bulletin. International Bar Association [*A publication*] (DLA)
Bull ICJ....... Bulletin. International Commission of Jurists [*A publication*] (DLA)
BULLIENT .... Bullientis [*Boiling*] [*Pharmacy*] (ROG)
Bull III .... Bulletin. Institut Intermediaire International [*A publication*] (DLA)
Bull Int Sc Soc... Bulletin International des Sciences Sociales [*A publication*] (DLA)
Bull JAG ..... Bulletin. Judge Advocate General of the Army [*United States*] [*A publication*] (DLA)
Bull JAGA.... Bulletin of the Judge Advocate General of the Army [*Now LAAWS BBS*] (AAGC)
Bull Legal Devel... Bulletin of Legal Developments [*A publication*] (DLA)
Bull Leg Dev... Bulletin of Legal Developments [*A publication*] (DLA)
Bull L Science & Tech... Bulletin of Law, Science, and Technology [*A publication*] (DLA)
Bull Mediev Canon L... Bulletin of Medieval Canon Law [*A publication*] (DLA)
Bull Monaro Conserv Soc... Monaro Conservation Society. Bulletin [*A publication*]
Bull Nat Tax Assoc... Bulletin. National Tax Association [*A publication*] (DLA)
Bull NP........ Buller's Law of Nisi Prius [*England*] [*A publication*] (DLA)
Bull NP (Eng)... Buller's Law of Nisi Prius [*England*] [*A publication*] (DLA)
Bull NSW Inst Ed Res... New South Wales Institute for Educational Research. Bulletin [*A publication*]
Bull NTA...... Bulletin. National Tax Association [*A publication*] (DLA)
Bull O........ Weekly Law Bulletin [*Ohio*] [*A publication*] (DLA)
Bull (Ohio).. Weekly Law Bulletin (Ohio) [*A publication*] (DLA)
Bull Que Soc Crim... Bulletin. Quebec Society of Criminology [*A publication*] (DLA)
Bull Reserve Bank Aust... Reserve Bank of Australia. Bulletin [*A publication*]
Bull Run ...... Bull Run Corp. [*Associated Press*] (SAG)
Bull Rylands Libr... Bulletin. John Rylands Library [*A publication*] (OCD)
Bull Syd Div Instn Eng Aust... Bulletin. Sydney Division. Institution of Engineers of Australia [*A publication*]
Bull Us .... Bulletin Usuel des Lois et Arretes [*A publication*] (ILCA)
Bull Waseda Univ Inst of Comp Law... Waseda University. Institute of Comparative Law. Bulletin [*Tokyo, Japan*] [*A publication*] (DLA)
Buls .... Bulstrode's English King's Bench Reports [*1610-25*] [*A publication*] (DLA)
Bulst .... Bulstrode's English King's Bench Reports [*1610-25*] [*A publication*] (DLA)
Bulstr.......... Bulstrode's English King's Bench Reports [*1610-25*] [*A publication*] (DLA)
BUM........... Bargaining Unit Member [*of a faculty union*]
BUM........... Break-Up Missile (MCD)
BUM........... Bulletin. Societe "Union Musicologique" [*A publication*]
BuM............ Bureau of Mines [*Department of the Interior*]
BUM............ Butler, MO [*Location identifier FAA*] (FAAL)

BUM & S ..... Bureau of Medicine and Surgery [Navy]

BUMED .... Bureau of Medicine and Surgery [Obsolete Navy]

BUMEDINST... Bureau of Medicine and Surgery Instructions [Navy]

BUMF .... Bum-Fodder [Toilet paper] [Slang British] (DSUE)

BUMINES.... Bureau of Mines [Department of the Interior]

BUM Int ...... BUM International, Inc. [Associated Press] (SAG)

BUMM .... BUM International, Inc. [NASDAQ symbol] (SAG)

BUMP .... Basic Update Matrix Program

BUMP .... Boston University Marine Program [Boston University] [Research center]

BUMP .... Bottom-Up Modular Programming

BUMP .... Bumpstead [England]

Bump B'k'cy... Bump on Bankruptcy [A publication] (DLA)

Bump Comp... Bump on Composition in Bankruptcy [A publication] (DLA)

Bump Const Dec... Bump's Notes on Constitutional Decisions [A publication] (DLA)

Bump Fed Pr... Bump. Federal Procedure [A publication] (DLA)

Bump Fraud Conv... Bump on Fraudulent Conveyances [A publication] (DLA)

Bump Fr Conv... Bump on Fraudulent Conveyances [A publication] (DLA)

Bump Int Rev... Bump's Internal Revenue Laws [A publication] (DLA)

Bump NC ...... Bump's Notes on Constitutional Decisions [A publication] (DLA)

Bump Pat..... Bump's Law of Patents, Trade-Marks, Etc. [A publication] (DLA)

Bump's Int Rev Law... Bump's Internal Revenue Laws [A publication] (DLA)

Bump St L ... Bump. United States Stamp Laws [A publication] (DLA)

BUMS .... Bachelor of Unani Medicine and Surgery

BUN .... Blood Urea Nitrogen [Medicine]

BUN .... Buenaventura [Colombia] [Airport symbol] (AD)

BUN .... Bulletin (NTCM)

BUN .... Bunion [Orthopedics and podiatry] (DAVI)

BUN .... Bunnythorpe [New Zealand] [Seismograph station code, US Geological Survey Closed] (SEIS)

BUNAC........ British Universities North America Club (EA)

BUNAV........ Bureau of Navigation [Later, Bureau of Naval Personnel] [Navy]

Bunb .... Bunbury. English Exchequer Reports [145 English Reprint] [A publication] (DLA)

BUNCH........ Burroughs, UNIVAC, NCR, Control Data, Honeywell [IBM competitors in computer manufacture]

BUNG .... Bungalow [Classified advertising] (ADA)

BUNK .... Bunkum [Nonsense] [Slang] (DSUE)

BUNO .... Bureau Number [Aircraft identification] [Obsolete Navy]

BUNS .... Block Unit Numbers (MCD)

BUNT .... British Underground Nuclear Test (MCD)

BUNY .... Board of Underwriters of New York (EA)

Buny Dom L... Bunyon. Domestic Law [1875] [A publication] (DLA)

Buny Fire Ins... Bunyon. Fire Insurance [7th ed.] [1923] [A publication] (DLA)

Buny Life Ass... Bunyon on Life Assurance [A publication] (DLA)

Buny Life Ins... Bunyon. Life Insurance [5th ed.] [1914] [A publication] (DLA)

BUNZ .... Schlotzskys, Inc. [NASDAQ symbol] (SAG)

BUNZ .... Schlotzsky's Inc. [NASDAQ symbol] (TTSB)

BUO .... Beaumont, CA [Location identifier FAA] (FAAL)

BUO .... Bilirubin of Unknown Origin [Gastroenterology] (DAVI)

BUO .... Bleeding [or Bruising] of Undetermined Origin [Medicine]

BUO .... Burao [Somalia] [Airport symbol] (OAG)

BUORD .... Bureau of Ordnance [Functions transferred to Bureau of Naval Weapons, 1960, and later to Naval Ordnance Systems Command] [Navy]

BUORDINST... Bureau of Ordnance Instructions [Later, NAVORDINST]

BUOU .... Backup Optical Unit (NASA)

B/UP .... Back Up [Automotive engineering]

BUP .... Backup Plate

BUP .... Basotho Unity Party [South Africa] [Political party] (PPW)

BUP .... Bend Up [Technical drawings]

BUP .... Bristol United Press Ltd., Bristol, United Kingdom [Library symbol Library of Congress] (LCLS)

BUP .... British United Press

BUP .... Buprenorphine [Analgesic]

BUP .... Pittsfield, ME [Location identifier FAA] (FAAL)

BUPA .... British United Provident Association (DCTA)

BUPERS .... Bureau of Naval Personnel [Also, BNP, NAVPERS]

BUPERSCONINSTRBIL... Bureau of Naval Personnel Controlled Instructor Billets

BUPP .... Backup Plate, Perforated

Buppie .... Black Urban Professional [Lifestyle classification]

BUPS .... Beacon, Ultra Portable "S" Band [Navy]

BUPX .... Beacon, Ultra Portable X Band [Navy] (IAA)

BUQ .... Bulawayo [Zimbabwe] [Airport symbol] (OAG)

BUR .... Backup Rate [Ventilator] [Medicine] (DAVI)

BUR .... Back Up Register

BUR .... Bottom-Up Review

BUR .... Builder, Concrete [Navy rating]

BUR .... Built-Up Roofing

BUR .... Burbank [California] [Airport symbol]

BUR .... Bureau (AFM)

bur............. Bureau (WDMC)

BUR .... Bureau

BUR .... Buried

bur............. Burlap (VRA)

BUR .... Burlington [Vermont] [Seismograph station code, US Geological Survey Closed] (SEIS)

BUR .... Burlington Industries [NYSE symbol] (TTSB)

BUR .... Burlington Industries, Inc. [NYSE symbol] (SPSG)

BUR .... Burlington Public Library [UTLAS symbol]

BUR .... Burma [ANSI three-letter standard code] (CNC)

bur............. Burmese [MARC language code Library of Congress] (LCCP)

Bur............. Burnett's Wisconsin Supreme Court Reports [1841-43] [A publication] (DLA)

BUR .... Burnt Island Gold Ltd. (NPL) [Vancouver Stock Exchange symbol]

Bur............. Burrow. English King's Bench Reports [A publication] (DLA)

BUR .... Business Air AG [Switzerland ICAO designator] (FAAC)

Bur & Gres Eq Pl... Burroughs and Gresson's Irish Equity Pleader [A publication] (DLA)

Bur Ass ...... Burrill on Voluntary Assignments [A publication] (DLA)

B Urb Pl ...... Bachelor of Urban Planning

BUrbRegPlan... Bachelor of Urban and Regional Planning

Bur Chy...... Burrough's History of the Chancery [A publication] (DLA)

Bur Circ Ev... Burrill on Circumstantial Evidence [A publication] (DLA)

BURD .... Biplane Ultra-Light Research Device (PDAA)

BURD .... Burdick [Suction] [Surgery] (DAVI)

Burd.......... Burdick Suction [Medicine] (BABM)

Burdick Crime... Burdick's Law of Crime [A publication] (DLA)

Burdick Roman Law... Burdick's Principles of Roman Law [A publication] (DLA)

BURDS........ Burroughs Distribution Scheduling System [Computer science] (BUR)

BUREC .... Bureau of Reclamation [Later, WPRS] [Department of the Interior]

BurEl.......... Bureau of Electronic Publishing, Inc. [Associated Press] (SAG)

BurEIP........ Bureau of Electronic Publishing, Inc. [Associated Press] (SAG)

Burf........... Burford's Reports [6-18 Oklahoma] [A publication] (DLA)

Bur Forms ... Burrill's Forms [A publication] (DLA)

BURG .... Burg [Commonly used] (OPSA)

BURG .... Burgess

BURG .... Burgher (ROG)

Burg........... Burglary

BURG .... Burgomaster (ROG)

Burg Col & For Law... Burge on Colonial and Foreign Law [A publication] (DLA)

Burg Dig ...... Burgwyn's Digest Maryland Reports [A publication] (DLA)

Burge App ... Burge on Appellate Jurisdiction [1841] [A publication] (DLA)

Burge Col Law... Burge on Colonial and Foreign Law [A publication] (DLA)

Burge Confl Law... Burge on the Conflict of Laws [A publication] (DLA)

Burge Mar Int L... Burge on Maritime International Law [A publication] (DLA)

Burgen......... Burgess' Reports [16-49 Ohio] [A publication] (DLA)

Burgess .... Burgess' Reports [16-49 Ohio] [A publication] (DLA)

Burge Sur ... Burge on Suretyship [A publication] (DLA)

BURGL........ Burglary (DLA)

BURGS........ Burgs [Commonly used] (OPSA)

Burgw MD Dig... Burgwyn's Digest Maryland Reports [A publication] (DLA)

BURISA........ British Urban and Regional Information System Association

Burke .... Burke Mills, Inc. [Associated Press] (SAG)

Burke Cel Tr... Burke's Celebrated Trials [A publication] (DLA)

Burke Cop... Burke. Copyright [1842] [A publication] (DLA)

Burke Cr L ... Burke. Criminal Law [2nd ed.] [1845] [A publication] (DLA)

Burke Int Cop... Burke. International Copyright [1852] [A publication] (DLA)

Burke Pub Sch... Burke on the Law of Public Schools [A publication] (DLA)

Burke Tr ...... Burke's Celebrated Trials [A publication] (DLA)

Burks .... Burks' Reports [91-98 Virginia] [A publication] (DLA)

BURL .... Bradford University Research Ltd. [British] (IRUK)

BURL .... Burlesque (ROG)

Burlamaqui... Burlamaqui's Natural and Political Law [A publication] (DLA)

Bur Law Dic... Burrill's Law Dictionary [A publication] (DLA)

BurlCoat...... Burlington Coat Factory Warehouse Corp. [Associated Press] (SAG)

Burlesque Reps... Skillman's New York Police Reports [A publication] (DLA)

BurlInds....... Burlington Industries, Inc. [Formerly, Burlington Industries Equity] [Associated Press] (SAG)

Bur LJ.......... Burma Law Journal [A publication] (DLA)

Burl Nat....... Burlamaqui's Natural and Political Law [A publication] (DLA)

Burl Natural & Pol Law... Burlamaqui's Natural and Political Law [A publication] (DLA)

BurINSF....... Burlington Northern Santa Fe Corp. [Associated Press] (SAG)

Bur LR......... Burma Law Reports [A publication] (DLA)

BurlRsCl....... Burlington Resources Coal Seam Gas Royalty Trust [Associated Press] (SAG)

Bur LT .... Burma Law Times [A publication] (DLA)

BURM .... Burma (WDAA)

BURM .... Burmah Castrol Ltd. [NASDAQ symbol] (SAG)

Bur M .... Burrow's Reports Tempore Mansfield [England] [A publication] (DLA)

BURMA........ Be Undressed, Ready, My Angel [Correspondence] (DSUE)

Burma Law Inst J... Burma Law Institute. Journal [A publication] (DLA)

Burma L Inst J... Burma Law Institute. Journal [A publication] (DLA)

Burma LR .... Burma Law Reports [A publication] (DLA)

BurmhC........ Burmah Castrol Ltd. [Associated Press] (SAG)

Burm LJ....... Burma Law Journal [A publication] (DLA)

Burm LR ...... Burma Law Reports [A publication] (DLA)

Burm LT ...... Burma Law Times [A publication] (DLA)

BURMY........ Burmah Castrol plc ADR [NASDAQ symbol] (TTSB)

BURN .... British Unemployment Resource Network (PDAA)

Burn........... Burnett's Wisconsin Reports [A publication] (DLA)

BURN .... Burnham [England]

burn............ Burnished (VRA)

Burn............ High Commission Court [1865] [England] [A publication] (DLA)

Burn............ Star Chamber Proceedings [England] [A publication] (DLA)

BURN .... Water-Jel Tech [NASDAQ symbol] (TTSB)

BURN .... Water-Jel Technologies [NASDAQ symbol] (SAG)

Burn Att Pr... Burn's Attorney's Practice [A publication] (DLA)

Burn Cr L .... Burnet. Criminal Law of Scotland [A publication] (DLA)

Burn Dict ..... Burn's Law Dictionary [A publication] (DLA)

Burn Eccl ..... Burn's Ecclesiastical Law [A publication] (DLA)

Burn Ecc Law... Burn's Ecclesiastical Law [A publication] (DLA)

Burnet......... Burnet. Manuscript Decisions, Scotch Court of Session [A publication] (DLA)

Burnett........ Burnett's Reports [20-22 Oregon] [A publication] (DLA)

Burnett........ Burnett's Wisconsin Reports [A publication] (DLA)

Burnett's Rep... Burnett's Wisconsin Reports [A publication] (DLA)

Burnett (Wis)... Burnett's Wisconsin Reports [A publication] (DLA)

Burn JP........ Burn's Justice of the Peace [England] [A publication] (DLA)

Burn Law Dict... Burn's Law Dictionary [*A publication*] (DLA)
Burn Mar Ins... Burn's Marine Insurance [*A publication*] (DLA)
BurnPP .... Burnham Pacific Properties [*Associated Press*] (SAG)
Burns' Ann St... Burns' Annotated Statutes [*Indiana*] [*A publication*] (DLA)
Burns-Begg... Southern Rhodesia Reports [*A publication*] (DLA)
Burn's Ecc Law... Burn's Ecclesiastical Law [*A publication*] (DLA)
Burn's JP (Eng)... Burn's Justice of the Peace [*England*] [*A publication*] (DLA)
Burns Pract... Burns. Conveyancing Practice [*Scotland*] [*A publication*] (DLA)
Burns' Rev St... Burns' Annotated Statutes [*Indiana*] [*A publication*] (DLA)
Burn St Job... Burn on Stock Jobbing [*A publication*] (DLA)
BURNZ........ Water-Jel Technol Wrrt'A' [*NASDAQ symbol*] (TTSB)
BURP .... Bachelor of Urban and Regional Planning
BURP .... Backup Rate of Pitch
BURPIES..... Boozing Urban-Rural Parasites [*Lifestyle classification*]
Bur Pr......... Burrill's New York Practice [*A publication*] (DLA)
BURR.......... Backup Rate of Roll
Burr .... Burrow. English King's Bench Reports Tempore Lord Mansfield [*97, 98 English Reprint*] [*A publication*] (DLA)
Burr Adm .... Burrell's Admiralty Cases [*1584-1839*] [*A publication*] (DLA)
Burr & Gr Eq Pl... Burroughs and Gresson's Irish Equity Pleader [*A publication*] (DLA)
Burr Ass ...... Burrill on Assignments [*A publication*] (DLA)
BurrBr......... Burr-Brown Corp. [*Associated Press*] (SAG)
Burr Ch .... Burroughs' History of the Chancery [*A publication*] (DLA)
Burr Circ Ev... Burrill on Circumstantial Evidence [*A publication*] (DLA)
Burr Dict...... Burrill's Law Dictionary [*A publication*] (DLA)
Burrell .... Burrell's Reports, Admiralty, Edited by Marsden [*167 English Reprint*] [*A publication*] (DLA)
Burrell (Eng)... Burrell's Reports, Admiralty, Edited by Marsden [*167 English Reprint*] [*A publication*] (DLA)
Burr (Eng).... Burrow. English King's Bench Reports Tempore Lord Mansfield [*97, 98 English Reprint*] [*A publication*] (DLA)
Burr Forms... Burrill's Forms [*A publication*] (DLA)
Burrill .... Burrill's Law Dictionary [*A publication*] (DLA)
Burrill Ass ... Burrill on Voluntary Assignments [*A publication*] (DLA)
Burrill Assignm... Burrill on Assignments [*A publication*] (DLA)
Burrill Circ Ev... Burrill on Circumstantial Evidence [*A publication*] (DLA)
Burrill Pr ...... Burrill's Practice [*A publication*] (DLA)
Burr Law Dict... Burrill's Law Dictionary [*A publication*] (DLA)
Burrow........ Burrow's Reports, English King's Bench [*A publication*] (DLA)
Burrow Sett Cas... Burrow's English Settlement Cases [*A publication*] (DLA)
Burr Pr......... Burrill's New York Practice [*A publication*] (DLA)
Burr Pub Sec... Burroughs on Public Securities [*A publication*] (DLA)
Burr SC........ Burrow's English Settlement Cases [*A publication*] (DLA)
Burr S Cas... Burrow's English Settlement Cases [*A publication*] (DLA)
Burr S Cases... Burrow's English Settlement Cases [*A publication*] (DLA)
Burr Sett Cas... Burrow's English Settlement Cases [*A publication*] (DLA)
Burr Sett Cas (Eng)... Burrow's English Settlement Cases [*A publication*] (DLA)
Burr Tax ...... Burroughs on Taxation [*A publication*] (DLA)
Burr TM .... Burrow's Reports Tempore Mansfield [*England*] [*A publication*] (DLA)
Burr Tr........ Burr's Trial, Reported by Robertson [*A publication*] (DLA)
Burr Tr Rob... Burr's Trial, Reported by Robertson [*A publication*] (DLA)
BURS .... Bursar
Bur SC........ Burrow's English Settlement Cases [*A publication*] (DLA)
Bur Tax .... Burroughs on Taxation [*A publication*] (DLA)
Burt Bank..... Burton on Bankruptcy [*A publication*] (DLA)
Burt Cas ...... Burton's Collection of Cases and Opinions [*England*] [*A publication*] (DLA)
Burt Man ..... Burton. Manual of the Laws of Scotland [*A publication*] (DLA)
Burt Parl...... Burton's Parliamentary Diary [*A publication*] (DLA)
Burt Real Prop... Burton on Real Property [*A publication*] (DLA)
Burt RP .... Burton on Real Property [*A publication*] (DLA)
Burt Sc Tr.... Burton's Scotch Trials [*A publication*] (DLA)
Buru........... Burundi (VRA)
BURY .... Backup Rate of Yaw
BUS .... Bachelor of Urban Studies
BUS .... Backscatter Ultraviolet Spectrometer
BUS .... Bank of the United States
BUS .... Bartholin's, Urethral, Skene's [*Glands*] [*Medicine*]
BUS .... Batumi [*Former USSR Airport symbol*] (OAG)
BUS .... Beilstein Unique Sequence [*Chemistry*]
BUS .... BOMARC [*Boeing-Michigan Aeronautical Research Center*] Universal SAGE [*Semiautomatic Ground Environment*] (IAA)
BUS .... Broadcast Unknown Server [*Telecommunications*] (ACRL)
BUS .... Building Use Studies [*Research firm*] [*British*]
BUS .... Burmac Energy Corp. [*Vancouver Stock Exchange symbol*]
BUS .... Bushel
BUS .... Business (AFM)
BUS .... Business
bus............. Business (DD)
BUS .... Business Division [*Census*] (OICC)
Bus .... Busiris [*of Isocrates*] [*Classical studies*] (OCD)
BUS .... Busulfan [*Also, BSF*] [*Antineoplastic drug*]
BUS .... Greyhound Lines [*AMEX symbol*] (SPSG)
BUSA .... British Universities Society of Arts
BUSAC .... Bureau of Ships Analog Computer [*Obsolete Navy*]
Bus Admin... Business Administration (DLA)
BUSAK .... Bus Acknowledgement [*Computer science*] (TEL)
BUSAN........ Business Analyst Skills Evaluation [*Test*]
BUSANDA .... Bureau of Supplies and Accounts [*Later, NSUPSC*] [*Navy*]
Bus & Com... Business and Commerce [*A publication*] (DLA)
Bus & L .... Business and Law [*A publication*] (DLA)
Bus & Prof... Business and Professions [*A publication*] (DLA)
Bus & Prof C... Business and Professions Code (DLA)
BUSARB...... British-United States Amateur Rocket Bureau

Busb .... Busbee's North Carolina Law Reports [*A publication*] (DLA)
BUSBC......... Brazil-US Business Council (EA)
Busb Cr Dig... Busbee's Criminal Digest [*North Carolina*] [*A publication*] (DLA)
Busbee Eq (NC)... Busbee's North Carolina Equity Reports [*A publication*] (DLA)
Busb Eq ...... Busbee's North Carolina Equity Reports [*A publication*] (DLA)
Bus Bk R ..... Business Book Review [*A publication*] (BRI)
Busb L......... Busbee's North Carolina Law Reports [*A publication*] (DLA)
BUSCI .... British-United States Convoy Instructions
BUSCON ...... Microcomputer Bus Users' Show and Conference [*MultiDynamics, Inc.*] (TSPED)
BUSEG .... Bartholin's, Urethral, and Skene's Glands and External Genitalia [*Gynecology*] (DAVI)
BUSEN .... Beilstein Unique Sequence Number [*Chemistry*]
Bus Eq .... Busbee's North Carolina Equity Reports [*A publication*] (DLA)
BUSF .... British Universities Sports Federation
BUSG .... Burns United Support Group (EA)
BUSH .... Bushel
BUSH .... Bushing (MSA)
Bush .... Bush's Kentucky Reports [*64-77 Kentucky*] [*A publication*] (DLA)
BUSH .... Bush Terminal R. R. [*AAR code*]
BUSH .... Buy United States Here [*Program to procure US-made supplies from overseas subsidiaries of US firms*] (AFM)
Bush BA....... Bush Boake Allen, Inc. [*Associated Press*] (SAG)
Bush Dig...... Bush's Digest of Florida Laws [*A publication*] (DLA)
Bush Elec ... Bushby. Parliamentary Elections [*5th ed.*] [*1880*] [*A publication*] (DLA)
BushInd .... Bush Industries [*Associated Press*] (SAG)
BUSHIPS..... Bureau of Ships [*Later, Naval Sea Systems Command*]
Bush (KY).... Bush's Kentucky Reports [*64-77 Kentucky*] [*A publication*] (DLA)
BUSI .... Bring-Up Security Investigation [*Military*]
Business LJ... Business Law Journal (DLA)
BusinObj..... Business Objects SA [*Associated Press*] (SAG)
BUSIVISIT.... Business Visit [*Program*] [*United States Travel Service*]
Busk Pr....... Buskirk. Indiana Practice [*A publication*] (DLA)
BUSL .... Boston University School of Law (DLA)
BUSL .... Buoy Boat, Stern Loading
Bus LJ .... Business Law Journal (DLA)
BusLR......... Business Library Review [*A publication*] (BRI)
Bus L Rep .. Business Law Reports (DLA)
BUSM .... British United Shoe Machinery [*Commercial firm*]
BusMgmt .... Business Management (DD)
BUS MGR .... Business Manager (WDAA)
Busn .... Business (BARN)
BusnObj...... Business Objects SA [*Associated Press*] (SAG)
BusnRc .... Business Records Holding Corp. [*Associated Press*] (SAG)
BusnRs .... Business Resource Group [*Associated Press*] (SAG)
BUSP .... Butt Splice (MCD)
BUSRA .... British-United States Routing Agreement [*Shipping*]
BUSRAT....... Battle-Unit Short-Range Antitank Weapon System (NATG)
Bus Reg...... Business Regulation (DLA)
Bus Reg L Rep .. Business Regulation Law Report [*A publication*] (DLA)
BUSRQ........ Bus Request [*Computer science*] (TEL)
BUSS .... Backup Scram System [*Nuclear energy*] (NRCH)
BUSS .... Backup Study Sheets [*Military*]
BUSS .... Balloon-Borne Ultraviolet Stellar Spectrometer
BUSS .... Biomedical Urine Sampling System (KSC)
BUSS .... Bradford University Software Services Ltd. [*British*] (IRUK)
BUSS .... Buoy Underwater Sound Signal (NG)
Bus Soc ...... Business and Society [*A publication*] (BRI)
BUS STOP ... Breathers United to Stop Standing Time of Passenger-Buses [*Student legal action organization*]
BusStudies... Business Studies (DD)
BUSTC .... Backup System Test Console
BUSTDS....... Bureau of Standards
Bus W .... Business Week [*A publication*] (BRI)
Busw & Wol Pr... Buswell and Wolcott. Massachusetts Practice [*A publication*] (DLA)
Bus Wk .... Business Week [*A publication*] (AAGC)
BUSWREC... Ban Unsafe Schoolbuses Which Regularly Endanger Children [*Student legal action organization*]
BUSY .... Budget System
BUT............ Basic Unit Training
BUT............ Breakup Time [*Ophthalmology*]
BUT............ British United Traction Co.
BUT............ Broadband Unbalanced Transformer [*Telecommunications*] (OA)
BUT............ Bureau of University Travel [*Defunct*]
BUT............ Business Air Taxi [*Switzerland ICAO designator*] (FAAC)
BUT............ Butanol [*Organic chemistry*]
BUT............ Butte [*Montana*] [*Seismograph station code, US Geological Survey*] (SEIS)
BUT............ Butter (AAMN)
BUT............ Button
BUT............ Butyrum [*Butter*] [*Pharmacy*] (ROG)
Bute .... Buteshire [*County in Scotland*] (BARN)
BUTE.......... Phenylbutazone (DAVI)
BUTEC .... British Universities Transatlantic Exchange Committee (AIE)
BUTI.......... BeautiControl Cosmetics [*NASDAQ symbol*] (TTSB)
BUTI.......... BeautiControl Cosmetics, Inc. [*NASDAQ symbol*] (NQ)
BUTL.......... Butler International [*Formerly, North American Ventures, Inc.*] [*NASDAQ symbol*] (SPSG)
But Law & Cl... Butler's Lawyer and Client [*A publication*] (DLA)
Butler.......... Butler County Legal Journal [*Pennsylvania*] [*A publication*] (DLA)
Butler.......... Butler International, Inc. [*Associated Press*] (SAG)
Butler Co Litt... Butler's Notes to Coke on Littleton [*A publication*] (DLA)
Butler Hor Jur... Butler's Horae Juridicae [*A publication*] (DLA)

ButlerMfg .... Butler Manufacturing [*Associated Press*] (SAG)
Butler U .... Butler University (GAGS)
ButlrMf .... Butler Manufacturing Co. [*Associated Press*] (SAG)
ButlrNt .... Butler National Corp. [*Associated Press*] (SAG)
BUTM .... Baring Unit Trust Management Service [*Finance British*]
BUTN .... Butane (MSA)
BUTN .... Button
BUTR .... Butter
butr .... Buttress (VRA)
Butrey .... Buttrey Food & Drug Stores Co. [*Associated Press*] (SAG)
BUTT .... Buttock [*Slang*] (DSUE)
Butterworth's SA Law Review... Butterworth's South African Law Review
          [*A publication*] (DLA)
Butterworth's South Afr L Rev... Butterworth's South African Law Review
          [*A publication*] (DLA)
Butt RA .... Butterworth's Rating Appeals [*1913-31*] [*England*] [*A publication*]
          (DLA)
Butt Rat App... Butterworth's Rating Appeals [*1913-31*] [*England*] [*A publication*]
          (DLA)
Butt SA Law Rev... Butterworth's South African Law Review [*A publication*] (DLA)
Butts Sh .... Butts' Edition of Shower's English King's Bench Reports
          [*A publication*] (DLA)
Butt WCC ..... Butterworth's Workmen's Compensation Cases [*A publication*] (DLA)
Butt Work Comp Cas... Butterworth's Workmen's Compensation Cases
          [*A publication*] (DLA)
BuTx .... Bungarotoxin [*Also, BGT, BTX*] [*Biochemistry*]
BUU .... Basic User Unit (MCD)
BUU .... Burlington, WI [*Location identifier FAA*] (FAAL)
BUV .... Backscatter Ultraviolet [*Spectrometry*] (MCD)
BUV .... Buchan [*Australia Seismograph station code, US Geological Survey
          Closed*] (SEIS)
BUVS .... Backscatter Ultraviolet Spectrometer
BUW .... Bau Bau [*Indonesia*] [*Airport symbol*] (OAG)
BUWA .... Business Who's Who of Australia [*Database*] [*R.G. Riddell Pty. Ltd.*]
BUWEAPS .... Bureau of Weapons [*Navy*]
BUWEPS ..... Bureau of Naval Weapons [*Obsolete*]
BUWEPS ..... Bureau of Naval Weapons (AAGC)
BUWEPSFLEREADREP... Bureau of Naval Weapons Fleet Readiness
          Representative [*Obsolete*] (MCD)
BUWEPSFLEREADREPCEN... Bureau of Naval Weapons Fleet Readiness
          Representative, Central [*Obsolete*] (MCD)
BUWEPSFLEREADREPLANT... Bureau of Naval Weapons Fleet Readiness
          Representative, Atlantic [*Obsolete*] (MCD)
BUWEPSFLEREADREPPAC... Bureau of Naval Weapons Fleet Readiness
          Representative, Pacific [*Obsolete*] (MCD)
BUWEPSFLTREADREP... Bureau of Naval Weapons Fleet Readiness
          Representative [*Obsolete*] (MUGU)
BUWEPS FR... Bureau of Naval Weapons Fleet Readiness [*Obsolete*] (MCD)
BUWEPSINST... Bureau of Naval Weapons Instruction [*Obsolete*] (MCD)
BUWEPSNOTE... Bureau of Naval Weapons Notice [*Obsolete*]
BUWEPSREP... Bureau of Naval Weapons Representative [*Obsolete*] (MCD)
BUWEPSREPS... Bureau of Naval Weapons Representatives (AAGC)
BUWEPSRESREP... Bureau of Naval Weapons Resident Representative [*Obsolete*]
BUWEPSTECHREP... Bureau of Naval Weapons Technical Representative
          [*Obsolete*] (MUGU)
BUWEPSTLO... Bureau of Naval Weapons Technical Liaison Office [*Obsolete*]
          (MUGU)
BUWNE .... Brotherhood of Utility Workers of New England (EA)
BUX .... Bunia [*Zaire*] [*Airport symbol*] (OAG)
BUX .... Bunia [*Zaire*] [*Airport symbol*] (AD)
Buxton .... Buxton's Reports [*123-129 North Carolina*] [*A publication*] (DLA)
Buxton (NC)... Buxton's Reports [*123-129 North Carolina*] [*A publication*] (DLA)
BUY .... Bunbury [*Australia Airport symbol*] (OAG)
BUY .... Burlington, NC [*Location identifier FAA*] (FAAL)
BUYAC .... Buying Activity [*Air Force*] (AFM)
BUY & D ...... Bureau of Yards and Docks [*Later, NFEC*] [*Navy*]
BUYARD ...... Bureau of Yards and Docks [*Later, NFEC*] [*Navy*] (KSC)
BUYDSDOCKS... Bureau of Yards and Docks [*Later, NFEC*] [*Navy*]
BUYR .... Buyer
BUYV .... Burdock Yellows Virus [*Plant pathology*]
BUZ .... Budakeszi [*Hungary*] [*Later, TYH*] [*Geomagnetic observatory code*]
BUZ .... Bushehr [*Iran*] [*Airport symbol*] (OAG)
BUZ .... Bushire [*Iran*] [*Airport symbol*] (AD)
BUZ .... Buzzer (MSA)
BUZ .... Columbus, OH [*Location identifier FAA*] (FAAL)
Buzz E J ...... Buzzworm's Earth Journal [*A publication*]
BV .... Babylonian Vocalization (BJA)
BV .... Bacitracin V [*Antibacterial compound*]
BV .... Back View (MSA)
BV .... Bacterial Vaginosis [*Medicine*]
BV .... Balanced Voltage
BV .... Balneum Vaporis [*Vapor Bath*] [*Medicine*]
BV .... Baltimore Vegetarians [*Later, VRG*] (EA)
BV .... Bank of Valletta [*Malta*]
BV .... Basilic Vein [*Anatomy*] (AAMN)
BV .... Baudot-Verdan Differential Analyzer [*Electronics*] (IAA)
BV .... Bayerische Vereinsbank [*Union Bank of Bavaria*] [*Munich, West
          Germany*]
BV .... Beata Virgo [*Blessed Virgin*] [*Latin*]
BV .... Beatitudo Vestra [*Your Holiness*] [*Latin*]
BV .... Bee Venom [*Entomology*]
BV .... Before Video
BV .... Bellows Valve
BV .... Bene Vale [*Farewell*] [*Latin*]
BV .... Bene Vixit [*He Lived a Good Life*] [*Latin*]

BV .... Berkeley Version (BJA)
BV .... Besloten Vennootschap [*Private or Closed Limited Company*] [*Dutch*]
BV .... Betamethasone Valerate [*Glucocorticoid*]
BV .... Beverage (KSC)
BV .... Bible Version [*As opposed to the Prayer Book version of the Psalms*]
BV .... Biological Value
BV .... Biological Variation
BV .... Birth Visit (ROG)
BV .... Black Veterans, Inc. (EA)
BV .... Bleed Valve (MCD)
BV .... Blessed Virgin
BV .... Blood Vessel [*Medicine*]
BV .... Blood Volume [*Medicine*]
BV .... Blow Valve
B-V .... Blue-Visual [*Color index*]
BV .... Boeing-Vertol Division [*The Boeing Co.*] [*ICAO aircraft manufacturer
          identifier*] (ICAO)
BV .... Bonnet Valve
BV .... Bons Vivants [*An association*] (EA)
BV .... Book Value [*Business term*]
bv .... Bouvet Island [*MARC country of publication code Library of
          Congress*] (LCCP)
BV .... Bouvet Island [*ANSI two-letter standard code*] (CNC)
BV .... Bowl Vent [*Automotive engineering*]
BV .... Breakdown Voltage
BV .... Brick Veneered [*Insurance classification*]
BV .... Bronchovesicular [*Breath sounds*] [*Medicine*]
BV .... Bureau Veritas [*International register for the classification of shipping
          and aircraft*]
BV .... Bureau Voucher [*Army*] (AABC)
BV .... Busy Verification [*Telecommunications*] (TEL)
BV .... Butterfly Valve (DAC)
BV .... Bypass Valve (MCD)
bv .... Cover (VRA)
bv .... Covered (VRA)
BV .... Northwest Skyways [*ICAO designator*] (AD)
BV .... Vernon Library, British Columbia [*Library symbol National Library of
          Canada*] (NLC)
BVA .... Bachelor of Visual Arts
BVA .... Bachelor of Vocational Agriculture
BVA .... Beauvais [*France*] [*Airport symbol*] (AD)
BVA .... Best Corrected Visual Acuity [*Ophthalmology*]
BVA .... Billing Validation Application
BVA .... Bioimpedance Venous Analysis [*Biochemistry*] (DAVI)
BVA .... Biventricular Assistance [*Cardiology*]
BVA .... Blinded Veterans Association (EA)
BVA .... Board of Veterans Appeals [*Veterans Administration*]
BVA .... Boundary Value Analysis [*Computer program test*]
BVA .... British Veterinary Association
BVA .... British Videogram Association
BVA .... British Vigilance Association (BI)
BVA .... Buena Vista [*Guatemala*] [*Seismograph station code, US Geological
          Survey*] (SEIS)
BVA .... Buffalo Airways [*ICAO designator*] (FAAC)
BVA .... Business Volunteers for the Arts (NFD)
BVA .... Vancouver Public Library, British Columbia [*Library symbol National
          Library of Canada*] (NLC)
BVAA .... Vancouver City Archives, British Columbia [*Library symbol National
          Library of Canada*] (NLC)
BVAABS .... Synod Office, Ecclesiastical Province of British Columbia, Anglican
          Church of Canada, Vancouver, British Columbia [*Library symbol
          National Library of Canada*] (NLC)
BVAABSA ..... Archives, British Columbia Provincial Synod, Anglican Church of
          Canada, Vancouver, British Columbia [*Library symbol National
          Library of Canada*] (NLC)
BVAAD .... Alcoholism and Drug Abuse Commission, Vancouver, British
          Columbia [*Library symbol National Library of Canada*] (NLC)
BVAADP .... Alcohol and Drug Programs, Vancouver, British Columbia [*Library
          symbol National Library of Canada*] (NLC)
BVAAE .... Associated Engineering Services Ltd., Vancouver, British Columbia
          [*Library symbol National Library of Canada*] (NLC)
BVAAG .... Agriculture Canada, Vancouver, British Columbia [*Library symbol
          National Library of Canada*] (NLC)
BVAAM .... Fifteenth Field Artillery Regiment, Royal Canadian Artillery Museum
          and ArchivesSociety, Vancouver, British Columbia [*Library
          symbol National Library of Canada*] (NLC)
BVAAP .... Information Services, Asia Pacific Foundation of Canada, Vancouver,
          British Columbia [*Library symbol National Library of Canada*]
          (NLC)
BVABCR .... Corporate Information, BC Rail, Vancouver, British Columbia [*Library
          symbol National Library of Canada*] (NLC)
BVABCS .... British Columbia Sports Hall of Fame and Museum, Vancouver,
          British Columbia [*Library symbol National Library of Canada*]
          (NLC)
BVABOT .... Vancouver Board of Trade Library, British Columbia [*Library symbol
          National Library of Canada*] (NLC)
BVABS .... Brown Strachan Associates, Vancouver, British Columbia [*Library
          symbol National Library of Canada*] (NLC)
BVABSM ..... British Columbia Museum, Vancouver, British Columbia [*Library
          symbol National Library of Canada*] (NLC)
BVABT .... British Columbia Telephone Co., Burnaby, British Columbia [*Library
          symbol National Library of Canada*] (NLC)
BVABY .... British Columbia and Yukon Chamber of Mines, Vancouver, British
          Columbia [*Library symbol National Library of Canada*] (NLC)

BVAC .... Capilano College, Vancouver, British Columbia [*Library symbol National Library of Canada*] (NLC)

BVACAA .... Archives, Archdiocese of Vancouver, Catholic Church, British Columbia [*Library symbol National Library of Canada*] (NLC)

BVACBA .... CBA Engineering Ltd., Vancouver, British Columbia [*Library symbol National Library of Canada*] (NLC)

BVACBV .... VTR Library, Canadian Broadcasting Corp. [*Videotheque, Societe Radio-Canada*], Vancouver, British Columbia [*Library symbol National Library of Canada*] (BIB)

BVACCA .... Cancer Control Agency of British Columbia, Vancouver, British Columbia [*Library symbol National Library of Canada*] (NLC)

BVACCU .... British Columbia Central Credit Union, Vancouver, British Columbia [*Library symbol National Library of Canada*] (NLC)

BVACF .... Council of Forest Industries of British Columbia, Vancouver, British Columbia [*Library symbol National Library of Canada*] (NLC)

BVACG .... Regional Library, Canadian Coast Guard [*Bibliotheque Regionale, Garde CotiereCanadienne*] North Vancouver, British Columbia [*Library symbol National Library of Canada*] (NLC)

BVACI .... Chemetics International Ltd., Vancouver, British Columbia [*Library symbol National Library of Canada*] (NLC)

BVACILS ...... British Columbia College and Institute Library Services Clearinghouse for the Print Impaired (CILS), Vancouver, British Columbia [*Library symbol National Library of Canada*] (NLC)

BVACM .... Centennial Museum, Vancouver, British Columbia [*Library symbol National Library of Canada*] (NLC)

BVACOM .... Cominco Ltd., Vancouver, British Columbia [*Library symbol National Library of Canada*] (NLC)

BVAD .... Biventricular Assist Device [*Medicine*] (DMAA)

BVADC .... Coal Division, Denison Mines Ltd., Vancouver, British Columbia [*Library symbol National Library of Canada*] (BIB)

BVAEAE .... Atmospheric Environment Service, Environment Canada [*Service de l'Environnement Atmospherique, Environnement Canada*] Vancouver, British Columbia [*Library symbol National Library of Canada*] (NLC)

BVAEC .... British Columbia Energy Commission, Vancouver, British Columbia [*Library symbol National Library of Canada*] (NLC)

BVAEN .... Envirocon Ltd., Vancouver, British Columbia [*Library symbol National Library of Canada*] (NLC)

BVAEP .... Environmental Protection Service, Environment Canada/Pacific Region [*Service de la Protection de l'Environnement, Environnement Canada/Region du Pacifique*] West Vancouver, British Columbia [*Library symbol National Library of Canada*] (NLC)

BVAF .... Vancouver Laboratory, Fisheries and Oceans Canada [*Laboratoire de Vancouver, Peches et Oceans Canada*], British Columbia [*Library symbol Obsolete National Library of Canada*] (NLC)

BVAFA .... Fine Arts, Music, and Films Division, Vancouver Public Library, British Columbia [*Library symbol National Library of Canada*] (NLC)

BVAFI .... Fisheries Management Regional Library, Fisheries and Oceans Canada [*Bibliotheque Regionale de la Gestion des Pecheries, Peches et Oceans Canada*] Vancouver, British Columbia [*Library symbol National Library of Canada*] (NLC)

BVAFP .... Forintek Canada Corp., Vancouver, British Columbia [*Library symbol National Library of Canada*] (NLC)

BVAFV .... Farris, Vaughan, Wills & Murphy Law Firm, Vancouver, British Columbia [*Library symbol National Library of Canada*] (NLC)

BVAG .... Geological Survey of Canada [*Commission Geologique du Canada*] Vancouver, British Columbia [*Library symbol National Library of Canada*] (NLC)

BVAGB .... Golder Brawner & Associates Ltd., Vancouver, British Columbia [*Library symbol National Library of Canada*] (NLC)

BVAGF .... Staff Medical Library, G. F. Strong Rehabilitation Centre, Vancouver, British Columbia [*Library symbol National Library of Canada*] (BIB)

BVAH .... British Columbia Hydro and Power Authority, Vancouver, British Columbia [*Library symbol National Library of Canada*] (NLC)

BVAHD .... Vancouver Health Department, British Columbia [*Library symbol National Library of Canada*] (NLC)

BVAHE .... British Columbia Hydro Engineering Library, Vancouver, British Columbia [*Library symbol National Library of Canada*] (NLC)

BVAHP .... Historic Photographic Collection, Vancouver Public Library, British Columbia [*Library symbol National Library of Canada*] (NLC)

BVAHS .... H. A. Simons Ltd., Vancouver, British Columbia [*Library symbol National Library of Canada*] (NLC)

BVAI .... International North Pacific Fisheries, Vancouver, British Columbia [*Library symbol National Library of Canada*] (NLC)

BVAIB .... IBIS Information & Research Services, Vancouver, British Columbia [*Library symbol National Library of Canada*] (NLC)

BVAINA .... Resource Center, Information Services, Indian and Northern Affairs Canada, British Columbia Region [*Centre de Ressources, Services d'Information, Affaires I ndiennes et du Nord Canadien, Bureau Regional de la CB*] Vancouver, British Columbia [*Library symbol National Library of Canada*] (NLC)

BVAJ .... Canada Department of Justice [*Ministere de la Justice*] Vancouver, British Columbia [*Library symbol National Library of Canada*] (NLC)

BVAJH .... Jewish Historical Society, Vancouver, British Columbia [*Library symbol National Library of Canada*] (BIB)

BVAJI .... Justice Institute of British Columbia, Vancouver, British Columbia [*Library symbol National Library of Canada*] (NLC)

BVAJR .... Jewish Resource Centre, Vancouver, British Columbia [*Library symbol National Library of Canada*] (BIB)

BVAL .... BC [*British Columbia*] Court House Library Society, Vancouver, British Columbia, [*Library symbol National Library of Canada*] (NLC)

BVAL .... Blackman's Volunteer Army of Liberation [*An association*] (EA)

BVALD .... Ladner, Downs, Barristers & Solicitors, Vancouver, British Columbia [*Library symbol National Library of Canada*] (NLC)

BVALE .... Valemount Public Library, British Columbia [*Library symbol National Library of Canada*] (NLC)

BVALMW ..... L. M. Warren, Inc., Vancouver, British Columbia [*Library symbol National Library of Canada*] (NLC)

BVALS .... Legal Resource Centre, Legal Services Society, Vancouver, British Columbia [*Library symbol National Library of Canada*] (NLC)

BVAM .... British Columbia Medical Library Service, Vancouver, British Columbia [*Library symbol National Library of Canada*] (NLC)

BVAMA .... British Valve and Actuators Manufacturers Association (DBA)

BVAMB .... MacMillan Bloedel Research Ltd., Vancouver, British Columbia [*Library symbol National Library of Canada*] (NLC)

BVAMBL ...... MacMillan Bloedel Ltd., Vancouver, British Columbia [*Library symbol National Library of Canada*] (NLC)

BVAME .... McElhanney Engineering, Vancouver, British Columbia [*Library symbol National Library of Canada*] (NLC)

BVAMI .... Employment and Immigration Canada [*Emploi et Immigration Canada*] Vancouver, British Columbia [*Library symbol National Library of Canada*] (NLC)

BVAMM .... Maritime Museum, Vancouver, British Columbia [*Library symbol National Library of Canada*] (NLC)

BVAMOE ...... Mobil Oil Estates Ltd., Vancouver, British Columbia [*Library symbol National Library of Canada*] (NLC)

BVAMUM ..... British Columbia Museum of Medicine, Vancouver, British Columbia [*Library symbol National Library of Canada*] (NLC)

BVAMV .... Military Vehicle Historical Society of British Columbia and Museum, Vancouver, British Columbia [*Library symbol National Library of Canada*] (NLC)

BVAN .... Western Laboratory, National Research Council [*Laboratoire de l'Ouest, Conseil National de Recherches*] Vancouver, British Columbia [*Library symbol National Library of Canada*] (NLC)

BVANH .... Health Protection Branch, Canada Department of National Health and Welfare [*Direction Generale de la Protection de la Sante, Ministere de la Sante Nationale et du Bien-Etre Social*] Vancouver, British Columbia [*Library symbol National Library of Canada*] (NLC)

BVANHC .... Northwest History Collection, Vancouver Public Library, British Columbia [*Library symbol National Library of Canada*] (NLC)

BVAOCA .... Oblate Resource Centre and Archives, Vancouver, British Columbia [*Library symbol National Library of Canada*] (NLC)

BVAOL .... Open Learning Institute, Richmond, British Columbia [*Library symbol National Library of Canada*] (NLC)

BVAP .... BCNU [*Carmustine*], Vincristine, Adriamycin, Prednisone [*Antineoplastic drug regimen*] (NLC)

BVAP .... Placer Development Library, Vancouver, British Columbia [*Library symbol National Library of Canada*] (NLC)

BVAPAD .... Product Assurance & Development, British Columbia Packers Ltd., Vancouver, British Columbia [*Library symbol National Library of Canada*] (NLC)

BVAPC .... Phillips Cables Ltd., Vancouver, British Columbia [*Library symbol National Library of Canada*] (NLC)

BVAPD .... Planning Development Library, Greater Vancouver Regional District, Vancouver, British Columbia [*Library symbol National Library of Canada*] (NLC)

BVAPDA .... P/DAUM Information Services, Vancouver, British Columbia [*Library symbol National Library of Canada*] (BIB)

BVAPE .... West Vancouver Laboratory, Fisheries and Oceans Canada [*Laboratoire de West-Vancouver, Peches et Oceans Canada*] British Columbia [*Library symbol National Library of Canada*] (NLC)

BVAPP .... Pacific Press Library, Vancouver, British Columbia [*Library symbol National Library of Canada*] (NLC)

BVAPPC .... Pulp and Paper Centre, University of British Columbia, Vancouver, British Columbia [*Library symbol National Library of Canada*] (NLC)

BVAPPR .... Vancouver Laboratory, Pulp and Paper Research Institute of Canada, British Columbia [*Library symbol National Library of Canada*] (NLC)

BVAPR .... Resource Centre, Pacific Rim Institute for Tourism, Vancouver, British Columbia [*Library symbol National Library of Canada*] (BIB)

BVAPVI .... Provincial Resource Centre for the Visually-Impaired, Vancouver, British Columbia [*Library symbol National Library of Canada*] (NLC)

BVAPW .... Price, Waterhouse & Co., Vancouver, British Columbia [*Library symbol National Library of Canada*] (NLC)

BVAPWP ..... Pacific Region Library, Public Works Canada [*Bibliotheque de la Region du Pacifique, Travaux Publics Canada*] Vancouver, British Columbia [*Library symbol National Library of Canada*] (NLC)

BVAR .... British Columbia Research Council, Vancouver, British Columbia [*Library symbol National Library of Canada*] (NLC)

BVARD .... Russell & Dumoulin, Vancouver, British Columbia [*Library symbol National Library of Canada*] (NLC)

BVARE .... Archives of the Ecclesiastical Province of British Columbia, Vancouver, British Columbia [*Library symbol National Library of Canada*] (NLC)

BVAREC .... Regent College, Vancouver, British Columbia [*Library symbol National Library of Canada*] (NLC)

BVARJ .... Rolf Jensen & Associates Ltd., Vancouver, British Columbia [*Library symbol National Library of Canada*] (NLC)

BVARN .... Registered Nurses Association of British Columbia, Vancouver, British Columbia [*Library symbol National Library of Canada*] (NLC)

BVAS .... Bio-Vascular, Inc. [*NASDAQ symbol*] (NQ)

BVAS .... Simon Fraser University, Burnaby, British Columbia [*Library symbol National Library of Canada*] (NLC)

BVASA .... Archives and Special Collections, Simon Fraser University, Burnaby, British Col umbia [*Library symbol National Library of Canada*] (NLC)

BVASC .... Sandwell & Co., Vancouver, British Columbia [*Library symbol National Library of Canada*] (NLC)

BVASEC .... British Columbia Securities Commission, Vancouver, British Columbia [*Library symbol National Library of Canada*] (BIB)

BVASG .... Simon Fraser Gallery, Simon Fraser University, Burnaby, British Columbia [*Library symbol National Library of Canada*] (NLC)

BVASLA .... F. F. Slaney & Co. Ltd., Vancouver, British Columbia [*Library symbol National Library of Canada*] (NLC)

BVASM .... Map Library, Simon Fraser University, Burnaby, British Columbia [*Library symbol National Library of Canada*] (NLC)

BVASP .... Social Planning and Research Council of British Columbia, Vancouver [*Library symbol National Library of Canada*] (BIB)

BVASPH ...... Health Sciences Library, St. Paul's Hospital, Vancouver, British Columbia [*Library symbol National Library of Canada*] (NLC)

BVAST .... Vancouver School of Theology, British Columbia [*Library symbol National Library of Canada*] (NLC)

BVASW .... Swan Wooster Engineering Co., Vancouver, British Columbia [*Library symbol National Library of Canada*] (NLC)

BVAT .... Blood-Stage Variant Antigen Type [*Immunology*]

BVATAN .... Noise Library, Air Navigation Systems Requirements, Transport Canada [*Bibliotheque Normes de Bruit, Exigences du Systeme de Navigation Aerienne, Transports Canada*], Vancouver, British Columbia [*Library symbol National Library of Canada*] (NLC)

BVATAS .... Aviation Safety Programs, Transport Canada [*Programme de la Securite Aerienne, Transports Canada*], Vancouver, British Columbia [*Library symbol National Library of Canada*] (NLC)

BVATCA .... Air Regional Library (PGSL), Transport Canada [*Bibliotheque Regionale de l'Air (PGSL), Transports Canada*] Vancouver, British Columbia [*Library symbol National Library of Canada*] (NLC)

BVATE .... Elizabeth Watson Library, Teck Mining Group Ltd., Vancouver, British Columbia [*Library symbol National Library of Canada*] (NLC)

BVATF .... British Columbia Teachers' Federation Resources Centre, Vancouver, British Columbia [*Library symbol National Library of Canada*] (NLC)

BVATM .... Trans Mountain Pipe Line Co. Ltd., Vancouver, British Columbia [*Library symbol National Library of Canada*] (NLC)

BVATPF .... Towers, Perrin, Forster & Crosby, Vancouver, British Columbia [*Library symbol National Library of Canada*] (NLC)

BVATPT .... Professional and Technical Services Library, Transport Canada [*Bibliotheque des Services Professionnels et Techniques, Transports Canada*], Vancouver, British Columbia [*Library symbol National Library of Canada*] (NLC)

BVAU .... University of British Columbia, Vancouver, British Columbia [*Library symbol National Library of Canada*] (NLC)

BVAUBCA ..... Archives, British Columbia Conference, United Church, Vancouver, British Columbia [*Library symbol National Library of Canada*] (NLC)

BVAUCA .... Archives, Unitarian Church of Vancouver, British Columbia [*Library symbol National Library of Canada*] (NLC)

BVAUCC .... Charles Crane Memorial Library, University of British Columbia, Vancouver, British Columbia [*Library symbol National Library of Canada*] (NLC)

BVAUG .... Department of Geography, University of British Columbia, Vancouver, British Columbia [*Library symbol National Library of Canada*] (NLC)

BVAUL .... Law Library, University of British Columbia, Vancouver, British Columbia [*Library symbol National Library of Canada*] (NLC)

BVAULS .... School of Library, Archival, and Information Studies, University of British Columbia, Vancouver, British Columbia [*Library symbol National Library of Canada*] (NLC)

BVAUM .... Map Division, University of British Columbia, Vancouver, British Columbia [*Library symbol National Library of Canada*] (NLC)

BVAUS .... Special Collections Division, University of British Columbia, Vancouver, BritishColumbia [*Library symbol National Library of Canada*] (NLC)

BVAUW .... Woodward Biomedical Library, University of British Columbia, Vancouver, British Columbia [*Library symbol National Library of Canada*] (NLC)

BVAUWGV ... United Way of Greater Vancouver, British Columbia [*Library symbol National Library of Canada*] (NLC)

BVAVA .... Vancouver Art Gallery, British Columbia [*Library symbol National Library of Canada*] (NLC)

BVAVCL .... Vancouver Community College, Langara Campus, Vancouver, British Columbia [*Library symbol National Library of Canada*] (NLC)

BVAVCLT ...... Library Technician Program, Vancouver Community College, British Columbia [*Library symbol National Library of Canada*] (NLC)

BVAVSA .... [*The*] Emily Carr College of Art, Vancouver, British Columbia [*Library symbol National Library of Canada*] (NLC)

BVAWC .... Workers Compensation Board of British Columbia, Vancouver, British Columbia [*Library symbol National Library of Canada*] (NLC)

BVAWCT ...... West Coast Transmission Ltd., Vancouver, British Columbia [*Library symbol National Library of Canada*] (NLC)

BVAWH .... Warnock Hersey International Ltd., Vancouver, British Columbia [*Library symbol National Library of Canada*] (NLC)

BVB .... Boa Vista [*Brazil*] [*Airport symbol*] (OAG)

BVB .... Bridge View Bancorp [*AMEX symbol*] (SAG)

BVBC .... Bobby Vinton Booster Club (EA)

BVBRF .... Blood Vessel of Branchial Filament

BVC .... Bear Valley Observatory [*California*] [*Seismograph station code, US Geological Survey Closed*] (SEIS)

BVC .... Black Varnish Cambric [*Insulation*] (MSA)

BVC .... Boa Vista [*Cape Verde Islands*] [*Airport symbol*] (OAG)

BVC .... British Vacuum Council (DBA)

BVC .... British Veterinary Code

BVC .... Buena Vista College [*Storm Lake, IA*]

BVC .... Bushveldt Carabineers [*British military*] (DMA)

BVCA .... British Venture Capital Association (DBA)

BVCPP .... BCNU [*Carmustine*], Vinblastine, Cyclophosphamide, Procarbazine, Prednisone [*Antineoplastic drug regimen*]

BVD .... BCNU [*Carmustine*], Vincristine, and arbazine [*DTIC*] [*Antineoplastic drug regimen*] (DAVI)

BVD .... Beacon Video Digitizer

BVD .... Beverly Development, Inc. [*Toronto Stock Exchange symbol*]

BVD .... Bonus Vacation Days [*United Auto Workers*]

BVD .... Bovine Viral Diarrhea

BVD .... Bradley, Voorhees, & Day [*A brand name underwear*]

BvD .... Bureau +van Dijk, SA (IID)

BVD .... BVD Co. [*Initials stand for Bradley, Voorhies, and Day, organizers of the company*]

BVDH .... Vanderhoof Public Library, British Columbia [*Library symbol National Library of Canada*] (NLC)

BVDS .... Bleomycin, Vinblastine, Doxorubicin, Streptozocin [*Antineoplastic drug regimen*]

BVDT .... Brief Vestibular Disorientation Test

BVDU .... Bromovinyldeoxyuridine [*Biochemistry*]

BVDV .... Bovine Viral Diarrhea Virus

BVE .... Bachelor of Vocational Education

BVE .... Batallon Vasco Espanol [*Spanish Basque Battalion*] (PD)

BVE .... Before Your Very Eyes (DGA)

BVE .... Binocular Visual Efficiency

BVE .... Bivariate Exponential [*Distribution*] [*Statistics*]

BVE .... Bootheville, LA [*Location identifier FAA*] (FAAL)

BVE .... Brandevor Enterprises Ltd. [*Toronto Stock Exchange symbol Vancouver Stock Exchange symbol*]

BVE .... Breadboard Verification Equipment [*NASA*]

BVE .... Brive-La-Gaillarde [*France*] [*Airport symbol*] (OAG)

BVE .... Butyl Vinyl Ether [*Organic chemistry*]

B Verf G ...... Bundesverfassungsgericht [*Federal Constitutional Court*] [*German*] (DLA)

B Verw G ..... Bundesverwaltungsgericht [*Federal Supreme Administrative Court*] [*German*] (DLA)

BVET .... Board of Vocational Education and Training [*New South Wales, Australia*]

BVetC .... British Veterinary Codex [*A publication*]

B Vet Med ... Bachelor of Veterinary Medicine

BVetSc .... Bachelor of Veterinary Science (ADA)

BVetSci .... Bachelor of Veterinary Science (NADA)

BVetSur .... Bachelor of Veterinary Surgery (NADA)

BVF .... Biovail Corp. International [*AMEX symbol*] (SAG)

BVF .... Biovail Corp. Intl. [*AMEX symbol*] (TTSB)

BVF .... Bua [*Fiji*] [*Airport symbol Obsolete*] (OAG)

BVFS .... Bay View Capital [*NASDAQ symbol*] (TTSB)

BVFS .... Bay View Capital Corp. [*NASDAQ symbol*] (NQ)

BVG .... Banco Bilbao Vizcaya [*NYSE symbol*] (SPSG)

BVG .... Battlefield Visualization Graphics (AABC)

BVG .... Berlevag [*Norway*] [*Airport symbol*] (OAG)

BVG .... Berliner Verkehrs-Gesellschaft [*Later, Berliner Verkehrs-Betriebe*] [*Berlin Transport West Berlin*]

BVG .... Bureau du Verificateur General du Canada [*Office of the Auditor-General of Canada*]

BVG .... Enterprise, AL [*Location identifier FAA*] (FAAL)

BVGA .... British Videogram Association (NITA)

BVGE .... Beverage (MSA)

BVGPr .... BancoBilbaoVizcaya9.75% ADS [*NYSE symbol*] (TTSB)

BVGPrB .... Banco Bilbao Vizcaya 9% ADS [*NYSE symbol*] (TTSB)

BVGPrC .... BancoBilbaoVizcaya8.00%ADS [*NYSE symbol*] (TTSB)

BVH .... Beaverhead Resources [*Vancouver Stock Exchange symbol*]

BVH .... Biventricular Hypertrophy [*Cardiology*]

BVH .... Vilhena [*Brazil*] [*Airport symbol*] (AD)

BVHA .... British Veterinary Hospitals Association (DBA)

BVI .... Beaver Falls, PA [*Location identifier FAA*] (FAAL)

BVI .... Better Vision Institute (EA)

BVI .... Birdsville [*Australia Airport symbol*] (OAG)

BVI .... Blood Vessel Invasion [*Medicine*] (MAE)

BVI .... British Virgin Islands

BVI .... Greater Victoria Public Library, British Columbia [*Library symbol National Library of Canada*] (NLC)

BVI .... Virgin Islands Airways [*British*] [*FAA designator*] (FAAC)

BVIA .... Art Gallery of Greater Victoria, Victoria, British Columbia [*Library symbol National Library of Canada*] (NLC)

BVIABS .... Synod Office, Diocese of British Columbia, Anglican Church of Canada, Victoria, British Columbia [*Library symbol National Library of Canada*] (NLC)

BVIADP .... Alcohol and Drug Programs, Victoria, British Columbia [*Library symbol National Library of Canada*] (BIB)

BVIAGC........ CLEU Library, British Columbia Ministry of Attorney General, Victoria, British Columbia [*Library symbol National Library of Canada*] (NLC)

BVIAGL........ Law Library, British Columbia, Ministry of the Attorney General, Victoria, British Columbia [*Library symbol National Library of Canada*] (NLC)

BVIB............ British Columbia Barkerville Restoration Advisory Committee, Victoria, British Columbia [*Library symbol National Library of Canada*] (NLC)

BVIC............ Camosun College, Victoria, British Columbia [*Library symbol National Library of Canada*] (NLC)

BVICA .... Victoria City Archives, British Columbia [*Library symbol National Library of Canada*] (NLC)

BVIDE .... British Columbia Ministry of Education, Victoria, British Columbia [*Library symbol National Library of Canada*] (NLC)

BVIED .... British Columbia Ministry of Industry and Small Business Development, Victoria, British Columbia [*Library symbol National Library of Canada*] (NLC)

BVIEM......... Institute of Ocean Sciences, Fisheries and Oceans Canada [*Institut des Sciences Oceanographiques, Peches et Oceans Canada*] Sidney, British Columbia [*Library symbol National Library of Canada*] (NLC)

BVIF............ Pacific Forest Research Centre, Agriculture Canada [*Centre de Recherches Forestieres du Pacifique, Agriculture Canada*] Victoria, British Columbia [*Library symbol National Library of Canada*] (NLC)

BVIFC.......... Bobby Vinton International Fan Club (EA)

BVIFC.......... British Columbia Ferry Corp., Victoria, British Columbia [*Library symbol National Library of Canada*] (NLC)

BVIFO .... British Columbia Ministry of Forests, Victoria, British Columbia [*Library symbol National Library of Canada*] (NLC)

BVIFS.......... British Columbia Forest Service, Victoria, British Columbia [*Library symbol National Library of Canada*] (NLC)

BVIGH .... Victoria General Hospital, British Columbia [*Library symbol National Library of Canada*] (NLC)

BVIH .... British Columbia Ministry of Highways and Public Works, Victoria, British Columbia [*Library symbol National Library of Canada*] (NLC)

BVIHCA........ British Virgin Islands Hotel and Commerce Association (EAIO)

BVIHCR........ Ministry Library, Ministry of Municipal Affairs, Recreation, and Culture, Victoria, British Columbia [*Library symbol National Library of Canada*] (NLC)

BVIHE .... British Columbia Ministry of Health, Victoria, British Columbia [*Library symbol National Library of Canada*] (NLC)

BVIHRS........ British Columbia Ministry of Human Resources, Vancouver, British Columbia [*Library symbol National Library of Canada*] (NLC)

BVIHRS........ British Columbia Ministry of Social Services and Housing, Vancouver, British Columbia [*Library symbol National Library of Canada*] (NLC)

BVIL............ Law Library Foundation, Victoria, British Columbia [*Library symbol National Library of Canada Obsolete*] (NLC)

BVILBP .... Lester B. Pearson College of the Pacific, Victoria, British Columbia [*Library symbol National Library of Canada*] (NLC)

BVILFW........ British Columbia Ministry of Environment, Victoria, British Columbia [*Library symbol National Library of Canada*] (NLC)

BVILPHP ...... Parks Library, Ministry of Parks, Victoria, British Columbia [*Library symbol National Library of Canada*] (NLC)

BVILSB .... Library Services Branch, Ministry of Provincial Secretary and Governement Services, Victoria, British Columbia [*Library symbol National Library of Canada*] (NLC)

BVIM........... British Columbia Ministry of Energy, Mines and Petroleum Resources, Victoria, British Columbia [*Library symbol National Library of Canada*] (NLC)

BVIMH .... Maltwood Art Museum, University of Victoria, British Columbia [*Library symbol National Library of Canada*] (NLC)

BVIML .... British Columbia Ministry of Labour, Victoria, British Columbia [*Library symbol National Library of Canada*] (NLC)

BVIMM........ Maritime Museum of British Columbia, Victoria, British Columbia [*Library symbol National Library of Canada*] (NLC)

BVIP .... Legislative Library, Victoria, British Columbia [*Library symbol National Library of Canada*] (NLC)

BVIPA .... Provincial Archives of British Columbia, Victoria, British Columbia [*Library symbol National Library of Canada*] (NLC)

BVIPM .... British Columbia Provincial Museum, Victoria, British Columbia [*Library symbol National Library of Canada*] (NLC)

BVIPME....... Ethnology Division, British Columbia Provincial Museum, Victoria, British Columbia [*Library symbol National Library of Canada*] (NLC)

BVIPR .... Victoria Press Ltd., British Columbia [*Library symbol National Library of Canada*] (NLC)

BVIRJ.......... Victoria Medical and Hospital Libraries, Royal Jubilee Hospital Site, British Columbia [*Library symbol National Library of Canada*] (NLC)

BVISC.......... British Columbia Systems Corp., Victoria, British Columbia [*Library symbol National Library of Canada*] (NLC)

BVIT............ Thurber Consultants Ltd., Victoria, British Columbia [*Library symbol National Library of Canada*] (NLC)

BVITRA........ Thalassa Research Associates, Victoria, British Columbia [*Library symbol National Library of Canada*] (NLC)

BVIUCN........ Union Catalogue of British Columbia Newspapers, Victoria, British Columbia [*Library symbol National Library of Canada*] (NLC)

BVIV........... University of Victoria, British Columbia [*Library symbol National Library of Canada*] (NLC)

BVIVA .... Department of History in Art, University of Victoria, British Columbia [*Library symbol National Library of Canada*] (NLC)

BVIVG .... Geography Department, University of Victoria, British Columbia [*Library symbol National Library of Canada*] (NLC)

BVIVL .... Law Library, University of Victoria, British Columbia [*Library symbol National Library of Canada*] (NLC)

BVL............. Bear Valley [*California*] [*Seismograph station code, US Geological Survey*] (SEIS)

BVL............. Bellevue Ventures Ltd. [*Vancouver Stock Exchange symbol*]

BVL............. Beveled [*Technical drawings*]

BVL............. Bilateral Vas Ligation [*Medicine*]

BVL............. Bonneville, UT [*Location identifier FAA*] (FAAL)

BVL............. BVL [*Bowlers' Victory Legion*] Fund (EA)

BVLA........... British Volunteers, Latin America [*British military*] (DMA)

BVLS........... Battery-Voltage Limit System

BVM............ Bachelor of Veterinary Medicine

BVM............ Beata Virgo Maria [*Blessed Virgin Mary*] [*Latin*]

BVM............ Beau Val Mines [*Vancouver Stock Exchange symbol*]

BVM............ Belmonte [*Brazil*] [*Airport symbol*] (OAG)

BVM............ Bibliotheques Vertes pour le Monde [*Green Library - GL*] [*Saint Egreve, France*] (EAIO)

BVM............ Blessed Virgin Mary

BVM............ Boussinesq Viscosity Model (MCD)

BVM............ Bronchovascular Marking [*Medicine*] (MAE)

BVM............ Bureau of Veterinary Medicine [*FDA*]

BVM............ Business Visitors Memorandum [*British Overseas Trade Board*] (DS)

BVM............ Sisters of Charity of Blessed Virgin Mary (TOCD)

BVM............ Sisters of Charity of the Blessed Virgin Mary [*Roman Catholic religious order*]

BVMA.......... British Valve Manufacturers Association (PDAA)

BVMA.......... Vernon Museum, Archives and Art Gallery, British Columbia [*Library symbol National Library of Canada*] (NLC)

BVM & S ..... Bachelor of Veterinary Medicine and Surgery

BVMC.......... Blessed Virgin Missionaries of Carmel (TOCD)

BVMG .... Bender Visual-Motor Gestalt [*Test*] [*Psychology*] (DAVI)

BVMGT .... Bender Visual-Motor Gestalt Test [*Education*]

BVMS.......... Bachelor of Veterinary Medicine and Science [*Academic degree*] (DMAA)

BVMS.......... Bachelor of Veterinary Medicine and Surgery

BVN .... Baron Aviation Services, Inc. [*ICAO designator*] (FAAC)

BVN .... Bivariate Normal Mixture [*Statistics*]

BVN .... Bow Valley Naturalists (AC)

BVN .... Compania de Minas Buenaventura SA [*NYSE symbol*] (SAG)

BVN .... Comp de Minas Buenaventura ADS [*NYSE symbol*] (TTSB)

BVNA .... British Veterinary Nursing Association (DBA)

BVO .... Bartlesville [*Oklahoma*] [*Airport symbol*] (AD)

BVO .... Bartlesville, OK [*Location identifier FAA*] (FAAL)

BVO .... Branch Vein Occlusion [*Medicine*] (DMAA)

BVO .... Bravo Resources [*Vancouver Stock Exchange symbol*]

BVO .... Brominated Vegetable Oil [*Soft drink additive*]

BVocArts...... Bachelor of Vocational Arts

BVocEd .... Bachelor of Vocational Education

BVON .... Blending Value Octane Number [*Petroleum technology*]

BVOR.......... O'Keefe Ranch and Interior Heritage Society, Vernon, British Columbia [*Library symbol National Library of Canada*] (NLC)

BVP............. Bayerische Volkspartei [*Bavarian People's Party*] [*Germany Political party*] (PPE)

BVP............. Beacon Video Processor

BVP............. Benzyl(vinyl)pyridinium Bromide [*Organic chemistry*]

BVP............. Blood Vessel of Pinnule

BVP............. Blood Vessel Prosthesis [*Medicine*]

BVP............. Booster Vacuum Pump

BVP............. Boundary Value Problem

BVP............. British Visitor's Passport

BVP............. British Volunteer Programme

BVP............. Burst of Ventricular Pacing [*Medicine*] (DMAA)

BVP............. Burton Public Library, Burton, OH [*OCLC symbol*] (OCLC)

BVP............. Business Venture Profiles [*TECHSTART International, Inc.*] [*Information service or system*] (CRD)

BVPP .... BCNU [*Carmustine*], Vincristine, Procarbazine, Prednisone [*Antineoplastic drug regimen*]

BVPP .... Blood Vessel of Palp

BVPS .... Beacon Video Processing System

BVPS .... Beaver Valley Power Station (NRCH)

BVPS .... Booster Vacuum Pump System

BVQ .... Glasgow, KY [*Location identifier FAA*] (FAAL)

BVR .... Balanced Valve Regulator

BVR .... Bangalore Volunteer Rifles [*British military*] (DMA)

BVR .... Beaver

BVR .... Beyond Visual Range (MCD)

BVR .... Black Void Reactor

BVR .... Bloque de la Vanguardia Revolucionaria [*Bolivia*] [*Political party*] (PPW)

BVR .... Bureau of Vocational Rehabilitation (OICC)

BVR .... BVR Technologies Ltd. [*Associated Press*] (SAG)

BVR .... Byggvaruregistret [*Building Commodity File*] [*Swedish Building Center Stockholm*] [*Information service or system*] (IID)

BVRA .... British Veterinary Radiology Association (DBA)

BVRAAM ...... Beyond Visual Range Air-to-Air Missile

BVRB .... Bernard van Risenbergh [*Label stamped on works by the master ebeniste*]

BVRLA .... British Vehicle Rental and Leasing Association (DBA)

BVRM .... Beyond Visual Range Missile (MCD)

BVRO .... Base Vehicle Reporting Officer

BVRR .... Bureau of Veterans Reemployment Rights [*Department of Labor*]

BVRS .... Breadboard Visual Reference System [*NASA*]

BVRT .... Benton Visual Retention Test [*Psychology*] (DAVI)

BVRT	Benton Visual Retention Time [*Psychiatry*]
BVRT	BVR Technologies Ltd. [*NASDAQ symbol*] (SAG)
BVRTF	BVR Technologies Ltd [*NASDAQ symbol*] (TTSB)
BVRTR	Benton Visual Retention Test, Revised [*Psychology*] (DAVI)
BVS	Bachelor of Veterinary Science
BVS	Bachelor of Veterinary Surgery
BVS	Battery Vehicle Society [*British*]
BVS	Bela Vista [*Brazil*] [*Airport symbol*] (AD)
BVS	Best Value Selection (AAGC)
BVS	Bevier & Southern Railroad Co. [*AAR code*]
BVS	Bibliothek-Verbund-System [*Library Network System*] [*Siemens AG*] [*Information service or system*] (IID)
BVS	Biodegradable Volatile Solids [*Analytical chemistry*]
BVS	Blanked Ventricular Sense [*Medicine*] (DMAA)
BVS	Bond Valence Sum [*Physical chemistry*]
BVS	Brethren Volunteer Service (EA)
BVS	British Vexillological Society
BVS	Buddhist Vihara Society (EA)
BVS	Bulk Verification Services [*British*]
BVS	Buoyant Venus Station [*NASA*]
BVS	Bureau of Vital Statistics (AFM)
BVS	Business Vehicle Survey
BV Sc	Bachelor of Veterinary Science
BVSc & AH	Bachelor of Veterinary Science and Animal Husbandry
BVSI	Brite Voice System, Inc. [*NASDAQ symbol*] (NQ)
BVSI	Brite Voice Systems [*NASDAQ symbol*] (TTSB)
BVSN	BroadVision, Inc. [*NASDAQ symbol*] (SAG)
BVSNSW	Board of Veterinary Surgeons of New South Wales [*Australia*]
BVSP	Basaltic Volcanism Study Project [*Planetary science*]
BVSV	Bimetal Vacuum Switching Valve [*Automotive engineering*]
BVT	Bouvet Island [*ANSI three-letter standard code*] (CNC)
BVT	Brevet [*Military*]
BVT	Lafayette, IN [*Location identifier FAA*] (FAAL)
BVTM	Bivariate Thematic Mapping
BVU	Bellevue, WA [*Location identifier FAA*] (FAAL)
BVU	Bromoisovalerylurea [*Pharmacology*]
BVU	(Bromovinyl)uracil [*Antiviral compound*]
BVV	Bovine Vaginitis Virus [*Veterinary medicine*] (MAE)
BVV	Brookhaven, MS [*Location identifier FAA*] (FAAL)
BVVFA	Barossa Valley Vintage Festival Association [*Australia*]
BVW	Backward Volume Wave [*Telecommunications*] (TEL)
BVW	Binary Voltage Weigher
BVX	Bacitracin V and X [*Antibacterial compound*]
BVX	Batesville [*Arkansas*] [*Airport symbol*] (OAG)
BVX	Batesville, AR [*Location identifier FAA*] (FAAL)
BVY	Beverly, MA [*Location identifier FAA*] (FAAL)
BVZ	Beverly Springs [*Australia Airport symbol Obsolete*] (OAG)
BVZS	British Veterinary Zoological Society (DBA)
b/w	Backed With [*Used by record companies and trade papers to indicate music on the alternative side of a disk*]
BW	Backward Wave [*Telecommunications*] (IAA)
BW	Bacteriological Warfare
BW	Bacteriological Warhead
BW	Baltischer Weltrat [*Baltic World Council*] (EAIO)
BW	Bandwidth [*Frequency range*]
bw	Bandwidth (IDOE)
BW	Bango Whiplash [*Military*]
BW	Baroclinic Waves [*Astronomy*]
BW	Barrack Warden [*British military*] (DMA)
BW	Basal Web
BW	Beam Width (CET)
BW	Beautiful Wife (IIA)
BW	Bell Wire
BW	Below Waist [*Medicine*]
BW	Below Watch
BW	Below Water (NG)
BW	Bendix-Westinghouse Automotive Air Brake Co.
BW	Best of Winners [*Dog show term*]
BW	Bewusstein [*Consciousness*] [*Psychology*]
BW	Bibles for the World (EA)
BW	Bid Wanted [*Business term*]
BW	Bijbels Woordenboek [*A publication*] (BJA)
BW	Binary Workstation [*Computer science*]
BW	Biological Warfare
BW	Biological Weapons [*Military*]
BW	Birth Weight [*Medicine*]
BW	Biweekly
BW	Black and White [*Photography, television, etc.*] (KSC)
b/w	Black and White [*Photography*] [*Art*] (WDMC)
B/W	Black and White [*Photography*] [*Art*] (WDMC)
b/w	Black and White (IDOE)
bw	Black-and-White (IDOE)
BW	Black Watch [*Military unit*] [*British*]
BW	Black Writers [*A publication*]
BW	Bladder Washout [*Urology*]
BW	Blood Wassermann [*Medicine*]
BW	Blue Wove [*Paper*] (DGA)
BW	Bluie West [*US air bases in Greenland*] [*World War II*]
BW	Blunted Wedge
BW	Board of Works [*British*]
BW	Body Water [*Medicine*]
BW	Body Weight
BW	Body Whorl
BW	Body Wing (KSC)
BW	Bombardment Wing [*Air Force*]

BW	Bonded Warehouse
BW	Bonded Winery
BW	Book World [*A publication*] (BRI)
BW	Borg-Warner Corp.
BW	Both Ways [*Technical drawings*]
BW	Botswana [*ANSI two-letter standard code*] (CNC)
BW	Bottom Withdrawal [*Tube*]
BW	Bound With (ROG)
BW	Bradbury Wilkinson (DGA)
BW	Braided Wire Armor (AAG)
BW	Brain Water
BW	Bridgewire (NASA)
BW	British Waterways [*State-owned company*]
BW	British West Indian Airways Ltd. [*ICAO designator*] (OAG)
BW	Brush Wellman [*NYSE symbol*] (TTSB)
BW	Brush Wellman, Inc. [*NYSE symbol*] (SPSG)
BW	Burgerlijk Wetboek [*Civil Code*] [*Netherlands*] (ILCA)
BW	Buried Wire [*Telecommunications*] (TEL)
BW	Burroughs Wellcome & Co.
BW	Burroughs Wellcome Research Institute [*Great Britain*] [*Research code symbol*]
BW	Business Week [*A publication*]
BW	Butler's Wharf [*Shipping*] [*British*] (ROG)
BW	Butt Weld (DNAB)
BW	Butt Welded (IAA)
BW	BWIA International [*ICAO designator*] (AD)
BW	Kurzes Bibelwoerterbuch [*A publication*] (BJA)
BW	Trinidad and Tobago Airways Corp. [*Trinidad and Tobago*] [*ICAO designator*] (ICDA)
BWA	Backward Wave Amplifier
BWA	Baptist World Aid (EA)
BWA	Baptist World Alliance (EA)
BWA	Barossa Winemakers' Association [*Australia*]
BWA	Bedstead Workmens Association [*A union*] [*British*]
BWA	Bent Wire Antenna
BWA	Bhairawa [*Nepal*] [*Airport symbol*] (OAG)
BWA	Black Women's Association (EA)
BWA	Borg-Warner Automotive [*NYSE symbol*] (TTSB)
BWA	Borg-Warner Automotive, Inc. [*NYSE symbol*] (SPSG)
BWA	Botswana [*ANSI three-letter standard code*] (CNC)
BWA	Boxing Writers Association
BWA	Branch Warehouse Association (EA)
BWA	British Waterfowl Association (BI)
BWA	British Waterworks Association
BWA	British West Africa
BWA	British Wildlife Appeal (EAIO)
BWA	Building Waterproofers Association [*Defunct*] (EA)
BWA	Trinidad and Tobago Airways Corp. [*ICAO designator*] (FAAC)
BWAA	Baseball Writers Association of America (EA)
BWAA	Bowling Writers Association of America (EA)
BWAHDA	British Warm Air Hand Drier Association (DBA)
BWAI	Builders Warehouse Assn [*NASDAQ symbol*] (TTSB)
BWAI	Builders Warehouse Association, Inc. [*NASDAQ symbol*] (SAG)
BWAid	Baptist World Aid (EA)
BWANJ	Beer Wholesalers Association of New Jersey (SRA)
BWAR	Budget Workload Analysis Report [*Navy*] (NG)
BWARF	Baptist World Relief [*Later, Baptist World Aid*] (EA)
BWAS	Barron-Welsh Art Scale [*Psychology*]
BWASA	Blind Welfare Society of South Australia
BWatch	Bookwatch [*A publication*] (BRI)
B'WAY	Broadway [*A street name*]
BWAY	Brockway Standard Holdings, Inc. [*NASDAQ symbol*] (SAG)
BWAY	BWAY Corp. [*Associated Press*] (SAG)
BWAY	BWAY Corp. [*NASDAQ symbol*] (TTSB)
BWB	Blended Wing Body [*Megaplane*]
BWB	Boere Weerstandsbeweging [*South Africa Political party*] (EY)
BWB	British Waterways Board
BWB	Bryan, OH [*Location identifier FAA*] (FAAL)
BWBA	Blue Water Bridge Authority
BWBA	North American District of the Belgian Warmblood Breeding Association (EA)
BWBR	Bureau of Naval Weapons Branch Representative [*Obsolete*] (MCD)
BWBS	British Warm-Blood Society (DBA)
BWC	Backward Wave Converter (CET)
BWC	Baldwin-Wallace College [*Berea, OH*]
BWC	Baltic Women's Council (EA)
BWC	Baltic World Council [*Defunct*] (EA)
BWC	Basic Weight Controller
BWC	Battle Watch Captain (MCD)
BWC	Beauty without Cruelty USA (EA)
BWC	Belden, Inc. [*NYSE symbol*] (SPSG)
BWC	Big West Conference (EA)
BWC	Biological Weapons Command (DOMA)
BWC	Biological Weapons Convention
BWC	Board of War Communications [*World War II*]
B/WC	Bomb-to-Warhead Conversion (MCD)
BWC	Bonded Wine Cellar
BWC	Bowhunters Who Care (EA)
BWC	Brawley, CA [*Location identifier FAA*] (FAAL)
BWC	Bretton Woods Committee (EA)
BWC	Brisbane Women's Club [*Australia*]
BWC	British War Cabinet
BWC	Broadband Waveguide Circulator
BWC	Buffer Word Counter [*Computer science*]
BWC	Bureau of Water Carriers

BWC............ Bureau Weather Control
BWCA.......... Boundary Waters Canoe Area [*Minnesota*]
BWCC.......... Bomb-to-Warhead Conversion Components (CINC)
BWCC.......... British Weed Control Council (BI)
BWCC.......... Butterworth's Workmen's Compensation Cases [*A publication*] (DLA)
BWCC (Eng)... Butterworth's Workmen's Compensation Cases [*A publication*] (DLA)
BWCMA........ British Wood Chipboard Manufacturers Association (PDAA)
BWCMG....... British Watch and Clockmakers Guild (DBA)
BWCP.......... Base Wire Communications Program [*Air Force*]
BWCP.......... Bench Welder Control Panel
BWCR.......... National Black Women's Consciousness Raising Association (EA)
BWCS.......... Bagged White Cell Study [*Cytology*] (DAVI)
BWCS.......... Base Wire Communications System [*Air Force*] (CET)
BWCS.......... Beauty Without Cruelty Society [*Australia*]
BWCS.......... Black Women in Church and Society (EA)
BWCSA........ Blue Willow Collectors Society (EA)
BWCSA........ British White Cattle Society of Australia
BW/CW........ Biological Warfare/Chemical Warfare (NG)
BWD........... Babcock Woodall-Duckham Ltd. [*British*] (IRUK)
BWD........... Bacillary White Diarrhea [*Veterinary medicine*]
BWD........... Backward [*Telecommunications*] (TEL)
BW(D)......... Bacteriological Warfare, Defence [*British World War II*]
BWD........... Basic Work Data (MHDB)
BWD........... Biological Warfare Defense
BWD........... Bridgewest Development [*Vancouver Stock Exchange symbol*]
BWD........... Brownwood [*Texas*] [*Airport symbol*] (OAG)
BWD........... Bulk Wet Density
BWDA.......... Bicycle Wholesale Distributors Association (EA)
BWE........... Bachelor of Welding Engineering
BWE........... Brewmaster Systems Ltd. [*Vancouver Stock Exchange symbol*]
BWE........... Bucket Wheel Excavator (DICI)
BWE........... BUWEPS [*Bureau of Naval Weapons, now obsolete*] Evaluation
BWE........... Weston School of Theology, Cambridge, MA [*OCLC symbol*] (OCLC)
BWEA.......... Black Women's Educational Alliance (EA)
BWEA.......... British Wind Energy Association (IRUK)
BWEM.......... Westbank Museum, British Columbia [*Library symbol National Library of Canada*] (NLC)
BWEPRN....... Black Women's Educational Policy and Research Network (EA)
BWETPA....... British Water and Effluent Treatment Plant Association (PDAA)
BWF........... Bailett Weighting Function
BWF........... Beyond War Foundation (EA)
BWF........... Biblical Witness Fellowship (EA)
BWF........... Black World Foundation (EA)
BWF........... Breit-Wigner-Fano [*Spectra interference*]
BWF........... Breit-Wigner Formula
BWF........... Bretton Woods Fund (EA)
BWF........... Brisbane Warana Festival [*Australia*]
BWF........... British Whiting Federation (BI)
BWF........... British Woodworking Federation (DBA)
BWF........... British Wool Federation
BWF........... Building Wake Factor [*Nuclear energy*] (NRCH)
BWF........... Burroughs Wellcome Fund
BWF........... Burst Waveform
BWF........... Butt Welded Filter
BWF........... BWIP, Inc. [*NYSE symbol*] (SAG)
BWFC.......... Bank West Financial [*NASDAQ symbol*] (TTSB)
BWFC.......... Bank West Financial [*NASDAQ symbol*] (SAG)
BWFC.......... Benny Wilson Fan Club (EA)
BWFC.......... Betty White Fan Club (EA)
BWFI........... Bacteriostatic Water for Injection [*Medicine*]
BWFRR........ Bureau of Naval Weapons Fleet Readiness Representative [*Obsolete*] (MCD)
BWFRRCEN... Bureau of Naval Weapons Fleet Readiness Representative, Central [*Obsolete*] (MUGU)
BWFRRLANT... Bureau of Naval Weapons Fleet Readiness Representative, Atlantic [*Obsolete*] (MUGU)
BWFRRPAC... Bureau of Naval Weapons Fleet Readiness Representative, Pacific [*Obsolete*] (MUGU)
BW/FWT & TT... Boiler Water/Feedwater Test and Treatment Training (DNAB)
BWG........... Biphenyl Work Group (EA)
BWG........... Birmingham Wire Gauge
BWG........... Bouygues Offshore SA [*NYSE symbol*] (SAG)
BWG........... Bowling Green [*Kentucky*] [*Airport symbol*] (AD)
BWG........... Bowling Green, KY [*Location identifier FAA*] (FAAL)
BWGMSB..... Bright Wire Goods Manufacturers Service Bureau [*Defunct*] (EA)
BWH........... Blower Wheel Housing
BWHA.......... Brisbane Women's Hockey Association [*Australia*]
BWHB.......... Black and White Horizontal Bands [*Navigation markers*]
BWHBC........ Boston Women's Health Book Collective
BWHC.......... Heiltsuk Cultural Education Centre, Waglisla, British Columbia [*Library symbol National Library of Canada*] (NLC)
BWHP.......... Black Women's Health Project [*Later, NBWHP*] (EA)
BWI............ Baltimore [*Maryland*] [*Name derived from Baltimore-Washington International Airport*] [*Airport symbol*]
BWI............ Battle Wound Injury (CINC)
BWI............ BioWhittaker, Inc. [*NYSE symbol*] (SPSG)
BWI............ Boating While Intoxicated (BARN)
BWI............ Boating Writers International (EA)
BWI............ British Water International
BWI............ British West Indies [*Later, WI*]
BWI............ British Workmen's Institute (BI)
BWI............ Budget Workload Indicators
BWIA.......... British West Indian Airways Ltd.
BWIG.......... British Water Industries Group (DBA)

BWIN.......... Baldwin & Lyons, Inc. [*NASDAQ symbol*] (NQ)
BWINA........ Baldwin & Lyons CI'A' [*NASDAQ symbol*] (TTSB)
BWINB........ Baldwin & Lyons CI'B' [*NASDAQ symbol*] (TTSB)
BWIP.......... Basalt Waste Isolation Project [*Department of Energy*]
BWIP.......... Black Women in Publishing (EA)
BWIP.......... BWIP Holding, Inc. [*Associated Press*] (SAG)
BWIP.......... BWIP, Inc. [*NASDAQ symbol*] (SAG)
BWIP.......... BW/IP Inc. [*NASDAQ symbol*] (TTSB)
BWIR.......... Black-White Infrared [*Film*]
BWIU.......... Building Workers' Industrial Union [*British*]
BWIUA........ Building Workers' Industrial Union of Australia
BWJ........... Butt Welded Joint
BWK........... Batch Weighing Kit
BWK........... Belt Weather Kit (MCD)
BWK........... Bowker Out of Print Books [*Source file*] [*UTLAS symbol*]
BWK........... Brickwork
BWK........... Brillouin-Wentzel-Kramers [*Physics*]
BWK........... Bulwark
B Wksp....... Base Workshop [*British and Canadian*] [*Military*]
BWL........... Belt Work Line
BWL........... Belt Work Line
BWL........... Biological Warfare Laboratory
BWL........... Blackwell, OK [*Location identifier FAA*] (FAAL)
BWL........... Bowl America, Inc. [*AMEX symbol*] (SPSG)
BWL........... British World Airlines Ltd. [*FAA designator*] (FAAC)
BWLC.......... Cariboo-Chilcotin Archives, Williams Lake, British Columbia [*Library symbol National Library of Canada*] (NLC)
BWLK.......... Boardwalk Casino [*NASDAQ symbol*] (SAG)
BWLKW....... Boardwalk Casino Wrrt [*NASDAQ symbol*] (TTSB)
BWLM.......... William Lake Museum, British Columbia [*Library symbol National Library of Canada*] (NLC)
BWLN.......... Bowlin Outdoor Advertising & Travel Ctr., Inc. [*NASDAQ symbol*] (SAG)
BwlOtdr....... Bowlin Outdoor Advertising & Travel Ctr., Inc. [*Associated Press*] (SAG)
BWLT.......... Bow Light
BWM........... Backward Wave Magnetron (MSA)
BWM........... Best Western Motels [*Motel chain*]
BWM........... Block-Write Mode [*Computer graphics*] (BYTE)
BWM........... Brenwest Mining [*Vancouver Stock Exchange symbol*]
BWM........... British War Medal
BWM........... Broom and Whisk Makers (MHDB)
BWM........... Bursts with Memory [*Physics*]
BWM........... International Broom and Whisk Makers' Union of America [*Defunct*] (EA)
BWM........... Wells Museum, British Columbia [*Library symbol National Library of Canada*] (NLC)
BWMA......... Baptist Women's Missionary Auxilliary [*British*] (BI)
BWMA......... British Woodwork Manufacturers' Association (BI)
BWMB......... British Wool Marketing Board
BWMC......... British Working Men's Club
BWMS........ Baseline Waste Management Strategy (NUCP)
BWMS........ British Wireless Marine Service (DEN)
BWN........... Bandar Seri Begawan [*Brunei*] [*Airport symbol*] (OAG)
BWN........... Benefit Week Number [*Unemployment insurance*] (OICC)
BWN........... Black Women's Network [*An association*] (EA)
BWN........... Brown [*Telecommunications*] (TEL)
BWN........... Brownsville [*Diocesan abbreviation*] [*Texas*] (TOCD)
BWNIC........ British Withdrawal from Northern Ireland Campaign
BWNMA...... British Wire Netting Manufacturers Association (DBA)
BwnSh........ Brown & Sharpe Manufacturing Co. [*Associated Press*] (SAG)
BWO........... Backward Wave Oscillator
BW(O)......... Bacteriological Warfare, Operational Panel [*British World War II*]
BWO........... Base Work Order (AAG)
BWO........... Blue-Winged Olive [*Insect*]
BWO........... Bridge Wireless Officer [*British military*] (DMA)
BWO........... BW Air Services Ltd. [*British ICAO designator*] (FAAC)
BWOC........ Big Woman on Campus [*Slang*]
BWOED....... Black Women Organized for Educational Development (EA)
BWOS........ Backward Wave Oscillator Synchronizer
BWOT......... Backward Wave Oscillator Tube
BWOY......... British Wheel of Yoga [*An association*] (DBA)
BW(P)......... Bacteriological Warfare, Policy Panel [*British World War II*]
BWP........... Bahawalpur [*Pakistan*] [*Airport symbol*] (AD)
BWP........... Ballistic Wind Plotter
BWP........... Banco Wiese ADS [*NYSE symbol*] (TTSB)
BWP........... Banco Wiese Limitado [*NYSE symbol*] (SAG)
BWP........... Barrier, Waterproof (MSA)
BWP........... Basic War Plan [*Navy*]
BWP........... Belgische Werkliedenpartij [*Belgian Workers' Party*] [*Later, Belgian Socialist Party*] [*Political party*] (PPE)
BWP........... Bewani [*Papua New Guinea*] [*Airport symbol*] (OAG)
BWP........... [*The*] Birds of Western Palearctic [*Book series*] [*British A publication*]
BWP........... Brown Wrapping Paper (OA)
BWP........... Wahpeton, ND [*Location identifier FAA*] (FAAL)
BWPA......... Backward Wave Power Amplifier
BWPA......... British Waste Paper Association (PDAA)
BWPA......... British Women Pilots Association (PDAA)
BWPA......... British Wood Preserving Association
BWPA......... British Wood Pulp Association (DBA)
BWPC......... Blue/White Pottery Club (EA)
BWPE......... Biased World Paw Entry [*Testing of left and right laterality in mice*]
BWPS......... Bus Workers' Protection Society [*A union*] [*British*]
BWPUC...... British Waste Paper Utilisation Council (BI)
BWQ........... Brewarrina [*Australia Airport symbol*] (OAG)

BWQ	Buzz Word Quotient [Computer science] (NHD)
BWR	Alpine, TX [Location identifier FAA] (FAAL)
BWR	Bandwidth Radio (MCD)
BWR	Bandwidth Ratio
bwr	Belorussian Soviet Socialist Republic [MARC country of publication code Library of Congress] (LCCP)
BWR	Benedict-Webb-Rubin [Equation of state]
BWR	Biweekly Report (MCD)
bwr	Blackware (VRA)
BWR	Boiling Water Reactor
BWR	Breakwater Resources Ltd. [Toronto Stock Exchange symbol Vancouver Stock Exchange symbol]
BWR	Bureau of Naval Weapons Representative [Obsolete]
BWRA	British Welding Research Association [Later, WI] (MCD)
BWRL	Boll Weevil Research Laboratory [Department of Agriculture] [Mississippi State, MS] [Research center]
BWRL	Bureau of War Risk Litigation
BWRM	City of White Rock Museum and Archives, British Columbia [Library symbol National Library of Canada] (NLC)
BWROG	Boiling Water Reactor Owners Group [Nuclear energy] (NRCH)
BWRR	Bureau of Naval Weapons Resident Representative [Obsolete] (MUGU)
BWRRA	British Wire Rod Rollers' Association (BI)
BWRS	British War Relief Society [in US]
BWRU	Boll Weevil Research Unit [Mississippi State, MS] [Agricultural Research Service] [Department of Agriculture] (GRD)
BWRVP	Black Women's Roundtable on Voter Participation (EA)
BWRWS	Biological Warfare Rapid Warning System [Army]
BWS	Bank of Western Samoa
BWS	Base Weather Station (MCD)
BWS	Batch Weighing System
BWS	Battered Woman [or Wife] Syndrome [Medicine Defunct]
BWS	Battlefield Weapons System
BWS	Beaufort Wind Scale
BWS	Beckwith-Wiedemann Syndrome [Medicine]
BWS	Better World Society [Defunct] (EA)
BWS	Beveled Wood Siding [Technical drawings]
BWS	Big White Set [Type of lush movie set used in 1930's musical-comedy films]
BWS	Biological Weapons System [Military]
BWS	British Water Colour Society (BI)
BWSA	British Wheat Starch Association (DBA)
BWSC	Boys of Woodcraft Sportsmen's Clubs [Later, Woodmen Rangers and Rangerettes] (EA)
BWSC	British War Supplies Committee [Combined Production and Resources Board] [World War II]
BWSF	British Water Ski Federation
BWSL	Battlefield Weapons System Laboratory
BWSN	Beckwith-Wiedemann Support Network (EA)
BWSO	Backward Wave Sweep Oscillator
BWSRT	Bureau of Naval Weapons Support Representative, Naval Air Training Command [Obsolete] (MUGU)
BWST	Back Widow Spider Toxin [Medicine] (DMAA)
BWST	Borated Water Storage Tank [Nuclear energy] (NRCH)
BWSTMA	British Welded Steel Tube Manufacturers Association (PDAA)
BWSTRN	Bowstring
BWSTx	Black Widow Spider Toxin
BWSV	Black Widow Spider Venom
BWT	Backward Wave Tube [Physics]
BWT	Bandwidth Ratio [Telecommunications] (NITA)
BWT	Bermuda-Schwortz Industries, Inc. [Vancouver Stock Exchange symbol]
BWT	Birth Weight [Medicine]
BWT	Boeing Wind Tunnel
BWT	Bohr-Wheeler Theory
BWT	Both Way Trunk
BWT	Bottom Water Temperature [Oceanography]
BWT	British Winter Time (IAA)
BWTA	Boston Wool Trade Association (EA)
BWTA	British Wholesale Traders Association (DBA)
BWTA	British Women's Temperance Association (BI)
BWTA	British Wood Turners' Association
BWT Bull	Butterworth's Weekly Tax Bulletin [Australia A publication]
BWTF	Bank Wire Transfer of Funds
BWTP	Bureau of Work-Training Programs [Terminated, 1969] [Department of Labor]
BWTR	Babcock & Wilcox Test Reactor
BWTS	Base Wire and Telephone System [Air Force] (MCD)
BWTS	Bayonet Workers' Trade Society [A union] [British]
BWTSDS	Base Wire and Telephone System Development Schedule [Air Force]
BWU	Blue-Whale-Unit [Whaling industry]
BWUSA	Blind Workers' Union of South Australia
BWUSWP	Baptist Women's Union of the South West Pacific [Australia]
BWUV	Blind Workers' Union of Victoria [Australia]
BWV	Bach Werke-Verzeichnis [Music]
BWV	Back-Water Valve
BWV	West Vancouver Memorial Library, British Columbia [Library symbol National Library of Canada] (NLC)
BWVA	British War Veterans of America (EA)
BWVB	Black and White Vertical Blinds [Navigation markers] (DNAB)
BWVHC	Hatfield Consultants Ltd., West Vancouver, British Columbia [Library symbol National Library of Canada] (NLC)
BWVS	Black and White Vertical Stripes [Navigation markers]
BWW	Barter Worldwide, Inc. [Information service or system] (IID)
BWW	Biggers, Whitten, and Whittingham [Growth medium] [Gynecology]
BWW	Buses Worldwide [British] [An association] (DBA)
BWWEA	British Woven Wire Export Association (DBA)
BWY	Blast Wave Yield
BWY	Bowes Lyon Resources Ltd. [Vancouver Stock Exchange symbol]
BWY	Broadway Stores [Formerly, Carter Hawley, Hale] [NYSE symbol] (SAG)
BWY	Fleet Requirement Air Direction Unit [British ICAO designator] (FAAC)
BWYV	Beet Western Yellows Virus
BWY.WS	Broadway Stores Wrrt [NYSE symbol] (TTSB)
BWZ	Schooley's Mountain, NJ [Location identifier FAA] (FAAL)
BX	Bacitracin X [Antibacterial compound]
BX	Base Exchange
BX	Base Register [Computer science]
BX	Basic Exercises
BX	Biopsy [Medicine]
BX	Box
bx	Box (VRA)
bx	Box Container [Shipping] (DS)
BX	Branch Exchange [Telecommunications]
Bx	Bronx [New York] (BARN)
bx	Brunei [MARC country of publication code Library of Congress] (LCCP)
BX	Builders' Exchange Association of Texas (SRA)
BX	Compania SPANTAX (Servicios y Transportes Aereos Air Charter) [Spain ICAO designator] (ICDA)
BXA	Bogalusa, LA [Location identifier FAA] (FAAL)
BXA	Bureau of Export Administration [Department of Commerce]
BXB	Babo [Indonesia] [Airport symbol] (OAG)
BXBD	Boxboard (DGA)
BX BS	Blue Cross and Blue Shield [Insurance plan] (DAVI)
BXC	Biotin-X Cadaverine [Biochemical labelling compound]
BX-C	Bithorax Complex [Gene cluster in fruit fly]
BXD	Bade [Indonesia] [Airport symbol] (OAG)
BXD	Boxed
BXDT	Boxcar Detector (MSA)
BXE	Bakel [Senegal] [Airport symbol] (OAG)
BXE	Bowtex Energy (Canada) Corp. [Toronto Stock Exchange symbol]
BXF	Box Fin
BXG	Bluegreen Corp. [NYSE symbol] (SAG)
BXG	Bluegreen Corp. [NYSE symbol] (TTSB)
BXG	BRX Mining & Petroleum [Vancouver Stock Exchange symbol]
BXG	Waynesboro, GA [Location identifier FAA] (FAAL)
BXH	British Independent Airways [ICAO designator] (FAAC)
BXH	Martha's Vineyard, MA [Location identifier FAA] (FAAL)
BXI	Boundiali [Ivory Coast] [Airport symbol] (OAG)
BXK	Broadband X-Band Klystron
BXK	Buckeye, AZ [Location identifier FAA] (FAAL)
BXL	Air Exel Belgique [Belgium ICAO designator] (FAAC)
BXL	Boston College Law School, Newton, MA [OCLC symbol] (OCLC)
BXM	Boston College, Chestnut Hill, MA [OCLC symbol] (OCLC)
BXMN	Bre-X Minerals Ltd. [NASDAQ symbol] (SAG)
BXN	Bauxite & Northern Railway Co. [AAR code]
BXN	Dallas-Fort Worth, TX [Location identifier FAA] (FAAL)
BXO	Balanitis Xerotica Obliterans (DMAA)
BXO	Bissau [Portuguese Guinea] [Airport symbol] (OAG)
BXR	Barexor Minerals, Inc. [Vancouver Stock Exchange symbol]
BXR	Siren, WI [Location identifier FAA] (FAAL)
BXS	Base Excess [Medicine]
BXS	Borrego Springs [California] [Airport symbol] (OAG)
BXS	Compania Spantax [Spain ICAO designator] (FAAC)
BXT	American Municipal Term Trust II [NYSE symbol] (SAG)
BXT	Amer Muni Term Trust II [NYSE symbol] (TTSB)
BX/TK	Boxed or Tanked
BXU	Butuan [Philippines] [Airport symbol] (OAG)
BXV	Breiddalsvik [Iceland] [Airport symbol] (OAG)
bxwd	Boxwood (VRA)
BXY	Allentown, PA [Location identifier FAA] (FAAL)
BY	Base Year (DOMA)
BY	Bay (ADA)
BY	Bedfordshire Yeomanry [British military] (DMA)
BY	Billion Years
BY	Blowing Spray [ICAO] (FAAC)
BY	Born Young [An association] (EA)
BY	Britannia Airways [Airline flight code] (ODBW)
BY	Budget Year (AFM)
BY	Busy [Telecommunications] (TEL)
BY	BWAY Corp. [NYSE symbol] (SAG)
BY	Byelorussian Soviet Socialist Republic [ISO two-letter standard code] (CNC)
BY1	Byrd - Stanford Research Institute [Antarctica] [Seismograph station code, US Geological Survey Closed] (SEIS)
BYA	Bay Ann Resources, Inc. [Vancouver Stock Exchange symbol]
BYA	Bay Apartment Communities [NYSE symbol] (SAG)
BYA	Boundary, AK [Location identifier FAA] (FAAL)
BYA	Byrd Station, Antarctica
BYAA	Byelorussian Youth Association of America [Later, BAYO] (EA)
Byb	Byblian (BJA)
ByB	Byblos Librairie Bookshop, Beirut, Lebanon [Library symbol Library of Congress] (LCLS)
BYBB	Backyard Boat Builders [USCG] (TAG)
BYBI	Back Yard Burgers [NASDAQ symbol] (TTSB)
BYBI	Back Yard Burgers, Inc. [NASDAQ symbol] (SAG)
BYC	Bengal Yeomanry Cavalry [British military] (DMA)
BYC	Berkshire Yeomanry Cavalry [British military] (DMA)

BYC.............	Brewers Yeast Council [*Later, Brewers Yeast and Grains Council*] [*Defunct*] (EA)
BYC.............	British Youth Council (EAIO)
BYC.............	Northern Airlines Sanya Lts. [*China*] [*FAA designator*] (FAAC)
BYC.............	Yacuiba [*Bolivia*] [*Airport symbol*] (OAG)
BYD.............	Barley Yellow Dwarf [*Plant pathology*]
BYD.............	Bayridge Development [*Vancouver Stock Exchange symbol*]
BYD.............	Beyond (FAAC)
BYD.............	Bicentennial Youth Debates [*National Endowment for the Humanities program*]
BYD.............	Boyd Gaming [*NYSE symbol*] (SPSG)
BYD.............	Bureau of Yards and Docks [*Later, NFEC*] [*Navy*] (MCD)
BYDIR.........	By Direction (NVT)
BYDS	Boyds Wheels [*NASDAQ symbol*] (TTSB)
BYDS	Boyds Wheels, Inc. [*NASDAQ symbol*] (SAG)
BYDV	Barley Yellow Dwarf Virus
BydWhls	Boyds Wheels, Inc. [*Associated Press*] (SAG)
BYE.............	Barile-Yaguchi-Eveland [*Growth medium*] [*Microbiology*]
BYE.............	Bear Stearns Companies, Inc. [*AMEX symbol*] (SAG)
BYE.............	Benefit Year Ending [*Unemployment insurance*]
Bye.............	Byelorussia [*Belarus*] (BARN)
BYF.............	Bloody Young Fool [*Officer under the age of 30*] [*British*] (DSUE)
BYFC...........	Broadway Financial [*NASDAQ symbol*] (TTSB)
BYFC...........	Broadway Financial Corp. [*NASDAQ symbol*] (SAG)
BYG	Buffalo, WY [*Location identifier FAA*] (FAAL)
BYG	BYG Natural Resources, Inc. [*Toronto Stock Exchange symbol*]
BYH	Blytheville, AR [*Location identifier FAA*] (FAAL)
BYI.............	Burley, ID [*Location identifier FAA*] (FAAL)
BYI.............	Burley-Rupert [*Idaho*] [*Airport symbol*] (AD)
BYK	Bouake [*Ivory Coast*] [*Airport symbol*] (OAG)
Byl Bills......	Byles on Bills of Exchange [*A publication*] (DLA)
Byles	Byles on Bills of Exchange [*A publication*] (DLA)
Byl Exch	Byles' Law of Exchange [*A publication*] (DLA)
BYLINE	Brigham Young Libraries Information Network [*Brigham Young University*] [*Provo, UT*] [*Information service or system*] (IID)
Byl Us L	Byles on the Usury Laws [*A publication*] (DLA)
BYM	Bayamo [*Cuba*] [*Airport symbol*] (OAG)
BYM............	Historic Yale Museum, British Columbia [*Library symbol National Library of Canada*] (NLC)
BYM-AG	Bornu Youth Movement - Action Group Alliance [*Nigeria*]
BYMS...........	British Yard Motor Minesweepers
BYMUX	Byte-Multiplexer Channel
BYMV..........	Bean Yellow Mosaic Virus
BYN	Bangor Public Library, Bangor, ME [*OCLC symbol*] (OCLC)
BYN	Bear Stearns Companies, Inc. [*AMEX symbol*] (SAG)
BYN	Bryan, OH [*Location identifier FAA*] (FAAL)
BYN	Byron Resources, Inc. [*Vancouver Stock Exchange symbol*]
BYNA	British Young Naturalists Association (BI)
BYNT	Buoyant (MSA)
Byn War	Bynkershoek's Law of War [*A publication*] (DLA)
BYO	Bring Your Own [*Liquor*] [*Party invitation notation*]
BYOB	Bring Your Own Beef [*Phrase popularized during 1973 beef shortage*]
BYOB	Bring Your Own Boat
BYOB	Bring Your Own Booze [*or Bottle*] [*Party invitation notation*]
BYOG	Bring Your Own Girl (IIA)
BYOG	Bring Your Own Grog [*British*] (ADA)
BYOTV	Bring Your Own TV
BYOV	Bring Your Own Vehicle
BYOW	Bring Your Own Wine (ADA)
BYP.............	Bypass (KSC)
BYP.............	Bypass
BYPA	Bypass [*Commonly used*] (OPSA)
BYPAS	Bypass [*Commonly used*] (OPSA)
BYPASS	Bypass [*Commonly used*] (OPSA)
BYPCAP	Bypass Capacitor [*Electronics*] (IAA)
BYPCOND	Bypass Condenser [*Electronics*] (IAA)
BYPS	Bypass [*Commonly used*] (OPSA)
BYPU	Baptist Young People's Union
BYR	Billion Years
BYR	Byrd [*Antarctica*] [*Seismograph station code, US Geological Survey Closed*] (SEIS)
BYrbLin.......	Bank of Yorba Linda [*Associated Press*] (SAG)
ByrdAE........	Byrd Antarctic Expedition [*1928-30, 1933-35*]
Byrne BS	Byrne. Bills of Sale [*2nd ed.*] [*1870*] [*A publication*] (DLA)
Byrne Pat....	Byrne on Patents [*A publication*] (DLA)
BYRS	Buyers
BYS	Barstow, CA [*Location identifier FAA*] (FAAL)
BYS	Base Year Dollars (MCD)
BYS.............	British Yugoslav Society (DBA)
BYS.............	Byelorussian Soviet Socialist Republic [*ISO three-letter standard code*] (CNC)
BYSMV	Barley Yellow Striate Mosaic Virus [*Plant pathology*]
BYSV	Beet Yellow Stunt Virus [*Plant pathology*]
BYT.............	Bentley Resources Ltd. [*Vancouver Stock Exchange symbol*]
BYT.............	Bright Young Thing (DSUE)
BYT.............	Bytom [*Poland*] [*Seismograph station code, US Geological Survey*] (SEIS)
byte	Binary Term [*Computer science*]
Byth Conv	Bythewood. Precedents in Conveyancing [*4th ed.*] [*1884-90*] [*A publication*] (DLA)
Byth Prec.....	Bythewood. Precedents in Conveyancing [*4th ed.*] [*1884-90*] [*A publication*] (DLA)
BYU	Barksdale, LA [*Location identifier FAA*] (FAAL)
BYU	Bayou

BYU	Bayou
BYU	Bayreuth [*Germany Airport symbol*] (OAG)
BYU	Bayu Indonesia Air PT [*ICAO designator*] (FAAC)
BYU	Brandy Resources [*Vancouver Stock Exchange symbol*]
BYU	Brigham Young University [*Utah*]
BYU	Brigham Young University, Hawaii Campus, Laie, HI [*OCLC symbol*] (OCLC)
BYUP	Brigham Young University Press
BYV.............	Baiyer River [*New Guinea*] [*Airport symbol*] (AD)
BYV.............	Beet Yellows Virus
BYVBV	Bean Yellow Vein Banding Virus [*Plant pathology*]
BYW	Blakely Island [*Washington*] [*Airport symbol*] (OAG)
BYX.............	Barymin Explorations Ltd. [*Toronto Stock Exchange symbol*]
BYX.............	Bayou Steel 'A' [*AMEX symbol*] (TTSB)
BYX.............	Bayou Steel Corp. of La Place [*AMEX symbol*] (SPSG)
BYY.............	Bay City, TX [*Location identifier FAA*] (FAAL)
BYZ.............	Byzantine
Byz.............	Byzantine (VRA)
Byzan.........	Byzantine
Byz und Neugr Jahrb...	Byzantinisch-Neugriechische Jahrbucher [*A publication*] (OCD)
Byz Zeitschr...	Byzantinische Zeitschrift [*A publication*] (OCD)
BZ...............	Audible Signal Devices [*JETDS nomenclature*] [*Military*] (CET)
BZ...............	Bairnco Corp. [*NYSE symbol*] (SPSG)
BZ...............	Belize [*ANSI two-letter standard code*] (CNC)
BZ...............	Belousov-Zhabotinskii [*Physical chemistry*]
BZ...............	Benzene [*Organic chemistry*] (ADA)
BZ...............	Benzodiazepine [*Also, BZD*] [*Organic chemistry*]
BZ...............	Benzopyrene [*or Benzpyrene*] [*Also, BP Carcinogen*]
Bz...............	Benzoyl [*Organic chemistry*]
BZ...............	Bild Zeitung [*Picture newspaper*] [*German*]
BZ...............	Blank when Zero
BZ...............	Bnai Zion (EA)
BZ...............	Branch Zip Code [*Database Terminology*] (NITA)
BZ...............	Bravo Zulu [*Signal for "job well done"*] [*Navy*] (DOMA)
BZ...............	Brillouin Zone [*Physics*]
BZ...............	Bronze
bz...............	Bronze (VRA)
BZ...............	Buckled Zone (SAA)
BZ...............	Buzzer [*Electronics*] (IAA)
BZ...............	Capital Airlines [*ICAO designator*] (AD)
BZ...............	Iraq [*Formerly, TS*] [*License plate code assigned to foreign diplomats in the US*]
BZ...............	Phenylbutazone [*Organic chemistry*] (DAVI)
BZ...............	Quinuclidinyl Benzilate [*Also, QNB*] [*Army symbol*]
BZ...............	Skyfreighters [*ICAO designator*] (AD)
Bza.............	Benzimidazole [*Biochemistry*]
Bza.............	Benzimidazolyl [*Biochemistry*]
BZA.............	Board of Zoning Adjustment
BZA.............	Bombenzielapparat [*Bomb sight*] [*German military - World War II*]
BZA.............	British Zeolite Association
BZA.............	Yuma, AZ [*Location identifier FAA*] (FAAL)
BZAC...........	Benzoylacetone [*Organic chemistry*]
BZAC...........	Brazing Accessory [*Tool*] (AAG)
BZ & C........	Bellaire, Zanesville & Cincinnati Railroad [*Nickname: Bent, Zigzagged, and Crooked*]
BzAnth	Benzanthracene [*Also, BA*] [*Organic chemistry*]
BZC.............	Hyannis, MA [*Location identifier FAA*] (FAAL)
BZD.............	Benzidine [*Carcinogen*]
BZD.............	Benzodiazepine [*Also, BZ*] [*Organic chemistry*]
BZD.............	Blizzard Resources, Inc. [*Vancouver Stock Exchange symbol*]
BZDZ...........	Benzodiazepine [*Pharmacology*] (DAVI)
BZE.............	Belize City [*Belize*] [*Airport symbol*] (OAG)
BZE.............	Benzoylecgonine [*Biochemistry*]
BZE.............	Bozeman [*Montana*] [*Seismograph station code, US Geological Survey Closed*] (SEIS)
BZET	Biofield Corp. [*NASDAQ symbol*] (SAG)
BZET	Biofield Corp. [*NASDAQ symbol*] (TTSB)
BZF.............	Brazil Fund [*NYSE symbol*] (TTSB)
BZF.............	Brazil Fund, Inc. [*NYSE symbol*] (SPSG)
BZF.............	Clinton, OK [*Location identifier FAA*] (FAAL)
BZFX..........	Brazing Fixture
BZG.............	Bombenzielgeraet [*Bomb sight*] [*German military - World War II*]
BZG.............	Bydgoszcz [*Poland*] [*Airport symbol Obsolete*] (OAG)
BZGL...........	Bezueglich [*In Regard To, With Reference To*] [*German*]
BZH.............	Beazer Homes USA [*NYSE symbol*] (SAG)
Bzh.............	Benzhydryl [*Biochemistry*]
BZH.............	Britair SA [*France ICAO designator*] (FAAC)
BZHPrA........	Beazer HomesUSA$2.00CvExPfd [*NYSE symbol*] (TTSB)
BZI.............	Balikesir [*Turkey*] [*Airport symbol*] (AD)
BZI.............	Beam Zero Indication (MCD)
BZI.............	Benyzlimidazole [*Organic chemistry*]
BZion.........	Der Bote aus Zion [*Berlin*] [*A publication*] (BJA)
BZJ.............	Indiantown Gap, PA [*Location identifier FAA*] (FAAL)
BZK.............	Brookfield, MO [*Location identifier FAA*] (FAAL)
BZL.............	Barisal [*Bangladesh*] [*Airport symbol*] (AD)
Bzl.............	Benzyl [*Organic chemistry*]
BZL.............	Brazilian Equity Fund [*NYSE symbol*] (SPSG)
BZM.............	Beit Zeiroth Mizrachi (BJA)
BZM.............	Boston University, School of Theology, Boston, MA [*OCLC symbol*] (OCLC)
BZM.............	Bozeman [*Montana*] [*Seismograph station code, US Geological Survey Closed*] (SEIS)
BZM.............	Hickory, NC [*Location identifier FAA*] (FAAL)
BZN.............	Bozeman [*Montana*] [*Airport symbol*] (OAG)

BZN............. Brize Norton, FTU [*British*] [*FAA designator*] (FAAC)
BZNS .... Bulgarski Zemedelski Naroden Soyuz [*Bulgarian Agrarian People's Union-United*] [*Political party*] (EY)
BZO............. Bolzano [*Italy*] [*Airport symbol*] (AD)
BZO............. Bonanza Oil & Gas Ltd. [*Toronto Stock Exchange symbol*]
BZP............. Bizant [*Australia Airport symbol Obsolete*] (OAG)
BZP............. Galena, AK [*Location identifier FAA*] (FAAL)
BZPCA .... British Zone Petroleum Coordinating Authority [*Post-World War II, Germany*]
BZQ............. Benzquinamide [*Pharmacology*]
BZR............. Bazaar
BZR............. Baz Resources Ltd. [*Vancouver Stock Exchange symbol*]
BZR............. Beziers [*France*] [*Airport symbol*] (OAG)

BZR............. Buzzer (FAAC)
BZ Sc........... Bachelor of Zoological Science
BZStF.......... Biblische Zeit-und Streitfragen (BJA)
BZT .... Brazoria, TX [*Location identifier FAA*] (FAAL)
Bz-Ty-PABA... Benzoyl-Tyrosyl-Para-Aminobenzoic Acid [*Test*] (MEDA)
BZU............. Buta [*Zaire*] [*Airport symbol*] (OAG)
BZV............. Berliner Zionistische Vereinigung [*A publication*] (BJA)
BZV............. Brazzaville [*People's Republic of the Congo*] [*Airport symbol*] (OAG)
BZW............. Barclays de Zoete Wedd [*Investment firm*] [*British*]
BZW............. Bare Zirconium Wire
BZW............. Beziehungsweise [*Respectively*] [*German*]
BZX............. Bismarck, ND [*Location identifier FAA*] (FAAL)
BZY............. Brasileia [*Brazil*] [*Airport symbol*] (AD)
BZZ............. Butane Buzzard Aviation Corp. [*British ICAO designator*] (FAAC)

C
By Acronym

C.................. 100 (WDMC)
C.................. Acceleration Correction
C.................. All India Reporter, Calcutta Series [*A publication*] (DLA)
C.................. Ampere [*Unit of electric current*] (ROG)
C.................. Ascorbic Acid [*Vitamin C*] (DAVI)
C.................. Basso Continuo [*Continued Bass*] [*Music*] (ROG)
C.................. Business Class [*Also, J*] [*Airline fare code*]
C.................. Byk-Gulden Lomberg [*Germany*] [*Research code symbol*]
C.................. Cabinet [*Technical drawings*] (NFPA)
C.................. Cable
C.................. Cactus [*Horticulture*]
C.................. Cadet [*British military*] (DMA)
C.................. Caecum
C.................. Caesarean [*or Cesarean*] [*Section Obstetrics*] (DAVI)
C.................. Cage Container (DCTA)
C.................. Caius (ROG)
C.................. Calculus (MAE)
C.................. Caledonian [*Railway*] [*Scotland*] (ROG)
C.................. Calendae [*Calends*] [*The First Day of the Month*] [*Latin*]
C.................. California Reports [*A publication*] (DLA)
C.................. California State Library, Sacramento, CA [*Library symbol Library of Congress*] (LCLS)
C.................. California Supreme Court Reports [*A publication*] (DLA)
C.................. Call (IAA)
C.................. Calling-On [*Railroad signal arm*] [*British*]
C.................. Calm [*i.e., no wind*]
C.................. Calorie
c.................. Calorie [*Small Calorie*] [*Dietetics*] (DAVI)
C.................. Calyx [*Botany*] (ROG)
C.................. Cambridge [*Municipal borough in England*]
C.................. Can [*Buoy*] [*Maps and charts*]
C.................. Canada
C.................. Canceled
C.................. Cancer
C.................. Candela [*Formerly, Candlepower*] [*See also cd*] (MDG)
C.................. Candidatus [*Academic degree*] [*Latin*]
C.................. Candle [*Illumination*]
c.................. Candle (IDOE)
C.................. Canine [*Deciduous*] [*Dentistry*]
C.................. Cannon Street Station [*London*] (ROG)
C.................. Canoe
C.................. Canon
C.................. Canto (ROG)
C.................. Canvas (VRA)
C.................. Capacitance [*Symbol*] [*IUPAC*]
c.................. Capacitance (IDOE)
C.................. Capacitor (CET)
C.................. Capacity [*Medicine*]
c.................. Capacity [*Electricity*] (DAS)
C.................. Cape [*Maps and charts*]
C.................. Cape Provincial Division Reports [*South Africa*] [*A publication*] (DLA)
c.................. Capillary (AAMN)
C.................. Capillary Blood [*Medicine*] (DAVI)
C.................. Capitals [*Printing*]
C.................. Capitulum [*Chapter*] [*Latin*] (ROG)
C.................. Capo [*The Beginning*] [*Music*]
C.................. Captain
C.................. Captain [*Worn on captain's uniform*] [*Hockey*]
C.................. Caput [*Head*] [*Latin*]
C.................. Carat [*Unit of measure for precious stones or gold*]
C.................. Carbohydrate [*Dietetics*]
C.................. Carbon [*Chemical element*]
C.................. Card [*Manuscript descriptions*]
C.................. Cargo (WGA)
C.................. Cargo/Transport [*Designation for all US military aircraft*]
C.................. Carnian [*Geology*]
C.................. Carrier [*JETDS nomenclature*]
C.................. Carry
C.................. Carton
C.................. Case
C.................. Case Packaging [*Shipping*] (DS)
C.................. Cash [*Stock exchange term*] (SPSG)
C.................. Cassenne [*France*] [*Research code symbol*]
C.................. Cast (AAG)
C.................. Castle
C.................. Casualty [*Insurance*]

C.................. Catalog
C.................. Catalyst
C.................. Catch [*Pisciculture*]
C.................. Catcher [*Baseball*]
C.................. Catechism
C.................. Cathode [*or Cathodal*] [*Radiology*] (DAVI)
C.................. Catholic
C.................. Cattle (ROG)
C.................. Caucasian
C.................. Caudal [*Anatomy*]
C.................. Caught [*by*] [*In cricket*]
C.................. Caught Out
C.................. Causa [*Case or Cause*]
C.................. Cause
C.................. Cavalry [*British military*] (DMA)
C.................. Cavern (ROG)
C.................. Cedi [*Monetary unit*] [*Ghana*]
C.................. Ceiling [*Hazard limit*]
C.................. Cell
C.................. Celsius [*Centigrade*] [*Temperature scale*]
C.................. Celtic (ROG)
C.................. Cenomanian [*Paleontology*]
C.................. Censor (ROG)
C.................. Cent [*Monetary unit*]
C.................. Cental [*Short hundredweight*] [*British*] (WGA)
C.................. Centavo [*Monetary unit in many Spanish-American countries*]
C.................. Center [*A position in football, lacrosse, basketball*]
C.................. Centerline (WDMC)
c.................. Centi [*A prefix meaning divided by 100*] [*SI symbol*]
C.................. Centigrade [*Celsius*] [*Temperature scale*]
C.................. Centigram
C.................. Centime [*Monetary unit*] [*France*]
C.................. Centimeter
C.................. Centissime (ROG)
C.................. Cento [*Composition compiled from other works*]
C.................. Central
C.................. Centrifugal
C.................. Centum [*Hundred*]
C.................. Centum Milia [*One Hundred Thousand*] [*Latin*]
C.................. Century
c.................. Century (VRA)
C.................. Cerebrospinal Fluid [*Medicine*] (AAMN)
C.................. Certified (AAG)
C.................. Cervical [*Medicine*]
C.................. Cervus [*Deer*] (ROG)
C.................. Cessna Aircraft Co. [*ICAO aircraft manufacturer identifier*] (ICAO)
C.................. Chairman [*or Chairwoman or Chairperson*]
C.................. Chancellor
C.................. Chancery
C.................. Change [*Used in combinations only*] [*Army*] (AABC)
C.................. Chapel
C.................. Chapter
C.................. Character (BUR)
C.................. Charge (ROG)
C.................. Charge Conjugation [*Atomic physics*]
C.................. Charles Curtis [*Genotype of Phlox paniculata*]
C.................. Charlie [*Phonetic alphabet*] [*International since 1956*] (DSUE)
C.................. Charlotte [*North Carolina*] [*Mint mark, when appearing on US coins*]
c.................. Charmed (Quark) [*Atomic physics*]
C.................. Chemical (NFPA)
C.................. Chemistry [*Secondary school course*] [*British*]
C.................. Chest [*Medicine*]
C.................. Chest [*Tea trade*] (ROG)
C.................. Chief
C.................. Child
C.................. Chirp (IAA)
C.................. Chlorambucil [*Also, CHL, CMB*] [*Antineoplastic drug*]
C.................. Chloramphenicol [*Antimicrobial compound*]
C.................. Cholesterol [*Also, Ch, Cho, CHOL*] [*Biochemistry*] (AAMN)
C.................. Choppy, Short, or Cross Sea [*Navigation*]
C.................. Christ (WDAA)
C.................. Christian
C.................. Chrominance [*Video monitor*]
C.................. Chronium (ROG)
C.................. Chronometer Time [*Navigation*]

C................ Chrysler Corp. [*NYSE symbol Toronto Stock Exchange symbol*] (SPSG)
C................ Church
C................ Churchwarden
C................ Ciba-Geigy AG [*Switzerland*] [*Research code symbol*]
C................ Cibus [*Meal*] [*Latin*]
C................ Cilag-Chemie AG [*Switzerland*] [*Research code symbol*]
C................ Cimetidine [*Pharmacology*]
C................ Cimex [*Genus of microorganisms*] (MAH)
C................ Cinemas [*Public-performance tariff class*] [*British*]
c................ Circa [*or Circiter or Circum*] [*About (used with dates denoting approximate time)*] [*Latin*] (GPO)
C................ Circle [*Freemasonry*] (ROG)
C................ Circling [*Approach and landing charts*] [*Aviation*]
C................ Circuit
C................ Circular
C................ Circum
C................ Circumference
C................ Circumlocution [*Used in correcting manuscripts, etc.*]
C................ Cirrus [*Meteorology*]
C................ Cited (DLA)
C................ City [*Maps and charts*]
C/................ City Limits [*In outdoor advertising*] (WDMC)
c................ Civil [*Legal term*] (DLA)
C................ Class [*Used with number for Navy rating as: 1c; i.e., first class*]
C................ Class "C" Preferred or Common Stock [*Investment term*]
C................ Classical
C................ Clean
C................ Clear [*Calculators*]
C................ Clearance
C................ Clearance Rate [*Renal*] [*Nephrology*] (DAVI)
C................ Cleverness Factor [*Psychology*]
C................ Cliff (ROG)
C................ Clipped [*Ecology*]
C................ Clock
C................ Clockwise
C................ Clonus
C................ Closed
C................ Clostridium [*Genus of microorganism*] (CPH)
C................ Closure [*Medicine*]
C................ Cloudy [*Meteorology*]
C................ Club
C................ Coagulase [*An enzyme*]
C................ Coarse [*Appearance of bacterial colony*]
C................ Coarse [*Agronomy*]
C................ Coastal-Nonrigid Airship [*Royal Naval Air Service*] [*British*]
C................ Cobalt [*Chemical symbol is Co*]
C................ Cobbly [*Agronomy*]
C................ Cocaine [*Slang*]
C................ Code (DLA)
C................ Codex
C................ Codex Ephaemi [*Ephraem the Syrian*] [*A publication*] (ROG)
C................ Codex Juris Civilis [*A publication*] (ILCA)
C................ Coefficient
C................ Coffin [*Missile launch environment symbol*]
C................ Cognate
C................ Cognitive
C................ Coil [*Genetics*]
C................ Col [*With The*] [*Music*]
C................ Cold
C................ Colla [*With The*] [*Music*] (ROG)
C................ Collateral
C................ Collector [*Electronics*]
c................ Collector (IDOE)
C................ College
C................ Colon [*Monetary unit*] [*Costa Rica, El Salvador*]
C................ Colonel (ROG)
C................ Color
C................ Colorado [*Dark-colored cigar*]
C................ Color Detail [*Rorschach*] [*Psychology*]
C................ Color Index
C................ Color Sense (AAMN)
C................ Colt [*Thoroughbred racing*]
C................ Columbia [*Record Label*] [*Great Britain, Europe, Australia, etc.*]
C................ Combat [*In unit designations and symbols only*]
C................ Command (ROG)
C................ Commandant [*Coast Guard*]
C................ Commander [*Usually in combination, as: CNAB for Commander, Naval Air Bases*]
C................ Commanding Officer
C................ Command Paper
C................ Commerce Department
C................ Commercial [*FCC*] (NTCM)
C................ Commercial Bank (ROG)
C................ Commissary [*Marine Corps*]
C................ Commodore [*Navy British*] (ROG)
C................ Common [*Ecology*]
C................ Common Carrier [*FCC*] (NTCM)
C................ Common Entrance [*Examination for entry into public school*] [*British*]
C................ Common Meter [*Music*]
C................ Common (Noun) [*Linguistics*]
C................ Common Time
C................ Communications
C................ Compact [*Car size*]
C................ Companion

C................ Compass
C................ Compatible
C................ Complement [*Immunochemistry*]
C................ Complement [*Linguistics*]
C................ Complete (NASA)
C................ Complex
C................ Complexity
C................ Compliance [*Volume change per unit of applied pressure*] [*Medicine*] (DAVI)
C................ Component (DAVI)
C................ Composite (ROG)
C................ Compositus [*Compound*] [*Pharmacy*]
C................ Compound [*Engines*] [*Lloyd's Register Shipping*]
C................ Comprehensive School [*British*]
C................ Compression
C................ Comptroller
C................ Compulsory
C................ Compute [*or Computer*] (MDG)
C................ Computer Language (NITA)
C................ Computer Programming Language [*for small computers*] (BARN)
C................ Con [*With*] [*Music*] (ROG)
C................ Concealed [*Ecology*]
C................ Concentration [*in the blood phase*] [*Medicine*] (DAVI)
c................ Concentration by Volume [*Chemistry*]
C................ Concisus [*Cut*] [*Medicine*]
C................ Conclusion (WGA)
C................ Concurrent
c................ Condemnation [*Legal term*] (DLA)
C................ Condemned
C................ Condemno [*I Condemn*] [*Used by Romans in criminal trials*] [*Latin*]
c................ Condenser
C................ Conditioning [*Neurophysiology*]
C................ Conductivity
C................ Conductor
C................ Confessor
C................ Confidential
C................ Congius [*Gallon*] [*Pharmacy*]
C................ Congregation
C................ Congress
C................ Congressional (ROG)
C................ Conjugation (WGA)
C................ Connection (NFPA)
C................ Conservative [*Politics*]
C................ Consonant [*Linguistics*]
C................ Consortium
C................ Constable
C................ Constant
C................ Constant Region [*Immunochemistry*]
C................ Constructor [*Freemasonry*] (ROG)
C................ Consul [*License plate code assigned to foreign diplomats in the US*]
C................ Consul [*or Consulate*]
C................ Consultant in Dental Surgery [*Medical Officer designation*] [*British*]
C................ Consultation [*Medicine*]
C................ Consumption
C................ Contact
C................ Contact Publishers [*Holland*]
C................ Container (DCTA)
C................ Content [*of gas in blood phase*] (AAMN)
C................ Continental [*Air mass*]
C................ Continuous [*Botany*]
C................ Continuous Operation during Hours Shown [*Broadcasting*]
C................ Contra [*Against*] [*Latin*]
C................ Contraction
C................ Contracture [*or Contraction*] [*Orthopedics*] (DAVI)
C................ Contralateral [*Anatomy*]
C................ Contralto [*Music*]
C................ Contrast (ADA)
C................ Control [*Referring to a group in an experiment*] (DAVI)
C................ Control [*Officer's rating*] [*British Royal Navy*]
C................ Controlled [*Currency exchange rate*] [*British*]
C................ Controller (ECII)
C................ Controls [*JETDS nomenclature*] [*Military*] (CET)
C................ Contusus [*Bruised*] [*Medicine*]
C................ Convection (ADA)
C................ Convict (ADA)
C................ Cook [*Ranking title*] [*British Women's Royal Naval Service*]
C................ Cooker
C................ Cooling (PS)
C................ Copper [*Chemical symbol is Cu*]
C................ Coppered
C................ Copy
C................ Copyhold [*British Legal term*] (ROG)
C................ Copyright
C................ Cord
C................ Cordoba [*Monetary unit*] [*Nicaragua*]
C................ Core (IAA)
C................ Corinthians [*New Testament book*] (BJA)
C................ Corolla
C................ Corps
C................ Corpus [*Body*] [*Latin*] (DLA)
C................ Correct [*or Correction*]
C................ Correct [*In marking school papers*] (BARN)
C................ Cortex [*Anatomy*]
C................ Corundum [*CIPW classification*] [*Geology*]
C................ Corynebacterium [*Genus of microorganisms*] (MAH)

C	Cost
C	Costa [*Rib*] [*Anatomy*]
C	Cotton (AAG)
C	Cotyledon [*Botany*]
C	Cough [*Medicine*]
C	Coulomb [*Symbol*] [*SI unit of electric charge*]
C	Council [*Australia*]
C	Councillor (ROG)
C	Count
C	Counter
C	Counter-Tenor [*Music*]
C	Country
c	Country Music [*Radio station format*] (WDMC)
C	County
C	Coupon
C	Course
C	Course Angle [*Navigation*]
C	Course Winner [*Horse racing*]
C	Court
C	Cousin
C	Cove [*Maps and charts*]
C	Cover [*of a magazine*]
C	Coxsackie [*Virus*] (MAE)
C	Crane Engines [*Trains*] [*British*]
C	Created
C	Creosote [*Telecommunications*] (TEL)
c	Criticised [*Soundness of decision or reasoning in cited case criticised for reasons given*] [*Used in Shephard's Citations*] [*Legal term*] (DLA)
C	Cross (ADA)
C	Crossed [*Stereo images*]
C	Crowned
C	Cruiser
C	Cryptococcus [*Genus of microorganism*] (CPH)
C	Crystalline
C	Cuba
C	Cubic
C	Culex [*Genus of microorganisms*] (MAH)
C	Cum [*With*] [*Latin*]
C	Cumulus [*Cloud*] [*Meteorology*]
C	Cup
C	Curacy [*or Curate*]
C	Curie [*Unit of radioactivity*] [*See Ci*]
c	Curie (IDOE)
C	Currency
C	Current
C	Current Expenditure [*Economics*]
C	Currentis [*Of the Current Month or Year*] [*Latin*]
C	Cushion Lift (AAG)
C	Cuticle
C	Cyan (WDMC)
C	Cyanosis [*Medicine*] (DAVI)
C	Cycle [*Electricity*]
C	Cycles per Second [*See also HZ*] (IAA)
c	Cyclic [*Biochemistry*]
C	Cyclohexane [*Organic chemistry*]
C	Cyclophosphamide [*Cytoxan*] [*Antineoplastic drug*]
C	Cylinder
C	Cylindrical [*Leaf characteristic*] [*Botany*]
C	Cyprus (BARN)
C	Cysteine [*One-letter symbol*] [*Also, Cys, CySH*]
C	Cytidine [*One-letter symbol; see Cyd*]
C	Cytochrome [*Biochemistry*] (MAE)
C	Cytosine [*Also, Cyt*] [*Biochemistry*]
c	Deaza [*As substituent on nucleoside*] [*Biochemistry*]
C	Degrees Celsius
C	Electrical Equipment [*Fire classification*]
C	E. R. Squibb & Sons [*Research code symbol*]
C	Fairly Reliable Source of Intelligence Information
C	Heat Capacity [*Symbol*] [*IUPAC*]
C	Imperfect Time [*Represents an incomplete circle and refers to 4/4 time*] [*Music*]
C	Income Not Paying Interest [*Standard & Poor's bond rating*]
C	Indian Law Reports, Calcutta Series [*A publication*] (DLA)
C	Institut Pasteur [*France*] [*Research code symbol*]
c-----	Intercontinental Areas (Western Hemisphere) [*MARC geographic area code Library of Congress*] (LCCP)
C	Lab. Sopharga [*France*] [*Research code symbol*]
C	Liquidating Dividend [*Investment term*] (DFIT)
C	Lord Chancellor (DLA)
C	Lowest [*Moody's bond rating*] [*Investment term*]
C	Medium Narrow [*Men's shoe width*]
C	Medium Wide [*Women's shoe width*]
C	One Hundred [*Roman numeral*]
C	One Hundred Dollar Bill [*C Note*] [*Slang*]
C	Philadelphia [*Branch in the Federal Reserve regional banking system*] (BARN)
C	Protected Cruiser [*Navy symbol Obsolete*]
C	Series "C" Bonds or Debentures [*Investment term*]
C	Shape Descriptor [*C-clamp, for example. The shape resembles the letter for which it is named*]
C	Shoe Width Greater than B and Less than D (BARN)
c	Specific Heat Capacity [*Symbol*] [*IUPAC*]
c	Speed of Light in Vacuum [*Symbol*]
c	Velocity of Sound [*Symbol*] [*IUPAC*]

C	Velocity of Sound of Blood [*on Doppler Study*] [*Cardiology*] (DAVI)
C1	Canadian Canoe, Single Person (ADA)
C1	Chief Petty Officer, First Class [*Canadian*] [*Navy*]
C-1	[*Readiness status*] [*Fully*] Combat Capable [*Military*] (DOMA)
C_1	Costa I [*First rib*] [*Costa II, second rib is C_2, etc., through C12 Orthopedics*] (DAVI)
C-1	First Cervical Nerve [*Second cervical nerve is C-2, etc., through C-7*] [*Medicine*] (DAVI)
C-1	First Cervical Vertebra [*Second cervical vertebra is C-2, etc., through C-7*] [*Medicine*]
C10	Canto Primo [*First Soprano*] [*Music*]
c1s	Coated One Side [*Paper*] (WDMC)
C1S	Coated One Size [*Paper*]
C2	Canadian Canoe, Two Person (ADA)
C2	Chief Petty Officer, Second Class [*Canadian*] [*Navy*]
C^2	Command and Control [*Pronounced "see-squared"*]
C2	Command and Control (AAGC)
C2	Nauru [*Aircraft nationality and registration mark*] (FAAC)
C_2	Second Rib [*Anatomy*] (DMAA)
C2CSE	Connected Two-Color Simulated Photon Echo [*Spectroscopy*]
C2d	California Supreme Court Reports, Second Series [*A publication*] (DLA)
C2D	Chrysler Collision Detection [*Automotive safety and electronics*]
C^2E	Continuous Comprehensive Evaluation [*Army*] (RDA)
C2F2	Crew Compartment Fit and Function [*NASA*] (KSC)
C2H5OH	Ethanol [*DOE*] (TAG)
C2I	Command, Control, and Intelligence [*Military*] (RDA)
C^2I	Command, Control, and Intelligence [*Network*] [*Military*] (DOMA)
C^2IS	Command and Control Information System [*Military*]
C^2MUG	Command and Control Micro-Computer Users Group [*Fort Leavenworth, KS*] [*Army*] (INF)
C^2S	Command and Control System (DOMA)
C2SC	Command and Control Steering Committee
C^2 SID	Command, Control, and Systems Integration Directorate [*Army and NASA joint operation*] (RDA)
C^2V	Command and Control Vehicle [*Army*]
C2W	Command and Control Warfare [*Military*] (RDA)
C2X	Command and Control Exercise
C3	Ceramic Chip Carrier
C_3	Collin's Solution (MAE)
C^3	Command and Control Center
C^3	Command, Control, and Communications [*Pronounced "see-cubed"*]
C^3	Command, Control, and Communications (AAGC)
C3	Complement Component Three [*Hematology*]
C3	Third Cervical Nerve [*Anatomy*] (DMAA)
C3	Third Cervical Vertebra [*Anatomy*] (DMAA)
C3	Third Component of Complement (DMAA)
C3A-JTO	Command, Control, and Communications Agency Joint Test Organization [*Fort Huachuca, AZ*]
C^3/BM	Command, Control, and Communications Battle Management [*Military*]
C^3BM	Command, Control, and Communications for Battle Management [*Military*] (DOMA)
C^3CM	C^3 [*Command, Control, and Communications*] Countermeasures [*Pronounced "see-cubed see-m"*]
C3CM	Command, Control, and Communications Countermeasures [*Warfare*]
C3CM	Command, Control, and Communications Countermeasures (AAGC)
C^3CM	Command, Control, and Communications Counter-Measures (DOMA)
C3CM	Command, Control, and Communications Countermeasures (LAIN)
C3CM-JTF	Command, Control, and Communications Countermeasures Joint Test Force [*Kirtland Air Force Base, NM*]
C3d	California Supreme Court Reports, Third Series [*A publication*] (DLA)
C3D	Cascade Charge Coupled Device [*Electronics*]
C3DP	Complement 3 Degradation Product [*Immunology*]
C3FE	Collection, Classification, Cannibalization, and Field Expedients [*Military*]
C3FM	Case Center for Complex Flow Measurements [*Case Western Reserve University*] [*Research center*] (RCD)
C3I	Center for Command, Control, Communications, and Intelligence [*George Mason University*] [*Research center*] (RCD)
C^3I	Command, Control, Communications, and Intelligence [*Pronounced "see-cubed eye"*]
C^3I	Command, Control, Communications, and Intelligence (DOMA)
C^3I	Communications, Command, Control, and Intelligence (PDAA)
C^3I	Computer-Controlled Coil Ignition [*Automotive engineering*]
C^3I2	Command, Control, Communications, Intelligence, and Interoperability
C3IAC	Command, Control, Communications and Intelligence Acquisition Center [*Army*] (RDA)
C^3IC	Coalition, Coordination, Communications, and Integration Center (DOMA)
C^3L	Complementary Constant Current Logic [*Computer science*] (MCD)
C^3MP	Command, Control, and Communications Master Plan (DOMA)
C3RAM	Continuously Charge-Coupled Random Access Memory [*Computer science*] (PDAA)
C3S	College Chemistry Consultants Service
C^3S	Command, Control, Communications Systems (DOMA)
C^3SYS DIR	Command, Control, Communications Systems Directorate (DOMA)
C4	Census Community Communications Council [*US Census Bureau*]
C4	Channel 4 [*Television*] [*British*]
C4	Command and Control, Communications and Computers (PDAA)
C4	Command, Control Communication, and Computer Systems (USGC)
C^4	Command, Control, Communications, and Computer Systems (NVT)
C-4	Composition-4 [*Explosive*]

C-4	Computer-Controlled Catalytic Converter [*Automotive engineering*]
C₄D	Conductivity-Connected Charge-Coupled Device [*Electronics*] (EECA)
C4I	Command, Control, Communications, Computer, and Intelligence [*Army*]
C⁴I	Command, Control, Communications, Computers, and Intelligence (DOMA)
C4I	Command, Control, Communications, Computers and Intelligence
C⁴I²	Command, Control, Communications, Computers, Intelligence, and Interoperability [*Marine Corps*] (DOMA)
C⁴I2	Command, Control, Communications, Computing/Information and Intelligence
C⁴ICM	Command, Control, Communications, Computers, Intelligence, and Counter-Measures (DOMA)
C₄IFTW	Command, Control, Communications Computer and Intelligence for the Warrior [*Army*]
C⁴S	Command, Control, Communications, and Computer Systems (DOMA)
C⁴S2	Command, Control, Communications, and Combat Service Support [*Military*] (INF)
C5	Gambia [*Aircraft nationality and registration mark*] (FAAC)
C5I3	Coordinated Command, Control, Communications and Computing for Integrated Information and Intelligence [*Military*]
C6	Bahamas [*Aircraft nationality and registration mark*] (FAAC)
C-6	Hexamethonium [*Biochemistry*] (DAVI)
C 8VA	Coll'Ottava [*With the Octave*] [*Music*] (ROG)
C9	Mozambique [*Aircraft nationality and registration mark*] (FAAC)
C10	Decamethonium [*Organic chemistry*] (DAVI)
C13-NMR	Carbon 13 Nuclear Magnetic Resonance [*Informations system Karlsrube*] (NITA)
C¹⁴	Radioactive Carbon [*Key substance for determination of age of objects by measurement of radioactivity*]
C31	Command, Control, Communications, and Intelligence (USGC)
C31	Command, Control, Communications and Intelligence Systems (AAGC)
C33	Prisoner identification number assigned to Oscar Wilde in Reading Gaol [*Used as pseudonym*]
C41	Communication, Command, Control, Computer, and Intelligence (USGC)
C63	Cinemists 63 (EA)
C200	Committee of 200 [*An association*]
CA	Assistant Commandant [*Coast Guard*]
CA	Cable (MSA)
CA	Cable Assembly
CA	Cable Authority [*British*]
CA	Cab to Axle [*GSA*] (TAG)
CA	Cab-to-Rear Axle [*Automotive engineering*]
CA	Cadmium Association [*British*] (EAIO)
CA	Caffeic Acid [*Organic chemistry*]
Ca	Calcareous [*Quality of the bottom*] [*Nautical charts*]
Ca	Calcium [*Chemical element*]
CA	Calibrated Altitude [*Navigation*]
CA	California [*Postal code*]
CA	California Appellate Reports [*A publication*] (DLA)
CA	Callable Bond [*Investment term*]
CA	Camanachd Association (EA)
CA	Cambodian Appeal [*Defunct*] (EA)
CA	Canada [*ANSI two-letter standard code*] (CNC)
CA	Canadian Airlines [*TS Symbol*] (TTSB)
CA	Canadian Army
CA	Canamin Resources [*Vancouver Stock Exchange symbol*]
CA	Cancer [*or Carcinoma*] [*Medicine*]
Ca	Candle
CA	Candy Apple [*Bowdlerized version*]
CA	Cant [*or Canting*] [*Heraldry*]
CA	Cantors Assembly (EA)
CA	Capacitor (IAA)
CA	Cape
CA	Capital Account [*Finance*]
CA	Capital Accumulation [*Business term*]
CA	Capital Airlines, Inc.
CA	Capital Appreciation [*Business term*]
CA	Capital Asset
CA	Car Accountant
CA	Car Assembly
CA	Carbohydrate Antigen [*A tumor marker*] (CDI)
ca	Carbonate Accumulation [*Archeology*]
CA	Carbonic Anhydrase [*An enzyme*]
CA	Carcinoma
CA	Card Alert [*Database terminology*] (NITA)
CA	Cardiac Arrest [*Medicine*]
CA	Cardinal
CA	Cargo Ship
CA	Caribbean Area [*Services to the Armed Forces*] [*Red Cross*]
CA	Carotid Artery [*Anatomy*] (DAVI)
CA	Carrier Aircraft (MCD)
CA	Carries Ampholytes [*Chemistry*]
CA	Carry
CA	Cartographic Assistant [*Ministry of Agriculture, Fisheries, and Food*] [*British*]
CA	Cascade Amplifier (DEN)
Ca	Case [*Legal term*] (ILCA)
C-4	Case Aide [*Red Cross*]
CA	Caserio
CA	Cash Account [*Banking*]
CA	Cashier and Accountant [*British*] (ROG)

CA	Castles Association (EA)
CA	Cat Allergen [*Immunology*]
CA	Catboat Association (EA)
CA	Catch per Angler [*Pisciculture*]
CA	Catecholamine [*or Catecholaminergic*] [*Biochemistry*]
CA	Category
CA	Catenarian Arch [*Freemasonry*] (ROG)
CA	Caterer [*Military British*]
CA	Catering Accountant [*British military*] (DMA)
CA	Cathode
CA	Catholic Action
Ca	Caudality Scale [*Psychology*]
Ca	Causa [*Decretum Gratiani*] [*A publication*] (DSA)
CA	Cause of Action (MHDB)
CA	Cavan [*County in Ireland*] (ROG)
CA	Celiac Axis [*Anatomy*]
CA	Cell Attached [*Microbiology*]
CA	Cellular Automation [*Computer science*] (IAA)
CA	Cellulose Acetate [*Organic chemistry; plastics*]
CA	Census Agglomeration [*Canada*]
CA	Centacare Australia
CA	Centare [*Unit of area in metric system*]
CA	Center for Astrophysics [*Harvard-Smithsonian*]
C/A	Central Air Conditioning [*Classified advertising*] (CDAI)
CA	Central Airways Corp. (AAG)
CA	Central America
CA	Central Area
CA	Cephalic Artery
CA	Cerebral Aqueduct [*Brain anatomy*]
CA	Cerebrovascular Amyloid [*Medicine*]
CA	Certificate of Airworthiness
CA	Certification Authority (ACRL)
CA	Certified Acupuncturist [*Medicine*] (DAVI)
CA	Certified Acupuncturist [*Medicine*]
CA	Cervicoaxial [*Dentistry*]
CA	Chancery Appeal Cases, English Law Reports [*A publication*] (DLA)
CA	Chances Accepted [*Baseball*]
CA	Change Administration
CA	Change of Address (WDMC)
C/A	Change of Address [*Postal term*] [*United States*] (WDMC)
CA	Channel Adapter [*Computer science*] (IBMDP)
CA	Chargeable to Accidents (MCD)
CA	Charge Amplifier (NRCH)
CA	Charge d'Affaires [*Foreign Service*]
CA	Chartered Accountant
C/A	Chartered Agent [*Business term*]
CA	Checks Anonymous
CA	Chemical Addition and Sampling System [*Nuclear energy*] (NRCH)
CA	Chemistry Associates [*Australia*]
C/A	Cheque Account [*British Banking*] (ADA)
CA	Chief Accountant
CA	Chief Advisor
CA	Children of the Americas (EA)
CA	Chile Alert [*Defunct*] (EA)
CA	Chinese Army (CINC)
CA	Chloramphetamine [*Neurochemistry*]
CA	Chloranil [*Organic chemistry*]
CA	Chlorendic Acid [*Organic chemistry*]
CA	Chlorendic Anhydride [*Also, CAN*] [*Organic chemistry*]
CA	Chlorogenic Acid [*Organic chemistry*]
CA	Cholamine (PDAA)
CA	Cholic Acid [*Biochemistry*] (AAMN)
CA	Choline-Adrenalin [*Test*] [*Medicine*]
CA	Christ Alongside (EA)
CA	Christian Army (ROG)
CA	Chromic Acid [*Inorganic chemistry*] (OA)
CA	Chronological Age [*Psychology*]
CA	Church Army [*An association*] (EA)
CA	Church Association [*British*]
CA	Churchman Associates (EA)
CA	Cinnamic Acid [*Organic chemistry*] (OA)
ca	Circa [*or Circiter or Circum*] [*About (used with dates denoting approximate time)*] [*Latin*]
CA	Circuitry Adapter [*Electronics*] (IAA)
CA	Circular Arc [*Aviation*]
CA	cis-Aconityl [*Organic radical*]
CA	Cited Authors [*Database terminology*] (NITA)
CA	Citizens Advocacy
CA	Citizens for Animals [*Defunct*] (EA)
CA	Civic Action
CA	Civil Affairs
CA	Civil Affairs (DOMA)
CA	Civil Agency
CA	Civil Authorities
CA	Civil Aviation
CA	Claim Agent [*Insurance*]
CA	Clamshell Alliance (EA)
CA	Classical America (EA)
CA	Classical Association (EAIO)
CA	Classics of Art [*A publication*]
CA	Clear Above [*Aviation*] (FAAC)
CA	Clear and Add
CA	Clear Aperture (MSA)
CA	Clerical Aptitude [*Test*]
CA	Clerical Assistant [*Civil Service*] [*British*]

CA	Clipped and Ash [*Ecology*]
CA	Clipping Amplifier
CA	Close Annealed [*Metal industry*]
CA	Closest Approach [*Aerospace*]
CA	Clothing Allowance [*British military*] (DMA)
CA	Clowns of America [*Later, CAI*] (EA)
CA	Club Anri [*Commercial firm*] (EA)
CA	Club Aquarius (EA)
CA	Cluster Analysis [*Data analysis*]
CA	Coagulation [*Test*]
CA	Coalitions for America (EA)
CA	Coarctation of the Aorta [*Medicine*] (DMAA)
C/A	Coarse Acquisition Code [*Computer science*] (RDA)
CA	Coarse Alignment
CA	Coast Alliance [*Defunct*] (EA)
CA	Coast Artillery
CA	Coastwatchers' Association [*Australia*]
C/A	Coat of Arms (AABC)
CA	Coaxial (AAG)
CA	Cocaine Anonymous (EA)
CA	Codex Aleppensis (BJA)
CA	Coeliac Axis (BABM)
CA	Coelieac [*or Celiac*] Axis [*Gastroenterology*] (DAVI)
CA	Cold Acclimated [*Physiology*]
CA	Cold Agglutination [*Test*] [*Clinical chemistry*]
CA	Cold Air
CA	Collagen Antigen [*Immunology*] (DAVI)
CA	Coll'arco [*With the Bow*] [*Music*]
CA	Colloid Antigen [*Immunology*]
CA	Colonial Allowance [*British military*] (DMA)
CA	Color Association of the United States
CA	Combat Aircrew [*or Aircrewman*]
CA	Combat Arms
CA	Combat Assault
CA	Combined Arms (AABC)
CA	Command Accountant [*Military British*]
CA	Command Action (NATG)
CA	Commandant Assistant [*Coast Guard*]
CA	Commercial Activities
CA	Commercial Agent
CA	Commercial Air
CA	Commercial Announcement (NTCM)
CA	Commercial Art Program [*Association of Independent Colleges and Schools specialization code*]
CA	Commercial Aviation (IAA)
CA	Commercially Available (DNAB)
CA	Commissioner of Accounts
CA	Commissural and Association [*Anatomy*]
CA	Commitment Authorization
CA	Common Antigen [*Immunochemistry*]
CA	Communications Adapter
CA	Communist Activities [*British*]
CA	Commutator Assemblies [*SONAR*] (MCD)
CA	Compensation Act [*Forms*]
CA	Competent Authority
CA	Complex Angle (PDAA)
CA	Compressed Air (AAG)
CA	Compressed Analog [*Sound processing strategies*]
CA	Comptroller of Accounts
CA	Comptroller of the Army
CA	Computer Access (IAA)
CA	Computer-Aided [*or Assisted*] (HGAA)
CA	Computer Assembly
CA	Computer Associates [*A company*] [*Islandia, New York*] (WDMC)
CA	Computer Associates International, Inc. [*NYSE symbol*] (SPSG)
CA	Computer Assoc Intl. [*NYSE symbol*] (TTSB)
CA	Computer Automation, Inc. [*Richardson, TX*] (TSSD)
CA	Computers and Automation (BUR)
CA	Concept Approval [*Automotive project management*]
CA	CONCERN/America (EA)
CA	Concert Artist [*Record label*] [*Great Britain*]
CA	Conchologists of America (EA)
CA	Conditional Authorization [*Environmental science*]
CA	Conditioned Abstinence (AAMN)
CA	Condylomata Acuminata [*Medicine*]
CA	Cone Angle [*NASA*] (NASA)
CA	Confederate Army
CA	Configuration Alternative (MCD)
CA	Configured Article
CA	Conflict Alert [*Aviation*]
CA	Connecting Arrangement [*Telecommunications*]
CA	Constant Amplitude
CA	Constituent Assembly [*Vietnam*]
CA	Construction Authorization (NRCH)
CA	Constructionman, Apprentice [*Navy rating*]
CA	Constructive Availability (CAAL)
CA	Consular Agent
CA	Consultant-Adviser
CA	Consultant Agreement (MCD)
CA	Consumer Alert (EA)
CA	Consumers' Association (EAIO)
CA	Contact Adhesive
CA	Contact Area, Articular [*Medicine*]
CA	Container Agreement (DNAB)
CA	Contemporary Authors [*A publication*]
CA	Content-Addressable Memory [*Computer science*] (IAA)
CA	Continental Airways (AAG)
CA	Continental Assurance Co.
CA	Contingencies of the Army
CA	Contingency Abort [*NASA*] (NASA)
CA	Continue-Any [*Mode*] [*Computer science*] (IBMDP)
CA	Continuous-Action [*Pharmacy*]
CA	Contract Administration [*or Administrator*] [*DoD*]
CA	Contract Air (TAG)
CA	Contract Appeals [*Department of the Interior pre-1954*] (AAGC)
CA	Contract Authorization
CA	Contract Award
CA	Contracting Activity
CA	Contractor-Assisted
CA	Control Accelerometer (IAA)
C/A	Control Accumulator
CA	Control Area [*Computer science*]
CA	Control Armourer [*British military*] (DMA)
CA	Control Assembly
CA	Control Augmentation
CA	Controlled Approach (IAA)
CA	Controlled Atmosphere
CA	Controller of Accounts
CA	Convening Authority
CA	Convention Africaine [*African Covenant*]
CA	Conventional Alloy (OA)
CA	Cooperating Administrator [*Education*] (AEE)
CA	Cooperative Agreement
CA	Coopers Appreciation [*An association*] (EA)
CA	Coracoacromial [*Anatomy*]
CA	Cor Anglais [*English Horn*]
CA	Coriolis Absorber
CA	Cornu Ammonis [*Anatomy*]
CA	Coronary Artery [*Medicine*]
CA	Corpora Alata [*Insect anatomy*]
CA	Corpora Amylacea [*Neurology*]
CA	Corps Adjutant [*British military*] (DMA)
CA	Corps Area [*Army*]
CA	Corpus Allatum
CA	Corrective Action (MCD)
CA	Correct [*an error*] or Amplify [*information*] [*US Copyright Office form*]
CA	Correlator Acquisition [*Military*]
CA	Correspondence Aid [*A publication*]
CA	Correspondence Analysis [*Statistical analysis*]
CA	Cortisone Acetate [*Endocrinology*]
CA	Cosmopolitan Associates [*Later, OC*]
ca	Cost About
CA	Cost Account [*Accounting*]
CA	Cost Accountant [*Accounting*] (AABC)
C/A	Cost of Arms [*Army*] (AABC)
CA	Council Accepted [*Medicine*]
CA	Council of the Alleghenies (EA)
CA	Counselor Association (EA)
CA	Counter Air (MCD)
C/A	Counterattack
CA	Counterpoise Antenna (IAA)
CA	Countryside Act [*Town planning*] [*British*]
CA	County Alderman [*British*]
CA	County Architect [*British*]
CA	County Attorney
CA	Coupe Automatic [*Model designation of an automobile*]
CA	Coupons-Attached [*Business term*]
CA	Courant Alternatif [*Alternating Current*] [*French*]
CA	Course Alignment
CA	Courtesy Announcement (NTCM)
CA	Court of Appeal
CA	Court of Appeals Reports [*New Zealand*] [*A publication*] (DLA)
CA	Court of Arches [*England*] (DLA)
CA	Court of Customs and Patent Appeals Reports [*A publication*] (DLA)
CA	Court of Customs Appeals Reports [*1919-29*] [*A publication*] (DLA)
CA	Courtship Analysis [*Psychology*]
CA	Cover Aft
CA	Crab Apple [*Defunct*] (EA)
CA	Cranial Academy (EA)
CA	Crank Angle (MCD)
CA	Cranking Amperes [*Battery*] [*Automotive engineering*]
CA	Credit Account [*Business term*]
CA	Credit Agricole [*France*]
CA	Credit Associate [*Society of Certified Consumer Credit Executives*] [*Designation awarded by*]
CA	Creel Associates, Inc. [*Oak Brook, IL*] (TSSD)
CA	Cricket Association
CA	Critical Assembly [*Nuclear energy*] (NRCH)
CA	Criticality Analysis (KSC)
CA	Cromwell Association (EA)
CA	Croquet Association [*British*]
CA	Crossword Association [*British*] (DBA)
CA	Crotonaldehyde (PDAA)
CA	Croup-Associated [*Virus*]
CA	Crown Agent
CA	Cruise Altitude [*Aviation*]
CA	Cruisermen's Association (EA)
CA	Cruising Association [*British*] (EAIO)
CA	Ctenidial Analog [*Biology*]
CA	Cuadra Associates, Inc. [*Information service or system*] (IID)

CA...............	Cuenta Abierta [*Open Account*] [*Spanish Business term*]
CA...............	Cultists Anonymous [*British*] (DBA)
CA...............	Cumulative Amount (DNAB)
CA...............	Curates' Alliance [*British*]
CA...............	Curing Agent
CA...............	Current Account [*Business term*]
CA...............	Current Address (DNAB)
CA...............	Current Analysis [*Program*] [*Department of State*]
CA...............	Current Asset [*Business term*]
CA...............	Curriculum Association (AIE)
CA...............	Curse of Agade (BJA)
CA...............	Custodian Account [*Banking*]
CA...............	Customs Act [*Canada*]
CA...............	Cyanoacrylate Adhesive
CA...............	Cyclohexenedicarboxylic Acid [*Organic chemistry*]
CA...............	Cypriote Archaic (BJA)
CA...............	Cyproterone Acetate [*Endocrinology*]
CA...............	Cyprus Airways Ltd. (IMH)
CA...............	Cytarabine [*Cytosine arabinoside*] [*Also, ara-C, CAR*] [*Antineoplastic drug*]
CA...............	Cytosine Arabinoside [*Medicine*] (DMAA)
CA...............	Gun Cruiser [*Navy symbol*]
CA...............	Office of Congressional Affairs [*Energy Research and Development Administration*] (NRCH)
CA...............	SONAR Commutator Assemblies [*JETDS nomenclature*] [*Military*] (CET)
Ca...............	Speculative - Often in Default [*Moody's bond rating*]
CA...............	United States Court of Appeals [*Formerly, United States Circuit Court of Appeals*]
CA 2d.........	California Appellate Reports, Second Series [*A publication*] (DLA)
CA 2d Supp...	California Appellate Reports, Second Series, Supplement [*A publication*] (DLA)
CA 3d.........	California Appellate Reports, Third Series [*A publication*] (DLA)
CA 3S	California Appellate Reports, Third Series, Supplement [*A publication*] (DLA)
CA: 80's......	Congressional Agenda: 80's [*Later, CA: 90's*] (EA)
CA: 90's......	Congressional Agenda: 90's (EA)
CA 125........	Carbohydrate Antigen 125 [*Immunology*] (DAVI)
CAA.............	Caging Amplifier Assembly
CAA.............	California Alarm Association (SRA)
CAA.............	California Ambulance Association (SRA)
CAA.............	California Apartment Association (SRA)
CA A	California Appellate Reports [*A publication*] (DLA)
CAA.............	California Autobody Association (SRA)
CAA.............	Cambridge Acoustical Associates, Inc. (MCD)
CAA.............	Canadian Acoustical Association
CAA.............	Canadian Archaeological Association [*SA ACA*]
CAA.............	Canadian Association of Anatomists (AC)
CAA.............	Canadian Authors Association
CAA.............	Canadian Automobile Association
CAA.............	Canadian Avalanche Association [*Also, Canadian Avalanche Centre*] (AC)
CAA.............	Canberra [*Australia Geomagnetic observatory code*]
CAA.............	Cantors Assembly of America [*Later, CA*] (EA)
CAA.............	Carbon Adsorption/Absorption [*for vapor recovery*]
CAA.............	Caribbean Australian Association
CAA.............	Carnival Air [*ICAO designator*] (FAAC)
CAA.............	Carotid Audiofrequency Analysis [*Medicine*] (DMAA)
CAA.............	Carriage Association of America (EA)
CAA.............	Casamino Acids [*Biochemistry*]
CAA.............	Catear Resources Ltd. [*Vancouver Stock Exchange symbol*]
CAA.............	Cathedral Architects Association [*British*] (DBA)
CAA.............	Catholic Aid Association (EA)
CAA.............	Catholic Anthropological Association [*Defunct*] (EA)
CAA.............	Catholic Art Association [*Defunct*] (EA)
CAA.............	Cement Admixtures Association (EAIO)
CAA.............	Center for American Archeology
CAA.............	Central African Airways Corp.
CAA.............	Central Assets Account [*Finance*]
CAA.............	Centre Against Apartheid [*United Nations*] (DUND)
CAA.............	Cerebral Amyloid Angiopathy [*Medicine*]
CAA.............	Chanaral [*Chile*] [*Seismograph station code, US Geological Survey*] (SEIS)
CAA.............	Chaplains' Aid Association [*Later, CAA/SEF*] (EA)
CAA.............	Chemical Agent Alarm
CAA.............	Chester Alan Arthur [*US president, 1829-1886*]
CAA.............	Chicken Anaemia Agent [*Australia*]
CAA.............	Chief Aircraft Artificer [*British military*] (DMA)
CAA.............	Chief of Army Aviation
CAA.............	Chile-American Association (EA)
CAA.............	Chinese for Affirmative Action (EA)
CAA.............	Chiropractic Advancement Association [*British*]
CAA.............	Chiropractors' Association of Australia
CAA.............	Cigar Association of America (EA)
CAA.............	Cinema Advertising Association [*British*]
CAA.............	Circular Aperture Antenna
CAA.............	Citizens Assessment Administration
CAA.............	Civil Aeronautics Administration [*Later, part of FAA*]
CAA.............	Civil Aeronautics Authority (AAGC)
CAA.............	Civil Aeronautics Authority Reports [*A publication*] (DLA)
CAA.............	Civil Affairs Association (EA)
CAA.............	Civil Air Attache [*British*]
CAA.............	Civil Aviation Administration [*Marine science*] (OSRA)
CAA.............	Civil Aviation Administration (USDC)
CAA.............	Civil Aviation Authority [*British*]

CAA.............	Clean Air Act [*1963, 1990*]
CAA.............	Coalition of Automotive Associations [*Defunct*] (EA)
CAA.............	Collection Agencies Association [*British*] (DBA)
CAA.............	Collectors of American Art (EA)
CAA.............	College Art Association (EA)
CAA.............	Collision Avoidance Aid
CAA.............	Colombian American Association (EA)
CAA.............	Colorado Assessors' Association (SRA)
CAA.............	Comandos Autonomos Anti-Capitalistas [*Spain Political party*] (EY)
CAA.............	Combined Arms Army (MCD)
CAA.............	Comite des Amities Acadiennes [*Acadian Friendship Committee - AFC*] (EAIO)
CAA.............	Commission on Art and Antiquities
CAA.............	Commonwealth Accreditation Agency [*Australia*]
CAA.............	Commonwealth Archivists Association [*Later, ACARM*] (EA)
CAA.............	Commonwealth Association of Architects [*British*] (EAIO)
CAA.............	Community Action Agencies [*Community Services Administration*]
CAA.............	Compliance Assurance Agreement [*Environmental Protection Agency*] (GFGA)
CAA.............	Computational Aeroacoustics [*Laser technology*]
CAA.............	Computer-Aided Analysis (SSD)
CAA.............	Computer Amplifier Alarm
CAA.............	Computer-Assisted Accounting (BUR)
CAA.............	Computing Across America [*From book title, "Computing Across America: The Bicycle Odyssey of a High-Tech Nomad" by Steven K. Roberts*]
CAA.............	Concept Analysis (MCD)
CAA.............	Concepts Analysis Agency [*Bethesda, MD*] [*Army*] (AABC)
CAA.............	Concert Artists Association [*British*] (BI)
CAA.............	Confederation Arabe d'Athletisme [*Arab Amateur Athletic Federation - AAAF*] (EAIO)
CAA.............	Conference of the American Armies
CAA.............	Conference on Asian Affairs [*Later, AS*] (MCD)
CAA.............	Conformal-Array Antenna (PDAA)
CAA.............	Connecticut Ambulance Association (SRA)
CAA.............	Conseil Africain de l'Arachide [*African Groundnut Council*] (EAIO)
CAA.............	Constitutional Aplastic Anemia [*Medicine*]
CAA.............	Contaminant Analysis Automation
CAA.............	Controlled Access Area (MCD)
CAA.............	Cooperative Alumni Association (EA)
CAA.............	Coronary Artery Aneurysm [*Cardiology*]
CAA.............	Correctional Administrators Association of America [*Later, ASCA*] (EA)
CAA.............	Council of African Affairs (IIA)
CAA.............	Council of Association Attorneys (EA)
CAA.............	Cowboy Artists of America (EA)
CAA.............	Creative Artists Agency
CAA.............	Cremation Association of America [*Later, CANA*] (EA)
CAA.............	Crime Aboard Aircraft
CAA.............	Croatian Academy of America (EA)
CAA.............	Croatian Australian Association
CAA.............	Cryonics Association of Australia
CAA.............	Crypto Access Authorization [*Military*] (AABC)
CAA.............	Crystalline Amino Acid [*Biochemistry*] (DAVI)
CAA.............	Cyanoacrylate Adhesive
Caa	Poor Standing [*Moody's bond rating*]
CA A 2d	California Appellate Reports, Second Series [*A publication*] (DLA)
CA A 3d	California Appellate Reports, Third Series [*A publication*] (DLA)
CAAA	California Agricultural Aircraft Association (EA)
CAAA	California Applicants Attorney Association (SRA)
CAAA	Canadian Academic Accounting Association [*See also ACPC*]
CAAA	Canadian Association of Advertising Agencies (NTCM)
CAAA	Chief of Army Audit Agency
CAAA	Clean Air Act Amendment
CAAA	Coast Artillery Antiaircraft
CAAA	College Art Association of America [*Later, CAA*] (EA)
CAAA	Commuter Airline Association of America [*Later, RAA*] (EA)
CAAA	Composers, Authors, and Artists of America
CAAA	Crane Army Ammunition Activity (AABC)
CaAAAR	Alberta Department of Agriculture, Regional Office, Airdrie, AB, Canada [*Library symbol Library of Congress*] (LCLS)
CAAACT	Chiropractors' Association of Australia, Australian Capital Territory
CaAAiM........	Airdrie Municipal Library, Airdrie, AB, Canada [*Library symbol Library of Congress*] (LCLS)
CAAAL	Classified Abstract Archive of the Alcohol Literature
CaAAM........	Acme Municipal Library, Acme, AB, Canada [*Library symbol Library of Congress*] (LCLS)
CAAA-MWD...	Commanding Army Audit Agency - Midwestern District
CaAAn.........	Andrew Public Library, Andrew, AB, Canada [*Library symbol*] [*Library of Congress*] (LCLS)
CaAAs.........	Ashmont Public Library, Ashmont, AB, Canada [*Library symbol*] [*Library of Congress*] (LCLS)
CaAAth........	Athabasca Public Library, Athabasca, AB, Canada [*Library symbol*] [*Library of Congress*] (LCLS)
CAAAV	Coalition Against Anti-Asian Violence (EA)
CaAB...........	Banff Library, Banff, AB, Canada [*Library symbol Library of Congress*] (LCLS)
CAAB	California Apricot Advisory Board (EA)
CAAB	California Artichoke Advisory Board (EA)
CAAB	California Asparagus Advisory Board [*Defunct*] (EA)
CAAB	California Avocado Advisory Board [*Later, CAC*]
CAAB	Canadian Advertising Advisory Board
CAAB	Canadian Association of Animal Breeders [*Association Canadienne des Eleveurs de Betail*] (AC)

CAAB .... Commandement Allie des Approches de la Baltique [*Baltic Approaches Allied Command*] [*NATO*] (NATG)

CAAB .... Contract Administration Advisory Board [*DoD*]

CaABA .... Archives of the Canadian Rockies, Banff, AB, Canada [*Library symbol Library of Congress*] (LCLS)

CaABaAR ..... Alberta Department of Agriculture, Regional Office, Barrhead, AB, Canada [*Library symbol Library of Congress*] (LCLS)

CaABAC .... Alpine Club, Banff, AB, Canada [*Library symbol Library of Congress*] (LCLS)

CaABAH .... Alberta Horticultural Research Centre, Brooks, AB, Canada [*Library symbol Library of Congress*] (LCLS)

CaABcBC ...... Bear Point Community Library, Bear Canyon, AB, Canada [*Library symbol*] [*Library of Congress*] (LCLS)

CaABdM....... Black Diamond Municipal Library, Black Diamond, AB, Canada [*Library symbol Library of Congress*] (LCLS)

CaABdSRC ... Sheep River Community Library, Black Diamond, AB, Canada [*Library symbol*] [*Library of Congress*] (LCLS)

CaABeaAr ..... Alberta RCMP Century Library, Beaverlodge, AB, Canada [*Library symbol*] [*Library of Congress*] (LCLS)

CaABeAg...... Canada Department of Agriculture, Research Station, Beaverlodge, AB, Canada [*Library symbol Library of Congress*] (LCLS)

CaABeM....... Beiseker Municipal Library, Beiseker, AB, Canada [*Library symbol Library of Congress*] (LCLS)

CaABerWM... Berwyn W.I. Municipal Library, Berwyn, AB, Canada [*Library symbol*] [*Library of Congress*] (LCLS)

CaABi........... Bow Island Public Library, Bow Island, AB, Canada [*Library symbol Library of Congress*] (LCLS)

CaABIDM ..... Banff Municipal Library, Improvement District No. 9, Banff, AB, Canada [*Library symbol Library of Congress*] (LCLS)

CaABoa........ Bon Accord Public Library, Bon Accord, AB, Canada [*Library symbol*] [*Library of Congress*] (LCLS)

CaABoy........ Boyle Public Library, Boyle, AB, Canada [*Library symbol*] [*Library of Congress*] (LCLS)

CaABPWG.... Peter Whyte Gallery, Banff, AB, Canada [*Library symbol Library of Congress*] (LCLS)

CaABrC .... Browndale Community Library, Browndale, AB, Canada [*Library symbol*] [*Library of Congress*] (LCLS)

CaABruM ..... Bruderheim Municipal Library, Bruderheim, AB, Canada [*Library symbol*] [*Library of Congress*] (LCLS)

CaABSFA ..... Banff School of Fine Arts, Banff, AB, Canada [*Library symbol Library of Congress*] (LCLS)

CAABU .... Council for the Advancement of Arab-British Understanding [*London, England*]

CaAC........... Calgary Public Library, Calgary, AB, Canada [*Library symbol Library of Congress*] (LCLS)

CAAC .... Center for Academic & Administrative Computing [*George Washington University*] [*Research center*] (RCD)

CAAC .... Chinese American Arts Council (EA)

CAAC .... Chinese American Association of Commerce (EA)

CAAC .... Civil Aviation Administration of China

CAAC .... Civil Aviation Authority of China (GAVI)

CAAC .... Civilian Agency Acquisition Council (AAGC)

CAAC .... Civilian Aviation Advisory Committee [*Air Defense Planning Board*] (AAG)

CAAC .... College Admissions Assistance Center [*Defunct*]

CAAC .... Combat Alert Aircrew [*Air Force*]

CAAC .... Committee to Assure the Availability of Casein [*Defunct*] (EA)

CAAC .... Counseling and Assistance Center [*Military*] (NVT)

CaACAC ...... AMOCO Canada Petroleum Co. Ltd., Calgary, AB, Canada [*Library symbol Library of Congress*] (LCLS)

CaACACH.... Alberta Children's Hospital, Calgary, AB, Canada [*Library symbol*] [*Library of Congress*] (LCLS)

CaACaCJC.... Church of Jesus Christ of Latter-Day Saints, Genealogical Society Library, Cardston Branch, Cardston, AB, Canada [*Library symbol Library of Congress*] (LCLS)

CAACACT ..... Consumer Affairs Advisory Committee of the Australian Capital Territory

CaACAD .... Alcoholism and Drug Abuse Commission, Calgary, AB, Canada [*Library symbol Library of Congress*] (LCLS)

CaACAE....... Alberta Energy Co., Calgary, AB, Canada [*Library symbol Library of Congress*] (LCLS)

CaACAEL...... Alsands Energy Ltd., Library and Records Centre, Calgary, AB, Canada [*Library symbol Library of Congress*] (LCLS)

CaACAG ...... Alberta Gas Ethylene Co., Calgary, AB, Canada [*Library symbol Library of Congress*] (LCLS)

CaACAH .... Alberta Department of Agriculture, Horse Industry Branch, Calgary, AB, Canada [*Library symbol Library of Congress*] (LCLS)

CaACAI .... Arctic Institute of North America, Calgary, AB, Canada [*Library symbol Library of Congress*] (LCLS)

CaACAL........ Camrose Lutheran College, Camrose, AB, Canada [*Library symbol Library of Congress*] (LCLS)

CaACaM....... Canmore Municipal Library, Canmore, AB, Canada [*Library symbol Library of Congress*] (LCLS)

CaACAO .... Ashland Oil Canada Ltd., Calgary, AB, Canada [*Library symbol Library of Congress*] (LCLS)

CaACAqE...... Aquatic Environments Ltd., Calgary, AB, Canada [*Library symbol Library of Congress*] (LCLS)

CaACARC .... Arctec Ltd., Calgary, AB, Canada [*Library symbol Library of Congress*] (LCLS)

CaACarM...... Carbon Municipal Library, Carbon, AB, Canada [*Library symbol Library of Congress*] (LCLS)

CaACas........ Caslan Public Library, Caslan, AB, Canada [*Library symbol*] [*Library of Congress*] (LCLS)

CaACB .... Brascon Resources Ltd., Calgary, AB, Canada [*Library symbol Library of Congress*] (LCLS)

CaACBB .... Berean Bible College, Calgary, AB, Canada [*Library symbol Library of Congress*] (LCLS)

CaACBC .... Biotechnica Canada, Calgary, AB, Canada [*Library symbol*] [*Library of Congress*] (LCLS)

CaACBPE ..... BP Exploration Canada Ltd., Calgary, AB, Canada [*Library symbol*] [*Library of Congress*] (LCLS)

CaACCEL...... Canuck Engineering Ltd., Calgary, AB, Canada [*Library symbol*] [*Library of Congress*] (LCLS)

CaACCES ..... Cenior Services Ltd., Calgary, AB, Canada [*Library symbol*] [*Library of Congress*] (LCLS)

CaACCH .... Calgary Herald, Calgary, AB, Canada [*Library symbol Library of Congress*] (LCLS)

CaACCJC...... Church of Jesus Christ of Latter-Day Saints, Genealogical Society Library, Calgary Branch, Calgary, AB, Canada [*Library symbol Library of Congress*] (LCLS)

CaACCL....... Calgary Library Service Centre, Calgary, AB, Canada [*Library symbol Library of Congress*] (LCLS)

CaACCP ...... Canadian Petroleum Association, Calgary, AB, Canada [*Library symbol Library of Congress*] (LCLS)

CaACCS ...... Canadian Superior Oil Ltd., Calgary, AB, Canada [*Library symbol Library of Congress*] (LCLS)

CaACDG .... Devonian Group of Charitable Foundations, Calgary, AB, Canada [*Library symbol Library of Congress*] (LCLS)

CaACDP .... Dome Petroleum Ltd., Calgary, AB, Canada [*Library symbol Library of Congress*] (LCLS)

CAACE .... Christian Association for Adult and Continuing Education [*British*]

CaACeC....... Cessford Community Library, Cessford, AB, Canada [*Library symbol Library of Congress*] (LCLS)

CaACEC....... Montreal Engineering Co. Ltd., Calgary, AB, Canada [*Library symbol Library of Congress*] (LCLS)

CaACEM....... Alberta Education Materials Resources Centre, Calgary, AB, Canada [*Library symbol Library of Congress*] (LCLS)

CaACEN .... Alberta Department of the Environment, Calgary, AB, Canada [*Library symbol Library of Congress*] (LCLS)

CaACER .... Alberta Energy Resources Conservation Board, Calgary, AB, Canada [*Library symbol Library of Congress*] (LCLS)

CaACERC .... ESSO [*Standard Oil*] Resources Canada Ltd., Calgary, AB, Canada [*Library symbol Library of Congress*] (LCLS)

CaACERI ..... ESSO [*Standard Oil*] Resources Canada Ltd., Library Information Center, Calgary, AB, Canada [*Library symbol Library of Congress*] (LCLS)

CaACerM ..... Cereal Municipal Library, Cereal, AB, Canada [*Library symbol Library of Congress*] (LCLS)

CaACERR .... Energy Resources Research, Calgary, AB, Canada [*Library symbol Library of Congress*] (LCLS)

CaACES........ City of Calgary Electric System, Resource Centre, Calgary, AB, Canada [*Library symbol Library of Congress*] (LCLS)

CaACF.......... Foothills Pipe Lines (Yukon) Ltd., Calgary, AB, Canada [*Library symbol Library of Congress*] (LCLS)

CaACFC........ Fluor Canada Ltd., Calgary, AB, Canada [*Library symbol*] [*Library of Congress*] (LCLS)

CaACFH .... Foothills Hospital, Calgary, AB, Canada [*Library symbol*] [*Library of Congress*] (LCLS)

CaACG .... Glenbow Alberta Institute, Calgary, AB, Canada [*Library symbol Library of Congress*] (LCLS)

CaACGO .... Gulf Oil Canada Ltd., Calgary, AB, Canada [*Library symbol Library of Congress*] (LCLS)

CaACGP....... Great Plains Development Co. of Canada Ltd., Calgary, AB, Canada [*Library symbol Library of Congress*] (LCLS)

CaACGTL .... Alberta Gas Trunk Line Co. Ltd., Calgary, AB, Canada [*Library symbol Library of Congress*] (LCLS)

CaACH .... Home Oil Co. Ltd., Calgary, AB, Canada [*Library symbol Library of Congress*] (LCLS)

CaACHaS ..... Haverlift Systems Ltd., Calgary, AB, Canada [*Library symbol Library of Congress*] (LCLS)

CaACHB .... Hudson's Bay Oil & Gas Co. Ltd., Calgary, AB, Canada [*Library symbol Library of Congress*] (LCLS)

CaAChCU ..... Canadian Union College, College Heights, AB, Canada [*Library symbol Library of Congress*] (LCLS)

CaACHE .... Canadian Hunter Exploration Ltd., Calgary, AB, Canada [*Library symbol*] [*Library of Congress*] (LCLS)

CaACHO .... Husky Oil Operation, Calgary, AB, Canada [*Library symbol Library of Congress*] (LCLS)

CaACHS ...... Chevron Standard Ltd., Calgary, AB, Canada [*Library symbol Library of Congress*] (LCLS)

CaACI.......... Imperial Oil Ltd., Calgary, AB, Canada [*Library symbol Library of Congress*] (LCLS)

CaACIA .... Canada Department of Indian Affairs and Northern Development, Parks Canada, Western Regional Office, Calgary, AB, Canada [*Library symbol Library of Congress*] (LCLS)

CaACIPRD.... ESSO [*Standard Oil*] Resources Canada Ltd., Production Research Division, Calgary, AB, Canada [*Library symbol Library of Congress*] (LCLS)

CaACIS .... Infocon Information Services Ltd., Calgary, AB, Canada [*Library symbol*] [*Library of Congress*] (LCLS)

CaACL.......... Law Society of Alberta, Calgary, AB, Canada [*Library symbol Library of Congress*] (LCLS)

CaACLa........ Lavalin Services, Inc., Calgary, AB, Canada [*Library symbol*] [*Library of Congress*] (LCLS)

CaACLM...... Cold Lake Municipal Library, Cold Lake, AB, Canada [*Library symbol Library of Congress*] (LCLS)

CaACLS........ Calgary Public School Board, Calgary, AB, Canada [*Library symbol Library of Congress*] (LCLS)

CaACM........ Mobil Oil Canada Ltd., Exploration Library, Calgary, AB, Canada [*Library symbol Library of Congress*] (LCLS)

CaACMC ...... Manalta Coal Ltd., Information Centre, Calgary, AB, Canada [*Library symbol*] [*Library of Congress*] (LCLS)

CaACMD ...... Macleod Dixon Library, Calgary, AB, Canada [*Library symbol Library of Congress*] (LCLS)

CaACME .... Montreal Engineering Co. Ltd., Monenco Library, Calgary, AB, Canada [*Library symbol Library of Congress*] (LCLS)

CaACMM ...... I. N. McKinnon Memorial Library, Calgary, AB, Canada [*Library symbol Library of Congress*] (LCLS)

CaACMO ...... Monenco Consultants Ltd., Calgary, AB, Canada [*Library symbol*] [*Library of Congress*] (LCLS)

CaACMR ...... Mount Royal Junior College, Calgary, AB, Canada [*Library symbol Library of Congress*] (LCLS)

CaACNA .... Nova, an Alberta Corp., Calgary, AB, Canada [*Library symbol*] [*Library of Congress*] (LCLS)

CaACNC .... Novacor Chemicals Ltd., Calgary, AB, Canada [*Library symbol*] [*Library of Congress*] (LCLS)

CaACNE .... Northern Engineering Services Co. Ltd., Calgary, AB, Canada [*Library symbol Library of Congress*] (LCLS)

CaACNER ..... Norcen Energy Resources Ltd., Calgary, AB, Canada [*Library symbol Library of Congress*] (LCLS)

CaACNOC ..... Novatel Communications Ltd., Technical Library, Calgary, AB, Canada [*Library symbol*] [*Library of Congress*] (LCLS)

CaACNP .... Northern Pipeline Agency, Calgary, AB, Canada [*Library symbol Library of Congress*] (LCLS)

CaACNWS .... Nowsco Well Service Ltd., Calgary, AB, Canada [*Library symbol Library of Congress*] (LCLS)

CaACoM .... Cochrane Municipal Library, Cochrane, AB, Canada [*Library symbol Library of Congress*] (LCLS)

CaAConM ...... Consort Municipal Library, Consort, AB, Canada [*Library symbol Library of Congress*] (LCLS)

CaACP .... Pacific Petroleums Ltd., Calgary, AB, Canada [*Library symbol Library of Congress*] (LCLS)

CaACPC .... Petro-Canada, Calgary, AB, Canada [*Library symbol Library of Congress*] (LCLS)

CaACPCE ...... Petro-Canada Exploration, Calgary, AB, Canada [*Library symbol Library of Congress*] (LCLS)

CaACPCR ..... Petro-Canada, Research Laboratory, Calgary, AB, Canada [*Library symbol Library of Congress*] (LCLS)

CaACPF .... Plasti-Fab Ltd., Calgary, AB, Canada [*Library symbol Library of Congress*] (LCLS)

CaACPL .... Planning Library and Resource Centre, City of Calgary, Calgary, AB, Canada [*Library symbol Library of Congress*] (LCLS)

CaACPMC ...... Alberta Petroleum Marketing Commission, Calgary, AB, Canada [*Library symbol Library of Congress*] (LCLS)

CaACPO .... Panarctic Oils Ltd., Calgary, AB, Canada [*Library symbol Library of Congress*] (LCLS)

CaACPow ..... Calgary Power Ltd., Calgary, AB, Canada [*Library symbol Library of Congress*] (LCLS)

CaACPP .... PanCanadian Petroleum Ltd., Calgary, AB, Canada [*Library symbol Library of Congress*] (LCLS)

CaACR .... Calgary Research Center, Calgary, AB, Canada [*Library symbol*] [*Library of Congress*] (LCLS)

CaACRB .... Royal Bank of Canada, Calgary, AB, Canada [*Library symbol*] [*Library of Congress*] (LCLS)

CaACRDM .... Center for Research and Development in Masonry, Calgary, AB, Canada [*Library symbol*] [*Library of Congress*] (LCLS)

CaACrM .... Crossfield Municipal Library, Crossfield, AB, Canada [*Library symbol Library of Congress*] (LCLS)

CaACRS .... Alberta Research Council, Southern Branch Library, Calgary, AB, Canada [*Library symbol*] [*Library of Congress*] (LCLS)

CaACRV .... Rocky View School Division No. 41, Calgary, AB, Canada [*Library symbol*] [*Library of Congress*] (LCLS)

CaACS .... J. C. Sproule & Associates Ltd., Calgary, AB, Canada [*Library symbol Library of Congress*] (LCLS)

CaACSA .... Southern Alberta Institute of Technology, Calgary, AB, Canada [*Library symbol Library of Congress*] (LCLS)

CaACSAA ..... Alberta College of Art, Calgary, AB, Canada [*Library symbol Library of Congress*] (LCLS)

CaACSC .... Shell Canada Ltd., Calgary, AB, Canada [*Library symbol Library of Congress*] (LCLS)

CaACSCL ..... Shell Canada Ltd., Research Center Library, Calgary, AB, Canada [*Library symbol*] [*Library of Congress*] (LCLS)

CaACSDI ...... Sulphur Development Institute of Canada, Calgary, AB, Canada [*Library symbol Library of Congress*] (LCLS)

CaACSM ...... Stockmen's Memorial Foundation, Calgary, AB, Canada [*Library symbol*] [*Library of Congress*] (LCLS)

CaACSO .... Sun Oil Co., Calgary, AB, Canada [*Library symbol Library of Congress*] (LCLS)

CaACSP .... Institute of Sedimentary and Petroleum Geology, Calgary, AB, Canada [*Library symbol Library of Congress*] (LCLS)

CaACSTA ..... Society for Treatment of Autism, Calgary, AB, Canada [*Library symbol*] [*Library of Congress*] (LCLS)

CaACT .... Treehouse Books, Calgary, AB, Canada [*Library symbol*] [*Library of Congress*] (LCLS)

CaACTBC ..... Tom Baker Cancer Centre, Medical Library, Calgary, AB, Canada [*Library symbol Library of Congress*] (LCLS)

CaACTC .... TCPL Resources Ltd., Calgary, AB, Canada [*Library symbol*] [*Library of Congress*] (LCLS)

CaACTCP ...... Trans-Canada Pipelines, Calgary, AB, Canada [*Library symbol Library of Congress*] (LCLS)

CaACTCR ..... Texaco Canada Resources Ltd., Calgary, AB, Canada [*Library symbol Library of Congress*] (LCLS)

CaACTE .... Techman Engineering Ltd., Calgary, AB, Canada [*Library symbol Library of Congress*] (LCLS)

CaACTP .... Total Petroleum (North American) Ltd., Calgary, AB, Canada [*Library symbol Library of Congress*] (LCLS)

CaACTR ...... Touche Ross & Co., Calgary, AB, Canada [*Library symbol*] [*Library of Congress*] (LCLS)

CaACTU .... Transalta Utilities, Calgary, AB, Canada [*Library symbol Library of Congress*] (LCLS)

CAACU .... Civilian Anti-Aircraft Co-Operation Unit [*British military*] (DMA)

CaACU .... University of Calgary, Calgary, AB, Canada [*Library symbol Library of Congress*] (LCLS)

CaACUAI ..... University of Calgary, Arctic Institute of North America, Calgary, AB, Canada [*Library symbol Library of Congress*] (LCLS)

CaACUCES .... University of Calgary, Research Centre for Canadian Ethnic Studies, Calgary, AB,Canada [*Library symbol Library of Congress*] (LCLS)

CaACUFE .... University of Calgary, Faculty of Education, Calgary, AB, Canada [*Library symbol Library of Congress*] (LCLS)

CaACUM ..... University of Calgary, Medical Library, Calgary, AB, Canada [*Library symbol Library of Congress*] (LCLS)

CaACUMA .... University of Calgary, Maps Library, Calgary, AB, Canada [*Library symbol Library of Congress*] (LCLS)

CaACUMC .... University of Calgary, Department of Education, Materials Centre Library, Calgary, AB, Canada [*Library symbol Library of Congress*] (LCLS)

CaACUNO .... Union Oil of Canada Ltd., Calgary, AB, Canada [*Library symbol Library of Congress*] (LCLS)

CaACVC .... Alberta Vocational Centre, Calgary, AB, Canada [*Library symbol Library of Congress*] (LCLS)

CaACVZS .... V. Zay Smith Associates Ltd., Calgary, AB, Canada [*Library symbol Library of Congress*] (LCLS)

CaACW .... Western Canada High School, Calgary, AB, Canada [*Library symbol Library of Congress*] (LCLS)

CaACWB ..... Williams Brothers Canada Ltd., Calgary, AB, Canada [*Library symbol Library of Congress*] (LCLS)

CaACWR ...... William Roper Hull Home, Calgary, AB, Canada [*Library symbol*] [*Library of Congress*] (LCLS)

CaACWRD .... Western Research and Development Ltd., Calgary, AB, Canada [*Library symbol Library of Congress*] (LCLS)

CAAD .... Computer-Aided Architectural Design (MCD)

CAAD .... Computer Aided Art and Design (NITA)

CAAD .... Computer Air-Air Dispenser (MCD)

CAAD .... Counseling and Assistance Director [*Military*] (DNAB)

CAADAC ...... California Association of Alcoholism and Drug Abuse Counselors (SRA)

CaADeC ...... Debolt Community Library, Debolt, AB, Canada [*Library symbol*] [*Library of Congress*] (LCLS)

CaADer .... Derwent Public Library, Derwent, AB, Canada [*Library symbol*] [*Library of Congress*] (LCLS)

CaADM .... Delia Municipal Library, Delia, AB, Canada [*Library symbol Library of Congress*] (LCLS)

CaADoM ..... Donnelly Municipal Library, Donnelly, AB, Canada [*Library symbol*] [*Library of Congress*] (LCLS)

CaADrM .... Drumheller Municipal Library, Drumheller, AB, Canada [*Library symbol Library of Congress*] (LCLS)

CAADRP ...... Civil Aircraft Airworthiness Data Recording Program [*British*] (MCD)

CAADS .... California Association for Adult Day Services (SRA)

CAAE .... Canadian Association for Adult Education

CaAE .... Edmonton Public Library, Edmonton, AB, Canada [*Library symbol Library of Congress*] (LCLS)

CaAEA .... Alberta Historical Resources, Edmonton, AB, Canada [*Library symbol Library of Congress*] (LCLS)

CAAEA .... Citizens Against Airport Environment Association

CaAEacC ...... East Coulee Community Library, East Coulee, AB, Canada [*Library symbol*] [*Library of Congress*] (LCLS)

CaAEacC ...... East Coulee Community Library, East Coulee, AB, Canada [*Library symbol*] [*Library of Congress*] (LCLS)

CaAEAD .... Alcoholism and Drug Abuse Commission, Edmonton, AB, Canada [*Library symbol Library of Congress*] (LCLS)

CaAEAE .... Alberta Department of Advanced Education and Manpower, Edmonton, AB, Canada [*Library symbol Library of Congress*] (LCLS)

CaAEAg .... Alberta Department of Agriculture, Edmonton, AB, Canada [*Library symbol Library of Congress*] (LCLS)

CaAEAgL .... Alberta Department of Agriculture, Laboratory, Edmonton, AB, Canada [*Library symbol Library of Congress*] (LCLS)

CaAEAGS .... Alberta Government Services, Operating and Maintenance Division, Edmonton, AB, Canada [*Library symbol*] [*Library of Congress*] (LCLS)

CaAEAH ...... Alberta Hospital, Edmonton, AB, Canada [*Library symbol*] [*Library of Congress*] (LCLS)

CaAEAHA .... Alberta Hospital Association, Resource Library, Edmonton, AB, Canada [*Library symbol*] [*Library of Congress*] (LCLS)

CaAEaM ...... Eaglesham Municipal Library, Eaglesham, AB, Canada [*Library symbol*] [*Library of Congress*] (LCLS)

CaAEAME .... Allsopp, Morgan Engineering Ltd., Edmonton, AB, Canada [*Library symbol Library of Congress*] (LCLS)

CaAEAO .... Alberta Department of Agriculture, O. S. Longman Building, Edmonton, AB, Canada [*Library symbol Library of Congress*] (LCLS)

CaAEAOS ..... Alberta Oil Sands Information Centre, Edmonton, AB, Canada [*Library symbol Library of Congress*] (LCLS)

CaAEAPA ...... Alberta Personnel Administration, Edmonton, AB, Canada [*Library symbol Library of Congress*] (LCLS)

CaAEARN ...... Alberta Association of Registered Nurses, Edmonton, AB, Canada [*Library symbol*] [*Library of Congress*] (LCLS)

CaAEASC ..... Alberta Securities Commission, Edmonton, AB, Canada [*Library symbol Library of Congress*] (LCLS)

CaAEAtG ..... Alberta Department of the Attorney General, Edmonton, AB, Canada [*Library symbol Library of Congress*] (LCLS)

CaAEAU .... Athabasca University, Edmonton, AB, Canada [*Library symbol Library of Congress*] (LCLS)

CaAEAUC ..... Alberta Government Union Catalogue, Edmonton Concordia College, Edmonton, AB, Canada [*Library symbol Library of Congress*] (LCLS)

CaAEC.......... Concordia College, Edmonton, AB, Canada [*Library symbol Library of Congress*] (LCLS)

CaAECA........ Alberta Department of Consumer and Corporate Affairs, Edmonton, AB, Canada [*Library symbol Library of Congress*] (LCLS)

CaAECC........ Alberta Cancer Clinic, Edmonton, AB, Canada [*Library symbol Library of Congress*] (LCLS)

CaAECCH ..... Charles Camsell Hospital, Peter Wilcock Library, Edmonton, AB, Canada [*Library symbol Library of Congress*] (LCLS)

CaAECCI ...... Cross Cancer Institute, Edmonton, AB, Canada [*Library symbol Library of Congress*] (LCLS)

CaAECJC...... Church of Jesus Christ of Latter-Day Saints, Genealogical Society Library, Edmonton Branch, Edmonton, AB, Canada [*Library symbol Library of Congress*] (LCLS)

CaAECL........ Alberta Culture, Edmonton, AB, Canada [*Library symbol Library of Congress*] (LCLS)

CaAECLS...... Alberta Culture Library Services, Edmonton, AB, Canada [*Library symbol Library of Congress*] (LCLS)

CaAECS........ Alberta Union of Civil Service Employees, Edmonton, AB, Canada [*Library symbol Library of Congress*] (LCLS)

CaAECSD ..... Edmonton Catholic School District, Edmonton, AB, Canada [*Library symbol Library of Congress*] (LCLS)

CaAECU .... Canadian Utilities Ltd., Edmonton, AB, Canada [*Library symbol*] [*Library of Congress*] (LCLS)

CaAECYR ..... Alberta Culture, Edmonton, AB, Canada [*Library symbol Library of Congress*] (LCLS)

CaAECYRH... Alberta Culture, Heritage Resources Development, Edmonton, AB, Canada [*Library symbol Library of Congress*] (LCLS)

CaAEDC .... Alberta Department of Government Services, Computing and Systems Division, Edmonton, AB, Canada [*Library symbol Library of Congress*] (LCLS)

CaAEdg........ Edgerton Public Library, Edgerton, AB, Canada [*Library symbol*] [*Library of Congress*] (LCLS)

CaAEDN .... Distribution Networks, Edmonton, AB, Canada [*Library symbol Library of Congress*] (LCLS)

CaAEE.......... Alberta Department of Education, Edmonton, AB, Canada [*Library symbol Library of Congress*] (LCLS)

CAAEE.......... Coast and Antiaircraft Experimental Establishment [*British World War II*]

CaAEEA........ City of Edmonton Archives, Edmonton, AB, Canada [*Library symbol Library of Congress*] (LCLS)

CaAEEAE...... Environment Canada, Atmospheric Environment Service, Edmonton, AB, Canada [*Library symbol Library of Congress*] (LCLS)

CaAEEAV...... Alberta Department of Education, Audio Visual Services Branch, Edmonton, AB, Canada [*Library symbol Library of Congress*] (LCLS)

CaAEEC........ Alberta Department of Economic Development, Edmonton, AB, Canada [*Library symbol Library of Congress*] (LCLS)

CaAEECA...... Environment Council of Alberta, Edmonton, AB, Canada [*Library symbol Library of Congress*] (LCLS)

CaAEECW .... Canada Department of the Environment, Canadian Wildlife Service, Edmonton, AB, Canada [*Library symbol Library of Congress*] (LCLS)

CaAEEI......... Employment and Immigration Canada, Edmonton, AB, Canada [*Library symbol*] [*Library of Congress*] (LCLS)

CaAEEM .... Alberta Education Materials Resource Centre, Edmonton, AB, Canada [*Library symbol Library of Congress*] (LCLS)

CaAEEN........ Alberta Department of the Environment, Edmonton, AB, Canada [*Library symbol Library of Congress*] (LCLS)

CaAEENR ..... Alberta Energy and Natural Resources Library, Edmonton, AB, Canada [*Library symbol Library of Congress*] (LCLS)

CaAEEP........ Edmonton Power Co., Edmonton, AB, Canada [*Library symbol Library of Congress*] (LCLS)

CaAEEPS...... Environment Canada, Environmental Protection Service, Northwest Region, Edmonton, AB, Canada [*Library symbol Library of Congress*] (LCLS)

CaAEESE...... Alberta Department of Education, Special Education, Materials Resource Centre, Edmonton, AB, Canada [*Library symbol Library of Congress*] (LCLS)

CaAEF.......... Canada Department of the Environment, Northern Forest Research Centre, Edmonton,AB, Canada [*Library symbol Library of Congress*] (LCLS)

CAAEF.......... Central Asian-American Enterprise Fund [*Commercial firm*] [*Republic of Kazakstan*]

CaAEFIA....... Alberta Department of Federal and Intergovernmental Affairs, Edmonton, AB, Canada [*Library symbol Library of Congress*] (LCLS)

CaAEG .... Glenrose Provincial General Hospital, Staff Library, Edmonton, AB, Canada [*Library symbol*] [*Library of Congress*] (LCLS)

CaAEGH .... Edmonton General Hospital, Edmonton, AB, Canada [*Library symbol Library of Congress*] (LCLS)

CaAEGM .... Grant MacEwan Community College, Edmonton, AB, Canada [*Library symbol Library of Congress*] (LCLS)

CaAEGMCR... Grant MacEwan Community College, Cromdall Campus Learning Resource Centre, Edmonton, AB,Canada [*Library symbol*] [*Library of Congress*] (LCLS)

CaAEGMJP... Grant MacEwan Community College, Jasper Place Campus Learning Resource Centre, Edmonton,AB,Canada [*Library symbol*] [*Library of Congress*] (LCLS)

CaAEGMMW... Grant MacEwan Community College, Mill Woods Campus Learning Resource Centre, Edmonton, AB, Canada [*Library symbol*] [*Library of Congress*] (LCLS)

CaAEGMSS... Grant MacEwan College, Edmonton, AB, Canada [*Library symbol Library of Congress*] (LCLS)

CaAEGS .... Alberta Department of Government Services, Edmonton, AB, Canada [*Library symbol Library of Congress*] (LCLS)

CaAEGSA ..... Good Samaritan Auxiliary Hospital, Edmonton, AB, Canada [*Library symbol Library of Congress*] (LCLS)

CaAEGT........ Alberta Government Telephones Commission, Edmonton, AB, Canada [*Library symbol Library of Congress*] (LCLS)

CaAEHA .... Hardy Associates Ltd., Edmonton, AB, Canada [*Library symbol Library of Congress*] (LCLS)

CaAEHC ...... Alberta Housing Corp., Edmonton, AB, Canada [*Library symbol Library of Congress*] (LCLS)

CaAEHCI ...... Health Care Insurance Commission, Edmonton, AB, Canada [*Library symbol Library of Congress*] (LCLS)

CaAEHH .... Handicapped Housing Society of Alberta, Edmonton, AB, Canada [*Library symbol*] [*Library of Congress*] (LCLS)

CaAEHO .... Alberta Hospital, Oliver, AB, Canada [*Library symbol Library of Congress*] (LCLS)

CaAEHR .... Alberta Human Rights Commission, Edmonton, AB, Canada [*Library symbol Library of Congress*] (LCLS)

CaAEHSC..... Hospital Services Commission, Edmonton, AB, Canada [*Library symbol Library of Congress*] (LCLS)

CaAEHSD .... Alberta Department of Social Services and Community Health, Edmonton, AB, Canada [*Library symbol Library of Congress*] (LCLS)

CaAEHT........ Alberta Department of Transportation, Edmonton, AB, Canada [*Library symbol Library of Congress*] (LCLS)

CaAEHTT...... Alberta Department of Transportation, Highways Testing Laboratory, Edmonton, AB,Canada [*Library symbol Library of Congress*] (LCLS)

CaAEIC......... Alberta Department of Business Development and Tourism, Edmonton, AB, Canada [*Library symbol Library of Congress*] (LCLS)

CaAEINE ...... Indian and Northern Affairs Canada, Engineering and Architecture, Edmonton, AB, Canada [*Library symbol*] [*Library of Congress*] (LCLS)

CaAEJ .... Canada Department of Justice, Edmonton, AB, Canada [*Library symbol Library of Congress*] (LCLS)

CaAEL .... Luscar Ltd., Edmonton, AB, Canada [*Library symbol*] [*Library of Congress*] (LCLS)

CaAELBS..... Alberta Labour-Building Standards Library, Edmonton, AB, Canada [*Library symbol Library of Congress*] (LCLS)

CaAELF........ Alberta Department of Energy and Natural Resources, Renewable Resources Division, Edmonton, AB, Canada [*Library symbol Library of Congress Obsolete*] (LCLS)

CaAElk .... Elk Point Public Library, Elk Point, AB, Canada [*Library symbol*] [*Library of Congress*] (LCLS)

CaAELL .... Province of Alberta Law Library System, Edmonton, AB, Canada [*Library symbol Library of Congress*] (LCLS)

CaAELN........ Local Networks, Edmonton, AB, Canada [*Library symbol*] [*Library of Congress*] (LCLS)

CaAEM .... Empress Municipal Library, Empress, AB, Canada [*Library symbol Library of Congress*] (LCLS)

CaAEMA....... Alberta Department of Municipal Affairs, Edmonton, AB, Canada [*Library symbol Library of Congress*] (LCLS)

CaAEMAN .... Alberta Manpower, Edmonton, AB, Canada [*Library symbol*] [*Library of Congress*] (LCLS)

CaAEMB....... Multilingual Biblioservice, Edmonton, AB, Canada [*Library symbol Library of Congress*] (LCLS)

CaAEMH .... Misericordia Hospital, Edmonton, AB, Canada [*Library symbol*] [*Library of Congress*] (LCLS)

CaAEML....... Alberta Department of Labour, Edmonton, AB, Canada [*Library symbol Library of Congress*] (LCLS)

CaAEMLOH... Alberta Department of Labour, Occupational Health and Safety Division, Edmonton,AB, Canada [*Library symbol Library of Congress*] (LCLS)

CaAEMM...... Alberta Department of Energy and Natural Resources, Edmonton, AB, Canada [*Library symbol Library of Congress Obsolete*] (LCLS)

CaAEMR ...... Myrias Research Corp., Edmonton, AB, Canada [*Library symbol*] [*Library of Congress*] (LCLS)

CaAEMT....... Ministry of Transport, Canadian Air Transportation Administration, Edmonton, AB,Canada [*Library symbol Library of Congress*] (LCLS)

CaAEMTC..... Ministry of Transport, Canadian Air Transportation Administration, Construction Branch, Edmonton, AB, Canada [*Library symbol*] [*Library of Congress*] (LCLS)

CaAEMTCA... Ministry of Transport, Canadian Air Transportation Administration, Civil Aviation Branch, Edmonton, AB, Canada [*Library symbol*] [*Library of Congress*] (LCLS)

CaAENA .... Northern Alberta Institute of Technology, Edmonton, AB, Canada [*Library symbol Library of Congress*] (LCLS)

CaAENABC... North American Baptist College and Divinity School, Edmonton, AB, Canada [*Library symbol Library of Congress*] (LCLS)

CaAENF........ Network Facilities-Development, Edmonton, AB, Canada [*Library symbol*] [*Library of Congress*] (LCLS)

CaAENI .... Technical Data Control Centre, Edmonton, AB, Canada [*Library symbol Library of Congress*] (LCLS)

CaAENR .... Alberta Department of Energy and Natural Resources, Edmonton, AB, Canada [*Library symbol Library of Congress*] (LCLS)

CaAEO .... Oblate Archives of Alberta-Saskatchewan, Edmonton, AB, Canada [*Library symbol Library of Congress*] (LCLS)

CaAEOH .... Alberta Worker's Health, Safety, and Compensation, Edmonton, AB, Canada [*Library symbol Library of Congress*] (LCLS)

CaAEOM ...... Alberta Ombudsman, Edmonton, AB, Canada [*Library symbol Library of Congress*] (LCLS)

CaAEP .... Alberta Legislature Library, Edmonton, AB, Canada [*Library symbol Library of Congress*] (LCLS)

CaAEP .... Cassell's Anthology of English Poetry [*A publication*]

CaAEPA .... Alberta Public Affairs Bureau, Bibliography Section, Edmonton, AB, Canada [*Library symbol*] [*Library of Congress*] (LCLS)

CaAEPAA ..... Provincial Archives of Alberta, Edmonton, AB, Canada [*Library symbol Library of Congress*] (LCLS)

CaAEPC .... Alberta Provincial Courts, Edmonton, AB, Canada [*Library symbol Library of Congress*] (LCLS)

CaAEPL .... Edmonton Catholic School District, Professional Library, Edmonton, AB, Canada [*Library symbol Library of Congress*] (LCLS)

CaAEPRD ..... Alberta Department of the Attorney General, Planning, Research, and Development Division, Edmonton, AB, Canada [*Library symbol Library of Congress*] (LCLS)

CaAEPU .... Alberta Public Utilities Board, Edmonton, AB, Canada [*Library symbol Library of Congress*] (LCLS)

CaAEPW ...... Alberta Department of Housing and Public Works, Edmonton, AB, Canada [*Library symbol Library of Congress*] (LCLS)

CaAEPWW ... Public Works Canada, Western Regional Library, Edmonton, AB, Canada [*Library symbol*] [*Library of Congress*] (LCLS)

CaAER .... Alberta Research, Edmonton, AB, Canada [*Library symbol Library of Congress*] (LCLS)

CaAERA .... Royal Alexandra Hospital, Edmonton, AB, Canada [*Library symbol Library of Congress*] (LCLS)

CaAERASN... Royal Alexandra Hospital, School of Nursing, Edmonton, AB, Canada [*Library symbol*] [*Library of Congress*] (LCLS)

CaAERC .... Alberta Research Council, Clover Bar Branch, Edmonton, AB, Canada [*Library symbol Library of Congress*] (LCLS)

CaAERM ...... R. M. Hardy & Associates Ltd., Edmonton, AB, Canada [*Library symbol Library of Congress*] (LCLS)

CaAERPW .... Alberta Department of Recreation, Parks, and Wildlife, Edmonton, AB, Canada [*Library symbol Library of Congress*] (LCLS)

CaAERSWE... Alberta Research Council, Solar and Wind Energy Research Program Information Centre, Edmonton, AB, Canada [*Library symbol Library of Congress*] (LCLS)

CaAERTP ..... Alberta Research Council, Terrace Plaza Branch Library, Edmonton, AB, Canada [*Library symbol*] [*Library of Congress*] (LCLS)

CaAERU .... Alberta Research Council, University Branch, Edmonton, AB, Canada [*Library symbol Library of Congress*] (LCLS)

CaAES .... Statistics Canada, Edmonton, AB, Canada [*Library symbol Library of Congress*] (LCLS)

CaAESAE...... Stanley Associates Engineering Ltd., Edmonton, AB, Canada [*Library symbol Library of Congress*] (LCLS)

CaAESC .... Syncrude Canada Ltd., Edmonton, AB, Canada [*Library symbol Library of Congress*] (LCLS)

CaAESD .... Alberta School for the Deaf, Edmonton, AB, Canada [*Library symbol Library of Congress*] (LCLS)

CaAESG .... Alberta Solicitor General's Department, Edmonton, AB, Canada [*Library symbol Library of Congress*] (LCLS)

CaAESIS ...... Schick Information Systems, Edmonton, AB, Canada [*Library symbol Library of Congress*] (LCLS)

CaAET .... Alberta Treasury Department, Edmonton, AB, Canada [*Library symbol Library of Congress*] (LCLS)

CaAETA .... Travel Alberta, Edmonton, AB, Canada [*Library symbol Library of Congress Obsolete*] (LCLS)

CaAETATE.... Transport Canada, Canadian Air Transportation Administration, Telecommunicationsand Electronics, Edmonton, AB, Canada [*Library symbol Library of Congress*] (LCLS)

CaAETBS..... Alberta Treasury Department, Bureau of Statistics, Edmonton, AB,Canada [*Library symbol Library of Congress*] (LCLS)

CaAETCT...... Alberta Treasury Department, Corporate Tax Administration, Edmonton, AB, Canada [*Library symbol Library of Congress*] (LCLS)

CaAEU .... University of Alberta, Edmonton, AB, Canada [*Library symbol Library of Congress*] (LCLS)

CaAEUA .... University of Alberta, Archives, Edmonton, AB, Canada [*Library symbol Library of Congress*] (LCLS)

CaAEUAG..... University of Alberta, Department of Agricultural Engineering, Edmonton, AB, Canada [*Library symbol*] [*Library of Congress*] (LCLS)

CaAEUB .... University of Alberta, Boreal Institute for Northern Studies, Edmonton, AB, Canada [*Library symbol Library of Congress*] (LCLS)

CaAEUL....... University of Alberta, Law Library, Edmonton, AB, Canada [*Library symbol Library of Congress*] (LCLS)

CaAEULS ..... University of Alberta, Faculty of Library Science, Edmonton, AB, Canada [*Library symbol Library of Congress*] (LCLS)

CaAEUM ...... University of Alberta, University Map Collection, Edmonton, AB, Canada [*Library symbol Library of Congress*] (LCLS)

CaAEUN .... Unifarm Association, Edmonton, AB, Canada [*Library symbol Library of Congress*] (LCLS)

CaAEUS .... University of Alberta, Special Collections Department, Edmonton, AB, Canada [*Library symbol Library of Congress*] (LCLS)

CaAEUSJ..... University of Alberta, Faculte Saint-Jean, Edmonton, AB, Canada [*Library symbol Library of Congress*] (LCLS)

CaAEUT....... Alberta Department of Utilities and Telephones, Edmonton, AB, Canada [*Library symbol Library of Congress*] (LCLS)

CaAEVC....... Alberta Vocational Centre, Edmonton, AB, Canada [*Library symbol Library of Congress*] (LCLS)

CaAExC........ Exshaw Community Library, Exshaw, AB, Canada [*Library symbol Library of Congress*] (LCLS)

CAAF........... Campbell Army Airfield [*Fort Campbell, Kentucky*]

CAAF........... Chief of the Army Air Forces [*World War II*]

CAAF........... Combined Allied Air Forces

CAAF........... Conseil Asiatique d'Analystes Financiers [*Asian Council of Securities Analysts - ASAC*] [*Tokyo, Japan*] (EAIO)

CaAFAAR .... Alberta Department of Agriculture, Regional Office, Fairview, AB, Canada [*Library symbol Library of Congress*] (LCLS)

CaAFAAV .... Alberta Department of Agriculture, Veterinary Laboratory, Fairview, AB, Canada [*Library symbol Library of Congress*] (LCLS)

CaAFAC....... Fairview College, Fairview, AB, Canada [*Library symbol Library of Congress*] (LCLS)

CaAFalD ...... Dentinger Library, Falher, AB, Canada [*Library symbol*] [*Library of Congress*] (LCLS)

CaAFcM ...... Fox Creek Municipal Library, Fox Creek, AB, Canada [*Library symbol*] [*Library of Congress*] (LCLS)

CAAFDP ...... Central American Association of Families of Disappeared Persons [*See also ACAFADE*] [*San Jose, Costa Rica*] (EAIO)

CaAFk .... Fort Kent Public Library, Fort Kent, AB, Canada [*Library symbol Library of Congress*] (LCLS)

CaAFmH ...... Fort McMurray Regional Hospital, Fort McMurray, AB, Canada [*Library symbol*] [*Library of Congress*] (LCLS)

CaAFmK...... Keyona College, Fort McMurray, AB, Canada [*Library symbol Library of Congress*] (LCLS)

CaAFmSI...... SUNCOR, Inc., Resources Group, Information Centre, Fort McMurray, AB, Canada [*Library symbol Library of Congress*] (LCLS)

CAAFS .... Institute of Chemical Analysis, Applications, and Forensic Science [*Northeastern University*] [*Research center*] (RCD)

CaAFSM...... Fort Saskatchewan Municipal Library, Fort Saskatchewan, AB, Canada [*Library symbol Library of Congress*] (LCLS)

CaAFsSG.... Sherritt Gordon Mines Ltd., Fort Saskatchewan, AB, Canada [*Library symbol Library of Congress*] (LCLS)

CaAFV .... Fairview Public Library, Fairview, AB, Canada [*Library symbol*] [*Library of Congress*] (LCLS)

CaAFvC....... Fort Vermilion Community Library, Fort Vermilion, AB, Canada [*Library symbol*] [*Library of Congress*] (LCLS)

CAAG .... Civil Aviation Advisory [*or Assistance*] Group [*FAA*]

CaAGcM ...... Grand Centre Municipal Library, Grand Centre, AB, Canada [*Library symbol Library of Congress*] (LCLS)

CaAGcNL .... Northern Lights Library Co-Operative, Grand Centre, AB, Canada [*Library symbol Library of Congress*] (LCLS)

CaAGi .... Gibbons Public Library, Gibbons, AB, Canada [*Library symbol*] [*Library of Congress*] (LCLS)

CaAGM .... Gleichen Municipal Library, Gleichen, AB, Canada [*Library symbol Library of Congress*] (LCLS)

CaAGP .... Grande Prairie Public Library, Grande Prairie, AB, Canada [*Library symbol*] [*Library of Congress*] (LCLS)

CaAGPC ...... Grande Prairie College, Grande Prairie, AB, Canada [*Library symbol Library of Congress*] (LCLS)

CaAGPH...... Grande Prairie Regional Hospital, Grande Prairie, AB, Canada [*Library symbol*] [*Library of Congress*] (LCLS)

CaAGras ..... Grassland Public Library, Grassland, AB, Canada [*Library symbol*] [*Library of Congress*] (LCLS)

CaAGrWM .... Grimshaw W.I. Municipal Library, Grimshaw, AB, Canada [*Library symbol*] [*Library of Congress*] (LCLS)

CAAGS........ Caseless Ammunition Aerial Gun System (MCD)

CaAGVC ...... Alberta Vocational Centre, Grouard, AB, Canada [*Library symbol Library of Congress*] (LCLS)

CaAGvM....... Girouxville Municipal Library, Girouxville, AB, Canada [*Library symbol*] [*Library of Congress*] (LCLS)

CAAH .... Chronic Active Autoimmune Hepatitis [*Medicine*] (DMAA)

CAAH .... Chronology of African-American History [*A publication*]

CAAHA........ Council on Arteriosclerosis of the American Heart Association (EA)

CaAHcM....... Hines Creek Municipal Library, Hines Creek, AB, Canada [*Library symbol*] [*Library of Congress*] (LCLS)

CaAHe .... Heinsburg Public Library, Heinsburg, AB, Canada [*Library symbol*] [*Library of Congress*] (LCLS)

CAAHEP....... Commission on Accreditations of Allied Health Education Programs (PGP)

CaAHh .... Hairy Hill Public Library, Hairy Hill, AB, Canada [*Library symbol*] [*Library of Congress*] (LCLS)

CaAHM .... Hanna Municipal Library, Hanna, AB, Canada [*Library symbol Library of Congress*] (LCLS)

CaAHrM ...... High River Municipal Library, High River, AB, Canada [*Library symbol Library of Congress*] (LCLS)

CAAHTT ...... Canadian Association of Animal Health Technologists & Technicians (AC)

CaAHuM ...... Hussar Municipal Library, Hussar, AB, Canada [*Library symbol Library of Congress*] (LCLS)

CaAHyM...... Hythe Municipal Library, Hythe, AB, Canada [*Library symbol*] [*Library of Congress*] (LCLS)

CaAIr .... Iron River Public Library, Iron River, AB, Canada [*Library symbol Library of Congress*] (LCLS)

CaAIrmC ...... Irma Community Library, Irma, AB, Canada [*Library symbol*] [*Library of Congress*] (LCLS)

CAAJ .... Civil Aeronautics Authority Journal [*A publication*] (AAGC)

CaAJ .... Jasper Public Library, Jasper, AB, Canada [*Library symbol Library of Congress*] (LCLS)

CAAJA......... Council of Affiliated Associations of Jewelers of America (EA)

CAAK .... Civil Aviation Administration of Korea [*North Korea*]

CaAK .... Kitscoty Public Library, Kitscoty, AB, Canada [*Library symbol Library of Congress*] (LCLS)

CaAKM......... Kinuso Municipal Library, Kinuso, AB, Canada [*Library symbol*] [*Library of Congress*] (LCLS)

CaAKrC .... Keg River Community Library, Keg River, AB, Canada [*Library symbol*] [*Library of Congress*] (LCLS)

CAAL............ Canadian Association of Applied Linguistics
CAAL............ COMOPTEVFOR Acronym and Abbreviation List [*A publication*] (CAAL)
CAAL............ Computer-Aided Adult Learning (HGAA)
CAAL............ Corporate Author Authority List
CaAL............ Lethbridge Public Library, Lethbridge, AB, Canada [*Library symbol Library of Congress*] (LCLS)
CaALaAF...... Alberta Department of Agriculture, Field Crops Branch, Lacombe, AB, Canada [*Library symbol Library of Congress*] (LCLS)
CaALaAg...... Canada Department of Agriculture, Research Station, Lacombe, AB, Canada [*Library symbol Library of Congress*] (LCLS)
CaALADR..... Canada Department of Agriculture, Animal Diseases Research Institute (West), Lethbridge, AB, Canada [*Library symbol Library of Congress*] (LCLS)
CaALaf........ Lafond Public Library, Lafond, AB, Canada [*Library symbol*] [*Library of Congress*] (LCLS)
CaALAg....... Canada Department of Agriculture, Lethbridge, AB, Canada [*Library symbol Library of Congress*] (LCLS)
CaALAi........ Alberta Department of Agriculture, Irrigation Division, Lethbridge, AB, Canada [*Library symbol Library of Congress*] (LCLS)
CaALam...... Lamont Public Library, Lamont, AB, Canada [*Library symbol*] [*Library of Congress*] (LCLS)
CaALaP....... Parkland Regional Library, Lacombe, AB, Canada [*Library symbol Library of Congress*] (LCLS)
CaALAR...... Alberta Department of Agriculture, Regional Office, Lethbridge, AB, Canada [*Library symbol Library of Congress*] (LCLS)
CAALAS...... Central Australian Aboriginal Legal Aid Scheme
CaALC........ Lethbridge College, Lethbridge, AB, Canada [*Library symbol Library of Congress*] (LCLS)
CaALcC....... La Crete Community Library, La Crete, AB, Canada [*Library symbol*] [*Library of Congress*] (LCLS)
CaALCJC..... Church of Jesus Christ of Latter-Day Saints, Genealogical Society Library, Lethbridge Branch, Stake Center, Lethbridge, AB, Canada [*Library symbol Library of Congress*] (LCLS)
CaALEG....... Legal Public Library, Legal, AB, Canada [*Library symbol*] [*Library of Congress*] (LCLS)
CaALEn....... Alberta Department of the Environment, Lethbridge, AB, Canada [*Library symbol Library of Congress*] (LCLS)
CaALgC....... La Glace Community Library, La Glace, AB, Canada [*Library symbol*] [*Library of Congress*] (LCLS)
CaALiM...... Linden Municipal Library, Linden, AB, Canada [*Library symbol Library of Congress*] (LCLS)
CAALL........ Canadian Association of Administrators of Labour Legislation
CaALlb........ Lac La Biche Public Library, Lac La Biche, AB, Canada [*Library symbol*] [*Library of Congress*] (LCLS)
CaALLbVC.... Alberta Vocational Centre, Lac La Biche, AB, Canada [*Library symbol Library of Congress*] (LCLS)
CaALoM...... Longview Municipal Library, Longview, AB, Canada [*Library symbol Library of Congress*] (LCLS)
CAALS .... Consortium on Automated Analytical Laboratory Systems [*National Institute of Standards & Technology*]
CaALU .... University of Lethbridge, Lethbridge, AB, Canada [*Library symbol Library of Congress*] (LCLS)
CaALUG ...... University of Lethbridge, Department of Geography, Lethbridge, AB, Canada [*Library symbol Library of Congress*] (LCLS)
CAAM.......... Canadian Association of Artists Managers (AC)
CAAM.......... Civil Aeronautics Administration Manual
CAAM.......... Conventional Airfield Attack Missile (MCD)
CaAMai....... Mallaig Public Library, Mallaig, AB, Canada [*Library symbol*] [*Library of Congress*] (LCLS)
CaAMaM...... Manning Municipal Library, Manning, AB, Canada [*Library symbol*] [*Library of Congress*] (LCLS)
CaAMan...... Mannville Public Library, Mannville, AB, Canada [*Library symbol*] [*Library of Congress*] (LCLS)
CaAMar....... Marwayne Public Library, Marwayne, AB, Canada [*Library symbol*] [*Library of Congress*] (LCLS)
CaAMCH ...... Crescent Heights High School, Medicine Hat, AB, Canada [*Library symbol Library of Congress*] (LCLS)
CaAMe......... Medley Public Library, Medley, AB, Canada [*Library symbol Library of Congress*] (LCLS)
CAAMF........ Cowboy Artists of America Museum Foundation (EA)
CaAMG .... Medicine Hat General Hospital, Medicine Hat, AB, Canada [*Library symbol Library of Congress*] (LCLS)
CaAMHS ...... Medicine Hat High School, Medicine Hat, AB, Canada [*Library symbol Library of Congress*] (LCLS)
CaAMiC....... Millarville Community Library, Millarville, AB, Canada [*Library symbol Library of Congress*] (LCLS)
CaAMLM..... McLennan Municipal Library, McLennan, AB, Canada [*Library symbol*] [*Library of Congress*] (LCLS)
CaAMM....... Medicine Hat College, Medicine Hat, AB, Canada [*Library symbol Library of Congress*] (LCLS)
CaAMoM..... Morrin Municipal Library, Morrin, AB, Canada [*Library symbol Library of Congress*] (LCLS)
CaAMor....... Morinville Public Library, Morinville, AB, Canada [*Library symbol*] [*Library of Congress*] (LCLS)
CaAMP........ Medicine Hat Public Library, Medicine Hat, AB, Canada [*Library symbol Library of Congress*] (LCLS)
CaAMsIF...... International Fertilizer Development Center, Muscle Shoals, AB, Canada [*Library symbol*] [*Library of Congress*] (LCLS)
CaAMyr....... Myrnam Public Library, Myrnam, AB, Canada [*Library symbol*] [*Library of Congress*] (LCLS)
CAAN.......... Combined Arms Assessment Network [*DoD*]
CAAN.......... Continental Advertising Agency Network [*Later, Advertising and Marketing International Network*] (EA)
CAAN .... Contracting and Acquisition Newsletter [*A publication*]

CaANE .... Newbrook Public Library, Newbrook, AB, Canada [*Library symbol*] [*Library of Congress*] (LCLS)
CaANM .... Nampa Municipal Library, Nampa, AB, Canada [*Library symbol*] [*Library of Congress*] (LCLS)
CAANS .... Canadian Association for the Advancement of Netherlandic Studies G2 [*See also ACAEN*]
CAANS .... Cenral Alberta AIDS Network Society (AC)
CAAO .... Canadian Association of Amateur Oarsmen
CaAOAC ...... Olds Agricultural College, Olds, AB, Canada [*Library symbol Library of Congress*] (LCLS)
CaAOAF ...... Alberta Department of Agriculture, Farm Business Management Branch, Olds, AB, Canada [*Library symbol Library of Congress*] (LCLS)
CAAOM .... California Association of Acupuncture and Oriental Medicine (SRA)
CaAOM .... Okotoks Municipal Library, Okotoks, AB, Canada [*Library symbol Library of Congress*] (LCLS)
CAA Op .... Civil Aeronautics Authority Opinions [*A publication*] (DLA)
CaAOyM ...... Oyen Municipal Library, Oyen, AB, Canada [*Library symbol Library of Congress*] (LCLS)
CAAP .... Certified Advertising Agency Practitioner
CAAP .... Child and Adolescent Adjustment Profile [*Child development test*] [*Psychology*]
CAAP .... Community Action Association of Pennsylvania (SRA)
CAAP .... Cornhusker Army Ammunition Plant (AABC)
CAAP .... Council for the Advancement of the African People [*British*]
CaAPH .... Alberta Hospital, Staff Library, Ponoka, AB, Canada [*Library symbol Library of Congress*] (LCLS)
CaAPi.......... Plamondon Public Library, Plamondon, AB, Canada [*Library symbol*] [*Library of Congress*] (LCLS)
CAAPP .... Content-Addressable Array Parallel Processor [*Computer science*]
CaAPrEN ..... Alberta Department of the Environment, Peace River, AB, Canada [*Library symbol Library of Congress*] (LCLS)
CaAPrM ...... Peace River Municipal Library, Peace River, AB, Canada [*Library symbol*] [*Library of Congress*] (LCLS)
CaAPrPLS .... Peace Library System, Peace River, AB, Canada [*Library symbol*] [*Library of Congress*] (LCLS)
CaAPv .... Paradise Valley Public Library, Paradise Valley, AB, Canada [*Library symbol*] [*Library of Congress*] (LCLS)
CAAQ .... Customs Agents' Association of Queensland [*Australia*]
CAAR .... Compressed Air Accumulator Rocket
CaAR .... Ralston Public Library, Ralston, AB, Canada [*Library symbol*] [*Library of Congress*] (LCLS)
CaARaC .... Alcoma Community Library, Rainier, AB, Canada [*Library symbol*] [*Library of Congress*] (LCLS)
CaARad....... Radway Public Library, Radway, AB, Canada [*Library symbol*] [*Library of Congress*] (LCLS)
CAARC........ Commonwealth Advisory Aeronautical Research Council [*British*] (EAIO)
CaARd .... Red Deer Public Library, Red Deer, AB, Canada [*Library symbol Library of Congress*] (LCLS)
CaARDAR ... Alberta Department of Agriculture, Regional Office, Red Deer, AB, Canada [*Library symbol Library of Congress*] (LCLS)
CaARDC....... Red Deer College, Red Deer, AB, Canada [*Library symbol Library of Congress*] (LCLS)
CaARDMC... Michener Centre, Red Deer, AB, Canada [*Library symbol Library of Congress*] (LCLS)
CaARe .... Redcliff Public Library, Redcliff, AB, Canada [*Library symbol*] [*Library of Congress*] (LCLS)
CaARed........ Redwater Public Library, Redwater, AB, Canada [*Library symbol*] [*Library of Congress*] (LCLS)
CaARGC....... Graham Community Library, Ralston, AB, Canada [*Library symbol*] [*Library of Congress*] (LCLS)
CAARH .... California Association of Alcoholic Recovery Homes (SRA)
CaARh .... Rolling Hills Public Library, Rolling Hills, AB, Canada [*Library symbol*] [*Library of Congress*] (LCLS)
CAARI .... Cyprus American Archaeological Research Institute [*Research center*] (IRC)
CaARIM ...... Rainbow Lake Municipal Library, Rainbow Lake, AB, Canada [*Library symbol*] [*Library of Congress*] (LCLS)
CaARM .... Rockyford Municipal Library, Rockyford, AB, Canada [*Library symbol Library of Congress*] (LCLS)
CaARo .... Rosemary Public Library, Rosemary, AB, Canada [*Library symbol*] [*Library of Congress*] (LCLS)
CaARoc .... Rochester Public Library, Rochester, AB, Canada [*Library symbol*] [*Library of Congress*] (LCLS)
CAARRS........ Contract Administration Automated Records Retrieval System (MCD)
CaARS .... Canada Department of National Defence, Defence Research Establishment Suffield, Ralston, AB, Canada [*Library symbol*] [*Library of Congress*] (LCLS)
CaARuM ...... Rumsey Municipal Library, Rumsey, AB, Canada [*Library symbol Library of Congress*] (LCLS)
CaARy......... Ryley Public Library, Ryley, AB, Canada [*Library symbol*] [*Library of Congress*] (LCLS)
CaARyM...... Rycroft Municipal Library, Rycroft, AB, Canada [*Library symbol*] [*Library of Congress*] (LCLS)
CAAS .... Canadian Association for American Studies (EA)
CAAS .... Canadian Association of African Studies [*See also ACEA*]
CAAS .... Capital Brands, Inc. [*NASDAQ symbol*] (SAG)
CAAS .... Center for Afro-American and African Studies [*University of Michigan*] [*Research center*] (RCD)
CAAS .... Center for Afro-American Studies [*University of California, Los Angeles*] [*Research center*] (RCD)
CAAS .... Chet Atkins Appreciation Society (EA)
CAAS .... Chinese Association for the Advancement of Science
CAAS .... Class A Airspace [*Aviation*] (FAAC)

CAAS .... Combined Arms and Support [*Army*] (AABC)
CAAS .... Combined Artillery/Aviation Simulator (DWSG)
CAAS .... Computer-Aided Alerting Subsystem (CAAL)
CAAS .... Computer-Aided Approach Spacing [*Aviation*]
CAAS .... Computer-Assisted Acquisition System [*for libraries*]
CAAS .... Contemporary Authors Autobiography Series [*A publication*]
CAAS .... Continence Aids Assistance Scheme [*Australia*]
CAAS .... Contracted Advisory and Assistance Services [*DoD*]
CAAS .... Conventional Airfield Attack System [*Army*]
CAAS .... Council of American Artist Societies (EA)
CaASA .... St. Albert Public Library, St. Albert, AB, Canada [*Library symbol Library of Congress*] (LCLS)
CaASAMLM... MLM Groundwater Engineering, St. Albert, AB, Canada [*Library symbol Library of Congress*] (LCLS)
CAASD .... Capital Brands [*NASDAQ symbol*] (TTSB)
CAASE .... Computer-Aided Analytical Solution for Engineers
CAASE .... Computer-Assisted Area Source Emissions [*Environmental Protection Agency*]
CAA/SEF ...... Chaplains' Aid Association/Seminary Education Fund (EA)
CaASeSM ... Shannon Municipal Library, Sexsmith, AB, Canada [*Library symbol*] [*Library of Congress*] (LCLS)
CAASF .... Canadian Army Active Service Force
CaASg .... Spruce Grove Public Library, Spruce Grove, AB, Canada [*Library symbol*] [*Library of Congress*] (LCLS)
CaASgY .... Yellowhead Regional Library, Spruce Grove, AB, Canada [*Library symbol Library of Congress*] (LCLS)
CaASh .... Swan Hills Public Library, Swan Hills, AB, Canada [*Library symbol*] [*Library of Congress*] (LCLS)
CAASHHE ..... Canadian Association Against Sexual Harassment in Higher Education [*Association Canadienne Contre le Harcelement Sexuel en Milieu d'Ensignement Superieur*] (AC)
CaASiC .... Saint Isidore Community Library, Saint Isidore, AB, Canada [*Library symbol*] [*Library of Congress*] (LCLS)
CaASl .... Smoky Lake Public Library, Smoky Lake, AB, Canada [*Library symbol*] [*Library of Congress*] (LCLS)
CaASM .... Strathmore Municipal Library, Strathmore, AB, Canada [*Library symbol Library of Congress*] (LCLS)
CaASMLS .... Marigold Library System, Strathmore, AB, Canada [*Library symbol Library of Congress*] (LCLS)
CaASpEMRCM... Energy, Mines, and Resources Canada, Western Research Laboratory, CANMET Library, Sherwood Park, AB, Canada [*Library symbol Library of Congress*] (LCLS)
CaASpl .... Stony Plain Public Library, Stony Plain, AB, Canada [*Library symbol*] [*Library of Congress*] (LCLS)
CaASpS .... County of Strathcona Library, Sherwood Park, AB, Canada [*Library symbol Library of Congress*] (LCLS)
CAASR .... Canadian Association of Applied Social Research [*See also ACRSA*]
CaASrM ...... Spirit River Municipal Library, Spirit River, AB, Canada [*Library symbol Library of Congress*] (LCLS)
CAAST .... Canadian Alliance Against Software Theft [*Alliance Canadienne Contre le vol de Logiciels*] (AC)
CaAStM .... Standard Municipal Library, Standard, AB, Canada [*Library symbol Library of Congress*] (LCLS)
CaASTP .... St. Paul Public Library, St. Paul, AB, Canada [*Library symbol*] [*Library of Congress*] (LCLS)
CaASvSC ..... Savanna Municipal Library, Silver Valley, AB, Canada [*Library symbol*] [*Library of Congress*] (LCLS)
CAAT .... Campaign Against Arms Trade [*British*] (EAIO)
CAAT .... Center for Alternatives to Animal Testing [*At Johns Hopkins*]
CAAT .... Centre Afro-Americain du Travail [*Afro-American Labor Center*] (AF)
CAAT .... College of Applied Arts and Technology
CAAT .... Computer-Assisted Audit Techniques
CAAT .... Computer-Assisted Axial Tomography [*Also, CAT, CT*] [*Roentgenography*]
CAATC .... Civil Aeronautics Administration Type Certificate
CaAThi .... Two Hills Public Library, Two Hills, AB, Canada [*Library symbol*] [*Library of Congress*] (LCLS)
CaAThM ...... Three Hills Municipal Library, Three Hills, AB, Canada [*Library symbol Library of Congress*] (LCLS)
CaAThoM ...... Thorhild Municipal Library, Thorhild, AB, Canada [*Library symbol*] [*Library of Congress*] (LCLS)
CaATi .... Tilley Public Library, Tilley, AB, Canada [*Library symbol*] [*Library of Congress*] (LCLS)
CAATO .... Combined Army Air Transport Organization [*World War II*]
CaATof .... Tofield Public Library, Tofield, AB, Canada [*Library symbol*] [*Library of Congress*] (LCLS)
Ca-ATPase... Calcium-Dependent Adenosine Triphophatase (PDAA)
CaATrM .... Trochu Municipal Library, Trochu, AB, Canada [*Library symbol Library of Congress*] (LCLS)
CAATS .... Canadian Automated Air Traffic System
CAAV .... Central Association of Agricultural Valuers [*British*]
CAAV .... Civil Aviation Administration of Vietnam
CaAVAR ...... Alberta Department of Agriculture, Regional Office, Vermilion, AB, Canada [*Library symbol Library of Congress*] (LCLS)
CaAVC .... Lakeland College, Vermilion, AB, Canada [*Library symbol Library of Congress*] (LCLS)
CaAVe.......... Vegreville Public Library, Vegreville, AB, Canada [*Library symbol*] [*Library of Congress*] (LCLS)
CaAVeE .... Alberta Environmental Centre, Vegreville, AB, Canada [*Library symbol Library of Congress*] (LCLS)
CaAVER .... Vermilion Public Library, Vermilion, AB, Canada [*Library symbol*] [*Library of Congress*] (LCLS)
CaAVi .... Vilna Public Library, Vilna, AB, Canada [*Library symbol*] [*Library of Congress*] (LCLS)

CaAVik .... Viking Public Library, Viking, AB, Canada [*Library symbol*] [*Library of Congress*] (LCLS)
CaAVLF .... Alberta Labour, Alberta Fire Training School, Vermilion, AB, Canada [*Library symbol*] [*Library of Congress*] (LCLS)
CaAVM .... Veteran Municipal Library, Veteran, AB, Canada [*Library symbol Library of Congress*] (LCLS)
CaAVvM .... Valleyview Municipal Library, Valleyview, AB, Canada [*Library symbol*] [*Library of Congress*] (LCLS)
CAAW .... Customer Authorization for Additional Work
CaAW.......... Wetaskiwin Municipal Library, Wetaskiwin, AB, Canada [*Library symbol Library of Congress*] (LCLS)
CaAWaC ...... Wanham Community Library, Wanham, AB, Canada [*Library symbol*] [*Library of Congress*] (LCLS)
CaAWAD ...... Alberta Department of Agriculture, Dairy Division, Wetaskiwin, AB, Canada [*Library symbol Library of Congress*] (LCLS)
CaAWaiC ..... Wainwright Community Library, Wainwright, AB, Canada [*Library symbol*] [*Library of Congress*] (LCLS)
CaAWas....... Waskatenau Public Library, Waskatenau, AB, Canada [*Library symbol*] [*Library of Congress*] (LCLS)
CAAWEX ...... Canned Antiair Warfare Exercise (NVT)
CaAWil .... Willingdon Public Library, Willingdon, AB, Canada [*Library symbol*] [*Library of Congress*] (LCLS)
CaAWr .... Wandering River Public Library, Wandering River, AB, Canada [*Library symbol*] [*Library of Congress*] (LCLS)
CAAWS .... Canadian Association for the Advancement of Women & Sport & Physical Activity [*Association Canadienne pour l'Avancement des Femmes du Sport et de l'Activite Physique*] (AC)
CAA-WTS ..... Civil Aviation Authority - War Training Service
CAAX .... Central American Airways [*Air carrier designation symbol*]
CaAYM .... Youngstown Municipal Library, Youngstown, AB, Canada [*Library symbol Library of Congress*] (LCLS)
CaAZcC .... Zama City Community Library, Zama City, AB, Canada [*Library symbol*] [*Library of Congress*] (LCLS)
CAB.............. Cabalistic (ROG)
CAB.............. Caballero [*Cavalier*] [*Spanish*] (DSUE)
CAB.............. Cabin (MSA)
CAB.............. Cabinda [*Angola*] [*Airport symbol*] (OAG)
CAB.............. Cabinet (KSC)
CAB.............. Cables [*Business term*]
CAB.............. Cabletelevision Advertising Bureau [*New York, NY*] (EA)
CAB.............. Cabramurra [*Australia Seismograph station code, US Geological Survey Closed*] (SEIS)
CAB.............. Cabriolet (ROG)
CAB.............. Calibrate
CaB.............. Cambridge Bible for Schools and Colleges [*A publication*] (BJA)
CAB.............. Campaign Against US Military Bases in the Philippines (EA)
CAB.............. Canadian Armoured Brigade
CAB.............. Canadian Association of Broadcasters
CAB.............. Capco Automotive Products [*Formerly, Clark Automotive Products*] [*NYSE symbol*] (SAG)
CAB.............. Capped Argon Bubbling [*Steelmaking*]
CAB.............. Captured Air Bubble (MCD)
CAB.............. Carbon Arc Brazing
CAB.............. Career Adaptive Behavior Inventory [*Vocational guidance test*]
CAB.............. Case at Bar [*Legal shorthand*] (LWAP)
CAB.............. Cellulose Acetate Butyrate [*Organic chemistry*]
CAB.............. Cement-Asbestos Board (DAC)
CAB.............. Centralized Accounting and Billeting [*Military*] (DNAB)
CAB.............. Centralized Accounting and Billing (MCD)
CAB.............. Ceramic Awareness Bulletin [*Defense Ceramic Information Center*] [*A publication*]
CAB.............. Change Analysis Board
CAB.............. Chemical-Atomic-Biological (BARN)
CAB.............. Chesapeake Air Services [*ICAO designator*] (FAAC)
CAB.............. Circuit Assurance Block (SSD)
CAB.............. Citizens' Advice Bureau [*British*]
CAB.............. Citizen's Advisory Board (OICC)
CAB.............. Civil Aeronautics Board [*Independent government agency*] [*Terminated, 1984, functions transferred to Department of Transportation*]
CAB.............. Civil Aeronautics Board Reports [*A publication*] (DLA)
CAB.............. Civil Aeronautics Bulletin
CAB.............. Civil Air Branch [*Air Force*]
CAB.............. CNO [*Chief of Naval Operations*] Advisory Board
CAB.............. Collating and Binding
CAB.............. Combat Aviation Battalion [*or Brigade*]
CAB.............. Combined Arms Battalion (MCD)
CAB.............. Command Advisory Board
CAB.............. Commonwealth Agricultural Bureaux [*Database producer*] (EA)
CAB.............. Commonwealth Bureau of Soils [*British*]
CAB.............. Communications Adaptor Board (NITA)
CAB.............. Comprehensive Ability Battery [*Test*]
CAB.............. Computer-Aided Building (PDAA)
CAB.............. Consequential Arc Back
CAB.............. Consortium on Advanced Biosensors (EA)
CAB.............. Consumers' Advisory Board
CAB.............. Contract Adjustment Board (AAGC)
CAB.............. Contract Appeals Board [*Veterans Administration*]
CAB.............. Contractor's Advisory Board (SAA)
CAB.............. Controlled Amortization Bond
CAB.............. Controlled Atmosphere Brazing [*Metallurgy*]
CAB.............. Cooperative Analysis of Broadcasting [*Term used in TV rating*]
CAB.............. Coronary Artery Bypass [*Medicine*]
CAB.............. Corrective Action Board
CAB.............. Corrosion Advice Bureau [*British Steel Corp.*] (PDAA)

CAB............. Cost Analysis Brief (MCD)
CAB............. Cost Audit Board (NASA)
CAB............. Critical Air Blast [Test]
CAB............. Cultural Association of Bengal (EA)
CAB............. Current Awareness Bibliographies [DTIC]
CAB............. Cytoplasmic Androgen Binder [Endocrinology]
CABA......... California Aviation Business Association (SRA)
CABA......... Canadian American Business Association (AC)
CABA......... Canadian Automated Buildings Association [Association Canadienne pour l'Automatisation des Batiments] (AC)
CABA.......... Charge Account Bankers Association [Later, ABA]
CABA.......... Citizens' Advice Bureau, Adelaide [Australia]
CABA.......... Compressed Air Breathing Apparatus
CaBAbF....... Fraser Valley Union Library, Abbotsford, BC, Canada [Library symbol Library of Congress] (LCLS)
CaBAbFV...... Fraser Valley College, Abbotsford, BC, Canada [Library symbol Library of Congress] (LCLS)
CaBAbFVL.... Fraser Valley College, Library Technician Program, Abbotsford, BC, Canada [Library symbol] [Library of Congress] (LCLS)
CABACT ...... Citizen's Advice Bureau, Australian Capital Territory
CABAF .... Currency Adjustment and Bunkering Adjustment Factors [British] (DCTA)
CaBAgAg...... Canada Department of Agriculture, Research Station, Agassiz, BC, Canada [Library symbol Library of Congress] (LCLS)
CABAL .... Calcium-Boron-Aluminum [Glasses]
CABAL .... Clifford, Arlington, Buckingham, Ashley, Lauderdale [Ministers of Charles II of England] [Some claim that the word "cabal" is derived from this acronym; others, that it comes from the Hebrew "cabala"]
Cab & E ...... Cababe and Ellis' Queen's Bench Reports [1882-85] [England] [A publication] (DLA)
Cab & El ..... Cababe and Ellis' Queen's Bench Reports [1882-85] [England] [A publication] (DLA)
Cab & El (Eng)... Cababe and Ellis' Queen's Bench Reports [1882-85] [England] [A publication] (DLA)
Cab & Ell .... Cababe and Ellis' Queen's Bench Reports [1882-85] [England] [A publication] (DLA)
CAB-ATM .... Civil Aeronautics Board Air Transport Mobilization Standby Order
CaBB........... Burnaby Public Library, Burnaby, BC, Canada [Library symbol Library of Congress] (LCLS)
CABB .... Captured Air Bubble Boat [Navy]
CABB .... Citizens' Advice Bureau, Brisbane [Australia]
CaBBA .... Burnaby Art Gallery, Burnaby, BC, Canada [Library symbol Library of Congress] (LCLS)
CaBBBCM .... British Columbia Microelectronics, Burnaby, BC, Canada [Library symbol] [Library of Congress] (LCLS)
CaBBCJC .... Church of Jesus Christ of Latter-Day Saints, Genealogical Society Library, Vancouver Branch, Stake Center, Vancouver, BC, Canada [Library symbol Library of Congress] (LCLS)
CaBBCM ...... Bella Coola Museum, Bella Coola, BC, Canada [Library symbol] [Library of Congress] (LCLS)
CaBBCRN.... Registered Nurses Association of British Columbia, Kootenay District Nursing Archives, Blueberry Creek, BC, Canada [Library symbol] [Library of Congress] (LCLS)
CaBBIT........ British Columbia Institute of Technology, Burnaby, BC, Canada [Library symbol Library of Congress] (LCLS)
CaBBK .... Burnaby Public Library, Kingsway Branch, Kingsway, BC, Canada [Library symbol] [Library of Congress] (LCLS)
CaBBL......... Lenkurt Electric Co., Burnaby, BC, Canada [Library symbol Library of Congress] (LCLS)
CaBBLA....... British Columbia Library Services Branch, Audiobook Service to the Handicapped, Burnaby, BC, Canada [Library symbol] [Library of Congress] (LCLS)
CaBBLM...... Lakes District Museum, Burns Lake, BC, Canada [Library symbol] [Library of Congress] (LCLS)
CaBBPM...... Bralorne Pioneer Museum, Bralorne, BC, Canada [Library symbol] [Library of Congress] (LCLS)
CaBBPVI..... Pacific Vocational Institute, Burnaby, BC, Canada [Library symbol Library of Congress] (LCLS)
CaBBT......... British Columbia Telephone Co., Burnaby, BC, Canada [Library symbol Library of Congress] (LCLS)
CaBBUC....... British Columbia Union Catalogue, Burnaby, BC, Canada [Library symbol Library of Congress] (LCLS)
CABC .... Canada-Arab Business Council (AC)
CABC .... Canadian Amenian Business Council Inc. [Conseil Commercial Canadien-Armenien Inc.] (AC)
CaBC........... Caribbean Broadcasting Corp.
CaBCDVM .... Doukhobor Village Museum, Castlegar, BC, Canada [Library symbol] [Library of Congress] (LCLS)
CaBCFVA...... Fraser Valley Antique Farm Machinery Association, Cleabrook, BC, Canada [Library symbol] [Library of Congress] (LCLS)
CaBCh......... Chilliwack Public Library, Chilliwack, BC, Canada [Library symbol Library of Congress] (LCLS)
CaBCIF....... Fraser Valley College, Clearbrook, BC, Canada [Library symbol Library of Congress] (LCLS)
CaBCLM...... Clinton Museum, Clinton, BC, Canada [Library symbol] [Library of Congress] (LCLS)
CaBCoM...... Courtenay and District Museum, Courtenay, BC, Canada [Library symbol Library of Congress] (LCLS)
CaBComN.... North Island College, Comox, BC, Canada [Library symbol Library of Congress] (LCLS)
CaBCrEK .... East Kootenay Community College, Cranbrook, BC, Canada [Library symbol Library of Congress] (LCLS)
CaBCS .... Selkirk College, Castlegar, BC, Canada [Library symbol Library of Congress] (LCLS)

CABD .... Computer-Aided Building Design (PDAA)
CaBDC .... Dawson Creek Public Library, Dawson Creek, BC, Canada [Library symbol Library of Congress] (LCLS)
CaBDCL ...... Library Advisory Council, Dawson Creek, BC, Canada [Library symbol Library of Congress] (LCLS)
CaBDCNL.... Northern Lights College, Dawson Creek, BC, Canada [Library symbol Library of Congress] (LCLS)
CaBDCWW.. Walter Wright Pioneer Village, Dawson Creek, BC, Canada [Library symbol] [Library of Congress] (LCLS)
CaBDEAF ..... American Foundrymen's Society Archives and Museum, British Columbia Chapter, Delta, BC, Canada [Library symbol] [Library of Congress] (LCLS)
CaBDeCW .... Environment Canada, Pacific and Yukon Region Canadian Wildlife Service, Delta, BC, Canada [Library symbol] [Library of Congress] (LCLS)
CaBDEOA ..... British Columbia Orchard Archives Society, Delta, BC, Canada [Library symbol] [Library of Congress] (LCLS)
CABDS .... Computer-Aided Building-Design System [Computer science]
CaBDUCVM... Cowichan Valley Museum, Duncan, BC, Canada [Library symbol Library of Congress] (LCLS)
CaBDUFM .... British Columbia Forest Museum, Duncan, BC, Canada [Library symbol] [Library of Congress] (LCLS)
CABE........... California Association for Bilingual Education (SRA)
CABE........... Canadian Alliance of Black Educators [See also ACEN]
CABE........... Canadian Association for Business Economics
CABE........... Christian Association of Business Executives [British]
CABE........... Coalition Against Black Exploitation (EA)
CABE........... Companion of the Association of Business Executives [British] (DBQ)
CABE........... Computers and Adult Basic Education [Liverpool Institute of Higher Education] [British] (AIE)
CABE........... Connecticut Association of Boards of Education (SRA)
CaBEC......... Crease Clinic Library, Essondale, BC, Canada [Library symbol Library of Congress] (LCLS)
CABEI......... Central American Bank for Economic Integration
Cabeltel...... Cabletel Communications Corp. [Associated Press] (SAG)
CaBEM........ Enderby and District Museum, Enderby, BC, Canada [Library symbol] [Library of Congress] (LCLS)
CaBEPN ...... Canada Department of National Defence, Defence Research Establishment, Esquimalt, BC, Canada [Library symbol Library of Congress] (LCLS)
CABFAA ...... Coach and Bus First Aid Association [British] (DBA)
CAB file ...... Cabinet File (CDE)
CaBFLFMM... British Columbia Farm Machinery Museum, Fort Langley, BC, Canada [Library symbol] [Library of Congress] (LCLS)
CaBFIPC ...... Parks Canada, Fort Langley National Historic Park, BC, Canada [Library symbol] [Library of Congress] (LCLS)
CABFM .... Canadian Association for Business Forms Management
CaBFM........ Fernie Museum, Fernie, BC, Canada [Library symbol] [Library of Congress] (LCLS)
CaBFSJA...... Fort St. James Public Library, Fort St. James, BC, Canada [Library symbol] [Library of Congress] (LCLS)
CaBFSJHS ... Fort St. James National Historic Site, Fort St. James, BC, Canada [Library symbol] [Library of Congress] (LCLS)
CABFSPHP... Fort Steele Provincial Historic Park, Fort Steele, BC, Canada [Library symbol] [Library of Congress] (LCLS)
CABG .... Coronary Artery Bypass Graft [Medicine]
CaBGFBM .... Boundary Museum, Grand Forks, BC, Canada [Library symbol] [Library of Congress] (LCLS)
CaBGIPM .... Ephinstone Pioneer Museum, Gibsons, BC, Canada [Library symbol] [Library of Congress] (LCLS)
CaBGM .... Greenwood Museum, Greenwood, BC, Canada [Library symbol] [Library of Congress] (LCLS)
CaBGRM...... Groundbirch Museum, Groundbirch, BC, Canada [Library symbol] [Library of Congress] (LCLS)
CaBGRNS .... Nootka Sound Historical Society, Gold River, BC, Canada [Library symbol] [Library of Congress] (LCLS)
CABGS .... Coronary Artery Bypass Graft Surgery [Medicine]
CaBGS .... Gulf Islands Secondary School, Ganges, BC, Canada [Library symbol Library of Congress] (LCLS)
CaBGSI .... Saltspring Island Public Library, Mary Hawkins Memorial Library, Ganges, BC, Canada [Library symbol] [Library of Congress] (LCLS)
CAB(H)........ Combined Arms Battalions (Heavy) [Army]
CaBH .... Houston Public Library, Houston, BC, Canada [Library symbol Library of Congress] (LCLS)
CaBHA .... Hazelton Public Library, Hazelton, BC, Canada [Library symbol] [Library of Congress] (LCLS)
CaBHKIM .... Ksan Indian Village and Museum, Haselton, BC, Canada [Library symbol] [Library of Congress] (LCLS)
CaBI............ Calcium Bone Index [Medicine] (DAVI)
CABI............ Calif Bancshares [NASDAQ symbol] (TTSB)
CABI............ California Bancshares, Inc. [NASDAQ symbol] (SAG)
CABI............ Commonwealth Agricultural Bureaux International [Research center British] (IRC)
Cab Int........ Cababe. Interpleader and Attachment of Debts [1900] [A publication] (ILCA)
CABIOS........ Computer Applications in the Biosciences [A publication]
CABK .... Capital Bancorp [NASDAQ symbol] (SPSG)
CaBK .... Kamloops Public Library, Kamloops, BC, Canada [Library symbol Library of Congress] (LCLS)
CaBKAg....... Canada Department of Agriculture, Research Station, Kamloops, BC, Canada [Library symbol Library of Congress] (LCLS)
CaBKAS .... ALCAN Smelters Chemical Ltd., Technical Library, Kitimat, BC, Canada [Library symbol Library of Congress] (LCLS)

CaBKASL ..... Kaslo Public Library, Kaslo, BC, Canada [*Library symbol*] [*Library of Congress*] (LCLS)

CaBKCC .... Cariboo College, Kamloops, BC, Canada [*Library symbol Library of Congress*] (LCLS)

CaBKCT .... Cariboo-Thompson Nicola Library System, Kamloops, BC, Canada [*Library symbol Library of Congress*] (LCLS)

CaBKEM ...... Keremeos Museum, Keremeos, BC, Canada [*Library symbol*] [*Library of Congress*] (LCLS)

CaBKESVM .. Similkameen Valley Museum, Keremeos, BC, Canada [*Library symbol*] [*Library of Congress*] (LCLS)

CaBKIHM ..... Kimberley and District Heritage Museum, Kimberley, BC, Canada [*Library symbol*] [*Library of Congress*] (LCLS)

CaBKIT .... Kitimat Public Library, Kitimat, BC, Canada [*Library symbol*] [*Library of Congress*] (LCLS)

CaBKKA ...... Diocese of Kootenay Archives, Kelowna, BC, Canada [*Library symbol*] [*Library of Congress*] (LCLS)

CaBKM .... Kamloops Museum, Kamloops, BC, Canada [*Library symbol Library of Congress*] (LCLS)

CaBKNW ...... B.C. Native Women's Society, Kamloops, BC, Canada [*Library symbol*] [*Library of Congress*] (LCLS)

CaBKO .... Okanagan Regional Library, Kelowna, BC, Canada [*Library symbol Library of Congress*] (LCLS)

CaBKOC .... Okanagan College, Kelowna, BC, Canada [*Library symbol Library of Congress*] (LCLS)

CaBKOM ..... Kelowna Centennial Museum and Archives, Kelowna, BC, Canada [*Library symbol Library of Congress*] (LCLS)

CaBKRM ..... Kettle Valley Railway Museum, Kelowna, BC, Canada [*Library symbol*] [*Library of Congress*] (LCLS)

CABKZ .... Capital Bancorp $2 Dep'C'Pfd [*NASDAQ symbol*] (TTSB)

CABL .... Cable

CABL .... Citizens Against Bad Law (AC)

CAB(L) .... Combined Arms Battalions (Light) [*Army*]

CABL .... Communication Cable, Inc. [*NASDAQ symbol*] (NQ)

CABL .... Consolidation above Battalion Level [*Army*] (RDA)

CABL .... Contemporary American Business Leaders [*A publication*]

Cab Lawy .... Cabinet Lawyer, by John Wade [*England*] [*A publication*] (DLA)

CABLE .... Cardington Atmospheric Boundary Layer Experiment (PDAA)

CABLE .... Collaborative Atmospheric Boundary Layer Experiment (PDAA)

CABLE .... Computer Associates Basic Language Extended [*Computer Associates International, Inc.*] (PCM)

CABLE .... Consolidation of Administration at Battalion Level [*Army*]

CableCo .... Cable & Co. Worldwide, Inc. [*Associated Press*] (SAG)

Cabletel ...... Cabletel Communications Corp. [*Associated Press*] (SAG)

CaBLIHS ...... Lasqueti Island Historical Society, Hawkshaw Ranch, Hawkshaw, BC, Canada [*Library symbol*] [*Library of Congress*] (LCLS)

CaBLIM .... Lillooet Museum, Lillooet, BC, Canada [*Library symbol*] [*Library of Congress*] (LCLS)

CABLIS .... Current Awareness Bulletin for Librarians and Information Scientists [*British*] [*A publication*] (NITA)

Cablmax ...... CableMaxx Holdings, Inc. [*Associated Press*] (SAG)

Cabltrn .... Cabletron Systems, Inc. [*Associated Press*] (SAG)

CaBLTW .... Trinity Western College, Langley, BC, Canada [*Library symbol Library of Congress*] (LCLS)

Cablvsn .... CableVision Systems Corp. [*Associated Press*] (SAG)

CablWire ...... Cable & Wireless Ltd. [*Associated Press*] (SAG)

CABM .... Center for Advanced Biotechnology and Medicine [*Rutgers University*] [*Research center*] (RCD)

C-ABM .... Chinese-Oriented Antiballistic Missile System (AABC)

CABMA .... Canadian Association of British Manufacturers and Agencies

CABMA .... College Athletic Business Management Association (EA)

CaBMIM .... Mayne Island Museum, Mayne Island, BC, Canada [*Library symbol*] [*Library of Congress*] (LCLS)

CABMKR ...... Cabinetmaker

CaBMKRM ... Kettle River Museum, Midway, BC, Canada [*Library symbol*] [*Library of Congress*] (LCLS)

CaBMRM ..... Maple Ridge Museum, Maple Ridge, BC, Canada [*Library symbol*] [*Library of Congress*] (LCLS)

CaBMrP .... Pacific Vocational Institute, Maple Ridge, BC, Canada [*Library symbol Library of Congress*] (LCLS)

CABMV .... Cowpea Aphid-Borne Mosaic Virus [*Plant pathology*]

CABN .... Cabinet Card (VRA)

CABN .... Canadian Association of Burn Nurses (AC)

CaBNA .... Nakusp Public Library, Nakusp, BC, Canada [*Library symbol*] [*Library of Congress*] (LCLS)

CaBNAKM ... Nakusp Museum, Nakusp, BC, Canada [*Library symbol*] [*Library of Congress*] (LCLS)

CaBNAM ..... Naramata Museum, Naramata, BC, Canada [*Library symbol*] [*Library of Congress*] (LCLS)

CaBNaMBL ... MacMillan Bloedel Ltd., Nanaimo, BC, Canada [*Library symbol Library of Congress*] (LCLS)

CaBNCM ...... Nanaimo Centennial Museum, Nanaimo, BC, Canada [*Library symbol*] [*Library of Congress*] (LCLS)

CaBNEM ...... Nelson Museum, Nelson, BC, Canada [*Library symbol*] [*Library of Congress*] (LCLS)

CaBNM .... Malaspina College, Nanaimo, BC, Canada [*Library symbol Library of Congress*] (LCLS)

CaBNND ...... David Thompson University Centre [*Formerly, Notre Dame University of Nelson*], Nelson, BC, Canada [*Library symbol Library of Congress*] (LCLS)

CaBNP .... Canada Department of the Environment, Fisheries and Marine Service, Research and Development Directorate, Pacific Biological Station, Nanaimo, BC, Canada [*Library symbol Library of Congress*] (LCLS)

CaBNSV .... Selkirk College, Vocational Division, Nelson, BC, Canada [*Library symbol Library of Congress*] (LCLS)

CaBNT .... Cabinet

CaBNv .... North Vancouver City Library, North Vancouver, BC, Canada [*Library symbol Library of Congress*] (LCLS)

CaBNvBR .... Ballard Research, Inc., North Vancouver, BC, Canada [*Library symbol Library of Congress*] (LCLS)

CaBNvD .... District of North Vancouver Library, North Vancouver, BC, Canada [*Library symbol Library of Congress*] (LCLS)

CaBNVI .... Vancouver Island Regional Library, Nanaimo, BC, Canada [*Library symbol Library of Congress*] (LCLS)

CaBNvPM ... Pacific Marine Training Institute, North Vancouver, BC, Canada [*Library symbol Library of Congress*] (LCLS)

CaBNvSL ..... Special Libraries Cataloguing, Inc., North Vancouver, BC, Canada [*Library symbol*] [*Library of Congress*] (LCLS)

CaBNW .... New Westminster Public Library, New Westminster, BC, Canada [*Library symbol Library of Congress*] (LCLS)

CaBNWB ..... British Columbia Library, New Westminster, BC, Canada [*Library symbol Library of Congress*] (LCLS)

CaBNWCR ... CanOcean Resources Ltd., New Westminster, BC, Canada [*Library symbol Library of Congress*] (LCLS)

CaBNWD ..... Douglas College, New Westminster, BC, Canada [*Library symbol Library of Congress*] (LCLS)

CaBNWHC ... New Westminster Historic Centre and Museum, New Westminster, BC, Canada [*Library symbol Library of Congress*] (LCLS)

CaBNWL ...... Lower Mainland Regional Planning Board, New Westminster, BC, Canada [*Library symbol Library of Congress*] (LCLS)

CaBNWLP .... Lockhead Petroleum Services Ltd., New Westminster, BC, Canada [*Library symbol Library of Congress*] (LCLS)

CaBNWRC ... Royal Columbian Hospital, New Westminster, BC, Canada [*Library symbol Library of Congress*] (LCLS)

cabo .... Cabochon (VRA)

CABO .... Canadian Association of Basketball Officials

CABO .... Cisplatin, Methotrexate, Bleomycin, Oncovin (Vincristine) [*Antineoplastic drug regimen*]

CABO .... Council of American Building Officials (EA)

CaBOM .... Osoyoos Museum, Osoyoos, BC, Canada [*Library symbol*] [*Library of Congress*] (LCLS)

CABOP .... Cyclophosphamide, Adriamycin, Bleomycin, Oncovin [*Vincristine*], Prednisone [*Antineoplastic drug regimen*]

CABOS .... Carbon Absorption Bio-oxidation System (PDAA)

Cabot .... Cabot Corp. [*Associated Press*] (SAG)

CABOWV ..... Captured Air Bubble Over Water Vehicle [*Military*] (IAA)

CaBP .... Calcium Binding Protein [*Biochemistry*]

CABP .... Cameron Ashley Bldg Prod [*NASDAQ symbol*] (TTSB)

CABP .... Cameron Ashley Building Products, Inc. [*NASDAQ symbol*] (SAG)

CABP .... Campaign Against Book Piracy [*British*] (NITA)

CABP .... Carboxyarabitol Bisphosphate [*Biochemistry*]

CABP .... Conjugate Acid-Base Pair [*Chemistry*]

CaBP .... Penticton Public Library, Penticton, BC, Canada [*Library symbol Library of Congress*] (LCLS)

CaBPaM ...... Alberni Valley Museum, Port Alberni, BC, Canada [*Library symbol Library of Congress*] (LCLS)

CaBPc .... Port Coquitlam Public Library, Port Coquitlam, BC, Canada [*Library symbol Library of Congress*] (LCLS)

CaBPcI .... ISI Infosearch, Port Coquitlam, BC, Canada [*Library symbol*] [*Library of Congress*] (LCLS)

CaBPcRH ..... Riverview Hospital, Port Coquitlam, BC, Canada [*Library symbol Library of Congress*] (LCLS)

CaBPEM ...... Peachland Museum, Peachland, BC, Canada [*Library symbol*] [*Library of Congress*] (LCLS)

CaBPEMM ... Pemberton Museum, Pemberton, BC, Canada [*Library symbol*] [*Library of Congress*] (LCLS)

CaBPG .... Prince George Public Library, Prince George, BC, Canada [*Library symbol Library of Congress*] (LCLS)

CaBPGC .... College of New Caledonia, Prince George, BC, Canada [*Library symbol Library of Congress*] (LCLS)

CaBPGRM .... Fraser Fort George Regional Museum, Prince George, BC, Canada [*Library symbol*] [*Library of Congress*] (LCLS)

CaBPM .... Penticton Museum and Archives, Penticton, BC, Canada [*Library symbol Library of Congress*] (LCLS)

CaBPMM ...... Port Moody Station Museum, Port Moody, BC, Canada [*Library symbol*] [*Library of Congress*] (LCLS)

CaBPmP ...... Port Moody Public Library, Port Moody, BC, Canada [*Library symbol Library of Congress*] (LCLS)

CaBPO .... Dominion Radio Astrophysical Observatory, Penticton, BC, Canada [*Library symbol Library of Congress*] (LCLS)

CaBPOC ...... Pouce Coupe Public Library, Pouce Coupe, BC, Canada [*Library symbol*] [*Library of Congress*] (LCLS)

CaBPorH ..... Powell River Historical Museum, Powell River, BC, Canada [*Library symbol Library of Congress*] (LCLS)

CABPP .... Commission for Acceleration of Black Participation in Psychology

CaBPR .... Prince Rupert Public Library, Prince Rupert, BC, Canada [*Library symbol Library of Congress*] (LCLS)

CaBPRACS ... Anglican Church of Canada, Diocese of Caledonia, Synod Office, Victoria, BC, Canada [*Library symbol Library of Congress*] (LCLS)

CaBPrD .... Powell River District Libraries, Powell, BC, Canada [*Library symbol Library of Congress*] (LCLS)

CaBPrDP ..... Powell River District Public Library, Powell River, BC, Canada [*Library symbol*] [*Library of Congress*] (LCLS)

CaBQM .... Quesnel and District Museum, Quesnel, BC, Canada [*Library symbol*] [*Library of Congress*] (LCLS)

CABR .... Cabre Corp. [*NASDAQ symbol*] (SAG)

CABR .... Cabrillo National Monument

CABR .... Children's Adaptive Behavior Report [*Child development test*] [*Psychology*]

CABRA .... Copper and Brass Research Association [*Later, CDA*]

CaBraDE ...... Dollman Electronics Ltd., Brampton, ON, Canada [*Library symbol Library of Congress*] (LCLS)

CaBRC .... Royal Roads Military College, Royal Roads, BC, Canada [*Library symbol Library of Congress*] (LCLS)

Cabre .... Cabre Corp. [*Associated Press*] (SAG)

CaBRi .... Richmond Public Library, Richmond, BC, Canada [*Library symbol Library of Congress*] (LCLS)

CaBRi .... Richmond Public Library, Richmond, BC, Canada [*Library symbol*] [*Library of Congress*] (LCLS)

CaBRM .... Rossland Historical Museum, Rossland, BC, Canada [*Library symbol Library of Congress*] (LCLS)

CaBRRPC ..... Rogers Pass Centre, Revelstoke, BC, Canada [*Library symbol*] [*Library of Congress*] (LCLS)

CABS .... Carrier Access Billing System [*Telecommunications*] (ACRL)

CABS .... CCNU [*Lomustine*], Adriamycin, Bleomycin, Streptozotocin [*Antineoplastic drug regimen*]

CABS .... Center for the Applied Behavioral Sciences [*St. Louis University*] [*Research center*] (RCD)

CABS .... Children's Assertiveness Behavior Scale

CABS .... Command Automated Budget System [*Army*]

CABS .... Computer-Aided Batch Scheduling

CABS .... Computer Aided Batch Searching (NITA)

CABS .... Computer-Assisted Bibliographic Service [*University of South Dakota*] (OLDSS)

CABS .... Computer-Augmented Block System (MHDB)

CABS .... Computerized Annotated Bibliography System [*Alberta University*] [*Canada*]

CABS .... Conservation Association of Botanical Societies (DBA)

CABS .... Consolidated Ammunition Bulk Shippers (MCD)

CABS .... Consortium for the Advancement of Building Sciences [*Pennsylvania State University*] [*Research center*] (RCD)

CABS .... Contemporary Authors Bibliographical Series [*A publication*]

CABS .... Coronary Artery Bypass Surgery [*Medicine*]

CABS .... Current Awareness in Biological Sciences [*Pergamon Press*] [*Information service or system*] (IID)

CaBS .... Smithers Public Library, Smithers, BC, Canada [*Library symbol*] [*Library of Congress*] (LCLS)

CaBSAAM .... Salmon Arm Museum and Heritage Association, Salmon Arm, BC, Canada [*Library symbol*] [*Library of Congress*] (LCLS)

CABSADS ..... Computerized, Automated, Bus Spacing and Dispatching System

CaBSAg .... Canada Department of Agriculture, Research Station, Saanichton, BC, Canada [*Library symbol Library of Congress*] (LCLS)

CaBSH .... British Columbia Hydro and Power Authority, Surrey, BC, Canada [*Library symbol Library of Congress*] (LCLS)

CaBSIOS ...... Canada Department of Fisheries and Oceans, Institute of Ocean Studies, Sidney, BC, Canada [*Library symbol Library of Congress*] (LCLS)

CaBSKC .... Kwantlen College, Surrey, BC, Canada [*Library symbol Library of Congress*] (LCLS)

CaBSLHS ..... Shawinigan Lake Historical Society, Shawinigan, BC, Canada [*Library symbol*] [*Library of Congress*] (LCLS)

CaBSOM ...... Sointula Museum, Sointula, BC, Canada [*Library symbol*] [*Library of Congress*] (LCLS)

CaBSPSM ... Saanich Pioneer Society Museum, Saanichton, BC, Canada [*Library symbol*] [*Library of Congress*] (LCLS)

CaBSS .... School District 88, Skeena-Terrace, BC, Canada [*Library symbol Library of Congress*] (LCLS)

CaBSuAg ...... Canada Department of Agriculture, Research Station, Summerland, BC, Canada [*Library symbol Library of Congress*] (LCLS)

CaBSur .... Surrey Public Library, Surrey, BC, Canada [*Library symbol*] [*Library of Congress*] (LCLS)

CABSUS ...... Committee of Atomic Bomb Survivors in the US (EA)

CABT .... Cabinet

CABT .... Cesium Atomic Beam Tube (IAA)

CaBTC .... Consolidated Mining & Smelting Co., Central Technical Library, Trail, BC, Canada [*Library symbol Library of Congress*] (LCLS)

CaBTeNW .... North West College, Terrace, BC, Canada [*Library symbol Library of Congress*] (LCLS)

CaBTM .... Trail Museum, Trail, BC, Canada [*Library symbol*] [*Library of Congress*] (LCLS)

CaBTOMM ... West Coast Maritime Museum, Tofino, BC, Canada [*Library symbol*] [*Library of Congress*] (LCLS)

CABV .... Canadian Association of Business Valuators

CaBV .... Vernon Library, Vernon, BC, Canada [*Library symbol Library of Congress*] (LCLS)

CaBVa .... Vancouver Public Library, Vancouver, BC, Canada [*Library symbol Library of Congress*] (LCLS)

CaBVaA .... Vancouver City Archives, Vancouver, BC, Canada [*Library symbol Library of Congress*] (LCLS)

CaBVaABS ... Anglican Church of Canada, Ecclesiastical Province of British Columbia, Vancouver, BC, Canada [*Library symbol*] [*Library of Congress*] (LCLS)

CaBVaABSA ... Anglican Church of Canada, British Columbia Provincial Synod, Archives, Vancouver, BC, Canada [*Library symbol Library of Congress*] (LCLS)

CaBVaADP ... Alcohol and Drug Programs, Vancouver, BC, Canada [*Library symbol Library of Congress*] (LCLS)

CaBVaAE ...... Associated Engineering Services Ltd., Vancouver, BC, Canada [*Library symbol Library of Congress*] (LCLS)

CaBVaAg ...... Canada Department of Agriculture, Entomological Society of British Columbia Library, Vancouver, BC, Canada [*Library symbol Library of Congress*] (LCLS)

CaBVaAP ..... Asia Pacific Foundation of Canada, Information Services, Vancouver, BC, Canada [*Library symbol*] [*Library of Congress*] (LCLS)

CaBVaBCR ... British Columbia Rail, Corporate Information, Vancouver, BC, Canada [*Library symbol*] [*Library of Congress*] (LCLS)

CaBVaBS ..... Brown Strachan Associates, Vancouver, BC, Canada [*Library symbol*] [*Library of Congress*] (LCLS)

CaBVaBT ..... British Columbia Telephone Co., Vancouver, BC, Canada [*Library symbol Library of Congress*] (LCLS)

CaBVaBY ..... British Columbia and Yukon Chamber of Mines, Vancouver, BC, Canada [*Library symbol Library of Congress*] (LCLS)

CaBVaC .... Capilano College, Vancouver, BC, Canada [*Library symbol Library of Congress*] (LCLS)

CaBVaCAA ... Catholic Church, Archdiocese of Vancouver, Archives, Vancouver, BC, Canada [*Library symbol Library of Congress*] (LCLS)

CaBVaCBA ... CBA Engineering Ltd., Vancouver, BC, Canada [*Library symbol Library of Congress*] (LCLS)

CaBVaCBV ... Canadian Broadcasting Corp., VTR Library, Vancouver, BC, Canada [*Library symbol*] [*Library of Congress*] (LCLS)

CaBVaCCU ... BC Central Credit Union, Vancouver, BC, Canada [*Library symbol Library of Congress*] (LCLS)

CaBVaCF ...... Council of Forest Industries of British Columbia, Vancouver, BC, Canada [*Library symbol Library of Congress*] (LCLS)

CaBVaCI ...... Chemetics International Ltd., Vancouver, BC, Canada [*Library symbol Library of Congress*] (LCLS)

CaBVaCM ..... Centennial Museum, Vancouver, BC, Canada [*Library symbol Library of Congress*] (LCLS)

CaBVaCOM ... Cominco Ltd., Vancouver, BC, Canada [*Library symbol Library of Congress*] (LCLS)

CaBVaEAE ... Environment Canada, Atmospheric Environment Service, Vancouver, BC, Canada [*Library symbol*] [*Library of Congress*] (LCLS)

CaBVaEC ...... British Columbia Energy Commission, Vancouver, BC, Canada [*Library symbol Library of Congress*] (LCLS)

CaBVaEN ...... Envirocon Ltd., Vancouver, BC, Canada [*Library symbol Library of Congress*] (LCLS)

CaBVaEP ...... Canada Department of the Environment, Environmental Protection Service, Vancouver, BC, Canada [*Library symbol Library of Congress*] (LCLS)

CaBVaF .... Canada Department of the Environment, Fisheries and Marine Service, Research andDevelopment Directorate, Vancouver Laboratory, Vancouver, BC, Canada [*Library symbol Library of Congress*] (LCLS)

CaBVaFA ...... Vancouver Public Library, Fine Arts, Music, and Films Division, Vancouver, BC, Canada [*Library symbol Library of Congress*] (LCLS)

CaBVaFi ...... Canada Department of Fisheries and Oceans, Vancouver, BC, Canada [*Library symbol Library of Congress*] (LCLS)

CaBVaFP ...... Canada Department of the Environment, Forest Products Laboratory, Vancouver, BC,Canada [*Library symbol Library of Congress*] (LCLS)

CaBVaFV ...... Farris, Vaughan, Wills & Murphy Law Firm, Vancouver, BC, Canada [*Library symbol Library of Congress*] (LCLS)

CaBVaG .... Canada Geological Survey, Vancouver, BC, Canada [*Library symbol Library of Congress*] (LCLS)

CaBVaGB ..... Golder, Brawner & Associates Ltd., Vancouver, BC, Canada [*Library symbol Library of Congress*] (LCLS)

CaBVaH .... British Columbia Hydro and Power Authority [*Formerly, British Columbia Electric C o. Ltd.*], Vancouver, BC, Canada [*Library symbol Library of Congress*] (LCLS)

CaBVaHD ..... Vancouver Health Department, Vancouver, BC, Canada [*Library symbol*] [*Library of Congress*] (LCLS)

CaBVaHE ..... British Columbia Hydro Engineering Library, Vancouver, BC, Canada [*Library symbol Library of Congress*] (LCLS)

CaBVaHP ..... Vancouver Public Library, Historic Photographic Collection, Vancouver, BC, Canada [*Library symbol Library of Congress*] (LCLS)

CaBVaHS ..... H. A. Simons Ltd., Vancouver, BC, Canada [*Library symbol Library of Congress*] (LCLS)

CaBVaI .... International North Pacific Fisheries, Vancouver, BC, Canada [*Library symbol Library of Congress*] (LCLS)

CaBVaIB ...... IBIS Information & Research Services, Vancouver, BC, Canada [*Library symbol*] [*Library of Congress*] (LCLS)

CaBVaINA .... Indian and Northern Affairs, B.C. Region, Resource Center Information Services, Vancouver, BC, Canada [*Library symbol*] [*Library of Congress*] (LCLS)

CaBVaJ .... Canada Department of Justice, Vancouver, BC, Canada [*Library symbol Library of Congress*] (LCLS)

CaBVaJH ...... Jewish Historical Society, Vancouver, BC, Canada [*Library symbol*] [*Library of Congress*] (LCLS)

CaBVaJI ...... Justice Institute of British Columbia, Vancouver, BC, Canada [*Library symbol Library of Congress*] (LCLS)

CaBVAJR .... Jewish Resource Centre, Vancouver, BC, Canada [*Library symbol Library of Congress*] (LCLS)

CaBVaL .... Law Society of British Columbia, Vancouver, BC, Canada [*Library symbol Library of Congress*] (LCLS)

CaBVaLMW ... L. M. Warren, Inc., Vancouver, BC, Canada [*Library symbol Library of Congress*] (LCLS)

CaBVaM .... British Columbia Medical Library Service, Vancouver, BC, Canada [*Library symbol Library of Congress*] (LCLS)

CaBVaMB .... MacMillan Bloedel Research Ltd., Vancouver, BC, Canada [*Library symbol Library of Congress*] (LCLS)

CaBVaMBL ... MacMillan Bloedel Research Ltd., Vancouver, BC, Canada [*Library symbol Library of Congress*] (LCLS)

CaBVaME ..... McElhanney Engineering, Vancouver, BC, Canada [*Library symbol*] [*Library of Congress*] (LCLS)

CaBVaMI ...... Canada Employment and Immigration Department, Vancouver, BC, Canada [*Library symbol Library of Congress*] (LCLS)

CaBVaMM....   Maritime Museum, Vancouver, BC, Canada [*Library symbol Library of Congress*] (LCLS)

CaBVaMOE...   Mobil Oil Estates Ltd., Vancouver, BC, Canada [*Library symbol Library of Congress*] (LCLS)

CaBVaMUM...   British Columbia Museum of Medicine, Vancouver, BC, Canada [*Library symbol*] [*Library of Congress*] (LCLS)

CaBVaNH.....   Canada Department of National Health and Welfare, Health Protection Branch, Vancouver, BC, Canada [*Library symbol Library of Congress*] (LCLS)

CaBVaNHC...   Vancouver Public Library, Northwest History Collection, Vancouver, BC, Canada [*Library symbol Library of Congress*] (LCLS)

CaBVAOCA...   Oblate Resource Center and Archives, Vancouver, BC, Canada [*Library symbol*] [*Library of Congress*] (LCLS)

CaBVaOL.....   Open Learning Institute, Richmond, BC, Canada [*Library symbol*] [*Library of Congress*] (LCLS)

CaBVaP........   Placer Development Library, Vancouver, BC, Canada [*Library symbol Library of Congress*] (LCLS)

CaBVaPAD...   British Columbia Packers Ltd., Product Assurance and Development, Vancouver, BC,Canada [*Library symbol Library of Congress*] (LCLS)

CaBVaPC.....   Phillips Cables Ltd., Vancouver, BC, Canada [*Library symbol Library of Congress*] (LCLS)

CaBVaPD.....   Greater Vancouver Regional District, Planning Development Library, Vancouver, BC, Canada [*Library symbol Library of Congress*] (LCLS)

CaBVaPE......   Canada Department of the Environment, Pacific Environment Institute, Vancouver, BC, Canada [*Library symbol Library of Congress*] (LCLS)

CaBVaPPC...   University of British Columbia, Pulp and Paper Centre, Vancouver, BC, Canada [*Library symbol*] [*Library of Congress*] (LCLS)

CaBVaPPR...   Pulp and Paper Research Institute of Canada, Vancouver Laboratory, Vancouver, BC, Canada [*Library symbol*] [*Library of Congress*] (LCLS)

CaBVaPVI....   Provincial Resource Centre for the Visually-Impaired, Vancouver, BC, Canada [*Library symbol*] [*Library of Congress*] (LCLS)

CaBVaPWP...   Public Works Canada, Pacific Region Library, Vancouver, BC, Canada [*Library symbol*] [*Library of Congress*] (LCLS)

CaBVaR.......   British Columbia Research Council, Vancouver, BC, Canada [*Library symbol Library of Congress*] (LCLS)

CaBVaRB....   Royal Bank of Canada, Vancouver, BC, Canada [*Library symbol Library of Congress*] (LCLS)

CaBVaRC.....   Rayonier Canada, Research Division, Vancouver, BC, Canada [*Library symbol Library of Congress Obsolete*] (LCLS)

CaBVaRE.....   Archives of the Ecclesiastical Province of British Columbia, Vancouver, BC, Canada [*Library symbol Library of Congress*] (LCLS)

CaBVaREC...   Regent College, Vancouver, BC, Canada [*Library symbol*] [*Library of Congress*] (LCLS)

CaBVaRN...   Registered Nurses Association, Vancouver, BC, Canada [*Library symbol Library of Congress*] (LCLS)

CaBVaS........   Simon Fraser University, Vancouver, BC, Canada [*Library symbol Library of Congress*] (LCLS)

CaBVaSC.....   Sandwell & Co., Vancouver, BC, Canada [*Library symbol Library of Congress*] (LCLS)

CaBVaSG.....   Simon Fraser University, Simon Fraser Gallery, Burnaby, BC, Canada [*Library symbol Library of Congress*] (LCLS)

CaBVaSLA ...   F. F. Slaney & Co. Ltd., Vancouver, BC, Canada [*Library symbol Library of Congress*] (LCLS)

CaBVaSM ....   Simon Fraser University, Map Library, Vancouver, BC, Canada [*Library symbol Library of Congress*] (LCLS)

CaBVaSPH ...   Saint Paul's Hospital, Health Sciences Library, Vancouver, BC, Canada [*Library symbol Library of Congress*] (LCLS)

CaBVaST.....   Vancouver School of Theology, Vancouver, BC, Canada [*Library symbol Library of Congress*] (LCLS)

CaBVaSW ....   Swan Wooster Engineering Co., Vancouver, BC, Canada [*Library symbol Library of Congress*] (LCLS)

CaBVaTE.....   Teck Mining Group Ltd., Elizabeth Watson Library, Vancouver, BC, Canada [*Library symbol Library of Congress*] (LCLS)

CaBVaTF......   British Columbia Teachers' Federation Resources Centre, Vancouver, BC, Canada [*Library symbol Library of Congress*] (LCLS)

CaBVaTPF....   Towers Perrin Forster & Crosby, Vancouver, BC, Canada [*Library symbol*] [*Library of Congress*] (LCLS)

CaBVaTR .....   Touche Ross & Co., Vancouver, BC, Canada [*Library symbol*] [*Library of Congress*] (LCLS)

CaBVaU ....   University of British Columbia, Vancouver, BC, Canada [*Library symbol Library of Congress*] (LCLS)

CaBVaUBCA...   United Church, British Columbia Conference, Archives, Vancouver, BC, Canada [*Library symbol Library of Congress*] (LCLS)

CaBVaUCC ...   University of British Columbia, Charles Crane Memorial Library, Vancouver, BC, Canada, [*Library symbol Library of Congress*] (LCLS)

CaBVaUG.....   University of British Columbia, Department of Geography, Vancouver, BC, Canada [*Library symbol Library of Congress*] (LCLS)

CaBVaUL .....   University of British Columbia, Law Library, Vancouver, BC, Canada [*Library symbol Library of Congress*] (LCLS)

CaBVaULS ...   University of British Columbia, School of Library, Archival, and Information Studies, Vancouver, BC, Canada [*Library symbol Library of Congress*] (LCLS)

CaBVaUM ....   University of British Columbia, Map Division, Vancouver, BC, Canada [*Library symbol Library of Congress*] (LCLS)

CaBVaUS .....   University of British Columbia, Special Collections Division, Vancouver, BC, Canada [*Library symbol Library of Congress*] (LCLS)

CaBVaUW ....   University of British Columbia, Woodward Library, Vancouver, BC, Canada [*Library symbol Library of Congress*] (LCLS)

CaBVaUWGV...   United Way of Greater Vancouver, Vancouver, BC, Canada [*Library symbol Library of Congress*] (LCLS)

CaBVaVA .....   Vancouver Art Gallery, Vancouver, BC, Canada [*Library symbol Library of Congress*] (LCLS)

CaBVaVCL ...   Vancouver City College, Langara, Vancouver, BC, Canada [*Library symbol Library of Congress*] (LCLS)

CaBVaVCLT...   Vancouver Community College, Library Technician Program, Vancouver, BC, Canada [*Library symbol*] [*Library of Congress*] (LCLS)

CaBVaVSA ...   Vancouver School of Art, Vancouver, BC, Canada [*Library symbol Library of Congress*] (LCLS)

CaBVaWC ...   Workers Compensation Board of British Columbia, Vancouver, BC, Canada [*Library symbol Library of Congress*] (LCLS)

CaBVaWH ...   Warnock Hersey International Ltd., Vancouver, BC, Canada [*Library symbol Library of Congress*] (LCLS)

CaBVaWT ...   West Coast Transmission Ltd., Vancouver, BC, Canada [*Library symbol Library of Congress*] (LCLS)

CaBVi..........   Greater Victoria Public Library, Victoria, BC, Canada [*Library symbol Library of Congress*] (LCLS)

CaBViA ....   Art Gallery of Greater Victoria, Victoria, BC, Canada [*Library symbol Library of Congress*] (LCLS)

CaBViAGC...   British Columbia Ministry of Attorney General, CLEU Library, Victoria, BC, Canada [*Library symbol Library of Congress*] (LCLS)

CaBViAGL...   British Columbia Ministry of the Attorney General, Law Library, Victoria, BC, Canada [*Library symbol*] [*Library of Congress*] (LCLS)

CaBViB ....   British Columbia Barkerville Restoration Advisory Committee, Victoria, BC, Canada [*Library symbol Library of Congress*] (LCLS)

CaBViBE ......   British Columbia Bureau of Economics and Statistics, Business-Finance Library, Victoria, BC, Canada [*Library symbol Library of Congress*] (LCLS)

CaBViC ....   Camosun College, Victoria, BC, Canada [*Library symbol Library of Congress*] (LCLS)

CaBViDE .....   British Columbia Ministry of Education, Victoria, BC, Canada [*Library symbol Library of Congress*] (LCLS)

CaBViED .....   British Columbia Ministry of Economic Development, Victoria, BC, Canada [*Library symbol Library of Congress*] (LCLS)

CaBViEM.....   Canada Department of the Environment, Institute of Ocean Sciences, Victoria, BC,Canada [*Library symbol Library of Congress*] (LCLS)

CaBViEP ......   British Columbia Ministry of the Environment, Environmental Protection, Pollution Control Branch, Victoria, BC, Canada [*Library symbol Library of Congress*] (LCLS)

CaBViEPR ....   British Columbia Ministry of Environment, Planning and Resource Management Division, Victoria, BC, Canada [*Library symbol*] [*Library of Congress*] (LCLS)

CaBViF........   Canada Department of the Environment, Forest Research Laboratory, Victoria, BC, Canada [*Library symbol Library of Congress*] (LCLS)

CaBViFS ......   British Columbia Forest Service, Victoria, BC, Canada [*Library symbol Library of Congress*] (LCLS)

CaBViH ....   British Columbia Ministry of Highways and Public Works, Victoria, BC, Canada [*Library symbol Library of Congress*] (LCLS)

CaBViHCR....   British Columbia Heritage Conservation, Branch Resource Information Centre, Victoria, BC, Canada [*Library symbol*] [*Library of Congress*] (LCLS)

CaBViHe .....   British Columbia Ministry of Health, Victoria, BC, Canada [*Library symbol Library of Congress*] (LCLS)

CaBViHI ......   British Columbia Ministry of Health, Health Information, Victoria, BC, Canada [*Library symbol Library of Congress*] (LCLS)

CaBViHPP...   British Columbia Ministry of Health, Health Promotion Programmes, Victoria, BC, Canada [*Library symbol Library of Congress*] (LCLS)

CaBViHRS....   British Columbia Ministry of Human Resources, Staff Development Division, Victoria, BC, Canada [*Library symbol Library of Congress*] (LCLS)

CaBViL........   Law Library Foundation, Victoria, BC, Canada [*Library symbol Library of Congress*] (LCLS)

CaBViLBP ...   Lester B. Pearson College of the Pacific, Victoria, BC, Canada [*Library symbol Library of Congress*] (LCLS)

CaBViLC ......   Public Library Commission, Victoria, BC, Canada [*Library symbol Library of Congress*] (LCLS)

CaBViLDC ...   Library Development Commission, Victoria, BC, Canada [*Library symbol Library of Congress*] (LCLS)

CaBViLFW ...   British Columbia Ministry of the Environment, Victoria, BC, Canada [*Library symbol Library of Congress*] (LCLS)

CaBViLPHP...   British Columbia Ministry of Lands, Parks, and Housing, Parks Library, Victoria,BC, Canada [*Library symbol Library of Congress*] (LCLS)

CaBViLSB ....   Ministry of the Provincial Secretary and Government Services, Library Services Branch, Victoria, BC, Canada [*Library symbol Library of Congress*] (LCLS)

CaBViM........   British Columbia Ministry of Mines and Petroleum Resources, Victoria, BC, Canada [*Library symbol Library of Congress*] (LCLS)

CaBViMH .....   University of Victoria, Maltwood Art Museum, Victoria, BC, Canada [*Library symbol Library of Congress*] (LCLS)

CaBViML.....   British Columbia Ministry of Labour, Victoria, BC, Canada [*Library symbol*] [*Library of Congress*] (LCLS)

CaBViMM ...   Maritime Museum of British Columbia, Victoria, BC, Canada [*Library symbol Library of Congress*] (LCLS)

CaBViO ....   Dominion Astrophysical Observatory, Victoria, BC, Canada [*Library symbol Library of Congress*] (LCLS)

CaBViP ....   Legislative Library, Victoria, BC, Canada [*Library symbol Library of Congress*] (LCLS)

CaBViPA ...... Provincial Archives, Victoria, BC, Canada [*Library symbol Library of Congress*] (LCLS)

CaBViPM ..... British Columbia Provincial Museum, Victoria, BC, Canada [*Library symbol*] [*Library of Congress*] (LCLS)

CaBViPME ... British Columbia Provincial Museum, Ethnology Division, Victoria, BC, Canada [*Library symbol Library of Congress*] (LCLS)

CaBViPR ..... Victoria Press Ltd., Victoria, BC, Canada [*Library symbol Library of Congress*] (LCLS)

CaBViRC ...... British Columbia Ministry of Recreation and Conservation, Fish and Game Branch, Victoria, BC, Canada [*Library symbol Library of Congress*] (LCLS)

CaBViT .... R. Thuber & Associates, Victoria, BC, Canada [*Library symbol Library of Congress*] (LCLS)

CaBViTRA .... Thalassa Research Associates, Victoria, BC, Canada [*Library symbol*] [*Library of Congress*] (LCLS)

CaBViUCN .... Union Catalogue of British Columbia's Newspapers, Victoria, BC, Canada [*Library symbol*] [*Library of Congress*] (LCLS)

CaBViV .... University of Victoria, Victoria, BC, Canada [*Library symbol Library of Congress*] (LCLS)

CaBViVA ...... University of Victoria, Department of History in Art, Victoria, BC, Canada [*Library symbol Library of Congress*] (LCLS)

CaBViVG ...... University of Victoria, Geography Department, Victoria, BC, Canada [*Library symbol Library of Congress*] (LCLS)

CaBViVL ..... University of Victoria, Law Library, Victoria, BC, Canada [*Library symbol Library of Congress*] (LCLS)

CaBVMA ..... Vernon Museum, Archives and Art Gallery, Vernon, BC, Canada [*Library symbol Library of Congress*] (LCLS)

CaBVOR ...... O'Keefe Ranch and Interior Heritage Society, Vernon, BC, Canada [*Library symbol*] [*Library of Congress*] (LCLS)

CABWA .... Copper and Brass Warehouse Association (PDAA)

CaBWEM ..... Westbank Museum, Westbank, BC, Canada [*Library symbol*] [*Library of Congress*] (LCLS)

CaBWLM ..... Williams Lake Museum, Williams Lake, BC, Canada [*Library symbol*] [*Library of Congress*] (LCLS)

CaBWM .... Wells Museum, Wells, BC, Canada [*Library symbol*] [*Library of Congress*] (LCLS)

CaBWv .... West Vancouver Memorial Library, West Vancouver, BC, Canada [*Library symbol Library of Congress*] (LCLS)

CaBWvHC .... Hatfield Consultants Ltd., West Vancouver, BC, Canada [*Library symbol Library of Congress*] (LCLS)

CABx .... Citizens' Advice Bureaux [*British*] (ILCA)

CAC .... Cable Access Cover

CAC .... Cacwhuacintle [*Race of maize*]

CAC .... Calama [*Chile*] [*Seismograph station code, US Geological Survey*] (SEIS)

CAC .... Calcium Aluminate Cement (PDAA)

CAC .... Calibration and Certification (IAA)

CAC .... Calibration and Checkout (IAA)

CAC .... California Association of Collectors (SRA)

CAC .... California Avocado Commission (EA)

CAC .... California State University and Colleges, Tape Profile, Long Beach, CA [*OCLC symbol*] (OCLC)

CAC .... Campaign Against Censorship [*British*] (DBA)

CAC .... Canada Art Council [*Conseil des Arts du Canada*]

CAC .... Canadian Airports Council [*Conseil des Aeroports du Canada*] (AC)

CAC .... Canadian-American Committee (EA)

CAC .... Canadian Armoured Corps

CAC .... Canadian Art Club, Toronto [*1907-15*] (NGC)

CAC .... Canaveral Administration Complex [*NASA*] (SAA)

CAC .... Caravan America-China [*Defunct*] (EA)

CAC .... Carbon Arc Cutting [*Welding*]

CAC .... Cardiac Accelerator Center [*Physiology*]

CAC .... Cardiac Arrest Code [*Medicine*]

CAC .... Career Assistance Counseling [*Air Force*] (AFM)

CAC .... Caribbean Air Command [*Air Force*]

CAC .... Cascadia Mines [*Vancouver Stock Exchange symbol*]

CAC .... Cascavel [*Brazil*] [*Airport symbol*] (OAG)

CAC .... Casino Advisory Committee [*Tasmania*] [*Australia*]

CAC .... Cathedrals Advisory Committee [*Church of England*]

CAC .... Catholic Anthropological Conference

CAC .... Cell Affinity Chromatography

CAC .... Center Accessory Compartment (MCD)

CAC .... Central Advisory Committee [*British*]

CAC .... Central Air Conditioning [*Classified advertising*]

CAC .... Central American Club of New York (EA)

CAC .... Central Arbitration Committee [*British*] (ILCA)

CAC .... Centre for Advancement of Counselling [*British*]

CAC .... Centre for Agricultural Commerce [*University of New England*] [*Australia*]

CAC .... Centre for the Analysis of Conflict [*Research center British*] (IRC)

CAC .... Cessna Aircraft Co.

CAC .... Cessna Airmaster Club (EA)

CAC .... Champion Aircraft Co.

CAC .... Change Administration Conference

CAC .... Change Analysis Commitment (SAA)

CAC .... Change to Approach Control (FAAC)

CAC .... Channel Amplitude Class [*Electrical engineering*]

CAC .... Charge-Air Cooling [*Automotive engineering*]

CAC .... Chase Aircraft Co.

CAC .... Chemical Abstracts Condensates [*A publication*] (IID)

CAC .... Chemical Addiction Certification (BARN)

CAC .... Chief Artillery Controller (NATG)

CAC .... Chief of Air Corps [*World War II*]

CAC .... Children's Advocacy Center (EA)

CAC .... Chlorinated Aromatic Compound [*Organic chemistry*]

CAC .... Chloroacetyl Chloride [*Organic chemistry*]

CAC .... Christian Action Council (EA)

CAC .... Cigarette Advertising Code, Inc. (EA)

CAC .... Circulating Anticoagulant [*Medicine*] (MEDA)

CAC .... Citizens Advocate Center [*Antipoverty organization*] [*Defunct*]

CAC .... Citrus Administrative Committee [*Florida*] (SRA)

CAC .... Civic Action Centers [*Military*] (CINC)

CAC .... Civil Administration Committee [*US Military Government, Germany*]

CAC .... Classical Association of Canada [*See also SCEC*]

CAC .... Classroom Adjustment Code

CAC .... Clear All Channels

CAC .... Clear and Add Clock (SAA)

CAC .... Clerical Administrative Class (ADA)

CAC .... Climate - Altitude Chamber

CAC .... Climate Analysis Center [*National Weather Service*]

CAC .... Coaching Association of Canada

CAC .... [*The*] Coal Association of Canada (AC)

CAC .... Coast Artillery Corps [*Army*]

CAC .... Codex Alimentarius Commission [*United Nations*] (PDAA)

CAC .... Coffee Association of Canada [*Association du Cafe du Canada*] (AC)

CAC .... Collection Advisory Center (MCD)

CAC .... College Admissions Center (EA)

CAC .... Colonial Aircraft Co.

CAC .... Combat Air Crew

CAC .... Combat Alert Center (SAA)

CAC .... Combat Analysis Capability (MCD)

CAC .... Combined Action Company [*Formerly, Joint Action Co.*] [*Military*]

CAC .... Combined Additional Coverage [*Insurance*]

CAC .... Combined Arms Center (AABC)

CAC .... Comite Administratif de Coordination [*Administrative Committee on Coordination - ACC*] [*United Nations French*] (ASF)

CAC .... Comite Administrativo de Coordinacion [*Administrative Committee on Coordination - ACC*] [*United Nations Spanish*] (MSC)

CAC .... Command Analysis Center

CAC .... Command and Control (NVT)

CAC .... Commander Air Center

CAC .... Commercial Arbitration Centre [*Northern Territory*] [*Australia*]

CAC .... Commission du Codex Alimentarius [*Joint FAO-WHO Codex Alimentarius Commission*] (EA)

CAC .... Commission of Assembly of the Church of Scotland (DAS)

CAC .... Communication and Control (IAA)

CAC .... Communications Analysis Corp. [*Framingham, MA*] [*Telecommunications*] (TSSD)

CAC .... Community Activity Center (MCD)

CAC .... Commuting Area Candidates [*Civil Service*]

CAC .... Compagnie des Agents de Change [*French Stockbrokers Association*] [*Information Service or System*] (EAIO)

CAC .... Complete Address Constant

CAC .... Computer Access Corp. [*Information service or system*] (IID)

CAC .... Computer Advisory Committee [*Marine science*] (OSRA)

CAC .... Computer Advisory Committee (USDC)

CAC .... Computer-Aided Calibration (ACII)

CAC .... Computer-Aided Classification

CAC .... Computer-Assisted Counseling [*Proposed for Air Force*]

CAC .... Computer Augmented Communication

CAC .... Congressional Arts Caucus (EA)

CAC .... Congressional Automotive Caucus (EA)

CAC .... Connection Admission Control [*Telecommunications*] (ACRL)

CAC .... Conquest Airlines Corp. [*ICAO designator*] (FAAC)

CAC .... Conseil Africain-Canadien (AC)

CAC .... Conseil des Arts du Canada [*Canada Council*] (EAIO)

CAC .... Consolidated Aircraft Corp. [*Later, General Dynamics Corp.*] (AAG)

CAC .... Consolidated Athletic Commission (EA)

CAC .... Constant Alert Cycle

CAC .... Constitutional Acts of Canada [*Database*] [*Federal Department of Justice*] [*Information service or system*] (CRD)

CAC .... Constitution and Ancient Charges [*Freemasonry*] (ROG)

CAC .... Consumer Attorneys of California (SRA)

CAC .... Consumer's Advisory Council

CAC .... Consumers' Association of Canada

CAC .... Contact Approach Control (FAAC)

CAC .... Contact Area Commander

CAC .... Containment Atmosphere Control [*Monitor, or System*] [*Nuclear energy*] (IEEE)

CAC .... Continental Air Command

CAC .... Continental Army Command [*See CONARC*]

CAC .... Continuous Aim Correction [*Military*] (CAAL)

CAC .... Continuous Air Circulation (IIA)

CAC .... Continuous Annular Chromatograph

CAC .... Contract Administration Control (DNAB)

CAC .... Contract Auditor Coordinator

CAC .... Control and Analysis Centers [*ERADCOM*] (RDA)

CAC .... Control and Coordination [*Army*]

CAC .... CONVAIR [*Consolidated-Vultee Aircraft Corp.*] Astronautics Corp. [*Later, General Dynamics Corp.*] (AAG)

CAC .... Cooperation and Coordination

CAC .... Corps Aviation Company [*Army*] (VNW)

CAC .... Correction Action Committee

CAC .... Corrugated Asbestos Cement (ADA)

CAC .... Cosmetology Accrediting Commission [*Later, NACCAS*] (EA)

CAC .... Cost Account Code [*Accounting*]

CAC .... Council for Arms Control [*British*] (DBA)

CAC .... Council for the Advancement of Citizenship (EA)

CAC .... County Agricultural Committee (BARN)

CAC............. Critical Aggregation Concentration [*Electrolyte induced aggregation of dispersed species*]
CAC............. Crosley Automobile Club (EA)
CAC............. Crown Agents for the Colonies [*British*]
CAC............. Crusade Against Corruption (EA)
CAC............. Cultural Action Committee
CAC............. Currency Adjustment Charge [*Business term*]
CAC............. Current Account [*Business term*] (IAA)
CAC............. Current Actions Center
CAC............. Curriculum Advisory Committee [*American Occupational Therapy Association*]
CAC............. Customer Applicability Code (MCD)
CAC............. Customs Additional Code (DS)
CAC............. Czechoslovak Association of Canada (EAIO)
CAC............. Heavy Cruiser, Guided Missile [*Navy symbol*]
CAC............. Newton, KS [*Location identifier FAA*] (FAAL)
CAC2 .... Combined Arms Command and Control [*Army*] (RDA)
CACA .... Cambodian Advisory Council of Australia
CACA .... Canada Academy & Association of Chinese Acupuncture/Medicine (AC)
CACA .... Canadian Agricultural Chemics Association
CACA .... Canadian Amateur Cowboys Association
CACA .... Carlsbad Caverns National Park
CACA .... Central After Care Association [*British*]
CACA .... Chartered Association of Certified Accountants [*British*] (EAIO)
CACA .... Chinese American Citizens Alliance (EA)
CACA .... Citizens Against Crime Association [*Australia*]
CACA .... Citizens Association for the Care of Animals (EA)
CACA .... Collision Alert [*Air traffic control*]
CACA .... Computer-Aided Circuit Analysis [*Electronics*]
CACA .... Continuous Accumulation of Coriolis Acceleration [*Bioscience*]
CACA .... Council Against Communist Aggression [*Later, CDF*] (EA)
CACAC .... Civil Aircraft Control Advisory Committee [*British*] (AIA)
CACAM .... Communications of the Association for Communicating Machinery (HGAA)
CAC & W .... Continental Aircraft Control and Warning (MUGU)
CACAS .... Chemical Agent Casualty Assessment System (MCD)
CACAW .... Canadian Association of Communications & Allied Workers [*Association Canadienne des Employes de Communications et Travailleurs Connexes*] (AC)
CACB .... Calcium Carbonate [*Pharmacology*] (DAVI)
CACB .... Cascade Bancorp [*NASDAQ symbol*] (SAG)
CACB .... Center Aisle Connector Bracket (MCD)
CACB .... Compressed Air Circuit Breaker (MSA)
CACC .... Canadian Association of Captioning Consumers (AC)
CaCC .... Cathodal Closure Contraction [*Also, CCC*] [*Physiology*]
CACC .... Chinese American Civic Council (EA)
CACC .... Christian Anti-Communism Crusade (EA)
CACC .... Civil Aviation Communication Center [*Canada*]
CACC .... Colombian-American Chamber of Commerce (EA)
CACC .... Communications and Configuration Console (MCD)
CACC .... Computer Application Control Code
CACC .... Conseil Acadien de Cooperation Culturelle en Atlantique [*Acadian Council of Cultural Cooperation in Atlantic Canada*]
CACC .... Continental Africa Chamber of Commerce (EA)
CACC .... Corps Area Communications Center [*Army*]
CACC .... Cossack-American Citizens' Committee (EA)
CACC .... Council for the Accreditation of Correspondence Colleges [*British*]
CACC .... Credit Acceptance [*NASDAQ symbol*] (TTSB)
CACC .... Credit Acceptance Corp. [*NASDAQ symbol*] (SAG)
CACCA .... Connecticut Association of Child Caring Agencies (SRA)
CACCB .... Colorado Association of Community Centered Boards (SRA)
CAC-CDR ..... Comite d'Action et de Concertation du Conseil Democratique Revolutionnaire [*Chad*] [*Political party*] (EY)
CACCE .... Carolinas Association of Chamber of Commerce Executives (SRA)
CACCE .... Council of American Chambers of Commerce in Europe [*Later, European Council of American Chambers of Commerce*] (EA)
CACCI .... Confederation of Asian-Pacific Chambers of Commerce and Industry [*Taipei, Taiwan*] (EAIO)
CACCL .... Colorado Association of Campgrounds, Cabins, and Lodges (SRA)
CACCN .... Canadian Association of Critical Care Nurses [*Association Canadienne des Infirmieres et Infirmiers de Soins Intensifs*] [*Formerly, National Society of Critical Care Nurses*] (AC)
CACD .... California Association for Counseling and Development (SRA)
CACD .... Canadian Association of Chemical Distributors [*Association Canadienne des Distributeurs de Produits Chimiques*] (AC)
CACD .... Computer-Aided Circuit Design
CACD .... Computer Automated Cargo Documentation (IAA)
CACDA .... Combined Arms Combat Development Activity [*Fort Leavenworth, KS*] [*Army*] (AABC)
CACDA/C3I... Combined Arms Combat Development Activity C3I [*Command, Control, Communications, and Intelligence*] Directorate [*Fort Leavenworth, KS*] [*Army*]
CACE........... Canadian Association for Co-Operative Education [*Association Canadienne de l'Enseignement Cooperatif*] (AC)
CACE........... Canadian Association of Chairmen of English Departments
CACE........... Computer-Aided Cost Estimating (BTTJ)
CACE........... Counteracting Chromatographic Electrophoresis
CACEA .... Canadian Association of Certified Executive Accountants [*Formerly, Association of Cost & Executive Acconants in Canada*] (AC)
CACEED .... Conference of Americans of Central and Eastern European Descent [*Defunct*] (EA)
Ca Celeb...... Causes Celebres [*Quebec Provincial Reports*] [*A publication*] (DLA)
CACEP .... Congressional Arts Caucus Education Program (EA)
CACEQ .... Citizens Advisory Committee on Environmental Quality

CACF........... Case Assignment Control File [*IRS*]
CAC/FHS ..... Casualty Assistance Calls and Funeral Honors Support Program [*Military*] (DNAB)
CACFOA ...... Chief and Assistant Chief Fire Officers' Association [*British*]
CACGA .... Canadian Association on Charitable Gift Annuities (NFD)
CACGP .... Commission on Atmospheric Chemistry and Global Pollution [*British*]
CACGS .... Computer Assisted Careers Guidance System (AIE)
CACGV .... Community Arts Council of Greater Victoria (AC)
CACH .... Cache, Inc. [*NASDAQ symbol*] (NQ)
CACH .... California Association of Catholic Hospitals (SRA)
CACH .... Canyon de Chelly National Monument
Cach .... Carmelite Sisters of Charity (TOCD)
CACH .... Consumer Affairs Clearinghouse
CaCh........... Sorores Carmelitae a Caritate [*Carmelite Sisters of Charity*] [*Roman Catholic religious order*]
CACHA .... Calwestern Automated Clearing House Association (MHDB)
CACHAC ...... Community Athenaeum Colleges of the Hellenic Advancement Council [*Australia*]
Cache .... Cache, Inc. [*Associated Press*] (SAG)
CACHE .... Chicago Area Computer Hobbyist Exchange
CACHE .... Computer Aids for Chemical Engineering Education [*National Academy of Engineering*]
CACHE .... Computer-Controlled Automated Cargo Handling Envelope
CACHR .... Central American Committee for Human Rights [*British*] (EAIO)
CACHR .... El Salvador and Guatemala Committees for Human Rights [*British*] (EAIO)
CACI........... Cacia International [*Associated Press*] (SAG)
CACI........... Cacia International, Inc. [*NASDAQ symbol*] (NQ)
CACI........... CACI Int'l [*NASDAQ symbol*] (TTSB)
CACI........... California Analysis Centers, Inc. [*A management consulting company*] [*Arlington, Virginia*] (WDMC)
CACI........... Canadian Academic Centre in Italy
CACI........... Catholic Alumni Clubs International (EA)
CACI........... Centre Academique Canadien en Italie [*Canadian Academic Centre in Italy*]
CACI........... Civil Aviation Chaplains International (EAIO)
CACI........... Classic AMX Club International (EA)
CACI........... Colorado Association of Commerce and Industry (SRA)
CACI........... Community Arts Councils, Inc. [*Later, American Council for the Arts*] (EA)
CACI........... Computer Assisted Continuous Infusion [*Pharmacology*] (DAVI)
CACI........... Consolidated Analysis Centers, Inc.
CACL .... California-Arizona Citrus League (SRA)
CACL .... Canadian Association for Community Living
CACL .... Canadian Association for Community Living (EAIO)
CACL .... Canadian Association of Children's Librarians
CACL .... Castle Clinton National Monument
CACL .... Computer & Aerospace Components Ltd. [*British*]
CACL .... Computer-Assisted Computer Language (SSD)
CaCl2 .... Calcium Chloride [*Pharmacology*] (DAVI)
CACLALS .... Canadian Association for Commonwealth Literature and Language Studies [*See also ACELLC*]
CACLD .... Canadian Association for Children with Learning Disabilities
CACM.......... California Association of Community Managers (SRA)
CACM.......... Central American Common Market (BARN)
CACM.......... Certified Associate Contracts Manager [*Exam*] (AAGC)
CACM.......... Communications. Association for Computing Machinery
CACMDBMC... Community Advisory Committee of the Murray-Darling Basin Ministerial Council [*Australia*]
CACMID .... Canadian Association for Clinical Microbiology & Infectious Diseases [*Association Canadienne de Microbiologie Clinique et des Maladies Contagieuses*] (AC)
CACMS .... Committee for the Accreditation of Canadian Medical Schools [*Canada*] (PGP)
CACNB .... Comite Associe du Code National du Batiment [*Associate Committee of the National Building Code*] [*National Research Council of Canada*]
CACNIQ........ Centre d'Arbitrage Commerical National et International du Quebec [*Quebec National & International Commerical Arbitration Centre*] (AC)
CACNRWC ... Cuban-American Committee for Normalization of Relations with Cuba (EA)
CACNT .... Consumer Affairs Council, Northern Territory [*Australia*]
CACO .... Cape Cod National Seashore [*National Park Service designation*]
CACO .... Casualty Assistance Calls Officer
CACO .... Casualty Assistance Control Officer [*Navy*] (DOMA)
CACO .... [*The*] Cato Corp. [*NASDAQ symbol*] (NQ)
CACO .... Corporate Administrative Contracting Officer [*DoD*]
CACO .... Corporate Home Office Administrative Contracting Officer (AAGC)
CaCO3 .... Calcium Carbonate [*Pharmacology*] (DAVI)
CACOA .... Canadian Association for Children of Alcoholics (AC)
CACOA .... Cato Corp.'A' [*NASDAQ symbol*] (TTSB)
CACOM .... Central American Common Market
CACOM .... Chief Aircraft Communicator [*British military*] (IAA)
CACON .... Cargo Container (KSC)
CACON .... Chemical Abstracts Condensates [*Database*]
CACP .... Canadian Association of Chiefs of Police
CACP .... Cartridge-Actuated Compaction Press (PDAA)
CACP .... Casualty Assistance Calls Program (CINC)
CACP .... Central Arbitration Control Point (BYTE)
CACP .... Cisplatin [*Antineoplastic drug*] (DAVI)
CACP .... Corrosion and Cathodic Protection (IAA)
CACP .... Council for the Advancement of Consumer Policy (EA)
CACPAF .... Continental Association of CPA [*Certified Public Accountant*] Firms (EA)

CAC/PL	Canadian Advisory Committee on Programming Languages
CACPT	Canadian Association of Cardio-Pulmonary Technologists (AC)
CACPT	Canadian Association of Certified Planning Tecnicians (AC)
CACR	Clean Air Car Race
CACR	Contract Acquisition Cost Report (MCD)
CACR	Council for Agricultural and Chemurgic Research (EA)
CACREP	Council for Accreditation of Counseling and Related Educational Programs (AEE)
CA/CRL	Custody Authorization/Custody Receipt Listing
CACS	California Aqueduct Control System
CACS	California Association of College Stores (SRA)
CACS	Centralized Alarm and Control System [Telecommunications] (TEL)
CA/CS	Change Administration Cover Sheet
CACS	Comprehensive Airport Communications System (PDAA)
CACS	Computer-Aided [or -Assisted] Communication System
CACS	Content Addressable Computing System
CACS	Continental Airways and Communications Service [Air Force]
CACS	Contract Audit Closing Statements (AAGC)
CACS	Controller Active State (IAA)
CACS	Core Auxiliary Cooling System [Nuclear energy] (NRCH)
CACS	Corps Area Communications System [Vietnam] (MCD)
CACSA	Contemporary Art Centre of South Australia
CACSD	Computer-Aided Control System Design (PDAA)
CACSMA	Canadian Association for Composite Structures & Materials (AC)
CACSO	Central American and Caribbean Sports Organization (EAIO)
CACST	Central Advisory Council for Science and Technology [British]
CACSW	Canadian Advisory Council on the Status of Women (AC)
CACSW	Citizens' Advisory Council on the Status of Women
CACT	Civil Air Carrier Turbojet (FAAC)
CACT	Command Automatic Card Tester
CACTIS	Computer Assistant to a Community Telephone Information Service (PDAA)
CAC-TNG	Combined Arms Command-Training [Fort Leavenworth, KS] [Army] (INF)
CACTO	Cactoblastis [South American moth brought to Australia to destroy the prickly pear] (DSUE)
CACTOS	Computation and Communication Trade-Off Study [ARPA]
CACTS	Canadian Air Cushion Technology Society (AC)
CACTUS	Cartridge Access Controller-to-Update System [Primary Rate, Inc.]
CACUCS	Conference of Administrators of College and University Counseling Services (EA)
CACUL	Canadian Association of College and University Libraries
CACUSS	Canadian Association of College and University Student Services
CaCV	Calicivirus [Medicine] (DMAA)
CACV	Cooperstown & Charlotte Valley Railway Corp. [AAR code]
CACW	Central American Confederation of Workers (EAIO)
CACW	Chinese-American Composite Wing [Air Force]
CACW	Core Auxiliary Cooling Water [Nuclear energy] (NRCH)
CACWS	Core Auxiliary Cooling Water System [Nuclear energy] (NRCH)
CACWV	Committee to Aid Cold War Veterans (EA)
CACX	Cancer of the Cervix [Medicine]
CACY	Calcyclin [Medicine] (DMAA)
CAD	Cabling Diagram
Cad	Cadaver [Medicine]
cad	Caddo [MARC language code Library of Congress] (LCCP)
CAD	Cadenza [Cadence] [Music]
CAD	Cadet
CAD	Cadger (ROG)
CAD	Cadillac, MI [Location identifier FAA] (FAAL)
CAD	Cadiz Railroad Co. [AAR code]
CAD	Cadmium [Chemical symbol is Cd] (KSC)
CAD	Cady Mountains [California] [Seismograph station code, US Geological Survey Closed] (SEIS)
CAD	Canadian Air Division (MCD)
CAD	Canadian Almanac and Directory [A publication]
CAD	Canadian Annual Digest [A publication] (DLA)
CAD	Canadian Association of the Deaf (EAIO)
CAD	Capital Acquisition Deduction [Business term]
CADAC	Capital Adequacy Directive [European Union] (ECON)
CAD	Cartridge-Actuated Device [Military] (NVT)
CAD	Cash Against Disbursement [Sales] (MHDW)
CAD	Cash Against Documents [Sales]
CAD	Center Aiming Disc (NATG)
CAD	Center for Affective Disorders [University of Wisconsin, Madison] [Research center] (RCD)
CAD	Center for Astronomical Data [Academy of Sciences of the USSR] [Information service or system] (IID)
CAD	Central Aircraft Dispatch
CAD	Central Ammunition Depot (NATG)
C-A-D	C'Est-a-Dire [That Is to Say] [French]
CAD	Channel Address [Military]
CAD	Character Assemble/Disassemble
CAD	Characterization and Assessment Division [Environmental Protection Agency] (GFGA)
CAD	Chicago Assyrian Dictionary [A publication] (BJA)
CAD	Chief of Air Defense
CAD	Chilliwack Aviation Ltd. [Canada ICAO designator] (FAAC)
CAD	Cinnamyl Alcohol Dehydrogenase [An enzyme]
CAD	Circulatory Assist Device (PDAA)
CAD	Civil Action Detachment [Military] (DNAB)
CAD	Civil Affairs Division [Military]
CAD	Clear and Add (SAA)
CAD	Cold Agglutinin Disease [Medicine] (DMAA)
CAD	Collective Address Directory [Navy] (NVT)
CAD	Collision-Activated Dissociation [Spectrometry]

CAD	Collisionally Activated Dissociation
CAD	Colorado Association of Distributors (SRA)
CAD	Combat Arms Division (INF)
CAD	Comite d'Aide au Developpement [OCDE]
CAD	Command Address [Computer science] (IAA)
CAD	Commercial Advance Design [Reports] (MCD)
CAD	Committee for Agricultural Development [Iowa State University] [Research center] (RCD)
CAD	Communication and Data (IAA)
CAD	Communications Access Device (CET)
CAD	Commutated Aerial Direction
CAD	Company of American Dance
CAD	Compensated Avalanche Diode
CAD	Computation and Analysis Division [NASA] (MCD)
CAD	Computer Access Device
CAD	Computer Adaptor Display
CAD	Computer Address Decoder [Navy Navigation Satellite System] (DNAB)
CAD	Computer-Aided Design
CAD	Computer-Aided Detection
CAD	Computer Aided Dispatch [Police communications]
CAD	Computer-Aided Dispatching [Vehicle fleet management]
CAD	Computer-Aided Drafting [or Drawing]
CAD	Computer-Assisted Design
CAD	Computer-Assisted Diagnosis
CAD	Computer-Assisted Dialog
CAD	Computer-Associated [or -Assisted] Device
CAD	Concepts and Analysis Division [US Army Engineer Topographic Laboratories]
CAD	Conseil des Assurances de Dommages (AC)
CAD	Conserved ATPase [Adenosine Triphosphatase] Domain [Biochemistry]
CAD	Consolidate Acquisition Directive [DoD]
CAD	Containment Atmosphere Dilution [Nuclear energy] (NRCH)
CAD	Continuous Acceleration Device
CAD	Contract Action Directive (MCD)
CAD	Contract Administration Data [DoD]
CAD	Contract Award Date (AAG)
CAD	Control and Display (IAA)
CAD	Coronary Artery Disease [Medicine]
CAD	Corps Advisory Detachment
CAD	Corrective Action Directive [or Disposition]
CAD	Council on Anxiety Disorders (EA)
CAD	Course Administrative Data [DoD]
CAD	Creating an Automatic Design
CAD	Current Account Deficit [Economics]
CAD	Customs Appeals Decisions [A publication] (DLA)
CAD	Cyclophosphamide, Adriamycin, Dacarbazine [Antineoplastic drug regimen]
CAD	Cytarabine, Daunorubicin [Antineoplastic drug regimen]
CADA	CAM Data Systems [NASDAQ symbol] (SAG)
CADA	Campus Americans for Democratic Action [Defunct] (EA)
CADA	Canadian Academic Decathlon Associations (AC)
CADA	Canadian Amateur Diving Association Inc. [Association Candienne du Plongeon Amateur Inc.] (AC)
CADA	Canadian Antique Dealers Association (AC)
CADA	Canadian Automobile Dealers Association [Formerly, Federation of Automobile Dealer Associations of Canada] (AC)
CADA	Cellulose Acetate Diethylaminoacetate (OA)
CADA	Center for Advanced Digital Applications [New York University School of Continuing Education]
CADA	Clear Air Dot Angle
CADA	Colorado Automobile Dealers Association (SRA)
CADA	Computer-Aided Design and Analysis
CADA	Computer-Assisted Development Aids
CADA	Computer-Assisted Distribution and Assignment (NVT)
CADA	Confederation of Art and Design Associations (AIE)
CADAC	Crossbow Archery Development Association (EAIO)
CADAC	Clean Arithmetic with Decimal Base and Controlled Precision (MCD)
CADACS	Computer-Aided Design and Construction System (PDAA)
CADAE	Computer-Aided Design and Engineering (MHDI)
CADAI	Center Apollo Documentation Administration Instructions [NASA] (KSC)
CADAL	Centro di Azione e Documentazione sull'America Latina
CADAM	Computer-Aided Design and Manufacturing
CADAM	Computer-Augmented Design and Manufacturing [Trademark of Cadam, Inc.] [Aviation]
CADAM	Computer-Graphics-Augmented Design and Manufacturing (MCD)
CADAMS	Laboratory for Computer-Aided Design and Analysis in the Molecular Sciences [Washington State University] [Research center] (RCD)
CADANCE	Computer-Aided Design and Numerical Control Effort
CADAPSO	Canadian Association of Data and Professional Service Organizations [Information service or system] (IID)
CADAPSO	Canadian Association of Data Processing Organizations (IAA)
CADAPSO	Canadian Association of Data Processing Service Organizations (NITA)
CADAR	Computer-Aided Design, Analysis, and Reliability (IEEE)
CADAS	Coventry and District Archaeological Society [British] (DBA)
CADASIL	Cerebral Autosomal Dominant Arteriopathy with Subcortical Infarcts and Leukoencephalopathy [Medicine]
CADAT	Computer-Aided Design and Test [System]
CADAV	Cadaver [Medicine] (ROG)
CADAVRS	Computer-Assisted Dial Access Video Retrieval System (MHDI)
CADB	Cadbury [England]
CADB	Cadbury Schweppes Ltd. [NASDAQ symbol]

CADB .... Climate Assessment Data Base [*National Meteorological Center*] [*Database*]
CADBY .... Cadbury Schweppes PLC (MHDW)
CadbyS .... Cadbury Schwepps Ltd. [*Associated Press*] (SAG)
CADC .... Cambridge Automatic Digital Computer (IEEE)
CADC .... Canadian Army Dental Corps (DMA)
CADC .... Central Air Data Computer
CADC .... Centro Academico da Democracia Crista [*Academic Center for Christian Democracy*] [*Portugal Political party*] (PPE)
CADC .... Combined Administrative Committee
CADC .... Computer-Aided Design Centre [*British*] (EECA)
CADC .... Computer-Aided Design Centre [*Department of Trade and Industry*] [*British*] (NITA)
CADC .... Computer Automated Diameter Control (PDAA)
CADC .... Connecticut Art Directors Club (SRA)
CADC .... Continental Air Defense Command [*Discontinued, 1975*]
CADC .... Court of Appeals for the District of Columbia Circuit (AAGC)
CADC .... Crown Asset Disposal Corp. [*Canada*]
CADC .... District of Columbia Court of Appeals (DLA)
CADCA .... Community Anti-Drug Coalitions of America
CAD/CAM ..... Computer-Aided Design/Computer-Aided Manufacturing
CADCC .... Central American Development Coordination Council
CADC/CC ..... Central Air Data Computer / Central Computer (PDAA)
CADCO .... Core and Drum Corrector
CADCOM ...... Computer-Aided Design for Communications (PDAA)
CADCTS .... Central Air Data Computer Test Set
CADD .... Canadians Against Drunk Driving [*Canadiens Contre l'Alcool au Volant*] (AC)
Cadd .... Cheap Analyzer of Demographic Data [*Term coined by William F. Doescher, publisher of "D & B Reports"*]
CADD .... Code Address [*Telecommunications*] (ECII)
CADD .... Combat Air Delivery Division [*Air Force*] (AFM)
CADD .... Computer-Aided Design and Drafting [*Software package*] (MCD)
CADD .... Computer-Aided Design and Drafting
CADD .... Computer Aided Design and Draughting (NITA)
CADD .... Computer-Aided Design Development
CADD .... Computer Assisted Document Drafting
CADD .... Computer-Assisted Drug Design
CADDA .... Computer-Aided Design and Design Automation
CADDAC ...... Central Analog Data Distributing and Computing System (KSC)
CADDE .... Canadian Association of Deans and Directors of Education
CADDE .... Central Automatic Digital Data Encoder [*NASA*]
CADDIA .... Cooperation in Automation of Data and Documentation for Imports/ Exports and Agriculture [*EC*] (ECED)
CADDMAS .... Computer-Assisted Dynamic Data Monitoring and Analysis System
CADDS .... Center Apollo Document Description Standards [*NASA*] (KSC)
CADD/TEK .... Computer-Aided Design Drafting via Tektronix (MCD)
CADDY .... Committee to Aid Democratic Dissidents in Yugoslavia [*Defunct*] (EA)
CADE .... Cade Industries [*NASDAQ symbol*] (TTSB)
CADE .... Cade Industries, Inc. [*NASDAQ symbol*] (NQ)
CADE .... Canadian Association for Distance Education
CADE .... Canadian Association of Drilling Engineers (AC)
CADE .... Caution Against Dangerous Exports [*Shipping*]
CADE .... Center for Analysis of Developing Economies [*University of Pennsylvania*] [*Research center*] (RCD)
CADE .... Coalition Against Dangerous Exports
CADE .... Combined Allied Defense Experiment [*Military*] (SDI)
CADE .... Computer-Aided [*or Assisted*] Data Entry (IAA)
CADE .... Computer-Aided Design and Evaluation (MCD)
CADE .... Computer-Aided Design Engineering (RDA)
CADE .... Computer Aided Document Engineering [*Computer software*] (PCM)
CADE .... Computer-Assisted Data Entry (GFGA)
CADE .... Computer-Assisted Data Evaluation (ODBW)
CADE .... Confused and Disabled Elderly Patient
CADE .... Controller/Attitude-Direct Electronics (NASA)
CADEA .... Chloroacetaldehyde Diethyl Acetal [*Organic chemistry*]
CADEC .... Christian Action for Development in the Caribbean [*Caribbean Conference of Churches*]
CadeIn .... Cade Industries, Inc. [*Associated Press*] (SAG)
CADEM .... Computer-Aided Design Engineering and Manufacturing (IAA)
CADEM .... CONUS [*Continental United States*] Air Defense Effectiveness Model (MCD)
Cadence ...... Cadence Design Systems, Inc. [*Associated Press*] (SAG)
CADENS .... CONUS [*Continental United States*] Air Defense Engagement Simulation
CADEP .... Computer-Aided Design of Electronic Products (IEEE)
CADEP .... Computer-Assisted Description of Patterns (PDAA)
CADES .... COMIREX [*Committee on Imagery Requirements and Exploitation*] Advanced Exploitation System (MCD)
CADES .... Computer-Aided Development and Evaluation System (MHDI)
CADET .... Can't Add, Doesn't Even Try [*Computer science*]
CADET .... City Air Defense Evaluation Tool
CADET .... Computer-Aided Design and Electrical Test
CADET .... Computer-Aided Design and Evaluation Technology (MCD)
CADET .... Computer-Aided Design Experiment Translator
CADET .... Computer-Associated Diagnostic and Evaluation Tests (CAAL)
CADETRON ... Cadet Practice Squadron
CADETS .... Classroom-Aided Dynamic Educational Time-Sharing System (IEEE)
CADEUL .... Confederation des Associations des Etudiants de l'Universite Laval (AC)
CADEX .... Combination and Dissemination of Experiment Data System [*Army*] (RDA)
CADF .... Cathode-Ray Tube Automatic Direction Finding (IEEE)
CADF .... Central Air Defense Force

CADF .... Commutated Antenna Direction Finder (IEEE)
CADF .... Computer-Aided Design and Fabrication (MCD)
CADF .... Contract Administration Data File [*DoD*] (AFM)
CADFISS ...... Computation and Data Flow Integrated Subsystem [*Simulated flight tests*] [*NASA*]
CAD-I .... Adriamcin, Cyclophosphamide, Cisplatin [*Antineoplastic drug regimen*] (DAVI)
CADI .... Call Diverter (NITA)
CADI .... Central Apollo Data Index [*NASA*] (MCD)
CADI .... Computer Access Device Input (CET)
CADI .... Computer-Assisted Diabetic Instruction [*System*] [*Endocrinology*] (DAVI)
CADIA .... Computer-Assisted Densitometric Image Analysis [*Microbiology*]
CADIAP .... Comment and Data Integration and Printing (IAA)
CADIC .... Chemical Analysis Detection Instrumentation Control
CADIC .... Compagnie Africaine des Ingenieurs-Conseils
CADIC .... Computer-Aided Design of Integrated Circuits (MCD)
CADIC .... Cyclophosphamide, Adriamycin, Dacarbazine [*DTIC*] [*Antineoplastic drug regimen*] (DAVI)
CADICS .... Computer-Aided Design of Industrial Cabling Systems (PDAA)
CADIN .... Continental Air Defense Integration, North
CADIS .... Computer-Aided Design Interactive System (IAA)
CADIS .... Computer-Aided Design of Information System (IAA)
CADISIM ...... Computer-Assisted Disposal Simulation [*Game*]
Cadiz .... Cadiz Land Co., Inc. [*Associated Press*] (SAG)
CADIZ .... Canadian Air Defence Identification Zone
CADIZ .... Civil Air Defense Identification Zone (MCD)
CADJ .... Counter Angle Deception Jammer [*Military*] (CAAL)
CADL .... Communications and Data Link (KSC)
CADL .... Communicative Ability in Daily Living
CADLAB .... Computer Aided Design and Graphics Laboratory [*Purdue University*] [*Research center*] (RCD)
CAD-LAB ..... Computer-Aided Design Laboratory [*Pennsylvania State University*] [*Research center*] (RCD)
CADLAS .... Computer Assisted Depreciation and Life Analysis System [*BTS*] (TAG)
CADLIC .... Computer-Aided Design of Linear Integrated Circuits (MHDB)
CADM .... Center Apollo Data Manager [*NASA*] (KSC)
CADM .... Central German Administrative Department [*Economic*] Committee [*US Military Government, Germany*]
CAdm .... Chartered Administrator (DD)
CADM .... Clustered Airfield Defeat Munition (MCD)
CADM .... Clustered Airfield Depot Munition (MCD)
CAD/M .... Computer-Aided Design/Manufacturing [*Army*] (RDA)
CADM .... Configuration and Data Management (DNAB)
CADM .... Content-Addressable Data Manager
CADM .... CONUS [*Continental United States*] Air Defense Modernization
CADMA .... Chloroacetaldehyde Dimethyl Acetal [*Organic chemistry*]
CADMAC ...... Computer-Aided Document Management and Control System (HGAA)
CADMAC ...... Computer Assisted Drawing Management and Control [*Infodetics Co.*] (NITA)
CADMAP ...... Computer-Assisted Dispatching/Mapping
CADMAT ...... Computer-Aided Design, Manufacture, and Test (MCD)
CADMINI ...... Computer Administrative Instruction (AABC)
CADMP .... Computer-Aided Data Management Procedure (MCD)
CADMS .... Costing and Data Management System
CADMSS ...... Configuration and Data Management Support System
Cadmus .... Cadmus Communicatons Corp. [*Associated Press*] (SAG)
CADMUS ...... Cadmus Group, Inc. (GAAI)
CADNAM ...... Computer Aided Design and Numerical Analysis for Manufacture Group
CADNC .... Computer-Aided Design and Numerical Control (DNAB)
CADNET .... Chemical Agent Detection Network
CADNPH ...... Chloroacetaldehydedinitrophenylhydrazone [*Fungicide*]
CADO .... Central Air Documents Office [*Air Force*]
CADO .... Chief, Air Doctrine and Operations (MCD)
CADO .... Colorado Association of D.A.R.E. [*Drug Abuse Resistance Education*] Officers (SRA)
CADO .... Computer Access Device Output (CET)
CADO .... Computer-Aided Document Origination (MHDI)
CADO .... Current Actions Duty Officer [*Air Force*]
CADOB .... Consolidate Air Defense Order of Battle (MCD)
CADOCR ...... Computer-Aided Design of Optical Character Recognition (MHDI)
CADOCS ...... Carrier Aircraft Deck Operations Control System [*Navy*] (NG)
CADOP .... Continental Air Defense Objectives Plan (AABC)
CADOPCART .. Computer-Aided Design of Printed Circuit Artwork (PDAA)
CADORA .... Canadian Dressage Owners and Riders Association
CADOS .... Computer-Aided Design of Optical Systems [*Energy Soft Computer Systems Ltd.*] [*Software package*] (NCC)
CADOXEN .... Cadmium Oxide - Ethylenediamine [*Cellulose solvent*]
CADP .... Central Annunciator Display Panel (MCD)
CADPA .... Cystic Adventitial Degeneration of the Popliteal Artery [*Medicine*]
CADPI .... Computer Assisted Diagnostic and Prescription Instruction (EDAC)
CADPIN .... Customs Automatic Data Processing Intelligence Network [*US Customs Service*]
CADPL .... Communications/Automatic Data Processing Laboratory [*Army Electronics Command*] [*Fort Monmouth, NJ*]
CADPO .... Canadian Association of Professional Dance Organizations (AC)
CADPO .... Communications and Data Processing Operation
CADPR .... Cyclic Adenosine Diphosphoribose [*Biochemistry*]
CADR .... Clean Air Delivery Rate [*of air purifiers*]
CADR .... Computer-Aided Design Reliability
CADR .... Contract Appeals Decision Reporter [*CCH*] [*A publication*] (AAGC)
CADRBT .... Coalition to Abolish the Draize Rabbit Blinding Tests (EA)
CADRC .... Combined Air Documents Research Center

CADRE	Center for Aerospace Doctrine, Research, and Education [*Air University*] [*Research center*] (RCD)
CADRE	Centre d'Animation de Developpement et de Recherche en Education (AC)
CADRE	Coalition Advocating for Disability Refoerm in Education
CADRE	Collectors, Artists, and Dealers for Responsible Equity
CADRE	Collegial Association for the Development and Renewal of Educators (EDAC)
CADRE	Complete ADR [*Applied Data Research, Inc.*] Environment (EA)
CADRE	Completed Active Duty Requirements, Enlisted [*Military*]
CADRE	Cooperative Advanced Digital Research Experiment (MCD)
CADRE	Current Awareness and Document Retrieval for Engineers (DIT)
CADRIC	Calculation of Drilling Coordinates (MCD)
CADS	Canadian Association for Disable Skiing [*Association Canadienne des Sports pour Skieurs Handicapes*] (AC)
CADS	Cellular Absorbed Dose Spectrometer
CADS	Center for Assessment and Demographic Studies [*Gallaudet College*] [*Research center*] (RCD)
CADS	Central Air Data System [*Air Force*]
CADS	Centralized Air Defense System (SAA)
CADS	Chemical Agent Decontamination Simulant (MCD)
CADS	Chemical Agent Disclosure Solution [*Toxicology*]
CADS	Civil Air Defense Services
CADS	Combined Air-Defense System [*Military*] (DOMA)
CADS	Command and Data Simulator (NASA)
CADS	Commando Anticomunista del Sur [*Southern Anticommunist Commando*] [*Guatemala*] (PD)
CADS	Computer-Aided Design System
CADS	Computer Analysis and Design System (NITA)
CADS	Computer-Assisted Dispatching System [*IBM Corp.*]
CADS	Computer-Assisted Display Systems (MCD)
CADS	Computerized Attack/Defense System [*Title of a science fiction novel by John Sievert*]
CADS	Consolidated Actuarial Data System [*Health insurance*] (GHCT)
CADS	Containerized Ammunition Distribution System
CADS	Containment Atmosphere Dilution System [*Nuclear energy*] (IEEE)
CADS	Content Addressable File Store [*Computer science*] (PDAA)
CADS	Continental Air Defense System
CADS	Control Air Data System (MCD)
CADS	Conversational Analyzer and Drafting System (PDAA)
CADS	Cooperative Air Defense System (MCD)
CADS	Crustal Accretion-Differentiation Supervent [*Geology*]
CADSAME	Call Signs and/or Address Group Remain Same (MUGU)
CADSAT	Computer-Aided Design and System Analysis Tool (MCD)
CadScD	Cadbury Schweppes Delaware LP [*Associated Press*] (SAG)
CADSI	Communications and Data Systems Integration (NASA)
CADSS	Combined Analog-Digital Systems Simulator [*Computer science*]
CADSS	Communications and Data Subsystem (IAA)
CADSVAN	Containerized Ammunition Distribution System Van (DOMA)
CADSWES	Center for Advanced Decision Support for Water and Environmental Systems [*University of Colorado at Boulder*] [*Research center*] (RCD)
CADT	(Carboxamidophenyl)dimethyltriazene [*Biochemistry*]
CADT	Coalition Against Double Taxation [*Defunct*] (EA)
CaDTe	Cathodal Duration Tetanus [*Physiology*]
CADTES	Computer-Aided Design and Test (MHDB)
Ca-DTPA	Chelating Agent - Diethylenetriaminepentaacetic Acid (PDAA)
CADU	Control and Display Unit (NASA)
CADUS	Census and Data Users Services [*Illinois State University*] [*Information service or system*] (IID)
CadusPh	Cadus Pharmaceutical Corp. [*Associated Press*] (SAG)
CADV	Cash Advance (DCTA)
CADW	Civil Air Defense Warning [*System*]
Cadwalader	Cadwalader's Cases, United States District Court, Eastern District of Pennsylva nia [*A publication*] (DLA)
Cadw Dig	Cadwalader's Digest of Attorney-General's Opinions [*A publication*] (DLA)
CAE	Cab Alongside Engine [*Automotive engineering*]
CAE	CAE Industries Ltd. [*Toronto Stock Exchange symbol*]
Cae	Caelum [*Constellation*]
CaE	Calcium Excretion [*Medicine*] (DMAA)
CAE	California Association of Employers (SRA)
CAE	Canadian Academy of Endodontics (EAIO)
CAE	Canadian Academy of Engineering (EAIO)
CAE	Canadian Association of Exhibitions [*Association des Expositions du Canada*] (AC)
CAE	Canadian Aviation Electronics
CAE	CANMARC [*Canadian Machine-Readable Cataloging*] English Authority File [*Source file*] [*UTLAS symbol*]
CAE	Capillary Array Electrophoresis [*Analytical biochemistry*]
CAE	Caprine Arthritis-Encephalitis [*Veterinary medicine*]
CAE	Carrier Aircraft Equipment
CAE	Cascade Corp. [*NYSE symbol*] (SAG)
CAE	Cellulose Acetate Electrophoresis [*Organic chemistry*] (MAE)
CAE	Center for Academic Ethics (EA)
CAE	Central African Empire [*Later, CAR*]
CAE	Central Associated Engineers, Inc. [*Versailles, KY*] [*Telecommunications service*] (TSSD)
CAE	Centro Anglo-Espanol (EA)
CAE	Certified Association Executive [*American Society of A ssociation Executives*] [*Designation awarded by*]
CAE	Chemical Abstracts, Even-Numbered Issue
CAE	Chicago, Aurora & Elgin Railroad Corp. [*AAR code*]
CAE	Chief Activation Engineer
CAE	Chief Administrative Engineer
CAE	Chloroacetate Esterase [*An enzyme*]
CAE	Cholesterol Epoxide [*Biochemistry*]
CAE	Columbia [*South Carolina*] [*Airport symbol*]
CAE	Common Application Environment [*Computer science*] (BTTJ)
CAE	Common Applications Environment [*Computer science*] (BARN)
CAE	Communications and Electronics (IAA)
CAE	Compagnie Europeenne d'Automatisme [*Became part of Compagnie Internationale d'Informatique*]
CAE	Compare Alphabetic Equal [*Computer science*] (OA)
CAE	Component Acquisition Executive (DOMA)
CAE	Computer-Aided Education (BUR)
CAE	Computer-Aided Engineering
CAE	Computer-Aided Engineering Center [*University of Wisconsin - Madison*] [*Research center*] (RCD)
CAE	Computer-Aided Engineering Centre [*Heriot-Watt University*] [*British*] (CB)
CAE	Computer-Assisted Enrollment [*IBM Corp.*] (IEEE)
CAE	Computer-Assisted Entry
CAE	Computer-Assisted Estimating
CAE	Confederation of American Educators
CAE	Continental Aviation & Engineering Corp.
CAE	Contingent Aftereffects [*Visual*]
CAE	Corrective Action Effectiveness (MCD)
CAE	Council for Aid to Education [*Formerly the Council for Financial Aid to Education*] (NFD)
CAE	Council of American Embroiderers (EA)
CAE	Council on Anthropology and Education (EA)
CAE	Criterion Action Element [*Army*] (ADDR)
CAEA	California Aviation Education Association
CAEA	Canadian Actors' Equity Association [*Canada*] (WWLA)
CAEA	Canadian Automotive Electric Association
CAEA	Central American Economics Association
CAEAI	Chartered Auctioneers' and Estate Agents' Institute [*British*] (BI)
CAEAL	Canadian Association for Environmental Analytical Laboratories (AC)
CAEB	Canadian Association of Ethnic (Radio) [*Association Canadienne des Radiodiffuseurs Ethniques*] (AC)
CAEB	Combat Arms Enlistment Bonus [*Military*]
CAEC	Center for Analysis of Environmental Change [*Oregon State University*] [*Research center*] (RCD)
CAEC	Central American Energy Commission (EAIO)
CAEC	Comite des Associations Europeennes de Cafe [*Committee of European Coffee Associations*] [*EC*] (ECED)
CAEC	Committee of the Acta Endocrinologica Countries
Caecin	Pro Caecina [*of Cicero*] [*Classical studies*] (OCD)
CAECS	Computer-Aided Environmental Control System (MCD)
CAEDA	Compressed Air Equipment Distributors Association [*British*] (DBA)
CAEDET	Commandable Audio Engine Detector (MCD)
CAEDETS	Commandable Acoustic Engine Ignition Detectors (MCD)
CAEDM	Community/Airport Economic Development Model [*FAA*]
CAEDO	Canadian Association of Educational Development Officers (NFD)
CAEDO	Canadian Association of Education Development Officers
CAEDS	Computer-Aided Emulation Design System
CAEDS	Computer-Aided Engineering and Architectural Design System (RDA)
CAEDS	Computer Aided Engineering Design System (NITA)
CaEDTA	Calcium Disodium Ethylenediaminetetraacetate [*Chelating agent*]
CAEE	Committee on Aircraft Engine Emissions [*ICAO*] (DA)
CAEF	Chinese-American Educational Foundation (EA)
CAEF	Comite des Associations Europeennes de Fonderie [*Committee of European Foundry Associations*] (EA)
CAEF	Computer-Aided Exercise Facility (MCD)
CAEFMS	Canadian Agricultural Economics and Farm Management Society
CAEFS	Canadian Association of Elizabeth Fry Societies [*Association Canadienne des Societes Elizabeth Fry*] (AC)
CAEG	Computer Aided Engineering Graphics [*FAA*] (TAG)
CAEI	Canadian Aeronautical Institute (IAA)
CAEJ	Communaute des Associations d'Editeurs de Journaux [*Community of Associations of Newspaper Publishers*] [*EEC Belgium*] (PDAA)
CAEJC	[*The*] Commonwealth Association for Education in Journalism & Communication (AC)
CAEJ-CEE	Communaute des Associations d'Editeurs de Journaux de la CEE [*Community of the Newspaper Publishing Associations of the EEC*] [*Belgium*] (EAIO)
CAEL	Caelebs [*Unmarried*] [*Latin*] (ROG)
Cael	Caelum [*Constellation*]
CAEL	Consolidated Aerospace Equipment List (MCD)
CAEL	Cooperative Assessment of Experiential Learning Project (EDAC)
CAEL	Council for Adult and Experiential Learning (EA)
Cael	De Caelo [*of Aristotle*] [*Classical studies*] (OCD)
Cael	Pro Caelio [*of Cicero*] [*Classical studies*] (OCD)
CAE LAB	Computer-Aided Engineering Laboratory [*Lawrence Institute of Technology*] [*Research center*] (RCD)
CAEM	Association Canadienne des Educateurs de Musique [*Canadian Music Educators' Association*]
CAEM	Canadian Association of Exposition Managers
CAEM	Cargo Airline Evaluation Model (PDAA)
CAEM	Centre Africaine d'Etudes Monetaires [*African Centre for Monetary Studies*] [*Senegal*] (EAIO)
CAEM	Certified Assistant Export Manager [*American Society of International Executives*] [*Designation awarded by*]
CAeM	Commission for Aeronautical Meteorology [*WMO*] (MSC)
CAEM	Conseil d'Assistance Economique Mutuelle [*Council for Mutual Economic Assistance - CMEA*] [*French*] (AF)
CAEM	Controlled Atmosphere Electron Microscopy
CAE/MIS	Computer-Assisted Estimating and Management Information Systems
CAEMS	Computer-Aided Embarkation Management System [*Navy*]

CAENEX Complete Atmospheric Energetics Experiment [*Marine science*] (OSRA)
CAENEX Complex Atmospheric Energetics Experiment [*National Science Foundation and USSR*]
CAEO Coalition of Adult Education Organizations (EA)
CAEP Canadian Association of Emergency Physicians
CAEP Connecticut Assessment of Educational Progress (EDAC)
CAEP Cortical Auditory Evoked Potential [*Medicine*] (DMAA)
CAEP Custodian of Allied and Enemy Property [*British World War II*]
CAEPS Computer Aided Estimating and Planning System (NITA)
CAER Caere Corp. [*NASDAQ symbol*] (NQ)
CAER Chemical Awareness and Emergency Response [*Program for handling hazards*]
CAER Chief Aerographer [*Navy rating Obsolete*]
CAER Community Awareness and Emergency Response Program [*Environmental Protection Agency*] (GFGA)
CAER Conservative Action for Electoral Reform [*British*]
Caere Caere Corp. [*Associated Press*] (SAG)
CAERL Caerulcus [*Blue*] [*Pharmacy*] (ROG)
CAERM Chief Aerographer's Mate [*Navy rating Obsolete*]
Caern Caernarvonshire [*Wales*] (BARN)
Caerns Caernarvonshire [*County in Wales*]
CAERS Canadian Anti-Racism Education & Research Society (AC)
caerul Caeruleus [*Dark Blue, Dark Green*] [*Pharmacy*] (DAVI)
Caes Caesar [*of Plutarch*] [*Classical studies*] (OCD)
CAES Canadian Agricultural Economics Society
CAES Center for Action on Endangered Species (EA)
CAES Center for Air Environment Studies [*Pennsylvania State University*] [*Research center*] (RCD)
CAES Certificate of Advanced Educational Specialization (PGP)
CAES Compressed Air Energy Storage (MCD)
CAES Connecticut Agricultural Experiment Station
CAESAR Centre of Advanced European Studies and Research [*Germany*]
CAESCO Canadian Association of Energy Service Companies (AC)
Caes Contar Caesar Contardus [*Deceased, 1585*] [*Authority cited in pre-1607 legal work*] (DSA)
CAESO Computer Aided Engineering Support Office (NITA)
CAESQ Communications and Electronics Squadron (IAA)
CAET Canadian Association for Enterostomal Therapy (AC)
CAET Canadian Association of Electroencephalograph Technologists
CAETA Commonwealth Association for Education and Training of Adults
CAET PAR Caeteris Paribus [*Other Things Being Equal*] [*Latin*] (ROG)
CAETR Center for Acquisition Education, Training, and Research [*Military*] (RDA)
CAETS Council of Academies of Engineering and Technological Sciences [*National Academyof Engineers*]
CAEU Casualty Air Evacuation Unit [*RAF*] [*British*]
CAEV Caprine Arthritis Encephalitis Virus [*Veterinary medicine*]
CAEWIS Computer-Aided Electronic Warfare Information Systems [*Air Force*] (GFGA)
CAEWW Carrier Airborne Early Warning Wing [*Navy*] (NVT)
CAEX Community Automatic Exchange [*Telephone*] (BUR)
CAEX Computer-Aided Exploration (BTTJ)
CAF Cable Arts Foundation, Inc. (NTCM)
caf Cafeteria (BARN)
CAF Caffeine
CAF Calcium-Activated Factor [*Meat science*]
CAF Calviac [*France*] [*Seismograph station code, US Geological Survey*] (SEIS)
CAF Canadian Advertising Foundation
CAF Canadian Air Force [*1920-1923*]
CAF Canadian Apparel Federation [*Federation Canadienne du Vetement*] (AC)
CAF Canadian Arab Federation [*Federation Canado-Arabe*] (AC)
CAF Canadian Armed Forces
CAF Canadian Futurity Oils Ltd. [*Toronto Stock Exchange symbol*]
CAF CANMARC [*Canadian Machine-Readable Cataloging*] French Authority File [*Source file*] [*UTLAS symbol*]
CAF Capital American Financial [*NYSE symbol*] (SPSG)
CAF Capitol American Financial Cp. [*NYSE symbol*] (SAG)
CAF Capitol American Finl [*NYSE symbol*] (TTSB)
CAF Carauari [*Brazil*] [*Airport symbol*] (AD)
CAF Cell Adhesion Factor [*Cytochemistry*]
CAF Cell Antiviral Factor [*Immunochemistry*]
CAF Central African Federation [*Disbanded Dec. 31, 1963*]
CAF Central African Republic [*ANSI three-letter standard code*] (CNC)
CAF Centralized Authorized File [*IRS*]
CAF Centre d'Animation des Femmes de Hull (AC)
CAF Charities Aid Foundation [*Information service or system*] (IID)
CAF Charities Aid Fund [*British*]
CAF Chemical Analysis Facility (NRCH)
CAF Chief Air Fitter [*British military*] (DMA)
CAF Children of Alcoholics Foundation (EA)
CAF Children's Art Foundation (EA)
CAF Chinese Air Force [*Nationalist*]
CAF Chinese American Forum (EA)
CAF Chromatin Assembly Factor [*Genetics*]
CAF Citizen Action Fund (EA)
CAF Citric Acid Fermentation (DMAA)
CAF Citric Acid Fermenter [*Microbiology*]
CAF Clean Assembly Facility
CAF Clerical, Administrative, and Fiscal [*Used with number, as, CAF-6, to indicate grade of position*] [*Civil Service*]
CAF Cloth Assistance Factor [*Textiles*]
CAF Coastal Air Force [*British*]
CAF College of Agriculture and Forestry (AIE)
CAF Colloidal Array Filters [*for LASER applications*]
CAF Combined Action Forces [*Military*] (DNAB)
CAF Combined Aviation Force
CAF Comicorum Atticorum Fragmenta [*A publication*] (OCD)
CAF Complete Assembly for Ferry [*Air Force*]
CAF Computer Aided-Fraud (NITA)
CAF Confederate Air Force (EA)
CAF Confederation Africaine de Football [*African Football Confederation - AFC*] (EAIO)
CAF Congressional Action Fund (EA)
CAF Conjunctive Alteration File
CAF Conservative Action Foundation (EA)
caf Consider All Factors (BARN)
CAF Continental Air Forces
CAF Continuous Atrial Fibrillation [*or Flutter*] [*Cardiology*] (DAVI)
CAF Contract Administration Function (DNAB)
CAF Contraction Augmenting Factor [*Medicine*]
CAF Conversion Adjustment Factor
CAF Cooley's Anemia Foundation (EA)
CAF Cooperative Assistance Fund (EA)
CAF Corporacion Andina de Fomento [*Commercial firm Colorado*] (ECON)
CAF Cost Adjustment Factor
CAF Cost and Freight [*Shipping*]
CAF Council on Alternate Fuels (EA)
CAF Cout, Assurance, Fret [*Cost, Insurance, Freight - CIF*] [*Shipping*] [*French*]
CAF Critical Area Flag
CAF Cuban American Foundation (EA)
CAF Curates' Augmentation Fund [*British*]
CAF Currency Adjustment Factor [*Business term*]
CAF Customer Access Facilities [*Telecommunications*]
CAF Cyclophosphamide, Adriamycin, Fluorouracil [*Antineoplastic drug regimen*]
CAF Guided Missile Heavy Cruiser (MCD)
CAFA Canadian Amateur Football Association
CAFA Canadian Arab Friendship Association
CAFA Chicago Academy of Fine Arts
CAFA Coated Abrasives Fabricators Association [*Defunct*] (EA)
CAFAC Commander, All Forces, Aruba-Curacao
CAFAC Commission Africaine de l'Aviation Civile [*African Civil Aviation Commission - AFCAC*] (EAIO)
CAFAF Commander, Amphibious Force, Atlantic Fleet
CAFALSIS Canadian Addiction Foundation, Addictions Librarians Special Interest Section
CAFB Canadian Association of Food Banks [*Association Canadienne des Banques Alimentaires*] (AC)
CAFB Chanute Air Force Base [*Illinois*] (SAA)
CAFB Charleston Air Force Base [*South Carolina*]
CAFB Chemically Active Fluidized Bed [*Fuel gas*]
CAFB Cooke Air Force Base [*Later, VAFB*] (AAG)
CAFC Canadian Association of Fire Chiefs
CAFC Carolina First Corp. [*NASDAQ symbol*] (NQ)
CAFC Computer-Automated Frequency Control (MHDB)
CAFC Congressional Alcohol Fuels Caucus (EA)
CAFC Court of Appeals for the Federal Circuit [*Highest US patent court*]
CAFCA Citizens Against Foreign Control of America (EA)
CAFCA Conventional Armed Forces and Conventional Armaments
CAFCAL Contact a Family Computer Assisted Learning (AIE)
CAF/CANA Conservative Action Foundation/Coalition Against Nuclear Annihilation [*Research center*] (RCD)
CAFD Contact Analog Flight Display
CAFD Council for Academic Freedom and Democracy [*British*]
CAFDA Commandement Aerien des Forces de Defense Aerienne [*Air Defense Forces Air Command*] (NATG)
CAFE Canadian Association for Free Expression
CAFE Canadian Association of Family Enterprise [*Association Canadienne des Enterprises Familiales*] (AC)
CAFE Canadian Association of Fish Exporters (AC)
CAFE Canadian Association of Foundations of Education
CAFE Chemically-Assisted Field Evaporation [*Materials science*]
CAFE Computer-Aided Design of Fire Escapes [*Micro Core Ltd.*] [*Software package*] (NCC)
CAFE Computer-Aided Film Editor
CAFE Conventional Armed Forces in Europe (ECON)
CAFE Cooperative Average Fuel Economy (BARN)
CAFE Corporate Average Fuel Economy [*Automobile industry*]
CAFE Corporate Average Fuel Efficiency [*Automobile Industry*]
CAFE Council of American Forensic Entomologists
CAFE Country Star Restaurants [*NASDAQ symbol*] (TTSB)
CAFE Country Star Restaurants, Inc. [*NASDAQ symbol*] (SAG)
CAFE Negotiations on Conventional Armed Forces in Europe
CAFEA-ICC Commission on Asian and Far Eastern Affairs of the International Chamber of Commerce
CAFEC Consumer Action for Energy Conservation [*British*]
CAFEE Chemical Assembly Fuel Element Exchange (NUCP)
CAFEE Critical Assembly Fuel Element Exchange [*Nuclear energy*]
CAFEP Country Star Rest Cv'A' Pfd [*NASDAQ symbol*] (TTSB)
CAFES Computer-Aided Function Allocation and Evaluation System
CAFF Canadian Association of Firefighters [*Association Canadienne des Pompiers*] (AC)
CAFF Computer-Aided Fault Finding (PDAA)
CAFFI Cyclophosphamide, Adriamycin [*Doxorubicin*], Fluorouracil by Continuous Infusion [*Antineoplastic drug regimen*] (DAVI)
C AFFS for COLS Commissioner for Affidavits for Colonies [*British*] (ROG)

CAFG	Commander, Air Forces, Gulf [British military] (DMA)
CAFGA	Computer Applications for the Graphic Arts
CAFG&S	California Association of Flower Growers and Shippers (SRA)
CAFI	Camco Financial [NASDAQ symbol] (TTSB)
CAFI	Camco Financial Corp. [NASDAQ symbol] (SAG)
CAFI	Canadian Association of Footwear Importers Inc. (AC)
CAFI	Ceramic Arts Federation International (EA)
CAFICS	Canadian Association of Former International Civil Servants [Association Canadienne des Anciens Fonctionnaires Internationaux] (AC)
CAFIG	Circuit Analyzer - Fault Isolation Generator (PDAA)
CAFIP	Canadian Association for Israel Philately
CAFIT	Computer-Assisted Fault Isolation Test
CAFLIS	Coalition for the Advancement of Foreign Languages and International Studies
CAFM	Cable FM [Radio] (NTCM)
CAFM	Commercial Air Freight Movement
CAFM	Computer-Aided Facility Management
CAFMC	Combined Agricultural and Food Machinery Committee [World War II]
CAFMCO	Chief, Air Force Modernization Coordination Office (MCD)
CAFMS	Computer-Assisted Force Management System [Air Force] (PDAA)
CAFMS	Continental Association of Funeral and Memorial Societies
CAFMV	Commissioner's Adjusted Fair Market Value [Business term] (EMRF)
CAFO	Command Accounting and Finance Office (AFM)
CAFO	Confidential Admiralty Fleet Order [British military] (DMA)
CAFO	Confidential Air Force Order [British military] (DMA)
CAFO	Consent Agreement/Final Order (GFGA)
CAFOB	Combined Air Force Operating Base (CINC)
CAFOC	Computer-Aided Flight Operations Center
CAFOD	Catholic Fund for Overseas Development [British]
CAFP	California Academy of Family Physicians (SRA)
CAFP	Colorado Academy of Family Physicians (SRA)
CAFP	Connecticut Academy of Family Physicians (SRA)
CAFP	Cyclophosphamide, Adriamycin, Fluorouracil, Prednisone [Antineoplastic drug regimen]
CAFPF	Commander, Amphibious Force, Pacific Fleet (DNAB)
CAFPME	Canadian Association for Peace in the Middle East
CAFPRS	Canadian Academy of Facial Plastic & Reconstructive Surgery [Academie Canadienne de Chirurgie Plastique et Reconstructive Faciale] [Formerly, Canadian Institute of Facial Plastic Surgery] (AC)
CAfr	Central Africa
CAFR	Comprehensive Annual Financial Report
CAFRAD	Centre Africain de Formation et de Recherche Administratives pour la Developpement [African Training and Research Center in Administration for Development] (IID)
CAFRADES	Centre Africain de Recherche Appliquee et de Formation en Matiere de Developpement Social [African Center for Applied Research and Training in Social Development - ACARTSD] (EAIO)
CAFRIC	Campaign for Real Ice Cream [British] (DI)
CAfrRep	Central African Republic
CAFS	Canadian Arab Friendship Society of Toronto (AC)
CAFS	Canadian Association for Future Studies
CAFS	Cartridge-Actuated Flame System [Terminated Military] (MCD)
CAFS	Center for Advanced Feminist Studies [University of Minnesota] [Research center] (RCD)
CAFS	Central Australian Folk Society
CAFS	Centre for African Family Studies [Kenya] (EAIO)
CAFS	Centre for African Studies [International Planned Parenthood Federation] (ECON)
CAFS	Chinese American Food Society (EA)
CAFS	Content-Addressable File Store [Computer science] (IEEE)
CAFS	Content-Addressable File Store [Computer science] (NITA)
CAFS	Content-Addressed Film System [Computer science] (PDAA)
CAFSAC	Canadian Atlantic Fisheries Scientific Advisory Committee (ASF)
CAFSC	Control Air Force Specialty Code
CAFSMNA	Compound Animal Feeding Stuffs Manufacturers National Association [British] (BI)
CAFSU	Carrier and Field Service Unit (NVT)
CAFT	California, Arizona, Florida, and Texas
CAFT	Center for Advanced Food Technology [Rutgers University]
CAFT	Center for Anti-Fratricide Technology [Army] (DOMA)
CAFT	Clinitron Air Fluidized Therapy [Medicine] (DAVI)
CAFT	Combined Agencies Field Team [US Military Government, Germany]
CAFT	Consolidated Advance Field Team [Navy]
CAFTA	Canadian-American Free Trade Area
CAFTA	Central American Free Trade Area
CAFTD	Commercially Available/Fabricated Training Device
CAFTDR	Commercially Available/Fabricated Training Device Requirement
CAFTN	Commonwealth Air Force Telecommunications Network (IAA)
CAFTR	Commercially Available/Fabricated Training Device Requirement
CAFTRA	Cafeteria
CAFU	Civil Aviation Flying Unit [British] (AIA)
CAFV	Combined Arms Fighting Vehicle (MCD)
CAFVP	Cyclophosphamide, Adriamycin, Fluorouracil, Vincristine, Prednisone [Antineoplastic drug regimen]
CAG	Cagliari [Italy] [Airport symbol] (OAG)
CAG	Caguas [Puerto Rico] [Seismograph station code, US Geological Survey] (SEIS)
CAG	Canadian Air Group (MCD)
CAG	Canadian Association of Geographers
CAG	Canadian Association on Gerontology [Association Canadienne de Gerontologie] (AC)
CAG	Canopus Acquisition Gate [NASA]
CAG	Cap and Gown; a Treasury of College Verse [A publication]

CAG	Carcinogen Assessment Group [Environmental Protection Agency]
CAG	Carrier Air Group [Navy]
CAG	Catapult and Arresting Gear [Aviation] (DNAB)
CAG	Catholic Accountants Guild (EA)
CAG	Catholic Actors Guild of America (EA)
CAG	Ceratobasidium Anastomosis Group [Phytopathology]
CAG	Change Analysis Group
CAG	Chronic Atrophic Gastritis [Medicine]
CAG	Citizen Action Group [Defunct] (EA)
CAG	Civic Action Group [Military] (CINC)
CAG	Civil Affairs Group [Military] (DNAB)
CAG	Civil Air Guard [British]
CAG	Collective Address Group [Navy] (NVT)
CAG	Combat Analysis Group [Joint Chiefs of Staff]
CAG	Combat Arms Group [Army] (AABC)
CAG	Combat Aviation Group
CAG	Combined Action Group [Senior command of all Combined Action Companies] [Military]
CAG	Combined Arms Group [Army]
CAG	Commander, Air Group [Navy]
CAG	Command System Operations Analysis Group Area [Space Flight Operations Facility, NASA]
CAG	Commercial Artists' Guild
CAG	Committee on Autonomous Groups (EA)
CAG	Competition Advocate General [Army]
CAG	Composers-Authors Guild (EA)
CAG	Comptroller and Auditor General
CAG	Computer-Aided Gear Changing [Automotive engineering]
CAG	Computer Applications Group [Air Force]
CAG	Computer Applications Group [Aslib] (NITA)
CAG	Conagra Capital [NYSE symbol] (SAG)
CAG	ConAgra, Inc. [NYSE symbol] (SPSG)
CAG	Concepts Analysis Group [Army]
CAG	Concert Artists Guild (EA)
CAG	Consort Art Graphics [British]
CAG	Constant Altitude Glide
CAG	Cooperative Automation Group [British Library] [Information service or system Defunct] (IID)
CAG	Coronary Angiography [Cardiology] (DMAA)
CAG	Cost Advisory Group [Army]
CAG	Craig, CO [Location identifier FAA] (FAAL)
CAG	Creative Art Group [Australia]
CAG	Crisis Assessment Group [NATO] (NATG)
CAG	Guided Missile Heavy Cruiser [Navy symbol Obsolete]
CAGA	Calgranulin A (DMAA)
CAGA	Catholic Actors Guild of America (EA)
CAGA	Church Architectural Guild of America [Later, IFRAA] (EA)
CAG/ACG	Canadian Association of Geographers/Association Canadienne des Geographes
CAGB	Calgranulin B (DMAA)
CAGB	Coronary Artery Graft Bypass [Cardiology] (DAVI)
CAGC	Canadian Association of Geophysical Contractors (AC)
CAGC	Clutter Automatic Gain Control
CAGC	Coded Automatic Gain Control
CAGC	Continuous-Access Guided Communication [Computer science] (PDAA)
CA GCL	California General Corporation Law [A publication] (DLA)
CAGD	California Academy of General Dentistry (SRA)
CAGD	Computer-Aided Geometric Design (MCD)
CAGE	California Almond Growers Exchange [Later, BDG] (EA)
CAGE	Canadian Air-Ground Environment
CAGE	Commercial and Government Entity (MCD)
CAGE	Compiler and Assembler by General Electric
CAGE	Computer-Aided Genetic Engineering
CAGE	Computerized Aerospace Ground Equipment (MCD)
CAGE	Convicts' Association for a Good Environment [Defunct]
CAGE	Cut Down, Annoyed, Guilty, Eye-Opener [Clinical questions asked to detect alcoholism]
CAGEE	Canadians for Accessible Governmetn & Equal Employment Inc. (AC)
CAGEL	Consolidated Aerospace Ground Equipment List
CAGEL	Consolidated AGE Ground Equipment List (MCD)
CAGFU	Civilian Armed Force Geographical Units [Paramilitary security force] [Philippines] (ECON)
CAGI	Compressed Air and Gas Institute (EA)
CAGIS	Chicago Area Geographic Information Study [University of Illinois at Chicago] [Also, an information service or system] (IID)
Cagle	Cagle's, Inc. [Associated Press] (SAG)
CAgM	Commission for Agricultural Meteorology [WMO] (MSC)
CAG(N)	Guided Missile Heavy Cruiser (Nuclear Propulsion) [Navy symbol]
CAGNE	Commerce Action Group for the Near East [Terminated, 1981]
CAGNY	Chemical Advertisers Group of New York [Inactive] (EA)
CAGO	Cargo Apparent Good Order [Shipping]
CAGP	Canadian Association of Gift Planners (NFD)
CAGP	Canadian Association of Gift Planners
CAGPL	Canadian Arctic Gas Pipeline Ltd.
CAGPrA	ConAgra Cap L.C. 9% Pfd [NYSE symbol] (TTSB)
CAGPrB	ConAgra Cap L.C.Adj Pfd'B' [NYSE symbol] (TTSB)
CAGPrC	ConAgra Cap L.C.9.35% Pfd [NYSE symbol] (TTSB)
CAGR	Casa Grande Ruins National Monument [National Park Service designation]
CAGR	Civil Advanced Gas-Cooled Reactor (NUCP)
CAGR	Commercial Advanced Gas-Cooled Reactor (NUCP)
CAGR	Comparison of Annual Growth Rate
CAGR	Compound Annual Growth Rate [Business term]

CAGR	Cumulative Annual Growth Rate [*Business term*]
CAGS	Canadian Association for Graduate Studies (AC)
CAGS	Canadian Association of General Surgeons
CAGS	Certificate of Advanced Graduate Study
CAGS	Chet Atkins Guitar Society [*British*] (EAIO)
CAGS	Chinese Academy of Geological Science
CAGSB	Certificate in Advanced Study in Business (GAGS)
CAGW	Citizens Against Government Waste (EA)
CAGW	Committee Against Government Waste (EA)
CAGY	Columbus & Greenville Railway Co. [*AAR code*]
CAH	Cambridge Ancient History [*1st edition, 1923-39*] [*A publication*] (OCD)
CAH	Canadian Association of Hispanists [*See also ACH*]
CAH	Canadian Automotive Historians (AC)
CAH	Canarchon Holdings Ltd. [*Toronto Stock Exchange symbol*]
CAH	Cardinal Health [*NYSE symbol*] (TTSB)
CAH	Cardinal Health, Inc. [*NYSE symbol*] (SAG)
CAH	Center for American History [*University of Texas, Austin*] [*Research center*] (RCD)
CAH	Center for Attitudinal Healing (EA)
CAH	Chronic Active Hepatitis [*Medicine*]
CAH	Chronic Aggressive Hepatitis [*Medicine*] (MEDA)
CAH	College of Agriculture and Horticulture [*British*] (DI)
CAH	Command Airways [*South Africa ICAO designator*] (FAAC)
CAH	Community of All Hallows [*Anglican religious community*]
CAH	Conference on Asian History (EA)
CAH	Congenital Adrenal Hyperplasia [*Medicine*]
CAH	Council of American Homeowners (EA)
CAH	Cyanacetic Acid Hydrazine [*Organic chemistry*] (DAVI)
CAH	Cyanocethydrazide [*Antihelminthic*] (ADA)
CAH	Valparaiso, FL [*Location identifier FAA*] (FAAL)
CAH²	Cambridge Ancient History [*2nd edition*] [*A publication*] (OCD)
CAHA	Canadian Administrative Housekeepers Association (AC)
CAHA	Canadian Amateur Hockey Association
CAHA	Canadian Association of Health-Care Auxiliaries [*Associations des Auxiliaires Benevoles des Etablissements de Sante du Canada*] [*Formerly, Canadian Association of Hospital Auxiliaries*] (AC)
CAHA	Cape Hatteras National Seashore [*National Park Service designation*]
CAHALS	Catapult Hookup and Launch Surveillance
CAHB	Chronic Active Hepatitis Type B [*Medicine*]
CAHB	Colorado Association of Home Builders (SRA)
CAHC	Center for the Advancement of Human Co-Operation (EA)
CAHC	Coalition for Affordable Health Care
CAHC	Compagnie d'Assurance d'Hypotheques du Canada [*Mortgage Insurance Co. of Canada - MICC*]
CAHC	Connecticut Association for Home Care (SRA)
CAHCL	Capitol Area Health Consortium Libraries [*Library network*]
CAHD	Coronary Artery Heart Disease [*Cardiology*] (DAVI)
CAHD	Coronary Atherosclerotic Heart Disease [*Medicine*] (MAE)
Cah de la Fac de Droit Nancy	Cahiers. Faculte de Droit et des Sciences Economiques de Nancy [*A publication*] (DLA)
CAHDRT	Center Ad Hoc Data Review Team [*NASA*] (KSC)
CAHE	Core Auxiliary Heat Exchanger [*Nuclear energy*] (NRCH)
CAHEA	Committee on Allied Health Education and Accreditation (EA)
CAHF	California Association of Health Facilities (SRA)
CAHF	Campaign Against Health Fraud [*British*] (DBA)
CAHI	Canadian Animal Health Institute [*Institut Canadien de la Sante Animale*] (AC)
CAHI	Canadian Association of Home Inspectors (AC)
CAHI	Central Aero-Hydrodynamical Institute [*Former USSR*]
Cahier Dr Fiscal	Cahiers de Droit Fiscal International [*A publication*] (DLA)
Cahill's Ill St	Cahill's Illinois Statutes [*A publication*] (DLA)
CAHIPE	Committee of the Associations of Honey Importers and Packers of Europe (EAIO)
CAHIS	California Association of Hearing Instrument Specialists (SRA)
CAHJP	Central Archives for the History of the Jewish People [*Jerusalem*] [*A publication*] (BJA)
CAHN	Canadian Association for the History of Nursing (AC)
CAHP	California Association of Highway Patrolmen (SRA)
CAHP	Canadian Academy of the History of Pharmacy [*Academie Canadienne d'Histoire de la Pharmacie*] (AC)
CAHP	Certified by the Association for Healthcare Philanthropy (NFD)
CAHP	Certified Member of AHP [*Association of Healthcare Philanthropy*]
CAHPER	Canadian Association for Health, Physical Education, and Recreation
CAHPERD	California Association for Health, Physical Education, Recreation, and Dance (SRA)
CAHPERD	Canadian Association for Health, Physical Education, Recreation & Dance [*Association Canadienne pour la Sante, l'Education Physique, les Loisirs et la Danse*] (AC)
CAHR	Center for Advanced Heart Research
CAHR	Council for the Advancement of Hospital Recreation [*Defunct*] (EA)
CAHRC	Central American Human Rights Committee [*British*]
CAHRO	Canadian Association of Housing and Renewal Officials
CAHRS	Compass Altitude Heading Reference System (DWSG)
CAHS	Canadian Association of Hungarian Studies [*See also ACEH*]
CAHS	Canadian Aviation Historical Society (AC)
CAHS	Centre for Applied Health Studies [*University of Ulster at Coleraine*] [*British*] (CB)
CAHS	Civil Aviation Historical Society [*Australia*]
CAHS	Comprehensive Automation of the Hydrometeorological Service
CAHS	Connecticut Association for Human Services (SRA)
CAHS	Council of Australian Humanist Societies
CAHSA	California Association of Homes and Services for the Aging (SRA)
CAHSA	Colorado Association of Homes and Services for the Aging (SRA)
CAHSAH	California Association for Health Services at Home (SRA)

CAHSL	Connecticut Association of Health Sciences Libraries [*Library network*]
CAHSLA	Cincinnati Area Health Sciences Library Association [*Library network*]
CAHSP	Center for the Advancement of Human Service Practice (EA)
CAHT	Canadian Associate for Humane Trapping (AC)
CAHT	Computer Aids for Human Translation [*Carnegie-Mellon University*] (NITA)
CAHUMC	Commission on Archives and History of the United Methodist Church (EA)
Cai	Caines' New York Cases in Error [*A publication*] (DLA)
Cai	Caines' Reports, New York Supreme Court [*A publication*] (DLA)
Cai	Caines' Term Reports, New York Supreme Court [*A publication*] (DLA)
CAI	Cairo [*Egypt*] [*Airport symbol*] (OAG)
CAI	Caithness [*County in Scotland*] (ROG)
CAI	Calcium-Aluminum-Rich Inclusion [*Meteorite composition*]
CAI	Canadian Aeronautical Institute
CAI	Canadian Airlines International Ltd. [*Canadian Pacific Airlines Ltd. and Pacific Western Airlines Ltd.*] [*Formed by a merger of*]
CAI	Canadian Arctic Island
CAI	Canlan Investment Corp. [*Vancouver Stock Exchange symbol*]
CAI	Canvas Awning Institute [*Later, American Canvas Institute*] (EA)
CAI	Carboxyamidoimidazole [*Organic chemistry*]
CAI	Carcinogenic Activity Indicator (FFDE)
CAI	Career Apparel Institute (EA)
CAI	Career Assessment Inventory [*Vocational guidance test*]
CAI	Career Awareness Inventory [*Vocational guidance test*]
CAI	Center for Archaeological Investigations [*Southern Illinois University at Carbondale*] [*Research center*] (RCD)
CAI	Center for Arts Information [*Defunct*] (EA)
cai	Central American Indian [*MARC language code Library of Congress*] (LCCP)
CAI	Chemical and Allied Industries [*Department of Employment*] [*British*]
CAI	Children's Aid International (EA)
CAI	Children's Authors and Illustrators [*A publication*]
CAI	Chinese Army in India
CAI	Civic Action Institute [*Defunct*] (EA)
CAI	Civil Aeromedical Institute [*FAA*]
CAI	Close Approach Indicator (IEEE)
CAI	Clowns of America International (EA)
CAI	Coded Acoustic Interrogator
CAI	Codon Adaptation Index [*Genetics*]
CAI	Combined Arms Initiative [*Army*]
CAI	Comite Arctique International [*International Arctic Committee*] [*Monte Carlo, Monaco*] (EAIO)
CAI	Commission d'Appel de l'Immigration [*Immigration Appeal Board - IAB*] [*Canada*]
CAI	Common Air Interface [*Telecommunications*]
CAI	Common Air Interference
CAI	Communication Advisors, Inc. [*Southfield, MI*] [*Telecommunications*] (TSSD)
CAI	Community Associations Institute (EA)
CAI	Compagnia Aeronautica Italiana SPA [*Italy ICAO designator*] (FAAC)
CAI	Compressed Air Institute (KSC)
CAI	Computer-Administered [*or Assisted*] Instruction (RDA)
CAI	Computer-Aided Industry (IAA)
CAI	Computer-Aided Inspection (BTTJ)
CAI	Computer-Aided [*or -Assisted*] Instruction
CAI	Computer Analog Input
CAI	Computer Applications, Inc. (MCD)
CAI	Computer-Assisted Image
CAI	Computer Assisted Instruction (AIE)
CAI	Computer-Assisted Instruction Project [*Army-Signal Center and School*] [*Fort Monmouth, NJ*]
CAI	Computer-Assisted Interviewing (GFGA)
CAI	Computer Automation, Inc.
CAI	Confederation of Aerial Industries [*British*] (DBA)
CAI	Confederation of American Indians (EA)
CAI	Confederation of Ariel Industries (NITA)
CAI	Conference Aeronautique Internationale [*International Aeronautical Conference*]
CAI	Configuration Acceptance Inspection
CAI	Configuration Audit Inspection [*Army*] (AABC)
CAI	Configured Article Identifier
CAI	Confused Artificial Insemination
CAI	Conjunctive Alteration Indicator
CAI	Connectionless Acknowledged Information
CAI	Constructive Action, Inc. [*Whittier, CA*] (EA)
CAI	Continental Airlines, Inc. [*NYSE symbol*] (SPSG)
CAI	Control Area Indicator (MCD)
CAI	Control and Acquisition Interface (KSC)
CAI	Corporacion Aereo Internacional SA de CV [*Mexico ICAO designator*] (FAAC)
CAI	Corporate Agents, Inc. [*Information service or system*] (IID)
CAI	Counselor Activity Inventory [*Guidance*]
CAI	Crochet Association International (EA)
CAI	Croquet Association of Ireland (EAIO)
CAI	Current Annual Increment (DICI)
CAIA	California Apparel Industries Association [*Later, CFC*] (EA)
CAIA	Clock Assemblers and Importers Association (EA)
CAIA	Council of American Indian Artists (EA)
CAIB	California Association of Independent Business (SRA)
CAIB	Canadian Accredited Insurance Broker (DD)
CAIB	Certified Associate of the Institute of Bankers [*Canada*] (DD)
CAIB	Certified Associate of the Institute of Bankers (ODBW)

CAIBE.........	Chemically-Assisted Ion Beam Etching (MCD)
CAIC...........	Canadian Association of Investment Clubs
CAIC...........	Central America Information Center [*An association*] (EA)
CAIC...........	Chemical Accident/Incident Control (MCD)
CAIC...........	Civil Aviation Information Circular [*British*] (AIA)
CAIC...........	Coalition of Apparel Industries in California (SRA)
CAIC...........	Commission Internationale des Activites Commerciales [*International Commission on Commercial Activities*] (EAIO)
CAIC...........	Computer-Assisted Indexing and Categorizing [*or Classification*]
CAIC...........	Computer-Assisted Instruction Center
Cai Ca........	Caines' Cases [*New York*] [*A publication*] (DLA)
Cai Cas........	Caines' New York Cases in Error [*A publication*] (DLA)
Cai Cas........	Caines' Reports, New York Supreme Court [*A publication*] (DLA)
Cai Cas.......	Caines' Term Reports, New York Supreme Court [*A publication*] (DLA)
Cai Cas Err...	Caines' New York Cases in Error [*A publication*] (DLA)
CAICB	Conseil des Associations d'Ingenieurs du Commonwealth Britannique [*Commonwealth Engineers Council*] (EAIO)
CAICO	Chemical Accident/Incident Control Officer [*Military*] (AABC)
CAICYT	Centro Argentino de Informacion Cientifica y Tecnologica [*Argentine Center for Scientific and Technological Information*] [*Information service or system*] (IID)
CAID	Canadian Agency for International Development [*Defunct*]
CAID	Civil Affairs Inland Depot [*for relief supplies to liberated territory*] [*British World War II*]
CAID	Computer Aid
CAID	Computer-Aided Industrial Design (BTTJ)
CAID	Convention of American Instructors of the Deaf (EA)
CAIE..........	Centro de Analisis e Investigacion Economica [*Participant in the Inter-American Bank Research Network*] [*Mexico*] (CROSS)
CAIE..........	Standing Committee on Archival Information Exchange [*Society of American Archivists*] [*Information service or system*] (IID)
CAIFI.........	Committee for Artistic and Intellectual Freedom in Iran (EA)
Cai Forms...	Caines' Practical (New York) Forms [*A publication*] (DLA)
CAIG	Canadian Aircraft Insurance Group
CAIG	Cost Analysis Improvement Group [*DoD*] (DOMA)
CAII...........	Capital Associates [*NASDAQ symbol*] (TTSB)
CAII...........	Capital Associates, Inc. [*NASDAQ symbol*] (NQ)
CAII...........	Carbonic Anhydrase II [*Analytical chemistry*]
CAIIA	California Association of Independent Insurance Adjusters (SRA)
CAIL..........	Canadian Airlines International Ltd. [*Canadian Pacific Airlines Ltd. and Pacific Western Airlines Ltd.*] [*Formed by a merger of*]
CAIL..........	Computer-Aided Information Logistics (IAA)
CAILC.........	Canadian Association of Independent Living Centres (AC)
Cai Lex Mer...	Caines' Lex Mercatoria Americana [*A publication*] (DLA)
CAILS.........	Certified American Indian Lineage Specialist
CAIMAF.......	Canadian Advanced Industrial Materials Forum [*Forum Canadien des Materiaux Industriels de Haute Qualite*] (AC)
CAIMAW......	Canadian Association of Industrial, Mechanical, and Allied Workers
CAIMS	CONUS [*Continental United States*] Army Installation Management Study
CAIMS	Conventional Ammunition Integrated Management System
Cain...........	Caines' New York Cases in Error [*A publication*] (DLA)
Cain...........	Caines' Reports, New York Supreme Court [*A publication*] (DLA)
Cain...........	Caines' Term Reports, New York Supreme Court [*A publication*] (DLA)
CAIN	Calculation of Inertia (IAA)
CAIN	Cataloging and Indexing Number [*Later, AGRICOLA*] [*National Agricultural Library Database*]
CAIN	Computer Algebra Information Network [*Computer science*]
CAIN	Computer Anxiety Index (EDAC)
CAIN	Computerised AIDS [*Acquired Immune Deficiency Syndrome*] Network [*Medicine Australia*]
CAIN	Computerized AIDS [*Acquired Immune Deficiency Syndrome*] Information Network [*Los Angeles Gay and Lesbian Community Services Center*] [*Database*]
Cain Cas in Error...	Caines' New York Cases in Error [*A publication*] (DLA)
Cain CE.......	Caines' New York Cases in Error [*A publication*] (DLA)
Cain E........	Caines' New York Cases in Error [*A publication*] (DLA)
Caine R	Caines' Reports [*New York*] [*A publication*] (DLA)
Caines	Caines' New York Cases in Error [*A publication*] (DLA)
Caines	Caines' Reports, New York Supreme Court [*A publication*] (DLA)
Caines	Caines' Term Reports, New York Supreme Court [*A publication*] (DLA)
Caines Ca in E...	Caines' New York Cases in Error [*A publication*] (DLA)
Caines' Ca in Er...	Caines' New York Cases in Error [*A publication*] (DLA)
Caines Cas...	Caines' New York Cases in Error [*A publication*] (DLA)
Caines Cas...	Caines' Reports, New York Supreme Court [*A publication*] (DLA)
Caines Cas...	Caines' Term Reports, New York Supreme Court [*A publication*] (DLA)
Caines' Cas in Er...	Caines' New York Cases in Error [*A publication*] (DLA)
Caines (NY)...	Caines' New York Cases in Error [*A publication*] (DLA)
Caines (NY)...	Caines' Reports, New York Supreme Court [*A publication*] (DLA)
Caines (NY)...	Caines' Term Reports, New York Supreme Court [*A publication*] (DLA)
Caines' R.....	Caines' Reports [*New York*] [*A publication*] (DLA)
Caines Rep...	Caines' Reports [*New York*] [*A publication*] (DLA)
Caines Term Rep (NY)...	Caines' Term Reports, New York Supreme Court [*A publication*] (DLA)
CAINS	Carrier Aircraft [*or Alignment*] Inertial Navigation System (MCD)
CAINS	Computer-Aided Instruction System (MHDB)
Cains C.......	Caines' Cases [*New York*] [*A publication*] (DLA)
Cains R.......	Caines' Reports [*New York*] [*A publication*] (DLA)
CAINSW......	Chamber of Automotive Industries of New South Wales [*Australia*]
CAINT	Computer-Assisted Interrogation (IAA)
CAINT	Counter-Air and Interdiction
Cai (NY)	Caines' Reports [*New York*] [*A publication*] (DLA)
CAIO	Caribbean American Intercultural Organization (EA)
CAI/O	Computer Analog Input/Output (DEN)
CAIO	Corps Artillery Intelligence Officer [*British*]
CAIOGP.......	Council of Active Independent Oil and Gas Producers (EA)
CA ION.......	Calcium, Ionized [*Organic chemistry*] (DAVI)
CAIOP	Computer Analog Input/Output
CAIP..........	Catholic Association for International Peace [*Defunct*] (EA)
CAIP..........	Center for Computer Aids for Industrial Productivity [*Rutgers University*] [*Research center*] (RCD)
CAIP..........	Civil Aircraft Inspection Procedure (DA)
CAIP..........	Computer Assisted Indexing Program (NITA)
CAIP..........	Concerned American Indian Parents (EA)
Cai Pr	Caines' Practice [*A publication*] (DLA)
Cai R	Caines' New York Cases in Error [*A publication*] (DLA)
Cai R	Caines' Reports, New York Supreme Court [*A publication*] (DLA)
Cai R	Caines' Term Reports, New York Supreme Court [*A publication*] (DLA)
CAIR	Child Abuse Institute of Research (EA)
CAIR	Comprehensive Assessment Information Rule [*Environmental Protection Agency*]
CAIR	Concerned Americans for Individual Rights (EA)
CAIR	Conquest Industries Corp. [*NASDAQ symbol*] (SAG)
CAIR	Cost Analysis Information Report [*Air Force*] (MCD)
CAIR	Council on American-Islamic Relations
CAIR	Countermeasures, Airborne Infrared
CAIRA	Central Automated Inventory and Referral Activity [*Organization for operation of CAIRS*] [*Air Force*]
CAIRC	Caribbean Air Command [*Air Force*]
Cairn..........	Cairn Energy USA, Inc. [*Associated Press*] (SAG)
Cairns Dec...	Cairns. Decisions in the Albert Arbitration (Reilly) [*1871-75*] [*England*] [*A publication*] (DLA)
CAIRS	Canadian Institute for Radiation Safety [*Institut Canadien de Radioprotection*] (AC)
CAIRS	Central Automated Inventory and Referral System [*Air Force*]
CAIRS	Close Air Support
CAIRS	Computer-Aided Analysis and Information Recovery Systems (MCD)
CAIRS	Computer-Assisted Information Retrieval Service [*Mississippi State University*] (OLDSS)
CAIRS	Computer Assisted Information Retrieval System (NITA)
CAIRS	Computer-Assisted Interactive Resources Scheduling System
CAIRW........	Conquest Inds Wrrt [*NASDAQ symbol*] (TTSB)
CAIS..........	Canadian Association for Information Science [*Ottawa, ON*]
CAIS..........	Canadian Association for Irish Studies
CAIS..........	Canadian Association of Independent Schools (EAIO)
CAIS..........	Center for Applied Isotope Studies [*University of Georgia*] [*Research center*] (RCD)
CAIS..........	Center for Arab-Islamic Studies (EA)
CAIS..........	Central Abstracting and Indexing Service [*American Petroleum Institute*] [*Information service or system*] (IID)
CAIS..........	Centre for Aboriginal and Islander Studies [*Northern Territory*] [*Australia*]
CAIS..........	Common Ada Interface Standard [*British*]
CAIS..........	Common APSE [*Ada Program Support Environment*] Interface Set [*Computer science*]
CAIS..........	Communication and Information Systems [*Micro-Electronics Programme*] [*British*] (NITA)
CAIS..........	Complete Androgen Insensitivity Syndrome [*Medicine*] (DMAA)
CAIS..........	Computer-Aided Instruction (IEEE)
CAIS..........	Computer-Assisted Action Information System [*NATO*]
CAIS..........	Computer-Assisted Introduction System (SSD)
CAIS..........	Congress of Arabic and Islamic Studies [*Madrid, Spain*] (EA)
CAISA	Campaign Against Investment in South Africa [*Defunct*] (EA)
CAIS/ACSI....	Canadian Association for Information Science/Association Canadienne des Sciencesde l'Information (IID)
CAISF.........	Chemical Abstracts Integrated Subject File [*Chemical Abstracts Service*] [*Database*] [*A publication*] (IID)
CAISH	Computer Assisted Instruction and Support for the Handicapped (EDAC)
CAISIM	Computer-Assisted Industrial Simulation [*Army*]
CAISM	Central Association of Irish Schoolmistresses (BI)
CAISMS	Computer-Assisted Instruction Study Management System (MCD)
CAISR	Center for Automation and Intelligent Systems Research [*Case Western Reserve University*] [*Research center*] (RCD)
CAISYS	Computer-Aided Instruction System [*Programming language*] [*1971*] (CSR)
CAIT...........	Canadian Association of Immersion Teachers (AC)
CAITE.........	Computer Aided Instruction for Teacher Education (EDAC)
caith	Caithness County [*Scotland*] (BARN)
Cai TR	Caines' Term Reports, New York Supreme Court [*A publication*] (DLA)
CAITS.........	Centre for Alternative Industrial and Technological Systems [*British*] (CB)
CAITS.........	Chemical Agent Identification Training Set
CAITS.........	Computer-Aided Interactive Testing System (EDAC)
CAITS.........	Computerized Automatic Inertial Test Set (MCD)
CAITT.........	Construction Acquisition Improvement Implementation Team (AAGC)
CAIV..........	Computer-Assisted Interactive Video
CAIV..........	Cost as an Independent Variable (AAGC)
CAIVman......	Computer Audio Interactive Video Manipulator [*Designed by Christopher Conley*]
CAIVR	Computer-Assisted Instruction with Voice Response (MHDI)
CAI Wre	CAI Wireless Systems, Inc. [*Associated Press*] (SAG)
CAIX..........	Central American International [*Air carrier designation symbol*]

CAJ	Canadian Association of Journalists [*L'Association Canadienne des Journalistes*] (AC)
CAJ	Canaima [*Venezuela*] [*Airport symbol*] (OAG)
CAJ	Canasia Industries Corp. [*Vancouver Stock Exchange symbol*]
CAJ	Caulked Joint
CAJ	Center for Administrative Justice [*Later, NCAJ*] (EA)
CAJ	Comision Andina de Juristas [*Andean Commission of Jurists - ACJ*] (EAIO)
CAJ	Committee on the Administration of Justice [*British*] (DBA)
CAJ	Consumers' Association of Jamaica
CAJ	Cougar Air, Inc. [*Canada ICAO designator*] (FAAC)
CAJAD	Canadian Association of Japanese Automovbile Dealers (AC)
CAJAD	Center po Atomn. i Jadernum Dannym [*Center for Nuclear Structure and Reaction Data*] [*USSR State Committee on the Utilization of Atomic Energy*] [*Information service or system*] (IID)
CAJC	California Jury Instructions, Criminal [*A publication*] (DLA)
CAJE	Coalition for Alternatives in Jewish Education (EA)
CAJE	Coalition for the Advancement of Jewish Education (EA)
CAJE	Comprehensive Antijam Equipment (MCD)
CAJE	Computer-Assisted Job Evaluation [*Human resources*] (WYGK)
CAJE	Consolidated Anti-Jam Equipment (MCD)
CAJI	California Jury Instructions, Civil [*A publication*] (DLA)
CAJIR	Association Canadienne d'Assistance Juridique, d'Information et de Recherche desHandicapes [*Canadian Legal Advocacy Information and Research Association of the Disabled*]
CAJL	Central-Anzeiger fuer Juedische Litteratur [*A publication*] (BJA)
CAJLE	Canadian Association for Japanese Language Education (AC)
CAJM	Council of American Jewish Museums (EA)
CAJP	Central Archives of the Jewish People [*Jerusalem*] [*A publication*] (BJA)
CAJP	Christian Anti-Jewish Party (BJA)
CAJR	New York State Commission on Administration of Justice, Report [*A publication*] (DLA)
CAK	Akron/Canton [*Ohio*] [*Airport symbol*]
CAK	Canadian Arctic Petroleum [*Vancouver Stock Exchange symbol*]
CAK	CDK (Cyclin Dependent Kinae) Activating Kinae [*An enzyme*]
CAK	Command Access Keys
CAK	Command Acknowledge (BUR)
CAK	Concept Assessment Kit [*Child development test*]
CAK	Conical Alignment Kit
CAK	County Air Services Ltd. [*British ICAO designator*] (FAAC)
CAK	Cube Alignment Kit
CAKE	Cheesecake Factory [*NASDAQ symbol*] (TTSB)
CAKE	[*The*] Cheesecake Factory, Inc. [*NASDAQ symbol*] (SAG)
Cal	All India Reporter, Calcutta Series [*A publication*] (DLA)
Cal	Calando [*Dying Away*] [*Music*]
CALC	Calcium [*Symbol is Ca*] [*Chemical element*] (ROG)
CAL	Calcium [*Test*] [*Dentistry*] (DAVI)
CAL	Calcraft [*Hangman*] [*Slang British*] (DSUE)
cAL	Calcrete [*Geology*]
CAL	Calculated Average Life (AAG)
CAL	Calcutta [*India*] [*Seismograph station code, US Geological Survey*] (SEIS)
Cal	Caldecott's English Settlement Cases [*1776-85*] [*A publication*] (DLA)
CAL	Caldwell College for Women, Caldwell, NJ [*OCLC symbol*] (OCLC)
CAL	Caledonia [*Scotland*] (ROG)
CAL	Calendae [*Calends*] [*The First Day of the Month*] [*Latin*] (ROG)
CAL	Calendar
cal	Calendar (VRA)
cal	Calendar (WDMC)
Cal	Calendars of the Proceedings in Chancery, Record Commission [*A publication*] (DLA)
Cal	Calendered Paper (BARN)
CAL	Cal Fed Bancorp [*NYSE symbol*] (TTSB)
CAL	Caliber (AFM)
Cal	Caliber (DMAA)
CAL	Calibrate (CET)
CAL	Calibration (MSA)
CAL	California
CAL	California Federal Bank [*NYSE symbol*] (SPSG)
Cal	California Reports [*A publication*] (DLA)
CALS	Call Aircraft Co.
CAL	Callus [*Medicine*] (DAVI)
CAL	Calomel [*Pharmacy*] (ROG)
CAL	Calorie (MSA)
cal	Calorie (IDOE)
CAL	Calspan Corp. [*Formerly, Cornell Aeronautical Laboratory*]
Cal	Calthrop's English King's Bench Reports [*80 English Reprint*] [*A publication*] (DLA)
CAL	Campbeltown [*Scotland*] [*Airport symbol*] (OAG)
CAL	Canadian Airways Ltd.
CAL	Canadian Arsenals Limited
CAL	CAN [*Controller Area Network*] Application Layer (ACII)
CAL	Capella Resources Ltd. [*Vancouver Stock Exchange symbol*]
CAL	Capitol Air Lines
CAL	Cargo Air Lines [*Israel*] (BJA)
CAL	Caribbean Action Lobby (EA)
CAL	Carter-Atkinson Lurmann Mechanism [*Air pollution*]
CAL	Center for Applied Linguistics (EA)
CAL	Center for Army Leadership [*Fort Leavenworth, KS*] (INF)
CAL	Certificate in Applied Linguistics (PGP)
CAL	Certificate of Advanced Librarianship (PGP)
CAL	China Airlines [*Taiwan*] [*ICAO designator*] (FAAC)
CAL	Chiropractic Association of Louisiana (SRA)
CAL	Chronic Airflow Limitation [*Medicine*]

CAL	Colonial Air Lines
CAL	Comandos Armados de Liberacion [*Armed Liberation Commandos*] [*Puerto Rico*] (PD)
CAL	Command Authorization List
CAL	Common Assembler Language [*Computer science*] (NITA)
CAL	Common Assembly Language (MCD)
CAL	Component Action List [*NASA*] (KSC)
CAL	Composite Assessment of Leverage (EDAC)
CAL	Compressed Air Loudspeaker
CAL	Computer-Aided [*or -Assisted*] Learning (BUR)
CAL	Computer-Aided Lighting [*Automotive engineering*]
CAL	Computer-Aided Logistics [*Army*]
CAL	Computer Animation Language
CAL	Computer Assisted Learning (AIE)
CAL	Computer Augmented Learning (CMD)
CAL	Confined Area Landing
CAL	Conservation Analytical Laboratory [*Smithsonian Institution*]
CAL	Continental Airlines, Inc. (MCD)
CAL	Continuity Accept Limit
CAL	Continuous Annealing Line (PDAA)
CAL	Contractor Alert List (AAGC)
CAL	Contractor Attention List
CAL	Conversational Algebraic Language [*Adaptation of JOSS language*] [*Computer science*]
CAL	Copy and Add Logical Word (CET)
CAL	Cornell Aeronautical Laboratory (KSC)
CAL	Course Author Language [*Computer science*]
Cal	Large Calorie (DMAA)
CAL	Romance Writers of America. Chapter Advisory Letter [*A publication*] (EAAP)
Cal 2d	California Reports, Second Series [*A publication*] (DLA)
Cal 3d	California Reports, Third Series [*A publication*] (DLA)
CAla	Alameda Free Library, Alameda, CA [*Library symbol Library of Congress*] (LCLS)
Cala	Calcified Alluvium [*Archeology*]
CALA	Canadian Association of Legal Assistants (AC)
CALA	Charles A. Lindbergh Association [*Defunct*] (EA)
CALA	Chinese-American Librarians Association (EA)
CALA	Citizens Against Lawyer Abuse (EA)
CALA	Civil Aviation Licensing Act (DLA)
CALA	Combined Administrative Liquidating Agency [*Microfilmed SHAEF documents for each participating country after SHAEF was disbanded*] [*Post-World War II*]
CALA	Community Action on Latin America (EA)
CALA	Computer-Aided Loads Analysis (MCD)
CALA	Contemporary Archive on Latin America [*Defunct British*]
CALAC	Lockheed-California Co. [*Division of Lockheed Aircraft Corp.*] (MCD)
CALACS	Canadian Association of Latin American and Caribbean Studies
Cal Adm Code	California Administrative Code [*A publication*] (DLA)
Cal Admin Code	California Administrative Code [*A publication*] (DLA)
Cal Admin Reg	California Administrative Register [*A publication*] (DLA)
Cal Adv Legis Serv	California Advance Legislative Service (Deering) [*A publication*] (DLA)
CALAFCO	California Association of Local Agency Formation Commissions (SRA)
Cal Agric Code	California Agriculture Code [*A publication*] (DLA)
CALALT	Calculated Altitude
CalAmp	California Amplifier, Inc. [*Associated Press*] (SAG)
Cal App	California Appellate Reports [*A publication*] (DLA)
Cal App 2d	California Appellate Reports, Second Series [*A publication*] (DLA)
Cal App 2d Supp	California Appellate Reports, Second Series, Supplement [*A publication*] (DLA)
Cal App 3d	California Appellate Reports, Third Series [*A publication*] (DLA)
Cal App 3d Supp	California Appellate Reports, Third Series, Supplement [*A publication*] (DLA)
Cal App Dec	California Appellate Decisions [*A publication*] (DLA)
Cal App Supp	California Appellate Reports, Supplement [*A publication*] (DLA)
CALAR	Cooperative Arid Lands Agriculture Research Program [*Established by Egypt, Israel, and the US at the University of San Diego in 1981*]
CalArts	California Institute of the Arts [*Valencia, CA*]
CALAS	Canadian Association for Laboratory Animal Science
CALAS	Canadian Association of Latin American Studies
CALAS	Computer-Aided Laboratory Automation System (IAA)
CALAS	Computer-Assisted Language Analysis System (PDAA)
CaLaSOAP	Calcium Lanthanum Silicate Oxyapatite (IEEE)
calasp	Cytosine Arabinoside, Vincristine, L-Asparaginase, Prednisone [*Antineoplastic drug regimen*] (DAVI)
CAlaUN	United States Naval Air Station, Alameda, CA [*Library symbol Library of Congress*] (LCLS)
CAlb	Albany Free Public Library, Albany, CA [*Library symbol Library of Congress*] (LCLS)
Calb	Albumin Clearance [*Biochemistry*] (DAVI)
CALB	Computer-Aided Line Balance
CAlbA	United States Department of Agriculture, Western Regional Research Laboratory, Albany, CA [*Library symbol Library of Congress*] (LCLS)
CAL-BIO	California Biotechnology, Inc.[*Later, Scios, Inc.*]
CALBLK	Calibration Blank [*Spectroscopy*]
CalBnc	California Bancshares, Inc. [*Associated Press*] (SAG)
CALBR	Calibration (AABC)
CAL Bull	Association of the Bar of the City of New York. Committee on Amendment of the Law. Bulletin [*A publication*] (DLA)
CALC	Calculate [*or Calculated*]
CALC	Calculator (WDAA)

CALC........... Calculus (WDAA)
CALC........... Calcutta [*India*] (ROG)
CALC........... Cargo Allocation and Load Control [*Aviation*]
CALC........... Chicago Academic Library Council [*Library network*]
CALC........... Clergy and Laity Concerned (EA)
CALC........... Commonwealth Aluminum [*NASDAQ symbol*] (TTSB)
CALC........... Commonwealth Aluminum Corp. [*NASDAQ symbol*] (SAG)
CALC........... Commonwealth Association of Legislative Counsel (AC)
CALC........... Computer Aided Learning Centre [*Victoria University*] [*Australia*]
CALC........... Curl's Algorithm for Logic Compression
CALC........... Customer Access Line Charge [*Telecommunications*]
Calc........... Indian Law Reports, Calcutta Series [*A publication*] (DLA)
Cal C Arts & Crafts... California College of Arts and Crafts (GAGS)
CALCAV........ Clergy and Laymen Concerned about Vietnam [*Later, CALC*] (EA)
CALCC .... Charles A. Lindbergh Collectors Club (EA)
CALCD .... Calculated (ADA)
CAL/CERT ... Calibration/Certification (SAA)
Cal Ch .... Calendar of Proceedings in Chancery Tempore Elizabeth [*1827-32*] [*A publication*] (DLA)
Calc LJ ...... Calcutta Law Journal [*A publication*] (DLA)
CalCmB....... California Community Bancshares Corp. [*Associated Press*] (SAG)
CALCN........ Calculation (IAA)
CALCO........ Capitol Area Library Consortium, Inc. [*Library network*]
Cal Code...... Deering's Annotated California Code [*A publication*] (DLA)
Cal Code Regs... California Code of Regulations [*Also CCR*] [*A publication*] (AAGC)
CALCOFI...... California Cooperative Oceanic Fishery Investigations [*Also, CCOFI*]
CALCOMP .... California Computer Products, Inc. (MCD)
Cal Comp Cases... California Compensation Cases [*A publication*] (DLA)
CALCON....... California Connections [*Information service or system*] (CRD)
Cal Const..... California Constitution [*A publication*] (DLA)
CAL-COPS.... California Council of Police and Sheriffs (SRA)
CALCQ .... Confederation des Associations Linguistiques et Culturelles du Quebec (EA)
Calc Ser ...... Calcutta Series, Indian Law Reports [*A publication*] (DLA)
Calcutta LJ... Calcutta Law Journal [*A publication*] (DLA)
Calcutta WN... Calcutta Weekly Notes [*A publication*] (DLA)
Calc WN ...... Calcutta Weekly Notes [*A publication*] (DLA)
Cald........... Caldecott's Magistrates' and Settlement Cases [*1776-85*] [*England*] [*A publication*] (DLA)
CALD .... Calderon [*Spanish dramatist, 1600-1682*] (ROG)
Cald........... Caldwell's Reports [*25-36 West Virginia*] [*A publication*] (DLA)
CALD .... Chronic Active Liver Disease [*Medicine*]
CALD .... Computer-Assisted Logic Design (PDAA)
CALDA........ Canadian Air Line Dispatchers' Association [*See also ACRV*]
Cald Arb ...... Caldwell. Arbitration [*2nd ed.*] [*1825*] [*A publication*] (DLA)
Cal Dec....... California Decisions [*A publication*] (DLA)
CALDEF....... Cuban American Legal Defense and Education Fund (EA)
Cald (Eng) ... Caldecott's Magistrates' and Settlement Cases [*1776-85*] [*England*] [*A publication*] (DLA)
CALDEPOP... California Depopulation Commission [*Defunct*] (EA)
CALDIS .... Calderdale Information Service [*Library cooperative*] [*British*] (NITA)
Cald JP....... Caldecott's Magistrates' and Settlement Cases [*1776-85*] [*England*] [*A publication*] (DLA)
caldm .... Caldarium (VRA)
Cald Mag Cas... Caldecott's Magistrates' and Settlement Cases [*1776-85*] [*England*] [*A publication*] (DLA)
Cald M Cas... Caldecott's Magistrates' and Settlement Cases [*1776-85*] [*England*] [*A publication*] (DLA)
CALDOC...... Calgary Public Library Government Documents [*Information service or system*] (IID)
Caldor......... Caldor Corp. [*Associated Press*] (SAG)
CaLDRA ...... Canadian Long Distance Riding Association (AC)
Cald SC ...... Caldecott's Magistrates' and Settlement Cases [*1776-85*] [*England*] [*A publication*] (DLA)
Cald Set Cas... Caldecott's Magistrates' and Settlement Cases [*1776-85*] [*England*] [*A publication*] (DLA)
Cald Sett Cas... Caldecott's Magistrates' and Settlement Cases [*1776-85*] [*England*] [*A publication*] (DLA)
CAL-E......... Calibration Equipment [*Military*]
CALE.......... Canadian Army Liaison Executive
CALEA........ Canadian Air Lines Employees Association
CALEA........ Commission on Accreditation for Law Enforcement Agencies (EA)
CALED .... Caledonia [*Scotland*]
CALED .... California Association for Local Economic Development (SRA)
Caledon...... Caledonia Mining [*Associated Press*] (SAG)
CALEF........ Calefiat [*Warm It*] [*Pharmacy*]
CALEFACT.... Calefactus [*Made Warm*] [*Pharmacy*] (ROG)
Calenergy ... Calenergy Co., Inc. [*Associated Press*] (SAG)
CalEng........ California Energy Co. [*Associated Press*] (SAG)
CALEW........ Common Assembly Language for Electronic Warfare (MCD)
CALEXICO.... California and Mexico (IIA)
CALF.......... Calfskin [*Book cover material*] (NTCM)
CALF.......... Charles A. Lindbergh Fund [*An association*] (EA)
CALF.......... Combined Allied Land Forces
CALFAA....... Canadian Air Line Flight Attendants Association
CALFAB....... Computer-Aided Layout and Fabrication (MCD)
CalFd......... California Federal Bank [*Associated Press*] (SAG)
CalFdCt....... California Federal Bank [*Associated Press*] (SAG)
CalFedl....... California Federal Bank [*Associated Press*] (SAG)
CALFEX....... Capabilities Live Fire Exercise [*Military*]
CALFEX....... Combined Arms Live Fire Exercises (INF)
CALFIN .... California Fisheries Information Network [*Marine science*] (OSRA)
CALFIN .... California Fisheries Information Network (USDC)
CalFncl........ California Financial Holding Co. [*Associated Press*] (SAG)

CalFSecCt... California Federal Bank [*Associated Press*] (SAG)
CALG.......... Calgary [*Canada*] (ROG)
CALG .... California Federal Bank [*NASDAQ symbol*] (SAG)
CALGB .... Cancer and Leukemia, Group B [*Medicine*]
CALGEN...... Courseware Authoring Language Generator [*Computer science*] (MCD)
Calgene....... Calgene, Inc. [*Associated Press*] (SAG)
Cal Gen Laws Ann (Deering)... Deering's California General Laws, Annotated [*A publication*] (DLA)
CALGI .... Calcium Alginate [*Swab*] [*Medicine*] (DAVI)
Calgon .... Calgon Carbon Corp. [*Associated Press*] (SAG)
CAlh.......... Alhambra Public Library, Alhambra, CA [*Library symbol Library of Congress*] (LCLS)
CAlhB.......... C. F. Braun & Co., Alhambra, CA [*Library symbol Library of Congress*] (LCLS)
Cali.......... California
CALI.......... California Association of Licensed Investigators (SRA)
CALI.......... Canadian Association for Labour Israel (AC)
CALI.......... Chromophore-Assisted LASER Inactivation [*Analytical biochemistry*]
CALI.......... Concerned Agoraphobics Learning to Live [*An association*] (PAZ)
CALI.......... Cornell Aeronautical Laboratory, Inc. (SAA)
Cal IAC ...... Decisions of the Industrial Accident Commission of California [*A publication*] (DLA)
Cal IACCC.... California Industrial Accident Commission, Compensation Cases [*A publication*] (DLA)
Cal IAC Dec... California Industrial Accident Decisions [*A publication*] (DLA)
CALIB.......... Calibrate (AAG)
Caliber........ Caliber Systems, Inc. [*Associated Press*] (SAG)
CALIBN....... Cafibration (AAG)
CALIBR .... Calibration
CALICO .... Computer Assisted Language Learning and Instruction Consortium (EA)
CALICO .... Computer Assisted Library Instruction Co., Inc. [*Information service or system*] (AID)
CALICON ...... California Contract Show [*Western Merchandise Mart*] (TSPED)
CALID .... Calidus [*Warm*] [*Pharmacy*] (ROG)
CALIF......... California (AFM)
Calif........... California (ODBW)
Calif........... California Reports [*A publication*] (DLA)
CalifCul....... California Culinary Academy, Inc. [*Associated Press*] (SAG)
CalifInd....... California Independant Bancorp [*Associated Press*] (SAG)
Calif Ind Accdt Com Dec... Decisions of the Industrial Accident Commission of California [*A publication*] (DLA)
Calif SBJ ..... California State Bar Journal [*A publication*] (DLA)
calig .... Calligraphy (VRA)
Calig .... Gaius Caligula [*of Suetonius*] [*Classical studies*] (OCD)
CALIM......... Consortium of Academic Libraries in Manchester [*British*] (AIE)
Cal Ind Acc Com... Decisions of the Industrial Accident Commission of California [*A publication*] (DLA)
Cal Ind Acc Com Dec... Decisions of the Industrial Accident Commission of California [*A publication*] (DLA)
Cal Ind Acci Dec... California Industrial Accident Decisions [*A publication*] (DLA)
Cal Ind Com... Decisions of the Industrial Accident Commission of California [*A publication*] (DLA)
CALINE .... California Line Source Model [*Environmental Protection Agency*] (GFGA)
CALINET ...... California Information Network [*Library network*]
CALIP.......... Campaign Against Lead in Petrol [*British*]
CALIP.......... Computer Aptitude, Literacy, and Interest Profile [*Vocational guidance test*]
CALIPER ...... Cost Analysis of LASER Investment, Production, Engineering, and Research Cost Mode (MCD)
CALIPS .... Calibrated Pressure Switch (KSC)
CaliRlty....... Cali Realty Corp. [*Associated Press*] (SAG)
CaliRty........ Cali Realty Corp. [*Associated Press*] (SAG)
Calis........... Callistratus [*Flourished, 3rd century*] [*Authority cited in pre-1607 legal work*] (DSA)
CALIT.......... California Institute of Technology [*Also, CALT, CALTECH, CIT*] [*Pasadena*] (MCD)
calit .... Callitype (VRA)
Cal JIC .... California Jury Instructions, Criminal [*A publication*] (DLA)
Cal Jur........ California Jurisprudence [*A publication*] (DLA)
Cal Jur 2d ... California Jurisprudence, Second Edition [*A publication*] (DLA)
CALL.......... Callington [*England*]
Call........... Call's Virginia Reports [*5-10 Virginia*] [*1797-1825*] [*A publication*] (DLA)
CALL.......... Canadian Association of Law Libraries
CALL.......... Cancer Aid Listening Line [*British*] (DI)
CALL.......... Carat Assembled Logical Loader (IAA)
CALL.......... Center for Army Lessons Learned (INF)
CALL.......... Centre for Australian Languages and Linguistics [*Batchelor College*]
CALL.......... Common Null Cell Acute Lymphoblastic Leukemia [*Medicine*]
CALL.......... Communications Alert and Liaison System [*Office of Fisheries*] (MSC)
CALL.......... Composite Aeronautical Load List
CALL.......... Computer-Aided LOFT Lines (MCD)
CALL.......... Computer-Assisted Language Learning (ADA)
CALL.......... Computer-Augmented Loft Lines [*Graphic arts*] (MCD)
CALL.......... Conservative Alliance (EA)
CALL.......... Counseling at the Local Level [*Small Business Administration*]
CALL.......... Nextel Communications [*NASDAQ symbol*] (SAG)
CALL.......... NEXTEL Communic'ns'A' [*NASDAQ symbol*] (TTSB)
CALLA......... Common Acute Lymphoblastic Leukemia Antigen [*or Antiserum*] [*Immunochemistry*]
Cal Leg Adv... Calcutta Legal Adviser [*India*] [*A publication*] (DLA)

Cal Legis Serv... California Legislative Service (West) [*A publication*] (DLA)

Cal Leg Obs... Calcutta Legal Observer [*A publication*] (DLA)

Cal Leg Rec... California Legal Record [*A publication*] (DLA)

CALLEV........ California Low-Emission Vehicle [*Automotive industry*]

CALLG........ Calling (ROG)

CallGolf....... Callaway Golf Co. [*Associated Press*] (SAG)

Callim.......... Callimachus [*Third century BC*] [*Classical studies*] (OCD)

CALLIOPE ... Computer-Assisted Legislative Liaison; On-Line Political Evaluation

Callis.......... Callis on Sewers [*A publication*] (DLA)

Callis Sew... Callis on Sewers [*A publication*] (DLA)

Cal LJ.......... Calcutta Law Journal Reports [*A publication*] (DLA)

Cal LJ.......... California Law Journal [*A publication*] (DLA)

Callman Unfair Comp... Callman on Unfair Competition and Trade Marks [*A publication*] (DLA)

Call Mil L...... Callan's Military Laws of the United States [*A publication*] (DLA)

CallNet...... Call Net Enterprises [*Associated Press*] (SAG)

CallonP...... Callon Petroleum Co. [*Associated Press*] (SAG)

Cal LR .... Calcutta Law Reporter [*A publication*] (DLA)

CALLS.......... California Academic Libraries Lists of Serials (EDAC)

Call Sew ..... Callis on Sewers [*A publication*] (DLA)

Cal Luth U ... California Lutheran University (GAGS)

Call (VA)..... Call's Virginia Reports [*5-10 Virginia*] [*1797-1825*] [*A publication*] (DLA)

CALM.......... Cafe-au-Lait Macules (DMAA)

CALM.......... Call Monitor (NOAA)

CALM.......... Calmato [*More Calm*] [*Music*]

CalM.......... Calmodulin [*Also, CaM*] [*Biochemistry*]

CALM.......... Campaign Against Lorry Menace [*British*]

CALM.......... Canadian Association of Labour Media

CALM.......... Canadian Association of Logistics Management (EAIO)

CALM.......... Catapult Arresting Gear and Landing Aids Maintenance [*Aviation*] (NG)

CALM.......... Catenary Anchor Leg Mooring

CALM.......... Center for Alternative Living Medicine

CALM.......... Centralized Accounting for Local Management [*Veterans Administration*]

CALM.......... Child Abuse Listening Mediation (EA)

CALM.......... Citizens Against Legalized Murder [*Opposes death penalty for criminals*] [*Defunct*]

CALM.......... COBOL [*Common Business-Oriented Language*] Automatic Language Modifier [*Computer science*]

CALM.......... Cognitive and Affective Learning Model [*Psychology*]

CALM.......... Collected Algorithm for Learning Machines [*Computer science*]

CALM.......... Combined Allowance for Logistics Management

CALM.......... Computer-Aided Layout of Masks (PDAA)

CALM.......... Computer Aided Learning in Mathematics (AIE)

CALM.......... Computer-Aided Livestock Marketing

CALM.......... Computer Archive of Language Materials [*Stanford University*] (NITA)

CALM.......... Computer-Assisted Library Mechanization

CALM.......... Continuously-Advancing Longwall Mining (PDAA)

CALM.......... Crane Attachment Lorry Mounted (PDAA)

CALM.......... Custody Action for Lesbian Mothers (EA)

CALMAC ...... Caledonia MacBrayne [*Commercial firm British*]

Calmat........ CalMat Co. [*Associated Press*] (SAG)

CALMET....... Computer Aided Learning in Meteorology

CalMic........ California Microwave, Inc. [*Associated Press*] (SAG)

CalMicr........ California Micro Devices Corp. [*Associated Press*] (SAG)

Cal Mil Laws... Callan's Military Laws of the United States [*A publication*] (DLA)

CALMMS........ Computerized Air-Launched Missile Management System (MCD)

CALMS........ Combined Allowance for Logistics and Maintenance Support System [*Coast Guard*] (MCD)

CALMS........ Continuous Automatic Line Monitoring System

CALMS........ Credit and Load Management System [*Software*] [*British*]

CALN .... Calnetics Corp. [*NASDAQ symbol*] (NQ)

CALN .... Computer-Assisted Learning Network

CALNET........ California Network [*US Geological Survey*]

Calnetcs...... Calnetics Corp. [*Associated Press*] (SAG)

CALO .... Cape Lookout National Seashore [*National Park Service designation*]

CALO .... Capitulo [*Chapter*] [*Latin*] (ROG)

CALOGSIM... Computer-Assisted Logistics Simulation [*Navy*]

CALOLL........ Catholic Aviation League of Our Lady of Loreto [*Defunct*] (EA)

CALOT .... Calotype (VRA)

CALOW .... Contingency Action/Limited Objective Warfare (DOMA)

Caloway...... Calloways Nursery, inc. [*Associated Press*] (SAG)

CALP.......... California Pro Sports, Inc. [*NASDAQ symbol*] (SAG)

CALP.......... Calif Pro Sports [*NASDAQ symbol*] (TTSB)

Calp.......... Calpurnius Siculus [*First century AD*] [*Classical studies*] (OCD)

CALP.......... Congenital Absence of Left Pericardium [*Medicine*] (DMAA)

CALPA .... Canadian Airline Pilots Association

Cal P Ch ..... Calendar of Proceedings in Chancery Tempore Elizabeth [*1827-32*] [*A publication*] (DLA)

Cal Penal Code... California Penal Code [*A publication*] (DLA)

CalPERS...... California Public Employees' Retirement System

CalPERS...... California Public Employees Retirement System [*Pension fund*]

Calpine....... Calpine Corp. [*Associated Press*] (SAG)

CALPr .... Cal Fed Bk 7.75% CvPfd'A' [*NYSE symbol*] (TTSB)

Cal Prac ...... California Practice [*A publication*] (DLA)

CALPrB........ Calif Fed'l Bk10.625%'B'Pfd [*NYSE symbol*] (TTSB)

CalPro .... California Pro Sports, Inc. [*Associated Press*] (SAG)

Calprop....... Calprop Corp. [*Associated Press*] (SAG)

Cal PUC...... Decisions of the California Public Utilities Commission [*A publication*] (DLA)

CALPW .... California Pro Sports Wrrt [*NASDAQ symbol*] (TTSB)

CALR .... Computer-Assisted Legal Research (DLA)

CALR .... Computer Assisted Legal Retrieval (NITA)

CALRAB...... California Raisin Advisory Board (EA)

Cal RC Dec... California Railroad Commission Digest of Decisions [*A publication*] (DLA)

Cal RC Dec Dig... California Railroad Commission Digest of Decisions [*A publication*] (DLA)

Cal R Com... Opinions and Orders of the Railroad Commission of California [*A publication*] (DLA)

CalRE.......... California Real Estate Investment Trust [*Associated Press*] (SAG)

Cal Reg Notice Reg... California Regulatory Notice Register [*A publication*] (AAGC)

CALREN ...... California Research and Education Network [*Computer science*] (TNIG)

Cal Rep ...... California Reports [*A publication*] (DLA)

Cal Rep ...... Calthrop's English King's Bench Reports [*80 English Reprint*] [*A publication*] (DLA)

CALRFE........ Association for Asian Studies, Committee on American Library Resources on the Far East, Center for Research Libraries, Chicago, IL [*Library symbol Library of Congress*] (LCLS)

CALROC........ Calibration Rocket [*NASA*]

CALROSA..... Committee on American Library Resources on South Asia [*Later, CORMOSE A*] (EA)

CALROSEA.... Committee on American Library Resources on Southeast Asia [*Later, CORMOSEA*] (EA)

CAL ROT PAT... Calendarium Rotulorum Patentium [*Calendar of the Patent Rolls*] [*Latin*]

Cal Rptr ...... California Reporter (West) [*A publication*] (DLA)

CALRS .... Centralized Automatic Loop Reporting System [*Telecommunications*] (TEL)

CALS.......... Canadian Association of Library Schools

CALS.......... Centre for Applied Language Studies [*Carleton University*] [*Canada Research center*] (RCD)

CALS.......... Certified American Lineage Specialist

CALS.......... Christadelphian Auxiliary Lecturing Society [*British*] (BI)

CALS.......... Committee for Ammunition Logistics Support [*Army*] (MCD)

CALS.......... Communications Area Local Station (NVT)

CALS.......... Comprehensive Automated Learning Resources System [*Elgin Community College*] [*Information service or system*] (IID)

CALS.......... Computer-Aided Acquisition and Logistics Support (MCD)

CALS.......... Computer-Aided Acquisition and Logistics System (AAGC)

CALS.......... Computer-Aided Logistics Support [*Army*]

CALS.......... Computer-Aided Logistics System [*Air Force*] (DOMA)

CALS.......... Computer-Assisted Logistics Simulation [*Navy*] (MCD)

CALS.......... Computer-Automated Laboratory System

CALS.......... Connecticut Association of Land Surveyors (SRA)

CALS.......... Contingency Airfield Logistic System (DWSG)

CALS.......... Continuous Acquisition and Life-Cycle Support [*Military*] (RDA)

CALS.......... Continuous Acquisition and Life-Cycle Support (AAGC)

CALS.......... Current Awareness Literature Service [*Department of Agriculture*] [*Beltsville, MD*]

CALS.......... Customs Acts Legislation Service [*Australia A publication*]

CAL/SAP ..... Computer Adaptive Language for Development of Structural Analysis Programs [*University of California at Berkeley*] (NITA)

Cal SBJ........ California State Bar Journal [*A publication*] (DLA)

CalSBk........ California State Bank [*Associated Press*] (SAG)

CALS/CE ..... Computer-Aided Acquisition and Logistic Support/Concurrent Engineer (USGC)

Cal SDA...... Calcutta Sadr Diwani Adalat Reports [*India*] [*A publication*] (DLA)

CAL-SEIA .... California Solar Energy Industries Association (SRA)

Cal Ser........ Calcutta Series, Indian Law Reports [*A publication*] (DLA)

Cal Sew ...... Callis on Sewers [*A publication*] (DLA)

CAL-SOAP.... California Student Opportunity and Access Program (EDAC)

CALSPHERE... Calibration Sphere (MCD)

CALSS .... Canadian Association of Legal Support Staff (AC)

CALSSR ...... Common Assembly Language Scientific Subroutine Package [*Computer science*] (MHDI)

CALST.......... Cornell Aeronautical Laboratory Shock Tunnel (SAA)

Cal Stat ...... Statutes and Amendments to the Code of California [*A publication*] (DLA)

Cal Stats...... Statutes of California [*A publication*] (DLA)

Cal St Poly U (Pomona)... California State Polytechnic University at Pomona (GAGS)

Cal St Poly U (San Luis Obispo)... California State Polytechnic University at San Luis Obispo (GAGS)

Cal St U (Chico)... California State University at Chico (GAGS)

Cal St U (Dominguez Hills)... California State University at Dominguez Hills (GAGS)

Cal St U (Fresno)... California State University at Fresno (GAGS)

Cal St U (Fullerton)... California State University at Fullerton (GAGS)

Cal St U (Hayward)... California State University at Hayward (GAGS)

Cal St U (Humboldt)... Humboldt State University (GAGS)

Cal St U (LA)... California State University at Los Angeles (GAGS)

Cal St U (Long Beach)... California State University at Long Beach (GAGS)

Cal St U (Northridge)... California State University at Northridge (GAGS)

Cal St U (Sacramento)... California State University at Sacramento (GAGS)

Cal St U (San Bernardino)... California State University at San Bernardino (GAGS)

Cal St U (San Francisco)... San Francisco State University (GAGS)

Cal St U (San Jose)... San Jose State University (GAGS)

Cal St U (Sonoma)... Sonoma State University (GAGS)

Cal St U (Stanislaus)... California State University at Stanislaus (GAGS)

CALSU .... Combat Airlift Support Unit [*Air Force*]

Cal (subject) Code (Deering)... Deering's Annotated California Code [*A publication*] (DLA)

Cal (subject) Code (West)... West's Annotated California Codes [*A publication*] (DLA)

Cal Sup........ California Superior Court, Reports of Cases in Appellate Departments [*A publication*] (DLA)

Cal Sup........ California Supplement [*A publication*] (DLA)
Cal Sup (Cal)... California Superior Court, Reports of Cases in Appellate Departments [*A publication*] (DLA)
CAlt............. Altadena Library District, Altadena, CA [*Library symbol Library of Congress*] (LCLS)
CALT............ California Institute of Technology [*Also, CALIT, CALTECH, CIT*] [*Pasadena*]
CALT............ Canadian Association of Law Teachers [*See also ACPD*]
CALT............ Cleared Altitude (IAA)
CALT............ Computer Assisted Language Teaching (AIE)
CALT............ Contracting Lead Time (AAGC)
CAltaC......... Chaffey College, Alta Loma, CA [*Library symbol Library of Congress*] (LCLS)
CALTECH ..... California Institute of Technology [*Also, CALIT, CALT, CIT*] [*Pasadena*]
Cal Tech...... California Institute of Technology (GAGS)
CALTEL........ California Association of Long Distance Telephone Companies (SRA)
CALTEX........ California Texas Oil Co.
Calth........... Calthrop's City of London Cases, King's Bench [*England*] [*A publication*] (DLA)
Calth........... Calthrop's English King's Bench Reports [*80 English Reprint*] [*A publication*] (DLA)
Calth Copyh... Calthrop on Copyholds [*A publication*] (DLA)
Calth (Eng)... Calthrop's City of London Cases, King's Bench [*England*] [*A publication*] (DLA)
Calth (Eng)... Calthrop's English King's Bench Reports [*80 English Reprint*] [*A publication*] (DLA)
Calthr.......... Calthrop's City of London Cases, King's Bench [*England*] [*A publication*] (DLA)
Calthr.......... Calthrop's English King's Bench Reports [*80 English Reprint*] [*A publication*] (DLA)
CALTIA........ California Travel Industry Association (SRA)
CAL/TIMS .... Computer-Aided Logistics/Technical Information Management System [*Military*] (GFGA)
Calton......... Calton, Inc. [*Associated Press*] (SAG)
CALTRANS.... California Department of Transportation [*BTS*] (TAG)
CAltT........... Theosophical University, Altadena, CA [*Library symbol Library of Congress*] (LCLS)
CAltu........... Modoc County Free Library, Alturas, CA [*Library symbol Library of Congress*] (LCLS)
CALU .... California Association of Life Underwriters (SRA)
CALU .... Colorado Association of Life Underwriters (SRA)
CALULEV...... California Ultra-Low-Emission Vehicle [*Automotive industry*]
Calumet....... Calumet Bancorp, Inc. [*Associated Press*] (SAG)
Cal Unrep .... California Unreported Cases [*1855-1910*] [*A publication*] (DLA)
Cal Unrep Cas... California Unreported Cases [*1855-1910*] [*A publication*] (DLA)
Cal U (Pa) ... California University of Pennsylvania
CALUPL....... Council of Administrators of Large Urban Public Libraries [*Canada*]
CALURA....... Corporations and Labor Union Returns Act
Cal Urep ..... California Unreported Cases [*1855-1910*] [*A publication*] (DLA)
CALUS .... Centre for Advanced Land Use Studies [*College of Estate Management*] [*British*] (CB)
CALUSA....... Centre for Applied Linguistics, University of South Australia
CALUTRON.... California University Cyclotron
CALV........... Caledonia Mining [*NASDAQ symbol*] (SAG)
CALV........... Carrot Latent Virus [*Plant pathology*]
CALV........... Cassava Latent Virus [*Plant pathology*]
CALVADA..... Carl Reiner, Sheldon Leonard, Dick Van Dyke, Danny Thomas [*Acronym is name of production company of TV series "The Dick Van Dyke Show"*]
CALVF......... Caledonia Mining [*NASDAQ symbol*] (TTSB)
Calv Par ..... Calvert's Parties to Suits in Equity [*A publication*] (DLA)
Calv Parties... Calvert's Parties to Suits in Equity [*A publication*] (DLA)
Cal West Sch of Law... California Western School of Law (GAGS)
Cal WN .... Calcutta Weekly Notes [*A publication*] (DLA)
Cal WR .... Calcutta Weekly Reporter [*A publication*] (DLA)
CalWtr .... California Water Service Co. [*Associated Press*] (SAG)
CALY........... Calypte Biomedical Corp. [*NASDAQ symbol*] (SAG)
Calypte .... Calypte Biomedical Corp. [*Associated Press*] (SAG)
CAM........... Administrative Management Division [*Coast Guard*]
C$_{am}$............. Amylase Clearance [*Biochemistry*] (DAVI)
CAM........... Calculated Access Method (PDAA)
CaM............ Calmodulin [*Also, CalM*] [*Biochemistry*]
CAM........... Cam-and-Claw [*Pulldown mechanism in a camera or projector*]
CAM........... Camber [*Aerospace engineering*]
cam........... Cambodian [*MARC language code Library of Congress*] (LCCP)
CAM........... Cambridge [*Municipal borough in England*]
CAM........... Cambridge [*Massachusetts*] [*Seismograph station code, US Geological Survey Closed*] (SEIS)
CAM........... Cambridge, NY [*Location identifier FAA*] (FAAL)
CAM........... Camco International [*NYSE symbol*] (SPSG)
Cam........... Camden [*Division of Victor*] [*Record label*]
CAM........... Camden [*Diocesan abbreviation*] [*New Jersey*] (TOCD)
Cam........... Camelopardalis [*Constellation*]
CAM........... Camera (KSC)
cam .... Camera (VRA)
CAM........... Camera
Cam........... Cameron. Reports, Upper Canada Queen's Bench [*A publication*] (DLA)
CAM........... Cameron's Privy Council Decisions [*1832-1929*] [*Canada*] [*A publication*] (DLA)
CAM........... Cameron's Supreme Court Cases [*Canada*] [*A publication*] (DLA)
CAM........... Cameroon (WDAA)
Cam........... Camillus [*of Plutarch*] [*Classical studies*] (OCD)
CAM........... Camino

CAM............ CAM [*Central American Mission*] International (EA)
CAM............ Camiri [*Bolivia*] [*Airport symbol*] (OAG)
CAM............ Camisole (DSUE)
CAM............ Camoens [*Portuguese poet, 1524-1579*] (ROG)
CAM............ Camosun College Library [*UTLAS symbol*]
CAM............ Camouflage (AFM)
CAM............ Campus
CAM............ Camshaft [*Automotive engineering*]
CA(M)......... Canadian Army (Militia)
CAM............ Canam Manac Group, Inc. [*Toronto Stock Exchange symbol*]
CAM............ Cancellation of Amplitude Modulation (MCD)
CAM............ Capsule Assembly Machine (MCD)
Cam............ Carbamylmethyl [*Biochemistry*]
CAM............ Carboxamidomethyl [*Organic chemistry*]
CAM............ Care Aggregated Module
CAM............ Care and Maintenance [*British military*] (IAA)
CAM............ Cargo Module (MCD)
CAM............ Carrier Aircraft Modification (NASA)
CAM............ Cartographic Automatic Mapping (PDAA)
CAM............ Cascade Access Method [*Computer science*] (NITA)
CAM............ Catapult Aircraft Merchantship [*Used by British RAF to catapult Hurricane fighter planes from ships to defend convoys from enemy bombers*] [*World War II*]
CAM............ Catchment Area Management [*Army medical term*]
CAM............ Cell Adhesion Molecule [*Cytology*]
CAM............ Cell Associating Molecule [*Cytology*]
CAM............ Cellular-Automata Machine [*Computer science*] (BARN)
CAM............ Cellulose Acetate Methacrylate
CAM............ Cement Aggregate Mixture (OA)
CAM............ Center for Advanced Materials [*Lawrence Berkeley Laboratory*] [*Berkeley, CA*] [*Department of Energy*] (GRD)
CAM............ Center for Advanced Materials [*Pennsylvania State University*] [*Research center*] (RCD)
CAM............ Center for Applied Mathematics [*University of Georgia*] [*Research center*] (RCD)
CAM............ Center for Applied Microbiology [*University of Texas at Austin*] [*Research center*] (RCD)
CAM............ Central Address Memory [*Computer science*]
CAM............ Certified Administrative Manager [*Administrative Management Society*] [*Designation awarded by*]
CAM............ Championship Association of Mechanics (EA)
CAM............ Character Address Module [*Computer science*] (PDAA)
CAM............ Check Authorization Method
CAM............ Checkout and Automatic Monitoring (MSA)
CAM............ Checkout and Maintenance
CAM............ Chemical Agent Monitor [*Military*] (RDA)
CAM............ Chief, Aircraft Maintenance
CAM............ Chloramphenicol [*Antimicrobial compound*]
CAM............ Chorioallantoic Membrane [*Embryology*] [*Assay for chemical irritability*]
CAM............ Christian Aid Mission (EA)
CAM............ Christian Amendment Movement [*Later, CGM*] (EA)
CAM............ Christ in Action Ministries (EA)
CAM............ Church Assembly Measure (DLA)
CAM............ Circular Area Method
CAM............ Civil Aeronautics Manual
CAM............ Civil Air Movement
CAM............ Classified Advertising Manager (IIA)
CAM............ Clean Air Movement
CAM............ Clear and Add Magnitude (IAA)
CAM............ Coalition for the Apostolic Ministry [*Later, ECM*]
CAM............ Cockpit Area Microphone (MCD)
CAM............ Combined Arms Modeling [*Military*]
CAM............ Comite d'Action Musulman [*Mauritian political party*]
CAM............ Commercial Air Movement
CAM............ Commercial Assets Mobilization [*Navy*] (DOMA)
CAM............ Commission for Agricultural Meteorology [*WMO*] (ASF)
CAM............ Committee for Aquatic Microbiology [*United Nations*] (ASF)
CAM............ Committee on Aviation Medicine [*NAS/NRC*]
CAM............ Common Access Method [*Computer programming*] (BYTE)
CAM............ Commonwealth Association of Museums [*Calgary, AB*] (EAIO)
CAM............ Commonwealth Association of Museums (AC)
CAM............ Communication Access Method (IAA)
CAM............ Communication, Advertising, and Marketing Education Foundation [*British*]
CAM............ Communications Access Manager (MHDB)
CAM............ Complementary/Alternative Medicine [*Medicine*]
CAM............ Complete Answering Machine
CAM............ Compliance Assurance Monitoring [*Environmental science*] [*Environmental Protection Agency*]
CAM............ Compliance Assurance Monitoring [*Environmental Protection Agency*]
CAM............ Composite Army-Marine
CAM............ Composition and Make-Up
CAM............ Composition and Markup [*Graphic arts*] (DGA)
CAM............ Computer Access Matrix (NITA)
CAM............ Computer Achievement Monitoring (MCD)
CAM............ Computer Addressed Memory (NITA)
CAM............ Computer Address Matrix
CAM............ Computer-Aided Makeup [*Graphic arts*]
CAM............ Computer-Aided Manufacturing
CAM............ Computer-Aided Mathematics
CAM............ Computer Annunciation Matrix (MCD)
CAM............ Computer-Assisted Mailing (IAA)
CAM............ Computer-Assisted Maintenance
CAM............ Computer-Assisted Makeup [*Graphic arts*]

CAM	Computer-Assisted Manufacturing (PCM)
CAM	Computerized Alert Monitor (LAIN)
CAM	Computerized Anatomical Man [*NASA*]
CAM	Consolidated Aircraft Maintenance
CAM	Constant Air Monitor [*Nuclear energy*] (NRCH)
CAM	Construction Association of Michigan (SRA)
CAM	Containment Atmospheric Monitoring [*Nuclear energy*] (NRCH)
CAM	Content-Addressable Memory [*Computer science*]
CAM	Contingency Analysis Model (KSC)
CAM	Continuous Air Monitor [*Nuclear energy*] (NRCH)
CAM	Contract Air Mail
CAM	Contract Audit Manual
CAM	Contractor-Acquired Materiel (AFM)
CAM	Contralateral Axillary Metastasis [*Medicine*] (MAE)
CAM	Control Access Manager (BUR)
CAM	Conventional Airfield Attack Munitions [*Army*]
CAM	Cooperative Atomic Migration
CAM	Cost Account Manager (MCD)
CAM	Crane, Aircraft Maintenance (MCD)
CAM	Crassulacean Acid Metabolism [*Biochemistry*]
CAM	Cruise and Maintain [*Aviation*]
CAM	Cryogenic Acoustic Microscopy (MCD)
CAM	Cybernetic Anthropomorphous Machine [*Robot*] [*Army*]
CAM	Cyclophosphamide, Adriamycin, Methotrexate [*Antineoplastic drug regimen*]
CAM	Cystic Adenomatoid Malformation
CAM	Cytotoxic Activated Macrophage [*Biochemistry*]
CAM	Engineering Center for Automated Manufacturing Technology [*Clemson University*] [*Research center*] (RCD)
CAM	Los Angeles County Museum of Art, Los Angeles, CA [*OCLC symbol*] (OCLC)
CAM	Village Aviation, Inc. [*ICAO designator*] (FAAC)
CAMA	Canadian Appliance Manufacturers Association (AC)
CAMA	Canadian Association of Municipal Administrators (AC)
CAMA	Canadian Automatic Merchandising Association (AC)
CAMA	Central Australian Motels Association
CAMA	Centralized Automatic Message Accounting [*Bell System*]
CAMA	Children's Apparel Manufacturers' Association [*Canada*]
CAMA	Civil Aviation Medical Association (EA)
CAMA	Coastal Area Management Act [*1974*] (MSC)
CAMA	Coated Abrasive Manufacturers' Association [*British*] (BI)
CAMA	Computer-Assisted Method Assembly [*Analytical method writing*]
CAMA	Critical Agricultural Materials Act [*1984*]
CAMAA	Combined Arms Mission Area Analysis [*Army*]
CAMAC	Center for Agricultural Meteorology and Climatology [*University of Nebraska - Lincoln*] [*Research center*] (RCD)
CAMA-C	Centralized Automatic Message Accounting - Computerized [*Bell System*] (TEL)
CAMAC	Combinatorial and Algebraic Machine-Aided Computation (WGA)
CAMAC	Computer-Aided Measurement and Control [*NASA*]
CAMAC	Computer-Automated Measurement and Control (MSA)
CAMACC	Campaign Against Council Corruption [*British*] (DBA)
CaMACMH	Altona Community Memorial Health Centre, Altona, MB, Canada [*Library symbol Library of Congress*] (LCLS)
CAMAE	Central Air Materiel Area, Europe
CAMAK	Cataract-Microcephaly-Arthrogryposis-Kyphosis [*Syndrome*] [*Medicine*] (DMAA)
CAMAL	Cambridge Algebraic System [*Programming language*] [*1975*] (CSR)
CaMAMC	Altona Medical Centre, Altona, MB, Canada [*Library symbol Library of Congress*] (LCLS)
Cam Am LJ	Canadian-American Law Journal [*A publication*] (DLA)
Cam & N	Cameron and Norwood's North Carolina Conference Reports [*A publication*] (DLA)
Cam & Nor	Cameron and Norwood's North Carolina Conference Reports [*1800-04*] [*A publication*] (DLA)
CAMA-ONI	Centralized Automatic Message Accounting - Operator Number Identification [*Telecommunications*] (TEL)
CAMAQ	Centre d'Adaptation de la Main-d'Oeuvre Aerospatiale du Quebec (AC)
CAMAR	Common Aperture Multifunction Array RADAR
CAMAS	Central Automatic Message Accounting System (CET)
CAMAS	Commander, South Atlantic Maritime Area
CAMAS	Computer-Assisted Manpower Analysis System (MCD)
CAMAS	Confederation of African Medical Associations and Societies [*Nigeria*] (EAIO)
CAMB	California Association of Mortgage Brokers (SRA)
Camb	Cambior, Inc. [*Associated Press*] (SAG)
CAMB	Cambistry [*Finance*]
CAMB	Cambodia (WDAA)
Camb	Cambodia (VRA)
CAMB	Camborne [*Urban district in England*]
CAMB	Cambrian [*Period, era, or system*] [*Geology*]
Camb	Cambridge [*Record label*]
CAMB	Cambridge [*Municipal borough in England*]
CAMB	Cambridge University [*England*]
Camb	Cambyses (BJA)
CAMB	Canadian Association of Medical Biochemists (AC)
CAMB	Civilian Acquisition Management Branch [*Army*] (RDA)
CAMB	Colorado Association of Mortgage Brokers (SRA)
CAMB	Combined Arms Maneuver Battalion [*Experiment*] [*Army*] (INF)
CAMB	Continued Automated Multi-Baseline (MCD)
CAMB	Cyclophosphamide, Adriamycin, Methotrexate, Bleomycin [*Antineoplastic drug regimen*]
CaMBa	Rural Municipality of Argyle Public Library, Baldur, MB, Canada [*Library symbol*] [*Library of Congress*] (LCLS)

CaMBABS	Anglican Church of Canada, Diocese of Brandon, Synod Office, Brandon, MB, Canada [*Library symbol Library of Congress*] (LCLS)
CaMBAC	Assiniboine Community College, Brandon, MB, Canada [*Library symbol Library of Congress*] (LCLS)
CaMBAg	Canada Department of Agriculture, Research Station, Brandon, MB, Canada [*Library symbol Library of Congress*] (LCLS)
CambB	Cambridge Bible [*A publication*] (BJA)
CaMBBR	Brokenhead River Regional Library, Beausejour, MB, Canada [*Library symbol Library of Congress*] (LCLS)
CaMBC	Brandon University, Brandon, MB, Canada [*Library symbol Library of Congress*] (LCLS)
CaMBCA	Brandon University, Archives, Brandon, MB, Canada [*Library symbol*] [*Library of Congress*] (LCLS)
CaMBCAM	Commonwealth Air Training Plan Museum, Inc., Brandon, MB, Canada [*Library symbol*] [*Library of Congress*] (LCLS)
CaMBCG	Brandon University, Department of Geography, Brandon, MB, Canada [*Library symbol Library of Congress*] (LCLS)
Camb Co LJ	Cambria County Reports [*Pennsylvania*] [*A publication*] (DLA)
Cambex	Cambex Corp. [*Associated Press*] (SAG)
CaMBGH	Brandon General Hospital, School of Nursing, Brandon, MB, Canada [*Library symbol Library of Congress*] (LCLS)
CambHrt	Cambridge Heart, Inc. [*Associated Press*] (SAG)
Cambior	Cambior, Inc. [*Associated Press*] (SAG)
CAMBL	Continuous Automatic Multi-Base Propellant Line (MCD)
CaMBMH	Brandon Mental Health Centre, Brandon, MB, Canada [*Library symbol Library of Congress*] (LCLS)
CambNe	Cambridge NeuroScience, Inc. [*Associated Press*] (SAG)
CaMBoM	Boissevain and Morton Regional Library, Boissevain, MB, Canada [*Library symbol Library of Congress*] (LCLS)
CaM-BP	Calmodulin Binding Protein [*Biochemistry*]
Cambria	Cambria County Legal Journal [*Pennsylvania*] [*A publication*] (DLA)
Cambria Co LJ	Cambria County Legal Journal [*Pennsylvania*] [*A publication*] (DLA)
Cambria Co (PA)	Cambria County Legal Journal [*Pennsylvania*] [*A publication*] (DLA)
Cam Brit	Camden's Britannia [*A publication*] (DLA)
Cambrx	Cambrex Corp. [*Associated Press*] (SAG)
CAMBS	Cambridgeshire [*County in England*]
Cambs	Cambridgeshire [*County in England*] (ODBW)
CAMBS	Command Active Multi-Beam Sonobuoy (PDAA)
CambSnd	Cambridge Soundworks, Inc. [*Associated Press*] (SAG)
CambTch	Cambridge Technology Partners [*Associated Press*] (SAG)
CaMBW	Western Manitoba Regional Library, Brandon, MB, Canada [*Library symbol Library of Congress*] (LCLS)
CAMBY	Cambridge Instrument Co. PLC (MHDW)
CAMC	Canadian Army Medical Corps
CAMC	Canadian Association of Management Consultants
CAMC	Carlsberg Automated Meridian Circle [*Astronomy*]
CAMC	Central American Monetary Council
CAMCA	Canadian-American Motor Carriers Association (EA)
Cam Cas	Cameron's Supreme Court Cases [*Canada*] [*A publication*] (DLA)
CaMCB	Boyne Regional Library, Carman, MB, Canada [*Library symbol Library of Congress*] (LCLS)
CAMCC	Canadian Air Mail Collectors Club (EA)
CaMCh	Churchill Public Library, Churchill, MB, Canada [*Library symbol Library of Congress*] (LCLS)
CaMChE	Eskimo Museum, Churchill, MB, Canada [*Library symbol Library of Congress*] (LCLS)
CaMChPC	Parks Canada, Churchill, MB, Canada [*Library symbol Library of Congress*] (LCLS)
Camco	Camco International [*Associated Press*] (SAG)
CamcoFn	Camco Financial Corp. [*Associated Press*] (SAG)
Camcorder	Camera and Recorder
CAMCORE	Central American and Mexico Coniferous Resources Cooperative (GNE)
CAMCOS	Computer-Assisted Maintenance Planning and Control System
CAMD	Calif Micro Devices [*NASDAQ symbol*] (TTSB)
CAMD	California Micro Devices Corp. [*NASDAQ symbol*] (SAG)
CAMD	Center for Advanced Macrostructures and Devices [*Louisiana State University*]
CAMD	Computer-Aided Mechanical Drafting
CAMD	Computer-Assisted Molecular Design
CAMD	Craft and Amphibious Material Department [*British military*] (DMA)
CAMDA	Car and Motorcycle Drivers Association Ltd. [*British*] (BI)
CaMDa	Dauphin Public Library, Dauphin, MB, Canada [*Library symbol Library of Congress Obsolete*] (LCLS)
CAMDAP	Computers and Medieval Data Processing [*Canada*] [*A publication*] (NITA)
CaMDaP	Parkland Regional Library, Dauphin, MB, Canada [*Library symbol Library of Congress*] (LCLS)
CaMDB	Bren Del Win Centennial Library, Deloraine, MB, Canada [*Library symbol Library of Congress*] (LCLS)
Camd Brit	Camden's Britannia [*A publication*] (DLA)
CAMDEC	Ceramics Advanced Manufacturing Development Engineering Center [*Defunct*] (EA)
Camden	Camden's Britannia [*A publication*] (DLA)
CAMDEV	Canadian Management Associates for Global Development (AC)
CAMDF	Canadian Agricultural Market Development Fund
CAMDG	Civil Assistant to Medical Director-General [*Navy British*]
CamdnP	Camden Property Trust [*Associated Press*] (SAG)
CAMDO	Canadian Art Museum Directors Organization
CAMDP	Center for Alternative Mining Development Policy (EA)
CamDs	Cam Designs Co. [*Associated Press*] (SAG)
CAMDS	Chemical Agent Munition Disposal System [*Army*]

CAM Dt....... CAM Data Systems, Inc. [*Associated Press*] (SAG)
Cam Duc...... Camera Ducata [*Duchy Chamber*] [*Latin Legal term*] (DLA)
CaMDW ...... Delta Waterfowl Research Station, Delta, MB, Canada [*Library symbol Library of Congress*] (LCLS)
CAME........ Certification of Air Moving Equipment [*British*] (IRUK)
CAME.......... Corps Airspace Management Element (MCD)
CAME.......... Cost Analysis Monthly Exchange [*Army*]
CAMECEC .... Computer-Aided Machine Loading (MHDB)
Cameco ...... Cameco Corp. [*Associated Press*] (SAG)
CaMeCo...... Catholic Media Council [*Aachen, Federal Republic of Germany*] (EAIO)
CAMEL........ Call Management Language [*Telecommunications*] (ACRL)
CAMEL........ Capital Adequacy, Asset Quality, Management, Earnings, Liquidity [*Formula used by the Federal Deposit Insurance Corp. to evaluate banks*]
CAMEL........ Collapsible Airborne Military Equipment Lifter
CAMEL........ Component and Material Evaluation Loop [*Nuclear energy*] (NRCH)
CAMEL........ Critical Aeronautical Material and Equipment List
CAMELEON... Cytarabine, Methotrexate, Leucovorin [*Folinic acid-SF*], Oncovin [*Vincristine*] [*Antineoplastic drug regimen*]
CAMELF...... Camelford [*Rural district in England*]
Camelot...... Camelot Corp. [*Associated Press*] (SAG)
CAMELOT .... Computerization and Mechanization of Local Office Tasks (MHDB)
CAMELOT .... Cultural Auction of Many Extraordinary Lots of Treasure [*St. Louis, Missouri*]
CAMEO .... Capitol Area Motion Pictures Education Organization [*Washington, DC*]
CAMEO .... Chemically Active Material Ejected in Orbit (MCD)
CAMEO .... Computer Aided Management of Emergency Operations [*Marine science*] (OSRA)
CAMEO .... Computer-Assisted Management for Emergency Operations [*Database*]
CAMEO .... Computer Assisted Mechanistic Evaluation of Organic Reactions [*Data analysis*]
CAMEO .... Council of Affiliated Marriage Enrichment Organizations [*Defunct*] (EA)
CAMEO .... Covert Active Modular Electro-Optical System (MCD)
CAMEO .... Creative Audio and Music Electronics Organization (EA)
CAMEO .... Cyclophosphamide, Adriamycin, Methotrexate, Etoposide, Oncovin [*Vincristine*] [*Antineoplastic drug regimen*]
Camer........ Cameroon
CAMERA ...... Canadian Association of Motion Picture and Electronic Recording Artists
CAMERA ...... Command Management Review and Analysis [*Army*]
CAMERA ...... Committee for Accuracy in Middle East Reporting in America (EA)
CAMERA ...... Computer-Aided Maneuver Evaluation, Reconstruction, and Analysis [*British*]
CAMERA ...... Cooperating Agency Method for Event Reporting and Analysis (IAA)
Cameron...... Cameron's Supreme Court Cases [*Canada*] [*A publication*] (DLA)
Cameron (Can)... Cameron's Supreme Court Cases [*Canada*] [*A publication*] (DLA)
Cameron Cas (Can)... Cameron's Supreme Court Cases [*Canada*] [*A publication*] (DLA)
Cameron Pr... Cameron's Practice [*Canada*] [*A publication*] (DLA)
Cameron Pr (Can)... Cameron's Practice [*Canada*] [*A publication*] (DLA)
Cameron SC... Cameron's Supreme Court Cases [*Canada*] [*A publication*] (DLA)
CAMES........ Colorado Association of Medical Equipment Services (SRA)
CAMES........ Combined Agency for Middle East Supplies [*World War II*]
CAMESA ...... Canadian Military Electronics Standards Agency (MCD)
CAMESE...... Canadian Association of Mining Equipment & Services for Export (AC)
CAMET........ Centre for the Advancement of Mathematical Education in Technology [*Loughborough University of Technology*] [*Research center British*] (CB)
CAMEX........ Coastal AMOS [*Automated Meteorological Observing Station*] Experiment
CAMF.......... Canadian Association of Metal Finishers
CAMF.......... Connecticut Association of Metal Finishers (SRA)
CAMF.......... Course Approval and Monitoring Form [*Inner London Education Authority*] [*British*] (AIE)
CAMF.......... Cyclophosphamide, Adriamycin, Methotrexate, Fluorouracil [*Antineoplastic drug regimen*] (DAVI)
CAMF.......... Cyclophosphamide, Adriamycin, Methotrexate, Folinic acid-SF [*Antineoplastic drug regimen*]
CAMFAX ...... Civil Aviation Meteorological Facsimile Network (PDAA)
CAMFET...... CAMEL [*Critical Aeronautical Material and Equipment List*] Gate Field Effe ct Transistors (MCD)
CaMFF........ Flin Flon Public Library, Flin Flon, MB, Canada [*Library symbol Library of Congress*] (LCLS)
CaMFFHB .... Hudson Bay Mining & Smelting Co. Ltd., Flin Flon, MB, Canada [*Library symbol Library of Congress*] (LCLS)
CAMFT........ California Association of Marriage and Family Therapists (SRA)
CA/MG .... Civil Affairs/Military Government
CAMG .... Consolidated Aircraft Maintenance Group [*Air Force*]
CaMGE........ Evergreen Regional Library, Gimli, MB, Canada [*Library symbol Library of Congress*] (LCLS)
CaMGi .... Gillam Municipal Library, Gillam, MB, Canada [*Library symbol Library of Congress*] (LCLS)
CaMGPC ..... Grandview Personal Care Home, Grandview, MB, Canada [*Library symbol Library of Congress*] (LCLS)
CAMH .... Cambridge Heart, Inc. [*NASDAQ symbol*] (SAG)
CAMHDD...... Commonwealth Association of Mental Handicap and Developmental Disabilities (EA)
CAMI.......... Camisole (DSUE)
CAMI.......... Canadian Apparel Manufacturers Institute (EAIO)

CAMI.......... Citizens Against Military Injustice [*Defunct*] (EA)
CAMI.......... Civil Aeromedical Institute [*FAA*]
CAMI.......... Civil Aviation Medical Institute (MCD)
CAMI.......... Coated Abrasives Manufacturers Institute (EA)
CAMI.......... Columbia Artists Management, Inc.
CAM-I......... Computer Aided Manufacturing International (EA)
CAMI.......... Concerned Americans for Military Improvements (EA)
CAMI.......... Continuing Action Maintenance Instruction
CAMIC........ Canadian Association of Mutual Insurance Companies (AC)
CAMIFA...... Campaign for Independent Financial Advice [*British*] (ECON)
CAMIL........ Computer-Assisted/Managed Instructional Language (CSR)
CAMILA....... Chicanos Against Military Intervention in Latin America [*Promotes understanding between Mexico and the US at the grassroots level*] (CROSS)
Camil Plaut... Camillus Plautius [*Flourished, 1533-66*] [*Authority cited in pre-1607 legal work*] (DSA)
CAMINO...... Central America Information Office [*Defunct*] (EA)
Cam Int Suc... Cameron. Intestate Succession in Scotland [*A publication*] (DLA)
CAMIS .... Cadet Administrative Management Information System [*Air Force*] (GFGA)
CAMIS .... Commercial Activities Management Information System (AAGC)
CAMIS .... Computer-Assisted Makeup and Imaging Systems
CAMIS .... Continental Army Management Information System (RDA)
CAMJ.......... Council of Arab Ministers of Justice [*See also CMAJ*] [*Rabat, Morocco*] (EAIO)
Cam JS Comp... Cameron on Joint Stock Companies [*Scotland*] [*A publication*] (DLA)
CaMKL........ Lakeland Regional Library, Killarney, MB, Canada [*Library symbol Library of Congress*] (LCLS)
CaMKTLH .... Tri-Lake Health Centre, Killarney, MB, Canada [*Library symbol Library of Congress*] (LCLS)
Caml........... Camelopardalis [*Constellation*]
CAML.......... Camelot Corp. [*NASDAQ symbol*] (NQ)
CAML.......... Canadian Association of Music Libraries
CAML.......... Cargo Aircraft Mine Laying (MCD)
CAML.......... Coarticulation Assessment in Meaningful Language [*Speech evaluation test*]
CaMLdB...... Regional Library, Lac Du Bonnet, MB, Canada [*Library symbol Library of Congress*] (LCLS)
CAMLEJ...... Camp Lejeune [*North Carolina*] [*Marine Corps*]
CAMLR .... Conservation of Antarctic Marine Living Resources [*International agreement signed in 1982*]
CaMLR........ Leaf Rapids Public Library, Leaf Rapids, MB, Canada [*Library symbol Library of Congress*] (LCLS)
CAMLS........ Cleveland Area Metropolitan Library System [*Library network*]
CAMLT........ California Association for Medical Laboratory Technology (SRA)
CAMM.......... Canadian Association of Medical Microbiologists [*Association Canadienne des Medecins Microbiologistes*] (AC)
CAMM.......... Canadian Association of Moldmakers [*Formerly, Windsor Association of Moldmakers*] (AC)
CAMM.......... Central Association of the Miraculous Medal (EA)
CAMM.......... Chlor-Alkali-Market Model
CAMM.......... Computer-Aided Maintenance Management
CAMM.......... Computer-Assisted Molecular Modeling [*Chemistry*]
CAMM.......... Council of American Maritime Museums (EA)
CAMM.......... Council of American Master Mariners (EA)
CAMMAC ..... Canadian Amateur Musicians (EAIO)
CAMMD........ Canadian Association of Manufacturers of Medical Devices
CaMMcS...... Southwestern Manitoba Regional Library, Melita, MB, Canada [*Library symbol Library of Congress*] (LCLS)
CaMMiR ...... Minnedosa Regional Library, Minnedosa, MB, Canada [*Library symbol Library of Congress*] (LCLS)
CAMMIS ..... Command Aerospace Maintenance Manpower Information System
CaMMoAg.... Canada Department of Agriculture, Research Station, Morden, MB, Canada [*Library symbol Library of Congress*] (LCLS)
CaMMoW..... Morden-Winkler Regional Library, Morden, MB, Canada [*Library symbol Library of Congress*] (LCLS)
CAMMS....... Combined Arms Multipurpose Missile System [*Army*]
CAMMS....... Computer-Aided Materials Management System [*Canadian provincial governments*]
CAMMS....... Computer-Assisted Map Maneuver Simulation (MCD)
CAMMS....... Computer-Assisted Map Maneuver System [*Military*] (INF)
CAMMU....... Cache/Memory Management Unit (BYTE)
CAMN .... Canadian Directory of Completed Master's Theses in Nursing [*University of Alberta*] [*Information service or system*] (IID)
CAMN .... Chief Aircraft Mechanician [*British military*] (DMA)
CaMNCI ...... Neepawa Collegiate Institute, Neepawa, MB, Canada [*Library symbol Library of Congress*] (LCLS)
CAMNET ...... Computer Applications for Ministry Network (EA)
CamNt .... Cam-Net Communicatoins Network [*Associated Press*] (SAG)
CAMO .... Camouflage
CAMO .... Capulin Mountain National Monument [*National Park Service designation*]
CAMO .... Chief Administrative Medical Officer [*British*]
CAMO .... Consolidated Administrative Management Organization [*AID*]
cam obs ..... Camera Obscura (VRA)
CAMOF .... Camouflage (MSA)
CAMOL .... Computer-Assisted Management of Learning (PDAA)
Cam Op ...... Cameron's Legal Opinions [*Toronto*] [*A publication*] (DLA)
CAMO-P...... Central Ammunition Management Office - Pacific [*Army*] (MCD)
CAMO-PAC... Central Ammunition Management Office - Pacific [*Army*] (AABC)
CAMOS .... Computer-Aided Abrasive Machining Oscillation Studies (PDAA)
CaMoV........ Carnation Mottle Virus
CaMOWBC... Winnipeg Bible College, Otterburne, MB, Canada [*Library symbol Library of Congress*] (LCLS)

CAMP.......... Cabin Air Manifold Pressure [*Aviation*]
CAMP.......... Calibrated Airborne Measurements Program (MCD)
CAMP.......... Calif Amplifier [*NASDAQ symbol*] (TTSB)
CAMP.......... California Amplifier, Inc. [*NASDAQ symbol*] (NQ)
CAMP.......... CAMP [*Commonly used*] (OPSA)
CAMP.......... Campaign Against Marijuana Planting
Camp.......... Campanian
Camp.......... Campbell's Compendium of Roman Law [*A publication*] (DLA)
Camp.......... Campbell's English Nisi Prius Reports [*A publication*] (DLA)
Camp.......... Campbell's Legal Gazette Reports [*Pennsylvania*] [*A publication*] (DLA)
Camp.......... Campbell's Reports [*27-58 Nebraska*] [*A publication*] (DLA)
Camp.......... Campbell's Reports of Taney's United States Circuit Court Decisions [*A publication*] (DLA)
CAMP.......... Campden [*England*]
Camp.......... Campeche [*Mexico*] (BARN)
Camp.......... Camp's Reports [*1 North Dakota*] [*A publication*] (DLA)
CAMP.......... Center for Acquisition Management Policy [*DSMC*] (AAGC)
CAMP.......... Center for Advanced Management Programs [*University of Houston at Clear Lake*] [*Research center*] (RCD)
CAMP.......... Center for Advanced Manufacturing and Production [*Southern Illinois University at Edwardsville*] [*Research center*] (RCD)
CAMP.......... Center for Advanced Materials Processing [*Clarkson University*] [*Research center*] (RCD)
CAMP.......... Central Access Monitor Program (NITA)
CAMP.......... Christie, Atkins, Munch-Peterson Test [*Bacteriology*]
CAMP.......... Classified Advertisement Management Program [*British*] (DGA)
CAMP.......... Coalition for the Abolition of Marijuana Prohibition (EA)
CAMP.......... College Assistance Migrant Program
CAMP.......... Command and Management Presentation [*Marine Corps*]
CAMP.......... Common ADA Missile Packages (MCD)
CAMP.......... Companies, Agencies, Markets, Positions (IIA)
CAMP.......... Compiler for Automatic Machine Programming (BUR)
CAMP.......... Comprehensive Analytical Methods of Planning
CAMP.......... Computer-Aided Mask Preparation (DNAB)
CAMP.......... Computer-Aided Message Processing (LAIN)
CAMP.......... Computer Applications of Military Problems [*Computer users' group*]
CAMP.......... Computer-Assisted Management of Portfolios
CAMP.......... Computer-Assisted Match Program [*Military*]
CAMP.......... Computer-Assisted Mathematics Program [*Scott, Foresman, 1968-1969*] [*Textbook series*] (BUR)
CAMP.......... Computer-Assisted Menu Planning
CAMP.......... Computer-Assisted Metabolic Prediction [*Biochemistry*]
CAMP.......... Computer-Assisted Movie Production (IEEE)
CAMP.......... Computerized Aircraft Maintenance Program
CAMP.......... Concentration of Adenosine Monophosphate [*Medicine*] (DMAA)
CAMP.......... Continuous Air Monitoring Program [*or Project*] [*Environmental Protection Agency*]
CAMP.......... Control and Monitoring Processor (IEEE)
CAMP.......... Control and Monitor Panel
CAMP.......... Cost of Alternative Military Programs (SAA)
CAMP.......... Council on America's Military Past (EA)
CAMP.......... Cyclic Adenosine Monophosphate [*Also, cAMP*] [*Biochemistry*]
CAMP.......... Cyclophosphamide, Adriamycin, Methotrexate, Procarbazine [*Antineoplastic drug regimen*]
CaMP.......... Pinawa Public Library, Pinawa, MB, Canada [*Library symbol Library of Congress*] (LCLS)
Campb.......... Campbell's Compendium of Roman Law [*A publication*] (DLA)
Campb.......... Campbell's English Nisi Prius Reports [*A publication*] (DLA)
Campb.......... Campbell's Legal Gazette Reports [*Pennsylvania*] [*A publication*] (DLA)
Campb.......... Campbell's Reports [*27-58 Nebraska*] [*A publication*] (DLA)
Campb.......... Campbell's Reports of Taney's United States Circuit Court Decisions [*A publication*] (DLA)
Campb Dec... Campbell's Reports of Taney's United States Circuit Court Decisions [*A publication*] (DLA)
Campbell..... Campbell's Compendium of Roman Law [*A publication*] (DLA)
Campbell..... Campbell's English Nisi Prius Reports [*A publication*] (DLA)
Campbell..... Campbell's Legal Gazette Reports [*Pennsylvania*] [*A publication*] (DLA)
Campbell..... Campbell's Lives of the Chief Justices [*A publication*] (DLA)
Campbell..... Campbell's Lives of the Lord Chancellors [*A publication*] (DLA)
Campbell..... Campbell's Reports [*27-58 Nebraska*] [*A publication*] (DLA)
Campbell..... Campbell's Reports of Taney's United States Circuit Court Decisions [*A publication*] (DLA)
Campbell U... Campbell University (GAGS)
Campb (Eng)... Campbell's English Nisi Prius Reports [*A publication*] (DLA)
Campb (PA)... Campbell's Legal Gazette Reports [*Pennsylvania*] [*A publication*] (DLA)
CaMPCFP .... Canadian Food Products Development Center, Portage La Prairie, MB, Canada [*Library symbol Library of Congress*] (LCLS)
Camp Ch Jus... Campbell's Lives of the Chief Justices [*A publication*] (DLA)
Camp Cit ...... Campbell on Citation and Diligence [*A publication*] (DLA)
Camp Dec.... Campbell's Reports of Taney's United States Circuit Court Decisions [*A publication*] (DLA)
CampDsg...... Cam Designs Co. [*Associated Press*] (SAG)
CAMPEN...... Camp Pendleton [*California*] [*Marine Corps*]
Camp Ex...... Campbell on Executors and Administrators in Pennsylvania [*A publication*] (DLA)
CAMPFIRE ... Communal Areas Management Program for Indigenous Resources
CAMPH........ Camphora [*Camphor*] [*Pharmacy*] (ROG)
CAM-PK....... Calmodulin-Dependent Protein Kinase [*An enzyme*]
Camp Ld Ch... Campbell's Lives of the Lord Chancellors [*A publication*] (DLA)
Camp LG ..... Campbell's Legal Gazette Reports [*Pennsylvania*] [*A publication*] (DLA)

Camp Lives Ld Ch... Campbell's Lives of the Lord Chancellors [*A publication*] (DLA)
CaMPlp........ Portage La Prairie Public Library, Portage La Prairie, MB, Canada [*Library symbol Library of Congress*] (LCLS)
CaMPlpM..... Manitoba School, Portage La Prairie, MB, Canada [*Library symbol Library of Congress*] (LCLS)
Camp Merc L... Campbell. Mercantile Law [*3rd ed.*] [*1904*] [*A publication*] (DLA)
Camp Neg ... Campbell. Negligence [*2nd ed.*] [*1878*] [*A publication*] (DLA)
Camp NP ... Campbell's English Nisi Prius Reports [*A publication*] (DLA)
CAMPO .... Committee to Award Miss Piggy the Oscar [*Defunct*]
CampoEl...... Campo Electronics, Appliances & Computers, Inc. [*Associated Press*] (SAG)
CAMPP .... Canadian Association of Motion Picture Producers
CAMP-PDE... Cyclic Adenosine Monophosphate Phosphodiesterase (PDAA)
CAMPPS ..... Conventional Ammunition Maintenance, Preservation, and Packaging Set (MCD)
Cam Prac.... Cameron's Supreme Court Practice [*Canada*] [*A publication*] (DLA)
CAMPRAD... Computer-Assisted Message Preparation Relay and Distribution (PDAA)
Camp Rom L... Campbell's Compendium of Roman Law [*A publication*] (DLA)
Camp Rom L Comp... Campbell's Compendium of Roman Law [*A publication*] (DLA)
CAMPS .... California Association of Medical Products Suppliers (SRA)
CAMPS .... Centralized Automated Military Pay System
CAMPS .... Computer-Assisted Message Processing System (MCD)
CAMPS .... Computer-Assisted Mission Planner System (MCD)
CAMPS .... Cooperative Area Manpower Planning System [*Environmental Protection Agency*]
CAMPS .... Cost and Material Position System (MCD)
CAMPS .... Cumulative Auction-Market Preferred Stock [*Investment term*]
Camp Sale... Campbell. Sale of Goods and Commercial Agency [*2nd ed.*] [*1891*] [*A publication*] (DLA)
CampSp...... Campbell Soup Co. [*Associated Press*] (SAG)
CAMPUS ..... Coalition of American Pro-Life University Students [*Later, ACL*] (EA)
CAMPUS ..... Comprehensive Analytical Method of Planning in the University Sphere [*Cost simulation technique*]
CAMPUT ..... Canadian Association of Members of Public Utility Tribunals (AC)
CaMPW....... Atomic Energy of Canada, Whiteshell Nuclear Research Establishment, Pinawa, MB, Canada [*Library symbol Library of Congress*] (LCLS)
CaMPW....... Provincial Library of Manitoba, Winnipeg, MB, Canada [*Library symbol*] [*Library of Congress*] (LCLS)
CAM R .... Cambrian Railway [*British*]
CAMR.......... Camera (MSA)
CamR.......... Campbell Reproductions Ltd., Ottawa, ON, Canada [*Library symbol Library of Congress*] (LCLS)
CAMR .... Canadian Association for the Mentally Retarded
CAMR .... Centre for Applied Microbiology and Research [*Public Health Laboratory Service*] [*British*]
CAMR .... Computer-Assisted Micrographic Retrieval (PDAA)
CAMR .... Configuration Accounting and Management Report (MCD)
CAMRA .... Campaign for Real Ale
CAMRA .... Consolidated Air Mission Results Analysis (CINC)
CaMRa........ Rapid City Regional Library, Rapid City, MB, Canada [*Library symbol Library of Congress*] (LCLS)
CAMRAS ..... Computer-Assisted Mapping and Records Activities System (IEEE)
CAMRAS ..... Counter Artillery and Mortar RADAR Acquisition Simulation (MCD)
CAMRB .... Central Aircrew Medical Review Board [*Military*] (AFM)
CaMRD .... Russell and District Regional Library, Russell, MB, Canada [*Library symbol Library of Congress*] (LCLS)
CAMRDC..... Central African Mineral Resources Development Centre [*Congo*] (EAIO)
CaMReP ...... Reston and District Regional Library, Reston, MB, Canada [*Library symbol Library of Congress*] (LCLS)
CaMRiP ...... Prairie Crocus Regional Library, Rivers, MB, Canada [*Library symbol Library of Congress*] (LCLS)
CAMRL .... Canadian Association of Medical Record Librarians
CamrnAsh... Cameron Ashley [*Associated Press*] (SAG)
CamrnF........ Cameron Financial Corp. [*Associated Press*] (SAG)
CAMRO .... Canadian Association of Marketing Research Organization [*Association Canadienne des Organismes de Recherche en Marketing*] (AC)
CaMRo......... Rossburn Regional Library, Rossburn, MB, Canada [*Library symbol Library of Congress*] (LCLS)
CAMROC..... Cambridge Radio Observatory Committee
CaMRoH ...... Rossburn District Hospital, Rossburn, MB, Canada [*Library symbol Library of Congress*] (LCLS)
CAMRSS ..... Center for Autonomous and Man-Controlled Robotic and Sensing Systems [*Research center*] (RCD)
CAMRT .... Canadian Association of Medical Radiation Technologists (EAIO)
CAMS .... Cabin Atmosphere Monitoring System [*NASA*]
CAMS .... Calibrated Airborne Multispectral Scanner [*Instrumentation*]
CAMS .... Canadian Applied Mathematics Society (MCD)
CAMs.......... Cell-Cell Adhesion Molecules [*Genetics*] (DOG)
CAMS .... Central Atmosphere Monitoring System [*Military*] (CAAL)
CAMS .... Certificate of Advanced Management Studies (PGP)
CAMS .... Chinese American Medical Society (EA)
CAMS .... Coastal Antimissile System (MCD)
CAMS .... Color Appearance Monitoring System [*Automotive quality control*]
CAMS .... COMIREX [*Committee on Imagery Requirements and Exploitation*] Automated Management System (MCD)
CAMS .... Commissioning Accession Management System [*Military*] (DNAB)
CAMS .... Common Aperture Multispectrum Seeker [*Army*] (MCD)
CAMS .... Communications Area Master Station (NVT)

CAMS.......... Comprehensive Agrimedia Measurement Study [*Database*] [*Doane Marketing Research, Inc.*] [*Information service or system*] (CRD)
CAMS.......... Computer-Aided Milestone Schedule
CAMS....... Computer-Aided Missile Synthesis [*Army*] (MCD)
CAMS....... Computer-Assisted Messaging Services [*Electronic mail*] [*Computer science*]
CAMS.......... Computerized Arrythmia Monitoring System [*Medicine*] (CPH)
CAMS.......... Computerized Automotive Maintenance System [*Buick's factory to dealership communication system*]
CAMS.......... Computers for the Advancement of Medicine & Science [*Information service or system*] (IID)
CAMS.......... Consolidated Aircraft Maintenance Squadron [*Air Force*]
CAMS.......... Constant-Angle Mie Scattering [*Optics*]
CAMS......... Consumer and Marketing Service [*Later, AMS*] [*Department of Agriculture*] (IAA)
CAMS.......... Container Automated Marking Systems
CAMS.......... Containerized Avionics Maintenance System (NG)
CAMS.......... Control of Aircraft Maintenance and Servicing
CAMS.......... Core Automated Maintenance System (MCD)
CAMS.......... Crisis Action Management System
CAMS.......... Cybernetic Anthropomorphous Machine System [*Robot*] [*Army*]
Cam Sal ...... Camillus Salernus [*Flourished, 16th century*] [*Authority cited in pre-1607 legal work*] (DSA)
Cam Salern... Camillus Salernus [*Flourished, 16th century*] [*Authority cited in pre-1607 legal work*] (DSA)
CA/MSAW .... Conflict Alert/Minimum Safe Altitude Warning [*FAA*] (TAG)
Cam SC ...... Cameron's Supreme Court Cases [*Canada*] [*A publication*] (DLA)
CaMSC........ College de St. Boniface, St. Boniface, MB, Canada [*Library symbol Library of Congress*] (LCLS)
CAM SCAC... Camera Scaccari [*Exchequer Chamber*] [*Latin Legal term*] (DLA)
Cam Scacc... Camera Scaccarii [*Exchequer Chamber*] [*Latin Legal term*] (DLA)
CaMSEC...... Selkirk Community Library, Selkirk, MB, Canada [*Library symbol Library of Congress*] (LCLS)
CaMSeL....... Lord Selkirk Regional School, Selkirk, MB, Canada [*Library symbol Library of Congress*] (LCLS)
CaMSeMH ... Selkirk Mental Health Centre, Selkirk, MB, Canada [*Library symbol Library of Congress*] (LCLS)
CaMSePCL... Parks Canada, Lower Fort Garry National Historic Park, Selkirk, MB, Canada [*Library symbol Library of Congress*] (LCLS)
CaMSePN .... School of Psychiatric Nursing, Selkirk, MB, Canada [*Library symbol Library of Congress*] (LCLS)
CAMSEQ ...... Conformational Analysis of Molecules in Solution by Empirical and Quantum Techniques
CaMShCFAM... Canadian Forces Base, Royal Canadian Army Museum, Shilo, MB, Canada [*Library symbol Library of Congress*] (LCLS)
CAMSI .... Canadian-American Merchant Shipping Instructions
CAMSI .... Canadian Association of Medical Students and Interns
CAMSI .... Carrier Aircraft Maintenance Support Improvement (DNAB)
CAMSI .... Confidential Admiralty Merchant Shipping Instructions
CAMSIM ...... Computer-Assisted Maintenance Simulation [*Army*]
CaMSL........ Snow Lake Community Library, Snow Lake, MB, Canada [*Library symbol Library of Congress*] (LCLS)
CaMSoG...... Glenwood and Souris Regional Library, Souris, MB, Canada [*Library symbol Library of Congress*] (LCLS)
CAMSPF ...... Catholic Archdiocese of Melbourne Schools' Provident Fund [*Australia*]
CAMSq........ Consolidated Aircraft Maintenance Squadron [*Air Force*]
CaMSrNW.... North-West Regional Library, Swan River, MB, Canada [*Library symbol Library of Congress*] (LCLS)
CAMSTA ...... Cameron Station [*Virginia*] [*Army*] (AABC)
CaMSte........ Steinbach Public Library, Steinbach, MB, Canada [*Library symbol Library of Congress*] (LCLS)
Cam Stell .... Camera Stellate [*Star Chamber*] [*Latin Legal term*] (DLA)
CaMSteM..... Mennonite Village Museum, Steinbach, MB, Canada [*Library symbol Library of Congress*] (LCLS)
CaMStJ........ Public Library, St. James, MB, Canada [*Library symbol Library of Congress*] (LCLS)
CaMStoS...... South Interlake Regional Library, Stonewall, MB, Canada [*Library symbol Library of Congress*] (LCLS)
CaMStPJ...... Jolys Regional Library, St. Pierre, MB, Canada [*Library symbol Library of Congress*] (LCLS)
CaMStR .... Sainte Rose Regional Library, Sainte Rose, MB, Canada [*Library symbol Library of Congress*] (LCLS)
CAMT.......... Canadian Association for Music Therapy
CAMT.......... Centre for Advanced Materials Technology [*Monash University*] [*Australia*]
CAMT.......... Consolidated Aircraft Maintenance Training
CaMT.......... Transcona Public Library, Transcona, MB, Canada [*Library symbol Library of Congress*] (LCLS)
CAMTEC...... Camouflage Technology Center [*Battelle Columbus Division, OH*]
CAMTEC....... Canadian Marine Trade Exhibition and Congress [*SHOWBEX*] (TSPED)
CaMTh .... Thompson Public Library, Thompson, MB, Canada [*Library symbol Library of Congress*] (LCLS)
CAMTMTS.... Central Area, Military Traffic Management and Terminal Service (AABC)
CaMTp .... The Pas Public Library, The Pas, MB, Canada [*Library symbol Library of Congress*] (LCLS)
CaMTPK...... Keewatin Community College, The Pas, MB, Canada [*Library symbol Library of Congress*] (LCLS)
CAMTRON.... Council of Australian Machine Tool and Robotics Manufacturers
CAMTT........ Civil Affairs Mobile Training Team [*Military*] (CINC)
CAMU .... Cardiac Ambulatory Monitoring Unit [*Cardiology*] (DAVI)
CAMU .... Coronary Arrhythmia Monitoring Unit [*Cardiology*] (DAVI)
CAMU .... Corrective Action Management Unit [*Environmental science*]

CAMUS .... Commitment Accounting and Management of Unit Supplies (MCD)
CaMV.......... Cauliflower Mosaic Virus [*Also, CLMV*]
CAMV.......... Cowpea Aphid-Borne Mosaic Virus
CAMVAC ...... Centro de Apoyo para Mujeres Violadas [*An association Mexico*] (EAIO)
CAMVAP ...... Canadian Motor Vehicle Arbitration Program
CaMVE........ Virden-Elkhorn Regional Library, Virden, MB, Canada [*Library symbol Library of Congress*] (LCLS)
CAMW .... Consolidated Aircraft Maintenance Wing [*Air Force*]
CaMW .... Winnipeg Public Library, Winnipeg, MB, Canada [*Library symbol Library of Congress*] (LCLS)
CaMWA........ Canada Department of Agriculture, Winnipeg, MB, Canada [*Library symbol Library of Congress*] (LCLS)
CaMWAG ..... Canada Department of Agriculture, Research Station, Winnipeg, MB, Canada [*Library symbol Library of Congress*] (LCLS)
CaMWAMA... Manitoba Department of Municipal Affairs, Administration Branch, Winnipeg, MB, Canada [*Library symbol Library of Congress*] (LCLS)
CaMWAMT... Aikens, Macaulay & Thorauldson Law Firm, Winnipeg, MB, Canada [*Library symbol Library of Congress*] (LCLS)
CaMWaPCR... Parks Canada, Riding Mountain National Park, Wasagaming, MB, Canada [*Library symbol Library of Congress*] (LCLS)
CaMWARN... Manitoba Association of Registered Nurses, Winnipeg, MB, Canada [*Library symbol Library of Congress*] (LCLS)
CaMWAS ..... Arthritis Society, Winnipeg, MB, Canada [*Library symbol Library of Congress*] (LCLS)
CaMWBM .... Bethania Mennonite Personal Care Home, Winnipeg, MB, Canada [*Library symbol Library of Congress*] (LCLS)
CaMWC....... Canadian Broadcasting Corp., Music and Record Library, Winnipeg, MB, Canada [*Library symbol Library of Congress*] (LCLS)
CaMWCA ..... Cantetech, Inc., Winnipeg, MB, Canada [*Library symbol Library of Congress*] (LCLS)
CaMWCCA ... Manitoba Department of Consumer and Corporate Affairs, Winnipeg, MB, Canada [*Library symbol Library of Congress*] (LCLS)
CaMWCCH ... Health Science Centre, Children's Centre, Winnipeg, MB, Canada [*Library symbol Library of Congress*] (LCLS)
CaMWCCI .... Manitoba Department of Consumer, Corporate, and Internal Services, Consumers' Bureau, Winnipeg, MB, Canada [*Library symbol Library of Congress*] (LCLS)
CaMWCCIR... Canada Department of Communications, Central Region Information Resources Center, Winnipeg, MB, Canada [*Library symbol Library of Congress*] (LCLS)
CaMWCF..... Canadian Forces Base Winnipeg, Canadian Forces Aerospace and Navigation School, Westwin, MB, Canada [*Library symbol*] [*Library of Congress*] (LCLS)
CaMWCH ..... Concordia Hospital, Winnipeg, MB, Canada [*Library symbol Library of Congress*] (LCLS)
CaMWCHA ... Charles Howard & Associates, Winnipeg, MB, Canada [*Library symbol Library of Congress*] (LCLS)
CaMWCHD... Charleswood Public Library, Winnipeg, MB, Canada [*Library symbol*] [*Library of Congress*] (LCLS)
CaMWCI ...... Canertech, Inc., Winnipeg, MB, Canada [*Library symbol*] [*Library of Congress*] (LCLS)
CaMWCM .... Canadian Mennonite Bible College, Winnipeg, MB, Canada [*Library symbol Library of Congress*] (LCLS)
CaMWCT...... Manitoba Cancer Treatment and Research Foundation, Winnipeg, MB, Canada [*Library symbol Library of Congress*] (LCLS)
CaMWCU ..... Credit Union Central of Manitoba, Winnipeg, MB, Canada [*Library symbol Library of Congress*] (LCLS)
CaMWCWB... Canadian Wheat Board, Winnipeg, MB, Canada [*Library symbol Library of Congress*] (LCLS)
CaMWDL ..... Deer Lodge Hospital, Winnipeg, MB, Canada [*Library symbol Library of Congress*] (LCLS)
CaMWDRR... Manitoba Department of Renewable Resources, Winnipeg, MB, Canada [*Library symbol Library of Congress*] (LCLS)
CaMWDU .... Ducks Unlimited, Winnipeg, MB, Canada [*Library symbol Library of Congress*] (LCLS)
CaMWE........ Manitoba Department of Education, Winnipeg, MB, Canada [*Library symbol Library of Congress*] (LCLS)
CaMWEAE... Environment Canada, Atmospheric Environment Service, Central Region Headquarter, Winnipeg, MB,Canada [*Library symbol*] [*Library of Congress*] (LCLS)
CaMWECW... Environment Canada, Canadian Wildlife Service, Winnipeg, MB, Canada [*Library symbol Library of Congress*] (LCLS)
CaMWEEP... Environment Canada, Environmental Protection Service, Winnipeg, MB, Canada [*Library symbol*] [*Library of Congress*] (LCLS)
CaMWEM .... Manitoba Environmental Management Division, Winnipeg, MB, Canada [*Library symbol Library of Congress*] (LCLS)
CaMWESM... Manitoba Department of Education, Special Materials Services, Winnipeg, MB, Canada [*Library symbol*] [*Library of Congress*] (LCLS)
CaMWEWSH... Manitoba Department of Environment and Workplace Safety and Health, Winnipeg, MB, Canada [*Library symbol*] [*Library of Congress*] (LCLS)
CaMWFD ..... Fred Douglas Lodge Nursing Home, Winnipeg, MB, Canada [*Library symbol Library of Congress*] (LCLS)
CaMWFI....... Manitoba Department of Finance, Winnipeg, MB, Canada [*Library symbol Library of Congress*] (LCLS)
CaMWFP..... Winnipeg Free Press Co. Ltd., Winnipeg, MB, Canada [*Library symbol Library of Congress*] (LCLS)
CaMWFRS ... Manitoba Department of Fitness, Recreation and Sport, Winnipeg, MB, Canada [*Library symbol*] [*Library of Congress*] (LCLS)
CaMWFW .... Fresh Water Institute, Canada Fisheries Research Board, Winnipeg, MB, Canada [*Library symbol Library of Congress*] (LCLS)

CaMWGBP ... Guertin Brothers Paint Library, Winnipeg, MB, Canada [*Library symbol Library of Congress*] (LCLS)

CaMWGCH ... Health Sciences Centre, General Centre, Winnipeg, MB, Canada [*Library symbol Library of Congress*] (LCLS)

CaMWGH ... Grace Hospital, Winnipeg, MB, Canada [*Library symbol Library of Congress*] (LCLS)

CaMWGHA ... Gunn, Hoffer & Associates, Winnipeg, MB, Canada [*Library symbol Library of Congress*] (LCLS)

CaMWGR ..... Canada Department of Agriculture, Canadian Grain Commission, Winnipeg, MB, Canada [*Library symbol Library of Congress*] (LCLS)

CaMWGW .... Great West Life Assurance Co., Winnipeg, MB, Canada [*Library symbol Library of Congress*] (LCLS)

CaMWH .... Manitoba Hydro, Winnipeg, MB, Canada [*Library symbol Library of Congress*] (LCLS)

CaMWHM ..... Health Sciences Centre, Medical Library, Winnipeg, MB, Canada [*Library symbol Library of Congress*] (LCLS)

CaMWHP ..... Manitoba Department of Health and Community Service, Winnipeg, MB, Canada [*Library symbol Library of Congress*] (LCLS)

CaMWHR ..... Henderson Regional Library, Winnipeg, MB, Canada [*Library symbol Library of Congress*] (LCLS)

CaMWHSC ... Manitoba Health Services Commission, Winnipeg, MB, Canada [*Library symbol Library of Congress*] (LCLS)

CaMWI .... Insurance Institute of Winnipeg, Winnipeg, MB, Canada [*Library symbol Library of Congress*] (LCLS)

CaMWIAP .... Parks Canada, Prairie Regional Office, Winnipeg, MB, Canada [*Library symbol*] [*Library of Congress*] (LCLS)

CaMWIC ...... Manitoba Department of Industry and Commerce, Winnipeg, MB, Canada [*Library symbol Library of Congress*] (LCLS)

CaMWIDE .... IDE Engineering Co., Winnipeg, MB, Canada [*Library symbol Library of Congress*] (LCLS)

CaMWIE .... Indus Electronic, Winnipeg, MB, Canada [*Library symbol Library of Congress*] (LCLS)

CaMWIN ...... Indian and Northern Affairs Canada, Winnipeg, MB, Canada [*Library symbol*] [*Library of Congress*] (LCLS)

CaMWinBH ... Bethel Hospital, Winkler, MB, Canada [*Library symbol Library of Congress*] (LCLS)

CaMWJ .... Canada Department of Justice, Winnipeg, MB, Canada [*Library symbol Library of Congress*] (LCLS)

CaMWK .... Kelvin High School, Winnipeg, MB, Canada [*Library symbol Library of Congress*] (LCLS)

CaMWL .... Law Society of Manitoba, Winnipeg, MB, Canada [*Library symbol Library of Congress*] (LCLS)

CaMWLC ...... Library Service Centre, Winnipeg School Division No. 1, Winnipeg, MB, Canada [*Library symbol Library of Congress*] (LCLS)

CaMWLCC ... Lutheran Council in Canada, Winnipeg, MB, Canada [*Library symbol Library of Congress*] (LCLS)

CaMWLR ..... Manitoba Department of Labour, Labour Research Library, Winnipeg, MB, Canada [*Library symbol Library of Congress*] (LCLS)

CaMWLS ...... University of Manitoba, Faculty of Law Library, Winnipeg, MB, Canada [*Library symbol Library of Congress*] (LCLS)

CaMWM .... University of Manitoba, Medical Library, Winnipeg, MB, Canada [*Library symbol Library of Congress*] (LCLS)

CaMWMBC ... Mennonite Brethren College, Winnipeg, MB, Canada [*Library symbol Library of Congress*] (LCLS)

CaMWME ..... MacLaren Engineering, Winnipeg, MB, Canada [*Library symbol Library of Congress*] (LCLS)

CaMWMG ..... Misericordia General Hospital, Winnipeg, MB, Canada [*Library symbol Library of Congress*] (LCLS)

CaMWMH .... Winnipeg Municipal Hospital, Winnipeg, MB, Canada [*Library symbol Library of Congress*] (LCLS)

CaMWMI ...... Canada Department of Manpower and Immigration, Winnipeg, MB, Canada [*Library symbol Library of Congress*] (LCLS)

CaMWMM ..... Manitoba Museum of Man and Nature, Winnipeg, MB, Canada [*Library symbol Library of Congress*] (LCLS)

CaMWMMP ... Meadowood Manor Personal Care Home, Winnipeg, MB, Canada [*Library symbol Library of Congress*] (LCLS)

CaMWMR ..... Manitoba Department of Mines, Resource and Environmental Management, Mineral Resources Division, Winnipeg, MB, Canada [*Library symbol*] [*Library of Congress*] (LCLS)

CaMWMRC ... Manitoba Research Council, Winnipeg, MB, Canada [*Library symbol Library of Congress*] (LCLS)

CaMWMTC ... Manitoba Theater Center, Winnipeg, MB, Canada [*Library symbol Library of Congress*] (LCLS)

CaMWMTS ... Manitoba Teachers Society, Winnipeg, MB, Canada [*Library symbol Library of Congress*] (LCLS)

CaMWNR ..... Manitoba Department of Mines, Natural Resources and Environment, Natural Resources and Environment Division, Winnipeg, MB, Canada [*Closed*] [*Library symbol*] [*Library of Congress*] (LCLS)

CaMWO .... Rev. Peres Oblats, Winnipeg, MB, Canada [*Library symbol Library of Congress*] (LCLS)

CaMWP .... Provincial Library of Manitoba, Winnipeg, MB, Canada [*Library symbol Library of Congress*] (LCLS)

CaMWPA ..... Provincial Archives of Manitoba, Winnipeg, MB, Canada [*Library symbol Library of Congress*] (LCLS)

CaMWPCPA ... Parks Canada, Prairie Region Library, Archaeology Subsection Office, Winnipeg, MB, Canada [*Library symbol Library of Congress*] (LCLS)

CaMWPCPH ... Parks Canada, Prairie Region Library, Historic Resources Conservation SubsectionOffice, Winnipeg, MB, Canada [*Library symbol Library of Congress*] (LCLS)

CaMWPL ...... Department of Tourism, Recreation, and Cultural Affairs, Public Library Services, Winnipeg, MB, Canada [*Library symbol Library of Congress*] (LCLS)

CaMWPNR ... Manitoba Department of Natural Resources, Park Management Library, Winnipeg, MB,Canada [*Library symbol Library of Congress*] (LCLS)

CaMWPPH ... Provincial Public Health Nursing Services, Winnipeg, MB, Canada [*Library symbol Library of Congress*] (LCLS)

CaMWPS ..... Manitoba Probation Services, Winnipeg, MB, Canada [*Library symbol Library of Congress*] (LCLS)

CaMWQCG ... Quadraplegic Communications Group, Inc., Media and Information Services, Winnipeg, MB, Canada [*Library symbol*] [*Library of Congress*] (LCLS)

CaMWR .... Royal Winnipeg Ballet, Winnipeg, MB, Canada [*Library symbol Library of Congress*] (LCLS)

CaMWRC .... Royal Canadian Mounted Police, Crime Laboratory, Winnipeg, MB, Canada [*Library symbol Library of Congress*] (LCLS)

CaMWRCC ... Roman Catholic Chancery Office, Winnipeg, MB, Canada [*Library symbol*] [*Library of Congress*] (LCLS)

CaMWRR ..... Red River Community College, Learning Resources Centre, Winnipeg, MB, Canada [*Library symbol Library of Congress*] (LCLS)

CaMWRRL .... Red River Community College, Library Technician Program, Winnipeg, MB, Canada [*Library symbol*] [*Library of Congress*] (LCLS)

CaMWRS ..... Richardson Securities of Canada, Winnipeg, MB, Canada [*Library symbol Library of Congress*] (LCLS)

CaMWSA ..... Saint Andrew's College, Winnipeg, MB, Canada [*Library symbol Library of Congress*] (LCLS)

CaMWSAC ... Saint Amant Center, Winnipeg, MB, Canada [*Library symbol Library of Congress*] (LCLS)

CaMWSB ..... St. Boniface Public Library, Winnipeg, MB, Canada [*Library symbol Library of Congress*] (LCLS)

CaMWSBM ... St. Boniface General Hospital, Medical Library, Winnipeg, MB, Canada [*Library symbol Library of Congress*] (LCLS)

CaMWSBN ... St. Boniface General Hospital, School of Nursing, Winnipeg, MB, Canada [*Library symbol Library of Congress*] (LCLS)

CaMWSC .... Society for Crippled Children and Adults, Winnipeg, MB, Canada [*Library symbol Library of Congress*] (LCLS)

CaMWSD ..... Winnipeg School Division No. 1, Teachers' Library and Resource Centre, Winnipeg,MB, Canada [*Library symbol Library of Congress*] (LCLS)

CaMWSJ ...... Saint John's College, Winnipeg, MB, Canada [*Library symbol Library of Congress*] (LCLS)

CaMWSM ..... Stony Mountain Institution Library, Winnipeg, MB, Canada [*Library symbol Library of Congress*] (LCLS)

CaMWSN ..... Winnipeg School of Nursing, Health Science Centre, Winnipeg, MB, Canada [*Library symbol Library of Congress*] (LCLS)

CaMWSOGH ... Seven Oaks General Hospital, Education Services, Winnipeg, MB, Canada [*Library symbol Library of Congress*] (LCLS)

CaMWSP ..... Saint Paul's College, Winnipeg, MB, Canada [*Library symbol Library of Congress*] (LCLS)

CaMWSPA ... Spiece Associates, Winnipeg, MB, Canada [*Library symbol*] [*Library of Congress*] (LCLS)

CaMWSPC ... Social Planning Council of Winnipeg, Winnipeg, MB, Canada [*Library symbol Library of Congress*] (LCLS)

CaMWSV ..... Saint Vital Public Library, Winnipeg, MB, Canada [*Library symbol Library of Congress*] (LCLS)

CaMWT .... Winnipeg Tribune, Winnipeg, MB, Canada [*Library symbol Library of Congress*] (LCLS)

CaMWTC ...... Teshmount Consultants, Winnipeg, MB, Canada [*Library symbol Library of Congress*] (LCLS)

CaMWTE ...... Templeton Engineering, Winnipeg, MB, Canada [*Library symbol Library of Congress*] (LCLS)

CaMWTRC ... Manitoba. Department of Tourism, Recreation, and Cultural Affairs, Winnipeg, MB,Canada [*Library symbol Library of Congress*] (LCLS)

CaMWTS ...... Manitoba Telephone System, Winnipeg, MB, Canada [*Library symbol Library of Congress*] (LCLS)

CaMWU .... University of Manitoba, Winnipeg, MB, Canada [*Library symbol Library of Congress*] (LCLS)

CaMWUAF ... University of Manitoba, Architecture and Fine Arts Library, Winnipeg, MB, Canada [*Library symbol Library of Congress*] (LCLS)

CaMWUC ..... University of Winnipeg, Winnipeg, MB, Canada [*Library symbol Library of Congress*] (LCLS)

CaMWUD ..... University of Manitoba, Dental Library, Winnipeg, MB, Canada [*Library symbol Library of Congress*] (LCLS)

CaMWUG ..... University of Manitoba, Department of Geography, Winnipeg, MB, Canada [*Library symbol Library of Congress*] (LCLS)

CaMWUGG ... United Grain Growers, Winnipeg, MB, Canada [*Library symbol Library of Congress*] (LCLS)

CaMWUM ..... University of Manitoba, Map and Atlas Collection, Winnipeg, MB, Canada [*Library symbol Library of Congress*] (LCLS)

CaMWUML ... Underwood McLellan Ltd., Winnipeg, MB, Canada [*Library symbol Library of Congress*] (LCLS)

CaMWVGH ... Victoria General Hospital, Winnipeg, MB, Canada [*Library symbol Library of Congress*] (LCLS)

CaMWVS ..... Manitoba Veterinarian Services, Branch Library, Winnipeg, MB, Canada [*Library symbol Library of Congress*] (LCLS)

CaMWW ...... Winnipeg Public Library, William Avenue Branch, Winnipeg, MB, Canada [*Library symbol*] [*Library of Congress*] (LCLS)

CaMWWA .... Winnipeg Art Gallery, Winnipeg, MB, Canada [*Library symbol Library of Congress*] (LCLS)

CaMWWC .... Winnipeg Clinic, Winnipeg, MB, Canada [*Library symbol Library of Congress*] (LCLS)

CaMWWLW ... W. L. Wardrop & Associates, Winnipeg, MB, Canada [*Library symbol Library of Congress*] (LCLS)

CAM-X .... Canadian Association of Message Exchanges, Inc. [*Association Canadienne d'Echange de Messages, Inc.*] (AC)
CAN .... Air Canarias S. Coop Ltd. [*Spain ICAO designator*] (FAAC)
CAN .... Bremerton, WA [*Location identifier FAA*] (FAAL)
CAN .... Cajun Nike [*US Navy missile*]
CaN .... Calcineurin [*Biochemistry*]
CAN .... Calcium-Ammonium Nitrate [*Fertilizer*]
CAN .... Calculator-Aware Number [*Project*] (AIE)
CAN .... California Association of Nonprofits (SRA)
CAN .... California Association of Nurserymen (SRA)
CAN .... Campus Action Network [*Defunct*] (EA)
Can .... Canaanite (BJA)
CAN .... Canada [*ANSI three-letter standard code*] (CNC)
Can .... Canada (VRA)
Can .... Canada (ODBW)
Can .... Canadian (ODBW)
Can .... Canadian (ROG)
CAN .... Canadian Action for Nicaragua (AC)
CAN .... Canadian MARC [*Machine-Readable Cataloging*] [*Source file*] [*UTLAS symbol*]
CAN .... Canal (ROG)
CAN .... Canaveral [*Obsolete NASA*] (KSC)
CAN .... Canberra [*Australia Seismograph station code, US Geological Survey*] (SEIS)
CAN .... Cancel (AABC)
can.............. Cancel [*Publishing*] (WDMC)
CAN .... Cancel Character [*Keyboard*] [*Computer science*]
can.............. Canceled (WDMC)
Can .... Cancer [*Oncology*] (DAVI)
CAN .... Cancer [*Constellation*]
CAN .... Cancrinite [*A zeolite*]
CAN .... Candida [*Genus of fungi*] (AAMN)
CAN .... Canister (AAG)
CAN .... Cannabis Action Network (EA)
CAN .... Cannery
CAN .... Cannon (WDAA)
CAN .... [*The*] Cannon Group, Inc. (MHDW)
CAN .... Canon
CAN .... Canonicorum [*England*]
CAN .... Canopy (MSA)
CAN .... Canto [*Melody*] [*Music*]
CAN .... Canton [*City in China*] (ROG)
CAN .... Canton [*China*] [*Airport symbol*] (AD)
CAN .... Cantoris [*Of the Cantor*] [*Music*]
Can .... Canute [*King of England, Denmark, and Norway, 994-1035*] (ILCA)
Can .... Canvas (DAC)
CAN .... Career Advancement Network (EA)
CAN .... Cascade Activity Numbering (PDAA)
CAN .... Central Autentica Nacionalista [*Nationalist Authentic Central*] [*Guatemala*] [*Political party*] (PPW)
CAN .... Centralforbundet for Alkohol- och Narkotikaupplysning [*Swedish Council for Information on Alcohol and Other Drugs*] [*Information service or system*] (IID)
CAN .... Ceric Ammonium Nitrate [*Inorganic chemistry*]
CAN .... Certification Analysis Network (NASA)
CA/N .... Child Abuse and Neglect
CAN .... Children's Action Network [*Defunct*] (EA)
CAN .... Chlorendic Anhydride [*Also, CA*] [*Organic chemistry*]
CAN .... Christians in the Arts Networking (EA)
CAN .... Citizens Against Noise
CAN .... Citizens Against Nuclear War [*Defunct*] (EA)
CAN .... Claim Account Number [*Social Security Administration*] (GFGA)
CAN .... Climate Action Network [*An alliance of groups that includes Greenpeace, the World Wide Fund for Nature, and The Natural Resources Defense Council*]
CAN .... Command Aviation Net [*Military*] (INF)
CAN .... Committee on Aircraft Noise [*ICAO*] (DA)
CAN .... Common Account Number [*Environmental Protection Agency*] (GFGA)
CAN .... Community Arts Network [*Australia*]
CAN .... Computer Architecture News [*A publication*]
CAN .... Configuration Accounting Number
CAN .... Conservation Administration News [*A publication*]
CAN .... Consumer Action Now (EA)
CAN .... Continental Can [*Formerly, Viatech, Inc.*] [*NYSE symbol*] (SPSG)
CAN .... Contl Can [*NYSE symbol*] (TTSB)
CAN .... Controlled Area Network [*Communication engineering*]
CAN .... Cord Around Neck [*Neonatology and obstetrics*] (DAVI)
CAN .... Corporate Angel Network (EA)
CAN .... Correlation Air Navigation
CAN .... Cosmopolitan Area Network [*Telecommunications*] (ACRL)
CAN .... Cost Account Number [*Accounting*] (NG)
CAN .... Cult Awareness Network (EA)
CAN .... Cure AIDS [*Acquired Immune Deficiency Syndrome*] Now [*An association*] (EA)
CAN .... Customer Access Network
CAN .... Customs Assigned Number [*Shipping*] [*British*]
CAN .... Guangzhou [*China*] [*Airport symbol*] (OAG)
CAna .... Anaheim Public Library, Anaheim, CA [*Library symbol Library of Congress*] (LCLS)
CANA .... California Association of Nurse Anesthetists (SRA)
CANA .... Canadian Army (NATG)
CANA .... Canadian Association of Nurse Administrators (AC)
CANA .... Christian Anti-Narcotic Association [*Later, SFM*]
CANA .... Cider Association of North America (EA)

CANA .... Clergy Against Nuclear Arms [*British*] [*An association*] (DBA)
CANA .... Convalescent Antidote for Nerve Agent (DOMA)
CANA .... Cremation Association of North America (EA)
CANA .... Czech American National Alliance (EA)
CAnaA .... North American Rockwell Corp., Autonetics Technical Library, Anaheim, CA [*Library symbol Library of Congress*] (LCLS)
CAnaA-R ...... North American Rockwell Corp., A. R. Rechnitzer Oceanographic Collection, Anaheim, CA [*Library symbol Library of Congress*] (LCLS)
Can Abr ...... Canadian Abridgment [*A publication*] (DLA)
Can Abr (2d)... Canadian Abridgment [*2nd ed.*] [*A publication*] (DLA)
CANAC .... Canadian Association of Nurses in AIDS Care (AC)
CANACT .... Canadian African Newcomer Aid Centre of Toronto (AC)
CANAD .... Canada (WGA)
Canada Commerce... Canadian Department of Industry, Trade, and Commerce (DLA)
Canada LT... Canadian Law Times [*A publication*] (DLA)
CANAEP .... Council on Accreditation of Nurse Anesthetists Educational Programs (PGP)
CANAGREX... Canadian Agricultural Export Corp.
CAnaGS .... Church of Jesus Christ of Latter-Day Saints, Genealogical Society Library, Anaheim Branch, Anaheim, CA [*Library symbol Library of Congress*] (LCLS)
CAnaI .... Interstate Electronics Corp., Anaheim, CA [*Library symbol Library of Congress*] (LCLS)
CANAIR .... Air-Cushion Vehicle built by Canadian Cushion Craft [*Usually used in comb ination with numerals*] [*Canada*]
CANAIRDEF... Air Defense Command Headquarters, St. Hubert, Province of Quebec, Canada
CANAIRDIV... Canadian Air Division Headquarters [*Allied Air Forces in Europe*]
CANAIRFAX... Maritime Group Headquarters, Halifax, Nova Scotia, Canada
CANAIRHED... Air Force Headquarters, Ottawa, Ontario, Canada
CANAIRLIFT... Air Transport Command Headquarters, Rockcliffe, Ontario, Canada
CANAIRLON... Air Member, Canadian Joint Staff, London, England
CANAIRMAT... Air Material Command Headquarters, Ottawa, Ontario, Canada
CANAIRNEW... Senior Royal Canadian Air Force Liaison Officer, St. Johns, Newfoundland, Canada
CANAIRNORWEST... North-West Air Command Headquarters, Edmonton, Alberta, Canada
CANAIRPEG... Canadian Fourteenth Air Training Group Headquarters, Winnipeg
CANAIRTAC... Canadian Tactical Air Command Headquarters
CANAIRTRAIN... Canadian Air Training Command Headquarters
CANAIRVAN... Twelfth Air Defense Group Headquarters, Vancouver, British Columbia, Canada
CANAIRWASH... Air Member, Canadian Joint Staff, Washington, DC
CANAL .... Campaign for Action on Navigation and Locks [*British*] (DI)
CANAL .... Command Analysis [*Telecommunications*] (TEL)
CANAL .... Kanizkar Le'eyl [*As Mentioned Above*] [*Hebrew*]
Canal Zone Sup Ct... Canal Zone Supreme Court Reports [*A publication*] (DLA)
CAN-AM ...... Canadian-American Center [*University of Maine at Orono*] [*Research center*] (RCD)
CAN-AM ...... Canadian-American Challenge Cup Series [*Auto racing*]
CAnaN-N ...... Nortronics Corp., Anaheim, CA [*Library symbol Library of Congress*] (LCLS)
Can App ...... Canadian Reports, Appeal Cases [*1828-1913*] [*A publication*] (DLA)
Can App Cas... Canadian Appeal Cases [*A publication*] (DLA)
CANARI .... Caribbean Natural Resources Institute (EAIO)
CANARI .... Communications and Navigation Airborne Radio Instrumentation [*Military*] (IAA)
CANARIE ..... Canadian Network for the Advancement of Research, Industry and Education (IID)
CANAS .... Canadian Naval Air Station
CANASA ...... Canadian Alarm & Security Association [*Association Canadienne de l'Alarme et de la Securite*] (AC)
CANATA ...... Canada-Australia Trade Agreement
CAnaU .... United States Borax Research Corp., Anaheim, CA [*Library symbol Library of Congress*] (LCLS)
CANAVAT..... Naval Attache [*Canadian Navy*]
CANAVBRIT... Naval Member, Canadian Joint Staff, London, England
CANAVCHARGE... Senior Officer [*or Officer in Charge*] at ____ [*Navy Canada*]
CANAVHED... Naval Headquarters, Ottawa, ON, Canada
CANAVMODS... Canadian Naval Modifications
CANAVSTORES... Naval Stores Officer [*Canadian Navy*]
CANAVUS .... Canadian Member, Canadian Joint Staff, Washington, DC
CANB .... Construction Association of New Brunswick Inc. (AC)
CANB .... Council of Archives New Brunswick [*Conseil des Archives du Nouveau-Brunswick*] (AC)
Can BA ...... Canadian Bar Association. Proceedings [*A publication*] (DLA)
CaNBAB ...... Canada Department of the Environment, Fisheries and Marine Service, Research and Development Directorate Biological Station, St. Andrews, NB, Canada [*Library symbol*] [*Library of Congress*] (LCLS)
CaNBACCH... Charlotte County Historical Society, Inc., St. Andrews, NB, Canada [*Library symbol Library of Congress*] (LCLS)
Can BAJ...... Canadian Bar Association. Journal [*A publication*] (DLA)
Can Bankr Ann... Canadian Bankruptcy Reports, Annotated [*A publication*] (DLA)
Can Bankr Ann (NS)... Canadian Bankruptcy Reports, Annotated, New Series [*A publication*] (DLA)
Can Bar Year Book... Year Book. Canadian Bar Association [*A publication*] (DLA)
Can B Ass'n YB... Canadian Bar Association. Year Book [*A publication*] (DLA)
CaNBBB .... Bathurst College, Bathurst, NB, Canada [*Library symbol Library of Congress*] (LCLS)
CaNBBCC...... College Communautaire du New Brunswick, Bathurst, NB, Canada [*Library symbol Library of Congress*] (LCLS)
CANBBE .... Curriculum Adaptation Network for Bilingual, Bicultural Education

CaNBBN....... Nepisiguit Library Region, Bathurst, NB, Canada [*Library symbol Library of Congress*] (LCLS)

CaNBCa .... Campbellton Centennial Public Library, Campbellton, NB, Canada [*Library symbol Library of Congress*] (LCLS)

CaNBCaC ..... Chaleur Library Region, Campbellton, NB, Canada [*Library symbol Library of Congress*] (LCLS)

CaNBCAM .... Campobello Public Library, Campobello, NB, Canada [*Library symbol*] [*Library of Congress*] (LCLS)

CaNBCCC ..... NEw Brunswick Community College, Miramichi Campus, Chatham, NB, Canada [*Library symbol*] [*Library of Congress*] (LCLS)

CaNBCH .... Historical Society Nicholas Denis, Caraquet, NB, Canada [*Library symbol Library of Congress*] (LCLS)

CaNBChM .... Miramichi Natural History Society, Chatham, NB, Canada [*Library symbol*] [*Library of Congress*] (LCLS)

CaNBCISH.... La Societe Historique de Clair, Inc., Clair, NB, Canada [*Library symbol Library of Congress*] (LCLS)

CaNBCS .... Saint Thomas University, Fredericton, NB, Canada [*Library symbol Library of Congress*] (LCLS)

CaNBCVHA.. Le Village Historique Acadien, Caraquet, NB, Canada [*Library symbol Library of Congress*] (LCLS)

CaNBDRRM... Restigouche Regional Museum, Dalhousie, NB, Canada [*Library symbol*] [*Library of Congress*] (LCLS)

CaNBEBR ..... Bibliotheque Regionale du Haut Saint-Jean, Edmundston, NB, Canada [*Library symbol Library of Congress*] (LCLS)

CaNBECC ..... New Brunswick Community College, Edmundston, NB, Canada [*Library symbol Library of Congress*] (LCLS)

CaNBEMM .... Musee de Madawaska, Edmundston, NB, Canada [*Library symbol*] [*Library of Congress*] (LCLS)

Canberra Hist J... Canberra Historical Journal [*A publication*]

CaNBESLM... College Saint-Louis-Maillet, Edmundston, NB, Canada [*Library symbol Library of Congress*] (LCLS)

CaNBFA .... New Brunswick Provincial Archives, Fredericton, NB, Canada [*Library symbol Library of Congress*] (LCLS)

CaNBFAFA ... Anglican Church of Canada, Diocese of Fredericton, Archives, Fredericton, NB, Canada [*Library symbol Library of Congress*] (LCLS)

CaNBFAg ..... Canada Department of Agriculture, Research Station, Fredericton, NB, Canada [*Library symbol Library of Congress*] (LCLS)

CaNBFB .... New Brunswick Archives, Beaverbrook Collection, Fredericton, NB, Canada [*Library symbol Library of Congress*] (LCLS)

CaNBFBS ..... New Brunswick Barristers Society, Fredericton, NB, Canada [*Library symbol Library of Congress*] (LCLS)

CaNBFC .... New Brunswick Library Service, Fredericton, NB, Canada [*Library symbol Library of Congress*] (LCLS)

CaNBFE....... Canada Department of the Environment, Maritimes Forest Research Centre, Fredericton, NB, Canada [*Library symbol Library of Congress*] (LCLS)

CaNBFED ..... New Brunswick Department of Education, Fredericton, NB, Canada [*Library symbol*] [*Library of Congress*] (LCLS)

CaNBFEn ..... New Brunswick Department of the Environment, Fredericton, NB, Canada [*Library symbol Library of Congress*] (LCLS)

CaNBFHR..... New Brunswick Department of Historical Resources, Fredericton, NB, Canada [*Library symbol Library of Congress*] (LCLS)

CaNBFKL .... Kings Landing Historical Settlement, Fredericton, NB, Canada [*Library symbol Library of Congress*] (LCLS)

CaNBFL........ New Brunswick Legislative Library, Fredericton, NB, Canada [*Library symbol Library of Congress*] (LCLS)

CaNBFLM ... New Brunswick Department of Lands and Mines, Photogrammetry Branch, Fredericton,NB, Canada [*Library symbol Library of Congress*] (LCLS)

CaNBFMA .... New Brunswick Department of Municipal Affairs, Fredericton, NB, Canada [*Library symbol Library of Congress*] (LCLS)

CaNBFMM .... Medley Memorial Library, Christ Church Cathedral, Fredericton, NB, Canada [*Library symbol Library of Congress*] (LCLS)

CaNBFNR..... New Brunswick Department of Natural Resources and Energy, Fredericton, NB, Canada [*Library symbol*] [*Library of Congress*] (LCLS)

CaNBFP .... New Brunswick Power, Fredericton, NB, Canada [*Library symbol Library of Congress*] (LCLS)

CaNBFPO ..... Province of New Brunswick, Premier's Office, Fredericton, NB, Canada [*Library symbol Library of Congress*] (LCLS)

CaNBFRP..... New Brunswick Research and Productivity Council, Fredericton, NB, Canada [*Library symbol Library of Congress*] (LCLS)

CaNBFSS .... New Brunswick Department of Social Services, Fredericton, NB, Canada [*Library symbol Library of Congress*] (LCLS)

CaNBFT........ Government of New Brunswick, Translation Bureau, Fredericton, NB, Canada [*Library symbol*] [*Library of Congress*] (LCLS)

CaNBFU .... University of New Brunswick, Fredericton, NB, Canada [*Library symbol Library of Congress*] (LCLS)

CaNBFUA..... University of New Brunswick, Archives and Special Collections Department, Fredericton, NB, Canada [*Library symbol Library of Congress*] (LCLS)

CaNBFUL ..... University of New Brunswick, Law Library, Fredericton, NB, Canada [*Library symbol Library of Congress*] (LCLS)

CaNBFUM .... University of New Brunswick, Government Documents Department, Map Room, Fredericton, NB, Canada [*Library symbol Library of Congress*] (LCLS)

CaNBFY .... York-Sunbury Historical Society, Fredericton, NB, Canada [*Library symbol Library of Congress*] (LCLS)

CaNBFYR.... York Regional Library, Fredericton, NB, Canada [*Library symbol Library of Congress*] (LCLS)

CaNBGACF... Canadian Forces Base, Gagetown, NB, Canada [*Library symbol Library of Congress*] (LCLS)

CaNBGfCC... New Brunswick Community College, Grand Falls Campus, Grand Falls, NB, Canada [*Library symbol Library of Congress*] (LCLS)

CaNBGfH..... Grand Falls Historical Society, Grand Falls, NB, Canada [*Library symbol Library of Congress*] (LCLS)

CaNBGG....... Gerrish House Society, Grand Harbour, Grand Manan Island, NB, Canada [*Library symbol Library of Congress*] (LCLS)

CaNBGMM... Grand Manan Museum, Grand Harbour, Grand Manon Island, NB, Canada [*Library symbol*] [*Library of Congress*] (LCLS)

CaNBMCM... Minto Coal Museum, Minto, NB, Canada [*Library symbol*] [*Library of Congress*] (LCLS)

CaNBMoCC... New Brunswick Community College, Moncton, NB, Canada [*Library symbol Library of Congress*] (LCLS)

CaNBMoF .... Fisheries and Oceans Canada, Moncton, NB, Canada [*Library symbol Library of Congress*] (LCLS)

CaNBMoHD... Hopital Docteur Georges-L. Dumont, Moncton, NB, Canada [*Library symbol Library of Congress*] (LCLS)

CaNBMoLM... Lutz Mountain Heritage Foundation, Inc., Moncton, NB, Canada [*Library symbol*] [*Library of Congress*] (LCLS)

CaNBMoM ... Moncton Civic Museum, Moncton, NB, Canada [*Library symbol Library of Congress*] (LCLS)

CaNBMoRE... Canada Department of Regional Economic Expansion, Moncton, NB, Canada [*Library symbol Library of Congress*] (LCLS)

CaNBMoU... Universite de Moncton, Moncton, NB, Canada [*Library symbol Library of Congress*] (LCLS)

CaNBMoUA... Universite de Moncton, Archives Acadiennes, Moncton, NB, Canada [*Library symbol Library of Congress*] (LCLS)

CaNBMOUD... Universite de Moncton, Bibliotheque de Droit, Moncton, NB, Canada [*Library symbol Library of Congress*] (LCLS)

CaNBMoW ... Albert-Westmorland-Kent Regional Library, Moncton, NB, Canada [*Library symbol Library of Congress*] (LCLS)

CaNBN........ Old Manse Library, Newcastle, NB, Canada [*Library symbol Library of Congress*] (LCLS)

CaNBNAM... Miramichi Historical Society Archives, Newcastle, NB, Canada [*Library symbol Library of Congress*] (LCLS)

CaNBNdH... New Denmark Historical Museum, New Denmark, NB, Canada [*Library symbol Library of Congress*] (LCLS)

CaNBO........ Oromocto Public Library, Oromocto, NB, Canada [*Library symbol Library of Congress*] (LCLS)

CaNBPaSV... Southern Victoria Historical Society, Perth-Andover, NB, Canada [*Library symbol*] [*Library of Congress*] (LCLS)

CaNBReH..... L'Eglise Historique St-Henri-de-Barachois, Robichaud, NB, Canada [*Library symbol Library of Congress*] (LCLS)

CaNBRN...... Nestart Library, Richibucto, NB, Canada [*Library symbol Library of Congress*] (LCLS)

CaNBS .... Saint John Regional Library, Saint John, NB, Canada [*Library symbol Library of Congress*] (LCLS)

CaNBSaB ..... Fort Beausejour Museum, Sackville, NB, Canada [*Library symbol Library of Congress*] (LCLS)

CaNBSaCW... Canada Department of the Environment, Canadian Wildlife Service, Sackville, NB, Canada [*Library symbol Library of Congress*] (LCLS)

CaNBSaM .... Mount Allison University, Sackville, NB, Canada [*Library symbol Library of Congress*] (LCLS)

CaNBSCU..... Centre Universitaire de Shippagan, Shippagan, NB, Canada [*Library symbol Library of Congress*] (LCLS)

CaNBShCM... Centre Marin, Shippagan, NB, Canada [*Library symbol Library of Congress*] (LCLS)

CaNBSM ...... New Brunswick Museum, Saint John, NB, Canada [*Library symbol Library of Congress*] (LCLS)

CaNBSmQH... Quaco Historical and Library Society, St. Martins, NB, Canada [*Library symbol*] [*Library of Congress*] (LCLS)

CaNBStiM .... Le Musee de St-Isidore, Inc., St. Isidore, NB, Canada [*Library symbol*] [*Library of Congress*] (LCLS)

CaNBSU....... University of New Brunswick in Saint John, Saint John, NB, Canada [*Library symbol Library of Congress*] (LCLS)

CaNBSuH..... Kings County Historical Society, Sussex, NB, Canada [*Library symbol Library of Congress*] (LCLS)

CaNBSuS..... Sussex Public Library, Sussex, NB, Canada [*Library symbol*] [*Library of Congress*] (LCLS)

CaNBSVS..... Saint John Vocational School, Saint John, NB, Canada [*Library symbol Library of Congress*] (LCLS)

CaNBTM ...... Le Musee Historique de Tracadie, Tracadie, NB, Canada [*Library symbol*] [*Library of Congress*] (LCLS)

CaNBW........ Woodstock Public (Fisher Memorial) Library, Woodstock, NB, Canada [*Library symbol Library of Congress*] (LCLS)

CaNBWV ...... Victoria-Carleton Courthouse, Woodstock, NB, Canada [*Library symbol Library of Congress*] (LCLS)

CaNBWY ...... York Regional Library Headquarters No. 2, Woodstock, NB, Canada [*Library symbol Library of Congress*] (LCLS)

CANC .... Canceled

CANC .... Cancellation

Canc .... Cancer [*Constellation*]

CANC .... Cuban American National Council (EA)

CANCAM...... Canadian Congress of Applied Mechanics (PDAA)

CANCARAIRGRP... Carrier Air Group [*Canadian military*]

CANCASS..... Canadian Command Active Sonobuoy System (PDAA)

CAN/CAT...... Canadiana/Cataloguing Subsystem

Can CC .... Canada Criminal Cases, Annotated [*A publication*] (DLA)

CANCEE ...... Canadian National Committee for Earthquake Engineering

CANCERLIT... Cancer Literature [*National Cancer Institute*] [*Information service or system*]

CANCERPROJ... Cancer Research Projects [*National Cancer Intitute*] [*Information service or system Defunct*]

CANCES .... Centre for Advanced Numerical Computation in Engineering and Science [*Australia*]

CAN Charlie Chan... Coalition of Asians to Nix Charlie Chan (EA)

CANC INSTR... Cancellation of Instruments [*Legal term*] (DLA)

CANCIRCO ... Cancer International Research Cooperative
Can CL........ Canadian Children's Literature [*A publication*] (BRI)
CANCL .... Canceling (DCTA)
CANCLG .... Canceling
CANCLN .... Cancellation (ROG)
CANCOM....... Canadian Satellite Communications, Inc. [*Mississauga, ON*] [*Telecommunications*] (TSSD)
CANCOMARLANT... Canadian Maritime Commander, Atlantic (NATG)
CANCOMARPAC... Canadian Commander, Army, Pacific (CINC)
Can Com Cas... Canadian Commercial Law Reports [*1901-05*] [*A publication*] (DLA)
CANCOMDESFE... Commander, Canadian Destroyers, Far East
CANCOMDESFLOT 1... Commander, First Canadian Destroyer Flotilla
CANCOMDESLANT... Commander, Canadian Destroyers, Atlantic
CANCOMDESPAC... Commander, Canadian Destroyers, Pacific
CANCOMFLT... Senior Officer Afloat [*Navy Canada*]
CANCOMFLTLANT... Senior Officer Afloat Atlantic [*Navy Canada*]
CANCOMFLTPAC... Senior Officer Afloat Pacific [*Navy Canada*]
Can Com L Guide (CCH)... Canadian Commercial Law Guide (Commerce Clearing House) [*A publication*] (DLA)
Can Com LJ... Canadian Community Law Journal [*A publication*] (DLA)
Can Com LR... Canadian Commercial Law Reports [*1901-05*] [*A publication*] (DLA)
Can Com L Rev... Canadian Communications Law Review [*A publication*] (DLA)
CANCOMNEW... Canadian Naval Commander Newfoundland
Can Com R... Canadian Commercial Law Reports [*1901-05*] [*A publication*] (DLA)
CANCON .... Canadian Control System [*For convoys in Canadian Coastal Zone*]
CanCorp....... Canadian Corporations [*Micromedia Ltd.*] [*Canada Information service or system*] (CRD)
Can Cr Acts... Canada Criminal Acts, Taschereau's Edition [*A publication*] (DLA)
Can Cr Cas... Canadian Criminal Cases [*A publication*] (DLA)
Can Crim Cas... Canadian Criminal Cases, Annotated [*A publication*] (DLA)
Can Crim Cas Ann... Canadian Criminal Cases, Annotated [*A publication*] (DLA)
Can Crim Cas (NS)... Canadian Criminal Cases, New Series [*A publication*] (DLA)
Can Cr R... Canadian Criminal Reports [*A publication*] (DLA)
CAN/CRS...... Canadian Computer-Based Reference Service [*National Library of Canada*] [*Information service or system*] (IID)
Can CS .... Cour Supreme du Canada [*Supreme Court of Canada*] (DLA)
CancTr........ Cancer Treatment Holdings, Inc. [*Associated Press*] (SAG)
CAND .... Canadian Association of Numismatic Dealers (AC)
CAND .... Candidate (AFM)
CAND .... Candies, Inc. [*NASDAQ symbol*] (SAG)
CAND .... Cantate Domino [*Sing Unto the Lord*] [*Music*]
C & A.......... Chicago & Alton Railroad Co. [*Also known as Alton*]
C & A.......... Classification and Audit (AFM)
C & A.......... Clinitest and Acitest [*Trademarked clinical laboratory tests*]
C & A.......... Command and Administration
C & A.......... Compartment and Access [*Technical drawings*]
CANDA........ Computer Assisted New Drug Application [*Medicine Australia*]
C & A.......... Configuration and Administration
C & A.......... Cooke and Alcock's Irish King's Bench Reports [*1833-34*] [*A publication*] (DLA)
C & B.......... Caught and Bowled [*Cricket*]
C & B.......... Chair and Bed Rest [*Medical directive*] (CPH)
C & B.......... Concurrency Control Bus [*Computer science*] (NITA)
C and B ...... Cropper and Burgess [*Bank in "He Knew He Was Right" by Anthony Trollope*]
C & B.......... Crown and Bridge [*Dentistry*] (DAVI)
C & Btr....... Grade C and Better (DAC)
C & C.......... Canton & Carthage Railroad (IIA)
C & C.......... Cantrell and Cochrane [*Initials used as brand name of soft drink*]
C & C.......... Capital & Counties [*Property development company*] [*British*]
C & C.......... Carpets and Curtains (ADA)
C & C.......... Cars & Concepts [*Auto industry supplier*]
C & C.......... Cash and Carry (IIA)
C & C.......... Coal and Coke
C & C.......... Coleman and Caines' Cases [*New York*] [*A publication*] (DLA)
C & C.......... Command and Control
C & C.......... Communication and Cognition (EA)
C & C.......... Computers and Communications
c&c........... Computers and Communications (WDMC)
C & C.......... Confirmed and Compatible (MEDA)
C & CA .... Cement and Concrete Association [*British Research center*] (IRUK)
C & CI .... Contingency and Confidential Intelligence (CINC)
C & CL........ Coating and Chemical Laboratory [*Aberdeen Proving Ground, MD*] [*Army*] (RDA)
C & CS .... Command and Control System
C & CSIT ..... Command and Control System Interface Test [*Military*] (CAAL)
C & D .... Cats and Dogs [*i.e., low selling items or speculative stock*] [*Slang Business term*]
C & D .... Cease and Desist [*Legal shorthand*] (LWAP)
C & D .... Chemist and Druggist
C & D .... Collection and Delivery [*Shipping*]
C & D .... Collection and Distribution [*Transportation*]
C & D .... Command and Decision [*Military*] (CAAL)
C & D .... Communications and Data
C & D .... Construction and Development
C & D .... Control and Display (GFGA)
C & D .... Corbett and Daniell's English Election Cases [*1819*] [*A publication*] (DLA)
C & D .... Cover and Deception (CINC)
C & D .... Crawford and Dix's Irish Circuit Court Cases [*A publication*] (DLA)
C & D .... Curettage and Desiccation [*Gynecology*] (DAVI)
C & D .... Cystoscopy and Dilatation [*Medicine*]
C & DAC ..... Crawford and Dix's Irish Abridged Cases [*A publication*] (DLA)
C & DB .... Cough and Deep-Breathe [*Medicine*]

C & DCC ..... Crawford and Dix's Irish Circuit Court Cases [*A publication*] (DLA)
C & DDAC.... Cover and Deception, Direction, and Coordination
C & DH .... Command and Data Handling (NASA)
C & DH .... Communications and Data Handling (SSD)
C & DM RGA... Cornwall and Devon Miners Royal Garrison Artillery [*British military*] (DMA)
C & DS .... Command and Data Simulator (NASA)
C & DS .... Controls and Displays System [*or Subsystem*] [*Aerospace*]
C & DSS ...... Communication and Data Subsystem
C & E.......... Cababe and Ellis' Queen's Bench Reports [*1882-85*] [*England*] [*A publication*] (DLA)
C & E.......... Chicago & Erie Railroad Co.
C and E....... Christmas and Easter [*Refers to Church of England members who attend church only on those days*] (DSUE)
C & E.......... Clothing and Equipage
CANDE........ Command and Edit Language (NITA)
CANDE........ Command and Edit Program [*Burroughs Corp.*] [*Computer science*] (BUR)
CANDE........ Communications and Electronics [*SHAPE*] (MCD)
C & E.......... Communications and Electronics
C & E.......... Construction and Equipment
C & E.......... Consultation and Education
C & E.......... Control and Evaluation
C & E.......... Coordination and Equipment
CANDE........ Culvert Analysis and Design (MHDB)
C & EI........ Chicago & Eastern Illinois Railroad Co. [*Absorbed into Missouri Pacific System*]
Candela...... Candela Laser Corp. [*Associated Press*] (SAG)
CANDEP....... Royal Canadian Navy Depot
C & ER........ Combustion and Explosives Research (AAG)
CANDESFE... Canadian Destroyers Far East
CANDESFLOT 1... First Canadian Destroyer Flotilla
CANDESLANT... Canadian Destroyers Atlantic
CANDESPAC... Canadian Destroyers Pacific
CANDESRON 4... Fourth Canadian Destroyer Squadron [*Canadian Navy*]
C & F.......... Clark and Finnelly's English House of Lords Reports [*6-8 English Reprint*] [*A publication*] (DLA)
C & F.......... Commerce and Finance
C & F.......... Cost and Freight [*Shipping*]
C&F........... Cost and Freight (DFIT)
C & F.......... Costo y Flete [*Cost and Freight*] [*Shipping*] [*Spanish*]
C & F.......... Cout et Fret [*Cost and Freight*] [*Shipping*] [*French*]
C & F.......... Curettage and Electrodesiccation [*Fulguration*] [*Medicine*] (DAVI)
C & FA........ Culinary and Fine Arts Club [*Later, Culinary Arts Club*] (EA)
C & G.......... Ceramic and Graphite Information Center [*Air Force*] (MCD)
C & G.......... Cheltenham and Gloucester [*A British Building Society*] (ECON)
C & G.......... City and Guilds of London [*British*]
C & G.......... Columbus & Greenville Railway Co.
C & G.......... Control and Guidance (MCD)
C&GC......... Climate and Global Change Program (USDC)
C&GC......... Climate and Globe Change Program [*Marine science*] (OSRA)
C&GLI........ City & Guilds of London Institute (ACII)
C & GS .... Charting and Geodetic Services Office [*National Oceanic and Atmospheric Administration*] (PDAA)
C & GS .... Coast and Geodetic Survey [*Later, NOAA*] [*Rockville, MD*]
C & GS .... Command and General Staff [*Military*]
C&GS.......... Office of Charting and Geodetic Services [*National Ocean Service*] (USDC)
C & GSC ...... Command and General Staff College [*Fort Leavenworth, KS*] [*Military*]
C & GSS ...... Command and General Staff School [*Army*]
C & GS Sch... Command and General Staff School [*Army*]
C & GTR ...... Canada & Gulf Terminal Railway (MHDB)
C & GWRY... Chicago Great Western Railway
C & H .... Calvin and Hobbes [*Comic strip*]
C & H .... Cocaine and Heroin
C & H Char Tr... Cooke and Harwood's Charitable Trusts [*2nd ed.*] [*1867*] [*A publication*] (DLA)
C & H Dig.... Coventry and Hughes' Digest of the Common Law Reports [*A publication*] (DLA)
C & H Elec Cas... Clarke and Hall's Cases of Contested Elections in Congress [*1789-1834*] [*United States*] [*A publication*] (DLA)
C & HP .... Chemistry and Health Physics (GFGA)
Candi.......... Candies, Inc. [*Associated Press*] (SAG)
C & I........... Classification and Index [*Air Force*] (AFM)
C & I........... Commercial and Industrial (GFGA)
C & I........... Communication and Instrumentation [*NASA*] (KSC)
C & I........... Compatibility and Interoperability (RDA)
C & I........... Control and Indication (MCD)
C & I........... Control and Instrumentation (NRCH)
C & I........... Cost and Insurance [*Shipping*]
C & IA .... Counterintelligence and Investigative Activities [*Military*]
CANDID....... Candida Yeast [*Biochemistry*] (DAVI)
CANDIDE..... Canadian Disaggregated Interdepartmental Economic Model
Candies ...... Candies, Inc. [*Associated Press*] (SAG)
C & IM........ Chicago & Illinois Midland Railway Co.
CANDIS....... Canadian Disarmament Information Service
C & IS .... Communication and Instrumentation System [*CIS is preferred*] [*NASA*] (KSC)
C & J.......... Carpentry and Joinery
C & J.......... Collection and Jamming
C & J.......... Crime and Justice Bulletin [*A publication*]
C & J.......... Crompton and Jervis' English Exchequer Reports [*1830-32*] [*A publication*] (DLA)
CAND JUR ... Candidatus Juris [*Doctor of Law*] [*Latin*] (WDAA)

C & K.......... Carrington and Kirwan's English Nisi Prius Reports [*174, 175 English Reprint*] [*A publication*] (DLA)
C & L.......... Cagney and Lacey [*Television series*]
C and L........ Canal and Lake
CANDL........ Candies Inc. Wrrt'B' [*NASDAQ symbol*] (TTSB)
C & L.......... Conner and Lawson's Irish Chancery Reports [*1841-43*] [*A publication*] (DLA)
C & L.......... Control and Line (AABC)
C & L.......... Coopers & Lybrand USA [*New York, NY Telecommunications*] (TSSD)
C & L.......... Culture and Life [*A publication*]
Candla........ Candela Laser Corp. [*Associated Press*] (SAG)
C & LA........ Cargo and Loading Analysis [*Shipping*]
c & lc.......... Capital and Lower Case (WDMC)
C & LC........ Capitals and Lower Case [*Printing*]
C & LCC...... Caines and Leigh. Crown Cases [*England*] [*A publication*] (DLA)
C & L Dig..... Cohen and Lee's Maryland Digest [*A publication*] (DLA)
CANDLE...... Childhood Aphasia, Neurological Disorders, Landau-Klefner, and Epilepsy
CANDLES..... Children of Auschwitz - Nazis' Deadly Lab Experiments Survivors [*Acronym is used as name of association*] (EA)
C & LSE...... Clothing and Life Support Equipment [*Military*]
C & M.......... Care and Maintenance [*British military*] (DMA)
C & M.......... Carrington and Marshman's English Nisi Prius Reports [*1840-42*] [*A publication*] (DLA)
C & M.......... Coal and Mining
C & M.......... Cocaine and Morphine (MAE)
C & M.......... Construction and Machinery
C & M.......... Contract and Material
C & M.......... Control and Monitoring (NASA)
C & M.......... Crompton and Meeson's English Exchequer Reports [*1832-34*] [*A publication*] (DLA)
C&MA.......... [*The*] Cristian & Missionary Alliance in Canada [*Alliance Chretienne et Missionaire au Canada*] [*Also, The Alliance Church*] (AC)
C & Mar...... Carrington and Marshman's English Nisi Prius Reports [*1840-42*] [*A publication*] (DLA)
C & Marsh... Carrington and Marshman's English Nisi Prius Reports [*1840-42*] [*A publication*] (DLA)
C & MB....... Dressed and Matched Beaded [*Lumber*] (DAC)
C & M Bills... Collier and Miller on Bills of Sale [*A publication*] (DLA)
C & ME....... Civil and Mining Engineer
C & MS....... Consumer and Marketing Service [*Later, AMS*] [*Department of Agriculture*]
C & MSSRA... Consumer and Marketing Service, Service and Regulatory Announcements [*Later, AMS*] [*Department of Agriculture*]
C & N.......... Cameron and Norwood's North Carolina Conference Reports [*A publication*] (DLA)
CANDN........ Canadian
CANDN........ Candies Inc. Wrrt'C' [*NASDAQ symbol*] (TTSB)
C & N.......... Communication and Navigation (MCD)
C & NPRR.... Chicago & Northern Pacific Railroad
C & NW........ Carolina & North Western [*Railroad*] (MHDB)
C & NW....... Carolina & Northwestern Railroad (IIA)
CANDO........ Canaveral District Office [*Obsolete NASA*] (KSC)
C & O.......... [*The*] Chesapeake & Ohio Railway Co. [*Later, Chessie System, Inc.*]
CAN DO....... Computer Analyzed Newspaper Data On-Line [*Newspaper Advertising Bureau, Inc.*] [*Information service or system*] (IID)
CAN DO....... Consolidated Accelerated Navy Documentation Organization
C & O.......... Controllability and Observability
CANDOC...... Canadian Documentation [*National Research Council*] (NITA)
CANDOFD.... Computer Analysis of Networks with Design Orientation in the Frequency Domain (PDAA)
C & OM....... Clothing and Organic Materials [*Army*] (MCD)
C & OR Cas... Carrow and Oliver's English Railway and Canal Cases [*A publication*] (DLA)
C & P.......... Capabilities and Procedures
C & P.......... Care and Preservation [*Army*] (AABC)
C & P.......... Carriage and Packing [*Shipping*] (ADA)
C & P.......... Carrington and Payne's English Nisi Prius Reports [*1823-41*] [*A publication*] (DLA)
C & P.......... Chemicals and Polymers Group [*British*]
C & P.......... Collated and Perfect (ADA)
C & P.......... Compensation and Pension
C&P............ Conditions and Performance [*Report to Congress*] [*FHWA*] (TAG)
C & P.......... Control and Processing [*Company*] [*INSCOM*]
C & P.......... Craig and Phillips' English Chancery Reports [*1840-41*] [*A publication*] (DLA)
C & P.......... Cumberland & Pennsylvania Railroad (IIA)
C & P.......... Cut and Paste
C & P.......... Cystoscopy and Panendoscopy [*Medicine*]
C & P.......... Cystoscopy and Pyelogram [*Medicine*]
Cand Pharm... Candidate of Pharmacy
C&P press.... Chandler and Price Letterpress Printing Press (WDMC)
C & R.......... Bureau of Construction and Repair [*Until 1940*] [*Navy*]
C & R.......... Canal and Rail [*Transportation*]
C & R.......... Clifford and Richard's English Locus Standi Reports [*1873-84*] [*A publication*] (DLA)
C & R.......... Cockburn and Rowe's English Election Cases [*1833*] [*A publication*] (DLA)
C and R....... Construction and Repair [*Coast Guard*]
CANDR........ Construction and Repair [*Military*]
C and R....... Control and Reporting (NATG)
C & R.......... Convalescent and Rehabilitation [*Military*]
C & R.......... Convoy and Routing [*Section*] [*US Fleet*]
CANDR........ Convoy and Routing [*Section*] [*US Fleet*]

C & R.......... Curriculum and Research (ADA)
C & RE........ Conservation and Renewable Energy Program [*Department of Energy*]
C & S.......... Calvarium and Scalp [*Anatomy*] (DAVI)
C & S.......... Changes and Specifications
C & S.......... Citizens & Southern Corp.
C & S.......... Clarke and Scully's Drainage Cases [*Canada*] [*A publication*] (DLA)
C and S....... Clean and Sober [*Slang*]
C and S....... Clear and Secure [*Military*] (VNW)
C & S.......... Clerk and Steward [*British*]
C & S.......... Clifford and Stephens' English Locus Standi Reports [*1867-72*] [*A publication*] (DLA)
C & S.......... [*The*] Colorado & Southern Railway Co.
C & S.......... Command and Staff
C & S.......... Computers and Systems (IEEE)
C & S.......... Conjunctiva and Sclera [*Ophthalmology*]
C & S.......... Cordon and Search [*Military*]
C & S.......... Culture and Sensitivity
C & S.......... Culture and Susceptibility [*Medicine*] (MEDA)
C & S App... Clifford and Stephens' English Locus Standi Reports, Appendix [*A publication*] (ILCA)
C & SB........ Correspondence and Service Branch [*BUPERS*]
CANDSC...... Candelabra Screw (IAA)
c&sc.......... Capital and Small Capitals (WDMC)
C & SC........ Capitals and Small Capitals [*Printing*]
C & SC........ Caps and Small Caps (IIA)
C & SC........ Chicago and South Consortium [*Library network*]
C & sc........ Large and Small Capital Letters (WDMC)
C & SD........ Corporate and Staff Development
C & S Dig.... Connor and Simonton's South Carolina Digest [*A publication*] (DLA)
C & S DIP.... City and State Directories in Print [*A publication*]
C & SLJ....... Company and Securities Law Journal [*Australia A publication*]
C & SLR....... City and South London Railway [*"The Tube"*] (ROG)
C & SS........ Clothing and Small Stores [*Military*] (DNAB)
C & T.......... Classification and Testing [*Air Force*] (AFM)
C & T.......... Clothing and Textiles
C and T....... Commencement and Termination [*British railroad term*]
C & T.......... Communication and Tracking [*NASA*] (NASA)
C & T.......... Contingency and Training [*Army*] (AABC)
Cand Techn Sci... Candidate of Technical Science
C & TM....... Clothing and Textile Materiel [*Army*] (AABC)
CANDU........ Canadian Deuterium Reactor (GAAI)
CANDU........ Canadian Deuterium Uranium [*Family of nuclear reactors developed in Canada*]
C & U.......... College and University [*A publication*] (BRI)
C & U.......... Construction and Use (DCTA)
CANDU BLW... Canadian Deuterium Uranium Boiling Light-Water [*Nuclear reactor*]
CANDU PHW... Canadian Natural Deuterium Uranium Pressurized Heavy-Water [*Nuclear reactor*]
C & VB........ Convention and Visitors Bureau
C & W.......... Cable and Wireless Ltd. [*Telecommunications*] (TEL)
C and W....... Carriage and Wagon Work [*British railroad term*]
C & W.......... Caution and Warning [*Aerospace*] (KSC)
C & W.......... Country and Western [*Music*]
C & W.......... Cunningham & Walsh [*Advertising agency*]
C & WC....... Charleston & Western Carolina Railway Co. [*Seaboard Coast Line Railroad*]
C & WM...... Chicago & West Michigan Railroad
C & WS....... Caution and Warning System [*NASA*] (KSC)
C & Y.......... Children and Youth
CANDY........ Cigarette Advertising Normally Directed to Youth [*Student legal action organization*]
CANDY........ Continuously Advertised Nutritionally Deficient Yummies [*In cookbook title, "The Taming of the CANDY Monster"*]
Candy......... Printed Judgments of Sind, by Candy and Birdwood [*India*] [*A publication*] (DLA)
Candy MC.... Candy. Mayor's Court Practice [*1879*] [*A publication*] (DLA)
CANE......... Cationic Asphalt-Neoprene Emulsion [*Dust control*]
CANE......... Chemical Applications of Nuclear Explosions (PDAA)
CANE......... Classical Association of New England (EDAC)
CANE......... Combined Arms in a Nuclear/Chemical Environment [*Military*] (RDA)
CANE......... Computer-Aided Navigation Equipment (MCD)
CANE......... Connecticut Aircraft Nuclear Experiment (NRCH)
Cane & L..... Cane and Leigh. Crown Cases Reserved [*England*] [*A publication*] (DLA)
CANEL........ Connecticut Advanced Nuclear Engineering Laboratory
Can Environ LN... Canadian Environmental Law News [*A publication*] (DLA)
Can Env L News... Canadian Environmental Law News [*A publication*] (DLA)
CANES........ Corpus of Ancient Near Eastern Seals in North American Collections [*Washington, DC*] (BJA)
CAnet........ Canada Network [*Computer science*] (TNIG)
CANEW....... Canewdon [*England*]
CANEWS...... Canadian Naval Electronic Warfare System
Can Ex........ Canada Law Reports, Exchequer Court [*A publication*] (DLA)
CANEX........ Canadian Flight Experiment [*NASA*]
CANEX........ Canadian Forces Exchange [*Military*]
Can Exch..... Canada Law Reports, Exchequer Court [*A publication*] (DLA)
Can Ex CR... Canada Law Reports, Exchequer Court [*A publication*] (DLA)
Can Ex R.... Canada Law Reports, Exchequer Court [*A publication*] (DLA)
CANF......... Combined Account Number File [*IRS*]
CANF......... Combined Allied Naval Forces
CANF......... Cuban American National Foundation (EA)
CaNfAC....... Arnolds Cove Public Library, Arnolds Cove, NF, Canada [*Library symbol Library of Congress*] (LCLS)

CanFar .... Canadian Foundation for AIDS Research [*Fondation Canadienne de Recherche sur le SIDA*] (AC)

CaNfBF .... Bishops Falls Public Library, Bishops Falls, NF, Canada [*Library symbol*] [*Library of Congress*] (LCLS)

CaNfBI .... Bell Island Public Library, Bell Island, NF, Canada [*Library symbol Library of Congress*] (LCLS)

CaNfBo .... Bonavista Public Library, Bonavista, NF, Canada [*Library symbol Library of Congress*] (LCLS)

CaNfBot .... Botwood Public Library, Botwood, NF, Canada [*Library symbol Library of Congress*] (LCLS)

CaNfBQ .... Rural District Memorial Library, Badgers Quay, NF, Canada [*Library symbol Library of Congress*] (LCLS)

CaNfBR .... Bay Roberts Public Library, Bay Roberts, NF, Canada [*Library symbol Library of Congress*] (LCLS)

CaNfBri .... Brigus Public Library, Brigus, NF, Canada [*Library symbol Library of Congress*] (LCLS)

CaNfBu .... Buchans Public Library, Buchans, NF, Canada [*Library symbol Library of Congress*] (LCLS)

CaNfBuri ...... Burin Public Library, Burin, NF, Canada [*Library symbol Library of Congress*] (LCLS)

CaNfBV .... Baie Verte Public Library, Baie Verte, NF, Canada [*Library symbol Library of Congress*] (LCLS)

CaNfC .... Carbonear Public Library, Carbonear, NF, Canada [*Library symbol Library of Congress*] (LCLS)

Can FC .... Federal Court of Canada [*A publication*] (DLA)

CaNfCa .... Carmanville Public Library, Carmanville, NF, Canada [*Library symbol Library of Congress*] (LCLS)

CaNfCat ...... Joseph E. Clouter Memorial Library, Catalina, NF, Canada [*Library symbol Library of Congress*] (LCLS)

CaNfCB .... Corner Brook City Library, Corner Brook, NF, Canada [*Library symbol Library of Congress*] (LCLS)

CaNfCBF ...... Newfoundland Department of Forest Resources and Lands, Corner Brook, NF, Canada [*Library symbol*] [*Library of Congress*] (LCLS)

CaNfCBM ..... Memorial University Regional College at Corner Brook, Corner Brook, NF, Canada [*Library symbol Library of Congress*] (LCLS)

CaNfCBr .... Regional Library, Corner Brook, NF, Canada [*Library symbol Library of Congress*] (LCLS)

CaNfCBrW .... Western Memorial Hospital, Corner Brook, NF, Canada [*Library symbol Library of Congress*] (LCLS)

CaNfCe .... Centreville Public Library, Centreville, NF, Canada [*Library symbol Library of Congress*] (LCLS)

CaNfCF .... Churchill Falls Public Library, Churchill Falls, NF, Canada [*Library symbol Library of Congress*] (LCLS)

CaNfCGH ...... Carbonear General Hospital, Carbonear, NF, Canada [*Library symbol Library of Congress*] (LCLS)

CaNfCH .... Cow Head Public Library, Cow Head, NF, Canada [*Library symbol Library of Congress*] (LCLS)

CaNfCI .... Changes Islands Public Library, Changes Islands, NF, Canada [*Library symbol Library of Congress*] (LCLS)

CaNfCl .... Clarenville Public Library, Clarenville, NF, Canada [*Library symbol Library of Congress*] (LCLS)

CaNfCo .... Cormack Public Library, Cormack, NF, Canada [*Library symbol Library of Congress*] (LCLS)

CaNfCP .... Channel/Port Aux Basques Public Library, Channel/Port Aux Basques, NF, Canada [*Library symbol Library of Congress*] (LCLS)

Can FCR ...... Canada Federal Court Reports [*A publication*] (DLA)

CaNfDC .... Dark Cove Public Library, Dark Cove, NF, Canada [*Library symbol Library of Congress*] (LCLS)

CaNfDH .... Daniels Harbour Public Library, Daniels Harbour, NF, Canada [*Library symbol Library of Congress*] (LCLS)

CaNfDL .... Deer Lake Public Library, Deer Lake, NF, Canada [*Library symbol Library of Congress*] (LCLS)

CaNfF .... Fogo Public Library, Fogo, NF, Canada [*Library symbol Library of Congress*] (LCLS)

CaNfFH .... Fox Harbour Public Library, Fox Harbour, NF, Canada [*Library symbol Library of Congress*] (LCLS)

CaNfFo .... Fortune Public Library, Fortune, NF, Canada [*Library symbol Library of Congress*] (LCLS)

CaNfFr .... Freshwater Public Library, Freshwater, NF, Canada [*Library symbol Library of Congress*] (LCLS)

CaNfG .... Gander Public Library, Gander, NF, Canada [*Library symbol Library of Congress*] (LCLS)

CaNfGa .... Garnish Public Library, Garnish, NF, Canada [*Library symbol Library of Congress*] (LCLS)

CaNfGB .... Grand Bank Public Library, Grand Bank, NF, Canada [*Library symbol Library of Congress*] (LCLS)

CaNfGfC .... Central Region Libraries, Grand Falls, NF, Canada [*Library symbol Library of Congress*] (LCLS)

CaNfGfH .... Central Newfoundland Hospital, Grand Falls, NF, Canada [*Library symbol Library of Congress*] (LCLS)

CaNfGfHa ..... Harmsworth Public Library, Grand Falls, NF, Canada [*Library symbol Library of Congress*] (LCLS)

CaNfGJPH .... James Paton Memorial Hospital, Gander, NF, Canada [*Library symbol Library of Congress*] (LCLS)

CaNfGl .... Glenwood Public Library, Glenwood, NF, Canada [*Library symbol Library of Congress*] (LCLS)

CaNfGlo .... Glovertown Public Library, Glovertown, NF, Canada [*Library symbol Library of Congress*] (LCLS)

CaNfGr .... Greenspond Public Library, Greenspond, NF, Canada [*Library symbol Library of Congress*] (LCLS)

CaNfHB .... Harbour Breton Public Library, Harbour Breton, NF, Canada [*Library symbol Library of Congress*] (LCLS)

CaNfHBa ...... Hare Bay Public Library, Hare Bay, NF, Canada [*Library symbol Library of Congress*] (LCLS)

CaNfHe .... Hermitage Public Library, Hermitage, NF, Canada [*Library symbol Library of Congress*] (LCLS)

CaNfHG .... Harbour Grace Public Library, Harbour Grace, NF, Canada [*Library symbol Library of Congress*] (LCLS)

CaNfHH .... Harrys Harbour Public Library, Harrys Harbour, NF, Canada [*Library symbol Library of Congress*] (LCLS)

CaNfHV .... Happy Valley Public Library, Happy Valley, NF, Canada [*Library symbol Library of Congress*] (LCLS)

CaNfKP .... Kings Point Public Library, Kings Point, NF, Canada [*Library symbol Library of Congress*] (LCLS)

CaNfL .... Labrador City Regional Library, Labrador City, NF, Canada [*Library symbol Library of Congress*] (LCLS)

CaNfLa .... L'Anse Au Loup Public Library, L'Anse Au Loup, NF, Canada [*Library symbol Library of Congress*] (LCLS)

CANFLAGLANT... Flag Officer, Atlantic Coast [*Canada*]

CANFLAGPAC... Flag Officer, Pacific Coast [*Canada*]

CaNfLe .... Lewisporte Public Library, Lewisporte, NF, Canada [*Library symbol Library of Congress*] (LCLS)

CaNfLHB ...... Blow Me Down School/Public Library, Lark Harbour, NF, Canada [*Library symbol Library of Congress*] (LCLS)

CaNfLIO .... Iron Ore Co. of Canada, Training Department, Labrador City, NF, Canada [*Library symbol Library of Congress*] (LCLS)

CaNfLo .... Lourdes Public Library, Lourdes, NF, Canada [*Library symbol Library of Congress*] (LCLS)

CaNfLs .... La Scie Public Library, La Scie, NF, Canada [*Library symbol Library of Congress*] (LCLS)

CaNfLu .... Lumsden Public Library, Lumsden, NF, Canada [*Library symbol Library of Congress*] (LCLS)

CaNfM .... Conception Bay South Public Library, Manuels, NF, Canada [*Library symbol Library of Congress*] (LCLS)

CaNfMa .... Marystown Public Library, Marystown, NF, Canada [*Library symbol Library of Congress*] (LCLS)

CaNfMG .... Memorial University of Newfoundland, Department of Geography, St. John's, NF, Canada [*Library symbol Library of Congress*] (LCLS)

CaNfMHJ ...... John B. Wheeler Memorial Library, Musgrave Harbour, NF, Canada [*Library symbol Library of Congress*] (LCLS)

CaNfMP .... Mount Pearl Public Library, Mount Pearl, NF, Canada [*Library symbol Library of Congress*] (LCLS)

CaNfNA .... Norris Arm Public Library, Norris Arm, NF, Canada [*Library symbol Library of Congress*] (LCLS)

CaNfNaLI ...... Labrador Inuit Association, Nain, NF, Canada [*Library symbol*] [*Library of Congress*] (LCLS)

CaNfNP .... Norris Point Public Library, Norris Point, NF, Canada [*Library symbol Library of Congress*] (LCLS)

CaNfOP .... Old Perlican Public Library, Old Perlican, NF, Canada [*Library symbol Library of Congress*] (LCLS)

CANFORCEHED... Canadian Forces Headquarters [*NATO*] (NATG)

CaNfP .... Placentia Public Library, Placentia, NF, Canada [*Library symbol Library of Congress*] (LCLS)

CaNfPa .... Pasadena Public Library, Pasadena, NF, Canada [*Library symbol Library of Congress*] (LCLS)

CaNfPc .... Pouch Cove Public Library, Pouch Cove, NF, Canada [*Library symbol Library of Congress*] (LCLS)

CaNfPeC ...... Curran Memorial Library, Port Au Port East, NF, Canada [*Library symbol Library of Congress*] (LCLS)

CaNfPL .... Point Leamington Public Library, Point Leamington, NF, Canada [*Library symbol Library of Congress*] (LCLS)

CaNfPS .... Port Saunders Public Library, Port Saunders, NF, Canada [*Library symbol Library of Congress*] (LCLS)

CaNfPw .... Port Au Port West School/Public Library, Port Au Port West, NF, Canada [*Library symbol Library of Congress*] (LCLS)

Can Fr .... Canadian French [*Language*] (BARN)

CaNfRH .... Rocky Harbour Public Library, Rocky Harbour, NF, Canada [*Library symbol Library of Congress*] (LCLS)

CaNfRP .... Marie S. Penney Memorial Library, Ramea, NF, Canada [*Library symbol Library of Congress*] (LCLS)

CaNfSA .... Newfoundland Archives, St. John's, NF, Canada [*Library symbol Library of Congress*] (LCLS)

CaNfSAg ...... Canada Department of Agriculture, Research Station, St. John's, NF, Canada [*Library symbol Library of Congress*] (LCLS)

CaNfSaIC ...... Charles Curtis Memorial Hospital, International Grenfell Association, St. Anthony, NF, Canada [*Library symbol Library of Congress*] (LCLS)

CaNfSal .... St. Albans Public Library, St. Albans, NF, Canada [*Library symbol Library of Congress*] (LCLS)

CaNfSan .... St. Anthony Public Library, St. Anthony, NF, Canada [*Library symbol Library of Congress*] (LCLS)

CaNfSANS ..... Naskapi School/Public Library, Sops Arms, NF, Canada [*Library symbol Library of Congress*] (LCLS)

CaNfSB .... Spaniards Bay Public Library, Spaniards Bay, NF, Canada [*Library symbol Library of Congress*] (LCLS)

CaNfSBC ...... Boy's Club, St. John's, NF, Canada [*Library symbol Library of Congress*] (LCLS)

CaNfSbCS .... Cape Shore Public Library, St. Brides, NF, Canada [*Library symbol Library of Congress*] (LCLS)

CaNfSC .... Seal Cove Public Library, Seal Cove, NF, Canada [*Library symbol Library of Congress*] (LCLS)

CaNfSCA ...... Children's and Adults' Library, St. John's, NF, Canada [*Library symbol Library of Congress*] (LCLS)

CaNfSCAEE... Newfoundland Department of Consumer Affairs and Environment, Environment Division, St. John's, NF, Canada [*Library symbol Library of Congress*] (LCLS)

CaNfSCF ...... College of Fisheries, St. John's, NF, Canada [*Library symbol Library of Congress*] (LCLS)

CaNfSCJ ...... Charles A. Janeway Child Health Centre, St. John's, NF, Canada [*Library symbol Library of Congress*] (LCLS)

CaNfSCR ..... Children's Rehabilitation Centre, St. John's, NF, Canada [*Library symbol Library of Congress*] (LCLS)

CaNfSCT ..... College of Trades and Technology, St. John's, NF, Canada [*Library symbol Library of Congress*] (LCLS)

CaNfSCTM .. College of Trades and Technology, Medical Sciences Library, St. John's, NF, Canada [*Library symbol Library of Congress*] (LCLS)

CaNfSEC ..... Canada Department of Fisheries and Oceans, St. Johns, NF, Canada [*Library symbol Library of Congress*] (LCLS)

CaNfSF .... Canada Department of Fisheries and Ocean, St. John's, NF, Canada [*Library symbol*] [*Library of Congress*] (LCLS)

CaNfSFBD .... Federal Business Development Bank, St. John's, NF, Canada [*Library symbol Library of Congress*] (LCLS)

CaNfSFJG .... Saint Judes Central High School Public Library/Bay St. George South Public Library, St. Fintans, NF, Canada [*Library symbol Library of Congress*] (LCLS)

CaNfSG .... Newfoundland Public Libraries Board, St. John's, NF, Canada [*Library symbol Library of Congress*] (LCLS)

CaNfSGe ...... St. Georges Public Library, St. Georges, NF, Canada [*Library symbol Library of Congress*] (LCLS)

CaNfSGGH ... Grace General Hospital, C. A. Pippy, Jr. Medical Library, St. John's, NF, Canada [*Library symbol Library of Congress*] (LCLS)

CaNfSGGHN... Grace General Hospital, School of Nursing, St. John's, NF, Canada [*Library symbol Library of Congress*] (LCLS)

CaNfSGH ...... General Hospital, St. John's, NF, Canada [*Library symbol Library of Congress*] (LCLS)

CaNfSGHN ... General Hospital, Nursing Education, St. John's, NF, Canada [*Library symbol Library of Congress*] (LCLS)

CaNfSGo ...... Gosling Library, St. John's, NF, Canada [*Library symbol Library of Congress*] (LCLS)

CaNfSH .... Southern Harbour Public Library, Southern Harbour, NF, Canada [*Library symbol*] [*Library of Congress*] (LCLS)

CaNfSHE ...... Newfoundland Department of Health, Health Education Division, St. John's, NF, Canada [*Library symbol Library of Congress*] (LCLS)

CaNfSHPH ... Newfoundland Department of Health, Public Health Nursing Division, St. John's, NF, Canada [*Library symbol Library of Congress*] (LCLS)

CaNfSICA ..... Institute of Chartered Accountants of Newfoundland, St. John's, NF, Canada [*Library symbol Library of Congress*] (LCLS)

CaNfSJL .... Newfoundland Department of Justice, Law Library, St. John's, NF, Canada [*Library symbol Library of Congress*] (LCLS)

CaNfSK .... Kindale Public Library, Stephenville, NF, Canada [*Library symbol Library of Congress*] (LCLS)

CaNfSL .... Legislative Library, St. John's, NF, Canada [*Library symbol Library of Congress*] (LCLS)

CaNfSLa ...... St. Lawrence Public Library, St. Lawrence, NF, Canada [*Library symbol Library of Congress*] (LCLS)

CaNfSLG ...... Saint Lunaire-Griquet Public Library, St. Lunaire, NF, Canada [*Library symbol Library of Congress*] (LCLS)

CaNfSLP ...... Newfoundland Light & Power Co., Central Records Library, St. John's, NF, Canada [*Library symbol Library of Congress*] (LCLS)

CaNfSLS ...... Law Society of Newfoundland, St. John's, NF, Canada [*Library symbol Library of Congress*] (LCLS)

CaNfSM .... Memorial University of Newfoundland, St. John's, NF, Canada [*Library symbol Library of Congress*] (LCLS)

CaNfSMA ..... Newfoundland Department of Municipal Affairs, St. John's, NF, Canada [*Library symbol Library of Congress*] (LCLS)

CaNfSME ..... Newfoundland Department of Mines and Energy, St. John's, NF, Canada [*Library symbol Library of Congress*] (LCLS)

CaNfSMEC ... Memorial University, Education Library, Curriculum Materials Centre, St. John's,NF, Canada [*Library symbol Library of Congress*] (LCLS)

CaNfSMEd ... Memorial University, Education Library, St. John's, NF, Canada [*Library symbol Library of Congress*] (LCLS)

CaNfSMEM... Newfoundland Department of Mines and Energy, Mineral Development Division, St. John's, NF, Canada [*Library symbol Library of Congress*] (LCLS)

CaNfSMM ..... Memorial University of Newfoundland, Faculty of Medicine Library, St. John's, NF, Canada [*Library symbol Library of Congress*] (LCLS)

CaNfSMO ..... Memorial University, Ocean Engineering Centre, St. John's, NF, Canada [*Library symbol Library of Congress*] (LCLS)

CaNfSNL ...... Newfoundland and Labrador Hydro, St. John's, NF, Canada [*Library symbol Library of Congress*] (LCLS)

CaNfSNLD .... Newfoundland & Labrador Development Corp., St. John's, NF, Canada [*Library symbol Library of Congress*] (LCLS)

CaNfSNM ..... National Research Council, Canada Institute for Scientific and Technical Information, Marin Dynamics Branch, St. Johns, NF, Canada [*Library symbol*] [*Library of Congress*] (LCLS)

CaNfSp .... Springdale Public Library, Springdale, NF, Canada [*Library symbol Library of Congress*] (LCLS)

CaNfSPR ...... Provincial Reference Library, St. John's, NF, Canada [*Library symbol Library of Congress*] (LCLS)

CaNfSPRV ... Pictou Regional Vocational School, St. John's, NF, Canada [*Library symbol Library of Congress*] (LCLS)

CaNfSQ .... Queen's College, St. John's, NF, Canada [*Library symbol Library of Congress*] (LCLS)

CaNfSRD ...... Newfoundland Department of Rural Development, St. John's, NF, Canada [*Library symbol Library of Congress*] (LCLS)

CaNfSREx .... Canada Department of Regional Economic Expansion, St. John's, NF, Canada [*Library symbol Library of Congress*] (LCLS)

CaNfSSC ...... Saint Clare's Mercy Hospital, St. John's, NF, Canada [*Library symbol Library of Congress*] (LCLS)

CaNfSSCN ... Saint Clare's Mercy Hospital, School of Nursing, St. John's, NF, Canada [*Library symbol Library of Congress*] (LCLS)

CaNfSSW ..... Newfoundland Status of Women Council, St. John's, NF, Canada [*Library symbol Library of Congress*] (LCLS)

CaNfST .... Newfoundland Department of Tourism, St. John's, NF, Canada [*Library symbol Library of Congress*] (LCLS)

CaNfSTA ...... Newfoundland Teachers' Association, St. John's, NF, Canada [*Library symbol Library of Congress*] (LCLS)

CaNfStC .... Stephenville Crossing Public Library, Stephenville Crossing, NF, Canada [*Library symbol Library of Congress*] (LCLS)

CaNFSTR ...... Sir Thomas Roddick Hospital, Medical Library, Stephenville, NF, Canada [*Library symbol*] [*Library of Congress*] (LCLS)

CaNfSu .... Summerford Public Library, Summerford, NF, Canada [*Library symbol Library of Congress*] (LCLS)

CaNfSWH ..... Waterford Hospital, Health Services, St. John's, NF, Canada [*Library symbol Library of Congress*] (LCLS)

CANFSWPA... Combined Allied Naval Forces, Southwest Pacific Area

CANFSWPAOPPLAN... Combined Allied Naval Forces, Southwest Pacific Ocean Area Operating Plan

CaNfTo .... Torbay Public Library, Torbay, NF, Canada [*Library symbol Library of Congress*] (LCLS)

CaNfTr .... Trepassey Public Library, Trepassey, NF, Canada [*Library symbol Library of Congress*] (LCLS)

CaNfTw .... Twillingate Public Library, Twillingate, NF, Canada [*Library symbol Library of Congress*] (LCLS)

CaNfUF ...... Codroy Valley Public Library, Upper Ferry, NF, Canada [*Library symbol Library of Congress*] (LCLS)

CaNfUI .... Upper Island Cove Public Library, Upper Island Cove, NF, Canada [*Library symbol Library of Congress*] (LCLS)

CaNfV .... Victoria Public Library, Victoria, NF, Canada [*Library symbol Library of Congress*] (LCLS)

CaNfWa .... Wabush Public Library, Wabush, NF, Canada [*Library symbol Library of Congress*] (LCLS)

CaNfWE .... Edgar L. M. Roberts Memorial Library, Woodypoint, NF, Canada [*Library symbol Library of Congress*] (LCLS)

CaNfWh .... Whitbourne Public Library, Whitbourne, NF, Canada [*Library symbol Library of Congress*] (LCLS)

CaNfWi .... Windsor Memorial Public Library, Windsor, NF, Canada [*Library symbol Library of Congress*] (LCLS)

CaNfWin ...... Winterton Public Library, Winterton, NF, Canada [*Library symbol Library of Congress*] (LCLS)

CaNfWv .... Wesleyville Public Library, Wesleyville, NF, Canada [*Library symbol Library of Congress*] (LCLS)

Can Gaz .... Canada Gazette (Regulations) [*A publication*] (DLA)

CAngP .... Pacific Union College, Angwin, CA [*Library symbol Library of Congress*] (LCLS)

Can Green Bag... Canadian Green Bag [*A publication*] (DLA)

Can Hist R ... Canadian Historical Review [*A publication*] (BRI)

Can HJ .... Canberra Historical Journal [*A publication*]

Can Human Rights Rep... Canadian Human Rights Reporter [*A publication*] (DLA)

CANI .... Consultants Association for the Natural Industry

CANINE .... Computer Analysis of Networks via Inversion of Network Equations (PDAA)

Can in Wld Aff... Canada in World Affairs [*A publication*] (DLA)

Canisius C .... Canisius College (GAGS)

Can J Correct... Canadian Journal of Corrections [*A publication*] (ILCA)

Can J Criminol... Canadian Journal of Criminology [*A publication*] (DLA)

CANL .... Canadian Association for Nursing Law (AC)

CANLA .... Canadian Library Association [*Also known as ACB and CLA*]

CanLA .... Canadian Library Association, Ottawa, ON, Canada [*Library symbol Library of Congress*] (LCLS)

CanLabINSPIRE... Canadian Laboratory for Integrated Spatial Information Research and Engineering [*University of New Brunswick*] [*Research center*] (RCD)

CANLANT ..... Canadian Atlantic Subarea [*Canadian Navy*]

Can Leg N ... Canada Legal News [*A publication*] (DLA)

Can Leg Stud ... Canadian Legal Studies [*A publication*] (DLA)

Can Leg Studies... Canadian Legal Studies [*A publication*] (DLA)

CANLF .... United States Committee to Aid the National Liberation Front of South Vietnam

Can Lit .... Canadian Literature [*A publication*] (BRI)

Can LJ .... Canada Law Journal [*A publication*] (DLA)

Can LJ NS ... Canada Law Journal, New Series [*A publication*] (DLA)

Can LR .... Canada Law Reports, Exchequer Court and Supreme Court [*A publication*] (DLA)

Can LRBR ..... Canadian Labour Relations Board Reports [*A publication*] (DLA)

Can L Rev ... Canadian Law Review [*A publication*] (DLA)

Can LS .... Canadian Legal Studies [*A publication*] (ILCA)

Can LT .... Canadian Law Times [*A publication*] (DLA)

Can L Times ... Canadian Law Times [*A publication*] (DLA)

Can LT Occ N ... Canadian Law Times. Occasional Notes [*A publication*] (DLA)

CanM .... Canadian Microfilming Co., Montreal, PQ, Canada [*Library symbol Library of Congress*] (LCLS)

CANMAP ...... Canada Marketing Assistance Program

CAN/MARC ... Canadian Machine-Readable Cataloguing [*National Library of Canada*] [*Information service or system*]

CANMARCOM... Canadian Maritime Command

Can Mat .... CM: A Reviewing Journal of Canadian Materials for Young People [*A publication*] (BRI)

Canmax .... Canmax, Inc. [*Associated Press*] (SAG)

CANMET ...... Canada Centre for Mineral and Energy Technology [*Department of Energy, Mines, and Resources*] [*Ottawa, ON*]

CANMINDEX... Canadian Mineral Occurrence Index [*Department of Energy, Mines, and Resources*] [*Information service or system*] (IID)

Can Mun J ... Canadian Municipal Journal [*A publication*] (DLA)

CANN .... Canadian Association of Neuroscience Nurses [*Association Canadienne des infirmieres el Infirmiers en Sciences Neurologiques*] (AC)
CANN .... Cannon [*Freight*]
CANN .... Canon, Inc. [*NASDAQ symbol*] (NQ)
CANNAC ...... Canadian National Asbestos Council [*Formerly, The Canadian Chapter of the National Asbestos Council*] (AC)
Can Native L Rep... Canadian Native Law Reporter. Native Law Centre. University of Saskatchewan [*A publication*] (DLA)
CannEx .... Cannon Express, Inc. [*Associated Press*] (SAG)
CannExp ...... Cannon Express, Inc. [*Associated Press*] (SAG)
CANNY .... Canon, Inc. (MHDW)
CANO .... Catalog Number
CANOCO ...... Canonical Correspondence Analysis [*Statistical analysis*]
Can Oil & Gas... Canadian Oil and Gas Handbook [*A publication*] (DLA)
CANOLA .... Canada Oil Low Acid [*Variety of rapeseed*]
CAN/OLE ...... Canadian Online Enquiry System [*Pronounced "can-olay"*] [*National Research Council of Canada Ottawa, ON*]
Canondle ..... Cannondale Corp. [*Associated Press*] (SAG)
CanonI .... Canon, Inc. [*Associated Press*] (SAG)
CANP .... Calcium Activated Neutral Protease [*An enzyme*]
CANP .... Canister Purge Solenoid [*Automotive engineering*]
CANP .... Civil Aircraft Notification Procedure (PDAA)
CANPAC .... Canadian National Power Alcohol Conference
CANPAT .... Canadian Patent (IAA)
Can Pat Off Rec... Canadian Patent Office. Record [*A publication*] (DLA)
Can Persp.... Canadian Perspectives on International Law and Organization [*A publication*] (DLA)
CANPFA .... Connecticut Association of Not-for-Profit Providers for the Aging (SRA)
CANPLATES... Chrome and Nickel Plating Logistics Automated Test Electronics System (MCD)
CANPO .... Colorado Association of Nonprofit Organizations (SRA)
Can Pub Ad... Canadian Public Administration [*A publication*] (DLA)
CANQUA .... Canadian Quaternary Association
CANR .... Canadian NORAD Region [*Aviation*] (FAAC)
CANR .... Contemporary Authors New Revision Series [*A publication*]
CANRA .... Committee on Army and Navy Religious Activities [*National Jewish Welfare Board*]
Can RAC ..... Canadian Reports, Appeal Cases [*1828-1913*] [*A publication*] (DLA)
Can R App Cas... Canadian Reports, Appeal Cases [*1828-1913*] [*A publication*] (DLA)
Can RC .... Railway Commission of Canada (DLA)
Can R Cas ... Canadian Railway Cases [*A publication*] (DLA)
CANRESLANT... Senior Officer Reserve Fleet East Coast [*Navy Canada*]
CANRESPAC... Senior Officer Reserve Fleet West Coast [*Navy Canada*]
Can Rev Stat... Revised Statutes of Canada [*A publication*] (DLA)
CANRIS .... Child Abuse and Neglict Reprint and Inquiry Systems (EDAC)
CANRQ .... Canisco Resources [*NASDAQ symbol*] (TTSB)
Can Ry & T Cas... Canadian Railway and Transport Cases [*A publication*] (DLA)
Can Ry Cas... Canada Railway Cases [*A publication*] (DLA)
CANS .... Central Auditory Nervous System (DMAA)
CANS .... Citizens' Advice Notes [*British*] (DI)
CANS .... Civilian Air Navigation School
CANS .... Coastal Air Navigation Supplement (MCD)
CANS .... Computer-Assisted Network Scheduling System (IEEE)
cans .... Headphones [*Slang*] (WDMC)
CaNSAAC ..... Atlantic Co-Operator, Antigonish, NS, Canada [*Library symbol*] [*Library of Congress*] (LCLS)
CaNSADN .... Daily News, Amherst, NS, Canada [*Library symbol*] [*Library of Congress*] (LCLS)
CaNSAF ...... Canadian Sales Finance Long Form Report
CaNSAH ...... Heritge Association of Antigonish, Antogonish, NS, Canada [*Library symbol*] [*Library of Congress*] (LCLS)
CaNSAIN ..... Indian and Northern Affairs Canada, Amherst, NS, Canada [*Library symbol*] [*Library of Congress*] (LCLS)
Can Sales Tax Rep (CCH)... Canadian Sales Tax Reporter (Commerce Clearing House) [*A publication*] (DLA)
CaNSAMC .... Cumberland Regional Library, Amherst, NS, Canada [*Library symbol Library of Congress*] (LCLS)
CaNSAMRMS... Maritime Resource Management Service, Amherst, NS, Canada [*Library symbol Library of Congress*] (LCLS)
CANSAP ...... Canadian Network for Sampling Precipitation
CaNSAR ...... Annapolis Valley Regional Library, Annapolis Royal, NS, Canada [*Library symbol Library of Congress*] (LCLS)
CaNSARF .... Fort Anne Museum, Annapolis Royal, NS, Canada [*Library symbol*] [*Library of Congress*] (LCLS)
CaNSAS ...... Saint Francis Xavier University, Antigonish, NS, Canada [*Library symbol Library of Congress*] (LCLS)
CaNSASC .... Saint Francis Xavier University, Chemistry Department, Antigonish, NS, Canada [*Library symbol Library of Congress*] (LCLS)
CANSAVE ..... Canadian Save the Children Fund
CaNSBaCSH... Cape Sable Historical Society, Barrington, NS, Canada [*Library symbol*] [*Library of Congress*] (LCLS)
CaNSBadVCA... Victoria County Archives and Museum, Baddeck, NS, Canada [*Library symbol*] [*Library of Congress*] (LCLS)
CaNSBDM .... DesBrisay Museum and National Exhibit Centre, Bridgewater, NS, Canada [*Library symbol*] [*Library of Congress*] (LCLS)
CaNSBeAE ... Environment Canada, AES Regional Library, Bedford, NS, Canada [*Library symbol*] [*Library of Congress*] (LCLS)
CaNSBeLE ... Leader, Berwick, NS, Canada [*Library symbol*] [*Library of Congress*] (LCLS)
CaNSBeR .... Register, Berwick, NS, Canada [*Library symbol*] [*Library of Congress*] (LCLS)

CaNSBL .... Lighthouse Publishing Ltd., Bridgewater, NS, Canada [*Library symbol*] [*Library of Congress*] (LCLS)
CaNSBrH ..... Bear River Historical Society, Bear River, NS, Canada [*Library symbol*] [*Library of Congress*] (LCLS)
CaNSBrJH .... James House, Bridgetown, NS, Canada [*Library symbol*] [*Library of Congress*] (LCLS)
CaNSBrM ..... Monitor, Bridgetown, NS, Canada [*Library symbol*] [*Library of Congress*] (LCLS)
CaNSBS ...... South Shore Regional Library, Bridgewater, NS, Canada [*Library symbol Library of Congress*] (LCLS)
CaNSBSSN ... South Shore News, Bridgewater, NS, Canada [*Library symbol*] [*Library of Congress*] (LCLS)
Can SC .... Canada Supreme Court (DLA)
Can SC .... Canada Supreme Court Reports [*A publication*] (DLA)
CaNSCaH .... Canso Historical Society, Canso, NS, Canada [*Library symbol*] [*Library of Congress*] (LCLS)
CANSCAIP .... Canadian Society of Children's Authors, Illustrators, and Performers
CaNSCaNQH... North Queens Historical Society, Caledonia, NS, Canada [*Library symbol*] [*Library of Congress*] (LCLS)
CaNSCCM .... Cumberland County Museum, Amherst, NS, Canada [*Library symbol*] [*Library of Congress*] (LCLS)
CaNSCeAS ... Archelaus Smith Museum, Shelburne County, NS, Canada [*Library symbol*] [*Library of Congress*] (LCLS)
CaNSCoCF ... Canadian Forces Base, Cornwallis, NS, Canada [*Library symbol*] [*Library of Congress*] (LCLS)
CaNSCoCFE... Canadian Forces Base, Ensign, Cornwallis, NS, Canada [*Library symbol*] [*Library of Congress*] (LCLS)
Can SCR ..... Canada Supreme Court Reports [*A publication*] (DLA)
Can SC Rep.. Canada Supreme Court Reports [*A publication*] (DLA)
CaNSCS ...... Universite Sainte Anne, Church Point, NS, Canada [*Library symbol Library of Congress*] (LCLS)
Can S Ct ..... Canada Law Reports, Supreme Court [*A publication*] (DLA)
Can S Ct ..... Canada Supreme Court Reports [*A publication*] (DLA)
CaNSD .... Dartmouth Regional Library, Dartmouth, NS, Canada [*Library symbol Library of Congress*] (LCLS)
CaNSDB ...... Canada Department of the Environment, Bedford Institute of Oceanography, Dartmouth, NS, Canada [*Library symbol Library of Congress*] (LCLS)
CaNSDE ...... Environment Canada, Dartmouth, NS, Canada [*Library symbol Library of Congress*] (LCLS)
CaNSDGH .... Dartmouth General Hospital, Dartmouth, NS, Canada [*Library symbol Library of Congress*] (LCLS)
CaNSDH ...... Hermes Electronics Ltd., Dartmouth, NS, Canada [*Library symbol Library of Congress*] (LCLS)
CAN/SDI ...... Canadian Service for the Selective Dissemination of Information [*National Research Council of Canada*] [*Information service or system*] (IID)
CaNSDiC ..... Courier, Digby, NS, Canada [*Library symbol*] [*Library of Congress*] (LCLS)
CaNSDiM ..... Mirror, Digby, NS, Canada [*Library symbol*] [*Library of Congress*] (LCLS)
CaNSDiNHM... North Highlands Museum, Dingwall, NS, Canada [*Library symbol*] [*Library of Congress*] (LCLS)
CaNSDMM... MacLaren Marex, Dartmouth, NS, Canada [*Library symbol Library of Congress*] (LCLS)
CaNSDMP ... MacLaren Plansearch Ltd., Dartmouth, NS, Canada [*Library symbol*] [*Library of Congress*] (LCLS)
CaNSDNSH... Nova Scotia Hospital, Dartmouth, NS, Canada [*Library symbol Library of Congress*] (LCLS)
CANSERVCOL... Canadian Services College
CaNSGbCC... Coastal Courier, Glace Bay, NS, Canada [*Library symbol*] [*Library of Congress*] (LCLS)
CaNSGCFA... Canadian Forces Base, Greenwood, NS, Canada [*Library symbol*] [*Library of Congress*] (LCLS)
CaNSGuOC... Old Court House Museum, Guysborough, NS, Canada [*Library symbol*] [*Library of Congress*] (LCLS)
CaNSH .... Halifax City and Regional Library, Halifax, NS, Canada [*Library symbol Library of Congress*] (LCLS)
CaNSHAE ..... Nova Scotia Department of Education, Adult Education Division, Halifax, NS, Canada [*Library symbol Library of Congress*] (LCLS)
CaNSHAG .... Art Gallery of Nova Scotia, Halifax, NS, Canada [*Library symbol Library of Congress*] (LCLS)
CaNSHaHS... Hantsport and Area Historical Society, Hantsport, NS, Canada [*Library symbol*] [*Library of Congress*] (LCLS)
CaNSHAI ..... Atlantic Institute of Education, Halifax, NS, Canada [*Library symbol Library of Congress*] (LCLS)
CaNSHALMH... Abbie J. Lane Memorial Hospital, Halifax, NS, Canada [*Library symbol Library of Congress*] (LCLS)
CaNSHANSS... Anglican Church of Canada, Diocese of Nova Scotia, Synod Office, Halifax, NS, Canada [*Library symbol Library of Congress*] (LCLS)
CaNSHAR .... Algas Resources Ltd., Halifax, NS, Canada [*Library symbol Library of Congress*] (LCLS)
CaNSHAVI .... [*The*] Atlantic Provinces Resource Centre for the Visually-Impaired, Hal ifax, NS, anada [*Library symbol*] [*Library of Congress*] (LCLS)
CaNSHBS .... Nova Scotia Barristers Society, Halifax, NS, Canada [*Library symbol Library of Congress*] (LCLS)
CaNSHC ...... Cambridge Military Library, Halifax, NS, Canada [*Library symbol*] [*Library of Congress*] (LCLS)
CaNSHCA .... Nova Scotia College of Art, Halifax, NS, Canada [*Library symbol Library of Congress*] (LCLS)
CaNSHCB .... Canadian Broadcasting Corp., Music and Record Library, Halifax, NS, Canada [*Library symbol Library of Congress*] (LCLS)
CaNSHCBC... Canadian British Consultants Ltd., Halifax, NS, Canada [*Library symbol Library of Congress*] (LCLS)

CaNSHCDD... Nova Scotia Commission on Drug Dependency, Halifax, NS, Canada [*Library symbol Library of Congress*] (LCLS)

CaNSHCH Camp Hill Hospital, Halifax, NS, Canada [*Library symbol Library of Congress*] (LCLS)

CaNSHCIC... Nova Scotia Communications and Information Centre, Halifax, NS, Canada [*Library symbol Library of Congress*] (LCLS)

CaNSHD....... Dalhousie University, Halifax, NS, Canada [*Library symbol Library of Congress*] (LCLS)

CaNSHDA.... Dalhousie University, Archives, Halifax, NS, Canada [*Library symbol*] [*Library of Congress*] (LCLS)

CaNSHDAG... Nova Scotia Department of the Attorney-General, Halifax, NS, Canada [*Library symbol Library of Congress*] (LCLS)

CaNSHDCA.. Nova Scotia Department of Consumer Affairs, Halifax, NS, Canada [*Library symbol Library of Congress*] (LCLS)

CaNSHDD .... Nova Scotia Department of Development, Halifax, NS, Canada [*Library symbol Library of Congress*] (LCLS)

CaNSHDE... Nova Scotia Department of the Environment, Halifax, NS, Canada [*Library symbol Library of Congress*] (LCLS)

CaNSHDF..... Nova Scotia Department of Fisheries, Halifax, NS, Canada [*Library symbol Library of Congress*] (LCLS)

CaNSHDH .... Nova Scotia Department of Highways, Halifax, NS, Canada [*Library symbol Library of Congress*] (LCLS)

CaNSHDIP .. Dalhousie University, Institute of Public Affairs, Halifax, NS, Canada [*Library symbol Library of Congress*] (LCLS)

CaNSHDL... Dalhousie University, Law School, Halifax, NS, Canada [*Library symbol Library of Congress*] (LCLS)

CaNSHDM... Dalhousie University, W. K. Kellog Health Sciences Library, Halifax, NS, Canada [*Library symbol Library of Congress*] (LCLS)

CaNSHDMA.. Dalhousie University, Map Library, Halifax, NS, Canada [*Library symbol Library of Congress*] (LCLS)

CaNSHDOL.. Nova Scotia Department of Labour, Halifax, NS, Canada [*Library symbol Library of Congress*] (LCLS)

CaNSHDOM.. Nova Scotia Department of Mines, Halifax, NS, Canada [*Library symbol Library of Congress*] (LCLS)

CaNSHDR .... Nova Scotia Department of Recreation, Halifax, NS, Canada [*Library symbol Library of Congress*] (LCLS)

CaNSHDT .... Nova Scotia Department of Tourism, Halifax, NS, Canada [*Library symbol Library of Congress*] (LCLS)

CaNSHE ..... Nova Scotia Provincial Library, Teachers' Library, Halifax, NS, Canada [*Library symbol Library of Congress*] (LCLS)

CaNSHF....... Canada Department of the Environment, Fisheries and Marine Service, Halifax, NS, Canada [*Library symbol*] [*Library of Congress*] (LCLS)

CaNSHH....... Nova Scotia Department of Health, Halifax, NS, Canada [*Library symbol Library of Congress*] (LCLS)

CaNSHHC ... Halifax County Regional Library, Halifax, NS, Canada [*Library symbol Library of Congress*] (LCLS)

CaNSHHI...... Halifax Infirmary, Health Services Library, Halifax, NS, Canada [*Library symbol Library of Congress*] (LCLS)

CaNSHHR .... Nova Scotia Human Rights Commission, Halifax, NS, Canada [*Library symbol Library of Congress*] (LCLS)

CaNSHIAP... Canada Department of Indian Affairs and Northern Development, Parks Canada, Atlantic Regional Office, Halifax, NS, Canada [*Library symbol*] [*Library of Congress*] (LCLS)

CaNSHJ .... Canada Department of Justice, Halifax, NS, Canada [*Library symbol Library of Congress*] (LCLS)

CaNSHK....... University of King's College, Halifax, NS, Canada [*Library symbol Library of Congress*] (LCLS)

CaNSHKH .... Izaak Walton Killam Hospital for Children, Halifax, NS, Canada [*Library symbol Library of Congress*] (LCLS)

CaNSHKJ ..... University of King's College, School of Journalism, Halifax, NS, Canada [*Library symbol*] [*Library of Congress*] (LCLS)

CaNSHKMGM... Kitz, Matheson, Green & MacIsaac Law Firm, Halifax, NS, Canada [*Library symbol Library of Congress*] (LCLS)

CaNSHL .... Legislative Library, Halifax, NS, Canada [*Library symbol Library of Congress*] (LCLS)

CaNSHLP ..... Liberal Party of Nova Scotia, Halifax, NS, Canada [*Library symbol*] [*Library of Congress*] (LCLS)

CaNSHM ..... National Research Council, Halifax, NS, Canada [*Library symbol Library of Congress*] (LCLS)

CaNSHMA.... Nova Scotia Department of Municipal Affairs, Halifax, NS, Canada [*Library symbol Library of Congress*] (LCLS)

CaNSHMI..... Canada Department of Manpower and Immigration, Halifax, NS, Canada [*Library symbol Library of Congress Obsolete*] (LCLS)

CaNSHMM ... Maritime Museum of the Atlantic Library, Halifax, NS, Canada [*Library symbol Library of Congress*] (LCLS)

CaNSHMS.... Nova Scotia Museum of Science, Halifax, NS, Canada [*Library symbol Library of Congress*] (LCLS)

CaNSHMT .... Canada Ministry of Transport, Marine Library, Halifax, NS, Canada [*Library symbol Library of Congress*] (LCLS)

CaNSHMTT... Maritime Telegraph & Telephone, Information Resource Centre, Halifax, NS, Canada [*Library symbol Library of Congress*] (LCLS)

CaNSHN....... Canada Department of National Defence Research Establishment Atlantic, Dartmouth, NS, Canada [*Library symbol Library of Congress*] (LCLS)

CaNSHN....... Defence Research Establishment, Atlantic Defence Research Board, Halifax, NS, Canada [*Library symbol Library of Congress*] (LCLS)

CaNSHND .... Canada Department of National Defence, Reference and Recreational Library [*Stadacona*], Halifax, NS, Canada [*Library symbol Library of Congress*] (LCLS)

CaNSHNS .... Canadian Forces Base Halifax, Ships Recreational Library, Halifax, NS, Canada [*Library symbol*] [*Library of Congress*] (LCLS)

CaNSHP....... Nova Scotia Public Archives, Halifax, NS, Canada [*Library symbol Library of Congress*] (LCLS)

CaNSHPC.... Nova Scotia Power Corp., Halifax, NS, Canada [*Library symbol Library of Congress*] (LCLS)

CaNSHPH ... Atlantic School of Theology, Halifax, NS, Canada [*Library symbol Library of Congress*] (LCLS)

CaNSHPL..... Nova Scotia Provincial Library, Nova Scotia Union Catalogue, Halifax, NS, Canada [*Library symbol Library of Congress*] (LCLS)

CaNSHPLP... Nova Scotia Provicial Library, Public Library Services, Halifax, NS, Canada [*Library symbol*] [*Library of Congress*] (LCLS)

CaNSHPLX... Nova Scotia Provincial Library, Reference Services, Halifax, NS, Canada [*Library symbol Library of Congress*] (LCLS)

CaNSHPW... Public Works Canada, Atlantic Regional Library, Halifax, NS, Canada [*Library symbol Library of Congress*] (LCLS)

CaNSHR ..... Nova Scotia Research Foundation, Halifax, NS, Canada [*Library symbol Library of Congress*] (LCLS)

CaNSHRC ... Nova Scotia Rehabilitation Centre, Halifax, NS, Canada [*Library symbol Library of Congress*] (LCLS)

CaNSHRCA.. Roman Catholic Archdiocesan Archivers, Halifax, NS, Canada [*Library symbol*] [*Library of Congress*] (LCLS)

CaNSHRL.... Nova Scotia Regional Libraries, Halifax, NS, Canada [*Library symbol Library of Congress*] (LCLS)

CaNSHRP ... Nova Scotia Research Foundation, Photogrammetry Division, Halifax, NS, Canada [*Library symbol Library of Congress*] (LCLS)

CaNSHS....... Saint Mary's University, Halifax, NS, Canada [*Library symbol Library of Congress*] (LCLS)

CaNSHSMC. Stewart, MacKeen & Covert, Halifax, NS, Canada [*Library symbol Library of Congress*] (LCLS)

CaNSHSPT... Saint Mary's University, Patrick Power Library, Community Tape Resource, Halifax, NS, Canada [*Library symbol*] [*Library of Congress*] (LCLS)

CaNSHSS.... Nova Scotia Department of Social Services, Halifax, NS, Canada [*Library symbol Library of Congress*] (LCLS)

CaNSHSW... Maritime School of Social Work, Halifax, NS, Canada [*Library symbol Library of Congress*] (LCLS)

CaNSHT...... Nova Scotia Technical College, Halifax, NS, Canada [*Library symbol Library of Congress*] (LCLS)

CaNSHTI...... Nova Scotia Institute of Technology, Halifax, NS, Canada [*Library symbol Library of Congress*] (LCLS)

CaNSHTU.... Nova Scotia Teachers Union, Halifax, NS, Canada [*Library symbol Library of Congress*] (LCLS)

CaNSHTU.... Tuns Library, Halifax, NS, Canada [*Library symbol Library of Congress*] (LCLS)

CaNSHV..... Mount Saint Vincent University, Halifax, NS, Canada [*Library symbol Library of Congress*] (LCLS)

CaNSHVA.... Mount Saint Vincent University, Art Gallery, Halifax, NS, Canada [*Library symbol Library of Congress*] (LCLS)

CaNSHVGH.. Victoria General Hospital, Health Sciences Library, Halifax, NS, Canada [*Library symbol Library of Congress*] (LCLS)

CaNSHVH ... Halifax Regional Vocational School, Halifax, NS, Canada [*Library symbol Library of Congress*] (LCLS)

CaNSHVTT ... Nova Scotia Department of Vocational and Technical Training, Halifax, NS, Canada [*Library symbol*] [*Library of Congress*] (LCLS)

CaNSHW...... Canada Department of the Environment, Atmospheric Environment Service, Atlantic Region, Halifax, NS, Canada [*Library symbol Library of Congress*] (LCLS)

CANSI......... Canadian Association of Nordic Ski Instructors (AC)

CanSIA........ Canadian Solar Industries Association Inc. [*Association des Industries Solaires du Canada Inc.*] (AC)

CANSIM...... Canadian Socio-Economic Information Management System [*Statistics Canada*] [*Database Ottawa, ON*] (IID)

CanSIS........ Canadian Soil Information System [*Land Resource and Research Institute*] [*Ottawa, ON*] [*Information service or system*] (IID)

CaNSKER .... Efamol Research Institute, Kentville, NS, Canada [*Library symbol*] [*Library of Congress*] (LCLS)

CaNSKOK.... Old Kings Courthouse Heritage Museum, Kentville, NS, Canada [*Library symbol*] [*Library of Congress*] (LCLS)

CaNSKR...... Canada Department of Agriculture, Research Station, Kentville, NS, Canada [*Library symbol Library of Congress*] (LCLS)

CaNSKS...... Nova Scotia Sanatorium, Kentville, NS, Canada [*Library symbol Library of Congress*] (LCLS)

CaNSLA...... Louisbourg Archives, Louisbourg, NS, Canada [*Library symbol Library of Congress*] (LCLS)

CaNSLF....... Fortress of Louisbourg, Canada Department of Indian Affairs and Northern Development, Fortress of Louisbourg, NS, Canada [*Library symbol Library of Congress*] (LCLS)

CaNSLhFP ... Fort Point Museum, La Have, NS, Canada [*Library symbol*] [*Library of Congress*] (LCLS)

CaNSLiQCM... Queens County Museum, Liverpool, NS, Canada [*Library symbol*] [*Library of Congress*] (LCLS)

CaNSLoLS... Lockeport Little School Museum, Lockeport, NS, Canada [*Library symbol*] [*Library of Congress*] (LCLS)

CaNSLuFM... Fisheries Museum of the Atlantic, Lunenburg, NS, Canada [*Library symbol*] [*Library of Congress*] (LCLS)

CaNSLuHS... Lunenburg Heritage Society, Lunenburg, NS, Canada [*Library symbol*] [*Library of Congress*] (LCLS)

CaNSLuPE... Progress-Enterprise, Lunenburg, NS, Canada [*Library symbol*] [*Library of Congress*] (LCLS)

CaNSMCA.... Maritime Conference Archives, Halifax, NS, Canada [*Library symbol Library of Congress*] (LCLS)

CaNSME ...... Eastern Counties Regional Library, Mulgrave, NS, Canada [*Library symbol Library of Congress*] (LCLS)

CaNSMiEX... Examiner, Middleton, NS, Canada [*Library symbol*] [*Library of Congress*] (LCLS)

CaNSMiM .... Macdonald Museum, Middleton, NS, Canada [*Library symbol*] [*Library of Congress*] (LCLS)

CaNSMiV ..... Valley Mirror, Middleton, NS, Canada [*Library symbol*] [*Library of Congress*] (LCLS)

CAN/SND ..... Scientific Numeric Database Service [*National Research Council of Canada*] [*Information service or system*] (IID)

CaNSNE ...... Nappan Experimental Farm, Nappan, NS, Canada [*Library symbol*] [*Library of Congress*] (LCLS)

CaNSNgP ..... Pictou-Antigonish Regional Library, New Glasgow, NS, Canada [*Library symbol Library of Congress*] (LCLS)

CaNSNhC.... Cabot Archives, Neil's Harbour, NS, Canada [*Library symbol*] [*Library of Congress*] (LCLS)

CaNSNmK.... Kentville Publishing, New Minas, NS, Canada [*Library symbol*] [*Library of Congress*] (LCLS)

CaNSOJ .... Journal, Oxford, NS, Canada [*Library symbol*] [*Library of Congress*] (LCLS)

CaNSoPt...... Canada Southern Petroleum Ltd. [*Associated Press*] (SAG)

CANSPA ...... Canadian Swimming Pool Association

CaNSPA .... Pictou Advocate, Pictou, NS, Canada [*Library symbol*] [*Library of Congress*] (LCLS)

CaNSPaR .... Record, Parrsboro, NS, Canada [*Library symbol*] [*Library of Congress*] (LCLS)

CaNSPaSH... Parrsboro Shore Historical Society, Parrsboro, NS, Canada [*Library symbol*] [*Library of Congress*] (LCLS)

CaNSPBB .... Burning Bush Museum, Pictou, NS, Canada [*Library symbol*] [*Library of Congress*] (LCLS)

CaNSPMH.... McCulloch House, Pictou, NS, Canada [*Library symbol*] [*Library of Congress*] (LCLS)

CaNSPNC.... North Cumberland Historical Society, Pugwash, NS, Canada [*Library symbol*] [*Library of Congress*] (LCLS)

CaNSSC .... Cape Breton Regional Library, Sydney, NS, Canada [*Library symbol Library of Congress*] (LCLS)

CaNSSCB .... Cape Breton Post, Sydney, NS, Canada [*Library symbol*] [*Library of Congress*] (LCLS)

CaNSSCG .... Canada Coast Guard College, Sydney, NS, Canada [*Library symbol Library of Congress*] (LCLS)

CaNSShCF ... Canadian Forces Base Barrington, Stone Horse, NS, Canada [*Library symbol*] [*Library of Congress*] (LCLS)

CaNSShCM... Shelburne County Museum, Shelburne, NS, Canada [*Library symbol*] [*Library of Congress*] (LCLS)

CaNSSheCO... Coast Guard, Shelburne, NS, Canada [*Library symbol*] [*Library of Congress*] (LCLS)

CaNSSmM ... Memorial High School, Sidney Mines, NS, Canada [*Library symbol Library of Congress*] (LCLS)

CaNSSmMM... Memorial High School Sidney Mines, NS, Canada [*Library symbol*] [*Library of Congress*] (LCLS)

CaNSSpR ..... Record, Springhill, NS, Canada [*Library symbol*] [*Library of Congress*] (LCLS)

CaNSSrM ..... South Rawdon Museum, South Rawdon, NS, Canada [*Library symbol*] [*Library of Congress*] (LCLS)

CaNSSSRH... Saint Rita's Hospital, Sydney, NS, Canada [*Library symbol Library of Congress*] (LCLS)

CaNSSX .... College of Cape Breton, Sydney, NS, Canada [*Library symbol Library of Congress*] (LCLS)

CaNSSXA..... College of Cape Breton, Archives and General Library, Sydney, NS, Canada [*Library symbol Library of Congress*] (LCLS)

CaNSTA .... Nova Scotia Agricultural College, Truro, NS, Canada [*Library symbol Library of Congress*] (LCLS)

CaNSTaF..... Fraser Culture Centre, Tatamagouche, NS, Canada [*Library symbol*] [*Library of Congress*] (LCLS)

CANSTAN..... Canadian Standards [*Standards Council of Canada*] [*Information service or system*] (CRD)

Can Stat ...... Statutes of Canada [*A publication*] (DLA)

Can Stat O & Regs... Statutory Orders and Regulations [*Canada A publication*]

CaNSTC .... Colchester-East Hants Regional Library, Truro, NS, Canada [*Library symbol Library of Congress*] (LCLS)

CaNSTDN..... Daily News, Truro, NS, Canada [*Library symbol*] [*Library of Congress*] (LCLS)

CANSTEP ..... Canadian Society for Titanic Education & Preservation (AC)

CaNSTiIM .... Islands Museum and Tourist Bureau, Tiverton, NS, Canada [*Library symbol*] [*Library of Congress*] (LCLS)

CaNSTT....... Nova Scotia Teachers' College, Truro, NS, Canada [*Library symbol Library of Congress*] (LCLS)

Can Sup Ct... Canada Supreme Court Reports [*A publication*] (DLA)

CANSW....... Careers' Association of New South Wales [*Australia*]

CANSW........ Chess Association of New South Wales [*Australia*]

CANSW........ Christian Assembly of New South Wales [*Australia*]

CaNSWA...... Acadia University, Wolfville, NS, Canada [*Library symbol Library of Congress*] (LCLS)

CaNSWAG.... Acadia University, Department of Geography, Wolfville, NS, Canada [*Library symbol Library of Congress*] (LCLS)

CaNSWH...... Wolfville Historical Museum, Wolfville, NS, Canada [*Library symbol Library of Congress*] (LCLS)

CaNSWiHJ... Hants Journal, Windsor, NS, Canada [*Library symbol*] [*Library of Congress*] (LCLS)

CaNSWiKE... King's-Edgehill School, Windsor, NS, Canada [*Library symbol*] [*Library of Congress*] (LCLS)

CaNSY .... Western Counties Regional Library, Yarmouth, NS, Canada [*Library symbol Library of Congress*] (LCLS)

CaNSYC ...... Courrier de la Nouvelle-Ecosse, Yarmouth, NS, Canada [*Library symbol*] [*Library of Congress*] (LCLS)

CaNSYFG.... Fundy Group Publications, Yarmouth, NS, Canada [*Library symbol*] [*Library of Congress*] (LCLS)

CaNSYHM.... Yarmouth County Historical Society, Yarmouth, NS, Canada [*Library symbol Library of Congress*] (LCLS)

CanT .... Canadian Telefunken [*Record label*]

Can T........... Canberra Times [*A publication*]

CANT .... Cantabile [*Flowing Style*] [*Music*]

CANT .... Cantabrigiensis [*Of Cambridge University*] [*Latin*] (ROG)

CANT .... Canterbury [*City in England*]

Cant............ Canterbury [*Record label*]

CANT .... Canticle of Canticles [*Old testament book*] [*Douay version*]

Cant............ Canticles [*Song of Solomon*] [*Old Testament book*]

CANT .... Cantilever

CANT .... Canto [*Melody*] [*Music*]

CANT .... Cantonese

CANT .... Cantor

CANT .... Cat Association of the Northern Territory [*Australia*]

CANT .... Chinese Atmospheric Nuclear Test (MCD)

CANT .... Coalition Against Noneffective Lightning Protection Technologies (EA)

CANTAB ..... Cantabile [*Flowing Style*] [*Music*]

Cantab .... Cantab Pharmaceuticals Ltd. [*Associated Press*] (SAG)

CANTAB ..... Cantabrigiensis [*Of Cambridge University*] [*Latin*]

CAN/TAP ..... Canadian Technical Awareness Programme (HGAA)

CANTASS .... Canadian Towed Array SONAR System

CANTAT ...... Canadian Transatlantic Telephone Cable [*Between Canada and England*]

Cantaur....... Cantuariensis [*of Canterbury*] [*Latin*] (BARN)

Can Tax App Bd... Canada Tax Appeal Board Cases [*A publication*] (DLA)

Can Tax Cas... Canada Tax Cases [*A publication*] (DLA)

Can Tax Cas Ann... Canada Tax Cases, Annotated [*A publication*] (DLA)

Can Tax Found... Canadian Tax Foundation. Conference Report [*A publication*] (DLA)

Can Tax Found Rep Proc Tax Conf... Canadian Tax Foundation. Report of Proceedings of the Tax Conference [*A publication*] (DLA)

Can Tax LJ... Canadian Tax Law Journal [*A publication*] (DLA)

Can Tax Rep (CCH)... Canadian Tax Reporter (Commerce Clearing House) [*A publication*] (DLA)

CantbrPk..... Canterbury Park Holdings [*Associated Press*] (SAG)

Cantbry....... Canterbury Corporate Services [*Associated Press*] (SAG)

CANTCO ...... Cannot Comply (NVT)

Cantel......... Cantel Industries, Inc. [*Associated Press*] (SAG)

CANTELCAS... Cantilevered Elevated Causeway [*Army*]

CANTERB .... Canterbury [*City and county borough in England*]

Can Terr ..... Territories Law Reports [1885-1907] [*Canada*] [*A publication*] (DLA)

CANTHA...... Cantharides [*Spanish Fly*] [*Pharmacy*] (ROG)

CANTHARD.. Cantharides [*Spanish Fly*] [*Pharmacy*] (ROG)

CANTIL .... Cantilever (MSA)

CANTO .... Cantando [*In a Singing Manner*] [*Music*] (ROG)

CANTO .... Concern Against Nuclear Technology Organisations [*British*] (DI)

CANTON...... Cantonments [*Military*] (ROG)

Cantor Med & Surg... Cantor's Traumatic Medicine and Surgery for the Attorney [*A publication*] (DLA)

CANTOT ...... Computer Analysis of Troubles on Trunk Circuits (PDAA)

CantP .... Canterbury Park Holdings [*Associated Press*] (SAG)

CANTR .... Cantor

CANTRAC.... Catalog of Navy Training Courses (NVT)

CANTRAINDIV... Canadian Training Division [*Canadian Navy*]

CANTRAINRON... Canadian Training Squadron [*Canadian Navy*]

CANTRAN ... Canceled Transmission (CET)

Can TS........ Canada Treaty Series [*A publication*] (DLA)

CANTUAR ... Cantuaria [*Canterbury*] [*Latin*]

Cantuar ...... Cantuariensis [*Of Canterbury*] [*Latin*] (ILCA)

CANTV .... Compania Anonima Nacional Telefonos de Venezuela [*Associated Press*] (SAG)

Cantwell ...... Cantwell's Cases on Tolls and Customers [*Ireland*] [*A publication*] (DLA)

CANUC:H ..... Canadian Union Catalogue of Library Materials for the Handicapped [*National Library of Canada*] [*Information service or system*] (IID)

CANUCS....... Union List of Serials in the Social Sciences and Humanities Held by Canadian Libraries

CAN-UK........ Canada-United Kingdom

CAN-UK JCEC... Canada-United Kingdom-Joint Communications Electronics Committees

CANUKUS .... Canada-United Kingdom-United States [*Agreement*]

CANUKUS JCECS... Canada-United Kingdom-United States Joint Communications-Electronics Committees

CANUNET..... Canadian University Computer Network (MCD)

CAN-US........ Canada-United States (AFM)

CANUSE...... Canadian-United States Eastern Power Complex

CANV .... Canvas

CANV .... Canvas

CANW .... Campaign Against Nuclear War (EA)

CANWEA...... Canadian Wind Energy Association Inc. [*Association Canadienne d'Energie Ecolienne*] (AC)

CANWEC...... Canadian National Committee, World Energy Conference

CANWEL ...... Canadian Water Supply Energy Loop

CaNWFsPCN... Parks Canada, Nahanni National Park, Fort Simpson, NT, Canada [*Library symbol Library of Congress*] (LCLS)

CaNWFSPCW... Parks Canada, Wood Buffalo National Park, Fort Smith, NT, Canada [*Library symbol Library of Congress*] (LCLS)

CaNWHRN..... Northwest Territories Public Library Services, Hay River, NT, Canada [*Library symbol Library of Congress*] (LCLS)

CaNWII .... Canada Department of Indian Affairs and Northern Development, Inuvik Research Laboratory, Inuvik, NT, Canada [*Library symbol Library of Congress*] (LCLS)

CaNWIIE ...... Indian and Northern Affairs Canada, Eastern Artic Research Laboratory, Igloolik, NT, Canada [*Library symbol*] [*Library of Congress*] (LCLS)

CaNWPPCA... Parks Canada, Auyuittuq National Park, Pangnirtung, NT, Canada [*Library symbol Library of Congress*] (LCLS)

Canwst......... Canwest Global Communications Corp. [*Associated Press*] (SAG)

CaNWY .... Yellowknife Public Library, Yellowknife, NT, Canada [*Library symbol*] [*Library of Congress*] (LCLS)

CaNWYECW... Environment Canada, Canadian Wildlife Service, Yellowknife, NT, Canada [*Library symbol Library of Congress*] (LCLS)

CaNWYEEP... Environment Canada, Environmental Protection Service, Assessment and Coordination, Yellowknife, NT, Canada [*Library symbol*] [*Library of Congress*] (LCLS)

CaNWYGI..... Government In-Service Library, Yellowknife, NT, Canada [*Library symbol Library of Congress*] (LCLS)

CaNWYIM .... Canada Department of Indian and Northern Affairs, Yellowknife, NT, Canada [*Library symbol Library of Congress*] (LCLS)

CaNWYND ... Canada Department of National Defence, Northern Region Information System, [*NORIS*], Yellowknife, NT, Canada [*Library symbol Library of Congress*] (LCLS)

CaNWYOS.... Doctor Otto Schaefer Health Resource Centre, Yellowknife, NT, Canada [*Library symbol*] [*Library of Congress*] (LCLS)

CaNWYPC.... Parks Canada, Yellowknife, NT, Canada [*Library symbol Library of Congress*] (LCLS)

CANX .... Calnexin (DMAA)

CANX .... Cannon Express [*NASDAQ symbol*] (TTSB)

CANX .... Cannon Express, Inc. [*NASDAQ symbol*] (NQ)

CANY .... Canyonlands National Park

Cany .... Canyon Resources Corp. [*Associated Press*] (SAG)

CANYN........ Canyon [*Commonly used*] (OPSA)

CANYON ...... Canyon [*Commonly used*] (OPSA)

CanyonRs ... Canyon Resources [*Associated Press*] (SAG)

CANYPS....... Canadian National Yellow Pages Service

CanyRs........ Canyon Resources Corp. [*Associated Press*] (SAG)

CANYS......... Correctional Association of New York State (SRA)

CANZ .... Canada, Australia and New Zealand

CaO............. Calcium Oxide [*Organic chemistry*] (DAVI)

CAO .... California Association of Ophthalmology (SRA)

CAO .... Canadian Army Orders

CAO .... Canadian Association of Orthodontists [*Association Canadienne des Orthodontists*] (AC)

CAO .... Cara Operations Ltd. [*Toronto Stock Exchange symbol*]

CAO .... Carolina Freight Corp. [*NYSE symbol*] (SPSG)

CAO .... Carotid Artery Occlusion [*Medicine*]

CAO .... Casualty Assistance Officer [*Army*] (ADDR)

CAO .... Central Accounting Office [*Military*] (AFM)

CAO .... Central Action Office [*Army*]

CAO .... Central Applications Office [*Ireland*]

CAO .... Change of Appointing Office (FAAC)

CAO .... Chemical Abstracts, Odd-Numbered Issue

CAO .... Chief Accountant Officer [*RAF*] [*British*]

CAO .... Chief Administrative Officer

CAO .... Chief Agency Officer [*Insurance*]

CAO .... Chiropractic Association of Oklahoma (SRA)

CAO .... Chiropractic Association of Oregon (SRA)

CAO .... Chronic Airway Obstruction [*Medicine*]

CAO .... Circuit Activation Order

CAO .... Circum-Atlantic Project [*Marine science*] (OSRA)

CAO .... City Administrative Office

CAO .... Civil Affairs Officer [*Navy*]

CAO .... Civil Aviation Order

CAO .... Clayton, NM [*Location identifier FAA*] (FAAL)

CAO .... Collateral Action Officer [*Army*] (AABC)

CAO .... Collective Analysis Only (IAA)

CAO .... Committee on Amphibious Operations (SAA)

CAO .... Commonwealth Arts Organization (EA)

CAO .... Communications Allocation Order (CINC)

CAO .... Community Affairs Officer

CAO .... Completed as Ordered (ECII)

CAO .... Complex Assessment Officer

CAO .... Computer-Aided Office (IAA)

CAO .... Computer-Aided Optimization

CAO .... Conception Assistee par Ordinateur [*Computer-Assisted Design - CAD*] [*French*]

CAO .... Congress of Astrological Organizations [*Defunct*] (EA)

CAO .... Connecticut Association of Optometrists (SRA)

CAO .... Consumer Affairs Office [*Federal Energy Administration*]

CAO .... Contract Administration Office [*or Officer*] [*Navy*]

CAO .... Cooperative Agreement Officer [*Department of Housing and Urban Development*] (GFGA)

CAO .... Coordinated Atomic Operations (CINC)

CAO .... Copper Amine Oxidase [*An enzyme*]

CAO .... Coronary Artery Obstruction [*Cardiology*] (DMAA)

CAO .... Corrective Action Order [*Environmental Protection Agency*] (ERG)

CAO .... Cost Analysis Office [*Army*] (RDA)

CAO .... Cost of Analysis Organization [*Navy*] (NG)

CAO .... Cretans' Association "Omonoia" (EA)

CAO .... Crimean Astrophysical Observatory

CAO .... Cultural Affairs Officer [*United States Information Service*]

CAO .... Customer Assistance Office

CAO .... Cyclophosphamide, Adriamycin, Oncovin [*Vincristine*] [*Antineoplastic drug regimen*]

CaOAc......... Action Public Library, Action, ON, Canada [*Library symbol Library of Congress*] (LCLS)

CaOAcH....... Acton High School, Acton, ON, Canada [*Library symbol Library of Congress*] (LCLS)

CaOAgCP..... Canada Publishing Corp., Agincourt, ON, Canada [*Library symbol*] [*Library of Congress*] (LCLS)

CaOAgG .... Gage Educational Publishing Ltd., Agincourt, ON, Canada [*Library symbol Library of Congress*] (LCLS)

CaOAj .... Ajax Public Library, Ajax, ON, Canada [*Library symbol Library of Congress*] (LCLS)

CaOAL .... Alliston Public Library, Alliston, ON, Canada [*Library symbol Library of Congress*] (LCLS)

CaOALAC ..... Lennox & Addington County Public Library, Amherstview Branch, Amherstview, ON, Canada [*Library symbol*] [*Library of Congress*] (LCLS)

CaOAmF .... Fort Malden National Historic Park, Amherstburg, ON, Canada [*Library symbol Library of Congress*] (LCLS)

CaOANT .... Normanby Township Community & School Library, Ayton, ON, Canada [*Library symbol*] [*Library of Congress*] (LCLS)

CaOARB....... Arnprior Public Library, Arnprior, ON, Canada [*Library symbol*] [*Library of Congress*] (LCLS)

CaOARB....... Rayside-Balfour Public Library, Azilda Branch, Azilda, ON, Canada [*Library symbol*] [*Library of Congress*] (LCLS)

CaOArBC...... Boeing of Canada Ltd., Arnprior, ON, Canada [*Library symbol*] [*Library of Congress*] (LCLS)

CaOArM .... Middlesex County Public Library, Arva, ON, Canada [*Library symbol Library of Congress*] (LCLS)

CaOARMS..... Armstrong Public Library, Armstrong, ON, Canada [*Library symbol*] [*Library of Congress*] (LCLS)

CaOASDG .... Stomount, Dundas & Glengarry County Public Library, Alexandria Branch, Alexandria, ON, Canada [*Library symbol*] [*Library of Congress*] (LCLS)

CaOAtD .... Arthur District High School, Arthur, ON, Canada [*Library symbol*] [*Library of Congress*] (LCLS)

CaOAtH....... Atikokan High School, Atikokan, ON, Canada [*Library symbol Library of Congress*] (LCLS)

CaOAttB .... Attawapiskat Band Library, Attawapiskat, ON, Canada [*Library symbol*] [*Library of Congress*] (LCLS)

CaOAu .... Aurora Public Library, Aurora, ON, Canada [*Library symbol Library of Congress*] (LCLS)

CaOAuH....... Aurora Historical Society, Aurora, ON, Canada [*Library symbol*] [*Library of Congress*] (LCLS)

CaOAuHS..... Aurora High School, PRECIS Project, Aurora, ON, Canada [*Library symbol*] [*Library of Congress*] (LCLS)

CaOAUM...... Aurora Museum, Aurora, ON, Canada [*Library symbol*] [*Library of Congress*] (LCLS)

CaOAuYCE ... York County Board of Education, Aurora, ON, Canada [*Library symbol Library of Congress*] (LCLS)

CaOAwOP ... Ontatio Police College, Aylmer West, ON, Canada [*Library symbol*] [*Library of Congress*] (LCLS)

CaOAYM ...... Aylmer District Museum, Aylmer, ON, Canada [*Library symbol*] [*Library of Congress*] (LCLS)

CaOB .... Brockville Public Library, Brockville, ON, Canada [*Library symbol Library of Congress*] (LCLS)

CaOBa .... Barrie Public Library, Barrie, ON, Canada [*Library symbol Library of Congress*] (LCLS)

CaOBaG....... Georgian Bay Regional Library, Barrie, ON, Canada [*Library symbol Library of Congress*] (LCLS)

CaOBaGC..... Georgian College of Applied Arts and Technology, Barrie, ON, Canada [*Library symbol Library of Congress*] (LCLS)

CaOBan........ Bancroft Public Library, Bancroft, ON, Canada [*Library symbol Library of Congress*] (LCLS)

CaOBarF....... Frontenac County Public Library, Barriefield, ON, Canada [*Library symbol Library of Congress*] (LCLS)

CaOBaS .... Simcoe County Co-op, Barrie, ON, Canada [*Library symbol Library of Congress*] (LCLS)

CaOBBMV..... Madawaska Valley District High School, Barry's Bay, ON, Canada [*Library symbol*] [*Library of Congress*] (LCLS)

CaOBC......... Barwick Community Library, Barwick, ON, Canada [*Library symbol*] [*Library of Congress*] (LCLS)

CaOBCAB..... Town of Caledon Public Libraries, Albion-Bolton Branch, Bolton, ON, Canada [*Library symbol Library of Congress*] (LCLS)

CaOBCCL..... Canada Cement Lafarge Ltd., Belleville, ON, Canada [*Library symbol Library of Congress*] (LCLS)

CaOBCS .... Chromatographic Specialties Ltd., Brockville, ON, Canada [*Library symbol*] [*Library of Congress*] (LCLS)

CaOBE .... Belleville Public Library, Belleville, ON, Canada [*Library symbol Library of Congress*] (LCLS)

CaOBEAB..... Brock Township Public Library, Beaverton Branch, Beaverton, ON, Canada [*Library symbol*] [*Library of Congress*] (LCLS)

CaOBeaTE.... Thorah Eldon Historical Society, Inc., Beaverton, ON, Canada [*Library symbol Library of Congress*] (LCLS)

CaOBeD....... Beamsville District Secondary School, Beamsville, ON, Canada [*Library symbol Library of Congress*] (LCLS)

CaOBeLF..... Lincoln Public Library, Fleming Branch, Beamsville, ON, Canada [*Library symbol*] [*Library of Congress*] (LCLS)

CaOBeIL...... Loyalist College of Applied Arts and Technology, Belleville, ON, Canada [*Library symbol Library of Congress*] (LCLS)

CaOBEM ...... Beachville Ye Olde Museum, Beachville, ON, Canada [*Library symbol*] [*Library of Congress*] (LCLS)

CaOBESA ..... Stephens-Adamson, Belleville, ON, Canada [*Library symbol*] [*Library of Congress*] (LCLS)

CaOBfAR...... Burks Falls, Armour & Ryerson Union Library, Burks Falls, ON, Canada [*Library symbol*] [*Library of Congress*] (LCLS)

CaOBfNO..... Northern Ontario Public School Principals' Association, Burks Falls, ON, Canada [*Library symbol Library of Congress*] (LCLS)

CAOBISCO ... Association des Industries de la Chocolaterie, Biscuiterie-Biscotterie et Confiserie de la CEE [*Association of the Chocolate, Biscuit and Confectionery Industries of the EEC*] (ECED)

CaOBIWR..... Whitefish River Band Public Library, Birch Island, ON, Canada [*Library symbol*] [*Library of Congress*] (LCLS)

CaOBLAC ..... Lennox & Addington County Public Library, Bath Branch, Bath, ON, Canada [*Library symbol*] [*Library of Congress*] (LCLS)

CaOBLR .... Blind River Public Library, Blind River, ON, Canada [*Library symbol*] [*Library of Congress*] (LCLS)

CaOBMP ...... Bruce Mines & Plummer Additional Union Public Library, Bruce Mines, ON, Canada [*Library symbol*] [*Library of Congress*] (LCLS)

CaOBNE .... Northern Electric Co., Belleville, ON, Canada [*Library symbol Library of Congress*] (LCLS)

CaOBobV ...... Victoria County Public Library, Bobcaygeon Branch, Bobcaygeon, ON, Canada [*Library symbol*] [*Library of Congress*] (LCLS)

CaOBolC ...... Caledon Public Libraries, Bolton, ON, Canada [*Library symbol Library of Congress*] (LCLS)

CaOBoN .... Newcastle Public Library Board, Bowmanville, ON, Canada [*Library symbol Library of Congress*] (LCLS)

CaOBONF ..... Bonfield Public Library, Bonfield, ON, Canada [*Library symbol*] [*Library of Congress*] (LCLS)

CaOBP .... Canada Department of Agriculture, Research Institute, Belleville, ON, Canada [*Library symbol Library of Congress Obsolete*] (LCLS)

CaOBr .... Bradford Public Library, Bradford, ON, Canada [*Library symbol Library of Congress*] (LCLS)

CaOBra .... Brampton Public Library, Brampton, ON, Canada [*Library symbol Library of Congress*] (LCLS)

CaOBrac ...... Bracebridge Public Library, Bracebridge, ON, Canada [*Library symbol Library of Congress*] (LCLS)

CaOBraDE .... Dollman Electronics Ltd., Brampton, ON, Canada [*Library symbol*] [*Library of Congress*] (LCLS)

CaOBram ..... Chinguacousy Township Public Library, Bramalea, ON, Canada [*Library symbol Library of Congress*] (LCLS)

CaOBramB .. Bell Northern Research, Bramalea, ON, Canada [*Library symbol Library of Congress*] (LCLS)

CaOBraNT .... Northern Telecom, Brampton, ON, Canada [*Library symbol Library of Congress*] (LCLS)

CaOBrER ...... Eldorado Resources Ltd., Blind River Refinery, Blind River, ON, Canada [*Library symbol Library of Congress*] (LCLS)

CaOBRO .... Oxford-on-Rideau Township Public Library, Burritt's Rapids, ON, Canada [*Library symbol*] [*Library of Congress*] (LCLS)

CaOBRPH .... Brockville Psychiatric Hospital, Library Resources and Informtion Centre, Brockville, ON, Canada [*Library symbol*] [*Library of Congress*] (LCLS)

CaOBrt .... Brantford Public Library, Brantford, ON, Canada [*Library symbol Library of Congress*] (LCLS)

CaOBrtBM .... Brant County Historical Museum, Brantford, ON, Canada [*Library symbol Library of Congress*] (LCLS)

CaOBrtM ...... W. Ross MacDonald School, Brantford, ON, Canada [*Library symbol*] [*Library of Congress*] (LCLS)

CaOBrtP .... Pauline Johnson College, Brantford, ON, Canada [*Library symbol Library of Congress*] (LCLS)

CaOBrtWI .... Woodland Indian Cultural Educational Centre, Brantford, ON, Canada [*Library symbol Library of Congress*] (LCLS)

CaOBSL .... Saint Lawrence College of Applied Arts and Technology, Brockville, ON, Canada [*Library symbol Library of Congress*] (LCLS)

CaOBU .... Burlington Public Library, Burlington, ON, Canada [*Library symbol Library of Congress*] (LCLS)

CaOBUC .... Canada Department of Mines and Resources, Centre for Inland Waters, Burlington, ON, Canada [*Library symbol Library of Congress*] (LCLS)

CaOBUCC ..... Canadian Canners Ltd., Burlington, ON, Canada [*Library symbol Library of Congress*] (LCLS)

CaOBUL .... Lord Elgin High School, Burlington, ON, Canada [*Library symbol Library of Congress*] (LCLS)

CaOC .... Cathodal Opening Contraction [*Also, COC*] [*Physiology*]

CAOC .... Combat Air Operations Center (CINC)

CAOC .... Constant Axial Offset Control (NRCH)

CaOC .... Cornwall Public Library, Cornwall, ON, Canada [*Library symbol Library of Congress*] (LCLS)

CAOC .... Counter Air Operations Center (DNAB)

CaOCAB .... Brock Township Public Library, Cannington Branch, Cannington, ON, Canada [*Library symbol*] [*Library of Congress*] (LCLS)

CaOCam ...... Campbellford Public Library, Campbellford, ON, Canada [*Library symbol Library of Congress*] (LCLS)

CaOCaOCC .. Ontario CAD/CAM Centre, Cambridge, ON, Canada [*Library symbol*] [*Library of Congress*] (LCLS)

CaOCARD .... Cardinal Public Library, Cardinal, ON, Canada [*Library symbol*] [*Library of Congress*] (LCLS)

CaOCauHM ... Haldimand County Museum Board, Cayuga, ON, Canada [*Library symbol Library of Congress*] (LCLS)

CaOCaW ...... Waterloo Regional Library, Cambridge, ON, Canada [*Library symbol Library of Congress*] (LCLS)

CaOCC .... Courtaulds Ltd., Cornwall, ON, Canada [*Library symbol Library of Congress Obsolete*] (LCLS)

CaOCCIN ...... Inco Ltd., Process Technology Department, Copper Cliff, ON, Canada [*Library symbol Library of Congress*] (LCLS)

CaOCCT .... Collingwood Township Public Library, Brockville, ON, Canada [*Library symbol*] [*Library of Congress*] (LCLS)

CaOCELAC ... Lennox & Addington County Library, Camden East Branch, Camden East, ON, Canada [*Library symbol*] [*Library of Congress*] (LCLS)

CaOCGH .... Cornwall General Hospital, Cornwall, ON, Canada [*Library symbol Library of Congress*] (LCLS)

CaOCha .... Chatham Public Library, Chatham, ON, Canada [*Library symbol Library of Congress*] (LCLS)

CaOChaFMFP .... Ontario Center for Machinery and Food Processing Technology, Chatham, ON, Canada [*Library symbol*] [*Library of Congress*] (LCLS)

CaOChaH .... Chatham Public General Hospital, Chatham, ON, Canada [*Library symbol Library of Congress*] (LCLS)

CaOChaK ..... Chatham-Kent Museum, Chatham, ON, Canada [*Library symbol Library of Congress*] (LCLS)

CaOChaKC ... Kent County Public Library, Chatham, ON, Canada [*Library symbol Library of Congress*] (LCLS)

CaOChaT ...... Thames Arts Centre, Chatham, ON, Canada [*Library symbol Library of Congress*] (LCLS)

CaOChaUG ... Union Gas Ltd., Chatham, ON, Canada [*Library symbol*] [*Library of Congress*] (LCLS)

CaOCHCB ..... Huron County Board of Education, Clinton, ON, Canada [*Library symbol*] [*Library of Congress*] (LCLS)

CaOCheRB ... Rayside-Balfour Public Library, Chelmsford, ON, Canada [*Library symbol Library of Congress*] (LCLS)

CaOChiN ...... Norton Electric Co., Chippewa, ON, Canada [*Library symbol Library of Congress*] (LCLS)

CAOCI .... Commercially Available Organic Chemicals Index [*Chemical Notation Association*] [*Databank*] [*British*]

CaOCkA .... Atomic Energy of Canada, Chalk River, ON, Canada [*Library symbol Library of Congress*] (LCLS)

CaOCkE .... Canada Department of the Environment, Petawawa Forest Experiment Station, Chalk River, ON, Canada [*Library symbol Library of Congress*] (LCLS)

CaOClFC ...... Frontenac County Library, Cloyne Branch, Cloyne, ON, Canada [*Library symbol*] [*Library of Congress*] (LCLS)

CaOCN .... National Historic Park, Cornwall, ON, Canada [*Library symbol Library of Congress*] (LCLS)

CaOCNGH .... Northumberland County Public Library, Garden Hill Branch, Campbellcroft, ON, Canada [*Library symbol*] [*Library of Congress*] (LCLS)

CaOCo .... Cobourg Public Library, Cobourg, ON, Canada [*Library symbol Library of Congress*] (LCLS)

CaOCoA .... Art Gallery of Cobourg, Cobourg, ON, Canada [*Library symbol Library of Congress*] (LCLS)

CaOCob .... Cobalt Public Library, Cobalt, ON, Canada [*Library symbol*] [*Library of Congress*] (LCLS)

CaOCoBD .... Cobden Public Library, Cobden, ON, Canada [*Library symbol*] [*Library of Congress*] (LCLS)

CaOCoc .... Cochrane Public Library, Cochrane, ON, Canada [*Library symbol Library of Congress*] (LCLS)

CaOCoGF ..... General Foods Ltd., Cobourg, ON, Canada [*Library symbol Library of Congress*] (LCLS)

CaOCol .... Collingwood Public Library, Collingwood, ON, Canada [*Library symbol Library of Congress*] (LCLS)

CAOCOMNET ... Coordination of Atomic Operations Communications Net

CaOCoN .... Northumberland and Newcastle Board of Education, Cobourg, ON, Canada [*Library symbol*] [*Library of Congress*] (LCLS)

CaOCp .... Carleton Place Public Library, Carleton Place, ON, Canada [*Library symbol Library of Congress*] (LCLS)

CaOCpG ...... Goodwood Data Systems Ltd., Carleton Place, ON, Canada [*Library symbol Library of Congress*] (LCLS)

CaOCpL .... Leigh Instruments Ltd., Carleton Place, ON, Canada [*Library symbol Library of Congress*] (LCLS)

CaOCpS .... I. P. Sharp Associates Ltd., Carleton Place, ON, Canada [*Library symbol Library of Congress*] (LCLS)

CaOCrSDG ... Stormount, Dundas and Glengarry County Library, Crysler Branch, Crysler, ON, Canada [*Library symbol*] [*Library of Congress*] (LCLS)

CAOCS .... Carrier Aircraft Operational Compatibility System [*Navy*]

CaOCSDG .... Seaway Valley Libraries [*Formerly, Stormont, Dundas, and Glengarry Counties Publi c Library*], Cornwall, ON, Canada [*Library symbol Library of Congress*] (LCLS)

CaOCSL .... Saint Lawrence College, Cornwall, ON, Canada [*Library symbol Library of Congress*] (LCLS)

CaOCTH .... Town of Haldimand Public Libraries, Caledonia, ON, Canada [*Library symbol Library of Congress*] (LCLS)

CAOD .... Coronary Artery Occlusive Disease [*Medicine*] (DMAA)

CaOD .... Dundas Public Library, Dundas, ON, Canada [*Library symbol Library of Congress*] (LCLS)

CAODC .... Canadian Association of Oilwell Drilling Contractors

CaODe .... Delhi Public Library, Delhi, ON, Canada [*Library symbol Library of Congress*] (LCLS)

CaODeAg ...... Canada Department of Agriculture, Research Station, Delhi, ON, Canada [*Library symbol Library of Congress*] (LCLS)

CaODH .... Highland Secondary School, Dundas, ON, Canada [*Library symbol Library of Congress*] (LCLS)

CaODmD ...... Delcan, Don Mills, ON, Canada [*Library symbol*] [*Library of Congress*] (LCLS)

CaODmWS ... Wyda Sysstems Canada Inc., Don Mills, ON, Canada [*Library symbol*] [*Library of Congress*] (LCLS)

CaODO .... Opeongo High School, Douglas, ON, Canada [*Library symbol Library of Congress*] (LCLS)

CaODob .... Dobie Public Library, Dobie, ON, Canada [*Library symbol*] [*Library of Congress*] (LCLS)

CaODr .... Dryden Public Library, Dryden, ON, Canada [*Library symbol Library of Congress*] (LCLS)

CaODu .... Dunnville Public Library, Dunnville, ON, Canada [*Library symbol Library of Congress*] (LCLS)

CaODUN .... Dundalk Public Library, Dundalk, ON, Canada [*Library symbol*] [*Library of Congress*] (LCLS)

CaODur .... Durham Public Library, Durham, ON, Canada [*Library symbol Library of Congress*] (LCLS)

CAOE .... Contractor-Acquired Operational Equipment

CaOE .... Exeter Public Library, Exeter, ON, Canada [*Library symbol Library of Congress*] (LCLS)

CaOEA .... City of Etobicoke Archives, Etobicoke, ON, Canada [*Library symbol*] [*Library of Congress*] (LCLS)

CAO-EC .... Committee of Agricultural Organizations in the European Communities (EAIO)

CaOEf .... Ear Falls Public Library, Ear Falls, ON, Canada [*Library symbol Library of Congress*] (LCLS)

CaOEL .... Elliot Lake Public Library, Elliot Lake, ON, Canada [*Library symbol Library of Congress*] (LCLS)

CaOElk .... Elk Lake Public Library, Elk Lake, ON, Canada [*Library symbol*] [*Library of Congress*] (LCLS)

CaOELS .... Elliot Lake Secondary School, Elliot Lake, ON, Canada [*Library symbol Library of Congress*] (LCLS)

CaOEng .... Englehart Public Library, Englehart, ON, Canada [*Library symbol*] [*Library of Congress*] (LCLS)

CaOENLA ...... Lennox & Addington County Library, Enterprise Branch, Enterprise, ON, Canada [*Library symbol*] [*Library of Congress*] (LCLS)

CaOErD .... Erin District High School, Erin, ON, Canada [*Library symbol*] [*Library of Congress*] (LCLS)

CaOERT .... Russell Township Public Library, Embrun Branch, Embrun, ON, Canada [*Library symbol*] [*Library of Congress*] (LCLS)

CaOEsE .... Essex County Public Library, Essex, ON, Canada [*Library symbol Library of Congress*] (LCLS)

CaOEtHL ...... Hoffman-Laroche Ltd., Etobicoke, ON, Canada [*Library symbol*] [*Library of Congress*] (LCLS)

CAOF .... Catholic Association of Foresters (EA)

CaOFaF .... Falconbridge Nickel Mines Ltd., Metallurgical Research Library, Falconbridge, ON, Canada [*Library symbol Library of Congress*] (LCLS)

CaOFauS ...... Fauquier-Strickland Public Library, Fauquier, ON, Canada [*Library symbol*] [*Library of Congress*] (LCLS)

CaOFeHM ..... Fort Reie Historical Museum, Fort Erie, ON, Canada [*Library symbol*] [*Library of Congress*] (LCLS)

CaOFER .... Fergus Public Library, Fergus, ON, Canada [*Library symbol*] [*Library of Congress*] (LCLS)

CaOFerC ...... Centre Wellington District High School, Fergus, ON, Canada [*Library symbol*] [*Library of Congress*] (LCLS)

CaOFerW ..... Wellington County Public Library, Fergus, ON, Canada [*Library symbol Library of Congress*] (LCLS)

CaOFerWM... Wellington County Museum and Archives, Fergus, ON, Canada [*Library symbol*] [*Library of Congress*] (LCLS)

CaOFF .... Fort Frances Public Library, Fort Frances, ON, Canada [*Library symbol Library of Congress*] (LCLS)

CaOFFM .... Fort Frances Museum and Cultural Centre, Fort Frances, ON, Canada [*Library symbol*] [*Library of Congress*] (LCLS)

CaOFl .... Flesherton Public Library, Flesherton, ON, Canada [*Library symbol Library of Congress*] (LCLS)

CaOFsB .... Fort Severn Band Library, Fort Severn, ON, Canada [*Library symbol*] [*Library of Congress*] (LCLS)

CaOFtaB ...... Fort Albany Band Library, Fort Albany, ON, Canada [*Library symbol*] [*Library of Congress*] (LCLS)

CaOFWN ...... Northwestern Regional Library System, Thunder Bay, ON, Canada [*Library symbol Library of Congress*] (LCLS)

CAOG .... Central Association of Obstetricians and Gynecologists (PDAA)

CAOG .... Crown Agents for Overseas Governments [*British*]

CaOG .... Guelph Public Library, Guelph, ON, Canada [*Library symbol Library of Congress*] (LCLS)

CaOGal .... Cambridge Public Library, Cambridge, ON, Canada [*Library symbol Library of Congress*] (LCLS)

CaOGalC ...... Galt Collegiate Institute, Cambridge, ON, Canada [*Library symbol Library of Congress*] (LCLS)

CaOGB .... Gloucester Public Library, Beriault Branch, Beriault, ON, Canada [*Library symbol*] [*Library of Congress*] (LCLS)

CaOGC .... Centennial Collegiate Vocational Institute, Guelph, ON, Canada [*Library symbol*] [*Library of Congress*] (LCLS)

CaOGCF .... Canada Department of Agriculture, Canadian Farm Management Data System, Guelph, ON, Canada [*Library symbol Library of Congress*] (LCLS)

CaOGCH .... College Heights Secondary School, Guelph, ON, Canada [*Library symbol*] [*Library of Congress*] (LCLS)

CaOGCV .... Guelph Collegiate Vocational Institute, Guelph, ON, Canada [*Library symbol*] [*Library of Congress*] (LCLS)

CaOGDR .... Uniroyal Ltd., Guelph, ON, Canada [*Library symbol Library of Congress*] (LCLS)

CaOGE .... Entomological Society of Ontario, Guelph, ON, Canada [*Library symbol Library of Congress*] (LCLS)

CaOGEDJ ..... Gloucester Public Library, E.D. Jones Branch, Gloucester, ON, Canada [*Library symbol*] [*Library of Congress*] (LCLS)

CaOGeG .... Georgetown District High School, Georgetown, ON, Canada [*Library symbol Library of Congress*] (LCLS)

CaOGEH .... Halton Hills Public Libraries, Georgetown Branch, Georgetown, ON, Canada [*Library symbol*] [*Library of Congress*] (LCLS)

CaOGeo .... Georgetown Public Library, Georgetown, ON, Canada [*Library symbol Library of Congress*] (LCLS)

CaOGeV .... Varian Canada, Inc., Georgetown, ON, Canada [*Library symbol Library of Congress*] (LCLS)

CaOGIAP ...... Canada Department of Indian Affairs and Northern Development, Parks Canada, Ontario Regional Office, Cornwall, ON, Canada [*Library symbol*] [*Library of Congress*] (LCLS)

CaOGIG .... GasTOPS Ltd., Gloucester, ON, Canada [*Library symbol*] [*Library of Congress*] (LCLS)

CaOGJFR ..... John F. Ross Collegiate Vocational Institute, Guelph, ON, Canada [*Library symbol*] [*Library of Congress*] (LCLS)

CaOGmSD.... South Dumfries Township Public Library, Glen Morris Branch, Glen Morris, ON, Canada [*Library symbol*] [*Library of Congress*] (LCLS)

CaOGoH .... Huron County Public Library, Goderich, ON, Canada [*Library symbol Library of Congress*] (LCLS)

CaOGra .... Gravenhurst Public Library, Gravenhurst, ON, Canada [*Library symbol Library of Congress*] (LCLS)

CaOGri .... Grimsby Public Library and Art Gallery, Grimsby, ON, Canada [*Library symbol Library of Congress*] (LCLS)

CaOGriSM.... Stone Shop Museum, Grimsby, ON, Canada [*Library symbol Library of Congress*] (LCLS)

CaOGRV .... Grand Valley Public Library, Grand Valley, ON, Canada [*Library symbol*] [*Library of Congress*] (LCLS)

CaOGU .... University of Guelph, Guelph, ON, Canada [*Library symbol Library of Congress*] (LCLS)

CaOGWE ...... Wellington County Board of Education, Education Library, Guelph, ON, Canada [*Library symbol*] [*Library of Congress*] (LCLS)

CaOH .... Hamilton Public Library, Hamilton, ON, Canada [*Library symbol Library of Congress*] (LCLS)

CaOHAG .... Art Gallery of Hamilton, Hamilton, ON, Canada [*Library symbol Library of Congress*] (LCLS)

CaOHaH .... Haliburton County Public Library, Hastings, ON, Canada [*Library symbol Library of Congress*] (LCLS)

CaOHai .... Haileybury Public Library, Haileybury, ON, Canada [*Library symbol Library of Congress*] (LCLS)

CaOHal .... Haliburton Public Library, Haliburton, ON, Canada [*Library symbol Library of Congress*] (LCLS)

CaOHalM ...... Haliburton Highlands Museum, Haliburton, ON, Canada [*Library symbol*] [*Library of Congress*] (LCLS)

CaOHan .... Hanover Public Library, Hanover, ON, Canada [*Library symbol Library of Congress*] (LCLS)

CaOHarAg .... Canada Department of Agriculture, Research Station, Harrow, ON, Canada [*Library symbol Library of Congress*] (LCLS)

CaOHasN ...... Northumberland County Public Library, Hastings Branch, Hastings, ON, Canada [*Library symbol*] [*Library of Congress*] (LCLS)

CAOHC......... Council for Accreditation in Occupational Hearing Conservation (EA)

CaOHDF .... Dominion Foundries & Steel Ltd., Hamilton, ON, Canada [*Library symbol Library of Congress*] (LCLS)

CaOHDFR .... DOFASCO, Inc., Research Information Center, Hamilton, ON, Canada [*Library symbol*] [*Library of Congress*] (LCLS)

CaOHe .... Hearst Public Library, Hearst, ON, Canada [*Library symbol Library of Congress*] (LCLS)

CaOHEC .... Hamilton Education Centre, Hamilton, ON, Canada [*Library symbol Library of Congress*] (LCLS)

CaOHESC.... Ontario Libraries Service Escarpment, Hamilton, ON, Canada [*Library symbol*] [*Library of Congress*] (LCLS)

CaOHET .... Erin Township Public Library, Hillsburgh, ON, Canada [*Library symbol*] [*Library of Congress*] (LCLS)

CaOHk .... Hawkesbury Public Library, Hawkesbury, ON, Canada [*Library symbol Library of Congress*] (LCLS)

CaOHkC .... International Cellulose Research Ltd., Hawkesbury, ON, Canada [*Library symbol*] [*Library of Congress*] (LCLS)

CaOHIEG ...... East Gwillimbury Public Libraries, Holland Landing, ON, Canada [*Library symbol*] [*Library of Congress*] (LCLS)

CaOHM .... McMaster University, Hamilton, ON, Canada [*Library symbol Library of Congress*] (LCLS)

CaOHMA ...... McMaster University, Archives and Special Collections Division, Hamilton, ON, Canada [*Library symbol Library of Congress*] (LCLS)

CaOHMB ...... McMaster University, Biomedical Library, Hamilton, ON, Canada [*Library symbol*] [*Library of Congress*] (LCLS)

CaOHMC...... Mohawk College of Applied Arts and Technology, Hamilton, ON, Canada [*Library symbol*] [*Library of Congress*] (LCLS)

CaOHMCL.... Mohawk College of Applied Arts and Technology, Library Technician Program, Hamilton, ON, Canada [*Library symbol*] [*Library of Congress*] (LCLS)

CaOHMDBA... McMaster University, McMaster Divinity College, Canadian Baptist Archives, Hamilton, ON, Canada [*Library symbol*] [*Library of Congress*] (LCLS)

CaOHMM ...... McMaster University, Map Library, Hamilton, ON, Canada [*Library symbol Library of Congress*] (LCLS)

CaOHOHS .... Canadian Centre for Occupational Health and Safety, Hamilton, ON, Canada [*Library symbol Library of Congress*] (LCLS)

CaOHRB....... Royal Botanical Gardens, Hamilton, ON, Canada [*Library symbol Library of Congress*] (LCLS)

CaOHS .... Hamilton Spectator, Hamilton, ON, Canada [*Library symbol Library of Congress*] (LCLS)

CaOHSC...... South Central Regional Library, Hamilton, ON, Canada [*Library symbol Library of Congress*] (LCLS)

CaOHSCC.... Steel Co. of Canada, Hamilton, ON, Canada [*Library symbol Library of Congress*] (LCLS)

CaOHTR....... Theological College of the Canadian Reformed Churches, Hamilton, ON, Canada [*Library symbol*] [*Library of Congress*] (LCLS)

CaOHU......... Huntsville Public Library, Huntsville, ON, Canada [*Library symbol Library of Congress*] (LCLS)

CaOHuM ...... Muskoka Pioneer Village, Huntsville, ON, Canada [*Library symbol*] [*Library of Congress*] (LCLS)

CaOHW........ Canadian Westinghouse Library, Hamilton, ON, Canada [*Library symbol Library of Congress*] (LCLS)

CaOHWL...... Wentworth Library, Hamilton, ON, Canada [*Library symbol Library of Congress*] (LCLS)

CaOI............ Ingersoll Public Library, Ingersoll, ON, Canada [*Library symbol Library of Congress*] (LCLS)

CaOIf .... Iroquois Falls Public Library, Iroquois Falls, ON, Canada [*Library symbol Library of Congress*] (LCLS)

CaOIg .... Ignace Public Library, Ignace, ON, Canada [*Library symbol Library of Congress*] (LCLS)

CaOInSDG.... Stormount, Dundas and Glengarry County Library, Ingleside Branch, Ingleside, ON,Canada [*Library symbol*] [*Library of Congress*] (LCLS)

CaOIR .... Iroquois Public Library, Iroquois, ON, Canada [*Library symbol*] [*Library of Congress*] (LCLS)

CaOIsE........ ERCO Industries Ltd., Islington, ON, Canada [*Library symbol Library of Congress*] (LCLS)

CaOIsMSJ... Micropower/St. Joseph's High School, Islington, ON, Canada [*Library symbol*] [*Library of Congress*] (LCLS)

CaOK .... Kingston Public Library, Kingston, ON, Canada [*Library symbol Library of Congress*] (LCLS)

CaOKA .... ALCAN Research & Development Ltd., Kingston, ON, Canada [*Library symbol Library of Congress*] (LCLS)

CaOKAL .... Aluminum Co. of Canada Ltd., Kingston, ON, Canada [*Library symbol Library of Congress*] (LCLS)

CaOKAN .... Kanata Public Library, Kanata, ON, Canada [*Library symbol*] [*Library of Congress*] (LCLS)

CaOKanA ..... Arctec Canada Ltd., Kanata, ON, Canada [*Library symbol Library of Congress*] (LCLS)

CaOKanLU ... Lumonics, Inc., Kanata, ON, Canada [*Library symbol*] [*Library of Congress*] (LCLS)

CaOKanM .... Mitel Corp., Kanata, ON, Canada [*Library symbol*] [*Library of Congress*] (LCLS)

CaOKanMC... Miller Communications Systems Ltd., Kanata, ON, Canada [*Library symbol Library of Congress*] (LCLS)

CaOKanMD... Mitel Corp., Digital Systems, Kanata, ON, Canada [*Library symbol Library of Congress*] (LCLS)

CaOKanNC ... Newbridge Communication Neywork Corp., Kanata, ON, Canada [*Library symbol*] [*Library of Congress*] (LCLS)

CaOKAOS ..... Anglican Church of Canada, Diocese of Ontario, Synod Office, Kingston, ON, Canada [*Library symbol Library of Congress*] (LCLS)

CaOKap........ Kapuskasing Public Library, Kapuskasing, ON, Canada [*Library symbol Library of Congress*] (LCLS)

CaOKap........ Kapuskasing Public Library, Kapuskasing, ON, Canada [*Library symbol*] [*Library of Congress*] (LCLS)

CaOKasB ..... Kashechewan Band Library, Kashechewan, ON, Canada [*Library symbol*] [*Library of Congress*] (LCLS)

CaOKASG ..... Anglican Church of Canada, St. George's Cathedral, Kingston, ON, Canada [*Library symbol Library of Congress*] (LCLS)

CaOKCAA ..... Catholic Church, Archdiocese of Kingston, Archives, Kingston, ON, Canada [*Library symbol Library of Congress*] (LCLS)

CaOKCIL ...... Millhaven Fibers Ltd., Kingston, ON, Canada [*Library symbol Library of Congress*] (LCLS)

CaOKcKT..... King Township Public Library, King City, ON, Canada [*Library symbol Library of Congress*] (LCLS)

CaOKD .... Du Pont of Canada Ltd., Research Centre Library, Kingston, ON, Canada [*Library symbol Library of Congress*] (LCLS)

CaOKe .... Kenora Public Library, Kenora, ON, Canada [*Library symbol Library of Congress*] (LCLS)

CaOKeAKS ... Anglican Church of Canada, Diocese of Keewatin, Synod Office, Kenora, ON, Canada [*Library symbol Library of Congress*] (LCLS)

CaOKemAF... Ontario Ministry of Agriculture and Food, Kemptville, ON, Canada [*Library symbol Library of Congress*] (LCLS)

CaOKes........ Georgina Township Public Library, Keswick, ON, Canada [*Library symbol Library of Congress*] (LCLS)

CaOKF .... Canadian Land Forces Command and Staff College, Kingston, ON, Canada [*Library symbol Library of Congress*] (LCLS)

CaOKFC .... Frontenac County Library, Kingston, ON, Canada [*Library symbol Library of Congress*] (LCLS)

CaOKFCSM... Frontenac County Schools Museum Association, ON, Canada [*Library symbol*] [*Library of Congress*] (LCLS)

CaOKHD....... Hotel Dieu Hospital, Kingston, ON, Canada [*Library symbol*] [*Library of Congress*] (LCLS)

CaOKit .... Kitchener Public Library, Kitchener, ON, Canada [*Library symbol Library of Congress*] (LCLS)

CaOKITC ...... Conestoga College of Applied Arts & Technology, Learning Resource Centre, Kitchener, ON, Canada [*Library symbol*] [*Library of Congress*] (LCLS)

CaOKitM ...... Midwestern Regional Library, Kitchener, ON, Canada [*Library symbol Library of Congress*] (LCLS)

CaOKitW ...... Kitchener-Waterloo Record, Kitchener, ON, Canada [*Library symbol Library of Congress*] (LCLS)

CaOKitWC.... Waterloo County Board of Education, Kitchener, ON, Canada [*Library symbol*] [*Library of Congress*] (LCLS)

CaOKitXS..... Xenotech Systems, Inc., Kitchener, ON, Canada [*Library symbol*] [*Library of Congress*] (LCLS)

CaOKL .... Lake Ontario Regional Library System, Kingston, ON, Canada [*Library symbol Library of Congress*] (LCLS)

CaOKleM ..... McMichael Canadian Collection, Kleinburg, ON, Canada [*Library symbol Library of Congress*] (LCLS)

CaOKIN........ Northeastern Regional Library, Kirkland Lake, ON, Canada [*Library symbol Library of Congress*] (LCLS)

CaOKINC...... Northern College, Kirkland Lake Campus, Kirkland Lake, ON, Canada [*Library symbol Library of Congress*] (LCLS)

CaOKIT .... Teck Centennial Public Library, Kirkland Lake, ON, Canada [*Library symbol Library of Congress*] (LCLS)

CaOKME ...... Metro Canada Ltd., Kingston, ON, Canada [*Library symbol*] [*Library of Congress*] (LCLS)

CaOKMM ..... Marine Museum of the Great Lakes at Kingston, Kingston, ON, Canada [*Library symbol Library of Congress*] (LCLS)

CaOKOH....... Ongwanada Hospital, Penrose Division, Kingston, ON, Canada [*Library symbol*] [*Library of Congress*] (LCLS)

CaOKQ......... Queen's University, Kingston, ON, Canada [*Library symbol Library of Congress*] (LCLS)

CaOKQA....... Queen's University, Agnes Ethrington Art Centre, Kingston, ON, Canada [*Library symbol Library of Congress*] (LCLS)

CaOKQAR..... Queen's University, Archives, Kingston, ON, Canada [*Library symbol Library of Congress*] (LCLS)

CaOKQCI...... Queen's University, Canadian Institute of Guided Ground Transport, Kingston, ON,Canada [*Library symbol*] [*Library of Congress*] (LCLS)

CaOKQG...... Queen's University, Department of Geography, Kingston, ON, Canada [*Library symbol Library of Congress*] (LCLS)

CaOKQGS..... Queen's University, Department of Geological Sciences, Kingston, ON, Canada [*Library symbol Library of Congress*] (LCLS)

CaOKQH....... Queen's University, Health Sciences Library, Kingston, ON, Canada [*Library symbol Library of Congress*] (LCLS)

CaOKQL....... Queen's University, Law Library, Kingston, ON, Canada [*Library symbol Library of Congress*] (LCLS)

CaOKQM....... Queen's University, McArthur College of Education, Kingston, ON, Canada [*Library symbol Library of Congress*] (LCLS)

CaOKQMA..... Queen's University, Douglas Library, Map Collection, Kingston, ON, Canada [*Library symbol Library of Congress*] (LCLS)

CaOKR .... Royal Military College, Kingston, ON, Canada [*Library symbol Library of Congress*] (LCLS)

CaOKRC....... Regiopolis College, Kingston, ON, Canada [*Library symbol Library of Congress*] (LCLS)

CaOKRS....... Royal Military College of Canada, Science Engineering Library, Kingston, ON, Canada [*Library symbol*] [*Library of Congress*] (LCLS)

CaOKSL .... Saint Lawrence College of Applied Arts and Technology, Kingston, ON, Canada [*Library symbol Library of Congress*] (LCLS)

CaOKUTD..... Urban Transportation Development Corp., Kingston, ON, Canada [*Library symbol Library of Congress*] (LCLS)

CaOL............ London Public Library and Art Museum, London, ON, Canada [*Library symbol Library of Congress*] (LCLS)

CaOLAg........ Canada Department of Agriculture, Research Institute, London, ON, Canada [*Library symbol Library of Congress*] (LCLS)

CaOLAL........ Alfred Township Public Library, Bibliotheque Publique du Canton d'Alfred, Lefaivre, ON, Canada [*Library symbol*] [*Library of Congress*] (LCLS)

CaOLaTN ...... Township of Norfolk Public Library, Langston, ON, Canada [*Library symbol Library of Congress*] (LCLS)

CaOLB .... London Board of Education, London, ON, Canada [*Library symbol Library of Congress*] (LCLS)

CaOLBR .... Brescia College, London, ON, Canada [*Library symbol*] [*Library of Congress*] (LCLS)

CaOLC .... Catholic Central High School, London, ON, Canada [*Library symbol Library of Congress*] (LCLS)

CaOLCC .... Ontario Cancer Clinic, London, ON, Canada [*Library symbol*] [*Library of Congress*] (LCLS)

CaOLCR .... Clark Road Secondary School, London, ON, Canada [*Library symbol Library of Congress*] (LCLS)

CaOLCSSCP... Ontario Ministry of Community and Social Services, Children's Psychiatric Research Institute, London, ON, Canada [*Library symbol Library of Congress*] (LCLS)

CaOLel........ Canada Department of Indian Affairs and Northern Development, Point Pelee National Park, Leamington, ON, Canada [*Library symbol Library of Congress*] (LCLS)

CaOLFC........ Fanshawe College of Applied Arts and Technology, London, ON, Canada [*Library symbol Library of Congress*] (LCLS)

CaOLfSCG .... Latchford Senior Citizens Group, Latchford, ON, Canada [*Library symbol*] [*Library of Congress*] (LCLS)

CaOLgCV ..... Century Village, Lang, ON, Canada [*Library symbol*] [*Library of Congress*] (LCLS)

CaOLH .... Huron College, London, ON, Canada [*Library symbol Library of Congress*] (LCLS)

CaOLHM ...... London Historical Museums, London, ON, Canada [*Library symbol*] [*Library of Congress*] (LCLS)

CaOLi........... Lindsay Public Library, Lindsay, ON, Canada [*Library symbol Library of Congress*] (LCLS)

CaOLiRM .... Ross Memorial Hospital, Medical Library, Lindsay, ON, Canada [*Library symbol*] [*Library of Congress*] (LCLS)

CaOLIS .... Listowel Public Library, Listowel, ON, Canada [*Library symbol*] [*Library of Congress*] (LCLS)

CaOLiSF ...... Sir Sandford Fleming College, Frost Campus, Lindsay, ON, Canada [*Library symbol*] [*Library of Congress*] (LCLS)

CaOLiV .... Victoria County Public Library, Lindsay, ON, Canada [*Library symbol Library of Congress*] (LCLS)

CaOLivW...... Walden Public Library, Liverly, ON, Canada [*Library symbol*] [*Library of Congress*] (LCLS)

CaOLK .... King's College, London, ON, Canada [*Library symbol Library of Congress*] (LCLS)

CaOLLCR ..... Labatt's Central Research Library, London, ON, Canada [*Library symbol Library of Congress*] (LCLS)

CaOLLE........ Lake Erie Regional Library, London, ON, Canada [*Library symbol Library of Congress*] (LCLS)

CaOLOS .... Oakridge Secondary School, London, ON, Canada [*Library symbol Library of Congress*] (LCLS)

CaOLPT........ Pinchas Troester Library, Congregation B'nai Israel, London, ON, Canada [*Library symbol Library of Congress*] (LCLS)

CaOLRAG ..... London Regional Art Gallery, London, ON, Canada [*Library symbol*] [*Library of Congress*] (LCLS)

CaOLS .... Sparton of Canada Ltd., London, ON, Canada [*Library symbol*] [*Library of Congress*] (LCLS)

CaOLSDG..... Stormount, Dundas & Glengarry County Library, Lancaster Branch, Lancaster, ON, Canada [*Library symbol*] [*Library of Congress*] (LCLS)

CaOLSJ........ Saint Joseph's Hospital, London, ON, Canada [*Library symbol Library of Congress*] (LCLS)

CaOLSP....... Saint Peter's Seminary, London, ON, Canada [*Library symbol*] [*Library of Congress*] (LCLS)

CaOLT.......... United Lodge of Theosophists, London, ON, Canada [*Library symbol Library of Congress*] (LCLS)

CaOLTMC .... Three M Canada, Inc., Technical Information Centre, London, ON, Canada [*Library symbol Library of Congress*] (LCLS)

CaOLU .... University of Western Ontario, London, ON, Canada [*Library symbol Library of Congress*] (LCLS)

CaOLUE ...... University of Western Ontario, Engineering Library, London, ON, Canada [*Library symbol*] [*Library of Congress*] (LCLS)

CaOLUG....... University of Western Ontario, Department of Geography, London, ON, Canada [*Library symbol Library of Congress*] (LCLS)

CaOLUH...... University Hospital, London, ON, Canada [*Library symbol Library of Congress*] (LCLS)

CaOLUL ...... University of Western Ontario, Law Library, London, ON, Canada [*Library symbol Library of Congress*] (LCLS)

CaOLUM ..... University of Western Ontario, Health Science Centre, London, ON, Canada [*Library symbol Library of Congress*] (LCLS)

CaOLUMG ... University of Western Ontario, MacIntosh Gallery, London, ON, Canada [*Library symbol Library of Congress*] (LCLS)

CaOLURC..... London Urban Resource Centre, London, ON, Canada [*Library symbol Library of Congress*] (LCLS)

CaOLUS .... University of Western Ontario, School of Library and Information Science, London, ON, Canada [*Library symbol Library of Congress*] (LCLS)

CaOLUVA .... University of Western Ontario, Visual Arts Department, London, ON, Canada [*Library symbol Library of Congress*] (LCLS)

CaOLVH .... Victoria Hospital, London, ON, Canada [*Library symbol Library of Congress*] (LCLS)

CaOM........... Mississauga Public Library, Mississauga, ON, Canada [*Library symbol Library of Congress*] (LCLS)

CaOMa......... Markham Public Library, Markham, ON, Canada [*Library symbol Library of Congress*] (LCLS)

CaOMABP ... Abitibi-Price, Inc., Mississauga, ON, Canada [*Library symbol Library of Congress*] (LCLS)

CaOMAC ...... Alkaril Chemicals Ltd., Mississauga, ON, Canada [*Library symbol Library of Congress*] (LCLS)

CaOMAECL... AECL International, Mississauga, ON, Canada [*Library symbol Library of Congress*] (LCLS)

CAOMAF ...... Command Analysis of Office of Military Assistance Funding (MCD)

CaOMaGL .... Gartner Lee Associates Ltd., Markham, ON, Canada [*Library symbol*] [*Library of Congress*] (LCLS)

CaOMaH ...... Markham High School, Markham, ON, Canada [*Library symbol Library of Congress*] (LCLS)

CaOMaHM .. Markham District Historical Museum, Markham, ON, Canada [*Library symbol*] [*Library of Congress*] (LCLS)

CaOMAI .... Allelix, Inc., Mississauga, ON, Canada [*Library symbol Library of Congress*] (LCLS)

CaOMan....... Manitouwadge Public Library, Manitouwadge, ON, Canada [*Library symbol*] [*Library of Congress*] (LCLS)

CaOMap....... Vaughan Public Library, Maple, ON, Canada [*Library symbol Library of Congress*] (LCLS)

CaOMat........ Matheson Public Library, Matheson, ON, Canada [*Library symbol Library of Congress*] (LCLS)

CaOMBC ..... Beak Consultants, Mississauga, ON, Canada [*Library symbol Library of Congress*] (LCLS)

CaOMCCS .... Centraide, Montreal, PQ, Canada [*Library symbol Library of Congress*] (LCLS)

CaOMCG ...... Ciba/Geigy Canada Ltd., Mississauga, ON, Canada [*Library symbol Library of Congress*] (LCLS)

CaOMCSG .... Canada Systems Group, Mississauga, ON, Canada [*Library symbol Library of Congress*] (LCLS)

CaOMD .... Du Pont of Canada Ltd., Maitland, ON, Canada [*Library symbol Library of Congress*] (LCLS)

CaOMDCPL... Du Pont Canada, Inc., Patent and Legal Library, Mississauga, ON, Canada [*Library symbol*] [*Library of Congress*] (LCLS)

CaOMDG...... Dominion Glass Co. Ltd., Mississauga, ON, Canada [*Library symbol Library of Congress*] (LCLS)

CaOMDO...... Domglas, Inc., Corporate Library, Mississauga, ON, Canada [*Library symbol Library of Congress*] (LCLS)

CaOMDR...... Dunlop Research Centre, Sheridan Park, Mississauga, ON, Canada [*Library symbol Library of Congress*] (LCLS)

CaOMDS ..... Delphax Systems, Mississauga, ON, Canada [*Library symbol Library of Congress*] (LCLS)

CaOME........ University of Toronto, Erindale College, Mississauga, ON, Canada [*Library symbol Library of Congress*] (LCLS)

CaOMfD .... Mount Forest District High School, Mount Forest, ON, Canada [*Library symbol*] [*Library of Congress*] (LCLS)

CaOMGA...... Golder Associates, Mississauga, ON, Canada [*Library symbol*] [*Library of Congress*] (LCLS)

CaOMGO...... Gulf Oil Canada Ltd., Mississauga, ON, Canada [*Library symbol Library of Congress*] (LCLS)

CaOMi .... Midland Public Library, Midland, ON, Canada [*Library symbol Library of Congress*] (LCLS)

CaOMiH .... Huronia Historical Park, Midland, ON, Canada [*Library symbol Library of Congress*] (LCLS)

CaOMIHS..... Institute for Hydrogen Systems, Mississauga, ON, Canada [*Library symbol*] [*Library of Congress*] (LCLS)

CaOMil .... Milton Central Library, Milton, ON, Canada [*Library symbol Library of Congress*] (LCLS)

CaOMILV ..... Milverton Public Library, Milverton, ON, Canada [*Library symbol*] [*Library of Congress*] (LCLS)

CaOMIN ...... International Nickel Co. of Canada, Mississauga, ON, Canada [*Library symbol Library of Congress*] (LCLS)

CaOMinSA ... Simcoe County Archives, Minesing, ON, Canada [*Library symbol Library of Congress*] (LCLS)

CaOMIT........ Mitchell Public Library, Mitchell, ON, Canada [*Library symbol*] [*Library of Congress*] (LCLS)

CaOMJAT..... H.J.A. Brown Education Centre, J. A. Turner Professional Library, Mississauga, ON, Canada [*Library symbol*] [*Library of Congress*] (LCLS)

CaOMLT...... [*The*] Learning Tree, Mississauga, ON, Canada [*Library symbol*] [*Library of Congress*] (LCLS)

CaOMNT ..... Northern Telecom, Mississauga, ON, Canada [*Library symbol Library of Congress*] (LCLS)

CaOMorUC... Upper Canada Village, Morrisburg, ON, Canada [*Library symbol Library of Congress*] (LCLS)

CaOMPW..... Pratt & Whitney Aircraft Ltd., Mississauga, ON, Canada [*Library symbol Library of Congress*] (LCLS)

CaOMSK...... Smith, Kline & French Canada Ltd., Niagara Falls, ON, Canada [*Library symbol Library of Congress*] (LCLS)

CaOMSM .... Syntex, Inc., Medical Library, Mississauga, ON, Canada [*Library symbol Library of Congress*] (LCLS)

CaOMuCR ... Chippewa Resource Center, Muncey, ON, Canada [*Library symbol*] [*Library of Congress*] (LCLS)

CaONaLAC ... Lennox and Addington Counties Public Libraries, Napanee, ON, Canada [*Library symbol Library of Congress*] (LCLS)

CaONaLAM... Lennox and Addington Museum, Napanee, ON, Canada [*Library symbol Library of Congress*] (LCLS)

CaONB .... North Bay Public Library, North Bay, ON, Canada [*Library symbol Library of Congress*] (LCLS)

CaONbNU .... Nipissing University College, North Bay, ON, Canada [*Library symbol Library of Congress*] (LCLS)

CaONBWF ... West Ferris Secondary School, North Bay, ON, Canada [*Library symbol Library of Congress*] (LCLS)

CaONCB....... Nepean Public Library, Centennial Branch, Centennial, ON, Canada [*Library symbol*] [*Library of Congress*] (LCLS)

CaONCU...... Cumberland Township Library, Navan, ON, Canada [*Library symbol*] [*Library of Congress*] (LCLS)

CaONe .... Newmarket Public Library, Newmarket, ON, Canada [*Library symbol Library of Congress*] (LCLS)

CaONeP .... Pickering College, Newmarket, ON, Canada [*Library symbol*] [*Library of Congress*] (LCLS)

CaONEU....... Neustadt Village Public Library, Neustadt, ON, Canada [*Library symbol*] [*Library of Congress*] (LCLS)

CaONf .... Niagara Falls Public Library, Niagara Falls, ON, Canada [*Library symbol Library of Congress*] (LCLS)

CaONfA........ Acres Consulting Services Ltd., Niagara Falls, ON, Canada [*Library symbol Library of Congress*] (LCLS)

CaONfCy ..... Cyanamid, Niagara Falls, ON, Canada [*Library symbol Library of Congress*] (LCLS)

CaONfLC...... Lanmer Consultants Ltd., Niagara Falls, ON, Canada [*Library symbol Library of Congress*] (LCLS)

CaONfWPL... W. P. London & Associates, Niagara Falls, ON, Canada [*Library symbol Library of Congress*] (LCLS)

CaONHi........ Niagara Historical Society, Niagara-On-The-Lake, ON, Canada [*Library symbol Library of Congress*] (LCLS)

CaONl .... New Liskeard Public Library, New Liskeard, ON, Canada [*Library symbol Library of Congress*] (LCLS)

CaONoDA.... Norwich nd District Archives, Norwich, ON, Canada [*Library symbol*] [*Library of Congress*] (LCLS)

CaONOL....... Niagara-on-the-Lake Public Library, Niagara-on-the-Lake, ON, Canada [*Library symbol*] [*Library of Congress*] (LCLS)

CaONpEMRCM... Energy, Mines, and Resources Canada, CANMET, BCC Library, Nepean, ON, Canada [*Library symbol*] [*Library of Congress*] (LCLS)

CaONRDB ... Nepean Public Library, Ruth E. Dickinson Branch, Nepean, ON, Canada [*Library symbol*] [*Library of Congress*] (LCLS)

CaONSM ..... St. Mark's Church, Niagara-On-The-Lake, ON, Canada [*Library symbol Library of Congress*] (LCLS)

CaOOA......... Public Archives of Canada, Ottawa, ON, Canada [*Library symbol Library of Congress*] (LCLS)

CaOOAC....... Algonquin College, Ottawa, ON, Canada [*Library symbol Library of Congress*] (LCLS)

CaOOACC.... Algonquin College, Colonel By Campus, Ottawa, ON, Canada [*Library symbol*] [*Library of Congress*] (LCLS)

CaOOACF..... Ontario Cancer Foundation, Alta Vista Branch, Ottawa, ON, Canada [*Library symbol Library of Congress*] (LCLS)

CaOOACH ... Algonquin College of Applied Arts and Technology, Heron Park Campus, Ottawa, ON,Canada [*Library symbol*] [*Library of Congress*] (LCLS)

CaOOACL.... Algonquin College of Applied Arts and Technology, Library Technician Program, Ottawa, ON, Canada [*Library symbol*] [*Library of Congress*] (LCLS)

CaOOACR ... Algonquin College, Rideau Campus, Ottawa, ON, Canada [*Library symbol Library of Congress*] (LCLS)

CaOOAD....... Archives Deschatelets [*Oblates de Marie-Immaculee*], Ottawa, ON, Canad a [*Library symbol*] [*Library of Congress*] (LCLS)

CaOOAE ...... Atomic Energy of Canada, Ottawa, ON, Canada [*Library symbol Library of Congress*] (LCLS)

CaOOAEA..... Public Archives, Ethnic Archives of Canada, Ottawa, ON, Canada [*Library symbol Library of Congress*] (LCLS)

CaOOAEC..... Atomic Energy of Canada Chemical Co., Ottawa, ON, Canada [*Library symbol Library of Congress*] (LCLS)

CaOOAECB... Atomic Energy Control Board, Ottawa, ON, Canada [*Library symbol Library of Congress*] (LCLS)

CaOOAER..... Atomic Energy of Canada Ltd., Research Co., Ottawa, ON, Canada [*Library symbol Library of Congress*] (LCLS)

CaOOAF....... Bibliotheque de l'Ambassade de France, Ottawa, ON, Canada [*Library symbol*] [*Library of Congress*] (LCLS)

CaOOAg....... Canada Department of Agriculture, Ottawa, ON, Canada [*Library symbol Library of Congress*] (LCLS)

CaOOAgA..... Department of Agriculture, Animal Disease Research Institute, Ottawa, ON, Cana da [*Library symbol Library of Congress*] (LCLS)

CaOOAgAR... Department of Agriculture, Animal Research Institute, Ottawa, ON, Canada [*Library symbol Library of Congress*] (LCLS)

CaOOAgB..... Department of Agriculture, Plant Research Institute, Ottawa, ON, Canada [*Library symbol Library of Congress*] (LCLS)

CaOOAgC..... Department of Agriculture, Central Experimental Farm Reference Library, Ottawa, ON, Canada [*Library symbol Library of Congress Obsolete*] (LCLS)

CaOOAgCh... Department of Agriculture, Chemistry Division, Ottawa, ON, Canada [*Library symbol Library of Congress Obsolete*] (LCLS)

CaOOAGCH... Department of Agriculture, Neatby Library, Ottawa, ON, Canada [*Library symbol Library of Congress*] (LCLS)

CaOOAgE..... Department of Agriculture, Entomology Research Institute, Ottawa, ON, Can ada [*Library symbol Library of Congress*] (LCLS)

CaOOAgER... Department of Agriculture, Engineering Research Service, Ottawa, ON, Canada [*Library symbol Library of Congress*] (LCLS)

CaOOAgFP... Department of Agriculture, Food Production and Marketing Branch, Laboratory Services Section, Ottawa, ON, Canada [*Library symbol Library of Congress*] (LCLS)

CaOOAgH..... Department of Agriculture, Horticultural Division, Ottawa, ON, Canada [*Library symbol Library of Congress Obsolete*] (LCLS)

CaOOAgL..... Department of Agriculture, Legal Library, Ottawa, ON, Canada [*Library symbol Library of Congress Obsolete*] (LCLS)

CaOOAgO..... Department of Agriculture, Research Station, Ottawa, ON, Canada [*Library symbol Library of Congress*] (LCLS)

CaOOAgSR... Department of Agriculture, Soil Research Institute, Ottawa, ON, Canada [*Library symbol Library of Congress*] (LCLS)

CaOOAI....... AMCA International Ltd., Ottawa, ON, Canada [*Library symbol Library of Congress*] (LCLS)

CaOOak....... Oakville Public Library, Oakville, ON, Canada [*Library symbol Library of Congress*] (LCLS)

CaOOakA..... Appleby College, Oakville, ON, Canada [*Library symbol Library of Congress*] (LCLS)

CaOOakSC .. Sheridan College, Oakville, ON, Canada [*Library symbol Library of Congress*] (LCLS)

CaOOAM...... Canada Department of National Defence, Ottawa, ON, Canada [*Library symbol Library of Congress Obsolete*] (LCLS)

CaOOAMA.... Public Archives of Canada, National Map Collection, Ottawa, ON, Canada [*Library symbol Library of Congress*] (LCLS)

CaOOAMS.... Public Archives, Manuscript Division, Ottawa, ON, Canada [*Library symbol Library of Congress*] (LCLS)

CaOOANF..... Public Archives, National Film Archives, Ottawa, ON, Canada [*Library symbol Library of Congress*] (LCLS)

CaOOAOA ... Anglican Church of Canada, Diocese of Ottawa, Archives, Ottawa, ON, Canada [*Library symbol Library of Congress*] (LCLS)

CaOOAR....... Canadian Broadcasting Corp., Ottawa, ON, Canada [*Library symbol Library of Congress*] (LCLS)

CaOOASH .... Ashbury College, Ottawa, ON, Canada [*Library symbol*] [*Library of Congress*] (LCLS)

CaOOAT....... Canadian Transport Commission, Air Transport Committee, Ottawa, ON, Canada [*Library symbol Library of Congress Obsolete*] (LCLS)

CaOOB .... Bank of Canada, Ottawa, ON, Canada [*Library symbol Library of Congress*] (LCLS)

CaOOBC....... Bowmar Canada Ltd., Ottawa, ON, Canada [*Library symbol Library of Congress*] (LCLS)

CaOOBDR .... Bell Canada Data Resource Center, Ottawa, ON, Canada [*Library symbol Library of Congress*] (LCLS)

CaOOBE....... Ottawa Board of Education, Ottawa, ON, Canada [*Library symbol Library of Congress*] (LCLS)

CaOOBM...... Bartonian Metaphysical Society, Ottawa, ON, Canada [*Library symbol Library of Congress*] (LCLS)

CaOOBMC.... Canada Department of Supply and Services, Bureau of Management and Consulting, Ottawa, ON, Canada [*Library symbol Library of Congress*] (LCLS)

CaOOBMI..... Bell Canada Market Information Centre, Ottawa, ON, Canada [*Library symbol*] [*Library of Congress*] (LCLS)

CaOOC .... Ottawa Public Library, Ottawa, ON, Canada [*Library symbol Library of Congress*] (LCLS)

CaOOCAC..... Canada Art Council, Ottawa, ON, Canada [*Library symbol Library of Congress*] (LCLS)

CaOOCACSW... Canadian Advisory Council on the Status of Women, Documentation Centre, Ottawa, ON, Canada [*Library symbol*] [*Library of Congress*] (LCLS)

CaOOCANM... Canadian Museum Association, Ottawa, ON, Canada [*Library symbol*] [*Library of Congress*] (LCLS)

CaOOCAP..... Canadian Periodical Reference Services, Ottawa, ON, Canada [*Library symbol Library of Congress Obsolete*] (LCLS)

CaOOCAR .... Canadian Arctic Resources Committee, Ottawa, ON, Canada [*Library symbol Library of Congress*] (LCLS)

CaOOCAS.... Children's Aid Society, Ottawa, ON, Canada [*Library symbol*] [*Library of Congress*] (LCLS)

CaOOCB....... Colonel By Secondary School, Ottawa, ON, Canada [*Library symbol Library of Congress*] (LCLS)

CaOOCBC..... Conference Board in Canada, Ottawa, ON, Canada [*Library symbol Library of Congress*] (LCLS)

CaOOCBE..... Carleton Board of Education, Ottawa, ON, Canada [*Library symbol Library of Congress*] (LCLS)

CaOOCC ...... Carleton University, Ottawa, ON, Canada [*Library symbol Library of Congress*] (LCLS)

CaOOCCAH... Carleton University, Department of Art History, Ottawa, ON, Canada [*Library symbol Library of Congress*] (LCLS)

CaOOCCFA... Canadian Centre for Films on Art, Ottawa, ON, Canada [*Library symbol Library of Congress*] (LCLS)

CaOOCCG .... Carleton University, Geography Department, Ottawa, ON, Canada [*Library symbol Library of Congress*] (LCLS)

CaOOCCR .... Canada Department of Energy, Mines, and Resources, Canada Centre for Remote Sensing, Ottawa, ON, Canada [*Library symbol Library of Congress*] (LCLS)

CaOOCCSS... Carleton University, Social Sciences Division, Ottawa, ON, Canada [*Library symbol Library of Congress Obsolete*] (LCLS)

CaOOCD....... Canadian International Development Agency, Ottawa, ON, Canada [*Library symbol Library of Congress*] (LCLS)

CaOOCDA .... Canadian Dental Association, Ottawa, ON, Canada [*Library symbol Library of Congress*] (LCLS)

CaOOCDC .... Computing Devices of Canada, Ottawa, ON, Canada [*Library symbol Library of Congress*] (LCLS)

CaOOCDP .... College Dominicain de Philosophie et de Theologie, Ottawa, ON, Canada [*Library symbol Library of Congress*] (LCLS)

CaOOCES .... Combustion Engineering Superheater Ltd., Ottawa, ON, Canada [*Library symbol*] [*Library of Congress*] (LCLS)

CaOOCF .... Canadian Film Institute, Ottawa, ON, Canada [*Library symbol Library of Congress*] (LCLS)

CaOOCH....... Children's Hospital, Ottawa, ON, Canada [*Library symbol Library of Congress*] (LCLS)

CaOOCHR .... Canadian Human Rights Commission, Ottawa, ON, Canada [*Library symbol Library of Congress*] (LCLS)

CaOOCI....... Canada Department of Consumer and Corporate Affairs, Ottawa, ON, Canada [*Library symbol Library of Congress*] (LCLS)

CaOOCIHM... Canadian Institute for Historical Microreproductions, Ottawa, ON, Canada [*Library symbol*] [*Library of Congress*] (LCLS)

CaOOCLA .... Canadian Library Association, Ottawa, ON, Canada [*Library symbol*] [*Library of Congress*] (LCLS)

CaOOCLC .... Canadian Labour Congress, Ottawa, ON, Canada [*Library symbol Library of Congress*] (LCLS)

CaOOCM...... Central Mortgage & Housing Corp., Ottawa, ON, Canada [*Library symbol Library of Congress*] (LCLS)

CaOOCMA ... Canadian Medical Association, Ottawa, ON, Canada [*Library symbol Library of Congress*] (LCLS)

CaOOCMC.... Central Mortgage & Housing Corp., Children's Environments Advisory Service, Ottawa, ON, Canada [*Library symbol Library of Congress*] (LCLS)

CaOOCMS.... Central Mortgage & Housing Corp., Standards Information Centre, Ottawa, ON, Canada [*Library symbol Library of Congress*] (LCLS)

CaOOCN...... Canadian Nurses' Association, Ottawa, ON, Canada [*Library symbol Library of Congress*] (LCLS)

CaOOCNP .... Energy, Mines, and Resources Canada, CNP Resource Centre, Ottawa, ON, Canada [*Library symbol Library of Congress*] (LCLS)

CaOOCO....... Canada Department of Communications, Ottawa, ON, Canada [*Library symbol Library of Congress*] (LCLS)

CaOOCOG .... COGLA [*Canada Oil and Gas Lands Administration*] Ocean Mining Resource Centre, APGTC , Ottawa, ON, Canada [*Administration du Petrole et du Gaz des Terres du Canada*] [*Library symbol Library of Congress*] (LCLS)

CaOOCOL..... Commissioner of Official Languages, Ottawa, ON, Canada [*Library symbol Library of Congress*] (LCLS)

CaOOCP....... Community Planning Association of Canada, Ottawa, ON, Canada [*Library symbol Library of Congress*] (LCLS)

CaOOCPC .... Canadian Police College, Royal Canadian Mounted Police, Ottawa, ON, Canada [*Library symbol Library of Congress*] (LCLS)

CaOOCRC .... Canadian Red Cross Society, Ottawa, ON, Canada [*Library symbol Library of Congress*] (LCLS)

CaOOCRI...... Canadian Research Institute for the Advancement of Women, Ottawa, ON, Canada [*Library symbol*] [*Library of Congress*] (LCLS)

CaOOCRLF... Canadian Rights and Liberties Federation, Ottawa, ON, Canada [*Library symbol Library of Congress*] (LCLS)

CaOOCRM.... Canadian Royal Mint, Ottawa, ON, Canada [*Library symbol Library of Congress*] (LCLS)

CaOOCS....... Public Service Commission, Ottawa, ON, Canada [*Library symbol Library of Congress*] (LCLS)

CaOOCSC..... Canada Safety Council, Ottawa, ON, Canada [*Library symbol*] [*Library of Congress*] (LCLS)

CaOOCSL..... Public Service Commission, Training Centres Libraries, Ottawa, ON, Canada [*Library symbol Library of Congress*] (LCLS)

CaOOCT .... Canadian Teachers Federation, Ottawa, ON, Canada [*Library symbol Library of Congress*] (LCLS)

CaOOCU....... Association of Universities and Colleges of Canada, Ottawa, ON, Canada [*Library symbol Library of Congress*] (LCLS)

CaOOCUI...... Canadian Unity Information Centre, Ottawa, ON, Canada [*Library symbol Library of Congress*] (LCLS)

CaOOCUS .... Canadian University Service Overseas, Ottawa, ON, Canada [*Library symbol Library of Congress*] (LCLS)

CaOOCW...... Canadian Council on Social Development, Ottawa, ON, Canada [*Library symbol Library of Congress*] (LCLS)

CaOOCWC.... Canadian Wood Council, Ottawa, ON, Canada [*Library symbol*] [*Library of Congress*] (LCLS)

CaOOCz........ Ottawa Citizen, Ottawa, ON, Canada [*Library symbol Library of Congress*] (LCLS)

CaOODCH .... DCH Consultants, Inc., Ottawa, ON, Canada [*Library symbol*] [*Library of Congress*] (LCLS)

CaOODLAC... Lennox & Addington County Library, Odessa Branch, Odessa, ON, Canada [*Library symbol*] [*Library of Congress*] (LCLS)

CaOODLC .... Data Logic Canada, Library Education Services, Ottawa, ON, Canada [*Library symbol Library of Congress*] (LCLS)

CaOODP....... Canada Department of Supply and Services, Ottawa, ON, Canada [*Library symbol Library of Congress*] (LCLS)

CaOODPS ... Canada Department of Supply and Services, Compensation Branch, Superannuation Division, Ottawa, ON, Canada [*Library symbol Library of Congress*] (LCLS)

CaOODRC .... Canada Department of National Defence, Defence Research Establishment, Ottawa, ON, Canada [*Library symbol Library of Congress*] (LCLS)

CaOOE .... Canada Department of External Affairs, Ottawa, ON, Canada [*Library symbol Library of Congress*] (LCLS)

CaOOEAPT... Environment Canada, Air Pollution Technology Centre, Ottawa, ON, Canada [*Library symbol Library of Congress*] (LCLS)

CaOOEAR.... Environment Canada, Archaeological Research, Ottawa, ON, Canada [*Library symbol Library of Congress*] (LCLS)

CaOOEC .... Economic Council of Canada, Ottawa, ON, Canada [*Library symbol Library of Congress*] (LCLS)

CaOOECD.... Environment Canada, Conservation Division, Ottawa, ON, Canada [*Library symbol Library of Congress*] (LCLS)

CaOOECS ..... Energy Conversion Systems, Ottawa, ON, Canada [*Library symbol*] [*Library of Congress*] (LCLS)

CaOOECW .... Canada Department of the Environment, Canadian Wildlife Service, Ottawa, ON, Canada [*Library symbol Library of Congress*] (LCLS)

CaOOECWN... Environment Canada, Canadian Wildlife Service, National Wildlife Research Centre, Ottawa, ON, Canada [*Library symbol*] [*Library of Congress*] (LCLS)

CaOOED....... Ministry of State for Economic Development, Ottawa, ON, Canada [*Library symbol Library of Congress*] (LCLS)

CaOOEDC..... Export Development Corp., Ottawa, ON, Canada [*Library symbol Library of Congress*] (LCLS)

CaOOEF .... Canada Department of the Environment, Fontaine Branch Library, Ottawa, ON, Canada [*Library symbol Library of Congress*] (LCLS)

CaOOELB ..... Canada Department of External Affairs, Legal Branch, Ottawa, ON, Canada [*Library symbol Library of Congress*] (LCLS)

CaOOELS ..... Environment Canada, Legal Services, Ottawa, ON, Canada [*Library symbol*] [*Library of Congress*] (LCLS)

CaOOEME .... Canada Department of Energy, Mines, and Resources, Energy Development Sector, Ottawa, ON, Canada [*Library symbol Library of Congress Obsolete*] (LCLS)

CaOOEN....... Eldorado Nuclear Ltd., Ottawa, ON, Canada [*Library symbol Library of Congress*] (LCLS)

CaOOEO .... Eastern Ontario Regional Library, Ottawa, ON, Canada [*Library symbol Library of Congress*] (LCLS)

CaOOEPC...... Emergency Planning Canada, Ottawa, ON, Canada [*Library symbol Library of Congress*] (LCLS)

CaOOERE..... Canada Department of the Environment, Resource and Environmental Law Library, Ottawa, ON, Canada [*Library symbol Library of Congress Obsolete*] (LCLS)

CaOOEy........ Eyretechnics Ltd., Ottawa, ON, Canada [*Library symbol Library of Congress*] (LCLS)

CaOOF .... Canada Department of Finance, Ottawa, ON, Canada [*Library symbol Library of Congress*] (LCLS)

CaOOFC .... Federal Court of Canada, Ottawa, ON, Canada [*Library symbol Library of Congress*] (LCLS)

CaOOFD....... Canada Department of National Health and Welfare, Food and Drug Directorate, Ottawa, ON, Canada [*Library symbol Library of Congress*] (LCLS)

CaOOFF .... Canada Department of the Environment, Ottawa, ON, Canada [*Library symbol Library of Congress*] (LCLS)

CaOOFFR..... Canada Department of the Environment, Forest Fire Research Institute, Ottawa, ON, Canada [*Library symbol Library of Congress*] (LCLS)

CaOOFL .... Federal Liberal Agency of Canada, Ottawa, ON, Canada [*Library symbol*] [*Library of Congress*] (LCLS)

CaOOFM ...... Falconbridge Ltd., Mining Library, Onaping, ON, Canada [*Library symbol*] [*Library of Congress*] (LCLS)

CaOOFP .... Canada Department of the Environment, Forest Products Laboratory, Ottawa, ON, Canada [*Cl osed*] [*Library symbol*] [*Library of Congress*] (LCLS)

CaOOFS .... Canadian Documentation Centre, Fitness and Sport, Ottawa, ON, Canada [*Library symbol Library of Congress*] (LCLS)

CaOOG......... Geological Survey of Canada, Ottawa, ON, Canada [*Library symbol Library of Congress*] (LCLS)

CaOOGDC .... Gandalf Data Communications Ltd., Ottawa, ON, Canada [*Library symbol Library of Congress*] (LCLS)

CaOOGE....... Department of Supply and Services, Canadian Government Expositions Centre, Ottawa, ON, Canada [*Library symbol Library of Congress*] (LCLS)

CaOOGGH .... Grace General Hospital, Ottawa, ON, Canada [*Library symbol Library of Congress*] (LCLS)

CaOOGH ...... Government House, Reference Library, Inttawa, ON, Canada [*Library symbol Library of Congress*] (LCLS)

CaOOH......... Laboratory of Hygiene, Ottawa, ON, Canada [*Library symbol Library of Congress Obsolete*] (LCLS)

CaOOHB....... National Harbours Board, Ottawa, ON, Canada [*Library symbol Library of Congress*] (LCLS)

CaOOHC....... Heritae Canada Foundation, Ottawa, ON, Canada [*Library symbol*] [*Library of Congress*] (LCLS)

CaOOHI....... Historical Society of Ottawa Library and the Bytown Historical Museum, Ottawa, ON, Canada [*Library symbol Library of Congress*] (LCLS)

CaOOhSN.... Six Nations Public Library, Ohsweken, ON, Canada [*Library symbol*] [*Library of Congress*] (LCLS)

CaOOI .... Canada Department of Industry, Ottawa, ON, Canada [*Library symbol Library of Congress Obsolete*] (LCLS)

CaOOIAB..... Immigration Appeal Board, Ottawa, ON, Canada [*Library symbol*] [*Library of Congress*] (LCLS)

CaOOIB........ Imperial Ballet of Canada, Ottawa, ON, Canada [*Library symbol Library of Congress*] (LCLS)

CaOOIC....... Investment Canada, Information Centre, Ottawa, ON, Canada [*Library symbol*] [*Library of Congress*] (LCLS)

CaOOICC..... Indian Claims Commission, Ottawa, ON, Canada [*Library symbol Library of Congress*] (LCLS)

CaOOICP..... National Film Board, Phototheque, Ottawa, ON, Canada [*Library symbol Library of Congress*] (LCLS)

CaOOID........ International Development Research Centre, Ottawa, ON, Canada [*Library symbol Library of Congress*] (LCLS)

CaOOIJC .... International Joint Commission, Ottawa, ON, Canada [*Library symbol*] [*Library of Congress*] (LCLS)

CaOOIn .... Canada Department of Insurance, Ottawa, ON, Canada [*Library symbol Library of Congress*] (LCLS)

CaOOIPC..... Offices of the Information and Privacy Commissioners of Canada, Ottawa, ON, Canada [*Library symbol*] [*Library of Congress*] (LCLS)

CaOOIRP...... Institute for Research on Public Policy, Ottawa, ON, Canada [*Library symbol*] [*Library of Congress*] (LCLS)

CaOOIT .... Inuit Tapirisat of Canada, Ottawa, ON, Canada [*Library symbol*] [*Library of Congress*] (LCLS)

CaOOJ .... Canada Department of Justice, Ottawa, ON, Canada [*Library symbol Library of Congress*] (LCLS)

CaOOL .... Canada Department of Labour, Ottawa, ON, Canada [*Library symbol Library of Congress*] (LCLS)

CaOOLAP.... Canada Department of Labour, Occupational Safety and Health Branch, Ottawa, ON, Canada [*Library symbol Library of Congress*] (LCLS)

CaOOLC .... Labour College of Canada, Ottawa, ON, Canada [*Library symbol Library of Congress*] (LCLS)

CaOOLR .... Law Reform Commission, Ottawa, ON, Canada [*Library symbol Library of Congress*] (LCLS)

CaOOLRB.... Canada Labour Relations Board, Ottawa, ON, Canada [*Library symbol Library of Congress*] (LCLS)

CaOOLWB .... Department of Labour, Women's Bureau, Ottawa, ON, Canada [*Library symbol Library of Congress*] (LCLS)

CaOOM .... Department of Energy, Mines, and Resources, Canada Center for Mineral and EnergyTechnology, Ottawa, ON, Canada [*Library symbol Library of Congress*] (LCLS)

CaOOMAD.... Michael A. Dagg Associates, Ottawa, ON, Canada [*Library symbol*] [*Library of Congress*] (LCLS)

CaOOMC...... Metric Commission Reference Unit, Ottawa, ON, Canada [*Library symbol Library of Congress*] (LCLS)

CaOOMHS.... Merivale High School, Ottawa, ON, Canada [*Library symbol Library of Congress*] (LCLS)

CaOOMI....... Canada Employment and Immigration Department, Ottawa, ON, Canada [*Library symbol Library of Congress*] (LCLS)

CaOOMJ ...... Macera & Jarzyna, Ottawa, ON, Canada [*Library symbol*] [*Library of Congress*] (LCLS)

CaOOML ...... Metropolitan Life Insurance Co., Ottawa, ON, Canada [*Library symbol Library of Congress*] (LCLS)

CaOOMNA.... Energy, Mines and Resources Canada, National Air Photo Library, Ottawa, ON, Canada [*Library symbol*] [*Library of Congress*] (LCLS)

CaOOMP...... Canada Department of Energy, Mines, and Resources, Physical Metallurgy Division,Ottawa, ON, Canada [*Library symbol Library of Congress*] (LCLS)

CaOOMR...... Canada Department of Energy, Mines, and Resources, Resources Economic Library, Ottawa, ON, Canada [*Library symbol Library of Congress*] (LCLS)

CaOOMSD.... Ministry of State for Social Development, Ottawa, ON, Canada [*Library symbol Library of Congress*] (LCLS)

CaOOMSS.... Canada Ministry of State for Science and Technology, Ottawa, ON, Canada [*Library symbol Library of Congress*] (LCLS)

CaOOMUA.... Canada Ministry of State for Urban Affairs, Ottawa, ON, Canada [*Library symbol Library of Congress*] (LCLS)

CaOON........ Canada Institute for Scientific and Technical Information, National Research Council, Ottawa, ON, Canada [*Library symbol Library of Congress*] (LCLS)

CaOONAB .... Canada Institute for Scientific and Technical Information, Administration Building Library, Ottawa, ON, Canada [*Library symbol Library of Congress*] (LCLS)

CaOONAM.... Canada Institute for Scientific and Technical Information, Aeronautical and Mechanical Engineering Branch, Ottawa, ON, Canada [*Library symbol Library of Congress*] (LCLS)

CaOONBR .... Canada Institute for Scientific and Technical Information, Division of Building Research, Ottawa, ON, Canada [*Library symbol Library of Congress*] (LCLS)

CaOONC.... Canada Institute for Scientific and Technical Information, Chemistry Library, Ottawa, ON, Canada [*Library symbol Library of Congress*] (LCLS)

CaOONCC .... National Capital Commission, Ottawa, ON, Canada [*Library symbol Library of Congress*] (LCLS)

CaOOND ...... Department of National Defence, Ottawa, ON, Canada [*Library symbol Library of Congress*] (LCLS)

CaOONDAT... Department of National Defence, Air Technical Library, Ottawa, ON, Canada [*Library symbol*] [*Library of Congress*] (LCLS)

CaOONDC .... Department of National Defence, Chief Computer Services, Ottawa, ON, Cana da [*Library symbol Library of Congress*] (LCLS)

CaOONDCG... Department of National Defence, General Engineering and Maintenance, Dire ctorate of Clothing, Ottawa, ON, Canada [*Library symbol Library of Congress*] (LCLS)

CaOONDCP... Department of National Defence, Chief Construction and Properties, Ottawa, ON, Canada [*Library symbol Library of Congress*] (LCLS)

CaOONDEM... Department of National Defence, Chief Engineering and Maintenance, Ottawa, ON, Canada [*Library symbol Library of Congress*] (LCLS)

CaOONDH .... Department of National Defence, Historical Section, Ottawa, ON, Canada [*Library symbol Library of Congress*] (LCLS)

CaOONDIS ... Department of National Defence, Directorate of Information Services, Ottawa, ON, Canada [*Library symbol Library of Congress*] (LCLS)

CaOONDJ..... Department of National Defence, Judge Advocate General's Library, Ottawa, ON, Canada [*Library symbol Library of Congress*] (LCLS)

CaOONDLT... Department of National Defence, Land Technical Library, Ottawa, ON, Canada [*Library symbol Library of Congress*] (LCLS)

CaOONDM ... Department of National Defence, Medical Library, Ottawa, ON, Canada [*Library symbol Library of Congress*] (LCLS)

CaOONDMC... Department of National Defence, Mapping and Charting Establishment, Ottawa, ON, Canada [*Library symbol Library of Congress*] (LCLS)

CaOONDMT... Department of National Defence, Marine Technical Library, Ottawa, ON, Canada [*Library symbol Library of Congress*] (LCLS)

CaOONDORAE... Department of National Defence, Operational Research and Analysis Establishment, Ottawa, ON, Canada [*Library symbol Library of Congress*] (LCLS)

CaOONDR .... Directorate of Scientific Information Service, Defence Research Board, Ottawa, ON, Canada [*Library symbol Library of Congress*] (LCLS)

CaOONDT .... Department of National Defence, Translation Bureau, Ottawa, ON, Canada [*Library symbol*] [*Library of Congress*] (LCLS)

CaOONE....... National Energy Board, Ottawa, ON, Canada [*Library symbol Library of Congress*] (LCLS)

CaOONF....... National Film Board, Montreal, PQ, Canada [*Library symbol Library of Congress*] (LCLS)

CaOONFP..... National Farm Products Marketing Council, Ottawa, ON, Canada [*Library symbol*] [*Library of Congress*] (LCLS)

CaOONG ...... National Gallery of Canada, Ottawa, ON, Canada [*Library symbol Library of Congress*] (LCLS)

CaOONH ...... National Health and Welfare Library, Ottawa, ON, Canada [*Library symbol Library of Congress*] (LCLS)

CaOONHBR... Department of National Health and Welfare, Banting Research Centre, Ottawa, ON, Canada [*Library symbol Library of Congress*] (LCLS)

CaOONHH .... Health and Welfare Canada, Environmental Health Directorate, Health Protection Branch, Ottawa, ON, Canada [*Library symbol*] [*Library of Congress*] (LCLS)

CaOONHHP... Health and Welfare Canada, Health Protection Branch, Library Services Division, Ottawa, ON, Canada [*Library symbol*] [*Library of Congress*] (LCLS)

CaOONHHS... Department of National Health and Welfare, Health Services and Promotion Branch, Ottawa, ON, Canada [*Library symbol Library of Congress*] (LCLS)

CaOONHL .... Canada Department of National Health and Welfare, Health Protection Branch, Laboratory Centre for Disease Control, Ottawa, ON, Canada [*Library symbol*] [*Library of Congress*] (LCLS)

CaOONHP .... Department of National Health and Welfare, Health Protection Board, Place Vanier, Vanier Reading Room, Ottawa, ON, Canada [*Library symbol*] [*Library of Congress*] (LCLS)

CaOONHPP... Health and Welfare Canada, Policy Planning and Information Library, Ottawa, ON, Canada [*Library symbol*] [*Library of Congress*] (LCLS)

CaOONL....... National Library of Canada, Ottawa, ON, Canada [*Library symbol Library of Congress*] (LCLS)

CaOONLB..... National Library, Union Catalogue of Books, Ottawa, ON, Canada [*Library symbol*] [*Library of Congress*] (LCLS)

CaOONLC..... National Library, Canadiana Acquisitions, Ottawa, ON, Canada [*Library symbol*] [*Library of Congress*] (LCLS)

CaOONLD .... National Library, Library Systems Centre, Ottawa, ON, Canada [*Library symbol*] [*Library of Congress*] (LCLS)

CaOONLP.... National Library, Public Service Branch, Ottawa, ON, Canada [*Library symbol Library of Congress*] (LCLS)

CaOONLR .... National Library of Canada, Retrospective Bibliography, Ottawa, ON, Canada [*Library symbol*] [*Library of Congress*] (LCLS)

CaOONLS..... National Library, Union Catalogue of Serials, Ottawa, ON, Canada [*Library symbol Library of Congress*] (LCLS)

CaOONM...... National Museum of Canada, Ottawa, ON, Canada [*Library symbol Library of Congress*] (LCLS)

CaOONMC.... Canadian War Museum, Ottawa, ON, Canada [*Library symbol Library of Congress*] (LCLS)

CaOONMCC... National Museums of Canada, Canadian Conservation Institute, Ottawa, ON, Canada [*Library symbol Library of Congress*] (LCLS)

CaOONMM... National Museums of Canada, National Museum of Man, Ottawa, ON, Canada [*Library symbol Library of Congress*] (LCLS)

CaOONMS.... National Museum of Science and Technology, Ottawa, ON, Canada [*Library symbol Library of Congress*] (LCLS)

CaOONorE.... Bell Northern Research, Ottawa, ON, Canada [*Library symbol Library of Congress*] (LCLS)

CaOONorE.... Bell Northern Research, Ottawa, ON, Canada [*Library symbol*] [*Library of Congress*] (LCLS)

CaOONR ...... Canada Department of National Revenue, Customs and Excise Division, Ottawa, ON, Canada [*Library symbol Library of Congress*] (LCLS)

CaOONRE .... Canada Institute for Scientific and Technical Information, Radio and Electrical Engineering Division, Ottawa, ON, Canada [*Library symbol Library of Congress*] (LCLS)

CaOONRT .... Canada Department of National Revenue, Taxation Division, Ottawa, ON, Canada [*Library symbol Library of Congress*] (LCLS)

CaOONRTC... Revenue Canada-Taxation, Centre for Career Development, Ottawa, ON, Canada [*Library symbol Library of Congress*] (LCLS)

CaOONS....... Canada Institute for Scientific and Technical Information, Sussex Library, Ottawa, ON, Canada [*Library symbol Library of Congress*] (LCLS)

CaOONSF..... National Science Film Library, Ottawa, ON, Canada [*Library symbol Library of Congress*] (LCLS)

CaOONU ...... Canada Institute for Scientific and Technical Information, Uplands Library, Ottawa, ON, Canada [*Library symbol Library of Congress*] (LCLS)

CaOONUL .... Union List of Scientific Serials in Canadian Libraries, Ottawa, ON, Canada [*Library symbol Library of Congress*] (LCLS)

CaOONVRC... National Victims Resource Centre, Ottawa, ON, Canada [*Library symbol*] [*Library of Congress*] (LCLS)

CaOOO......... Canada Department of Energy, Mines, and Resources, Earth Physics Branch, Ottawa, ON, Canada [*Library symbol Library of Congress*] (LCLS)

CaOOOA...... Canada Department of Justice, Occupational Analysis Library, Ottawa, ON, Canada [*Library symbol Library of Congress Obsolete*] (LCLS)

CaOOOAG .... Office of the Auditor General, Ottawa, ON, Canada [*Library symbol Library of Congress*] (LCLS)

CaOOOCF..... Ontario Cancer Foundation, Ottawa Clinic, Ottawa, ON, Canada [*Library symbol Library of Congress*] (LCLS)

CaOOOCH .... Ottawa Civic Hospital, Ottawa, ON, Canada [*Library symbol Library of Congress*] (LCLS)

CaOOOCM.... Ontario Centre for Microelectronics, Information Services, Ottawa, ON, Canada [*Library symbol*] [*Library of Congress*] (LCLS)

CaOOP......... Library of Parliament, Ottawa, ON, Canada [*Library symbol Library of Congress*] (LCLS)

CaOOPA....... National Arts Centre, Ottawa, ON, Canada [*Library symbol Library of Congress*] (LCLS)

CaOOPAC..... Environment Canada, Parks Canada, Ottawa, ON, Canada [*Library symbol Library of Congress*] (LCLS)

CaOOPC....... Canada Privy Council Office, Management Information, Ottawa, ON, Canada [*Library symbol Library of Congress*] (LCLS)

CaOOPCF.... Parliamentary Centre for Foreign Affairs and Foreign Trade, Ottawa, ON, Canada [*Library symbol*] [*Library of Congress*] (LCLS)

CaOOPH....... Perley Hospital, Ottawa, ON, Canada [*Library symbol Library of Congress*] (LCLS)

CaOOPI........ Department of Energy, Mines, and Resources, Petroleum Incentives Program, Ottawa, ON, Canada [*Library symbol Library of Congress*] (LCLS)

CaOOPIP...... Professional Institute of the Public Service of Canada, Ottawa, ON, Canada [*Library symbol*] [*Library of Congress*] (LCLS)

CaOOPM...... National Postal Museum, Ottawa, ON, Canada [*Library symbol Library of Congress*] (LCLS)

CaOOPO....... Post Office Library, Ottawa, ON, Canada [*Library symbol Library of Congress*] (LCLS)

CaOOPOR .... Ports Canada, Ottawa, ON, Canada [*Library symbol*] [*Library of Congress*] (LCLS)

CaOOPS....... Public Service Staff Relations Board, Ottawa, ON, Canada [*Library symbol Library of Congress*] (LCLS)

CaOOPSAC... Public Service Alliance of Canada, Ottawa, ON, Canada [*Library symbol Library of Congress*] (LCLS)

CaOOPW...... Canada Department of Public Works, Ottawa, ON, Canada [*Library symbol Library of Congress*] (LCLS)

CaOOPWC.... Canada Department of Public Works, Capital Region Library, Ottawa, ON, Canada [*Library symbol Library of Congress*] (LCLS)

CaOOPWD ... Canada Department of Public Works, Office of the Dominion Fire Commissioner, Ottawa, ON, Canada [*Library symbol Library of Congress Obsolete*] (LCLS)

CaOOPWR ... Canada Department of Public Works, Research and Development Laboratories, Ottawa, ON, Canada [*Library symbol Library of Congress*] (LCLS)

CaOOQA...... Canada Department of National Defence, Quality Assurance Division, Ottawa, ON, Canada [*Library symbol Library of Congress*] (LCLS)

CaOOQP....... Information Canada, Publishing Division, Ottawa, ON, Canada [*Library symbol Library of Congress Obsolete*] (LCLS)

CaOOr.......... Orillia Public Library, Orillia, ON, Canada [*Library symbol Library of Congress*] (LCLS)

CaOOR........ Royal Canadian Mounted Police Headquarters Reference Library, Ottawa, ON, Canada [*Library symbol Library of Congress*] (LCLS)

CaOORCS .... Ottawa Roman Catholic Seperate School Board, Ottawa, ON, Canada [*Library symbol*] [*Library of Congress*] (LCLS)

CaOORD ...... Canada Department of Indian Affairs and Northern Development, Ottawa, ON, Canada [*Library symbol*] [*Library of Congress*] (LCLS)

CaOORE....... Canadian Council for Research in Education, Ottawa, ON, Canada [*Library symbol Library of Congress Obsolete*] (LCLS)

CaOOREx..... Canada Department of Regional Economic Expansion, Ottawa, ON, Canada [*Library symbol Library of Congress*] (LCLS)

CaOORExR... Canada Department of Regional Economic Expansion, Reference and Enquiries Unit, Ottawa, ON, Canada [*Library symbol Library of Congress Obsolete*] (LCLS)

CaOOrGC..... Georgian College of Applied Arts and Technology, Learning Resources Centre, Orillia, ON, Canada [*Library symbol*] [*Library of Congress*] (LCLS)

CaOORH...... Riverside Hospital, Ottawa, ON, Canada [*Library symbol Library of Congress*] (LCLS)

CaOrHUR... Huronia Regional Centre, Orillia, ON, Canada [*Library symbol*] [*Library of Congress*] (LCLS)

CaOORIA..... J.L. Richardson Associates, Ltd., Ottawa, ON, Canada [*Library symbol*] [*Library of Congress*] (LCLS)

CaOORM...... Regional Municipality of Ottawa-Carleton, Ottawa, ON, Canada [*Library symbol Library of Congress*] (LCLS)

CaoORMT ... Regional Municipality of Ottawa-Carleton, Transportation-Works Department, Ottawa, ON, Canada [*Library symbol*] [*Library of Congress*] (LCLS)

CaOORO...... Royal Ottawa Hospital, Ottawa, ON, Canada [*Library symbol Library of Congress*] (LCLS)

CaOORORR... Royal Ottawa Regional Rehabilitation Centre, Royal Ottawa Hospital, Ottawa, ON, Canada [*Library symbol Library of Congress*] (LCLS)

CaOORPL.... Canada Department of Communications, Communications Research Centre, Ottawa, ON, Canada [*Library symbol Library of Congress*] (LCLS)

CaOORS...... RCMP, Scientific Information Centre, Ottawa, ON, Canada [*Library symbol*] [*Library of Congress*] (LCLS)

CaOOrSMH.. Orilla Soldiers' Memorial Hospital, Health Sciences Library, Orilla, ON, Canada [*Library symbol*] [*Library of Congress*] (LCLS)

CaOORT....... Canadian Radio-Television and Telecommunications Commission, Ottawa, ON, Canada [*Library symbol Library of Congress*] (LCLS)

CaOORTA..... Roads and Transportation Association of Canada, Ottawa, ON, Canada [*Library symbol Library of Congress*] (LCLS)

CaOOS .... Statistics Canada, Ottawa, ON, Canada [*Library symbol Library of Congress*] (LCLS)

CaOOSC...... Supreme Court of Canada, Ottawa, ON, Canada [*Library symbol Library of Congress*] (LCLS)

CaOOSCA..... Archives des Soeurs de la Charite d'Ottawa, Ottawa, ON, Canada [*Library symbol*] [*Library of Congress*] (LCLS)

CaOOSCC.... Science Council of Canada, Ottawa, ON, Canada [*Library symbol Library of Congress*] (LCLS)

CaOOSCL.... Statistics Canada, Census Library, Ottawa, ON, Canada [*Library symbol Library of Congress*] (LCLS)

CaOOSCM.... Statistics Canada, Census Map Library, Ottawa, ON, Canada [*Library symbol Library of Congress*] (LCLS)

CaOOSG....... Canada Department of the Solicitor General, Ottawa, ON, Canada [*Library symbol Library of Congress*] (LCLS)

CaOOsh........ Oshawa Public Library, Oshawa, ON, Canada [*Library symbol Library of Congress*] (LCLS)

CaOOshD ..... Durham College of Applied Arts and Technology, Oshawa, ON, Canada [*Library symbol Library of Congress*] (LCLS)

CaOOSHH.... Oshawa General Hospital, Eduction Resource Centre, Oshawa, ON, Canada [*Library symbol*] [*Library of Congress*] (LCLS)

CaOOshR.... Robert McLaughlin Gallery, Oshawa, ON, Canada [*Library symbol Library of Congress*] (LCLS)

CaOOSHT..... Systemhouse Ltd., Technical Library, Ottawa, ON, Canada [*Library symbol*] [*Library of Congress*] (LCLS)

CaOOSJ .... Bibliotheque Deschatelets, Peres Oblats, Ottawa, ON, Canada [*Library symbol Library of Congress*] (LCLS)

CaOOSLM..... Saint Louis De Montfort Hospital, Ottawa, ON, Canada [*Library symbol Library of Congress*] (LCLS)

CaOOSM...... Canada Department of Energy, Mines, and Resources, Surveys and Mapping Branch, Ottawa, ON, Canada [*Library symbol Library of Congress*] (LCLS)

CaOOSMM ... Canada Department of Energy, Mines, and Resources, Map Library, Ottawa, ON, Canada [*Library symbol Library of Congress*] (LCLS)

CaOOSP....... Patent and Copyright Office, Ottawa, ON, Canada [*Library symbol Library of Congress*] (LCLS)

CaOOSS....... Canada Department of the Secretary of State, Ottawa, ON, Canada [*Library symbol Library of Congress*] (LCLS)

CaOOSST..... Canada Department of the Secretary of State, Translation Bureau, Multilingual Services Division, Ottawa, ON, Canada [*Library symbol Library of Congress Obsolete*] (LCLS)

CaOOSSTE... Department of Secretary of State, Translation Bureau, Terminology and Documentation Branch, Ottawa, ON, Canada [*Library symbol*] [*Library of Congress*] (LCLS)

CaOOSSTM... Department of the Secretary of State, Translation Bureau, Multilingual Services, Ottawa, ON, Canada [*Library symbol*] [*Library of Congress*] (LCLS)

CaOOSSTR... Department of the Secretary of State, Translation Bureau, Translation Services, Ottawa, ON, Canada [*Library symbol*] [*Library of Congress*] (LCLS)

CaOOSSTT... Canada Department of the Secretary of State, Translation Bureau, Terminology Centre Library, Ottawa, ON, Canada [*Library symbol Library of Congress*] (LCLS)

CaOOSTI...... Canada Department of Revenue, Canada Customs and Excise, Scientific and Technical Information Centre, Laboratory and Scientific Services Division, Ottawa, ON, Canada [*Library symbol Library of Congress*] (LCLS)

CaOOSU....... Saint Paul University, Ottawa, ON, Canada [*Library symbol Library of Congress*] (LCLS)

CaOOSUA .... Saint Paul University, Oblate Fathers Archives, Ottawa, ON, Canada [*Library symbol Library of Congress*] (LCLS)

CaOOSV...... Saint Vincent Hospital, Ottawa, ON, Canada [*Library symbol Library of Congress*] (LCLS)

CaOOT......... Ministry of Transport, Ottawa, ON, Canada [*Library symbol Library of Congress*] (LCLS)

CaOOTAC.... Ministry of Transport, Airports and Construction Services, Ottawa, ON, Canada [*Library symbol Library of Congress*] (LCLS)

CaOOTAS.... Ministry of Transport, Aviation Safety Bureau, Ottawa, ON, Canada [*Library symbol Library of Congress*] (LCLS)

CaOOTB...... Canadian Government Travel Bureau, Reference Library, Ottawa, ON, Canada [*Library symbol Library of Congress*] (LCLS)

CaOOTC...... Canada Department of Industry, Trade, and Commerce, Ottawa, ON, Canada [*Library symbol Library of Congress*] (LCLS)

CaOOTCT.... TransCanada Telephone System, Ottawa, ON, Canada [*Library symbol Library of Congress*] (LCLS)

CaOOTEC.... Ottawa Teachers' College, Ottawa, ON, Canada [*Library symbol Library of Congress*] (LCLS)

CaOOTI........ Canada Ministry of Transport Training Institute, Ottawa, ON, Canada [*Library symbol Library of Congress*] (LCLS)

CaOOTN...... External Affairs Canada, Trade Negotiations Office, Ottawa, ON, Canada [*Library symbol*] [*Library of Congress*] (LCLS)

CaOOTR...... Tax Review Board, Ottawa, ON, Canada [*Library symbol Library of Congress*] (LCLS)

CaOOTRB.... Treasury Board, Ottawa, ON, Canada [*Library symbol Library of Congress*] (LCLS)

CaOOTRT..... Ministry of Transport, Railway Transportation Directorate, Ottawa, ON, Canada [*Library symbol Library of Congress*] (LCLS)

CaOOTT .... Canadian Transport Commission, Ottawa, ON, Canada [*Library symbol Library of Congress*] (LCLS)

CaOOTTE .... Ministry of Transport, Telecommunications and Electronics Directorate, Ottawa, ON, Canada [*Library symbol Library of Congress*] (LCLS)

CaOOU........ University of Ottawa, Ottawa, ON, Canada [*Library symbol Library of Congress*] (LCLS)

CaOOUC...... University of Ottawa, Department of Criminology, Ottawa, ON, Canada [*Library symbol Library of Congress*] (LCLS)

CaOOUD...... University of Ottawa, Faculty of Law, Ottawa, ON, Canada [*Library symbol Library of Congress*] (LCLS)

CaOOUH ...... University of Ottawa, Health Sciences Library, Ottawa, ON, Canada [*Library symbol Library of Congress*] (LCLS)

CaOOUI....... Unemployment Insurance Commission, Ottawa, ON, Canada [*Library symbol Library of Congress Obsolete*] (LCLS)

CaOOUIC.... University of Ottawa, Institute of International Cooperation, Ottawa, ON, Canada [*Library symbol Library of Congress*] (LCLS)

CaOOULT.... United Lodge of Theosophists, Ottawa, ON, Canada [*Library symbol Library of Congress Obsolete*] (LCLS)

CaOOUM..... University of Ottawa, Vanier Library, Ottawa, ON, Canada [*Library symbol Library of Congress*] (LCLS)

CaOOUMA... University of Ottawa, Map Library, Ottawa, ON, Canada [*Library symbol Library of Congress*] (LCLS)

CaOOUP...... University of Ottawa, Faculty of Psychology and Education, Ottawa, ON, Canada [*Library symbol Library of Congress Obsolete*] (LCLS)

CaOOUSA .... United States Embassy, Ottawa, ON, Canada [*Library symbol Library of Congress*] (LCLS)

CaOOUSI..... United States International Communications Agency, Ottawa, ON, Canada [*Library symbol Library of Congress*] (LCLS)

CaOOV........ Canada Department of Veterans Affairs, Ottawa, ON, Canada [*Library symbol Library of Congress*] (LCLS)

CaOOVIF...... Vanier Institute of the Family, Ottawa, ON, Canada [*Library symbol Library of Congress*] (LCLS)

CaOOVV...... Versatile Vickers Systems, Inc., Ottawa, ON, Canada [*Library symbol*] [*Library of Congress*] (LCLS)

CaOOw........ Owen Sound Public Library, Owen Sound, ON, Canada [*Library symbol Library of Congress*] (LCLS)

CaOOwGC.... Georgian College Resource Centre, Owen Sound, ON, Canada [*Library symbol Library of Congress*] (LCLS)

CaOOwGM... General and Marine Hospital, Health Sciences Library, Owen Sound, ON, Canada [*Library symbol Library of Congress*] (LCLS)

CaOOWIC.... West Island College of Ontario, Ottawa, ON, Canada [*Library symbol*] [*Library of Congress*] (LCLS)

CaOOWLS.... Carleton Board of Education, Sir Wilfrid Laurier High School Library, Ottawa, ON, Canada [*Library symbol*] [*Library of Congress*] (LCLS)

CaOOwT....... Tom Thomson Memorial Gallery, Owen Sound, ON, Canada [*Library symbol Library of Congress*] (LCLS)

CAOP .... Canadian Association of Occupational Therapy (HGAA)

CaOPAC .... Algonquin College of Applied Arts and Technology, School of Lanark County, Resource Centre, Perth, ON, Canada [*Library symbol*] [*Library of Congress*] (LCLS)

CAOPAL .... Lakehead University, Thunder Bay, ON, Canada [*Library symbol Library of Congress*] (LCLS)

CaOPALE ..... Lakehead University, Faculty of Education, Thunder Bay, ON, Canada [*Library symbol Library of Congress*] (LCLS)

CaOPALG.... Lakehead University, Department of Geography, Thunder Bay, ON, Canada [*Library symbol Library of Congress*] (LCLS)

CaOpalN ...... Norwell District Secondary School, Palmerston, ON, Canada [*Library symbol*] [*Library of Congress*] (LCLS)

CaOPar........ Paris Public Library, Paris, ON, Canada [*Library symbol*] [*Library of Congress*] (LCLS)

CaOPC .... Perth Courier, Perth, ON, Canada [*Library symbol Library of Congress*] (LCLS)

CaOPd .... Port Dover Centennial Public Library, Port Dover, ON, Canada [*Library symbol Library of Congress*] (LCLS)

CaOPeEPB ... Eastern Pentecostal Bible College, Peterborough, ON, Canada [*Library symbol Library of Congress*] (LCLS)

CaOPem ...... Pembroke Public Library, Pembroke, ON, Canada [*Library symbol Library of Congress*] (LCLS)

CaOPemAC... Algonquin College, Upper Ottawa Valley Campus Resource Centre, Pembroke, ON, Canada [*Library symbol Library of Congress*] (LCLS)

CaOPemO .... Ottawa Valley Historical Society, Pembroke, ON, Canada [*Library symbol*] [*Library of Congress*] (LCLS)

CaOPenE ...... Ecole Secondaire le Caron, Penetanguishene, ON, Canada [*Library symbol*] [*Library of Congress*] (LCLS)

CaOPenM ...... Mental Health Centre, Penetanguishene, ON, Canada [*Library symbol Library of Congress*] (LCLS)

CaOPeT .... Trent University, Peterborough, ON, Canada [*Library symbol Library of Congress*] (LCLS)

CaOPeTA ..... Trent University Archives, Peterborough, ON, Canada [*Library symbol Library of Congress*] (LCLS)

CaOPeTAL ... Trent University, Trent Audio Library Services, Peterborough, ON, Canada [*Library symbol*] [*Library of Congress*] (LCLS)

CaOPeTCG ... Canadian General Electric Co. Ltd., Peterborough, ON, Canada [*Library symbol Library of Congress*] (LCLS)

CaOPeTM ..... Trent University, Map Library, Peterborough, ON, Canada [*Library symbol Library of Congress*] (LCLS)

CaOPeTP ..... Peterborough Public Library, Peterborough, ON, Canada [*Library symbol Library of Congress*] (LCLS)

CaOPeTSF ... Sir Sandford Fleming College of Applied Arts and Technology, Peterborough, ON, Canada [*Library symbol Library of Congress*] (LCLS)

CaOPh .... Public Library, Port Hope, ON, Canada [*Library symbol Library of Congress*] (LCLS)

CaOPhE........ Eldorado Mining & Refining Co., Port Hope, ON, Canada [*Library symbol Library of Congress*] (LCLS)

CaOPhWA .... Westinghouse Canada Inc., Atomic Tower Division, Port Hope, ON, Canada [*Library symbol Library of Congress*] (LCLS)

CaOPic......... Pickering Public Library, Pickering, ON, Canada [*Library symbol Library of Congress*] (LCLS)

CaOPicET..... ECO-TEC Ltd., Pickering, ON, Canada [*Library symbol*] [*Library of Congress*] (LCLS)

CaOPiG .... Picton Gazette, Picton, ON, Canada [*Library symbol Library of Congress*] (LCLS)

CaOPiNM...... North Marysburgh Museum, Picton, ON, Canada [*Library symbol*] [*Library of Congress*] (LCLS)

CaOPM .... Perth Museum, Perth, ON, Canada [*Library symbol Library of Congress*] (LCLS)

CaOPmn ...... Port McNicoll Public Library, Port McNicoll, ON, Canada [*Library symbol Library of Congress*] (LCLS)

CaOPoC .... Port Colborne Public Library, Port Colborne, ON, Canada [*Library symbol Library of Congress*] (LCLS)

CaOPpP .... Port Perry High School, Port Perry, ON, Canada [*Library symbol Library of Congress*] (LCLS)

CaOPr .... Port Rowan Public Library, Port Rowan, ON, Canada [*Library symbol Library of Congress*] (LCLS)

CaOPs.......... Parry Sound Public Library, Parry Sound, ON, Canada [*Library symbol Library of Congress*] (LCLS)

CaOPsA........ Algonquin Regional Library, Parry Sound, ON, Canada [*Library symbol Library of Congress*] (LCLS)

CAOPT .... Council of American Official Poultry Tests (EA)

CaOPteB ...... Bruce County Public Library, Port Elgin, ON, Canada [*Library symbol Library of Congress*] (LCLS)

CaOPteOEB... Port Elgin Branch Library, Port Elgin, ON, Canada [*Library symbol*] [*Library of Congress*] (LCLS)

CaOQC .... Queensway-Carleton Hospital, Ottawa, ON, Canada [*Library symbol Library of Congress*] (LCLS)

CAOR .... Canadian Academy of Oral Radiology [*Academie Canadienne de Radiologie Buccale*] (AC)

CAORA........ Combined Arms Operations Research Activity [*Fort Leavenworth, KS*]

CAORC........ Council of American Overseas Research Centers (EA)

CAORE .... Canadian Army Operational Research Establishment

CaOREC....... Eramosa Community Library, Rockwood, ON, Canada [*Library symbol*] [*Library of Congress*] (LCLS)

CAORF........ Computer-Aided Operations Research Facility [*Kings Point, NY*] [*National Maritime Research Center Department of Transportation*] (MCD)

CAORG........ Canadian Army Operational Research Group (DMA)

CaORh .... Richmond Hill Public Library, Richmond Hill, ON, Canada [*Library symbol Library of Congress*] (LCLS)

CaORhCO..... Central Ontario Regional Library, Richmond Hill, ON, Canada [*Library symbol Library of Congress*] (LCLS)

CaORhT .... Ontario Library Service-Trent, Richmond Hill, ON, Canada [*Library symbol*] [*Library of Congress*] (LCLS)

CaORr.......... Red Rock Public Library, Red Rock, ON, Canada [*Library symbol Library of Congress*] (LCLS)

CAOS .... Completely Automatic Operational System [*UNIVAC*]

CAOS .... Computer-Augmented Oscilloscope System (PDAA)

CAOS .... Cost Analysis Organization (SAA)

CaOS .... Sarnia Public Library, Sarnia, ON, Canada [*Library symbol Library of Congress*] (LCLS)

CaOSAMS .... Anglican Church of Canada, Diocese of Moosonee, Synod Office, Schumacher, ON, Canada [*Library symbol Library of Congress*] (LCLS)

CaOSbM ...... Morrison Library Outpost, Severn Bridge, ON, Canada [*Library symbol Library of Congress*] (LCLS)

CaOSc.......... Scugog Public Library, Scugog, ON, Canada [*Library symbol Library of Congress*] (LCLS)

CaOSD........ Dow Chemical Co., Sarnia, ON, Canada [*Library symbol Library of Congress*] (LCLS)

CaOSE .... Edwardsburg Township Public Library, Spencerville, ON, Canada [*Library symbol*] [*Library of Congress*] (LCLS)

CaOSfAR ...... Algonquin Regional Library System, Sturgeon Falls Branch, Sturgeon Falls, ON, Canada [*Library symbol Library of Congress*] (LCLS)

CaOSFC .... Fiberglass Ltd., Sarnia, ON, Canada [*Library symbol Library of Congress*] (LCLS)

CaOSFCSR... Ministry of Community and Social Services, Rideau Regional Centre, Smith Falls, ON, Canada [*Library symbol*] [*Library of Congress*] (LCLS)

CaOSH .... Shelburne Public Library, Shelburne, ON, Canada [*Library symbol*] [*Library of Congress*] (LCLS)

CaOShT........ Sharon Temple, Sharon, ON, Canada [*Library symbol*] [*Library of Congress*] (LCLS)

CaOSI .... Imperial Oil Enterprises Ltd., Sarnia, ON, Canada [*Library symbol Library of Congress*] (LCLS)

CaOSiDM ...... Eva Brook Donly Museum, Simcoe, ON, Canada [*Library symbol Library of Congress*] (LCLS)

CaOSIE .... Imperial Oil Enterprises Ltd., Engineering Division, Sarnia, ON, Canada [*Library symbol Library of Congress Obsolete*] (LCLS)

CaOSiL .... Lynnwood Arts Centre, Simcoe, ON, Canada [*Library symbol Library of Congress*] (LCLS)

CaOSiNH...... Norfolk Historical Society, Simcoe, ON, Canada [*Library symbol Library of Congress*] (LCLS)

CaOSiP .... Simcoe Public Library, Simcoe, ON, Canada [*Library symbol Library of Congress*] (LCLS)

CaOSl .... Sioux Lookout Public Library, Sioux Lookout, ON, Canada [*Library symbol Library of Congress*] (LCLS)

CaOSLA .... Lennox & Addington County Library, Stella Branch, Stella, ON, Canada [*Library symbol Library of Congress*] (LCLS)

CaOSLC .... Lambton College of Applied Arts and Technology, Sarnia, ON, Canada [*Library symbol Library of Congress*] (LCLS)

CaOSmf .... Smith Falls Public Library, Smith Falls, ON, Canada [*Library symbol Library of Congress*] (LCLS)

CaOSML ...... McNeil Laboratories (Canada) Ltd., Stouffville, ON, Canada [*Library symbol Library of Congress*] (LCLS)

CaOSNC....... Sarnia Northern Collegiate, Sarnia, ON, Canada [*Library symbol Library of Congress*] (LCLS)

CAO-SOP ..... Coordination of Atomic Operations - Standard Operating Procedures

CaOSP .... Polysar Ltd., Sarnia, ON, Canada [*Library symbol Library of Congress*] (LCLS)

CaOSpNC..... Northern College of Applied Arts and Technology, Porcupine Campus, South Porcupine, ON, Canada [*Library symbol Library of Congress*] (LCLS)

CaOSpTM .... Timmins Museum, South Porcupine, ON, Canada [*Library symbol*] [*Library of Congress*] (LCLS)

CaOSrf......... Smooth Rock Falls Public Library, Smooth Rock Falls, ON, Canada [*Library symbol*] [*Library of Congress*] (LCLS)

CaOST .... Stratford Public Library, Stratford, ON, Canada [*Library symbol Library of Congress*] (LCLS)

CaOSTAC ..... Bibliotheque Publique Cambridge-St-Albert, St.-Albert, ON, Canada [*Library symbol*] [*Library of Congress*] (LCLS)

CaOStC .... St. Catharines Public Library, St. Catharines, ON, Canada [*Library symbol Library of Congress*] (LCLS)

CaOStCB ...... Brock University, Saint Catharines, ON, Canada [*Library symbol Library of Congress*] (LCLS)

CaOStCBG.... Brock University, Department of Geography, Saint Catharines, ON, Canada [*Library symbol Library of Congress*] (LCLS)

CaOStCG...... Grantham High School, Saint Catharines, ON, Canada [*Library symbol Library of Congress*] (LCLS)

CaOStCGL..... Genaire Ltd., Saint Catharines, ON, Canada [*Library symbol Library of Congress*] (LCLS)

CaOStCMEC... Montreal Engineering Co. Ltd., St. Catharines, ON, Canada [*Library symbol Library of Congress*] (LCLS)

CaOStCNR ... Niagara Regional Library, Saint Catharines, ON, Canada [*Library symbol Library of Congress Obsolete*] (LCLS)

CaOStCT ...... St. Catharines Teachers' College, St. Catharines, ON, Canada [*Library symbol Library of Congress*] (LCLS)

CaOStCTR .... St. Catharines Teachers' College, Reference Library, St. Catharines, ON, Canad a [*Library symbol Library of Congress*] (LCLS)

CaOStG .... South Dunfries Public Library, St. George Branch, St. George, ON, Canada [*Library symbol*] [*Library of Congress*] (LCLS)

CaOStJeCR... Conseil Regional de la Sante et des Services Sociaux Laurentides Lanaudiere, Saint-Jerome, ON, Canada [*Library symbol Library of Congress*] (LCLS)

CaOStM .... Sault Ste. Marie Public Library, Sault Ste. Marie, ON, Canada [*Library symbol Library of Congress*] (LCLS)

CaOStMA ..... Algoma College, Sault Ste. Marie, ON, Canada [*Library symbol Library of Congress*] (LCLS)

CaOStMAAS... Anglican Church of Canada, Diocese of Algoma, Synod Office, Sault Ste. Marie, ON, Canada [*Library symbol*] [*Library of Congress*] (LCLS)

CaOStMAS ... Algoma Steel Corp., Quality Control and Research Department, Sault Ste. Marie, ON, Canada [*Library symbol Library of Congress*] (LCLS)

CaOStMC ..... Sault College of Applied Arts and Technology, Sault Ste. Marie, ON, Canada [*Library symbol Library of Congress*] (LCLS)

CaOStMEF ... Canada Department of the Environment, Sea Lamprey Control Centre, Sault Ste. Marie, ON, Canada [*Library symbol Library of Congress*] (LCLS)

CaOStMF ..... Canada Department of the Environment, Research Station, Sault Ste. Marie, ON, Canada [*Library symbol Library of Congress*] (LCLS)

CaOStMGH... General Hospital, Sault Ste. Marie, ON, Canada [*Library symbol*] [*Library of Congress*] (LCLS)

CaOStMH..... Sault Ste. Marie and 49th (SSM) Field Regiment, RCA Historical Society, Sault Ste. Marie, ON, Canada [*Library symbol Library of Congress*] (LCLS)

CaOStMPH... Plummer Public Hospital, Sault Ste. Marie, ON, Canada [*Library symbol Library of Congress*] (LCLS)

CaOStr......... Streetsville Public Library, Streetsville, ON, Canada [*Library symbol Library of Congress*] (LCLS)

CaOStrAG .... Rothmans Art Gallery, Stratford, ON, Canada [*Library symbol Library of Congress*] (LCLS)

CaOStro....... Stround Branch Library, Stround, ON, Canada [*Library symbol Library of Congress*] (LCLS)

CaOStrP....... Strathroy Public Library, Strathroy, ON, Canada [*Library symbol Library of Congress*] (LCLS)

CaOStT .... St. Thomas Public Library, St. Thomas, ON, Canada [*Library symbol Library of Congress*] (LCLS)

CaOStTE .... Elgin County Public Library, St. Thomas, ON, Canada [*Library symbol Library of Congress*] (LCLS)

CaOStu .... Sturgeon Falls Public Library, Sturgeon Falls, ON, Canada [*Library symbol Library of Congress*] (LCLS)

CaOSu .... Sudbury Public Library, Sudbury, ON, Canada [*Library symbol Library of Congress*] (LCLS)

CaOSUC ...... Cambrian College, Sudbury, ON, Canada [*Library symbol*] [*Library of Congress*] (LCLS)

CaOSUCS..... Sudbury Public Library, Information and Reference, Sudbury, ON, Canada [*Library symbol*] [*Library of Congress*] (LCLS)

CaOSuGH..... Sudbury General Hospital, Sudbury, ON, Canada [*Library symbol Library of Congress*] (LCLS)

CaOSuL....... Laurentian University, Sudbury, ON, Canada [*Library symbol Library of Congress*] (LCLS)

CaOSuN .... North Central Regional Library, Sudbury, ON, Canada [*Library symbol Library of Congress*] (LCLS)

CaOSunB ..... Brock Township Public Library, Sunderland, ON, Canada [*Library symbol Library of Congress*] (LCLS)

CaOSuU .... University of Sudbury, Sudbury, ON, Canada [*Library symbol*] [*Library of Congress*] (LCLS)

CaOSyFC...... Frontenac County Library, Sydenham Branch, Sydenham, ON, Canada [*Library symbol*] [*Library of Congress*] (LCLS)

CAOT .... Canadian Association of Occupational Therapists [*Association Canadienne des Ergotherapeutes*] (AC)

CaOTA .... Academy of Medicine, Toronto, ON, Canada [*Library symbol Library of Congress*] (LCLS)

CaOTAC .... Acres Consulting Services Ltd., Toronto, ON, Canada [*Library symbol Library of Congress*] (LCLS)

CaOTAD .... Addiction Research Foundation, Toronto, ON, Canada [*Library symbol*] [*Library of Congress*] (LCLS)

CaOTAE....... Atomic Energy of Canada, Toronto, ON, Canada [*Library symbol Library of Congress*] (LCLS)

CaOTAF....... Ontario Ministry of Agriculture and Food, Toronto, ON, Canada [*Library symbol Library of Congress*] (LCLS)

CaOTAG .... Art Gallery of Ontario, Toronto, ON, Canada [*Library symbol Library of Congress*] (LCLS)

CaOTAGAV... Art Gallery of Ontario, Audiovisual Library, Toronto, ON, Canada [*Library symbol Library of Congress*] (LCLS)

CaOTAGC..... Attorney General of Ontario, Crown Law Office, Toronto, ON, Canada [*Library symbol Library of Congress*] (LCLS)

CaOTAH .... Ontario Ministry of Agriculture and Food, Home Economics Branch, Toronto, ON, Canada [*Closed*] [*Library symbol Library of Congress*] (LCLS)

CaOTAL....... Arts and Letters Club, Toronto, ON, Canada [*Library symbol Library of Congress*] (LCLS)

CaOTAP .... Alternative Press Centre, Toronto, ON, Canada [*Library symbol Library of Congress*] (LCLS)

CaOTAr .... Ontario Department of Public Records and Archives, Toronto, ON, Canada [*Library symbol Library of Congress*] (LCLS)

CaOTARC ..... Centennial College of Applied Arts and Technology, Scarborough, ON, Canada [*Library symbol Library of Congress*] (LCLS)

CaOTB .... Thunder Bay Public Library, Thunder Bay, ON, Canada [*Library symbol Library of Congress*] (LCLS)

CaOTbA....... Terrace Bay Public Library, Terrace Bay, ON, Canada [*Library symbol Library of Congress*] (LCLS)

CaOTBBR ..... Brodie Resource Library, Thunder Bay, ON, Canada [*Library symbol Library of Congress*] (LCLS)

CaOTBC .... Canadian Broadcasting Corp., Toronto, ON, Canada [*Library symbol Library of Congress*] (LCLS)

CaOTBCC ..... Confederation College, Thunder Bay, ON, Canada [*Library symbol Library of Congress*] (LCLS)

CaOTBCG ..... Blake, Cassels & Graydon, Law Library, Toronto, ON, Canada [*Library symbol Library of Congress*] (LCLS)

CaOTBCIR.... Bell Canada Information Resource Centre, Toronto, ON, Canada [*Library symbol Library of Congress*] (LCLS)

CaOTBCO..... Bank of Commerce, Technical Information Facility, Toronto, ON, Canada [*Library symbol*] [*Library of Congress*] (LCLS)

CaOTBCP ..... Canadian Broadcasting Corp., Program Archives, Toronto, ON, Canada [*Library symbol Library of Congress*] (LCLS)

CaOTBDHC... Thunder Bay District Health Council, Thunder Bay, ON, Canada [*Library symbol Library of Congress*] (LCLS)

CaOTBH .... Thunder Bay Historical Society, Thunder Bay, ON, Canada [*Library symbol Library of Congress*] (LCLS)

CaOTBLA .... Lakehead University, Audio Library Services of Northwestern Ontario, Thunder Bay, ON, Canada [*Library symbol*] [*Library of Congress*] (LCLS)

CaOTBLL...... Lakehead University, School of Library Technology, Thunder Bay, ON, Canada [*Library symbol*] [*Library of Congress*] (LCLS)

CaOTBLP ..... Lakehead Psychiatric Hospital, Staff Library, Thunder Bay, ON, Canada [*Library symbol Library of Congress*] (LCLS)

CaOTBM ...... Bank of Montreal, Technical Information Centre, Willowdale, ON, Canada [*Library symbol Library of Congress*] (LCLS)

CaOTBMB .... Mary J. L. Black Library, Thunder Bay, ON, Canada [*Library symbol Library of Congress*] (LCLS)

CaOTBMC .... McKellar General Hospital, Medical Library, Thunder Bay, ON, Canada [*Library symbol Library of Congress*] (LCLS)

CaOTBNL ..... Canadian National Institute for the Blind, National Library Division, Toronto, ON, Canada [*Library symbol*] [*Library of Congress*] (LCLS)

CaOTBNS..... Bell Northern Software Research, Toronto, ON, Canada [*Library symbol Library of Congress*] (LCLS)

CaOTBOC..... Ontario Cancer Treatment and Research Foundation, Thunder Bay, ON, Canada [*Library symbol Library of Congress*] (LCLS)

CaOTBP .... Blaney, Pasternak, Smela, Eagleson & Watson, Toronto, ON, Canada [*Library symbol Library of Congress*] (LCLS)

CaOTBR ...... Barringer Research Ltd., Rexdale, ON, Canada [*Library symbol Library of Congress*] (LCLS)

CaOTC .... Ontario College of Education, Toronto, ON, Canada [*Library symbol Library of Congress*] (LCLS)

CaOTCA ...... Ontario College of Art, Toronto, ON, Canada [*Library symbol Library of Congress*] (LCLS)

CaOTCAE .... Canadian Association for Adult Education, Toronto, ON, Canada [*Library symbol Library of Congress*] (LCLS)

CaOTCAG.... Canada Arctic Gas Study Ltd., Toronto, ON, Canada [*Library symbol Library of Congress*] (LCLS)

CaOTCAS .... Canadian Association in Support of the Native Peoples, Toronto, ON, Canada [*Library symbol Library of Congress*] (LCLS)

CaOTCC .... United Church of Canada Archives, Toronto, ON, Canada [*Library symbol Library of Congress*] (LCLS)

CaOTCCC .... Cross Cultural Communication Centre, Toronto, ON, Canada [*Library symbol*] [*Library of Congress*] (LCLS)

CaOTCCL .... Currie, Coopers & Lybrand Ltd., Toronto, ON, Canada [*Library symbol Library of Congress*] (LCLS)

CaOTCCP ..... Canadian Centre for Philanthropy, Toronto, ON, Canada [*Library symbol Library of Congress*] (LCLS)

CaOTCCRT ... Ministry of Consumer and Commercial Relations, Technical Standards Division, Toronto, ON, Canada [*Library symbol Library of Congress*] (LCLS)

CaOTCe........ Central Library, North York, ON, Canada [*Library symbol Library of Congress*] (LCLS)

CaOTCEA .... Canadian Education Association, Toronto, ON, Canada [*Library symbol Library of Congress*] (LCLS)

CaOTCF....... Centre of Forensic Sciences, Ontario Solicitor General, Toronto, ON, Canada [*Library symbol Library of Congress*] (LCLS)

CaOTCGL .... Campbell, Godfrey & Lewtas, Toronto, ON, Canada [*Library symbol Library of Congress*] (LCLS)

CaOTCGR.... Canadian Gas Research Institute, Don Mills, ON, Canada [*Library symbol Library of Congress*] (LCLS)

CaOTCGW... Clarkson, Gordon & Co.: Woods, Gordon & Co., Toronto, ON, Canada [*Library symbol Library of Congress*] (LCLS)

CaOTCH ...... Anglican Church House, Toronto, ON, Canada [*Library symbol Library of Congress*] (LCLS)

CaOTCHA .... Canadian Hospital Association, Toronto, ON, Canada [*Library symbol Library of Congress*] (LCLS)

CaOTCHAr.... Anglican Church of Canada, Archives, Toronto, ON, Canada [*Library symbol Library of Congress*] (LCLS)

CaOTCIA ...... Canadian Institute of International Affairs, Toronto, ON, Canada [*Library symbol Library of Congress*] (LCLS)

CaOTCIB ...... Canadian Imperial Bank of Commerce, Toronto, ON, Canada [*Library symbol Library of Congress*] (LCLS)

CaOTCJC...... Church of Jesus Christ of Latter-Day Saints, Genealogical Society Library, Toronto Branch, Etobicoke, ON, Canada [*Library symbol Library of Congress*] (LCLS)

CaOTCL........ Connaught Medical Research Laboratories, Toronto, ON, Canada [*Library symbol Library of Congress*] (LCLS)

CaOTCLA .... Confederation Life Association, Toronto, ON, Canada [*Library symbol Library of Congress*] (LCLS)

CaOTCM ...... Canadian School of Missions and Ecumenical Institute, Toronto, ON, Canada [*Library symbol Library of Congress*] (LCLS)

CaOTCMC .... Canadian Memorial Chiropractic College, Toronto, ON, Canada [*Library symbol Library of Congress*] (LCLS)

CaOTCMLA... Canadian Music Library Association, Toronto, ON, Canada [*Library symbol Library of Congress*] (LCLS)

CaOTCom .... Cominco Ltd., Toronto, ON, Canada [*Library symbol Library of Congress*] (LCLS)

CaOTCOU.... Council of Ontario Universities, Toronto, ON, Canada [*Library symbol Library of Congress*] (LCLS)

CaOTCPB ..... Toronto City Planning Board, Toronto, ON, Canada [*Library symbol Library of Congress*] (LCLS)

CaOTCR .... Ontario Ministry of Culture and Recreation, Toronto, ON, Canada [*Library symbol Library of Congress*] (LCLS)

CaOTCS .... Correctional Services of Ontario, Toronto, ON, Canada [*Library symbol Library of Congress*] (LCLS)

CaOTCSA .... Canadian Standards Association, Toronto, ON, Canada [*Library symbol Library of Congress*] (LCLS)

CaOTCSC ..... Civil Service Commission of Ontario, Toronto, ON, Canada [*Library symbol Library of Congress*] (LCLS)

CaOTCSS ..... Canebsco Subscription Service Ltd., Toronto, ON, Canada [*Library symbol*] [*Library of Congress*] (LCLS)

CaOTCT........ Canadian Tax Foundation, Toronto, ON, Canada [*Library symbol Library of Congress*] (LCLS)

CaOTCTA ..... Canadian Telebook Agency, Toronto, ON, Canada [*Library symbol Library of Congress*] (LCLS)

CaOTCTAR... City of Toronto, Division of Records and Archives, Toronto, ON, Canada [*Library symbol*] [*Library of Congress*] (LCLS)

CaOTCTVN... CTV Television Network, CTV News Research Library, Toronto, ON, Canada [*Library symbol*] [*Library of Congress*] (LCLS)

CaOTCW ...... Canada Wire & Cable Co. Ltd., Toronto, ON, Canada [*Library symbol Library of Congress*] (LCLS)

CaOTCWB... Canadian Welding Development Institute, Toronto, ON, Canada [*Library symbol Library of Congress*] (LCLS)

CaOTDAR... Doctors Hospital, Alexander Raxlen Memorial Library, Toronto, ON, Canada [*Library symbol Library of Congress*] (LCLS)

CaOTDE .... Ontario Department of Education, Curriculum Division, Toronto, ON, Canada [*Library symbol Library of Congress*] (LCLS)

CaOTDH ...... Ontario Ministry of Health, Toronto, ON, Canada [*Library symbol Library of Congress*] (LCLS)

CaOTDHA..... De Havilland Aircraft of Canada Ltd., Downsview, Toronto, ON, Canada [*Library symbol Library of Congress*] (LCLS)

CaOTDHL..... Ontario Department of Health, Laboratories Branch, Toronto, ON, Canada [*Library symbol Library of Congress*] (LCLS)

CaOTDL .... Ontario Department of Labour, Toronto, ON, Canada [*Library symbol Library of Congress*] (LCLS)

CaOTDM ...... Ontario Ministry of Natural Resources, Mines Library, Toronto, ON, Canada [*Library symbol Library of Congress*] (LCLS)

CaOTDP .... Ontario Department of Public Works, Toronto, ON, Canada [*Library symbol Library of Congress Obsolete*] (LCLS)

CaOTDR....... Department of National Defence, Defence and Civil Institute of Environmental Medicine, Toronto, ON, Canada [*Library symbol Library of Congress*] (LCLS)

CaOTDRE.... Ontario Ministry of Treasury, Economics, and Inter-governmental Affairs, Toronto, ON, Canada [*Library symbol Library of Congress*] (LCLS)

CaOTDT .... Ontario Ministry of Transportation and Communications, Toronto, ON, Canada [*Library symbol Library of Congress*] (LCLS)

CaOTDU .... Ontario Ministry of Colleges and Universities, Toronto, ON, Canada [*Library symbol Library of Congress*] (LCLS)

CaOTE.......... Emmanuel College, Victoria University, Toronto, ON, Canada [*Library symbol Library of Congress*] (LCLS)

CaOTEC........ Toronto Board of Education, Education Centre, Toronto, ON, Canada [*Library symbol Library of Congress*] (LCLS)

CaOTECU..... Ontario Ministry of Education, Colleges and Universities, Toronto, ON, Canada [*Library symbol*] [*Library of Congress*] (LCLS)

CaOTEM ...... ESSO [*Standard Oil*] Minerals of Canada, Toronto, ON, Canada [*Library symbol Library of Congress*] (LCLS)

CaOTEMC ... Elizabeth McRae Associates, Toronto, ON, Canada [*Library symbol*] [*Library of Congress*] (LCLS)

CaOTEMR .... Energy, Mines and Resources Canada, Conservation and Renewable Energy Office, Toronto, ON, Canada [*Library symbol*] [*Library of Congress*] (LCLS)

CaOTEP........ Ontario Department of Education, Provincial Library Service, Toronto, ON, Canada [*Library symbol Library of Congress*] (LCLS)

CaOTEPS ..... Environment Canada, Environmental Protection Service, Toronto, ON, Canada [*Library symbol Library of Congress*] (LCLS)

CaOTEPSE ... Environment Canada, Environmental Protection Service, Environmental Emergency Library, Toronto, ON, Canada [*Library symbol Library of Congress*] (LCLS)

CaOTER ...... Ontario Institute for Studies in Education, Toronto, ON, Canada [*Library symbol Library of Congress*] (LCLS)

CaOTERM .... Ontario Department of Energy and Resources Management, Toronto, ON, Canada [*Library symbol Library of Congress Obsolete*] (LCLS)

CaOTET........ Ontario Educational Communications Authority, Toronto, ON, Canada [*Library symbol Library of Congress*] (LCLS)

CaOTEtPL ... Etobicoke Public Library, Etobicoke, ON, Canada [*Library symbol Library of Congress*] (LCLS)

CaOTEY........ East York Public Library, Toronto, ON, Canada [*Library symbol Library of Congress*] (LCLS)

CaOTF.......... University of Toronto, Environmental Sciences and Engineering, Toronto, ON, Canada [*Library symbol Library of Congress*] (LCLS)

CaOTFC........ Ontario Ministry of Consumer and Commercial Relations, Toronto, ON, Canada [*Library symbol Library of Congress*] (LCLS)

CaOTFH .... Forest Hill Public Library, Toronto, ON, Canada [*Library symbol Library of Congress*] (LCLS)

CaOTFM....... Fire Marshal of Ontario, Toronto, ON, Canada [*Library symbol Library of Congress*] (LCLS)

CaOTFN ...... Falconbridge Nickel Mines Ltd., Information Centre, Toronto, ON, Canada [*Library symbol Library of Congress*] (LCLS)

CaOTFT........ Financial Times, Don Mills, Toronto, ON, Canada [*Library symbol Library of Congress*] (LCLS)

CaOTGE .... Canadian General Electric Co. Ltd., Toronto, ON, Canada [*Library symbol Library of Congress*] (LCLS)

CaOTGFM .... General Foods, Inc., Management Science Department, Don Mills, ON, Canada [*Library symbol*] [*Library of Congress*] (LCLS)

CaOTGM ...... Globe and Mail, Toronto, ON, Canada [*Library symbol Library of Congress*] (LCLS)

CaOTGOH ... Gowling & Henderson, Toronto, ON, Canada [*Library symbol*] [*Library of Congress*] (LCLS)

CaOTGSB.... Ontario Ministry of Government Services, Bibliographic Centre, Toronto, ON, Canada [*Library symbol Library of Congress*] (LCLS)

CaOTH .... Hydro-Electric Power Commission of Ontario, Toronto, ON, Canada [*Library symbol Library of Congress*] (LCLS)

CaOTHA...... Hatch Associates Ltd., Toronto, ON, Canada [*Library symbol*] [*Library of Congress*] (LCLS)

CaOTHC....... Humber College of Applied Arts and Technology, Rexdale, Toronto, ON, Canada [*Library symbol Library of Congress*] (LCLS)

CaOTHL .... Honeywell Ltd., Advanced Technology Centre, Willowdale, ON, Canada [*Library symbol*] [*Library of Congress*] (LCLS)

CaOTHMC ... Hay Management Consultants, Information Resources, Toronto, ON, Canada [*Library symbol*] [*Library of Congress*] (LCLS)

CaOTHMH ... Humber Memorial Hospital, Weston, ON, Canada [*Library symbol Library of Congress*] (LCLS)

CaOTHO....... Thornbury Public Library, Thronbury, ON, Canada [*Library symbol*] [*Library of Congress*] (LCLS)

CaOThoP...... Ontario Paper Co. Ltd., Thorold, ON, Canada [*Library symbol Library of Congress*] (LCLS)

CaOThor ..... Thornhill Public Library, Thornhill, ON, Canada [*Library symbol Library of Congress*] (LCLS)

CaOThorF .... Falconbridge Nickel Mines Ltd., Metallurgical Laboratory, Thornhill, ON, Canada [*Library symbol Library of Congress*] (LCLS)

CaOTHP .... Ontario Department of Highways, Planning and Design Branch, Toronto, ON, Canada [*Library symbol Library of Congress Obsolete*] (LCLS)

CaOTHu .... Huntec Ltd., Toronto, ON, Canada [*Library symbol Library of Congress*] (LCLS)

CaOTi.......... Timmins Public Library, Timmins, ON, Canada [*Library symbol Library of Congress*] (LCLS)

CaOTIAP ...... IAPA [*Industrial Accident Prevention Association*] Library, Toronto, ON, Canada [*Library symbol Library of Congress*] (LCLS)

CaOTIC .... Idea Corp., Toronto, ON, Canada [*Library symbol*] [*Library of Congress*] (LCLS)

CaOTICA ...... Institute of Chartered Accountants of Ontario, Toronto, ON, Canada [*Library symbol Library of Congress*] (LCLS)

CaOTiHM ..... Tillonsburg and District Historical Museum Society, Tillonsburg, ON, Canada [*Library symbol*] [*Library of Congress*] (LCLS)

CaOTil .... Tilbury Public Library, Tilbury, ON, Canada [*Library symbol Library of Congress*] (LCLS)

CaOTIM........ Pontifical Institute of Mediaeval Studies, University of Toronto, Toronto, ON, Canada [*Library symbol Library of Congress*] (LCLS)

CaOTIN .... International Nickel Co. of Canada, Toronto, ON, Canada [*Library symbol Library of Congress*] (LCLS)

CaOTINF ...... Informart, Toronto, ON, Canada [*Library symbol Library of Congress*] (LCLS)

CaOTIO .... United Kingdom Information Office, Toronto, ON, Canada [*Library symbol Library of Congress*] (LCLS)

CaOTIOL ...... Imperial Oil Ltd., Toronto, ON, Canada [*Library symbol Library of Congress*] (LCLS)

CaOTiP .... Tillsonburg Public Library, Tillsonburg, ON, Canada [*Library symbol Library of Congress*] (LCLS)

CaOTiSMG ... Saint Mary's General Hospital, Timmins, ON, Canada [*Library symbol*] [*Library of Congress*] (LCLS)

CaOTJ.......... Canada Department of Justice, Toronto, ON, Canada [*Library symbol Library of Congress*] (LCLS)

CaOTJFM ..... James F. MacLaren Ltd., Willowdale, Toronto, ON, Canada [*Library symbol Library of Congress*] (LCLS)

CaOTJL........ Ontario Ministry of the Attorney General, Judges Library, Toronto, ON, Canada [*Library symbol Library of Congress*] (LCLS)

CaOTJPS...... Jerram Pharmaceuticals Ltd., Sands Pharmaceutical Division, Toronto, ON, Canada [*Library symbol Library of Congress*] (LCLS)

CaOTJS........ Jesuit Seminary, Toronto, ON, Canada [*Library symbol Library of Congress*] (LCLS)

CaOTK .... Knox College, University of Toronto, Toronto, ON, Canada [*Library symbol Library of Congress*] (LCLS)

CaOTKC .... Kidd Creek Mines Ltd., Toronto, ON, Canada [*Library symbol*] [*Library of Congress*] (LCLS)

CaOTL.......... Ontario Legislative Library, Toronto, ON, Canada [*Library symbol Library of Congress*] (LCLS)

CaOTLC........ Ontario Ministry of Natural Resources, Information Section, Reference Library, Toronto, ON, Canada [*Library symbol Library of Congress*] (LCLS)

CaOTLCC ..... Lummus Co. Canada Ltd., Willowdale, ON, Canada [*Library symbol Library of Congress*] (LCLS)

CaOTLF........ Ontario Ministry of Natural Resources, Natural Resources Library, Toronto, ON, Canada [*Library symbol Library of Congress*] (LCLS)

CaOTLL........ Ontario Ministry of Natural Resources, Lands and Surveys Branch, Toronto, ON, Canada [*Library symbol Library of Congress*] (LCLS)

CaOTLP........ Ledbury Park Junior High School, Toronto, ON, Canada [*Library symbol Library of Congress*] (LCLS)

CaOTLR .... Ontario Ministry of Natural Resources, Research Branch, Toronto, ON, Canada [*Library symbol Library of Congress*] (LCLS)

CaOTLS........ Law Society of Upper Canada, Toronto, ON, Canada [*Library symbol Library of Congress*] (LCLS)

CaOTLSC ..... Litton Systems Canada Ltd., Rexdale, ON, Canada [*Library symbol*] [*Library of Congress*] (LCLS)

CaOTM........ Canada Department of the Environment, Atmospheric Environment Service, Toronto, ON, Canada [*Library symbol Library of Congress*] (LCLS)

CaOTMAG .... Ontario Ministry of the Attorney General, Toronto, ON, Canada [*Library symbol*] [*Library of Congress*] (LCLS)

CaOTMB ...... McMillen Birch, Toronto, ON, Canada [*Library symbol Library of Congress*] (LCLS)

CaOTMC ...... Massey College in the University of Toronto, Toronto, ON, Canada [*Library symbol Library of Congress*] (LCLS)

CaOTMCL .... Metropolitan Toronto Central Library, Toronto, ON, Canada [*Library symbol Library of Congress Obsolete*] (LCLS)

CaOTME....... Ontario Ministry of Energy, Toronto, ON, Canada [*Library symbol Library of Congress*] (LCLS)

CaOTMEN .... Ontario Ministry of the Environment, Toronto, ON, Canada [*Library symbol Library of Congress*] (LCLS)

CaOTMENL.. Ontario Ministry of the Environment, Laboratory, Toronto, ON, Canada [*Library symbol Library of Congress*] (LCLS)

CaOTMF....... McIntyre-Falconbridge Library, Toronto, ON, Canada [*Library symbol Library of Congress*] (LCLS)

CaOTMH ...... MacLean-Hunter Ltd., Toronto, ON, Canada [*Library symbol Library of Congress*] (LCLS)

CaOTMI........ Royal Canadian Military Institute, Toronto, ON, Canada [*Library symbol Library of Congress*] (LCLS)

CaOTMIO ..... Canada Employment and Immigration Department, Toronto, ON, Canada [*Library symbol Library of Congress*] (LCLS)

CaOTMM..... McCarthy & McCarthy, Barristers and Solicitors, Toronto, ON, Canada [*Library symbol Library of Congress*] (LCLS)

CaOTMMB .. Ontario Milks Marketing Board, Toronto, ON, Canada [*Library symbol Library of Congress*] (LCLS)

CaOTMML.... Micromedia Ltd., Toronto, ON, Canada [*Library symbol*] [*Library of Congress*] (LCLS)

CaOTMOF .... MacDonald Ophthalmic Foundation, Toronto, ON, Canada [*Library symbol Library of Congress*] (LCLS)

CaOTMS ...... Mount Sinaid Hospital, Toronto, ON, Canada [*Library symbol*] [*Library of Congress*] (LCLS)

CaOTMSS .... Metropolitan Separate School Board, Professional Library, Willowdale, ON, Canada [*Library symbol*] [*Library of Congress*] (LCLS)

CaOTMT....... Monetary Times, Toronto, ON, Canada [*Library symbol Library of Congress*] (LCLS)

CaOTMTS ..... Metropolitan Toronto School Board, Toronto, ON, Canada [*Library symbol Library of Congress*] (LCLS)

CaOTMTSS... Metropolitan Toronto School Board, Secondary Schools, Toronto, ON, Canada [*Library symbol*] [*Library of Congress*] (LCLS)

CaOTN .... Newtonbrook Secondary School, Willowdale, ON, Canada [*Library symbol Library of Congress*] (LCLS)

CaOTNA .... Ontario Ministry of Northern Affairs, Toronto, ON, Canada [*Library symbol Library of Congress*] (LCLS)

CaOTNH....... National Heritage Ltd., Toronto, ON, Canada [*Library symbol Library of Congress*] (LCLS)

CaOTNHH .... Canada Department of National Health and Welfare, Health Protection Branch, Toronto, ON, Canada [*Library symbol*] [*Library of Congress*] (LCLS)

CaOTNIMR... National Institute on Mental Retardation, Toronto, ON, Canada [*Library symbol Library of Congress*] (LCLS)

CaOTNM ...... Northern Mines, Toronto, ON, Canada [*Library symbol Library of Congress*] (LCLS)

CaOTNS .... Bank of Nova Scotia, Toronto, ON, Canada [*Library symbol Library of Congress*] (LCLS)

CaOTNY .... North York Public Library, Toronto, ON, Canada [*Library symbol Library of Congress*] (LCLS)

CaOTNYE ..... North York Board of Education, F. W. Minkler Library, Willowdale, Toronto, ON, Canada [*Library symbol Library of Congress*] (LCLS)

CaOTo.......... Tottenham Public Library, Tottenham, ON, Canada [*Library symbol Library of Congress*] (LCLS)

CaOTOC .... Ontario Cancer Institute, Toronto, ON, Canada [*Library symbol Library of Congress*] (LCLS)

CaOTOE .... Omnispace Environments Ltd., Toronto, ON, Canada [*Library symbol*] [*Library of Congress*] (LCLS)

CaOTOEB ..... Ontario Energy Board, Toronto, ON, Canada [*Library symbol*] [*Library of Congress*] (LCLS)

CaOTOEC ..... Ontario Economic Council, Toronto, ON, Canada [*Library symbol Library of Congress*] (LCLS)

CaOTOGR .... Ontario Geriatrics Research Society, Toronto, ON, Canada [*Library symbol Library of Congress*] (LCLS)

CaOTOH....... Ontario Housing Corp., Toronto, ON, Canada [*Library symbol Library of Congress*] (LCLS)

CaOTOHOR... Ontario Hydro, Central Records, Toronto, ON, Canada [*Library symbol Library of Congress*] (LCLS)

CaOTOMA .... Ontario Medical Association, Toronto, ON, Canada [*Library symbol Library of Congress*] (LCLS)

CaOTOMR.... Ontario Ministry of Revenue, Toronto, ON, Canada [*Library symbol Library of Congress*] (LCLS)

CaOTOPC ..... Ortho Pharmaceutical Canada Ltd., Don Mills, Toronto, ON, Canada [*Library symbol Library of Congress*] (LCLS)

CaOTOPCT ... Ontario Police Commission, Technical Services Branch, Planning and Research Library, Toronto, ON, Canada [*Library symbol*] [*Library of Congress*] (LCLS)

CaOTOSC..... Ontario Securities Commission, Toronto, ON, Canada [*Library symbol*] [*Library of Congress*] (LCLS)

CaOTOSS..... Ontario Secondary School Teachers Federation, Toronto, ON, Canada [*Library symbol*] [*Library of Congress*] (LCLS)

CaOTP .... Toronto Public Library, Metropolitan Bibliographic Centre, Toronto, ON, Canada [*Library symbol Library of Congress*] (LCLS)

CaOTPA .... Institute of Public Administration of Canada, Toronto, ON, Canada [*Library symbol Library of Congress*] (LCLS)

CaOTPAL ..... PAL Reading Service, Toronto, ON, Canada [*Library symbol*] [*Library of Congress*] (LCLS)

CaOTPB .... Metropolitan Toronto Central Library, Baldwin Room, Toronto, ON, Canada [*Library symbol Library of Congress*] (LCLS)

CaOTPFA ..... Toronto Public Libraries, Fine Arts Libraries, Northern District, Toronto, ON, Canada [*Library symbol Library of Congress*] (LCLS)

CaOTPG....... Polar Gas Library, Toronto, ON, Canada [*Library symbol Library of Congress*] (LCLS)

CaOTPH .... Metropolitan Toronto Central Library, History Section, Toronto, ON, Canada [*Library symbol Library of Congress*] (LCLS)

CaOTPM ...... Municipal Reference Library, Toronto, ON, Canada [*Library symbol*] [*Library of Congress*] (LCLS)

CaOTPP .... Ontario Provincial Police, Toronto, ON, Canada [*Library symbol Library of Congress*] (LCLS)

CaOTPPC .... Ontario Provincial Police College, Toronto, ON, Canada [*Library symbol Library of Congress*] (LCLS)

CaOTPR ...... Proctor & Redfern Group, Toronto, ON, Canada [*Library symbol Library of Congress*] (LCLS)

CaOTPW ...... Ontario Ministry of Community and Social Services, Toronto, ON, Canada [*Library symbol Library of Congress*] (LCLS)

CaOTPWC .... Public Works Canada, Ontario Regional Library, Toronto, ON, Canada [*Library symbol Library of Congress*] (LCLS)

CaOTQE .... Queen Elizabeth Hospital, Toronto, ON, Canada [*Library symbol*] [*Library of Congress*] (LCLS)

CaOTQRM.... Queen's Own Rifles of Canada Regimental Museum, Toronto, ON, Canada [*Library symbol Library of Congress*] (LCLS)

CaOTQSM .... Queen Street Mental Health Centre, Toronto, ON, Canada [*Library symbol Library of Congress*] (LCLS)

CaOTR .... Ryerson Institute, Toronto, ON, Canada [*Library symbol Library of Congress*] (LCLS)

CaOTRA .... Royal Astronomical Society, Toronto, ON, Canada [*Library symbol Library of Congress*] (LCLS)

CaOTRAL ..... Rio Algom Ltd., Toronto, ON, Canada [*Library symbol*] [*Library of Congress*] (LCLS)

CaOTRBI ..... Royal Bank of Canada, Information Resources, Toronto, ON, Canada [*Library symbol*] [*Library of Congress*] (LCLS)

CaOTRC .... Canadian Forces College, Toronto, ON, Canada [*Library symbol Library of Congress*] (LCLS)

CaOTRCL .... Reichhold Chemicals Ltd., Weston, Toronto, ON, Canada [*Library symbol Library of Congress*] (LCLS)

CaOTRCS ..... Canada Department of National Defence, Canadian Forces Staff School, Toronto, ON, Canada [*Library symbol Library of Congress*] (LCLS)

CaOTREC ..... Regis College, Toronto, ON, Canada [*Library symbol Library of Congress*] (LCLS)

CaOTREx..... Canada Department of Regional Economic Expansion, Toronto, ON, Canada [*Library symbol Library of Congress*] (LCLS)

CaOTRF .... Ontario Research Foundation, Toronto, ON, Canada [*Library symbol Library of Congress*] (LCLS)

CaOTRIC ...... Rockwell International, Collins Canada Division, Toronto, ON, Canada [*Library symbol Library of Congress*] (LCLS)

CaOTRL .... Reed Ltd., Toronto, ON, Canada [*Library symbol Library of Congress*] (LCLS)

CaOTRM ...... Royal Ontario Museum, Toronto, ON, Canada [*Library symbol Library of Congress*] (LCLS)

CaOTRMC .... Royal Ontario Museum, Canadiana Department, Toronto, ON, Canada [*Library symbol Library of Congress*] (LCLS)

CaOTRMF .... Royal Ontario Museum, Far Eastern Department, Toronto, ON, Canada [*Library symbol Library of Congress*] (LCLS)

CaOTS .... Statistics Canada, Toronto, ON, Canada [*Library symbol Library of Congress*] (LCLS)

CaOTSA .... Salvation Army Library, Toronto, ON, Canada [*Library symbol Library of Congress*] (LCLS)

CaOTSAC .... Sanco Consultants Ltd., Toronto, ON, Canada [*Library symbol*] [*Library of Congress*] (LCLS)

CaOTSAP ..... Spar Aerospace Products, Toronto, ON, Canada [*Library symbol Library of Congress*] (LCLS)

CaOTSC .... Seneca College, Willowdale, ON, Canada [*Library symbol Library of Congress*] (LCLS)

CaOTSCC .... Scarborough College, Scarborough, ON, Canada [*Library symbol Library of Congress*] (LCLS)

CaOTSCI ...... Sulzer Canada, Inc., Toronto, ON, Canada [*Library symbol*] [*Library of Congress*] (LCLS)

CaOTSCL ..... Shell Canada Ltd., Toronto, ON, Canada [*Library symbol Library of Congress*] (LCLS)

CaOTSE........ Toronto Stock Exchange Library, Toronto, ON, Canada [*Library symbol*] [*Library of Congress*] (LCLS)

CaOTSED ..... Scarborough Borough Board of Education, Toronto, ON, Canada [*Library symbol Library of Congress*] (LCLS)

CaOTSLR ..... Sun Life of Canada, Reference Library, Toronto, ON, Canada [*Library symbol Library of Congress*] (LCLS)

CaOTSM ...... Saint Michael's Hospital, Toronto, ON, Canada [*Library symbol Library of Congress*] (LCLS)

CaOTSMC .... Sunnybrook Medical Centre, Toronto, ON, Canada [*Library symbol Library of Congress*] (LCLS)

CaOTSML .... Selco Mining Corp., Toronto, ON, Canada [*Library symbol*] [*Library of Congress*] (LCLS)

CaOTSP .... Scarborough Public Library, Scarborough, ON, Canada [*Library symbol Library of Congress*] (LCLS)

CaOTSPA ..... Scarborough Public Library, Albert Campbell Branch, Scarborough, ON, Canada [*Library symbol Library of Congress*] (LCLS)

CaOTSPC .... Scarborough Public Library, Cedarbrae Branch, Scarborough, ON, Canada [*Library symbol Library of Congress*] (LCLS)

CaOTST........ Ontario Science Centre, Toronto, ON, Canada [*Library symbol Library of Congress*] (LCLS)

CaOTStA ...... Saint Augustine's Seminary, Toronto, ON, Canada [*Library symbol Library of Congress*] (LCLS)

CaOTSTF....... Ontario Film Institute, Science Centre Library, Toronto, ON, Canada [*Library symbol Library of Congress*] (LCLS)

CaOTSTG .... St. George's College, Toronto, ON, Canada [*Library symbol*] [*Library of Congress*] (LCLS)

CaOTSTJ....... St. Joseph's Health Centre, George Pennal Library, Toronto, ON, Canada [*Library symbol*] [*Library of Congress*] (LCLS)

CaOTStM ..... University of Saint Michael's College, Toronto, ON, Canada [*Library symbol Library of Congress*] (LCLS)

CaOTT......... Toronto Transportation Commission, Toronto, ON, Canada [*Library symbol Library of Congress*] (LCLS)

CaOTTC....... University of Trinity College, Toronto, ON, Canada [*Library symbol Library of Congress*] (LCLS)

CaOTTCA..... University of Trinity College, Archives, Toronto, ON, Canada [*Library symbol Library of Congress*] (LCLS)

CaOTTDB..... Toronto Dominion Bank, Toronto, ON, Canada [*Library symbol Library of Congress*] (LCLS)

CaOTTeC..... Toronto Teachers' College, Toronto, ON, Canada [*Library symbol Library of Congress*] (LCLS)

CaOTTex...... Texaco Canada Inc., Don Mills, Toronto, ON, Canada [*Library symbol Library of Congress*] (LCLS)

CaOTTI......... Ontario Ministry of Industry and Tourism, Toronto, ON, Canada [*Library symbol Library of Congress*] (LCLS)

CaOTTOA..... Canada Ministry of Transport, Canadian Air Transportation Administration, Ontario Region, Toronto, ON, Canada [*Library symbol Library of Congress*] (LCLS)

CaOTTR....... Thomson & Rogers, Barristers and Solicitors, Toronto, ON, Canada [*Library symbol Library of Congress*] (LCLS)

CaOTTRC.... Touche Ross and Co., Toronto, ON, Canada [*Library symbol*] [*Library of Congress*] (LCLS)

CaOTTRCC.. Thistletown Regional Centre for Children and Adolescents, Rexdale, ON, Canada [*Library symbol*] [*Library of Congress*] (LCLS)

CaOTU .... University of Toronto, Toronto, ON, Canada [*Library symbol Library of Congress*] (LCLS)

CaOTUA....... University of Toronto, Institute of Aerophysics, Toronto, ON, Canada [*Library symbol Library of Congress*] (LCLS)

CaOTUAn..... University of Toronto, Department of Anatomy, Toronto, ON, Canada [*Library symbol Library of Congress*] (LCLS)

CaOTUAP..... University of Toronto, Department of Applied Physics, Toronto, ON, Canada [*Library symbol Library of Congress*] (LCLS)

CaOTUAr...... University of Toronto, Archives, Toronto, ON, Canada [*Library symbol Library of Congress*] (LCLS)

CaOTUAV..... University of Toronto, Audiovisual Library, Toronto, ON, Canada [*Library symbol Library of Congress*] (LCLS)

CaOTUB....... University of Toronto, Department of Biochemistry, Toronto, ON, Canada [*Library symbol Library of Congress*] (LCLS)

CaOTUBP..... University of Toronto, Banting-Best Physiology Library, Toronto, ON, Canada [*Library symbol Library of Congress*] (LCLS)

CaOTUC....... University of Toronto, Department of Chemistry, Toronto, ON, Canada [*Library symbol Library of Congress*] (LCLS)

CaOTUCC.... University of Toronto, Institute of Computer Science, Toronto, ON, Canada [*Library symbol Library of Congress*] (LCLS)

CaOTUCE..... University of Toronto, Department of Chemical Engineering and Applied Chemistry, Toronto, ON, Canada [*Library symbol Library of Congress*] (LCLS)

CaOTUCi...... University of Toronto, Department of Civil Engineering, Toronto, ON, Canada [*Library symbol Library of Congress*] (LCLS)

CaOTUCr...... University of Toronto, Centre of Criminology, Toronto, ON, Canada [*Library symbol Library of Congress*] (LCLS)

CaOTUCS..... University of Toronto, Institute of Child Study, Toronto, ON, Canada [*Library symbol Library of Congress*] (LCLS)

CaOTUD....... University of Toronto, David Dunlap Observatory, Toronto, ON, Canada [*Library symbol Library of Congress*] (LCLS)

CaOTUDB..... University of Toronto, Department of Botany, Toronto, ON, Canada [*Library symbol Library of Congress*] (LCLS)

CaOTUDM.... University of Toronto, Department of Mathematics, Toronto, ON, Canada [*Library symbol Library of Congress*] (LCLS)

CaOTUDP..... University of Toronto, Clarke Institute of Psychiatry, Toronto, ON, Canada [*Library symbol Library of Congress*] (LCLS)

CaOTUEE..... University of Toronto, Department of Electrical Engineering, Toronto, ON, Canada [*Library symbol Library of Congress*] (LCLS)

CaOTUFA..... University of Toronto, Department of Fine Arts, Toronto, ON, Canada [*Library symbol Library of Congress*] (LCLS)

CaOTUFD..... University of Toronto, Faculty of Dentistry, Toronto, ON, Canada [*Library symbol Library of Congress*] (LCLS)

CaOTUFM.... University of Toronto, Faculty of Music, Toronto, ON, Canada [*Library symbol Library of Congress*] (LCLS)

CaOTUFP..... University of Toronto, Faculty of Pharmacy, Toronto, ON, Canada [*Library symbol Library of Congress*] (LCLS)

CaOTUG....... University of Toronto, Department of Geological Sciences, Toronto, ON, Canada [*Library symbol Library of Congress*] (LCLS)

CaOTUGL..... University of Toronto, Geophysics Laboratory, Toronto, ON, Canada [*Library symbol Library of Congress*] (LCLS)

CaOTUH....... University of Toronto, School of Hygiene, Toronto, ON, Canada [*Library symbol Library of Congress*] (LCLS)

CaOTUHO.... University of Toronto, Science Medicine Library, Occupational and Environmental Health Unit, Toronto, ON, Canada [*Library symbol*] [*Library of Congress*] (LCLS)

CaOTUINC.... University of Toronto, Innis College, Toronto, ON, Canada [*Library symbol*] [*Library of Congress*] (LCLS)

CaOTUIRN... University of Toronto, Center for Industrial Relations, the Jean and Dorothy Newman Industrial Relations Library, Toronto, ON, Canada [*Library symbol Library of Congress*] (LCLS)

CaOTUL....... University of Toronto, Faculty of Law, Toronto, ON, Canada [*Library symbol Library of Congress*] (LCLS)

CaOTULAS... University of Toronto, Library Automation Systems, Toronto, ON, Canada [*Library symbol Library of Congress*] (LCLS)

CaOTULS..... University of Toronto, School of Library Science, Toronto, ON, Canada [*Library symbol Library of Congress*] (LCLS)

CaOTUM...... University of Toronto, Department of Mechanical Engineering, Toronto, ON, Canada [*Library symbol Library of Congress*] (LCLS)

CaOTUMa.... University of Toronto, Map Library, Toronto, ON, Canada [*Library symbol Library of Congress*] (LCLS)

CaOTUME.... University of Toronto, Department of Metallurgical Engineering, Toronto, ON, Canada [*Library symbol Library of Congress*] (LCLS)

CaOTUMi.... University of Toronto, Department of Mining Engineering, Toronto, ON, Canada [*Library symbol Library of Congress*] (LCLS)

CaOTUN....... University of Toronto, School of Nursing, Toronto, ON, Canada [*Library symbol Library of Congress*] (LCLS)

CaOTUNC.... Union Carbide Canada Ltd., Toronto, ON, Canada [*Library symbol Library of Congress*] (LCLS)

CaOTUNWC... University of Toronto, New College, Toronto, ON, Canada [*Library symbol*] [*Library of Congress*] (LCLS)

CaOTUP....... University of Toronto, Department of Physics, Toronto, ON, Canada [*Library symbol Library of Congress*] (LCLS)

CaOTUPa..... University of Toronto, Department of Pathology, Banting-Best Institute, Toronto, ON, Canada [*Library symbol Library of Congress*] (LCLS)

CaOTURS..... University of Toronto, Department of Rare Books and Special Collections, Toronto, ON, Canada [*Library symbol Library of Congress*] (LCLS)

CaOTUSA..... University of Toronto, School of Architecture, Toronto, ON, Canada [*Library symbol Library of Congress*] (LCLS)

CaOTUSP..... University of Toronto, School of Physical and Health Education, Toronto, ON, Canada [*Library symbol Library of Congress*] (LCLS)

CaOTUSW.... University of Toronto, School of Social Work, Toronto, ON, Canada [*Library symbol Library of Congress*] (LCLS)

CaOTUTD.... Urban Transportation Development Corp., Toronto, ON, Canada [*Library symbol Library of Congress*] (LCLS)

CaOTUTF..... University of Toronto, Thomas Fisher Rare Book Library, Toronto, ON, Canada [*Library symbol Library of Congress*] (LCLS)

CaOTUTP..... University of Toronto Press, University of Toronto, Toronto, ON, Canada [*Library symbol Library of Congress*] (LCLS)

CaOTUUC.... University of Toronto, University College, Toronto, ON, Canada [*Library symbol*] [*Library of Congress*] (LCLS)

CaOTUZ....... University of Toronto, Department of Zoology, Toronto, ON, Canada [*Library symbol Library of Congress*] (LCLS)

CaOTV .... Victoria University, Toronto, ON, Canada [*Library symbol Library of Congress*] (LCLS)

CaOTVL....... V&L Enterprises, Downsview, ON, Canada [*Library symbol*] [*Library of Congress*] (LCLS)

CaOTW .... Wycliffe College, Toronto, ON, Canada [*Library symbol Library of Congress*] (LCLS)

CaOTWC ...... Workmen's Compensation Board, Toronto, ON, Canada [*Library symbol Library of Congress*] (LCLS)

CaOTWCA .... Ontario Workers' Compensation Appeals Tribunal, Toronto, ON, Canada [*Library symbol*] [*Library of Congress*] (LCLS)

CaOTWCV .... Worker's Compensation Board, Vocatioal Rehabilitation Library, Toronto, ON, Canada [*Library symbol*] [*Library of Congress*] (LCLS)

CaOTWH ...... [*The*] Wellesley Hospital, Toronto, ON, Canada [*Library symbol*] [*Library of Congress*] (LCLS)

CaOTWL ...... William Lyon MacKenzie Collegiate Institute, Downsview, ON, Canada [*Library symbol Library of Congress*] (LCLS)

CaOTWLC .... Warner-Lambert Canada Ltd., Sheridan Park, ON, Canada [*Library symbol Library of Congress*] (LCLS)

CaOTWM .... William M. Mercer Ltd., Toronto, ON, Canada [*Library symbol Library of Congress*] (LCLS)

CaOTWY ...... Wyeth Ltd., Medical Library, Downsview, ON, Canada [*Library symbol*] [*Library of Congress*] (LCLS)

CaOTXRA.... X-Ray Assay Laboratories Ltd., Don Mills, Toronto, ON, Canada [*Library symbol Library of Congress*] (LCLS)

CaOTY .... York University, Toronto, ON, Canada [*Library symbol Library of Congress*] (LCLS)

CaOTYA ...... York University Archives, Toronto, ON, Canada [*Library symbol*] [*Library of Congress*] (LCLS)

CaOTYBE ..... York Borough Board of Education, Toronto, ON, Canada [*Library symbol Library of Congress*] (LCLS)

CaOTYBES ... Board of Education for the City of York, Schools, Toronto, ON, Canada [*Library symbol*] [*Library of Congress*] (LCLS)

CaOTYCE ..... York County Board of Education, Toronto, ON, Canada [*Library symbol Library of Congress*] (LCLS)

CaOTYL....... York University, Law Library, Toronto, ON, Canada [*Library symbol Library of Congress*] (LCLS)

CaOTYP .... York Public Library, Toronto, ON, Canada [*Library symbol Library of Congress*] (LCLS)

CaOUSH....... Uxbridge-Scott Historical Society, Uxbridge, ON, Canada [*Library symbol*] [*Library of Congress*] (LCLS)

CaOUT .... Uxbridge Township Public Library, Uxbridge, ON, Canada [*Library symbol*] [*Library of Congress*] (LCLS)

CaOVAg .... Ontario Ministry of Agriculture and Food, Horticultural Research Institute, Vineland Station, ON, Canada [*Library symbol Library of Congress*] (LCLS)

CaOVAgR..... Canada Department of Agriculture, Research Station, Vineland Station, ON, Canada [*Library symbol Library of Congress*] (LCLS)

CaOVan........ Vanier Public Library, Vanier, ON, Canada [*Library symbol Library of Congress*] (LCLS)

CaOVc.......... Valley East Public Library, Val Caron, ON, Canada [*Library symbol Library of Congress*] (LCLS)

CaOW .... Windsor Public Library, Windsor, ON, Canada [*Library symbol Library of Congress*] (LCLS)

CaOWA .... University of Windsor, Windsor, ON, Canada [*Library symbol Library of Congress*] (LCLS)

CaOWAG...... Art Gallery of Windsor, Windsor, ON, Canada [*Library symbol Library of Congress*] (LCLS)

CaOWAL	University of Windsor, Law Library, Windsor, ON, Canada [*Library symbol Library of Congress*] (LCLS)
CaOWall	Wallaceburg Public Library, Wallaceburg, ON, Canada [*Library symbol Library of Congress*] (LCLS)
CaOWaP	Waterford Public Library, Waterford, ON, Canada [*Library symbol Library of Congress*] (LCLS)
CaOWar	Warkworth Public Library, Warkworth, ON, Canada [*Library symbol Library of Congress*] (LCLS)
CaOWaT	Wainfleet Township Library, Wainfleet, ON, Canada [*Library symbol*] [*Library of Congress*] (LCLS)
CaOWBC	Bloorview Children's Hospital, Health Sciences Library, Willowdale, ON, Canada [*Library symbol*] [*Library of Congress*] (LCLS)
CaOWBE	Windsor Board of Education, Windwor, ON, Canada [*Library symbol*] [*Library of Congress*] (LCLS)
CaOWC	Centennial Secondary School, Windsor, ON, Canada [*Library symbol Library of Congress*] (LCLS)
CaOWCC	Cape Croker Public Library, Wiarton, ON, Canada [*Library symbol Library of Congress*] (LCLS)
CaOWdOBC...	Ontario Bible College-Ontario Theological College, J. William Horsey Library, Willowdale, ON, Canada [*Library symbol*] [*Library of Congress*] (LCLS)
CaOWe	Welland Public Library, Welland, ON, Canada [*Library symbol Library of Congress*] (LCLS)
CaOWeC	Centennial Secondary School, Welland, ON, Canada [*Library symbol Library of Congress*] (LCLS)
CaOWeN	Niagara College of Applied Arts and Technology, Welland, ON, Canada [*Library symbol Library of Congress*] (LCLS)
CaOWENC	Westport-North Crosby Public Library, Westport, ON, Canada [*Library symbol*] [*Library of Congress*] (LCLS)
CaOWeNL	Niagara College of Applied Arts and Technology, Library Technician Program, Welland, ON, Canada [*Library symbol*] [*Library of Congress*] (LCLS)
CaOWesBC...	Borden Chemical, Westhill, ON, Canada [*Library symbol Library of Congress*] (LCLS)
CaOWH	Herman Collegiate Institute, Windsor, ON, Canada [*Library symbol Library of Congress*] (LCLS)
CaOWhP	Whitby Public Library, Whitby, ON, Canada [*Library symbol Library of Congress*] (LCLS)
CaOWhPH	Whitby Psychiatric Hospital, Whitby, ON, Canada [*Library symbol*] [*Library of Congress*] (LCLS)
CaOWIJC	International Joint Commission, Windsor, ON, Canada [*Library symbol Library of Congress*] (LCLS)
CaOWISDG...	Stormount, Dundas & Glengarry County Library, Williamstown Branch, Williamstown,ON, Canada [*Library symbol*] [*Library of Congress*] (LCLS)
CaOWL	Lowe Technical School, Windsor, ON, Canada [*Library symbol Library of Congress*] (LCLS)
CaOWNC	North Crosby Union Library, Westport, ON, Canada [*Library symbol*] [*Library of Congress*] (LCLS)
CaOWo	Woodstock Public Library, Woodstock, ON, Canada [*Library symbol Library of Congress*] (LCLS)
CaOWoM	Woodstock Museum, Woodstock, ON, Canada [*Library symbol*] [*Library of Congress*] (LCLS)
CaOWoO	Oxford County Public Library, Woodstock, ON, Canada [*Library symbol Library of Congress*] (LCLS)
CaOWR	Riverside Secondary School, Windsor, ON, Canada [*Library symbol Library of Congress*] (LCLS)
CaOWS	Southwestern Regional Library, Windsor, ON, Canada [*Library symbol Library of Congress*] (LCLS)
CaOWSA	Spar Aerospace Ltd., Weston, ON, Canada [*Library symbol Library of Congress*] (LCLS)
CaOWSC	Saint Clair College, Windsor, ON, Canada [*Library symbol Library of Congress*] (LCLS)
CaOWt	Waterloo Public Library, Waterloo, ON, Canada [*Library symbol Library of Congress*] (LCLS)
CaOWtA	Kitchener-Waterloo Academy of Medicine, Waterloo, ON, Canada [*Library symbol Library of Congress*] (LCLS)
CaOWtG	Kitchener-Waterloo General Hospital, Waterloo, ON, Canada [*Library symbol Library of Congress*] (LCLS)
CaOWtL	Wilfrid Laurier University, Waterloo, ON, Canada [*Library symbol Library of Congress*] (LCLS)
CaOWtO	Ontario Library Services Center, Waterloo, ON, Canada [*Library symbol*] [*Library of Congress*] (LCLS)
CaOWtS	Saint Mary's General Hospital, Waterloo, ON, Canada [*Library symbol Library of Congress*] (LCLS)
CaOWtU	University of Waterloo, Waterloo, ON, Canada [*Library symbol Library of Congress*] (LCLS)
CaOWtUE	University of Waterloo, Environmental Studies Library, Waterloo, ON, Canada [*Library symbol Library of Congress*] (LCLS)
CaOWVM	Vincent Massey Secondary School, Windsor, ON, Canada [*Library symbol Library of Congress*] (LCLS)
CaOWW	Walkerville Collegiate Institute, Windsor, ON, Canada [*Library symbol Library of Congress*] (LCLS)
CaOWyL	Lambton County Public Library, Wyoming, ON, Canada [*Library symbol Library of Congress*] (LCLS)
CaOWyOL	Ontario Library Co-Operative, Wyoming, ON, Canada [*Library symbol*] [*Library of Congress*] (LCLS)
CA OX.........	Calcium Oxalate [*Organic chemistry*] (AAMN)
CAP.............	Azusa Pacific College, Azusa, CA [*OCLC symbol*] (OCLC)
CAP.............	Cable Access Point [*Telecommunications*] (TSSD)
Ca/P............	Calcium-to-Phosphorus [*Molar ratio*] (DAVI)
CAP.............	Camas Prairie [*Railroad*] (MHDW)
CAP.............	Camas Prairie Railroad Co. (IIA)
CAP.............	Campaign Against Pollution
CAP.............	Campaign Against Pornography [*British*]

CAP.............	Canada Assistance Plan
CAP.............	Canadian Air Publication
CAP.............	Canadian Association of Palynologists [*Association Canadienne des Palynologues*] (AC)
CAP.............	Canadian Association of Pathologists
CAP.............	Canadian Association of Physicists (MCD)
CAP.............	Canadian Association of Principals (AC)
CaP.............	Canadian Poetry in English [*A publication*]
CAP.............	Cancer of Prostate [*Oncology and urology*] (DAVI)
CAP.............	Capacitance (DEN)
cap.............	Capacitance (IDOE)
cap.............	Capacitor (IDOE)
CAP.............	Capacitor (MSA)
CAP.............	Capacity (AFM)
CAP.............	Capacity Assurance Plan [*Environmental regulation*]
CAP.............	Cap Haitien [*Haiti*] [*Airport symbol*] (OAG)
CAP.............	Capiat [*Let the Patient Take*] [*Pharmacy*]
CAP.............	Capilano College Media Centre [*UTLAS symbol*]
CAP.............	Capital (EY)
cap.............	Capital (VRA)
cap.............	Capital (WDMC)
CAP.............	Capital Airlines, Inc. [*ICAO designator*] (FAAC)
CAP.............	Capital Dynamics [*Vancouver Stock Exchange symbol*]
cap.............	Capitalisation
CAP.............	Capitalization [*Real estate*]
CAP.............	Capital Letter [*Typography*] (WDAA)
CAP.............	Capitation
Cap.............	Capitol [*Record label*]
CAP.............	Capitol
CAP.............	Capitol International Airways (MCD)
Cap.............	Capitolo [*Chapter*] [*Italian*] (ILCA)
CAP.............	Capitulum [*Chapter*] [*Latin*]
CAP.............	Capodimonte [*Italy*] [*Seismograph station code, US Geological Survey Closed*] (SEIS)
Cap.............	Capricornus [*Constellation*]
CAP.............	Capsula [*Capsule*] [*Pharmacy*]
CAP.............	Captain
CAP.............	Capture
CAP.............	Caput [*Head*] [*Latin*]
CAP.............	Carbamyl Phosphate [*Also, CP*] [*Organic chemistry*]
CAP.............	Card Assembly Program
CAP.............	Cardioacceleratory Peptide [*Biochemistry*]
CAP.............	Career Analysis Procedure [*LIMRA*]
CAP.............	Career Assistance Program [*Department of Labor*]
CAP.............	Carrierless Amplitude/Phase Modulation (ACRL)
Ca P............	Cases in Parliament [*A publication*] (DLA)
CAP.............	Cash Against Policy [*Insurance*]
CAP.............	Catabolite Activator Protein [*Biochemistry, genetics*]
CAP.............	Catabolite Gene Activator Protein [*Biochemistry, genetics*]
CAP.............	Catalog of American Portraits [*Smithsonian Institution*] [*Washington, DC*]
CAP.............	Cataloguing in Advance of Publication [*British Library Bibliographic Services Division*] (NITA)
CAP.............	Catapult and Arresting Gear Pool [*Navy*]
CAP.............	Catch All Phaults [*Quality control*]
CAP.............	CAVDA [*Citizens Alliance for Venereal Disease Awareness*]-Citizens AIDS Project (EA)
CAP.............	CCMS [*Checkout, Control and Monitor Systems*] Application Program
CAP.............	CCMS [*Checkout, Control, and Monitor Subsystem*] Application Programs [*NASA*] (NASA)
CAP.............	Cell Attachment Protein [*Cytochemistry*]
CAP.............	Cellular Array Processor [*Computer science*] (NITA)
CAP.............	Cellulose Acetate Phthalate [*Organic chemistry*] (MAE)
CAP.............	Cellulose Acetate Propionate [*Organic chemistry*]
CAP.............	Center for Academic Precocity [*Arizona State University*] [*Research center*] (RCD)
CAP.............	Center for Accountability to the Public (EA)
CAP.............	Central Africa Party [*Southern Rhodesia*]
CAP.............	Central Africa Protectorate [*British government*]
CAP.............	Central America and Panama (IID)
CAP.............	Central Arbitration Point [*Computer science*] (PCM)
CAP.............	Central Arizona Project [*Federal water-and-power project, similar to TVA*]
CAP.............	Centralized Assignment Procedures [*Military*] (INF)
CAP.............	Ceramide-Activated Protein [*Biochemistry*]
CAP.............	Certificat d'Aptitude Professionelle [*Certificate of Professional Ability*] [*French*] (BARN)
CAP.............	Chief Ancient Philosophies [*A publication*]
CAP.............	Chief Aviation Pilot [*Navy, Coast Guard*]
CAP.............	Children of Alcoholic Parents [*An association*] (EA)
CAP.............	Chloramphenicol [*Antimicrobial compound*]
CAP.............	Chloraromatic Compound [*Organic chemistry*]
CAP.............	Chloroacetophenone [*Also, CN*] [*Tear gas*]
CAP.............	Cholesteric Analysis Profile Test [*Thermography*] [*Radiology*] (DAVI)
CAP.............	Christian Appalachian Project
CaP.............	Church and Peace [*Schoeffengrund, Federal Republic of Germany*] (EAIO)
CAP.............	Circuit Access Point [*Telecommunications*] (TEL)
CAP.............	Citation Abstract Procurement
CAP.............	Citizens Against PAC's [*Political Action Committees*] [*Defunct*] (EA)
CAP.............	Citizens Against Pornography (EA)
CAP.............	Civil Air Patrol (EA)
CAP.............	Civil Air Publication [*British*] (DEN)
CAP.............	Clathrin-Associated Protein [*Cytology*]
CAP.............	Clean Air Package

CAP	Clean Air Projector
CAP	Client Assistance Program [*Department of Education Department of Health and Human Services*] (GFGA)
CAP	Clinical Articulation Profile [*Speech evaluation test*]
CAP	Closing Agreement Program (WYGK)
CAP	Coalition Against Pipeline Pollution (EA)
CAP	Coarse Aim Positioning
CAP	Coastal America Partnership [*US Army Corps of Engineers*]
CAP	Code of Advertising Practices [*British*]
CAP	Codes and Paging (NRCH)
CAP	Collection Agency Practices
CAP	Collection Agency Project [*Student legal action organization*] (EA)
CAP	College of American Pathologists (EA)
CAP	Combat Aircraft Prototype (MCD)
CAP	Combat Air Patrol
CAP	Combined Action Platoon
CAP	Comite d'Action de la Pomme de Terre [*Potato Action Committee*] [*Canadian Department of Agriculture*]
CAP	Command Action Plan (NVT)
CAP	Command Analysis Pattern (KSC)
CAP	Commencing at a Point
CAP	Commercial Activities Program (AAGC)
CAP	Commission for Accountability to the Public (EA)
CAP	Committee on Accounting Procedure (TDOB)
CAP	Common Agricultural Policy [*Common Market*]
CAP	Commonwealth Association of Planners [*British*] (EAIO)
CAP	Communication Application Platform [*Computer science*] (PCM)
CAP	Communication Association of the Pacific [*Later, WCA*] (EA)
CAP	Communications Afloat Program [*Military*] (DNAB)
CAP	Community-Acquired Pneumonia
CAP	Community Action Party [*Thailand*] [*Political party*] (FEA)
CAP	Community Action Program [*Community Services Administration*]
CAP	Community Alert Patrol
CAP	Competitive Access Provider [*Telecommunications*]
CAP	Compliance Advisory Panel [*Environmental Protection Agency*]
CAP	Compliance Aid for Pharmaceuticals
CAP	Compliance Audit Program [*Environmental technology*]
CAP	Component Acceptance Procedure (IAA)
CAP	Composers' Autograph Publications [*Defunct*] (EA)
CAP	Composite Aircraft Program [*Military*] (RDA)
CAP	Compound Action Potential [*Biology*]
CAP	Computational Arithmetic Program
CAP	Computer Address Panel (CAAL)
CAP	Computer-Aided Planning
CAP	Computer-Aided Presentation (IAA)
CAP	Computer-Aided [*or Assisted*] Production
CAP	Computer-Aided Programming
CAP	Computer-Aided [*or Assisted*] Publishing
CAP	Computer-Aided Purchasing (HGAA)
CAP	Computer Analysts & Programmers Ltd. [*British*]
CAP	Computer Application Program (NASA)
CAP	Computer-Assisted Printing
CAP	Computerized Assignment of Personnel [*Military*]
CAP	Computerized Automated Psychophysiological Device
CAP	Computing Assistance Program [*Taylor University*] [*Information service or system*] (IID)
CAP	Concepts About Print Test (EDAC)
CAP	Concurrent Algorithmic Programming Language [*Computer science*] (CSR)
CAP	Condenser Absolute Pressure
CAP	Confederate Action Party of Australia [*Political party*]
CAP	Configuration Audit Plan
CAP	Congress of African Peoples
CAP	Console Action Processor
CAP	Contact Approach [*Aviation*] (DA)
CAP	Contemporary American Patriot Club (EA)
CAP	Contemporary Authors: Permanent Series [*A publication*]
CAP	Continental Africa Project [*National Academy of Sciences*]
CAP	Contingency Amphibious Plan [*NATO*] (NATG)
CAP	Continuing Airworthiness Panel [*ICAO*] (DA)
CAP	Continuous Air Patrol [*Proposed defense for missiles*] [*Military*]
CAP	Continuous Audit Program [*Finance*] [*Computer science*] (IEEE)
CAp	Contra Apionem [*Against Apion*] [*Josephus*] (BJA)
CAP	Contract Administration Panel [*Military*]
CAP	Contract Administration Plan
CAP	Contract Amendment Proposal
CAP	Contractor-Acquired Property (AFM)
CAP	Control and Authorization Process (KSC)
CAP	Control Anticipation Parameter (PDAA)
CAP	Control Assembly Program (BUR)
CAP	Controlled Acceleration Propulsion (SSD)
CAP	Controlled Atmosphere Packaging
CAP	Convertible Adjustable Rate Preferred Stock (MHDB)
CAP	Cordic Arithmetic Processor (IAA)
CAP	Coriolis Acceleration Platform
CAP	Corporate Action Project [*Defunct*] (EA)
CAP	Corrective Action Plan [*Department of Health and Human Services*] (GFGA)
CAP	Cost Account Package [*Accounting*] (NASA)
CAP	Cost Account Plan
CAP	Cost Allocation Procedure [*Environmental Protection Agency*] (GFGA)
CAP	Cost Analysis Plan
CAP	Council Against Poverty (IIA)
CAP	Council on Advanced Programming
CAP	Council on Alcohol Policy (EA)
CAP	Cover, Artillery Protection [*Military*] (PDAA)
CAP	Creative Computer Applications, Inc. [*AMEX symbol*] (SAG)
CAP	Crew Activity Plan (MCD)
CAP	Crisis Action Package (AAGC)
CAP	Criteria Air Pollutant [*Environmental Protection Agency*] (GFGA)
CAP	Critical Acquisition Position [*Military*] (RDA)
CAP	Cropland Adjustment Program
CAP	Cryotron Associative Processor (IEEE)
CAP	Cultural Awareness Program
CAP	Current Approval Plan [*Army*]
CAP	Current Assessment Plan
CAP	Customer Assistance Program (PCM)
CAP	Customized Assurance Plans [*Automotive engineering*]
CAP	Cyclic-AMP [*Adenosine Monophosphate*] Receptor Protein [*Also, CRP*] [*Genetics*]
CAP	Cyclophosphamide, Adriamycin, Platinol [*Cisplatin*] [*Antineoplastic drug regimen*]
CAP	Cyclophosphamide, Adriamycin, Prednisone [*Antineoplastic drug regimen*]
CAP	Cystylaminopeptidase [*An enzyme*]
CAP	Faulty Capitalization [*Used in correcting manuscripts, etc.*]
CAP	Foolscap [*Paper*] (ROG)
CAP	National Cap and Patch Association (EA)
CAP	Springfield, IL [*Location identifier FAA*] (FAAL)
CAPA	Caffeine, Alcohol, Pepper, and Aspirin [*As in CAPA-free diet*] [*Medicine*] (DAVI)
CAPA	California Academy of Physician Assistants (SRA)
CAPA	California Association of Port Authorities (SRA)
CAPA	Canada-Caribbean-Central America Policy Alternatives [*An association*]
CAPA	Canadian Animation Producers Association
CAPA	Canadian Association for Physical Anthropology
CAPA	Canadian Association of Purchasing Agents (HGAA)
CAPA	Cancer-Associated Polypeptide Antigen [*Medicine*] (DMAA)
CAPA	Carolina Asphalt Pavement Association (SRA)
CAPA	Central Airborne Performance Analyzer (MCD)
CAPA	Central Arizona Project Association (EA)
CAPA	Closet Accordion Players of America
CAPA	Colorado Academy of Physician Assistants (SRA)
CAPA	Colorado Asphalt Pavement Association (SRA)
CAPA	Comics Amateur Press Alliance
CAPA	Comite d'Action du Personnel Autochtone [*Native Employees Action Team*] [*Canada*]
CAPA	Commission on Asian and Pacific Affairs [*International Chamber of Commerce*]
CAPA	Commonwealth Association of Polytechnics in Africa [*Nairobi, Kenya*] (EAIO)
CAPA	Connecticut Association of Professional Accountants (SRA)
CAPA	Corrosion and Protection Association
CAPA	Creative and Performing Arts
CAPA	Critical Aquifer Protection Area [*Environmental Protection Agency*] (FFDE)
CAPAB	Council of Australian Public Abattoir Authorities
CAPAB	Capability (KSC)
CAPAB	Capetown Performing Arts Board
CAPABLE	Controls and Panel Arrangement by Logical Evaluation (PDAA)
CAPAC	Cathodic Protection by Automatically-Controlled Impressed Current (PDAA)
CAPAC	Composers, Authors, and Publishers Association of Canada
CAPACOA	Canadian Arts Presenters Association [*Association Candienne des Organismes Artistiques*] (AC)
CAPAFSA	Child Abuse Prevention, Adoption, and Family Services Act of 1988
CAPAL	Computer and Photographic Assisted Learning
CapAm	Capital American Financial Co. [*Associated Press*] (SAG)
CapAm	Capitol American Financial Cp. [*Associated Press*] (SAG)
CAPAP	Confederation of Australasian Performing Arts Presenters [*Australia*]
CAPAR	Combined Active/Passive RADAR
Ca Parl	Cases in Parliament (Shower) [*1694-99*] [*A publication*] (DLA)
CAPARS	Computer-Aided Placement and Routing System (PDAA)
CapAsc	Capital Bancorp, Inc. [*Associated Press*] (SAG)
CAPAV	Committee on Atmospheric Problems of Aerospace Vehicles [*American Meteorological Society*]
CAPB	Canadian Association of Police Boards (AC)
CAPB	Child Abuse Protection Board [*Tasmania*] [*Australia*]
CAPB	Compression-Annealed Pyrolytic Boron Nitride (PDAA)
CapBFL	Capital Bancorp (Florida) [*Associated Press*] (SAG)
CapBn	Capital Bancorp, Inc. [*Associated Press*] (SAG)
CapBnc	Capital Bancorp, Inc. [*Associated Press*] (SAG)
CAP-BOP	Cyclophosphamide, Adriamycin, Procarbazine, Bleomycin, Oncovin [*Vincristine*], Prednisone [*Antineoplastic drug regimen*]
CapBrnd	Capital Brands, Inc. [*Associated Press*] (SAG)
CApC	Cabrillo College, Aptos, CA [*Library symbol Library of Congress*] (LCLS)
CAPC	Calcium Phosphate [*Organic chemistry*] (DAVI)
CAPC	California Association of Parking Controllers (EA)
CAPC	California Association of Public Cemeteries (SRA)
CAPC	Canadian Aquaculture Producers' Council [*Conseil Canadien des Aquiculteurs*] (AC)
CAPC	Canadian Army Pay Corps (DMA)
CAPC	Canadian Association of Professional Conservators
CAPC	Central America Peace Campaign [*Defunct*] (EA)
CAPC	City of Adelaide Planning Commission [*Australia*]
CAPC	Civil Aviation Planning Committee (AFM)
CAPC	Computer-Aided Production Control (MHDB)

CaPC............ Prince Edward Island Libraries, Charlottetown, PE, Canada [*Library symbol Library of Congress*] (LCLS)

CAPCA........ California Agricultural Production Consultants Association (SRA)

CaPCA........ Public Archives, Charlottetown, PE, Canada [*Library symbol Library of Congress*] (LCLS)

CaPCAg........ Canada Department of Agriculture, Research Station, Charlottetown, PE, Canada [*Library symbol Library of Congress*] (LCLS)

CAPCAR...... Command Assessment Review [*Air Force*] (AAGC)

CAPCAS...... Computer Aided Production for Current Awareness Services [*Information service or system*] (IID)

CAPCATS..... Capability Categories (RDA)

CAPCC........ Canadian Association of Poison Control Centres

CaPCCA...... Confederation Art Gallery and Museum, Charlottetown, PE, Canada [*Library symbol Library of Congress*] (LCLS)

CaPCCOA..... Coles Associates Ltd., Charlottetown, PE, Canada [*Library symbol Library of Congress*] (LCLS)

CaPCE.......... Prince Edward Island Department of Education, Charlottetown, PE, Canada [*Library symbol Library of Congress*] (LCLS)

CAPCFT....... Prince Edward Island Food Technology Centre, Information Centre, Charlottetown, PE, Canada [*Library symbol*] [*Library of Congress*] (LCLS)

CaPCHC....... Holland College, Charlottetown, PE, Canada [*Library symbol Library of Congress*] (LCLS)

CAPCHE....... Component Automatic-Program Checkout Equipment [*Aerospace*] (AAG)

CaPCIMR..... Institute of Man and Resources, Charlottetown, PE, Canada [*Library symbol Library of Congress*] (LCLS)

CapCities..... Capital Cities/ABC, Inc. [*Associated Press*] (SAG)

CaPCL.......... Confederation Centre Library, Charlottetown, PE, Canada [*Library symbol Library of Congress*] (LCLS)

CaPCLS........ Law Society of Prince Edward Island, Charlottetown, PE, Canada [*Library symbol Library of Congress*] (LCLS)

CaPCMA ...... Prince Edward Island Department of Municipal Affairs, Charlottetown, PE, Canada [*Library symbol Library of Congress*] (LCLS)

CAPCO......... Capital & Counties [*Property development company*] [*British*]

CAPCO......... Central Area Power Coordination Group [*Nuclear Regulatory Commission*] (GFGA)

CAPCO......... China American Petrochemical Co. Ltd. [*Taiwan*]

CAPCO......... Consumer Aerosol Products Council

CapcoA........ Capco Automotive Products [*Formerly, Clark Automotive Products*] [*Associated Press*] (SAG)

CAPCOM...... Capsule Communications [*or Communicator*] [*NASA*]

CAPCOM...... Capture/Compare [*Electronics*] [*Automotive engineering*]

CAPCON....... Capitol Consortium Network [*of CUMWA*] [*Information service or system*]

CAPCON...... Capsule Control [*NASA*] (KSC)

CAPCP .... Civil Air Patrol Coastal Patrol [*Wartime*]

CaPCPL........ Planning Library, Charlottetown, PE, Canada [*Library symbol Library of Congress*] (LCLS)

CaPCQEH..... Queen Elizabeth Hospital, Charlottetown, PE, Canada [*Library symbol*] [*Library of Congress*] (LCLS)

CAPCRA...... Cooperative Agricole des Producteurs de Cereales de la Region d'Arras

CaPCT .... Canadian Association of Psychoanalytic Child Therapists (AC)

CaPCU .... University of Prince Edward Island, Charlottetown, PE, Canada [*Library symbol Library of Congress*] (LCLS)

CAP D.......... Capitular Degrees [*Freemasonry*] (ROG)

CAPD.......... Cathodic Arc Plasma Deposition [*Coating technology*]

CAPD.......... Chronic Ambulatory Peritoneal Dialysis [*Medicine*]

CAPD.......... Climb at Pilot's Discretion [*Aviation*] (FAAC)

CAPD.......... Computer-Aided Parameter Design

CAPD.......... Computer-Aided Process Design (MCD)

CAPD.......... Continuous Ambulatory Peritoneal Dialysis [*Medicine*]

CAPDAC...... Computer-Aided Piping Design and Construction (MCD)

CAPDAS...... Computer-Aided Polymer Data System (IID)

CAPDET...... Commercial Activities Program Detachment [*Military*] (DNAB)

CAPDETREGOFF... Commercial Activities Program Detachment Regional Office [*Military*] (DNAB)

CaPDi .... Calcium Pyrophosphate Dihydrate [*Inorganic chemistry*]

CAPE............ Canadian Association for Pastoral Education (AC)

CAPE............ Canadian Association of Professors of Education

CAPE............ Capability and Proficiency Evaluation

CAPE............ Cape [*Commonly used*] (OPSA)

CAPE............ Cape Kennedy Precipitation Experiment [*Marine science*] (OSRA)

CAPE............ Cape Kennedy Precipitation Experiment (USDC)

CAPE............ Center for Advanced Professional Education [*Canada*]

CAPE............ Center for Propellant and Missile Completion [*France*]

CAPE............ Children's Alliance for Protection of the Environment (EA)

CAPE............ China Association of Plant Engineering (EAIO)

CAPE............ Clifton Assessment Procedures for the Elderly [*Personality development test*] [*Psychology*]

CAPE............ Coalition of American Public Employees

CAPE............ Colorado Association of Public Employees (SRA)

CAPE............ Comite d'Appui au Peuple Espagnol [*Committee of Support for Spanish People*] [*Canada*]

CAPE............ Committee on Assessing the Progress of Education [*Later, NAEP*] (EA)

CAPE............ Communication Automatic Processing Equipment

CAPE............ Complete Anthropomorphic Protective Enclosure (SAA)

CAPE............ Computer-Aided Planning and Estimating [*Marlow Microplan National Engineering Laboratory*] [*Software package*] (NCC)

CAPE............ Computer-Aided Process Engineering

CAPE............ Computer-Assisted Policy Evaluation (MCD)

CAPE............ Computer-Assisted Psychosocial Evaluation

CAPE............ Conduction Analysis Program Using Eigenvalues [*NASA*]

CAPE............ Consortium for the Advancement of Physics Education

CaPE............ Convective and Precipitation/Electrification [*Experiment*] [*Marine science*] (OSRA)

CaPE............ Convective and Precipitation/Electrification [*Experiment*] (USDC)

CAPE............ Convective Available Potential Energy

CAPE............ Council for American Private Education (EA)

CAPEI.......... Coaches Association of PEI (AC)

capel .... Capella [*Chapel*] [*Latin*] (BARN)

Cape Law J.. Cape Law Journal [*South Africa*] [*A publication*] (DLA)

Cape LJ...... Cape Law Journal [*South Africa*] [*A publication*] (DLA)

Cape P Div.. Cape Provincial Division Reports [*South Africa*] [*A publication*] (DLA)

CAPER .... Canadian Association of Publishers' Educational Representatives

CAPER .... Canadian Post-MD Education Registry [*Systeme Informatise sur les Stagiaires Post-MD en Formation Clinique*] (AC)

CAPER .... Civilian Authority for the Protection of Everybody, Regardless [*Crime-fighting unit in TV series "The Kids From C.A.P.E.R."*]

CAPER .... Combined Active/Passive Emitter Rangings

CAPER .... Computer-Aided Pattern Evaluation and Recognition (KSC)

CAPER .... Computer-Aided Preparation of Electrical Routing (MCD)

CAPER .... Computer-Assisted Pathology Encoding and Reporting System [*Medicine*] (DHSM)

CAPER .... Configuration Analysis and Performance (MCD)

CAPER .... Cost of Attaining Personnel Requirement

CAPERS ...... Computer-Assisted Psychiatric Evaluation and Review System [*Medicine*] (DMAA)

CAPERS ...... Cost and Performance Effectiveness Ratios

CAPERTSIM... Computer-Assisted Program Evaluation Review-Technique Simulation [*Army*]

CAPES .... Controlled Alternating Parachute Exit System (PDAA)

Cape SCR ... Supreme Court Reports, Cape Colony [*1880-1910*] [*South Africa*] [*A publication*] (DLA)

CAPETN ...... Cape Town [*South Africa*] (ROG)

Cape TR ..... Cape Times Supreme Court Reports, Cape Of Good Hope [*South Africa*] [*A publication*] (DLA)

CAPEX .... Capability Exercise

CAPF............ Capacity Factor (IAA)

CAPF............ Capital Factors Holding, Inc. [*NASDAQ symbol*] (SAG)

CAPF............ Chemical Age Project File [*Pergamon ORBIT InfoLine Inc.*] [*Information service or system*]

CapFact .... Capital Factors Holding, Inc. [*Associated Press*] (SAG)

CAPFG .... Capacitor Flashgun [*Photography*]

CAPG .... Capital Goods [*Finance*]

CAPG .... Civil Air Patrol Guard

CAPG .... Compression-Annealed Pyrolytic Graphite (PDAA)

CapGty......... Capital Guaranty Corp. [*Associated Press*] (SAG)

CAPH .... California Association of Public Hospitals (SRA)

CAPH .... Colt Automatic Pistol Hammerless (DICI)

CAPH .... Committee on Application of Polarized Headlights [*OECD*]

CAPHC .... Canadian Association of Professional Heritage Consultants [*Association Canadienne des Consultants Patrimoine*] (AC)

CAPHE .... Consortium for the Advancement of Private Higher Education (EA)

CAPI............. Center for the Analysis of Public Issues [*Princeton, NJ*]

CAPI............. Computer-Administered Programmed Instruction (OA)

CAPI............. Computer-Assisted Personal Interviewing (GFGA)

CAP-I........... Cyclophosphamide, Adriamycin, Cisplatin [*Antineoplastic drug regimen*] (DAVI)

CAPIA .... Carolina Association of Professional Insurance Agents (SRA)

CAPIANT...... Capiantur [*Let Them Be Taken*] [*Pharmacy*] (ROG)

CAPIC .... Canadian Association for Production and Inventory Control

CAPIC .... Canadian Association of Photographers & Illustrators in Communications [*Association Canadienne de Photographes et Illustrateurs de Publicite*] (AC)

CAPICS .... Computer-Aided Processing of Industrial Cabling Systems (PDAA)

CAPIEL......... Comite de Coordination des Associations de Constructeurs d'Appareillage [*Coordinating Committee for Common Market Associations of Manufacturers of Electrical Switchgear and Controlgear*] [*EC*] (ECED)

CAPIEND...... Capiendus [*To Be Taken*] [*Pharmacy*]

CAP-II .... Cyclophosphamide, Adriamycin, High-dose Cisplatin [*Antineoplastic drug regimen*] (DAVI)

CAP-II .... Cyclophosphamide, Adriamycin, High-Dose Platinol [*Cisplatin*] [*Antineoplastic drug regimen*]

CAP III .... Centralized Assignment Procedures Computer System [*Military*]

CAPIO .... Commission for the Advancement of Public Interest Organizations (EA)

CAPIR .... Computer-Assisted Photo-Interpretation Research (MCD)

CAPIS .... Canadian Association of Plastic Surgery (HGAA)

CAP/IS .... Combined Approach Control/International Station (FAAC)

CAPIS .... Customs Accelerated Passenger Inspection System [*US Customs Service*]

Capit............ Capital

Capita.......... Capita Preferred Trust [*Associated Press*] (SAG)

CAPITA .... Center for Air Pollution Impact and Trend Analysis [*Washington University*] [*Research center*] (RCD)

Capital U ..... Capital University (GAGS)

CAPITB .... Clothing and Allied Products Industry Training Board (AIE)

cAPK............ Cyclic AMP [*Adenosine Monaphorphate*] -Dependent Protein Kinase [*Biochemistry*]

CAPL............ Canadian Association of Public Libraries

CAPL............ Capital [*Accounting; Finance; Economics*] (ROG)

CAPL............ Civilian Acquisition Position List [*Army*] (RDA)

CAPL............ Coastal Anti-Pollution League [*British*]

CAPL............ Commission for the Accreditation of Public Libraries [*Proposed*]

CAPL............ Continuous Annealing and Processing Line [*Steel manufacture*]

CAPL............ Controlled Assembly Parts List [*Aerospace*] (AAG)

CAPLA	Computer-Aided Product Launch Application
CAPLA	Council of Australian Public Library Associations
CAPLAR	Computer Assisted PLA [*Product License Application*] Review [*FDA*]
Caplet	Capsule/Tablet [*Medicine*]
CAPLO	Council of Australian Power Lifting Associations
CAPM	Capital-Asset Pricing Model
CapM	Capstead Mortgage Corp. [*Associated Press*] (SAG)
CAPM	Computer-Aided Patient Management
CAPM	Computer-Aided Plant Management
CAPM	Computer-Aided Production Management (IAA)
CAPM	Connecticut Association of Purchasing Management (SRA)
CAPMA	Cairns Agricultural, Pastoral, and Mining Association [*Australia*]
CapMAC	Capital Marketers Assurance Corporation (TDOB)
CapMAC	CapMAC Holdings [*Associated Press*] (SAG)
CAPM & R ...	Canadian Association of Physical Medicine and Rehabilitation (EAIO)
CAPMAR	Cost Account Performance Measurement and Analysis Report (MCD)
CapMdia	Capital Media Group Ltd. [*Associated Press*] (SAG)
CAPME	Committee of Americans for Peace in the Middle East [*Defunct*] (EA)
CAPMI	Computer-Assisted Post Mortem Identification (RDA)
CapMI	Capitol MultiMedia, Inc. [*Associated Press*] (SAG)
CAPMO	Carrefour des Agents de Pastorale en Monde Ouvrier [*Crossroads of Pastoral Agents and Workers of the World*] [*Canada*]
CAP MOLL ...	Capsula Mollis [*Soft Capsule*] [*Pharmacy*]
CAPMP	Committee Against the Political Misuse of Psychiatry (EA)
CapMult	Capitol MultiMedia, Inc. [*Associated Press*] (SAG)
CAPN	Canadian Association of Pediatric Nurses (AC)
CAPN	Captain (ROG)
CAPNA	Canadian Association of Practical Nursing Assistants
CAPO	Canadian Army Post Office (DMA)
CAPO	Canadian Association of Prosthetists and Orthotists
CAPO	Capistrano [*Hazardous test facility*]
CAPO	Center Apollo Program Offices [*NASA*] (KSC)
CAPO	Civil Affairs Police Officer [*British World War II*]
CAPO	Contract Acceptance and Purchase Order
CapOne	Capital One Financial Corp. [*Associated Press*] (SAG)
CAPOS	Cargo Performance Overview System [*BTS*] (TAG)
CAPOSS	Capacity Planning and Operations Sequencing System [*IBM Corp.*]
CAPOSS-E...	Capacity Planning and Operations Sequencing System - Extended [*IBM Corp.*]
CAPP	California Association of Pet Professionals (EA)
CAPP	Canadian Association of Petroleum Producers (IID)
CAPP	Canadian Association of Prawn Producers [*Association Canadienne des Producteurs de Crevette*] (AC)
Capp	Cappadocian (BJA)
CAPP	Captopril Prevention Project [*Study*] [*Medicine*] (DMAA)
CAPP	Census Awareness and Products Program [*Bureau of the Census*] (GFGA)
CAPP	Center for Animals and Public Policy (GNE)
CAPP	Center for Applied Parallel Processing [*University of Colorado, Boulder*] [*Research center*] (RCD)
CAPP	Ceramide Activated Protein Phosphatase [*An enzyme*]
CAPP	Clinical Applications and Prevention Program [*Bethesda, MD*] [*National Heart, Lung, and Blood Institute*] [*Department of Health and Human Services*] (GRD)
CAPP	Computer-Aided Process Planning (MCD)
CAPP	Computer-Aided Pulse Plating [*Electrochemistry*]
CAPP	Conference for the Advancement of Private Practice [*in social work*]
CAPP	Conference of Actuaries in Public Practice [*Itasca, IL*] (EA)
CAPP	Content-Addressable Parallel Processor [*Computer science*]
C App	Sentenza della Corte di Appello [*Decision of the Court of Appeal*] [*Italian*] (ILCA)
CAPPA	Caffeine, Alcohol, Pepper, Peppermint, and Alcohol [*As in CAPPA-free diet*] (DAVI)
CAPPA	Crusher and Portable Plant Association [*Defunct*] (EA)
CAPPAC	Computer-Aided Production Planning and Control [*John Yates & Associates*] [*Software package*] (NCC)
CapPcHI......	Capital Pacific Holdings [*Associated Press*] (SAG)
C App R	Criminal Appeal Reports [*England*] [*A publication*] (DLA)
CAPPRO.......	Capital Property Accounting and Control (MCD)
CAPPS	California Association of Photocopiers and Process Servers (SRA)
CAPPS	Center for Aseptic Processing and Packaging Studies [*North Carolina State University*] [*Research center*] (RCD)
CAPPS	Centralized Army Passenger Port Call System (AABC)
CAPPS	Computer-Assisted Pricing Proposal System (MCD)
CAPPS	Council for the Advancement of the Psychological Professions and Sciences [*Later, AAP*]
CAPPS	Current and Past Psychopathology Scales [*Psychology*]
CAPQ	Conseil des Artistes Peintres du Quebec [*1982, founded 1966 as SAPQ*] [*Canada*] (NGC)
CAP QUANT VULT...	Capiat Quantum Vult [*Let the Patient Take as Much as He Will*] [*Pharmacy*]
CAPR	Calcium Pyrophosphate [*Organic chemistry*] (DAVI)
Capr.............	Capricornus [*Constellation*]
CAPR	Catalog of Programs
Ca Prac CP...	Cooke's Practice Cases [*1706-47*] [*England*] [*A publication*] (DLA)
CAP Rate.....	Co-op Action Action Plan [*Advertising*] (WDMC)
CAPRCA.......	Chronic, Acquired, Pure Red Cell Aplasia [*Medicine*] (DMAA)
CapRe..........	Capital Re Corp. [*Associated Press*] (SAG)
CAPRI.........	Captive Reset Ignitor (NASA)
CAPRI	Card and Printer Remote Interface
CAPRI	Cardiopulmonary Research Institute (DAVI)
CAPRI	Center for Applied Polymer Research [*Case Western Reserve University*] [*Research center*] (RCD)
CAPRI	Coded Address Private Radio Intercommunication (MCD)
CAPRI	Compact All-Purpose Range Instrument [*RADAR*] (MCD)
CAPRI	Computer-Aided Passive Ranging Indicator [*Military*] (CAAL)
CAPRI	Computer Aided Personal Reference Index System [*Automic Energy Authority*] [*British*] (NITA)
CAPRI	Computerized Administration of Patent Documents Reclassified According to the IPC [*International Patent Classification*] [*INPADOC*] [*Information service or system*] (ADA)
CAPRI	Computerized Advance Personnel Requirements Information [*or Inventory*] [*Navy*]
CAPRI	Computerized Analysis for Programming Investments (MHDI)
CAPRI	Computerized Area Pricing [*Telecommunications*] (TEL)
CapRI2........	Capital Realty Investors Tax Exempt Fund Ltd. [*Associated Press*] (SAG)
CapRI3........	Capital Realty Investors Tax Exempt Fund Ltd. [*Associated Press*] (SAG)
CAPRIS	Combat Active and Passive RADAR Identification System (MCD)
CAPRISTOR...	Capacitor-Resistor (IAA)
CAPRO.........	Canadian Association of Profession Radio Operators [*Association Canadienne des Professionnels de l'Exploitation Radio*] (AC)
CAPRT	Center for Aquatic Plant Research and Technology [*Army*]
CapRtyl.......	Capital Realty Investors Tax Exempt Ltd. [*Associated Press*] (SAG)
CAPS	Caffeine, Alcohol, Pepper, Spicy Foods [*Nutrition*]
CAPS	Call Attempts per Second [*Telecommunications*] (TEL)
CAPS	Capitals [*Printing*]
CAPS	Capital Savings Bancorp [*NASDAQ symbol*] (SAG)
CAPS	Capsula [*Capsule*] [*Pharmacy*]
CAPS	Capsule
CAPS	Captive Animals Protection Society [*British*] (DI)
CAPS	Career Ability Placement Survey [*Vocational guidance test*]
CAPS	Cashiers' Automatic Processing System (DIT)
CAPS	Cassette Programming System [*Digital Equipment Corp.*]
CAPS	Cavity Alternated Phase Shift (MCD)
CAPS	Cell Atmosphere Processing System [*Nuclear energy*] (NRCH)
CAPS	Census Awareness and Products Staff [*Bureau of the Census*] (GFGA)
CAPS	Center for Advanced Purchasing Studies [*Arizona State University*] [*Research center*] (RCD)
CAPS	Center for AIDS Prevention Studies [*University of California, San Francisco*] [*Research center*] (RCD)
CAPS	Center for Analysis and Prediction of Storms [*University of Oklahoma*] [*Research center*] (RCD)
CAPS	Centralized Accounting and Polling Software [*Computer science*] (PCM)
CAPS	Centralized Automated Pay System
CAPS	Certificate of Advanced Professional Studies (PGP)
CAPS	Children of Ageing Parents (EA)
CAPS	Christian Association for Psychological Studies (EA)
CAPS	Civil Assistant Personal Services [*Navy British*]
CAPS	Civil Aviation Purchasing Service [*ICAO*] (DA)
CAPS	Clearinghouse on Counseling and Personnel Services [*ERIC*]
CAPS	Coalition for Asian Peace and Security (EA)
CAPS	Coastal Aerial Photo-LASER Survey (PDAA)
CAPS	Combat Air Patrol Support [*Aircraft*] (PDAA)
CAPS	Command Automated Procurement System (MCD)
CAPS	Commitment and Payment System (MCD)
CAPS	Common Attitude Pointing System (MCD)
CAPS	Community Adjustment Profile System (DMAA)
CAPS	Competitive Access Provider
CAPS	Computer-Aided Personnel Scheduling
CAPS	Computer-Aided Pipe Sketching [*System*] [*Du Pont*]
CAPS	Computer Aided Problem Solving (NITA)
CAPS	Computer-Aided Process Synthesis
CAPS	Computer-Aided Programming System
CAPS	Computer-Aided Program Simulator
CAPS	Computer-Assisted Picking System (WDMC)
CAPS	Computer-Assisted Placement Service [*British*]
CAPS	Computer-Assisted Problem Solving (IEEE)
CAPS	Computer-Assisted Product Search [*Information service or system*] (IID)
CAPS	Computer-Assisted Prosthesis Selection [*Orthopedic surgery*]
CAPS	Computerized Agency Processing System (IAA)
CAPS	Computerized Aircraft Performance System (MCD)
CAPS	Computing and Data Processing Services [*University of Maine*] [*Research center*] (RCD)
CAPS	Consolidation Aerial Port System [*or Subsystem*] [*Air Force*] (MCD)
CAPS	Construction Advanced Planning and Sequencing [*Nuclear energy*] (NRCH)
CAPS	Contents, Abstracts, and Photocopies Services [*India*] [*Information service or system*]
CAPS	Continuous Automated Placement Survey [*Department of Labor*]
CAPS	Control and Auxiliary Power Supply System
CAPS	Conventional Armaments Planning System (DOMA)
CAPS	Convertible Adjustable Preferred Stock [*Investment term*] (DFIT)
CAPS	Cooperative Agricultural Pest Survey Program [*Information service or system*] (IID)
CAPS	Cooperative Association of Professional Salespeople [*Defunct*] (EA)
CAPS	Cooperative Awards in Pure Science [*British*]
CAPS	Corporate Affairs Processing System
CAPS	Cost per Average Pound Saved
CAPS	Counseling and Personnel Services [*Educational Resources Information Center*] [*Information retrieval*] (AEBS)
CAPS	Courtauld's All-Purpose Simulator (IEEE)
CAPS	Creative Artists Public Service Program (EA)
CAPS	Crew Activity Planning System (SSD)
CAPS	Critical Angle Prism Sensor (KSC)
CAPS	Current Advances in Plant Science [*A database*] [*Pergamon*] (NITA)

CAPS .... Cyclohexylaminopropanesulfonic Acid [*A buffer*]
CAPSA .... Canadian Association of Pension Supervisory Authorities [*Association Canadienne des Organismes de Controle des Regimes de Retraite*] (AC)
CAPS AMYLAC... Capsula Amylacea [*A Cachet*] [*Pharmacy*]
CAPSCR...... Capscrew [*Technical drawings*]
CapsCT .... Capstone Capital Trust, Inc. [*Associated Press*] (SAG)
CAPSE .... Computer-Assisted Power System Engineering (MCD)
CAPSEP .... Capsule Separation [*Aerospace*] (AAG)
CAPS GELAT... Capsula Gelatina [*A Gelatine Capsule*] [*Pharmacy*]
cap sheet..... Caption Sheet [*Television*] [*Publishing*] (WDMC)
CAPSHIPFOR... Capacity Ships Force
CAPSIM .... Captive Simulation (NASA)
CAPSIN........ Civil Aviation Packet Switching Integrated Network (DA)
CAPSK .... Combined Amplitude Phase Shift Keying (MCD)
CaPSL .... Canon Printer System Language [*Computer application*] (PCM)
CAPSLE........ Canadian Association for the Practical Study of Law in Education [*Association Canadienne pour une Etude Pratique de la Loi Dan le Systeme Educatif*] (AC)
CAPSM .... Canadian Academy of Podiatric Sports Medicine
CAPSO-N .... Capital Area, Personnel Service Office (Navy)
CapsPh .... Capstone Pharmacy Services, Inc. [*Associated Press*] (SAG)
CapsPhm ...... Capstone Pharmacy Services, Inc. [*Associated Press*] (SAG)
CAPSR .... Cost Account Performance Status Report [*Accounting*] (MCD)
CAPSS .... Canadian Automated Pilot Selection System
CAPSS .... Connecticut Association of Public School Superintendents (SRA)
CAPST .... Capacitor-Start [*Motor*] [*Electricity*]
CAPSTAR..... Capacitor Start and Run (IAA)
Capstar........ Capstar Hotel Co. [*Associated Press*] (SAG)
CapstCT .... Capstone Capital Trust, Inc. [*Associated Press*] (SAG)
Capstd .... Capstead Mortgage Corp. [*Associated Press*] (SAG)
CAPSTONE... Central Automated Personnel Security Transaction or Notification Exchange [*DoD*]
capsul.......... Capsula [*Capsule*] [*Pharmacy*] (DAVI)
Capsure .... Capsure Holdings [*Associated Press*] (SAG)
CapSvgs ...... Capital Savings Bancorp [*Associated Press*] (SAG)
CapSw .... Capital Southwest Corp. [*Associated Press*] (SAG)
CAPT.......... Canadian Association of Pharmacy Technicians (AC)
CAPT.......... Capiat [*Let the Patient Take*] [*Pharmacy*] (ROG)
CAPT.......... Captain (AAG)
Capt............ Captain (ODBW)
CAPT.......... Captain
Capt............ Captain (DD)
CAPT.......... Caption (ADA)
Capt............ Captivi [*of Plautus*] [*Classical studies*] (OCD)
CAPT.......... Center for Applications of Psychological Type (EA)
CAPT.......... Conversational Parts Programming Language [*Computer science*] (IEEE)
CAPTA .... Child Abuse Prevention and Treatment Act
CAPTAC .... Conference des Administrations des Postes et Telecommunications de l'Afrique Centrale [*Conference of Posts and Telecommunications Administrations of Central Africa*] (PDAA)
CAPTAIN...... Carter's Adaptation Procesor to Aid Interception (SAA)
CAPTAIN...... Computer-Aided Processing and Terminal Access Information Network [*Rutgers University*] [*New Brunswick, NJ Library computer network*]
CAPTAIN...... Covariance Analysis Program for the Study of Augmented Inertial Navigators (MCD)
CAPTAINS.... Character and Pattern Telephone Access Information Network System [*Viewdata system*] [*Japan*]
CAPTALC ..... Control and Protection of Transoceanic Air Lanes of Communication
CAPTEAO ..... Conference Administrative des Postes et Telecommunications des Etats de l'Afrique de l'Ouest [*Conference of Posts and Telecommunications Administrations of the States of West Africa*]
Capt-Gen ..... Captain-General [*British military*] (DMA)
CAPTIS .... Computer-Assisted Prisoner Transportation Index Service [*National Sheriffs' Association*]
CAPTIVE ...... Collaborative Authoring Production and Transmission of Interactive Video for Education (AIE)
CaptlBc........ Capitol Bancorp Ltd. [*Associated Press*] (SAG)
Capt (N)....... Captain (Naval)
CAPTOR....... Encapsulated Torpedo [*Antisubmarine*] [*Navy*]
CapTrns....... Capitol Transamerica [*Associated Press*] (SAG)
CAPTV .... Computer-Animated Photographic Terrain View (MCD)
CAPU .... Coast African People's Union [*Kenya*]
CAPUC........ Coordinating Area Production Urgency Committee
Capv........... Capoverso [*Paragraph*] [*Italian*] (ILCA)
CAPVI .... Catholic Association of Persons with Visual Impairment (EA)
CapWest...... Capital Corp. of the West [*Associated Press*] (SAG)
CAPWIRE...... Capitol Wireless, Inc. [*Telecommunications service*] (TSSD)
CAPWSK ...... Collision Avoidance, Proximity Warning, Station Keeping Equipment [*Military*] (NG)
CAPX .... Capitol International Airways [*Air carrier designation symbol*]
CAPY .... Capacity [*Insurance; Finance; Transportation*]
CAQ .... Caucasia [*Colombia*] [*Airport symbol*] (OAG)
CAQ .... Change Agent Questionnaire [*Interpersonal skills and attitudes test*]
CAQ .... Chess Association of Queensland [*Australia*]
CAQ .... Class Activities Questionnaire [*Teacher evaluation test*]
CAQ .... Clinical Analysis Questionnaire
CAQ .... Computer-Aided [*or Assisted*] Quality
CAQ .... Computer Aptitude Quotient (EDAC)
CAQ .... Constant Area Quantization (MCD)
CA(Q).......... Council of Agriculture, Queensland [*Australia*]
CAQ .... Selma, AL [*Location identifier FAA*] (FAAL)
CAQA .... Computer-Aided Quality Assurance

CaQAA .... Aluminum Co. of Canada Ltd., Arvida, PQ, Canada [*Library symbol Library of Congress*] (LCLS)
CaQALC .... College d'Alma, Lac St.-Jean, PQ, Canada [*Library symbol Library of Congress*] (LCLS)
CAQAP .... Canadian Association of Quality Assurance Professionals
CaQArM .... Bibliotheque Municipale, Arthabaska, PQ, Canada [*Library symbol Library of Congress*] (LCLS)
CaQAsAg...... Canada Department of Agriculture, Experimental Farm, L'Assomption, PQ, Canada [*Library symbol Library of Congress*] (LCLS)
CaQAsB....... Bibliotheque Municipale, Asbestos, PQ, Canada [*Library symbol Library of Congress*] (LCLS)
CaQBE .... Beaconsfield Public Library, Beaconsfield, PQ, Canada [*Library symbol Library of Congress*] (LCLS)
CaQBEC .... Bibliotheque Municipale, Becancour, PQ, Canada [*Library symbol Library of Congress*] (LCLS)
CaQBJ......... Juniorat des Freres du Sacre-Coeur, Bromptonville, PQ, Canada [*Library symbol Library of Congress*] (LCLS)
CaQBO........ Bibliotheque Municipale, Boucherville, PQ, Canada [*Library symbol Library of Congress*] (LCLS)
CaQBRG...... Centre Hospitalier Robert Giffard, Quebec, PQ, Canada [*Library symbol Library of Congress*] (LCLS)
CaQBrMS...... Mitel Semiconductor, Bromont, PQ, Canada [*Library symbol*] [*Library of Congress*] (LCLS)
CaQBSPH.... Centre Hospitalier de Charlevoix, Baie St. Paul, PQ, Canada [*Library symbol*] [*Library of Congress*] (LCLS)
CaQCB .... Bibliotheque Municipale, Coaticook, PQ, Canada [*Library symbol Library of Congress*] (LCLS)
CaQCbL....... Logilab, Inc., Charlebois, PQ, Canada [*Library symbol*] [*Library of Congress*] (LCLS)
CaQCC .... Bibliotheque Gaspesienne, Cap-Chat, PQ, Canada [*Library symbol Library of Congress*] (LCLS)
CaQCCRS..... Conseil Regional de la Sante et des Services Sociaux, Chicoutimi, PQ, Canada [*Library symbol Library of Congress*] (LCLS)
CaQChaAG... Ministere de l'Agriculture, des Percheries et de l'Alimentation, Chateauguay, PQ, Canada [*Library symbol*] [*Library of Congress*] (LCLS)
CaQChJC..... Jewish Convalescent Hospital, Chomedy, PQ, Canada [*Library symbol Library of Congress*] (LCLS)
CaQCIPC...... Parks Canada, National Historic Park, Coteau-du-lac, PQ, Canada [*Library symbol*] [*Library of Congress*] (LCLS)
CaQCmM...... Bibliotheque Municipale, Cap-De-La Madeleine, PQ, Canada [*Library symbol Library of Congress*] (LCLS)
CaQCRCN..... Campus Notre-Dame de Foy, Cap-Rouge, PQ, Canada [*Library symbol Library of Congress*] (LCLS)
CaQCRS...... Seminaire Saint Augustine, Cap Rouge, PQ, Canada [*Library symbol Library of Congress*] (LCLS)
CaQCSH...... Societe Historique du Saguenay, Chicoutimi, PQ, Canada [*Library symbol Library of Congress*] (LCLS)
CaQCU .... Universite du Quebec, Chicoutimi, PQ, Canada [*Library symbol Library of Congress*] (LCLS)
CaQCUG...... Universite du Quebec, Departement de Geographie, Chicoutimi, PQ, Canada [*Library symbol Library of Congress*] (LCLS)
CaQCUGC.... Universite du Quebec, Cartotheque, Chicoutimi, PQ, Canada [*Library symbol Library of Congress*] (LCLS)
CaQDC........ Canadian Celanese Ltd., Drummondville, PQ, Canada [*Library symbol Library of Congress*] (LCLS)
CaQDCE...... College Bourgchemin (CEGEP) [*College d'Enseignement General et Professionnel*], Drummondville, PQ, Canada [*Library symbol Library of Congress*] (LCLS)
CaQDHSC.... Hopital Sainte-Croix, Drummondville, PQ, Canada [*Library symbol*] [*Library of Congress*] (LCLS)
CaQDM........ Bibliotheque Municipale, Drummondville, PQ, Canada [*Library symbol Library of Congress*] (LCLS)
CaQDOPH.... Office des Personnes Handicapees du Quebec, Drummondville, PQ, Canada [*Library symbol Library of Congress*] (LCLS)
CaQGaH...... Hotel-Dieu de Gaspe, Gaspe, PQ, Canada [*Library symbol Library of Congress*] (LCLS)
CaQGaP....... Ministere de l'Agriculture, des Pecheries, et de l'Alimentation, Centre de Documentation en Peches Maritimes, Gaspe, PQ, Canada [*Library symbol*] [*Library of Congress*] (LCLS)
CaQGatCH.... Centre Hospitalier de Gatineau, Gatineau, PQ, Canada [*Library symbol*] [*Library of Congress*] (LCLS)
CaQGC........ College de la Gaspesie, Gaspe, PQ, Canada [*Library symbol Library of Congress*] (LCLS)
CaQGL........ Granby Leader, Granby, PQ, Canada [*Library symbol Library of Congress*] (LCLS)
CaQGM....... Bibliotheque Municipale, Granby, PQ, Canada [*Library symbol Library of Congress*] (LCLS)
CaQGMG..... Musee de la Gaspesie, Gaspe, PQ, Canada [*Library symbol*] [*Library of Congress*] (LCLS)
CaQGmM..... Bibliotheque Municipale, Grand'Mere, PQ, Canada [*Library symbol Library of Congress*] (LCLS)
CaQH.......... Bibliotheque Municipale, Hull, PQ, Canada [*Library symbol Library of Congress*] (LCLS)
CaQHaC....... College d'Enseignement General et Professionnel de Regional Cote Nord, Hauterive, PQ, Canada [*Library symbol Library of Congress*] (LCLS)
CaQHaCR.... Conseil Regional de la Sante et des Services Sociaux de la Region Cote-Nord, Hauterive, PQ, Canada [*Library symbol Library of Congress*] (LCLS)
CaQHB .... Bell Canada Documentation Resource Center, Hull, PQ, Canada [*Library symbol*] [*Library of Congress*] (LCLS)
CaQHBE .... Bell Canada, Headquarters Economics Library, Hull, PQ, Canada [*Library symbol*] [*Library of Congress*] (LCLS)

CaQHBEER... Bell Canada, Headquarters Engineering Economics Reference Centre, Hull, PQ, Canada [*Library symbol*] [*Library of Congress*] (LCLS)

CaQHBRM.... Bell Canada Headquarters Regulatory Matters-Regulatory Information Bank, Hull, PQ, Canada [*Library symbol*] [*Library of Congress*] (LCLS)

CAQHC......... Canadian Association for Quality in Health Care [*Association Canadienne pour la Qualite dans les Services de Sante*] (AC)

CaQHC......... College d'Enseignement General et Professionnel de l'Outaouais, Hull, PQ, Canada [*Library symbol Library of Congress*] (LCLS)

CaQHCH...... CEGEP [*College d'Enseignement General et Professionnel*] de l'Outaouais, Heritage Campus, Hull, PQ, Canada [*Library symbol Library of Congress*] (LCLS)

CaQHCL...... CLSC de Hull, Centre de Documentation, Hull, PQ, Canada [*Library symbol*] [*Library of Congress*] (LCLS)

CaQHCRS .... Conseil Regional de la Sante et des Services Sociaux de la Region Outaouais-Hull, Hull, PQ, Canada [*Library symbol Library of Congress*] (LCLS)

CaQHE .... E. B. Eddy Co., Research and Technical Library, Hull, PQ, Canada [*Library symbol Library of Congress*] (LCLS)

CaQHEn .... Environment Canada, Hull, PQ, Canada [*Library symbol Library of Congress*] (LCLS)

CaQHESJ ..... Ecole Secondaire St. Joseph, Hull, PQ, Canada [*Library symbol*] [*Library of Congress*] (LCLS)

CaQHPJ ..... Centre Hospitalier Pierre Janet, Hull, PQ, Canada [*Library symbol Library of Congress*] (LCLS)

CaQHSA ...... Societe d'Amenagement de l'Outaouais, Hull, PQ, Canada [*Library symbol Library of Congress*] (LCLS)

CaQHSC....... Centre Hospitalier du Sacre-Coeur, Hull, PQ, Canada [*Library symbol Library of Congress*] (LCLS)

CaQHU......... Universite du Quebec-Outaouais, Hull, PQ, Canada [*Library symbol Library of Congress*] (LCLS)

CaQIFMA ..... Archives des Freres Maristes, Iberville, PQ, Canada [*Library symbol*] [*Library of Congress*] (LCLS)

CaQJC.......... College de Joliette, Joliette, PQ, Canada [*Library symbol Library of Congress*] (LCLS)

CaQJH .... Hopital Saint-Charles, Joliette, PQ, Canada [*Library symbol Library of Congress*] (LCLS)

CaQJJ .... Seminaire de Joliette, Joliette, PQ, Canada [*Library symbol Library of Congress*] (LCLS)

CaQJMA...... Musee d'Art de Joliette, Joliette, PQ, Canada [*Library symbol Library of Congress*] (LCLS)

CaQJoC........ College de Jonquiere, Jonquiere, PQ, Canada [*Library symbol Library of Congress*] (LCLS)

CaQKB .... Brome County Historical Society, Knowlton, PQ, Canada [*Library symbol Library of Congress*] (LCLS)

CaQKi .... Kirkland Municpal Library, Kirkland, PQ, Canada [*Library symbol*] [*Library of Congress*] (LCLS)

CaQKiPC ..... Pfizer Canada, Inc., Medical Library, Kirkland, PQ, Canada [*Library symbol*] [*Library of Congress*] (LCLS)

CaQKITA ...... Institut de Technologie Agricole, Kamouraska, PQ, Canada [*Library symbol Library of Congress*] (LCLS)

CaQKlBW...... Burroughs Wellcome, Inc., Kirkland Lake, ON, Canada [*Library symbol*] [*Library of Congress*] (LCLS)

CaQLA .... Bibliotheque Municipale, Laval, PQ, Canada [*Library symbol Library of Congress*] (LCLS)

CaQLAC .... CEGEP [*College d'Enseignement General et Professionnel*] Montmorency-Chomedy, Laval, PQ, Canada [*Library symbol Library of Congress*] (LCLS)

CaQLACS ..... Cite de la Sante de Laval, Laval, PQ, Canada [*Library symbol Library of Congress*] (LCLS)

CaQLaCW .... Canadian Workplace Automation Research Centre, Laval, PQ, Canada [*Library symbol*] [*Library of Congress*] (LCLS)

CaQLAIAF .... Universite du Quebec, Institut Armand-Frappier, Laval, PQ, Canada [*Library symbol Library of Congress*] (LCLS)

CaQLaM ...... Bibliotheque Municipale, Lachine, PQ, Canada [*Library symbol*] [*Library of Congress*] (LCLS)

CaQLaPED ... Pylon Electronic Development Co., Ltd., Lachine, PQ, Canada [*Library symbol*] [*Library of Congress*] (LCLS)

CaQLASC .... College de l'Assomption, L'Assomption, PQ, Canada [*Library symbol Library of Congress*] (LCLS)

CaQLASGPT... Canada Ministry of the Solicitor General, Penitentiary, Federal Training Centre,Laval, PQ, Canada [*Library symbol Library of Congress*] (LCLS)

CaQLB .... Bishop's University, Lennoxville, PQ, Canada [*Library symbol Library of Congress*] (LCLS)

CaQLBG .... Bishop's University, Department of Geography, Lennoxville, PQ, Canada [*Library symbol Library of Congress*] (LCLS)

CaQLCLL...... Cegep de Levis-Lauzon, Lauzon, PQ, Canada [*Library symbol*] [*Library of Congress*] (LCLS)

CaQLe.......... Bibliotheque Municipale, Levis, PQ, Canada [*Library symbol Library of Congress*] (LCLS)

CaQLeC........ College de Levis, Levis, PQ, Canada [*Library symbol Library of Congress*] (LCLS)

CaQLeCCP ... Confederation des Caisses Populaires et d'Economie Desjardins du Quebec, Levis, PQ, Canada [*Library symbol*] [*Library of Congress*] (LCLS)

CaQLFECA ... Ville de Laval, Archives des Freres des Ecoles Chretienne, Laval, PQ, Canada [*Library symbol*] [*Library of Congress*] (LCLS)

CaQLHD....... Hotel-Dieu de Levis, Levis, PQ, Canada [*Library symbol*] [*Library of Congress*] (LCLS)

CaQLo.......... Bibliotheque Municipale, Longueuil, PQ, Canada [*Library symbol Library of Congress*] (LCLS)

CaQLoCE...... College Edouard-Montpetit, Longueuil, PQ, Canada [*Library symbol Library of Congress*] (LCLS)

CaQLoCRS ... Conseil Regional de la Sante et des Services Sociaux, Longueuil, PQ, Canada [*Library symbol Library of Congress*] (LCLS)

CaQLoGM .... Institut de Genie des Materiaux, Longueuil, PQ, Canada [*Library symbol Library of Congress*] (LCLS)

CaQLoNLB ... Institut Nazareth et Louis-Braille, Longueuil, PQ, Canada [*Library symbol*] [*Library of Congress*] (LCLS)

CaQLoPB ..... Centre Hospitalier Pierre Boucher, Longueuil, PQ, Canada [*Library symbol Library of Congress*] (LCLS)

CaQLoPS ..... Petro-Sun International, Inc., Longueuil, PQ, Canada [*Library symbol*] [*Library of Congress*] (LCLS)

CaQLoU .... Pratt & Whitney Aircraft, Longueuil, PQ, Canada [*Library symbol Library of Congress*] (LCLS)

CaQLs.......... Bibliotheque Municipale, La Salle, PQ, Canada [*Library symbol Library of Congress*] (LCLS)

CaQLsO........ L'Octogone, Centre de la Culture, La Salle, PQ, Canada [*Library symbol*] [*Library of Congress*] (LCLS)

CaQLt........... Bibliotheque Municipale, La Tuque, PQ, Canada [*Library symbol Library of Congress*] (LCLS)

CaQMA .... Aluminum Secretariat Ltd., Montreal, PQ, Canada [*Library symbol Library of Congress*] (LCLS)

CaQMAA ..... Archives de la Chancellerie, Montreal, PQ, Canada [*Library symbol Library of Congress*] (LCLS)

CaQMAB ...... Montreal Association for the Blind, Montreal, PQ, Canada [*Library symbol*] [*Library of Congress*] (LCLS)

CaQMABB .... Asselin, Benoit, Boucher, Ducharme & Lapointe, Inc., Montreal, PQ, Canada [*Library symbol Library of Congress*] (LCLS)

CaQMaC ...... McGill University, Macdonald College, Montreal, PQ, Canada [*Library symbol Library of Congress*] (LCLS)

CaQMACAR... Carmel de Montreal, Montreal, PQ, Canada [*Library symbol Library of Congress*] (LCLS)

CaQMACL .... Quebec Association for Children with Learning Disabilities, Montreal, PQ, Canada [*Library symbol Library of Congress*] (LCLS)

CaQMACN ... Archives de la Congregation de Notre-Dame, Montreal, PQ, Canada [*Library symbol Library of Congress*] (LCLS)

CaQMADMA... Anglican Church of Canada, Diocese of Montreal, Archives, Montreal, PQ, Canada [*Library symbol Library of Congress*] (LCLS)

CaQMAE ...... Aviation Electric Ltd., Montreal, PQ, Canada [*Library symbol Library of Congress*] (LCLS)

CaQMAEC .... Atomic Energy of Canada, Montreal, PQ, Canada [*Library symbol Library of Congress*] (LCLS)

CaQMAI .... Arctic Institute of North America, Montreal, PQ, Canada [*Library symbol Library of Congress Obsolete*] (LCLS)

CaQMAL ...... Air Liquide, Montreal, PQ, Canada [*Library symbol Library of Congress*] (LCLS)

CaQMALL .... Abbott Laboratories Ltd., Montreal, PQ, Canada [*Library symbol Library of Congress*] (LCLS)

CaQMAM ..... McGill University, Allan Memorial Institute of Psychiatry, Montreal, PQ, Canada [*Library symbol Library of Congress*] (LCLS)

CaQMAMA ... Andre Marsan & Associes, Inc., Montreal, PQ, Canada [*Library symbol Library of Congress*] (LCLS)

CaQMAPO .... Centre de Documentation, APO Quebec, Montreal, PQ, Canada [*Library symbol*] [*Library of Congress*] (LCLS)

CaQMAPS .... Quebec Aid for the Partially-Sighted, Montreal, PQ, Canada [*Library symbol*] [*Library of Congress*] (LCLS)

CaQMaPTI ... Potton Technical Industries, Mansonville, PQ, Canada [*Library symbol Library of Congress*] (LCLS)

CaQMArC ..... Archives Provinciales des Capucins, Montreal, PQ, Canada [*Library symbol Library of Congress*] (LCLS)

CaQMAS ...... Archives du Seminaire de Saint-Sulpice, Montreal, PQ, Canada [*Library symbol Library of Congress*] (LCLS)

CaQMASI ..... Ministere des Affaires Sociales, Informatheque-Laboratoires, Ste.-Anne-De-Bellevue, PQ, Canada [*Library symbol Library of Congress*] (LCLS)

CaQMASIN... Informatheque des Affaires Sociales du Quebec, Montreal, PQ, Canada [*Library symbol Library of Congress*] (LCLS)

CaQMaSRC... Space Research Corp., Masonville, PQ, Canada [*Library symbol Library of Congress*] (LCLS)

CaQMASSAS... Association pour la Sante et la Securite du Travail, Secteur Affaires Sociales, Centre de Documentation, Montreal, PQ, Canada [*Library symbol Library of Congress*] (LCLS)

CaQMAv....... Barreau de Montreal, Bibliotheque des Avocats, Montreal, PQ, Canada [*Library symbol Library of Congress*] (LCLS)

CaQMAy....... Ayerst, McKenna & Harrison Ltd., Montreal, PQ, Canada [*Library symbol Library of Congress*] (LCLS)

CaQMB .... Bell Telephone Co. of Canada, Montreal, PQ, Canada [*Library symbol Library of Congress*] (LCLS)

CaQMBA ...... Ecole des Beaux-Arts, Montreal, PQ, Canada [*Library symbol Library of Congress*] (LCLS)

CaQMBAE .... Bristol Aero Engines Ltd., Montreal, PQ, Canada [*Library symbol Library of Congress*] (LCLS)

CaQMBAN ... Banque Nationale du Canada, Centre de Documentation, Montreal, PQ, Canada [*Library symbol*] [*Library of Congress*] (LCLS)

CaQMBB ...... College Bois-De-Boulogne, Montreal, PQ, Canada [*Library symbol Library of Congress*] (LCLS)

CaQMBBL .... Beauchemin, Beaton, LaPointe, Inc., Montreal, PQ, Canada [*Library symbol Library of Congress*] (LCLS)

CaQMBD ...... Canada Department of the Secretary of State, Translation Bureau, Montreal, PQ, Canada [*Library symbol Library of Congress*] (LCLS)

CaQMBI .... Bibliotheque des Instituteurs, Montreal, PQ, Canada [*Library symbol Library of Congress*] (LCLS)

CaQMBL ...... Bell Telephone Co. of Canada, Law Department Library, Montreal, PQ, Canada [*Library symbol Library of Congress*] (LCLS)

CaQMBM ..... Bibliotheque de la Ville de Montreal, Montreal, PQ, Canada [*Library symbol Library of Congress*] (LCLS)

CaQMBMo ... Bank of Montreal, Montreal, PQ, Canada [*Library symbol Library of Congress*] (LCLS)

CaQMBN ...... Bibliotheque Nationale du Quebec, Montreal, PQ, Canada [*Library symbol Library of Congress*] (LCLS)

CaQMBNR ... Bell Northern Research, Montreal, PQ, Canada [*Library symbol Library of Congress*] (LCLS)

CaQMBP ...... Building Products Ltd., Montreal, PQ, Canada [*Library symbol Library of Congress*] (LCLS)

CaQMBR ...... Bio-Research Laboratories Ltd., Pointe-Claire, PQ, Canada [*Library symbol Library of Congress*] (LCLS)

CaQMBT ...... Montreal Board of Trade, Montreal, PQ, Canada [*Library symbol Library of Congress*] (LCLS)

CaQMC .... College de Montreal, Montreal, PQ, Canada [*Library symbol Library of Congress*] (LCLS)

CaQMCa ...... Canadair Ltd., Engineering Library, Montreal, PQ, Canada [*Library symbol Library of Congress*] (LCLS)

CaQMCAD .... Centre d'Animation, de Developpement, et de Recherche en Education, Montreal, PQ, Canada [*Library symbol Library of Congress*] (LCLS)

CaQMCADQ ... Conservatoire d'Art Dramatique de Quebec, Montreal, PQ, Canada [*Library symbol Library of Congress*] (LCLS)

CaQMCAE .... Canadian Aviation Electronics, Montreal, PQ, Canada [*Library symbol Library of Congress*] (LCLS)

CaQMCAG .... College Andre Grasset, Montreal, PQ, Canada [*Library symbol Library of Congress*] (LCLS)

CaQMCAI ..... Canadian Asbestos Information Centre, Montreal, PQ, Canada [*Library symbol*] [*Library of Congress*] (LCLS)

CaQMCam .... Canadair Ltd., Missiles and Systems Library, Montreal, PQ, Canada [*Library symbol Library of Congress*] (LCLS)

CaQMCAT .... Commission des Accidents du Travail, Montreal, PQ, Canada [*Library symbol Library of Congress*] (LCLS)

CaQMCAV .... Ministere des Communications du Quebec, Direction Generale du Cinema et de l'Audiovisuel, Montreal, PQ, Canada [*Library symbol Library of Congress*] (LCLS)

CaQMCB ...... Canadian Broadcasting Corp., Montreal, PQ, Canada [*Library symbol Library of Congress*] (LCLS)

CaQMCBE .... Canadian Broadcasting Corp., Engineering Headquarters Library, Montreal, PQ, Canada [*Library symbol Library of Congress*]

CaQMCBH .... Catherine Booth Hospital, Montreal, PQ, Canada [*Library symbol*] [*Library of Congress*] (LCLS)

CaQMCBM .... Canadian Broadcasting Corp., Music Library, Montreal, PQ, Canada [*Library symbol*] [*Library of Congress*] (LCLS)

CaQMCC ...... Canada Cement Co. Ltd., Montreal, PQ, Canada [*Library symbol Library of Congress*] (LCLS)

CaQMCCL .... Currie, Coopers & Lybrand Ltd., Montreal, PQ, Canada [*Library symbol Library of Congress*] (LCLS)

CaQMCCR .... Canadian Council of Resource Ministers, Montreal, PQ, Canada [*Library symbol Library of Congress*] (LCLS)

CaQMCCS .... Centraide, Montreal, PQ, Canada [*Library symbol*] [*Library of Congress*] (LCLS)

CaQMCD ...... Centrale des Bibliotheques, Centre Documentaire, Montreal, PQ, Canada [*Library symbol Library of Congress*] (LCLS)

CaQMCDM .... College de Maisonneuve, Montreal, PQ, Canada [*Library symbol Library of Congress*] (LCLS)

CaQMCDP .... Caisse de Depot de Placement du Quebec, Montreal, PQ, Canada [*Library symbol Library of Congress*] (LCLS)

CaQMCE ...... Celanese Canada Ltd., Montreal, PQ, Canada [*Library symbol Library of Congress*] (LCLS)

CaQMCEA .... Canadian Export Association, Montreal, PQ, Canada [*Library symbol Library of Congress*] (LCLS)

CaQMCEC .... Catholic School Commission, Montreal, PQ, Canada [*Library symbol Library of Congress*] (LCLS)

CaQMCECI ... Centre Canadien d'Etudes et de Cooperation Internationle, Montreal, PQ, Canada [*Library symbol*] [*Library of Congress*] (LCLS)

CaQMCF ...... Charles E. Frosst & Co., Montreal, PQ, Canada [*Library symbol Library of Congress*] (LCLS)

CaQMCFH .... Charette, Fortier, Hawey, Touche, Ross, Centre de Documentation, Montreal, PQ, Canada [*Library symbol*] [*Library of Congress*] (LCLS)

CaQMCG ...... Ciba-Geigy Canada Ltd., Dorval, PQ, Canada [*Library symbol Library of Congress*] (LCLS)

CaQMCh ...... Chemcell Ltd., Montreal, PQ, Canada [*Library symbol Library of Congress*] (LCLS)

CaQMCHC .... Montreal Chest Hospital, Montreal, PQ, Canada [*Library symbol Library of Congress*] (LCLS)

CaQMCHF .... Centre de Documentation, Centre Hospitalier Fleury, Montreal, PQ, Canada [*Library symbol*] [*Library of Congress*] (LCLS)

CaQMCHL .... Centre Hospitalier de Lachine, Montreal, PQ, Canada [*Library symbol Library of Congress*] (LCLS)

CaQMCi .... Ciba Co. Ltd., Montreal, PQ, Canada [*Library symbol Library of Congress*] (LCLS)

CaQMCih ..... Ville de Montreal, Bibliotheque de Documentation des Archives, Montreal, PQ, Canada [*Library symbol Library of Congress*] (LCLS)

CaQMCIL .... Canadian Industries Ltd., Montreal, PQ, Canada [*Library symbol Library of Congress*] (LCLS)

CaQMCILL .... Canadian Industries Ltd., Legal Department, Montreal, PQ, Canada [*Library symbol Library of Congress*] (LCLS)

CaQMCILR ... Canadian Industries Ltd., Central Research Laboratory, McMasterville, PQ, Canada [*Library symbol Library of Congress*] (LCLS)

CaQMCIM .... Canadian Institute of Mining and Metallurgy, Montreal, PQ, Canada [*Library symbol Library of Congress*] (LCLS)

CaQMCJ ...... Canadian Jewish Congress Library, Montreal, PQ, Canada [*Library symbol Library of Congress*] (LCLS)

CaQMCL ..... CanAtom Ltd., Montreal, PQ, Canada [*Library symbol Library of Congress*] (LCLS)

CaQMCM .... Canadian Marconi Co., Montreal, PQ, Canada [*Library symbol Library of Congress*] (LCLS)

CaQMCN ..... Canadian National Railways, Montreal, PQ, Canada [*Library symbol Library of Congress*] (LCLS)

CaQMCNC ... Canadian National Railways, Chemical Library, Montreal, PQ, Canada [*Library symbol Library of Congress*] (LCLS)

CaQMCOM ... Conservatoire de Musique de Montreal, Montreal, PQ, Canada [*Library symbol Library of Congress*] (LCLS)

CaQMCP ..... Canadian Pacific Railway Co., Montreal, PQ, Canada [*Library symbol Library of Congress*] (LCLS)

CaQMCR ..... Canadian Copper Refiners Ltd., Montreal, PQ, Canada [*Library symbol Library of Congress*] (LCLS)

CaQMCRI .... Centre de Recherche Industrielle du Quebec, Montreal, PQ, Canada [*Library symbol*] [*Library of Congress*] (LCLS)

CaQMCRP .... Conference des Recteurs et des Principaux des Universites du Quebec, Montreal, PQ, Canada [*Library symbol Library of Congress*] (LCLS)

CaQMCS ..... Christian Science Reading Room, Montreal, PQ, Canada [*Library symbol Library of Congress*] (LCLS)

CaQMCSCA ... Archives de la Congregation de Sainte-Croix, Montreal, PQ, Canada [*Library symbol*] [*Library of Congress*] (LCLS)

CaQMCSSMM ... C.S.S.M.M. [*Centre de Services Sociaux du Montreal Metropolitan*], Mon treal, PQ, Canada [*Library symbol*] [*Library of Congress*] (LCLS)

CaQMCSSS ... Conseil de la Sante et des Services Sociaux de la Region de Montreal Metropolitain, Service de Reference, Montreal, PQ, Canada [*Library symbol*] [*Library of Congress*] (LCLS)

CaQMCSVA .... Archives des Clercs de Saint-Viateur, Province de Montreal, Outremont, PQ, Canada [*Library symbol*] [*Library of Congress*] (LCLS)

CaQMCT ...... Commission de Transport de la Communaute Urbaine de Montreal, Montreal, PQ, Canada [*Library symbol Library of Congress*] (LCLS)

CaQMCTM ... Canadian Tobacco Manufacturers' Council, Montreal, PQ, Canada [*Library symbol Library of Congress*] (LCLS)

CaQMCVM .... Commission des Valeurs Mobilieres de Quebec, Quebec, PQ, Canada [*Library symbol Library of Congress*] (LCLS)

CaQMCW .... Canada Wire & Cable Co. Ltd., Montreal, PQ, Canada [*Library symbol Library of Congress*] (LCLS)

CaQMD .... Institut Genealogique Drouin, Montreal, PQ, Canada [*Library symbol Library of Congress*] (LCLS)

CaQMDB ..... College Jean-De-Brebeuf, Montreal, PQ, Canada [*Library symbol Library of Congress*] (LCLS)

CaQMDE ..... Dominion Engineering Works Ltd., Montreal, PQ, Canada [*Library symbol Library of Congress*] (LCLS)

CaQMDH ..... Douglas Hospital, Montreal, PQ, Canada [*Library symbol Library of Congress*] (LCLS)

CaQMDL ..... Domtar Ltd., Montreal, PQ, Canada [*Library symbol Library of Congress*] (LCLS)

CaQMDM .... Montreal Association for the Mentally Retarded, Montreal, PQ, Canada [*Library symbol Library of Congress*] (LCLS)

CaQMDom ... Dominion Bridge Co. Ltd., Montreal, PQ, Canada [*Library symbol Library of Congress*] (LCLS)

CaQMDP ..... Du Pont of Canada Ltd., Economist's Office Library, Montreal, PQ, Canada [*Library symbol Library of Congress*] (LCLS)

CaQMDPL .... Du Pont of Canada Ltd., Legal Library, Montreal, PQ, Canada [*Library symbol Library of Congress*] (LCLS)

CaQMDT ..... Dominion Textile, Montreal, PQ, Canada [*Library symbol Library of Congress*] (LCLS)

CaQME .... Engineering Institute of Canada, Montreal, PQ, Canada [*Library symbol Library of Congress Obsolete*] (LCLS)

CaQMEA ..... Environment Canada, Atmospheric Environment Service, Dorval, PQ, Canada [*Library symbol Library of Congress*] (LCLS)

CaQMEC ..... Montreal Engineering Co. Ltd., Montreal, PQ, Canada [*Library symbol Library of Congress*] (LCLS)

CaQMECB .... Quebec Ministere de l'Education, Centrale des Bibliotheques, Montreal, PQ, Canada [*Library symbol Library of Congress*] (LCLS)

CaQMECS .... Experts-Conseils Shawinigan, Montreal, PQ, Canada [*Library symbol*] [*Library of Congress*] (LCLS)

CaQMEE ...... Canada Department of the Environment, Environmental Protection Services, Montreal, PQ, Canada [*Library symbol*] [*Library of Congress*] (LCLS)

CaQMEN ..... Ministere de l'Environnement, Montreal, PQ, Canada [*Library symbol Library of Congress*] (LCLS)

CaQMENT .... Ecole Nationale de Theatre, Montreal, PQ, Canada [*Library symbol Library of Congress*] (LCLS)

CaQMEP ...... Ecole Polytechnique, Montreal, PQ, Canada [*Library symbol Library of Congress*] (LCLS)

CaQMES ..... Ecole Secondaire Saint-Stanislas, Montreal, PQ, Canada [*Library symbol Library of Congress*] (LCLS)

CaQMF .... Fraser-Hickson Institute, Montreal, PQ, Canada [*Library symbol Library of Congress*] (LCLS)

CaQMFA ..... Montreal Museum of Fine Arts, Montreal, PQ, Canada [*Library symbol Library of Congress*] (LCLS)

CaQMFBD .... Federal Business Development Bank, Montreal, PQ, Canada [*Library symbol Library of Congress*] (LCLS)

CaQMFC ...... First Church of Christ, Scientist, Montreal, PQ, Canada [*Library symbol Library of Congress*] (LCLS)

CaQMFER .... Forest Engineering Research Institute of Canada, Pointe-Claire, PQ, Canada [*Library symbol Library of Congress*] (LCLS)

CaQMFH ..... Frank W. Horner Ltd., Montreal, PQ, Canada [*Library symbol Library of Congress*] (LCLS)

CaQMFLCP... Ministere du Loisir de la Chasse et de la Peche du Quebec, Bibliotheque de la Faune, Montreal, PQ, Canada [*Library symbol Library of Congress*] (LCLS)

CaQMFMO ... Federation des Medecins Omnipracticiens du Quebec, Montreal, PQ, Canada [*Library symbol Library of Congress*] (LCLS)

CaQMFMS ... Federation des Medecins Specialistes du Quebec, Montreal, PQ, Canada [*Library symbol Library of Congress*] (LCLS)

CaQMFR ...... Canada Department of the Environment, Fisheries and Marine Service, Ste.-Anne-De-Bellevue, PQ, Canada [*Library symbol Library of Congress*] (LCLS)

CaQMFRA .... Archives des Franciscains, Montreal, PQ, Canada [*Library symbol*] [*Library of Congress*] (LCLS)

CaQMFran ... Studium Franciscain de Theologie, Montreal, PQ, Canada [*Library symbol Library of Congress*] (LCLS)

CaQMFSGA... Archives des Freres de Saint-Gabriel, Montreal, PQ, Canada [*Library symbol*] [*Library of Congress*] (LCLS)

CaQMG .... Concordia University, Sir George Williams Campus, Montreal, PQ, Canada [*Library symbol Library of Congress*] (LCLS)

CaQMGa ...... Montreal Gazette, Montreal, PQ, Canada [*Library symbol Library of Congress*] (LCLS)

CaQMgB ..... Bibliotheque Municipale, Magog, PQ, Canada [*Library symbol Library of Congress*] (LCLS)

CaQMGB ..... Grands Ballets Canadiens, Montreal, PQ, Canada [*Library symbol Library of Congress*] (LCLS)

CaQMGDH ... Grace Dart Hospital Center, Montreal, PQ, Canada [*Library symbol*] [*Library of Congress*] (LCLS)

CaQMGG ..... Concordia University, Sir George Williams Campus, Department of Geography, Montreal, PQ, Canada [*Library symbol Library of Congress*] (LCLS)

CaQMGGM... Concordia University, Sir George Williams Campus, Department of Geography, University Map Collection, Montreal, PQ, Canada [*Library symbol Library of Congress*] (LCLS)

CaQMGH ..... Montreal General Hospital, Montreal, PQ, Canada [*Library symbol Library of Congress*] (LCLS)

CaQMGHC.... Montreal General Hospital, Community Health Department, Montreal, PQ, Canada [*Library symbol*] [*Library of Congress*] (LCLS)

CaQMGHN ... Montreal General Hospital, Nurses' Library, Montreal, PQ, Canada [*Library symbol*] [*Library of Congress*] (LCLS)

CaQMGLS .... Concordia University, Librry Studies Program, Montreal, PQ, Canada [*Library symbol*] [*Library of Congress*] (LCLS)

CaQMGP ..... Gerard Parizeau Ltee., Montreal, PQ, Canada [*Library symbol Library of Congress*] (LCLS)

CaQMGS ...... Grand Seminaire, Montreal, PQ, Canada [*Library symbol Library of Congress*] (LCLS)

CaQMH .... Hydro-Quebec, Bibliotheque, Montreal, PQ, Canada [*Library symbol Library of Congress*] (LCLS)

CaQMHC ...... Hoechst Canada, Inc, Medical Library, Montreal, PQ, Canada [*Library symbol*] [*Library of Congress*] (LCLS)

CaQMHCL .... Hopital Charles Lemoyne, Bibliotheque Medical, Montreal, PQ, Canada [*Library symbol*] [*Library of Congress*] (LCLS)

CaQMHCLC... Hospital Charles Lemoyne, Department de Sante Communutaire, Montreal, PQ, Canada [*Library symbol*] [*Library of Congress*] (LCLS)

CaQMHD ...... Hotel-Dieu Hospital, Montreal, PQ, Canada [*Library symbol Library of Congress*] (LCLS)

CaQMHDE .... Direction de l'Environnement, Hydro-Quebec, Montreal, PQ, Canada [*Library symbol Library of Congress*] (LCLS)

CaQMHE ...... Ecole des Hautes Etudes Commerciales, Montreal, PQ, Canada [*Library symbol Library of Congress*] (LCLS)

CaQMHGC.... Centre Hospitalier de Verdun, Montreal, PQ, Canada [*Library symbol Library of Congress*] (LCLS)

CaQMHGF .... Hopital General Fleury, Montreal, PQ, Canada [*Library symbol Library of Congress*] (LCLS)

CaQMHJT .... Hopital Jean Talon, Montreal, PQ, Canada [*Library symbol Library of Congress*] (LCLS)

CaQMHM ..... Centre Hospitalier Jacques Viger, Montreal, PQ, Canada [*Library symbol Library of Congress*] (LCLS)

CaQMHME ... Hopital Marie-Enfant, Montreal, PQ, Canada [*Library symbol Library of Congress*] (LCLS)

CaQMHMR... Hopital Maisonneuve-Rosemont, Montreal, PQ, Canada [*Library symbol Library of Congress*] (LCLS)

CaQMHND ... Notre Dame Hospital, Medical Library, Montreal, PQ, Canada [*Library symbol Library of Congress*] (LCLS)

CaQMHNDI... Hopital Notre-Dame, Bibliotheque des Services Infirmiers, Montreal, PQ, Canada [*Library symbol Library of Congress*] (LCLS)

CaQMHRP.... Hopital Riviere-Des-Prairies, Montreal, PQ, Canada [*Library symbol Library of Congress*] (LCLS)

CaQMHSC ... Hopital du Sacre-Coeur, Montreal, PQ, Canada [*Library symbol Library of Congress*] (LCLS)

CaQMHSCA... Hopital Santa Cabrini, Montreal, PQ, Canada [*Library symbol Library of Congress*] (LCLS)

CaQMHSJ .... Hopital Louis-H.-LaFontaine, Montreal, PQ, Canada [*Library symbol Library of Congress*] (LCLS)

CaQMHSJA... Hopital Ste-Jeanne-D'Arc, Montreal, PQ, Canada [*Library symbol Library of Congress*] (LCLS)

CaQMHSL .... Hopital Saint-Luc, Montreal, PQ, Canada [*Library symbol Library of Congress*] (LCLS)

CaQMI .... Insurance Institute of the Province of Quebec, Montreal, PQ, Canada [*Library symbol Library of Congress*] (LCLS)

CaQMIA .... International Air Transport Association, Montreal, PQ, Canada [*Library symbol Library of Congress*] (LCLS)

CaQMIAA ..... Institut des Arts Appliques, Montreal, PQ, Canada [*Library symbol Library of Congress*] (LCLS)

CaQMIAG ..... Institut des Arts Graphiques, Montreal, PQ, Canada [*Library symbol Library of Congress*] (LCLS)

CaQMIAP ..... Institut Albert Prevost, Montreal, PQ, Canada [*Library symbol Library of Congress*] (LCLS)

CaQMIC .... International Civil Aviation Organization, Montreal, PQ, Canada [*Library symbol Library of Congress*] (LCLS)

CaQMICA ..... Institute of Chartered Accountants of Quebec, Montreal, PQ, Canada [*Library symbol Library of Congress*] (LCLS)

CaQMICE ..... Canadian Institute of Adult Education, Montreal, PQ, Canada [*Library symbol Library of Congress*] (LCLS)

CaQMICM .... Institut de Cardiologie de Montreal, Montreal, PQ, Canada [*Library symbol Library of Congress*] (LCLS)

CaQMIFQ ..... Informatech France-Quebec, Montreal, PQ, Canada [*Library symbol Library of Congress*] (LCLS)

CaQMIG .... Industrial Grain Products Ltd., Montreal, PQ, Canada [*Library symbol Library of Congress*] (LCLS)

CaQMII .... Instituto Italiano di Cultura, Montreal, PQ, Canada [*Library symbol Library of Congress*] (LCLS)

CaQMIIS ...... McGill University, Institute of Islamic Studies, Montreal, PQ, Canada [*Library symbol Library of Congress*] (LCLS)

CaQMILO .... International Labour Office, Montreal, PQ, Canada [*Library symbol Library of Congress*] (LCLS)

CaQMIM ..... Institut de Microbiologie et d'Hygiene de Montreal, Montreal, PQ, Canada [*Library symbol Library of Congress*] (LCLS)

CaQMIMM ... Institut National de Productivite, Montreal, Montreal, PQ, Canada [*Library symbol Library of Congress*] (LCLS)

CaQMIMO ... Travail-Quebec, Montreal, PQ, Canada [*Library symbol Library of Congress*] (LCLS)

CaQMINCA... Institut National Canadien pour les Aveugles, Montreal, PQ, Canada [*Library symbol*] [*Library of Congress*] (LCLS)

CaQMIP ...... McGill University, Macdonald College, Institute of Parasitology, Montreal, PQ, Canada [*Library symbol Library of Congress*] (LCLS)

CaQMIPP ..... Institut Philippe Pinel de Montreal, Montreal, PQ, Canada [*Library symbol Library of Congress*] (LCLS)

CaQMIRC .... Institut de Recherches Cliniques, Montreal, PQ, Canada [*Library symbol Library of Congress*] (LCLS)

CaQMIRS .... Informatheque IRSST [*Institut de Recherche en Sante et Securite au Travail*], Montreal, PQ, Canada [*Library symbol*] [*Library of Congress*] (LCLS)

CaQMISM .... Institution des Sourds de Montreal, Centre de Ressources Multimedia, Montreal, PQ, Canada [*Library symbol Library of Congress*] (LCLS)

CaQMIT........ Imperial Tobacco Co. of Canada Ltd., Montreal, PQ, Canada [*Library symbol Library of Congress*] (LCLS)

CaQMITR ..... Imperial Tobacco Co. of Canada Ltd., Research Library, Montreal, PQ, Canada [*Library symbol Library of Congress*] (LCLS)

CaQMJ........ Jewish Public Library, Montreal, PQ, Canada [*Library symbol Library of Congress*] (LCLS)

CaQMJB ...... Jardin Botanique de Montreal, Montreal, PQ, Canada [*Library symbol Library of Congress*] (LCLS)

CaQMJES .... Joseph E. Seagram & Sons Ltd., Technical Services, Lasalle, PQ, Canada [*Library symbol Library of Congress*] (LCLS)

CaQMJFM ... Fisheries and Oceans Canada, Maurice Lamontagne Institute, Mont-Joli, PQ, Canada [*Library symbol*] [*Library of Congress*] (LCLS)

CaQMJG ..... Jewish General Hospital, Montreal, PQ, Canada [*Library symbol Library of Congress*] (LCLS)

CaQMJGI .... Jewish General Hospital, Institute of Community and Family Psychiatry, Montreal,PQ, Canada [*Library symbol Library of Congress*] (LCLS)

CaQMJGL .... Jewish General Hospital, Lady Davis Institute for Medical Research, Montreal, PQ, Canada [*Library symbol Library of Congress*] (LCLS)

CaQMjH .... Hopital de Mont-Joli, Inc., Mont-Joli, PQ, Canada [*Library symbol Library of Congress*] (LCLS)

CaQMJJ .... Johnson & Johnson Ltd., Montreal, PQ, Canada [*Library symbol Library of Congress*] (LCLS)

CaQMJL .... John Lovell & Son, City Directories Ltd., Montreal, PQ, Canada [*Library symbol Library of Congress*] (LCLS)

CaQMJM ...... Canada Department of Justice, Montreal, PQ, Canada [*Library symbol Library of Congress*] (LCLS)

CaQMJSJ ..... Ministere de la Justice, Commission des Services Juridiques, Montreal, PQ, Canada [*Library symbol Library of Congress*] (LCLS)

CaQML........ Concordia University, Loyola Campus, Montreal, PQ, Canada [*Library symbol Library of Congress*] (LCLS)

CaQMLA ...... Laboratoires Abbott Ltee, Montreal, PQ, Canada [*Library symbol*] [*Library of Congress*] (LCLS)

CaQMLCA.... Lower Canada Arms Collectors Association, Montreal, PQ, Canada [*Library symbol Library of Congress*] (LCLS)

CaQMLCC .... Lower Canada College, Montreal, PQ, Canada [*Library symbol Library of Congress*] (LCLS)

CaQMLG ...... Lakeshore General Hospital, Pointe-Claire, PQ, Canada [*Library symbol Library of Congress*] (LCLS)

CaQMLGC .... Lakeshore General Hospital, Community Health Department, Montreal, PQ, Canada [*Library symbol*] [*Library of Congress*] (LCLS)

CaQMLQ ...... Loto-Quebec, Centre de Documentation, Montreal, PQ, Canada [*Library symbol*] [*Library of Congress*] (LCLS)

CaQMLR ...... Lethbridge Rehabilitation Centre, Montreal, PQ, Canada [*Library symbol Library of Congress*] (LCLS)

CaQMM........ McGill University, Montreal, PQ, Canada [*Library symbol Library of Congress*] (LCLS)

CaQMMAC ... Musee d'Art Contemporain, Montreal, PQ, Canada [*Library symbol Library of Congress*] (LCLS)

CaQMMAQ ... La Magnetotheque des Aveugles du Quebec, Montreal, PQ, Canada [*Library symbol*] [*Library of Congress*] (LCLS)

CaQMMB ..... McGill University, Blackader/Lauterman Library of Architecture and Art, Montreal, PQ, Canada [*Library symbol Library of Congress*] (LCLS)

CaQMMBG ... McGill University, Botany-Genetics Library, Montreal, PQ, Canada [*Library symbol Library of Congress*] (LCLS)

CaQMMBZ ... McGill University, Blacker-Wood Library, Montreal, PQ, Canada [*Library symbol Library of Congress*] (LCLS)

CaQMMC ..... Miron Co. Ltd., Montreal, PQ, Canada [*Library symbol Library of Congress*] (LCLS)

CaQMMCH ... Montreal Children's Hospital, Montreal, PQ, Canada [*Library symbol Library of Congress*] (LCLS)

CaQMMCR ... Musee du Chateau de Ramezay, Montreal, PQ, Canada [*Library symbol Library of Congress*] (LCLS)

CaQMMD ..... McGill University, Religious Studies Library, Montreal, PQ, Canada [*Library symbol Library of Congress*] (LCLS)

CaQMME...... McGill University, Engineering Library, Montreal, PQ, Canada [*Library symbol Library of Congress*] (LCLS)

CaQMMFD ... McGill University, Dentistry Library, Montreal, PQ, Canada [*Library symbol Library of Congress*] (LCLS)

CaQMMG ..... McGill University, Department of Geography, University Map Collection, Montreal,PQ, Canada [*Library symbol Library of Congress*] (LCLS)

CaQMMGS ... McGill University, Department of Geological Sciences, Montreal, PQ, Canada [*Library symbol Library of Congress*] (LCLS)

CaQMMH ..... Mental Hygiene Institute, Montreal, PQ, Canada [*Library symbol Library of Congress*] (LCLS)

CaQMMHH ... Maimonides Hospital and Home for the Aged, Montreal, PQ, Canada [*Library symbol Library of Congress*] (LCLS)

CaQMMI ...... Atwater Library, Montreal, PQ, Canada [*Library symbol Library of Congress*] (LCLS)

CaQMMIQ .... Canada Employment and Immigration Department, Quebec Regional Office, Montreal, PQ, Canada [*Library symbol Library of Congress*] (LCLS)

CaQMML...... McGill University, Law Library, Montreal, PQ, Canada [*Library symbol Library of Congress*] (LCLS)

CaQMMLS ... McGill University, Graduate School of Library Science, Montreal, PQ, Canada [*Library symbol Library of Congress*] (LCLS)

CaQMMM .... McGill University, Medical Library, Montreal, PQ, Canada [*Library symbol Library of Congress*] (LCLS)

CaQMMMa ... McGill University, Map Collection, Montreal, PQ, Canada [*Library symbol Library of Congress*] (LCLS)

CaQMMMcM... McGill University, McCord Museum, Montreal, PQ, Canada [*Library symbol Library of Congress*] (LCLS)

CaQMMN ..... McGill University, Nursing Library, Montreal, PQ, Canada [*Library symbol Library of Congress*] (LCLS)

CaQMMNS ... McGill University, Northern Studies Library, Montreal, PQ, Canada [*Library symbol Library of Congress*] (LCLS)

CaQMMO ..... McGill University, Osler Collection, Montreal, PQ, Canada [*Library symbol Library of Congress*] (LCLS)

CaQMMoC ... Monsanto Canada Ltd., Montreal, PQ, Canada [*Library symbol Library of Congress*] (LCLS)

CaQMMoS ... Montreal Star, Montreal, PQ, Canada [*Library symbol Library of Congress*] (LCLS)

CaQMMPB ... MPB Technologies, Dorval, PQ, Canada [*Library symbol*] [*Library of Congress*] (LCLS)

CaQMMPS ... McGill University, Physical Sciences Centre, Montreal, PQ, Canada [*Library symbol Library of Congress*] (LCLS)

CaQMMRB ... McGill University, Department of Rare Books and Special Collections, Montreal, PQ, Canada [*Library symbol Library of Congress*] (LCLS)

CaQMMRS ... Mendelsohn Rosentzveig Schacter, Montreal, PQ, Canada [*Library symbol*] [*Library of Congress*] (LCLS)

CaQMMS ..... McGill University, Social Work Library, Montreal, PQ, Canada [*Library symbol Library of Congress*] (LCLS)

CaQMMSC ... McGill University, Howard Ross Library of Management, Montreal, PQ, Canada [*Library symbol Library of Congress*] (LCLS)

CaQMMSR ... Ministe de la Main-d'Oeuvre et de la Securite du Revenu du Quebec, Centre de Documentation, Montreal, PQ, Canada [*Library symbol*] [*Library of Congress*] (LCLS)

CaQMn......... Bibliotheque Municipale, Montreal-Nord, PQ, Canada [*Library symbol Library of Congress*] (LCLS)

CaQMNA ...... Canadian Pulp and Paper Association, Montreal, PQ, Canada [*Library symbol Library of Congress*] (LCLS)

CaQMNDE .... Hopital Notre-Dame-De-L'Esperance-De-St-Laurent, Montreal, PQ, Canada [*Library symbol Library of Congress*] (LCLS)

CaQMNE ...... Northern Electric Co., Montreal, PQ, Canada [*Library symbol Library of Congress*] (LCLS)

CaQMNF ...... National Film Board, Montreal, PQ, Canada [*Library symbol*] [*Library of Congress*] (LCLS)

CaQMNFNI... National Film Board, National Information and Distribution System, Montreal, PQ,Canada [*Library symbol Library of Congress*] (LCLS)

CaQMNHH ... Canada Department of National Health and Welfare, Health Protection Branch, Montreal, PQ, Canada [*Library symbol Library of Congress*] (LCLS)

CaQMNI .... National Industrial Conference Board, Montreal, PQ, Canada [*Library symbol Library of Congress*] (LCLS)

CaQMNIH..... Montreal Neurological Institute and Hospital, Montreal, PQ, Canada [*Library symbol Library of Congress*] (LCLS)

CaQMNOT.... Northern Telecom Canada Ltd., Montreal, PQ, Canada [*Library symbol*] [*Library of Congress*] (LCLS)

CaQMNR...... Noranda Research Centre, Montreal, PQ, Canada [*Library symbol Library of Congress*] (LCLS)

CaQMNT ...... Nesbitt, Thomson & Co. Ltd., Montreal, PQ, Canada [*Library symbol Library of Congress*] (LCLS)

CaQMO .... Oratoire Saint-Joseph du Mont-Royal, Montreal, PQ, Canada [*Library symbol Library of Congress*] (LCLS)

CaQMOB ..... Ministere des Pecheries et de la Chasse, Office de Biologie, Montreal, PQ, Canada [*Library symbol Library of Congress*] (LCLS)

CaQMOCQ... Office de la Construction du Quebec, Montreal, PQ, Canada [*Library symbol Library of Congress*] (LCLS)

CaQMOF ..... Ogilvie Flour Mills Co. Ltd., Montreal, PQ, Canada [*Library symbol Library of Congress*] (LCLS)

CaQMOFJ ... Office Franco-Quebecois pour la Jeunesse, Montreal, PQ, Canada [*Library symbol Library of Congress*] (LCLS)

CaQMOI ...... Ordre des Infirmieres et Infirmiers du Quebec, Montreal, PQ, Canada [*Library symbol Library of Congress*] (LCLS)

CaQMOLF .... Office de la Langue Francaise, Montreal, PQ, Canada [*Library symbol Library of Congress*] (LCLS)

CaQMPA ...... Project Archipel de Montreal, Centre de Documentation Project Archipel de Montreal, Centre de Documentation, Montreal, PQ, Canada [*Library symbol*] [*Library of Congress*] (LCLS)

CaQMPC ...... Presbyterian College, Montreal, PQ, Canada [*Library symbol Library of Congress*] (LCLS)

CaQMPE ...... Pezaris Electronics Co., Research Library, Montreal, PQ, Canada [*Library symbol Library of Congress*] (LCLS)

CaQMPI .... Polish Institute of Arts and Sciences in Canada, Montreal, PQ, Canada [*Library symbol Library of Congress*] (LCLS)

CaQMPM ..... Peat, Marwick & Associes, Montreal, PQ, Canada [*Library symbol Library of Congress*] (LCLS)

CaQMPp ...... Pulp and Paper Research Institute of Canada, Pointe Claire, PQ, Canada [*Library symbol Library of Congress*] (LCLS)

CaQMPRA.... Archives Providence, Montreal, PQ, Canada [*Library symbol*] [*Library of Congress*] (LCLS)

CaQMPSM ... Protestant School Board of Greater Montreal, Montreal, PQ, Canada [*Library symbol Library of Congress*] (LCLS)

CaQMPSR ... P. S. Ross & Partners, Montreal, PQ, Canada [*Library symbol Library of Congress*] (LCLS)

CaQMPW ..... Price, Waterhouse & Co. Library, Vancouver, BC, Canada [*Library symbol Library of Congress*] (LCLS)

CaQMPWQ... Public Works Canada, Quebec Region Library, Montreal, PQ, Canada [*Library symbol*] [*Library of Congress*] (LCLS)

CaQMQ .... Queen Mary Veterans Hospital, Montreal, PQ, Canada [*Library symbol Library of Congress*] (LCLS)

CaQMQAr..... Quebec Archives, Montreal, PQ, Canada [*Library symbol Library of Congress*] (LCLS)

CaQMQDP.... Quebec Commission des Droits de la Personne, Montreal, PQ, Canada [*Library symbol Library of Congress*] (LCLS)

CaQMQE ..... Queen Elizabeth Hospital, Montreal, PQ, Canada [*Library symbol Library of Congress*] (LCLS)

CaQMR .... Royal Bank of Canada, Montreal, PQ, Canada [*Library symbol Library of Congress*] (LCLS)

CaQMRA ...... Railway Association of Canada, Montreal, PQ, Canada [*Library symbol Library of Congress*] (LCLS)

CaQMRAD.... Institut de Recherche Appliquee sur le Travail, Centre de Documentation, Montreal, PQ, Canada [*Library symbol Library of Congress*] (LCLS)

CaQMRAQ... Recherches Amerindiennes au Quebec, Montreal, PQ, Canada [*Library symbol*] [*Library of Congress*] (LCLS)

CaQMRC ...... Royal Canadian Air Force Library, Montreal, PQ, Canada [*Library symbol Library of Congress*] (LCLS)

CaQMRCM ... Raymond, Chabot, Martin, Pare, Montreal, PQ, Canada [*Library symbol*] [*Library of Congress*] (LCLS)

CaQMRD ...... Reader's Digest of Canada Ltd., Montreal, PQ, Canada [*Library symbol Library of Congress*] (LCLS)

CaQMRE ...... Revenue Canada, Montreal, PQ, Canada [*Library symbol Library of Congress*] (LCLS)

CaQMREG ... Regie de l'Electricite et du Gaz, Montreal, PQ, Canada [*Library symbol Library of Congress*] (LCLS)

CaQMRH...... Centre de Recherches en Relations Humaines, Montreal, PQ, Canada [*Library symbol Library of Congress*] (LCLS)

CaQMRI .... Rehabilitation Institute of Montreal, Montreal, PQ, Canada [*Library symbol Library of Congress*] (LCLS)

CaQMRL ...... Centre de Documentation de la Regie du Logement, Montreal, PQ, Canada [*Library symbol Library of Congress*] (LCLS)

CaQMRM ..... Reddy Memorial Hospital, Montreal, PQ, Canada [*Library symbol Library of Congress*] (LCLS)

CaQMRP ...... Rhone-Poulenc Pharma, Inc., Montreal, PQ, Canada [*Library symbol*] [*Library of Congress*] (LCLS)

CaQMRQ ...... Radio-Quebec, Montreal, PQ, Canada [*Library symbol Library of Congress*] (LCLS)

CaQMRR ...... Rolls-Royce of Canada Ltd., Montreal, PQ, Canada [*Library symbol Library of Congress*] (LCLS)

CaQMRS ...... C.S.I.S. [*Canadian Security Intelligence Service*], Information Centre , Montreal, PQ, Canada [*Library symbol*] [*Library of Congress*] (LCLS)

CaQMRSJA... Archives des Religieuses Hospitalieres de Saint-Joseph, Montreal, PQ, Canada [*Library symbol*] [*Library of Congress*] (LCLS)

CaQMRV ...... Royal Victoria Hospital Library, Montreal, PQ, Canada [*Library symbol Library of Congress*] (LCLS)

CaQMRVW... Royal Victoria Hospital, Women's Pavillion, Montreal, PQ, Canada [*Library symbol Library of Congress*] (LCLS)

CaQMS .... Sun Life Assurance Co. of Canada, Montreal, PQ, Canada [*Library symbol Library of Congress*] (LCLS)

CaQMSa ...... Province de Quebec, Ministere des Affaires Sociales, Montreal, PQ, Canada [*Library symbol Library of Congress*] (LCLS)

CaQMSAC ... Sandoz Canada, Inc., Dorval, PQ, Canada [*Library symbol*] [*Library of Congress*] (LCLS)

CaQMSAP ... Societe des Artistes Professionels du Quebec, Montreal, PQ, Canada [*Library symbol Library of Congress*] (LCLS)

CaQMSC ...... Southern Canada Power Co. Library, Montreal, PQ, Canada [*Library symbol Library of Congress*] (LCLS)

CaQMSCa ... Statistics Canada, Montreal, PQ, Canada [*Library symbol Library of Congress*] (LCLS)

CaQMSD ...... Systems Development (Montreal), Information Resource Centre (Systemes-Applications Practiques (Montreal), Centre d'Information Specialise), Montreal, PQ, Canada [*Library symbol*] [*Library of Congress*] (LCLS)

CaQMSDB .... Societe de Developpement de la Baie James, Montreal, PQ, Canada [*Library symbol Library of Congress*] (LCLS)

CaQMSDL .... Sidbec-Dosco Ltd., Montreal, PQ, Canada [*Library symbol Library of Congress*] (LCLS)

CaQMSEB .... Societe d'Energie de la Baie James, Montreal, PQ, Canada [*Library symbol Library of Congress*] (LCLS)

CaQMSEBJ ... Societe d'Energie de la Baie James, Centre de Documentation, Montreal, PQ, Canada [*Library symbol Library of Congress*] (LCLS)

CaQMSGE .... Office des Services de Garde a l'Enfance, Montreal, PQ, Canada [*Library symbol Library of Congress*] (LCLS)

CaQMSGME ... Gouvernement du Quebec, Ministere de l'Education, Service General des Moyens d'Enseignement, Montreal, PQ, Canada [*Library symbol Library of Congress*] (LCLS)

CaQMSH ...... Societe Historique de Montreal, Montreal, PQ, Canada [*Library symbol Library of Congress*] (LCLS)

CaQMSHE .... Stadler Herter, Montreal, PQ, Canada [*Library symbol Library of Congress*] (LCLS)

CaQMSI .... Scolasticat de l'Immaculee-Conception, Montreal, PQ, Canada [*Library symbol Library of Congress*] (LCLS)

CaQMSJ .... Saint Joseph's Teachers' College, Montreal, PQ, Canada [*Library symbol Library of Congress*] (LCLS)

CaQMSK ...... Smith, Kline & French Co. [*Later, SmithKline Corp.*], Montreal, PQ, Canada [*Library symbol Library of Congress*] (LCLS)

CaQMSM ..... College Sainte-Marie, Montreal, PQ, Canada [*Library symbol Library of Congress*] (LCLS)

CaQMSMa ... Saint Mary's Hospital, Montreal, PQ, Canada [*Library symbol Library of Congress*] (LCLS)

CaQMSNC .... Surveyer, Nenninger & Chenevert, Inc., Montreal, PQ, Canada [*Library symbol Library of Congress*] (LCLS)

CaQMSO ...... Shell Oil Co. of Canada, Montreal, PQ, Canada [*Library symbol Library of Congress*] (LCLS)

CaQMSOB .... Le Groupe SOBECO, Montreal, PQ, Canada [*Library symbol Library of Congress*] (LCLS)

CaQMSQC .... Squibb Canada, Inc., Montreal, PQ, Canada [*Library symbol*] [*Library of Congress*] (LCLS)

CaQMStC ..... College Sainte-Croix, Montreal, PQ, Canada [*Library symbol Library of Congress*] (LCLS)

CaQMSTJ ..... Hopital Sainte-Justine, Centre d'Information sur la Sante de l'Enfant, Montreal,PQ, Canada [*Library symbol Library of Congress*] (LCLS)

CaQMSTJC ... Hopital Sainte-Justine, Centre d'Information sur l'Enfance et l'Adolescence Inadaptees, Montreal, PQ, Canada [*Library symbol Library of Congress Obsolete*] (LCLS)

CaQMSTJS ... Hopital Sainte-Justine, Departement de Sante Communautaire, Montreal, PQ, Canada [*Library symbol*] [*Library of Congress*] (LCLS)

CaQMSU ...... Surete du Quebec, Montreal, PQ, Canada [*Library symbol Library of Congress*] (LCLS)

CaQMSW ..... Sherwin-Williams Co. of Canada, Montreal, PQ, Canada [*Library symbol Library of Congress*] (LCLS)

CaQMSWP ... Shawinigan Engineering Co. Ltd., Montreal, PQ, Canada [*Library symbol Library of Congress*] (LCLS)

CaQMT .... Montreal Trust Co., Montreal, PQ, Canada [*Library symbol Library of Congress*] (LCLS)

CaQMTA ...... Tomenson-Aletander Ltd., Montreal, PQ, Canada [*Library symbol Library of Congress*] (LCLS)

CaQMTC ...... Air Canada, Montreal, PQ, Canada [*Library symbol Library of Congress*] (LCLS)

CaQMTCP .... Quebec Ministere du Tourisme, de la Chasse, et de la Peche, Montreal, PQ, Canada [*Library symbol Library of Congress*] (LCLS)

CaQMTD ...... Canada Ministry of Transport, Transportation Development Agency, Montreal, PQ, Canada [*Library symbol Library of Congress*] (LCLS)

CaQMTGC ... Teleglobe Canada, Montreal, PQ, Canada [*Library symbol Library of Congress*] (LCLS)

CaQMTH ...... Institut de Tourisme et d'Hotellerie du Quebec, Montreal, PQ, Canada [*Library symbol Library of Congress*] (LCLS)

CaQMTMO ... Ministere du Travaile et de la Main-D'Oeuvre, Montreal, PQ, Canada [*Library symbol Library of Congress*] (LCLS)

CaQMTQM ... Trans-Quebec & Maritimes, Montreal, PQ, Canada [*Library symbol Library of Congress*] (LCLS)

CaQMTR ...... Canada Ministry of Transport, Waterways Development, Montreal, PQ, Canada [*Library symbol Library of Congress*] (LCLS)

CaQMU .... Universite de Montreal, Montreal, PQ, Canada [*Library symbol Library of Congress*] (LCLS)

CaQMUA ...... Service des Archives de l'Universite de Montreal, Montreal, PQ, Canada [*Library symbol Library of Congress*] (LCLS)

CaQMUC ...... Union Carbide Canada Ltd., Pointe-Aux-Trembles, PQ, Canada [*Library symbol Library of Congress*] (LCLS)

CaQMUDD ... Universite de Montreal, Departement de Demographie, Montreal, PQ, Canada [*Library symbol Library of Congress*] (LCLS)

CaQMUE .... Institut des Etudes Medievales, Universite de Montreal, Montreal, PQ, Canada [*Library symbol Library of Congress*] (LCLS)

CaQMUEB ... Universite de Montreal, Ecole de Bibliotheconomie, Montreal, PQ, Canada [*Library symbol*] [*Library of Congress*] (LCLS)

CaQMUEC ... Universite de Montreal, l'Ecole de Criminologie, Montreal, PQ, Canada [*Library symbol Library of Congress*] (LCLS)

CaQMUG ..... Universite de Montreal, Departement de Geographie, Montreal, PQ, Canada [*Library symbol Library of Congress*] (LCLS)

CaQMUGC ... Universite de Montreal, Departement de Geographie, Cartotheque, Montreal, PQ, Canada [*Library symbol Library of Congress*] (LCLS)

CaQMUGL .... Universite de Montreal, Cartotheque de l'Institut de Geologie, Montreal, PQ, Canada [*Library symbol Library of Congress*] (LCLS)

CaQMUM ..... Universite de Montreal, Bibliotheque Medicale, Montreal, PQ, Canada [*Library symbol Library of Congress Obsolete*] (LCLS)

CaQMUO ..... Universite de Montreal, Bibliotheque d'Optometrie, Montreal, PQ, Canada [*Library symbol Library of Congress*] (LCLS)

CaQMUP ...... Universite de Montreal, Bibliotheque Paramedicale, Montreal, PQ, Canada [*Library symbol Library of Congress*] (LCLS)

CaQMUQ ..... Universite du Quebec a Montreal, Montreal, PQ, Canada [*Library symbol Library of Congress*] (LCLS)

CaQMUQA ... Service des Archives de l'Universite du Quebec a Montreal, Montreal, PQ, Canada [*Library symbol*] [*Library of Congress*] (LCLS)

CaQMUQC ... Universite du Quebec a Montreal, Cartotheque, Montreal, PQ, Canada [*Library symbol Library of Congress*] (LCLS)

CaQMUQDSJ ... Universite du Quebec a Montreal, le Centre de Documentation des Sciences Juridiques, Montreal, PQ, Canada [*Library symbol Library of Congress*] (LCLS)

CaQMUQEN ... Universite du Quebec, Ecole Nationale d'Aministration Publique, Montreal, PQ, Canada [*Library symbol*] [*Library of Congress*] (LCLS)

CaQMUQET ... Universite du Quebec, Ecole de Technologie Superieure, Montreal, PQ, Canada [*Library symbol Library of Congress*] (LCLS)

CaQMUQIC ... Universite du Quebec a Montreal, INRS-Urbanisation, Cartotheque, Montreal, PQ, Canada [*Library symbol Library of Congress*] (LCLS)

CaQMUQIS ... Universite du Quebec, INRS-Sante, Centre de Documentation, Montreal, PQ, Canada [*Library symbol*] [*Library of Congress*] (LCLS)

CaQMUQPA ... Universite du Quebec a Montreal, Pavillon des Arts, Montreal, PQ, Canada [*Library symbol Library of Congress*] (LCLS)

CaQMUQS ... Universite du Quebec, Bibliotheque des Sciences, Montreal, PQ, Canada [*Library symbol*] [*Library of Congress*] (LCLS)

CaQMUQTM ... Universite du Quebec, Tele-Universite, Montreal, PQ, Canada [*Library symbol*] [*Library of Congress*] (LCLS)

CaQMUSC ... Universite de Montreal, Bibliotheque des Sciences Sociales, Cartotheque, Montreal, PQ, Canada [*Library symbol Library of Congress*] (LCLS)

CaQMUSHS ... Universite de Montreal, Bibliotheque des Sciences Humaines et Sociales, Section de Criminologie, Montreal, PQ, Canada [*Library symbol Library of Congress*] (LCLS)

CaQMV .... RCA Victor Co. Ltd., Montreal, PQ, Canada [*Library symbol Library of Congress*] (LCLS)

CaQMVC ...... Vanier College, Media Resources Centre, Montreal, PQ, Canada [*Library symbol Library of Congress*] (LCLS)

CaQMW .... Warnock Hersey Co. Ltd., Montreal, PQ, Canada [*Library symbol Library of Congress*] (LCLS)

CaQMWM ... William M. Mercer, Montreal, PQ, Canada [*Library symbol Library of Congress*] (LCLS)

CaQMY .... YWCA Library, Montreal, PQ, Canada [*Library symbol Library of Congress*] (LCLS)

CaQMYH ...... YM-YWHA Library, Montreal, PQ, Canada [*Library symbol Library of Congress*] (LCLS)

CaQNCHRN ... Centre Hospitalier Rouyn-Noranda, Noranda, PQ, Canada [*Library symbol Library of Congress*] (LCLS)

CaQNCRS ... Conseil Regional de la Sante et des Services Sociaux Rouyn-Noranda, Noranda, PQ,Canada [*Library symbol Library of Congress*] (LCLS)

CaQNicA ..... Soeurs de l'Assomption, Nicolet, PQ, Canada [*Library symbol Library of Congress*] (LCLS)

CaQNicS ...... Seminaire de Nicolet, Nicolet, PQ, Canada [*Library symbol Library of Congress*] (LCLS)

CaQNIP .... Institut de Police du Quebec, Nicolet, PQ, Canada [*Library symbol Library of Congress*] (LCLS)

CaQOTCP .... Ministere du Tourisme, de la Chasse, et de la Peche, Orsainville, PQ, Canada [*Library symbol Library of Congress*] (LCLS)

CaQPA .... Bibliotheque Municipale, Port-Alfred, PQ, Canada [*Library symbol Library of Congress*] (LCLS)

CaQPAg ...... Canada Department of Agriculture, Experimental Farm, La Pocatiere, PQ, Canada [*Library symbol Library of Congress*] (LCLS)

CaQPC .... College de Sainte-Anne, La Pocatiere, PQ, Canada [*Library symbol Library of Congress*] (LCLS)

CaQPES .... Institut de Technologie Agricole, La Pocatiere, PQ, Canada [*Library symbol Library of Congress*] (LCLS)

CaQPfD .... Bibliotheque Intermunicipale de Pierrefonds et Dollard-des-Ormeaux, Pierrefonds,PQ, Canada [*Library symbol*] [*Library of Congress*] (LCLS)

CaQPIM ...... Bibliotheque Municipale, Plessisville, PQ, Canada [*Library symbol Library of Congress*] (LCLS)

CaQPOC .... Pointe Claire Public Library, Pointe Claire, PQ, Canada [*Library symbol Library of Congress*] (LCLS)

CaQPrM ...... Bibliotheque Municipale, Princeville, PQ, Canada [*Library symbol Library of Congress*] (LCLS)

CaQQ .... Bibliotheque Municipale, Quebec, PQ, Canada [*Library symbol Library of Congress*] (LCLS)

CaQQA .... Bibliotheque des Archives de la Province de Quebec, Quebec, PQ, Canada [*Library symbol Library of Congress*] (LCLS)

CaQQAA ...... Archives de l'Archeveche de Quebec, Quebec, PQ, Canada [*Library symbol Library of Congress*] (LCLS)

CaQQAC ...... Quebec Ministere des Affaires Culturelles, Quebec, PQ, Canada [*Library symbol Library of Congress*] (LCLS)

CaQQACJ ..... Province du Canada-Francais, Archives de la Compagnie de Jesus, Quebec, PQ, Canada [*Library symbol Library of Congress*] (LCLS)

CaQQAg .... Ministere de l'Agriculture et de la Colonisation, Quebec, PQ, Canada [*Library symbol Library of Congress*] (LCLS)

CaQQAI .... Quebec Ministere des Affaires Intergouvernementales, Bibliotheque Administrative, Quebec, PQ, Canada [*Library symbol Library of Congress*] (LCLS)

CaQQAM ..... Ministere des Affaires Municipales, Centre de Documentation, PQ, Canada [*Library symbol Library of Congress*] (LCLS)

CaQQAND .... Archives du Monastere Notre-Dame-Des-Anges, Quebec, PQ, Canada [*Library symbol Library of Congress*] (LCLS)

CaQQAPC ..... Cerebral Palsy Association of Quebec, Inc., Quebec, PQ, Canada [*Library symbol Library of Congress*] (LCLS)

CaQQAQS .... Anglican Church of Canada, Diocese of Quebec, Synod Office, Quebec, PQ, Canada [*Library symbol Library of Congress*] (LCLS)

CaQQAS .... Archives du Seminaire de Quebec, Quebec, PQ, Canada [*Library symbol Library of Congress*] (LCLS)

CaQQASF ... Conseil des Affaires Sociales et de la Famille, Quebec, PQ, Canada [*Library symbol Library of Congress*] (LCLS)

CaQQBJNQ .. Bureau de la Baie James et du Nord Quebecois, Ste.-Foy, PQ, Canada [*Library symbol Library of Congress*] (LCLS)

CaQQBL ...... Bibliotheque Lasallienne, Quebec, PQ, Canada [*Library symbol*] [*Library of Congress*] (LCLS)

CaQQBQ .... Ministere des Communications du Quebec, Bibliotheque Administrative, Quebec, PQ, Canada [*Library symbol Library of Congress*] (LCLS)

CaQQBS .... Bureau de la Statistique du Quebec, Quebec, PQ, Canada [*Library symbol Library of Congress*] (LCLS)

CaQQBST ..... Bureau de la Science et de la Technologie, Quebec, PQ, Canada [*Library symbol Library of Congress*] (LCLS)

CaQQC .... Defence Research Establishment, Valcartier, Canada Department of National Defence, Quebec, PQ, Canada [*Library symbol Library of Congress*] (LCLS)

CaQQCA .... Centre Antonien, Quebec, PQ, Canada [*Library symbol Library of Congress*] (LCLS)

CaQQCAD ..... Conservatoire d'Art Dramatique de Quebec, Quebec, PQ, Canada [*Library symbol Library of Congress*] (LCLS)

CaQQCAI ..... Commission de l'Acces a l'Information, Centre de Documentation, Quebec, PQ, Canada [*Library symbol*] [*Library of Congress*] (LCLS)

CaQQCDP .... Quebec Commission des Droits de la Personne, Quebec, PQ, Canada [*Library symbol Library of Congress*] (LCLS)

CaQQCE .... CEGEP [*College d'Enseignement General et Professionnel*] de Limoilou, Quebec, PQ, Canada [*Library symbol Library of Congress*] (LCLS)

CaQQCGI ..... Conseillers en Gestion et Informatique CGI, Inc., Centre de Documentation, Quebec, PQ, Canada [*Library symbol*] [*Library of Congress*] (LCLS)

CaQQCH .... Departement des Archives et Statistiques de la Ville de Quebec, Quebec, PQ, Canada [*Library symbol Library of Congress*] (LCLS)

CaQQCLF ..... Conseil de la Langue Francaise, Quebec, PQ, Canada [*Library symbol Library of Congress*] (LCLS)

CaQQCM ..... College Merici, Quebec, PQ, Canada [*Library symbol Library of Congress*] (LCLS)

CaQQCMQ .... Conservatoire de Musique du Quebec, Quebec, PQ, Canada [*Library symbol Library of Congress*] (LCLS)

CaQQCPS ..... Conseil de la Politique Scientifique du Quebec, Quebec, PQ, Canada [*Library symbol Library of Congress*] (LCLS)

CaQQCRH .... Centre des Recherches Historiques, Quebec, PQ, Canada [*Library symbol Library of Congress Obsolete*] (LCLS)

CaQQCRS .... Centre de Documentation de la Regie du Logement, Montreal, PQ, Canada [*Library symbol Library of Congress*] (LCLS)

CaQQCS .... Service de Documentation et de Bibliotheque, Quebec, PQ, Canada [*Library symbol Library of Congress*] (LCLS)

CaQQCSF ..... Conseil du Statut de la Femme, Quebec, PQ, Canada [*Library symbol Library of Congress*] (LCLS)

CaQQCT .... Commission de Toponymie, Quebec, PQ, Canada [*Library symbol Library of Congress*] (LCLS)

CaQQCU .... Conseil des Universites du Quebec, Quebec, PQ, Canada [*Library symbol Library of Congress*] (LCLS)

CaQQDTI ...... Ministere des Finances, Service du Traitement de l'Information, Duberger, PQ, Canada [*Library symbol Library of Congress*] (LCLS)

CaQQE .... Canada Department of the Environment, Quebec Region, Ste.-Foy, Quebec, PQ, Canada [*Library symbol Library of Congress*] (LCLS)

CaQQEDOP ... Ministere de l'Education, Office des Professions du Quebec, PQ, Canada [*Library symbol Library of Congress*] (LCLS)

CaQQEN .... Quebec Ministere de l'Environnement, Quebec, PQ, Canada [*Library symbol Library of Congress*] (LCLS)

CaQQEPC ..... Department of the Environment, Parks Canada, Ste.-Foy, PQ, Canada [*Library symbol Library of Congress*] (LCLS)

CaQQER .... Ministere de l'Energie et des Ressources du Quebec, Quebec, PQ, Canada [*Library symbol Library of Congress*] (LCLS)

CaQQERE ..... Ministere de l'Energie et des Ressources, Secteur Energie, Centre de Documentation et de Renseignements, Quebec, PQ, Canada [*Library symbol Library of Congress*] (LCLS)

CaQQF .... Bibliotheque Franciscaine, Quebec, PQ, Canada [*Library symbol Library of Congress*] (LCLS)

CaQQFPCE ... Ministere de la Fonction Publique, Direction de la Classification et de l'Evaluation des Emplois, Quebec, PQ, Canada [*Library symbol Library of Congress*] (LCLS)

CaQQFTI ...... Ministere des Finances, Service du Traitement de l'Information, Duberger, PQ, Canada [*Library symbol Library of Congress*] (LCLS)

CaQQGR ...... Bibliotheque Gabrielle-Roy, Quebec, PQ, Canada [*Library symbol*] [*Library of Congress*] (LCLS)

CaQQHD ...... Hotel-Dieu de Quebec, Quebec, PQ, Canada [*Library symbol Library of Congress*] (LCLS)

CaQQHDM ... Musee des Augustines de l'Hotel-Dieu de Quebec, Quebec, PQ, Canada [*Library symbol Library of Congress*] (LCLS)

CaQQHDS .... Hotel-Dieu du Sacre-Coeur, Quebec, PQ, Canada [*Library symbol Library of Congress*] (LCLS)

CaQQHSS .... Hopital du Saint-Sacrement, Quebec, PQ, Canada [*Library symbol Library of Congress*] (LCLS)

CaQQIAP ..... Canada Department of Indian Affairs and Northern Development, Parks Canada, Quebec Regional Office, Ste-Foy, Quebec, PQ, Canada [*Library symbol Library of Congress*] (LCLS)

CaQQIAS ..... Informatheque des Affaires Sociales du Quebec, Quebec, PQ, Canada [*Library symbol Library of Congress*] (LCLS)

CaQQIC .... Ministere de l'Industrie et du Commerce du Quebec, Quebec, PQ, Canada [*Library symbol Library of Congress*] (LCLS)

CaQQIF .... Ministere des Institutions Financieres, Compagnies, et Cooperatives, Quebec, PQ, Canada [*Library symbol Library of Congress*] (LCLS)

CaQQIM .... Institut Maritime du Quebec, CEGEP de Rimouski, Quebec, PQ, Canada [*Library symbol Library of Congress*] (LCLS)

CaQQIN .... Indian and Northern Affairs Canada, Quebec, PQ, Canada [*Library symbol*] [*Library of Congress*] (LCLS)

CaQQIQRC ... Institut Quebecois de Recherche sur la Culture, Quebec, PQ, Canada [*Library symbol Library of Congress*] (LCLS)

CaQQJ .... Ministere de la Justice du Quebec, Ste.-Foy, PQ, Canada [*Library symbol Library of Congress*] (LCLS)

CaQQL .... Bibliotheque de la Legislature de la Province de Quebec, Quebec, PQ, Canada [*Library symbol Library of Congress*] (LCLS)

CaQQLa ...... Universite Laval, Quebec, PQ, Canada [*Library symbol Library of Congress*] (LCLS)

CaQQLaA ..... Universite Laval, Faculte des Sciences de l'Agriculture et de l'Alimentation, Quebec, PQ, Canada [*Library symbol Library of Congress*] (LCLS)

CaQQLaAA ... Universite Laval, Secteur Art et Architecture, Quebec, PQ, Canada [*Library symbol Library of Congress*] (LCLS)

CaQQLaAV ... Universite Laval, Ecole des Arts Visuelles, Quebec, PQ, Canada [*Library symbol Library of Congress*] (LCLS)

CaQQLaCa ... Universite Laval, Cartotheque, Quebec, PQ, Canada [*Library symbol Library of Congress*] (LCLS)

CaQQLaCI ... Universite Laval, Centre International de Recherches sur le Bilinguisme, Quebec, PQ, Canada [*Library symbol Library of Congress*] (LCLS)

CaQQLaD ..... Universite Laval, Faculte de Droit, Quebec, PQ, Canada [*Library symbol Library of Congress*] (LCLS)

CaQQLaFG ... Universite Laval, Faculte de Foresterie et de Geodesie, Quebec, PQ, Canada [*Library symbol Library of Congress*] (LCLS)

CaQQLaG .... Universite Laval, Institut de Geographie, Quebec, PQ, Canada [*Library symbol Library of Congress*] (LCLS)

CaQQLaGM ... Universite Laval, Departement de Geologie et de Mineralogie, Quebec, PQ, Canada [*Library symbol Library of Congress*] (LCLS)

CaQQLaI ...... Universite Laval, Societe Dante Aleghieri, Quebec, PQ, Canada [*Library symbol Library of Congress*] (LCLS)

CaQQLaS ..... Universite Laval, Faculte des Sciences, Quebec, PQ, Canada [*Library symbol Library of Congress*] (LCLS)

CaQQLCP ..... Ministere du Loisir de la Chasse et de la Peche, Quebec, PQ, Canada [*Library symbol Library of Congress*] (LCLS)

CaQQLH .... Literary and Historical Society of Quebec, Quebec, PQ, Canada [*Library symbol Library of Congress*] (LCLS)

CaQQMAA .... Archives du Monastere des Augustines, Quebec, PQ, Canada [*Library symbol Library of Congress*] (LCLS)

CaQQMAB .... Bibliotheque du Monastere des Augustines, Quebec, PQ, Canada [*Library symbol*] [*Library of Congress*] (LCLS)

CaQQMAGA ... Archives des Augustines du Monastere de l'Hopital General de Quebec, Quebec, PQ, Canada [*Library symbol*] [*Library of Congress*] (LCLS)

CaQQMC ...... Ministere des Communications du Quebec, Bibliotheque Administrative, Quebec, PQ, Canada [*Library symbol Library of Congress*] (LCLS)

CaQQMF ...... Canada Department of the Environment, Forest Research Laboratory, Quebec, PQ, Canada [*Library symbol Library of Congress*] (LCLS)

CaQQMQ ...... Musee du Quebec, Quebec, PQ, Canada [*Library symbol Library of Congress*] (LCLS)

CaQQMR ...... Musee du Royal 22e Regiment et la Regie du Royal 22e Regiment, Quebec, PQ, Canada [*Library symbol Library of Congress*] (LCLS)

CaQQMSRD ... Ministere de la Main-d'Oeuvre et de la Securite du Revenu, Direction du Developpement du Systeme, Centre de Documentation, Quebec, PQ, Canada [*Library symbol*] [*Library of Congress*] (LCLS)

CaQQOLF..... Office de la Langue Francaise, Quebec, PQ, Canada [*Library symbol Library of Congress*] (LCLS)

CaQQOP....... Office de Planification et de Developpement du Quebec, Quebec, PQ, Canada [*Library symbol Library of Congress*] (LCLS)

CaQQOPC .... Office de la Protection du Consommateur, Quebec, PQ, Canada [*Library symbol Library of Congress*] (LCLS)

CaQQOPD .... Office des Promotions du Quebec, Direction de la Documentation, Quebec, PQ, Canada [*Library symbol Library of Congress*] (LCLS)

CaQQPC...... Parks Canada, Ste. Foy, PQ, Canada [*Library symbol*] [*Library of Congress*] (LCLS)

CaQQPEA..... Archives des Peres Eudistes, Charlesbourg, PQ, Canada [*Library symbol*] [*Library of Congress*] (LCLS)

CaQQPSM... Canada Department of Fisheries and the Environment, Fisheries and Marine Service, Quebec, PQ, Canada [*Library symbol Library of Congress*] (LCLS)

CaQQQE...... Universite du Quebec, Centre Quebecois des Sciences de l'Eau, Quebec, PQ, Canada [*Library symbol Library of Congress*] (LCLS)

CaQQR........ Reed Ltd., Technical Information Centre, Quebec, PQ, Canada [*Library symbol Library of Congress*] (LCLS)

CaQQRA...... Roche Associes Ltee., Groupe-Conseil, Ste.-Foy, PQ, Canada [*Library symbol Library of Congress*] (LCLS)

CaQQRAA..... Regie de l'Assurance Automobile du Quebec, Sillery, PQ, Canada [*Library symbol Library of Congress*] (LCLS)

CaQQRAMQ... Regie de l'Assurance-Maladie du Quebec, Quebec, PQ, Canada [*Library symbol Library of Congress*] (LCLS)

CaQQRE...... Ministere du Revenu, Ste.-Foy, PQ, Canada [*Library symbol Library of Congress*] (LCLS)

CaQQRN...... Ministere des Richesses Naturelles du Quebec, Quebec, PQ, Canada [*Library symbol Library of Congress*] (LCLS)

CaQQRNC.... Centre de Documentation de la Direction Generale de l'Energie du Ministere des Richesses Naturelles du Quebec, Quebec, PQ, Canada [*Library symbol Library of Congress Obsolete*] (LCLS)

CaQQRQ ...... Regie des Rentes du Quebec, Quebec, PQ, Canada [*Library symbol Library of Congress*] (LCLS)

CaQQRRQ.... Regie des Rentes du Quebec, Quebec, PQ, Canada [*Library symbol Library of Congress*] (LCLS)

CaQQRSP .... Regie des Services Publics, Ste.-Foy, PQ, Canada [*Library symbol Library of Congress*] (LCLS)

CaQQRV...... Regie des Ventes du Quebec, Quebec, PQ, Canada [*Library symbol Library of Congress Obsolete*] (LCLS)

CaQQS......... Seminaire de Quebec, Quebec, PQ, Canada [*Library symbol Library of Congress*] (LCLS)

CaQQSIP...... Societe Quebecoise d'Initiatives Petrolieres, Ste-Foy, PQ, Canada [*Library symbol Library of Congress*] (LCLS)

CaQQT .... Ministere des Terres et Forets du Quebec, Quebec, PQ, Canada [*Library symbol Library of Congress*] (LCLS)

CaQQTCG..... Canadian Coast Guard, Quebec, PQ, Canada [*Library symbol*] [*Library of Congress*] (LCLS)

CaQQTO....... Ministere du Tourisme du Quebec, Quebec, PQ, Canada [*Library symbol*] [*Library of Congress*] (LCLS)

CaQQTR...... Ministere des Transports, Quebec, PQ, Canada [*Library symbol Library of Congress*] (LCLS)

CaQQTRD .... Ministere des Trasports-Rue Dorchester, Centre de Documentation, Quebec, PQ, Canada [*Library symbol*] [*Library of Congress*] (LCLS)

CaQQU......... Couvent des Ursulines, Quebec, PQ, Canada [*Library symbol Library of Congress*] (LCLS)

CaQQUA....... Archives du Monastere des Ursulines de Merici, Quebec, PQ, Canada [*Library symbol*] [*Library of Congress*] (LCLS)

CaQQUED .... Universite du Quebec, Institut National de la Recherche Scientifique (Education), Quebec, PQ, Canada [*Library symbol Library of Congress*] (LCLS)

CaQQUIE...... Universite du Quebec, Institut Nationale de la Recherche Scientifique (Eau), Quebec, PQ, Canada [*Library symbol Library of Congress*] (LCLS)

CaQQUQ ...... Universite du Quebec a Quebec, Quebec, PQ, Canada [*Library symbol Library of Congress*] (LCLS)

CaQQUQEN... Universite du Quebec, Ecole Nationale d'Administration Publique, Quebec, PQ, Canada [*Library symbol Library of Congress*] (LCLS)

CaQQUQT .... Universite du Quebec, Tele-Universite, Ste.-Foy, Quebec, PQ, Canada [*Library symbol Library of Congress*] (LCLS)

CaQQUS....... University Seminary, Quebec, PQ, Canada [*Library symbol Library of Congress*] (LCLS)

CaQQZ .... Jardin Zoologique de Quebec, Quebec, PQ, Canada [*Library symbol Library of Congress*] (LCLS)

CaQRC......... College de Rouyn, Rouyn, PQ, Canada [*Library symbol Library of Congress Obsolete*] (LCLS)

CaQRCB....... College Bourget, Rigaud, PQ, Canada [*Library symbol Library of Congress*] (LCLS)

CaQRCN....... College du Nord Ouest, Rouyn, PQ, Canada [*Library symbol Library of Congress*] (LCLS)

CaQRCRS .... Conseil Regional de la Sante et des Services Sociaux, Rimouski, PQ, Canada [*Library symbol Library of Congress*] (LCLS)

CaQRe .... Bibliotheque Municipale, Repentigny, PQ, Canada [*Library symbol*] [*Library of Congress*] (LCLS)

CaQRECHL... Centre Hospitalier Le Gardeur, Repentigny, PQ, Canada [*Library symbol*] [*Library of Congress*] (LCLS)

CaQRIB........ Bibliotheque Municipale, Rock Island, PQ, Canada [*Library symbol Library of Congress*] (LCLS)

CaQRiC........ College de Rimouski, Rimouski, PQ, Canada [*Library symbol Library of Congress*] (LCLS)

CaQRIM....... Institut Maritime, CEGEP de Rimouski, PQ, Canada [*Library symbol Library of Congress*] (LCLS)

CaQRo .... Sources Public Library, Roxboro, PQ, Canada [*Library symbol Library of Congress*] (LCLS)

CaQRobHD... Hotel-Dieu de Roberval, Bibliotheque Medicale, Roberval, PQ, Canada [*Library symbol*] [*Library of Congress*] (LCLS)

CaQRU......... Universite du Quebec a Rimouski, Rimouski, PQ, Canada [*Library symbol Library of Congress*] (LCLS)

CaQRUC...... Universite du Quebec a Rimouski, Cartotheque, Rimouski, PQ, Canada [*Library symbol Library of Congress*] (LCLS)

CaQRUQR... Universite du Quebec a Rouyn, Rouyn, PQ, Canada [*Library symbol Library of Congress*] (LCLS)

CaQSABS .... Laboratoire de Sante Publique du Quebec, Ste. Anne de Bellevue, PQ, Canada [*Library symbol*] [*Library of Congress*] (LCLS)

CaQSeD ...... Domtar Ltd., Research Centre, Senneville, PQ, Canada [*Library symbol Library of Congress*] (LCLS)

CaQSF .... Bibliotheque Municipale, Ste.-Foy, PQ, Canada [*Library symbol Library of Congress*] (LCLS)

CaQSFAg ..... Canada Department of Agriculture, Research Station, Ste.-Foy, PQ, Canada [*Library symbol Library of Congress*] (LCLS)

CaQSFC ...... College d'Enseignement, Ste.-Foy, PQ, Canada [*Library symbol Library of Congress*] (LCLS)

CaQSFCAE ... Clinique d'Aide a l'Enfance, Ste.-Foy, PQ, Canada [*Library symbol Library of Congress*] (LCLS)

CaQSFCM .... College Marguerite d'Youville, Ste.-Foy, PQ, Canada [*Library symbol Library of Congress*] (LCLS)

CaQSFCP .... Commission de Police du Quebec, Ste.-Foy, PQ, Canada [*Library symbol Library of Congress*] (LCLS)

CaQSFCR .... Ministere de l'Industrie, du Commerce, et du Tourisme, Centre de Recherche Industrielle du Quebec, Complexe Scientifique, Ste.-Foy, PQ, Canada [*Library symbol Library of Congress*] (LCLS)

CaQSFCRO... Commission Rochon, Centre de Documentation, Ste. Foy, PQ, Canada [*Library symbol*] [*Library of Congress*] (LCLS)

CaQSFIG ...... Institut National de la Recherche Scientifique-Georessources, Ste. Foy, PQ, Canada [*Library symbol*] [*Library of Congress*] (LCLS)

CaQSFS ...... SOQUEM [*Societe Quebecoise d'Exploration Miniere*], Ste.-Foy, PQ, Canada [*Library symbol Library of Congress*] (LCLS)

CaQSH .... Stanstead Historical Society, Stanstead, PQ, Canada [*Library symbol Library of Congress*] (LCLS)

CaQSHC...... CEGEP [*College d'Enseignement General et Professionnel*] de Shawinigan, Shawinigan, PQ, Canada [*Library symbol Library of Congress*] (LCLS)

CaQSherA.... Archeveche de Sherbrooke, Sherbrooke, PQ, Canada [*Library symbol Library of Congress*] (LCLS)

CaQSherC.... Universite de Sherbrooke, Centre Hospitalier Universitaire, Sherbrooke, PQ, Canada [*Library symbol Library of Congress*] (LCLS)

CaQSherCR... Conseil Regional de la Sante et des Services Sociaux des Cantons de l'Est, Sherbrooke, PQ, Canada [*Library symbol Library of Congress*] (LCLS)

CaQSherD.... Sherbrooke Daily Record, Sherbrooke, PQ, Canada [*Library symbol Library of Congress*] (LCLS)

CaQSherE.... College de Sherbrooke (CEGEP) [*College d'Enseignement General et Professionnel*], Sherbrooke, PQ, Canada [*Library symbol Library of Congress*] (LCLS)

CaQSherG.... Grand Seminaire des Saints-Apotres, Sherbrooke, PQ, Canada [*Library symbol Library of Congress*] (LCLS)

CaQSherH.... Huntingdon Gleaner, Sherbrooke, PQ, Canada [*Library symbol Library of Congress*] (LCLS)

CaQSherHD... Centre Hospitalier Hotel-Dieu, Sherbrooke, PQ, Canada [*Library symbol Library of Congress*] (LCLS)

CaQSherL .... Sherbrooke Library, Sherbrooke, PQ, Canada [*Library symbol Library of Congress*] (LCLS)

CaQSherM.... Monastere de Peres Redemptoristes, Sherbrooke, PQ, Canada [*Library symbol Library of Congress*] (LCLS)

CaQSherN.... Bibliotheque Municipale de Sherbrooke, Sherbrooke, PQ, Canada [*Library symbol Library of Congress*] (LCLS)

CaQSherS.... Seminaire de Sherbrooke, Sherbrooke, PQ, Canada [*Library symbol Library of Congress*] (LCLS)

CaQSherSB... Les Conseillers Samson Belair, Inc., Sherbrooke, PQ, Canada [*Library symbol*] [*Library of Congress*] (LCLS)

CaQSherSC... College du Sacre-Coeur, Sherbrooke, PQ, Canada [*Library symbol Library of Congress*] (LCLS)

CaQSherSF... Ecole Secondaire Saint-Francois, Sherbrooke, PQ, Canada [*Library symbol Library of Congress*] (LCLS)

CaQSherSH... Societe Historique des Cantons de l'Est, Sherbrooke, PQ, Canada [*Library symbol Library of Congress*] (LCLS)

CaQSherSS... Seminaire de Sherbrooke, Sherbrooke, PQ, Canada [*Library symbol Library of Congress Obsolete*] (LCLS)

CaQSherSV... Centre Hospitalier St.-Vincent-De-Paul, Sherbrooke, PQ, Canada [*Library symbol Library of Congress*] (LCLS)

CaQSherU.... Universite de Sherbrooke, Sherbrooke, PQ, Canada [*Library symbol Library of Congress*] (LCLS)

CaQSherUA... Universite de Sherbrooke, Galerie d'Art et Centre Culturel, Sherbrooke, PQ, Canada [*Library symbol Library of Congress*] (LCLS)

CaQSherUD... Universite de Sherbrooke, Faculte de Droit, Sherbrooke, PQ, Canada [*Library symbol Library of Congress*] (LCLS)

CaQSherUG... Universite de Sherbrooke, Departement de Geographie, Sherbrooke, PQ, Canada [*Library symbol Library of Congress*] (LCLS)

CaQSherUGC... Universite de Sherbrooke, Departement de Geographie, Cartotheque, Sherbrooke, PQ, Canada [*Library symbol Library of Congress*] (LCLS)

CaQSherURA... Universite de Sherbrooke, Programme de Recherche sur l'Amiante, Centre de Documentation, Sherbrooke, PQ, Canada [*Library symbol*] [*Library of Congress*] (LCLS)

CaQSherUS... Universite de Sherbrooke, Faculte des Sciences, Sherbrooke, PQ, Canada [*Library symbol*] [*Library of Congress*] (LCLS)

CaQSHERY... Hopital d'Youville de Sherbrooke, Centre de Documentation et d'Audio-Viseul, Sherbrooke, PQ, Canada [*Library symbol*] [*Library of Congress*] (LCLS)

CaQSHM...... Municipal Library, Shawinigan, PQ, Canada [*Library symbol Library of Congress*] (LCLS)

CaQSHS...... Seminaire Ste.-Marie, Shawinigan, PQ, Canada [*Library symbol Library of Congress*] (LCLS)

CaQSi......... Bibliotheque Municipale, Sept-Iles, PQ, Canada [*Library symbol Library of Congress*] (LCLS)

CaQSiIOM.... Iron Ore Co., Mineralogy Laboratory, Sept-Illes, PQ, Canada [*Library symbol Library of Congress*] (LCLS)

CaQSiIC...... College Jesus-Marie de Sillery, Sillery, PQ, Canada [*Library symbol Library of Congress*] (LCLS)

CaQSJ......... Stanstead Journal, Stanstead, PQ, Canada [*Library symbol Library of Congress*] (LCLS)

CaQSICR..... Champlain Regional College, Campus 1, St.-Lambert, PQ, Canada [*Library symbol Library of Congress*] (LCLS)

CaQSo......... Bibliotheque Municipale, Sorel, PQ, Canada [*Library symbol Library of Congress*] (LCLS)

CaQSoIT...... Quebec Iron & Titanium Corp., Sorel, PQ, Canada [*Library symbol Library of Congress*] (LCLS)

CaQSTAH..... Ste. Anne's Hospital, Ste.-Anne-De-Bellevue, PQ, Canada [*Library symbol Library of Congress*] (LCLS)

CaQSTAIAS... Ministere des Affaires Sociales, Informatheque-Laboratoires, Ste.-Anne-De-Bellevue, PQ, Canada [*Library symbol Library of Congress*] (LCLS)

CaQSTAJ...... John Abbott College, Ste.-Anne-De-Bellevue, PQ, Canada [*Library symbol Library of Congress*] (LCLS)

CaQSTAS ..... Spar Technology Ltd., Ste.-Anne-De-Bellevue, PQ, Canada [*Library symbol Library of Congress*] (LCLS)

CaQStBL ...... Abbaye de Saint-Benoit-Du-Lac, Comte De Brome, PQ, Canada [*Library symbol Library of Congress*] (LCLS)

CaQSTFRA.... Roche Associes Ltee., Centre de Documentation, Ste.-Foy, PQ, Canada [*Library symbol Library of Congress*] (LCLS)

CaQStHAG ... Agriculture Canada, Saint Hyacinthe Food Research Centre, Saint Hyacinthe, PQ, Canada [*Library symbol*] [*Library of Congress*] (LCLS)

CaQStHHR ... Societe d'Histoire Regionale de St.-Hyacinthe, St.-Hyacinthe, Canada [*Library symbol Library of Congress*] (LCLS)

CaQStHS ..... Seminaire de St.-Hyacinthe, St.-Hyacinthe, PQ, Canada [*Library symbol Library of Congress*] (LCLS)

CaQStHuM... Canada Department of National Defence, Headquarters Mobile Command, St. Hubert, PQ, Canada [*Library symbol Library of Congress*] (LCLS)

CaQStHV...... Faculte de Medecine Veterinaire de l'Universite de Montreal, St.-Hyacinthe, PQ, Canada [*Library symbol Library of Congress*] (LCLS)

CaQStJ......... College Militaire Royal de Saint-Jean, Saint-Jean, PQ, Canada [*Library symbol Library of Congress*] (LCLS)

CaQStJAg ..... Canada Department of Agriculture, Research Station, Saint-Jean, PQ, Canada [*Library symbol Library of Congress*] (LCLS)

CaQStJB ...... Bibliotheque Municipale, Saint-Jean, PQ, Canada [*Library symbol Library of Congress*] (LCLS)

CaQStJC ...... College Saint-Jean-Sur-Richelieu, Saint-Jean, PQ, Canada [*Library symbol Library of Congress*] (LCLS)

CaQStJe....... Bibliotheque Municipale, Saint-Jerome, PQ, Canada [*Library symbol Library of Congress*] (LCLS)

CaQStJeJ...... Jesuites/Bibliotheque, Saint-Jerome, PQ, Canada [*Library symbol Library of Congress*] (LCLS)

CaQStJS ...... Seminaire de Saint-Jean, Saint-Jean, PQ, Canada [*Library symbol Library of Congress Obsolete*] (LCLS)

CaQStL .... Bibliotheque Municipale, Saint-Laurent, PQ, Canada [*Library symbol Library of Congress*] (LCLS)

CaQStLe ...... Bibliotheque Municipale, Saint-Leonard, PQ, Canada [*Library symbol Library of Congress*] (LCLS)

CaQStR .... Bibliotheque Municipale de Saint Raphael de l'Ile Bizard, Saint Raphael de l'IleBizard, PQ, Canada [*Library symbol*] [*Library of Congress*] (LCLS)

CaQSttH....... Les Industries Harnois, St. Thomas de Joliette, PQ, Canada [*Library symbol*] [*Library of Congress*] (LCLS)

CaQT........... Bibliotheque Municipale, Trois-Rivieres, PQ, Canada [*Library symbol Library of Congress*] (LCLS)

CaQTA .... Archives Nationales du Quebec, Trois-Rivieres, PQ, Canada [*Library symbol Library of Congress*] (LCLS)

CaQTB .... Editions du Boreal Express, Montreal, PQ, Canada [*Library symbol Library of Congress*] (LCLS)

CaQTBC .... Bibliotheque Centrale de Pret de la Mauricie, Trois-Rivieres, PQ, Canada [*Library symbol Library of Congress*] (LCLS)

CaQTCE....... CEGEP [*College d'Enseignement General et Professionnel*], Trois-Rivieres, PQ, Canada [*Library symbol Library of Congress*] (LCLS)

CaQTCL....... College Lafleche, Trois-Rivieres, PQ, Canada [*Library symbol Library of Congress*] (LCLS)

CaQTCO....... Communication-Quebec, Trois-Rivieres, PQ, Canada [*Library symbol Library of Congress*] (LCLS)

CaQTCPB .... Corporation Pierre-Boucher, Trois-Rivieres, PQ, Canada [*Library symbol Library of Congress*] (LCLS)

CaQTCRD.... Conseil Regional de Developpement, Trois-Rivieres, PQ, Canada [*Library symbol Library of Congress*] (LCLS)

CaQTCRS..... Conseil Regional de la Sante et des Services Sociaux, Trois-Rivieres, PQ, Canada [*Library symbol Library of Congress*] (LCLS)

CaQTCSRV... Commission Scolaire Regionale des Vieilles-Forges, Trois-Rivieres, PQ, Canada [*Library symbol Library of Congress*] (LCLS)

CaQTCSS..... Centre de Services Sociaux, Trois-Rivieres, PQ, Canada [*Library symbol Library of Congress*] (LCLS)

CaQTE........ Ecole Normale M. L. Duplessis, Trois-Rivieres, PQ, Canada [*Library symbol Library of Congress*] (LCLS)

CaQTeTF...... Temifibre, Inc., Temiscaming, PQ, Canada [*Library symbol*] [*Library of Congress*] (LCLS)

CaQTHSJ ..... Hopital Saint-Joseph, Trois-Rivieres, PQ, Canada [*Library symbol Library of Congress*] (LCLS)

CaQTHSM .... Hopital Sainte-Marie, Trois-Rivieres, PQ, Canada [*Library symbol Library of Congress*] (LCLS)

CaQTI........... Institut Albert Tessier, Trois-Rivieres, PQ, Canada [*Library symbol Library of Congress*] (LCLS)

CaQTO .... Institut Agricole d'Oka, LaTrappe, PQ, Canada [*Library symbol Library of Congress Obsolete*] (LCLS)

CaQTOPDQ.. Office de Planification et de Developpement du Quebec, Trois-Rivieres, PQ, Canada [*Library symbol Library of Congress*] (LCLS)

CaQTS .... Seminaire des Trois-Rivieres, Trois-Rivieres, PQ, Canada [*Library symbol Library of Congress*] (LCLS)

CaQTT......... Trois-Rivieres High School, Trois-Rivieres, PQ, Canada [*Library symbol Library of Congress*] (LCLS)

CaQTU .... Universite du Quebec a Trois-Rivieres, Trois-Rivieres, PQ, Canada [*Library symbol Library of Congress*] (LCLS)

CaQTUAH..... Universite du Quebec a Trois-Rivieres, Archives Historiques, Trois-Rivieres, PQ,Canada [*Library symbol Library of Congress*] (LCLS)

CaQTUGC..... Universite du Quebec a Trois-Rivieres, Departement de Geographie, Cartotheque, Trois-Rivieres, PQ, Canada [*Library symbol Library of Congress*] (LCLS)

CaQTUIH...... Universite du Quebec a Trois-Rivieres, Imprimes Historiques, Trois-Rivieres, PQ , Canada [*Library symbol Library of Congress*] (LCLS)

CaQTUrA...... Archives des Ursulines, Trois-Rivieres, PQ, Canada [*Library symbol Library of Congress*] (LCLS)

CaQTUTH.... Centre de Documentation en Theatre Quebecois, Trois-Rivieres, PQ, Canada [*Library symbol Library of Congress*] (LCLS)

CaQV .... Bibliotheque Municipale, Victoriaville, PQ, Canada [*Library symbol Library of Congress*] (LCLS)

CaQVaH ...... Institut de Recherche d'Hydro-Quebec, Varennes, PQ, Canada [*Library symbol Library of Congress*] (LCLS)

CaQVal .... Institut National de la Recherche Scientifique (Energie), Varennes, PQ, Canada [*Library symbol*] [*Library of Congress*] (LCLS)

CaQVauH ..... Hoffman-La Roche Ltd., Vaudreuil, PQ, Canada [*Library symbol Library of Congress*] (LCLS)

CaQVC .... College de Victoriaville, Victoriaville, PQ, Canada [*Library symbol Library of Congress*] (LCLS)

CaQVCEMBO... College de Victoriaville, Ecole du Meuble et du Bois Ouvre, Victoriaville, PQ, Canada [*Library symbol Library of Congress*] (LCLS)

CaQVeC ...... Centre Culturel, Verdun, PQ, Canada [*Library symbol Library of Congress*] (LCLS)

CaQVsLEA.... Environment Canada, Atmospheric Environment Service, Ville St. Laurent, PQ, Canada [*Library symbol*] [*Library of Congress*] (LCLS)

CaQW .... Waterloo Public Library, Waterloo, PQ, Canada [*Library symbol Library of Congress*] (LCLS)

CaQWsmM... Westmount Public Library, Westmount, PQ, Canada [*Library symbol Library of Congress*] (LCLS)

CaQWsmSH... Congregation Shaar Hashomayim Library-Museum, Westmount, PQ, Canad [*Library symbol*] [*Library of Congress*] (LCLS)

CAr.............. Arcadia Public Library, Arcadia, CA [*Library symbol Library of Congress*]

CAR .... Cable Television Relay (NTCM)

CAR .... Cadena Azul de Radiodifusion [*Radio network*] [*Spain*]

CAR .... California Association of Realtors (SRA)

CA R .... California Reporter [*A publication*] (DLA)

CAR .... Canadian Airborne Regiment (MCD)

CA(R).......... Canadian Army (Regular)

CAR .... Canadian Artists' Representation

CAR .... Canadian Association of Radiologists

CAR .... Canam Industry Corp. [*Vancouver Stock Exchange symbol*]

CAR .... Capital Adequacy Ratio

CAR .... Capital Appropriation Request (TDOB)

CAR .... Capital Authorization Request

CAR .... Caracas [*Venezuela*] [*Seismograph station code, US Geological Survey*] (SEIS)

CAR .... Carat [*Unit of measure for precious stones or gold*]

Car.............. Carbohydrate [*Dietetics*]

CAR .... Carboxylic Acid Reductase [*An enzyme*]

Car.............. Cardinalis [*Authority cited in pre-1607 legal work*] (DSA)

CAR .... Career

CAR .... Cargill Information Center, Wayzata, MN [*OCLC symbol*] (OCLC)

CAR .... Cargo (MSA)

car.............. Carib [*MARC language code Library of Congress*] (LCCP)

CAR .... Caribbean

CAR .... Caribbean Region [*USTTA*] (TAG)

CAR .... Cariboo College Library [*UTLAS symbol*]

CAR .... Caribou, ME [*Location identifier FAA*] (FAAL)

Car.............. Carina [*Constellation*]

CAR .... Carlow [*County in Ireland*] (ROG)

CAR	Carminative [*Expelling Wind*] [*Pharmacy*] (ROG)
CAR	Carmine (ROG)
CAR	Carolina [*United States*] [*Obsolete*] (ROG)
CAR	Carolus [*Charles*] [*Numismatics*] (ROG)
CAR	Carpenter [*Navy British*] (ROG)
car	Carre (DD)
CAR	Carrier (CINC)
CAR	Carronade
CAR	Carta [*Music*]
CAR	Carter-Wallace [*NYSE symbol*] (TTSB)
CAR	Carter-Wallace, Inc. [*NYSE symbol*] (SPSG)
CAR	Caruscan Corp. [*Toronto Stock Exchange symbol*]
CAR	Cell Adhesion Regulator [*Genetics*]
CAR	Center for Aging Research
CAR	Center for Alcohol Research [*University of Florida*] [*Research center*] (RCD)
CAR	Center for Architectural Research [*Rensselaer Polytechnic Institute*] [*Research center*] (RCD)
CAR	Center for Automotive Research [*Wayne State University*] [*Research center*] (RCD)
CAR	Central African Regiment [*British military*] (DMA)
CAR	Central African Republic
CAR	Central Apparatus Room (DEN)
CAR	Certificate for Automobile Receivables [*Investment term*] (DFIT)
CAR	Certification Approval Request (NASA)
CAR	Change Agent Research (PDAA)
CAR	Channel Address Register [*Computer science*]
CAR	Check Authorization Record [*IBMDP*]
CAR	Chief Airship Rigger [*Navy rating Obsolete*]
CAR	Chief, Army Reserve (AABC)
CAR	Christian Aid for Romania (EA)
CAR	cis-Acting REV-Responsive Sequence [*Genetics*]
CAR	Cis Anti-Repression Sequence [*Genetics*]
CAR	Civil Aeronautical Regulation (MCD)
CAR	Civil Air Regulation [*FAA*]
CAR	Civil Air Reserve (AAG)
CAR	Cloud-Top Altitude Radiometer
CAR	Cockpit Assessment of Reach [*Aviation*] (PDAA)
CAR	Collection Activity Reports [*IRS*]
CAR	Colorado Association of Realtors (SRA)
CAR	Combat Action Ribbon [*Military decoration*] (VNW)
CAR	Combined Arms Regiment [*Marine Corps*] (DOMA)
CAR	Command Action Report [*Army*]
CAR	Command Assessment Review (MCD)
CAR	Commanders Availability Report (CINC)
CAR	Commerce Acquisition Regulation [*Department of Commerce*]
CAR	Commission on Administrative Review [*House of Representatives*]
CAR	Committee for Automobile Reform
CAR	Community Antenna Relay [*Service*] [*FCC*]
CAR	Compound Annual Return (ODBW)
car	Compounded Annual Rate [*Finance*] (ODBW)
CAR	Computer-Aided Repair (IAA)
CAR	Computer-Assisted Reporting [*Journalism*] (WDMC)
CAR	Computer-Assisted Research (BUR)
CAR	Computer-Assisted Retrieval
CAR	Concentrated Area Review [*US Postal Service*]
CAR	Condenser Air Removal [*Nuclear energy*] (NRCH)
CAR	Conditional Antimicrobial Reporting [*Microbiology*]
CAR	Condition and Recommendation (AABC)
CAR	Conditioned Avoidance Response [*Psychometrics*]
CAR	Configuration and Acceptance Review (MCD)
CAR	Configuration Audit Review
CAR	Connecticut Association of Realtors (SRA)
CAR	Containment Air Removal [*Recirculation fan*] (IEEE)
CAR	Contemporary Authors First Revision Series [*A publication*]
CAR	Contract Administration Report [*DoD*]
CAR	Contract Appraisal Report
CAR	Contract Authorization Request (AAG)
CAR	Contractor All Risk (AIA)
CAR	Control Advisory Release (NRCH)
CAR	Control of Advertisements Regulations [*Town planning*] [*British*]
CAR	Conversion, Alteration, and Repair [*Navy*]
CAR	Corps Automation Requirements [*Army*]
CAR	Corrective Action Reply
CAR	Corrective Action Report
CAR	Corrective Action Request
CAR	Cost Allocation Report [*DoD*]
CAR	Cost Allocation Review
CAR	Criminal Appeal Reports [*England*] [*A publication*] (DLA)
CAR	Customer Account Representative (AFM)
CAR	Cytarabine [*Cytosine arabinoside*] [*Also, ara-C, CA*] [*Antineoplastic drug*]
CAR	Cytosolic Androgen Receptor [*Endocrinology*]
CAR	Inter RCA [*Central African Republic*] [*ICAO designator*] (FAAC)
CAR	United States Army, Caribbean
CARA	Caraco Pharmaceutical Labs [*NASDAQ symbol*] (SAG)
CARA	Caraco Pharm Labs [*NASDAQ symbol*] (TTSB)
CARA	Cargo and Rescue Aircraft
CARA	Center for Applied Research in the Apostolate (EA)
CARA	Center for Astrophysical Research in Antarctica [*National Science Foundation*]
CARA	Centers and Regional Associations (EA)
CARA	Centre for Astrophysical Research in Antarctica (ECON)
CARA	Check Area Airports (FAAC)
CARA	Chinese American Restaurant Association (EA)

CARA	Christian Addiction Rehabilitation Association (EA)
CARA	Circular Active Reflector Antenna (PDAA)
CARA	Civilian Appellation Review Agency [*Army*] (MCD)
CARA	Classification and Rating Administration [*For movies*]
CARA	Classification and Ratings Administration [*Motion Picture Association of America*] (WDMC)
CARA	Combat Aircrew Recovery [*or Rescue*] Aircraft [*Later, ARRS, ARS*]
CARA	Combined Altitude RADAR Altimeter [*Electronic defense system*]
CARA	Computer-Aided Requirements Analysis (MCD)
CARA	Coordinated Agency-Wide Research Activities [*National Science Foundation*]
CARA	Current Aerospace Research Activities (KSC)
Caraco	Caraco Pharmaceutical Labs [*Associated Press*] (SAG)
CARAD	Computer-Aided Reliability and Design (MHDB)
CARAE	Caribbean Regional Council for Adult Education [*University of the West Indies*] (EAIO)
CARAEWRON	Carrier Airborne Early Warning Squadron [*Navy*]
CARAEWTRARON	Carrier Airborne Early Warning Training Squadron [*Navy*] (DNAB)
CARAIRGROUP	Carrier Air Group [*Navy*]
CARAL	Canadian Abortion Rights Action League
CARALA	Conference of American Renting and Leasing Associations (EA)
CARALOC	Children's Attribution of Responsibility and Locus of Control (EDAC)
CARAM	Content-Addressable Random Access Memory [*Computer science*] (HGAA)
Car & K	Carrington and Kirwan's English Nisi Prius Reports [*174, 175 English Reprint*] [*A publication*] (DLA)
Car & K (Eng)	Carrington and Kirwan's English Nisi Prius Reports [*174, 175 English Reprint*] [*A publication*] (DLA)
Car & Kir	Carrington and Kirwan's English Nisi Prius Reports [*174, 175 English Reprint*] [*A publication*] (DLA)
Car & M	Carrington and Marshman's English Nisi Prius Reports [*1840-42*] [*A publication*] (DLA)
Car & Mar	Carrington and Marshman's English Nisi Prius Reports [*1840-42*] [*A publication*] (DLA)
Car & M (Eng)	Carrington and Marshman's English Nisi Prius Reports [*1840-42*] [*A publication*] (DLA)
Car & O	English Railway and Canal Cases, by Carrow, Oliver, and Others [*1835-55*] [*A publication*] (DLA)
Car & Ol	English Railway and Canal Cases, by Carrow, Oliver, and Others [*1835-55*] [*A publication*] (DLA)
Car & P	Carrington and Payne's English Nisi Prius Reports [*1823-41*] [*A publication*] (DLA)
Car & P (Eng)	Carrington and Payne's English Nisi Prius Reports [*1823-41*] [*A publication*] (DLA)
CARANTISUBGRU	Carrier Antisubmarine Warfare Group [*Navy*] (DNAB)
CARAS	Canadian Academy of Recording Arts and Sciences
CARAT	Cargo Agents Reservation Airwaybill Insurance and Tracking System (DA)
CARAT	Coating Ageing-Resistant Aluminum Technology [*Materials science*]
CARAT	Congestion Avoidance and Reduction for Automobiles and Trucks [*FHWA*] (TAG)
Caraustr	Caraustar Industries, Inc. [*Associated Press*] (SAG)
CARAW	Caraco Pharm Labs Wrrt [*NASDAQ symbol*] (TTSB)
CARB	California Air Resources Board
CARB	Capital Assets Review Board
CARB	Carbamazepine [*Also, CBZ*] [*An analgesic*]
CARB	Carbide
CARB	Carbohydrate [*Dietetics*]
CARB	Carbon
CARB	Carbonate
CARB	Carbonated
CARB	Carburetor (MSA)
CARB	Center for Advanced Research in Biotechnology [*Jointly sponsored by the US National Bureau of Standards and the University of Maryland*]
CArb	Certified Arbitrator [*Canada*] (DD)
CARB	Commercial Airlift Review Board [*DOD*] (AAGC)
CARB	Consortium for Advanced Residential Buildings
CARB	Coronary Artery Bypass Graft [*Cardiology*] (DMAA)
CARB	Current Australian Reference Books [*A publication*]
CARBAGAIR	Baggage for Air Cargo
CARBAM	Carbamazepine [*Pharmacology*] (DAVI)
CARBASORD	Carry Out Remainder Basic Orders
CARBINE	Computer-Automated Real-Time Betting Information Network (IEEE)
CARBO	Carbohydrate [*Dietetics*]
CarboCe	Carbo Ceramics, Inc. [*Associated Press*] (SAG)
CARBOPOL	Carboxypolymethylene [*Organic chemistry*]
carbor	Carborondum (VRA)
CARBTR	Carburetor
CArc	Arcata Public Library, Arcata, CA [*Library symbol Library of Congress*] (LCLS)
CARC	Canadian Agricultural Research Council
CARC	Canadian Arctic Resources Committee [*Ottawa, ON*] [*Research center*]
CARC	Carcano Rifle
CARC	Censo de Archivos [*Database*] [*Ministerio de Cultura*] [*Spanish*] [*Information service or system*] (CRD)
CARC	Central America Resource Center (EA)
CARC	Chemical Agent Resistant Coating [*A paint*]
CARC	Coalition for Auto Repair Choice [*Defunct*] (EA)
CARC	Coast Artillery Reserve Corps
CARC	Computer-Assisted Reference Center [*Information service or system*] (IID)
CARCAE	Caribbean Regional Council for Adult Education [*Barbados*] (EAIO)

CARCAH....... Chief, Aerial Reconnaissance Coordination, All Hurricanes [*National Hurricane Center*]
CARCAV....... Conceptual Armored Cavalry (MCD)
CARCD......... California Association of Resourse Conservation Districts (SRA)
CArcHT........ Humboldt State College, Arcata, CA [*Library symbol Library of Congress*] (LCLS)
Car Cr L....... Carrington. Criminal Law [*3rd ed.*] [*1828*] [*A publication*] (DLA)
CARCSLR..... Career Counselor [*Military*] (AABC)
CARCV......... Carnation Cryptic Virus [*Plant pathology*]
CARD........... Campaign Against Racial Discrimination [*British*]
CARD........... Canadian Advertising Rates and Data
CARD........... Canadian Advertising Rates and Data
CARD........... Card Automated Reproduction and Distribution System (ECII)
CARD........... Cardiganshire [*County in Wales*] (ROG)
CARD........... Cardinal
CARD........... Cardinal
CARD........... Cardinal Bancshares [*NASDAQ symbol*] (TTSB)
CARD........... Cardinal Bancshares, Inc. [*NASDAQ symbol*] (SAG)
Card............. Cardinalis [*Authority cited in pre-1607 legal work*] (DSA)
card............. Cardiology (MAE)
CARD........... Caribbean Association for the Rehabilitation of the Disabled [*Defunct*] (EAIO)
CARD........... Center for Agricultural and Rural Development [*Iowa State University*] [*Research center*] (RCD)
CARD........... Center for Anthropometric Research Data (IID)
CARD........... Certificate for Amortizing Revolving Debts [*Salomon Brothers*] [*Accounting*]
CARD........... Channel Allocation and Routing Data (IEEE)
CARD........... Civil Aviation Research and Development [*NASA*]
CARD........... Coastal and Arctic Research Division [*Formerly, Marine Services Research Division*] [*Marine science*] (OSRA)
CARD........... Coastal and Arctic Research Division [*Formerly, Marine Service Research Division*] (USDC)
CARD........... Coded Automatic Reading Device
CARD........... Comet and Asteroid Rendezvous Docking (MCD)
CARD........... Committee Against Registration and the Draft (EA)
CARD........... Community Association for Riding for the Disabled (AC)
CARD........... Compact Automatic Retrieval Device [*Massachusetts Institute of Technology*] [*Computer science*]
CARD........... Compact Automatic Retrieval Display [*Computer science*] (IID)
CARD........... Computer-Aided RADAR Design (KSC)
CARD........... Computer-Aided Remote Driving [*for robotic command vehicles*] (RDA)
CARD........... Computer-Assisted Route Development (IAA)
CARD........... Computing Australia Recruiting Directory [*A publication*]
CARD........... Crash Avoidance Research Data File [*NHTSA*] (TAG)
CARDA......... Computer-Aided Reliability Data Analysis (MHDB)
CARDA......... CONUS [*Continental United States*] Airborne Reconnaissance for Damage Assessment (MCD)
CARDAMAP... Cardiovascular Data Analysis by Machine Processing (AEBS)
CARDAN...... Centre d'Analyse et de Recherche Documentaires pour l'Afrique Noire
CardBnc....... Cardinal Bancshares, Inc. [*Associated Press*] (SAG)
CARDCODER... Card Automatic Code System [*IBM Corp.*] (IEEE)
CARDE......... Canadian Armament Research and Development Establishment
Card Flor..... Cardinalis Florentinus [*Franciscus Zabarella*] [*Deceased, 1417*] [*Authority cited in pre-1607 legal work*] (DSA)
CardGen...... CardioGenesis Corp. [*Associated Press*] (SAG)
CARDI.......... Cardigan (DSUE)
Cardi............ Cardinalis [*Authority cited in pre-1607 legal work*] (DSA)
CARDIA........ Coronary Artery Risk Development in Young Adults [*Epidemiologic study*]
CARDIAC...... Cardboard Illustrative Aid to Computation [*Bell Telephone Co.*] [*Computer science*]
CardiDiag.... Cardiovascular Diagnostics, Inc. [*Associated Press*] (SAG)
CardiDy........ Cardiovascular Dynamics, Inc. [*Associated Press*] (SAG)
CARDIGS..... Cardiganshire [*County in Wales*] (ROG)
CardinlH...... Cardinal Health, Inc. [*Associated Press*] (SAG)
CARDIO........ Cardiology
cardiol......... Cardiology
Cardiom....... Cardiometrics, Inc. [*Associated Press*] (SAG)
CardioTh...... CardioThoracic Systems, Inc. [*Associated Press*] (SAG)
CARDIS........ Cargo Data Interchange System (MCD)
Car Dis Ab... Careers and the Disabled [*A publication*]
CAR DI SYS... Carbon Dioxide System [*of a ship*] (DS)
CARDIV........ Carrier Division [*Navy*]
CardnHlt...... Cardinal Health, Inc. [*Associated Press*] (SAG)
CARDO......... Centre for Architectural Research and Development Overseas [*University of Newcastle upon Tyne*] [*British*] (CB)
CARDPAC.... Card Packet System (AABC)
CARDPLMNRY... Cardiopulmonary
CardPth....... Cardiac Pathways Corp. [*Associated Press*] (SAG)
Cardpul........ Cardiopulmonary Corp. [*Associated Press*] (SAG)
CardRlt........ Cardinal Realty Services, Inc. [*Associated Press*] (SAG)
CardRlty...... Cardinal Realty Services, Inc. [*Associated Press*] (SAG)
CARDS......... Card-Automated Reproduction and Distribution System [*Library of Congress*]
CARDS......... Cardiganshire [*County in Wales*]
CARDS......... Catalog of Approved Requirement Documents [*Army*] (RDA)
CARDS......... Certificates for Amortizing Revolving Debts [*Finance*] (DFIT)
CARDS......... Combat Aircraft Recording and Data System
CARDS......... Comprehensive Approach for Reusable Defense Systems [*DoD*]
CARDS......... Computer-Aided Reliability Data Systems [*Bell System*]
CARDS......... Computer-Aided Requirements Definition Software
CARDS......... Contract Award Rates Delivery Study [*Army*]

Card Stritch C... Cardinal Stritch College (GAGS)
Cardtch........ Cardiotech International, Inc. [*Associated Press*] (SAG)
Card Zabarel... Cardinalis Florentinus (Franciscus Zabarella) [*Deceased, 1417*] [*Authority cited in pre-1607 legal work*] (DSA)
CARE........... Campaign for All Employees to Reduce Errors (SAA)
CARE........... Cancer Aftercare and Rehabilitation Society [*British*] (DBA)
CARE........... Capias ad Respondendum [*That You Take to Answer*] [*A judicial writ*] [*Latin*] [*Legal term*] (ADA)
CARE........... Capitol Reef National Monument
CARE........... Care Group [*NASDAQ symbol*] (TTSB)
CARE........... [*The*] Care Group, Inc. [*NASDAQ symbol*] (NQ)
CARE........... Center for Advanced Rehabilitation Engineering [*University of Texas at Arlington*] [*Research center*] (RCD)
CARE........... Center for Athletes' Rights and Education [*Defunct*] (EA)
CARE........... Centre for Applied Research in Education [*University of East Anglia*] [*British*] (CB)
CARE........... Ceramics Applications in Reciprocating Engines [*Research group*] [*British*]
CARE........... Challenging Adults to Read Effectively (EDAC)
CARE........... Christian Action, Research, and Education [*British*]
CARE........... Citizens Against a Radioactive Environment [*An association*] (ECON)
CARE........... Citizens for Animals, Resources, and Environment (EA)
CARE........... Clinical and Administrative Record [*System*]
CARE........... Clothing Articles Require Explanation [*Student legal action organization*]
CARE........... Coalition for Auto Repair Equality [*Automotive aftermarket parts lobbying group*]
CARE........... Combined Accident Reduction Effort
CARE........... Communicating Alarm Response Equipment [*British Telecom*]
CARE........... Community Action to Reach the Elderly
CARE........... Computer-Aided Reliability Estimation
CARE........... Computer-Aided Risk Evaluation (ODBW)
CARE........... Computerized Audit and Record Evaluation System [*Medical records*] (DHSM)
CARE........... Consolidated Assistance and Relocation Efforts (MCD)
CARE........... Continental Association of Resolute Employers [*Washington, DC*] (EA)
CARE........... Continuous Affinity Recycle Extraction [*Chemical engineering*]
CARE........... Continuous Aircraft Reliability Evaluation (PDAA)
CARE........... Conversion and Recording Equipment (MCD)
CARE........... Cooperative Alliance for Refuge Enhancement
CARE........... Cooperative for American Relief Everywhere [*Formerly, Cooperative for American Remittances Everywhere*] (AEBS)
CARE........... Cooperative for American Remittances Everywhere [*Former name*]
CARE........... Coronary Artery Risk Evaluation Program [*Air Force*]
CARE........... Cottage and Rural Enterprises [*British*] (DI)
CAREBACO... Caribbean Regional Badminton Confederation [*Aruba*] (EAIO)
CARECEN..... Central American Refugee Center (EA)
CARED......... Centre for Applied Research and Engineering Design [*McMaster University, Hamilton, ON*]
CAREE......... Christians Associated for Relationships with Eastern Europe (EA)
CareerHz...... Career Horizons, Inc. [*Associated Press*] (SAG)
CAREERS..... Career Airmen Reenlistment Reservation System [*Air Force*]
CAREF......... Cooking Advancement Research and Education Foundation (EA)
CareGp........ Care Group, Inc. [*Associated Press*] (SAG)
CAREIRS...... Conservation and Renewable Energy Inquiry and Referral Service [*Department ofEnergy*] [*Information service or system*] (IID)
CAREL......... Central Atlantic Regional Educational Laboratory
Caremk........ Caremark International, Inc. [*Associated Press*] (SAG)
Caremtx....... Carematrix Corp. [*Associated Press*] (SAG)
CARES......... Cancer Rehabilitation Evaluation System [*Medicine*] (DMAA)
CARES......... Certification Authority for Reinforcing Steels (PDAA)
CARES......... Civil Air Rescue Emergency Services (AC)
CARES......... Civil Air Rescue Emergency Services - AAC Project [*Also, Alberta Aviation Council Project*] (AC)
CARES......... Combined Automated Resource System [*Department of Health and Human Services*] (GFGA)
CARES......... Computer-Aided Railway Engineering System (MCD)
CARESIM..... Computer-Assisted Repair Simulation [*Game*]
CA RESP...... Capias ad Respondendum [*That You Take to Answer*] [*A judicial writ*] [*Latin*] [*Legal term*] (ROG)
CARESS....... Career Retrieval Search System [*Pittsburgh University*] (NITA)
CARESS....... Center for Analytic Research in Economics and the Social Sciences [*University of Pennsylvania*] [*Research center*] (RCD)
Caretnd........ Caretenders Healthcorp. [*Associated Press*] (SAG)
CARETS....... Central Atlantic Regional Ecological Test Site [*Department of the Interior*]
Carey........... Manitoba Reports, by Carey [*1875*] [*A publication*] (ILCA)
Carey MR..... Manitoba Reports, by Carey [*1875*] [*A publication*] (DLA)
CARF........... Campaign Against Racism and Fascism [*British*] (DI)
CARF........... Canadian Advertising Research Foundation [*Founded 1949*]
CARF........... Canadian Amateur Radio Federation (PDAA)
CARF........... Center Airman Record File [*Air Force*]
CARF........... Central Altitude Reservation Facility [*or Function*]
CARF........... Central Altitude Reservation Function [*FAA*] (TAG)
CARF........... Christian Amateur Radio Fellowship [*Defunct*] (EA)
CARF........... Commission on Accreditation of Rehabilitation Facilities (EA)
CARF........... Community Affairs and Regulatory Functions [*HUD*] (OICC)
CARF........... Compartmented Consolidated Analysis Report Final (MCD)
CARF........... Connecticut Association of Residential Facilities (SRA)
CARFAC....... Canadian Artists' Representation/Front des Artistes Canadiens
CARG........... Caribbean Amphibious Ready Group [*Navy*] (NVT)
CARG........... Carrier Air Group
CARG........... Catering
CARG........... Commander, Amphibious Ready Group [*Navy*] (NVT)

CARG......... Community Action Research Group (OICC)

CARG......... Corporate Accountability Research Group [Formed by consumer-advocate Ralph Nader]

CARGO........ Careers Guidance Observed (AIE)

CARGO........ Consolidated Afloat Requisitioning Guide (DNAB)

CarGot........ Carr Gottstein Foods [Associated Press] (SAG)

CarGrpt....... [The] Carbide/Graphite Group, Inc. [Associated Press] (SAG)

CARH......... Career Horizons, Inc. [NASDAQ symbol] (SAG)

CARH......... Citizens Against Rationing Health [An association]

Car H & A.... Carrow, Hamerton, and Allen's New Sessions Cases [1844-51] [England] [A publication] (DLA)

CARHE........ Canadian Association for Research in Home Economics [See also ACREF]

CARI......... Canadian Association of Recycling Industries (AC)

CARI......... Canadian Association of Regulated Importers [Association Canadienne des Importateurs Reglementes] (AC)

Cari........... Carina [Constellation]

CARI......... Civil Aeromedical Research Institute [FAA]

CARI......... Committee for Action for Rural Indians (EA)

CARI......... Comparative Administration Research Institute [Kent State University, Ohio]

CARI......... Council of Air-Conditioning and Refrigeration Industry (EA)

CARIAC....... Cardboard Illustrative Aid to Computation [Computer science] (PDAA)

CARIB........ Caribbean (AFM)

CARIBAIR .... Caribbean Atlantic Airlines [Puerto Rico]

CARIBANK .... Caribbean Development Bank

Caribbean LJ.. Caribbean Law Journal [A publication] (DLA)

CaribCig ...... Caribbean Cigar Co. [Associated Press] (SAG)

CARIBCOM.... Caribbean Command [Military]

CARIBDIV .... Caribbean Division [Navy] (DNAB)

Caribinr ...... Caribiner Intl., Inc. [Associated Press] (SAG)

Carib LJ....... Caribbean Law Journal [A publication] (DLA)

CARIBNAVFACENGCOM... Caribbean Division Naval Facilities Engineering Command

CARIBSEAFRON... Caribbean Sea Frontier [Navy]

CARIC......... Carica [A Fig] [Pharmacology] (ROG)

caric .... Caricature [or Caricaturist]

CARIC......... Computerized Automation and Robotics Information Center [Society of Manufacturing Engineers] [Information service or system] (IID)

CARIC......... Contractor All-Risk Incentive Contract [Air Force]

CARICARGO... Caribbean Air Cargo Ltd. [Barbados] (EY)

CARICOM..... Caribbean Community [or Common Market] [Barbados, Jamaica, Trinidad-Tobago, Guyana, Belize, Dominica, Grenada, St. Kitts-Nevis-Anguilla, St. Lucia, St. Vincent Guyana]

CARICOMP... Caribbean Coastal Marine Productivity [Marine science] (OSRA)

CARID......... Customer Acceptance Review Item Disposition (NASA)

CARIFTA...... Caribbean Free Trade Association

CARIH........ Children's Asthma Research Institute and Hospital [Denver, CO]

CARIN......... Car Information and Navigation System [Compact disc technology]

CARIN......... Central America Research Institute (EA)

CARINFOCEN... Career Information Center (DNAB)

Caringtn....... Carrington Labs [Associated Press] (SAG)

CARIOL....... Bishop of Carlisle [British]

CARIRI........ Caribbean Industrial Research Institute [Trinidad and Tobago] [Research center] (IRC)

CARIS .... Computerized Agricultural Research Information System (NITA)

CARIS .... Computerized Audio Report Information and Status (IAA)

CARIS .... Constant-Angle Reflection Interference Spectroscopy

CARIS .... Current Agricultural Research Information System [Food and Agriculture Organization] [United Nations Information service or system] (IID)

CARISMA..... Computer-Aided Research into Stock Market Applications

CARISMA..... Corrections to Applied Research Laboratories Ion-Sputtering Mass Analyzers [Computer science]

CARISPLAN... Caribbean Information System for Economic and Social Planning [ECLAC] [United Nations] (DUND)

CARITAS...... International Confederation of Catholic Organizations for Charitable and Social Action [Vatican] [Acronym is based on foreign phrase]

CARL .... Calibration Requirements List (NG)

CARL .... Canadian Academic Research Libraries

CARL .... Canadian Association of Research Libraries [Also, ABRC]

Carl............ Carleton's New Brunswick Reports [A publication] (DLA)

CARL .... Category Assignment Responsibility List (MCD)

CARL .... Chemical Algorithm for Reticulation Linearization (NITA)

CARL .... Code Analysis Recording by Letters (PDAA)

CARL .... Colorado Alliance of Research Libraries [Denver, CO] [Library network]

CARL .... Comparative Animal Research Laboratory [Department of Energy] (GRD)

CARL .... Computer Audio Research Laboratory [Research center] (RCD)

CArIA .... Arlington College, Arlington, CA [Library symbol Library of Congress] (LCLS)

CARLA .... Center for Applied Research in the Language Arts [Texas Tech University] [Research center] (RCD)

CARLA .... Code Actuated Random Load Apparatus (MCD)

Car Law Repos.. Carolina Law Repository [North Carolina] [A publication] (DLA)

Car Laws ..... Caruther's History of a Lawsuit. Cases in Chancery [A publication] (DLA)

CarlCm .... Carlton Communications Ltd. [Associated Press] (SAG)

CARLIS .... Canadian Art Libraries

Carlisle........ Carlisle Companies [Associated Press] (SAG)

CarlisIP....... Carlisle Plastics, Inc. [Associated Press] (SAG)

Car LJ........ Carolina Law Journal [A publication] (DLA)

CARLJS........ Council of Archives and Research Libraries in Jewish Studies (EA)

Car LR .... Carolina Law Repository (Reprint) [North Carolina] [A publication] (DLA)

Car L Rep.... Carolina Law Repository [North Carolina] [A publication] (DLA)

Car L Repos... Carolina Law Repository (Reprint) [North Carolina] [A publication] (DLA)

CArIS .... La Sierra College, Arlington, CA [Library symbol Library of Congress] (LCLS)

CarltCm ...... Carlton Communications Ltd. [Associated Press] (SAG)

CARLV .... Carrot Red Leaf Virus [Plant pathology]

CARM .... Carmarthen [Welsh depot code]

CARM .... Carmarthenshire [County in Wales]

CARM .... Carmelite

Carm.......... Carmina [or Odes] [of Sidonius Apollinaris] [Classical studies] (OCD)

CARM .... Computer-Aided Reliability Model (MCD)

CARMA .... Canadian Rock Mechanics Association [Association Candienne de Mechanique des Roches] (AC)

CARMAN..... Canadian Artists' Representation Manitoba [Also, CARFAC Manitoba] (AC)

CARMAND... Civilian Application of the Results of Military Research and Development (PDAA)

CARMARTHS... Carmarthenshire [County in Wales] (ROG)

Carm Arv .... Carmen Arvale [of Calpurnius Siculus] [Classical studies] (OCD)

CARMC .... Cumulative Annual Regular Military Compensation (MCD)

Carmel........ Carmel Container Systems Ltd. [Associated Press] (SAG)

CarmelDCJ... Carmelite Sisters of the Divine Heart of Jesus (TOCD)

Carm Epigr... Carmina Epigraphica [of Calpurnius Siculus] [Classical studies] (OCD)

Carm Epigr... Carmina Latina Epigraphica [A publication] (OCD)

Carmik........ Carmike Cinemas, Inc. [Columbus, GA] [Associated Press] (SAG)

CARML .... County & Regional Municipality Librarians of Ontario (AC)

CARMOCS.... Continental Army and Major Overseas Commands Systems [Later, ASMIS]

Carmody-Wait NY Prac... Carmody-Wait. Cyclopedia of New York Practice [A publication] (DLA)

Carm Pop .... Carmina Popularia [of Calpurnius Siculus] [Classical studies] (OCD)

CARMS .... Carmarthenshire [County in Wales]

C-ARMS ...... Commercial-Accounts Receivable Management System (PDAA)

Carm Saec.... Carmen Saeculare [of Horace] [Classical studies] (OCD)

Carm Sal .... Carmen Saliare [of Calpurnius Siculus] [Classical studies] (OCD)

CARMSIM..... Computer-Assisted Reliability and Maintainability Simulation [Game]

CarMV .... Carnation Mottle Virus

CARN .... Carnarvonshire [County in Wales]

CARN .... Carnation (DSUE)

CARN .... Carnival

CARN .... Carrington Laboratories [NASDAQ symbol] (TTSB)

CARN .... Carrington Laboratories, Inc. (MHDW)

CARN .... Carrington Labs [NASDAQ symbol] (SAG)

CARH .... Conditional Analysis for Random Networks [Electronics] (OA)

CARNA .... CMV [Cucumber Mosaic Virus] Associated Ribonucleic Acid [Biochemistry, genetics]

CARNARVS... Carnarvonshire [County in Wales] (ROG)

CarnB......... Carnegie Bancorp [Associated Press] (SAG)

CarnCp........ Carnival Corp. [Formerly, Carnival Cruise] [Associated Press] (SAG)

CARNDE...... Canadian Association for Research in Nondestructive Evaluation (AC)

CarnegBc.... Carnegie Bancorp [Associated Press] (SAG)

Carnegie...... Carnegie Group, Inc. [Associated Press] (SAG)

Carnegie Mellon U... Carnegie Mellon University (GAGS)

CARNEID...... Caribbean Network of Educational Innovation for Development [UNESCO] [United Nations] (DUND)

CARNET .... Canadian Aging Research Network [University of Toronto] [Research center] (RCD)

CARNI......... Carnival (DSUE)

carnl .... Carnelian (VRA)

CARNM .... Carnmarth [England]

CARNS .... Carnarvonshire [County in Wales] (ROG)

CARNS .... Collision Avoidance RADAR and Navigation System [Military]

CarnvCp ...... Carnival Corp. [Associated Press] (SAG)

CARO .... Canadian Artists' Representation Ontario [Front des Artistes Canadiens del'Ontario] (AC)

CARO .... Canadian Association of Radiation Oncologists [Association Canadienne des Radio-Oncologues] (AC)

CARO .... Centre d'Analyse et de Recherche Operationnelle [Operational Research and Analysis Establishment] [Canadian Department of National Defense]

CARO .... Combined Arms Research Office

Car O & B.... English Railway and Canal Cases, by Carrow, Oliver, Beavan, and Others [1835-55] [A publication] (DLA)

CaroF.......... Carolina First Corp. [Associated Press] (SAG)

CaroFin........ Carolina Fincorp., Inc. [Associated Press] (SAG)

CaroFst........ Carolina First Corp. [Associated Press] (SAG)

CaroFt......... Carolina First Corp. [Associated Press] (SAG)

CAROL .... Computer-Assisted Research On-Line [Information service or system] (IID)

Carolina LJ... Carolina Law Journal [A publication] (DLA)

Carolina L Repos... Carolina Law Repository [North Carolina] [A publication] (DLA)

Carol Molin... Carolus Molinaeus [Deceased, 1566] [Authority cited in pre-1607 legal work] (DSA)

CAROM........ Career Area Rotation Model [Air Force]

Caro Molin... Carolus Molinaeus [Deceased, 1566] [Authority cited in pre-1607 legal work] (DSA)

CaroP.......... Carolina Power & Light Co. [Associated Press] (SAG)

CaroPw .... Carolina Power & Light Co. [Associated Press] (SAG)

CAROSEL..... Consumable-Anode, Radial, One-Side, Electrolytic [Automotive engineering]

CaroSth........ Carolina Southern Bank [*Associated Press*] (SAG)
CAROT......... Carotene [*Biochemistry*] (DAVI)
CAROT........ Centralized Automatic Recording on Trunks [*Bell System*]
CARP.......... Call Accounting Reconciliation Process [*Telecommunications*] (TEL)
CARP.......... Canadian Association of Rehabilitation Personnel
CARP.......... Canadian Association of Retired Persons [*Association Canadienne des Individus Retraites*] (AC)
Carp............. Carpathian Mountains (BARN)
CARP........... Carpentaria (ROG)
CARP.......... Carpenter [*or Carpentry*]
carp............. Carpenter [*Theater*] [*Slang*] (WDMC)
Carp............. Carpenter's Reports [*52-53 California*] [*A publication*] (DLA)
CARP........... Carpet (MSA)
Carp............. Carpmael's Patent Cases [*1602-1842*] [*England*] [*A publication*] (DLA)
CarP............. Carrollton Press, Inc., Washington, DC [*Library symbol Library of Congress*] (LCLS)
CARP.......... Cast Arrested Repeating Persons [*Fictitious fishing term*]
CARP.......... Center for Advanced Research in Phenomenology [*Defunct*] (EA)
CARP.......... Clean Annapolis River Project (AC)
CARP.......... Collegiate Association for the Research of Principles (DICI)
CARP.......... Commissary Accounting and Reporting System [*Army*]
CARP.......... Comprehensive Agrarian Reform Programme [*Philippines*] (ECON)
CARP.......... Comprehensive Areal Rainfall Program [*British*]
CARP.......... Computed Air-Release Point
CARP.......... Computer-Aided Rapid Prototyping
CARP.......... Computer-Aided Release Point (MCD)
CARP.......... Construction of Aircraft and Related Procurement
CARP.......... Cooperative Agricultural Research Program [*Tennessee State University*] [*Research center*] (RCD)
CARP.......... Cooperative Auto Research Program [*Department of Transportation*]
CarP8.55..... Carolina Power & Light Co. [*Associated Press*] (SAG)
CARPA........ Committee Against Repression in the Pacific and Asia [*Australia*] (EAIO)
CARPAC....... Carriers, Pacific Fleet [*Navy*]
CARPAS....... Comision Asesora Regional de Pesca para el Atlantico Sudoccidental [*Regional Fisheries Advisory Commission for the South-West Atlantic*] [*Inactive*] (EAIO)
Carpenter .... Carpenter's Reports [*52-53 California*] [*A publication*] (DLA)
CARPG......... Committee for the Advancement of Role-Playing Games (EA)
CARP M-L.... Comite de Apoio de Reconstrucao do Partido Marxista-Leninista [*Support Committee for the Reconstruction of the Marxist-Leninist Party*] [*Portugal Political party*] (PPE)
Carp Pat Cas... Carpmael's Patent Cases [*1602-1842*] [*England*] [*A publication*] (DLA)
Carp PC .... Carpmael's Patent Cases [*1602-1842*] [*England*] [*A publication*] (DLA)
CARPS......... Calculus Rate Problem Solver (PDAA)
CarpTech..... Carpenter Technology Corp. [*Associated Press*] (SAG)
CARPTR....... Carpenter
CARQUAL .... Carrier Qualification [*Navy*] (NG)
CARR.......... Cahners Advertising Research Reports [*A publication*]
CAR R......... Cardiff Railway [*Wales*]
CARR.......... Carretera
CARR.......... Carriage
CARR.......... Carriage (ROG)
CARR.......... Carried (ADA)
CARR.......... Carrier [*Telecommunications*] (AFM)
CARR.......... [*The*] Carrollton Railroad [*AAR code*]
CARR.......... Computer-Assisted Records Retrieval (ADA)
CARR.......... Conference Administrative Regionale de Radiodiffusion a Ondes Hectometriques [*Regional Administrative FM Broadcasting Conference*] [*Canada*]
CARR.......... Customer Acceptance Readiness Review [*Apollo*] [*NASA*]
CarrAmR...... Carr America Realty Corp. [*Associated Press*] (SAG)
Carr & M ..... Carrington and Marshman's English Nisi Prius Reports [*1840-42*] [*A publication*] (DLA)
Carrau .... Carrau's Edition of Summary Cases [*Bengal*] [*A publication*] (DLA)
CARRC......... Central Aerospace Rescue and Recovery Center [*Air Force*]
Carr Cas ...... Carran's Summary Cases [*India*] [*A publication*] (DLA)
carr fwd...... Carriage Forward [*Finance*] (ODBW)
CarrGott...... Carr Gottstein Foods [*Associated Press*] (SAG)
Carr Ham & Al... Carrow, Hamerton, and Allen's New Sessions Cases [*1844-51*] [*England*] [*A publication*] (DLA)
CarrollB....... Carrollton Bancorp [*Associated Press*] (SAG)
CARROTC .... Chief, Army Reserve and Reserve Officers Training Corps Affairs
CarrRlty....... Carr Realty [*Associated Press*] (SAG)
CARRS......... Close-In Automatic Route Restoral System [*NORAD*]
CARRS......... Coherent Anti-Stokes Resonance Raman Scattering [*Spectrometry*]
CarrSrv........ Carriage Services, Inc. [*Associated Press*] (SAG)
CAR-RT........ Carrier Route (WGA)
Car-rt-sort.... Carrier Route Sort [*Postal Service*] [*United States*] (WDMC)
CARRV......... Challenger Armored Repair and Recovery Vehicle [*British*]
CARS.......... Autolend Group, Inc. [*NASDAQ symbol*] (SAG)
CARS.......... Cable Relay Service [*or Station*] [*Television transmission*]
CARS.......... Canadian Arthritis and Rheumatism Society
CARS.......... Canadian Association of Rhodes Scholars
CARS.......... Canadian Association of Rural Studies
CARS.......... Careers
CARS.......... Center for Applications of Remote Sensing [*Oklahoma State University*] [*Research center*] (RCD)
CARS.......... Center for Atomic Radiation Studies (EA)
CARS.......... Central Alarm System (NUCP)
CARS.......... Centralized Automotive Reporting System [*DARCOM*] (MCD)
CARS.......... Certificate For Automobile Receivables [*Business term*] (EMRF)

CAR's........... Certificates of Automobile Receivables [*Salomon Bros.*]
CARS.......... Certified Automotive Repairmen's Society [*Defunct*] (EA)
CARS.......... Children's Affective Reading Scale
CARS.......... Classroom Adjustment Rating Scale
CARS.......... Climate and Remote Sensing Group [*University of California, San Diego*] [*Research center*] (RCD)
CARS.......... Coherent Anti-Stokes Raman Spectroscopy
CARS.......... Collateralized Automobile Receivable Security
CARS.......... Collision Avoidance RADAR Simulator [*Maritime*]
CARS.......... Combat Arms Regimental System [*Army*]
CARS.......... Commissary Accounting and Reporting System [*Army*]
CARS.......... Committee Against Revising Staggers [*Group opposed to changes in the Staggers Act*]
CARS.......... Common Accounting Reporting System (ADA)
CARS.......... Community Aerodrome Radio Station (DA)
CARS.......... Community Antenna Relay Service [*FCC Telecommunications*]
CARS.......... Comprehensive Automotive Release System [*3M Corp.*] [*Computer software*]
CARS.......... Compressed Air System (NUCP)
CARS.......... Computer-Aided Reference Service [*University of Arizona Library, University of Utah*] [*Information service or system*]
CARS.......... Computer-Aided Routing System
CARS.......... Computer Assisted Referee Selection (NITA)
CARS.......... Computer-Assisted Reference Service [*Indiana University Libraries*] (OLDSS)
CARS.......... Computer-Assisted Research Services [*Brigham Young University*] [*Information service or system*] (IID)
CARS.......... Computer Audit Retrieval System [*Trade name for Sage Systems, Inc., computer software product*]
CARS.......... Computerized Application and Reference System
CARS.......... Computerized Automotive Replacement Scheduling [*Bell System*]
CARS.......... Computerized Automotive Reporting Service (BUR)
CARS.......... Congress for Automotive Repair and Service
CARS.......... Consolidated Acquistion Reporting System [*Army*]
CARS.......... Containment Atmosphere Recirculation System [*Nuclear energy*] (NRCH)
CARS.......... Continuous Alarm Reporting Service [*Telecommunications*] (TEL)
CARS.......... Correction Action Reporting System
CARS.......... Country and Regional Specialist [*Navy*] (MCD)
CARSE.......... Centre for Alcohol and Road Safety Education [*British*] (AIE)
Carsh.......... Carshaltown's Court Rolls [*England*] [*A publication*] (DLA)
CARSO........ Carnegie Southern Observatory [*Later, Las Campanas Observatory*]
CARSO........ Country, Area, or Regional Staff Officer [*Military*] (DNAB)
Carson........ Carson, Inc. [*Associated Press*] (SAG)
CarsPir........ Carson Pirie Scott & Co. [*Associated Press*] (SAG)
CARSRA....... Computer-Aided Redundant System Reliability Analysis (MCD)
CARSTAT...... Carrier State
CARSTRIKFOR... Carrier Striking Force [*Tactical Air Command*] (NATG)
CARSTRIKGRU... Carrier Striking Group [*NATO*]
CARSUIT....... Carrier Suitability
CART.......... Canadian Amateur Radio Teletype Group (HGAA)
CART.......... Caribbean Association of Rehabilitation Therapists [*Guyana*] (EAIO)
CART.......... Carta [*Music*]
CART.......... Cartage [*Shipping*]
Cart............. Carter's English Common Pleas Reports [*1664-76*] [*A publication*] (DLA)
Cart............. Carter's Reports [*1, 2 Indiana*] [*A publication*] (DLA)
Cart............. Carthew's English King's Bench Reports [*1686-1701*] [*A publication*] (DLA)
CART.......... Cartography
CART.......... Cartridge
Cart............. Cartwright's Cases on the British North America Act [*Canada*] [*A publication*] (DLA)
CART.......... Central Automated Replenishment Technique (IEEE)
CART.......... Central Automatic Reliability Tester (IEEE)
CART.......... Centralized Automatic Recorder and Tester
CART.......... Championship Auto Racing Teams (EA)
CART.......... Children's Associative Responding Test (EDAC)
CART.......... Classification and Regression Trees
CART.......... Cloud and Radiation Testbed [*Network*] [*Department of Energy*] (OSRA)
CART.......... Cloud and Radiation Testbed Network [*Department of Energy*] (USDC)
CART.......... Coalition Against Regressive Taxation (EA)
CART.......... Collision Avoidance RADAR Trainer (PDAA)
CART.......... Combat Assessment of Readiness and Training (DOMA)
CART.......... Command, Arming, Recording, and Timing (PDAA)
CART.......... Community Artists Residency Training (DICI)
CART.......... Complete Automatic Reliable Testing
CART.......... Completion and Ready for Test (MCD)
CART.......... Computer-Aided Real Time Transcription [*Medical records*] (DAVI)
CART.......... Computer-Assisted Radiotherapy [*Medicine*] (DMAA)
CART.......... Computerized Automatic Rating Technique (DEN)
CART.......... Conditions of Assembly and Release Transfer
CART.......... Construction and Road Transport (ADA)
CART.......... Cultural Attitudes Repertory Technique (EDAC)
CART.......... Custom Asynchronous Receiver/Transmitter [*Automotive engineering*]
CART.......... Cytosine Arabinoside [*ara-C*], L-Asparaginase, Rubidomycin , Thioguanine [*Daunorubicin*] [*Antineoplastic drug regimen*]
CARTA.......... Canadian Association of Retail Travel Agents
CARTA.......... Catholic Apostolate of Radio, Television, and Advertising (NTCM)
CARTA.......... Computer-Aided Reorder Trap Analysis [*Bell Laboratories*]
CARTA.......... Contour Analysis by Random Triangulation Algorithm (IAA)
CARTA.......... Regional Transit Authority [*Advanced vehicle*]
CARTASKFOR... Carrier Task Force [*Navy*]

CARTB	Canadian Association of Radio and Television Broadcasters
Cart BNA	Cartwright's Constitutional Cases [1868-96] [Canada] [A publication] (DLA)
CArtC	Cerritos Junior College, Artesia, CA [Library symbol Library of Congress] (LCLS)
Cart Cas (Can)	Cartwright's Cases [Canada] [A publication] (DLA)
CARTE	Contact and Repair Test Equipment (MCD)
CarTec	Carpenter Technology Corp. [Formerly, Carpenter Steel Co.] [Associated Press] (SAG)
Cartel	Cartel. Review of Monopoly, Developments, and Consumer Protection [London, England] [A publication] (DLA)
Carter	Carter's English Common Pleas Reports Tempore Orlando Bridgman [A publication] (DLA)
Carter	Carter's Reports [1, 2 Indiana] [A publication] (DLA)
CARTH	Carthage
Carth	Carthage (VRA)
CARTH	Carthaginia (ROG)
Carth	Carthew's English King's Bench Reports [1686-1701] [A publication] (DLA)
CARTH	Carthusian
Carth (Eng)	Carthew's English King's Bench Reports [1686-1701] [A publication] (DLA)
Cartm	Cartmell's Trade Mark Cases [1876-92] [England] [A publication] (DLA)
CARTOG	Cartography (MUGU)
Cart Sax	Cartularium Saxonicum [A publication] (ILCA)
CartWal	Carter-Wallace, Inc. [Associated Press] (SAG)
Cartw CC	Cartwright's Constitutional Cases [1868-96] [Canada] [A publication] (DLA)
Cartwr Cas	Cartwright's Cases [Canada] [A publication] (DLA)
CARU	Canadian Airspace Reservation Unit [Aviation] (FAAC)
CARU	Computer Architecture Research Unit [York University] [Canada Research center] (RCD)
CARV	Carver Federal Svgs Bank [NASDAQ symbol] (TTSB)
CARV	Carver FSB [NASDAQ symbol] (SAG)
Carv Carr	Carver's Treatise on the Law Relating to the Carriage of Goods by Sea [1885-1957] [A publication] (DLA)
Carver	Carver Corp. [Associated Press] (SAG)
Carver	Carver's Treatise on the Law Relating to the Carriage of Goods by Sea [1885-1957] [A publication] (DLA)
CarverFS	Carver Federal Savings Bank [Associated Press] (SAG)
CARW	Carolina Western [AAR code]
Car Wom	Career Woman [A publication]
Cary	Cary's English Chancery Reports [1537-1604] [A publication] (DLA)
Cary Jur	Cary on Juries [A publication] (DLA)
Cary Lit	Cary's Commentary on Littleton's Tenures [A publication] (DLA)
Cary Part	Cary. Partnership [1827] [A publication] (ILCA)
CAS	Cabin Address System [Aviation] (AIA)
CAS	Cable Activity System [Telecommunications] (TEL)
CAS	Cable Assembly Set (KSC)
CAS	Calcarine Sulcus [Medicine] (DMAA)
CAS	Calcific Aortic Stenosis [Medicine] (DMAA)
CAS	Calculated Air Speed (MSA)
CAS	Calibrated Air Speed
CAS	California Academy of Sciences
CAS	California Avocado Society (EA)
CAS	Call Accounting System [or Subsystem] [Telecommunications]
CAS	Cambrian Airways Ltd.
CAS	Canadian Aerophilatelic Society (AC)
CAS	Canadian Anaesthetists Society
CAS	Canadian Association of Slavists [See also ACS]
CAS	Canadian Astronautical Society
CAS	Canadian Astronomical Society
CAS	Canadian Atherosclerosis Society [Societe Canadienne d'Atherosclerose] (AC)
CAS	Canadian Cooperative Applications Satellite (HGAA)
CAS	Canberra Archaeological Society [Australia]
CAS	Cancer Attitude Survey [Oncology and psychiatry] (DAVI)
CAS	Cardiac Adjustment Scale [Psychology]
CAS	Cardiac Surgery [Medicine] (MAE)
CAS	Carotid Artery System [Medicine]
CAS	Casablanca [Morocco] [Airport symbol] (OAG)
CAS	Casamari [Italy] [Seismograph station code, US Geological Survey Closed] (SEIS)
CAS	Cascade (MSA)
CAS	Cascades, Inc. [Toronto Stock Exchange symbol]
CAS	Casein
cas	Casein (VRA)
Cas	Casey's Reports [25-36 Pennsylvania] [A publication] (DLA)
CAS	Cashier (ROG)
CAS	Cashier
Cas	Casina [of Plautus] [Classical studies] (OCD)
CAS	Casing (WGA)
Cas	Cassiopeia [Constellation]
CAS	Cast Aluminum Structure
CAS	Castle (MSA)
CAS	Castle [A. M.] & Co. [AMEX symbol] (SPSG)
CAS	Casual
CAS	Casualty (AFM)
CAS	Casualty Actuarial Society (EA)
CAS	Casualty Assessment System [Army]
CAS	Catgut Acoustical Society (EA)
CAS	Cell Analysis System [Microscopy]
CAS	Center for Alcohol Studies (EA)
CAS	Center for Austrian Studies (EA)
CAS	Center for Auto Safety (EA)
CAS	Central Alarm Station (IEEE)
CAS	Central Alarm System (NRCH)
CAS	Central Amplifier Station [Telecommunications] (OA)
CAS	Central Asian States (ECON)
CAS	Centralized Attendants Service [Bell System]
CAS	Centre for Aging Studies [Flinders University] [Australia]
CAS	Centre for Agricultural Strategy [University of Reading] [British] (CB)
CAS	Centre for Atmospheric Science
CAS	Cerebral Arteriosclerosis [Medicine] (MAE)
CAS	Certificate in Advanced Standing (GAGS)
CAS	Certificate of Advanced Study (WGA)
CAS	Change Analysis Section
CAS	Channel Associated Signaling [Telecommunications] (ACRL)
CAS	Charge Air-Temperature Sensor [Automotive engineering]
CAS	Chemical Abstracts Service [American Chemical Society] [Columbus, OH Database producer]
CAS	Chemical Abstracts Service, Columbus, OH [OCLC symbol] (OCLC)
CAS	Chicago Academy of Science
CAS	Chief of Air Staff [World War II]
CAS	Child Anxiety Scale [Child development test] [Psychology]
CAS	Child Attitudes Survey [Education]
CAS	Children Against Smoking [British]
CAS	Children's Aid Society (BARN)
CAS	China Association of Standardization [INFOTERM]
CAS	Chinese Academy of Sciences
CAS	Christian Airmen's Fellowship International [Defunct] (EA)
CAS	Christman Air System [ICAO designator] (FAAC)
CAS	Chronic Anovulation Syndrome [Medicine] (MEDA)
CAS	Church Army Society (EA)
CAS	Circuits and Systems [IEEE] (MCD)
CAS	Citizens Alarm System (MCD)
CAS	Citizenship Automated System [Australia]
CAS	Civil Affairs Section
CAS	Civil Air Surgeon [of FAA]
CAS	Clean Air Society [Australia]
CAS	Cleaner Air System [Automotive engineering]
CAS	Close Air Support [Military]
CAS	Cluster Activation Systems Specialist [NASA]
CAS	Coarse Alignment Servo
CAS	Coast Artillery School [British]
CAS	Coded Armaments System
CAS	Codifying Act of Sederunt (DLA)
CAS	Coherent Acquisition System (MCD)
CAS	Cold Agglutinin Syndrome [Medicine] (DMAA)
CAS	Collected Alongside Ship [Shipping]
CAS	Collision Avoidance System [Aviation]
CAS	Column-Address Strobe (IEEE)
CAS	Combat Applications Squadron [Air Force]
CAS	Combined Activities System [Vietnam] [Air Force]
CAS	Combined Air Support [Army] (DOMA)
CAS	Combined Antenna System (CAAL)
CAS	Command Augmentation System
CAS	Commission for Atmospheric Sciences [WMO] (MSC)
CAS	Commission on American Shipbuilding
CAS	Committee on Atlantic Studies (EA)
CAS	Committee on Atmospheric Sciences [Marine science] (OSRA)
CAS	Communicating Applications Specifications
CAS	Communication Access System (IAA)
CAS	Communication Analysis Section
CAS	Communications Antenna Sleeve
CAS	Community Adaptation Schedule [Psychology]
CAS	Compare Accumulator with Storage [Computer science] (IAA)
CAS	Compensating Air Supply
CAS	Complaint Administration System [Office of Federal Contract Compliance] (GFGA)
CAS	Complete Assembly for Strike
CAS	Compressed Air Spraying
CAS	Compressed Air System (NRCH)
CAS	Computer Accounting System [Boole & Babbage, Inc.]
CAS	Computer-Aided Scheduling
CAS	Computer-Aided Selling (IAA)
CAS	Computer-Aided Styling
CAS	Computer Aid System (NITA)
CAS	Computer Algebra Systems (PDAA)
CAS	Computer Application Summary (IAA)
CAS	Computer Arts Society (EAIO)
CAS	Computer-Assisted Search (CAAL)
CAS	Computer Audit Specialist [IRS]
CAS	Computer or Computerized Acquisition System (NITA)
CAS	Computers and Systems (IAA)
CAS	Concept Alternative Selection [Automotive project management]
CAS	Conflict Alert System [Aviation]
CAS	Congenital Alcoholic Syndrome [Medicine] (DMAA)
CAS	Connecticut Association of Schools (SRA)
CAS	Connecticutensis Academiae Socius [Fellow of the Connecticut Academy of Arts and Sciences]
CAS	Consortium for Atlantic Studies [Arizona State University] [Research center]
CAS	Consumer Aid Series [National Highway Traffic Safety Administration]
CAS	Contemporary Art Society
CAS	Continental Air Services
CAS	Contract Accounting Standard
CAS	Contract Administration Services [DoD]

CAS..............	Control Actuation System
CAS..............	Control Adjustment Strap
CAS..............	Control Assembly Set (MCD)
CAS..............	Control Augmentation System
CAS..............	Control Automation System [IBM Corp.]
CAS..............	Controlled Access System (IAA)
CAS..............	Controlled Airspace
CAS..............	Controlled American Source [Military] (CINC)
CAS..............	Controls Assembly Set
CAS..............	Cooperative Applications Satellite [France] [NASA]
CAS..............	Coordination of Allied Supplies [World War II]
CAS..............	Coordinator of Army Studies (AABC)
CAS..............	Cost Accounting Schedule (MCD)
CAS..............	Cost Accounting Standards [Accounting] (MCD)
CAS..............	Cost Accumulation System
CAS..............	Council for the Advancement of Standards for Student Services/Development Programs (EA)
CAS..............	Council of Academic Societies (DAVI)
CAS..............	Council of Adult Stutterers [Later, NCS] (EA)
CAS..............	Council on Atmospheric Studies
CAS..............	County Architects Society [British] (BI)
CAS..............	Courier Air Service
CAS..............	Course Alignment Servo
CAS..............	Court of Arbitration of Sport [See also TAS] [Lausanne, Switzerland] (EAIO)
CAS..............	Creativity Attitude Survey [Educational test]
CAS..............	Crisis Action System (MCD)
CAS..............	Current Awareness Service [Cryogenic literature bibliography] [Cryogenic Data Center]
CAS..............	Curriculum and Accreditation Secretariat [Victoria] [Australia]
CAS..............	Customer Application Summary (IAA)
CAS3............	Combined Arms and Services Staff School [Army] (RDA)
CAS3	Combined Arms and Service Staff School (DOMA)
CASA	California Association of Sanitation Agencies (SRA)
CASA	Callisthenic Association of South Australia
CASA	Canadian Advertising and Sales Association
CASA	Canadian Amateur Speed Skating Association
CASA	Canadian Amputee Sports Association
CASA	Canadian Amputee Sports Association [Association Canadienne des Sports Pour Amputes] (AC)
CASA	Canadian Asian Studies Association [See also ACEA]
CASA	Canadian Association of School Administrators (AC)
CASA	Canadian Automatic Sprinkler Association (AC)
CA SA	Capias ad Satisfaciendum [A writ of execution] [Latin Legal term] (ROG)
CASA	Car Audio Specialists Association (EA)
CASA	Casa Ole-Restaurants [NASDAQ symbol] (TTSB)
CASA	Casa Ole Restaurants, Inc. [NASDAQ symbol] (SAG)
CasA	Cassiopeia A [Constellation]
CASA	Castillo de San Marcos National Monument
CASA	Centre Alliance Students' Association [Australia]
CASA	Chinese Art Society of America [Later, AS] (EA)
CASA	Christian AIDS Services Alliance (EA)
CASA	Civil Affairs Staging Area [World War II]
CASA	Close Air Support Aircraft [Military]
CASA	Commander, Antarctic Support Activities [Military] (DNAB)
CASA	Committee for Anglophone Social Action [Canada]
CASA	Computer-Aided Systems Analysis (MCD)
CASA	Computer and Automated Systems Association [Later, CASA/SME]
CASA	Computer-Assisted Self Assessment [Medicine] (DMAA)
CASA	Computer Assisted Sperm Analyzer
CASA	Computer-Assisted [or Assisted] Self-Assessment [British]
CASA	Confederation des Associations Latino-Americaines (AC)
CASA	Configuration Accountability Systems, Aerospace
CASA	Contemporary Acapella Society of America (EA)
CASA	Controller Automated Spacing Aid [FAA] (TAG)
CASA	Cornish Association of South Australia
CASA	Court Appointed Special Advocates [In association name National CASA Association]
CA(SA)........	Member of the Accountants' Society (South Africa)
CASAA	Combined Arms Studies and Analysis Activity [Fort Leavenworth, KS]
CASAC	Canadian Anti-Soviet Action Committee (AC)
CASAC	Canadian Association of Sexual Assault Centres [Association Canadienne des Centres Contre le Viol] (AC)
CASAC	Clean Air Scientific Advisory Committee
CASAC	Clean Air Scientific Advisory Committee [Environmental Protection Agency Washington, DC]
CASADA......	Close Air Support Aircraft Design Alternative [Military]
CASAE	Canadian Association for the Study of Adult Education [See also ACEEA]
CASAFA	Interunion Commission on the Application of Science to Agriculture, Forestry, and Aquaculture [ICSU] [Ottawa, ON] (EAIO)
CASAG	Computer Assisted Synthetic Analysis Group (NITA)
CasaOle.......	Casa Ole Restaurants, Inc. [Associated Press] (SAG)
Cas App.......	Cases of Appeal to the House of Lords [A publication] (DLA)
CASAR........	Communications Acquisition Status and Assessment Report (MCD)
CASARA......	Canadian Search and Rescue Association
CASARA......	Civil Air Search & Rescue Association (AC)
Cas Arg & Dec...	Cases Argued and Decreed in Chancery, English [A publication] (DLA)
CASAS	Canadian Association for South Asian Studies
CASAS	Commonwealth Association of Scientific Agricultural Societies [Canada]
CASA/SME ...	Computer and Automated Systems Association of Society of Manufacturing Engineers (EA)

CASAW........	Canadian Association of Smelter and Allied Workers
CASB	Canadian Aviation Safety Board
CASB	Cascade Financial Corp. [Washington] [NASDAQ symbol] (SAG)
CAS(B)........	Civil Affairs Service (Burma) [British]
CASB	Colorado Association of School Boards (SRA)
CASB	Cost Accounting Standards Board [US] [Terminated]
CAS/BAI	Close Air Support/Battlefield Air Interdiction (DOMA)
CASBAR	Collision Avoidance System Using Baseband Reflectrometry [Aviation] (PDAA)
CAS/BAT	Close Air Support/Battlefield Air Interdiction
CASB-CMF...	Cost Accounting Standards Board's Cost of Money Factors [Form] (AAGC)
CaSBe..........	Beauval Public Library, Beauval, SK, Canada [Library symbol] [Library of Congress] (LCLS)
CaSBIN	Canada Department of Indian Affairs and Northern Development, Battleford National HistoricPark, Battleford, SK, Canada [Library symbol] [Library of Congress] (LCLS)
CASBL	Continuous Automated Single Base Line [Automated control system]
CASBO	Conference of American Small Business Organizations [AFSB] [Absorbed by] (EA)
Cas BR	Cases Banco Regis Tempore William III [12 Modern Reports] [A publication] (DLA)
Cas BR Holt...	Cases and Resolutions (of Settlements; not Holt's King's Bench Reports) [England] [A publication] (DLA)
CASBS	Center for Advanced Study in the Behavioral Sciences (EA)
CaSBuN	Buffalo Narrows Public Library, Buffalo Narrows, SK, Canada [Library symbol] [Library of Congress] (LCLS)
CASBY	Canadian Artists Selected by You [Music award alternative to the Canadian Juno Award] [Established 1985]
CASC	California Association of Student Councils (BARN)
CASC	Canadian Army Service Corps [British military] (DMA)
CASC	Canadian Association for Studies in Cooperation [See also ACEC]
CASC	Canadian Automobile Sports Club
CASC	Capital Area Support Center [Military]
CASC	Captive Air Spacecraft (MCD)
CASC	Cascade
CASC	Cascade Corp. [NASDAQ symbol] (NQ)
casc............	Cascara [A cathartic] [Pharmacy] (DAVI)
CASC	Cataloging and Standardization Center [Air Force]
CASC	Center for Adhesives, Sealants, and Coatings [Case Western Reserve University] [Research center] (RCD)
CASC	Central Administrative Support Center [Marine science] (OSRA)
CASC	Central Administrative Support Center (USDC)
CASC	Certified Alfalfa Seed Council (EA)
CASC	Ceylon Army Service Corps [British military] (DMA)
CASC	China Aero-Space Corp. (ECON)
CASC	Corps Area Signal Center (MCD)
CASC	Council for the Advancement of Small Colleges [Later, CIC] (EA)
CaSCA	Archibald Library, Caronport, SK, Canada [Library symbol Library of Congress] (LCLS)
CASCADE....	Centralized Administrative Systems Control and Design (PDAA)
CASCADE....	Combined Airborne Surveillance and Control for Aerospace Defense
CASCADE....	Computer-Aided Scantling Determination (PDAA)
CASCADE....	Content and Source of Cataloging Data for Local Use (PDAA)
CASCAN......	Casualty Canceled [Navy]
CascBcp......	Cascade Bancorp [Associated Press] (SAG)
CASCC........	Canadian Agricultural Services Coordinating Committee
CASCC........	Current Awareness System in Coordination Chemistry
CascCm.......	Cascade Communications [Associated Press] (SAG)
CASCD	Cascade [Meteorology] (FAAC)
CASCD	Colorado Association of Soil Conservation Districts (SRA)
Cascde........	Cascade Corp. [Associated Press] (SAG)
CascdeCp.....	Cascade Corp. [Associated Press] (SAG)
CascFin.......	Cascade Financial Corp [Washington] [Associated Press] (SAG)
Cas Ch........	Cases in Chancery [England] [A publication] (DLA)
Cas Ch........	Select Cases in Chancery [1724-33] [England] [A publication] (DLA)
Cas Ch 1 2 3...	Cases in Chancery Tempore Car. II [A publication] (DLA)
Cas CL........	Cases in Crown Law [England] [A publication] (DLA)
CascNG........	Cascade Natural Gas Corp. [Associated Press] (SAG)
CASCO	Canada Starch Co.
CASCO	Canadian Australian Line
Cas Com	Arret de la Section Commerciale de la Cour de Cassation [Decision of the Commercial Section of the Court of Appeal] [French] (ILCA)
CASCOM	Combined Arms Support Command [DoD] (RDA)
CASCOM	Combined Arms Support Command (DOMA)
CASCOMP...	Comprehensive Airship Sizing and Performance Computer Program
CASCON......	Casualty Control Station [Military] (DNAB)
CASCON......	Close Air Support Control [Military] (NVT)
CASCOR......	Casualty Corrected [Navy]
CASCOR......	Casualty Correction Report
CASCP	Caribbean Area Small Craft Project
CAS/CPA	Computer Accounting System / Computer Performance Analysis (MHDB)
Cas CR	Cases Tempore William III [12 Modern Reports] [A publication] (DLA)
CaSCR	Chinook Regional Library, Swift Current, SK, Canada [Library symbol Library of Congress] (LCLS)
CASCU	Commander, Aircraft Support Control Unit [Navy]
CASD	Carrier Aircraft Service Detachment [Marine Corps]
CASD	Carrier Aircraft Service Division [Navy]
CASD	Computer-Aided Software Development [Computer science]
CASD	Computer-Aided Structural Design (MCD)
CASD	Computer-Aided System Design [Programming language] (BUR)
CASDAC.......	Computer-Aided Ship Design and Construction

CASDAT...... Computer-Aided System for the Development of Aircrew Training (MCD)
CASDC........ Computer-Aided Ship Design and Construction
CAS DDS ..... Chemical Abstracts Service Document Delivery Service [*American Chemical Society*] (NITA)
CASDIV....... Carrier Aircraft Service Division [*Navy*]
CASDO........ Computer Applications Support and Development Office [*Navy*]
CASDOS....... Computer-Assisted Detailing of Ships
CASDS........ Cascades [*NWS*] (FAAC)
CASDS........ Centre for Advanced Study in the Developmental Sciences [*British*]
CASDS........ Computer-Aided Structural Detailing of Ships (DNAB)
CASE.......... Campaign for the Advancement of State Education [*British*]
CASE.......... Center for Advanced Study in Education [*City University of New York*] [*Research center*] (RCD)
CASE.......... Citizens Association for Sound Energy (EA)
CASE.......... Clerical and Allied Service Employees (DICI)
CASE.......... Coalition of America to Save the Economy (EA)
CASE.......... Coatings, Adhesives, Sealants, and Elastomers [*Polyurethanes*]
CASE.......... Cognitive Acceleration through Science Education (AIE)
CASE.......... Colorado Association of School Executives (SRA)
CASE.......... Combined Arms Systems Engineering
CASE.......... Commission on Accreditation of Service Experiences [*Later, OECC*]
CASE.......... Committee for the Absorption of Soviet Emigres
CASE.......... Committee on Academic Science and Engineering [*Federal Council for Science and Technology*]
CASE.......... Committee on the Atlantic Salmon Emergency
CASE.......... Common Access Switching Equipment (AAG)
CASE.......... Commonality and Standardization Effort (MCD)
CASE.......... Common Application Service Element [*Telecommunications*] (OSI)
CASE.......... Common Application Service Element [*Computer science*] (NITA)
CASE.......... Communications, Analysis, Simulation, and Evaluation [*Army*] (MCD)
CASE.......... Complete Affinity Server Enclosure [*Computer science*]
CASE.......... Computer-Aided Software Engineering
CASE.......... Computer-Aided System Engineering (MCD)
CASE.......... Computer-Aided System Evaluation
CASE.......... Computer and System Engineering (IAA)
CASE.......... Computer-Assisted Sensory Examination
CASE.......... Computer-Automated Structure Evaluator [*Database*]
CASE.......... Computer-Automated Support Equipment
CASE.......... Confederation for the Advancement of State Education
CASE.......... Conference of Association Society Executives (EA)
CASE.......... Connecticut Academy of Science and Engineering (SRA)
CASE.......... Consolidated Aerospace Supplier Evaluation (NRCH)
CASE.......... Cooperative Awards in Science and Engineering [*British*]
CASE.......... Coordinated Air-Sea Experiment [*Marine science*] (OSRA)
CASE.......... Coordinated Air-Sea Experiment (USDC)
CASE.......... Coordinating Agency for Supplier Evaluation
CASE.......... Council for Advancement and Support of Education (EA)
CASE.......... Council for Advancement of Secondary Education [*Defunct*] (EA)
CASE.......... Council for Alternatives to Stereotyping in Entertainment [*Defunct*] (EA)
CASE.......... Council for the Advancement and Support of Education
CASE.......... Council of Administrators of Special Education (EA)
CASE.......... Counselling Assistance to Small Enterprises [*Canada*]
CASE.......... Counter-Agency for Sabotage and Espionage [*Military*] (DNAB)
CASE.......... Crew Accommodations and Support Equipment (SSD)
CASE.......... New York State Center for Advanced Technology in Computer Applications and Software Engineering [*Syracuse University*] [*Research center*] (RCD)
CASEA .... Center for the Advanced Study of Educational Administration
CASEAC .... Civilian Affairs Supports for Echelon above Corps [*Military*]
CASEAREA(ONR)... Contract Administration Southeast Area (Office of Naval Research)
CASEC .... Centre for the Advancement and Study of the European Currency [*France*] (EAIO)
CASEC .... Confederation of Associations of Specialist Engineering Contractors (DBA)
CaseCp .... Case Corp. [*Formerly, Case Equipment*] [*Associated Press*] (SAG)
CASEE........ Canadian Army Signals Engineering Establishment (IAA)
CASEE........ Carrier Aircraft Squadron Effectiveness Evaluation
CASEE........ Comprehensive Aircraft Support Effectiveness Evaluation (MCD)
CASEP........ Canadian Altitude Sensing Experiment Package (MCD)
CASEP........ Cognitive Acceleration through Science Education Project (AIE)
Cas Eq .... Cases and Opinions in Law, Equity, and Conveyancing [*A publication*]
Cas Eq .... Cases in Equity, Gilbert's Reports [*A publication*] (DLA)
Cas Eq Abr... Cases in Equity Abridged [*1667-1744*] [*England*] [*A publication*] (DLA)
Cas Err .... Caines' New York Cases in Error [*A publication*] (DLA)
CASERTZ .... Corridor Aerogeophysics of the Southeastern Ross Transect Zone [*Geology*]
CASES .... Center for Alternative Sentencing and Employment Services [*Research center*] (RCD)
CASES .... Computer Assisted Simulation and Education System [*Simulation of doctor's decision making*] [*Netherlands*] (NITA)
CASES .... Computerized Applicant Search, Evaluation, and Selection (SAA)
Cases in Ch... Select Cases in Chancery [*England*] [*A publication*] (DLA)
CASETS....... Computer Assisted Spanish English Transition Sequence (EDAC)
Ca Sett .... Cases of Settlements and Removals [*1710-42*] [*England*] [*A publication*] (DLA)
CASEUR....... Controller Administration Service, Europe [*Air Force*]
CASEVAC ..... Casualty Evacuation
Case West Res U... Case Western Reserve University (GAGS)
CASEX .... Close Air Support Exercise [*Military*] (NVT)
CASEX .... Combined Aircraft Submarine Exercise [*NATO*] (NATG)

Casey.......... Casey's Reports [*25-36 Pennsylvania*] [*A publication*] (DLA)
Caseys........ Casey's General Stores, Inc. [*Associated Press*] (SAG)
CASF.......... Calcium-Activated Sarcoplasmic Factor [*A proteolytic enzyme*]
CASF.......... Canadian Amateur Sports Federation
CASF.......... Canadian Association of Specialty Foods [*L'Association Canadienne des Aliments Fins*] [*Formerly, Canadian Specialty Food Association*] (AC)
CASF.......... Composite Air Strike Force [*Air Force*]
CASF.......... Crew Augmented Stability Factor [*Boating*]
CasFd........ Castle Convertible Fund, Inc. [*Associated Press*] (SAG)
Cas FT .... Cases Tempore Talbot, English Chancery (Forrester) [*A publication*] (DLA)
CASG .... Cost Accounting Standards Guide [*CCH*] [*A publication*] (AAGC)
CaSGM........ College Mathieu, Gravelbourg, SK, Canada [*Library symbol Library of Congress*] (LCLS)
CASGP........ Close Air Support Gun Program [*Military*] (MCD)
CASGS........ Close Air Support Gun System [*Military*] (MCD)
CASH .... Call Accounting System for Hotels [*Telecommunications*] (IAA)
CASH .... Canadian Association for Sport Heritage [*Association Canadienne pour l'Heritage Sportif*] (AC)
CASH .... Cashel [*City in Ireland*] (ROG)
CASH .... Cashier
CASH .... Catalog of Available and Standard Hardware [*NASA*]
CASH .... Charge-Amplified Sample and Hold (PDAA)
CASH .... Chronic Affliction Serum Hepatitis [*Medicine*]
CASH .... Citizens Alliance for Self-Help (EA)
CASH .... Coalition Against Sexist-Racist Hiring [*Student legal action organization*]
CASH .... Collection Agent System for Hospitals [*Navy*] (GFGA)
CASH .... Committee on Administrative Services of Hospitals
CASH .... Committee to Abolish Sport Hunting (EA)
CASH .... Computer-Aided Stock Holdings (PDAA)
CASH .... Computer-Aided System Hardware (MHDI)
CASH .... Correct Age Stocking and Height [*Inventory*] [*Forestry*]
CASH .... Costing and Assessing via Substantial History
CASH .... First Midwest Financial [*NASDAQ symbol*] (SAG)
CashAm....... Cash America International, Inc. [*Associated Press*] (SAG)
CASHD....... Coronary Arteriosclerotic Heart Disease
Cas HL........ Cases in the House of Lords [*England*] [*A publication*] (DLA)
cashm......... Cashmere (VRA)
CaSHPA...... Prairie Agricultural Machinery Institute, Humboldt, SK, Canada [*Library symbol Library of Congress*] (LCLS)
CASHR........ Cashier
CASHRA...... Canadian Association of Statutory Human Rights Agencies [*Association Canadienne des Organismes Statutaires pour la Protection des Droits de la Personne*] (AC)
CASI............ Canadian Aeronautics and Space Institute
CASI............ Center for Aerospace Information (AAGC)
CASI............ Chili Appreciation Society International (EA)
CASI............ Cognitive Abilities Screening Instrument [*Medicine*] (DMAA)
CASI............ Cognitive Abilities Screening Instrument
CASI............ Combined Approach System Investigation (SAA)
CASI............ Computer Application Services, Inc. [*Los Alamitos, CA*] [*Telecommunications*] (TSSD)
CASI............ Conditional Amount of Sample Information [*Statistics*]
CASI............ Convenient Automotive Services Institute (EA)
CA/SI .... Office of Consumer Affairs and Special Impact [*Federal Energy Administration*]
CASIA .... Chemical Abstracts Subject Index Alert [*Database*] [*A publication*]
CASIB .... Center for Advanced Studies in International Business
CASID .... Canadian Association for the Study of International Development [*L'Association Canadienne d'Etudes du Developpement International*] (AC)
CASID .... Center for Advanced Study of International Development [*Michigan State University*] [*Research center*] (RCD)
CASIE......... Coalition for Advertising Supported Information and Entertainment
CaSIL.......... Ile a la Crosse Public Library, Ile a la Crosse, SK, Canada [*Library symbol*] [*Library of Congress*] (LCLS)
CASIMS ...... Calibrated Airborne Special Infrared Measurement Systems (PDAA)
CASIN .... Center for Applied Studies in International Negotiations [*Switzerland*] (EAIO)
Cas in C ..... Cases in Chancery [*England*] [*A publication*] (DLA)
Cas in C ..... Select Cases in Chancery [*England*] [*A publication*] (DLA)
Cas in Ch..... Cases in Chancery [*England*] [*A publication*] (DLA)
CASINFOSUPPSYS... Casualty Information Support System [*Military*] (DNAB)
CASING....... Cross Linking by Activated Species of Inert Gases (MCD)
CasinoAm....... Casino America, Inc. [*Associated Press*] (SAG)
CasinoD....... Casino Data Systems [*Commercial firm Associated Press*] (SAG)
CASIQ .... Conseil des Agences de Securite et d'Investigation du Quebec Inc. (AC)
CASK .... Canadian Associated School of Karate-Doh
Cas KB........ Cases in King's Bench [*8 Modern Reports*] [*England*] [*A publication*] (DLA)
Cas KBTH ... Cases Tempore Hardwicke (W. Kelynge's English King's Bench Reports) [*A publication*] (DLA)
Cas KBT Hard... Cases Tempore Hardwicke (W. Kelynge's English King's Bench Reports) [*A publication*] (DLA)
CASL........... Canadian Association of Special Libraries (EAIO)
CASL........... Committee of American Steamship Lines [*Later, AIMS*] (EA)
CASL........... Computer Architecture Specification Language (CSR)
CASL........... Crosstalk Application Script Language [*Programming language*] [*1987*] [*Computer science*]
CaSL........... Lloydminster Public Library, Lloydminster, SK, Canada [*Library symbol Library of Congress*] (LCLS)
Cas L & Eq... Gilbert's Cases in Law and Equity [*A publication*] (DLA)

CASLE......... Commonwealth Association of Surveying and Land Economy [*British*] (EAIO)
Cas L Eq...... Cases in Law and Equity [*10 Modern Reports*] [*A publication*] (DLA)
CASLIM........ Consortium of Academic and Special Libraries in Montana [*Library network*]
CASLIS .... Canadian Association of Special Libraries and Information Services (HGAA)
CaSLL.......... La Loche Public Library, La Loche, SK, Canada [*Library symbol*] [*Library of Congress*] (LCLS)
CaSIM......... Slave Lake Municipal Library, Slave Lake, AB, Canada [*Library symbol*] [*Library of Congress*] (LCLS)
CASLP........ Conference on Alternative State and Local Policies [*Later, CPA*] (EA)
CASLPA .... Canadian Association of Speech-Language Pathologists & Audiologists [*Association Canadienne des Orthophonistes et Audiologistes*] (AC)
CASLPP .... Conference on Alternative State and Local Public Policies [*Later, CPA*] (EA)
CaSLrPRF .... Parks and Renewable Resources, Fisheries Branch, La Ronge, SK, Canada [*Library symbol*] [*Library of Congress*] (LCLS)
CaSLrTB ...... Saskatchewan Tourism and Small Business, La Ronge, SK, Canada [*Library symbol*] [*Library of Congress*] (LCLS)
CASLT.......... Canadian Association of Second Language Teachers (AC)
CASM......... Canadian Academy of Sport Medicine (AC)
CASM......... Canadian Academy of Sport Medicine [*See also CCMS*]
CAS(M)....... Civil Affairs Service (Malaya) [*British*]
CASM......... Close Air Support Missile [*Military*] (MCD)
CASM......... Combined Arms Simulation Model (MCD)
CASM......... Command and Service Module [*NASA*] (IAA)
CASM......... Communications and Systems Management [*Software module*] [*Stratus Computer, Inc.*]
CASM......... Cyclic Air Sampling Monitor
CASMA .... Calgary Air Conditioning & Sheet Metal Association (AC)
CASMA .... Confederation des Associations et Societies Medicales d'Afrique [*Confederation of African Medical Associations and Societies - CAMAS*] [*Nigeria*] (EAIO)
CASMAC ...... Core Australian Specification for Management and Administrative Computing
CasMagic .... Casino Magic Corp. [*Associated Press*] (SAG)
CASMAP ...... Command Area Study and Mission Analysis Program [*Military*] (INF)
CaSMcPCF... Parks Canada, Fort Walsh National Historic Park, Maple Creek, SK, Canada [*Library symbol Library of Congress*] (LCLS)
CASMD .... Congenital Atonic Sclerotic Muscular Dystrophy [*Medicine*] (DMAA)
CASME........ Commonwealth Association of Science and Mathematics Educators [*British*]
CASMIT....... Control Automation System Manufacturing Interface Tape (IAA)
CaSMJ......... Moose Jaw Public Library, Moose Jaw, SK, Canada [*Library symbol Library of Congress*] (LCLS)
CaSMJAEM... Saskatchewan Department of Advanced Education and Manpower, Moose Jaw, SK, Canada [*Library symbol*] [*Library of Congress*] (LCLS)
CaSMJP....... Palliser Regional Library, Moose Jaw, SK, Canada [*Library symbol Library of Congress*] (LCLS)
CaSMJT .... Saskatchewan Technical Institute, Moose Jaw, SK, Canada [*Library symbol Library of Congress*] (LCLS)
CASMOS...... Computer Analysis and Simulation of Metaloxide Semiconductor Circuit (IAA)
CASMS .... Computer-Controlled Area Sterilization Multisensor System
CASMT........ Central Association of Science and Mathematics Teachers [*Later, SSMA*]
CaSMuSP .... Saint Peter's Abbey and College, Muenster, SK, Canada [*Library symbol Library of Congress*] (LCLS)
CASN .... Command Automated Support Network [*Marine Corps*] (DOMA)
CaSNB .... Lakeland Library Region, North Battleford, SK, Canada [*Library symbol Library of Congress*] (LCLS)
CASNET .... Casual-Associative Network [*for medical applications*] [*Computer science*]
CASNP........ Canadian Alliance in Solidarity with the Native People (EA)
CasnRsc ...... Casino Resource Corp. [*Associated Press*] (SAG)
CASO .... Canada Southern Railway [*Penn Central*] [*AAR code*]
CASO .... Cancellation Addendum Sales Order (NASA)
CASO .... Cataloging and Standardization Office [*Air Force*] (AFIT)
CASO .... Civil Affairs Staff Officer [*British*]
CASO .... Computer-Assisted System Operation (PDAA)
CASO .... Council of American Flag-Ship Operators (EA)
CASOC .... California Arabian Standard Oil Co.
CASOE .... Computer Accounting System for Office Expenditure (MHDB)
CASOFF .... Control and Surveillance of Friendly Forces (MCD)
Cas Op........ Burton. Cases and Opinions [*A publication*] (DLA)
CASOR .... Civil Mediator Organisation [*British*] (DA)
CA-SP .... Calcium Urine Spot [*Test*] [*Biochemistry*] (DAVI)
CASP .... California Association of School Psychologists (SRA)
CASP .... Canadian Association for Suicide Prevention [*L'Association Canadienne pour la Prevention du Suicide*] (AC)
CASP .... Canadian Atlantic Storms Program [*Meteorology*]
CASP .... Capability Support Plan
Cas P .... Cases in Parliament [*A publication*] (DLA)
CASP .... CDS Application Support Programs [*NASA*] (NASA)
CASP .... Central American Society of Pharmacology [*Panama*] (EAIO)
CASP .... Centre for the Analysis of Social Policy [*University of Bath*] [*British*] (CB)
CASP .... Civil Aviation Statistics Programme [*ICAO*] [*United Nations*] (DUND)
CASP .... Civilian Acquired Skills Program [*Military*]
CASP .... Comprehensive Area Service Plan
CASP .... Computer-Assisted Search Planning (MCD)

CASP .... Country Analysis Strategy Paper [*Bureau of Inter-American Affairs*] [*Department of State*]
CASP .... Crew Activities Scheduling Program [*NASA*] (KSC)
CASP .... Cysteamine-S-Phosphate [*Biochemical analysis*]
CASPA .... Certificate of Advanced Study in Public Administration (PGP)
CaSPAASS ... Anglican Church of Canada, Diocese of Saskatchewan, Synod Office, Prince Albert,SK, Canada [*Library symbol Library of Congress*] (LCLS)
CaSPAC .... Canadian Seniors Packaging Advisory Council [*Conseil Consultatif Canadien pour l'Adaptation de l'Emballage aux Besoins des Aines*] (AC)
CaSPAF .... Saskatchewan Department of Natural Resources, Forestry Branch, Prince Albert, SK, Canada [*Library symbol Library of Congress*] (LCLS)
CaSPAIN ..... Canada Department of Indian and Northern Affairs, Prince Albert, SK, Canada [*Library symbol Library of Congress*] (LCLS)
CaSPAMI ..... Canada Department of Manpower and Immigration, Prince Albert, SK, Canada [*Library symbol Library of Congress Obsolete*] (LCLS)
CaSPANC ..... Wapiti Regional Library, Prince Albert, SK, Canada [*Library symbol Library of Congress*] (LCLS)
CaSPANI ..... Northern Institute of Technology, Prince Albert, SK, Canada [*Library symbol*] [*Library of Congress*] (LCLS)
CASPAR....... Cambridge Analog Simulator for Predicting Atomic Reactions [*British*] (DIT)
CASPAR....... Cushion Air System Parametric Assessment Rig (PDAA)
Cas Parl ...... Cases in Parliament [*A publication*] (DLA)
CaSPAS ...... Social Service Department, Prince Albert, SK, Canada [*Library symbol Library of Congress*] (LCLS)
CASPER .... Computer-Assisted Pericardiac Surgery [*Cardiology*] (DMAA)
CASPER .... Consolidated Army System for Processing Entitlements to Reservists
CASPER .... Contact Area Summary Position Estimate Report [*Military*] (NVT)
CASPERS ..... Computer-Automated Speech Perception System (PDAA)
Casp For Med... Casper's Forensic Medicine [*A publication*] (DLA)
CASPMT ...... Casual Payment
Cas Pr .... Cases of Practice, English King's Bench [*A publication*] (DLA)
CASPR........ Command Automated System for Procurement [*Army*]
CASPR........ Computer Advanced Software Products [*Database producer*] (IID)
Cas Prac CP... Cases of Practice, English Common Pleas [*1702-27*] [*A publication*] (DLA)
Cas Prac KB... Cases of Practice, English King's Bench [*A publication*] (DLA)
Cas Pra CP... Cases of Practice, English Common Pleas [*1702-27*] [*A publication*] (DLA)
Cas Pra KB... Cases of Practice, English King's Bench [*A publication*] (DLA)
Cas Pr CP.... Cases of Practice, English Common Pleas [*Cooke's Reports*] [*A publication*] (DLA)
Cas Pr KB.... Cases of Practice, English King's Bench [*A publication*] (DLA)
CASPRO....... Casualty Procedure
Cas Proc ..... Cassel. Procedure in the Court of Canada [*A publication*] (DLA)
CAS/PWI...... Collision Avoidance System / Pilot Warning Indicator [*Aviation*] (PDAA)
CASPWI...... Collision Avoidance System Proximity Warning Indicator [*Aviation*] (IAA)
CASQ .... Calsequestrin (DMAA)
CASQ .... Children's Attributional Style Questionnaire
Cas R.......... Casey's Reports [*25-36 Pennsylvania*] [*A publication*] (DLA)
CASR .... Centre for Applied Social Research [*Macquarie University*] [*Australia*]
CASR .... Certificate in Advanced Social Research (PGP)
CASR .... Chemical Activity Status Report [*Chemical Information Systems, Inc.*] [*Information service or system*] (CRD)
CASR .... Controller of American Supplies and Repair [*Ministry of Aircraft Production*] [*British World War II*]
CaSR .... Regina Public Library, Regina, SK, Canada [*Library symbol Library of Congress*] (LCLS)
CaSRA .... Legislative Library of Saskatchewan, Office of the Archives Division, Regina, SK, Canada [*Library symbol Library of Congress*] (LCLS)
CaSRAB .... Allan Blair Memorial Clinic, Regina, SK, Canada [*Library symbol*] [*Library of Congress*] (LCLS)
CaSRAC .... Alcoholism Commission of Saskatchewan, Regina, SK, Canada [*Library symbol Library of Congress*] (LCLS)
CaSRAEL ..... Saskatchewan Department of Advanced Education and Manpower, Labour Market Plan, Regina, SK, Canada [*Library symbol*] [*Library of Congress*] (LCLS)
CaSRAEW .... Saskatchewan Department of Advanced Education, Women's Services Branch, Regina, SK, Canada [*Library symbol*] [*Library of Congress*] (LCLS)
CaSRAF .... Archibald Foundation, Regina, SK, Canada [*Library symbol Library of Congress*] (LCLS)
CaSRAg ...... Saskatchewan Department of Agriculture, Regina, SK, Canada [*Library symbol Library of Congress*] (LCLS)
CaSRAgE ..... Canada Department of Agriculture, Economics Branch, Regina, SK, Canada [*Library symbol Library of Congress*] (LCLS)
CaSRAgR ..... Canada Department of Agriculture, Research Station, Regina, SK, Canada [*Library symbol Library of Congress*] (LCLS)
CaSRAS .... Albert South Library, Regina, SK, Canada [*Library symbol*] [*Library of Congress*] (LCLS)
CaSRBMI ..... BMI Finance, Regina, SK, Canada [*Library symbol Library of Congress*] (LCLS)
CaSRCA .... Saskatchewan Department of Consumer Affairs, Regina, SK, Canada [*Library symbol Library of Congress*] (LCLS)
CaSRCB .... Canadian Bible College, Regina, SK, Canada [*Library symbol Library of Congress*] (LCLS)
CaSRCR .... Saskatchewan Culture and Recreation, Regina, SK, Canada [*Library symbol*] [*Library of Congress*] (LCLS)

CaSRCU .... Credit Union Central, Regina, SK, Canada [*Library symbol Library of Congress*] (LCLS)

CaSRDA .... Dunlop Art Gallery, Regina, SK, Canada [*Library symbol Library of Congress*] (LCLS)

CaSRDL .... Saskatchewan Department of Labour, Regina, SK, Canada [*Library symbol Library of Congress*] (LCLS)

CaSRE .... Saskatchewan Department of the Environment, Regina, SK, Canada [*Library symbol Library of Congress*] (LCLS)

CaSREAE ..... Environment Canada, AES Regina Weather Office, Regina, SK, Canada [*Library symbol*] [*Library of Congress*] (LCLS)

CaSREC .... Executive Council, Regina, SK, Canada [*Library symbol Library of Congress*] (LCLS)

CaSREd .... Saskatchewan Department of Education, Regina, SK, Canada [*Library symbol Library of Congress*] (LCLS)

CaSREEP ..... Environment Canada, Environmental Protection Service, Regina, SK, Canada [*Library symbol*] [*Library of Congress*] (LCLS)

CAS-REGN ... Chemical Abstracts Service Registry Number [*Medicine*] (DMAA)

CaSREIW ..... Environment Canada, Inland Waters Directorate, Regina, SK, Canada [*Library symbol Library of Congress*] (LCLS)

CASREP .... Casualty Report [*Navy*]

CASREPT ..... Casualty Report [*Navy*]

CaSRG .... Regina General Hospital, Regina, SK, Canada [*Library symbol Library of Congress*] (LCLS)

CaSRGE .... Saskatchewan Government Employees Association, Regina, SK, Canada [*Library symbol Library of Congress*] (LCLS)

CaSRGH .... Pasqua Hospital, Regina, SK, Canada [*Library symbol Library of Congress*] (LCLS)

CaSRGI .... Saskatchewan Government Insurance, Regina, SK, Canada [*Library symbol Library of Congress*] (LCLS)

CaSRHP .... Saskatchewan Department of Highways and Transportation, Regina, SK, Canada [*Library symbol Library of Congress*] (LCLS)

CaSRHS .... Plains Health Centre, Health Sciences Library, Regina, SK, Canada [*Library symbol Library of Congress*] (LCLS)

CaSRIA .... Saskatchewan Intergovernmental Affairs, Regina, SK, Canada [*Library symbol Library of Congress*] (LCLS)

CaSRIFC ..... Saskatchewan Indian Federated College, Regina, SK, Canada [*Library symbol*] [*Library of Congress*] (LCLS)

CaSRIN .... Indian and Northern Affairs Canada, Regina, SK, Canada [*Library symbol*] [*Library of Congress*] (LCLS)

CaSRISP ...... Interprovincial Steel & Pipe Corp. Ltd., Regina, SK, Canada [*Library symbol Library of Congress*] (LCLS)

CaSRJC .... Saskatchewan Department of Justice, Communications Policy Branch, Regina, SK, Canada [*Library symbol*] [*Library of Congress*] (LCLS)

CaSRL .... Legislative Library of Saskatchewan, Regina, SK, Canada [*Library symbol Library of Congress*] (LCLS)

CaSRLC .... Luther College, Regina, SK, Canada [*Library symbol Library of Congress*] (LCLS)

CaSRLP .... Leader-Post, Regina, SK, Canada [*Library symbol Library of Congress*] (LCLS)

CaSRMA ..... Saskatchewan Department of Municipal Affairs, Regina, SK, Canada [*Library symbol Library of Congress*] (LCLS)

CaSRMR ...... Saskatchewan Department of Mineral Resources, Regina, SK, Canada [*Library symbol Library of Congress*] (LCLS)

CASRN .... Chemical Abstracts Service Registry Number

CaSRN .... Saskatchewan Registered Nurses Association, Regina, SK, Canada [*Library symbol Library of Congress*] (LCLS)

CASRO .... Combined Arms and Support Research Office [*Fort Leavenworth, KS*]

CASRO .... Council of American Survey Research Organizations (EA)

CaSRO .... Saskatchewan Oil Co., Regina, SK, Canada [*Library symbol*] [*Library of Congress*] (LCLS)

CaSROH .... Occupational Health Library, Regina, SK, Canada [*Library symbol Library of Congress*] (LCLS)

CASROS .... Campaign Against Secret Records on Schoolchildren (AIE)

CASRP .... Close Air Support Request Processing [*Military*]

CaSRP .... Saskatchewan Provincial Library and Union Catalogue, Regina, SK, Canada [*Library symbol Library of Congress*] (LCLS)

CaSRPC .... Saskatchewan Power Corp., Regina, SK, Canada [*Library symbol Library of Congress*] (LCLS)

CaSRPCRD ... Saskatchewan Power Corp., Research and Development Center, Regina, SK, Canada [*Library symbol Library of Congress*] (LCLS)

CaSRPH .... Saskatchewan Department of Health, Regina, SK, Canada [*Library symbol Library of Congress*] (LCLS)

CaSRPS .... Saskatchewan Public Service Commission, Regina, SK, Canada [*Library symbol Library of Congress*] (LCLS)

CaSRRC .... Royal Canadian Mounted Police Academy, Resource Centre, Regina, SK, Canada [*Library symbol Library of Congress*] (LCLS)

CaSRREE ..... Canada Department of Regional Economic Expansion, Prairie Farm Rehabilitation Administration, Regina, SK, Canada [*Library symbol Library of Congress*] (LCLS)

CaSRRI .... Wascana Institute of Applied Arts and Sciences, Regina, SK, Canada [*Library symbol Library of Congress*] (LCLS)

CasRs .... Casino Resource Corp. [*Associated Press*] (SAG)

CASRS .... Countdown and Status Receiving Station [*or System*] [*NASA*] (KSC)

CaSRS .... Saskoil, Regina, SK, Canada [*Library symbol Library of Congress*] (LCLS)

CaSRSA .... Saskatchewan Arts Board, Regina, SK, Canada [*Library symbol Library of Congress*] (LCLS)

CaSRSEMG ... Sask Energy and Mines, Geological Laboratory, Regina, SK, Canada [*Library symbol*] [*Library of Congress*] (LCLS)

CaSRSG .... Subsurface Geological Laboratory, Regina, SK, Canada [*Library symbol Library of Congress*] (LCLS)

CaSRSH .... Wascana Hospital, Regina, SK, Canada [*Library symbol Library of Congress*] (LCLS)

CaSRSSPT ... Saskatchewan Department of Social Services, Personnel and Training Library, Regina, SK, Canada [*Library symbol Library of Congress*] (LCLS)

CaSRSSRC ... Saskatchewan Department of Social Services, Resource Centre, Regina, SK, Canada [*Library symbol*] [*Library of Congress*] (LCLS)

CASRT .... Corrected Adjusted Sinus Node Recovery Time [*Medicine*] (DMAA)

CaSRU .... University of Regina, Regina, SK, Canada [*Library symbol Library of Congress*] (LCLS)

CaSRUA .... Saskatchewan Urban Affairs, Regina, SK, Canada [*Library symbol*] [*Library of Congress*] (LCLS)

CaSRUC .... University of Saskatchewan, Regina Campus, Campion College, Regina, SK, Canada [*Library symbol Library of Congress*] (LCLS)

CaSRUE .... University of Regina, Education Library, Regina, SK, Canada [*Library symbol*] [*Library of Congress*] (LCLS)

CaSRUFA ..... University of Regina, Faculty of Fine Arts, Regina, SK, Canada [*Library symbol Library of Congress*] (LCLS)

CaSRUG .... University of Regina, Department of Geography, Regina, SK, Canada [*Library symbol Library of Congress*] (LCLS)

CaSRUNM ... University of Regina, Norman MacKenzie Art Gallery, Regina, SK, Canada [*Library symbol Library of Congress*] (LCLS)

CaSRW .... Saskatchewan Wheat Pool, Research Library, Regina, SK, Canada [*Library symbol Library of Congress*] (LCLS)

CaSRWP ...... Saskatchewan Department of Social Services, Regina, SK, Canada [*Library symbol Library of Congress*] (LCLS)

CaSRWR ...... Saskatchewan Water Resources Commission, Regina, SK, Canada [*Library symbol Library of Congress*] (LCLS)

Cass .... Arret de la Cour de Cassation [*Decision of the Court of Appeal*] [*Belgium*] (ILCA)

CASS .... Canadian Association for Scottish Studies [*See also ACEE*]

CASS .... Canadian Association for the Social Studies

CASS .... Canadian Association of Sports Sciences

CASS .... Cargo Accounts Settlement System [*IATA*] (DS)

CASS .... Carrier Aircraft Support Study [*Navy*] (NG)

Cass .... Cassatie [*Appeal to High Court of Justice*] [*Netherlands*] (ILCA)

CASS .... Cassette (MSA)

Cass .... Cassiopeia [*Constellation*]

Cass .... Cassite (BJA)

CASS .... Center for Applied Social Science [*Boston University*] [*Research center*] (RCD)

CASS .... Center for Astrophysics and Space Sciences [*University of California, San Diego*] [*Research center*] (RCD)

CASS .... Center for Atmospheric and Space Sciences [*Utah State University*] [*Research center*] (RCD)

CASS .... Center for Auditory and Speech Sciences [*Gallaudet University*] [*Research center*] (RCD)

CASS .... Central Australian Show Society

CASS .... Central Automated Support System (DNAB)

CASS .... Chartered Accountant Students' Society [*Australia*]

CASS .... CITE Augmentation Support System (MCD)

CASS .... Closed Area Security System (MCD)

CASS .... Cluster Activation Systems Specialist [*NASA*] (KSC)

CASS .... Coarse Alignment Subsystem

CASS .... Collection Analysis Support Subsystem (MCD)

CASS .... Combat Area Surveillance System (PDAA)

CASS .... Command Active Sonobuoy System [*Navy*]

CASS .... Computer Access Security System (NITA)

CASS .... Computer-Automated Social Simulation

CASS .... Computer Automatic Scheduling System

CASS .... Computerized Algorithmic Satellite Scheduler [*NASA*]

CASS .... Consolidated Automated Support Station (MCD)

CASS .... Contract Administration Subservice

CASS .... Coronary Artery Surgery Study [*Medicine*]

Cass .... Corte di Cassazione [*Court of Appeal*] [*Italian*] (DLA)

CASS .... Country Assistance Strategy Statement [*Military*] (CINC)

Cass .... Cour de Cassation [*Court of Appeal*] [*French*] (DLA)

CASS .... Course Alignment Subsystem

CASS .... Crab Angle Sensing System (MCD)

CaSS .... Saskatoon Public Library, Saskatoon, SK, Canada [*Library symbol Library of Congress*] (LCLS)

C Ass .... Sentenza della Corte d'Assise [*Decision of the Assize Court*] [*Italian*] (ILCA)

Cass .... Sentenza della Corte Suprema di Cassazione [*Decision or Judgment of the Supreme Court of Appeals*] [*Italian*] (ILCA)

CASSA .... Canadian Amateur Speed Skating Association

CASSA .... Canadian Amateur Synchronized Swimming Association

CASSA .... CONARC [*Continental Army Command*] Automated System Support Agency [*Obsolete*] (AABC)

CaSSA .... University of Saskatchewan, Office of the Saskatchewan Archives, Saskatoon, SK, Canada [*Library symbol Library of Congress*] (LCLS)

CaSSAA ...... Saskatchewan Institute of Applied Arts, Saskatoon, SK, Canada [*Library symbol Library of Congress*] (LCLS)

CaSSAC .... Armak Chemicals, Saskatoon, SK, Canada [*Library symbol Library of Congress*] (LCLS)

CaSSAgR ..... Canada Department of Agriculture, Research Station, Saskatoon, SK, Canada [*Library symbol Library of Congress*] (LCLS)

CaSSAMR .... Saskatchewan Association for the Retarded, John Dolan Resource Library, Saskatoon, SK, Canada [*Library symbol*] [*Library of Congress*] (LCLS)

CASSANDRA ... Chromatogram Automatic Soaking, Scanning, and Digital Recording Apparatus

CASSARS ..... Computer-Assisted Simulation of Supply and Related Systems

Cass Ass Plen .... Cour de Cassation, Assemblee Pleniere [*France*]

CaSSBE....... Saskatoon Board of Education, Saskatoon, SK, Canada [*Library symbol*] [*Library of Congress*] (LCLS)

CASSC........ Clinical Academic Staff Salaries Committee [*Committee of Vice Chancellors and Principals*] (AIE)

CaSSC........ Cooperative College of Canada, Saskatoon, SK, Canada [*Library symbol Library of Congress*] (LCLS)

CaSSCAg ..... Canada Department of Agriculture, Research Station, Swift Current, SK, Canada [*Library symbol Library of Congress*] (LCLS)

Cas SC (Cape GH)... Cases in the Supreme Court, Cape Of Good Hope [*A publication*] (DLA)

CASSCF ...... Complete Active Space Self Consistent Field (MCD)

Cass Ch Reun... Cour de Cassation, Chambres Reunies [*France*] (ILCA)

CaSSCI .... Saskatoon Collegiate Institute, Saskatoon, SK, Canada [*Library symbol Library of Congress*] (LCLS)

Cass Civ ..... Arret de la Chambre Civile de la Cour de Cassation [*Decision of the Court of Appeal, Civil Division*] [*French*] (ILCA)

Cass Civ ..... Sentenza della Sezione Civile della Corte di Cassazione [*Decision of the Court of Appeal, Civil Division*] [*Italian*] (ILCA)

Cass Civ 1re... Cour de Cassation, Premiere Section Civile [*French*] (ILCA)

Cass Civ 3e... Cour de Cassation, Troisieme Section Civile [*French*] (ILCA)

Cass Civ Com... Cour de Cassation, Commerciale [*French*] (ILCA)

Cass Cive 2e... Cour de Cassation, Deuxieme Section Civile [*French*] (ILCA)

Cass Civ Soc... Cour de Cassation, Sociale [*French*] (ILCA)

CASSCM ...... Close Air Support Standoff Munition (MCD)

Cass Com ... Cour de Cassation, Commerciale [*French*] (ILCA)

Cass Crim.... Arret de la Chambre Criminelle de la Cour de Cassation [*Decision of the Court of Appeal, Criminal Division*] [*French*] (ILCA)

Cass Dig..... Cassel's Digest [*Canada*] [*A publication*] (DLA)

CASSE .... Close Air Support Survivability Enhancement System [*Military*] (MCD)

CaSSECW .... Canada Department of the Environment, Canadian Wildlife Service, Prairie Migratory Bird Research Centre, Saskatoon, SK, Canada [*Library symbol Library of Congress*] (LCLS)

CaSSEDA ..... SED Systems Ltd., Aerospace Products Division, Saskatoon, SK, Canada [*Library symbol Library of Congress*] (LCLS)

CaSSEH .... Environment Canada, National Hydrology Research Centre, Saskatchewan, SK, Canada [*Library symbol*] [*Library of Congress*] (LCLS)

Cas Self Def... Horrigan and Thompson's Cases on Self-Defense [*A publication*] (DLA)

CaSSESC ..... College of Emmanuel and St. Chad, Saskatoon, SK, Canada [*Library symbol Library of Congress*] (LCLS)

Cas Sett...... Cases of Settlements and Removals [*1710-42*] [*England*] [*A publication*] (DLA)

CaSSGC .... Saskatoon Gallery and Conservatory, Saskatoon, SK, Canada [*Library symbol Library of Congress*] (LCLS)

CASSI .... Chemical Abstracts Service Source Index [*American Chemical Society*] [*Information service or system*]

CaSSIC .... Saskatchewan Indian Cultural College, Saskatoon, SK, Canada [*Library symbol Library of Congress*] (LCLS)

Cassingle ... Cassette Single [*Trademark of IRS Records*]

Cassiod........ Cassiodorus [*Sixth century AD*] [*Classical studies*] (OCD)

Cassiod Var... Cassiodori Variarum [*A publication*] (DLA)

CASSIP .... Computer-Assisted Study Skills Improvement Program (EDAC)

CASSIS .... Classification and Research Support Information System (AAGC)

CASSIS .... Classification and Search Support Information System [*Patent and Trademark Office*] [*Information service or system*]

CASSIS .... Communication and Social Science Information Service [*Canadian research collection network*]

CASSIT .... Casualty Situation Report

Cas Six Cir... Cases on the Six Circuits [*1841-43*] [*Ireland*] [*A publication*] (DLA)

CaSSKIL ...... Kelsey Institute of Applied Arts and Sciences, Library Technician Program, Saskatoon, SK, Canada [*Library symbol*] [*Library of Congress*] (LCLS)

Cass LGB.... Casson's Local Government Board Decisions [*1902-16*] [*England*] [*A publication*] (DLA)

Cas SM........ Cases of Settlement, King's Bench [*1713-15*] [*England*] [*A publication*] (DLA)

C/ASSM ...... Cents per Available Seat Statute Mile [*Aviation*]

CASSM .... Context Addressed Segment Sequential Memory [*Computer science*]

CaSSM......... Saint Thomas More College, Saskatoon, SK, Canada [*Library symbol Library of Congress*] (LCLS)

CaSSMD ...... Saskatchewan Mining Development Corp., Saskatoon, SK, Canada [*Library symbol Library of Congress*] (LCLS)

CaSSOS .... One Sky, the Saskatchewan Cross Culture Centre, Saskatoon, SK, Canada [*Library symbol*] [*Library of Congress*] (LCLS)

CASSP .... Central Ammunition Supply Status Point

CaSSP .... Prairie Regional Laboratory, National Research Council, Saskatoon, SK, Canada [*Library symbol Library of Congress*] (LCLS)

Cass Pen .... Sentenza della Sezione Penale della Corte di Cassazione [*Decision of the Court of Appeal, Criminal Division*] [*Italian*] (ILCA)

CaSSPP .... POS Pilot Plant Corp., Saskatoon, SK, Canada [*Library symbol Library of Congress*] (LCLS)

Cass Prac .... Cassel's Practice Cases [*Canada*] [*A publication*] (DLA)

Cass Prac Cas... Cassel's Practice Cases [*Canada A publication*] (DLA)

Cass Proc .... Cassel. Procedure in the Court of Canada [*A publication*] (DLA)

CaSSR .... Saskatchewan Research Council, Saskatoon, SK, Canada [*Library symbol Library of Congress*] (LCLS)

Cass Req..... Arret de la Chambre des Requetes de la Cour de Cassation [*Decision of the Court of Appeal, Chamber of Requests*] [*French*] (ILCA)

CaSSSA .... Saint Andrew's College, Saskatoon, SK, Canada [*Library symbol Library of Congress*] (LCLS)

Cass SC...... Cassel's Supreme Court Decisions [*A publication*] (DLA)

CaSSSI .... Kelsey Institute of Applied Arts and Sciences, Saskatoon, SK, Canada [*Library symbol Library of Congress*] (LCLS)

Cass Soc ..... Arret de la Section Sociale de la Cour de Cassation [*Decision of the Social Security and Labor Division of the Court of Appeal*] [*French*] (ILCA)

Cass Sup C Prac... Cassel's Supreme Court Practice [*2nd ed., by Masters*] [*A publication*] (DLA)

CaSST.......... Saskatchewan Teachers' Federation, Saskatoon, SK, Canada [*Library symbol Library of Congress*] (LCLS)

CASSTT .... Cassette

CaSSU .... University of Saskatchewan, Saskatoon, SK, Canada [*Library symbol Library of Congress*] (LCLS)

CaSSUEM ..... Uranerz Exploration & Mining Ltd., Saskatoon, SK, Canada [*Library symbol Library of Congress*] (LCLS)

CaSSUGP..... University of Saskatchewan, Government Publications, Saskatoon, SK, Canada [*Library symbol Library of Congress*] (LCLS)

CaSSUJD..... University of Saskatchewan, the Right Honourable John G. Diefenbaker Centre, Saskatoon, SK, Canada [*Library symbol Library of Congress*] (LCLS)

CaSSUL .... University of Saskatchewan, Law Library, Saskatoon, SK, Canada [*Library symbol Library of Congress*] (LCLS)

CaSSULS ..... Lutheran Seminary, University of Saskatchewan, Saskatoon, SK, Canada [*Library symbol Library of Congress*] (LCLS)

CaSSUM ...... University of Saskatchewan, Medical Library, Saskatoon, SK, Canada [*Library symbol Library of Congress*] (LCLS)

CaSSUMC..... Ukrainian Museum of Canada, Saskatoon, SK, Canada [*Library symbol*] [*Library of Congress*] (LCLS)

CASSW .... Canadian Association of Schools of Social Work [*See also ACESS*]

CaSSW .... Wheatland Regional Library, Saskatoon, SK, Canada [*Library symbol Library of Congress*] (LCLS)

CASSWAC.... Canadian Association of School Social Workers & Attendance Counsellors (AC)

CaSSWD ...... Western Development Museum, Saskatoon, SK, Canada [*Library symbol Library of Congress*] (LCLS)

CAST .... Cable and Satellite Television (NITA)

CAST........... Canadian Air/Sea Transportable Combat Group

CAST........... Canadian Association of Senior Travellers (AC)

CAST........... Capillary Action Shaping Technique (MCD)

CAST........... Cardiac Arrhythmia Suppression Trial [*National Heart, Lung, and Blood Institute*]

CAST........... Cast Aluminum Structure Technology

CAST........... Castinet

CAST........... Casting

CAST........... Castle

CAST........... Castrate

CAST........... Catalogue of Approved Scientific and Technical Intelligence Tasks (MCD)

CAST........... Center for Advanced Studies in Telecommunications [*Ohio State University*] (TSSD)

CAST........... Center for Aerospace Technology [*Weber State College*] [*Research center*] (RCD)

CAST........... Center for Application of Sciences and Technology

CAST........... Center for Applied Special Technology

CAST........... Center for Assessment and Training [*Peace Corps*]

CAST........... Chemical Abstract Searching Terminal (NITA)

CAST........... Chemical Automated Search Terminal [*Computer Corp. of America*] [*Information service or system*] (IID)

CAST........... China Association for Science and Technology

CAST........... Chinese Academy of Space Technology

CAST........... Citation Corp. [*NASDAQ symbol*] (TTSB)

CAST........... Citation Corp. Alabama [*NASDAQ symbol*] (SAG)

CAST........... Clearinghouse Announcements in Science and Technology [*of CFSTI*] [*Later, WGA*]

CAST........... Coatings and Surfaces Technology [*National Centre for Tribology*] [*British*]

CAST........... Color Allergy Screen Test

CAST........... Common Access Security Terminal

CAST........... Computer-Aided Software Testing (MCD)

CAST........... Computer-Aided Structural Technology (MCD)

CAST........... Computer-Assisted Scanning Techniques

CAST........... Computerized Adaptive Screening Test (MCD)

CAST........... Computerized Automatic Systems Tester (MCD)

CAST........... Consortium for an Advanced Silent Transport (MCD)

CAST........... Coordinated ASW [*Antisubmarine Warfare*] Services and Training [*Navy*] (NVT)

CAST........... Coronary Artery Surgery Trial [*Medicine*]

CAST........... Council for Agricultural Science and Technology (EA)

CAST........... [*The*] Creative and Supportive Trust [*British*] (DI)

CaSTA......... Campionati Sciistici della Truppe Alpini [*Alpini Ski Championships*] [*Italian*]

CASTA .... Candida Albicans Skin Test Antigen [*Immunology*]

CASTA .... Center for Advanced Study in Theatre Arts [*City University of New York*] [*Research center*] (RCD)

CASTA .... Colorado Association of Transit Agencies (SRA)

CASTAFRICA... Conference on the Application of Science and Technology to the Development of Africa

Cas Tak & Adj... Cases Taken and Adjudged [*First Edition of Reports in Chancery*] [*England*] [*A publication*] (DLA)

CASTALA..... Conference on the Application of Science and Technology to the Development of Latin America

Cas Tax ..... Canada Tax Cases, Annotated [*A publication*] (DLA)

Cas T Ch II... Cases Tempore Charles II [*A publication*] (DLA)

CastCk........ Castle & Cooke [*Associated Press*] (SAG)

Cast Com..... Castle's Law of Commerce in Time of War [*A publication*] (DLA)

CASTE......... Civil Aviation Signal Training Establishment (IAA)

CASTE......... Collision Avoidance System Technical Evaluation [*Aviation*] (MCD)

Castech........ Castech Aluminum Group, Inc. [*Associated Press*] (SAG)

Cas Temp F... Cases Tempore Finch, English Chancery [1673-81] [23 English Reprint] [A publication] (DLA)

Cas Temp H... Cases Tempore Hardwicke, English King's Bench [95 English Reprint] [1733-38] [A publication] (DLA)

Cas Temp Hardw... Cases Tempore Hardwicke [A publication] (DLA)

Cas Temp Lee... Cases Tempore Lee (English Ecclesiastical) [A publication] (DLA)

Cas Temp Talb... Cases Tempore Talbot [A publication] (DLA)

CASTEX....... Coordinator ASW [Antisubmarine Warfare] Services and Training (DOMA)

Cas T F....... Cases Tempore Finch, English Chancery [1673-81] [23 English Reprint] [A publication] (DLA)

Cas T Finch (Eng)... Cases Tempore Finch, English Chancery [1673-81] [23 English Reprint] [A publication] (DLA)

CASTFOREM... Combined Arms and Support Task Force Evaluation Model [Army] (RDA)

Cas T Geo I... Cases Tempore George I, English Chancery [8, 9 Modern Reports] [A publication] (DLA)

Cas T H ...... Cases Tempore Hardwicke, English King's Bench (Ridgway, Lee, or Annaly) [1733-38] [A publication] (DLA)

Cas T H ...... Cases Tempore Holt, English King's Bench [A publication] (DLA)

Cas T H ...... West's Chancery Reports Tempore Hardwicke [A publication] (DLA)

Cas T Hard by Lee... Cases Tempore Hardwicke, by Lee [England] [A publication] (DLA)

Cas T Hardw... Cases Tempore Hardwicke, English King's Bench (Ridgway, Lee, or Annaly) [1733-38] [A publication] (DLA)

Cas T Hardw... West's Chancery Reports Tempore Hardwicke [England] [A publication] (DLA)

Cas T Holt ... Cases Tempore Holt, English King's Bench [A publication] (DLA)

CASTI.......... Centers for the Analysis of Science and Technical Information (NITA)

Cas T K .... Moseley's English Chancery Reports Tempore King [A publication] (DLA)

Cas T K .... Select Cases in Chancery Tempore King, Edited by Macnaghten [1724-33] [England] [A publication] (DLA)

Cas T King... Moseley's English Chancery Reports Tempore King [A publication] (DLA)

Cas T King... Select Cases in Chancery Tempore King, Edited by Macnaghten [1724-33] [England] [A publication] (DLA)

CASTL......... Castle

CastlAM...... Castle AM & Co. [Associated Press] (SAG)

CASTLE....... Computer Assisted Student Tutorial Learning Environment (EDAC)

CASTLE....... Computer-Assisted System for Theater Level Engineering [Army] (AABC)

CastleAM..... Castle [A. M.] & Co. [Associated Press] (SAG)

Cas T Lee.... Phillimore's English Ecclesiastical Cases Tempore Lee [A publication] (DLA)

CastleEn ..... Castle Energy Corp. [Associated Press] (SAG)

Cas T Mac... Cases Tempore Macclesfield [10 Modern Reports] [1710-25 England] [A publication] (DLA)

Cas T Maccl... Cases Tempore Macclesfield [10 Modern Reports] [1710-25 England] [A publication] (DLA)

CASTME...... Commonwealth Association of Science, Technology, and Mathematics Educators [London, England] (EAIO)

Cas T Nap .. Drury's Irish Chancery Reports Tempore Napier [1858-59] [A publication] (DLA)

CASTNO...... Cast Number [In urinalysis] [Biochemistry] (DAVI)

Cas T North... Eden's English Chancery Reports Tempore Northington [28 English Reprint] [1757-66] [A publication] (DLA)

CASTOR...... Castoreum [Castor] [Pharmacy] (ROG)

CASTOR...... College Applicant Status Report [Honeywell, Inc.] [Computer science]

CASTOR...... Corps Airborne Stand-Off RADAR (MCD)

Cas T Plunk... Lloyd and Goold's Irish Chancery Reports Tempore Plunkett [A publication] (DLA)

Cas T QA ..... Cases Tempore Queen Anne [11 Modern Reports] [1702-30 England] [A publication] (DLA)

Cas T Q Anne... Cases Tempore Queen Anne [11 Modern Reports] [1702-30 England] [A publication] (DLA)

Cast Rat ...... Castle on Rating [4th ed.] [1903] [A publication] (DLA)

CASTS .... Canal Safe Transit System

CASTS .... Computers for Advanced Space Transportation System (MCD)

CASTS .... Countdown and Status Transmission System [NASA] (KSC)

Cas T Sugd... Cases Tempore Sugden, Irish Chancery [A publication] (DLA)

Cas T Tal.... Cases Tempore Talbot, English Chancery [1734-38] [A publication] (DLA)

Cas T Talb... Cases Tempore Talbot [A publication] (DLA)

CASTWG...... Converging Approach Standards Technical Working Group [FAA] (TAG)

Cas T Wm III... Cases Tempore William III [12 Modern Reports] [A publication] (DLA)

CASU .... Canadian Association of SAS Users (AC)

CASU .... Carrier Aircraft Service Unit [Navy]

CASU .... Combat Aircraft Service Unit [Navy] (MUGU)

CASU(F)...... Combat Aircraft Service Unit (Fleet) [Navy] (DNAB)

CASUM .... Civil Affairs Summary [Navy]

CASUM .... Coalition of Steel-Using Manufacturers

CA Supp ..... California Appellate Reports, Supplement [A publication] (DLA)

CaSVmPCG... Parks Canada, Grasslands National Park, Val Marie, SK, Canada [Library symbol Library of Congress] (LCLS)

CASW .... Canadian Association of Social Workers [See also ACTS]

CASW .... Church Association for Seamen's Work [Later, SCI] (EA)

CASW .... Close Air Support Weapon [Military] (MCD)

CASW .... Council for the Advancement of Science Writing (EA)

CASW .... Counter Anti-Submarine Warfare (PDAA)

CASWAHF.... Canadian Association of Social Work Administrators in Health Facilities [Associations Canadienne des Administrateurs de Services Sociaux en Milieu de Sante] (AC)

CaSWaPCP... Parks Canada, Prince Albert National Park, Waskesiu Lakes, SK, Canada [Library symbol Library of Congress] (LCLS)

Casw Cop .... Caswall. Copyholds [3rd ed.] [1841] [A publication] (DLA)

Cas Wm I ... Bigelow's Cases, William I to Richard I [A publication] (DLA)

CaSWN .... Notre Dame College, Wilcox, SK, Canada [Library symbol Library of Congress] (LCLS)

CASWO........ Confidential and Secret Weekly Orders [Naval Air Stations]

Cas w Op..... Cases with Opinions by Eminent Counsel [1700-75] [A publication] (DLA)

CASWS .... Close Air Support Weapon System [Military] (MCD)

CaSWSE ...... Southeast Regional Library, Weyburn, SK, Canada [Library symbol Library of Congress] (LCLS)

CASX .... Cryderman Air Service [Air carrier designation symbol]

CASY .... Casey's General Stores, Inc. [NASDAQ symbol] (NQ)

CaSYP .... Parkland Regional Library, Yorkton, SK, Canada [Library symbol Library of Congress] (LCLS)

Cat .... Bellum Catilinae [or De Catilinae Coniuratione] [of Sallust] [Classical studies] (OCD)

CAT.............. Cabin Air Temperature [Aviation] (NG)

CAT.............. Cable Avoiding Tool (PDAA)

CAT.............. CADO [Computer Access Device Output] Actions-Terminal (IAA)

CAT.............. California Achievement Test

CAT.............. California Associated Truckers (SRA)

CAT.............. California Association of Tiger-Owners (EA)

CAT.............. Camper Alert Team [for missile sites] [Air Force]

CAT.............. Canadian Anti-Acoustic Torpedo Gear [World War II]

CAT.............. Canadian Army Trophy

CAT.............. Canadian Automotive Trade [A publication]

CAT.............. Canon Auto Tuning [Photography] (OA)

CAT.............. Capacity Activated Transducer [Electronics] (NITA)

CAT.............. Capillary Agglutination Test [Medicine] (DMAA)

CAT.............. Carbon Adsorber Tube (PDAA)

CAT.............. Carburetor Air Temperature [Aviation]

CAT.............. Cartridge Assembly Test (NG)

CAT.............. Cases Temporary [Legal term British]

CAT.............. Catadioptric [Optics]

CAT.............. Catafalque

cat .... Catalan [MARC language code Library of Congress] (LCCP)

CAT.............. Catalan [Language, etc.]

CAT.............. Catalase [Also, CTS] [An enzyme]

CAT.............. Catalog (KSC)

cat .... Catalog (VRA)

cat .... Catalog (WDMC)

CAT.............. Catalonian [Language, etc.] (ROG)

CAT.............. Catalyst (WGA)

cat .... Catamaran (ADA)

CAT.............. Catania [Italy] [Seismograph station code, US Geological Survey] (SEIS)

CAT.............. Cataplasma [Poultice] [Pharmacy]

CAT.............. Catapult (NG)

Cat.............. Cataract [Ophthalmology]

CAT.............. Catechism

CAT.............. Catecholamine [Biochemistry]

Cat.............. Categoriae [of Aristotle] [Classical studies] (OCD)

CAT.............. Category (AFM)

CAT.............. Caterpillar, Inc. [Wall Street slang name: "Cat"] [NYSE symbol] (SPSG)

CAT.............. Cathedral Gold Corp. [Toronto Stock Exchange symbol]

CAT.............. Catholic (ADA)

CAT.............. Cat Island [Bahamas] [Airport symbol] (AD)

CAT.............. Catonsville Community College, Baltimore, MD [OCLC symbol] (OCLC)

CAT.............. Cattle

CAT.............. Caught

CAT.............. Celestial Atomic Trajectile

CAT.............. Center for Advanced Technologies [Focus: HOPE]

CAT.............. Central American Tropical [In CATHOUSES, a reference to temporary US Army barracks in Honduras, 1984]

CAT.............. Centralized Automatic Testing

CAT.............. Centre for Alternative Technology [British] (CB)

CAT.............. Certificado de Abono Tributario [Tax Credit Certificate] [Spanish]

CAT.............. Character Assignment Table [Computer science] (IAA)

CAT.............. Chatham, NJ [Location identifier FAA] (FAAL)

CAT.............. Chemical Addition Tank (NRCH)

CAT.............. Children's Apperception Test [Psychology]

CAT.............. Chloramphenicol Acetyltransferase [An enzyme]

CAT.............. Chlormerodrin Accumulation Test [Medicine] (MAE)

CAT.............. Choline Acetyl Transferase [Also, ChA, ChAc, ChAT] [An enzyme]

CAT.............. Chronic Abdominal Tympany [Medicine] (AAMN)

CAT.............. City Air Terminal (IAA)

CAT.............. Civil Action Team (AFM)

CAT.............. Civil Affairs Team

CAT.............. Civil Air Transport [Free China's international airline]

CAT.............. Civilian Actress Technician [Term for professional actresses who worked under Army Special Services Division in soldier shows] [World War II]

CAT.............. Civilian Air Transport

CAT.............. Classical Analytic Technique

CAT.............. Classical Anaphylatoxin [Immunology]

CAT.............. Classified Anaphylatoxin [Pharmacology] (DAVI)

CAT.............. Clean Air Transport [Commercial firm Sweden]

CAT.............. Clear Air Temperature

CAT............. Clear Air Turbulence [*Aviation*]
CAT............. Clerical Aptitude Test
CAT............. Closest Approach Time (SAA)
CAT............. Cockpit Automation Technology [*Air Force*]
CAT............. Cognitive Abilities Test [*Education*]
CAT............. Collaborative Access Team
CAT............. Collect and Transmit (DNAB)
CAT............. Collective Art Technology
CAT............. College Ability Test
CAT............. College Advanced Technology [*British technical colleges*]
CAT............. College of Art and Technology (AIE)
CAT............. Color Adjusted Transmission [*Optical coating to facilitate use of binoculars in low light*] [*Steiner-Optik of West Germany*]
CAT............. Combat Aircraft Technology
CAT............. Combat Artist Team
CAT............. Combat Assistance Team [*US military advisory team, Vietnam*] (VNW)
CAT............. Combined Acceptance Trials
CAT............. Combined Arms Team (MCD)
CAT............. Command and Triangulation
CAT............. Commander, Amphibious Troops
CAT............. Commercial Air Transport (DA)
CAT............. Committee Against Torture [*See also CCT*] [*Geneva, Switzerland*] (EAIO)
CAT............. Committee of the Associated Trades [*A union*] [*British*]
CAT............. Common Assessment Test [*Education*]
CAT............. Communications Advisory Team (OICC)
CAT............. Communications Assist Team (NVT)
CAT............. Community Action Team [*Department of Labor*]
CAT............. Community Antenna Television [*Later, CTV*] (IAA)
CAT............. Community Arts Teachers [*Australia*]
CAT............. Commuters Air Transport, Inc.
CAT............. Compile and Test (BUR)
CAT............. Complementary Analysis Team [*NASA*] (KSC)
CAT............. Component Acceptance Test (IAA)
CAT............. Compressed Air Tunnel [*British*]
CAT............. Computer Adaptive Testing
CAT............. Computer-Aided Teaching
CAT............. Computer-Aided Technology (MCD)
CAT............. Computer-Aided Test [*Telecommunications*] (TEL)
CAT............. Computer-Aided Testing [*Hoskyns Group Ltd.*] [*Software package*] (NCC)
CAT............. Computer-Aided Tomography (ACRL)
CAT............. Computer-Aided Training (RDA)
CAT............. Computer-Aided Transceiver
CAT............. Computer-Aided Transcription
CAT............. Computer-Aided Translation (IEEE)
CAT............. Computer-Aided Tree (PDAA)
CAT............. Computer-Aided Typesetting (OA)
CAT............. Computer Analysis of Transistors (IAA)
CAT............. Computer Assisted Televideo [*Commercial firm*] [*Netherlands*] (NITA)
CAT............. Computer-Assisted Testing (BUR)
CAT............. Computer-Assisted Tomography
CAT............. Computer-Assisted Training
CAT............. Computerized Axial Tomography [*Also, CAAT, CT*] [*Usually used in combination, as CATscan*] [*Roentgenography*]
CAT............. Computer of Average Transients [*Spectroscopy*]
cat............. Concatenate (CDE)
CAT............. Concerned about Trident [*Ecology group*]
CAT............. Conditionally Accepted Tag (NRCH)
CAT............. Configuration Accountability Transmittal
CAT............. Configuration Analysis Tool (MCD)
CAT............. Configuration and Traceability (KSC)
CAT............. Consolidated Atomic Time
CAT............. Construction Appraisal Team (NRCH)
CAT............. Contacts, Activities, Time [*Computer science*]
CAT............. Container Anchorage Terminal (NVT)
CAT............. Contractor Acceptance Test (AABC)
CAT............. Control and Assessment Team [*Military*] (GFGA)
CAT............. Control Attenuator Timer (KSC)
CAT............. Controlled Avalanche Transistor (IAA)
CAT............. Conventional Arms Transfers
CAT............. Converted Aerial Targets (NG)
CAT............. Cooled-Anode Transmitting (DEN)
CAT............. Copenhagen Airtaxi [*Denmark ICAO designator*] (FAAC)
CAT............. Copper Alloy Tubing
CAT............. Cosmic Anisotropy Telescope
CAT............. Counter-Assault Tactical [*In television movie "C.A.T. Squad"*]
CAT............. Courseware Authoring Tools [*Stanford University computer software project*]
CAT............. Crack Arrest Temperature [*Nuclear energy*] (NRCH)
CAT............. Craft-Access Terminal [*Computer science*]
CAT............. Credit Authorization Terminal
CAT............. Crisis Action Team (MCD)
CAT............. Cumulative Abbreviated Trouble File [*Telecommunications*] (TEL)
CAT............. Current Adjusting Type
CAT............. Curriculum Analysis Taxonomy [*Education*] (AIE)
CAT............. Customer Activated Terminal
CAT............. Cytosine Arabinoside [*ara-C*], Adriamycin, Thioguanine [*Antineoplastic drug regimen*]
CAT............. Cytosine Arabinoside and Thioguanine [*Antineoplastic drug regimen*] (DAVI)
Cat............. In Catilinam [*of Cicero*] [*Classical studies*] (OCD)
CATA............. California Agricultural Teachers Association (SRA)

CATA...: Canadian Advanced Technology Association [*Association Canadienne de Technologie de Pointe*] (AC)
CATA Canadian Advanced Technology Association [*Ottawa, ON*] [*Telecommunications service*]
CATA Canadian Air Transportation Administration
CATA Canadian Art Therapy Association-Eastern Chapter (AC)
CATA Canadian Athletic Therapists Association
CATA Capitol Transamerica [*NASDAQ symbol*] (TTSB)
CATA Capitol Transamerica Corp. [*NASDAQ symbol*] (NQ)
CATA Catalog
CATA Catalytic [*Automotive engineering*]
CATA Center for Atmospheric Theory and Analysis [*Research center*] (RCD)
CAT-A Children's Apperception Test [*Child development test*] [*Psychology*]
CATA Civil Air Training Academy [*Australia*]
CATA Combined Arms Training Activity [*Fort Leavenworth, KS*] (INF)
CATA Commonwealth Association of Tax Administrators [*British*] (EAIO)
CATA Community Antenna Television Association (EA)
CATA Computer-Aided Travel Assistant
CATA Computer-Assisted Test Assembly [*Microcomputer program*]
CATA Connecticut Automotive Trades Association (SRA)
CA/TA Cortical Area/Total Area (Ratio)
CATA Cushion Air Tread Articulate [*Vehicle*] [*Army*]
CATAB Centre d'Analyse et de Traitement Automatique de la Bible [*Centre of Analysis and Automatic Treatment of the Bible*]
CATAC Commandement Aerien Tactique [*French Tactical Air Command*]
CAtaGS San Luis Obispo County Genealogical Society, Atascadero, CA [*Library symbol*] [*Library of Congress*] (LCLS)
CAtaH Atascadero State Hospital, Atascadero, CA [*Library symbol Library of Congress*] (LCLS)
Cata ILt Catalina Lighting [*Associated Press*] (SAG)
CAT-A-KIT Catecholamines Radioenzymic Assay Kit [*Clinical chemistry*] [*Acronym is trademark*]
Catal Catalepton [*of Vergil*] [*Classical studies*] (OCD)
CATAL Catalog (ROG)
CatalSem Catalyst Semiconductor, Inc. [*Associated Press*] (SAG)
Catalyst Catalyst International, Inc. [*Associated Press*] (SAG)
CATALYST Computer-Assisted Teaching and Learning System (PDAA)
Catalyt Catalytica, Inc. [*Associated Press*] (SAG)
CATAM Computer Aided Teaching of Applied Mathematics [*Cambridge University, England*] (EDAC)
CATAPL Cataplasma [*Poultice*] [*Pharmacy*] (ROG)
Catapl Cataplus [*of Lucian*] [*Classical studies*] (OCD)
CATAPLAS Cataplasma [*Poultice*] [*Pharmacy*] (ROG)
CATAPLSM Cataplasma [*Poultice*] [*Pharmacy*]
CATARAC Central Area Training Aboriginal Resource Accounting Committee [*Australia*]
CATAS Center for Accelerator Technology and Applied Sciences [*University of Texas at Arlington*] [*Research center*] (RCD)
CATAZINE Catalogue Magazine
CATB Canadian Air Transport Board
CATB Catalase B (DMAA)
CATB Catskill Financial [*NASDAQ symbol*] (TTSB)
CATB Coast Artillery Training Battalion
CATB Combined Arms Training Board [*Military*]
CATC Canadian Air Transport Command (MUGU)
CATC Canadian Association of Token Collectors
CATC Carrier Air Traffic Controller (MCD)
CATC Circular-Arc-Toothed Cylindrical (PDAA)
CATC Civil Affairs Training Center [*World War II*]
CATC Coast Artillery Training Centre [*British military*] (DMA)
CATC Combat Air Traffic Controller [*Air Force*] (VNW)
CATC Combined Arms Training Center [*Army*]
CATC Commonwealth Air Transport Council [*British*] (EAIO)
CATC Computer Access Technology Corp. (PCM)
CATC Computer-Assisted Test Construction (EDAC)
CATC Confederation of All Type Canaries [*Defunct*] (EA)
CATC Continental Oil, Atlantic Refining, Tidewater Oil, and Cities Service [*Group of companies joined together for mutual drilling ventures*]
CATCA Canadian Air Traffic Control Association
CATCALL Completely Automated Technique for Cataloguing and Acquisition of Literature forLibraries (NITA)
CATCC Canadian Association of Textile Colourists and Chemists (HGAA)
CATCC Carrier Air Traffic Control Center [*Navy*]
CATCC Carrier Air Traffic Control Center [*Navy*] (DOMA)
CATCC-DAIR Carrier Air Traffic Control Center - Direct Altitude Identity Readout [*Navy*] (MCD)
CATCH Canadian Association of Teachers of Community Health [*Association Canadienne des Professeurs de Sante Communautaire*] (AC)
CATCH Character Allocated Transfer Channel [*Computer science*] (IAA)
CATCH Citizens Against the Concorde Here
CATCH Community Action to Control High Blood Pressure [*HEW*]
CATCH Computer Analysis of Thermochemical Data Tables [*University of Sussex*] [*Sussex, England*]
CATCH Countering Attack Helicopter (MCD)
Ca T Ch 2 Cases Tempore Charles 2 [*A publication*] (DLA)
CATCH-22 Cardiac Defects, Abnormal Facies, Thymic Hypoplasia, Cleft Palate, and Hypocalcemia from Deletions in Chromosome 22 [*Medical syndrome*]
CATCO Carrier Air Traffic Control Officer [*Navy*]
CATCO Catalytic Construction Co.
CATCO CSM [*Command and Service Module*] and ATM Communications Specialist [*Apollo Telescope Mount*] [*NASA*]
CATCUSAF Commander, Amphibious Training Command, United States Atlantic Fleet

CATD	Cold Air Turbine Drive (MCD)
CATD	Combined Arms and Tactics Department [*Military*] (INF)
CATD	Cooperative Association of Tractor Dealers (EA)
CATDO	Chief Airways Technical District Office
CATDS	Commission of Accredited Truck Driving Schools (EA)
CATE	Canadian Achievement Test in English [*Education*] (AEBS)
CATE	Canadian Association for Teacher Education (AC)
CATE	Centre for Advanced Technology Education [*Ryerson Polytechnical Institute*] [*Canada Research center*] (RCD)
CATE	Citizens for Alternatives to Trident and ELF [*Extremely Low Frequency System*] [*Defunct*] (EA)
CATE	Commercial, Automatic Test System [*Military*]
CATE	Computer-Aided Test Equipment (MSA)
CATE	Computer-Controlled Automatic Test Equipment
CATE	Council for the Accreditation of Teacher Education (AIE)
CATE	Current ARDC [*Air Research and Development Command*] Technical Efforts [*DoD program*]
CATEG	Category
CAT-EIS	Center of Advanced Technology in Electronic Imaging Systems [*New York State Science and Technology Foundation*] (RDA)
Catelu	Catellus Development Corp. [*Associated Press*] (SAG)
Catelus	Catellus Development Corp. [*Associated Press*] (SAG)
CATEM	Cost Analysis Technical Manual
Ca Temp F...	Cases Tempore Finch, English Chancery [*1673-81*] [*23 English Reprint*] [*A publication*] (DLA)
Ca Temp H...	Cases Tempore Hardwicke, English King's Bench [*95 English Reprint*] [*1733-38*] [*A publication*] (DLA)
Ca Temp Hard...	Cases Tempore Hardwicke, English King's Bench [*95 English Reprint*] [*1733-38*] [*A publication*] (DLA)
Ca Temp Holt...	Cases Tempore Holt, English King's Bench [*A publication*] (DLA)
Ca Temp K...	Cases in Chancery Tempore King, King's Bench [*1724-33*] [*England*] [*A publication*] (DLA)
Ca Temp King...	Cases in Chancery Tempore King [*25 English Reprint*] [*1724-33*] [*A publication*] (DLA)
Ca Temp Talb...	Cases in Chancery Tempore Talbot, King's Bench [*1734-38*] [*England*] [*A publication*] (DLA)
Ca Temp Talbot...	Cases Tempore Talbot [*A publication*] (DLA)
Caterp..........	Caterpillar, Inc. [*Wall Street slang name: "Cat"*] [*Associated Press*] (SAG)
Cates	Cates' Reports [*109-127 Tennessee*] [*A publication*] (DLA)
CATES	Centralized Automatic Test System [*Navy*] (MCD)
CATES	Computer-Aided Training Evaluation and Scheduling (MCD)
CATESOL	California Association of Teachers of English to Speakers of Other Languages (EDAC)
CATF..........	Canadian Achievement Test in French [*Education*] (AEBS)
CATF..........	Central America Task Force (EA)
CATF..........	Chinese Air Task Force
CATF..........	Combined Amphibious Task Force (NVT)
CATF..........	Commander, Amphibious Task Force (NVT)
CATF	Cost Analysis Task Force [*NASA*] (KSC)
Ca T F	Finch's English Chancery Reports [*1673-81*] [*A publication*] (DLA)
CATFAE	Catapult Launched Fuel Air Expendable Round (DWSG)
Cat Fan........	Cat Fancy [*A publication*] (BRI)
CATFO	Chief Airways Technical Field Office
CATG	Commander, Amphibious Task Group (DNAB)
CATGEN	Computer-Aided Test Generator (PDAA)
Ca TH	Cases Tempore Hardwicke, English King's Bench [*95 English Reprint*] [*1733-38*] [*A publication*] (DLA)
Ca TH	Cases Tempore Holt [*11 Modern Reports*] [*88 English Reprint 1702-10*] [*A publication*] (DLA)
CATH	Cathartic [*Pharmacy*]
CATH	Cathedral
cath	Cathedral (VRA)
Cath...........	[*St.*] Catherine's College [*Oxford University*] (BARN)
CATH	Catherines Stores [*NASDAQ symbol*] (TTSB)
CATH	Catherines Stores Corp. [*NASDAQ symbol*] (SPSG)
CATH	Catheter [*Medicine*]
CATH	Catheterization [*or Catheterize*] [*Cardiology and urology*] (DAVI)
CATH	Cathode (MSA)
CATH	Catholic
CATH	Catholic
CAT-H	Children's Apperception Test - Human Figures [*Child development test*] [*Psychology*]
CATH	Common Anti-Tank Helicopter (MCD)
Ca T Hard....	Cases Tempore Hardwicke, English King's Bench [*95 English Reprint*] [*1733-38*] [*A publication*] (DLA)
CATHART	Cathartica [*Cathartic*] [*Pharmacy*] (ROG)
CathBcp	Cathay Bancorp, Inc. [*Associated Press*] (SAG)
CATHDRL	Cathedral
CathEp	Catholic Epistles (BJA)
CATHFOL	Cathode Follower (IAA)
CATHL	Cathedral
CathMC	Catholic Microfilm Center, Berkeley, CA [*Library symbol Library of Congress Obsolete*] (LCLS)
CATHOL	Catholic
Catholic U ...	[*The*] Catholic University of America (GAGS)
Catholic U of PR...	Catholic University of Puerto Rico (GAGS)
Catholic Wkly...	Catholic Weekly [*A publication*]
Ca T Holt.....	Cases Tempore Holt [*11 Modern Reports*] [*88 English Reprint 1702-10*] [*A publication*] (DLA)
CathStr	Catherines Stores Corp. [*Associated Press*] (SAG)
Cath W	Catholic World [*A publication*] (BRI)
CATI............	Colorado Advanced Technology Institute
CATI............	Computer-Aided Technical Illustration (MCD)
CATI............	Computer-Assisted Telephone Inquiry

CATI............	Computer-Assisted Telephone Interviewing
CATIA..........	Central Australian Tourism Industry Association
CATIA..........	Charlottetown Area Tourism Industry Association (AC)
CATIA..........	Computer-Assisted Three-Dimensional Interactive Application (ACRL)
CATIA..........	Computer-Graphics Aided Three-Dimensional Interactive Application System [*IBM Corp.*]
CATIE..........	Centro Agronomico Tropical Investigacion y Ensenanza [*Tropical Agricultural Research and Training Center*] [*Turrialba, Costa Rica*] (EAIO)
CATIE..........	Community AIDS Treatment Information Exchange [*Reseau Communautaire d'Infotraitement SIDA*] (AC)
CATIE..........	Computer Aided Three [*Dimensional*] Interactive Application
CATIES........	Combined Arms Training Integrated Evaluation System [*Military*]
CATIES........	Common Aperture Technique for Imaging Electro-Optical Sensors (MCD)
CATIS..........	Computer-Aided Tactical Information System (IEEE)
CATIS..........	Computer-Assisted Tactical Intelligence System (MCD)
CATITB........	Civil Air Transport Industry Training Board (MCD)
CATIWAR......	Combat Attrition and Intensity of War (MCD)
Ca TK	Cases Tempore King, Chancery [*A publication*] (DLA)
CATK..........	Counterattack (AABC)
Ca T King ...	Cases Tempore King, Chancery [*A publication*] (DLA)
CATL..........	Canadian Association of Toy Libraries and Parent Resource Centers (EAIO)
CATLA.........	Catholic Library Association
CATLAS.......	Centralized Automatic Trouble-Locating and Analysis System [*AT & T*] (TEL)
CATLC.........	California Association of Thrift and Loan Companies (SRA)
Ca T Lee......	Cases Tempore Lee [*1752-58*] [*A publication*] (DLA)
Catleman	Cattlemans, Inc. [*Associated Press*] (SAG)
CATLG........	Catalog (BUR)
CATLG........	Catalog
CATLHD	Cattle Hide
CATLINE	Catalog On-Line [*National Library of Medicine*] [*Bibliographic database*]
Cat Lit Pap...	Catalogue of the Literary Papyri in the British Museum [*A publication*] (OCD)
CATM..........	Canadian Achievement Test in Mathematics [*Education*] (AEBS)
CATM..........	Captive Airborne Training Missile (DOMA)
CATM..........	Computer-Aided Technical Management (DOMA)
CATM..........	Consolidated Air Tour Manual [*Air travel term*]
Ca T Mac	Cases in Law and Equity [*10 Modern Reports*] [*A publication*] (DLA)
Cat Mai	Cato Maior [*of Plutarch*] [*Classical studies*] (OCD)
CATMAT......	Computer-Assisted Terrain Mobility Analysis Techniques (MCD)
CATMDV	Catamaran Mine Disposal System (MCD)
Cat Min.......	Cato Minor [*of Plutarch*] [*Classical studies*] (OCD)
CatMkt	Catalina Marketing Corp. [*Associated Press*] (SAG)
CATMN	Consolidated Air Target Material Notices [*NOO*]
Ca T N	Eden's English Chancery Reports Tempore Northington [*28 English Reprint*] [*1757-66*] [*A publication*] (DLA)
Ca T Nap	Drury's Irish Chancery Reports Tempore Napier [*1858-59*] [*A publication*] (DLA)
CATNI.........	Catchword and Trade Name Index [*A publication*]
CATNIP	Computer-Assisted Technique for Numerical Indexing Purposes
Ca T North...	Eden's English Chancery Reports Tempore Northington [*28 English Reprint*] [*1757-66*] [*A publication*] (DLA)
CATNYP	Catalog of the New York Public Library
CATO	Canadian Association for the Treatment of Offenders
CATO	Catapult-Assisted Takeoff
CATO	Catoctin Mountain Park [*National Park Service designation*]
CATO	Civil Air Traffic Operations (AIA)
CATO	Compiler for Automatic Teaching Operation (IEEE)
CATO	Computer for Automatic Teaching Operations (DNAB)
CATOC........	Carrier Air Traffic Control
CATOCOMP...	Computer for Automatic Teaching Operations-Compiler (DNAB)
CatoCp	Cato Corp. [*Associated Press*] (SAG)
CaTOHOR	Ontario Hydro, Central Records, Toronto, ON, Canada [*Library symbol Library of Congress*] (LCLS)
CATOR........	Chemical Abuse Addiction Treatment Outcome Registry
CATOR........	Combined Air Transport Operations Room [*Allied office, World War II*]
CATOR........	Comprehensive Assessment of Treatment Outcome Research (BARN)
CATORES.....	Computer for Automatic Teaching Operations-Resident (DNAB)
CAT-OX.......	Catalytic Oxidation
CATP..........	Cambridge Technology Partners [*NASDAQ symbol*] (SAG)
CATP..........	Cambridge Technology Ptnrs [*NASDAQ symbol*] (TTSB)
CATP..........	Classified Area Term Pass (AAG)
CATP..........	Computer-Aided Text Processing (IAA)
CATP..........	Computer-Aided Typesetting Process
CATPA	Connecticut Association of Third Party Administrators (SRA)
CATPASS	Computer-Aided Telephony Performance Assessment (PDAA)
CATPCE.......	Comite d'Action des Transports Publics des Communautes Europeennes [*Action Committee of Public Transport of the European Communities - ACPTEC*] (EAIO)
Ca T Plunk...	Cases in Chancery Tempore Plunkett [*1834-39*] [*Ireland*] [*A publication*] (DLA)
CATQ	Conseil des Arts Textiles du Quebec (AC)
Ca T QA	Cases Tempore Holt [*11 Modern Reports*] [*88 English Reprint 1702-10*] [*A publication*] (DLA)
CATR	Caterer
CATR	Central Air Transport
CATRA	Combined Aircraft Transfer and Release Assembly (MCD)
CATRA	Cutlery and Allied Trades Research Association [*British*] (IRUK)

CATRADA..... Combined Arms Training Developments Activity [or Agency] [Army] (RDA)
CATRADAR... Combined Acquisition and Tracking RADAR [NASA] (MCD)
CATRALA ..... Car and Truck Renting and Leasing Association (EA)
CATS.......... Care about the Strays (EA)
CATS.......... Catalog Access System [Project for automated library systems]
CATS.......... Catalyst Semiconductor [NASDAQ symbol] (TTSB)
CATS.......... Catalyst Semiconductor, Inc. [NASDAQ symbol] (SAG)
CATS.......... Category Switch [Electronics] (IAA)
CATS.......... CATS Software, Inc. [Associated Press] (SAG)
CATS.......... Center for Advanced Television Studies [British] (NTCM)
CATS.......... Center for Applied Thermodynamic Studies [University of Idaho] [Research center] (RCD)
CATS.......... Centralized Automatic Test System [Navy] (MCD)
CATS.......... Certificate of Accrual on Treasury Securities [Salomon Brothers] [Finance]
CATS.......... Chicago Area Transportation Study
CAT-S .... Children's Apperception Test - Supplement [Child development test] [Psychology]
CATS.......... Citizens Against Tobacco Smoke (EA)
CATS.......... Citizens for an Alternative Tax System (EA)
CATS.......... Civic Action Team [Navy] (VNW)
CATS.......... Civil Affairs Training School [Navy]
CATS.......... Coded-Access Teleconferencing System [Telecommunications]
CATS.......... Coherent Acoustic Torpedo System (MCD)
CATS.......... Combined Arms Training Strategy [Army] (DOMA)
CATS.......... Common Assessment Tasks
CATS.......... Communications and Tracking System [or Subsystem]
CATS.......... Comprehensive Analytical Test System
CATS.......... Compute Air-Trans Systems, Inc.
CATS.......... Computer-Accessed [or-Aided] Telemetry System
CATS.......... Computer-Aided Teaching System (IEEE)
CATS.......... Computer-Aided Time Standard (PDAA)
CATS.......... Computer Aided Trading System
CATS.......... Computer-Aided Training System
CATS.......... Computer-Aided Troubleshooting
CATS.......... Computer-Assisted Test Shop
CATS.......... Computer-Assisted Trading System [American Meat Exchange, Inc.] [Information service or system]
CATS.......... Computer-Assisted Training System [IRS]
CATS.......... Computer-Automated Test System [AT & T]
CATS.......... Computer-Automated Transit Systems
CATS.......... Consortium for Assessment and Testing in Schools (AIE)
CATS.......... Conventional and Alternative Transportation Systems Laboratory [University of Florida] [Research center] (RCD)
CATS.......... Corrective Action Tracking System [Environmental Protection Agency] (GFGA)
CATS.......... Cost Assignment to Telecommunication Services [Telecommunications]
CATS.......... Courier and Transport Service Ltd. [British]
CATS.......... Criteria of Teacher Selection [Project] (AIE)
CATSA......... Confectionery and Allied Trades Sports Association [British] (BI)
CATSCAN...... Computer-Assisted Tomography Scanner [Radiology] (DAVI)
CATscan ...... Computerized Axial Tomography Scanner [Roentgenography]
CATSS .... California Association of Temporary and Staffing Services (SRA)
CATSS .... Catalog Support System [UTLAS International Canada] [Information service or system]
CATSS .... Communication Analysis Tool for Space Station (MCD)
Ca T Sugd ... Drury's Irish Chancery Reports Tempore Sugden [A publication] (DLA)
CATT.......... Calcium Tolerance Test [Medicine] (DMAA)
CATT.......... Card Agglutination Trypanosomiasis Test [Clinical chemistry]
CATT.......... Center for Advanced Technology in Telecommunications [Polytechnic Institute of New York] [Brooklyn] [Telecommunications service] (TSSD)
CATT.......... Centralized Automatic Toll Ticketing [Telecommunications] (TEL)
CATT.......... Ceramic Audio Tone Transducer (PDAA)
CATT.......... Colorado Advanced Technology Institute
CATT.......... Combined Arms Tactical Trainer [Army] (RDA)
CATT.......... Combined Army Tactical Training [System] (DOMA)
CATT.......... Consumers' Association of Trinidad and Tobago
CATT.......... Controlled Avalanche Transit Time [Electronics]
CATT.......... Conveyorized Automatic Tube Tester [Computer science]
CATT.......... Cooled-Anode Transmitting Tube
Ca T Talb..... Cases Tempore Talbot, English Chancery [1734-38] [A publication] (DLA)
CATTB......... Component Advanced Technology Test Bed [US Army Tank-Automotive Command] (RDA)
CATTCM....... Canadian Achievement Test in Technical and Commercial Mathematics [Education] (AEBS)
CATTS .... Combined Arms Tactical Training Simulator [Army] (MCD)
CATTS .... Committee on Advanced Television Transmission Systems [Australia]
CATTT .... Curriculum Assessment and Teacher/Trainer Training
CATTw........ Canadian Association of Teachers of Technical Writing
C Atty .... [The] Complete Attorney [A publication] (DLA)
CATU.......... Ceramic and Allied Trade Union [British] (DCTA)
CATU.......... Combat Aircrew Training Unit [Navy]
CATU.......... Confederation of Arab Trade Unions
Catull......... Catullus [First century BC] [Classical studies] (OCD)
CATV.......... Cabin Air Temperature Valve [Aviation]
CATV.......... Cable Antenna Television (IAA)
CATV.......... Cable Television [Later, CTV]
CATV.......... Canadian All-Terrain Vehicle Distributors Council [Conseil Canadien des Distributeurs de Vehicules Tout Terrain] (AC)
CATV.......... Community Access Television (WDAA)

CATV.......... Community Antenna Television [Later, CTV]
CATV.......... Community Antenna Television [Also, cable television] (WDMC)
CATV.......... Cooled-Anode Transmitting Valve (IAA)
CATVA......... Computer-Assisted Total Value Assessment [Army] (MCD)
CATVCMA .... Cable Television Cable Makers Association (PDAA)
CATVCMA .... Cable Television Cable Makers Association [British] (NITA)
CATVS .... Community Antenna Television System (IAA)
CATW.......... Catwalk [Technical drawings] (DAC)
Ca T Wm 3.. Cases Tempore William 3 [12 Modern Reports] [A publication] (DLA)
CATX.......... C.ATS Software [NASDAQ symbol] (TTSB)
CATX.......... CATS Software, Inc. [NASDAQ symbol] (SAG)
CA TX .... Civil Appeals, Texas [A publication] (DLA)
CATX.......... Climb and Cross [Aviation] (FAAC)
CATY.......... Cathay Bancorp [NASDAQ symbol] (TTSB)
CATY.......... Cathay Bancorp, Inc. [NASDAQ symbol] (SAG)
cau............. California [MARC country of publication code Library of Congress] (LCCP)
CA U .... California Unreported Cases [1855-1910] [A publication] (DLA)
CAU .... Cancun Avioturismo SA [Mexico ICAO designator] (FAAC)
CAU .... Canyon Resources [AMEX symbol] (SAG)
CAU .... Capital University, Columbus, OH [OCLC symbol] (OCLC)
CAU .... Carbon Absorption Unit (GFGA)
CAU .... Cassia Petroleum [Vancouver Stock Exchange symbol]
cau............. Caucasian [MARC language code Library of Congress] (LCCP)
CAU .... Caucasian (AFM)
CAU .... Civil Affairs Unit [British]
CAU .... Coarse Alignment Unit
CAU .... Command Acquisition Unit (NASA)
CAU .... Command Activation Unit (MCD)
CAU .... Command Arithmetic Unit
CAU .... Compare Alphabetic Unequal [Computer science] (OA)
CAU .... Congress of American Unions
CAU .... Consolidated Undrained Shear with Pore Pressure Measurement [Nuclear energy] (NUCP)
CAU .... Controlled Access Unit [Computer science]
CAU .... Controller Adaptor Unit [Computer science] (NITA)
CAU .... Converter Amplifier Unit (MCD)
CAU .... Counter Accelerometer Unit (MCD)
CAU .... Course Alignment Unit
CAU .... Cryptoancillary Unit (AABC)
CAU .... Customer Acquisition Unit (NASA)
CAUBO .... Canadian Association of University Business Officers
CAUC .... Calculated Area under the Curve [Statistics]
Cauc .... Caucasian (MAE)
CAUC .... Cumulative Average Unit Cost
CAUCE .... Canadian Association for University Continuing Education
CAUCE .... Coalition Against Unsolicited Commercial Email [An association] [Computer science]
CAUD .... Caudal [Anatomy] (DAVI)
CAuD .... DeWitt State Hospital, Auburn, CA [Library symbol Library of Congress] (LCLS)
CAUDAR...... Computer-Assisted Unit Data Acquisition/Reduction (PDAA)
CAUEOI....... Caucasian Except as Otherwise Indicated [Army]
CAUFN........ Caution Advised Until Further Notice [Aviation] (FAAC)
CAUIS .... Computer-Automated Ultrasonic Inspecting Systems (MCD)
CAULI .... Cauliflower (DSUE)
CAUML....... Computers and Automation Universal Mailing List (IEEE)
CAUN .... Cuban Association for the United Nations (EAIO)
CAuN .... Native Sons of the Golden West, Auburn Parlor, Auburn, CA [Library symbol Library of Congress] (LCLS)
CAuP.......... Auburn-Placer County Library, Auburn, CA [Library symbol Library of Congress] (LCLS)
CAUPR........ Center for Architecture and Urban Planning Research [University of Wisconsin - Milwaukee] [Research center] (RCD)
CAURA........ Canadian Association of University Research Administrators [See also ACARU]
CAUS .... Causation
Caus .... Causative (BJA)
CAUS .... Citizens Against UFO [Unidentified Flying Object] Secrecy (EA)
CAUS .... Color Association of the United States (EA)
CAUS .... Computer-Automated Ultrasonic System (MCD)
CAUSE .... California Union of Safety Employees (SRA)
CAUSE .... College and University Systems Exchange [Acronym is now used as name of association]
CAUSE .... Comprehensive Assistance to Undergraduate Science Education [National Science Foundation]
CAUSE .... Computer-Assisted Utility System Evaluation (MCD)
CAUSE .... Counselor Advisor University Summer Education [Department of Labor program]
CAUSEWAY... Causeway [Commonly used] (OPSA)
CAUSM....... Canadian Association of University Schools of Music
CAUSN........ Canadian Association of University Schools of Nursing [See also ACEUN]
Caus Pl....... De Causis Plantarum [of Theophrastus] [Classical studies] (OCD)
CAUSPS....... Canadian Association of University Student Personnel Services
CAUSR........ Canadian Association of University Schools of Rehabilitation (AC)
CAUSWAY.... Causeway [Commonly used] (OPSA)
CAUT .... Canadian Association of University Teachers
caut .... Cauterization [Medicine] (DMAA)
CAUT .... Cauterize [or Cauterization] (CPH)
CAUT .... Caution (IAA)
CAUTG .... Canadian Association of University Teachers of German
C Auth .... Civil Authorities [Army]
CAUTION..... Citizens Against Unneccessary Tax Increases and Other Nonsense [St. Louis organization]

CAUTRA....... Coordinateur Automatique de Traffic
CAV............ Calm Air [Canada ICAO designator] (FAAC)
CAV............ Cambodian Association of Victoria [Australia]
CAV............ Canine Adenovirus [Veterinary medicine]
CAV............ Capital University, Law Library, Columbus, OH [OCLC symbol] (OCLC)
CAV............ Cavalier [Knight title]
CAV............ Cavalier Homes [NYSE symbol] (TTSB)
CAV............ Cavalier Homes Co. [NYSE symbol] (SAG)
CAV............ Cavalry
CAV............ Cavan [County in Ireland] (ROG)
CAV............ Caveat [Let Him Beware] [A judicial writ] [Latin Legal term]
CAV............ Cavern (ROG)
CAV............ Cavitation
cav............ Cavity [Dentistry] (DAVI)
CAV............ Cavity (MSA)
CAV............ Chinese Association of Victoria [Australia]
CAV............ Clarion, IA [Location identifier FAA] (FAAL)
CAV............ Classical Association of Victoria [Australia]
CAV............ Commando Association, Victoria [Australia]
CAV............ Component Analog Video (NTCM)
CAV............ Composite Analog Video
CAV............ Composite Armored Vehicle [Army] (RDA)
CAV............ Congenital Absence of Vagina [Medicine]
CAV............ Congenital Adrenal Virilism [Medicine]
CAV............ Constant Angular Velocity [Videodisk format]
CAV............ Construction Assistance Vehicle [Navy] (MCD)
CAV............ Continuous Airworthiness Visit
CAV............ Coordinate, Anticipate, and Verify (MCD)
CAV............ Credit Account Voucher (DCTA)
CAV............ Crotalus Adamanteus Venom
CAV............ Curia Advisari Vult [The Court Wishes to Consider] [Latin Legal term]
CAV............ Cyclophosphamide, Adriamycin [Doxorubicin], Vincristine [Antineoplastic drug regimen]
CAV............ Czechoslovak Association of Victoria [Australia]
CAVALCADE... Calibrating, Amplitude-Variation, and Level-Correcting Analog-Digital Equipment (DEN)
CAVALIER.... Cooperatively Assembled Virginia Low Intensity Educational Reactor (NRCH)
CAVALIR...... Catalog of Virginia Library Resources (EDAC)
CavalIrH...... Cavalier Homes Co. [Associated Press] (SAG)
CavalrH....... Cavalier Homes [Associated Press] (SAG)
CAVAMP-V... Centralized Asset Visibility and Management Program for Vietnam [Army] (RDA)
CAVAT .... Carrow Auditory-Visual Abilities Test
CAV ATD...... Composite Armored Vehicle Advanced Technology Demonstrator (RDA)
CAVB .... Canadian Association of Volunteer Bureaux Centres (AC)
CAVB .... Complete Atrioventricular Block [Medicine] (DMAA)
CAVC .... Canadian Army Veterinary Corps (DMA)
CAVC .... Common Arterioventricular Canal [Cardiology] (DAVI)
Cavco......... Cavco Industries, Inc. [Associated Press] (SAG)
CAVCO .... Consolidated Audio-Visual Coordinating Office [Military] (DNAB)
CAVCTS ...... Combined Acceleration Vibration Climatic Test System
CAVD .... Completion, Arithmetic, Vocabulary, Directions [Psychology]
CAVDA .... Citizens Alliance for VD [Venereal Disease] Awareness (EA)
Cav Deb...... Cavendish's Debates, House of Commons [A publication] (DLA)
Cav Deb Can... Cavender's Debates on Canada [A publication] (DLA)
CAVE........... Catholic Audio-Visual Educators Association (EA)
CAVE........... Cave Automatic Virtual Environment [Virtual reality]
CAVe........... CCNU [Lomustine], Adriamycin, Vinblastine [Antineoplastic drug regimen]
CAVE........... Company Average VOC [Volatile Organic Compound] Emission [Environmental Protection Agency]
CAVE........... Computer Aided Design for VLSI [Very Large Scale Integration] in Europe [British]
CAVE........... Computer Assisted Virtual Environment
CAVE........... Computer Augmented Video Education [US Naval Academy] (NITA)
CAVE........... Computer Automatic Virtual Environment [Virtual reality system] (CDE)
CAVE........... Conduction Analysis via Eigenvalues [NASA] (MCD)
CAVE........... Consolidated Aquanauts Vital Equipment
CAVEAT....... Code and Visual Entry Authorization Technique [Closed-circuit TV] (MCD)
CAVEAT....... Coronary Angioplasty Versus Excisional Atherectomy Trial [Cardiology study]
Caveat Emptor... Caveat Emptor Consumer Report [A publication] (AAGC)
CAVEWA ...... Canadian Association for Vocational Evaluation & Work Adjustment [Association Canadienne des Evaluateur de Capacites de Travail] (AC)
CAVF........... Coronary Arteriovenous Fistula [Cardiology]
CAVG .... Coronary Artery Vein Graft [Medicine] (DMAA)
CAVH .... Continuous Arteriovenous Hemofiltration [Medicine]
CAVHD .... Continuous Arteriovenous Hemodialysis [Medicine] (DMAA)
CaVIC......... Canadian Volunteers in Corrections Training Project
CAV-ID....... Computer-Aided Victim Identification [Computer software]
Cav Mon Sec... Cavanagh's Law of Money Securities [A publication] (DLA)
CAVMV....... Cassava Vein Mosaic Virus [Plant pathology]
CAVNAV...... Combat Air Vehicle Navigation and Vision
CAVNAVS.... Cavalry Navigation System (MCD)
CAVO......... Common Atrioventricular Orifice [Medicine] (DMAA)
C(a-v)O₂...... Arteriovenous Oxygen Content Difference [Medicine] (DAVI)
CAVOK....... Cloud and Visibility Okay [NWS] (FAAC)
CAVORT...... Coherent Acceleration and Velocity Observations in Real Time
CAVP .... Census of Australian Vascular Plants

CAVP .... Complex Arithmetic Vector Processor (RDA)
CAVP .... Cyclophosphamide, Adriamycin, VM-26, Prednisone [Antineoplastic drug regimen] (DAVI)
CAVP-I........ Cyclophosphamide, Adriamycin, Vincristine, Prednisone [Antineoplastic drug regimen] (DAVI)
CAVPM........ Cyclophosphamide, Adriamycin, VP-16, Prednisone, Methotrexate [Antineoplastic drug regimen] (DAVI)
CAVR .... Carver Corp. [NASDAQ symbol] (NQ)
CAVRA .... Child Abuse Victims' Rights Act of 1986
CAVS .... Calibrated Armor Vehicle Simulator (MCD)
CAVS .... Center for Advanced Visual Studies [Massachusetts Institute of Technology] [Research center]
CAVT.......... Caveat [Let Him Beware] [A judicial writ] [Latin Legal term] (ROG)
CAVT.......... Constant Absolute Vorticity Trajectory
CAVU......... Ceiling and Visibility Unrestricted [or Unlimited] [Aviation] (MCD)
CAVU......... Continuous Arteriovenous Ultrafiltration [Medicine] (DMAA)
CAW.......... Cable and Wireless Ltd. [Telecommunications] (IAA)
CAW.......... Cam Action Wheel
CAW.......... Campos [Brazil] [Airport symbol] (OAG)
CAW.......... Canadian Auto Workers Union
CAW.......... Carbon Arc Welding
CAW.......... Carrier Air Wing [Navy]
CAW.......... Central Airways [Medicine] (DMAA)
CAW.......... Central America Week
CAW.......... Central Aural Warning System (MCD)
CAW.......... Channel Address Word [Computer science]
CAW.......... Close Assault Weapon (INF)
CAW.......... Commericial Air Services (Pty) Ltd. [South Africa ICAO designator] (FAAC)
CAW.......... Commission on Agricultural Workers (ECON)
CAW.......... Common Aerial Working [Telecommunications] (TEL)
CAW.......... Computer-Aided Writing
CAW.......... Computer-Assisted War [Slang] (DNAB)
CAW.......... Co-Ordinating Animal Welfare [British]
CAWA .... California Automotive Wholesalers' Association (SRA)
CAWA .... Canadian Amateur Wrestling Association [Association Canadienne de Lutte Amateur] (AC)
CAWA .... Chesapeake Automotive Wholesalers Association (SRA)
CAWA .... Closing Abductory Wedge Osteotomy [Orthopedics] (DAVI)
CAWA .... Consumers' Association of Western Australia
CAWAAS ..... Canadian-American Women's Association, American Section (EA)
CAWAWL .... Crusade to Abolish War and Armaments by World Law (EA)
CAWC .... Committee on Air and Water Conservation [Later, Committee for Environmental Affairs] [American Petroleum Institute]
CAWC .... Computer-Aided Written Communication
CAWCF....... Conventional Ammunition Working Capital Fund [DoD]
CAWDS........ Canadian Association of Warehousing & Distribution Services [Association Canadienne des Entreposeurs et des Distributeurs] [Formerly, Canadian Warehousing Association] (AC)
CAWEE........ Canadian Association of Women Executives & Entrepreneurs [Association Canadienne des Femmes Cadres et Entrepreneurs] (AC)
CAWEX .... Conventional Air Warfare Exercise (DNAB)
CAWF......... Carrier All-Weather Flying
CAWFGB...... Coopers' and Allied Workers' Federation of Great Britain [A union]
CAWG .... California Association of Wheat Growers (SRA)
CAWG .... California Association of Winegrape Growers (EA)
CAWG .... Canada Asia Working Group
CAWG .... Christian Alliance of Women and Girls [British] (BI)
CAWG .... Clean Air Working Group [An association Defunct] (EA)
CAWG .... Coaxial Adapter Waveguide
CAWG .... Colorado Association of Wheat Growers (SRA)
CAWG .... Construction Acquisition Work Group (AAGC)
CAWGS........ Covert All-Weather Gun System
CAWK .... Cautious Hawk [Description of President Reagan's position on foreign affairs, used in book "Gambling with History: Reagan in the White House"]
CAWKI .... Civilization As We Know It [An association British]
Cawl .... Cawley's Laws Concerning Jesuits, Etc. [1680] [A publication] (DLA)
CAWL.......... Centre for Advancement in Work & Living (AC)
CAWM .... California Association of Window Manufacturers (SRA)
CAWMC ...... Canadian Association of Wooden Money Collectors (AC)
CAWP .... Center for the American Woman and Politics (EA)
CAWPR .... Committee for the Aid to West Papuan Refugees [Netherlands] (EAIO)
CAWPRC...... Canadian Association on Water Pollution Research and Control (EAIO)
CAWQ .... Canadian Association on Water Quality [Also, Canadian National Committee of the International Association on Water Quality] [Formerly, Canadian Association on Water Pollution Research & Control] (AC)
CAWR .... Carrier Air Wing Reserve [Navy]
CAWR .... Combined Annual Wage Reporting [IRS]
CAWS .... CAI Wireless Systems [NASDAQ symbol] (TTSB)
CAWS .... CAI Wireless Systems, Inc. [NASDAQ symbol] (SAG)
CAWS .... Cannon Artillery Weapon Systems (MCD)
CAWS .... Central Aural Warning System (MCD)
CAWS .... Close-Assault Weapon System
CAWS .... Cockpit Alerting and Warning System (MCD)
CAWS .... Computer-Aided Work Sampling
CAWSE .... Casualty Analysis for Determining Weapon System Effectiveness [Army] (AABC)
CAWSS .... Crisis Action Weather Support System (MCD)
CAWTS .... Chemical Attack Warning Transmission System (MCD)
CAWTU .... Church Action with the Unemployed [Church of England]

CAWU .... Clerical and Administrative Workers Union [*British*]
CAWU .... Commercial and Allied Workers' Union [*Somali Republic*]
CAWV .... Contractors Association of West Virginia (SRA)
CAX .... Canpax-Air AG [*Switzerland ICAO designator*] (FAAC)
CAX .... Capricorn Resources Ltd. [*Vancouver Stock Exchange symbol*]
CAX .... Carlisle [*England*] [*Airport symbol*] (OAG)
CAX .... Cheltenham Annex [*Military*] (DNAB)
CAX .... Combined Arms Exercise (MCD)
CAX .... Combined Arms Exercise [*Marine Corps*] (DOMA)
CAX .... Commercial Assets [*AMEX symbol*] (SPSG)
CAX .... Community Automatic Exchange [*Telephone*]
CAXB .... Composite Auxiliary Boiler [*of a ship*] (DS)
CAXBS .... Composite Auxiliary Boiler Survey [*of a ship*] (DS)
CAY .... Cayenne [*French Guiana*] [*Airport symbol*] (OAG)
CAY .... Cayman Airways Ltd. [*British ICAO designator*] (FAAC)
CAY .... Come-All-Ye [*A publication*] (BRI)
Cay Abr .... Cay's Abridgment, or the English Statutes [*A publication*] (DLA)
CAYAS .... Children's and Young Adult Services
CAYC .... Canadian Association for Young Children
CAYC .... Centro de Arte y Communicacion [*Center of Art and Communication*] [*Argentina*] (EAIO)
CaYDaw .... Dawson Public Library, Dawson, YT, Canada [*Library symbol Library of Congress*] (LCLS)
CaYDPCK .... Parks Canada, Klondike Historic Site, Dawson City, YT, Canada [*Library symbol Library of Congress*] (LCLS)
CayenneSf .... Cayenne Software, Inc. [*Associated Press*] (SAG)
CaYHjPCK .... Parks Canada, Kluane National Park, Haines Junction, YT, Canada [*Library symbol Library of Congress*] (LCLS)
CAYMV .... Canna Yellow Mottle Virus [*Plant pathology*]
CAYN .... Cayenne Software, Inc. [*NASDAQ symbol*] (SAG)
CAYO .... Canadian Association of Youth Orchestras
CaYW .... Whitehorse Public Library, Whitehorse, YT, Canada [*Library symbol*] [*Library of Congress*] (LCLS)
CaYWA .... Yukon Archives, Whitehorse, YT, Canada [*Library symbol Library of Congress*] (LCLS)
CaYWED ...... Government of the Yukon, Department of Economic Development: Mines and Small Business, Whitehorse, YT, Canada [*Library symbol*] [*Library of Congress*] (LCLS)
CaYWEEP .... Environment Canada, Environmental Protection Service, Whitehorse, YT, Canada [*Library symbol*] [*Library of Congress*] (LCLS)
CaYWHHR ... Government of the Yukon, Department of Health and Human Resources, Whitehorse, YT, Canada [*Library symbol*] [*Library of Congress*] (LCLS)
CaYWHS ...... Whitehorse Historical Society, Whitehorse, YT, Canada [*Library symbol Library of Congress*] (LCLS)
CaYWIN .... Indian and Northern Affairs Canada, Northern Program, Whitehorse, YT, Canada [*Library symbol*] [*Library of Congress*] (LCLS)
CaYWL........ Yukon Law Library, Whitehorse, YT, Canada [*Library symbol Library of Congress*] (LCLS)
CaYWLS ...... Government of the Yukon, Library Services Branch, Whitehorse, YT, Canada [*Library symbol Library of Congress*] (LCLS)
CaYWPCN .... Parks Canada, National Historic Sites, Whitehorse, YT, Canada [*Library symbol Library of Congress*] (LCLS)
CaYWR .... Yukon Regional Library, Whitehorse, YT, Canada [*Library symbol Library of Congress*] (LCLS)
CaYWRR...... Government of the Yukon, Department of Renewable Resources, Whitehorse, YT, Canada [*Library symbol*] [*Library of Congress*] (LCLS)
CaYWTA ...... Government of the Yukon, Department of Territorial Affairs, Whitehorse, YT, Canada [*Library symbol Library of Congress*] (LCLS)
CayWtr......... Cayman Water Co. Ltd. [*Associated Press*] (SAG)
CAz .... Azusa Public Library, Azusa, CA [*Library symbol Library of Congress*] (LCLS)
CAZ .... Can Am Gold Resources [*Vancouver Stock Exchange symbol*]
CAZ .... Castlepoint [*New Zealand*] [*Seismograph station code, US Geological Survey*] (SEIS)
CAZ .... Cat Aviation, AG [*Switzerland ICAO designator*] (FAAC)
CAZ .... Cazador Explorations [*Vancouver Stock Exchange symbol*]
CAZ .... Cobar [*Australia Airport symbol*] (OAG)
CAzA .... Aerojet Electrosystems Co., Azusa, CA [*Library symbol Library of Congress*] (LCLS)
CAzC .... Citrus College, Azusa, CA [*Library symbol Library of Congress*] (LCLS)
CAZPA .... Canadian Association of Zoological Parks & Aquariums (AC)
CAzPC......... Azusa Pacific College, Azusa, CA [*Library symbol Library of Congress*] (LCLS)
CAZS .... Centre for Arid Zone Studies [*University College of North Wales*] [*British*] (CB)
CB .... Allen & Hanburys [*Great Britain*] [*Research code symbol*]
C$_B$ .... Base Capacitance (IDOE)
CB .... Battle Cruiser [*Navy symbol*]
CB .... Belgian Congo
CB .... Berkeley Public Library, Berkeley, CA [*Library symbol Library of Congress*] (LCLS)
CB .... Cadet Battalion [*British military*] (DMA)
CB .... Cadmium Bronze
CB .... Caesarean [*or Cesarean*] Birth [*Obstetrics*] (DAVI)
CB .... Cafeteria Benefits [*Health insurance*] (GHCT)
CB .... Callable Bond [*Investment term*]
CB .... Call Back [*Word processing*]
cb .... Cambodia [*Democratic Kampuchea*] [*MARC country of publication code Library of Congress*] (LCCP)
CB .... Campaign Brief [*A publication*]
C/B.............. Cancel on Back [*Deltiology*]

CB .... Cannery Board [*Queensland*] [*Australia*]
CB .... Capacitor Bank
CB .... Cape Ballet [*South Africa*]
CB .... Cape Breton Island
CB .... Carbenicillin [*Bactericide*]
Cb .... Carbobenzoxy [*Also, CBZ*] [*Organic chemistry*]
CB .... Carbon Bond [*Chemistry*]
CB .... Carboy (MCD)
cb .... Cardboard (MAE)
cb .... Cardboard Film Holder Without Intensifying Screens [*Radiology*] (DAVI)
CB .... Caribair [*Airlines*] (OAG)
CB .... Carrier-Based
CB .... Carte Blanche [*Credit card*]
CB .... Cash Book
CB .... Cast Brass
CB .... Cast Bronze (IIA)
CB .... Casualty Branch [*BUPERS*]
CB .... Cataclysmic Binary [*Computer science*]
CB .... Catapult Bulletin (MCD)
CB .... Catch Basin [*Technical drawings*]
CB .... Catheterized Bladder [*Urology*] (DAVI)
CB .... Cavalry Brigade
C/B .... C-Band [*3900-6200 MHz*]
CB .... C-Battery
CB .... Ceased Breathing [*Medicine*] (DAVI)
CB .... Cement Base [*Technical drawings*]
CB .... Census Bureau [*Department of Commerce*]
CB .... Center Back [*Soccer*]
CB .... Center of Buoyancy
CB .... Centibar
Cb .... Centibels [*Telecommunications*]
CB .... Central Bank [*Philippines*] (IMH)
CB .... Central Battery (NATG)
CB .... Central Board
CB .... Century Bible [*A publication*]
CB .... Cerebellum [*Brain anatomy*]
CB .... Certain Borough [*British*]
CB .... Certification Body (IAA)
CB .... Chain Break [*Broadcasting*] (WDMC)
CB .... Chairman of the Board
CB .... Change Board (MCD)
CB .... Change Bulletin
CB .... Channel Bank (ACRL)
CB .... Charles Bruning Reproduction Processes
CB .... Chemical and Biological [*Warfare*] [*Formerly, CBR, CEBAR*] [*Military*]
CB .... Chemically Benign [*Medicine*]
CB .... Chest-Back [*Medicine*]
CB .... Chester Beatty Research Institute [*Great Britain*] [*Research code symbol*]
CB .... Chief Baron [*British*]
CB .... Chief Boilermaker [*Navy rating Obsolete*]
CB .... Children's Bureau [*of SSA*]
CB .... Chinch Bug [*Entomology*]
CB .... Chirurgiae Baccalaureus [*Bachelor of Surgery*]
CB .... Chlorobiphenyl [*Chemistry*]
CB .... Chlorobromomethane [*Also, CBM*] [*Organic chemistry*] (MCD)
CB .... Chocolate Blood [*Agar*] [*Biochemistry*] (MAE)
CB .... Choke Breaker [*Automotive engineering*]
CB .... Chorale Book [*Music*] (ROG)
CB .... Christian Businessman [*Christian Business Men's Committee of United States of America*] [*A publication*]
CB .... Chronic Bronchitis [*Medicine*]
CB .... [*The*] Chubb Corp. [*NYSE symbol*] (SPSG)
CB .... Cinema Board [*Tasmania*] [*Australia*]
CB .... Circle Bed [*Medicine*]
CB .... Circuit Board (DWSG)
CB .... Circuit Breaker
CB .... Citizens Band [*A radio frequency band for limited-range, two-way voice communications by persons without technical training or standard operator licenses*]
CB .... Clear Back [*Telecommunications*] (TEL)
CB .... Clin-Byla [*France*] [*Research code symbol*]
CB .... Clipped and Burned [*Ecology*]
CB .... Clydesdale Bank [*British*]
CB .... Coach Builder (ROG)
cb .... Coated Back [*Paper*] (WDMC)
CB .... Coated on the Back Side [*Carbonless paper*]
CB .... Cobalt Bomb [*Nuclear*] (AAG)
CB .... Code Blue [*Emergency hospital code*] (DAVI)
CB .... Code Book (AFM)
CB .... Coin Box [*Telecommunications*] (TEL)
CB .... Col Basso [*With the Bass*] [*Music*]
CB .... Collective Bargaining (DCTA)
CB .... Collector-Base (DNAB)
CB .... Colombia [*IYRU nationality code*] (IYR)
CB .... Colored-Bordered [*Paper*] (DGA)
Cb .... Columbium [*A chemical element; modern name is niobium, see Nb*]
CB .... Column Base
CB .... Combination Block [*Engraving*] (DGA)
CB .... Commanderie de Bordeaux (EA)
CB .... Commander of the Most Excellent Order of the Bath [*British*]
CB .... Commercial Bank
CB .... Common Base [*Computer science*] (MSA)
CB .... Common Battery [*Electronics; technical drawings*]

CB	Common Bench [*Legal term*]
CB	Common Bench Reports [*A publication*]
CB	Common Bias (IAA)
cb	Common Brick [*Construction*] (BARN)
CB	Communications Buffer [*Computer science*]
CB	Communications Bus
CB	Commuter Airlines [*Airline code*]
CB	Companion of the [*Order of the*] Bath [*British*]
CB	Comparator Buffer [*Computer science*] (MUGU)
CB	Compass Bearing [*Navigation*]
Cb	Complement [*Immunochemistry*] (DAVI)
CB	Component Board (MSA)
CB	Composite Boson [*Physics*]
CB	Concrete Block
CB	Conditional Branch
CB	Condition BIT [*Binary Digit*] [*Computer science*]
CB	Conduction Band [*Electronics*]
CB	[*The*] Conference Board [*Formerly, National Industrial Conference Board*]
CB	Confidential Book [*Navy British*]
CB	Confidential Bulletin
CB	Configuration Baseline
CB	Confinement to Barracks [*A military punishment*]
CB	Conjugate (Counter) Base [*Chemistry*]
CB	Connecting Block [*Telecommunications*] (TEL)
CB	Consolidated-Bathurst, Inc. [*Toronto Stock Exchange symbol*]
CB	Constant Bandwidth (MCD)
CB	Construction Battalion [*SEABEE*] [*Navy*]
CB	Construction Briefing Paper [*A publication*] (AAGC)
CB	Contact Breaker
CB	Container Base (DS)
CB	Containment Building [*Nuclear energy*] (NRCH)
CB	Contemporary Books [*Publisher's imprint*]
CB	Continental Breakfast
CB	Continuous Blowdown (AAG)
CB	Continuous Breakdown (WDAA)
CB	Contrabass [*Music*]
CB	Contract Brief
CB	Contrast Baths [*Physical therapy*] (DAVI)
CB	Control Board
CB	Control Booth
CB	Control Branch [*Military*]
CB	Control Break
CB	Control Buffer [*Computer science*] (IAA)
CB	Control Building [*Nuclear energy*] (NRCH)
CB	Control Button
CB	Conus Branch [*Anatomy*]
CB	Coomb [*Combe*] [*British*] (ROG)
CB	Corned Beef [*Restaurant slang*]
CB	Cornerback [*Football*]
CB	Corps Brandenburgia (EA)
C/B	Cost/Benefit [*Accounting*]
CB	Cottony Blight [*of turf grass*]
CB	Coulomb [*Unit of electric charge*]
CB	Coulomb Blockade [*Physics*]
CB	Counter Battery
CB	Counter Bombardment [*British military*] (DMA)
CB	CountryBaskets [*Associated Press*] (SAG)
CB	Country Bill [*Banking*]
CB	County Borough
CB	Coupled Biquad [*Electronics*] (OA)
CB	Coupon Bond [*Investment term*]
CB	Crash Boat
CB	Credit Balance
C/B	Creosote Bushes [*Ecology*]
CB	Crew Boat
CB	Cubic (IAA)
CB	Cumulative Bulletin [*US Internal Revenue Service*] [*A publication*] (AAGC)
CB	Cumulonimbus [*Cloud*] [*Meteorology*]
CB	Currency Bond
CB	Current Background
CB	Current Biography [*A publication*]
CB	Current BIT [*Binary Digit*] [*Computer science*] (IAA)
CB	Customs Bureau
CB	Cytochalasin B [*Biochemistry*]
CB	English Common Bench Reports [*1840-56*] [*A publication*] (DLA)
CB	Large Cruiser [*Navy symbol Obsolete*]
CB	SEABEE [*Construction Battalion*] [*Navy*] (MCD)
CB	Suckling Airways [*Airline flight code*] (ODBW)
CB1	Coal Bug One [*Microbe used to remove sulfur from coal*]
CB1S	Center Beam One Side [*Lumber*] (DAC)
CB2S	Center Beam Two Sides [*Lumber*] (DAC)
CB4	Carbon Bond Mechanism - Version 4 [*Air pollution*]
CB$_{11}$	Phenadoxone Hydrochloride [*An analgesic and hypnotic*] [*Pharmacy*] (DAVI)
CBA	Association for Bright Children [*Canada*]
CBA	Brilliance China Automotive [*NYSE symbol*] (SPSG)
CBA	Cake and Biscuit Alliance [*British*]
CBA	California Bankers Association (SRA)
CBA	California Broadcasters Association (SRA)
CBA	California State College, Bakersfield, CA [*OCLC symbol*] (OCLC)
CBA	Cambridge Buddhist Association (EA)
CBA	Canadian Badminton Association
CBA	Canadian Band Association (EAIO)

CBA	Canadian Bankers Association
CBA	Canadian Bar Association
CBA	Canadian Battery Association (AC)
CBA	Canadian Bison Association [*Association Canadienne du Bison*] (AC)
CBA	Canadian Booksellers Association
CBA	Canadian Botanical Association
CBA	Canadian Bus Association [*Association Canadienne de l'Autobus*] [*Formerly, Canadian Motor Coach Association*] (AC)
CBA	Candy Brokers Association of America [*Later, NCBSA*] (EA)
CBA	Capital Builder Account [*Merrill Lynch & Co., Inc.*] [*Finance*]
CBA	Carcinoma-Bearing Animal (AAMN)
CBA	Caribbean Atlantic Airlines [*Puerto Rico*] [*ICAO designator*]
CBA	Cast Bullet Association (EA)
CBA	Catholic Biblical Association of America (EA)
CBA	Catholic Broadcasters Association (EA)
CBA	C-Band Transponder Antenna [*Radio*] (CET)
CBA	Center for Book Arts (EA)
CBA	Central [*Common*] Battery Apparatus [*Electronics*]
CBA	Central Borrowing Authorities
CBA	Central Broadcasting Administration [*China*]
CBA	Certificated Bailiffs Association [*British*] (DBA)
CBA	Certificate in Business Administration [*Academic degree*] (AIE)
CBA	Certified Business Appraiser [*Institute of Business Appraisers*] [*Designation awarded by*]
CBA	Chemical Blowing Agent [*Plastics technology*]
CBA	Chemical Bond Approach
CBA	Chesapeake Bay Agreement (GNE)
CBA	Chesapeake Bay Annex [*Navy*]
CBA	Chinese Biopharmaceutical Association
CBA	Chlorobenzoic Acid [*Organic acid*]
CBA	Christian Boaters Association (EA)
CBA	Christian Bodybuilding Association (EA)
CBA	Christian Booksellers Association (EA)
CBA	Christian Brethren Assemblies [*Australia*]
CBA	Christian Broadcasting Association (EA)
CBA	Christian Brothers' Association of Australia
CBA	Chronic Bronchitis and Asthma [*Medicine*]
CBA	Circuit Board Assembly (MCD)
CBA	Citizens Bar Association (EA)
CBA	Citizens for a Better America (EA)
CBA	Civil Aviation Inspectorate of the Czech Republic [*ICAO designator*] (FAAC)
CBA	Classified by Association (DNAB)
CBA	Clydesdale Breeders Association of the United States [*Later, CBUS*] (EA)
Cba	Cobamide [*Biochemistry*]
CBA	Cocoa Beach Apollo [*NASA*] (MCD)
CBA	Coin Box Adapter [*Computer science*] (ECII)
CBA	Cold Bay [*Alaska*] [*Seismograph station code, US Geological Survey Closed*] (SEIS)
CBA	Collective-Bargaining Agreement
CBA	Collective Black Artists (EA)
CBA	Colliding Beam Accelerator [*High-energy physics*]
CBA	Colorado Bankers Association (SRA)
CBA	Colorado Bar Association (SRA)
CBA	COMLINE Business Analysis [*COMLINE International Corp.*] [*Japan Information service or system*] (CRD)
CBA	Commercial Bank of Australia
CBA	Common Battery System (MCD)
CBA	Commonwealth Broadcasting Association [*London, England*] (EAIO)
CBA	Community Bankers Association of Georgia (SRA)
CBA	Community Broadcasters Association [*Defunct*] (EA)
CBA	Community Broadcasters of America [*Defunct*] (EA)
CBA	Competitive-Binding Assay
CBA	Component Board Assembly (MSA)
CBA	Computer-Based Accounting
CBA	Computer-Based Automation
CBA	Concrete Block Association (MHDB)
CBA	Confederation of British Associations (DBA)
CBA	Congressional Black Associates [*An association*] (EA)
CBA	Connecticut Bankers Association (SRA)
CBA	Connecticut Bar Association (SRA)
CBA	Connecticut Broadcasters Association (SRA)
CBA	Constants Board Assembly
CBA	Consumer Bankers Association [*Arlington, VA*] (EA)
CBA	Continental Basketball Association (EA)
CBA	Continuous-Beam Analysis [*Jacys Computing Services*] [*Software package*] (NCC)
CBA	Cost-Benefit Analysis [*Accounting*]
CBA	Council for British Archaeology
CBA	Criminal Bar Association [*British*] (DBA)
CBA	Current Biotechnology Abstracts [*Royal Society of Chemistry*] [*Information service or system*] (IID)
CBA	Curriculum-Based Assessment [*Education*]
CBA	Cytochemical Bioassay
CBA	Moncton, NB [*AM radio station call letters*]
CBAA	Canadian Business Aircraft Association (EAIO)
CB(AA)	Cavalry Brigade (Air Attack) [*Army*]
CBAA	Cleveland Bay Association of America [*Later, Cleveland Bay Society of America*] (EA)
CBAA	Combat Brigade Air Attack
CBAA	Conservative Baptist Association of America (EA)
CBAA	Corset and Brassiere Association of America [*Later, AAMA*] (EA)
CBAB	California Brandy Advisory Board [*Defunct*] (EA)

CBABG .... CAB [*Commonwealth Agricultural Bureaux*] International Bureau of Animal Breeding and Genetics (EAIO)

CBABS .... [*The*] Conference Board Abstract Database [*The Conference Board, Inc.*] [*Information service or system*] (CRD)

CBAC .... Catholic Biblical Association of Canada [*Formerly, Canadian Catholic Biblical Association*] (AC)

CBAC .... Chemical-Biological Activities [*Information service or system A publication*]

CB/ac .... Circuit Break/Alternating Current

CBAC .... Clay Brick Association of Canada [*Association Canadienne de Brique d'Argile Cuite*] [*Formerly, Canadian Structural Clay Asssociation*] (AC)

CBAC .... Combat Brigade Air Cavalry

CBAC .... Commander Base Area Command [*Australia*]

CBAC .... Council for Business and the Arts in Canada

CBACT .... Chiropractic Board of the Australian Capital Territory [*Medicine*]

CBADS .... Chemical and Biological Agent Delivery System (MCD)

CBAE .... Commonwealth Board of Architectural Education [*British*] (EAIO)

CBAE .... Competency-Based Adult Education

CBAF .... Cobalt Base Alloy Foil

CBAF .... Commercial Bank Address File [*IRS*]

CBAF-FM .... Moncton, NB [*FM radio station call letters*]

CBA-FM .... Moncton, NB [*FM radio station call letters*]

CBAFT .... Moncton, NB [*Television station call letters*]

CBAG .... Children's Book Action Group [*National Book League*] [*British*]

CBAG .... Crested Corp. [*NASDAQ symbol*] (SAG)

CBaGS .... Church of Jesus Christ of Latter-Day Saints, Genealogical Society Library, Bakersfield Branch, Bakersfield, CA [*Library symbol Library of Congress*] (LCLS)

CBAH .... Commonwealth Bureau of Animal Health [*British*]

CBaH .... Kern Medical Center, Bakersfield, CA [*Library symbol Library of Congress*] (LCLS)

CBA Handbook... Commonwealth Broadcasting Association. Handbook [*A publication*]

CBAI .... Community Bankers Association of Illinois (SRA)

CBAI .... Community Bankers Association of Indiana (SRA)

CBAIC .... Chemical and Biological Accident and Incident Control [*Army*] (AABC)

CBAICP .... Chemical and Biological Accident and Incident Control Plan [*Army*] (AABC)

CBaK .... Kern County Library, Bakersfield, CA [*Library symbol Library of Congress*] (LCLS)

CBaKH .... Kern County Department of Health, Bakersfield, CA [*Library symbol Library of Congress*] (LCLS)

CBaKM .... Kern County Museum, Reference Library, Bakersfield, CA [*Library symbol Library of Congress*] (LCLS)

CBA-KS .... Community Bankers Association of Kansas (SRA)

CBAL .... Counterbalance (KSC)

CBAL .... Moncton, NB [*FM radio station call letters*]

CBALS .... Carrier-Borne Air Liaison Section [*Navy*]

CBAM .... Calcein Blue Acetoxymethyl Ester [*Organic chemistry*]

CBAM .... Concerns-Based Adoption Model (EDAC)

CBan .... Banning Union Public Library, Banning, CA [*Library symbol Library of Congress*] (LCLS)

CBAN .... Commonwealth Bureau of Animal Nutrition [*British*]

CB & H .... Continent between Bordeaux and Hamburg [*Business term*]

CB & I .... Chicago Bridge & Iron Co. [*Later, CBI Industries*]

CB & Q .... Chicago, Burlington & Quincy Railroad [*Also known as Burlington Route*]

CBANY .... Covered Button Association of New York (EA)

CBANYS ...... Community Bankers Association of New York State (SRA)

CBAO .... Community Bankers Association of Ohio (SRA)

CBAO .... Community Bankers Association of Oklahoma (SRA)

CBAP .... (Carboxyphenyl)benzoyl-Aminopenicillanic Acid [*Biochemistry*]

CBAQ .... Clay Brick Association of Queensland [*Australia*]

CBAR .... Center for Bioanalytical Research [*University of Kansas*]

CBAR .... Change Board Analysis Record (SAA)

CBAR .... Counterbore Arbor [*Tool*]

C/BAR .... Cross Bar [*Automotive engineering*]

CBARC .... Columbia Basin Agricultural Research Center [*Oregon State University*] [*Research center*] (RCD)

CBARC .... Conference Board of Associated Research Councils (EA)

CBarGS .... Church of Jesus Christ of Latter-Day Saints, Genealogical Society Library, Barstow Branch, Barstow, CA [*Library symbol Library of Congress*] (LCLS)

CBarUSA ...... United States Army, Fort Irwin Post Library, Barstow, CA [*Library symbol Library of Congress*] (LCLS)

CBaS .... California State College, Bakersfield, CA [*Library symbol Library of Congress*] (LCLS)

CBAS .... Central [*Common*] Battery Alarm Signaling [*Electronics*]

CBAS .... Chemical Bond Approach Study

CBAS .... Class B Airspace [*Aviation*] (FAAC)

CBAS .... Combat Augmentation Subsystem (MCD)

CBAS .... Command Budget Automated System [*Air Force*] (GFGA)

C-BASIC ...... Commercial BASIC

CBAST .... Concentrated Boric Acid Storage Tank [*Nuclear energy*] (NRCH)

CBAT .... Central Bureau for Astronomical Telegrams (EA)

CBAT .... College Board Admission Test (WDAA)

CBAT .... Saint John, NB [*AM radio station call letters*]

CBAT-1 .... Bon Accord, NB [*Television station call letters*] (RBYB)

CBAT-2 .... Moncton, NB [*Television station call letters*]

CBAT-4 .... Campbellton, NB [*Television station call letters*]

CB/ATCS ...... Carrier-Based Airborne Tactical Control System (SAA)

CB/ATDS ...... Carrier-Based Airborne Tactical Data System (MCD)

CBAT-TV ...... Bon Accord, NB [*TV station call letters*] (RBYB)

CBAV .... Cambodian Buddhist Association of Victoria [*Australia*]

CBAVD .... Congenital Bilateral Absence of the Vas Deferens [*Medicine*]

CBAVE .... Competency-Based Adult Vocational Education (EDAC)

CBb .... Burbank Public Library, Burbank, CA [*Library symbol Library of Congress*] (LCLS)

CBB .... Caliber System [*NYSE symbol*] (TTSB)

CBB .... Caliber Systems, Inc. [*NYSE symbol*] (SAG)

CBB .... Cambridge Bay [*Canada*] [*Geomagnetic observatory code*]

CBB .... Catholic Big Brothers (EA)

CBB .... Citizens for a Balanced Budget (EA)

CBB .... Cobra Enterprises [*Vancouver Stock Exchange symbol*]

CBB .... Cochabamba [*Bolivia*] [*Airport symbol*] (OAG)

CBB .... Commercial Blanket Bond [*Insurance*]

CBB .... Computerized Bulletin Board

CBB .... Contract Budget Baseline (MCD)

CBB .... Control Block Data Base (ECII)

CBB .... Coomassie Brilliant Blue [*A stain*]

CBBA .... Christian Brothers Boys Association (EA)

CBBAG .... Canadian Bookbinders & Book Artist Guild [*Guide Canadienne des Relieurs et des Artisans du Livre*] (AC)

CBBB .... Council of Better Business Bureaus [*Arlington, VA*] (EA)

CBBC .... Council of Bible Believing Churches (EA)

CB Bcp .... CB Bancorp, Inc. [*Associated Press*] (SAG)

CBBD .... California Beer and Beverage Distributors (SRA)

CBBF .... Children's Brittle Bone Foundation

CBBFC .... Cooder Brown Band Fan Club (EA)

CBBG .... Canadian Bookbinders and Book Artists Guild

CBbGS .... Southern California Genealogical Society, Burbank, CA [*Library symbol*] [*Library of Congress*] (LCLS)

CBbH .... Hydro-Air Library, Burbank, CA [*Library symbol Library of Congress*] (LCLS)

CBBI .... Cast Bronze Bearings Institute [*Later, NFFS*]

CBBI .... CB Bancshares [*NASDAQ symbol*] (TTSB)

CBBI .... CB Bancshares, Inc. [*NASDAQ symbol*] (SAG)

CBBII .... Council of the Brass and Bronze Ingot Industry (EA)

CBBK-FM ..... Kingston, ON [*FM radio station call letters*]

CBbL .... Lockheed-California Co., Burbank, CA [*Library symbol Library of Congress*] (LCLS)

CBBL-FM ..... London, ON [*FM radio station call letters*]

CBBM .... Color Blindness, Blue Monocone-Monochromatic Type [*Medicine*] (DMAA)

CBBMMA ..... Canada Brush, Broom & Mop Manufacturers Association [*Association Candienne des Fabricants de Brosses, Balais et Vadrouilles*] (AC)

CB Bnc .... CB Bancshares, Inc. [*Associated Press*] (SAG)

CBBS .... Center for Biochemical and Biophysical Studies [*Northern Illinois University*] [*Research center*] (RCD)

CBBS .... Community Bulletin Board System

CBBS .... Computer-Based Behavioral Studies (MCD)

CBBS .... Computer-Based Bibliographic Search Services

CBBS .... Computer Bulletin Board System

CBbT .... Technicolor, Inc., Burbank, CA [*Library symbol Library of Congress*] (LCLS)

CBBU .... Construction Battalion Base Unit [*Obsolete Navy*]

CBbW .... Warner Brothers, Inc., Research Library, Burbank, CA [*Library symbol Library of Congress*] (LCLS)

CBbWD .... Walt Disney Productions, Burbank, CA [*Library symbol Library of Congress*] (LCLS)

CBC .... Anahuac, TX [*Location identifier FAA*] (FAAL)

CBC .... Biola College, La Mirada, CA [*OCLC symbol*] (OCLC)

CBC .... Cadmium Bronze Connector

CBC .... [*The*] Cambridge Bible Commentary: New English Bible [*A publication*] (BJA)

CBC .... Cambridge Bicycle Club [*British*]

CBC .... Canadian Broadcasting Corp. [*Ottawa, ON*] [*Also facetiously translated as Casual Broadcasting Corp. and Communist Broadcasting Corp.*] [*Telecommunications*]

CBC .... Canberra Bridge Club [*Australia*]

CBC .... Canberra Bushwalkers' Club [*Australia*]

CBC .... Canberra Business Council [*Australia*]

CBC .... Can't Be Called [*Telecommunications*] (TEL)

CBC .... Carbenicillin [*Bactericide*]

CBC .... Carbon County Railway Co. [*AAR code*]

CBC .... Caribbean Resources Corp. [*Vancouver Stock Exchange symbol*]

CBC .... Carteret Bancorp, Inc. (MHDW)

CBC .... Catholic Bushwalking Club [*Australia*]

CBC .... Cauchy Boundary Condition [*Mathematics*]

CBC .... Cementitious Barrier Coat [*Anticorrosive coating*]

CBC .... Central Bureau of Compensation [*See also BCC*] [*Belgium*] (EAIO)

CBC .... Centura Banks [*NYSE symbol*] (SPSG)

CBC .... Cerebro-Buccal Commissure [*Medicine*]

CBC .... Chain Block Character [*Computer science*] (NITA)

CBC .... Chamberlain [*California*] [*Seismograph station code, US Geological Survey*] (SEIS)

CBC .... Chatto, Bodley Head, and Jonathan Cape Group [*Publishers*] [*British*]

CBC .... Chemically Bonded Ceramic [*Materials science*]

CBC .... Chicago Book Clinic

CBC .... Child Behavior and Characteristics

CBC .... Childless by Choice [*An association*]

CBC .... Children by Choice [*Australia*]

CBC .... Children's Behavior Checklist

CBC .... Children's Book Circle [*British*]

CBC .... Children's Book Council (EA)

CBC .... Christian Brothers College [*Tennessee*]

CBC............ Christian Brothers Conference (EA)
CBC............ Christian Businessman's Committees [Australia]
CBC............ Christmas Bird Count [National Audubon Society]
CBC............ Cipher Block Chaining [Computer science] (HGAA)
CBC............ Circuit Board Card
CBC............ Circulation Bed Combustor [Chemical engineering]
CBC............ Citizens for Better Care in Nursing Homes, Homes for the Aged, and Other After- Care Facilities (EA)
CBC............ Civil Budget Committee [NATO] (NATG)
CBC............ Closed Brayton Cycle [Thermodynamics]
CBC............ Collier's Bankruptcy Cases [A publication] (DLA)
CBC............ Colorado Beef Council (SRA)
CBC............ Columbia Bible College [South Carolina]
CBC............ Combined Blood Count (WDAA)
CBC............ Commercial Banking Co. of Sydney [Australia]
CBC............ Commonwealth Banking Corporation [Australia]
CBC............ Community Based Corrections (OICC)
CBC............ Complete Blood Count [Medicine]
CBC............ Computer-Based Conferencing (PDAA)
CBC............ Computer-Based Consultant (MCD)
CBC............ Confederation of Building Contractors [British] (DBA)
CBC............ Conference Board of Canada
CBC............ Congressional Black Caucus (EA)
CBC............ Congressional Border Caucus [An association] (EA)
CBC............ Connecticut Building Congress (SRA)
CBC............ Conservative Book Club
CBC............ Construction Battalion Center [Navy] (MCD)
CBC............ [The] Construction Briefing Collection [A publication] (AAGC)
CBC............ Continuous Boresight Correction (MCD)
CBC............ Contraband Control [Navy]
CBC............ Control Blocks Configuration [Computer science] (ECII)
CBC............ Coordinated Bargaining Committee (DICI)
CBC............ Coordinated Building Communication (PDAA)
CBC............ Corset and Brassiere Council [Defunct] (EA)
CBC............ Couldn't Be Cuter [Slang]
CBC............ Country Bound Connection [An association] (EA)
CBC............ County Borough Council [British] (ROG)
CBC............ Cyprus Broadcasting Corp. (IMH)
CBC............ Large Tactical Command Ship [Navy symbol Obsolete]
CBCA .... Canadian Badminton Coaches Association
CBCA .... Canadian Business and Current Affairs [Micromedia Ltd.] [Information service or system] (CRD)
CBCA .... Caribbean Basin Corrections Association [Cayman Islands] (EAIO)
CBCA .... Chancellor Broadcstg'A' [NASDAQ symbol] (TTSB)
CBCA .... Chancellor Corp. [NASDAQ symbol] (SAG)
CBCA .... Customs Brokers' Council of Australia
CBCBC ...... Corn-Soybeans-Corn-Soybeans-Corn [Crop rotation]
CB-CC .... Centroblastic/Centrocytic [Biochemistry]
CBCC .... Chemical-Biological Coordination Center [NAS/NRC]
CBCC .... Common Bias, Common Control
CBCC .... Conviction by Civil Court
CBCCUA .... Central Bureau, Catholic Central Union of America (EA)
CBCD .... Citrus Bacterial Canker Disease [Plant pathology]
CBCE......... Comite de Bourses de la Communaute Europeenne [Committee of Stock Exchanges in the European Community - CSEE] (EAIO)
CBCE......... Competency-Based Career Education (OICC)
CBCES ...... Chesapeake Bay Center for Environmental Studies [Smithsonian Institution]
CBCEW ...... Catholic Bishops' Conference of England and Wales (EAIO)
CBCF......... Carbon-Bonded Carbon Fiber
CBCF......... Citizens Banking [NASDAQ symbol] (TTSB)
CBCF......... Citizens Banking Corp. [NASDAQ symbol] (NQ)
CBCG .... CB Commercial Real Estate Services Group, Inc. [NASDAQ symbol] (SAG)
CBCHA ...... Clearinghouse on Business Coalitions for Health Action [Defunct] (EA)
CBChest...... County Bank of Chesterfield [Associated Press] (SAG)
CBCI......... Calumet Bancorp [NASDAQ symbol] (SAG)
CBCL......... Capitol Bancorp Ltd. [NASDAQ symbol] (NQ)
CBCL......... Child Behavior Checklist
CBCL......... Cutter Laboratories, Berkeley, CA [Library symbol Library of Congress] (LCLS)
CBCL-FM .... London, ON [FM radio station call letters]
CBCM......... Confederation of Brewers in the Common Market [Belgium] (EAIO)
CBCMA .... Carbonated Beverage Container Manufacturers Association [Later, CMI] (EA)
CBCMC ...... Carbonated Beverage Can Makers Committee [Division of CBCMA] (EA)
CBCMIS ...... Construction Battalion Center Management Information System [Navy] (DNAB)
CBCN .... Carbenicillin [Medicine] (DMAA)
CBCO .... CB Bancorp [NASDAQ symbol] (TTSB)
CBCO .... CB Bancorp, Inc. [NASDAQ symbol] (SAG)
CBCO .... Certified Building Code Official [Canada] (AAGC)
CB CoRI ..... CB Commercial Real Estate Services Group, Inc. [Associated Press] (SAG)
CBCP .... Capital Bancorp (Florida) [NASDAQ symbol] (SAG)
CBCP-1 ...... Shaunavon, SK [Television station call letters]
CBCP-2 ...... Cypress Hills, SK [Television station call letters]
CBCP-3 ...... Ponteix, SK [Television station call letters]
CBCPQ .... Christian Brethren Church in the Province of Quebec [l'Eglise des Freres Chretiens dans la Province du Quebec] [Also, Plymouth Brethren] (AC)
CBCR .... Change Board Comment Record
CBCS .... C-Band Checkout System (KSC)

CBCS .... Chemical-Biological Computer System
CBCS .... Chinese Banknote Collectors Society [Defunct] (EA)
CBCS .... Sudbury, ON [FM radio station call letters]
CBCSM ...... Council of British Ceramic Sanitaryware Manufacturers
CBCT......... Charlottetown, PE [Television station call letters]
CBCT......... Circuit Board Card Tester
CBCT......... Community-Based Clinical Trial [Medicine]
CBCT......... Council of British Cotton Textiles (DBA)
CBCT......... Customer-Bank Communication Terminal [Computerized banking]
CBCT-FM .... Charlottetown, PE [FM radio station call letters]
CBCU .... Counterbore Cutter [Tool] (AAG)
CBD .... Call Box Discrimination [Telecommunications] (TEL)
CBD .... Cannabidiol [Organic chemistry]
CBD .... Carbide (MSA)
CBD .... Cash before Delivery
C-BD .... C-Band [3900-6200 MHz] (NASA)
CBD .... Cellulose-Binding Domain [Genetics]
CBD .... Center for Biomedical Design [University of Utah] [Research center] (RCD)
CBD .... Central Business District
CBD .... Certificate of Bank Deposit
CBD .... Chemical-Biological Defense [Military]
CBD .... Chesapeake Bay Detachment [Washington, DC Navy] (GRD)
CBD .... Chester, CA [Location identifier FAA] (FAAL)
CBD .... Chief Benefits Director [Department of Veterans Affairs]
CBD .... Children before Dogs (EA)
CBD .... Christian Book Distributors [An association]
CBD .... Chronic Beryllium Disease [Medicine] (MCD)
CBD .... Closed Bladder Drainage [Medicine]
CBD .... Coffee Berry Disease
CBD .... Commerce Building Daily [Marine science] (OSRA)
CBD .... Commerce Building Daily (USDC)
CBD .... Commerce Business Daily [A publication] (AAGC)
CBD .... Common Bile Duct [Medicine]
CBD .... Configuration Block Diagram [Telecommunications] (TEL)
CBD .... Constant BIT [Binary Digit] Density [Control feature of magnetic tape recorders] [Computer science]
CBD .... Construction Battalion Detachment [Navy]
CBD .... Convention on Biological Diversity [1992] [United Nations] [Marine science] (OSRA)
CBD .... Convergent Beam Diffraction
CBD .... Corepressor Binding Domain [Genetics]
CBD .... Cumberland Resources Ltd. [Vancouver Stock Exchange symbol]
CBD .... Current Bibliographic Directory of the Arts and Sciences [A publication]
CBDA .... Cannabidiolic Acid [Organic chemistry]
CBDA .... Chemical Biological Defense Agency [Army]
CBDB .... [The] Conference Board Data Base [The Conference Board, Inc.] [Information service or system] (CRD)
CBDC .... Chronic Bullous Disease of Children [Medicine] (DMAA)
CB/dc .... Circuit Breaker/Direct Current
CBDC .... County Bank of Chesterfield [NASDAQ symbol] (SAG)
CBDCA........ Carboplatin [Antineoplastic drug] (CDI)
CBDCOM ..... Chemical and Biological Defense Command [Army] (RDA)
CBDE .... Common Bile Duct Exploration [Medicine] (DAVI)
CBD-FM ...... St. John, NB [FM radio station call letters]
CBDI .... Control Red Bank Demand Indicator (IEEE)
CB Dig .... United States Customs Bureau, Digest of Customs and Related Laws [A publication] (DLA)
CBDL .... Cross Branch Data Link (MCD)
CBDN .... Canadian Bacterial Diseases Network (AC)
CBDNA........ College Band Directors National Association (EA)
CBDQ .... Labrador City, NF [AM radio station call letters]
CBDR.......... Citizens for Better Driving Records [Later, CSD] (EA)
CBDS .... Carcinogenesis Bioassay Data System [National Cancer Institute] (IID)
CBDS .... Circuit Board Design System [IBM Corp.]
CBDS .... Common Bile Duct Stenosis [Medicine]
CBDS .... Connectionless Broadband Data Service [Telecommunications]
CBDST........ Commonwealth Bureau of Dairy Science and Technology [British]
CBDT .... Can't Break Dial Tone [Telecommunications] (TEL)
CBDT .... Citizenship of British Dependent Territories
CBDV .... Colocasia Bobone Disease Virus [Plant pathology]
CBE .... Aerovias Caribe SA [Mexico ICAO designator] (FAAC)
CBE .... Cab Behind Engine [Automotive engineering]
CBE .... Cabre Exploration Ltd. [Toronto Stock Exchange symbol]
CBE .... Calgary Board of Education, Acquisition and Technical Services [UTLAS symbol]
CBE .... Carbon Black Export (EA)
CBE .... Center for Biofilm Engineering [Montana State University]
CBE .... Central Battery Exchange [Electronics] (IAA)
CBE .... Central Bomber Establishment [British military] (DMA)
CBE .... Centralized Branch Exchange [Telecommunications] (TEL)
CBE .... Certified Bank Examiner
CBE .... Cesium Bombardment Engine
CBE .... Changes Being Effected [Food and Drug Administration]
CBE .... Chemical Beam Epitaxy [Solid state physics]
CBE .... Chemical Binding Effect
CBE .... [The] Chilswell Book of English Poetry [A publication]
CBE .... Chlorobromoethane [Organic chemistry]
CBE .... Circuit Board Extractor
CBE .... Citizens for a Better Environment (EA)
CBE .... Clinical Breast Examination [Medicine] (DMAA)
CBE .... [The] Coalition for Brand Equity [An organization of advertisers, agencies, and media]

CBE............. Combined Book Exhibit
CBE............. Command Budget Estimates [*Military*] (AABC)
CBE............. Commander of the [*Order of the*] British Empire [*Facetious translation: Can't Be Everywhere*]
CBE............. Companion of the Order of the British Empire (ADA)
CBE............. Competency Based Education
CBE............. Compression Bonding Encapsulation
CBE............. Computer Aided Education (ECII)
C-BE............ Computer-Based Education [*Project*]
CBE............. Computer Brokers Exchange [*Information service or system*] (IID)
CBE............. Conference of Business Economists (EA)
CBE............. Connector Bracket Experiment (MCD)
CBE............. Constant Blow Energy [*Teledyne Roxon 400*] [*Hydraulics*]
CBE............. Consumer Buying Expectations Survey [*Formerly, Quarterly Survey of Intentions*] [*Bureau of the Census*]
CBE............. Contract Budget Estimate (MCD)
CBE............. Cooper Indus [*NYSE symbol*] (TTSB)
CBE............. Cooper Industries, Inc. [*Formerly, Cooper-Bessemer Corp.*] [*NYSE symbol*] (SPSB)
CBE............. Corporacion Bancaria de Espana [*Spain*] (ECON)
CBE............. Costs, Budgeting, and Economics
CBE............. Council for Basic Education (EA)
CBE............. Council of Biology Editors (EA)
CBE............. Counselor Behavior Evaluation Form (EDAC)
CBE............. Crude Barrel Equivalent [*Oil*]
CBE............. Cumberland [*Maryland*] [*Airport symbol*] (OAG)
CBE............. International Commercial Business Establishment [*Saudi Arabia*]
CBea............ Windsor, ON [*AM radio station call letters*]
CBea............ Beaumont Library District Library, Beaumont, CA [*Library symbol Library of Congress*] (LCLS)
CBEA........... California Business Education Association (SRA)
CBEA........... Catholic Business Education Association [*Later, NCBEA*] (EA)
CBEA........... Christian Brothers Education Association [*Later, RECCB*] (EA)
CBEA........... Commonwealth Banana Exporters Association [*Saint Lucia*] (EAIO)
CBEA........... Council for a Black Economic Agenda (EA)
CBEC........... Canadian Book Exchange Centre (IID)
CBEC........... Concentration-Based Exemption Criteria [*Environmental science*]
CBECS......... Control Building Environmental Control System [*Nuclear energy*] (NRCH)
CBED.......... Center for Business and Economic Development [*Auburn University at Montgomery*] [*Research center*] (RCD)
CBED.......... Children with Behavioral and Emotional Difficulty
CBED.......... Convergent Beam Electron Diffraction [*Analytical technique*]
CBEEP......... Commercial Building Energy Efficiency Program [*Australia*]
CBEF.......... Windsor, ON [*AM radio station call letters*]
CBE-FM....... Windsor, ON [*FM radio station call letters*]
CBEFT......... Windsor, ON [*Television station call letters*]
CBEG.......... Sarnia, ON [*FM radio station call letters*]
CBEL.......... [*The*] Cambridge Bibliography of English Literature [*A publication*]
CBEL.......... Current Balance Earth Leakage (PDAA)
CBelmD....... Textron, Inc., Dalmo Victor Co., Belmont, CA [*Library symbol Library of Congress*] (LCLS)
CBelmN....... College of Notre Dame, Belmont, CA [*Library symbol Library of Congress*] (LCLS)
CBelmP....... Peninsula Library System, Belmont, CA [*Library symbol Library of Congress*] (LCLS)
CBelmS....... San Mateo County Free Library, Belmont, CA [*Library symbol Library of Congress*] (LCLS)
CBELT......... Computer Based English Language Testing (AIE)
CBEM.......... Computer-Based Electronic Mail (MCD)
CBEMA........ Canadian Business Equipment Manufacturers Association (HGAA)
CBEMA........ Computer and Business Equipment Manufacturers Association [*Washington, DC*] (EA)
CBEMR....... Commercial Bank of Ethiopia. Market Report [*A publication*]
CBen.......... Benicia Free Public Library, Benicia, CA [*Library symbol Library of Congress*] (LCLS)
CBEN.......... Commonwealth Banking Corporation. Economic Newsletter [*A publication*] (ADA)
CB (Eng)...... English Common Bench Reports (Manning, Granger, and Scott) [*135-139 English Reprint*] [*A publication*] (DLA)
CBENT........ Catholic Biblical Encyclopedia. New Testament [*A publication*] (BJA)
CBEOT........ Catholic Biblical Encyclopedia. Old Testament [*A publication*] (BJA)
CBER.......... Center for Biochemical Engineering Research [*New Mexico State University*] [*Research center*] (RCD)
CBER.......... Center for Biologics Evaluation and Research [*FDA*]
CBER.......... Center for Business and Economic Research [*University of Alabama*] [*University, AL*] [*Information service or system*] (IID)
CBER.......... Center for Business & Economics Research [*University of Nevada - Las Vegas*] [*Research center*] (RCD)
CBERA........ Caribbean Basin Economic Recovery Act
CBET.......... Certified Biomedical Equipment Technician (RDA)
CBET.......... Competency-Based Education and Training
CBET.......... Computer-Based Education and Training
CBET.......... Windsor, ON [*Television station call letters*]
CBETV........ Conditioned Bald Eagle Total Value
CBev.......... Beverly Hills Public Library, Beverly Hills, CA [*Library symbol Library of Congress*] (LCLS)
CBevA......... American Film Institute, Center for Advanced Film Studies, Beverly Hills, CA [*Library symbol Library of Congress*] (LCLS)
CBEVE........ Central Bureau for Educational Visits and Exchanges
CBevL......... Litton Industries, Inc., Beverly Hills, CA [*Library symbol Library of Congress*] (LCLS)
CBevT......... Twentieth Century-Fox Film Corp., Beverly Hills, CA [*Library symbol Library of Congress*] (LCLS)
CBEX........... Cambex Corp. [*NASDAQ symbol*]

CB EX......... Chief Baron of the Exchequer [*British*] (ROG)
CBF............. Canadian Bridge Federation
CBF............. Canbra Foods Ltd. [*Toronto Stock Exchange symbol*]
CBF............. Cancer Breaking Factor [*Antineoplastic drug*]
CBF............. Capillary Blood Flow [*Medicine*] (MAE)
CBF............. Central British Fund for World Jewish Relief (EAIO)
CBF............. Centreboard Factor [*IOR*]
CBF............. Centrifugal Barrel Finishing [*of metal surfaces*]
CBF............. Cerebral Blood Flow [*Medicine*]
CBF............. Chesapeake Bay Foundation [*Marine science*] (OSRA)
CBF............. Chesapeake Bay Foundation (USDC)
CBF............. Children's Blood Foundation (EA)
CBF............. China Northern Airlines [*FAA designator*] (FAAC)
CBF............. Colonial Bishoprics' Fund [*British*]
CBF............. Common Beam Former
CBF............. Community Bankers of Florida (SRA)
CBF............. Confectioners Benevolent Fund [*British*] (BI)
CBF............. Coronary Blood Flow [*Medicine*]
CBF............. Cortical Blood Flow [*Urology*]
CBF............. Council Bluffs, IA [*Location identifier FAA*] (FAAL)
CBF............. Counter-Battery Fire
CBF............. County Boundary File [*Bureau of the Census*] (GFGA)
CBF............. Montreal, PQ [*AM radio station call letters*]
CBF............. Shenyang Regional Administration of CAA of China [*ICAO designator*] (FAAC)
CBFA.......... Canadian Business Forms Association (DGA)
CBFA.......... Cerebral Blood Flow Autoregulation
CBFAP........ Commander, British Forces, Arabian Peninsula [*British military*] (DMA)
CBFB.......... Core Binding Factor Beta [*Genetics*]
CBFC.......... Cathy Buchanan Fan Club (EA)
CBFC.......... Clyde Bowling Fan Club [*Defunct*] (EA)
CBFC.......... Copper and Brass Fabricators Council (EA)
CBFCA........ Commander, British Forces, Caribbean Area [*NATO*] (NATG)
CBF-FM....... Montreal, PQ [*FM radio station call letters*]
CBF-FM-1.... Trois Rivieres, PQ [*FM radio station call letters*]
CBFFTA....... Copper and Brass Fabricators Foreign Trade Association [*Later, CBFC*]
CBFG.......... Commander, British Forces, Gulf [*British military*] (DMA)
CBF Labs.... Cerebral Blood Flow Laboratories [*Research center*] (RCD)
CBFM.......... Constant Bandwidth Frequency Modulation (MHDB)
CBFM.......... Continuous Business Forms Manufacturers (DGA)
CBFMS........ Conservative Baptist Foreign Mission Society (EA)
CBFRJ........ Carol Burnett Fund for Responsible Journalism (EA)
CBFS.......... Caesium Beam Frequency Standard (IAA)
CBFS.......... Carbon Black Feedstock
CBFS.......... Cerebral Blood Flow Studies [*Cardiology*] (DAVI)
CBFSEI....... Clearinghouse for Community Based Free Standing Educational Institutions (EA)
CBFST-2...... Temiscaming, PQ [*Television station call letters*]
CBFT.......... Montreal, PQ [*Television station call letters*]
CBFT-2....... Mont-Laurier, PQ [*Television station call letters*]
CBFV.......... Cerebral Blood Flow Velocity [*Cardiology*] (DAVI)
CBG........... Cambridge [*England*] [*Airport symbol Obsolete*] (OAG)
CBG........... Cambridge, MN [*Location identifier FAA*] (FAAL)
CBG........... Cambridge Shopping Centres Ltd. [*Toronto Stock Exchange symbol*]
CBG........... Capillary Blood Gas [*Biochemistry*] (DAVI)
CBG........... Capillary Blood Glucose [*Biochemistry*] (DAVI)
CBG........... Color Business Graphics (HGAA)
CBG........... Committee to Bridge the Gap (EA)
CBG........... Corticosteroid-Binding Globulin [*Transcortin*] [*Endocrinology*]
CBG........... Craniofacial Biology Group of the International Association for Dental Research (EA)
CBG........... Gander, NF [*AM radio station call letters*]
CBGA.......... California Beet Growers Association (SRA)
CBGA.......... Matane, PQ [*AM radio station call letters*]
CBGA-8....... Iles De La Madeleine, PQ [*FM radio station call letters*]
CBGAT........ Matane, PQ [*Television station call letters*]
CBGB.......... Country, Bluegrass, Blues [*New York nightclub*] [*Later, CMGB & OMFUG*]
CBGF......... Conseil des Bibliotheques du Gouvernement Federal (AC)
CBGHN....... Coalition on Block Grants and Human Needs (EA)
CBGLO........ Carrier-Borne Ground Liaison Officer [*Military British*]
CBGM......... Committee of Black Gay Men (EA)
CBgmstr...... Chief Buglemaster [*Navy*]
CBGN......... Ste. Anne Des Monts, PQ [*AM radio station call letters*]
CBGTU........ Graduate Theological Union, Berkeley, CA [*Library symbol Library of Congress*] (LCLS)
CBGTU-B...... American Baptist Seminary of the West, Berkeley, CA [*Library symbol Library of Congress*] (LCLS)
CBGv.......... Corticosteroid-Binding Globulin Variant [*Medicine*] (DMAA)
CBGY......... Bonavista Bay, NF [*AM radio station call letters*]
CBH........... Bechar [*Algeria*] [*Airport symbol*] (OAG)
CBH........... Camp Beverly Hills [*California clothing store*]
CBH........... Can't Be Heard [*Telecommunications*] (TEL)
CBH........... CB Exective Helicopters [*British ICAO designator*] (FAAC)
CBH........... Cellobiohydrolase [*An enzyme*]
CBH........... Center for Borderline History (EA)
CBH........... Central Board of Health [*South Australia*] [*Australia*]
CBH........... Childbearing Hips
CBH........... Circuit Board Holder
CBH........... Colomb Bechar [*Algeria*] [*Airport symbol*] (AD)
CBH........... Commerce Bancorp New Jersey [*NYSE symbol*] (SAG)
CBH........... Commonwealth Bureau of Helminthology (BI)

CBH .... Congregatie Broeders van Huybergen [*Brothers of the Immaculate Conception of the Mother of God - BICMG*] [*Huybergen, Netherlands*] (EAIO)
CBH .... Cutaneous Basophil Hypersensitivity [*Immunology*]
CBH .... Halifax, NS [*FM radio station call letters*]
CBH .... Hexcel Products, Technical Library, Berkeley, CA [*Library symbol Library of Congress*] (LCLS)
CBHA .... Council for Biology in Human Affairs
CBHA .... Cross Border Humanitarian Assistance (DOMA)
CBHA .... Halifax, NS [*FM radio station call letters*]
CBHFT .... Halifax, NS [*Television station call letters*]
CBHFT-1 ...... Yarmouth, NS [*Television station call letters*]
CBHFT-2 ...... Mulgrave, NS [*Television station call letters*]
CBHFT-3 ...... Sydney, NS [*Television station call letters*]
CBHFT-4 ...... Cheticamp, NS [*Television station call letters*]
CBHHA .... [*The*] Church of the Brethren Homes and Hospitals Association [*Later, BHOAM*] (EA)
CBHi .... Berkeley Historical Society, Berkeley, CA [*Library symbol*] [*Library of Congress*] (LCLS)
CBHI .... Brewer,C Homes'A' [*NASDAQ symbol*] (TTSB)
CBHI .... C Brewer Homes [*NASDAQ symbol*] (SAG)
CBHK .... Captive Boresight Harmonization Kit (MCD)
CBHL .... Council on Botanical and Horticultural Libraries (EA)
CBHM .... Coso Basin North [*California*] [*Seismograph station code, US Geological Survey*] (SEIS)
CBHMA .... Custer Battlefield Historical and Museum Association (EA)
CBHMS .... Conservative Baptist Home Mission Society (EA)
CBHPC .... Commonwealth Bureau of Horticulture and Plantation Crops [*British*]
CBHS .... Certificate in Basic Health Sciences (PGP)
CBHSA .... Cleveland Bay Horse Society of America (EA)
CBHSM .... Council for Better Hearing and Speech Month (EA)
CBHT .... Cedarholm, Bland, Havens, and Townes [*Ether drift experiment*] (MUGU)
CBHT .... Halifax, NS [*Television station call letters*]
CBHT-3 .... Yarmouth, NS [*Television station call letters*]
CBHT-4 .... Sheet Harbour, NS [*Television station call letters*]
CBHT-11 ...... Mulgrave, NS [*Television station call letters*]
CBi .... Biggs Free Public Library, Biggs, CA [*Library symbol Library of Congress*] (LCLS)
CBI .... Cache Bus Interface [*Computer science*] (BYTE)
CBI .... Cahners Books International, Inc. [*Later, CBI Publishing Co., Inc.*]
CBI .... Canine Behavior Institute (EA)
CBI .... Carbonated Beverage Institute (EA)
CBI .... Caribbean Basin Initiative [*Financial aid package proposed by President Reagan for Central American and Caribbean countries*]
CBI .... Cast Bronze Institute [*Defunct*] (EA)
CBI .... CBI Industries, Inc. [*Formerly, Chicago Bridge & Iron Co.*] [*Associated Press*] (SAG)
CBI .... Center for Business Information [*Information service or system*] (IID)
CBI .... Central Bible Institute [*Missouri*]
CBI .... Central Bureau of Identification (WDAA)
CBI .... Charles Babbage Institute for the History of Information Processing (EA)
CBI .... Chesapeake Bay Institute [*Johns Hopkins University*]
CBI .... Chesbar Resources, Inc. [*Toronto Stock Exchange symbol*]
CBI .... Chichijima [*Bonin Islands*] [*Seismograph station code, US Geological Survey*] (SEIS)
CBI .... Children's Behavior Inventory [*Medicine*] (DMAA)
CBI .... Children's Broadcast Institute [*Canada*]
CBI .... China-Burma-India Theater [*World War II*]
CBI .... Christopher Burns, Inc. [*Also, an information service or system*] (IID)
CBI .... Client Behavior Inventory [*Psychology*] (AEBS)
CBI .... Close-Binding-Intimate [*Biochemistry*]
Cbi .... Cobinamide [*Biochemistry*]
CBI .... Collective Bargaining Institute [*New York, NY*]
CBI .... Columbia, MO [*Location identifier FAA*] (FAAL)
CBI .... Committee on Biological Information [*British*] (DIT)
CBI .... Common Batch Identification [*Computer science*] (EECA)
CBI .... Competency-Based Instruction
CBI .... Complete Background Investigation
CBI .... Compliance Biomonitoring Inspection [*Environmental Protection Agency*] (GFGA)
CBI .... Compound Batch Identification [*Computer science*]
CBI .... Computer-Based Instruction [*Education*]
CBI .... Conditional Breakpoint Instruction
CBI .... Confederation of British Industry
CBI .... Confidential Business Information [*Environmental Protection Agency*]
CBI .... Confidential Business Information [*Government regulations*]
CBI .... Continuous Bladder Irrigation [*Urology*]
CBI .... Cooperative Business International [*Washington, DC*] (EA)
CBI .... Corriente Batllista Independiente [*Uruguay*] [*Political party*] (EY)
CBI .... Council for a Beautiful Israel (EA)
CBI .... Information Unltd., Berkeley, CA [*Library symbol Library of Congress*] (LCLS)
CBI .... Sydney, NS [*AM radio station call letters*]
CBIA .... California Building Industry Association (SRA)
CBIA .... Canadian Bar Insurance Association [*Association d'Assurance du Barreau Canadien*] (AC)
CBIA .... Connecticut Business and Industry Association (SRA)
CBIAC .... Chemical Warfare/Chemical Biological Defense Information Analysis Center [*DoD*]
CBIAC .... Columbia Basin Inter-Agency Committee [*Department of Commerce*] (NOAA)
CBIB .... Censo de Bibliotecas [*Database*] [*Ministerio de Cultura*] [*Spanish*] [*Information service or system*] (CRD)

CBIB .... Checkerboard Immunoblotting Technique [*Immunology*]
CBIC .... Canadian Book Information Centre
CBIC .... Caribbean Basin Business Information Center (IMH)
CBIC .... Complementary Bipolar Integrated Circuit [*Telecommunications*] (TEL)
CBIC .... Computer-Based Information Center [*Free Library of Philadelphia*] (OLDSS)
CBIE .... Canadian Bureau for International Education [*See also BCEI*]
CBI-FM .... Sydney, NS [*FM radio station call letters*]
CBIH .... Chemical and Biological Information Handling [*National Institutes of Health*]
CBIHPA .... China-Burma-India Hump Pilots Association (EA)
CBIL .... China Book Information Letter [*A publication*]
CBIL .... Common and Bulk Items List
CBIM .... Canadian Baptist International Ministries (EAIO)
CBIM .... Companion of the British Institute of Management (DBQ)
CBIMT .... Iles De La Madeleine, PQ [*Television station call letters*]
CBIN .... Caribbean Basin Information Network [*Caribbean/Central American Action*] [*Information service or system*] (IID)
CBIN .... Community Bank Shares(Ind) [*NASDAQ symbol*] (TTSB)
CBIN .... Community Bank Shares of Indiana, Inc. [*NASDAQ symbol*] (SAG)
CBIO .... Counterbattery Intelligence Officer [*Army*] (AABC)
CBiP .... Biggs Free Public Library, Biggs, CA [*Library symbol*] [*Library of Congress*] (LCLS)
CBIP .... Canter Background Interference Procedure [*For the Bender Gestalt Test*] [*Psychology*] (DAVI)
CBIPBG .... Canter Background Interference Procedure for Bender Gestalt [*Test*] [*Psychology*] (DAVI)
CBIPO .... Custom-Built Installation Process Offering [*Computer science*] (HGAA)
CBIRF .... Chemical/Biological Incident Response Force [*Marine Corps*]
CBIS .... Campus-Based Information System [*National Science Foundation*]
CBIS .... Communist Bloc Intelligence Service (NATG)
CBIS .... Computer-Based Instruction System (IEEE)
CBisI .... Inyo County Free Library, Bishop, CA [*Library symbol Library of Congress*] (LCLS)
CBISSSH ...... Committee on Bibliography and Information Services for the Social Sciences and Humanities [*National Library of Canada*]
CBIT .... China-Burma-India Theater [*World War II*]
CBIT .... Contract Bulk Inclusive Tour [*Airline fare*]
CBIT .... Sydney, NS [*Television station call letters*]
CBIT-2 .... Cheticamp, NS [*Television station call letters*]
CBIVA .... China-Burma-India Veterans Association (EA)
CBJ .... Cambior, Inc. [*AMEX symbol*] (SAG)
CBJ .... Caribjet, Inc. [*Antigua and Barbuda*] [*ICAO designator*] (FAAC)
CBJ .... Chicoutimi, PQ [*AM radio station call letters*]
CBJ .... Common Bulkhead Joint
CBJA .... Central Bureau for the Jewish Aged (EA)
CBJE-FM ..... Chicoutimi, PQ [*FM radio station call letters*]
CBJET .... Chicoutimi, PQ [*Television station call letters*]
CBJ-FM ...... Chicoutimi, PQ [*FM radio station call letters*]
CBJO .... Coordinating Board of Jewish Organizations (EA)
CBK .... CB Pak, Inc. [*Toronto Stock Exchange symbol*]
C Bk .... Cheque Book [*British*] (DAS)
CBK .... Citizens First Financial Corp. [*AMEX symbol*] (SAG)
CBK .... Citizens First Finl [*AMEX symbol*] (TTSB)
CBK .... Colby, KS [*Location identifier FAA*] (FAAL)
CBK .... Commercial Bank of Korea
CBK .... Community Bankers of Kentucky (SRA)
CBK .... Regina, SK [*AM radio station call letters*]
CBKA .... La Ronge, SK [*FM radio station call letters*]
CBKA-FM ..... La Ronge, SK [*FM radio station call letters*]
CBKF-1 .... Gravelbourg, SK [*AM radio station call letters*]
CBKF-2 .... Saskatoon, SK [*AM radio station call letters*]
CBKF-FM ..... Regina, SK [*FM radio station call letters*]
CBK-FM ...... Regina, SK [*FM radio station call letters*]
CBKFT .... Regina, SK [*Television station call letters*]
CBKFT-3 ..... Debden, SK [*Television station call letters*]
CBKFT-4 ..... St. Brieux, SK [*Television station call letters*]
CBKFT-5 ..... Zenon Park, SK [*Television station call letters*]
CBKFT-6 ..... Gravelbourg, SK [*Television station call letters*]
CBKFT-9 ..... Bellegarde, SK [*Television station call letters*]
CBKI .... Community Banks, Inc. [*NASDAQ symbol*] (NQ)
CBKS .... Saskatoon, SK [*FM radio station call letters*]
CBKST .... Saskatoon, SK [*Television station call letters*]
CBKST-1 ..... Stranraer, SK [*Television station call letters*]
CBKT .... Regina, SK [*Television station call letters*]
CBKT-2 .... Willow Bunch, SK [*Television station call letters*]
CBL .... Cable (AAG)
CBL .... Cabline
CBL .... Calwer Bibellexikon (BJA)
CBL .... Camara Brasileira do Livro [*Brazilian Chamber of Publishing*] (EAIO)
CBL .... Canadian Broadcasting League
CBL .... Carlyle Barton Laboratory (MCD)
CBL .... Carte Blanche [*Freedom of Action*] [*French*]
CBL .... Caustic Boundary Layer [*Acoustics*]
CBL .... CBL & Associates Prop [*NYSE symbol*] (TTSB)
CBL .... CBL & Associates Properties [*NYSE symbol*] (SPSG)
CBL .... Central Bidder's List
CBL .... Chesapeake Biological Laboratories [*University of Maryland*]
CBL .... Ciudad Bolivar [*Venezuela*] [*Airport symbol*] (OAG)
CBL .... Cleared Bidder's List
Cbl .... Cobalamin [*Biochemistry*]
CBL .... Collect Bill of Lading (AAGC)
CBL .... Commercial Bill of Lading [*Shipping*]

CBL............. Community Business Lothian [*British*]
CBL............. Competency-Based Learning [*Education*]
CBL............. Computer-Based Learning
CBL............. Conemaugh & Black Lick Railroad Co. [*AAR code*]
CBL............. Configuration Breakdown List
CBL............. Convective Boundary Layer [*Marine science*] (OSRA)
CBL............. Convective Boundary Layer (USDC)
CBL............. Cord [*Umbilical*] Blood Leukocytes [*Hematology*]
CBL............. Crown Bute Resources Ltd. [*Vancouver Stock Exchange symbol*]
CBL............. Nichols Air Service, Inc. [*ICAO designator*] (FAAC)
CBl............. Palo Verde Valley District Library, Blythe, CA [*Library symbol Library of Congress*] (LCLS)
CBL............. San Bernardino County Free Library, San Bernardino, CA [*OCLC symbol*] (OCLC)
CBL............. Toronto, ON [*AM radio station call letters*]
CBLA............ Central Blood Laboratories Authority [*British*]
CBLANT .... Construction Battalions, Atlantic [*Navy*]
CBL Asc...... CBL & Associates Properties [*Associated Press*] (SAG)
CBLAT......... Geraldton, ON [*Television station call letters*]
CBLAT-1 ..... Manitouwadge, ON [*Television station call letters*]
CBLAT-3 ..... Wawa, ON [*Television station call letters*]
CBLAT-4 ..... Marathon, ON [*Television station call letters*]
CBLC.......... Center for the Book in the Library of Congress (EA)
CblCar .... Cable Car Beverage Corp. [*Associated Press*] (SAG)
CblDsgn...... Cable Design Technologies [*Associated Press*] (SAG)
CbleCo....... Cable & Co. Worldwide, Inc. [*Associated Press*] (SAG)
CBLFA......... Corn Belt Livestock Feeders Association [*Later, NCA*]
CBL-FM........ Toronto, ON [*FM radio station call letters*]
CBLFT......... Toronto, ON [*Television station call letters*]
CBLFT-1....... Sturgeon Falls, ON [*Television station call letters*]
CBLFT-2....... Sudbury, ON [*Television station call letters*]
CBLFT-3....... Timmins, ON [*Television station call letters*]
CBLFT-4....... Kapuskasing, ON [*Television station call letters*]
CBLFT-5....... Hearst, ON [*Television station call letters*]
CBLFT-6....... Elliot Lake, ON [*Television station call letters*]
CBLHI .... California Brief Life History Inventory [*Personality development test*] [*Psychology*]
CBLJ........... Corporate Business Law Journal [*A publication*]
CBLM.......... Cluster-Bethe-Lattice Method (MCD)
CBLMN....... Cableman (IAA)
CBLNE .... Community Bank League of New England (SRA)
CBLO .... Chief Bombardment Liaison Officer [*Navy*]
CBLRD .... Cable Reed
CBLS........... Carrier Bombs Light Store [*Military*] (PDAA)
CBLS........... Carrier-Borne Air Liaison Section [*Navy*]
CBLS........... Corn Belt Library System [*Library network*]
CBLT........... Character Block Transfer (BYTE)
CBLT........... Toronto, ON [*Television station call letters*]
CBM........... Calcium-Based Minerals [*Inorganic chemistry*]
CBM........... California Beverage Merchants (SRA)
CBM........... Cambrex Corp. [*AMEX symbol*] (SPSG)
CBM........... Caribou [*Maine*] [*Seismograph station code, US Geological Survey*] (SEIS)
CBM........... Carrierband MODEM [*Motorola, Inc.*]
CBM........... Center for Biological Macromolecules [*State University of New York at Albany*] [*Research center*] (RCD)
CBM........... Central Bank Money
CBM........... Central Bank of Malta
CBM........... Central Battle Manager
CBM........... Ceramic-Based Microcircuit
CBM........... Certified Ballast Manufacturers Association (EA)
CBM........... Chemical-Biological Munitions (AFM)
CBM........... Cherokee Leasing, Inc. [*ICAO designator*] (FAAC)
CBM........... Chief Boatswain's Mate [*Navy rating Obsolete*]
CBM........... Chlorobromomethane [*Also, CB*] [*Organic chemistry*]
CBM........... Cigar Box Manufacturers [*Defunct*] (EA)
CBM........... Cognitive-Behavior Modification [*Psychology*]
CBM........... Columbus, MS [*Location identifier FAA*] (FAAL)
CBM........... Commemorative Bucks of Michigan
CBM........... Commodore Business Machines [*Commercial firm*] (NITA)
CBM........... Common Bill of Material (MCD)
CBM........... Communications Buffer Memory [*Computer science*]
CBM........... Condition-Based Maintenance [*Army*]
CBM........... Conduction Band Minimum [*Electronics*]
CBM........... Confidence-Building Measure
CBM........... Consolidated Boulder Mountain [*Vancouver Stock Exchange symbol*]
CBM........... Constant Boiling Mixture
CBM........... Continental Ballistic Missile
CBM........... Continental Baptist Mission (EA)
CBM........... Contour Blind & Shade (Canada) Ltd. [*Toronto Stock Exchange symbol*]
CBM........... Conventional Buoy Mooring (DS)
CBM........... Corn, Beans, Miami [*Tongue-in-cheek description of a crop rotation system, allowing farmers to spend winter in Florida*]
CBM........... Cruise Ballistic Missile (MCD)
CBM........... Cubic Meter (ROG)
CBM........... Judah L. Magnes Memorial Museum, Rabbi Morris Goldstein Library, Berkeley, CA [*Library symbol Library of Congress*] (LCLS)
CBM........... Montreal, PQ [*AM radio station call letters*]
CBMA.......... Canadian Book Manufacturing Association
CBMA.......... Canadian Business Manufacturers Association (MCD)
CBMA.......... Certified Ballast Manufacturers Association
CBMA.......... Chief Boatswain's Mate, Acting [*Navy rating Obsolete*]
CBMA.......... Christian Bookstall Managers Association (EA)
CBMA.......... Concrete Brick Manufacturers Association [*British*] (DBA)

CBMA.......... Country Bread Manufacturers' Association [*Western Australia*] [*Australia*]
CBMAM....... Cumulonimbus Mamma [*NWS*] (FAAC)
CBMAWA .... Clay Brick Manufacturers' Association of Western Australia
CBMC.......... Canadian Book Marketing Centre [*Formerly, Canadian Book Information Centre*] (AC)
CBMC.......... Christian Business Men of Canada
CBMC.......... Christian Business Men's Committee of USA (EA)
CBMC.......... Communaute de Travail des Brasseurs du Marche Commun [*Working Committee of Common Market Brewers*]
CBMC.......... Confederation des Brasseurs du Marche Commun [*Belgium*] (EAIO)
CBMC.......... Corregidor-Bataan Memorial Commission [*Government agency*] [*Terminated, 1967*]
CBMCA .... Christian Business Men's Committees Australia
CBMCBB ..... Chief Boatswain's Mate, Construction Battalion, Boatswain [*Navy rating Obsolete*]
CBMCBS ..... Chief Boatswain's Mate, Construction Battalion, Stevedore [*Navy rating Obsolete*]
CBMCI .... Christian Business Men's Committee International [*Later, CBMC*] (EA)
CBMD .... Calcified Bone Mineral Density
CBMD .... Columbia Bancorp [*NASDAQ symbol*] (SAG)
CBMDA .... California Building Material Dealers Association (SRA)
CBME .... Combined Bureau, Middle East [*British military*] (DMA)
CBM-FM ..... Montreal, PQ [*FM radio station call letters*]
CBMI........... Baie Comeau, PQ [*FM radio station call letters*]
CBMI........... Christian Blind Mission International [*Bensheim, Federal Republic of Germany*] (EAIO)
CBMI........... Creative BioMolecules [*NASDAQ symbol*] (TTSB)
CBMI........... Creative BioMolecules, Inc. [*NASDAQ symbol*] (SAG)
CBMIS .... Comprehensive Budget and Management Information System (MHDI)
CBMIS .... Computer-Based Management Information System (MHDB)
CBMKR .... Chief Boilermaker [*Coast Guard*]
CBMM......... Chief Boatswain's Mate, A [*Master-at-Arms*] [*Navy rating Obsolete*]
CBMMP....... Chronic Benign Mucous Membrane Pemphigoid [*Medicine*]
CBMP......... Conference Board of Major Printers [*Defunct*] (EA)
CBMPE....... Council of British Manufacturers of Petroleum Equipment
CBMPP....... Cargo Bay Module Personnel Provisions [*NASA*] (KSC)
CBMPTU ..... Cigar Box Makers' and Paperers' Trade Union [*British*]
CBMR......... Fermont, PQ [*FM radio station call letters*]
CBMS......... Computer-Based Management System (IAA)
CBMS......... Computer-Based Medical System
CBMS......... Computer-Based Message System [*Electronic mail*]
CBMS......... Conference Board of the Mathematical Sciences (EA)
CBM's........ Confidence-Building Measure [*for European military security*]
CBMSRC ..... Chief Boatswain's Mate, Ship Repair, Crane Operator [*Navy rating Obsolete*]
CBMSRR ..... Chief Boatswain's Mate, Ship Repair, Rigger [*Navy rating Obsolete*]
CBMSRS ..... Chief Boatswain's Mate, Ship Repair, Canvasman [*Navy rating Obsolete*]
CBMT .... Certification Board for Music Therapists (EA)
CBMT .... Cross-Linked Biotinylated Microtubule [*Biochemistry*]
CBMT .... Montreal, PQ [*Television station call letters*]
CBMU .... Canadian Board of Marine Underwriters
CBMU .... Construction Battalion Maintenance Unit [*Navy*]
CBMU .... Current BIT [*Binary Digit*] Monitor Unit [*Computer science*]
CBMUA .... Canadian Boiler and Machinery Underwriters Association
CBMUDET ... Construction Battalion Maintenance Unit Detachment [*Navy*] (DNAB)
CBMWA .... Country Bread Manufacturers of Western Australia
CBN .... Cabarien [*Cuba*] [*Airport symbol*] (AD)
CBN .... Cabin
CBN .... Cannabinol [*A component of marijuana*]
CBN .... Carbine (AABC)
CBN .... Chemical/Bacterial/Nuclear [*Military*] (MCD)
CBN .... Christian Broadcasting Network [*Cable-television system*]
CBN .... Chronic Benign Neutropenia [*Hematology*] (DAVI)
CBN .... Cirebon [*Indonesia*] [*Airport symbol*] (OAG)
CBN .... Commission on Biochemical Nomenclature [*IUPAC*]
CBN .... Commonwealth Broadcasting Network [*British*] (NTCM)
CBN .... Consolidated Marbenor Mines Ltd. [*Toronto Stock Exchange symbol*]
CBN .... Construction Battalion [*Navy*]
CBN .... Corbin [*Virginia*] [*Seismograph station code, US Geological Survey*] (SEIS)
CBN .:.......... Cornerstone Bank [*AMEX symbol*] (SAG)
CbN............. Courses by Newspaper (EDAC)
CBN............. Cubic Boron Nitride [*Cutting tool edges*]
CBN .... St. John's, NF [*AM radio station call letters*]
CBNAT .... Grand Falls, NF [*Television station call letters*]
CBNAT-1 ..... Baie Verte, NF [*Television station call letters*]
CBNAT-4 ..... St. Anthony, NF [*Television station call letters*]
CBNAT-9...... Mount St. Margaret, NF [*Television station call letters*]
CBNB .... Chemical Business NewsBase [*Royal Society of Chemistry*] [*Information service or system*]
CBNC .... Collective Bargaining Negotiations and Contracts [*Bureau of National Affairs*] [*Information service or system*]
CBNDET ...... Construction Battalion Detachment [*Navy*] (DNAB)
CBNEV .... Constitution Bancorp of New England, Inc. (MHDW)
CB NEWS.... Community Business Scotland News [*A publication*]
CBN-FM ...... St. John's, NF [*FM radio station call letters*]
CBNH .... Community Bankshares, Inc. [*NASDAQ symbol*] (NQ)
CBNH .... Community Bankshares (NH) [*NASDAQ symbol*] (TTSB)
CBNJ .... Carnegie Bancorp [*NASDAQ symbol*] (SAG)
CBNJW .... Carnegie Bancorp Wrrt [*NASDAQ symbol*] (TTSB)
CBNLT .... Labrador City, NF [*Television station call letters*]

CBNM	Central Bureau of Nuclear Measurements [*European Atomic Energy Community*]
CBNRC	Communications Branch, National Research Council
CBNS	Center for the Biology of Natural Systems [*Washington University*]
CBNS	Commander, British Naval Staff
CBNS	Common Bench, New Series [*A publication*]
CB (NS)	English Common Bench Reports, New Series (Manning, Granger, and Scott) [*140-144 English Reprint*] [*A publication*] (DLA)
CB NS (Eng)	English Common Bench Reports, New Series (Manning, Granger, and Scott) [*140-144 English Reprint*] [*A publication*] (DLA)
CBNT	Cabinet
CBNT	St. John's, NF [*Television station call letters*]
CBNT-1	Port Rexton, NF [*Television station call letters*]
CBNT-2	Placentia, NF [*Television station call letters*]
CBNT-3	Marystown, NF [*Television station call letters*]
CBNY	Commercial Bank of New York [*NASDAQ symbol*] (SAG)
CBO	Canadian Continental Oil [*Vancouver Stock Exchange symbol*]
CBO	Cancel Back Order
CBO	Carrier Balloon/Omegasonde System [*National Center for Atmospheric Research*]
CBO	Certificate of Beneficial Ownership
CBO	Characteristics of Business Owners [*Bureau of the Census*] (GFGA)
CBO	Chesbro Reservoir [*California*] [*Seismograph station code, US Geological Survey*] (SEIS)
CBQ	Clarksville Branch Office [*AEC*]
CBO	Coding Board Officer
CBO	Collateralized Bond Obligation [*Investment term*] (DFIT)
CBO	Collective Bargaining Organization
CBO	Combined Bomber Offensive [*World War II*]
CBO	Community-Based Order (ADA)
CBO	Community-Based Organization [*Organization which provides employment and training services*] [*CETA*]
CBO	Components Business Operations [*Chrysler campaign to increase sales*]
CBO	Computer Burst Order (AABC)
CBO	Conference of Baltic Oceanographers [*Germany*] (EAIO)
CBO	Confirmation of Broadcast Order (WDMC)
CBO	Congressional Budget Office [*Washington, DC*]
CBO	Control Board Operator [*Lighting*] (NTCM)
CBO	Convertible Bond Option [*Finance*] (EMRF)
CBO	Cotabato [*Philippines*] [*Airport symbol*] (OAG)
CBO	Counter-Battery Officer
CBO	Cycles between Overhaul (MCD)
CBO	Ottawa, ON [*FM radio station call letters*]
CBOA	Citizens Band Operating Area
CBOB	Collegiate Basketball Officials Bureau [*Later, Eastern College Basketball Association*] (EA)
CBOC	Canada Business Opportunity Centre [*1986*]
CBoC	Central Bank of China
CBOC	Completion of Bed Occupancy Care [*Veterans Administration*]
CBOC	County Bank of Chesterfield [*NASDAQ symbol*] (TTSB)
CBOD	Carbonaceous Biochemical Oxygen Demand [*Environmental chemistry*]
CBOE	Chicago Board Options Exchange [*Chicago, IL*] (EA)
CBOE	Committee of Butchery Organizations of the EEC (EAIO)
CBOF	Competitive Business Operation Fund (AAGC)
CBOF	Ottawa, ON [*AM radio station call letters*]
CBOF-1	Maniwaki, PQ [*AM radio station call letters*]
CBOF-FM	Ottawa, ON [*FM radio station call letters*]
CBOFT	Ottawa, ON [*Television station call letters*]
CBOI	Complete Basis of Issue [*Military*] (AABC)
CBOIP	Complete Basis of Issue Plan [*Military*] (AABC)
CBOK-ACES	Christelijke Bond van de Ondergrondse Kerk/Action Chretienne pour l'Eglise du Silence [*Belgium*]
CBOM	Current Break-Off and Memory (OA)
CBOMB	Canadian Baptist Overseas Mission Board
C (Bomb)	Cobalt Bomb [*Nuclear*]
CBON	Sudbury, ON [*FM radio station call letters*]
CBOQ	Ottawa, ON [*FM radio station call letters*]
CBORE	Counterbore (KSC)
CBOREO	Counterbore Other Side
CBOS	Chesapeake Bay Observing System [*Marine science*] (OSRA)
CBOS	Chesapeake Bay Observing System (USDC)
CBOSS	Count Back Order and Sample Select [*Computer science*]
CBOT	Chicago Board of Trade [*Chicago, IL*] (EAIO)
CBOT	Commissions Board of Trade
CBOT	Ottawa, ON [*Television station call letters*]
CBOV	[*The*] College Book of Verse [*A publication*]
CBOX	Ottawa, ON [*FM radio station call letters*]
CBp	Buena Park Library District Library, Buena Park, CA [*Library symbol Library of Congress*] (LCLS)
CBP	Calgary Board of Education, Professional Library [*UTLAS symbol*]
CBP	Campbellpur [*Pakistan*] [*Seismograph station code, US Geological Survey*] (SEIS)
CBP	Canadian Business Press
CBP	Caribe Petroleums [*Vancouver Stock Exchange symbol*]
CBP	Catholic Book Publishers [*Later, CBPA*] (EA)
CBP	Ceramic Beam Pentode
CBP	Charm Bracelet Polymer [*Organic chemistry*]
CBP	Cholesterol Binding Protein [*Biochemistry*]
CBP	Class of Blue Copper Proteins [*Crystallography*]
CBP	Colchicine-Binding Protein [*Biochemistry*]
CBP	Columbus, OH [*Location identifier FAA*] (FAAL)
CBP	Combined Black Publishers [*Defunct*] (EA)
CBP	Condensate Booster Pump [*Nuclear energy*] (NRCH)

CBP	Connector Bracket (Power) (MCD)
CBP	Constant Boiling Point
CBP	Construction Briefing Paper [*A publication*] (AAGC)
CBP	County Business Patterns [*Bureau of the Census*] [*Information service or system A publication*]
CBPA	California Business Properties Association (SRA)
CBPA	Catholic Book Publishers Association (EA)
CBPAC	Construction Battalions, Pacific [*Navy*]
CBPac	Pacific School of Religion, Berkeley, CA [*Library symbol Library of Congress*] (LCLS)
CBPANSW	Clay Brick and Paver Association of New South Wales [*Australia*]
CBPC	[*The*] Cambridge Book of Poetry for Children [*A publication*]
CBPC	Canadian Book Publishers' Council
CBPDC	Canadian Book and Periodical Development Council
CBPDF	Canadian Broadcast Program Development Fund
CBPF	Pacific Film Archives, University Art Museum, Berkeley, CA [*Library symbol Library of Congress*] (LCLS)
CBPFC	Commonwealth Bureau of Pastures and Field Crops [*British*]
CBPI	Conditional Breakpoint Instruction
CBPISA	Clay Brick and Paver Institute of South Australia
CBPMP	Cold Brine Pump
CBpN	Nutrilite Products, Inc., Technical Library, Buena Park, CA [*Library symbol Library of Congress*] (LCLS)
CBPO	Consolidated Base Personnel Office [*Air Force*]
CBPOL	Consolidated Base Personnel Office Letter [*Air Force*]
CBPP	Center on Budget and Policy Priorities (EA)
CBPP	Contagious Bovine Pleuropneumonia [*Veterinary medicine*]
CBPPA	Cytoxan, Bleomycin, Procarbazine Prednisone, Adriamycin [*Antineoplastic drug regimen*] (DAVI)
CBPQ	Corporation des Bibliothecaires Professionnels du Quebec [*Corporation of Professsional Librarians of Quebec*] (AC)
CBPS	Chemically and Biologically Protected Shelter [*Army*]
CBPT	Carbonprint (VRA)
CBPT	CLIRA [*Closed-Loop In-Reactor Assembly*] Backup Plug Tool [*Nuclear energy*] (NRCH)
CBPTC	Carbon Black Producers Traffic Committee
CBQ	Calabar [*Nigeria*] [*Airport symbol*] (OAG)
CBQ	Chicago, Burlington & Quincy Railroad [*Also known as Burlington Route*] [*AAR code*]
CBQ	Civilian Bachelor Quarters [*Air Force*] (AFM)
CBQ	CLass Based Queuing [*Computer science*]
CBQ	Competence-Based Qualification [*Education*] (AIE)
CBQ	Conseil de la Boulangerie du Quebec [*Quebec Bakery Council*] (AC)
CBQ	Thunder Bay, ON [*FM radio station call letters*]
CBQCA	(Carboxybenzoyl)quinolinecarboxaldehyde [*Organic chemistry*]
CBQL	Savant Lake, ON [*FM radio station call letters*]
CBQN	Osnaburgh, ON [*FM radio station call letters*]
CBQP	Pickle Lake, ON [*FM radio station call letters*]
CBQR	Rankin Inlet, NT [*FM radio station call letters*]
CBQS	Sioux Narrows, ON [*FM radio station call letters*]
CBQT	Thunder Bay, ON [*FM radio station call letters*]
CBQX	Kenora, ON [*FM radio station call letters*]
C_{BR}	Bilirubin Clearance [*Gastroenterology*] (DAVI)
CBr	Brawley Public Library, Brawley, CA [*Library symbol Library of Congress*] (LCLS)
CBR	Calgary, AB [*AM radio station call letters*]
CBR	California Bearing Ratio [*Aviation*]
CBR	Campaign for a British Referendum (ECON)
CBR	Canadian Bankruptcy Reports, Annotated [*A publication*] (DLA)
CBR	Canadian Barranca Corp. [*Vancouver Stock Exchange symbol*]
CBR	Canberra [*Australia Airport symbol*] (OAG)
CBR	Carotid Bodies Resected [*Medicine*] (AAMN)
CBR	Case-Based Reasoning
CBR	Cast Brass
CBR	Center for Blood Research [*Research center*] (RCD)
CBR	Center for Brain Research [*University of Rochester*] [*Research center*] (RCD)
CBR	Centre for Business Research [*Manchester Business School*] [*British*] (CB)
CBR	Change Board Register
CBR	Charger Battery Relay (MCD)
CBR	Chemical, Biological, and Radiological [*Warfare*] [*Later, CB*] [*Military*]
CBR	Chemically-Bound Residue [*Medicine*] (DMAA)
CBR	China Business Resources Co. Ltd. (ECON)
CBR	China Business Review [*A publication*]
CBR	Chronic Bed Rest [*Medicine*]
CBR	Circuit Board Rack
CBR	Citizens Band Radio (IAA)
CBR	Cloud Base Recorder (PDAA)
CBR	Colonial Bird Register [*Cornell University*] [*Information service or system*] (IID)
CBR	Commercial Breeder Reactor
CBR	Complete Bed Rest [*Medicine*]
CBR	Comprehensive Beacon RADAR
CBR	Computer-Based Reference (CDE)
CBR	Computer Book Review [*Comber Press*] [*Information service or system*] (CRD)
CBR	Computerized Bibliographic Retrieval [*Hope College*] (OLDSS)
CBR	Concurrent Budget Resolution (AAGC)
CBR	Constant Bit Rate [*Telecommunications*] (CDE)
CBR	Contract Baseline Report (MCD)
CBR	Cosmic Background Radiation
CBR	Cosmic Black-Body Radiation [*Astrophysics*]
C/BR	Cost/Burden Reduction

CBR .... Cour du Banc de la Reine [*Court of Queen's Bench*] [*Quebec*] [*Canada*] (ILCA)
CBR .... Crude Birth Rate [*Medicine*]
CBR .... Current Balance Record [*Banking*] (IAA)
CBRA .... Canadian Book Review Annual [*A publication*] (BRI)
CBRA .... Chemical, Biological, Radiological Agency [*Military*]
CBRA .... Cobra Golf, Inc. [*NASDAQ symbol*] (SAG)
CBRA .... Copper and Brass Research Association [*Later, CDA*]
CBRA .... Critical Bibliography to Religion in America [*A publication*] (BJA)
CBRA .... Library of Congress COBRA [*Source file*] [*UTLAS symbol*]
CBRC .... Chemical, Biological, and Radiological Center [*Military*]
CBRCC .... Chemical, Biological, Radiological Control Center [*Military*] (AABC)
C/BRD .... Circuit Board [*Automotive engineering*]
CBRD .... Construction Battalion Replacement Depot [*Navy*]
CBRE .... Canadian Brotherhood of Railway Employees and Other Transport Workers
CBRE .... Chemical, Biological, and Radiological Element [*Military*] (AABC)
CBreA .... Ameron, Inc. Corrosion Control Division, Brea, CA [*Library symbol Library of Congress*] (LCLS)
CBRED .... Closed Bomb Data Reduction Program (MCD)
CBREG .... Chemical-Biological-Radiological Engineering Group [*Army*] (MCD)
CBreU .... Union Oil Co. of California, Brea, CA [*Library symbol Library of Congress*] (LCLS)
CBrewer ...... C Brewer Homes [*Associated Press*] (SAG)
CBRF .... Community-Based Residential Facility
CBR-FM ...... Calgary, AB [*FM radio station call letters*]
CBRI .... Chemistry and Biology Research Institute [*Agriculture Canada Research Branch*] [*Research center*] (RCD)
CBRI .... Comic Book Retailers International [*An association*] (EA)
CBri .... Mono County Free Library, Bridgeport, CA [*Library symbol Library of Congress*] (LCLS)
CBRL .... Cracker Barrel Old Country Store [*NASDAQ symbol*] (SAG)
CBRL .... Cracker Brl Old Ctry [*NASDAQ symbol*] (TTSB)
CBRM .... Cash by Return Mail [*Business term*] (IAA)
CBRM .... Charger-Battery-Regulator Module [*NASA*]
CBRN .... Carribean Basin Radar Network [*Military*] (DOMA)
CBRN .... Chemical, Biological, Radiological, and Nuclear [*Army*] (AABC)
CBR (NS) ..... Canadian Bankruptcy Reports, Annotated, New Series [*A publication*] (DLA)
CBRO .... Chemical, Biological, Radiological Officer [*Army*]
CBRP .... CB [*Citizens Band*] Radio Patrol of American Federation of Police (EA)
CBRP .... Chemical, Biological, and Radiological Protection (DNAB)
CBRPT .... Confederation of British Road Passenger Transport (ILCA)
CBRS .... Chemical, Biological, and Radiological Section [*Military*]
CBRS .... Child Behavior Rating Scale [*Devereaux*] [*Psychology*]
CBRS .... Children's Book Review Service [*A publication*] (BRI)
CBRS .... Chiropody Bibliographical Research Society
CBRS .... Coastal Barrier Resources System [*Department of the Interior*]
CBRS .... Computer-Based Reference Service [*Information service or system*]
CBRS .... Concepts-Based Requirements System
CBRT .... Cabaret
CBRT .... Calgary, AB [*Television station call letters*]
CBRT .... Canadian Brotherhood of Railway Transport and General Workers
CBRU .... Computer-Based Resource Units [*Education*]
CBrug .... Collationes Brugenses (BJA)
CBRY .... Northland Cranberries, Inc. [*NASDAQ symbol*] (NQ)
CBRYA .... Northland Cranberries'A' [*NASDAQ symbol*] (TTSB)
CBS .... Caborca [*Mexico*] [*Seismograph station code, US Geological Survey*] (SEIS)
CBS .... Call Box Station (MSA)
CBS .... Cambodian Buddhist Society (EA)
CBS .... Cambridge Biological Series [*A publication*]
CBS .... Cambridge BioScience Corp.
CBS .... Canadian Biochemical Society (HGAA)
CBS .... Canadian Boiler Society [*Societe Canadienne de Manufacturiers Chaudieres*] (AC)
CBS .... Canberra Blind Society [*Australia*]
CBS .... Canberra Bonsai Society [*Australia*]
CBS .... Carrier and Sideband (IAA)
CBS .... Carrier Balloon System (MCD)
CBS .... Catalogue of the Babylonian Section [*University Museum, Philadelphia*] [*Formerly, CBM*] (BJA)
CBS .... CBS, Inc. [*Formerly, Columbia Broadcasting System, Inc.*] [*NYSE symbol*] (SPSG)
CBS .... CBS, Inc. [*Formerly, Columbia Broadcasting System, Inc.*] [*Associated Press*] (SAG)
CBS .... Center Back Stage [*A stage direction*]
CBS .... Center for Bibliographical Services [*Modern Language Association*] (BARN)
CBS .... Center for Bigfoot Studies [*An association*] (EA)
CBS .... Central Battery Signaling (NATG)
CBS .... Central [*Common*] Battery Supply [*Electronics*]
CBS .... Central [*Common*] Battery Switchboard [*Electronics*]
CBS .... Central [*Common*] Battery System [*Electronics*]
CBS .... Central Bibliographic System [*Library of Congress*]
CBS .... Central Bureau of Statistics [*Information service or system*] (IID)
CBS .... Certified Business Solutions
CBS .... Channel Base Section [*World War II*]
CBS .... Channel Status Byte [*Computer science*] (IAA)
CBS .... Christian Brethren School [*Australia*]
CBS .... Christian Brothers School [*Ireland*]
CBS .... Chronic Brain Syndrome [*Medicine*]
CBS .... Church Building Society [*British*]
CBS .... Cinder-Block on Concrete Slab [*Construction*]

CBS .... Cinnabar Resources Ltd. [*Vancouver Stock Exchange symbol*]
CBS .... City Business System [*British Telecom*] (NITA)
CBS .... Civilian Budgeting System [*Military*]
CBS .... Clarity, Brevity, Sharpness [*Objectives of good editing, as set forth in Barry Tarshis' book "How to Write without Pain"*]
CBS .... Close Boundary Sentry [*Military*] (AFM)
CBS .... Coarse Bearing Servo
CBS .... Coastal Base Section [*Name changed to Continental Advance Section*] [*World War II*]
CBS .... Colloidal Bismuth Subcitrate [*Pharmacy*]
CBS .... Columbia Broadcasting System [*Later, CBS, Inc.*]
CBS .... Columbus Avia [*Ukraine*] [*FAA designator*] (FAAC)
CBS .... Command Battle Simulation (MCD)
CBS .... Commission for Basic Systems [*WMO*] (MSC)
CBS .... Committee on Boarding Schools (EA)
CBS .... Commodity Bookform Standard (MCD)
CBS .... Common Battery Signaling [*Telecommunications*] (TEL)
CBS .... Common Battery System
CBS .... Commonwealth Bureau of Soils [*British*]
CBS .... Compact Buoy System
CBS .... Company Buyer Study [*Life Insurance Management and Research Association*]
CBS .... Complete Band Shape (MCD)
CBS .... Complex Behavior Simulator
CBS .... Conference on British Studies (EA)
CBS .... Confraternity of the Blessed Sacrament (EA)
CBS .... Congregation of Bon Secours (TOCD)
CBS .... Connector Backing Shell
CBS .... Connector Bracket Signal (MCD)
CBS .... Conservative Baptist Theological Seminary, Englewood, CO [*OCLC symbol*] (OCLC)
CBS .... Consolidated Balance Sheet [*Accounting*]
CBS .... Consolidated Business System (IAA)
C-B-S .... Contact-Bend-Stretch (PDAA)
CBS .... Continental Base Section
CBS .... Continuing Balance System [*Army*] (MCD)
CBs .... Contrabass [*Music*]
CBS .... Controlled Barrier System
CBS .... Controlled Blip Scan (CET)
CBS .... Conventional Boom Sprayer
CBS .... Copenhagen Business School [*Denmark*] (ECON)
CBS .... Corps Battle Simulation [*Army*]
CBS .... Correlation Bombing System [*Air Force*] (MCD)
CBS .... Cort Business Services [*NYSE symbol*] (TTSB)
CBS .... Cost Breakdown Structure (MCD)
CBS .... Crew Ballistic Shelter (MCD)
CBS .... Cyclohexylbenzothiazole Sulfenamide [*Organic chemistry*]
CBS .... Sisters of Bon Secours [*Roman Catholic religious order*]
CBS .... W. T. Bandy Center for Baudelaire Studies (EA)
CBSA .... Cargo Bay Stowage Assembly (NASA)
CBSA .... Catholic Bible Society of America (EA)
CBSA .... Centre for Business Systems Analysis [*City University*] [*British*] (CB)
CBSA .... Chiropody Board of South Australia [*Medicine*]
CBSA .... Chiropractors' Board of South Australia [*Medicine*]
CBSA .... Citrus Board of South Australia
CBSA .... Class B Surface Area [*Aviation*] (FAAC)
CBSA .... Clay Bird Shooting Association [*British*] (DI)
CBSA .... Cleveland Bay Society of America (EA)
CBSA .... Coastal Bancorp [*NASDAQ symbol*] (SAG)
CBSA .... Copper and Brass Servicenter Association (EA)
CBSAA .... Christian Book Selling Association of Australia
CBSAP .... Coastal Bancorp 9% 'A' Pfd [*NASDAQ symbol*] (TTSB)
CBSB .... Charter Bank Shares, Inc. [*NASDAQ symbol*] (SAG)
CBSB .... Charter Financial [*NQS*] (TTSB)
CBSC .... Cambridge Bible for Schools and Colleges [*A publication*] (BJA)
CBSC .... Common Bias, Single Control
CBSD .... Cassanova Brown Streak Disease [*Plant pathology*]
CBSE .... Caboose [*Freight*]
CBSE .... Certified Building Society Executive [*Canada*] (DD)
CBSE .... Commonwealth Board of Surveying Education [*London, England*] (EAIO)
CBSH .... Commerce Bancshares [*NASDAQ symbol*] (TTSB)
CBSH .... Commerce Bancshares, Inc. [*NASDAQ symbol*] (NQ)
CBSHP .... Cobbler Shop
CBSI .... Chartered Building Societies Institute [*British*] (DBA)
CBSI .... Community Bank System, Inc. [*NASDAQ symbol*] (NQ)
CBSI .... Community Bank Systems [*NASDAQ symbol*] (TTSB)
CBSI .... Computer Business Services, Inc.
CBSI .... Council on Biological Sciences Information (DIT)
CBSI .... Sept-Iles, PQ [*FM radio station call letters*]
CBSISH .... Comite de la Bibliographie et des Services d'Information en Sciences Humaines [*Committee on Bibliography and Information Services for the Social Sciences and Humanities - CBISSSH*] [*National Library of Canada*]
CBSLE .... Center for Bilingual Research and Second Language Education [*Later, CLEAR*] (GRD)
CBSM .... Comprehensive Behavioral Services Model
CBSO .... City of Birmingham Symphony Orchestra [*British*]
CBSO .... Counter Battery Staff Officer [*World War I*] [*Canada*]
CBSR .... Carcinogen Bioassay in Small Rodents
CBSR .... Chief Boilermaker, Ship Repair [*Navy*]
CBSR .... Coupled Breeding Superheating Reactor
CBSS .... Churches at Bosra and Samaria-Sebaste [*A publication*] (BJA)
CBSS .... Closed Breech Scavenging System (MCD)
CBSS .... Combustible Case Ammunition [*Weaponry*] [*Military*] (VNW)

CBSS	Compass Bancshares [*NASDAQ symbol*] (TTSB)	CBU	Construction Battalion Unit [*Navy*]
CBSS	Compass Bancshares, Inc. [*NASDAQ symbol*] (SAG)	CBU	Contact Back-Up (DNAB)
CBST	Colchicine Binding Site on Tubulin [*Biochemistry*]	CBU	Court of Bankruptcy, Undischarged [*British*]
CBST	Cubist Pharmaceuticals, Inc. [*NASDAQ symbol*] (SAG)	CBU	Vancouver, BC [*AM radio station call letters*]
CBST	Sept-Iles, PQ [*Television station call letters*]	CBUBT-1	Canal Flats, BC [*Television station call letters*]
CBStM	Saint Margaret's House, Berkeley, CA [*Library symbol Library of Congress*] (LCLS)	CBUBT-7	Cranbrook, BC [*Television station call letters*]
		CBuCTA	California Teachers Association, Burlingame, CA [*Library symbol Library of Congress*] (LCLS)
CBSV	Cycles between Scheduled Visits (MCD)	CBUDFIN	Chief of Budget and Finance Division [*Supreme Headquarters Allied Powers Europe*] (NATG)
CBS-X	Continuing Balance System - Expanded [*Army*] (AABC)		
CBT	Cabinet (WGA)	CBUF	United States Forest Service, Pacific Southwest Forest and Range Experiment Station, Berkeley, CA [*Library symbol Library of Congress*] (LCLS)
CBT	Cabot Corp. [*NYSE symbol*] (SPSG)		
CBT	Cape Breton Island [*Nova Scotia*] (BARN)		
CBT	Catalina Flying Boats, Inc. [*FAA designator*] (FAAC)	CBUF	Vancouver, BC [*FM radio station call letters*]
CBT	Catheter Balloon Valvuloplasty [*Medicine*] (CPH)	CBU-FM	Vancouver, BC [*FM radio station call letters*]
CBT	CBT Group PLC [*Associated Press*] (SAG)	CBUFT	Vancouver, BC [*Television station call letters*]
CBT	Cembratriene-diol [*Organic chemistry*]	CBUFT-2	Kamloops, BC [*Television station call letters*]
CBT	Center for Building Technology [*Gaithersburg, MD*] [*National Institute of Standards and Technology*]	CBUFT-3	Terrace, BC [*Television station call letters*]
		CBUIVTF	Concerned Broadcasters Using Inter-City Video Transmission Facilities (EA)
CBT	Central Battery Telephone [*Telecommunications*]		
CBT	Cesium Beam Tube	CBUK	Cutter & Buck [*NASDAQ symbol*] (TTSB)
CBT	Chicago Board of Trade [*A futures exchange*] [*Investment term*]	CBUK	Cutter & Buck, Inc. [*NASDAQ symbol*] (SAG)
CBT	Cincinnati Board of Trade [*Defunct*] (EA)	CBUS	Clydesdale Breeders of the United States (EA)
CBT	Clean Ballast Tanks [*Transportation*]	CBUT	Vancouver, BC [*Television station call letters*]
CBT	Coin Box Telephone [*Telecommunications*]	CBV	Cabin Bleed Valve [*Aviation*] (MCD)
CBT	Combat (AABC)	CBV	Canadian Beaver Resources [*Vancouver Stock Exchange symbol*]
CBT	Committee for Better Transit (EA)	CBV	Carburetor Bowl Vent [*Automotive engineering*]
CBT	Competency Based Teaching (AIE)	CBV	Central Blood Volume [*Medicine*]
CBT	Comprehensive Business Tax	CBV	Chartered Business Valuator [*Canada*] (DD)
CBT	Computed Body Tomography [*Medicine*] (CPH)	CBV	Christliche Bayerische Volkspartei - Bayerische Patriotenbewegung [*Christian Bavarian People's Party - Movement of Bavarian Patriots*] [*Germany Political party*] (PPW)
CBT	Computer-Based Terminal		
CBT	Computer-Based Training		
CBT	Connecticut Ballet Theatre		
CBT	Connecticut Bank & Trust Co. (MHDW)	CBV	Circulating Blood Volume [*Medicine*]
CBT	Consolidated Bel-Air [*Vancouver Stock Exchange symbol*]	CBV	Classroom Business Venture (EDAC)
CBT	Continuous Boat Track [*Navy*] (CAAL)	CBV	Clover Blotch Virus [*Plant pathology*]
CBT	Contractor Bonding Tape [*3M Co.*]	CBV	Conseil des Bourses de Valeurs [*French*] (ECON)
CBT	Cooperative Bureau for Teachers [*Superseded by IES*] (EA)	CBV	Containment Building Ventilation [*Nuclear energy*] (NRCH)
CBT	Core Block Table [*Computer science*] (OA)	CBV	Corrected Blood Volume [*Medicine*]
CBT	Grand Falls-Windsor, NF [*AM radio station call letters*]	CBV	Quebec, PQ [*AM radio station call letters*]
CBT	Institute of Transportation Studies Library, University of California, Berkeley, CA [*OCLC symbol*] (OCLC)	CBV-6	La Malbaie, PQ [*FM radio station call letters*]
		CBVD	CCNU [*Lomustine*], Bleomycin, Vinblastine, Dexamethasone [*Antineoplastic drug regimen*]
CBTA	Canadian Business Telecommunications Alliance (AC)		
CBTA	Canadian Business Travel Association [*Association Canadienne des Charges de Voyages*] (AC)	CBVD	Cerebrovascular Disease [*Medicine*] (DMAA)
		CBVD	Malartic, PQ [*Television station call letters*]
CBTA	Central Battery Telephone Apparatus [*Telecommunications*]	CBVE	Quebec, PQ [*FM radio station call letters*]
CBTC	CBT Corp. [*NASDAQ symbol*] (SAG)	CBV-FM	Quebec, PQ [*FM radio station call letters*]
CBT Cp	CBT Corp. [*Associated Press*] (SAG)	CBVI	Coin Bill Validator [*NASDAQ symbol*] (TTSB)
CBTDC	China Building Technology Development Centre [*Beijing*] [*Information service or system*] (IID)	CBVI	Coin Bill Validator, Inc. [*NASDAQ symbol*] (SAG)
		CBVM	Community of the Blessed Virgin Mary [*Anglican religious community*]
CBTDEV	Combat Developer		
Cbt Dev	Combat Developer (AAGC)	CBVT	Quebec City, PQ [*Television station call letters*]
CBTE	Advisory Committee for Chemical, Biochemical, and Thermal Engineering [*Washington, DC*] [*National Science Foundation*] (EGAO)	CBVT-2	La Tuque, PQ [*Television station call letters*]
		CBVWS	Combat Vehicle Weapons System [*Army*] (AFIT)
		CBW	Bureau of the Census, Field Division Library, Washington, DC [*OCLC symbol*] (OCLC)
CBTE	Competency-Based Teacher Education		
CBTE	Crawford Bay, BC [*FM radio station call letters*]	CBW	Canadian Broadcasting Winnipeg [*Canadian Broadcasting Co. record series pref ix*]
CBTENGRBN	Combat Engineer Battalion (DNAB)		
CBTF	Chlorobenzotrifluoride [*Organic chemistry*]	CBW	Catholic Book Week
CBT Gp	CBT Group PLC [*Associated Press*] (SAG)	CBW	Chelan Butte [*Washington*] [*Seismograph station code, US Geological Survey*] (SEIS)
CBTI	Combat Intelligence		
CBTK	Kelowna, BC [*FM radio station call letters*]	CBW	Chemical and Biological Warfare [*Military*]
CbtOG	Cabot Oil & Gas [*Associated Press*] (SAG)	CBW	Chemical and Biological Weapons [*Military*]
CBTP	Competency-Based Teacher Preparation	CBW	Children's Book Week
CBTR	Carrier and Bit Timing Recovery [*Computer science*] (LAIN)	CBW	CITIBASE-Weekly [*Citicorp Database Services*] [*Information service or system*] (IID)
CBTR	Center for Biomedical and Toxicological Research [*Florida State University*] [*Research center*] (RCD)		
		CBW	Commerical Bank of Wales [*British*]
CBTR	Clinical Behavior Therapy Review [*A publication*]	CBW	Community Bankers of Wisconsin (SRA)
CBTRY	Counterbattery	CBW	Consolidated Brinco Ltd. [*Toronto Stock Exchange symbol*]
CBTS	California Baptist Theological Seminary	CBW	Constant Bandwidth (MCD)
CBTS	CBT Group PLC [*NASDAQ symbol*] (SAG)	CBW	Continuous Butt-Weld [*Metal industry*]
CBTS	Central Battery Telephone Set [*Telecommunications*]	CBW	Control by Wire (MCD)
CBTS	Cesium Beam Time Standard	CBW	Critical Bandwidth [*of noise*]
CBTS	Computer-Based Training System (MCD)	CBW	[*A*] Translation in the Language of the People (1950) [*Charles B. Williams*] [*A publication*] (BJA)
CBTS	Cyclohexylbenzothiazyl Sulphenamide (PDAA)		
CBTSIG	Child Behavior Therapy Special Interest Group [*Defunct*] (EA)	CBW	Winnipeg, MB [*AM radio station call letters*]
CBTSY	CBT Group ADS [*NASDAQ symbol*] (TTSB)	CBW	Women's History Research Center, Inc., Berkeley, CA [*Library symbol Library of Congress*] (LCLS)
CBTT	Competency-Based Teacher Training		
CBTTA	Coordinating Board of Tobacco Trade Associations [*Later, NATD*] (EA)	CBWA	Copper and Brass Warehouse Association [*Later, CBSA*] (EA)
		CBWAT	Kenora, ON [*Television station call letters*]
CBTU	Coalition of Black Trade Unionists (EA)	CBWBT	Flin Flon, MB [*Television station call letters*]
CBTU	Companhia Brasileira de Trens Urbanos [*Railway system*] [*Brazil*] (EY)	CBWC	Corset and Brassiere Women's Club [*Later, UC*] (EA)
		CBWCA	Classic Bicycle and Whizzer Club of America (EA)
CBTV	Coalition for Better Television	CBWCT	Fort Frances, ON [*Television station call letters*]
CBU	Bureau of the Census, Washington, DC [*OCLC symbol*] (OCLC)	CBWDT	Dryden, ON [*Television station call letters*]
CBu	Burlingame Public Library, Burlingame, CA [*Library symbol Library of Congress*] (LCLS)	CBWF	Canada Bottle Water Federation [*Federation Canadienne des Eaux Embouteillees*] (AC)
CBU	Caribbean Broadcasting Union	CBW-FM	Winnipeg, MB [*FM radio station call letters*]
CBU	CBO Resources Corp. [*Vancouver Stock Exchange symbol*]	CBWFT	Winnipeg, MB [*Television station call letters*]
CBU	Character Buffer Unit [*Computer science*] (ECII)	CBWFT-4	Ste. Rose Du Lac, MB [*Television station call letters*]
CBU	Chemical/Biological Unit (DWSG)	CBWFT-10	Brandon, MB [*Television station call letters*]
CBU	Cluster Bomb Unit [*Military*]	CBWG	Children's Book Writers' Group [*Australia*]
CBU	Coefficient of Beam Utilization [*Floodlighting*]	CBWGT	Fisher Branch, MB [*Television station call letters*]
CBU	Collective Bargaining Unit (MCD)	CBWI	Wright Institute, Berkeley, CA [*Library symbol Library of Congress*] (LCLS)
CBU	Completely Built Up (ADA)		
CBU	Completely Built Up [*Automotive manufacturing*]	CBWK	Thompson, MB [*FM radio station call letters*]

CBWR	Coos Bay Wagon Road [Lands] [Department of the Interior]
CBWST	Baldy Mountain, MB [Television station call letters]
CBWT	Winnipeg, MB [Television station call letters]
CBWT-2	Lac Du Bonnet, MB [Television station call letters]
CBWYT	Mafeking, MB [Television station call letters]
CBX	Cam Box
CBX	C-Band Transponder [Radio]
CBX	Centralized Branch Exchange [Telecommunications] (NITA)
CBX	Computer-Based Examination
CBX	Computerized [or Computer-Controlled] Branch Exchange [Telecommunications]
CBX	Condobolin [Australia Airport symbol] (OAG)
CBX	Consolidated Boundary Explorations [Vancouver Stock Exchange symbol]
CBX	Continuous Belt Xanthator [Rayon technology]
CBX	Edmonton, AB [AM radio station call letters]
CBXAT	Grande Prairie, AB [Television station call letters]
CBXAT-2	High Prairie, AB [Television station call letters]
CBXAT-3	Manning, AB [Television station call letters]
CBXC	Cybex Computer Products [NASDAQ symbol] (TTSB)
CBXC	Cybex Corp. [NASDAQ symbol] (SAG)
CBX-FM	Edmonton, AB [FM radio station call letters]
CBXFT	Edmonton, AB [Television station call letters]
CBXFT-1	Bonnyville, AB [Television station call letters]
CBXFT-6	Fort McMurray, AB [Television station call letters]
CBXFT-8	Grande Prairie, AB [Television station call letters]
CBXT	Edmonton, AB [Television station call letters]
CBY	Canobie [Australia Airport symbol Obsolete] (OAG)
CBY	Carboy
CBY	Children's Book of the Year [British]
Cby	Cobyric Acid [Biochemistry]
CBY	Colby College, Waterville, ME [OCLC symbol] (OCLC)
CBY	Coningsby FTU [British ICAO designator] (FAAC)
CBY	Corner Brook, NF [AM radio station call letters]
C by B	Collected [or Delivered] by Barge [Shipping]
CBYG	Prince George, BC [FM radio station call letters]
CBYH	Christian Brethren Youth Hostel [Australia]
C by T	Collected [or Delivered] by Truck [Shipping]
CBYT	Corner Brook, NF [Television station call letters]
CBYT-1	Stephenville, NF [Television station call letters]
CBYT-3	Bonne Bay, NF [Television station call letters]
CBZ	Campbell Island [New Zealand] [Seismograph station code, US Geological Survey] (SEIS)
CBZ	Carbamazepine [Also, CARB] [An analgesic]
CBZ	Carben Energy, Inc. [Vancouver Stock Exchange symbol]
CBZ	Carbobenzoxy [Also, Cb] [Organic chemistry]
CBz	Carbobenzoxychloride [Organic chemistry] (DAVI)
CBZ	Cucui [Brazil] [Airport symbol] (AD)
CBZ	Fredericton, NB [AM radio station call letters]
CBZ-E	Carbamazepine-Epoxide [An analgesic]
CBZF	Fredericton-St. John, NB [FM radio station call letters]
CBZ-FM	Fredericton, NB [FM radio station call letters]
CC	Air-Cushion Vehicle built by Cushioncraft [England] [Usually used in combination with numerals]
CC	Battle Cruiser [Navy]
CC	Cable Connector (IAA)
CC	Cadet Captain
CC	Cadet Corps [British military] (DMA)
CC	Cadmium Council (EA)
CC	Caius College [Cambridge University] (ROG)
CC	Cajal Club (EA)
cc	Calcite [CIPW classification] [Geology]
CC	Calcium Cyclamate [Sweetener]
CC	Calculator (MDG)
CC	Calcutta Computers [Software manufacturing company] [India] (ECON)
CC	Calibration Cycle (AFIT)
CC	California Compensation Cases [A publication] (DLA)
CC	Call Check [Telecommunications] (NITA)
CC	Call Contract
CC	Calorimetry Conference (EA)
CC	Camera Copy [or Camera-Ready Copy]
CC	Camouflage Critical [Designation] [Army] (RDA)
CC	Camp Century [Greenland] [Seismograph station]
CC	Camp Chair
CC	Camp Commandant
CC	Canada Council (EAIO)
CC	Canadian Club [A whiskey]
CC	Canberra Consumers Incorporated [Australia]
CC	Cancelation Clause [Business term]
CC	Canceled Check [Banking]
CC	Cancer Care (EA)
CC	Cans or Cartons [Freight]
CC	Canvas Covers [Shipping] (DS)
CC	Capacity Coupling
CC	Cape Colony [British Empire]
CC	Cape Corps [British military] (DMA)
CC	Capita [Chapters] [Latin]
CC	Capsule Communications [or Communicator] [NASA]
CC	Caption Code (DNAB)
CC	Carbamylcholine [Organic chemistry]
CC	Carbohydrate Craver [Nutrition]
CC	Carbonaceous Chondrite
CC	Carbonate Crust [Archeology]
C-C	Carbon-Carbon (NASA)

CC	Carbon Copy
CC	Car Craft [A publication]
CC	Card Code
CC	Card Column
CC	Card Count [Computer science]
CC	Cardiac Catheterization [Cardiology] (DAVI)
CC	Cardiac Cycle [Medicine]
CC	Cardinal Club (EA)
CC	Career Control (AFM)
CC	Cargo Capacity [Shipping] (DCTA)
CC	Cargo Control
CC	Caribbeana Council [Defunct] (EA)
cc----	Caribbean Area [MARC geographic area code Library of Congress] (LCCP)
CC	Caribbean Commission [Later, Caribbean Organization]
CC	Carmel Community [Roman Catholic women's religious order]
CC	Carpenters' Co. (EA)
CC	Carriage Control
CC	Carrier Current (IAA)
CC	Carrying Capacity (EA)
CC	Carson City [Nevada] [Mint mark, when appearing on US coins] [Obsolete]
Cc	Carya cardioformis [Butternut hickory tree]
CC	Cases in Chancery [England] [A publication] (DLA)
CC	Cash Commodity [Business term]
CC	Cash Credit [British]
CC	Cashier's Check
CC	Casinos Czechoslovakia (ECON)
CC	Cassidy Class (EA)
CC	Cast Coated [Paper] (DGA)
CC	Cast Copper
CC	Catalytic Converter [Automotive engineering]
CC	Catalytic Cracker [Chemical engineering]
CC	Cat Collectors [Commercial firm] (EA)
CC	Catecholamine Club (EA)
CC	Category Code [Online database field identifier]
CC	Caterpillar Club (EA)
CC	Cathartic Compound (IIA)
CC	Cathodochromic [Cathode-ray tube]
CC	Catholic Clergyman
CC	Catholic Confraternity Version [1941, 1952] (BJA)
CC	Catholic Curate
CC	Cause for Concern [Defunct] (EA)
CC	Causes Celebres [Quebec Provincial Reports] [A publication] (DLA)
CC	Celestial Canopy [Freemasonry]
CC	Cell Cap [Botany]
CC	Cell Culture [Cytology]
CC	Center of Concern (EA)
C-C	Center to Center
CC	Centigrams (ROG)
CC	Central Canal [Anatomy]
CC	Central Coast [ADA]
CC	Central Committee
CC	Central Computer
CC	Central Console
CC	Central Control (KSC)
CC	Central Control Channel Command (MCD)
CC	Centrifugal Coating
CC	Centristas de Cataluna [Political party Spain] (EY)
CC	Centuries
CC	Cepi Corpus [Latin Legal term] (DLA)
CC	Ceramic Capacitor (IAA)
CC	Cerebral Commissure [Brain anatomy]
CC	Certified Check [Banking]
CC	Cervical Connective [Neuroanatomy]
CC	Chain of Command (IAA)
CC	Challenge Certificate [In dog shows] (BARN)
CC	Chamber of Commerce
CC	Change Code (MCD)
cc	Change Column Measure [Typesetting] (WDMC)
CC	Change Course
CC	Change for Children [An association] (EA)
C/C	Change of Course [Aviation]
CC	Channel Command [Refers to English Channel] [Military]
CC	Channel Controller (MCD)
CC	Channel Coordinator [Telecommunications] (NITA)
CC	Chapters (WGA)
CC	Character Count [Typography]
CC	Charbonneau Connection (EA)
CC	Charcoal Canister (GNE)
CC	Chargeable to Crew (MCD)
CC	Charge Conveyor [Electronics] (EECA)
CC	Charge Coupled (IAA)
CC	Charged Current [Physics]
CC	Charges Collect [Business term]
CC	Charity Commission [British]
CC	Chartered Cartographer
CC	Checker Club (EA)
CC	Chemical Closet
CC	Chemical Composition [Of precious stones]
CC	Chemical Corps [Army] (GFGA)
CC	Chemistry Consortium (EA)
CC	Chemists' Club [New York] (SRA)
CC	Chess Club
cc	Chest Circumference [Neonatology and pediatrics] (DAVI)

CC	Chest Complaint [*Medicine*] (ADA)
CC	Chief Clerk
CC	Chief Complaint [*Medicine*]
CC	Chief Constable [*Scotland Yard*]
CC	Chief Controller (NATG)
CC	Chief Counsel (KSC)
CC	Chief Court [*Freemasonry*] (ROG)
CC	Chief of Chaplains [*Later, CCH*] [*Army*]
CC	Child Care (ADA)
CC	Children's Committee 10 (EA)
CC	Children's Court [*Australia*]
CC	China Council [*An association*] (EA)
CC	Chip Carrier [*Electronics*] (EECA)
CC	Chiral Chromatography
CC	Chocolate-Coated [*Pharmacy*]
CC	Choke Coil
CC	Chondrocalcinosis [*Orthopedics*] (DAVI)
CC	Choriocarcinoma [*Oncology*]
CC	Christian Century [*A publication*] (BRI)
CC	Christian Coalition (EA)
CC	Christian Crusade (EA)
CC	Christians in Crisis (EA)
CC	Christmas Club (EA)
CC	Chronic Complainer [*Medicine*] (DMAA)
CC	Chronocoulometry [*Electrochemistry*]
CC	Chronometer Correction [*Navigation*]
CC	Chrysler Corp.
CC	Church of Christ
CC	Circuit City Stores [*NYSE symbol*] (TTSB)
CC	Circuit City Stores, Inc. [*NYSE symbol*] (SPSG)
CC	Circuit Closing
C/C	Circuit Control
CC	Circuit Court
CC	Circulating Copy
CC	Circulation Council of DMA [*Direct Marketing Association*] [*New York, NY*] (EA)
CC	Circulatory Collapse [*Cardiology*]
CC	Circumnavigators Club (EA)
CC	Cirrocumulus [*Meteorology*]
CC	Citizen's Call (EA)
CC	Citizen's Choice [*Defunct*] (EA)
CC	City Corp. [*of London*]
CC	City Council [*or Councillor*]
CC	City Court (DLA)
CC	Civil Code [*A publication*] (DLA)
CC	Civil Commotion
CC	Civil Court
CC	Civilian Congress (EA)
CC	Class Code [*Database terminology*] (NITA)
CC	Classical Conditioning
CC	Classification Code [*IRS*] [*Online database field identifier*]
CC	Classification of Characteristics [*Navy*] (NG)
CC	Clean Catch [*of urine*] [*Medicine*]
CC	Clerk of the Chapel [*Unions*] [*British*] (DGA)
CC	Clerk of the Crown [*British*]
CC	Clerk of the Privy Council [*British*]
CC	Clindamycin [*Antibacterial compound*]
CC	Clinical Center [*National Institutes of Health*] (GRD)
CC	Clinical Course [*Medicine*]
CC	Clipper Club [*Pan American Airlines' club for frequent flyers*] (EA)
C/C	Clock Coercion
CC	Clock Control (IAA)
CC	Clomiphene Citrate [*Fertility drug*]
CC	Close-Coupled [*Electricity*]
CC	Closed Captioned [*Refers to captioning of television programs for the deaf*]
CC	Closed Circuit [*Transmission*] (DEN)
CC	Closed Container [*Packaging*] (DCTA)
CC	Closing Capacity
CC	Closing Coil
CC	Cloud Chamber [*Physics*]
CC	Cloud Cover (KSC)
CC	Cluster Controller
CC	Coaching Club (EA)
CC	Coarse Control [*Nuclear energy*] (NRCH)
CC	Coastal Command [*Air Force British*]
CC	Coat Cupboard [*Classified advertising*] (ADA)
CC	Coated Cartridge [*Paper*] (DGA)
CC	Cobra Club [*Later, SAAC*] (EA)
CC	Cocos [*Keeling*] Islands [*ANSI two-letter standard code*] (CNC)
CC	Code Control (AFM)
CC	Code Converter
CC	Code of Canon Law
CC	Codex Prophetarum Cairensis (BJA)
CC	Codice Civile [*Civil Code*] [*Italian*] (ILCA)
CC	Coefficient of Contingency [*Statistics*]
CC	Coefficient of Correlation [*Statistics*]
CC	Coincident-Current (IAA)
·CC	Coin Collect [*Telecommunications*] (TEL)
CC	Coin Completing [*Telecommunications*] (TEL)
CC	Cold Canvassing [*Business term*]
CC	Coleman's Cases [*New York*] [*A publication*] (DLA)
CC	Coliform Count [*Microbiology*] (OA)
CC	Collect Call [*Telecommunications*] (TEL)
C$_c$	Collector Capacitance (IDOE)
CC	Collector Circle [*Defunct*] (EA)
CC	Collector's Chronicle [*A publication*]
CC	Collectors Club (EA)
CC	College of Commerce (AIE)
CC	Colon Classification [*Library science*]
CC	Colorado-Claro [*Medium-colored cigar*]
CC	Color Code [*as, for types of wire*] [*Technical drawings*]
CC	Color Compensation [*Photography*]
CC	Color Contrast
CC	Color Correction [*Color printing*]
CC	Column Chromatography [*Analytical chemistry*]
CC	Combat Center [*Military*]
CC	Combat Clothing [*NATO*]
CC	Combat Command [*Initialism may be followed by a number as, CC2, to indicate a specific, numbered command*] [*Army*]
CC	Combat Commandant [*Military*]
CC	Combat Consumption [*Military*]
CC	Combat Control [*Army*]
CC	Combat Correspondent
CC	Combination Companies [*Insurance*]
CC	Combustion Chamber (KSC)
CC	Comic Crusader [*A publication*]
CC	Command Car (SAA)
CC	Command Center (AAG)
CC	Command Chain [*Computer science*]
CC	Command Code [*IRS*]
CC	Command Computer (AAG)
CC	Command Conference [*Viking lander mission*] [*NASA*]
CC	Command Console (IAA)
CC	Command Ship [*Navy symbol Obsolete*]
CC	Commercial Cable Co. (MHDW)
CC	Commercial Carrier
CC	Commercial Consumables (CINC)
CC	Commercial Continuity [*Broadcasting*] (NTCM)
CC	Commerical Control (SAA)
CC	Commission Certified [*Bacteriology*]
CC	Committee Charter (MCD)
C/C	Committees of Correspondence [*National Center for Science Education*]
CC	Common Carrier
CC	Common Cause (EA)
CC	Common Code (IAA)
CC	Common Cold (HGAA)
CC	Common Collector [*Amplifier*]
CC	Common Control [*Telecommunications*] (TEL)
CC	Common Council [*or Councilman*]
CC	Common Cycle
CC	Commonwealth Aircraft Corp. Ltd. [*Australia ICAO aircraft manufacturer identifier*] (ICAO)
CC	Communication Center
CC	Communication Commission (EA)
CC	Communication Comptroller
CC	Communications Central [*Military*]
CC	Communications Computer (IAA)
CC	Communications Control (MCD)
CC	Communications Council (EA)
CC	Community College
CC	Community Communications [*Independent Local Radio*] [*British*]
CC	Compact Cassette (IAA)
CC	Companion of the Order of Canada
CC	Companion of the Order of Canada (DD)
CC	Company Commander
CC	Comparison Circuit [*Telecommunications*] (OA)
CC	Compass Course
CC	Compensation Court [*Australia*]
CC	Completion Code (ECII)
CC	Complex Conjugate (MCD)
CC	Component Check [*Nuclear energy*] (NRCH)
CC	Component Commander [*Military*]
CC	Component Cooling [*Nuclear energy*] (NRCH)
CC	Composite Cross [*Genetics*]
CC	Composition Caster [*Monotype*] (DGA)
CC	Compound Carburetion [*Automotive engineering*]
CC	Compound Cathartic [*Pills*]
CC	Compte Courant [*Current Account*] [*French Business term*]
CC	Compulsory Censorship [*British World War II*]
CC	Computational Component (MCD)
CC	Computation Center
CC	Computer-Calculated (DAVI)
CC	Computer Calculator
CC	Computer Center [*Telecommunications*] (TEL)
CC	Computer Community (IEEE)
CC	Computer Complex
CC	Computer Conferencing
CC	Computer Consulting (IAA)
CC	Computer Controlled (IAA)
CC	Comunn na Clarsaich [*Clarsach Society*] (EAIO)
Cc	Concave
CC	Concentration Camp
CC	Concept Chart (AFIT)
CC	Concept Code [*Database terminology*] (NITA)
CC	Conciliation Committees [*Australia*]
CC	Conclusion [*Broadcasting*] (WDMC)
CC	Concord Council [*Defunct*] (EA)

CC............ Concrete Cancer [*Refers to disintegration caused by weathering and pollutants*]
CC............ Concrete Ceiling
CC............ Concurrency Controller [*Computer science*]
CC............ Concurrent Concession (MDG)
CC............ Condemned [*Prisoners'*] Cell (IIA)
CC............ Condition Code
CC............ Conditioning Container (AAG)
CC............ Conductive Channel (IAA)
CC............ Conductive Coating
cc............ Condylocephalic [*Medicine*] (DAVI)
CC............ Configuration Control (AAG)
CC............ Confined to Camp [*Military*]
CC............ Congressional Caucus for Women's Issues (EA)
CC............ Congressional Club (EA)
CC............ Connect Confirmation (ACRL)
cc............ Connected Case [*Different case from case cited but arising out of same subject matter or intimately connected therewith*] [*Used in Shepard's Citations*] [*Legal term*] (DLA)
CC............ Connecting Carrier
CC............ Connector Circuit
CC............ Consolidated Computer (IAA)
CC............ Consolidation of [*Telecommunications*] Center (MCD)
CC............ Constant Conditions
CC............ Constant Current [*Electronics*] (IAA)
CC............ Constitutional Commission [*An association*] (EA)
C/C............ Constraint Control
CC............ Constructing Contractor (AAG)
CC............ [*The*] Construction Contractor [*A publication*] (AAGC)
CC............ Construction Corps
CC............ Consular Clerk [*British*] (ROG)
CC............ Consular Corps
CC............ Consules [*Consuls*] [*Latin*]
CC............ Consumer Council [*American National Standards Institute*]
CC............ Contact Center (EA)
CC............ Contact Closure (KSC)
CC............ Container Control (DCTA)
C/C............ Conte Corrente [*Running Account*]
CC............ Contemporary Christian [*Music*] (WDMC)
CC............ Contemporary Civilization [*University course*]
CC............ Continuation Clause
CC............ Continuing Calibration
CC............ Continuing Care [*Medicine*] (DAVI)
CC............ Continuous Casting [*Metalworking*]
CC............ Continuous Current
CC............ Contra Credit [*Banking*]
CC............ Contractor Company Code [*Database terminology*] (NITA)
CC............ Control Cabin
CC............ Control Center
CC............ Control Chamber [*Diving apparatus*]
CC............ Control Circuit
CC............ Control Code (IAA)
CC............ Control Computer (KSC)
CC............ Control Connector (IAA)
CC............ Control Console
CC............ Control Converter (MCD)
CC............ Control Counter [*Computer science*]
C/C............ Controlled-Circulation [*Boiler*]
CC............ Controlled Circulation [*Newspaper and magazine distribution*] (NTCM)
CC............ Controllers Council (EA)
CC............ Convective Combustion (MCD)
CC............ Conventional Color (OA)
C-C............ Convexo-Concave [*Replacement heart valves*] [*Cardiology*]
CC............ Convoy Commodore [*Navy*] (NVT)
CC............ Cooling Coil (AAG)
CC............ Coordinate Converter (AAG)
CC............ Coordinates Computed (MUGU)
CC............ Copper Chromite
CC............ Coracoclavicular [*Anatomy*] (MAE)
CC............ Corben Club (EA)
CC............ Cord Compression [*Medicine*]
CC............ Cornu Cervi [*Hartshorn*] [*Pharmacy*] (ROG)
CC............ Coronary Club (EA)
CC............ Coronary Collateral [*Medicine*] (AAMN)
CC............ Corpora Cardiaca [*Endocrinology*]
CC............ Corporate Communication (WDMC)
CC............ Corporate Conversions [*Information service or system*] (IID)
CC............ Corporation Commission
CC............ Corps Commander [*British military*] (DMA)
CC............ Corpus Callosum [*Brain anatomy*]
CC............ Corpus Cardiacum (PDAA)
CC............ Corpus Christi (ROG)
CC............ Correct Code (MCD)
CC............ Corrected Copy
CC............ Correlation Coefficient (MCD)
CC............ Correspondence Course
CC............ Correspondent Committee [*Defunct*] (EA)
CC............ Corriente Critica [*Mexico Political party*] (EY)
CC............ Corrosion Control [*Lloyds Register*] (DS)
CC............ Corrugated or Cupped [*Freight*]
CC............ Cortico-Cortical Connection [*Neurology*]
CC............ Cost Center (AFM)
CC............ Cost Code (MCD)
CC............ Costochondral [*Anatomy*]
CC............ Cotton Covered [*Wire insulation*] (IAA)

CC............ Coulter Counter [*Medicine*] (DMAA)
CC³............ Council of Churches
CC............ Council of Conservationists (EA)
CC............ Council on Competitiveness (EA)
CC............ Counterclockwise
CC............ Countercurrent
CC............ Country Cheque [*Banking*] [*British*]
CC............ Country Clearing
CC............ Country Club
CC............ Country Code (AFM)
CC............ Countryside Commission [*British*]
CC............ County Circuit [*As in "CC Rider," i.e., a traveling preacher*]
CC............ County Clerk [*British*] (ROG)
CC............ County Commissioner
CC............ County Constituency [*British*]
CC............ County Council [*or Councillor*] [*British*]
CC............ County Court
CC............ Coupled Channel [*Electronics*]
CC............ Coupled Cluster [*Physical chemistry*]
CC............ Courant Continu [*Direct Current*] [*French*]
CC............ Coventry Climax [*Auto racing engine manufacturer*] [*British*]
CC............ Craniocaudal [*Anatomy*]
CC............ Craniocervical [*Anatomy*] (HGAA)
C/C............ Crankcase [*Automotive engineering*]
CC............ Creatinine Clearance [*Clinical chemistry*]
CC............ Credentialing Commission (EA)
CC............ Credit Card [*Business term*] (ADA)
Cc............ Creek Chub [*Ichthyology*]
CC............ Crew Certified (MCD)
CC............ Crew Chief (MCD)
CC............ Crew Compartment (MCD)
CC............ Cricket Club
CC............ Critical Care [*Medicine*]
CC............ Critical Condition [*Medicine*]
CC............ Croquet Club [*British*]
CC............ Cross Channel
CC............ Cross Correlation
CC............ Cross Couple
CC............ Crossword Club [*Romsey, Hampshire, England*] (EAIO)
CC............ Crown Aviation [*ICAO designator*] (AD)
CC............ Crown Cases
CC............ Crown Clerk [*British*] (ROG)
CC............ Crown Colony
CC............ Crown Court (ILCA)
CC............ Cruisers (NATG)
CC............ Cruising Club [*British*]
CC............ Crusaders for Christ (EA)
CC............ Crus Cerebri [*Medicine*] (DMAA)
CC............ Crystal Control
CC............ Crystal Current
CC............ Cubic Capacity (DS)
cc............ Cubic Centimeter
CC............ Cubic Contents
CC............ Cucurbita Cruenta [*Cupping Glass*] [*Pharmacy*]
CC............ Cultural Council [*Australia*]
CC............ Culver Club (EA)
CC............ Cumberland Railway & Coal (MHDB)
cc............ Cum Correction [*With lenses*] [*Ophthalmology*]
CC............ Cumulative Changes (NATG)
CC............ Curling Club
CC............ Current Cases [*1965-71*] [*Ghana*] [*A publication*] (DLA)
CC............ Current Challengers
CC............ Current Complaints [*Medicine*]
CC............ Current Cost
CC............ Curriculum Corporation [*Commercial firm Australia*]
CC............ Cursor Centered [*Automotive engineering*]
CC............ Cursor Control [*Computer science*] (BUR)
CC............ Cushion Craft
CC............ Custodian Contractor
CC............ Custom Chip [*Personal computers*]
cc............ Customer within Country (AAGC)
CC............ Cuthbert Cudgel [*Pseudonym used by T. Houston*]
CC............ Cycle Count (MCD)
CC............ Cyclic Check [*Computer science*] (IAA)
CC............ Cyclic Code (BUR)
CC............ Cycling Club
CC............ Cyfeillion Cymru [*Friends of Wales*] [*Australia*]
cc............ Cylindrical with Adaxial Channel [*Leaf characteristics*] [*Botany*]
CC............ Cymdeithas y Cymmrodorion [*Honorable Society of Cymmrodorion*] [*British*]
CC............ Cypriot Classical (BJA)
CC............ Federal Carriers Cases [*Commerce Clearing House*] [*A publication*] (DLA)
CC............ Federal Carriers Reporter (Commerce Clearing House) [*A publication*] (DLA)
cc............ Mainland China [*MARC country of publication code Library of Congress*] (LCCP)
CC............ Ohio Circuit Court Reports [*A publication*] (DLA)
CC............ R. A. Bloch Cancer Foundation [*Formerly, Cancer Connection*] (EA)
CC............ Tactical Command Ship [*Navy symbol*]
CC............ Uniform Commercial Code [*Also UCC*] (AAGC)
CC............ Versatile Corp. [*Vancouver Stock Exchange symbol*]
CC³............ Counter-C³ [*Command, Control, and Communications*] [*Pronounced "see-see-cubed"*]
CC 1992....... Columbus: Countdown 1992 [*An association*] (EA)

CCA	Air China [ICAO designator] (FAAC)
CCA	Calgary Construction Association (AC)
CCA	California Cattlemen's Association (SRA)
CCA	California Central Airlines
CCA	California Chiropractic Association (SRA)
CCA	California Cosmetology Association (SRA)
CCA	Canadian Camping Association (AC)
CCA	Canadian Canoe Association
CCA	Canadian Cartographic Association [Association Canadienne de Cartographie] (AC)
CCA	Canadian Cat Association
CCA	Canadian Cattlemen's Association
CCA	Canadian Celiac Association [Association Canadienne de la Maladie Coeliaque] [Also, Celiac Canada] (AC)
CCA	Canadian Centre for Architecture
CCA	Canadian Charolais Association
CCA	Canadian Chemical Association (HGAA)
CCA	Canadian Chiropractic Association
CCA	Canadian Colonial Airways
CCA	Canadian Commonwealth Association
CCA	Canadian Communication Association
CCA	Canadian Conference of the Arts
CCA	Canadian Construction Association
CCA	Canadian Co-Operative Association (AC)
CCA	Canadian Council of Archives [Conseil Canadien des Archives] (AC)
CCA	Canadian Cowboys Association
CCA	Canadian Cycling Association
CCA	Canberra Classical Association [Australia]
CCA	Cannonical Correlation Analysis (PDAA)
CCA	Canonical Correlation Analysis [Mathematics]
CCA	Capital Consumption Adjustment [or Allowance] [Accounting]
CCA	Capital Cost Allowance [Accounting]
CCA	Capri Class Association (EA)
CCA	Caribbean Conservation Association [St. Michael, Barbados]
CCA	Carrier Controlled Approach [Aircraft carrier RADAR landing system]
CCA	Cash Clothing Allowance
CCA	Catholic Committee of Appalachia (EA)
CCA	CCA Industries, Inc. [Associated Press] (SAG)
CCA	Cecchetti Council of America (EA)
CCA	Celktic Council of Australia
CCA	Cell Cycle Analyzer [Instrumentation]
CCA	Cellular Cellulose Acetate [Organic chemistry]
CCA	Cellular Concrete Association (EA)
CCA	Cement and Concrete Association [British Research center]
CCA	Central Computer Accounting
CCA	Central Computer Agency [Civil Service Department] [British] (NITA)
CCA	Cephalin Cholesterol Antigen [Immunochemistry]
CCA	Channel-to-Channel Adapter [Computer science]
CCA	Charter Cruise Air Ltd. [Australia]
CCA	Chemical Coaters Association (EA)
CCA	Chemical Communications Association (EA)
CCA	Chess Collectors Association [Defunct] (EA)
CCA	Chick Cell Agglutination [Vaccine potency test]
CCA	Chief Clerk of the Admiralty [British]
CCA	Chief of Civil Affairs [Army]
CCA	Chihuahua Club of America (EA)
CCA	Child Care Assistance
CCA	Child Care Association of Illinois (SRA)
CCA	Chimpanzee Coryza Agent [A virus]
CCA	Chinese Communist Army (CINC)
CCA	Chinese Culture Association (EA)
CCA	Choriocarcinoma [Oncology]
CCA	Christian Chiropractors Association (EA)
CCA	Christian Conference of Asia (EA)
CCA	Christie's Contemporary Art [Reproductions] [London, England]
CCA	Chromated Copper Arsenate [Wood preservative]
cca	Circa [About, Approximately] [Latin]
CCA	Circuit Card Assembly (MCD)
CCA	Circuit Court of Appeals (GPO)
CCA	Circumflex Coronary Artery [Medicine] (MEDA)
CCA	Citizens' Commission on AIDS [Acquired Immune Deficiency Syndrome] (EA)
CCA	Citizens' Councils of America (EA)
CCA	Citizens for a Competitive America (EA)
CCA	Citizens for Cable Awareness (NTCM)
CCA	Citizens for Clean Air
CCA	City Center Arts [A publication]
CCA	Civic Catering Association [British] (BI)
CCA	Civilian Control Agency
CCA	Classic Comet Club of America (EA)
CCA	Close Contact Annealing (MCD)
CCA	Cloud Chamber Analysis
CCA	Clown Club of America [Later, CAI] (EA)
CCA	Cluster Compression Algorithm (MCD)
CCA	Coamo [Puerto Rico] [Seismograph station code, US Geological Survey] (SEIS)
CCA	Coastal Conservation Association (EA)
CCA	Cold Cranking Ampere
CCA	College Caterers Association [British] (DBA)
CCA	College Characteristics Analysis
CCA	Collegiate Commissioners Association (EA)
CCA	Collie Club of America (EA)
CCA	Colorado Cattlemen's Association (SRA)
CCA	Colorado Chiropractic Association (SRA)
CCA	Colorado Contractors Association (SRA)

CCA	Combat Center Active [Military] (SAA)
CCA	Combat Command A
CCA	Comics Code Authority [Regulatory body for comic book and comic magazine publishing industry]
CCA	Comites Communistes pour l'Autogestion [Communist Committees for Self-Management] [France Political party] (PPW)
CCA	Commission on Crystallographic Apparatus [International Council of Scientific Unions]
CCA	Committee for Conventional Armaments
CCA	Committee of Concerned Africans [Defunct] (EA)
CCA	Common Carotid Artery [Anatomy]
CCA	Common Carrier Motor Freight Association, Dallas TX [STAC]
CCA	Common Communication Adapter [Computer science]
CCA	Common Cryptographic Architecture [IBM encryption software] (CDE)
CCA	Commonwealth Chess Association (EA)
CCA	Commonwealth Correspondents' Association (BI)
CCA	Communication Carrier Assembly [Spaceship]
CCA	Communications Channel Adapter (IAA)
CCA	Communications Control Area (IAA)
CCA	Company Chemists' Association [British]
CCA	Company-to-Company Agreement (MCD)
CCA	Compass Control Alarm
CCA	Compatible Communications Architecture [Telecommunication protocol] (CDE)
CCA	Complete Cell Analysis [Medicine]
CCA	Complmentary Chromatic Adaptation [Plant Biology]
CCA	Component Checkout Area (AAG)
CCA	Comprehensive Cooperative Agreement (MHDB)
CCA	Computer Corp. of America
CCA	Comtec Cable Accessories Ltd. [British] (NITA)
CCA	Conceptual Communications Area [Computer science] (TNIG)
CCA	Concerned Citizens of America [Defunct] (EA)
CCA	Conference Canadienne des Arts [Canadian Conference of the Arts - CCA]
CCA	Configuration Control Action (KSC)
CCA	Congenital Contracture Arachnodactyly [Medicine]
CCA	Conseil Canadien des Aveugles [Canadian Council of the Blind] (EAIO)
CCA	Conseil Consultatif des Athletes [Athletes' Advisory Council] [Canada]
CCA	Conservative Clubs of America (EA)
CCA	Consolidated Canarctic Industries Ltd. [Vancouver Stock Exchange symbol]
CCA	Consumer and Corporate Affairs Canada [UTLAS symbol]
CCA	Consumer Credit Association [British] (EAIO)
CCA	Consumers Cooperative Association [Later, Farmland Industries] (EA)
CCA	Container Corp. of America [Later, Marcor, Inc.]
CCA	Contamination Control Area [Army] (ADDR)
CCA	Continental Control Area [FAA]
CCA	Continuously Contemporary Accounting (ADA)
CCA	Contract Change Authorization (KSC)
CCA	Controlled Circulation Audit [Name changed to Business Publications Audit of Circulation]
CCA	Coolant Control Assembly (NASA)
CCA	Cooperative Communicators Association (EA)
CCA	Copper-Chrome Arsenate [Wood preservative] (ADA)
CCA	Copywriter's Council of America (EA)
CCA	Corduroy Council of America [Defunct] (EA)
CCA	Corpus Christi Public Library, Corpus Christi, TX [OCLC symbol] (OCLC)
CCA	Corrections Corp. of America
CCA	Cougar Club of America (EA)
CCA	Council of Chemical Associations [Defunct] (EA)
CCA	Council of Consumer Advisers
CCA	County Chasers of America (EA)
CCA	County Councils Association [British] (BI)
CCA	County Court Appeals [A publication] (DLA)
CCA	Coupled Cluster Approach (MCD)
CCA	Covered Conductors Association [British] (BI)
CCA	Credit Control Act [1969]
CCA	Crop Condition Assessment
CCA	Cruising Club of America (EA)
CCA	Crystal Colloidal Array [Chemistry]
CCA	Crystalline Colloidal Array [Chemistry]
CCA	Current-Controlled Amplifier [Electronics] (ECII)
CCA	Current Cost Accounting
CCA	Cushman Club of America (EA)
CCA	Customer Cost Analysis [Business term] (MHDW)
CCA	Customs Consolidation Act [British]
C-C-A	Cytidyl-Cytidyl-Adenyl [Biochemistry] (BABM)
CCA	Fort Chaffee, AR [Location identifier FAA] (FAAL)
CCA	United States Circuit Court of Appeals (AAGC)
CCAA	Canadian Clean Air Act (GNE)
CCAA	Canadian Colleges Athletic Association
CCAA	Canadian Consulting Agrologists Association [L'Assiciation Canadienne des Agronomes-Conseils] (AC)
C/CAA	Caribbean/Central American Action
CCAA	Chefs de Cuisine Association of America (EA)
CCAA	Citizens' Civic Action Association [Canada] (BARN)
CCAA	Collector Car Appraisers Association (EA)
CCAA	Contract Clearance Approval Authority (AAGC)

CCAAC	Child Care Advocacy Association of Canada [*Association Canadienne pour la Promotion des Services de Garde a l'Enfance*] [*Formerly, Canadian Day Care Advocacy Association*] (AC)
CCAAFB	Cape Canaveral Auxiliary Air Force Base [*Obsolete*] (AAG)
CCAAP	Central Committee for the Architectural Advisory Panels [*British*]
CCAATF	Close Combat Antiarmor Task Force (MCD)
CCAAWS	Close Combat Antiarmor Weapon System (MCD)
CCAB	Canadian Circulations Audit Board [*Founded 1937*]
CCAB	Commandant, Civil Affairs Branch [*British World War II*]
CCAB	Consultative Committee of Accountancy Bodies [*United Kingdom and Ireland*]
CCABC	Cancer Control Agency of British Columbia (PDAA)
CCABC	Cemetery & Crematorium Association of British Columbia (AC)
CCABC	Chris-Craft Antique Boat Club (EA)
CCABF	Common Carotid Artery Blood Flow [*Medicine*]
CCAC	California College of Arts and Crafts [*Oakland*]
CCAC	Canadian Casualty Assembly Centre (DMA)
CCAC	Canadian Council on Animal Care
CCAC	Central Computer Accounting Corp.
CCAC	Central Council for Agricultural and Horticultural Co-Operation [*British*]
CCAC	Child Care Action Campaign (EA)
CCAC	Children's Court Advisory Committee [*Australia*]
CCAC	Close Combat Armament Center [*Dover, NJ*] [*Army*] (GRD)
CCAC	Combined Civil Affairs Committee [*World War II*]
CCAC	Continuing Care Accreditation Commission [*American Association of Homes for Aging*]
CCAC/L	Combined Civil Affairs Committee, London Subcommittee [*World War II*]
CCACN	Command and Control Alert/Conferencing Network (CINC)
CCAC/S	Combined Civil Affairs Committee, Supply Subcommittee [*World War II*]
CCAD	Carnegie Council on Adolescent Development (EA)
CCAD	Center for Computer Aided Design [*University of Iowa*] [*Research center*] (RCD)
CCAD	Computer and Communications Access Device (AAGC)
CCAD	Corpus Christi Army Depot (AABC)
CCAE	Canada Committee on Agricultural Engineering
CCAE	Canadian Council for the Advancement of Education [*Le Conseil Canadien pour l'Avancement de l'Education*] (AC)
CCAE	Canadian Council for the Advancement of Education (NFD)
CCAE	Canadian Council for the Advancement of Education
CCAE	Council of Canning Association Executives [*Later, CFPAE*] (EA)
CCAEP	Computer-Controlled Action Entry Panel (DNAB)
CCAF	Canadian Comprehensive Auditing Foundation (HGAA)
CCAF	Chinese Communist Air Force
CCAF	Community College of the Air Force (AFM)
CCAFS	Cape Canaveral Air Force Station (NASA)
CCAFT	Citizens Concerned About Free Trade [*Canadian organization opposed to the US/Canadian free trade agreement*] (CROSS)
CCAG	Canadian Correspondence Art Gallery
CCAG	Catalogus Codicum Astrologorum Graecorum [*A publication*] (OCD)
CCAG	COEA [*Cost and Operational Effectiveness Analysis*] Cost Advisory Group [*Military*]
CCAG	Conseil Canadien des Arpenteurs-Geometres [*Canadian Council of Land Surveyors - CLS*]
CCAG	Cost Committee Advisory Group
CCAG	Cost Control and Action Group
CCAHS	Consumer Commission on the Accreditation of Health Services [*Defunct*] (EA)
CCAI	Chamber of Commerce of the Apparel Industry (EA)
CC-AI	Communication and Cognition - Artificial Intelligence (EA)
CCAI	Community Care of America [*NASDAQ symbol*] (SAG)
CCAI	Continental Confederation of Adopted Indians (EA)
CCAIC	Catholic College Admissions and Information Center (EA)
CCAID	Charge-Coupled Area Imaging Device (PDAA)
CCAIE	Commission Canadienne de l'Annee Internationale de l'Enfant [*Canadian Commission for the International Year of the Child*]
CCAIR	CCAIR, Inc. [*Associated Press*] (SAG)
CCAIT	Community College Association for Instruction and Technology (EA)
CCal	Calexico Public Library, Calexico, CA [*Library symbol Library of Congress*] (LCLS)
CCAL	Christensen Canadian African Line [*Steamship*] (MHDW)
CCAL	Community Care of Amer [*NASDAQ symbol*] (TTSB)
CCALA	Combined Civil Affairs Liquidating Agency [*World War II*]
CCali	Calistoga Free Public Library, Calistoga, CA [*Library symbol Library of Congress*] (LCLS)
CCALI	Center for Computer-Assisted Legal Instruction (EA)
CCAM	Canadian Congress of Applied Mechanics (HGAA)
CCAM	CCA Industries [*NASDAQ symbol*] (TTSB)
CCAM	CCA Industries, Inc. [*NASDAQ symbol*] (NQ)
CCAM	Certified Clinic Account Manager [*American Guild of Patient Account Manag ement*] [*Designation awarded by*]
CCAM	Computer Communications Access Method (DNAB)
CCAM	Connection Co-Processor Application Manager [*Computer science*]
CCAM	Conversational Communication Access Method
CCAM	Council for Complementary Alternative Medicine [*British*]
CCamarH	Camarillo State Hospital, Camarillo, CA [*Library symbol Library of Congress*] (LCLS)
CCamarSJ	Saint John's Seminary, Camarillo, CA [*Library symbol Library of Congress*] (LCLS)
CCAMLR	Commission for the Conservation of the Antarctic Marine Living Resources [*Australia*] (EAIO)

CCAMLR	Convention of the Conservation of Antarctic Marine Living Resources (USDC)
CCAN	Construction Computer Applications Newsletter [*Database*] [*Construction Industry Press*] [*Information service or system*] (CRD)
CC & BB	Cepi Corpus and Bail Bond [*Legal term*] (DLA)
CC & C	Cepi Corpus and Committitur [*Legal term*] (ILCA)
CC & C	Colony Count and Culture [*Bacteriology*] (DAVI)
CC & C	Command, Control, and Communications [*Air Force*]
CC & C	Cowlitz, Chehalis & Cascade Railroad (IIA)
CC & CP	Command Control and Communications Program [*Air Force*]
CC & DF	Central Computer and Display Facility [*Air Force*] (CET)
CC & GTCC	Casino Chips and Gaming Tokens Collectors Club (EA)
CC & L	Chicago, Cincinnati & Louisville Railway
CC & NF	Cell Culture and Nitrogen Fixation Laboratory [*Department of Agriculture*]
CC & R	Conditions, Covenants, and Restrictions [*On condominiums*]
CC & R	Convenant, Condition, and Restriction [*Business term*] (EMRF)
CC & S	Central Computer and Sequencer [*NASA*]
CC & S	Cornea, Conjunctiva, and Sclera [*Ophthalmology*] (DAVI)
CC & S	Nuclear Weapons Command, Control, and Security Requirements (MCD)
CC & T	Combat Center and Crosstell (SAA)
CCANE	Conseil Cooperatif Acadien de la Nouvelle-Ecosse (AC)
CCANI	Clearinghouse on Child Abuse and Neglect Information (EA)
CCANSW	Campers and Caravanners' Association of New South Wales [*Australia*]
CCAO	Chambre de Compensation de l'Afrique de l'Ouest [*West African Clearing House - WACH*] (EAIO)
CCAO	Chief Civil Affairs Officer [*Navy*]
CCAO	Contract Cost Analysis Organization [*Navy*] (AFIT)
CCAO	County Commissioners Association of Ohio (SRA)
CCAO(B)	Chief Civil Affairs Officer (Burma) [*British*]
CCAP	Capsule Cartilage Articular Preservation [*Orthopedics*] (DAVI)
CCAP	Census Community Awareness Program [*Bureau of the Census*] (GFGA)
CCAP	Center for Clean Air Policy (EA)
CCAP	Citizens Crusade Against Poverty [*Absorbed by Center for Community Change*]
CCAP	Commercial Commodity Acquisition Program [*DoD*] (RDA)
CCAP	Committee of Concerned Artists and Professionals (EA)
CCAP	Communications Control Applications Program
CCAP	Community College Assessment Program [*Academic achievement and aptitude test*]
CCAP	Conventional Circuit Analysis Program (DNAB)
CCAP	County Commissioners Association of Pennsylvania (SRA)
CCAP	Crustacean Cardioactive Peptide [*Biochemistry*]
CCAP	Culture Centre of Algae and Protozoa [*Freshwater Biological Association*] [*British*] (CB)
CCAPP	[*The*] Canadian Council for Accreditation of Pharmacy Programs [*Le Conseil Canadien de l'Agrement des Programmes de Pharmacie*] (AC)
CCAPS	Closed Cycle ADCAP [*Advanced Capability*] Propulsion System [*Mk48 torpedo improvement*] (DOMA)
CCAQ	Consultative Committee on Administrative Questions [*United Nations*]
CCAQ	Corporation des Concessionnaires d'Automobiles du Quebec Inc. (AC)
CCAR	CCAIR, Inc. [*NASDAQ symbol*] (NQ)
CCAR	Central Conference of American Rabbis (EA)
CCAR	Colorado Center for Astrodynamics Research [*University of Colorado at Boulder*] [*Research center*] (RCD)
CCarl	Carlsbad City Library, Carlsbad, CA [*Library symbol Library of Congress*] (LCLS)
CCarm	Harrison Memorial Library, Carmel, CA [*Library symbol Library of Congress*] (LCLS)
CCarmJ	Robinson Jeffers Home [*Tor House*], Carmel, CA [*Library symbol Library of Congress*] (LCLS)
CCarpHi	Carpinteria Valley Historical Association, Carpinteria, CA [*Library symbol*] [*Library of Congress*] (LCLS)
CCarsP	Purex Corp., Carson, CA [*Library symbol Library of Congress*] (LCLS)
CCAS	Cape Canaveral Air Station
CCAS	Carrier-Controlled Approach System
CCAS	Center for Contemporary Arab Studies [*Georgetown University*] [*Research center*] (RCD)
CCAS	Central Computer and Sequencer [*NASA*] (IAA)
CCAS	Christian Comic Arts Society (EA)
CCAS	Citizens Council of America for Segregation [*Defunct*] (EA)
CCAS	Class C Airspace [*Aviation*] (FAAC)
CCAS	Community College Activities Survey (EDAC)
CCAS	Comprehensive Close Air Support [*Military*]
CCAS	Containment Cooling Actuation Signal [*Nuclear energy*] (NRCH)
CCAS	Convention for the Conservation of Antarctic Seals [*Australia*]
CCASS	Council of Colleges of Arts and Sciences (EA)
CCASS	Construction Contractor Appraisal Support System (AAGC)
CCAST	China Center for Advanced Science and Technology
CCAT	Cambridgeshire College of Arts and Technology [*British*] (AIE)
CCAT	Canadian Cognitive Abilities Test [*Academic achievement and aptitude test*]
CCAT	Chick Cell Agglutination Test (DMAA)
CCAT	Comite de Coordination de l'Assistance Technique [*ONU*]
CCAT	Conglutinating Complement Absorption Test [*Immunochemistry*]
CCAT	Cooperative College Ability Test (WGA)
CCATF	Commander, Combined Amphibious Task Force [*Military*] (NVT)

CCATM........	Conference Canadienne des Administrateurs en Transport Motorise [*Canadian Conference of Transport Administrators*]
CCATNA	Combined Committee on Air Training in North America
CCATS	Communications, Command, and Telemetry Systems (MCD)
CCATTD	Common Chassis Advanced Technology Transition Demonstrator
CCAU	Career Criminal Apprehension Unit (LAIN)
CCAU	Cell Cover Arming Unit (MCD)
CCA (US)	Circuit Court of Appeals (United States) [*A publication*] (DLA)
CCA-UWM....	Center for Consumer Affairs, University of Wisconsin-Milwaukee (EA)
CCAV	Community Council Against Violence [*Australia*]
C-CAVE	Canadians Concerned About Violence in Entertainment (AC)
CCAVV	CCNU [*Lomustine*], Cyclophosphamide, Adriamycin, Vincristine, VP-16 [*Antineoplastic drug regimen*] (DAVI)
CCAWA	Cleaning Contractors' Association of Western Australia
CCAWS	Close Combat Anti-Armor Weapon System [*Army*] (RDA)
CCB.............	Calcium Channel Blocker [*Medicine*] (CPH)
CCB.............	CAM Control Block [*Computer science*]
CCB.............	Campbell Colpitts Bridge [*Electronics*]
CCB.............	Canadian Commercial Bank
CCB.............	Canadian Council of the Blind
CCB.............	Canadian Custom Bonded
CCB.............	Capital Cities/ABC, Inc. [*NYSE symbol*] (SPSG)
CCB.............	Carroll Center for the Blind (EA)
CCB.............	CCB Financial [*NYSE symbol*] (SAG)
CCB.............	Cell-Cycle Box [*Genetics*]
CCB.............	Change Control Board [*Social Security Administration*]
CCB.............	Channel Command [*or Control*] Block [*Computer science*] (IAA)
CCB.............	Character Control Block [*Computer science*] (IBMDP)
CCB.............	Chemical Cleaning Building [*Nuclear energy*] (NRCH)
CCB.............	Chicago City Ballet
CCB.............	Circuit Concentration Bay (IEEE)
CCB.............	Civil Cooperation Bureau [*South African covert-operations team*] (ECON)
CCB.............	Clear Creek Butte [*Alaska*] [*Seismograph station code, US Geological Survey Closed*] (SEIS)
CCB.............	Close Control Bombing [*Air Force*]
CCB.............	Code de Commerce Belge (DLA)
CCB.............	Coin Collecting Box [*Telecommunications*] (TEL)
CCB.............	[*The*] Collective Catalogue of Belgium [*Database*] (IID)
CCB.............	Combat Command B
CCB.............	Combined Communications Board [*World War II*]
CCB.............	Command and Control Boat [*Navy symbol*]
CCB.............	Command Communications Boat
CCB.............	Command Control Block [*Computer science*] (BUR)
CCB.............	Commission Canadienne du Ble [*Canadian Wheat Board - CWB*]
CCB.............	Common Carrier Bureau [*of FCC*]
CCB.............	Communications Control Block [*Computer science*]
CCB.............	Competence in Clearing Bacilli [*Test for leprosy bacilli*]
CCB.............	Concrete Block
CCB.............	Configuration Change Board [*NASA*] (MCD)
CCB.............	Configuration Control Board [*DoD*]
CCB.............	Conseil Canadien du Bois (AC)
CCB.............	Console to Computer Buffer (MUGU)
CCB.............	Construction Criteria Base [*Information service or system*] (IID)
CCB.............	Continuing Calibration Blank [*Laboratory analysis*]
CCB.............	Contraband Control Base [*Navy*]
CCB.............	Contract Change Board
CCB.............	Contre Complications Bronchiques [*Vaccine for "bronchial complaints"*] [*Medicine*]
CCB.............	Convertible Circuit Breaker
CCB.............	Co-Operative and Commerce Bank [*Nigeria*]
CCB.............	Co-Operative Central Bank [*Malaysia*]
CCB.............	Coordination Control Board (MCD)
CCB.............	Cubic Capacity of Bunkers [*British*] (ADA)
CCB.............	Cyclic Check BIT [*Binary Digit*] [*Computer science*] (IAA)
CCB.............	Upland, CA [*Location identifier FAA*] (FAAL)
CCBA	Canadian Cattle Breeders' Association (AC)
CCBA	Central Canada Broadcasting Association
CCBA	Chinese Consolidated Benevolent Association (EA)
CCBA	Christian Classic Bikers Association [*Later, ICCM*] (EA)
CCBAI	Christian Classic Bikers Association International [*Later, ICCM*] (EA)
CCB-B	Center for Children's Books. Bulletin [*A publication*] (BRI)
CCBB	Clinical Center Blood Bank
CCBBB	Canadian Council of Better Business Bureaus [*Conseil Canadien des Bureaux d'Ethique Commerciale*] (AC)
CCBC	California Commun Bancshs [*NASDAQ symbol*] (TTSB)
CCBC	California Community Bancshares Corp. [*NASDAQ symbol*] (SAG)
CCBC	Council of Community Blood Centers (EA)
CCBD	Change Control Board Directive [*NASA*] (MCD)
CCBD	Configuration Control Board Data [*or Directive*] [*DoD*]
CCBD	Contract Change Board Directive (SAA)
CCBD	Council for Children with Behavioral Disorders (EA)
CCBDA	Canadian Copper and Brass Development Association
CCBE	Certified Credit Bureau Executive [*Society of Certified Consumer Credit E xecutives*] [*Designation awarded by*]
CCBE	Conseil des Barreaux de la Communaute Europeenne [*Council of the Bars and Law Societies of the European Community*] (EAIO)
CCBE	Consultative Committee of the Bars and Law Societies of the European Community (ILCA)
CCBF.........	CCB Financial [*NASDAQ symbol*] (TTSB)
CCBF.........	CCB Financial Corp. [*NASDAQ symbol*] (NQ)
CCBF.........	Cell-Cycle Box Factor [*Genetics*]
CCBF.........	Commanderie des Cordons Bleus de France (EA)
CCBFC	Cole Country Band Fan Club (EA)
CCB Fn	CCB Financial Co. [*Associated Press*] (SAG)
CCBG	Canberra Craft Bookbinders' Guild [*Australia*]
CCBI............	Council of Churches for Britain and Ireland (EAIO)
CCBL...........	C-COR Electronics, Inc. [*NASDAQ symbol*] (NQ)
CCBL...........	C-COR Electrs [*NASDAQ symbol*] (TTSB)
CCBM..........	Chemically Contaminated Biological Mask (MCD)
CCBM..........	Copper Cylinder and Boiler Manufacturers' Association [*British*] (BI)
CCBMM........	Comac Condition Base Monitor Module [*Comac Systems Ltd..*] [*Software package*] (NCC)
CCBN	Central Council for British Naturism (BI)
CCBN	Commission des Champs de Bataille Nationaux [*National Battlefields Commission - NBC*] [*Canada*]
CCBncsh	Corpus Christi Bancshares [*Associated Press*] (SAG)
CCBOM	Certificant, Canadian Board of Occupational Medicine (DD)
CCBP	Combined Communications Board Publications
CCBS	Center for Computer-Based Behavioral Studies [*Research center*] (RCD)
CCBS	Change Control Board Summary [*NASA*] (MCD)
CCBS	Clear Channel Broadcasting Service (EA)
CCBS	Commodore, Contract-Built Ships [*British military*] (DMA)
CCBS	Completion of Calls to Busy Subscriber [*Telecommunications*] (DOM)
CCBT..........	Cape Cod Bank & Trust [*Associated Press*] (SAG)
CCBT..........	Cape Cod Bank & Trust Co. [*NASDAQ symbol*] (NQ)
CCBV..........	Central Circulating Blood Volume [*Physiology*]
CCC............	Calcium Cyanamide Citrated [*or Citrated Calcium Carbimide*] [*Pharmacology*]
CCC............	Calculator Collectors Club [*British*] (DBA)
CCC............	Calgon Carbon [*NYSE symbol*] (TTSB)
CCC............	Calgon Carbon [*NYSE symbol*] (SAG)
CCC............	Calibration Check Compound
CCC............	California Chamber of Commerce (SRA)
CCC............	California College of Chiropody
CCC............	Calorie Control Council (EA)
CCC............	Calverton, NY [*Location identifier FAA*] (FAAL)
CCC............	Cambodia Crisis Center [*Defunct*] (EA)
CCC............	Cambodian Crisis Committee (EA)
CCC............	Cambridge Communication Corp. (MCD)
CCC............	Campus Crusade for Christ International (EA)
CCC............	Canadian Catholic Conference
CCC............	Canadian Climate Center
CCC............	Canadian Commercial Corp. [*Government-owned*] (RDA)
CCC............	Canadian Committee on Cataloguing [*Librarianship*]
CCC............	Canadian Computer Complex (NITA)
CCC............	Canadian Computer Conference (MCD)
CCC............	Canadian Conservative Centre (EAIO)
CCC............	Canadian Council of Churches (EAIO)
CCC............	Canadian Crafts Council
CCC............	Canadian Criminal Cases [*Law Book, Inc.*] [*Information service or system*]
CCC............	Canberra Canoe Club [*Australia*]
CCC............	Canberra Chamber of Commerce [*Australia*]
CCC............	Canberra Children's Choir [*Australia*]
CCC............	Canberra Churches Centre [*Australia*]
CCC............	Canine Control Council [*Australia*]
CCC............	Canoe-Camping Club [*British*] (BI)
CCC............	Cape Cod Central Railroad
CCC............	Cape Communications Control [*NASA*]
CCC............	Capricorn Conservation Council [*Australia*]
CCC............	Car Care Council (EA)
CCC............	Care-Cure Coordination [*Medicine*] (DMAA)
CCC............	Care Custody and Control
CCC............	Caribbean Conference of Churches (EAIO)
CCC............	Caribbean Conservation Corp. (EA)
CCC............	Carpet Cushion Council (EA)
CCC............	Carriage Control Character [*Computer science*]
CCC............	Carrington Cotton Corporation [*Australia*]
CCC............	Case Collectors Club (EA)
CCC............	Catalog Card Corp. of America [*Information service or system*] (IID)
CCC............	Catalytic Construction Co. (MCD)
CCC............	Cathodal Closure Contraction [*Also, CaCC*] [*Physiology*]
CCC............	CCATS [*Communications, Command, and Telemetry Systems*] Command Controller [*NASA*]
CCC............	Cedar Crest College [*Pennsylvania*]
CCC............	Cellules Combattantes Communistes [*Communist Combatant Cells*] [*Belgium*]
CCC............	Cellules Communistes Combattantes [*Terrorist organization*] [*Belgium*] (EY)
CCC............	Center for Community Change (EA)
CCC............	Centerville Community College [*Iowa*]
CCC............	Central Citroen Club [*Defunct*] (EA)
CCC............	Central Classification Committee [*International Federation for Documentation*]
CCC............	Central Communications Controller
CCC............	Central Computational Computer
CCC............	Central Computer Center
CCC............	Central Computer Complex
CCC............	Central Counteradaptive Change (AAMN)
CCC............	Central Criminal Court [*Old Bailey*] [*British*]
CCC............	Cercle Culturel Camerounais
CCC............	Certificate of Clinical Competence
CCC............	Certified Collateral Corp. (IID)
CCC............	Challenger Communications Consultants Ltd. [*British Telecommunications service*] (TSSD)
CCC............	Channel Command or Control [*Computer science*] (IAA)
CCC............	Channel Control Check [*Electronics*] (IAA)
CCC............	Cherry Central Cooperative (EA)

CCC............. Chicago City College [*Illinois*] (AEBS)
CCC............. Chicago Clinical Chemist [*A publication*]
CCC............. Chief Cable Censor [*Navy rating Obsolete*]
CCC............. China Christian Council
CCC............. Chlorocholine Chloride [*Organic chemistry*]
CCC............. Chow Chow Club (EA)
CCC............. Choyce's Cases in Chancery [*1557-1606*] [*England*] [*A publication*] (DLA)
CCC............. Christian Chamber of Commerce (EA)
CCC............. Christian Citizens' Crusade (EA)
CCC............. Christian City Church [*Australia*]
CCC............. Christian College Coalition (EA)
CCC............. Christian College Consortium (EA)
CCC............. Christian Community Church [*Australia*]
CCC............. Christian Community Concern [*Australia*]
CCC............. Christ's College (Cambridge University) (ROG)
CCC............. Chronic Calculous Cholecystitis [*Medicine*] (MAE)
CCC............. CINC [*Commander in Chief*] Command Center (DOMA)
CCC............. Circo Craft Co., Inc. [*Toronto Stock Exchange symbol*]
CCC............. Citizens' Committee for Children of New York (EA)
CCC............. Citizens Communication Center (NTCM)
CCC............. Citizens for Constitutional Concerns (EA)
CCC............. Citrated Calcium Cyanamide (IIA)
CCC............. Citroen Car Club (EA)
CCC............. City Communications Centre [*British*] (CB)
CCC............. Civilian Conservation Centers [*Job Corps*]
CCC............. Civilian Conservation Corps [*Created, 1937; liquidated, 1943*]
CCC............. Claro [*Light-colored cigar*]
CCC............. Classified Control Clerk [*Army*]
CCC............. Clean Coal Coalition [*Defunct*] (EA)
CCC............. Clear, Cancel, or Complete (MCD)
CCC............. Cloisonne Collectors Club (EA)
CCC............. Closed-Cycle Cooler
CCC............. Club Cricket Conference [*British*] (BI)
CCC............. Clue Computing Co. [*British*]
CCC............. Coalition for Common Courtesy [*Defunct*] (EA)
CCC............. Collection/Classification/Cannibalization [*Military*]
CCC............. Colorado Cooperative Council (SRA)
CCC............. Combat Cargo Command
CCC............. Combat Command C
CCC............. Combined Case Control [*IRS*]
CCC............. Command and Control Center [*Air Force*] (AFM)
CCC............. Command Communications Console
CCC............. Command Control Console (KSC)
CCC............. Commercial Contract Change
CCC............. Commercial Credit Corp. (MHDW)
CCC............. Committee of Chinese Correspondence (EA)
CCC............. Committee of Concerned Catholics [*Defunct*] (EA)
CCC............. Committee on the Care of Children [*Defunct*] (EA)
CCC............. Commodity Credit Corp. [*Department of Agriculture*]
CCC............. Common Control Circuit [*Telecommunications*] (IAA)
CCC............. Commonwealth Communications Council [*British World War II*]
CCC............. Communication Center Console
CCC............. Communications Center of Clarksburg [*Clarksburg, MD*] [*Telecommunications*] (TSSD)
CCC............. Communications, Command, and Control
CCC............. Communications Control Console (MCD)
CCC............. Community Conference Crew [*World online service referees*]
CCC............. Comparative Capital Cost (TEL)
CCC............. Competition and Credit Control [*British*]
CCC............. Complex Control Center (KSC)
CCC............. Component Change Control [*Navy*] (NG)
CCC............. Component Control Committee [*DoD*]
CCC............. Comprehensive Cancer Center [*Ohio State University*] [*Research center*] (RCD)
CCC............. Compucats' Computer Club [*Defunct*] (EA)
CCC............. Computer Command Control [*General Motors Corp.*]
CCC............. Computer Communications Console (AFM)
CCC............. Computer Communications Converter (MCD)
CCC............. Computer Composition Corp. [*Also, an information service or system*] (IID)
CCC............. Computer Control Communication (BUR)
CCC............. Computer Control Complex
CCC............. Computer Control Corp.
CCC............. Concerned Citizens for Charity (DICI)
CCC............. Concrete Ceiling
CCC............. Concurrent Care Concern [*Medicine*]
CCC............. Congressional Competitiveness Caucus (EA)
CCC............. Congressional Crime Caucus [*Defunct*] (EA)
CCC............. Consecutive Case Conference (MAE)
CCC............. Conservative Central Council [*British*]
CCC............. Conservatives for a Constitutional Convention (EA)
CCC............. Console Control Circuit
CCC............. Consommation et Corporations Canada [*Consumer and Corporate Affairs Canada-CCA*]
CCC............. Constitutio Carolina Criminalis [*A publication*] (DSA)
CCC............. Constitutional Consultative Committee on the Political Future of Nigeria [*Political party*]
CCC............. Consultative Committee on the Curriculum [*British*]
CCC............. Consumer Consultative Committee [*British*]
CCC............. Consumer Credit Counselors [*Banking*]
CCC............. Consumers' Consultative Committee [*EC*] (ECED)
CCC............. Contaminant Control Cartridge (MCD)
CCC............. Continuing Community Care [*Psychology*] (DAVI)
CCC............. Contract Carrier Conference [*Later, ICC*] (EA)

CCC............. Control Core Cell (PDAA)
CCC............. Controller Checkout Console (NASA)
CCC............. Convert Character Code (OA)
CCC............. Coordinate Conversion Computer (MCD)
CCC............. Copy Control Character [*Computer science*] (IAA)
CCC............. Copyright Clearance Center (EA)
CCC............. Copyright Collective of Canada (AC)
CCC............. Core College Curriculm (EDAC)
CCC............. Corporate Capital Charge (MCD)
CCC............. Corporate Conservation Council (EA)
CCC............. Corpus Christi Campaign (EA)
CCC............. Corpus Christi College [*Cambridge and Oxford*]
CCC............. Cost Category Code (MCD)
CCC............. Council for Cultural Co-Operation [*Council of Europe*] (EY)
CCC............. Council for the Care of Churches [*British*]
CCC............. Council of Community Churches [*Later, National Council of Community Churches*] (EA)
CCC............. Council of Conservative Citizens (EA)
CCC............. Council of Container Carriers
CCC............. Council on Clinical Classifications (HCT)
CCC............. Countercurrent Chromatography
CCC............. County Counseling Center [*Psychology*] (DAVI)
CCC............. Covalently Closed Circular [*Configuration of DNA*] [*Microbiology*]
CCC............. Cox's English Criminal Cases [*A publication*] (DLA)
CCc............. Crescent City Public Library, Crescent City, CA [*Library symbol Library of Congress*] (LCLS)
CCC............. Critical Coagulation Concentration [*Colloidal chemistry*]
CCC............. Critical Control Circuit
CCC............. Cube-Connected Cycle (MCD)
CCC............. Curriculum Coordinating Committees (EDAC)
CCC............. Cusp Creek [*British Columbia*] [*Seismograph station code, US Geological Survey Closed*] (SEIS)
CCC............. Customer Coordination Center (SSD)
CCC............. Customs Co-Operation Council [*See also CCD*] [*Brussels, Belgium*] (EAIO)
ccc............. Cwmni Cyfyngedig Cyhoeddus [*Public Limited Company*] [*Welsh*] (ODBW)
CCC............. Cyclic Check Character [*Computer science*]
CCC............. Cycocel (BARN)
CCC............. European Aviation Services Ltd. [*British ICAO designator*] (FAAC)
CCC............. Honnold Library, Claremont, CA [*Library symbol Library of Congress*] (LCLS)
CCC............. MIT [*Massachusetts Institute of Technology*] Cell Culture Center [*Research center*] (RCD)
CCC............. One Hundred Call Seconds [*A unit of television call measurement*] (WDMC)
CCC............. Vanguarda de Comando de Caca aos Comunistas [*Vanguard of the Commando for Hunting Communists*] [*Brazil*] (PD)
CCCA .... California Contract Cities Association (SRA)
CCCA .... California Court Clerks Association (SRA)
CCCA .... Canadian Cosmetics Careers Association
CCCA .... Canadian Criminology and Corrections Association
CCCA .... Catholic Civics Clubs of America [*Defunct*] (EA)
CCC-A......... Certificate of Clinical Competence in Audiology
CCCA .... Checker Car Club of America (EA)
CCCA .... Classic Car Club of America (EA)
CCCA .... Classic Comet Club of America (EA)
CCCA .... Cocoa, Chocolate, and Confectionary Alliance [*British*]
CCCA .... Commission on Critical Choices for Americans
CCCA .... Committee of Concern for Central America (EA)
CCCA .... Comprehensive Crime Control Act [*1984*] (GFGA)
CCCA .... Conseil de Commerce Canada-Arabe (AC)
CCCA .... Corps Commander Coast Artillery [*British*]
CCCADA...... Carolus Cordell, Catholicae Academicae Duacenae Alumnus [*Pseudonym used by Charles Cordell*]
CCC & StL ... Cleveland, Cincinnati, Chicago & St. Louis Railway
CCCAV....... Child Care Centres Association, Victoria [*Australia*]
CCCB .... Canadian Conference of Catholic Bishops
CCCB .... Component Change Control Board [*DoD*]
CCCB .... Component Configuration Control Board (AFIT)
CCCB .... Configuration Change Control Board [*NASA*] (KSC)
CCCBR........ Central Council of Church Bell Ringers [*British*]
CCC Bull ..... Bulletin. Committee on Criminal Courts' Law and Procedure. Association of the B ar. City of New York [*A publication*] (DLA)
CCCC .... Canada-California Chamber of Commerce (SRA)
CCCC .... Canadian Council of Christian Charities (AC)
CCCC .... Cape Cod Community College [*West Barnstable, MA*]
CCCC .... Cape Colony Cyclist Corps [*British military*] (DMA)
CCCC .... Centralized COMINT Communications Center [*National Security Agency*]
CCCC .... Centrifugal Countercurrent Chromatography
CCCC .... Charity Christmas Card Council [*British*] (DI)
CCCC .... Charles County Community College [*La Plata, MD*]
CCCC .... Chrome Car Collectors Club [*Later, D of A*] (EA)
CCCC .... Chrysler Car Club Council
CCCC .... Colonel Coon Collectors Club (EA)
CCCC .... Committee for Conservation and Care of Chimpanzees (EA)
CCCC .... Community Child Care Cooperative [*Australia*]
CCCC .... Computer-Controlled Catalytic Converter [*Automotive engineering*]
CCCC .... Computerized Conferencing and Communications Center [*New Jersey Institute of Technology*] [*Research center*] (RCD)
CCCC .... Conference on College Composition and Communication (EA)
CCCC .... Consolidated Computer and Control Center
CCCC .... Cookie Cutter Collectors Club (EA)
CCCC .... Coordinating Council for Computers in Construction (EA)

CCCC .... Council of Car Care Centers (EA)
CCCC .... Countercurrent Cooling Crystallization [*Tsukishima Kikai Co., Tokyo*] [*Chemical engineering*]
CCCC .... Cover Collectors Circuit Club (EA)
CCCC .... Cross-Channel Coordination Center [*NATO*] (NATG)
CCCC .... Cut, Carat, Clarity, Color [*Factors in determining the value of a diamond*]
CCC Cas ..... Central Criminal Court Cases, Sessions Papers [*1834-1913*] [*England*] [*A publication*] (DLA)
CCCCD .... Conductivity-Connected Charge-Coupled Device [*Electronics*] (EECA)
CCCCE .... Conseil de la Cooperation Culturelle du Conseil de l'Europe [*Council for Cultural Cooperation of the Council of Europe*] (EAIO)
CCCD .... Canadian Co-Ordinating Council on Deafness
CCCD .... Citizens' Council on Civic Development [*Canada*]
CCCD .... Combating Childhood Communicable Diseases Project [*Agency for International Development*]
CCCDA .... Conseil Canadien de Coordination de la Deficience Auditive [*Canadian Co-Ordinating Council on Deafness - CCCD*]
cccDNA .... Covalently Closed Circular DNA [*Deoxyribonucleic Acid*] [*Genetics*] (DOG)
CCCE .... Canadian Community of Computer Educators (AC)
CCCE .... Certified Consumer Credit Executive [*International Con sumer Credit Association*] [*Designation awarded by*]
CCCE .... Closed-Cycle Cryogenic Equipment
CCCE .... Community Cancer Care Evaluation [*Department of Health and Human Services*] (GFGA)
CCCE .... Consulting Chemists and Chemical Engineers
CCCE .... Cross-Cultural Cognitive Examination (DMAA)
CCCE .... Cumann Cluiche Corr na hEireann [*Rounders Association of Ireland*] (EAIO)
CCCEP .... Commissary Civilian Career Enhancement Program [*Air Force*]
CCCET .... Comite Canadien de la Classification Ecologique du Territoire [*Canadian Committee on Ecological (Biophysical) Land Classification - CCELC*]
CCCF .... Canadian Child Care Federation [*Formerly, Canadian Child Day Care Federation*] (AC)
CCCF .... Candlelighters Childhood Cancer Foundation (EA)
CCCF .... Central Committee on Communications Facilities
CCCF .... Chai Na Ta Corp. [*NASDAQ symbol*] (SAG)
CCCFC .... Candlelighters Childhood Cancer Foundation Canada [*Fondation des Eclaireurs pour le Cancer dans l'Enfance Canada*] [*Also, Candlelighters Canada*] (AC)
CCCFF .... Chai-Na-Ta Corp. [*NASDAQ symbol*] (TTSB)
CCCG .... CCC Information Services Group, Inc. [*NASDAQ symbol*] (SAG)
CCCH .... Chinese Chamber of Commerce of Hawaii (SRA)
CC Chr .... Chancery Cases Chronicle [*Ontario*] [*A publication*] (DLA)
CC Chron .... Chancery Cases Chronicle [*Ontario*] [*A publication*] (DLA)
CCCHRON .... County Courts Chronicle [*1847-1920*] [*England*]
CCCI .... Campus Crusade for Christ International (EA)
CCCI .... Candy, Chocolate and Confectionery Institute (EA)
CCCI .... Capital Cities Communications, Inc.
CCCI .... Cathodal Closure Clonus [*Medicine*] (DMAA)
CCCI .... Classic Chevy Club International (EA)
CCCI .... Coca-Cola Collectors Club International (EA)
CCCI .... Command, Control, Communications, and Intelligence [*Telecommunications*] (TEL)
CCCI .... Computer-Controlled Coil Ignition [*Automotive engineering*]
CCCI .... Conceal-Control-Command-Instruction [*NATO*]
CCCI .... Conseil Canadien pour la Cooperation Internationale [*Canadian Council for International Cooperation - CCIC*]
CCCI .... Continental Choice Care, Inc. [*NASDAQ symbol*] (SAG)
CCCI .... Contl Choice Care [*NASDAQ symbol*] (TTSB)
CCC Info .... CCC Information Services Group, Inc. [*Associated Press*] (SAG)
CCCIPR .... Citizens Communication Center of the Institute for Public Representation [*Later, CCCPIPR*] (EA)
CCCIW .... Continental Choice Care Wrrt [*NASDAQ symbol*] (TTSB)
CCCJ .... [*The*] Canadian Council of Christians & Jews [*Conseil Canadien des Chretiens et des Juifs*] (AC)
CCCL .... Canadian and Catholic Confederation of Labour
CC Cl .... Cathodal Closure Clonus [*Medicine*]
CCCL .... Catholic Council on Civil Liberties [*Defunct*] (EA)
CCCL .... Citizens Committee for Constitutional Liberties [*Defunct*]
CCCL .... Cleveland, Cincinnati, Chicago & St. Louis Railway [*AAR code*]
CCCL .... CMOS [*Complementary Metal Oxide Semiconductor*] Compact Cell Logic [*Electronics*] (NITA)
CCCL .... Complementary Constant Current Logic [*Computer science*] (BUR)
CCcL .... Crescent City Public Library, Crescent City, CA [*Library symbol*] [*Library of Congress*] (LCLS)
CCCLA .... Coordination Council on Control of Liquor Abuse
CCCLC .... Command Control Communications Laboratory Center (SAA)
CCCLS .... Clackamas Cooperative County-Wide Library Services [*Library network*]
CCCM.......... Canadian Consultative Council on Multiculturalism
C/CCM .... Counter/Counter-Countermeasure [*Military*]
CCCMA .... Central Coast Country Music Association
CCCMD .... Comprehensive Cancer Center of Metropolitan Detroit [*National Cancer Institute*] [*Research center*] (RCD)
CCCMMM .... Closed Chest Cardiac Massage and Mouth-to-Mouth Resuscitation [*Medicine*] (AABC)
CCCN .... Canadian Council Cardiovascular Nurses [*Conseil Canadien des Infirmieres en Nursing Cardiovasculaire*] (AC)
CCCN .... Cost Change Commitment Notice
CCCN .... Customs Co-Operation Council Nomenclature [*See also BTN*]
CCCNA .... Congregational Christian Churches National Association (EA)
CCCO .... Catalytically Cracked Clarified Oil [*Petroleum technology*]

CCCO .... Catalytic Construction Co. (KSC)
CCCO .... CCCO [*Central Committee for Conscientious Objectors*]/An Agency for Military and Draft Counseling (EA)
CCCO .... Committee on Climatic Changes and the Ocean [*Defunct Paris, France*] (EAIO)
CCCOGP...... Conservation Committee of California Oil and Gas Producers (SRA)
CC Com Proc... Code of Civil and Commercial Procedure (DLA)
CCCOWE-NA... Chinese Coordination Centre of World Evangelism (North America) (EA)
CCCP .... Carbonylcyanide-meta-chlorophenylhydrazone [*Also, CCP*] [*Organic chemistry*]
CCCP .... Comprehensive Cancer Center Program [*National Cancer Institute*]
CCCP .... Consolidated Command, Control, and Communications Program (MCD)
CCCP .... Council on Cooperative College Projects [*Later, CCP*] (EA)
CCCP .... Union of Soviet Socialist Republics [*Initialism represents Russian phrase, Soyuz Sotsialistiches Kikh Respublik*]
CCCPIPR...... Citizens Communications Center Project of the Institute for Public Representation (EA)
CCCPR .... Client-Centered Counseling Progress Record [*Psychology*]
CCCR .... Citizens' Commission on Civil Rights (EA)
CCCR .... Closed Chest Cardiac Resuscitation [*Medicine*]
CCCR .... Command Classified Control Register
CCCR .... Communication and Command Control Requirements (AAG)
CCCR .... Coordinator of Commercial and Cultural Relations [*New Deal*]
CCCRAM ...... Continuously Charge-Coupled Random Access Memory [*Computer science*] (IAA)
CCCRC .... Connecticut Chemosensory Clinical Research Center [*University of Connecticut*] [*Research center*] (RCD)
CCCS .... Canadian Cooperative Credit Society
CCCS .... Canadian Critical care Society [*Societe Canadienne de Soins Intensifs*] (AC)
CCCS .... Caratage, Color, Clarity, and Shape [*Factors in determining the value of a diamond*]
CCCS .... Central Control Computer System
CCCS .... Centre for Contemporary Cultural Studies [*University of Birmingham*] [*British*] (CB)
CCC-S .... Certificate of Clinical Competence in Speech
CCCS .... Colonial [*or Commonwealth*] and Continental Church Society [*British*]
CCCS .... Command, Control, and Communications System (NATG)
CCCS .... Condom Catheter Collecting System [*Medicine*] (DMAA)
CCCS .... Consumer Credit Counseling Services [*Banking*]
CCCS .... Core Component Cleaning System [*Nuclear energy*] (NRCH)
CCCS .... Core Component Conditioning Station [*Nuclear energy*] (NRCH)
CC/CS .... Current Contents/Chemical Sciences [*A publication*]
CCC Sess Pap... Central Criminal Court Cases, Sessions Papers [*1834-1913*] [*England*] [*A publication*] (DLA)
CCCT.......... Cabinet Council on Commerce and Trade [*Reagan administration*]
CCCT.......... Canadian Centre for Creative Technology [*Centre Canadien de Technologie Creative*] (AC)
CCCT.......... Closed Craniocerebral Trauma [*Medicine*] (DMAA)
CCCT.......... Compound Cyclic Corrosion Test [*Materials science*]
CC Ct Cas .... Central Criminal Court Cases [*1834-1913*] [*England*] [*A publication*] (DLA)
CCCTU .... Central Council of Ceylon Trade Unions
CCCU .... Comprehensive Cardiac Care Unit [*Medicine*] (DMAA)
CCCU .... Crew Compartment Cooling Unit [*NASA*] (KSC)
CCCUN .... Communications Coordination Committee for the United Nations (EA)
CCCUNY...... City College of City University of New York
CCCV .... Chevrolet Car Club of Victoria [*Australia*]
CCCV .... Coconut Cadang-Cadang Viroid [*Also, CCV*]
CCCWA .... Central Citrus Council of Western Australia
CCCY .... Canadian Council on Children and Youth [*Research center*] (RCD)
CCD .... Calcite Compensation Depth [*Oceanography*]
CCD .... Calibration Curve Data
CCD .... Cambridge Crystallographic Database [*England*]
CCD .... Camera Concealment and Deception (DWSG)
CCD .... Camouflage, Concealment, and Deception (MCD)
CCD .... Canadian Car Demurrage Bureau, The, Montreal PQ CDA [*STAC*]
CCD .... Carbonate Compensation Depth [*Oceanography*]
CCD .... Carlos Cervantes del Rio [*Mexico ICAO designator*] (FAAC)
CCD .... Cash Concentration and Disbursement
CCD .... Cell Current Density
CCD .... Census County Division [*Bureau of Census*]
CCD .... Center for Community Development [*Humboldt State University*] [*Research center*] (RCD)
CCD .... Center for Curriculum Design [*Information service or system Defunct*] (IID)
CCD .... Central Command Decoder [*Spacecraft assembly*] (MCD)
CCD .... Central Commissioning Detail [*Navy*]
CCD .... Central Composite Design [*Statistical design of experiments*]
CCD .... Central Corporate Design
CCD .... Change Control Determine (MCD)
CCD .... Charge-Coupled Device [*Data storage device*]
CCD .... Checkout Command Decoder [*NASA*]
CCD .... Chemical Composition Distribution
CCD .... Chemical Control Division [*Environmental Protection Agency*] (GFGA)
CCD .... Childhood Celiac Disease [*Medicine*] (DMAA)
CCD .... Circumscribing Circle Diameter (MCD)
CCD .... City [*or County*] Civil Defense Director
CCD .... Civil Censorship Division [*US Military Government, Germany*]
CCD .... Civil Coordination Detachment [*General Air Traffic Element at Operational Traffic and Defense Centers*] [*NATO*]
CCD .... Cleidocranial Dysplasia [*Medicine*]
CCD .... Coarse Control Damper [*Nuclear energy*] (NRCH)

CCD .... Cold Cathode Discharge
CCD .... Combat Center Director
CCD .... Combat Command D
CCD .... Combustion Chamber Deposits [*Fuels and lubricants testing*]
CCD .... Command and Control Director [*Air Force*]
CCD .... Command and Control Division [*SHAPE Technical Center*] (NATG)
CC/D .... Command Control/Destruct (MUGU)
CCD .... Commander, Coast Defenses
CCD .... Commander, Cruiser-Destroyer Force [*Navy*] (DNAB)
CCD .... Committee for the Care of the Diabetic
CCD .... Common Core of Data [*National Center for Educational Statistics*] [*Department of Education*] (OICC)
CCD .... Community College of Denver [*Colorado*]
CCD .... Complementary Coded Decimal [*Computer science*] (HGAA)
CCD .... Computer-Controlled Display
CCD .... Concord Energy [*Vancouver Stock Exchange symbol*]
CCD .... Condensed Chemical Dictionary [*A publication*]
CCD .... Conference of the Committee on Disarmament [*Formerly, ENDC*] [*NATO*]
CCD .... Configuration Change Directive (KSC)
CCD .... Confraternity of Christian Doctrine
CCD .... Conseil de Cooperation Douaniere [*Customs Co-Operation Council - CCC*] (EAIO)
CCD .... Considerable Conduct Disorder
CCD .... Constants Change Display (MCD)
CCD .... Construction Completion Date (AFM)
CCD .... Consumer Computing Device (PCM)
CCD .... Continental Communications Division [*Military*]
CCD .... Contract Change Directive (DNAB)
CCD .... Contract Completion Date [*Telecommunications*] (TEL)
CCD .... Controlled Current Distribution [*Telecommunications*] (OA)
CCD .... Coordinated Cockpit Display (MCD)
CCD .... Copolymer Composition Distribution (PDAA)
CCD .... Core Current Driver
CCD .... Corona Current Detector
CCD .... Cost Center Determination (AAG)
CCD .... Council for Computer Development [*British*] (NITA)
CCD .... Countercurrent Decantation [*Engineering*]
CCD .... Countercurrent Digestion [*Ore leach process*]
CCD .... Countercurrent Distribution [*Analytical chemistry*]
CCD .... Czechoslovak Christian Democracy (EA)
CCDA .... Canadian Computer Dealer Association (EAIO)
CCDA .... Canadian Council of Grocery Distributors [*Conseil Canadien de la Distribution Alimentaire*] (AC)
CCDA .... Charge Coupled Diode Array [*Liquid chromatography*]
CCDA .... Commercial Chemical Development Association [*Later, CDA*] (EA)
CCDA .... Committee on Cataloging: Description and Access [*Association for Library Collections and Technical Services*]
CC-DAD .... Command and Control - Division Air Defense (MCD)
CCDB .... Carbon-Carbon Data Base [*Battelle Columbus Laboratories*] [*Database*]
CCDB .... Contractor's Control Data Bank (DNAB)
CCDB .... County and City Data Book [*Bureau of the Census*] (GFGA)
CCDC .... Cambridge Crystallographic Data Centre [*University of Cambridge*] [*Information service or system*] (IID)
CCDC .... Canadian Communicable Disease Center
CCDC .... Cape Cod Direction Center [*Air Force*]
CCDC .... Central Citizens' Defence Committee [*Northern Ireland*]
CCDC .... Central Control and Display Console
CC/DC .... Combined Combat Center, Direction Center [*Military*] (SAA)
CCDC .... Connecticut Census Data Center [*Connecticut State Office of Policy and Management*] [*Information service or system*] (IID)
CcdCam ...... Concord Camera Corp. [*Associated Press*] (SAG)
CCDD .... Coalition Concerned with Developmental Disabilities [*American Occupational Therapy Association*]
CCDD .... Command and Control Development Division [*Air Force*]
CCDD .... Controller of Chemical Defence Department [*Ministry of Supply*] [*British*]
CCDF .... Cambridge Crystallographic Data File [*Database*]
CCDF .... Catholic Church Development Fund [*Australia*]
CCDF .... Complementary Cumulative Distribution Function [*Mathematics*]
CCDF .... Co-ordinating Committee of Democratic Forces [*Ghana*] [*Political party*] (EY)
CCDG .... Civil Coordination Detachment General [*NATO*] (NATG)
C/CDGE .... Coated Cartridge [*Paper*] (DGA)
CCDHAL ...... Comite Chretien pour les Droits Humains en Amerique Latine [*Christian Committee for Human Rights in Latin America*] [*Canada*] (EAIO)
CCDJ .... Conseil Canadien de la Documentation Juridique [*Canadian Law Information Council*]
CCDL .... CAINS [*Carrier/Aircraft Inertial Navigation System*] Covert Data Link (MCD)
CCDL .... Commander, Cruiser-Destroyer Forces, Atlantic (MCD)
CCDL .... Cross-Channel Data Link (MCD)
CCDLG .... Coalition Canadienne pour les Droits des Lesbiennes et des Gais [*Canadian Lesbian and Gay Rights Coalition*]
CCDLNE .... Commission for Controlling the Desert Locust in the Near East [*United Nations*] (EA)
CCDLNWA .... Commission for Controlling the Desert Locust in North-West Africa [*United Nations*] (EA)
CC-DLTS ...... Constant Capacitance - Deep Level Transient Spectroscopy (PDAA)
CCDM .... Cause Consequence Diagram Method [*Engineering*]
CCDM .... Consultative Committee on the Definition of the Meter [*International Bureau of Weights and Measures*]
CCDM .... Continuing Committee of Deputy Ministers [*Canada*]

CCDM .... Council on Career Development for Minorities (EA)
CCDMRB ...... Command Contractor Data Management Review Board [*Air Force*] (AFIT)
CCdmS .... Sherman Library and Gardens, Corona Del Mar, CA [*Library symbol*] [*Library of Congress*] (LCLS)
CCDN .... Centre de Compilation de Donnees Neutroniques [*Neutron Data Compilation Center*] [*France Information service or system*] (IID)
CCDN .... Corporate Consolidated Data Network [*IBM Corp.*] [*Telecommunications*]
CCDO .... Canadian Classification and Dictionary of Occupations [*A publication*]
CCDO .... Combat Center Duty Officer [*Military*] (SAA)
CCD(OCCE)... Commonwealth Committee for Defence (Operational Clothing and Combat Equipment) (ADA)
CCDP .... Churchmen's Commission for Decent Publications [*Defunct*] (EA)
CCDP .... Climate Change Detection Project [*Marine science*] (OSRA)
CCDP .... Command Control Dial Panel
CCDP .... Commander, Cruiser-Destroyer Forces, Pacific [*Navy*] (DNAB)
CCDP .... Commission Canadienne des Droits de la Personne [*Canadian Human Rights Commission - CHRC*]
CCDP .... Computer Control and Display Panel (MCD)
CCDP .... Cooperative College Development Program
CCDP .... Croatian Christian Democratic Party [*Political party*] (EY)
CCDPH .... Conseil Canadien des Droits des Personnes Handicapees (AC)
CCDQ .... Counselling and Career Development Organisation [*British*] (AIE)
CCDR .... Container Cost Data Reporting
CCDR .... Contract Cost Data Reports (AAGC)
CCDR .... Contractor Cost Data Reporting (MCD)
CCDR .... Contractor Critical Design Review (MCD)
CCDR .... Cross-Cultural Dance Resources (EA)
CCDS .... Canadian Centre for Drug-Free Sport [*Centre Candien Sur le Dopage Sportif*] (AC)
CCDS .... Centers for the Commercial Development of Space
CCDS .... Command, Control, and Detection System [*Military*]
CCDS .... Command Control Destruct System (MUGU)
CCDS .... Commercial Computer Documentation Set (MCD)
CCDS .... Conseil Canadien de Developpement Social [*Canadian Council on Social Development*] (EAIO)
CCDS .... Consultative Committee for the Definition of the Second
CCDS .... Control Circuits Design Section
CCDS .... Control, Communication, and Display Subsystem (MCD)
CCDS .... Corpus Cultus Deae Syriae (BJA)
CCDSO .... Command and Control Defense Systems Office
CCDT .... Calcium Carbonate Deposition Test [*Organic chemistry*] (DICI)
CCDU .... Coastal Command Defence Unit [*British*]
CCDU .... Coastal Command Development Unit [*British*]
CCDW .... Carrying Concealed Deadly Weapon [*Police term*]
CCE .... Caines' New York Cases in Error [*A publication*] (DLA)
CCE .... Cairo Air Transport Co. [*Egypt*] [*ICAO designator*] (FAAC)
CCE .... Campaign for Comprehensive Education [*British*] (DI)
CCE .... Cape Cod Experiment [*Oceanography*]
CCE .... Carboline Carboxylic Acid Ester [*Medicine*] (DMAA)
CCE .... Carbon-Chloroform Extract (PDAA)
CCE .... Cases of Contested Elections [*A publication*] (DLA)
CCE .... Cathode Current Efficiency [*Electrochemistry*]
CCE .... CCC Coded Communications [*Vancouver Stock Exchange symbol*]
CCE .... Cell-Cycle Element [*Cytology*]
CCE .... Center for Conscious Evolution (EA)
CCE .... Centre for Environmental Education [*British*] (AIE)
CCE .... Centro de Calculo Electronico Universidad Nacional Autonoma de Mexico [*National Autonomous University of Mexico, Data Processing Center*] [*Mexico*]
CCE .... Certified Chamber Executive [*American Chamber of Comme rce Executives*] [*Designation awarded by*]
CCE .... Cesium Contact Engine
CCE .... Chamois Contagious Ecthyma [*Medicine*] (DMAA)
CCE .... Change Control Engineer
CCE .... Channel Command [*or Control*] Entry [*Computer science*] (IAA)
CCE .... Charge Composition Explorer [*Spacecraft*]
CCE .... Chief Construction Engineer (OA)
CCE .... Chief, Corps of Engineers [*Army*]
CCE .... Chief of Communications - Electronics
CCE .... Civil Communications Element [*Military*] (NATG)
CCE .... Clapeyron-Clausius Equation [*Physics*]
CCE .... Clear-Cell Carcinoma of Endometrium [*Medicine*]
CCE .... Clubbing, Cyanosis, or Edema [*Medicine*]
CCE .... Coca-Cola Enterprises [*NYSE symbol*] (TTSB)
CCE .... Coca-Cola Enterprises, Inc. [*NYSE symbol*] (SPSG)
CCE .... Collaborative Computing Environment
CCE .... College Canadien des Enseignants [*Canadian College of Teachers - CCT*]
CCE .... Combat Communications Equipment [*Military*]
CCE .... Combat Control Elements [*Army*]
CCE .... Comhaltas Ceoltoiri Eireann [*Traditional Irish Singing and Dancing Society*] (EA)
CCE .... Comite de Cooperacion Economica del Istmo Centroamericano [*Central American Economic Cooperation Committee*]
CCE .... Command Control Equipment (KSC)
CCE .... Commercial Construction Equipment [*Plan*] [*Army*]
CCE .... Commission des Communautes Europeennes [*Commission of the European Communities - CEC*] [*Belgium*] (EAIO)
CCE .... Communications Control Equipment (MCD)
CCE .... Complex Control Equipment [*NASA*] (IAA)
CCE .... Computer Command Engineer (MCD)
CCE .... Confederation des Compagnonnages Europeens [*European Companions - EC*] [*France*] (EAIO)

CCE............ Conseil Canadien des Eglises [*Canadian Council of Churches*] (EAIO)

CCE............ Conseil des Communes d'Europe [*Council of European Municipalities*]

CCE............ Console Communications Equipment (MCD)

CCE............ Consultative Committee on Electricity [*International Bureau of Weights and Measures*]

CCE............ Consulting Communications Engineers, Inc. [*Villanova, PA*] (TSSD)

CCE............ Continuing Criminal Enterprise

CCE............ Contract Change Estimate

CCE............ Contract Closeout Extension (AFIT)

CCE............ Contractor Change Evaluation (AAG)

CCE............ Control Creation Edition [*Microsoft Corp.*] [*Computer science*] (PCM)

CCE............ Controlled Configuration Explosive [*Military*]

CCE............ Council for a Competitive Economy (EA)

CCE............ Council for Court Excellence (EA)

CCE............ Council of Construction Employers [*Defunct*] (EA)

CCE............ Council on Chiropractic Education (EA)

CCE............ Counsel and Care for the Elderly [*British*]

CCE............ Countercurrent Electrophoresis [*Also, CE*] [*Analytical chemistry*]

CCE............ Counterflow Centrifugal Elutriation [*Analytical biochemistry*]

CCE............ Crusade for a Cleaner Environment [*Defunct*] (EA)

CCE............ Current Cash [*or Cost*] Equivalent (ADA)

CCE............ Cyanosis, Clubbing, or Edema [*Medicine*] (MAE)

CCE............ Naples, FL [*Location identifier FAA*] (FAAL)

CCEA.......... Cabinet Council on Economic Affairs [*Reagan administration*]

CCEA.......... Canadian Council for European Affairs [*Conseil Canadien des Affaires Europeenes*] (AC)

CCEA.......... Center for Climatic and Environmental Assessment [*National Oceanic and Atmospheric Administration*] (IID)

CCEA.......... Central Canada Exhibition Association

CCE/A......... Certified Cost Estimator/Analyst (AAGC)

CCEA.......... Chief Control Electrical Artificer [*British military*] (DMA)

CCEA.......... Commission de Controle de l'Energie Atomique [*Atomic Energy Control Board - AECB*]

CCEA.......... Commonwealth Council for Educational Administration [*British*] (AIE)

CCEA.......... Conventional Combustion Environmental Assessment [*Environmental Protection Agency*] (GFGA)

CCEAD........ Consultative Committee on Exotic Animal Diseases [*Australia*]

CCEAFS....... Conference of Central and East African States

CCE & HR.... Charing Cross, Euston & Highgate (Underground) Railway [*British*] (ROG)

CCEB.......... Centre for Clinical Epidemiology and Biostasis [*University of Newcastle*] [*Australia*]

CCEB.......... Continuing Legal Education of the Bar, University of California Extension (DLA)

CCEBI......... Centre for Continuing Education in the Building Industry [*Polytechnic of the South Bank*] [*British*] (CB)

CCEBK........ Chronicles Concerning Early Babylonian Kings [*A publication*] (BJA)

CCEBL........ Cold Cathode Electron Beam LASER (MCD)

CCEBS........ Committee for the Collegiate Education of Black Students

CCEC.......... Chairman, Communications-Electronics Committee [*NATO*] (NATG)

CCEC.......... Command and Control Engineering Center [*Washington, DC*]

CCED.......... Center for Community Economic Development

CCED.......... Center for Compatible Economic Development [*Leesburg, VA*]

CCEDMRI.... Consultative Committee for the Standards of Measurement of Ionizing Radiations [*International Bureau of Weights and Measures*]

CCEE.......... Computer Concepts [*NASDAQ symbol*] (TTSB)

CCEE.......... Computer Concepts Corp. [*NASDAQ symbol*] (SAG)

CCEE.......... Consilium Conferentiarum Episcopalium Europae [*Council of European Bishops' Conferences*] (EAIO)

CCEEP........ Committee for Coordination of Emergency Economic Planning [*US/Canada*]

CCEER........ Canadian Coalition for Ecology, Ethics & Religion (AC)

CCEF.......... Communication Countermeasures Evaluation Facility [*Air Force*] (MCD)

CCEF.......... Consumer Credit Education Foundation (EA)

CCEFP........ Center for Community Education Facility Planning [*Inactive*] (EA)

CCEGR........ Coolant-Controlled Exhaust Gas Recirculation [*Automotive engineering*]

CCEI.......... Caisse Commune d'Epargne et d'Investissement [*Finance institutions*] [*Cameroon*] (EY)

CCEI.......... Composite Cost Effectiveness Index (PDAA)

CCEI.......... Coordinating Committee for Ellis Island (EA)

CCEI.......... Crown-Crisp Experimental Index [*Personality development test*] [*Psychology*]

CCEIA........ Carnegie Council on Ethics and International Affairs (EA)

CCEJ.......... Conseil Canadien d'Experimentation des Jouets [*Canadian Toy Testing Council*]

CCEL.......... Chief Control Electrician [*British military*] (DMA)

CCEL.......... Coolidge Center for Environmental Leadership (EA)

CCELC........ Canada Committee on Ecological (Biophysical) Land Classification G2 [*See also CCCET*]

CCELF........ Conference des Communautes Ethniques de Langue Francaise [*Standing Committee of French-Speaking Ethnical Communities - SCFSEC*] (EA)

CCEM.......... Construction, Civil Engineering, Mining [*A publication*]

CCEM.......... Consulting Committee on Educational Matters (AIE)

CCE/MACI.... Commercial Construction Equipment and Military Adaptation of Commercial Items (MCD)

CCEMI......... Conseil Canadien pour l'Education Multiculturelle et Interculturelle (AC)

CCEML........ Canon-Caliber Electromagnetic Launcher

CCEMN .... Chief Control Electrical Mechanician [*British military*] (DMA)

CCEMRI ...... Comite Consultatif pour les Standards des Mesurement Radiations Ionizant [*Consultative Committee for the Standards of Measurement of Ionizing Radiations*] [*International Standards Organization*] [*French*] (BARN)

CCEMWD .... Close Combat, Engineering, and Mine Warfare Directorate [*Army*]

CCEO .... Controller of Communications Equipment Overseas [*British*]

CCEOBHA.... Conference of Chief Executive Officers of Bulk Handling Authorities [*Australia*]

CCEP.......... Cabinet Committee for Economic Policy [*Later, CEP*]

CCEP.......... Child Care Employee Project (EA)

CCEP.......... Commercial COMSEC [*Communications Security*] Endorsement Program [*NASA*]

CCEP.......... Comprehensive Clinical Evaluation Program [*For Gulf War veterans*]

CCEP.......... Comprehensive Clinical Evaluation Program [*Army*]

CCEP.......... Connecticut College of Emergency Physicians (SRA)

CCERD........ Cabinet Committee on Economic and Regional Development [*Canada*]

CCES.......... Canadian Council of Engineering Students

CCES.......... Case Center for Electrochemical Sciences [*Case Western Reserve University*] [*Research center*] (RCD)

CCES.......... Catholic Church Extension Society of the USA (EA)

CCESP........ Center-Clipping Echo Suppressor (MCD)

CCES.......... Center for Corporate Economics and Strategy [*Defunct*] (EA)

CCES.......... Common Control Echo Suppressor [*Telecommunications*] (TEL)

CCES.......... Council for Christian Education in Schools [*Australia*]

CCESC........ Citizens Committee on the El Salvador Crisis (EA)

CCE/SMHE ... Commercial Construction and Selected Materials Handling Equipment (RDA)

CCESO .... Committee on Contributions for Elective State Officials

CCESP........ Committee on Continuing Education for School Personnel (EA)

CCESUSA.... Catholic Church Extension Society of the United States of America (EA)

CCet............ Capitol-Cetra [*Record label*]

CCET.......... Centre for Computers in Education and Training [*University of Salford*] [*British*] (CB)

CCETSW ...... Central Council for Education and Training in Social Work [*British*]

CCETT........ Centre Commun d'Etudes de Television et de Telecommunications [*Videotex research center*] [*France*]

CCEU .... Council on the Continuing Education Unit [*Later, IACET*] (EA)

CCEVS .... Coolant Control Engine Vacuum Switch [*Automotive engineering*]

CCEW .... Center for Continuing Education for Women

CCEW .... Congregational Church in England and Wales (BI)

CCEWG........ Civil Communications-Electronics Working-Group [*Military*] (NATG)

CCEWP........ Combat Clothing and Equipment Working Party [*NATO*]

CCEWT........ Central Control Evaluation and Warning Team (CINC)

CCEX.......... Clad Controlled Expansion

CCF.......... Canadian Communications Foundation

CCF.......... Cancer Cytology Foundation of America [*Later, National Cancer Cytology Center*]

CCF.......... Capital Construction Fund [*FHWA*] (TAG)

CCF.......... Captain, Coastal Forces [*Navy British*]

CCF.......... Carbonaceous Chondrite Fission [*Geophysics*]

CCF.......... Carcassonne [*France*] [*Airport symbol*] (OAG)

CCF.......... Cardiolipin Complement Fixation [*Immunochemistry*] (DAVI)

CCF.......... Carotid Cavernous Fistula [*Medicine*]

CCF.......... Catholic Communications Foundation (NTCM)

CCF.......... CCF Holding Co. [*Associated Press*] (SAG)

CCF.......... Central Clearance Facility [*Military*] (GFGA)

CCF.......... Central Computing Facility [*NASA*]

CCF.......... Central Control Facility [*Military*] (AABC)

CCF.......... Central Control Function [*Aviation*] (DA)

CCF.......... Central Personnel Security Clearance Facility [*Army*] (MCD)

CCF.......... Centre for Conservation Farming [*Charles Sturt University*] [*Australia*]

CCF.......... Cephalin-Cholesterol Flocculation [*Clinical chemistry*]

CCF.......... Chain Command Flag (IAA)

CCF.......... Channel Control Field [*Telecommunications*] (ECII)

CCF.......... Chase Corp. [*AMEX symbol*] (SAG)

CCF.......... Chinese Communist Forces

CCF.......... Christian Century Foundation (EA)

CCF.......... Christian Children's Fund (EA)

CCF.......... Cilla's Circle of Fans (EAIO)

CCF.......... Cinema Center Films

CCF.......... Circular Crystal Facet

CCF.......... Citizens' Council Forum [*Defunct*] (EA)

CCF.......... Civilian Casualty Fund (EA)

CCF.......... COBOL [*Common Business-Oriented Language*] Communications Facility (IAA)

CCF.......... Collection Control File [*Bureau of the Census*] (GFGA)

CCF.......... Collection Coordination Facility (MCD)

CCF.......... Combat Center Function [*Military*] (SAA)

CCF.......... Combined Cadet Force [*British equivalent of US ROTC*]

CCF.......... Committee of Corporate Finance [*of the National Association of Securities Dealers*]

CCF.......... Common Cause Failure [*Nuclear energy*] (NRCH)

CCF.......... Common Claims File [*Health insurance*] (GHCT)

CCF.......... Common Cold Foundation [*Defunct*]

CCF.......... Common Communications Format [*International Standards Organization*] (NITA)

CCF.......... Communication Central Facility [*Air Force*]

CCF.......... Communications Control Facility [*Military*]

CCF.......... Communications Control Field

CCF.......... Commutated Capacitor Filter (PDAA)

CCF.......... Complex Coherence Function (PDAA)

CCF.......... Component Characteristic File (DNAB)

CCF.......... Compound Comminuted Fracture [*Medicine*]

CCF	Compressed Citation File
CCF	Concentrated Complete Fertilizer [*Imperial Chemical Industries*] [*British*]
CCF	Concrete Floor
CCF	Configuration Control Function [*Telecommunications*] (TEL)
CCF	Congestive Cardiac Failure [*Medicine*]
CCF	Conglutinating Complement Fixation (PDAA)
CCF	Congregational Churches Fellowship [*Australia*]
CCF	Congress for Cultural Freedom [*British*]
CCF	Congressional Clearinghouse on the Future (EA)
CCF	Conservative Collegiate Forum (AIE)
CCF	Consultants (Computer & Financial) [*Commercial firm*] [*British*]
CCF	Contract Cases, Federal (AFIT)
CCF	Converter Compressor Facility (KSC)
CCF	Cooperative Commonwealth Federation [*Later, New Democratic Party - NDP*] [*Political party Canada*]
CCF	Co-Operative Commonwealth Federation [*Later, NDP*] [*Canadian*] (PPW)
CCF	Corps Contingency Force [*Army*] (AABC)
CCF	Correctional Custody Facility [*Military*] (AABC)
CCF	Cross-Correlation Function
CCF	Crown Competition Factor (PDAA)
CCF	Crystal-Induced Chemotactic Factor [*Immunology*]
CCF	Curtis Completion Form [*Psychology*]
CCF	Custom Control Factory [*Desaware Co.*]
CCFA	Cancer Cytology Foundation of America [*Later, National Cancer Cytology Center*]
CCFA	Caribbean Cane Farmers' Association [*Kingston, Jamaica*] [*Inactive*] (EAIO)
CCFA	Cefoxitin Cycloserine Fructose Agar [*Medium*] [*Microbiology*] (DAVI)
CCFA	Cefoxitin Cycloserine Fructose Agar Medium [*Medicine*] (BABM)
CCFA	Center for Craniofacial Anomalies [*University of Illinois at Chicago*] [*Research center*] (RCD)
CCFA	Children's Cancer Fund of America [*Defunct*] (EA)
CCFA	Colorado Cattle Feeders Association (SRA)
CCFA	Combined Cadet Force Association [*British military*] (DMA)
CCFA	Common Cause Failure Analysis [*Nuclear energy*] (NRCH)
CCFA	Comptoir Commercial Franco-Africain [*Franco-African Trade Office*] [*Guinea*] (AF)
CCFA	Cost Contract Fee Appendix (SAA)
CCFA	Crohn's and Colitis Foundation of America, Inc. (PAZ)
CCFAC	Canadian Concerned Fathers Action Committee
CCFATU	Coastal Command Fighter Affiliation Training Unit [*British military*] (DMA)
CCFB	Francis Bacon Foundation, Inc., Claremont, CA [*Library symbol Library of Congress*] (LCLS)
CCFC	Circus Clown Friends Club [*British*]
CCFC	Citizens Committee for a Free Cuba
CCFC	Colleen Casey Fan Club [*Defunct*] (EA)
CCFC	Connie Causey Fan Club (EA)
CCFC	Continental Car Ferry Centre [*British*]
CCFC	Syndicat des Controleurs de Circulation Ferroviaire du Canada [*Union of Rail Canada Traffic Controllers - RCTC*]
CCFD	Comite Catholique Contre la Faim et pour le Developpement [*France*]
CCFDPC	Citizens Committee on Future Directions for the Peace Corps [*Defunct*] (EA)
CCFE	Commercial Contractor-Furnished Equipment (AAG)
CCFE	Commercial Customer-Furnished Equipment
CCFE	Communaute des Chemins de Fer Europeens [*Belgium*] (EAIO)
CCFE	Cyclophosphamide, Cisplatin, Fluorouracil, and Extramustine [*Medicine*] (DMAA)
CCFem	Coca Cola Femsa SA de CV [*Commercial firm Associated Press*] (SAG)
CCFemsa	Coca Cola Femsa SA de CV [*Associated Press*] (SAG)
CCFET	Captain, Coastal Forces, Eastern Theater [*Navy*]
CCFF	Canadian Cystic Fibrosis Foundation
CCFF	Cape Canaveral Forecast Facility [*NASA*] (NASA)
CCFF	Compensatory and Contingency Financing Facility [*International Monetary Fund*]
CCFF	Crew Compartment Fit and Function [*NASA*]
CCFF	Critical Color Flicker Frequency (PDAA)
CCFF	Crown Cat Fanciers Federation [*Defunct*] (EA)
CCFFR	Canadian Council for Fisheries Research (ASF)
CCFGANSW	Commercial Cut Flower Growers' Association of New South Wales [*Australia*]
CCFH	CCF Holding [*NASDAQ symbol*] (TTSB)
CCFH	CCF Holding Co. [*NASDAQ symbol*] (SAG)
CCFHA	Corson Family History Association (EA)
CCFHD	Chol Chol Foundation for Human Development (EA)
CCFI	Canadian Centre for Fisheries Innovation [*Centre Canadien d'Innovations des Peches*] [*Formerly, Centre for Fisheries Innovation*] (AC)
CCFIS	Coastal Command Flying Instructors School [*British military*] (DMA)
CCFL	Cold-Cathode Fluorescent Lamp (PCM)
CCFL	Conference on Consumer Finance Law (EA)
CCFL	Counter Current Flow Limit [*Nuclear energy*]
CCFLSA	Citizens Committee on the Fair Labor Standards Act (EA)
CCFLT	Colorado Congress of Foreign Language Teachers (EDAC)
CCFM	Council of Canadian Filmmakers
CCFM	Cryogenic Continuous Film Memory [*Computer science*] (DIT)
CCFMC	Center for the Coordination of Foreign Manuscript Copying [*Library of Congress*]
CCFOE	Central Committee for Forest Ownership in the EEC (EAIO)
CCFP	Certificate of the College of Family Physicians of Canada (DD)

CCFP	Child Care Food Program [*Washington, DC*]
CCFPT	Conseil Canadien des Fabricants des Produits du Tabac [*Canadian Tobacco Manufacturers' Council*]
CCFQ	Conference des Cooperatives Forestieres du Quebec (AC)
CCFR	Commonwealth Committee on Fuel Research [*British*]
CCFR	Constant Current Flux Reset
CCFRU	Comite Canadien sur le Financement de la Recherche dans les Universites [*Canadian Committee on Financing University Research - CCFUR*]
CCFS	Continuous Contractor Field Service
CCFSA	Certified Cold Fur Storage Association (EA)
CCFSF	Chinese Culture Foundation of San Francisco (EA)
CCF-SS	Collection Coordination Facility Support System (MCD)
CCFT	Cold Cathode Fluorescent Technology
CCFT	Cold Cathode Fluorescent Tube
CCFT	Combat Communications Flight
CCFT	Controlled Current Feedback Transformer (MSA)
CCFUR	Canadian Committee on Financing University Research
CCFV	[*Le*] Centre Culturel Francophone de Vancouver [*Vancouver French Cultural Centre*] (AC)
CCFX	ContiCurrency Foreign Exchange and Money Market Database [*No longer available online*]
CCFXe	Carbonaceous Chondrite Fission Xenon [*Geophysics*]
CCG	California Carvers Guild (EA)
CCG	Camp Century [*Greenland*] [*Seismograph station code, US Geological Survey Closed*] (SEIS)
CCG	Canada College Library, Redwood City, CA [*OCLC symbol*] (OCLC)
CCG	Canada-United Kingdom-United States Cryptographic Systems General Publications (MCD)
CCG	Canadian Coast Guard
CCG	Cargo Center of Gravity (MSA)
CCG	Carrigan Industries Ltd. [*Vancouver Stock Exchange symbol*]
CCG	Cartesian Coordinate Grid (NVT)
CCG	Catalytic Coal Gasification [*Fuel technology*]
CCG	Central Clock Generator [*Telecommunications*] (ACRL)
CCG	Central Coast Gruens [*Political party Australia*]
CCG	Chelsea GCA Realty [*NYSE symbol*] (TTSB)
CCG	Childrens Cancer Group
CCG	Cholecystogram [*Radiology*] (DAVI)
CCG	Choral Conductors Guild (EA)
CCG	Combat Cargo Group (CINC)
CCG	Combat Center Group [*Military*] (SAA)
CCG	Combat Communications Group (AFIT)
CCG	Combat Control Group
CCG	Combinatory Categorical Grammar [*Artificial intelligence*]
CCG	Comite de Coordination des Experts Budgetaires Gouvernementaux [*Coordinating Committee of Government Budget Experts*] [*NATO*] (NATG)
CCG	Commandant of the Coast Guard
CCG	Command Control Group [*Air Force*]
CCG	Commission Canadienne des Grains [*Canadian Grain Commission*]
CCG	Commission on College Geography (AEBS)
CCG	Committee for Constitutional Government (EA)
CCG	Commodity Coordination Groups
CCG	Communications Change Group (SAA)
CCG	Computer Communications Group [*Canada*]
CCG	Computer Control Group [*Military*] (CAAL)
CCG	Conforms to Copyright Guidelines
CCG	Congressional Coal Group (EA)
CCG	Constant Current Generator
CCG	Construction Coordination Group [*NASA*] (KSC)
CCG	Consumer Complaint Guide
CCG	Control Commission for Germany [*World War II*]
CCG	Copyright Convergence Group [*Australia*]
CCG	Copyright Copying Guidelines (EDAC)
CCG	Corporation Consulting Group [*British*]
CCG	Crow Executive Air, Inc. [*FAA designator*] (FAAC)
CCGA	California Cactus Growers Association (EA)
CCGA	Canadian Computer Graphics Association (AC)
CCGA	Colorado Corn Growers Association (SRA)
CCGA	Communications Control Group Assembly [*Ground Communications Facility, NASA*]
CCGA	Custom Clothing Guild of America [*Defunct*] (EA)
CCGAA	Canadian Certified General Accountants' Association
CCGB	Confrerie des Chevaliers du Goute Boudin [*Brotherhood of Knights of the Black Pudding Tasters - BKBPT*] (EA)
CCGBI	Camping Council of Great Britain and Ireland, Ltd.
CCGC	Capillary Column Gas Chromatography
CCGCR	Closed-Cycle Gas-Cooled Reactor (DEN)
CCGCS	Containment Combustion Gas Control System [*Nuclear energy*] (IEEE)
CCGD	Canadian Council of Grocery Distributors [*Conseil Canadien de la Distribution Alimentaire*] (AC)
CCGD	Commander, Coast Guard District
CCGE	Cold Cathode Gauge Experiment [*Apollo*] [*NASA*]
CCGE	Copper-Cored Ground Electrode [*Automotive engineering*]
CCGEA	Community College General Education Association (EDAC)
CCGI	Commodity Coordinated Group Item (DNAB)
CCGI	Community College Goals Inventory [*Test*]
CCGM	Commission de la Carte Geologique du Monde [*Commission for the Geological Map of the World - GMW*] (EAIO)
CCGN	Commanding General, Ground Forces [*World War II*]
CCGNJ	Council on Compulsive Gambling of New Jersey (EA)
CCGP	Combat Communications Group [*Air Force*]

CCGS	Canadian Centre for Global Security [*Centre Canadien pour la Securite Mondiale*] [*Formerly, The Arms Control Centre*] (AC)
CCGS	Canadian Coast Guard Service
CCGT	Closed-Cycle Gas Turbine (PDAA)
CCGT	Combined-Cycle Gas Turbines (ECON)
CCH	Calcium Chloride Hexahydrate
CCH	California Association of Children's Homes (SRA)
CCH	California State University, Chico, Chico, CA [*OCLC symbol*] (OCLC)
CCH	Campbell Resources [*NYSE symbol*] (TTSB)
CCH	Campbell Resources, Inc. [*Formerly, Campbell Chibougamau Mines Ltd.*] [*NYSE symbol Toronto Stock Exchange symbol*] (SPSG)
CCh	Carbachol [*Cholinergic*]
CCH	CCH, Inc. [*Associated Press*] (SAG)
CCH	Certificate in Community Health (PGP)
CCH	Channel-Check Handler [*Japan*] (MCD)
CCH	Chief of Chaplains [*Formerly, CC, C of CH, COFCH*] [*Army*] (AABC)
CCH	Chilchota Taxi Aereo SA de CV [*Mexico ICAO designator*] (FAAC)
CCH	Chile Chico [*Chile*] [*Airport symbol*] (AD)
CCH	Citizenship Clearing House
CCH	Close Combat, Heavy
CCH	Cochabamba [*Bolivia*] [*Seismograph station code, US Geological Survey*] (SEIS)
CCH	Colchicine [*Biochemistry*]
CCH	Command Control Handover and Keying (SAA)
CCH	Commerce Clearing House (DFIT)
CCH	Commerce Clearing House, Inc. [*Publisher*] [*Chicago, IL*]
CCH	Committee on Cosmic Humanism (EA)
CCH	Computerized Criminal History [*FBI*]
CCH	Connections per Circuit per Hour [*Telecommunications*] (TEL)
CCH	Consumer Coalition for Health [*Inactive*] (EA)
CCH	Cost Comparison Handbook [*A publication*] (MCD)
CCH	Country Club Hotels [*British*] (ADA)
CCH	Creativity Checklist [*Educational test*]
CCH	Cross-Correlation Histogram [*Statistics*]
CCH	Cube Corner Holder
CCH	Cubic Capacity of Holds [*British*] (ADA)
CCH	Currency Clearinghouse
CCH	Cyclohexylidenecyclohexane [*Organic chemistry*]
CCH	Logan, UT [*Location identifier FAA*] (FAAL)
CCHA	California Children's Hospital Association (SRA)
CCHA	Canadian Catholic Historical Association [*See also SCHEC*]
CCHA	Canadian Corps Heavy Artillery [*World War I*]
CCHA	Canadian Council on Hospital Accreditation (HCT)
CCHA	Canadian Craft & Hobby Association (AC)
CCHA	Central Collegiate Hockey Association (EA)
CCHA	Community College Humanities Association (EA)
CCHAL	Commission on Chicago Historical and Architectural Landmarks
CCHAPG	Conference of Chaplains-General [*Australia*]
CCH Atom En L Rep...	Atomic Energy Law Reporter (Commerce Clearing House) [*A publication*] (DLA)
CCHBPPC.....	Canadian Coalition for High Blood Pressure Prevention & Control [*Coalition Canadienne pour la Prevention et le Controle de l'Hypertension Arterielle*] (AC)
CCHC	Connecticut Catholic Hospital Council (SRA)
C CH COLL...	Christ Church College [*Oxford University*] (ROG)
CCH Comm Mkt Rep...	Common Market Reporter (Commerce Clearing House) [*A publication*] (DLA)
CCHCOPALLANC...	Commissioner, Chancery Court, County Palatine of Lancaster [*British*] (ROG)
CCHD	Committee to Combat Huntington's Disease [*Later, HDFA*] (EA)
CCHD	Cyanotic Congenital Heart Disease (DAVI)
CCHE	Carnegie Commission on Higher Education
CCHE	Central Council for Health Education [*British*] (AEBS)
CChE	Certified Chemical Engineer
CCHE	Coordinating Council for Higher Education
CChem	Chartered Chemist [*British*]
CCHENV-LNC...	Consortium for Continuing Higher Education - Librarians' Networking Committee [*Library network*]
CCHEP	Cement-Coated Heavy Epoxy
CCHF	Children's Country Holiday Fund [*British*]
CCHF	Crimean-Congo Hemorrhagic Fever [*Medicine*]
CCHFA	Canadian Council on Health Facilities Accreditation
CCH Fed Banking L Rep...	Federal Banking Law Reports (Commerce Clearing House) [*A publication*] (DLA)
CCH Fed Sec L Rep...	Federal Securities Law Reporter (Commerce Clearing House) [*A publication*] (DLA)
CCHHS........	Center for Canadian Historical Horticultural Studies [*Hamilton, ON*]
CCHI	CCH, Inc. [*NASDAQ symbol*] (SAG)
CChi.............	Chico Public Library, Chico, CA [*Library symbol Library of Congress*] (LCLS)
CChiBP	Bidwell Mansion State Historic Park, Chico, CA [*Library symbol*] [*Library of Congress*] (LCLS)
CChiGS	Church of Jesus Christ of Latter-Day Saints, Genealogical Society Library, ChicoBranch, Stake Center, Chico, CA [*Library symbol Library of Congress*] (LCLS)
CChiS...........	California State University, Chico, Chico, CA [*Library symbol Library of Congress*] (LCLS)
CCHK	Continuity Check
CCHL	China Container Holdings
CCH Lab Arb Awards...	Labor Arbitration Awards (Commerce Clearing House) [*A publication*] (DLA)
CCH Lab Cas...	Labor Cases (Commerce Clearing House) [*A publication*] (DLA)
CCH Lab L Rep...	Labor Law Reporter (Commerce Clearing House) [*A publication*] (DLA)
CCH LLR.....	Labor Law Reporter (Commerce Clearing House) [*A publication*] (DLA)
CCHMS	Central Committee for Hospital Medical Services [*British*] (DAVI)
CCHN	Colorado Community Health Network (SRA)
CCHP	CCH [*Commerce Clearing House*] Publications Index (ADA)
CCHP	Consumer Choice Health Plan
CC-HPLC.....	Column Chromatography - High-Performance [*or Pressure*] Liquid Chromatography [*Analytical chemistry*]
CChR	Calendar of Charter Rolls [*British*]
CCHR	Chile Committee for Human Rights [*Institute for Policy Studies*] (EA)
CChr............	Corpus Christianorum [*Turnhout*] (BJA)
CCHRA	Church Committee for Human Rights in Asia (EA)
CCHREI	Canadian Council for Human Resources in the Environment Industry [*Le Conseil Canadien des Ressources Humaines de l'Industrie de L'Environnement*] (AC)
CCHRLA	Christian Committee for Human Rights in Latin America [*Canada*] (EAIO)
CCHRP	Church Coalition for Human Rights in the Philippines (EA)
CCHS	Christian Community High School [*Australia*]
CCHS	Coalition for Consumer Health and Safety (EA)
CCHS	Community and Child Health Service [*Australia*]
CCHS	Conference of California Historical Societies
CCHS	Congenital Central Hypoventilation Syndrome [*Medicine*]
CCHS	Congregational Christian Historical Society (EA)
CCHS	Cylinder-Cylinder-Head-Sector [*Computer science*] (IBMDP)
CCHSE	Canadian College of Health Service Executives [*College Canadien des Directeurs de Services de Sante*] (AC)
CCHST	Centre Canadien d'Hygiene et de Securite au Travail [*Canadian Centre for Occupational Health and Safety - CCOHS*]
CCH Stand Fed Tax Rep...	Standard Federal Tax Reporter (Commerce Clearing House) [*A publication*] (DLA)
CCH State Tax Cas Rep...	State Tax Cases Reports (Commerce Clearing House) [*A publication*] (DLA)
CCH State Tax Rev...	State Tax Review (Commerce Clearing House) [*A publication*] (DLA)
CCH Tax Ct Mem...	Tax Court Memorandum Decisions (Commerce Clearing House) [*A publication*] (DLA)
CCH Tax Ct Rep...	Tax Court Reporter (Commerce Clearing House) [*A publication*] (DLA)
CCHTS	Center for Carburization Heat Treatment Studies [*Worchester Polytechnic Institute*] [*Research center*]
CChu............	Chula Vista Public Library, Chula Vista, CA [*Library symbol Library of Congress*] (LCLS)
CCHW	Citizen's Clearinghouse for Hazardous Wastes (EA)
CCHX	Component Cooling Heat Exchanger (IEEE)
CCI	Cache d'Or Resources [*Vancouver Stock Exchange symbol*]
CCI	Calcium Chloride Institute [*Defunct*] (EA)
CCI	Calculated Cetane Index [*Fuel technology*]
CCI	Campaign Communications Institute [*Telemarketing*] (WDMC)
CCI	Canadian Carpet Institute (EAIO)
CCI	Canadian Circumpolar Institute [*University of Alberta*] (IRC)
CCI	Canadian Condominium Institute-National Chapter (AC)
CCI	Canadian Conservation Institute [*See also ICC*] [*National Museums of Canada*] [*Research center*] (RCD)
CCI	Canadian Copyright Institute
CCI	Canadian Credit Institute
CCI	Canadian Crossroads International
CCI	Canadian Culinary Institute (AC)
CCI	Cancer Care, Inc. (EA)
CCI	Canine Companions for Independence (EA)
CCI	Card Computer Interface [*Computer science*] (IID)
CCI	Cardiovascular Credentialing International (EA)
CCI	Carrefour Canadien International [*Canadian Crossroads International*] (EAIO)
CCI	Carrier-Controlled Intercept (DNAB)
CCI	Center for Compliance Information (EA)
CCI	Center for Creative Imaging [*Camden, Maine*] [*Computer art training*]
CCI	Central Control Indicator (MCD)
CCI	Centre de Creation Industrielle [*Center for Industrial Creation*] [*Information service or system*] (IID)
CCI	Centre du Commerce International [*International Trade Center - ITC*] [*Geneva, Switzerland*] [*French*] (EAIO)
CCI	Centro de Comercio Internacional [*International Trade Center - ITC*] [*Spanish*]
CCI	Certified Consultants International [*Defunct*] (EA)
CCI	Chambers of Commerce and Industry [*ASEAN*] (DS)
CCI	Chambers of Commerce of Ireland (EAIO)
CCI	Chambre de Commerce Internationale [*The International Chamber of Commerce - ICC*] [*Paris, France*] (EAIO)
CCI	Charge-Coupled Imager
CCI	Charleston, SC [*Location identifier FAA*] (FAAL)
CCI	Chess Collectors International (EA)
CCI	Christian Camping International [*Later, CCI/USA*] (EA)
CCI	Christian Communications, Inc. (EA)
CCI	Christians Concerned for Israel [*Superseded by NCLCI*] (EA)
CCI	Chronic Coronary Insufficiency [*Medicine*]
CCI	Circuit Condition Indicator
CCI	Citicorp [*NYSE symbol*] (SPSG)
CCI	Citrus College, Azusa, CA [*OCLC symbol*] (OCLC)
CCI	Clean Car Initiative
CCI	Climate Control International [*Auto industry supplier*]
CCI	Co-Channel Interface [*Telecommunications*] (NITA)
CCI	Co-Channel Interference (NTCM)
CCI	College Characteristics Index [*A questionnaire*]
CCI	Command Control Interface [*Army*] (AABC)

CCI.............. Commission for Climatology [*Marine science*] (OSRA)
CCI.............. Committee for Chilean Inquiry (EA)
CCI.............. Common Carrier Interface (MCD)
CCI.............. Communications Carrier, Inc. [*Austin, TX*] [*Telecommunications*] (TSSD)
CCI.............. Communications Concepts, Inc. [*Newport Beach, CA*] [*Telecommunications*] (TSSD)
CCI.............. Communications Consultants, Inc. [*Washington, NJ*] [*Telecommunications*] (TSSD)
CCI.............. Communications Control Interface (MCD)
CCI.............. Community Creativity, Inc. [*Defunct*] (EA)
CCI.............. Compactor Co., Inc.
CCI.............. Component Control Index [*Navy*] (AFIT)
CCI.............. Component Cost Index
CCI.............. Computer Communications, Inc.
CCI.............. Computer Communications Interface (IAA)
CCI.............. Computer Composition International [*Telecommunications*] (NITA)
CCI.............. Computer Control Indicator (CAAL)
CCI.............. Computer Controlled Inking [*Graphic arts*] (DGA)
CCI.............. Comshare Communications Interface (IAA)
CCI.............. Concordia [*Brazil*] [*Airport symbol Obsolete*] (OAG)
CCI.............. Concordia Collegiate Institute [*New York*]
CCI.............. Conseil Canadien des Ingenieurs [*Canadian Council of Engineers*]
CCI.............. Consortium Communications International, Inc. [*New York, NY*] [*Telecommunications*] (TSSD)
CCI.............. Construction Cost Index
CCI.............. Consumer Confidence Index [*Conference Board*]
CCI.............. Consumer Credit Insurance
CCI.............. Contract Change Identification (MCD)
CCI.............. Control Current Impedance
CCI.............. Controlled COMSEC [*Communications Security*] Items
CCI.............. Convert Clock Input [*Computer science*] (IAA)
CCI.............. Corrected Count Increment [*Hematology*]
CCI.............. Corrugated Container Institute [*Defunct*] (EA)
CCI.............. Corrugated, Cupped, or Indented [*Freight*]
CCI.............. Cost Category Input (SAA)
CCI.............. Cost Control Item (MCD)
CCI.............. Cotton Council International (EA)
CCI.............. Council for Cable Information [*Defunct*] (EA)
CCI.............. Council for Continuous Improvement
CCI.............. Council on Consumer Information [*Later, ACCI*] (EA)
CCI.............. Cour Canadienne de l'Impot [*Tax Review Board - TRB*]
CCI.............. Course Content Improvement
Ccl .... Cowles Communications, Inc., New York, NY [*Library symbol Library of Congress*] (LCLS)
CCI.............. Credit de la Cote-D'Ivoire [*Credit Bank of the Ivory Coast*]
CCI.............. Cross Cancer Institute [*Alberta Cancer Board*] [*Canada*] (IRC)
CCI.............. Current-Controlled Inductor [*Electronics*] (IAA)
CCIA.......... California Crop Improvement Association (SRA)
CCIA.......... Canadian Career Information Association (AC)
CCIA.......... Cellular Communications Industry Association [*Telecommunications*] (EA)
CCIA.......... Commission of the Churches on International Affairs [*Switzerland*] (EAIO)
CCIA.......... Computer and Communications Industry Association (EA)
CCIA.......... Connecticut Construction Industries Association (SRA)
CCIA.......... Console Computer Interface Adapter
CCIA.......... Consumer Credit Insurance Association [*Chicago, IL*] (EA)
CCIAESC ...... Coffee Commission of the Inter-American Economic and Social Council [*United States*]
CCIAH........ Clearinghouse Committee for Information on the Arts and Humanities
CCIANSW..... Caravan and Camping Industry Association of New South Wales [*Australia*]
CCIASA .... Caravan and Camping Industry Association of South Australia [*Australia*]
CCIA/WCC .... Commission of the Churches on International Affairs (of the World Council of Churches) (EA)
CCIB.......... Canadian Council for International Business [*Conseil Canadien pour le Commerce International*] [*Also, Canadian Secretariat ICC/BIAC*] (AC)
CCIBP .... Canadian Committee for the International Biological Programme
CCIC.......... Camden Council for International Cooperation [*British*]
CCIC.......... Campus Chemical Instrument Center [*Ohio State University*] [*Research center*] (RCD)
CCIC.......... Canadian Council for International Cooperation
CCIC.......... Centre Catholique International pour l'UNESCO [*France*]
CCIC.......... Club of Channel Islands Collectors (EA)
CCIC.......... Comite Catholique International de Coordination Aupres de l'UNESCO
CCIC.......... Comite Consultatif International du Coton [*International Cotton Advisory Committee*]
CCIC.......... Concerned Citizens Information Council [*Group opposing sex education in schools*]
CCIC.......... Conference of Casualty Insurance Companies [*Indianapolis, IN*] (EA)
CCIC.......... Constant Cost Integer Code [*Computer science*] (IAA)
CCICA.......... Catholic Commission on Intellectual and Cultural Affairs (EA)
CCICCC .... Canadian Chapter of the International Council of Community Churches [*Section Canadienne du Conseil International des Eglises Communautaires*] (AC)
CCID .... Community Colleges for International Development (EA)
CCID .... Confidential Chemicals Identification System (GNE)
CCID .... Control Channel Information Demodulator
CCID .... Countermine/Counterintrusion Department [*Army*] (RDA)
CCID .... Crew Command Input Device

CCIDA .... Canadian Centre for Information and Documentation on Archives [*National Archives of Canada*]
CCIDC .... California Council for Interior Design Certification (SRA)
CCIDES .... Command Control Interactive Display Experimentation System [*Army*] (MCD)
CCIE............ Cisco Certified Internetwork Expert (CDE)
CCIE............ Countercurrent Immunoelectrophoresis (PDAA)
CCIEM.......... Center for Computer Integrated Engineering and Manufacturing [*University of Tennessee at Knoxville*] [*Research center*] (RCD)
CCIF............ Comite Consultatif International Telephonique des Frequences [*International Telephone Consultative Committee*] (NATG)
CCIF............ Cost Category Input Form (SAA)
CCIFP.......... Chambre de Compensation des Instruments Financiers de Paris
CCIG .... Cold Cathode Ion Gauge
CCII............ Canadian Council on International Law [*Conseil Canadien de Droit International*] (AC)
CCII............ Crosscurrents International Institute (EAIO)
CCIL............ Canadian Council of Independent Laboratories [*Conseil Canadien des Laboratoires Independents*] (AC)
CCIL............ Cellular Communications International, Inc. [*NASDAQ symbol*] (SAG)
CCIL............ Cellular Commun Intl [*NASDAQ symbol*] (TTSB)
CCIL............ Commander's Critical Item List [*Army*] (AABC)
CCILMB.......... Interim Committee for Coordination of Investigations of the Lower Mekong Basi n [*of the United Nations Economic and Social Commission for Asia and the Pacific*] [*Thailand*] (EAIO)
CCIM.......... Certified Commercial Investment Member [*Realtors Natio nal Marketing Institute of the National Association of Realtors*] [*Designation awarded by*]
CCIM.......... Command Computer Input Multiplexer (MCD)
CCINC.......... Cabinet Committee on International Narcotics Control [*Terminated, 1977*]
CCINW .... Carpet Cleaners Institute of the Northwest (SRA)
CCIO .... Canadian Committee for Industrial Organization
CCIP.......... Canadian Cataloguing in Publication
CCIP.......... Chambre de Commerce et d'Industrie de Paris [*Paris Chamber of Commerce and Industry*] [*France*] [*Information service or system*] (IID)
CCIP.......... Command and Control Information Processing [*Computer science*] (MHDI)
CCIP.......... Commission du Commerce International des Produits de Base [*United Nations*]
CCIP.......... Continuously Computed Impact Point [*Type of bombing sighting system*] [*Air Force*]
CCIPP.......... Chinese Canadian Information Processing Professionals (EAIO)
CCIPr.......... Citicorp Adj Rt 2nd Pfd [*NYSE symbol*] (TTSB)
CCIPrA.......... Citicorp Adj Rt 3rd Pfd [*NYSE symbol*] (TTSB)
CCIPrD.......... Citicorp 9.08% Dep Pfd [*NYSE symbol*] (TTSB)
CCIPrE.......... Citicorp 8.00% Dep Pfd [*NYSE symbol*] (TTSB)
CCIPrF.......... Citicorp 7.50% Dep Pfd [*NYSE symbol*] (TTSB)
CCIPrG.......... Citicorp Adj Rt Dep Pfd [*NYSE symbol*] (TTSB)
CCIPrH.......... Citicorp Adj Rt Dep'H'Pfd [*NYSE symbol*] (TTSB)
CCIPrI.......... Citicorp 8.30% Dep Pfd [*NYSE symbol*] (TTSB)
CCIPrJ.......... Citicorp 8.50% Dep Pfd [*NYSE symbol*] (TTSB)
CCIPrK.......... Citicorp 7.75% Dep Sr 22 Pfd [*NYSE symbol*] (TTSB)
CCIR.......... Citizens' Committee for Immigration Reform [*Defunct*] (EA)
CCIR .... Comite Consultatif International des Radiocommunications [*International Radio Consultative Committee*] [*of the International Telecommunications Union*] [*Switzerland*]
CCIR .... Commander's Critical Information Requirement [*Army*] (INF)
CCIR .... Committed Change Incorporation Record (KSC)
CCIR .... Communications Change Initiation Request (IAA)
CCIR .... Computer-Controlled Information Readout
CCIR .... Consultative Committee on International Radio [*Australia*]
CCIR .... Continental Circuits Corp. [*NASDAQ symbol*] (SAG)
CCIR .... Contl Circuits [*NASDAQ symbol*] (TTSB)
CCIR .... International Radio Consultative Committee
CCIRD.......... Computers and Computing Information Resources Directory [*A publication*]
CCIRID.......... Charge-Coupled Infrared Information Device (PDAA)
CCIRRS.......... Container and Chassis Identification Reporting and Recording System [*DoD*] (PDAA)
CCIRS .... Container and Chassis Identification and Reporting System [*Military*] (MCD)
CCIS............ Center for Computer and Information Services [*Rutgers University, The State University of New Jersey*] [*Information service or system*] (IID)
CCIS............ Coaxial Cable Information System (NTCM)
CCIS............ Cold Cathode Ion Source
CCIS............ Command and Control Information System [*Hughes Aircraft Co.*]
CCIS............ Common-Channel Interface Signaling (IDOE)
CCIS............ Common Channel Interoffice Signaling [*Telecommunications*]
CCIS............ Common Control Interoffice Signaling
CCIS............ Communications and Information Systems Committee [*NATO*] (EAIO)
CCIS............ Computer-Controlled Interconnect System (MCD)
CCIS............ Computerized Clinical Information System [*Micromedex, Inc.*] [*Database*]
CCISA.......... Chamber of Commerce and Industry of South Australia
CCISS.......... Command, Control, Intelligence Support Squadron [*Air Force*]
CCIT............ California Council for International Trade (SRA)
CCIT............ Consultative Committee on International Telephony [*Later, CCITT*] [*ITU*]
CCITT.......... Comite Consultatif International Telegraphique et Telephonique [*Consultative Committee on International Telegraphy and Telephony*] [*of the International Telecommunications Union*] [*Switzerland*]

CCITT............	Consultative Committee International Telephony and Telegraphy
CCITU.........	Coordinating Committee of Independent Trade Unions
CCIU............	Command Channel Interface Unit (MHDI)
CCIU............	Command Control Information Utility [Military]
CCIU............	Component Control Issue Unit (DNAB)
CCIU............	Computer to Communications Interface Unit
CCI/USA......	Christian Camping International/USA (EA)
C Civ Ann	Code Civil Annote, Dalloz [A publication] (ILCA)
CCIVS..........	Coordinating Committee for International Voluntary Service [France] (EAIO)
CCIW..........	Canada Centre for Inland Waters
CCIWA.........	Chamber of Commerce and Industry of Western Australia
CCIX............	Climate Change Information Exchange
CCIX............	Communications Central [NASDAQ symbol] (SAG)
CCIX............	Communic Central [NASDAQ symbol] (TTSB)
CCIX............	Continuous Countercurrent Ion-Exchange [Chemistry]
CCIZT..........	Committee of Control of the International Zone of Tangier
CCJ.............	Cameco Corp. [NYSE symbol] (SAG)
CCJ.............	Cameco Corp. [NYSE symbol] (TTSB)
CCJ.............	Center for Community Justice (EA)
CCJ.............	Coalition for Consumer Justice [Defunct] (EA)
CCJ.............	Comite Europeen de Cooperation Juridique [French]
CCJ.............	Concert Resources, Inc. [Vancouver Stock Exchange symbol]
CCJ.............	Conference of Chief Justices (EA)
CCJ.............	Congregation of Charity of the Most Sacred Heart of Jesus [Roman Catholic religious order]
CCJ.............	Costochondral Junction [Medicine] (DAVI)
CCJ.............	County Court Judge (DLA)
CCJ.............	Springfield, OH [Location identifier FAA] (FAAL)
CCJA............	Canadian Criminal Justice Association [Association Canadienne de Justice Penale] (AC)
CCJA............	Certificate in Criminal Justice Administration (PGP)
CCJA............	Community College Journalism Association (EA)
CCJC............	Chicago City Junior College [Illinois]
CCJC............	Church Council on Justice & Corrections [Conseil des Eglises pour la Justice et la Criminologie] (AC)
CCJC............	Custer County Junior College [Montana]
CCJO............	Consultative Council of Jewish Organizations (EA)
CCJPP........	Cameco Corp. 1st Installment [NYSE symbol] (TTSB)
CCJR............	Citizens for Civil Justice Reform
CCJS............	Coalition for Constitutional Justice and Security (EA)
CCJW..........	Chuck Jaws [Tools]
CCK.............	Campbell's Creek R. R. [AAR code]
CCK.............	Central College of Kentucky
CCK.............	Channel Control Check [Electronics] (OA)
CCK.............	Chiang Ching-kuo [Son of Nationalist Chinese leader Chiang Kai-shek]
CCK.............	Chief Cook [Navy rating Obsolete]
CCK.............	Ching Chuan Kang Air Base [Vietnam]
CCK.............	Cholecystokinin [Also, PZ] [Endocrinology]
CCK.............	Clackamas Community College Library, Oregon City, OR [OCLC symbol] (OCLC)
CCK.............	Cocos Island [Keeling Islands, Australia] [Airport symbol] (AD)
CCK.............	Cocos [Keeling] Islands [Seismograph station code, US Geological Survey Closed] (SEIS)
CCK.............	Cocos [Keeling] Islands [ANSI three-letter standard code] (CNC)
CCK.............	Coherent Carrier Keying [Computer science] (IAA)
CCK.............	Crown Cork & Seal [NYSE symbol] (TTSB)
CCK.............	Crown Cork & Seal Co., Inc. [NYSE symbol] (SPSG)
CCK.............	Flight Trac, Inc. [FAA designator] (FAAC)
CCK(B).........	Chief Cook (Baker) [Navy rating Obsolete]
CCK-B.........	Cholecystokinin-Brain Type Receptor
CCK(C)........	Chief Cook (Commissary) [Navy rating Obsolete]
CCK-GB.......	Cholecystokinin-Gallbladder [Medicine] (MEDA)
CCK-OP.......	Cholecystokinin Octapeptide [Biochemistry] (DAVI)
CCKPr.........	Crown Cork&Seal 4.50% Cv Pfd [NYSE symbol] (TTSB)
CCKPT........	Cockpit
CCK-PZ........	Cholecystokinin-Pancreozymin [Endocrinology]
CCKRP.......	Cholecystokinin-Releasing Peptide [Biochemistry]
CCKW	Counterclockwise (WGA)
CCL.............	Cambridge Consultants Ltd.[Arthur D. Little Ltd.] [Research center British] (IRUK)
CCL.............	Canadian Congress of Labour
CCL.............	Cancer Checking Lipid [Oncology]
CCL.............	Candida Cylindracea [A yeast]
CCL.............	Capacitor Coupled Logic [Electronics] (NITA)
CCL.............	Carbonate Compensation Level [Oceanography]
CCL.............	Carcinoma Cell Line [Cytology]
CCL.............	Caribbean Congress of Labor
CCL.............	Carnival Corp. [NYSE symbol] (SAG)
CCL.............	Carnival Corp'A' [NYSE symbol] (TTSB)
CCL.............	Carolina, Clinchfield & Ohio [Railway] (MHDB)
CCL.............	Carrier Common Line [Telecommunications] (IT)
CCL.............	Catalytic Coal Liquefaction
CCL.............	Celanese Canada [TS Symbol] (TTSB)
CCL.............	Celanese Canada, Inc. [Toronto Stock Exchange symbol]
CCL.............	Centenary College of Louisiana [Shreveport]
CCL.............	Center for Computer/Law (EA)
CCL.............	Center for Creative Leadership (EA)
CCL.............	Certified Cell Line [ATCC]
CCL.............	Chemical and Coating Laboratory [Army] (MCD)
CCL.............	Chinchilla [Australia Airport symbol]
CCL.............	Clinical Chemistry Lookout [Medical Information Centre] [Defunct Information service or system] (CRD)

CCL.............	Clocked CMOS [Complementary Metal-Oxide Semiconductor] Logic [Electronics] (IAA)
CCL.............	Closed Circuit Loop (MCD)
CCI.............	Cloverdale Public Library, Cloverdale, CA [Library symbol Library of Congress] (LCLS)
CCL.............	Coal Contractors Ltd. [British]
CCL.............	Coating and Chemical Laboratory [Aberdeen Proving Ground, MD] [Army]
CCL.............	Color Center LASER (PDAA)
CCL.............	Combat Command L
CCL.............	Combat Configured Load [Military] (INF)
CCL.............	Commerce Control List (AAGC)
CCL.............	Commission Canadienne du Lait [Canadian Dairy Commission - CDC]
CCL.............	Commissioner of Crown Lands [British]
CCI.............	Commission for Climatology [WMO]
CCL.............	Commodity Control List [Office of Export Administration]
CCL.............	Commonality Candidate List [NASA] (NASA)
CCL.............	Common Carrier Line (HGAA)
CCL.............	Common Command Language [Computer science] (IT)
CCL.............	Common Control Language [Computer science] (NITA)
CCL.............	Commonwealth Countries' League [Middlesex, England] (EAIO)
CCL.............	Communications Change Log (IT)
CCL.............	Communications Circular Letter [Navy]
CCL.............	Communications Control Language
CCL.............	Communications Control Link (DNAB)
CCL.............	Compartment Checkoff List (DNAB)
CCL.............	Composite Cell Logic
CCL.............	Computer Control Loading
CCL.............	Concise Command Language [Computer science] (MHDI)
CCL.............	Conference for Catholic Lesbians (EA)
CCL.............	Conference on Christianity and Literature (EA)
CCL.............	Configuration Control Logic (NASA)
CCL.............	Conforms to Copyright Law
CCL.............	Connection Control Language [Computer science]
CCL.............	Conseil de la Culture des Laurentides (AC)
CCL.............	Consultec Canada Ltd. [Vancouver, BC] [Telecommunications] (TSSD)
CCL.............	Consumer Credit Letter [Business Publishers, Inc.] [Information service or system] (CRD)
CCL.............	Contact Clock (IAA)
CCL.............	Continental Aviation Ltd. [Ghana] [ICAO designator] (FAAC)
CCL.............	Control Card Listing [Computer science]
CCL.............	Convective Condensation Level [Meteorology]
CCL.............	Conversion and Check Limit (IAA)
CCL.............	Cooperative College Library Center, Atlanta, GA [OCLC symbol] (OCLC)
CCL.............	Core Current Layer (OA)
C/CL............	Counterclaim [Legal shorthand] (LWAP)
CCL.............	Couple to Couple League (EA)
C CI.............	Court of Claims Reports [United States] [A publication] (DLA)
CCL.............	Critical Carbohydrate Level [Nutrition]
CCL.............	Critical Commodities List [Department of Commerce]
CCL.............	Critical Components List
cc/l.............	Cubic Centimeter per Liter [Measurement] (DAVI)
CCL.............	Customs Clearance (DS)
CCL₄	CCl_4 Carbon Tetrachloride (GNE)
CCLA............	Canadian Civil Liberties Association
CCLA............	Canadian Comparative Literature Association [See also ACLC]
CCLA............	Committee on Cooperation in Latin America [of The National Council of Churches of Christ in the USA] (EA)
CCLA............	Coos County Library Association [Library network]
CCLA............	Corporate Council for the Liberal Arts [Defunct] (EA)
CCLA............	Correspondence Chess League of America (EA)
CCLAT........	Centre Canadien de Lutte Contre l'Alcoolisme et les Toxicomanies (AC)
C-CLAW......	Close Combat LASER Assault Weapon
CCLC...........	Carrier Common Line Charge [Computer science] (TNIG)
CCLC...........	Child Care Law Center (EA)
CCLC...........	Community College League of California (SRA)
CCLC...........	Cooperative College Library Center [Atlanta, GA] [Library network]
CCLCS	Centre for Comparative Literature and Cultural Studies [Monash University] [Australia]
CCLD	Chronic Cholestatic Liver Disease [Medicine]
CCLDS	Clear of Clouds [Aviation] (FAAC)
CCLE...........	Chronic Cutaneous (Discoid) Lupus Erythematosus [Medicine]
CCLED	Constant Current Light Emitting Diode (DICI)
CCLEPE......	Consultative Committee for Local Ecumenical Projects in England [Church of England]
CCLGF	Consultative Council on Local Government Finance [British]
CCLH	Committee on Canadian Labour History
CCLI...........	Composite Clinical and Laboratory Index [Medicine] (DMAA)
CCLJ...........	Central Committee of Lithuanian Jurists (EA)
CCLJ...........	Centre County Legal Journal [Pennsylvania] [A publication] (DLA)
CCLKOB......	Counterclockwise Orbit [Aviation] (FAAC)
CCLKWS	Counterclockwise (FAAC)
CCLM..........	Committee on Constitutional and Legal Matters [UN Food and Agriculture Organization]
CCLM..........	Computer Communications Line Monitor (MCD)
CCLM..........	Coordinating Council of Literary Magazines [Later, CLMP] (EA)
CCL(ML).......	Canadian Communist League (Marxist-Leninist)
CCLN	Consignment Note Control Label Number (DS)
CCLN	Council for Computerized Library Networks (IID)
CCLO	Classification and Classified List of Occupations
CCLOW	Canadian Congress for Learning Opportunities for Women

CCLP............ Common Carier Line Pool (HGAA)
CCLP............ National Coalition of Concerned Legal Professionals (EA)
CCLR............ Collaborative Clinical Research, Inc. [NASDAQ symbol] (SAG)
CCLS............ Canadian Canon Law Society (AC)
CCLS............ Canadian Centre for Learning Systems [Research center] (RCD)
CCLS............ Canadian Council of Land Surveyors [See also CCAG]
CCLS............ Canadian Council of Library Schools [Conseil Canadien des Ecoles de Bibliotheconomie] (AC)
CCLS............ Central Colorado Regional Library Service System [Library network]
CCLS............ Chautauqua-Cattaraugus Library System [Library network]
CCLS............ Computer-Controlled Launch Set [NASA] (KSC)
CCLS............ Conference on Critical Legal Studies (EA)
CCLS............ Court of Claims
CCLSR......... Court of Claims Reports
CCLT............ Canfield Centre for Logistics and Transportation
CCLU............ Canadian Civil Liberties Union
CCLV............ Council of Citizens with Low Vision (EA)
CCLV............ Crimson Clover Latent Virus [Plant pathology]
CCLWA........ Council for Civil Liberties in Western Australia
CCLWC........ Committee on Christian Literature for Women and Children (EA)
CCLWCMF ... Committee on Christian Literature for Women and Children in Mission Fields [Later, CCLWC] (EA)
CCM............ Augusta, ME [Location identifier FAA] (FAAL)
CCM............ California Citrus Mutual (SRA)
CCM............ California Conference of Machinists (SRA)
CCM............ Call Count Meter [Telecommunications] (NITA)
CCM............ Canadian Committee on MARC
CCM............ Canadian Corporate Management Co. Ltd. [Toronto Stock Exchange symbol]
CCM............ Canarc Resources [Vancouver Stock Exchange symbol]
CCM............ Cancel/Clarify Message (SSD)
CCM............ Capel-Cure Myers [Stockbrokers] [British]
CCM............ Carlton Communications [NYSE symbol] (SPSG)
CCM............ Celtic Club Melbourne [Australia]
CCM............ Center for Communications Media [University of Massachusetts-Boston] [Telecommunications service] (TSSD)
CCM............ Center for Communications Ministry [Formerly, NSCS] [Defunct] (EA)
CCM............ Center for Composite Materials [University of Delaware] [Research center] (RCD)
CCM............ Central Configuation Management
CCM............ Central Cultural Movement [China]
CCM............ Centre de Controle Mixte [Joint Control Center] [NATO] (NATG)
CCM............ Cerebrocostomandibular Syndrome [Medicine] (DMAA)
CCM............ Certified Cash Manager [National Corporate Cash Management Association] [Designation awarded by]
CCM............ Certified Club Manager [Club Managers Association of America] [Designation awarded by]
CCM............ Certified Configuration Manager
CCM............ Chain Crossing Model [Semiconductor technology] (OA)
CCM............ Chama Cha Mapinduzi [Revolutionary Party] [Tanzania] [Political party] (PPW)
CCM............ Charge-Coupled Memory [Computer science] (IAA)
CCM............ Chief Carpenter's Mate [Navy rating Obsolete]
CCM............ Chief of Budget and Finance Division [Supreme Headquarters Allied Powers Europe] (NATG)
CCM............ Chinese Christian Mission (EA)
CCM............ Chromatography Control Module [Instrumentation]
CCM............ Close Confinement Mesa [Electronics] (NITA)
CCM............ Cloud Camera Multiplexer
CCM............ Coincident-Current Memory
CCM............ Combat Cargo Mission [Air Force]
CCM............ Combined Cipher Machine
CCM............ Combined Coding Machine
CCM............ Commodity Class Manager
CCM............ Communications Controller Multichannel [Computer science]
CCM............ Communications Control Module [Telecommunications] (TEL)
CCM............ Community Climate Model [Meteorology]
CCM............ Companions of the Celtic Mission (EAIO)
CCM............ Completed Contract Method (AAGC)
CCM............ Computer Color Matching
CCM............ Computer-Controlled Monitor [Philips Consumer Electronics Co.] (PCM)
CCM............ Computer-Controlled Multiplexer (MCD)
CCM............ Computer Coupled Machines (NITA)
CCM............ Concerned Citizens' Movement [St. Christopher and Nevis] [Political party] (EY)
CC/M............ Configuration Control and Management (MCD)
CCM............ Congestive Cardiomyopathy [Medicine] (CPH)
CCM............ Connecticut Conference of Municipalities (SRA)
CCM............ Conseil Canadien de la Musique [Canadian Music Council] (EAIO)
CCM............ Conseil Canadien du Multiculturalisme [Canadian Multicultural Council]
CCM............ Constant Current Modulation
CCM............ Construction Claims Monthly [Business Publishers, Inc.] [A publication] (AAGC)
CCM............ Continuous Care Manikin [Medical training] [Navy]
CCM............ Continuous Casting Machine [Metalworking]
CCM............ Contro-Clusive Magnetism [Pest control concept]
CCM............ Control Civil and Military [British] (AIA)
CCM............ Control Communications Module [Telecommunications] (ECII)
CCM............ Controlled Carrier Modulation (KSC)
CCM............ Corse-Mediterranee Compagnie [France ICAO designator] (FAAC)
CCM............ Council of Communication Management (EA)
CCM............ Council of Cultural Ministers [Australia]

CCM............ Counter-Countermeasures [Military]
CCM............ Crew Cargo Module [NASA] (KSC)
CCM............ Crisciuma [Brazil] [Airport symbol] (OAG)
CCM............ Critical Care Manual
CCM............ Cross-Country Movement [Maps]
CCM............ Cross Cultural Medicine
CCM............ Crosstalk Communicator [Computer software] [Digital Communications Associates] (PCM)
CCM............ Crowell-Collier & Macmillan, Inc. [Later, Macmillan, Inc.] [Publishers]
CCM............ Cubic Centimeter (ROG)
CCM............ Cyclophosphamide, CCNU [Lomustine], Methotrexate [Antineoplastic drug regimen]
CCM............ Engineering Research Center for Composites Manufacturing Science and Engineering [Newark, DE] [Army] (GRD)
CCM............ Modesto Junior College, Modesto, CA [OCLC symbol] (OCLC)
CCMA............ Cabinet Council on Management and Administration [Executive Office of the President] (GFGA)
CCMA............ California Cast Metals Association (SRA)
CCMA............ Canadian Chicken Marketing Agency [Office Canadien de Commercialisation des Poulets] (AC)
CCMA............ Canadian Circulation Management Association [Association Canadienne des Chefs de Tirage] (AC)
CCMA............ Canadian Council of Management Associations (HGAA)
CCMA............ Canadian Country Music Association [Association de la Musique Country Canadienne] (AC)
CCMA............ Card Clothing Manufacturers Association [Defunct] (EA)
CCMA............ Carolinas Concrete Masonry Association (SRA)
CCMA............ Catholic Campus Ministry Association (EA)
CCMA............ CCNU [Lomustine], Cyclophosphamide, Methotrexate, Adriamycin [Antineoplastic drug regimen] (DAVI)
CCMA............ Certified Color Manufacturers Association (EA)
CCMA............ Civilian Clothing Maintenance Allowance [Army] (AABC)
CCMA............ Comite de Compradores de Material Aeronautico de America Latina (MCD)
CCMA............ Commander Corps Medium Artillery [British]
CCMA............ Conseil Canadien des Metiers d'Art (AC)
CCMA............ Contract Cleaning and Maintenance Associatioh [British]
CCMA............ Corrugated Case Materials Association [British] (DBA)
CCMA............ Cotton Canvas Manufacturers Association [British] (BI)
CCMA............ Crew Correctable Maintenance Action (MCD)
CCMAC......... Committee of Common Market Automobile Constructors [EEC]
CCMACPI...... Commission for Catholic Missions among the Colored People and the Indians (EA)
CCMB............ Completion of Calls Meeting Busy [Telecommunications] (NITA)
CCMC............ Canadian Creative Music Collective [Jazz group]
CCMC............ Civilian Career Management Center [Military] (DNAB)
CCMC............ Coincident-Current Magnetic Core
CCMC............ Comite des Constructeurs d'Automobiles du Marche Common [Common Market Automobile Manufacturers Committee] [French]
CCMC............ Committee on the Costs of Medical Care (DMAA)
CCMC............ Conseil des Communautes Musulmanes du Canada [Council of Muslim Communities of Canada] (EAIO)
CCMCA........ California Conference of Mason Contractor Associations (SRA)
CCMCBB....... Chief Carpenter's Mate, Construction Battalion, Builder [Navy rating Obsolete]
CCMCBD....... Chief Carpenter's Mate, Construction Battalion, Draftsman [Navy rating Obsolete]
CCMCBE....... Chief Carpenter's Mate, Construction Battalion, Excavation Foreman [Navy rating Obsolete]
CCMCBS....... Chief Carpenter's Mate, Construction Battalion, Surveyor [Navy rating Obsolete]
CCMCC........ Continuing Committee on Muslim-Christian Cooperation (EA)
CCMD........ Chrysler Corporation Missile Division (MCD)
C Cmd .... Coastal Command [Air Force British] (DMA)
CCMD........ Coded Command
CCMD........ Continuous Current-Monitoring Device
CCME............ Churches' Committee on Migrants in Europe (EAIO)
CCME............ Contract Change Mass Estimate (NASA)
CCME............ Coordinating Council on Medical Education [Superseded by CFMA] (EA)
CCMEU .... Camera de Comercio Mexico-Estados Unidos [United States-Mexico Chamber of Commerce] (EAIO)
CCMF............ Calvin Coolidge Memorial Foundation (EA)
CCMF............ Canadian Children's Multimedia Foundation (AC)
CCMF............ [The] Churches' Committee for Supplementing Religious Education Among Men in HM Forces [British military] (DMA)
CCMFA......... Civilian Career Management Field Agency (MCD)
CCMG .... Canadian College of Medical Geneticists [College Canadien de Geneticiens Medicaux] (AC)
CCMG .... Conseil Canadien de la Main-d'Oeuvre en Genie [Canadian Engineering Manpower Council]
CCMHC........ Comprehensive Community Mental Health Centers Inventory [Department of Health and Human Services] (GFGA)
CCMHF......... Coordinating Council on Manufactured Housing Finance [Defunct] (EA)
CCmHi .... Costa Mesa Historical Society, Costa Mesa, CA [Library symbol] [Library of Congress] (LCLS)
CCMHRL...... Consortium of Central Massachusetts Health Related Libraries [Library network]
CCMIA .... Canned and Cooked Meat Importers Association (EA)
CCMIE .... Canadian Council for Multicultural & Intercultural Education (AC)
CCMIS .... Commodity Command Management Information System [Army]
CCMIS .... Compliance Management Information System [FAA] (TAG)
CCMIS .... Contraceptive Commodity Management Information System [United Nations] (ECON)

CCML............ Comprehensive Core Medical Library [Database] [BRS Information Technologies] [Information service or system] (IID)
CCMLO .... Chief Chemical Officer [Army]
CCMM.......... Complete Correlation Matrix Memory [Computer science] (PDAA)
CCMM.......... Council on Children, Media, and Merchandising (NTCM)
CCmO .... Orange Coast College, Costa Mesa, CA [Library symbol Library of Congress] (LCLS)
CCMOS .... Clocked Complementary Metal Oxide Semiconductor [Electronics] (IAA)
CCMP.......... Ceylon Corps of Military Police [British military] (DMA)
CCMP.......... Computer Color Match Prediction
CCMP.......... Conversion Complete (IAA)
CCMP.......... Cooked Cured-Meat Pigment [Food technology]
cCMP.......... Cyclic Cytidine Monophosphate [Biochemistry]
CCMPA .... Canadian Concrete Masonry Producers' Association (EAIO)
CCMPr .... Carlton Commun'X-CAPS' [NYSE symbol] (TTSB)
CCMPTC ...... Central Computer Center (AABC)
CCMR .... Central Contract Management Region [Air Force]
CCMR .... Conseil Canadien des Ministres des Ressources [Canadian Council of Resource Ministers]
CCMRD........ Coordinating Committee on Materials Research and Development [Executive Office of the President]
CCMRE .... Conseil Canadien des Ministres des Ressources et de l'Environnement [Canadian Council of Resource and Environment Ministers - CCREM]
CCMRG........ Commonwealth Committee on Mineral Resources and Geology [British]
CCMS.......... Central Cardiac Monitoring System
CCMS.......... Central Control and Monitoring System [for managing buildings' heating, ventilation, and security needs]
CCMS.......... Checkout Control and Monitor Subsystem [NASA] (NASA)
CCMS.......... Clean Catch Midstream Urine [Medicine]
CCMS.......... Clinical Care Management System [Medicine] (DMAA)
CCMS.......... Command Control and Monitor System [NASA] (NASA)
CCMS.......... Committee on the Challenges of Modern Society [Brussels, Belgium] (EA)
CCMS.......... Commodity Configuration Management System (AFIT)
CCMS.......... Community Case Management Services
CCMS.......... Computer Center Management System (MHDB)
CCMS.......... Congress of County Medical Societies (EA)
CCMS.......... Conseil Canadien de la Medecine Sportive [Canadian Academy of Sport Medicine - CASM]
CCMS.......... Control Commission Military Section [British World War II]
CCmS.......... Southern California College, Costa Mesa, CA [Library symbol Library of Congress] (LCLS)
CCMSA .... Comite Consultatif Mondial de la Societe des Amis [World Consultative Committee of the Society of Friends] [British] (EAIO)
CCMSC .... Caribbean Common Market Standards Council [Georgetown, Guyana] (EAIO)
CCMSRB ..... Chief Carpenter's Mate, Ship Repair, Boatbuilder, Wood [Navy rating Obsolete]
CCMSRJ ..... Chief Carpenter's Mate, Ship Repair, Joiner [Navy rating Obsolete]
CCMSS .... Computer-Controlled Microfilm Search System (MCD)
CCMSU .... Clean Catch Midstream Urine [Medicine]
CCMSUA ...... Clean-Catch-Midstream Urinalysis [Medicine] (MEDA)
CCMT.......... Catechol Methyltransferase (DMAA)
CCMT.......... Catechol-O-Methyltransferase [An enzyme]
CCMT.......... Centre for Construction Market Information Ltd. [British] (CB)
CCMT.......... Computer-Controlled Machine Tool (MHDB)
CCMTA........ Canadian Council of Motor Transport Administrators [Conseil Canadien des Administrateurs en Transport Motorise] (AC)
CCMTA........ Cape Canaveral Missile Test Annex [Later, KSC]
CCMTC........ Cape Canaveral Missile Test Center [Later, KSC]
CCMTS........ Crown Cork Manufacturers' Technical Council [British] (BI)
CCMU .... Commander's Control and Monitoring Unit (DNAB)
CCMU .... Computer Controller Multiplexer Unit
CCMU .... Control Center Mock-Up
CCMU .... Critical Care Medical Unit (DMAA)
CCMV .... Cowpea Chloretic Mottle Virus
CCMW .... Council for Christian Medical Work [Later, CHH] (EA)
CCN .... Cachucha Ranch [New Mexico] [Seismograph station code, US Geological Survey Closed] (SEIS)
CCN .... Campus Conference Network [Services by Satellite, Inc.] [Washington, DC] [Telecommunications] (TSSD)
CCN .... Category Codes and Nomenclature (MCD)
CCN .... Central Command Network
CCN .... Cereal Cyst Nematode [Medicine]
CCN .... Certification Control Number (MCD)
CCN .... Certified Clinical Nutritionist [Medicine]
CCN .... Chakcharan [Afghanistan] [Airport symbol Obsolete] (OAG)
CCN .... Chinese Communist Navy (CINC)
CCN .... Chris-Craft Indus [NYSE symbol] (TTSB)
CCN .... Chris-Craft Industries, Inc. [NYSE symbol] (SPSG)
CCN .... Classification Change Notice (KSC)
CCN .... Closed Condensation Nuclei (MCD)
CCN .... Cloud Condensation Nuclei [Fog]
CCN .... Cluster Controller Node (IAA)
CCN .... Command Confirmation
CCN .... Command Control Number [Air Force] (AFM)
CCN .... Communication Control Number (AAG)
CCN .... Community Care Network [Medicine]
CCN .... Computer Call Network [Telemarketing]
CCN .... Configuration Change Notice (DOMA)
CCN .... Configuration Control Number (AAG)

CCN .... Consulta di i Cumitati Nationalisti [Corsica] (PD)
CCN .... Contract Change Negotiation (NASA)
CCN .... Contract Change Notice (MCD)
CCN .... Contract Completion Notices [DoD]
CCN .... Copper Concentric Neutral (PDAA)
CCN .... Coronary Care Nursing [Medicine] (MAE)
CCN .... Cost Charge Number (MCD)
CCN .... Cruzada Civica Nacionalista [Nationalist Civic Crusade] [Venezuela Political party] (PPW)
CCN .... Cruzada Civilista Nacional [Panama] [Political party] (EY)
CCNA .... Canadian Community Newspapers Association [Founded 1919]
CCNA .... Combined Committee for North Africa [World War II]
CCNA .... Council on Certification of Nurse Anesthetists (EA)
CCNAA .... Coordination Council for North American Affairs
CCNB .... Concerned Citizens for the Nuclear Breeder (EA)
CCNB .... Conservation Council of New Brunswick [Conseil de la Conservation du Nouveu-Brunswick] (AC)
CCNBC .... Committee for the Coordination of National Bibliographic Control [Defunct] (EA)
CCNC .... Chinese Canadian National Council [Conseil National des Canadiens Chinois] [Also, Chinese Canadian National Council for Equality] (AC)
CCNC .... Common Channel Network Controller [Telecommunications]
CCNC .... Common Channel Signaling Network Control [Telecommunications] (ACRL)
CCNC .... Cooperative Council of North Carolina (SRA)
CCNCE .... Chinese Canadian National Council for Equality
CCNCO .... Coordinating Council of National Court Organizations [Defunct] (EA)
CCND .... Children's Campaign for Nuclear Disarmament (EA)
CCND .... Committee to Cap the National Debt (EA)
CCNDT .... Canadian Council for Non-Destructive Technology (HGAA)
CC-NDT........ Can't Call - No Dial Tone [Telecommunications] (TEL)
CCNF .... Committee for Consumers No-Fault (EA)
CCNF .... Commodore Commanding Newfoundland Force [Navy Canada World War II]
CCNG .... Computer Communications Networks Group [University of Waterloo] [Canada Information service or system Research center] (IID)
CCNI .... Code Control Number Identifier [Department of Health and Human Services] (GFGA)
CCNMA .... California Chicano News Media Association (SRA)
CCNPP .... Calvert Cliffs Nuclear Power Plant (NRCH)
CCNPrA .... Chris-Craft Ind,$1 Pr Pfd [NYSE symbol] (TTSB)
CCNPrB .... Chris-Craft Ind,$1.40 Cv Pfd [NYSE symbol] (TTSB)
CCNR .... Canadian Coalition for Nuclear Responsibility
CCNR .... Central Commission for the Navigation of the Rhine [France] (EAIO)
CCNR .... Citizens Committee on Natural Resources [Defunct] (EA)
CCNR .... Consultative Committee for Nuclear Research [EEC] (PDAA)
CCNR .... Current Controlled Negative Resistance [Electronics] (IAA)
CCNRA .... Central Council of National Retail Associations (EA)
CCNRRH ...... Comite Consultatif National des Recherches sur les Ressources Hydrauliques [National Advisory Committee on Water Resources Research] [Canada]
CCNS .... Canadian Congress of Neurological Sciences [Congres Canadien des Sciences Neurologiques] (AC)
CCNS .... Cell Cycle Nonspecific [Antitumor agent]
CCNS .... Concerned Citizens for Nuclear Safety [Advocacy group, New Mexico]
CCNS .... Congressional Caucus on National Security (EA)
CCNS .... Ohio Circuit Court Reports, New Series [A publication] (DLA)
CCNSC .... Cancer Chemotherapy National Service Center [National Institutes of Health]
CCNSIG .... Canadian Clinical Nurse Specialist Interest Group (AC)
CCNSW .... Cancer Council, New South Wales [Australia]
CCNT .... Chief Controller
CCNT .... Conservation Commission of the Northern Territory [Australia]
CCNU .... (Chloroethyl)cyclohexylnitrosourea [Lomustine] [Antineoplastic drug regimen]
CCNU-OP ..... CCNU Lomustine, Oncovin [Vincristine], Prednisone [Antineoplastic drug regimen] (DAVI)
CCNV .... Community for Creative Non-Violence (EA)
CCNW .... Center on the Consequences of Nuclear War (EA)
CCNWC .... Continuing Committee of the National Women's Conference [Later, NW] (EA)
CCNY .... Canadian Club of New York (EA)
CCNY .... Carnegie Corp. of New York (EA)
CCNY .... Chemists' Club - of New York (EA)
CCNY .... City College of New York [Later, City University of New York]
CCNYA .... Campaign for the Creation of the National Youth Advisor (EA)
CCNY (CUNY)... City College of The City University of New York (GAGS)
CCO .... Aerolineas Coco Club Hoteles de Mexico SA de CV [ICAO designator] (FAAC)
CCO .... Calf Certifying Officer [Ministry of Agriculture, Fisheries, and Food] [British]
CCO .... Canadian College of Organists
CCO .... Carbohydrate-Craving Obesity [Medicine]
CCO .... Center for Contemporary Opera (EA)
CCO .... Centre for Chiropractic and Osteopathy [Macquarie University] [Australia]
CC/O .... Certificate of Consignment/Origin [Shipping] (DS)
CCO .... Chemicals Control Order [Australia]
CCO .... Chico [California] [Seismograph station code, US Geological Survey] (SEIS)
CCO .... Chief Chemical Officer [Army]
CCO .... Chief Commanding Officer
CCO .... Chief, Contracting Office (AAGC)

CCO	Chief of Combined Operations [British Army] [World War II]
CCO	Circuit Control Office [Automatic Digital Information Network] (CET)
CCO	Cisco Resources [Vancouver Stock Exchange symbol]
CCO	Classified Control Officer
CCO	Clinchfield Railroad Co. [AAR code]
CCO	Cocoa
CCO	Coconut Oil (PDAA)
CCO	Combat Cargo Officer [Military] (NVT)
CCO	Comite Canadien d'Oceanographie [Canadian Committee on Oceanography - CCO]
CCO	Command Control Order
CCO	Commercial Contracting Officer
CCO	Commodity Credit Corporation (TDOB)
CCO	Commonwealth Copyright Office (DGA)
CCO	Community Collaboration Office [Veterans Administration] (GFGA)
CCO	Component Change Order (MCD)
CC/O	Composite Checkout [Aerospace] (AAG)
CC-O	Composite Cutoff [Aerospace] (AAG)
CCO	Comprehensive Certificate of Origin [Department of Commerce] (BARN)
CCO	Configuration Change Order
CCO	Conseil de la Cooperation d'Ontario (AC)
CCO	Conservation Council of Ontario [Le Conseil de Conservation de l'Ontario] (AC)
CCO	Constant Control Oil (IAA)
CCO	Constant Current Operation (IAA)
CCO	Consultants and Consulting Organizations Directory [A publication]
CCO	Context Control Object [Telecommunications] (OSI)
CCO	Contingency Contracting Officers [Military] (RDA)
CCO	Contract Change Order
CCO	Contracts Compliance Regional Office [DoD]
CCO	Controlled Collection Objective (MCD)
CCO	Conversion Control Officer [Army]
CCO	Converter Clutch Override [Automotive engineering]
CCO	Convoy Control Officer [Navy]
CCO	Coordinating Committee on Oceanography
CCO	Corporate Contract Officer
CCO	Council of Consulting Organizations (EA)
CCO	Council on Chiropractic Orthopedics (EA)
CCO	Country Clearing Office
CCO	Credit Clearing Outward (DCTA)
CCO	Crystal-Controlled Oscillator
CCO	Current-Controlled Oscillator (IEEE)
CCO	Cytochrome C Oxidase (DMAA)
CCO	Newnan, GA [Location identifier FAA] (FAAL)
CCO	Occidental College, Los Angeles, CA [OCLC symbol] (OCLC)
CCOA	Cadillac Convertible Owners of America (EA)
CCoa	Coalinga Unified School District Library, Coalinga, CA [Library symbol Library of Congress] (LCLS)
CCOA	Connecticut Campground Owners Association (SRA)
CCOA	Controller Central Operating Authority (NATG)
CCoac	Coachella Municipal Public Library, Coachella, CA [Library symbol Library of Congress] (LCLS)
CCOAD	Churches' Council on Alcohol and Drugs [Church of England]
CCoaJC	West Hills College, Coalinga, CA [Library symbol Library of Congress] (LCLS)
CCOB	CCNU [Lomustine], Cyclophosphamide, Oncovin , Bleomycin [Vincristine] [Antineoplastic drug regimen] (DAVI)
CCOC	Canadian Children's Opera Chorus (AC)
CCOC	Command Center Operations Chief (MCD)
CCOC	Command Control Operations Center [Army] (AABC)
CCOC	Council on Clinical Optometric Care (EA)
CCOCP	Corporate Customer Order Control Program (IAA)
CCOD	Consultants and Consulting Organizations Directory [Gale Research Co.] [Detroit, MI] [Information service or system] [A publication]
CCOF	California Certified Organic Farmers
CCOFI	California Cooperative Oceanic Fisheries Investigations [Also, CALCOFI] (MSC)
CCOH	Combined Contaminants, Oxygen, and Humidity (MCD)
CCOH	Corrosive Contaminants, Oxygen, and Humidity (MCD)
CCOHS	Canadian Centre for Occupational Health and Safety [Ministry of Labour]
CCOHS	Canadian Centre for Occupational Health & Safety [Centre Canadien d'Hygiene et de Securite au Travail] (AC)
CCOI	Committee for Crescent Observation International (EA)
CCol	Chartered Colorist (DD)
CCol	Chartered Colourist [British] (DBQ)
CCol	Colton Public Library, Colton, CA [Library symbol Library of Congress] (LCLS)
CCOL	Compartment Checkoff List [Navy] (NVT)
CCOL	Coordinating Committee on the Ozone Layer [United Nations] (OSRA)
C (Colds)	Catarrhal Colds [Medicine]
CColu	Colusa County Free Library, Colusa, CA [Library symbol Library of Congress] (LCLS)
CColuGS	Colusa County Genealogical Society, Colusa, CA [Library symbol] [Library of Congress] (LCLS)
CColumC	Columbia Junior College, Columbia, CA [Library symbol Library of Congress] (LCLS)
CCOM	Chicago College of Osteopathic Medicine
C COM	Code de Commerce [Commercial Code] [French]
CCOM	Colonial Coml [NASDAQ symbol] (TTSB)
CCOM	Colonial Commercial Corp. [NASDAQ symbol] (NQ)
C Com C	Civil and Commercial Code [A publication] (DLA)

CComC	Compton College, Compton, CA [Library symbol Library of Congress] (LCLS)
CComD	Dominquez Seminary, Compton, CA [Library symbol Library of Congress] (LCLS)
C Comm	Codice Commerciale [Commercial Code] [A publication] (ILCA)
CCOMM	Corn, Corn, Oats, Meadow, Meadow [Crop rotation]
C Comm C	Civil and Commercial Code [A publication] (DLA)
CCOMMRGN	Central Communications Region [Air Force]
CCOMP	Colonial Comml Cv Pfd [NASDAQ symbol] (TTSB)
CCOMSRS	Corps Communications Support Requirement Simulations (MCD)
CCON	Catalogus Codicum Orientalium [The Netherlands] [A publication] (BJA)
CCON	Circon Corp. [NASDAQ symbol] (NQ)
CCONAS	Coordinating Council of National Archaeological Societies (EA)
CConE	Diablo Valley College, Concord, CA [Library symbol Library of Congress] (LCLS)
cCOP	Calculated Colloidal Osmotic Pressure [Clinical chemistry]
CCOP	Chlorine-Catalyzed Oxidative-Pyrolysis [Chemical engineering]
CCOP	Community Clinical Oncology Program [Department of Health and Human Services] (GFGA)
CCOP	Consolidated Customer Order Processing (IAA)
CCOP	Constant-Control Oil Pressure (MSA)
CCOP	Current Cost Operating Profits [Accounting]
CCOPE	Cooperative Convection Precipitation Experiment [Meteorology]
CCOPEA	Committee for Coordination of Joint Prospecting for Mineral Resources in Asian Offshore Areas, East Asia [United Nations]
CCOPS	Coordination and Control of Personnel Surveys [Military] (DNAB)
CCOP/SOPAC	Committee for Co-Ordination of Joint Prospecting for Mineral Resources in South Pacific Offshore Areas (EAIO)
C COR	CCOR Electronics, Inc. [Associated Press] (SAG)
CCOR	Continuously-Computed Optimum Release (PDAA)
CCOR	Cubic Chain-of-Rotators [Equation of state]
C-CORE	Centre for Cold Ocean Resources Engineering [Memorial University of Newfoundland] [Research center] (RCD)
CCorn	Carnegie Public Library of Corning, Corning, CA [Library symbol Library of Congress] (LCLS)
CCoro	Corona Public Library, Corona, CA [Library symbol Library of Congress] (LCLS)
CCoron	Coronado Public Library, Coronado, CA [Library symbol Library of Congress] (LCLS)
CCoronUN	United States Naval Amphibious Base, Coronado, CA [Library symbol Library of Congress] (LCLS)
CCOS	Churches Commission on Overseas Students (EAIO)
CCOS	Combined Chiefs of Staff [DoD]
C/COS	Computer/Controlled Operating System [Computer science] (PDAA)
CCOSA	Cooperative Council for Oklahoma School Administration (SRA)
CCOSH	Canadian Center for Occupational Safety and Health (IID)
CCOSO	Coordinating Committee of Overseas Students Organization [British]
CCOSOP	Consultative Committee on Safety in the Offshore Petroleum Industry [Australia]
C Cost	Corte Costituzionale [Constitutional Court] [Italian] (DLA)
CC/OT	Caudate-Caudate to Outer Table (Ratio) [Neuroradiology]
CCOT	Cervical Compression Overloading Test [Medicine] (DMAA)
CCOT	Cycling Clutch-Orifice Tube [Automobile air-conditioning system]
CCov	Covina Public Library, Covina, CA [Library symbol Library of Congress] (LCLS)
CCovGS	Church of Jesus Christ of Latter-Day Saints, Genealogical Society Library, Covina Branch, Covina, CA [Library symbol Library of Congress] (LCLS)
CCOW	Capital Corp. of the West [NASDAQ symbol] (SAG)
CCOW	Capital Corp. of the West [NASDAQ symbol] (TTSB)
CCOW	Channel Control Orderwire (CAAL)
CCP	Cable Connector Panel
CCP	Call Control Processing [Telecommunications] (TEL)
CCP	Canadian Children's Project, Inc.
CCP	Canfor Capital Ltd. [Toronto Stock Exchange symbol]
CCP	Carbamoylcyclopropene [Organic chemistry]
CCP	Carbonless Copying Paper (IAA)
CCP	Carbonylcyanide-meta-chlorophenylhydrazone [Also, CCCP] [Organic chemistry]
CCP	Card Input-Preliminary Processing (SAA)
CCP	Carlsbad City Library, Carlsbad, CA [OCLC symbol] (OCLC)
CCP	Casualty Collecting-Post (NATG)
CCP	Casualty Collection Point [Army] (INF)
CCP	Casualty Control Panel (CAAL)
CCP	Catalogue Collectif des Periodiques [A bibliographic publication]
CCP	Cebu [Philippines] [Later, DAV] [Geomagnetic observatory code]
CCP	Cebu City [Philippines] [Seismograph station code, US Geological Survey] (SEIS)
CCP	Center Console Panel (MCD)
CCP	Center for Communication Programs (EA)
CCP	Center for Community Planning [HEW]
CCP	Central Charging Panel [Navy]
CCP	Central Control Point (AAGC)
CCP	Centre for Interdisciplinary Studies in Chemical Physics [University of Western Ontario] [Canada] (IRC)
CCP	Centrifugal Charging Pump (IEEE)
CCP	Centro Catolico Portugues [Portuguese Catholic Center] [Political party] (PPE)
CCP	Certificate in Computer Programming [Designation awarded by Institute for the Certification of Computer Professionals]
CCP	Certified Claims Professional
CCP	Cesium Chloride Polymerizable [Analytical chemistry]
CCP	Chance-Constrained Programming (PDAA)
CCP	Channel Control Processor [Computer science] (NITA)

CCP............. Character Controlled Protocol (HGAA)
CCP............. Character Count Protocol (HGAA)
CCP............. Charge Capacitance Probe (NASA)
CCP............. Chemical Control Procedure [*Nuclear energy*] (NRCH)
CCP............. Chevy Chase Preferred Capital Corp. [*NYSE symbol*] (SAG)
CCP............. Chief Commissioner of Police (DAS)
CCP............. Chilean Communist Party [*Political party*]
CCP............. China Clay Producers Trade Association (EA)
CCP............. Chinese Communist Party [*Political party*] (PD)
CCP............. Chronic Calcific Pancreatitis [*Medicine*]
CCP............. Cibachrome-Print [*Color photography*]
CCP............. Ciliocytopathoria [*Medicine*]
CCP............. Circulation Control Point (AABC)
CCP............. Code of Civil Procedure [*A publication*] (DLA)
CCP............. Collaborative Computational Projects [*Daresbury Laboratory*] [*British*] (IRUK)
CCP............. Command Control Panel
CCP............. Command Control Post
CCP............. Commercial Casualty Products [*Insurance*]
CCP............. Commercial Change Proposal (MCD)
CCP............. Commission Canadienne de Pedologie [*National Soil Survey Committee*] [*Canadian Department of Agriculture*]
CCP............. Commission on College Physics
CCP............. Committee on Commodity Problems [*Rome, Italy*] [*United Nations*] (ASF)
CCP............. Communication Check Point (DICI)
CCP............. Communication Control Program (BUR)
CCP............. Communications Career Program [*Military*]
CCP............. Communications Control Package
CCP............. Communications Control Panel
CCP............. Communications Control Processor
CCP............. Company Collection Point [*Army*] (INF)
CCP............. Compendium of Copyright Office Practices [*A publication*]
CCP............. Complete Count Program [*Bureau of the Census*] (GFGA)
CCP............. Composite Correction Plan [*Environmental Protection Agency*] (GFGA)
CCP............. Computer Central Processing [*Telecommunications*] (TEL)
CCP............. Computer-Controlled Polisher [*Instrumentation*]
CCP............. Computer Control Panel
CCP............. Comunity Care Plan [*Medicine*]
CCP............. Concepcion [*Chile*] [*Airport symbol*] (OAG)
CCP............. Conciliation Commission for Palestine [*of the UN*]
CCP............. Conditional Command Processor [*Computer science*] (MHDI)
CCP............. Confederation of Construction Professions [*British*] (DBA)
CCP............. Conference Chretienne pour la Paix [*Christian Peace Conference - CPC*] [*Prague, Czechoslovakia*] (EAIO)
CCP............. Configuration Change Plan (KSC)
CCP............. Configuration Change Point (NASA)
CCP............. Configuration Change Proposal (MCD)
CCP............. Configuration Control Panel
CCP............. Configuration Control Phase (MCD)
CCP............. Conseil Canadien du Porc [*Formerly, Canadian Swine Council*] (AC)
CCP............. Console Command Processor [*Digital Research*]
CCP............. Console Control Package
CCP............. Consolidated Command Post [*Military*]
CCP............. Consolidated Cryptologic Program [*DoD*] (AABC)
CCP............. Consolidation/Containerization Point
CCP............. Consumer Credit Project [*Defunct*] (EA)
CCP............. Continuous Correlation Processing
CCP............. Contract Configuration Process [*Telecommunications*] (TEL)
CCP............. Contractor Change Proposal (MCD)
CCP............. Control Command Processor (IAA)
CCP............. Control Configured Propulsion (MCD)
CCP............. Controlled Canister Purge [*Automotive engineering*]
CCP............. Cooperative Cardiovascular Project
CCP............. Coordinated Care Program [*Medicine*]
CCP............. Coordinated Commentary Programming [*Computer science*]
CCP............. Coordinated Containerization Point
CCP............. Core Component Pot [*Nuclear energy*] (NRCH)
CCP............. Corporate Control Procedure (MCD)
CCP............. Cost Control Program (NASA)
CCP............. Council for Career Planning [*Defunct*] (EA)
CCP............. Council of 1890 College Presidents (EA)
CCP............. Country Centres Project [*Australia*]
CCP............. County Court Practice (ILCA)
CCP............. Court of Common Pleas
CCP............. Credit Card Purchase (AFM)
CCP............. Critical Compression Pressure
CCP............. Critical Control Point [*Food technology*]
CCP............. Crockett, TX [*Location identifier FAA*] (FAAL)
CCP............. Cropland Conversion Program
CCP............. Cross-Check Procedure (NG)
CCP............. Cross Connection Point [*Telecommunications*] (TEL)
CCP............. Cryptologic Program [*Military*] (GFGA)
CCP............. Cuban Communist Party [*Political party*]
CCP............. Cubic Close Packing [*Crystallography*]
CCP............. Cushion Control Point [*Navy*] (ANA)
CCP............. Cytidine Cyclic Phosphate [*Medicine*] (DMAA)
CCP............. Cytochrome-c Peroxidase [*An enzyme*]
CCpA............ Atomics International, Canoga Park, CA [*Library symbol Library of Congress*] (LCLS)
CCPA .... California Canning Peach Association (EA)
CCPA .... Canadian Centre for Policy Alternatives (EAIO)
CCPA .... Canadian Chemical Producers Association
CCPA .... Canadian Concrete Pipe Association (AC)

CCPA .... Catholics for Christian Political Action [*Defunct*] (EA)
CCPA .... Cemented Carbide Producers Association (EA)
CCPA .... Cloud Chamber Photographic Analysis
CCPA .... Committee for Congested Production Areas [*1943-1944*]
CCPA .... Connecticut Community Providers Association (SRA)
CCPA .... Conseil Canadien de Protection des Animaux [*Canadian Council on Animal Care*]
CCPA .... Consumer Credit Protection Act [*1969*]
CCPA .... Court of Customs and Patent Appeals
CCPA .... United States Court of Customs and Patent Appeals [*Now CAFC*] (AAGC)
CCPAB .... California Cling Peach Advisory Board
CCPAC .... Certified Claims Professional Accreditation Council (EA)
CCPBI .... Comite Canadien pour le Programme Biologique International [*Canadian Committee for the International Biological Programme - CCIBP*]
CCPC .... Canadian-Controlled Private Corp.
CCPC .... Civil Communication Planning Committee [*Military*] (NATG)
CCPC .... Comite de Coordination des Plans Civils d'Urgence [*Civil Emergency Coordinating Committee*] [*NATO*] (NATG)
CCPC .... Committee on Crime Prevention and Control [*Economic and Social Council of the UN*] [*Vienna, Austria*] (EAIO)
CCPC .... Communication Computer Programming Center (AFM)
CCPC .... Control Center Programming Center [*NASA*] (KSC)
CCPC .... Cooperative Credit Purchasing Co. [*Company that buys banks' bad debts*] [*Japan*] (ECON)
CCPC .... Critical Collection Problems Committee [*United States Intelligence Board*] [*Obsolete*]
CCPD .... Charge-Coupled Photodiode Array
CCPD .... Continuous Cyclic Peritoneal Dialysis [*Medicine*]
CCPD .... Coupling Capacitor Potential Device (IEEE)
CCPDF .... Committee for the Co-Ordination of Patriotic and Democracy-Loving Forces [*Thailand*] (PD)
CCPDS .... Centralized Cancer Patient Data System
CCPDS .... Command Center Processing and Display Systems [*Air Force*] (MCD)
CCPDS-R ..... Command Center Processing and Display Systems Replacement [*Military*] (GFGA)
CCPE........... Canadian Council of Professional Engineers
CCPE........... College Certificate in Physical Education [*British*]
CCPEDQ....... Confederation des Caisses Populaires et d'Economie Desjardins du Quebec (AC)
CCPEF......... Congres Canadien pour la Promotion des Etudes chez la Femme [*Canadian Congress for Learning Opportunities for Women*]
CCPEW .... Combatant Craft Passive Electronic Warfare [*Navy*] (CAAL)
CCPF........... Children's Campaign for a Positive Future (EA)
CCPF........... Clergy Couples of the Presbyterian Family [*Defunct*] (EA)
CCPF........... Combined Cooling Performance Factor
CCPF........... Comite Central de la Propriete Forestiere [*Central Committee for Forest Ownership in the EEC - CCFOE*] (EAIO)
CCPF........... Commander-in-Chief, Pacific Fleet [*Navy*]
CCPG .... Chemical Corps Proving Ground [*Army*]
CCPGAB....... California Cling Peach Growers Advisory Board (SRA)
CCPGR .... Canada Committee on Plant Gene Resources
CCPI........... Center for Corporate Public Involvement (EA)
CCPI........... Communications Control Program Initialization (MCD)
CCPI........... Consultative Committee for Public Information [*United Nations*]
CCPIT.......... China Council for the Promotion of International Trade (PDAA)
CCPL........... Combat Center Programming Leader [*Military*] (SAA)
CCPL........... Cullman County Library [*Library network*]
CCPL........... Cuyahoga County Public Library (IID)
CCPM.......... Canadian College of Physicists in Medicine [*College Canadien des Physiciens en Medecine*] (AC)
CCPM.......... Command Career Program Management (MCD)
CCPM.......... Commissioned Corps Personnel Manual
CCPM.......... Constant-Choice Perceptual Maze Test
CCPM.......... Cubic Centimeter Per Minute (IAA)
CCPMO .... Consultative Council of Professional Management Organizations [*British*] (DBA)
CCPMS .... Cost Center Performance Measurement System (AFM)
CCPN .... Centre de Conditionnement Pre-Natal [*Pre-Natal Conditions Centre*] [*Canada*]
CCPO .... Central Civilian Personnel Office [*Military*]
CCPO .... Conseil Canadien des Producteurs d'Oeufs [*Canadian Egg Producers Council*]
CCPO .... Consolidated Civilian Personnel Office [*Air Force*]
CCPOA .... California Correctional Peace Officers Association (SRA)
CCPOFD....... Consolidated Civilian Personnel Office Field Division [*Air Force*] (DNAB)
CCPP .... Conseil Consultatif de la Politique du Personnel [*Advisory Council on Personnel Policy*] [*Canada Public Service Commission and Treasury Board*]
CCPR .... Cellular Communications Puerto Rico [*NASDAQ symbol*] (SAG)
CCPR .... Cellular Commun P.R. [*NASDAQ symbol*] (TTSB)
CCPR .... Central Council of Physical Recreation [*British*]
CCPR .... Codex Committee on Pesticide Residues [*Australia*]
CCPR .... Coherent Cloud Physics RADAR
CCPR .... Consultative Committee for Photometry and Radiometry [*International Committee on Weights and Measures*]
CCPR .... Crypt Cell Production Rate [*Medicine*]
CCpR .... Rockwell International, Rocketdyne Division, Technical Information Center, Canoga Park, CA [*Library symbol Library of Congress*] (LCLS)
CC Proc ...... Code of Civil Procedure [*A publication*] (DLA)
CCPS .... Center for Chemical Process Safety (EA)

CCPS .... Center for Consumer Product Safety [*National Institute of Standards and Technology*]
CCPS .... Centre for Canadian Population Studies
CCPS .... Christopher Columbus Philatelic Society (EA)
CCPS .... Comprehensive Country Programming System [*Department of State*]
CCPS .... Consolidated Container Processing System (MCD)
CCPS .... Consultative Council for Postal Studies [*Universal Postal Union*] (EY)
CCPSA .... Canadian Cerebral Palsy Sports Association [*Association Canadienne Sports de Paralysie Cerebrale*] (AC)
CCPSHE ...... Carnegie Council of Policy Studies in Higher Education [*Defunct*] (EA)
CCPT .... Center for Consumer Product Technology [*National Institute of Standards and Technology*] (GRD)
CCPT .... Comite de Coordination des Plans de Transport [*Coordinating Committee for Transport Planning*] [*NATO*] (NATG)
CCPT .... Council on Chiropractic Physiological Therapeutics (EA)
CCpT .... Thompson-Ramo-Wooldridge, Inc., Canoga Park, CA [*Library symbol Library of Congress*] (LCLS)
CC-PU .... Conference Reguliere sur les Problemes Universitaires [*Standing Conference on University Problems*] [*Council of Europe*] [*Strasbourg, France*] (EAIO)
CCQ .... Cachoeira do Sul [*Brazil*] [*Airport symbol*] (AD)
CCQ .... Cataloguing and Classification Quarterly [*A publication*]
CCQ .... CCL Industries, Inc. [*Toronto Stock Exchange symbol*]
CCQ .... Civil Code of Quebec [*A publication*] (DLA)
CCQ .... Classroom Climate Questionnaire (EDAC)
CCQ .... Conseil de la Cooperation du Quebec (AC)
CCR .... Calendar of Close Rolls [*British*]
CCR .... California Code of Regulations [*A publication*] (AAGC)
CCR .... Call Charge Record (ADA)
CCR .... Canadian Council for Refugees [*Conseil Canadien pour les Refugies*] [*Formerly, Standing Conference of Organizations Concerned for Refugees*] (AC)
CCR .... Capital Commitment Request (DNAB)
CCR .... Carga Aerea Venezolana Caraven SA [*Venezuela*] [*ICAO designator*] (FAAC)
CCR .... Cassette Camera Recorder (BARN)
CCR .... Catholic Committee for Refugees (EA)
CCR .... Center City Report [*A publication*] (EAAP)
CCR .... Center for Cereals Research [*Pennsylvania State University*] [*Research center*] (RCD)
CCR .... Center for Climatic Research [*University of Wisconsin - Madison*] [*Research center*] (RCD)
CCR .... Center for Constitutional Rights (EA)
CCR .... Central Communications Region [*Air Force*] (MCD)
CCR .... Central Control Room (DEN)
CCR .... Centre for Catalogue Research [*University of Bath*] [*British*] (CB)
CCR .... Centre for Conflict Resolution [*Macquarie University*] [*Australia*]
CCR .... Centre for Criminological Research [*University of Alberta*] [*Canada*] (IRC)
CCR .... Chacarita [*Argentina*] [*Seismograph station code, US Geological Survey Closed*] (SEIS)
CCR .... Change Commitment Record (SAA)
CCR .... Channel Command [*or Control*] Register [*Computer science*] (IAA)
CCR .... Channel Control Reconfiguration [*Computer science*] (MHDI)
CCR .... Circuit Court Reports [*A publication*] (DLA)
CCR .... Circulation Control Rotor [*Navy*]
CCR .... City Court Reports [*A publication*] (DLA)
CCR .... Closed-Circuit Radio
CCR .... Closed-Cycle Refrigerator
CCR .... Cluster-Catalyzed Reactivity [*Physics*]
CCR .... Coalition for Corporate Responsibility [*Defunct*] (EA)
CCR .... Coastal Confluence Region (DNAB)
CCR .... Coaxial Cavity Resonator (IAA)
CCR .... Code of Colorado Regulations [*A publication*]
CCR .... Coherent Crystal Radiation (PDAA)
CCR .... Color-to-Color Register [*Graphic arts*] (DGA)
CCR .... Combat Center Remoted [*Military*]
CCR .... Combat Command Reserve
CCr .... Combat Crew [*Air Force*] (AFM)
CCR .... Command Control Receiver
CCR .... Command Control Room
CCR .... Commission Centrale pour la Navigation du Rhin [*Central Commission for the Navigation of the Rhine*]
CCR .... Commission on Civil Rights
CCR .... Commitment, Concurrency and Recovery [*Computer science*] (TNIG)
CCR .... Commodity Classification Rates [*British*] (DS)
CCR .... Communications Change Request (IAA)
CCR .... Communications Control Room (IAA)
CCR .... Company Credit Reports [*Teikoku DataBank Ltd.*] [*Japan Information service or system*] (CRD)
CCR .... Complementary Color Removal [*Graphic arts*] (DGA)
CCR .... Complex Chemical Reaction
CCR .... Complex Control Room [*NASA*] (KSC)
CCR .... Component Catalog Review (IAA)
CCR .... Component Change Request (MCD)
CCR .... Component Characteristics Record
CCR .... Computer Character Recognition
CCR .... Computer Command Ride [*Automotive engineering*]
CCR .... Concord, CA [*Location identifier FAA*] (FAAL)
CCRS .... Condition Code Register
CCR .... Configuration Change Request
CCR .... Configuration Control Review (SSD)
CCR .... Configuration Control Room [*Social Security Administration*]
CCR .... Confrerie de la Chaine des Rotisseurs [*France*] (EAIO)

CCR .... Conradson Carbon Residue Test [*for petroleum products*]
CCR .... Construction Change Request
CCR .... Consumable Case Rocket
CCR .... Contactor Control Relay (MCD)
CCR .... Continuous Catalyst Regeneration [*Chemical engineering*]
CCR .... Continuous Complete Remission [*Oncology*] (DAVI)
CCR .... Contract Change Release
CCR .... Contract Change Request
CCR .... Contractor Change Request (NASA)
CCR .... Contractor Cost Reduction
CCR .... Control Center Rack (MCD)
CCR .... Control Circuit Resistance
CCR .... Control Contactor (IEEE)
CCR .... Cooperative College Registry [*Defunct*]
CCR .... [*The*] Corinth & Counce Railroad Co. [*AAR code*]
CCR .... Cosumnes River College, Sacramento, CA [*OCLC symbol*] (OCLC)
CCR .... Council for Chemical Research (EA)
CCR .... Countrywide Credit Indus [*NYSE symbol*] (TTSB)
CCR .... Countrywide Credit Industries, Inc. [*NYSE symbol*] (SPSG)
CCR .... County Court Rules (ILCA)
CCR .... County Courts Reports [*1860-1920*] [*England*] [*A publication*] (DLA)
CCR .... Court of Crown Cases Reserved [*England*] (DLA)
CCR .... Crack Resources Ltd. [*Vancouver Stock Exchange symbol*]
Ccr .... Creatinine Clearance [*Clinical chemistry*] (MAE)
CCR .... Credit Card Reader
CCR .... Creedence Clearwater Revival [*Rock music group*]
CCR .... Critical Compression Ratio
CCR .... Cross-Channel Rejection
CCR .... Crown Cases Reserved
CCR .... Crystal Can Relay
CCR .... Cube Corner Reflector
CCR .... Current Chemical Reactions [*A publication*]
CCR .... Current Control Relay (DNAB)
CCR .... Customer Controlled Reconfiguration [*Telecommunications*] (TSSD)
CCR .... Cyclic Catalytic Reforming [*Chemical engineering*] (IAA)
CCR .... Rancho Santa Ana Botanic Garden, Claremont, CA [*Library symbol Library of Congress*] (LCLS)
CCRA .... Canadian Carbonization Research Association (AC)
CCRA .... Cape Canaveral Reference Atmosphere [*NASA*] (NASA)
CCRA .... Carotid Chemoreceptor Activation [*Medicine*]
CCRA .... Colorado Court Reporters Association (SRA)
CCRA .... Commander Corps Royal Artillery [*British*]
CCRAB .... California Celery Research Advisory Board (SRA)
CCRAK .... Combined Command for Reconnaissance Activities in Korea
CCR&R .... Child Care Resource and Referral Program (WYGK)
CCR & R ...... Covenants, Conditions, Restrictions, and Reservations (MHDB)
CCRB .... Civilian Complaint Review Board
CCRC .... Canberra Civil Rehabilitation Committee [*Australia*]
CCRC .... Cataloging Code Revision Committee [*of ALA*]
CCRC .... Children's Creative Response to Conflict Program (EA)
CCRC .... Combat Crew Replacement Center [*World War II*]
CCRC .... Community Careers Resource Center (EA)
CCRC .... Complex Carbohydrate Research Center [*Athens, GA*]
CCRC .... Continuing-Care Retirement Communities
CCRC .... Continuing-Care Retirement Community
CCRC .... Core Component Receiving Container [*Nuclear energy*] (NRCH)
CCRCA .... Curly-Coated Retriever Club of America (EA)
CCRCT .... Commander Corps Royal Corps of Transport [*Military British*]
CCRD .... Controller of Chemical Research and Development [*Ministry of Supply*] [*British*]
CCRDC .... Chemical Corps Research and Development Command [*Army*] (AAG)
CCRDES ...... Concept for a Radiological Detection System (CINC)
CCRE .... Canadian Council for Research in Education
CCRE .... Commander Corps Royal Engineers [*Military British*]
CCRE .... Commitment, Concurrency, and Recovery Element [*Computer science*] (TNIG)
CCRE .... Conseil Canadien pour la Recherche en Education [*Canadian Council for Research in Education*]
CCREM .... Canadian Council of Resource and Environment Ministers
CC Rep .... County Courts Reporter [*in Law Journal*] [*London*] [*A publication*] (DLA)
CCRESPAC ... Current Cancer Research Project Analysis Center [*Database producer*]
CCRF .... Consolidated Communications Recording Facility (MCD)
CCRG .... Canadian Classification Research Group [*International Federation for Documentation*]
CCRH .... Canadian Council for Racial Harmony (AC)
CCRH .... Conseil Canadien de Recherches sur les Humanites [*Humanities Research Council of Canada - HRCC*]
CCRH .... Conseil Canadien pour la Readaptation des Handicapes [*Canadian Rehabilitation for the Disabled*] (EAIO)
CCRI .... California Civil Rights Initiative (ECON)
CCRI .... Colorado Casino Resorts [*NASDAQ symbol*] (TTSB)
CCRI .... Colorado Casino Resorts, Inc. [*NASDAQ symbol*] (SAG)
CCRI .... Community College of Rhode Island [*Formerly, RIJC*]
C Crim Proc... Code of Criminal Procedure [*A publication*] (DLA)
CCRIS .... Chemical Carcinogenesis Research Information System [*National Library of Medicine*] [*Information service or system*]
CCRKBA ...... Citizens Committee for the Right to Keep and Bear Arms (EA)
CCRLS .... Chemeketa Cooperative Regional Library Service [*Library network*]
CCRM .... Catholic Charismatic Renewal Movement
CCRM .... Center for Chinese Research Materials (EA)
CCRMA .... Center for Computer Research in Music and Acoustics [*Pronounced "karma"*] [*Stanford University*]

CCR M-L...... Comites Comunistas Revolucionarios, Marxistas-Leninistas [Marxist-Leninist Revolutionary Communist Committees] [Portugal Political party] (PPE)
CCRMP........ Canadian Certified Reference Materials Project (PDAA)
CCRN.......... Cardiac Care Registered Nurse (WGA)
CCRN.......... Centre Commun de Recherches Nucleaires [Joint Nuclear Research Center] [EURATOM]
CCRN.......... Critical Care Registered Nurse
CCRO.......... Clintrials Research [NASDAQ symbol] (SAG)
CCRO.......... Community Charge Registration Officer [British]
CCROS........ Card Capacitor Read-Only Storage [Computer science] (IEEE)
CCRP.......... Comite Consultatif de la Radioprotection [Advisory Committee on Radiological Protection] [Canada]
CCRP.......... Comprehensive Community Revitalization Project
CCRP.......... Continuously Computed Release Point (MCD)
CCRPR........ Centre Canadien de Recherche en Politiques de Rechange [Canadian Centre for Policy Alternatives] (EAIO)
C Cr Pr....... Code of Criminal Procedure [A publication] (DLA)
CCRR.......... Center for Community and Regional Research [University of Minnesota, Duluth] [Research center] (RCD)
CCRR.......... Conference Committee for Refugee Rabbis (EA)
CCRS.......... Canadian Centre for Remote Sensing [See also CCT]
CCRS.......... Carbonaceous Chondrite Reference Standard [Geophysics]
CCR(S)........ Chemical Compound Registry (System) (DIT)
CCRS.......... Computer-Controlled Receiving System (DNAB)
CCRS.......... Configuration Control Reporting System [Navy] (MCD)
CCRS.......... Cost Category Reporting System (MCD)
CCRSA........ Confederation of the Canons Regular of Saint Augustine [Italy] (EAIO)
CCRSFF....... Commander, Central Region SEATO [Southeast Asia Treaty Organization] FieldForces (CINC)
CCRSFF(D)... Commander, Central Region SEATO Field Forces (Designate)
CCRSS........ Conseil Canadien de Recherche en Sciences Sociales [Social Sciences Research Council of Canada - SSRCC]
CCRT .... Canadian Council on Rehabilitation & Work [Le Conseil Canadien de la Readaptation et du Travail] (AC)
CCRT .... Cathodochromic Cathode Ray Tube (PDAA)
CCRT .... Check Collectors Round Table [Later, ASCC] (EA)
CCRT ,......... Closed Circuit Radio Transmitter (NTCM)
CCRT ,......... Computer-Controlled Radiation Therapy [Medicine] (DMAA)
CCRT ,......... Core Conflictional Relationships Theme [Psychology]
CCRTL .... Citizens Coalition for Rational Traffic Laws [Later, NMA] (EA)
CC/RTS .... Chemical Collection/Request Tracking System [Environmental Protection Agency] (ERG)
CCRU.......... Common Cold Research Unit [British Medical Council]
CCRU.......... Complete Crew
CCRU.......... Critical Care Recovery Unit [Medicine] (DAVI)
CCRVDF....... Codex Committee on Residues of Veterinary Drugs in Food [Australia]
CCRW.......... Canadian Council on Rehabilitation & Work (AC)
CCRZ.......... Climb and Cruise [Aviation] (FAAC)
CCS.............. C (100) Call Seconds [Telecommunications] (NITA)
CCS.............. Cabin Communications System [Aviation]
CCS.............. CAD/CAM [Computer-Aided Design/Computer-Aided Manufacturing] Systems
CCS.............. California Current System [Oceanography]
CCS.............. Call Control Systems [San Clemente, CA] [Telecommunications] (TSSD)
CCS.............. Calling Card Service [Bell System]
CCS.............. Camera Control System (KSC)
CCS.............. Canadian Cancer Society (BARN)
CCS.............. Canadian Cardiovascular Society (EAIO)
CCS.............. Canadian Ceramic Society (AC)
CCS.............. Canadian Computer Show
CCS.............. Canbec Resources [Vancouver Stock Exchange symbol]
CCS.............. Cancer Control Society (EA)
CCS.............. Cape Chelyuskin [Former USSR Geomagnetic observatory code]
CCS.............. Cape Cod System [Air Force]
CCS.............. Caracas [Venezuela] [Airport symbol] (OAG)
CCS.............. Caroline Chisholm Society [Australia]
CCS.............. Carpentaria Community Services [Australia]
CCS.............. Carrier Color Signal
CCS.............. Cartographic Conversion Station (MCD)
CCS.............. Cartoon Conservation Scales [Educational test]
CCS.............. Cast Carbon Steel
CCS.............. Castle & Cooke [NYSE symbol] (SAG)
CCS.............. Castle & Cooke Inc. [NYSE symbol] (TTSB)
CCS.............. Castlecrag Conservation Society [Australia]
CCS.............. Casualty Clearing Station [Military]
CCS.............. Cataloging and Classification Section [of ALA]
CCS.............. Catholic Committee on Scouting [Later, NCCS]
CCS.............. Catholic Community Services Inc. [Services Communautaires Catholiques Inc.] (AC)
CCS.............. Cawcaw Swamp [South Carolina] [Seismograph station code, US Geological Survey] (SEIS)
CCS.............. Cell Cycle Specific [Antitumor agent]
CCS.............. Census Control System [Bureau of the Census] (GFGA)
CCS.............. Cent Call Seconds [Telecommunications]
CCS.............. Center for Chinese Studies [University of Michigan] [Research center] (RCD)
CCS.............. Center for Christian Studies (EA)
CCS-L.......... Center for Coastal Studies [University of California, San Diego] [Research center] (RCD)
CCS.............. Center for Community Study [University of Rochester] [Research center] (RCD)

CCS.............. Center for Comparative Sociology
CCS.............. Center for Computational Seismology [Berkeley, CA] [Lawrence Berkeley Laboratory] [Department of Energy] (GRD)
CCS.............. Center for Cuban Studies (EA)
CCS.............. Center for Cybernetic Studies [University of Texas at Austin] [Research center] (RCD)
CCS.............. Central Certificate Service [Stock exchange automation program]
CCS.............. Central Computer Station
CCS.............. Central Computing Site (IAA)
CCS.............. Central Computing System [Computer science]
CCS.............. Central Control Section (NASA)
CCS.............. Central Control Ship [Navy] (NVT)
CCS.............. Central Control Station (MCD)
CCS.............. Central Cooperative Society [United Arab Republic]
CCS.............. Central Co-Operative Society Council [Rangoon, Burma] (EY)
CCS.............. Centralized Computing Services
CC/S............ Centralized Correspondence Study [Alaska] (EDAC)
CCS.............. Centre for Child Study [University of Birmingham] [British] (CB)
CCS.............. Centre for Contemporary Studies [British] (CB)
CCS.............. Centre of Christian Spirituality [Australia]
CCS.............. Centro Calculo Sabadell [Sabadell Computing Center] [Information service or system] (IID)
CCS.............. Centum Call-Seconds [Telecommunications] (PCM)
CCS.............. Centurion COLIDAR [Coherent Light Detecting and Ranging] System
CCS.............. Certified Configuration Specialist
CCS.............. Certified Construction Specifier [Construction Specifications Institute] [Automotive engineering]
CCS.............. Ceylon Civil Service [Obsolete]
CCS.............. Change Control System
CCS.............. Chassis Compound-Control System [Automotive engineering]
CCS.............. Chemical Coordination Staff [Environmental Protection Agency] (GFGA)
CCS.............. Chief Commissary Steward [Navy rating Obsolete]
CCS.............. Choledocwo-Caval Shunt [Medicine]
CCS.............. Christian Chaplain Services (EA)
CCS.............. Christian Community Schools [Australia]
CCS.............. Chronic Cerebellar Stimulation [Medicine]
CCS.............. Church of Christ, Scientist
CCS.............. Circular Cylindrical Shell
CCS.............. Citizens for Common Sense [Defunct] (EA)
CCS.............. City College of San Francisco, San Francisco, CA [OCLC symbol] (OCLC)
CCS.............. Classification and Compensation Society (EA)
CCS.............. Clean Community System [Waste management program]
CCS.............. Clear-Channel Station [Telecommunications] (LAIN)
CCS.............. Clinical Sleep Society [Neurology] (DAVI)
CCS.............. Clock Coercion Signal
CCS.............. Cloudy Cornea Syndrome [Medicine] (DMAA)
CCS.............. Cockpit Control System (DWSG)
CCS.............. Cold Cranking Simulator Test [for petroleum products]
CCS.............. Collective Call Sign [Radio]
CCS.............. Collective Consciousness Society [Vocal and instrumental group]
CCS.............. Collector Coupled Structure (IAA)
CCS.............. College of Creative Studies [University of California, Santa Barbara]
CCS.............. Color Vision Constant Speed [Physiology] (IAA)
CCS.............. Column Code Suppression [Computer science] (IAA)
CCS.............. Combat Center Standby [Military] (SAA)
CCS.............. Combat Communications Squadron [Air Force] (AFIT)
CCS.............. Combat Control Squadron
CCS.............. Combat Control System [Military] (CAAL)
CCS.............. Combined Chiefs of Staff [DoD]
CCS.............. Combined CUSUM [Cumulative Sum]/Stewart Method [Laboratory analysis]
CCS.............. Command and Communications System [or Subsystem] [NASA]
CCS.............. Command and Control Segment [Air Force] (DOMA)
CCS.............. Command and Control Set (MCD)
CCS.............. Command and Control Subsystem (NASA)
CCS.............. Command and Control System [Army] (RDA)
CCS.............. Command and Control System
CCS.............. Command and Coordination Set
CCS.............. Command, Control, Support [Army]
CCS.............. Commemorative Collectors Society [Long Eaton, Nottinghamshire, England] (EAIO)
CCS.............. Commercial Cane Sugar
CCS.............. Commercial Communications Satellite [Japan]
CCS.............. Commitment Control System (NRCH)
CCS.............. Committee for Collective Security [Defunct] (EA)
CCS.............. Committee for Common Security (EA)
CCS.............. Committee of Concerned Scientists (EA)
CCS.............. Committee on Codes and Standards [Defunct] (EA)
CCS.............. Committee on the Constitutional System (EA)
C/CS............ Commodities - Coal and Steel (NATG)
CCS.............. Common Channel Signaling [Telecommunications] (TEL)
CCS.............. Common Command Set [Computer science]
CCS.............. Common Communications Support [Computer science] (PCM)
CCS.............. Communication Control System
CCS.............. Compass Control System
CCS.............. Complex Control Set (NASA)
CCS.............. Component Control Section
CCS.............. Component Cooling System [Nuclear energy] (NRCH)
CCS.............. Composers Cooperative Society [Later, Composers Theatre]
CCS.............. Computer Campaign Services [Data processing firm in field of politics]
CCS.............. Computer Chemical System

CCS............ Computer-Chemistry-System [*Yokogawa Hewlett Packard Ltd.*] [*Japan*]
CCS............ Computer Command Subsystem [*NASA*]
CCS............ Computer Consulting Service (BUR)
CCS............ Computer-Controlled Suspension [*Volvo*] [*Automotive engineering*]
CCS............ Computer Control Station (IAA)
CCS............ Computer Core Segment (NASA)
CCS............ Concentration Camp Syndrome [*Psychiatry*]
CCS............ Condensate Cleanup System [*Nuclear energy*] (NRCH)
CCS............ Condensate Cooling System [*Nuclear energy*] (NRCH)
CCS............ Confederation of Construction Specialists [*British*] (DBA)
CCS............ Confidential Cover Sheet (AAG)
CCS............ Configuration Control Secretariat (KSC)
CCS............ Conseil Canadien de la Securite (AC)
CCS............ Console Communication System (MCD)
CCS............ Consolidate-Cargo Container Service (DS)
CCS............ Consort Coarse Servo
CCS............ Contact Children's Services [*Australia*]
CCS............ Containment Cooling System [*Nuclear energy*] (NRCH)
CCS............ Contamination Control Station (MCD)
CCS............ Contamination Control System (NASA)
CCS............ CONTEL [*Continental Telecom Corp.*] Customer Support [*Telecommunications service*] (TSSD)
CCS............ Continuous Color Sequence [*Telecommunications*]
CCS............ Continuous Commercial Service [*Equipment specifications*]
CCS............ Continuous Composite Servo [*Optical disc recording format*] (BYTE)
CCS............ Contour Control System (IAA)
CCS............ Contract Change System (DNAB)
CCS............ Contract Completion Studies (MCD)
CCS............ Contrast Contour Seeker
CCS............ Control and Computation System [*or Subsystem*] [*Navy*] (MCD)
CCS............ Control Computer System [*or Subsystem*] (IAA)
CCS............ Controlled Combustion System [*Antipollution device for automobiles*]
CCS............ Controlled Communications Systems [*Chicago, IL*] [*Telecommunications*] (TSSD)
CCS............ Convention on the Continental Shelf (NOAA)
CCS............ Conversational Compiling System [*Xerox Corp.*] (IEEE)
CCS............ Conveyor Control System
CCS............ Cooperative Computing System [*Echo detection*]
CCS............ Cornell Computer Services [*Cornell University*] [*Information service or system*] (IID)
CCS............ Corporation of Certified Secretaries (AIE)
CCS............ Correlation Cancellation System
CCS............ Cost Control System
CCS............ Council of Communication Societies [*Defunct*] (EA)
CCS............ Council of the City of Sydney
CCS............ Countryside Commission for Scotland
C/CS............ County/Coverage Service [*ISI audience data*] (NTCM)
CCS............ Covert Camera Spy [*System*]
CCS............ Creative Computing Services [*Information service or system*] (IID)
CCS............ Crippled Children's Services
CCS............ Crippled Children's Society (DAVI)
CCS............ Critical Crevice Solution (PDAA)
CCS............ Custom Computer System (IEEE)
CCS............ Custom Contract Service [*IBM Corp.*]
CCS............ Customs Clearance Status [*British*] (DS)
CC/S............ Cycles per Second [*See also Hz*]
CCS............ One Hundred Call-Seconds [*Also, UC*] [*Bell System*] (TSSD)
CCS²............ Command, Control, and Subordinate Systems [*Telecommunications*] (TEL)
CCSA .... Canadian Centre on Substance Abuse (AC)
CCSA .... Children's Cognitive Style Assessment Instrument (EDAC)
CCSA .... Class C Surface Area [*Aviation*] (FAAC)
CCSA .... Common Carrier Special Application
CCSA .... Common Channel Signalling Arrangement [*Telecommunications*] (NITA)
CCSA .... Common Control Switching Arrangement [*AT & T*] [*Telecommunications*]
CCSA .... Council for Christian Social Action [*Later, OCIS*] [*United Church of Christ*]
CCSA .... Council of Churches, South Australia
CCSAA .... Cross Country Ski Areas Association (EA)
CCSAC .... Comite de Coordination des Services Agricoles Canadiens [*Canadian Agricultural Services Coordinating Committee*]
CCS&FCF.... Canada-Cuba Sports & Fitness Cultural Festivals (AC)
CCSAP .... Cancer Control Science Associates Program [*National Cancer Institute*]
CCSATU ...... Coordinating Council of South African Trade Unions
CCSAU .... Committee for Corporate Support of American Universities [*Later, Committee for Corporate Support of Private Universities*] (EA)
CCSB .... Change Control Sub-Board (DNAB)
CCSB .... Coca-Cola & Schweppes Beverages [*British*]
CCSB .... Control Commission Shipping Bureau [*Allied German Occupation Forces*]
CCSB .... Credit Card Service Bureau
CCSBA .... Credit Card Service Bureau of America [*Later, CCSB*]
CCSC .... Cemetery Consumer Service Council (EA)
CCSC .... Central Connecticut State College [*Later, Central Connecticut State University*] [*New Britain*]
CCS-C .... Central Coordinating Staff, Canada (AFM)
CCSC .... Civil Affairs Staff Center [*Wimbledon, England*]
CCSC .... Coherent Communications Systems Corp. [*NASDAQ symbol*] (SAG)
CCSC .... Coherent Communic Sys [*NASDAQ symbol*] (TTSB)
CCSC .... Combat Cryptological Support Console (MCD)
CCSC .... Commercial Computer Security Center [*British*]

CCSC .... Community Concern for Senior Citizens [*Defunct*] (EA)
CCSC .... Congregational Christian Service Committee [*Superseded by UCBWM*] (EA)
CCSC .... Coordinating Committee for Satellite Communication [*Switzerland*] (NITA)
CCSC .... School of Theology at Claremont, Claremont, CA [*Library symbol Library of Congress*] (LCLS)
CCSCE .... Center for Continuing Study of the California Economy [*Information service or system*] (IID)
CCSCS .... Central Cervical Spinal Cord Syndrome [*Medicine*] (DMAA)
CCSD .... Canadian Council on Social Development
CCSD .... Center for Computer Systems Design [*Washington University*] [*Research center*] (RCD)
CCSD .... Chrysler Corporation Space Division (KSC)
CCSD .... Command Communications Service Designator (CET)
CCSD .... Complex Carbohydrate Structural Database [*University of Georgia*]
CCSD .... Coupled-Cluster Singles and Doubles [*Quantum chemistry*]
CCS/DCC.... Cataloging and Classification Section's Descriptive Cataloging Committee [*of ALA*]
CCSDPT ...... Committee for the Coordination of Services to Displaced Persons in Thailand [*Australia*]
CCSDS .... Closed-Circuit Saturation Diving System [*Navy*] (CAAL)
CCSDS .... Consultative Committee for Space Data Systems (SSD)
CCSDT .... Coupled Cluster Singles Doubles and Triples [*Physical chemistry*]
CCSE .... Cognitive Capacity Screening Examination [*Psychology*]
CCSE .... Community Care Services, Inc. [*NASDAQ symbol*] (SAG)
CCSEAS ...... Canadian Council for Southeast Asian Studies [*Carleton University*] [*Research center*] (RCD)
CCSEM .... Computer-Controlled Scanning Electron Microscope
CCSEP .... Cement-Coated Single Epoxy
CCSERC ...... Conservation Council for the South East Region and Canberra [*Australia*]
CCSES .... Canada Committee on Socio-Economic Services [*See also CCSSE*]
CCSET........ Command and Control Standardization and Evaluation Team [*Military*]
CCSF.......... City College of San Francisco [*California*]
CCSF.......... Commander, Caribbean Sea Frontier
CCSF.......... Conseil Consultatif de la Situation de la Femme [*Advisory Council on the Status of Women*] [*Canada*]
CCSFI.......... Canned Chop Suey Foods Industry [*Defunct*]
CCSG .... Children's Cancer Study Group [*National Institutes of Health*]
CCSG .... Civil Censorship Study Group (EA)
CCSG .... Computer Components and System Group [*Massachusetts Institute of Technology*]
CCSGP .... Coalition for Common Sense in Government Procurement [*Later, CGP*] [*Washington, DC*] (EA)
CCSH .... Canadian Council on Smoking and Health
CCSHS .... Crippled Children's Seaside Home Society [*Australia*]
CCSI.......... Chromatics Color Sciences [*NASDAQ symbol*] (TTSB)
CCSI.......... Chromatics Color Sciences International, Inc. [*NASDAQ symbol*] (SAG)
CCSI.......... Crowncap Collectors Society International (EA)
CCSIL.......... Command, Control Simulation Integration Language [*ARPA*]
CCSIP .... Combat Control Systems Improvement Program [*Military*] (CAAL)
CCSIW .... Chromatics Color Sci Wrrt [*NASDAQ symbol*] (TTSB)
CCSJ.......... Congressional Coalition for Soviet Jews (EA)
CCSL.......... Cambridge Crystallography Subroutine Library [*Database*]
CCSL.......... Camp Coles Signal Laboratory [*Army*] (MCD)
CCSL.......... Citizens Conference on State Legislatures [*Later, Legis 50/The Center for Legislative Improvement*]
CCSL.......... Combat Center Status Indicator [*Military*] (SAA)
CCSL.......... Communications and Control Systems Laboratory
CCSL.......... Compatible Current-Sinking Logic (MSA)
CCSM.......... Cambridge Conference on School Mathematics [*National Science Foundation*]
CCSM.......... Corporate Customer Satisfaction Monitor
CCSMDG...... International Coordination Council of Societies of Mineral Deposits Geology
CCS MK2..... Combat Control System Mark 2 [*Navy*]
CCSN.......... Caroline Chisholm School of Nursing [*Monash University*] [*Australia*]
CCSN.......... Comite Consultatif de la Surete Nucleaire [*Advisory Committee on Nuclear Safety*] [*Canada*]
CCSN.......... Conference of Catholic Schools of Nursing (EA)
CCSN.......... Cross-Cultural Shamanism Network (EA)
CCSNYS...... Council of Community Services of New York State (SRA)
CCSO.......... Command and Control Systems Office [*Military*]
CCSO.......... Command and Control Systems Organization [*Defense Communications Agency*] [*Washington, DC*]
CCSO.......... Computing and Communications Services Office [*Telecommunications*]
CCSOC........ Character-Error Correcting Convolutional Self-Orthogonal Code (PDAA)
CCSOIM...... Chambre de Commerce du Sud-Ouest de l'Ile de Montreal (AC)
CCSP........ Canada Community Services Projects
CCSP........ Circuit Cellar Intelligent Serial EPROM Programmer [*Computer science*]
CCSP........ Clara Cell-Specific Protein (DMAA)
CCSP........ Coca Cola South Pacific [*Commercial firm*]
CCSP........ College Curriculum Support Project [*Bureau of the Census*] (GFGA)
CCSP........ Communications Concentrator Software Package [*Computer science*]
CCSP........ Consolidated Computer Security Program [*Military*] (GFGA)
CCSP........ Contractor Claims Settlement Program [*Military*] (DNAB)
CCSP........ University/Industry Cooperative Research Center for Communications and Signal Processing [*North Carolina State University*] [*Research center*] (RCD)

CCSPA .... Council of Canadian Studies Programme Administrators
CCSPP .... Clergy Counseling Service for Problem Pregnancies [*Defunct*] (EA)
CCSPSL ...... Centre for Criminology and the Social and Philosophical Study of Law [*University of Edinburgh*] [*British*] (CB)
CCSPU .... Committee for Corporate Support of Private Universities
CCSQ .... Consultative Committee on Substantive Questions [*United Nations*]
CCSR .... Canadian Consortium for Social Research (IID)
CCSR .... Center for Climate System Research [*Marine science*] (OSRA)
CCSR .... Center for Climate System Research (USDC)
CCSR .... Copper Cable Steel-Reinforced (IAA)
CCS/RTS ...... Chemical Collection System / Request Tracking [*Online database*] [*Environmental Protection Agency*]
CCSS .... Canada Centre for Space Science [*National Research Council of Canada*] [*Research center*] (RCD)
CCSS .... Canadian Committee of Scientists & Scholars [*Comite Canadien des Savants et Scientifiques*] (AC)
CCSS .... Central Coolant Supply Station (MCD)
CCSS .... Centralized Command Selection System (MCD)
CCSS .... Comanche Crew Support System [*Army*] (RDA)
CCSS .... Combat and Combat Support System (MCD)
CCSS .... Command and Control Simulation System (MCD)
CCSS .... Command and Control Switching System (DOMA)
CCSS .... Command Center Support System (MCD)
CCSS .... Commodity Command Standard System
CCSS .... Common Channel Signalling System [*Telecommunications*] (NITA)
CCSS .... Communications Collection Standard System (MCD)
CCSS .... Conversational Computer Statistical System (PDAA)
CCSS .... Cooperative College-School Science [*Program*] [*Defunct National Science Foundation*]
CCSS .... Cooperative College - School Service (OICC)
CCSS .... Coordination and Contract Summary Sheet
CCSSA .... Canadian Corporate Shareholder Services Association [*Association Canadienne des Services aux Actionnaires*] (AC)
CCSSA .... Community College Social Science Association (EA)
CCSSA .... Control and Command Systems Support Agency [*NATO*] (NATG)
CCSSE .... Comite Canadien sur les Services Socio-Economiques [*Canada Committee on Socio-Economic Services - CCSES*]
CCSSF .... Conseil Consultatif Canadien sur la Situation de la Femme (AC)
CCSSL .... Committee for Common Sense Speed Laws [*California*] [*Defunct*] (EA)
CCSS-MOD... Commodity Command Standard System - Modernization
CCSSO .... Council of Chief State School Officers (EA)
CCSSOI .... Commodity Command Standard System Operating Instructions [*Army*]
CCST .... Centennial Centre of Science and Technology
CCST .... Center for Computer Sciences and Technology [*Later, ICST*] [*National Institute of Standards and Technology*]
CCST .... Coordinating Committee on Science and Technology [*Australia*]
CCST .... CPG Cyclic Stick Trigger (MCD)
CCSTA .... Canadian Catholic School Trustees' Association [*Association Canadienne des Commissaires d'Ecoles Catolique*] (AC)
CCSTD .... Chief Commissary Steward [*Navy rating Obsolete*]
CCSTG .... Carnegie Commission on Science, Technology, and Government (EA)
CCSTP .... Cubic Centimeters at Standard Temperature and Pressure [*Also, CSTP*]
CCSU .... Captain Cook Study Unit [*American Topical Association*] (EA)
CCSU .... Computer Cross Select Unit
CCSU .... Configuration Control and Sensing Unit (CET)
CCSU .... Council of Civil Service Unions [*British*]
CC Supp ..... City Court Reports, Supplement [*New York*] [*A publication*] (DLA)
CCSVI .... Comite de Coordination du Service Voluntaire International [*Coordinating Committee for International Voluntary Service - CCIVS*] [*Paris, France*] (EA)
CCSW .... Component Cooling Service Water [*Nuclear energy*] (NRCH)
CCSW .... Copper-Clad Steel Wire (IAA)
CCSYS .... CAD/CAM [*Computer-Aided Design/Computer-Aided Manufacturing*] Systems (MCD)
CCSZ .... Coastal and Continental Shelf Zone [*Oceanography*]
CCT .... California Lutheran College, Thousand Oaks, CA [*OCLC symbol*] (OCLC)
CCT .... Canada Cement Lafarge Ltd. [*Toronto Stock Exchange symbol*]
CCT .... Canadian Centre for Toxicology [*Research center*] (RCD)
CCT .... Canadian College of Teachers [*See also CCE*]
CCT .... Capstone Capital [*NYSE symbol*] (TTSB)
CCT .... Capstone Capital Trust, Inc. [*NYSE symbol*] (SAG)
CCT .... Captive Carrier Test [*Military*]
CCT .... Carotid Compression Tomography [*Medicine*]
CCT .... Cathodal Closure Tetanus [*Physiology*]
CCT .... Cauchy Convergence Test [*Mathematics*]
CCT .... C-Band Communications Transponder
CCT .... Center-Cracked Tension (MCD)
CCT .... Center for Children and Technology [*Bank Street College of Education*] [*Research center*] (RCD)
CCT .... Central California Traction Co. [*AAR code*]
CCT .... Central City, KY [*Location identifier FAA*] (FAAL)
CCT .... Centre Canadien de Teledetection [*Canadian Centre for Remote Sensing - CCRS*]
CCT .... Certificati di Credito del Tesoro [*Italy*] (ECON)
CCT .... Certified Corrective Therapist
CCT .... Cesium Contact Thruster
CCT .... Chamber of Coal Traders [*British*] (DBA)
CCT .... Children's Checking Test (EDAC)
CCT .... Chilecito [*Argentina*] [*Seismograph station code, US Geological Survey Closed*] (SEIS)

CCT .... Chocolate-Coated [*or Covered*] Tablet [*Pharmacy*]
CCT .... Circle Cutting
CCT .... Circuit (NATG)
CCT .... Circuit Continuity Tester [*Electronics*] (IAA)
CCT .... Citty Taxi Aereo Nacional SA de CV [*Mexico ICAO designator*] (FAAC)
CCT .... Clarkson College of Technology [*Potsdam, NY*]
CCT .... Clear, Creamy Layer at Top [*Biochemistry*] (DAVI)
CCT .... Coal Combustion Technology
CCT .... Coated Cargo Tank (DNAB)
CCT .... Coated Compressed Tablet [*Pharmacy*]
CCT .... College of Commerce and Technology (AIE)
CCT .... Combat Controller [*Air Force*] (VNW)
CCT .... Combat Control Team [*Australia*]
CCT .... Combat Crew Training [*Air Force*] (AFM)
CCT .... Combined Cortical Thickness (DNAB)
CCT .... Comfort Cooling Tower [*Air conditioning*]
CCT .... Comite Contre la Torture [*Committee Against Torture - CAT*] [*Switzerland*] (EAIO)
CCT .... Comite de Coordination des Telecommunications [*Coordinating Committee for Communications*] [*NATO France*] (NATG)
CCT .... Command Cadet Team [*Military British*]
CCT .... Command Control Transmitter (MCD)
CCT .... Committee for Competitive Television (NTCM)
CCT .... Common Customs Tariff [*Common Market*]
CCT .... Communications Control Team [*Military*]
CCT .... Comparator Chart-Tooling (MCD)
CCT .... Complete Calls To [*Telecommunications*] (TEL)
CCT .... Complex Coordination Test (AAG)
CCT .... Composite Cyclic Therapy (MAE)
CCT .... Compound Card Terminal (CET)
CCT .... Comprehensive College Test
CCT .... Compulsory Competitive Tendering [*Australia*]
CCT .... Computer and Communications Technology Corporation (AAGC)
CCT .... Computer-Compatible Tape
CCT .... Computer-Compatible Terminal (MCD)
CCT .... Computer-Controlled Teletext
CCT .... Confrerie des Chevaliers du Tastevin (EA)
CCT .... Congenitally Corrected Transposition [*Of the great vessels*] [*Cardiology*] (DAVI)
CCT .... Connecting Circuit [*Electronics*] (IAA)
CCT .... Consolidated Change Table (MCD)
CCT .... Constant Current Transformer
CCT .... Consultative Committee on Thermometry [*International Bureau of Weights and Measures*]
CCT .... Contact Charge Transfer (MCD)
CCT .... Continuous Coding Transformation (MCD)
CCT .... Continuous Cooling Transformation
CCT .... Contour Check Template (MCD)
CCT .... Controlled Cord Traction [*Medicine*]
CCT .... Coordinated Caribbean Transport [*US shipping line*] (IMH)
CCT .... Coronary Care Team [*Medicine*]
CCT .... Correlated Color Temperature (IEEE)
CCT .... Cortical Collecting Tubule [*Anatomy*]
CCT .... Council for Clinical Training [*Later, ACPE*] (EA)
CCT .... Coupler Cut-Through
CCT .... Covered Carriage Trucks [*British railroad term*]
CCT .... Cranial Computed Tomography [*Medicine*] (DMAA)
CCT .... Craniocerebral Trauma [*Medicine*]
CCT .... Crimes Compensation Tribunal [*Victoria*] [*Australia*]
CCT .... Crude Coal Tar [*Medicine*] (CPH)
CCT .... Crystal-Controlled Transmitter
CCT .... Cuneiform Texts from Cappadocian Tablets in the British Museum (BJA)
CCT .... Current Clinical Trials [*A publication*]
CCT .... Cyclic Control Time (MCD)
CCT .... Cyclic Corrosion Test
CCTA .... California Cable Television Association (SRA)
CCTA .... Canadian Cable Television Association
CCTA .... Cape Canaveral Test Annex [*Obsolete Aerospace*] (AAG)
CCTA .... Central Computer and Telecommunications Agency [*British*]
CCTA .... Centre de Controle Tactique Aerien [*Air Tactical Control Center*] [*NATO*] (NATG)
CCTA .... Command Director of Administration (AAGC)
CCTA .... Commission de Cooperation Technique en Afrique [*Commission for Technical Cooperation in Africa*]
CCTA .... Coordinating Committee of Technical Assistance
CCTA .... Council of County Territorial Associations [*British military*] (DMA)
CCTB .... Consolidated Carriers Tariff Bureau
CCTC .... Canadian Communications and Transportation Commission
CCTC .... Chemical Corps Technical Command [*Army*] (MCD)
CCTC .... Command and Control Technical Center [*DoD*]
CCTC .... Computer-to-Computer Transfer Channel (ECII)
CCTCF .... Communication Circuit Technical Control Facility (MCD)
CCTC-WAD... Command and Control Technical Center WWMCCS [*Worldwide Military Command and Control System*] ADP Directorate [*Automatic Data Processing*] [*DoD*]
CCTD .... Coordinating Committee on Toxics and Drugs (EA)
CCTDE .... Compound Cycle Turbine Diesel Engine (MCD)
CCTDP .... Clean Coal Technology Demonstration Program [*Department of Energy*]
CCTE .... Canadian Council of Teachers of English
CCTE .... Cathodal Closure Tetanus [*Physiology*]
CCTE .... Certified Corporate Travel Executive [*National Passenger Traffic Association*] [*Designation awarded by*]

CCTE.......... Compound Cycle Turbofan Engine (PDAA)
CCTE.......... Council on Cooperation in Teacher Education [Defunct]
CCTE.......... Cumann Cheol Tíre Éireann [Folk Music Society of Ireland] (EAIO)
CCTELA....... Canadian Council of Teachers of English & Language Arts (AC)
CCTEP........ Cement-Coated Triple Epoxy
CC (Test)..... Component Check Test [Nuclear energy] (NRCH)
CCTF.......... Combat Cargo Task Force [British military] (DMA)
CCTF.......... Command and Control Test Facility
CCTFA........ Canadian Cosmetic, Toiletry & Fragrance Association [Association Canadienne des Cosmetiques, Produit de Toilette et Parfums] (AC)
CCTG .... California Christmas Tree Growers (SRA)
CCTG .... Connecting (ECII)
CCTGA....... Congenitally Corrected Transposition of the Great Arteries [Cardiology] (DAVI)
CCTGA....... Connecticut Christmas Tree Growers (SRA)
CCTI.......... Committee on Children's Television, Inc. (NTCM)
CCTI.......... Composite Can and Tube Institute (EA)
CCTI.......... Cooper & Chyan Technology [NASDAQ symbol] (TTSB)
CCTI.......... Cooper & Chyan Technology, Inc. [NASDAQ symbol] (SAG)
CCT in PET... Crude Coal Tar in Petroleum [Pharmacology] (DAVI)
CCTL.......... Casing Cooling Tank Level (IEEE)
CCTL.......... Code Clock Transfer Loop
CCTL.......... Core Component Test Loop [Nuclear energy] (NRCH)
CCTLR........ Chief Controller (FAAC)
CCTM......... Communication Connect Time Monitor [Computer science]
CCTM......... Communications Command Technical Manual [Army]
CCTM......... Council for Children's Television and Media (EA)
CCTMA....... Closed Circuit Television Manufacturers Association (EA)
CCTMM....... Commission Canadienne pour la Theorie des Machines et des Mecanismes [Canadian Committee for the Theory of Machines & Mechanisms] (AC)
CCTO......... Canadian Conference of Tourism Officials
CCTOV........ Conseil Canadien des Transformateurs d'Oeufs et de Volailles [Formerly, Canadian Produce Council] (AC)
CCTP.......... Center City Transportation Program
CCTP.......... Clean Coal Technology Program (GNE)
CCTP.......... Coordination Committee for Transport Planning [NATO] (NATG)
CCTP.......... Coronary Care Training Project [Cardiology] (DAVI)
CCTPP........ Churches' Center for Theology and Public Policy (EA)
CCTR .... Centre for Cell and Tissue Research [University of York] [Research center British] (CB)
CCTR .... Culham Conceptual Tokamak Reactor [Nuclear energy British] (NUCP)
CCTS.......... Canaveral Council of Technical Societies
CCTS.......... Carnegie Center for Transnational Studies
CCTS.......... Chicago Cluster of Theological Schools [Library network]
CCTS.......... Close Combat Training System [Army]
CCTS.......... Collaborative Corneal Transplantation Studies
CCTS.......... Combat Crew Training School [Air Force] (AFM)
CCTS.......... Combat Crew Training Squadron (MCD)
CCTS.......... Command Center Terminal System (MCD)
CCTS.......... Conseil Canadien sur le Tabagisme et la Santé [Canadian Council on Smoking and Health]
CCTS.......... Contour Check Template Set (MCD)
CCTSCH...... Combat Crew Training School [Air Force]
C Cts Chr .... County Courts Chronicle [1847-1920] [England] [A publication] (DLA)
CCTSIM....... Circuit Simulation [Electronics] (IAA)
C/CTSP .... Community/Corridor Traffic Safety Program
CCTSq......... Combat Crew Training Squadron [Air Force]
CCTT.......... Canadian Council of Technicians & Technologists [Conseil Canadien des Techniciens et Technologues] (AC)
CCTT.......... Close Combat Tactical Trainer
CCTU .... Committee of Corporate Telecommunications Users [An association] (EA)
CCTU .... Corporate Committee of Telecommunications Users (EA)
CCTUO........ Coordinating Committee of Trade Union Organizations [Ceylon]
CCTV.......... Carlton Communications Ltd. [NASDAQ symbol] (SAG)
CCTV.......... China Central Television [The national Chinese network]
CCTV.......... Closed-Circuit Television
CCTV.......... Closed Circuit Television (AIE)
CCTV.......... Command and Control Training Vehicles (MCD)
CCTV/LSD .... Closed Circuit Television / Large Screen Display (MHDI)
CCTVS......... Closed-Circuit Television System (IAA)
CCTVY .... Carton Communic ADS [NASDAQ symbol] (TTSB)
CCTW......... Combat Crew Training Wing [Air Force]
CCTWg........ Combat Crew Training Wing [Air Force] (AFM)
CCTWT........ Coupled Cavity Travelling Wave Tube (PDAA)
CCU .... Cabinet Casemakers' Union [British]
CCU .... Calcutta [India] [Airport symbol] (OAG)
CCU .... Camera Control Unit
CCU .... Canadian Commercial Bank [Toronto Stock Exchange symbol]
CCU .... Capillary Column Usage
CCU .... Cardiac Care Unit [Medicine]
CCU .... Caribbean Consumers Union [Antigua-Barbuda] (EAIO)
CCU .... Catalytic Cracking Unit [Chemical engineering]
CCU .... Catholic Central Union [Later, COF]
CCU .... Cedar City [Utah] [Seismograph station code, US Geological Survey] (SEIS)
CCU .... Central Computer Unit
CCU .... Central Control Unit
CCU .... Channel Control Unit (CMD)
CCU .... Chart Comparison Unit
CCU .... Cherry-Crandall Unit (MAE)
CCU .... Christian Computer Users [Defunct] (EA)

CCU .... Civil Contingency Unit [Cabinet Office] [British] (DI)
CCU .... Clear Channel Commun [NYSE symbol] (TTSB)
CCU .... Clear Channel, Inc. [NYSE symbol] (SAG)
CCU .... Cluster Control Unit
CCU .... Color Changing Unit [Medical technology]
CCU .... Commercial Casualty Underwriting [Insurance]
CCU .... Common Control Unit [Army] (AABC)
CCU .... Communication Control Unit
CCU .... Communications Coupling Unit (CET)
CCU .... Community Care Unit (MAE)
CCU .... Community College Unit [Office of Education]
CCU .... Component Control Unit (DNAB)
CCU .... Computer Control Unit
CCU .... Computer Coupling Unit (MCD)
CCU .... Concurrency Control Unit (NITA)
CCU .... Confederation of Canadian Unions
CCU .... Configuration Control Unit (MCD)
CCU .... Consultative Committee for Units [International Bureau of Weights and Measures]
CCU .... Containment Cooling Unit [Nuclear energy] (NRCH)
CCU .... Contaminant Collection Unit (OA)
CCU .... Control Communications Unit [Telecommunications] (ECII)
CCU .... Conversion Computer Unit
CCU .... Convolutional Coding Unit
CCU .... Cooker Control Unit
CCU .... Cornu Cervi Ustum [Burnt Hartshorn] [Pharmacy] (ROG)
CCU .... Coronary Care Unit [of a hospital]
CCU .... Correctional Custody Unit [Navy]
CCU .... Correspondence Control Unit [Environmental Protection Agency] (GFGA)
CCU .... Council on Christian Unity (EA)
CCU .... Coupling Control Unit
CCU .... Crew [or Crewman] Communications Umbilical [Apollo] [NASA]
CCU .... Critical Care Unit [Medicine]
CCU .... Croatian Catholic Union of the USA and Canada (EA)
CCU .... Cycle Control Unit [IRS]
CCU .... Czech Catholic Union (EA)
CCUA .... Catholic Central Union of America (EA)
CCUA .... Christian Computer Users Association (EA)
CCUA .... Credit Card Users of America [Beverly Hills, CA] (EA)
CCUAP........ Computerized Cable Upkeep Administrative Program [Bell System]
CCUBC........ Canadian Council of University Biology Chairs (AC)
C-CUBE .... C-CUBE Microsystems [Associated Press] (SAG)
CCUE .... Committee on Comparative Urban Economics (EA)
CCUGC........ Central Canada University Geological Conference
CCuH .... Hughes Aircraft Co., Culver City, CA [Library symbol Library of Congress] (LCLS)
CCuH-C .... Hughes Aircraft Co., Communications Division Library, Airport Site, Inglewood, CA [Library symbol Library of Congress] (LCLS)
CCuH-G .... Hughes Aircraft Co., Ground Systems Library, Fullerton, CA [Library symbol Library of Congress] (LCLS)
CCuH-M ...... Hughes Aircraft Co., Marketing Research Library, Airport Site, Inglewood, CA [Library symbol Library of Congress] (LCLS)
CCuH-R .... Hughes Aircraft Co., Research Laboratories Library, Malibu, CA [Library symbol Library of Congress] (LCLS)
CCuH-RC..... Hughes Aircraft Co., Santa Barbara Research Center, Santa Barbara, CA [Library symbol Library of Congress] (LCLS)
CCuH-S .... Hughes Aircraft Co., Semiconductor Division Library, Newport Beach, CA [Library symbol Library of Congress] (LCLS)
CCUL .... California Credit Union League (SRA)
CCUL .... Colorado Credit Union League (SRA)
CCUL .... Connecticut Credit Union League (SRA)
CCUM .... Catholic Committee on Urban Ministry (EA)
CCuM......... Metro-Goldwyn-Mayer, Research Department, Culver City, CA [Library symbol Library of Congress] (LCLS)
CCUML .... Comite Comunista Unificado Marxista-Leninista [Peru] [Political party] (EY)
CCUN .... Church Center for the United Nations (EA)
CCUN .... Collegiate Council for the United Nations (EA)
CCUP .... Colpocystourethropexy [Medicine]
CCuP .... Pacific Semiconductors, Inc., Culver City, CA [Library symbol Library of Congress] (LCLS)
CCUR .... Concurrent Computer [NASDAQ symbol] (TTSB)
CCUR .... Concurrent Computer Corp. [NASDAQ symbol] (NQ)
CCURR........ Canadian Council on Urban and Regional Research (EA)
CCUS .... Chamber of Commerce of the United States (EA)
CCUS .... Circuit Court of the United States (DLA)
CCUS .... Cleared Customs (FAAC)
CCUS .... Concerned Citizens for Universal Service [Defunct] (EA)
CCUSA .... Catholic Charities USA (EA)
CCUU .... Compania Cervecerias Unides [NASDAQ symbol] (SAG)
CCUUY .... Compania Cervecerias ADS [NASDAQ symbol] (TTSB)
CCV............ Canada Club of Victoria [Australia]
CCV............ Canadian Cariboo Resources Ltd. [Vancouver Stock Exchange symbol]
CCV............ Cape Charles, VA [Location identifier FAA] (FAAL)
CCV............ Cash Collection Voucher
CCV............ CCNU [Lomustine], Cyclophosphamide, Vincristine [Antineoplastic drug regimen] (DAVI)
CCV............ Chamber Coolant Valve (NASA)
CCV............ Channel Catfish Virus
CCV............ Chara Corallina Virus [Plant pathology]
CCV............ Chosen Coefficient of Variation [Statistics]
CCV............ Clark College, Library, Vancouver, WA [OCLC symbol] (OCLC)
CCV............ Close Combat Vehicle [Military]

CCV............	Clyde Cablevision [*Commercial firm*] [*British*] (NITA)
CCV............	Coal Corporation of Victoria [*Australia Commercial firm*]
CCV............	Coconut Cadang-Cadang Viroid [*Also, CCCV*]
CCV............	Code Converter (IAA)
CCV............	Color Contrast Value
CCV............	Combat Command V
CCV............	Composite Concept Vehicle
CCV............	Computer-Controlled Vehicle [*Public transit systems*]
CCV............	Conductivity Cell Volume [*Hematology*]
CCV............	Congregatio a Sacro Corde Jesu [*Congregation of the Priests of the Sacred Heart*] [*Roman Catholic religious order*]
CCV............	Continuing Calibration Verification [*Laboratory analysis*]
CCV............	Control Configured Vehicle [*Air Force*]
CCV............	Coolant Control Valve
CCV............	Coupe Concept Vehicle [*Austin Rover*]
CCV............	Craft Council of Victoria [*Australia*]
CCV............	Craig Cove [*Vanuatu*] [*Airport symbol*] (OAG)
CCVA	Chamber Coolant Valve Actuator (MCD)
CCVA	Citizens Committee for Victim Assistance (EA)
CCV-AV	CCNU [*Lomustine*], Cyclophosphamide, Vincristine, Alternating with Adriamycin, Vincristine [*Antineoplastic drug regimen*]
CCVB	CCNU [*Lomustine*], Cyclophosphamide, Vincristine, Bleomycin [*Antineoplastic drug regimen*] (DAVI)
CCVCS	Command and Control Voice Communications System [*Defense Supply Agency*]
CCVD	Cardiovascular Dynamics, Inc. [*NASDAQ symbol*] (SAG)
CCVD	Chronic Cerebrovascular Disease [*Medicine*] (DMAA)
CCVD	Combustion Chemical Vapor Deposition
CCVI............	Congregatio Caritatis Verbi Incarnati [*Congregation of the Sisters of Charity of the Incarnate Word*] [*Roman Catholic religious order*]
CCVI............	Sisters of Charity of Incarnate Word, Houston, TX (TOCD)
CCVID	Close Combat Vehicle Integration Diagnostic [*Army*] (RDA)
CCVL	Close Combat Vehicle - Light [*Army*]
CCVL	Configuration Control Verification List (MCD)
CCVPP	CCNU [*Lomustine*], Cyclophosphamide, Vincristine, Procarbazine, Prednisone [*Antineoplastic drug regimen*]
CCVRE	Churches' Committee for Voter Registration-Education (EA)
CCVS	COBOL [*Common Business-Oriented Language*] Compiler Validation System [*Computer science*]
CCVS	Combustion Control by Vortex Stratification [*Automotive engine design*]
CCVS	Current-Controlled Voltage Source (IEEE)
CCVT	Canadian Centre for Victims of Torture [*Formerly, Canadian Centre for Investigation & Prevention of Torture*] (AC)
CCVT	Coupling Capacitor Voltage Transformer
CCVV	Clarissimi Viri [*Illustrious Men*] [*Latin*] (BARN)
CCVV	Cyclophosphamide, CCNU [*Lomustine*] VP-16, Vincristine [*Antineoplastic drug regimen*] (DAVI)
CCVVP	Cyclophosphamide, CCNU [*Lomustine*], VP-16, Vincristine, Cisplatin [*Antineoplastic drug regimen*] (DAVI)
CCW............	Caldwell College for Women [*New Jersey*]
CCW............	Canadian Curtiss-Wright Ltd. [*Toronto Stock Exchange symbol*]
CCW............	Carbon Copy for Windows [*Symantec Corp.*] (PCM)
CCW............	Carmelite Community of the Word (TOCD)
CCW............	Carrying Concealed Weapon [*Police term*]
CCW............	Channel Command [*or Control*] Word [*Computer science*]
CCW............	Charles City Western Railway Co. [*AAR code*]
CCW............	Child Care Worker
CCW............	Children's Computer Workshop
CCW............	Circulation Control Wing (MCD)
CCW............	Close Combat Weapon System [*Army*] (MCD)
CCW............	Closed Cooling Water [*Nuclear energy*] (NRCH)
CCW............	Command Control and Weather (SAA)
CCW............	Command Control Word (IAA)
CCW............	Component Cooling Water [*Nuclear energy*] (NRCH)
CCW............	Condenser Circulating Water [*Nuclear energy*] (NRCH)
CCW............	Condenser Cooling Water [*Nuclear energy*] (NRCH)
CCW............	Constituent Concentrations in the Waste [*Environmental Protection Agency*]
CCW............	Continuous Composite Write (CDE)
CCW............	Cosmetic Career Women [*Later, CEW*]
CCW............	Counterclockwise
ccw	Counterclockwise (IDOE)
CCW............	Critical Care Workstation [*Medicine*] (DMAA)
CCW............	Curriculum Council for Wales (AIE)
CCW............	International Committee on Chemical Warfare
CCW............	United Church of Christ Coordinating Center for Women in Church and Society (EA)
CCWA	Catholic Construction Workers of America (EA)
CCWA	Conference of Churches of Western Australia [*Australia*]
CCWAA	Collegiate Council of Women's Athletic Administrators (EA)
CCWAD	Conference of Church Workers Among the Deaf [*Later, ECD*] (EA)
CCWBAD	Counterclockwise Bottom Angular Down (OA)
CCWBAU	Counterclockwise Bottom Angular Up (OA)
CCWBH	Counterclockwise Bottom Horizontal (OA)
CCWC	Cambodian Community Welfare Centre [*Australia*]
CCWC	Committee of Catholics Who Care (EA)
CCW(CD)	International Committee on Chemical Warfare, Crop Destruction
CCWCP	Coordinating Committee for the World Climate Program [*Marine science*] (OSRA)
CCWDB	Counterclockwise Down Blast (OA)
CCWE.........	Constituent Concentration in a Waste Extract
CCWEAC	Co-Operative, Career & Work Education Association of Canada [*Association Canadienne pour l'Alternance Travail-Etudes*] [*Also, National Co-Operative Education Centre*] (AC)

CCWHP........	Coordinating Committee on Women in the Historical Profession [*Later, CCWHP/CGWH*] (EA)
CCWHP/CGWH...	Coordinating Committee on Women in the Historical Profession/ Conference Group onWomen's History (EA)
CCWL..........	Catholic Council on Working Life (EA)
CCWM	Citizens' Clearinghouse on Waste Management (AC)
CCWO	Command Center Watch Officer (MCD)
CCWO	Commercial Communications Work Order [*Air Force*]
CCWO	Cryptocenter Watch Officer
CCWRH	Canvas-Covered Wire-Rope Handrail [*Aerospace*] (MSA)
CC WR HDR..	Canvas-Covered Wire-Rope Handrail [*Aerospace*] (AAG)
CCWS	Chief of the Chemical Warfare Service [*World War II*]
CCWS	Close Combat Weapon System [*Marine Corps*]
CCWS	Closed Cooling Water System [*Nuclear energy*] (NRCH)
CCWS	Component Cooling Water System [*Nuclear energy*] (NRCH)
CCWTAD......	Counterclockwise Top Angular Down (OA)
CCWTAU......	Counterclockwise Top Angular Up (OA)
CCWTH	Counterclockwise Top Horizontal (OA)
CCWUB.......	Counterclockwise Up Blast (OA)
CCWW	Cable & Co. Worldwide, Inc. [*NASDAQ symbol*] (SAG)
CCX............	Caceres [*Brazil*] [*Airport symbol*] (OAG)
CCX............	Cancom Industries, Inc. [*Vancouver Stock Exchange symbol*]
CCX............	Chapman College Library, Orange, CA [*OCLC symbol*] (OCLC)
CCX............	Complication [*Medicine*] (DAVI)
CCX............	Corporate Planning Office [*AFSC*]
CCX............	Customer Communications Exchange [*Bell System*]
CCX............	Indian Ocean Airlines [*Australia ICAO designator*] (FAAC)
CCXD	Computer-Controlled X-Ray Diffractometer
CCY............	Camping Club Youth [*British*]
CCY............	Charles City, IA [*Location identifier FAA*] (FAAL)
CCY............	Chief Communications Yeoman [*British military*] (DMA)
CCY............	Coalition for Children and Youth [*American Occupational Therapy Association*]
CCY............	Columbia College Library, Columbia, CA [*OCLC symbol*] (OCLC)
CCyC	Cypress Junior College, Cypress, CA [*Library symbol Library of Congress*] (LCLS)
CCYDA	Canadian Child and Youth Drama Association
CCYUA	Catholic Central Youth Union of America (EA)
CCZ............	Chub Cay [*Bahamas*] [*Airport symbol*] (OAG)
CCZ............	Coastal Confluence Zone [*Aviation*] (DA)
CCZ............	Command and Control Zone (SSD)
CCZ............	Pittsburgh, PA [*Location identifier FAA*] (FAAL)
CCZA	Canadian Coastal Zone Atlantic
CCZP	Canadian Coastal Zone Pacific
CD..............	Application for Certiorari Denied [*Legal term*] (DLA)
CD..............	Cable Duct (MSA)
CD..............	Cabling Data
CD..............	Cadaver Donor [*Medicine*]
Cd..............	Cadmium [*Chemical element*]
CD..............	Caesarean Delivered [*Medicine*]
CD..............	Calendar Day (AFM)
CD..............	Calibration Device (KSC)
CD..............	Call Deflection [*Telecommunications*] (DOM)
CD..............	Call Detector (IAA)
CD..............	Call Director (SAA)
CD..............	Call Disconnect [*Telecommunications*] (ACRL)
CD..............	Call Dispatch (IAA)
CD..............	Calling Device [*Telecommunications*]
CD..............	Calls per Day (IAA)
CD..............	Camouflage Detection [*Often, in regard to a special photographic film, as, "CD film"*] [*Military*]
CD..............	Campomelic Dysplasia [*Medicine*]
CD..............	Canadian Dollar [*Monetary unit*]
CD..............	Canadian Forces Decoration
CD..............	Cancer Dose (NUCP)
cd..............	Candela [*Formerly, Candlepower*] [*Symbol SI unit of luminous intensity*]
CD..............	Candle [*Illumination*]
CD..............	Canine Distemper [*Veterinary medicine*]
CD..............	Canine Dose [*Veterinary medicine*]
CD..............	Capabilities Data (SAA)
CD..............	Capacitative Discharge [*Voltage source*]
CD..............	Capacitor Diode
CD..............	Capacitor Discharge [*Automotive engineering*]
CD..............	Captain of the Dockyard [*Obsolete British*]
CD..............	Carbonate Dehydratase [*An enzyme*] (MAE)
CD..............	Card (MSA)
cd..............	Card (VRA)
CD..............	Card Deck (IAA)
CD..............	Card Distribution
CD..............	Car Deck
CD..............	Cardiac Disease [*Medicine*]
CD..............	Cardiac Dullness [*Physiology*]
CD..............	Cardinal Airlines (MHDB)
CD..............	Cardiovascular Deconditioning [*Medicine*] (MEDA)
CD..............	Cardiovascular Disease [*Medicine*]
CD..............	Career Development (WYGK)
CD..............	Carrel-Dakin [*Fluid*]
CD..............	Carried Down [*Bookkeeping*]
CD..............	Carrier Detect [*Electronics*] (ECII)
CD..............	Carrier Detector (BUR)
C/D.............	Cash Against Documents [*Sales*] (ADA)
CD..............	Cash Discount [*Sales*]
cd..............	Cash Discount (WDMC)
CD..............	Cash Dispenser [*Banking*] (BUR)

CD	Casting Division
CD	Castleman's Disease [*Oncology*]
CD	Casualty Department [*British police*]
CD	Catalogued
C-D	Catalytic-Dow (KSC)
CD	Cathedral
CD	Caudal [*Anatomy*]
cd	Caudal [*Medicine*] (DMAA)
CD	Cavalry Division [*Army*]
CD	Center Director [*John F. Kennedy Space Center Directorate*] [*NASA*] (NASA)
CD	Center Distance (MSA)
CD	Central Disc [*of flowers*] [*Botany*]
CD	Central District
CD	Centre Democratique [*Democratic Center*] [*Later, Center of Social Democrats*] [*France*] [*Political party*] (PPE)
CD	Centrum-Demokraterne [*Center Democrats*] [*Denmark Political party*] (PPE)
CD	Century Dictionary [*A publication*] (ROG)
CD	Century Edition of the American Digest System (West) [*A publication*] (DLA)
C/D	Certificate of Damage [*Tea trade*] (ROG)
C/D	Certificate of Delivery
CD	Certificate of Deposit [*Banking*]
CD	Certificate of Destruction (AFM)
CD	Certificate of Disposal (ADA)
CD	Certificate of Distribution
CD	Certification Data (AFIT)
CD	Certification Division [*Environmental Protection Agency*] (GFGA)
CD	Cesarean-Delivered [*Obstetrics*] (MAE)
cd	Chad [*MARC country of publication code Library of Congress*] (LCCP)
C/D	Chaff/Delivery (SAA)
CD	Chain Delivery [*Press*] (DGA)
CD	Chaining Data [*Computer science*] (IAA)
CD	Chancery Division
CD	Change Diameter (MCD)
CD	Change Directive (AAG)
CD	Change Directory [*Computer science*]
CD	Channel Down [*Biochemistry*] (DAVI)
CD	Chapter Director
CD	Charge/Discharge (IAA)
CD	Cheatham Dam [*TVA*]
CD	Check Correct (ECII)
CD	Check Digit [*IRS*]
CD	Chemically Diabetic [*Endocrinology*]
CD	Chemiluminescence Depletion [*Chemical kinetics*]
CD	Chief Draftsman (MCD)
CD	Chief of Detectives
CD	Chief of Division
CD	Childhood Disease (HGAA)
CD	Chilldown [*NASA*] (KSC)
CD	Chiroptical Discrimination [*Steroisomeric chemistry*]
CD	Chirp Duration [*Entomology*]
CD	Chlordan [*or Chlordane*] [*Insecticide*]
CD	Chlordecone (Kepone) [*Pesticide*]
CD	Chord
CD	Christian Democrats [*European political movement*] (ECON)
CD	Christian Dior [*Couturier*]
CD	Christopher Davies [*Publisher*] [*British*]
CD	Christus Dominus [*Decree on the Bishops' Pastoral Office in the Church*] [*Vatican II document*]
C/d	Cigarettes per Day [*Medicine*]
CD	Circuit Decisions [*A publication*] (DLA)
CD	Circuit Description (MSA)
CD	Circuit Diagrams
CD	Circular Dichroism [*Optics*]
CD	Circular Dispersion
CD	Citizen Diplomacy (EA)
CD	Civil Defense
CD	Civil Disobedience
CD	Claims, Defense (CAAL)
CD	Classification of Defects (AAG)
CD	Claude Dornier [*German aircraft designer, 1884-1969*]
CD	Clearance Diving [*Navy British*]
CD	[*The*] Clearinghouse Directory [*A publication*]
CD	Clock Driver
CD	Close Doublet (SAA)
CD	Closing Date
CD	Clothes Drier
CD	Club Delahaye [*An association France*] (EAIO)
CD	Cluster Designation [*Immunology*]
CD	Cluster of Differentiation [*Immunology*]
CD	Clutch Drive [*on a ship*] (DS)
CD	Coalicion del Centro Democratico [*Nicaragua*] [*Political party*] (EY)
CD	Coalicion Democratica [*Democratic Coalition*] [*Spain Political party*] (PPE)
CD	Coastal Defense RADAR (MUGU)
CD	Coast Defense
Cd	Coccygeal [*Anatomy*] (DAVI)
CD	Code (MCD)
CD	Code Definition
D	Coden [*Online database field identifier*]
D	Coefficient of Drag (MCD)
	Coherent Detector [*Electronics*] (OA)

CD	Coin Dimple
CD	Cold-Drawn [*Metal*]
CD	Colla Destra [*With the Right Hand*] [*Music*]
CD	College Discovery [*Educational project for disadvantaged youngsters*] (EA)
CD	Collision Detect [*Computer science*]
CD	Collision Detection [*Telecommunications*] (ACRL)
CD	Colonial Dames [*An association*] (IIA)
CD	Color Developer System [*Canon, Inc.*]
CD	Combat Development
CD	Combination Die (MCD)
CD	Combination Drug
CD	Command
CD	Command Decoder
C/D	Command Destruct (AAG)
CD	Commander of the Order of Distinction [*Jamaica*]
Cd	Command Papers [*A publication*] (DLA)
CD	Commerce Department
CD	Commercial Dock [*Shipping*]
CD	Commission du Danube [*Danube Commission - DC*] (EAIO)
CD	Commissioned
CD	Commissioner's Decisions [*US Patent and Trademark Office*]
CD	Committee Draft [*Telecommunications*] (OSI)
CD	Common Denominator (AAG)
CD	Common Digitizer [*FAA*]
CD	Common Duct [*Medicine*]
CD	Communicable Disease [*or a patient with such a disease*] [*Medicine*]
CD	Communicable Disease Report [*A publication*]
CD	Communicative Disorders
CD	Community Development
CD	Compact Design [*Automotive engineering*]
CD	Compact Disk [*Audio/video technology*] [*Philips*]
CD	Compact Disk [*Audio/Video Technology*] [*Philips*] (ACRL)
CD	Companion Dog [*Dog show term*]
CD	Compass Department [*British military*] (DMA)
CD	Competitive Design
CD	Competitive Development
CD	Complaint Docket [*Legal term*] (DLA)
CD	Complementary Distribution [*Linguistics*]
C/D	Complete Deal [*Coupon redemption*]
CD	Complete Drawing [*Animation*] (NTCM)
CD	Completely Denatured
CD	Compliance Division [*Environmental Protection Agency*] (GFGA)
CD	Complicated Delivery [*Obstetrics*]
CD	Computer-Controlled Dampers [*Automotive suspension feature*]
CD	Comyn's Digest of the Laws of England [*1762-1882*] [*A publication*] (ILCA)
CD	Concealment Device [*Criminology*] (LAIN)
CD	Concept Definition (MCD)
CD	Concept Development
CD	Concept to Division [*Automotive project management*]
CD	Condemned (WGA)
CD	Condition [*Automotive advertising*]
CD	Condition of Detail
cd	Conductance
CD	Conductivity Detector
CD	Conference on Disarmament
CD	Confessor, Doctor [*Ecclesiastical*] (ROG)
CD	Confidential Document [*Navy*]
CD	Configuration Definition
CD	Congressional District
CD	Conjugata Diagonalis [*Pelvic measurement*] [*Anatomy*]
CD	Connecting Device (IAA)
CD	Conning Director [*Navy*]
CD	Consanguineous Donor [*Medicine*]
CD	Constant Depression [*Automotive engineering*]
CD	Constant Drainage (WGA)
CD	Constrained Deconvolution Technique [*Computer science*]
CD	Construction Defect
CD	Constructive Dilemma [*Rule of inference*] [*Logic*]
CD	Consular Declaration
CD	Contact Dermatitis [*Medicine*]
CD	Contagious Diseases
CD	Continued Development
CD	Continuous Duty (IAA)
CD	Contract Definition [*Military*]
CD	Contract Demonstration [*Army*] (AFIT)
CD	Contract Design
CD	Control Data
CD	Control Diet
C/D	Control/Display Ratio [*Quality control*]
CD	Controlled Dissemination (MCD)
CD	Controlled Drug
CD	Control Rod Drive [*Nuclear energy*] (IEEE)
C-D	CONVAIR [*Consolidated-Vultee Aircraft Corp.*] Daingerfield [*Later, General Dynamics/Daingerfield*] (AAG)
CD	Conventional District [*Church of England*]
CD	Convergencia Democratica [*Democratic Convergence*] [*El Salvador*] [*Political party*] (EY)
CD	Converging-Diverging (MCD)
CD	Convulsive Disorder [*Medicine*]
CD	Convulsive Dose [*Medicine*]
C/D	Cooldown [*Nuclear energy*] (NRCH)
CD	Cooperation for Development [*British*] (EAIO)

CD.............. Coordinacion Democratica [*Democratic Coordination*] [*Spain Political party*] (PPE)
CD.............. Coordinadora Democratica [*Democratic Coordinating Board*] [*Nicaragua*] (PPW)
CD.............. Coordinating Draft [*of field manuals*] [*Military*] (INF)
CD.............. Coordination Document
CD.............. Coordination Drawing
CD.............. Cord
CD.............. Cordoba Durchmusterung [*Star chart*]
CD.............. Corneal Dystrophy [*Medicine*] (DMAA)
CD.............. Corollary Discharge Neuron [*Neurophysiology*]
CD.............. Corps Diplomatique [*Diplomatic Corps*]
C/D.............. Correction/Discrepancy (DNAB)
CD.............. Cosmo Dog
CD.............. Could
CD.............. Council Deputies (NATG)
CD.............. Council of Deliberation [*Freemasonry*] (ROG)
CD.............. Countdown [*Aerospace*] (AAG)
CD.............. Countdown [*Credit card*] [*British*]
C/D.............. Count Down
CD.............. Counting Device
CD.............. Court Druggist [*Foresters*] [*British*] (ROG)
CD.............. Crash Damage (MCD)
CD.............. Creative Director (DOAD)
CD.............. Criminal Deportee (ADA)
CD.............. Crohn's Disease [*Gastroenterology*] (DAVI)
CD.............. Cross Direction
CD.............. Crossed Diagonal [*Medicine*] (DMAA)
CD.............. Crossland Industries Corp. [*Vancouver Stock Exchange symbol*]
CD.............. Crusade for Decency (EA)
CD.............. Cryogenic Distillation (MCD)
CD.............. Crystal Diode
CD.............. Crystal Driver
CD.............. Cultural Deprivation [*Psychology*] (AEBS)
CD.............. Cultural Disadvantage
CD.............. Cum Dividendo [*With Dividend*] [*Latin Stock exchange term*]
C/D.............. Cup to Disk [*Ratio*] [*Opthalmology*] (DAVI)
CD.............. Curative Dose [*Medicine*]
CD.............. Current Density
CD.............. Current Digest [*A publication*]
CD.............. Current Discharge (IAA)
CD.............. Current Driver
CD.............. Customs Court Decisions [*A publication*] (DLA)
CD.............. Customs Decisions [*Department of the Treasury*] [*A publication*] (DLA)
C/D.............. Customs Declaration
CD.............. Cutaneous Discrimination [*Psychometric test*]
CD.............. Cutdown [*Cardiovascular and surgery*] (DAVI)
CD.............. Cyclodextrin [*Organic chemistry*]
CD.............. Cystic Duct [*Medicine*]
CD.............. Cytochalasin D [*Biochemistry*]
CD.............. Cytotoxic Dose [*Toxicology*]
CD.............. Department of Productivity [*Government Aircraft Factory*] [*Australia ICAO aircraft manufacturer identifier*] (ICAO)
Cd................ Drag Coefficient [*Automotive engineering*]
CD.............. Driver [*Navy rating*] (MUGU)
Cd................ Drug Coefficient [*Pharmacology*] (DAVI)
CD.............. Lewis D. and John J. Gilbert, Corporate Democracy (EA)
CD.............. Ohio Circuit Decisions [*A publication*] (DLA)
CD.............. Trans-Provincial Airlines [*ICAO designator*] (AD)
CD/50.......... Median Curative Dose [*Medicine*]
CDA.............. Aerocardal [*Chile*] [*FAA designator*] (FAAC)
CDA.............. California Dental Association (SRA)
CDA.............. California Dietetic Association (SRA)
CDA.............. California Distributors Association (SRA)
CDA.............. Canada
CDA.............. Canadian Dental Association
CDA.............. Canadian Department of Agriculture
CDA.............. Canadian Dermatology Association (EAIO)
CDA.............. Canadian Diabetic Association
CDA.............. Canadian Dietetic Association
CDA.............. Canadian Drilling Association [*Also, Canadian Diamond Drilling Association*] (AC)
CDA.............. Canadian Transtect Industries [*Vancouver Stock Exchange symbol*]
CDA.............. Cape Douglas [*Alaska*] [*Seismograph station code, US Geological Survey*] (SEIS)
CDA.............. Carbide Diamond Abrasive (IAA)
CDA.............. Casualty and Damage Assessment (MCD)
CDA.............. Catalog Data Activity [*Army*]
CDA.............. Catalog Data Agency (MCD)
CDA.............. Catholic Daughters of the Americas (EA)
CDA.............. Center for Democratic Alternatives [*Defunct*] (EA)
CDA.............. Central Design Activity (MCD)
CDA.............. Central Directed Audit [*Military*]
CDA.............. Centre de Documentation Astrologique (AC)
CDA.............. Ceramics Distributors of America (EA)
CDA.............. Certified Dental Assistant
CDA.............. Cesium Dihydrogen Arsenate
CDA.............. Chemists' Defence Association [*British*] (BI)
CDA.............. Chenodeoxycholic Acid [*Also, CDC, CDCA, CHENIC*] [*Biochemistry*]
CDA.............. Child Development Associate [*National certificate*] (OICC)
CDA.............. Chlorodeoxyadenosine [*Biochemistry*]
CDA.............. Christen Democratisch Appel [*Christian Democratic Appeal*] [*Netherlands Political party*] (PPW)

CDA.............. Christian Democratic Action for Social Justice [*Namibia*] [*Political party*] (EY)
CDA.............. Ciliary Dyskinesia Activity (PDAA)
CDA.............. Circuit Distribution Assembly [*Ground Communications Facility, NASA*]
CDA.............. City Demonstration Agency
CDA.............. Civic Democratic Alliance [*Former Czechoslovakia*] [*Political party*] (EY)
CDA.............. Civil Defense Agency
CDA.............. Classic Desk Accessories [*Apple Computer, Inc.*] [*Utility program*] [*Computer science*]
CDA.............. Coefficient of Drag-Area
CDA.............. Coin Detection and Announcement [*Telecommunications*] (TEL)
CDA.............. College Diploma in Agriculture [*British*] (DI)
CDA.............. Colonial Dames of America (EA)
CDA.............. Colorado Dental Association (SRA)
CDA.............. Combined Development Agency [*Anglo-American uranium procurement*]
CDA.............. Command and Data Acquisition (NASA)
CDA.............. Commercial Development Association (EA)
CDA.............. Common Dollar Accounting (ADA)
CDA.............. Communications Decency Act
CDA.............. Communications Decency Act
CDA.............. Communications Distribution Amplifier (MCD)
CDA.............. Community Development Administration [*HUD*]
CDA.............. Comparative Distribution Analysis [*Marketing*] (WDMC)
CDA.............. Completely Denatured Alcohol
CDA.............. Compound Department Architecture [*Digital Equipment Corp.*] [*Computer science*]
CDA.............. Compound Document Architecture
CDA.............. Comprehensive Dissertation Abstracts [*University Microfilms International*] [*Information service or system*]
CDA.............. Computer Dealers Association [*Later, CDLA*]
CDA.............. Computer Directions Advisors, Inc. [*Information service or system*] (IID)
CDA.............. Concept Development Associates, Inc. [*Information service or system*] (IID)
CDA.............. Conference of Defence Associations Institute [*Institut du Congres des Associations de la Defense*] (AC)
CDA.............. Configuration Design Audit (MCD)
CDA.............. Congenital Dyserythropoietic Anemia [*Hematology*]
CDA.............. Constant Dollar Accounting (ADA)
CDA.............. Contagious Diseases Act [*British*]
CDA.............. Containment Depressurization Actuation [*Nuclear energy*] (NRCH)
CDA.............. Containment Depressurization Alarm [*Nuclear energy*] (IEEE)
CDA.............. Continuous-Descent Approach (PDAA)
CDA.............. Contract Disputes Act of 1978 (AAGC)
CDA.............. Controlled Droplet Application (PDAA)
CDA.............. Convolutional Decoder Assembly
CDA.............. Cool Dehumidified Air (PDAA)
CDA.............. Copier Dealers Association (EA)
CDA.............. Copper Development Association (EA)
CDA.............. Cordiant ADS [*NYSE symbol*] (TTSB)
CDA.............. Cordiant PLC [*NYSE symbol*] (SAG)
CDA.............. Core Disruptive Accident [*Nuclear energy*] (NRCH)
CDA.............. Corporacion Dominicana de Aviacion [*Dominican Aviation Corporation*] [*Airline Dominican Republic*]
C d'A.......... Corps d'Afrique
CDA.............. Cost Driver Attribute
CDA.............. Council for Democracy in the Americas [*Defunct*] (EA)
CDA.............. Craft Digital Assistant [*Computer science*]
CDA.............. Critical Design Audit (MCD)
CDA.............. National Society of Colonial Dames of America (EA)
CDA.............. Southwest Regional Library Service System, Durango, CO [*OCLC symbol*] (OCLC)
CDAA.......... California District Attorneys Association (SRA)
CDAA.......... Canadian Dental Assistants Association (AC)
CDAA.......... Central Data Analysis Area (KSC)
CDAA.......... Chlorodiallylacetamide [*Herbicide*]
CDAA.......... Circularly Disposed Antenna Array [*Radio receiver*]
CDAAA........ Committee to Defend America by Aiding the Allies [*Active prior to US entry into World War II*]
CDAB.......... Crime and Delinquency Abstracts [*A publication*]
CDABO........ College of Diplomates of the American Board of Orthodontics (EA)
CDAC.......... California Date Administrative Committee (EA)
CDAC.......... Cetyldimethylbenzylammonium Chloride [*A surfactant*]
CDAC.......... Chicago Dance Arts Coalition
CDAC.......... Child Development Associate Consortium [*CDANCP*] [*Superseded by*] (EA)
CDAC.......... Civil Defense Advisory Council
CDAC.......... Clinical Data Abstraction Center [*Medicine*] (DMAA)
CDACL........ Carrer Development and Assessment Center for Librarians (EDAC)
CDAD.......... Clostridium Difficile-Associated Diarrhea [*Medicine*]
CDAD.......... Compact Digital Audio Disk (ADA)
CDAD.......... Computer Dual Access Driver (MCD)
CDAE.......... Civil Defense Adult Education [*Program*]
CDAEP........ Civil Defense Adult Education Program
CDAF.......... Configuration Development of Advanced Fighters [*Military*] (MCD)
CDAI.......... Crohn's Disease Activity Index [*Medicine*]
CDALB........ Concise Dictionary of American Literary Biography [*A publication*]
CDANC........ Committee for the Development of Art in Negro Colleges [*Later, CAA*]
CDANCP...... Child Development Associate National Credentialing Program (EA)
CD & CC...... Central Data and Cataloging Center (AFM)
CD & F........ Class Determination and Finding

CD & ME .... Combat Developments and Material Evaluation [*Program*] [*Army*]
CD & SC ..... Central Data and Switching Center [*NASA*] (KSC)
CD & SC ..... Communications, Distribution, and Switching Center [*NASA*] (KSC)
CDAP .... Civil Damage Assessment Program [*Army*] (AABC)
CDAP .... Climatic Data Analysis Program
CDAP .... Continuous Distending Airway Pressure [*Medicine*] (DMAA)
CDAPC .... Comprehensive Drug Abuse Prevention and Control Act (BARN)
CDAPSO ...... Canadian Data Processing Service Organisation (PDAA)
CDAS .... Catapult Data Acquisition System (DNAB)
CDAS .... Central Data Acquisition System
CDAS .... Centre for Developing-Area Studies [*McGill University*] [*Canada*] (IRC)
CDAS .... Civil Defense Ambulance Service (WDAA)
CDAS .... Class D Airspace [*Aviation*] (FAAC)
CDAS .... Command and Data Acquisition Station [*Aerospace*]
CD/AT .... Contrast Density/Appearance Time [*of images on a film*]
CDAT .... Control Data Systems [*NASDAQ symbol*] (SAG)
CDATA .... Census Data [*Database*]
CDATS .... Chemical Detection and Alarm Training Simulator (MCD)
CDAW .... Controlled Data Analysis Workshops [*Magnetospheric physics*]
CDB .... California Distance Table Bureau, San Francisco CA [*STAC*]
CDB .... Caliper Disk Brake
CDB .... Canberra Development Board [*Australia*]
CDB .... Capacitance Decode Box
CDB .... Cardinal Mineral Corp. Ltd. [*Vancouver Stock Exchange symbol*]
CDB .... Caribbean Development Bank [*St. Michael, Barbados*]
CDB .... Cast Double Base
CDB .... Center for Drugs and Biologics [*FDA*]
CDB .... Central Data Bank
CDB .... Central Data Buffer [*Computer science*] (MCD)
CDB .... Centralized Data Base (RDA)
CDB .... Charlie Daniels Band
CDB .... Childhood Disability Benefits [*Social Security Administration*] (OICC)
CDB .... City Development Board (OICC)
CDB .... Coal Data Base [*International Energy Agency*] [*British*] (NITA)
CDB .... Cognitive Diagnostic Battery [*Test*]
CDB .... Cold Bay [*Alaska*] [*Airport symbol*] (OAG)
CDB .... Cold Bay, AK [*Location identifier FAA*] (FAAL)
CDB .... Combat Development Branch
CDB .... Command Database (MCD)
CDB .... Command Data Buffer [*Air Force*] (MCD)
CdB .... Commanderie de Bordeaux (EA)
CDB .... Common Database [*Computer science*] (CAAL)
CDB .... Common Data Bus [*Computer science*]
CDB .... Community Development Bank
CDB .... Composite Double-Base [*Propellant*]
CDB .... Connector Data Base [*Aviation*]
CDB .... Consolidated Data Base (PDAA)
CDB .... Corporate Database [*Computer science*]
CDB .... Current Data BIT [*Binary Digit*] [*Computer science*]
CDB .... Cyclohexyldithiobenzothiazole [*Organic chemistry*]
CDBA .... Central Database Administrator (GFGA)
CDBA .... Clearance Diver's Breathing Apparatus
CDBA .... Commonwealth Development Bank of Australia
CDBA .... Containment Design Basis Accident [*Nuclear energy*] (NRCH)
CDBAB .... California Dry Bean Advisory Board (EA)
CDBD .... Cardboard (ADA)
cdbd .... Cardboard (VRA)
CDBD .... Common Database Design
CDBF .... Chlorinated Dibenzofuran [*Organic chemistry*] (FFDE)
CDBFR .... Command Data Buffer [*Air Force*] (MCD)
CDBFR .... Common Data Buffer (NASA)
CDBG .... Community Development Block Grant [*HUD*]
CDBI .... Consultants Directory for Business and Industry [*A publication*]
CDBI .... Cost Data Bank Index
CDBMS .... Cost Data Base Management System [*Air Force*]
CDBN .... Column-Digit Binary Network
CdBP .... Cadmium Binding Protein
CDBP .... Chlorodihydroxybenzopyranone [*Organic chemistry*]
CDBRA .... Canadian Deafblind & Rubella Association [*Association Canadienne de la Surdi-Cecite et de la Rubeole*] (AC)
CD/BRAC ..... Carmen Division of the Brotherhood of Railway, Airline and Steamship Clerks, Freight Handlers, Express and Station Employes (EA)
CDBS .... Central Data Base Server (DOMA)
CDBS .... Central Database System (DA)
CDBS .... Cost Data Bank System (AFIT)
CDC .... Cahiers de Droit Compare [*A publication*] (ILCA)
CDC .... Cairo Documents of the Damascus Covenanters [*A publication*] (BJA)
CDC .... Calculated Date of Confinement [*Obstetrics*] (DAVI)
CDC .... California Debris Commission [*Army*]
CDC .... California Defense Counsel (SRA)
CDC .... Call Address Code [*Telecommunications*] (ECII)
CDC .... Call Directing Character (IAA)
CDC .... Call Directing Code
CDC .... Calories Don't Count [*Title of a 1961 book by Dr. Herman Taller; initialism referred to the diet and diet capsules promoted by the book*]
CDC .... Canada Development Corp. [*Toronto Stock Exchange symbol - Vancouver Stock Exchange symbol*]
CDC .... Canada Road [*California*] [*Seismograph station code, US Geological Survey*] (SEIS)
CDC .... Canadian Dairy Commission
CDC .... Cancer Detection Centre [*British*]

CDC .... Capillary Diffusion Capacity [*Medicine*] (DMAA)
CDC .... Capsule Drive Core [*Aerospace*]
CDC .... Carbon from Dissolved Carbonates
CDC .... Carboplatin, Doxorubicin, Cytoxan [*Antineoplastic drug*] (CDI)
CDC .... Career Development Center (EA)
CDC .... Career Development Course (AFM)
CDC .... Carga del Caribe SA de CV [*Mexico*] [*FAA designator*] (FAAC)
CDC .... Caribbean Defense Command [*or Commander*]
CDC .... Cathodic Dichromate (PDAA)
CDC .... Caudodorsal Cells [*Anatomy*]
CDC .... Cedar City [*Utah*] [*Airport symbol*] (OAG)
CDC .... Cedarville College, Cedarville, OH [*OCLC symbol*] (OCLC)
CDC .... Cell Division Cycle [*Cytology*]
CDC .... Center for Developmental Change [*University of Kentucky*] [*Research center*] (RCD)
CDC .... Center on Destructive Cultism (EA)
CDC .... Centers for Disease Control [*Formerly, Communicable Disease Center*] [*Department of Health and Human Services Atlanta, GA*]
CDC .... Centers for Disease Control and Prevention
CDC .... Central Digital Computer
CDC .... Central Distribution Center [*Army*] (DOMA)
CDC .... Central Document Control [*Jet Propulsion Laboratory, NASA*]
CDC .... Ceramic Disk Capacitor
CDC .... Characteristic Distortion Compensation [*Telecommunications*] (TEL)
CDC .... Chemical Data Center, Inc. [*Information service or system*] (IID)
CDC .... Chemical Development Corp. [*Geneva, Switzerland*]
CDC .... Chenodeoxycholic Acid [*Also, CDA, CDCA, CHENIC*] [*Biochemistry*]
CDC .... Child Development Center
CDC .... Child Development Consultant
CDC .... Chinese Development Council (EA)
CDC .... Circuit Defense Counsel
CDC .... Citizens' Defense Corps
CDC .... Citizens Democracy Corps [*An association*] (EA)
CDC .... Civil Defense Committee (NATG)
CDC .... Civil Defense Coordinator (AAG)
CDC .... Clamped Dielectric Constant
CDC .... Classified Document Control
CDC .... Cleanly Designed Cigar
CDC .... Clearance Dock Club [*A union*] [*British*]
CDC .... Clearinghouse on Development Communication (EA)
CDC .... Climate Diagnostics Center [*Marine science*] (OSRA)
CDC .... Climate Diagnostics Center [*Environmental Research Laboratories*] (USDC)
CDC .... Coaxial Directional Coupler
CDC .... Code Directing Character [*Computer science*]
CDC .... Cold-Drawn Copper (MSA)
CDC .... Collision Damage Classification [*Insurance*]
CDC .... Colonial Development Corp.
CDC .... Combat Development Command [*Terminated, 1973*] [*Army*] (MCD)
CDC .... Combat Direction Center (NVT)
CDC .... Command and Data-Handling Console
CDC .... Command Decoder Coaxial (MCD)
CDC .... Command Destruct Control (AAG)
CDC .... Commissioners of District of Columbia
CDC .... Committee for a Democratic Consensus (EA)
CDC .... Common Distributable Change (DNAB)
CDC .... Commonwealth Development Corp. (ILCA)
CDC .... Communicable Disease Center
CDC .... Communications and Data Centre (NITA)
CDC .... Communications Design Center [*Carnegie-Mellon University*] [*Research center*] (RCD)
CDC .... Community Development Corp. [*Later, NCDC*]
CDC .... Companhia Danca Contemporanea [*Portugal*]
CDC .... Company Data Coordinator
CDC .... Complement-Dependent Cytotoxicity [*Immunology*]
CDC .... Complete Disk Checker [*Compact disks*]
CDC .... Component Design Confirmation
CDC .... Computer Development Center (KSC)
CDC .... Computer Directions Corp.
CDC .... Computer Display Channel
CDC .... Comunidad Democratica Centroamericana [*Central American Democratic Community*] (EAIO)
CDC .... Concertacion Democratica Cubana [*Political party*] (EY)
CDC .... Concert Dance Company
CDC .... Configuration Data Control (AAG)
CDC .... Confined Detonating Cord (MCD)
CDC .... Conservation Data Centers (GNE)
CDC .... Construction Design Criteria [*Telecommunications*] (TEL)
CDC .... Continental Dorset Club (EA)
CDC .... Contract Data Coordinator (NG)
CDC .... Contract Definition Concept (DNAB)
CDC .... Control Data Corp. [*Information service or system*] (IID)
CDC .... Control Distribution Center (AAG)
CD-C .... Controlled Drinker-Control [*Medicine*] (DMAA)
CDC .... Convergencia Democratica de Catalunya [*Democratic Convergence of Catalonia*] [*Spain Political party*] (PPE)
CDC .... Copper Data Center [*Inactive*] [*Battelle Memorial Institute*] [*Information service or system*]
CDC .... Corp. de Developpement du Canada [*Canada Development Corp. - CDC*]
CDC .... Council for Disabled Children (AIE)
CDC .... Count - Double Count (MUGU)
CDC .... Countdown Clock [*Aerospace*]
CDC .... Coupled Diffusion Control (MCD)
CDC .... Course and Distance Calculator [*or Computer*]

CDC .... Credit Code (DNAB)
CDC .... Criticallity Data Center
CDC .... Croatian Democratic Community [*Political party*]
CDC .... Crop Development Centre [*University of Saskatchewan*] [*Canada*] (IRC)
CDC .... Cryogenic Data Center [*National Institute of Standards and Technology*]
CDC .... Crystal Data Center [*National Institute of Standards and Technology*]
CDC .... Cumberland Railway & Coal Co. [*AAR code*]
CDc .... Daly City Public Library, Daly City, CA [*Library symbol Library of Congress*] (LCLS)
CDCA .... Canadian Dexter Cattle Association (AC)
CDCA .... Caudodorsal Cells Autotransmitter [*Zoology*]
CDCA .... Chefs de Cuisine Association of America
CDCA .... Chenodeoxycholic Acid [*Also, CDA, CDC, CHENIC*] [*Biochemistry*]
CD Cal .... United States District Court for the Central District of California (DLA)
CDCC .... Caribbean Development and Cooperation Committee [*Economic Commission for Latin America*]
CDCCP .... Control Data Communications Control Procedure [*Telecommunications*] (TEL)
CDCCV .... Carburetor Deceleration Combustion Controlled Valve [*Automotive engineering*]
CDCD .... Certificate of Disposition of Classified Documents (AAG)
CDCD .... Counter-Double-Current Distribution [*Analytical chemistry*]
CDCDA .... Community Design Center Directors Association (EA)
CDCDP .... Civil Defense Career Development Program
CDCDSCA .... Children's Dress, Cotton Dress, and Sportswear Contractors Association [*Later, MAAA*] (EA)
CDCE .... Central Data-Conversion Equipment
CDCE .... Commander, Disaster Control Element
CDCE .... Continuous Dress Creep Feed (PDAA)
CDCEC .... Combat Development Command Experimentation Center [*Terminated Army*] (MCD)
CDCF .... Commander, Disaster Control Force
CDCF .... Cosmic Dust Collection Facility (SSD)
CDCG .... Commander, Disaster Control Group
CDCH .... Caudodorsal Cell Hormone [*Zoology*]
CDCIA .... Combat Development Command Infantry Agency [*Terminated Army*]
CDC-INTA .... Combat Development Command - Intelligence Agency [*Terminated Army*] (MCD)
cdc kinases... Cell Division Cycle Kinases [*Genetics*] (DOG)
CDCL .... Citizens in Defense of Civil Liberties [*Defunct*] (EA)
CDCL .... Command Document Capability List (IAA)
CDCM .... Carbon Dioxide Concentrating [*or Concentrator*] Module
CDCMA .... Combat Development Command Maintenance Agency [*Terminated Army*]
CDCN .... Command Document Control Number (AFIT)
CDCN .... Contract Data Change Notice (MCD)
CDCN .... Contract Document Change Notice (MCD)
CDCN .... Controller Defence Communications Network [*Navy British*]
CDCNET ...... Control Data Corporation Distributed Communications Network [*Telecommunications*]
CDCO .... Cidco, Inc. [*NASDAQ symbol*] (SAG)
CDCO .... Combat Direction Center Officer [*Navy*] (DOMA)
CDCO .... Coupling Display Manual Control-Optics (SAA)
CDC-OCCE ... Commonwealth Defence Conference - Operational Clothing and Combat Equipment (EA)
CDCOM .... Coordinating Committee (MCD)
CDCP .... Center for Disease Control and Prevention (DHSM)
CDCP .... Central Data Collection Point [*Army*]
CDCP .... Command Display and Control Processor
CDCP .... Comprehensive Day Care Programs [*An association*] (EA)
CDCP .... Milstep Central Data Collection Point [*McClellan Air Force Base*]
CDCQ .... Child Development Center Q-Sort [*Personality development test*] [*Psychology*]
CDCR .... Center for Documentation and Communication Research [*Case Western Reserve University*]
CDCR .... Childrens Discovery Centers [*NASDAQ symbol*] (TTSB)
CDCR .... Children's Discovery Centers of America, Inc. [*NASDAQ symbol*] (NQ)
CDCR .... Control Drawing Change Request (AAG)
CDCRAFT ..... Compact Disc and Cathode Ray Tube Applied Format [*Automotive navigation systems*]
CDCS .... Central Data Collection System (AFM)
CDCS .... Centralized Digital Control System [*Computer science*] (PDAA)
CDCS .... Civil Defense Countermeasures System
CDCS .... Construction Dollar Control System [*AT & T*]
CDCS .... Customer Depot Complaint System (MCD)
CDCT .... Centro de Documentacao Cientifica e Tecnica [*Scientific and Technical Documentation Center*] [*Portugal*] [*Information service or system*] (IID)
CDCTA .... Combat Development Command Transportation Agency [*Terminated Army*]
CDCU .... Communications Digital Control Unit
CDCW .... Cymdeithas Diogelu Cymru Wledig [*Council for the Protection of Rural Wales*] (EAIO)
CDD .... Candela Resources Ltd. [*Vancouver Stock Exchange symbol*]
CDD .... Cardiodilatin [*Biochemistry*]
CDD .... Castilejo-Dalitz-Dyson
CDD .... Central Data Display
CDD .... Certificate of Disability for Discharge [*Military*]
CDD .... Chart Distribution Data
CDD .... Chlorinated Dibenzo-para-dioxin [*Organic chemistry*]
CDD .... Chronic Disabling Dermatoses [*Medicine*]
CDD .... Clostridium Difficile Disease [*Medicine*]

CDD .... Coded (IAA)
CDD .... Coded Decimal Digit
CDD .... Collateral Damage Distance (AABC)
CDD .... Color Data Display
CDD .... Combat Data Director [*Military*] (SAA)
CDD .... Command Destruct Decoder
CDD .... Command Document Discard (IAA)
CDD .... Common Data Dictionary (MCD)
CDD .... Computer-Directed Drawing
CDD .... Conference on Dual Distribution
CDD .... Congressional District Data [*Bureau of the Census*]
CDD .... Cosmic Dust Detector
CDD .... Cratering Demolition Device
CDD .... Current Discontinuity Device (IAA)
CDDA .... Canadian Diamond Drilling Association
CDDA .... Compact Data Disk Association [*Defunct*] (EA)
CD-DA .... Compact Disk Digital Audio [*Computer science*]
CDDAC .... Cover and Deception, Direction, and Coordination (MCD)
CDDB .... Central Demand Data Base Supply [*Army*]
CDDC .... Center Data Descriptions Catalog (KSC)
CD D/C .... Civil Defense Director/Coordinator
CDDD .... Comprehensive Dishonesty, Disappearance, and Destruction Policy [*Insurance*]
CDDF .... Central Data Distribution Facility [*National Oceanic and Atmospheric Administration*]
CDDGP .... Commander, Destroyer Development Group, Pacific [*Navy*] (MCD)
CDDI .... Computer-Directed Drawing Instrument
CDDI .... Copper Distributed Data Interface [*Computer science*] (TNIG)
CDDI .... Copper Distributed Digital Interface [*Computer science*]
CD-DIAL ...... Community Development - Data Information Analysis Laboratory (OICC)
CDDL .... Conference of Directors of Danube Lines [*Budapest, Hungary*] (EAIO)
CDDMAN ...... Cruiser-Destroyerman [*A publication*] (DNAB)
CDDO .... Coalition of Digestive Disease Organizations (EA)
CDDP .... Canadian Department of Defence Production
CDDP .... cis-Diamminadichloroplatinum [*Cisplatin*] [*Also, cis-DDP, CPDD, CPT, DDP, P*] [*Antineoplastic drug*]
CDDP .... College Discovery and Development Program [*New York City*] (EDAC)
CDDP .... Command Cruiser-Destroyer Force, Pacific (DNAB)
CDDP .... Console Digital Display Programmer (MUGU)
CDDR .... CD [*Compact Disc*] Data Report [*Langley Publications*] [*Information service or system A publication*] (IID)
CDDR .... Coordinated Design Data Required
CDDRB .... International Centre for Diarrhoeal Disease Research, Bangladesh (ECON)
CDDT .... Countdown Demonstration Test [*NASA*]
CDDT .... Cyclododecatriene [*Organic chemistry*]
CDE .... Caledonia [*Panama*] [*Airport symbol*] (OAG)
CDE .... Canine Distemper Encephalitis [*A disease*]
CDE .... Cape Decision, AK [*Location identifier FAA*] (FAAL)
CDE .... Carbon Dioxide Economizer
CDE .... Carbon Dioxide Equivalent [*Environmental science*]
CD-E .... CD [*Compact Disk*] - Erasable (CDE)
CDE .... Center for Demography and Ecology [*University of Wisconsin - Madison*] [*Research center*] (RCD)
CDE .... Certificate in Data Education (BUR)
CDE .... Certified Data Educator (HGAA)
CDE .... Certified Diabetes Educator (MEDA)
CDE .... Chemical Defence Establishment [*British*]
CDE .... Chemical Defense Equipment [*Military*] (INF)
CDE .... Chlordiazepoxide [*Librium*] [*Sedative*]
CDE .... Civil Director of Economics
CDE .... Clutter Doppler Error (MCD)
CDE .... Coal Development Establishment [*British*] (BI)
CDE .... Code
CDE .... Coeur d'Alene Mines [*NYSE symbol*] (TTSB)
CDE .... Coeur d'Alene Mines Corp. [*NYSE symbol*] (SPSG)
CDE .... Cognizant Development Engineer
CDE .... Colorado Department of Education (EDAC)
CDE .... Combat Developments Experimentation Command [*Army*]
CDE .... Comed Aviation Ltd. [*British*] [*FAA designator*] (FAAC)
CDE .... Comissao Democratica Eleitoral [*Democratic Electoral Committee*] [*Portugal Political party*] (PPE)
CDE .... Command Decision Echelon (MCD)
CDE .... Command-Destruct Epoxy [*A plastic resin*]
CDE .... Command Document End (IAA)
CDE .... Commission for Development and Exchange [*International Council of Scientific Unions*]
CDE .... Common Desktop Environment [*Graphical user interface*] (CDE)
CDE .... Common Duct Exploration [*Medicine*] (MAE)
CDE .... Condensate Demineralization Effluent [*Nuclear energy*] (NRCH)
CDE .... Conference on Confidence and Security-Building Measures and Disarmament in Europe
CDE .... Conserved DNA [*Deoxyribose Nucleic Acid*] Element [*Genetics*]
CDE .... Consolidated Sea Gold Corp. [*Vancouver Stock Exchange symbol*]
CDE .... Consumption Data Exchange
CDE .... Contamination-Decontamination Experiment [*Nuclear energy*]
CDE .... Contents Directory Entry [*Computer science*] (MHDI)
CDE .... Continuing Dental Education
CD-E .... Controlled Drinker-Experimental [*Chemical dependency*] (DAVI)
CDE .... CONUS [*Continental United States*] Depot Equipment [*Military*]
CDE .... Cooperative Defense Efforts (MCD)
CDE .... Cooperative Development Environment [*Computer science*] (PCM)

CDE	Cornell Dubilier Electronics (MUGU)
CDE	Corporate Data Exchange (EA)
CDE	Current Design Expendable [*Refers to payload type*] [*NASA*]
CDEA	Cetyl(dimethyl)ethylammonium Bromide [*A surfactant*]
CDEC	Chloroallyl Diethyldithiocarbamate [*Herbicide*]
CDEC	Combat Development Experimentation Center [*Fort Ord, CA*] (MCD)
CDEC	Combat Development Experimentation Center (AAGC)
CDEC	Combat Developments Evaluation Command (MCD)
CDEC	Combat Developments Experimentation Command [*Army*] (RDA)
CDEC	Combined Documents Exploitation Center [*Saigon, Vietnam*] (VNW)
CDEC	Comprehensive Developmental Evaluation Chart [*Child development test*] [*Psychology*]
C de CASS	Cour de Cassation [*Court of Appeal*] [*French*]
CDED	Cleveland Diesel Engine Division [*GM Corp.*]
CDEE	Canadian Defence Education Establishment (PDAA)
CDEE	Chemical Defence Experimental Establishment [*British*]
CDEET	Commonwealth Department of Employment, Education, and Training [*Australia*]
CDEF	Committee on the Development of Engineering Faculties
C de G	Croix de Guerre [*French military decoration*]
CDEI	Control Data Education Institutes
CDEK	Computer Data Entry Keyboard
CDEM	Civic Development Movement [*Sierra Leone*] [*Political party*] (EY)
CDEM	Continuous Dynode Electron Multiplier [*Instrumentation*]
CDEOS	Civil Defense Emergency Operations System
CDEP	Central Directorate on Environmental Protection [*British*] (DCTA)
CDEP	Civil Defense Education Program
CdePA	Club de Petanque d'Adelaide [*Australia*]
CDEPr	Coeur d'Alene Mines 'MARCS' [*NYSE symbol*] (TTSB)
CDER	Center for Death Education and Research (EA)
CDER	Center for Drug Evaluation and Research [*Food and Drug Administration*]
CDES	Chemical Defence Experimental Station [*British World War II*]
CDES	Computer Data Entry System (NITA)
CDET	Council for Dance Education and Training [*British*]
C de V	Carte de Visite [*Visiting Card*] [*French*]
cdev	Control-Device Resource [*Computer science*] (BYTE)
CDEV	Control Panel Device [*Computer science*] (DOM)
CDEVC	Computer Development Center (KSC)
CDEX	Casual Disability Exclusion [*Insurance*]
CDEX	Civil Defense Exercise
CDF	Cable Distribution Frame (NASA)
CDF	Cahiers de Droit Familial [*A publication*] (ILCA)
CDF	Canadian Foundation Co. Ltd. [*Toronto Stock Exchange symbol*]
CDF	Candidate Density Function (MCD)
CDF	Canine Defense Fund (EA)
CDF	Capital Development Fund [*United Nations*]
CDF	Cardiff [*Welsh depot code*]
CDF	Celiac Disease Foundation (EA)
CDF	Central Data Facility [*NASA*] (NASA)
CDF	Central Distribution Frame (CDE)
CDF	Champagne d'Argent Federation (EA)
CDF	Champ Du Feu [*France*] [*Seismograph station code, US Geological Survey*] (SEIS)
CDF	Channel Definition Format [*Microsoft Corp.*] [*Computer science*]
CDF	Channel Definition Format [*Computer science*]
CDF	Charities Deposit Fund [*Finance British*]
CDF	Children's Defense Fund (EA)
CDF	Chlordimeform [*Insecticide*]
CDF	Chlorinated Dibenzofuran [*Organic chemistry*]
CDF	Chlorodifluoroethylene [*Organic chemistry*]
CDF	Chondrodystrophia Foetalis [*Medicine*] (DMAA)
CDF	Chronic Disease Facility [*Medicine*]
CDF	Circuit Design Fabrication (NASA)
CDF	Civil Defence Force [*British military*] (DMA)
CDF	Class Determination and Finding
CDF	Clutter Discriminating Fuze (MCD)
CDF	Collider Detector at Fermilab [*Particle physics*]
CDF	Combat Defense Force
CDF	Combined Distribution Frame [*RADAR*]
CDF	Combined Distribution Function (MCD)
CDF	Command Decoder Filter
CDF	Common Data Format [*Computer science*]
CDF	Common Data Format
CDF	Common Weapon Control System Development Facility (MCD)
CDF	Communications-Data Field
CDF	Communications Data Formatter (MCD)
CDF	Community Development Foundation [*SCF*] [*Absorbed by*] (EA)
CDF	Compare and Difference Full Words (SAA)
CDF	Confined Detonating Fuze
CDF	Confined Disposal Facilities
CDF	Congregation for the Doctrine of the Faith
CDF	Conservative Democratic Forum (EA)
CDF	Constant Current Fringes
CDFr	Contained Disposal Facility
CDF	Contiguous-Disk File [*Computer science*] (PDAA)
CDF	Control Detonating Fuses (KSC)
CDF	Cool-Down Facility (NASA)
CDF	Core Damage Frequency [*Nuclear energy*] (NRCH)
CDF	Cortina d'Ampezzo [*Italy*] [*Airport symbol*] (AD)
CDF	Council for the Defense of Freedom
CDF	Critical Demulsification Temperature (PDAA)
CDF	Cumulative Damage Function [*Nuclear energy*] (NRCH)
CDF	Cumulative Distribution Function [*Statistics*]
CDF	Custom Defined Function [*Computer science*] (PCM)

CDFA	Christian Dance Federation of Australia
CDFA	Citizens for a Debt Free America (EA)
CDFA	Citizens for a Drug Free America (EA)
CDFA	Committee to Defend the First Amendment [*Later, FARI*] (EA)
CDFA	Council of Development Finance Agencies
CDFAA	Commission Dyers and Finishers' Association of Australia
CDFAB	California Dried Fig Advisory Board [*Later, CFAB*]
CDF & TDS	Circuit Design, Fabrication, and Test Data Systems (NASA)
CDFB	Contractor Design Freeze Baseline (MCD)
CDFC	Charlie Daniels Fan Club (EA)
CDFC	Cloud Depiction and Forecast System [*Marine science*] (OSRA)
CDFC	Cloud Depiction and Forecast System (USDC)
CDFC	Commonwealth Development Finance Co. Ltd. [*Joint government and private agency in London established to aid businesses elsewhere in British Commonwealth*]
CDFC	Count Dracula Fan Club (EA)
CDFCHB	Command Data Format Control Handbook [*NASA*] (KSC)
CDFCV	Charlie Daniels Fan Club Volunteers (EA)
CDFE	Center for the Defense of Free Enterprise [*Bellevue, WA*] (EA)
CDFEA	California Dried Fruit Export Association (EA)
CDFF	Command Distributor Flip-Flop (SAA)
CDFFA	California Department of Forestry Firefighters Association (SRA)
CDFFC	Controllable-Displacement-Factor Frequency Changer (DICI)
CDFGI	Charles Darwin Foundation for the Galapagos Isles (EA)
CDFHR	Coalition for Drug-Free Horse Racing (EA)
CDFISA	Canadian Dairy & Food Industries Supply Association [*Association Canadienne des Fournisseurs des Industries Laitierie et de l'Alimentation*] (AC)
CDFL	Capacitor Diode FET [*Field Effect Transistor*] Logic [*Electronics*] (NITA)
CDFM	Committee of Direction of Fruit Marketing [*Queensland*] [*Australia*]
CD-FM	Compact Disc File Manager [*Computer science*] (NTCM)
CDFNT	Cold Front [*NWS*] (FAAC)
CDFR	Commercial Demonstration Fast Reactor
CDFS	Chief of Defense Force Staff (MCD)
CDFS	Compact Disk File System [*Computer science*] (PCM)
CD/FT²	Candelas per Square Foot
cd fwd	Carried Forward [*Bookkeeping*] (ODBW)
CDG	Capacitance Diaphragm Gauge [*Instrumentation*]
CDG	Capacitor Diode Gate
CDG	Cardigan [*City and county in Wales*] (ROG)
CDG	Carters Dam [*Georgia*] [*Seismograph station code, US Geological Survey*] (SEIS)
CDG	Central Design Group
CDG	Central Developmental Groove [*Medicine*] (DMAA)
CDG	Central Display Generator (MCD)
CDG	Charles De Gaulle Airport [*France*]
CDG	Check Digit Verifier
CDG	Chloro-deoxy-glucose [*Biochemistry*]
CDG	Circular Diffraction Grating
CDG	Civil Disturbance Group [*Department of Justice intelligence unit*]
CDG	Coder-Decoder Group [*Army*] (AABC)
CDG	Coffee Development Group (EA)
CDG	Commanding (WGA)
CDG	Community Design Group [*North Carolina State University*] [*Research center*] (RCD)
CDG	Compact Disc Group [*Defunct*] (EA)
CD + G	Compact Disc Plus Graphics
CDG	Competitive Development Group [*Army*] (RDA)
CDG	Computer Directions Group, Inc. [*Information service or system*] (IID)
CDG	Consumers Distributing Co. Ltd. [*Toronto Stock Exchange symbol*]
CDG	Converter Display Group
CDG	Costume Designers Guild (EA)
CDG	Council for Democratic Government [*Japan*] (ECON)
CDG	Houston, TX [*Location identifier FAA*] (FAAL)
CDG	Paris [*France*] Charles De Gaulle Airport [*Airport symbol*] (OAG)
CDG	Shandong Airlines [*China*] [*FAA designator*] (FAAC)
CDGA	California Date Growers Association [*Defunct*] (EA)
CDGE	Constant Denaturing Gradient Electrophoresis [*Analytical biochemistry*]
CDGF	Cartilage-Derived Growth Factor [*Biochemistry*]
CDGRA	Colorado Dude/Guest Ranch Association (SRA)
CDH	Cable Distribution Head
CDH	California State University, Dominguez Hills, Carson, CA [*OCLC symbol*] (OCLC)
CDH	Camden [*Arkansas*] [*Airport symbol*] (OAG)
CDH	Canadian Hydrocarbons Ltd. [*Toronto Stock Exchange symbol*] (SPSG)
CDH	Center pour les Droits de l'Homme [*Center for Human Rights*] [*Switzerland*] (EAIO)
CDH	Ceramide Dihexoside [*Biochemistry*]
CDH	Chronic Daily Headache [*Neurology*] (DAVI)
CDH	Command and Data Handling (DEN)
CDH	Congenital Diaphragmatic Hernia [*Medicine*]
CDH	Congenital Dislocation [*or Dysplasia*] of the Hip [*Medicine*]
CDH	Constant Delta Height [*Aerospace*]
CDH	Constant Differential Height [*Aerospace*] (MCD)
CDH	Constricted Double Heterojunction (MCD)
CDH	Constricted Double Heterostructure [*Electronics*] (NITA)
CDHA	Canadian Dental Hygienists' Association [*Association Canadienne des Hygienistes Denteurs*] (AC)
CDHC	Canberra and District Home Care [*Australia*]
CDHC	Command and Data-Handling Console (KSC)
CDHES	Comision de Derechos Humanos de El Salvador [*Spain*]
CDHHF	Canadian Deaf & Hard of Hearing Forum (AC)

CDHIA	California Dairy Herd Improvement Association (SRA)
CDHNRU	Committee for the Defence of Human and National Rights in Ukraine [Australia]
CDHP	Carbamoyldihydropyridine [Organic chemistry]
CDHP	Catalytic Dehydrogenative Polycondensation [Organic chemistry]
CDHRCA	Commission for the Defense of Human Rights in Central America (EA)
CDHRM	Committee for Defense of Human Rights in Morocco (EA)
CDhS	California State College, Dominguez Hills [Later, California State University, Dominguez Hills], Dominguez Hills, CA [Library symbol Library of Congress] (LCLS)
CDHS	CERN [Conseil European pour la Recherche Nucleaire]-Dortmund-Heidelberg-Saclay Collaboration
CDHS	Comprehensive Data Handling System [Environmental Protection Agency]
CDHS	Continuous Disability History Sample [Social Security Administration] (GFGA)
CDHW	International Association of Cleaning and Dye House Workers
CDI	Cambridge, OH [Location identifier FAA] (FAAL)
CDI	Canadian Development Institute (AC)
CDI	Canadian Dollar Investments (Bermuda) Ltd. [Toronto Stock Exchange symbol]
CDI	Can Do It [Temporary-help agency]
CDI	Capacitor Discharge Ignition [Automotive technology]
CDI	Carbodiimide [Organic chemistry]
CDI	Carbonyldiimidazole [Organic chemistry]
CDI	Cargo Disposition Instructions [Shipping]
CDI	Cartilage-Derived Inhibitor [To vascularization] [Biochemistry]
CDI	Case Development Inspection
CDI	Category Development Index (WDMC)
CDI	CDI Corp. [NYSE symbol] (SPSG)
CDI	Cell-Directed Inhibitor [Medicine] (DMAA)
CDI	Cellular Directions, Inc. [Telecommunications service] (TSSD)
CDI	Center for Defense Information (EA)
CDI	Centre de Danse International [France]
CDI	Centre pour le Developpement Industriel [Centre for the Development of Industry] (EAIO)
CDI	Chief Draftsman's Instructions (MCD)
CDI	Children's Depression Inventory [Personality development test] [Psychology]
CDI	Children's Diagnostic Inventory
CDI	Christian Democrat International (EAIO)
CDI	Church Defence Institution [British]
CDI	Classification Document Index (DNAB)
CDI	Classified Defense Information [Military]
CDI	Clearinghouse on Disability Information (EA)
CDI	Cobalt Development Institute (EAIO)
C$_{Di}$	Coefficient of Induced Drag [Aviation] (DA)
CDI	Collateral Duty Inspector (MCD)
CDI	Collector Diffusion Isolation [Electronics]
CDI	College Descriptive Index (EDAC)
CDI	Command Display Indicator (MCD)
CDI	Commission du Droit International [United Nations]
CDI	Common Defense Installation (AFM)
CD-I	Compact Disc-Interactive [Computer science]
CD-I	Compact Disk - Interactive
CDI	Compass Direction Indicator (PDAA)
CDI	Comprehensive Dissertation Index [University Microfilms International] [Ann Arbor, MI Bibliographic database] [A publication]
CDI	Compudata, Inc. [Information service or system] (IID)
CDI	Computer-Developed Instruction
CDI	Computer Devices, Inc.
CDI	Computer-Directed Instrument
CDI	Computer Direct Input [Computer science] (DCTA)
CD-I	Computer Disk-Interactive
CDI	Concept Development Investigation
CDI	Consumer Demographics, Inc. [Information service or system] (IID)
CDI	Continuing Disability Investigation [Social Security Administration] (OICC)
CDI	Continuous Deionization
CDI	Contractor's Demonstration Inspection
CDI	Control Data Institute
CDI	Control Direction Indicator (MCD)
CDI	Control Director Intercept (CINC)
CDI	Controlled Direct Injection [Automotive engineering]
CDI	Conventional Defense Improvements (DOMA)
CDI	Conventional Defense Initiative [Military] (SDI)
CDI	Corollary Discharge Interneuron [Neurology]
CDI	Course Deviation Indicator [Aviation]
CDI	Current Difference Logic (DGA)
CDI	Cutting Die Institute (EA)
CDi	Dixon Unified School District Library, Dixon, CA [Library symbol Library of Congress] (LCLS)
Cdia	Concordia [Record label]
CDIAC	Carbon Dioxide Information and Analysis Center [Department of Energy Information service or system] (IID)
CDIB	Collector, Diffusion, Isolation, Bipolar [Electronics] (NITA)
CDIC	Canada Deposit Insurance Corp.
CDIC	Canada Development Investment Corp. [Corp. de Developpement des Inve stissements du Canada]
CDIC	Carbon Dioxide Information Center [Department of Energy] [Oak Ridge, TN Database]
CDIC	Collingwood & District Information Centre (AC)
CDIC	Combat Damage Information Center [Military]
CDIC	Combat Data Information Center [Army]
CDICS	Centralized Dealer Inventory Control System (MHDB)
CDIDC	Committee on Data Interchange and Data Centers (MSC)
CDIDS	Consolidated Deficiency and Improvement Data Systems
CDIF	CASE [Computer-Aided Software Engineering] Data Interchange Format (CDE)
CDIF	Component Development and Integration Facility [Butte, MT] [Department of Energy]
CDIF	Compound Document Interchange Format [Computer science]
CDIF	Consumer Drug Information [American Society of Hospital Pharmacists] [Database] [Information service or system] (IID)
CDIF	Consumer Drug Information Fulltext [American Society of Hospital Pharmacists] [Database] [Information service or system]
CDIF	Controller/Director Information File (AFM)
CDIIIU	Central Drugs and Illegal Immigration Intelligence Unit [British] (DI)
CDIL	Command Database Interface Language (MCD)
CDILD	Chronic Diffuse Interstitial Lung Disease [Medicine] (DMAA)
CDIM	Capitol Multimedia [NASDAQ symbol] (TTSB)
CDIM	Capitol MultiMedia, Inc. [NASDAQ symbol] (SAG)
CDIMW	Capitol Multimedia Wrrt 'A' [NASDAQ symbol] (TTSB)
CD/IN²	Candela per Square Inch (WDAA)
CDIO	Cardiotronics Inc. [NASDAQ symbol] (TTSB)
CDIP	Combined Defense Improvement Projects
CDIP	Community Development Infrastructure Program [Australia]
CDIP	Consolidated Defense Intelligence Program
CDIP	Consolidated Development Increment Package
CDIP	Continuously Displayed Impact Point (MCD)
CDIPAF	Sidebrazed Ceramic DIP [Dual In-line Package] (CDE)
CDipAF	Certified Diploma in Accounting and Finance [British] (DBQ)
CDIR	Chemical Demilitarization and Installation Restoration (MCD)
CDIR	Concepts Direct [NASDAQ symbol] (TTSB)
CDIR	Concepts Direct, Inc. [NASDAQ symbol] (SAG)
CDIS	Commandment, Defense Intelligence School (DNAB)
CDIS	Commodities Data Information Service [MJK Associates] [Santa Clara, CA] [Information service or system] (IID)
CDIS	Community Data Information System [MJK Associates] (NITA)
CDIS	Consumer Drug Information Service [Australia]
CDIUPA	Centre de Documentation Internationale des Industries Utilisatrices de Produits Agricoles [International Documentation Center for Industries Using Agricultural Products] [Database producer] [Information service or system] (IID)
CDIV	Cum Dividendo [With Dividend] [Stock exchange term] (ADA)
CDJ	American Adjustable Rate Term Trust 1997 [NYSE symbol] (SPSG)
CDJ	Cash Disbursements Journal [Accounting]
CDJ	Choledochoduodenal Junction [Anatomy]
CDJ	Conceicao Do Araguaia [Brazil] [Airport symbol] (OAG)
CDJ	Continental Datanet, Inc. [Vancouver Stock Exchange symbol]
CDJA	Canadian Disc Jockey Association (AC)
CDJI	Dow Jones Index - Commodity [Stock market]
CDK	Cedar Key, FL [Location identifier FAA] (FAAL)
CDK	Channel Data Check
CDK	Communication Desk (BUR)
CDK	Control Development Kit [Microsoft Corp.] (PCM)
CDK	Council for Democracy in Korea [Defunct] (EA)
CDK	Cyclin-Dependent Kinase [An enzyme]
cdks	Cyclin-Dependent Kinases [Genetics] (DOG)
CDL	Cable Delay Line
CDL	Call Description Language [Computer science] (PDAA)
CDL	Canal Defense Light
CDL	Candle, AK [Location identifier FAA] (FAAL)
CDL	Capacitor-Diode Logic (MSA)
CDL	Carbon Dioxide LASER
CDL	Cardinal
CDL	CCAir, Inc. [ICAO designator] (FAAC)
CDL	Central Dental Laboratories [Army]
CDL	Central Dockyard Laboratory [British]
CDL	Centre for Distance Learning [University of Central Queensland] [Australia]
CDL	Ceramic Delay Line
CDL	Chancellor of the Duchy of Lancaster [British]
CDL	Chlorodeoxylincomycin (MAE)
CDL	Christian Defense League (EA)
CDL	Circuit Descriptive Language
CDL	Citadel Holding [AMEX symbol] (TTSB)
CDL	Citadel Holding Corp. [AMEX symbol] (SPSG)
CDL	Citizens for Decency through Law [Later, CLF] (EA)
CDL	Citizens for Decent Literature [Later, Citizens for Decency through Law] (EA)
CDL	Civil Defence Legion [British military] (DMA)
CDL	Clock Delay
CDL	Coaxial Diode Limiter
CDL	Command Definition Language [Computer science] (IAA)
CDL	Commercial Driver's License
CDL	Common Bile Duct Ligation [Medicine]
CDL	Common Display Logic [Computer science]
CDL	Compare and Difference Left Half Words (SAA)
CDL	Computer Description Language (BUR)
CDL	Computer Design Language (CSR)
CDL	Computer Development Laboratory [Fujitsu Ltd., Hitachi Ltd., and Mitsubishi Corp.] [Japan]
CDL	Condor Data Link
CDL	Confidential Damage Level (SAA)
CDL	Configuration Deviation List (MCD)
CDL	Constant Delay Line
CDL	Container Deposit Legislation

CDL............ Contract Data List
CDL............ Contract Deficiency Listing (AFM)
CDL............ Corby Distilleries Ltd. [*Toronto Stock Exchange symbol Vancouver Stock Exchange symbol*]
CDL............ Core Diode Logic
CDL............ Cronar Dot Litho [*Du Pont*]
CDL............ Current Discharge Line (IAA)
CDL............ National Board for Certification of Dental Laboratories (EA)
CDL............ San Diego County Law Library, San Diego, CA [*OCLC symbol*] (OCLC)
CDLA .... Computer Dealers and Lessors Association (EA)
CDLB .... Carbon Dioxide LASER Beam (MCD)
CDLC .... Calgary & District Labour Council (AC)
CDLC .... Capital District Library Council for Reference and Research Resources [*Latham, NY*] [*Library network*]
CDLC .... Cellular Data Link Control [*Communications protocol*]
CDLDM .... Comite de Defense des Libertes Democratiques au Mali [*Committee for the Defense of Democratic Liberties in Mali*] (PD)
CDLE........... Chronic Discoid Lupus Erythematosus [*Medicine*]
CDLG .... Championship Drivers Licensing Group [*Automobile racing*]
CDLI........... Commercial Dental Laboratories of Indiana (SRA)
CDLI........... Consol Delivery & Logistics [*NASDAQ symbol*] (TTSB)
CDLI........... Consolidated Delivery & Logistis, Inc. [*NASDAQ symbol*] (SAG)
CDLIS .... Commercial Driver's License Information System [*FHWA*] (TAG)
CDLP .... Christian Democratic Labour Party [*Grenada*] [*Political party*] (EY)
CDLR .... Committee for the Defense of Legitimate Rights [*Saudi Arabia*] (ECON)
CDLRD........ Confirming Design Layout Report Date [*Bell System*] (TEL)
CDLS .... Commercial Driver's License Information System
CDLS .... Condor Data Link System
CDLS .... Conseil de Developpement du Loisir Scientifique (AC)
CdLS .... Cornelia De Lange Syndrome [*Medicine*]
CDLS .... Cost Document Library System [*Air Force*] (AFIT)
CdLSF .... Cornelia De Lange Syndrome Foundation (EA)
CDLS(W)..... Canadian Defence Liaison Staff (Washington) (AFM)
CDM............ Cadeguomycin Deazaguanosine [*Antineoplastic drug*]
CDM............ Carga Aerea Dominicana [*Dominican Republic*] [*ICAO designator*] (FAAC)
CDM............ Cash Dispensing Machine [*Banking*]
CDM............ Center for Dance Medicine (EA)
CDM............ Central Data Management (NRCH)
CDM............ Centre de Documentation de la Mecanique [*Documentation Center for Mechanics*] [*Technical Center for Mechanical Industries*] [*Information service or system*] (IID)
CDM............ Centro Democratico de Macau [*Macao Democratic Center*] (PPW)
CDM............ Certified Data Manager
CDM............ Certified Decal Manufacturers (EA)
CdM............ Chant du Monde [*Record label*] [*France*]
CDM............ Chemical Downwind Message [*Military*] (INF)
CDM............ Chemically Defined Medium [*Microbiology*]
CDMA .... Chief Decision Makers
CDM............ Chlordimeform [*Expectorant*]
CDM............ Christian Democratic Movement [*Former Czechoslovakia*] [*Political party*] (EY)
CdM............ Chrysler de Mexico SA [*Chrysler Corp.*]
CDM............ Circuit Directory Maintenance (IAA)
CDM............ Civil Defense Management
CDM............ Climatological Dispersion Model [*Environmental Protection Agency*] (GFGA)
CDM............ Clinical Decision Making [*Medicine*] (DMAA)
CDM............ Coalition for a Democratic Majority (EA)
CDM............ Coded Division Multiplex
CDM............ Cold Dark Matter [*Astronomy*]
CDM............ Color Difference Meter
CDM............ Communications/Data Manager (MCD)
CDM............ Companded Delta Modulation [*Telecommunications*] (TEL)
CDM............ Compare and Difference of Masked BIT [*Binary Digit*] [*Computer science*] (SAA)
CDM............ Comprehensive Data Management (GFGA)
CDM............ Computer-Assisted Decision Making System
CDM............ Concept Demonstration Model
CDM............ Condemn (MSA)
CDM............ Configuration Data Management
CDM............ Congestion/Demand Management [*TXDOT*] (TAG)
CDM............ Consumer Distribution Marketing
CDM............ Contractor Developed Material
CDM............ Control Data Mathematic Program (IAA)
CDM............ Core Division Multiplexing (IAA)
CDM............ Corona Diagnostic Mission (SSD)
CDM............ Curriculum Development Manager (MCD)
CD/M² .... Candela per Square Meter (WDAA)
cd/m² .... Candelas per Square Meter (IDOE)
CDMA .... Canadian Direct Mail Association
CDMA .... Canadian Direct Marketing Association
CDMA .... Canadian Donkey & Mule Association (AC)
CDMA .... Canadian Drug Manufactures Association (AC)
CDMA .... Cartridge Direct Memory Access
CDMA .... Code Division Multiple Access
CDMA .... Code-Division Multiple Access [*Navigation systems*]
CDMB .... Civil and Defense Mobilization Board [*Military*] (SAA)
CDMC .... Crop Dryer Manufacturers Council (EA)
CDMI .... Canadian Dun's Market Identifiers [*Dun & Bradstreet Canada Ltd.*] [*Information service or system*] (CRD)
CDML.......... Claris Dynamic Markup Language [*Computer science*]
CDML.......... Crash Damage Material List (MCD)

CDMLS .... Commutated Doppler Microwave Landing System (PDAA)
CDMMA .... Canadian Direct Mail/Marketing Association
CDMO .... Contract Data Management Officer (MCD)
CDMP .... Certified Direct Marketing Practitioner [*Direct Marketing Association Ins urance Council*] [*Designation awarded by*]
CDMP .... Contractor Data Management Program [*Air Force*] (AFIT)
CDMQ .... Conseil des Directeurs Medias du Quebec
CDMR .... Command Data Management Routine [*Computer science*]
CDMR .... Cyclic Data Management Routine [*Computer science*]
CDMS .... Cadmus Communication [*NASDAQ symbol*] (TTSB)
CDMS .... Cadmus Communications Corp. [*NASDAQ symbol*] (NQ)
CDMS .... Coherent Doppler Measurement System
CDMS .... Command Data Management System (NASA)
CDMS .... Commercial Data Management System [*Computer science*] (PDAA)
CDMS .... Communication and Data Management System (SSD)
CDMS .... COMRADE [*Computer-Aided Design Environment*] Data Management System
CDMS .... Continuous Deformation Monitoring System [*US Army Engineer Topographic Laboratories*] (RDA)
CDMS .... Contracting Data Management System [*Military*] (MCD)
CDMS .... Cryogenic Dark Matter Search [*Astrophysics*]
CDMS .... Crystal Document Management System [*Printer technology*]
CDMS .... Current Depth Measurement Subsystem [*National Ocean Survey*] (MSC)
CDMSCS ..... Committee for the Development and Management of Fisheries in the South China Sea [*Thailand*] (EAIO)
CDN .... Cadence Design Sys [*NYSE symbol*] (TTSB)
CDN .... Cadence Design Systems [*NYSE symbol*] (SPSG)
CDN .... California Data Network [*Claremont McKenna College, Rose Institue of State and Local Government*] [*Information service or system*] (IID)
CDN .... Camden, SC [*Location identifier FAA*] (FAAL)
CDN .... Canadian (NATG)
Cdn .... Canadian (DD)
CDN .... Canadian Airlines International Ltd. [*ICAO designator*] (FAAC)
CDN .... Carena-Bancorp, Inc. [*Toronto Stock Exchange symbol*]
CDN .... CDR Discrepancy Notice [*NASA*] (MCD)
CDN .... Cerro Del Durzno [*New Mexico*] [*Seismograph station code, US Geological Survey*] (SEIS)
CDN .... Coded Decimal Notation
CDN .... Community Dreamsharing Network (EA)
CDN .... Consumer Discount Network
CDN .... Convergent-Divergent Nozzle
CDN .... Coordinadora Democratica Nicaraguense Ramiro Sacasa [*Nicaragua*] [*Political party*] (EY)
CDN .... Coordination [*ICAO designator*] (FAAC)
CDN .... Coordination Message [*Aviation code*]
CDN .... To Be Continued [*Polish underground publishing house begun by author Czeslaw Bielecki*] [*Acronym represents Polish phrase*]
CDNA .... Canadian Daily Newspapers Association
cDNA .... Deoxyribonucleic Acid, Cloned [*Biochemistry, genetics*]
cDNA .... Deoxyribonucleic Acid, Complementary [*Biochemistry, genetics*]
CDNB .... Chlorodinitrobenzene [*Organic chemistry*]
CDNC .... Cadence Design Systems, Inc. (MHDW)
CDNC .... Communications Data Network Controller (MCD)
CD/NC .... Computer-Aided Design/Numerical Control (AABC)
CDND .... Canadian Department of National Defence
CDNET .... Consortium Data Network [*University of Michigan*] [*Ann Arbor*] [*Information service or system*] (IID)
CdnGn......... Canadian General Capital [*Associated Press*] (SAG)
CDNI .... Committee for the Defense National Interest (CINC)
CdnIGin....... Canadian Imperial Ginseng Products Ltd. [*Associated Press*] (SAG)
CDNLAO...... Conference of Directors of National Libraries in Asia and Oceania [*Australia*]
CDNnet .... Canadian Research and Education Network [*Computer science*] (TNIG)
CdnNRy....... Canadian National Railway Co. [*Associated Press*] (SAG)
CdnOc......... Canadian Occidental Petroleum Ltd. [*Associated Press*] (SAG)
CDNOPT...... Canadian Stock Options [*Toronto Stock Exchange*] [*Canada Information service or system*] (CRD)
CDNPA........ Canadian Daily Newspaper Publishers Association
CdnPc......... Canadian Pacific Ltd. [*Associated Press*] (SAG)
CDNR .... CDR Discrepancy Notice Record
CdnRy......... Canadian National Railway Co. [*Associated Press*] (SAG)
CDNS .... Climatological Data, National Summary (NOAA)
CD (NS) ...... Ohio Circuit Court Decisions, New Series [*A publication*] (DLA)
CDNT .... Congenital Disorders of Neuromuscular Transmission (PAZ)
CDO .... Canada Orient Resources [*Vancouver Stock Exchange symbol*]
CDO .... Cargo Dor Ltd. [*Ghana*] [*ICAO designator*] (FAAC)
CDO .... Cease and Desist Order [*Legal shorthand*] (LWAP)
CDO .... Change Design Order [*Navy*] (NG)
CDO .... Chief Development Officer (NFD)
CDO .... Civil Defense Organization [*United Nations*]
CDO .... College of Dieticians of Ontario [*L'Ordre des Dietetistes de l'Ontario*] (AC)
CDO .... Combat Development Office
CDO .... Comdisco, Inc. [*NYSE symbol*] (SPSG)
CDO .... Command Duty Officer [*Navy*]
CDO .... Commando (NATG)
CDO .... Communications Duty Officer (FAAC)
CDO .... Community Dial Office [*Small switching system*] [*Telecommunications*]
CDo............ Downey City Library, Downey, CA [*Library symbol Library of Congress*] (LCLS)
CDOA .... Car Department Officers Association (EA)

CDOA .... Christian Democratic Organisation of America [*Venezuela*] (EAIO)
CDOC .... Community Drying-Out Centre [*British*] (DI)
CDOC .... Company Doctor [*NASDAQ symbol*] (TTSB)
CDOC .... Company Doctor (The) [*NASDAQ symbol*] (SAG)
CDoctr .... Company Doctor (The) [*Associated Press*] (SAG)
CDOCW .... Company Doctor Wrrt [*NASDAQ symbol*] (TTSB)
CDOD .... Comptroller, Department of Defense (AAGC)
CdoFcsRM .... Commando Forces, Royal Marines [*British*]
CDOG .... Combat Development Objective Guide [*CDC*]
CDOH .... Coupling Display Optical Hand Controller (KSC)
CDOIPS .... Central Dispatching Organization of the Interconnected Power Systems [*Former Czechoslovakia*] (EAIO)
CDOL .... Customer Data and Operations Language (SSD)
CdoLogRegtRM... Commando Logistics Regiment, Royal Marines [*British*]
CDOM .... Chief Draftsman Office Memorandum (SAA)
CDoN .... North American Rockwell Corp., Downey, CA [*Library symbol Library of Congress*] (LCLS)
CDONSA ...... Coordinator, Department of the Navy Studies and Analyses (DNAB)
CDOOC .... Curved Dash Olds Owners Club (EA)
CDOPrA....... Comdisco 8.75% cm Ser'A'Pfd [*NYSE symbol*] (TTSB)
CDOPrB....... Comdisco 8.75% cm Ser'B'Pfd [*NYSE symbol*] (TTSB)
CDOS .... Combat Days of Supply (MCD)
CDOS .... Controlled Date of Separation [*Military*] (AFM)
CDOS .... Customer Data and Operations System (SSD)
CDOVHL...... Crash Damage Overhaul (MCD)
CDP .... Call Routine Display Panel (IAA)
CDP .... Canada Permanent Mortgage Corp. [*Toronto Stock Exchange symbol*]
CDP .... Canadian Pacer Petroleum [*Vancouver Stock Exchange symbol*]
CDP .... Capuchin Sisters (Spain) (TOCD)
CDP .... Carbon Design Partnership
CDP .... Career Development Program (OICC)
CDP .... Cask Decontamination Pit [*Nuclear energy*] (NRCH)
CDP .... Census Designated Place [*Bureau of the Census*] (GFGA)
CDP .... Center for Democratic Policy (EA)
CDP .... Center for Design Planning (EA)
CDP .... Center for Development Policy [*Later, ICDP*] (EA)
CDP .... Central Distribution Panel
CDP .... Central Distribution Point
CDP .... Central Distribution Programmer (IAA)
CDP .... Centralized Data Processing (IEEE)
CDP .... Centre pour Democratie et Progres [*Center for Democracy and Progress*] [*Later, Center of Social Democrats*] [*France*] [*Political party*] (PPE)
CDP .... Cerro De Punta [*Puerto Rico*] [*Seismograph station code, US Geological Survey*] (SEIS)
CDP .... Certificate in Data Processing [*Designation awarded by Institute for Certification of Computer Professionals*]
CDP .... Certified Data Processor (DD)
CDP .... Chandpur [*Bangladesh*] [*Airport symbol*] (AD)
CDP .... Charged-Drop Precipitator (PDAA)
CDP .... Checkout Data Processor [*RADAR*]
CDP .... Chemical Defense Program (MCD)
CDP .... Chief of Defence Procurement [*British*] (RDA)
CDP .... Child Development Programme [*British*]
CDP .... Christian Democratic Party [*Italy Political party*]
CDP .... Christian Democrat Party [*Australia Political party*]
CDP .... Chromosome Distribution Pattern [*Genetics*]
CDP .... Civic Democratic Party [*Former Czechoslovakia*] [*Political party*] (EY)
CDP .... Coded Description Pattern (AFIT)
C$_{Dp}$....... Coefficient of Profile Drag [*Aviation*] (DA)
CDP .... Collagenase-Digestible Protein
CDP .... Collection Development Policy [*Libraries*]
CDP .... Collett Dickenson Pearce [*British advertising agency*]
CDP .... Color Diaposition Plate
CDP .... Combat Developer Proponent (MCD)
CDP .... Combat Development Phase (MCD)
CDP .... Combat Development Plan (MCD)
CDP .... Combat Development Process (MCD)
CDP .... Combat Development Project [*Army*]
CDP .... Command Data Processor
CDP .... Committee of Directors of Polytechnics [*British*]
CDP .... Common Depth Point [*Seismology*]
CDP .... Communications Data Processor [*Electronics*]
CDP .... Company Distributing Point [*Army*]
CDP .... Competitive Development Phase
CDP .... Compound Diffraction Projector
CDP .... Compound Document Processor [*Computer science*]
CDP .... Comprehensive Drinker Profile [*Test*] [*Psychology*]
CDP .... Comprehensive Dwelling Policies [*Insurance*]
CDP .... Compressor Discharge Pressure
C-DP .... Comptroller-Director of Programs [*Army*]
CDP .... Concept Definition Proposal (MCD)
CDP .... Concept Development Phase (MCD)
CDP .... Concept Development Plan
CDP .... Concept Development Process (MCD)
CDP .... Confidence Development Plan
CDP .... Configuration Data Package (DNAB)
CDP .... Consolidated Papers [*NYSE symbol*] (TTSB)
CDP .... Consolidated Papers, Inc. [*NYSE symbol*] (SAG)
CDP .... Constant Deviation Prism
CDP .... Constant [*or Continuous*] Distending Pressure (AAMN)
CDP .... Continuous Distending Pressure [*Medicine*] (DAVI)
CDP .... Contract Data Package (AAGC)
CDP .... Contract Definition Phase [*DoD*]

CDP .... Contract Design Package (MCD)
CDP .... Control and Display Panel (MCD)
CDP .... Control Data Panel
CDP .... Control Diastolic Pressure [*Cardiology*]
CDP .... Convention Democratic Party [*Liberia*] [*Political party*] (EY)
CDP .... Cornu Double Prism
CDP .... Coronary Drug Project
CDP .... Correlated Data Processor
CDP .... Cost Data Plan
CDP .... Cresyl Diphenylphosphate
CDP .... Critical Decision Point
CDP .... Croatian Democratic Party [*Political party*] (EY)
CDP .... Cross Deck Pendant (MCD)
CDP .... Cross-Linked Dextran Polymer [*Organic chemistry*]
CDP .... Crustal Dynamics Project [*NASA*]
CDP .... Cumulative Detection Probability (CAAL)
CDP .... Cybernetic Data Products Corp. [*Telecommunications service*] (TSSD)
CDP .... Cytidine Diphosphate [*Biochemistry*]
CDP .... Cytosine Diphosphate [*Biochemistry*]
CDP .... Sisters of Divine Providence (TOCD)
CDP .... Sisters of Divine Providence of Kentucky (TOCD)
CDP .... Sisters of Divine Providence of San Antonio, TX (TOCD)
CDPA .... Canadian Decorating Products Association [*Association Canadienne de l'Industrie de Decoration*] (AC)
CDPA .... Canadian Defense Preparedness Association
CDPA .... Certified Data Processing Auditor [*EDP Auditors Foundation*] [*Designation awarded by*]
CDPA .... Coarse Diffraction Pattern Analysis (MCD)
CDPA .... Command and Data Processing Area (MCD)
CDPAbe .... Cytidine Diphosphoabequose [*Biochemistry*]
CDPAC .... Conservative Democratic Political Action Committee (EA)
CDPC .... Central Data Processing Center
CDPC .... Central Data Processing Computer
CDPC .... Comite de Defense du Peuple Canadien (Citoyens et Residents) [*Canadian People's (Citizens and Residents) Defence Committee*]
CDPC .... Commercial Data Processing Center (IEEE)
CDPC .... Computation and Data Processing Center (DIT)
CDPC .... Cytidine Diphosphate Choline [*Biochemistry*] (MAE)
CDPD .... Cellular Digital Packet Data [*Computer science*] (PCM)
CDPD .... Compressed Data Packet Data
CDPF .... Central Data Processing Facility [*NASA*]
CDPF .... Composed Document Printing Facility [*IBM Corp.*]
CDPG .... Center for Demographic and Population Genetics [*University of Texas*] [*Research center*] (RCD)
CDPG .... Combat Developments Planning Group (MCD)
CDPG .... Commander, Disaster-Preparedness Group [*Military*] (DNAB)
CDPG .... Coronary Drug Project Group [*Medicine*] (BABM)
CDPHE .... Colorado Department of Public Health and Environment (DOGT)
CDPHE .... Colorado Department of Public Health and Environment
CDPI .... Command, Data Processing, and Instrumentation [*NASA*]
CDPIE .... Command Data Processing Interface Equipment
CDPIM .... Conference des Directeurs des Bibliotheques Publiques de l'Ile de Montreal [*Conference of Public Library Directors of the Island of Montreal*] (AC)
CDPIR.......... Crash Data Position Indication Recorder (MCD)
CDPIRS........ Crash Data Position Indicator Recorder Subsystem (PDAA)
CDPIS .... Command, Data Processing, and Instrumentation System [*NASA*] (NASA)
CDPK .... Calcium-Dependent Protein Kinase [*An enzyme*]
CDPL .... Cadmium Plate [*Technical drawings*]
CDPL .... Command Designated Position List (MCD)
CDPLP .... Committee in Defense of the Palestinian and Lebanese Peoples [*Defunct*] (EA)
CDPM .... Colored Digital Panel Meter (EECA)
CDPO .... Director for Civil Disturbance Planning and Operations
CDPOC........ Committee for the Defense of Persecuted Orthodox Christians [*Defunct*] (EA)
CDPP .... Christian Democratic People's Party [*Hungary Political party*] (EY)
CDPPP .... Center for Development Planning, Projections, and Policies [*United Nations*]
CDPPV .... Committee for the Defense of Political Prisoners in Vietnam (EA)
CDPR .... Cathedral Priory
CDPR .... Chondrodysplasia Punctata, Rhizomelic [*Medicine*] (DMAA)
CDPR .... Customer Dial Pulse Receiver [*Telecommunications*] (TEL)
CD-PROM .... Compact Disk Programmable Read-Only Memory [*Computer science*]
CDPS .... Calcium-Dependent Protease Small Subunit [*Medicine*] (DMAA)
CDPS .... Communications Data Processing System (NVT)
CDPS .... Computing and Data Processing Society (HGAA)
CDPS .... Consolidated Decision Package Set [*Military*]
CDPX .... Combined Displaced Persons Executive [*World War II*]
CDQ .... Child Development Questionnaire (EDAC)
CDQ .... Core-Dominated Quasar [*Astronomy*]
CDQ .... Croydon [*Australia Airport symbol Obsolete*] (OAG)
CDQCP .... Civil Defense Quality Check Program [*Military*] (DNAB)
CDQD .... Collision-Dominated Quiescent Discharge
CDQR.......... Critical Design and Qualification Review (NASA)
CDR .... Cabin Discrepancy Report [*Report for airline log*]
CDR .... Cadarache [*France*] [*Seismograph station code, US Geological Survey*] (SEIS)
CDR .... Cadre
CDR .... Calcium-Ion Dependent Regulator [*Biochemistry*]
CDR .... Call Detail Recording [*Telecommunications*] (TEL)

CDR .... Call-Detail Routing [*Telecommunications*] (TSSD)
CDR .... Carbon Dioxide Reduction [*Factor for metabolism*]
CDR .... Card Reader [*Computer science*]
CDR .... Career Development Review [*Australia*]
CDR .... Cargo Delivery Receipt [*Shipping*]
CDR .... Cargo Drop Reel (NVT)
CDR .... CDR Resources [*Vancouver Stock Exchange symbol*]
CDR .... Center for Democratic Renewal
CDR .... Center for Documentation on Refugees [*United Nations High Commission for Refugees*] [*Switzerland Information service or system*] (IID)
CDR .... Central Data Recording
CDR .... Centre for Documentation on Refugees [*UNHCR*] [*Information service or system*] (IID)
CDR .... Chadron [*Nebraska*] [*Airport symbol*] (OAG)
CDR .... Child Development Research (BARN)
CDR .... Civil Defense Receiver
CDR .... Cleaning, Decontamination Request (MCD)
CDR .... Clinical Dementia Rating
CDR .... Collateralized Depository Receipt [*Finance*] (EMRF)
CDR .... Comitato per la Difesa della Repubblica [*Committee for the Defense of the Republic*] [*San Marino*] [*Political party*] (PPW)
CDR .... Command Destruct Receiver (AFM)
CDR .... Command Distribution Rack
CDR .... Command Document Resynchronization (IAA)
CDR .... Commander
CDR .... Commission des Reparations [*Reparation Commission*] [*France*]
CDR .... Committee for the Defense of the Revolution [*Cuba*]
CDR .... Communications and Distributed Resources Report [*International Data Corp.*] [*Defunct Information service or system*] (CRD)
CDR .... Communications Desk Reference [*A publication*] (TSSD)
CD-R .... Compact Disc Recordable
CD-R .... Compact Disc Recorder
CDR .... Compare and Difference Right-Half Words (SAA)
CDR .... Complementarity-Determining Region [*Immunology*]
CDR .... Complementarity-Determining Residue [*Genetics*]
CDR .... Complete Design Release [*Navy*] (NG)
CDR .... Composite Damage Risk
CDR .... Conceptual Design Requirement (NRCH)
CDR .... Conductor (ADA)
CDR .... Configuration Data Requirement (DNAB)
CDR .... Conseil Democratique Revolutionnaire [*Democratic Revolutionary Council*] [*Chad*] (PD)
CDR .... Constant Density Recording
CDR .... Constant Dose Range [*Radiation in atmosphere*]
CDR .... Construction Discrepancy Report
CDR .... Contents of Decrement Part of Register [*Computer science*] (NHD)
CDR .... Continental Depositary Receipt [*Banking*] (MHDW)
CDR .... Contract Data Requirement (MCD)
CDR .... Contractor Deficiency Report (AAGC)
CDR .... Contractor Design Review (DOMA)
CDR .... Controlled Dynamic Range
CDR .... Council on Documentation Research [*Defunct*]
CDR .... Countdown Deviation Request [*Aerospace*] (AAG)
CDR .... Crankcase Depression Regulator [*AC Spark Plug Co.*] [*Automotive engineering*]
CDR .... Crash Damage Rate (MCD)
CDR .... Critical Design Review (AFM)
CDR .... Crude Death Rate [*Medicine*]
CDR .... Crystal Diffusion Reflection
CDR .... Cumulative Data Report (MCD)
CDR .... Current Design Reusable [*Refers to payload type*] [*NASA*]
CDR .... Current Device Register
CDR .... Current Directional Relay
CDRA .... Canadian Drilling Research Association (HGAA)
CDRA .... Civil Defense Research Associates
CDRA .... Committee of Directors of Research Associations and Federation of Technology Centres [*British*]
CDRA .... Corps of Drivers Royal Artillery [*British military*] (DMA)
CDRad .... CD Radio, Inc. [*Associated Press*] (SAG)
CDRadio ...... CD Radio, Inc. [*Associated Press*] (SAG)
CDRAM .... Cache DRAM [*Dynamic Random Access Memory*] (CDE)
CD-RAW ..... Compact Disc Read and Write
CDRB .... Canadian Defence Research Board
CDRB .... Contract Dispute Resolution Board [*States*] (AAGC)
CDRC .... Canadian Disability Rights Council (AC)
CDRC .... Computation and Data Reduction Center [*Military*] (DNAB)
CDRC .... Conductivity-Recording Controller (IAA)
CDRC .... Critical Design Review Commercial (MCD)
CDRD .... Carbon Dioxide Research Division [*Oak Ridge National Laboratory*]
CDRD .... CD Radio, Inc. [*NASDAQ symbol*]
CDRD .... Computations and Data Reduction Division [*NASA*] (KSC)
CD/RDMS ... Controlled Depth/Rapid Deployment Moored Sweep [*Navy*] (CAAL)
CDRDW .... CD Radio Inc. Wrrt [*NASDAQ symbol*] (TTSB)
CDRE .... Chemical Defence Research Establishment [*British*]
CDRE .... Commodore
CDRF .... Canadian Dental Research Foundation (HGAA)
CDRH .... Center for Devices and Radiological Health [*FDA*]
CDRI .... Chihuahuan Desert Research Institute (EA)
CDRI .... Contemporary Deep Rack Interior (MCD)
CDRILL .... Counterdrill
CDRILLO ..... Counterdrill Other Side
CDRJPAA ..... Commander, Joint Military Postal Activity, Atlantic (DNAB)
CDRJPAALANT... Commander, Joint Military Postal Activity, Atlantic (DNAB)
CDRJTE .... Commander, Joint Task Element (DNAB)

CDRL .... Cedrol
CDRL .... Contract [*or Contractor*] Data Requirements List
CDRL .... Customer Data Requirements List (MCD)
CDRM .... Chatham Division Royal Marines [*Military unit*] [*British*]
CDRM .... Critical Design Review Meeting (SAA)
CDRM .... Preiss Byron Multimedia [*NASDAQ symbol*] (TTSB)
CDRM .... Preiss [*Byron*] Multimedia Co., Inc. [*NASDAQ symbol*] (SAG)
CdRMG .... Commissioned Royal Marine Gunner [*British*]
CDRMS .... Contract Data Requirements Management System [*Computer science*]
CDRMW .... Preiss Byron Multimedia Wrrt [*NASDAQ symbol*] (TTSB)
CDRO .... Concentration - Dependent Regulation of Oxygen
CD-ROM ..... Compact Disc-Read Only Memory [*Computer science*] (ACRL)
CD-ROM ..... Compact Disk Read-Only Memory [*Computer science*]
CD-ROM XA... Compact Disc Read-Only Memory Extended Architecture [*Computer science*] (PCM)
CDRR .... Committee to Defend Reproductive Rights (EA)
CDRR .... Contract Documentation Requirements Records [*NASA*] (NASA)
CDRS .... Charles Darwin Research Station [*Santa Cruz, Galapagos Islands*]
CDRS .... Children's Depression Rating Scale
CDRS .... Comdisco Disaster Recovery Services (HGAA)
CDRS .... Computer Data Recording System (KSC)
CDRS .... Conceptual Design and Rendering System [*Computer engineering*]
CDRS .... Container Design Retrieval System (MCD)
CDRS .... Control and Data Retrieval System [*Formerly, DCDRS*] [*Air Force*] (MCD)
CDRSC .... Children's Depression Rating Scale for Classrooms (EDAC)
CDR/SMDR... Call-Detail-Recording/Station-Message-Detail-Recording [*Telecommunications*]
CDRT .... Committee on Diagnostic Reading Tests [*Defunct*] (EA)
CDRTI .... Canadian Deafness Research & Training Institute [*Institut Canadien de Recherche et de Formation sur la Surdite*] (AC)
CD-RTOS ..... Compact Disk Real-Time Operating System
CDRTx .... Cadaveric Donor Renal Transplantation [*Medicine*]
CDRU .... Child Development Research Unit [*Nigeria*]
CDRV .... Crankcase Depression Regulator Valve [*Emissions*] [*Automotive engineering*]
CDRX .... Critical Damping Resistance External
CDS .... Alliance Entertainment [*NYSE symbol*] (TTSB)
CDS .... Alliance Entertainment Corp. [*NYSE symbol*] (SAG)
C/DS .... Cache/Disk System [*A storage device*] [*Computer science*] (NITA)
CdS .... Cadmium Sulfide [*Inorganic chemistry*] (WGA)
CDS .... Campaign for Democratic Socialism [*British*]
CDS .... Canadian Depository for Securities
CDS .... [*The*] Canadian Doukhobor Society (AC)
CDS .... Capability Design Specifications (AABC)
CDS .... Card Distribution Service [*Library of Congress*]
CDS .... Career Decision Scale (EDAC)
CDS .... Career Development Scheme
CDS .... Cargo Delivery System [*Shipping*]
CDS .... Carl Duisberg Society [*Later, CDSI*] (EA)
CDS .... Case Data System [*Computer science*] (PDAA)
CDS .... Cash on Delivery Service
CDS .... Cask Decontamination Station [*Nuclear energy*] (NRCH)
CDS .... Cataloging Distribution Service [*Library of Congress*] [*Washington, DC*]
CDS .... Cathode Dark Space
CDS .... Centaurus Distant Supercluster [*Astronomy*]
CDS .... Center for Demographic Studies [*Census*] (OICC)
CDS .... Center for Development Studies
CDS .... Center for Dispute Settlement (EA)
CDS .... Center for Research on Effective Schooling for Disadvantaged Students [*Johns Hopkins University*] [*Research center*] (RCD)
CDS .... Central Data Station
CDS .... Central Data System [*or Subsystem*] (MCD)
CDS .... Central Defence Staff [*British*]
CDS .... Central Distribution System [*Publications*] [*Navy*]
CDS .... Central Districts Airlines [*Former USSR*] [*FAA designator*] (FAAC)
CDS .... Central Dynamic Store (PDAA)
CDS .... Centre de Documentation pour le Sport [*Sport Information Resource Centre*] [*Coaching Association of Canada*]
CDS .... Centre de Donnees Stellaires [*Stellar Data Center*] [*France Information service or system*] (IID)
CDS .... Centre des Democrates Sociaux [*Center of Social Democrats*] [*France Political party*] (PPW)
CDS .... Centre for Development Studies [*Flinders University*] [*Australia*]
CDS .... Centro Democratico y Social [*Democratic and Social Center*] [*Spain Political party*] (PPE)
CDS .... Certificate of Deposit [*Banking*]
CDS .... Certified Data Specialist
CDS .... Certified Documentary Specialist [*Designation awarded by American Society of International Executives, Inc.*]
CDS .... Chaff Dispensing System [*or Subsystem*] (MCD)
CDS .... Chamber of Destination of Ships
CdS .... Character Disorder Sign [*Psychology*]
CDS .... Charge Data System [*Equal Employment Opportunity Commission*] (GFGA)
CDS .... Charged Droplet Scrubber
CDS .... Chemical Data System
CDS .... Chemical Delivery System [*Medicine*]
CDS .... Chemical Discriminator System
CDS .... Chief of Defence Staff [*British*] (NATG)
CDS .... Children's Depression Scale
CDS .... Childress, TX [*Location identifier FAA*] (FAAL)
CDS .... China Defense Supplies, Inc.

CDS	Chip Detector Sensor	(MCD)
CDS	Christian Dental Society	(EA)
CDS	Christian Doctors Sodality	(EA)
CDS	Cinema Digital Sound	
CDS	Circadian Data System	(MCD)
CDS	Circuit Data Sheet	
CDS	Circuit Design System	(MCD)
CDS	Circular Date Stamp [Postmark of a stamp cancellation]	
CDS	Civil Direction of Shipping	(NVT)
CDS	Cleaning and De-Icing System	(MCD)
CDS	Climatological Data Sheet [Air Force]	
CDS	Clonidine Displacing Substance [Biochemistry]	
CDS	Closeout Door System	(MCD)
CDS	Cold-Drawn Steel	
CDS	Collision Detector System	(NASA)
CDS	Color Data System	
CDS	Color Difference Signal	
CDS	Combat Direction Systems	(NVT)
CDS	Command and Decision System	(MCD)
CDS	Command Destruct System	(MCD)
CDS	Command Disable System [Air Force]	
CDS	Command Document Start	(IAA)
CDS	Commander, Destroyer Squadron	
CDS	Common Diagram System	(IAA)
CDS	Common Doppler System	(MCD)
CDS	Communication Deception System	(DWSG)
CDS	Communication Disorders Specialist	
CDS	Communications and Data Subsystems	
CDS	Communications and Distributed Systems [British]	
CDS	Community Development Society	(EA)
CDS	Community Development Support [Australia]	
CDS	Community Dispute Services	(EA)
CDS	Compact Sounder	
CDS	Companion of the Distinguished Service Order [British]	
CDS	Compatible Duplex System	
CDS	Compliance Data System [Environmental Protection Agency]	(MCD)
CDS	Component Disassembly Station [Nuclear energy]	(NRCH)
CDS	Comprehensive Data Systems	(OICC)
CDS	Comprehensive Display System	
CDS	Compressed Data Storage	
CDS	Computer Data Switchboard	
CDS	Computer Data System	
CDS	Computer Distribution System [FAA]	(TAG)
CDS	Computer Duplex System	(BUR)
CDS	Computerized Dispersive Spectroscopy	
CDS	Computerized Documentation System [UNESCO]	(IID)
CDS	Conceptual Data Store [Telecommunications]	(OSI)
CDS	Conceptual Design Study	
CDS	Condensate Demineralization Subsystem [Nuclear energy]	(NRCH)
CDS	Conference of Drama Schools [British]	
CDS	Configuration Development System	(MCD)
CDS	Congregation of the Divine Spirit [Roman Catholic women's religious order]	
CDS	Congressional Data Sheet	(MCD)
CDS	Congressional Descriptive Summaries	(RDA)
CDS	Consolidated Silver Standard Mines Ltd. [Vancouver Stock Exchange symbol]	
CDS	Construction-Differential Subsidy [Authorized by Merchant Marine Act of 1936]	
CDS	Construction Dollar Spreading [System] [AT & T]	
CDS	Container Delivery System [Military]	
CDS	Container Distribution System	(MCD)
cdst	Continuous Dynamical System	
CDS	Contractor Developed Specifications	(MCD)
CDS	Control and Display Subsystem	(MCD)
CDS	Control Data System	(NASA)
CDS	Control Distribution System	
CDS	Controlled Delivery System	
CDS	Control of Destination of Ships	
CDS	Cooperative Development Services [British]	
CDS	Corporate Data Sciences [Commercial firm]	(NITA)
CDS	Correlated Double Sampling	
CDS	Cost Data Sheet	(MCD)
CDS	Cotton Double Silk [Wire insulation]	(IAA)
CDS	Count Dracula Society	(EA)
CDS	Countermeasures Dispenser Set	(MCD)
CDS	Crashworthiness Data System [NHTSA]	(TAG)
CDS	Cross Spectral Density [Physics]	(IAA)
CDS	Crystal Diffraction Spectrometer	(MCD)
CDS	Cul-de-Sac [Medicine]	(MAE)
CDS	CUNY [City University of New York] Data Service [Information service or system]	(IID)
CDS	Current Directory Structure [Computer science]	(PCM)
CDS	Cutting Disposal System [Oil well drilling]	
CDs	Deep Springs College, Deep Springs, CA [Library symbol Library of Congress]	(LCLS)
CDS	Partido do Centro Democratico Social [Party of the Social Democratic Center] [Portugal Political party]	(PPE)
CDS	San Diego State College, San Diego, CA [OCLC symbol]	(OCLC)
CDS2	Compact Dimension 2-Stroke Engine [Automotive engineering]	
CDSA	Canadian Deaf Sports Association [Association des Sports des Sourds du Canada]	(AC)
CDSA	Canadian Driver and Safety Educators Association	
CDSA	Center for Data Systems and Analysis [Montana State University] [Research center]	(RCD)

CDSA	Circuit Distribution Assembly [Ground Communications Facility, NASA]	
CDSA	Class D Surface Area [Aviation]	(FAAC)
CDSA	Country Dance Society of America [Later, CDSSA]	(EA)
CDSB	Cargo Data Standards Board [IATA]	(DS)
CdSB	Commissioned Signals Boatswain [British]	
CDSC	Coastal District Surveillance Center [Military]	
CDSC	Communicable Disease Surveillance Centre [British]	
CDSC	Communications, Distribution, and Switching Center [NASA]	(KSC)
CDSC	Coupling Display Scanning Telescope Manual Control	(IAA)
CDSD	Civil Defense Support Detachments	(AABC)
CDSE	Computer-Driven Simulation Environment [FAA]	
CD-SEM	Critical Dimension Scanning Electron Microscopes	
CDSF	Combat Development Support Facility	
CDSF	Commercially Developed Space Facility [Proposed]	
CDSF	COMRADE [Computer-Aided Design Environment] Data Storage Facility	
CDSF	Customer Data Services Facility	(SSD)
CDSG	Coast Defense Study Group	(EA)
CDSH	Centre de Documentation Sciences Humaines [Documentation Center for Human Sciences] [France] [Information service or system]	(IID)
CDSHA	Country Day School Headmasters Association of the US	(EA)
CDSI	CDS [Carl Duisberg Society] International	(EA)
CDSI	Computer Data Systems [NASDAQ symbol]	(SAG)
CDSI	Computer Data Systems, Inc. [Information service or system]	(IID)
CDSI	Contemporary Digital Services, Inc. [New Rochelle, NY] [Telecommunications]	(TSSD)
CDSIDS	Command and Decision Sensor Interface Data System	(MCD)
CDS/ISIS	Computerized Documentation Service/Integrated Set of Information Systems [UNESCO]	(IID)
CDSL	Connect Data Set to Line [Computer science]	(IAA)
CDSL	Consumer Digital Subscriber Line [Telecommunications]	
CDSM	Cobra Dane System Modernization	(DWSG)
CDSM	Combat Development Support Manager [Army]	
CDSM	Committee on Dental and Surgical Materials [British]	(BABM)
CDSM	Consolidated Defense Supply Material	
CDSN	Chinese Digital Seismograph Network	
CdSO	Commissioned Supply Officer [British]	
CDSO	Commonwealth Defence Science Organisation [British]	
CDSO	Companion of the Distinguished Service Order [British]	
CDSORG	Civil Direction of Shipping Organization	(MCD)
CDSP	China Democratic Socialist Party [Political party]	(EY)
CDSPP	Committee for Defense of Soviet Political Prisoners	(EA)
CD/SR	Candela per Steradian	
CDSR	Centre for Deafness Studies and Research [Griffith University] [Research center Australia]	
CDSR	Consolidated Delivery Status Report	(MCD)
CDSR	Contractual Data Status Reporting System	(MCD)
CDSR	Controlled Deployment Specular Reflector [Army]	(AABC)
CDSRS	Consolidated Delivery Status Report System	(MCD)
CDSS	Canadian Department of Supply and Services	(MCD)
CDSS	Canadian Down Syndrome Society	
CDSS	Clinical Decision Support System	(MAE)
CDSS	Command Decision Subsystem [Military]	(CAAL)
CDSS	Compressed Data Storage System	
CDSS	Computer Digital Switching System	(NITA)
CDSS	Constitutionally Delayed Short Stature [Medicine]	
CDSS	Country Development Strategy Statement [Agency for International Development]	
CDSS	Customer Digital Switching System [Telecommunications]	(MHDI)
CDSSA	Country Dance and Song Society of America	(EA)
cdst	Card Stock	(VRA)
CDST	Central Daylight Saving Time	
CDT	Bishop, CA [Location identifier FAA]	(FAAL)
Cdt	Cadet [British military]	(DMA)
CDT	Cadet	
CDT	Cambridge Display Technology [British]	
CDT	Canadian Graphite [Vancouver Stock Exchange symbol]	
CDT	Canyon Diablo Troilite [Geophysics]	
CDT	Carbon Dioxide Therapy	
CDT	Center for Democracy and Technology	
CDT	Central Daylight Time	
CDT	Centre d'Excellence pour le Developpement de la Technologie Telidon [Telidon Technology Development Center] [Polytechnical School of Montreal Quebec] [Information service or system]	(IID)
CDT	Certified Dental Technician	
CDT	Chargeable Downtime [Navy]	
CDT	Clearance Diving Tender	
CDT	Coincidence Detection Program	(SAA)
CDT	Colonial Data Technologies Corp. [AMEX symbol]	(SPSG)
CDT	Combined Diptheria and Tetanus [Vaccine] [Medicine]	
CDT	Combined Double Tee [Engineering]	(IAA)
CDT	Commandant	(WGA)
CDT	Command Descriptor Table	(NASA)
CDT	Command Destruct Transmitter	(AFM)
CDT	Commissioners Disability Table [Insurance]	
CDT	Communications Data Terminal	(MCD)
CDT	Communications Display Terminal	(IAA)
CDT	Community Development Trust	(AIE)
CDT	Compressed Data Tape	
CDT	Concept Developments Talks	
CDT	Concept Developments Tasks	(MCD)
CDT	Conduct	(AABC)
CDT	Conduit	

CDT............ Configuration Data Table (MCD)
CDT............ Connectionless Data Transmission [Telecommunications] (OSI)
CDT............ Consecutive Duty Tour [Air Force]
CDT............ Continuous Duty Target
CDT............ Contract Definition Test
CDT............ Contractor's Development Testing (MUGU)
CDT............ Control Data Terminal
CDT............ Control Differential Transformer
CDT............ Controlled Departure Time [FAA] (TAG)
CDT............ Coordinate Data Terminal (MCD)
CDT............ Coordinate Data Transmission
CDT............ Countdown Demonstration Test [NASA]
CDT............ Countdown Time [Aerospace]
CDT............ Craft Design and Technology
CDT............ Critical Dissolution Time [Chemistry]
CDT............ Cyclododecatriene [Organic chemistry]
CDTA .... Canadian Dance Teachers Association [Association Canadienne des Professeurs de Danse] (AC)
CDTA .... Chemical Diversion and Trafficking Act [1988]
CDTA .... Confederation of Design and Technology Associations [British]
CDTA .... (Cyclohexylenedinitrilo)tetraacetic Acid [Organic chemistry]
CDT & E ...... Contractor Development Test and Evaluation
CDTC .... Cable Design Technologies [NASDAQ symbol] (SAG)
CDTC .... Combat Development Test Center (CINC)
CDTC .... Computer Detector Test Console (DNAB)
CDTC-V .... Combat Development Test Center - Vietnam
C-DTE .... Character-Mode Data Terminal Equipment [Computer science] (PDAA)
CDTE.......... Council for Distributive Teacher Education
CDTEC .... Combat Development Technical Evaluation Center
CDTF .... Chemical Decontamination Training Facility [Military]
CDTI........... Clean Diesel Technologies [NASDAQ symbol] (TTSB)
CDTI........... Cockpit Displayed Traffic Information
CDTI........... Cockpit-Display-of-Traffic Information [NASA]
CDTL .... Common Data Translation Language
CDTLBS ...... Computer-Directed Training Lesson Building System
CDTOA .... California Dump Truck Owners Association (SRA)
CDTPA .... Calcium Diethylene-Triamine-Pentaacetic Acid (PDAA)
CDTPM .... Campaign for the Defence of the Turkish Peace Movement [British]
CDTS .... Centralized Digital Telecommunications System [Telecommunications] (HGAA)
CDTS .... Computer-Directed Training System
CDTS .... Computer-Driven Tactical System (MCD)
CDTS .... Conductus, Inc. [NASDAQ symbol] (SAG)
CDTS .... Constant-Depth Temperature Sensor [Oceanography]
CDTS .... Continental Divide Trail Society (EA)
CDTS .... Continuous Duty Target Source
CDTT .... Committee on Domestic Technology Transfer [Federal Council for Science and Technology]
CDTV .... Commodore Dynamic Total Vision [Interactive TV]
CDTV .... Compact Disk Television (BARN)
CDTX .... Colonial Data Tech [NASDAQ symbol] (TTSB)
CDTY .... Continuous Duty (MSA)
CDU .... Cabin Display Unit [Aviation]
CDU .... Cable Distribution Unit [Aerospace] (AAG)
CDU .... Call Director Unit
CDU .... Cartridge Disk Unit [Computer science] (MHDI)
CDU .... Central Development Unit
CDU .... Central Display Unit
CDU .... Christelijk-Democratische Unie [Christian Democratic Union] [Netherlands] (PPE)
CDU .... Christian Democratic Union [Germany] [Political party]
CDU .... Christlich-Demokratische Union [Christian Democratic Union] [Germany Political party] (PPW)
CDU .... Classification Decimale Universelle [Universal Decimal Classification]
CDU .... Coastal Defense RADAR for Detecting U-Boats
CDU .... Coligacao Democratico Social [Portugal] [Political party] (ECED)
CDU .... Color Developing Unit (NITA)
CDU .... Command Destruct Unit (AABC)
CDU .... Command Detector Unit (MCD)
CDU .... Command Display Unit (MCD)
CDU .... Command Distribution Unit (IIA)
CDU .... Computer Display Unit (MCD)
CDU .... Condenser Discharge Unit
CDU .... Congress of Democratic Unions (AC)
CDU .... Control and Diagnostic Unit [Computer science]
CDU .... Control and Display Unit (NASA)
CDU .... Control Data Unit
CDU .... Convergencia Democratica en Uruguay [Democratic Convergence in Uruguay] (PD)
CDU .... Coolant Distribution Unit [Computer science]
CDU .... Counter Display Unit (MCD)
CDU .... Coupling Data Unit (MCD)
CDU .... Coupling Display Unit
CDU .... Creative Development Unit [Australian Film Commission]
CDU .... Croatian Democratic Union [Political party] (EY)
CDU .... Crotonylidene Diurea [Fertilizer]
CDU .... CRT [Cathode-Ray Tube] Display Unit (MCD)
CDU .... Crude Distillation Unit [Petroleum technology]
CDU .... University of San Diego, James S. Copley Library, San Diego, CA [OCLC symbol] (OCLC)
CDU-BH .... Croatian Democratic Union of Bosnia-Herzegovina [Political party] (EY)
CDUCE .... Christian Democratic Union of Central Europe [Former Czechoslovakia] (EAIO)

CDU/CSU .... Christlich Demokratische Union/Christlich Soziale Union [Christian Democratic Union/Christian Social Union] [Germany Political party] (PPE)
CD-UDF....... Compact Disc Universal Disk Format
CDUEP .... Civil Defense University Extension Program
CDuG .... Giannini Controls Corp., Duarte, CA [Library symbol Library of Congress] (LCLS)
CDuH .... City of Hope Medical Center, Duarte, CA [Library symbol Library of Congress] (LCLS)
CDUI .... Command Document User Information (IAA)
CDUM .... Coupling Display Unit - IMU [Inertial Measurement Unit] (SAA)
CDuM.......... Minneapolis-Honeywell Library, Duarte, CA [Library symbol Library of Congress] (LCLS)
CDUO .... Coupling Display Unit Optic (IAA)
CDUP .... Committee for the Defence of the Unjustly Prosecuted (EAIO)
CDU-PAV .... Civic Democratic Party - Public Against Violence [Former Czechoslovakia] [Political party] (EY)
CD-USA .... Civil Defense, United States of America [Home study course]
CDUSA .... Coalition for a Decent USA [Defunct] (EA)
CDUSC .... Committee to Defend the US Constitution [Defunct] (EA)
CDV .... Canine Distemper Virus [Veterinary medicine]
CDV .... Capacitance Discharge Vaporization [Nuclear energy] (NRCH)
CDV .... Carma Developers Ltd. [Toronto Stock Exchange symbol]
CDV .... Carte de Visite [Visiting Card] [French]
CDV .... Check Digit Verification (CMD)
CDV .... Commander's Distinguished Visitors [Program] [Air Force]
CDV .... Compact Disk Video [Audio/video technology]
CDV .... Compressed Digital Video [Telecommunications]
CD/V .... Concept Demonstration/Validation Phase (AAGC)
CDV .... Cordova [Alaska] [Airport symbol] (OAG)
CDV .... Council of Disabled Persons, Victoria [Australia]
CDV .... Current Domestic Value [of goods in the country of origin]
CDv .... Sierra County Free Library, Downieville, CA [Library symbol Library of Congress] (LCLS)
CDVFGFC.... Commonwealth Dried Vine Fruits Grade Fixing Committee [Australia]
CD-VI .... Compact Disk Video Interactive [Computer science]
CDVO .... Civilian Defense Volunteer Office
CDVT .... Carte-de-Visite (VRA)
CDVT .... Cell Delay Variation Tolerance [Telecommunications] (ACRL)
CDVU .... Composed Document Viewing Utility [IBM Corp.]
CDW .... Caldwell, NJ [Location identifier FAA] (FAAL)
CDW .... Carrying a Dangerous Weapon [Police term]
CDW .... Catalytic Dewaxing [Petroleum refining]
CDW .... Charge-Density Wave [Physics]
CDW .... Chilled Drinking Water [Aerospace] (AAG)
CDW .... Circumpolar Deep Water [Oceanography]
CDW .... Civil Defense Warning
CDW .... Collision Damage Waiver [Insurance]
CDW .... Command Data Word (MCD)
CDW .... Common Damage Waiver
CDW .... Computer Data Word (CET)
CDW .... Computer Discount Warehouse (PCM)
CDWC .... CDW Computer Centers [NASDAQ symbol] (TTSB)
CDWC .... CDW Computer Centers, Inc. [NASDAQ symbol] (SAG)
CDW Cpt..... CDW Computer Centers [Associated Press] (SAG)
CDWG .... Countdown Working Group [NASA] (KSC)
CDWI .... CD Warehouse, Inc. [NASDAQ symbol] (SAG)
CD-WO....... Compact Disc-Write Once [Computer science] (DOM)
CDWR .... Chest of Drawers
CDWR .... Chilled Drinking Water Return [Aerospace]
CD Wrhs ..... CD Warehouse, Inc. [Associated Press] (SAG)
CDWS .... Civil Defense Warning System
CDWSP .... Community Development Work Study Program [Department of Housing and Urban Development] (GFGA)
CDWT .... Cord Welt
CDWU .... Christian Democratic World Union (EA)
CDX .... Canadex Resources Ltd. [Toronto Stock Exchange symbol]
CDX .... Catellus Development [NYSE symbol] (TTSB)
CDX .... Catellus Development Corp. [NYSE symbol] (SPSG)
CDX .... Change Directory Extended [Computer science] (PCM)
CDX .... Companion Dog, Excellent [Dog show term]
CDX .... Compound Index File [Computer science] (PCM)
CDX .... Control Differential Transmitter
CDX .... Somerset, KY [Location identifier FAA] (FAAL)
CDXPrA....... Catellus Dvlp $3.75'A'Cv Pfd [NYSE symbol] (TTSB)
CDY .... Chevy Development Corp. [Vancouver Stock Exchange symbol]
CDYN .... Dynamic Compliance [Of lung on pulmonary function tests] [Medicine] (DAVI)
Cdyn .... Dynamic Lung Compliance [Medicine] (BABM)
CDZ............ Chef der Zivilverwaltung [Chief of Civil Affairs Section] [German military - World War II]
CE.............. Adult, Career, and Vocational Education [Educational Resources Information Center (ERIC) Clearinghouse] [Ohio State University] (PAZ)
CE.............. Air Virginia [ICAO designator] (AD)
CE.............. Avions Mudry & Cie. [France ICAO aircraft manufacturer identifier] (ICAO)
CE.............. Beames' Costs in Equity [A publication] (DLA)
CE.............. Cache Enable [Computer science] (PCM)
C/E............. Calculation/Experiment (NRCH)
CE.............. Calenergy Co., Inc. [NYSE symbol] (SAG)
CE.............. CalEngery Co. [NYSE symbol] (TTSB)
CE.............. California Encephalitis [Medicine]
CE.............. California Energy Co., Inc. [NYSE symbol] (SPSG)
CE.............. Cambridge Econometrics [British]

C-E	Campbell-Ewald Co. [Advertising agency]
CE	Canada East
CE	Canadian Energy Services Ltd. [Toronto Stock Exchange symbol]
CE	Canadian Engineers (DMA)
CE	Candidate Evaluation
CE	Capillary Electrophoresis [Physical chemistry]
CE	Capital Equipment (AFIT)
CE	Capital Expenditure [Accounting]
CE	Carbon Equivalent [Chemical engineering]
CE	Carboxylation Efficiency [Botany]
CE	Carboxylesterase [An enzyme]
CE	Card Error [Computer science] (IAA)
CE	Cardiac Emergency [Medicine] (MAE)
CE	Cardiac Enlargement [Medicine]
CE	Cardioesophageal [Junction] [Gastroenterology] (DAVI)
CE	Carotid Endarterectomy [Medicine]
CE	Cash Earnings [Business term]
CE	Cast Enamel [Classified advertising] (ADA)
CE	Catalog Events [Exhibition of US company product catalogs, etc., in foreign markets] [Department of Commerce]
C/E	Catch per Unit Effort [Pisciculture]
CE	Caveat Emptor [Let the Buyer Beware] [Latin]
CE	Celestial Equator
CE	Cellular Envelope [Embryology]
CE	Cellulose Ester [Organic chemistry]
CE	Center of Effort [Sailing]
CE	Central (SSD)
CE	Central Engine [Galactic radio source]
CE	Central Engineering (IIA)
CE	Central Episiotomy [Obstetrics] (DAVI)
CE	Central Europe (NATG)
CE	Cerebral Edema [Medicine] (CPH)
Ce	Cerium [Chemical element]
CE	Certainty Equivalent Coefficient [Finance]
CE	Certified Exchangor [International Exchangors Association] [Designation awarded by]
CE	Certified Exchangors [An association] (EA)
ce	Ceylon [Sri Lanka] [MARC country of publication code Library of Congress] (LCCP)
CE	Chancellor of the Exchequer [British]
CE	Change Evaluation (NASA)
CE	Channel End (OA)
CE	Chartered Engineer [British]
CE	Chemical Energy
CE	Chemical Engineer
CE	Chicken Embryo
CE	Chief Engineer [Navy]
CE	Chief Executive
CE	Chief of Engineers [Later, COE] [Army]
CE	Childhood Education [A publication] (BRI)
CE	Chip Enable [Computer science] (NITA)
CE	Chip Enable Input [Computer science]
CE	Chloroform and Ether [Mixture]
CE	Cholesterol Esters [Clinical chemistry]
CE	Christian Endeavor (IIA)
CE	Christian Era
CE	Chronometer Error [Navigation]
CE	Church of England
CE	Cincinnati Electronics Corp. [Information service or system Defunct] (IID)
CE	Circles of Exchange [Later, COE] [An association] (EA)
CE	Circuit Edges [Bookbinding] (DGA)
CE	Circular Error [Military]
CE	Civil Engineer
CE	Civil Enterprise [Publishing program]
CE	Civilian Enterprise
CE	Clear-Entry [Calculators]
CE	Clinical Emphysema [Medicine] (MAE)
CE	Clinoenstatite [A mineral]
CE	Close Encounter [with a UFO]
CE	Club Elite of North America (EA)
CE	Coal Equivalent
CE	Coarse Erection
CE	Cognizant Engineer
CE	Collision Elimination [Wiring hub] [Computer science] (PCM)
CE	Columbia Encyclopedia [A publication]
CE	Combat Element [Marine Corps] (DOMA)
CE	Combustion Engineering [Navy]
CE	Commercial Engineer
CE	Commercial Enterprise
CE	Commercial Equipment
CE	Commodity Exchange [Investment term]
CE	Common Emitter
CE	Common Entrance [Examination for entry into public school] [British]
CE	Common Era
CE	Communaute EURAIL [EURAIL Community] [An association Netherlands] (EAIO)
CE	Communaute Europeenne [European Community]
C-E	Communications-Electronics
CE	Communications Equipment
CE	Community of the Epiphany [Anglican religious community]
CE	Commutator End (MSA)
CE	Compacted Earth (PDAA)
CE	Compact Edition [Windows] [Computer science] (PCM)
CE	Comparative Estimating

CE	Comparing Element (IAA)
CE	Compass Error [Navigation]
CE	Competitive Equilibrium [Mathematics]
C/E	Component/Equipment (MCD)
CE	Composition Exploding (PDAA)
CE	Compression Engine
CE	Computational Element (NITA)
CE	Compute Element (IAA)
CE	Computer Engineer
CE	Concept Exploration
CE	Concurrent Engineering
CE	Conditional Exemption [Environmental science]
CE	Conducted Emission (IEEE)
CE	Conductivity Element [Nuclear energy] (NRCH)
CE	Cone
CE	Configuration Element (AFIT)
CE	Conjugated Estrogens [Endocrinology]
CE	Conseil de l'Entente [Entente Council - EC] (EAIO)
CE	Conseil de l'Europe [Council of Europe] (EAIO)
CE	Conseil d'Etat [Council of State] [French] (ILCA)
CE	Conspicuity Enhancement [Aviation]
CE	Constant Error [Psychology]
CE	Construction Electrician [Navy rating]
CE	Consultative Examination [Social Security Administration] (OICC)
CE	Consulting Engineer
CE	Consumatum Est [It Is Finished] [Freemasonry] [Latin] (ROG)
CE	Consumption Entry [Economics]
CE	Continuing Education
CE	Continuous Estrus [Endocrinology]
CE	Continuous Evaluation [DoD]
CE	Contract Engineers (MCD)
CE	Contract Exploration (MCD)
CE	Contractile Element [of skeletal muscle]
CE	Contrast Echocardiology [Cardiology] (DAVI)
CE	Control Electrician [British military] (DMA)
CE	Control Element (MCD)
CE	Control Engineering
CE	Control Equipment (IAA)
CE	Control Error (IAA)
CE	Controlled Environment
CE	Conversational English
CE	Converting Enzyme
CE	Copy Editor (WDMC)
ce	Copy Editor (WDMC)
CE	Corps Eligible [Army] (RDA)
CE	Corps of Engineers [Army]
CE	Corps of Engineers Command [Army] (AAGC)
CE	Cost Effectiveness [Accounting]
CE	Cost Element (MCD)
CE	Cotton Effect
CE	Coulomb Excitation [Nuclear physics] (OA)
CE	Council of Europe (NUCP)
CE	Countercurrent Electrophoresis [Also, CCE] [Analytical chemistry]
CE	Counterespionage
CE	Coupe Einspritz [Coupe Fuel-Injection] [German]
CE	Crew Evaluator [Military] (INF)
CE	Criminal Evidence (LAIN)
CE	Critical Examination (CAAL)
CE	Cum Entitlement [With Entitlement] [Latin Legal term] (ADA)
C/E	Currency Exploitation
CE	Current Efficiency [Electrochemistry]
CE	Current Estimate (AFIT)
CE	Current Expendable (NASA)
CE	Current Exploitation (MCD)
CE	Customer Engineer [Computer science]
CE	Customs and Excise
CE	Cuvee Extra
CE	Cyanoethyl [Organic chemistry]
CE	Cytopathic Effect [Medicine]
C_E	Emitter Capacitance (IDOE)
CE	Eureka City Library, Eureka, CA [Library symbol Library of Congress] (LCLS)
CE	International Society of Christian Endeavor
CE	Republic of Singapore Air Force [ICAO designator] (ICDA)
CE1	Construction Electrician, First Class [Navy rating]
CE2	Construction Electrician, Second Class [Navy rating]
CE3	Close Encounters of the Third Kind [Movie title]
CE3	Construction Electrician, Third Class [Navy rating]
CEA	Association of Consulting Engineers of Alberta (AC)
CEA	California Eastern Airways
CEA	California Escrow Association (SRA)
CEA	Cambridge Electron Accelerator
CEA	Canadian Economics Association [See also ACE]
CEA	Canadian Education Association
CEA	Canadian Electrical Association
CEA	Canadian Export Association
CEA	Canadian Exporters' Association [Association des Exportateurs Canadiens] (AC)
CEA	Carcinoembryonic Antigen [Immunochemistry]
CEA	Carcinoembryonic Antigen [Medicine] (CDI)
CEA	Carotid Endarterectomy [Cardiology] (DAVI)
CEA	Catholic Economic Association [Later, ASE] (EA)
CEA	Cement Employers Association (EA)
CEA	Center for Early Adolescence (EA)
CEA	Central Electricity Authority [British]

CEA............ Centre for Electronics in Agriculture [*University of New England*] [*Australia*]
CEA............ Certified Environmental Auditor [*Environmental science*]
CE/A.......... Change Evalution/Analysis [*Engineering*]
CEA............ Chemical Engineering Abstracts [*Royal Society of Chemistry*] [*Information service or system*]
CEA............ Chief Electrical Artificer [*British military*] (DMA)
CEA............ Children's Emotions Anonymous (EA)
CEA............ Chinese Exclusion Act
CEA............ Chlorendic Aldehyde [*Organic chemistry*]
CEA............ Cholesterol-Esterifying Activity [*Biochemistry Medicine*] (DMAA)
CEA............ Church Evangelism Association [*Later, Masterkey Association*] (EA)
CEA............ Church Extension Association [*British*]
CEA............ Cinematograph Exhibitioners' Association of Great Britian and Ireland
CEA............ Cinematograph Exhibitors' Association [*Australia*]
CEA............ Circular Error Average [*Military*]
CEA............ Cisco Enterprise Accounting [*Computer science*]
CEA............ Citizen Education Association [*Defunct*] (EA)
CEA............ Citizens Environment Alliance of Southwestern Ontario (AC)
CEA............ Clearinghouse on Educational Administration [*ERIC*]
CEA............ Clearinghouse on Election Administration [*Federal Election Commission*]
CEA............ Coal Exporters Association of the United States (EA)
CEA............ College English Association (EA)
CEA............ Colorado Education Association (SRA)
CEA............ Colt Car Co. [*British ICAO designator*] (FAAC)
CEA............ Combustion Engineering Association [*British*]
CEA............ Commissariat a l'Energie Atomique [*Atomic Energy Commission - AEC*] [*France Research center*]
CEA............ Commission Economique pour l'Afrique [*Economic Commission for Africa - ECA*] (EAIO)
CEA............ Commissioner for Enterprise Agreements [*New South Wales*] [*Australia*]
CEA............ Committee for Energy Awareness [*Later, USCEA*] (EA)
CEA............ Commodity Exchange Act
CEA............ Commodity Exchange Authority [*Later, CFTC*] [*Department of Agriculture*]
CEA............ Common Error Analysis (MCD)
C-EA.......... Communications-Electronics Agency [*Army*]
CEA............ Community Electoral Assistant [*Australia*]
CEA............ Conductive Education Association (AIE)
CEA............ Confederation des Educateurs Americains [*Confederation of American Educators*]
CEA............ Confederation Europeenne de l'Agriculture [*European Confederation of Agriculture*] (EAIO)
CEA............ Congressional Education Associates [*Private, nonpartisan consulting group*]
CEA............ Connecticut Education Association (SRA)
CEA............ Connecticut Electric Association (SRA)
CEA............ Conservation Education Association (EA)
CEA............ Constant Extinction Angle (IAA)
CEA............ Construction Equipment Advertisers [*Later, CEA PRC*] (EA)
CEA............ Control Electrical Artificer [*Navy rating British*]
CEA............ Control Electronics Assembly [*Aerospace*]
CEA............ Control Element Assembly [*Nuclear energy*] (NRCH)
CEA............ Controlled Environment Agriculture
CEA............ Cooperative Education Association (EA)
CEA............ Cooperative Enforcement Agreement [*Environmental Protection Agency*] (GFGA)
CEA............ Correctional Education Association (EA)
CEA............ Cost-Effectiveness Analysis [*Economics*]
CEA............ Council for Educational Advance [*British*]
CEA............ Council of Economic Advisers [*to the President*]
CEA............ Council on Environmental Alternatives (EA)
CEA............ Crystalline Egg Albumin (MAE)
CEA............ Wichita, KS [*Location identifier FAA*] (FAAL)
CEAA.......... Canadian Environmental Auditing Association (AC)
CEAA.......... Center for Editions of American Authors [*Later, CSE*]
CEAA.......... Centre Europeen d'Aviation Agricole
CEAA.......... Childbirth Education Association of Australia
CEAA.......... Council of European-American Associations [*Later, FEAO*]
CEAAC........ Catholic Education Aboriginal Advisory Committee [*Australia*]
CEAAL........ Consejo de Educacion de Adultos de America Latina [*Santiago, Chile*] (EAIO)
CEABA........ Chemical Engineering and Biotechnology Abstracts [*A publication*]
CEABREP..... Cost Effectiveness Analysis of Bonuses and Reenlistment Policies
CEAC.......... Citizens Educational Advisory Committee
CEAC.......... Clinical Education and Assessment Center [*Medicine*] (DMAA)
CEAC.......... Commission Europeenne de l'Aviation Civile [*European Civil Aviation Conference - ECAC*] (EAIO)
CEAC.......... Committee for European Airspace Coordination [*NATO*]
CEAC.......... Control Element Assembly Calculator [*Nuclear energy*] (NRCH)
CEAC.......... Cost and Economic Analysis Center (DOMA)
CEACO........ Committee for Equitable Access to Crude Oil (EA)
CEAD.......... Centre des Auteurs Dramatiques (AC)
CEAD.......... Chief Engineer and Superintendent of Armaments Design [*British military*] (DMA)
CEADI........ Colored Electronic Attitude Director Indicator (MCD)
CEADS........ Central European Air Defense Sector
CEAE.......... Centre d'Etudes de l'Asie de l'Est [*University of Montreal*] [*Research center*] (RCD)
CEAF.......... Centre d'Education et d'Action des Femmes de Montreal (AC)
CEAFU........ Concerned Educators Against Forced Unionism (EA)
CEAH.......... Conference on Early American History (EA)

CEAI.......... Chase Econometrics Associates, Inc. [*Information service or system*] (IID)
CEAI.......... Christian Educators Association International (EAIO)
CEAIO........ Comite Europeen de l'Association Internationale de l'Ozone [*European Committee of the International Ozone Association*] (EAIO)
CEAL.......... Cambridge Electron Accelerator Laboratories [*Massachusetts Institute of Technology*]
CEAL.......... Carcinoembryonic Antigen-Like [*Protein*] [*Medicine*] (DMAA)
CEAL.......... Comite Europe-Amerique Latine [*Belgium*]
CEAL.......... Committee on East Asian Libraries
CEAM.......... Center for Exposure Assessment Modeling [*Athens, GA*] [*Environmental Protection Agency*] (GRD)
CEAM.......... Cost-Effectiveness Analysis Methodology [*Economics*] (MCD)
CEAM-TU..... Advanced Materials at Tuskegee University (RDA)
CEANAR....... Commission on Education in Agriculture and Natural Resources [*National Research Council*] [*Defunct*]
CE & IS...... Combined Elements and Integrated Systems (SSD)
CE & R....... Central Episiotomy and Repair [*Obstetrics*] (DAVI)
CEAO.......... Camouflage Effectiveness Assessment Office [*Army*] (RDA)
CEAO.......... County Engineers Association of Ohio (SRA)
CEAP.......... Clinical Efficacy Assessment Project [*Medicine*] (DMAA)
CEAP.......... Corps of Engineers Automation Plan [*DoD*] (GFGA)
CEAPD........ Central Air Procurement District
CEA PRC..... Construction Equipment Advertisers and Public Relations Council [*Milwaukee, WI*] (EA)
CEAPS........ Conventional Engine Anti-Pollution System [*Automotive engineering*]
CEAR.......... Center for Engineering Applications of Radioisotopes [*North Carolina State University*] [*Research center*] (RCD)
CEARC........ Canadian Environmental Assessment Research Council
CEARC........ Computer Education and Applied Research Center
CEAREX....... Coordinated Eastern Arctic Experiment [*Marine science*] (OSRA)
CEAREX....... Coordinated Eastern Arctic Experiment (USDC)
CEARP........ Continuing Education Approval and Recognition Program (DMAA)
CEARS........ COMSEC [*Communications Security*] Equipment Asset Reporting System (MCD)
CEAS.......... Center for Environmental Assessment Services [*National Oceanic and Atmospheric Administration Information service or system*] (IID)
CEAS.......... Centre Ecologique Albert Schweitzer [*Albert Schweitzer Ecological Centre*] [*Switzerland*] (EAIO)
CEAS.......... Centre for European Agricultural Studies [*British*] (ARC)
CEAS.......... Class E Airspace [*Aviation*] (FAAC)
CEAS.......... Composite Educational Abilites Scale (AIE)
CEASA........ Canadian Electronic & Appliance Service Association [*Organisation Canadienne de Service d'Appareils Domestique*] (AC)
CEASC........ Committee for European Airspace Coordination [*NATO*] (NATG)
CEASD........ Conference of Educational Administrators Serving the Deaf (EA)
CEASD........ Corporate Engineering and Sales Directive
CEASE........ Citizens to End Animal Suffering and Exploitation (EA)
CEASE........ Concerned Educators Allied for a Safe Environment (EA)
CEASPECT ... Camera Europea degli Arbitri Stragiudiziali e dei Periti Esperti Consulenti Tecnici [*European Chamber of Extra-Judicial Adjudicators and Expert Technical Advisors*] (EAIO)
CEASRS....... Civil Engineer Automated Specification Retrieval System [*Air Force*]
CEAT.......... Canadian-English Achievement Test [*Education*] (AEBS)
CEAT.......... Chronic Ectopic Atrial Tachycardia [*Medicine*] (DMAA)
CEAT.......... Contractor Evidence Audit Team [*Environmental Protection Agency*] (ERG)
CEATOS....... Cost Effectiveness Analysis of the Tactical Operations System [*Military*] (MCD)
CEAU.......... Continuing Education Achievement Unit (IEEE)
CEAV.......... Career Education Association of Victoria [*Australia*]
CEB............ Calcium Entry Blocking [*Agent*] [*Physiology*]
CEB............ Cebu [*Philippines*] [*Airport symbol*] (OAG)
CEB............ Cellulolytic Enzyme Biodegradability [*Biochemistry*]
CEB............ Central Electricity Board [*British*]
CEB............ Change Evaluation Board [*NASA*] (SSD)
CEB............ Chemical Element Balance (GFGA)
CEB............ Cluster Effects Bomblet
CEB............ CNO [*Chief of Naval Operations*] Evaluation Board
CEB............ CNO [*Chief of Naval Operations*] Executive Board
CEB............ Combined Effects Bomb (MCD)
CEB............ Comite Euro-International du Beton [*Euro-International Committee for Concrete*]
CEB............ Comite Europeen des Constructeurs de Broleurs [*European Committee of Manufacturers of Burners*] (EA)
CEB............ Comite Europeen du Beton [*European Committee for Concrete*]
CEB............ Communications-Electronics Board (NATG)
CEB............ Comunidades Eclesiales de Base [*Spanish*]
CEB............ Confederation Europeenne de Billard
CEB............ Consolidated Omab Enterprises Ltd. [*Vancouver Stock Exchange symbol*]
CEB............ Continuous Election Beam [*Accelerator facility*]
CEB............ Cotton Elastic Bandage (DAVI)
CEB............ Council on Employee Benefits (EA)
CEB............ Cryogenic Expulsive Bladder
CEB............ Edwards Air Force Base Library, Edwards AFB, CA [*OCLC symbol*] (OCLC)
CEBA.......... Circuitless Electron Beam Amplifier (MCD)
CEBA.......... Communications Excellence to Black Audiences [*An award*]
CEBA.......... Competitive Equality Banking Act [*1987*]
CEBA.......... Confederation Europeenne de Baseball Amateur [*European Amateur Baseball Confederation - EABC*] (EA)
CEBAF........ Continuous Electron Beam Accelerator Facility [*Physics*]

CEBAR	Chemical, Biological, Radiological Warfare [*Later, CB*] [*Military*]
CEBC	Centennial Bancorp [*NASDAQ symbol*] (SAG)
CEBC	Consulting Engineers of British Columbia (AC)
CEBEMO	Centrale Bemiddeling bij Medefinanciering Ontuikkelingsprogramma's [*Netherlands*]
CEBER	Center for Built Environment Research [*Morgan State University*] [*Research center*] (RCD)
CEBJ	Commission of Editors of Biochemical Journals
CEBK	Central Co-Operative Bank [*NASDAQ symbol*] (NQ)
CEBLS	Comprehensive Evaluation of Basic Living Skills
CEBM	Corona, Eddy Current, Beta Ray, Microwave
CEBMCA	Corps of Engineers Ballistic Missile Construction Agency [*Army*]
CEBMCO	Corps of Engineers Ballistic Missile Construction Office [*Army*]
CEBN	Combat Equipment Battalion, North [*Military*]
CEBOE	National Association of Classroom Educators in Business and Office Education (EA)
CEBQ	Conseil de l'Enveloppe du Batiment du Quebec (AC)
CEBR	Cedar Breaks National Monument
CEBS	Certified Employee Benefit Specialist [*Trademark of the International Foundation of Employee Benefit Plans, Inc.*]
CEBST	Church of England Boys' School in Tasmania [*Australia*]
CEBus	Confirmed Exposure but Unconscious [*Advertising*]
CEBus	Consumer Electronics Bus [*Residential wiring standard*]
CEBV	Chronic Epstein-Barr Virus [*Medicine*]
CEBV	Communaute Economique du Betail et de la Viande [*Economic Community for Livestock and Meat - ECLM*] (EAIO)
CEC	Cambridge Education Consultants Ltd. [*British*]
CEC	Cambridge English Classics [*A publication*]
CEC	Canada Employment Centre
CEC	Canadian Electrical Code
CEC	Canberra Entertainment Centre [*Australia*]
CEC	Canteen for Extreme Climate [*Army*]
CEC	Capillary Electrochromatography [*Computer science*]
CEC	Capital Equipment Corp. [*Burlington, MA*]
CEC	Capsule End Cover [*Aerospace*]
CEC	Caribbean Economic Community
CEC	Caribbean Employers Confederation [*Trinidad and Tobago*] (EAIO)
CEC	Catholic Enquiry Centre [*Australia*]
CEC	Cation-Exchange Capacity [*Chemical technology*]
CEC	Cation Exchange Chromography (NUCP)
CEC	CEC Resources Ltd. [*Associated Press*] (SAG)
CEC	Celebrity Engineering [*Vancouver Stock Exchange symbol*]
CEC	Center for Economic Conversion (EA)
CEC	Center for Educational Change [*University of California, Berkeley*]
CEC	Central East Coast
CEC	Central Economic Committee
CEC	Centralized Electronic Control [*Navy*]
CEC	Centre Europeen de la Culture [*European Cultural Centre - ECC*] (EAIO)
CEC	Centre for Economic Cooperation (AC)
CE C	Cepi Corpus [*I Have Taken the Body*] [*Latin Legal term*] (DLA)
CEC	Ceramic Educational Council (EA)
CEC	Certification of Equipment Completion (SAA)
CEC	Chemical Engineering Catalog [*A publication*]
CEC	Chicano Employment Committee (DICI)
CEC	Childress [*Texas*] [*Seismograph station code, US Geological Survey*] (SEIS)
CEC	Cholesteryl Erucyl Carbonate (PDAA)
CEC	Ciliated Epithelial Cells [*Medicine*]
CEC	Circular Exhaust Cloud (PDAA)
CEC	Citizen Exchange Council (EA)
CEC	Citizens Electoral Council [*Political party Australia*]
CEC	Citizens Energy Corp. [*Nonprofit*]
CEC	Citizen's Energy Council (EA)
CEC	Civil Engineer Corps [*Army*]
CEC	Clark Equipment Co. (MCD)
CEC	Clothing Export Council [*British*] (DS)
CEC	Coal Experts Committee [*Allied German Occupation Forces*]
CEC	Commission Europeenne de la Corseterie [*European Corsetry Commission - ECC*] (EAIO)
CEC	Commission of the European Communities [*See also CCE*] (EAIO)
CEC	Committee for Equitable Compensation [*Defunct*] (EA)
CEC	Commodities Exchange Center [*New York, NY*]
CEC	Commodity Exchange Commission [*Functions transferred to CFTC*]
CEC	Commons Expenditure Committee [*British*]
CEC	Commonwealth Economic Committee [*British*]
CEC	Commonwealth Edison Co. (MHDB)
CEC	Commonwealth Education Conferences [*British*]
CEC	Commonwealth Engineering Conference (MCD)
CEC	Commonwealth Engineers Council [*See also CAICB*] [*British*] (EAIO)
CEC	Communication Effectiveness Centre [*Canada*]
CEC	Communications and Electronics Command [*Formerly, ASC*] [*Army*]
CEC	Communications-Electronics Committee (AFM)
CEC	Community Environmental Council (EA)
CEC	Complex Equipment Contract (MCD)
CEC	Compound Elliptic Concentrator (PDAA)
CEC	Compromising Emanations Control (MCD)
CEC	Computer Engineer Console
CEC	Computers, Electronics and Control Symposium (MHDI)
CEC	Confederation Europeenne de l'Industrie de la Chaussure [*European Confederation of the Footwear Industry*] [*EC*] (ECED)
CEC	Confederation Europeenne des Cadres [*European Confederation of Managers*] [*EC*] (ECED)
CEC	Conference of European Churches (EA)

CEC	Conseil Europeen de Coordination pour le Developpement des Essais de Performancedes Combustibles et des Lubrifiants pour Moteurs [*Coordinating European Council for the Development of Performance Tests for Lubricants and Engine Fuels - CEC*] (EAIO)
CEC	Consolidated Edison Co. (MHDB)
CEC	Consolidated Electrodynamics Corp.
CEC	Consolidated Electronics Corp.
CEC	Constant Electric Contact (IAA)
CEC	Construction Electrician, Chief [*Navy rating*]
CEC	Consulting Engineers Council [*Later, ACEC*] (EA)
CEC	Continental Entry Charts [*Air Force*]
CEC	Continuing Education Center [*Veterans Administration*] (GFGA)
CEC	Continuing Education Council [*Later, CNCE*] (EA)
CEC	Continuing Education Credit (DAVI)
CEC	Contractor Establishment Code (AAGC)
CEC	Control Encoder Coupler (NASA)
CEC	Controlled Element Computer
CEC	Cooperative Engagement Capability [*Navy*] (DOMA)
CEC	Coordinating European Council for the Development of Performance Tests for Lubricants and Engine Fuels (EA)
CEC	Corneal Endothelial Cell [*Medicine*] (CPH)
CEC	Council for Education in the Commonwealth (EAIO)
CEC	Council for Exceptional Children (EA)
CEC	Council of the European Communities
CEC	Coupon Exchange Club [*Commercial firm*] (EA)
CEC	Crescent City [*California*] [*Airport symbol*] (OAG)
CEC	Crew Equipment Compartment (MCD)
CEC	Crown Estate Commissioner [*British*]
CEC	Cryogenic Engineering Conference (EA)
CEC	Customs Entry Charge (DCTA)
CEc	El Centro Free Public Library, El Centro, CA [*Library symbol Library of Congress*] (LCLS)
CEC	European Council for Education by Correspondence
CEC	National Council on the Evaluation of Foreign Educational Credentials (EA)
CECA	Carolinas Electrical Contractors Association (SRA)
CECA	Committee of European Coffee Associations (EAIO)
CECA	Communaute Europeenne du Charbon et de l'Acier [*European Coal and Steel Community*]
CECA	Community Emergency Care Association [*Defunct*] (EA)
CECA	Constructionman Apprentice, Construction Electrician, Striker [*Navy rating*]
CECA	Consumer Energy Council of America (EA)
CECA	Council on Economic and Cultural Affairs [*Later, ADC*] [*Rockefeller Brothers Fund, Ford Foundation activity*]
CEcaE	El Camino College, Torrance, CA [*Library symbol Library of Congress*] (LCLS)
CECAF	Fishery Committee for the Eastern Central Atlantic [*See also COPACE*]
CEcajC	Christian Heritage Library, El Cajon, CA [*Library symbol Library of Congress*] (LCLS)
CECAL	Commission Episcopale de Cooperation Apostolique Canada-Amerique Latine
CECAPI	Commission Europeenne des Constructeurs d'Appareillage Electrique d'Installations [*European Commission of Manufacturers of Electrical Installation Equipment*] (EAIO)
CECA/RF	Consumer Energy Council of America Research Foundation (EA)
CECATS	CSB [*Chemical Species Balance*] Existing Chemicals Assessment Tracking System [*Environmental Protection Agency*] (EPA)
CECAVI	Confederation Europeenne des Categories Auxiliaires des Activites Viti-Vinicole [*European Confederation of Auxiliary Occupations in the Wine Trade*] [*Common Market*]
CECB	Conseil Europeen du Cuir Brut [*European Untanned Leather Council*]
CECC	California Educational Computing Consortium (EA)
CECC	CENELEC [*Comite Europeen de Normalisation Electrotechnique*] Electronic Components Committee (DS)
CECC	Commonwealth Economic Consultative Council [*British*]
CECC	Communaute Europeenne de Credit Communal [*European Municipal Credit Community*]
CECCAM	Centro de Estudios para el Cambio del campo en Mexico [*A Mexican think tank which works on policies and training for growers*] (CROSS)
CECCP	Combustion Equilibrium Calculation Computer Program (MCD)
CECD	Confederation Europeenne du Commerce de Detail [*European Federation for Retail Trade*] (EAIO)
CECDC	Cost Estimate Control Data Center (AABC)
CECE	Ceco Environmental [*NASDAQ symbol*] (SAG)
CECE	Combined Electrolysis and Catalytic Exchange [*CANDU-reactor advantage*]
CECE	Committee for European Construction Equipment [*British*] (EAIO)
CECED	Conseil Europeen de la Construction Electrodomestique [*European Committee of Manufacturers of Electrical Domestic Equipment*] (EA)
CECEEB	Commission on English of the College Entrance Examination Board (EA)
CEC EIT	Civil Engineer Corps, Engineer-in-Training [*Army*] (DNAB)
CEcerB	Western Baptist Bible College, El Cerrito, CA [*Library symbol Library of Congress*] (LCLS)
CECF	Children's Eye Care Foundation [*Later, NCECF*] (EA)
CECF	Chinese Export Commodities Fair
CECF	Corrective Eye Care Foundation [*Later, CLMA*] (EA)
CECG	Consumers in the European Community Group
CECH	Comite Europeen de la Culture du Houblon [*European Hop Growers Committee*]

CECI............. Centre d'Etude et de Cooperation International [*International Study and Cooperation Centre*] [*Canada*]

CEcI............. Imperial County Free Library, El Centro, CA [*Library symbol Library of Congress*] (LCLS)

CECIF........... Chambre Europeenne pour le Developpement du Commerce, de l'Industrie, et des Finances [*European Chamber for the Development of Trade, Industry, and Finances*] [*Brussels, Belgium*] (EAIO)

CECIL............ Compact Electronic Components Inspection Laboratory

CECIMO .... Comite Europeen de Cooperation des Industries de la Machine Outil [*European Committee for Cooperation of the Machine Tool Industries*] [*EC*] (ECED)

CECIOS........ Conseil Europeen du Comite International de l'Organisation Scientifique [*European Council of International Committee of Scientific Management*]

CECIP........... Comite Europeen des Constructeurs d'Instruments de Pesage [*European Committee of Weighing Instrument Manufacturers - ECWIM*] (EAIO)

CECL............ Civil Engineering Computer Laboratory [*MIT*] (MCD)

CECL............ Comite d'Etude sur les Conditions du Logement [*Study Committee Study on Housing Conditions*] [*Canada*]

CECL............ Conference of Eastern College Librarians

CECLA......... Comision Especial de Coordinacion Latinoamericana

CECLANT .... French Commander-in-Chief, Atlantic [*NATO*]

CECLB......... Comite Europeen de Controle Laitierbeurrier

CECLES........ Conseil Europeen pour la Construction de Lanceures d'Engins Spatiaux [*European Council for the Construction of Spacecraft Launching Areas*] [*France*]

CECM........... Clarke Memorial Museum, Eureka, CA [*Library symbol*] [*Library of Congress*] (LCLS)

CECM........... Composite Engineering Change Memo [*NASA*] (KSC)

CECM........... Concurrent Engineering for Composites Materials Program [*University of Delaware, Center for Composite Materials*] (RDA)

CECM........... Construction Electrician, Master Chief [*Navy rating*]

CECM........... Convention Europeenne de la Construction Metallique [*EC*] (ECED)

CECMED ...... French Commander-in-Chief, Mediterranean [*NATO*]

CEC-MR ...... Division on Mental Retardation of the Council for Exceptional Children [*EA*]

CECMRL ...... Communications-Electronics Consolidated Mobilization Reserve List

CECMV........ Cereal Chlorotic Mottle Virus [*Plant pathology*]

CECN .... Constructionman, Construction Electrician, Striker [*Navy rating*]

CECO .... Center Engine Cutoff [*NASA*] (KSC)

CECO .... Chandler Evans Corp.

CECO .... Commission d'Enquete pour le Crime Organise [*Organized Crime Investigating Commission*] [*Canada*]

CECO .... Communications & Entertainment Corp. [*NASDAQ symbol*] (SAG)

CECO .... Cost Estimate Change Order (NRCH)

CECOD .... Comite de Fabricants Europeens d'Installations et de Distribution de Petrole [*Committee of European Manufacturers of Petroleum Measuring and Distributing Equipment*] [*EC*] (ECED)

CECODE ...... Centre Europeen du Commerce de Detail [*European Center of the Retail Trade*] [*Common Market*]

CecoEnv...... Ceco Environmental [*Associated Press*] (SAG)

CECOF .... European Committee of Industrial Furnace and Heating Equipment Associations [*EC*] [*Germany*] (EAIO)

CECOFFSCOL... Civil Engineer Corps Officer's School [*Army*] (DNAB)

CECOGp....... Civil Engineer Construction Operations Group [*Air Force*] (AFM)

CECOM .... Communications-Electronics Command [*Fort Monmouth, NJ*] [*Army*] (GRD)

CECOMAF .... Comite Europeen des Constructeurs de Materiel Frigorifique [*European Committee of Manufacturers of Refrigeration Equipment*] (EAIO)

CECOP .... Comite Europeen des Cooperatives de Production et de Travail Associe [*European Committee of Workers' Cooperatives*] [*EC*] (ECED)

CECOPE .... Centro Coordinador de Proyectos Ecumenicos [*Promotes exchanges between Mexico, US, and Canada*] (CROSS)

CECOS .... Civil Engineer Corps Officer's School [*Army*] (DNAB)

CECOS .... Civil Engineers Corps Officers School [*Navy*]

CECP........... Compatibility Engineering Change Proposal [*NASA*] (NASA)

CECPA .... Comite Europeen du Commerce des Produits Amylaces et Derives [*European Center for Trade in Starch Products and Derivatives*] [*Common Market*]

CEC-PD .... CEC [*Council for Exceptional Children*] Pioneers Division (PAZ)

CEC PE .... Civil Engineer Corps, Professional Engineer [*Army*] (DNAB)

CECR .... Central European Communication Region [*Air Force*] (MCD)

CECR .... Committee for Effective Capital Recovery [*Defunct*] (EA)

CEC RA....... Civil Engineer Corps, Registered Architect [*Army*] (DNAB)

CECRA .... Comite Europeen du Commerce et de la Reparation Automobiles [*European Committee for Motor Trades and Repairs*] [*EC*] (ECED)

CECS........... Casualty Evacuation and Control Ship [*Navy*] (NVT)

CECS........... Center for Evaluative Clinical Sciences

CECS........... Charge Exchange Cross Section

CECS........... Church of England Children's Society

CECS........... Civil Engineering Computing System (PDAA)

CECS........... Closed-Loop Environmental Control System

CECS........... Communications-Electronics Coordinating Section [*NATO*]

CECS........... Construction Electrician, Senior Chief [*Navy rating*]

CECS........... Containment Environmental Control System [*Nuclear energy*] (NRCH)

CECSD .... Citizens for Energy Conservation and Solar Development

CECSET....... Committee for Enlisted Classification Selection and Testing [*Navy*] (NVT)

CECSR .... Contractor Employee Compensation System Review [*DoD*]

CECT............ Comite Europeen de la Chaudronnerie et de la Tolerie [*European Committee for Boilermaking and Kindred Steel Structures*]

CECT............ Contrast Enhancement Computed Tomography [*Radiology*] (DAVI)

CECTAL........ Centre for English Cultural Tradition and Language [*University of Sheffield*] [*British*] (CB)

CECU .... Concursos y Certamenes Culturales [*Database*] [*Ministerio de Cultura*] [*Spanish*] (CRD)

CECUA......... Confederation of European Computer Users Associations (EAIQ)

CECX........... Castle Energy Corp. [*NASDAQ symbol*] (NQ)

CED............. Campaign for Economic Democracy

CED............. Canadian Encyclopedic Digest [*A publication*] (DLA)

CED............. Capacitance Electronic Disk

CED............. Captured Enemy Documents [*Military*] (AFM)

CED............. Carbon-Equivalent-Difference (PDAA)

CED............. Cardiff East Docks [*Welsh depot code*]

CED............. Cedar Springs [*California*] [*Seismograph station code, US Geological Survey Closed*] (SEIS)

CED............. Ceduna [*Australia Airport symbol*] (OAG)

CED............. Center for Educational Development [*University of Illinois at Chicago*] [*Research center*] (RCD)

CED............. Center for Entrepreneurial Development [*Carnegie-Mellon University*]

CED............. Centre for Information and Advice on Educational Disadvantage [*British*]

CED............. Centro de Encuentros y Dialogos [*Member of RMALC*] (CROSS)

CED............. Centro de Esploro kaj Dokumentado pri la Monda Lingvo-Problemo [*Center for Research and Documentation on International Language Problems*] (EAIO)

CED............. CERCLA [*Comprehensive Environmental Response, Compensation, and Liability Act*] Enforcement Division [*Environmental Protection Agency*] (GFGA)

CED............. Chemical Exchange Directory SA [*Information service or system*] (IID)

CED............. Chief Executive Dockyard [*Navy British*]

CED............. Chondroectodermal Dysplasia [*Medicine*] (DMAA)

CED............. Chronic Enthusiasm Disorder [*Medicine*] (MEDA)

CEd............. Classic Editions [*Record label*]

C/ED............ Clothing and Equipment Development Branch [*Army Natick Laboratories, MA*]

CED............. Cohesive Energy Density [*Solubility parameter*]

CED............. Collins English Dictionary [*A publication British*]

CED............. Committee for Economic Development (EA)

CED............. Common European Demonstrator [*Automotive engineering*]

CED............. Communaute Europeenne de Defense [*European Defense Community*]

CED............. Communications-Electronics Directive

CED............. Communications-Electronics Doctrine [*Series of Air Force manuals*]

CED............. Communications-Electronics Document

CED............. Communications Engineering Department [*Military*] (DNAB)

CED............. Community and Economic Development Division (AAGC)

CED............. Community Employment Development [*Department of Labor*]

CED............. Competitive Engineering Definition (PDAA)

CED............. Computer Entry Device [*Computer science*] (PDAA)

CED............. Concept Exploration and Definition [*Military*]

CED............. Concept Exploration Development Phase [*DoD*]

CED............. Condition Education Division [*Department of Education*] (GFGA)

CED............. Constant Energy Differences

CED............. Cost Estimate Dispersion (KSC)

CED............. Council of Education of the Deaf [*Australia*]

CED............. Council on Education of the Deaf (EA)

CED............. County Education District

CED............. Criminal Enforcement Division [*Office of Enforcement and Compliance Monitoring*] [*Environmental Protection Agency*] (EPA)

CED............. Critical Error Detection (MCD)

CED............. Cultural / Ethnic Diversity (MEDA)

CED............. Current Enlistment Date [*Military*]

CED............. United States Air Force, Edwards Air Force Base, AFFTC Technical Library, Edwards AFB, CA [*OCLC symbol*] (OCLC)

CEDA .... Canadian Electrical Distributors Association, Inc.

CEDA .... Catering Equipment Distributors Association [*British*] (DBA)

CEDA .... Central Dredging Association (EA)

CEDA .... Comite d'Etude des Droits des Autochtones [*Committee for Original Peoples' Entitlement*] [*Canada*]

CEDA .... Communications Equipment Distributors Association (MHDI)

CEDA .... Community Economic Development Act of 1981

CEDA .... Confederacion Espanola de Derechas Autonomas [*Spanish Confederation of Autonomous Rightist Forces*] [*Political party*] (PPE)

CEDA .... Cross-Examination Debate Association (EA)

CEdA........... United States Air Force, Flight Test Center Technical Library, Edwards AFB, CA [*Library symbol Library of Congress*] (LCLS)

CEDAC .... Central Differential Analyzer Control

CEDAC .... Computer Energy Distribution and Automated Control (MHDB)

CEDAC .... Cooling Effect Detection and Control

CEDADE ...... Circulo Espanol de Amigos de Europa [*Spanish Circle of Friends of Europe*] (PD)

CEDAL .... Centre d'Etudes et de Documentation d'Amerique Latine (AC)

CEDAL .... Centro de Estudios Democraticos de America Latina

CEDAM .... Casa Editrice Dott. A. Milani [*Italian publisher*]

CEDAM .... Conservation Education Diving Archeology Museums

CEDAM .... Conservation, Exploration, Diving, Archeology, Museums [*Acronym is used as name of an international organization interested in these five subjects*] (EA)

CEDAR .... Center for Engineering Development and Research [*University of South Florida*] [*Research center*] (RCD)

CEDAR........ Center for Entrepreneurial Development, Advancement, Research, and Support [*University of Texas, El Paso*] [*Research center*] (RCD)

CEDAR........ Centre for Educational Development, Appraisal and Research [*University of Warwick*] [*British*] (AIE)

CEDAR........ Computer-Aided Environmental Design Analysis and Realization (MHDB)

CEDAR........ Construction of Embedded Dedicated Real-Time System [*Computer science*]

CEDaR........ Council for Educational Development and Research (EA)

CEdA-R...... United States Air Force, Air Force Rocket Propulsion Laboratory, Edwards AFB, CA [*Library symbol Library of Congress*] (LCLS)

CEDARC...... Confluent Education Development and Research Center [*Defunct*] (EA)

CedarGp .... Cedar Group, Inc. [*Associated Press*] (SAG)

CedarI........ Cedar Income Fund Ltd. [*Associated Press*] (SAG)

CEDAT .... Centre for Educational Development and Training [*Manchester Polytechnic*] [*British*] (CB)

CEDAU....... Cruise/Entry Data Acquisition Unit [*NASA*]

CEDAW ...... Committee on the Elimination of Discrimination Against Women [*United Nations*]

CEDB .... Church Executive Development Board

CEDB .... Currency Exchange Database [*GE Information Services*] [*Information service or system*] (CRD)

CEDBR....... Center for Economic Development and Business Research [*Wichita State University*] [*Kansas*] [*Information service or system*] (IID)

CEDC .... Central European Development Corp.

CEDC .... (Chloroethyl)deoxycytidine [*Antiviral*]

CEDC .... Cost Estimating Data Center

CEDC .... Cyclic Error Detection Code (MCD)

CEDDA .... Center for Experiment Design and Data Analysis [*National Oceanic and Atmospheric Administration*]

CEDE......... Centre d'Etudes et de Documentation Europeennes [*Montreal*]

CEDE......... Certificate Depository [*New York Stock Exchange*]

CEDE......... Committed Effective Dose Equivalent [*Radioactivity*]

CEDEC .... Centre Europeen de Documentation et de Compensation

CEDEFOP .... Centre Europeen pour le Developpement de la Formation Professionnelle [*European Centre for the Development of Vocational Training*] (EAIO)

CEDEL......... Centrale de Livraison de Valeurs Mobilieres

CEDER .... Center for Environmental Design Education and Research [*University of Colorado*] [*Research center*] (RCD)

CEDETIM...... Centre d'Etudes Anti-Imperialistes [*France*]

CEDF......... Canadian Environmental Defence Fund (AC)

CEDH .... Commission Europeenne des Droits de l'Homme [*European Commission of Human Rights - ECHR*] (EA)

CEDI........... Confederation Europeenne des Independants [*European Confederation of the Self Employed*] [*EC Germany*] (ECED)

CEDIA .... Custom Electronic Design Installation Association (EA)

CEDIC .... Comite Europeen des Ingenieurs-Conseils [*European Committee of Consulting Engineers*] [*EC*] (ECED)

CEDIGAZ ..... Centre International d'Information sur le Gaz Naturel et tous Hydrocarbures Ga zeux [*International Information Center on Natural Gas and Gaseous Hydrocarbons*] [*France*] (PDAA)

CEDIM .... Comite Europeen des Federations Nationales de la Maroquinerie, Articles de Voyages, et Industries Connexes (EAIO)

CEDM.......... Committee on Environmental Decision Making [*National Research Council*]

CEDM.......... Control Element Drive Mechanism [*Nuclear energy*] (NRCH)

CEDMCS ..... Control Element Drive Mechanism Control System [*Nuclear energy*] (NRCH)

CEDN .... Classic English Detective Novel

CEDO .... Captured Enemy Documents Organization (NATG)

CEDO .... Centre for Educational Development Overseas

CEDP .... Committee for the Employment of Disabled People (AIE)

CEDPA .... Centre for Development and Population Activities (EA)

CEDPA .... Certificate in Electronic Data Processing Auditing (IAA)

CEDPA .... Correction Education Demonstration Project Act of 1978

CEDPO .... Communications-Electronics Doctrinal Projects Office [*Air Force*]

CEDPS .... College Eye Data Processing System [*Air Force*] (MCD)

CEDR .... Cedar

CEDR .... Cedar Income Fund [*NASDAQ symbol*] (TTSB)

CEDR .... Cedar Income Fund Ltd. [*NASDAQ symbol*] (NQ)

CEDR .... Comite Europeen de Droit Rural [*France*]

CEDRA........ Community Emergency Drought Relief Act of 1977

CEDREP ...... Communications - Electronics Deployment Report (MCD)

CedrFr .... Cedar Fair Ltd. [*Associated Press*] (SAG)

CEDRIC....... Customs and Excise Departmental Reference and Information Computer (PDAA)

CEDRS .... Capabilities Engineering Data Report System (MCD)

CEDS .... Center for Econometrics and Decision Sciences [*University of Florida*] [*Research center*] (RCD)

CEDS .... Continuing Education Delivery Systems

CEDS .... Control Element Drive System [*Nuclear energy*] (NRCH)

CEDS .... Council for Educational Diagnostic Services [*Council for Exceptional Children*]

CEDT.......... Comite Europeen du The [*European Tea Committee*] [*EC*] (ECED)

CEDT.......... Confederation Europeenne des Detaillants en Tabac [*European Federation of Tobacco Retail Organizations*] (EAIO)

CEDU .... (Chloroethyl)deoxyuridine [*Biochemistry*]

CEE .... Advisory Committee for Civil and Environmental Engineering [*Terminated, 1 985*] [*National Science Foundation*] (EGAO)

CEE .... C-Air [*Former USSR*] [*FAA designator*] (FAAC)

CEE .... Cancorp Enterprises [*Vancouver Stock Exchange symbol*]

CEE .... Captured Enemy Equipment [*Military*] (AFM)

CEE .... Carbon Electrode Equipment

CEE .... Career Employment Experience [*Office of Youth Programs*] [*Department of Labor*]

CEE .... Center for Environmental Education [*Research center*] (EA)

CEE .... Central and Eastern Europe

CEE .... Central European Eq Fd [*NYSE symbol*] (TTSB)

CEE .... Central European Equity Fund [*NYSE symbol*] (SAG)

CEE .... Centro de Estudios Estrategicos [*Center for Strategic Studies*] [*Mexico*] (CROSS)

CEE .... Certificate of Extended Education [*British*] (DI)

CEE .... Chartered Electrical Engineer [*British*] (DAS)

CEE .... Chick Embryo Extract [*Culture media*]

CEE .... Civil and Environmental Engineering

CEE .... Clear Mines Ltd. [*Vancouver Stock Exchange symbol*]

CEE .... Cleveland, OH [*Location identifier FAA*] (FAAL)

CEE .... Combat Emplacement Excavator

CEE .... Commercial Electronic Equipment [*Military*]

CEE .... Commercial Equivalent Equipment

CEE .... Commission Economique pour l'Europe [*Economic Commission for Europe - ECE*] [*French*]

CEE .... Commissioner of Election Expenses [*Canada*]

CEE .... Commission Internationale de Certification de Conformite de l'Equipement Electrique [*International Commission for Conformity Certification of Electrical Equipment*] [*French*] (EA)

CEE .... Commission Internationale de Reglementation en veu de l'Approbation de l'Equipement Electrique [*International Commission on Rules for the Approval of Electrical Equipment*] (PDAA)

CEE .... Committee on Energy and the Environment [*National Research Council*]

CEE .... Common Entrance Examination (BARN)

CEE .... Communaute Economique Europeenne [*European Economic Community*]

CEE .... Communication Electronic Equipment [*Military*]

CEE .... Communication Electronics Element [*Army*] (AABC)

CEE .... Comprehensive Environmental Evaluation [*British Antarctic Survey*]

CEE .... Conference on English Education (EA)

CEE .... Conjugated Equine Estrogen [*Endocrinology*]

CEE .... Conseil d'Expansion Economique [*Economic Expansion Council*] [*Canada*]

CEE .... Controlled Experimental Ecosystem [*Study technique*]

CEE .... Cooperative Educational Enterprises

CE-E........... Corps of Engineers Guide Specifications for Emergency Type Construction [*Army*]

CEE .... Cost per Entered Employment [*Job Training and Partnership Act*] (OICC)

CEE .... Council for Environmental Education [*British*]

CEE .... Council on Electrolysis Education (EA)

CEEA........... Canadian Earth Energy Association [*Association Canadienne de l'Energie du Sol*] (AC)

CEEA........... Catholic Educational Exhibitors Association [*Later, NCEE*]

CEEA........... Charging Electrical Effects Analyzer (MCD)

CEEA........... Communaute Europeenne de l'Energie Atomique

CEEA........... Curved End-to-End Anastomosis [*Stapler*] [*Medicine*] (DMAA)

CEEA........... Cyanoethylethylamine [*Organic chemistry*]

CEEAC......... Communaute Economique des Etats de l'Afrique Centrale [*Economic Community of Central African States - ECCAS*] [*Bangui, Central African Republic*] (EAIO)

CEEAS......... Centre Europeen d'Etudes de l'Acide Sulfurique [*European Center for Studies of Sulfuric Acid*] (EAIO)

CEEB.......... College Entrance Examination Board [*Known as The College Board; acronym no longer used*] (EA)

CEEC.......... Central and Eastern European Country (ECON)

CEEC.......... Comite Europeen pour l'Enseignement Catholique [*European Committee for Catholic Education*] (EAIO)

CEEC.......... Committee for European Economic Cooperation [*Marshall Plan*] [*Post-World War II*]

CEEC.......... Construction Economics European Committee (EAIO)

CEECT......... Centre for Editing Early Canadian Texts

CEED.......... Center for Energy and Economic Development [*US Bureau of Mines*]

CEED.......... Center for Entrepreneurship and Economic Development [*Pan American University*] [*Research center*] (RCD)

CEED.......... Centre for Economic and Environmental Development [*British*] (CB)

CEED.......... Council for Economic and Environmental Development (BARN)

CEEDE......... Center for Educational Experimentation, Development, and Evaluation [*University of Iowa*] [*Research center*] (RCD)

CEEDO .... Civil and Environmental Engineering Development Office [*Tyndall Air Force Base, FL*]

CEEDS .... Community Enhancement & Economic Development Society (AC)

CEEF .... Clergy Economic Education Foundation [*Later, EEFC*]

CEEFAX........ See Facts [*BBC "dial-a-page" news broadcast*] [*British*]

CEEG .... Computer Electroencephalogram

CEEI .... Center for Energy and Environmental Information [*Department of Energy*] (GRD)

CEEIA.......... Communications-Electronics Engineering Installation Agency [*DoD*]

CEEIA-NCC... Communications-Electronics Engineering Installation Agency-National Communications Command [*DoD*] (RDA)

CEEM .... Council for Education on Electronic Media (NTCM)

CEEMA .... Conference Europeenne des Experts Meteorologistes de l'Aeronautique

CEEMAT....... Centre d'Etudes et d'Experimentation du Machinisme Agricole Tropical [*Center for the Study and Experimentation of Tropical Agriculture Machinery*] [*International Cooperation Center of Agricultural Research for Development*] [*Information service or system*] [*France*] (IID)

CEEMAT...... Converter Enhanced, Electronically Managed Automatic Transmission
CEEMT........ Cyanoethyl Ethyl-M-Toluidine [*Organic chemistry*]
CEENU .... Chloroethyl-Cyclohexyl-Nitrosoures [*Also called Lomustine*] [*Antineoplastic drug*] (DAVI)
CEE/ONU..... Commission Economique pour l'Europe/Organisation des Nations Unies [*Economic Commission for Europe/United Nations Organization*] (EAIO)
CEEOP......... Contracts Equal Employment Opportunity Program (AAGC)
CEEP........... Centre Europeen de l'Entreprise Publique [*European Center of Public Enterprise - ECPE*] (EAIO)
CEEP........... Centre Europeen d'Etudes de Population [*European Center for Population Studies*]
CEEP........... Coastal Engineering Education Program [*U.S. Army Engineer Waterways Experiment Station*]
CEEP........... Committee for Environmentally Effective Packaging (EA)
CEEP........... Confederation des Educateurs Physiques du Qubec (AC)
CEEP........... Crustal Evolution Education Project [*National Association of Geology Teachers*] (EDAC)
CEEPR......... Center for Energy and Environmental Policy Research [*Formerly, Center for Energy Policy and Research*]
CEER .... Center for Energy and Environmental Research [*University of Puerto Rico*]
CEER .... Cost Estimate Error Report
CEERA .... Conference Europeenne des Experts Radiotelegraphistes de l'Aeronautique
CEES .... Center for Energy and Environmental Studies [*Carnegie-Mellon University*] [*Research center*] (RCD)
CEES........... Center for Environmental and Estuarine Studies [*University of Maryland*] [*Research center*]
CEES........... Comite Europeen d'Etude du Sel [*European Committee for the Study of Salt - ECSS*] (EA)
CEES........... Committee on Earth and Envionmental Sciences [*Marine science*] (OSRA)
CEES........... Committee on Earth and Environmental Sciences (USDC)
CEESAC....... Central and East European Studies Association of Canada [*See also AEECEEC*]
CEESTEM.... Centro de Estudios Economicos y Sociales del Tercer Mundo [*Center for Economic and Social Studies of the Third World*] [*Canada*]
CEETA.......... Communications Electronics Evaluation and Test Agency (MCD)
CEETB......... Comite Europeen des Equipements Techniques du Batiment [*European Committee for Building Technical Equipment - ECBTE*] (EAIO)
CE et S .... Conseil Economique et Social [*United Nations*]
CEEUSA ...... Commission for Educational Exchange between the United States of America and Afghanistan
CEEV.......... Central European Encephalitis Virus [*Medicine*] (MAE)
CEEWOC ...... Computer Enhanced Electronic Warfare Operations Centre [*Military Canada*]
CEF............. California Engineering Foundation (EA)
CEF............. Canadian Equestrian Federation [*Federation Equestre Canadienne*] (AC)
CEF............. Canadian Expeditionary Forces
CEF............. Captain [*Commanding*] Escort Forces [*Navy*]
CEF............. Career Executive Force [*Air Force*]
CEF............. Carrier Elimination Filter
CEF............. Catalogue de l'Edition Francaise
CeF............. Centrala Filmarkivet Ab, Stockholm, Sweden [*Library symbol Library of Congress*] (LCLS)
CEF............. Central Fund,Cda'A' [*AMEX symbol*] (TTSB)
CEF............. Central Fund of Canada Ltd. [*AMEX symbol Toronto Stock Exchange symbol*]
CEF............. Centralized Environmental Facility
CEF............. Centre for Economic Forecasting [*London Business School*] [*British*] (CB)
CEF............. Centrifugal Electrostatic Focusing [*Engineering*] (IAA)
CEF............. Centrifugation Extractable Fluid
CEF............. Channeling Effect Factor
CEF............. Chick Embryo Fibroblast
CEF............. Chicken Embryo Fibroblast [*Cell line*]
CEF............. Chicopee Falls, MA [*Location identifier FAA*] (FAAL)
CEF............. Chief Executives Forum [*Later, CEO*]
CEF............. Childbirth Education Foundation (EA)
CEF............. Child Evangelism Fellowship (EA)
CEF............. Children's Express Foundation (EA)
CEF............. Chinese Expeditionary Force
CEF............. Chlorine Efficiency Factor
CEF............. Christian Educators Fellowship [*Later, CEAI*] (EA)
CEF............. Citizens for Educational Freedom (EA)
CEF............. Civil Engineering File (DOMA)
CEF............. Civil Engineering Flight [*Military*]
CEF............. Clearinghouse on Educational Facilities [*ERIC*]
CEF............. Closed-End Fund [*Investment term*]
CEF............. Cloth Elongation Factor [*Textiles*]
CEF............. Commission Europeenne des Forets
CEF............. Committee for Education Funding (EA)
CEF............. Complementary Emitter Follower
CEF............. Computer Execute Function (KSC)
CEF............. Constant Electric Field [*Medicine*] (DMAA)
CEF............. Contemporary Evaluation Form [*Army*]
CEF............. Controlled Environmental Forestry
CEF............. Controlled Environment Facilities
CEF............. Corps Expeditionaire Francais
CEF............. Council on Educational Finance [*National Education Association*] (AEBS)
CEF............. Creative Education Foundation (EA)

CEF .... Critical Experiments Facility [*Nuclear energy*] (OA)
CEF .... Cross-Range Error Function
CEF .... Cryptographic Equipment Facility (MCD)
CEF .... Czech Air Force [*ICAO designator*] (FAAC)
CEFA .... Child Evangelism Fellowship of Australia
CEFA .... Council for Educational Freedom in America (EA)
CEFAC......... Civil Engineering Field Activities Center
CEFACD....... Comite Europeen des Fabricants d'Appareils de Chauffage et de Cuisine Domestiques [*European Committee of Manufacturers of Domestic Heating and Cooking Appliances*]
CEFACEF...... Comite Europeen des Fabricants d'Appareils de Chauffage en Fonte (PDAA)
CEFC........... Country Edition Fan Club [*Defunct*] (EA)
CEFCO .... Centre d'Etudes Franco-Canadiennes de l'Ouest [*Centre of Studies of French-Canadians of Western Canada*]
CEFCO .... Cooperative Export Financing Corp. (MHDW)
CEFCTU....... Central European Federation of Christian Trade Unions (EA)
CEFCUT....... Conseil des Ecoles Francaises de la Communaute Urbaine de Toronto [*Metro Toronto French-Language School Council*] (AC)
CEFDA .... Central European Forces Distribution Agency [*NATO*] (NATG)
CEFEI.......... Committee of European Financial Executives Institutes [*EC*] (ECED)
CEFEPAL..... Centro de Estudos Franciscanos e Pastorais para a America Latina
CEFF........... Controlled Energy Flow Forming
CEFHR......... Civil Engineering Flight, Heavy Repair [*Military*]
CEFI........... Child Evangelism Fellowship International [*Later, CEF*] (EA)
CEFI........... Contractor Engineer - Furnish and Install
CEFIC.......... Conseil Europeen des Federations de l'Industrie Chimique [*European Council of Chemical Manufacturers Federations - ECCMF*] [*Belgium*] (EAIO)
CEFIM......... Cercle de la Finance Internationale de Montreal (AC)
CEFIP.......... Communications-Electronics Facility Inoperative for Parts (MCD)
C-E-F L .... Clifton-Essex-Franklin Library [*Library network*]
CEFMG........ Council on Education for Foreign Medical Graduates (BABM)
CEFO .... Complete Equipment Fighting Order [*British military*] (DMA)
CEFOAM....... Checkout Equipment for Onboard Automatic Maintenance
CEFP........... Council of Educational Facility Planners (EA)
CEFPI.......... Council of Educational Facility Planners, International (EA)
CEFRAS ...... Centre Europeen de Formation et de Recherche en Action Sociale [*European Centre for Social Welfare Training and Research - ECSWTR*] [*United Nations*] (EAIO)
CEFRIO .... Centre Francophone de Recherche en Informatisation des Organisations (AC)
CE Frnk....... CE Franklin Ltd. [*Associated Press*] (SAG)
CEFS........... Comite Europeen des Fabricants de Sucre [*European Committee of Sugar Manufacturers*] [*Common Market*]
CEFSR......... Committee for Evaluating the Feasibility of Space Rocketry [*Navy Bureau of Aeronautics*] [*Obsolete*]
CEFT .... Children's Embedded Figures Test [*Psychology*]
CEFT .... Concord EFS [*NASDAQ symbol*] (TTSB)
CEFT .... Concord EFS, Inc. [*NASDAQ symbol*] (NQ)
CEFU .... Continuing Education Field Unit [*Veterans Administration*] (GFGA)
CEFYM......... Central European Federal Youth Movement
CEG............ Cahners Exposition Group [*Telecommunications service*] (TSSD)
CEG............ Camel Oil & Gas Ltd. [*Toronto Stock Exchange symbol*]
CEG............ Canadian Giant Explorations [*Vancouver Stock Exchange symbol*]
CEG............ Career Employment Group [*British military*] (DMA)
CEG............ Careers Education and Guidance (AIE)
CEG............ Catholic Evidence Guild [*Defunct*] (EA)
CEG............ Cave Exploration Group [*Australia*]
CEG............ Cega Aviation Ltd. [*British ICAO designator*] (FAAC)
CEG............ Central Emergency Government Headquarters (MCD)
CEG............ Central Equipment Group [*Military*] (CAAL)
CEG............ Certified Engineering Geologist [*Environmental science*]
CEG............ Chester [*England*] [*Airport symbol*] (AD)
CEG............ Civil Engineering Group [*Air Force*]
CEG............ Combat Evaluation Group [*Strategic Air Command*] (SAA)
CEG............ Competitive Events Guidelines [*A publication*] (EAAP)
CEG............ Computer Education Group [*British*] (BI)
CEG............ Consumer Electronics Group [*Education Industries Association*] (NTCM)
CEG............ Continuous Edge Graphics [*Edson Laboratories*] [*Computer science*]
CEGB.......... Council for Excellence in Government (EA)
CEGB.......... Central Electricity Generating Board [*British*]
CEG-DSP..... Continuous Edge Graphics-Digital Signal Processor [*Edson Laboratories*] [*Computer science*] (PCM)
CEGE.......... Cell Genesys [*NASDAQ symbol*] (TTSB)
CEGE.......... Cell Genesys, Inc. [*NASDAQ symbol*] (SAG)
CEGE.......... Combat Equipment Group, Europe (MCD)
CEGEP .... College d'Enseignement General et Professionnel [*College of General and Professional Instruction*] [*Canada*]
CEGET......... Centre d'Etudes en Geographie Tropicale [*Centre of Studies in Tropical Geography*] [*France*]
CEG-I .... Committee for the Economic Growth of Israel (EA)
CEGJA......... Coalition to End Grand Jury Abuse [*Later, CPR*] (EA)
CEGL........... Cause-Effect Graph Language [*Computer science*] (IBMDP)
CEGNY........ Catholic Evidence Guild of New York [*Defunct*] (EA)
CEGROB...... Communaute Europeenne des Associations du Commerce de Gros de Biere des Pays Membres de la CEE [*European Community of Associations of the Wholesale Beer Trade of the EEC*]
CEGS .... Centre of European Governmental Studies [*University of Edinburgh*] [*British*] (CB)
CEGS .... Church of Jesus Christ of Latter-Day Saints, Genealogical Society Library, Eureka Branch, Eureka, CA [*Library symbol Library of Congress*] (LCLS)
CEGS .... Committee to Establish the Gold Standard (EA)

CEGS	Council for Economic Growth and Security [Defunct]
CEGS	Council on Education in the Geological Sciences
CEGTS	Controlled Environment Gravity Tube System (PDAA)
CEH.............	Center for Environmental Health [Atlanta, GA] [Department of Health and Human Services] (GRD)
CEH.............	Center for Equine Health
CEH.............	Central Capital Corp. [Toronto Stock Exchange symbol]
CEH.............	Central European History [A publication] (BRI)
CEH.............	Centre on Environment for the Handicapped [British] (CB)
CEH.............	Chapel Hill [North Carolina] [Seismograph station code, US Geological Survey] (SEIS)
CEH.............	Characteristic Event Hypothesis [For earthquake occurence]
CEH.............	Chemical Economics Handbook [SRI International] [Database]
CEH.............	Conference Euorpeenne des Horaires et des Services Directs [European Conference of Time-tables and Direct Services] (PDAA)
CEH.............	Conference Europeenne des Horaires des Trains de Voyageurs [European Passenger Timetable Conference] [Switzerland]
CEH.............	Humboldt County Free Library, Eureka, CA [Library symbol Library of Congress] (LCLS)
CEHA	Contact Equipment Handling Area [Nuclear energy] (NRCH)
CEHC	Canever English History Club
CEHF	Centre for Ergonomics and Human Factors [Australia]
CEHI............	Centre d'Etudis Historics Internationals [Center for International Historical Studies] (EA)
CEHi............	Humboldt County Historical Society, Eureka, CA [Library symbol] [Library of Congress] (LCLS)
CEHIC	Center for Environmental Health and Injury Control [Atlanta, GA] [Centers for Disease Control] [Department of Health and Human Services] (GRD)
CEHILA	Comision de Estudios de Historia de la Iglesia en Latinoamerica [Commission of the Studies of History of the Church in Latin America] [Mexico]
CEHP	Comite Europeen de l'Hospitalisation Privee [European Committee of Private Hospitalization] [EC] [Belgium] (ECED)
CEHP	Conservation Environment and Historic Preservation [Commercial firm]
CEHS	Church of England Historical Society (ADA)
CEHS	Civilian Employee Health Service
CEHSA	Consumer and Environmental Health Services Administration [HEW]
CEI.............	Cabin Equipment Interface [Aviation]
CEI.............	Cambridge Electronic Industries [British]
CEI.............	Center for Education Improvement [U.S. Department of Education] (EDAC)
CEI.............	Center for Education in International Management [Canada]
CEI.............	Center for Energy Information [Defunct]
CEI.............	Center for Environmental Information, Inc. [Information service or system] (IID)
CEI.............	Centre d'Etudes Industrielles [Center for education in international management] [Switzerland] (DCTA)
CEI.............	Centre for Employment Initiatives Ltd. [British] (CB)
CEI.............	Centre for Environmental Interpretation [Manchester Polytechnic] [British] (CB)
CEI.............	Centro de Estudios Interplanetarios [Spain] (EAIO)
CEI.............	Character Education Institute (EA)
CEI.............	Chiang Rai [Thailand] [Airport symbol] (OAG)
CEI.............	Chicago & Eastern Illinois Railroad Co. [Absorbed into Missouri Pacific System]
CEI.............	Chicago Evangelistic Institute
CEI.............	Chip Enable Input [Computer science] (MHDI)
CEI.............	Claremont Economics Institute [Information service or system] (IID)
CEI.............	Classroom Environment Index [Student attitude test]
CEI.............	Coated Electrodes International [British]
CEI.............	Commission Electrotechnique Internationale [International Electrotechnical Commission - IEC] [Switzerland] (EAIO)
CEI.............	Committee for Environmental Information (IID)
CEI.............	Communication Electronic Instructions
CEI.............	Communications Engineering and Installation Department [Army]
CEI.............	Community Economics, Inc. (EA)
CEI.............	Comparably Efficient Interconnection [Telecommunications]
CEI.............	Compliance Evaluation Inspection [Environmental Protection Agency] (GFGA)
CEI.............	Computer-Enhanced Instruction
CEI.............	Computer-Extended Instruction (IEEE)
CEI.............	Conference of the Electronics Industry [British] (BI)
CEI.............	Configuration End Item (AFIT)
CEI.............	Connection Endpoint Identifier [Telecommunications] (ACRL)
CEI.............	Continuous Extravascular Infusion [Medicine]
CEI.............	Contract End Item (MCD)
CEI.............	Contractor End Item (MCD)
CEI.............	Converting-Enzyme Inhibitor [Biochemistry]
CEI.............	Correct End Item (KSC)
CEI.............	Co-Steel, Inc. [Toronto Stock Exchange symbol]
CEI.............	Cost Effectiveness Index [Economics]
CEI.............	Coulomb Explosion Imaging [Nuclear physics]
CEI.............	Council of Engineering Institutions [British]
CEI.............	Crescent Real Estate Eq [NYSE symbol] (TTSB)
CEI.............	Critical Engine Inoperative (MCD)
CEI.............	Cycle Engineers' Institute
CEIA	Canadian Environment Industry Association [Association Canadienne des Industries de l'Environnement] (AC)
CEIA	Centro Economico Italia Africa [Italian-African Economic Center] (AF)
CEIA	Communications Engineering and Installation Agency
CEIAC..........	Canada Employment and Immigration Advisory Council (EDAC)
CEIAC..........	Coastal Engineering Information Analysis Center [Vicksburg, MS] [DoD] (GRD)
CEIB............	Computer Equipment Information Bureau [Information service or system] (IID)
CEIB............	Confederation Europeenne des Industries du Bois [European Confederation of Woodworking Industries]
CEI-BOIS.....	Confederation Europeenne des Industries du Bois [European Confederation of Woodworking Industries] (EAIO)
CEIBS..........	China Europe International Business School
CEIBS..........	China Europe International Business School
CEIC...........	Canada Employment and Immigration Commission
CEIC...........	Census and Economic Information Center [Montana State Department of Commerce] [Helena] [Information service or system] (IID)
CEIC...........	Chemical Effects Information Center [Department of Energy] (IID)
CEIC...........	Closed-End Investment Company [Business term]
CEICI...........	Centre d'Education Interculturelle et de Comprehension Internationale [Centre for Intercultural Education & International Understanding] (AC)
CEID...........	Crossed Electroimmunodiffusion [Analytical biochemistry]
CE/IDC.........	Chase Econometrics/Interactive Data Corp. [Database vendor]
CEIDD	Committee on the Economic Impact of Defense and Disarmament (KSC)
CEIDP	Conference on Electrical Insulation and Dielectric Phenomena [National Academy of Sciences]
CEIF............	Council of European Industrial Federations
CEIL............	Ceiling [Aviation]
ceil	Ceiling (VRA)
CEIL............	Combat Essential Items List [Army]
CEIL............	Consumer Education and Information Liaison [Federal interagency group]
CEIN............	Contract End Item Number
CEIP............	Carnegie Endowment for International Peace (EA)
CEIP............	Center for Environmental Intern Programs (EA)
CEIP............	Coastal Energy Impact Program [National Oceanic and Atmospheric Administration]
CEIP............	Communications-Electronics Implementation Plan [For major air command requirements within the communications-electronics area] [Air Force]
CEIPA..........	Communications-Electronics Implementation Plan Amendment [See CEIP] [Air Force] (AFM)
CEIPI...........	Centre d'Etudes Internationales de la Propriete Industrielle
CEIR...........	Civil Emergency Information Room [NATO] (NATG)
CEIR...........	Comite Europeen de l'Industrie de la Robinetterie [European Committee for the Valves and Fittings Industry] [EC] [Germany] (ECED)
CEIR...........	Cooperative Economic Insect Report [Department of Agriculture] [A publication]
CEIR...........	Corporation for Economics and Industrial Research [Subsidiary of Control Data Corporation]
CEIRD	Confirming Engineering Information Report Date [Bell System] (TEL)
CEIRPP	Committee on the Exercise of the Inalienable Rights of the Palestinian People (EA)
CEIRS	Conservation and Renewable Energy Inquiry and Referral Service [Database]
CEIS...........	Candidate Environmental Impact Statement (MCD)
CEIS...........	Caribbean Energy Information System [UNESCO] (DUND)
CEIS...........	Central Economic Information Service [British]
CEIS...........	Centre for European Industrial Studies [University of Bath] [British] (CB)
CEIS...........	Committee on Evaluation and Information Systems (OICC)
CEIS...........	Cost and Economic Information System [DoD] (MCD)
CEIS...........	Cost Estimate Input Sheet [Jet Propulsion Laboratory, NASA]
CEIT............	Crew Equipment Integration [or Interface] Test (MCD)
CEITG..........	Chemical Effects Information Task Group [Department of Energy Information service or system] (IID)
CEIU............	Canada Employment and Immigration Union
CE/IWT........	Central Europe Inland Waterways Transport [NATO] (NATG)
CEJ	Cardioesophageal Junction [Gastroenterology] (DAVI)
CEJ	Cement-Enamel Junction [Dentistry]
CEJ	Compagnie Europeenne de la Jeunesse
CEJ	Confederation Europeenne du Jouet [France] (EAIO)
CEJ	Cooperative Expendable Jammer
CEJ	Corporacion Area Ejecutiva SA de CV [Mexico ICAO designator] (FAAC)
CEJ	Wildwood, NJ [Location identifier FAA] (FAAL)
CEJA	Conseil Europeen des Jeunes Agriculteurs [European Committee of Young Farmers] [Common Market]
CEJEDP.......	Central Europe Joint Emergency Defense Plan [NATO] (NATG)
CEK............	Cetec Engineering Co., Inc. [Vancouver Stock Exchange symbol]
CEK............	Chick Embryo Kidney [Medicine] (DMAA)
CEK............	Computer Entry Keyboard
CEK............	Societe Seca [France ICAO designator] (FAAC)
CEL............	Carbon Equilibrium Loop
CEL............	Carbon-Equivalent, Liquidus (OA)
CEL............	Carboxyl-Ester Lipase (DMAA)
cel	Celadon (VRA)
CEL............	Celaya [Race of maize]
CEL............	Celebrated
CEL............	Celesta [Music]
CEL............	Celestial (AFM)
CEL............	Celibate
CEL............	Celico Resources [Vancouver Stock Exchange symbol]
CEL............	Celluloid
CEL............	Cellulose [Botany]

CEL .... Celsius [*Centigrade*] [*Temperature scale*]
CEL .... Celtic
cel .... Celtic Group [*MARC language code Library of Congress Obsolete*] (LCCP)
CEL .... Ceneast Airlines Ltd. [*Kenya*] [*ICAO designator*] (FAAC)
CEL .... Central European Line [*Oil pipeline*]
CEL .... Channels of English Literature [*A publication*]
CEL .... Child-Centered Experience-Based Learning [*An association Canada*]
CEL .... Civil Engineering Laboratory [*Also, CIVENGRLAB*] [*Port Hueneme, CA*] [*Navy*] (MCD)
CEL .... Civilian Education Level [*Military*] (INF)
CEL .... Coastal Ecology Laboratory [*Louisiana State University*] [*Research center*] (RCD)
CEL .... Combat Elevation Launch
CEL .... Committee for an Extended Lifespan [*Defunct*] (EA)
CEL .... Compressor Endurance Loops (MCD)
CEL .... Computer Economics Ltd. [*British*] (NITA)
CEL .... Constitutional Educational League
CEL .... Contractor Experience List [*DoD*]
CEL .... Contrast Enhanced Lithography
CEL .... Contrast-Enhancement Layer [*Photoprocessing*]
CEL .... Conversational Extensible Language [*Computer science*] (CSR)
CEL .... Cooley Electronics Laboratory [*University of Michigan*] [*Research center*] (RCD)
CEL .... Cosine Emission Law [*Optics*]
CEL .... Council on Engineering Laws [*Defunct*] (EA)
CEL .... Crew Evaluation Launcher (SAA)
CEL .... Critical Experiment Laboratory
CEL .... Crop Evolution Laboratory [*University of Illinois*]
CEL .... Crowding Effect LASER (IAA)
CEL .... Cryogenic Engineering Laboratory [*National Institute of Standards and Technology*]
CEL .... Customer Engineering Letter (MCD)
CEL .... Customs and Excise Laboratory [*Canada*]
CEI .... Elsinore Free Public Library, Elsinore, CA [*Library symbol Library of Congress*] (LCLS)
CEL .... Grupo Iusacell SA de CV [*NYSE symbol*] (SAG)
CEL .... Grupo Iusacell S.A.'L ADS [*NYSE symbol*] (TTSB)
CELA .... Canadian Environmental Law Association
CEL(A) ...... Chief Electrician (Air) [*British military*] (DMA)
CELACS ..... Confidential Employment Listing [*American Chemical Society*]
CELADE ...... Centro Latinoamericana de Demografia [*Latin American Demographic Center*] [*Economic Commission for Latin America and the Caribbean Chile*] [*United Nations*]
Celadon ...... Celadon Group [*Associated Press*] (SAG)
CELAM .... Consejo Episcopal Latinoamericano [*Latin American Episcopal Council*] (EAIO)
CELA Newsletter... Canadian Environmental Law Association. Newsletter [*A publication*] (DLA)
CELAT .... Centre d'Etudes sur la Langue, les Arts, et les Traditions Populaires des Francophones en Amerique du Nord [*Laval University*] [*Canada Research center*] (RCD)
CEL(AW) ...... Chief Electrician (Air Weapon) [*British military*] (DMA)
CELC .... Commonwealth Education Liaison Committee [*British*]
CELCAA .... Comite Europeen de Liaison des Commerces Agro-Alimentaires [*European Liaison Committee for Agricultural and Food Trades*] (EAIO)
CelCmA ...... Cellular Communications, Inc. [*Associated Press*] (SAG)
CelCmPR ..... Cellular Communications Puerto Rico [*Associated Press*] (SAG)
CELD .... Cause-Effect Logic Diagram [*Engineering*]
CELD .... Central External Liaison Department [*Chinese Secret Service*]
CEL.D .... Grupo Iusacell S.A.'D'ADS [*NYSE symbol*] (TTSB)
CELDIC .... Commission on Emotional and Learning Disorders in Children [*Canada*]
CELDS .... Computerized Environmental Legislative Data System [*Army*]
CelebEn ...... Celebrity Entertainment, Inc. [*Associated Press*] (SAG)
CelebInc ...... Celebrity, Inc. [*Associated Press*] (SAG)
CEleQ .... Club d'Electricite du Quebec Inc. (AC)
CELESCAN ... Cell Scanning System [*Cytology*] (SAA)
CELESCO ..... Celestial Research Corp. (KSC)
CELESCOPE... Celestial Telescope [*OAO*]
Celestial ...... Celestial Seasonings, Inc. [*Associated Press*] (SAG)
Celex .... Celex Group, Inc. [*Associated Press*] (SAG)
CELEX .... Communitatis Europae Lex [*European Community Law*] [*Commission of the European Communities*] [*Information service or system*] (IID)
CELF .... Clinical Evaluation of Language Functions [*Speech evaluation test*]
CELG .... Celgene Corp. [*NASDAQ symbol*] (NQ)
Celgene ...... Celgene Corp. [*Associated Press*] (SAG)
CELI .... Carrow Elicited Language Inventory [*Education*]
CELI .... Cel-Sci Corp. [*NASDAQ symbol*] (NQ)
CELI .... Congressional Economic Leadership Institute (EA)
CELI .... Contingent Employee Liability Insurance
CELIA .... Computer Enhanced Language Instruction Archive (AIE)
CELIA .... Continuous Electrocardiogram in Ambulatory Patients [*Medicine*]
CELIBRIDE.... Comite de Liaison International des Broderies, Rideaux, et Dentelles [*International Liaison Committee for Embroideries, Curtains, and Laces*]
CELIMAC...... Comite Europeen de Liaison des Industries de la Machine a Coudre [*European Liaison Committee for the Sewing Machine Industries - ELCSMI*] [*Defunct*] (EAIO)
CELINTREP... Accelerated Intelligence Report (NATG)
CELIS .... Conservation and Environment Library Information System
CELISA .... Competitive Enzyme-Linked Immunosorbent Assay
CELIW .... Cel-Sci Corp. Wrrt [*NASDAQ symbol*] (TTSB)

CELL .... Brightpoint, Inc. [*NASDAQ symbol*] (SAG)
CELL .... Cellular
Cell .... Celluloid [*Dentistry*] (DAVI)
CELL .... Continuing Education Learning Laboratory (EA)
Cellegy .... Cellegy Pharmaceuticals [*Associated Press*] (SAG)
CellegyPh .... Cellegy Pharmaceuticals [*Associated Press*] (SAG)
CellexB ...... Cellex Biosciences, Inc. [*Associated Press*] (SAG)
CellGens ..... Cell Genesys, Inc. [*Associated Press*] (SAG)
Cellgy .... Cellegy Pharmaceuticals [*Associated Press*] (SAG)
Celli .... Violoncelli [*Cellos*] [*Music*]
Cell Intl ...... Cellular Communications International, Inc. [*Associated Press*] (SAG)
CellNet .... CellNet Data Systems, Inc. [*Associated Press*] (SAG)
CELLO .... Violoncello [*Music*]
CellPro .... CellPro, Inc. [*Associated Press*] (SAG)
CellrTch ...... Cellular Technical Services [*Associated Press*] (SAG)
CELLSIM ..... Cell Simulation [*Programming language*] [*1973*] (CSR)
Cellstar .... Cellstar Corp. [*Associated Press*] (SAG)
CELLUL .... Cellular
CellVisin ..... CellularVision USA, Inc. [*Associated Press*] (SAG)
Cellx .... Cellex Biosciences, Inc. [*Associated Press*] (SAG)
CELMN .... Chief Electrical Mechanician [*British military*] (DMA)
CELNAV ...... Celestial Navigation (FAAC)
CELNUCO.... Comite Europeen de Liaison des Negociants et Utilisateurs de Combustibles [*European Liaison Committee of Fuel Merchants and Users*]
CELO .... Chicken Embryo Lethal Orphan [*Virus*]
CELOGS ...... Combat Effectiveness with Logistics Support (MCD)
CeloxLab ..... Celox Laboratories, Inc. [*Associated Press*] (SAG)
CELP .... Civilian Employment Level Plan [*DoD*]
CELP .... Code Excited Linear Prediction [*Computer science*] (ACRL)
CELP .... College Employers Links Project (AIE)
celph .... Cellophane (VRA)
CELPLO ...... Chief Executives of Large Public Libraries of Ontario (AC)
CELPP .... Colleges of Education Learning Programme Project [*British*]
CELR .... Canadian Environmental Law Reports [*A publication*] (DLA)
CELRA .... Conference of Latin Bishops of Arab Regions [*Jersalem, Israel*] (EAIO)
CELRF .... Canadian Environmental Law Research Foundation (GNE)
CELS .... Celsius (ROG)
CELS .... Centre for European Legal Studies [*University of Exeter*] [*British*] (CB)
CELS .... CommNet Cellular [*NASDAQ symbol*] (TTSB)
CELS .... CommNet Cellular, Inc. [*NASDAQ symbol*] (SAG)
CelSc .... Cel-Sci Corp. [*Associated Press*] (SAG)
CelSci .... Cel-Sci Corp. [*Associated Press*] (SAG)
CELSCOPE ... Celestial Telescope [*OAO*] (DNAB)
Cel Sep ...... Cell Separation [*Cytology*]
CELSF .... Committee to Eliminate Legal-Size Files [*Defunct*] (EA)
CELSS .... Closed Ecological Life Support System [*NASA*]
Celsus Med.. Celsus, De Medicina [*First century AD*] [*Classical studies*] (OCD)
CELT .... Celtic
CELT .... Celtic Investment [*NASDAQ symbol*] (TTSB)
CELT .... Celtic Investment, Inc. [*NASDAQ symbol*] (SAG)
CELT .... Centre for English Language Teaching [*University of Stirling*] [*British*] (CB)
CELT .... Classified Entries in Lateral Transposition [*Indexing*]
CELT .... Coherent Emitter Location Testbed (IEEE)
CELT .... Consolidated Entry Level Training (MCD)
CELT .... Continuing Education for Laboratory Technicians [*Union Carbide Co.*]
CELTE .... Constructeurs Europeens de Locomotives Thermiques et Electriques [*European Manufacturers of Thermal and Electric Locomotives*]
CELTIC........ Cell Transport Integral Calculation (PDAA)
CelticInv ..... Celtic Investment, Inc. [*Associated Press*] (SAG)
Cel Tr .... Burke's Celebrated Trials [*A publication*] (DLA)
Celtrx .... Celtrix Pharmaceuticals [*Associated Press*] (SAG)
celtx.......... Celotex (VRA)
CELV .... Complementary Expendable Launch Vehicle [*Space technology*]
CELX .... Celox Laboratories [*NASDAQ symbol*] (TTSB)
CELX .... Celox Laboratories, Inc. [*NASDAQ symbol*] (SAG)
CEM .... Captured Enemy Material [*Military*]
CEM .... CEM Corp. [*Associated Press*] (SAG)
CEM .... Cement (KSC)
cem .... Cement (VRA)
CEM .... Cement
CEM .... Cement Conduit [*Telecommunications*] (TEL)
CEM .... Cemetery (AABC)
CEM .... Center for Electromechnics [*University of Texas at Austin*] [*Research center*] (RCD)
CEM .... Center for Entrepreneurial Management [*New York, NY*] (EA)
CEM .... Center for the Environment and Man, Inc. [*Research center*] (RCD)
CEM .... Central [*Alaska*] [*Airport symbol*] (OAG)
CEM .... Central Error Module (CAAL)
CeM .... Central Microfilm Service Corp., St. Louis, MO [*Library symbol Library of Congress*] (LCLS)
CEM .... Centre for Environmental Management [*University of Newcastle*] [*Australia*]
CEM .... Certified Exposition Manager [*National Association of Exposition Managers , Inc.*] [*Designation awarded by*]
CEM .... Channel Electron Multiplier (MCD)
CEM .... Chief Electrician's Mate [*Navy rating Obsolete*]
CEM .... Chief Enlisted Manager
CEM .... Christian Education Movement [*British*]
CEM .... Circular Electric Mode
CEM .... CITL [*Crew-in-the-Loop*] Encapsulated Methodology [*Army*]

CEM............ Coastal Engineering Manual [*A publication Army*]
CEM............ College of Estate Management [*British*] (BI)
CEM............ Combat Earthmover [*Army*]
CEM............ Combat Effectiveness Measure [*Military*] (CAAL)
CEM............ Combat Evaluation Model (MCD)
CEM............ Combination Export Management [*Small Business Administration*]
CEM............ Combined Effects Munition (MCD)
CEM............ Comissao Eleitoral Monarquica [*Monarchy Electoral Committee*] [*Portugal*] (PPE)
CEM............ Commission on Education for Mission [*National Council of Churches*] (EA)
CEM............ Communications-Electronics-Meteorological [*Equipment*]
CEM............ Complex Electromechanical Device
CEM............ Compromising Emanations (AABC)
CEM............ Computer-Assisted Electron Microscope
CEM............ Computer Education for Management
CEM............ Computerized Exercise Machine
CEM............ CONAF [*Conceptual Design for the Army in the Field*] Evaluation Model
CEM............ Concepts Evaluation Model [*Military*]
CEM............ Confederacion Evangelica Mundial [*World Evangelical Fellowship*]
CEM............ Conference Europeenne des Horaires des Trains de Marchandises [*European Freight Timetable Conference*] (EAIO)
CEM............ Contagious Equine Metritis
CEM............ Continuous Electrocardiographic Monitoring [*Medicine*] (CPH)
CEM............ Continuous Emission Monitoring [*Environmental Protection Agency*] (GFGA)
CEM............ Continuous Emissions Monitor [*Environmental Protection Agency*]
CEM............ Contract Energy Managers [*British*]
CEM............ Contrast Enhancement Material [*Photoprocessing*]
CEM............ Control Electrical Mechanic [*British military*] (DMA)
CEM............ Conventional-Transmission Electron Microscope
CEM............ Cost Element Monitor [*Air Force*]
CEM............ Council of European Municipalities
CEM............ Counter Electromotive Cell
CEM............ Cream Silver Mines Ltd. [*Vancouver Stock Exchange symbol*]
CEM............ Crops Estimating Memorandum [*Department of Agriculture*] (GFGA)
CEM............ Current Evangelism Ministries (EA)
CEM3.......... Combat Engineer Mission Management Module [*Software*]
CEMA.......... Canadian Egg Marketing Agency
CEMA.......... Canadian Electrical Manufacturers' Association
CEMA.......... Catering Equipment Manufacturers' Association [*British*] (BI)
CEMA.......... Channel Electron Multiplier Array (MCD)
CEMA.......... Cleaning Equipment Manufacturers Association [*Later, CETA*] (EA)
CEMA.......... Comite Europeen des Groupements de Constructeurs du Machinisme Agricole [*European Committee of Associations of Manufacturers of Agricultural Machinery*] (EAIO)
CEMA.......... Committee of European Promotors of Exhibitions of Measurement and Automation (ACII)
CEMA.......... Converting Equipment Manufacturers Association (EA)
CEMA.......... Conveyor Equipment Manufacturers Association (EA)
CEMA.......... Council for Economic Mutual Assistance [*Also known as CMEA, COMECON*] [*Communist-bloc nations: Poland, Russia, East Germany, Czechoslovakia, Romania, Bulgaria, Hungary Dissolved 1991*]
CEMA.......... Council for the Encouragement of Music and the Arts [*Later, Arts Council*]
CEMA.......... Customs and Excise Management Act (DS)
CEMA.......... Cyanoethyl Methylaniline [*Organic chemistry*]
Cem Ab....... Cement-Asbestos Board (DAC)
CEMAD........ Coherent Echo Modulation and Detection (MCD)
CEMAFON ... Comite Europeen des Materiels et Produits pour la Fonderie [*European Committee of Foundry Materials and Products*] (EAIO)
CEMAID ...... Centres of Excellence in Molecular and Interfacial Dynamics [*Research center*] (RCD)
CEMAL........ Consejo Empresarial Mexicano para Asuntos Internacionales [*The Mexican Business Council for International Affairs*] (CROSS)
CEMAP........ Cotton Export Market Acreage Program
CEMARS ...... COMSEC [*Communications Security*] Equipment Modification Application and Reporting System [*Army*] (MCD)
CEMAS........ Complete Element Matrix Analysis from Scatter [*Spectrometry*]
CEMAST....... Control of Engineering Material, Acquisition, Storage and Transport (IAA)
CEMATEX..... Comite Europeen des Constructeurs de Materiel Textile [*European Committee of Textile Machinery Manufacturers*] (EAIO)
CEMB.......... Cembalo [*Cymbals*] [*Music*] (ROG)
CEMB.......... Civilian Executive Management Board [*Military*] (DNAB)
CEMB.......... Comite Europeen pour le Mini-Basketball [*European Committee for Mini-Basketball - ECMB*] [*Munich, Federal Republic of Germany*] (EAIO)
CEMB.......... Communication-Electronic-Meteorological Board [*Air Force*]
CEMBI......... Conference to Explore Machine Readable Bibliographic Interchange
CEMBUREAU... European Cement Association (EAIO)
CEMC.......... Canadian Engineering Manpower Council
CEMC.......... Combined Exports Market Committee [*World War II*]
CEMC.......... Communications Electronics Management Center [*Air Force*] (AFIT)
CEMC.......... Counter Electromotive Cell
CEMC.......... Curriculum Evaluation and Management Centre [*University of Newcastle upon Tyne*] [*British*] (CB)
CEMCBC ..... Chief Electrician's Mate, Construction Battalion, Communications [*Navy rating Obsolete*]
CEMCBD ..... Chief Electrician's Mate, Construction Battalion, Draftsman [*Navy rating Obsolete*]
CEMCBG ...... Chief Electrician's Mate, Construction Battalion, General [*Navy rating Obsolete*]

CEMCBL....... Chief Electrician's Mate, Construction Battalion, Line and Station [*Navy rating Obsolete*]
CEMCO .... Continental Electronics Manufacturing Co. (AAG)
CEME .... Comite des Eglises Aupres des Migrants en Europe [*Churches' Committee on Migrants in Europe*] (EA)
CEMEC........ Committee of European Associations of Manufacturers of Electronic Components [*EC*] [*Italy*] (ECED)
CEMEL........ Clothing, Equipment, and Materials Engineering Laboratory [*Army Natick Research and Development Laboratories, MA*] (RDA)
CEMEP........ European Committee of Manufacturers of Electrical Machines and Power Electronics [*France*] (EAIO)
CEMERS ...... Center for Medieval and Early Renaissance Studies (EA)
CEMET........ Cemetery (ROG)
cemet .... Cemetery (VRA)
CEMF.......... Counter Electromotive Force (MCD)
Cem Fin .... Cement Finish (DAC)
Cem Fl......... Cement Floor [*Technical drawings*] (DAC)
CEMGC .... Comite Europeen des Materiels de Genie Civil [*Committee for European Construction Equipment - CECE*] (EAIO)
CE/MHE....... Construction Equipment and Materials Handling Equipment [*Military*] (RDA)
CEMI .... China-Europe Management Institute
CEMI .... Commission Europeenne de Marketing Industriel [*European Commission for Industrial Marketing*] [*Brixham, Devonshire, England*] (EAIO)
CEMI .... Committee on Emergency Medical Identification (EA)
CEMICH ...... Michoacan Information Center on the Mexico-US Future (EA)
CEMICS........ Central Equipment Management and Inventory Control System (MCD)
CEMIRT........ Civil Engineering Maintenance, Inspection, Repair, and Training Team [*Air Force*]
CEMIS.......... Client-Employee Management Information System (MHDB)
CEML.......... Central Electron Microscopy Laboratory [*University of Georgia*] [*Research center*] (RCD)
CEML.......... Committee to End the Marion Lockdown (EA)
CEMLA........ Centro de Estudios Monetarios Latinoamericanos [*Center for Latin American Monetary Studies*] [*Mexico City, Mexico*] (EAIO)
CEMM.......... Compaq Extended Memory Manager [*Software*]
Cem Mort .... Cement Mortar [*Technical drawings*] (DAC)
CEMN.......... Center for Endocrinology, Metabolism, and Nutrition [*Northwestern University*]
CEMN.......... Control Electrical Mechanician [*Navy rating British*]
CEM/NET...... Centro de Epidemiologia Molecular, Network for Epidemiologic Tracking [*An international alliance of hospitals that track drug resistance*]
CEMO.......... Canada Emergency Measures Organization [*Civil defense*]
CEMO.......... Command Equipment Management Office [*Military*] (AFM)
CEMO.......... Communications Electronics Mission Order (MCD)
CEMON .... Customer Engineering Monitor [*IBM Corp.*]
CEMOS........ Complementary Enhanced Metal Oxide Semiconductor [*Electronics*] (NITA)
CeMP.......... Central Maine Power Co. [*Associated Press*] (SAG)
CEMP.......... Coastal Environmental Management Plan [*Advisory Committee on Pollution of the Sea*]
CEMP.......... Commonwealth Energy Management Program
CEMPAC ...... Communications-Electronics-Meteorological Program Aggregate Code [*Air Force*] (AFM)
CEMPIMS .... Communications-Electronics-Meteorological Program Implementation Management System [*Air Force*] (CET)
Cem Plas.... Cement Plaster [*Technical drawings*] (DAC)
CEMPR........ Command Equipment Management Program Review [*Military*] (MCD)
CeMPw........ Central Maine Power Co. [*Associated Press*] (SAG)
CEMQ.......... Corporation des Entrepreneurs en Maconnerie du Quebec (AC)
CEMR.......... Center for Economic and Management Research [*University of Oklahoma*] [*Norman*] [*Information service or system*] (IID)
CEMR.......... Center for Energy and Mineral Resources [*Texas A & M University*] [*Research center*]
CEMR.......... Continuing Education in Mental Retardation Program [*American Associaton on Mental Deficiency*] (EDAC)
CEMR.......... Contractor Estimating Methods Review [*DoD*]
CEMR.......... Council of European Municipalities and Regions
CEMREL........ Central Midwest Regional Educational Laboratory
CEMS.......... Calgary Early Music Society (AC)
CEMS.......... Central Electronic Management System
CEMS.......... Church of England Men's Society
CEMS.......... Civil Engineer Management System (AFM)
CEMS.......... Commission on Emergency Medical Services [*Defunct*] (EA)
CEMS.......... Communications and Electronics Maintenance Squadron [*Air Force*]
CEMS.......... Communications Electronics Management Systems
CEMS.......... Comprehensive Engine Management System
CEMS.......... Construction Equipment Management System
CEMS.......... Continuous Emissions Monitoring System
CEMS.......... Conversion Electron Mossbauer Spectroscopy
CEMSq........ Communications and Electronics Maintenance Squadron (AFM)
CEMSRG ...... Chief Electrician's Mate, Ship Repair, General Electrician [*Navy rating Obsolete*]
CEMSRS ...... Chief Electrician's Mate, Ship Repair, Shop Electrician [*Navy rating Obsolete*]
CEMSRT ...... Chief Electrician's Mate, Ship Repair, IC Repairman [*Navy rating Obsolete*]
CEMSS........ Current Engineering and Manufacturing Services Staff [*Automotive industry*]
CEMT.......... Cement
CEMT.......... Command Equipment Management Team [*Military*]

CEMT	Conference Europeenne des Ministres des Transports [*European Conference of Ministers of Transport - ECMT*] [*France*]
CEMTE	Common Experiments Monitoring and Test Equipment (MCD)
CEMTEX	Central Magnetic Tape Exchange [*Computer science*] (ADA)
CEMV	Celery Mosaic Virus [*Plant pathology*]
CEMX	CEM Corp. [*NASDAQ symbol*] (NQ)
CEMYF	Charles Edison Memorial Youth Fund [*Later, FAS*] (EA)
CEN	Canadian Environmental Network (GNE)
CEN	Canterra Energy Ltd. [*Toronto Stock Exchange symbol*]
CEN	Captive European Nations (NATG)
CEN	Cenozoic [*Period, era, or system*] [*Geology*]
CEN	Centaur [*Rocket*] [*NASA*] (KSC)
Cen	Centaurus [*Constellation*]
CEN	Centenary College of Louisiana, Magale Library, Shreveport, LA [*OCLC symbol*] (OCLC)
CEN	Centennial (ROG)
CEN	Center [*or Central*] (AFM)
CEN	Central Airlines, Inc.
CEN	Central Airways Corp. [*Canada ICAO designator*] (FAAC)
CEN	Central Datum
CEN	Central Education Network [*Des Plaines, IL*] [*Telecommunications service*] (TSSD)
CEN	Centro Nacionalista [*Nationalist Center*] [*Bolivia*] [*Political party*] (PPW)
CEN	Century
CEN	Century
CEN	Ceridian Corp. [*Formerly, Control Data Corp.*] [*NYSE symbol*] (SPSG)
CEN	Cerro-Negro [*Argentina*] [*Seismograph station code, US Geological Survey*] (SEIS)
CEN	Certification for Emergency Nursing
CEN	Church of England Newspaper
CEN	Ciudad Obregon [*Mexico*] [*Airport symbol*] (OAG)
CEN	Comite Europeen de Coordination des Normes [*European Committee for Coordination of Standards*]
CEN	Comite Europeen de Normalisation [*European Committee for Standardization*] [*Belgium*]
CEN	Commission pour l'Etude des Nuages [*OMI*]
CEN	Communications Electronics Navigation [*Military*]
CEN	Computer Equipment News [*A publication*] (APTA)
CEN	Copper Ethanolamine
CEN	Cultural Expression in the Navy Workshop (DNAB)
CEN	La Centrale des Bibliotheques [*Source file*] [*UTLAS symbol*]
CENA	Centred' Etudes de la Navigation Aerienne [*France*] (GAVI)
CENA	Charge Exchange Neutralo Analyzer (MCD)
CENA	Coalition of Eastern Native Americans [*Defunct*] (EA)
CENADEM	Centro Nacional de Desenvolvimento do Gerenciamento da Informacao [*National Center for Information Management Development*] [*Brazil Information service or system*] (IID)
CEN AFR REP	Central African Republic (WDAA)
CENAGRI	Centro Nacional de Informacao Documental Agricola [*National Center for Agricultural Documentary Information*] [*Ministry of Agriculture Brazil*] [*Information service or system*] (IID)
CE/NAVFAC	Army Corps of Engineers/Naval Facilities Engineering Command
CENB	Consulting Engineers of New Brunswick (AC)
CENC	Convergent Exhaust Nozzle Control (MCD)
CENCATS	Central Pacific Combat Air Transport Service
CENCER	Association Cerification Comite European de Normalisation (OSI)
CENCOMMRGN	Central Communications Region [*Air Force*] (AFM)
CENCOMS	Center for Communications Systems [*CADPL*] [*Army*] (RDA)
CEND	Combustion Engineering Nuclear Division [*AEC*] (MCD)
CENDHRRA	Center for the Development of Human Resources in Rural Asia (EAIO)
CENDI	Department of Commerce/National Technical Information Service, Department of Energy/Office of Scientific and Technical Information, National Aeronautics and Space Administration Scientific and Technical Information Branch, and Department ofDefense/Defense Technical Information Center
CENDIS	Centre de Documentation et d'Information Interuniversitaire en Sciences Sociales[*Interuniversity Documentation and Information Center for the Social Science s*] [*Information service or system*] (IID)
CENDIT	Centre for Development of Instructional Technology
CENDRAFT	Central Drafting Officer [*Navy*]
CENECA	Centre National des Expositions et Concours Agricoles
CENEL	Comite Europeen de Coordination des Normes Electriques [*European Electrical Standards Coordinating Committee*]
CENELEC	Comite Europeen de Normalisation Electrotechnique [*European Committee for Electrotechnical Standardization*] (EAIO)
CENESC	Committee for Exchange with Non-English Speaking Countries (AIE)
CENEUR	Central European (AFM)
CENEX	Complex Energetics Experiment
CENF	CENFED Financial [*NASDAQ symbol*] (TTSB)
CENF	Cenfed Financial Corp. [*NASDAQ symbol*] (SAG)
CenFAcc	Central Financial Acceptance Corp. [*Associated Press*] (SAG)
Cenfed	Cenfed Financial Corp. [*Associated Press*] (SAG)
C Eng	Chartered Engineer [*British*]
CenGardn	Central Garden & Pet Co. [*Associated Press*] (SAG)
CENGR	Civil Engineer (FAAC)
CenHud	Central Hudson Gas & Electric Corp. [*Associated Press*] (SAG)
CenHV	[*A*] Century of Humorous Verse [*A publication*]
CENI	Conestoga Enterprises [*NASDAQ symbol*] (TTSB)
CENI	Conestoga Enterprises, Inc. [*NASDAQ symbol*] (SAG)

CENID	Centro Nacional de Informacion y Documentacion [*National Center for Information and Documentation*] [*Chile*] [*Information service or system*]
CENIDS	Centro Nacional de Informacion y Documentacion en Salud [*National Center for Health Information and Documentation*] [*Mexico*] [*Information service or system*] (IID)
CenitBcp	Cenit Bancorp [*Associated Press*] (SAG)
CenL	[*A*] Century of Lyrics [*A publication*]
CENL	Community Equivalent Noise Level (PDAA)
CenLAEI	Central Louisiana Electric Co., Inc. [*Associated Press*] (SAG)
CenM	Central Maine Power Co. [*Associated Press*] (SAG)
CENO	Central Naval Ordnance Management Information System
CENOG	Computerized Electro Neuro-Ophthalmograph
CENOMISO	Central Naval Ordnance Management Information System Office (DNAB)
CENP	Centromere Protein (DMAA)
CENPAC	Central North Pacific [*Aviation*] (FAAC)
CENPAC	Central Pacific Area [*Navy*]
CENPACFOR	Central Pacific Forces
CENPACSARCOORD	Central Pacific Search and Rescue Coordinator [*Coast Guard*] (DNAB)
CENPAT	Central Patch and Test [*Facility*]
CENPr	Ceridian Cp Cv Ex Dep Pfd [*NYSE symbol*] (TTSB)
CENPRO	Census Projections [*Database*] (IT)
CENR	Committee on Environment and Natural Resources [*National Science and Technology Council*]
CENR	Committee on Environment and Natural Resources (USDC)
CENRIVSARCOORD	Central Rivers Search and Rescue Coordinator [*Coast Guard*] (DNAB)
CENS	Censor [*or Censorship*] (AFM)
CENS	Council on Economics and National Security [*Defunct*] (EA)
CENSA	Council of European and Japanese National Shipowners Associations [*England*] (EAIO)
CENSAC	Census Access System [*Urban Decision Systems, Inc.*] [*Information service or system Defunct*] (CRD)
CEN/SCK	Centre d'Etude de l'Energie Nucleaire/Studiecentrum voor Kernenergie [*Belgium*] (EY)
CENSEI	Center for Systems Engineering and Integration [*Army*] (GRD)
CENSER	Census Servomechanism and Tape Handler
CENSHARE	Center to Study Human-Animal Relationships and Environments [*University of Minnesota*] [*Research center*] (RCD)
CenSoWst	Central & South West Corp. [*Associated Press*] (SAG)
CENSPAC	Census Bureau Software Package (GFGA)
CENT	Cental [*Short hundredweight*] [*British*] (ROG)
CENT	Centaur [*Rocket*] [*NASA*] (KSC)
Cent	Centaurus [*Constellation*]
Cent	Centenary [*or Centennial*]
CENT	Centennial
CENT	Center [*Commonly used*] (OPSA)
CENT	Centigrade [*Celsius*] [*Temperature scale*] (KSC)
CENT	Centime [*Monetary unit*] [*France*]
cent	Centimeter (MAE)
CENT	Central
Cent	Central (AAGC)
CENT	Central Garden & Pet [*NASDAQ symbol*] (TTSB)
CENT	Central Garden & Pet Co. [*NASDAQ symbol*] (SAG)
Cent	Central Reporter [*A publication*] (DLA)
CENT	Centrifugal (KSC)
CENT	Centum [*Hundred*]
CENT	Century
CENT	Consulting Engineers of NWT (AC)
CENTA	Combined Edible Nut Trade Association [*British*] (DBA)
CENTAC	Central Tactical Unit [*Drug Enforcement Administration*]
CENTACS	Center for Tactical Computer Systems [*CADPL*] [*Army*] (MCD)
Cent Afr Rep	Central African Republic (VRA)
CENTAG	Central [*European*] Army Group [*NATO*]
CentAl	Century Aluminum Co. [*Associated Press*] (SAG)
CENTAM	Central America
Cent Am	Central American (VRA)
CENTAMP	Central Treaty Organization Allied Military Publication
CENTAUM	Committee on Education Needs for Teen-Age Unwed Mothers
CentB	Century Bible [*A publication*] (BJA)
CentBk	Centura Banks [*Associated Press*] (SAG)
CentC	Century Casinos, Inc. [*Associated Press*] (SAG)
CentCas	Century Casinos, Inc. [*Associated Press*] (SAG)
CentCel	Centennial Cellular Corp. [*Associated Press*] (SAG)
CENTCOM	Central Command [*Persian Gulf War*]
CENTCOM	Central Pacific Communications Instructions
CENTCOM	United States Central Command (INF)
CENTCON	Centralized Control Facility
Cent Conn St U	Central Connecticut State University (GAGS)
Cent Crim C Cas	Central Criminal Court Cases, Sessions Papers [*1834-1913*] [*England*] [*A publication*] (DLA)
Cent Crim CR	Central Criminal Court Reports [*England*] [*A publication*] (DLA)
Cent Dict	Century Dictionary [*A publication*] (DLA)
Cent Dict and Cyc	Century Dictionary and Cyclopedia [*A publication*] (DLA)
Cent Dict & Ency	Century Dictionary and Encyclopedia [*A publication*] (DLA)
Cent Dig	Century Edition of the American Digest System (West) [*A publication*] (DLA)
CENTED	Center for Technology, Environment, and Development [*Clark University*]
CentEn	Centerior Energy Corp. [*Associated Press*] (SAG)
CentenT	Centennial Technologies, Inc. [*Associated Press*] (SAG)
CENTER	Center [*Commonly used*] (OPSA)
CenterFn	Center Financial Corp. (Connecticut) [*Associated Press*] (SAG)

CENTERS ..... Centers [*Commonly used*] (OPSA)
CentEur......... Central European Equity Fund [*Associated Press*] (SAG)
Centex .... Centex Corp. [*Associated Press*] (SAG)
CENTF......... Centrifugal
CentFin......... Century Financial Corp. [*Associated Press*] (SAG)
Centgrm......... Centigram Communications Corp. [*Associated Press*] (SAG)
CENTIG .... Centigrade [*Celsius*] [*Temperature scale*] (ROG)
CENTLANT ... Central Subarea, Atlantic [*NATO*]
Cent Law J. ... Central Law Journal [*A publication*] (DLA)
CentlBc......... Centennial Bancorp [*Associated Press*] (SAG)
Cent LJ......... Central Law Journal [*A publication*] (DLA)
Cent L Mo ... Central Law Monthly [*A publication*] (DLA)
Cent Mich U... Central Michigan University (GAGS)
Cent Mo St U... Central Missouri State University (GAGS)
Cent Nupt ... Cento Nuptialis [*of Ausonius*] [*Classical studies*] (OCD)
CENTO .... Central European Treaty Organization (MCD)
CENTO .... Central Treaty Organization [*Also, CTO*] [*Formerly, Baghdad Pact*]
Centocor...... Centocor, Inc. [*Associated Press*] (SAG)
CENTPACBACOM... Central Pacific Base Command [*Navy*]
CentPkg......... Central Parking Corp. [*Associated Press*] (SAG)
Cent Prov LR... Central Provinces Law Reports [*India*] [*A publication*] (DLA)
CENTR .... Center [*Commonly used*] (OPSA)
CENTR .... Central (ROG)
CENTRA......... Centralized Training [*Material management subsystem*] (MCD)
CENTRA....... Central Nova Therapeutic Riding Association (AC)
Central LJ... Central Law Journal [*A publication*] (DLA)
Centr Cr Ct R... Central Criminal Court Cases, Sessions Papers [*1834-1913*] [*England*] [*A publication*] (DLA)
Centr Cr Ct R... Central Criminal Court Reports [*England*] [*A publication*] (ILCA)
CENTRE .... Center [*Commonly used*] (OPSA)
CENTREDOC... Swiss Center of Documentation in Microtechnology [*Information service or system*] (IID)
Cent Rep ... Central Reporter [*A publication*] (DLA)
CENTREX......... Central Exchange
Centr LJ......... Central Law Journal [*A publication*] (DLA)
CENTRO....... Central New York Library Resources Council [*Syracuse, NY*] [*Library network*]
Cent R (PA)... Central Reporter [*Pennsylvania*] [*A publication*] (DLA)
CentrpPr ...... Centerpoint Properties Corp. [*Associated Press*] (SAG)
CENTS .... Consortium for the Education of Non-Traditional Students (BARN)
CentSE .... Central Securities Corp. [*Associated Press*] (SAG)
CentTc .... Centennial Technologies, Inc. [*Associated Press*] (SAG)
CenturaSft ... Centura Software Corp. [*Associated Press*] (SAG)
Cent Wash U... Central Washington University (GAGS)
CentxCn .... Centex Construction Products [*Associated Press*] (SAG)
centy........ Century (BARN)
CENU .... Chloroethylnitrosourea [*A class of antineoplastic agents*]
CENV .... Canadian Environment [*Database*] [*WATDOC*] [*Information service or system*] (CRD)
C Environ LN... Canadian Environmental Law News [*A publication*] (DLA)
CENX .... Century Aluminum [*NASDAQ symbol*] (TTSB)
CENX .... Century Aluminum Co. [*NASDAQ symbol*] (SAG)
CENYC .... Council of European National Youth Committees (EA)
CEO............ Association of Consulting Engineers of Ontario (AC)
CEO............ Casualty Evacuation Officer
CEO............ Center for Electron Optics [*Michigan State University*] [*Research center*] (RCD)
CEO............ Central Oregon Community College, Library, Bend, OR [*OCLC symbol*] (OCLC)
CEO............ Chemical Engineering Operations [*MIT*] (MCD)
CEO............ Chick Embryo Origin
CEO............ Chief Education Officer (AIE)
CEO............ Chief Elected Official (OICC)
CEO............ Chief Electoral Officer [*Canada*]
CEO............ Chief Engineer's Office (SAA)
CEO............ Chief Executive Officer
CEO............ Chief Executives Organization (EA)
CEO............ Chip Enable Output [*Computer science*]
CEO............ Collective-Electronic Oscillator [*Physics*]
CEO............ Comite Europeen de l'Outillage [*European Tool Committee - ETC*] (EA)
CEO............ Command Education Officer [*Military British*]
CEO............ Command Entertainments Officer [*Military British*]
CEO............ Communications-Electronics Officer [*Air Force*]
CEO............ Community Education Officer (ADA)
CEO............ Comprehensive Electronic Office [*Data General Corp.*]
CEO............ Council for Economic Advisors (AAGC)
CEO............ Covert Entrepreneurial Organization [*Term used by Carl S. Taylor in his book on street gangs, Dangerous Society*]
CEO............ Cultural Exchange Officer [*United States Information Service*]
CEO............ Customs Enforcement Officer [*US Customs Service*]
CEO............ Waco Kungo [*Angola*] [*Airport symbol*] (OAG)
CEOA .... Central Europe Operating Agency [*Versailles, France*] [*NATO*]
CEOA .... Civic Entertainment Officers' Association [*British*] (BI)
CEOAH......... Comite Europeen de l'Outillage Agricole et Horticole [*European Committee for Agricultural and Horticultural Tools and Implements - ECAHTI*] (EA)
CEOAS .... Corps of Engineers Office of Appalachian Studies [*Army*] (AABC)
CEOC .... Confederation Europeenne d'Organismes de Controle (EAIO)
CEOCOR....... Comite d'Etude de la Corrosion et de la Protection des Canalisations [*Committee for the Study of Pipe Corrosion and Protection*] (EAIO)
CEOCOR....... Commission Europeenne de Corrosion des Conduites Souterraines [*Brussels, Belgium*] (EAIO)
CEODP......... Committee to Expose, Oppose, and Depose Patriarchy (EA)

CEOE............ Certified Engineering Operations Executive [*American Hotel and Motel Asso ciation*] [*Designation awarded by*]
CEOF........... Complex Empirical Orthogonal Function [*Mathematics*]
CEOI........... Communications-Electronics Operating Instruction (CINC)
CEOM........... Catholic Education Office, Melbourne [*Australia*]
CEON .... Cerion Technologies, Inc. [*NASDAQ symbol*] (SAG)
CEON .... CevionTechnologies [*NASDAQ symbol*] (TTSB)
CEOP........... Communaute Europeenne des Organisations de Publicitaires [*European Community of Advertising Organizations*]
CEOR........... Certainty Equivalent of Revenues [*Business term*]
CEORS .... Center for Earth Observations and Remote Sensing [*Boulder, CO*] [*Cooperative Institute for Research in Environmental Sciences*] [*National Oceanic and Atmospheric Administration*] (GRD)
CEOS .... Civil Engineering Operations Squadron [*Air Force*]
CEOS .... Committee on Earth Observations Satellites [*NASA*]
CEOS .... County Education Officers' Society [*British*]
CEOST .... Committee on Equal Opportunities in Science and Technology [*National Science Foundation*]
CEOT .... Calcifying Epithelial Odontogenic Tumor [*Medicine*] (DMAA)
CEOWA .... Catholic Education Office of Western Australia
CEOYLA .... Council of Eastern Orthodox Youth Leaders of the Americas [*Defunct*] (EA)
CEP............ Calculated Error Probable
CEP............ Capability Evaluation Plan
CEP............ Capital Expenditure Proposal
CEP............ Career Exploration Profile [*Vocational guidance test*]
CEP............ Caribbean Environment Program [*Marine science*] (OSRA)
CEP............ Caribbean Environment Program (USDC)
CEP............ Catalytic Extraction Process [*Engineering*]
CEP............ Catalytic Extraction Processing [*Recycling*]
CEP............ Cathode Electrodeposited Paint [*Environmental science*]
CEP............ CCNU [*Lomustine*], Etoposide, Prednimustine [*Antineoplastic drug regimen*]
CEP............ Center of Experimentation in the Pacific Ocean (BARN)
CEP............ Central East Pacific [*Region*]
CEP............ Centralized Employment Program
CEP............ [*A*] Century of Excavation in Palestine [*A publication*] (BJA)
Cep............ Cepheus [*Constellation*]
CEP............ Certified Environmental Professional [*Environmental science*]
CEP............ Character Education Partnership [*An association*]
CEP............ Chicano Education Project [*Defunct*] (EA)
CEP............ Chretiens pour Une Eglise Populaire [*Christians for One Common Church*] [*Canada*]
CEP............ Christian Education Publications [*Australia*]
CEP............ Circle End Point
CEP............ Circle of Equal Probability
CEP............ Circular Error Probability [*Military*]
CEP............ Circular Error Probable (AAGC)
CEP............ Citizens' Energy Project [*Defunct*] (EA)
CEP............ Civil Emergency Planning [*NATO*] (NATG)
CEP............ Civil Engineering Package (IEEE)
CEP............ Civilian Employment Projection (MCD)
CEP............ Coal Employment Project (EA)
CEP............ [*A*] Collection of English Poems [*A publication*]
CEP............ Color Evaluation Program
CEP............ Combat Engineer Party [*Army*] (VNW)
CEP............ Command Executive Procedure [*Computer science*] (OA)
CEP............ Commercial Exchange of Philadelphia [*Defunct*] (EA)
CEP............ Committee for Energy Policy [*Organization for Economic Cooperation and Development*] (MCD)
CEP............ Committee on Environmental Protection [*Marine science*] (OSRA)
CEP............ Common Electronic Parts
CEP............ Communications, Energy & Paperworkers Union of Canada (AC)
CEP............ Community Energy Program [*Office of Volunteer Liaison*] [*ACTION*]
CEP............ Community Enterprise Program [*British*]
CEP............ Company Export Planning
CEP............ Compensatory Equipment Package (MCD)
CEP............ Competition Engineering Program [*Air Force*]
CEP............ Complementary Even Parity (PDAA)
CEP............ Component Error Propagation
CEP............ Computed Ephemeris Position
CEP............ Computer Entry Punch
CEP............ Concentrated Employment Program [*Also known as CIEP*] [*Department of Labor*]
CEP............ Concepcion [*Bolivia*] [*Airport symbol*] (OAG)
CEP............ Concept Evaluation Program [*Army*]
CEP............ Condensate Extraction Pump [*Chemical engineering*]
CEP............ Conduction Electron Polarization
CEP............ Confederation Europeenne d'Etudes Phytosanitaires [*European Confederation for Plant Protection Research*]
CEP............ Conference on Economic Progress [*Defunct*] (EA)
CEP............ Congenital Erythropoietic Porphyria [*Medicine*]
CEP............ Consolidated Explorer Petroleum Corp. [*Vancouver Stock Exchange symbol*]
CEP............ Construction Electrician, Power [*Navy rating*]
CEP............ Contact Evaluation Plot (NVT)
CEP............ Continuing Education Program [*State University of New York at Albany*] [*Research center*]
CEP............ Continuous Estimation Program
CEP............ Contract Estimating and Pricing (MCD)
CEP............ Contractual Engineering Project (AFIT)
CEP............ ConVest Energy Partners Ltd. (MHDW)
CEP............ Cooperative Engineering Program [*Automotive industry*]
CEP............ Coordinated Examination Program [*Internal Revenue Service*]
CEP............ Corporate Electronic Publishing (HGAA)

CEP............ Cortical Evoked Potential [*Neurophysiology*]
CEP............ Cost Evaluation Plan (AAGC)
CEP............ Cotton Equalization Program
CEP............ Council on Economic Policy [*Inactive*]
CEP............ Council on Economic Priorities (EA)
CEP............ Council on Energy Policy [*Proposed Presidential council*]
CEP............ Council on Environmental Pollutants
CEP............ Countercurrent Electrophoresis [*Analytical chemistry*] (DAVI)
CEP............ Counterelectrophoresis [*Analytical chemistry*]
CEP............ Country Economic Profiles [*I. P. Sharp Association Pty. Ltd.*] [*Australia Information service or system*] (CRD)
CEP............ Court Employment Project (EA)
CEP............ Crossed Electrophoresis (MCD)
CEP............ Current Energy Patents [*A publication*]
CEP............ Cylinder Escape Probability (PDAA)
CEP............ Cylindrical Electrostatic Probe [*NASA*] (MCD)
CEP............ Executive Privatization Commission
CEP1.......... Construction Electrician, Power, First Class [*Navy rating*] (DNAB)
CEP2.......... Construction Electrician, Power, Second Class [*Navy rating*] (DNAB)
CEP3.......... Construction Electrician, Power, Third Class [*Navy rating*] (DNAB)
CEPA.......... Canadian Energy Pipeline Association
CEPA.......... Canadian Environmental Protection Act
CEPA.......... Central Europe Pipeline Agency [*Later, CEOA*] [*NATO*] (NATG)
CEPA.......... Chaleur Environment Protection Association (AC)
CEPA.......... Chloroethane Phosphoric Acid [*Organic chemistry*] (DAVI)
CEPA.......... Chloroethylphosphonic Acid [*Maturation compound for fruits*]
CEPA.......... Civil Engineering Program Applications (MCD)
CEPA.......... Commercial Egg Producers' Association [*Australia*]
CEPA.......... Committee on Educational Policy in Agriculture [*National Academy of Sciences*]
CEPA.......... Conseil Europeen pour la Protection des Animaux [*European Council for Animal Welfare - ECAW*] (EA)
CEPA.......... Consolidated Electric Power Asia (ECON)
CEPA.......... Consumers Education and Protective Association International (EA)
CEPA.......... Coupled Electron Pair Approximation [*Physics*]
CEPA.......... Society for Computer Applications in Engineering, Planning, and Architecture (EA)
CEPAC........ Confederation Europeenne de l'Industrie de Pates, Papiers, et Cartons [*European Confederation of Pulp, Paper, and Board Industries*] (EAIO)
CEPAC........ Conferentia Episcopalis Pacifici [*Episcopal Conference of the Pacific*] (EAIO)
CEPACC....... Chemical Education Planning and Coordinating Committee [*American Chemical Society*]
CEPACS....... Customs Entry Processing and Cargo System (PDAA)
CEPAL......... Comision Economica para America Latina y el Caribe [*Economic Commission for Latin America and the Caribbean - ECLAC*] [*Santiago, Chile*] [*United Nations*] (EAIO)
CEPAQ........ Centre d'Etudes Politiques et Administratives du Quebec [*University of Quebec*] [*Research center*] (RCD)
CEPAQ........ Centre pour l'Avancement des Associations du Quebec (AC)
CEPAR........ Curing, Extrusion, Plasticity, and Recovery (PDAA)
CEPB.......... Civil Emergency Planning Bureau [*NATO*] (NATG)
CEPC.......... Canadian Egg Producers Council
CEPC.......... Chief Engineer Port Construction [*British military*] (DMA)
CEPC.......... Civil Emergency Planning Committee [*US/Canada*]
CEPC.......... Comite Europeen pour les Problemes Criminels [*Council of Europe*]
CEPC.......... Committee of Engineering Professors' Conference (ACII)
CEPCA........ Construction Electrician, Power, Construction Apprentice [*Navy rating*] (DNAB)
CEPCAD....... Committee to Eliminate Premature Christmas Advertising and Display [*Defunct*] (EA)
CEPCEO....... Comite d'Etude des Producteurs de Charbon d'Europe Occidentale [*Association of the Coal Producers of the European Community*] (EAIO)
CEPCIES...... Comision Ejecutiva Permanente del Consejo Interamericano Economico y Social [*Permanent Executive Committee of the Inter-American Economic and Social Council*] (EA)
CEPCN........ Construction Electrician, Power, Constructionman [*Navy rating*] (DNAB)
CEPD .... Communications-Electronics Policy Directives [*NATO*] (NATG)
CEPE.......... Central Experimental and Proving Establishment [*Canada*] (MCD)
CEPE.......... Chain-Extended Polyethylene (PDAA)
CEPE.......... Comite Europeen des Associations des Fabricants de Peinture, d'Encres d'Imprimerie, et de Couleurs [*European Committee of Paint, Printing Ink, and Artists' Colours Manufacturers Associations*] (EAIO)
CEPE.......... Cylindrical Electrostatic Probe Experiment [*NASA*]
CEPEI......... Child Find PEI Inc. (AC)
CEPEIGE...... Centro Panamericano de Estudios e Investigaciones Geograficas [*Pan American Center for Geographical Studies and Research - PACGSR*] (EAIO)
CEPEP......... Centre Europeen des Parents de l'Ecole Publique (AIE)
CEPER........ Combined Engineering Plant Exchange Record [*Telecommunications*] (TEL)
CEPES......... Centre Europeen pour l'Enseignement Superieur [*European Centre for Higher Education*] (EAIO)
CEPES......... Comite Europeen pour le Progres Economique et Social [*European Committee for Economic and Social Progress*]
CEPEX........ Central Equatorial Pacific Experiment [*Marine science*] (OSRA)
CEPEX........ Central Equatorial Pacific Experiment (USDC)
CEPEX........ Controlled Ecosystem Pollution Experiment [*National Science Foundation project*]

CEPFAR ...... Centre Europeen pour la Promotion de la Formation Milieu Agricole et Rural [*European Training and Development Centre for Farming and Rural Life - ETDCFRL*] (EAIO)
CEPFR .... Critical Experiment Pulsed Fast Reactor
CEPG .... Cambridge Economic Policy Group [*British*]
CEPGL .... Communaute Economique des Pays des Grands Lacs [*Economic Community of the Great Lakes Countries - ECGLC*] [*Gisenye, Rwanda*] (EAIO)
CEPH .... Centre d'Etude du Polymorphisme Humain [*Paris, France*] (ECON)
CEPH .... Cephalic (ROG)
CEPH .... Cephalon, Inc. [*NASDAQ symbol*] (SPSG)
CEPH .... Cephalosporin [*Pharmacology*] (DAVI)
Ceph .... Cepheus [*Constellation*]
CEPH .... Council on Education for Public Health (EA)
CEPH-FLOC.. Cephalin Flocculation [*Clinical chemistry*] (AAMN)
CephIn .... Cephalon, Inc. [*Associated Press*] (SAG)
CEPI.......... Capital Expenditure Price Index
CEPI.......... Circulo de Escritores y Poetas Iberoamericanos [*An association*] (EA)
CEPIS.......... Centro Panamericano de Ingenieria Sanitaria y Ciencias del Ambiente [*Pan American Center for Sanitary Engineering and Environmental Sciences*] [*Peru*] [*Research center*] (IRC)
CEPL.......... Conference Europeenne des Pouvoirs Locaux
CEPM.......... Center for Educational Policy and Management [*Department of Education*] (GRD)
CEPM.......... Civil Engineer Preventive Maintenance [*Air Force*]
CEPMS........ Compensation, Employment, and Performance Management Staff [*Department of Agriculture*] (GFGA)
CEPO.......... Central Eastern Personnel Organization [*Computerized scouting combine for professional football teams*]
CEPO.......... Central Engineering Projects Office [*NATO*] (NATG)
CEPO.......... Central Europe Pipeline Office [*NATO*]
CEPO.......... Centralized Excess Personal Property [*Department of Agriculture*] (GFGA)
CEPO.......... County Emergency Planning Officers Society [*British*]
CEPOD........ Catalyzed Electrolytic Plutonium Oxide Dissolution [*Chemistry*]
CEPOM........ Centre d'Etudes des Problemes d'Outre-Mer [*Center for the Study of Overseas Problems*] [*France*] (AF)
CEPP.......... Chemical Emergency Preparedness Plan (GNE)
CEPP.......... Chemical Emergency Preparedness Program [*Environmental Protection Agency*]
CEPP.......... Contractor Employee Protection Program [*DOE*] (AAGC)
CEPPC........ Central Europe Pipeline Policy Committee [*NATO*]
CEPR.......... Center for Energy Policy and Research (EA)
CEPR.......... Centre for Economic Policy Research [*Australian National University*] [*Economics Australia*]
CEPR.......... Centre for Economic Policy Research [*British*] (ECON)
CEPR.......... Certified in Education for Public Relations [*Public Relations Society of America*] [*New York, NY*] (WDMC)
CEPR.......... College of Engineers of Puerto Rico
CEPR.......... Council on Education in Professional Responsibility [*Later, CLEPR*] (EA)
CEPRAP....... Center for Engineering Plants for Resistance Against Pathogens [*University of California*] [*Research center*] (RCD)
CEPRC........ Chemical Emergency Planning and Response Commission
CEPS.......... Center for Educational Policy Studies (EA)
CEPS.......... Central Europe Pipeline System [*NATO*] (NATG)
CEPS.......... Centre for European Policy Studies (ECON)
CEPS.......... Civil Engineering Problems
CEPS.......... Color Electronic Prepress Systems [*Printing technology*]
CEPS.......... Combined Exercise Planning Staff [*Military*] (MCD)
CEPS.......... Command Module Electrical Power System [*NASA*]
CEPS.......... Components Evaluation Propulsion System (MCD)
CEPS.......... Computerized Equipment Pricing System [*Council of Petroleum Accountants Societies*] [*Information service or system*] (CRD)
CEPS.......... Congress for the Education of the Partially Seeing (AEBS)
CEPS.......... Continuous Explosion-Puffing System [*Food technology*]
CEPS.......... Corporate Electronic Publishing Systems Exhibition [*or Exposition*] (ITD)
CEPS.......... Council for the Education of the Partially Seeing [*Later, Division for the Visually Handicapped*] (EA)
CEPT.......... Chemically Enhanced Primary Treatment [*Water treatment*]
CEPT.......... Common Effective Preferential Tariff
CEPT.......... Conference Europeenne des Administrations des Postes et des Telecommunications [*Conference of European Postal and Telecommunications Administrations*] [*Telecommunications*] (EAIO)
CEPT.......... European Conference of Postal and Telecommunications Administration (OSRA)
CEPTIA........ Committee to End Pay Toilets in America [*Defunct*]
CEPUP .... Chemical Education for Public Understanding Program [*University of California, Berkley*]
CEQ............ Cannes [*France*] [*Airport symbol*] (AD)
CEQ............ Centrale de l'Enseignement du Quebec [*Quebec Teaching Congress*] (AC)
CEQ............ Centrale de l'enseignment du Quebec [*Canada An association*] (CROSS)
CEQ............ Cinequity Corp. [*Toronto Stock Exchange symbol*]
CEQ............ Council on Environmental Quality [*of Federal Council on Science and Technology*] [*Washington, DC*]
CEQA.......... California Environmental Quality Act (DOGT)
CEQB .... Collinear Exact Quantum Bend [*Kinetics*]
CER............ Caesar Resources Ltd. [*Vancouver Stock Exchange symbol*]
CER............ Capital Expenditure Request
CER............ Capital Expenditure Review (DHSM)

CER............	Carbon Dioxide Exchange Rate [*Plant biochemistry*]
CER............	Carriage of Explosives Regulations
CER............	Cation-Exchange Resin [*Chemical technology*]
CER............	Celanese Engineering Resins Division [*Celanese Corp.*]
CER............	Celmar Servicios Aereos SA de CV [*Mexico ICAO designator*] (FAAC)
CER............	Center for Economic Research [*University of Texas at Austin*] [*Research center*] (RCD)
CER............	Center for Educational Reform (EA)
CER............	Central Illinois Light Co. [*NYSE symbol*] (SAG)
CER............	Centre for Endangered Reptiles [*Centre Pour Reptiles Menaces*] [*Formerly, The Reptile Breeding Foundation*] (AC)
CER............	Ceramic (MSA)
cer............	Ceramics (VRA)
Cer............	Ceramide [*Biochemistry*]
CER............	Cereal Agar
CER............	Ceres [*South Africa*] [*Seismograph station code, US Geological Survey*] (SEIS)
cer............	Cerise [*Philately*]
CER............	Cerrada
CER............	Certification Evaluation Review
CER............	Cervicothoracic Orthosis [*Also, CTO*] [*Medicine*]
CER............	Cherbourg [*France*] [*Airport symbol*] (OAG)
CER............	Chief of Establishments and Research [*British*]
CER............	Cilcorp [*NYSE symbol*] (SAG)
CER............	CILCORP ,Inc. [*NYSE symbol*] (TTSB)
CER............	Citicorp Economic Report [*Database*] [*Citicorp Information Services*] [*Information service or system*] (CRD)
CER............	Citizens for Eye Research (EA)
CER............	Civil Engineering Report
CER............	Climb en Route [*Aviation*] (FAAC)
CER............	Closer Economic Relations (ADA)
CER............	Coarse Element Refinement (IAA)
CER............	Coastal and Estuarine Regimes [*Oceanography*] (MSC)
CER............	Cohesive Energy Ratio (MCD)
CER............	Colonizing Efficiency Ratio [*Forestry*]
CER............	Combat Effectiveness Report (NATG)
CER............	Command and Expenditure Report
CER............	Commanders Evaluation Report [*Army*]
CER............	Committee on Educational Reconstruction
CER............	Community Educational Resources
CER............	Complete Engineering Release
CER............	Complete Engine Repair (NG)
CER............	Component Engineering Request
CER............	Conditioned Emotional Response [*Psychology*]
CER............	Consultative Environmental Review [*Australia*]
CER............	Contact End Resistance [*Photovoltaic energy systems*]
CER............	Controlled Environment Room [*Agricultural science*] (OA)
CER............	Controller of Research and Development Establishments and Research [*British*] (RDA)
CER............	Coordinated Ecosystem Research [*Marine science*] (OSRA)
CER............	Coordinated Ecosystem Research (USDC)
CER............	Coordinated Experimental Research [*Program*] [*National Science Foundation*]
CER............	Coordinating Equipment Research Committee
CER............	Corotation Eccentricity Resonance [*Planetary science*]
CER............	Cost-Effective Ratio [*Economics*]
CER............	Cost Estimate Request
CER............	Cost Estimating Relation [*or Relationship*] (AFM)
CER............	Cost-Exchange Ratio [*DoD*]
CER............	Council of European Regions (EAIO)
CER............	Council on Environmental Remediation (AAGC)
CER............	Crew Environment Requirements (SAA)
CER............	Critical Experiment Reactor (NRCH)
CER............	Cross-linking Electron Resist (PDAA)
CEr............	Eagle Rock Public Library, Eagle Rock, CA [*Library symbol Library of Congress*] (LCLS)
Cer............	Hymnus in Cererem [*of Callimachus*] [*Classical studies*] (OCD)
CERA........	Canadian Educational Researchers Association [*See also ACCE*]
CERA	Central Electric Railfans' Association (EA)
CERA	Chief Engine Room Artificer [*British military*] (DMA)
CERA	Civil Engineering Research Association
CERA	Comision Especial de Expertos para el Estudio de las Necesidades Financieras quePlantea la Ejecucion de Planes de Reforma Agraria [*Consejo Interamericano Economico y Social*] [*Washington, DC*]
CERA	Conard [*Henry S.*] Environmental Research Area [*Grinnell College*] [*Research center*] (RCD)
CERA	Council for Equal Rights in Adoption
CERAD........	Consortium to Establish a Registry for Alzheimer's Disease
CERAM........	British Ceramic Research Ltd. [*Research center*] (IRC)
CERAM........	Ceramic (ROG)
CERAMAL....	Ceramic and Alloy [*NASA*]
CERAMBRUX...	European Centre for Medical Application and Research (EAIO)
CERAMETERM...	Ceramic Metal Terminal [*NASA*] (IAA)
Ceram Mo ...	Ceramics Monthly [*A publication*] (BRI)
CERAP........	Combined Center Radar Approach Control [*FAA*] (TAG)
CERAT........	Ceratum [*Wax Ointment*] [*Pharmacy*]
CERATF.......	Communications Era Task Force [*Defunct*] (EA)
CERB........	CERBCO, Inc. [*NASDAQ symbol*] (NQ)
CERB........	Coastal Engineering Research Board [*Vicksburg, MS*] [*Army*] (AABC)
Cerbco	Cerbco, Inc. [*Associated Press*] (SAG)
CERBOM......	Centre d'Etudes et de Recherches de Biologie et d'Oceanographie Medicale
CERC	Central Engine Room Control

CERC	Coastal Engineering Research Center [*Vicksburg, MS*] [*Army*] (AABC)
CERC	Coastal Engineering Research Council (EA)
CERC	Computer Entry and Read-Out Control [*Computer science*] (PDAA)
CERC	Consumer Education Research Center (EA)
CERC	Corporate Emergency Response Center [*Nuclear emergency planning*]
CERCA	Commonwealth and Empire Radio for Civil Aviation [*British*]
CERCLA	Comprehensive Environmental Response, Compensation, and Liability Act [*1980*]
CERCLIS	CERCLA Information System
CERCLIS	Comprehensive Environmental Responsibility, Compensation, and Liability System
CERCOM......	Communications and Electronics Materiel Readiness Command [*Army*]
CERD	Center for Educational Research and Development [*University of Maryland*] [*Research center*] (RCD)
CERD	Central Evidence of Research and Development Reports
CERD	Chronic Endstage Renal Disease [*Nephrology*]
CERDAC......	Centre d'Etudes et de Recherches Documentaires sur l'Afrique Centrale
CERDEC......	Center for Research and Documentation on the European Community [*American University*] [*Research center*] (RCD)
CERDIC.......	Centre de Recherches et de Documentation des Institutions Chretiennes [*Christian Institutions Research and Documentation Center*] [*France*] [*Information service or system*] (IID)
CERDIP.......	Ceramic DIP [*Dual In-line Package*] (CDE)
CER-DIP.......	Ceramic Dual In-Line Package
CERDO........	Consortium of Evangelical Relief and Development Organizations (DICI)
CERDP........	Centre Europeen de Recherche et de Documentation Parlementaires [*European Centre for Parliamentary Research and Documentation - ECPRD*] [*Luxembourg*] (EAIO)
CERDS	Charter of Economic Rights and Duties of States [*United Nations*]
Cerdyn........	Ceradyne, Inc. [*Associated Press*] (SAG)
CERE........	Center for Environmental Research Education [*State University of New York College, Buffalo*] [*Research center*] (RCD)
CERE........	Centre d'Essais Regional Europeen [*European Regional Test Center*] [*NATO*] (NATG)
Cer E	Ceramic Engineer
CERE........	Comite Europeen pour les Relations Economiques
CERE........	Computer Entry and Readout Equipment (KSC)
CEREA........	Centre de Regroupement Africain [*Center for African Regroupment*] [*Congo - Leopoldville*]
CEREL........	Civil Engineering and Evaluation Laboratory [*Navy*] (MCD)
CEREOL	Cereolus [*An urethral bougie*] [*Pharmacy*]
CEREQ	Centre d'Etudes et de Recherches sur les Qualifications (AIE)
CERES	Center for Research and Education in Sexuality [*San Francisco State University*] [*Research center*] (RCD)
CERES	Circles Effect Research Group [*British*] (DBA)
CERES	Cloud and the Earth's Radiant Energy System
CERES	Coalition for Environmentally-Responsible Economies (EA)
CERES	Computer-Enhanced Radio Emission Surveillance [*British*]
CERES	Cross-Polarization Evaluation Radio Echo System (PDAA)
CERESIS	Centro Regional de Sismologia para America del Sur [*Regional Seismology Center for South America*] [*Peru*] [*Research center*] (IRC)
CERF........	Canine Eye Registration Foundation [*Defunct*] (EA)
CERF........	Commander, Emergency Recovery Force
CERF........	Corps of Engineers Reserve Fleet
CERF........	Council of Europe Resettlement Fund
CERFE........	Center for Education and Research in Free Enterprise [*College Station, TX*] (EA)
CERFIRO.......	Countermeasures Evaluation - Infrared and Optical
CERFnet......	[*The*] California Education & Research Federation Network [*Computer science*] (TNIG)
CERFS	Community Educational Radio Fixed Service (MSA)
CERG	Cambridge Energy Research Group [*University of Cambridge*] [*British*] (IRUK)
CERG	Commander, Emergency Recovery Group
CERG	Consumer Education Research Group [*Later, CERC*] (EA)
CERGE........	[*The*] Center for Economic Research and Graduate Education [*Prague*] (ECON)
CERH	Comite Europeen de Rink Hockey [*European Committee for Rink Hockey*] (EAIO)
CERHU........	Centre d'Etudes en Relations Humaines [*Centre of Studies in Human Relations*] [*Canada*]
CERI........	Canadian Energy Research Institute [*University of Calgary*] [*Research center*] (RCD)
CERI........	Center for Earthquake Research and Information [*Memphis State University*] [*Research center*] (RCD)
CERI........	Center for Environmental Research Information [*Environmental Protection Agency*] (EPA)
CERI........	Central Electrochemical Research Institute
CERI........	Centre Europeen de Recherches sur l'Investissement (EAIO)
CERI........	Centre for Educational Research and Innovation (EAIO)
CERI........	Clean Energy Research Institute [*University of Miami*] [*Research center*]
CERI........	Computational Engineering Research Institute, Inc. [*Research center*]
CERIC	Committee of Ecological Research for the Interoceanic Canal [*National Academy of Science*] (MSC)
Ceridian.......	Ceridian Corp. [*Associated Press*] (SAG)
Ceridn..........	Ceridian Corp. [*Associated Press*] (SAG)

CERIES .... Centre de Recherches et Investigations Eridermiques et Sensorielles [*The Epidermal and Sensory Research and Investigation Center*] [*Funded by Chanel*] [*France*]
CerionT .... Cerion Technologies, Inc. [*Associated Press*] (SAG)
CERIS .... Chinese Educational Resources Information System [*Database*] [*National Taiwan Normal University Library*] [*Information service or system*] (CRD)
CERL .... Cambridge Electronic Research Laboratory (KSC)
CERL .... Central Electricity Research Laboratories [*British*]
CERL .... Commercial Equipment Requirement List
CERL .... Computer-Based Education Research Laboratory [*University of Illinois*] [*Research center*]
CERL .... Construction Engineering Research Laboratory [*Champaign, IL*] [*Army*]
CERL .... Corvallis Environmental Research Laboratory [*Oregon*] [*Environmental Protection Agency*]
CERLAC ...... Centre for Research on Latin America and the Caribbean [*York University*] [*Canada Research center*] (RCD)
CERLAL .... Centro Regional para el Fomento del Libro en America Latina
CERLI .... Cooperative Educational Research Laboratory, Inc.
CERM .... Centre Europeen de Recherches Mauvernay [*France*] [*Research code symbol*]
CERMET ...... Ceramic Metal Element [*NASA*]
CERMET ...... Ceramic Metal Fuel [*NASA*] (IAA)
CERMET ...... Ceramic-to-Metal Seal
CERMS .... Continuous Emission Rate Monitoring System [*Environmental science*]
CERN .... Centre European de Recherches Nucleaires [*Switzerland*] (USDC)
CERN .... Cerner Corp. [*NASDAQ symbol*] (NQ)
CERN .... China Environmental Research Network
CERN .... Consumer Education Resource Network
CERN .... European Laboratory for Particle Physics
CERN .... Organisation Europeenne pour la Recherche Nucleaire [*European Organization for Nuclear Research*] [*Acronym represents previous name, Conseil Europeen pour la Recherche Nucleaire*] (EAIO)
CERNA .... Conference des Eveques de la Region Nord de l'Afrique [*North African Episcopal Conference*] (EAIO)
Cerner .... Cerner Corp. [*Associated Press*] (SAG)
CERnet .... China Education and Research Network [*Computer science*]
CERO .... Coastal Engineering Research Office (SAA)
CERO .... Corps Epidemiological Reference Office [*Military*]
CERP .... Civil Engineering Report of Performance (AFM)
CERP .... COCORP Extended Research Project [*Geology*]
CERP .... Confederation Europeenne des Relations Publiques [*European Confederation of Public Relations*] (EAIO)
CERP .... Conservation Education and Research Program (GNE)
CERP .... Continuing Education Recognition Program [*For nurses*]
CERP .... Continuing Education Re-Education Program (DAVI)
CERP .... Current Economic Reporting Program [*Department of State*]
CERPACK ..... Ceramic Package [*NASA*] (IAA)
CERPB .... Citizens for Eye Research to Prevent Blindness [*Defunct*] (EA)
Cerplex .... Cerplex Group [*Associated Press*] (SAG)
CERPr .... Central I11 Lt4 1/2% cm Pfd [*NYSE symbol*] (TTSB)
Cerprbe .... Cerprobe Corp. [*Associated Press*] (SAG)
CERPS .... Centralized Expenditure/Reimbursement Processing System (NVT)
CERR .... Centre for Earth Resources Research [*Memorial University of Newfoundland*] [*Research center*] (RCD)
CERR .... Comite Europeen de Reflexion sur les Retraites [*European Pension Committee*] [*Paris, France*] (EAIO)
CERR .... Configuration Enhanced Radiation Rejection [*Space technology*]
CERRC .... Complete Engine Repair Requirements Card [*DoD*]
CE/RRT .... Central Europe Railroad Transport [*NATO*] (NATG)
CERS .... Carrier Evaluation and Reporting System
CERS .... Commander, Emergency Recovery Section
CERS .... Communications Engineering Research Satellite (NITA)
CERS .... Counseling Effectiveness Rating Scale (EDAC)
CERT .... Centers for Education and Research in Therapeutics [*FDA*]
CE/RT .... Central Europe Road Transport [*NATO*] (NATG)
CERT .... [*A*] Certainty
CERT .... Certificate [*or Certification*] (AFM)
Cert .... Certificate (DD)
CERT .... Certified
cert .... Certified From [*or Certified To*] [*Legal term*] (DLA)
cert .... Certify (DLA)
CERT .... Certiorari [*Legal term*] (DLA)
cert .... Certiorari [*To be certified*] [*A writ from a superior to an inferior court*] [*Latin*] (AAGC)
CERT .... Character Error Rate Test
CERT .... Combined Environmental Reliability Testing [*Air Force*] (RDA)
CERT .... Composite Electrical Readiness Test (KSC)
CERT .... Computer Emergency Response Team (PCM)
CERT .... Computer Emergency Response Team
CERT .... Constant Extension Rate Tensile Test
CERT .... Corporate Equity-Reducing Transaction
CERT .... Council of Energy Resource Tribes (EA)
CertAIB .... Certificated Associate of the Institute of Bankers [*British*] (DI)
CERTAIN ...... Cost Effectiveness and Reliability Technology for the Automotive Industry
CertArchDraft... Certificate in Architectural Drafting
CertArt .... Certificate in Art
CertArtStud... Certificate in Art Studies
CertAst .... Certificate in Astrology
CertBusMan... Certificate in Business Management
CertBusStud... Certificate in Business Studies

CERTC .... Certificate (ROG)
Cert CAM ..... Certificate in Communication, Advertising, and Marketing (ODBW)
CertComDev... Certificate in Community Development
CertCouns .... Certificate in Counselling
CERTD .... Certified
cert den .... Certiorari Denied [*Legal term*] (DLA)
CertDesRCA... Certificate of Designer of the Royal College of Art [*British*] (DBQ)
CertDiet .... Certificate in Dietetics
cert dis .... Certiorari Dismissed [*Legal term*] (DLA)
CertECTEd... Certificate in Early Childhood Teacher Education
CertEd .... Certificate in Education [*British*] (DBQ)
Cert Ed .... Certificate in Education (ODBW)
CertElecComm... Certificate in Electronics and Communication
CertElecEng... Certificate in Electrical Engineering
CertFA .... Certificate in Fine Arts
CERTFD .... Certified (ROG)
CertFSStud... Certificate in Family Systems Studies
CERT GR ..... Certiorari Granted [*Legal term*] (DLA)
Cert Granted.... Petition to United States Supreme Court for Writ of Certiorari Granted [*Legal term*] (DLA)
CertHE .... Certificate of Health Education [*British*] (DI)
CertHEd .... Certificate in Higher Education
CertHisPhilSc... Certificate in History and Philosophy of Science
CertHort .... Certificate in Horticulture
CertHSM ...... Certificate in Health Services Management [*Academic degree*] (AIE)
CERTICO ...... Certification Committee [*American National Standards Institute*] (IEEE)
CERTIF .... Certificate
CertJourn ..... Certificate in Journalism
CertMarkMan... Certificate in Marketing Management
CertMFTh ..... Certificate in Marriage and Family Therapy
CERTN .... Certain (ROG)
CertNNICU ... Certificate of Neo-Natal Intensive Care Nursing
CertPacAdm... Certificate in Pacific Administration
CertPR .... Certificate in Public Relations
CertProWriEd... Certificate in Professional Writing and Editing
CertPsychTh... Certificate in Psychotherapy
Cert RAS ..... Royal Academy Schools Certificate [*British*]
Certron .... Certron Corp. [*Associated Press*] (SAG)
CERTS .... Certification Test System (MCD)
CERTS .... Consolidated Eglin Real-Time System (MCD)
CERTSUB ...... Certain Submarine [*Navy*] (NVT)
CERTT .... Center for Economic Renewal and Technology Transfer [*Montana State University*]
CertTeach .... Certificate in Teaching
CertTESL ..... Certificate in Teaching English as a Second Language
CertTesol ..... Certificate in Teaching English to Speakers of Other Languages [*Australia*]
CertText .... Certificate in Textiles
CertTour ...... Certificate in Tourism
CertTransAdm... Certificate in Transport Administration
CertUniEd ..... Certificate in University Education
CERU .... Commander, Emergency Recovery Unit
CERULO .... Ceruloplasmin [*Biochemistry*] (DAVI)
CERV .... Carnation Etched Ring Virus
CERV .... Cervix [*Anatomy*]
cerv .... Cervix [*Gynecology*] (DMAA)
CERV .... Controlled Energy Relief Valve (MCD)
CERV .... Corporate Experimental Research Vehicle [*General Motors Corp.*] [*Automotive engineering*]
CERV .... Crew Emergency Vehicle (MCD)
Cervecer ...... Compania Cervecerias Unides [*Associated Press*] (SAG)
CERVED .... Centri Elettronici Reteconnessi Valutazione Elaborazione Dati [*Central Electronic Network for Data Processing and Analysis*] [*Information service or system*] (IID)
CERVED .... Societa Nazionale di Informatica delle Camere di Commerces Italiane [*National Information Company of Italian Chambers of Commerce*] [*Information service or system*] (IID)
CES .... Canadian Evaluation Society [*Societe Canadienne l'Evaluation*] (AC)
CES .... Candelabra Edison Screw (IAA)
CES .... Capillary Electrophoresis System [*In CES I, manufactured by Dionex Corp.*] [*Analytical biochemistry*]
CES .... Career Exploration Series [*Vocational guidance test*]
CES .... Caribbean Educational Service
CES .... Carrefour des Employees de Secretariat [*Crossroads of Secretariat Employees*] [*Canada*]
CES .... Casa El Salvador (EA)
CES .... Casualty Estimation Study [*Military*]
CES .... Cat Eye Syndrome [*Medicine*]
CES .... Center for Economic Studies [*Washington, DC Department of Commerce*] (GRD)
CES .... Center for Education Statistics [*Washington, DC Department of Education Also, an information service or system*] (IID)
CES .... Center for Energy Studies [*University of Texas at Austin*] [*Research center*] (RCD)
CES .... Center for Energy Studies [*Louisiana State University*] [*Information service or system*] (IID)
CES .... Center for Entrepreneurial Studies [*New York University*] [*Research center*] (RCD)
CES .... Center for Environmental Sciences [*University of Colorado at Denver*] [*Research center*] (RCD)
CES .... Center for Environmental Studies [*Arizona State University*] [*Research center*] (RCD)
CES .... Center for Environmental Studies [*Williams College*] [*Research center*] (RCD)

ces.............. Centimes [*Monetary unit*] [*France*] (GPO)
CES.............. Central Electronics System (KSC)
CES.............. Central [*Nervous System*] Excitatory State
CES.............. Central Executive System
CES.............. Centre Europeen des Silicones [*of the European Council of Chemical Manufacturers' Federations*] (EAIO)
CES.............. Centre for Educational Sociology [*University of Edinburgh*] [*British*] (CB)
CES.............. Centre for Educational Studies [*King's College, London*] [*British*] (CB)
CES.............. Centre for Energy Studies [*Technical University of Nova Scotia*] [*Research center*] (RCD)
CES.............. Centre for Environmental Studies [*British*]
CES.............. Centre for European Studies [*Monash University*] [*Australia*]
CES.............. Certified Exhibit Specialist (WDMC)
CES.............. Cessnock [*Australia Airport symbol*] (OAG)
CES.............. Chick Embryonic Skin
CES.............. China Eastern Airlines [*ICAO designator*] (FAAC)
CES.............. Christian Evidence Society [*British*] (DBA)
CES.............. Circuit Emulation Service [*Electronics*] (ACRL)
CES.............. Circus Education Specialists [*In association name, CES, Inc.*] (EA)
CES.............. Citicorp Economic Services [*Information service or system*] (IID)
CES.............. Civil Engineering Squadron [*Air Force*]
CES.............. Classroom Environment Scale [*Teacher evaluation test*]
CES.............. Closed Ecological System
CES.............. Coalition for Economic Survival (EA)
CES.............. Coalition of Essential Schools (EA)
CES.............. Coast Earth Station [*INMARSAT*]
CES.............. Cognitive Environmental Stimulation [*Medicine*] (DAVI)
CES.............. Combined Effects Submissile (MCD)
CES.............. Combined English Stores [*Commercial firm British*]
CES.............. Comite Economique et Social [*Economic and Social Committee*] [*of CEE*]
CES.............. Commercial Earth Station
CES.............. Commission on Epidemiological Survey [*Armed Forces Epidemiological Board*] (DNAB)
CES.............. Committee on Earth Sciences [*President's Office of Science & Technology Policy*]
CES.............. Committee on Economic Security [*Terminated as formal agency, 1936, but continued informally for some time thereafter*]
CES.............. Committee to Eradicate Syphilis [*Defunct*] (EA)
CES.............. Common-Equipment System (IAA)
CES.............. Commonwealth Energy Sys [*NYSE symbol*] (TTSB)
CES.............. Commonwealth Energy System [*NYSE symbol*] (SPSG)
CES.............. Communication Engineering Standard
CES.............. Communications Errors Statistics (CMD)
CES.............. Comparative Education Society [*Later, CIES*] (EA)
CES.............. Comprehensive Export Schedule [*US*]
CES.............. Compressor End Seal
CES.............. Computer Election Systems, Inc.
CES.............. Computer Engineering Service
CES.............. Confederation Europeenne de Scoutisme [*European Confederation of Scouts - ECS*] (EAIO)
CES.............. Conferentia Episcopalis Scandiae [*Scandinavian Episcopal Conference - SEC*] (EAIO)
CES.............. Constant Elasticity of Substitution [*Industrial production*]
CES.............. Construction Electrician, Shop [*Navy rating*]
CES.............. Constructive Error Score (EDAC)
CES.............. Consumer Electronics Show [*Computer industry*]
CES.............. Consumer Expenditure Survey [*Bureau of Labor Statistics*] (GFGA)
CES.............. Continuous Electrical Stimulation
CES.............. Control Electronics Section [*Apollo*] [*NASA*]
CES.............. Control Electronics System (MCD)
CES.............. Controlled Environmental System [*NASA*]
CES.............. Cooperative Educational Services
CES.............. Cooperative Extension Service [*Department of Agriculture*]
CES.............. Coordinated Evaluation System [*National Institute of Standards and Technology*]
CES.............. Corporate Engineering Standard (IAA)
CES.............. Cosmos Resources, Inc. [*Vancouver Stock Exchange symbol*]
CES.............. Cost Effectiveness Study [*Economics*]
CES.............. Cost-Estimating System (ODBW)
CES.............. Council for European Studies (EA)
CES.............. County Extension Service [*Agriculture*]
CES.............. Court of Exchequer [*Scotland*] (DLA)
CES.............. Creative Electronic Systems
CES.............. Crew Escape System (MCD)
CES.............. Critical Experiment Station [*Nuclear energy*] (GFGA)
CES.............. Croatian Ethnic School [*Australia*]
CES.............. Current Employment Statistics [*Bureau of Labor Statistics*] (OICC)
CES.............. Current Employment Status
CES.............. Cyanoethylsucrose
CEs.............. El Segundo Public Library, El Segundo, CA [*Library symbol Library of Congress*] (LCLS)
CES.............. IEEE Consumer Electronics Society (EA)
CES1............ Construction Electrician, Shop, First Class [*Navy rating*] (DNAB)
CES2............ Construction Electrician, Shop, Second Class [*Navy rating*] (DNAB)
CES3............ Construction Electrician, Shop, Third Class [*Navy rating*] (DNAB)
CEsA............ Aerospace Corp., El Segundo, CA [*Library symbol Library of Congress*] (LCLS)
CESA............ Canadian Engineering Standards Association [*Later, Canadian Standards Association*]
CESA............ Canadian Ethnic Studies Association
CESA............ Canberra Ex-Servicewomen's Association [*Australia*]
CESA............ Class E Surface Area [*Aviation*] (FAAC)

CESA.......... Comite Europeen des Syndicats de l'Alimentation, du Tabac, et de l'Industrie Hoteliere [*European Trade Union Committee of Food and Allied Workers*] [*Common Market*]
CESA.......... Committee of EEC [*European Economic Community*] Shipbuilders' Associations (EAIO)
CESA.......... Cooperative Educational Service Agency [*National Science Foundation*]
CESA.......... Council of Estonian Societies in Australia
CESA.......... Cultural Exchange Society of America (EA)
CESA.......... Czechoslovak Ex-servicemen's Association [*Australia*]
CESAC .... Commonwealth Employment Service Advisory Committee [*Australia*]
CESAC .... Communications-Electronics Scheme Accounting and Control [*Air Force*]
CESAC .... Conference of Executives of State Associations of Counties [*Later, National Council of County Association Executives*] (EA)
CESAO .... Commission Economique et Sociale pour l'Asie Occidentale [*Economic and Social Commission for Western Asia - ESCWA*] (EAIO)
CESAP .... Commission Economique et Sociale pour l'Asie et le Pacifique [*Economic and Social Commission for Asia and the Pacific*] [*French United Nations*] (DUND)
CESAR .... Canadian Expedition to Study the Alpha Ridge [*1983*]
CESAR .... Capsule Escape and Survival Applied Research [*Aerospace*]
CESAR .... Center for Engineering Systems Advanced Research [*Oak Ridge National Laboratory*] [*Oak Ridge, TN*] [*Department of Energy*]
CESAR .... Combustion Engineering Safety Analysis Report [*Nuclear energy*] (IAA)
CESARS .... Chemical Evaluation Search and Retrieval System [*Michigan Department of Natural Resources*] [*Information service or system*] (CRD)
CESB .... Center for Experimental Studies in Business [*University of Minnesota*]
CESC .... Centre for European Security and Cooperation [*Netherlands*]
CEsC .... Computer Sciences Corp., Technical Library, El Segundo, CA [*Library symbol Library of Congress*] (LCLS)
CESC .... Conference on European Security and Cooperation
CESC .... Continuing Education for Senior Citizens
CESC .... Continuing Education Standing Committee (AIE)
CEsc........... Escondido Public Library, Escondido, CA [*Library symbol Library of Congress*] (LCLS)
CESCA .... Construction Electrician, Shop, Construction Apprentice [*Navy rating*] (DNAB)
CE-SCB .... Capillary Electrophoresis-Single Cell Biosensor [*Analytical biochemistry*]
CESCE.......... Comite Europeen des Services des Conseillers [*European Committee for Consultant Services - ECCS*] (EAIO)
CESCH .... Communications Electronics School [*Air Force*]
CESCN .... Construction Electrician, Shop, Constructionman [*Navy rating*] (DNAB)
CESCO .... Community Economic Stabilization Corporation [*Member of FIRR*] (CROSS)
CEsCS .... Computer Sciences Corp., Technical Library, El Segundo, CA [*Library symbol*] [*Library of Congress*] (LCLS)
CES-D .... Center for Epidemiologic Studies - Depression Scale [*Personality development test*] [*Psychology*]
CESD .... Centre Europeen de Formation des Statisticiens Economistes des Pays en Voie de Developpement [*European Center for Training Statisticians and Economists from Developing Countries*]
CESD .... Cholesterol Ester Storage Disease [*Medicine*]
CESD .... Composite External Symbol Dictionary (BUR)
CESD .... Continental Electronic Security Division [*Military*]
CESE .... Captured Enemy Signal Equipment [*Military*] (MCD)
CESE .... Centre Economique de Secours Europeens [*European Economic Relief Committee*] [*NATO*] (NATG)
CESE .... Civil Engineer Support Equipment [*Army*]
CESE .... Communications Equipment Support Element (MCD)
CESE .... Comparative Education Society in Europe (EAIO)
CESEMI....... Computer Evaluation of Scanning Electron Microscope Image
CESF .... Civil Engineering Support Flight [*Military*]
CESF .... College of Environmental Science and Forestry [*SUNY*]
CESF .... Commander, Eastern Sea Frontier [*Navy*]
CESF .... Community Educational Services Foundation (IID)
CESG .... Communications-Electronics Security Group [*British*]
CESG .... Cryogenic Electrically Suspended Gyroscope
CESGM .... Corporation des Entrepreneurs Specialises du Grand Montreal (AC)
CESH .... CE Software Hldgs [*NASDAQ symbol*] (TTSB)
CESH .... CE Software Holdings, Inc. [*NASDAQ symbol*] (SAG)
CESHR .... Civil Engineering Squadron, Heavy Repair [*Air Force*]
CESI .... Canadian Educational Standards Institute (AC)
CESI .... Centre for Economic and Social Information [*United Nations*]
CESI .... Closed Entry Socket Insulator
CESI .... Communications-Electronics Standing Instruction (AABC)
CESI .... Council for Elementary Science International (EA)
CESIA .... Centre d'Etudes des Systemes d'Information des Administrations [*Center for the Study on Information Systems in Government*] [*Information service or system*] (IID)
CESK.......... Cable End Sealing Kit
CESL .... Camp Evans Signal Laboratory [*Army*]
CESL .... Civil Engineering Systems Laboratory [*University of Illinois*]
CESLS......... Constant Energy Synchronous Luminescence Spectroscopy
CESM.......... Continuous Electro-Slag Melting (PDAA)
CESMET .... Civil Engineering and Services Management Evaluation Team [*Military*]
CESMIS........ Civil Engineer Support Management Information System [*Military*] (DNAB)

CESNEF........ Centro di Studi Nucleari Enrico Fermi [*Nuclear Engineering Institute - Enrico Fermi Nuclear Center*] [*Italy*] (NRCH)
CESNU .... Conseil Economique et Social des Nations-Unies [*United Nations Economic and Social Council*]
CESO .... Canadian Executive Service Organization
CESO .... Centrum voor de Studie van het Onderwijs in Ontwikkelingslanden [*Centre for Study of Education in Developing Countries*] [*Netherlands*] (EAIO)
CESO .... Civil Engineer Support Office [*Navy*]
CESO .... Communication Electronics Staff Officer (MCD)
CESO .... Council of Engineers and Scientists Organizations
CE Soft .... CE Software Holdings, Inc. [*Associated Press*] (SAG)
CESOP .... Contributory Employee Stock Ownership Plan
CESP .... Centre d'Etude des Supports Publicitaires [*Center for the Study of Advertising Support*] [*Database producer Paris, France*]
CESP .... Civil Engineer Support Plan
CESP .... Confederation of European Specialists in Pediatrics (EAIO)
CESP .... Correlation Echo Sound Processor [*Oceanography*]
CESPAO ...... Comision Economica y Social para Asia Occidental [*Economic and Social Commission for Western Asia*] [*Spanish United Nations*] (DUND)
CESPAP .... Comision Economica y Social para Asia y el Pacifico [*Economic and Social Commission for Asia and the Pacific*] [*Spanish United Nations*] (DUND)
CESPE......... Centro Studi Politica Economica [*of the Italian Communist Party*]
CESPG .... Civil Engineering Support Plan Generator (DOMA)
CESPM........ Commission de l'Enseignement Superieur des Provinces Maritimes [*Maritime Provinces Higher Education Commission*] [*Canada*]
C ESPR .... Con Espressione [*With Expression*] [*Music*] (ROG)
CESq .... Combat Evaluation Squadron [*Air Force*]
CESQG .... Conditionally Exempt Small Quantity Generator
CESR .... Canadian Electronic Sales Representatives
CESR .... Colliding Electron-Beam Storage Ring [*Nuclear energy*] (NRCH)
CESR .... Conduction Electron Spin Resonance
CESR .... Consumer Economic Study Report [*Department of Agriculture*]
CESR .... Cornell Electron Storage Ring [*Atomic physics*]
CESRF .... Christian Economic and Social Research Foundation [*British*] (DI)
CESS.......... Children's Fear Survey Schedule [*Psychology*] (EDAC)
CESS.......... Civil Engineering Support Squadron [*Air Force*]
CESS.......... Council of Engineering Society Secretaries [*Later, CESSE*] (EA)
CESSA .... Church of England Soldiers', Sailors', and Airmen's Club
CESSAC .... Church of England Soldiers', Sailors', and Airmen's Clubs
CESSAM ...... Computer Equipment System for Surface-to-Air Missiles (MCD)
CESSAR .... Combustion Engineering Standard Safety Analysis Report [*Nuclear energy*] (NRCH)
CESSE......... Council of Engineering and Scientific Society Executives (EA)
CESSI.......... Church of England Sunday School Institute
CESSLGO..... Continuing Education Service for State and Local Government Officials
CEST .... Center for the Exploitation of Science and Technology [*British*]
CEST .... Centre for Exploitation of Science and Technology [*British*] (ECON)
CEST .... Compacted Earth Sodium Treated (PDAA)
CEST .... Cost-Effective Shape Technology (MCD)
CEST .... Cost Effective Surface Torpedo (MCD)
CESTA......... Centre d'Etudes Scientifiques et Techniques d'Aquitaine [*France*]
CESTR .... Cestriensis [*Signature of the Bishops of Chester*] (ROG)
CESTR .... Chichester [*City in England*] (ROG)
CESTRIEN.... Cestriensis [*Signature of the Bishops of Chester*] (ROG)
CESUS .... Estonian School Center in the United States (EA)
CESV.......... Combat Engineer Supply Vehicle (MCD)
CESV.......... Communications-Electronics Survivability and Vulnerability
CESW.......... Conditionally Exempt Specified Wastestream [*Environmental science*]
CESX.......... Contemporary Entertainment Services [*Air carrier designation symbol*]
CET .... Calibrated Engine Testing
CET .... Canadian Equestrian Team
CET .... Capital Expenditure Threshold (DMAA)
CET .... Capsule Elapsed Time [*Aerospace*]
CET .... Casualty Evacuation Train [*British*]
CET .... Ceeta-Kel Air [*France ICAO designator*] (FAAC)
CET .... Center for Educational Technology [*Florida State University*] [*Research center*]
CET .... Center for Environmental Toxicology [*Michigan State University*] [*Research center*] (RCD)
CET .... Central England Temperature [*Record since 1659*]
CET .... Central European Time (DEN)
CET .... Central Securities [*AMEX symbol*] (TTSB)
CET .... Central Securities Corp. [*AMEX symbol*] (SPSG)
CET .... Central Trust Co. [*Toronto Stock Exchange symbol*]
CET .... Centre Europeen de Traduction [*European Translation Center*]
Cet .... Centus [*Constellation*]
CET .... Certified Engineering Technologist [*Environmental science*]
CET .... Certified Environmental Trainer
Cet .... Cetane [*Organic chemistry*]
Cet .... Cetra [*Record label*] [*Italy*]
Cet .... Cetus [*Whale constellation*] [*Latin*] (BARN)
CET .... CITL [*Crew-in-the-Loop*] Encapsulation Template [*Army*]
CET .... Combat Engineer Team [*Army*] (VNW)
CET .... Combat Engineer Tractor [*British*] (RDA)
CET .... Combustor Exit Temperature (MCD)
CET .... Commission Europeenne de Tourisme [*European Travel Commission - ETC*] [*Paris, France*]
CET .... Common External Tariff [*for EEC countries*] [*Also, CXT*]
CET .... Community Enterprise Trust (AIE)

CET .... Comprehensive External Trade Policy [*Export Credits Guarantee Department*] [*British*]
CET .... Computerized Emission Tomogram (WGA)
CET .... Concentration/Exposure Time [*Herbicides*]
CET .... Concept Evaluation Technique [*Psychometrics*]
CET .... Concept Evaluation Test (MCD)
CET .... Confederation Europeene dex Taxis [*Belgium*] (EAIO)
CET .... Congenital Eyelid Tetrad [*Medicine*] (DMAA)
CET .... Consolidated Environmental Technologies [*Commercial firm British*] (ECON)
CET .... Construction Electrician, Telephone [*Navy rating*]
CET .... Continuing Education and Training (ACII)
CET .... Controlled Environment Testing
CET .... Cooperative English Test
CET .... Corrected Effective Temperature (IEEE)
CET .... Council for Educational Technology [*London, England*] [*Telecommunications Information service or system*] (TSSD)
CET .... Critical Emulsification Temperature (PDAA)
CET .... Critical Experiment Tank
CET .... Cumulative Elapsed Time
CEt .... Etna Free Library, Etna, CA [*Library symbol Library of Congress*] (LCLS)
CET1 .... Construction Electrician, Telephone, First Class [*Navy rating*] (DNAB)
CET2 .... Construction Electrician, Telephone, Second Class [*Navy rating*] (DNAB)
CET3 .... Construction Electrician, Telephone, Third Class [*Navy rating*] (DNAB)
CETA......... China Economic & Technology Alliance [*Sponsored by international chemical firms*]
CETA......... Chinese-English Translation Assistance Group (EA)
CETA......... Civilian Electronics Technician Afloat [*Navy*] (NVT)
CETA......... Cleaning Equipment Trade Association (EA)
CETA......... Comprehensive Employment and Training Act [*1973*] [*Formerly, MDTA Expired, 1982 Department of Labor*]
CETA......... Conference des Eglises de Toute l'Afrique [*All Africa Conference of Churches - AACC*] (EAIO)
CETA......... Corrosion Evaluation and Test Area [*NASA*]
CETA......... Crew and Equipment Translation Aids [*NASA*]
CETAB......... Cetyltrimethylammonium Bromide [*Also, CTAB, CTBM*] [*Antiseptic*]
CETAC......... Careers, Education, and Training Advice Centre [*British*] (CB)
CETAF......... Corporation des Maitres Entrepreneurs en Refrigeration du Quebec [*Corporation of Air Treatment & Cold Processing Entreprises*] (AC)
CETAI......... Centre d'Etudes en Administration Internationale [*Canada*]
CETAP......... Cetacean and Turtle Assessment Program [*University of Rhode Island*] [*Research center*] (RCD)
CETAS......... Compass Equal Target Acquisition System
CETATS....... Cetyltrimethylammonium Toluenesulfonate [*Organic chemistry*]
CETC......... Centralized Electrification and Traffic Control (MCD)
CETC......... Corps of Engineers Technical Committee [*Army*]
CETC......... Council for Export Trading Companies [*Washington, DC*] (EA)
CETCA......... Construction Electrician, Telephone, Construction Apprentice [*Navy rating*] (DNAB)
CETCN .... Construction Electrician, Telephone, Constructionman [*Navy rating*] (DNAB)
CETD......... Calculated Estimated Time of Departure [*Aviation*] (DA)
CETDC .... China External Trade Development Council [*Taiwan*]
CETEC......... Consolidated Engineering Technology Corp. (MCD)
CET EnvS ... CET Environmental Services [*Associated Press*] (SAG)
CET ES .... CET Environmental Services [*Associated Press*] (SAG)
CETEX......... Committee on Contamination of Extra-Terrestrial Exploration [*NASA*]
CETF......... Clothing and Equipment Test Facility [*Army*] (RDA)
CETFA......... Canadians for Ethical Treatment of Food Animals (AC)
CETG......... Civil Effects Test Group [*DASA and AEC*]
CETHEDEC.. Centre d'Etudes Theoriques de la Detection et des Communications
Ceti .... Centus [*Constellation*]
CETI......... Communication with Extraterrestrial Intelligence [*Later, SETI*] [*Radioastronomy*]
CETI......... Continuously Expecting Transfer Interface [*IBM Corp.*]
CETIA......... Computer Electronics Telecommunications Instruments Automation (ADA)
CETICE......... Centre d'Ecologie et de Toxicologie de l'Industrie Chimique Europeenne [*European Chemical Industry Ecology and Toxicology Center - ECETOC*] (EAIO)
CETIE......... Centre Technique International de l'Embouteillage [*International Technical Center of Bottling*]
CETIL......... Committee of Experts for the Transfer of Information between Community Languages [*EEC*] (PDAA)
CETIM......... Centre Europe-Tiers Monde [*Switzerland*]
CETIS......... Centre Europeen de Traitement de l'Information Scientifique [*EURATOM*]
CETIS......... Complex Effluent Toxicity Information System [*Environmental Protection Agency*]
CETO......... Calculated Estimated Time of Overflight [*Aviation*] (DA)
CETO......... Centre for Educational Television Overseas [*British*]
CETO......... Civil Effects Test Operations [*DASA and AEC*]
CETOR......... Commission on Education of Teachers of Reading (EDAC)
CETOS......... Corporate Engineering Transfer and Obsoletion System (IAA)
CETP......... Cholesterol Ester Transport Protein [*Biochemistry*]
CETP......... Cholesteryl Ester Transfer Protein [*Biochemistry*]
CETP......... Comprehensive Employment and Training Plan [*Department of Labor*]
CETP......... Confederation Europeenne Therapeutique Physique [*European Confederation for Physical Therapy*] (EAIO)
CET PAR ...... Ceteris Paribus [*Other Things Being Equal*] [*Latin*]

CETR............	Consolidated Edison Thorium Reactor
CETRAL.......	Centre de Recherche sur l'Amerique Latine et le Tiers-Monde [*France*]
CETRAMAR...	Consortium Europeen de Transports Maritimes [*Shipping company*] [*France*] (EY)
CETRM........	Combat Effective Training Management (MCD)
CETRrD.......	Central Sec$2cmCv D Pfd [*AMEX symbol*] (TTSB)
CETS...........	Church of England Temperance Society
CETS...........	Civilian Engineering Technical Service [*Navy*] (NVT)
CETS...........	Communicative Electronic Training System
CETS...........	Conference Europeenne des Telecommunications par Satellite [*European Conference on Satellite Communications*]
CETS...........	Conference Europeenne des Telecommunications par Satellites [*Benelux*]
CETS...........	Contractor Engineering and Technical Services (AFM)
CETS...........	Contractor Engineering and Technical Support
CETS...........	Control Element Test Stand [*Nuclear energy*] (NRCH)
CETSA........	Cost Estimating Techniques for System Acquisition [*Army*]
CETSP.........	Contract Engineering and Technical Services Personnel [*Air Force*] (AFIT)
CETU...........	Computer Energy Time Unit (MCD)
CETUS	Computerized Exploration and Technical Underwater Surveyor (PDAA)
CETV...........	Central Euro Media Enter'A' [*NASDAQ symbol*] (TTSB)
CETV...........	Central European Media Enterprises Ltd. [*NASDAQ symbol*] (SAG)
CETYCW	Council for Education and Training in Youth and Community Work (AIE)
CEU.............	Camera Electronic Unit (MCD)
CEU.............	Central European University [*Hungary*]
CEU.............	Central Executive Unit (DA)
CEU.............	Centurion Gold Ltd. [*Vancouver Stock Exchange symbol Toronto Stock Exchange symbol*]
CEU.............	Ceuta Unida [*Political party*] (EY)
CEU.............	Channel Extension Unit
CEU.............	Christian Endeavor Union
CEU.............	Clemson, SC [*Location identifier FAA*] (FAAL)
CEU.............	Communications Expansion Unit
CEU.............	Confederation of Entertainment Unions [*British*]
CEU.............	Congenital Ectropion Uveae [*Medicine*] (DMAA)
CEU.............	Consolidated Edison Uranium (GAAI)
CEU.............	Constructional Engineering Union [*British*]
CEU.............	Continuing Education Unit [*American Management Association*]
CEU.............	Control Electronics Unit (MCD)
CEU.............	Coupler Electronics Unit
CEU.............	Cyanoethylurea [*Immunochemistry*]
CEUCA	Customs and Economic Union of Central Africa
CEUD	Comissao Eleitoral para a Unidade Democratico [*Electoral Committee for Democratic Unity*] [*Portugal Political party*] (PPE)
CEUF	Cost Estimate and Updating Form (MCD)
CEUR	Cellular [*Freight*]
CEURC	Coal Extraction and Utilization Research Center [*Southern Illinois University at Carbondale*] [*Research center*] (RCD)
CEurMda	Central European Media Enterprises Ltd. [*Associated Press*] (SAG)
CEUS	Cairn Energy USA [*NASDAQ symbol*] (TTSB)
CEUS	Cairn Energy USA, Inc. [*NASDAQ symbol*] (SAG)
CEUS	Commission for the Exploration and Utilization of Space [*Former USSR*]
CEUSP	Consolidated Edison Uranium Solidification Program [*Oak Ridge National Laboratory*]
CEV.............	Cal Denver Resources [*Vancouver Stock Exchange symbol*]
CEV.............	Carbon Equivalent Value (PDAA)
CEV.............	Centre d'Essais en Vol [*France ICAO designator*] (FAAC)
CEV.............	Chromosomal Expression Vector [*Genetics*]
CEV.............	Citrus Exocortis Viroid
CEV.............	Combat Engineer Vehicle [*Army*]
CEV.............	Contemporary English Version [*Of the Bible*]
CEV.............	Controlled Environmental Vault (ACRL)
CEV.............	Convoy Escort Vessel [*Navy*]
CEV.............	Corona Extinction Voltage (IEEE)
CEV.............	Cryogenic Explosive Valve
CEv.............	Emeryville Public Library, Emeryville, CA [*Library symbol Library of Congress*] (LCLS)
CEV.............	Evergreen Valley College, San Jose, CA [*OCLC symbol*] (OCLC)
CEVA..........	Centre d'Essaies Vehicule Automobile [*Motor Vehicle Test Center*] [*French*]
CEVAR	Consumable-Electrode Vacuum-Arc Remelt [*Nuclear energy*] (NRCH)
CEVAT.........	Combined Environmental, Vibration, Acceleration, Temperature [*Aerospace*] (AAG)
CEVD	CCNU [*Lomustine*], Etoposide, Vindesine, Dexamethasone [*Antineoplastic drug regimen*]
CEVG..........	Combat Evaluation Group [*Strategic Air Command*]
CEVM..........	Consumable Electrode Vacuum Melting
CEVMA........	Christian European Visual Media Association (EAIO)
CEVNO	Centre for International Education [*Netherlands*] (EAIO)
CEvS	Shell Development Co., Emeryville, CA [*Library symbol Library of Congress Obsolete*] (LCLS)
CEVT...........	Contingency Extravehicular Transfer [*NASA*] (KSC)
CEW...........	Caravan of East and West
CEW...........	Church Employed Women (EA)
CEW...........	Circular Electric Wire
CEW...........	Clinton Engineer Works (SAA)
CEW...........	Coextrusion Welding
CEW...........	Consort Energy Corp. [*Vancouver Stock Exchange symbol*]
CEW...........	Construction Electrician, Wiring [*Navy rating*]
CEW............	Copi-Elgot-Wright [*Electronics*]
CEW............	Cosmetic Executive Women (EA)
CEW............	Crestview, FL [*Location identifier FAA*] (FAAL)
CEW1..........	Construction Electrician, Wiring, First Class [*Navy rating*] (DNAB)
CEW2..........	Construction Electrician, Wiring, Second Class [*Navy rating*] (DNAB)
CEW3..........	Construction Electrician, Wiring, Third Class [*Navy rating*] (DNAB)
CEWA..........	Combined Economic Warfare Agencies
CEWC.........	Council for Education in World Citizenship [*British*]
CEWCA	Construction Electrician, Wiring, Construction Apprentice [*Navy rating*] (DNAB)
CEWCN	Construction Electrician, Wiring, Constructionman [*Navy rating*] (DNAB)
CEWCSC	Corps of Engineers Waterborne Commerce Statistics Center [*Army*] (AABC)
CEWHS	Church of England Women's Help Society [*British*]
CEWI..........	Combat Electronic Warfare Intelligence
CEWISCON...	Combat Electronic Warfare and Intelligence O & S [*Operations and Support*] Concept Development
CEWLRA	Commission on Education of the World Leisure and Recreation Association (EAIO)
CEWMS.......	Church of England Working Men's Society
CEWR	Centimetric Early Warning RADAR (IAA)
CEWRC	Civilian Employee Welfare and Recreation Committee [*Military*] (DNAB)
CEWRM	Communications-Electronics War Readiness Materiel (SAA)
CEWS..........	Contractor's Early Warning System (MCD)
CEWT	Central England Winter Temperature (PDAA)
CEX.............	Canadian Environmental Exposition [*Heating, Refrigerating, and Air Conditioning Institute of Canada*] (TSPED)
CEX.............	Capitol Air Express [*ICAO designator*] (FAAC)
CEX.............	Charge Exchange
CEX.............	Chena Hot Springs, AK [*Location identifier FAA*] (FAAL)
CEX.............	Civil Effects Exercise [*NASA*] (KSC)
CEX.............	Civil Effects Experiments [*DASA and AEC*]
CEX.............	Clinical Evaluation Exercise [*Medicine*] (DMAA)
CEX.............	Combat Excavator [*Military*]
CEX.............	Conwest Exploration Co. Ltd. [*Toronto Stock Exchange symbol*]
CEXC..........	Conwest Exploration Company Ltd. [*NASDAQ symbol*] (SAG)
CEXP..........	Corporate Express [*NASDAQ symbol*] (TTSB)
CEXP..........	Corporate Express, Inc. [*NASDAQ symbol*] (SAG)
CEY.............	Association of Consulting Engineers of the Yukon (AC)
CEY.............	Cerknica [*Yugoslavia*] [*Seismograph station code, US Geological Survey*] (SEIS)
Cey	Ceylon
CEY.............	Murray [*Kentucky*] [*Airport symbol*] (OAG)
CEYC...........	Church of England Youth Council (BI)
Ceyl	Ceylon (VRA)
Cey Lab LJ...	Ceylon Labour Law Journal [*A publication*] (DLA)
Ceyl Cr App R...	Ceylon Criminal Appeal Reports [*A publication*] (DLA)
Ceyl Leg Misc...	Ceylon Legal Miscellany [*A publication*] (DLA)
Ceyl LJ........	Ceylon Law Journal [*A publication*] (DLA)
Ceyl LR.......	Ceylon Law Recorder [*A publication*] (DLA)
Ceyl L Rec...	Ceylon Law Recorder [*A publication*] (DLA)
Ceyl L Rev...	Ceylon Law Review [*A publication*] (DLA)
Ceyl LW.......	Ceylon Law Weekly [*A publication*] (DLA)
Ceylon Law Rec...	Ceylon Law Recorder [*A publication*] (DLA)
Ceylon LR...	Ceylon Law Review and Reports [*A publication*] (DLA)
Ceylon L Soc J...	Ceylon Law Society. Journal [*A publication*] (DLA)
Ceylon NLR...	New Law Reports (Ceylon) [*A publication*] (ILCA)
CEYMS........	Church of England Young Men's Society
CEYPA........	Church of England Young People's Assembly [*British*]
CEYW..........	Continuing Education for Young Women
CEZ............	Cefazolin [*Antibacterial compound*]
CEZ............	Cefazolin (DMAA)
CEZ............	Central Economic Zone
CEZ............	Cortez [*Colorado*] [*Airport symbol*] (OAG)
CEZA..........	Comite Europeen d'Etudes de Zoologie Agricole
CEZMS........	Church of England Zenana Missionary Society [*British*]
CF..............	Cable Firing [*or Fuzing*] (NG)
CF..............	Cable, Functional
CF..............	Calf
cf...............	Calf [*Calfskin*] [*Bookbinding*] (WDMC)
CF..............	Calibration Factor
C-F.............	California State Department of Fish and Game, Marine Technical Information Center, San Pedro, CA [*Library symbol Library of Congress*] (LCLS)
Cf...............	Californium [*Chemical element*]
CF..............	Call Finder [*Telecommunications*]
CF..............	Came Free (ADA)
CF..............	Canadian Forces (AABC)
CF..............	Canadian Forum [*A publication*] (BRI)
C/F.............	Cancel on Face [*Deltiology*]
CF..............	Cancer Free [*Medicine*]
CF..............	Candle Foot [*Illumination*] (IAA)
CF..............	Candlelighters Childhood Cancer Foundation (EA)
CF..............	Cannot Find
CF..............	Cantus Firmus [*Plain Chant*] [*Music*]
CF..............	Capacity Factor (IAA)
CF..............	Cape Fear Railways, Inc. [*AAR code*]
CF..............	Capital Formation [*Later, NCCD*] (EA)
CF..............	Carbolfuchsin [*A dye*]
cf...............	Carbonate of Flake [*Archeology*]
CF..............	Carbon Fiber
CF..............	Carbon Film
CF..............	Carbon Filtered
CF..............	Carbon Furnace

CF	Carboxyfluorescein [*Fluorophore*]
CF	Card Feed [*Computer science*] (IAA)
CF	Cardiac Failure [*Medicine*]
C/F	Carried Forward (WGA)
CF	Carried Forward [*Finance*] (DFIT)
cf	Carried Forward [*Bookkeeping*] (ODBW)
CF	Carrier-Free [*Radioisotope*]
CF	Carrier Frequency [*Radio*]
Cf	Carrier of Iron (Ferrum) (MAE)
CF	Carry Flag [*Computer science*] (PCM)
C/F	Carry Forward [*Accounting*] (MUGU)
CF	Cascade Filtration [*Medicine*] (DMAA)
CF	Cash Flow
CF	Castalia Foundation [*Defunct*] (EA)
CF	Cat Fund (EA)
CF	Cathode Follower
CF	Cationized Ferritin [*Biochemistry*]
CF	Caucasian Female
CF	Cell Factor [*Biology*]
CF	Cement Floor [*Technical drawings*]
CF	Center Field [*or Fielder*] [*Baseball*]
CF	Center Fire
CF	Center Focus [*Binoculars*]
CF	Center Forward [*Soccer*]
CF	Center Frequency
CF	Center of Flotation
CF	Central African Republic [*ANSI two-letter standard code*] (CNC)
CF	Central Field [*Ophthalmology*] (CPH)
CF	Central Files
CF	Centrally Funded (AFM)
CF	Centrifugal Force
CF	Centripetal Force
CF	Cephalothin [*Medicine*] (CPH)
CF	Certainty Factor [*Mathematics*] (BARN)
CF	Certificates [*in bond listings of newspapers*] [*Investment term*]
CF	CFCF, Inc. [*Toronto Stock Exchange symbol*]
C/F	Chaff/Flare (MCD)
CF	Chalcedon Foundation (EA)
cf	Change Font [*Typesetting*] (WDMC)
CF	Change in Formula
CF	Chaplain of the Fleet [*Navy British*]
CF	Chaplain to the Forces [*British*]
CF	Characteristic Frequency [*Acoustics*]
CF	Chemotactic Factor [*Immunology*]
CF	Chemotherapy Foundation (EA)
CF	Chiari-Frommel (Syndrome) [*Medicine*]
CF	Chick Fibroblast [*Cytology*]
CF	Chief of Finance [*Army*]
CF	Child Find [*Later, CFA*] [*An association*] (EA)
CF	Chosin Few (EA)
CF	Christian Feminists (EA)
CF	Christians in Futures [*Defunct*] (EA)
CF	Christmas Factor [*Also, PTC*] [*Hematology*]
CF	Chromatic Aberration-Free [*Optics*]
CF	Chromosomal Fraction
CF	Circuit Finder
CF	Cisplatin, Fluorouracil [*Antineoplastic drug*] (CDI)
CF	Citrovorum Factor [*Biochemistry*]
CF	Clamping Fixture (MCD)
C/F	Clarissima Femina [*Most Illustrious Woman*] [*Latin*]
CF	Clastogenic Factor [*Medicine*]
CF	Climbing Fiber [*Cytology*]
CF	Clinician Full Time [*Chiropody*] [*British*]
CF	Clothing and Footwear [*Department of Employment*] [*British*]
CF	Club Ford [*Class of racing cars*]
CF	Coastal Frontier [*Military*]
CF	Coasting Flight
cf	Coated-Front Paper (WDMC)
CF	Coated on the Front Side [*Carbonless paper*]
CF	Coefficient of Friction [*Physics*] (BARN)
CF	Coformycin [*Biochemistry*]
CF	Coil Finish (MSA)
CF	Cold-Finished [*Metal*] (MSA)
CF	Cold Fluid (DICI)
CF	Cold Front [*Meteorology*]
CF	Colicine Factor [*Immunology*]
CF	Colony Forming [*Cytology*]
C-F	Colored Female
CF	Column Feed [*Nuclear energy*] (NRCH)
CF	Comb Filter [*Military*] (CAAL)
CF	Combined Function (OA)
CF	Common Fund
CF	Commonwealth Foundation (EAIO)
CF	Communications Facility (IAA)
CF	Communications Factor (IAA)
CF	Commutation Factor
CF	Comorian Franc [*Monetary unit*] (ODBW)
CF	Compania de Aviacion "Faucett" SA [*Peru*] [*ICAO designator*] (ICDA)
CF	Company First [*A mealtime whimsicality for use when guests are present*]
cf	Compare (DAVI)
CF	Compassionate Friends [*British*] [*An association*] (DBA)
CF	Compensation Factor
CF	Compensation Fee
CF	Complement-Fixation [*Immunology*]
CF	Complete Fabrication
CF	Completion Flag [*Computer science*] (IAA)
CF	Computer Fraud [*A publication*] (NITA)
CF	Concentration Factor [*Nuclear energy*] (NUCP)
CF	Concept Feasibility (AABC)
CF	Concept Formulation [*DoD*]
CF	Concrete Floor [*Technical drawings*]
CF	Condensation Figure [*Surface physical chemistry*]
CF	Conditional Freedom (ADA)
CF	Confer [*Compare, Consult*] [*Latin*]
CF	Confessions
CF	Confinement Factor [*Nuclear energy*] (NRCH)
cf	Congo [*MARC country of publication code Library of Congress*] (LCCP)
CF	Conjugation Factor [*Plant genetics*]
CF	Conservation Foundation (EA)
CF	Conservation Fund [*An association*] (EA)
CF	Consolidated Freightways, Inc.
CF	Constant Frequency [*Electronics*]
CF	Constant Funding (MCD)
CF	Consumption Function [*Economics*]
CF	Container Fumigated (ADA)
cf	Contemporary Force (OA)
CF	Context Free (BUR)
CF	Continuous Flow [*Chemical engineering*] [*Nuclear energy*] (NRCH)
CF	Contract Formulation
CF	Contract Furnished (MCD)
CF	Contractile Force [*Medicine*]
CF	Control Flag [*Computer science*] (IAA)
CF	Control Footing
CF	Control Function [*Computer science*] (IAA)
CF	Controlled Facility [*Aerospace*] (AAG)
CF	Controlled Fragmentation (SAA)
CF	Conversation Factor [*Computer science*]
CF	Conversion Factor (MCD)
CF	Cooling Fan (MSA)
CF	Copper Fastened
CF	Copy Furnished [*Army*] (AABC)
CF	Core Flooding System [*Nuclear energy*] (NRCH)
CF	Corn Flour (OA)
CF	Coro Foundation (EA)
CF	Coronary Flow [*Medicine*]
CF	Correction Factor
CF	Correction Field (MCD)
CF	Correlation Factor (AABC)
CF	Corresponding Fellow
CF	Corrosion Fatigue (PDAA)
CF	Corrugated Furnace (DS)
CF	Cosanti Foundation [*Later, Arcosanti*] (EA)
CF	Cost and Freight [*Shipping*]
CF	Cottonseed Flour
CF	Council on Foundations (EA)
CF	Counterfire [*Military*] (AFM)
CF	Counter Force (MCD)
CF	Count Forward [*Computer science*]
CF	Counting Fingers [*Also, FC*]
CF	Coupling Factor [*Cytology*]
CF	Cover Forward
CF	Covering Force (MCD)
CF	Crash Finish [*of paper*] [*Graphic arts*] (DGA)
CF	Cresol Formaldehyde
CF	Crestar Financial [*NYSE symbol*] (TTSB)
CF	Crest Factor [*Physics*] (IAA)
CF	Critical Fusion Frequency [*Optics*] (IAA)
CF	Cross Fade
CF	Cross Front [*Photography*]
cf	Cross-Reference (WDMC)
CF	Crude Fiber
CF	Cryofixation [*Electron microscopy*]
CF	Cryogenic Focusing [*Instrumentation*]
CF	Crystal Field [*Ionic Model*]
CF	Crystal Filter (IAA)
CF	Cubic Feet (AFM)
CF	Culture Filtrate [*Analytical biochemistry*]
CF	Cumulative Frequency
CF	Cumulus Fractus [*Type of cloud*] [*Meteorology*] (DNAB)
CF	Current Feedback (IAA)
CF	Current Force (IAA)
CF	Customer File (MCD)
CF	Customer Furnished (MCD)
CF	Customs Form
CF	Cut Film [*Photography*]
CF	Cutting Fluid [*Metallurgy*]
CF	Cycling Fibroblast [*Cytology*]
CF	Cystic Fibrosis [*Medicine*]
CF	Cystinosis Foundation (EA)
CF	Faucett [*ICAO designator*] (AD)
CF	Faucett Peruvian Airlines [*Airline flight code*] (ODBW)
CF	Flying-Deck Cruiser [*Navy symbol Obsolete*]
cF	Form Clearance [*Manufacturing term*]
CF	Fresno County Free Library, Fresno, CA [*Library symbol Library of Congress*] (LCLS)
CF3	Computer Form, Fit, and Function (MCD)
CFA	Alexian Brothers (TOCD)
cfa	Alexian Brothers (TOCD)

CFA............	Association Canadienne de Vexillologie (AC)
CFA............	California Fertilizer Association (SRA)
CFA............	California Forestry Association (SRA)
CFA............	California Freezers Association [*AFFI*] [*Absorbed by*] (EA)
CFA............	California Gold Mines Ltd. [*Toronto Stock Exchange symbol Vancouver Stock Exchange symbol*]
CFA............	Call for Action [*An association*] (NTCM)
CFA............	Canadian Federation of Agriculture
CFA............	Canadian Fencing Association
CFA............	Canadian Field Artillery
CFA............	Canadian Forces Attache
CFA............	Canadian Forestry Association [*See also AFC*]
CFA............	Canadian Foundry Association [*Association des Fonderies Canadiennes*] (AC)
CFA............	Canadian Fraternal Association [*Association Canadienne des Societes Fraternelles*] (AC)
CFA............	Canadian Freight Association
CFA............	Cancer Fund of America
CFA............	Caribbean Federation of Aeroclubs (EA)
CFA............	Carrier Frequency Alarm [*Telecommunications*] (TEL)
CFA............	Cascade-Failure Analysis (IEEE)
CFA............	Cash-Flow Accounting
CFA............	Cash Free America [*An association*] (EA)
CFA............	Cat Fanciers' Association (EA)
CFA............	Catfish Farmers of America (EA)
CFA............	Causal Factors Analysis [*Engineering*]
CFA............	Center for Astrophysics [*Harvard-Smithsonian*]
CFA............	Central Facilities Area
CFA............	Central Freight Association
CFA............	Centrifugal Fast Analyzer [*Analytical chemistry*]
CFA............	Certified Fitness Appraiser [*Canadian Association of Sports Sciences*]
CFA............	Chartered Financial Analyst [*Institute of Chartered Fi nancial Analysts*] [*Designation awarded by*]
CFA............	Chartier Family Association (EA)
CFA............	Chian Federation of America (EA)
CFA............	Chief of Field Artillery
CFA............	Child Find Alberta [*Formerly, Friends of Child Find Society*] (AC)
CFA............	Child Find of America (EA)
CFA............	Chilled Foods Association (EA)
CFA............	China Flying Dragon Aviation Co. [*FAA designator*] (FAAC)
CFA............	Circus Fans Association of America (EA)
CFA............	Citizens' Flag Alliance [*An association*]
CFA............	Citizens for America [*Later, CFAEF*] (EA)
CFA............	City Facts and Abstracts [*EDIC*] [*Ringmer Near Lewes, East Sussex, England*] [*Information service or system*] (IID)
CFA............	Cleared for Approach [*Aviation*]
CFA............	Club Francais d'Amerique (EA)
CFA............	Coconut Fatty Alcohol [*Organic chemistry*]
CFA............	Cognizant Field Activity
CFA............	College Football Association (EA)
CFA............	Collocation Flutter Analysis
CFA............	Colonization Factor Antigen [*Analytical biochemistry*]
CFA............	Colony-Forming Ability [*Microbiology*]
CFA............	Color Filter Array (IAA)
CFA............	Color Forming Ability [*Food technology*]
CFA............	Combination Fabrication and Assembly (SAA)
CFA............	Combined Field Army (MCD)
CFA............	Commission of Fine Arts [*Independent government agency*]
CFA............	Committee for a Free Afghanistan (EA)
CFA............	Committee for the Future of America (EA)
C/FA..........	Commodities - Food and Agriculture (NATG)
CFA............	Common Femoral Artery [*Anatomy*] (DAVI)
CFA............	Commonwealth Forestry Association [*Oxford, England*] (EAIO)
CFA............	Communaute Financiere Africaine [*Currency*] (ECON)
CFA............	Community Facilities Administration [*of HHFA*] [*Terminated*]
CFA............	Companions of the Forest of America (EA)
CFA............	Compass Failure Annunciator
CFA............	Complement-Fixing Antibody [*Immunology*]
CFA............	Complete Freund's Adjuvant [*Immunology*]
CFA............	Complex Field Amplitude
CFA............	Component Flow Analysis [*Business term*] (MHDW)
CFA............	Computer Family Architecture
CFA............	Computerized Fleet Analysis, Inc.
CFA............	Concept Feasibility Analysis
CFA............	Conformal Array (CAAL)
CFA............	Congregatio Fratrum Cellitarum seu Alexianorum [*Alexian Brothers*] [*Roman Catholic religious order*]
CFA............	Connecticut Florists Association (SRA)
CFA............	Connecticut Food Association (SRA)
CFA............	Consumer Federation of America (EA)
CFA............	Continuous Flow Analysis
CFA............	Contract Flooring Association [*British*] (DBA)
CFA............	Contractor-Furnished Accessories (AFIT)
CFA............	Controlled Field Actuator [*Computer science*] (NITA)
CFA............	Controlled Firing Area [*Aviation*] (FAAC)
CFA............	Cookery and Food Association [*British*] (BI)
CFA............	Cooley Family Association of America (EA)
CFA............	Core Flood Alarm [*Nuclear energy*] (IEEE)
CFA............	Coronel Fontana [*Argentina*] [*Seismograph station code, US Geological Survey*] (SEIS)
CFA............	Correctional Facilities Association [*Defunct*] (EA)
CFA............	Correspondence Factor Analysis
CFA............	Cost, Freight, Assurance [*Shipping*]
CFA............	Council for Acupuncture [*British*] (DBA)

CFA............	Council of Iron Foundry Associations
CFA............	Council on Fertilizer Application [*Defunct*]
CFA............	Covering Force Area (AABC)
CFA............	Covert Family Association (EA)
CFA............	Cowl-Flap Angle [*Air Force*]
CFA............	Croquet Foundation of America (EA)
CFA............	Crossed-Field Amplifier [*Air Force*]
CFA............	Cross-Functional Analysis (ADA)
CFA............	Current Files Area
CFA............	Cyclic Fatty Acid [*Organic chemistry*]
CFA............	Cyprus Federation of America
CFa............	Solano County Library, Fairfield, CA [*Library symbol Library of Congress*] (LCLS)
CFAA..........	Cooperative Finance Association of America (EA)
CFAB..........	Baseball Canada [*Also, Canadian Federation of Amateur Baseball*] (AC)
CFAB..........	California Fig Advisory Board (EA)
CFAB..........	Windsor, NS [*AM radio station call letters*]
CFABC........	Canadian Forestry Association of British Columbia
CFAC..........	Calgary, AB [*AM radio station call letters*]
CFAC..........	Central Financial Acceptance Corp. [*NASDAQ symbol*] (SAG)
CFAC..........	Citizens Foreign Aid Committee [*Defunct*] (EA)
CFAC..........	Complement-Fixing Antibody Consumption [*Immunology*] (DAVI)
CFAD	Commander, Fleet Air Defense (NATG)
CFAD	Commander, Fleet Air Detachment
CFAD	Composite Flight Data Processing (FAAC)
CFADC........	Canadian Forces Air Defense Command [*ICAO designator*] (FAAC)
CFADC........	Controlled Fusion Atomic Data Center [*Department of Energy*] (IID)
CFADD........	Canadian Foundation on Alcohol and Drug Dependencies
CFAE..........	Contractor-Furnished Aircraft Equipment (AFM)
CFAE..........	Contractor-Furnished and Equipped
CFAE..........	Council for Financial Aid to Education (EA)
CFAEF........	Citizens for America Educational Foundation (EA)
CFAG	Cystic Fibrosis Antigen [*Medicine*] (DMAA)
CFAI	Call for Action, Inc. (EA)
CFAI	Edmundston, NB [*FM radio station call letters*]
CFAM..........	Altona, MB [*AM radio station call letters*]
CFAM..........	Coupled Fuselage-Aiming Mode (MCD)
CFAN	Miramichi, NB [*AM radio station call letters*]
CF & A......	Chief of Finance and Accounting [*Army*] (AABC)
CF & AD	Counterfire and Air Defense (MCD)
CF and E.....	Cost, Freight, and Exchange [*Shipping*]
CF & I........	Contractor Furnish and Install (MSA)
CF & I........	Cost, Freight, and Insurance [*Shipping*]
CFANS........	Canadian Forces Air Navigation School
CFAO	Canadian Forces Administrative Order
CFAO	Concrete Forming Association of Ontario (AC)
CFAP	Cleared for Approach [*Aviation*] (FAAC)
CFAP	Committee for American Principles (EA)
CFAP	Constant-Adjustment Matrix, Flexible-Accelerator Path [*Economic theory*]
CFAP	Constant False Alarm Probability [*Military*]
CFAP	Council on Fine Art Photography (EA)
CFAP	Quebec City, PQ [*Television station call letters*]
CFAR	Center for AIDS Research [*National Institutes of Health*]
CfAR	Center for Automation Research [*University of Maryland*] [*Research center*] (RCD)
CFAR	Citizens for Foreign Aid Reform [*Canada*]
C-FAR	Citizens for Foreign Aid Reform Inc. (AC)
CFAR	Collaborative Forecasting and Replenishment [*Computer science*]
CFAR	Constant False Alarm Rate [*or Ratio*] [*Military*]
CFAR	Flin Flon, MB [*AM radio station call letters*]
C-FARR.......	Center for Fertility and Reproductive Research [*Vanderbilt University*] [*Research center*] (RCD)
CFAS..........	Canadian Fertility & Andrology Society [*Societe Canadienne de Fertilite et d'Andrologie*] (AC)
CFAS..........	Catholic Fine Arts Society (EA)
CFAS..........	Charge-Free Anticontamination System
CFaS..........	Solano College, Fairfield, CA [*Library symbol*] [*Library of Congress*] (LCLS)
CFASI........	Club of the Friends of Ancient Smoothing Irons (EA)
CFAT..........	Carnegie Foundation for the Advancement of Teaching (EA)
CFAV..........	Canadian Forces Auxiliary Vessels [*Military*]
CFAW..........	Canadian Food and Allied Workers
CFAW..........	Commander, Fleet Air Wing
CFAW..........	Committee of French American Wives [*Later, FAAC*] (EA)
CFAWL........	Commander, Fleet Air Wing, Atlantic
CFAWP........	Commander, Fleet Air Wing, Pacific
CFAX..........	Victoria, BC [*AM radio station call letters*]
CFB............	Call Forwarding Busy [*Telecommunications*] (DOM)
CFB............	Camfrey Resources Ltd. [*Vancouver Stock Exchange symbol*]
CFB............	Canadian Forces Base (NATG)
CFB............	Carey Foster Bridge [*Electronics*]
CFB............	Cash-To-Futures Basis [*Business term*] (EMRF)
CFB............	Center for Family Business [*Cleveland, OH*] (EA)
CFB............	Central Fibrous Body [*Medicine*] (DMAA)
CFB............	Central Freight Bureau (DS)
CFB............	Centrifugal Fluidized Bed [*Chemical engineering*]
CFB............	Cipher Feedback
CFB............	Circulating Fluid Bed [*Chemical engineering*]
CFB............	Coated Front and Back [*Carbonless paper*]
CFB............	Combat Fitness Badge [*Army*] (INF)
CFB............	Combined Food Board [*United States, United Kingdom, and Canada*] [*World War II*]
CFB............	Commercial Federal [*NYSE symbol*] (TTSB)

CFB............ Commercial Federal Corp. [*NYSE symbol*] (SAG)
CFB............ Commonwealth Forestry Bureau [*Oxford, England*]
CFB............ Coniferous Forest Biome [*Ecological biogeographic study*]
CFB............ Continental Flood Basalt [*Geology*]
CFB............ Creep Form Block (MCD)
CFb............ Fort Bragg Public Library, Fort Bragg, CA [*Library symbol Library of Congress*] (LCLS)
CFBA........... Canadian Food Brokers Association [*Association Canadienne des Courtiers en Alimentation*] (AC)
CFBA........... Chinchilla Fur Breeders' Association [*British*] (BI)
CFBA........... Connecticut Farm Bureau Association (SRA)
CFBAC......... Central Fire Brigades Advisory Council [*British*]
CFB Bcp....... CFB Bancorp, Inc. [*Associated Press*] (SAG)
CFBC.......... CF Bancorp [*NASDAQ symbol*] (SAG)
CFBC.......... St. John, NB [*AM radio station call letters*]
CF Bcp........ CF Bancorp [*Associated Press*] (SAG)
CFBE.......... Certified Food and Beverage Executive [*Educational Institute of the Ameri can Hotel and Motel Association*] [*Designation awarded by*]
CFBG .... Bracebridge, ON [*FM radio station call letters*]
CFBG .... Camp Fire Boys and Girls (EA)
CFBI........... Cullen Frost Bankers [*NASDAQ symbol*] (TTSB)
CFBI........... Cullen/Frost Bankers, Inc. [*NASDAQ symbol*] (NQ)
CFBK.......... Citizens Federal Bank, a Federal Savings Bank [*NASDAQ symbol*] (SAG)
CFBK.......... Huntsville, ON [*FM radio station call letters*]
CFBN .... CFB Bancorp [*NASDAQ symbol*] (TTSB)
CFBN .... CFB Bancorp, Inc. [*NASDAQ symbol*] (SAG)
CFBP.......... Continental Flood Basalt Province [*Geology*]
CFBPS........ Canada [*or Canadian*] Farm Building Plan Service
CFBPWC ..... Canadian Federation of Business and Professional Women's Clubs [*Established 1930*]
CFBR.......... Continuously Fed Batch Reactor [*Chemical engineering*]
CFBR .... Edmonton, AB [*FM radio station call letters*]
CFBS......... Canadian Federation of Biological Societies
CFBS......... Central Fidelity Banks [*NASDAQ symbol*] (TTSB)
CFBS......... Central Fidelity Banks, Inc. [*NASDAQ symbol*] (NQ)
CFBS......... Colostrum-Free Bovine Serum
CFBT.......... Creep Form Block Template (MCD)
CFBUS........ Consortium of Fire Brigade Uniform Supplies [*British*]
CFBV.......... Smithers, BC [*AM radio station call letters*]
CFBX.......... Community First Bankshares [*NASDAQ symbol*] (SAG)
CFBXZ......... Community First 7% Cv Dep Pfd [*NASDAQ symbol*] (TTSB)
CFC............ California Fashion Creators (EA)
CFC............ California Fashion Creators (EA)
CFC............ Campus-Free College
CFC............ Canadian Armed Forces [*ICAO designator*] (FAAC)
CFC............ Canadian Film Centre [*Centre Canadien du Film*] [*Formerly, Canadian Centre for Advanced Film Studies*] (AC)
CFC............ Canadian Forestry Corps [*World War I*]
CFC............ Capillary Filtration Coefficient (IEEE)
CFC............ Capital Formation Counselors [*Service mark of Capital Formation Counselors, Inc.*]
CFC............ Carbon Fiber Reinforced Composite
CFC............ Career Factor Checklist (EDAC)
CFC............ Caribbean Food Corp. [*An association*] (EAIO)
CFC............ Cash Flow Component
CFC............ C-Band Frequency Converter
CFC............ Central Data Flow Control
CFC............ Central Fire Control [*Military*]
CFC............ Central Forms Committee [*Defunct*] (EA)
CFC............ Centre Francais de la Couleur [*Online service*]
CFC............ CFC Financial Communications [*An association*] (EA)
CFC............ Chamber Flow-Field Code (MCD)
CFC............ Channel Flow Control
CFC............ Channel Frequency Class [*Electrical engineering*]
CFC............ Chartered Financial Consultant (MHDB)
CFC............ Chartered Financial Counselor (DFIT)
CFC............ Chess Federation of Canada
CFC............ Chicago Fan Club (EA)
CFC............ Chicano Family Center (EA)
CFC............ Chief Fire Controlman [*Navy rating Obsolete*]
CFC............ Chlorinated Fluorocarbon (GAAI)
CFC............ Chlorofluorocarbon [*Organic chemistry*]
CFC............ Chrysler Financial Corp.
CFC............ Cinematograph Films Council [*British*]
CFC............ Claflin College, Orangeburg, SC [*OCLC symbol*] (OCLC)
CFC............ Coin and Fee Checking [*Telecommunications*] (TEL)
CFC............ Colony-Forming Cell [*Cytology*]
CFC............ Combined Federal Campaign [*Federal government*] (AABC)
CFC............ Combined Field Command (MCD)
CFC............ Combined Forces Command [*Korea*] (MCD)
CFC............ Commercial Finance Company [*Generic term*]
CFC............ Committee for a Free China [*Defunct*] (EA)
CFC............ Committee for Children (EA)
CFC............ Committee on Foreign Correspondence [*Freemasonry*]
CFC............ Company Fire Control [*Net*] (MCD)
CFC............ Complex Facility Console [*Aerospace*] (AAG)
CFC............ Congregation of Christian Brothers [*Formerly, Christian Brothers of Ireland*] [*Roman Catholic religious order*]
CFC............ Connecticut Film Circuit [*Library network*]
CFC............ Consolidated Freight Classification
CFC............ Continuous-Flow Centrifuging [*Clinical chemistry*]
CFC............ Contract Finance Committee [*Military*]
CFC............ Contract Furnishings Council (EA)
CFC............ Controlled Force Circulation [*Boilers*]

CFC............ Controlled Foreign Company [*or Corporation*]
CFC............ Coolant Fan Control [*Automotive engineering*]
CFC............ Cooperative Finance Corp. [*of National Rural Utilities*]
CFC............ Cost of Facilities Capital (AAGC)
CFC............ Council of Free Czechoslovakia (EA)
CFC............ Court of Federal Claims (AAGC)
CFC............ Cowboys for Christ (EA)
CFC............ Cowsills Fan Club (EA)
CFC............ Crewcuts Fan Club (EA)
CFC............ Critical Flocculation Concentration [*Electrolyte induced flocculation of dispersed species*]
CFC............ Crossed-Film Cryotron
CFC............ Fresno City College, Fresno, CA [*Library symbol Library of Congress*] (LCLS)
CFCA........... California Fish Canners Association [*Later, TRF*] (EA)
CFCA........... Camp Fire Club of America (EA)
CFCA........... Change for Children Association (AC)
CFCA........... Christian Foundation for Children and Aging (EA)
CFCA........... Communications Fraud Control Association (EA)
CFCA........... Confederation Francaise de la Cooperation Agricole
CFCA........... Crested Fowl Club of America [*Later, CFFA*] (EA)
CFCA........... Kitchener, ON [*FM radio station call letters*]
CFCB.......... Computer Format Control Buffer
CFCB.......... Corner Brook, NF [*AM radio station call letters*]
CFCC.......... Canadian Federation of Chefs & Cooks [*Federation Canadienne des Chefs et Cuisiniers*] (AC)
CFCC.......... Canadian Forces Communication Command (NATG)
CFCC.......... Continuous-Filament Ceramic Composite [*Materials science*]
CFCCOM ..... Contractor Facilities and Capital Cost of Money
CFCCS .... Condensate and Feedwater Chemistry Control System [*Nuclear energy*] (NRCH)
CFCCT......... Committee for Freedom of Choice in Cancer Therapy [*Later, CFCM*] (EA)
CFCD.......... Canadian Federal Corporations and Directors [*Canada Systems Group*] [*Information service or system*] (IID)
CF/CD .... Concept Formulation/Contract Definition [*Procurement procedure*]
CFCda......... Central Fund of Canada Ltd. [*Associated Press*] (SAG)
CFCE.......... Conseil des Federations Commerciales d'Europe [*Council of European Commercial Federations*]
CFCF.......... Camp Fire Conservation Fund (EA)
CFCF.......... Central Flow Control Facility [*or Function*] (MCD)
CFCF.......... Montreal, PQ [*Television station call letters*]
CFCG .... Canadian Foundation on Compulsive Gambling (AC)
CFCGR........ Corrosion-Fatigue Crack Growth Rate (PDAA)
CFCH .... North Bay, ON [*Station begun by Lord Roy Thomson in March, 1931*] [*AM radio station call letters*]
CFCI........... CFC International, Inc. [*NASDAQ symbol*] (SAG)
CFCI........... CFC Intl. [*NASDAQ symbol*] (TTSB)
CFCIntl........ CFC International, Inc. [*Associated Press*] (SAG)
CFCL.......... Timmins, ON [*Television station call letters*]
CFCL-2........ Kearns, ON [*Television station call letters*]
CFCM.......... Chief Consolidated Mining Co. [*NASDAQ symbol*] (NQ)
CFCM.......... Chief Consol Mining [*NASDAQ symbol*] (TTSB)
CFCM.......... Committee for Freedom of Choice in Medicine (EA)
CFCM.......... Quebec City, PQ [*Television station call letters*]
CFCN-TV...... Calgary, AB [*Television station call letters*]
CFCN-TV-1... Drumheller, AB [*Television station call letters*]
CFCN-TV-5... Lethbridge, AB [*Television station call letters*]
CFCN-TV-8... Medicine Hat, AB [*Television station call letters*]
CFCO .... Chatham, ON [*AM radio station call letters*]
CFCO .... Chief Fire Controlman, Operator [*Navy rating Obsolete*]
CFCP.......... Coastal Financial [*NASDAQ symbol*] (SAG)
CFCP.......... Coastal Finl Del [*NASDAQ symbol*] (TTSB)
CFCP.......... Corrosion Fatigue Crack Propagation (PDAA)
CFCP.......... Courtenay, BC [*AM radio station call letters*]
CFCRA........ Coronado 15 Class Racing Association (EA)
CFCRFC ...... Chewings Fescue and Creeping Red Fescue Commission (EA)
CFCR-FM .... Saskatoon, SK [*FM radio station call letters*] (RBYB)
CFCS.......... Canadian Force Communications System
CFCS.......... Caribbean Food Crops Society [*Isabela, Puerto Rico*] (EAIO)
CFCS.......... Chief Fire Controlman, Submarines [*Navy rating Obsolete*]
CFCS.......... Crossed Field Closing Switch (MCD)
CFCT.......... Tuktoyaktuk, NT [*AM radio station call letters*]
CFCV.......... St. Andrews, NF [*FM radio station call letters*]
CFCW.......... Camrose, AB [*AM radio station call letters*]
CFCW.......... Canadian Federation of Communications Workers [*See also FCC*]
CFCW.......... Composers' Forum for Catholic Worship [*Defunct*] (EA)
CFCX.......... Center Financial [*NASDAQ symbol*] (TTSB)
CFCX.......... Center Financial Corp. (Connecticut) [*NASDAQ symbol*] (SAG)
CFCY.......... Charlottetown, PE [*AM radio station call letters*]
CFCYP......... Centre of Films for Children and Young People [*British*] (DI)
CFD............ Bryan [*Texas*] [*Airport symbol*] (AD)
CFD............ Bryan, TX [*Location identifier FAA*] (FAAL)
CFD............ Call Forward Directive [*World War II*]
CFD............ Canadian Financial Database [*The Globe and Mail*] [*Toronto, ON*] [*Information service or system*] (IID)
CFD............ Canadians for Decency (AC)
CFD............ Candidate for Disposal (MCD)
CFD............ Center for Faith Development [*Later, CRFMD*] (EA)
CFD............ Cephalo-Facial Deformity [*Medicine*] (DMAA)
CFD............ Clad Failure Detection [*Nuclear energy*] (NUCP)
CFD............ Clifton Star Resources, Inc. [*Vancouver Stock Exchange symbol*]
CFD............ Club Francais du Disque [*Record label*] [*France*]
CFD............ Coalition for Decency [*Later, NFF*] (EA)
CFD............ Cockfield Brown, Inc. [*Toronto Stock Exchange symbol*]

CFD............	Cold Fog Dissipation System
CFD............	Compact Floppy Disk [*Computer science*] (EECA)
CFD............	Company of Fifers and Drummers (EA)
CFD............	Computational Fluid Dynamics [*Chemical engineering*]
CFD............	Computational Fluids Dynamics [*Organic chemistry*]
CFD............	Computation Fluid Dynamics
CFD............	Concern for Dying (EA)
CFD............	Congress for Democracy [*India*]
CFD............	Constant Fraction Discriminator [*Electronics*] (OA)
CFD............	Continuous Flow Diffusion (SSD)
CFD............	Contractor Functional Demonstration (KSC)
CFD............	Control Flow Diagram (MCD)
CFD............	Control Functional Diagram
CFD............	Converter, Frequency to DC [*Direct Current*] Voltage (MCD)
CFD............	Corporate Finance Director
CFD............	Corporate Fund for Dance
CFD............	Crainfield Institute of Technology [*British ICAO designator*] (FAAC)
CFD............	Cubic Feet per Day
CFD............	Cumulative Frequency Distribution (KSC)
CFDA..........	Carboxyfluorescein Diacetate [*Organic chemistry*]
CFDA..........	Catalog of Federal Domestic Assistance [*A publication*]
CFDA..........	Christian Film Distributors Association (NTCM)
CFDA..........	Cooperative Food Distributors of America [*Later, NGA*] (EA)
CFDA..........	Council of Fashion Designers of America (EA)
CFDA..........	Victoriaville, PQ [*AM radio station call letters*]
CFDB..........	Concept Formulation Data Bank (DNAB)
CFDB..........	Conventional Force Data Base [*Model*]
CFDC..........	Canadian Film Development Corp.
CFDC..........	Canadian Film-Makers Distribution Centre
CFDC..........	Central File Document Control
CFDC..........	Clean Fuels Development Coalition (EA)
CFDD..........	Compact Floppy Disk Drive [*Computer science*] (EECA)
CFDE..........	Call Failure Detection Equipment [*Telecommunications*] (NITA)
CFDH..........	Fresno County Department of Health, Fresno, CA [*Library symbol Library of Congress*] (LCLS)
CFDL..........	Confederation Francaise Democratique du Travail [*French Democratic Confederation of Labor*] (BARN)
CFDL..........	Deer Lake, NF [*FM radio station call letters*]
CFDMAS	Canadian Federation of Deans of Management & Administrative Studies [*Federation Canadienne des Doyens de Gestion et d'Administration*] (AC)
CFDMH	Fresno County Department of Mental Health Services, Fresno, CA [*Library symbol Library of Congress*] (LCLS)
CFDMM........	Comite de Formation et de Developpement Municipaux des Maritimes [*Maritime Municipal Training and Development Board*] [*Canada*]
CFDR	Dartmouth, NS [*AM radio station call letters*]
CFDS	Centrifugal Fault Display System
CFDS	Congested Freeway Driving Schedule [*For vehicle emission measurements*]
CFDS	Craniofacial Dyssynostosis [*Medicine*] (DMAA)
CFDTS	Cold Flow Development Test System [*AEC*]
CFE	California Fruit Exchange [*Later, BAI*] (EA)
CFE	Canadian Forces in Europe (NATG)
CFE	Carbide-Forming Element [*Metal treating*]
CFE	Carbon-Fibre Electrode
CFE	Cathode Flicker Effect
CFE	Cell Free Extract [*Microbiology*]
CFE	Central Fighter Establishment [*British*]
CFE	Certified Financial Examiner [*Society of Financial Examiners*] [*Designation awarded by*]
CFE	Certified Fraud Examiner [*Canada*] (DD)
CFE	Characteristic Function Estimator
CFE	Chlorotrifluoroethylene [*Organic chemistry*]
CFE	Cityflyer Express [*British ICAO designator*] (FAAC)
CFE	Clandestine Fission Explosive [*Nuclear energy*] (NRCH)
CFE	Clermont-Ferrand [*France*] [*Airport symbol*] (OAG)
CFE	College of Further Education (AIE)
CFE	Colony-Forming Efficiency [*Cytology*]
CFE	Committee for a Free Estonia [*Defunct*] (EA)
CFE	Communications Front End (SSD)
CFE	Confederation Fiscale Europeenne [*European Fiscal Confederation*] (EAIO)
CFE	Conference on Forces in Europe
CFE	Continued Fraction Expansion (IAA)
CFE	Continuous Flow Electrophoresis [*Physical chemistry*]
CFE	Contractor-Furnished Engineers (MCD)
CFE	Contractor-Furnished Equipment
CFE	Controlled Flash Evaporation
CFE	Conventional Forces in Europe [*Military*]
CFE	Cost-Free Evaluation
CFe	Ferndale Public Library, Ferndale, CA [*Library symbol Library of Congress*] (LCLS)
CFE	Negotiations on Conventional Armed Forces in Europe
CFEA..........	Collective Front-End Analysis (MCD)
CFEA..........	College Fraternity Editors Association (EA)
CF(EC)........	Chaplain to the Forces - Emergency Commission [*British*]
CFE/CFAE....	Contractor-Furnished Equipment / Contractor-Furnished Aircraft Equipment (SAA)
CFED..........	Chapais, PQ [*AM radio station call letters*]
CFED..........	Committee for Elimination of Death [*Later, CEL*] (EA)
CFED..........	Corporation for Enterprise Development (EA)
CFEE..........	Canadian Foundation for Economic Education [*Fondation d'Education Economique*] (AC)
CFEE	Carnegie Forum on Education and the Economy (EA)

CFEG..........	Canadian Film Editors Guild
CFEI............	St. Hyacinthe, PQ [*FM radio station call letters*]
CFEK..........	Fernie, BC [*AM radio station call letters*]
CFEL..........	Cold Flow Electric LASER (MCD)
CFEL..........	Montmagny, PQ [*FM radio station call letters*]
CFEN..........	Contractor Furnished Equipment Notice [*Military*] (DOMA)
CFEP..........	Cell-Free Elicitor Preparation [*Plant pathology*]
CFEP..........	Committee on Fair Employment Practices [*World War II*]
CFEP..........	Continuous Flow Electrophoresis [*Physical chemistry*] (SSD)
CFEP..........	Council on Foreign Economic Policy [*Functions transferred to Secretary of State, 1961*]
C-FER	Centre for Frontier Engineering Research [*University of Alberta*] [*Canada*] (IRC)
CFER..........	Collector Field Effect Register [*Electronics*] (OA)
CFER..........	Rimouski, PQ [*Television station call letters*]
CFER-2........	Gaspe-Nord, PQ [*Television station call letters*]
CFE-RISS....	Contractor-Furnished Equipment - Repairable Items Support System (MCD)
CFES..........	Canadian Federation of Engineers and Scientists
CFES..........	Center for Energy Systems [*General Electric Information Services Co.*] (NITA)
CFES..........	Continuous Flow Electrophoresis in Space [*Physical chemistry*]
CFES..........	Continuous Flow Electrophoresis System [*Chemical separation*]
CFESA........	Commercial Food Equipment Service Association (EA)
CFET..........	Common Field Effect Transistor [*Computer science*] (ADA)
CFEWB........	Colonial, Fish-Eating Water Bird
CFF............	Canadian Fencing Federation [*Federation Canadienne d'Escrime*] (AC)
CFF............	Capuchin Franciscan Friary
CFF............	Carry Flip-Flop [*Computer science*] (IAA)
CFF............	Cat Fanciers' Federation (EA)
CFF............	Change Film Frame (SAA)
CFF............	Children's Film Foundation Ltd. [*British*] (BI)
CFF............	Christian Freedom Foundation (EA)
CFF............	Citizens Freedom Foundation (EA)
CFF............	Clean Fuel Fleet [*VDOT*] (TAG)
CFF............	Clermont-Ferrand [*France*] [*Seismograph station code, US Geological Survey*] (SEIS)
CFF............	Compensatory Financing Facility [*International Monetary Fund*]
CFF............	Compressible Flow Facility [*NASA*]
CFF............	Concessional Finance Facility
CFF............	Conical Flow Field
CFF............	Consolidated Callinan Flin Flon Mines Ltd. [*Vancouver Stock Exchange symbol*]
CFF............	Contract Furnishings Forum (EA)
CFF............	Convergent Force Field [*Neuromechanics*]
CFF............	Cooperative Financing Facility [*Export-Import Bank*]
CFF............	Counter Flip-Flop [*Computer science*]
CFF............	Critical Flicker Frequency [*Optics*] (AAMN)
CFF............	Critical Flicker Fusion [*Ophthalmology*]
CFF............	Critical Fusion Frequency [*Optics*]
CFF............	Crossflow Filtration [*Process engineering*]
CFF............	Current Fault File [*Telecommunications*] (TEL)
CFF............	Cystic Fibrosis Foundation (EA)
CFFA..........	Chemical Fabrics and Film Association (EA)
CFFA..........	Crested Fowl Fanciers' Association (EA)
CFFA..........	Cystic Fibrosis Factor Activity [*Medicine*] (AAMN)
CF-FAB........	Continuous-Flow Fast Atom Bombardment [*Spectroscopy*]
CFFAFR.......	Center for Financial Freedom and Accuracy in Financial Reporting (EA)
CFFB..........	Iqaluit, NT [*AM radio station call letters*]
CFFC..........	Carter Family Fan Club (EA)
CFFC..........	Catholics for a Free Choice (EA)
CFFC..........	Community Financial Corp. [*NASDAQ symbol*] (SAG)
CFFC..........	Community Finl VA [*NASDAQ symbol*] (TTSB)
CFFC..........	Connie Francis Fan Club [*Defunct*] (EA)
CFFC..........	Counterflow Film Cooling
CFFC..........	Country Fire Fan Club (EA)
CF-Fe..........	Carrier-Bound [*Ferrum Iron*] (DAVI)
CFFEP........	Committee for Full Funding of Education Programs (EA)
CFFF..........	Coal Fluid Flow Facility
CFFF..........	Peterborough, ON [*FM radio station call letters*]
CFFM..........	Canadian Federation of Friends of Museums (AC)
CFFM..........	Williams Lake, BC [*FM radio station call letters*]
CFFMA........	Canadian Flexible Foam Manufacturers' Association (AC)
CFFO..........	Christian Farmers Federation of Ontario [*Federation des Agriculteurs Chretien de l'Ontario*] (AC)
CFFP..........	Cooperative Forest Fire Prevention [*Forest Service, Department of Agriculture*]
CFFR..........	Calgary, AB [*AM radio station call letters*]
CFFR..........	Coiffeur
CFFR..........	Consolidated Federal Fund Report [*Bureau of the Census*] (GFGA)
CFFR..........	Cushman Foundation for Foraminiferal Research (EA)
CFFS..........	Canadian Federation of Film Societies
CFFS..........	Coiffeuse
CFFS..........	Combat Field Feeding System [*Army*] (INF)
CFFS..........	Committee on Food from the Sea [*National Council on Marine Resources and Engineering Development*] (GFGA)
CFFT..........	Critical Flicker Fusion Threshold [*Ophthalmology*] (PDAA)
CFFTP........	Canadian Fusion Fuels Technology Project
CFFX..........	Kingston, ON [*AM radio station call letters*]
CFG............	Camp Fire Girls [*Later, CFBG*] (EA)
CFG............	Canadian Film Group
CFG............	Change for Good [*An association*] (EA)
CFG............	Cherry Lane Fashion [*Vancouver Stock Exchange symbol*]

CFG.............. Childrens Fashion Group [British] (BI)
CFG.............. Christian Focus on Government (EA)
CFG.............. Cienfuegos [Cuba] [Airport symbol Obsolete] (OAG)
CFG.............. Compact-Flake-Graphite [Type of Iron]
CFG.............. Computerized Fuel Gauge (DWSG)
CFG.............. Condor Flugdienst GmbH [Germany ICAO designator] (FAAC)
CFG.............. Constant Frequency Generator (MCD)
CFG.............. Context-Free Grammar [Computer science]
CFG.............. Corporate and Foundation Givers [A publication]
CFGB .... Canadian Foodgrains Bank Association Inc. [Association de la Banque Candienne de Grains Inc.] (AC)
CFGB .... Happy Valley, NF [FM radio station call letters]
CFGBI .... Coopers' Federation of Great Britain and Ireland [A union]
CFG file ...... Configuration File (CDE)
CFGI............ Community Financial Group [NASDAQ symbol] (SAG)
CFGI............ Community Finl Group [NASDAQ symbol] (TTSB)
CFGIW .... Community Finl Group Wrrt [NASDAQ symbol] (TTSB)
CFGL............ Laval, PQ [FM radio station call letters]
CFGM........... Committee for a Free Gold Market (EA)
CFGO........... Ottawa, ON [AM radio station call letters]
CFGP .... Grande Prairie, AB [AM radio station call letters]
CFGS .... Church of Jesus Christ of Latter-Day Saints, Genealogical Society Library, Fresno Branch, Fresno, CA [Library symbol Library of Congress] (LCLS)
CFGS .... Hull, PQ [Television station call letters]
CFGT........... Alma, PQ [AM radio station call letters]
CFGX .... Sarnia, ON [FM radio station call letters]
CFH.............. Canadian Federation for the Humanities [See also FCEH] [Research center] (RCD)
CFH.............. Canadian Forces Hospital
CFH.............. Carmelita Petroleum [Vancouver Stock Exchange symbol]
CFH.............. Chloroplasts, Ferredoxin, and Hydrogenase [Photoreactant system]
CFH.............. Citizens for Health
CFH.............. Clifton Hills [Australia Airport symbol Obsolete] (OAG)
CFH.............. COBOL [Common Business-Oriented Language] File Handler (IAA)
CFH.............. Conference on Faith and History (EA)
CFH.............. Council on Family Health (EA)
CFH.............. Cubic Feet per Hour
CFH.............. Fresno Community Hospital, Fresno, CA [Library symbol Library of Congress] (LCLS)
CFHA .... Canadian Field Hockey Association
CFHC .... Calif Finl Hldg [NASDAQ symbol] (TTSB)
CFHC .... California Financial Holding Co. [NASDAQ symbol] (NQ)
CFHC .... Canadian Field Hockey Council
CFHC .... Canmore, AB [AM radio station call letters]
CFHC .... Cornell Feline Health Center [Cornell University] [Research center] (RCD)
CFHE .... College of Further and Higher Education (AIE)
CFHK .... St. Thomas, ON [FM radio station call letters]
CFHL .... Complement Factor H-Like [Protein] [Medicine] (DMAA)
CF/HP .... Constant-Flow/High Pressure [Oxygen system]
CFHP .... Council on Federal Health Programs (DMAA)
CFHQ .... Canadian Forces Headquarters [NATO]
CFHRM .... Congressional Friends of Human Rights Monitors (EA)
CFHS .... Canadian Federation of Humane Societies [Federation des Societes Candiennes d'Assistance aux Animaux] (AC)
CFHS .... Coherent Frequency-Hopping Signal
CFHT........... Canada-France-Hawaii Telescope [Mauna Kea, Hawaii]
CFHT........... Continuous Flow Hypersonic Tunnel [NASA]
CFI.............. California Fig Institute (EA)
CFI.............. California State University, Fullerton, Fullerton, CA [OCLC symbol] (OCLC)
CFI.............. Camp Fire, Inc. (AEE)
CFI.............. Canadian Film Institute [See also ICF]
CFI.............. Cancer Federation, Inc. (EA)
CFI.............. Canyonlands Field Institute [An association] (EA)
CFI.............. Card Format Identifier (NASA)
CFI.............. Central Fuel Injection [Automotive engineering]
CFI.............. Centro Filatelico Internazionale
CFI.............. Ceramic Foam Insulation
CFI.............. Certification for Issue (MCD)
CFI.............. Certified Flight Instructor [Aviation]
CFI.............. Chaplain to Foreign Immigrants [British] (DI)
CFI.............. Chemotactic Factor Inactivator [Immunology]
CFI.............. Chief Flying Instructor [RAF] [British]
CFI.............. Chloroform Fumigation-Incubation Technique
CFI.............. Christian Friends of Israel [British] (BI)
CFI.............. Closed-Fist Injury
CFI.............. Clothing and Footwear Institute [British] (EAIO)
CFI.............. Coalition for Food Irradiation [Defunct] (EA)
CFI.............. Coastal Fisheries Institute [Louisiana State University]
CFI.............. College Fiord [Alaska] [Seismograph station code, US Geological Survey] (SEIS)
CFI.............. Commonwealth Forestry Institute [British]
CFI.............. Community Fluorosis Index
CFI.............. Company Form Instruction (MCD)
CFI.............. Complement Fixation Inhibition [Test] [Immunology]
CFI.............. Computer Fault Isolation (MCD)
CFI.............. Consolidated Film Industries [Commercial firm]
CFI.............. Continuous Flow Intersection [Automated traffic management]
CFI.............. Continuous Forest Inventory (DICI)
CFI.............. Continuous Fuel Injection
CFI.............. Contractor Final Inspection (MCD)
CFI.............. Contractor-Furnished Information (MCD)
CFI.............. Controlled Fuel Injection [Engineering]

CFI.............. Core Flooding System Isolation Valve Interlock [Nuclear energy] (NRCH)
CFI.............. Cost, Freight, and Insurance [Shipping]
CFI.............. Court of First Instance (BARN)
CFI.............. Credit Factoring International [Commercial firm British]
CFI.............. Crestbrook Forest Industries Ltd. [Toronto Stock Exchange symbol Vancouver Stock Exchange symbol]
CFI.............. Crossfire Injection [Automotive engineering]
CFI.............. Crystal Frequency Indicator
CFI.............. Cumulative Form Inception (MCD)
CFIA .... Canadian Feed Industry Association [Association Canadienne des Industries de l'Alimentation Animale] (AC)
CFIA .... Center for Independent Action (EA)
CFIA .... Center for International Affairs [Harvard University] [Research center] (RCD)
CFIA .... Collective-Focusing Ion Accelerator (MCD)
CFIA .... Component Failure Impact Analysis [IBM Corp.]
CFIA .... Core Flood Isolation Valve Assembly [Nuclear energy] (IEEE)
CFIAB .... Canadian Federation of Insurance Agents and Brokers
CFIAM .... Canadian Forces Institute of Aviation Medicine (PDAA)
CFIB .... Canadian Federation of Independent Business
CFIB .... CFI Industries [NASDAQ symbol] (NQ)
CFIC .... Canadian Feed Information Centre (AC)
CFIC .... Canned Food Information Council (EA)
CFIC .... Central Flight Instructor Course [Military]
CFIC .... Community Financial Corp. (Illinois) [NASDAQ symbol] (SAG)
CFIC .... Community Financial (IL) [NQS] (TTSB)
CF-ICA .... Complement-Fixing Islet Cell Antibodies [Immunochemistry]
CFID .... Catalytic Flame Ionization Detector
CFIdBk .... Central Fidelity Bank [Associated Press] (SAG)
CFIDS .... Chronic Fatigue Immune Dysfunction Syndrome [Medicine]
CFIDSA .... Chronic Fatigue Immune Dysfunction Syndrome Association (EA)
CFIE .... Conseil des Federations Industrielles d'Europe [Council of European Industrial Federations]
CFIEI .... Canadian Farm and Industrial Equipment Institute
CFIEM .... Canadian Armed Forces Institute of Environmental Medicine (PDAA)
CFIF .... Continuous Flow Isoelectric Focusing [Materials processing]
CFIG .... Canadian Federation of Independent Grocers [Federation Canadienne des Epiciers Independants] (AC)
CFII .... Certified Flight Instructor, Instrument [Aviation]
CFI Ind....... CFI Industries [Associated Press] (SAG)
CFIL .... Gillam, MB [FM radio station call letters]
CFIM .... Confocal Flourescence Imaging Microscopy [Medicine]
CFIM .... Iles-de-la-Madeline, PQ [FM radio station call letters]
CFIN .... Consumers Financial Corp. [NASDAQ symbol] (NQ)
CFIN .... Consumers Finl [NASDAQ symbol] (TTSB)
CFIN .... Lac-Etchemin, PQ [FM radio station call letters]
CFINP .... Consumers Finl 8.50% Cv Pfd [NASDAQ symbol] (TTSB)
CFI Pro ...... CFI Proservices, Inc. [Associated Press] (SAG)
CFIRB .... Cosmic Far-Infrared Background
CFIRS .... Central Florida Information Research Service, Inc. [Information service or system] (IID)
CFIT .... Controlled Flight into Terrain
CFIUS .... Committee on Foreign Investment in the United States
CFJ.............. Center for Foreign Journalists (EA)
CF(J)........... Chaplain to the Forces (Jewish) [British]
CFJ.............. Cobi Foods, Inc. [Toronto Stock Exchange symbol]
CFJ.............. Control Flow Jet
CFJ.............. Crawfordsville, IN [Location identifier FAA] (FAAL)
CFJ.............. Cross-Field Jammer
CFJ.............. Fujian Airlines [China] [FAA designator] (FAAC)
CFJB .... Barrie, ON [FM radio station call letters]
CFJC .... Kamloops, BC [AM radio station call letters]
CFJC .... Merritt, BC [FM radio station call letters]
CFJC-TV ..... Kamloops, BC [Television station call letters]
CFJO .... Council of Federated Jewish Organizations [Defunct] (EA)
CFJO .... Thetford Mines, PQ [FM radio station call letters]
CFJP .... Montreal, PQ [Television station call letters]
CFJQ .... Nipigon-Red Rock, ON [FM radio station call letters]
CFJR .... Brockville, ON [AM radio station call letters]
CFK.............. CE Franklin Ltd. [AMEX symbol] (SAG)
CFK.............. CE Franklin Ltd [AMEX symbol] (TTSB)
CFK.............. Citizens for Free Kuwait [Defunct] (EA)
CFK.............. Cliff Resources Corp. [Toronto Stock Exchange symbol]
CFK.............. Confidence Firing Kit
CFKC .... Creston, BC [AM radio station call letters]
CFKM .... Trois-Rivieres, PQ [Television station call letters]
CFKR .... Center for Fast Kinetics Research [University of Texas at Austin] [Research center] (RCD)
CFKS .... Sherbrooke, PQ [Television station call letters]
CFL.............. Calibrated Focal Length (MSA)
CFL.............. Call Failed [or Failure] [Telecommunications] (TEL)
CFL.............. Canadian Federation of Labour
CFL.............. Canadian Football League
CFL.............. Canadian Forces College Library [UTLAS symbol]
CFL.............. Care for Life [An association] (EA)
CFL.............. Central Film Library [British]
CFL.............. Ceylon Federation of Labor [Obsolete]
CFL.............. Chinese Federation of Labor [Nationalist China]
CFL.............. Christian Family Life (EA)
CFL.............. Cisplatin, Fluorourncil, Leucovorin Calcium [Antineoplastic drug] (CDI)
CFL.............. Citizens for Farm Labor [Defunct] (EA)
CFL.............. Clear Flight Level
CFL.............. Close Focus Lens

CFL............ Club Francais du Livre [French Book Club]
CFL............ Cold-Cathode Fluorescent Lamp
CFL............ Cold Flow Laboratory [Martin Marietta Corp.]
CFL............ Committee for a Free Latvia (EA)
CFL............ Committee for a Free Lithuania [Defunct] (EA)
CFL............ Committee on Federal Laboratories [Federal Council for Science and Technology] [Terminated, 1976]
CFL............ Compact Fluorescent Lamp
CFL............ Compact Fluorescent Light
CFL............ Conflict (MSA)
CFL............ Consort Aviation [British ICAO designator] (FAAC)
CFL............ Constant Feed Lubricator
CFL............ Context-Free Language [Computer science]
CFL............ Continental Football League
CFL............ Coordinated Fire Line (AABC)
CFL............ Core States Financial [NYSE symbol] (SAG)
CFL............ CoreStates Financial [NYSE symbol] (TTSB)
CFL............ CoreStates Financial Corp. [NYSE symbol] (SPSG)
CFL............ Corporate Foods Ltd. [Toronto Stock Exchange symbol]
CFL............ Corps Front Luxembourgeois [Resistance organization in Luxembourg] [World War II]
CFL............ Council of Federal Libraries (AC)
CFL............ Counterflashing [Technical drawings]
CFL............ Critical Field Length (MCD)
CFl............ Fullerton Public Library, Fullerton, CA [Library symbol Library of Congress] (LCLS)
CFL............ Stanislaus County Free Library, Modesto, CA [OCLC symbol] (OCLC)
CFLA........... Canadian Finance & Leasing Association (AC)
CFLA........... Catholics for Latin America
CFLAG........ Citizens for a Lakeshore Greenway (AC)
CFlB........... Beckman Instruments, Inc., Fullerton, CA [Library symbol Library of Congress] (LCLS)
CFLC........... Churchill Falls, NF [FM radio station call letters]
CFlCO......... Southern California College of Optometry, Fullerton, CA [Library symbol Library of Congress] (LCLS)
CFLD........... Burns Lake, BC [AM radio station call letters]
CFLETC....... Consolidated Federal Law Enforcement Training Center [Later, FLETC] [Department of the Treasury]
C-FLEX........ Cobra Fleet Life Extension Program [Military]
CFLG........... Cornwall, ON [FM radio station call letters]
CFLG........... Counterflashing (MSA)
CFLI........... Catholic Family Life Insurance (EA)
CFLI........... Clay Flue Lining Institute [Defunct] (EA)
CFLIS......... Canadian Foresters Life Insurance Society (EA)
CFlJ........... Fullerton Junior College, Fullerton, CA [Library symbol Library of Congress] (LCLS)
CFLLADS..... Canadian Forces Low Level Air Defense System [Military]
CFLLP......... Commission on Folk Law and Legal Pluralism [of the International Union of Anthropological and Ethnological Sciences] (EAIO)
CFLM.......... La Tuque, PQ [AM radio station call letters]
CFLN.......... Comite Francais de Liberation Nationale [Algeria]
CFLN.......... Goose Bay, NF [AM radio station call letters]
CFLO.......... Cardiometrics, Inc. [NASDAQ symbol] (SAG)
CFLO.......... Mont-Laurier, PQ [FM radio station call letters] (RBYB)
CFLOS........ Cloud-Free Line of Sight
CFLP.......... Canada Farm Labor Pool
CFLP.......... Code of Fair Labor Practices (NOAA)
CFlP........... Pacific Christian College, Fullerton, CA [Library symbol Library of Congress] (LCLS)
CFLP.......... Rimouski, PQ [AM radio station call letters]
CFLPA........ Canadian Football League Players' Association [Association des Joueurs de la Ligue de Football Canadienne] (AC)
CFLRI......... Canadian Fitness & Lifestyle Research Institute [Institut Canadien de la Recherche sur la Condition Physique et le Mode de Vie] (AC)
CFlS.......... California State University, Fullerton, Fullerton, CA [Library symbol Library of Congress] (LCLS)
CFLS.......... Levis, PQ [FM radio station call letters]
C/FLT......... Captive Flight (MUGU)
CFLW......... Wabush, NF [AM radio station call letters]
CFLX.......... Sherbrooke, PQ [FM radio station call letters]
CFLY.......... Kingston, ON [FM radio station call letters]
CFM............ Cadet Forces Medal [British military] (DMA)
CFM............ Canadian Friends of Mine (EA)
CFM............ Captive Flight Model [Military] (CAAL)
CFM............ Carbon-Free Medium [Cytology]
CFM............ Cassells' Family Magazine [A publication] (ROG)
CFM............ Cathode Follower Mixer
CFM............ Center Frequency Modulation
CFM............ Cerebral Function Monitor (PDAA)
CFM............ Chemical Force Microscope
CFM............ Chilldown Flow Meter
CFM............ Chlorofluoromethane [Propellant]
CFM............ Christiane Fabre de Morlhon [Information service name CFM Documentazione] (IID)
CFM............ Christian Family Movement (EA)
CFM............ Cliffside [Montana] [Seismograph station code, US Geological Survey Closed] (SEIS)
CFM............ Closed Flux Memory [Computer science]
CFM............ Close-Fitting Mask [Medicine] (DMAA)
CFM............ Code Fragment Manager [Computer science]
CFM............ Collision-Force Method (PDAA)
CFM............ Comision Femenil Mexicana Nacional (EA)
CFM............ Committee for a Free Mozambique [Defunct] (EA)
CFM............ Companding and Frequency Modulation [Telecommunications] (TEL)

CFM............ Computer Facilities Management (MCD)
CFM............ Computer Field Maintenance [British]
CFM............ Confirm (AAG)
CFM............ Consumers for the Free Market [Pittsburgh, PA] (EA)
CFM............ Containment Failure Mode [Nuclear energy] (NRCH)
CFM............ Contamination Free Manufacturing [Semiconductor manufacturing]
CFM............ Contingency Financing Mechanism [International Monetary Fund]
CFM............ Contingency for Movement [Army]
CFM............ Continuous Filament Mat
CFM............ Continuous Flow Manufacturing [Automotive engineering]
CFM............ Continuous Functional Monitoring
CFM............ Contractor Financial Management (DOMA)
CFM............ Contractor-Furnished Material
CFM............ CONUS [Continental United States] Freight Management System [DoD]
CFM............ Council of Foreign Ministers
CFM............ Covering Fire Mine (MCD)
CFM............ Craniofacial Microsomia [Medicine] (DMAA)
CFM............ Critical Flow Model
CFM............ Crown Life Properties, Inc. [Toronto Stock Exchange symbol]
CFM............ Crystal Frequency Multiplier
CFM............ Cubic Feet per Minute
CFM............ Customer-Furnished Material (NASA)
CFM............ Cytoxan, Fluorouracil, Methotrexate [Antineoplastic drug] (CDI)
CFM............ Roman Catholic Bishop of Fresno, Monterey-Fresno Diocesan Library, Fresno, CA [Library symbol Library of Congress] (LCLS)
CFMA.......... Canadian Fibreboard Manufacturers' [Association Canadienne des Manufacturiers d'Isolant de Fibre de Bois] (AC)
CFMA.......... Catholic Family Missionary Alliance [Later, MEW] (EA)
CFMA.......... Central Financial Management Activities [Military] (AABC)
CFMA.......... Chair Frame Manufacturers' Association [British] (BI)
CFMA.......... Church Furniture Manufacturers Association [Defunct] (EA)
CFMA.......... Coal Fuel Mixtures Association (EA)
CFMA.......... Construction Financial Management Association (EA)
CFMA.......... Council for Medical Affairs (EA)
CFMA.......... Cutting Fluid Manufacturers Association [Defunct] (EA)
CFMAS........ Calcium, Ferrous, Magnesium, Aluminum, Silicon [Oxide system in geology]
CFMB.......... Montreal, PQ [AM radio station call letters]
CFMC.......... Canned Food Marketing Committee (EA)
CFMC.......... Caribbean Fishery Management Council [National Oceanic and Atmospheric Administration] (GFGA)
CFMC.......... Saskatoon, SK [FM radio station call letters]
CFMDC .... Canadian Film-Makers Distribution Centre
CFME.......... Cryogenic Fluid Management Experiment (MCD)
CFMen........ Mennonite Brethren Biblical Seminary, Fresno, CA [Library symbol Library of Congress] (LCLS)
CFMF.......... Crip Flow Management Facility [NASA] (GFGA)
CFMF.......... Cryogenic Fluid Management Facility (MCD)
CFMF.......... Fermont, PQ [FM radio station call letters]
CFMG.......... St. Albert, AB [FM radio station call letters]
CFMHS........ Commission on Family Ministries and Human Sexuality (EA)
CFMI.......... New Westminster, BC [FM radio station call letters]
CFMK.......... Kingston, ON [FM radio station call letters]
CFML.......... Cold Fusion Markup Language [Computer science] (PCM)
CFML.......... Computational Fluid Mechanics Laboratory [University of Arizona] [Research center] (RCD)
CFMM.......... Brothers of Our Lady, Mother of Mercy (TOCD)
CFMM.......... Brothers of Our Lady of Mercy [Roman Catholic religious order]
cfmm.......... Brothers of the Poor of St. Francis (TOCD)
CFMM.......... Canadian Federation of Mayors and Municipalities
CFMM.......... Congregatio Filiarum Minimarum Mariae [Minim Daughters of Mary Immaculate] [Roman Catholic religious order]
CFMM.......... Minim Daughters of Mary Immaculate (TOCD)
CFMM.......... Prince Albert, SK [FM radio station call letters]
CFMO.......... Smiths Falls, ON [FM radio station call letters]
CFMQ.......... Hudson Bay, SK [FM radio station call letters]
CFMS.......... Canadian Folk Music Society
CFMS.......... Chained File Management System [IBM Corp.]
CFMS.......... Combined Field Maintenance Shop [Army] (AABC)
CFMS.......... Computer-Based Financial Management System [Harper & Shuman, Inc.] [Cambridge, MA] [Information service or system] (IID)
CFMS.......... Contractor Field Maintenance Service [Army]
CFMS.......... Crip Flow Management Facility [NASA]
CFM/S........ Cubic Feet per Minute/Second (DEN)
CFMS.......... Victoria, BC [FM radio station call letters]
CFMSA........ Catholic Foreign Mission Society of America (EA)
CFMT.......... CFM Technologies, Inc. [NASDAQ symbol] (SAG)
CFM T........ CFM Technologies, Inc. [Associated Press] (SAG)
CFMT.......... Toronto, ON [Television station call letters]
CFMTA........ Canadian Federation of Music Teachers' Associations
CFMU.......... Centralized Flow Management Unit (DA)
CFMU.......... Chinese Foreign Missionary Union (EA)
CFMU.......... Hamilton, ON [FM radio station call letters]
CFMUA .... Cotton Fire and Marine Underwriters Association
CFMWFS...... Canadian Forces Maritime Warfare School [Canadian Navy]
CFMWP........ Central Flow Weather Service Unit [FAA] (TAG)
CFMX.......... Cobourg, ON [FM radio station call letters]
CFMX-FM-1... Mississauga, ON [FM radio station call letters]
CFN............ Christ for the Nations (EA)
CFN............ Church Family Newspaper [A publication] (ROG)
CFN............ Clifton Herbarium [British]
CFN............ Committee for a Free Namibia [Defunct] (EA)
CFN............ Confine (FAAC)

CFN.............. Consolidated Fredonia Resources Ltd. [*Vancouver Stock Exchange symbol*]
CFN.............. Contifinancial Corp. [*NYSE symbol*] (SAG)
CFN.............. ContiFinancial Corp. [*NYSE symbol*] (TTSB)
CFN.............. Craftsman [*Military British*]
CFN.............. Los Angeles, CA [*Location identifier FAA*] (FAAL)
CFN&HCP ... Centre for Nursing and Health Care Practices [*Southern Cross University*] [*Medicine Australia*]
CFNB .... Fredericton, NB [*AM radio station call letters*]
CFNC .... Carolina Fincorp., Inc. [*NASDAQ symbol*] (SAG)
CFNC .... Cross Lake, MB [*AM radio station call letters*]
CFND .... Communicators for Nuclear Disarmament (EA)
CFND .... Craniofrontonasal Dysostosis [*Medicine*] (DMAA)
CFNI .... Port Hardy, BC [*AM radio station call letters*]
CFNJ .... St. Gabriel De Brandon, PQ [*FM radio station call letters*]
CFNK .... Pinehouse Lake, SK [*FM radio station call letters*]
CFNL.......... Fort Nelson, BC [*AM radio station call letters*]
CF/NML........ Citizens Forum on Self-Government/National Municipal League [*Information service or system*] (IID)
CFNN .... St. Anthony, NF [*FM radio station call letters*]
CFNO .... Common Fund for Nonprofit Organizations [*Fairfield, CT*] (EA)
CFNO .... Marathon, ON [*FM radio station call letters*]
CFNP .... Committee on Federalism and National Purpose [*Defunct*] (EA)
CFNP .... Community Food and Nutrition Programs [*Community Services Administration*]
CFNR .... Call Forwarding No Reply [*Telecommunications*] (DOM)
CF-NRTS ...... Central Facilities - National Reactor Test Station (SAA)
CFNS .... Calgary Field Naturalists' Society [*Societe des Champs Etat de Nature de Calgary*] [*Formerly, Calgary Bird Club*] (AC)
CFNW .... Port Au Choix, NF [*AM radio station call letters*]
CFNY .... Brampton, ON [*FM radio station call letters*]
CFO.............. Association of Camps Farthest Out (EA)
CFO.............. Calling for Orders [*Shipping*]
CFO.............. Canceling Former Order
C/FO............ Cartoon/Fantasy Organization [*Defunct*] (EA)
CFO.............. Central Forecast Office (DA)
CFO.............. Ceramic Fiber Optics
CFO.............. Channel for Orders [*Business term*]
CFO.............. Chapman Freeborn [*British*] [*FAA designator*] (FAAC)
CFO.............. Chief Financial Officer [*Business term*]
CFO.............. Chief Financial Official (AAGC)
CFO.............. Chief Fire Officer [*British*] (ADA)
CFO.............. Chief Flight Operator (AAGC)
CFO.............. Coast for Orders [*Chartering*]
CFO.............. Commissioning and Fitting Out
CFO.............. Complex Facility Operator [*Aerospace*] (AAG)
CFO.............. Connection Fitting Out [*Navy*]
CFO.............. Consolidated Function Ordinary [*IBM Corp.*]
CFO.............. Consolidated Funds Ordinary [*Insurance*]
CFO.............. Contract Financing Office (AAGC)
CFO.............. Council of Film Organizations (EA)
CFO.............. Critical Flashover [*Voltage*] (IEEE)
CFO.............. Critical Flow Orifice [*Engineering*]
CFOA .... Champion Fleet Owners Association (EA)
CFOA .... Chief Financial Officer Act of 1990
CFoA.......... United States Army, Fort Ord Library System, Fort Ord, CA [*Library symbol Library of Congress*] (LCLS)
CFoA-M....... United States Army, Presidio of Monterey Library, Monterey, CA [*Library symbol Library of Congress*] (LCLS)
CFOB .... Fort Frances, ON [*AM radio station call letters*]
CFOC .... Contractor Fin Opener Crank (NG)
CFOCCF ...... Concerned Friends of Ontario Citizens in Care Facilities (AC)
CFOF........... Centre Franco-Ontarien de Folklore [*Formerly, Institut de Folklore*] [*Research center*] (RCD)
CFOK .... Westlock, AB [*AM radio station call letters*]
CFON .... Target Tech Inc. [*NASDAQ symbol*] (TTSB)
CFON .... Target Technologies, Inc. [*NASDAQ symbol*] (SAG)
CFonK.......... Kaiser Steel Corp., Fontana, CA [*Library symbol Library of Congress*] (LCLS)
CFOR .... Command Forces
CFOR .... COMSEC [*Communications Security*] Field Office of Record [*Army*] (AABC)
CFOR .... Conversional FORTRAN [*Formula Translating System*] (IAA)
CFORP......... Centre Franco-Ontarien de Ressources Pedagogiques (AC)
CFOS .... CNARESTRA [*Chief of Naval Air Reserve Training*] Fleet Operating Squadrons
CFOS .... Owen Sound, ON [*AM radio station call letters*]
CFOT........... Crossed-Field Output Tube
CFOX .... Vancouver, BC [*FM radio station call letters*]
CFOZ........... Argentia, NF [*FM radio station call letters*]
cfp .... Brothers of the Poor of St. Francis (TOCD)
CFP.............. Canadian Forces Publication
CFP.............. Canadian Foundation for the Advancement of Pharmacy [*Fondation Canadienne pour l'Avancement de la Pharmacie*] [*Also, Canadian Foundation for Pharmacy*] (AC)
CFP.............. Canfor Corp. [*Toronto Stock Exchange symbol Vancouver Stock Exchange symbol*]
CFP.............. Cardiac Filling Pressure [*Cardiology*]
CFP.............. Carrier Frequency Pulse
CFP.............. Casualty Firing Panel
CFP.............. Center of Filtering and Plotting (NATG)
CFP.............. Center of Fruiting Period [*Ecology*]
CFP.............. Cerebrospinal Fluid Protein [*Biochemistry*] (DAVI)
CFP.............. Certified Financial Planner [*College of Financial Planning*] [*Designation awarded by Business term*]

CFP.............. Change Flight Plan
CFP.............. Chartered Financial Planner
CFP.............. Chinese Freedom Party [*Political party*] (EY)
CFP.............. Chronic False Positive [*Test*] [*Medicine*]
CFP.............. Ciguatera Fish Poisoning [*Medicine*]
CFP.............. Cold Front Passage [*NWS*] (FAAC)
CFP.............. Combined Filter and Plot (NATG)
CFP.............. Commission on Federal Paperwork [*Terminated, 1978*]
CFP.............. Common Fisheries Policy [*EEC*]
CFP.............. Community Fellows Program (EA)
CFP.............. Compania de Aviacion Faucett SA [*Peru*] [*ICAO designator*] (FAAC)
CFP.............. Completion Fitting-Out Period
CFP.............. Computer Flight Plan
CFP.............. Computer Forms Printer (IAA)
CFP.............. Concentracion de Fuerzas Populares [*Concentration of Popular Forces*] [*Ecuador*] [*Political party*] (PPW)
CFP.............. Concentric Flight Plan (KSC)
CFP.............. Concept Formulation Package [*Military*]
CFP.............. Conceptual Flight Profile (MCD)
CFP.............. Congregatio Fratrum Pauperum [*Brothers of the Poor of St. Francis*] [*Roman Catholic religious order*]
CFP.............. Congressional Fact Paper [*Army*]
CFP.............. Contingency Force Pool
CFP.............. Contractor-Furnished Product (AAGC)
CFP.............. Contractor-Furnished Property [*Air Force*]
CFP.............. Control Filter Post (NATG)
CFP.............. Coordinated Financial Planning
CFP.............. Corporate Finance Partner
CFP.............. Covenant Fellowship of Presbyterians (EA)
CFP.............. Creation Facilities Program [*Computer science*] (IBMDP)
CFP.............. Cyclophosphamide, Fluorouracil, Prednisone [*Antineoplastic drug regimen*]
CFP.............. Cystic Fibrosis of the Pancreas [*Medicine*]
CFP.............. Cystic Fibrosis Protein [*Biochemistry*] (DAVI)
CFP.............. Feminine Congregation of the Passion (TOCD)
CFP.............. Mexican Passionist Sisters (TOCD)
CFP.............. Pacific College, Fresno, CA [*Library symbol Library of Congress*] (LCLS)
CFPA.......... Canadian Fluid Power Association [*Association Canadienne d'Energie Fluide*] (AC)
CFPA.......... Canadian Food Processors Association
CFPA.......... Caribbean Family Planning Affiliation (EAIO)
CFPA.......... Cationic Flocculant Producers Association [*Defunct*] (EA)
CFPAE........ Council of Food Processors Association Executives (EA)
CFPC.......... College of Family Physicians of Canada (EAIO)
CFPC.......... Commission de la Fonction Publique du Canada [*Public Service Commission - PSC*] [*Canada*]
C-F/PCM ..... Coarse-Fine/Pulse Code Modulator
CFPD.......... Center for Foreign Policy Development (EA)
CFPDMS ...... Californium-252 Plasma Desorption Mass Spectrometry
CFPF.......... Central Food Preparation Facility [*Military*] (AABC)
CFPFT......... Committee on Free Press and Fair Trial [*of the American Newspaper Publishers Association*] (EA)
CFPG.......... Coalition to Free Petkus and Gajauskas [*Defunct*] (EA)
CFPG.......... Context-Free Programmed Grammar (PDAA)
CFPI........... Cystic Fibrosis Pancreatic Insufficiency [*Medicine*]
CFPL........... Carryover from Previous Log [*Aviation*] (FAAC)
CFPL........... London, ON [*AM radio station call letters*]
CFPL-FM...... London, ON [*FM radio station call letters*]
CFPL-TV...... London, ON [*Television station call letters*]
CFPM.......... Crossed-Field Photomultiplier (IAA)
CFP-MB .... Fresno Pacific College, Center for Mennonite Brethren Studies, Fresno, CA [*Library symbol*] [*Library of Congress*] (LCLS)
CFPMO .... Canadian Forces Project Management Office (HGAA)
CFPNI .... Children's Friendship Project for Northern Ireland (EA)
CFPP.......... Coal-Fired Power Plant
CFPP.......... Cold Filter Plugging Point
CFPP.......... Craniofacial Pattern Profile [*Medicine*] (DMAA)
CFPPU .... Comite de Familiares de Presos Politicos Uruguayos [*Relatives' Committee for Uruguayan Political Prisoners*] [*Malmo, Sweden*] (EAIO)
CFPR .... Canadian Familial Polyposis Registry (DMAA)
CFPR .... Center for Federal Policy Review (EA)
CFPR .... Prince Rupert, BC [*AM radio station call letters*]
CFPRA .... Campden Food Preservation Research Association [*British*] (DBA)
CFPS........... Canadian Forces Postal System
CFPS........... Captain, Fishery Protection Squadron [*NATO*]
CFPS........... Central Food Preparation System [*Military*] (AABC)
CFPS........... Centre for Foreign Policy Studies [*Dalhousie University*] [*Canada*] (IRC)
CFPS........... Crossed-Field Plasma Sheath
CFPS........... Cystic Fibrosis Pancreatic Sufficiency [*Medicine*]
CFPS........... Port Elgin, ON [*AM radio station call letters*]
CFPSG .... Context-Free Phrase Structure Grammar [*Computer science*] (PDAA)
CFPSJ.......... Capuchin-Franciscans (Province of St. Joseph) (EA)
CFPT........... Cytoxan, Flurouracil, Prednisone, Methotrexate [*Antineoplastic drug*] (CDI)
CFP/TDP...... Concept Formulation Package - Technical Development Plan [*Air Force*]
CFQ............. CH Financial Co. [*Vancouver Stock Exchange symbol*]
CFQ............. Cognitive Failure Questionnaire [*Education*] (AIE)
CFQ............. Cooperative Federee du Quebec (AC)
CFQC .... Saskatoon, SK [*FM radio station call letters*]
CFQC-1 .... Stranraer, SK [*Television station call letters*]
CFQC-2 .... North Battleford, SK [*Television station call letters*]

CFQC-TV	Saskatoon, SK [*Television station call letters*]
CFQM...........	Moncton, NB [*FM radio station call letters*]
CFQR	Montreal, PQ [*FM radio station call letters*]
CFQX	Selkirk, MB [*FM radio station call letters*]
CFR..............	Caen [*France*] [*Airport symbol*] (OAG)
CFR..............	Caile Ferate Romane [*Romanian Railways Board*] [*Department of Railways*]
CFR..............	Carbon-Film Resistor
CFR..............	Carrier-Free Radar (LAIN)
CFR..............	Case Fatality Ratio [*Medicine*]
CFR..............	Catastrophic Failure Rate
CFR..............	Center for Field Research (EA)
CFR..............	Central Files Repository
CFR..............	Chance Failure Rate (IAA)
CFR..............	Chauffair Ltd. [*British ICAO designator*] (FAAC)
Cfr...,,........	Chauffeur [*Army*]
CFR..............	Christian Family Renewal (EA)
CFR..............	Citizens for Reagan (EA)
CFR..............	Citrovorum-Factor Rescue [*Cancer treatment*]
CFR..............	Civil Fast Reactor (PDAA)
CFR..............	Code of Federal Regulation (DOMA)
CFR..............	Code of Federal Regulations (ACII)
CFR..............	Cold Filament Resistance
CFR..............	Commander of Federal Republic of Nigeria
CFR..............	Commercial Fast Reactor [*British*]
CFR..............	Commissioned from the Ranks [*Canadian Navy*]
CFR..............	Committee on Foreign Resistance [*War Cabinet*] [*British World War II*]
CFR..............	Committee on Friendly Relations among Foreign Students [*Later, ISS*] (EA)
CFR..............	Compilation of the Federal Register
CFR..............	Computerized Facial Recognition
CFR..............	Concept Feasibility Report
CFR..............	Condensate Filter Demineralizer [*Nuclear energy*] (NRCH)
CFR..............	Confirmation to Receive [*Computer science*]
CFR..............	Confraternity (ROG)
CFR..............	Consolidated Five Star Resources [*Vancouver Stock Exchange symbol*]
CFR..............	Constant Flow Rate
CFR..............	Contact Flight Rules [*Same as VFR*] [*Meteorology*]
CFR..............	Contractor Furnished Requirements
CFR..............	Cooperative Fuels Research [*Committee*]
CFR..............	Coordinating Fuel Research (MCD)
CFR..............	Cost and Freight ["*INCOTERM,*" *International Chamber of Commerce official code*] [*Business term*]
CFR..............	Council on Foreign Relations (EA)
CFR..............	Counterflow Reactor [*Chemical engineering*]
CFR...,,........	CRI Liquidating Real Estate Investment Trust [*NYSE symbol*] (SPSG)
CFR...,,........	CRI Liquidating REIT [*NYSE symbol*] (TTSB)
CFR..............	Crossfire (MSA)
CFR..............	Cumulative Failure Rate
CFR..............	Cumulative Financial Requirements (MCD)
CFR..............	Franciscan Friars of the Renewal (TOCD)
cfr...............	Franciscan Friars of the Renewal (TOCD)
CFr..............	Queen of the Rosary College, Fremont, CA [*Library symbol Library of Congress*] (LCLS)
CFrA.............	Alameda County Library, Fremont, CA [*Library symbol Library of Congress*] (LCLS)
CFRA	Ottawa, ON [*AM radio station call letters*]
CFRB	Toronto, ON [*AM radio station call letters*]
CFRC	Canadian Forces Recruiting Centre
CFRC	Community and Family Program Review Committee [*DoD*]
CFRC	Consolidated Flight Record Custodian [*Air Force*] (AFM)
CFRC	Kingston, ON [*FM radio station call letters*]
CFRD	Confidential, Formerly Restricted Data
CFRDA	Commercial Fisheries Research and Development Act
CFRE...........	Certified Fund-Raising Executive
CFRE...........	Circulating Fuel Reactor Experiment [*Nuclear energy*]
CFRE...........	Contract Financial Requirements Estimate [*NASA*] (KSC)
CFRE...........	Regina, SK [*Television station call letters*]
CFR(EP).......	Committee on Foreign Resistance, Economic Policy [*Ministry of Supply*] [*British World War II*]
CFRF	Christian Forum Research Foundation [*Later, CC*] (EA)
CFRG	Canadians for Responsible Government (EAIO)
CFRG	Carbon Fiber-Reinforced Glass (PDAA)
CFRGC	Carbon Fiber-Reinforced Glass-Ceramic (PDAA)
CFRJ...........	Center for Russian and East European Jewry [*Later, CREEJ*] (EA)
CFRM...........	Continuous Fiber Reinforcing Mat [*Fiberglass*]
CFRM...........	Contract Financial Reporting Manual
CFRMF........	Coupled Fast Reactivity Measurement Facility [*Idaho Falls, ID*] [*Department of Energy*] (NRCH)
CFRMS	Chesnut Fencing Manufacturers Society [*British*] (DBA)
CFRN	Edmonton, AB [*AM radio station call letters*]
CFRN-1........	Grande Prairie, AB [*Television station call letters*]
CFRN-2........	Peace River, AB [*Television station call letters*]
CFRN-3........	Whitecourt, AB [*Television station call letters*]
CFRN-4........	Ashmont, AB [*Television station call letters*]
CFRN-5........	Lac La Biche, AB [*Television station call letters*]
CFRN-6........	Red Deer, AB [*Television station call letters*]
CFRN-7........	Lougheed, AB [*Television station call letters*]
CFRN-8........	Grouard Mission-High Prairie, AB [*Television station call letters*]
CFRN-9........	Slave Lake, AB [*Television station call letters*]
CFRN-TV......	Edmonton, AB [*Television station call letters*]
CFRO...........	Vancouver, BC [*FM radio station call letters*]
CF(R of O)...	Chaplain to the Forces - Reserve of Officers [*British*]
CFROI	Cash Flow Return on Investment
CFRP	Carbon Fiber Reinforced Plastic
CFRP	Carbon Fiber-Reinforced Polymer (PDAA)
CFRP	Central Florida Research Park
CFRP	Consolidated Fuel Reprocessing Program [*Oak Ridge National Laboratory*]
CFRP	Forestville, PQ [*AM radio station call letters*]
CFRQ	Dartmouth, NS [*FM radio station call letters*]
CFRRIIA	Council on Foreign Relations and Royal Institute of International Affairs [*British*]
CFRS	Canada-France Redshift Survey [*Astronomy*]
CFRS	Jonquiere, PQ [*Television station call letters*]
CFRSL	Center for Reflection on the Second Law (EA)
CFR Supp	Code of Federal Regulations Supplement [*A publication*] (GFGA)
CFRT	Cystic Fibrosis Research Trust [*British*]
CFRTP	Carbon Fiber Reinforced Thermoplastic [*Plastics technology*]
CFRU	Combat Fitness Retraining Unit
CFRU	Guelph, ON [*FM radio station call letters*]
CFRV	Lethbridge, AB [*FM radio station call letters*]
CFRW	Campaign Fund for Republican Women [*Defunct*] (EA)
CFRY	Portage La Prairie, MB [*AM radio station call letters*]
CFS.............	California State University, Fresno, Fresno, CA [*Library symbol Library of Congress OCLC symbol*] (LCLS)
CFS.............	Calls for Service Signal [*Telecommunications*] (TEL)
CFS.............	Canadian Federation of Students
CFS.............	Canadian Forces Station
CFS.............	Canadian Forestry Service
CFS.............	Cancer Family Syndrome [*Oncology*] (DAVI)
CFS.............	Canted Fuselage Station (MCD)
CFS.............	Carrier Frequency Shift
CFS.............	Cassegrain Feed System
CFS.............	Center for Family Support (EA)
CFS.............	Center for Standards
CFS.............	Center Frequency Stabilization [*Radio*]
CFS.............	Central Flying School [*RAF*] [*British Australia*]
CFS.............	Central Forecasting Station (IAA)
CFS.............	Central Frequency Synthesizer
CFS.............	Centre for Fiscal Studies [*University of Bath*] [*British*] (CB)
CFS.............	Cesium Feed System
CFS.............	Chief of Fleet Support [*Navy British*]
CFS.............	Christians for Socialism in the United States (EA)
CFS.............	Chronic Fatigue Syndrome [*Medicine*]
CFS.............	Coffs Harbour [*Australia Airport symbol*] (OAG)
CFS.............	Coherent Forward Scattering [*Spectrometry*]
CFS.............	Coherent Frequency Synthesizer
CFS.............	Cold-Finished Steel (MSA)
CFS.............	Combined File Search [*IBM program*] [*Computer science*]
CFS.............	Comforce Corp. [*AMEX symbol*] (SAG)
CFS.............	Comforce Corp. [*AMEX symbol*] (TTSB)
CFS.............	Commercial Financial Services Inc.
CFS.............	Committee for Food and Shelter [*Later, NAEH*] (EA)
CFS.............	Committee on World Food Security [*United Nations*] (EA)
CFS.............	Commodity Flow Survey [*BTS*] (TAG)
CFS.............	Commodity Flow System
CFS.............	Common File System [*Computer science*]
CFS.............	Community, Family, and Soldier [*Support Command*] [*Korea*] (DOMA)
CFS.............	Completely Finished Sets
CFS.............	Component Failure Summary (KSC)
CFS.............	Composite Feed System
CFS.............	Computerized Forwarding System [*US Postal Service*]
CFS.............	Concept Formulation Studies
CFS.............	Condensate and Feedwater System [*Nuclear energy*] (NRCH)
CFS.............	Confuse (MSA)
CFS.............	Congregation de la Fraternite Sacerdotale [*Congregation of the Sacerdotal Fraternity*] [*Canada*] (EAIO)
CFS.............	Congressional Flying Service (SAA)
CFS.............	Consolidated Financial Statement (HGAA)
CFS.............	Constant Final State Spectroscopy (MCD)
CFS.............	Container Freight Station [*Shipping*]
CFS.............	Contoured Femoral Stem [*Total hip prosthesis*] [*Orthopedics*] (DAVI)
CFS.............	Contract [*or Contractor*] Field Service (AFM)
CFS.............	Contract Field Support
CFS.............	Contract Financial Status (AFM)
CFS.............	Controlled Foods International Ltd. [*Toronto Stock Exchange symbol*]
CFS.............	Core Former Structure [*Nuclear energy*] (NRCH)
CFS.............	Council of Fleet Specialists (EA)
CFS.............	Counter Filling System
CFS.............	Critical Field Strength (AAG)
CFS.............	Cryogenic Fluid Storage
CFS.............	CT Financial Services, Inc. [*Toronto Stock Exchange symbol*]
CFS.............	CT Fini Services [*TS Symbol*] (TTSB)
CFS.............	Cubic Feet per Second
cfs...............	Cubic Foot per Second [*Marine science*] (OSRA)
CFS.............	Cystic Fibrosis Society
CFS.............	Empire Airlines, Inc. [*ICAO designator*] (FAAC)
CFSA	California Flyers School of Aeronautics
CFSA	Canadian Figure Skating Association
CFSA	Canadian Fire Safety Association (AC)
CFSA	College Fraternity Secretaries Association [*Later, FEA*] (EA)
CFSA	Saint Agnes Hospital and Medical Center, Fresno, CA [*Library symbol Library of Congress*] (LCLS)
CFSAN	Center for Food Safety and Applied Nutrition [*Washington, DC Department of Health and Human Services*] (GRD)
CFSB...........	CFSB Bancorp [*NASDAQ symbol*] (TTSB)

CFSB	CFSB Bancorp, Inc. [*NASDAQ symbol*] (SAG)
CFSB	Cold-Finished Steel Bar
CFSBI	Cold Finished Steel Bar Institute (EA)
CFSC	Canadian Friends Service Committe [*Also, Religious Society of Friends*] (AC)
CFSC	Community and Family Support Center [*Army*]
CFSC	Cryogenic Fluid Storage Container
CF-SCAN	Canadian Forces - Second Career Assistance Network
CFSCP	Centrally Funded Short Course Program
CFSD	Citizens for Space Demilitarization (EA)
CFSDT	Centrally Funded Second Destination Transportation [*Army*]
CFSE	Carmelite Brothers of the Holy Eucharist [*Roman Catholic religious order*]
CFSE	Crystal Field Stabilization Energy
C/FSE	Customer/Field Support Elements (RDA)
CFSEA	Canadian Food Service Executives Association
CFSEB	Conference of Funeral Service Examining Boards of the United States (EA)
CFSG	Cometary Feasibility Study Group [*European Space Research Organization*] (IEEE)
CFSG/NML	Citizens Forum on Self-Government/National Municipal League [*Information service or system*] (IID)
CFSID	Canadian Foundation for the Study of Infant Deaths [*Fondation Canadienne sur l'Etude de la Mortalite Infantile*] (AC)
CFSJ	Coalition to Free Soviet Jews (EA)
CFSK	Coherent Frequency Shift Keying
CFSK	Saskatoon, SK [*Television station call letters*]
CFSL	Weyburn, SK [*AM radio station call letters*]
CFSLP	Center for Short-Lived Phenomena [*Cambridge, MA*]
CFSN	Confusion (MSA)
CFSO	Canadian Forces Supplementary Order
CFSOA	College Fraternity Scholarship Officers Association
CFSO-BEBO	Crystal Field Surface Orbital-Bond Energy Bond Order [*Model for chemisorption*]
CFSOCQ	Change Facilitator Stages of Concern Questionnaire [*Educational test*]
CFSP	California School of Professional Psychology, Fresno, CA [*Library symbol Library of Congress*] (LCLS)
CFSP	Common Foreign and Security Policy [*European Union*]
CFSP	Contractor Field Services Personnel
CFSPL	Canadian Forces Special Projects Laboratory · (HGAA)
CFSR	Abbotsford-Matsqui, AB [*FM radio station call letters*]
CFSR	Citizens for Social Reponsibility [*Citoyen pour la Conscience Sociale*] [*Formerly, Citizens for Nuclear Responsibility*] (AC)
CFSR	Commission on Financial Structure and Regulation [*White House*]
CFSR	Contract Fund Status Report [*Army*] (AABC)
CFSR	Control Funds Status Report (SSD)
CFSS	Canadian Forces Supply System (MCD)
CFSS	Chronic Fatigue Syndrome Society, International (EA)
CFSS	Combined File Search Strategy [*Computer science*]
CFSS	Committee of French Speaking Societies (EA)
CFSS	Contractor Field Services Support
CFSSA	Canadian Food Service Supervisors Association
CFSSB	Central Flight Status Selection Board [*Air Force*]
CFSSC-K	Community, Family, and Soldier Support Command - Korea [*Army*]
CFSSE	Contractor-Furnished Special Support Equipment (AFIT)
CFSSU	Canadian Forces Supply System Upgrade
CFST	Context-Free Syntactical Translator
CFSTI	Clearinghouse for Federal Scientific and Technical Information [*Later, NTIS*] [*National Institute of Standards and Technology*]
CFSTR	Continuous-Flow Stirred Tank Reactor [*Chemical engineering*]
CFSX	Stephenville, NF [*AM radio station call letters*]
CFT	Canadian Foremost Ltd. [*Toronto Stock Exchange symbol*]
CFT	Captive Flight Trainer
CFT	Caster and Floor Truck Manufacturers Association [*Later, ICM*]
CFT	Charge-Flow Transistor (PDAA)
CFT	Chem. Fabr. Tempelhof [*Germany*] [*Research code symbol*]
CFT	Children's Film Theatre [*Later, Media Center for Children*]
CFT	Clean Fuel Oil Tank (MSA)
CFT	Clifton-Morenci, AZ [*Location identifier FAA*] (FAAL)
CFT	Clinical Full-Time [*Medicine*] (MAE)
CFT	Coated Foam Tape
CFT	Cockpit Familiarization Trainer (MCD)
CFT	Cold Flow Test
CFT	Cold Fluctuating Temperature
CFT	Common Facilities Test [*NASA*] (NASA)
CFT	Complement-Fixation Test [*Immunology*]
CFT	Complex Fourier Transform
CFT	Computer Flight Testing (MCD)
CFT	Concealed Figures Test (EDAC)
CFT	Concept Formation Test [*Psychology*]
CFT	Conformal Fuel Tank (MCD)
CFT	Constant Fraction Trigger (OA)
CFT	Continuous Fourier Transport
CFT	Contract Field Technician
CFT	Contractor Field Team (MCD)
CFT	Contractor/Foreign Testing [*Air Force*]
CFT	Contractor-Furnished Technicians (MCD)
CFT	Core Flood Tank [*Nuclear energy*] (NRCH)
CFT	Craft (AABC)
CFT	Craftsman
CFT	Cray Fortran [*Programming language*] (NITA)
CFT	Crew Factor (SSD)
CFT	Crossed-Field Tube
CFT	Crystal Field Theory [*Chemistry*]

CFT	Cubic Foot (DAS)
CFT	Curd Firmness Tester [*For milk products*]
CFT	Fuller Theological Seminary, Pasadena, CA [*OCLC symbol*] (OCLC)
CFT	Jet Freighters, Inc. [*ICAO designator*] (FAAC)
CFTA	Canadian Film and Television Association
CFTA	Canadian Free Trade Agreement (ECON)
CFTA	CECOM Flight Test Activity [*Lakehurst, NJ*] [*Later, AERA*] [*Army*] (GRD)
CF(TA)	Chaplain to the Forces (Territorial Army) [*British*]
CFTB	Central Freight Tariff Bureau
CFTB	Control Flight Test Bed
CFTB	Cylindrical Fire Tube Boiler [*of a ship*] (DS)
CFTBS	Cylindrical Fire Tube Boiler Survey [*of a ship*] (DS)
CFTC	Canadian Feed the Children (AC)
CFTC	Central Flying Training Command [*AAFCFTC*]
CFTC	Committee on Fair Trade with China [*Medina, WA*] (EA)
CFTC	Commodity Futures Trading Commission [*Formerly, CEA*] [*Independent government agency*]
CFTC	Commonwealth Fund for Technical Co-Operation [*British*] (EAIO)
CFTC	Cooler Flusher Tank Cell [*Nuclear energy*] (NRCH)
CFTCA	Children's Film and Television Center of America (EA)
CFTE	Cooler Flusher Tank Equipment [*Nuclear energy*] (NRCH)
CFTF	Children's Film and Television Foundation [*British*]
CFTG	Context-Free Transduction Grammar (MHDI)
CFTH	Harrington Harbour, PQ [*FM radio station call letters*]
CFTI	Cape Fear Technical Institute [*Wilmington, NC*] (ASF)
CFTK	Terrace, BC [*AM radio station call letters*]
CFTK-TV	Terrace, BC [*Television station call letters*]
CFTM	Captive Flight Test Missiles (MCD)
CFTM	Conversion to Full-Time Manning
CFTM	Montreal, PQ [*Television station call letters*]
CFTMA	Caster and Floor Truck Manufacturers Association [*Later, ICM*] (EA)
CFTMN	Craftsman (MUGU)
CFTMN	Craftsman
Cftn	Craftsman [*Military British*] (DMA)
CFTO	Canadian Forces Technical Orders (MCD)
CFTO	Committee for the Furtherance of Torah Observance (EA)
CFTO	Toronto, ON [*Television station call letters*]
CFTP	Community Federal Bancorp, Inc. [*NASDAQ symbol*] (SAG)
CFTPA	Canadian Film & Television Production Association [*Association Canadienne de Production de Film et Television*] (AC)
CFTR	Citizens for the Republic (EA)
CFTR	Community Federal Bancorp [*NASDAQ symbol*] (TTSB)
CFTR	Crafter
CFTR	Cystic Fibrosis Transmembrane-Conductance Regulator [*Genetics*]
CFTR	Toronto, ON [*AM radio station call letters*]
CFTRI	Central Food Technology Research Institute [*India*]
CFTS	Captive Firing Test Set [*Aerospace*] (AAG)
CFTS	Computerized Flight Test System (PDAA)
CFTT	Controlled Flight Toward Terrain (PDAA)
CFTU	Confederation of Free Trade Unions [*India*]
CFTU	Montreal, PQ [*Television station call letters*]
CFU	CAA Flying Unit [*British ICAO designator*] (FAAC)
CFU	Call Forwarding Unconditional [*Telecommunications*] (DOM)
CFU	Canadian Farmworkers Union (AC)
CFU	Central Firing Unit
CFU	Chartered Financial Underwriter
CFU	Chesterfield, VA [*Location identifier FAA*] (FAAL)
CFU	Colony-Forming Unit [*Cytology*]
CFU	Color Forming Units [*Food technology*]
CFU	Color-Forming Units [*Biochemistry*] (DAVI)
CFU	Control Functional Unit [*Data link*] (NG)
CFU	Corfu [*Greece*] [*Airport symbol*] (OAG)
CFU	Corn-Equivalent Feed Unit
CFU	Covefort [*Utah*] [*Seismograph station code, US Geological Survey*] (SEIS)
CFU	Croatian Fraternal Union of America (EA)
CFU	Current File User [*Computer science*] (OA)
CFU	Fullerton Junior College Library, Fullerton, CA [*OCLC symbol*] (OCLC)
CFUA	Canadian Fire Underwriters' Association [*Later, Canadian Underwriters' Association*]
CFU-C	Colony-Forming Unit - Culture [*Cytology*]
CFU-E	Colony-Forming Unit/Erythroid [*Cytology*]
CFU-Eo	Colony-Forming Unit - Eosinophil [*Cytology*]
CFUeos	Colony-Forming Unit Eosinophil [*Cytology*] (MAE)
CFU-G	Colony Forming Unit-Granulocyte [*Cytology*]
CFU-GEMM	Colony-Forming Unit - Granulocyte-Erythrocyte-Monocyte-Megakaryocyte [*Cytology*]
CFU-GM	Colony-Forming Unit/Granulocyte Macrophage [*Cytology*]
CFUJCF	CFU [*Croatian Fraternal Union of America*] Junior Cultural Federation (EA)
CFU-L	Colony-Forming Unit/Lymphoid [*Cytology*]
CFU-M	Colony-Forming Unit/Megakaryocyte [*Cytology*]
CFU$_{MEG}$	Colony-Forming Unit - Megakaryocyte [*Cytology*] (DAVI)
CFU-mL	Colony-Forming Unit per Milliliter [*Cytology*] (DAVI)
CFUN	Vancouver, BC [*AM radio station call letters*]
CFUnm	Colony-Forming Unit Neutrophil-Monocyte [*Cytology*] (MAE)
CFU-S	Colony-Forming Unit - Single Cell [*Cytology*]
CFUS	Colony-Forming Unit - Spleen [*Cytology*]
CFUSAFA	Committee to Form a US-Albania Friendship Association (EA)
CFUV	Victoria, BC [*FM radio station call letters*]
CFUV-FM	Victoria, BC [*Radio station call letters*]
CFUW	Canadian Federation of University Women

CFV	Cadillac Fairview Corp. Ltd. [*Toronto Stock Exchange symbol Vancouver Stock Exchange symbol*]
CFV	Cavalry Fighting Vehicle
CFV	Clean Fleet Vehicle [*VDOT*] (TAG)
CFV	Clean Fuel Vehicle
CFV	Coffeyville, KS [*Location identifier FAA*] (FAAL)
CFV	Comite des Forces Vives - Hery Velona [*Madagascar*] [*Political party*] (EY)
CFV	Continuous Flow Ventilation [*Medicine*] (DMAA)
CFV	Conventional Friend Virus
CFV	Conventionally Fueled Vehicle [*Automotive engineering*]
CFV	Critical Flow Venturi [*Engineering*]
CFVA	United States Veterans Administration Hospital, Fresno, CA [*Library symbol Library of Congress*] (LCLS)
CFVCO	Canadian Film and Videotape Certification Office
CFV-CVS	Critical Flow Venture-Constant Volume Sampler (ERG)
CFVD	Constant Frequency Variable Dot
CFVD	Degelis, PQ [*FM radio station call letters*]
CFVD-1	Cabano, PQ [*FM radio station call letters*]
CFVD-2	Pohenegamook, PQ [*FM radio station call letters*]
CFVI	Council of Families with Visual Impairment (EA)
CFVI	San Joaquin Valley Information Service, Fresno, CA [*Library symbol Library of Congress*] (LCLS)
CFVM	Amqui, PQ [*AM radio station call letters*]
CFVM	Valley Medical Center, Fresno, CA [*Library symbol Library of Congress*] (LCLS)
CFVS	Council for Fishing Vessel Safety (EA)
CFVS	Val D'Or, PQ [*Television station call letters*]
CFVS-1	Rouyn, PQ [*Television station call letters*]
CFW	Calcofluor White [*A cotton whitener*]
CFW	Cancer-Free White Mouse [*Medicine*] (MEDA)
CFW	Carworth Farm Mouse, Webster Strain [*Medicine*] (DMAA)
CFW	Committee for the Free World (EA)
CFW	Condensate and Feedwater [*Nuclear energy*] (NRCH)
CFW	CONVAIR [*Consolidated-Vultee Aircraft Corp.*] Fort Worth [*Later, General Dynamics/Fort Worth*] (AAG)
CFWB	Campbell River, BC [*AM radio station call letters*]
CFWC	Canadian Federal Warning Center
CFWC	CFW Communications [*NASDAQ symbol*] (TTSB)
CFWC	CFW Communications Co. [*NASDAQ symbol*] (SAG)
CFW Cm	CFW Communications Co. [*Associated Press*] (SAG)
CFWD	Canadian Foundation for World Development (AC)
CFWE	Lac La Biche, AB [*FM radio station call letters*]
CFWE-FM	Regina, SK [*FM radio station call letters*] (RBYB)
CFWH	Whitehorse, YT [*AM radio station call letters*]
CFWH-TV	Whitehorse, YT [*Television station call letters*]
CFWIS	Central Fighter Weapons Instructor School (NATG)
CFWM	Cancer-Free White Mouse [*Medicine*] (MAE)
CFWM	Cancer-Free White Mouse (DMAA)
CFWM	Carworth Farm Mice (Webster strain) [*Research*] (DAVI)
CFWM-FM	Winnipeg, MB [*FM radio station call letters*] (RBYB)
CFWRU	Florida Cooperative Fish and Wildlife Research Unit [*University of Florida*] [*Research center*] (RCD)
CFWS	Condensate and Feedwater System [*Nuclear energy*] (NRCH)
CFWS	Coordinated Federal Wage System (MCD)
CFWSU	Central Flow Weather Service Unit (FAAC)
CFWT	Compressible Flow Wind Tunnel (MCD)
CFWY	Consolidated Freightways [*NASDAQ symbol*] (SAG)
cfx	Brothers of St. Francis Xavier (TOCD)
CFX	Brothers of St. Francis Xavier (TOCD)
CFX	Cadiz, OH [*Location identifier FAA*] (FAAL)
CFX	CFX Corp. [*Formerly, Chesire Financial*] [*AMEX symbol*] (SAG)
CFX	Circumflex [*Coronary artery*] [*Cardiology*] (DAVI)
CFX	Colfax Energy [*Vancouver Stock Exchange symbol*]
CFX	Command Field Exercise [*Military*] (INF)
CFX	Congregatio Fratrum Sancti Francisci Xaverii [*Brothers of St. Francis Xavier*] [*Xaverian Brothers*] [*Roman Catholic religious order*]
CFX	Credit for Exports [*Bank*] [*British*]
CFX	Flexair Ltd. [*British ICAO designator*] (FAAC)
CFX Cp	CFX Corp. [*Formerly, Cheshire Financial*] [*Associated Press*] (SAG)
CFXL	Calgary, AB [*AM radio station call letters*]
CFY	Clarify (FAAC)
CFY	Clinical Fellow Year (BARN)
CFY	Company Fiscal Year (NASA)
CFY	Contractor Fiscal Year (AAGC)
CFY	Current Fiscal Year (AFM)
CFY	Faraday Resources, Inc. [*Toronto Stock Exchange symbol*]
CFYK	Yellowknife, NT [*AM radio station call letters*]
CFYK-TV	Yellowknife, NT [*Television station call letters*]
CFYM	Kindersley, SK [*AM radio station call letters*]
CFZ	Capillary Free Zone [*Medicine*] (DMAA)
CFZ	CFS Group, Inc. [*Toronto Stock Exchange symbol*]
CFZ	Chefornak, AK [*Location identifier FAA*] (FAAL)
CFZ	Contiguous Fisheries Zone [*Offshore*]
CFZ	Critical Friendly Zone [*Army*] (ADDR)
CFZ	Zhongfei General Aviation Co. [*China*] [*FAA designator*] (FAAC)
CFZZ	St. Jean sur Richelieu, PQ [*FM radio station call letters*]
CG	Cage (MSA)
CG	Cairensis Gnosticus [*Nag Hammadi Codices*] (BJA)
CG	Cairo Geniza (BJA)
Cg	Called Game [*Baseball*]
CG	Camera Gun
CG	Canadian Geographic [*A publication*] (BRI)
CG	Capacitance Grid [*Electronics*] (IAA)
CG	Capital Gain [*Accounting*]

CG	Capital Goods [*Business term*]
CG	Capital Guaranteed [*Business term*]
CG	Captain-General
CG	Captain of Gun [*British military*] (DMA)
CG	Captain of the Guard [*Freemasonry*]
CG	Carbonic Dichloride [*Phosgene*] [*Poison gas Army symbol*]
CG	Cardio-Green (Dye) [*Trademark*]
CG	Cargo Glider [*Military*]
CG	Carl Gustav [*King of Sweden*]
CG	Cartoonists Guild (EA)
Cg	Carya glabra [*Pignut hickory*]
CG	Catalogue General des Antiquites Egyptiennes du Musee du Caire (BJA)
CG	Categorical Grammar
CG	Ceiling Grille [*Technical drawings*] (DAC)
CG	Cement Gland [*Embryology*]
CG	Centerless Ground (DNAB)
CG	Center of Gravity
Cg	Centigram
CG	Central Gland [*of the prostate*]
CG	Central Gray [*Brain anatomy*]
CG	Central of Georgia Railroad Co.
Cg	Cephalosporium gramineum [*Plant pathology*]
CG	Cerebral Ganglion [*Medicine*]
CG	Certificate in Gerontology (PGP)
CG	Certificate of Gameness [*Purebred canine award*]
CG	Certified Genealogist
CG	Chain Grate (MSA)
CG	Chairman's Guidance (DOMA)
CG	Change for Good (EA)
CG	Character-Generated [*Refers to electronically produced text*] (WDMC)
CG	Character Generator [*Telecommunications*]
CG	Chemical Gas (MCD)
CG	Chemie Gruenenthal GmbH [*Germany*] [*Research code symbol*]
cg	Chemoglobulin [*Biochemistry*] (DAVI)
CG	[*The*] Children's Garland [*A publication*]
CG	Choking Gas [*US Chemical Corps symbol*]
CG	Choreographers Guild (EA)
CG	Chorionic Gonadotrophin [*Endocrinology*]
CG	Choristers Guild (EA)
CG	Christians in Government (EA)
Cg	Chromogranin [*Biochemistry*]
CG	Chronic Glomerulonephritis [*Medicine*]
CG	Cigar
CG	Ciliary Ganglion [*Neurology*]
CG	Civil Guard [*Air Force*] (MCD)
CG	Clearance Group [*Customs*] (DS)
CG	Clear Glass
CG	Cloud to Ground [*Marine science*] (OSRA)
CG	Cloud to Ground (USDC)
CG	Cloud-to-Ground Lightning [*Meteorology*]
CG	Clubair [*ICAO designator*] (AD)
CG	Clutter Gate
CG	Coalicion Galega [*Spain Political party*] (EY)
CG	Coalition des Gauches [*Left Unity*] [*Transnational party group in the European Parliament*] (ECED)
CG	Coarse Grain (DAC)
CG	Coast Guard
CG	Coconut Grove [*Florida*]
CG	Code Generator (IAA)
CG	Coincidence Gate
C/G	Coincidence Guidance
CG	Coldstream Guards [*British military*]
CG	Collagen-Glycosaminoglycan [*Physiology*]
CG	Colloidal Gold [*Chemistry*]
CG	Color Graphics (MHDI)
CG	Columbia Gas System [*NYSE symbol*] (TTSB)
CG	Columbia Gas System, Inc. [*NYSE symbol Toronto Stock Exchange symbol*] (SPSG)
CG	Combat Group
CG	Commandant General [*British military*] (DMA)
CG	Command Group (MCD)
CG	Command Guidance [*Aerospace*] (AAG)
CG	Commanding General
CG	Commercial Ground (IAA)
CG	Commissary-General
CG	Committee for the Game (EA)
CG	Communications Group [*Air Force*]
CG	Comparison Group
CG	Complete Games [*Baseball*]
CG	Completion Guarantor [*Motion picture financing*] (NTCM)
CG	Compressed Gas (DNAB)
CG	Comptroller General
CG	Computer Graphics (MCD)
CG	Conditional Grant
CG	Congo [*ANSI two-letter standard code*] (CNC)
cg	Congo (Kinshasa) [*Zaire*] [*MARC country of publication code Library of Congress*] (LCCP)
CG	Conjugate Gradient (IAA)
CG	Connradh na Gaedhilge [*The Gaelic League, founded in 1893*]
CG	Consolidated Guidance (RDA)
CG	Consul General
CG	Consultative Group [*NATO*]
CG	Contemporary Games [*A publication*]
CG	Contracted Ground [*Personnel*] (OSRA)

CG	Contract/Grant Numbers [*Database terminology*] (NITA)
CG	Contrast Gate (MCD)
CG	Contributions Greater Than [*Database terminology*] (NITA)
CG	Control Grid
CG	Control Group
CG	Coral Gables [*Florida*]
CG	Corner Guard [*Technical drawings*]
CG	Cost Growth (DNAB)
CG	Counseling and Student Services [*Educational Resources Information Center (ERIC) Clearinghouse*] [*University of North Carolina at Greensboro*] (PAZ)
CG	Course Generator
CG	Covent Garden [*Royal Opera or Royal Ballet*] [*British*]
CG	Cowper Greens [*Political party Australia*]
CG	Cruiser, Guided Missile [*NATO*]
CG	Crushed or Ground
CG	Cryoglobulin [*Clinical medicine*]
CG	Current Gain
CG	Cypriote Geometric (BJA)
CG	Cystine Guanine [*Medicine*] (DMAA)
CG	Glaxo Laboratories Ltd. [*Great Britain*] [*Research code symbol*]
CG	Guided Missile Cruiser [*Navy symbol*]
CG	Phosgene [*Organic chemistry*]
CG	Radio Frequency Component Cable Assemblies [*JETDS nomenclature*] [*Military*] (CET)
CG²	Coconut Grove and Coral Gables [*Florida*]
CG2E	Center Groove Two Edges [*Lumber*] (DAC)
CGA	California Glass Association (SRA)
CGA	California Grocers Association (SRA)
CGA	California Groundwater Association (SRA)
CGA	Canadian Garrison Artillery
CGA	Canadian Gas Association
CGA	Canadian Guard Association [*Association Canadienne des Gardiens*] (AC)
CGA	Cape Garrison Artillery [*British military*] (DMA)
CGA	Cargo's Proportion of (General) Average [*Shipping*]
CGA	Caribbean Gamefishing Association
CGA	Carrier Group Alarm [*Telecommunications*]
CGA	Catabolite Gene Activator [*Medicine*] (DMAA)
CGA	Catholic Golden Age (EA)
CGA	Center for Growth Alternatives [*Defunct*] (EA)
CGA	Central Grant Aid [*British*]
CGA	Central Guaranty Trustco Ltd. [*Toronto Stock Exchange symbol*]
CGA	Central of Georgia Railroad Co. [*AAR code*]
CGA	Certified General Accountant
CGA	Certified Graphoanalyst
CGA	Chlorogenic Acid [*Organic chemistry*]
CGA	Chromogranin A [*Biochemistry*]
CGA	Citizens Global Action (EA)
CGA	Clutter Gate Amplifier (MCD)
CGA	Coal-Gas Atmosphere (MCD)
CGA	Coast Guard Academy
CGA	Coast Guard Auxiliary
CGA	Colloidal Gas Aphron [*Physical chemistry*]
CGA	Color/Graphics Adapter [*Computer technology*]
CGA	Color Guild Associates (EA)
CGA	Cornerstone Natural Gas [*Formerly, Endevco, Inc.*] [*AMEX symbol*] (SPSG)
CGA	Community of the Glorious Ascension [*Anglican religious community*]
CGA	Compensator Group Adapter [*Military*] (CAAL)
CGA	Comprehensive Geriatric Assessment [*Medicine*] (CPH)
CGA	Compressed Gas Association (EA)
CGA	Compressed Gas Association, Inc. (AAGC)
CGA	Concord Grape Association (EA)
CGA	Congressional Air Ltd. [*ICAO designator*] (FAAC)
CGA	Contemporary Graphic Artists [*A publication*]
CGA	Contrast Gate Amplifier
CGA	Control Group Adapter (MCD)
CGA	Converging Guide Accelerator (MCD)
CGA	Council on Gift Annuities [*Informal name for the American Council on Gift Annuities*] (NFD)
CGA	Country Gentlemen's Association [*British*]
CGA	Craig [*Alaska*] [*Airport symbol*] (OAG)
CGA	Cylinder Gas Audit
CGA	United States Coast Guard Academy, New London, CT [*OCLC symbol*] (OCLC)
CGAA	Computer Graphics for Aerodynamic Analysis (MCD)
CGAA	Copa Girls Alumnae Association (EA)
CGAAF	Commanding General, Army Air Forces
CGAB	Coast Guard Air Base
CGAC	China General Aviation Corp. [*ICAO designator*] (FAAC)
CGAC	[*The*] Commonwealth Games Association of Canada Inc. [*Association Canadienne des Jeux du Commonwealth Inc.*] (AC)
CGACTEUR	Coast Guard Activities Europe
CGADC	Commanding General, Air Defense Command (NATG)
CGADS	Computer-Generated Acquisition Documents System (AAGC)
CGAES	Coffee Growers' Association of El Salvador [*Defunct*] (EA)
CGAIRDET	Coast Guard Air Detachment
CGAIRFMFPAC	Commanding General, Aircraft Fleet Marine Force, Pacific (MUGU)
CGAIRFMLANT	Commanding General, Aircraft Fleet Marine Force, Atlantic (NATG)
CGAL	Central Georgia Associated Libraries [*Library network*]
CGAL	Comprehensive General and Automobile Liability [*Insurance*]
CGAM	Coast Guard Achievement Medal [*Military decoration*]

CGAMEEC	Committee of Glutamic Acid Manufacturers of the European Economic Community (EAIO)
CGANC	Corn Growers Association of North Carolina (SRA)
CGand	Collationes Gandavenses (BJA)
CG & TFL	California Grape and Tree Fruit League (EA)
CGAP	Cancer Genome Anatomy Project [*A Cooperative database*]
CGARA	Commission Generale de l'Assurance du Risque Atomique [*Paris, France*] (EAIO)
CGARADCOM	Commanding General, United States Army Air Defense Command (MUGU)
CGARF	CGA - Canada Research Foundation (AC)
CGARP	Committee for the Global Atmospheric Research Program
CGarP	Professional Media Service Corp., Gardena, CA [*Library symbol*] [*Library of Congress*] (LCLS)
CGARY	Central of Georgia Railroad Co.
CGAS	Class G Airspace [*Aviation*] (FAAC)
CGAS	Clinton Gas System [*NASDAQ symbol*] (TTSB)
CGAS	Clinton Gas Systems, Inc. [*NASDAQ symbol*] (NQ)
CGAS	Coast Guard Air Station
CGAS	Cooled-Grating Array Spectrometer [*Instrumentation*]
CGASC	Cornell-Guggenheim Aviation Safety Center (SAA)
CGAT	Chromaffin Granule Amine Transporter [*Biochemistry*]
CGAU	Cabin Gas Analysis Unit [*Aviation*] (NASA)
CGB	Air Cargo Belize Ltd. [*FAA designator*] (FAAC)
CGB	Central Gear Box (MCD)
CGB	Ceramics and Graphite Branch [*Air Force*]
CGB	Chronic Gastrointestinal [*Tract*] Bleeding [*Gastroenterology*] (DAVI)
CGB	Chronic Gonadotropin, Beta-Unit [*Medicine*] (DMAA)
CGB	Coldspring Resources [*Vancouver Stock Exchange symbol*]
CGB	Commonwealth Geographical Bureau (EA)
CGB	Convert Gray to Binary
CGB	Corpus Glossariorum Biblicorum (BJA)
CGB	Cuiaba [*Brazil*] [*Airport symbol*] (OAG)
CGBASE	Coast Guard Base
CGBCA	Coast Guard Board of Contract Appeals [*A publication*] (AAGC)
CGBR	Central Government Borrowing Requirement [*British*]
CGC	Caenorhabditis [*Nematode*] Genetics Center
CGC	Calavo Growers of California (EA)
CGC	Canadian Geophysics Congress (AC)
CGC	Canadian Geoscience Council [*Conseil Geoscientifique Canadien*] (AC)
CGC	Canine Good Citizen [*Purebred canine award*]
CGC	Cape Gloucester [*Papua New Guinea*] [*Airport symbol*] (OAG)
CGC	Capillary Gas Chromatograph
CGC	Cascade Natural Gas [*NYSE symbol*] (TTSB)
CGC	Cascade Natural Gas Corp. [*NYSE symbol*] (SPSG)
CGC	Cathode-Grid Capacitance
CGC	Census Grievance Committee [*Vietnam*]
CGC	Ceramic Gold Coating
CGC	Certified Gastrointestinal Clinician (MEDA)
CGC	Church Growth Center (EA)
CGC	Circuit Group Congestion [*Telecommunications*] (TEL)
CGC	Clebsch-Gordan Coefficients [*Mathematics*]
CGC	Coast Guard Cutter
CGC	Color Graphics Converter [*Computer science*]
CGC	Combat Gap Crosser [*Army*]
CGC	Command Guidance Computer (NASA)
CGC	Computer Guidance Corp.
CGC	Computerized Gas Chromatography
CGC	Connecticut Guild of Craftsmen (SRA)
CGC	Consumers Packaging, Inc. [*Toronto Stock Exchange symbol*]
CGC	Craig [*Colorado*] [*Seismograph station code, US Geological Survey Closed*] (SEIS)
CGC	Critical Grid Current
CGC	Cross-Guide Coupler
CGC	Cruise Guidance Control [*Aviation*]
CGC	Cruiser, Guided Missile and Command [*NATO*]
CGC	Cryogenic Gas Chromatography
CGCA	Canadian Guidance and Counselling Association
CGCA	Controller General of Civil Aviation [*British*]
CGCARC	Commanding General, Continental Army Command (NATG)
CGCCL	Cutaneous Germinal Center Cell-Derived Lymphomas
CGCF	Canadian Guidance & Counselling Foundation (AC)
CGCM	Coast Guard Commendation Medal [*Military decoration*]
CGCM	Coupled General Circulation Model
CGCM	Coupled Global Climate Model
CGCM	Court Martial Reports, Coast Guard Cases [*New York*] [*A publication*] (DLA)
CGCMM	Coast Guard Court-Martial Manual [*A publication*] (DLA)
CGCMS	Special Court-Martial, Coast Guard [*United States*] (DLA)
CGCO	Commerce Group [*NASDAQ symbol*] (TTSB)
CGCO	Commerce Group Corp. [*NASDAQ symbol*] (NQ)
CGCONARC	Commanding General, Continental Army Command (NATG)
CGCP	CardioGenesis Corp. [*NASDAQ symbol*] (SAG)
CGCP	CardioGenesis Corp. [*NASDAQ symbol*] (TTSB)
CGCP	Catalogue of the Greek Coins of Palestine [*A publication*] (BJA)
CGCP	Climate and Global Change Program [*Marine science*] (OSRA)
CGCP	Climate and Global Change Program [*National Oceanic and Atmospheric Administration*] (USDC)
CGCP	Combined Ground Command Post (MCD)
CGCRUITSTA	Coast Guard Recruiting Station
CGCS	Combustion Gas Control System [*Nuclear energy*] (NRCH)
CGCS	Council of the Great City Schools (EA)
CGCS	Cover Gas Clean-Up System [*Nuclear energy*] (NUCP)
CGCV	Ceramic Gravitational Containment Vessel [*i.e., cup*] [*Slang*]

CGCVA .... Coast Guard Combat Veterans Association (EA)
CGD .... Canguard Health Technologies, Inc. [*Vancouver Stock Exchange symbol*]
CGD .... Center of Genetic Diversity
CGD .... Charlotte, NC Air National Guard [*FAA designator*] (FAAC)
CGD .... Chromosomal Gonadal Dysgenesis [*Genetics*] (AAMN)
CGD .... Chronic Granulomatous Disease [*Medicine*]
CGD .... Coast Guard District
CGD .... Coast Guard Docket
CGD .... Commissural Gastric Driver [*Neurology*]
CGD .... Commonwealth Government Directory [*Australia A publication*]
CGD .... Comptroller General's Decision
CGDB .... Canadian Guide Dogs for the Blind (AC)
CGDE .... Contact Glow Discharge Electrolysis
CGDina .... Consorcio G Grupo Dina SA de CV [*Commercial firm Associated Press*] (SAG)
CGDIST .... Coast Guard District
CGDK .... Coalition Government of Democratic Kampuchea
CGDN .... Canadian Genetic Diseases Network (AC)
CGDN .... Comptroller General's Decision (AAGC)
CGD-NAGC .. North American Gladiolus Council, Commercial Growers Division [*Defunct*] (EA)
CGDO .... Coast Guard District Office
CGDS .... Computer Graphics Display System [*Army*] (MCD)
CGDV .... Canine Gastric Dilatation-Volvulus [*Veterinary medicine*]
CGE .... Cambridge, MD [*Location identifier FAA*] (FAAL)
CGE .... Canadian General Electric Co. Ltd. [*Toronto Stock Exchange symbol*]
CGE .... Capillary Gel Electrophoresis
CGE .... Carriage
CGE .... Center for Global Education (EA)
CGE .... Certificate of General Education
CGE .... Chadwick-Goldhaber Effect [*Physics*]
CGE .... Charge
CGE .... Children of the Green Earth (EA)
CGE .... Cobalt Gray Equivalent [*Radiology*]
CGE .... Cockpit Geometry Evaluation [*Computer program*] [*Boeing Co.*]
CGE .... Compagnie Generale d'Electricite [*General Electric Company*] [*France*]
CGE .... Compagnie Generale des Eaux
CGE .... Compagnie Generale Electrique du Canada [*Canadian General Electric Co. Ltd.*]
CGE .... Controller General of Economy [*Military British*]
CGE .... Cortical Granule Exocytosis [*Cytology*]
CGE .... Cresyl Glycidyl Ether [*Organic chemistry*]
CGE .... European Business Information
CGE .... Nelson Aviation College [*New Zealand*] [*ICAO designator*] (FAAC)
CGEA .... California Geotechnical Engineers Association (SRA)
CGED .... Caribbean Group for Cooperation in Economic Development (EA)
CGEL .... Cover Gas Evaluation Loop [*Nuclear energy*] (NRCH)
CGen .... Chaplain General [*British*] (DAS)
CGEN .... Collagen Corp. [*NASDAQ symbol*] (NQ)
CGEN .... Comptroller General Decisions [*CCH*] [*A publication*] (AAGC)
CGEN .... Consul General
CGEOSq .... Cartographic Geodetic Squadron [*Air Force*]
CGER .... Caisse Generale d'Epargne et de Retraite [*State-owned bank*] [*Belgium*] (EY)
CGES .... Colonial Gas [*NASDAQ symbol*] (TTSB)
CGES .... Colonial Gas Co. [*NASDAQ symbol*] (NQ)
CGF .... Carr Gottstein Foods [*NYSE symbol*] (SAG)
CGF .... Carr-Gottstein Foods [*NYSE symbol*] (TTSB)
CGF .... Carr-Gottstein Foods, Inc. [*NYSE symbol*] (SPSG)
CGF .... Carrier Gas Fusion [*Chemistry*]
CGF .... Central Group of Forces (MCD)
CGF .... Centre of Gravity Factor [*Yachting*]
CGF .... Chemotaxis-Generating Factor
CGF .... Child Growth Foundation [*British*] (DBA)
CGF .... Chondrocyte Growth Factor [*Biochemistry*]
CGF .... Cleveland, OH [*Location identifier FAA*] (FAAL)
CGF .... Coarse Glass Frit
CGF .... College of Great Falls [*Montana*]
CGF .... Comicorum Graecorum Fragmenta [*A publication*] (OCD)
CGF .... Commonwealth Games Federation [*British*] (EAIO)
CGF .... Computer Generated Forces [*Army*]
CGF .... Consolidated Gold Fields [*British*]
CGF .... Czech Government Flying Service [*ICAO designator*] (FAAC)
CGFA .... California Grain annd Feed Association (SRA)
CGFA .... Colorado Grain and Feed Association (SRA)
CGFAB .... Catholic Guild for All the Blind [*Later, CCB*] (EA)
CGFC .... Crystal Gayle Fan Club [*Defunct*] (EA)
CGFMF .... Commanding General, Fleet Marine Force (DNAB)
CGFMFLANT... Commanding General, Fleet Marine Force, Atlantic (NATG)
CGFMFPAC... Commanding General, Fleet Marine Force, Pacific (MUGU)
CGFNS .... Commission on Graduates of Foreign Nursing Schools (EA)
CGFP .... Calcined Gross Fission Product
CGFPI .... Consultative Group on Food Production and Investment in Developing Countries [*United Nations*]
CGFPS .... Conference Group on French Politics and Society (EA)
CGG .... Canadian General Capital [*NYSE symbol*] (SAG)
CGG .... Chicken Gamma-Globulin [*Immunology*]
CGG .... Continuous Grinding Gauge
CGGA .... China, Glass, and Giftware Association (EA)
CGGA .... Colorado Greenhouse Growers Association (SRA)
CGGB .... Composers' Guild of Great Britain (EAIO)
CGGBT .... China, Glass, Giftware Board of Trade [*Later, CGGA*] (EA)
CGGC .... Constitution General Grand Chapter [*Freemasonry*] (ROG)

CGGCM .... Coast Guard Good Conduct Medal
CGGE .... Constant Gradient Gel Electrophoresis [*Medicine*] (DMAA)
CGGI .... Carbide/Graphite Group [*NASDAQ symbol*] (TTSB)
CGGI .... [*The*] Carbide/Graphite Group, Inc. [*NASDAQ symbol*] (SAG)
CGGLF .... Canadian Give the Gift of Literacy Foundation (AC)
CGGP .... Conference Group on German Politics (EA)
CGGPrT .... Canadian Genl Cp 9.125%'TOPrS' [*NYSE symbol*] (TTSB)
CGH .... Cape of Good Hope [*South Africa*] [*Seismograph station code, US Geological Survey Closed*] (SEIS)
CGH .... Chorionic Gonadotrophin Hormone [*Endocrinology*] (AAMN)
CGH .... Chorionic Gonadotrophin, Human [*Endocrinology*]
CGH .... Commercial Ground High (IAA)
CGH .... Comparative Genomic Hybridization [*Biochemistry*]
CGH .... Computalog Gearhart Ltd. [*Toronto Stock Exchange symbol*]
CGH .... Computer-Generated Hologram
CGH .... Computer-Generated Hologram
CGH .... Congenital Generalized Hypertrichosis [*Medicine*]
CGH .... Congenital Generalized Hypertrichosis [*Werewolf syndrome*] [*Medicine*]
CGH .... Cough [*Medicine*]
CGH .... Guizhon Airlines [*China*] [*FAA designator*] (FAAC)
CGH .... Sao Paulo [*Brazil*] Congonhas Airport [*Airport symbol*] (OAG)
CGHL .... Cutaneous Genuine Histiocytic Lymphoma
CGHS .... Computer-Generated Holographic Scanner [*Instrumentation*]
CGI .... Canadian General Investments Ltd. [*Toronto Stock Exchange symbol*]
CGI .... Cancer Guidance Institute (EA)
CGI .... Cape Girardeau [*Missouri*] [*Airport symbol*] (OAG)
CGI .... Capital Guaranty Insurance
CGI .... Carbimazole [*Pharmacology*] (DAVI)
CGI .... Certified Genealogical Instructor
CGI .... Chief Ground Instructor [*British military*] (DMA)
CGI .... Chief Gunnery Instructor [*British military*] (DMA)
CGI .... City and Guilds [*of London*] Institute (BARN)
CGI .... Clinical General Impression [*Psychiatric testing*]
CGI .... Clinical Global Impression [*Scale*] PY (DAVI)
CGI .... Coalition on Government Information (EA)
CGI .... Cognizant Government Inspector (SAA)
CGI .... Color Graphics Indicator (HGAA)
CGI .... Commerce Group, Inc. [*NYSE symbol*] (SAG)
CGI .... Common Gateway Interface [*Standard that extends the functionality of Web servers*] [*Computer science*]
CGI .... Communications Group, Inc. [*Concord, MA*] [*Telecommunications*] (TSSD)
CGI .... Compacted Graphite Iron [*Metallurgical engineering*]
CGI .... Computer-Generated Imagery
CGI .... Computer Graphics Interface
CGI .... Computer-Guided Instruction (IAA)
CGI .... Conseillers en Gestion et Informatique [*Montreal, PQ*] [*Telecommunications service*] (TSSD)
CGI .... Corrugated Galvanized Iron
CGI .... Cruise Guide Indicator [*Aviation*]
CGi .... Gilroy Free Public Library, Gilroy, CA [*Library symbol Library of Congress*] (LCLS)
CGIA .... City and Guilds of London Insignia Award [*British*]
CGIAR .... Consultative Group on International Agricultural Research (EA)
CGIBT .... Commanding General, India-Burma Theater [*World War II*]
CGIC .... Ceramics and Graphite Information Center [*Air Force*]
CGIC .... Clinical Global Impression of Change
CGIC .... Compressed-Gas-Insulated Cable
CGIF .... Cherry Growers and Industries Foundation (EA)
CGIIP .... Coast Guard International Ice Patrol (NOAA)
CGIP .... Compagnie Generale d'Industrie et de Participations
CGIP .... Computer Graphics and Image Processing (MCD)
CGIP .... Conference Group on Italian Politics (EDAC)
CGIS .... Canada Geographic Information System [*Canada Land Data Systems Division*] [*Environment Canada*] [*Information service or system*] (IID)
CGIS .... COMSAT [*Communications Satellite Corp.*] General Integrated System (NITA)
CGIT .... Compressed-Gas-Insulated Transmission Line
CGIVS .... Computer-Generated Image Visual System (MCD)
CGIX .... Camegie Group [*NASDAQ symbol*] (TTSB)
CGIX .... Carnegie Group, Inc. [*NASDAQ symbol*] (SAG)
C$_{GK}$ .... Grid Cathode Capacitance (IDOE)
CGKT .... Confederation Generale Kamerounaise du Travail [*Cameroonian General Confederation of Workers*]
CGL .... Cagle's, Inc. [*AMEX symbol*] (SPSG)
CGL .... Center-of-Gravity Locator
CGL .... Centro Gerontologico Latino [*An association*] (EA)
CGL .... Certified Genealogical Lecturer
CGL .... Charge Generation Layer (MCD)
CGL .... Children of Gays/Lesbians [*Later, CGP*] (EA)
CGL .... Chronic Granulocytic Leukemia [*Medicine*]
CGL .... Circling Guidance Light [*Aviation*] (FAAC)
CGL .... Coast Guard League (EA)
CGL .... Coghlan Island, AK [*Location identifier FAA*] (FAAL)
CGL .... Command Guard List [*Navy*] (CAAL)
CGL .... Comprehensive General Liability [*Insurance*]
CGL .... Computer Generated Letter
CGL .... Conglomerate [*Lithology*]
CGL .... Continuous Gas LASER
CGL .... Controlled Ground Landing (AAG)
CGL .... Coral Energy Corp. [*Vancouver Stock Exchange symbol*]
CGL .... Corpus Glossariorum Latinorum (BJA)

CGL............ Corrected Geomagnetic Latitude
cgl .... Correction with Glasses [*Optometry*] (MAE)
CGI............ Glendale Public Library, Glendale, CA [*Library symbol Library of Congress OCLC symbol*] (LCLS)
CGLA .... Cagle's Inc. 'A' [*AMEX symbol*] (TTSB)
CGLA .... Columbia Gay and Lesbian Alliance (EA)
CGLAS .... Center for Great Lakes and Aquatic Sciences [*University of Michigan*]
CGLASTA..... Coast Guard Light Attendant Station
CGLAT .... Cassel Group Level of Aspiration Test [*Psychology*]
CGLBSTA.... Coast Guard Lifeboat Station
CGL Bull...... Coast Guard Law Bulletin [*A publication*] (DLA)
CGIC .... Glendale College, Glendale, CA [*Library symbol Library of Congress*] (LCLS)
CGICC .... Los Angeles College of Chiropractic, Glendale, CA [*Library symbol Library of Congress*] (LCLS)
CGLE........... Complex Ginzburg-Landau Equation [*Physics*] [*For study of spatio temporal chaos*]
CGle........... Glendora Public Library, Glendora, CA [*Library symbol Library of Congress*] (LCLS)
CGIF........... Forest Lawn Museum, Glendale, CA [*Library symbol Library of Congress*] (LCLS)
CGL/GLT ...... Corrected Geomagnetic Latitude and Geomagnetic Local Time (DICI)
CGLI........... City and Guilds of London Institute [*British*] (AIE)
CGLIHA....... Coastwise-Great Lakes and Inland Hull Association [*Defunct*] (EA)
CGLKR......... Cleaning Gear Locker
CGIL........... General Precision, Inc., Librascope Division, Glendale, CA [*Library symbol Library of Congress*] (LCLS)
CGLM........... Classical General Linear Model [*Statistics*]
CGLORSTA... Coast Guard LORAN [*Long-Range Aid to Navigation*] Transmitting Station
CGLS .... Center for Great Lakes Studies [*University of Wisconsin - Milwaukee*] [*Research center*] (RCD)
CGLS .... Coast Guard LORAN [*Long-Range Aid to Navigation*] Station
CGIS .... Glendale Sanitarium and Hospital, Glendale, CA [*Library symbol Library of Congress*] (LCLS)
CGLSP .... Consortium of Graduate Liberal Studies Programs (EA)
CGLTG .... Cloud-to-Ground Lightning [*Meteorology*] (KSC)
CGLTSTA..... Coast Guard Light Station
CGIWD........ WED [*Walt E. Disney*] Enterprises, Inc., Research Library, Glendale, CA [*Library symbol Library of Congress*] (LCLS)
CGM........... Cairngorm [*Type of quartz*] (ROG)
CGM........... Cape Girardeau [*Missouri*] [*Seismograph station code, US Geological Survey*] (SEIS)
CGM........... Cargoman [*Oman*] [*ICAO designator*] (FAAC)
CGM........... Centigram
CGM........... Central Gray Matter [*Physiology*]
CGM........... Chief Gunner's Mate [*Navy rating Obsolete*]
CGM........... Christian Government Movement [*Defunct*] (EA)
CGM........... Ciliated Groove to Mouth
CGM........... Coarse-Grained Material (MCD)
CGM........... Coffin Ground-Attack Missile
CGM........... Computer Graphics Metafile
CGM........... Congoleum Corp. [*NYSE symbol*] (SAG)
CGM........... Congoleum Corp.'A' [*NYSE symbol*] (TTSB)
CGM........... Conspicuous Gallantry Medal [*British*]
CGM........... Corn Gluten Meal
CGM........... Corrected Geomagnetic Time
CGM........... Grant MacEwan Community College Library Technology Program, Edmonton, AB, Canada [*OCLC symbol*] (OCLC)
CGMA .... Casein Glue Manufacturers Association [*British*] (BI)
CGMAG........ Commanding General, Marine Aircraft Group
CGMAP....... Conjugate Gradient Method of Approximate Programming
CGMARBRIG... Commanding General, Marine Brigade
CGMAW....... Commanding General, Marine Aircraft Wing
CGMB .... Commanding General, Marine Base
CGMCBG..... Chief Gunner's Mate, Construction Battalion, Armorer [*Navy rating Obsolete*]
CGMCBP..... Chief Gunner's Mate, Construction Battalion, Powderman [*Navy rating Obsolete*]
CGMCU....... Council of General Motors Credit Unions [*Warren, MI*] (EA)
CGMI .... Church of God, Men International (EA)
CGMIS .... Commanding General's Management Information System [*Army*]
CGMMV....... Cucumber Green Mottle Mosaic Virus [*Plant pathology*]
CGMO........ Coast and Geodetic Magnetic Observatory
CGMP .... Controller General of Munitions Production [*Ministry of Supply*] [*British*]
CGMP .... Current Good Manufacturing Practice [*Food and Drug Administration*]
cGMP......... Cyclic Guanosine Monophosphate [*Biochemistry*]
CGMS......... Coordination of Geostationary Meteorological Satellites [*National Oceanic and Atmospheric Administration*]
CGMS .... Cover Gas Monitoring Subsystem [*Nuclear energy*] (NRCH)
CGMT........ Census of Graduate Medical Trainees
CGMT........ Controller General of Machine Tools [*Ministry of Supply*] [*British*]
CGMTO .... Commanding General, Mediterranean Theater of Operations [*World War II*]
CGMV........ Cedar Group [*NASDAQ symbol*] (TTSB)
CGMV........ Cedar Group, Inc. [*NASDAQ symbol*] (SAG)
CGMW........ Commission for the Geological Map of the World [*Marine science*] (OSRA)
CGN........... Changan Airlines [*China*] [*FAA designator*] (FAAC)
CGN........... Chronic Glomerulonephritis [*Medicine*]
CGN........... Cognitronics Corp. [*AMEX symbol*] (SPSG)
CGN........... Cologne/Bonn [*Germany Airport symbol*] (OAG)
CGN........... Convalescent Growing Nursery (MEDA)

CGN .... Coordinadora Guerrillera Nacional [*Colorado*] (EY)
CGN .... CTG Compression Technology Group, Inc. [*Vancouver Stock Exchange symbol*]
CGN .... Glendale College Library, Glendale, CA [*OCLC symbol*] (OCLC)
CGN .... Guided Missile Cruiser (Nuclear Propulsion) [*Navy symbol*]
CGNA .... Canadian Gerontological Nursing Association (AC)
CGNB .... Composite Ganglioneuroblastoma [*Oncology*]
CGNE .... Calgene, Inc. [*NASDAQ symbol*] (NQ)
CGNG .... Collodion Glass Negative (VRA)
CGNSE .... Changes in Global National Security Environment (DOMA)
CGNX .... Cognex Corp. [*NASDAQ symbol*] (NQ)
CGO .... Canadian Gold Resources [*Vancouver Stock Exchange symbol*]
CGO .... Can Go Over [*Newspapers*]
cgo........... Can Go Over (WDMC)
CGO .... Can Go Over (WDMC)
CGO .... Cargo (AABC)
CGO .... Chengchow [*China*] [*Airport symbol*] (AD)
CGO .... Chicago Air, Inc. [*ICAO designator*] (FAAC)
CGO .... Cogeco, Inc. [*Toronto Stock Exchange symbol*]
CGO .... Coker Gas Oil
CGO .... Committee on Government Operations
CGO .... Comptroller General Opinion
CGO .... Comptroller General's Opinion (AAGC)
CGO .... Contango [*Premium or interest paid*] [*London Stock Exchange*]
CGO .... Contracts Group Office
CGO .... Conventional Grain-Oriented Product (MCD)
CGO .... Council of Georgist Organizations (EA)
CGO .... Zhengzhou [*China*] [*Airport symbol*] (OAG)
CGOAP......... Conjugate Gradient Optimization Algorithm Program [*Lighting system design*]
CGOB .... Coast Guard Operating Base
CGOFE .... CONVAIR [*Consolidated-Vultee Aircraft Corp.; later, General Dynamics Corp.*] Government-Owned Facilities and Equipment (AAG)
CGoGS .... Church of Jesus Christ of Latter-Day Saints, Genealogical Society Library, SantaBarbara Branch, Goleta, CA [*Library symbol Library of Congress*] (LCLS)
CGOPHEOSE... Consultative Group on Potentially Harmful Effects of Space Experiments
CG/OQ .... Cerebral Glucose Oxygen Quotient [*Medicine*] (MAE)
CGOR .... Computer Guided Optical Registration [*VISCOM Optical Products, Inc.*]
CGoR .... Raytheon Co., Goleta, CA [*Library symbol Library of Congress*] (LCLS)
CGOS .... Combat Gunnery Officers School [*Army Air Forces*]
CGOS .... Computervision Graphics Operating System (MHDI)
CGOT .... Canadian Government Office of Tourism
CGOU .... Coast Guard Oceanographic Unit
CGP .... Cal Graphite Corp. [*Vancouver Stock Exchange symbol*]
CGP .... Canadian Group of Painters [*1933-69*] (NGC)
CGP .... Capacitance Grid Plate [*Electronics*] (IAA)
CGP .... Captain-General and President (ROG)
CGP .... Central Graphics Processor [*Computer science*] (NITA)
CGP .... Central Grounding Point (NASA)
CGP .... Certified Guitar Player [*Monogram used by Chet Atkins*]
CGP .... Chicago Public Library, Chicago, IL [*OCLC symbol*] (OCLC)
CGP .... Children of Gay Parentage (EA)
CGP .... Chittagong [*Bangladesh*] [*Airport symbol*] (OAG)
CGP .... Choline Glycerophosphatide (MAE)
CGP .... Chorionic Growth Hormone - Prolactin [*Also, HCS, HPL*] [*Endocrinology*]
CGP .... Circulating Granulocyte Pool [*Hematology*]
CGP .... Coalition for Government Procurement (EA)
CGP .... [*The*] Coastal Corp. [*Formerly, Coastal States Gas Producing Co.*] [*NYSE symbol*] (SPSG)
CGP .... Coast Guard Pension [*British*] (ROG)
CGP .... College of General Practitioners [*British*] (BI)
CGP .... Color Graphics Printer
CGP .... Comando Guerrilleros del Pueblo [*Guerrilla group*] [*Guatemala*] (EY)
CGP .... Commission on Government Procurement [*Terminated, 1973*]
CGP .... Comparative Guidance and Placement Program (EDAC)
CGP .... Computer Graphics Processing (HGAA)
C$_{GP}$........... Grid Plate Capacitance (IDOE)
CGP .... N-Carbobenzoxy-Glycyl-L-Phenylalanine (BABM)
CGPA .... Canadian Gas Processors Association (AC)
CGPA .... Canadian Group Psychotherapy Association (AC)
CGPA .... Council of Governors Policy Advisors (EA)
CGPAA......... China, Glass, and Pottery Association of America [*Later, CGGA*] (EA)
CGPC .... Canadian Government Photo Centre
CGPC .... Cellular General Purpose Computer
CGPC .... Coast Guard Patrol Cutter
CGPF .... Church of God Peace Fellowship (EA)
CGPI .... CollaGenex Pharmaceuticals, Inc. [*NASDAQ symbol*] (SAG)
CGPL .... Conversational Graphical Programming Language (PDAA)
CGPM .... Conseil General des Peches pour la Mediterranee [*General Fisheries Council for the Mediterranean*]
CGPM .... General Conference on Weights and Measures (ACII)
CGPP .... Comparative Guidance and Placement Program [*College Entrance Examination Board*]
CGPPrA........ Coastal Corp. $1.19 Cv A Pfd [*NYSE symbol*] (TTSB)
CGPPrB........ Coastal Corp. $1.83 Cv B Pfd [*NYSE symbol*] (TTSB)
CGPPrH........ Coastal Corp.$2.125 cm Pfd [*NYSE symbol*] (TTSB)
CGPR .... Coast Guard Procurement Regulations
CGPR .... Computer-Generated Purchase Request

CGPS	Canadian Government Purchasing Service (PDAA)
CGPSq	Cartographic and Geodetic Processing Squadron [*Air Force*] (AFM)
CGQ	Changchun [*China*] [*Airport symbol*] (OAG)
CGQ	Conseil de la Gravure du Quebec [*1978, founded 1971 as AGQ, CQE from 1984*] [*Canada*] (NGC)
CGQ	Consolidated Gold Standard Resources, Inc. [*Vancouver Stock Exchange symbol*]
CGQ	Corsicana, TX [*Location identifier FAA*] (FAAL)
CGR	Campo Grande [*Brazil*] [*Airport symbol*] (OAG)
CGR	Canadian Arrow Mines Ltd. [*Toronto Stock Exchange symbol*]
CGR	Canadian Garrison Regiment (DMA)
CGR	Captured Gamma Ray
CGR	Center for Governmental Research, Inc. [*Research center*] (RCD)
CGR	Citizens for Governmental Restraint (EA)
CGR	Coast Guard Regulations [*A publication*] (DLA)
CGR	Coast Guard Reserve
CGR	Coliform Growth Response [*Bioassay*]
CGR	Compagnia Generale Ripreseaeree, SPA [*Italy*] [*FAA designator*] (FAAC)
CGR	Cooker Restaurant [*NYSE symbol*] (TTSB)
CGR	Cooker Restaurant, Inc. [*NYSE symbol*] (SAG)
CGR	Crime on Government Reservation
CGR	Crop Growth Rate (OA)
CGr	Grass Valley Free Public Library, Grass Valley, CA [*Library symbol Library of Congress*] (LCLS)
CGR	United States Coast Guard Research and Development Center Library, Groton, CT [*OCLC symbol*] (OCLC)
CGRA	Canadian Good Roads Association
CGRA	China and Glass Retailers Association [*British*] (DBA)
CGRADSTA	Coast Guard Radio Station
CGRAM	Clock Generator Random-Access Memory [*Computer science*] (OA)
CGR & MOT for S	Captain-General of the Religious and Military Order of the Temple for Scotland [*Freemasonry*] (ROG)
CGR/DC	Coast Guard Research and Development Center [*Groton, CT*]
CGRDO	Coast Guard Radio (NOAA)
CGRG	Computer Graphics Research Group [*Ohio State University*] [*Research center*] (RCD)
CGRI	Canadian Gas Research Institute [*Canadian Gas Association*] (IRC)
CGRI	Center for Governmental Research Inc. (EA)
CGrI	Gridley Public Library, Gridley, CA [*Library symbol Library of Congress*] (LCLS)
CGrIGS	Church of Jesus Christ of Latter-Day Saints, Genealogy Society Library, Gridley Branch, Gridley, CA [*Library symbol Library of Congress*] (LCLS)
CGRM	Centigram Communications [*NASDAQ symbol*] (SPSG)
CGRM	Containment Gaseous Radiation Monitor [*Nuclear energy*] (IEEE)
CGRM	Department of the Commandant-General, Royal Marines [*British*]
CGRN	Coarsely Granular [*Organic chemistry*] (DAVI)
CGRO	Compton Gamma Ray Observatory [*Satellite*]
CGRO	Crop Growers [*NASDAQ symbol*] (TTSB)
CGRO	Crop Growers Corp. [*NASDAQ symbol*] (SAG)
CGRP	Calcitonin Gene-Related Peptide [*Endocrinology*]
CGRP	Circuit Group [*Telecommunications*] (TEL)
CGRPR	Calcitonin Gene Related Peptide Receptor [*Medicine*] (DMAA)
CGRS	Canadian Geriatrics Research Society
CGRS	Central Gyro Reference System
CGRS	Certified Genealogical Record Searcher
CGRS	Compact Gamma Ray Spectrometer
CGS	Caguas [*Diocesan abbreviation*] [*Puerto Rico*] (TOCD)
CGS	Cambridge Geographical Series [*A publication*]
CGS	Cambridge Graphic Systems [*Computer science*] (HGAA)
CGS	Canadian Geographical Society (BARN)
CGS	Canadian Geotechnical Society
CGS	Canadian Goat Society
CGS	CAP-Gemini-Sogeti [*Software manufacturer*]
CGS	Cardiogenic Shock [*Cardiology*] (DMAA)
CGS	Catgut Suture [*Medicine*]
CGS	Catholic Guardian Society (EA)
CGS	CEC Resources [*AMX*] (TTSB)
CGS	CEC Resources Ltd. [*AMEX symbol*] (SAG)
CGS	Center for Government Service [*Rutgers University*] [*Research center*] (RCD)
CGS	Centimeter-Gram-Second [*System of units*] (AAG)
cgs	Centimeter-Gram-Second (IDOE)
CGS	Central Gliding School [*British military*] (DMA)
CGS	Central Gunnery School [*British military*] (DMA)
CGS	Certificate of Graduate Studies (PGP)
CGS	Champagne Gift Service [*De Courcy Pere et Fils*] [*British*]
CGS	Chef des Generalstabs des Heeres [*Chief of General Staff of the Army*] [*German military - World War II*]
CGS	Chief of the General Staff [*in the field*] [*Formerly, CIGS*] [*Military*] [*British*]
CGS	Cholesterol Gallstones [*Medicine*]
CGS	Chromatographic Separation
CGS	Circuit Group Congestion Signal [*Telecommunications*] (IAA)
CGS	Clinical Genetical Society [*British*]
CGS	Coast and Geodetic Survey [*Later, NOAA*] [*Rockville, MD*] (AFM)
CGS	Coast Guard Specification
CGS	College Park, MD [*Location identifier FAA*] (FAAL)
CGS	Colorado Genealogical Society (EA)
CGS	Command Ground Station [*Army*] (RDA)
CGS	Commissary-General of Subsistence [*Army British*]
CGS	Commission on Government Security [*Terminated, 1957*]
CGS	Committee on Geological Sciences [*Marine science*] (OSRA)

CGS	Committee on Geological Sciences [*National Academy of Sciences*] (USDC)
CGS	Common Graphics System (MCD)
CGS	Common Ground Station [*Military*] (RDA)
CGS	Community Guidance Service (EA)
CGS	Concerned Guatemala Scholars [*Defunct*] (EA)
CGS	Contemplatives of Good Shepherd (TOCD)
CGS	Continuous-Grain Silicon
CGS	Control Guidance Subsystem (OA)
CGS	CONUS [*Continental United States*] Ground Station (MCD)
CGS	Cost of Goods Sold (AAGC)
CGS	Cottage Garden Society [*British*] (DBA)
CGS	Council of Graduate Schools (EA)
CGS	Country Grammar School [*British*]
CGS	Crew Gunnery Simulator (PDAA)
CGS	Czechoslovak Genealogical Society (EA)
CGSA	Canadian Golf Superintendents Association [*Association Canadienne des Surintendants de Golf*] (AC)
CGSA	Cellular Geographic Serving Area [*Telecommunications*]
CGSA	Computer Graphics Structural Analysis
CGSA	Connecticut General Statutes, Annotated [*A publication*] (DLA)
CGSAC	Commanding General, Strategic Air Command (NATG)
CGSB	Canadian General Standards Board [*Formerly, Canadian Government Specifications Board*]
CGSB	Coordinadora Guerrillera Simon Bolivar [*Colorado Political party*] (EY)
CGSBN	Consortium for Graduate Study in Business for Negroes [*Later, CGSM*]
CGSC	Cancer Genetics Studies Consortium
CG(S)C	Civilian Goods (Supply) Committee [*British World War II*]
CGSC	Coli Genetic Stock Center
CGSC	Command and General Staff College [*Fort Leavenworth, KS*] [*Military*]
CGSE	Centimeter-Gram-Second-Electrostatic
CGSE	Common Ground Support Equipment (MCD)
CGSEL	Common Ground Support Equipment List (NVT)
CGSFU	Ceramic [*or Clear*] Glazed Structural Facing Units [*Technical drawings*]
CGSI	Computer-Generated/Synthesized Imagery (MCD)
CGSL	California Guaranteed Student Loans (EDAC)
CGSM	Centimeter-Gram-Second-Electromagnetic
CGSM	Consortium for Graduate Study in Management [*St. Louis, MO*] (EA)
CGSMCM	Coast Guard Supplement to Manual for Courts-Martial [*A publication*] (DLA)
CGSOC	Command and General Staff Officer Course [*Military*] (INF)
CGSP	Conventional Geometry Smart Projectile
CGSS	Ceramics, Glass, and Solid State Science Division [*National Institute of Standards and Technology*] (GRD)
CGSS	Copilot/Gunner Stabilized Sight (MCD)
CGSS	Cryogenic Gas Storage System (MCD)
CGSSC	Columbia Gas System Service Corp. [*of Columbia Gas System, Inc.*]
CGSTA	Coast Guard Station
CGSTN	Congestion (FAAC)
CGSU	Centimeter-Gram-Second Unit
CGSUB	Ceramic [*or Clear*] Glazed Structural Unit Base [*Technical drawings*]
CGSUPCEN	Coast Guard Supply Center
CGSUS	Council of Graduate Schools in the United States (EA)
CGT	[*The*] Cambridge Greek Testament [*A publication*] (BJA)
CGT	[*The*] Canada & Gulf Terminal Railway Co. [*AAR code*]
CGT	Capital Gains Tax
CGT	Cheguitti [*Mauritania*] [*Airport symbol*] (OAG)
CGT	Chicago Heights, IL [*Location identifier FAA*] (FAAL)
CGT	Chorionic Gonadotropin [*Endocrinology*] (MAE)
CGT	Chuian-Garon [*Former USSR Seismograph station code, US Geological Survey Closed*] (SEIS)
CGT	Color Graphics Terminal (MCD)
CGT	Command Generator Tracker (MCD)
CGT	Compensated Gross Tons [*Measure of shipbuilding capacity*]
CGT	Computer-Guided Teaching (EDAC)
CGT	Consumers' Gas Co. Ltd. [*Toronto Stock Exchange symbol*]
CGT	Corrected Geomagnetic Time
CGT	Current Gate Tube
CGT	Cyclodextrin Glucanotransferase (DMAA)
CGTAC	Commanding General, Tactical Air Command (NATG)
CGTase	Cyclodextrin Glycosyltransferase [*An enzyme*]
CGTB	Clinical Gene Therapy Branch
CGTB	Colombian Government Trade Bureau (EA)
CGTC	Cambridge Greek Testament Commentary [*A publication*] (BJA)
CGTEL	Coast Guard Teletype (NOAA)
CGTHIRDMAW	Commanding General, Third Marine Air Wing (MUGU)
CGTM	Command Guided Tactical Missile
CGTO	Consolidated Group of Tribes and Organizations
CGTO	Contracted Gaussian-Type Orbital [*Atomic physics*]
CGTRASTA	Coast Guard Training Station
CGTS	Coast and Geodetic Tide Station
CGTS	Coast Guard Training Station
CGTSC	Cambridge Greek Testament for Schools and Colleges [*A publication*] (BJA)
CGTSS	Command Group Training Support System (MCD)
CGTSS	Command Guidance-Training Support System [*Military*]
CGTT	Cortisol Glucose Tolerance Test [*Medicine*] (DAVI)
CGTT	Cortisone Glucose Tolerance Test [*Medicine*]
CGTV	Command Guidance Test Vehicle
CGU	Canadian Geophysical Union
CGU	Ceramic Glazed Unit [*Technical drawings*]

CGU .... Church Guilds Union [British]
CGU .... Corning Resources [Vancouver Stock Exchange symbol]
CGUA .... Compu/Graphics Users Association [Defunct] (EA)
CGUL .... Margate Industries [NASDAQ symbol] (TTSB)
CGUL .... Margate Ventures [NASDAQ symbol] (NQ)
CGUP .... Comite Guatemalteco de Unidad Patriotica [Guatemalan Committee of Patriotic Unity] (PD)
CGUSA .... Common Ground - USA (EA)
CGUSACOMZEUR... Commanding General, United States Army Communications Zone, Europe (NATG)
CGUSADC .... Commanding General, United States Army Combat Developments Command
CGUSAMC .... Commanding General, United States Army Material Command
CGUSARADCOM... Commanding General, United States Army Air Defense Command
CGUSARAL... Commanding General, United States Army, Alaska (MUGU)
CGUSARCDC... Commanding General, United States Army Combat Developments Command (MUGU)
CGUSARF .... Commanding General, United States Army Forces (CINC)
CGUSARMAC... Commanding General, United States Army Material Command (CINC)
CGUSARMC... Commanding General, United States Army Material Command (MUGU)
CGUSARYIS... Commanding General, United States Army, Ryukyu Islands (CINC)
CGUSCONARC... Commanding General, United States Continental Army Command [Obsolete]
CGUSFET ..... Commanding General, United States Forces, European Theater [World War II]
CGV .... Cadena Garcia Valseca [Press agency] [Mexico]
CGV .... Centre de Gravite Verticale [Vertical Center of Gravity] [Shipping] [French]
CGV .... Critical Grid Voltage
CGVH .... Computer-Generated Volume Hologram
CGVH .... Computer-Generate Volume Hologram (PDAA)
CGVHD .... Chronic Graft-Versus-Host Disease [Medicine]
CGVS .... Ciliated Groove to Ventral Sac
CGVT .... Commission Gastronomique, Vinicole, et Touristique (EA)
CGW .... Air Great Wall [CHINA] [FAA designator] (FAAC)
CGW .... Chattanooga, TN [Location identifier FAA] (FAAL)
CGW .... Chicago Great Western Railroad (IIA)
CGW .... Citco Growth Investment [Vancouver Stock Exchange symbol]
CGW .... Corning Glass Works
CGW .... Cristalerias de Chile ADS [NYSE symbol] (SPSG)
CGW .... Golden West College Library, Huntington Beach, CA [OCLC symbol] (OCLC)
CGW .... Great Wall Airlines [China] [ICAO designator] (FAAC)
CGWA .... Canadian Ground Water Association [Association Canadienne des Eaux Souterraine] [Formerly, Canadian Water Well Contractors Association] [Formerly, Canadian Water Well Association] (AC)
CGWT .... Cylindrically Guided Wave Technique [Nuclear energy equipment]
CGX .... Chicago [Illinois] Meigs Field [Airport symbol] (OAG)
CGX .... Guided Missile Cruiser (MCD)
CGY .... Cagayan De Oro [Philippines] [Airport symbol] (OAG)
CGY .... Calgary Centre Holdings Ltd. [Toronto Stock Exchange symbol]
CGY .... Capital Guaranty Corp. [NYSE symbol] (SPSG)
CGY .... Centigray [Radiation therapy] (ADDR)
CGYD .... Coast Guard Yard
CGZ .... Casa Grande, AZ [Location identifier FAA] (FAAL)
CGZ .... Casa Grande Engineering & Mines [Vancouver Stock Exchange symbol]
CH .... Air-Cushion Vehicle built by Commercial Hovercraft Industries [New Zealand] [Usually used in combination with numerals]
CH .... A. Nattermann & Cie [Germany] [Research code symbol]
CH .... Aviation Cruiser (MCD)
CH .... Bellanca Aircraft Corp., Champion Aircraft Corp. [ICAO aircraft manufacturer identifier] (ICAO)
CH .... Caeharris [Cardiff] [Welsh depot code]
CH .... Calcium Hydroxide [Inorganic chemistry] (OA)
CH .... Cancer Hot Line [of Cancer Connection] (EA)
CH .... Candle-Hour [Illumination]
CH .... Can't Hear [Telecommunications] (TEL)
CH .... Captain of Horse [British]
CH .... Captain of the Host [Freemasonry] (ROG)
CH .... Caravan House [An association] (EA)
C/H .... Cards per Hour [Computer science]
CH .... Cargo Helicopter (AABC)
CH .... Carriers Haulage [Shipping] (DS)
CH .... Case Harden [Metal] [Technical drawings]
CH .... Casein Hydrolyzate [Cell growth medium]
CH .... Ceiling Height (OA)
CH .... Center Halfback [Soccer]
CH .... Central Heating
CH .... Century Hutchinson [Publisher] [British]
CH .... Certified Herbalist
CH .... Chain
ch .... Chain (WDMC)
CH .... Chain Home [Aviation]
CH .... Chair
CH .... Chairman
CH .... Chaldea (ROG)
CH .... Chaldron [Unit of measure] [Obsolete]
Ch .... Chalmers' Colonial Opinions [England] [A publication] (DLA)
CH .... Chamber (ADA)
CH .... Chamfer [Design engineering] (IAA)
CH .... Champion [Dog show term]

CH .... Chancellor (ADA)
CH .... Chancellor's Court [England] (DLA)
CH .... Chancery [British]
CH .... Change (AABC)
CH .... Channel
ch .... Channel (WDMC)
CH .... Chaplain (AFM)
CH .... Chapter
ch .... Chapter (WDMC)
Ch .... Chapter (AAGC)
CH .... Chapter House [British] (ROG)
CH .... Character [Computer science] (BUR)
CH .... Charcoal [Automotive advertising]
CH .... Charcoal Hemoperfusion [Medicine]
CH .... Chargeable to Hardware
CH .... Chart
CH .... Charter Rolls [British]
CH .... Chasmogamous [Botany]
CH .... Chassemaree [Ship's rigging] (ROG)
CH .... Chatham House (DAS)
CH .... Check
CH .... Checkered (WGA)
CH .... Chediak-Higashi Syndrome [Medicine] (DMAA)
CH .... Cheese (ROG)
CH .... Chemical Hazards
ch .... Chemin (DD)
ch .... Chervonets [Monetary unit; 1922-1947] [Russian]
CH .... Chest [Medicine]
ch .... Chest (DMAA)
CH .... Chestnut [Horse racing]
CH .... Chicago [Illinois] (ROG)
CH .... Chicago Helicopter Airways, Inc. [ICAO designator Obsolete]
Ch .... Chido [Antibodies] [Immunology] (DAVI)
CH .... Chief (AFM)
ch .... Chief (WDMC)
CH .... Chiffonier
CH .... Child [or Children]
ch .... Child (DMAA)
CH .... Children's Hospital [Philadelphia, PA]
CH .... Child's Fare [Airline fare code]
CH .... Chile Fund, Inc. [NYSE symbol] (SPSG)
CH .... China [IYRU nationality code] (ROG)
ch .... China, Republic of [Taiwan] [MARC country of publication code Library of Congress] (LCCP)
Ch .... Chinese
CH .... Chirurgia [Surgery] [Latin]
CH .... Chlorpheniramine [Pharmacology]
ch .... Chocolate
CH .... Choice (ADA)
Ch .... Choir (ROG)
CH .... Choir Organ
CH .... Choke (MSA)
Ch .... Cholesterol [Also, C, Cho, CHOL] [Biochemistry]
Ch .... Choline [Also, Cho] [Biochemistry]
CH .... Christ
CH .... Christchurch Chromosome [Genetics] (DAVI)
CH .... Chromogenic (WGA)
CH .... Chronic [Medicine]
ch .... Chronic [Medicine] (DMAA)
Ch .... Chronicles [Old Testament book] (BJA)
CH .... Church
ch .... Church (VRA)
CH .... Church Heritage [A publication] (APTA)
CH .... Church History [A publication] (BRI)
CH .... Church Pennant [Navy British]
CH .... C. Hurst & Co. [Publisher] [British]
CH .... Chute
CH .... City of Hope (EA)
CH .... Cladosporium Herbarum [A fungus]
CH .... Clearinghouse [Banking]
CH .... Clearing House Code [Database terminology] (NITA)
CH .... Clock Hour (KSC)
CH .... Clothing and Housing Research Division [of ARS, Department of Agriculture]
CH .... Cluster Headache [Neurology] (DAVI)
CH .... Coach
CH .... Coach House
CH .... Coastal Harbor [Telecommunications] (TEL)
CH .... Coat Hook
CH .... Codex Hammurabi (BJA)
CH .... Come Hither [A publication]
CH .... Companion of Honour [British]
CH .... Compass Heading
CH .... Competition Hot [In "Harley-Davidson XLCH"]
CH .... Conductor Head (KSC)
CH .... Congenital Hypomyelination [Medicine]
CH .... Conquering Hero [British, for returning soldiers]
CH .... Constant Human Immunoglobulin
CH .... Contact Handled
CH .... Continental Group, Inc. [Toronto Stock Exchange symbol]
CH .... Control Heading (BUR)
CH .... Control Hole (BUR)
CH .... Controlled Hardening [Ferrous metallurgy]
CH .... Controlled Humidity (MCD)
CH .... Controlled Hypertension [Medicine]

CH	Convalescent Hospital (DAVI)
CH	Corptech Industry, Inc. [*Vancouver Stock Exchange symbol*]
CH	Country Handbooks [*A publication*]
CH	Court House
Ch	Court of Chancery [*New Jersey*] (DLA)
CH	Covenant House [*An association*] (EA)
CH	Critical Height (DA)
CH	Critical Hours [*Broadcasting term*]
CH	Crown-Heel [*Length of fetus*] [*Medicine*]
CH	Custom House [*Business term*]
C/H	Cycles per Hour
CH	Cyclohexanone [*Organic chemistry*]
CH	Cycloheximide [*Also, CHX, CXM, Cyh*] [*Fungicide*]
ch	Cylindrical Horizontal Tank [*Liquid gas carriers*]
CH	Cytoplasmic Hypovirulence [*Pathology*]
Ch	English Law Reports, Chancery Appeals [*1891 onwards*] [*A publication*] (DLA)
Ch	English Law Reports, Chancery Division [*A publication*] (DLA)
CH	Express Airways [*ICAO designator*]
CH	Hayward Public Library, Hayward, CA [*Library symbol Library of Congress*] (LCLS)
cH	Hydrogen Ion Concentration [*Organic chemistry*] (DAVI)
CH	Switzerland [*ANSI two-letter standard code*] (CNC)
CH	Wheelchair (DAVI)
Ch¹c	Christchurch Chromosome
CH₂0	Formaldehyde (GNE)
CH3OH	Methanol [*DOE*] (TAG)
CH4	Methane [*BTS*] (TAG)
CH5	Clark Hill Reservoir [*Georgia*] [*Seismograph station code, US Geological Survey*] (SEIS)
CH6	Clark Hill Reservoir [*Georgia*] [*Seismograph station code, US Geological Survey*] (SEIS)
CH50	Complement Hemolyzing 50 [*Immunology*]
CHA	Alameda County Public Library, Hayward, CA [*Library symbol Library of Congress*] (LCLS)
CHA	Cable-Harness Analyzer
CHA	California Healthcare Association (SRA)
CHA	Camp Horsemanship Association (EA)
CHA	Canadian Handball Association [*Federation de Balle au mur du Canada*] (AC)
CHA	Canadian Health Association
CHA	Canadian Historical Association [*See also SHC*]
CHA	Canadian Hospital Association
CHA	Canadian Hydrographic Association [*Association Canadienne d'Hydrographie*] (AC)
CHA	Caribbean Hotel Association (EA)
CHA	Catholic Health Association of the United States (EA)
CHA	Catholic Hospital Association [*Canada*]
CHA	Center for Health Action (EA)
CHA	Certified Hotel Administrator [*Educational Institute of the American Hote l and Motel Association*] [*Designation awarded by*]
CHA	Chabazite [*A zeolite*]
Cha	Chamaeleon [*Constellation*]
Cha	Chamber
CHA	Champion International Corp. [*NYSE symbol*] (SPSG)
CHA	Champion Intl. [*NYSE symbol*] (TTSB)
cha	Chasing (VRA)
CHA	Chassis
CHA	Chatra [*Nepal*] [*Seismograph station code, US Geological Survey*] (SEIS)
CHA	Chattanooga [*Tennessee*] [*Airport symbol*]
CHA	Chauvco Resources Ltd. [*Toronto Stock Exchange symbol*]
CHA	Chest and Heart Association [*British*] (BI)
CHA	Chicago Helicopter Airways, Inc.
CHA	Chickasaw Horse Association (EA)
CHA	Chiltern Airways [*British ICAO designator*] (FAAC)
ChA	Choline Acetylase [*Also, CAT, ChAc, ChAT*] [*An enzyme*]
CHA	Christian Herald Association (EA)
CHA	Christian Holiness Association (EA)
CHA	Chronic Hemolytic Anemia [*Medicine*]
CHA	Colorado Hospital Association (SRA)
CHA	Committee of Heads of Administration [*NATO*] (NATG)
CHA	Community Health Association
CHA	Concentric Hemispherical Analyzer [*Surface analysis*]
CHA	Concise Handbooks of Art [*A publication*]
CHA	Congenital Hypoplastic Anemia [*Hematology*]
CHA	Connecticut Hospital Association (SRA)
CHA	Countrywide Holidays Association [*British*] (DBA)
CHA	Crop Husbandry Adviser [*Ministry of Agriculture, Fisheries, and Food*] [*British*]
CHA	Crosier Heritage Association [*Defunct*] (EA)
CHA	Cyclohexyladenosine [*Biochemistry*]
CHA	Cyclohexylamine [*Organic chemistry*]
CHAA	Catholic Health Association of Alberta [*Formerly, Catholic Health Care Conference of Alberta*] (AC)
CHAA	Combined Health Appeal of America (EA)
Cha Add	Chapman's Addenda [*A publication*] (DLA)
CHAA-FM	Longueuil, PQ [*FM radio station call letters*] (RBYB)
CHAALS	Communications High-Accuracy Airborne Location System [*Military*]
Cha App	Chancery Appeal Cases, English Law Reports [*A publication*] (DLA)
CHAART	Center for Health Applications of Aerospace Related Technologies
CHAB	Moose Jaw, SK [*AM radio station call letters*]
CHABA	Committee on Hearing and Bio-Acoustics
CHABAD	Chochma, Bina, Daat [*Wisdom, Understanding, Knowledge*] [*Philosophy of the Lubavitch Movement, a Hasidic sect*]

CHABC	Catholic Health Association of British Columbia (AC)
CHAC	Catholic Health Association of Canada
CHAC	Catholic Hospital Association of Canada
CHAC	Chicano Humanities and Arts Council (EDAC)
ChAc	Choline Acetylase [*Also, CAT, ChA, ChAT*] [*An enzyme*]
Ch Acc Aust	Chartered Accountant in Australia [*A publication*]
CHACF	California Hungarian American Cultural Foundation (EA)
CHACOM	Chain of Command
CHAD	Amos, PQ [*AM radio station call letters*]
CHAD	Change Display [*Utility*]
CHAD	Change of Address [*Direct marketing*] (WDMC)
CHAD	Charleston Army Depot [*South Carolina*] [*Closed*] (AABC)
CHAD	Code to Handle Angular Data (IEEE)
CHAD	Cyclophosphamide, Adriamycin, Cisplatin Hexamethylmelamire [*Antineoplastic drug regimen*] (DAVI)
CHAD	Cyclophosphamide, Hexamethylmelamine, Adriamycin, Diamminedichloroplatinum [*Cisplatin*] [*Antineoplastic drug regimen*]
ChadArch	Chadashoth Archeologioth [*Israel*] [*A publication*] (BJA)
CHADD	Children and Adults with Attention Deficit Disorder (PAZ)
ChADD	Children with Attention-Deficit Disorders (EA)
CHADECJA	Stronnictwo Chrzescijanskiej Demokracji [*Christian Democratic Party*] [*Poland*] (PPE)
Cha Dig	Chaney's Digest, Michigan Reports [*A publication*] (DLA)
Chadron St C	Chadron State College (GAGS)
ChadThr	Chad Therapeutics, Inc. [*Associated Press*] (SAG)
CHAE	Centre d'Histoire de l'Aeronautique et de l'Espace [*Aeronautics and Space Historical Center - ASHC*] (EAIO)
CH AE	Chief Artificer Engineer [*Navy British*] (ROG)
CHAER	Chief Aerographer [*Navy rating Obsolete*]
CHAF	Chafford [*England*]
CHAFAG	Chief, Air Force Advisory Group
CHAFB	Chanute Air Force Base [*Illinois*] (AAG)
CHAFFROC	Chaff Rocket [*Military*] (NVT)
CHAFSEC	Chief, Air Force Section (CINC)
CHAG	Chain Arrester Gear (MCD)
C-HAG	Community Health Awareness Group
CHAG	Compact High-Performance Aerial Gun (MCD)
CHAG	Consumer Housing Assistance Grants
ChaH	Chadwyck-Healey Ltd., Bishops Stortford, Herts., United Kingdom [*Library symbol Library of Congress*] (LCLS)
CHAH	Chronology of Hispanic-American History [*A publication*]
CHAI	Concern for Helping Animals in Israel (EA)
CHAI	Continuous Hepatic Artery Infusion [*Medicine*] (DAVI)
CHAI	Life Medical Sciences [*NASDAQ symbol*] (SAG)
CHAI	Life Med Sciences [*NASDAQ symbol*] (TTSB)
CHAI	Newberry Library/D'Arcy McNickle Center for the History of the American Indian [*Research center*] (RCD)
CHAID	Chi-Squared Automatic Interaction Detector
CHAI-FM	Chateauquay, PQ [*FM radio station call letters*] (RBYB)
CHAIN	Computerized Head-End Access Information Network (HGAA)
ChaiNaTa	Chai-Na-Ta Ginsing Products Ltd. [*Associated Press*] (SAG)
ChaiNT	Chai Na Ta Corp. [*Associated Press*] (SAG)
CHAIR	Chairman (EY)
CHAIS	Consumer Hazards Analytical Information Service [*Laboratory of the Government Chemist*] [*British*] (NITA)
CHAIW	Life Med Sciences Wrrt 'A' [*NASDAQ symbol*] (TTSB)
CHAIZ	Life Med Sciences Wrrt'B' [*NASDAQ symbol*] (TTSB)
CHAK	Inuvik, NT [*AM radio station call letters*]
CHAK-TV	Inuvik, NT [*Television station call letters*]
CHAL	Chaldron [*Unit of measure*] [*Obsolete*]
CHAL	Challenge (AABC)
CHAL	Chalmette National Historical Park
CHAL	Chalumeau [*Reed*] [*Music*]
Cha L & T	Chambers. Landlord and Tenant [*1823*] [*A publication*] (DLA)
CHALD	Chaldea [*or Chaldean or Chaldaic*]
CHALICE	Compressional Heating and Linear Injection Cusp Experiment
ChalInt	Challanger International Ltd. [*Associated Press*] (SAG)
Challis	Challis on Real Property [*1885-1911*] [*A publication*] (DLA)
CHALM	Chalumeau [*Reed*] [*Music*] (ROG)
Chalmers	Chalmers on Bills of Exchange [*1878-1952*] [*A publication*] (DLA)
Chalone	Chalone Wine Group Ltd. [*Associated Press*] (SAG)
Chal Op	Chalmers' Opinions, Constitutional Law [*1669-1809*] [*England*] [*A publication*] (DLA)
CHAM	Catholic Health Association of Manitoba (AC)
Cham	Chamaeleon [*Constellation*]
Cham	Chambers' Upper Canada Reports [*1849-82*] [*A publication*] (DLA)
CHAM	Chamfer [*Design engineering*]
CHAM	Chamizal National Memorial
cham	Chamois [*Philately*]
CHAM	Chamomile [*Pharmacology*] (ROG)
CHAM	Champagne (ROG)
CHAM	Combustion, Heat, and Mass (PDAA)
CHAM	Hamilton, ON [*AM radio station call letters*]
Cham & PRR	Chambers and Parsons' Railroad Laws [*A publication*] (DLA)
CHAMB	Chamber (MSA)
CHAMB	Chamberlain (ROG)
Chamb	Chambers' Upper Canada Reports [*1849-82*] [*A publication*] (DLA)
Chamb Dig PHC	Chambers' Digest of Public Health Cases [*A publication*] (DLA)
Chamb Ency	Chambers's Encyclopaedia [*A publication*] (ROG)
Chamber	Chamber Reports, Upper Canada [*A publication*] (DLA)
Chamb R	Upper Canada Chancery Chambers Reports [*1857-72*] [*Ontario*] [*A publication*] (DLA)
Chamb Rep	Chancery Chambers Reports, Ontario [*A publication*] (DLA)

Chamb Rep... Upper Canada Chambers Reports [*1846-52*] [*Ont.*] [*A publication*] (DLA)

Cham Chy Jur... Chambers' Chancery Jurisdiction as to Infants [*A publication*] (DLA)

Cham Com... Chambers. Commons and Open Spaces [*1877*] [*A publication*] (DLA)

Cham Com Law... Chamberlin's American Commercial Law [*A publication*] (DLA)

Cha Men...... Changing Men [*A publication*] (BRI)

Cham Est...... Chambers. Estates and Tenures [*A publication*] (DLA)

CHAMIL...... Chameleon Micro Implementation Language [*1978*] [*Computer science*] (CSR)

Cham L & T... Chambers. Landlord and Tenant [*1823*] [*A publication*] (DLA)

Cham Leas... Chambers. Leases [*1819*] [*A publication*] (DLA)

CHAMMP..... Computer Hardware, Advanced Mathematics, and Model Physics Initiative [*Department of Energy*]

CHAMOMA... Cyclophosphamide, Hydroxyurea, Dactinomycin Oncovin [*Vincristine*], Methotrexate, Adriamycin [*Antineoplastic drug regimen*]

CHAMP....... Canard Homing Antimaterial Projectile

Champ........ Champerty and Maintenance [*A publication*] (DLA)

CHAMP....... Champion (DSUE)

CHAMP....... Champion

Champ........ Champion's Cases, Wine and Beer-Houses Act [*England*] [*A publication*] (DLA)

champ .... Champleve (VRA)

CHAMP....... Character Manipulation Procedures

CHAMP....... Child Amputee Program [*Canada*]

CHAMP....... Children's Hospital Automated Medical Program (DMAA)

CHAMP....... Comet Halley Active Monitoring Program

CHAMP....... Communications Handler for Automatic Multiple Programs

CHAMP....... Community Health Air Monitoring Program [*Environmental Protection Agency*]

CHAMP....... Competitive Health and Medical Plan [*Proposed*]

CHAMP....... Computer Hardware Acquisition and Modernization Program [*Department of Agriculture*] (GFGA)

CHAMPION... Compatible Hardware and Milestone Program for Integrating Organizational Needs [*AFSC*]

Champps ..... Champps Entertainment, Inc. [*Associated Press*] (SAG)

Cham Pr ...... Chambers Practice [*A publication*] (DLA)

CHAMPUS.... Civilian Health and Medical Program of the Uniformed Services [*Military*]

CHAMPVA.... Civilian Health and Medical Program of the Veterans Administration [*Military*]

Cham Rat .... Chambers. Rates and Rating [*2nd ed.*] [*1889*] [*A publication*] (DLA)

Cham Rep ... Chambers' Upper Canada Reports [*1849-82*] [*A publication*] (DLA)

CHAN......... Center for the History of American Needlework (EA)

Chan .... Chancellor (DLA)

CHAN .... Chancery

CHAN .... Chandler Insurance Co. Ltd. [*NASDAQ symbol*]

Chan .... Chaney's Michigan Reports [*37-58 Michigan*] [*A publication*] (DLA)

CHAN .... Channel [*Computer science*] (AABC)

chan.......... Channel (WDMC)

CHAN .... Clearing House Accession Number [*Online database field identifier*]

Chan .... Gloria Chandler Recordings [*Record label*]

CHan.......... Hanford Public Library, Hanford, CA [*Library symbol Library of Congress*] (LCLS)

CHAN .... Vancouver, BC [*Television station call letters*]

CHAN-1....... Chilliwack, BC [*Television station call letters*] (RBYB)

CHAN-2....... Bowen Island, BC [*Television station call letters*] (RBYB)

CHAN-3....... Squamish, BC [*Television station call letters*] (RBYB)

CHAN-4....... Courtenay, BC [*Television station call letters*] (RBYB)

CHAN-5....... Brackendale, BC [*Television station call letters*] (RBYB)

CHAN-7....... Whistler, BC [*Television station call letters*] (RBYB)

CHANC....... Chancellor

CHANC....... Chancery (ROG)

Chan Cas..... Cases in Chancery [*England*] [*A publication*] (DLA)

CHANCE....... Coalition for Handicapped Children's Education (DAVI)

Chanc Ex .... Chancellor of the Exchequer [*British*] (DLA)

Chan Chamb... Chancery Chambers Reports, Upper Canada [*1857-72*] [*A publication*] (DLA)

CHANCLLR... Chancellor

CHANCOM.... Channel Committee [*NATO*] (NATG)

CHANCOMTEE... Channel Committee [*NATO*] (NATG)

Chanc Pow... Chance on Powers [*1831*] [*Supplement, 1841*] [*A publication*] (DLA)

Chan Ct....... Chancery Court [*England*] (DLA)

Chand .... Chandler's Reports [*20, 38-44 New Hampshire*] [*A publication*] (DLA)

Chand .... Chandler's Wisconsin Reports [*1849-52*] [*A publication*] (DLA)

CH & A .... Carrow, Hamerton, and Allen's New Sessions Cases [*1844-51*] [*England*] [*A publication*] (DLA)

Ch & Cl Cas... Cripp's Church and Clergy Cases [*1847-50*] [*England*] [*A publication*] (DLA)

Chand Crim Tr... Chandler's American Criminal Trials [*A publication*] (DLA)

Chand Cr T... Chandler's American Criminal Trials [*A publication*] (DLA)

C(H & D) ..... Center (Hospital and Domiciliary) [*Veterans Administration*]

CH and D..... Cold, Hungry, and Dry [*Slang*]

CH & H....... Continent between Havre and Hamburg [*Business term*]

Chandl .... Chandler's Reports [*20, 38-44 New Hampshire*] [*A publication*] (DLA)

Chandl .... Chandler's Wisconsin Reports [*1849-52*] [*A publication*] (DLA)

CH&LA........ Colorado Hotel and Lodging Association (SRA)

Chandler...... Chandler's Wisconsin Reports [*1849-52*] [*A publication*] (DLA)

Chandler Wis... Chandler's Wisconsin Reports [*1849-52*] [*A publication*] (DLA)

CH&MA........ California Hotel and Motel Association (SRA)

Chand (NH)... Chandler's Reports [*20, 38-44 New Hampshire*] [*A publication*] (DLA)

Ch & P........ Chambers and Pretty. Cases on Finance Act [*1909-10*] [*England*] [*A publication*] (DLA)

CH & P .... Crew Habitability and Protection [*NASA*] (KSC)

CH & R....... Catch a Horse and Ride [*Fictitious railroad initialism used to indicate one of the most reliable modes of rural transportation*]

Chand R ...... Chandler's Wisconsin Reports [*1849-52*] [*A publication*] (DLA)

Chand (Wis)... Chandler's Wisconsin Reports [*1849-52*] [*A publication*] (DLA)

Chaney .... Chaney's Michigan Reports [*37-58 Michigan*] [*A publication*] (DLA)

Chaney (Mich)... Chaney's Michigan Reports [*37-58 Michigan*] [*A publication*] (DLA)

CHANF........ Chandler Insurance Ltd. (MHDW)

CHANG C .... Chang Conjunctiva Cells [*Medicine*] (DMAA)

CHANG L .... Chang Liver Cells [*Medicine*] (DMAA)

ChanIn........ Chandler Insurance Co. Ltd. [*Associated Press*] (SAG)

CHanK .... Kings County Free Library, Hanford, CA [*Library symbol Library of Congress*] (LCLS)

CHANL....... Chandler

Channell...... Channell Commercial Corp. [*Associated Press*] (SAG)

CHAN PROC... Chancery Proceedings [*British*] (ROG)

Chan Rep C... Reports in Chancery [*21 English Reprint*] [*1615-1710*] [*A publication*] (DLA)

CHANS....... Chanson [*Song*] [*Music*]

CHANSEC.... Channel Committee Secretary [*NATO*] (NATG)

Chan Sentinel... Chancery Sentinel [*New York*] [*A publication*] (DLA)

CHANSY...... Charleston Naval Shipyard [*South Carolina*] (DNAB)

Chantal ...... Chantal Pharmaceutical Corp. [*Associated Press*] (SAG)

CHANT CERT... Chantry Certificates [*British*] (ROG)

Chan Toon ... Leading Cases on Buddhist Law [*A publication*] (DLA)

CHAO.......... Catholic Health Association of Ontario (AC)

CHAO......... Cooperative Housing Association of Ontario Inc. [*L'Association de l'Habitation Co-Operative de l'Ontario*] [*Formerly, Ontario Co-Op Housing Committee*] (AC)

CHAOS........ Cannon Hunters Association of Seattle [*Defunct*] (EA)

CHAOS........ Chain Handling Automated Overlay System (SAA)

CHAOTIC...... Computer and Human-Assisted Organization of a Technical Information Center [*National Institute of Standards and Technology*]

CHAP .... Certified Hospital Admission Program (DAVI)

CHAP .... Challenge Handshake Authentication Protocol [*Telecommunications*] (PCM)

CHAP .... Champion International Corp. (MHDW)

CHAP .... Chapel

CHAP .... Chapelry [*Geographical division*] [*British*]

CHAP .... Chaplain

CHAP .... Chaplain

CHAP .... Chapman [*One who sells in a cheaping or market*] [*Said to be origin of "chap," meaning "fellow"*]

Chap .... Chappell [*Record label*] [*Great Britain*]

CHAP .... Chapter (AFM)

chap.......... Chapter (WDMC)

CHAP .... Charring Ablation Program [*NASA*]

CHAP .... Child Health Assessment Program

CHAP .... Children Have a Potential [*Program for handicapped or disturbed children of Air Force personnel*] (AFM)

CHAP .... Commission for Historical Architectural Preservation

CHAP .... Composite HTGR [*High-Temperature Gas-Cooled Reactor*] Analysis Program [*Nuclear energy*] (NRCH)

CHAP .... Comprehensive Health Assessments and Primary Care for Children [*Proposed*]

CHAP .... Comprehensive Homeless Assistance Plan [*Homeless Assistance Act*] (GFGA)

CHAP .... Contractor-Held Air Force Property (AFM)

CHAP .... Controlled Helium Atmosphere Plant (PDAA)

CHAP .... Convective Heating and Ablative Program [*Army*]

Chap & Sh... Chappell and Shoard. Copyright [*1863*] [*A publication*] (DLA)

CHAPAR...... Chaplain Area Representative [*Air Force*]

CHAP/FAAR... Chaparral/Forward Area Alert RADAR [*Military*] (RDA)

CHAP-GEN... Chaplain-General to the Forces [*British*] (ROG)

CHAPGRU... Cargo Handling and Port Group [*Navy*] (NVT)

CHAP HO .... Chapter House [*British*] (ROG)

CHAPI......... Compact Helicopter Approach Path Indicator (DA)

CHAP I of S... Chapter Illuminators of Sweden [*Freemasonry*] (ROG)

CHAPL........ Chaplain

Chapman U... Chapman University (GAGS)

Ch App........ Chambre d'Appel [*French Legal term*] (DLA)

Ch App........ Court of Appeal in Chancery [*England*] (DLA)

Chapp .... Customers Having Abundant Product Possibilities [*Term coined by William F . Doescher, publisher of "D & B Reports"*] [*Lifestyle classification*]

Ch App........ Law Reports, Chancery Appeal Cases [*1865-75*] [*England*] [*A publication*] (DLA)

Ch App Cas... Chancery Appeal Cases, English Law Reports [*A publication*] (DLA)

Cha Pr .... Chapman. Practice of the Court of King's Bench [*2nd ed.*] [*1831*] [*A publication*] (DLA)

Chapral........ Chaparral Resources, Inc. [*Associated Press*] (SAG)

CHAPS........ Center for Health and Advanced Policy Studies [*Boston University*] [*Research center*] (RCD)

CHAPS........ ((Cholamidopropyl)dimethylammonio)propanesulfonate [*Biochemistry*]

CHAPS........ Clearinghouse Automated Payments System [*Banking*] [*London*]

CHAPS........ Community Health Action Planning Service

CHAP-S....... Cyclophosphamide, Hexamethylmelamine, Adriamycin, Cisplatin [*Antineoplastic drug regimen*] (DAVI)

CHAPSO...... (Cholamidopropyl)dimethylammonio(hydroxy) Propanesulfonate [*Organic chemistry*]

Chap St J.... Chaplain of the Order of St. John of Jerusalem

CHAR.......... Alert, NT [*FM radio station call letters*]

CHAR.......... Campaign for the Homeless and Rootless [*British*] (DI)

CHAR.......... Chaparral Resources [*NASDAQ symbol*] (TTSB)

CHAR .... Chaparral Resources, Inc. [*NASDAQ symbol*] (NQ)
CHAR .... Character (KSC)
CHAR .... Character
Char .... Characteres [*of Theophrastus*] [*Classical studies*] (OCD)
CHAR .... Characteristic (AABC)
CHAR .... Charcoal
CHAR .... Charcoal Accumulation Rate [*Ecology*]
CHAR .... Charity
CHAR .... Charter
CHAR .... Charwoman [*Slang British*] (DSUE)
CHAR .... Committee for Hispanic Arts and Research (EA)
CHARA .... Center for High Angular Resolution Astronomy [*Georgia State University*] [*Research center*]
CHARA .... Charabanc [*Bus used for sightseeing trips*] [*Slang British*] (DSUE)
CHARAC ...... Character [*or Characteristic*] [*Computer science*] (IAA)
Char Cham Cas... Charley's Chamber Cases [*1875-76*] [*England*] [*A publication*] (DLA)
Chard .... Chardon du Dol et de la Fraude [*A publication*] (DLA)
char del .... Character Delete [*Computer science*] (WDMC)
CHARGE ...... Coloforma, Heart Disease, Arrested Growth or Development, Genital Hypoplasia, and Ear Abnormalities [*Medicine*]
CHARGUID... Character Guidance [*Army*] (AABC)
CHARIBDIS... Chalk River Bibliographic Data Information System [*Atomic Energy of Canada Ltd.*] (NITA)
CHARISMA... Chicago-Argonne Resonant Ionization Spectrometer for Microanalysis [*Astronomy*]
CHARL .... Charlton Kings [*Urban district in England*]
Charl Cha Cas... Charley's Chamber Cases [*1875-76*] [*England*] [*A publication*] (DLA)
Charley Ch Cas... Charley's Chamber Cases [*1875-76*] [*England*] [*A publication*] (DLA)
Charley Pr Cas... Charley's Practice Cases [*1875-81*] [*England*] [*A publication*] (DLA)
Charl Pl .... Charley's Pleading under the Judicature Acts [*A publication*] (DLA)
Charl Pr Cas... Charley's Practice Cases [*1875-81*] [*England*] [*A publication*] (DLA)
Charl RP Stat... Charley's Real Property Statutes [*A publication*] (DLA)
CharlsFS ...... Charles, [*J. W.*] Financial Services [*Associated Press*] (SAG)
CHARM .... CAA [*Civil Aeronautics Authority*] High-Altitude Remote Monitoring
CHARM .... Checking, Accounting and Reporting for Member Firm [*Banking*] (IAA)
CHARM .... Checking, Accounting, and Reporting for Member Firms [*London Stock Exchange*] (MHDW)
CHARM .... Coastal Habitat Fisheries Assessment Research Mensuration [*National Oceanic and Atmospheric Administration*]
CHARM .... Complex Hazardous Air Release Model
CHARM .... Composite High-Altitude Radiation Model (MCD)
CHARM .... Coupled Hydrosphere Atmosphere Research Model [*Marine science*] (OSRA)
CHARM .... Coupled Hydrosphere-Atmosphere Research Model (USDC)
Char Merc ... Charta Mercatoria [*Latin A publication*] (DLA)
Char Pr Cas... Charley's Practice Cases [*1875-81*] [*England*] [*A publication*] (DLA)
CHARR .... Cabaret, Hotel, Restaurant and Retailers Association [*Alaska*] (SRA)
CHARSEC..... Characters per Second [*Computer science*] (IAA)
CHART .... Charta [*Paper*] [*Pharmacy*]
Chart .... Chart Industries [*Associated Press*] (SAG)
CHART .... Chesapeake Highway Advisories Routing Traffic
CHART .... Children's Attitude toward Reading Test (EDAC)
CHART .... Clearinghouse for Augmenting Resources for Training [*DoD*]
CHART .... Computerized Hierarchy and Relationship Table
CHART .... Continuous Hormones as Replacement Therapy [*Medicine*]
CHART .... Council of Hotel and Restaurant Trainers (EA)
Chart .... Rotulus Chartarum [*Charter Roll*] [*Latin A publication*] (DLA)
CHARTAC ..... Chartered Accountant
Chart Acc Aust... Chartered Accountant in Australia [*A publication*]
Chart Antiq.. Chartae Antiquae [*A publication*] (DLA)
CHART BIB... Charta Bibula [*Blotting Paper*] [*Latin*]
CHART CERAT... Charta Cerata [*Waxed Paper*] [*Pharmacy*]
Chart Engr ... Chartered Engineer [*A publication*]
ChartFdl ...... Charter Federal Savings & Loan Virginia [*Associated Press*] (SAG)
Chart Forest... Charta de Foresta [*Charter of the Forest*] [*Latin A publication*] (DLA)
Chart Foresta... Charta de Foresta [*Charter of the Forest*] [*Latin A publication*] (DLA)
Chart Secretary... Chartered Secretary [*A publication*]
CHARTUL ..... Chartula [*A Small Paper*] [*Pharmacy*]
ChartwellL... Chartwell Leisure, Inc. [*Associated Press*] (SAG)
ChartwllRe... Chartwell Re Corp. [*Associated Press*] (SAG)
CHAS .... Catholic Health Association of Saskatchewan (AC)
CHAS .... Catholic Housing Aid Society [*British*] (DBA)
CHAS .... Center for Health Administration Studies [*University of Chicago*] [*Research center*] (RCD)
CHAS .... Chambers
CHAS .... Chassis (MSA)
CHAS .... Comprehensive Housing Affordability Strategy
CHAS .... Sault Ste. Marie, ON [*FM radio station call letters*]
CHASA .... Committee of Heads of Architecture Schools of Australasia [*Australia*]
CHASA .... Council of Hungarian Associations in South Australia
Chase .... [*The*] Chase Manhattan Corp. [*Associated Press*] (SAG)
Chase .... Chase's United States Circuit Court Decisions [*A publication*] (DLA)
CHASE .... Children's Heart Association for Support & Education (AC)
CHASE .... Comet Halley American Southern-Hemisphere Expedition
CHASE .... Cornell Hotel Administration Simulation Exercise [*Computer-programmed management game*]
CHASE .... Cut Holes and Sink 'Em [*Navy ammunition disposal project*]
ChaseBr ...... Chase Brass Industries, Inc. [*Associated Press*] (SAG)

ChaseBrs ..... Chase Brass Industries, Inc. [*Associated Press*] (SAG)
Chase C Law... Salmon P. Chase College of Law of Northern Kentucky State College (GAGS)
ChaseCp ..... Chase Corp. [*Associated Press*] (SAG)
Chase Dec.... Chase's United States Circuit Court Decisions [*A publication*] (DLA)
Chase's Bl.... Chase's Blackstone [*A publication*] (DLA)
Chase's St.... Chase's Statutes at Large [*Ohio*] [*A publication*] (DLA)
Chase Steph Dig Ev... Chase on Stephens' Digest of Evidence [*A publication*] (DLA)
Chase Tr...... Chase's Trial (Impeachment) by the United States Senate [*A publication*] (DLA)
CHASG .... Advise Individual Concerned of Change of Assignment [*Military*]
CHASNAVSHIPY... Charleston Naval Shipyard [*South Carolina*]
CHASSIS ..... Cheshire Achievement of Scientific Skills in Schools [*British*] (AIE)
CHASTEN .... Canadian Health Alliance to Stop Therapist Exploitation Now (AC)
CHAT .... ChatCom [*NASDAQ symbol*] (SAG)
CHAT .... ChatCom Inc. [*NASDAQ symbol*] (TTSB)
CHAT .... Chattel [*Legal shorthand*] (LWAP)
CHAT .... Cheap Access Terminal [*Computer science*] (MHDI)
ChAT .... Choline Acetyl-Transferase [*Also, CAT, ChA, ChAc*] [*An enzyme*]
CHAT .... CLIRA [*Closed-Loop In-Reactor Assembly*] Holddown Assembly Tool [*Nuclear energy*] (NRCH)
CHAT .... Coalition to Halt Auto Theft (EA)
CHAT .... Computer-Harmonized, Application-Tailored (MCD)
CHAT .... Crisis Home Alert Technique
CHAT .... Medicine Hat, AB [*AM radio station call letters*]
CHAT-1 .... Pivot, AB [*Television station call letters*]
ChatCom ..... ChatCom [*Associated Press*] (SAG)
ChateauP .... Chateau Properties [*Associated Press*] (SAG)
CHATNE ...... Chatelaine [*Jewelry*] (ROG)
CHATS .... Call Handler for Advanced Telephone Services [*Telecommunications*] (NITA)
CHATS .... Crabtree-Horsham Affective Trait Scale (EDAC)
CHATT .... Chatteris [*Urban district in England*]
Chattm .... Chattem, Inc. [*Associated Press*] (SAG)
CHAT-TV ...... Medicine Hat, AB [*Television station call letters*]
CHAU .... Carleton, PQ [*Television station call letters*]
CHAUC .... Chaucer [*Fourteenth century English poet*] (ROG)
CHAUFF .... Chauffeur (DSUE)
CHAUFFEUR... Car Handling Automation for Fail-Safe European Roadway
CHA-US .... Catholic Health Association of the United States (EA)
Chaus .... Chaus [*Bernard*], Inc. [*Associated Press*] (SAG)
CHAVMAINTECH... Chief Aviation Maintenance Technician (DNAB)
CHAW .... Command Home All the Way [*Military*] (CAAL)
CHAW .... Cuspidore Hitters Association Worldwide [*Defunct*] (EA)
CHAWA .... Council of Hungarian Associations in Western Australia
CHawN .... National Cash Register Co., Electronics Division, Hawthorne, CA [*Library symbol Library of Congress*] (LCLS)
CHawNo....... Northrop Corp., Aircraft Division, Hawthorne, CA [*Library symbol Library of Congress*] (LCLS)
CHAY .... Barrie, ON [*FM radio station call letters*]
CHaZaL .... Chakhamenu Zikhronam Livrakhah [*A publication*] (BJA)
Ch B .... Bachelor of Chemistry
ChB .... Bachelor of Surgery (DD)
CHB .... Bay Area Library and Information System, Hayward, CA [*Library symbol Library of Congress*] (LCLS)
CHB .... Cargo Handling Battalion [*Obsolete Army*]
CHB .... Center Halfback [*Soccer*]
CHB .... Chain Home Beamed [*Aviation*]
CHB .... Champion Enterprises [*NYSE symbol*] (SAG)
CHB .... Champion Enterprises [*NYSE symbol*] (TTSB)
CHB .... Champion Enterprises, Inc. [*AMEX symbol*] (SPSG)
CHB .... Chelyabinsk Air Enterprise [*Former USSR*] [*FAA designator*] (FAAC)
chb .... Chibcha [*MARC language code Library of Congress*] (LCCP)
Ch B .... Chirurgiae Baccalaureus [*Bachelor of Surgery*]
CHB .... Cholera Toxin B [*Medicine*]
CHB .... Chronic Hepatitis B [*Medicine*]
CHB .... Chronic Hepatitis B [*Medicine*] (DMAA)
CHB .... Church [*Alaska*] [*Seismograph station code, US Geological Survey*] (SEIS)
CHB .... Commission on Highway Beautification
CHB .... Commonwealth Heraldry Board [*Papatoetoe, New Zealand*] (EAIO)
CHB .... Complete Heart Block [*Medicine*]
CHB .... Composted Hardwood Barks
CHB .... Congenital Heart Block [*Medicine*] (DMAA)
CHB .... Cooperative Housing Bulletin [*A publication*] (EAAP)
CHB .... Cyanohydroxybutene [*Organic chemistry*]
CHBA .... Canadian Home Builders' Association
CHBA .... Congenital Heinz Body Hemolytic Anemia [*Medicine*]
CHBC .... Capitol Hill Burro Club (EA)
CHBC .... Cleveland Hockey Booster Club (EA)
CHBC .... Kelowna, BC [*Television station call letters*]
CHBD .... Chalk Board [*Technical drawings*]
CHBDL-ST.... Common High Bandwith Data Link - Shipboard Terminal (DWSG)
Ch B Ex...... Chief Baron of the Exchequer [*British*] (DLA)
CHBHA .... Congenital Heinz Body Hemolytic Anemia [*Medicine*] (DMAA)
Ch Bills....... Chitty on Bills [*A publication*] (DLA)
ChBk.......... Chemical Banking Corp. [*Associated Press*] (SAG)
Ch Bk News... Children's Book News [*A publication*] (BRI)
Ch Black...... Chase's Blackstone [*A publication*] (DLA)
Ch Black...... Chitty's Edition of Blackstone's Commentaries [*A publication*] (DLA)
CHBOSN ...... Chief Boatswain [*Navy rating. Obsolete*]
chbr .... Chamber (VRA)
CHBR .... Chlorobromide Print Process (VRA)
CHBUAER .... Chief of the Bureau of Aeronautics [*Obsolete Navy*]

CHBUDOCKS... Chief of the Bureau of Yards and Docks [*Obsolete Navy*]
CHBUMED.... Chief of the Bureau of Medicine and Surgery [*Navy*]
CHBUORD.... Chief of the Bureau of Ordnance [*Obsolete Navy*]
CHBUPERS.... Chief of the Bureau of Naval Personnel
Ch Burn's J... Chitty's Edition of Burn's Justice [*A publication*]   (DLA)
CHBUSANDA... Chief of the Bureau of Supplies and Accounts [*Obsolete Navy*]
CHBUSHIPS... Chief of the Bureau of Ships [*Obsolete Navy*]
Ch BWatch.... Children's Bookwatch [*A publication*]   (BRI)
CHBX .... Sault Ste. Marie, ON [*Television station call letters*]
CHC .... California Housing Council   (SRA)
CHC .... Canadian Horticultural Council [*Conseil Canadien de l'Horticulture*]
           (AC)
CHC .... Cargo Handling Charge [*Shipping*]   (DS)
CHC .... Cell Hemoglobin Concentration [*Biochemistry, medicine*]
CHC .... Cell Host Computer
CHC .... Centro Hispano Catolico [*Catholic Spanish Center*]   (EA)
CHC .... Chabot College, Hayward, CA [*Library symbol Library of Congress*]
           (LCLS)
CHC .... Champion Healthcare [*AMEX symbol*]   (TTSB)
CHC ...,,...... Champion Healthcare Corp. [*AMEX symbol*]   (SAG)
CHC .... Chance   (FAAC)
CHC .... Chancellor Energy Resources, Inc. [*Toronto Stock Exchange symbol*]
CHC .... Channel Control   (BUR)
CHC .... Chapel Hill [*North Carolina*] [*Seismograph station code, US
           Geological Survey Closed*]   (SEIS)
CHC .... Chaplain Corps
CHC .... Check Coil
CHC .... Chestnut Hill College [*Pennsylvania*]
CHC .... Child Health Centre [*Australia*]
CHC .... China Ocean Helicopter Corp. [*ICAO designator*]   (FAAC)
CHC .... Chlorinated Hydrocarbon
CHC .... Choke Coil   (AAG)
CHC .... Christchurch [*New Zealand*] [*Airport symbol*]   (OAG)
CHC .... Christian Heritage Center   (EA)
CHC .... Christian Heritage College [*El Cajon, CA*]
CHC .... Clathrin Heavy Chain [*Genetics*]
CHC .... Clean Harbors Cooperative   (EA)
CHC .... Clerk to the House of Commons   (DLA)
CHC .... Coalitions for Health Care   (EA)
CHC .... College of the Holy Cross [*Worcester, MA*]
CHC .... Committee for Handgun Control   (EA)
CHC .... Community Health Center
CHC .... Community Health Computing
CHC .... Community Health Council [*British*]
CHC .... Community of the Holy Cross [*Anglican religious community*]
CHC .... Comprehensive Health Center [*Medicine*]
CHC .... Confederate High Command, International [*Later, AT*] [*An
           association*]   (EA)
CHC .... Congressional Hispanic Caucus   (EA)
CHC .... Corrected Head Count
CHC .... Craftsman Homeowner Club   (EA)
CHC .... Crouse-Hinds Co.
CHC .... Cyclohexylamine Carbonate [*Corrosion prevention*]
CHCA .... Canadian Home Care Association [*Association Canadienne de Soins
           et Services a Domicile*]   (AC)
Ch Ca.......... Cases in Chancery [*England*] [*A publication*]   (DLA)
CHCA .... Chaco Canyon National Monument
CHCA .... Colorado Health Care Association   (SRA)
CHCA .... Consolidated Health Care Associates, Inc. [*NASDAQ symbol*]   (SAG)
CHCA .... Consolidated Hlth Care Assoc [*NASDAQ symbol*]   (TTSB)
Ch Ca Ch ..... Choyce's Cases in Chancery [*1557-1606*] [*England*] [*A publication*]
           (DLA)
CHCANYS .... Community Health Care Association of New York State   (SRA)
CHCARP....... Chief Carpenter [*Navy rating Obsolete*]
Ch Cas......... Cases in Chancery [*England*] [*A publication*]   (DLA)
Ch Cas Ch .... Choyce's Cases in Chancery [*1557-1606*] [*England*] [*A publication*]
           (DLA)
Ch Cas (Eng)... Cases in Chancery [*England*] [*A publication*]   (DLA)
Ch Cas in Ch... Choyce's Cases in Chancery [*1557-1606*] [*England*]
           [*A publication*]   (DLA)
CHCBP........ Continued Health Care Benefit Program [*DoD*]
CHCC .... Connecticut Heating and Cooling Contractors Association   (SRA)
CHCC .... Montefiore-Morrisania Comprehensive Health Care Center [*Research
           center*]   (RCD)
CHCE .... Choice
CHCF .... Component Handling and Cleaning Facility [*Energy Research and
           Development Administration*]
ChCft........... Chris-Craft Industries, Inc. [*Associated Press*]   (SAG)
CHCH .... Chickamauga and Chattanooga National Military Park
CHCH .... Church   (ROG)
CHCH .... (Cyclohexenyl)cyclohexanone [*Organic chemistry*]
CHCH .... Hamilton, ON [*Television station call letters*]
Ch Ch.......... Upper Canada Chancery Chambers Reports [*A publication*]   (DLA)
Ch Cham....... Upper Canada Chancery Chambers Reports [*A publication*]   (DLA)
Ch Chamb..... Chancery Chambers [*Upper Canada*]   (DLA)
Ch Chamb (Can)... Chancery Chambers [*Upper Canada*]   (DLA)
CHCHel........ CHC Helicopter Corp. [*Associated Press*]   (SAG)
ChchTch....... Churchill Technology [*Associated Press*]   (SAG)
ChChW....... Chronik der Christlichen Welt [*A publication*]   (BJA)
CHCIVENG ... Chief of Civil Engineers [*Army*]   (DNAB)
CHCIVENGS... Chief of Civil Engineers [*Army*]
CHCK .... Chief Cook [*Navy rating Obsolete*]
ChckExp...... Check Express, Inc. [*Associated Press*]   (SAG)
Ch Clk......... Chief Clerk   (BARN)
CHCLS .... Canister Harpoon Control and Launch System   (MCD)

CHCM .... Cell Hemoglobin Concentration Mean [*Biochemistry, medicine*]
CHCM .... Marystown, NF [*AM radio station call letters*]
ChCMV....... Chrysanthemum Chlorotic Mottle Viroid
CHCNSW..... Catholic Health Care Association of New South Wales [*Australia*]
CHCO .... City Holding [*NASDAQ symbol*]   (TTSB)
CHCO .... City Holding Co. [*NASDAQ symbol*]   (NQ)
CH COLL ..... Christ's College [*Cambridge University*]   (ROG)
Ch Col Op..... Chalmers' Colonial Opinions [*England*] [*A publication*]   (DLA)
CHCOMNAVAIRSYS... Chief, Command Naval Air Systems [*Later, NAVAIR*]
CHCP .... Cargo Handling Cooperative Program [*MARAD*]   (TAG)
CHCP .... Chemical Hazard Communication Policy [*Stanford University*]
CHCP .... Chief Justice of the Common Pleas [*British*]   (DLA)
CHCP .... Correctional Health Care Program
CHCQ .... Congres Haitien Canada-Quebec   (AC)
Ch Cr L .... Chitty's Criminal Law [*A publication*]   (DLA)
CHCS .... Cabin Humidity Control Subsystem [*Aviation*]   (NASA)
CHCS .... Canadian Highland Cattle Society [*Societe Canadienne des Eleveurs
           de Bovins Highland*]   (AC)
CHCS .... Chico's FAS [*NASDAQ symbol*]   (TTSB)
CHCS .... Chicos Fas, Inc. [*NASDAQ symbol*]   (SAG)
CHCS .... Composite Health Care System [*DoD*]
CHCSS .... Chief Central Security Service
CHCT .... Caffeine Halothane Challenge Test [*Clinical chemistry*]
CHCT .... Halothane-Caffeine Contracture Test [*Medical test*]   (PAZ)
CHCU .... Channel Control Unit
CHCW .... Conference for Health Council Work [*Later, Conference on
           Community Health Planning*]
CHD .... Campaign for Human Development   (EA)
CHD .... Centre for Human Development [*British*]   (CB)
CHD .... Chaldron [*Unit of measure*] [*Obsolete*]
CHD .... Chandler, AZ [*Location identifier FAA*]   (FAAL)
CHD .... Chediak-Higashi Disease [*Medicine*]
CHD .... Chelsea Resources [*Vancouver Stock Exchange symbol*]
CHD .... Child   (ROG)
CHD .... Childhood Disease [*Medicine*]
ChD............ Chile Democratico   (EA)
ChD............ Chirurgiae Doctor [*Doctor of Surgery*]
CHD .... Chord   (KSC)
CHD .... Chronic Hemodialysis [*Nephrology*]
CHD .... Church & Dwight [*NYSE symbol*]   (TTSB)
CHD .... Church & Dwight Co., Inc. [*NYSE symbol*]   (SPSG)
CHD .... Committee for Handicapable Dancers   (EA)
CHD .... Common Hepatic Duct [*Gastroenterology*]   (DAVI)
CHD .... Congenital Heart Disease [*Medicine*]
CHD .... Congestive Heart Disease [*Cardiology*]   (DAVI)
CHD .... Cordell Hull Dam [*TVA*]
CHD .... Coronary Heart Disease [*Medicine*]
CHD .... Correctional Holding Detachment [*Military*]   (AABC)
CHD .... Cyclohexadiene [*Organic chemistry*]
CHD .... Cyclophosphamide, Hexamethylmelamine, Cisplatin [*Antineoplastic
           drug regimen*]   (DAVI)
Ch D .... Doctor of Chemistry
Ch D .... English Law Reports, Chancery Division [*A publication*]   (DLA)
Ch D 2d ...... English Law Reports, Chancery Division, Second Series
           [*A publication*]   (DLA)
CHDB .... Compatible High-Density Bipolar Code [*Telecommunications*]   (TEL)
CHDC .... Canadian Housing Design Council [*CMHC*]
CHDC .... Cyclohexenedicarboxylic Acid [*Organic chemistry*]
CHDDS........ Committee of Heads of Drama Departments in Scotland   (AIE)
CHDI .... Cyclohexylene Diisocyanate [*Organic chemistry*]
Ch Dig .... Chaney's Digest, Michigan Reports [*A publication*]   (DLA)
CHDIR......... Change Directory [*Computer science*]
Ch Div .... English Law Reports, Chancery Division [*A publication*]   (DLA)
Ch Div (Eng)... English Law Reports, Chancery Division [*A publication*]   (DLA)
Ch Div'l Ct... Chancery Divisional Court [*England*]   (DLA)
CHDL .... Computer Hardware Description Language
CHDLG........ Chief, Defense Liaison Group   (CINC)
CHDLG-INDO... Chief, Defense Liaison Group-Indonesia   (DNAB)
CHDM .... Cyclohexanedimethanol [*Organic chemistry*]
CHDN .... Children   (ROG)
CHDN .... Churchill Downs, Inc. [*NASDAQ symbol*]   (SAG)
chDNA .... Chloroplast DNA [*Deoxyribonucleic Acid*] [*Genetics*]   (DOG)
CHDO.......... Community Housing Development Organization [*Department of
           Housing and Urban Development*]
ChDock .... Chicago Dock & Canal Trust [*Associated Press*]   (SAG)
CHD-R .... Cyclophosphamide, Hexamethylmelamine, Cisplatin plus
           Radiotherapy [*Antineoplastic drug regimen*]   (DAVI)
CHDX .... U.S.-China Indl Exchange [*NASDAQ symbol*]   (TTSB)
CHDXW....... US-China Indl Exchange Wrrt'A' [*NASDAQ symbol*]   (TTSB)
CHDXZ........ US-China Indl Exchange Wrrt'B' [*NASDAQ symbol*]   (TTSB)
CHE .... Campaign for Homosexual Equality [*British*]   (DBA)
CHE .... Cargo Handling Equipment [*Army*]
CHE .... Channel End   (BUR)
CHE .... Chapel of Ease [*Church of England*]
CHE..... Cheb [*Eger*] [*Czechoslovakia*] [*Seismograph station code, US
           Geological Survey*] [*Closed*]   (SEIS)
che............ Chechen [*MARC language code Library of Congress*]   (LCCP)
CHE............ Chemed Corp. [*NYSE symbol*]   (SPSG)
Ch E .... Chemical Engineer
CHE............ Cheque [*British*]   (ROG)
che............ Cherry   (VRA)
CHE............ Chestnut Hill College, Philadelphia, PA [*OCLC symbol*]   (OCLC)
Ch E .... Chief Engineer [*British military*]   (DMA)
CHE............ Chip Enable [*Computer science*]   (MHDI)
ChE........... Cholinesterase [*An enzyme*]

CHE.............	Chronicle of Higher Education [*A publication*] (BRI)
CHE.............	Coalition for Health and the Environment (EA)
CHE.............	Commonwealth Human Ecology Council [*British*]
CHE.............	Container Handling Equipment
CHE.............	Continuing Health Education (MCD)
CHE.............	Council for Higher Education [*US and Israel*]
CHE.............	Hayden, CO [*Location identifier FAA*] (FAAL)
CHe.............	Healdsburg Carnegie Public Library, Healdsburg, CA [*Library symbol Library of Congress*] (LCLS)
CHE.............	Switzerland [*ANSI three-letter standard code*] (CNC)
CHE.............	Top Flight Air Service, Inc. [*ICAO designator*] (FAAC)
CHEA	Canadian Home Economics Association [*Association Canadienne d'Economie Familiale*] (AC)
CHEA	Children's Home-Based Education Association [*British*] (DBA)
CHEA	Christian Home Educators Association (EA)
CHEA	Commonwealth Hansard Editors Association (EAIO)
CHEAD	Conference for Higher Education in Art and Design [*British*]
CHEAF	Canadian Home Economics Association Foundation [*Fondation de l'Association Canadienne d'Economie Familiale*] (AC)
CHeaFF	Children's Health and Fitness Fund
CHEAM	Centre des Hautes Etudes Administratives sur l'Afrique et l'Asie Modernes [*Center for Advanced Administrative Studies on Modern Africa and Asia*] [*French*] (AF)
CHEAO	Coalition of Higher Education Assistance Organizations (EA)
CHEAR	Council on Higher Education in the American Republics [*Later, ICHE*]
CHEAR	National Foundation for Children's Hearing Education and Research (EA)
CHEC	Cascade Holistic Economic Consultants (EA)
CHEC	Channel Evaluation and Call (IEEE)
CHEC	Checkered [*Navigation markers*]
CHEC	Coalition for Hypertension Education and Control
CHEC	Commonwealth Human Ecology Council [*British*] (EAIO)
CHEC	Community Hypertension Evaluation Clinic [*New Jersey*]
CHEC	Comprehensive Health and Emergency Care [*Medicine*]
Check.........	Checkpoint [*A publication*]
Checkers......	Checkers Drive In Restaurants [*Associated Press*] (SAG)
Checkmte	Checkmate Electronics, Inc. [*Associated Press*] (SAG)
CHECKSUM...	Summation Check [*Communications transmissions*]
CHECMATE...	Compact High-Energy Capacitor Module Advanced Technology Experiment [*For development of the rail gun*]
CHECO	Contemporary Historical Examination Current Operations [*Air Force*] (AFM)
CHED	Edmonton, AB [*AM radio station call letters*]
CHEEF	Center for Hydrogen Embrittlement of Electroplated Fasteners [*Worchester Polytechnic Institute*] [*Research center*] (RCD)
CHEESE.......	Cheshire Experiment in Educational Software [*British*] (AIE)
Cheeseck......	[*The*] Cheesecake Factory, Inc. [*Associated Press*] (SAG)
Cheev Med Jur...	Cheever's Medical Jurisprudence for India [*A publication*] (DLA)
CHEF	Chefs International, Inc. [*NASDAQ symbol*] (NQ)
CHEF	Chefs Intl. [*NASDAQ symbol*] (TTSB)
CHEF	Chelation-Enhanced Fluorescence [*Chemistry*]
CHEF	Chemistry of High Elevation Fog Project [*Environment Canada*]
CHEF	Chicken Embryo Fibroblast [*Cytology*]
CHEF	Chinese Hamster Embryo Fibroblast [*Cytology*]
CHEF	Citizens Honest Elections Foundation
CHEF	Clamped Homogeneous Electric Field
CHEF	Comprehensive Health Education Foundation (EA)
CHEF	Contour-Clamped Homogeneous Electric Field [*Instrumentation*]
C-HEF	Corporate-Higher Education Forum [*Forum Entreprises-Universites*] (AC)
CHEF	Granby, PQ [*AM radio station call letters*]
ChefsInt	Chefs International, Inc. [*Associated Press*] (SAG)
CHEFU	Cooled High-Energy Firing Unit
CHEHA	Centre for Human Ecology and Health Advancement [*University of Newcastle*] [*Australia*]
CHeHM	Healdsburg Museum, Healdsburg, CA [*Library symbol*] [*Library of Congress*] (LCLS)
CHE INC.......	Center for Human Environments Associates, Inc. [*City University of New York*] [*Research center*] (RCD)
CHEK	Victoria, BC [*Television station call letters*]
CHEK-5	Campbell River, BC [*Television station call letters*]
CHEKA	Chrezvychainaya Komissiya po Borbe s Kontrrevolutisiei i Sabotazhem [*Extraordinary Commission for Combating Counterrevolution and Sabotage; Soviet secret police organization, 1917-1921*]
CHEL...........	Cambridge History of English Literature
CHEL...........	Chain Home Extra Low [*Aviation*]
Chel...........	Chelsea [*A publication*] (BRI)
CHELEC........	Chief Electrician [*Navy rating Obsolete*]
CHELECTECH...	Chief Electronics Technician (DNAB)
ChelGCA	Chelsea GCA Realty [*Associated Press*] (SAG)
CHELM.........	Chelmsford [*City in England*]
CHELMSF ...	Chelmsford [*City in England*] (ROG)
CHELT.........	Cheltenham [*Typeface*] (DGA)
CHELT.........	Cheltenham [*City in England*]
CHELTM.......	Cheltenham [*City in England*] (ROG)
CHEM..........	Chemical [*or Chemistry*] (AFM)
CHEM..........	Chemist
CHEM..........	Chemist
Chem..........	Chemistry (DD)
Chem..........	Chemotherapy [*Medicine*] (MAE)
CHEM..........	Chempower, Inc. [*NASDAQ symbol*] (NQ)
CHEM..........	Containerized Hospital Emergency Mobile (PDAA)
CHem..........	Hemet Public Library, Hemet, CA [*Library symbol Library of Congress*] (LCLS)

CHEM..........	Trois Rivieres, PQ [*Television station call letters*]
CHEMASIA...	Asian International Chemical and Process Engineering and Contracting Show and Conference
CHEM DEMIL...	Chemical Demilitarization [*Military*] (RDA)
ChemDep.......	Chemical Dependency (OICC)
CHEMDEX.......	Chemical Index [*Database*]
Chem E........	Chemical Engineer
Chemed........	Chemed Corp. [*Associated Press*] (SAG)
Chem Eng....	Chemical Engineer
Chem Engng Mining Rev...	Chemical Engineering and Mining Review [*A publication*]
CHEMFET.......	Chemically Sensitive Field Effect Transistor
CHEMFICO......	Chemical International Finance & Consulting [*Belgium*]
CHEMI	Chemical Engineering Modular Instruction [*Project*]
ChemID........	Chemical Identification File [*National Library of Medicine*] [*Information service or system*] (IID)
Chem Ing....	Chemischer Ingenieur [*Chemical Engineer*] [*German*]
ChemIntl......	Chem International, Inc. [*Associated Press*] (SAG)
CHEML.........	Chemical (ROG)
CHEML.........	Chemical
CHEMLAB	Chemical Modeling Laboratory [*NIH/EPA Chemical Information System*] [*Database*]
CHEMLINE ...	Chemical Dictionary On-Line [*National Library of Medicine*] [*Bethesda, MD Database*]
CHEMLY	Chemically [*Freight*]
CHEMNAME...	Chemical Name Dictionary [*Dialog Information Services, Inc.*] [*Database*]
CHEMNET ...	Chemical Network [*Chemical Transportation Emergency Center*] (ERG)
CHEMO	Chemotherapy [*Medicine*] (WDAA)
Chem/PetEng...	Chemical/Petroleum Engineering (DD)
CHEMPID......	Chemical & Petroleum Division (ACII)
CHEMRAWN...	Chemical Research Applied to World Need [*IUPAC*]
CHEMRiC....	Chemical Monograph Referral Center [*Consumer Product Safety Commission*] [*Information service or system*] (IID)
CHEMS	Chemical Education Material Study [*American Chemical Society*] (AEE)
CHEMSDI......	Chemical Abstracts Selective Dissemination of Information (NITA)
CHEMSEARCH...	Chemicals Selected for Equal, Analogous, or Related Character (DIT)
ChemSEP.....	Chemical Special Emphasis Program [*Occupational Safety and Health Administration*]
CHEMSIS	CHEM Singly Indexed Substances [*DIALOG Information Services, Inc.*] [*Database*]
ChemSTAR...	Chemical Structure Analysis Routine
ChemTeC....	Chemical Technicians Curriculum [*Project*]
CHEMTIC	Chemistry Test Item Collection (ADA)
CHEMTIPS	Chemistry Teaching Information Processing System
CHEMTRACK...	Chemical Information and Tracking System (GNE)
CHEMTREC...	Chemical Transportation Emergency Center [*Chemical Manufacturers Association*]
ChemTrl.....	Chemi-Trol Chemical Co. [*Associated Press*] (SAG)
CHEMU	Chemical Hazards and Emergency Management Unit [*Queensland*] [*Australia*]
CHEMVVAM...	Chemical Vehicle Vulnerability Analysis Model (MCD)
CHENIC......	Chenodeoxycholic Acid [*Also, CDA, CDC, CDCA*] [*Biochemistry*]
CHEOPS......	Chemical Information Systems Operators [*Later, EUSIDIC*]
CHEOPS......	Chemical Operations System
CHEOPS......	Cyclically Harvested Earth-Orbit Production System
CHEP	Community Health Education Project
CHEP	Cuban/Haitian Entrant Program [*Department of Health and Human Services*] (GFGA)
CHEPP	Catastrophic Health Expense Protection Plan [*Insurance*]
CHEPS	Centre for Higher Education Policy Studies [*British*] (AIE)
CHEPSOP.....	Charitable / Employee Stock Ownership Plan [*Tax plan*] (MHDW)
CHEQ	Chelation-Enhanced Quenching [*Chemistry*]
CHEQ	Cheque [*British*] (ROG)
CHER	Centre for Habilitation Education and Research [*University of Waterloo*] [*Research center*] (RCD)
CHER	Cherry Corp. [*NASDAQ symbol*] (NQ)
Cher...........	De Cherubim [*Philo*] (BJA)
CHER	Sydney, NS [*AM radio station call letters*]
CHERA	Canadian Health Economics Research Association [*See also ACRES*]
CHERA	Cherry Corp. 'A' [*NASDAQ symbol*] (TTSB)
CHERB	Cherry Corp. 'B' [*NASDAQ symbol*] (TTSB)
Cher Ca	Cherokee Case [*A publication*] (DLA)
Cheroke......	Cherokee, Inc. [*Associated Press*] (SAG)
Cherry........	Cherry Corp. [*Associated Press*] (SAG)
CHERSS.......	Continuous High-Amplitude EEG [*Electroencephalogram*] Rhythmical Synchronous Slowing [*Medicine*] (DMAA)
CHERUB.......	Chemical Engineering Database
CHES	Canadian Hospital Engineering Society
CHES	Cheese
CHES	Chesapeake Bay [*Virginia and Maryland*]
CHES	Chesham [*Urban district in England*]
CHES	Cheshire [*County in England*]
Ches	Cheshire [*County in England*] (ODBW)
CHES	Chester Hldgs Ltd [*NASDAQ symbol*] (TTSB)
CHES	Chestnut (ROG)
CHES	Cyclohexylaminoethanesulfonic Acid [*A buffer*]
CHESBAYGRU...	Chesapeake Bay Group [*Navy*] (DNAB)
ChesBio	Chesapeake Biological Laboratories, Inc. [*Associated Press*] (SAG)
Ches Ca......	Report of the Chesapeake Case, New Brunswick [*A publication*] (DLA)

Ches Co.......	Chester County Reports [*Pennsylvania*] [*A publication*] (DLA)
Ches Co Rep...	Chester County Reports [*Pennsylvania*] [*A publication*] (DLA)
CHESDIVNAVFACENGCOM...	Chesapeake Division Naval Facilities Engineering Command (DNAB)
CHESDIVSUPPAC...	Chesapeake Division Support Facility [*Navy*] (DNAB)
ChesEn	Chesapeake Energy Corp. [*Associated Press*] (SAG)
CHESH........	Cheshire [*County in England*] (ROG)
Cheshire......	Smith's New Hampshire Reports [*A publication*] (DLA)
CHES/NAVFAC...	Chesapeake Division Naval Facilities Engineering Command [*Washington, DC*]
CHESNAVFACENGCOM...	Chesapeake Division Naval Facilities Engineering Command [*Washington, DC*]
CHESOP......	Charitable/Employee Stock Ownership Plan [*Tax plan*]
CHESS........	Canadian Health Education Specialists Society
CHESS........	Centers for Health, Education, and Social Systems Studies [*Formerly, Center for H ealth and Social Systems Research*] [*Research center*] (RCD)
CHESS........	Chemical Shift Selective [*Medicine*] (DMAA)
CHESS........	Children's Health, Education, and Safety Services [*Australia*]
CHESS........	Clearing House Electronic Subregister System [*Australian Stock Exchange*]
ChESS........	Clearing House for Education and Social Studies/Social Science [*Department of Education*] (NITA)
CHESS........	Community Health and Environmental Surveillance System [*Environmental Protection Agency project*]
CHESS........	Cornell High-Energy Synchrotron Source Laboratory [*Cornell University*] [*Research center*]
Chess L......	Chess Life [*A publication*]
CHEST........	Chester [*City in England*] (ROG)
CHEST........	Chesterton [*England*]
CHEST........	Combined Higher Education Software Team (AIE)
Chest Ca.....	Case of the City of Chester on Quo Warranto [*A publication*] (DLA)
Chest Co......	Chester County Reports [*Pennsylvania*] [*A publication*] (DLA)
Chest Co (PA)...	Chester County Reports [*Pennsylvania*] [*A publication*] (DLA)
Chest Co Rep...	Chester County Reports [*Pennsylvania*] [*A publication*] (DLA)
Chester........	Chester County Reports [*Pennsylvania*] [*A publication*] (DLA)
Chester Co (PA)...	Chester County Reports [*Pennsylvania*] [*A publication*] (DLA)
Chester Co Rep...	Chester County Reports [*Pennsylvania*] [*A publication*] (DLA)
ChestrBc......	Chester Bancorp, Inc. [*Associated Press*] (SAG)
ChestrV.......	Chester Valley Bancorp [*Associated Press*] (SAG)
ChesUtl.......	Chesapeake Utilities Corp. [*Associated Press*] (SAG)
CHETAH......	Chemical Thermodynamics and Energy Hazard Evaluation [*American Society for Testing and Materials*]
Chetty........	Sadr Diwani Adalat Cases, Madras [*India*] [*A publication*] (DLA)
CHEV..........	Chevalier [*Knight title*]
Chev..........	Chevalier (DD)
CHEV..........	Cheveley [*England*]
Chev..........	Cheves' South Carolina Law Reports [*1839-1940*] [*A publication*] (DLA)
CHEV..........	Chevrolet [*Automotive engineering*]
CHEV..........	Chevron
Chev Ch......	Cheves' South Carolina Equity Reports [*1839-1940*] [*A publication*] (DLA)
Chev Eq......	Cheves' South Carolina Equity Reports [*1839-1940*] [*A publication*] (DLA)
Cheves........	Cheves' South Carolina Law Reports [*1839-1940*] [*A publication*] (DLA)
Cheves Eq (SC)...	Cheves' South Carolina Equity Reports [*1839-1940*] [*A publication*] (DLA)
Cheves L (SC)...	Cheves' South Carolina Equity Reports [*1839-1940*] [*A publication*] (DLA)
CHEVMA......	Canadian Heat Exchange & Vessel Manufacturers Association (AC)
Chevron.......	Chevron Corp. [*Associated Press*] (SAG)
CHEVY........	Chevrolet
ChevyC.......	Chevy Chase Preferred Capital Corp. [*Associated Press*] (SAG)
CHEX.........	Cheques [*British*] (ROG)
Ch Ex Off.....	Chief Executive Officer [*Also, CEO*]
CHEX-TV......	Peterborough, ON [*Television station call letters*]
CHEX-UP......	Cyclophosphamide, Hexamethylmelamine, Fluorouracil, Platinol [*Cisplatin*] [*Antineoplastic drug regimen*]
CHEY.........	Cheyenne [*City in Wyoming*] (ROG)
CHEY.........	Cheyenne Software, Inc. (MHDW)
CHEY.........	Trois Rivieres, PQ [*FM radio station call letters*]
CheySoft......	Cheyenne Software, Inc. [*Associated Press*] (SAG)
CHEZ.........	Ottawa, ON [*FM radio station call letters*]
CHEZ.........	Suprema Specialities, Inc. [*NASDAQ symbol*] (SAG)
CHEZ.........	Suprema Specialities [*NASDAQ symbol*] (TTSB)
CHF..........	Calhoun Falls [*South Carolina*] [*Seismograph station code, US Geological Survey*] (SEIS)
CHF..........	California Health Federation (SRA)
CHF..........	Canadian Hunger Foundation [*Fondation Canadienne Contre la Faim*] (AC)
ChF..........	Chaplain of the Fleet [*Navy British*]
CHF..........	Chatham House Foundation (EA)
CHF..........	Chemical Heritage Foundation [*Formerly, NFHC*]
CHF..........	Cherry Hill Free Public Library, Cherry Hill, NJ [*OCLC symbol*] (OCLC)
CHF..........	Chick Heart Fibroblast [*Cytology*]
CHF..........	Chief
CHF..........	Chief
CHF..........	Children's Heart Fund (EA)
CHF..........	Chitaavia [*Former USSR*] [*FAA designator*] (FAAC)
CHF..........	Chock Full O'Nuts [*NYSE symbol*] (TTSB)
CHF..........	Chock Full O'Nuts Corp. [*Wall Street slang name: "Nuts"*] [*NYSE symbol*] (SPSG)

CHF..........	Chronic Heart Failure [*Cardiology*] (DAVI)
CHF..........	Chrysler Historical Foundation
CHF..........	Coalition for Health Funding (EA)
CHF..........	Columba House Fund [*Later, CIM*] (EA)
CHF..........	Community of the Holy Family [*Anglican religious community*]
CHF..........	Congenital Hepatic Fibrosis [*Medicine*] (DMAA)
CHF..........	Congestive Heart Failure [*Medicine*]
CHF..........	Congregation of the Sisters of the Holy Faith [*Australia*]
CHF..........	Contract History File [*Military*] (AFIT)
CHF..........	Cooperative Housing Foundation (EA)
CHF..........	Coupled Hartree-Fock [*Quantum mechanics*]
CHF..........	Creation Health Foundation (EA)
CHF..........	Crimean Hemorrhagic Fever [*Medicine*] (PDAA)
CHF..........	Critical Heat Flux [*Nuclear energy*]
CHF..........	Cyclophosphamide, Hexamethylmelamine, Fluorouracil [*Antineoplastic drug regimen*]
CHF..........	Czech Heritage Foundation (EA)
CHFA	Canadian Health Food Association
CHFA	Carbonate Hydroxy Fluorapatite [*Inorganic chemistry*]
CHFA	Edmonton, AB [*AM radio station call letters*]
CHFB	Chase Federal Bank [*NASDAQ symbol*] (TTSB)
CHFC	Carnegie Hero Fund Commission (EA)
CHFC	Certified Financial Consultant [*Canada*] (DD)
ChFC	Chartered Financial Consultant [*The American College*] [*Designation awarded by*]
CHFC	Chemical Financial [*NASDAQ symbol*] (TTSB)
CHFC	Chemical Financial Corp. [*NASDAQ symbol*] (NQ)
CHFC	Cheryl Hale Fan Club [*Defunct*] (EA)
CHFC	Churchill, MB [*AM radio station call letters*]
CHFCI	Charlie Hodge Fan Club Internationale (EA)
ChfCon	Chief Consolidated Mining Co. [*Associated Press*] (SAG)
CHFD	Ceramic Hotform Die (MCD)
CHFD	Charter Federal Savings & Loan Virginia [*NASDAQ symbol*] (NQ)
CHFD	Controlled High Flux Dialysis [*Medicine*] (DMAA)
CHFD	Thunder Bay, ON [*Television station call letters*]
CHFFR	Chauffeur
CHFI	Toronto, ON [*FM radio station call letters*]
CHFIE	Cordell Hull Foundation for International Education (EA)
ChfInt	Chieftain International Fund [*Associated Press*] (SAG)
CHFM	Calgary, AB [*FM radio station call letters*]
CHFNS	Cooperative Housing Federation of Nova Scotia (AC)
ChFP	Chartered Financial Planner [*Insurance*]
CHFR	Critical Heat Flux Ratio [*Nuclear energy*] (NRCH)
CHFS	Central [*Atom*] Hyperfine Structure
CHFT	Canadian Home Fitness Test [*Medicine*]
CHFTN	Chieftain (ROG)
CHFV	Combined High Frequency of Ventilation [*Medicine*] (DAVI)
Ch Fwd	Charges Forward (DS)
CHFX	Halifax, NS [*FM radio station call letters*]
CHG	Challengair [*Belgium*] [*FAA designator*] (FAAC)
CHG	Change (AAG)
CHG	Charge (KSC)
CHG	Charge d'Affaires [*Foreign Service*]
CHG	Charlemagne Resources [*Vancouver Stock Exchange symbol*]
CHG	Chiang Mai [*Thailand*] [*Seismograph station code, US Geological Survey*] (SEIS)
CHG	Crosshatch Generator
CHG	Helicopter Ship, Missile-Armed [*NATO*]
CHG	Sisters of the Holy Ghost [*Roman Catholic religious order*]
CHGA	Maniwaki, PQ [*FM radio station call letters*]
CHGCB........	Change Control Board [*NASA*] (KSC)
CHGD.........	Center for Human Growth and Develoment [*University of Michigan*] [*Research center*] (RCD)
CHGD.........	Changed (WGA)
CHGD.........	Charged (ROG)
CHGE.........	Charge
CHGFA........	Costs Chargeable to Fund Authorization [*Army*]
CHGN.........	AES China Generating Co. [*NASDAQ symbol*] (SAG)
CHGN.........	AES China Generating Co. [*NASDAQ symbol*] (SAG)
Ch GN	Chronic Glomerulonephritis [*Nephrology*] (DAVI)
CHGNF........	AES China Generating'A' [*NASDAQ symbol*] (TTSB)
CHGO.........	Changing Over (FAAC)
CHGO.........	Chicago [*Illinois*]
CHGO.........	Chicago Pizza & Brewery, Inc. [*NASDAQ symbol*] (SAG)
CHGOV........	Change Over
CHGP.........	Charging Pump (IEEE)
CHGPAA.......	Costs Chargeable to Purchase Authorization Advice
CHGPH........	Choreography
CHGR.........	Charger (MSA)
CHGR.........	Chemogram (VRA)
CHGR.........	Concord Health Group, Inc. [*NASDAQ symbol*] (SAG)
CHGS.........	Charges
CHGUN........	Chief Gunner [*Navy rating Obsolete*]
CHH	Airlines of Hainan Province [*China*] [*ICAO designator*] (FAAC)
CHH	Cartilage-Hair Hypoplasia [*Medicine*] (MAE)
CHH	Chain Home High [*Aviation*]
CHH	Chaplain of His Holiness
CHH	Chatham, MA [*Location identifier FAA*] (FAAL)
CHH	Cheswick & Harmar [*AAR code*]
CHH	Chihuahua [*Mexico*] [*Seismograph station code, US Geological Survey*] (SEIS)
CHH	Choice Hotels International, Inc. [*NYSE symbol*] (SAG)
CHH	Commission d'Histoire de l'Historiographie [*Commission of the History of Historiography*] [*Ceret, France*] (EAIO)
CHH	Commission on Health and Healing [*Formerly, CCMW*] (EA)

CHH .... Consolidated Churchill Enterprises, Inc. [*Vancouver Stock Exchange symbol*]

CHH .... Contemporary Heroes and Heroines [*A publication*]

CHH .... Hainan Airlines [*China*] [*FAA designator*] (FAAC)

CHHA .... Canadian Hard of Hearing Association

CHHA/CHS ... Council of Home Health Agencies and Community Health Services [*Later, NAHC*]

CHHE .... Certified Hospitality Housekeeping Executive [*Educational Institute of th e American Hotel and Motel Association*] [*Designation awarded by*]

CHHi .... Hayward Area Historical Society, Hayward, CA [*Library symbol*] [*Library of Congress*] (LCLS)

CHHMA .... Canadian Hardware & Housewares Manufacturers' Association [*Association Canadienne des Fabricants en Quincaillerie et Article Menagers*] (AC)

CHHN .... Certificate in Home Health Nursing (PGP)

CHHO .... Coalition of Holistic Health Organizations [*Defunct*] (EA)

CHHR .... Committee on Health and Human Rights (EA)

CHHS .... Charles Homer Haskins Society (EA)

CHHS .... Chinese Historical Society of America (EA)

CHHSM .... Council for Health and Human Services Ministries (EA)

CHHVC .... Cairns and District Historic Vehicle Club [*Australia*]

CHi .... California Historical Society, San Francisco, CA [*Library symbol Library of Congress*] (LCLS)

CHI .... Catastrophic Health Insurance (GFGA)

CHI .... Chalcone Isomerase [*An enzyme*]

CHI .... Chapleau Resources Ltd. [*Vancouver Stock Exchange symbol*]

CHI .... Chemical Hazards in Industry [*Royal Society of Chemistry*] [*Information service or system*] (IID)

CHI .... Chicago [*Illinois*] [*Airport symbol*] (OAG)

CHI .... Chicago - Loyola [*Illinois*] [*Seismograph station code, US Geological Survey*] (SEIS)

CHI .... Children's Hospice International (EA)

CHI .... China

chi .... Chinese [*MARC language code Library of Congress*] (LCCP)

CHI .... City Hostess International (EA)

CHI .... Clearinghouse on Health Indexes [*Public Health Service*] [*Information service or system*] (IID)

CHI .... Closed Head Injury [*Medicine*]

CHI .... Coastal, Harbor, and Inland [*Waterways*] (MCD)

CHI .... Computer-Human Interaction (BUR)

CHI .... Computer-Human Interface

CHI .... Concordia Historical Institute (EA)

CHI .... Consortium for Health Information and Library Sciences [*Library network*]

CHI .... Cooperative High-Performance Sequential Inference Machine [*NEC Corp.*]

CHI .... Cougar Helicopter, Inc. [*Canada ICAO designator*] (FAAC)

CHI .... Creatinine Height Index [*Biochemistry*] (DAVI)

CHI .... Cyclohexyl Isocyanate [*Organic chemistry*]

CHI .... Furr's/Bishop's, Inc. [*NYSE symbol*] (SPSG)

CHIA .... California Health Information Association (SRA)

CHIA .... Canadian Health Insurance Association

CHIA .... Comprehensive Health Insurance Act

CHIAA .... Crop-Hail Insurance Actuarial Association [*Later, NCIS*] (EA)

chiaro .... Chiaroscuro (VRA)

Chi BA Rec.. Chicago Bar Association. Record [*A publication*] (DLA)

CHIBCHA..... Colombia Human Rights Information Committee (EA)

Chi Black..... Chitty's Edition of Blackstone's Commentaries [*A publication*] (DLA)

Chi B Record... Chicago Bar Record [*A publication*] (DLA)

CHIC .... Canadian Head Injury Coalition (AC)

CHIC .... CERMET [*Ceramic Metal Element*] Hybrid Integrated Circuit

CHIC .... Chicago [*Illinois*]

Chic .... Chihuahua [*Mexico*] (BARN)

CHIC .... Commonwealth Holiday Inns of Canada

CHIC .... Complex Hybrid Integrated Circuit [*Electronics*] (IAA)

Chicago LB... Chicago Law Bulletin [*A publication*] (DLA)

Chicago Leg News... Chicago Legal News [*Illinois*] [*A publication*] (ILCA)

Chicago Leg News (Ill)... Chicago Legal News [*Illinois*] [*A publication*] (DLA)

Chicago LJ... Chicago Law Journal [*A publication*] (DLA)

Chicago L Rec... Chicago Law Record [*Illinois*] [*A publication*] (DLA)

Chicago L Record (Ill)... Chicago Law Record [*Illinois*] [*A publication*] (DLA)

Chicago LT... Chicago Law Times [*A publication*] (DLA)

CHICAGORILLA... Chicago Gorilla [*Slang for a desperado gunman*]

Chicago St U... Chicago State University (GAGS)

ChicBy .... Chic By HIS, Inc. [*Associated Press*] (SAG)

CHICH .... Chichester [*City in England*] (ROG)

CHICK .... Chicken

Chic LB .... Chicago Law Bulletin [*A publication*] (DLA)

Chic Leg N... Chicago Legal News [*Illinois*] [*A publication*] (DLA)

Chic LJ .... Chicago Law Journal [*A publication*] (DLA)

Chic LR .... Chicago Law Record [*Illinois*] [*A publication*] (DLA)

Chic LT .... Chicago Law Times [*A publication*] (DLA)

CHICO .... Coordination of Hybrid and Integrated Circuit Operations (IAA)

CHICODER ... Chinese Language Encoder

CHICOM ...... Chinese Communist

Chicos .... Chicos Fas, Inc. [*Associated Press*] (SAG)

CHICS .... Computerized Hospital Information System (MCD)

CHID .... Combined Health Information Database [*Public Health Service*] [*Information service or system*] (IID)

CHID .... Community Human and Industrial Development, Inc. [*Office of Economic Opportunity*] [*Terminated*]

CHIDE .... Committee to Halt Indoctrination and Demoralization in Education [*Group opposing sex education in schools*]

CHIE .... Council on Health Information and Education (EA)

Chief .... Chieftain International [*Associated Press*] (SAG)

CHIEF .... Combined Helmholtz Integral Equation Formulation

CHIEF .... Controlled Handling of Internal Executive Functions [*UNIVAC*]

CHIEF .... Customs Handling of Import and Export Freight [*EC*] (ECED)

CHIF .... Channel Interface

CHIGW .... Chigwell [*Urban district in England*]

CHIK .... Golden Poultry Co. [*NASDAQ symbol*] (TTSB)

CHIK .... Golden Poultry Co., Inc. [*NASDAQ symbol*] (NQ)

CHIK-FM ...... Quebec, PQ [*FM radio station call letters*] (RBYB)

CHIL .... Child (ADA)

CHIL .... Chile

CHIL .... Consolidated Hazardous Item List (MCD)

CHIL .... Current-Hogging Injection Logic [*Electronics*] (IEEE)

CHIL .... Current-Hogging Injection Logic (IDOE)

Chi LB .... Chicago Law Bulletin [*A publication*] (DLA)

CHILD .... Chicago Institute for the Study of Learning Disabilities [*Research center*] (RCD)

CHILD .... Children's

CHILD .... Children's Healthcare Is a Legal Duty (EA)

CHILD .... Children's Health Information about Liver Disease

CHILD .... Cognitive Hybrid Intelligent Learning Device

CHILD .... Conductive Hearing Impairment Language Development Program (EDAC)

CHILD .... Congenital Hemidysplasia with Ichthyosiform Erythroderma and Limb Defects Syndr ome [*Medicine*] (DMAA)

CHILD .... Coordinated Helps in Language Development (ADA)

Child Ct ...... Children's Court (DLA)

ChildDis...... Childrens Discovery Centers of America [*Associated Press*] (SAG)

CHILDHD ..... Childhood

Child Legal Rts J... Children's Legal Rights Journal [*A publication*] (DLA)

Child Lit ...... Children's Literature [*A publication*] (BRI)

Childr......... Childrobics, Inc. [*Associated Press*] (SAG)

Childrbc...... Childrobics, Inc. [*Associated Press*] (SAG)

Chile .... Chile Fund, Inc. [*Associated Press*] (SAG)

Chi Leg N .... Chicago Legal News [*Illinois*] [*A publication*] (DLA)

ChileTel...... Compania de Telecommunicaciones de Chile SA [*Associated Press*] (SAG)

ChileTel...... Compania de Telefonos de Chile SA [*Associated Press*] (SAG)

CHILF......... Chilford [*England*]

Chilgener.... Cilgener SA [*Associated Press*] (SAG)

Chilian........ Chilianus Koenig [*Deceased, 1526*] [*Authority cited in pre-1607 legal work*] (DSA)

Chi LJ .... Chicago Law Journal [*A publication*] (DLA)

Chil Kon ..... Chilianus Koenig [*Deceased, 1526*] [*Authority cited in pre-1607 legal work*] (DSA)

CHILL.......... CCITT [*Consultative Committee on International Telegraphy and Telephony*] High-Level Language [*Telecommunications*] (TEL)

CHILL.......... Chicago-University of Illinois [*RADAR system*]

Chi LR .... Chicago Law Record [*Illinois*] [*A publication*] (DLA)

Chil Rts Rep... Children's Rights Report [*A publication*] (DLA)

Chi LT .... Chicago Law Times [*A publication*] (DLA)

CHIM .... Chief Inspector of Machinery [*Navy British*] (ROG)

Chim.......... Chimney [*Technical drawings*] (DAC)

ChiME........ Chemical Industry for Minorities in Engineering (EA)

ChiMini....... Chicago Miniature Lamp, Inc. [*Associated Press*] (SAG)

CHIN .... Canadian Heritage Information Network [*National Museums of Canada*] [*Ottawa, ON*] [*Information service or system*] (IID)

CHIN .... China

CHIN .... Chinese [*Language, etc.*] (ROG)

CHIN .... Chinese

CHIN .... Community Health Information Network [*Library network*]

CHIN .... Toronto, ON [*AM radio station call letters*]

CHINA .... Children in Need of Assistance (OICC)

CHINA .... Chronic Infectious Neuropathic Agents [*Medicine*]

ChinaFd ...... [*The*] China Fund [*Associated Press*] (SAG)

ChinaIndl..... China Industrial Group [*Associated Press*] (SAG)

China Law Rev... China Law Review [*A publication*] (DLA)

China L Rev... China Law Review [*A publication*] (DLA)

China T........ China Today [*A publication*]

CHINAT........ Chinese Nationalist

ChinaTr........ China Treasure, Inc. [*Associated Press*] (SAG)

CH-in-C........ Chaplain-in-Chief [*British*]

Chinese Soc'y Int'l L Annals... Annals. Chinese Society of International Law [*Taipei, Taiwan*] [*A publication*] (DLA)

CHIN-FM...... Toronto, ON [*FM radio station call letters*]

CHINFO........ Chief of Information [*Also, CINFO*] [*Navy*]

Chinl.......... China Industrial Group [*Associated Press*] (SAG)

Chino .... Chinoiserie (VRA)

CHINOPERL... Conference for Chinese Oral and Performing Literature (EA)

Chin P .... Chinese Pharmacopoeia [*A publication*]

ChinRs........ China Resources Development, Inc. [*Associated Press*] (SAG)

CHINS .... Child [*or Children*] in Need of Service [*Pediatrics and social services*] (DAVI)

CHINS .... Children in Need of Supervision [*Classification for delinquent children*] (OICC)

ChinTire....... China Tire Holdings Ltd. [*Associated Press*] (SAG)

CHIO .... Character-Oriented Input-Output Processor [*Computer science*] (IAA)

CHIP .... Allied Command Channel Intelligence Plan [*NATO*] (NATG)

CHIP .... Canada, Hungary, Indonesia, and Poland [*Countries comprising the International Commission of Control and Supervision, charged with supervising the cease-fire in Vietnam, 1973*]

CHIP .... Canadian Home Insulation Plan

CHIP .... Center for Human Information Processing [*Research center*] (RCD)

CHIP .... Central Hole in Pintle [*Diesel engineering*]

CHIP .... Chain Input Pointing [*Computer science*]

CHIP .... Channel-Forming Integral Protein [*Biochemistry*]
CHIP .... Chemical Hazard Information Profile [*Environmental Protection Agency*]
CHIP .... Children of High Intellectual Potential
CHIP .... Chip Hermeticity in Plastic [*Electronics*] (MDG)
Chip .... Chipman's New Brunswick Reports [*1825-35*] [*A publication*] (DLA)
CHIP .... Classification, Hazard Information and Packaging [*British*]
CHIP .... Cold and Hot Isostatic Pressing [*Materials science and technology*]
CHIP .... Community Help and Improvement Program
CHIP .... Community Housing and Infrastructure Program [*Australia*]
CHIP .... Comprehensive Health Insurance Plan [*or Proposal*]
CHIP .... Constraint Handling in Prolog [*A programming language*] [*Computer science*]
CHIP .... Customized Health Information Project [*Computer science*]
CHIP .... Fort Coulonge, PQ [*FM radio station call letters*]
Chip Cont..... Chipman on the Law of Contracts [*A publication*] (DLA)
CHIPF .... Children of High Intellectual Potential Foundation [*Australia*]
Chip Gov...... Chipman's Principles of Government [*A publication*] (DLA)
CHIPITTS ..... Chicago-Pittsburgh [*Proposed name for possible "super-city" formed by growth and mergers of other cities*]
ChiPizza....... Chicago Piza & Brewery, Inc. [*Associated Press*] (SAG)
Chip Ms....... Chipman's New Brunswick Manuscript Reports [*A publication*] (DLA)
CHiPS .... California Highway Patrol [*Acronym used as title of TV series*]
CHIPS .... Case Handling Information Processing System [*National Labor Relations Board*]
CHIPS .... Chemical Engineering Information Processing System
CHIPS .... Chromosome Interphase Staining [*Medicine*]
CHIPS .... Clearing House Interbank Payment System (BUR)
CHIPS .... Consumer Health Information Program and Services [*LSCA*]
CHIPSODB.... Chipping Sodbury [*England*]
ChipsTc....... Chips and Technologies, Inc. [*Associated Press*] (SAG)
Chip W .... Chipman's New Brunswick Reports [*1825-35*] [*A publication*] (DLA)
ChiPza .... Chicago Pizza & Brewery, Inc. [*Associated Press*] (SAG)
Chiq .... Chiquita Brands International [*Associated Press*] (SAG)
CHIQ .... Winnipeg, MB [*FM radio station call letters*]
Chiquta........ Chiquita Brands International [*Associated Press*] (SAG)
CHIR .... Chiricahua National Monument and Fort Bowie National Historic Site
CHIR .... Chiron Corp. [*NASDAQ symbol*] (NQ)
ChirDoc........ Chirurgiae Doctor [*Doctor of Surgery*] [*Latin*] (NADA)
Chir Doct .... Chirurgiae Doctor [*Doctor of Surgery*]
ChiRex......... ChiRex, Inc. [*Associated Press*] (SAG)
CHIRO .... Chiropractor
Chiron.......... Chiron Corp. [*Associated Press*] (SAG)
CHIROPRCTC... Chiropractic
CHIRP .... Chemical Engineering Investigation of Reaction Paths [*Computer science*]
CHIRURG..... Chirurgicalis [*Surgical*] [*Pharmacy*]
ChiRv.......... Chicago Rivet & Machine Co. [*Associated Press*] (SAG)
ChiRv.......... Chicago Rivet & Machine Co. [*Associated Press*] (SAG)
CHIS .... Channel Islands National Monument
CHIS .... Computerized Hospital Information System
CHisC.......... Central Hispano Capital Ltd. [*Associated Press*] (SAG)
CHisIn......... Central Hispano International, Inc. [*Associated Press*] (SAG)
CHISOX....... Chicago White Sox [*Baseball team*]
Ch Is Rolls... Rolls of the Assizes in Channel Islands [*A publication*] (DLA)
CHIT........... Chitarrone [*Large Guitar*] [*Music*]
Chit............. Chitty's English Bail Court Reports [*1770-1822*] [*A publication*] (DLA)
Chit............. Chitty's English King's Bench Practice Reports [*1819-20*] [*A publication*] (DLA)
Chit & H Bills... Chitty and Hulme on Bills of Exchange [*A publication*] (DLA)
Chit & M Dig... Chitty and Mew's Supplement to Fisher's English Digest [*A publication*] (DLA)
Chit & T Car... Chitty and Temple on Carriers [*A publication*] (DLA)
Chit Ap .... Chitty's Law of Apprentices [*A publication*] (DLA)
Chit Archb Pr... Chitty's Edition of Archbold's Practice [*A publication*] (DLA)
Chit Arch Pr... Chitty's Edition of Archbold's Practice [*A publication*] (DLA)
Chit B .... Chirurgiae Baccalaureus [*Bachelor of Surgery*] [*Latin*] (BARN)
Chit BC........ Chitty's English Bail Court Reports [*1770-1822*] [*A publication*] (DLA)
Chit Bills .... Chitty on Bills [*A publication*] (DLA)
Chit Bl .... Chitty's Edition of Blackstone's Commentaries [*A publication*] (DLA)
Chit Bl Comm... Chitty's Edition of Blackstone's Commentaries [*A publication*] (DLA)
Chit Burn's J... Chitty's Edition of Burn's Justice [*A publication*] (DLA)
Chit Car ..... Chitty's Treatise on Carriers [*A publication*] (DLA)
Chit Com L... Chitty on Commercial Law [*A publication*] (ILCA)
Chit Com Law... Chitty on Commercial Law [*A publication*] (DLA)
Chit Con ..... Chitty on Contracts [*A publication*] (DLA)
Chit Cont ..... Chitty on Contracts [*A publication*] (DLA)
Chit Crim Law... Chitty's Criminal Law [*A publication*] (DLA)
Chit Cr L..... Chitty's Criminal Law [*A publication*] (DLA)
Chit Cr Law... Chitty's Criminal Law [*A publication*] (DLA)
Chit Des ...... Chitty on the Law of Descents [*A publication*] (DLA)
Chit Eq Dig... Chitty's Equity Digest [*A publication*] (DLA)
Chit Eq Ind... Chitty's Equity Index [*A publication*] (DLA)
Chit F......... Chitty's English King's Bench Forms [*A publication*] (DLA)
Chit Gen Pr... Chitty's General Practice [*A publication*] (DLA)
Chit GL ...... Chitty on the Game Laws [*A publication*] (DLA)
Chit Jun B ... Chitty, Junior, on Bills [*A publication*] (DLA)
Chit Lawy ... Chitty's Commercial and General Lawyer [*A publication*] (DLA)
Chit L of N... Chitty. Law of Nations [*1812*] [*A publication*] (DLA)
Chit Med Jur... Chitty on Medical Jurisprudence [*A publication*] (DLA)
Chit Nat ..... Chitty. Law of Nations [*1812*] [*A publication*] (DLA)
CHITO .... Container Handling in Terminal Operations [*Army study*] (RDA)
Chit Pl .... Chitty on Pleading [*A publication*] (DLA)
Chit Pr .... Chitty's General Practice [*A publication*] (DLA)

Chit Prec .... Chitty's Precedents in Pleading [*A publication*] (DLA)
Chit Prer...... Chitty's Prerogatives of the Crown [*A publication*] (DLA)
Chit R .... Chitty's English Bail Court Reports [*1770-1822*] [*A publication*] (DLA)
Chi Trib .... Chicago Tribune (BARN)
Chit St .... Chitty's Statutes of Practical Utility [*1235-1948*] [*England*] [*A publication*] (DLA)
Chit St A..... Chitty's Stamp Act [*A publication*] (DLA)
Chit Stat ..... Chitty's Statutes of Practical Utility [*1235-1948*] [*England*] [*A publication*] (DLA)
Chit Sum P... Chitty's Summary of the Practice of the Superior Courts [*A publication*] (DLA)
Chitt............ Chitty's English Bail Court Reports [*1770-1822*] [*A publication*] (DLA)
Chitt & Pat... Chitty and Patell's Supreme Court Appeals [*India*] [*A publication*] (DLA)
Chittend...... Chittenden Corp. [*Associated Press*] (SAG)
Chitt LJ....... Chitty's Law Journal [*A publication*] (DLA)
Chitty .... Chitty on Bills [*A publication*] (DLA)
Chitty BC ..... Chitty's English Bail Court Reports [*1770-1822*] [*A publication*] (DLA)
Chitty BC (Eng)... Chitty's English Bail Court Reports [*1770-1822*] [*A publication*] (DLA)
Chitty Bl Comm... Chitty's Edition of Blackstone's Commentaries [*A publication*] (DLA)
Chitty Com Law... Chitty on Commercial Law [*A publication*] (DLA)
Chitty Eq Ind... Chitty's Equity Index [*A publication*] (DLA)
CHIV .... Chivalry (ROG)
ChiYuc........ China Yuchai International Ltd. [*Associated Press*] (SAG)
CHJ............. Charger Resources Ltd. [*Vancouver Stock Exchange symbol*]
CHJ............. Chichibu [*Japan*] [*Seismograph station code, US Geological Survey*] (SEIS)
CHJ............. Chief Justice [*British*] (ROG)
CHJ............. Chino, CA [*Location identifier FAA*] (FAAL)
CHJ............. Colel Hibath Jerusalem [*Society of the Devotees of Jerusalem*] (EA)
CHJ............. Cooperative Housing Journal [*A publication*] (EAAP)
CHJB........... Contribution a l'Histoire Juridique de la Ire Dynastie Babylonienne [*A publication*] (BJA)
CHJCP......... Chief Justice of the Common Pleas [*British*] (ROG)
CH-JM......... Carnegie Hall - Jeunesses Musicales [*Defunct*] (EA)
CHJUB......... Chief Justice of the Upper Bench [*British*] (ROG)
CHJUSMAG... Chief, Joint United States Military Advisory Group [*Followed by name of country*] (CINC)
CHK .... Chablis Resources Ltd. [*Vancouver Stock Exchange symbol*]
CHK .... Chalan Kanoa [*Diocesan abbreviation*] (TOCD)
CHK .... Check (KSC)
chk............. Check (WDMC)
CHK .... Check
CHK .... Check Register Against Bounds [*Computer science*]
CHK .... Chemeketa Community College, Salem, OR [*OCLC symbol*] (OCLC)
CHK .... Chesapeake Energy [*NYSE symbol*] (TTSB)
CHK .... Chesapeake Energy Corp. [*NYSE symbol*] (SAG)
CHK .... Chicago [*Illinois*] [*Seismograph station code, US Geological Survey Closed*] (SEIS)
CHK .... Chickasha, OK [*Location identifier FAA*] (FAAL)
CHK .... Christ the King
CHK .... Flying Boat, Inc. [*ICAO designator*] (FAAC)
CHKB........... Check Bit
CHKDSK...... Check Disk [*Computer science*]
CHKE.......... Cherokee Group [*NASDAQ symbol*] (NQ)
CHKE.......... Cherokee Inc. [*NASDAQ symbol*] (TTSB)
ChkEx......... Check Express, Inc. [*Associated Press*] (SAG)
CHKFRAG ... Checks Fragmentation [*Computer science*] (PCM)
Chkfree....... Checkfree Corp. [*Associated Press*] (SAG)
ChkFull........ Chock Full O'Nuts Corp. [*Wall Street Slang Name: "Nuts"*] [*Associated Press*] (SAG)
CHKG .... Checking
CHKL........... Kelowna, BC [*Television station call letters*]
CHKL-1 .... Penticton, BC [*Television station call letters*]
CHKL-2 .... Vermon, BC [*Television station call letters*] (RBYB)
CHKL-3 .... Revelstoke, BC [*Television station call letters*] (RBYB)
CHKM.......... Kamloops, BC [*Television station call letters*]
CHKM-1 .... Pritchard, BC [*Television station call letters*] (RBYB)
CHKMAG...... Chief, Korea Military Assistance Group
CHKN.......... Chicken
CHKP........... Check Point Software Technologies Ltd. [*NASDAQ symbol*] (SAG)
ChkPnt........ Check Point Software Technologies Ltd. [*Associated Press*] (SAG)
CHKPT .... Checkpoint [*Computer science*] (BUR)
ChkPt.......... Checkpoint Systems, Inc. [*Associated Press*] (SAG)
CHKR........... Checker (MSA)
CHKR........... Checkers Drive-In Restaurants [*NASDAQ symbol*] (SPSG)
CHKR........... Checkers Drive-In Restr [*NASDAQ symbol*] (TTSB)
ChkTch........ Check Technology Corp. [*Associated Press*] (SAG)
Chl............. Biblioteca Nacional de Chile, Santiago, Chile [*Library symbol Library of Congress*] (LCLS)
CHL............. Cambridge Higher Local Examination [*British*] (ROG)
CHL............. Central Hockey League
CHL............. Certified Hardware List (MCD)
CHL............. Chain Home Low [*Aviation*]
CHL............. Chaldron [*Unit of measure*] [*Obsolete*] (ROG)
CHL............. Chalna [*Bangladesh*] [*Airport symbol*] (AD)
CHL............. Chalqueno [*Race of maize*]
CHL............. Channel (NASA)
chl............. Charcoal (VRA)
CHL............. Charlotte [*Diocesan abbreviation*] [*North Carolina*] (TOCD)
CHL............. Charterhall Oil Canada [*Vancouver Stock Exchange symbol*]
CHL............. Chemical Banking Corp. [*NYSE symbol*] (SPSG)
CHL............. Chicken Hepatic Lectin

CHL	Chile [*ANSI three-letter standard code*] (CNC)
CHL	Chilik [*Former USSR Seismograph station code, US Geological Survey Closed*] (SEIS)
CHL	Chinese Hamster Lung [*Cell line*]
CHL	Chlorambucil [*Antineoplastic drug*]
CHL	Chloramphenicol [*Antimicrobial compound*] (MAE)
CHL	Chlorite [*A mineral*]
CHL	Chloroform [*Organic chemistry*] (WGA)
ChL	Chlorophyll
CHL	Clemson Hydraulics Laboratory [*Clemson University*] [*Research center*] (RCD)
CHL	Coastal and Hydraulics Laboratory [*U.S. Army Engineer Waterways Experiment Station*]
CHL	Cohlmia Aviation [*ICAO designator*] (FAAC)
CHL	Commentationes Humanorum Litterarum [*A publication*] (BJA)
CHL	Committee for Humane Legislation (EA)
CHL	Confinement at Hard Labor [*Army*] (AABC)
CHL	Cronar Halftone Litho [*Du Pont*]
CHL	Current-Hogging Logic [*Electronics*]
CHLA	Canadian Health Libraries Association
CHLA	Children's Hospital, Los Angeles, CA
ChLA	Children's Literature Association (EA)
CHLA	Cyclohexyllinoleic Acid [*Organic chemistry*]
ChLAQ	Children's Literature Association Quarterly [*A publication*] (BRI)
Chlb	Chlorobutanol [*Pharmacology*] (DAVI)
CHLC	Baie Comeau, PQ [*AM radio station call letters*]
CHLC	Cooperative Human Linkage Center [*Genetics research*]
CHLC	Cooperative Human Linkage Center
CHLC-FM	Baie Comeau, PQ [*FM radio station call letters*] (RBYB)
CHLD	Children
CHLD	Childrobics, Inc. [*NASDAQ symbol*] (SAG)
CHLD	Chilled (MSA)
CHLD	Chronic Hypoxic Lung Disease [*Medicine*] (DMAA)
ChldBrd	Childrens Broadcasting Corp. [*Associated Press*] (SAG)
ChldCmp	Childrens Comprehensive Services [*Associated Press*] (SAG)
Chl-DNA	Deoxyribonucleic Acid - Chloroplast [*Biochemistry, genetics*] [*Also, cpDNA, ctDNA*]
Chldtime	Childtime Learning Centers, Inc. [*Associated Press*] (SAG)
CHLDW	Childrobics Inc. Wrrt [*NASDAQ symbol*] (TTSB)
ChldWn	Childrens Wonderland, Inc. [*Associated Press*] (SAG)
ChldWon	Childrens Wonderland, Inc. [*Associated Press*] (SAG)
chldy	Chalcedony (VRA)
Ch Lit Ed	Children's Literature in Education [*A publication*] (BRI)
chlith	Chromolithograph (VRA)
CHLJ	Chaplain of the Order of St Lazarus of Jerusalem [*Australia*]
chlk	Chalky [*Philately*]
CHLL	Concurrent High-Level Language [*Computer science*] (MCD)
Chllr	Chancellor
CHLN	Chalone Wine Group [*NASDAQ symbol*] (NQ)
CHLN	Trois Rivieres, PQ [*AM radio station call letters*]
CHLO	Chloride [*Chemistry*] (ADA)
CHLO	Chloroform [*Organic chemistry*] (ADA)
CHLOR	Chloride [*Chemistry*] (ROG)
CHLOR	Chlorinated [*Freight*]
CHLOR	Chloroform [*Organic chemistry*] (ROG)
CHLOREP	Chlorine Emergency Plan [*Chlorine Institute*]
CHLP	Montreal, PQ [*Radio station call letters*] [*1930's*]
CHL + PRED	Chlorambucil and Prednisone [*Antineoplastic drug regimen*] (DAVI)
CHLQ	Charlottetown, PE [*FM radio station call letters*]
chlr	Chlorite (VRA)
Chl-rDNA	Deoxyribonucleic Acid, Ribosomal - Chloroplast [*Biochemistry, genetics*]
CHLT	Charter Long Term
CHLT	Chlorthalidone [*Diuretic*]
CHLT	Sherbrooke, PQ [*AM radio station call letters*]
CHLT-TV	Sherbrooke, PQ [*Television station call letters*]
ChlU	University of Chile, Valparaiso, Chile [*Library symbol Library of Congress*] (LCLS)
CHL VPP	Chlorambucil, Vinblastine, Procarbazine, Prednisone [*Antineoplastic drug regimen*]
CHLW	Commercial High Level Waste [*Nuclear energy*] (NUCP)
CHLW	St. Paul, AB [*AM radio station call letters*]
CHM	Aero Chombo SA [*Mexico ICAO designator*] (FAAC)
CHM	Canadian Institute for Historical Microreproductions [*Source file*] [*UTLAS symbol*]
CHM	Chairman
CHM	Chamber (AAG)
CHM	Charm [*Jewelry*] (ROG)
CHM	Checkmate
CHM	Chemical [*Freight*]
CHM	Chemical Machining [*Factory automation*] (BTTJ)
CHM	Children's Hospital of Michigan
CHM	Chimbote [*Peru*] [*Airport symbol Obsolete*] (OAG)
CHM	Chimkent [*Former USSR Seismograph station code, US Geological Survey Closed*] (SEIS)
Ch M	Chirurgiae Magister [*Master of Surgery*]
CHM	Choroideremia [*Ophthalmology*]
CHM	Christian Homesteading Movement (EA)
CHM	CHUM Ltd. [*Toronto Stock Exchange symbol*]
CHM	City of Hope Medical Center, Duarte, CA [*OCLC symbol*] (OCLC)
CHM	Compound Handling Machine
CHM	Congregation of Humility of Mary [*Roman Catholic women's religious order*]
CHM	Diploma of Choir Master of the Royal College of Organists [*British*]
ChM	Master of Surgery (DD)

CHM	Specialty Chemical Res [*AMEX symbol*] (TTSB)
CHM	Specialty Chemical Resources [*AMEX symbol*] (SAG)
CHMA	Canadian Holistic Medicine Association
CHMA	Comprehensive Health Manpower Training Act [*1971*]
CHMA	Cyclohexyl Methacrylate [*Organic chemistry*]
CHMA	Sackville, NB [*FM radio station call letters*]
CHMAAG	Chief, Military Assistance Advisory Group [*Followed by name of country*] (CINC)
CHMACH	Chief Machinist [*Navy rating Obsolete*]
CHMAN	Chairman
CHMB	Vancouver, BC [*AM radio station call letters*] (RBYB)
ChmBnk	Chemical Banking Corp. [*Associated Press*] (SAG)
CHMBR	Chamber (MSA)
CHMBR	Chamber
CHMC	Children's Hospital Medical Center [*Ohio*]
ChmCS	Chromatics Color Sciences International, Inc. [*Associated Press*] (SAG)
CHMD	Chronimed, Inc. [*NASDAQ symbol*] (SAG)
CHMD	Clinical Hyaline Membrane Disease [*Medicine*] (AAMN)
CHMEDT	Chief, Military Equipment Delivery Team (CINC)
CHMEP	Cooperative Health Manpower Education Program [*Veterans Administration*] (GFGA)
CHMF	Crazy Horse Memorial Foundation (EA)
Chmfab	Chemfab Corp. [*Associated Press*] (SAG)
ChmFin	Chemical Financial Corp. [*Associated Press*] (SAG)
CHMG	[*The*] Columbia University College of Physicians and Surgeons Complete HomeMedical Guide [*A publication*]
CHMG	St. Albert, AB [*AM radio station call letters*]
CHMI	Portage La Prairie, MB [*Television station call letters*]
CHMILTAG	Chief, Military Technical Advisory Group (CINC)
ChmInt	Chem International, Inc. [*Associated Press*] (SAG)
CHMK	Chung-Hau Min Kuo [*Republic of China*]
CHML	Chicago Miniature Lamp [*NASDAQ symbol*] (TTSB)
CHML	Chicago Miniature Lamp, Inc. [*NASDAQ symbol*] (SAG)
CHML	Hamilton, ON [*AM radio station call letters*]
CHMM	Certified Hazardous Materials Manager [*Environmental science*]
CHMN	Chairman (AFM)
CHMNY	Chimney
CHMO	Moosonee, ON [*AM radio station call letters*]
CHMOS	Complementary High-Performance Metal-Oxide Semiconductor
CHMP	Champion Industries [*NASDAQ symbol*] (TTSB)
CHMP	Champion Industries, Inc. [*NASDAQ symbol*] (SAG)
CHMP	Chan Hills Military Police [*British military*] (DMA)
ChmpE	Champion Enterprises [*Associated Press*] (SAG)
ChmpH	Champion Healthcare Corp. [*Associated Press*] (SAG)
ChmpIn	Champion Industries, Inc. [*Associated Press*] (SAG)
ChmpIn	Champion International Corp. [*Associated Press*] (SAG)
CHMPO	Chief, Military Planning Office (CINC)
ChmpPr	Champion Parts Rebuilders, Inc. [*Associated Press*] (SAG)
Chmpwr	Chempower, Inc. [*Associated Press*] (SAG)
CHMR	Center for Hazardous Materials Research (EA)
CHMR	St. John's, NF [*FM radio station call letters*]
CHMSA	Critical Health Manpower Shortage Areas
CHMSE	Canadian Hotel Marketing & Sales Executive (AC)
ChmSh	Charming Shoppes, Inc. [*Associated Press*] (SAG)
CHMSL	Center High-Mounted Stop Lamp [*Pronounced "chimsel"*] [*Automotive engineering*]
CHMT	Components Hybrids and Manufacturing Technology (MCD)
ChmTrk	ChemTrak, Inc. [*Associated Press*] (SAG)
CHMTS	IEEE Components, Hybrids, and Manufacturing Technology Society (EA)
CHMX	Regina, SK [*FM radio station call letters*]
CHN	Cable Health Network [*Cable-television system*] [*Viacom International, Inc.*]
CHN	Canadian Longhorn Petroleum [*Vancouver Stock Exchange symbol*]
CHN	Carbon, Hydrogen, Nitrogen
CHN	Central Hemorrhagic Necrosis [*Medicine*] (MAE)
CHN	Certified Hemodialysis Nurse (MEDA)
CHN	Chain [*Measure*]
CHN	Chain
CHN	Chairman (ROG)
CHN	Change [*Telecommunications*] (TEL)
CHN	Channel Island Aviation [*ICAO designator*] (FAAC)
CHN	Charan Industries, Inc. [*Toronto Stock Exchange symbol*]
CHN	Child Neurology
CHN	Children [*Genealogy*]
CHN	China [*ANSI three-letter standard code*] (CNC)
CHN	China Fund [*NYSE symbol*] (SPSG)
CHN	Chinchina [*Colombia*] [*Seismograph station code, US Geological Survey*] (SEIS)
CHN	Chinese Hamster [*Medicine*] (DMAA)
chn	Chinook Jargon [*MARC language code Library of Congress*] (LCCP)
CHN	Community Health Network (DHSM)
CHN	Community of the Holy Name of Jesus [*Anglican religious community*]
CHN	Council of the Haida Nation (AC)
CHN	Fort Wayne, IN [*Location identifier FAA*] (FAAL)
CHNA	Canadian Holistic Nurses Association (AC)
CHNA	China Pacific [*NASDAQ symbol*] (TTSB)
CHNA	China Treasure, Inc. [*NASDAQ symbol*] (SAG)
CHNAC	Community Health Nurses Association of Canada (AC)
CHNAVADGP	Chief, Naval Advisory Group
CHNAVADGRU	Chief, Naval Advisory Group [*Followed by name of country*] (CINC)
CHNAVAIRSHIPTRA	Chief, Naval Airships Training

CHNAVDEV...	Chief of Naval Development (DNAB)
CHNAVGP	Chief, Naval Advisory Group
CHNAVMARCORMARS...	Chief, Navy-Marine Corps Military Affiliate Radio Station (DNAB)
CHNAVMAT...	Chief of Naval Material (MCD)
CHNAVMAT ERS...	Chief of Naval Material Emergency Relocation Site Commander (DNAB)
CHNAVMIS...	Chief, Naval Mission
CHNAVPERS...	Chief of Naval Personnel (NVT)
CHNAVRES...	Chief of Naval Reserve (DOMA)
CHNAVSEC...	Chief, Navy Section (CINC)
CHNAVSECJUSMAGTHAI...	Chief, Navy Section, Joint United States Military Advisory Group, Thailand (DNAB)
CHNAVSECMAAG...	Chief, Navy Section, Military Assistance Advisory Group
CHNAVSECMTM...	Chief, Navy Section, Military Training Mission (DNAB)
CHNAVSECUSMILGP...	Chief, Navy Section, United States Military Group (DNAB)
CHNAVTRA...	Chief of Naval Training
CHNB	North Bay, ON [Television station call letters]
CHNC	New Carlisle, PQ [AM radio station call letters]
ChNCAM	Chicken Neural Cell Adhesion Molecule
Chncellr.......	Chancellor Corp. [Associated Press] (SAG)
CHNG	Change (MSA)
CHNG	Change
CHNL	Channel [Electrical transmission] (AFM)
CHNL	Channell Commercial Corp. [NASDAQ symbol] (SAG)
CHNL	Kamloops, BC [AM radio station call letters]
CHNL-1	Clearwater, BC [AM radio station call letters]
CHNNL	Channel
CHNO	Sudbury, ON [AM radio station call letters]
CHNOMISO...	Chief, Naval Ordnance Management Information System Office (DNAB)
CHNOPS	Carbon, Hydrogen, Nitrogen, Oxygen, Phosphorus, and Sulfur [Compounds]
CHNR	Simcoe, ON [AM radio station call letters]
CHNS	Halifax, NS [AM radio station call letters]
CHNSY........	Charleston Naval Shipyard [South Carolina]
chnt	Chestnut [Philately]
C/H/O	Cannot Hear Of [Bookselling]
CHO	Capstar Hotel Co. [NYSE symbol] (SAG)
CHO	Carbohydrate [Organic chemistry]
CHO	Charlim Explorations [Vancouver Stock Exchange symbol]
CHO	Charlottesville [Virginia] [Airport symbol] (OAG)
CH/O	Child Of [Genealogy]
CHO	Chinese Hamster Ovarian [or Ovary] [Cytology]
cho.............	Choctaw [MARC language code Library of Congress] (LCCP)
Cho	Choephori [of Aeschylus] [Classical studies] (OCD)
CHO	Chole Packet (ACRL)
Cho	Cholesterol [Also, C, Ch, CHOL] [Biochemistry]
Cho	Choline [Also, Ch] [Biochemistry]
CHO	Choral
Cho	Chorus [Music]
CHO	Choshi [Japan] [Seismograph station code, US Geological Survey] (SEIS)
CHO	Ciga Hotels Aviation SpA [Italy ICAO designator] (FAAC)
CHO	Cyclophosphamide, Hydroxydaunomycin [Adriamycin], Oncovin [Vincristine] [Antineoplastic drug regimen]
CHo.............	Hollister Public Library, Hollister, CA [Library symbol Library of Congress] (LCLS)
CHOA.........	Cooperative Home Care Associates
CHOA.........	Corporate Home Office Auditor (AAGC)
CHOA.........	Rouyn, PQ [FM radio station call letters]
CHOB.........	Cannon House Office Building
CHOB.........	Cyclophosphamide, Hydroxydaunomycin [Adriamycin], Oncovin , Bleomycin [Vincristine] [Antineoplastic drug regimen]
CHOBS........	Chief Observer [Navy] (NVT)
CHOC........	Center for History of Chemistry [Later, NFHC] (EA)
CHOC........	Chocolate
CHOC........	Chocolate
CHOC........	Consumer Health Organization of Canada (AC)
CHOC........	Jonquiere, PQ [FM radio station call letters]
Cho Ca Ca ...	Choyce's Cases in Chancery [1557-1606] [England] [A publication] (DLA)
Cho Ca Ch ...	Choyce's Cases in Chancery [1557-1606] [England] [A publication] (DLA)
CHoCL	San Benito County Free Library, Hollister, CA [Library symbol Library of Congress] (LCLS)
CHOD..........	Chief of Defense (NATG)
ChOd..........	Chilean Odeon [Record label]
CHOD..........	Cholesterol Oxidase [An enzyme]
CHOD..........	Cornwall, ON [AM radio station call letters] (RBYB)
CHOE.........	Matane, PQ [FM radio station call letters]
CH of F	Chaplain of the Fleet [Navy British]
CHOG.........	Richmond Hill, ON [AM radio station call letters]
CHOH.........	Chesapeake and Ohio Canal National Monument
CHOH.........	Hearst, ON [AM radio station call letters]
CHOI..........	Quebec, PQ [FM radio station call letters]
CHOICE.......	Center for Humane Options in Childbirth Experiences (EA)
CHOICE.......	Concern for Health Options: Information, Care and Education [An association] (EA)
CHOICE........	Consumer Help on the Individual's Conservation of Energy [Student legal action organization]
ChoiceH.......	Choice Hotels International, Inc. [Associated Press] (SAG)
CHOICES.......	Computerized Heuristic Occupational Information and Career Exploration System (EDAC)
Choirm........	Choirmaster [Music]
CHOK	Check Okay (FAAC)
CHOK	Sarnia, ON [AM radio station call letters]
CHOKE	Care How Others Keep the Environment [An association]
CHOKE	Concern for the Health of Our Kids and the Environment [Adelaide] [Australia]
CHOL	Cholesterol [Also, C, Ch, Cho] [Biochemistry]
CHOL	Common High-Order Language
chole	Cholecystectomy [Medicine] (MAE)
CHOL E........	Cholesterol Esters [Organic chemistry] (MAH)
Cholest	Cholestech Corp. [Associated Press] (SAG)
Chol Est	Cholesterol Ester [Clinical chemistry] (MAE)
chol est	Cholesterol Esters [Clinical chemistry] (CPH)
CHOM	Montreal, PQ [FM radio station call letters]
C Home	Clerk Home's Decisions, Scotch Court of Session [1735-44] [A publication]
CHOMPS.......	Canine Home Protection System [Acronym is title of 1979 movie]
CHOMS........	Canadian Hydrological Operational Multipurpose Subprogramme [Environment Canada] [Information service or system] (CRD)
CHON	Carbon, Hydrogen, Oxygen, Nitrogen [Composition of interstellar dust]
ChON	Chasti Osobogo Naznacheniia [Elements of Special Designation] [Political police units attached to the armed forces (1918-1924)] [Former USSR]
CHON..........	Whitehorse, YT [FM radio station call letters]
CHOP	Change of Operational Control [Military]
CHOP	Check-Out Procedure (CAAL)
CHOP	Chief Operator (NVT)
CHOP	Cyclophosphamide, Hydroxydaunomycin [Adriamycin], Oncovin , Prednisone [Vincristine] [Antineoplastic drug regimen]
CHOPAIR	Change of Operational Control of Air Cover [Military] (NVT)
CHOP-Bleo...	Cyclophosphamide, Hydroxydaunomycin [Adriamycin], Oncovin , Prednisone, Bleomycin [Vincristine] [Antineoplastic drug regimen]
CHOPLN	Change My Operation Plan [Military] (AABC)
CHOPP........	Columbia Homogenous Parallel Processor
CHOPP........	Cyclophosphamide, Hydroxydaunomycin [Adriamycin], Oncovin , Procarbazine, Prednisone [Vincristine] [Antineoplastic drug regimen]
CHOPPER	Combined Helicopter Outyear Procurement Package - Educational Requirement [Army]
CHOPS........	Chief of Operations
CHOPSUM....	Change of Operational Control Summary [Military] (NVT)
CHOR..........	Choir
CHOR..........	Choral
CHOR..........	Choreograph
CHOR..........	Chorus
CHOR..........	Cyclophosphamide, Hydroxydaunomycin [Adriamycin], Oncovin , Radiation therapy [Vincristine] [Antineoplastic drug regimen]
CHOR..........	Summerland, BC [AM radio station call letters]
CHORD	Change My Operation Order [Military]
CHORD CHIRURG...	Chorda Chirurgicalis [Surgical Catgut] [Pharmacy]
Choreog......	Choreography
CHORI........	Chief of Office of Research and Inventions [Navy]
CHORUS	Coalition for Harmony of Races in the US (EA)
CHOS	Rattling Brook, NF [FM radio station call letters]
CHOT	Hull, PQ [Television station call letters]
CHOV	Changeover [Aviation] (FAAC)
CHO/VAC.....	Cholera Vaccine [Medicine]
CHOVR........	Changeover (AAG)
CHOW	Welland, ON [AM radio station call letters]
CHOX	La Pocatiere, PQ [FM radio station call letters]
Choyce Cas Ch...	Choyce's Cases in Chancery [1557-1606] [England] [A publication] (DLA)
Choyce Cas (Eng)...	Choyce's Cases in Chancery [1557-1606] [England] [A publication] (DLA)
CHOZ	St. John's, NF [FM radio station call letters]
CHP	Aviacion de Chiapas [Mexico ICAO designator] (FAAC)
CHP	Canadian Humanist Publications (AC)
CHP	Capacitance Hole Probe
CHP	Center on Human Policy (EA)
CHP	Central Heating Plant (KSC)
CH-P	Challenge Position [Dancing]
CHP	Champion Oil & Gas [Vancouver Stock Exchange symbol]
CHP	Championship
CHP	Channel Processor
CHP	Chapalote [Race of maize]
CHP	Chemical Heat Pipe [Energy storage]
CHP	Chemical Hygiene Plan [Occupational Safety and Health Administration]
ChP	Chest Pysician (BABM)
CHP	Chicago Helicopter Airways, Inc. [Air carrier designation symbol]
CHP	Child Psychiatry [Medical specialty] (DHSM)
CH/P	Chondromalacia/Patella [Medicine]
CHP	Chopper (MSA)
CHP	Christian Heritage Party of Canada [Parti d'Heritage du Canada] (AC)
CHP	Chuchupate [California] [Seismograph station code, US Geological Survey Closed] (SEIS)
CHP	Circle Hot Springs [Alaska] [Airport symbol Obsolete] (OAG)
Chp	Clinohypersthene [Inorganic chemistry]
CHP	Coal Handling Plant
CHP	Cogeneration of Heat and Power
CHP	Combined Heat and Power [Generation]
CHP	Combined-Heat-and-Power Station [Energy production]
CHP	Comhuriyet Halk Partisi [Turkey]
CHP	Community Health Program (MCD)

CHP .... Comprehensive Health Planning [*A requirement for HEW grants to local agencies*]
CHP .... Conquest of Hunger Program [*Rockefeller Foundation*] (EA)
CHP .... Council of Housing Producers [*Defunct*] (EA)
CHP .... Cumene Hydroperoxide [*Organic chemistry*]
CHP .... Cyclohexylpyrrolidone [*Organic chemistry*]
CHP .... Cyril Hayes Press, Inc. [*Publisher*]
CHP .... Ferrocarril de Chihuahua al Pacifico, SA de CV [*AAR code*]
CHP .... Paymaster in Chief [*Navy British*] (ROG)
CHPA .... Canadian Hardwood Plywood Association (AC)
CHPA .... Combined Heart and Power Association [*British*] (DBA)
CHPAE .... Critical Human Performance and Evaluation (IEEE)
CHPCLK ..... Chief Pay Clerk [*Navy rating Obsolete*]
CHPDH........ Combined-Heat-and-Power District Heating [*British*] (DI)
CHPE .... Center for Health Promotion and Education [*Atlanta, GA*] [*Department of Health and Human Services*] (GRD)
ChpEn .... Champion Enterprises, Inc. [*Associated Press*] (SAG)
CHPF .... Combined Heating Performance Factor
CHPHAR ..... Chief Pharmacist [*Navy rating Obsolete*]
CHPHOT...... Chief Photographer [*Navy rating Obsolete*]
CHPI .... Characters per Inch [*Computer science*] (CMD)
Ch PI .... Chitty on Pleading [*A publication*] (DLA)
CHPLN .... Chaplain
CHPP .... Champps Entertainment, Inc. [*NASDAQ symbol*] (SAG)
CH PPD........ Charges Prepaid (WDAA)
CHPR .... Center for Health Policy Research [*University of Florida*] [*Research center*] (RCD)
Chpr........... Chairperson (BARN)
Ch Pr .... Chancery Practice [*A publication*] (DLA)
CHPR .... Hawkesbury, ON [*FM radio station call letters*]
CHPRD........ Center for Health Promotion Research and Development [*University of Texas*] [*Research center*] (RCD)
Ch Pre .... Precedents in Chancery, Edited by Finch [*1689-1723*] [*England*] [*A publication*] (DLA)
ChpRM........ Champion Road Machinery Ltd. [*Associated Press*] (SAG)
CHPROVMAAGK... Chief, Military Assistance Advisory Group, Korea (Provisional) (CINC)
CHPS .... Characters per Second [*Computer science*] (CMD)
CHPS .... Chips & Technologies, Inc. [*NASDAQ symbol*] (NQ)
CHPS .... Chips/Technologies [*NASDAQ symbol*] (TTSB)
CHPS .... Cold High Pressure Separator [*Chemical engineering*]
CHPS .... Comprehensive Health Planning Service [*Federal government*]
ChpStl .... Chaparral Steel Co. [*Associated Press*] (SAG)
chpt .... Chapter (VRA)
chpt hs .... Chapter House (VRA)
CHPTR .... Chapter
CHPX .... Chickenpox [*Also, Cp*] [*Medicine*]
CHQ .... Central Headquarters (DCTA)
CHQ .... Chania [*Greece*] [*Airport symbol*] (OAG)
CHQ .... Charlesbourg [*Quebec*] [*Seismograph station code, US Geological Survey*] (SEIS)
CHQ .... Charleston, MO [*Location identifier FAA*] (FAAL)
CHQ .... Chautauqua Airlines [*ICAO designator*] (FAAC)
CHQ .... Cheque [*British*]
CHQ .... China Sea Resources Corp. [*Vancouver Stock Exchange symbol*]
CHQ .... Chloroquinol [*Medicine*] (DMAA)
CHQ .... Company Headquarters [*British military*] (DMA)
CHQ .... Corps Headquarters [*Army*]
CHQB .... Chief Justice of the Queen's Bench (DLA)
CHQB .... Powell River, BC [*AM radio station call letters*]
CHQM .... Vancouver, BC [*FM radio station call letters*]
CHQMCLK... Chief Quartermaster Clerk [*Coast Guard*]
CHQR .... Calgary, AB [*AM radio station call letters*]
CHQT .... Edmonton, AB [*AM radio station call letters*]
CHR .... Air Charter Services [*Zaire*] [*ICAO designator*] (FAAC)
CHR .... Canadians for Health Research [*Canadiens pour la Recherche Medicale*] (AC)
C-HR .... Candle-Hour [*Illumination*] (AAG)
CHR .... Cargo Handling Rig (RDA)
CHR .... Catholic Historical Review [*A publication*] (BRI)
CHR .... Center for Health Research [*Wayne State University*] [*Research center*] (RCD)
CHR .... Center for Human Radiobiology
CHR .... Center for Human Resources [*Rutgers University*] [*Research center*] (RCD)
CHR .... Cercarienhullen Reaktion [*Medicine*]
CHR .... Chair
chr .... Chair of the Board (DD)
CHR .... Character (BUR)
CHR .... Character Register
CHR .... Charleston [*Diocesan abbreviation*] [*South Carolina*] (TOCD)
CHR .... Charter Oil Co. Ltd. [*Toronto Stock Exchange symbol*]
CHR .... Cheers International [*Vancouver Stock Exchange symbol*]
chr .... Cherokee [*MARC language code Library of Congress*] (LCCP)
CHR .... Chestnut Ridge Railway Co. [*AAR code*]
CHR .... Chilgener SA [*NYSE symbol*] (SAG)
CHR .... Chilgener S.A. ADS [*NYSE symbol*] (TTSB)
Ch R .... Chitty's English King's Bench Reports [*A publication*] (DLA)
Chr........... Chorismic Acid [*Biochemistry*]
chr .... Chrestomathy (BARN)
CHR .... Christ [*or Christian*]
CHR .... Christchurch [*New Zealand*] [*Later, EYR*] [*Geomagnetic observatory code*]
CHR .... Christened
Chr........... Christian

Chr........... Christschall [*Record label*] [*Austria*]
CHR .... Chrome (ROG)
chr .... Chrome (VRA)
CHR .... Chromium [*Chemical symbol is Cr*] (MSA)
Chr........... Chromobacterium (MAE)
CHR .... Chronic [*Medicine*]
Chr........... Chronicles [*Old Testament book*]
CHR .... Church (MCD)
CHR .... Coherent Heterodyne Receiver (PDAA)
CHR .... Commission on Human Resources [*National Research Council*]
CHR .... Commission on Human Rights [*Geneva, Switzerland*] (EAIO)
CHR .... Community Health Representative Program [*Department of Health and Human Services*] (GFGA)
CHR .... Community of the Holy Rood [*Anglican religious community*]
CHR .... Compositor Hourly Rate (DGA)
CHR .... Computer Hour
CHR .... Condenser Heat Rejection (IAA)
CHR .... Constant Hazard Ratio
CHR .... Contemporary Hit Radio
CHR .... Convent of the Holy Rood [*British*] (BI)
CHR .... Cooling Water/Hot Water Return [*Nuclear energy*] (NRCH)
CHR .... Cooper-Harper Rating [*NASA*] (NASA)
CHR .... Coordinated Hungarian Relief [*Defunct*] (EA)
CHR .... Council on Homosexuality & Religion [*Conseil de l'Homosexualite et la Region*] (AC)
c-hr........... Curie-Hour [*Measurement*] (DAVI)
Ch R .... Irish Chancery Reports [*A publication*] (DLA)
Ch-R .... National Central Library, Rare Book Collection, Taipei, Taiwan, China [*Library symbol Library of Congress*] (LCLS)
Ch R .... Reports in Chancery [*1615-1712*] [*England*] [*A publication*] (DLA)
Ch R .... Upper Canada Chancery Chambers Reports [*A publication*] (DLA)
CHRA .... Canadian Health Record Association
CHRA .... Canadian Holocaust Remembrance Association (AC)
CHRA .... Canadian Housing & Renewal Association (AC)
CHRA .... Center Housing Rotating Assembly [*Automotive engineering*]
CHRA .... Colorado Human Resource Association (SRA)
CHRA .... Committee for Human Rights in Argentina [*British*]
CHRB .... China Resource Dvlmt [*NASDAQ symbol*] (TTSB)
CHRB .... China Resources Development, Inc. [*NASDAQ symbol*] (SAG)
CHRB .... High River, AB [*AM radio station call letters*]
ChRBC .... Chicken Red Blood Cell [*Medicine*] (DMAA)
CHRBRSYN... Chronic Brain Syndrome [*Medicine*]
CHRC .... Canadian Human Rights Commission [*See also CCDP*]
CHRC .... Congressional Human Rights Caucus (EA)
CHRC .... Quebec, PQ [*AM radio station call letters*]
Chrcft .... Chromcraft Revington, Inc. [*Associated Press*] (SAG)
Chr Ch .... Christian's Charges to Grand Juries [*A publication*] (DLA)
ChrchlID ..... Churchill Downs, Inc. [*Associated Press*] (SAG)
CHRCL .... Charcoal
CHRCS........ Centre for Human Relations and Community Studies [*Concordia University*] [*Canada Research center*] (RCD)
CHRD......... Chaired
CHRD......... Drummondville, PQ [*AM radio station call letters*]
ChrDem ...... Christian Democrats (EY)
CHRDS........ Comprehensive Human Resources Data System (MCD)
CHRDT........ Committee for Human Rights and Democracy in Turkey (EA)
ChrDwt....... Church & Dwight Co., Inc. [*Associated Press*] (SAG)
CHRE .... St. Catherines, ON [*FM radio station call letters*]
CH Rec .... City Hall Recorder (Rogers) [*New York City*] [*A publication*] (DLA)
CHRELE ...... Chief Radio Electrician [*Navy rating Obsolete*]
CH Rep .... City Hall Reporter (Lomas) [*New York City*] [*A publication*] (DLA)
Ch Rep .... Irish Chancery Reports [*A publication*] (DLA)
Ch Rep .... Reports in Chancery [*A publication*] (DLA)
Ch Rep Ir..... Irish Chancery Reports [*A publication*] (DLA)
Ch Repts ..... Irish Chancery Reports [*A publication*] (DLA)
Ch Repts ..... Reports in Chancery [*A publication*] (DLA)
Chr Etoh ...... Chronic Ethanolism [*Chemical dependency*] (DAVI)
Ch Reun ...... Arret de la Cour de Cassation Toutes Chambres Reunies [*Decision of the Full Court of the Court of Appeal*] [*French*] (ILCA)
Ch Rev Int ... China Review International
Ch Rev Int ... China Review International [*A publication*] (BRI)
CHRF .... Children's Hospital Research Foundation [*Research center*] (RCD)
CHRG......... Charge (AFM)
CHRG......... Charge
CHRGN .... Character Generator [*Computer science*] (NITA)
CHRI .... Christiansted National Historic Site
CHRI .... COHR, Inc. [*NASDAQ symbol*] (SAG)
CHRI .... COHR Inc. [*NASDAQ symbol*] (TTSB)
CHRIE .... Council on Hotel, Restaurant, and Institutional Education (EA)
CHRI-FM ..... Ottawa, ON [*FM radio station call letters*] (RBYB)
CHRIS .... Cancer Hazards Ranking and Information System
CHRIS .... Chemical Hazards Response Information System [*Coast Guard Information service or system*]
CHRIS .... Cheque Reconciliation and Information System [*Australia*]
CHRIS .... Christened (ADA)
CHRIS .... Cloud Height Remote Indicating System (PDAA)
Chris BL ...... Christian's Bankrupt Law [*A publication*] (DLA)
ChrisCr .... Chris-Craft Industries, Inc. [*Associated Press*] (SAG)
CHRIS/HACS... Chemical Hazards Response Information System/Hazard Assessment Computer System [*Coast Guard*] (ERG)
Christ Lanfran... Christophorus Lanfranchinus [*Deceased, 1490*] [*Authority cited in pre-1607 legal work*] (DSA)
Christn........ Christiana Companies, Inc. [*Associated Press*] (SAG)
CHRL .... Roberval, PQ [*AM radio station call letters*]
CHRM .... Center for Holistic Resource Management (EA)

CHRM	Certificate in Human Resources Management (DD)
CHRM	Chairman
ChRM	Champion Road Machinery Ltd. [*Associated Press*] (SAG)
Chrm	Charmides [*of Plato*] [*Classical studies*] (OCD)
CHRM	Matane, PQ [*AM radio station call letters*]
CHRMN	Chairman
CHRMN	Chairman
ChrmSh	Charming Shoppes, Inc. [*Associated Press*] (SAG)
CHRN	Committee on Human Rights for Nicaragua [*Later, CHRPN*] (EA)
CHRNCL	Chronicle
CHRO	Chromolithograph (DSUE)
CHRO	Pembroke, ON [*Television station call letters*]
Ch Rob	Robinson's English Admiralty Reports [*1799-1808*] [*A publication*] (DLA)
CHROM	Chromium [*Chemical symbol is Cr*]
Chrom	Chromosome [*Genetics*]
ChromCS	Chromatics Color Sciences International, Inc. [*Associated Press*] (SAG)
Chromia	Chromatographia [*A publication*]
CHROMO	Chromolithograph (ROG)
chron	Chronic [*Medicine*] (AAMN)
Chron	Chronica [*of St. Jerome*] [*Classical studies*] (OCD)
CHRON	Chronicle
Chron	Chronicles [*Old Testament book*]
CHRON	Chronological
chron	Chronology
CHRON	Chronometer
Chron Div Cts	Chronicles of the Divorce Courts [*A publication*] (DLA)
Chronimed	Chronimed, Inc. [*Associated Press*] (SAG)
Chron Jur	Chronica Juridicalia [*A publication*] (DLA)
CHRONO	Chronological (AFM)
CHRONTER	Chronometer (ROG)
CHRO PLTD	Chrome Plated [*Freight*]
CHRP	Canadian Home Renovation Program
CHRP	Certified Human Resources Professional [*Canada*] (DD)
CHRP	Common Hardware Reference Platform [*Computer science*]
ChrP	National Palace Museum, Wai-shuang-hsi, Shih-lin, Taipei, Taiwan, China [*Library symbol*] [*Library of Congress*] (LCLS)
CHRPE	Congenital Hypertrophy of the Retinal Pigment Epithelium [*Medicine*] (DMAA)
CHRPI	Center for Health Resources Planning Information [*National Institutes of Health*]
CHRPN	Committee on Human Rights for the People of Nicaragua (EA)
CHRPRSN	Chairperson
CHRPRSN	Chairperson
Chr Pr W	Christie's Precedents of Wills [*A publication*] (DLA)
CH RPT	Cheap Reprint (DGA)
CHRR	Center for Human Resource Research [*Ohio State University*] [*Research center*] (RCD)
CHRR	Center for Human Rights and Responsibilities [*British*]
CHRR	Committee for Human Rights in Rumania (EA)
Chr Rep	Chamber Reports, Upper Canada [*A publication*] (DLA)
Chr Rob	Christopher Robinson's English Admiralty Reports [*165 English Reprint*] [*A publication*] (DLA)
CHRRS	Community Homefinding, Relocation, and Referral Services [*US Army Corps of Engineers*]
CHRS	Canadian Heritage River System [*NPPAC*]
CHRS	Capitol Hill Restoration Society (EA)
CHRS	Center for Hospitality Research and Service (EA)
CHRS	Cerebrohepatorenal Syndrome [*Medicine*]
CHRS	Chambers (ROG)
CHRS	Charming Shoppes [*NASDAQ symbol*] (TTSB)
CHRS	Charming Shoppes, Inc. [*NASDAQ symbol*] (NQ)
CHRS	Christian Syndrome [*Medicine*] (DMAA)
CHRS	Chrysoberyl [*Jewelry*] (ROG)
CHRS	Committee for Human Rights in Syria (EA)
CHRS	Congenital Hereditary Retinoschisis [*Ophthalmology*] (DAVI)
CHRS	Containment Heat Removal System [*Nuclear energy*] (NRCH)
chr scrn	Choir Screen (VRA)
ChrSoc	Christian Socialist (EY)
CHRST	Characteristic (MSA)
CHRST	Christ
CHRSTN	Christian
CHRSTN	Christian
CHRT	Chartwell Leisure, Inc. [*NASDAQ symbol*] (SAG)
CHRT	Coordinated Human Resource Technology (MCD)
CHRT	St. Eleuthere, PQ [*AM radio station call letters*]
ChrtBk	Charter Bank SB [*Associated Press*] (SAG)
CHRTBL	Charitable
ChrtMed	Charter Medical Corp. [*Associated Press*] (SAG)
CHRTR	Charter
CHRTRD	Chartered
CHRUSNAS	Committee on Human Rights of the US National Academy of Sciences (EA)
ChrW	Christentum und Wissenschaft [*A publication*] (BJA)
ChrW	Die Christliche Welt [*A publication*] (BJA)
CHRW	London, ON [*FM radio station call letters*]
CHRWMN	Chairwoman
ChrWo	Christianskii Wostok [*A publication*] (BJA)
CHRX	ChiRex, Inc. [*NASDAQ symbol*] (SAG)
CHRX	ChiRex Inc. [*NASDAQ symbol*] (TTSB)
CHRY	Cherry
CHRY	Chrysler Corp.
CHRY	Toronto, ON [*FM radio station call letters*]
CHRYSANT	Chrysanthemum [*Horticulture*] (DSUE)

CHRYSLR	Chrysler
Chryslr	Chrysler Corp. [*Associated Press*] (SAG)
CHRZ	Computer Horizons [*NASDAQ symbol*] (TTSB)
CHRZ	Computer Horizons Corp. [*NASDAQ symbol*] (NQ)
CHS	California State University, Hayward, Hayward, CA [*Library symbol Library of Congress*] (LCLS)
CHS	Cambridge Historical Series [*A publication*]
CHS	Canadian Hearing Society (AC)
CHS	Canadian Hemochromatosis Society [*Societe Canadienne de l'Hemochromatose*] (AC)
CHS	Canadian Hemophilia Society [*Societe Canadienne de l'Hemophilie*] (AC)
CHS	Canadian Hydrographic Service (MCD)
CHS	Canadian Hypertension Society [*Societe Canadienne d'Hypertension Arterielle*] (AC)
CHS	Canberra Horticultural Society [*Australia*]
CHS	Capitol Historical Society [*Washington, DC*]
CHS	Catholic Homiletic Society [*Later, CPC*] (EA)
CHS	Center for Holocaust Studies (EA)
CHS	Center for Human Services (EA)
CHS	Central Heading System (SAA)
CHS	Chalcone Synthase [*An enzyme*]
CHS	Challenge Aviation Pty Ltd. [*Australia ICAO designator*] (FAAC)
CHS	Channel Handicap System [*Yacht racing*]
CHS	Characters per Second [*Computer science*] (IAA)
CHS	Charleston [*South Carolina*] [*Airport symbol*]
CHS	Chaus [*Bernard*], Inc. [*NYSE symbol*] (SPSG)
CHS	Chediak-Higashi Syndrome [*Medicine*]
CHS	Chester [*British depot code*]
CHS	Cheswick Historical Society (EA)
CHS	Chicago Suburban Motor Carriers Association, Inc., Homewood IL [*STAC*]
CHS	Cholinesterase [*An enzyme*]
CHS	Chose
CHS	Church Historical Society [*Later, HSEC*] (EA)
CHS	Chusal [*Former USSR Seismograph station code, US Geological Survey Closed*] (SEIS)
CHS	Chutine Resources Ltd. [*Vancouver Stock Exchange symbol*]
CHS	Circular Hollow Section [*Metal industry*]
CHS	Circus Historical Society (EA)
CHS	Citizens for Highway Safety [*Defunct*] (EA)
CHS	Cleveland Health Sciences Library, Cleveland, OH [*OCLC symbol*] (OCLC)
CHS	Clydesdale Horse Society [*British*] (DBA)
CHS	College for Human Services [*Formerly, WTC*]
CHS	College of Health Sciences [*Iran*]
CHS	Collimated Holes Structure (PDAA)
CHS	Columbia Historical Society [*Later, HSWDC*] (EA)
CHS	Command Hardware/Software [*Army*]
CHS	Command Hardware System [*Army*]
CHS	Common Hardware and Software [*Army*]
CHS	Community Health Service [*HEW*]
CHS	Community of the Holy Spirit (TOCD)
CHS	Compression Hip Screw [*System*] [*Orthopedics*] (DAVI)
CHS	Concert Hall Society [*Record label*]
CHS	Confederate Historical Society [*British*]
CHS	Consolidated Headquarters Squadron [*Military*]
CHS	Constant Heat Summation
CHS	Crime on High Seas
CHS	Cripples' Help Society [*British*] (BI)
CHS	Cross Head Speed (MCD)
CHS	Cylinder, Head, and Sector [*Computer science*]
CHSA	Chest, Heart, and Stroke Association [*British*]
CHSA	Chinese Historical Society of America (EA)
CHSAA	Catholic High Schools Athletic Association
CHSAMS	Chief, Security Assistance Management and Staff [*Military*] (DNAB)
CHSANSW	Cooperative Housing Societies Association of New South Wales [*Australia*]
CHSB	Chief Signal Boatswain [*Navy British*] (ROG)
chsbl	Chasuble (VRA)
CHSC	Canadian Home Shopping Club
CHSC	Central Health Services Council (AIE)
CHSC	St. Catherines, ON [*AM radio station call letters*]
CHSCA	Colorado High School Coaches Association (SRA)
CHSCLK	Chief Ship's Clerk [*Navy rating Obsolete*]
CHSD	Children's Health Services Division [*HEW*]
CHSD	Council for Holocaust Survivors with Disabilities (EA)
CHSE	Central Health Services Executive [*British*] (DI)
Chse	[*The*] Chase Manhattan Corp. [*Associated Press*] (SAG)
CHSE	CHS Electronics [*NASDAQ symbol*] (TTSB)
CHSE	CHS Electronics, Inc. [*NASDAQ symbol*] (SAG)
CHSEC	Characters per Second [*Computer science*] (IAA)
Ch Sec	Chartered Secretary [*A publication*]
CHS El	CHS Electronics, Inc. [*Associated Press*] (SAG)
Ch Sent	Chancery Sentinel [*New York*] [*A publication*] (DLA)
Ch Sent (NY)	Chancery Sentinel [*New York*] [*A publication*] (DLA)
ChsePC	Chase Preferred Capital Corp. [*Associated Press*] (SAG)
CHSF	Cargo Handling and Storage Facility
CHSF	Cargo Hazardous Servicing Facility (MCD)
CHSI	Committee on the Health Services Industry [*Cost of Living Council*] [*Abolished, 1973*]
CHSJ	St. John, NB [*AM radio station call letters*]
CHSKED	Change My Operation Schedule [*Military*] (MUGU)
ChSkr	Chief Skipper [*Navy British*]

CHSM .... Centre for Health Services Management [*Leicester Polytechnic*] [*British*] (CB)
CHSM .... China Service Medal [*Military decoration*]
CHSM .... Steinbach, MB [*AM radio station call letters*]
CHSN .... Canadian Home Shopping Network [*Television*]
CHSN .... Saskatoon, SK [*FM radio station call letters*]
CHSP .... Clinton Health Security Plan [*Medicine*]
CHSP .... Congregate Housing Services Program [*HUD*]
Chspk. .... Chesapeake Corp. [*Associated Press*] (SAG)
CHSPR .... Center for Health Services and Policy Research [*Northwestern University*] [*Research center*] (RCD)
CHSPTF .... Canadian Home & School & Parent-Teacher Federation [*Federation Canadienne des Associations Foyer-Ecole et Parents-Maitres*] (AC)
CHSR .... Center for Health Services Research [*University of Iowa*] [*Research center*] (RCD)
CHSR .... Child Health Services Research
CHSR .... Fredericton, NB [*FM radio station call letters*]
CHSS .... Chess
CHSS .... Children's Hypnotic Susceptibility Scale [*Psychology*]
CHSS .... Cooperative Health Statistics System [*Medicine*]
CHSS .... Counseling and Human Services Specialist (PGP)
CHSS .... Wynyard, SK [*Television station call letters*]
CHSSR .... Chaussure
CHST .... Canadian Historical Production/Injection File [*Petroleum Information Corp.*] [*Information service or system*] (CRD)
CHST .... Check and Store
Ch St J .... Chaplain of the Order of St. John of Jerusalem
CHSTJJ .... Chaplain of the Order of St. John of Jerusalem
CHSTNT ...... Chestnut [*Horse racing*]
chstnt .... Chestnut (VRA)
CHSTNT ...... Chestnut
CHSTR .... Characteristics of Transportation Resources File
CHT .... Call Hold and Trace [*Telecommunications*] (TEL)
CHT .... Call Holding Time [*Telecommunications*] (TEL)
CHT .... Catadioptric-Herschelian Telescope (PDAA)
CHT .... Cathode Heating Time
CHT .... Ceiling Height [*Technical drawings*]
CHT .... Center for Human Toxicology [*University of Utah*] [*Research center*] (RCD)
CHT .... Ceramic-Heated Tunnel [*Langley Research Center*]
CHt. .... Certified Hypnotherapist [*Medicine*]
CHT .... Charactron Tube [*Electronics*]
CHT .... Chart House Enterpr [*NYSE symbol*] (TTSB)
CHT .... Chart House Enterprises [*NYSE symbol*] (SPSG)
CHT .... Chest [*Shipping*]
CHT .... Chillicothe, MO [*Location identifier FAA*] (FAAL)
CHT .... Chita [*USSR*] [*Airport symbol*] (AD)
CHT .... Chittagong [*Bangladesh*] [*Seismograph station code, US Geological Survey*] (SEIS)
CHT .... Chute (KSC)
CHT .... Closed Head Trauma [*Emergency medicine*] (DAVI)
CHT .... Collection, Holding, Transfer [*Shipboard waste disposal*] (MCD)
CHT .... Congenital Hypothyroidism [*Medicine*]
CHT .... Continuous Heating Transformation [*Chemical engineering*]
CHT .... Convective Heat Transfer
CHT .... Cycloheptatriene [*Organic chemistry*]
CHT .... Cylinder-Head Temperature
CHTA .... Contract Heat Treatment Association [*British*] (DBA)
ChTB .... Channel Terminal Bay
ChtBnc .... Charter Bancshares, Inc. [*Associated Press*] (SAG)
CHTG .... Charting (AFM)
ChTg .... Chymotrypsinogen [*Biochemistry*]
ChtHou .... Chart House Enterprises [*Associated Press*] (SAG)
ChTK .... Chicken Thymidine Kinase [*An enzyme*]
CHTK .... Prince Rupert, BC [*AM radio station call letters*]
CHTL .... Chantal Pharmaceutical [*NASDAQ symbol*] (TTSB)
CHTL .... Chantal Pharmaceutical Corp. [*NASDAQ symbol*] (NQ)
CHTM .... Thompson, MB [*AM radio station call letters*]
CHTN .... Charlottetown, PE [*AM radio station call letters*]
CHTN .... Cooperative Human Tissue Network
CHTO .... Chiang Mai [*Thailand*] [*Seismograph station code, US Geological Survey*] (SEIS)
Ch Today ..... Christianity Today [*A publication*] (BRI)
ChtOneF ...... Charter One Financial, Inc. [*Associated Press*] (SAG)
CHTORP ...... Chief Torpedoman [*Navy rating Obsolete*]
ChtPwr .... Charter Power Systems [*Associated Press*] (SAG)
CHTR .... Charter (FAAC)
CHTR .... Charter Power Systems [*NASDAQ symbol*] (SAG)
ChTr .... Chymotrypsin [*An enzyme*]
CHTT .... Chattem, Inc. [*NASDAQ symbol*] (NQ)
CHTT .... Chicago Heights Terminal Transfer Railroad Co. [*AAR code*]
CHTW .... Canadian High Technology Week [*Trade show*] (ITD)
CHTZ .... Chlorothiazide [*Diuretic*]
CHTZ-FM ..... St. Catharines, ON [*FM radio station call letters*] (RBYB)
CHU .... Caledonia, MN [*Location identifier FAA*] (FAAL)
CHU .... Caloric Heat Unit
CHU .... Celsius Heat Unit (ADA)
CHU .... Centigrade Heat Unit
CHU .... Chabua [*India*] [*Airport symbol*] (AD)
CHU .... Channel Resources Ltd. [*Vancouver Stock Exchange symbol*]
CHU .... Christelijk-Historische Unie [*Christian-Historical Union*] [*Netherlands Political party*] (PPW)
CHU .... Chur [*Coire*] [*Switzerland*] [*Seismograph station code, US Geological Survey*] [*Closed*] (SEIS)

CHU .... Church
CHU .... Church Aircraft Ltd. [*ICAO designator*] (FAAC)
CHU .... Churches Speak [*A publication*]
chu. .... Church Slavic [*MARC language code Library of Congress*] (LCCP)
CHU .... Closed Head Unit [*Neurology*] (DAVI)
CHU .... Humboldt State College, Arcata, CA [*OCLC symbol*] (OCLC)
CHu .... Huntington Beach Public Library, Huntington Beach, CA [*Library symbol Library of Congress*] (LCLS)
CHUA .... Canadian Hail Underwriters Association
CHUAS .... Cooperative Hurricane Upper Air Station [*National Weather Service*] (NOAA)
Chubb .... [*The*] Chubb Corp. [*Associated Press*] (SAG)
CHUC .... Cobourg, ON [*AM radio station call letters*]
CHUCK .... Committee to Halt Useless College Killings [*Acronym is now organization's official name*] (EA)
CHUD .... Cannibalistic Humanoid Underground Dwellers [*or Contaminated Hazard Underground Disposal*] [*Acronym used as title of movie*]
CHuG .... Golden West College, Huntington Beach, CA [*Library symbol Library of Congress*] (LCLS)
CHUM .... Center for the Humanities [*State University of New York at Albany*] [*Research center*] (RCD)
CHUM .... Chart Updating Manual [*Air Force*]
CHUM .... Chumleigh [*England*]
CHUM .... Toronto, ON [*AM radio station call letters*]
CHuMD .... McDonnell Douglas Astronautics Co., Western Division, Huntington Beach, CA [*Library symbol Library of Congress*] (LCLS)
CHUM-FM .... Toronto, ON [*FM radio station call letters*]
Chump .... Child of Upwardly Mobile Professionals [*Lifestyle classification*]
CHUMP .... Criminal Headquarters for Underworld Master Plan [*Organization in TV series "Lancelot Link"*]
CHUMS .... Cancer Hopefuls United for Mutual Support [*Defunct*] (EA)
CHUMS .... Computerized Homes Underwriting Management Systems [*Department of Housing and Urban Development*] (GFGA)
CHUNNEL ..... Channel Tunnel [*Joint British-French project in English Channel*]
CHUO .... Ottawa, ON [*FM radio station call letters*]
Chuppie .... Chinese Urban Professional [*Hong Kong Yuppie*] [*Lifestyle classification*]
CHUR .... Chondritic Uniform Reservoir [*Geology*]
CHUR .... Churchill Technology [*NASDAQ symbol*] (TTSB)
CHUR .... Churchill Technology, Inc. [*NASDAQ symbol*] (NQ)
CHUR .... North Bay, ON [*AM radio station call letters*]
Church & Br Sh... Churchill and Bruce. Office and Duties of Sheriff [*2nd ed.*] [*1882*] [*A publication*] (DLA)
CHUR-FM .... North Bay, ON [*FM radio station call letters*] (RBYB)
CHUSAOSASF... Chief, United States Army Overseas Supply Agency, San Francisco (CINC)
CHUSDLG ..... Chief, United States Defense Liaison Group (DNAB)
CHUSMSI ..... Chief, United States Military Supply Mission, India (CINC)
CHUSNAVMIS... Chief, United States Naval Mission (DNAB)
CHUT .... Cable Households Using Television [*Cable television ratings*] (NTCM)
CHUT .... Chutty [*Chewing gum*] [*Slang British*] (DSUE)
CHUTE .... Parachute (NASA)
Chute Eq ..... Chute's Equity under the Judicature Act [*A publication*] (DLA)
CHuW .... Christentum und Wissenschaft [*A publication*] (BJA)
CHUX .... O'Charley's, Inc. [*NASDAQ symbol*] (SAG)
CHV .... Callitrichid Hepatitis Virus
CHV .... Carl Hanser Verlag [*Publisher*]
CHV .... Chattahoochee Valley Railway Co. [*AAR code*]
CHV .... Check Valve (KSC)
CH-V .... Cheval-Vapeur [*Horsepower*] [*French*]
CHV .... Chevron Corp. [*Vancouver Stock Exchange symbol NYSE symbol*] (SPSG)
CHV .... Chiavari [*Italy*] [*Seismograph station code, US Geological Survey Closed*] (SEIS)
ChV .... Chilean Victor [*Record label*]
CHV .... Chivenor FTU [*British ICAO designator*] (FAAC)
chv. .... Chuvash [*MARC language code Library of Congress*] (LCCP)
CHVA .... Contemporary Historical Vehicle Association (EA)
CHVD .... Dolbeau, PQ [*AM radio station call letters*]
CHVD-FM .... Dolbeau, PQ [*FM radio station call letters*]
CHVO .... Carbonear, NF [*AM radio station call letters*]
CHVP .... Cyclophosphamide, Hydroxydaunomycin [*Adriamycin*], VM-26 , Prednisone [*Teniposide*] [*Antineoplastic drug regimen*]
CHVR .... Pembroke, ON [*AM radio station call letters*]
CHVR-1 .... Renfrew, ON [*AM radio station call letters*]
CHVR-2 .... Arnprior, ON [*AM radio station call letters*]
CHVR-FM .... Pembroke, ON [*FM radio station call letters*] (RBYB)
chvt. .... Chevet (VRA)
CHW .... Charleston [*West Virginia*] [*Airport symbol*] (AD)
CHW .... Charter Air Ges. MbH & Co. Kg [*Austria*] [*FAA designator*] (FAAC)
CHW .... Chatwood Resources [*Vancouver Stock Exchange symbol*]
CHW .... Chesapeake Western Railway [*AAR code*]
CHW .... Chilled Water [*Aerospace*] (AAG)
CHW .... Chowiet Island [*Alaska*] [*Seismograph station code, US Geological Survey*] (SEIS)
CHW .... Cold and Hot Water
CHW .... Cold Heading Wire
CHW .... Constant Hot Water [*British*]
CHW .... Jiuquan [*China*] [*Airport symbol*] (OAG)
CHWDN .... Churchwarden
CHWI .... Wheatley, ON [*Television station call letters*]
CHWK .... Chilliwack, BC [*AM radio station call letters*]
CHWO .... Oakville, ON [*AM radio station call letters*]
CHWPC .... Capitol Hill Women's Political Caucus (EA)
CHWR .... Cooling Water/Hot Water Return [*Nuclear energy*] (NRCH)

CHWS	Council for Health and Welfare Services, United Church of Christ [*Later, CHHSM*] (EA)
CHWTO	Chief, Western Pacific Transportation Office (CINC)
CHX	Air Charter Express [*France ICAO designator*] (FAAC)
CHX	Cabin Heat Exchanger [*Aviation*] (MCD)
CHX	Chaix Hill [*Alaska*] [*Seismograph station code, US Geological Survey*] (SEIS)
CHX	Changuinola [*Panama*] [*Airport symbol*] (OAG)
CHX	Chavin of Canada [*Vancouver Stock Exchange symbol*]
CHX	Chicago Stock Exchange (SRA)
CHX	Chiro-Xylographic [*Type of block book*]
CHX	Choteau, MT [*Location identifier FAA*] (FAAL)
CH-X	Condensate Heat Exchanger (MCD)
CHX	Cycloheximide [*Also, CH, CXM, Cyh*] [*Fungicide*]
CHX	Pilgrim's Pride [*NYSE symbol*] (TTSB)
CHX	Pilgrim's Pride Corp. [*NYSE symbol*] (SPSG)
CHXL	Brockville, ON [*FM radio station call letters*]
CHXS	Check Express, Inc. [*NASDAQ symbol*] (SAG)
CHY	Chancery
CHY	Charity
chy	Cheyenne [*MARC language code Library of Congress*] (LCCP)
CHY	Cheyenne [*Diocesan abbreviation*] [*Wyoming*] (TOCD)
CHY	Chiayi [*Republic of China*] [*Seismograph station code, US Geological Survey*] (SEIS)
CHY	Chimney
CHY	China Air Cargo [*ICAO designator*] (FAAC)
CHY	Choiseul Bay [*Solomon Islands*] [*Airport symbol*] (OAG)
CHY	Christian Heritage Year [*1984*] [*British*]
CHY	Chyron Corp. [*NYSE symbol*] (SPSG)
CHy	Commission for Hydrology [*World Meteorological Organization*] (GFGA)
CHY	Denver, CO [*Location identifier FAA*] (FAAL)
chya	Chaitya (VRA)
Chy App Rep	Wright's Tennessee Chancery Appeals Reports [*A publication*] (DLA)
CHYC	Sudbury, ON [*AM radio station call letters*]
Chy Ch	Upper Canada Chancery Chambers Reports [*A publication*] (DLA)
Chy Chrs	Upper Canada Chancery Chambers Reports [*A publication*] (DLA)
CHYD	Churchyard
CHYK	Kapuskasing, ON [*AM radio station call letters*]
CHYM	Kitchener, ON [*FM radio station call letters*]
CHYMV	Chicory Yellow Mottle Virus [*Plant pathology*]
CHYR	Leamington, ON [*FM radio station call letters*]
Chyron	Chyron Corp. [*Associated Press*] (SAG)
CHZ	Career Horizons [*NYSE symbol*] (TTSB)
CHZ	Cheshire Air Training School [*British ICAO designator*] (FAAC)
CHZ	Chisholm Resources [*Vancouver Stock Exchange symbol*]
CHZ	Chorzow [*Poland*] [*Seismograph station code, US Geological Survey*] (SEIS)
CHZ	Chymohelizyme [*Biochemistry*]
CHZ	Continuously Habitable Zone (DICI)
CI	Call Indicator [*Computer science*]
CI	Cambria & Indiana Railroad Co. [*AAR code*]
CI	Candover Investments [*Finance British*]
C/I	Canister/Interceptor
CI	Capability Inspection [*Air Force*] (AFM)
CI	Capital Intensive [*Finance*]
CI	Captain-Instructor [*Navy British*]
CI	Carcinogenic Index
CI	Cardiac Index [*Physiology*]
CI	Cardiac Insufficiency [*Medicine*] (MAE)
CI	Card Input [*Computer science*] (BUR)
CI	Caritas Internationalis [*International Confederation of Catholic Organizations for Charitable and Social Action*] [*Vatican City, Vatican City State*] (EAIO)
CI	Carnegie Institute [*New York*]
CI	Caroline Islands [*Diocesan abbreviation*] (TOCD)
C/I	Carrier-to-Interference Ratio [*Computer science*]
CI	Case Informant [*Criminology*] (LAIN)
CI	Cash Item [*Accounting*]
CI	Cast Iron
CI	Catfish Institute [*An association*] (EA)
CI	Cato Institute (EA)
CI	CAUSA Institute (EA)
CI	Cayman Islands
CI	Cell Interaction [*Immunology*]
CI	Cellular, Inc. [*Telecommunications service*] (TSSD)
CI	Center Island [*Nuclear energy*] (NRCH)
CI	Center of Impact
CI	Central Indiana Railroad (IIA)
CI	Central Institution [*Scotland*] (AIE)
CI	Central Interval
CI	Centrifugation Interaction
CI	Centromeric Indices [*Chromosomes*]
CI	Cephalic Index
CI	Cereal Institute [*Defunct*] (EA)
CI	Cerebral Infarction [*Medicine*]
C/I	Certificate of Indebtedness [*Finance*]
CI	Certificate of Insurance
CI	Certification Inspection (MCD)
CI	Cesium Implant [*Oncology and radiation therapy*] (DAVI)
CI	Cetane Index [*Fuel technology*]
CI	Chain Index (ADA)
CI	Change Indicator (SSD)
CI	Channel Islands

C/I	Channel to Interference Ratio [*Telecommunications*] (OSI)
CI	Chapters of Instruction [*Freemasonry*] (ROG)
CI	Characteristic Independence
C + I	Chemical and Insulating
CI	Chemical Injection [*Nuclear energy*] (NRCH)
CI	Chemical Inspectorate [*British*]
CI	Chemical Ionization [*Spectrometry*]
CI	Chemotherapeutic Index [*Medicine*]
CI	Cher'd Interest [*Fan club*] (EA)
CI	Chest Incision [*Medicine*]
CI	Chief Inspector
CI	Chief Instructor
CI	Chief of Information [*Army*]
CI	Children, Inc. [*An association*] (EA)
CI	China Airlines (GAVI)
CI	China Airlines [*Airline flight code*] (ODBW)
CI	China Airlines [*ICAO designator*] (AD)
CI	China Institute in America (EA)
CI	Chlorine Institute (EA)
CI	Cholesteryl Iopanoate [*Biochemistry*]
CI	Christic Institute (EA)
CI	Chromatid Interchange (PDAA)
CI	Chums, Inc. [*An association*] (EA)
CI	Ciesta Gold Exploration Ltd. [*Vancouver Stock Exchange symbol*]
CI	CIGNA Corp. [*NYSE symbol*] (SPSG)
CI	Cimetidine [*Pharmacology*]
CI	Cinus de Pistoia [*Deceased, 1336*] [*Authority cited in pre-1607 legal work*] (DSA)
CI	Circuit Interrupter (MCD)
CI	Cirrhosis [*Medicine*]
CI	Cirrus [*Meteorology*]
CI	Civilian Internee [*Military*] (INF)
CI	Civil Imprisonment
CI	Civitan International (EA)
CI	Clandestine Intelligence (LAIN)
CI	Classification Inventory [*Military*]
CI	Clinical Investigation [*Medicine*] (MAE)
CI	Clomipramine [*Medicine*] (DMAA)
CI	Clonus Index (MAE)
CI	Close-In
CI	Cochlear Implant [*Otorhinolaryngology*] (DAVI)
CI	Coefficient of Intelligence
CI	Cold-Iron Soldered Joint (IAA)
CI	Colloidal Iron (OA)
CI	Color Index
CI	Color Interior Film (MCD)
CI	Colour Index [*Used in the dye industry*] (DAVI)
CI	Combat Indoctrination (MCD)
CI	Combat Ineffective [*Military*] (NVT)
CI	Combat Interviews
CI	Combination Inventory [*LIMRA*]
CI	Combustion Institute (EA)
CI	Comfort Index
CI	Commander-Instructor [*Navy British*]
CI	Command Information (MCD)
CI	Command Interpreter (SSD)
CI	Comment Issue
CI	Commonwealth Institute [*British*] (DI)
CI	Communication and Instrumentation [*NASA*] (KSC)
CI	Communication Information
CI	Communications Interface (MCD)
CI	Community Information
CI	Community of Interest [*Telecommunications*] (TEL)
CI	Compassion International (EA)
CI	Competitive Intelligence [*Corporate libraries*]
CI	Complete Iridectomy [*Ophthalmology*]
CI	Composites Institute (EA)
CI	Compounded Interest [*Business term*]
CI	Compression Ignition Engine
CI	Compulsory Insurance
CI	Computer Indicator (AFM)
CI	Computer Industry
CI	Computer Inquiries
CI	Computer Intelligence Corp. [*Information service or system*] (IID)
CI	Computer Interconnect (ACRL)
CI	Computer Interrogator
CI	Computing Index [*Computer analysis*]
CI	Concept Identification [*Psychology*]
CI	Concept Initiation [*Automotive project management*]
CI	Concern, Inc. [*An association*] (EA)
CI	Confidence Interval [*Statistics*]
CI	Confidential Informant [*Department of Justice*]
CI	Configuration Identification (MCD)
CI	Configuration Index
CI	Configuration Inspection (NASA)
CI	Configuration Interaction [*Quantum mechanics*]
CI	Configuration Item
CI	Congressional Interference
CI	Conservation International (EA)
C/I	Consistency Index [*Botany*]
CI	Consular Invoice
CI	Consumer Information
CI	Consumer Interpol (EA)
CI	Consuming Interest [*A publication*] (ADA)
C + I	Containerization Institute [*Later, CII*]

CI............... Containment Integrity [Nuclear energy] (NRCH)
CI............... Containment Isolation [Nuclear energy] (NRCH)
CI............... Contamination Index [Medicine]
CI............... Continuous Injection [Automotive engineering]
CI............... Continuous Interlock (MCD)
CI............... Contract Items
CI............... Contractor Inventory
CI............... Contrast Index [Photography]
CI............... Control Indicator
CI............... Controlled Ionization
CI............... Controlled Item
CI............... Conventional Instruction (RDA)
CI............... Cooperating Individual [FBI]
CI............... Coordinate Index
CI............... Coordinating Installations (MCD)
CI............... Cordage Institute (EA)
CI............... Core Insulation [Nuclear energy]
CI............... Cornell Index [Psychology]
CI............... Coronary Insufficiency [Medicine]
CI............... Corrected Count Increment [Hematology]
Ci............... Cosine Integral
CI............... Cosmopolitan International (EA)
CI............... Cost and Insurance [Shipping]
CI............... Cost Index (GAVI)
CI............... Cost Inspector
CI............... Cotton Inc. [An association] (EA)
CI............... Cottonseed Protein Isolate
CI............... Counterinsurgency (CINC)
CI............... Counterintelligence (MCD)
CI............... Couples, Inc. [An association] (EA)
CI............... Course Indicator (IEEE)
CI............... Covert Investigation [Police term]
CI............... Craft Inclination [Aerospace] (AAG)
CI............... Cranberry Institute (EA)
CI............... Creative Initiative [Later, BWF] (EA)
CI............... Crew Interface (MCD)
CI............... Crime Intelligence [British] (DI)
CI............... Criminal Informant
CI............... Criminal Intelligence [Branch of the Metropolitan Police, London]
CI............... Criminal Investigation [or Investigator] [Military]
CI............... Critical Influence
CI............... Critical Intelligence
CI............... Critical Item
CI............... Cropping Index
CI............... Crucible Institute [Formerly, CMA] (EA)
CI............... Crystal Impedance
CI............... Crystalline Insulin
CI............... Cubic Inch (MCD)
CI............... Cumulative Index (DLA)
Ci............... Curie [Unit of radioactivity] [Preferred unit is Bq, Becquerel]
CI............... Current Interrupter [Electronics] (IAA)
CI............... Customer Integration (SSD)
CI............... Customer Item
CI............... Cut In
CI............... Cytoplasmic Incompatibility [Entomology]
CI............... Cytotoxic Index [Cytochemistry]
CI............... First Cranial Nerve [Anatomy] (DMAA)
CI............... Grand Cayman [IYRU nationality code] (IYR)
CI............... Imperial Order of the Crown of India [British]
CI............... Ivory Coast [ANSI two-letter standard code] (CNC)
CI............... Juedisch-Palaestinisches Corpus Inscriptionum [A publication] (BJA)
CI............... Parke, Davis & Co. [Research code symbol]
CI2............. Second Computer Inquiry (TSSD)
CIA............. California Institute of the Arts [Valencia] [OCLC symbol] (OCLC)
CIA............. Canadian Implant Association (EAIO)
CIA............. Canadian Importers Association
CIA............. Canadian Infantry Association [Association Canadienne de l'Infanterie] (AC)
CIA............. Canadian Institute of Actuaries
CIA............. Canberra Institute of the Arts [Australia]
CIA............. Capital Investment Analysis [Business term]
CIA............. Capitol Information Association (EA)
CIA............. Captured in Action [Military]
CIA............. Cariana International Industries, Inc. [Vancouver Stock Exchange symbol]
CIA............. Carpet Institute of Australia
CIA............. Casein Importers Association (EA)
CIA............. Cash in Advance
CIA............. Catholic Irish Attorneys [Fictional organization]
CIA............. CCNU [Lomustine], Ifosfamide, Adriamycin [Antineoplastic drug regimen]
CIA............. Center for Interreligious Affairs
CIA............. Central Intelligence Agency [Acronym has been facetiously translated "Casey in Action," a reference to the agency's former director]
CIA............. Centre for Image Analysis [Charles Sturt University] [Australia]
CIA............. Centre International des Antiparasitaires
CIA............. Ceramics International Association [Defunct] (EA)
CIA............. Certificate of Internal Auditing (TDOB)
CIA............. Certified Internal Auditor [The Institute of Internal Auditors, Inc.] [Designation awarded by]
CIA............. Chemical Industries Association
CIA............. Chemiluminescence Immunoassay (OA)
CIA............. Chief Inspector of Armaments
CIA............. China Institute in America (EA)
CIA............. Chloroisatoic Anhydride [Organic chemistry]

CIA............. Christmas Island Arbitrator
CIA............. Chronic Idiopathic Anhidrosis [Medicine] (DAVI)
CIA............. Chymotrypsin Inhibitor Activity
CIA............. Cigar Institute of America [Later, CAA] (EA)
CIA............. Citizens, Inc. [AMEX symbol] (SAG)
CIA............. Citizens Inc.'A' [AMEX symbol] (TTSB)
CIA............. Clumping Inducing Agent [Bacteriology, genetics]
CIA............. Coalition for Indian Education (EA)
CIA............. Collagen-Induced Arthritis [Medicine]
CIA............. Collegium Internationale Allergologicum [Berne, Switzerland] (EA)
CIA............. Collision-Induced Absorption (MCD)
CIA............. Color Image Assembly [Graphic arts]
CIA............. Colostomy and Ileostomy Association [Medicine]
CIA............. Comitato Italiano Atlantico [Italian Atlantic Committee] (EAIO)
CIA............. Comite International d'Auschwitz [International Auschwitz Committee]
CIA............. Commission Internationale d'Analyses
CIA............. Commission on International Affairs (EA)
CIA............. Communications Interface Assembly [Computer science]
CIA............. Communications Interrupt Analysis [Sperry UNIVAC] (IEEE)
CIA............. Compania [Company] [Spanish]
Cia............. Compania [Company] [Spanish] (DFIT)
CIA............. Composites Institute of Australia
CIA............. Computer Industry Association [Later, CCIA]
CIA............. Computer Interface Adapter
CIA............. Confederation Internationale des Accordeonistes [International Confederation of Accordionists]
CIA............. Conseil International des Archives [International Council on Archives]
CIA............. Consultant-Initiated Activity [LIMRA]
CIA............. Consumer Information Association
CIA............. Containment Isolation A [Nuclear energy] (NRCH)
CIA............. Control Indicator Assembly (MCD)
CIA............. Control Interface Assembly (MCD)
CIA............. Controllers Institute of America [Later, FEI]
CIA............. Cooperative Immunoassay
CIA............. Cork Institute of America [Defunct] (EA)
CIA............. Correctional Industries Association (EA)
CIA............. Cotton Importers Association (EA)
CIA............. Cotton Insurance Association [Defunct] (EA)
CIA............. Council on Islamic Affairs (EA)
CIA............. Culinary Institute of America [Hyde Park, NY]
CIA............. Rome [Italy] Ciampino Airport [Airport symbol Obsolete] (OAG)
CIAA........... Central Intercollegiate Athletic Association (EA)
CIAA........... Centre International d'Aviation Agricole [International Agricultural Aviation Center]
CIAA........... Cheese Importers Association of America (EA)
CIAA........... Christmas Island Administration and Assembly [Australia]
CIAA........... College Inventory of Academic Adjustment [Psychology]
CIAA........... Confederation des Industries Agro-Alimentaires de la CEE [Confederation of the Food and Drink Industries of the ECC] (EAIO)
CIAA........... Connecticut Industrial Arts Association (EDAC)
CIAA........... Coordinator of Inter-American Affairs
CIAA de l'UNICE... Confederation des Industries Agro-Alimentaires de l'Union des Industries de la Communaute Europeenne [Commission of the Agricultural and Food Industries of the Union of Industries of the European Community] (EAIO)
CIAB........... Coal Industry Advisory Board
CIAB........... Conseil International des Agences Benevoles [International Council of Voluntary Agencies - ICVA] (EA)
CIABS......... Center for Inter-American and Border Studies [University of Texas, El Paso] [Research center] (RCD)
CIAC........... Canadian Independent Adjusters Conference
CIAC........... Career Information and Counseling [Air Force]
CIAC........... Central Industrial Applications Center [Southeastern Oklahoma State University] [Information service or system] (IID)
CIAC........... Centre d'Inter-Action Culturelle [Center for Inter-Cultural Action] (EAIO)
CIAC........... Ceramics Information Analysis Center (IID)
CIAC........... Changchun Institute of Applied Chemistry [China]
CIAC........... Computer Incident Advisory Capability [Department of Energy] [Computer science]
CIAC........... Computer Incident Advisory Capability [Department of Energy]
CIAC........... Contributions in Aid of Construction [IRS]
CIAC........... Council for Inter-American Cooperation [Later, NFTC]
CIAC........... Cultural Information Analysis Center (SAA)
CIACA......... International Committee for Amateur-Built Aircraft (EA)
CIACS......... Coded Integrated Armament Control System (MCD)
CIACT......... CNO [Chief of Naval Operations] Industry Advisory Committee for Telecommunications [DoD] (EGAO)
CIA/C-TC...... Central Intelligence Agency / Counter-Terrorism Center (LAIN)
CIAD........... Climate Impact Assessment Division [National Enviromental Satellite, Data, and Information Service] (USDC)
CIAD........... Climate Impact Assessment Division [Marine science] (OSRA)
CIAD .... Coalition Internationale pour l'Action au Developpement [International Coalition for Development Action - ICDA] (EAIO)
CIAD........... Counterintelligence Analysis Division [DoD]
CIADA......... Carolinas Independent Automobile Dealers Association (SRA)
CIADEC....... Confederation Internationale des Associations de Diplomes en Sciences Economiques et Commerciales [International Confederation of Associations of Graduates in Economic and Commercial Sciences]
CIADFOR...... Centre Interafricain pour le Developpement de la Formation Professionnelle [Inter-African Center for the Development of Professional Training] [Abidjan, Ivory Coast] (EAIO)

CIADI .... Centro Internacional de Arreglo de Diferencias Relativas a Inversiones [*International Center for Settlement of Investment Disputes*]

CIADSR .... Comite International sur l'Alcool, les Drogues et la Securite Routiere [*International Committee on Alcohol, Drugs, and Traffic Safety*] (EAIO)

CIAE .... Chicago International Art Exhibition (ITD)

CIAE .... Crossed Immunoaffinoelectrophoresis [*Analytical biochemistry*]

CIAED .... Collagen-Induced Autoimmune Ear Disease [*Immunology and otorhinolaryngology*] (DAVI)

CIAF .... Centro Interamericano de Fotointerpretacion [*Bogota, Colombia*]

CIAFMA .... Centre International de l'Actualite Fantastique et Magique

CIAFT .... Conseil d'Intervention pour l'Acces des Femmes au Travail (AC)

CIAGA .... Confederacion Interamericana de Ganaderos

CIAGP .... Commission Internationale des Aumoniers Generaux des Prisons [*International Commission of Catholic Prison Chaplains - ICPC*] (EA)

CIAgrE .... Companion of the Institution of Agricultural Engineers [*British*]

CIAI .... Comite International d'Aide aux Intellectuels

CIAI .... Conference Internationale des Associations d'Ingenieurs [*International Federatiio of Engineering Associations*] (PDAA)

CIAJ .... Canadian Institue for the Admistration of Justice (AC)

CIAJ .... Communications Industries Association of Japan [*Telecommunications*]

CIAL .... Communaute Internationale des Associations de la Librairie [*International Community of Booksellers Associations*]

CIAL .... Corresponding Member of the International Institute of Arts and Letters

CIALANT ...... Central Intelligence Agency, Atlantic (MCD)

CIAM .... Cambridge, ON [*AM radio station call letters*]

CIAM .... Canadian Institute of Academic Medicine [*Institut Canadien de Medecine Academique*] (AC)

CIAM .... Commission International d'Aeromodelisme [*International Aeromodelling Commission*] (PDAA)

CIAM .... Computerized Integrated and Automated Manufacturing (IAA)

CIAMS .... Color Image Assembly and Manipulation System [*Graphic arts*] (DGA)

CIANDE .... Civil Information and Education Section of Allied Headquarters [*World War II*]

CI & R .... Community Information and Referral Service [*Library science*]

CI & W .... Cincinnati, Indiana & Western Railway

CIANS .... Collegium Internationale Activitatis Nervosae Superioris [*Milan, Italy*] (EAIO)

CIAO .... Brampton, ON [*AM radio station call letters*]

Ciao .... Columbia International Affairs Online [*Computer science*]

CIAO .... Conference Internationale des Africanistes de l'Ouest

CIAO .... Congress of Italian-American Organizations

CiaoCuc ..... Ciao Cucina Corp. [*Associated Press*] (SAG)

CIAP .... Cambodia-IRRI [*International Rice Research Institute*]-Australia Project

CIAP .... Climatic Impact Assessment Program [*for high altitude aircraft*]

CIAP .... Climatic Implications of Atmospheric Pollution

CIAP .... Comite Interamericano de la Alianza para el Progreso [*Inter-American Committee of the Alliance for Progress*]

CIAP .... Comprehensive Improvement Assistance Program [*HUD*]

CIAPG .... Confederation Internationale des Anciens Prisonniers de Guerre [*International Confederation of Former Prisoners of War*] [*Paris, France*] (EAIO)

CIAPHR .... Coalition for Information Access for Print Handicapped Readers [*An association*]

CIAPS .... Customer-Integrated Automated Procurement System (AFM)

CIAQ .... Committee on Indoor Air Quality [*Environmental Protection Agency*] (GFGA)

CIAR .... Canadian Institute for Advanced Research

CIAR .... Center for Inter-American Relations (EA)

CIARA .... Conference Internationale Administrative des Radiocommunications Aeronautiques

CIARA .... Conference Internationale sur l'Assistance aux Refugies en Afrique [*International Conference on Assistance for Refugees in Africa - ICARA*] [*United Nations Geneva, Switzerland*] (EAIO)

CIArb .... Chartered Institute of Arbitrators [*British*] (DBA)

CIARDS .... Central Intelligence Agency Retirement and Disability System

CIAS .... Calgary Immigrant Aid Society (AC)

CIAS .... California Institute of Asian Studies [*An evening graduate school*] (EA)

CIAS .... Central Ironmoulders Association of Scotland [*A union*]

CIAS .... Chicago International Antiques Show (ITD)

CIAS .... Conference of Independent African States (NATG)

CIAS .... Conseil Inter-Americain de Securite [*Inter-American Safety Council*]

CIAS .... Conseil International de l'Action Sociale [*International Council on Social Welfare - ICSW*] [*Vienna, Austria*] (EA)

CIAS .... Containment Isolation Actuation Signal [*Nuclear energy*] (NRCH)

CIAS .... Crash Impact Absorbing Structure [*Automotive safety*]

CIASE .... Computer Institute for Applications in Science and Engineering (MCD)

CIASTA .... Cooperative Institute for Aerospace Science and Terrestrial Applications [*University of Nevada*] [*Research center*] (RCD)

CIAT .... Centro Interamericano de Administracion del Trabajo [*Inter-American Center for Labor Administration*] [*Lima, Peru*] (EAIO)

CIAT .... Centro Interamericano de Administradores Tributarios [*Inter-American Center of Tax Administrators*] (EAIO)

CIAT .... Centro Internacional de Agricultura Tropical [*International Center for Tropical Agriculture*] [*Colombia*]

CIAT .... Ciatti's, Inc. [*NASDAQ symbol*] (NQ)

CIAT .... Comision Interamericana del Atun Tropical [*Interamerican Tropical Tuna Commission - IATTC*]

CIAT HA ...... Crew-Initiated Automatic Test

CIATF .... Comite International des Associations Techniques de Fonderie [*International Committee of Foundry Technical Associations*] (EAIO)

CIATO .... Centre International d'Alcoologie / Toixixomanies [*International Center of Alcohol/Drug Addiction*] (PDAA)

Ciattis .... Ciatti's, Inc. [*Associated Press*] (SAG)

CIAU .... Canadian Intercollegiate Athletic Union

CIAU .... Ciao Cucina Corp. [*NASDAQ symbol*] (SAG)

CIB .... Banco Indl Colombiano Pref ADS [*NYSE symbol*] (TTSB)

CIB .... Banco Industrial Columbiano SA [*NYSE symbol*] (SAG)

CIB .... CALS [*Customs Acts Legislation Service*] Information Bulletin [*Australia A publication*]

CIB .... Cambodian Investment Board (ECON)

CIB .... Canada Income Plus Fund Trust Units [*Toronto Stock Exchange symbol*]

CIB .... Canadian Infantry Brigade (DMA)

CIB .... Canadian Institute of Biotechnology [*Institut Canadien de la Biotechnologie*] (AC)

CIB .... Carnation Instant Breakfast [*Nestle Beverage Co.*] [*Tradename*] (DAVI)

CIB .... Catalina Island [*California*] Airport in the Sky [*Airport symbol*] (OAG)

CIB .... Central Intelligence Board

CIB .... Centralized Intercept Bureau [*Bell System*]

CIB .... Centrum voor Informatie Beleid [*Netherlands Center for Information Policy*] [*The Hague*] [*Information service or system*] (IID)

CIB .... Change Impact Board (NASA)

CIB .... Change Implementation Board [*NASA*] (GFGA)

CIB .... Channel Interface Bus (NITA)

CIB .... Charities Information Bureaux [*British*] (CB)

CIB .... Chartered Institute of Bankers [*London, England*] (EAIO)

CIB .... Chartered Insurance Broker

CIB .... Children's Interests Bureau [*South Australia*]

CIB .... China, India, Burma

CIB .... China Investment Bank

CIB .... Chloride Industrial Batteries [*Manufacturer*] [*British*]

CIB .... Cibus [*Meal*] [*Latin*]

CIB .... COBOL [*Common Business-Oriented Language*] Information Bulletin [*Air Force*]

CIB .... Cognac Information Bureau [*Commercial firm*] (EA)

CIB .... Combat Infantryman's Badge [*Military decoration*]

CIB .... Command Information Bureau [*Military*] (CINC)

CIB .... Command Input Block [*Computer science*]

CIB .... Command Input Buffer [*Computer science*] (IBMDP)

CIB .... Commercial and Industrial Bulletin [*Ghana*] [*A publication*] (DLA)

CIB .... Commonwealth Investigation Branch [*Australia*]

CIB .... Communaute Internationale Baha'ie [*Baha'i International Community*]

CIB .... Communication Information Bulletin (DNAB)

CIB .... Complaints Investigation Branch [*Scotland Yard*]

CIB .... Complementary Instruction Book [*Military*]

CIB .... Concrete Industry Board

CIB .... Conseil International du Batiment pour la Recherche, l'Etude, et la Documentation [*International Council for Building Research, Studies, and Documentation*] (EAIO)

CIB .... Conseil International du Ble [*International Wheat Council - IWC*] (EAIO)

CIB .... Containment Isolation B [*Nuclear energy*] (NRCH)

CIB .... Convective Instability Base (PDAA)

CIB .... Cosmic Infrared Background Radiation

CIB .... Counterfeiting Intelligence Bureau [*International Chamber of Commerce*] [*British*] (CB)

CIB .... Criminal Intelligence Bureau

CIB .... Current Intelligence Bulletin [*A publication*]

CIB .... Cytomegalic Inclusion Bodies [*Cytology*] (DAVI)

CIB .... ICC [*International Chamber of Commerce*] Counterfeiting Intelligence Bureau (EA)

CIBA .... Chemical Industry in Basle

CIBC .... CABI [*Commonwealth Agricultural Bureaux International*] Institute of Biological Control [*Research center British*] (IRC)

CIBC .... Canadian Imperial Bank of Commerce

CIBC .... Citizens Bancorp [*NASDAQ symbol*] (NQ)

CIBC .... Commonwealth Institute of Biological Control [*Trinidad*]

CIBC .... Confederation Internationale de la Boucherie et de la Charcuterie [*International Federation of Meat Traders' Associations*]

CIBC .... Council on Interracial Books for Children (EA)

CIBCH .... Cibachrome (VRA)

CIBCR .... Center for International Business Cycle Research [*Columbia University*] [*New York, NY Research center*] (RCD)

CIBD .... Chronic Inflammatory Bowel Disease [*Medicine*]

CIBE .... Confederation Internationale des Betteraviers Europeens [*International Confederation of European Sugar-Beet Growers*] (EAIO)

CIBEP .... Commission pour le Marche Commun du Commerce International de Bulbes a Fleurs etde Plantes [*Common Market Commission for International Trade in Flower Bulbs and Plants*]

CIBER .... Cellular Intercarrier Billing Exchange Record

CIBER .... Cellular Intercarrier Billing Exchange Roamer Record [*A publication*] (TSSD)

CIBER .... Ciber, Inc. [*Associated Press*] (SAG)

CIBFV .... Cinema Industry Benevolent Fund of Victoria [*Australia*]

CIBG .... Canadian Infantry Brigade Group [*British military*] (DMA)

CIB HA .... Congenital Inclusion Body Hemolytic Anemia [*Medicine*] (AAMN)

CI-BI .... Clinician Interview Based Impression

CIBI............	Community Investors Bancorp [*NASDAQ symbol*] (TTSB)
CIBI............	Community Investors Bancorp, Inc. [*NASDAQ symbol*] (SAG)
CIBI............	Continuous Intrathecal Baclofen Infusion [*Medicine*]
CIBI............	Council of Independent Black Institutions
CIBIC..........	Clinician's Interview Based Impression of Change
CIBICC........	Craftsman of the Incorporated British Institute of Certified Carpenters (DI)
CIBL............	Citicorp Investment Bank Ltd. [*England*]
CIBL............	Convective Internal Boundary Layer (GFGA)
CIBL............	Montreal, PQ [*FM radio station call letters*]
CIBLE..........	Critical Inspection of Bearings for Life Extension (MCD)
CIBM..........	Riviere du Loup, PQ [*FM radio station call letters*]
CIBN	California Independant Bancorp [*NASDAQ symbol*] (SAG)
CIBO	Council of Industrial Boiler Owners (EA)
CIBO	Senneterre, PQ [*FM radio station call letters*]
CIBP...........	Chronic Intractable Benign Pain [*Medicine*] (DMAA)
CIBP...........	Comite Interregional des Bibliotheques Publiques [*Interregional Committee of Public Libraries*] [*Canada*]
CIBPA	Canadian Italian Business & Professional Association Inc. [*Association des Gens d'Affaires & Professionnels Italo-Canadiens Inc.*] (AC)
CIBPA	Canadian Italian Business & Professional Association of British Columbia [*Formerly, Italian Canadian Business & Professional Association of British Columbia*] (AC)
CIBPA	Canadian Italian Business and Professional Men's Association
CIBPS	Chronic Intractable Benign Pain Syndrome [*Medicine*] (DMAA)
CIBQ	Brooks, AB [*AM radio station call letters*]
CIBR	California Institute of Biological Research [*La Jolla*]
CIBR	Ciber, Inc. [*NASDAQ symbol*] (SAG)
cibr	Ciborium (VRA)
CIBRM	Council for International Business Risk Management (EA)
CIBS...........	Center for Inter-American and Border Studies [*University of Texas, El Paso*] [*Research center*] (RCD)
CIBS...........	Center for International Business Studies [*Research center*] (RCD)
CIBS...........	Chartered Institution of Building Service (EAIO)
CIBS...........	Chicago International Boat Show (ITD)
CIBS...........	Coach and Independent Bus Sector [*British*] (DI)
CIBS...........	Conferencia Interamericana de Bienestar Social [*Interamerican Social Welfare Conference*]
CIBS...........	Cosmetic Industry Buyers and Suppliers (EA)
CIBSE..........	Chartered Institution of Building Services Engineers (EAIO)
CIBT...........	Contributions of Infantry to the Battle Test [*Combat Developments Experimentation Center*] [*Army*] (INF)
CIBV...........	Consejo Internacional de Buena Vecindad, AC [*International Good Neighbor Council - IGNC*] [*Monterrey, Mexico*] (EAIO)
CIBW-FM	Drayton Valley, AB [*FM radio station call letters*] (RBYB)
CIBX-FM	Fredericton, NB [*FM radio station call letters*] (RBYB)
CIC.............	Cable in the Classroom [*An association*] (ECON)
CIC.............	Canadian Infantry Corps
CIC.............	Canadian Intelligence Corps (DMA)
CIC.............	Cancer Information Clearinghouse [*National Cancer Institute*] [*Database*]
CIC.............	Capital Issues Committee [*British*] (BARN)
CIC.............	Carbon-in-Column [*Gold ore processing*]
CIC.............	Cardiac Inhibition Center [*Physiology*]
CIC.............	Card Identification Code [*DoD*] (AFIT)
CIC.............	Card Inventory Control
CIC.............	Career Information Center (OICC)
CIC.............	Carrier Identification Code
CIC.............	Carson, Inc. [*NYSE symbol*] (SAG)
CIC.............	Catholic Interracial Council of New York (EA)
CIC.............	Cedar Rapids & Iowa City Railway Co. [*AAR code*]
CIC.............	Celtic Inernational Ltd. [*British ICAO designator*] (FAAC)
CIC.............	Centre d'Informations Catholiques pour la France et l'Etranger
CIC.............	Centre for Industrial Control [*Concordia University*] [*Canada Research center*] (RCD)
CIC.............	Certified Infection Control (MEDA)
CIC.............	Certified Insurance Counselor [*Society of Certified Insurance Counselors*] [*Designation awarded by*]
CIC.............	Change Identification Control Number
CIC.............	Change Indicator Code (SAA)
CIC.............	Change of Initial Condition (MCD)
CIC.............	Chartered Investment Counsel (MHDB)
CIC.............	Chartered Investment Counsellor [*Canada*] (DD)
CIC.............	Chemical Industry Council
CIC.............	Chemical Information Center [*Indiana University*]
CIC.............	Chemical Institute of Canada
CIC.............	Chico [*California*] [*Airport symbol*] (OAG)
CIC.............	Chiropractic Information Centre Ltd. [*British*] (CB)
CIC.............	Christian Israelite Church [*Australia*]
Cic.............	Cicero [*of Plutarch*] [*Classical studies*] (OCD)
CIC.............	Cicero [*Marcus Tullius, Roman orator and author, 106-43BC*] [*Classical studies*]
CIC.............	Circulating Immune Complexes [*Medicine*]
CIC.............	City Investment Centres [*British*]
CIC.............	Clean Intermittent Catherization [*Medicine*]
CIC.............	Climatic Impact Committee [*National Academy of Sciences - National Academy of Engineering*]
CIC.............	Climatic Impacts Centre
CIC.............	Clinical Investigation Center [*Oakland, CA*]
CIC.............	Cloud in Cell
CIC.............	Coaxial Injection Combustion (MCD)
CIC.............	Cobalt Information Center [*Battelle Memorial Institute*] [*Information service or system*] (IID)

CIC.............	Code d'Instruction Criminelle [*Code of Criminal Procedure*] [*A publication*] (ILCA)
CIC.............	Codex Iuris Canonici [*Code of Canon Law*] [*Latin*]
CIC.............	Cogeneration Coalition [*Later, CIPCA*] (EA)
CIC.............	Cognac Information Centre [*British*] (CB)
CIC.............	Combat Information Center [*Navy*]
CIC.............	Combat Intelligence Center
CIC.............	Combat Intercept Control
CIC.............	Combined Industry Committee [*Australia*]
CIC.............	Combined Intelligence Center (DOMA)
CIC.............	Combined Intelligence Committee [*World War II*]
CIC.............	Comite International de Coordination pour l'Initiation a la Science et le Developpement des Activites Scientifiques Extra-Scolaires [*International Coordinating Committee for the Presentation of Science and the Development of Out-of-School Scientific Activities - ICC*] (EAIO)
CIC.............	Comite International de la Conserve
CIC.............	Commander-in-Chief [*Air Force*]
CIC.............	Command Information Center [*Military*]
CIC.............	Command Input Coupler (CET)
CIC.............	Command Intelligence (MCD)
CIC.............	Command Interface Control (MCD)
CIC.............	Commission Internationale du Chataignier
CIC.............	Committee for an Independent Canada
CIC.............	Committee for Industrial Co-Operation [*European Economic Community/African, Caribbean, and Pacific States*] (DS)
CIC.............	Committee on Institutional Cooperation (EA)
CIC.............	Committee on Israeli Censorship (EA)
CIC.............	Common-Impression Cylinder
CIC.............	Communication Intelligence Corp. (PCM)
CIC.............	Communication Interface Coordinator [*NASA*]
CIC.............	Communications Instructor Console (MCD)
CIC.............	Communications Intelligence Channel
CIC.............	Compensated Ion Chamber
CIC.............	Completely in-the-Canal [*Audiology*]
CIC.............	Complex Integrated Circuit
CIC.............	Comprehensive Inorganic Chemistry [*A publication*]
CIC.............	Computer Industry Council (EA)
CIC.............	Computer Innovations Distribution, Inc. [*Toronto Stock Exchange symbol*]
CIC.............	Computer Instruments Corp.
CIC.............	Computer Intelligence Corp. [*Information service or system*] (IID)
CIC.............	Computer Interface Control [*Part of digital television computer*]
CIC.............	Computers in the City Exhibition [*British*] (ITD)
CIC.............	Computers in the Curriculum [*Education*] (AIE)
CIC.............	Computing Information Center [*University of Washington*] [*Seattle*] [*Information service or system*] (IID)
CIC.............	Concrete Industries Council (EA)
CIC.............	Confederation Internationale de la Coiffure [*International Conference of the Hairdressing Trade*]
CIC.............	Confederation Internationale des Cadres [*International Confederation of Executive Staffs*] [*Paris, France*] (EAIO)
CIC.............	Conseil International de la Chasse et de la Conservation du Gibier [*International Council for Game and Wildlife Conservation*] (EAIO)
CIC.............	Conseil International des Compositeurs [*International Council of Composers*]
CIC.............	Construction Industry Commission [*Canada*]
CIC.............	Construction Information Center Co. Ltd. [*Information service or system*] (IID)
CIC.............	Consumer Information Center (EA)
CIC.............	Contemporary Issues Clearinghouse [*Defunct*] (EA)
CIC.............	Contemporary Issues Criticism [*A publication*]
CIC.............	Content Indication Codes (NG)
CIC.............	Control and Information Center (NASA)
CIC.............	Control Inquiry Card [*Computer science*] (IAA)
CIC.............	Control Installation Code [*Air Force*] (AFIT)
CIC.............	Control Instrument Co. (MCD)
CIC.............	Controlled Item Code [*Air Force*] (AFIT)
CIC.............	Coordination and Information Center [*Department of Energy*] [*Information service or system*] (IID)
CIC.............	Coordinator for Industrial Cooperation [*Functions ceased, 1937*]
CIC.............	Core Image Converter [*Computer science*]
CIC.............	Corn Items Collectors Association (EA)
CIC.............	Corporate Information Center [*Later, ICCR*]
CIC.............	Cost Indicator Code [*Army*] (AFIT)
CIC.............	Council of Independent Colleges (EA)
CIC.............	Council of Intergovernmental Coordinators (EA)
CIC.............	Counter Intelligence, Combat [*World War II*]
CIC.............	Counterintelligence Corps [*Military*]
CIC.............	Country Indicator Code [*Computer science*] (ACRL)
CIC.............	Creative Incentive Coalition
CIC.............	Criminal Investigation Command (MCD)
CIC.............	Crisis Intervention Clinic (HGAA)
CIC.............	Critical Issues Council [*Defunct*] (EA)
CIC.............	Critical Item Code
CIC.............	Cross Information Co. [*Boulder, CO*] [*Telecommunications*] (TSSD)
CIC.............	Curate in Charge [*Church of England*]
CIC.............	Current Indian Cases, Old Series [*India*] [*A publication*] (DLA)
CIC.............	Customer Identification Code
CIC.............	Customer-Initiated Call [*Marketing*] (IAA)
CIC.............	Custom Integrated Circuit (PDAA)
CIC.............	Sisters of the Immaculate Conception [*Roman Catholic religious order*]
CIC.............	Society of Certified Insurance Counselors [*Austin, TX*] (EA)

CICA	Canadian Institute of Chartered Accountants
CICA	Captive Insurance Companies Association (EA)
CICA	Cervical Internal Cartoid Artery [*Medicine*] (DMAA)
CICA	Chemical and Industrial Consultants Association (DBA)
CICA	Cogeneration Coalition of America [*Later, CIPCA*] (EA)
CICA	Comite International Catholique des Aveugles (EAIO)
CICA	Committee for International Collaborative Activities [*An association*]
CICA	Competition in Contracting Act [*1984*]
CICA	Confederation Internationale du Credit Agricole [*International Confederation of Agricultural Credit*] [*Zurich, Switzerland*] (EAIO)
CICA	Confederation of International Contractors' Associations [*Paris, France*] (EAIO)
CICA	Conference Internationale des Controles d'Assurances des Etats Africains [*International Conference of African States on Insurance Supervision*] (EAIO)
CICA	Configuration Identification Control and Accounting
CICA	Connecticut Irrigation Contractors (SRA)
CICA	Construction Industry Computing Association (EAIO)
CICA	Council of International Civil Aviation
CICA	Toronto, ON [*Television station call letters*]
CICADA	Central Instrumentation Control and Data (MCD)
CICAE	Confederation Internationale des Cinemas d'Art et d'Essai [*International Experimental and Art Film Theatres Confederation*] [*France*]
CICAM	Canadian Institute of Certified Administrative Managers (AC)
CICAR	Cooperative Investigation of the Caribbean and Adjacent Regions [*UNESCO*]
CICARDI	CICAR [*Cooperative Investigation of the Caribbean and Adjacent Regions*] Data Inventory [*Marine science*] (MSC)
CICAS	Computer Integrated Command and Attack Systems (PDAA)
CICATIRS	Comite International de Coordination et d'Action des Groupements de Techniciens des Industries de Revetements de Surface [*International Committee to Coordinate Activities of Technical Groups in Coatings Industry - ICCATCI*] (EAIO)
CICATS	Computer Industry Coalition for Advanced Television Service
CICB	Center International des Civilisations Bantu (EAIO)
CICB	Criminal Injuries Compensation Board [*British*]
CICBC	Construction Industry Collective Bargaining Commission [*Terminated, 1978*] [*Department of Labor*] (EGAO)
CICBV	Canadian Institute of Chartered Business Valuators [*Formerly, Canadian Association of Business Valuators*] (AC)
CICC	Cargo Integration Control Center (MCD)
CICC	Catholic Interracial Council of Chicago (EA)
CICC	Centre International de Criminologie Comparee [*International Center for Comparative Criminology - ICCC*] [*Montreal, PQ*] (EA)
CICC	Clinical Investigation Control Center [*Military*] (DNAB)
CICC	Conference Internationale des Charites Catholiques [*International Conference of Catholic Charities*]
CICC	Consolidated Intelligence Communication Center (MCD)
CICC	Yorkton, SK [*Television station call letters*]
CICC-1	Wynyard, SK [*Television station call letters*]
CICCA	Centre International de Coordination pour la Celebration des Anniversaires
CICCE	Comite des Industries Cinematographiques des Communautes Europeennes [*Committee of the Cinematography Industries in the European Communities*] (EAIO)
CICD	Collegium Internationale Chirurgiae Digestivae [*Rome, Italy*] (EAIO)
CICE	Centre d'Information des Chemins de Fer Europeens [*Information Center of the European Railways*]
CICE	Combined Intracapsular Cataract Extraction [*Opthalmology*] (DAVI)
CICE	Council for International Congresses of Entomology [*London, England*] (EA)
CICE	Cumann Innealtoiri Comhairle na hEirann [*Association of Consulting Engineers of Ireland*] (EAIO)
CICEO	China International Cultural Exchange Organization
CICEP	Conseil Interamericain du Commerce et de la Production
CICERO	Communications Integrated Control Engineering, Reporting, and Operations (MCD)
CICERO	The Center for International Climate and Environmental Research - Oslo [*University of Oslo*] [*Norway*]
CICESTR	Bishop of Chichester [*British*]
CICF	Competitive Industrial Concept Formulation
CICF	Confederation Internationale des Corps de Fonctionnaires [*International Confederation of Public Service Officers*]
CICF	Vernon, BC [*AM radio station call letters*]
CICG	Center for Interactive Computer Graphics [*Rensselaer Polytechnic Institute*] [*Research center*] (RCD)
CICG	Centre International de Conferences de Geneve [*International Conference Center of Geneva*] [*Switzerland*] (PDAA)
CICG	Centre International du Commerce de Gros [*International Center for Wholesale Trade*]
CICG	Conference Internationale Catholique du Guidisme [*International Catholic Conference of Guiding*] (EAIO)
CICH	Canadian Institute of Child Health
CICH	Centro de Informacion Cientifica y Humanistica [*Center for Scientific and Humanistic Information*] [*Mexico*] [*Information service or system*] (IID)
CICH	Comite International de la Culture du Houblon [*International Hop Growers Convention - IHGC*] (EAIO)
CICh	Corpus Inscriptionum Chaldaicarum (BJA)
CICHE	Consortium for International Cooperation in Higher Education [*Defunct*] (EA)
CICHS	Center for International Community Health Studies [*University of Connecticut*] [*Research center*] (RCD)
CICI	Cochlear Implant Club International (EA)
CICI	Combined Intelligence Center, Iraq [*World War II*]
CICI	Communication Intelligence Corp. [*NASDAQ symbol*] (SAG)
CICI	COMSAT [*Communications Satellite Corp.*] International Communications, Inc. (TSSD)
CICI	Confederation of Information Communication Industries [*British*]
CICI	Sudbury, ON [*Television station call letters*]
CICI-1	Elliot Lake, ON [*Television station call letters*]
CICIAMS	Comite International Catholique des Infirmieres et Assistantes Medico-Sociales [*International Committee of Catholic Nurses - ICCN*] [*Vatican City, Vatican City State*] (EAIO)
CICIBA	Centre International des Civilisations Bantu [*International Center for the Bantu Civilizations*] [*Gabon*] [*Research center*] (IRC)
CICIEM	Chambre Islamique de Commerce, d'Industrie et d'Echange des Marchandises [*Islamic Chamber of Commerce, Industry, and Commodity Exchange - ICCICE*] [*Karachi, Pakistan*] (EAIO)
CICIH	Confederation Internationale Catholique des Institutions Hospitalieres [*International Catholic Confederation of Hospitals*]
CICILS	Confederation Internationale du Commerce et des Industries des Legumes Secs [*International Pulse Trade and Industry Confederation*] [*EC*] (ECED)
CICIN	Conference on Interlibrary Communications and Information Networks [*September 28 - October 2, 1970*]
CICIREPATO	Committee for International Co-operation in Information Retrieval Among Examining Patent Offices
CICIS	Chemicals in Commerce Information System [*Environmental Protection Agency*]
CICL	Canadian Index of Computer Literature [*A publication*]
CICL	Computer in Control Logic (MCD)
CICLV	Citrus Crinkly Leaf Virus [*Plant pathology*]
CICM	Coaxial Injection Combustion Model (MCD)
CICM	Commission Internationale Catholique pour les Migrations [*International Catholic Migration Commission - ICMC*] [*Geneva, Switzerland*] (EAIO)
CICM	Congregatio Immaculati Cordis Mariae [*Congregation of the Immaculate Heart of Mary*] [*Roman Catholic men's religious order*]
cicm	Missionhurst Congregation of the Immaculate Heart of Mary (TOCD)
CICM	Missionhurst Congregation of the Immaculate Heart of Mary (TOCD)
CICMA	Canadian Insurance Claims Managers Association
CICNet	[*The*] Committee on Institutional Cooperation Network [*Computer science*] (TNIG)
CICNY	Catholic Interracial Council of New York (EA)
CICO	Combat Information Center Office [*or Officer*] [*Navy*] (MUGU)
CICO	Conference of International Catholic Organizations [*Geneva, Switzerland*] (EAIO)
CICO-9	Thunder Bay, ON [*Television station call letters*]
CICO-18	London, ON [*Television station call letters*]
CICO-19	Sudbury, ON [*Television station call letters*]
CICO-20	Sault Ste. Marie, ON [*Television station call letters*]
CICO-24	Ottawa, ON [*Television station call letters*]
CICO-28	Kitchener, ON [*Television station call letters*]
CICO-32	Windsor, ON [*Television station call letters*]
CICO-59	Chatham, ON [*Television station call letters*]
CICOM	Citizens for Informed Choices on Marijuana (EA)
CICOP	Catholic Inter-American Cooperation Program [*Defunct*]
CICOPA	Comite International des Cooperatives de Production et Artisanales [*International Committee of Producers' Cooperatives*] (EAIO)
CICP	Capital Investment Computer Program [*Economics*]
CICP	Coalition for International Cooperation and Peace (EA)
CICP	Committee to Investigate Copyright Problems
CICP	Communication Interrupt Control Program [*Computer science*] (IBMDP)
CICP	Complex Inorganic Color Pigment [*Chemistry*]
CICP	Confederation Internationale du Credit Populaire [*International Confederation of Popular Credit - ICPC*] [*Paris, France*] (EAIO)
CICPE	Comite d'Initiative pour le Congres du Peuple Europeen
CICPLB	Comite International pour le Controle de la Productivite Laitiere du Betail [*International Committee for Recording the Productivity of Milk Animals - ICRPMA*] (EAIO)
CICPR	Confederation Internationale pour la Chirurgie Plastique et Reconstructive [*International Confederation for Plastic and Reconstructive Surgery*] (EAIO)
CICR	Calcium-Induced Calcium Release [*Biochemistry*]
CICR	Canadian Institute for Conflict Resolution [*Institute Canadien pour la Resolution des Conflits*] (AC)
CICR	Comite International Contre la Repression [*International Committee Against Repression*] [*Paris, France*] (EAIO)
CICR	Comite International de la Croix-Rouge [*International Committee of the Red Cross*]
CICR	Committee on Information and Cultural Relations (EAIO)
CICRA	Centre International pour la Coordination des Recherches en Agriculture
CICRC	Commission Internationale Contre le Regime Concentrationnaire [*International Commission Against the Regime of Concentration Camps*] [*France*]
CICRED	Comite International de Cooperation dans les Recherches Nationales en Demographie [*Committee for International Cooperation in National Research in Demography*] (EAIO)
CICRIS	Cooperative Industrial and Commercial Reference and Information Service
CICS	Caledon Information & Community Services [*Formerly, Bolton Contact Centre*] [*Formerly, Caledon Information Centre*] (AC)
CICS	Canadian Intergovernmental Conference Secretariat
CICS	Center for Intelligent Computing Studies [*Washington University*] [*Research center*] (RCD)

CICS.......... Central Integrated Checkout System
CICS.......... Centre for Industrial Control Science [*University of Newcastle*] [*Australia*]
CICS.......... Citizens Bancshares [*NASDAQ symbol*] (TTSB)
CICS.......... Citizens Bancshares, Inc. [*NASDAQ symbol*] (SAG)
CICS.......... Client Information Control System (ECII)
CICS.......... Commercial or Industrial and Control Service Data System
CICS.......... Cooperative Institute fo Climate Studies [*Marine science*] (OSRA)
CICS.......... Cooperative Institute for Climate Studies (USDC)
CICS.......... Counselor Interview Competence Scale (EDAC)
CICS.......... Customer Information Control System [*Pronounced "kicks"*] [*IBM Corp.*] [*Computer science*]
CICS.......... Customer Interface Control System (GFGA)
CICSA........ Change Identification Control Schedule Analysis
CICSB........ Coalition of Indian Controlled School Boards (EDAC)
CIC-SS........ Change Identification Control Schedule Summary
CICS/VS....... Customer Information Control System Virtual Storage [*IBM Corp.*] [*Computer science*]
CICT.......... Calgary, AB [*Television station call letters*]
CICT.......... Commission on International Commodity Trade
CICT.......... Conseil International du Cinema et de la Television [*International Film and Television Council*]
CICTA.......... Commission Internationale pour la Conservation des Thonides de l'Atlantique [*International Commission for the Conservation of Atlantic Tunas - ICCAT*]
CICTEE........ China International Center for Technical and Economic Exchange
CICU .... Cardiac Intensive Care Unit [*of a hospital*] (AAMN)
CICU .... Cardiovascular In-Patient Care Unit
CICU .... Central Interface Converter Unit
CICU .... Children's Intensive Care Unit (ADA)
CICU .... Cirrocumulus [*Meteorology*]
CICU .... Commission on Independent Colleges and Universities [*Pennsylvania*]
CICU .... Computer Interface Conditioning Unit (MCD)
CICU .... Computer Interface Control Unit (NASA)
CICU .... Coronary Intensive Care Unit [*of a hospital*]
CICV.......... Combined Intelligence Center, Vietnam
CICWO........ Combat Information Center Watch Officer [*Navy*]
CICX.......... Orillia, ON [*FM radio station call letters*]
CICYP .... Consejo Interamericano de Comercio y Produccion [*Interamerican Council of Commerce and Production*]
CICYT.......... Inter-American Committee on Science and Technology [*Organization of American States*] (ASF)
CICZ.......... Midland, ON [*FM radio station call letters*]
CID.............. Association de Consultants Internationaux en Droits de l'Homme [*Association of International Consultants on Human Rights*] [*Geneva, Switzerland*] (EAIO)
CID.............. Cable Interconnection Diagram (KSC)
CID.............. Cabling Interface Drawing (MCD)
CID.............. Capital Investment Discard
CID.............. Cedar Rapids/Iowa City [*Iowa*] [*Airport symbol*] (OAG)
CID.............. CEIP [*Communications-Electronics Implementation Plan*] Implementation Directive [*Air Force*] (CET)
CID.............. Center for Industrial Development [*European Economic Community/African, Caribbean, and Pacific States*] (DS)
CID.............. Center for Infectious Diseases [*Department of Health and Human Services*] (GRD)
CID.............. Center for Innovative Diplomacy [*Defunct*] (EA)
CID.............. Center for Inquiry and Discovery [*Washington, DC, museum*]
CID.............. Central Institute for the Deaf (MCD)
CID.............. Central Instrumentation Department [*David W. Taylor Naval Ship Research and Development Center*] [*Bethesda, MD*]
CID.............. Centre for Information and Documentation [*EURATOM*] (MCD)
CID.............. Centre International de Documentation [*International Center for Documentation*]
CID.............. Centre International pour le Developpement [*International Center for Development*] [*French*] (AF)
CID.............. Centro de Informativo y Documentacion [*Press agency*] [*Argentina*]
CID.............. Centrum voor Informatie en Documentatie [*Center for Information and Documentation*] [*Netherlands Organization for Applied Scientific Research Delft*] [*Information service or system*] (IID)
CID.............. Change in Design
CID.............. Channel Identification (CET)
CID.............. Characteristic Item Description (MCD)
CID.............. Charge-Injection Device [*Electronics*]
CID.............. Chick Infective Dose (MAE)
CID.............. Chieftain International [*AMEX symbol Toronto Stock Exchange symbol*] (SPSG)
CID.............. Chieftain Intl. [*AMEX symbol*] (TTSB)
CID.............. Choice in Dying
CID.............. Circular Intensity Difference [*Spectrometry*]
CID.............. Civil Investigative Demand [*Department of Justice*]
CID.............. Cleanliness Identification [*Label*] [*Aerospace*] (AAG)
CID.............. Coalicion Institucionalista Democratica [*Democratic Institutional Coalition*] [*Ecuador*] [*Political party*] (PPW)
CID.............. Collision-Induced Decomposition [*or Dissociation*] [*Spectrometry*]
CID.............. Combat Identification [*Army*] (RDA)
CID.............. Combat Information and Detection (NVT)
CID.............. Combined Immunodeficiency Disease [*Immunology*]
CID.............. Comfortable Interpersonal Distance Scale (EDAC)
CID.............. Comite International de Dachau
CID.............. Comite International des Derives Tensio-Actifs [*International Committee of Tensio-Active Derivatives*]
CID.............. Commander's Integrated Display [*Military*] (RDA)
CID.............. Commander's Intelligent Display [*Military*] (RDA)

CID.............. Command Information Division (MCD)
CID.............. Commercial Import Division [*Vietnam*]
CID.............. Commercial Item Description
CID.............. Commercial Item Drawing (MCD)
CID.............. Commission for International Development (EA)
CID.............. Committee for Imperial Defence [*British*]
CID.............. Committee for Industrial Development [*United Nations*]
CID.............. Committee on Interest and Dividends [*Terminated, 1974*] [*Federal Reserve Board*]
CID.............. Communication Identifier [*Computer science*] (IBMDP)
CID.............. Communication Implementation Directive [*Air Force*]
CID.............. Communications Identification Directory [*Air Force*] (CET)
CID.............. Compact Indium Discharge (WDMC)
CID.............. Compact Iodide Daylight (WDMC)
CID.............. Compagnie Industrielle du Disque [*Record label*] [*France*]
CID.............. Compatibility Initialization Deck (IAA)
CID.............. Component Identification
CID.............. Component Identification Designation (CAAL)
CID.............. Compositional Interdiffusion [*Chemistry*] (IAA)
CID.............. Compound Interest Deposit [*Banking*] (DICI)
CID.............. Computer Industry Daily [*Zif-Davis*] [*A publication*] (NITA)
CID.............. Computer-Integrated Design
CID.............. Computer-Integrated Draughting [*Terminal Display Systems Ltd.*] [*Software package*] (NCC)
CID.............. Computer Interface Device (NASA)
CID.............. Confederation of Institute Directors (AIE)
CID.............. Configuration Identification Documentation
CID.............. Configuration Index Document (MCD)
CID.............. Configuration, Installation, and Distribution Architecture [*Computer science*] (PCM)
CID.............. Consortium on International Development
CID.............. Control Interface Document
CID.............. Controlled Impact Demonstration [*FAA, NASA*]
CID.............. Core Image Dictionary [*Computer science*] (IAA)
CID.............. Council for Independent Distribution [*Later, CPDA*]
CID.............. Council of Industrial Design [*British*]
CID.............. Creative Industries of Detroit, Inc. [*Warren, MI*] [*Telecommunications*] (TSSD)
CID.............. Criminal Investigation Department [*Often loosely referred to as Scotland Yard*] [*Facetious translation: Copper in Disguise*] [*British*]
CID.............. Criminal Investigation Detachment
CID.............. Criminal Investigation Division [*Army*]
CID.............. Critical Issues Demonstration (MCD)
CID.............. Cubic Inch Displacement [*in engines*]
CID.............. Current Image Diffraction (MCD)
CID.............. Current Information Database
CID.............. Curriculum and Instruction Development [*Program*] [*National Science Foundation*]
CID.............. Customized-Information-Delivery System [*Bell Communications Research Laboratory*]
CID.............. Cylinder Identification [*Automotive engineering*]
CID.............. Cytomegalic Inclusion Disease [*Ophthalmology*]
CID.............. Movement for an Independent and Democratic Cuba (EA)
CID.............. North Central Regional Library, Community Information Directory Project [*UTLAS symbol*]
CID$_{50}$........ Chimpanzee Infectious Dose for Half the Population
CIDA .... Canadian International Development Agency [*Formerly, External Aid Office*]
CIDA .... Centre d'Information et de Documentation Atlantique [*Brussels, Belgium*]
CIDA .... Centre d'Informatique et Documentation Automatique [*Center for Automated Information and Documentation*] [*France*] [*Information service or system*] (IID)
CIDA .... Centre International de Developpement de l'Aluminium
CIDA .... Centre International de Documentation Arachnologique [*International Centre for Arachnological Documentation*] (EAIO)
CIDA .... Change in Drawing Authorization (MCD)
CIDA .... Channel Indirect Data Addressing (IBMDP)
CIDA .... Christian Instrumental Directors Association (EA)
CIDA .... Comite Interamericano de Desarrollo Agricola [*Inter-American Committee for Agricultural Development*]
CIDA .... Comite Intergouvernemental du Droit d'Auteur [*Intergovernmental Copyright Committee - IGC*] [*UNESCO*] (EAIO)
CIDA .... Council of Intellectual Disability Agencies [*Victoria*] [*Australia*]
CIDA .... Current Input Differential Amplifier [*Electronics*] (OA)
CIDAC .... Cancer Information Dissemination and Analysis Center
CIDAC .... Centro de Informacao e Documentacao Amilcar Cabral [*Portugal*]
CIDAC .... Centro de Investigacion para el Desarrollo [*Mexican government funded political and economic research center*] (CROSS)
CIDADEC...... Confederation Internationale des Associations d'Experts et de Conseils [*International Confederation of Associations of Experts and Consultants*]
CIDAL .... Centro de Informacion, Documentacion, y Analisis Latinoamericano
CIDALC .... Comite International pour la Diffusion des Arts et des Lettres par le Cinema [*International Committee for the Diffusion of Arts and Literature through the Cinema*] (EAIO)
CIDAS .... Conversational Interactive Digital/Analog Simulator [*IBM Corp.*] (IEEE)
CIDAT .... Centre d'Informatique Appliquee au Developpement et a l'Agriculture Tropicale [*Center for Informatics Applied to Development and Tropical Agriculture*] [*Royal Museum of Central Africa*] [*Information service or system*] (IID)

CIDB .... Chemie-Information und Dokumentation Berlin [*Chemical Information and Documentation - Berlin*] [*Information service or system German*] (IID)
CIDB .... Co-Operative Insurance Development Bureau [*Canada*] (EAIO)
CIDC .... Centre Islamique pour le Developpement du Commerce [*Islamic Center for Development of Trade - ICDT*] [*Casablanca, Morocco*] (EAIO)
CIDC .... Construction Industry Development Council [*Canada*]
CIDC .... Criminal Investigation Command [*Army*] (DOMA)
CIDC .... Orangeville, ON [*FM radio station call letters*]
CIDCIM .... Computer-Integrated Design - Computer-Integrated Manufacturing (ADA)
Cidco .... Cidco, Inc. [*Associated Press*] (SAG)
CIDCOMED... Council for Interdisciplinary Communication in Medicine
CIDCON........ Civil Disturbance Readiness Conditions [*Army*] (AABC)
CIDE............. Cambridge International Dictionary of English [*A publication*]
CIDE............. Centro de Investigacion y Docencia Economica [*Institute which focuses on Mexica n/US relations*] (CROSS)
CIDE............. Commission Intersyndicale des Deshydrateurs Europeens [*European Dehydrators Association*] [*Common Market Paris, France*]
CIDEC .... Conseil International pour le Developpement du Cuivre [*International Copper Development Council*] (AF)
CIDECT .... Comite International pour l'Etude et le Developpement de la Construction Tubulaire [*International Committee for the Study and Development of Tubular Construction*] [*Canada*]
CIDEM .... Consejo Interamericano de Musica [*Inter-American Music Council*] (EA)
CIDEP .... Centre International de Documentation Concernant les Expressions Plastiques
CIDEP .... Chemically Induced Dynamic Electron Polarization [*Spectrometry*]
CIDER .... Center for Inherited Disease Research [*Genotyping facility, Maryland*]
CIDERE .... Civil Defense Report
CIDES .... Cente International de Documentation et d'Echanges de la Francophonie (AC)
CIDESA .... Centre International de Documentation Economique et Sociale Africaine [*International Center for African Social and Economic Documentation*]
CIDESCO...... Comite International d'Esthetique et de Cosmetologie [*International Committee for Esthetics and Cosmetology*]
CIDET........... Cooperation Internationale en Matiere de Documentation sur l'Economie des Transports [*International Cooperation in the Field of Transport Economics Documentation*] [*France*] [*Information service or system*] (IID)
CIDF............. Communication Intercept and Direction Finding (MCD)
CIDF............. Control Interval Definition Field [*Computer science*] (BUR)
CIDG .... Civilian Irregular Defense Group [*Military*]
CIDHAL .... Comunicacion, Intercambio, y Desarrollo Humano en America Latina
CIDHEC........ Centre Intergouvernemental de Documentation sur l'Habitat et l'Environnement [*Intergovernmental Center for Documentation on Dwellings and the Environment*] (PDAA)
CIDI .... Centre International de Documentation et d'Information
CIDI .... Compression Ignition-Direct Injection
CIDIA .... Centro Interamericano de Documentacion e Informacion Agricola [*Inter-American Center for Documentation and Agricultural Information*] [*Inter-American Institute for Cooperation on Agriculture*] [*Information service or system*] (IID)
CIDIE .... Centro Internacional de Informacion Economica
CIDIE .... Committee of International Development Institutions on the Environment (ECON)
CIDIN .... Common ICAO [*International Civil Aviation Organization*] Data Interchange Network
CIDITVA .... Centre International de Documentation de l'Inspection Technique des Vehicules Automobiles
CIDL............. Configuration Item Data List (NASA)
CIDM .... Canadian Institute for Development Management (AC)
CIDM .... Conseil International de Musique [*UNESCO*] [*Record label*]
CID-MAC...... Computer-Integrated Design - Manufacturing and Automation Center
CIDN .... Change in Drawing Notice
CIDN .... Computer Identics Corp. [*NASDAQ symbol*] (NQ)
CIDN .... Computer Indentics [*NASDAQ symbol*] (TTSB)
CIDNET .... CID [*Consortium on International Development*] Information Network
CIDNO.......... Contractor's Identification Number
CIDNP.......... Chemically Induced Dynamic Nuclear Polarization [*Spectrometry*]
CIDOC.......... Centro Intercultural de Documentacion [*Center for Intercultural Documentation*] [*Cuernavaca, Mexico*]
CIDOS .... Communications Security Interservice Depot Overhaul Standard (MCD)
CIDP .... Centre International de Documentation Parlementaire [*International Center for Parliamentary Documentation*] (EAIO)
CIDP .... Chronic Inflammatory Demyelinating Polyradiculoneuropathy [*Neurology*] (DAVI)
CIDP .... Computer Industry Development Potential (IAA)
CIDP .... Confederation Internationale pour le Desarmement et la Paix [*International Confederation for Disarmament and Peace - ICDP*] [*London, England*] (EA)
CIDPL .... Commission for International Due Process of Law (EA)
CIDPS .... Continental Intelligence Data Processing System (MCD)
CIDR .... Center for Inherited Disease Research [*Baltimore*] [*National Institutes of Health and Johns Hopkins University*]
CIDR .... Classless Inter-Domain Routing (CDE)
CIDR .... Critical Intermediate Design Review (NASA)
CIDR .... Windsor, ON [*FM radio station call letters*]
CIDRS .... Cascade Impactor Data Reduction System [*Environmental Protection Agency*] (GFGA)
CIDS .... Canadian Infectious Disease Society [*Societe Canadienne de Maladies Infectieuses*] (AC)
CIDS .... Career Information Delivery System (OICC)
CIDS .... Cellular Immunity Deficiency Syndrome [*Medicine*]
CIDS .... Chemical Information and Data System [*Army*]
CIDS .... Computer Information Delivery Service (BARN)
CIDS .... Concrete Island Drilling System [*Offshore oil exploration*]
CIDS .... Configuration Item Development Specifications (MCD)
CIDS .... Continuous Insulin Delivery System [*Endocrinology and pharmacology*] (DAVI)
CIDS .... Contractor Identification Data System (AAGC)
CIDS .... Coordination in Direct Support (NVT)
CIDS .... Critical Item Development Specification (CAAL)
CIDSE .... Cooperation Internationale pour le Developpement et la Solidarite [*International Cooperation for Development and Solidarity*] [*Formerly, Cooperation Internationale pour le Developpement Socio-Economique*] (EAIO)
CIDSS .... CINCPACAF [*Commander-in-Chief, Pacific Air Force*] Integrated Decision Support System
CIDSS .... Combat Identification Dismounted Soldier System [*Army*] (INF)
CIDSS .... Comite International pour l'Information et Documentation des Sciences Sociales [*International Committee for Social Sciences Documentation*]
CIDST .... Advisory Committee on Information Dissemination in Science and Technology
CIDST .... Committee for Information and Documentation on Science and Technology [*EEC*] (PDAA)
CIDSTAT ...... Civil Disturbance Status Reporting [*Army*] (AABC)
CIDT............. Cayman Islands Department of Tourism (EA)
CIDX .... Canadian International DX Radio Club (AC)
CIDX .... Chemical Industry Data Exchange [*Computer science*] (ACRL)
CIE............... CAB [*Commonwealth Agricultural Bureaux*] International Institute of Entomology [*British*] (IRUK)
CIE............... Canadian Institute of Energy (AC)
CIE............... Captain's Imperfect Entry [*Shipping*]
CIE............... Center for Independent Education [*Later, Cato Institute*] (EA)
CIE............... Center for Integrated Electronics [*Rensselaer Polytechnic Institute*] [*Research center*] (RCD)
CIE............... Central Information Exchange [*Community Service Council of Broward County, Inc.*] [*Information service or system*] (IID)
CIE............... Centre for Internationalising the Study of English
CIE............... Centre International de l'Enfance [*International Children's Centre*] [*Paris, France*] (EAIO)
CIE............... Certified International Executive [*American Society of International Exec utives*] [*Designation awarded by*]
CIE............... Cesium Ion Emission
CIE............... Citizens for Improved Education
CIE............... Cleveland Institute of Electronics [*Ohio*]
CIE............... Clothing and Individual Equipment [*Army*] (RDA)
CIE............... Cochise, AZ [*Location identifier FAA*] (FAAL)
CIE............... Coherent Infrared Energy (AAG)
CIE............... Comite International des Echanges pres la Chambre de Commerce Internationale
CIE............... Commission Internationale de l'Eclairage [*International Commission on Illumination*] [*Vienna, Austria*] (EA)
CIE............... Committee on Invisible Exports [*British*] (DS)
CIE............... Common Ion Effect
CIE............... Commonwealth Institute of Entomology [*British*] (MCD)
CIE............... Communications Interface Equipment (MCD)
Cie............... Compagnie [*Company*] [*French*]
CIE............... Companion of the [*Order of the*] Indian Empire [*British*]
CIE............... Computer-Integrated Environment (IAA)
CIE............... Computer Interrupt Equipment (MHDB)
CIE............... Congres International des Editeurs [*International Congress of Publishers*]
CIE............... Conseil International de l'Etain [*International Tin Council - ITC*] [*Defunct*] (EAIO)
CIE............... Consejo Interamericano do Escultismo [*Inter-American Scout Committee - IASC*] [*San Jose, Costa Rica*] (EAIO)
CIE............... Control and Indicating Equipment
CIE............... Controlled Internal Extension (MCD)
CIE............... Coras Iompair Eireann [*Irish Transport Co.*]
CIE............... Corpus Inscriptionum Elamicarum [*A publication*] (BJA)
CIE............... Corrected Infection Efficiency [*of plant pathogens*]
CIE............... Corrie Resources [*Vancouver Stock Exchange symbol*]
CIE............... Council for Indian Education (EA)
CIE............... Countercurrent Immunoelectrophoresis [*Immunology*] (DAVI)
CIE............... Counterimmunoelectrophoresis [*Also, CIEP*] [*Analytical biochemistry*]
CIE............... Crossed Immunoelectrophoresis [*Analytical biochemistry*]
CIE............... Customer Initiated Entry [*Banking*]
CIE............... Customs Information Exchange [*An arm of US Customs Service*]
CIE............... Czech Government Flying Service [*FAA designator*] (FAAC)
CIE............... Gould Laboratory Materials Research, Cleveland, OH [*OCLC symbol*] (OCLC)
CIE............... Itoh [*C.*] Electronics [*British*] (NITA)
CIEA............. Centre International pour Education Artistique [*International Centre for Art Education*] (EAIO)
CIEA............. College Institute Educators' Association of BC (AC)
CIEA............. Committee on International Environmental Affairs [*Department of State*] [*Washington, DC*] (EGAO)
CIEA............. Committee on International Ocean Affairs (USDC)
CIEA............. Conseil International d'Education des Adultes [*International Council for Adult Education*] [*Canada*]
CIE-AF .... Certified International Executive - Air Forwarding [*Am erican Society of International Executives, Inc.*] [*Designation awarded by*]

CIEAS........... Committee on International Education in Agricultural Sciences [*See also SVLB*] [*Deventer, Netherlands*] (EAIO)

CIEB............. Chilean Iodine Educational Bureau [*Defunct*] (EA)

CIEC............. Centre International des Engrais Chimiques [*International Center of Fertilizers*]

CIEC............. Centre International pour les Etudes Chimiques [*International Center for Chemical Studies - ICCS*] (EAIO)

CIEC............. Citizen's Internet Empowerment Coalition [*Sponsored by CDT - Center for Democracy and Technology*]

CIEC............. Commission Internationale de l'Etat Civil [*International Commission on Civil Status - ICCS*] (EAIO)

CIEC............. Confederation Interamericaine d'Education Catholique [*Inter-American Confederation of Catholic Education*]

CIEC............. Conference on International Economic Cooperation

CIEC............. Conseil International des Employeurs du Commerce [*International Council of Commerce Employers*]

CIEC............. Conseil International d'Etudes Canadiennes [*International Council for Canadian Studies - ICCS*]

CIECA........... Commission Internationale des Examens de Conduite Automobile [*International Driving Tests Committee*] (EAIO)

CIECA........... Current Injection Equivalent Circuit Approach (MCD)

CIECC........... Consejo Interamericano para la Educacion, la Ciencia, y la Cultura [*Inter-American Council for Education, Science, and Culture*] (EA)

CIED............. Card Input Editor [*Computer science*] (SAA)

CIED............. Centro Internacional de Educacion y Desarrollo [*Venezuela*]

CIEDA........... Center for Immunity Enhancement in Domestic Animals [*Iowa State University of Science and Technology*] [*Research center*] (RCD)

CIEDHAL...... Comite Inter-Eglises des Droits Humains en Amerique Latine [*Inter-Church Committee on Human Rights in Latin America*] [*Canada*] (EAIO)

CIEE............. Centre Interuniversitaire d'Etudes Europeennes [*Interuniversity Centre for European Studies*] [*Canada*]

CIEE............. Companion of the Institution of Electrical Engineers [*British*]

CIEE............. Council on International Educational Exchange (EA)

CIEEL........... Chemically Initiated Electron Exchange Luminescence

CIE-EM......... Certified International Executive - Export Management [*American Society of International Executives, Inc.*] [*Designation awarded by*]

CIEF............. Capillary Isoelectric Focusing

CIE-F............ Certified International Executive - Forwarding [*American Society of International Executives, Inc.*] [*Designation awarded by*]

CIEF............. Comite International d'Enregistrement des Frequences [*International Frequency Registration Board*]

CIEF............. Continuous Isoelectric Focusing [*Materials processing*]

CIEG............. Center for International Economic Growth [*Defunct*] (EA)

CIEG............. Egmont, BC [*FM radio station call letters*]

CIEH............. Comite Interafricain d'Etudes Hydrauliques [*Inter-African Committee for Hydraulic Studies - ICHS*] [*Ouagadougou, Burkina Faso*] (EAIO)

CIEHV .... Conseil International pour l'Education des Handicapes de la Vue [*International Council for Education of the Visually Handicapped - ICEVH*] (EAIO)

CIEI............. Center for International Environment Information [*Later, WEC*] (EA)

CI/EI............ Chemical Ionization/Electron Impact [*Spectroscopy*]

CIEI............. Classics International Entertainment, Inc. [*NASDAQ symbol*] (SAG)

CIEI............. Classics Intl. Entertainment [*NASDAQ symbol*] (TTSB)

CIEIA........... Competitive Inhibition Enzyme Immunoassay [*Analytical biochemistry*]

CIEL............. Centre International d'Etudes du Lindane [*International Research Centre on Lindane - IRCL*] (EAIO)

CIEL............. Computerized Industrial Environmental Legislation [*UNEP*] [*United Nations*] (DUND)

CIEL............. Longueuil, PQ [*FM radio station call letters*]

CIELP........... Canadian Institute for Environmental Law and Policy

CIEM............ Center for Information and Immigration Studies [*Mexico*] (CROSS)

CIEM............ Commission Internationale pour l'Enseignement des Mathematiques [*International Commission on Mathematical Instruction - ICMI*] (EA)

CIEM............ Conseil International d'Education Mesologique des Pays de Langue Francaise [*Established 1977*] [*Canada*]

CIEM............ Conseil International pour l'Exploration de la Mer [*International Council for the Exploration of the Sea*]

CIEMA.......... Centre International des Etudes de la Musique Ancienne [*International Center of Studies on Early Music*]

CIEMEN....... Centre Internacional Escarre per a les Minories Etniques i Nacionalitats (EAIO)

CIEMS.......... Catalog for Information Exchange and Message Standards (MCD)

CIEN............ Commission Interamericaine d'Energie Nucleaire [*Inter-American Nuclear Energy Commission*]

CIENES .... Centro Interamericano de Ensenanza de Estadistica

CIEO............ Catholic International Education Office [*Belgium*]

CIEO............ Centre International d'Exploitation des Oceans [*See also ICOD*] [*Canada*]

CIEP............ Coastal Energy Impact Program (USDC)

CIEP............ Commission Internationale de l'Enseignement de la Physique [*International Commission on Physics Education - ICPE*] (EAIO)

CIEP............ Committee on International Exchange of Persons

CIEP............ Concentrated Impact Employment Program [*Also known as CEP*] [*Department of Labor*]

CIEP............ Council on International Economic Policy [*Terminated, 1977*]

CIEP............ Counterimmunoelectrophoresis [*Also, CIE*] [*Analytical biochemistry*]

CIEPC........... Commission Internationale d'Etudes de la Police de Circulation [*International Study Commission for Traffic Police*]

CIEPCBC ..... Committee on International Exchange of Persons Conference Board of Associated Research Councils [*Later, Council for International Exchange of Scholars*] (EA)

CIEPLAN ..... Corporacion de Investigaciones Economicas para Latinoamerica

CIEPP........... Comite Illusionniste d'Expertise des Phenomenes Paranormaux [*International PSI Committee of Magicians - IPSICM*] (EAIO)

CIEPRC........ Confederation Internationale des Instituts Catholiques d'Education des Adultes Ruraux [*International Confederation of Catholic Rural People's Schools*]

CIEPS........... Conseil International de l'Education Physique et Sportive [*International Council of Sport and Physical Education*]

CIEPSS......... Conseil International pour l'Education Physique et la Science du Sport [*International Council of Sport Science and Physical Education - ICSSPE*] (EAIO)

CIEQ............. Conseil de l'Industrie Electronique du Quebec (AC)

CIER............. Centre Interamericain d'Education Rurale

CIER............. Comision de Integracion Electrica Regional [*Commission of Regional Electrical Integration*] (EAIO)

CIER............. Commission for International Educational Reconstruction

CIER............. Conseil International des Economies Regionales [*International Council for Local Development*] (EAIO)

CIERA .... Center for International Education and Research in Accounting [*University of Illinois, Urbana-Champaign*] [*Research center*] (RCD)

CIERSES...... Centre International d'Etudes et de Recherches en Socio-Economie de la Sante [*International Health Centre of Socioeconomics, Researches and Studies - IHCSERS*] [*Lailly En Val, France*] (EAIO)

CIES............. Comite International des Entreprises a Succursales [*International Associationof Chain Stores*] [*Later, International Center for Companies of the Food Trade and Industry*] (EAIO)

CIES............. Comparative and International Education Society (EA)

CIES............. Consejo Interamericano Economico-Social [*Inter-American Economic and Social Council*] (EA)

CIES............. Correctional Institutions Environment Scale [*Personality development test*] [*Psychology*]

CIES............. Council for International Exchange of Scholars (EA)

CIES............. International Center for Companies of the Food Trade and Industry [*Formerly, International Association of Chain Stores*] (EAIO)

CIESA........... Compania Internacional Editora, Sociedad Anonima

CIESC.......... Comparative and International Education Society of Canada

CIESIN......... Consortium for International Earth Science Information Network [*Information service or system*] (IID)

CIESJ........... Centre International d'Enseignement Superieur de Journalisme [*UNESCO*] (NTCM)

CIESM......... Commission Internationale pour l'Exploration Scientifique de la Mer Mediterranee[*International Commission for the Scientific Exploration of the Mediterranea n Sea - ICSEM*] [*Monaco*] [*Research center*] (IRC)

CIESPAL ..... Centro Internacional de Estudios Superiores de Periodisma para America Latina [*Press agency*] [*Ecuador*]

CIESS.......... Chief Inspector of Engineering and Signal Stores [*Military British*]

CIESTPM...... College International pour l'Etude Scientifique des Techniques de Production Mecanique [*International Institute for Production Engineering Research*]

CIET .... Canadian Institute for Energy Training Inc. [*L'Institut Canadien de Formation de l'Energie*] (AC)

CIET .... Center for Industrial and Engineering Technology [*Central Connecticut University*] [*Research center*] (RCD)

CIET............. Commissioners Industrial Extended Mortality Table [*Insurance*]

CIETA.......... Centre International d'Etude des Textiles Anciens [*International Center for the Study of Ancient Textiles*] [*France*] (SLS)

CIETA.......... Centre International d'Etudes des Textiles Anciens [*International Center for the Study of Ancient Textiles*] [*Lyon, France*]

CIE-TM........ Certified International Executive - Traffic Management [*American Society of International Executives, Inc.*] [*Designation awarded by*]

CIEU............ Carleton, PQ [*FM radio station call letters*] (RBYB)

CIEURP........ Conference Internationale pour l'Enseignement Universitaire des Relations Publiques [*International Conference on University Education for Public Relations*]

CIE-USA...... Chinese Institute of Engineers - USA (EA)

CIEW............ Warmley, SK [*Television station call letters*]

CIEZ............. Halifax, NS [*FM radio station call letters*]

CIF............... Calcium Influx Factor [*Neurobiology*]

CIF............... Canadian Institute of Forestry

CIF............... Candidate Item File

CIF............... Capacitor Input Filter

CIF............... Captive Installation Function [*Telecommunications*] (TEL)

CIF............... Carriage, Insurance, and Freight

CIF............... Cartilage Induction Factor [*Biochemistry*] (DAVI)

CIF............... Cash in Fist

CIF............... Cells in Frames [*Telecommunications*] (ACRL)

CIF............... Central Index File

CIF............... Central Information File

CIF............... Central Instrumentation Facility [*NASA*]

CIF............... Central Integration Facility

CIF............... Central Issue Facility [*Military*] (AABC)

CIF............... Certificate in International Finance (PGP)

CIF............... Channel Island Ferries [*British*]

CIF............... Chifeng [*China*] [*Airport symbol*] (OAG)

CIF............... China International Foundation [*Later, TIF*] (EA)

CIF............... CINC [*Commander-in-Chief*] Initiative Fund [*DoD*]

CIF............... Claims Inquiry Form (MEDA)

CIF............... Cloning Inhibiting Factor

CIF .... Cohesive Intermolecular Force
CIF .... Cold-Insoluble Fibrinogen [*Hematology*]
CIF .... Colonial Interim Hi Income [*NYSE symbol*] (TTSB)
CIF .... Colonial Intermediate High Income Fund [*NYSE symbol*] (SPSG)
CIF .... Command Information Flow [*Military*] (CAAL)
CIF .... Common Intermediate Format (CDE)
CIF .... Compiler Information File [*Computer science*]
CIF .... Computer-Integrated Factory
CIF .... Confederation Internationale des Fonctionnaires [*International Confederation of Public Service Officers*]
CIF .... Congressional Institute for the Future (EA)
CIF .... Conseil International des Femmes [*International Council of Women - ICW*] [*Paris, France*] (EA)
CIF .... Consolidated Indescor Corp. [*Formerly, Indescor Hydrodynamics, Inc.*] [*Vancouver Stock Exchange symbol*]
CIF .... Consolidation Incineration Facility
CIF .... Construction Industry Foundation [*Defunct*] (EA)
CIF .... Consumer Interests Foundation
CIF .... Core Instrumentation Facility [*Army*]
CIF .... Corporate Income Fund
CIF .... Cost, Insurance, and Freight [*Shipping*] [*"INCOTERM," International Chamber of Commerce official code*]
CIF .... Cost-Plus-Incentive Fee [*Business term*]
CIF .... Council of International Fellowship (EA)
CIF .... Critical Issues Fund [*National Trust for Historic Preservation*]
CIF .... Cultural Integration Fellowship (EA)
CIF .... Customer Information File [*Computer science*] (BUR)
CIF40 .... Conseil International Formule 40 [*International F-40 Council*] [*Paris, France*] (EAIO)
CIFA .... Campaign for Independent Financial Advice [*British*]
CIFA .... Comite International de Recherche et d'Etude de Facteurs de l'Ambiance [*International Committee for Research and Study on Environmental Factors*]
CIFA .... Committee for Inland Fisheries of Africa [*UN Food and Agriculture Organization*]
CIFA .... Corporation of Insurance and Financial Advisers [*British*]
CIFA .... Yarmouth, NS [*FM radio station call letters*]
CIFAE .... Canada-Israel Foundation for Academic Exchanges [*Foundation Canada-Israel pour les Exchanges Universitaires*] (AC)
CIF & C .... Cost, Insurance, Freight, and Commission [*Shipping*]
CIF & E .... Cost, Insurance, Freight, and Exchange [*Shipping*]
CIF & I .... Cost, Insurance, Freight, and Interest [*Shipping*]
CIFAR .... Center for International Financial Analysis and Research, Inc. [*Princeton, NJ*] [*Information service or system*] (IID)
CIFAR .... Central Institute of Foreign Affairs Research
CIFAR .... Cooperative Institute for Arctic Research [*Marine science*] (OSRA)
CIFAR .... Cooperative Institute for Arctic Research (USDC)
CIFAX .... Enciphered Facsimile Communications
CIFC .... Centre for Interfirm Comparison [*British*]
CIFC .... Cost, Insurance, Freight, and Commission [*Shipping*]
CIFC .... Council for the Investigation of Fertility Control [*Obstetrics*] (DAVI)
CIFCA .... Centro Internacional de Formacion en Ciencias Ambientales para Paises de Habla Espanol [*International Center for the Preparation of Personnel in Environmental Sciences in Spanish-Speaking Countries*] [*Spain*]
CIFC & I ..... Cost, Insurance, Freight, Commission, and Interest [*Shipping*]
CIFCE .... Cost, Insurance, Freight, Commission, and Exchange [*Shipping*]
CIFCE & I .... Cost, Insurance, Freight, Commission, Exchange, and Interest [*Shipping*]
CIFCI .... Cost, Insurance, Freight, Commission, and Interest [*Shipping*]
CIFCO .... Civilians in Foreign Communications Operations [*Military*]
CIFE .... Canadian International Footwear Exposition (ITD)
CIFE .... Center for Integrated Facility Engineering [*Stanford University*] [*Research center*] (RCD)
CIFE .... Central Index File - Europe (NATG)
CIFE .... Centre International de Formation Europeenne [*France*]
CIFE .... Comite International du Film Ethnographique
CIFE .... Conference for Independent Further Education [*British*]
CIFE .... Conseil International du Film d'Enseignement [*International Council for Educational Films*]
CIFE .... Cost, Insurance, Freight, and Exchange [*Shipping*]
CIFEG .... Centre International pour la Formation et les Echanges Geologiques [*International Center for Training and Exchanges in the Geosciences*] (EAIO)
CIFEJ .... Centre International du Film pour l'Enfance et la Jeunesse [*International Center of Films for Children and Young People*]
CIFF .... Central Identification, Friend or Foe [*DoD*]
CIFFA .... Canadian International Freight Forwarders Association, Inc. (AC)
CIFFO .... Cost, Insurance, Freight, Free Out [*Shipping*]
CIFG .... Prince George, BC [*Television station call letters*]
CIFI .... Catholic Institute of the Food Industry (EA)
CIFI .... Cost, Insurance, Freight, and Interest [*Shipping*]
CIFI & E ...... Cost, Insurance, Freight, Interest, and Exchange [*Shipping*]
CIFLT .... Cost, Insurance, Freight, London Terms [*Shipping*]
CIFM .... Computer Integrated Flexible Manufacturing (NITA)
CIFM .... Kamloops, BC [*FM radio station call letters*]
CIFO .... Criminal Investigation Field Office [*Military*]
CIFOR .... Center for International Forestry Research
CIFP .... Comite International pour le Fair Play [*International Fair Play Committee*] [*Paris, France*] (EAIO)
CIFP .... Committee on International Freedom to Publish (EA)
CIFPSE .... Catholic International Federation for Physical and Sports Education [*See also FICEP*] [*Paris, France*] (EAIO)
CIFREDH ...... Centre de Formation et de Recyclage des Enseignants des Droits de l'Homme [*France*]

CIFRS .... Common Market Group of International Rayon and Synthetic Fibres Committee (EAIO)
CIFT .... Canadian Institute of Fisheries Technology [*Technical University of Nova Scotia*] [*Research center*] (RCD)
CIFT .... Centro Internazionale di Fisica Teorica [*International Center for Theoretical Physics - ICTP*] (EAIO)
CIFT .... Committee on Invisibles and Financing Related to Trade [*United Nations Conference on Trade and Development*]
CIFT .... Contextual Indexing and Faceted Taxonomic Access System [*Computer science*] (BARN)
CIFT .... Contextual Indexing and Faceted Taxonomic System [*Modern Language Association of America*] [*A database*] (NITA)
CIFTA .... Comite International des Federations Theatrales d'Amateurs de Langue Francaise
CIFV .... Composite Infantry Fighting Vehicle [*Army*]
CIFX .... Winnipeg, MB [*AM radio station call letters*]
CIG .... Cable Integrity Group (NASA)
CIG .... Canadian Institute of Geomatics [*Association Canadienne des Sciences Geomatiques*] (AC)
CIG .... Ceiling (DA)
CIG .... Central Intelligence Group (LAIN)
CIG .... Centre Informatique Geologique [*Geological Information Centre*] [*Canada*]
CIG .... Chemical Ion Generator (AAG)
CIG .... Chief Intendent-General [*Freemasonry*] (ROG)
CIG .... Cigarette
CIG .... Citadel Gold Mines, Inc. [*Toronto Stock Exchange symbol*]
CIg .... Cold-Insoluble globulin [*Cytochemistry*]
CIG .... Comite International de Geophysique [*International Geophysical Committee*]
CIG .... Communications and Interface Group [*NASA*] (NASA)
CIG .... Compliance and Investigations Group [*U.S. Office of Personnel Management*] (BARN)
CIG .... Computer Image Generator [*or Generation*] (MCD)
CIG .... Computer-Informationsdienst Graz [*Graz Computer-Information Service*] [*Austria*] (IID)
CIG .... Computer Investment Group, Inc. (NITA)
CIG .... Computerized Interactive Graphics (MCD)
CIG .... Conference Internationale du Goudron [*International Tar Conference - ITC*] (EAIO)
CIG .... Consolidated Cigar Holdings, Inc. [*NYSE symbol*] (SAG)
CIG .... Contractor Interface Guide
CIG .... Coordinate Indexing Group [*ASLIB*] (DIT)
CIG .... Counterintelligence Group [*Military*]
CIG .... Creative Industries Group, Inc. [*Auburn Hills, MI*] (TSSD)
CIG .... Cryogenic In-Ground (OA)
CIG .... Current Intelligence, Group (NATG)
C-Ig .... Cytoplasmic Immunoglobulin [*Immunology*]
CIGAR .... Common Interactive Graphics Application Routine [*Army*]
CIGARS .... Committee Insuring and Guaranteeing Anyone's Right to Smoke
CIGARS .... Console Internally Generated and Refreshed Symbols (CAAL)
CIGB .... Commission Internationale des Grands Barrages [*International Commission on Large Dams - ICOLD*] (EAIO)
CIGB .... Trois Rivieres, PQ [*FM radio station call letters*]
CIGCOREP ... Counter Infiltration - Counter Guerilla Concept and Requirement Plan (CINC)
CIGFET .... Complementary Insulated-Gate Field-Effect Transistor (PDAA)
CIGGT .... Canadian Institute of Guided Ground Transport [*Queen's University at Kingston*] [*Research center*] (RCD)
CIGH .... Confederation Internationale de Genealogie et d'Heraldique [*International Confederation of Genealogy and Heraldry - ICGH*] [*Paris, France*] (EAIO)
CIGHi .... CIGNA High Income Shares [*Associated Press*] (SAG)
CIGI .... Canadian International Grains Institute
CIGL .... Belleville, ON [*FM radio station call letters*]
CIGM .... Sudbury, ON [*AM radio station call letters*]
CIGNA .... CIGNA Corp. [*Associated Press*] (SAG)
CIGO .... Port Hawkesbury, NS [*AM radio station call letters*]
CIGP .... Capital Investment Goal Programming
CIGP .... Comite Interministeriel de la Gestion du Personnel [*Personnel Administration Interdepartmental Committee*] [*Canada*]
CIGR .... Caribbean Cigar Co. [*NASDAQ symbol*] (SAG)
CIGR .... Commission Internationale du Genie Rural [*International Commission of Agricultural Engineering*] [*ICSU*] (EAIO)
CIGRE .... Conference Internationale des Grands Reseaux Electriques a Haute Tension [*International Conference on Large High Voltage Electric Systems*] (EAIO)
CIGS .... Centre International de Gerontologie Sociale [*International Center of Social Gerontology - ICSG*] [*Paris, France*] [*Defunct*]
CIGS .... Chief of the Imperial General Staff [*Later, CGS*] [*British*]
CIGS .... Copper, Indium, Gallium, and Selenium [*Photovoltaics*]
CIGTF .... Central Inertial Guidance Test Facility [*Air Force*]
CIGV .... Penticton, BC [*FM radio station call letters*]
CIH .... Canadian Institue of Hypnotism (AC)
CIH .... Carbohydrate-Induced Hyperglyceridemia [*Medicine*]
CIH .... Central India Horse [*British military*] (DMA)
CIH .... Certificate of Industrial Health
CIH .... Certified Industrial Hygienist
CIH .... Chain Ignition Hazard
CIH .... Changzhi [*China*] [*Airport symbol*] (OAG)
CIH .... Children in Hospitals (EA)
CIH .... CIS Technologies, Inc. [*Vancouver Stock Exchange symbol*]
CIH .... Colloidal Iron Hydroxide
CIH .... Committee for Italic Handwriting [*Defunct*] (EA)
CIH .... Commonwealth Institute of Helminthology [*St. Albans, England*]

CIH............. Corpus Inscriptionum Himjariticarum (BJA)
CIH............. Information Handling Services, Englewood, CO [OCLC symbol] (OCLC)
CIHA .... Comite International d'Histoire de l'Art (EAIO)
CIHB .... Canadian Inventory of Historic Building [Environment Canada] [Information service or system] (IID)
CIHE.......... Council for Industry and Higher Education (AIE)
CIHEAM .... Centre International de Hautes Etudes Agronomiques Mediterraneennes
CIHED .... Center for International Higher Education Documentation (EDAC)
CIHF.......... Canadian Icelandic Horse Federation (AC)
CIHF.......... Halifax, NS [Television station call letters]
CIHGLF .... Comite International d'Historiens et Geographes de Langue Francaise [International Committee of French-Speaking Historians and Geographers - ICFHG] (EAIO)
CIHI .... Fredericton, NB [AM radio station call letters]
CIHM .... Canadian Institute for Historical Microreproductions
CIHM .... Commission Internationale d'Histoire Militaire [International Commission of Military History] (EAIO)
CIHO .... St. Hilarion, PQ [FM radio station call letters]
Cihr............. Curie Hour (MAE)
CIHS .... Central Infantile Hypotonic Syndrome [Medicine] (DMAA)
CIHS .... Classified Information-Handling System [Department of State] (GFGA)
CIHU .... Canadian Infantry Holding Unit
CIHV .... Centre International Humanae Vitae [International Centre Humanae Vitae] [Paris, France] (EAIO)
CIHY .... Chambre Immobiliere de la Haute Yamaska Inc. [Haute Yamaska Real Estate Board] (AC)
CII............. Camrose International Institute [L'Institut International de Camrose] [Formerly, Camrose One World Institute] (AC)
CII............. Carnegie Interest Inventory [Medicine] (DMAA)
CII............. Cats in Industry [British] (DI)
CII............. Centre for Industrial Innovation [British] (ARC)
CII............. Centro Internacional de la Infancia [International Children's Center]
CII............. Chartered Insurance Institute [British]
CII............. Chitipa [Malawi] [Airport symbol] (AD)
CII............. Coady International Institute (AC)
CII............. Collective Investment Institution (MHDW)
CII............. Compagnie Internationale pour l'Informatique [Formed by merger of SEA and CAE]
CII............. Computer-Integrated Instruction (NVT)
CII............. Confederation of Irish Industry (EAIO)
CII............. Configuration Identification Index
CII............. Conseil International des Infirmieres [International Council of Nurses - ICN] [Geneva, Switzerland] (EA)
CII............. Construction Industry Institute [Australia]
CII............. Containerization and Intermodal Institute (EA)
CII............. Contolled Substance, Class Two [Department of Health and Human Services] (DAVI)
CII............. Controlled Interval Inspection (MCD)
CII............. Convention II (EA)
CII............. Cook Islands International [New Zealand] [ICAO designator] (FAAC)
CII............. Council of Institutional Investors [Washington, DC] (EA)
CII............. Council of International Investigators (EA)
CII............. Criminal Identification and Investigation
CII............. Critical Item Inspection [California Highway Patrol's accident inspection program]
CII............. Crosscurrents International Institute (EA)
CII............. CUG [Control Unit Group] Interrupt Inhibit
CII............. Current Indicator and Integrator
CII............. George M. Low Center for Industrial Innovation [Rensselaer Polytechnic Institute] [Research center] (RCD)
CIIA........... Canadian Information Industry Association [Information service or system Defunct] (IID)
CIIA........... Canadian Institute of International Affairs
CIIA........... Commission Internationale des Industries Agricoles et Alimentaires [International Commission for Food Industries] (EAIO)
CIIA........... Common Internal Iliac Artery [Medicine] (DMAA)
CIIAN .... Canadian International Institute of Applied Negotiation [L'Institut International Canadien de la Negociation Pratique] (AC)
CIIC........... Canadian Industrial Innovation Centre (AC)
CIIC........... Centro Internacional de Investigaciones sobre el Cancer [International Agency for Research on Cancer]
CIIC........... Chemical International Information Center
CIIC........... Counterintelligence Interrogation Center [Military]
CIIC........... Current Intelligence Indication Center (CINC)
CIIC/W........ Canadian Industrial Innovation Centre/Waterloo [University of Waterloo] [Research center] (RCD)
CIID .... Centre de Recherches pour le Developpement International [International Development Research Centre] [Canada]
CIID .... Commission Internationale des Irrigations et du Drainage [International Commission on Irrigation and Drainage - ICID] (EAIO)
CIII............ Paris, ON [Television station call letters]
CIII-1 .... Windsor, ON [Television station call letters]
CIII-2 .... Bancroft, ON [Television station call letters]
CIII-4 .... Owen Sound, ON [Television station call letters]
CIII-6 .... Ottawa, ON [Television station call letters]
CIII-7 .... Midland, ON [Television station call letters]
CIII-22 .... Stevenson, ON [Television station call letters]
CIII-27 .... Peterborough, ON [Television station call letters]
CIII-29 .... Oil Springs, ON [Television station call letters]
CIII-41 .... Toronto, ON [Television station call letters]
CI-III .... Computer Inquiry III [FCC]

CIIM........... Centre International d'Information de la Mutualite
CIIM........... Cyprus International Institute of Management (ECON)
CIIMS......... Canadian Information and Image Management Society [Information service or system] (IID)
CIIP .... Clothing Initial Issue Point [Military] (AABC)
CIIP .... Commander, International Ice Patrol [Coast Guard]
CIIPS .... Chronic Idiopathic Intesinal Pseudo-Obstruction Syndrome [Medicine] (DMAA)
CIIR .... Catholic Institute for International Relations [British] (EAIO)
CIIR .... Central Institute for Industrial Research (AAG)
CIIR .... Chloroisobutene Isoprene Rubber
CIIS .... Cattell Infant Intelligence Scale [Psychology] (DAVI)
CIIS .... Contemporary Issues in Science Program (EDAC)
CIIS .... Corporate Integrated Information System [Consumer and Corporate Affairs Canada] [Information service or system] (IID)
CIIT .... Chemical Industry Institute of Toxicology (EA)
CIITC......... Confederation Internationale des Industries Techniques du Cinema
CIIUAP .... Commission on Increased Industrial Use of Agricultural Products
CIJ............ Canadian Industrial Minerals Corp. [Vancouver Stock Exchange symbol]
CIJ............ Cobija [Bolivia] [Airport symbol] (OAG)
CIJ............ Commission Internationale de Juristes [International Commission of Jurists - ICJ] [Switzerland]
CIJ............ Corpus Inscriptionum Judaicarum [A publication] (BJA)
CIJ............ Corte Internacional de Justicia [International Court of Justice] [Spanish United Nations] (DUND)
CIJ............ Cour Internationale de Justice [International Court of Justice]
CIJ............ Sisters of the Infant Jesus [Nursing Sisters of the Sick Poor] [Roman Catholic religious order]
CIJA........... Centro para la Independencia de Jueces y Abogados [Switzerland]
CIJC........... Construction Industry Joint Conference (EA)
CIJL........... Centre for the Independence of Judges and Lawyers [See also CIMA] [Geneva, Switzerland] (EAIO)
CIJM .... Comite International des Jeux Mediterraneens [Athens, Greece] (EAIO)
CIJN........... Club International des Jeunes Naturistes [Paris, France] (EAIO)
CIJPECEW.... Committee for International Justice and Peace of the Episcopal Conference of England and Wales (EAIO)
CIK............ Canadian Insulock [Vancouver Stock Exchange symbol]
CIK............ Chalkyitsik [Alaska] [Airport symbol] (OAG)
CIKI.......... Rimouski, PQ [FM radio station call letters]
CIL............ Call Identification Line [Telecommunications] (NITA)
CIL............ Call Information Logging [Telecommunications] (NITA)
CIL............ Canadian Industries Ltd.
CIL............ Carbon-in-Leach [Gold ore processing]
CIL............ Cecil Aviation Ltd. [ICAO designator] (FAAC)
CIL............ Center for Independent Living [Rehabilitation] (DAVI)
CIL............ Central Identification Laboratory [Hawaii] [Army]
CIL............ Certificate in Lieu [of]
CIL............ Changes in Law (MCD)
CIL............ Chicago, Indianapolis & Louisville [Louisville & Nashville Railroad Co.] [AAR code]
CIL............ C-I-L, Inc. [Toronto Stock Exchange symbol]
CIL............ Clear Indicating Light (MSA)
CIL............ Cold Intermediate Layer [Oceanography]
CIL............ Commercial Instrument Landing
CIL............ Component Intergration Laboratories
C/I/L.......... Computer/Information/Library Sciences [Abstracts]
CIL............ Computer Interpreter Language (MHDB)
CIL............ Computer Investments Ltd. [British] (NITA)
CIL............ Configuration [or Contract] Inspection Log
CIL............ Contractor Involved in Litigation (AAGC)
CIL............ Controlled Items List
CIL............ Cooling-Induced Luminescence [In glass containing rare earth salts]
CIL............ Core Image Library (CMD)
CIL............ Council, AK [Location identifier FAA] (FAAL)
CIL............ Council for Interinstitutional Leadership (EA)
CIL............ Critical Item List (MCD)
CIL............ Current Injection Logic [Computer science]
CILA.......... Casualty Insurance Logistics Automated (PDAA)
CILA.......... Central Interior Logging Association (AC)
CILA.......... Centro Interamericano de Libros Academicos [Inter-American Scholarly Book Center]
CILA.......... Chartered Institute of Loss Adjusters [British] (BI)
CILA.......... Council of International Lay Associations [Defunct] (EA)
CI Labs .... Component Integration Labs [Sunnyvale, CA] (CDE)
CILAD .... Colegio Ibero-Latino-Americano de Dermatologia [Ibero Latin American College of Dermatology - ILACD] (EA)
CILAF .... Comite International de Liaison des Associations Feminines [International Liaison Committee of Women's Organizations] [French]
CILAS .... Centro de Investigacion Laboral y Asesoria Sindical [Member of RMALC] [Mexico] (CROSS)
CILB.......... Commission Internationale de Lutte Biologique Contre les Ennemis des Cultures
CILC.......... California Iceberg Lettuce Commission (EA)
CILC.......... Centralized Intermediate Logistics Concept (MCD)
CILC.......... Commonwealth International Law Cases [A publication] (DLA)
CILC.......... Confederation Internationale du Lin et du Chanvre [International Linen and Hemp Confederation] (EAIO)
Cilcorp........ Cilcorp., Inc. [Associated Press] (SAG)
CILE.......... Call Information Logging Equipment [Computer science] (PDAA)
CILE.......... Havre-Saint-Pierre, PQ [FM radio station call letters] (RBYB)

CILEA.......... Consorzio Interuniversitario Lombardo per l'Elaborazione Automatica [*Lombard Interuniversity Consortium for Data Processing*] [*Information service or system*] (IID)

CILECT........ Centre International de Liaison des Ecoles de Cinema et de Television [*International Liaison Centre for Film and Television Schools*] (EAIO)

CILER.......... Cooperative Institute for Limnology and Ecosystems Research [*Marine science*] (OSRA)

CILER.......... Cooperative Institute for Limnology and Ecosystems Research (USDC)

CILET.......... Circular Letter

CILF.......... Conseil International de la Langue Francaise [*International Council of the French Language - ICFL*] (EAIO)

CIL-HI.......... Central Identification Laboratory - Hawaii [*Army*]

CILIP.......... Civil Liberties and Police [*Germany*]

CILJSA........ Comparative and International Law Journal of Southern Africa [*A publication*] (DLA)

CILK.......... Kelowna, BC [*FM radio station call letters*]

CILM.......... Construction Injury Liability Monthly [*Business Publishers, Inc.*] [*A publication*] (AAGC)

CILMC......... Contingency Intermediate-Level Maintenance Center (DOMA)

CILOP.......... Conversion in Lieu of Procurement [*Military*]

CILOPGO..... Comite International de Liaison des Gynecologues et Obstetriciens

CILP.......... Current Index to Legal Periodicals [*University of Washington*] [*Information service or system*] (CRD)

CILPE.......... Conference Internationale de Liaison entre Producteurs d'Energie Electrique [*International Conference of Producers of Electrical Energy*]

CILQ.......... Conseil de l'Industrie Laitiere du Quebec Inc. [*Quebec Dairy Council Inc.*] (AC)

CILQ.......... Toronto, ON [*FM radio station call letters*]

CILRECO...... Comite International de Liaison pour la Reunification et la Paix en Coree [*International Liaison Committee for Reunification and Peace in Korea*] (EAIO)

CILRT.......... Containment Integrated Leak Rate Test [*Nuclear energy*] (NRCH)

CILRV .... Citrus Leaf Rugose Virus [*Plant pathology*]

CILS.......... Carrier Instrument Landing System [*Navy*] (CAAL)

CILS.......... Center for Independent Living Services

CILS.......... Centralized Intermediate Logistics System (MCD)

CILS.......... Collision-Induced Light Scattering (MCD)

CILS.......... Comite d'Information sur la Lutte Solidarite [*Portugal*]

CILS.......... Compatible Instrument Landing System [*Aviation*]

CILSA.......... Chief Inspector of Land Service Ammunition (NATG)

CILSDS........ Community Independent Living Service Delivery Systems (EDAC)

CILSMO ...... Command Integrated Logistics Management Office

CILSS.......... Comite Permanent Interetats de Lutte Contre la Secheresse dans le Sahel [*Permanent Interstate Committee for Drought Control in the Sahel*] (EAIO)

CILT.......... Centre for Independment Living in Toronto (AC)

CILT.......... Centre for Information on Language Teaching and Research [*Regent's College*] [*British*] (CB)

CILT.......... Centre for Information on Language Teaching and Research [*British*] (AIE)

CILT.......... Centre for Information on Language Training [*British*]

CIM.......... Canadian Institute of Management [*Institut Canadien de Gestion*] (AC)

CIM.......... Canadian Institute of Marketing [*Institut Canadien du Marketing*] (AC)

CIM.......... Canadian Institute of Metalworking [*McMaster University*] [*Research center*] (RCD)

CIM.......... Canadian Institute of Mining

CIM.......... Canadina Institute of Mining, Metallurgy & Petroleum [*Institut Canadien des Mines, de la Metallurgie et du Petrole*] [*Formerly, Canadian Institute of Mining & Metallurgy*] (AC)

CIM.......... Capital Investment Model [*Navy*]

CIM.......... Carina Minerals Resources Ltd. [*Vancouver Stock Exchange symbol*]

CIM.......... Cavitation Intensity Meter

CIM.......... Center for Integral Medicine [*Defunct*] (EA)

CIM.......... Certificate in Management

CIM.......... Certified Industrial Manager

CIM.......... Charge Imaging Matrix [*Electronics*]

CIM.......... Chartered Institute of Marketing [*British*] (EAIO)

CIM.......... Chicago & Illinois Midland Railway Co. [*AAR code*]

CIM.......... Chief Inspector of Machinery [*Navy British*] (ROG)

CIM.......... Children's Interaction Matrix [*Child development test*] [*Psychology*]

CIM.......... Chimachoy [*Guatemala*] [*Seismograph station code, US Geological Survey*] (SEIS)

CIM.......... China Inland Mission

CIM.......... Christian Ireland Ministries (EA)

CIM.......... Cimarron, NM [*Location identifier FAA*] (FAAL)

CIM.......... Cimbr Air, AS [*Denmark*] [*FAA designator*] (FAAC)

CIM.......... CIM High Yield Sec [*AMEX symbol*] (TTSB)

CIM.......... CIM High Yield Securities [*AMEX symbol*] (SPSG)

CIM.......... CIM High Yield Securities [*Associated Press*] (SAG)

CIM.......... Cimitarra [*Colombia*] [*Airport symbol*] (OAG)

Cim.......... Cimon [*of Plutarch*] [*Classical studies*] (OCD)

CIM.......... Cleveland Institute of Music [*Record label*]

CIM.......... CMOS Idustrial Microcomputer (NITA)

CIM.......... Code Impulse Modulation (IAA)

CIM.......... Code Interface Module (CAAL)

CIM.......... Coffin Intercept Missile

CIM.......... Colonic Intestinal Metaplasia [*Oncology*]

CIM.......... Comite International du Mini-Basketball [*International Committee for Mini-Basketball*] [*Munich, Federal Republic of Germany*] (EAIO)

CIM.......... COMLINE Industrial Monitor [*COMLINE International Corp.*] [*Japan Information service or system*] (CRD)

CIM.......... Commercial Industrial Marine [*Automotive engineering*]

CIM.......... Commission Internationale de Marketing [*International Marketing Commission - IMC*] [*Brixham, Devonshire, England*] (EAIO)

CIM.......... Communication Interface Monitor

CIM.......... Communications Improvement Memorandum [*Military*]

CIM.......... Communications Interface Modules [*Computer science*]

CIM.......... Component Item Manager [*Air Force*] (AFIT)

CIM.......... Compound Inserting Machine

CIM.......... CompuServe Information Manager [*CompuServe, Inc.*] (PCM)

CIM.......... Computer Input from Microfilm (ECII)

CIM.......... Computer Input Matrix (KSC)

CIM.......... Computer Input Microfilming (MCD)

CIM.......... Computer Input Multiplexer (KSC)

CIM.......... Computer Integrated Manufacturing

CIM.......... Computer Interface Module [*Computer science*]

CIM.......... [*The*] Computers in Manufacturing Show [*British*] (ITD)

CIM.......... Conductance Increase Mechanism

CIM.......... Congres International des Fabrications Mecaniques [*International Mechanical Engineering Congress*]

CIM.......... Congres Islamique Mondial

CIM.......... Conseil International de la Musique [*International Music Council*]

CIM.......... Consejo Internacional de Mujeres [*International Council of Women*]

CIM.......... Continuous Image Microfilm (IEEE)

CIM.......... Continuous Imprint Marking [*of medical linen*] (MCD)

CIM.......... Control Interface Module [*Chemistry*]

CIM.......... Convention Internationale Concernant le Transport des Marchandises par Chemins de Fer [*International Convention Concerning the Carriage of Goods by Rail*]

CIM.......... Cooperative Investigation of the Mediterranean

CIM.......... Cork Insulation Material

CIM.......... Corporate Information Management [*DoD*] (RDA)

CIM.......... Cortically Induced Movement [*Medicine*]

CIM.......... Council of Independent Managers [*Milwaukee, WI*] (EA)

CIM.......... Critical Index Management (HGAA)

CIM.......... Crystal Impedance Meter

CIM.......... Cubic Inches per Minute (IAA)

CIM.......... Cumulated Index Medicus [*A publication*]

CIM.......... Curtis Institute of Music [*Pennsylvania*]

CIM.......... University of California, Irvine, Medical Sciences Library, Irvine, CA [*OCLC symbol*] (OCLC)

CIMA.......... Centre pour l'Independance des Magistrats et des Avocats [*Centre for the Independence of Judges and Lawyers - CIJL*] (EA)

CIMA.......... Chartered Institute of Management Accountants [*British*] (EAIO)

CIMA.......... Chlorite-Iodide-Malonic-Acid [*Chemical reaction*]

CIMA.......... CIMA Labs [*NASDAQ symbol*] (TTSB)

CIMA.......... CIMA Labs, Inc. [*NASDAQ symbol*] (SAG)

CIMA.......... Construction Industry Manufacturers Association (EA)

CIMA.......... Creek Indian Memorial Association (EA)

CIMAC .... Cellulose Insulation Manufacturers Association of Canada (AC)

CIMAC .... Conseil International des Machines a Combustion [*International Council on Combustion Engines*] [*Paris, France*] (EAIO)

CIMADE ...... Comite Inter-Mouvement Aupres des Evacues [*France*]

CIMAe........ Commission Internationale de Meteorologie Aeronautique [*OMI*]

CIMAH .... Control of Industrial Major Accident Hazards [*British*]

CIMA Lb ..... CIMA Labs, Inc. [*Associated Press*] (SAG)

CIMAP .... Commission Internationale des Methodes d'Analyse des Pesticides [*Collaborative International Pesticides Analytic Council - CIPAC*] (EAIO)

CIMAR .... Center for Intelligent Machines and Robotics [*University of Florida*] [*Research center*] (RCD)

CIMarE........ Companion of the Institute of Marine Engineers [*British*]

CIMAS .... Conference Internationale de la Mutualite et des Assurances Sociales

CIMAS .... Cooperative Institute for Marine and Atmospheric Studies [*Coral Gables, FL*] [*NOAA, Rosenstiel School of Marine and Atmospheric Science of the University of Miami*] (GRD)

CIMAV .... Comite International de Medecine d'Assurances sur la Vie [*International Committee for Life Assurance Medicine*] [*France*] (EAIO)

CIMB.......... Cimbalom [*Music*]

CIMB.......... Construction Industry Management Board [*Defunct*] (EA)

CIMBA.......... Contractor Installation Make or Buy Authorization (AAG)

CIMC.......... CIMCO, Inc. [*NASDAQ symbol*] (NQ)

CIMC.......... Commanders' Internal Management Conference [*Air Force*]

CIMC.......... Committee for International Municipal Cooperation

CIMCEE....... Comite des Industries de la Moutarde de la CEE [*EEC Committee for the Mustard Industries*]

CIMCO .... Card Image Correction [*Computer science*]

Cimco .... Cimco, Inc. [*Associated Press*] (SAG)

CIMD .... Certified Institution for the Mental Defective [*British*]

CIM/DCS...... Computer Integrated Manufacture/Data Collection System (NITA)

CIME.......... Chartered Institute of Marine Engineers

CIME.......... Comite Intergouvernemental pour les Migrations Europeennes [*Intergovernmental Committee for European Migration*]

CIME.......... Computers in Mechanical Engineering [*American Society of Mechanical Engineers*] [*A publication*] (NITA)

CIME.......... Confederation Internationale de Musique Electroacoustique [*International Confederation for Electroacoustic Music - ICEM*] (EAIO)

CIME.......... Ste. Adele, PQ [*FM radio station call letters*]

CIMEA.......... Comite International des Mouvements d'Enfants et d'Adolescents [*International Committee of Children's and Adolescents' Movements*] [*Budapest, Hungary*] (EAIO)

CI Mech E.... Companion of the Institution of Mechanical Engineers [*British*]

CIMEX.......... Civil Military Exercise (MCD)

CIMF.......... Hull, PQ [*FM radio station call letters*]

CIMG .... Colloque International de Marketing Gazier [*International Colloquium about Gas Marketing - ICGM*] (EA)

CIMG .... Cut Image [*Computer science*] (PCM)

CIMG .... Swift Current, SK [*FM radio station call letters*]

CIMGTechE... Companion of the Institution of Mechanical and General Technician Engineers [*British*] (DBQ)

CIMH .... Comite International pour la Metrologie Historique [*International Committee for Historical Metrology*] (EAIO)

CIMI .... Chemical Information Management, Inc. [*Information service or system*] (IID)

CIMI .... Committee on Integrity and Management Improvement [*Environmental Protection Agency*] (EPA)

CIMI .... Computer Interchange of Museum Information Committee

CIMIC......... Civilian Military Cooperation (NATG)

CIMII.......... Continuous Intramuscular Insulin Infusion

CIMJ .... Guelph, ON [*FM radio station call letters*]

CIML .... Center for Improving Mountain Living [*Western Carolina University*] [*Research center*] (RCD)

CIML........... Contract Item Material List

CIMM .... Canadian Institute of Mining and Metallurgy

CIMM .... Comite International de Medecine Militaire [*International Committee of Military Medicine*] [*Belgium*] (EAIO)

CIMM .... Commodity Integrated Materiel Manager

CIMM .... Concours International de Musique de Montreal [*Montreal International Music Competition*] (AC)

CIMM .... Constant Impedance Mechanical Modulation (AAG)

CIM/ME....... Computer Integrated Manufacturing/Mechanical Engineering System (NITA)

CIMMO .... Chartered Institute of Marketing Management of Ontario (AC)

CIMMS........ Civilian Information Manpower Management System [*Navy*]

CIMMS........ Cooperative Institute for Mesoscale Meteorological Studies [*University of Oklahoma, NOAA*] [*Research center*] (RCD)

CIMMYT....... Centro Internacional de Mejoramiento de Maiz y Trigo [*International Maize and Wheat Improvement Center*] [*ICSU*] (EAIO)

CIMN .... Charlottetown, PE [*FM radio station call letters*] (RBYB)

CIMO .... Commission des Instruments et des Methodes d'Observation [*Commission for Instruments and Methods of Observation*] [*OMI*]

CIMO .... Confederation of Importers and Marketing Organizations in Europe of Fresh Fruit and Vegetables [*Brussels, Belgium*] (EA)

CIMO .... Magog, PQ [*FM radio station call letters*]

CImoH .... Napa State Hospital, Imola, CA [*Library symbol Library of Congress*] (LCLS)

CIM-OMF ..... China Inland Mission Overseas Missionary Fellowship [*Later, Overseas MissionaryFellowship*] (EA)

CIMOS .... Cast Iron Maintenance Optimization System [*for gas distribution mains*] [*A trademark*]

CIMP.......... Commission Internationale Medico-Physiologique [*International Medico-Physiological Commission*] (PDAA)

CIMP.......... Conseil International de la Musique Populaire [*International Folk Music Council*]

CIMP.......... Controlled Impulse (MCD)

CIMP.......... Curve Interpreter for Microprocessor (MCD)

CImp........... Imperial Public Library, Imperial, CA [*Library symbol Library of Congress*] (LCLS)

CIMPA .... Centre International de Mathematiques Pures et Appliquees [*International Center for Pure and Applied Mathematics - ICPAM*] [*United Nations*] (EA)

CIMPLE....... Card Image Manipulator for Large Entities [*Computer science*] (PDAA)

CIMPM........ Comite International de Medecine et de Pharmacie Militaires [*International Committee of Military Medicine and Pharmacy - ICMMP*] [*Liege, Belgium*] (EA)

CIMR .... Center for Interest Measurement [*University of Minnesota*] [*Research center*] (RCD)

CIMR .... Commanders' Internal Management Review [*Also known as Black Saturday*] [*Military*] (AAG)

CIMRA .... Colonialism and Indigenous Minorities Research and Action [*British*] (DI)

CIMRM .... Corpus Inscriptionum et Monumentorum Religionis Mithriacae [*A publication*] (BJA)

CIMRS .... Cooperative Institute for Marine Resources Studies [*Marine science*] (OSRA)

CIMRS .... Cooperative Institute for Marine Resources Studies (USDC)

CIMS........... Center for Innovation Management Studies [*Lehigh University*] [*Information service or system*] (IID)

CIMS........... Center for Integrated Manufacturing Studies [*Rochester Institute of Technology*] [*Research center*] (RCD)

CIMS........... Chemical Ionization Mass Spectrometry

CIMS........... Civilian Information Management System (AFIT)

CIMS........... Commercial Information Management System [*Department of Commerce*]

CIMS........... Communications Instructions for Merchant Ships [*Navy*]

CIMS........... Computer Installation Management System (PDAA)

CIMS........... Computer-Integrated Manufacturing System

CIMS........... Consociatio Internationalis Musicae Sacrae [*Rome, Italy*] (EAIO)

CIMS........... Countermeasures Internal Management System (PDAA)

CIMS........... Courant Institute of Mathematical Sciences [*New York University*] [*Research center*] (RCD)

CIMSCEE...... Comite des Industries des Mayonnaises et Sauces Condimentaires de la CEE [*Committee of the Industries of Mayonnaises and Table Sauces of the European Economic Community*]

CIMSS .... Cooperative Institute of Meteorology Satellite Studies [*Marine science*] (OSRA)

CIMSS .... Cooperative Institute of Meteorology Satellite Studies (USDC)

CIMT........... Centre International des Marees Terrestres [*International Centre for Earth Tides*] (EAIO)

CIMT........... Commission Internationale de la Medecine du Travail [*International Commissionof Occupational Health - ICOH*] [*Information service or system*] (IID)

CIMT........... Riviere du Loup, PQ [*Television station call letters*]

CIMTA......... Cottage Industry Miniaturists Trade Association (EA)

CIMTECH...... Centre for Information Media and Technology [*British*] (EAIO)

CIMTF......... Cimatron Ltd [*NASDAQ symbol*] (TTSB)

CIMTP......... Congres Internationaux de Medecine Tropicale et de Paludisme [*International Congresses on Tropical Medicine and Malaria*]

CIMU .... Compatibility-Integration Mock-Up (MCD)

CIMX.......... Windsor, ON [*FM radio station call letters*]

CIN............. Cargo Increment Number (DOMA)

CIN............. Carrier Input (MSA)

CIN............. Carroll, IA [*Location identifier FAA*] (FAAL)

CIN............. Center Information Network [*Support servicing center*] (SSD)

CIN............. Centro de Informacoes Nucleares [*Center for Nuclear Information*] [*Brazil*] [*Information service or system*] (IID)

CIN............. Cerebriform Intradermal Nevus [*Medicine*] (AAMN)

CIN............. Cervical Intraepithelial Neoplasia [*Medicine*]

CIN............. Change Identification Number (NASA)

CIN............. Change Incorporation Notice [*Business law*]

CIN............. Change Instrumentation Notice

CIN............. Chronic Interstitial Nephritis [*Medicine*] (MAE)

CIN............. Cincinnati [*Ohio*]

CIN............. Cincinnati Gas & Electric Co. [*NYSE symbol*] (SPSG)

CIN............. Cine [*Turkey*] [*Seismograph station code, US Geological Survey*] (SEIS)

CIN............. CINergy Corp. [*NYSE symbol*] (SAG)

CIN............. Code Identification Number (MSA)

CIN............. Combat Information Net

CIN............. Commission Internationale de Numismatique [*International Numismatic Commission*] [*Oslo, Norway*] (EA)

CIN............. Commodore Information Network [*Commodore Business Machines, Inc.*] [*Information service or system*] (TSSD)

CIN............. Common Interest Network (EA)

CIN............. Communication Identification Navigation

CIN............. Community Information Network [*Cable TV programming service*]

CIN............. Computer Information Network (SSD)

CIN............. Computers in Nursing (MEDA)

CIN............. Configuration Identification Number [*Military*]

CIN............. Contract Item Number (MCD)

CIN............. Cooperative Information Network [*Library network*]

CIN............. Corporation Index System [*Securities and Exchange Commission*] (GFGA)

CIN............. Council of Indian Nations [*An association*]

CIN............. Council of Indian Nations

CIN............. Criminal, Immoral, and Narcotic

Cin............. Insulin Clearance [*Medicine*] (MAE)

CIN............. United States Naval Weapons Center, China Lake, CA [*Library symbol Library of Congress*] (LCLS)

CIN............. University of Cincinnati, Cincinnati, OH [*OCLC symbol*] (OCLC)

CINA .... Canadian International Network Association (AC)

CINA .... Canadian Intravenous Nurses Association (AC)

CINA .... Centralinstitut for Nordisk Asienforskning [*Scandinavian Institute of Asian Studies*] [*Later, NIAS*] (EAIO)

CINA .... Commission Internationale de la Navigation Aerienne [*International Air Navigation Commission*]

CINA .... Cook Inlet Native Association [*Defunct*] (EA)

CINAA......... Cyclic Instrumental Neutron Activation Analysis

CINAHL....... Cumulative Index to Nursing and Allied Health Literature [*Database*]

CinarF........ Cinar Films, Inc. [*Associated Press*] (SAG)

CINAV......... Commission Internationale de la Nomenclature Anatomique Veterinaire [*International Committee on Veterinary Anatomical Nomenclature - ICVAN*] [*Zurich, Switzerland*] (EAIO)

Cin B Ass'n J... Cincinnati Bar Association. Journal [*A publication*] (DLA)

CINC .... Commander-in-Chief

C-in-C .... Commander-in-Chief (NATG)

CinC .... Commander in Chief (AAGC)

CINC .... Commander in Chief (AAGC)

C-in-C .... Curate-in-Charge [*Church of England*]

CINC .... Thompson, MB [*FM radio station call letters*] (RBYB)

CINCA......... Chronic Infantile Neurological Cutaneous and Auricular [*Syndrome*] [*Medicine*] (DMAA)

CINCA & WI... Commander-in-Chief, Atlantic and West Indies

CINCAC....... Commander-in-Chief, Continental Air Command (AFM)

CINCAF .... Commander-in-Chief, Allied Forces

CINCAF .... Commander-in-Chief, [*US*] Asiatic Fleet

CINCAFE ...... Commander-in-Chief, Air Forces, Europe (NATG)

CINCAFLANT... Commander-in-Chief, Air Force Atlantic Command (AFM)

CINCAFMED... Commander-in-Chief, Allied Forces, Mediterranean [*NATO*]

CINCAFPAC... Commander-in-Chief, [*US*] Army Forces in the Pacific

CINCAFSTRIKE... Commander-in-Chief, Air Force Strike Command (AFM)

CINCAIRCENT... Commander-in-Chief, Allied Air Forces, Central Europe (MCD)

CINCAIREASTLANT... Air Commander-in-Chief, Eastern Atlantic Area

CINCAL........ Commander-in-Chief, Alaskan Command

CINCALAIRCENEUR... Commander-in-Chief, Allied Air Forces, Central Europe

CINCANT....... Commander in Chief, Atlantic [*Military*] (DOMA)

CINCARIB .... Commander-in-Chief, Caribbean

CINCARLANT... Commander-in-Chief, [*US*] Army Forces, Atlantic (AABC)

CINCARPAC... Commander-in-Chief, [*US*] Army Forces, Pacific (AFM)

CINCARSTRIKE... Commander-in-Chief, Army Strike Command (AFM)

CINCATL ...... Commander-in-Chief, Atlantic

CINCAWI...... Commander-in-Chief, America West Indies Station [*British*]

CINCBPF...... Commander-in-Chief, British Pacific Fleet
CINCCENT..... Commander-in-Chief, Allied Forces, Central Europe [NATO]
CINCCHAN..... Allied Commander-in-Chief, Channel (MCD)
C in C CNA... Commander-in-Chief, Canadian Northwest Atlantic [World War II]
CINCEASTLANT... Commander-in-Chief, Eastern Atlantic Area [NATO]
CINCEI........ Commander-in-Chief, East Indies Station [British]
CINCENT...... Commander-in-Chief, Allied Forces, Central Europe (MCD)
CINCEUR...... Commander-in-Chief, Europe
CINCFE .... Commander-in-Chief, Far East
CINCFES...... Commander-in-Chief, Far East Station [British]
CINCFESTA.... Commander-in-Chief, Far East Station [British]
CINCFLT...... Commander-in-Chief, Fleet [British]
CINCFOR...... Commander in Chief, [US] Forces [Command] (DOMA)
Cinch.......... Cinchona [Quinine] [Pharmacology] (ROG)
CINCH......... Components of Inventory Change Survey [Bureau of the Census]
  (GFGA)
CINCHAN ..... Commander-in-Chief Channel and Southern North Sea
C-in-CHF..... Commander-in-Chief, Home Forces [British]
CINCHF....... Commander-in-Chief, United Kingdom Home Fleet [Also,
  CINCHOMEFLT] (NATG)
CINCHOMEFLT... Commander-in-Chief, United Kingdom Home Fleet [Also,
  CINCHF] (NATG)
CINCIBERLANT... Commander-in-Chief, Iberian Atlantic Area (NATG)
CINCJAPA.... Commander-in-Chief, Japan Area [World War II]
CINCLANDCENT... Commander-in-Chief, Allied Land Forces, Central Europe (MCD)
CINCLANT..... Commander-in-Chief, Atlantic
CINCLANT..... Commander in Chief, Atlantic Forces (AAGC)
CINCLANT ABNCP... Commander-in-Chief, Atlantic Airborne Command Post
  (DNAB)
CINCLANT CAO... Commander-in-Chief, Atlantic Coordination of Atomic
  Operations (DNAB)
CINCLANTFLT... Commander-in-Chief, Atlantic Fleet [Navy]
CINCLANT/PAC... Commander-in-Chief, Atlantic and Pacific (AFIT)
CINCLANTREP... Commander-in-Chief, Atlantic Representative (DNAB)
Cinc L Bul ... Cincinnati Law Bulletin [A publication] (DLA)
CINCMAC..... Commander-in-Chief, Military Airlift Command
CINCMAIRCHAN... Allied Maritime Air Commander-in-Chief, Channel
CINCMEAFSA... Commander-in-Chief, Middle East/Southern Asia and Africa South
  of the Sahara [Military]
CINCMED..... Commander-in-Chief, Mediterranean
CINCMELF ... Commander-in-Chief, Middle East Land Forces (NATG)
CINCNAVEASTLANTMED... Commander-in-Chief, Naval Forces, Eastern Atlantic
  and Mediterranean
CINCNE...... Commander-in-Chief, [US] Northeast Command
CINCNEDE... Commander-in-Chief, Netherlands Forces in the East
CINCNELM... Commander-in-Chief, Naval Forces, Eastern Atlantic and
  Mediterranean
CINCNORAD... Commander-in-Chief, North American Air Defense
CINCNOREUR... Commander-in-Chief, Northern Europe
CINCNORTH... Commander-in-Chief, Allied Forces, Northern Europe [NATO]
Cinc (Ohio)... Cincinnati Superior Court Reports [Ohio] [A publication] (DLA)
CINCONAD... Commander-in-Chief, Continental Air Defense Command
CINCPAC...... Commander-in-Chief, Pacific
CINCPACAF... Commander-in-Chief, Pacific Air Forces
CINCPAC-CINCPOA... Commander-in-Chief, [US] Pacific Fleet and Pacific Ocean
  Areas
CINCPACFLT... Commander-in-Chief, Pacific Fleet [Navy]
CINCPACFLT ACE... Commander-in-Chief, Pacific Fleet, Alternate Command
  Element Commander (DNAB)
CINCPACFLT ECC... Commander-in-Chief, Pacific Fleet, Emergency Command
  Center Commander (DNAB)
CINCPACFLT ERS... Commander-in-Chief, Pacific Fleet, Emergency Relocation Site
  Commander (DNAB)
CINCPACFLT OAC... Commander-in-Chief, Pacific Fleet, Oceanic Airspace
  Coordinator (DNAB)
CINCPACFLTREP... Commander-in-Chief, Pacific Fleet Representative (DNAB)
CINCPACHEDPEARL... Commander-in-Chief, [US] Pacific Fleet Headquarters, Pearl
  Harbor
CINCPACREP... Commander-in-Chief, Pacific Representative (AABC)
CINCPACREPPHIL... Commander-in-Chief, Pacific Representative, Philippines
CINCPACSTAFFINSTR... Commander-in-Chief, Pacific Staff Instruction (CINC)
CINCPOA..... Commander-in-Chief, Pacific Ocean Areas
CINCPOAHEDPEARL... Commander-in-Chief, Pacific Ocean Areas Headquarters,
  Pearl Harbor
CINCRDAF ... Commander-in-Chief, Royal Danish Air Force (NATG)
CINCRDN ..... Commander-in-Chief, Royal Danish Navy (NATG)
CINCRED...... Commander-in-Chief, Readiness Command
CINCREDCOM... Commander-in-Chief, Readiness Command
CINCRNAF ... Commander-in-Chief, Royal Norwegian Air Force (NATG)
CINCRNORN... Commander-in-Chief, Royal Norwegian Navy (NATG)
CINCSA...... Commander-in-Chief, South Atlantic Station [British]
CINCSAC...... Commander-in-Chief, Strategic Air Command
CINCSO....... Commander-in-Chief, Southern Command (AFM)
CINCSOC..... Commander in Chief, [US] Special Operations [Command] (DOMA)
CINCSOUTH... Commander-in-Chief, Allied Forces, Southern Europe [NATO]
CINCSOUTH... Commander in Chief, Southern Command (AAGC)
CINCSPACE... Commander in Chief, [US] Space [Command] (DOMA)
CINCSPECOMME... Commander-in-Chief, Specified Command, Middle East
CINCSTRAT... Commander in Chief, [US] Strategic [Command] (DOMA)
CINCSTRIKE... Commander-in-Chief, Strike Command
Cinc Sup Ct Rep... Cincinnati Superior Court Reporter [Ohio] [A publication] (DLA)
Cinc Super... Cincinnati Superior Court Reporter [Ohio] [A publication] (DLA)
CINCSWPA... Commander-in-Chief, Southwest Pacific Area [World War II]
CINCTAC .... Commander-in-Chief, Tactical Air Command
CINCTRANS... Commander in Chief, [US] Transportation [Command] (DOMA)

CINCUKAIR... Commander-in-Chief, United Kingdom Air Force (NATG)
CINCUNC ..... Commander-in-Chief, United Nations Command
CINCUNCKOREA... Commander-in-Chief, United Nations Command, Korea
CINCUNK....... Commander-in-Chief, United Nations Forces in Korea (MCD)
CINCUS....... Commander-in-Chief, United States Fleet [Later, COMINCH]
CINCUSACOM... Commander in Chief, USA Command [Established in 1993]
  (DOMA)
CINCUSAFE... Commander-in-Chief, United States Air Forces in Europe
CINCUSAFLANT... Commander-in-Chief, United States Air Force, Atlantic (AFM)
CINCUSAFNSCO... Commander-in-Chief, United States Army Forces, Naval Supply
  Center, Oakland [California]
CINCUSAFSTRIKE... Commander-in-Chief, United States Air Force Strike (AFM)
CINCUSAREUR... Commander-in-Chief, United States Army, Europe
CINCUSARPAC... Commander-in-Chief, United States Army, Pacific (AABC)
CINCUSARRED... Commander in Chief, US Army Forces, Readiness [Command]
  (DOMA)
CINCUSEUCOM... Commander in Chief, US European Command (DOMA)
CINCUSNAVEUR... Commander-in-Chief, United States Naval Forces, Europe
CINCUSNAVEUR... Commander in Chief, US Naval Forces Europe (DOMA)
CINCUSNAVEUR ERS... Commander-in-Chief, United States Naval Forces, Europe,
  Emergency Relocation Site Commander (DNAB)
CINCUSNAVEUR IDHS... Commander-in-Chief, United States Naval Forces, Europe,
  Intelligence Data-Handling System (DNAB)
CINCUSTAF... Commander-in-Chief, United States/Thai Forces
CINCVNN... Commander-in-Chief, Vietnamese Navy
C in C WA ... Commander-in-Chief, Western Approaches [British World War II]
CINCWESPAC... Commander-in-Chief, Western Pacific [World War II]
CINCWESTLANT... Commander-in-Chief, Western Atlantic Area [NATO]
CIND........... Central Indiana Railway Co. [Absorbed into Consolidated Rail Corp.]
  [AAR code]
CIND........... Chief Intercept Director
CIND........... China Industrial Group [NASDAQ symbol] (SAG)
CIND........... Computer Index of Neutron Data [Atomic Energy Authority]
  [Databank] [British]
CInd........... Indio Public Library, Indio, CA [Library symbol Library of Congress]
  (LCLS)
CINDA......... Chrysler Improved Numerical Differencing Analyzer [Computer
  science]
CINDA......... Computer Index for Neutron Data [Information service or system]
  (NITA)
CINDA......... Computer Index of Neutron Data [Brookhaven National Laboratory]
  [Information service or system] (CRD)
CINDA-3G... Chrysler Improved Numerical Differencing Analyzer for Third-
  Generation Computers [Computer science]
CINDAS........ Center for Information and Numerical Data Analysis and Synthesis
  [West Lafayette, IN] [Department of Commerce] (MCD)
CINDER....... Centro Interamericano para el Desarrollo Regional [Inter-American
  Center for Regional Development] [Venezuela] (EAIO)
CINDER....... Counter Improvised Nuclear Device Emergency Response [British]
CINDI......... Central Information Dispatch [Genesis Electronics Corp.] [Folsom,
  CA] [Telecommunications] (TSSD)
CINDW........ China Industrial Grp Wrrt'A' [NASDAQ symbol] (TTSB)
CINDZ........ China Industrial Grp Wrrt'B' [NASDAQ symbol] (TTSB)
CINE......... Chemotherapy-Induced Nausea and Emesis [Medicine] (DMAA)
CINE........ Cinema (NTCM)
cine .... Cinema (WDMC)
CINE......... Cinema
CINE........ Cinematografia [Ministerio de Cultura] [Spain Information service or
  system] (CRD)
CINE........ Cinematographic (MSA)
CINE........ Cinergi Pictures Entertain [NASDAQ symbol] (TTSB)
CINE........ Cinergi Pictures Entertainment, Inc. [NASDAQ symbol] (SAG)
CINE........ Council on International Nontheatrical Events (EA)
CINECA....... Cooperative Investigation of the Northern Part of the Eastern Central
  Atlantic
CineOd........ Cineplex Odeon Corp. [Associated Press] (SAG)
CINEP .... Centre d'Ingenierie Nordique [University of Montreal] [Research
  center] (RCD)
Cinergi........ Cinergi Pictures Entertainment, Inc. [Associated Press] (SAG)
CINergy....... CINergy Corp. [Associated Press] (SAG)
CineRide...... Cinema Ride [Associated Press] (SAG)
CINF.......... Cincinnati Financial [NASDAQ symbol] (TTSB)
CINF.......... Cincinnati Financial Corp. [NASDAQ symbol] (NQ)
CINF.......... Division of Chemical Information [American Chemical Society]
  [Information service or system] (IID)
CINFAC .... Cultural [formerly, Counterinsurgency] Information Analysis Center
  [Discontinued] (MCD)
CINFO .... Chief of Information [Also, CHINFO] [Navy]
CING .... Burlington, ON [FM radio station call letters]
CinG.......... Cincinnati Gas & Electric Co. [Associated Press] (SAG)
CIng.......... Inglewood Public Library, Inglewood, CA [Library symbol Library of
  Congress] (LCLS)
CIngN.......... Northrop Institute of Technology, Inglewood, CA [Library symbol
  Library of Congress] (LCLS)
CInI............ Inyo County Free Library, Independence, CA [Library symbol Library
  of Congress] (LCLS)
CINIME .... Centro de Informacion de Medicamentos [Spanish Drug Information
  Center] [Information service or system] (IID)
Cin Law Bul... Cincinnati Law Bulletin [A publication] (DLA)
Cin Law Bull... Weekly Cincinnati Law Bulletin [Ohio] [A publication] (DLA)
Cin L Bull ... Cincinnati Law Bulletin [A publication] (DLA)
CinMic........ Cincinnati Microwave, Inc. [Associated Press] (SAG)
CinMil......... Cincinnati Milacron, Inc. [Associated Press] (SAG)
Cin Mun Dec... Cincinnati Municipal Decisions [A publication] (DLA)
Cinn......... Cincinnati [Ohio] (WGA)

Cinnam........ Cinnamomum [*Cinnamon*] [*Pharmacology*] (ROG)
CinnBel........ Cincinnati Bell, Inc. [*Associated Press*] (SAG)
CinnFin........ Cincinnati Financial Corp. [*Associated Press*] (SAG)
CINN-FM...... Hearst, ON [*FM radio station call letters*] (RBYB)
CINO............ Chief Inspector of Naval Ordnance [*British*]
CINOA.......... Confederation Internationale des Negociants en Oeuvres d'Art [*International Confederation of Art Dealers*] (EAIO)
CINOS.......... Centralized Input/Output System (DNAB)
CINP............ Collegium Internationale Neuro-Psychopharmacologicum (EA)
CINP............ Collegium International Neuro-Psychopharmacologicum
CINP............ Comite International de Liaison pour la Navigation de Plaisance [*Pleasure Navigation International Joint Committee - PNIC*] [*The Hague, Netherlands*] (EAIO)
CINPrA......... Cincinnati G & E,4% Pfd [*NYSE symbol*] (TTSB)
CINPrB......... Cincinnati G & El 4 3/4% Pfd [*NYSE symbol*] (TTSB)
CINPrG......... Cincinnati G&E 7.375% Pfd [*NYSE symbol*] (TTSB)
CINPrI.......... Cincinnati G&E 7.875% Pfd [*NYSE symbol*] (TTSB)
CINPROS..... Commission Internationale des Professionals de la Sante (EAIO)
CINPROS..... Commission Internationale des Professionels de la Sante [*International Commission of Health Professionals for Health and Human Rights - ICHP*] (EA)
CINQ............ Montreal, PQ [*FM radio station call letters*]
CINR............ Cinar Films, Inc. [*NASDAQ symbol*] (SAG)
Cin R........... Cincinnati Superior Court Reports [*Ohio*] [*A publication*] (DLA)
CinRd........... Cinema Ride [*Associated Press*] (SAG)
Cin Rep....... Cincinnati Superior Court Reports [*Ohio*] [*A publication*] (DLA)
CINRF.......... Cinar Films Cl'B' [*NASDAQ symbol*] (TTSB)
CINS............ CENTO [*Central Treaty Organization*] Institute of Nuclear Science (EY)
CINS............ Children in Need of Supervision
CINS............ Circle Income Shares, Inc. [*NASDAQ symbol*] (NQ)
CINS............ Collegium Internationale Activitatis Nervosae Superioris
CINS............ Cryogenic Inertial Navigating System
CINS............ CSIRO [*Commonwealth Scientific and Industrial Research Organization*] Infolink News [*Database*]
CINSA.......... Canadian Indian/Native Studies Association
Cin SCR....... Cincinnati Superior Court Reports [*Ohio*] [*A publication*] (DLA)
Cin SC Rep... Cincinnati Superior Court Reports [*Ohio*] [*A publication*] (DLA)
CINSGCY...... Counterinsurgency (AABC)
CinStar........ CinemaStar Luxury Theaters, Inc. [*Associated Press*] (SAG)
C Inst Crim... Code d'Instruction Criminelle [*Code of Criminal Procedure*] [*A publication*] (ILCA)
CinStr.......... CinemaStar Luxury Theaters, Inc. [*Associated Press*] (SAG)
C Instr Cr..... Code d'Instruction Criminelle [*Code of Criminal Procedure*] (DLA)
C Instr Crim... Code d'Instruction Criminelle [*Code of Criminal Procedure*] [*A publication*] (ILCA)
Cin Sup Ct... Cincinnati Superior Court Reports [*Ohio*] [*A publication*] (DLA)
Cin Sup Ct R... Cincinnati Superior Court Reporter [*Ohio*] [*A publication*] (DLA)
Cin Sup Ct Rep... Cincinnati Superior Court Reports [*Ohio*] [*A publication*] (DLA)
Cin Super Ct... Cincinnati Superior Court Reporter [*Ohio*] [*A publication*] (DLA)
Cin Super Ct Rep'r... Cincinnati Superior Court Reports [*Ohio*] [*A publication*] (DLA)
Cin Super (Ohio)... Cincinnati Superior Court Reports [*Ohio*] [*A publication*] (DLA)
C Insurance... College of Insurance (GAGS)
CINTA.......... Compania Nacional de Turismo Aereo [*Chilean airline*]
Cintas.......... Cintas Corp. [*Associated Press*] (SAG)
C Int C......... Canadian Intelligence Corps
CINTC.......... Chief, Intelligence Corps
CINTEL......... Computer Interface for Television (MCD)
CINTERFOR... Centro Interamericano de Investigacion y Documentacion sobre Formacion Profesional [*Inter-American Centre for Research and Documentation on Vocational Training - IACRDVT*] (EAIO)
CINTEX........ Catalogue Interoperability Experiment [*Marine science*] (OSRA)
CINTEX........ Catalogue Interoperability Experiment (USDC)
CINTEX........ CICAR [*Cooperative Investigation of the Caribbean and Adjacent Regions*] Intercalibration Experiment [*Marine science*] (MSC)
CINTEX........ Combined In-Port Tactical Exercise [*Navy*] (NVT)
CINTRAFOR... Center for International Trade in Forest Products [*University of Washington*]
CINU............ Centre d'Information des Nations Unies
CINVA.......... Centro Interamericano de Vivienda
CINW........... Committee for Immediate Nuclear War (EA)
CINWMD...... Committee on Interpretation of the Nation-Wide Marine Definition [*Later, COI*] (EA)
CINZ............ Commission Internationale de Nomenclature Zoologique [*International Commission on Veterinary Anatomical Nomenclature*] [*British*] (EAIO)
CIO............... Career is Over [*Business term*] (MHDB)
CIO............... Carrier Insertion Oscillator [*Telecommunications*] (EECA)
CIO............... Carrots in Oil [*Health food capsules*] [*British*]
CIO............... Central Imagery Office [*DoD*]
CIO............... Central Imagery Office [*Formerly, NRO; changed in 1992*] [*DoD*] (DOMA)
CIO............... Central Input-Output Multiplexer [*Computer science*]
CIO............... Central Intelligence Organizations [*South Vietnam*]
CIO............... Charriot Resources [*Vancouver Stock Exchange symbol*]
CIO............... Chief Immigration Officer (DS)
CIO............... Chief Information Officer [*Business term*]
CIO............... Church Information Office [*British*]
CIO............... Combat Intelligence Officer [*Navy*]
CIO............... Comite International Olympique [*International Olympic Committee*]
CIO............... Command Issuing Office [*or Officer*]
CIO............... Commission Internationale d'Optique [*International Commission for Optics - ICO*] (EAIO)
CIO............... Common Item Order (AFM)
CIO............... Community Investment Officer [*Federal Home Loan Bank Board*]
CIO............... Confederation of Indian Organizations [*British*] (DBA)
CIO............... Confirming Informal Order [*Telecommunications*] (TEL)
CIO............... Congress of Industrial Organizations [*Later, AFL-CIO*] (GPO)
CIO............... Congressus Internationalis Ornithologicus [*International Ornithological Congress - IOC*] (EA)
CIO............... Conventional International Origin
CIO............... Corporate Information Officer
CIO............... Customer Integration Office (SSD)
CIOA............ Center for Information on America [*Defunct*] (EA)
CIOA............ Committee on International Ocean Affairs [*Department of State*] (NOAA)
CIOAC.......... Central Independiente de Obreros Agricolas y Campesinos [*Member of RMALC*] [*Mexico*] (CROSS)
CIOB............ Chartered Institute of Building [*British Research center*] (DI)
CIOC............ Combat Intelligence Operations Center (MCD)
CIOC............ Craftsman of the Institute of Carpenters [*British*] (DBQ)
CIOC............ Current Intelligence Operations Center (MCD)
CIOC-FM...... Victoria, BC [*FM radio station call letters*] (RBYB)
CIOCS.......... Communications Input and Output Control System (BUR)
CIOCS.......... Communications Input-Output Control System [*Computer science*] (ECII)
CIOFF.......... Comite International des Organisateurs de Festivals de Folklore [*International Committee of Folklore Festival Organizers*] [*Canada*]
CIOFF.......... Conseil International des Organisations de Festivals de Folklore et d'Arts Traditionnels [*International Council of Folklore Festival Organizations and Folk Art - ICFFO*] (EAIO)
CIOK............ St. John, NB [*FM radio station call letters*]
CIOKKK........ Confederation of Independent Orders, Ku Klux Klan (EA)
CIOL............ Chemical Information On-Line [*Ministry of Labour*] [*Hamilton, ON*] [*Information service or system*] (IID)
CIOM............ Canadian Institute for Organization Management (AC)
CIOM............ Communications Input/Output Multiplexer
CIOMR.......... Comite Interallie des Officiers Medecins de Reserve [*Interallied Committee of Medical Reserve Officers*]
CIOMS.......... Council for International Organizations on Medical Sciences [*Geneva, Switzerland*] (EA)
CION............ Quebec, PQ [*FM radio station call letters*] (RBYB)
CIOO............ Halifax, NS [*FM radio station call letters*]
CIOP............ CAMAC [*Computer-Aided Measurement and Control*] Input-Output Processor [*Computer*]
CIOP............ Communications Input/Output Processor [*Computer science*] (NITA)
CIoP............ Preston School of Industry, Ione, CA [*Library symbol Library of Congress*] (LCLS)
CIOPAC........ Congress of Industrial Organizations, Political Action Committee [*Later, COPE*]
CIOPORA..... Communaute Internationale des Obtenteurs de Plantes Ornementales et Fruitieres aReproduction Asexuee [*International Community of Breeders of Asexually Reproduced Fruit Trees and Ornamental Varieties*] [*Geneva, Switzerland*] (EAIO)
CIOPW.......... Charcoal, Ink, Oil, Pencil, and Watercolor [*Acronym is used as title of 1931 volume containing art works by e.e. cummings*]
CIOR............ Confederation Interalliee des Officiers de Reserve [*Interallied Confederation of Reserve Officers*] (EAIO)
CIOR............ Princeton, BC [*AM radio station call letters*]
CIOS............ Combined Intelligence Objectives Subcommittee [*World War II*]
CIOS............ Conseil International pour l'Organization Scientifique [*World Management Council*] (EA)
CIOS............ Stephenville, NF [*FM radio station call letters*]
CIOSL.......... Confederacion Internacional de Organizaciones Sindicales Libres [*International Confederation of Free Trade Unions*]
CIOSTA........ Commission Internationale pour l'Organisation Scientifique du Travail en Agriculture [*International Committee of Scientific Management in Agriculture*]
CIOSYS........ Concurrent Input/Output System [*Computer science*] (PCM)
CIOTF.......... Conseil International des Organismes de Travailleuses Familiales [*International Council of Home-Help Services*]
CIOU............ Custom Input/Output Unit [*Computer science*] (IEEE)
CIOZ............ Marystown, NF [*FM radio station call letters*]
CIP............... CABI [*Commonwealth Agricultural Bureaux International*] Institute of Parasitology [*Research center British*] (IRC)
CIP............... Calf Intestinal Phosphatase [*An enzyme*]
CIP............... Canadian Insolvency Practitioner (DD)
CIP............... Canadian Institute of Planners (PDAA)
CIP............... Canadian International Paper Co.
CIP............... Canadian Premium Resources Corp. [*Vancouver Stock Exchange symbol*]
CIP............... Capital Improvements Program
CIP............... Capital Investment Plan [*FAA*] (TAG)
CIP............... Capital Investment Program
CIP............... Capsule Internal Programmer [*Aerospace*]
CIP............... Carbon-in-Pulp [*Gold ore processing*]
CIP............... Carcinogen Information Program (EA)
CIP............... Career Intern Program (MCD)
CIP............... Cargo Investigation Panel [*IATA*] (DS)
CIP............... Carriage and Insurance Paid to Named Point [*Shipping*] (DS)
CIP............... Cascade Improvement Program [*AEC*]
CIP............... Cash Index Participation [*Investment term*] (DFIT)
CIP............... Cast-Iron Pipe [*Technical drawings*]
CIP............... Cataloging in Publication [*Pronounced "sip"*] [*Formerly, CIS Library science*]
CIP............... Catholic Institute of the Press [*Later, Catholic Alliance for Communications*] (EA)
CIP............... Catholic Intercontinental Press

CIP.............. Center for Interactive Programs [*University of Wisconsin-Extension*] [*Madison*] [*Information service or system*] [*Telecommunications*] (TSSD)
CIP.............. Center for International Policy (EA)
CIP.............. Central Information Processor (MCD)
CIP.............. Central Investment Program [*Army*] (MCD)
CIP.............. Centre d'Information de Presse [*Press agency*] [*Belgium*]
CIP.............. Centro Internacional de la Papa [*International Potato Center*] [*ICSU*] (EAIO)
CIP.............. Channel Interface Processor [*Telecommunications*] (ACRL)
CIP.............. Chief Industrial Property
CIP.............. Childhood in Poetry [*A publication*]
CIP.............. Chipata [*Zambia*] [*Airport symbol*] (OAG)
CIP.............. Cipolletti [*Argentina*] [*Seismograph station code, US Geological Survey Closed*] (SEIS)
CIP.............. CIPSCO, Inc. [*NYSE symbol*] (SPSG)
CIP.............. Citizens in Politics [*Defunct*] (EA)
CIP.............. Citizen's Party (EA)
CIP.............. Civilian Instruction Program (MUGU)
CIP.............. Clarion, PA [*Location identifier FAA*] (FAAL)
CIP.............. Clarke Institute of Psychiatry [*Research center*] (RCD)
CIP.............. Classification of Instructional Programs [*Department of Education*] (OICC)
CIP.............. Class Improvement Plan [*Navy*]
CIP.............. Classroom Instruction Program [*Dialog Information Services, Inc.*]
CIP.............. Cleaning-in-Place [*Microbiology*]
CIP.............. Coast-in-Point (NVT)
CIP.............. COBOL [*Common Business-Oriented Language*] Instrumentation Package [*Computer science*]
CIP.............. Cold Isostatically Pressed [*Materials processing*]
CIP.............. College International de Podologie [*International College of Podology*]
CIP.............. Colour Image Processor [*Computer science*] (NITA)
CIP.............. Combat Intelligence Plot (NATG)
CIP.............. Combined Instrument Panel
CIP.............. Comite International de Photobiologie [*International Committee of Photobiology*]
CIP.............. Command Information Program [*Military*] (AABC)
CIP.............. Command Inspection Program [*Army*] (INF)
CIP.............. Commercial Import Program
CIP.............. Commercial Instruction Processor [*Honeywell, Inc.*]
CIP.............. Commercially Important Person
CIP.............. Commercial-Type Product (AAGC)
CIP.............. Commission Internationale du Peuplier [*International Poplar Commission*]
CIP.............. Commission Internationale Permanente pour l'Epreuve des Armes a Feu [*Permanent International Commission for the Proof of Small-Arms - PICPSA*] (EAIO)
CIP.............. Commodities Import Program [*Military*]
CIP.............. Common Input Processor
CIP.............. Common Integrated Processor [*Hughes Air Corp.*]
CIP.............. Common Intersection Point [*Graphical representation*]
CIP.............. Communications Interface and Processing System (MCD)
CIP.............. Communications Interrupt Program
CIP.............. Community Improvement Program (EA)
CIP.............. Compagnie Internationale de Papier du Canada [*Canadian International Paper Co.*]
CIP.............. Compatible Independent Peripherals (IEEE)
CIP.............. Complex Information Processing (PDAA)
CIP.............. Component Improvement Program (DOMA)
CIP.............. Component Improvement Testing
CIP.............. Composite Interface Program (SAA)
CIP.............. Comprehensive Identification Process [*Child development test*]
CIP.............. Comprehensive Index to the Publications [*A bibliographic publication*]
CIP.............. Compressor Inlet Pressure (MSA)
CIP.............. Computer Information Processing (IAA)
CIP.............. Computer-Integrated Processing (ECON)
CIP.............. Configuration Identification Package (SAA)
CIP.............. Consolidated Instrument Package [*Atmospheric research*]
CIP.............. Consolidated Intelligence Program [*Military*] (AFM)
CIP.............. Construction Industry Press [*Information service or system*] (IID)
C/IP............. Construction/Inspection Procedure (NRCH)
CIP.............. Contact Ion-Pair [*Physical chemistry*]
CIP.............. Continuation-in-Part [*Patent application*]
CIP.............. Continuous Improvement Process
CIP.............. Continuous Inflating Pressure
CIP.............. Continuous Intravenous Infusion of Propranolol [*Medicine*]
CIP.............. Contract Implementation Plan (MCD)
CIP.............. Contract Information Processor
CIP.............. Contractor Improvement Program (AAGC)
CIP.............. Control Inlet Panel [*Aerospace*] (AAG)
CIP.............. Conversion in Place [*Aerospace*] (AAG)
CIP.............. Cook Islands Party [*Political party*] (PPW)
CIP.............. Corps of Intelligence Police [*Army*] (DOMA)
CIP.............. Cost Improvement Program
CIP.............. Cost Improvement Proposal (MCD)
CIP.............. Council of International Programs (EA)
CIP.............. Council of Iron Producers [*British*] (BI)
CIP.............. Counterinsurgency Plan (CINC)
CIP.............. Country Information Package (MCD)
CIP.............. Critical Intelligence Parameter (CAAL)
CIP.............. Cured in Place [*Gaskets and seals*]
CIP.............. Current Injection Probe
CIP.............. Customer Integration Panel (SSD)
CIP.............. Custom Interest Profile

CIP.............. Freight or Carriage and Insurance Paid To _____ [*"INCOTERM," International Chamber of Commerce official code*]
CIPA........... California Independent Petroleum Association (SRA)
CIPA........... Canadian Industrial Preparedness Association (HGAA)
CIPA........... Canadian Insolvency Practitioners Association [*Association Canadienne des Professionnels de l'Insolvabilite*] (AC)
CIPA........... Canadian Institute of Public Affairs
CIPA........... Chartered Institute of Patent Agents [*British*] (BI)
CIPA........... Classified Information Procedures Act [*1980*]
CIPA........... Comite Interamericano de Proteccion Agricola [*Interamerican Committee for Crop Protection*]
CIPA........... Comite Interamericano Permanente Antiacridiana
CIPA........... Comite International de Photogrammetrie Architecturale [*International Committee of Architectural Photogrammetry*] (EAIO)
CIPA........... Comite International de Plastiques en Agriculture [*International Committee of Plastics in Agriculture*] (EAIO)
CIPA........... Committee for Independent Political Action
CIPA........... Couchiching Institue on Public Affairs (AC)
CIPA........... Council on International and Public Affairs Program (EA)
CIPA........... Prince Albert, SK [*Television station call letters*]
CIPAC......... Christians' Israel Public Action Campaign (EA)
CIPAC......... Collaborative International Pesticides Analytical Council Ltd. [*See also CIMAP*] [*Wageningen, Netherlands*] (EAIO)
CIPAE......... Cente d'Inspection et de Prevention Automobile de l'Estrie (AC)
CIPA/ICPA.... Comite International de Prevention des Accidents du Travail de la Navigation Interieure/International Committee for the Prevention of Work Accidents in Inland Navigation (EAIO)
CIPAP......... Changes in Itinerary to Proceed to Additional Places [*Military*]
CIPAS......... Center for International Programs and Studies [*University of Missouri - Rolla*] [*Research center*] (RCD)
CIPASE....... Commission Internationale des Peches de l'Atlantique Sud-Est [*International Commission for the Southeast Atlantic Fisheries - ICSEAF*] [*Madrid, Spain*] (EAIO)
CIPASH....... Committee for an International Program in Atmospheric Sciences and Hydrology [*United Nations*]
CIPC........... Canadian Institute on Pollution Control
CIPC........... Cast-in-Place Concrete [*Technical drawings*]
CIPC........... Centre International de Phenomenologie Clinique (EAIO)
CIPC........... Centre International Provisoire de Calcul
CIPC........... Combat Intelligence Proficiency Course [*Military*] (INF)
CIPC........... Combined Intelligence Priorities Committee [*Later, CIU*] [*US and British London, World War II*]
CIPC........... Comite International Permanent de la Conserve [*International Permanent Committee on Canned Foods*]
CIPC........... Comprehensive Industrywide Program of Communication [*Defunct*] (EA)
CIPC........... Port-Cartier, PQ [*AM radio station call letters*]
CIPCA......... Cogeneration and Independent Power Coalition of America (EA)
CIPCI......... Conseil International des Praticiens du Plan Comptable International [*International Council of Practitioners of the International Plan of Accounts*]
C/IPD......... Concept/International Programs Definitions [*Military*]
CIPDU......... Control Indicator Power Distribution Unit [*Military*] (CAAL)
CIPE........... Canadian Institute of Personalized Education Inc. (AC)
CIPE........... Center for International Private Enterprise [*Washington, DC*] (EA)
CIPE........... Centro Interamericano de Promocion de Exportaciones [*Inter-American Export Promotion Center*]
CIPE........... Conseil International de la Preparation a l'Enseignement [*International Council on Education for Teaching*]
CIPE........... Consejo Internacional de la Pelicula de Ensenaza [*International Council for Educational Films*]
CIPEC......... Canadian Industry Program for Energy Conservation
CIPEC......... Conseil Intergouvernemental des Pays Exportateurs de Cuivre [*Intergovernmental Council of Copper Exporting Countries - ICCEC*] (EAIO)
CIPEM......... Comite International pour les Etudes Myceniennes [*Standing International Committee for Mycenaean Studies*] (EAIO)
CIPEMAT...... Centre International pour l'Etude de la Marionnette Traditionnelle [*International Center for Research on Traditional Marionettes*]
CIPER......... Central Inventory of Production Equipment Records [*Army*]
CIPF........... Canadian Injury Prevention Foundation (AC)
CIPF........... Confederation Internationale du Commerce des Pailles, Fourrages, Tourbes et Derives [*International Straw, Fodder and Peat Trade Confederation*] [*EC*] (ECED)
CIPFA......... Chartered Institute of Public Finance and Accountancy [*Formerly, IMTA*] [*British*]
CIPFS......... Configuration Item Product Fabrication Specification (MCD)
CIPG........... Communications and Information Processing Group [*Rensselaer Polytechnic Institute*] [*Research center*] (RCD)
CIPG........... Cure-In-Place Gasket
CIPH........... Canadian Institute of Plumbing & Heating [*L'Institut Canadien de Plomberie et de Chauffage*] (AC)
CIPH........... Comite International des Pharmaciens Homeopathiques [*International Committee of Homeopathic Pharmacists*] [*Karlsruhe, Federal Republic of Germany*] (EAIO)
CIPHI......... Canadian Institute of Public Health Inspectors [*Institut Canadien des Inspecteurs en Hygiene Publique*] (AC)
CIPHONY..... Cipher and Telephony Equipment [*Military*]
CIPIC......... Center for Image Processing and Integrated Computing [*University of California at Davis*] [*Research center*] (RCD)
CIPL........... Comite International Permanent des Linguistes [*Permanent International Committee of Linguists*] (EAIO)
CIPM.......... Comite International des Poids et Mesures [*International Committee on Weights and Measures*]

CIPM............ Companion of the Institute of Personnel Management [Formerly, FIPM] [British]
CIPM............ Council for International Progress in Management (EA)
CIPME.......... Committee on International Policy in the Marine Environment [National Council on Marine Resouces and Engineering Development] (GFGA)
CIPMP .... Commission Internationale pour la Protection de la Moselle Contre la Pollution [International Commission for the Protection of the Moselle Against Pollution - ICPMP] (EA)
CIPN .... Chronic Inflammatory Polyneuropathy [Medicine] (DMAA)
CIPN .... Pender Harbour, BC [FM radio station call letters]
CIPO .... Criminal Investigations Policy and Oversight (AAGC)
CIPOM .... Computers, Information Processing, and Office Machines
CIPP............ Commission Indo-Pacific des Peches [Indo-Pacific Fishery Commission - IPFC] (EAIO)
CIPP............ Comprehensive Incomes and Prices Policy (DICI)
CIPP............ Context, Input, Process, Product [Computer science]
CIPP............ Cured-In- Place Pipe [Civil Engineering]
CIPPP .... Cooperative International Pupil-to-Pupil Program (EA)
CIPPRS........ Canadian Image Processing and Pattern Recognition Society
CIPR............ Command Indicator Performance Review (MCD)
CIPR............ Consolidated Intelligence Periodic Summary
CIPR............ Continuous In-Flight Performance Recorder [Aviation] (PDAA)
CIPR............ Contractor Insurance and Pension Review [DoD]
CIPR............ Corporate Industrial Preparedness Representative [Military]
CIPR............ Cubic Inches per Revolution (MCD)
CIPRA.......... Cast Iron Pipe Research Association [Later, DIPRA] (EA)
CIPRA.......... Commission Internationale pour la Protection des Regions Alpines [International Commission for the Protection of Alpine Regions] (EAIO)
CIPREC .... Conversational and Interactive Project Evaluation and Control System [IBM Corp.]
Ciprico.......... Ciprico, Inc. [Associated Press] (SAG)
CIPS............ Canadian Information Processing Society [Toronto, ON]
CIPS............ Cesium Ion Propulsion System
CIPS............ Childhood in Poetry Supplement [A publication]
CIPS............ Commonwealth International Philatelic Society [Defunct] (EA)
CIPS............ Corporate Information Processing Standards (MCD)
CIPS............ Counterintelligence Periodic Summary (MCD)
CIPSCO........ CIPSCO, Inc. [Associated Press] (SAG)
CIPSH .... Conseil International de la Philosophie et des Sciences Humaines [International Council for Philosophy and Humanistic Studies] (EAIO)
CIPT............ Comite International des Telecommunications de Presse (EAIO)
CIPTO .... Centre d'Intervention et de Prevention en Toxicomanie de l'Outaouais (AC)
CIPTPP .... Cooperative International Pupil-to-Pupil Program (EA)
CIPW .... Cross, Iddings, Pirsson, and Washington [Norms] [Geology]
CIQ.............. Confoederatio Internationalis ad Qualitates Plantarum Edulium Perquirendas [International Association for Quality Research on Food Plants]
CIQ.............. Customs, Immigration, and Quarantine
CIQB .... Barrie, ON [FM radio station call letters] (RBYB)
CIQC .... Montreal, PQ [AM radio station call letters]
CIQM .... London, ON [FM radio station call letters]
CIR.............. Arctic Circle Service, Inc. [ICAO designator] (FAAC)
CIR.............. Cage Inventory Record [Shipping] (DS)
CIR.............. Cairo [Illinois] [Airport symbol] (AD)
CIR.............. Cairo, IL [Location identifier FAA] (FAAL)
CIR.............. Canada-India Reactor
CIR.............. Canadian Institute for Research
CIR.............. Cardiac Inward Rectifier [Biochemistry]
CIR.............. Cargo Integration Review (MCD)
CIR.............. Carrier-to-Interference Ratio [Computer science]
CIR.............. Center for Immigrants Rights (EA)
CIR.............. Center for Information Research [Research center] (IID)
CIR.............. Center for Inter-American Relations
CIR.............. Center for International Relations [University of California, Los Angeles] [Research center] (RCD)
CIR.............. Center for International Research [Bureau of the Census] [Information service or system] (IID)
CIR.............. Center for Investigative Reporting (EA)
CIR.............. Centre International de l'Eau et l'Assainissement [IRC International Water and Sanitation Centre] (EAIO)
CIR.............. Change Initiation Request (KSC)
CIR.............. Change to Initial Release (MCD)
CIR.............. Characteristic Instants of Restitution [Telecommunications] (OA)
CIR.............. Chiredzi [Rhodesia] [Seismograph station code, US Geological Survey] (SEIS)
CIR.............. Cimarron Petroleum Ltd. [Toronto Stock Exchange symbol]
CIR.............. Circa [or Circiter or Circum] [About (used with dates denoting approximate time)] [Latin]
Cir............... Circimus [Constellation]
CIR.............. Circle
cir............... Circle (WDMC)
Cir............... Circle (DD)
CIR.............. Circle
CIR.............. Circuit (AFM)
Cir............... Circuit Court (DLA)
Cir............... Circuit Court of Appeals (DLA)
CIR.............. Circular (AABC)
cir............... Circular (WDMC)
cir............... Circulation (WDMC)
CIR.............. Circulation (ADA)
cir............... Circumference (WDMC)

CIR.............. Circus
CIR.............. Circus Circus Enterp [NYSE symbol] (TTSB)
CIR.............. Circus Circus Enterprises, Inc. [NYSE symbol] (SPSG)
CIR.............. Cirrhosis [Medicine]
Cir............... Cirripedia [Quality of the bottom] [Nautical charts]
CIR.............. Citizen Initiated Referendums [Political party Australia]
CIR.............. Coherent Imaging RADAR
CIR.............. Collection Intelligence Requirements (NVT)
CIR.............. Color Infrared [Image]
CIR.............. Commissie voor Internationaal Recht [United Nations]
CIR.............. Commissioners of Inland Revenue [British]
CIR.............. Commission Internationale du Riz [International Rice Commission - IRC] [United Nations] (EAIO)
CIR.............. Commission on Industrial Relations [Department of Employment] [British]
CIR.............. Commission on Intergovernmental Relations
CIR.............. Committed Information Rate [Telecommunications]
CIR.............. Committee of Interns and Residents (EA)
CIR.............. Committee on Changing International Realities (EA)
CIR.............. Committee on International Relations [National Education Association] (AEBS)
CIR.............. Communications Industries Report [A publication] (EAAP)
CIR.............. Computer Information Resources
CIR.............. Computer-Integrated Research
CIR.............. Computerized Information Research (IAA)
CIR.............. Configuration Inspection Report (MCD)
CIR.............. Conformance Inspection Record (SAA)
Cir............... Connecticut Circuit Court Reports [A publication] (DLA)
CIR.............. Consignment Item Request (MCD)
CIR.............. Consortium for Information Resources, Framingham, MA [OCLC symbol] (OCLC)
CIR.............. Consumer Information Regulation [National Highway Traffic Safety Administration]
CIR.............. Continuing Intelligence Requirement (MCD)
CIR.............. Continuous Infrared (MCD)
CIR.............. Controlled Impact Reentry (MCD)
CIR.............. Controlled Intact Reentry (IAA)
CIR.............. Convention des Institutions Republicaines [Convention of Republican Institutions] [France Political party] (PPE)
CIR.............. Cooled Infrared Radiometer (PDAA)
CIR.............. Coordinator for International Relations [Australia]
CIR.............. Corotating Interaction Region [Planetary science]
CIR.............. Corotation Inclination Resonance [Planetary science]
CIR.............. Cosmetic Ingredient Review (EA)
CIR.............. Cost Information Reports [DoD]
CIR.............. Courant-Isaacson-Rees [Method]
CIR.............. Court of Industrial Relations [Philippines]
CIR.............. Crime on Indian Reservation
CIR.............. Current Industrial Reports [Census Bureau]
CIR.............. Current Instruction Register
CIR.............. Customer Inspection Record
CIR.............. Cycle Time and Inventory Reduction (MCD)
CIR.............. Cylindrical Internal Reflection [Spectroscopy]
Cir............... United States Court of Appeals [For the Circuit indicated] (AAGC)
CIRA .... Canadian Industrial Relations Association [See also ACRI]
CIRA .... Central Intelligence Retirees Association (EA)
CIRA .... Centre International de Recherches sur l'Anarchisme [International Research Center on Anarchism] [Geneva, Switzerland] (EAIO)
CIRA .... Citizen Initiated Referendum Alliance [Australia Political party]
CIRA .... Comite International Radioaeronautique
CIRA .... Command Information Requirement Analysis (MCD)
CIRA .... Commission Internationale pour la Reglementation des Ascenseurs et Monte-Charge [International Committee for Lift Regulations - ICLR] (EAIO)
CIRA .... Committee on International Reference Atmosphere
CIRA .... Computerised Instrumented Residential Audit [Energy auditing]
CIRA .... Conference of Industrial Research Associations (DGA)
CIRA .... Cooperative Institute for Research in the Atmosphere [Colorado State University, NOAA] [Research center] (RCD)
CIRA .... COSPAR [Committee on Space Research] International R eference Atmosphere
CIRA .... Montreal, PQ [FM radio station call letters] (RBYB)
CIRAC .... Canadian Independent Recording Artists in Concert [Pronounced "kerrack"]
CIRAC .... Canadian Institute for Research in Atmospheric Chemistry [York University]
CIRAD .... Corporation for Information Systems Research and Development (MCD)
CIRADS........ Counterinsurgency Research and Development System (MCD)
CIRAF .... Conseil International pour la Recherche en Agroforesterie [International Council for Research in Agroforestry] (EAIO)
CIRAG.......... Career Information Resource Advisory Group [Canada]
CIRAL .... Centre International de Recherche en Amenagement Linguistique (AC)
CIRANT........ Circular Antenna [Electromagnetism] (IAA)
CIRAS .... Center for Industrial Research and Service
CIRAST........ Centre d'Intervention et de Recherche pour l'Amelioration des Situations de Travail [University of Quebec at Rimouski] [Research center] (RCD)
CIRB .... Canadian Industrial Renewal Board [Montreal, PQ]
CIRB .... Centre International de Recherches sur le Bilinguisme [International Center for Research on Bilingualism] [Universite Laval, Quebec] [Canada]
CIRB .... Corpus Inscriptionum Regni Bosporani (BJA)
CIRB .... Crop Insurance Research Bureau [Indianapolis, IN] (EA)

CIR BKR ...... Circuit Breaker [*Technical drawings*] (DAC)
CIRC .... Central Information Reference and Control (DIT)
CIRC .... Central Intelligence Retrieval Center (MCD)
CIRC .... Central Iowa Railway Co. [*AAR code*]
CIRC .... Centralized Information Reference and Control
CIRC .... Chrysler Information Resources Center [*Pronounced "serk"*]
CIRC .... Circa [*or Circiter or Circum*] [*About (used with dates denoting approximate time)*] [*Latin*]
Circ .... Circimus [*Constellation*]
CIRC .... Circle
circ .... Circle (WDMC)
CIRC .... Circuit
CIRC .... Circular (AFM)
circ .... Circular (WDMC)
CIRC .... Circularization Burn [*Orbital Maneuvering Subsystem 2*] [*NASA*] (NASA)
CIRC .... Circulation (EY)
CIRC .... Circulation Input Recording Center [*Data processing system*]
CIRC .... Circulation System [*Computer science*] (NITA)
Circ .... Circulatory [*Medicine*] (DAVI)
CIRC .... Circumcision [*Medicine*]
CIRC .... Circumference
circ .... Circumference (WDMC)
CIRC .... Circumflex Coronary Artery [*Anatomy*]
CIRC .... Circumstance (AABC)
CIRC .... Circus (WDAA)
CIRC .... Comite Internacional de la Cruz Roja [*Switzerland*]
CIRC .... Critical Item Review Committee [*Air Force*] (AFIT)
CIRC .... Cross-Interleaved Reed-Solomon Code [*Computer science*]
circ .... Input Capacitance (IDOE)
CIRCA .... Center for Instructional and Research Computing Activities [*University of Florida*] [*Research center*] (RCD)
CIRCA .... Centre International de Recherche, de Creation, et d'Animation [*France*]
CIRCA .... Computerized Information Retrieval and Current Awareness (MHDI)
CIRCAL .... Circuit Analysis [*Computer science*]
CIRCARC .... Circular Arc
CIRCCE .... Confederation Internationale de la Representation Commerciale de la Communaute Europeenne [*International Confederation of Commercial Representation in the European Community*]
CIRCCO .... Cente d'Information et de Recherche en Consommation de Charlevoix-Ouest (AC)
Circ Dec ...... Ohio Circuit Decisions [*A publication*] (DLA)
CIRCE .... Catalogo Italiano Riviste su Calcolatore Elettronico [*Database*] [*Editrice Bibliografica*] [*Italian*] [*Information service or system*] (CRD)
CIRC E .... Circuit Edges [*Bookbinding*] (DGA)
CIRCE .... Circumstance
CIRCE .... Computerized Information Retrieval and Contract Entry [*Computer science*]
CIRCE .... Computerized Issue of Results and Certificates for Entries (PDAA)
CIRCFCE .... Circumference (ROG)
CircFn .... Circle Financial Corp. [*Associated Press*] (SAG)
CircInc .... Circle Income Shares [*Associated Press*] (SAG)
CIR/CIRD .... Circle/Dashed Circle (MCD)
CIRCL .... Center for Interdisciplinary Research in Computer-Based Learning [*University of Delaware*] [*Research center*] (RCD)
CIRCL .... Circle [*Commonly used*] (OPSA)
CIRCL .... Circular
CIRCLE .... Circle [*Commonly used*] (OPSA)
CircleK .... Circle K Corp. [*Associated Press*] (SAG)
CIRCLES .... Circles [*Commonly used*] (OPSA)
CIRCLTR .... Circular Letter [*Military*]
CIRCM .... Circumference
CIRCOL .... Central Information Reference and Control On-Line System (MCD)
CIRCOM .... Centre International de Recherches sur les Communautes Cooperatives Rurales [*International Research Center on Rural Cooperative Communities*]
CIRCOM .... Cooperative Internationale de Recherche et d'Action en Matiere de Communication (EAIO)
Circon .... Circon Corp. [*Associated Press*] (SAG)
CircRsh .... Circuit Research [*Associated Press*] (SAG)
CIRCS .... Circumstances [*Slang*] (DSUE)
CircSy .... Circuit Systems, Inc. [*Associated Press*] (SAG)
Circt .... Circuit (DD)
Cir Ct App .... Circuit Court of Appeals (DLA)
Cir Ct Dec.... Circuit Court Decisions [*A publication*] (DLA)
Cir Ct Dec (Ohio)... Circuit Court Decisions [*Ohio*] [*A publication*] (DLA)
Cir Ct R Ohio .... Ohio Circuit Court Reports [*A publication*] (DLA)
Cir Ct R .... Circuit Court Reports [*Ohio*] [*A publication*] (DLA)
CirCty .... Circuit City Stores, Inc. [*Associated Press*] (SAG)
CIRCUIT .... Curriculum Improvement Resulting from Creative Utilization of Instructional Two-Way Television Project [*Wisconsin*] (EDAC)
CIRCUM .... Circumambulation [*Freemasonry*] (ROG)
circum .... Circumcision [*Urology*] (DAVI)
CIRCUM .... Circumference (KSC)
CIRCUMJAC... Circumjacent [*Military*]
CIRCUS .... Calculation of Indirect Resources and Conversion to Unit Staff [*Computer science*]
CIRCUS .... Central Information Retrieval and Cartridge Update System [*Computer science*] (NITA)
CIRCUS .... Circuit Simulator (MHDB)
Circus .... Circus Circus Enterprises, Inc. [*Associated Press*] (SAG)
CIRDAP .... Centre for Integrated Rural Development for Asia and the Pacific

CIRDI .... Centre International pour le Reglement des Differends Relatifs aux Investissements [*International Center for Settlement of Investment Disputes*]
CIRE .... City of Refuge National Historic Park
CIRE .... Companion, Institute of Radio Engineers
CIREC .... Center for the Improvement of Reasoning in Early Childhood (EA)
CIREC .... Commercial-Investment Real Estate Council (EA)
CIREEH .... Carolina Institute for Research on Early Education for the Handicapped (EDAC)
CIREJ .... Commercial Investment Real Estate Journal [*Commercial-Investment Real Estate Council*] [*A publication*]
CI Rel .... Certificate in Industrial Relations
CIRELFA .... Conseil International pour le Recherche en Linguistique Fondamentale et Appliquee [*International Research Council on Pure and Applied Linguistics - IRCPAL*] (EA)
CIREM .... Centre International de Recherches et d'Etudes en Management [*International Centre for Research and Studies in Management*] [*Canada*]
CIREN .... Crash Injury Research and Engineering Network [*Medicine*] (DMAA)
CIRENC .... Cirencester [*Urban district in England*]
CIREP .... Circular Error Probability [*Military*] (DNAB)
CIREQ .... Cooperative d'Information et de Recherche Ecologiste du Quebec [*Environmental Information & Research Group*] (AC)
CIRES .... Chief Inspector of Royal Engineer Stores [*British military*] (DMA)
CIRES .... Communication Instructions for Reporting Enemy Sightings [*Navy*]
CIRES .... Computerized Information Retrieval Service [*University of Houston Libraries*] (OLDSS)
CIRES .... Cooperative Institute for Research in Environmental Sciences
CIRF .... Centralized Intermediate Repair Facility
CIRF .... Centre International d'Information et de Recherche sur la Formation Professionnelle
CIRF .... Consolidated Intermediate Repair Facility
CIRF .... Corn Industries Research Foundation [*Later, CRA*] (EA)
CIRF .... Customer Integrated And/Or Reference File System (IAA)
CIRFS .... Comite International de la Rayonne et des Fibres Synthetiques [*International Rayon and Synthetic Fibres Committee - IRSFC*] (EAIO)
CIRG .... Commonwealth Internet Reference Group [*Information service or system*]
CIRG .... Contract Information Reporting Groups [*Navy*] (AFIT)
CIRGA .... Critical Isotope Reactor, General Atomics
CIRHS .... Critical Items and Residual Hazards List (MCD)
CIRI .... Canadian Investor Relations Institute [*Institut Canadien de Relations Avec les Investisseurs*] [*Formerly, National Investor Relations Institute Canada*] (AC)
CIRI .... Caribbean Industrial Research Institute
CIRI .... Construction Industries of Rhode Island (SRA)
CIRIA .... Construction Industry Research and Information Association [*Research center British*] (IRC)
CIRID .... Center for Interdisciplinary Research on Immunologic Diseases [*Department of Health and Human Services*] (GRD)
CIRIL .... College International de Recherches Implantaires et Lariboisiere [*Rouen, France*] (EAIO)
CIR-IR .... Cylindrical Internal Reflectance - Infrared Spectroscopy
CIRIS .... Central Inertial Reference Instrumentation System (MCD)
CIRIS .... Completely Integrated Range Instrumentation System [*NASA*]
CIRIS .... Computerised Information Retrieval in Schools [*Project*] (AIE)
CIRIS .... Consolidated Intelligence Resource Information System [*Air Force*] (MCD)
CIRK .... Edmonton, AB [*FM radio station call letters*]
CIRKS .... Under the Circumstances [*Slang*] (ROG)
CIRL .... Canadian Institute of Resources Law [*University of Calgary*] [*Research center*] (RCD)
CIRL .... Central Iowa Regional Library [*Library network*]
CIRL .... Current Intelligence Requirement List (MCD)
CIRM .... Celestial Infrared Mapping [*Air Force*] (MCD)
CIRM .... Centro Internazionale Radio-Medico [*International Radio Medical Center; gives emergency medical advice to ships at sea*]
CIRM .... Comite International Radio Maritime [*International Maritime Radio Association*] (EAIO)
CIRMIL .... Circular Mil [*Wire measure*] (IAA)
cir mil .... Circular Mil (IDOE)
CIRMS .... Celestial Infrared Measurement System
CIRO .... Consolidated Industrial Relations Office (MUGU)
CIRO .... Crash Injury Research Organization [*Cornell University*]
CIRO .... St. Georges De Beauce, PQ [*FM radio station call letters*]
Cir Od NWP... Circular Orders, Northwestern Provinces [*India*] [*A publication*] (ILCA)
Cir Ord NWP... Circular Orders, Northwestern Provinces [*India*] [*A publication*] (DLA)
CIRP .... Canadian Industrial Renewal Program
CIRP .... College International de Recherches pour la Production [*Later, CIESTPM*] (EAIO)
CIRP .... Conseil International des Ressources Phytogenetiques [*International Board for Plant Genetic Resources - IBPGR*] (EAIO)
CIRP .... Cooperative Institutional Research Program [*UCLA*]
CIRPA .... Canadian Independent Record Producers Association
CIRPA .... Canadian Independent Record Production Association (AC)
CIRQ .... Cirque Energy Ltd. [*NASDAQ symbol*] (SAG)
CIRQF .... Cirque Energy Ltd [*NASDAQ symbol*] (TTSB)
CirqueE .... Cirque Energy Ltd. [*Associated Press*] (SAG)
CIRR .... Center on International Race Relations [*University of Denver*]
CIRR .... Chattahoochee Industrial Railroad [*AAR code*]
CIRR .... CorFile on Disc, Corporate and Industry Research Reports (IID)

CIRR .... Corporate and Industry Research Reports Index [*JA Micropublishing, Inc.*] [*Database*]

CIRRPC .... Committee on Interagency Radiation Research and Policy Coordination

Cirrus.......... Cirrus Logic, Inc. [*Associated Press*] (SAG)

CIRS .... Chemical Information Retrieval System [*Army*] (IID)

CIRS .... Chesapeake Information Retrieval Service (IID)

CIRS .... Circles [*Postal Service standard*] (OPSA)

CIRS .... Circles

CIRS .... Community Information and Referral Service [*United Way/Crusade of Mercy*] [*Information service or system*] (IID)

CIRS .... Computerized Information Retrieval Service [*California State University, Fullerton*] (OLDSS)

CIRS .... Construction Industry Reform Strategy

CIRS .... Containment Iodine Removal System [*Nuclear energy*] (NRCH)

CIRS .... Contractor Inventory Redistribution System (MCD)

CIRSA .... Canadian In-Line & Roller Skating Association (AC)

CIRSE .... Cardiovascular and Interventional Radiology Society of Europe (EA)

CIRSSE .... NASA Center for Intelligent Robotic System for Space Exploration [*Rensselaer Polytechnic Institute*] [*Research center*] (RCD)

CIRSV .... Carnation Italian Ringspot Virus [*Plant pathology*]

CIRSYS .... Circulation System (ADA)

CIRT .... Conference on Industrial Robot Technology

CIRT .... International Transboundary Resource Center [*University of New Mexico Law School*] (CROSS)

CIRTEF .... Conseil International des Radios-Televisions d'Expression Francaise [*International Association of Broadcasting Manufacturers - IABM*] (EAIO)

CIRTS .... Centre of Information Resource & Technology, Singapore [*Information service or system*] (IID)

CIRUR .... Comite Intergouvernemental de Recherches Urbaines et Regionales [*Intergovernmental Committee on Urban and Regional Research*] [*Canada*]

CIRV .... Toronto, ON [*FM radio station call letters*]

CIRVIS .... Communications Instructions for Reporting Vital Intelligence Sightings [*Military*]

CIRX .... Prince George, BC [*FM radio station call letters*]

CIS.............. Canadian Institute for Scientific and Technical Information - CISTI [*UTLAS symbol*]

CIS.............. Canadian Institute of Surveying

CIS.............. Canadian Iris Society

CIS.............. Cancer Information Service [*HEW*]

CIS.............. Cane Invert Syrup [*Food sweetener*]

CIS.............. Canfield Instructional Styles Inventory [*Teacher evaluation test*]

CIS.............. Canton Island [*Phoenix Islands*] [*Airport symbol*] (AD)

CIS.............. Carcinoma In Situ [*Oncology*]

CIS.............. Card Information Structure [*Computer science*]

CIS.............. Career Information System [*National Career Information System*] [*Eugene, OR*] [*Information service or system*] (IID)

CIS.............. Cargo Information System [*Aviation*] (DA)

CIS.............. Cassette Information Services

CIS.............. Casualty Information System (MCD)

CIS.............. Catalina Island [*California*] [*Seismograph station code, US Geological Survey*] (SEIS)

CIS.............. Cataloging in Source [*Later, CIP*] [*Library science*]

CIS.............. Catholic Information Society [*Defunct*] (EA)

CIS.............. CDIS Software, Inc. [*Vancouver Stock Exchange symbol*]

CIS.............. CD-ROM [*Compact Disk Read-Only Memory*] Continuous Information Service [*International Data Group - IDG*] [*Information service or system*] (IID)

CIS.............. Center for Imaging Science [*University of Chicago*] [*Research center*] (RCD)

CIS.............. Center for Immigration Studies (CROSS)

CIS.............. Center for Information Sciences (KSC)

CIS.............. Center for Instructional Services [*Purdue University*] [*Research center*] (RCD)

CIS.............. Center for Integrated Systems [*Stanford University*] [*Research center*] (RCD)

CIS.............. Center for Intelligence Studies (EA)

CIS.............. Center for International Security [*Defunct*] (EA)

CIS.............. Center-of-Inertia System

CIS.............. Center of International Studies [*MIT*] [*Research center*] (MCD)

CIS.............. Central Information Service [*The British Council*] (IID)

CIS.............. Central Information Service [*University of London*] (IID)

CIS.............. Central Inhibitory State [*Neurology*] (DAVI)

CIS.............. Central Installation Supply [*Air Force*]

CIS.............. Central Instructor School

CIS.............. Central Integration Site (NASA)

CIS.............. Centre d'Informations Spectroscopiques [*Spectroscopic Information Center*] [*Group for the Advancement of Spectroscopic Methods and Physicochemical Analysis*] [*Information service or system*] (IID)

CIS.............. Centre for Information on Standardization and Metrology [*Information service or system*] (IID)

CIS.............. Centre for Information Services [*Council for Scientific and Industrial Research - CSIR*] [*South Africa*] [*Information service or system*] (IID)

CIS.............. Centre for Institutional Studies [*North East London Polytechnic*] [*British*] (CB)

CIS.............. Centre for International Studies [*Canada*] (CROSS)

CIS.............. Centre International d'Informations de Securite et d'Hygiene du Travail [*International Occupational Safety and Health Information Center*] [*International Labour Office*] (IID)

CIS.............. Centro Internacional de Informacion sobre Seguridad e Higiene del Trabajo [*International Occupational Safety and Health Information Center*] [*Spain*]

CIS.............. Certificate Issuing System (ACRL)

CIS.............. Cesium Ion Source

CIS.............. Chaillotine Air Service [*France ICAO designator*] (FAAC)

CIS.............. Change Impact Summary (NASA)

CIS.............. Channel and Isolation Supervision [*Telecommunications*] (TEL)

CIS.............. Character Instruction Set (IEEE)

CIS.............. Charles Ives Society (EA)

CIS.............. Chartered Institute of Secretaries [*British*] (BI)

CIS.............. Chemical Information Services [*Stanford Research Institute*] (IID)

CIS.............. Chemical Information Systems, Inc. [*Fein-Marquart Associates*] [*Information service or system*] (IID)

CI(S) .... Chemical Injection (System) [*Nuclear energy*] (NRCH)

CIS.............. Chemically-Powered Interorbital Space Shuttle (MCD)

CIS.............. Chinese Industrial Standards

CIS.............. Christmas Island Station [*Military*] (SAA)

CIS.............. Chromosome Information System [*Genetics*]

CIS.............. Cingulate Sulcus (DMAA)

CIS.............. Cities in Schools (EA)

CIS.............. Clinical Immunology Society (EA)

CIS.............. Clinical Information System (MCD)

CIS.............. Close-In Support [*Military*] (AFM)

CIS.............. Coal Industry Society [*British*] (BI)

CIS.............. College of the Siskiyous Library, Weed, CA [*OCLC symbol*] (OCLC)

CIS.............. Combat Identification System

CIS.............. Combat Intelligence System (MCD)

CIS.............. Combined Intelligence Staff [*World War II*]

CIS.............. Command Information Systems [*Army*]

CIS.............. Command Instrument System

CIS.............. Commercial Industrial Services Program [*Navy*]

CIS.............. Commercial Instruction Set

CIS.............. Commonwealth of Independent States [*Formerly, Soviet Union*]

CIS.............. Communication and Instrumentation System [*Also, C & IS*] [*NASA*]

CIS.............. Communication Industrial Services

CIS.............. Communication Information System (IEEE)

CIS.............. Communications Interface System (MCD)

CIS.............. Community Improvement Scale [*Psychology*]

CIS.............. Community Industry Scheme [*Department of Employment*] [*British*]

CIS.............. Community Information Section [*Public Library Association*]

CIS.............. Community Information Services

CIS.............. Compensated Imaging System (MCD)

CIS.............. Complex Impedance Spectroscopy

CIS.............. Component Identification Sheet (MCD)

CIS.............. Composition Information Services [*Commercial firm*]

CIS.............. CompuServe Information Service [*CompuServe, Inc.*] (IID)

CIS.............. Computer and Information Sciences Research Laboratory [*University of Alabama in Birmingham*] [*Research center*] (RCD)

CIS.............. Computer-Based Information Services [*Information service or system*] (IID)

CIS.............. Computer Independent Specification

CIS.............. Computer Information Services [*Corp. for Public Broadcasting - CPB*] [*Information service or system*] (IID)

CIS.............. Computerized Information Service [*Public Library of Columbus and Franklin County*] (OLDSS)

CIS.............. Computing and Information Services [*McMaster University*] [*Canada*] (IRC)

CIS.............. Computing & Information Systems [*East Carolina University*] [*Research center*] (RCD)

CIS.............. Concord Fabrics CI'A' [*AMEX symbol*] (TTSB)

CIS.............. Concord Fabrics, Inc. [*AMEX symbol*] (SPSG)

CIS.............. Conductor, Insulator, Semiconductor (IAA)

CIS.............. Conference of Internationally-Minded Schools

CIS.............. Configuration Information System

CIS.............. Configuration Item Specification

CIS.............. Congressional Information Service [*Publisher*] (AAGC)

CIS.............. Congressional Information Service, Inc. [*Bethesda, MD*] [*Database producer*] [*Information service or system*]

CIS.............. Constant Initial State Spectroscopy (MCD)

CIS.............. Constant Injection System [*Automotive engineering*]

CIS.............. Consumer Information Series [*National Institute of Standards and Technology*]

CIS.............. Consumer Information Service [*Electronic mail*]

CIS.............. Consumer Information System

CIS.............. Contact Image Sensing [*Reprography*]

CIS.............. Containment Isolation Signal [*Nuclear energy*] (NRCH)

CIS.............. Containment Isolation System [*Nuclear energy*] (NRCH)

CIS.............. Continuous Injection System [*Automotive engineering*]

CIS.............. Continuous Interleaved Sampling

CIS.............. Contract Information System [*Environmental Protection Agency*] (GFGA)

CIS.............. Contract Items Specification (MCD)

CIS.............. Contractor's Information Submittal [*or Submitted*] (MCD)

CIS.............. Control Indicator Set (MCD)

CIS.............. Convention Information System (IAA)

CIS.............. Cooperative Independent Surveillance (DA)

CIS.............. Cooperative Insurance Society [*British*]

CIS.............. Copper-Indium-Diselenide [*Inorganic chemistry*]

CIS.............. Core Instrumentation Subsystem (MCD)

CIS.............. Corporate Information System (MCD)

CIS.............. Corrosion Interception Sleeve

CIS.............. Cost Information System

CIS.............. Cost Inspection Service [*Navy*]

CIS.............. Council for Inter-American Security (EA)

CIS............. Council for Intersocietal Studies (EA)
CIS............. Counter Information Services [*British*]
CIS............. Country Intelligence Study (MCD)
CIS............. Coupled Impedance Synthesis
CIS............. Court Information Service [*South Australia*]
CIS............. Creative Imagination Scale [*Psychology*] (EDAC)
CI's............. Crossability Indices [*Botany*]
CIS............. Cross Industry Standard
CIS............. Cryogenic Instrumentation System
CIS............. Cryogenic Interferometer Spectrometer (MCD)
CIS............. Cue Indexing System (IEEE)
CIS............. Cultural Information Service (EA)
CIS............. Current Index to Statistics [*MathSci database subfile*] (IT)
CIS............. Current Information Section (ADA)
CIS............. Current Information Selection [*IBM Technical Information Retrieval Center*] [*White Plains, NY*]
CIS............. Current Information Service [*Australia*]
CIS............. Curriculum and Instructional Standards [*Military*] (DNAB)
CIS............. Customer Information Squawk Sheet
CIS............. Customer Information System [*IBM Corp.*]
CIS............. Customer Item Squawks
CIS............. Custom Integrated System [*Computer science*] (PDAA)
CIS............. NIH [*National Institutes of Health*]-EPA Chemical Information System [*Falls Church*] [*Environmental Protection Agency Information service or system*] (IID)
CISA............ Canadian Industrial Safety Association (PDAA)
CISA............ Canadian Intercollegiate Sailing Association
CISA............ Casting Industry Suppliers Association (EA)
CISA............ Center for International and Strategic Affairs [*Research center*] (RCD)
CISA............ Certified Information Systems Auditor [*EDP Auditors Foundation*] [*Designation awarded by*]
CISA............ Commission Internationale pour le Sauvetage Alpin [*International Commission for Alpine Rescue*]
CISA............ Council for Independent School Aid (EA)
CISA-7 .... Lethbridge, AB [*Television station call letters*]
CISAC .... Changchu International Symposium on Analytical Chemistry [*1990*]
CISAC .... Committee on International Security and Arms Control [*National Academy of Sciences*]
CISAC .... Confederation Internationale des Societes d'Auteurs et Compositeurs [*International Confederation of Societies of Authors and Composers*]
CISAF........... Conseil International des Services d'Aide Familiale [*International Council of Homehelp Services - ICHS*] [*Driebergen-Rijsenburg, Netherlands*] (EAIO)
CISAI .... Comite International de Soutien aux Antifascistes Iberiques
CISAM .... Compressed Index Sequential Access Method
CIS & DB .... Comprehensive Information System and Database
CIS & P ...... Canadian Institute of Surveying and Photogrammetry
CISAP .... Congres International des Sciences de l'Activite Physique [*International Congress of Physical Activity Sciences*] [*Canada*]
CIS B .... CompuServe Information Service B [*Communications protocol*] (CDE)
CISBH .... Comite International de Standardisation en Biologie Humaine [*International Committee for Standardization in Human Biology*]
CISC............ Canadian Institute of Steel Construction
CISC............ Christmas Island Services Corp.
CISC............ Clearinghouse for Innovation in Scientific Communication
CISC............ Comite International de Sociologie Clinique [*International Committee on Clinical Sociology - ICCS*] (EA)
CISC............ Complex Instruction Set Computer (MCD)
CISC........... Compound Induction Step Control (PDAA)
CISC............ Confederation Internationale des Syndicats Chretiens [*International Federation of Christian Trade Unions*]
CISC............ Conference Internationale du Scoutisme Catholique [*International Conference of Catholic Scouting*]
CISC............ Construction Industry Stabilization Committee [*Abolished, 1974*]
CISC............ Continental Information Systems Corp. [*NASDAQ symbol*] (SAG)
CISC............ Continental Info Sys [*NASDAQ symbol*] (TTSB)
CISC............ Gibsons, BC [*FM radio station call letters*]
CISC............ Groupe International de Sociologie (EAIO)
CISCA .... Cast Iron Seat Collectors Association (EA)
CISCA .... Ceilings and Interior Systems Construction Association (EA)
CISCA .... Cisplatin, Cyclophosphamide, Adriamycin [*Antineoplastic drug regimen*]
CISCE.......... Comite International pour la Securite et la Cooperation Europeennes [*International Committee for European Security and Co-Operation - ICESC*] (EAIO)
Cisco .... Cisco Systems, Inc. [*Associated Press*] (SAG)
CISCO .... Civil Service Catering Organization [*British*]
CISCO .... Commodity Information Services Co. (IID)
CISCO .... Compass Integrated System Compiler (IEEE)
CIS-COBOL... Compact Interactive Standard for Common Business-Oriented Language [*Computer science*] (HGAA)
CIS-COMMS... Communications and Information Services - Communications
CISCS .... Construction Interface Surveillance Control Section (SAA)
CISD .... Critical Incident Stress Debriefing
cis-DDP .... cis-Diamminodichloroplatinum [*Cisplatin*] [*Also, CDDP, CPDD, CPT, DDP, P*] [*Antineoplastic drug*]
CISE............ Colleges, Institutes, and Schools in Education (AIE)
CISE............ Consortium for International Studies Education (EA)
CISE............ Sechelt, BC [*FM radio station call letters*]
CISem........... Corpus Inscriptionum Semiticarum [*A publication*] (OCD)
CISEP.......... Cellulose Industry Standards Enforcement Program (EA)
CISER .... Cornell Institute for Social and Economic Research [*Cornell University*] [*Research center*] (RCD)

CI/SERE .... Counterinsurgency/Survival, Evasion, Resistance, and Escape (DNAB)
CISET .... Centro Internazionale di Studi sull'Economia Turistica [*International Center of Studies on the Tourist Economy*] [*University of Venice*] [*Italy*]
CISET .... Committee on International Science, Engineering, and Technology [*US government interagency committee*] [*Washington, DC*]
CISEUA .... Centro de Investigaciones sobre Estados Unidos de America [*Mexico/US relations*] [*Member of UNAM*] (CROSS)
CISF............ Combat Information Systems Flight [*Military*]
CISF............ Confederation Internationale des Sages Femmes
CISH .... Comite International des Sciences Historiques [*International Committee of Historical Sciences*]
CISH .... Comite International de Standardisation en Hematologie [*International Committee for Standardization in Haematology*] (EAIO)
CISH .... Competitive in Situ Hybridization (DMAA)
CISHEC .... Chemical Industries Association's Safety and Health Council [*British*]
CISI............. C.I.S. Technologies [*NASDAQ symbol*] (TTSB)
CISI............. CIS Technologies, Inc. [*NASDAQ symbol*] (NQ)
CISI............. Compagnie Internationale de Services et Informatique [*International Information Services Company*] [*Information service or system France*] (IID)
CISID .... Congressional Information Sources, Inventories, and Directories (MCD)
CISI-ELECNUL... Compagnie Internationale de Services en Informatique-Electrical and Nuclear Energy [*France*] [*Information service or system*] (NITA)
CISI-IAI........ Compagnie Internationale de Services en Informatique [*Information service or system*] [*France*] (NITA)
CISIL........... Centralized Integrated System Compiler (MCD)
CISIL........... Centralized Integrated Systems for International Logistics
CISIL........... Consolidated Interchangeable and Substitute Item List
CISILI.......... Crash Injury Scale Intermediate Level Investigation (PDAA)
CISJA........... Comite International de Solidarite avec la Jeuness Algerienne
CISK............ Conditional Instability of the Second Kind
CISL............ Confederation Internationale des Syndicats Libres [*International Confederation of Free Trade Unions*]
CISL............ Richmond, BC [*AM radio station call letters*]
CISLANM ..... Committee in Solidarity with Latin American Nonviolent Movements (EA)
CISLB.......... Comite International pour la Sauveguarde de la Langue Bretonne [*International Committee for the Defense of the Breton Language - ICDBL*] (EAIO)
CISLE.......... Centre International des Syndicalistes Libres en Exil [*International Center of Free Trade Unionists in Exile*] [*Defunct*]
CISM........... Canadian Institute of Surveying and Mapping (EAIO)
CISM........... Centre International des Sciences Mecaniques
CISM........... Confederation Internationale des Societes Musicales [*International Confederation of Societies of Music - ICSM*] (EA)
CISM........... Conseil International du Sport Militaire [*International Military Sports Council*] [*Belgium*]
CISM........... Montreal, PQ [*FM radio station call letters*]
CISN........... Edmonton, AB [*FM radio station call letters*]
CISNU.......... Confederation of Iranian Students [*Germany*] (PD)
CISO........... Centre International de Solidarite Ouvriere (AC)
CISO........... Comite International des Sciences Onomastiques [*International Committee of Onomastic Sciences*]
CISOB .... Counsellor of the Incorporated Society of Organ Builders [*British*] (DI)
CISOC .... Computerized Information System of Organic Chemistry [*Developed in China*] [*Computer science*]
CISP............ Cast-Iron Soil Pipe (DNAB)
CISP............ Centro de Informacion y Solidaridad con el Paraguay [*Switzerland*]
CISP............ Commercial Item Support Program [*DoD*] (RDA)
CISP............ Council for Intercultural Studies and Programs [*Defunct*] (EA)
CISP............ Pemberton, BC [*FM radio station call letters*]
CISPCI .... Commission Internationale pour la Sauvegarde du Patrimoine Culturel Islamique [*International Commission for the Preservation of Islamic Cultural Heritage - ICPICH*] (EA)
CISPEC .... Configuration Item Specification (MCD)
CISPES .... US Committee in Solidarity with the People of El Salvador (EA)
CISPF.......... Cast Iron Soil Pipe Foundation [*Defunct*] (EA)
CISPI .... Cast Iron Soil Pipe Institute (EA)
CISPM .... Confederation Internationale des Societes Populaires de Musique
CISPO .... Combat Identification System Program Officer (MCD)
CISPO .... Combat Identification Systems Project Office [*Army*]
CISPR .... Comite International Special des Perturbations Radioelectriques [*International Special Committee on Radio Interference*] (EAIO)
CISq........... Communication Installation Squadron [*Air Force*]
CISQ........... Squamish, BC [*FM radio station call letters*]
CISR........... Canadian Institute for Synchrotron Radiation
CISR........... Center for Information Systems Research [*Massachusetts Institute of Technology*] [*Research center*] (RCD)
CISR........... Center for Instructional Services and Research [*Memphis State University*] [*Research center*] (RCD)
CISR .... Center for International Systems Research
CISR .... Communication Intelligence Security Regulation (MCD)
CISR .... Conference Internationale de Sociologie Religieuse [*International Conference of Sociology of Religion*]
CISR .... Configuration Index and Status Report (KSC)
CISR .... Santa Rosa, BC [*Television station call letters*]
CISRC .... Computer and Information Science Research Center [*Ohio State University*] [*Columbus, OH*]
CISRG .... Cartographic Information Systems Research Group [*Hull University*] [*British*] (NITA)

CISRI .... Central Iron and Steel Research Institute [China]
CISS .... Canadian Information Sharing Service
CISS .... Canadian Institute of Strategic Studies (EAIO)
CISS .... Casualty Information Support System [Military] (DNAB)
CISS .... Centaur Integrated Support Structure (MCD)
CISS .... Center for Information Systems Security [DoD] (DOMA)
CISS .... Centre for International and Strategic Studies [York University] [Research center] (RCD)
CISS .... Chromosomal In Situ Suppression [Genetics]
CISS .... Collectif d'Informations Sexuelles et Sexologiques [Collective of Sexual Information and Sexology] [Canada]
CISS .... Colonie Interim Storage Site [Colonie, NY] (GAAI)
CISS .... Colonie Interim Storage Site (DOGT)
CISS .... Colonie Interim Storage Site [Department of Energy]
CISS .... Comite International des Sports des Sourds [International Committee of Sports for the Deaf] (EAIO)
CISS .... Common Internet Scheme Syntax (DMAA)
CISS .... Communication and Instrumentation Support Services [NASA] (KSC)
CISS .... Computer Industry Software, Services, and Products [Information service or system] (IID)
CISS .... Conference Internationale de Service Social [International Conference of Social Service]
CISS .... Conferencia Interamericana de Seguridad Social [Inter-American Conference on Social Security - IACSS] (EAIO)
CISS .... Conseil International des Sciences Sociales [International Social Science Council - ISSC] (EAIO)
CISS .... Contract Information Subsystem (MCD)
CISS .... Contract Items Specification and Schedule (MCD)
CISS .... Toronto, ON [FM radio station call letters]
CISST .... Center for Interdisciplinary Study of Science and Technology [Northwestern University] [Research center] (RCD)
CISSY .... Campaign to Impede Sex Stereotyping in the Young [British] (DI)
CIST .... Canadian Institute of Science and Technology Ltd.
CIST .... Centro Internazionale di Studi sui Trasporti [International Center for Transportation Studies - ICTS] (EAIO)
CIST .... Chief Inspector of Supplementary Transport [British military] (DMA)
Cist .... Cistellaria [of Plautus] [Classical studies] (OCD)
CIST .... Command Instrument System Trainer [Army]
CIST .... Coorbital Interceptor Scoring Technique
CISTC .... Council on International Scientific and Technological Cooperation
CIS Tch .... CIS Technologies, Inc. [Associated Press] (SAG)
CISTI .... Canada Institute for Scientific and Technical Information [National Research Council of Canada] (IID)
CISTIP .... Committee on International Scientific and Technical Information Programs [Commission on International Relations] (PDAA)
CISTIP .... Committee on International Scientific and Technical Information Programs [National Academy of Sciences - National Research Council]
CISTISER ..... CISTI [Canada Institute for Scientific and Technical Information] Serials [Information service or system] (CRD)
CISTOD .... Confederation of International Scientific and Technological Organizations for Development [ICSU] [Paris, France] [Defunct] (EAIO)
CISTR .... Continuous Ideally Stirred Tank Reactor [Chemical engineering]
CISU .... Canadian Industrial Sweetener Users (AC)
CISV .... Children's International Summer Villages International Association [Newcastle-Upon-Tyne, England] (EAIO)
CISW .... California Institute of Social Welfare
CISW .... Whistler, BC [FM radio station call letters]
CISWO .... Coal Industry Social Welfare Organisation [British]
CISYO .... Committee for the Implementation of the Standardized Yiddish Orthography (EA)
CIT .... Advisory Committee for Innovation and Technology Transfer [EC] (ECED)
CIT .... Caliente Resources Ltd. [Vancouver Stock Exchange symbol]
CIT .... California Institute of Technology [Also, CALIT, CALT, CALTECH]
CIT .... Call-In Time [Military communications]
CIT .... Canadian Import Tribunal [QL Systems Ltd.] [Information service or system] (CRD)
CIT .... Canberra Institute of Technology [Australia]
CIT .... Career Interest Test [Vocational guidance test]
CIT .... Carnegie Institute of Technology [Later, Carnegie-Mellon University] [Pennsylvania]
CIT .... Case Institute of Technology [Later, Case Western Reserve University] [Ohio]
CIT .... Catalog Input Transmittal (DNAB)
CIT .... Center for Information Technology [Stanford University] [Stanford, CA] (CSR)
CIT .... Center for Irrigation Technology [California State University, Fresno] [Research center] (RCD)
CIT .... Central Independent Television [British] (DI)
CIT .... Centro de Informacion Tecnica [Technical Information Center] [University of Puerto Rico] [Information service or system] (IID)
CIT .... Charcoal Inhalation Tester (PDAA)
CIT .... Chartered Institute of Transport (EAIO)
CIT .... Chita [Former USSR Seismograph station code, US Geological Survey] (SEIS)
CIT .... Citadel (ROG)
CIT .... Citation (AFM)
cit .... Citation (WDMC)
CIT .... Citato [Cited] [Latin] (ADA)
cit .... Citator [or Cited In or Citing] [Legal term] (DLA)
Cit .... Citator and Indian Law Journal [1908-14] [A publication] (DLA)
cit .... Cited (WDMC)
CIT .... Citizen (AFM)

CIT .... Citrate
cit .... Citron [Philately]
Cit .... Citrulline [An amino acid]
CIT .... City-Jet Luftverklehrsges, GmbH [Austria ICAO designator] (FAAC)
CIT .... Cleaned in Transit
CIT .... Coherent Interpretation Time (MCD)
CIT .... Combined Intermittent Therapy (DAVI)
CIT .... Comite Interministeriel des Terres [Interdepartmental Committee on Land] [Canada]
CIT .... Comite International des Transports Ferroviaires [International Rail Transport Committee] (EAIO)
CIT .... Comite International de Television [International Television Committee]
CIT .... Comite International Tzigane [International Gypsy Committee]
CIT .... Command Interface Test (KSC)
CIT .... Commission on Instructional Technology (EA)
CIT .... Commission on Insurance Terminology of the American Risk and Insurance Association
CIT .... Communications and Information Technology Research [British]
CIT .... Communications Interface Table (MCD)
CIT .... Compact Ignition TOKAMAK [Toroidal Kamera Magnetic] [Plasma physics]
CIT .... Compagnie Industrielle de Telecommunication [Computer manufacturer] [France]
CIT .... Component Improvement Testing [Military]
CIT .... Compression in Transit
CIT .... Compressor Inlet Temperature (NG)
CIT .... Computer-Integrated Telephony [Computer science]
CIT .... Computer Interface Technology (IEEE)
CIT .... Computer Interface Terminal (CET)
CIT .... Computerized Industrial Tomography [Nondestructive testing method]
CIT .... Computing and Information Technology [Princeton University] [Research center] (RCD)
CIT .... Conductivity Indicator Transmitter [Nuclear energy] (NRCH)
CIT .... Configuration Identification Tables (AABC)
CIT .... Conseil International des Tanneurs [International Council of Tanners - ICT] (EAIO)
CIT .... Consejo Internacional del Trigo [International Wheat Council - IWC] (EAIO)
CIT .... Contact Ion Thruster
CIT .... Controlled Interceptor Trainer [Aerospace] (AAG)
CIT .... Convective Instability Top (PDAA)
CIT .... Conventional Insulin Treatment [Medicine]
CIT .... Cornell Information Technologies [Information service or system] (IID)
CIT .... Corporate Income Tax [Economics]
CIT .... Corporate Information Technology
CIT .... Counselor-in-Training [for summer camps]
CIT .... Counterintelligence Team (NVT)
CIT .... Court of International Trade. Reports [A publication] (DLA)
CIT .... Crack Initiation Temperature (PDAA)
CIT .... Cranfield Institute of Technology [British] (ARC)
CIT .... Cranfield Institute of Technology [California]
CIT .... Critical Incident Technique [Department of Health and Human Services] (GFGA)
CIT .... Critical Item Tag (MCD)
CIT .... Inter-American Travel Congresses (EA)
CITA .... Canadian Independent Telephone Association
CITA .... Canadian Institute for Theoretical Astrophysics [University of Toronto] [Research center] (RCD)
CITA .... Canadian International Trade Association (AC)
CITA .... Chartered Institute of Transport in Australia
CITA .... Citation (AABC)
CITA .... CITATION Computer Sys [NASDAQ symbol] (TTSB)
CITA .... Citation Computer Systems [NASDAQ symbol] (SAG)
CITA .... Collectif d'Information et de Travail Anti-Imperialiste [Collective of Information and Anti-Imperialist Labour] [Canada]
CITA .... Comite International de l'Inspection Technique Automobile [International Motor Vehicle Inspection Committee] [Verviers, Belgium] (EAIO)
CITA .... Commercial and Industrial-Type Activity (AABC)
CITA .... Commercial or Industrial-Type Activities (AAGC)
CITA .... Commission Internationale de Tourisme Aerien
CITA .... Committee for the Implementation of Textile Agreements
CITA .... Confederation Internationale des Ingenieurs Agronomes [International Confederation of Technical Agricultural Engineers]
CITA .... Confederation Internationale des Ingenieurs et Techniciens de l'Agriculture [International Confederation of Agricultural Engineers and Technicians] [Switzerland]
CITA .... Conference Internationale des Trains Speciaux d'Agences de Voyages [International Conference on Special Trains for Travel Agencies] (EAIO)
CITA .... Court Interpreters and Translators Association (EA)
CITAB .... Computer Information and Training Assistance for the Blind
Citadel .... Citadel Holding Corp. [Associated Press] (SAG)
CITAM .... Centre International de la Tapisserie Ancienne et Moderne [Switzerland]
CITAR .... Center for Interactive Technology, Applications, and Research [University of South Florida] [Research center] (RCD)
CITAR .... Computers in Training as a Resource (AIE)
CITARS .... Crop Identification Technology Assessment for Remote Sensing [NASA]
CITAT .... Container Inspection Training and Assistance Team [RSPA] (TAG)
Citation .... Citation Corp. Alabama [Associated Press] (SAG)
CitatnCpt...... Citation Computer Systems [Associated Press] (SAG)

CITB............ Construction Industry Training Board (MCD)
CITBA.......... Customs and International Trade Bar Association (EA)
CITC............ Canadian Institute of Travel Counsellors
CITC............ Centre for Information Technology and Communications
    [*Queensland*] [*Australia Information service or system*]
CITC............ Computer Indicator Test Console (DNAB)
CITC............ Construction Industry Training Center (MCD)
CITCE.......... Comite International de Thermodynamique et de Cinetique Electro-
    Chimiques [*International Committee of Electro-Chemical
    Thermodynamics and Kinetics*]
CITCM......... Canberra Income Tax Circular Memorandum [*Australia A publication*]
CiTCM......... Chinese Materials and Research Aids Service Center, Inc., Taipei,
    Taiwan, China [*Library symbol Library of Congress*] (LCLS)
Citcp .... Citicorp [*Associated Press*] (SAG)
CITCP.......... Civil Industrial Technologies Cooperation Plan [*Framework
    agreement for conducting cooperative global research*]
CITD............ Center for International Trade Development [*Oklahoma State
    University*] [*Research center*] (RCD)
CITE............. Canadian Institute of Technology for the Environment (AC)
CITE............. Capsule Integrated Test Equipment [*Aerospace*]
CITE............. Cargo Integration Test Equipment (NASA)
CITE............. Certified Incentive Travel Executive [*Society of Incentive Travel
    Executi ves*] [*Designation awarded by*]
CITE............. Chemical Instrumentation Test and Evaluation [*Marine science*]
    (OSRA)
CITE............. Chemical Instrumentation Test and Evaluation [*NASA*] (USDC)
CITE............. Coalition for International Trade Equity
CITE............. Compression Ignition and Turbine Engine
CITE............. Computer-Integrated Test Equipment
CITE............. Consolidated Index of Translations into English
CITE............. Contractor Independent Technical Effort [*DoD*]
CITE............. Controller Input Test Equipment
CITE............. Coordinated Information Transfer for Education (AEBS)
CITE............. Coordinating Information for Texas Educators [*Texas State Education
    Agency*] [*No longer available*] [*Information service or system*]
    (IID)
CITE............. Council of Institute of Telecommunication Engineers
CITE............. Current Information Tapes for Engineering
CITE............. Current Information Transfer in English
CITE............. Institute of Transportation Engineers [*District 7*] [*Canada*]
CITE............. Montreal, PQ [*FM radio station call letters*]
CITE-1......... Sherbrooke, PQ [*FM radio station call letters*]
CITEC.......... Contractor Independent Technical Effort (IEEE)
CITECH .... Cawkell Information & Technology Services, Ltd.
    [*Telecommunications*] (IID)
CITED.......... Copyright in Transmitted Electronic Documents
CITEJA........ Comite International Technique d'Experts Juridiques Aeriens
    [*International Technical Committee of Aerial Legal Experts*]
CITEL .... Conference on Inter-American Telecommunications [*Organization of
    American States*] [*Telecommunications*]
CITEN.......... Comite International de la Teinture et du Nettoyage [*International
    Committee for Dyeing and Dry Cleaning*]
CITEP.......... Community Integrated Training and Education Program
CITERE........ Centre d'Information en Temps Reel pour l'Europe [*European Center
    for Information in Real Time*] [*France*] [*Information service or
    system*] (IID)
CITES.......... Convention on International Trade in Endangered Species [*Of wild
    fauna and flora*]
CITES.......... Current Intelligence Traffic Exploitation System (PDAA)
CITF............ CDOS [*Customer Data and Operations System*] Integration and Test
    Facility (SSD)
CITF............ City Industry Task Force [*Confederation of British Industry*]
CITF............ Combat Identification Tank Force [*Army*]
CITF............ Combat Identification Task Force [*Army*] (DOMA)
CITF............ Commercial and Industrial-Type Functions [*Army*] (MCD)
CITF............ Community Integrated Training Type Functions
CITF............ Quebec, PQ [*FM radio station call letters*]
CitFed.......... CitFed Bancorp, Inc. [*Associated Press*] (SAG)
CitFFin......... Citizens First Financial Corp. [*Associated Press*] (SAG)
CITG............ Current Intelligence Targets Groups [*Military*]
CITH............ Centre d'Information Textile Habillement [*Textile and Clothing
    Information Center*] [*Information service or system*] (IID)
CITHA .... Confederation of International Trading Houses Associations [*The
    Hague, Netherlands*] (EAIO)
CITI............. Center for Information Technology Integration [*University of Michigan*]
    [*Research center*] (RCD)
CITI............. Citicasters, Inc. [*NASDAQ symbol*] (SAG)
CITI............. Citicasters Inc.'A' [*NASDAQ symbol*] (TTSB)
CITI............. Confederation Internationale des Travailleurs Intellectuels
    [*International Confederation of Professional and Intellectual
    Workers*]
CITI............. Congress of the International Theater Institute
CITI............. Winnipeg, MB [*FM radio station call letters*]
CITIBASE ..... Citibank Economic Database [*Citibank, NA*] [*New York, NY*]
    [*Information service or system*] (IID)
CitiBnc........ Citi Bancshares, Inc. [*Associated Press*] (SAG)
CITIC........... China International Trust Investment Corp.
Citicast........ Citicasters, Inc. [*Associated Press*] (SAG)
Citicorp........ Citicorp [*Associated Press*] (SAG)
Cities E Rom Prov... [*The*] Cities of the Eastern Roman Provinces [*A publication*]
    (OCD)
CITIGO .... Citizens for Good Government [*Political fund of Ling-Temco-Vought,
    Inc.*]
CITIN .... Citation Insurance [*NASDAQ symbol*] (TTSB)

CIT in Canada... Chartered Institute of Transport in Canada [*Institut Agree des
    Transports du Canada*] (AC)
CITIS........... Centralized Integrated Technical Information System (DIT)
CITIS........... Construction Industry Translation and Information Services [*Dublin,
    Ireland*]
CITIS........... Contractor Integrated Technical Information Systems [*Military*]
Citisave....... Citisave Financial Corp. [*Associated Press*] (SAG)
CitizBkg ...... Citizens Banking Corp. [*Associated Press*] (SAG)
CitizInc .... Citizens, Inc. [*Associated Press*] (SAG)
CITL........... Canadian Industrial Traffic League
CITL........... Crew-in-the-Loop
CITL........... Lloydminster, AB [*Television station call letters*]
CITLV.......... Citrus Tatter Leaf Virus [*Plant pathology*]
CITM........... Certified International Traffic Manager [*American Society of
    Internationa l Executives, Inc.*] [*Designation awarded by*]
CITM........... Charge Injection Transistor Memory [*Electronics*] (NITA)
CITM........... One Hundred Mile House, BC [*Television station call letters*]
CITM-1........ Williams Lake, BC [*Television station call letters*] (RBYB)
CITM-2........ Quesnel, BC [*Television station call letters*] (RBYB)
CITN........... CitnIns [*NASDAQ symbol*] (SAG)
CitnIns .... CitnIns [*Associated Press*] (SAG)
CITO........... Ceramics Industry Training Organisation [*British*] (AIE)
CITO........... Timmins, ON [*Television station call letters*]
CITO-2 .... Kearns, ON [*Television station call letters*]
CITO DISP .. Cito Dispensateur [*Dispense Quickly*] [*Pharmacy*]
CITP........... Capillary Isotachophoresis [*Biochemistry*]
CITP........... Chronic Idiopathic Thrombocytopenic Purpura [*Medicine*]
CITP........... Citizen Involvement Training Program (EA)
CITP........... Comite International des Telecommunications de Presse
    [*International Press Telecommunications Council - IPTC*] (EAIO)
CITP........... Community Infrastructure Training Program
CITP........... Contractor Input to Total Performance [*DoD*]
CITP........... Corporate Information Technology Plan
CITPA.......... International Committee of Paper and Board Converters in the
    Common Market (ECED)
CITPA.......... International Confederation of Paper and Board Converters in the
    European Commuity [*Germany*] (EA)
CITR........... Canadian Institute for Telecommunications Research [*Research
    center*] (RCD)
CITR........... Court of International Trade. Rules [*A publication*] (DLA)
CITR........... Vancouver, BC [*FM radio station call letters*]
CITRAC .... Central Integrated Traffic Control (PDAA)
CITRE.......... Cooperative Investigations of Tropical Reef Ecosystems [*Smithsonian
    Institution*] (MSC)
CITRIC .... Citriculture
CITS........... Central Integrated Test System
CITS........... Certificate of Individual Theological Studies (PGP)
CITS........... China International Travel Service
CITS........... Commission Internationale Technique de Sucrerie [*International
    Commission of Sugar Technology*] (EAIO)
CITS........... Corporate Information Technology Strategy
CITS........... Current Imaging Tunneling Spectroscopy
CITS-Mux.... Central Integrated Test System Multiplex (PDAA)
CITSS.......... Centre International pour la Terminologie des Sciences Sociales
    [*France*] (EAIO)
CITT .... Canadian Institute for Theatre Technology (AC)
CITT .... Canadian Institute of Traffic and Transportation
CITT .... Coping in Tough Times (AC)
CITTA .... Confederation Internationale des Fabricants de Tapis et de Tissus
    d'Ameublement [*International Confederation of Manufacturers of
    Carpets and Furnishing Fabrics*] (EAIO)
CITTC.......... Computer Industry Training and Technology Corp., Inc. [*Commercial
    firm Australia*]
CITU........... Centre of Indian Trade Unions
CITU........... Confederation of Independent Trade Unions (EAIO)
CITUC .... Council of International Trade Union Cooperation [*Sweden*] (EAIO)
CITV........... Commander's Independent Thermal Viewer [*Military*] (RDA)
CITV........... Edmonton, AB [*Television station call letters*]
CITW........... Canadian Institute of Treated Wood
CITY........... Avalon Community Services, Inc. [*NASDAQ symbol*] (SAG)
CITY........... Avalon Community Svcs [*NASDAQ symbol*] (TTSB)
CITY........... Toronto, ON [*Television station call letters*]
City Civ Ct Act... New York City Civil Court Act (DLA)
City Crim Ct Act... New York City Criminal Court Act (DLA)
City Ct .... City Court (DLA)
City Ct R...... City Court Reports [*New York*] [*A publication*] (DLA)
City Ct Rep... City Court Reports [*New York*] [*A publication*] (DLA)
City Ct Rep Supp... City Court Reports, Supplement [*New York*] [*A publication*]
    (DLA)
City Ct R Supp... City Court Reports, Supplement [*New York*] [*A publication*] (DLA)
City Ct Supp (NY)... City Court Reports, Supplement [*New York*] [*A publication*]
    (DLA)
City Hall Rec (NY)... City Hall Recorder [*New York City*] [*A publication*] (DLA)
City Hall Rep... City Hall Reporter (Lomas) [*New York City*] [*A publication*] (DLA)
City Hall Rep (NY)... City Hall Reporter (Lomas) [*New York City*] [*A publication*]
    (DLA)
City H Rec ... New York City Hall Recorder [*A publication*] (DLA)
City H Rep... City Hall Reporter (Lomas) [*New York City*] [*A publication*] (DLA)
CityNC .... City National Corp. [*Associated Press*] (SAG)
City Rec....... New York City Record [*A publication*] (DLA)
City Rec (NY)... New York City Record [*A publication*] (DLA)
CitzFnCp..... Citizens Financial Corp. [*Associated Press*] (SAG)
CITZN.......... Citizen
CitzUt.......... Citizens Utilities [*Associated Press*] (SAG)
CitzUt.......... Citizens Utilities Trust [*Associated Press*] (SAG)

CIU............	Cable Interface Unit (DGA)
CIU............	Career Information Unit (OICC)
CIU............	Central Interpretation Unit [Military]
CIU............	Chlorella International Union [Later, MIU]
CIU............	Chronic Idiopathic Urticaria [Dermatology] (DAVI)
CIU............	Cima Resources Ltd. [Vancouver Stock Exchange symbol]
CIU............	Club & Institute Union Ltd. [British] (BI)
CIU............	Combined Intelligence Unit [Formerly, CIPC] [RAF] [British]
CIU............	Command Interface Unit (KSC)
CIU............	Communications Interface Unit
CIU............	Community Information Utility (BUR)
CIU............	Computer Interface Unit
CIU............	Congress of Independent Unions (EA)
CIU............	Congress of Irish Unions
CIU............	Console Intelligence Unit (MCD)
CIU............	Consolidated Undrained Triaxial Test with Pore Pressure Measurements [Nuclear energy] (NUCP)
CIU............	Control Indicator Unit (OA)
CIU............	Controller Interface Unit (MCD)
CIU............	Convergencia i Unio [Convergence and Union] [Spain Political party] (PPE)
CIU............	Coopers' International Union of North America
CIU............	Council for International Understanding (EA)
CIU............	Coupler Interface Unit (MCD)
CIU............	Sault Ste. Marie [Michigan] [Airport symbol] (OAG)
CIUC..........	Chronic Idiopathic Ulcerative Colitis [Gastroenterology]
CIUC..........	Commission of International Union of Crystallography [British]
CIUG..........	Cognos International Users' Group (AC)
CIUG..........	Contractor Inventory Utilization Group (MCD)
CIUL..........	Council for International Urban Liaison (EA)
CIUNA........	Coopers' International Union of North America (EA)
CIUS	Canadian Institute of Ukrainian Studies [Institut Canadien d'Etudes Ukrainiennes] (AC)
CIUS	Conseil International des Unions Scientifiques [International Council of Scientific Unions]
CIUS	Corps Interim Upgrade System (MCD)
CIUS	County Intermediate Unit Superintendents [of NEA] [Later, AASA] (EA)
CIUSS	Catholic International Union for Social Service
CIUT..........	Toronto, ON [FM radio station call letters]
CIUTI	Conference Internationale Permanente de Directeurs d'Instituts Universitaires pour la Formation de Traducteurs et d'Interpretes [Standing International Conference of the Directors of University Institutes for the Training of Translators and Interpreters] (EAIO)
Civ	Arret de la Chambre Civile de la Cour de Cassation [Decision of the Court of Appeal, Civil Division] [French] (ILCA)
CIV............	Capital Improved Value (ADA)
CIV............	Center Island Vessel [Nuclear energy] (NRCH)
CIV............	Central Inspectorate of Vehicles [British military] (DMA)
CIV............	City Imperial Volunteers [Military unit] [British]
CIV............	Civil (AFM)
Civ	Civil Appeals [A publication] (DLA)
CIV............	Civil Aviation Authority of New Zealand [ICAO designator] (FAAC)
Civ	Civile [Civil] [Latin] (DLA)
CIV............	Civilian (AFM)
CIV............	Civilisations [A publication]
CIV............	Civilization (ROG)
CIV............	Code Inserter Verifier [Air Force]
CIV............	Combined Intercept Valve [Nuclear energy] (NRCH)
CIV............	Combined Intermediate Valve [Nuclear energy] (NRCH)
CIV............	Commander's Independent Viewer [Army] (INF)
CIV............	Commission Internationale du Verre [International Commission on Glass - ICG] (EAIO)
CIV............	Containment Isolation Valve [Nuclear energy] (IEEE)
CIV............	Convention Internationale Concernant le Transport des Voyageurs et des Bagages par Chemins de Fer [International Convention Concerning the Carriage of Passengers and Luggage by Rail]
CIV............	Corona Inception Voltage (PDAA)
CIV............	Critical Impact Velocity (MCD)
CIV............	CRREL [Cross-Leveling, Redistribution, Replenishment, and Excessing] Instrumented Vehicle [Automobile traction testing]
CIV............	Fourth Cranial Nerve [Anatomy] (DMAA)
CIV............	Indian Valley Colleges Library, Novato, CA [OCLC symbol] (OCLC)
CIV............	Ivory Coast [ANSI three-letter standard code] (CNC)
Civ	Texas Civil Appeals Reports [A publication] (DLA)
CIVA..........	Charge-Induced Voltage Alteration [Electronics]
CIVA..........	Rouyn, PQ [Television station call letters]
CIVACTGP....	Civic Action Group [Military] (CINC)
CIVAD	Civil Administrator (CINC)
Civ & Cr LS...	Civil and Criminal Law Series [India] [A publication] (DLA)
CIVB..........	Rimouski, PQ [Television station call letters]
CIVC..........	Civic Bancorp [NASDAQ symbol] (SAG)
CIVC..........	Trois-Rivieres, PQ [Television station call letters]
CIVCLO	Civilian Clothing
Civ Code Prac...	Civil Code of Practice [A publication] (DLA)
CIV CONF.....	Civilian Confinement [Military] (DNAB)
Civ Ct.........	Civil Court (DLA)
Civ Ct Rec ...	Civil Court of Record (DLA)
CIVD	Cold-Induced Vasodilation
Civ D Ct ...	Civil District Court (DLA)
CIVDEF.......	Civil Defence
CIVEMP.......	Civilian Employee (MCD)
CIVENG.......	Civil Engineering
CIVENGLAB...	Civil Engineering Laboratory [Navy] (DNAB)
CIVENGRLAB...	Civil Engineering Laboratory [Also, CEL] [Navy] (MUGU)
CIVENGSq...	Civil Engineering Squadron [Air Force]
CIVEX.........	Civilian Extraction [Nuclear energy]
CIVF..........	Baie-Trinite, PQ [Television station call letters]
CIVG	Sept-Iles, PQ [Television station call letters]
CIVH.........	Vanderhoof, BC [AM radio station call letters]
CIVIC	Civic Issues Voluntary Information Council [Michigan]
CivicBc	Civic Bancorp [Associated Press] (SAG)
CiViDiC	Cisplatin, Vindesine, Dacarbazine [Antineoplastic drug regimen]
Civil Pro R...	Civil Procedure Reports [New York] [A publication] (DLA)
CIVIS	Center for Intelligent Vision and Information Systems
CIVISION......	Enciphered Television (MCD)
CIVITAS	Center for Scientific Information on Vivisection (EA)
CIVITEX.......	Civic Information & Techniques Exchange [Citizens Forum on Self-Government/National Municipal League] [Information service or system] (IID)
Civ Just Q....	Civil Justice Quarterly [A publication] (DLA)
CIVL..........	Center International de Vol Libre [Aguessac, France] (EAIO)
CIV LIB	Civil Liberty (DLA)
Civ Lib Dock...	Civil Liberties Docket (DLA)
Civ Litigation Rep...	Civil Litigation Reporter [A publication] (DLA)
CIVM..........	Collision-Imparted Velocity Method
CIVM-MARP...	Montreal, PQ [Television station call letters]
CIV-M-MARP...	Civilian Mobilization Manpower Allocation/Requirements Plan
Civ No	Civil Number [Docket number] (AAGC)
CIVO	Hull, PQ [Television station call letters]
CIVP..........	Chapeau, PQ [Television station call letters]
CIVPERCEN...	United States Army Civilian Personnel Center (AABC)
CIVPERSADMSYS...	Civilian Personnel Administration Services Record System [Military] (DNAB)
CIVPERS/EEODIRSYS...	Civilian Personnel/Equal Employment Opportunity Directives System [Military] (DNAB)
CIVPERSINS...	Civilian Personnel Information System [Army]
Civ Pr	Civil Procedure Reports [New York] [A publication] (DLA)
Civ Prac......	Civil Practice Law and Rules [A publication] (DLA)
Civ Prac (NY)...	New York Civil Practice [A publication] (DLA)
Civ Pro	Civil Procedure Reports [New York] [A publication] (DLA)
Civ Proc......	Civil Procedure [Legal term] (DLA)
Civ Proc (NS)...	Civil Procedure Reports, New Series [1908-13] [New York] [A publication] (DLA)
Civ Proc (NY)...	New York Civil Procedure [A publication] (DLA)
Civ Proc R ...	Civil Procedure Reports [New York] [A publication] (DLA)
Civ Proc Rep...	Civil Procedure Reports [New York] [A publication] (DLA)
Civ Proc Rep NS...	Civil Procedure Reports, New Series [1908-13] [New York] [A publication] (DLA)
Civ Proc R (NS)...	Civil Procedure Reports, New Series [1908-13] [New York] [A publication] (DLA)
Civ Pro R.....	Civil Procedure Reports [New York] [A publication] (DLA)
Civ Pro Reports...	Civil Procedure Reports [New York] [A publication] (DLA)
Civ Pro R (NS)...	Civil Procedure Reports, New Series [1908-13] [New York] [A publication] (DLA)
Civ Pr Rep...	Civil Procedure Reports [New York] [A publication] (DLA)
CIVQ	Quebec City, PQ [Television station call letters]
CIV R.........	Civil Rights (DLA)
CIVR	Configuration Item Validation [or Verification] Review
CIVRES	Congres International des Techniques de Vide en Recherche Spatiale [International Congress for Vacuum Techniques in Space Research] (PDAA)
CIV S	Civil Service (DLA)
CIVS..........	Sherbrooke, PQ [Television station call letters]
Civ Serv......	Civil Service (DLA)
CIVSITREP ...	Civil Situation Reporting System (NATG)
CIVSUB........	Civilian Substitution Program [Navy] (NVT)
CIVT..........	Cargo Interface Verification Test (MCD)
CIVV..........	Chicoutimi, PQ [Television station call letters]
CIVV..........	Compressor Inlet Variable Vane (MCD)
CIW...........	California Institution for Women
CIW...........	Carnegie Institution of Washington (EA)
CIW...........	Ceramic Insulated Wire
CIW...........	Chicago & Illinois Western Railroad [AAR code]
CIW...........	Cities of the World [A publication]
CIW...........	Collingwood Energy [Vancouver Stock Exchange symbol]
CIW...........	Command Intelligence and Weather (SAA)
CIWA	Canadian Injured Workers Alliance [L'Alliance Canadienne des Victimes d'Accidents et de Maladies du Travail] (AC)
CIWA	Condition Identification Work Authorization [Business term] (NRCH)
CIWA	[The] Cuneiform Inscriptions of Western Asia [A publication] (BJA)
Ciwec.........	Canadian International Water and Energy Consultants
CIWF..........	Clearinghouse International of the Women's Forum (EA)
CIWF..........	Compassion in World Farming [British]
CIWG	Camera Industries of West Germany [Defunct]
CIWLT........	Cie. Internationale des Wagons-Lits et du Tourisme [International Sleeping Car Co.]
CIWNP........	Clinical Information Was Not Provided [Medicine]
CIWP	Counterintelligence Working Party [US Military Government, Germany]
CIWS	Central Instrument Warning System [Aviation] (DA)
CIWS	Close-In Weapon System (NATG)
CIWS	Concentrator Isolation Working Subsystem [Telecommunications] (TEL)
CIWW	Ottawa, ON [AM radio station call letters]
CIX...........	Chiclayo [Peru] [Airport symbol] (OAG)
CIX...........	Commercial Internet Exchange (PCM)
CIX...........	Consolidated BRX Mining & Petroleum Ltd. [Vancouver Stock Exchange symbol]
CIXA..........	Constant Infusion Excretory Urogram [Medicine] (DMAA)

CIX-CXII	Ninth to Twelfth Cranial Nerves [*Anatomy*] (DMAA)
CIXK	Owen Sound, ON [*FM radio station call letters*]
CIXU	Constant Infusion Excretory Urogram [*Medicine*] (MAE)
CIXX	London, ON [*FM radio station call letters*]
CIY	Camino Energy Corp. [*Vancouver Stock Exchange symbol*]
CIY	Comiso [*Italy*] [*Airport symbol*] (AD)
CIY	Consolidated Cyll Industry [*Vancouver Stock Exchange symbol*]
CIY	Siskiyou County Public Library, Yreka, CA [*OCLC symbol*] (OCLC)
CIYMS	Church of Ireland Young Men's Society
CIYR	Hinton, AB [*AM radio station call letters*]
CIZ	Central Initial Zone [*in inflorescence*] [*Botany*]
CIZ	Chatham Islands [*New Zealand*] [*Seismograph station code, US Geological Survey*] (SEIS)
CIZ	City Resources (Canada) Ltd. [*Vancouver Stock Exchange symbol Toronto Stock Exchange symbol*]
CIZL	Regina, SK [*FM radio station call letters*]
CIZZ	Red Deer, AB [*FM radio station call letters*]
CJ	Amador County Free Library, Jackson, CA [*Library symbol Library of Congress*] (LCLS)
CJ	Bay Meadows Operating Co. [*AMEX symbol*] (SPSG)
CJ	Bay Meadows Oper(Unit) [*AMEX symbol*] (TTSB)
CJ	Catholic Journalist [*A publication*] (EAAP)
cj	Cayman Islands [*MARC country of publication code Library of Congress*] (LCCP)
CJ	Ceiling Joist
CJ	Chapman-Jouquet [*Pressures*] (MCD)
CJ	Chief Judge [*Sports*]
CJ	Chief Justice [*Various supreme courts*]
CJ	Circuit Judge (DLA)
CJ	Civilian Jeep
CJ	Classical Journal [*A publication*] (BRI)
CJ	Cobra Jet [*Automotive engineering*]
CJ	Code of Justinian [*A publication*] (DSA)
CJ	Codex Justinianus (BJA)
CJ	Cold Junction
CJ	Colgan Airways [*ICAO designator*] (AD)
CJ	Congregatio Iosephitarum [*Josephite Fathers*] [*Roman Catholic religious order*]
CJ	Conjectural (ADA)
CJ	Conjunction
CJ	Conjunctivitis [*Medicine*] (DMAA)
CJ	Construction Joint [*Technical drawings*]
CJ	Control Joint (MCD)
CJ	Corpus Juris [*Body of Law*] [*Latin*]
CJ	Court of Justice of the European Communities
CJ	Creutzfeldt-Jakob Disease [*Neurological disorder*]
CJ	Josephite Fathers (TOCD)
cj	Josephite Fathers (TOCD)
CJ	Journal of the House of Commons [*A publication*] (DLA)
CJ	Lord Chief Justice [*British A publication*] (DLA)
CJA	Cajamarca [*Peru*] [*Airport symbol*] (OAG)
CJA	Campbell-Johnston Associates [*Commercial firm British*]
CJA	Canadians Jewellers Association (AC)
CJA	Carpenters and Joiners of America (MHDB)
CJA	Chess Journalists of America (EA)
CJA	Classic Jaguar Association (EA)
CJA	Colima Resources Ltd. [*Vancouver Stock Exchange symbol*]
CJA	Commonwealth Journalists Association [*British*] (EAIO)
CJA	Conseil de la Jeunesse d'Afrique [*African Youth Council*] [*Senegal*]
CJA	United Brotherhood of Carpenters and Joiners of America
CJA & HSA	Council of Justice to Animals and Humane Slaughter Association (EAIO)
CJAB	Chicoutimi, PQ [*FM radio station call letters*]
CJAC	Central Joint Advisory Committee on Tutoral Classes [*British*]
CJACS	Chemical Journals of the American Chemical Society [*Information service or system*] (CRD)
CJAD	Montreal, PQ [*AM radio station call letters*]
CJAF	Cabano, PQ [*AM radio station call letters*]
CJAIN	Criminal Justice Archive and Information Network [*Department of Justice*] (GFGA)
CJAL	Edmonton, AB [*Television station call letters*]
CJAM	Windsor, ON [*FM radio station call letters*]
CJAN	Asbestos, PQ [*AM radio station call letters*]
CJ Ann	Corpus Juris Annotations [*A publication*] (DLA)
CJAOAC	Chemical Journal of the Association of Official Analytical Chemists [*Association of Official Analytical Chemists*] [*Information service or system*] (CRD)
CJAR	Classified Job Accountability Record (MCD)
CJAR	The Pas, MB [*AM radio station call letters*]
CJaS	Sierra Conservation Center, Jamestown, CA [*Library symbol Library of Congress*] (LCLS)
CJASB	Country Joe and His All Star Band [*Pop music group*]
CJAT	Trail, BC [*AM radio station call letters*]
CJAT-FM	Trail, BC [*FM radio station call letters*] (RBYB)
CJAV	Port Alberni, BC [*AM radio station call letters*]
CJAY	Calgary, AB [*FM radio station call letters*]
CJB	Chief Judge in Bankruptcy (DLA)
CJB	Coimbatore [*India*] [*Airport symbol*] (OAG)
CJB	Cold Junction Box (MHDI)
CJBC	Toronto, ON [*AM radio station call letters*]
CJBC-4	London, ON [*FM radio station call letters*]
CJBK	London, ON [*AM radio station call letters*]
CJBL	Centre for Japanese Business Language [*Australia*]
CJBM	Causapscal, PQ [*AM radio station call letters*]
CJBN	Kenora, ON [*Television station call letters*]

CJBQ	Belleville, ON [*AM radio station call letters*]
CJBR	Rimouski, PQ [*AM radio station call letters*]
CJBR-FM	Rimouski, PQ [*FM radio station call letters*]
CJBRT	Rimouski, PQ [*Television station call letters*]
CJBT	Costume Jewelry Board of Trade of New York [*Inactive*]
CJBX	London, ON [*FM radio station call letters*]
CJC	Calama [*Chile*] [*Airport symbol*] (OAG)
CJC	Cambridge Junior College [*Massachusetts*]
CJC	Canadian Jewish Congress [*Congres Juif Canadien*] (AC)
CJC	Cancapital Corp. [*Toronto Stock Exchange symbol*]
CJC	Carver, J. C., Neptune NJ [*STAC*]
CJC	Charles J. Colgan & Associates, Inc. [*FAA designator*] (FAAC)
CJC	Chipola Junior College [*Marianna, FL*]
CJC	Cisco Junior College [*Texas*]
CJC	Citrus Junior College [*California*]
CJC	Coahoma Junior College [*Clarksdale,MS*]
CJC	Community Junior College
CJC	Compagnie des Jeunes Canadiens [*Company of Young Canadians*] [*Federal crown corporation to employ young people, 1966-75*]
CJC	Congres Juif Canadien [*Canadian Jewish Congress*]
CJC	Congress for Jewish Culture (EA)
CJC	Corpus Juris Civilis [*The Body of the Civil Law*] [*Latin*] (DLA)
CJC	Couper's Judiciary Cases [*1868-85*] [*Scotland*] [*A publication*] (DLA)
CJC	Poor Sisters of Jesus Crucified and the Sorrowful Mother [*Roman Catholic religious order*]
CJCA	Edmonton, AB [*AM radio station call letters*]
CJ Can	Corpus Juris Canonici [*The Body of the Canon Law*] [*Latin*] (DLA)
CJCB	Commonwealth Joint Communication Board [*British military*] (DMA)
CJCB	Sydney, NS [*AM radio station call letters*]
CJCB-1	Inverness, NS [*Television station call letters*]
CJCB-2	Antigonish, NS [*Television station call letters*]
CJCB-TV	Sydney, NS [*Television station call letters*]
CJCC	Coordinating Justice for Cyprus Committee [*Australia*]
CJCD	Yellowknife, NT [*AM radio station call letters*]
CJCD-1	Hay River, NT [*FM radio station call letters*]
CJCF	Cumberland House, SK [*FM radio station call letters*] (RBYB)
CJCH	Halifax, NS [*AM radio station call letters*]
CJCH-1	Canning, NS [*Television station call letters*]
CJCH-6	Caledonia, NS [*Television station call letters*]
CJCH-TV	Halifax, NS [*Television station call letters*]
CJCI	Conseil de la Jeunesse de Cote d'Ivoire [*Ivory Coast Youth Council*]
CJCI	Prince George, BC [*AM radio station call letters*]
CJ Civ	Corpus Juris Civilis [*The Body of the Civil Law*] [*Latin*] (DLA)
CJCJ	Woodstock, NB [*AM radio station call letters*]
CJCL	Toronto, ON [*AM radio station call letters*]
CJCLS	Community and Junior College Libraries Section [*Association of College and Research Libraries*]
CJCM	Grand Centre, AB [*AM radio station call letters*]
CJCN	Grand Falls, NF [*Television station call letters*]
CJCP	Chief Justice of the Common Pleas (DLA)
CJCS	Chairman, Joint Chiefs of Staff (AFM)
CJCS	Conference of Jewish Communal Service (EA)
CJCS	Stratford, ON [*AM radio station call letters*]
CJCW	Colby Junior College for Women [*Later, CSC*] [*New Hampshire*]
CJCW	Sussex, NB [*AM radio station call letters*]
CJCY	Medicine Hat, AB [*AM radio station call letters*]
CJD	Campaign for Justice in Divorce [*British*] (DI)
CJD	Canadian Journalism Data Base [*University of Western Ontario*] (IID)
CJD	Candilejas [*Colombia*] [*Airport symbol*] (OAG)
CJD	Candol Developments Ltd. [*Toronto Stock Exchange symbol*]
CJD	Creutzfeldt-Jakob Disease [*Neurological disorder*]
CJD	Doctor of Criminal Jurisprudence
CJD	Variant of Human Creutzfeldt-Jakob Disease [*Medicine*]
CJDC	Dawson Creek, BC [*AM radio station call letters*]
CJDC-FM	Dawson Creek, BC [*FM radio station call letters*]
CJDC-TV	Dawson Creek, BC [*Television station call letters*]
CJDM	Drummondville, PQ [*FM radio station call letters*]
CJDV	Committee for Justice for Domingo and Viernes [*Defunct*] (EA)
CJE	Carolina Gold [*Vancouver Stock Exchange symbol*]
CJE	Cookeville, TN [*Location identifier FAA*] (FAAL)
CJE	Council for Jewish Education (EA)
CJE	Critical Job Element (GFGA)
CJEC	Court of Justice of the European Communities (DLA)
CJEM	Edmundston, NB [*AM radio station call letters*]
CJEN	Jenpeg, MB [*FM radio station call letters*]
CJerFin	Central Jersey Financial Corp. [*Associated Press*] (SAG)
CJES	Centre for Japanese Economic Studies [*Macquarie University*] [*Australia*]
CJET	Committee on Jobs, Environment, and Technology [*Defunct*] (EA)
CJET	Smiths Falls, ON [*AM radio station call letters*]
CJEZ	Toronto, ON [*FM radio station call letters*]
CJF	Canadian Journalism Foundation [*La Fondation pour le Journalisme Canadien*] (AC)
CJF	Council of Jewish Federations (EA)
CJF	Country Joe and the Fish [*Pop music group*]
CJFB	Swift Current, SK [*Television station call letters*]
CJFC	Central Jersey Financial Corp. [*NASDAQ symbol*] (NQ)
CJFC	Central Jersey Finl [*NASDAQ symbol*] (TTSB)
CJFC	Chuck Jennings Fan Club [*Defunct*] (EA)
CJFCB	Conseil Jeunesse Francophone de la Colombie-Britannique (AC)
CJFM	Montreal, PQ [*FM radio station call letters*]
CJFP	Riviere du Loup, PQ [*AM radio station call letters*]
CJFW	Terrace, BC [*FM radio station call letters*]
CJFWF	Council of Jewish Federations and Welfare Funds [*Later, CJF*] (EA)
CJFX	Antigonish, NS [*AM radio station call letters*]

CJG	Canady, J. G., Charlotte NC [STAC]
CJG	Chai-Na-Ta-Ginseng [Vancouver Stock Exchange symbol]
CJG	Council of Jews from Germany [British] (EAIO)
CJG	Zhejiang Airlines [China] [ICAO designator] (FAAC)
CJGC	London, ON [Radio station call letters] [1930's]
CJGS	Chief of the Joint General Staff [Vietnam]
CJGS	Community of the Companions of Jesus the Good Shepherd [Anglican religious community]
CJGX	Yorkton, SK [AM radio station call letters]
CJH	Caddev Industry, Inc. [Vancouver Stock Exchange symbol]
CJH	Muskegon, MI [Location identifier FAA] (FAAL)
CJHS	Canadian Jewish Historical Society [See also SCHJ]
CJI	Canadian Jewellers Institute
CJI	Central Juvenile Index
CJI	Committee for the Jewish Idea (EA)
CJI	Concrete Joint Institute [Defunct] (EA)
CJI	Criminal Justice Institute (BARN)
CJIA	Comite Juridique International de l'Aviation
CJIB	Vernon, BC [AM radio station call letters]
CJIC	Sault Ste. Marie, ON [Television station call letters]
CJIS	Canadian Journal of Information Science [A publication] (NITA)
CJIS	Criminal Justice Information System
CJJ	Cresco, IA [Location identifier FAA] (FAAL)
CJJR	Vancouver, BC [FM radio station call letters]
CJK	Chinese, Japanese, and Korean [Library of Congress computer system]
CJKB	Chief Justice of the King's Bench (DLA)
CJKK-FM	Clarenville, NF [FM radio station call letters] (RBYB)
CJKL	Kirkland Lake, ON [AM radio station call letters]
CJKR	Winnipeg, MB [FM radio station call letters]
CJKX	Ajax, ON [FM radio station call letters] (RBYB)
CJL	Chitral [Pakistan] [Airport symbol Obsolete] (OAG)
CJL	Claimer Resources [Vancouver Stock Exchange symbol]
CJL	Committee for Justice and Liberty Foundation
CJLA	Lachute, PQ [FM radio station call letters]
CJLB	Thunder Bay, ON [AM radio station call letters]
CJLF	Criminal Justice Legal Foundation
CJLI	Command Job Language Interpreter [Computer science] [Telecommunications]
CJLM	Contemporary Jewish Learning Materials [A publication] (BJA)
CJLM	Joliette, PQ [AM radio station call letters]
CJLMC	Chicago-Joliet Livestock Marketing Center (EA)
CJLR-FM	La Ronge, SK [FM radio station call letters] (RBYB)
CJLS	Yarmouth, NS [AM radio station call letters]
CJLS-1	Shelburne, NS [FM radio station call letters]
CJLS-2	Digby, NS [FM radio station call letters]
CJLS/RCDS	Canadian Journal of Law and Society/Revue Canadienne de Droit et Societe [A publication]
CJLX	Belleville, ON [FM radio station call letters]
CJM	Cell-Junctional Molecule [Embryology]
CJM	Coalition for Justice in the Maquiladoras (CROSS)
CJM	Congregatio Jesu et Mariae [Congregation of Jesus and Mary] [Eudist Fathers] [Roman Catholic religious order]
CJM	Congregation of Jesus and Mary (TOCD)
cjm	Congregation of Jesus and Mary, Eudist Fathers (TOCD)
CJM	Congres Juif Mondial [World Jewish Congress]
CJM	Johns-Manville Corp., Corporate Information Center, Denver, CO [OCLC symbol] (OCLC)
CJMA	Communications Junction Module Assembly [Ground Control Facility, NASA]
CJMC	Ste. Anne Des Monts, PQ [AM radio station call letters]
CJMCAG	Conference on Jewish Material Claims Against Germany (EA)
CJMD	Chibougamau, PQ [AM radio station call letters]
CJME	Regina, SK [AM radio station call letters]
CJMF	Quebec, PQ [FM radio station call letters]
CJMG	Penticton, BC [FM radio station call letters]
CJMJ	Ottawa, ON [FM radio station call letters]
CJMM	Rouyn-Noranda, PQ [FM radio station call letters]
CJMO	Moncton, NB [FM radio station call letters]
CJMR	Mississauga, ON [AM radio station call letters]
CJMV	Val D'Or, PQ [FM radio station call letters]
CJMX	Sudbury, ON [FM radio station call letters]
CJN	Chelan Resources, Inc. [Vancouver Stock Exchange symbol]
CJN	Community of Jesus of Nazareth [Anglican religious community]
CJN	El Cajon [California] [Airport symbol Obsolete] (OAG)
CJN	Les Cercles des Jeunes Naturalistes (AC)
CJNB	North Battleford, SK [AM radio station call letters]
CJNH	Bancroft, ON [AM radio station call letters]
CJNL	Merritt, BC [AM radio station call letters]
CJNR	Blind River, ON [AM radio station call letters]
CJNS	Meadow Lake, SK [AM radio station call letters]
CJNT-TV	Montreal, PQ [TV station call letters] (RBYB)
CJO	Chemical Journals Online [American Chemical Society] [Database]
CJO	Communications Jamming Operator [Military]
CJO	Corporate Jobs Outlook [Information service or system] (IID)
CJO	Council of Jewish Organizations in Civil Service
CJOA	Consortium of Jazz Organizations and Artists [Later, AJA] (EA)
CJOB	Winnipeg, MB [AM radio station call letters]
CJOC	Lethbridge, AB [AM radio station call letters]
CJOCS	Council of Jewish Organizations in Civil Service (EA)
CJOEP	Coordinated Joint Outline Emergency Plan [Military] (CINC)
CJOH	Ottawa, ON [Television station call letters]
CJOH-6	Deseronto, ON [Television station call letters]
CJOH-8	Cornwall, ON [Television station call letters]
CJOJ	Belleville, ON [FM radio station call letters]
CJOK	Fort McMurray, AB [AM radio station call letters]
CJOM	Argentia, NF [Television station call letters] (RBYB)
CJON	St. John's, NF [Television station call letters]
CJOR	Osoyoos, BC [AM radio station call letters]
CJOS	Caronport, SK [FM radio station call letters] (RBYB)
CJOX-1	Grand Bank, NF [Television station call letters]
CJOY	Guelph, ON [AM radio station call letters]
CJOZ	Bonavista Bay, NF [FM radio station call letters]
CJP	Combined Jewish Philanthropies
CJP	Communication Jamming Processor (IEEE)
CJP	Conseil Jeunesse Provincial [Manitoba] (AC)
CJP	Conseil Jeunesse Provincial [Nouvelle-Ecosse] (AC)
CJP	Cornu-Jellet Prism
CJPCMA	Commonwealth Jam Preserving and Condiment Manufacturers' Association [Australia]
CJPF	Corporation for Jefferson's Poplar Forest (EA)
CJPFA	Coalition for Jobs, Peace, and Freedom in America (EA)
CJPM	Chicoutimi, PQ [Television station call letters]
CJPR	Blairmore, AB [AM radio station call letters]
CJPS	Carpenters and Joiners Protection Society [A union] [British]
CJPST	Canadian Journal of Political and Social Theory [A publication]
CJQ	[Les] Centres Jeunesse de Quebec (AC)
CJQ	Conference des Juges du Quebec (AC)
CJQB	Chief Justice of the Queen's Bench (DLA)
CJQM	Sault Ste. Marie, ON [FM radio station call letters]
CJQQ	Timmins, ON [FM radio station call letters]
CJR	Centric Jaw Relationship [Dentistry] (DAVI)
CJR	Chaurjahari [Nepal] [Airport symbol] (OAG)
CJR	Colray Resources, Inc. [Toronto Stock Exchange symbol]
CJR	Columbia Journalism Review [A publication] (BRI)
CJR	Columbia Journalism Review [A publication] [Columbia University] [New York, NY] (WDMC)
CJR	Secretariat for Catholic-Jewish Relations (EA)
CJR	Study Centre for Christian-Jewish Relations [Roman Catholic Church] [British] (CB)
CJRB	Boissevain, MB [AM radio station call letters]
CJRC	Gatineau, PQ [AM radio station call letters]
CJRE	Riviere au Renard, PQ [FM radio station call letters]
CJRG	Gaspe, PQ [FM radio station call letters]
CJRL	Criminal Justice Reference Library [University of Texas]
CJRL	Kenora, ON [AM radio station call letters]
CJRM	Labrador City, NF [FM radio station call letters]
CJRN	Niagara Falls, ON [AM radio station call letters]
CJRQ	Sudbury, ON [FM radio station call letters]
CJRRU	Casey Jones Railroad Unit (EA)
CJRSC	Chemical Journals of the Royal Society of Chemistry [British Information service or system] (CRD)
CJRT	Toronto, ON [FM radio station call letters]
CJRW	Summerside, PE [AM radio station call letters]
CJS	Canadian Jobs Strategy [Employment and Immigration Canada program launched in 1986]
CJS	Canadian Joint Staff
CJS	Center for Japanese Studies [University of Michigan] [Research center] (RCD)
CJS	Center for Judicial Studies (EA)
CJS	Centre for Journalism Studies [British] (CB)
CJS	Ciudad Juarez [Mexico] [Airport symbol] (OAG)
CJS	Commonwealth Jet Services, Inc. [ICAO designator] (FAAC)
CJS	Copper Jacketed Steel
CJS	Corpus Juris Secundum [A publication]
CJS	Cotton, Jute, or Sisal [Freight]
CJS	Criminal Justice System
CJSA	Costume Jewelry Salesmen's Association (EA)
CJSA	Criminal Justice Statistics Association (EA)
CJSANS	Committee on Joint Support of Air Navigation Services [International Civil Aviation Organization]
CJSD	Thunder Bay, ON [FM radio station call letters]
CJSL	Estevan, SK [AM radio station call letters]
CJSMF	Captain James Smith Memorial Foundation (EA)
CJSN	Shaunavon, SK [AM radio station call letters]
CJSO	Sorel, PQ [FM radio station call letters]
CJSPA	Conference of Jesuit Student Personnel Administrators [Later, JASPA] (EA)
CJSR	Edmonton, AB [FM radio station call letters]
CJSS	Conference on Jewish Social Studies (EA)
CJSS	Cornwall, ON [AM radio station call letters]
CJS Supp	Corpus Juris Secundum Supplement [West] [A publication] (AAGC)
CJSV	Stephenville, NF [Television station call letters]
CJSW	Calgary, AB [FM radio station call letters]
CJT	Civil Jet Transport
CJT	Control Joint [Technical drawings]
CJT	CTI Technologies Corp. [Vancouver Stock Exchange symbol]
CJTA	Costume Jewelry Trade Association [Defunct]
CJTF	Combined Joint Task Forces [NATO] (ECON)
CJTF	Commander, Joint Task Force
CJTF	Commander Joint Task Force (DOMA)
CJTF	Crossroads Joint Task Force [Atomic weapons testing]
CJTG	Commander, Joint Task Group
CJTN	Trenton, ON [AM radio station call letters]
CJTT	New Liskeard, ON [AM radio station call letters]
CJU	Cheju [South Korea] [Airport symbol] (OAG)
CJU	Chuan Hup Canada [Vancouver Stock Exchange symbol]
CJUB	Chief Justice of the Common (Upper) Bench (DLA)
C Jud Proc	Code of Judicial Procedure [A publication] (DLA)
CJV	Charlie O Beverage [Vancouver Stock Exchange symbol]

CJVA............	Caraquet, NB [*AM radio station call letters*]
CJVB...........	Vancouver, BC [*AM radio station call letters*]
CJVI............	Victoria, BC [*AM radio station call letters*]
CJVL....	Ste. Marie De Beauce, PQ [*AM radio station call letters*]
CJVR............	Melfort, SK [*AM radio station call letters*]
CJW.............	Canyon Junction [*Wyoming*] [*Seismograph station code, US Geological Survey Closed*] (SEIS)
CJW.............	Christian Jail Workers (EA)
CJWA...........	Wawa, ON [*AM radio station call letters*]
CJWA-FM	Wawa, ON [*FM radio station call letters*] (RBYB)
CJWB...........	Bonavista, NF [*Television station call letters*]
CJWILEY......	Chemical Journals of John Wiley & Sons [*John Wiley & Sons, Inc.*] [*Information service or system*] (CRD)
CJWN..........	Corner Brook, NF [*Television station call letters*]
CJWW.........	Saskatoon, SK [*AM radio station call letters*]
CJX.............	Canadian Jorex Ltd. [*Toronto Stock Exchange symbol*]
CJXX...........	Grande Prairie, AB [*AM radio station call letters*]
CJXY...........	Hamilton, ON [*FM radio station call letters*]
CJY.............	Utica, NY [*Location identifier FAA*] (FAAL)
CJYC...........	St. John, NB [*FM radio station call letters*]
CJYM..........	Rosetown, SK [*AM radio station call letters*]
CJYQ..........	St. John's, NF [*AM radio station call letters*] (RBYB)
CJYR..........	Edson, AB [*AM radio station call letters*]
CJZ.............	Cable Jacket Zipper
CJZ.............	Cajazeiras [*Brazil*] [*Airport symbol*] (AD)
CK..............	Cake
CK..............	Call Key [*Telecommunications*]
CK..............	Calvin Klein [*Fashion designer, 1942-*]
CK..............	Canine Kidney [*Physiology*]
CK..............	Cape Kennedy [*NASA*] (KSC)
CK..............	Caremark International [*NYSE symbol*] (SPSG)
CK..............	Carnal Knowledge [*FBI standardized term*]
CK..............	Cask
ck..............	Centistoke (BARN)
CK..............	Certified Kosher [*Food labeling*] (IIA)
Ck	Chalk [*Quality of the bottom*] [*Nautical charts*]
ck..............	Chalk (VRA)
CK..............	Check (AFM)
ck..............	Check (WDMC)
CK..............	Chesterfield Kings [*An association*] (EA)
CK..............	Chicken Kidney
CK..............	Choline Kinase [*An enzyme*]
CK..............	Circuit Check [*Electronics*] (IAA)
CK..............	Clerk (ROG)
CK..............	Clock
ck..............	Colombia [*ucu (United States Miscellaneous Caribbean Islands) used in records cataloged before January 1978*] [*MARC country of publication code Library of Congress*] (LCCP)
CK..............	Connair [*ICAO designator*] (AD)
CK..............	Console Keyset (MCD)
CK..............	Construction Keyed Lock (ADA)
C-K.............	Contact Karate
CK..............	Conversion Kit (MCD)
CK..............	Cook [*Navy British*]
CK..............	Cookery Officer [*Navy British*]
CK..............	Cookie
CK..............	Cook Islands [*ANSI two-letter standard code*] (CNC)
CK..............	Cork (MSA)
CK..............	Countersink (WGA)
CK..............	Creatine Kinase [*Also, CPK*] [*An enzyme*]
CK..............	Creek (ADA)
CK..............	Crystal Kit
CK..............	Cyanogen Chloride [*Poison gas*] [*Army symbol*]
CK..............	Cytokeratin [*Cytology*]
CK..............	Cytokinin [*Biochemistry*]
CK..............	King City Public Library, King City, CA [*Library symbol Library of Congress*] (LCLS)
CK..............	School Sisters of Christ the King (TOCD)
CKA.............	Catholic Knights of America (EA)
CKA.............	Cherokee, OK [*Location identifier FAA*] (FAAL)
CKA.............	Condaka Metals Corp. [*Vancouver Stock Exchange symbol*]
CKA.............	Cook Inlet Aviation, Inc. [*ICAO designator*] (FAAC)
CKAC	Montreal, PQ [*AM radio station call letters*]
CKAD	Middleton, NS [*AM radio station call letters*]
CKAFS	Cape Kennedy Air Force Station
CKAM	Upsalquitch Lake, NB [*Television station call letters*]
CKAO	Coalition to Keep Alaska Oil (EA)
CKAP	Kapuskasing, ON [*AM radio station call letters*]
CKAQ	Creche and Kindergarten Association of Queensland [*Australia*]
CKAT	North Bay, ON [*FM radio station call letters*]
CKAY	Duncan, BC [*AM radio station call letters*]
CKB.............	Cacquot Kite Balloon
CKB.............	Clarksburg [*West Virginia*] [*Airport symbol*] (OAG)
CKB.............	Clarksburg, WV [*Location identifier FAA*] (FAAL)
CKB.............	Cork Base
CKB.............	Creatine Kinase B [*An enzyme*]
CKBA	Athabasca, AB [*AM radio station call letters*]
CK-BB	Isoenzyme of Creatine Kinase with Brain Subunits [*Medicine*] (MEDA)
CKBC	Bathurst, NB [*AM radio station call letters*]
CKBD	Cork Board (AAG)
CKBD	Vancouver, BC [*AM radio station call letters*]
CKBI............	Prince Albert, SK [*AM radio station call letters*]
CKBI-3	Greenwater Lake, SK [*Television station call letters*]
CKBI-4	Nipawin, SK [*Television station call letters*]
CKBI-TV	Prince Albert, SK [*Television station call letters*]

CKBL...........	Kelowna, BC [*FM radio station call letters*] (RBYB)
CKBQ	Melfort, SK [*Television station call letters*]
CKBW	Bridgewater, NS [*AM radio station call letters*]
CKBW-1	Liverpool, NS [*FM radio station call letters*]
CKBW-2	Shelburne, NS [*FM radio station call letters*]
CKBX	One Hundred Mile House, BC [*AM radio station call letters*]
CKBY	Ottawa, ON [*FM radio station call letters*]
CKC.............	California Kamchatka Companies (ECON)
CKC.............	California Kiwifruit Commission (EA)
CKC.............	Canadian Kennel Club
CKC.............	Canberra Kennel Club [*Australia*]
CKC.............	Canuck Resources Corp. [*Vancouver Stock Exchange symbol*]
CKC.............	Cold Knife Conization [*Gynecology*] (DAVI)
CKC.............	Collins & Aikman [*NYSE symbol*] (TTSB)
CKC.............	Collins & Aikman Holdings Corp. [*NYSE symbol*] (SAG)
CKC.............	Kings County Free Library, Hanford, CA [*OCLC symbol*] (OCLC)
CKCA	Canadian Kitchen Cabinet Association (AC)
CKCB	Collingwood, ON [*AM radio station call letters*]
CKCD	Campbellton, NB [*Television station call letters*]
CKCI...........	Parksville, BC [*AM radio station call letters*] (RBYB)
CKCK	Regina, SK [*AM radio station call letters*]
CKCK-1	Colgate, SK [*Television station call letters*]
CKCK-2	Willow Bunch, SK [*Television station call letters*]
CKCK-TV	Regina, SK [*Television station call letters*]
CKCL	Chicago-Kent College of Law
ckcl	Crackle (VRA)
CKCL	Truro, NS [*AM radio station call letters*]
CKCM..........	Grand Falls-Windsor, NF [*AM radio station call letters*]
CKCN	Sept-Iles, PQ [*AM radio station call letters*]
CKCO	Kitchener, ON [*Television station call letters*]
CKCO-2	Wiarton, ON [*Television station call letters*]
CKCO-3	Sarnia, ON [*Television station call letters*]
CKCO-4	The Muskokas, ON [*Television station call letters*]
CKCQ	Quesnel, BC [*AM radio station call letters*]
CKCR	Revelstoke, BC [*AM radio station call letters*]
CKCSC	Cavalier King Charles Spaniel Club of America (EA)
CKCU	Ottawa, ON [*FM radio station call letters*]
CKCV	Clarenville, NF [*FM radio station call letters*]
CKCW	Moncton, NB [*AM radio station call letters*]
CKCW-1	Charlottetown, PE [*Television station call letters*]
CKCW-2	St. Edward, PE [*Television station call letters*]
CKCW-TV	Moncton, NB [*Television station call letters*]
CKD	Certified Kitchen Designer
CKD	Completely Knocked Down [*i.e., disassembled, as a toy or piece of furniture which must be assembled before use*] [*Freight*]
CKD	Cooked
CKD	Cooked
CKD	Count-Key-Data Device [*Computer science*]
CKD	Crooked Creek [*Alaska*] [*Airport symbol*] (OAG)
CKD	Crooked Creek, AK [*Location identifier FAA*] (FAAL)
CKDH	Amherst, NS [*AM radio station call letters*]
CKDIG	Check Digit [*Computer science*] (EECA)
CKDJ	Ottawa, ON [*FM radio station call letters*] (RBYB)
CKDK	Woodstock, ON [*FM radio station call letters*]
CKDM	Dauphin, MB [*AM radio station call letters*]
CKDO	Oshawa, ON [*AM radio station call letters*]
CKDQ	Drumheller, AB [*AM radio station call letters*]
CKDR	Dryden, ON [*AM radio station call letters*]
CKDR-5	Red Lake, ON [*AM radio station call letters*]
CKDR-6	Atikokan, ON [*AM radio station call letters*]
CKDU	Halifax, NS [*FM radio station call letters*]
CKDX	Newmarket, ON [*AM radio station call letters*]
CKDY	Digby, NS [*AM radio station call letters*]
CKE.............	Carl Karcher Enterprises
CKE.............	Carmike Cinemas'A' [*NYSE symbol*] (TTSB)
CKE.............	Carmike Cinemas Inc. [*NYSE symbol*] (SPSG)
CKE.............	Corporate Aviation Services, Inc. [*ICAO designator*] (FAAC)
CKEC	New Glasgow, NS [*AM radio station call letters*]
CKEG	Nanaimo, BC [*AM radio station call letters*]
CKEK	Cranbrook, BC [*AM radio station call letters*]
CKel	Kelseyville Free Library, Kelseyville, CA [*Library symbol Library of Congress*] (LCLS)
CKEN	Kentville, NS [*AM radio station call letters*]
CKenM	College of Marin, Kentfield, CA [*Library symbol Library of Congress*] (LCLS)
CKER	Edmonton, AB [*AM radio station call letters*]
CKE Rst	CKE Restaurants [*Associated Press*] (SAG)
CKEY	Fort Erie, ON [*FM radio station call letters*]
CKF.............	Canadian Fiber Foods [*Vancouver Stock Exchange symbol*]
CKF.............	Centerns Kvinnoforbund [*Women's Association of the Centre Party*] [*Sweden Political party*] (EAIO)
CKF.............	Check Fixture (MCD)
CKF.............	Christ the King Foundation [*Defunct*] (EA)
CKF.............	Cork Floor (AAG)
CKFB	CKF Bancorp [*NASDAQ symbol*] (TTSB)
CKFB	CKF Bancorp, Inc. [*NASDAQ symbol*] (SAG)
CKF Bc........	CKF Bancorp, Inc. [*Associated Press*] (SAG)
CKFC	Cub Koda Fan Club [*Defunct*] (EA)
CKFF	Cape Kennedy Forecast Facility [*NASA*] (KSC)
CKFL	Lac Megantic, PQ [*AM radio station call letters*]
CKFM..........	Check Form [*Tool*] (AAG)
CKFM..........	Toronto, ON [*FM radio station call letters*]
CKFR	Checkfree Corp. [*NASDAQ symbol*] (SAG)
CKFR-FM	Big White Ski Village, BC [*FM radio station call letters*] (RBYB)
CKFX-FM	North Bay, ON [*FM radio station call letters*] (RBYB)

CKG .... Cardiokymograph (BARN)
CKG .... Central Kalgoorlie Gold [*Australia*]
CKG .... Chongqing [*China*] [*Airport symbol*] (OAG)
CKG .... Chungking [*China*] [*Airport symbol*] (AD)
C/KG .... Coulombs per Kilogram
CKGA .... Check Gauge [*Tool*] (AAG)
CKGA .... Gander, NF [*AM radio station call letters*]
CKGB .... Timmins, ON [*AM radio station call letters*]
CKGE .... Oshawa, ON [*FM radio station call letters*]
CKGF .... Grand Forks, BC [*AM radio station call letters*]
CKGL .... Kitchener, ON [*AM radio station call letters*]
CKGM-AM .... Montreal, PQ [*AM radio station call letters*] (RBYB)
CKGO .... Hope, BC [*AM radio station call letters*]
CKGO-1 .... Boston Bar, BC [*FM radio station call letters*]
CKGR .... Golden, BC [*AM radio station call letters*]
CKGY .... Red Deer, AB [*AM radio station call letters*]
CKH .... Koko Head, HI [*Location identifier FAA*] (FAAL)
CKH .... Seacor Holdings [*NYSE symbol*] (SAG)
CKHJ .... Fredericton, NB [*AM radio station call letters*]
CKHR .... Hay River, NT [*FM radio station call letters*]
CKI .... Check Issued
CKI .... Cheung Kong Infrastructure
CKI .... Child Keyppers' International (EA)
CKI .... Circle K International (EA)
CKI .... Cockpit Kill Indicator [*Military*]
CKI .... Consolidated Stikine Silver Ltd. [*Vancouver Stock Exchange symbol*]
CKI .... Cyclin Kinase Inhibitor [*Biochemistry*]
CKI .... Kingstree, SC [*Location identifier FAA*] (FAAL)
CKIA .... Quebec, PQ [*FM radio station call letters*]
C(K)IAC .... Cocos (Keeling) Islands Administration and Council [*Australia*]
CKIC .... Chemical Kinetics Information Center [*National Institute of Standards and Technology*]
C(K)ICS .... Ccos (Keeling) Islands Cooperative Society [*Australia*]
CKIK .... Calgary, AB [*FM radio station call letters*]
CKIM .... Baie Verte, NF [*AM radio station call letters*]
CKIQ .... Big White Ski Village, BC [*FM radio station call letters*]
CKIQ .... Kelowna, BC [*AM radio station call letters*]
CKIR .... Invermere, BC [*AM radio station call letters*]
CKIS .... Catholic Knights Insurance Society (EA)
CKIS .... Montreal, PQ [*AM radio station call letters*]
CKIS-FM ...... Calgary, AB [*AM radio station call letters*] (RBYB)
CKIT .... Regina, SK [*FM radio station call letters*]
CKIX .... St. John's, NF [*FM radio station call letters*]
CKJM-FM ..... Cheticamp, NS [*FM radio station call letters*] (RBYB)
CKJR .... Wetaskiwin, AB [*AM radio station call letters*]
CKJS .... Winnipeg, MB [*AM radio station call letters*]
CKK .... Chekok [*Alaska*] [*Seismograph station code, US Geological Survey*] (SEIS)
CKK .... Miami, FL [*Location identifier FAA*] (FAAL)
CKKC .... Nelson, BC [*AM radio station call letters*]
CKKC-FM ..... Crawford Bay, BC [*FM radio station call letters*]
CKKL .... Ottawa, ON [*FM radio station call letters*]
CKKM .... Oliver-Osoyoos, BC [*Television station call letters*]
CKKN .... Prince George, BC [*FM radio station call letters*] (RBYB)
CKKQ .... Victoria, BC [*FM radio station call letters*]
CKKR .... Cranbrook, BC [*AM radio station call letters*] (RBYB)
CKKS .... Vancouver, BC [*FM radio station call letters*]
CKKW .... Kitchener, ON [*AM radio station call letters*]
CKKY .... Wainwright, AB [*AM radio station call letters*]
CKL .... CEL Industry Ltd. [*Vancouver Stock Exchange symbol*]
CKL .... Centreville, AL [*Location identifier FAA*] (FAAL)
CKL .... Chickasaw Library System, Ardmore, OK [*OCLC symbol*] (OCLC)
CKLB .... Yellowknife, NT [*FM radio station call letters*]
CKLC .... Kingston, ON [*AM radio station call letters*]
CKLD .... Thetford Mines, PQ [*AM radio station call letters*]
CKLE .... Bathurst, NB [*FM radio station call letters*]
CKLG .... Vancouver, BC [*AM radio station call letters*]
CKLH .... Hamilton, ON [*FM radio station call letters*]
CKLN .... Toronto, ON [*FM radio station call letters*] (RBYB)
CKLP .... Parry Sound, ON [*FM radio station call letters*]
CKLQ .... Brandon, MB [*AM radio station call letters*]
CKLS .... Central Kansas Library System [*Library network*]
CKLS .... La Sarre, PQ [*AM radio station call letters*]
CKLT .... St. John, NB [*Television station call letters*]
CKLW .... Windsor, ON [*AM radio station call letters*]
CKLY .... Lindsay, ON [*AM radio station call letters*]
CKLZ .... Kelowna, BC [*FM radio station call letters*]
CKM .... Checkmate Resources [*Vancouver Stock Exchange symbol*]
CKM .... Clarksdale, MS [*Location identifier FAA*] (FAAL)
CKM .... Clark University, Worcester, MA [*OCLC symbol*] (OCLC)
CKM .... Coopers Lake [*Montana*] [*Seismograph station code, US Geological Survey Closed*] (SEIS)
CKM .... Creatine Kinase, Muscle Type (DMAA)
CKMA .... Abbotsford-Matsqui, BC [*AM radio station call letters*]
CK-MB .... Isoenzyme of Creatine Kinase with Muscle and Brain Subunits [*Medicine*] (MEDA)
CKMC .... Swift Current, SK [*Television station call letters*]
CKMC-1 .... Golden Prairie, SK [*Television station call letters*]
CKMF .... Montreal, PQ [*FM radio station call letters*]
CKMG .... Maniwaki, PQ [*AM radio station call letters*]
CKMI .... Quebec City, PQ [*Television station call letters*]
CKMIC .... Class and Kind Made in Canada [*Business term*]
CKMJ .... Marquis, SK [*Television station call letters*]
CKMK .... Mackenzie, BC [*AM radio station call letters*]

CK-MM .... Isoenzyme of Creatine Kinase with Muscle Subunits [*Medicine*] (MEDA)
CKMM .... Winnipeg, MB [*FM radio station call letters*]
CKMN-FM ..... Rimouski-Mont Joli, PQ [*FM radio station call letters*] (RBYB)
CKMO-FM ..... Victoria, BC [*FM radio station call letters*] (RBYB)
CKMS .... Waterloo, ON [*FM radio station call letters*]
CKMTA .... Cape Kennedy Missile Test Annex [*NASA*] (KSC)
CKMV .... Grand Falls, NB [*AM radio station call letters*]
CKMW .... Winkler-Morden, MB [*AM radio station call letters*]
CKMX .... Calgary, AB [*AM radio station call letters*] (RBYB)
CKN .... Consolidated Nord Resources Ltd. [*Vancouver Stock Exchange symbol*]
CKN .... Crookston, MN [*Location identifier FAA*] (FAAL)
CKNB .... Campbellton, NB [*AM radio station call letters*]
CKNC .... Sudbury, ON [*Television station call letters*]
CKNC-1 .... Elliot Lake, ON [*Television station call letters*]
CKND .... Winnipeg, MB [*Television station call letters*]
CKND-2 .... Minnedosa, MB [*Television station call letters*]
CKNG .... Edmonton, AB [*FM radio station call letters*]
CKNL .... Fort St. John, BC [*AM radio station call letters*]
CKNMIC .... Class and Kind Not Made in Canada [*Business term*]
CKNR .... Elliott Lake, ON [*AM radio station call letters*]
CKNS .... Espanola, ON [*AM radio station call letters*]
CKNW .... New Westminster, BC [*AM radio station call letters*]
CKNX .... Wingham, ON [*AM radio station call letters*]
CKNX-FM ...... Wingham, ON [*FM radio station call letters*]
CKNX-TV ...... Wingham, ON [*Television station call letters*]
CKNY .... North Bay, ON [*Television station call letters*]
CKO .... Check Operator (DEN)
CKO .... Consolidated Knobby Lake Mines Ltd. [*Vancouver Stock Exchange symbol*]
CKO .... Cornelio Procopio [*Brazil*] [*Airport symbol*] (OAG)
CKOC .... Hamilton, ON [*AM radio station call letters*]
CKOD .... Valleyfield, PQ [*FM radio station call letters*]
CK of FC ...... Carnal Knowledge of Female Child [*FBI standardized term*]
CKOI .... Verdun, PQ [*FM radio station call letters*]
CKOM .... Saskatoon, SK [*AM radio station call letters*]
CKON .... Akwesasne, ON [*FM radio station call letters*]
CKOR .... Penticton, BC [*AM radio station call letters*]
CKOR .... Seacor Holdings [*NASDAQ symbol*] (SAG)
CKOS .... Yorkton, SK [*Television station call letters*]
CKOT .... Tillsonburg, ON [*AM radio station call letters*]
CKOT-FM ...... Tillsonburg, ON [*FM radio station call letters*]
CKOUT .... Checkout
CKOV .... Kelowna, BC [*AM radio station call letters*]
CKOY .... Timmins, ON [*AM radio station call letters*]
CKOZ .... Corner Brook, NF [*FM radio station call letters*]
CKP .... Cayley-Klein Parameter [*Mathematics*]
CKP .... Checkpoint Sys [*NYSE symbol*] (TTSB)
CKP .... Checkpoint Systems, Inc. [*NYSE symbol*] (SAG)
CKP .... Cherokee, IA [*Location identifier FAA*] (FAAL)
CKP .... Consolidated Pace II Industries Ltd. [*Vancouver Stock Exchange symbol*]
CKPC .... Brantford, ON [*AM radio station call letters*]
CKPC-FM ...... Brantford, ON [*FM radio station call letters*]
CKPE .... Sydney, NS [*FM radio station call letters*]
CKPG .... Containerboard and Kraft Paper Group (EA)
CKPG .... Prince George, BC [*AM radio station call letters*]
CKPG-TV ...... Prince George, BC [*Television station call letters*]
CKPR .... Thunder Bay, ON [*AM radio station call letters*]
CKPR-TV ...... Thunder Bay, ON [*Television station call letters*]
CKPT .... Checkpoint (MCD)
CKPT .... Cockpit
CKPT .... Peterborough, ON [*AM radio station call letters*]
CKQB .... Ottawa, ON [*FM radio station call letters*]
CKQM .... Peterborough, ON [*FM radio station call letters*]
CKQN .... Baker Lake, NT [*FM radio station call letters*]
CKQR .... Castlegar, BC [*AM radio station call letters*]
CKR .... Check Received
CKR .... Chesapeake Computer [*Vancouver Stock Exchange symbol*]
CKR .... CKE Restaurants [*NYSE symbol*] (TTSB)
CKR .... CKE Restaurants Ltd. [*Formerly, Carl Karcher Enterprise*] [*NYSE symbol*] (SAG)
CKR .... Cometary Kilometric Radiation [*Astrophysics*]
CKR .... Crown Air Systems [*ICAO designator*] (FAAC)
CKRA .... Cape Kennedy Reference Atmosphere [*Later, CCRA*] [*NASA*] (NASA)
CKRA .... Edmonton, AB [*FM radio station call letters*]
CKRB .... St. Georges de Beauce, PQ [*AM radio station call letters*]
CKRC .... Council of the Knights of the Red Cross [*Freemasonry*] (ROG)
CKRC .... Winnipeg, MB [*AM radio station call letters*]
CKRD .... Red Deer, AB [*AM radio station call letters*]
CKRD-1 .... Coronation, AB [*Television station call letters*]
CKRD-TV ...... Red Deer, AB [*Television station call letters*]
CKRK .... Kahnawake, PQ [*FM radio station call letters*]
CKRL .... Quebec, PQ [*FM radio station call letters*]
CKRM .... Regina, SK [*AM radio station call letters*]
CKRN .... Rouyn, PQ [*AM radio station call letters*]
CKRN-3 .... Bearn-Fabre, PQ [*Television station call letters*]
CKRN-TV ...... Rouyn, PQ [*Television station call letters*]
CKRO-FM ...... Pokemouche, NB [*FM radio station call letters*] (RBYB)
CKRP-FM ...... Falher, AB [*FM radio station call letters*] (RBYB)
CKRS .... Jonquiere, PQ [*AM radio station call letters*]
CKRSO .... Cape Kennedy Range Safety Officer [*NASA*] (KSC)
CKRT .... Riviere du Loup, PQ [*Television station call letters*]

CKRU	Peterborough, ON [*AM radio station call letters*]		CKXD	Gander, NF [*AM radio station call letters*]
CKRV	Kamloops, BC [*FM radio station call letters*]		CKX-FM	Brandon, MB [*FM radio station call letters*]
CKRW	Whitehorse, YT [*AM radio station call letters*]		CKXG	Grand Falls, NF [*AM radio station call letters*]
CKRX	Lethbridge, AB [*AM radio station call letters*]		CKXL	St. Boniface, MB [*FM radio station call letters*]
CKRY	Calgary, AB [*FM radio station call letters*]		CKXM	Victoria, BC [*AM radio station call letters*] (RBYB)
CKRY	Crockery		CKXR	Salmon Arm, BC [*AM radio station call letters*]
CKRZ	Ohsweken, ON [*FM radio station call letters*]		CKX-TV	Brandon, MB [*Television station call letters*]
CKS	American International Airways, Inc. [*FAA designator*] (FAAC)		CKX-TV-1	Foxwarren, MB [*Television station call letters*]
CKS	Cell Kinetics Society (EA)		CKXX	Corner Brook, NF [*AM radio station call letters*]
CKS	Centistokes [*Unit of kinematic viscosity*]		CKY	Conakry [*Guinea*] [*Airport symbol*] (OAG)
CKS	Chiang Kai-shek		CKY	Consolidated McKinney Resources, Inc. [*Vancouver Stock Exchange symbol*]
CKS	Chicago, Kalamazoo & Saginaw Railway [*AAR code*]		CKY	Winnipeg, MB [*Television station call letters*]
CKS	Christian Knowledge Society [*Also known as Society for Promoting Christian Knowledge*]		CKYB	Brandon, MB [*Television station call letters*]
CKS	Classic Form of Kaposi Sarcoma [*Medicine*] (DMAA)		CKYC	Toronto, ON [*AM radio station call letters*]
CKS	Coseka Resources Ltd. [*Toronto Stock Exchange symbol*]		CKYK-FM	Alma, PQ [*FM radio station call letters*] (RBYB)
CKSA	Catholic Kolping Society of America (EA)		CKYL	Peace River, AB [*AM radio station call letters*]
CKSA	Lloydminster, AB [*AM radio station call letters*]		CKYQ-FM	Plessisville, PQ [*FM radio station call letter*] (RBYB)
CKSA-TV	Lloydminster, AB [*Television station call letters*]		CKYR	Jasper, AB [*AM radio station call letters*]
CKSB	St. Boniface, MB [*AM radio station call letters*]		CKYR-1	Grand Cache, AB [*AM radio station call letters*]
CKSG	Catholic Knights of St. George (EA)		CKY-TV	Winnipeg, MB [*Television station call letters*]
CKSG	CKS Group [*NASDAQ symbol*] (TTSB)		CKYX	Fort McMurray, AB [*FM radio station call letters*]
CKSG	CKS Group, Inc. [*NASDAQ symbol*] (SAG)		CKZX	New Denver, BC [*FM radio station call letters*]
CKS Gr	CKS Group, Inc. [*Associated Press*] (SAG)		CKZX-1	Kaslo, BC [*FM radio station call letters*]
CKSH	Sherbrooke, PQ [*Television station call letters*]		CKZZ	Vancouver, BC [*FM radio station call letters*]
CKSL	London, ON [*AM radio station call letters*]		CL	Cabbage Looper [*Entomology*]
CKSM	Shawinigan, PQ [*AM radio station call letters*]		CL	Cable Link [*Telecommunications*] (OA)
CKSNI	Cape Kennedy Space Network, Inc. [*NASA*]		C-L	Cain-Levine Social Competency Scale [*Psychology*]
CKSO	Condon, Kinzua & Southern Railroad Co. [*AAR code*]		CL	Calamus Length
CKSQ	Stettler, AB [*AM radio station call letters*]		C-L	California State Law Library, Sacramento, CA [*Library symbol Library of Congress*] (LCLS)
CKSR	Chilliwack, BC [*FM radio station call letters*]		CL	Call Loan [*Banking*]
CKSS	Red Rocks, NF [*FM radio station call letters*]		CL	Canadair Ltd. [*Canada ICAO aircraft manufacturer identifier*] (ICAO)
CKST	Vancouver, BC [*AM radio station call letters*]		C/L	Canister/Launcher [*Strategic Defense Initiative*]
CKSW	Swift Current, SK [*AM radio station call letters*]		CL	Canron, Inc. [*Toronto Stock Exchange symbol*]
CKSY	Chatham, ON [*FM radio station call letters*]		CL	Capital Loss [*Accounting*]
CKT	Caledonian Airways Ltd. [*British ICAO designator*] (FAAC)		CL	Capitol International Airways [*ICAO designator*] (AD)
CKT	Cape Resources, Inc. [*Vancouver Stock Exchange symbol*]		CL	Carapace Length [*Pisciculture*]
CKT	Check Template		CL	Cardiolipin [*Immunochemistry*]
CKT	Circuit (AAG)		CL	Carload
CKT	Commandery of Knights Templar [*Freemasonry*] (ROG)		cl	Carload (WDMC)
CKT	Crocker Realty Investors, Inc. [*AMEX symbol*] (SAG)		CL	Carload Lot [*Commerce*]
CKT	Crocker Realty Trust [*AMEX symbol*] (TTSB)		CL	Carted Luggage (ROG)
CKTA	Taber, AB [*AM radio station call letters*]		C/L	Cash Letter [*Banking*]
CKTB	St. Catherines, ON [*AM radio station call letters*]		CL	Cathodoluminescence [*Geophysics*]
CKT BKR	Circuit Breaker (MSA)		CL	Ceiling Level
CKTF	Circuit Finder (MSA)		CL	Cell Line [*Cytology*]
CKTF	Gatineau, PQ [*FM radio station call letters*]		CL	Celtic League [*Peel, Isle of Man, England*] (EAIO)
CKT-ID	Circuit Identification [*Telecommunications*] (TEL)		CL	Center Left [*Theatrical term*] (WDMC)
CKTK	Kitimat, BC [*AM radio station call letters*]		C/L	Center Light [*Aviation*] (DA)
CKTL	Plessisville, PQ [*AM radio station call letters*]		CL	Center Line
CKTM	Trois-Rivieres, PQ [*Television station call letters*]		CL	Centerline Light [*Aviation*] (DA)
CKTN	Trail, BC [*Television station call letters*]		CL	Center of Lift
CKTN-3	Nelson, BC [*Television station call letters*] (RBYB)		CL	Centiliter (GPO)
CKTO	Truro, NS [*FM radio station call letters*]		CL	Centralis Lateralis [*Neuroanatomy*]
CKTS	Sherbrooke, PQ [*AM radio station call letters*]		CL	Centralized Lubrication [*Automotive engineering*]
CKTY	Sarnia, ON [*AM radio station call letters*]		CL	Central Laboratory
CKU	Cordova, AK [*Location identifier FAA*] (FAAL)		CL	Central Line
CKUA	Edmonton, AB [*AM radio station call letters*]		CL	Central Locking [*Automotive accessory*]
CKUA-1	Calgary, AB [*FM radio station call letters*]		CL	Centre Left [*Australian Labor Party*] [*Political party*]
CKUA-2	Lethbridge, AB [*FM radio station call letters*]		CL	Centrolateral [*Nucleus of thalamus*] [*Neuroanatomy*]
CKUA-3	Medicine Hat, AB [*FM radio station call letters*]		CL	Ceylon [*Sri Lanka*]
CKUA-4	Grande Prairie, AB [*FM radio station call letters*]		CL	Ceylon Lines [*Steamship*] (MHDW)
CKUA-5	Peace River, AB [*FM radio station call letters*]		CL	Change Leading [*Typography*] (WDMC)
CKUA-13	Drumheller, AB [*FM radio station call letters*]		cl	Change Leading [*Typesetting*] (WDMC)
CKUA-FM	Edmonton, AB [*FM radio station call letters*]		CL	Change List
CKUM	Moncton, NB [*FM radio station call letters*]		CL	Chartered Librarian [*British*]
CKUT	Montreal, PQ [*FM radio station call letters*]		CL	Chator-Lea Sidecar [*Early motorcars*] (ROG)
CKV	Chelik Resources, Inc. [*Vancouver Stock Exchange symbol*]		C/L	Checklist (KSC)
CKV	Clarksville [*Tennessee*] [*Airport symbol*] (OAG)		CL	Chemical Laboratory
CKV	Clarksville, TN [*Location identifier FAA*] (FAAL)		CL	Chemical LASER (MCD)
CKVD	Val D'Or, PQ [*AM radio station call letters*]		CL	Chemical Literature [*A publication*]
CKVH	High Prairie, AB [*AM radio station call letters*]		CL	Chemiluminescence
CKVL	Verdun, PQ [*AM radio station call letters*]		CL	Chest and Left Arm [*Cardiology*]
CKVM	Ville-Marie, PQ [*AM radio station call letters*]		CL	Chile [*ANSI two-letter standard code*] (CNC)
CKVO	Clarenville, NF [*AM radio station call letters*]		cl	Chile [*MARC country of publication code Library of Congress*] (LCCP)
CKVR	Barrie, ON [*Television station call letters*]			
CKVU	Vancouver, BC [*Television station call letters*]		Cl	Chloride (DAVI)
CKW	Cherokee, WY [*Location identifier FAA*] (FAAL)		Cl	Chlorine [*Chemical element*]
CKW	Clockwise (ADA)		Cl	Chlorite [*A mineral*]
CKW	[*A*] New Translation in Plain English (1963) [*Charles K. Williams*] [*A publication*] (BJA)		cl	Chloro [*As substituent on nucleoside*] [*Biochemistry*]
CKWA	Slave Lake, AB [*AM radio station call letters*]		CL	Cholesterol-Lecithin Test [*Medicine*] (MAE)
CKWF	Peterborough, ON [*FM radio station call letters*]		CL	Christos Lavatus [*An association*] (EA)
CKWFC	Cheryl K. Warner Fan Club (EA)		CL	Chronic Leukemia [*Hematology and oncology*] (DAVI)
CKWL	Williams Lake, BC [*AM radio station call letters*]		CL	Churchman's Library [*A publication*]
CKWM	Kentville, NS [*FM radio station call letters*]		CL	Chutz La'aretz (BJA)
CKWR	Kitchener, ON [*FM radio station call letters*]		CL	Cilium [*Zoology*]
CKWS	Kingston, ON [*Television station call letters*]		CL	Circuit Layout [*AT & T*]
CKWV	Nanaimo, BC [*FM radio station call letters*]		CL	Circular Letter
CKWW	Windsor, ON [*AM radio station call letters*]		CL	City of London [*British*]
CKWX	Vancouver, BC [*AM radio station call letters*]		CL	Civil Law
CKX	Brandon, MB [*AM radio station call letters*]		CL	Civil Liberties (ILCA)
CKX	Chicken, AK [*Location identifier FAA*] (FAAL)		CL	Claim (WGA)
CKX	Copper Lake Explorations Ltd. [*Vancouver Stock Exchange symbol*]		CL	Clandestine Lodges [*Freemasonry*] (ROG)
CKXB	Musgravetown, NF [*AM radio station call letters*]		CL	Clarendon Laboratory [*Oxford University*] (MCD)

cl	Claret [Philately]
CL	Clarinet
CL	Class (AFM)
cl	Class (WDMC)
CL	Classical
Cl	Classical Latin (BARN)
Cl	Classical Music [Radio station format] (WDMC)
Cl	Classical Strain [Of RNA]
CL	Classics (ADA)
CL	Classification
cl	Classification (WDMC)
CL	Classification Code (NITA)
CL	Classification Group [Database terminology] (NITA)
CL	Classification List [Military]
CL	Clause
cl	Clause (WDMC)
CL	Clavicle [Anatomy]
Cl	Clay [Quality of the bottom] [Nautical charts]
cl	Clay (VRA)
CL	Cleaner [Automotive engineering]
CL	Clear
CL	Clearance (MSA)
cl	Clearance [Broadcasting] (WDMC)
CL	Clear Liquid [Medicine]
CL	Cleistogamous [Botany]
CL	Clergy
Cl	Cleric (BARN)
CL	Clerical Aptitude Area (AABC)
CL	Clerk
CL	Cliff Leader [British military] (DMA)
CL	Climatic Laboratory [Military]
Cl	Clinic
CL	Clinical Laboratory (DAVI)
CL	Clip (MSA)
Cl	Clone
CL	Close (AAG)
CL	Closed Loop (KSC)
CL	Close Rolls [British]
CL	Closet
Cl	Clostridium [Genus of microorganisms]
CL	Closure [Physiology]
CL	Cloth
cl	Cloudy [Biochemistry] (DAVI)
cl	Clove [Seven pounds] [Unit of weight] [British] (ROG)
CL	Cluster (NASA)
CL	Clutch (MSA)
CL	Coalition for Literacy (EA)
CL	Coast Lines [Steamship] (MHDW)
CL	Codex Leningradensis (BJA)
CL	Coefficient of Lift
CL	Coil
CL	Colgate-Palmolive [NYSE symbol] (TTSB)
CL	Colgate-Palmolive Co. [NYSE symbol] (SPSG)
CL	Colistin [Also, CO] [Generic form] [An antibiotic]
CL	Collection Entry [Banking]
CL	College Letter [British]
CL	Col Legno [With the Back of the Bow] [Music]
CL	Collocated
CL	Color Line [Illustration] (DGA)
CL	Combat and Liaison (CINC)
C/L	Combat Loss
C/L	Combined Limit [Insurance]
CL	Commander of the Order of Leopold
CL	Command Language
CL	Command Line [Military]
CL	Commission Leaflets, American Telephone and Telegraph Cases [A publication] (DLA)
CL	Common Law
CL	Common Law Reports [1853-85] [A publication] (DLA)
CL	Communication Lieutenant [British military] (DMA)
CL	Competency Level
CL	Compiled Laws [A publication] (DLA)
CL	Compiler Language [Computer science] (DIT)
CL	Compliance Level [Automotive emissions standards]
CL	Component List [DoD]
CL	Computational Linguistics (IEEE)
CL	Computer Language (IAA)
CL	Concentration Length
CL	Conceptual Level (EDAC)
CL	Conceptual Network-Based Language [NEC Corp.]
CL	Conditional Lease (ADA)
CL	Conference Location (NITA)
CL	Conference Lodges [Freemasonry] (ROG)
CL	Confidence Level [Statistical mathematics]
CL	Confidence Limits
CL	Congressional Liaison
CL	Connecting Line
CL	Conservation League (EA)
CL	Consolidated Listing (AFM)
CL	Consolidation Lodges [Freemasonry] (ROG)
CL	Contact Lens [Ophthalmology]
CL	Contact Lost [RADAR]
CL	Containment Leakage [Nuclear energy] (NRCH)
CL	Continuous Liner [Fitting for a propeller shaft]
CL	Contract Law

CL	Contralateral [Anatomy]
CL	Contributions Less Than [Database terminology] (NITA)
CL	Control Language [Computer science] (BUR)
CL	Control Leader [Computer science]
CL	Control Logic
CL	Conventional Landing (MCD)
CL	Convention Liberale [Cameroon] [Political party] (EY)
CL	Conversion Loss
CL	Convertible Lens [Photography]
CL	Cooperative Logistics
CL	Coordination Line (NVT)
Cl	Coprinus laniger [A fungus]
CL	Corporation of Lloyds [Also, Lloyd's of London] [Insurance] (DS)
CL	Corpus Luteum [Endocrinology]
CL	Cost of Living [Economics] (AAG)
CL	Council (ADA)
CL	Counter Logic (IAA)
CL	Country Living [A publication]
C/L	Craft Loss [Shipping]
CL	Craik-Leibovich [Physics]
CL	Crane Load
CL	Cream Laid [Paper] (DGA)
CL	Credit Limit (DCTA)
CL	Critical List [Medicine]
CL	Cruiser, Light [British military] (DMA)
CL	Crystallographic Laboratory [MIT] (MCD)
cl	Cum Laude Approbatur [Latin]
CL	Cumulative List [Internal Revenue code with names of exempt organizations]
CL	Current Layer (OA)
CL	Current Liabilities [Insurance]
CL	Current Logic [Electronics] (IAA)
CL	Current Loop: Interface Standard (NITA)
CL	Cut Length (ADA)
CL	Cutter Laboratories [Research code symbol]
CL	Cutter Location File
CL	Cyclotron Laboratory
CL	Cylinder (MCD)
CL	Derwent Classes [Database terminology] (NITA)
CL	Derwent Classification [Database terminology] (NITA)
CL	English Common Law Reports [A publication] (DLA)
CL	Irish Common Law Reports [A publication] (DLA)
cl----	Latin America [MARC geographic area code Library of Congress] (LCCP)
CL	Lederle Laboratories [Research code symbol]
CL	Les Codes Larcier [A publication] (ILCA)
CL	Light Cruiser [Navy symbol]
CL	Los Angeles Public Library, Los Angeles, CA [Library symbol Library of Congress] (LCLS)
CL	Patent Classification Number [Database terminology] (NITA)
Cl	Rotulus Clausarum [Close Roll] [England] [A publication] (DLA)
CL/1	Connectivity Language/1 [Apple] (CDE)
CL1	Papanicolaau Class I [Biochemistry] (DAVI)
CL9	Cloud Nine [Manufacturer of remote control devices for home electronics] [Company founded by Stephen Wozniak]
CLA	California State University, Los Angeles, Los Angeles, CA [OCLC symbol] (OCLC)
CLA	Camden Library [A publication]
CLA	Canadian Lacrosse Association (AC)
CLA	Canadian Library Association [Also known as ACB and CANLA]
CLA	Canadian Linguistic Association [See also ACL]
CLA	Canadian Lumbermen's Association
CLA	Canadian Lung Association [Association Pulmonaire du Canada] (AC)
CLA	Carry Lookahead (MHDI)
CLA	Catholic Library Association (EA)
CLA	Center Line Average
CLA	Certified Laboratory Assistant (WGA)
CLA	Certified Legal Assistant
CLA	Cervicolinguoaxial [Dentistry]
CLA	Chala [Peru] [Seismograph station code, US Geological Survey Closed] (SEIS)
CLA	Chartered Loss Adjuster (DD)
CLA	Chinese Laundry Association (EA)
CLA	Chinese Librarians Association (EA)
CLA	Christian Labor Association of the USA (EA)
CLA	Christian Law Association (EA)
CLA	Christian Literacy Associates (EA)
CLA	Church League of America [Defunct] (EA)
CLA	Church Literature Association [British] (BI)
CLA	Class [Freight]
CLA	Cleaning, Lubrication, and Adjustment [Camera repair]
CLA	Clearance Array (MSA)
CLA	Clear and Add
CLA	Clear Ice [Aviation] (DA)
CLA	Closed-Loop Trainer Aid (MCD)
CLA	Club de las Americas [Defunct] (EA)
CLA	Clutter Acquisition
CLA	Coaxial Line Attenuator
CLA	Coin Laundry Association (EA)
CLA	College Language Association (EA)
CLA	Columbia [Italy ICAO designator] (FAAC)
CLA	Combined Language Age [of the hearing-impaired]
CLA	Comilla [Bangladesh] [Airport symbol] (AD)
CLA	Commission for Local Administration [British] (BARN)

CLA............ Common Leucocyte Antigen [*Immunology*]
CLA............ Commonwealth Lawyers' Association [*British*] (EAIO)
CLA............ Commonwealth Library Association
CLA............ Communication Line Adapters
CLA............ Communication Link Analyzer (IEEE)
CLA............ Communications Line Adaptor (NITA)
CLA............ Community Legal Aid
CLA............ Community Living Arrangement [*For the handicapped*]
CLA............ Comparative Literature Association (EA)
CLA............ Computer Law Association (EA)
CLA............ Computer Lessors Association [*Later, CDLA*] (EA)
CLA............ Computers Lawyers Association (EA)
CLA............ Conjugated Linoleic Acid [*Antineoplastic drug*]
CLA............ Conservative Library Association [*Defunct*]
CLA............ Contingency Landing Area [*NASA*]
CLA............ Contralateral Local Anesthesia [*Medicine*] (DMAA)
CLA............ Control Logic Array
CLA............ Copyright Licensing Agency [*Government body*] [*British*]
CLA............ Council for Latin America [*Later, COA*]
CLA............ Country Landowners' Association [*British*]
CLA............ Cover Layer Assembly (KSC)
CLA............ Credit Licensing Authority [*Victoria*] [*Australia*]
CLA............ Crew-Loading Analysis (DNAB)
CLA............ Cross Launcher Assign [*Navy*] (CAAL)
CLA............ Cross-Linking Agent
CLA............ Crown Life Insurance Co. [*Toronto Stock Exchange symbol*]
CLA............ Custom Logic Array [*Electronics*] (IAA)
CLA............ Cutaneous Lymphocyte-Associated Antigen [*Immunology*]
CLA............ Cyclic Lysine Anhydride [*Medicine*] (DMAA)
CLA............ Cypriot Liberation Army
CLA............ San Juan, PR [*Location identifier FAA*] (FAAL)
CLA............ University of California at Los Angeles. Law Review [*A publication*] (DLA)
CLAA........... Antiaircraft Light Cruiser [*Navy symbol*]
CLAAB......... Commercial Law Association of Australia. Bulletin [*A publication*]
CLAA Bulletin... Commercial Law Association of Australia. Bulletin [*A publication*]
CLAAMP...... Continuous LASER Argon-Age Microprobe
CLA(ASCP)... Clinical Laboratory Assistant (American Society of Clinical Pathologists) (DAVI)
CLAB.......... Celtic League, American Branch (EA)
CLAB.......... Centro Latinoamericano de Ciencias Biologicas [*Latin American Center of Biological Sciences*] [*Research center Venezuela*] (IRC)
CLABC........ Congregational Libraries Association of British Columbia (AC)
CLAc.......... Academy of Motion Picture Arts and Sciences, Los Angeles, CA [*Library symbol Library of Congress*] (LCLS)
ClAc........... Chloroacetyl [*Organic chemistry*] (DAVI)
CLAC.......... Christian Labour Association of Canada
CLAC.......... Closed-Loop Approach Control
CLAC.......... Combined Liberated Areas Committee [*World War II*]
CLAC.......... Comision Latinoamericana de Aviacion Civil [*Latin American Civil Aviation Commission - LACAC*] (EAIO)
CLAC.......... Commonwealth Legal Aid Commision [*Australia*]
CLACA........ American College for the Applied Arts, Los Angeles, CA [*Library symbol*] [*Library of Congress*] (LCLS)
CLACJ......... Confederacion Latinoamericana de Asociaciones Cristianas de Jovenes [*Latin American Confederation of YMCAs - LACYMCA*] (EAIO)
CLACK........ Clackmannanshire [*County in Scotland*]
CLAC(S)....... Combined Liberated Areas Committee, Supply Subcommittee [*World War II*]
CLACS........ Latin American and Caribbean Studies Center [*University of Illinois*] [*Research center*] (RCD)
CLACSO...... Consejo Latinoamericano de Ciencias Sociales [*Latin American Social Sciences Council - LASSC*] (EAIO)
CLACW....... Conference of Liberal Arts Colleges for Women (EA)
CLAD.......... Centro Latinoamericano de Administracion para el Desarrollo [*Latin American Center for Development Administration*] [*Research center Venezuela*] (IRC)
Clad........... Cladosporium [*A fungus*]
CLAD.......... Clerical Administration
CLAD.......... Collect Adapter
CLAD.......... Cover Layer Automated Design (MHDI)
CLADES....... Centro Latinoamericano de Documentacion Economica y Social [*Latin American Center for Economic and Social Documentation*] [*Economic Commission for Latin America and the Caribbean*] [*United Nations*] [*Information service or system*] (IID)
CL(ADO)...... Diploma in Contact Lens Fitting of the Association of Dispensing Opticians [*British*] (DBQ)
CLADR........ Class Life Asset Depreciation Range [*Insurance*] (DICI)
CLAE.......... Council of Library Association Executives (EA)
CLAES........ Cryogenic Limb Array Etalon Spectrometer (MCD)
CLAEU........ Comite de Liaison des Architectes de l'Europe Unie [*Liaison Committee of the Architects of United Europe*] [*EC*] (ECED)
CLAFIC........ Class Featuring Information Compression (PDAA)
CLAG......... Conference of Latin Americanist Geographers
CLAGS........ Center for Lesbian and Gay Studies (EA)
CLAH......... Conference on Latin American History (EA)
CLAH......... Congenital Lipoid Adrenal Hyperplasia [*Medicine*] (DMAA)
CLAH......... Container Lift Adapter for Helicopter (MCD)
CLahF......... Foothill College, Los Altos, CA [*Library symbol Library of Congress*] (LCLS)
CLAi.......... Airsearch Manufacturing Co., Los Angeles, CA [*Library symbol Library of Congress*] (LCLS)

CLAI............ Consejo Latinoamericano de Iglesias [*Latin American Council of Churches*] (EAIO)
CLAIM......... Centre for Library and Information Management [*Loughborough University of Technology*] [*British Information service or system*] (IID)
CLAIMS........ Class Code, Assignee, Index Method, Search [*IFI/Plenum Data Co.*] [*Patent database*] (NITA)
CLAIMS........ Conventional Ammunition Integrated Management System (DNAB)
CLAIMS/CHEM... Class Code, Assignee, Index, Method, Search/Chemistry [*Patent database*] [*IFI/Plenum Data Co. Arlington, VA*]
CLAIMS/CLASS... Class Code, Assignee, Index Method, Search/Classification [*Patent database*] (NITA)
CLAIMS/GEM... Class Code, Assignee, Index, Method, Search/General, Electrical, Mechanical [*Patent database*] [*IFI/Plenum Data Co. Arlington, VA*]
CLAIMS/GEN... Class Code, Assignee, Index Method, Search/General [*IFI/Plenum Data Co.*] [*Patent database*] (NITA)
CLAIMS/US Pats Abs... Class Code, Assignee, Index Method, Search/US Patent Abstracts (NITA)
CLAIR .... Canadian Legal Advocacy Information and Research Association of the Disabled
CLAIRE .... County Links Access to Information about Resources and Expertise [*Education*] (AIE)
ClairSt .... Claire's Stores, Inc. [*Associated Press*] (SAG)
ClairStr .... Claire's Stores [*Associated Press*] (SAG)
CLAIS .... Center for Latin American and Iberian Studies [*Vanderbilt University*] [*Research center*] (RCD)
CLAIS.......... Committee on Latin American and Iberian Studies [*Harvard University*] [*Research center*]
CLAIT .... Constitutions and Laws of the American Indian Tribes [*A publication*] (DLA)
CLALS .... Centre for Latin American Linguistic Studies [*University of St. Andrews*] [*British*] (CB)
CLAM .... Carline Assignment Model [*General Motors Corp.*]
C LAM .... Cervical Laminectomy [*Neurology and orthopedics*] (DAVI)
CLAM.......... Chemical Low-Altitude Missile [*Air Force program*]
CLAM.......... Child Language Ability Measures [*Child development test*]
CLAM.......... Classification Management (DNAB)
CLAM.......... Clear Air Mass
CLAM.......... Coalition for Life for All Mollusks
CLAM.......... Comite de Liaison de l'Agrumiculture Mediterraneenne [*Liaison Committee for Mediterranean Citrus Fruit Culture - LCMCFC*] (EAIO)
CLAM.......... Command Load Acceptance Message
CLamB........ Biola Library, La Mirada, CA [*Library symbol Library of Congress*] (LCLS)
ClamB......... La Sainte Bible [*Pirot-Clamer*] [*Paris*] [*A publication*] (BJA)
CLAMP........ Chemical Low-Altitude Missile Puny [*Air Force program*] (MCD)
CLAMP........ Closed-Form Solutions Applied to a Mesh-Point-Field [*Mathematics*]
CLAMP........ Closed-Loop Aiming Mechanism Prototype
CLAMP........ Computer Listing and Analysis of Maintenance Programs (MHDB)
CLAMS........ Clear Lane Marking System [*Army*] (RDA)
CLAMS........ Countermeasures Launcher Modular System [*Navy*] (CAAL)
CLAMTI....... Clutter-Locked Airborne Moving Target Indicator [*Air Force*]
CLAMUC ..... Consejo Latinoamericano de Mujeres Catolicas [*Latin American Council of Catholic Women*] (EAIO)
CLAN .... Core Local Area Network (SSD)
Clancy Husb & W... Clancy's Treatise of the Rights, Duties, and Liabilities of Husband and Wife [*A publication*] (DLA)
Clancy Rights... Clancy's Treatise of the Rights, Duties, and Liabilities of Husband and Wife [*A publication*] (DLA)
CL & CGB .... Church Lads and Church Girls Brigade [*British*] [*An association*] (DBA)
Cl & F.......... Clark and Finnelly's English House of Lords Cases [*1831-46*] [*A publication*] (DLA)
Cl & Fin....... Clark and Finnelly's English House of Lords Cases [*1831-46*] [*A publication*] (DLA)
Cl & H .... Clarke and Hall's Cases of Contested Elections in Congress [*1789-1834*] [*United States*] [*A publication*] (DLA)
CL & P........ CL & P Capital LP [*Associated Press*] (SAG)
CL & P........ CL & P Capital LP [*Associated Press*] (SAG)
CL & P........ Cleft Lip and Palate [*Medicine*] (DAVI)
CL & P........ Connecticut Light & Power Co.
CL & R .... Canal, Lake, and Rail
Cl & Sc Dr Cas... Clarke and Scully's Drainage Cases [*Canada*] [*A publication*] (DLA)
CLANG........ Concurrent Language [*Computer science*]
CLANS .... Computerized Link Analysis System
CLANSW....... Corporate Lawyers' Association of New South Wales [*Australia*]
CLAO .... Contact Lens Association for Optometry (EA)
CLAO .... Contact Lens Association of Ophthalmologists (EA)
CLAO .... Council of Lebanese American Organizations (EA)
CLAP.......... Chemical LASER Analysis Program (MCD)
CLAP.......... Clapham [*England*]
CLAPA........ Cleft Lip and Palate Association [*British*] (DI)
Cl App .... Clark's Appeal Cases, House of Lords [*England*] [*A publication*] (DLA)
CLAPTUR..... Confederacion Latinoamericana de Prensa Turistica [*Latin American Confederation of Touristic Press*] [*Medellin, Colombia*] (EAIO)
CLAQ .... Centro Latinoamericano de Quimica [*Latin American Center for Chemistry*] (PDAA)
CLAR .... Clarendon [*Type*] (ROG)
CLAR .... Clarification [*or Clarify*] (AFM)
CLAR .... Clarinet
CLAR .... Clarino [*Clarion*] [*Music*] (ROG)

CLar............	Larkspur Public Library, Larkspur, CA [*Library symbol Library of Congress*] (LCLS)
CLARA........	Citizens Law and Research Association [*Defunct*] (EA)
CLARA........	Computer Load and Resource Analysis (MCD)
CLARA........	Cornell Learning and Recognizing Automaton
CLARB........	Council of Landscape Architectural Registration Boards (EA)
CLARC........	Canada-Latin American Resource Centre (AC)
CLARC........	Consejo Latino-Americano de Radiacon Cosmica [*Latin-American Council on Cosmic Radiation*] [*Bolivia*] (PDAA)
Clarcor........	Clarcor, Inc. [*Associated Press*] (SAG)
Clare............	Clare [*C.P.*] Corp. [*Associated Press*] (SAG)
Claremont Grad Sch...	Claremont Graduate School (GAGS)
ClareTch......	Claremont Technology Group, Inc. [*Associated Press*] (SAG)
Clarify..........	Clarify, Inc. [*Associated Press*] (SAG)
Clarion U......	Clarion University of Pennsylvania (GAGS)
Clark..........	Clark's Reports [*58 Alabama*] [*A publication*] (DLA)
CLARK........	Combat Launch and Recovery Kit (AFM)
Clark..........	English House of Lords Cases, by Clark [*A publication*] (DLA)
Clark..........	Pennsylvania Law Journal Reports, Edited by Clark [*A publication*] (DLA)
Clark..........	Supreme Court Judgments by Clark [*1917-32*] [*Jamaica*] [*A publication*] (DLA)
Clark (Ala)...	Clark's Reports [*58 Alabama*] [*A publication*] (DLA)
Clark & F.....	Clark and Finnelly's English House of Lords Reports [*6-8 English Reprint*] [*A publication*] (DLA)
Clark & F (Eng)...	Clark and Finnelly's English House of Lords Reports [*6-8 English Reprint*] [*A publication*] (DLA)
Clark & Fin...	Clark and Finnelly's English House of Lords Cases [*1831-46*] [*A publication*] (DLA)
Clark & Fin (NS)...	Clark and Finnelly's English House of Lords Reports, New Series [*9-11 English Reprint*] [*1847-66*] [*A publication*] (DLA)
Clark & F (NS)...	Clark and Finnelly's English House of Lords Reports, New Series [*9-11 English Reprint*] [*1847-66*] [*A publication*] (DLA)
Clark & F (NS) Eng...	Clark and Finnelly's English House of Lords Cases, New Series [*A publication*] (DLA)
Clark App.....	Clark's Appeal Cases, House of Lords [*England*] [*A publication*] (DLA)
Clark Atl U...	Clark Atlanta University (GAGS)
Clark Col Law...	Clark. Colonial Law [*1834*] [*A publication*] (ILCA)
Clark Dig......	Clark's Digest, House of Lords Reports [*A publication*] (DLA)
Clarke..........	Clarke's Edition of 1-8 Iowa [*A publication*] (DLA)
Clarke..........	Clarke's New York Chancery Reports [*A publication*] (DLA)
Clarke..........	Clarke's Notes of Cases [*Bengal*] [*A publication*] (DLA)
Clarke..........	Clarke's Pennsylvania Reports [*5 vols.*] [*A publication*] (DLA)
Clarke..........	Clarke's Reports [*19-22 Michigan*] [*A publication*] (DLA)
Clarke Adm Pr...	Clarke's Admiralty Practice [*A publication*] (DLA)
Clarke & H Elec Cas...	Clarke and Hall's Cases of Contested Elections in Congress [*1789-1834*] [*United States*] [*A publication*] (DLA)
Clarke & S Dr Cas...	Clarke and Scully's Drainage Cases [*Canada*] [*A publication*] (DLA)
Clarke B	Clarke on Bills and Notes [*Canada A publication*] (DLA)
Clarke Bib Leg...	Clarke's Bibliotheca Legum [*A publication*] (DLA)
Clarke C	Clarke College (GAGS)
Clarke Ch.....	Clarke's New York Chancery Reports [*A publication*] (DLA)
Clarke Ch (NY)...	Clarke's New York Chancery Reports [*A publication*] (DLA)
Clarke Const...	Clarke's Constable's Manual [*Canada A publication*] (DLA)
Clarke CR	Clarke's New York Chancery Reports [*A publication*] (DLA)
Clarke Cr L...	Clarke's Criminal Law [*Canada A publication*] (DLA)
Clarke Extr...	Clarke on Extradition [*A publication*] (DLA)
Clarke (IA)...	Clarke's Edition of 1-8 Iowa [*A publication*] (DLA)
Clarke Insol...	Clarke's Insolvent Acts [*Canada A publication*] (DLA)
Clarke Insur...	Clarke's Insurance Law [*Canada A publication*] (DLA)
Clarke (Mich)...	Clarke's Reports [*19-22 Michigan*] [*A publication*] (DLA)
Clarke Not ...	Clarke's Notes of Cases, in His "Rules and Orders" [*Bengal*] [*A publication*] (DLA)
Clarke (PA)...	Clarke's Pennsylvania Reports [*5 vols.*] [*A publication*] (DLA)
Clarke R & O...	Clarke's Notes of Cases, in His "Rules and Orders" [*Bengal*] [*A publication*] (DLA)
Clarke Rom L...	Clarke's Early Roman Law [*A publication*] (DLA)
Clarke's Chy (NY)...	Clarke's New York Chancery Reports [*A publication*] (DLA)
Clark (Jam)...	Judgments, Jamaica Supreme Court of Judicature [*A publication*] (DLA)
Clark (PA)...	Clark's Pennsylvania Law Journal Reports [*A publication*] (DLA)
Clarkson U...	Clarkson University (GAGS)
Clark's Summary...	Clark's Summary of American Law [*A publication*] (DLA)
Clark U	Clark University (GAGS)
CLARM........	International Center for Living Aquatic Resources Management (EAIO)
CLARNICO ...	Clarke, Nichols & Co. [*British*] (ROG)
CLARO	Clarino [*Clarion*] [*Music*]
Clar Parl Chr...	Clarendon's Parliamentary Chronicle [*A publication*] (DLA)
CLArt	Art Center College of Design, Los Angeles, CA [*Library symbol Library of Congress*] (LCLS)
CLARTTO	Clarinetto [*Clarinet*] [*Music*] (ROG)
CLAS............	Arnold Schoenberg Institute, Los Angeles, CA [*Library symbol Library of Congress*] (LCLS)
CLAS............	California Loans to Assist Students (EDAC)
CLAS............	Canadian Labour Arbitration Summaries [*Canada Law Book, Inc.*] [*Information service or system*] (CRD)
CLAS............	Catholic Ladies Aid Society
CLAS............	Centre of Latin American Studies [*University of Cambridge*] [*British*] (CB)
CLAS............	Cholesterol-Lowering Atherosclerosis Study [*National Heart, Lung, and Blood Institute - NHLBI*]
CLAS............	Chromatography Laboratory Automatic Software

CLAS............	Class
Clas	Classical Music [*Radio station format*] (WDMC)
CLAS............	Classic Bancshares [*NASDAQ symbol*] (TTSB)
CLAS............	Classification [*or Classified*] (DNAB)
CLAS............	Classify (AFM)
CLAS............	Clinical Laboratory Automated System (PDAA)
CLAS............	Clinical Ligand Assay Society (EA)
CLAS............	Communications Link Analyzer System
CLAS............	Computerized Lesson-Authoring System (EDAC)
CLAS............	Computerized Library Acquisitions System [*Lukac Data Systems*] [*Lewis and Clark College Discontinued*] [*Information service or system*] (IID)
CLAS............	Congenital Localized Absence of Skin [*Medicine*] (MAE)
CLAS............	Congress of Lung Association Staff (EA)
CLAS............	Cross-Lines Alternative School
CLAS............	Crowd, Lift, Actuate, Swing [*Backhoe controls for tractors*]
CLASB........	Citizens League Against the Sonic Boom [*Defunct*]
CLASIA	ASIA Project, Los Angeles, CA [*Library symbol Library of Congress*] (LCLS)
CLASIX	Computer/LASER Access Systems for Information Exchange
CLASP	Center for Law and Social Policy (EA)
CLASP	Chemical LASER Analytical System Program (MCD)
CLASP	Circuit Layout, Automated Scheduling and Production (PDAA)
CLASP	Civil Liberties Action Security Project [*Canada*]
CLASP	Claimant Advisory Service Program [*Unemployment insurance*]
CLASP	Clients Lifetime Advisory Service Program [*Insurance*]
CLASP	Closed Line Assembly for Single Particles (IEEE)
CLASP	Closed-Loop Adaptive Single Parameter (MCD)
CLASP	College Level Academic Skills Project [*Florida*] (EDAC)
CLASP	Community & Legal Aid Services Program (AC)
CLASP	Composite Launch and Spacecraft Program System (MCD)
CLASP	Computer Language for Aeronautics and Space Programming [*NASA*]
CLASP	Computer Launch and Separation Problem (MCD)
CLASP	Connecting Link for Application and Source Peripherals [*Computer science*]
CLASP	Consortium of Latin American Studies Programs
CLASP	Consortium of Local Authorities Special Programme [*British*]
CLASP	Cylindrical LASER Plasma
CLASS	California Library Authority for Systems and Services [*Library network*]
CLASS	Canadian Ladies Association of Shooting Sports
CLASS	Canadian L and Surface Scheme
CLASS	Capacity Loading and Schedule System
CLASS	Carrier Landing-Aid Stabilization System [*Navy*]
CLASS	Chemical Laboratory Analysis and Scheduling System [*Computer science*]
CLASS	Chrysler LASER Atlas Satellite System [*Automotive engineering*]
CLASS	Class Action Study and Survey [*Student legal action organization*]
CLASS	Classic (ROG)
class...........	Classic (WDMC)
class...........	Classical
CLASS	Classification (AFM)
class...........	Classification (WDMC)
CLASS	Classification
class...........	Classified (WDMC)
class...........	Classify (WDMC)
CLASS	Close Air Support System [*Military*]
CLASS	Closed Loop Accounting for Stores Sales (IEEE)
CLASS	Closed Loop Artillery Simulation System [*Army*]
CLASS	Cognitive, Linguistic, and Social-Communicative Scales [*Speech evaluation test*]
CLASS	Collection of Labor by Serial System (MCD)
CLASS	Communications Link Analysis and Simulation System (MCD)
CLASS	Community Learning through America's Schools [*National Education Association*]
CLASS	Composite Laminate Automated Sizing for Strength (MCD)
CLASS	Computer-Based Laboratory for Automated School Systems [*System Development Corp. project*]
CLASS	Computerized Laser-Assisted Sight System [*Military*] (INF)
CLASS	Computerized Librarian-Assisted Search Service [*Nicholls State University*] (OLDSS)
CLASS	Computerized Literature Access Search Service [*Colorado State University Libraries*] [*Information service or system*]
CLASS	Computer Literacy and Studies in Schools (AIE)
CLASS	Concrete Lintel Association [*British*] (DBA)
CLASS	Containerized Lighter Aboard Ship System (IAA)
CLASS	Cooperative Library Agency for Systems and Services [*San Jose, CA*] [*Telecommunications*] (TSSD)
CLASS	Cross-Chain LORAN [*Long-Range Navigation*] Atmospheric Sounding System (USDC)
CLASS	Cross-Charm LORAN [*Longe-Range Navigation*] Atmospheric Sounding System [*Marine science*] (OSRA)
CLASS	Current Literature Alerting Search Service [*Biological Abstracts*] (NITA)
CLASS	Current Literature Awareness Search Service [*BIOSIS*] [*Database*]
CLASS	Customer Local Area Signal Service (HGAA)
CLASS	Custom Local Area Signaling Services [*Telecommunications*] (ACRL)
Class	Custom Local Area Signaling Services
Class Act Rep...	Class Action Reports [*A publication*] (DLA)
CLASSIC	Circulation Library Automated System for Inventory Control [*Cincinnati Electronics Corp.*] [*Discontinued*] [*Information service or system*] (IID)
CLASSIC	Covert Local Area Sensor System for Intrusion Classification (LAIN)

CLASSIC ...... Custom Logic and Array Simulation Systems for Integrated Circuits (PDAA)
Classics .... Classics International Entertainment, Inc. [*Associated Press*] (SAG)
CLASSICS .... Classification of Identification of Covert Satellites
CLASSIF .... Classification
CLASSMATE... Computer Language to Aid and Stimulate Scientific, Mathematical, and Technical Education
CLASSN .... Classification
Class Out ..... Classical Outlook [*A publication*] (BRI)
Class R .... Classical Review [*A publication*] (BRI)
CLAST .... College Level Academic Skills Test
CLASYC .... Chemical LASER System Code (MCD)
CLAT .... Central Latinamericana de Trabajadores [*Latin American Central of Workers*] (EA)
CLAT .... Communication Line Adapters for Teletype
CLAT .... Conventional Land Attack Tomahawk Missile (MCD)
CLatA .... Sharpe Army Depot Library, Lathrop, CA [*Library symbol Library of Congress*] (LCLS)
CLATEC .... Comision Latinoamericana de Trabajadores de la Educacion [*Venezuela*]
CLATT .... Comite Latinoamericano de Textos Teologicos
Clau .... Claustrum [*Neuroanatomy*]
Claud .... Claudianus [*Fourth century AD*] [*Classical studies*] (OCD)
Claud .... Divus Claudius [*of Suetonius*] [*Classical studies*] (OCD)
CLAUDIUS ... Coopers & Lybrand Accounting and Distributive Inventory System (MHDB)
CLAV .... Antelope Valley Junior College, Lancaster, CA [*Library symbol Library of Congress*] (LCLS)
CLAV .... Clavering [*England*]
Clav .... Clavichord [*Music*]
CLAV .... Clavicle [*Anatomy*] (DHSM)
clav .... Clavicle [*Medicine*] (DMAA)
CLAV .... Clavier [*Keyboard*] [*Music*]
CLavA .... Archaeological Survey Association of Southern California, La Verne, CA [*Library symbol Library of Congress*] (LCLS)
CLavC .... La Verne College, La Verne, CA [*Library symbol Library of Congress*] (LCLS)
Clavi .... Clavichord [*Music*]
CLavO .... Occidental Research Corp., La Verne, CA [*Library symbol Library of Congress*] (LCLS)
CLAVR .... Clavicular [*Medicine*] (ROG)
CLAW .... Close Air Support Weapon [*Military*] (MCD)
C-LAW .... Close Combat LASER Assault Weapon [*Military*] (PDAA)
CLAW .... Clustered Atomic Warhead
CLAW .... Concept for Low-Cost Air-to-Air Weapon (MCD)
CLAW .... Consortium of Local Authorities in Wales
CLAWP .... Commander, Light Attack Wing - Pacific Fleet (MCD)
CLAWS .... Canine Livestock Animals Welfare Service [*Australia*]
CLAWS .... Classify, Locate, and Avoid Wind Shear [*National Center for Atmospheric Research*]
CLAWS .... Controlled Large Aperture Wavefront Sampling (MCD)
CLAY .... Claydon [*England*]
Clay .... Clayton's English Reports, York Assizes [*A publication*] (DLA)
Clay Conv .... Clayton on Conveyancing [*A publication*] (DLA)
ClayEng .... Clayton Williams Energy, Inc. [*Associated Press*] (SAG)
Clay L & T ... Claydon. Landlord and Tenant [*A publication*] (DLA)
Clay's Dig .... Clay's Digest of Laws of Alabama [*A publication*] (DLA)
Clayt .... Clayton's English Reports, York Assizes [*A publication*] (DLA)
ClaytH .... Clayton Homes [*Associated Press*] (SAG)
ClaytHm .... Clayton Homes, Inc. [*Associated Press*] (SAG)
Clayton .... Clayton's English Reports, York Assizes [*A publication*] (DLA)
Clayton (Eng)... Clayton's English Reports, York Assizes [*A publication*] (DLA)
CLB .... Bachelor of Civil Law
CLB .... CAA Calibration Flight [*British ICAO designator*] (FAAC)
CLB .... Center Line Bend (MSA)
CLB .... Center Line Block [*Philately*]
CLB .... Central Logic Bus [*Computer science*]
CLB .... Chlorambucil [*Antineoplastic drug*]
CLB .... Chlorambucil [*Antineoplastic drug*] (CDI)
CLB .... Church Lads' Brigade [*Church of England*]
CLB .... Civil Liberties Bureau [*Forerunner of the American Civil Liberties Union*]
CIB .... Claiborne Industries Ltd. [*Toronto Stock Exchange symbol*]
Cl B .... Clarinette Basse [*Bass Clarinet*] [*Music*]
CLB .... Clear Both [*Computer science*]
CLB .... Climb (FAAC)
CLB .... Climb Detent of the Thrust Levers (GAVI)
CLB .... Club
CLB .... Club
CLB .... Columbus Realty Trust [*NYSE symbol*] (SPSG)
CLB .... Combat Lessons Bulletin
CLB .... Commercial Law Bulletin [*Commercial Law League of America*] [*A publication*]
CIB .... Connaitre la Bible [*Bruges*] [*A publication*] (BJA)
CLB .... Consortia of London Boroughs [*British*]
CLB .... Constant Level Balloon
CLB .... Continuous Line Bucket [*Deep mining system*]
CLB .... Contract Labour Branch [*Admiralty*] [*British*]
CLB .... Crash Locator Beacon [*Aviation*] (AFM)
CLB .... Curvilinear Body [*in Batten disease*]
CLB .... Long Beach Public Library, Long Beach, CA [*OCLC symbol*] (OCLC)
CLB .... Wilmington, NC [*Location identifier FAA*] (FAAL)
CLBA .... Closed-Loop Boresight Alignment (MCD)
CLBA .... Current Logical Byte Address (IAA)
CLBANY ...... Collateral Loan Brokers Association of New York (EA)

CLBBB .... Complete Left Bundle Branch Block [*Medicine*] (MAE)
CLBC .... Canadian Lawn Bowling Council
CLBC .... Christian Literature and Bible Center (EA)
CLBC .... Confederacion Latinoamericana de Bioquimica Clinica [*Latin American Confederation of Clinical Biochemistry - LACCB*] (EAIO)
CL BDS .... Cloth Boards [*Bookbinding*] (ROG)
CLBHS .... Clubhouse
CLBI .... Climb Immediately [*Aviation*] (FAAC)
Cl Bills .... Clarke on Bills and Notes [*Canada A publication*] (DLA)
CLBK .... Commercial Bancshares [*NASDAQ symbol*] (TTSB)
CLBK .... Commercial Bankshares, Inc. [*NASDAQ symbol*] (SAG)
CLBN .... Crash Locator Beacon [*Aviation*] (FAAC)
CLBN .... Credit Lyonnais Bank Nederland [*Credit Lyonnais' Dutch subsidiary*] (ECON)
CLBP .... Chronic Low Back Pain [*Medicine*] (DMAA)
CLBPA .... Canadian Latvian Business & Professional Association (AC)
CLBR .... Calibration
CLBraille ..... Braille Institute of America, Los Angeles, CA [*Library symbol Library of Congress*] (LCLS)
CLBRP .... Cannon-Launched Beam Rider Projectile (MCD)
CLBRTY .... Celebrity
CLBU .... China Law and Business Update [*A publication*]
CLBW .... Closed-Loop Bandwidth
CLC .... Cadillac-LaSalle Club (EA)
CLC .... Canadian Labour Congress
CLC .... Canadian League of Composers
CLC .... Capacity Limiting Constituents (GNE)
clc .... Capital and Lower Case (WDMC)
CLC .... Carrier Liaison Committee [*An association*] (EA)
CLC .... Catholic Ladies of Columbia
CLC .... Central Crude Ltd. [*Vancouver Stock Exchange symbol*]
CLC .... Central Labour College [*Railroad*] [*British*] (ROG)
CLC .... Central Logic Control [*Computer science*]
CLC .... Central Logistics Command [*Republic of Vietnam Armed Forces*]
CLC .... Centrifugal Lockup Converter [*Automotive engineering*]
CLC .... Change Letter Control (NASA)
CLC .... Channel Level Control (MCD)
CLC .... Cheshire Lines Committee Railway [*British*] (ROG)
CLC .... Child Life Council (EA)
CLC .... Children's Legal Centre (EAIO)
CLC .... Chile Legislative Center [*An association*] (EA)
CLC .... China Lake [*California*] [*Seismograph station code, US Geological Survey*] (SEIS)
CLC .... Cholesteric Liquid Crystal (PDAA)
CLC .... Christian Life Centre [*Australia*]
CLC .... Christian Life Communities [*English Canada*] (AC)
CLC .... Christian Literature Crusade [*British*]
CLC .... Church of the Lutheran Confession
CLC .... Civil Liability Convention [*British*]
CLC .... Clackmannan [*Town and county in Scotland*] (ROG)
CLC .... CLARCOR, Inc. [*NYSE symbol*] (SPSG)
CLC .... CLARCOR Inc. [*NYSE symbol*] (TTSB)
CLC .... Claritas Corp. [*Information service or system*] (IID)
CLC .... Clark College, Atlanta, GA [*OCLC symbol*] (OCLC)
Clc .... Classic [*Record label*] [*France*]
CLC .... Classic Air AG [*Switzerland ICAO designator*] (FAAC)
CLC .... Clear Carry
CLC .... Clear Lake City [*Texas*] [*Airport symbol*] (OAG)
CLC .... Clear Lake City, TX [*Location identifier FAA*] (FAAL)
CLC .... Closed-Loop Condensate [*Nuclear energy*] (NRCH)
CLC .... Closed-Loop Control [*Automotive engineering*]
CLC .... Columbia & Cowlitz Railway Co. [*AAR code*]
CLC .... Column Liquid Chromatography
CLC .... Comite de Liaison des Industries Cimentieres de la CEE [*Liaison Committee of the Cement Industries in the EEC*] (ECED)
CLC .... Command Load Controller
CLC .... Communications Law Centre [*Australia*]
CLC .... Communications Line Control
CLC .... Communications Link Controller [*International Computers Ltd.*] [*Telecommunications*]
CLC .... Compressive Load Cell
CLC .... Computerized Lubrication Control [*Sun Oil Co.*]
CLC .... Computer Learning Center (HGAA)
CLC .... Computer Literacy Council (EA)
CLC .... Condenser Load Compensation [*Portable electric generators*]
CLC .... Conseil pour la Liberation du Congo-Kinshasa [*Council for the Liberation of the Congo-Kinshasa*] [*Zaire*] (PD)
CLC .... Constant Light Compensating (OA)
CLC .... Contact Literacy Center (EA)
CLC .... Containment Leakage Control [*Nuclear energy*] (IEEE)
CLC .... Contemporary Literary Criticism [*Reference publication; often pronounced "click"*]
CLC .... Continued Lymphocyte Culture [*Immunology*]
CLC .... Contrast Light Compensation (IAA)
CLC .... Control Launch Center (MUGU)
CLC .... Convection Loss Cone (MCD)
CLC .... Convention Liaison Council (EA)
CLC .... Convention on Civil Liability for Oil Pollution Damage (DS)
CLC .... Cork Leather and Celastic [*Orthotic*] [*Orthopedics*] (DAVI)
CLC .... Cost of Living Council [*Also, COLC*] [*Terminated, 1974 Pronounced "click"*]
CLC .... Cotton Leaf Crumple [*Plant pathology*]
CLC .... Counter-Lock-Cord [*Tennis shoe technology*] [*Autry Industries, Inc.*]
CLC .... Course-Line Computer [*Aviation*] (MCD)

CLC.............	Current Law Consolidation [England] [A publication] (DLA)
CLC.............	Current Leading Component (PDAA)
CLC.............	Tactical Command Ship [Navy symbol]
CLCA...........	Comite de Liaison de la Construction Automobile [Liaison Committee for the Motor Industry in the EEC Countries] [Brussels, Belgium] (EAIO)
CLCan..........	Cannan Electric Co., Los Angeles, CA [Library symbol Library of Congress] (LCLS)
Cl Can Ins ...	Clarke's Canada Insolvent Acts [A publication] (DLA)
CLCAPF........	Los Angeles County Air Pollution Control District Library, Los Angeles, CA [Library symbol Library of Congress] (LCLS)
Cl CB	Clarinette Contre Basse [Contrabass Clarinet] [Music]
CLCB...........	Committee of London Clearing Bankers [British]
CLCC...........	Ceramic Leaded Chip Carrier (NITA)
CLCC...........	Closed-Loop Continuity Check [Aerospace] (AAG)
CLCC...........	Los Angeles Chamber of Commerce, Research Library, Los Angeles, CA [Library symbol Library of Congress] (LCLS)
CLCCR	Comite de Liaison de la Construction de Carrosseries et de Remorques [Liaison Committee of the Body- and Trailer-Building Industry] (EAIO)
CLCCS	Los Angeles County Civil Service Commission, Los Angeles, CA [Library symbol Library of Congress] (LCLS)
CLCD	Clearinghouse and Laboratory for Census Data [Defunct]
CLCD	Clearly Canadian Beverage Corp. [NASDAQ symbol] (SAG)
CLCD	Cleidocranial Dysostosis [Medicine] (DMAA)
CLCDF	Clearly Canadian Beverage [NASDAQ symbol] (TTSB)
CLCE...........	Communications Link Characterization Experiment [Communications Technology Satellite] (MCD)
CLCF	Children's Leukemia and Cancer Foundation [Australia]
CLCGH	Los Angeles County General Hospital, Los Angeles, CA [Library symbol Library of Congress] (LCLS)
CLCGM	Closed-Loop Cover Gas Monitor [Nuclear energy] (NRCH)
CLCH	Children's Hospital Society, Doctor's Library, Los Angeles, CA [Library symbol Library of Congress] (LCLS)
Cl Ch	Clarke's New York Chancery Reports [A publication] (DLA)
CL Ch	Common Law Chamber Reports [Ontario] [A publication] (DLA)
CL Chamb....	Chambers' Common Law [Upper Canada] [A publication] (DLA)
CL Chamb....	Common Law Chamber Reports [Ontario] [A publication] (DLA)
CL Chambers...	Chambers' Common Law [Upper Canada] [A publication] (DLA)
CL Chamb Rep...	Common Law Chamber Reports [Ontario] [A publication] (DLA)
CLCI...........	Cadiz Land [NASDAQ symbol] (TTSB)
CLCI...........	Cadiz Land Co., Inc. [NASDAQ symbol] (SAG)
CLC(I).........	Christian Literature Crusade (International) [Australia]
CLCiC..........	Los Angeles City College, Los Angeles, CA [Library symbol Library of Congress] (LCLS)
CLCIS..........	Closed-Loop Control and Instrumentation System [Nuclear energy] (NRCH)
CLCK..........	Clock
CLCLH	Cedars-Sinai Medical Center, Los Angeles, CA [Library symbol Library of Congress] (LCLS)
CLCM..........	Communication Line Concentrator Module (MHDI)
CLCM..........	Council of Lutheran Church Men [Defunct] (EA)
CLCM..........	Los Angeles County Museum of Natural History, Los Angeles, CA [Library symbol Library of Congress] (LCLS)
CLCMAr	Los Angeles County Museum of Art, Los Angeles, CA [Library symbol Library of Congress] (LCLS)
CLCN	Chloride Channel (DMAA)
CLCO	Claremont & Concord Railway Co., Inc. [AAR code]
CLCO	Los Angeles College of Optometry, Los Angeles, CA [Library symbol Library of Congress] (LCLS)
CLCo	Los Angeles County Public Library, Los Angeles, CA [Library symbol Library of Congress] (LCLS)
Cl Col	Clark's Colonial Laws [A publication] (DLA)
CLCol..........	Colorado River Board of California, Los Angeles, CA [Library symbol Library of Congress] (LCLS)
CLCON........	Class Convening
CLCONE.......	Closed Cone at Maturity [Botany]
CLCoP.........	Los Angeles County Public Library, Los Angeles, CA [Library symbol Library of Congress] (LCLS)
CL/CP..........	Cleft Lip and Cleft Palate [Medicine] (MAE)
CLCP..........	Command Launch Computer (DWSG)
CLCP..........	Los Angeles County Health Department, Los Angeles, CA [Library symbol Library of Congress] (LCLS)
CLCR	Cheshire Lines Committee Railway [British] (ROG)
CLCR	Communication Lieutenant-Commander [British military] (DMA)
CLCR	Controlled Letter Contract Reduction (IEEE)
CLCS..........	Cable Launch Control System (SAA)
CLCS..........	Chinese Language Computer Society (EA)
CLCS..........	Closed-Loop Control System [Nuclear energy] (IAA)
CLCS..........	Colchicine Sensitivity [Medicine] (DMAA)
CLCS..........	Consequence Limiting Control System [Nuclear energy] (NRCH)
CLCS..........	Current-Logic-Current-Switching [Electronics]
CLCSBC	Christian Life Commission of the Southern Baptist Convention (EA)
CLCSE.........	Center for Life Cycle Software Engineering [Communications-Electronics Command] [Army]
Cl Ct	[United States] Claims Court [Now Court of Federal Claims] (AAGC)
Cl Ct	Claims Court Reporter [West] [A publication] (AAGC)
CLCT..........	Collector [Freight]
Cl Ct R........	United States Claims Court Rules [A publication] (DLA)
CLCU..........	Civil Labour Control Unit [British]
CLCV..........	Clergy and Laity Concerned About Vietnam [An association] (VNW)
CLCV..........	Cold Leg Check Valve [Nuclear energy] (NRCH)
CLCVN	Class Convening
CLCW..........	Closed-Loop Cooling Water [Nuclear energy] (NRCH)
CLCX..........	Computer Learning Centers, Inc. [NASDAQ symbol] (SAG)

CLCX...........	Computer Learning Ctrs [NASDAQ symbol] (TTSB)
CLD.............	Caldera [Chile] [Seismograph station code, US Geological Survey Closed] (SEIS)
CLD.............	Caldor Corp. [NYSE symbol] (SPSG)
CLD.............	Called [In stock listings of newspapers] [Business term]
CLD.............	Called Line (ECII)
CLD.............	Cancelled (BARN)
CLD.............	Carlsbad [California] [Airport symbol] (OAG)
CLD.............	Center for Leadership Development (EA)
CLD.............	Center for Living Democracy (EA)
CLD.............	Central Library and Documentation Branch [International Labor Organization] (IEEE)
CLD.............	Centre for Learning and Development [British] (AIE)
CLD.............	Chemiluminescence Detector
CLD.............	Children with Learning Disabilities
CLD.............	Chloride Leak Detector (IEEE)
CLD.............	Cholestatic Liver Disease [Medicine]
CLD.............	Chronic Liver Disease [Medicine]
CLD.............	Chronic Lung Disease [Medicine]
CLD.............	Civil Liaison Division [Army]
CLD.............	Cleared
CLD.............	Cloud
CLD.............	Clydesdale [Valley in Scotland] (ROG)
CLD.............	Coincidence-Ledge-Dislocation (PDAA)
CLD.............	Colored
CLD.............	Comite de Liaison Commerce de Detail [Liaison Committee of European Retail Trade Associations] (EAIO)
CLD.............	Compression Load Deflection (PDAA)
CLD.............	Compulaw Digest [A publication] (ADA)
CLD.............	Computerland Corp. (MHDW)
CLD.............	Computer Logic Demonstrator
CLD.............	COMSAT [Communications Satellite Corp.], Washington, DC [OCLC symbol] (OCLC)
CLD.............	Concentrated Liquor Discharge (DICI)
CLD.............	Condensed Logic Diagram [Electronics] (IAA)
CLD.............	Constant Level Discriminator [Electronics] (OA)
CLD.............	Control Science [Vancouver Stock Exchange symbol]
CLD.............	Cooled (MSA)
CLD.............	Cost Laid Down
CLD.............	Could (ADA)
CLD.............	Council for Learning Disabilities (EA)
CLD.............	Crown Law Department [Western Australia]
CLD.............	Crystal Lattice Dislocation (PDAA)
CLD.............	Current-Limiting Device [Short-circuit limiter]
CLD.............	Doctor of Civil Law
CLDA	Control Logic and Drive Assembly
CLDAS	Clinical Laboratory Data Acquisition System [Computer science]
CLDC	COMSEC [Communications Security] Logistics Data Center (AABC)
CLDL..........	Canadian Labour Defence League
C/LDMO	Chief, Logistics Data Management Office [Army]
CLDN	Celadon Group [NASDAQ symbol] (SAG)
CLDO	Central Load Dispatching Office [US Military Government, Germany]
CLDo...........	Documentation Associates, Los Angeles, CA [Library symbol Library of Congress] (LCLS)
CLDR	Cliffs Drilling [NASDAQ symbol] (TTSB)
CLDR	Cliffs Drilling Co. [NASDAQ symbol] (NQ)
CLDRV	Cliffs Drilling Co. (MHDW)
CLDS	Canada Land Data System
CLDST	Closed-Loop Dynamic Stability Test (NASA)
CLDWN........	Cool Down (AAG)
CLDY	Cloudy
CLDZ...........	Cadillac-Larder Lake [Geology]
CLE.............	Barlow Sanatorium, Elks Tuberculosis Library, Los Angeles, CA [Library symbol Library of Congress] (LCLS)
CLE.............	Canadian Lencourt Mines Ltd. [Toronto Stock Exchange symbol]
CLE.............	Canister/Launcher Electronics
CLE.............	Cardinal Leger & His Endeavours (AC)
CLE.............	Center for Law and Education (EA)
CLE.............	Centre Europeen pour les Loisirs et l'Education [European Centre for Leisure and Education - ECLE] (EAIO)
CLE.............	Centrifugal Liquid Extraction [Chemistry]
CLE.............	Centrilobular Emphysema [Medicine] (MAE)
CLE.............	Chicago Livestock Exchange
CLE.............	Citizen's Library of Economics [A publication]
CLE.............	City of London Engineers [British military] (DMA)
CLE.............	Claire's Stores [NYSE symbol] (TTSB)
CLE.............	Claire's Stores, Inc. [NYSE symbol] (SPSG)
Cle.............	Clementinae Constitutions [A publication] (DSA)
CLE.............	Cleveland [Ohio] [Airport symbol]
CLE.............	Cleveland [Ohio] [Seismograph station code, US Geological Survey] (SEIS)
CLE.............	Cleveland Public Library, Cleveland, OH [OCLC symbol] (OCLC)
CLE.............	Closed End
CLE.............	Committee of Liberal Exiles [British] (EAIO)
CLE.............	Communications Line Expander [Electrodata, Inc.] [Telecommunications]
CLE.............	Console Local Equipment (MCD)
CLE.............	Consumption Levels Enquiry [British]
CLE.............	Continuing Legal Education
CLE.............	Contract Lineage Equivalent [Formula used by certain publications for calculating number of lines of advertising copy]
CLE.............	Council of Legal Education [British]
CLE.............	Crew Loose Equipment [Aerospace] (MCD)
CLE.............	Key Word [Online database field identifier]
CLEA...........	Canadian Library Exhibitors' Association

CLEA........... Commonwealth Legal Education Association (EAIO)
CLEA........... Community Legal Education Association (Manitoba) Inc. [*Association d'Education Juridique Communautaire (Manitoba) Inc.*] (AC)
CLEA .... Conference of LASER Engineering and Applications
CLEAA......... Comite de Liaison Entr'Aide et Action [*Help and Action Coordinating Committee*] (EAIO)
CLEAN .... California League Enlisting Action Now [*Antiobscenity group*]
CLEAN .... Committee for Leaving the Environment of America Natural
CLEAN .... Commonwealth Law Enforcement Assistance Network [*Pennsylvania*]
CleanH........ Clean Harbors, Inc. [*Associated Press*] (SAG)
CLEANS .... Clinical Laboratory for Evaluation and Assessment of Noxious Substances [*Environmental Protection Agency*] (GFGA)
CLEAPSE...... Consortium of Local Education Authorities for the Provision of Science Equipment [*British*]
CLEAR .... Campaign for Lead-Free Air [*British*]
CLEAR .... Center for Labor Education and Research [*University of Hawaii*] [*Research center*] (RCD)
CLEAR .... Center for Labor Education and Research [*University of Alabama at Birmingham*] [*Research center*] (RCD)
CLEAR .... Center for Labor Education and Research [*University of Colorado*]
CLEAR .... Center for Lake Erie Area Research [*Ohio State University*]
CLEAR .... Center for Language Education and Research [*Los Angeles, CA*] [*Department of Education*] (GRD)
CLEAR .... Closed-Loop Evaluation and Reporting System (MCD)
CLEAR .... Compiler, Executive Program, Assembler Routines
CLEAR .... Components Life Evaluation and Reliability
CLEAR .... County Law Enforcement Applied Regionally
CLEAR .... National Clearinghouse on Licensure, Enforcement and Regulation (EA)
ClearC .... Clear Channel, Inc. [*Associated Press*] (SAG)
ClearCh........ Clear Channel, Inc. [*Associated Press*] (SAG)
Clearinghouse Rev... Clearinghouse Review [*A publication*] (AAGC)
Clearnet....... Clearnet Communications, Inc. [*Associated Press*] (SAG)
CLEARS .... Cornell Laboratory for Environmental Applications of Remote Sensing [*Cornell University*] [*Information service or system*] (IID)
CLeaR-TV .... Christian Leaders for Responsible Television (NTCM)
Cleary RC .... Cleary's Registration Cases [*England*] [*A publication*] (DLA)
Cleary Reg Cas... Cleary's Registration Cases [*Ireland*] [*A publication*] (DLA)
CLEA/ST....... Council of Local Education Authorities/School Teacher Committee (AIE)
CLEAT......... Computer Language for Engineers and Technologists (MHDB)
CLEATS........ Clinical Laboratory of Evaluation and Assessment of Tox Substances (GNE)
Cleav Bank L... Cleaveland's Banking Laws of New York [*A publication*] (DLA)
CLEB.......... Celebrity Entertainment, Inc. [*NASDAQ symbol*] (SAG)
C/LEC......... Citizen/Labor Energy Coalition [*Defunct*] (EA)
CLEC.......... Closed-Loop Ecological Cycle [*Aerospace*] (AAG)
CLEC.......... Competitive Local Exchange Carrier
CLEC.......... Cross-Linked Enzyme Crystal
CLEC.......... Cross Linked Enzyme Crystal
CLECAT....... Comite de Liaison Europeen des Commissionnaires et Auxiliaires de Transport [*European Liaison Committee of Forwarders*] (EAIO)
CLED.......... Cystine-Lactose-Electrolyte Deficient [*Clinical chemistry*]
CLEDIPA ...... Comite de Liaison Europeen de la Distribution Independante de Pieces de Rechangeet Equipements pour Automobiles [*European Liaison Committee for the Independent Distribution of Spare Parts and Equipment for Motor Cars*] [*EC*] (ECED)
CL/EDS .... Cathodoluminescence/Energy Dispersive Spectroscopy
CLEE .... Canister/Launcher Electronic Equipment
CLEET......... Council on Law Enforcement Education and Training [*An association*]
CLEF.......... Civil Liberties Educational Foundation [*Defunct*] (EA)
CLEFS......... Commercial Licensed Evaluation Facilities [*British*]
CLEFT......... Cleavage of Lateral Epitaxial Film for Transfer [*Photovoltaic energy systems*]
C Leg Rec ... California Legal Record [*A publication*] (DLA)
CLEHA......... Conference of Local Environmental Health Administrators [*Later, NCLEHA*] (EA)
Cl Elec........ Clark's Treatise on Elections [*A publication*] (DLA)
CLELJ .... East Los Angeles College, Los Angeles, CA [*Library symbol Library of Congress*] (LCLS)
CLEM.......... Cargo Lunar Excursion Module
CLEM.......... Central Laboratory Equipment Management (MCD)
Clem.......... Clemens' Reports [*57-59 Kansas*] [*A publication*] (DLA)
Clem.......... Clementinae Constitutiones [*A publication*] (DSA)
Clem.......... Clement of Alexandria (BJA)
CLEM.......... Closed-Loop Ex-Vessel Machine [*Formerly, EVHM*] [*Nuclear energy*] (NRCH)
CLEM.......... Composite for the Lunar Excursion Module [*NASA*] (IEEE)
CLEM.......... Continuing Legal Education, University of Montana (DLA)
Clem.......... De Clementia [*of Seneca the Younger*] [*Classical studies*] (OCD)
Clem Al .... Clemens Alexandrinus [*First century AD*] [*Classical studies*] (OCD)
Clem Corp Sec... Clemens on Corporate Securities [*A publication*] (DLA)
ClemGlb ..... Clemente Global Growth Fund, Inc. [*Associated Press*] (SAG)
Clemson U... Clemson University (GAGS)
CLEN.......... Monoclinic Enstatite [*Geology*]
CLENE........ Continuing Library Education Network and Exchange [*American Library Association Information service or system*] (EA)
CLENERT ..... Continuing Library Education Network and Exchange Round Table (EA)
CLENOM...... Crew Loose Equipment Nomenclature [*Aerospace*] (MCD)
CLEO .... Clear Language for Expressing Orders [*Computer science*] (IEEE)
CLEO.......... Collateralized Lease Equipment (TDOB)
CLEO.......... Comite de Liaison Europeen des Osteopathes [*European Liaison Committee for Osteopaths - ELCO*] (EA)
CLEO.......... Community Legal Education Ontario (AC)

CLEO.......... Computer Listings of Employment Opportunities [*The Copley Press, Inc.*] [*Database*]
CLEO.......... Conference on LASERs and Electro-Optics (MCD)
CLEO.......... Council on Legal Education Opportunity (EA)
Cleom........ Cleomenes [*of Plutarch*] [*Classical studies*] (OCD)
CLEOP........ Cleopatra [*Queen of Egypt, 69-30BC*] (ROG)
CLEOPATRA... Comprehensive Language for Elegant Operating System and Translator Design (PDAA)
CLEOS .... Conference on LASER and Electro-Optical Systems
CLEP.......... College-Level Examination Program [*Trademark/service mark of the College Entrance Examination Board*]
CLEPA........ Comite de Liaison de la Construction d'Equipements et de Pieces d'Automobiles [*Liaison Committee of Manufacturers of Motor Vehicle Parts and Equipment*] (EAIO)
CLEPR........ Council on Legal Education for Professional Responsibility (EA)
CLER.......... Celebrity Entertainment [*NASDAQ symbol*] (TTSB)
CLER.......... Classification and Labelling of Explosives Regulations
CLER.......... Clear [*Biochemistry*] (DAVI)
CLER.......... Clergy
CLER.......... Clergy
CLER.......... Clerical
CLER.......... Clerical Test [*Military*]
CLER.......... Critical Laboratory Evaluation Roast [*Food technology*]
ClerCd .... Clearly Canadian Beverage Corp. [*Associated Press*] (SAG)
CLERG .... Clergyman
Clerke Am L... Clerke's American Law and Practice [*A publication*] (DLA)
Clerke & Br Conv... Clerke and Brett on Conveyancing, Etc. [*A publication*] (DLA)
Clerke Dig.... Clerke's Digest [*New York*] [*A publication*] (DLA)
Clerke Pr.... Clerke's Praxis Curiae Admiralitatis [*A publication*] (DLA)
Clerke Prax... Clerke's Praxis Curiae Admiralitatis [*A publication*] (DLA)
Clerk Home... Clerk Home's Decisions, Scotch Court of Session [*1735-44*] [*A publication*] (DLA)
CLER PARL... Clericus Parliamentariorum [*Clerk of Parliaments*] [*British*] (ROG)
CLES........... Centre for Local Economic Strategies Ltd. [*British*] (CB)
CLET.......... Cooler Liquid Electron Tube
CLETS......... California Law Enforcement Telecommunications System
CLEV.......... Cleveland [*District in Yorkshire, England*] (ROG)
Clev BJ....... Journal. Cleveland Bar Association [*A publication*] (DLA)
Cleve.......... Cleveland (BARN)
Cleve Bank... Cleaveland on the Banking System [*A publication*] (DLA)
Cleveland SLJ... Cleveland State Law Journal [*A publication*] (DLA)
Cleve Law R... Cleveland Law Reporter [*Ohio*] [*A publication*] (DLA)
Cleve Law Rec... Cleveland Law Record [*Ohio*] [*A publication*] (DLA)
Cleve Law Reg... Cleveland Law Register [*Ohio*] [*A publication*] (DLA)
Cleve Law Rep... Cleveland Law Reporter [*Ohio*] [*A publication*] (DLA)
Cleve L Rec... Cleveland Law Record [*Ohio*] [*A publication*] (DLA)
Cleve L Rec (Ohio)... Cleveland Law Record [*Ohio*] [*A publication*] (DLA)
Cleve L Reg... Cleveland Law Register [*Ohio*] [*A publication*] (DLA)
Cleve L Reg (Ohio)... Cleveland Law Register [*Ohio*] [*A publication*] (DLA)
Cleve L Rep... Cleveland Law Reporter [*Ohio*] [*A publication*] (DLA)
Cleve LR (Ohio)... Cleveland Law Reporter (Ohio) [*A publication*] (ILCA)
CLEVER....... Clinical Laboratory for Evaluation and Validation of Epidemiologic Research [*Environmental Protection Agency*] (GFGA)
Cleve Rep... Cleveland Law Reporter (Reprint) [*Ohio*] [*A publication*] (DLA)
Cleve St U... Cleveland State University (GAGS)
Clev Insan ... Clevenger's Medical Jurisprudence of Insanity [*A publication*] (DLA)
CLEVITE....... Cleveland Graphite [*American Cleveland Graphite Corp.*] [*Automotive parts supplier*]
Clev Law Rep... Cleveland Law Reporter (Reprint) [*Ohio*] [*A publication*] (DLA)
Clev L Rec... Cleveland Law Record [*Ohio*] [*A publication*] (DLA)
Clev L Reg... Cleveland Law Register [*Ohio*] [*A publication*] (DLA)
Clev L Rep... Cleveland Law Reporter [*Ohio*] [*A publication*] (DLA)
Clev R .... Cleveland Law Reporter (Reprint) [*Ohio*] [*A publication*] (DLA)
ClevtRt....... Clevetrust Realty Investors [*Associated Press*] (SAG)
CLEW......... Community Leadership Workshop
CLEWP........ Cleared Land Explosion Widening and Proofing (MCD)
CL EX......... Cloth Extra [*Bookbinding*] (ROG)
Cl Extr .... Clarke on Extradition [*A publication*] (DLA)
CLF........... Bristol Flying Centre Ltd. [*British ICAO designator*] (FAAC)
CLF........... Calendar of Literary Facts [*A publication*]
CLF........... Canadian Liver Foundation [*Fondation Canadienne du Foie*] (AC)
CLF........... Capacitive Loss Factor (IEEE)
CLF........... Capital Legal Foundation (EA)
CLF........... Central Liquidity Facility [*National Credit Union Administration*]
CLF........... Chambon-La-Foret [*France*] [*Seismograph station code, US Geological Survey Closed*] (SEIS)
CLF........... Children's Legal Foundation (EA)
CLF........... Children's Liver Foundation (EA)
CLF........... Cholesterol-Lecithin Flocculation [*Biochemistry*] (DAVI)
CLF........... Christian Librarians' Fellowship (EA)
CLF........... Citizens Leadership Foundation [*Defunct*] (EA)
CLF........... Civilian Labor Force [*DoD*]
CLF........... Clear [*Alaska*] [*Airport symbol*] (AD)
CLF........... Clear, AK [*Location identifier FAA*] (FAAL)
CLF........... Clear Forward [*Telecommunications*] (TEL)
CLF........... Clear Forward Signal [*Telecommunications*] (NITA)
CLF........... Cleveland-Cliffs [*NYSE symbol*] (TTSB)
CLF........... Cleveland-Cliffs, Inc. [*NYSE symbol*] (SPSG)
CLF........... Cleveland Cliffs, Inc. Holding Co. [*NYSE symbol*] (SAG)
CLF........... Cliff
CLF........... Cliff
CLF........... Clifton Resources Ltd. [*Vancouver Stock Exchange symbol*]
CLF........... Colorado Union Catalog, Denver Public Library, Denver, CO [*OCLC symbol*] (OCLC)
CLF........... Combat Logistics Force [*Navy*] (GFGA)

CLF............ Commander, Landing Force [*Navy*] (NVT)
CLF............ Common Log File [*Computer science*]
CLF............ Community Living Fund
CLF............ Comparative LOFAR Fixing [*Military*] (CAAL)
CLF............ Connecting Line Freight
CLF............ Conservation Law Foundation (ECON)
CLF............ Critical Link Factor
CLF............ Current Legal Forms with Tax Analysis [*A publication*] (DLA)
CLF............ Farmer's Insurance Group, Los Angeles, CA [*Library symbol Library of Congress*] (LCLS)
CLFA.......... California Licensed Foresters Association (SRA)
CLFB.......... Canadian Livestock Feed Board
CLFC.......... Carol Lawrence National Fan Club (EA)
CLFC.......... Closed-Loop Fire Control [*Army*] (MCD)
CLFDB........ Canadian Labour Force Development Board [*La Commission Canadienne de Mise en Valeur de la Main-d'Oeuvre*] (AC)
ClfDr.......... Cliffs Drilling Co. [*Associated Press*] (SAG)
CLFFK........ Company Level Field Feeding Kitchen [*Army's Combat System Test Activity*] (INF)
CLFIC......... Center Launch and Flight Instrumentation Center [*NASA*] (KSC)
CLFM.......... Coherent Linear Frequency Modulated (IAA)
CLFMI........ Chain Link Fence Manufacturers Institute (EA)
CLFP.......... California League of Food Processors (SRA)
CLFS.......... Cliffs
CLFS.......... Cliffs (MCD)
CLFY.......... Clarify, Inc. [*NASDAQ symbol*] (SAG)
CLG............ Calling (DEN)
CLG............ Calling Line (ECII)
CLG............ Cancelling (IAA)
CLG............ Ceiling [*Aviation*] (KSC)
CLG............ Center Landing Gear (MCD)
CLG............ Chalice Mining, Inc. [*Vancouver Stock Exchange symbol*]
CLG............ Change to Lower Grade [*Army*]
CLG............ Civilian Labor Group (MCD)
CLG............ Closed-Loop Gain
CLG............ Coalinga, CA [*Location identifier FAA*] (FAAL)
CLG............ College (MCD)
clg............. College (VRA)
CLG............ Cologne [*West Germany*] [*Seismograph station code, US Geological Survey*] (SEIS)
CLG............ Combat Leader's Guide (INF)
CLG............ Compile, Load, and Go [*Computer science*] (BUR)
CLG............ Cooling (MSA)
CLG............ Cumann Luthchleas Gael [*Gaelic Athletic Association*] (EAIO)
CLG............ Cymdeithas yr Laith Gymraeg [*Welsh Language Society*] (EAIO)
CLG............ Guided Missile Light Cruiser [*Navy symbol*]
CLg............ Los Gatos Memorial Library, Los Gatos, CA [*Library symbol Library of Congress*] (LCLS)
CLG............ Societe Chaleng Air [*France ICAO designator*] (FAAC)
CLGA.......... Canadian Ladies' Golf Association [*Association Canadienne des Golfeuses*] (AC)
CLGA.......... Composers and Lyricists Guild of America (EA)
CLGAWD...... Cement, Lime, Gypsum, and Allied Workers Division (EA)
CLGC.......... Civilian Labor Group Center [*Army*] (AABC)
CLgD........... Duncan & Associates Library Management Consultants and Looseleaf Filing Service, Los Gatos, CA [*Library symbol*] [*Library of Congress*] (LCLS)
CLGDC........ Gibson, Dunn & Crutcher, Los Angeles, CA [*Library symbol Library of Congress*] (LCLS)
CLGES........ California Life Goals Evaluation Schedules [*Psychology*]
CLGL.......... Church of Jesus Christ of Latter-Day Saints, Genealogical Society Library, Los Angeles Temple, Los Angeles, CA [*Library symbol Library of Congress*] (LCLS)
CLGLE........ Church of Jesus Christ of Latter-Day Saints, Genealogical Society Library, Los Angeles East Branch, Los Angeles, CA [*Library symbol Library of Congress*] (LCLS)
clgM.......... Cytoplasmic Immunoglobulin M [*Immunology*] (DAVI)
CLGN.......... Guided Missile Light Cruiser (Nuclear Propulsion) [*Navy symbol Obsolete*]
CLgN.......... Novitiate of Los Gatos, Los Gatos, CA [*Library symbol Library of Congress*] (LCLS)
CLGNM........ Citizens for a Lebanon-Grenada National Memorial [*Defunct*] (EA)
CLGO.......... Getty Oil Co., Los Angeles, CA [*Library symbol Library of Congress*] (LCLS)
CLGP.......... Cannon-Launched Guided Projectile
CLGP.......... General Petroleum Corp., Los Angeles, CA [*Library symbol Library of Congress*] (LCLS)
CLGPC........ George Pepperdine College, Los Angeles, CA [*Library symbol Library of Congress*] (LCLS)
CLGRC........ Canadian Lesbian and Gay Rights Coalition
CLGRO........ Coalition for Lesbian & Gay Right in Ontario [*Coalition pour les Droits des Lesbiennes et Personnes Gaies en Ontario*] [*Formerly, Coalition for Gay Rights in Ontario*] (AC)
CLGS.......... Compressed Limit Gauging Sampling (PDAA)
CLGS.......... Cooperating Libraries of Greater Springfield [*Library network*]
CLGS.......... Golden State Mutual Life Insurance Co., Los Angeles, CA [*Library symbol Library of Congress*] (LCLS)
CLGSFU....... Clear Glazed Structural Facing Units [*Technical drawings*]
CLGSO........ Civilian Labor Group Special Orders [*Army*] (AABC)
CLGSUB...... Clear Glazed Structural Unit Base [*Technical drawings*]
CLGT.......... Center for Local Government Technology [*Oklahoma State University*] [*Research center*] (RCD)
CL GT........ Cloth Gilt [*Bookbinding*] (ROG)
CLGW.......... United Cement, Lime, and Gypsum Workers International Union
CLGY.......... Cellegy Pharmaceutical [*NASDAQ symbol*] (TTSB)

CLGY.......... Cellegy Pharmaceuticals [*NASDAQ symbol*] (SAG)
CLGYW........ Cellegy Pharmaceuticals Wrrt [*NASDAQ symbol*] (TTSB)
CLH............ Calcutta Light Horse [*British military*] (DMA)
CLH............ Cedars of Lebanon Hospital (MCD)
CLH............ Cheltenham [*Maryland*] [*Seismograph station code, US Geological Survey Closed*] (SEIS)
CLH............ Christian League for the Handicapped (EA)
CLH............ Chronic Lobular Hepatitis [*Medicine*] (MAE)
CL H.......... Clare Hall [*Cambridge University*] (ROG)
CLH............ Common Lodging House [*British*] (ROG)
CLH............ Coolah [*New South Wales*] [*Airport symbol*] (AD)
CLH............ Coral Gold Corp. [*Vancouver Stock Exchange symbol*]
CLH............ Hyland Laboratories, Los Angeles, CA [*Library symbol Library of Congress*] (LCLS)
CLH............ Lufthansa Cityline [*Germany ICAO designator*] (FAAC)
CLHA.......... Common Lodging Houses Act [*1851*] [*British*] (ROG)
CLHB.......... Clean Harbors [*NASDAQ symbol*] (TTSB)
CLHB.......... Clean Harbors, Inc. [*NASDAQ symbol*] (NQ)
CLhC.......... Chevron Oil Field Research Co., La Habra, CA [*Library symbol Library of Congress*] (LCLS)
CLHC.......... Congregation of Our Lady, Help of the Clergy [*Roman Catholic women's religious order*]
ClHgBzO...... Chloromercuribenzoate [*Biochemistry*]
CLHi.......... Historical Society of Southern California, Los Angeles, CA [*Library symbol Library of Congress*] (LCLS)
CLHIA.......... Canadian Life & Health Insurance Association Inc. [*Association Canadienne des Compagnies d'Assurances de Personnes Inc.*] [*Formerly, Canadian Life Insurance Association*] (AC)
CLHJ.......... Los Angeles Harbor Junior College, Wilmington, CA [*Library symbol Library of Congress*] (LCLS)
CL HL........ Clerk of the House of Lords [*British*] (ROG)
CLHMC........ Centennial Legion of Historic Military Commands (EA)
CL HO COM... Clerk of the House of Commons [*British*] (ROG)
Cl Home..... Clerk Home's Scotch Session Cases [*A publication*] (DLA)
CLHU.......... Computer Laboratory of Harvard University
CLHU.......... Hebrew Union College - Jewish Institute of Religion, Los Angeles, CA [*Library symbol Library of Congress*] (LCLS)
CLI............ Air Club International [*Canada*] [*FAA designator*] (FAAC)
CLI............ Calamus Length Index
CLI............ Cali Realty [*NYSE symbol*] (TTSB)
CLI............ Cali Realty Corp. [*NYSE symbol*] (SAG)
CLI............ Calling Line Identification [*or Identity*] [*Telecommunications*] (TEL)
CLI............ Call Level Interface [*Computer science*]
CLI............ Canada Land Inventory
CLI............ Canadian Lifeboat Institution Inc. (AC)
CLI............ Capacitor Leakage Indicator
CLI............ Card and Light Gun Input (SAA)
CLI............ Celtic Resources Ltd. [*Vancouver Stock Exchange symbol*]
CLI............ Christian Law Institute (EA)
CLI............ Clear Interrupt [*PC instruction*] (PCM)
CLI............ Clintonville, WI [*Location identifier FAA*] (FAAL)
CLI............ Coach Lace Institute [*Defunct*] (EA)
CLI............ Coaliquid, Inc. (MCD)
CLI............ Coefficient of Luminous Intensity
CLI............ Coherent LASER Illumination
CLI............ Coin Level Indicator [*Telephone communications*]
CLI............ Command Language Interpreter [*Computer science*]
CLI............ Command Line Interface [*For Amiga computers*]
CLI............ Command Line Interpret [*Military*] (CAAL)
CLI............ Commercial Liability Insurance [*International Risk Management Institute*] [*A publication*]
CLI............ Communication Line Interface (MCD)
CLI............ Complement Lysis Inhibitor (DMAA)
CLI............ Compression Labs, Inc. [*San Jose, CA*] [*Telecommunications*] (TSSD)
CLI............ Connaught Laboratories, Inc.
CLI............ Contractor Line Item (MCD)
CLI............ Control Level Item
CLI............ Core Logic Intervalometer
CLI............ Cornwall Light Infantry [*British military*] (DMA)
CLI............ Corpus Luteum Insufficiency [*Medicine*] (DMAA)
CLI............ Corticoliberin-Like Immunoreactivity
CLI............ Cost-of-Living Index [*Economics*]
CLI............ Cutaneous Lymphoid Infiltrates
CLI............ Immaculate Heart College, Los Angeles, CA [*Inactive*] [*OCLC symbol*] (OCLC)
CLi............ Lincoln Public Library, Lincoln, CA [*Library symbol Library of Congress*] (LCLS)
CLIA.......... American Institute of Aeronautics and Astronautics, Pacific Aerospace Library, Los Angeles, CA [*Library symbol Library of Congress*] (LCLS)
CLIA.......... California Lodging Industry Association (SRA)
CLIA.......... Canadian Lawyers Insurance Association [*Association d'Assurances des Juristes Canadiens*] (AC)
CLIA.......... Clinical Laboratory Improvement Act
CLIA.......... Cruise Lines International Association (EA)
CLIBOC....... Chinese Linguistics Bibliography on Computer [*Cambridge University Press*] [*England*]
CLIC.......... Canadian Law Information Council [*Information service or system*] (IID)
CLIC.......... Canadian Legal Information Centre (EAIO)
CLIC.......... Center for Low-Intensity Conflict [*Army*]
CLIC.......... CERN [*Conseil Europeen pour la Recherche Nucleaire*] Linear Collider [*Particle physics*]
CLIC.......... Closed-Loop, Lock-In Compensation

CLIC............	Command Language for Interrogating Computers [*Royal RADAR Establishment*] [*British*]
CLIC............	Commercial Loan Insurance Corp.
CLIC............	Communication Linear Integrated Circuit (IAA)
CLIC............	Communication Line Interface Computer (MCD)
CLIC............	Computer Layout of Integrated Circuits (PDAA)
CLIC............	Conversational Language for Interactive Computing
CLIC............	Cooperating Libraries in Consortium [*St. Paul, MN*] [*Library network*]
CLIC............	Council of Life Insurance Consultants (EA)
CLICC..........	Cooperative Libraries in Central Connecticut [*Library network*]
CLICEC........	Comite de Liaison International des Cooperatives d'Epargne et de Credit [*International Liaison Committee on Co-Operative Thrift and Credit - ILCCTC*] [*Paris, France*] (EA)
CLICO	Colonial Life Co. [*Trinidad*]
CLICOM	Climate Computing (USDC)
CLICOM	Climate Computing [*Marine science*] (OSRA)
CLID............	Calling Line Identification [*Telecommunications*] (ACRL)
CLID............	Curriculum Led Institutional Development (AIE)
CLIDE..........	Chemical Literature Data Extraction
CLIETA........	Comite de Liaison de l'Industrie Europeenne des Tubes d'Acier [*Liaison Committee of the EEC Steel Tube Industry*] (EAIO)
Clif..............	Clifford's United States Circuit Court Reports, First Circuit [*A publication*] (DLA)
CLIF............	Cliffside Railroad Co. [*AAR code*]
CLIF............	Cloning Inhibitory Factor [*Medicine*] (DMAA)
Clif & R	Clifford and Richard's English Locus Standi Reports [*1873-84*] [*A publication*] (DLA)
Clif & Rich..	Clifford and Richard's English Locus Standi Reports [*1873-84*] [*A publication*] (DLA)
Clif & St	Clifford and Stephens' English Locus Standi Reports [*1867-72*] [*A publication*] (DLA)
Clif & Steph...	Clifford and Stephens' English Locus Standi Reports [*1867-72*] [*A publication*] (DLA)
CLIFC..........	Cecilia Lee International Fan Club (EA)
CLIFC..........	Chris LeDoux International Fan Club (EA)
ClifDr..........	Cliffs Drilling Co. [*Associated Press*] (SAG)
Clif El	Clifford's English Southwick Election Cases [*1796-97*] [*A publication*] (DLA)
Clif El Cas ...	Clifford's English Southwick Election Cases [*1796-97*] [*A publication*] (DLA)
CLIFF..........	Cliff [*Commonly used*] (OPSA)
Cliff.............	Clifford's English Southwick Election Cases [*1796-97*] [*A publication*] (DLA)
Cliff.............	Clifford's United States Circuit Court Reports, First Circuit [*A publication*] (DLA)
Cliff & Rich...	Clifford and Richard's English Locus Standi Reports [*1873-84*] [*A publication*] (DLA)
Cliff & Steph...	Clifford and Stephens' English Locus Standi Reports [*1867-72*] [*A publication*] (DLA)
Cliff (CC)	Clifford's United States Circuit Court Reports, First Circuit [*A publication*] (DLA)
Cliff El Cas...	Clifford's English Southwick Election Cases [*1796-97*] [*A publication*] (DLA)
CLIFFS........	Cliffs [*Commonly used*] (OPSA)
Clif Prob	Clifford's Probate Guide [*A publication*] (DLA)
CLIFS..........	Cost, Life, Interchangeability, Function, and Safety [*Navy*] (NG)
Clif South El...	Clifford's English Southwick Election Cases [*1796-97*] [*A publication*] (DLA)
Clif South El Cas...	Clifford's English Southwick Election Cases [*1796-97*] [*A publication*] (DLA)
Clift............	Clift's Entries [*1719*] [*England*] [*A publication*] (DLA)
CLIH............	Chicago Lying-In Hospital
CLIM...........	Cellular Logic-In Memory [*Telecommunications*] (IAA)
CLIM...........	Climatic (AFM)
CLIM...........	Common LISP [*List Processing Language*] Interface Management [*Computer science*]
CLIMAP........	Climate: Long-Range Investigation, Mapping, and Prediction [*National Science Foundation*]
CLIMAP........	Climate Modeling Prediction (USDC)
CLIMAT........	Climate
CLIMATE......	Computer and Language Independent Modules for Automatic Test Equipment (MHDI)
CLIMATOL ...	Climatology
CLIMB..........	Center for Loss in Multiple Birth
CLIMMAR	Centre de Liaison International des Marchands de Machines Agricoles et Reparateurs [*International Liaison Center for Agricultural Machinery Distributors and Maintenance*] [*Common Market*]
CLIMOA	Canadian Life Insurance Medical Officers Association [*Association Canadienne des Directeurs Medicaux en Assurance-Vie*] (AC)
CLIMPO	Contract Liaison and Master Planning Office [*Military*]
CLIN............	Clinic [*Medicine*] (WDAA)
CLIN............	Clinical
CLIN............	Contract Line Item Number [*Army*] (AABC)
CLIN............	Los Angeles Neurological Medical Group, Inc., Los Angeles, CA [*Library symbol Library of Congress*] (LCLS)
Clin Dig	Clinton's Digest [*New York*] [*A publication*] (DLA)
CᴸINE..........	Carpet Information Network [*Tapistree Group, Inc.*] [*Information service or system*] (IID)
clini............	Clinitest [*Miles Inc.*] [*Endocrinology*] (DAVI)
CLINIC........	Clinical
CLIN JL	Clinical Journal [*A publication*] (ROG)
Clin Path	Clinical Pathology (DAVI)
Clin Proc	Clinical Procedure [*Medicine*] (DAVI)
CLINPROT....	Clinical Protocols [*National Cancer Institute*] [*Information service or system*]
Cl Ins	Clarke on Law of Insurance [*Canada A publication*] (DLA)
CLINS..........	Climatic Laboratory Instrumentation System (MCD)
Clint...........	Intrinsic Clearance [*Physiology*]
ClintGs........	Clinton Gas Systems, Inc. [*Associated Press*] (SAG)
Clintrials.....	Clintrials Research, Inc. [*Associated Press*] (SAG)
CLIO............	Chelsea, London, Islington, Office [*Denoting a location where a manuscript was written*] [*Acronym used as pseudonym of Joseph Addison, British author, 1672-1719*]
Clio..............	Clio: A Journal of Literature, History and the Philosophy of History [*A publication*] (BRI)
CLIO............	Conversational Language for Input/Output [*Computer science*]
CLIP............	Calling Line Identification Presentation [*Telecommunications*] (DOM)
CLIP............	Cancel Launch in Progress [*Air Force*]
CLIP............	Cellular Logic Image Processor [*Telecommunications*] (TEL)
CLIP............	Centralized Library Information Processor [*United States Computer Corp.*] [*Information service or system*] (IID)
CLIP............	Cerebral Lipidosis [*Medicine*] (AAMN)
CLIP............	Class II-Associated Invariant Chain Peptides [*Biochemistry*]
Clip.............	Clipping [*Medicine*]
CLIP............	Close-In Improvement Program [*to increase torpedo effectiveness*] (MCD)
CLIP............	Combined LASER Instrumentation Package (NASA)
CLIP............	Common Law Institute of Intellectual Property [*British*] (DBA)
CLIP............	Compiler Language for Information Processing [*System Development Corp.*] [*Programming language*]
CLIP............	Computer Language for Information Processing (NITA)
CLIP............	Computer Launch Interference Problems
CLIP............	Computer Layout Installation Planner (MHDB)
CLIP............	Corticotrophin-Like Intermediate-Lobe Peptide [*Endocrinology*]
CLIP............	Country Logistics Improvement Program [*Air Force*]
CLiP............	Lincoln Public Library, Lincoln, CA [*Library symbol*] [*Library of Congress*] (LCLS)
CLIPER	Climatology and Persistence
CLIPI...........	Center for Law in the Public Interest (EA)
CLIPPR	Consolidated Logistics Information Planning and Programming Requirements
CLIPR	Computer Laboratory for Instruction in Psychological Research [*University of Colorado - Boulder*] [*Research center*] (RCD)
CLIPS..........	Calculation Link Processing System [*Military*] (CAAL)
CLIPS..........	Careers Literature and Information Prescription Service (AIE)
CLIPS..........	Chemical List Index and Processing System [*Environmental Protection Agency*] (ERG)
CLIPS..........	Coincident Light Information Photographic Strips
CLIR............	Calling Line Identification Restriction [*Telecommunications*] (DOM)
CLIR............	Center for Labor and Industrial Relations [*New York Institute of Technology*] [*Research center*] (RCD)
CLIRA	Closed-Loop In-Reactor Assembly [*Nuclear energy*] (NRCH)
CLIRS	Computerised Legal Information Retrieval System [*CLIRS Ltd.*] [*Information service or system*] (IID)
CLIRS	Computerized Legal Information Retrieval System (ADA)
CLIS............	Certificate of Library and Information Science (PGP)
CLIS............	Clearinghouse for Library and Information Sciences
CLIS............	Computer-Linked Information for Container Shipping (IAA)
CLIS............	Contract Line Item Status (MCD)
CLIS............	Criminalistic Laboratory Information Systems [*FBI*]
CLit.............	Companion of Literature [*Royal Society of Literature award*] [*British*]
CLITAM........	Centre de Liaison des Industries de Traitement des Algues Marines de la CEE [*Liaison Center of the Industries for the Treatment of Seaweeds in the European Economic Community*]
CLITRAVI	Centre de Liaison des Industries Transformatrices de la CEE [*Liaison Center of the Meat Processing Industries of the EEC*] [*Belgium*]
C Litt	Companion of Literature [*Royal Society of Literature Award*] [*British*] (BARN)
CLIU............	Catholic Life Insurance Union (EA)
CLIV............	Cold Leg Isolation Valve [*Nuclear energy*] (NRCH)
CLIV............	Core Logic Intervalometer
CLiv	Livermore Library, Livermore, CA [*Library symbol Library of Congress*] (LCLS)
CLIVAR	Climate Variability and Predictability Study
CLIVAR	Climate Variability and Prediction [*Program*] (USDC)
CLIVAR	Climate Variability and Prediction [*Program*] [*Marine science*] (OSRA)
CLivS	Sandia Laboratories, Livermore, CA [*Library symbol Library of Congress*] (LCLS)
CLivV	United States Veterans Administration Hospital, Livermore, CA [*Library symbol Library of Congress*] (LCLS)
CLIX............	Compression Labs [*NASDAQ symbol*] (TTSB)
CLIX............	Compression Labs, Inc. [*NASDAQ symbol*] (NQ)
CLIXS..........	Class IX Study
CLJ	Calais Resources Ltd. [*Toronto Stock Exchange symbol*]
CLJ	Calcutta Law Journal [*A publication*] (DLA)
CLJ	California Law Journal [*A publication*] (DLA)
CLJ	Canada Law Journal [*A publication*] (DLA)
CLJ	Cantrell Resources [*Vancouver Stock Exchange symbol*]
CLJ	Cape Law Journal [*South Africa*] [*A publication*] (DLA)
CLJ	Central Law Journal [*A publication*] (DLA)
CLJ	Ceylon Law Journal [*A publication*] (DLA)
CLJ	Chicago Law Journal [*A publication*] (DLA)
CLJ	Cluj-Napoca [*Romania*] [*Airport symbol*] (OAG)
CLJ	Colonial Law Journal Reports [*A publication*] (DLA)
CLJ	Commander of the Order of St. Lazarus of Jerusalem
CLJ	Commercial Law Journal [*Commercial Law League of America*] [*A publication*]
CLJ	Control Joint (AAG)

CLJ	University of Judaism, Los Angeles, CA [*Library symbol Library of Congress*] (LCLS)
CLJA	Closed-Loop Jumper Assembly [*Nuclear energy*] (NRCH)
CLJ & Lit Rev	California Law Journal and Literary Review [*A publication*] (DLA)
CLJC	Copiah-Lincoln Junior College [*Wesson, MS*]
CLjC	Copley Newspapers, Inc., James S. Copley Library, La Jolla, CA [*Library symbol Library of Congress*] (LCLS)
CLjFS	United States National Marine Fisheries Service, Southwest Fisheries Center, La Jolla, CA [*Library symbol Library of Congress*] (LCLS)
CLjHi	La Jolla Historical Society, La Jolla, CA [*Library symbol*] [*Library of Congress*] (LCLS)
CLjL	Library Association of La Jolla, La Jolla, CA [*Library symbol Library of Congress Obsolete*] (LCLS)
CLK	Cadillac & Lake City Railway Co. [*AAR code*]
CLK	Chileka [*Malawi*] [*Seismograph station code, US Geological Survey*] (SEIS)
CLK	Clark Aviation Corp. [*ICAO designator*] (FAAC)
CLK	Clerk (AFM)
CLK	Clinton, OK [*Location identifier FAA*] (FAAL)
CLK	Clock (AAG)
CLK	Colchis Resources Ltd. [*Vancouver Stock Exchange symbol*]
CLK	Contact-Lens-Induced Keratoconjunctivitis [*Ophthalmology*]
CLK	Craton, Lodge and Knight [*British*]
CLK	Hunter-Killer Ship [*Navy symbol Obsolete*]
CLK	Kaiser Foundation Hospital, Los Angeles, CA [*Library symbol Library of Congress*] (LCLS)
ClkCorp	CluckCorp International, Inc. [*Associated Press*] (SAG)
CLK CT	Clerks of Court [*Legal term*] (DLA)
CLK-D	Kaiser Foundation Hospital, Doctor's Library, Los Angeles, CA [*Library symbol Library of Congress*] (LCLS)
CLKG	Caulking (MSA)
CLKH	Comptoir du Livre [*Keren Hasefer*] [*A publication*] (BJA)
CLKJ	Caulked Joint
CLKO	Clerk in Orders [*Church of England*]
CLKOB	Clockwise Orbit [*Aviation*] (FAAC)
Clk's Mag	Clerk's Magazine [*A publication*] (DLA)
CLKW	Clockwise (ADA)
CLKWS	Clockwise
CLKWZ	Clockwise (AFM)
CLL	Aerovias Castillo SA [*Mexico ICAO designator*] (FAAC)
CLL	Calle
cll	Calligrapher [*MARC relator code*] [*Library of Congress*] (LCCP)
CLL	Carolin Mines Ltd. [*Toronto Stock Exchange symbol Vancouver Stock Exchange symbol*]
CLL	Catholic Listener Library [*Later, Maynard Listener Library*] (EA)
CLL	Centerline Lighting Will be Provided [*Aviation*] (DA)
CLL	Central Light Loss (OA)
CLL	Chicken Lactose-Lectin [*Biochemistry*]
CLL	Chief of Legislative Liaison [*Army*]
CLL	Chippewa Library League [*Library network*]
CLL	Cholesterol Lowering Lipid [*Biochemistry*]
CLL	Chronic Lymphatic [*or Lymphocytic*] Leukemia [*Medicine*]
CLL	Circulation Lift Limit
CL L	Classical Latin [*Language, etc.*] (ROG)
CLL	Clauses (ADA)
CLL	College Station [*Texas*] [*Airport symbol*] (OAG)
CLL	College Station, TX [*Location identifier FAA*] (FAAL)
CLL	Collmberg [*German Democratic Republic*] [*Seismograph station code, US Geological Survey*] (SEIS)
CLL	Consolidated Load List (DNAB)
CLL	Contact Limit Line [*Technical drawings*]
CLL	Contingent Liability Ledger [*DoD*]
CLL	Council for Liberal Learning [*Defunct*] (EA)
CLL	Creighton University, Law Library, Omaha, NE [*OCLC symbol*] (OCLC)
CLL	Critical Labor Level (ADA)
CLL	Critical Load Level
CLL	Crown Laboratories, Inc. [*AMEX symbol*] (SAG)
CLL	Los Angeles County Law Library, Los Angeles, CA [*Library symbol Library of Congress*] (LCLS)
CLLA	Commercial Law League of America [*Chicago, IL*] (EA)
Cl Lat	Classical Latin (BARN)
CLLBC	Canadian Ladies Lawn Bowling Council
CLLBRTV	Collaborative
CLLC	Canadian Labour Law Cases [*A publication*] (DLA)
CLLC	Centre for Literacy and Linguistic Computing [*University of Newcastle*] [*Australia*]
CLLCTABL	Collectable
CLLCTIBL	Collectible
CLLCTV	Collective
CLLDF	Civil Liberties Legal Defense Fund (EA)
CLLE	Center for Lifelong Education [*Ball State University*] [*Research center*] (RCD)
CLLE	Columnar-Lined Lower Esophagus [*Gastroenterology*] (DAVI)
CLLEC	Crown Laboratories [*ECM, exchange symbol*] (TTSB)
CLLGRPHR	Calligrapher
CLLI	Common Language location Identifier [*Telecommunications*] (TSSD)
CLLI	LIFE Bible College, Los Angeles, CA [*Library symbol Library of Congress*] (LCLS)
cl liq	Clear Liquid [*Dietetics*] (DAVI)
Cl liq	Clear Liquid (BABM)
CLLL	Calyx Lateral Lobe Length [*Botany*]
CLLM	Consolidated Link Layer Management [*Telecommunications*] (ACRL)
CLLoy	Loyola Marymount University, Los Angeles, CA [*Library symbol Library of Congress*] (LCLS)
CL LP	Cloth Limp [*Bookbinding*] (ROG)
CLLR	Councillor
Cllr	Councillor (ODBW)
CLLS	Calyx Lateral Lobe Shape [*Botany*]
CLLS	Country Life Library of Sport [*A publication*]
CLLSN	Collision
CLLT	Collation [*Online database field identifier*]
CLLTRL	Collateral
CLLU	Canadian League for the Liberation of Ukraine
CLLW	Calyx Lateral Lobe Width [*Botany*]
CLLW	Council for Lay Life and Work
CllxBio	Cellex Biosciences, Inc. [*Associated Press*] (SAG)
CL LYS	Clot Lysis [*Hematology*] (DAVI)
CLM	Career Limiting Move (MCD)
CLM	Care Logic Module (NASA)
CLM	Carlin Resources Corp. [*Vancouver Stock Exchange symbol*]
CLM	Certified Laundry Manager
CLM	Christian Life and Ministry [*Canada*]
CLM	Christian Life Movement
CLM	Circumlunar Mission (KSC)
CLM	Claim
CLM	Claiming Race [*Horse racing*]
CLM	Clemente Global Gr [*NYSE symbol*] (TTSB)
CLM	Clemente Global Growth Fund, Inc. [*NYSE symbol*] (SPSG)
CLM	Cognitive Levels Matching [*Psychology*] (EDAC)
CLM	Coleman [*Alberta*] [*Seismograph station code, US Geological Survey Closed*] (SEIS)
CLM	Column (IAA)
clm	Column (VRA)
clm	Column [*Typesetting*] (WDMC)
CLM	Communications Line Multiplexer
CLM	Commutatorless Motor (PDAA)
CLM	Computer Language Magazine [*Miller Freeman Publications*] [*Information service or system*] (CRD)
CLM	Contained-Liquid Membranes [*Chemical engineering*]
CLM	Continental Lithospheric Mantle [*Geology*]
CLM	Council of Logistics Management
CLM	Crane-Load Moment-Indicator (PDAA)
CLM	Croatian Liberation Movement [*Australia*]
CLM	Culham Laboratory Reports [*United Kingdom Atomic Energy Authority*]
CLM	Current Law Monthly [*A publication*] (DLA)
CLM	Los Angeles County Medical Association, Los Angeles, CA [*Library symbol Library of Congress*] (LCLS)
CLM	Port Angeles [*Washington*] [*Airport symbol*] (OAG)
CLM	Port Angeles, WA [*Location identifier FAA*] (FAAL)
CLMA	Cariboo Lumber Manufacturers' Association (AC)
CLMA	Certified Livestock Marketing Association [*Later, Livestock Marketing Association*]
CLMA	Cigarette Lighter Manufacturers Association (EA)
CLMA	Clinical Laboratory Management Association (EA)
CLMA	Clothing Monetary Allowance
CLMA	Contact Lens Manufacturers Association (EA)
CLMas	Masonic Library of Southern California, Los Angeles, CA [*Library symbol Library of Congress*] (LCLS)
CLMB	Center for Loss in Multiple Birth (EA)
CLMC	Canadian Learning Materials Centre
CLMC	Catholic Lay Mission Corps (EA)
CLMC	Central Logistics Management Center (NASA)
CLMC	Chemical LASER Mode Control
CLMeW	Metropolitan Water District of Southern California, Los Angeles, CA [*Library symbol Library of Congress*] (LCLS)
CLMG	Claiming (WGA)
CLML	Chicago Linear Music Language
CLML	Current List of Medical Literature
CLMLC	Mulholland Library of Conjuring & the Applied Arts, Los Angeles, CA [*Library symbol*] [*Library of Congress*] (LCLS)
CLMN	Complete Lower Motor Neuron [*Lesion*] [*Neurology*] (DAVI)
CLMO	Chief Labour Management Officer [*Ministry of Supply*] [*British*]
CLMP	Clumped [*Biochemistry*] (DAVI)
CLMP	Council of Literary Magazines and Presses (EA)
CL-MP	Los Angeles Public Library, Police Department Library, Los Angeles, CA [*Library symbol Library of Congress*] (LCLS)
CLMPC	Canadian Labour Market & Productivity Centre [*Centre Canadien du Marche du Travail et de la Productivite*] (AC)
CL-MR	Los Angeles Public Library, Municipal Reference Library, Los Angeles, CA [*Library symbol Library of Congress*] (LCLS)
CLMS	California League of Middle Schools (SRA)
Clms	Claims (DLA)
CLMS	Clinical Laboratory Management System [*Computer science*]
CLMS	Cluster Mission Simulator [*NASA*] (KSC)
CLMS	Company Lightweight Mortar System [*Army*]
CLMS	Continuous Longitudinal Manpower Survey [*Department of Labor*]
CLMSM	Mount St. Mary's College, Los Angeles, CA [*Library symbol Library of Congress*] (LCLS)
CLMT	Claremont Technology Group, Inc. [*NASDAQ symbol*] (SAG)
CLMV	Cauliflower Mosaic Virus [*Also, CaMV*]
CL-MW	Los Angeles Public Library, Water and Power Department Library, Los Angeles, CA [*Library symbol Library of Congress*] (LCLS)
CLN	Barns Olson Aeroleasing Ltd. [*British ICAO designator*] (FAAC)
CLN	Caledonia Resources Ltd. [*Vancouver Stock Exchange symbol*]
CLN	Carlsbad [*New Mexico*] [*Seismograph station code, US Geological Survey*] (SEIS)
CLN	Carolina [*Brazil*] [*Airport symbol*] (AD)
CLN	Cellulose Nitrate (PDAA)

CLN .... Central Library Network [*Library network*]
CLN .... Cervical Lymph Node [*Anatomy*]
CLN .... Chicago Legal News [*Illinois*] [*A publication*] (DLA)
CLN .... Clann Ltd., Sydney, NSW, Australia [*OCLC symbol*] (OCLC)
CLN .... Clean (MSA)
CLN .... Clean
CLN .... Clearance (KSC)
CLN .... Clinometer [*Engineering*]
CLN .... Clipper Negative
CLN .... Coleman Co. [*NYSE symbol*] (TTSB)
CLN .... Coleman Co., Inc. [*NYSE symbol*] (SPSG)
CLN .... Colon (AABC)
CLN .... Commercial Lending Newsletter [*Robert Morris Associates (National Association of Bank Loan and Credit Offices)*] [*A publication*]
CLN .... Computerized Laboratory Notebook
CLN .... Computer Liaison Nurse (MEDA)
CLN .... Connecticut League for Nursing (SRA)
C LN .... Corrective Lens [*Freight*]
CLNC .... Clearance (AFM)
CLNC .... Clinic
CLNG .... City of London National Guard [*British military*] (DMA)
CLNG .... Cleaning
CLNG .... Cleaning
CLNh .... Cumann Leabharann na hEireann [*Library Association of Ireland*] (EAIO)
CLNK .... Complink Ltd. [*NASDAQ symbol*] (SAG)
CLNL .... Colonial
CLNP .... Callon Petroleum [*NASDAQ symbol*] (TTSB)
CLNP .... Callon Petroleum Co. [*NASDAQ symbol*] (SAG)
CLNP .... Connectionless Mode Network Protocol [*Telecommunications*] (OSI)
CLNP .... Connectionless Network Protocol
CLNP .... Connectionless Network Protocol (DOMA)
CLNPP .... Callon Petroleum Cv Exch 'A' Pfd [*NASDAQ symbol*] (TTSB)
CLNR .... Cleaner (NASA)
CLNR .... Cleaner
CLNS .... Connectionless Mode Network Service [*Telecommunications*] (OSI)
CLNS .... Connectionless Network Service [*Telecommunications*] (ACRL)
CLNSR .... Cleanser
CLNT .... Clearnet Communications, Inc. [*NASDAQ symbol*] (SAG)
CLNT .... Coolant (AAG)
CLNTF .... Clearnet Communic 'A' [*NASDAQ symbol*] (TTSB)
CLNY .... Colony
CLO .... Alpena, MI [*Location identifier FAA*] (FAAL)
CLO .... Cali [*Colombia*] [*Airport symbol*] (OAG)
CLO .... California State University, Long Beach, Long Beach, CA [*OCLC symbol*] (OCLC)
CLO .... Campus Liaison Officer [*Military*] (DNAB)
CLO .... Campylobacter-Like Organism (PDAA)
CLO .... [*Le*] Cardinal Leger et Ses Oeuvres (AC)
CLO .... Cellular Logic Operation [*Telecommunications*] (IAA)
CLO .... Centerline of Occupant [*Automotive engineering*]
CLO .... Center Line of Occupant
CLO .... Chapter Liaison Officer
CLO .... Citizens for Law and Order (DICI)
CLO .... Civil Liaison Officer [*Army*] (AABC)
CLO .... Clean Lube Oil (AAG)
CLO .... Client Liaison Officer
CLO .... Close
CLO .... Closet (MSA)
CLO .... Cloth [*Bookbinding*] (ROG)
CLO .... Clothing (AABC)
CLO .... Cod Liver Oil
CLO .... Collateralized Loan Obligation (TDOB)
CLO .... Comet-Like Object
CLO .... Command Liaison Officer [*Military*] (DNAB)
CLO .... Community Law Offices
CLO .... Community Living Oakville (AC)
CLO .... Complex Layered Oxide [*Physical chemistry*]
CLO .... Computerized Loan Origination [*for mortgages*]
CLO .... Computer Lock-On
CLO .... Concentrated Liquor Outlet (DICI)
CLO .... Concentric Line Oscillator
CLO .... Congenital Lobar Overinflation
CLO .... Congressional Liaison Office
CLO .... Consular Liaison Officer
CLO .... Copyright Licensing Organisation [*British*] (AIE)
CLO .... Occidental College, Los Angeles, CA [*Library symbol Library of Congress*] (LCLS)
CLOA .... Chief Leisure Officers Association [*British*] (DBA)
CLOA .... Otis Art Institute of Parsons School of Design, Los Angeles, CA [*Library symbol*] [*Library of Congress*] (LCLS)
CLOAS .... Computations Life Office Administrations System (NITA)
CLoaS .... Southwest Regional Laboratory for Educational Research and Development, Los Alamitos, CA [*Library symbol Library of Congress*] (LCLS)
CLOAX .... Corrugated-Laminated Coaxial [*Cable*]
CLOB .... Composite [*or Consolidated*] Limit Order Book [*Stock exchange term*]
CLOB .... Core Load Overlay Builder [*General Automation, Inc.*]
CLob .... Long Beach Public Library, Long Beach, CA [*Library symbol Library of Congress*] (LCLS)
CLobB .... Bauer Hospital-Saint Mary Medical Center, Long Beach, CA [*Library symbol Library of Congress*] (LCLS)
CLobC .... Long Beach City College, Long Beach, CA [*Library symbol Library of Congress*] (LCLS)

CLobC-B .... Long Beach City College, Business and Technology Division, Long Beach, CA [*Library symbol Library of Congress*] (LCLS)
CLobD .... Douglas Aircraft Co., Technical Library, Long Beach, CA [*Library symbol Library of Congress*] (LCLS)
CLobGS .... Church of Jesus Christ of Latter-Day Saints, Genealogical Society Library, Long Beach East Branch, Stake Center, Long Beach, CA [*Library symbol Library of Congress*] (LCLS)
CLobHi .... Historical Society of Long Beach, Inc., Long Beach, CA [*Library symbol*] [*Library of Congress*] (LCLS)
CLobM .... Long Beach Memorial Hospital, Long Beach, CA [*Library symbol Library of Congress*] (LCLS)
CLobP .... Pacific Hospital of Long Beach, Long Beach, CA [*Library symbol Library of Congress*] (LCLS)
CLobS .... California State University, Long Beach, Long Beach, CA [*Library symbol Library of Congress*] (LCLS)
CLobT .... Trustees of the California State University and Colleges, Chancellor's Office Library, Long Beach, CA [*Library symbol Library of Congress*] (LCLS)
CLobUN .... United States Naval Station Library, Long Beach, CA [*Library symbol Library of Congress*] (LCLS)
CLobVA .... United States Veterans Administration Hospital, Long Beach, CA [*Library symbol Library of Congress*] (LCLS)
CLOC .... Clean Letter of Credit [*Banking*]
CLOC .... Collocation [*Computer software package*] [*University of Birmingham*] [*British*] (NITA)
CLOC .... Commodity Letter of Credit
CLOC .... Comparative Library Organization Committee [*American Library Association*]
CLOCCI .... Comite de Liaison des Organismes Chretiens de Cooperation Internationale (EAIO)
CLOCE .... Contingency Lines of Communication, Europe [*Military*] (AABC)
Clod .... Clodius [*of Scriptores Historiae Augustae*] [*Classical studies*] (OCD)
CLOD .... Coralline Lethal Orange Disease
CLod .... Lodi Public Library, Lodi, CA [*Library symbol Library of Congress*] (LCLS)
CLODA .... Closing Date
Clode ML .... Clode's Martial Law [*A publication*] (DLA)
CLODO .... Comite Liquidant ou Detournant les Ordinateurs [*Committee to Liquidate or Neutralize Computers*] [*France*] (PD)
CLODS .... Computerized Logic-Oriented Design System [*Air Force*]
CLOF .... Clofibrate (DMAA)
CLOF .... Complete Loss of Feedwater [*Nuclear energy*] (NRCH)
CLOFNAM .... International Committee for the Check-List of the Fishes of the North-Eastern Atlantic and Mediterranean
CL of P .... Clerk of the Peace [*British*] (ROG)
CLOGH .... Clogher [*Town in Northern Ireland*] (ROG)
CLOI .... Cloister (DSUE)
clois. .... Cloisonne (VRA)
CLOIS .... Cornette Library Online Information Service [*West Texas State University*] (OLDSS)
CLOIS .... Council for Languages and Other International Studies [*Later, NCLIS*] (EA)
CLoiC .... Loma Linda University, Loma Linda, CA [*Library symbol Library of Congress*] (LCLS)
CLom .... Lompoc Public Library, Lompoc, CA [*Library symbol Library of Congress*] (LCLS)
CLOM .... O'Melveny & Myers, Los Angeles, CA [*Library symbol Library of Congress*] (LCLS)
CLomGS .... Church of Jesus Christ of Latter-Day Saints, Genealogical Society Library, SantaMaria Branch, Lompoc, CA [*Library symbol Library of Congress*] (LCLS)
CLOMM .... O'Melveny & Myers, Los Angeles, CA [*Library symbol*] [*Library of Congress*] (LCLS)
CLON .... Clonidine (DMAA)
Clon .... Clonorchis [*A liver fluke*] [*Gastroenterology*] (DAVI)
CLONF .... Clonfert [*Village in Ireland*] (ROG)
CLONG-CE .... Comite de Liaison des Organisations Non-Gouvernmentales de Developpement aupres des Communautes Europeennes [*Liaison Committee of Development Non-Governmental Organizations to the European Communities*] (EAIO)
CLONGV .... Comite de Liaison des OrganizationSs Non-Gouvernmentales de Volontariat [*Committee for the Liaison of Non-Governmental Voluntary Organizations*] [*France*] (EAIO)
CLOOGE .... Continuous Log of Ongoing Events (PDAA)
CLOPP .... Continuous Level of Production Plan
Clorox .... Clorox Co. [*Associated Press*] (SAG)
CLOS .... Amer Safety Closure [*NASDAQ symbol*] (TTSB)
CLOS .... Clear Line-of-Sight (MCD)
CLOS .... Closet
CLOS .... Closure (MSA)
CLOS .... Command to Line of Sight [*Military British*]
CLOS .... Common LISP Object System [*Computer science*] (BYTE)
ClosMed .... Closure Medical Corp. [*Associated Press*] (SAG)
CLOST .... Canadian Lake & Ocean Salvage Team [*Commercial firm*]
Clostr .... Clostridium [*Medicine*] (DMAA)
CLOT .... Combined Loads Orbiter Test (MCD)
CLOT .... Cost, Lawsuits, On-Air Requirements, and Time Available
Cloth .... Clothes Time, Inc. [*Associated Press*] (SAG)
CLOTH .... Clothing
CLOTO .... Close This Office (FAAC)
CLOW .... Current Literature on Water [*Database*] [*South African Water Information Centre*] [*Information service or system*] (CRD)
Clow LC on Torts .... Clow's Leading Cases on Torts [*A publication*] (DLA)
CLOZ .... Clozapine [*Organic chemistry*]
CLP .... Caecum Ligation and Puncture [*Medicine*]

CLP	Calpine Resources, Inc. [*Vancouver Stock Exchange symbol*]
CLP	Campbell-Larsen Potentiometer
CLP	Canadian Labour Party
CLP	Cell Loss Priority [*Computer science*]
CLP	Center on Law and Pacifism [*Defunct*] (EA)
CLP	Certified Lenders Program [*Small Business Administration*]
CLP	City of London Police (ROG)
CLP	Clamp (MSA)
CLP	Clara Peak [*New Mexico*] [*Seismograph station code, US Geological Survey*] (SEIS)
CLP	[*The*] Clarendon & Pittsford Railroad Co. [*AAR code*]
CLP	Clarks Point [*Alaska*] [*Airport symbol*] (OAG)
CLP	Clarks Point, AK [*Location identifier FAA*] (FAAL)
CLP	Clasp
CLP	Cleaner/Lubricant/Preservation [*for firearms*] (MCD)
CLP	Clinical Pathology
CIP	Clinical Pathology [*Medicine*] (DMAA)
CLP	Clipper Positive
CLP	Colonial Properties Tr [*NYSE symbol*] (TTSB)
CLP	Colonial Properties Trust [*NYSE symbol*] (SPSG)
CLP	Color Layout Programmer (DGA)
CLP	Combined Lease Plan
CLP	Command Language Processor
CLP	Common Law Procedure [*England*] [*A publication*] (DLA)
CLP	Commonwealth Land Party [*British*] (DAS)
CLP	Communication Line Processor
CLP	Communist Labor Party (EA)
CLP	Comprehensive Language Program [*Test*]
CLP	Conference of the Labour Party [*British*]
CLP	Congress Liberation Party [*Nyasaland*] [*Political party*]
CLP	Console Lighting Panel (MCD)
CLP	Consolidation Loan Program [*Department of Education*] (GFGA)
CLP	Constituency Labour Party [*British*] (BARN)
CLP	Constraint Logic Programming
CLP	Contact Lens Practitioners (PDAA)
CLP	Continuous Line Plotter
CLP	Contract Laboratory Program [*Environmental Protection Agency*]
CLP	Cornell List Processor [*Computer science*]
CLP	Council for Livestock Protection [*Defunct*] (EA)
CLP	Country Liberal Party [*Australia*] (ADA)
C/LP	Courtesy Lamp [*Automotive engineering*]
CLP	Criminal Law and Procedure
CLP	Cross-Linked Polyethylene [*Organic chemistry*]
CLP	Current Laboratory Practice [*A publication*]
CLp	Current Line Pointer [*Computer science*] (IBMDP)
CLp	Lakeport Carnegie Public Library, Lakeport, CA [*Library symbol Library of Congress*] (LCLS)
CLPA	Common Law Procedure Acts (DLA)
CLPAC	Conservative Leadership Political Action Committee (EA)
CLP Act	English Common Law Procedure Act (DLA)
CL PAL	Cleft Palate [*Medicine*]
CLPC	Los Angeles Pacific College, Los Angeles, CA [*Library symbol Library of Congress*] (LCLS)
CLPCE	Comite de Liaison des Podologues de la CE [*Liaison Committee of Podologists of the Common Market*] (ECED)
CLPD	Campaign for Labour Party Democracy [*British*]
CLPE	Cross-Linked Polyethylene [*Organic chemistry*] (MCD)
CLPF	Chlorine Pentafluoride [*Inorganic chemistry*] (MCD)
CLPG	Chretiens pour la Liberation du Peuple Guadeloupeen [*Guadeloupe*] (PD)
CLPG	Cornelia de Lange Parents Group [*Later, Cornelia de Lange Syndrome Foundation*] (EA)
CL-PGM	Cannon-Launched Precision Guided Munition (MCD)
CLPHA	Council of Large Public Housing Authorities (EA)
CLPhil	Philosophical Research Society, Los Angeles, CA [*Library symbol Library of Congress*] (LCLS)
CLPI	Canadian Literary Periodical Index [*Information service or system*] (IID)
CLPI	Creative Learning Products [*NASDAQ symbol*] (TTSB)
CLPI	Creative Learning Products, Inc. [*NASDAQ symbol*] (NQ)
CLPI	Prudential Insurance Co. of America, Business, Recreation, and Field Management Libraries, Los Angeles, CA [*Library symbol Library of Congress*] (LCLS)
CLPL	Citizens Legal Protective League [*Defunct*] (EA)
CLPLOT	Center-Line Plotting (MCD)
CLPM	Canalicular Liver Plasma Membrane [*Anatomy*]
CLPoC	R. L. Polk & Co. of California, Los Angeles, CA [*Library symbol Library of Congress*] (LCLS)
CLPP	Paramount Pictures Corp., Research Department, Los Angeles, CA [*Library symbol Library of Congress*] (LCLS)
CLPPR	Clipper
CLPR	Caliper
CLPR	Clamper (MSA)
CLPR	Clapper [*Electricity*]
CLPr	Colgate-Palmolive,$4.25 Pfd [*NYSE symbol*] (TTSB)
CLPT	Collodion Print (VRA)
CLPT	Computer Languages for the Processing of Text (DGA)
CLPT	Pacific Telephone & Telegraph Co., Los Angeles, CA [*Library symbol Library of Congress*] (LCLS)
CLPZF	Colossal Resources [*NASDAQ symbol*] (TTSB)
CLQ	Check List Question (CAAL)
CLQ	Cold Metal Products [*NYSE symbol*] (SAG)
CLQ	Commercial Law Quarterly [*Australia A publication*]
CLQ	Compleat Health Corp. [*Vancouver Stock Exchange symbol*]
CLQ	Crown Land Reports, Queensland [*A publication*] (DLA)

CLQ	Queen of Angels School of Nursing, Los Angeles, CA [*Library symbol Library of Congress*] (LCLS)
CLR	Calcium, Lime, Rust Remover [*Cleaning product*]
CLR	Calcutta Law Reporter [*A publication*] (DLA)
CLR	Calendar of Liberate Rolls [*British*]
CLR	Calipatria, CA [*Location identifier FAA*] (FAAL)
CLR	Canada Law Reports [*A publication*] (DLA)
CLR	Canadian Law Review and Corporation Legal Journal [*A publication*] (DLA)
CLR	Cape Law Reports [*South Africa*] [*A publication*] (DLA)
CLR	Center of Lateral Resistance (IAA)
CLR	Central Logic Rack [*Telecommunications*] (TEL)
CLR	Central London Underground Railway
CLR	Centurion LASER Range-Finder
CLR	Ceylon Law Reports [*A publication*] (DLA)
CLR	Chloride Test [*Dentistry*] (BABM)
CLR	City of London Rifles [*British*]
CI R	Clarke's New York Chancery Reports [*A publication*] (DLA)
CLR	Clean Liquid RADwater [*Nuclear energy*] (IEEE)
CLR	Clear [*Alaska*] [*BMEWS Site 1*] (MCD)
clr	Clear (WDMC)
CLR	Clear to Zero [*Computer science*]
CLR	Cleveland Law Record [*Ohio*] [*A publication*] (DLA)
CLR	Collar (MSA)
CLR	Collurania [*Italy*] [*Seismograph station code, US Geological Survey Closed*] (SEIS)
CLR	Color (MSA)
clr	Color (VRA)
CLR	Color
CLR	Colortech Corp. [*Toronto Stock Exchange symbol*]
CLR	Columbia Law Review [*A publication*] (BRI)
CLR	Combined Line and Recording Trunk (IEEE)
CLR	Combustible Limit Relay (IAA)
CLR	Common Law Reports [*British*]
CLR	Common Line Receiver (IAA)
CLR	Computer Language Recorder
CLR	Computer Language Research (IEEE)
CLR	Conference Letter Report (SAA)
CLR	Constant Load Rupture (OA)
CLR	Construction Labor Report (AAGC)
CLR	Construction Law Reports (AAGC)
CLR	Construction Litigation Reporter (AAGC)
CLR	Contact Load Resistor (IAA)
CLR	Control Line Register
CLR	Cooler (MSA)
CLR	Coordinating Lubricant and Equipment Research Committee [*Coordinating Research Council*]
CLR	Coordination Letter Report (SAA)
CLR	Cornell Law Review [*A publication*] (ILCA)
CLR	Councillor (ADA)
CLR	Council of Law Reporting [*Australia*]
CLR	Council on Library Resources (EA)
CLR	Crater-Lamp Recorder
CLR	CST Entertainment [*AMEX symbol*] (TTSB)
CLR	CST Entertainment Imaging [*Formerly, Color Systems Technology, Inc.*] [*AMEX symbol*] (SPSG)
CLR	Current Law Reports [*Palestine*] [*A publication*] (DLA)
CLR	Current-Limiting Resistor (MSA)
CLR	Cycle Log Reduction [*Time required for a given amount of bacteriological kill*]
CLR	Cyprus Law Reports [*A publication*] (DLA)
CLR	New York State School of Industrial and Labor Relations, Cornell University, Ithaca, NY [*OCLC symbol*] (OCLC)
CLR	Trans American Airways, Inc. [*ICAO designator*] (FAAC)
CLRA	Construction Labour Relations - An Alberta Association (AC)
CLRA	Consumers' Law Reform Association [*Australia*]
CLRA	Inter-Corporate Ownership [*Canada Systems Group*] [*Information service or system*] (IID)
CLRAP	Catholic League for Religious Assistance to Poland (EA)
CLRAP	Cleared as Planned (FAAC)
CLRAQ	Consumers' Law Reform Association, Queensland [*Australia*]
CLRB	Canada Labour Relations Board
CLRB	Cost Limit Review Board
CLRC	Canada Law Reform Commission (DLA)
CLRC	Canadian Livestock Records Corporation [*Societe Canadienne d'Enregistrement des Animaux*] (AC)
CLRC	Central Labor Relations Commission [*Japan*]
CLRC	Circuit Layout Record Card [*Telecommunications*] (TEL)
CLR (Can)	Canada Law Reports, Exchequer Court and Supreme Court [*A publication*] (DLA)
CLR (Can)	Common Law Reports [*1835-55*] [*Canada*] [*A publication*] (DLA)
CLRCR	Catholic League for Religious and Civil Rights (EA)
CLRD	Criminal Law Review Division [*New South Wales*] [*Australia*]
CLRE	Contact Lens Registry Examination [*National Contact Lens Examiners*]
CL Rec	Cleveland Law Record [*Ohio*] [*A publication*] (DLA)
CL Reg	Cleveland Law Register [*Ohio*] [*A publication*] (DLA)
CL Rep	Cleveland Law Reporter [*Ohio*] [*A publication*] (DLA)
CLRF	Center for Law and Religious Freedom (EA)
CLRG	Clearing (MSA)
CLRG	Collector Ring [*Electricity*]
CLRI	Central Leather Research Institute [*British*]
CLRI	Computer Language Research, Inc. [*NASDAQ symbol*] (SAG)
CLRI	Computer Language Rsch [*NASDAQ symbol*] (TTSB)

CLRIT.......... Children's Legal Rights Information and Training [*An association*] (EA)
CLRK .... Clerk
Cl RL .... Clarke's Early Roman Law [*A publication*] (DLA)
Clrm.......... Classroom (BARN)
CLRM.......... Cool Room
CLRNDX....... Control Logic Read Index [*Computer science*] (ECII)
CLRNG.......... Clearing
CLRNSW....... Council of Law Reporting of New South Wales [*Australia*]
CLRO .... Clark Lake Radio Observatory [*University of Maryland*] [*Research center*] (RCD)
CLRO-E........ Richfield Oil Corp., Economic Research Department, Los Angeles, CA [*Library symbol Library of Congress*] (LCLS)
CLRO-R........ Richfield Oil Corp., Research and Development Library, Anaheim, CA [*Library symbol Library of Congress*] (LCLS)
CLRO-T........ Richfield Oil Corp., Technical Library, Wilmington, CA [*Library symbol Library of Congress*] (LCLS)
CLRP .... Color Prints [*Not tinted*] (VRA)
CLRP .... Command Logistics Review Program [*DoD*]
CLRP .... Cornell Local Roads Program [*Cornell University*] [*Research center*] (RCD)
CLRS .... Center for Labor Research and Studies [*Florida International University*] [*Research center*] (RCD)
CLRS .... Clear and Smooth [*NWS*] (FAAC)
CLRT.......... Command Logistics Review Team (MCD)
CLRTX .... Command Logistics Review Teams Expanded (MCD)
CLRU .... Cambridge Language Research Unit
CLRV .... Canadian Light Rail Vehicle
CLRV .... Cherry Leafroll Virus [*Plant pathology*]
CLRV .... County of London Regiment (Volunteers) [*British military*] (DMA)
CLRWS .... Clean Liquid Radioactive Waste System (NRCH)
CLS .... Cable Laying Ship
CLS .... California State University, Los Angeles, Los Angeles, CA [*Library symbol Library of Congress*] (LCLS)
CLS.............. Calistoga [*California*] [*Seismograph station code, US Geological Survey Closed*] (SEIS)
CLS.............. Callex Enterprises Ltd. [*Vancouver Stock Exchange symbol*]
CLS.............. Cambridge Life Sciences [*British*]
CLS.............. Cam Limit Switch
CLS.............. Canada Land Surveyor
CLS.............. Canadian Long Term Care Assciation [*Association Canadienne de Soins a Long Terme*] (AC)
CLS.............. Canadian Lumber Size (DAC)
CLS.............. Canfield Learning Styles Inventory [*Educational test*]
CLS.............. Canon Law Society of America (EA)
CLS.............. Carleton Library System [*Carleton University*] [*Information service or system*] (IID)
CLS.............. Carolina Library Services, Inc. (IID)
CLS.............. Cask Loading Station [*Nuclear energy*] (NRCH)
CLS.............. Center for Libertarian Studies (EA)
CLS.............. Centralized Lighting System [*Automotive engineering*]
CLS.............. Centre for Language Studies [*University of Newcastle*] [*Australia*]
Cls.............. Certificate in Library Science (BARN)
CLS.............. Characteristic Loss Spectroscopy
CLS.............. Charles Lamb Society [*British*]
CLS.............. Chehalis, WA [*Location identifier FAA*] (FAAL)
CLS.............. Chemical LASER Study [*or System*]
CLS.............. Chicago LASER Systems, Inc. (NITA)
CLS.............. Chicago Library System [*Chicago Public Library*] [*Chicago, IL Library network*]
CLS.............. Christian Legal Society (EA)
CLS.............. Cislunar Space
CLS.............. Citrus Label Society (EA)
Cls.............. Claims (DLA)
CLS.............. Classify (MSA)
Cls.............. Clauses (DLA)
CLS.............. Clear and Subtract (IEEE)
CLS.............. Clear Screen [*Computer science*]
CLS.............. Clerical Support
CLS.............. Clinical Laboratory Scientist (MAE)
CLS.............. Close [*Computer science*] (BUR)
CLS.............. Closed-Loop Support [*Army*] (AABC)
CLS.............. Closed-Loop System [*Chemical engineering*] [*Nuclear energy*] (NRCH)
CLS.............. Close Lunar Satellite
CLS.............. Closure [*Technical drawings*]
CLS.............. Cloud LIDAR System (MCD)
CLS.............. Coffin-Lowry Syndrome [*Medicine*]
CLS.............. Coils [*Freight*]
CLS.............. Collected Least Squares [*Statistics*]
CLS.............. College Libraries Section [*Association of College and Research Libraries*]
CLS.............. Combat Logistics System [*Air Force*] (GFGA)
CLS.............. Command and Launch Subsystem (MCD)
CLS.............. Command Liaison and Surveillance and Keying (SAA)
CLS.............. Committee on Life Sciences [*Federal interagency group*]
CLS.............. Common Language System [*Computer science*] (BUR)
CLS.............. Common Leaf Spot [*Plant pathology*]
CLS.............. Communications Line Switch
CLS.............. Community Liaison Staff [*Environmental Protection Agency*] (GFGA)
CLS.............. Comparative Literature Studies [*A publication*] (BRI)
CLS.............. Compatible LASER System
CLS.............. Computerized Litigation Support (HGAA)
CLS.............. Computer Letter Service (HGAA)

CLS.............. Computer Listing Service [*Computer Listing Service, Inc.*] [*Information service or system*] (IID)
CLS.............. Concept Learning System [*Computer science*] (BUR)
CLS.............. Constant Level Speech
CLS.............. Constrained Least Squares (PDAA)
CLS.............. Consular Law Society (EA)
CLS.............. Containment Leakage System [*Nuclear energy*] (IEEE)
CLS.............. Contingency Landing Site [*NASA*] (NASA)
CLS.............. Contractor Logistics Support [*DoD*]
CLS.............. Control Language Services [*Computer science*] (IAA)
CLS.............. Control Launch Subsystem (OA)
CLS.............. Controlled Leakage System (SAA)
CLS.............. Cornell Law School (DLA)
CLS.............. Courts of London Sessions [*British*] (BARN)
CLS.............. Creative List Services, Inc. [*Information service or system*] (IID)
CLS.............. Critical Legal Studies Philosophy
CLS.............. Cross-Linked Smectites [*Inorganic chemistry*]
CLS.............. Cum Laude Society (EA)
CLS.............. Harvard University, Cabot Science Library, Cambridge, MA [*OCLC symbol*] (OCLC)
CLS.............. New York Consolidated Laws Service [*A publication*]
CLSA.......... Canadian Law and Society Association [*See also ACDS*]
CLSA.......... Canon Law Society of America (EA)
CLSA.......... Closed-Loop Stripping Analysis [*Analytical chemistry*]
CLSA.......... Conservation Law Society of America [*Defunct*]
CLSA.......... Contact Lens Society of America (EA)
CLSA.......... Cooperative Logistic Support Arrangement [*Military*] (AFM)
CLSA-DB....... California Library Services Act Statewide Data Base [*California Library Services Board*] [*Information service or system*] (IID)
CLSB.......... Committee of London and Scottish Bankers [*British*]
CLSC.......... Chautauqua Literary and Scientific Circle (EA)
CLSC.......... Classic
CLSC.......... Coalesce
CLSC.......... Community Language in the Secondary Curriculum [*Project*] (AIE)
CLSC.......... Community Living Stormont County [*Integration Communautaire Comte de Stormont*] (AC)
CLSC.......... COMSEC [*Communications Security*] Logistic Support Center [*Army*] (AABC)
CLSCE.......... Southern California Edison Co., Los Angeles, CA [*Library symbol Library of Congress*] (LCLS)
CLSCS .... Cain-Levine Social Competency Scale [*Psychology*]
CLSD .... Closed (AAG)
CLSD .... Collaborative Library System Development
CLSE.......... Calf Lung Surfactant Extract [*Medicine*] (DMAA)
CLSES.......... Center for Lake Superior Environmental Studies [*Universtiy of Wisconsin - Superior*] [*Research center*] (RCD)
CLSF.......... Combined Logistics Stores Facility (DOMA)
CLSF.......... Security Pacific National Bank, Los Angeles, CA [*Library symbol Library of Congress*] (LCLS)
CLSG .... Closing (AAG)
CLSG .... Common Logistic Support Group [*Military*]
CLSH .... Corpus Luteum Stimulating Hormone (BARN)
CLSI .... Computer Library Services, Inc. [*Wellesley Hills, MA*]
CLSIR .... Cryogenic Limb Scanning Interferometer Radiometer (MCD)
CLSL .... Chronic Lymphosarcoma Cell Leukemia [*Medicine*] (MAE)
CLSL .... Southwestern University, School of Law, Los Angeles, CA [*Library symbol Library of Congress*] (LCLS)
CLSM.......... Confocal LASER Scanning Microscope [*or Microscopy*]
CLSM.......... Controlled Low-Strength Material
CLSM.......... Crew Life-Support Monitor [*NASA*] (KSC)
CLSM.......... Southwest Museum, Los Angeles, CA [*Library symbol Library of Congress*] (LCLS)
CLSM-B .... Southwest Museum, Braum Research Library, Los Angeles, CA [*Library symbol*] [*Library of Congress*] (LCLS)
CLSMDA ...... Closed-Loop System Melt-Down Accident [*Nuclear energy*] (NRCH)
CLSNG......... Closing
CLSO .... Contingency Landing Support Officer (MCD)
CLSP.......... Center for Law and Social Policy (EPA)
CLSP.......... Clinical Laboratory Specialist (MEDA)
CLSP.......... Composite Launch Sequence Plan (MCD)
CLSP.......... Contract Logistic Support Plan (MCD)
CLSP.......... Cooperative [*or Coordinated*] Logistics Support Program [*Air Force*] (MCD)
CLSR .... Closure (AAG)
CLSR .... Closure Medical Corp. [*NASDAQ symbol*] (SAG)
CLSR .... Computer Law Service Reporter
CLSS.......... Combat Logistics Support Squadron [*Air Force*]
CLSS.......... Combat Logistic Support System (AABC)
CLSS.......... Communication Link Subsystem
CLSS.......... Computerized Literature Searching Service
CLSS.......... Contractor Logistics Support Services (MCD)
CLSSA .... Cooperative Logistic Supply Support Arrangement [*Military*] (AFIT)
CLSSL.......... Colossal
CLSS MIS .... Contractor Logistics Support Services Management Information System (MCD)
CLST.......... Celestial
CLST.......... Cellstar Corp. [*NASDAQ symbol*] (SAG)
Clst.......... Clarinetist (BARN)
clst.......... Clerestory (VRA)
CL Stats....... Current Law Statutes, Annotated [*A publication*] (DLA)
CLSTBB........ Cluster Bomb [*Military*]
clstr .... Cloister (VRA)
CLStV.......... Saint Vincent College of Nursing, Los Angeles, CA [*Library symbol Library of Congress*] (LCLS)
CLSU .... Communications [*Security*] Logistics Support Unit (DOMA)

CLSU	COMSEC [*Communications Security*] Logistic Support Unit [*Army*] (AABC)
CLSU	University of Southern California, Los Angeles, CA [*Library symbol Library of Congress*] (LCLS)
CLSU-A........	University of Southern California, Architecture and Fine Arts Department, Los Angeles, CA [*Library symbol Library of Congress*] (LCLS)
CLSU-B........	University of Southern California, Biochemical Library, Los Angeles, CA [*Library symbol Library of Congress*] (LCLS)
CLSU-Bodd...	University of Southern California, H. G. Boddington Collection, Los Angeles, CA [*Library symbol Library of Congress*] (LCLS)
CLSU-Craig...	University of Southern California, Gordon Craig Collection, Los Angeles, CA [*Library symbol Library of Congress*] (LCLS)
CLSU-D........	University of Southern California, School of Dentistry, Los Angeles, CA [*Library symbol Library of Congress*] (LCLS)
CLSU-Ed	University of Southern California, Education Department, Los Angeles, CA [*Library symbol Library of Congress*] (LCLS)
CLSU-Farm...	University of Southern California, Farmington Plan Collection, Los Angeles, CA [*Library symbol Library of Congress*] (LCLS)
CLSU-Fe	University of Southern California, Feuchtwanger Library, Los Angeles, CA [*Library symbol*] [*Library of Congress*] (LCLS)
CLSU-Feucht...	University of Southern California, Feuchtwanger Memorial Collection, Los Angeles, CA [*Library symbol Library of Congress*] (LCLS)
CLSU-H........	University of Southern California, Hancock Library of Biology and Oceanography, Los Angeles, CA [*Library symbol Library of Congress*] (LCLS)
CLSU-Hefner...	University of Southern California, Lee Hefner Memorial Collection, Los Angeles, CA [*Library symbol Library of Congress*] (LCLS)
CLSU-Ho......	University of Southern California, Hoose Library of Philosophy, Los Angeles, CA [*Library symbol*] [*Library of Congress*] (LCLS)
CLSU-Hoose...	University of Southern California, Hoose Library of Philosophy, Los Angeles, CA [*Library symbol Library of Congress*] (LCLS)
CLSU-L........	University of Southern California, Law Library, Los Angeles, CA [*Library symbol Library of Congress*] (LCLS)
CLSU-Low....	University of Southern California, Kurt Lowenstein Collection, Los Angeles, CA [*Library symbol Library of Congress*] (LCLS)
CLSU-LTorch...	University of Southern California, Gregg Lane College, Torchieu Collection, Los Angeles, CA [*Library symbol Library of Congress*] (LCLS)
CLSU-M	University of Southern California, School of Medicine Library, Los Angeles, CA [*Library symbol Library of Congress*] (LCLS)
CLSU-Music...	University of Southern California, Music Library, Los Angeles, CA [*Library symbol Library of Congress*] (LCLS)
CLSU-R........	University of Southern California, Ruther Technology Library, Los Angeles, CA [*Library symbol Library of Congress*] (LCLS)
CLSU-Richm...	University of Southern California, Carl A. Richmond Collection, Los Angeles, CA [*Library symbol Library of Congress*] (LCLS)
CLSU-VKSmit...	University of Southern California, Von Kleinsmit Library of World Affairs, Los Angeles, CA [*Library symbol Library of Congress*] (LCLS)
CLSU-Vo	University of Southern California, Von KleinSmid Library of World Affairs, Los Angeles, CA [*Library symbol*] [*Library of Congress*] (LCLS)
CLSX...........	Closed-Loop Support Extended [*Army*] (AABC)
CLT	Calculated Landing Time [*FAA*] (TAG)
CLT	Canadian Law Times [*A publication*] (DLA)
CLT	Cargo Left Trailer (KSC)
CLT	Caribbean Air Transport Co., Inc. [*Netherlands ICAO designator*] (FAAC)
CLT	Center for Learning and Telecommunications [*American Association for Higher Education*] [*Information service or system*] (IID)
CLT	Central Limit Theorem [*Statistics*]
CLT	Charitable Lead Trust
CLT	Charlotte [*North Carolina*] [*Airport symbol*] (OAG)
CLT	Charlottesville [*Virginia*] [*Seismograph station code, US Geological Survey Closed*] (SEIS)
CLT	Chronic Lymphocytic Thyroiditis [*Medicine*]
CLT	Claimant (WGA)
CLT	Clark Technical College, Library Resource Center, Springfield, OH [*OCLC symbol*] (OCLC)
CLT	Clathan Literary Institute [*British*]
CLT	Cleat
CLT	Clerical Technician, Medical [*Navy*]
CLT	Client (ROG)
CLT	Clinical Laboratory Technician
CLT	Closed-Loop Telemetry
CLT	Closed-Loop Test (NASA)
CLT	Clot Lysis Time [*Hematology*]
CLT	Clotted [*Biochemistry*] (DAVI)
CLT	Code Language Telegram (IAA)
CLT	Collateral Trust [*Bond*]
CLT	Cominco Ltd. [*AMEX symbol Toronto Stock Exchange symbol Vancouver Stock Exchange symbol*] (SPSG)
CLT	Communication Line Terminal [*Computer science*]
CLT	Community Land Trust [*Agricultural economics*]
CLT	Computer Language Translator
CLT	Computer Line Terminal (HGAA)
CLT	Constant Load Tensile Test
CLT	Council of the Living Theatre [*Defunct*] (EA)
CLT	Cuttack Law Times [*India*] [*A publication*] (ILCA)
CLT	Los Angeles Times, Los Angeles, CA [*Library symbol Library of Congress*] (LCLS)
CLT	Total Lung Compliance [*Medicine*] (DAVI)
CLTA...........	Canadian Library Trustees' Association

CLTA...........	Chinese Language Teachers Association (EA)
CLTC...........	Central and Local Trades Committees [*Australia*]
CLTC...........	Chief Launch Vehicle Test Conductor [*NASA*] (KSC)
CLTC...........	Twentieth Century-Fox Film Corp., Research Library, Los Angeles, CA [*Library symbol Library of Congress*] (LCLS)
CLTCH	Clutch
CLTD...........	Computalog Ltd. [*NASDAQ symbol*] (SAG)
CLTDB.........	Clinical Laboratory Test Database [*Computer science*]
CLTDF.........	Computalog Ltd [*NASDAQ symbol*] (TTSB)
CLTE	Coefficient of Linear Thermal Expansion
CLTE	Coefficient of Linear Thermal Expansion
CLTE	Commissioned Loss to Enlisted Status [*Revocation of an officer's appointment*]
CLTG	Collecting (MSA)
CLTGL.........	Climatological (AABC)
CLTH..........	Clothes
CLTH..........	Cut Length (MSA)
CLTHG	Clothing (MSA)
CLTHNG......	Clothing
CLTHR	Clothier
CLTHS	Clothes
CLTI...........	Title Insurance & Trust Co., Los Angeles, CA [*Library symbol Library of Congress*] (LCLS)
CLTK..........	Celeritek Inc. [*NASDAQ symbol*] (TTSB)
CLT Occ N ...	Canadian Law Times. Occasional Notes [*A publication*] (DLA)
CL to MAGS...	Clerk to Magistrates [*British*] (ROG)
CL to VEST...	Clerk to Vestry [*British*] (ROG)
CLTR...........	Center for Local Tax Research (EA)
C/LTR..........	Cigarette [*or Cigar*] Lighter [*Automotive engineering*]
CLTR...........	Clutter (MSA)
CLTR...........	Continuous Loop Tubular Reactor [*Chemical engineering*]
CLTRL.........	Cultural
CLTRM........	Clutter Map (MSA)
CLTS	Chicago Lutheran Theological Seminary
CLTS	Connectionless-Mode Transport Service [*Telecommunications*] (ACRL)
CLTS	Connectionless Transport Service [*Computer science*] (TNIG)
CLTV	Closed-Loop Television
CLTV	Collective (MSA)
CLU	Canadian Labour Union
CLU	Capitol Line-Up [*A publication*] (EAAP)
CLU	Central Logic Unit [*Computer science*]
CLU	Certified Life Underwriter [*Insurance*]
CLU	Ceylon Labor Union [*Obsolete*]
CLU	Chartered Life Underwriter [*Solomon S. Huebner School of CLU Studies, The American College*] [*Designation awarded by*]
CLU	Chartered Life Underwriter (AAGC)
CLU	Circuit Line Up
CLU	Civil Liberties Union (IIA)
CLU	Club Air Europe Ltd. [*British ICAO designator*] (FAAC)
CLU	Cluj [*Kolozvar*] [*Romania*] [*Seismograph station code, US Geological Survey*] [*Closed*] (SEIS)
CLU	Cluster [*Programming language*] [*1973*] (CSR)
CLU	Clusterin (DMAA)
CLU	Command Launch Unit [*Military*]
CLU	Command Logic Unit (MCD)
CLU	Compatible Land Use [*FAA*] (TAG)
CLU	Competence Level Unit [*Education*]
CLU	Consolidated Louanna Gold Mines Ltd. [*Toronto Stock Exchange symbol*]
CLU	Corporate Library Update [*A publication*]
CLU	Institute of Chartered Life Underwriters of Canada
Clu	Pro Cluentio [*of Cicero*] [*Classical studies*] (OCD)
CLU	University of California, Los Angeles, Biomedical, Law, Physical Science, and Technology, Los Angeles, CA [*OCLC symbol*] (OCLC)
CLU	University of California, Los Angeles, Main Library, Los Angeles, CA [*Library symbol Library of Congress*] (LCLS)
CLU-ART......	University of California, Los Angeles, Art Library, Los Angeles, CA [*Library symbol Library of Congress*] (LCLS)
CLU-AUP......	University of California, Los Angeles, Architecture and Urban Planning Library, Los Angeles, CA [*Library symbol Library of Congress*] (LCLS)
CLUB	Club [*Commonly used*] (OPSA)
CLUB	HealthTech International, Inc. [*NASDAQ symbol*] (SAG)
CLUBZINE	Club Magazine [*Generic term for a publication covering the activities of a science-fiction fan club*]
CLUC	Combined Library Unions Committee [*Australia*]
CLU-C	University of California, Los Angeles, William Andrews Clark Memorial Library, Los Angeles, CA [*Library symbol Library of Congress*] (LCLS)
CLU-CHM....	University of California, Los Angeles, Chemistry Library, Los Angeles, CA [*Library symbol Library of Congress*] (LCLS)
CLU-COL......	University of California, Los Angeles, College Library, Los Angeles, CA [*Library symbol Library of Congress*] (LCLS)
CLUDACTDAT...	Include Accounting Data
CLUE...........	Career Laboratories Utilizing Experience (OICC)
CLUE...........	Clinical Literature Untoward Effects [*Service published by International Information Institute*]
CLUE...........	Computer Language Utility Extension (PDAA)
CLUE...........	Computer League for Users in Education (EDAC)
CLUE...........	Computer Learning under Evaluation (IAA)
CLUE...........	Computer Logging Unit and Editor (NITA)

CLU-EMS ..... University of California, Los Angeles, Engineering and Mathematical Sciences Library, Los Angeles, CA [*Library symbol Library of Congress*] (LCLS)

CLU-E/P ...... University of California, Los Angeles, Education and Psychology Library, Los Angeles, CA [*Library symbol Library of Congress*] (LCLS)

CLUES .... Computers, Learners, Users, Educators Association [*New Jersey*] (EDAC)

CLUG .... Community Land Use Game [*Urban-planning game*]

CLU-G/G ..... University of California, Los Angeles, Geology-Geophysics Library, Los Angeles, CA [*Library symbol Library of Congress*]

CLU-GRS .... University of California, Los Angeles, Graduate Reserve Service, Los Angeles, CA [*Library symbol Library of Congress Obsolete*] (LCLS)

CLU-L .... University of California, Los Angeles, Law Library, Los Angeles, CA [*Library symbol Library of Congress*] (LCLS)

CLU-M .... University of California, Los Angeles, Biomedical Library, Los Angeles, CA [*Library symbol Library of Congress*] (LCLS)

CLU-MAP .... University of California, Los Angeles, Map Library, Los Angeles, CA [*Library symbol Library of Congress*] (LCLS)

CLU-MGT .... University of California, Los Angeles, Management Library, Los Angeles, CA [*Library symbol Library of Congress*] (LCLS)

CLUMIS .... Cadastral and Land-Use Mapping Information System (PDAA)

CLUMP .... Compool Look-Up Memory Print

CLU-MUS .... University of California, Los Angeles, Music Library, Los Angeles, CA [*Library symbol Library of Congress*] (LCLS)

CLUnB .... United California Bank, Los Angeles, CA [*Library symbol Library of Congress*] (LCLS)

CLU-N/C ...... University of California, Los Angeles, Non-Circulating Reading Center, Los Angeles, CA [*Library symbol Library of Congress*] (LCLS)

CLU-O .... University of California, Los Angeles, Oriental Library, Los Angeles, CA [*Library symbol Library of Congress*] (LCLS)

CLUP .... Comprehensive Land Use Plan

CLUP .... Consolidated Labor Union of the Philippines

CLU-P .... University of California, Los Angeles, Physical Science and Technical Library, Los Angeles, CA [*Library symbol Library of Congress*] (LCLS)

CLU-PAS ..... University of California, Los Angeles, Public Affairs Service, Los Angeles, CA [*Library symbol Library of Congress*] (LCLS)

CLU-PHY .... University of California, Los Angeles, Physics Library, Los Angeles, CA [*Library symbol Library of Congress Obsolete*] (LCLS)

CLU-REF ..... University of California, Los Angeles, URL-Reference Department, Los Angeles, CA [*Library symbol Library of Congress*] (LCLS)

CLURT .... Come, Let Us Reason Together [*Labor mediators' slogan*]

CLUS .... Cluster of Stones [*Jewelry*] (ROG)

CLUS .... Continental Limits, United States

CLUSA .... Continental Limits, United States of America [*Navy*]

CLUSA .... Cooperative League of the United States of America (EA)

CLUSAF ...... United States Air Force, Technical Library, Los Angeles, CA [*Library symbol Library of Congress*] (LCLS)

CLU-S/C ...... University of California, Los Angeles, Department of Special Collections, Los Angeles, CA [*Library symbol Library of Congress*] (LCLS)

Clusk Pol TB... Cluskey's Political Text Book [*A publication*] (DLA)

CLUT .... Color Look-Up Table [*Computer graphics*]

CLUT .... Computer Logic Unit Tester (MCD)

CLU-T/A ...... University of California, Los Angeles, Theater Arts Reading Room, Los Angeles, CA [*Library symbol Library of Congress*] (LCLS)

CLUU .... College of Law, University of Utah (DLA)

CLU-U/A ...... University of California, Los Angeles, University Archives, Los Angeles, CA [*Library symbol Library of Congress*] (LCLS)

CLU-UES ..... University of California, Los Angeles, University Elementary School Library, LosAngeles, CA [*Library symbol Library of Congress*] (LCLS)

CLU-URL ..... University of California, Los Angeles, University Research Library, Los Angeles,CA [*Library symbol Library of Congress*] (LCLS)

CLUW .... Coalition of Labor Union Women (EA)

CLUWCER ... Coalition of Labor Union Women Center for Education and Research (EA)

CLV .... Cal Aviation SA [*Greece*] [*ICAO designator*] (FAAC)

CLV .... Carnation Latent Virus [*Plant pathology*]

CLV .... Ceiling Limit Value [*Investment term*] (MHDW)

CLV .... Clarissimus Vir [*Most Illustrious Man*] [*Latin*]

CLV .... Cleve [*Australia Seismograph station code, US Geological Survey*] (SEIS)

CLV .... Cleveland (BARN)

CLV .... Clevis [*Metal shackle*] (KSC)

CLV .... Combat Logistics Vehicle [*Army*]

CLV .... Constant Linear Velocity [*Videodisk format*]

CLV .... La Verne University, La Verne, CA [*OCLC symbol*] (OCLC)

CLV .... Library of Vehicles, Los Angeles, CA [*Library symbol Library of Congress*] (LCLS)

CLVA .... United States Veterans Administration Center, Medical Research Library, Los Angeles, CA [*Library symbol Library of Congress*] (LCLS)

CLVA-B .... United States Veterans Administration Center, Brentonwood Medical Library, Los Angeles, CA [*Library symbol Library of Congress*] (LCLS)

CLVCHD ...... Clavichord [*Music*]

ClvClf .... Cleveland-Cliffs, Inc. [*Associated Press*] (SAG)

ClvClf .... Cleveland Cliffs, Inc. Holding Co. [*Associated Press*] (SAG)

CLVD .... Clavichord [*Music*]

CLVd .... Columnea Latent Viroid [*Plant pathology*]

CLVD .... Compensated Linear Vector Dipole [*Seismology*]

ClvEl .... Cleveland Electric Illuminating Co. [*Associated Press*] (SAG)

CL VOID ...... Clean Voided [*Specimen*] [*Biochemistry*] (DAVI)

CIVPP .... Chlorambucil, Vinblastine, Procarbazine, Prednisone [*Antineoplastic drug regimen*]

CLVR .... Cliche Verre (VRA)

CLVRY .... Cavalry

CLW .... Capital Library Wholesale [*ACCORD*] [*UTLAS symbol*]

CLW .... Catholic Library World [*A publication*] (BRI)

CLW .... Ceylon Law Weekly [*A publication*] (ILCA)

CLW .... Clearwater, FL [*Location identifier FAA*] (FAAL)

CLW .... Clockwise (IAA)

CLW .... College of Librarianship Wales [*British*] (NITA)

CLW .... Colville [*Washington*] [*Seismograph station code, US Geological Survey Closed*] (SEIS)

CLW .... Commercial Laws of the World [*A publication*] (DLA)

CLW .... Council for a Livable World (EA)

CLWEF .... Council for a Livable World Education Fund (EA)

CLWelf .... Welfare Planning Council, Los Angeles, CA [*Library symbol Library of Congress*] (LCLS)

CLWestO ..... Western Oil and Gas Association, Los Angeles, CA [*Library symbol Library of Congress*] (LCLS)

CLWG .... Clear Wire Glass [*Technical drawings*]

CLWJ .... Western Jewish Institute, Los Angeles, CA [*Library symbol Library of Congress*] (LCLS)

CLWM .... Company Lightweight Mortar System [*Army*] (MCD)

CLWM .... White Memorial Medical Center, Los Angeles, CA [*Library symbol Library of Congress*] (LCLS)

CLWP .... Committee for Liquidation of German War Potential [*Allied German Occupation Forces*]

CLWP .... Western Precipitation Corp., Los Angeles, CA [*Library symbol Library of Congress*] (LCLS)

CLWS .... Clockwise

CLWY .... Calloway's Nursery [*NASDAQ symbol*] (SPSG)

CLX .... Cargolux Airline International [*Luxembourg*] [*ICAO designator*] (FAAC)

CLX .... Carlson Mines Ltd. [*Vancouver Stock Exchange symbol*]

CLX .... Clorox Co. [*NYSE symbol*] (SPSG)

CLX .... Continuous Lightweight Exterior

CLXG .... Celex Group [*NASDAQ symbol*] (TTSB)

CLXG .... Celex Group, Inc. [*NASDAQ symbol*] (SAG)

CLXX .... Cellex Biosciences [*NASDAQ symbol*] (TTSB)

CLXX .... Cellex Biosciences, Inc. [*NASDAQ symbol*] (SAG)

CLXXZ .... Cellex Biosciences Wrrt 2000 [*NASDAQ symbol*] (TTSB)

CLY .... Calvi [*Corsica*] [*Airport symbol*] (OAG)

CLY .... Clay-Mill Technical Systems, Inc. [*Toronto Stock Exchange symbol*]

CLY .... Clyde Surveys Ltd. [*British ICAO designator*] (FAAC)

CLY .... Cotton Valley [*Vancouver Stock Exchange symbol*]

CLY .... Crystal Lake [*New York*] [*Seismograph station code, US Geological Survey*] (SEIS)

CLY .... Current Law Year Book [*A publication*] (ILCA)

CLY .... Worcester, MA [*Location identifier FAA*] (FAAL)

CLY .... Yoshitomi Pharmaceutical Ind. Co. Ltd. [*Japan*] [*Research code symbol*]

CLYDE .... Computer-Graphics Language for Your Design Equations (PDAA)

CLYMV .... Clover Yellow Mosaic Virus [*Plant pathology*]

CLYS .... Catalyst International, Inc. [*NASDAQ symbol*] (SAG)

CLYS .... Catalyst Intl. [*NASDAQ symbol*] (TTSB)

CLySF .... Saint Francis Hospital, Health Science Library, Lynwood, CA [*Library symbol Library of Congress*] (LCLS)

Clysis .... Hypodermoclysis [*Medicine*] (DHSM)

CLY T C ...... Clay or Terra Cotta [*Freight*]

CLYVV .... Clover Yellow Vein Virus [*Plant pathology*]

CLZ .... Aerotaxis Calzada SA de CV [*Mexico ICAO designator*] (FAAC)

CLZ .... Baton Rouge, LA [*Location identifier FAA*] (FAAL)

CLZ .... Calabozo [*Venezuela*] [*Airport symbol*] (OAG)

CLZ .... Canasil Resources, Inc. [*Vancouver Stock Exchange symbol*]

CLZ .... Chlorozotocin [*Antineoplastic drug*] (CDI)

CLZ .... Clausthal [*Federal Republic of Germany*] [*Seismograph station code, US Geological Survey*] (SEIS)

CLZ .... Clozapine [*A drug*]

CLZ .... Copper, Lead, or Zinc [*Freight*]

CLZ .... Craft Landing Zone [*Military*] (DOMA)

CLZ .... Cristalandia [*Brazil*] [*Airport symbol*] (AD)

CLZ .... Cushion Landing Zone [*Navy*] (ANA)

CLZR .... Candela Corp. [*NASDAQ symbol*] (TTSB)

CLZR .... Candela Laser Corp. [*NASDAQ symbol*] (NQ)

CLZRW .... Candela Corp. Wrrt [*NASDAQ symbol*] (TTSB)

CM .... Calibrated Magnification (MSA)

CM .... Calibration Marker

CM .... California Mastitis Test [*Medicine*] (DMAA)

CM .... Call Money [*Investment term*]

C/M .... Call of More [*Stock exchange term British*] (ROG)

CM .... Camair [*Division of Cameron Iron Works, Inc.*] [*ICAO aircraft manufacturer identifier*] (ICAO)

cm .... Cameroon [*MARC country of publication code Library of Congress*] (LCCP)

CM .... Cameroon [*ANSI two-letter standard code*] (CNC)

CM .... Canada Medal

CM .... Canadian Imperial Bank of Commerce [*Toronto Stock Exchange symbol Vancouver Stock Exchange symbol*]

CM .... Canadian Imperial Bk [*TS, exchange symbol*] (TTSB)

CM .... Canadian Militia

CM .... Canberra Income Tax Circular Memorandum [*A publication*]

CM .... Candidate Material

CM .... Capitular Masonry [*Freemasonry*] (ROG)

CM .... Capreomycin [*An antibiotic*] (MAE)
CM .... Carat, Metric
CM .... Carboxymethyl [*Also, Cm, Cme*] [*Biochemistry*]
CM .... Carcinomatous Meningitis [*Oncology*]
CM .... Cardiac Monitor [*Medicine*] (MAE)
CM .... Cardiomyography [*Cardiology*]
CM .... Cardiomyopathy [*Medicine*]
CM .... Cards per Minute [*Computer science*]
CM .... Career Minister [*Department of State*]
CM .... Career Motivation (AFM)
CM .... Cargo Management (MCD)
CM .... Carmelite Missionaries [*Rome, Italy*] (EAIO)
CM .... Carnegie Museum of Natural History [*Pittsburgh, PA*]
CM .... Carpenter's Mate [*Navy*]
CM .... Cartographic Materials [*International Federation of Library Associations*]
CM .... Case Monitoring [*Air Force*] (AFIT)
CM .... Casomorphin [*Biochemistry*]
CM .... Casualty Mode [*Military*] (CAAL)
CM .... Caucasian Male
CM .... Caudal Magnocellular [*Nuclei*] [*Neuroanatomy*]
CM .... Causa Mortis [*On Occasion of Death*] [*Latin*]
CM .... Celestial Mechanics
CM .... Cell Membrane
CM .... Center Matched [*Technical drawings*]
CM .... Center of Mass [*Atomic physics*]
cm .... Centimeter (GPO)
cM .... Centimorgan [*Unit of genetic map distance*]
CM .... Central Memory [*Computer science*] (BUR)
CM .... Cerebral Malaria [*Medicine*]
CM .... Certificated Master [*or Mistress*] [*British*]
CM .... Certified Master [*British*]
CM .... Certified Midwife
CM .... Cervical Mucus [*Obstetrics*]
CM .... Chairman's Memorandum
CM .... Chargeable to Manuals (MCD)
CM .... Chart Maker [*Computer Design*] [*Software package*] (NCC)
C/M .... Chattel Mortgage [*Legal term*] (DLA)
CM .... Cheap Money [*Banking*]
CM .... Chelmsford (ODBW)
CM .... Chemical Corps [*Army*] (RDA)
CM .... Chemically-Induced Mutants [*Genetics*]
CM .... Chemically Malignant [*Medicine*]
CM .... Chemical Manufacture [*Department of Employment*] [*British*]
CM .... Chemical Milling (MSA)
CM .... Chick-Martin [*Test*] [*Microbiology*]
CM .... Chief Mechanic
CM .... Chief Metalsmith [*Navy rating Obsolete*]
CM .... Chirurgiae Magister [*Master of Surgery*] [*Latin*]
CM .... Chloramphenicol [*Antimicrobial compound*]
CM .... Chlorinated Methane [*Organic chemistry*]
CM .... Chloroquine-Mepacrine [*Antimalarial drugs*] (MAE)
CM .... Choirmaster [*Music*]
CM .... Chondromalacia [*Medicine*] (MAE)
CM .... Chopped Meat [*Medium*] [*Microbiology*]
CM .... Christian Mission (EA)
cm .... Chromite [*CIPW classification*] [*Geology*]
CM .... Chrom-Moly (MCD)
CM .... Church Missionary (IIA)
CM .... Circuit Master (MSA)
CM .... Circuit Modeller [*Seasim Engineering Software Ltd.*] [*Software package*] (NCC)
CM .... Circular Mail
CM .... Circular Measure
CM .... Circular Mil [*Wire measure*]
cm .... Circular Mil (IDOE)
CM .... Circular Muscle [*Anatomy*]
CM .... Circulation Manager (IIA)
CM .... Civic Movement [*Former Czechoslovakia*] [*Political party*] (EY)
CM .... Claims Manual [*Social Security Administration*] (OICC)
CM .... Classical Mechanics [*Physics*]
CM .... Classified Message
CM .... Class Marks [*Telecommunications*] (TEL)
CM .... Class of Material (MCD)
CM .... Clear Memory (IAA)
CM .... Clerical Medical [*Insurance firm*] [*British*]
CM .... Clinical Modification
CM .... Closed Mouth [*Doll collecting*]
CM .... Club Management [*Club Managers Association of America*] [*A publication*]
CM .... Club Mediterranee (EA)
CM .... Cochlear Microphonics [*Response*] [*Auditory testing*]
CM .... Coles Myer Ltd. [*NYSE symbol*] (CTT)
CM .... Coles Myer Ltd ADR [*NYSE symbol*] (TTSB)
CM .... Collection Management [*A publication*]
CM .... Colorado-Maduro [*Very dark-colored cigar*]
CM .... Colorado Midland
CM .... Columellar Muscle
CM .... Combat Material
CM .... Combat Mission [*Military*]
CM .... Combustion Metamorphism [*Geology*]
CM .... Command
CM .... Commander's Manual [*Military*]
CM .... Command Module [*NASA*]
CM .... Command Money [*British military*] (DMA)

CM .... Commentary on the Mishnah [*Maimonides*] (BJA)
CM .... Commercial [*Rate*] [*Value of the English pound*]
CM .... Commercial Manager (DCTA)
CM .... Commercial Manual [*DoD*]
CM .... Common Measure [*Music*] (IIA)
CM .... Common Meter [*Music*]
CM .... Common Migraine [*Neurology*] (DAVI)
CM .... Common Mode (IAA)
CM .... Communications Manager
CM .... Communications Module [*AT&T*] (ACRL)
CM .... Communications Monitor (BTTJ)
CM .... Communications Multiplexer [*Computer science*]
CM .... Community Code [*Database terminology*] (NITA)
CM .... Community Market Catalog
CM .... Comparators [*JETDS nomenclature*] [*Military*] (CET)
CM .... Compassionate Case [*Airline notation*]
CM .... Complementary Manual [*Military*]
CM .... Completed
CM .... Complete Medium [*Microbiology*]
CM .... Complication [*Medicine*] (AAMN)
CM .... Component Manufacturer [*Foundry Business Systems*] [*Software package*] (NCC)
CM .... Composite Merge
CM .... Computer Management [*British A publication*]
CM .... Computer Microtechnology (IAA)
CM .... Computer Module
CM .... Computing Media
Cm .... Concentration, minimal [*Medicine*] (DMAA)
CM .... Concerns of Motherhood (EA)
CM .... Conciertos Mexicanos [*Record label*] [*Mexico*]
CM .... Conditioned Medium [*For growing microorganisms*]
CM .... Condition Monitoring (DS)
CM .... Confidential Memorandum
CM .... Configuration Management
CM .... Congenital Malformation [*Medicine*]
CM .... Congestive Myocardiopathy [*Medicine*]
CM .... Congregatio Mariae [*Fathers of the Company of Mary*] [*Roman Catholic religious order*]
CM .... Congregatio Missionis Sancti Vicentii a Paulo [*Congregation of the Mission of St. Vincent de Paul*] [*Vincentians*] [*Roman Catholic men's religious order*]
CM .... Congregationis Missionum [*The Congregation of Lazarists*] (ROG)
CM .... Congregation of the Mission [*Vincentians*] (DAS)
cm .... Congregation of the Mission, Vincentian Fathers (TOCD)
CM .... Connecticut Mutual Life Insurance Co.
CM .... Connecting Machine (IAA)
CM .... Connection Machine [*Naval Research Laboratory*] (PS)
CM .... Connection Manager (ACRL)
CM .... Constant Misery [*Slang*]
CM .... Construction and Machinery
CM .... Construction Management
CM .... Construction Mechanic [*Navy rating*]
CM .... Consumables Management (NASA)
CM .... Contact Maker
CM .... Contamination Mode [*NASA*] (KSC)
CM .... Contemporary Musicians [*A publication*]
CM .... Continental Marines
CM .... Continuity Message [*Telecommunications*] (TEL)
CM .... Continuous Monitor
CM .... Continuous Murmur [*Cardiology*] (DAVI)
CM .... Contract Management
CM .... Contract Modification
CM .... Contrast Media [*Radiology*]
CM .... Contribution Margin [*Accounting*]
CM .... Controlled Minefield [*Navy*]
CM .... Control Mark (DEN)
CM .... Control Memory [*Telecommunications*] (TEL)
CM .... Control Mode (MCD)
CM .... Control Module
CM .... Control Monitor (MCD)
Cm .... Coprinus Micaceous [*A fungus*]
CM .... Copulatory Mechanism [*Medicine*]
CM .... Core Memory
CM .... Cornmeal
CM .... Correction Memo (MCD)
CM .... Corrective Maintenance
CM .... Corrective Management (MCD)
CM .... Corresponding Member
CM .... Costal Margin [*Medicine*]
CM .... Cotton Mather [*Initials used as pseudonym*]
CM .... Countermarked
CM .... Countermeasure
CM .... Countermortar
C/M .... Counts per Minute
CM .... Court-Martial
CM .... Court Martial Reports, Army Cases [*United States*] [*A publication*] (DLA)
CM .... Cow's Milk
CM .... Craft Masonry [*Freemasonry*] (ROG)
CM .... Cras Mane [*Tomorrow Morning*] [*Pharmacy*]
CM .... Credit Memo
CM .... Crewman (KSC)
CM .... Crew Module [*NASA*] (NASA)
CM .... Criminal Matters
CM .... CRISTA Ministries [*Later, CRISTA*] (EA)

CM.............	Critical Mass [*Later, CMEP*] [*An association*] (EA)
CM.............	Crosier Missions (EA)
CM.............	Cross Modulation [*Telecommunications*] (OA)
CM.............	Cruciform Monument (BJA)
CM.............	Crude Myosin [*Food technology*]
CM.............	Cruise Missile (MCD)
CM.............	Cruiser Minelayer
CM.............	Cryptic Masonry [*Freemasonry*] (ROG)
CM.............	Cub Master [*Scouting*]
CM.............	Culture Media [*Bacteriology*] (DAVI)
CM.............	Cumulative (WGA)
CM.............	Cumulative Mortality [*Radiology*]
CM.............	Cumulonimbus Mammatus [*Cloud*] [*Meteorology*]
Cm.............	Curium [*Chemical element*]
CM.............	Current Meter [*Marine science*] (OSRA)
CM.............	Current Monitor [*Instrumentation*]
C/M.............	Cycles per Minute (ADA)
CM.............	Cytoplasmic Membrane [*Botany*]
CM.............	Mariana Islands (VRA)
CM.............	Master of Surgery (DD)
Cm.............	Maximum Clearance (AAMN)
CM.............	Member of the Order of Canada
CM.............	Metric Carat [*200 milligrams*] (ADA)
cm----	Middle America [*MARC geographic area code Library of Congress*] (LCCP)
CM.............	Minelayer [*Navy symbol NATO*]
C-M.............	North Atlantic Council Memorandum [*NATO*]
CM.............	Northern Mariana Islands [*Postal code*]
CM1.............	Construction Mechanic, First Class [*Navy rating*]
c/m²	Candles per Square Meter [*Optics*]
CM/2.............	Communications Manager/2 [*Software*] (CDE)
CM2.............	Construction Mechanic, Second Class [*Navy rating*]
CM².............	Square Centimeter
cm².............	Square Centimeter (IDOE)
CM3.............	Construction Mechanic, Third Class [*Navy rating*]
C/M³.............	Coulombs per Cubic Meter
cm³.............	Cubic Centimeter (AAMN)
CM6.............	Central Minnesota Seismic Array [*Minnesota*] [*Seismograph station code, US Geological Survey*] (SEIS)
CMA.............	Cable Makers' Association [*British*] (BI)
CMA.............	Calcium Magnesium Acetate
CMA.............	Calcium Methanearsonate [*Herbicide*]
CMA.............	Calendar Marketing Agreement
CMA.............	Calendar Marketing Association (EA)
CMA.............	California Maritime Academy [*Vallejo*]
CMA.............	Campus Ministries of America (EA)
CMA.............	Canadian Manufacturers Association
CMA.............	Canadian Marconi Co. [*Aerospace*]
CMA.............	Canadian Medical Association
CMA.............	Canadian Metric Association
CMA.............	Canadian Mineral Analysts [*Analystes des Mineraux Canadiens*] (AC)
CMA.............	Canadian Motorcycle Association [*Association Motocycliste Canadienne*] (AC)
CMA.............	Canadian Museums Association
CMA.............	Candle Manufacturers Association [*Later, NCA*] (EA)
CMa.............	Canis Major [*Constellation*]
CMA.............	Career Management and Assignment [*Department of State*]
CMA.............	Carmac Resources [*Vancouver Stock Exchange symbol*]
CMA.............	Case Makers Association [*British*] (DBA)
CMA.............	Cash Management Account [*Merrill Lynch*]
CMA.............	Casket Manufacturers Association of America (EA)
CMA.............	Catering Managers Association of Great Britain and Northern Ireland (BI)
CMA.............	Cathodoluminescence Microscope Attachment
CMA.............	Cellulose Manufacturers Association (EA)
CMA.............	Census Metropolitan Area [*Canada*]
CMA.............	Center for Marine Affairs [*Scripps Institution of Oceanography*]
CMA.............	Central European Airlines [*Czechoslovakia*] [*ICAO designator*] (FAAC)
CMA.............	Centre of Management in Agriculture [*British*] (CB)
CMA.............	Certificate in Management Accounting [*Institute of Man agement Accounting of the National Association of Accountants*] [*Designation awarded by*]
CMA.............	Certified Management Accountant (DD)
CMA.............	Certified Medical Assistant
CMA.............	Chamber Music America (EA)
CMA.............	Channel Multiplier Array
CMA.............	Chemical Manufacturers Association (EA)
CMA.............	Chief Medical Adviser
CMA.............	Childrenswear Manufacturers Association (EA)
CMA.............	Chinese Merchants Association (EA)
CMA.............	Chocolate Manufacturers Association of the USA (EA)
CMA.............	Christian and Missionary Alliance
CMA1.............	Christian Management Association (EA)
CMA.............	Christian Motorcyclist Association (EA)
CMA.............	Church Music Association [*British*]
CMA.............	Cigar Manufacturers Association of America [*Later, CAA*] (EA)
CMA.............	Circular Mil Area
CMA.............	Civilian Material Assistance (EA)
CMA.............	Civil-Military Affairs
CMA.............	Classified Mail Address
CMA.............	Clear Mews [*Alaska*] [*Seismograph station code, US Geological Survey Closed*] (SEIS)
CMA.............	Closure Manufacturers Association (EA)

CMA.............	Clothespin Manufacturers of America (EA)
CMA.............	Clothing Maintenance Allowance [*Military*]
CMA.............	Clothing Manufacturers Association of the USA (EA)
CMA.............	Club Managers' Association [*Australia*]
CMA.............	Collection Management Authority (MCD)
CMA.............	College Media Advisers (EA)
CMA.............	Colleges of Mid-America (EA)
CMA.............	Colon Mucoprotein Antigen [*Immunochemistry*]
CMA.............	Colorado Mining Association (EA)
CMA.............	Comerica, Inc. [*NYSE symbol*] (SPSG)
CMA.............	Comma (FAAC)
CMA.............	Command Modulator Assembly [*NASA*]
CMA.............	Commercial Market Appraisal
CMA.............	Commissariat for Montagnard Affairs
CMA.............	Commonwealth Magistrates' Association [*British*] (EAIO)
CMA.............	Commonwealth Medical Association [*British*] (EAIO)
CMA.............	Communications Management Agency
CMA.............	Communications Managers Association [*Bernardsville, NJ*] [*Telecommunications service*] (TSSD)
CMA.............	Communications Market Association (EA)
CMA.............	Compania Mexicana de Aviacion [*Mexican airline*]
CMA.............	Competitive Market Analysis [*Real estate*]
CMA.............	Complement Accumulator
CMA.............	Complex Modulus Apparatus
CMA.............	Computer Management Association
CMA.............	Computer-Marked Assignment [*Education*] [*British*]
CMA.............	Computer Monitor Adapter
CMA.............	Confederate Memorial Association
CMA.............	Configuration Management Accounting (NASA)
CMA.............	Congres Mondial Acadien (AC)
CMA.............	Conical Monopole Antenna
CMA.............	Conseil Mondial de l'Alimentation [*World Food Council*] [*French United Nations*] (DUND)
CMA.............	Consejo Mundial de la Alimentacion [*World Food Council*] [*Spanish United Nations*] (DUND)
CMA.............	Consolidated Metropolitan Area [*Later, CMSA*] [*Census Bureau*] (WDMC)
CMA.............	Construction Mechanic, Automotive [*Navy rating*]
CMA.............	Contact-Making Ammeter (KSC)
CMA.............	Contact Motion Analysis (CAAL)
CMA.............	Contract Machine Accessory (MCD)
CMA.............	Contract Maintenance Activity (AFM)
CMA.............	Contract Managers' Association [*A union*] [*British*]
CMA.............	Contract Manufacturers Association (EA)
CMA.............	Contractor's Manual Prepared after Negotiated Authorization for Contract
CMA.............	Contractors Mutual Association [*Defunct*] (EA)
CMA.............	Controller Military Accounts [*British military*] (DMA)
CMA.............	Control Message Automation [*Aviation*]
CMA.............	Convert Makers of America [*Later, CMOA*] (EA)
CMA.............	Cookware Manufacturers Association (EA)
CMA.............	Cooperative Merchandising Agreement (DOAD)
CMA.............	Corn Meal Agar [*Growth medium*]
CMA.............	Corps Maintenance Area
CMA.............	Corps of Military Accountants [*British military*] (DMA)
CMA.............	Corrective Maintenance Action [*Military*] (CAAL)
CMA.............	Council for Museum Anthropology (EA)
CMA.............	Countermission Analysis (MCD)
CMA.............	Country Mayors' Association [*New South Wales*] [*Australia*]
CMA.............	Country Music Association (EA)
CMA.............	Court of Military Appeals
CMA.............	Court of Military Appeals Reports [*A publication*] (DLA)
CMA.............	Cow's Milk Allergy [*Medicine*] (DMAA)
CMA.............	Crucible Manufacturers Association [*Later, CI*]
CMA.............	Cunnamulla [*Australia Airport symbol*] (OAG)
CMA.............	Currency Market Analysis [*MMS International*] [*Information service or system*] (CRD)
CMA.............	Current Market Appraisal
CMA.............	Cyclic Multilayered Alloy [*Electroplating technology*]
CMA.............	Cylinder Manufacturers Association [*Defunct*] (EA)
CMA.............	Cylindrical Mirror Analyzer [*Analytical instrumentation*]
CMa.............	Madera County Free Public Library, Madera, CA [*Library symbol Library of Congress*] (LCLS)
CMA.............	Oxnard, CA [*Location identifier FAA*] (FAAL)
CMAA.............	Canadian Maine-Anjou Association (AC)
CMAA.............	Ceramic Manufacturers' Association of Australia
CMA-A.............	Certified Medical Assistant-Administrative (WGA)
CMAA.............	Chief Master at Arms [*Navy rating*]
CMAA.............	Church Music Association of America (EA)
CMAA.............	Cigar Manufacturers Association of America [*Later, CAA*]
CMAA.............	Club Managers Association of America (EA)
CMAA.............	Cocoa Merchants' Association of America (EA)
CMAA.............	Comics Magazine Association of America (EA)
CMAA.............	Construction Management Association of America (EA)
CMAA.............	Courts-Martial (Appeals) Act [*British military*] (DMA)
CMAA.............	Crane Manufacturers Association of America (EA)
CMA-AC.............	Certified Medical Assistant-Administrative and Clinical (WGA)
CMAAC.............	Chinese Medicine & Acupuncture Association Canada [*L'Association de Medecine Chinoise et d'Acupuncture du Canada*] (AC)
CMAAC.............	Concrete Masonry Association of Australia Cooperative
CMAB.............	Canadian Mutual Aid Board [*World War II*]
CMAB.............	Clothing Maintenance [*or Monetary*] Allowance, Basic [*Army*]
CMAB.............	Combined Munitions Assignments Board [*World War II*]
CMAC.............	Capital Military Assistance Command (AABC)
CMAC.............	Catchment Management Advisory Committee [*Australia*]

CMAC.......... Central Management Army Commissaries (AABC)
CMAC.......... Cerebellar Model Articulation Control [*System*] [*National Institute of Standards and Technology*]
CMA-C........ Certified Medical Assistant-Clinical
C-MAC........ Champagne-Mumm Admiral's Cup [*Yacht racing*]
CMAC.......... CMAC Investment Corp. [*Associated Press*] (SAG)
CMAC.......... Computer Monitor and Control (MCD)
CMAC.......... Confectionery Manufacturers Association of Canada [*Association Canadienne des Fabricants de Confiseries*] (AC)
CMAC.......... Contingency Maintenance Allocation Chart (MCD)
CMAC.......... Court-Martial Appeal Court of Canada
CMACL........ Composite Mode Adjective Check List [*FAA*]
CMACP........ Conseil Mondial pour l'Assemblee Constituante des Peuples [*World Council for the Peoples World Convention*]
CMACS........ Central Monitor and Control System (MCD)
CMAE.......... Contigency Movement After-Effect (PDAA)
CMAEC........ Conseil Mondial des Associations d'Education Comparee [*World Council of Comparative Education Societies - WCCES*] (EA)
CMAF.......... Canadian Master Athlete Federation
CMAFP........ Committee on Medical Aspects of Food Policy [*British*]
CMAFS........ Cheyenne Mountain Air Force Station
CMAFSS...... Cheyenne Mountain Air Force Software Support [*Army*]
CMAG .... Casino Magic [*NASDAQ symbol*] (TTSB)
CMAG .... Casino Magic Corp. [*NASDAQ symbol*] (SAG)
CMAG .... Cruise Missile-Advanced Guidance (MCD)
CMAGTF ...... Contingency MAGTF [*Marine Air Ground Task Force*] (DOMA)
CMAI.......... Chemical Market Associates, Inc. [*Information service or system*] (IID)
CMAIISS ...... Clothing Monetary Allowance, Initial Issue [*Army*]
C Mail........ Courier Mail [*Brisbane*] [*A publication*]
CMAIWAC... Clothing Monetary Allowance, Initial (Women's Army Corps)
CMaj.......... Canis Major [*Constellation*]
CMAJ.......... Conseil des Ministres Arabes de la Justice [*Council of Arab Ministers of Justice - CAMJ*] [*Rabat, Morocco*] (EAIO)
CMAK.......... Conical Monopole Antenna Kit
CMAL.......... Clothing Monetary Allowance List [*Military*] (AFM)
CMAL.......... Controlled Multiple Address Letter (AFM)
CMalG .... J. Paul Getty Museum, Malibu, CA [*Library symbol Library of Congress*] (LCLS)
CMalG-A ...... J. Paul Getty Center, Arts Archives, Santa Monica, CA [*Library symbol*] [*Library of Congress*] (LCLS)
CMalG-CI .... J. Paul Getty Center, Conservation Institute, Santa Monica, CA [*Library symbol*] [*Library of Congress*] (LCLS)
CMalG-P ...... J. Paul Getty Center for the History of Arts and the Humanities, Photo Archives,Santa Monica, CA [*Library symbol*] [*Library of Congress*] (LCLS)
CMalG-V ...... J. Paul Getty Center for the History of Art & the Humanities, Vocabulary Coordination Group, Santa Monica, CA [*Library symbol*] [*Library of Congress*] (LCLS)
CMalH .... Hughes Research Library, Malibu, CA [*Library symbol Library of Congress*] (LCLS)
CMalHi .... Los Angeles City Historical Society, Malibu, CA [*Library symbol*] [*Library of Congress*] (LCLS)
CMalP.......... Pepperdine University, Malibu, CA [*Library symbol Library of Congress*] (LCLS)
CMAM.......... Chief Mailman [*Navy rating Obsolete*]
C-MAN........ Coastal Marine Automated Network [*Marine science*] (OSRA)
C-MAN........ Coastal Marine Automated Network [*National Weather Service*] (USDC)
CM & D .... Countermeasures and Deception [*RADAR*]
CM & E....... Chemical Marketing and Economics
CM & G....... Chicago, Milwaukee & Gary Railroad [*Nickname: Cold, Miserable, and Grouchy*]
CM & H .... Cox, Macrae, and Hertslet's English County Court Reports [*1847-58*] [*A publication*] (DLA)
CM & JA..... Commonwealth Magistrates and Judges' Association (EAIO)
CM & M....... Carroll, McEntee & McGinley [*Commercial firm*]
CM & PS .... Chicago, Milwaukee & Puget Sound Railroad
CM & R .... Compton, Meeson, and Roscoe's English Exchequer Reports [*1834-36*] [*A publication*] (DLA)
CM & RDT ... Corris, Machynlleth & River Dovey Tramway [*Wales*]
CM & S....... Communications Maintenance and Storage (NASA)
CM & StP .... Chicago, Milwaukee & St. Paul Railway
CMANSW..... Ceramic Manufacturers' Association of New South Wales [*Australia*]
CMANSW..... Country Meatworks Association of New South Wales [*Australia*]
CMAO .... Consejo Mundial de Artes y Oficios [*World Crafts Council*]
CMAO .... Contract Management Assistance Officer [*NASA*] (NASA)
CMAO .... Court-Martial Appointing Order
C-MAP .... Career Motivation and Achievement Planning Inventory (EDAC)
CMAP.......... Central Memory Access Priority [*Computer science*]
CMAP.......... Charge Material Allocation Processor
CMAP.......... Commission Mondiale d'Action Professionnelle [*World Committee for Trade Action - WCTA*] (EA)
CMAP.......... Compound Muscle Action Potential [*Medicine*] (DMAA)
CMAP.......... Compound Muscle Action Potential [*Neurophysiology*]
CMAP.......... Contrast Media Appearance Picture [*Also known as coronary arteriography*] [*Radiology*]
CMAPS .... Council for Military Aircraft Propulsion Standards
CMAQ .... Congestion Mitigation and Air Quality [*Improvement program*] [*VDOT*] (TAG)
CMAQ .... Congestion Mitigation & Air Quality [*An association*]
CMAR .... Canadian Court Martial Appeal Reports [*1957-*] [*A publication*] (DLA)
CMAR .... Can't Manage a Rifle [*Formed by reversing the initials of Royal Army Medical Corps*] [*World War I*] [*British*]
CMAR .... Cell Matrix Adhesion Regulator [*Medicine*] (DMAA)

CMAR .... Control Memory Access Register [*Computer science*] (NITA)
CMAR .... Control Memory Address Register [*Computer science*]
CMAR .... Courts-Martial Appeal Rules [*British military*] (DMA)
CMar.......... Mariposa County Free Library, Mariposa, CA [*Library symbol Library of Congress*] (LCLS)
CMarc........ Canadian Marconi Co. [*Associated Press*] (SAG)
CM-ARI........ Contrast Media-Induced Acute Renal Insufficiency [*Medicine*]
CMarM........ Mariposa Museum and History Center, Resource Library, Mariposa, CA [*Library symbol*] [*Library of Congress*] (LCLS)
CMARS .... Cable Monitoring and Rating System (MHDI)
CMartCH...... Contra Costa Historical Society, Martinez, CA [*Library symbol Library of Congress*] (LCLS)
CMartVA ..... United States Veterans Administration Hospital, Martinez, CA [*Library symbol Library of Congress*] (LCLS)
CMary.......... Marysville City Library, Marysville, CA [*Library symbol Library of Congress*] (LCLS)
CMaryY........ Yuba College, Marysville, CA [*Library symbol Library of Congress*] (LCLS)
CMAS.......... Calcium, Magnesium, Aluminum, Silicon [*Oxide system in geology*]
CMAS.......... Children's Manifest Anxiety Scale [*Psychology*] (AEBS)
CMAS.......... Circular Map Accuracy Standard (PDAA)
CMAS.......... Clergy Mutual Assurance Society [*British*]
CMAS.......... Clothing Maintenance Allowance, Standard [*Air Force*]
CMAS.......... Clothing Maintenance Allowance System [*Military*]
CMAS.......... Clothing Monetary Allowance, Standard [*Army*]
CMAS.......... Complete Mixing Activated Sludge
CMAS.......... Computer-Based Maintenance Aid Presentation System (MCD)
CMAS.......... Confederation Mondiale des Activites Subaquatiques [*World Underwater Federation - WUF*] [*ICSU Paris, France*] (EAIO)
CMAS.......... Construction Management Accounting System (MHDI)
CMAS.......... Council for Military Aircraft Standards
CMAS.......... Cruise Missile Alarm System (MCD)
CMA/SME .... Composites Manufacturing Association of the Society of Manufacturing Engineers (EA)
CM-ASTT .... Certified Member, American Society of Traffic and Transportation [*America n Society of Transportation and Logistics*] [*Designation awarded by*]
CMAT.......... Canadian Mathematics Achievement Test [*Education*] (AEBS)
CMAT.......... Compatible Materials List (NASA)
CMathes ...... Curtis Mathes Holding Corp. [*Associated Press*] (SAG)
CMAV.......... Coalition Mondiale pour l'Abolition de la Vivisection [*World Coalition for the Abolition of Vivisection*]
CMAWA .... Cabinetmakers' Association of Western Australia
CMAX.......... Cablemaxx, Inc. [*NASDAQ symbol*] (SAG)
C$_{max}$ .... Maximum Capacitance (IDOE)
CMB............ Carbolic Methylene Blue [*Clinical chemistry*]
CMB............ Cellular and Molecular Biology
CMB............ Central Medical Board (BARN)
CMB............ Central Midwives Board
CMB............ Central States Motor Freight Bureau, Chicago IL [*STAC*]
CMB............ Chase Manhattan [*NYSE symbol*] (TTSB)
CMB............ [*The*] Chase Manhattan Corp. [*New York, NY NYSE symbol*] (SPSG)
CMB............ Chase Preferred Capital Corp. [*NYSE symbol*] (SAG)
CMB............ Chemical Mass Balance
CMB............ Chief Motor Boatman [*British military*] (DMA)
CMB............ Chlorambucil [*Antineoplastic drug*]
CMB............ Chloromercuribenzoic [*Organic chemistry*]
CMB............ Christian Mission to Buddhists [*See also NKB*] [*Arhus, Denmark*] (EAIO)
CMB............ Circus Model Builders, International (EA)
CMB............ Climb [*or Climbing*] [*Aviation*] (FAAC)
CMB............ CMAC Computer Systems Ltd. [*Vancouver Stock Exchange symbol*]
CMB............ Coal Mines Board (DAS)
CMB............ Coastal Motorboat [*Obsolete British*]
CMB............ Code Matrix Block (DNAB)
CMB............ Colombo [*Sri Lanka*] [*Airport symbol*] (OAG)
CMB............ Combat Maneuver Battalion [*Army*]
CMB............ Combat Medical Badge [*Military decoration*] (AABC)
CMB............ Composite Minimum Brightness (PDAA)
CMB............ Comstock Mealybug [*Plant pest*]
CMB............ Concrete Median Barrier (OA)
CMB............ Conductivity Modulated Bipolar [*Computer science*]
CMB............ Configuration Management Branch [*NASA*] (KSC)
CMB............ Continental Merchant Bank [*Nigeria*]
CMB............ Core-Mantle Boundary [*Geology*]
CMB............ Corrective Maintenance Burden
CMB............ Cosmic Microwave Background [*Of radiation*]
CMB............ Cotton Marketing Board [*Australia*]
CMB............ Crossed Molecular Beam [*Instrumentation*]
CMB............ Modesto Bee, Modesto, CA [*Library symbol Library of Congress*] (LCLS)
CMBA.......... Canada Mink Breeders Association [*Association des Eleveurs de Visions du Canada*] (AC)
CMBA.......... Concert Music Broadcasters Association (EA)
CMBA.......... Confectionery and Mixed Business Association of Australia
CMBANZ ...... Confectionery and Mixed Business Association of Australia and New Zealand
CMBARMTNG... Combined Arms Training [*Military*] (NVT)
CMBBT........ Cervical Mucous Basal Body Temperature [*Gynecology and obstetrics*] (DAVI)
CMBC.......... Canadian Mennonite Bible College
CMBD .... Cellular and Molecular Basis of Disease [*Program*] [*National Institutes of Health*]
CMBD .... Combined
CMBES.......... Canadian Medical and Biological Engineering Society

CMBF	Cow's Milk Base Formula
CMBG	Canadian Mechanized Brigade Group (MCD)
CMBHI	Craft Member of the British Horological Institute (DBQ)
CmbHld	Cumberland Holdings, Inc. [Associated Press] (SAG)
CMBI	Caribbean Marine Biological Institute (BARN)
CmBkIN	Community Bank Shares of Indiana, Inc. [Associated Press] (SAG)
CmBkPa	Community Banks, Inc. [Associated Press] (SAG)
CMBL	Commercial Bill of Lading [Shipping] (DNAB)
CMBM	Centre for Molecular Biology and Medicine [Monash University] [Australia]
CMBMC	Conservative Mennonite Board of Missions and Charities [Later, RMM] (EA)
CMBNY	China Medical Board of New York (EA)
CMBPfK	Chase Manhattan 7.50% Dep Pfd [NYSE symbol] (TTSB)
CMBPrA	Chase Manhattan 10 1/2%'A'Pfd [NYSE symbol] (TTSB)
CMBPrB	Chase Manhattan 9.76%'B'Pfd [NYSE symbol] (TTSB)
CMBPrC	Chase Manhattan 10.84%'C'Pfd [NYSE symbol] (TTSB)
CMBPrD	Chase Manhattan 9.08%'D'Pfd [NYSE symbol] (TTSB)
CMBPrE	Chase Manhattan 8.50%'E'Pfd [NYSE symbol] (TTSB)
CMBPrF	Chase Manhattan 8.32%'F'Pfd [NYSE symbol] (TTSB)
CMBPrG	Chase Manhattan 10.96% Pfd [NYSE symbol] (TTSB)
CMBPrH	Chase Manhattan 8.375% Pfd [NYSE symbol] (TTSB)
CMBPrI	Chase Manhattan 7.92% Dep Ptd [NYSE symbol] (TTSB)
CMBPrJ	Chase Manhattan 7.58% Dep Pfd [NYSE symbol] (TTSB)
CMBPrL	Chase Manhattan Adj Rt'L'Pfd [NYSE symbol] (TTSB)
CMBPrM	Chase Manhattan 8.40% M Pfd [NYSE symbol] (TTSB)
CMBPrN	Chase Manhattan Adj N Pfd [NYSE symbol] (TTSB)
CMBR	Component Meantime Between Removals (MCD)
CMBR	Cosmic Microwave Background Radiation
C/MBR	Cross Member [Automotive engineering]
CMBS	Conventional Mortgage-Backed Security
CMBSTR	Combustor (MSA)
CMBT	Combat (AFM)
CmbTch	Cambridge Technology Partners [Associated Press] (SAG)
CMBTSPTSq	Combat Support Squadron [Air Force]
CMB.WS	Chase Manhattan Wrrt [NYSE symbol] (TTSB)
CMC	Cable Maintenance Center [Telecommunications] (TEL)
CmC	California Microfilm Co., Fresno, CA [Library symbol Library of Congress] (LCLS)
CMC	Canada Manpower Centre
CMC	Canadian Marconi Co. [Toronto Stock Exchange symbol]
CMC	Canadian Meat Council [Conseil des Viandes du Canada] [Formerly, Meat Packers Council of Canada] (AC)
CMC	Canadian Meteorological Centre [Marine science] (MSC)
CMC	Canadian Music Centre
CMC	Canadian Music Council [Defunct] (EAIO)
CMC	Carboxymethylcellulose [Organic chemistry]
CMC	Carboxymethylcysteine [Biochemistry]
CMC	Carpometacarpal [Anatomy]
CMC	Catholic Microfilm Center [Defunct]
CMC	Cell-Mediated Cytolysis
CMC	Cellular Mobile Carrier
CMC	Center for Marine Conservation (EA)
CMC	Center for Marketing Communications [Later, Advertising Research Foundation] (EA)
CMC	Center for Mass Communication [Columbia University]
CMC	Center for Medical Consumers and Health Care Information (EA)
CMC	Center for Microcontamination Control [Research center]
CM C	Centimeter-Candle
CMC	Central Maintenance Computer (GAVI)
CMC	Central Master Control (MCD)
CMC	Central Military Commission [China]
CMC	Ceramic Matrix Composite [Materials science]
CMC	Certified Management Consultant [Institute of Management Consultants, Inc .] [Designation awarded by]
CMC	Chemech Aviation Ltd. [Pakistan] [FAA designator] (FAAC)
CMC	Chemical Materials Catalog
CMC	Cheyenne Mountain Complex [NORAD] (MCD)
CMC	Chloramphenicol [Antimicrobial compound]
CMC	Chopped Meat Carbohydrate [Medium] [Microbiology]
CMC	Christian Medical Commission (EA)
CMC	Christian Medical Council [Defunct] (EA)
CMC	Christian Ministry Centre [Australia]
CMC	Chronic Mucocutaneous Candidiasis [Medicine]
CMC	Chronic Mucocutaneous Moniliasis [Medicine] (DAVI)
CMC	Citizen Mobilization Campaign [Defunct] (EA)
CMC	Claremont Men's College [California]
CMC	Clark Memorial College [Mississippi]
CMC	Clutter Mapper Card
CMC	Coastal Minelayer [Navy symbol]
CMC	Code for Magnetic Characters (IEEE)
CMC	Co-Fired, Multilayer Ceramic [Materials science]
CMC	Coherent Multi-Channel (IAA)
CMC	Coherent Multichannel Communication
CMC	Collective Measures Commission [United Nations] (DLA)
CMC	Collins Motor Corp. [Alternative engine technology]
CMC	Color Mixture Curve
CMC	COMARC [Cooperative Machine-Readable Cataloging Program] [Source file] [UTLAS symbol]
CMC	Combat Maintenance Capability (MCD)
CMC	Combined Meteorological Committee
CMC	Commandant of the Marine Corps
CMC	Command Management Center [Military]
CMC	Command Master Chief [Navy] (DOMA)
CMC	Command Module Computer [NASA] (MCD)

CMC	Commerce [Legal shorthand] (LWAP)
CMC	Commercial Metals [NYSE symbol] (TTSB)
CMC	Commercial Metals Co. [NYSE symbol] (SPSG)
CMC	Commission Medicale Chretienne [Christian Medical Commission] [Geneva, Switzerland] (EA)
CMC	Commission on Marine and Coastal Resources [California]
CMC	Committee for Modern Courts (EA)
CMC	Commodity Manager Code [Military]
CMC	Common Messaging Calls [Computer science]
CMC	Communicating Magnetic Card (HGAA)
CMC	Communication Multiplexor Channel (DNAB)
CMC	Communications Channel (NITA)
CMC	Communications Management Configuration
CMC	Communications Mode Control
CMC	Compact Molecular Cloud [Chemistry] (BARN)
CMC	Compagnie Maritime Camerounaise SA [Shipping line] (EY)
CMC	Comparison Measuring Circuit (PDAA)
CMC	Complement Carry
CMC	Complete Missile Container
CMC	Component Modification Cards [Nuclear energy] (NRCH)
CMC	Computer and Management Show for Contractors (TSPED)
CMC	Computer Machinery Corp. Ltd. [Subsidiary of Microdata] (MCD)
CMC	Computer Mediated Communication
CMC	Computer-Mediated Conferencing (IT)
CMC	Computer Microfilm Corp. [Information service or system] (IID)
CMC	Computer Musician Coalition (EA)
CMC	Concurrent Media Conversion (IAA)
CMC	Conference of Mennonites in Canada (AC)
CMC	Congregation de la Mere du Carmel [Congregation of Mother of Carmel] [Alwaye Kerala, India] (EAIO)
cmc	Congregation of Mother Coredemptrix (TOCD)
CMC	Congregation of Mother Coredemptrix (TOCD)
CMC	Conservation Monitoring Centre [World trade of endangered species products]
CMC	Consolidated Maintenance Center (MCD)
CMC	Consolidated Mercantile Corp. [Toronto Stock Exchange symbol]
CMC	Consolidated Midland Corp. (DAVI)
CMC	Constant Mean Curvature [Mathematics]
CMC	Construction Mechanic, Chief [Navy rating]
CMC	Contact-Making Clock
CMC	Continental Motosport Club (EA)
CMC	Continuous Membrane Column [Chemical engineering]
CMC	Control Magnetization Curve
CMC	Coordinated Manual Control
CMC	Copper Mine [Northwest Territories] [Seismograph station code, US Geological Survey Closed] (SEIS)
CMC	Core Monitoring Computer [Nuclear energy] (NRCH)
CMC	Corporate Management Committee [Australia]
CMC	Corporate Mountaineers Cult
CMC	Corrective Maintenance Card (MCD)
CMC	Correlation Metric Construction [Analysis of chemical reaction]
CMC	Council of Mennonite Colleges (EA)
CMC	Council of Motorcycle Clubs
CMC	Creative Multimedia Corp. [Database producer] (IID)
CMC	Crew Module Computer (MCD)
CMC	Critical Micelle Concentration
CMC	Cruise Missile Carrier Aircraft
CMC	Curved Motion Cutter
CMC	Customized Multimedia Connection
CMC	Cyclophosphamide, Methotrexate, CCNU [Lomustine] [Antineoplastic drug regimen]
CMC	Groupement des Producteurs de Carreaux Ceramiques du Marche Commun [Grouping of Ceramic Tile Producers of the Common Market] (ECED)
CMC	National Institute of Certified Moving Consultants (EA)
CMCA	Canadian Masonry Contractors' Association (AC)
CMCA	Character Mode Communications Adapter
CMCA	Comcast UK Cable Partners Ltd. [NASDAQ symbol] (SAG)
CMCA	Construction Mechanic, Construction Apprentice [Navy rating] (DNAB)
CMCA	Cruise Missile Carrier Aircraft (MCD)
CMCAF	Comcast UK Cable Partners'A' [NASDAQ symbol] (TTSB)
CM/CAI	Computer Management/Computer-Assisted Instruction (MCD)
CMCB	Carpenter's Mate, Construction Battalion [Navy]
CMCBB	Carpenter's Mate, Construction Battalion, Builder [Navy]
CMCBD	Carpenter's Mate, Construction Battalion, Draftsman [Navy]
CMCBE	Carpenter's Mate, Construction Battalion, Excavation Foreman [Navy]
CmcBHb	Commerce Bank (Harrisburg) [Associated Press] (SAG)
CmCbINC	Communication Cable, Inc. [Associated Press] (SAG)
CmcBMO	Commerce Bancshares, Inc. [Associated Press] (SAG)
CmcBNJ	Commerce Bancorp New Jersey [Associated Press] (SAG)
CmcBNY	Commercial Bank of New York [Associated Press] (SAG)
CMCC	Central Magistrates' Court Committee [British]
CMCC	Central Marine Chamber of Commerce [Defunct] (EA)
CMCC	Chronic Mucocutaneous Candidiasis [Medicine] (DMAA)
CMCC	Classified Matter Control Center (AAG)
CMCC	Coastal Management and Coordination Committee [Victoria] [Australia]
CMCC	Computer Monitor and Control Console (CAAL)
CMCC	Conference of Mutual Casualty Companies [Later, CCIC] (EA)
CMCCA	Conference of the Methodist Church in the Caribbean and the Americas (EAIO)
CMCCJ	Confederation Mondiale de Centres Communautaires Juifs [World Confederation of Jewish Community Centers] (EAIO)
CM/CCM	Countermeasures/Counter Countermeasures [Army] (RDA)

CMCCS .... Configuration Management and Change Control System [*Social Security Administration*]
CMC-CT .... [*Sodium*] Carboxymethylcellulose (BARN)
CMCD .... Cadillac Motor Car Division [*General Motors Corp.*]
CMCD .... Carboxymethyl Cyclodextrin [*University of Arizona, Tucson*]
CMCD .... Chopped Meat Glucose Broth with Digoxin [*Medium*] [*Microbiology*]
CMCD .... COMSEC [*Communications Security*] Mode Control Device [*Army*] (DWSG)
CmceG .... Commerce Group, Inc. [*Associated Press*] (SAG)
CmceGp .... Commerce Group, Inc. [*Associated Press*] (SAG)
CmcFdl .... Commercial Federal Corp. [*Associated Press*] (SAG)
CMcGSA ...... Clan McGillivray Society, Australia
CMCH .... Company of Military Collectors and Historians [*Later, CMH*] (EA)
CMCHCI .... Center for Medical Consumers and Health Care Information (EA)
CMCHS .... Civilian-Military Contingency Hospital System [*DoD*]
CMCI .... Children's Medical Center of Israel [*Tel Aviv*]
CMCI .... CMC Industries [*NASDAQ symbol*] (TTSB)
CMCI .... CMC Industries, Inc. [*NASDAQ symbol*] (NQ)
CMCI .... Computed Mission Coverage Index (MCD)
CMC Ind ...... CMC Industries, Inc. [*Associated Press*] (SAG)
CMCJ .... Carpometacarpal Joint [*Medicine*] (DMAA)
CMCL .... Command Management Control List
CmclAst .... Commercial Assets, Inc. [*Associated Press*] (SAG)
CmclBsh .... Commercial Bankshares, Inc. [*Associated Press*] (SAG)
CmclMtl .... Commercial Metals Co. [*Associated Press*] (SAG)
CmclNL .... Commercial Net Lease Realty, Inc. [*Associated Press*] (SAG)
CMCM .... Centre for Machine Condition Monitoring [*Monash University*] [*Australia*]
CMCM .... Chairman, Military Committee Memorandum [*NATO*]
CMCM .... Commandant of the Marine Corps Memorandum
CMCM .... Construction Mechanic, Master Chief [*Navy rating*]
CMCM .... Croatian Male Choir, Melbourne [*Australia*]
CMCN .... Constructionman, Construction Mechanic, Striker [*Navy rating*]
CMCO .... Classified Material Control Officer (AFIT)
CMCO .... Columbus McKinnon [*NASDAQ symbol*] (TTSB)
CMCO .... Confidential Material Control Officer (DNAB)
CMCO .... Corps Movement Control Organization [*Royal Corps of Transport*] [*British*]
CMCOLL ...... Church Missionary College [*Church of England*]
CMCP .... Canadian Museum of Contemporary Photography
CMCP .... Chemically-Modified Carbon Paste [*Electrode*]
CMCP .... CPG Missile Control Panel (MCD)
CMCPPG ...... Commandant, Marine Corps Program Policy and Planning Guidance (MCD)
CMCQ .... Commercial Mariculture Council of Queensland [*Australia*]
CMCR .... Centre for Mass Communication Research [*University of Leicester*] [*British*] (CB)
CMCR .... Committee for Mother and Child Rights (EA)
CMCR .... Conservative Majority for Citizen's Rights (EA)
CMCR .... Continuous Melting, Casting and Rolling (MHDB)
CMCRL .... Consolidated Master Cross-Reference List [*Defense Supply Agency*]
CMCRP .... Center for Mass Communications Research and Policy [*University of Denver*] [*Research center*] (RCD)
CMCS .... Cam Case
CMCS .... Canadian Man-Computer Communications Society
CMCS .... Canadian Manufacturers of Chemical Specialties Association (EAIO)
CMCS .... CENTO [*Central Treaty Organization*] Military Communications System (MCD)
CMCS .... Comcast Corp. [*NASDAQ symbol*] (NQ)
CMCS .... Commandant, Marine Corps Schools [*Quantico, VA*]
CMCS .... Communications Monitoring and Control Subsystem (NVT)
CMCS .... Comprehensive Manufacturing Control System
CMCS .... COMSAT [*Communications Satellite Corp.*] Maritime Communications Satellite (MCD)
CMCS .... Construction Management Control System [*General Services Administration*]
CMCS .... Construction Mechanic, Senior Chief [*Navy rating*]
CMCSA .... Canadian Manufacturers of Chemical Specialties Association
CMCSA .... Canadian Masters Cross-Country Ski Association [*Association Canadienne des Maitres en Ski de Fond*] (AC)
CMCSA .... Comcast Cl'A' [*NASDAQ symbol*] (TTSB)
CMCSK .... Comcast Cl'A'Spl(non-vtg) [*NASDAQ symbol*] (TTSB)
CmcstUK ...... Comcast UK Cable Partners Ltd. [*Associated Press*] (SAG)
CMCT .... Communicate (MDG)
CMCT .... Communicating Magnetic Card Typewriter (AFIT)
CMCTL .... Current-Mode Complementary Transistor Logic [*Computer science*] (IEEE)
CMCV .... Classic Motorcycle Club of Victoria [*Australia*]
CMC-VAP ..... Cyclophosphamide, Methotrexate, CCNU [*Lomustine*], Vincristine, Adriamycin,Procarbazine [*Antineoplastic drug regimen*]
CMCW .... Christian Missions to the Communist World (EA)
CMCW .... Christian Mission to the Communist World [*Australia*]
CMD........... Capital Military District [*Vietnam*]
CMD........... Carboxymethyldextran [*Organic chemistry*]
CMD........... Carboxymuconolactone Decarboxylase [*An enzyme*]
CMD........... Carematrix Corp. [*AMEX symbol*] (SAG)
CMD........... Cartridge Module Drive (PDAA)
CMD........... Cataloging Management Data [*Army*]
CMD........... Center for Management Development [*American Management Association*] (EA)
CMD........... Center for Massachusetts Data [*Information service or system*] (IID)
CMD........... Central Meridian Distance [*NASA*]
CMD........... Cerebral Motor Dysfunction [*Medicine*]
CMD........... Certified Marketing Director [*International Council of Shopping Centers*] [*Designation awarded by*]

CMD........... Charter Medical Corp. [*AMEX symbol*] (SPSG)
CMD........... Chevrolet Motor Division [*General Motors Corp.*]
CMD........... Chickamauga Dam [*TVA*]
CMD........... Chief Medical Director [*Department of Veterans Affairs*]
CMD........... Chief Minister's Department [*Australian Capital Territory*] [*Australia*]
CMD........... Childhood Muscular Dystrophy
CMD........... Christian Mission for the Deaf (EA)
CMD........... Chronic Mental Defective [*British*] (ADA)
CMD........... City Merchant Developers [*British*]
CMD........... Colcemid [*Demecolcine*] [*Antineoplastic drug*]
CMD........... Colonial Medical Department [*British*]
CMD........... Color Magnitude Diagrams
CMD........... Comandor Avia [*Ukraine*] [*FAA designator*] (FAAC)
CMD........... Command (EY)
Cmd........... Command Papers (DLA)
CMD........... Commendation (AABC)
CMD........... Common Meter Double [*Music*]
CMD........... Compression Mold Dies (MCD)
CMD........... COMSAT [*Communications Satellite Corp.*], Washington, DC [*OCLC symbol*] (OCLC)
CMD........... Congenital Muscular Dystrophy [*Medicine*]
CMD........... Congenital Myotonic Dystrophy [*Medicine*]
CMD........... Contract Maintenance Data
CMD........... Contract Management District
CMD........... Contracts Management Division [*Environmental Protection Agency*] (GFGA)
CMD........... Conventional Munition Disposal (PDAA)
CMD........... Core Memory Driver
CMD........... Corporation for Menke's Disease (EA)
CMD........... Council of Music and Drama [*Queensland*] [*Australia*]
CMD........... Countermeasures Dispenser (MCD)
CMD........... Count Median Diameter (MAE)
CMD........... Creative Modern Design
CMD........... Current Meter Data Base [*National Ocean Survey*] (MSC)
CMDA .... Cam Designs [*NASDAQ symbol*] (TTSB)
CMDA .... Cam Designs Co. [*NASDAQ symbol*] (SAG)
CMDAC .... Current-Mode Digital-to-Analog Converter [*Computer science*]
CMDAW ...... Cam Designs Wrrt [*NASDAQ symbol*] (TTSB)
CMDB .... Composite-Modified Double-Base [*Propellant*]
CMDC .... Central Milk Distributive Committee [*British*]
CMDC .... Christian-Muslim Dialogue Committee (EA)
CMDCC .... Command Computer Console
CMDD .... Commanded
CMDDC .... City Merchant Developers Development Coordination [*British*]
CMD DCDR... Command Decoder (GFGA)
CMDE .... Center for Modern Dance Education [*Hackensack, NJ*]
CMDF .... Canadian Medical Discovery Fund
CMDF .... Catalog Master Data File
CMDF .... Combined Miniature Deterrent Forces [*Organization in film "Fantastic Voyage"*]
CMDG .... Commanding
CMDH .... Doctor's Hospital, Modesto, CA [*Library symbol*] [*Library of Congress*] (LCLS)
CMDI .... Creative Med Dev [*NASDAQ symbol*] (TTSB)
Cmdial........ Comdial Corp. [*Associated Press*] (SAG)
CMDINSP..... Command Inspection [*Military*] (NVT)
CMD/INV...... Command Involvement Report [*Army*]
CMDIS .... Computer-Management Distributed Information Software (MHDI)
CMDJA .... Country Music Disk Jockeys Association [*Defunct*] (EA)
CMDL.......... Climate Monitoring and Diagnostics Laboratory [*National Oceanic and Atmospheric Administration*]
CMDL.......... Comdial Corp. [*NASDAQ symbol*] (NQ)
CMDMS .... Chloromethyldimethylchlorosilane [*Organic chemistry*]
CMDMSG .... Command Message
CMDN .... Catalog Management Data Notification [*Army*] (AABC)
CMDNJ........ College of Medicine and Dentistry of New Jersey [*Newark*]
CMDO .... Chloromethyldioxolane [*Organic chemistry*]
CMDO .... Commando (CINC)
CMDO .... Consolidated Material Distribution Objectives [*Air Force*]
CMDP .... Civil Member for Development and Production [*British*]
CMDP .... Cleobury, Mortimer, and Ditton Prior Light Railway [*Wales*]
CMDR .... Coherent Monopulse Doppler RADAR
CMDR .... Commander (EY)
CMDR .... Commander
CMDR .... Commander Aircraft [*NASDAQ symbol*] (TTSB)
CMDR .... Commander Aircraft Co. [*NASDAQ symbol*] (SAG)
CMDR .... Command Reject (IAA)
CMDR .... Council for Microphotography and Document Reproduction [*British*] (DIT)
CmdrA .... Commodore Applied Technologies, Inc. [*Associated Press*] (SAG)
CmdrAp....... Commodore Applied Technologies, Inc. [*Associated Press*] (SAG)
Cmdre .... Commodore [*British military*] (DMA)
CMdrR .... R & D Associates, Marina Del Rey, CA [*Library symbol Library of Congress*] (LCLS)
CMDRS .... Contractor Maintenance Data Reporting System [*Department of State*]
CMDS .... Centralized Message Data System [*Bell System*]
CMDS .... Central Mine Data Systems
CMDS .... Chaff/Flare Countermeasures Dispenser System (PDAA)
CMDS .... Christian Medical and Dental Society (EA)
CMDS .... Collection, Management, and Dissemination Section
CMDS .... Command Manpower Data System
CMDS .... Countermeasures Dispenser Set (MCD)
CMDSA .... Corps Material Direct Support Activity (MCD)

CMDSW .... Command Software Subsystem [*Space Flight Operations Facility, NASA*]

CMDT .... Comdata Holdings Corp. [*NASDAQ symbol*] (NQ)

CMDT .... Commandant

CMDT .... Corrective Maintenance Downtime (MCD)

Cmdt Gen .... Commandant General [*British military*] (DMA)

CMDTY .... Commodity (AABC)

CMDV .... Carrot Mottle Dwarf Virus

Cme .... Carboxymethyl [*Also, CM, Cm*] [*Biochemistry*]

CME .... Center for Management Effectiveness [*Pacific Palisades, CA*] (EA)

CME .... Center for Marine Exploration (GNE)

CME .... Center for Media Education

CME .... Center for Metric Education [*Western Michigan University*]

CME .... Central European Media Enterprises

CME .... Central Mail Exchange [*British*] (ADA)

CME .... Central Memory Extension [*Computer science*]

CME .... Centre for Multicultural Education [*University of London Institute of Education*] [*British*] (CB)

CME .... Centrifuge Moisture Equivalent

CME .... Cervical Mediastinal Exploration (AAMN)

CME .... Chemically Modified Electrode [*Electrochemistry*]

CME .... Chicago Mercantile Exchange (EA)

CME .... Chief Mechanical Engineer [*Military British*]

CME .... Chloromethyl Ether [*Organic chemistry*]

CME .... Christian Methodist Episcopal Church

CME .... Ciudad Del Carmen [*Mexico*] [*Airport symbol*] (OAG)

CME .... CME Capital, Inc. [*Toronto Stock Exchange symbol*]

CME .... College of Medical Evangelists [*Los Angeles, CA*]

CME .... Colloid Microthruster Experiment

CME .... Colored Methodist Episcopal Church (IIA)

CME .... Commercial Measuring Equipment (SAA)

CME .... Commercial Multi-Engine [*Aviation*] (AIA)

CME .... Commission on Missionary Education [*Later, Department of Education for Missions*] (EA)

CME .... Committee on Militarism in Education [*Defunct*] (EA)

CME .... Common Mode Error

CME .... Community Modelling Effort [*Oceanography*]

CME .... Comprehensive (Ground Water) Monitoring Evaluation [*Environmental Protection Agency*] (ERG)

CME .... Comprehensive Monitoring Evaluation

CME .... Computerizing Medical Examination [*IBM Corp.*]

CME .... Computer Measurement and Evaluation

CME .... Computer Memory Element

CME .... Concurrent Machine Environment [*International Computers Ltd.*] [*British*] (NITA)

CME .... Condor Minerals and Energy Ltd. [*Australia*]

CME .... Conference Mondiale de l'Energie [*World Energy Conference - WEC*] (EAIO)

CME .... Conference of Ministers of Education [*World War II*]

CME .... Conseil Mondial d'Education [*World Council for Curriculum and Instruction*]

CME .... Continuing Medical Education

CMES .... Controlled Mission Equipment (MCD)

CME .... Core Materials Corp. [*AMEX symbol*] (SAG)

CME .... Coronal Mass Ejection [*Astrophysics*]

CME .... Coronal Mass Ejection [*Cosmology*]

CME .... Countermeasures Evaluation (CAAL)

CME .... Courtesy Motorboat Examination [*Coast Guard*] (IIA)

CME .... Crucible Melt Extraction [*Metal fiber technology*]

CME .... Crude Marijuana Extract

CME .... Cumann Muinteoiri Eireann [*Irish National Teachers' Organization*] (EAIO)

CME .... Cystoid Macular Edema [*Ophthalmology*]

CME .... [*The*] Monthly Journal of the Institution of Mechanical Engineers [*A publication*]

CME .... Prince Edward Air Ltd. [*Canada ICAO designator*] (FAAC)

CMEA .... Canadian Music Educators' Association

CMEA .... Central Medical Establishment, Aviation [*Air Force*]

CMEA .... Chief Marine Engineering Artificer [*British military*] (DMA)

CMEA .... Council for Middle Eastern Affairs [*Defunct*] (EA)

CMEA .... Council for Mutual Economic Assistance [*Also known as CEMA, COMECON*] [*Communist-bloc nations: Poland, Russia, East Germany, Czechoslovakia, Romania, Bulgaria, Hungary Dissolved 1991*] [*Former USSR*]

CMEAA .... Construction and Mining Equipment Association of Australia

CME-AMA .... Council on Medical Education - of the American Medical Association (EA)

CMEAOC ...... Conference Ministerielle des Etats d'Afrique de l'Ouest et du Centre sur les Transports Maritimes [*Ministerial Conference of West and Central African States on Maritime Transportation - MCWCS*] [*Abidjan, Ivory Coast*] (EAIO)

CMEC .... Canadian Managing Editors' Conference

CMEC .... Chemical Marketing and Economics

CMEC .... Christian Methodist Episcopal Church

CMEC .... Combat Materiel Exploitation Center [*Military*] (VNW)

CMEC .... Combined Military Exploitation Center

CMEC .... Convectron-Microsyn Erection Circuit (SAA)

CMED .... Colorado Medtech [*NASDAQ symbol*] (TTSB)

CMED .... Colorado MEDtech, Inc. [*NASDAQ symbol*] (SAG)

CMED .... Council for Management Education and Development (AIE)

C/MEDIA ...... Corporation for Maintaining Editorial Diversity in America (EA)

CMEE .... Chief Mechanical and Electrical Engineer [*Air Force British*]

CMEF .... Commander, Middle East Force (DOMA)

C-meiosis .... Colchicine-Blocked Meiosis [*Biology*] (DOG)

CMEIS .... Centre for Middle Eastern and Islamic Studies [*University of Durham*] [*British*] (CB)

CMEL .... Checkmate Electronics [*NASDAQ symbol*] (TTSB)

CMEL .... Checkmate Electronics, Inc. [*NASDAQ symbol*] (SAG)

CMEL .... Compliance Monitor Evaluation Log

CMEL .... Comprehensive (Ground Water) Monitoring Evaluation Log [*Environmental Protection Agency*] (ERG)

CMEM .... Chief Marine Engineering Mechanic [*British military*] (DMA)

CMEM .... Complete Minimum Essential Medium

CMEMA .... Chicago and Midwest Envelope Manufacturers Association [*Defunct*]

CMen .... Menlo Park Public Library, Menlo Park, CA [*Library symbol Library of Congress*] (LCLS)

CMenC .... Menlo School and College, Menlo Park, CA [*Library symbol Library of Congress*] (LCLS)

CMenS .... Sunset Magazine Reference Library, Menlo Park, CA [*Library symbol Library of Congress*] (LCLS)

CMenSP ...... Saint Patrick's Seminary, Menlo Park, CA [*Library symbol Library of Congress*] (LCLS)

CMenSR ...... Stanford Research Institute Library, Menlo Park, CA [*Library symbol Library of Congress*] (LCLS)

CMenUG ...... United States Geological Survey, Menlo Park, CA [*Library symbol Library of Congress*] (LCLS)

CMEP .... Critical Mass Energy Project (EA)

CMEQ .... Corporation des Maitres Electriciens du Quebec [*Corporation of Master Electricians of Quebec*] (AC)

CMER .... Component and Material Engineering Request

CMER .... Curtis, Milburn & Eastern Railroad Co. [*AAR code*]

CMERA .... Conference Mondiale des Experts Radiotelegraphistes de l'Aeronautique

CMerC .... Merced County Free Library, Merced, CA [*Library symbol Library of Congress*] (LCLS)

CMerCC ...... Merced Community College, Merced, CA [*Library symbol Library of Congress*] (LCLS)

CMerCL .... Merced County Bar Association Law Library, Merced, CA [*Library symbol Library of Congress*] (LCLS)

CMERI .... Central Mechanical Engineering Research Institute (MCD)

CMerUSAF ... United States Air Force, Castle Grate Air Force Base Library, Merced, CA [*Library symbol Library of Congress*] (LCLS)

CMerUSAH ... United States Air Force, Castle Air Force Base Hospital, Merced, CA [*Library symbol Library of Congress*] (LCLS)

CMES .... Center for Middle Eastern Studies [*Harvard University*] [*Research center*] (RCD)

CMES .... Center for Middle Eastern Studies [*University of California, Berkeley*] [*Research center*] (RCD)

CMES .... Contractor Maintenance Engineering Support (MCD)

CMET .... Certified Medical Electroencephalographic Technician (WGA)

CMET .... Coated Metal (AAG)

CMET .... Continental Mortgage & Equity Trust [*NASDAQ symbol*] (NQ)

C-metaphase ... Colchicine-Blocked Metaphase [*Biology*] (DOG)

CM-ETO .... Court-Martial, European Theater of Operations [*United States*] (DLA)

CMETS .... Contl Mtg & Eg Tr SBI [*NASDAQ symbol*] (TTSB)

CMEV .... Civilian Marine Emergency Volunteers

CMEWA .... Chamber of Mines and Energy of Western Australia

CMEWS .... Concrete Missile Entry Warning System (MCD)

CMF .... Calcium- and Magnesium-Free

CMF .... Cannet Des Maures [*France*] [*Seismograph station code, US Geological Survey Closed*] (SEIS)

CMF .... Capital Maintenance Fund

CMF .... Carbon Micro-Fiber [*Materials science*]

CMF .... Carbon Monofluoride [*Inorganic chemistry*]

CMF .... Cardinal Mindszenty Foundation (EA)

CMF .... Career Management Field [*Military*] (AABC)

CMF .... Cartesian Mapping Function

CMF .... Cast Metals Federation [*Later, NFA*] (EA)

CMF .... C-Band Monopulse Feed

CMF .... Central Maintenance Facility (NRCH)

CMF .... Central Mediterranean Force [*Later, AAI*] [*British World War II*]

CMF .... Chambery [*France*] [*Airport symbol*] (OAG)

CMF .... Chloromethylfurfuraldehyde [*Organic chemistry*]

CMF .... Chocolate Milk Foundation [*Defunct*] (EA)

CMF .... Chondromyxoid Fibroma [*Medicine*]

CMF .... Christian Medical Fellowship [*British*] (DAVI)

CMF .... Christian Medical Foundation International (EA)

CMF .... Christian Military Fellowship (EA)

CMF .... Christian Missionary Fellowship (EA)

CMF .... Circular Mil Foot

CMF .... Citizen Military Forces [*New Guinea*]

CMF .... Claretian Missionaries (TOCD)

cmf .... Claretian Missionaries, Missionary Sons of the Immaculate Heart of Mary (TOCD)

CMF .... Cluster Maintenance Facility [*Military*]

CMF .... Coal Merchants Federation [*British*] (DBA)

CMF .... Coherent Memory Filter

CMF .... Colonial Military Forces [*British*]

CMF .... Color Mixture Function

CMF .... Combat Mission Failure (AABC)

CMF .... Combat Mission Folder (AFM)

CMF .... Combined Master File [*Computer science*]

CMF .... Command File (IAA)

CMF .... Command Message Formulator (SAA)

CMF .... Commercial Financial Corp. Ltd. [*Toronto Stock Exchange symbol*]

CMFIS .... Commercial Fishing [*Type of water project*]

CMF .... Common Mode Failure [*Nuclear energy*] (NRCH)

CMF .... Commonwealth Military Forces [*British*]

CMF .... Compare Full Words (SAA)

CMF .... Complex Maintenance Facility [*Deep Space Instrumentation Facility, NASA*]
CMF .... Composite Medical Facility (AFM)
CMF .... Comprehensive Management Facility (IAA)
CMF .... Compressed Mortality File [*Medicine*]
CMF .... Congregatio Missionariorum Filiorum Immaculati Cordis Beatae Maria Virginia [*Congregation of Missionary Sons of the Immaculate Heart of the Blessed Virgin Mary*] [*Claretians*] [*Roman Catholic religious order*]
CMF .... Congressional Management Foundation (EA)
CMF .... Constant Magnetic Field (MHDB)
CMF .... Continuous Multibay Frames [*Jacys Computing Services*] [*Software package*] (NCC)
CMF .... Conventional Military Fuels (RDA)
CMF .... Cortical Magnification Factor
CMF .... Cost of Money Factor (SSD)
CMF .... Council of Michigan Foundations (SRA)
CMF .... Countermortar Fire
CMF .... Country Music Foundation (EA)
CMF .... Court-Martial Forfeiture
CMF .... Creative Music Foundation (EA)
CMF .... Critical Mission Function [*Army*] (RDA)
CMF .... Cross-Modulation Factor (DEN)
CMF .... Customer Master File
CMF .... Cyclophosphamide, Methotrexate, Fluorouracil [*Antineoplastic drug regimen*]
CMF .... Cylindrical Magnetic Film
CMF .... Cymomotive Force [*Telecommunications*] (TEL)
CMF .... Cytoplasmic Metabolic Factor (PDAA)
CMF .... Facilities Capital Cost of Money Factors Computation [*DoD*]
CMF .... Sisters of the Immaculate Heart of Mary [*Roman Catholic religious order*]
CMFA .... Common Mode Failure Analysis [*Nuclear energy*] (NRCH)
CMF/AV .... Cyclophosphamide, Methotrexate, Fluorouracil, Adriamycin, Oncovin (Vincristine) [*Antineoplastic drug regimen*]
CMFAVP ...... Cyclophosphamide, Methotrexate, Fluorouracil, Adriamycin, Vincristine, Prednisone [*Antineoplastic drug regimen*]
CMFB .... Chemfab Corp. [*NASDAQ symbol*] (NQ)
CMF-BLEO ... Cyclophosphamide [*Cytoxan*], Methotrexate, 5-Fluorouracil, Bleomycin [*Antineoplastic drug regimen*] (DAVI)
CMFC .... China Man-Made Fiber Corp. [*Taiwan*]
CMFC .... College des Medecins de Famille du Canada (EAIO)
CMFC .... Country Music Fan Club [*Defunct*] (EA)
CMFD .... Christian Mission for the Deaf (EA)
CMFD .... Color Multifunction Display
CMF-FLU ..... Cyclophosphamide [*Cytoxan*], Methotrexate, 5-Fluorouracil, Fluoxymesterone [*Antineoplastic drug regimen*] (DAVI)
CMFH .... Community Financial Holding Corp. [*NASDAQ symbol*] (SAG)
CMFH .... Community Finl Hldg [*NASDAQ symbol*] (TTSB)
CMFH .... Cyclophosphamide [*Cytoxan*], Methotrexate, 5-Fluorouracil, Hydroxyurea [*Antineoplastic drug regimen*] (DAVI)
C/MFI .... Conversion, Memory, and Fault Indication [*Telecommunications*] (TEL)
CMFK .... Camouflage Mobile Field Kitchen [*Military*] (MCD)
CMFL .... Commission on Marriage and Family Life [*of NCC*] [*Defunct*]
CMFLPD ...... Core Maximum Fraction of Limiting Power Density [*Nuclear energy*] (NRCH)
CMFLR .... Cam Follower
CMfNASA .... National Aeronautics and Space Administration, Ames Research Center, Technical Library, Moffett Field, CA [*Library symbol Library of Congress*] (LCLS)
CmFnIl .... Community Financial Corp. (Illinois) [*Associated Press*] (SAG)
CMFP .... Capstone Material Fielding Plan [*Army*]
CMFP .... Cyclophosphamide, Methotrexate, Fluorouracil, Prednisone [*Antineoplastic drug regimen*]
CMFP-VA ..... Cyclophosphamide, Methotrexate, 5-Fluorouracil, Prednisone, Vincristine, Adriamycin [*Antineoplastic drug regimen*] (DAVI)
CMFRT .... Comfort
CMFSW .... Calcium- and Magnesium-Free Synthetic Seawater
CMFT .... Canadian Museum of Flight and Transportation
CMFT .... Cardiolipin Microflocculation Test [*Medicine*] (DMAA)
CMFT .... Cyclophosphamide, Methotrexate, Fluorouracil, Tamoxifen [*Antineoplastic drug regimen*]
CMF-TAM .... Cyclophosphamide [*Cytoxan*], Methotrexate, 5-Fluorouracil, Tamoxifen [*Antineoplastic drug regimen*] (DAVI)
CMFV .... Cyclophosphamide [*Cytoxan*] Methotrexate, 5-Fluorouracil, Vincristine [*Antineoplastic drug regimen*] (DAVI)
CMFVAT ...... Cyclophosphamide, Methotrexate, Fluorouracil, Vincristine, Adriamycin, Testosterone [*Antineoplastic drug regimen*]
CMFVP .... Cyclophosphamide, Methotrexate, Fluorouracil, Vincristine, Prednisone [*Antineoplastic drug regimen*]
CMG .... Camargue Air Transport [*France ICAO designator*] (FAAC)
CMG .... Canada Malting Co. Ltd. [*Toronto Stock Exchange symbol*]
CMG .... Canadian Media Guild [*La Guilde Canadienne des Medias*] (AC)
CMG .... Candidatus Magisterii [*Academic Degree*] [*Latin*]
CMG .... Case Mix Grouping
CMG .... Central Machine Gun
CMG .... Chief Marine Gunner [*Navy rating*]
CMG .... Chopped Meat Glucose [*Medium*] [*Microbiology*]
CMG .... Church of Jesus Christ of Latter-Day Saints, Genealogical Society Library, Modesto, CA [*Library symbol Library of Congress*] (LCLS)
CMG .... Color Marketing Group [*Washington, DC*] (EA)
CMG .... Commission for Marine Geology [*of the International Union of Geological Sciences*] (EAIO)

CMG .... Committee for the Monument of Garibaldi (EA)
CMG .... Companion of the Order of St. Michael and St. George [*Facetiously translated "Call Me God"*] [*British*]
CMG .... Composite Maintenance Group [*Military British*]
CMG .... Compressed Medical Gas [*Food and Drug Administration*]
CMG .... Computer Management Group [*British*] (NITA)
CMG .... Computer Measurement Group (EA)
CMG .... Computer Modelling Group [*Research center*] (RCD)
CMG .... Conflict Management Group [*An association*]
CMG .... Control Moment Gyroscope [*Aerospace*]
CMG .... Corpus Medicorum Graecorum [*A publication*] (OCD)
CMG .... Corumba Mato Grosso [*Brazil*] [*Airport symbol*] (OAG)
CMG .... Corvair Model Group (EA)
CMG .... Cost Management Group [*An association*] (EA)
CMG .... Course Made Good [*Navy*]
CMG .... Cystometrogram [*or Cystometrography*] [*Urology*]
CMGA .... Control Moment Gyro Assembly [*Aerospace*]
CMGA .... Country Music Guild of Australasia [*Australia*]
CMGC .... Canadian Machine Gun Corps [*World War I*]
Cm Gds .... Coldstream Guards [*British military*] (DMA)
CMgE .... Certified Manufacturing Engineer (DD)
CMGEA .... Control Moment Gyro Electrical Assembly [*Aerospace*]
CMGI .... CMG Information Services [*NASDAQ symbol*] (SAG)
CMGI .... CMG Info Services [*NASDAQ symbol*] (TTSB)
CMGIA .... Control Moment Gyro Inverter Assembly [*Aerospace*] (MCD)
CMG Inf .... CMG Information Services [*Associated Press*] (SAG)
CMGM .... Center for Molecular and Genetic Medicine [*Stanford University*] [*Research center*]
CMGM .... Chronic Megakaryocytic Granulocytic Myelosis [*Medicine*]
CMGN .... Chronic Membranous Glomerulonephritis [*Medicine*] (MAE)
CMGS .... Chopped Meat-Glucose-Starch Medium [*Medicine*] (DMAA)
CMGS .... Control Moment Gyro System [*or Subsystem*] [*Aerospace*] (KSC)
CMGS .... Cruise Missile Guidance Set (MCD)
CMGS .... Cruise Missile Guidance System (MCD)
CMGSA .... Congressional Monitoring Group on Southern Africa (EA)
cm-g-s-Bi .... Centimeter-Gram-Second-Biot [*System of units*]
cm-g-s-Fr .... Centimeter-Gram-Second-Franklin [*System of units*]
CMGT .... Chromosome-Mediated Gene Transfer [*Biochemistry*]
CMGV .... Codling Moth Granulosis Virus
CMGW .... E. & J. Gallo Winery, Modesto, CA [*Library symbol Library of Congress*] (LCLS)
CMH .... Cambridge Modern History [*A publication*] (ROG)
CMH .... Campaign for the Mentally Handicapped [*British*]
CMH .... Center of Military History (AABC)
CMH .... Centimeter Height-Finder [*RADAR*]
CMH .... Ceramide Monohexoside [*Biochemistry*]
CMH .... Certificate in Medical Humanities (PGP)
CMH .... Chemehuevi Mountains [*California*] [*Seismograph station code, US Geological Survey*] (SEIS)
CMH .... Chief of Military History [*Army*]
CMH .... China Merchant Holdings (ECON)
CMH .... Clayton Homes [*NYSE symbol*] (TTSB)
CMH .... Clayton Homes, Inc. [*NYSE symbol*] (SPSG)
CMH .... Collapsible Maintenance Hangar (MCD)
CMH .... Collapsible Mobile Hangar (MCD)
CMH .... Columbus [*Ohio*] [*Airport symbol*] (OAG)
CMH .... Company of Military Historians (EA)
CMH .... Congenital Malformation of Heart [*Medicine*]
CMH .... Congressional Medal of Honor
CMH .... Construction Mechanic, Construction [*Navy rating*]
CMH .... Corporal-Major of Horse [*British*]
C/MH .... Cost per Man-Hour (MCD)
CMH .... Countermeasures Homing (CET)
CMH .... Modesto State Hospital, Staff Library, Modesto, CA [*Library symbol Library of Congress*] (LCLS)
CmH₂0 .... Centimeters of Water [*Cuff pressure*] [*Medicine*] (DAVI)
CMHA .... California Mental Health Analysis [*Testing*]
CMHA .... Canadian Mental Health Association
CMHA .... Canadian Mobile Home Association
CMHA .... Canadian Morgan Horse Association Inc. [*Association des Chevaux Morgan Canadien Inc.*] (AC)
CMHA .... Christian Maternity Home Association (EA)
CMHA .... Community Mental Health Activities
CMHA .... Comprehensive Mental Health Assessment
C-MHA .... Confidential - Modified Handling Authorized [*Army*] (AFM)
CMHC .... Canada Mortgage and Housing Corp. [*Government agency*]
CMHC .... Central Mortgage and Housing Corp. [*Canada*] (BARN)
CMHC .... Community Mental Health Center [*or Clinic*]
CMHCA .... Community Mental Health Centers Act [*1975*]
CMHEC .... Carboxymethyl Hydroxyethyl Cellulose [*Organic chemistry*]
CMHERA ..... Community and Mental Handicap Educational Research [*British*] (DBA)
CMHI .... Baker-Schulberg Community Mental Health Ideology Scale [*Psychology*]
CMHIF .... Cooperative Management Housing Insurance Fund [*Federal Housing Administration*]
CMHN .... Community Mental Health Nurse (DAVI)
CMHP .... Community Mental Health Program
CMHQ .... Canadian Military Headquarters (DMA)
CMHS .... Canadian Musical Heritage Society [*Societe pour le Patrimoine Musical Canadien*] (AC)
CMHS .... Center for Mental Health Services (USGC)
CMHS .... Congressional Medal of Honor Society (EA)
CMI .... CAB [*Commonwealth Agricultural Bureaux*] International Mycological Institute [*British*] (IRUK)

CMI............ Cambridge Memories, Inc.
CMI............ Canadian Magazine Index [*Micromedia Ltd.*] [*Information service or system*] (IID)
CMI............ Canadian Mediterranean Institute [*Research center*] (RCD)
CMi............. Canis Minor [*Constellation*]
CMI............ Can Manufacturers Institute (EA)
CMI............ Carbohydrate Metabolism Index [*Biochemistry*]
CMI............ Care and Maintenance Instruction [*Nuclear energy*] (NRCH)
CMI............ Career Maturity Inventory [*Vocational guidance test*]
CMI............ Caribbean Institute for Meteorology and Hydrology [*Caribbean Meteorologic al Institute*] [*Acronym is based on former name,*] (EAIO)
CMI............ Caribbean Meteorological Institute [*Marine science*] (OSRA)
cmi............. Carmelites of Mary Immaculate (TOCD)
CMI............ Carmelites of Mary Immaculate (TOCD)
CmI............ Cascade Microfilm Systems, Inc., Portland, OR [*Library symbol Library of Congress*] (LCLS)
CMI............ Case-Mix Index [*Medicare*] (DHSM)
CMI............ Cash Management Institute (EA)
CMI............ Cell [*or Cellular*]-Mediated Immunity [*Immunochemistry*]
CMI............ Cell-Mediated Immunity (DOG)
CMI............ Cell Multiplication Inhibition
CMI............ Center for Machine Intelligence [*Research center*] (RCD)
CMI............ Champaign [*Illinois*] [*Airport symbol*] (OAG)
CMI............ Champaign/Urbana, IL [*Location identifier FAA*] (FAAL)
CMI............ Chemotactic Index [*Immunology*]
CMI............ Cherry Marketing Institute (EA)
CMI............ China Market Intelligence [*National Council for US-China Trade*] [*A publication*]
CMI............ Chronically Mentally Ill [*Medicine*]
CMI............ Chronic Mesenteric Ischemia [*Medicine*]
CMI............ Cincinnati Microwave, Inc.
CMI............ Civil-Military Integration (AAGC)
CMI............ Classified Military Information (MCD)
CMI............ Cleaning Management Institute (EA)
CMI............ Clerical Medical International [*British*]
CMI............ Clomipramine [*An antidepressant*] [*Medicine*]
CMI............ Code Mark Inversion [*Telecommunications*] (TEL)
CMI............ Comite Maritime International [*International Maritime Committee - IMC*] [*Antwerp, Belgium*] (EAIO)
CMI............ Comite Meteorologique International
CMI............ Command Maintenance Inspection [*Army*]
CMI............ Commission Mixte Internationale pour les Experiences Relatives a la Protection des Lignes de Telecommunication et des Canalisations Souterraines [*Joint International Commission for the Protection of Telecommunication Lines and Underground Ducts*] [*Switzerland*]
CMI............ Commodity Microanalysis, Inc. [*Information service or system*] (IID)
CMI............ Common Mode Interface (IAA)
CMI............ Commonwealth Mycological Institute [*Research center British*] (IRC)
CMI............ Complete Management [*AMEX symbol*] (TTSB)
CMI............ Complete Management, Inc. [*AMEX symbol*] (SAG)
CMI............ Component Management Interface [*Computer science*]
CMI............ Computer-Managed Instruction
CMI............ Computer-Mediated Interaction (PDAA)
CMI............ Computer Memories, Inc. (NITA)
CMI............ Consejo Mundial de Iglesias [*Switzerland*]
CMI............ Continental Micronesia, Inc. [*Guam*] [*ICAO designator*] (FAAC)
CMI............ Contractor Missile Installation
CMI............ Conventions, Meetings, Incentive Travel [*Of CMI World, a publication aimed at those markets*]
CMI............ Cordage Manufacturers Institute [*British*] (DBA)
CMI............ Core Element Assembly Motion Inhibit [*Nuclear energy*] (IEEE)
CMI............ Cornell Medical Index [*Psychology*]
CMI............ Corrective Measures Implementation
CMI............ Cruise Missile Integration
CMI............ Cultured Marble Institute (EA)
CMI............ Cumulative Monthly Issue [*Material*] (AAG)
CMI............ Cytomegalic Inclusion Disease [*Ophthalmology*]
CMIA.......... Canadian Maritime Industries Association [*Association Canadienne des Industries Maritimes*] [*Formerly, Canadian Shipbuilding & Ship Repairing Association*] (AC)
CMIA.......... Coal Mining Institute of America [*Later, PCMIA*] (EA)
CMIA.......... Command Management Inventory Accounting [*Army*]
CMIA.......... Cultivated Mushroom Institute of America
CMIC.......... Calif Microwave [*NASDAQ symbol*] (TTSB)
CMIC.......... California Microwave, Inc. [*NASDAQ symbol*] (NQ)
CMIC.......... Canadian Meat Importers Committee (AC)
CMIC.......... Catalog of Material Improvement Cards (MCD)
CMIC.......... Chicken Meat Industry Committee [*Queensland*] [*Australia*]
CMIC.......... Combined Military Interrogation Center
CMIC.......... Computer Microfilm International Corp. [*Information service or system*] (IID)
CMIC.......... Controlled Monitor Interface Calibrator (PDAA)
CMICE........ Current Meter Intercomparison Experiment [*National Ocean Survey*] (MSC)
CMI Cp ...... CMI Corp. [*Associated Press*] (SAG)
CMID......... Commodity Manager Input Data (MCD)
CM-ID........ Crew Member Identification
CMID........ Cytomegalic Inclusion Disease [*Ophthalmology*] (MAE)
CMID........ Cytomegalic Inclusion Disease [*Medicine*] (DMAA)
CMid.......... Middletown Library, Middletown, CA [*Library symbol Library of Congress*] (LCLS)
CMIDR....... Compressed Mosiacked Image Data Record [*Geology*]
CMIE.......... Centre for Monitoring the Indian Economy (ECON)

CMIEA........ Conference of Minister for Immigration and Ethnic Affairs [*Australia*]
CMIEB........ Centre Mondial d'Information sur l'Education Bilingue [*World Information Centre for Bilingual Education - WICBE*] (EAIO)
CMI-EC...... Committee for the Mustard Industry of the European Communities [*Belgium*] (EAIO)
CMIF.......... Career Management Individual Files [*Military*] (INF)
CMIF.......... Career Management Information File [*Military*] (AABC)
CMIL.......... Circular Mil [*Wire measure*] (MSA)
CMIL.......... Comtech Telecommns [*NASDAQ symbol*] (TTSB)
CMIM......... Centre for Measurement and Information in Medicine [*City University*] [*British*] (CB)
CMin.......... Canis Minor [*Constellation*]
CMIN .... Cards per Minute [*Computer science*] (IAA)
C/MIN........ Counts per Minute
C/MIN........ Cycles per Minute
C$_{min}$...... Minimum Capacitance (IDOE)
CMIO .... COMSEC [*Communications Security*] Material Issuing Office [*Military*] (NVT)
CMIP.......... Common Management Information Protocol (PCM)
CMIP.......... Cost Management Improvement Program
CMIP.......... Coupled Model Intercomparison Project [*Marine science*] (OSRA)
CMIPDU...... Common Management Information Protocol Data Unit [*Telecommunications*] (OSI)
CMIR .... Cell-Mediated Immune Response [*Immunology*] (AAMN)
CMIR .... Common Mode Input Resistance
CMIS.......... Cane Medium Invert Syrup [*Food sweetener*]
CMIS.......... Classroom Management Improvement Study (EDAC)
CMIS.......... Command Management Information System [*Air Force*]
CMIS.......... Common Manufacturing Information System (IAA)
CMIS.......... Common Military Intelligence Skills (NVT)
CMIS.......... Computerized Medical Imaging Society (EA)
CMIS.......... Computerized Microscopic Imaging System [*Genetics*]
CMIS.......... Computer-Oriented Management Information System (IAA)
CMIS.......... Contract Management Information System (MCD)
CMIS.......... Control Monitor and Isolation Subsystem (MCD)
CMIS.......... Court-Martial Index and Summary (DNAB)
CMIS.......... Crisis Management INTERCOM System (MCD)
CMISE........ Common Management Information Service Element [*Telecommunications*] (OSI)
CMIST........ Configuration Management Integrated Support Tool [*Marine science*] (OSRA)
CMIST........ Configuration Management Integrated Support Tool (USDC)
CMIT.......... Canada Manpower Industrial Training
CMIT.......... Current Medical Information and Technology (DAVI)
CMIT.......... Current Medical Information and Terminology
C-mitosis.... Colchicine-Blocked Mitosis [*Biology*] (DOG)
CMITS........ Central Main Interactive Telecommunications System (EDAC)
CMiUN....... United States Naval Shipyard, Technical Library, Mare Island, CA [*Library symbol Library of Congress*] (LCLS)
CMIU of A... Cigar Makers' International Union of America (EA)
CMIUW...... Coal Miners' Industrial Union of Workers [*Australia*]
CMIWHTE ... Companion Member of the Institution of Works and Highways Technician Engineers [*British*] (DBQ)
CMIWSc...... Certified Member of the Institute of Wood Science [*British*] (DBQ)
CMJ .... Canadian Municipal Journal [*A publication*] (DLA)
CMJ .... Carpometacarpal Joint [*Anatomy*] (DAVI)
CMJ .... Church's Ministry among Jews [*Church of England*]
CMJ .... Code of Military Justice
CMJ .... College Media Journal [*A publication*] [*Alternative music*] (WDMC)
CMJ .... College of Mount St. Joseph-On-The-Ohio, Mount St. Joseph, OH [*OCLC symbol*] (OCLC)
CMJ .... Committee on Medical Journalism (DAVI)
CMJ .... Craniomandibular Joint [*Anatomy*]
CMJ .... Ketchikan, AK [*Location identifier FAA*] (FAAL)
CMJ .... Modesto Junior College, Modesto, CA [*Library symbol Library of Congress*] (LCLS)
CMJ .... Mudanjiang General Aviation Co. [*China*] [*FAA designator*] (FAAC)
CMJHL........ Canadian Major Junior Hockey League
CMJS .... Committee for the Maintenance of Jewish Standards (EA)
CMK .... Carmel, NY [*Location identifier FAA*] (FAAL)
CMK .... Chassis Marking Kit
CMK .... Chloromethyl Ketone [*Medicine*] (DMAA)
CMK .... College of Marin, Kentfield, CA [*OCLC symbol*] (OCLC)
CMK .... Colonial Intermarket Income Trust I [*NYSE symbol*] (SPSG)
CMK .... Colonial InterMkt Inc. Tr I [*NYSE symbol*] (TTSB)
CMK .... Congenital Multicystic Kidney [*Nephrology*] (DAVI)
CMK .... Core-Mark International, Inc. [*Toronto Stock Exchange symbol Vancouver Stock Exchange symbol*]
CMK .... Cynomolgus Monkey Kidney [*Medicine*]
CMKA......... Christopher Morley Knothole Association (EA)
CML .... Cammooweal [*Queensland*] [*Airport symbol*] (AD)
CML .... Canaanite Myths and Legends [*A publication*] (BJA)
CML .... Canthomeatal Line [*Anatomy*]
CML .... Cell Management Language [*Software*] (BYTE)
CML .... Cell-Mediated Lympholysis [*Immunology*]
CML .... Central Meridian Longitude [*Planetary science*]
CML .... Chemical (AABC)
CML .... Chemical Corps (AAGC)
CML .... Chicago Midway Laboratory [*Army*] (MCD)
CML .... Chief Moulder [*Navy rating Obsolete*]
CML .... Choice Magazine Listening [*An "aural magazine" for the blind and visually handicapped*]
CML .... Chronic Myelocytic [*or Myeloid or Myelogenous*] Leukemia [*Oncology*]

CML............ Cincinnati Milacron, Inc., Corporate Information Center, Cincinnati, OH [*OCLC symbol*] (OCLC)
CML............ Classical and Modern Literature [*A publication*] (BRI)
CML............ Clinical Medical Librarian
CML............ Clinical Microbiology Laboratory
CML............ CML Group [*NYSE symbol*] (TTSB)
CML............ CML Group, Inc. [*NYSE symbol*] (SPSG)
CML............ Coles Myer Ltd. [*Australia*]
CML............ Collimated Monochromatic Light
CML............ Commander Air Carter Ltd. [*Canada ICAO designator*] (FAAC)
CML............ Commercial
cml............. Commercial (WDMC)
CML............ Common Machine Language [*Computer science*]
CML............ Common Mode Logic
CmL............ Commonwealth Microfilm Library Ltd., Calgary, AB, Canada [*Library symbol Library of Congress*] (LCLS)
CML............ Compare Left Half Words (SAA)
CML............ Complement Mediated Cell Lysis [*Immunology*]
CML............ Components and Materials Laboratory
CML............ Computer-Managed Laboratory
CML............ Computer-Managed Learning (ADA)
CML............ Concordia Mutual Life Association (EA)
CML............ Consolidated Material List (MCD)
CML............ Contemporary Men of Letters [*A publication*]
CML............ Contracts Maintenance Log (MCD)
CML............ Conversational Modeling Language [*Computer science*]
CML............ Corpus Medicorum Latinorum [*A publication*] (OCD)
CML............ Council Moslem League [*Pakistan*] [*Political party*]
CML............ Council of Mortgage Lenders [*British*] (DBA)
CML............ Critical Mass Laboratory
CML............ Current-Mode Logic [*Computer science*]
CML............ Cutaneous Malignant Lymphomas
CMl............ Mill Valley Public Library, Mill Valley, CA [*Library symbol Library of Congress*] (LCLS)
CML............ Stanislaus County Law Library, Modesto, CA [*Library symbol Library of Congress*] (LCLS)
CMLA.......... Communications and Media Law Association [*Australia*]
CMLAWA ..... Civilian Maimed and Limbless Association of Western Australia
CMLB.......... Citrus Mealybug [*Plant pest*]
CMLC.......... Chemical Corps [*Army*]
CMLC.......... Civilian/Military Liaison Committee
CMLC.......... Classical and Medieval Literature Criticism [*A publication*]
CMLCBL....... Chemical Corps Biological Laboratories [*Army*]
CMLCENCOM... Chemical Corps Engineering Command [*Army*]
CMLCMATCOM... Chemical Corps Material Command [*Army*]
CMLCRDCOM... Chemical Corps Research and Development Command [*Army*]
CMLCRECOM... Chemical Corps Research and Engineering Command [*Army*]
CMLCTNGCOM... Chemical Corps Training Command [*Army*]
CMLDEF....... Chemical Defense
CMLE.......... Classical Music Lovers' Exchange (EA)
CMlG .... Golden Gate Baptist Theological Seminary, Mill Valley, CA [*Library symbol Library of Congress*] (LCLS)
CML Gp .... CML Group, Inc. [*Associated Press*] (SAG)
CMLHO .... Chemical Corps Historical Office [*Army*]
CmLL.......... Commonwealth Microfilm Library Ltd., Calgary, AB, Canada [*Library symbol*] [*Library of Congress*] (LCLS)
CMLM.......... [*The*] Congregation of Maronite Lebanese Missionaries (TOCD)
CMLOPS....... Chemical Operations [*Army*] (AABC)
CM-LP .... Comite Marxista-Leninista Portugues [*Portuguese Marxist-Leninist Committee*] (PPE)
CMLR.......... Common Market Law Review [*A publication*] (DLA)
CML Rev...... Common Market Law Review [*A publication*] (DLA)
CMLS.......... Cellular and Molecular Life Sciences [*A publication*] [*Formerly Experientia*]
CMLS.......... Central Michigan Library System [*Library network*]
CMLS.......... Comprehensive Mailing List System [*Library of Congress*]
CMLS.......... Computer Multiple Listing Service [*Information service or system*] (IID)
CMLS.......... Confederate Memorial Literary Society (EA)
CMLTEE ...... Classified Ministry Lists of Types of Educational Establishments [*British*]
CmlTek........ Commercial Intertech Corp. [*Associated Press*] (SAG)
CMLTO........ College of Medical Laboratory Technologists of Ontario (AC)
CMM........... Air 2000 Airlines Ltd. [*Canada ICAO designator*] (FAAC)
CMM........... Caldera Mines Ltd. [*Vancouver Stock Exchange symbol*]
CMM........... Capability Maturity Model
CMM........... Center for Molecular Medicine [*Germany*]
CMM........... Century Minerals and Mining [*Australia*]
CMM........... Chemical Milling Machine
CMM........... Chief Machinist's Mate [*Navy rating Obsolete*]
CMM........... Chief Merchanist's Mate [*Navy British*]
CMM........... Chief Motor Mechanic [*British military*] (DMA)
CMM........... Coal-Methane Mixture
CMM........... Coherent Microwave Memory
CMM........... Comma (AABC)
CMM........... Commander of the Order of Military Merit
CMM........... Commander of the Order of Military Merit [*Canada*] (DD)
cmm........... Commentator [*MARC relator code*] [*Library of Congress*] (LCCP)
Cmm........... Commission [*Business term*]
CMM........... Commission for Marine Meteorology [*Marine science*] (OSRA)
CMM........... Commission for Maritime Meteorology [*World Meteorological Organization*]
CMM........... Common Memory Manager (NITA)
CMM........... Communications Multiplexer Module [*Computer science*]
CMM........... Compare Mask (SAA)

CMM........... Component Maintenance Manual (MCD)
CMM........... Comprehensive Major Medical [*Health insurance*] (GHCT)
CMM........... Computerized Modular Monitoring (OA)
CMM........... Computer Main Memory [*Telecommunications*] (TEL)
CM/M.......... Computer Marketing/Mailing (SAA)
CMM........... Concentration Module Main [*Telecommunications*] (TEL)
CMM........... Conclave of Mystical Masons [*Freemasonry*] (ROG)
CMM........... Condition Monitored Maintenance (NASA)
CMM........... Configuration Management Manual (DNAB)
CMM........... Congregatio Missionariorum de Mariannhill [*Congregation of Mariannhill Missionaries*] [*Mariannhill Fathers*] [*Roman Catholic religious order*] [*Italy*]
CMM........... Congregation of Marianhill Missionaries Marianhill Fathers & Brothers (TOCD)
cmm .... Congregation of Mariannhill Missionaries, Mariannhill Fathers and Brothers (TOCD)
CMM........... Consistory of Masonic Magic [*Freemasonry*] (ROG)
CMM........... Converting Machinery and Materials (DGA)
CMM........... Coordinated Management of Meaning [*Communications theory*]
CMM........... Coordinate Measuring Machine
CMM........... Core Mechanical Mock-Up [*Nuclear energy*] (NRCH)
CMM........... CRI IMI MAE [*Formerly, Insured Mortgage Association*] [*NYSE symbol*] (SPSG)
CMM........... Criimi Mae, Inc. [*NYSE symbol*] (SAG)
CMM........... Cubic Millimeter
CMM........... Cutaneous Malignant Melanoma [*Medicine*] (MAE)
CMM........... Cutting or Molding Machine
CMM........... Mount St. Mary's College, Los Angeles, CA [*OCLC symbol*] (OCLC)
CMM........... Technical Commission for Marine Meteorology [*WHO*] [*Geneva, Switzerland*] (EAIO)
CMM........... US Region of Congregation of Mariannhill Missionaries (EA)
CMMA.......... Canadian Metal Mining Association
CMMA.......... Carpet Manufacturers Marketing Association (EA)
CMMA.......... Christian Ministries Management Association [*Later, CMA*] (EA)
CMMA.......... Cigar Makers' Mutual Association [*A union*] [*British*]
CMMA.......... Clock Manufacturers and Marketing Association (EA)
CMMA.......... Clothing Monetary Maintenance Allowance [*Military*] (AABC)
CMMA.......... Company of Master Mariners of Australia
CMMA.......... Concrete Mixer Manufacturers' Association [*British*] (BI)
CMMA.......... Custom Metallized Multigate Array [*NASA*]
CMMB.......... Catholic Medical Mission Board (EA)
CMMC.......... California Marine Mammal Center [*Research center*] (RCD)
CMMC.......... COMSEC [*Communications Security*] Material Management Center (MCD)
CMMC.......... Corps Material Management Center (MCD)
CMMC.......... Council of Muslim Communities of Canada (EAIO)
CMMCA........ Cruise Missile Mission Control Aircraft (MCD)
CMMCBE....... Chief Machinist's Mate, Construction Battalion, Equipment Operator [*Navy rating Obsolete*]
CMMD .... Command Security [*NASDAQ symbol*] (TTSB)
CMMD .... Command Security Corp. [*NASDAQ symbol*] (SAG)
CMMDA .... Command Module Multiple Docking Assembly [*NASA*] (KSC)
CMME......... Chloromethyl Methyl Ether [*Organic chemistry*]
CMME......... Compton's Multimedia Encyclopedia [*A publication*]
CMMEI......... Chamber of Mines, Metals, and Extractive Industries [*Australia*]
CMMF......... Component Maintenance and Mock-Up Facility [*Nuclear energy*] (NRCH)
CMMG .... Canadian Motor Machine Gun [*World War I*]
CMMG .... Chief Machinist's Mate, Industrial Gas Generating Mechanic [*Navy rating Obsolete*]
CMMG .... Civilian Manpower Management Guides [*Navy*] (NG)
CMMGB .... Canadian Motor Machine Gun Brigade (DMA)
CMMH .... Memorial Hospital Association, Modesto, CA [*Library symbol Library of Congress*] (LCLS)
CMMI.......... Civilian Manpower Management Instruction [*Navy*] (NG)
CMMI.......... Command Maintenance Management Inspection [*Army*]
CMMI.......... Council of Mining and Metallurgical Institutions [*British*] (EAIO)
CMMIO .... Communications Security Mobile Issuing Office [*Military*] (NVT)
CMML......... Christian Missions in Many Lands (EA)
CMML......... Chronic Myelomonocytic Leukemia [*Oncology*]
CMML......... Civilian Manpower Management Letters [*Navy*] (NG)
CMMLIT....... Chronic Myelomonocytic Leukemia in Transition [*Oncology*]
CMMM........ McHenry Museum, Modesto, CA [*Library symbol Library of Congress*] (LCLS)
CMMN .... Commission
CMMN .... Common
Cmmn......... Common
CMMNA .... Catholic Major Markets Newspaper Association (EA)
CMMND....... Commissioned
CMMNR .... Commissioner
CMMP........ Canada Manpower Mobility Program
CMMP........ Carnegie Multi-Mini Processor
CMMP........ Commodity Management Master Plan (MCD)
CMMP........ Conventional Munitions Master Plan (DOMA)
CMMP........ Convertible Money Market Preferred Stock [*Investment term*]
CMMP........ Corps of Military Mounted Police [*British military*] (DMA)
CMMPA........ Canadian Medical Malpractice Prevention Association (AC)
CMMR......... Chief Machinist's Mate, Refrigeration [*Navy rating Obsolete*]
Cmmr.......... Commissioner
CMMR......... Common Modular Multimode RADAR
CMMR......... Confirmed and Made a Matter of Record [*Army*] (AABC)
CMMRR....... Command Mode Rejection Ratio (HGAA)
CMMS......... Carbon Monoxide Measuring System
CMMS......... Center for Medical Manpower Studies [*Northeastern University*] [*Research center*] (RCD)

CMMS......... Chief Machinist's Mate, Shop [*Navy rating Obsolete*]
CMMS......... Columbia Mental Maturity Scale [*Psychology*]
CMMS......... Computerized Maintenance Management System
CMMS......... Congressionally Mandated Mobility Study [*DoD*]
CMMS......... Control Maintenance & Management Systems (ACII)
CMMS......... Corps Material Management System (MCD)
cmm/s .... Cubic Millimeters per Second [*Measurement*] (DAVI)
CMMSRO..... Chief Machinist's Mate, Ship Repair, Outside Machinist [*Navy rating Obsolete*]
CMMT......... Cold Month Mean Temperture [*Climatology*]
CMMT......... Columbia Mental Maturity Test [*Psychology*] (DAVI)
CMMTE .... Committee
CMMTQ....... Corporation des Maitres Mecaniciens en Tuyauterie du Quebec [*Corporation of Master Pipe Mechanics of Quebec*] (AC)
CMMU .... Cache Memory Management Unit [*Computer science*] (BYTE)
CMMWWII ... Combat Merchant Mariners World War II (EA)
cmmz .... Commercial Zone (BARN)
CMN......... Casablanca-Mohamed V [*Morocco*] [*Airport symbol*] (OAG)
CMN......... Caudal Mediastinal Node [*Medicine*] (DMAA)
CMN......... Cerium Magnesium Nitrate [*Inorganic chemistry*]
CMN......... Children's Miracle Network [*Medicine*]
CMN......... Coleman Collieries [*Vancouver Stock Exchange symbol*]
CMN......... Commission (DNAB)
CMN......... Common
CMN......... Common
CMN......... Computerized Management Network [*For Agricultural Cooperative Extension Service Education*] [*Virginia Polytechnic Institute Database*]
CMN......... Contract Management Network (MCD)
CMN......... Convention Relative au Contrat de Transport de Marchandises en Navigation Interieure [*Convention on the Carriage of Goods by Inland Waterways*]
CMN......... Corynebacteria, Mycobacteria, Nocardiae [*Trehalose containing genera*]
CMN......... Crewman (NASA)
CMN......... Crewman
CMN......... Crown Mine [*Nevada*] [*Seismograph station code, US Geological Survey Closed*] (SEIS)
CMN......... Cystic Medial Necrosis [*of aorta*] [*Medicine*]
CMNA .... Canadian Merchant Navy Association Inc. [*Association de la Marine Marchande Canadienne Inc.*] (AC)
CMNA .... Complement-Mediated Neutrophil Activation [*Medicine*] (DMAA)
CMN-AA...... Cystic Medial Necrosis of Ascending Aorta [*Medicine*] (MAE)
CMNC .... Comence (FAAC)
CMND .... Command (IBMDP)
CMND .... Command
Cmnd .... Command Papers [*A publication*] (DLA)
CmndSc ...... Command Security Corp. [*Associated Press*] (SAG)
CMNFB .... Church of Monday Night Football (EA)
CMNPO .... Common Market Newspaper Publishers' Organization [*See also CAEJ*] [*Brussels, Belgium*] (EAIO)
CMNPS .... Canadian Minimum Navigation Performance Specification Airspace [*FAA*] (TAG)
CMNR .... Committee on Military Nutrition Research
CMNS .... Committee on Mediterranean Neogene Stratigraphy
CMNT.......... Children's Miracle Network Telethon
CMNT.......... Children's Miracle Network Television
CMNT.......... Comment (MSA)
CMNT.......... Computer Network Technology [*NASDAQ symbol*] (TTSB)
CMNT.......... Computer Network Technology Corp. [*NASDAQ symbol*] (NQ)
CMNTY .... Community
CMNWLTH... Commonwealth
cmo .... Cameo (VRA)
CMO............ Canonical Molecular Orbital [*Physical chemistry*]
CMO............ Capstead Mortgage [*NYSE symbol*] (SPSG)
CMO............ Cardiac Minute Output [*Physiology*]
CMO............ Caribbean Meteorological Organisation [*Formerly, Caribbean Meteorological Service*] (EA)
CMO............ Caribbean Meteorological Organization [*Marine science*] (OSRA)
CMO............ Case Management Organization (WYGK)
cMo............ Centimorgan [*Unit of genetic map distance*] (MAE)
CMO............ Central Meteorological Observatory [*Japan*]
CMO............ Chicago, St. Paul, Minneapolis & Omaha R. R. [*AAR code*]
CMO............ Chief Maintenance Officer
CMO............ Chief Marketing Officer [*Insurance*]
CMO............ Chief Medical Officer [*Military*]
CMO............ Chief of Mission Operations [*NASA*]
CMO............ Civil-Military Operations (AABC)
CMO............ Clinical Medical Officer [*British*]
CMO............ Collateralized Mortgage Obligation [*Federal Home Loan Mortgage Corp.*]
CMO............ College - Fairbanks [*Alaska*] [*Seismograph station code, US Geological Survey Closed*] (SEIS)
CMO............ Comfort Measures Only [*Medicine*] (DAVI)
CMO............ Commercial Oil & Gas Ltd. [*Toronto Stock Exchange symbol*]
CMO............ Common Main Objective [*Stereomicroscope optical element*]
CMO............ Common Mode Operation [*Telecommunications*] (TEL)
CMO............ Configuration Management Office [*NASA*] (DNAB)
CMO............ Consolidated Management Office [*Military*]
CMO............ Contour Mapping On-Boresight (MCD)
CMO............ Contract Management Office [*Jet Propulsion Laboratory, NASA*]
CMO............ Controlled Materials Officer
CMO............ Cootamundra [*Australia Airport symbol*] (OAG)
CMO............ Corticosterone Methyl Oxidase [*An enzyme*]

CMO............ Countermeasure Office [*of Harry Diamond Laboratories*] [*Military*] (RDA)
CMO............ Court-Martial Officer
CMO............ Court-Martial Orders [*Navy*]
CMO............ Crisis Management Organization [*DoD*]
CMO............ Crystal Marker Oscillator
CMO............ Ocean Minelayer [*NATO*]
CMOA .... Commonwealth Medical Officers' Association [*Australia*]
CMOA .... Continental Mark II Owner's Association (EA)
CMOA .... Convert Movement Our Apostolate (EA)
CMODE........ Collisional Mode (MCD)
CMoL.......... Chronic Monoblastic Leukemia [*Hematology and oncology*] (DAVI)
CMoL.......... Chronic Monocytic Leukemia [*Medicine*] (MAE)
CMOL.......... Consumable Maintenance and Overhaul List (MCD)
CMOML........ Consumable Maintenance and Overhaul Material List [*Navy*] (MCD)
CMOMM ...... Chief Motor Machinist's Mate [*Navy rating Obsolete*]
CMOMSRD... Chief Motor Machinist's Mate, Ship Repair, Diesel Engineering Mechanic [*Navy rating Obsolete*]
CMOMSRG... Chief Motor Machinist's Mate, Ship Repair, Gasoline Engineering Mechanic [*Navy rating Obsolete*]
CMon .... Monrovia Public Library, Monrovia, CA [*Library symbol Library of Congress*] (LCLS)
CMont .... Monterey Public Library, Monterey, CA [*Library symbol Library of Congress*] (LCLS)
CMontFS...... Monterey Institute of Foreign Studies, Monterey, CA [*Library symbol Library of Congress*] (LCLS)
CMontM....... Monterey Peninsula College, Monterey, CA [*Library symbol Library of Congress*] (LCLS)
CMontNP .... United States Naval Postgraduate School, Monterey, CA [*Library symbol Library of Congress*] (LCLS)
CMontUSA... United States Army, Army Language School Technical Library, Monterey, CA [*Library symbol Library of Congress*] (LCLS)
CMontUSN... United States Navy, Environmental Prediction Research Facility, Monterey, CA [*Library symbol Library of Congress*] (LCLS)
CMOOW....... Company Midshipman Officer-of-the-Watch [*Navy*] (DNAB)
CMOP .... Charge Motion Oriented Process
CMOPE .... Confederation Mondiale des Organisations de la Profession Enseignante [*World Confederation of Organizations of the Teaching Profession - WCOTP*] (EAIO)
C-MOPP....... Cyclophosphamide, Mechlorethamine [*Mustargen*], Oncovin , Procarbazine, Prednisone [*Vincristine*] [*Antineoplastic drug regimen*]
CMOPrA....... Capstead Mtge $1.60cm Cv Pfd [*NYSE symbol*] (TTSB)
CMOPrB....... Capstead Mtge $1.26 cm Cv Pfd [*NYSE symbol*] (TTSB)
CMOR.......... Craniomandibular Orthepedic Repositioning Device [*Dentistry and oral surgery*] (DAVI)
CMOS .... Canadian Meteorological and Oceanographic Society
CMOS .... Capper Military Occupational Specialty [*Army*] (AABC)
CMOS .... Carbon Molybdenum Steel (MSA)
CMOS .... Cigarette Machine Operators' Society [*A union*] [*British*]
CMOS .... Classroom Management Observation Scale (EDAC)
CMOS .... Complementary Magnetic Oxide on Silicone [*Computer science*]
CMOS .... Complementary Metal-Oxide Semiconductor (PCM)
CMOS .... Complementary Metal-Oxide Semiconductor Transistor [*Electronics*]
CMOS .... Complementary Metal-Oxide Silicon (NASA)
CMOS .... Complimentary Metal Oxide Semiconductor [*Electronics*] (ACRL)
CMOS .... Credence Systems [*NASDAQ symbol*] (TTSB)
CMOS .... Credence Systems Corp. [*NASDAQ symbol*] (SAG)
CMOSM .... Configuration Management Operating Systems Manual (MCD)
CMosM .... Moss Landing Marine Laboratory, Moss Landing, CA [*Library symbol Library of Congress*] (LCLS)
CMOS/SOS... Complementary Metal-Oxide Semiconductor/Silicon-on-Sapphire [*Electronics*]
CMOST .... Complementary Metal-Oxide Semiconductor Transistor [*Electronics*]
CMOT.......... Caterpillar Micro Oxidation Test [*Automotive lubricant*]
CMOTV .... Carrot Mottle Virus [*Plant pathology*]
CMp............ Bruggemeyer Memorial Library, Monterey Park Public Library, Monterey Park, CA [*Library symbol*] [*Library of Congress*] (LCLS)
CMP............ Calcium-Binding Modulator Protein
CMP............ California Milk Producers (SRA)
CMP............ Camp (ABBR)
CMP............ Campeau Corp. [*Toronto Stock Exchange symbol*]
CMP............ Camp Military Police [*British military*] (DMA)
CMP............ Campo Alegre [*Brazil*] [*Airport symbol*] (OAG)
CMP............ Camp-On [*Telecommunications*] (TEL)
CMP............ Campulung [*Romania*] [*Seismograph station code, US Geological Survey*] (SEIS)
CMP............ Canadian Military Pattern (DMA)
CMP............ Canadian Mineral Processors (HGAA)
CMp............ Capacitively Coupled Microwave Plasma
CMP............ Cape Mounted Police [*British*] (ROG)
CMP............ Cardiomyopathy [*Medicine*] (MAE)
CMP............ Caseinomacropeptide [*Biochemistry*]
CMP............ Cast Metal Part
CMP............ CCNU [*Lomustine*], Methotrexate, Procarbazine [*Antineoplastic drug regimen*] (DAVI)
CMP............ Celestial Mapping Program [*Air Force*] (MCD)
CMP............ Cellular and Molecular Pharmacology (GNE)
CMP............ Center for Manufacturing Productivity and Technology Transfer [*Rensselaer Polytechnic Institute*] [*Research center*] (RCD)
CMP............ Center for Metals Production [*Carnegie Mellon University*] [*Research center*] (RCD)
CMP............ Central Monitoring Position (IAA)
CMP............ Certificate in Medical Parasitology (ADA)
CMP............ Chemical Mechanical Polishing [*Engineering*]

CMP............	Chemi-Mechanical Pulp
CMP............	Chloramphenicol [Antimicrobial compound]
CMP............	Chloro(methyl)phenol [Organic chemistry]
CMP............	Chondromalacia Patellae [Orthopedics] (DAVI)
CMP............	Christian Movement for Peace [See also MCP] [Brussels, Belgium] (EAIO)
CMP............	Circuit Modeller Plus [Seasim Engineering Software Ltd.] [Software package] (NCC)
CMP............	Civilian Marksmanship Program (MCD)
CMP............	Civil Monetary Penalties [Medicaid program] (GFGA)
CMP............	CLEM [Closed-Loop Ex-Vessel Machine] Maintenance Pit [Nuclear energy] (NRCH)
CMP............	Coastal Management Programs [Marine science] (OSRA)
CMP............	Coastal Management Programs (USDC)
CMP............	Color Mat Processor
CMP............	Command Module Pilot [Apollo] [NASA]
CMP............	Command Monitor Panel (SSD)
CMP............	Commercial Multi-Peril [Insurance]
CMP............	Commisioner of Metropolitan Police (BARN)
CMP............	Commodity Master Plan [Army]
CMP............	Common-Midpoint
CMP............	Communications Management Processor [Information technology]
CMP............	Communications Module Processor (ACRL)
CMP............	Compania Panamena de Aviacion SA [Panama] [ICAO designator] (FAAC)
CMP............	Compare [Computer science]
CMP............	Competitive Medical Plans
CMP............	Complete Meeting Package [Meetings industry]
CMP............	Compliance
CMP............	Component Metal Parts (MSA)
cmp	Composer [MARC relator code] [Library of Congress] (LCCP)
CMP............	Compound [Medicine] (DHSM)
CMP............	Comprehensive Care [NYSE symbol] (SPSG)
CMP............	Comprehensive Management Plan
CMP............	Comprehensive Manpower Planning (OICC)
CMP............	Comprehensive Medical Plan
CMP............	Comprehensive Migrant Program [Department of Labor]
CMP............	Compression (MUGU)
CMP............	Compromise (ADA)
CMP............	Computational (MDG)
CMP............	Computer (MUGU)
CMP............	Configuration Management Plan [or Program]
CMP............	Congruent Melting Point
CMP............	Conseil Mondial de la Paix [World Peace Council - WPC] (EAIO)
CMP............	Console Message Processor [Computer science]
CMP............	Contemporary Music Project [Defunct] (EA)
CMP............	Continental Margins Program [Australia]
CMP............	Contract Maintenance Plan
CMP............	Contract Management Plan [Military]
CMP............	Contract Monitoring Point (AFM)
CMP............	Contract Monitor of Progress [Air Force] (AFIT)
CMP............	Contractor Maintenance Personnel (MCD)
CMP............	Controlled Materials Plan [of War Production Board] [World War II]
CMP............	Controlled Materials Production [Nuclear energy]
CMP............	Conversion Master Plan (CAAL)
CMP............	Cornell Maritime Press (DGA)
CMP............	Corporate Manufacturing Practice (IAA)
CMP............	Corps of Military Police [British]
CMP............	Corrugated Metal Pipe [Technical drawings]
CMP............	Council of Maritime Premiers [See also CPMM] [Canada]
CMP............	Council on Municipal Performance
CMP............	Countermilitary Potential
CMP............	Coupled Microwave Plasma [Spectrometry]
CMP............	Cruise Missile Planning (MCD)
CMP............	Cytidine Monophosphate [Biochemistry]
CMP............	Cytosine Monophosphate [Biochemistry]
CMPA............	Calgary Milk Producers' Association [Formerly, United Milk & Cream Producers] (AC)
CMPA............	Canadian Magazine Publishers Association [Formerly, Canadian Periodical Publisher's Association] (AC)
CMPA............	Canadian Medical Protective Association
CMPA............	Canadian Music Publishers Association [See also ACEM]
CMPA............	Cash Management Practitioners Association [Later, NCCMA] (EA)
CMPA............	Center for Media and Public Affairs (EA)
CMPA............	Chain Makers' Providential Association [A union] [British]
CMPA............	Church Music Publishers Association (EA)
CMPAA............	Certified Milk Producers Association of America (EA)
CmpAsc	Computer Associates International, Inc. [Associated Press] (SAG)
CMPC............	CompuCoin Systems [NASDAQ symbol] (TTSB)
CMPC............	Compucom Systems [NASDAQ symbol] (SAG)
CMPC............	Compucom Systems, Inc. [NASDAQ symbol] (SAG)
Cmpcm	Compucom Systems [Associated Press] (SAG)
Cmpcm	Compucom Systems, Inc. [Associated Press] (SAG)
CMPCOM	Computer and Communications [Database] (IT)
CMPCS	Configuration Management and Project Control Staff [Social Security Administration]
CMPCT........	Compact (FAAC)
CMPCTR	Computer Center
CMPD	Chronic Myeloproliferative Disorder [Medicine] (DMAA)
CMPD	Compound
CMPD	CompuMed, Inc. [NASDAQ symbol] (SAG)
CMPDA........	Canadian Motion Picture Distributors Association
CmpData......	Computer Data Systems [Associated Press] (SAG)
CMPDW........	CompuMed Inc. Wrrt [NASDAQ symbol] (TTSB)
CMPE............	Contractors' Mechanical Plant Engineers [British] (BI)

CmpEnv	Comprehensive Environmental Systems, Inc. [Associated Press] (SAG)
CMPF............	Central Meat Processing Facility [Army] (AABC)
CMPF............	Commander, Maritime Prepositioned Force [Navy] (ANA)
CMPF............	Core Maximum Power Fraction [Nuclear energy] (IEEE)
CMPF............	Cumulative Preferred [A class of stock] [Investment term]
CMPF............	Cyclophosphamide, Methotrexate, Prednisone, 5-Fluorouracil [Antineoplastic drug regimen] (DAVI)
CMP-FX	Complement Fixation [Immunochemistry] (DAVI)
CMPG	Constant Miss Proportional Guidance
CmpGen......	Compare Generiks, Inc [Associated Press] (SAG)
CMPGN........	Campaign
CMPGN........	Chronic Membranoproliferative Glomerulonephritis [Immunology]
CMPGRND ...	Campground
CMPHE	Conference of Municipal Public Health Engineers [Later, NCLEHA] (EA)
CMPI............	Civilian Marine Personnel Instructions [Navy]
CMP(I)........	Corps of Military Police (India) [British military] (DMA)
CmpIdn......	Computer Identics Corp. [Associated Press] (SAG)
CMPKT........	Cam Pocket
CMPL............	Complement (IAA)
CMPL............	Complete (MUGU)
CMPL............	Critical Materials Parts List (MCD)
CMPLM........	Complement (MSA)
CmpLR........	Computer Language Research, Inc. [Associated Press] (SAG)
CMPLT........	Complete (FAAC)
CMPLT........	Complete
CMPM........	Catalog of Museum Publications and Media [A publication]
CMPM........	Computer-Managed Parts Manufacture
CmpMan......	Complete Management, Inc. [Associated Press] (SAG)
CmpMd......	CompuMed, Inc. [Associated Press] (SAG)
CMPNAN......	Cytidine Monophosphate-N-Acetylneuraminic Acid (PDAA)
CMPNG........	Camping
CmpnIAP......	Companion of the Institution of Analysts and Programmers [British] (DBQ)
cmpnl	Campanile (VRA)
CmpnSCP ...	Companion of the Society of Certified Professionals [British] (DBQ)
CMPNSTN	Compensation
CMPNT	Component (AFM)
CMPO	Campo Electr Appliances/Comp [NASDAQ symbol] (TTSB)
CMPO	Campo Electronics, Appliances & Computers, Inc. [NASDAQ symbol] (SAG)
CMPO	Chief, SEATO [Southeast Asia Treaty Organization] Military Planning Office (CINC)
CMPO	Cruise Missile Project Office (AAGC)
CMPP............	((Chloro(methyl)phenoxy))propionic Acid [Herbicide]
CMPP............	Computer-Managed Process Planning (MCD)
CMPP............	Configuration Management Program Plan [DoD]
CMPPA........	Computer-Matching Privacy and Protection Act
CmpPr	Computer Products, Inc. [Associated Press] (SAG)
CmpR........	Campbell Resources, Inc. [Formerly, Campbell Chibougarnau Mines Ltd.] [Associated Press] (SAG)
CMPR	Camper
CMPR	Compare (MSA)
CmpRD........	CompuRAD, Inc. [Associated Press] (SAG)
CMP Reg	Controlled Materials Plan Regulation (National Production) [of War Production Board] [World War II] (DLA)
CMPRHNSV...	Comprehensive
CMPRS........	Compress (ABBR)
CMPRSB......	Compressible (ABBR)
CMPRSBNS...	Compressibleness (ABBR)
CMPRSBT...	Compressibility (ABBR)
CMPRSD......	Compressed (ABBR)
CMPRSG......	Compressing (ABBR)
CmprsL........	Compression Labs, Inc. [Associated Press] (SAG)
CMPRSN......	Compression (ABBR)
CMPRSR......	Compressor (ABBR)
CMPRSV	Compressive (ABBR)
CMPRSVY	Compressively (ABBR)
CMPRT	Compartment (NASA)
CMPRTL	Compartmental (ABBR)
CMPRTLZ......	Compartmentalize (ABBR)
CMPRTLZD...	Compartmentalized (ABBR)
CMPRTLZG...	Compartmentalizing (ABBR)
CMPS........	Campus (ABBR)
CMPS........	Campus
CMPS........	Centimeters per Second
cmps........	Centimeters per Second (DMAA)
CMPS........	Colosseum of Motion Picture Salesmen (EA)
CMPS........	Command Module Procedures Simulator [NASA]
CMPS........	Common Mode Processing System (CAAL)
CMPS........	Compass (MSA)
CMPS........	Compost (ABBR)
CmpScrpt....	CompScript, Inc. [Associated Press] (SAG)
CMPSCTY	Computer Security (MSA)
CMPSF........	Composite Military Police Strike Force (VNW)
CMPSIT........	Composite (ABBR)
CMPSN........	Composition (MSA)
CMPSPrA	Consumers Pwr $4.16 Pfd [NYSE symbol] (TTSB)
CMPSR........	Compressor (ABBR)
CMPSR........	Compressor
CMPST........	Campsite
CMPST........	Composite (MSA)
CMPST........	Compost (ABBR)
CMPSTD	Composted (ABBR)

CMPSTG ...... Composting (ABBR)
CMPSU .... Composure (ABBR)
CMPT .... Component (AAG)
CMPT .... Compute [or Computer] (AABC)
CMPT .... Computone Corp. [NASDAQ symbol] (SAG)
CMPT .... Contempt [FBI standardized term]
CMPTD .... Computed
CmpTel .... Computer Telephone Corp. [Associated Press] (SAG)
CMPTG .... Computing
CMPTG .... Computing
CmptHz .... Computer Horizons Corp. [Associated Press] (SAG)
CMPTR .... Comptroller (ABBR)
CMPTR .... Computer (KSC)
CMPTR .... Computer
Cmptrc .... Computrac, Inc. [Associated Press] (SAG)
CmpTsk .... Computer Task Group, Inc. [Associated Press] (SAG)
Cmptvsn ...... Computervision Corp. [Associated Press] (SAG)
CMPU .... Compute (ABBR)
CMPUG .... Computing (ABBR)
CMPUL .... Compulsion (ABBR)
CMPULR ...... Compulsory (ABBR)
CMPULRY .... Compulsorily (ABBR)
CMPULV ...... Compulsive (ABBR)
CmpuMed .... CompuMed, Inc. [Associated Press] (SAG)
CMPUN .... Compunction (ABBR)
CMPUNSY ... Compunctiously (ABBR)
CMPUR .... Compurgation (ABBR)
CmpuSrv ..... CompuServe Corp. [Associated Press] (SAG)
Cmputa .... Computational Systems, Inc. [Associated Press] (SAG)
CMPUTAN ... Computation (ABBR)
CMPUTD ..... Computed (ABBR)
CMPUTG ..... Computing (ABBR)
CMPUTN ..... Computation (ABBR)
CMPUTR ..... Computer (ABBR)
Cmputrn ...... Computron Software, Inc. [Associated Press] (SAG)
CMPUTRZ .... Computerize (ABBR)
CMPUTRZD... Computerized (ABBR)
CMPUTRZG... Computerizing (ABBR)
CMPX .... COMPENDEX [Computerized Engineering Index, Inc.] [Bibliographic database] (NITA)
CMPX .... Complex
CMQ .... Anchorage, AK [Location identifier FAA] (FAAL)
CMQ .... Canadian Manoir Industries Ltd. [Toronto Stock Exchange symbol]
CMQ .... Clermont [Australia Airport symbol] (OAG)
CMQ .... Coal Mining and Quarrying
CMQB .... Coal Mining Qualifications Board [New South Wales] [Australia]
CMR .... California Manufacturers Register [Database Publishing] [Information service or system] (CRD)
CMR .... Cam Air Management Ltd. [British ICAO designator] (FAAC)
CMR .... Camerino [Italy] [Seismograph station code, US Geological Survey Closed] (SEIS)
CMR .... Cameroon [ANSI three-letter standard code] (CNC)
CMR .... Camreco, Inc. [Toronto Stock Exchange symbol]
CMR .... Canadian Mounted Rifles
CMR .... Cape Mounted Rifles [British]
CMR .... Capital Markets Report [Dow Jones & Co., Inc.] [Information service or system] (CRD)
CMR .... Capital Military Region
CMR .... Capture-Mark-Recapture [Demography]
CMR .... Carbon Magnetic Resonance [Also, CNMR]
CMR .... Catalytic Membrane Reactor [Chemical engineering]
CMR .... Center for Marine Resources [National Oceanic and Atmospheric Administration]
CMR .... Center for Marxist Research [Defunct] (EA)
CMR .... Center for Materials Research [Johns Hopkins University] [Research center] (RCD)
CMR .... Center for Materials Research [Stanford University] [Research center] (RCD)
CMR .... Center Materials Representative [NASA] (NASA)
CMR .... Centralized Mail Remittance [Telecommunications] (TEL)
CMR .... Centre for Manufacturing Renewal [University of Warwick] [British] (CB)
CMR .... Centre for Medicines Research [British] (CB)
CMR .... Cerebral Metabolic Rate [Medicine]
CMR .... Certified Medical Representative (MAE)
CMR .... Chemical Metallurgical Reporting
CMR .... Children's Medical Research
CMR .... Christian Management Report [Christian Ministries Management Association] [A publication]
CMR .... Classified Material Receipt
CMR .... Code Matrix Reader (PDAA)
CMR .... Code of Maine Rules (AAGC)
CMR .... Code of Massachusetts Regulations [A publication]
CMR .... College Militaire Royal [Canada]
CMR .... College Militaire Royal de Saint-Jean [UTLAS symbol]
CMR .... Colmar [France] [Airport symbol] (OAG)
CMR .... Colossal Magnetoresistance [Physics]
CMR .... Colossal Magnetoresistance [Physics]
CMR .... Commercial Marketing Representative (AAGC)
CMR .... Committee on Manpower Resources for Science and Technology
CMR .... Committee on Medical Research [Subdivision of OSRD] [World War II]
CMR .... Committee on Migration and Resettlement [Department of State] [World War II]

CMR .... Common Market Reporter [Commerce Clearing House] [A publication] (DLA)
CMR .... Common Mode Rejection
CMR .... Communications Monitoring Report
CMR .... Communications Moon Relay [System] [NASA]
CMR .... Compare Right Half Words (SAA)
CMR .... Competitive Media Reporting [An association] [Broadcasting] (WDMC)
CMR .... Configuration Management Review (AABC)
CMR .... Congregation of Mary Queen (TOCD)
CMR .... Consolidated Mail Room [Air Force] (AFM)
CMR .... Contact Microradiography (DICI)
CMR .... Continuous Maximum Rating [of equipment] (DEN)
CMR .... Contract Management Region
CMR .... Contract Management Review [DoD]
CMR .... Contractor Management Reserve (MCD)
CMR .... Convention on the Contract for the International Carriage of Goods by Road [Geneva] [19 May 1956] (DLA)
CMR .... Countdown Modification Request [Aerospace] (AAG)
CMR .... Countermortar RADAR
CMR .... Court-Martial Report (AFM)
CMR .... Court of Military Review (AFM)
CMR .... Crude Marriage Rate
CMR .... Crude Mortality Ratio (MAE)
CMR .... Customer Material Return
CMR₂ .... Square Centimeter (ROG)
CMR₃ .... Cubic Centimeter (ROG)
CMRA .... Camera (ABBR)
CMRA .... Canadian Maritime Rescue Auxiliary (PDAA)
CMRA .... Chemical Marketing Research Association (EA)
CMRA .... Committee on Migration and Refugee Affairs (EA)
CMRB .... California Melon Research Board (EA)
CMRB .... Composite Main Rotor Blade (MCD)
CMRB .... Contractor Material Review Board [NASA] (NASA)
CMRC .... Canadian Music Research Council
CMRC .... Coal Mining Research Centre [Canada]
CMRC .... Commerce (ABBR)
CMRC .... Crucible Materials Research Center (MCD)
CMR Cit & Ind... Court Martial Reports, Citators and Indexes [A publication] (DLA)
CMRCL .... Commercial (ABBR)
CMRCLSM ... Commercialism (ABBR)
CMRCLST ... Commercialist (ABBR)
CMRCLSTC... Commercialistic (ABBR)
CMRCLZ .... Commercialize (ABBR)
CMRCLZD ... Commercialized (ABBR)
CMRCLZG ... Commercializing (ABBR)
CMRD .... Committee on Migration, Refugees, and Demography (EA)
CMRD .... Comrade (ABBR)
CMRDC .... Chicken Meat Research and Development Council [Australia]
CMRDSP..... Comradeship (ABBR)
CMRE .... California Marriage Readiness Evaluation [Psychology]
CMRE .... Committee for Monetary Research and Education, Inc. [Research center] (RCD)
CMRE .... Comstock Resources [NASDAQ symbol] (TTSB)
CMRE .... Comstock Resources, Inc. [NASDAQ symbol] (NQ)
CMRED .... Council on Marine Resources and Engineering Development
CMREF........ Committee on Marine Research, Education, and Facilities [National Council on Marine Resources and Engineering Development] (GFGA)
CMREL .... Central Midwest Regional Educational Laboratory (AEBS)
CMRF.......... Capital Maintenance and Rental Funds (DNAB)
CMRF.......... Conditioned Medium Reconstituting Factor [Immunochemistry]
CMRG .... Cerebral Metabolic Rate of Glucose [Also, CMRglc] [Biochemistry]
CMRG .... Core Melt Review Group [Nuclear energy] (NRCH)
CMRGA .... Ceylon and Mauritius Royal Garrison Artillery [British military] (DMA)
CMRGF .... Canadian Modern Rhythmic Gymnastics Federation
CMRglc....... Cerebral Metabolic Rate of Glucose [Also, CMRG] [Biochemistry]
CMRI .... Cardiac Magnetic Resonance Imaging [Cardiology]
CMRI .... Cerebral Metabolic Rate of Lactate [Medicine] (DMAA)
CMRI .... Certified Medical Representatives Institute (EA)
CMRI .... Children's Medical Relief International [Defunct]
CMRI .... Children's Medical Research Institute [Australia]
CMRI .... Chloro(methyl)(ribityl)isoalloxazine [Biochemistry]
CMRI .... Combined Maintenance Removal Interval (AFIT)
CMRI .... Combined Removal Interval [Engine]
CMRI .... Command Maintenance Readiness Inspection [Army] (AABC)
CMR JAG AF... Court Martial Reports, Judge Advocate General of the Air Force [A publication] (DLA)
CMR JAG & US Ct of Mil App... Court Martial Reports, Judge Advocate General of the Armed Forces and United States Court of Military Appeals [A publication] (DLA)
CMRL.......... Combat Material Research Laboratory [Army]
CMRL.......... Consolidated Master Cross-Reference List [Defense Supply Agency]
CMRLR .... Cam Roller
CMRLS .... Central Massachusetts Regional Public Library System [Library network]
CMRLW .... Cape Mounted Rifles, Left Wing [British]
CMRN .... Cameron Financial [NASDAQ symbol] (TTSB)
CMRN .... Cameron Financial Corp. [NASDAQ symbol] (SAG)
CMRN .... Cooperative Meteorological Rocket Network [NASA]
CMRNG .... Chromosomally-Mediated Resistant Neisseria Gonorrhoeae [Medicine]
CMRNS .... Chamber of Mineral Resources of Nova Scotia (AC)
CMRO .... Cerebral Metabolic Rate of Oxygen [Biochemistry] (DAVI)
CMRO .... COMARCO, Inc. [NASDAQ symbol] (NQ)

CMRO₂........ Cerebral Metabolic Rate for Oxygen
CMRR .... Center for Magnetic Recording Research [*University of California, San Diego*] [*Research center*] (RCD)
CMRR .... Coal Mine Roof Rating [*US Bureau of Mines*]
CMRR .... Common Mode Rejection Ratio
CMRRA....... Canadian Musical Reproduction Rights Agency
CMRRW...... Cape Mounted Rifles, Right Wing [*British*]
CMRS .... Calibration/Measurement Requirements Summary
CMRS .... Center for Medieval and Renaissance Studies (EA)
CMRS .... Computerized Materials Retrieval System [*Computer science*] (ECII)
CMRS .... Countermeasures Receiving System
CMRST .... Committee on Manpower Resources for Science and Technology [*British*]
CMRT.......... Certified Material Test Report [*Nuclear energy*] (NRCH)
CMRW......... Coalition for the Medical Rights of Women [*Defunct*] (EA)
CMRWL .... Citizens for Media Responsibility without Law (EA)
CMS............ American Association of Councils of Medical Staffs [*Later, PDA*] (EA)
CMS............ Cabinet Makers' Society [*A union*] [*British*]
CMS............ Cable Marking System
CMS............ Calcium-Magnesium Silicate (OA)
CMS............ Calibration and Measurement Summaries [*Air Force*] (AFIT)
CMS............ California Macadamia Society (EA)
CMS............ California Medical Survey [*Psychology*]
CMS............ Call Management System [*Accounting package*] (CDE)
CMS............ Cambridge Mathematical Series [*A publication*]
CMS............ Cambridge Monitor System
CMS............ Camera Model System (MCD)
CMS............ Canadian Mathematical Society [*Societe Mathematique du Canada*] (AC)
CMS............ Canadian Micrographic Society
CMS............ Capital Market Statistics
cms............. Carbodiimide Residue [*As substituent on nucleoside*] [*Biochemistry*]
CMS............ Carbon Molecular Sieve [*Adsorption technology*]
CMS............ Carboxymethyl Starch [*Organic chemistry*]
CMS............ Case Management System [*Department of Justice*] (GFGA)
CMS............ Cashel Mercy Sisters (TOCD)
CMS............ Cash Management System (IAA)
CMS............ Catholic Missionary Society
CMS............ Cellular Management System [*Stratus Computer, Inc.*]
CMS............ Cement-Modified Soil (PDAA)
CMS............ Center for Management Systems (EA)
CMS............ Center for Manufacturing Systems [*New Jersey*]
CMS............ Center for Maritime Studies [*Later, MRD*] [*Webb Institute of Naval Architecture*] [*Research center*] (EA)
CMS............ Center for Materials Science [*Los Alamos, NM*] [*Los Alamos National Laboratory*] [*Department of Energy*] (GRD)
CMS............ Center for Measurement Science (BARN)
CMS............ Center for Metropolitan Studies [*University of Missouri - Saint Louis*] [*Research center*] (RCD)
CMS............ Center for Migration Studies of New York (EA)
CMS............ Center for Multinational Studies [*Defunct*] (EA)
cm/s............ Centimeter per Second [*Measurement*] (DAVI)
CMS............ Centralized Maintenance System [*Telecommunications*]
CMS............ Centralized Materials Section
CMS............ Cycloned Munitions Systems [*USARPAC*] (MCD)
CMS............ Central Material Section [*Medicine*] (DAVI)
CMS............ Central Material Supply [*Medicine*] (DAVI)
CMS............ Central Materiel Service Team [*Military*]
CMS............ Centre for Medieval Studies [*University of Toronto*] [*Canada*] (IRC)
CMS............ Centre for Multicultural Studies [*Flinders University*] [*Australia*]
CMS............ Certificate in Ministerial Studies (PGP)
CMS............ Certificate in Music Studies (PGP)
CMS............ Certified Metrication Specialist (DICI)
CMS............ Cervical Mucous Solution [*Gynecology*] (DAVI)
CMS............ Changeable Message Sign [*Highway engineering*]
CMS............ Charlotte-Mecklenburg School District
CMS............ Charlotte Motor Speedway [*Auto racing*]
CMS............ Chicago Map Society (EA)
CMS............ Chicago Medical School
CMS............ Chinese Masonic Society [*Australia*]
CMS............ Christian Medical Society [*Later, CMDS*] (EA)
CMS............ Chromographic Mode Sequencing [*Chromatography*]
CMS............ Chromosome Modification Site [*Genetics*] (DAVI)
CMS............ Church Missionary Society [*British*]
CMS............ Church Monuments Society (EA)
CMS............ Circuit Maintenance System [*AT & T*]
CMS............ Circulation, Motion, and Sensation (HGAA)
CMS............ Clarion Music Society (EA)
CMS............ Classified Materials System (LAIN)
CMS............ Classified Materials Systems (DOMA)
CMS............ Clay Minerals Society (EA)
CMS............ Cleaning Management Station
CMS............ Close Medium Shot [*A photograph or motion picture sequence taken from a relatively short distance*]
CMS............ Clyde Mood Scale [*Psychology*]
CMS............ CMS Energy [*Associated Press*] (SAG)
CMS............ CMS Energy Corp. [*NYSE symbol*] (SPSG)
CMS............ Cockpit Management System [*Aviation*]
CMS............ Coincidence Moessbauer Spectroscopy (OA)
CMS............ Collagen Matrix Support [*Cell culture*]
CMS............ Collapsible Maintenance Shelter (MCD)
CMS............ Collapsible Mobile Shelter (MCD)
CMS............ Collection Management System [*IRS*]
CMS............ Collectors Music Shop [*Record label*]
CMS............ College Music Society (EA)

CMS............ Color Management System [*Computer science*]
CMS............ Combat Mission Scenario [*Army*]
CMS............ Combat Mission Simulation (MCD)
CMS............ Combined Mixer Settler [*Chemical engineering*]
CMS............ Comboni Missionary Sisters (TOCD)
CMS............ Command Management System (MCD)
CMS............ Command Module Simulator [*NASA*]
CMS............ Common Manpower Standards (AFM)
CMS............ Common Mode Signal
CMS............ Common Mounting System (PDAA)
CMS............ Communication Management System [*Computer science*]
CMS............ Compensated Meatball Stabilization (PDAA)
CMS............ Compiler Monitor System (BUR)
CMS............ Complete Management Systems
CMS............ Complete Matched Set [*Philately*]
CMS............ Composite Multiplex Signal (MCD)
CMS............ Comprehensive Medical Society [*Defunct*] (EA)
CMS............ Computerized Manufacturing System (MCD)
CMS............ Computer Management System [*Burroughs Corp.*] (BUR)
CMS............ Computer Marketing Services [*Anaheim, CA*] [*Information service or system*] (IID)
CMS............ Computer-Modelling System [*Computer Modelling International Ltd.*] [*Software package*] (NCC)
CMS............ Condition Monitoring System (CAAL)
CMS............ Condor Missile System
CMS............ Configuration Management Staff [*Social Security Administration*]
CMS............ Configuration Management System
CMS............ Conflict Management Survey [*Interpersonal skills and attitudes test*]
CMS............ Congestion Management Systems [*VDOT*] (TAG)
CMS............ Conservation Materials and Services
CMS............ Consolidated Maintenance Squadron [*Air Force*]
CMS............ Consumer and Marketing Service [*Later, AMS*] [*Department of Agriculture*]
CMS............ Consumers Power Co. [*NYSE symbol*] (SAG)
CMS............ Consumers Power Co. Financing I [*NYSE symbol*] (SAG)
CMS............ Contemporary Music Society (EA)
CMS............ Continuous Measurement Survey [*US Census Bureau*]
CMS............ Contractor Maintenance Service [*or Support*] (MCD)
CMS............ Conventional Munitions System [*Military*]
CMS............ Conversational Monitor System [*IBM Corp.*] [*Computer science*]
CMS............ Corrective Maintenance System (NVT)
CMS............ Corrective Measure Study [*Environmental science*]
CMS............ Cost Management System
CMS............ Council of Medical Staffs (MEDA)
CMS............ Countermeasures Set (MCD)
CMS............ Countermeasures Subsystem (DWSG)
CMS............ Cras Mane Sumendus [*To Be Taken Tomorrow Morning*] [*Pharmacy*]
CMS............ Crisis Management System
CMS............ Cross-Section Measurement System
CMS............ Currency Market Service [*Database*] [*Money Market Services, Inc.*] [*Information service or system*] (CRD)
CMS............ Current-Mode Switching [*Computer science*] (MSA)
CMS............ Current Mortality Sample [*Department of Health and Human Services*] (GFGA)
CMS............ Cyclone Melting System [*Coal technology*]
CMS............ Cytoplasmic Male Sterility [*Botany*]
CMS............ Melodyland School of Theology, Anaheim, CA [*Inactive*] [*OCLC symbol*] (OCLC)
CMS............ Senior Enlisted Advisor [*AFSC*]
CMS............ , Sensation [*or Musculatory*] [*or Sensory Orthopedics and physical therapy*] (DAVI)
CMS............ Stanislaus County Free Library, Modesto, CA [*Library symbol Library of Congress*] (LCLS)
CMSA.......... Canning Machinery and Supplies Association [*Later, FPM & SA*] (EA)
CMSA.......... Chain Makers' and Strikers' Association [*A union*] [*British*]
CMSA.......... Church Missionary Society of Australia
CMSA.......... Consolidated Metropolitan Statistical Area [*Census Bureau*]
CMSA.......... Cruise Missile Support Activity (DOMA)
CMSAF........ Chief Master Sergeant of the Air Force (AFM)
CMSAR........ Commissar (ABBR)
CMSARY...... Commissary (ABBR)
CMSB.......... Commonwealth Savings [*NASDAQ symbol*] (TTSB)
CMSB.......... Commonwealth Savings Bank [*NASDAQ symbol*] (SAG)
CMSC.......... Cape Medical Staff Corps [*British military*] (DMA)
CMSC.......... Catalina Marine Science Center [*University of Southern California*] [*Research center*]
CMSC.......... Central Missouri State College [*Later, Central Missouri State University*]
CMSC.......... Communications Mode Selection Control (MCD)
CMSCI .... Council of Mechanical Specialty Contracting Industries [*Later, ASC*] (EA)
CMSD .... Congenital Myocardial Sympathetic Dysinnervation [*Medicine*] (DMAA)
CMSE.......... Center for Materials Science and Engineering [*MIT*] [*Research center*] (RCD)
CMSE.......... Conditional Mean Square Error [*Statistics*]
CM/SEC....... Centimeters per Second [*Telecommunications*] (TEL)
CMS Eng...... CMS Energy Corp. [*Associated Press*] (SAG)
CMSER .... Commission on Marine Science, Engineering, and Resources
CMSF.......... Centre for Molecular Structure and Function [*Australian National University*]
CMSG .... Canadian Merchant Service Guild
CMSG .... "C" Message Weighting [*Telecommunications*] (TEL)
CMSGT .... Chief Master Sergeant

CMSh............ Shell Development Co., Modesto, CA [*Library symbol Library of Congress*] (LCLS)
CMSHFT ...... Camshaft (MSA)
CMSI............ Checkout/Control and Monitor Subsystem Interface [*NASA*] (NASA)
CMSI............ Climatology Mission Success Indicators (MCD)
CMSI............ Corporate Memory Systems, Inc. [*Computer science*] (PCM)
CMSI............ Council of Mutual Savings Institutions [*New York, NY*] (EA)
CMSI............ Country Music Showcase International (EA)
CMSI............ Cryomedical Sciences [*NASDAQ symbol*] (TTSB)
CMSI............ Cryomedical Sciences, Inc. [*NASDAQ symbol*] (NQ)
CMSIO........ Communications Security Material Sub-Issuing Office [*Military*] (NVT)
CMSL............ Cambridge Manuals of Science and Literature [*A publication*]
CMSL............ CPG Missile Selection (MCD)
CMS/LC........ Chamber Music Society of Lincoln Center
CMSM........ Chemical Material Study Model [*Military*] (AFIT)
CM-SM........ Command Module - Service Module [*Combined*] [*NASA*] (MCD)
CMSM........ Committee on a Multimedium Approach to Sludge Management [*National Research Council*]
CMSM........ Conference of Major Superiors of Men (EA)
CMSM........ Stanislaus County Medical Library, Modesto, CA [*Library symbol Library of Congress*] (LCLS)
CMSN .... Commission (FAAC)
CMSNA .... Chinese Music Society of North America (EA)
CMSND .... Commissioned
CMSNG........ Commissioning (ABBR)
CMSNL .... Commissional (ABBR)
CMSNR .... Commissioner
CMSNY .... Commissionary (ABBR)
CMSO .... Chief Japanese Maritime Staff Office (CINC)
CMSP & P... Chicago, Milwaukee, St. Paul & Pacific Railroad (IIA)
CMSPrB ...... Consumers Pwr $4.50 Pfd [*NYSE symbol*] (TTSB)
CMSPrD ...... Consumers Pwr $7.45cmPfd [*NYSE symbol*] (TTSB)
CMSPrE ...... Consumers Pwr $7.72 Pfd [*NYSE symbol*] (TTSB)
CMSPrG ...... Consumers Pwr $7.76 Pfd [*NYSE symbol*] (TTSB)
CMSPrH ...... Consumers Pwr $7.68 Pfd [*NYSE symbol*] (TTSB)
CMSPrI .... Consumer Pwr $2.08'A'Pfd [*NYSE symbol*] (TTSB)
CMSPrJ........ Consumers Pwr Fin I 8.36%'TOPrS' [*NYSE symbol*] (TTSB)
CMSQ .... Communications Maintenance Squadron [*Air Force*]
CMSR .... Carpenter's Mate, Ship Repair [*Navy*]
CMSR .... Central Management Staff Record (PDAA)
CMSR .... Commercial/Military Spares Release (MCD)
CMSR .... Commissar (ABBR)
CMSR .... Continuous-Moment Sum Rules (PDAA)
CMSR .... Controller of Merchant Shipbuilding and Repairs [*Navy British*]
CMSRA .... Commiserate (ABBR)
CMSRAD...... Commiserated (ABBR)
CMSRAG...... Commiserating (ABBR)
CMSRAN ...... Commiseration (ABBR)
CMSRAR...... Commiserator (ABBR)
CMSRAV...... Commiserative (ABBR)
CMSRAVY.... Commiseratively (ABBR)
CMSRB .... Carpenter's Mate, Ship Repair, Boatbuilder-Wood [*Navy*]
CMSRB .... Chief Metalsmith, Ship Repair, Blacksmith [*Navy rating Obsolete*]
CMSRBA...... Conference of Major Superiors of Religious Brothers of Australia
CMSRC .... Carpenter's Mate, Ship Repair, Carpenter [*Navy*]
CMSRC .... Chief Metalsmith, Ship Repair, Coppersmith [*Navy rating Obsolete*]
CMSRJ........ Carpenter's Mate, Ship Repair, Joiner [*Navy*]
CMSRK .... Carpenter's Mate, Ship Repair, Caulker-Boat [*Navy*]
CMSRN .... Carpenter's Mate, Ship Repair, Cement Worker-Concrete [*Navy*]
CMSRS .... Carpenter's Mate, Ship Repair, Shipwright [*Navy*]
CMSRS .... Chief Metalsmith, Ship Repair, Sheet Metal Worker [*Navy rating Obsolete*]
CMSRY .... Commissary (ABBR)
CMSS.......... Circulation, Motor Ability, Sensation, and Swelling [*Medicine*]
CMSS.......... Commission on Molecular Structure and Spectroscopy
CMSS.......... Computerized Moment Stability System [*Navy*]
CMSS.......... Contractor Maintenance and Supply Services [*DoD*]
CMSS.......... Contractor Maintenance Supply and Support [*DoD*]
CMSS.......... Council of Medical Specialty Societies (EA)
CMSSN .... Commission (ABBR)
CMSSNR ...... Commissioner (ABBR)
CMST.......... Carmelite Missionaries of St. Theresa [*Roman Catholic women's religious order*]
CM ST P & P... Chicago, Milwaukee, St. Paul & Pacific Railroad Co.
CMSTRKFLT... Commander, Striking Fleet, Atlantic (MCD)
CMSTRKFLT-LANT... Commander Striking Fleet Atlantic [*Military*]
CmstRs .... Comstock Resources, Inc. [*Associated Press*] (SAG)
CMSU .... Central Missouri State University
CMSUA .... Clean Midstream Urinalysis [*Medicine*] (DAVI)
CMSV .... Community Savings FA [*NASDAQ symbol*] (SAG)
CMSW .... Conference of Major Religious Superiors of Women's Institutes of the United States of America [*Later, LCWR*]
CMSWA .... Conference of Major Superiors of Women's Religious Institutes of Australia
CMSWA .... Convention on the Conservation of Migratory Species of Wild Animals (ASF)
CMSX.......... Computer Management Sciences, Inc. [*NASDAQ symbol*] (SAG)
CMSX.......... Computer Mgmt Sciences [*NASDAQ symbol*] (TTSB)
CMSYS .... Combat Mobility System [*Army*] (RDA)
CMT............ Cadmium Mercury Telluride [*Solid state chemistry*]
CMT............ California Mastitis Test
CMT............ Caminito
CMT............ Cancer Multistep Therapy [*Medicine*] (DMAA)
CMT............ Cannon Maintenance Trainer
CMT............ Card Module Tester

CMT............ Casement Aviation [*ICAO designator*] (FAAC)
CMT............ Cash Management Trust (ADA)
CMT............ Cassette Magnetic Tape
CMT............ Cataloging Management Team [*American Library Association*]
CMT............ Catechol-O-Methyltransferase [*An enzyme*] (MAE)
CMT............ Cellular Mobile Telephone
CMT............ Cement [*Classified advertising*] (ADA)
CMT............ Center for Management Technology [*Commercial firm*] (EA)
CMT............ Center for the Ministry of Teaching (EA)
CMT............ Centroid-Moment Tensor [*Seismology*]
CMT............ Ceramic Mosaic Tile [*Technical drawings*]
CMT............ Certified Market Technician (DD)
CMT............ Certified Medical Transcriptionist
CMT............ Cervical Motion Tenderness [*Medicine*] (DAVI)
CM/T............ Change Management/Tracking [*IBM Corp.*]
CMT............ Charcot-Marie-Tooth [*Atrophy*] [*Medicine*]
CMT............ Chemical Machining Template (MCD)
CMT............ Chief Medical Technician [*British military*] (DMA)
CMT............ Child Migrants Trust
CMT............ Choline Magnesium Trisalicylate [*Pharmacy*]
CMT............ Church Music Trust [*British*] (BI)
CMT............ Circuit Master Tape [*Computer science*] (IAA)
CMT............ Circus Movement Tachycardia [*Medicine*] (DMAA)
CMT............ Class Music Teaching (AIE)
CMT............ CMAC Investment [*NYSE symbol*] (TTSB)
CMT............ CMAC Investment Corp. [*NYSE symbol*] (SPSG)
CMT............ Code Matching Technique
CMT............ College of San Mateo Library, San Mateo, CA [*OCLC symbol*] (OCLC)
CMT............ Combat Mission Trainer [*Air Force*]
CMT............ Combined Military Transportation [*British*]
CMT............ Command Military Training
CMT............ Comment (AABC)
CMT............ Commissary Technician, Medical
CMT............ Commit (MSA)
CMT............ Committee on Marine Technology [*British*]
CMT............ Common Maintenance Trainer (MCD)
CMT............ Common Market Travel Association (EAIO)
CMT............ Community Management Training Scheme [*Australia*]
CMT............ Company Maintenance Team (INF)
cmt............ Compositor [*MARC relator code*] [*Library of Congress*] (LCCP)
CMT............ Computer-Managed Training (MHDI)
CMT............ Computer-Mediated Teleconferencing (MHDB)
CMT............ Computer Memory Tester
CMT............ Computer Micrographics Technology [*An association Defunct*] (EA)
CMT............ Comterm, Inc. [*Toronto Stock Exchange symbol*]
CMT............ Concept Memory Test (EDAC)
CMT............ Concora Medium Test
CMT............ Confederation Mondiale du Travail [*World Confederation of Labour - WCL*] [*Brussels, Belgium*] (EAIO)
CMT............ Configuration Management Tool (SSD)
CMT............ Constant Maturity Treasury (TDOB)
CMT............ Construction Materials Testing (MHDI)
CMT............ Contract Maintenance Team (MCD)
CMT............ Contractor Maintenance Trainer [*Military*]
CMT............ Convection Microthermal Oven
CMT............ Conversational Mode Terminal [*Friden, Inc.*] (IEEE)
CMT............ Core Measurement Table (IAA)
CMT............ Core Melt Technology [*Metal casting*]
CMT............ Corporate Minimum Tax
CMT............ Corrected Mean Temperature
CMT............ Corrugating Medium Test [*For containerboard*]
CMT............ Council on Medical Television [*Later, HESCA*] (EA)
CMT............ Country Music Television [*Cable-television system*] (WDMC)
CMT............ Coupled Mode Theory (PDAA)
CMT............ Course Monitoring Tire [*Tire testing*]
CMT............ Craig Mountain Railway [*AAR code*]
CMT............ Creative Management Technologies (AAGC)
CMT............ Crew Member Trainee (DNAB)
CMT............ Crisis Management Team [*Army*] (INF)
CMT............ Critical Military Target
CMT............ Current Medical Terminology
CMT1B........ Charcot-Marie Tooth 1B [*Medicine*]
CMTA............ Canadian Marine Transportation Administration
CMTA............ Canadian Massage Therapist Alliance [*Alliance Candienne de Massotherapeutes*] (AC)
CMTA............ Canadian Music Therapy Association
CMTA............ Chinese Musical and Theatrical Association (EA)
CMTA............ Constant Momentum Transfer Average (MCD)
CMTC............ Carbondale Mining Technology Center [*Department of Energy*] (GRD)
CMTC............ Citizens Military Training Corps (AABC)
CMTC............ Civilian Military Training Camp (DNAB)
CMTC............ Combat Maneuver Training Center (INF)
CMTC............ Combat Maneuver Training Command
CMTC............ Combat Maneuver Training Complex [*Hohenfels Training Area*] [*Germany*]
CMTC............ Combined [*Arms*] Maneuver Training Center [*Hohenfels, Germany*] [*Army*] (DOMA)
CMTC............ Combined Military Transportation Committee
CMTC............ Conscience and Military Tax Campaign - US (EA)
CMTC............ Coupled Monostable Trigger Circuit [*Electronics*] (OA)
CMTC............ Cutis Marmorata Telangiectatica Congenita [*Medicine*] (DMAA)
CMTC-IS ..... Combat Maneuver Training Center - Instrumentation System [*Army*]
CMT CONC... Cement or Concrete [*Freight*]

CMTCU	Cigarette Makers' and Tobacco Cutters' Union [*British*]
CMTCU	Communications Message Traffic Control Unit [*Air Force*] (AFM)
CMTD	Center for Market and Trade Development [*China*]
CMTD	Charcot-Marie-Tooth Disease [*Medicine*] (DMAA)
CMTD	Commited (ABBR)
CMTD	Countermeasures and Test Directorate [*Army*] (RDA)
CMTDA	Canadian Machine Tool Distributors' Association (AC)
CMTE	Committee
CMTG	Commiting (ABBR)
CMthL	University of California, Santa Cruz, Lick Observatory Library, Santa Cruz, CA [*Library symbol Library of Congress*] (LCLS)
CMTI	Celestial Moving Target Indicator
CMTI	Community Medical Transport, Inc. [*NASDAQ symbol*] (SAG)
CMTI	Community Med Trans [*NASDAQ symbol*] (TTSB)
CMTIW	Community Med Trans Wrrt [*NASDAQ symbol*] (TTSB)
CMTK	Com-Tech Communication Technologies, Inc. [*NASDAQ symbol*] (SAG)
CMTK	Com/Tech Commun Tech [*NASDAQ symbol*] (TTSB)
CMTL	Chemical Machining Template Line (MCD)
CMTL	Comtech Telecommunications Corp. [*NASDAQ symbol*] (NQ)
CMTM	Capsule Mechanical Training Model [*Aerospace*] (MCD)
CMTM	Communications and Telemetry
CMTMT	Commitment (ABBR)
CMTN	Cytoplasmic Microtubule Network [*Cytology*]
CMTO	College of Massage Therapists of Ontario (AC)
CMTOCM	Common Mode-to-Common Mode (IAA)
CMTODM	Common Mode-to-Differential Mode (IAA)
CMTOS	Cassette Magnetic Tape Operating System [*Computer science*] (PDAA)
CMTP	Canada Manpower Training Program
CMTP	Cometary-Mass-to-Planets [*Astronomy*]
CMTPF	Current Months Total Program Forecast (MCD)
CMTR	Chemtrak, Inc. [*NASDAQ symbol*] (SAG)
CMTRLR	Comptroller (ABBR)
CMTRY	Cemetery (ABBR)
CMTS	Canadian Machine Tool Show (ITD)
CMTS	Cellular Mobile Telephone Service
CMTS	Centroid Moment Tensor Solutions [*A publication*]
CMTS	Charcot-Marie-Tooth Syndrome [*Medicine*] (DMAA)
CMTS	Community Management Training Service [*Australia*]
CMTS	Computer Maintenance Test Set
CMTT	Joint Committee on Television Transmission
CMTTCW	Christian Mission to the Communist World [*Australia*]
CMTTEE	Committee
CMTU	Cartridge Magnetic Tape Unit
CMTV	Country Music Television [*Cable-television system*]
CMTX	Charcot-Marie-Tooth, X-Linked [*Medicine*] [*Syndrome*] (DMAA)
CMTY	Community
CmtyBn	Community Bankshares, Inc. [*Associated Press*] (SAG)
CmtyBS	Community Bank System, Inc. [*Associated Press*] (SAG)
CmtyBSC	Community Bankshares, Inc. [*Associated Press*] (SAG)
CmtyCr	Community Care Services, Inc. [*Associated Press*] (SAG)
CmtyF	Community Financial Group [*Associated Press*] (SAG)
CmtyFin	Community Financial Holding Corp. [*Associated Press*] (SAG)
CmtyFncl	Community Financial Corp. [*Associated Press*] (SAG)
CmtyMd T	Community Medical Transport, Inc. [*Associated Press*] (SAG)
CmtyTrBc	Community Trust Bancorp, Inc. [*Associated Press*] (SAG)
CMU	Canadian Maritime Union (BARN)
CMU	Canadian Mineworkers Union
CMU	Carnegie-Mellon University [*Pittsburgh, PA*]
CMU	Central Michigan University [*Mount Pleasant*]
CMU	Ceylon Mercantile Union [*Obsolete*]
CMU	Cheyenne Mountain Upgrade
CMU	Chlorophenyldimethylurea [*Herbicide*]
CMU	Church Missionary Union [*British*]
CMU	Colliery Mazdoor Union [*India*]
CMU	Colonial Municipal Income Trust [*NYSE symbol*] (SPSG)
CMU	Colonial Muni Inc. Tr [*NYSE symbol*] (TTSB)
CMU	Comet Industries [*Vancouver Stock Exchange symbol*]
CMU	Communications Management Unit [*Aviation*]
CMU	Compatibility Mock-Up (KSC)
CMU	Complex Motor Unit [*Medicine*] (HGAA)
CMU	Computer Memory Unit
CMU	Concrete Masonry Unit [*Technical drawings*]
CMU	Control Maintenance Unit
CMU	Controls Mock-Up
CMU	Core Memory Unit (MCD)
CMU	Customer Memory Update [*Telecommunications*]
CMU	Kundiawa [*Papua New Guinea*] [*Airport symbol*] (OAG)
CMUA	Continuous Motor Unit Activity [*Medicine*] (DMAA)
CMUCZ	Committee on Multiple Use of the Coastal Zone [*National Council on Marine Resources and Engineering Development*] (GFGA)
CMU-DA	Carnegie-Mellon University-Design Automation (MCD)
CMUG	Christian Macintosh Users Group (EA)
CMUL	Cumulus (ABBR)
CMULA	Cumulate (ABBR)
CMULAD	Cumulated (ABBR)
CMULAG	Cumulating (ABBR)
CMULAN	Cumulation (ABBR)
CMULAV	Cumulative (ABBR)
CMULAVY	Cumulatively (ABBR)
CMULNBMS...	Cumulonimbus (ABBR)
CMULS	Cumulus (ABBR)
CMULU	Cumulus (ABBR)
CMUN	Commune (ABBR)

CMUNC	Communicate (ABBR)
CMUNCB	Communicable (ABBR)
CMUNCBNS...	Communicableness (ABBR)
CMUNCBT	Communicability (ABBR)
CMUNCBY	Communicably (ABBR)
CMUNCD	Communicated (ABBR)
CMUNCG	Communicating (ABBR)
CMUNCN	Communication (ABBR)
CMUNCNT	Communicant (ABBR)
CMUNCV	Communicative (ABBR)
CMUNCVY ...	Communicatively (ABBR)
CMUNCY	Communicatory (ABBR)
CMUND	Communed (ABBR)
CMUNG	Communing (ABBR)
CMUNG	Communique (ABBR)
CMUNN	Communion (ABBR)
CMUNSM	Communism (ABBR)
CMUNST	Communist (ABBR)
CMUNSTC	Communistic (ABBR)
CMUNT	Community (ABBR)
CMUNZ	Communize (ABBR)
CMUNZD	Communized (ABBR)
CMUNZG	Communizing (ABBR)
CMUNZN	Communization (ABBR)
CMUP	Clutter Map Update [*Military*]
CMUS	Censo de Museos de Espana [*Database*] [*Ministerio de Cultura*] [*Spanish*] [*Information service or system*] (CRD)
CMUS	Chief Musician [*Navy rating Obsolete*]
CMUS	Council of Masajid of United States (EA)
CMUT	Commute (ABBR)
CMUTA	Commutate (ABBR)
CMUTAB	Commutable (ABBR)
CMUTABT	Commutability (ABBR)
CMUTAD	Commutated (ABBR)
CMUTAG	Commutating (ABBR)
CMUTAR	Commutator (ABBR)
CMUTAV	Commutative (ABBR)
CMUTD	Commuted (ABBR)
CMUTG	Commuting (ABBR)
CMUTR	Commuter (ABBR)
CMU/WA	Committee on Man's Underwater Activities (EA)
CMUX	Converter Multiplexer (CAAL)
CMV	Cayo Mambi [*Cuba*] [*Airport symbol*] (AD)
CMV	Combat Mobility Vehicle [*Army*] (RDA)
CMV	Commercial Motor Vehicle (ADA)
CMV	Common Mode Voltage
CMV	Congenital Cytomegalovirus [*Medicine*]
CMV	Contact-Making Voltmeter
CMV	Continuous Mechanical Ventilation [*Medicine*] (DAVI)
CMV	Controlled Mechanical Ventilation
CMV	Controlled Multivibrator
CMV	Conventional Mechanical Ventilation
CMV	Cool Mist Vaporizer [*Medicine*] (DMAA)
CMV	Council of the Museum of Victoria [*Australia*]
CMV	Cucumber Mosaic Virus
CMV	Current Market Value [*Business term*] (ADA)
CMV	Cytomegalovirus [*A virus*]
CMV	Cytomegalovirus Infection
CMv	Mountain View Public Library, Mountain View, CA [*Library symbol Library of Congress*] (LCLS)
CMVC	Configuration Management Version Control [*Computer science*] (PCM)
cmvd	Mekhitarist Fathers (TOCD)
CMVd	Mekhitarist Order of Vienna [*Roman Catholic men's religious order*]
CMVE	Committee on Motor Vehicle Emissions [*National Academy of Sciences*]
CMVIG	Cytomegalovirus Immune Globulin [*Biochemistry*]
CMV-IGIV	Cytomegalovirus Immune Globulin Intravenous [*Immunology*]
CMVIO	Communications Security Material Van-Issuing Office [*Military*] (NVT)
CMVM	Contact-Making Voltmeter
CMVR	Common Mode Voltage Range
CMVS	Cavalry Mobile Veterinary Section [*British military*] (DMA)
CMVS	Contract Motor Vehicle Service
CMvS	Sylvania Electronics Systems, Inc., Mountain View, CA [*Library symbol Library of Congress*] (LCLS)
CMVSA	Commercial Motor Vehicle Safety Act [*1986*]
CMvSJ	Saint Joseph's College, Mountain View, CA [*Library symbol Library of Congress*] (LCLS)
CMVSS	Canadian Motor Vehicle Safety Standard
CMVSS	Canadian Motor Vehicle Safety Standard
CMVT	Comverse Technology [*NASDAQ symbol*] (TTSB)
CMVT	Comverse Technology, Inc. [*NASDAQ symbol*] (NQ)
CMVTSS	Canadian Motor Vehicle Tyre Safety Standard (PDAA)
CMW	Camaguey [*Cuba*] [*Airport symbol*] (OAG)
CMW	Campus Ministry Women (EA)
CMW	Canadian Marconi [*AMEX symbol*] (TTSB)
CMW	Canadian Marconi Co. [*AMEX symbol Toronto Stock Exchange symbol*] (SPSG)
CMW	Circular Magnetic Wave
CMW	Coal-Methanol-Water [*Fuel*]
CMW	Cold Molecular Weld
CMWA	Chamber of Mines of Western Australia
CmwAl	Commonwealth Aluminum Corp. [*Associated Press*] (SAG)
CMWB	Coalition of Minority Women in Business [*Washington, DC*] (EA)
CMWPT........	Coal Mine Workers' Pension Tribunal [*Victoria*] [*Australia*]

CMX..........	Cable Multiplexer [*Electronics*] (IAA)
CMX..........	Canamax Resources, Inc. [*Toronto Stock Exchange symbol*]
CMX..........	Cefmenoxime (DMAA)
CMX..........	Character Multiplexer [*Telecommunications*]
CMX..........	Chick Muscle Extract [*Embryology*]
CMX..........	CMI Corp. [*NYSE symbol*] (SAG)
CMX..........	CMI Corp. CI'A' [*NYSE symbol*] (TTSB)
CMX..........	Compania Mexicana de Taxis Aereos SA [*Mexico ICAO designator*] (FAAC)
CMX..........	Concentration Module Extension [*Telecommunications*] (TEL)
CMX..........	Hancock [*Michigan*] [*Airport symbol*] (OAG)
CMX..........	Hancock-Houghton [*Michigan*] [*Airport symbol*] (AD)
CMX..........	Hancock, MI [*Location identifier FAA*] (FAAL)
CM-XMP	Cloud Model with Explicit Microphysics [*Marine science*] (OSRA)
CM-XMP	Cloud Model with Explicit Microphysics (USDC)
CMY..........	Cape Mounted Yeomanry [*British military*] (DMA)
CMY..........	Cape Smyth Air [*ICAO designator*] (FAAC)
CMY..........	Civilian Man-Years [*Military*] (AABC)
CMY..........	Cockpit Motor Yacht
CMY..........	Commonwealth Minerals [*Vancouver Stock Exchange symbol*]
CMY..........	Community Psych Ctrs [*NYSE symbol*] (TTSB)
CMY..........	Community Psychiatric Centers [*NYSE symbol*] (SPSG)
CMY..........	Cyan, Magenta, and Yellow [*Color model*] (BYTE)
CMY..........	Sparta, WI [*Location identifier FAA*] (FAAL)
CmylBc......	Community Investors Bancorp, Inc. [*Associated Press*] (SAG)
CMYK........	Cyan, Magenta, Yellow, Black [*Color model*] (PCM)
CMZ..........	Central Molecular Zone [*Galactic science*]
CMZ..........	Chimera Resources Ltd. [*Vancouver Stock Exchange symbol*]
CMZ..........	Cincinnati Milacron [*NYSE symbol*] (TTSB)
CMZ..........	Cincinnati Milacron, Inc. [*NYSE symbol*] (SPSG)
CMZS........	Corresponding Member of the Zoological Society [*British*]
CN............	Absolute Coefficient of Yawing Moments
CN............	Calcineurin [*Biochemistry*]
CN............	Call Number [*Online database field identifier*]
CN............	Calton, Inc. [*AMEX symbol*] (SPSG)
CN............	Can
cn............	Canada [*MARC country of publication code Library of Congress*] (LCCP)
CN............	Canadian National Railways [*AAR code*]
CN............	Canet Nordenfelt Gun
CN............	Canister
CN............	Cannon Minerals Ltd. [*Vancouver Stock Exchange symbol*]
CN............	Canon
cn............	Carbonate Nodule [*Archeology*]
C/N..........	Carbon to Nitrogen Ratio
CN............	Careless and Negligent Driving [*Traffic offense charge*]
C/N..........	Carrier-to-Noise [*Ratio*]
C/N..........	Carrier-to-Noise Ratio [*Telecommunications*] (OSI)
CN............	Cascade Nozzle [*Aviation*] (OA)
CN............	Case of Need
CN............	Caudate Nucleus [*Anatomy*]
CN............	Cavity Nester [*Ornithology*]
CN............	Cellulose Nitrate [*Organic chemistry*]
CN............	Central Airlines, Inc.
CN............	Certified Nutritionist [*Medicine*]
CN............	Cetane Number [*Fuel technology*]
CMX..........	Change Notice
CN............	Charge Nurse [*Medicine*]
CN............	Check Not OK [*Telecommunications*] (TEL)
CN............	CHExchange Network [*An association*] (EA)
CN............	Child Nutrition
CN............	Children of the Night (EA)
CN............	China [*ANSI two-letter standard code*] (CNC)
CN............	Chinese Navy (CINC)
CN............	Chlorinated Naphthalene [*Organic chemistry*]
CN............	Chloroacetophenone [*Also, CAP*] [*Tear gas Army symbol*] (AAG)
C/N..........	Chloroplasts to Nuclei per Cell [*Botany*]
Cn............	Cinders [*Quality of the bottom*] [*Nautical charts*]
CN............	Circular Note [*Business term*]
CN............	Circulating Nurse (HGAA)
CN............	Citation Number [*Database terminology*] (NITA)
CN............	Clinical Nursing
CN............	Clipped and Nitrogen Added [*Ecology*]
CN............	Cneius (ABBR)
CN............	Coalicion Nacionalista [*Spain*] [*Political party*] (ECED)
CN............	Cochlear Nuclei [*Brain anatomy*]
CN............	Code Napoleon [*Napoleonic Code*] [*French Legal term*]
CN............	Coin Trunk [*Telecommunications*] (TEL)
CN............	Colin Energy Corp. [*Toronto Stock Exchange symbol*]
CN............	Collective Negotiations
CN............	Combined Nomenclature [*EC*] (ECED)
CN............	Common Name (ACRL)
CN............	Commonwealth Nation
CN............	Communes Network [*British*] (EAIO)
CN............	Communications Network
CN............	Commutated Network (IAA)
CN............	Company Name [*Database terminology*] (NITA)
CN............	Compass North
CN............	Compensators [*JETDS nomenclature*] [*Military*] (CET)
CN............	Concert Name [*Database terminology*] (NITA)
CN............	Condensation Nuclei
CN............	Condensation Nucleus [*Marine science*] (OSRA)
CN............	Congenital Nystagmus [*Ophthalmology*] (AAMN)
C-N..........	Conico Norteno [*Race of maize*]
CN............	Conjectanea Neotestamentica [*A publication*] (BJA)

CN............	Conservative Nationalist Party [*British*]
CN............	Conservative Network (EA)
CN............	Consignment Note [*Shipping*]
CN............	Consolidated [*Accounting*]
CN............	Consols [*Consolidateds*]
CN............	Constructionman [*Nonrated enlisted man*] [*Navy*]
C/N..........	Construction Number (LAIN)
CN............	Consultants' Network (EA)
CN............	Contaminated Normal [*Statistics*]
CN............	Contemporary Newsmakers [*Later, Newsmakers*] [*A publication*]
CN............	Continuous Noise
CN............	Contract/Grant Number [*Database terminology*] (NITA)
CN............	Contract Note [*Banking*]
CN............	Contract Number [*Computer science*]
CN............	Control Number
CN............	Convertible [*Rate*] [*Value of the English pound*]
CN............	Convertible Note
CN............	Coordination Number [*Chemistry*]
CN............	Corporate Source Name [*Database terminology*] (NITA)
CN............	Correction Notice (MCD)
CN............	Cosine
CN............	Counternarcotics [*Military*] (DOMA)
CN............	Country Name [*Database terminology*] (NITA)
CN............	Country National Party [*Political party Australia*]
CN............	Cover Note [*Insurance*]
CN............	Cranial Nerve [*Anatomy*]
CN............	Cras Nocte [*Tomorrow Night*] [*Pharmacy*]
CN............	Credit Note [*Business term*]
CN............	Cuban Navy
CN............	Cumulonimbus [*Cloud*] [*Meteorology*]
CN............	Cuneate Nucleus [*Neuroanatomy*]
CN............	Cupro Nickel
Cn............	Cyanide [*Organic chemistry*] (DAVI)
CN............	Cyanide Anion [*Organic chemistry*] (DAVI)
CN............	Cyanogen [*Toxic compound*] (AAMN)
CN............	Cyanogen Radical [*Organic chemistry*] (DAVI)
CN............	Cyanonaphthalene [*Organic chemistry*]
CN............	Morocco [*International civil aircraft marking*] (ODBW)
CN............	Napa City-County Library, Napa, CA [*Library symbol Library of Congress*] (LCLS)
CN............	Parke, Davis & Co. [*Research code symbol*]
CN............	Training and Riot Control Agent
CN............	Tropic Air [*ICAO designator*] (AD)
CN4..........	N4 Transportation Systems of Canada Ltd. [*Information service or system*] (IID)
CNA	Cadets Norfolk Artillery [*British military*] (DMA)
CNA	Calcium Nutrient Agar [*Medicine*] (DMAA)
CNA	California Nurses Association (SRA)
CNA	Camp New Amsterdam [*Netherlands*]
CNA	Canadian Naturopathic Association [*Association Canadienne de Naturopathie*] (AC)
CNA	Canadian Northwest Atlantic Area
CNA	Canadian Nuclear Association
CNA	Canadian Numismatic Association [*Association Canadienne de Numismatique*] (AC)
CNA	Canadian Nurses' Association [*See also AIC*]
CNA	Cananea [*Mexico*] [*Airport symbol*] (AD)
CNA	Capital Needs Analysis [*Finance*]
CNA	Centennial [*Spain ICAO designator*] (FAAC)
CNA	Center for Natural Areas (EA)
CNA	Center for Naval Analyses [*Alexandria, VA*] [*Navy*]
CNA	Center for Naval Analysis [*Marine science*] (OSRA)
CNA	Center for Numerical Analysis [*University of Texas at Austin*] [*Research center*] (RCD)
CNA	Central Neuropsychiatric Association (EA)
CNA	Central News Agency (DGA)
CNA	Central Nonprofit Agency (AAGC)
C/NA	Certification of Nonavailability [*DoD*]
CNA	Certified Nurse's Aide
Cna..........	Cessna [*Airplane code*]
CNA	Chart Not Available [*Medicine*] (DAVI)
CNA	Chemicals Notation Association [*British*]
CNA	Chevrolet Nomad Association (EA)
CNA	Chief Naval Adviser [*British*]
CNA	Chief of Naval Air
CNA	Chin National Army [*Myanmar*] [*Political party*] (EY)
CNA	Chlornaltrexamine [*Narcotic antagonist*] [*Pharmacochemistry*]
CNA	Chloronitroaniline [*Organic chemistry*]
CNA	Closed Numbering Area [*Telecommunications*]
CNA	CNA Financial [*NYSE symbol*] (TTSB)
CNA	CNA Financial Corp. [*NYSE symbol*] (SPSG)
CNA	Coalition of National Agreement [*Croatia*] [*Political party*]
CNA	Code Not Allocated
CNA	Colistin [*or Colimycin*] - Nalidixic Acid [*Antibacterial combination*] [*Clinical chemistry*]
CNA	Colorado Nursery Association (SRA)
CNA	Colorado Nurses Association (SRA)
CNA	Combined New Australia Party [*Political party*]
CNA	Comite National d'Action sur la Situation de la Femme du Canada [*National Action Committee on the Status of Women*] [*Canada*]
CNA	Commander's Narrative Analysis [*Military*]
CNA	Common Network Architecture (IAA)
CNA	Common Nozzle Assembly (MCD)
CNA	Communications Network Architects, Inc. [*Washington, DC Telecommunications service*] (TSSD)

CNA	Communications Network Architecture
CNA	Concerned Neighbors in Action (EA)
CNA	Connecticut Nurserymen's Association (SRA)
CNA	Connecticut Nurses Association (SRA)
CNA	Consolidated Cima Resources [Vancouver Stock Exchange symbol]
CNA	Continental National America [Insurance group]
CNA	Coordinator for Narcotics Affairs [Department of State]
CNA	Copper Nickel Alloy (MSA)
CNA	Cosmic Noise Absorption
CNA	Council on Nutritional Anthropology (EA)
CNA	Cyanide Amenable to Chlorination (EG)
CNA	Cyprus News Agency
CNA	Fairbanks, AK [Location identifier FAA] (FAAL)
CNa	National City Public Library, National City, CA [Library symbol Library of Congress] (LCLS)
CNAA	Chemical Neutron Activation Analysis
CNAA	Council for National Academic Awards [British]
CNAADTRA...	Chief of Naval Air Advanced Training [Also, CNAVANTRA] [Formerly, CNAOPTRA, CNAOT]
CNAAT	Chief, Naval Advanced Air Training
CNAB	Commander, Naval Air Bases
CNABATRA...	Chief of Naval Air Basic Training
CNABT	Chief, Naval Air Basic Training
CNABTRA.....	Chief, Naval Air Basic Training (DNAB)
CNAC	China National Aviation Corps
CNAD	Committee for National Arbor Day (EA)
CNAD	Conference of National Armaments Directors [NATO]
CNAF	Canadian Native Arts Foundation (AC)
CNAF	Chinese Nationalist Air Force
CNAF	Chronic Nonvalvular Atrial Fibrillation [Medicine] (DMAA)
CNAF	Combined Name and Address File [IRS]
CNA Fn	CNA Financial Corp. [Associated Press] (SAG)
CNAG	Chief [or Commander], Naval Advisory Group (DNAB)
CNAI	CNA Income Shares, Inc. [Associated Press] (SAG)
CNAI	Colorado Natural Areas Inventory [Colorado State Department of Natural Resources] [Denver] [Information service or system] (IID)
CNAINTERMTRA...	Chief of Naval Air Intermediate Training [Later, CNABATRA]
CNAIP	Council for Native American Indian Progress (EA)
CNAIT	Chief of Naval Air Intermediate Training [Later, CNABATRA]
CNAL	Chief of Naval Aviation Logistics (MCD)
CNAL	Commander, Naval Air Force, Atlantic
CNAM	Canadian Corporate Names [Canada Systems Group] [Information service or system] (IID)
CNAMB	Catholic Negro-American Mission Board (EA)
CNAN	Compagnie Nationale Algerienne de Navigation [Algerian National Shipping Company] (AF)
CNAOPTRA...	Chief of Naval Air Operational Training [Later, CNAADTRA, CNAVANTRA]
CNAOT	Chief of Naval Air Operational Training [Later, CNAADTRA, CNAVANTRA]
CNAP	Chief of Naval Air Pacific (MCD)
CNAP	Colorado Natural Areas Program [Colorado State Department of Natural Resources] [Information service or system] (IID)
CNAP	Combined New Australia Party [Political party]
CNAPRIMTRA...	Chief of Naval Air Primary Training [Later, CNARFSTRA]
CNAPS	Connected Network of Adaptive Processors System
CNAPT	Chief of Naval Air Primary Training [Later, CNARFSTRA]
CNAR	Commander, Naval Air Reserve (DNAB)
CNARESTRA...	Chief of Naval Air Reserve Training
CNARF	Commander, Naval Air Reserve Force (DNAB)
CNARFSTRA...	Chief of Naval Air Primary Training
CNAS	Chemical Nomenclature Advisory Service (PDAA)
CNAS	Chief of Naval Air Services [British]
CNAS	Civil Navigation Aids System
CNASA	Council of North Atlantic Shipping Associations [Also, CONASA]
CNASP	Chairman's Net Assesment of Strategic Planning (DOMA)
CNAT	Chief of Naval Air Training
CN-ATC	Cyanide Amenable to Chlorination
CNATE	Chief of Naval Airships Training and Experimentation
CNATECHTRA...	Chief of Naval Air Technical Training
CNATEC (LTA)...	Commander, Naval Air Technical Training (Lighter Than Air)
CNATRA	Chief of Naval Air Training
CNATRA	Chief of Naval Training (AAGC)
CNATT	Chief of Naval Air Technical Training
CNAVANTRA...	Chief of Naval Air Advanced Training [Also, CNAADTRA]
CNAVOP.......	Chief of Naval Operations [Also, CNO]
CNAVRES.....	Commander, Naval Reserves (NVT)
CNAVSTA.....	Charleston Naval Station [South Carolina]
CNB	Air Columbus SA [Portugal ICAO designator] (FAAC)
CNB	Canadian Naval Board
CNB	CNB Bancshares, Inc. [Associated Press] (SAG)
CNB	Colonial BancGroup [NYSE symbol] (TTSB)
CNB	Colonial Bankgroup [NYSE symbol] (SAG)
CNB	Commander, Naval Base
CNB	Coonamble [Australia Airport symbol] (OAG)
CNB	Coordinador Nacional de Bases [National Coordination of Bases] [Colorado] (PD)
CNB	Cutting Needle Biopsy [Medicine]
CNB	Cyclic-Nucleotide-Binding [Neurobiology]
CNb	Newport Beach Public Library, Newport Beach, CA [Library symbol Library of Congress] (LCLS)
CNBA	Chester Bancorp, Inc. [NASDAQ symbol] (SAG)
CNbAF	Aeronutronic Ford Corp., Newport Beach, CA [Library symbol Library of Congress] (LCLS)

CNB Bcsh....	CNB Bancshares, Inc. [Associated Press] (SAG)
CNBC	Center Bancorp, Inc. [NASDAQ symbol] (SAG)
CNBC	Congress of National Black Churches (EA)
CNBC	Consumer News and Business Channel [A cable division of NBC]
CNBD	Condensed Negative Binomial Distribution [Statistics]
CNBE	CNB Bancshares, Inc. [NASDAQ symbol] (NQ)
CNBF	CNB Financial Corp. [New York] [NASDAQ symbol] (SAG)
CNBF	CNB Financial(NY) [NASDAQ symbol] (TTSB)
CNB Fn	CNB Financial Corp NY [Associated Press] (SAG)
CNBI	CN Biosciences, Inc. [NASDAQ symbol] (SAG)
CN Biosc.....	CN Biosciences, Inc. [Associated Press] (SAG)
CNBK	Century BanCorp, Inc. [NASDAQ symbol] (NQ)
CNBKA	Century Bancorp(MA) [NASDAQ symbol] (TTSB)
CNBL	Citi-Bancshares [NASDAQ symbol] (TTSB)
CNBL	Citi Bancshares, Inc. [NASDAQ symbol] (SAG)
CNBLA	Commander, Naval Base, Los Angeles
CNbr	Chloroacetophenone in Chloroform (PDAA)
CNbr	Cyanogen Bromide (PDAA)
CNB-TV	Center for Non-Broadcast Television [Defunct] (EA)
CNB-TV	Custom Network Broadcasting, Inc. (TSSD)
CNC	Canadian Nut Council [Conseil Canadien des Noix] (AC)
Cnc	Cancer [Constellation]
CNC	Canuck Resources, Inc. [Toronto Stock Exchange symbol]
CNC	Captive Nations Committee (EA)
CNC	Carson-Newman College [Tennessee]
CNC	Center for New Creation (EA)
CNC	Center for Nonviolent Communication (EA)
CNC	Central Navigation Computer
CNC	Central State University, Wilberforce, OH [OCLC symbol] (OCLC)
CNC	Change Notice Card (AFIT)
CNC	Chariton, IA [Location identifier FAA] (FAAL)
CNC	Chief Naval Censor [Navy rating Obsolete]
CNC	Chief of Naval Communications [Formerly, DNC]
CNC	Clear, No Creamy Layer [Biochemistry] (DAVI)
CNC	Communications Network Controller (IAA)
CNC	Community Nursing Center (DMAA)
CNC	Computerized Numerical Control [Computer science]
CNC	Computer Numerical Control [Computer science]
CNC	Concord - Diablo Valley College [California] [Seismograph station code, US Geological Survey Closed] (SEIS)
CNC	Concordia University Library [UTLAS symbol]
CNC	Condensation Nuclei Counter
CNC	Confederate National Congress (EA)
CNC	Confederation Nationale de la Construction [Civil Engineering, Road and Building Contractors, and Auxiliary Trades Confederation] [Brussels, Belgium] (EY)
CNC	Configurable Network Computing [Software] [JD Edwards]
CNC	Configurable Network Computing [J.D. Edwards]
CNC	Congreso Nacional de Canarias [Spain Political party] (EY)
CNC	Conseco, Inc. [NYSE symbol] (SPSG)
CNC	Consecutive Number Control (IAA)
CNC	Corporacion Aereo Cencor SA de CV [Mexico ICAO designator] (FAAC)
CNC	Croatian National Congress (EA)
CNC	Napa College, Napa, CA [Library symbol Library of Congress] (LCLS)
CNc	Nevada City Free Public Library, Nevada City, CA [Library symbol Library of Congress] (LCLS)
CNCA	Council for National Cooperation in Aquatics (EA)
CNCA	Czechoslovak National Council of America (EA)
CNCAB	Caisse Nationale de Credit Agricole du Burkina (EY)
CnCap	ConAgra Capital [Associated Press] (SAG)
CNCbl	Cyanocobalamin [Biochemistry]
CNCC	Customer Network Control Center [Telecommunications] (TEL)
CNCC	Customer Networks Control Centre [Telecommunications]
CNCDG	Concluding (ABBR)
CNCE	Command NODAL [Network-Oriented Data Acquisition Language] Control Element
CNCE	Communications NODAL [Network-Oriented Data Acquisition Language] Control Element
CNCE	Council for Noncollegiate Continuing Education (EA)
CNCED	Concede (ABBR)
CNCED	Concentrated (ABBR)
CNCEDD.......	Conceded (ABBR)
CNCEDDY	Concededly (ABBR)
CNCEDG.......	Conceding (ABBR)
CNCEDR.......	Conceder (ABBR)
CncEFS	Concord EFS, Inc. [Associated Press] (SAG)
CNCEG	Concentrating (ABBR)
CNCEL	Conceal (ABBR)
CNCELB	Concealable (ABBR)
CNCELD	Concealed (ABBR)
CNCELG	Concealing (ABBR)
CNCELR	Concealer (ABBR)
CNCELT........	Concealment (ABBR)
CNCEN	Concentrate (ABBR)
CNCENC........	Concentric (ABBR)
CNCENCT....	Concentricity (ABBR)
CNCENCY....	Concentrically (ABBR)
CNCENN........	Concentration (ABBR)
CNCENR........	Concentrator (ABBR)
CNCENV........	Concentrative (ABBR)
CNCENVY....	Concentratively (ABBR)
CNCET	Conceit (ABBR)
CNCETD	Conceited (ABBR)

CNCETDY...... Conceitedly (ABBR)
CNCETG....... Conceiting (ABBR)
CN-CEU....... Council for Noncollegiate Continuing Education Units
CNCEV........ Conceive (ABBR)
CNCEVB....... Conceivable (ABBR)
CNCEVBT...... Conceivability (ABBR)
CNCEVBY..... Conceivably (ABBR)
CNCEVD....... Conceived (ABBR)
CNCEVG....... Conceiving (ABBR)
CNCEVR....... Conceiver (ABBR)
CNCHi........ Napa County Historical Society, Research Library, Napa, CA [*Library symbol*] [*Library of Congress*] (LCLS)
CNC/IAPS..... Canadian National Committee for the International Association on the Properties of Steam (PDAA)
CNC/IAWPRC... Canadian National Committee of the International Committee on Water Pollution Research and Control (EAIO)
CNCIAWPRC... Chilean National Committee of the International Association on Water Pollution Research and Control (EAIO)
CNCIAWPRC... Cyprus National Committee of the International Association on Water Pollution Research and Control (EAIO)
CNCIAWPRC... Czechoslovak National Committee of the International Association on Water Pollution Research and Control (EAIO)
CNC-IFAC..... Canadian National Committee for the International Federation of Automatic Control (EAIO)
CnCigar....... Consolidated Cigar Holdings, Inc. [*Associated Press*] (SAG)
CNC-IPS...... Canadian National Committee - International Peat Society
CNCIS........ Concise (ABBR)
CNCISN....... Concision (ABBR)
CNCISY....... Concisely (ABBR)
CNCL........ Cancel [*Computer science*] (BARN)
CNCL........ Characters in 19th Century Literature [*A publication*]
CNCL........ Concealed (MSA)
CNCL........ Council
CNCL........ Council
CNCLA........ Conciliate (ABBR)
CNCLAB...... Conciliable (ABBR)
CNCLAD...... Conciliated (ABBR)
CNCLAG...... Conciliating (ABBR)
CNCLAN...... Cancellation (ABBR)
CNCLAN...... Conciliation (ABBR)
CNCLAR...... Conciliator (ABBR)
CNCLARTRY... Conciliatory (ABBR)
CNCLARY..... Conciliatory (ABBR)
CNCLAV...... Conclave (ABBR)
CNCLB....... Cancelable (ABBR)
CNCLD........ Canceled (ABBR)
CNCLD........ Conclude (ABBR)
CNCLG........ Canceling (ABBR)
CNCLN....... Cancellation (ABBR)
CNCLNG...... Counciling
CNCLR........ Canceler (ABBR)
CNCLR........ Councillor
CNCLR........ Councilor (ABBR)
CNCLSN...... Conclusion (ABBR)
CNCLSV...... Conclusive (ABBR)
CNCLU........ Conclude (ABBR)
CNCLUD...... Concluded (ABBR)
CNCLUG...... Concluding (ABBR)
CNCLUN...... Conclusion (ABBR)
CNCLUR...... Concluder (ABBR)
CNCLUV...... Conclusive (ABBR)
CNCLUVY..... Conclusively (ABBR)
CNCLV........ Conclave (ABBR)
CNCM........ Council of Nature Conservation Ministers [*Australia*]
CNCMH....... Canadian National Committee for Mental Hygiene (BARN)
CN/CMS...... Counternarcotics Command Management System [*Army*] (RDA)
CN/CMS...... Counternarcotics Command Management System [*Army*] (RDA)
CNCMTNT..... Concomitant (ABBR)
CNCNSW...... Captive Nations' Council of New South Wales [*Australia*]
CNCNT........ Concurrently (FAAC)
CNCNTRA..... Concentrate (ABBR)
CNCNTRAG... Concentrating (ABBR)
CNCNTRC..... Concentric (ABBR)
CNCNTRN..... Concentration (ABBR)
CNCOC........ Concoct (ABBR)
CNCOCD...... Concocted (ABBR)
CNCOCG..... Concocting (ABBR)
CNCOCN..... Concoction (ABBR)
CNCOCR..... Concoctor (ABBR)
CNCOCV..... Concoctive (ABBR)
CNCOE........ California-Nevada Conference of Operating Engineers (SRA)
CNCOM....... Concomitance (ABBR)
CNCOMT..... Concomitant (ABBR)
CN Conf....... Cameron and Norwood's North Carolina Conference Reports [*A publication*] (DLA)
CNCOR........ Concourse (ABBR)
CNCP........ Canadian National-Canadian Pacific Railway
CNCP........ Center for New Corporate Priorities [*Defunct*] (EA)
CNCP........ Communications Network Control Processor (IAA)
CNCP........ Conceptronic, Inc. [*NASDAQ symbol*] (SAG)
CNCPN....... Conception (ABBR)
CNCPrD...... Conseco Inc. Series'D'Cv Pfd [*NYSE symbol*] (TTSB)
CNCPrE...... Conseco Inc. 7%'PRIDES' [*NYSE symbol*] (TTSB)
CN/CPT....... Canadian National/Canadian Pacific Telecommunications (NITA)
CNCPT........ Concept (ABBR)

CNCPT........ Concept
CNCPTL....... Conceptual (ABBR)
CNCPTLY..... Conceptually (ABBR)
CNCPTLZ..... Conceptualize (ABBR)
CNCPTLZD... Conceptualized (ABBR)
CNCPTLZG... Conceptualizing (ABBR)
CNCPTSM.... Conceptualism (ABBR)
CNCPTST..... Conceptualist (ABBR)
CNCPTV...... Conceptive (ABBR)
CNCQ........ Confederation Nationale des Cadres du Quebec (AC)
CNCR........ Cancer (ABBR)
CNCR........ Concern (ABBR)
CNCR........ Concurrent (AFM)
CNCRD....... Concord (ABBR)
CNCRDNC.... Concordance (ABBR)
CNCRDT...... Concordant (ABBR)
CNCRDTY.... Concordantly (ABBR)
CNCRG....... Concerning (ABBR)
CNCRG....... Concurring (ABBR)
CNCRI........ Choice-in-Currency Research Institute (EA)
CNCRN....... Concern (ABBR)
CNCRND..... Concerned (ABBR)
CNCRNG..... Concerning (ABBR)
CNCS........ Clearlink Network Control System [*AT & T Tridom*]
CNCS........ Computer Networking and Communications Systems Program [*Georgia Institute of Technology, School of Information and Computer Science*] [*Atlanta*] [*Telecommunications service*] (TSSD)
CNCSH....... Comite Nordique des Commissions des Sciences Humaines [*Nordic Committee of the Research Councils for the Humanities - NCRCH*] (EAIO)
CNCT........ Connect (FAAC)
CNCT........ Connective Therapeutics [*NASDAQ symbol*] (TTSB)
CNCT........ Connective Therapeutics, Inc. [*NASDAQ symbol*] (SAG)
CNCT........ Conseil National Canadien du Travail [*National Council of Canadian Labour - NCCL*]
CNCT........ Counter Control [*Military*]
CNCTRC...... Concentric (MSA)
CNCV........ Concave (MSA)
CND........ Calling Number Display [*Telecommunications*]
CND........ Campaign for Nuclear Disarmament
CND........ Cannot Duplicate (MCD)
C/N/d........ Carrier-to-Noise, Downlink
CND........ Center for a New Democracy (EA)
CND........ Centre National de Documentation [*National Documentation Center*] [*Morocco*] [*Information service or system*] (IID)
CND........ Chief of Naval Development
CND........ Cline Development Corp. [*Vancouver Stock Exchange symbol*]
CND........ Club National du Disque [*Record label*] [*France*]
CND........ Code Names Dictionary [*A publication*]
CND........ Commandant Nucleus Department [*Military British*]
CND........ Concord Airlines Nigeria Ltd. [*ICAO designator*] (FAAC)
CND........ Condemned (AABC)
CND........ Condensation Nuclei Detector (MCD)
CND........ Condition (MDG)
cnd........ Conductor [*MARC relator code*] [*Library of Congress*] (LCCP)
CNDPT...... Conduit (KSC)
CND........ Congregation of Notre Dame (TOCD)
CND........ Constanta [*Romania*] [*Airport symbol*] (OAG)
CND........ CONUS [*Continental United States*] Net Depot Method
CND........ Currant [*Nevada*] [*Seismograph station code, US Geological Survey*] (SEIS)
CND........ Sisters of the Congregation of Notre Dame [*Roman Catholic religious order*]
CNDA........ Cherished Numbers Dealers Association [*British*] (DBA)
CNDA........ Clapham Notre Dame Association [*British*] (BI)
CNDCT....... Conduct (MSA)
CNDDB........ California Natural Diversity Data Base [*California State Department of Fish and Game*] [*Information service or system*] (IID)
CNDF........ Complex-Valued Non-Linear Discriminant Function (PDAA)
CNDH........ Coalition Nationale pour les Droits des Homosexuals [*National Gay Rights Coalition*] [*Canada*]
CNDI........ Combination Die
CNDI........ Commercial Nondevelopment Items [*Military*] (AABC)
CNDI........ Congenital Nephrogenic Diabetes Insipidus [*Medicine*]
CNDI-LEE.... Commercial Nondevelopment Items of Law Enforcement Equipment (MCD)
CNDL........ Candlewood Hotel Co., Inc. [*NASDAQ symbol*] (SAG)
Cndlewd...... Candlewood Hotel Co., Inc. [*Associated Press*] (SAG)
CNDLLGHT... Candlelight
CNDM........ Composition Node Design Method [*For distillation*]
CNDN........ Canadian (FAAC)
CNDN........ Canadian
CNDN........ Canadian Reserve File [*Petroleum Information Corp.*] [*Information service or system*] (CRD)
CNDN........ Chittenden Corp. [*NASDAQ symbol*] (NQ)
CNDO........ Chief Navy Disbursing Officer
CNDO........ Complete Neglect of Differential Overlap [*Quantum mechanics*]
CNDP........ Centre National de Documentation Pedagogique [*National Center for Pedagogical Documentation*] [*Ministry of Education*] [*Information service or system*] (IID)
CNDP........ Centre National des Documents du Personnel [*National Personnel Records Center - NPRC*]
CNDP........ Communications Network Design Program
CNDP........ Continuing Numerical Data Projects

CNDP .... Cyano(dihydroxy)pyridine [Biochemistry]
CNDS .... CellNet Data Systems, Inc. [NASDAQ symbol] (SAG)
CNDS .... Condensate (KSC)
CNDST .... Centre National de Documentation Scientifique et Technique [National Scientific and Technical Documentation Center] [Royal Library of Belgium Belgium] [Information service or system] (IID)
CNDW .... Coalition for National Dance Week (EA)
CNDY .... Candy
CNE .... Air Toronto, Inc. [Canada ICAO designator] (FAAC)
CNE .... Canadian National Exhibition [Held annually in Toronto]
CNE .... Certified NetWare Engineer [Novell, Inc.] [Computer science] (PCM)
CNE .... Childress [Texas] [Seismograph station code, US Geological Survey] (SEIS)
CNE .... Chronic Nervous Exhaustion [Medicine]
CNE .... Combined Neutral and Earth (PDAA)
CNE .... Communications Network Emulator
CNE .... Compare Numeric Equal [Computer science]
CNE .... Connecticut Energy [NYSE symbol] (TTSB)
CNE .... Connecticut Energy Corp. [NYSE symbol] (SPSG)
CNEA .... Canadian Nurse Educators Association (AC)
CNEB .... Call Net Enterprises [NASDAQ symbol] (SAG)
CNEB .... Cambridge Bible Commentary: New English Bible [A publication] (BJA)
CNeBC .... Los Angeles Baptist College and Theological Seminary, Newhall, CA [Library symbol Library of Congress] (LCLS)
CNEBF .... Call-Net Enterprises 'B' [NASDAQ symbol] (TTSB)
CNEC .... Christian Nationals' Evangelism Council [Australia]
cnee .... Consignee [Business term] (DS)
CNEEMA .... Centre National d'Etudes et d'Experimentation du Machinisme Agricole
CNEF .... Canadian National Energy Forum
CNEGL .... Contributory Negligence [Legal shorthand] (LWAP)
CNeHi .... Santa Clarita Valley Historical Society, Newhall, CA [Library symbol] [Library of Congress] (LCLS)
CNEL .... Community Noise Equivalent Level
CNEL .... Cutaneous Non-Epidermotropic Lymphoma (PDAA)
CNEN .... Comissao Nacional de Energia Nuclear [National Commission for Nuclear Energy] [Brazil Information service or system] (IID)
CNENAS .... Center for Near Eastern and North African Studies [University of Michigan] [Research center] (RCD)
CNEO .... Chief Naval Engineering Officer [British]
CNEP .... Cable Network Engineering Program [Bell System]
CNES .... Centre National d'Etudes Spatiales [National Center for Space Studies] [France]
CNES .... Chronic Nervous Exhaustion Syndrome [Medicine] (DMAA)
CNET .... Centre National d'Etudes des Telecommunications [France ICAO designator] (FAAC)
CNET .... Chief of Naval Education and Training (MCD)
CNET .... Communication Network
CNET .... COMNET Corp. [Formerly, Computer Network Corp.] [NASDAQ symbol] (NQ)
C-NET .... Cromemco Local Area Network [Cromemco, Inc.] [Mountain View, CA] [Telecommunications] (TSSD)
CNETLANTREP... Commander, Naval Education and Training Command, Representative Coordinator for Atlantic (DNAB)
CNETP .... Consolidated New Equipment Training Plan (MCD)
CNETPACREP... Commander, Naval Education and Training Command, Representative Coordinator for Pacific (DNAB)
CNEWA .... Catholic Near East Welfare Association (EA)
CNEWS .... Canadian Northeast Wideband Systems [Air Force] (MCD)
CNEWS .... Consolidated Navy Electronic Warfare School (PDAA)
CNEWTP ...... Consolidated Navy Electronic Warfare Test Plan (CAAL)
CNF .... Canadian Income Plus Fund 1986 Trust Units [Toronto Stock Exchange symbol]
CNF .... Canadian Nature Federation [Federation Canadienne de la Nature] [Formerly, Canadian Audubon Society] (AC)
CNF .... Canadian Nurses Foundation [Fondation des Infirmieres et Infirmiers du Canada] (AC)
CNF .... Canifair Aviation, Inc. [Canada ICAO designator] (FAAC)
CNF .... Central NOTAM [Notice to Airmen] Facility [Military]
CNF .... Cerre Les Noroy [France] [Seismograph station code, US Geological Survey Closed] (SEIS)
CNF .... Child Nutrition Forum (EA)
CNF .... Chin National Front [Myanmar] [Political party] (EY)
CNF .... Chronic Nodular Fibrositis [Medicine] (DMAA)
CNF .... Citizens for a Nuclear Freeze [Defunct] (EA)
CNF .... Commander, [US] Naval Forces
CNF .... Commonwealth Nurses Federation (EA)
CNF .... Confine (AABC)
CNF .... Conjunctive Normal Formula
CNF .... Consolidated Freightways [NYSE symbol] (TTSB)
CNF .... Consolidated Freightways, Inc. [NYSE symbol] (SPSG)
C-NF .... Cost-No Fee [Type of contract] (AAGC)
CNF .... Cyclophosphamide, Mitoxantrone, Fluorouracil [Antineoplastic drug regimen] (DAVI)
CNF .... Cytotoxic Necrotizing Factor [Immunology]
CNF .... Fort Worth, TX [Location identifier FAA] (FAAL)
CNFA .... Citizens Network for Foreign Affairs (EA)
CNFA .... Commander, US Naval Forces, Azores (DNAB)
CNFC .... Canadian Native Friendship Centre (AC)
CNFDRTD .... Confederated
CNFH .... Coalition for a Nuclear Free Harbor (EA)
CNFIU .... Canadian National Federation of Independent Unions [See also FCNSI]

CNFL .... Central Nevada Field Laboratory [University of Nevada - Reno] [Research center] (RCD)
CNFL .... Citizens Financial Corp. [NASDAQ symbol] (SAG)
CNFL .... Citizens Finl Kentucky [NASDAQ symbol] (TTSB)
CNFP .... Coalition for a New Foreign Policy [Defunct] (EA)
CNFP .... Commercial Nuclear Fuel Plant (NRCH)
CNFR .... Confer
CNFRL .... Columbia National Fisheries Research Laboratory [Later, NFCRC] [Department of the Interior Columbia, MO] (GRD)
CNFRNC ...... Conference
CNFS .... California National Fuchsia Society [Later, NFS]
CNFSFACM... Committee of the National Ferrous Scrap Federations and Associations of the Common Market [See also COFENAF] (EAIO)
CNFUN .... Canada Income Plus Fund 1986 Trust Units [Toronto Stock Exchange symbol]
CNFV .... Carnation Necrotic Fleck Virus
CNG .... Calling Tone [Computer science]
CNG .... Central Norseman Gold Corp. Ltd. [Australia]
CNG .... Changalane [Mozambique] [Seismograph station code, US Geological Survey] (SEIS)
Cng .... Change [A publication] (BRI)
CNG .... Charge Number Grouping (MCD)
CNG .... Coalition of Northeastern Governors (EPA)
CNG .... Coastal Airways [ICAO designator] (FAAC)
CNG .... Commander, Northern Group
CNG .... Compressed Natural Gas
CNG .... Comten Network Gateway [NCR Corp.] [Computer science] (NITA)
CNG .... Concert Industry Ltd. [Vancouver Stock Exchange symbol]
CNG .... Connecticut Natural Gas Corp.
CNG .... Consolidated Nat Gas [NYSE symbol] (TTSB)
CNG .... Consolidated Natural Gas Co. [NYSE symbol] (SPSG)
CNG .... Cyclic Nucelotide-Gated [Neurobiology]
CNG .... Cyclic Nucleotide-Gated [Ion channels] [Neurobiology]
CNG .... Paducah, KY [Location identifier FAA] (FAAL)
CNGA .... California Natural Gas Association
CNGB .... Chief, National Guard Bureau [Army]
CNGB & OMFUG... Country, Bluegrass, Blues, and Other Music for Uplifting Gourmandizers [Formerly, CBGB] [New York nightclub]
CNGC .... Cyclic Nucleotide Gated Channel (DMAA)
CNGE .... Cummins Natural Gas Engines [Cummins Engine Co., Inc.]
CNGI .... Comite des Normes Gouvernementales en Informatique [Government Electronic Data Processing Standards Committee] [Canada]
CNGIAPL ...... Czechoslovak National Group of International Association of Penal Law (EAIO)
Cngln .... Conquest Industries Corp. [Associated Press] (SAG)
Cngrn .... Congregation (BJA)
CNGRS .... Congress
CNGRSNL ...... Congressional
CNGS .... Christlich-Nationaler Gewerkschaftsbund der Schweiz [Swiss Federation of National-Christian Trade Unions]
CNH .... Aquila Air, Inc. [FAA designator] (FAAC)
CNH .... Canhorn Mining Corp. [Toronto Stock Exchange symbol]
CN(h) .... Cellulose Nitrate with Hydrophobic Edge [Membrane filtration]
CNH .... Central Hudson Gas&El [NYSE symbol] (TTSB)
CNH .... Central Hudson Gas & Electric Corp. [NYSE symbol] (SPSG)
CNH .... Central Neurogenic Hyperpnea [Medicine] (DAVI)
CNH .... Central Neurogenic Hyperventilation [Medicine]
CNH .... Changchun [Republic of China] [Seismograph station code, US Geological Survey] (SEIS)
CNH .... Claremont, NH [Location identifier FAA] (FAAL)
CNH .... Community Nursing Home
CNH .... Contract Nursing Home (DAVI)
CNH .... Natural History Museum Foundation, Los Angeles County, Los Angeles, CA [OCLC symbol] (OCLC)
CNhB .... Bendix Aviation Corp. [Later, Bendix Corp.], Pacific Division, North Hollywood, CA [Library symbol Library of Congress] (LCLS)
CNHD .... Congenital Nonspherocytic Hemolytic Disease [Medicine] (MAE)
CNHI .... Committee for National Health Insurance (EA)
CNHM .... Chicago Natural History Museum
CNHO .... Consortium of National Hispanic Organizations [Defunct] (EA)
CNHS .... Center for Neo-Hellenic Studies (EA)
CNHS .... Cherokee National Historical Society (EA)
CNHS .... Coalition for a National Health System (EA)
CNHV .... Central Neurogenic Hyperventilation [Medicine]
CNI .... Call Number Identification (IAA)
CNI .... Canadian National Railway Co. [NYSE symbol] (SAG)
CNI .... Canadian News Index [Micromedia Ltd.] [Information service or system A publication]
CNI .... Center of Nuclear Image (DMAA)
CNI .... Centre National des Independants [National Center of Independents] [France Political party] (PPE)
CNI .... Centre National des Independants et des Paysans [National Centre of Independents and Peasants] (EAIO)
CNI .... Centro Nacional de Informaciones [National Information Center] [Supersedes DINA Chile]
CNI .... Changed Number Interception [Telecommunications] (TEL)
CNI .... Chief of Naval Information [Obsolete British]
CNI .... Chief of Naval Intelligence
CNI .... Chronic Nerve Irritation [Medicine] (DMAA)
CNI .... ChurchNews International [Database] [Resources for Communication] [Information service or system] (CRD)
CNI .... Coalition for Networked Information [Computer science] (TNIG)
CNI .... Columbus News Index [Public Library of Columbus and Franklin County] [Information service or system] (IID)

CNI............ Committee for a New Ireland [*Defunct*] (EA)
CNI............ Committee for Nuclear Information [*Later, Committee for Environmental Information*]
CNI............ Communicating NATO Intentions (MCD)
CNI............ Communication Navigation (NFPA)
CNI............ Communication, Navigation, and Identification
CNI............ Community Nutrition Institute (EA)
CNI............ Consolidated National Interveners [*An association*] (EA)
CNI............ Coordination Number Invariance [*Chemistry*]
CNI............ Council for the National Interest [*Australia*]
CNI............ Craven Resources Ltd. [*Vancouver Stock Exchange symbol*]
CNI............ Empresa Nacional de Servicios Aereos [*Cuba*] [*FAA designator*] (FAAC)
CNIB......... Canadian National Institute for the Blind
CNIB......... Champagne News and Information Bureau (EA)
CNIC......... Centre National de l'Information Chimique [*National Center for Chemical Information*] [*Information service or system*] (IID)
CNIC......... Clinical Neurology Information Center
CNIC......... Commander, Naval Intelligence Command (DNAB)
CNID......... Centro Nacional de Informacion y Documentacion [*National Information and Documentation Center*] [*Ministry of Labour*] [*Information service or system*] (IID)
CNID......... Congres National d'Initiative Democratique [*Mali*] [*Political party*] (EY)
CNIDR........ Center for Networked Information Discovery and Retrieval
CNIDR........ Clearinghouse for Network Information and Discovery and Retrieval [*Computer science*]
CNIE.......... Committee for the National Institute for the Environment [*Lobby group*]
CNIFC........ Chuck Norris International Fan Club (EA)
CNIL.......... Conseil National de l'Industrie Laitiere du Canada [*National Dairy Council of Canada*]
CnILt......... Central Illinois Light Co. [*Associated Press*] (SAG)
C/N/im....... Carrier-to-Noise, Intermodulation
CNIM.......... Consejo Nacional de la Industria Maquiladora [*National Council of the Maquiladora Industry*] [*Mexican/US business organization*] (CROSS)
CNIMZ....... Tsentar za Nauchna Informacija po Meditsina i Zdraveopazvane [*Center for Scientific Information in Medicine and Public Health*] [*Medical Academy*] [*Information service or system*] (IID)
CNIP.......... Centre National des Independants et des Paysans [*National Center of Independents and Peasants*] [*France Political party*] (PPW)
CNIPA........ Committee of National Institutes of Patent Agents [*Winchester, Hampshire, England*] (EA)
CNI PP........ Canadian Natl Railway [*NYSE symbol*] (TTSB)
CNIPTG....... Communications, Networks, and Information Processing Theory Group [*MIT*] (MCD)
CNIR.......... Cooperative Network of In-Service Resources (OICC)
CNIRA........ Centre National d'Information et de Recherche sur l'Aide Juridique [*National Legal Aid Research Centre*] [*Canada*]
CNIS.......... Channel Navigation Information Service [*British Coast Guard*] (PDAA)
CNIT.......... Cenit Bancorp [*NASDAQ symbol*] (SAG)
CNJ........... Catfish Pond [*New Jersey*] [*Seismograph station code, US Geological Survey Closed*] (SEIS)
CNJ........... Central Railroad Co. of New Jersey [*Absorbed into Consolidated Rail Corp.*] [*AAR code*]
CNJ........... Charleston Resources [*Vancouver Stock Exchange symbol*]
CNJ........... Cloncurry [*Australia Airport symbol*] (OAG)
CNJ........... Cole National [*NYSE symbol*] (TTSB)
CNJ........... Comite National de Jumelage [*National Committee for Town/City Twinning*] [*France*] (EAIO)
CNJ........... Copper Nickel Jacket (IAA)
CNJ........... Nanjing Airlines [*China*] [*FAA designator*] (FAAC)
CNJA......... Chief Naval Judge Advocate [*British*]
CNJC......... Cable Network Joint Committee
CNJFDC....... Food and Drug Administration, Notices of Judgment: Cosmetics [*A publication*] (DLA)
CNK.......... Cellular Natural Killing (PDAA)
CNK.......... Common Noun Keywords (PDAA)
CNK.......... Concordia, KS [*Location identifier FAA*] (FAAL)
CNK.......... Confederation of Khmer Nationalists [*Cambodia*] (PD)
CNK.......... Cortical Necrosis of Kidneys [*Medicine*] (DMAA)
CNK.......... Crompton & Knowles [*NYSE symbol*] (TTSB)
CNK.......... Crompton & Knowles Corp. [*NYSE symbol*] (SPSG)
CNK.......... Sunwest International Aviation [*Canada*] [*FAA designator*] (FAAC)
CNKP......... Committee for a New Korea Policy (EA)
CNKT......... Connect, Inc. [*NASDAQ symbol*] (SAG)
CNL.......... Canadian National Library (BARN)
CNL.......... Canal [*Board on Geographic Names*]
CNL.......... Canal
CNL.......... Cancel [*or Cancellation*] (AFM)
CNL.......... Cardiolipin Natural Lecithin [*Immunochemistry*] (MAE)
CNL.......... Carrier Noise Level
CNL.......... Centennial Airlines, Inc. [*ICAO designator*] (FAAC)
CNL.......... Central La Elec [*NYSE symbol*] (TTSB)
CNL.......... Central Louisiana Electric Co., Inc. [*NYSE symbol*] (SPSG)
CNL.......... Chemonucleolysis [*Surgery*]
CNL.......... Children's Nutrition Laboratory [*Baylor College of Medicine*]
CNL.......... Circuit Net Loss
CNL.......... Columbia, Newberry & Laurens Railroad Co. [*AAR code*]
CNL.......... Commonwealth National Library (DGA)
CNL.......... Computer Numerical Logic
CNL.......... Connel [*Washington*] [*Seismograph station code, US Geological Survey*] (SEIS)
CNL.......... Conservative and National Liberal Party [*British*]

CNL.......... Constant Net Loss [*Telecommunications*] (TEL)
CNL.......... Control (IAA)
CNL.......... Council on National Literatures (EA)
CNLA......... Council of National Library Associations [*Later, CNLIA*] (EA)
CNLCI........ Comite National pour la Liberation de la Cote d'Ivoire [*National Committee for the Liberation of the Ivory Coast*]
CNLDP........ Committee for National Land Development Policy [*Defunct*]
CNLFP........ Cancel Flight Plan (FAAC)
CNLG......... Conolog Corp. [*NASDAQ symbol*] (SAG)
CNLGP....... Cannon Nonlaunched Guided Projectile
CNLGU....... Conolog Corp. Unit [*NASDAQ symbol*] (TTSB)
CNLGW...... Conolog Corp. Wrrt'A' [*NASDAQ symbol*] (TTSB)
CNLI......... Irrigation Canal [*Board on Geographic Names*]
CNLIA........ Council of National Library and Information Associations (EA)
CNLN......... Navigation Canal [*Board on Geographic Names*]
CNLP......... Center on National Labor Policy (EA)
CNLS......... Center for Nonlinear Studies [*Los Alamos, NM*] [*Department of Energy*] (GRD)
CNLS......... Centre for Nonlinear Studies [*University of Leeds*] [*British*] (CB)
CNLS......... Comite Nationale de Lutte Contre le SIDA [*National Committee on the Fight Against AIDS*] [*Mauritania*] (EAIO)
CNL-SIDA .... Comite Nationale de Lutte Contre le SIDA [*National Committee on the Fight Against AIDS*] [*Burkina Faso*] (EAIO)
CNM.......... Canaveral-Mila [*Military*]
CNM.......... Canfic Resources Ltd. [*Vancouver Stock Exchange symbol*]
CNM.......... Carlsbad [*New Mexico*] [*Airport symbol*] (OAG)
CNM.......... Carlsbad, NM [*Location identifier FAA*] (FAAL)
CnM.......... Centro Nacional de Microfilm, Madrid, Spain [*Library symbol Library of Congress*] (LCLS)
CNM.......... Certificate in Nonprofit Management (PGP)
CNM.......... Certified Nurse Midwife
CNM.......... Certified Nurse Midwife [*Medicine*]
CNM.......... Chama [*New Mexico*] [*Seismograph station code, US Geological Survey Closed*] (SEIS)
CNM.......... Chief of Naval Material
CNM.......... Collection of the National Museum of Antiquities at Leiden (BJA)
CNM.......... Commander, US Naval Forces, Marianas (DNAB)
CNM.......... Communication Network Management (HGAA)
CNM.......... Continental Medical Systems [*NYSE symbol*] (SPSG)
CNM.......... Critical Nuclear Material
CNM.......... Cuban Nationalist Movement
CNM.......... Customer Network Management [*Telecommunications*] (ACRL)
CNMA........ Communications Network for Manufacturing Application [*Computer science*] (TNIG)
CNMA........ Customer Network Management Agent [*Telecommunications*] (ACRL)
CNMC........ Council of Nordic Master-Craftsmen [*Oslo, Norway*] (EAIO)
CNMD........ CONMED Corp. [*NASDAQ symbol*] (NQ)
CNME........ Council on Naturopathic Medicine (PGP)
CNMI......... Commonwealth Code, Commonwealth of the Northern Mariana Islands [*A publication*]
CNMI......... Communications Network Management Interface
CNMO........ Canadian Naval Mission Overseas
CNMR........ Carbon-13 Nuclear Magnetic Resonance [*Also, CMR*]
CNMR........ Carbon-13 Nuclear Magnetic Resonance Search System [*Netherlands Information Combine*] [*Database*]
CNMS........ Common Network Management System [*Unisys Corp.*]
CNMT........ Certified Nuclear Medicine Technologist (MAE)
cnmt......... Consignment [*Business term*] (DS)
CNMW...... Cincinnati Microwave [*NASDAQ symbol*] (TTSB)
CNMW...... Cincinnati Microwave, Inc. [*NASDAQ symbol*] (NQ)
CNMWW..... Cincinnati Microwave Wrrt [*NASDAQ symbol*] (TTSB)
CNMX........ Canmax, Inc. [*NASDAQ symbol*] (SAG)
CNN.......... Cable News Network [*Facetious translation: Chicken Noodle Network*] [*Cable-television system*]
CNN.......... Canada Trust Income Investments [*Toronto Stock Exchange symbol*]
CNN.......... Cincinnati [*Ohio*] [*Seismograph station code, US Geological Survey Closed*] (SEIS)
CNN.......... CNA Income Shares [*NYSE symbol*] (TTSB)
CNN.......... CNA Income Shares, Inc. [*NYSE symbol*] (SPSG)
CNN.......... Condensed Nearest Neighbor [*Mathematics*]
CNN.......... Congenital Nevomelanocytic Nevi [*Medicine*]
CNNA........ Clan Napier in North America [*An association*]
CNNA........ Culture-Negative Neutrocytic Ascite [*Bacteriology*]
CNNAH....... Chronology of Native North American History [*A publication*]
CNNNG....... Canning
CNNR........ Conner Peripherals, Inc. (MHDW)
CNNS........ Center for New National Security (EA)
CnNT........ Coniectanea Neotestamentica [*Uppsala*] [*A publication*] (BJA)
CNNW....... Coalition for a Non-Nuclear World [*Defunct*] (EA)
CNO.......... California State University, Northridge, Northridge, CA [*OCLC symbol*] (OCLC)
CNO.......... Carbon-Nitrogen-Oxygen [*Galactic molecular formation cycle*]
C/No......... Carrier-to-Noise Density
CNO.......... Center for Nonprofit Organizations [*Defunct*] (EA)
CNO.......... Chief Nursing Officer [*British*]
CNO.......... Chief of Naval Operations [*Also, CNAVOP*] [*Washington, DC*]
CNO.......... Childress [*Texas*] [*Seismograph station code, US Geological Survey*] (SEIS)
CNO.......... Chin National Organization [*Burma*]
CNO.......... Chino, CA [*Location identifier FAA*] (FAAL)
CNO.......... CML Industries Ltd. [*Toronto Stock Exchange symbol*]
CNO.......... Community Nursing Organization (DMAA)
CNO.......... Computer Not Operational (IAA)
CNO.......... Constitutional Officer (DNAB)
CNO.......... Cornerstone Propane Partners LP [*NYSE symbol*] (SAG)

CNOA	California Narcotics Officers Association (SRA)
CNO-AE	Council of National Organizations for Adult Education (EA)
CNO & TP	Cincinnati, New Orleans & Texas Pacific Railway Co.
CNO & TPR	Cincinnati, New Orleans & Texas Pacific Railroad (MHDB)
CNOB	Commander, Naval Operating Base
CNOBO	Chief of Naval Operations Budget Office
CNOC	Coordinadora Nacional de Organizaciones Cafetaleras [*National network of small coffee producers*] [*Mexico*] (CROSS)
C/NOCB	Cincinnati/New Orleans City Ballet
CNOCC	Chief of Naval Operations Communications Center (MCD)
CNOCOM/MIS	Chief of Naval Operations Command/Management Information System
CNOCS	Captain, Naval Operations Command Systems [*British military*] (DMA)
CNOCY	Council of National Organizations for Children and Youth [*Later, NCOCY*] (EA)
C/No/d	Carrier-to-Noise Density, Downlink
CNODC	China National Oceanographic Data Center [*Marine science*] (OSRA)
C/No/im	Carrier-to-Noise Density, Intermodulation
CNOL	Clinical Notes On-Line [*IRCS Medical Science*] [*Ceased operation*] [*Information service or system*] (IID)
CNOM	Chief of Naval Operations Memorandum
CNOM	Conseil National de l'Ordre des Medecins [*France*]
CNOM/CMCM	Chief of Naval Operations Memorandum and Commandant of the Marine Corps Memorandum [*Joint*]
CNOP	Conditional Nonoperation [*Computer science*]
CNoR	Canadian Northern Railway
CNOR	Certified Nurse, Operating Room (MEDA)
CNOR	Cincinnati Northern [*AAR code*]
CNOR	Command Not Operationally Ready [*Navy*] (NVT)
CNoR	Riker Laboratories, Inc., Northridge, CA [*Library symbol Library of Congress*] (LCLS)
CNO/RAAB	Chief of Naval Operations Reserve Affairs Advisory Board (DNAB)
CNORP	Chief of Naval Operational Requirement and Plans
CNoS	California State University, Northridge, Northridge, CA [*Library symbol Library of Congress*] (LCLS)
C/No/t	Carrier-to-Noise Density, Total
C Notre Dame	College of Notre Dame (GAGS)
C/No/u	Carrier-to-Noise Density, Uplink
CNovI	Indian Valley College, Novato, CA [*Library symbol Library of Congress*] (LCLS)
CNP	Canadian Northern Pacific Railway
CNP	Cases at Nisi Prius [*A publication*] (DLA)
CNP	Celestial North Pole (DNAB)
CNP	Center for National Policy (EA)
CNP	Central North Pacific
CNP	Central North Pacific Ocean
CNP	Chappell, NE [*Location identifier FAA*] (FAAL)
CNP	Chief of Naval Personnel [*The Second Sea Lord*] [*British*]
CNP	Chloro(nitro)phenol [*Organic chemistry*]
CNP	Chopped Nylon Phenolic (SAA)
CNP	Communications, Navigation, and Positioning [*Military*]
CNP	Communications Network Procedure [*Computer science*] (NITA)
CNP	Communications Network Processor
CNP	Community Nurse Practitioner
CNP	Consecutive Number Printer
CnP	Consumers Power Co. [*Associated Press*] (SAG)
CNP	Continuous Negative Pressure [*Medicine*]
CNP	Cornucopia Resources Ltd. [*Toronto Stock Exchange symbol Vancouver Stock Exchange symbol*]
CNP	Council for National Parks [*British*]
CNP	Country Nationalist Party [*Australia Political party*]
CNP	Crown Central Petroleum Corp. [*AMEX symbol*] (SPSG)
CNP	Customized Networking Platform
CNPA	Cossack National Press Association [*Defunct*] (EA)
CNP.A	Crown Centl Pet'A' [*AMEX symbol*] (TTSB)
CNPA-EEC	Community of the Newspaper Publishing Associations of the European Economic Communities [*Belgium*] (EAIO)
CNPB	Continuous Negative Pressure Breathing [*Physiology*]
CNP.B	Crown Central CI'B' [*AMEX symbol*] (TTSB)
CNPC	Campbell's English Nisi Prius Cases [*A publication*] (DLA)
CNPC	Comision Nacional Peruana de Cooperacion con la UNESCO [*Peruvian National Commission for the United Nations Educational, Scientific and Cultural Organization*] [*Peru*] (EAIO)
CNPC	Conference of National Park Concessioners
CNPC	Cuban National Planning Council [*Later, CANC*] (EA)
CNPD	Candidate/Nominee Protective Division [*US Secret Service*]
CnPF	Consumers Power Co. Financing I [*Associated Press*] (SAG)
CNPG	Cornucopia Resources Ltd. [*NASDAQ symbol*] (NQ)
CNPGF	Cornucopia Resources Ltd [*NASDAQ symbol*] (TTSB)
CNPM	Coalition of Non-Postal Media [*Defunct*] (EA)
CN/PNL	Contractors Panel [*Aerospace*] (AAG)
CNPP	Clinton Nuclear Power Plant (NRCH)
CNPPA	Commission on National Parks and Protected Areas [*of the International Union for Conservation of Nature and Natural Resources*] (EAIO)
CNPP-PSD	Convention Nationale des Patriotes Progressistes-Parti Social-Democrate [*Burkina Faso*] [*Political party*] (EY)
CNPPSDP	Cooperative National Plant Pest Survey and Detection Program [*Department of Agriculture*] [*Hyattsville, MD Database*]
CNPR	Center for National Policy Review [*Defunct*] (EA)
CNPR	Chatterji's Non-Language Preference [*Vocational guidance test*]
CNPS	Canadian Nurses Protective Society (AC)
CNPS	Caucus for a New Political Science (EA)
CNPTI	Centre National de Prevention et de Traitement des Intoxications [*National Poison Control Center*] [*Information service or system*] (IID)
CNPV	Continuous Negative Pressure Ventilation [*Medicine*] (DMAA)
CNPY	Canopy Cover [*Ecology*]
CNQ	Canadian Natural Resources Ltd. [*Toronto Stock Exchange symbol*]
CNQ	Corrientes [*Argentina*] [*Airport symbol*] (OAG)
CNQ	Roanoke, VA [*Location identifier FAA*] (FAAL)
CnqIn	Conquest Industries Corp. [*Associated Press*] (SAG)
CNQX	Cyano(nitro)quinoxalinedione [*Organic chemistry*]
CNR	Canadian National Railways [*Facetious translation: Certainly No Rush*]
CNR	Canadian Northern Railway (ROG)
CNR	Canadian Roxy Petroleum Ltd. [*Toronto Stock Exchange symbol*]
CNR	Carboxy Nitroso Rubber [*Organic chemistry*]
CNR	Carrier-to-Noise Ratio
CNR	Cellular Neoprene Rubber
CNR	Center for Nursing Research [*Ohio State University*] [*Research center*] (RCD)
CNR	Chanaral [*Chile*] [*Airport symbol*] (AD)
CNR	Change Notice Request (MCD)
CNR	Change to Navy Regulations
CNR	Chief Naval Representative [*British*]
CNR	Chief of Naval Research
CNR	Chief of Naval Reserve (DOMA)
CNR	Chonco [*Nicaragua*] [*Seismograph station code, US Geological Survey*] (SEIS)
CNR	Civil Nursing Reserve (DAVI)
CNR	Coalicion Nacional Republicana [*Ecuador*] [*Political party*] (EY)
CNR	Collection Nelson Rockefeller [*Identifying mark on art reproductions from the collection of Nelson Rockefeller*]
CNR	Collects No Revenue [*Humorous interpretation for Canadian National Railways*]
CNR	College of New Rochelle [*New York*]
CNR	Combat Net Radio [*Military*]
CNR	Commission on Natural Resources [*National Research Council*]
CNR	Committee for Nuclear Responsibility (EA)
CNR	Common Network Representation [*Telecommunications*] (OSI)
CNR	Community Noise Rating
CNR	Composite Noise Rating [*Aviation*]
CNR	COMSAT [*Communications Satellite Corp.*] Nonreflecting [*Solar cell*]
CNR	Condor Aero Services, Inc. [*ICAO designator*] (FAAC)
CNR	Conner Peripherals, Inc. [*NYSE symbol*] (SPSG)
CNR	Conseil Pationa de Recherches [*Canada*] [*Marine science*] (OSRA)
CNR	Consiglio Nazionale delle Ricerche [*National Research Council*] [*Italy*] [*Information service or system*] (IID)
CNR	Contractual Nontechnical Report (AAG)
CNR	Corner (ADA)
CNR	Council of National Representatives [*Of the International Council of Nurses*] (DAVI)
CNR	National Center for Atmospheric Research, Boulder, CO [*OCLC symbol*] (OCLC)
CNR	North Slope, AK [*Location identifier FAA*] (FAAL)
CNRA	Canadian National Recreation Association
CNRA	Commander, Navy Recruiting Area (DNAB)
CNRAG	Company Nuclear Review and Audit Group (NRCH)
CNRC	Commander, Navy Recruiting Command (DNAB)
CNRC	Conseil National de Recherches Canada [*National Research Council Canada*]
CNRE	Center for Nursing Research and Evaluation [*University of Wisconsin - Milwaukee*] [*Research center*] (RCD)
CN Regt	Chota Nagpur Regiment [*British military*] (DMA)
CNRET	Centre for Natural Resources, Energy, and Transport [*United Nations*]
CNRF	Chief, Naval Reserve Forces
CNRF	Cold Neutron Research Facility [*Physics*]
CNRG	Coastwide Energy Services [*NASDAQ symbol*] (SAG)
CNRG	Conseil National de la Resistance Guadeloupeenne [*Political party*] (EY)
CNRHSPP	Council for the National Register of Health Service Providers in Psychology (EA)
CNRI	National Research and Investigations Center [*Zaire*] (PD)
CNRL	Communication and Navigation Research Laboratory (NASA)
CNRM	Centre National de Recherches Meteorologiques [*Toulouse, France*] [*Marine science*] (OSRA)
CNRM	CNR [*Christian News Report*] Ministries (EA)
CNRMF	Cinram Ltd [*NASDAQ symbol*] (TTSB)
CNRN	Certified Neuroscience Registered Nurse (MEDA)
C N Rochelle	College of New Rochelle (GAGS)
CNRPTF	Canadian National Railways Pension Trust Fund [*Montreal-based pension fund*]
CNRS	Canadian Nautical Research Society [*Societe Canadienne pour la Recherche Nautique*] (AC)
CNRS	Canadian Numismatic Research Society
CNRS	Canadian Nurses Respiratory Society (AC)
CNRS	Centre National de la Recherche Scientifique [*France*] [*Marine science*] (OSRA)
CNRS	Centre National des Republicains Sociaux [*National Center of Social Republicans*] [*France Political party*] (PPE)
CNRS	Conseil National de Recherche Scientifique [*International Council of Scientific Unions*]
CNRT	Chief, Naval Reserve Training
CNRT	Corrected Sinus Node Recovery Time [*Medicine*] (DMAA)
CNRTC	Naval Reserve Training Command

CNRU.......... Clinical Nutrition Research Unit [*Medical College of Georgia*] [*Research center*] (RCD)
CNRU.......... Clinical Nutrition Research Unit [*Birmingham, AL*] [*Department of Health and Human Services*] (GRD)
CNRU.......... Cooperative Core Laboratories and Clinical Nutrition Research Unit [*Research center*] (RCD)
CNS .... Cairns [*Australia Airport symbol*] (OAG)
CNS .... Camp Newspaper Service
CNS .... Canada Safeway Ltd. [*Toronto Stock Exchange symbol*]
CNS .... Canadian National Steamships (MHDW)
CNS .... Canadian Naval Service
CNS .... Canadian Navigation Society (AC)
CNS .... Canadian Neurological Society [*Societe Canadienne de Neurologie*] (AC)
CNS .... Canadian News Service
CNS .... Canadian Nuclear Society (NUCP)
CNS .... Catawba Nuclear Station (NRCH)
cns............... Censor [*MARC relator code*] [*Library of Congress*] (LCCP)
CNS .... Centennial Flight Centre [*Canada ICAO designator*] (FAAC)
CNS .... Center for Nationalist Studies (EA)
CNS .... Center for Neuroscience [*Rutgers University*]
CNS .... Center for New Schools (EA)
CNS .... Center for Nonviolent Studies [*An association*] (EA)
CNS .... Center for Northern Studies [*Research center*] (RCD)
CNS .... Center for Nuclear Studies [*Memphis State University*] [*Research center*] (RCD)
CNS .... Central Navigation School
CNS .... Central Nervous System [*Physiology*]
CnS .... Central Securities Corp. [*Associated Press*] (SAG)
CNS .... Centre for Neuroscience [*University College, London*] [*British*] (CB)
CNS .... Channelled Narrow Stripe [*LASER diode technology*] (NITA)
CNS .... Charleston Naval Shipyard (DOGT)
CNS .... Charleston Naval Shipyard
CNS .... Cherokee Nuclear Station (NRCH)
CNS .... Chief, Nursing Services (DAVI)
CNS .... Chief of the Naval Staff [*Canada*]
CNS .... Child Neurology Society (EA)
CNS .... China News Service
CNS .... Chlorocetophenone Solution (AAG)
CNS .... Clinical Nurse Specialist
CNS .... CNS, Inc. [*Associated Press*] (SAG)
CNS .... Committee for National Security (EA)
CNS .... Commodity News Services, Inc. [*Information service or system*] (IID)
CNST .... Common Number System (AAG)
CNS .... Communication Network System (IAA)
CNS .... Communications, Navigation, and Surveillance
CNS .... Communications Network Service [*Satellite Business Systems*] [*McLean, VA*] [*Telecommunications*] (TSSD)
CNS .... Communications Network Services [*Virginia Polytechnic Institute and State University*] [*Blacksburg*] (TSSD)
CNS .... Communications Network Simulation [*Computer science*] (NITA)
CNS .... Complimentary Network Service [*Telecommunications*] (ACRL)
CNS .... CompuServe Network Services [*CompuServe, Inc.*] [*Columbus, OH*] [*Telecommunications*] (TSSD)
CNS .... Computerized Notation System (MEDA)
CNS .... Congress of Neurological Surgeons (EA)
CNS .... Consolidated Heron Resources [*Vancouver Stock Exchange symbol*]
CNS .... Consolidated Stores [*NYSE symbol*] (TTSB)
CNS .... Consolidated Stores Corp. [*NYSE symbol*] (SPSG)
CNS .... Continuous [*Aviation code*]
CNS .... Continuous National Survey [*National Opinion Research Center*]
CNS .... Continuous Net Settlement
CNS .... Control Network System [*Chiefly British*]
CNS .... Cooper Nuclear Station (NRCH)
CNS .... Copley News Service
CNS .... Council of Name Studies [*British*] (DBA)
CNS .... Cras Nocte Sumendus [*To Be Taken Tomorrow Night*] [*Pharmacy*]
CNS .... Cretaceous Normal Superchron [*Geology*]
CNS .... Crigler-Najjar Syndrome [*Medicine*]
CNS .... Czechoslovak Neurological Society (EAIO)
CNS .... Naval Ocean Systems Center, San Diego, CA [*OCLC symbol*] (OCLC)
CNS .... Sulfocyanate [*Organic chemistry*] (DAVI)
CNSA .... Chirurgiese Navorsingsvereniging van Suidelike Afrika [*Surgical Research Society of Southern Africa*] (EAIO)
CNSA .... Council of Nova Scotia Archives (AC)
CNSAF .... Contractor Non-SECOMO [*Software Engineering Cost Model*] Activity Factor
CNSB .... CNS Bancorp, Inc. [*NASDAQ symbol*] (SAG)
CNS Bcp ...... CNS Bancorp, Inc. [*Associated Press*] (SAG)
CNSC .... Carrying Nuclear-Strike Cruiser
CNSC .... Conesco Industries, Ltd. [*NASDAQ symbol*] (NQ)
CNSD .... Chronic Nonspecific Diarrhea [*Medicine*]
CNSD .... Computer and Network Services Division [*Marine science*] (OSRA)
CNSD .... Computer and Network Services Division [*Formerly, Computer Support Group*] (USDC)
CNS/EBU ..... Common Nacelle System/Engine Build-Up (MCD)
CNSF .... [*The*] Clean Nova Scotia Foundation (AC)
CNSF .... Cornell National Supercomputer Facility [*Cornell University*] [*Research center*] (RCD)
CnsFn .... Consumers Financial Corp. [*Associated Press*] (SAG)
CnsFrt......... Consolidated Freightways, Inc. [*Associated Press*] (SAG)
CnsFrtC....... Consolidated Freightways [*Associated Press*] (SAG)
CNSG .... Consolidated Nuclear Steam Generator
CNSHA........ Congenital Nonspherocytic Hemolytic Anemia [*Medicine*]

CNSI .... Cambridge NeuroScience [*NASDAQ symbol*] (TTSB)
CNSI .... Cambridge NeuroScience, Inc. [*NASDAQ symbol*] (SAG)
CNSI .... Computer Network Systems, Inc. (AAGC)
CNSIST .... Consistent
CNSISTY ..... Consistency
CNSK .... Covenant Bank for Savings [*NASDAQ symbol*] (SAG)
CNSL .... Cashew Nutshell Liquid
CNSL .... Console (KSC)
CNSL .... Counsel [*or Counseling or Counselor*] (AFM)
CNSL .... Counsel
CNSLD .... Chronic Nonspecific Lung Disease (CPH)
CNSLD .... Consolidate (MSA)
Cnsllr.......... Counsellor
CNSLLR ...... Counsellor
CNSLNG ...... Counseling
CNSLNR ...... Counselor
CNSLTN ...... Consultation
CNSLTNG .... Consulting
CNSM .... Cambridge Natural Science Manuals [*A publication*]
CNSM .... Chicago North Shore & Milwaukee R. R. [*AAR code*]
CnsMerc ...... Consolidated Mercatile Corp. [*Associated Press*] (SAG)
CNSMR .... Consumer
CNSN .... Canadian National Seismograph Network
CNSN .... Certified Nutrition Support Nurse (MEDA)
CNSO .... Conso Products [*NASDAQ symbol*] (TTSB)
CNSO .... Conso Products Co. [*NASDAQ symbol*] (SAG)
CNSP .... Central Sprinkler [*NASDAQ symbol*] (TTSB)
CNSP .... Central Sprinkler Corp. [*NASDAQ symbol*] (NQ)
CNSP .... Conspicuously
CnSprn........ Central Sprinkler Corp. [*Associated Press*] (SAG)
CNSR .... Canadian Network for Space Research (AC)
CNSR .... Combination Neutron Source Rod [*Nuclear energy*]. (NRCH)
CNSR .... Consumer
CNSRTM ..... Consortium
CNSS .... Canadian National Steamships [*AAR code*]
CNSS .... Center for National Security Studies (EA)
CNSS .... Core Nodal Switching Subsystems [*Electronics*] (ACRL)
CNSSC .... Conference of National Social Science Councils and Analogous Bodies
CNSSO........ Chief Naval Supply and Secretariat Officer [*British*]
CNST .... Coagulase-Negative Staphylococci [*Medicine*] (DMAA)
CNST .... Consiglio Nazionale Scienza Tecnologia [*Italy*]
CnStain....... Consolidated Stainless, Inc. [*Associated Press*] (SAG)
CNSTAT ...... Committee on National Statistics
CNSTNT ...... Consistent (FAAC)
CnsTom ...... Consolidated Tomoka Land Co. [*Associated Press*] (SAG)
CnStor .... Consolidated Stores Corp. [*Associated Press*] (SAG)
CNSWTG ..... Commander, Naval Special Warfare Task Group (NVT)
CNSY .... Charleston Naval Shipyard [*South Carolina*]
CNSYD........ Charleston Naval Shipyard [*South Carolina*]
CNT............. Canadian National Telecommunications
CNT............. Canadian National Telephone Co. (NITA)
CNT............. Canton [*Republic of China*] [*Seismograph station code, US Geological Survey*] (SEIS)
C/N/t .... Carrier-to-Noise, Total
CNT............. Celestial Navigation Trainer
CNT............. Center for Neighborhood Technology (EA)
CNT............. CenterPoint Properties [*AMEX symbol*] (SPSG)
CNT............. Centre National d'Etudes des Telecommunications [*France ICAO designator*] (FAAC)
CNT............. Certified Navy Twill (DNAB)
CNT............. Chief of Naval Training
CNT............. Coleoptile Node-Tillers of Wheat [*Plant pathology*]
CNT............. Commentaire du Nouveau Testament [*Neuchatel*] [*A publication*] (BJA)
CNT............. Commission to New Towns [*British*]
CNT............. Confraternity New Testament [*A publication*] (BJA)
CNT............. Container [*Shipping*] (DS)
CNT............. Could Not Test [*Laboratory*] (DAVI)
CNT............. Count
CNT............. Counter (MDG)
CNT............. Couny
CNT............. Cyanide Total (EG)
CNT............. Cyanotoluene [*Organic chemistry*]
CNTA .... Canadian Nursery Trades Association (AC)
CNTA .... Cenral Nova Tourist Association (AC)
CNTA .... Council of Nordic Teachers' Associations [*Copenhagen, Denmark*] (EAIO)
CNTB .... Cantab Pharmaceuticals Ltd. [*NASDAQ symbol*] (SAG)
CntBncp....... Center Bancorp, Inc. [*Associated Press*] (SAG)
CNTBRD ..... Centerboard (MSA)
CNTBY .... Cantab Pharmaceuticals ADS [*NASDAQ symbol*] (TTSB)
CNTC .... Canadian Network of Toxicology Centres (AC)
CNTC .... Contact (AABC)
CNTCLKWS... Counterclockwise
CNTCLKWZ... Counterclockwise (AFM)
CntCrd .... Countrywide Credit Industries, Inc. [*Associated Press*] (SAG)
CNTD .... Contained (MSA)
CNTD .... Controlled Nucleation Thermochemical Deposition (MCD)
cnte .... Conte (VRA)
cnte .... Conte Crayon (VRA)
CNTECHTRA... Chief of Navy Technical Training (DNAB)
CNTER .... Center [*Commonly used*] (OPSA)
CNTF........... Chick Neurotropic Factor [*Neurochemistry*]
CNTF........... Ciliary Neurotrophic Factor [*Biochemistry*]

CNTFGL.......	Centrifugal (MSA)
CNTGCY.......	Contingency (AABC)
CNTI...........	Cantel Industries [NASDAQ symbol] (TTSB)
CNTL...........	Cantel Industries, Inc. [NASDAQ symbol] (SAG)
CNTL...........	Central
CNTL...........	Command Nuclear Target List (MCD)
CNTL...........	Control (KSC)
CNTL...........	National Council of Tourism in Lebanon (EY)
CntlCir........	Continental Circuits Corp. [Associated Press] (SAG)
CntlInfo.......	Continental Information Systems Corp. [Associated Press] (SAG)
CNTLR........	Controller
CntMne........	Centurion Mines Corp. [Associated Press] (SAG)
CNTN.........	Contain (AABC)
CNTN.........	Contain
CNTNMNT....	Cantonment
CNTNR........	Container (MSA)
CNTO..........	Centocor, Inc. [NASDAQ symbol] (NQ)
CNTOR........	Contactor (MSA)
CNTP..........	Cincinnati, New Orleans & Texas Pacific Railway Co. [AAR code]
CNTP..........	Committee for a National Trade Policy [Defunct]
CNTP..........	Country and New Town Properties [British]
CntPk..........	Canterbury Park Holdings [Associated Press] (SAG)
CNTPS........	Consolidated Naval Telecommunications Program System (DNAB)
CNTR.........	Center
cntr............	Central (VRA)
CNTR.........	Centura Software Corp. [NASDAQ symbol] (SAG)
CNTR.........	Container (KSC)
CNTR.........	Contribute (AABC)
CNTR.........	Counter (MSA)
CNTR.........	Counter
CNTRCT.......	Contract
CNTRCTNG...	Contracting
CNTRF........	Centrifugal (AABC)
CNTRFUGL..	Centrifugal [Freight]
CNTRL........	Control
CNTRL........	Control
CNTRL........	Control Key [Electronics]
CNTRL........	Controller (NASA)
CNTRLLR....	Controller
CNTRLN.......	Centerline (FAAC)
CnTrnRtl......	Central Transport Rental Group Ltd. [Formerly, Tiphook Ltd. ADS] [Associated Press] (SAG)
cntrps..........	Contrapposto (VRA)
CNTRS BB ...	Containers in Barrels or Boxes [Freight]
CNTRWT......	Counterweight
CNTRY........	Cemetery
CNTRY........	Country
CNTRYSD....	Countryside
CNTS..........	Chief of Naval Technical Services [Canada]
CNTS..........	Chief of Naval Transportation Service
CNTST........	Contest
CNTT..........	Chief of Naval Technical Training (NVT)
CNTU..........	Confederation of National Trade Unions [Canada]
CNTW.........	Committee for National Theatre Week (EA)
CNTY..........	Century Casinos [NASDAQ symbol] (TTSB)
CNTY..........	Century Casinos, Inc. [NASDAQ symbol] (SAG)
CNTY..........	County
CntyBc........	Century Bancorp, Inc. [Associated Press] (SAG)
CntyCm.......	Century Telecommunications [Associated Press] (SAG)
CntyTl.........	Century Telephone Co. [Associated Press] (SAG)
CNTYW........	Century Casinos Wrrt [NASDAQ symbol] (TTSB)
CNU...........	Cameroon National Union [Political party]
CNU...........	Canadian Newspaper Unit
C/N/u..........	Carrier-to-Noise, Uplink
CNU............	Chanute, KS [Location identifier FAA] (FAAL)
CNU............	Chengdu [Republic of China] [Seismograph station code, US Geological Survey] (SEIS)
CNU...........	Committee for Nationalist Union [British]
CNU...........	Compare Numeric Unequal [Computer science]
CNU...........	Conscot Resources Ltd. [Vancouver Stock Exchange symbol] (SAG)
CNU...........	Continucare [AMEX symbol] (SAG)
CNU...........	Continuum Co. [NYSE symbol] (SPSG)
CNU...........	CSM [Command and Service Module] Navigation Update [NASA]
CNU...........	National University Library Cataloging Department, San Diego, CA [OCLC symbol] (OCLC)
CNUAH........	Centro de las Naciones Unidas para los Asentamientos Humanos [United Nations Centre for Human Settlements] [Spanish] (DUND)
CNUCD........	Conference des Nations Unies pour le Commerce et le Developpement [United Nations Conference on Trade and Development - UNCTAD] [French]
CNUCE........	Centro Nazionale Universitario di Calcalo Electronico [National University Center for Electronic Calculation] [Italy] (NITA)
CNUEH........	Centre des Nations Unies pour les Etablissements Humains [United Nations Centre for Human Settlements] [French] (DUND)
CNUIP........	Commission des Nations Unies pour l'Inde et le Pakistan
CNUJ..........	Committee for Nordic Universities of Journalism [See also RNJ] (EAIO)
CNUP..........	Center for Neuroscience, University of Pittsburgh
CNUR..........	Corriente Nacionalista de Unidad y Reconciliacion [Nicaragua] [Political party] (EY)
CNUURC.......	Commission des Nations Unies pour l'Unification et le Relevement de la Coree
CNV............	Cacao Necrosis Virus [Plant pathology]
CNV............	Canavieiras [Brazil] [Airport symbol] (OAG)

CNV	Cape Canaveral [Florida] (KSC)
CNV	Choroidal Neovascularization [Opthalmology]
CNV	Colistimethate-Nystatin-Vancomycin [Antibiotic mixture]
CNV	Conative Negative Variation (MAE)
CNV	Conditioned Nausea and Vomiting [Medicine]
CNV	Conduction Nerve Velocity [Neurology] (CPH)
CNV	Consolidated CSA Minerals, Inc. [Vancouver Stock Exchange symbol]
CNV	Contingent Negative Variation [Electrocortical measurement]
CNV	Convection
CNV	Converse
CNV	Convertible Hldgs [NYSE symbol] (TTSB)
CNV	Convertible Holdings [NYSE symbol] (SPSG)
CNVA	Center for Nonviolent Alternatives [Defunct] (EA)
CNVA	Committee for Nonviolent Action [Later, WRL] (EA)
CNVAA........	Combined National Veterans Association of America (EA)
CNVC	Convenience (MSA)
CNVEO........	Center for Night Vision and Electro-Optics [Fort Belvoir, VA] [Army] (INF)
CNVF	Coalition for Non-Violent Food (EA)
CNVF	Complex Notophyll Vine Forest
CNVG	Converge (FAAC)
CNVL	City Investing Co. Liquidating Trust [NASDAQ symbol] (NQ)
CNVLZ	City Investing Liq Tr [NASDAQ symbol] (TTSB)
CNVNT........	Convent
CNVNTN.......	Convention
CNVPr.........	Convertible Hldgs Inc Shrs [NYSE symbol] (TTSB)
CNVR	Conveyor (KSC)
CNVRSN	Conversion
CNVRT	Convert (FAAC)
CNVSN	Conversion (FAAC)
CnvstE	ConVest Energy Corp. [Associated Press] (SAG)
Cnvt	Convert (BARN)
CNVT	Convert (ECII)
CNVT	Converter [Electronics] (ECII)
CNVT	Convict (AABC)
CNVTS	Central Night Vision Training School [Military British]
CNVTV	Convective (FAAC)
CNVX	Convex Computer Corp. (MHDW)
CNVYG	Conveying
CNVYR	Conveyor
CNW	Canada News-Wire [Database] [Canada News-Wire Service] [Information service or system] (CRD)
CNW	Canada Northwest Energy Ltd. [Toronto Stock Exchange symbol]
CNW	Childress [Texas] [Seismograph station code, US Geological Survey] (SEIS)
CNW	China Northwest Airlines [ICAO designator] (FAAC)
CNW	CNW Corp. [NYSE symbol] (SPSG)
CNW	Combination Network [Graph theory]
CNW	Waco, TX [Location identifier FAA] (FAAL)
CNWA.........	Charleston Naval Weapons Annex [South Carolina]
CNWDI........	Critical Nuclear Weapons Design Information (MCD)
CNWF	Council for a Nuclear Weapons Freeze [Later, IFLN] (EA)
CNWM	Citizens Network on Waste Management (AC)
CNwMH.......	California State Department of Mental Hygiene, Metropolitan State Hospital Professional Staff Library, Norwalk, CA [Library symbol Library of Congress] (LCLS)
CNWRS.......	Centre for North-West Regional Studies [University of Lancaster] [British] (CB)
CNX	Allcanada Express Ltd. [Canada ICAO designator] (FAAC)
CNX	Canadian Northstar Corp. [Toronto Stock Exchange symbol]
CNX	Cancel (NVT)
CNX	Chiang Mai [Thailand] [Airport symbol] (OAG)
CNX	Convex Computer Corp. [NYSE symbol] (SPSG)
CNX	Corona, NM [Location identifier FAA] (FAAL)
CNXS	CNS, Inc. [NASDAQ symbol] (NQ)
CNY	City College of New York [New York] [Seismograph station code, US Geological Survey] (SEIS)
CNY	Moab [Utah] [Airport symbol] (OAG)
CNY	Moab, UT [Location identifier FAA] (FAAL)
CNYD	Croes Newydd [Welsh depot code]
CNYK	Central New York Railroad Corp. [AAR code]
CNYN.........	Canyon [Commonly used] (OPSA)
CNYT	Current New York Time (DOAD)
CNZ	Chateau [New Zealand] [Seismograph station code, US Geological Survey] (SEIS)
CNZ	Clarendon, TX [Location identifier FAA] (FAAL)
CO.............	Cabinet Office [New South Wales] [Australia]
CO.............	Call Option [Investment term]
CO.............	Camouflage Officer [British]
CO.............	Carbon Monoxide
C/O............	Carbon to Oxygen [Ratio]
CO.............	Cardiac Output [Cardiology]
C/O............	Care Of [Correspondence]
co.............	Care Of (WDMC)
C/O............	Care of County (WDMC)
co.............	Cargo Oil (DS)
CO.............	Cargo Operations [NASA] (MCD)
CO.............	Caribbean Organization [An international governmental body, of which the US was a member] [Terminated, 1965]
CO.............	Carried Over [Accounting]
Co.............	Carya ovata [Shagbark hickory]
C/O............	Case Of (AAG)
CO.............	Case Officer [Criminology] (LAIN)
C/O............	Case Oil

CO...............	Cash Order [*Business term*]
co...............	Cash Order (WDMC)
CO...............	Castor Oil
CO...............	Casualty Officer [*Military*] (DAVI)
CO...............	Cathodal Opening [*Medicine*] (ROG)
CO...............	Cathode-Ray Oscillator
CO...............	Cemented Only [*Of envelopes*]
CO...............	Central Office
CO...............	Centric Occlusion [*Dentistry*]
C/O...............	Cents-Off Coupon [*Advertising*]
CO...............	Certificate of Occupancy [*Business term*] (EMRF)
C/O...............	Certificate of Origin [*International trade*]
CO...............	Certificate of Origin [*Investment term*] (DFIT)
CO...............	Certification Office [*Trade union regulation*] [*British*]
CO...............	Certified Orthotist
CO...............	Cervical Orthosis [*Medicine*]
CO...............	Cervicoaxial [*Dentistry*] (DAVI)
CO...............	Chain Operator (AAG)
CO...............	Chain Overseas [*Aviation*]
C/O...............	Change Order (NG)
CO...............	Change [*of*] Order
C/O...............	Changeout (NASA)
CO...............	Change Over (DEN)
C/O...............	Channel Oscilloscope
C/O...............	Charging Order (DCTA)
CO...............	Check OK [*Telecommunications*] (TEL)
CO...............	Check Open [*Nuclear energy*] (NRCH)
CO...............	Checkout (KSC)
C/O...............	Check Out [*Medicine*] (DAVI)
C/O...............	Chief Officer [*Women's Royal Naval Service*] [*British*]
CO...............	Chief of Ordnance [*Army*]
CO...............	Chief Operator (NRCH)
CO...............	Choir Organ (ROG)
CO...............	Choline Oxidase [*An enzyme*]
CO...............	Christian Overcomers [*An association*] (EA)
CO...............	Ciclopirox Olamine [*Antifungal agent*]
CO...............	Classifier Overflow (IAA)
CO...............	Cleanout (AAG)
CO...............	Clergy Orphan Schools [*British*] (ROG)
CO...............	Clerical Officer [*Civil Service*] [*British*]
CO...............	Clock Oscillator
CO...............	Close-Open
CO...............	Closing Order (ROG)
CO...............	Coast
Co...............	Cobalt [*Chemical element*]
CO...............	COBOL [*Common Business-Oriented Language*] [*Computer science*] (IAA)
CO...............	Coden [*Online database field identifier*]
CO...............	Coefficient of Overestimation
Co...............	Coenzyme [*Biochemistry*]
CO...............	Coinbox Line [*Telecommunications*] (TEL)
CO...............	Coinsurance
CO...............	Coke Oven
Co...............	Coke's English King's Bench Reports [*1572-1616*] [*A publication*] (DLA)
Co...............	Coke's Institutes [*England*] [*A publication*] (DLA)
CO...............	Coldset Offset [*Printing*] (DGA)
CO...............	Colistin [*Also, CL*] [*Generic form An antibiotic*]
CO...............	Collation [*Online database field identifier*]
CO...............	Colombia [*ANSI two-letter standard code*] (CNC)
CO...............	Colon [*City in Panama*] (ROG)
CO₂...............	Colonial Office [*British*]
CO...............	Colorado [*Postal code*]
CO...............	Colorado Reports [*A publication*] (DLA)
Co...............	Colorado State Library, Denver, CO [*Library symbol Library of Congress*] (LCLS)
CO...............	Combat Aptitude Area (AABC)
CO...............	Combat Operation (INF)
CO...............	Combined Operations
CO...............	Come [*Like, As*] [*Music*] (ROG)
CO...............	Commanding Officer
CO...............	Command Operations [*Army*] (AABC)
CO...............	Command Orders
CO...............	Command Output
CO...............	Commercial
CO...............	Commissioner for Oaths
CO...............	Commissioner's Office [*Scotland Yard*]
CO...............	Common Orders (DLA)
CO...............	Commonwealth Office [*Formerly, CRO*] [*British*]
CO...............	Commonwealth Ombudsman [*Australia*]
CO...............	Communication (IAA)
CO...............	Communications Officer [*Navy*]
CO...............	Company [*Business term*] (AAG)
CO...............	Company
Co...............	Company (DD)
C-O...............	Company Owned (NTCM)
C/O...............	Complains Of [*Medicine*]
CO...............	Compliance Officer [*Department of Labor*]
CO...............	Components Only
CO...............	Compositus [*Compound*] [*Pharmacy*]
CO...............	Compound [*Medicine*] (AAMN)
c/o...............	Compte Ouvert [*Open Account*] [*French Business term*]
CO...............	Conceptual Organization [*Psychometrics*]
CO...............	Cone

CO...............	Congregation of the Oratory [*Oratorians*] [*Roman Catholic men's religious order*]
CO...............	Coniagas Mines Ltd. [*Toronto Stock Exchange symbol*]
co...............	Conical Tank [*Liquid gas carriers*]
CO...............	Conjugi Optimo [*To My Most Excellent Spouse*] [*Latin*]
CO...............	Connection-Oriented (ACRL)
CO...............	Conscientious Objector
C/O...............	Consist Of (MSA)
CO...............	Constantine Order [*Freemasonry*] (ROG)
CO...............	Constantly Operating
CO...............	Container
C/O...............	Contamination/Overpressure (MCD)
CO...............	Continental Airlines [*ICAO designator*] (AD)
CO...............	Continental Airlines, Inc. [*CAB official abbreviation*]
CO...............	Continuous Observation [*Nursing order*] (CPH)
CO...............	Contracting Officer [*Also, CONTRO, KO*]
CO...............	Control Order (MCD)
co...............	Copolymerized With [*Organic chemistry*]
CO...............	Copy (ROG)
CO...............	Copyright Office [*US*]
Co...............	Coral [*Quality of the bottom*] [*Nautical charts*]
CO...............	Corneal Opacity [*Medicine*] (MAE)
CO...............	Corn Oil
CO...............	Corporate Office (AAG)
CO...............	Corps Observation
CO...............	Corpus [*Referring to the uterus*] [*Gynecology*] (DAVI)
CO...............	Correction
CO...............	Correctional Officer
CO...............	Corrpro Co. [*NYSE symbol*] (TTSB)
Co...............	Costa [*Entomology*]
CO...............	Council Officer [*British*] (ROG)
CO...............	Country
CO...............	County (EY)
co...............	County (VRA)
c/o...............	County (WDMC)
CO...............	Coupled Oscillator (DEN)
CO...............	Course
CO...............	Course Pennant [*Navy British*]
CO...............	Covered Option [*Investment term*]
Co...............	Cowling Number [*IUPAC*]
C-0...............	Crew-Operated (SAA)
CO...............	Criminal Offence [*British*]
CO...............	Criminal Office
CO...............	Crossover [*Genetics*]
CO...............	Crown Office [*British*]
CO...............	Crystal Oscillator
CO...............	Customer Order Set (IAA)
CO...............	Cutoff (MSA)
CO...............	Cut Out
CO...............	Cycling Oiler [*Navy*] (MCD)
CO...............	Cyclophosphamide, Oncovin [*Vincristine*] [*Antineoplastic drug regimen*]
CO...............	Cytochrome Oxidase [*An enzyme*]
CO...............	Oakland Public Library, Oakland, CA [*Library symbol Library of Congress*] (LCLS)
CO...............	Oratorians (TOCD)
co...............	Oratorians (TOCD)
C₀...............	Output Capacitance (IDOE)
CO...............	Station Open to Official Correspondence Exclusively [*ITU designation*]
CO 1MO......	Canto Primo [*First Soprano*] [*Music*] (ROG)
CO10	Canto Primo [*First Soprano*] [*Music*]
CO₂...............	Carbon Dioxide (CDAI)
CO2 LRF......	Carbon Dioxide LASER Rangefinder [*Army*]
CO₃...............	Carbonate (GNE)
CO3...............	Carbonate
Co-60...............	Cobalt-60
COA	California Olive Association (EA)
COA	California Optometric Association (SRA)
COA	California Orthopaedic Association (SRA)
COA	Cal Owner's Association [*Defunct*] (EA)
COA	Camaro Owners of America [*Defunct*] (EA)
COA	Canadian Olympic Association
COA	Canadian Orthopaedic Association (DAVI)
COA	Carwash Operators Association (EA)
COA	Cathedral Organists' Association (EA)
COA	Cause of Action [*Legal shorthand*] (LWAP)
COA	Center on Aging [*University of Maryland*] [*Research center*] (RCD)
COA	Center Operations Area
COA	Central Operating Agency (NATG)
COA	Certificate of Authority
COA	Certified Office Administrator
COA	Change of Address
COA	Change of Assignment
COA	Change Order Account (AFM)
CO(A)	Change Order (Aircraft)
COA	Chief of Operations Analysis (MCD)
COA	Children of Alcoholic
CoA...............	Children of Alcoholics
COA	Children of the Americas (EA)
COA	Chloroxymorphamine [*Narcotic agonist*] [*Pharmacochemistry*]
COA	Christian Outdoorsman Association (EA)
COA	Clean Ocean Action (GNE)
COA	Coachella [*California*] [*Seismograph station code, US Geological Survey*] (SEIS)

COA	Coachmen Indus [*NYSE symbol*] (TTSB)
CoA	Coachmen Industries, Inc. [*NYSE symbol*] (SPSG)
CoA	Coagulation
CoA	Coarctation of the Aorta [*Cardiology*] (DAVI)
CoA	Coenzyme A [*Biochemistry*]
COA	Cognizant Operating Authority (MUGU)
COA	Coherent Optical Array
COA	College of Aeronautics [*British*]
COA	Colonial Order of the Acorn (EA)
CO A	Colorado Court of Appeals Reports [*A publication*] (DLA)
COA	Colorado Motor Carriers' Association, Denver CO [*STAC*]
COA	Colorado Optometric Association (SRA)
COA	Colorado Outfitters Association (SRA)
COA	Comanche Petroleums [*Vancouver Stock Exchange symbol*]
COA	Commissioned Officers Association of the United States Public Health Service (EA)
COA	Commission on the Aging (OICC)
COA	Committee for an Open Archives (EA)
COA	Committee on Accreditation [*American Library Association*]
COA	Commonwealth of Australia
COA	Compass Operation Alarm
COA	Comptroller of the Army
COA	Condition on Admission [*Medicine*] (ADA)
COA	Connecticut Opticians Association (SRA)
COA	Constant-Output Amplifier (MUGU)
COA	Continental Airlines, Inc. [*ICAO designator*] (FAAC)
COA	Contract of Affreightment [*Shipping*]
Co A	Cook's Lower Canada Admiralty Court Cases [*A publication*] (DLA)
COA	Cordova Airlines, Inc.
COA	Corporate Ombudsman Association (EA)
COA	Corps of Ordnance Artificers [*British military*] (DMA)
COA	Council of Agriculture [*Queensland*] [*Australia*]
CoA	Council of the Americas (EA)
COA	Council on Accreditation of Services for Families and Children (EA)
COA	Council on Aging
COA	Course-of-Action [*Military*]
COA	Crack-Opening Angle (MCD)
COA	Cruiser Olympia Association (EA)
COA	Current Operating Allowances
COA	Indianapolis, IN [*Location identifier FAA*] (FAAL)
COA	Shepard's Causes of Action [*A publication*]
COA	University of Colorado at Denver, Auraria Libraries, Denver, CO [*OCLC symbol*] (OCLC)
COAA	Customs Officers' Association of Australia
COAAL	Coordinated Activity Allowance List [*Military*] (NVT)
COAB	Computer Operator Aptitude Battery [*Test*]
COAC	Chief Operating Area Coordinator (DNAB)
COAC	Clutter-Operated Anticlutter
COAC	College Ouest Africaine des Chirurgiens [*West African College of Surgeons - WACS*] (EAIO)
COAC	Commanding Officer, Atlantic Coast
COAC	Council on Adoptable Children (EA)
COACH	Canadian Organization for Advancement of Computers in Health (EAIO)
COACH	Computer-Aided Chartroom
Coachm	Coachmen Industries, Inc. [*Associated Press*] (SAG)
COACT	Combat Activity Report [*Navy*]
CO-ACTION	Co-Operative Action Programme [*UNESCO*] (EA)
COAD	Chronic Obstructive Airway Disease [*Medicine*]
COAD	Chronic Obstructive Arterial Disease [*Cardiology*] (DAVI)
COAD	Coadjutor (ROG)
COAD	Coin-Operated Amusement Device
COAD	Columbus Army Depot [*Ohio*] (AABC)
COAD	Company Facts and Addresses [*EDIC*] [*Ringmer Near Lewes, East Sussex, England*] [*Information service or system*] (IID)
COAD	Continued on Active Duty (AABC)
COAD	Coordinate Adder (SAA)
COA(DAB)	Comptroller of the Army (Director of the Army Budget)
Co-ADD	Coalition for the Education and Support of Attention Deficit Disorder (PAZ)
COADJ	Coadjutor (ROG)
COADJ BP	Coadjutor Bishop (ROG)
COADS	Command and Administration System [*Army*]
COADS	Comprehensive Ocean Atmosphere Data Set
COADS	Conference on Application Development Systems (MHDI)
CoA/FMME	Council of the Americas/Fund for Multinational Management Education
CoAg	Aguilar Public Library, Aguilar, CO [*Library symbol Library of Congress*] (LCLS)
COAG	Chronic Open Angle Glaucoma [*Ophthalmology*]
coag	Coagulase [*An enzyme*]
COAG	Coagulation
COAG	Committee on Agriculture [*Food and Agricultural Organization*] [*United Nations*]
COAG PD	Coagulation Profile - Diagnosis [*Hematology*] (DAVI)
COAG PP	Coagulation Profile - Presurgery [*Hematology*] (DAVI)
COAHR	Committee on Appeal for Human Rights
COAIREVACRON	Commanding Officer, Air Evacuation Squadron
CoAk	Akron Public Library, Akron, CO [*Library symbol Library of Congress*] (LCLS)
COAL	Alameda County Law Library, Oakland, CA [*Library symbol Library of Congress*] (LCLS)
COAL	Amer Fuel [*NASDAQ symbol*] (TTSB)
COAL	Chronic Obstructive Airflow Limitation [*Medicine*] (DMAA)

CoAl	City of Alamosa-Southern Peaks Library, Alamosa, CO [*Library symbol Library of Congress*] (LCLS)
COAL	Coalition (ADA)
COAL	Consolidated Ordnance Allowance List [*Navy*]
COALA	Computer Aided Linguistic Analysis
CoAlC	Adams State College, Alamosa, CO [*Library symbol Library of Congress*] (LCLS)
COALDATA	European Coal Data Bank [*DECHEMA*] [*Germany Information service or system*] (IID)
COALPRO	Coal Research Projects [*IEA Coal Research*] [*Database*]
CoAlS	Southern Peaks Public Library, Alamosa, CO [*Library symbol*] [*Library of Congress*] (LCLS)
COALU	Amer Fuel Unit [*NASDAQ symbol*] (TTSB)
COAM	Client Owned and Maintained (ECII)
COAM	Coaming [*Naval architecture*]
COAM	Customer Owned and Maintained (OA)
COAMP	Computer Analysis of Maintenance Policies (MHDI)
COAMP	Cost Analysis of Maintenance Policy
COAMPS	Coupled Ocean Atmosphere Mesoscale Prediction System [*Marine science*] (OSRA)
COAMS	Computerization of Army Movement Schedules (CINC)
Co & Al	Cooke and Alcock's Great Britain Reports [*Ireland*] [*A publication*] (DLA)
CO & E	Crab Orchard & Egyptian Railroad [*American Rail Heritage Ltd.*]
CO & G	Chocktaw, Oklahoma & Gulf Railroad
Co & Sec Law Journal	Company and Securities Law Journal [*Australia A publication*]
CoAnG	Guadalupe Elementary School, Canejos School, Antonio, CO [*Library symbol*] [*Library of Congress*] (LCLS)
COANP	Cyclooctylamino-nitropyridine [*Organic chemistry*]
COAP	Center for Ocean Analysis and Prediction [*Monterey, CA*] [*NOAA*]
COAP	Center for Oceanic Analysis and Prediction [*Monterey, CA*] [*National Oceanic and Atmospheric Administration*]
COAP	Combat Optimization and Analysis Program [*Air Force*]
COAP	Cottonseed Oil Assistance Program [*Department of Agriculture*]
COAP	Cyclophosphamide, Oncovin [*Vincristine*], ara-C, Prednisone [*Antineoplastic drug regimen*]
COAP-BLEO	Cyclophosphamide, Oncovin [*Vincristine*], ara-C, Prednisone, Bleomycin [*Cytarabine*] [*Antineoplastic drug regimen*]
CoAr	Arvada Public Library, Arvada, CO [*Library symbol Library of Congress*] (LCLS)
COAR	COAR [*Comunidad Oscar A. Romero*] Peace Mission (EA)
COAR	Coherent Array RADAR (MSA)
COARC	Coarctation [*Cardiology*]
COARE	Coupled Ocean-Atmosphere Response Experiment [*Marine science*] (OSRA)
COARE	Coupled Ocean-Atmosphere Response Experiment [*Tropical Ocean-Global Atmosphere*] (USDC)
CoArGS	Church of Jesus Christ of Latter-Day Saints, Genealogical Society Library, Arvada Branch, Arvada, CO [*Library symbol Library of Congress*] (LCLS)
COAS	Canadian Osteopathic Aid Society (AC)
COAS	Coarse Optical Alignment Sight (NASA)
COAS	Columbia First Federal Savings & Loan Association (MHDW)
COAS	Council of the Organization of American States [*OAS*]
COAS	Council on Atmospheric Sciences
COAS	Crew [*or Crewman*] Optical Alignment Sight [*or Subsystem*] [*NASA*]
CoAs	Pitkin County Public Library, Aspen, CO [*Library symbol Library of Congress*] (LCLS)
CoAsL	Aspen Law Center, Aspen, CO [*Library symbol Library of Congress*] (LCLS)
COASP	Coordinated Aircraft/Stores Program [*Obsolete Navy*] (NG)
CoA-SPC	Coenzyme A-Synthetizing Protein Complex [*Medicine*] (DMAA)
COAST	Cambridge Optical Aperture Synthesis Telescope
Coast	Cambridge Optical Aperture Synthesis Telescope
COAST	Coastal Observation and Simulation with Topography [*Marine science*] (OSRA)
COAST	Coastal Observations and Simulations with Topography (USDC)
COASTA	Conference of Officers of Affiliated States and Territorial Associations
Coastal	[*The*] Coastal Corp. [*Formerly, Coastal State Gas Producing Co.*] [*Associated Press*] (SAG)
Coastcst	Coastcast Corp. [*Associated Press*] (SAG)
CoastD	Coast Distribution Systems [*Associated Press*] (SAG)
Coastl	[*The*] Coastal Corp. [*Formerly, Coastal State Gas Producing Co.*] [*Associated Press*] (SAG)
CoastSv	Coast Savings Financial, Inc. [*Associated Press*] (SAG)
COASYS	Crude Oil Analysis System [*National Institute for Petroleum and Energy Research*] (CRD)
COAT	Children's Orientation and Amnesia Test [*Medicine*] (DMAA)
COAT	Coherent Optical Adaptive Techniques
COAT	Coherent Optical Array Techniques
COAT	Continuous Oil Analysis Treatment [*Automotive maintenance*]
COAT	Corrected Outside Air Temperature
COATS	Canadian Over-the-Counter Automated Trading System
COATS	Communications-Oriented Automatic Test (MCD)
CoAul	Ault Public Library, Ault, CO [*Library symbol Library of Congress*] (LCLS)
CoAur	Aurora Public Library, Aurora, CO [*Library symbol Library of Congress*] (LCLS)
COAX	Coaxial (AAG)
COB	Aurora Public Library, Aurora, CO [*OCLC symbol*] (OCLC)
CoB	Boulder Public Library, Boulder, CO [*Library symbol Library of Congress*] (LCLS)
COB	Carry-On Box
COB	Ceramic Oceanographic Buoy

COB .... Change Order Board (AAG)

COB .... Chronic Obstructive Bronchitis [*Medicine*] (DMAA)

COB .... Cinematograph Operators' Board [*Victoria*] [*Australia*]

COB .... Cisplatin, Oncovin [*Vincristine*], Bleomycin [*Antineoplastic drug regimen*] (DAVI)

COB .... Cisplatin, Oncovin, Bleomycine [*Antineoplastic drug*] (CDI)

COB .... Clear over Base [*System of paint finishing*] [*Automotive engineering*]

COB .... Clip-on-Board [*Instrumentation*]

COB .... Close of Business [*With date*]

cob............. Cobalt [*Philately*]

COB .... Cobb [*New Zealand*] [*Seismograph station code, US Geological Survey*] (SEIS)

COB .... COBOL [*Common Business-Oriented Language*] Element Subtype [*Computer science*]

COB .... Collocated Operating Bases (MCD)

COB .... Colorado Motor Tariff Bureau, Inc., Denver CO [*STAC*]

Co-B............ Colorado State Library for the Blind and Physically Handicapped, Denver, CO [*Library symbol Library of Congress*] (LCLS)

COB .... Columbia Laboratories [*AMEX symbol*] (TTSB)

COB .... Columbia Laboratories, Inc. [*AMEX symbol*] (SPSG)

COB .... Comite Olimpico Boliviano [*Bolivian Olympic Committee*] (EAIO)

COB .... Command Operating Budget [*Army*]

COB .... Commission des Operations de Bourse

COB .... Committee of Combined Boards

COB .... Communications Office Building (NASA)

COB .... Complementary Offset Binary (HGAA)

COB .... Congregation of Oblates of Bethany [*Roman Catholic women's religious order*]

COB .... Congressional Office of the Budget

COB .... Conseil des Operations de Bourse [*French*] (ECON)

COB .... Continental-Oceanic [*Crust*] Boundary [*Geology*]

COB .... Continent-Ocean Boundary [*Geology*]

COB .... Coordination of Benefits [*Insurance*]

COB .... Cost Operating Budget (NOAA)

COB .... Current on Board (DNAB)

COB .... Cut Out Background [*Printing*]

CoBa............ Basalt Public Library, Basalt, CO [*Library symbol Library of Congress*] (LCLS)

COBA .... Commerce Bancorp [*NASDAQ symbol*] (TTSB)

COBA .... Commerce Bancorp New Jersey [*NASDAQ symbol*] (SAG)

COBA .... Coordinating Organization of Book Associations [*Defunct*]

CoBA............ National Center for Atmospheric Research, Boulder, CO [*Library symbol Library of Congress*] (LCLS)

COBAC .... Computer-Based Analytical Chemistry [*Conference*] [*Munich, 1982*]

CoBA-HA....... National Center for Atmospheric Research, High Altitude Observatory, Boulder, CO [*Library symbol Library of Congress*] (LCLS)

CoBai........... Park County Public Library, Bailey, CO [*Library symbol Library of Congress*] (LCLS)

Cobancp ...... Cobancorp, Inc. [*Associated Press*] (SAG)

COBAS......... Council of Black Architectural Schools [*Defunct*] (EA)

COBATAME... Committee of Black Americans for Truth about the Middle-East [*Defunct*]

CoBay .... Bayfield Public Library, Bayfield, CO [*Library symbol Library of Congress*] (LCLS)

COBAZ .... Council of Governing Bodies of Australian Zoos

COBB .... Cobbler

Cobb .... Cobb's New Digest, Laws of Georgia [*1851*] [*A publication*] (DLA)

Cobb .... Cobb's Reports [*121 Alabama*] [*A publication*] (DLA)

Cobb .... Cobb's Reports [*4-20 Georgia*] [*A publication*] (DLA)

Cobb Dig ..... Cobb's Digest of Statute Laws [*Georgia*] [*A publication*] (DLA)

Cobbey Repl... Cobbey's Practical Treatise on the Law of Replevin [*A publication*] (DLA)

Cobbey's Ann St... Cobbey's Annotated Statutes [*Nebraska*] [*A publication*] (DLA)

Cobb P & Pl... Cobbett on Pawns and Pledges [*A publication*] (DLA)

Cobb Parl Hist... Cobbett's Parliamentary History [*A publication*] (DLA)

Cobb Pol Reg... Cobbett's Political Register [*A publication*] (DLA)

CoBBRC....... Ball Brothers Research Corp., Boulder, CO [*Library symbol Library of Congress*] (LCLS)

COBBS .... Computer-Based Bibliographic Search Services [*Washington State University Libraries*] (OLDSS)

CoBBS .... United States National Oceanic and Atmospheric Administration, Environmental Research Laboratories Library, Boulder, CO [*Library symbol Library of Congress*] (LCLS)

Cobb Slav .... Cobb on Slavery [*A publication*] (DLA)

Cobb St Tr ... Cobbett's [*later, Howell's*] State Trials [*1163-1820*] [*England*] [*A publication*] (DLA)

COBCCEE ..... Comite des Organisations de la Boucherie-Charcuterie de la CEE [*Committee of Butchery and Cooked Meats Organizations of the EEC*]

COBCRM...... Cobalt-Chrome

COBE .... Command Operating Budget Estimate/Execution (MCD)

COBE .... Cosmic Background Explorer [*NASA*]

COBE .... Council on Broadcast Education [*Later, CEEM*] (NTCM)

CoBen.......... Adams County Public Library, Bennett, CO [*Library symbol Library of Congress*] (LCLS)

COBEO .... National Conference of Black Elected Officials (EA)

CoBer.......... Berthoud Public Library, Berthoud, CO [*Library symbol Library of Congress*] (LCLS)

COBESTCO... Computer-Based Estimating Technique for Contractors

COBET .... Common Basic Electronics Training (MCD)

COBFE .... Council of Black Federal Employees (EA)

CoBGS .... Church of Jesus Christ of Latter-Day Saints, Genealogical Society Library, Boulder Stake Branch, Boulder, CO [*Library symbol Library of Congress*] (LCLS)

COBH .... Commerce Bank (Harrisburg) [*NASDAQ symbol*] (SAG)

COBH .... Commerce Bk Harrisburg PA [*NASDAQ symbol*] (TTSB)

COBI .... Cobancorp, Inc. [*NASDAQ symbol*] (SAG)

COBI .... Coded Biphase

CoBIBM....... International Business Machines Corp., Systems Manufacturing Division, Boulder, CO [*Library symbol Library of Congress*] (LCLS)

COBICIL ...... Cooperative Bibliographic Center for Indiana Libraries

COBIDOC .... Commissie voor Bibliografie en Documentatie [*Netherlands Bibliographical and Documentary Committee*] [*Information service or system*] (IID)

COBIPUQ .... Comite des Bibliotheques Publiques de la Region de Quebec (AC)

COBIS .... Computer-Based Instruction System (IEEE)

CoBjBrE....... Broadway Elementary School, Grand Junction, CO [*Library symbol*] [*Library of Congress*] (LCLS)

COBK .... [*The*] Co-Operative Bank of Concord [*NASDAQ symbol*] (NQ)

Co BL.......... Coke's Bankrupt Law [*A publication*] (DLA)

COBLIB .... COBOL [*Common Business-Oriented Language*] Library [*Computer science*]

COBLOC....... CODAP [*Control Data Assembly Program*] Language Block-Oriented Compiler (MCD)

COBLOS....... Computer-Based Loans System (MHDI)

COBLSA .... Campaign to Oppose Bank Loans to South Africa [*Defunct*] (EA)

COBM .... Coded-Bias Mosaic (MCD)

COBOL........ Common Business-Oriented Language [*1959*] [*Computer science*]

COBOL/SF... COBOL Structured Facility [*IBM Corp.*] (NITA)

CoBolv .... Compania Boliviana de Energia Electrica [*Associated Press*] (SAG)

COBQ .... Chiropractors' and Osteopaths' Board of Queensland [*Australia*]

COBQ .... Cum Omnibus Bonis Quiescat [*May He, or She, Repose with All Good Souls*] [*Latin*]

COBR .... Cobra Electronics [*NASDAQ symbol*] (TTSB)

COBR .... Cobra Electronics Corp. [*NASDAQ symbol*] (SAG)

COBRA........ Cabinet Office Briefing Room [*British*]

COBRA........ Compatible On-Board Ranging

COBRA........ Comprehensive Omnibus Budget Reconciliation Act (GFGA)

COBRA........ Computer-Based Recruit Assignment (MCD)

COBRA........ Computer-Based Reference Assistance [*University of Northern Colorado*] (OLDSS)

COBRA........ Computerized Boolean Reliability Analysis [*Boeing*]

COBRA........ Computer Operated Branch Recording and Acquisition System (ADA)

COBRA........ Computer-Oriented Bearing Response Analysis [*Computer science*] (PDAA)

COBRA........ Conference for Basic Human Rights in the ASEAN [*Associaton of South East Asian Nations*] Countries [*British*]

COBRA........ Consolidated Omnibus Budget Reconciliation Act of 1985 [*Health insurance law*]

COBRA........ Continent, Britain & Asia [*Commercial firm*] (DS)

COBRA........ Coolant Boiling and Rod Arrays [*Nuclear energy*] (NRCH)

COBRA........ Copenhagen, Brussels, and Amsterdam [*Refers to a group of expressionist artists based in these three cities*]

COBRA........ Copper-Brazed Crosley [*Engine*] [*Automotive engineering*]

COBRA........ Cosmic Background Radiation Anisotropy [*Astronomy*] (ECON)

COBRA........ Counterbattery RADAR [*Military*]

CoBay .... Curved Orthotropic Bridge Analysis (PDAA)

CobraEl........ Cobra Electronics Corp. [*Associated Press*] (SAG)

CobraG........ Cobra Golf, Inc. [*Associated Press*] (SAG)

COBRAH .... Coin L-Band Ranging and Homing System [*Military*]

COBRAS....... Comprehensive Blast and Radiation Assessment System (MCD)

COBRE .... Committee on Basic Research in Education

CoBri .... Adams County Public Library, Brighton, CO [*Library symbol Library of Congress*] (LCLS)

CoBriH-M.... Brighton Community Hospital, Medical Library, Brighton, CO [*Library symbol Library of Congress*] (LCLS)

CoBriJ........... Adams County Juvenile Detention Center, Brighton, CO [*Library symbol Library of Congress*] (LCLS)

CoBro........... Mamie Doud Eisenhower Public Library, Broomfield, CO [*Library symbol Library of Congress*] (LCLS)

CoBru........... Brush Public Library, Brush, CO [*Library symbol Library of Congress*] (LCLS)

COBS .... Caesarean-Originated, Barrier-Sustained [*Rodent breeding*]

COBS .... Chronic Organic Brain Syndrome [*Medicine*]

COBSEA....... Co-Ordinating Body on the Seas of East Asia

COBSI......... Committee on Biological Sciences Information [*NAS/NRC*]

COBSRA....... Council for the British Societies for Relief Abroad (DAS)

Cob St Tr..... Cobbett's [*later, Howell's*] State Trials [*1163-1820*] [*England*] [*A publication*] (DLA)

COBT .... Chicago Open Board of Trade [*Later, MIDAM*]

COBT .... Chronic Obstruction of Biliary Tract [*Medicine*]

COBTU .... Combined Over-the-Beach Terminal Unit (NATG)

CoBue.......... Buena Vista Public Library, Buena Vista, CO [*Library symbol Library of Congress*] (LCLS)

CoBueR........ Colorado State Reformatory, Buena Vista, CO [*Library symbol Library of Congress*] (LCLS)

CoBueRL...... Colorado State Reformatory, Law Library, Buena Vista, CO [*Library symbol Library of Congress*] (LCLS)

CoBueRS...... Colorado State Reformatory, Staff Library, Buena Vista, CO [*Library symbol Library of Congress*] (LCLS)

COBUILD.... Collins Birmingham University International Language Database

CoBur.......... Burlington Public Library, Burlington, CO [*Library symbol Library of Congress*] (LCLS)

COBV .... Colocasia Bacilliform Virus [*Plant pathology*]

CoBVS .... Boulder Valley School, Boulder, CO [*Library symbol*] [*Library of Congress*] (LCLS)

CoBW.......... Western Interstate Commission for Higher Education, Boulder, CO [*Library symbol Library of Congress*] (LCLS)

COBY .... Current Operating Budget Year
COC .... Calgon Carbon [*NYSE symbol*] (SAG)
COC .... California College of Arts and Crafts, Oakland, CA [*Library symbol Library of Congress*] (LCLS)
COC .... Camco, Inc. [*Toronto Stock Exchange symbol*]
COC .... Canadian Opera Company
COC .... Carbon Monoxide Concentration
COC .... Cathodal Opening Clonus [*Physiology*] (MAE)
COC .... Cathodal Opening Contraction [*Also, CaOC*] [*Physiology*]
COC .... Central Office Connection [*Telecommunications*] (TSSD)
COC .... Certificate of Competency [*Small Business Administration*]
COC .... Certificate of Compliance [*FCC*] (NTCM)
COC .... Certificate of Conformance [*DoD*]
C/OC .... Certificate of Origin and Consignment [*Shipping*] (DS)
COC .... Certification of Completion
COC .... Chain of Custody
COC .... Chamber of Commerce
COC .... Change of Command
COC .... Change of Contract [*Business law*] (AAG)
COC .... Change Order Conference (AAG)
COC .... Chief of Chaplains [*Navy*]
COC .... Chlorate Oxygen Candle
COC .... CINCPAC [*Commander-in-Chief, Pacific*] Operation Center (CINC)
COC .... Circle of Companions [*Defunct*] (EA)
COC .... Civilian Orientation Cruise (DNAB)
COC .... Clergy Orphan Corp. [*British*]
COC .... Clerk of the Chapel [*Unions*] [*British*] (DGA)
COC .... Cleveland Open Cup [*Flash point determination*]
COC .... Climb on Course [*Aviation*] (FAAC)
COC .... Close-Open-Close (NASA)
COC .... Coccygeal [*Anatomy*]
COC .... Cocesna [*ICAO designator*] (FAAC)
COC .... Coded Optical Character [*Computer science*] (BUR)
COC .... Code of Conduct [*Military*] (AFM)
COC .... Code Operations Coordinator (MUGU)
COC .... Colloidal Organic Carbon [*Environmental chemistry*]
COC .... Colombo [*Sri Lanka*] [*Seismograph station code, US Geological Survey*] (SEIS)
COC .... Colorado College, Colorado Springs, CO [*OCLC symbol*] (OCLC)
COC .... Combat Operations Center [*Air Force*]
COC .... Combination Type Oral Contraceptive [*Medicine*]
COC .... Combined Operations Command [*British*]
COC .... Commandant of Cadets [*Military*]
COC .... Command of Camp [*Military*] (VNW)
COC .... Command Operations Center [*Military*] (NVT)
COC .... Commissioned Officer Corps [*National Oceanic and Atmospheric Administration*]
COC .... Committee of Concern
COC .... Committee on Carcinogenicity [*British*]
COC .... Committees of Correspondence (EA)
COC .... Companions of Christ (TOCD)
COC .... Compiler Object Code [*Telecommunications*] (TEL)
COC .... Complete Operational Capability
COC .... Comprehensive Organic Chemistry [*A publication*]
COC .... Comptroller of the Currency
COC .... Computer Operators' Course
COC .... Computer Oriented Classicists (EA)
COC .... Concordia [*Argentina*] [*Airport symbol*] (OAG)
COC .... Contempt of Court
COC .... Control Officers' Console
COC .... Conventional Oxidation Catalysis [*of gasoline engine exhausts*]
COC .... Corps of Cadets
COC .... Cost of Compliance [*Automotive emissions standards*]
COC .... Council of Canadians [*An association*]
CoC .... Council on Competitiveness (EA)
COC .... Cultuur-en Ontspanningscentrum [*Center for Culture and Recreation*] [*Netherlands*]
COC .... Customer-Originated Change (AAG)
COC .... Cycloolefin Copolymer
COC .... Cyprus Olympic Committee (EAIO)
COC .... Firma Conseta/Cirrus, Saabrucken [*Germany*] [*FAA designator*] (FAAC)
COc .... Oceanside Public Library, Oceanside, CA [*Library symbol Library of Congress*] (LCLS)
CoC .... Penrose Public Library, Colorado Springs, CO [*Library symbol Library of Congress*] (LCLS)
COCA .... Canadian Organization for Campus Activities
COCA .... Clearinghouse on Computer Accommodation [*General Services Administration*]
COCA .... Cooperative Contracts and Agreements [*Business term*]
COCA .... Council of Ontario Construction Associations (AC)
CoCa .... Gordon Cooper Library, Carbondale, CO [*Library symbol Library of Congress*] (LCLS)
CoCA .... United States Air Force Academy, Colorado Springs, CO [*Library symbol Library of Congress*] (LCLS)
CocaBtl .... Coca-Cola Bottling Co. Consolidated [*Associated Press*] (SAG)
COCAC .... California College of Arts and Crafts, Oakland, CA [*Library symbol*] [*Library of Congress*] (LCLS)
CocaCE .... Coca-Cola Enterprises, Inc. [*Associated Press*] (SAG)
CocaCl .... [*The*] Coca-Cola Co. [*Associated Press*] (SAG)
CoCaCM .... Carbondale Middle School, Carbondale, CO [*Library symbol*] [*Library of Congress*] (LCLS)
COCAG .... Commissioned Officer Corps Advisory Group [*National Oceanic and Atmospheric Administration*] (NOAA)

CoCA-H .... United States Air Force Academy, Hospital Library, Colorado Springs, CO [*Library symbol Library of Congress*] (LCLS)
COCAID .... Coupled Ocean-Land-Atmosphere One-Dimensional [*Model*] [*Marine science*] (OSRA)
COCAIN .... Cocaine (DAVI)
COCAMO ...... Cooperation Canada Mozambique (AC)
CoCAN .... American Numismatic Association, Colorado Springs, CO [*Library symbol Library of Congress*] (LCLS)
COC-APHA ... College of Chaplains [*of APHA*] (EA)
COCAS .... Customer Order Control Automated System (IAA)
COCAST .... Council for Overseas Colleges of Arts, Sciences, and TETOC [*British*]
COCATRAM... Comision Centroamericana de Transporte Maritimo [*Central American Commission of Maritime Transport*] [*Organization of Central American States*] [*San Salvador, El Salvador*] (EAIO)
COCB .... Crossed Olivocochlear Bundles [*Audiology*]
COCC .... California Concordia College, Oakland, CA [*Library symbol Library of Congress*] (LCLS)
CoCc .... Canon City Public Library, Canon City, CO [*Library symbol Library of Congress*] (LCLS)
COCC .... Center for Ocean Climate Chemistry [*Canada*] [*Marine science*] (OSRA)
CoCC........... Colorado College, Colorado Springs, CO [*Library symbol Library of Congress*] (LCLS)
CoCCC .... Colorado College, Colorado Springs, CO [*Library symbol*] [*Library of Congress*] (LCLS)
COCCEE ...... Comite des Organisations Commerciales des Pays de la CEE [*Committee of Commercial Organizations in the EEC Countries*]
cocci .... Coccidioidomycosis [*Bacteriology*] (DAVI)
CoCcP .... Colorado State Penitentiary, Canon City, CO [*Library symbol Library of Congress*] (LCLS)
CoCcPL .... Colorado State Penitentiary, Law Library, Canon City, CO [*Library symbol Library of Congress*] (LCLS)
CoCcPM ...... Colorado State Penitentiary, Medium Security Residents' Library, Canon City, CO [*Library symbol Library of Congress*] (LCLS)
CoCcPML .... Colorado State Penitentiary, Medium Security Law Library, Canon City, CO [*Library symbol Library of Congress*] (LCLS)
CoCcPMS .... Colorado State Penitentiary, Medium Security Staff Library, Canon City, CO [*Library symbol Library of Congress*] (LCLS)
CoCcPS .... Colorado State Penitentiary, Staff Library, Canon City, CO [*Library symbol Library of Congress*] (LCLS)
CoCcPW ...... Colorado State Penitentiary, Colorado Women's Correctional Institution, Residents' Library, Canon City, CO [*Library symbol Library of Congress*] (LCLS)
CoCcPWL .... Colorado State Penitentiary, Colorado Women's Correctional Institution, Law Library, Canon City, CO [*Library symbol Library of Congress*] (LCLS)
CoCcPWS .... Colorado State Penitentiary, Colorado Women's Correctional Institution, Staff Library, Canon City, CO [*Library symbol Library of Congress*] (LCLS)
COCD .... Canadian Ownership and Control Determination
COCD .... Center for Organizational and Community Development (EA)
CoCD .... Colorado School for the Deaf and Blind, Colorado Springs, CO [*Library symbol Library of Congress*] (LCLS)
COCDC........ Career Officer Candidate Development Course [*Air Force*]
CoCe .... Cedaredge Public Library, Cedaredge, CO [*Library symbol Library of Congress*] (LCLS)
COCE .... Commence (ROG)
CoCE .... El Paso Community College, Colorado Springs, CO [*Library symbol Library of Congress*] (LCLS)
COCEEE....... Committee on Captured Enemy Electronics Equipment
COCEMA ...... Comite des Constructeurs Europeens de Materiel Alimentaire [*Committee of European Plant Manufacturers for the Food Industry*] [*Common Market*]
CoCenS .... Saguache County Library, Center Branch, Center, CO [*Library symbol Library of Congress*] (LCLS)
Cocensys ..... Concensys, Inc. [*Associated Press*] (SAG)
CoCEP........ Pikes Peak Community College, Colorado Springs, CO [*Library symbol*] [*Library of Congress*] (LCLS)
COCERAL .... Comite du Commerce des Cereales et des Aliments du Betail de la Communaute Economique Europeenne [*Committee of the Cereals and Animal Feed Trade of the European Economic Community*]
COCESS .... Contractor-Operated Civil Engineer Supply Store
CoCF.......... Colorado Springs Fine Arts Center, Fine Arts and Anthropology of the Southwest, Library, Colorado Springs, CO [*Library symbol Library of Congress*] (LCLS)
CoCfC.......... Crawford Community Library, Crawford, CO [*Library symbol Library of Congress*] (LCLS)
CoCFc .... Fort Carson Library, Colorado Springs, CO [*Library symbol Library of Congress*] (LCLS)
CoCfCE........ Chatfield Elementary School, Clifton, CO [*Library symbol Library of Congress*] (LCLS)
CoCfCfE....... Clifton Elementary School, Clifton, CO [*Library symbol Library of Congress*] (LCLS)
CoCfCL........ Crawford Community Library, Crawford, CO [*Library symbol*] [*Library of Congress*] (LCLS)
CoCFc-M ...... Fort Carson Hospital, Medical Library, Colorado Springs, CO [*Library symbol Library of Congress*] (LCLS)
CoCGS .... Church of Jesus Christ of Latter-Day Saints, Genealogical Society Library, Colorado Springs Branch, Colorado Springs, CO [*Library symbol Library of Congress*] (LCLS)
COCh .... Chabot Observatory, Oakland, CA [*Library symbol Library of Congress*] (LCLS)
COCH .... Coaches [*Freight*]

COCH............ Cochin [*Region in India*] (ROG)
COCH............ Cochleare [*Spoonful*] [*Pharmacy*]
Coch............ Cochran's Nova Scotia Reports [*1859*] [*A publication*] (DLA)
COCH............ Concorde out, Concorde Home
CO CH............ Council Chambers [*Freemasonry*] (ROG)
Coch Apm.... Cochleare Amplum [*A tablespoonful*] [*Pharmacy*]
Coch Ch Ct... Chief Court of Cochin, Select Decisions [*A publication*] (DLA)
CoChey........ American Legion Auxiliary Library, Cheyenne Wells, CO [*Library symbol Library of Congress*] (LCLS)
Cochin .... Cochin Law Reports [*1909-48*] [*India*] [*A publication*] (DLA)
Coch Ind...... Cochin, India (ILCA)
COCH INFANT... Cochleare Infantum [*Teaspoonful*] [*Pharmacy*]
Cochin LJ.... Cochin Law Journal [*A publication*] (DLA)
Cochin LR.... Cochin Law Reports [*1909-48*] [*India*] [*A publication*] (DLA)
COCHL......... Cochleare [*Spoonful*] [*Pharmacy*]
COCHL AMP... Cochleare Amplum [*Heaping spoonful*] [*Pharmacy*] (MAH)
COCHL AMPL... Cochleare Amplum [*Tablespoonful*] [*Pharmacy*] (ROG)
COCHLEAT... Cochleatim [*Spoonfuls*] [*Pharmacy*] (ROG)
COCHL INFANT... Cochleare Infantum [*Teaspoonful*] [*Pharmacy*]
COCHL MAG... Cochleare Magnum [*Tablespoonful*] [*Pharmacy*] (ROG)
COCHL MED... Cochleare Medium [*Dessertspoonful*] [*Pharmacy*] (ROG)
COCHL MOD... Cochleare Modicum [*Dessertspoonful*] [*Pharmacy*] (ROG)
COCHL PARV... Cochleare Parvum [*Teaspoonful*] [*Pharmacy*] (ROG)
COCH MAG... Cochleare Magnum [*Tablespoonful*] [*Pharmacy*]
COCH MAX... Cochleare Maximum [*Tablespoonful*] [*Pharmacy*]
COCH MED... Cochleare Medium [*Dessertspoonful*] [*Pharmacy*]
COCH MIN ... Cochleare Minimum [*Teaspoonful*] [*Pharmacy*]
COCH MOD... Cochleare Modicum [*Dessertspoonful*] [*Pharmacy*]
Coch N Sc ... Cochran's Nova Scotia Reports [*1859*] [*A publication*] (DLA)
COCH PARV... Cochleare Parvum [*Teaspoonful*] [*Pharmacy*]
COCH PLEN... Cochleare Plenum [*Tablespoonful*] [*Pharmacy*]
cochr.......... Co-Chair of the Board (DD)
Cochr........... Cochran's Nova Scotia Reports [*1859*] [*A publication*] (DLA)
Cochr .... Cochran's Reports [*3-10 North Dakota*] [*A publication*] (DLA)
Cochran ...... Cochran's Reports [*3-10 North Dakota*] [*A publication*] (DLA)
Cochr Hind L... Cochrane's Hindu Law [*A publication*] (DLA)
COCI .... Consortium on Chemical Information [*British*]
COCiC......... Grove Street College, Oakland, CA [*Library symbol Library of Congress*] (LCLS)
COCINA....... Coordinadora Civilista Nacional [*Panama*] [*Political party*] (EY)
COCIR......... Coordinamento delle Industrie Radiologiche ed Elettromedicali [*Coordination Committee of the Radiological and Electromedical Industries*] [*EC*] (ECED)
CoCjFL....... Film Library of Mesa County, School District 51, Grand Junction, CO [*Library symbol*] [*Library of Congress*] (LCLS)
CoCK.......... Kaman Sciences Corp., Nuclear Library, Colorado Springs, CO [*Library symbol Library of Congress*] (LCLS)
Cock & R..... Cockburn and Rowe's English Election Cases [*1833*] [*A publication*] (DLA)
Cock & Rowe... Cockburn and Rowe's English Election Cases [*1833*] [*A publication*] (DLA)
Cockb & R... Cockburn and Rowe's English Election Cases [*1833*] [*A publication*] (DLA)
Cockb & Rowe... Cockburn and Rowe's English Election Cases [*1833*] [*A publication*] (DLA)
Cocke.......... Cocke. Reports [*16-18 Alabama*] [*A publication*] (DLA)
Cocke.......... Cocke. Reports [*14, 15 Florida*] [*A publication*] (DLA)
Cocke Const Hist... Cocke's Constitutional History of the United States [*A publication*] (DLA)
Cocke US Pr... Cocke's Common and Civil Law Practice of the US Courts [*A publication*] (DLA)
Cock Nat...... Cockburn on Nationality [*A publication*] (DLA)
Cock Tich Ca... Cockburn's Charge in the Tichborne Case [*A publication*] (DLA)
COCL.......... Cathodal Opening Clonus [*Physiology*]
COCl .... Cathodal Opening Clonus [*Medicine*] (DMAA)
COCLM .... Counterclaim [*Legal term*] (ROG)
CoCIM......... Mount Garfield Junior High School Library, Clifton, CO [*Library symbol Library of Congress*] (LCLS)
COcM.......... MiraCosta Community College, Oceanside, CA [*Library symbol*] [*Library of Congress*] (LCLS)
COCMIB....... Comite d'Organisation du Congres Mondial d'Implantologie des Biomateriaux [*Organizing Committee of the World Congress on Implantology and Bio-Materials - OCWCIB*] [*Rouen, France*] (EAIO)
COCN.......... Cocensys, Inc. [*NASDAQ symbol*] (SAG)
COCO.......... Cabinet Offices Cypher Office [*British World War II*]
CO-CO......... Central Office to Central Office [*Bell System*]
COCO .... Children's Oncology Care of Ontario Inc. [*Also, Ronald McDonald House*] (AC)
COCO .... COBOL [*Common Business-Oriented Language*] Conversion [*Computer science*] (MCD)
COCO .... Color Computer
COCO .... Commercially Owned, Commercially Operated (AFIT)
COCO .... Committee Code [*Database terminology*] (NITA)
COCO .... Committee on Contracting Out [*Defunct*] (EA)
COCO .... Communications. CSIRO [*A publication*]
COCO .... Community Colleges Data Base [*Information service or system*] (IID)
COCO .... Conference of Consumer Organizations (EA)
COCO .... Contractor-Owned, Contractor-Operated (AABC)
COCO .... Coordinate Conversion Routine
COCO .... Coordinator of Chain Operations [*Coast Guard*] (DNAB)
CoCo .... Cortez Public Library, Cortez, CO [*Library symbol Library of Congress*] (LCLS)
CoCo .... Cover Collectors Club (EA)
COCO .... Covert Communications

COCOA....... Cobra Owners Club of America (EA)
COCOA....... Continuously Contemporary Accounting (ADA)
COCOA....... Critical Terrain; Obstacles; Cover and Concealment; Observation and Fields of Fire; Avenues of Approach [*Military*]
COCOAS....... CONARC [*Continental Army Command*] Class One Automated System [*Later, BASOPS*] (MCD)
CoCOC-M..... United States Olympic Committee, Sports Medicine Division, Colorado Springs, CO [*Library symbol Library of Congress*] (LCLS)
COCODE...... Compressed Coherency Detection [*RADAR technique*]
CoCoGS .... Church of Jesus Christ of Latter-Day Saints, Genealogical Society Library, Durango Stake Branch, Cortez, CO [*Library symbol Library of Congress*] (LCLS)
CoCol.......... Collbran Public Library, Collbran, CO [*Library symbol Library of Congress*] (LCLS)
COCOM....... Combatant Command [*Military*]
COCOM....... Computer Cost Model
COCOM....... Controlled Commodity
COCOM....... Coordinating Committee
COCOM....... Coordinating Committee on Export Controls [*From Western to Eastern bloc nations*]
CoCOM .... Coordinating Committee on Export Controls (ACRL)
COCOM....... Coordinating Committee on Multilateral Export Controls (AAGC)
COCOMO...... Constructive Cost Model
Co-Co-Nuke... Coal, Conservation, and Nuclear [*Energy substitutes for oil*] [*British*]
Co Cop........ Coke's Compleat Copyholder [*5 eds.*] [*1630-73 England*] [*A publication*] (DLA)
COCOPEA...... Coordinating Council of Private Educational Associations
COCORP ...... Consortium for Continental Reflection Profiling [*Cornell University*] [*Ithaca, NY*]
COCOS......... Corporate Communications System [*Bell-Northern Research Ltd.*] [*Computer science*]
COCOSEERS... Coordinating Committee for Slavic and East European Library Resources
COCOT........ Customer-Owned Coin-Operated Telephone (WDMC)
CoCou.......... Co-Counsel, Inc. [*Associated Press*] (SAG)
CO COUNC... County Council [*British*] (ROG)
CoCounsl..... Co-Counsel, Inc. [*Associated Press*] (SAG)
COCP .... Crossed Olivocochlear Potential [*Audiology*]
CoCP-M ...... Penrose Hospital, Webb Memorial Library, Colorado Springs, CO [*Library symbol Library of Congress*] (LCLS)
CoCPP .... Penrose Public Library, Colorado Springs, CO [*Library symbol*] [*Library of Congress*] (LCLS)
COCQ-SIDA... Coalition des Organismes Communautaires Quebecois de Lutte Contre le Sida (AC)
CoCr........... Douglas County Public Library, Castle Rock, CO [*Library symbol Library of Congress*] (LCLS)
Co CR .... Pennsylvania County Court Reports [*A publication*] (DLA)
CoCra.......... Craig-Moffat County Public Library, Craig, CO [*Library symbol Library of Congress*] (LCLS)
CoCre.......... Creede Public Library, Creede, CO [*Library symbol Library of Congress*] (LCLS)
CoCri.......... Cripple Creek Public Library, Cripple Creek, CO [*Library symbol Library of Congress*] (LCLS)
COCRIL....... Council of City Research and Information Libraries [*British*] (NITA)
CoCroo........ Crook Community Library, Crook, CO [*Library symbol Library of Congress*] (LCLS)
COCS .... Camera Override Control System [*NASA*] (KSC)
COCS .... Container Operating Control System (PDAA)
COCSL .... California Spanish Language Data Base, Oakland, CA [*Library symbol*] [*Library of Congress*] (LCLS)
COCSP......... Contingency Operational Contracting Support Program [*Air Force*] (AAGC)
COCT .... Coctio [*Boiling*]
COCT .... Copper Oxidation Corrosion Test (PDAA)
Co Ct Cas ... County Court Cases [*England*] [*A publication*] (DLA)
Co Ct Ch ... County Courts Chronicle [*1847-1920*] [*England*] [*A publication*] (DLA)
Co Ct Chr... County Courts Chronicle [*1847-1920*] [*England*] [*A publication*] (DLA)
Co Ct ILT ... Irish Law Times, County Courts [*A publication*] (DLA)
Co Ct R....... County Courts Reports [*1860-1920*] [*England*] [*A publication*] (DLA)
Co Ct Rep.... County Courts Reports [*1860-1920*] [*England*] [*A publication*] (DLA)
Co Ct Rep.... Pennsylvania County Court Reports [*A publication*] (DLA)
Co Ct Rep (PA)... County Court Reports [*Pennsylvania*] [*A publication*] (DLA)
Co Cts.......... Coke on Courts [*or Fourth Institute*] [*England*] [*A publication*] (DLA)
COCTS........ County Courts [*Legal*] [*British*]
COCU.......... Consultation on Church Union (EA)
COCUSA....... Chamber of Commerce of the United States (EA)
COCWA....... Coin-Op Car Wash Association
CoCxC........ Climax Molybdenum Co., Technical Library, Climax, CO [*Library symbol Library of Congress*] (LCLS)
CoCZ.......... Zebulon Pike Detention Center, Colorado Springs, CO [*Library symbol Library of Congress*] (LCLS)
COD .... Cadkey Object Developer [*Computer science*]
COD .... Carrier Onboard Delivery [*Naval aviation*]
COD .... Carrier-on-Deck [*Navy carrier-based aircraft*]
COD .... Cash [*or Collect*] on Delivery [*Business term*]
COD .... Cause of Death [*Medicine*]
COD .... Center Operations Directorate (MCD)
COD .... Certificate of Deposit [*Banking*]
COD .... Chamber of Deputies (DAS)
COD .... Change Operations Directive (MCD)
COD .... Change-Over Delay (AEBS)
COD .... Chemical Oxygen Demand
COD .... Clean-Out Door (OA)
COD .... Close Order Drill (DNAB)

COD	Coalition de l'Opposition Democratique [Togo] [Political party] (EY)
COD	Coal-Oil Dispersion [Fuel technology]
Cod	Codeine (AAMN)
COD	Codex
cod.............	Codex (VRA)
cod.............	Codices (VRA)
COD	Codicil
Cod	Codification [Legal term] (ILCA)
COD	Coding (MSA)
COD	Cody [Wyoming] [Airport symbol] (OAG)
COD	Cody, WY [Location identifier FAA] (FAAL)
COD	Coefficient of Oxygen Delivery
COD	Coherent Optical Device
COD	Collect on Delivery (DFIT)
COD	Collect On Delivery (WDMC)
COD	Communications Operating Directive (KSC)
COD	Concise Oxford Dictionary [A publication]
COD	Condensed or Dried
COD	Condition on Discharge [Medicine] (DAVI)
COD	Consortium of Doctors (EA)
COD	Constrained Optimal Design [Computer science] (RDA)
COD	Consumer Organization of Diabled People of Newfoundland & Labrador (AC)
COD	Contract Operations Data [DoD]
COD	Cooperative Opportunities Document (AAGC)
COD	Coordinating Organization Director (SAA)
COD	Co-ordination de l'Opposition Democratique [Gabon] [Political party] (EY)
COD	Cordiale Resources, Inc. [Vancouver Stock Exchange symbol]
COD	Correction of Deficiency (MCD)
COD	Cost on Delivery (MCD)
COD	Council of Deans (DAVI)
COD	Council of Defence
COD	Country of Destination [International trade] (DCTA)
COD	Crack Opening Displacement
COD	Crane on Deck (MCD)
COD	Current Operations Division [Tactical Air Command]
COD	Cyclooctadiene [Organic chemistry]
CoD.............	Denver Public Library, Denver, CO [Library symbol Library of Congress] (LCLS)
Cod	Gibson's Codex Ecclesiastia [1715] [A publication] (DLA)
Cod	Gibson's Codex Juris Civilis [A publication] (DLA)
COD	University of Colorado, Boulder, CO [OCLC symbol] (OCLC)
CODA..........	Cash or Deferred Arrangement
CODA..........	Chemical On-Line Data Analyzer [Interactive Elements, Inc.]
CODA..........	Children of Deaf Adults (EA)
CODA..........	Coda Energy, Inc. [NASDAQ symbol] (NQ)
CoDA	Co-Dependents Anonymous (EA)
CODA..........	Committee on Drugs and Alcohol
CoDA	Common Destiny Alliance
CODA..........	Coulee Dam National Recreation Area
CODA..........	Council of Dance Administrators (EA)
CODA..........	Council on Drug Abuse [Canada]
CODA..........	Council on Drug Abuse (AC)
CODA..........	Crack Opening Displacement Application (PDAA)
CoDA	Denver Art Museum, Denver, CO [Library symbol Library of Congress] (LCLS)
CODAC........	Collateral Duty Alcoholism Counselor [Navy] (NVT)
CODAC........	Common Ownership Design and Construct [British]
CODAC........	Computer Design of Armoured Cables (PDAA)
CODAC........	Coordination of Operating Data by Automatic Computer
CoDAD	United States Department of Agriculture, Agricultural Research Service, Arthropod-Borne Animal Disease Research Laboratory, Denver, CO [Library symbol Library of Congress] (LCLS)
CodaEn	Coda Energy, Inc. [Associated Press] (SAG)
CODAF........	Concepts, Doctrine, and Force [Design]
CoDAFA	United States Air Force Accounting and Finance Center, Denver, CO [Library symbol Library of Congress] (LCLS)
CODAG........	Combined Diesel and Gas [Turbine]
CoDAH	American Humane Association, Denver, CO [Library symbol Library of Congress] (LCLS)
CODAI.........	Comite pour le Developpement des Alternatives a l'Incarceration [Committee for the Development of Alternatives to Incarceration] [Canada]
CODAI.........	Committee for the Development of Alternatives to Incarceration [Canada]
CODAM.......	Combat Damage/Assessment Model (MCD)
CODAM.......	Contractor-Oriented Data Abstract Modules [Air Force]
CoDAMC-M...	American Medical Center, Medical Library, Denver, CO [Library symbol Library of Congress] (LCLS)
CoDAmI	American Institute of Islamic Studies, Denver, CO [Library symbol Library of Congress] (LCLS)
CodaMu	Coda Music Technology, Inc. [Associated Press] (SAG)
CODAN........	Carrier-Operated Device, Antinoise [Radio]
CODAN........	Coded Analysis [Navy]
CODAP........	City of David Archaeological Project
CODAP........	Client-Oriented Data Acquisition Process [FDA]
CODAP........	Comprehensive Occupational Data Analysis Program [Military] (AABC)
CODAP........	Computer Occupational Data Analysis Program
CODAP........	Control Data Assembly Program [Control Data Corp.]
CODAR........	Coastal Ocean Dynamics Applications RADAR [Marine science] (OSRA)
CODAR........	Coastal Ocean Dynamics Applications Radar (USDC)

CoDAr..........	Colorado Division of State Archives, Denver, CO [Library symbol Library of Congress] (LCLS)
CODAR........	Correlation Data Analyzer Recorder (CAAL)
CODAR........	Correlation Detection and Ranging (MCD)
CODAR........	Correlation Display Analyzing and Recording
CODAS........	Consolidated Operations and Delay Analysis System [FAA] (TAG)
CODAS........	Control and Data Acquisition System (MCD)
CODAS........	Current Operational Data System
CODAS........	Customer-Oriented Data System (DIT)
CODASYL....	Conference on Data Systems Languages [Defunct] (EA)
CODATA......	Committee on Data for Science and Technology (EA)
CoDAW........	American Water Works Association, Denver, CO [Library symbol Library of Congress] (LCLS)
CoDB	Bibliographical Center for Research, Rocky Mountain Region, Denver, CO [Library symbol Library of Congress] (LCLS)
CoDBB	Baptist Bible College, Denver, CO [Library symbol Library of Congress] (LCLS)
CoDBCS	Blue Cross & Blue Shield of Colorado, Denver, CO [Library symbol Library of Congress] (LCLS)
CoDBH-M.....	Bethesda Hospital, Medical Library, Denver, CO [Library symbol Library of Congress] (LCLS)
CoDBI-M	Beth Israel Hospital, Medical Library, Denver, CO [Library symbol Library of Congress] (LCLS)
CoDBLM	United States Department of the Interior, Bureau of Land Management, Denver Service Center, Denver, CO [Library symbol Library of Congress] (LCLS)
CoDBM	United States Bureau of Mines, Denver, CO [Library symbol Library of Congress] (LCLS)
CoDBR	United States Bureau of Reclamation, Denver, CO [Library symbol Library of Congress] (LCLS)
CoDBW	United States Bureau of Sport Fisheries and Wildlife, Wildlife Research Center, Denver, CO [Library symbol Library of Congress] (LCLS)
CODC	Canadian Oceanographic Data Centre [Later, MEDS]
CoDC	Clayton College, Denver, CO [Library symbol Library of Congress] (LCLS)
CODC	Combined Operations Development Centre [British military] (DMA)
CoDc............	Dolores County Public Library, Dove Creek, CO [Library symbol Library of Congress] (LCLS)
CODCAVE.....	Committee on Decentralization of Controls after V-E Day [War Production Board]
CoDCB	Conservative Baptist Theological Seminary, Denver, CO [Library symbol Library of Congress] (LCLS)
CoDCC	Community College of Denver, Denver, CO [Library symbol Library of Congress] (LCLS)
CoDCC-A......	Community College of Denver, Auraria Campus, Denver, CO [Library symbol Library of Congress] (LCLS)
CoDCC-E......	Community College of Denver, Aurora Educational Learning Center, North Campus, Denver, CO [Library symbol Library of Congress] (LCLS)
CoDCC-N.....	Community College of Denver, North Campus, Denver, CO [Library symbol Library of Congress] (LCLS)
CoDCC-R.....	Community College of Denver, Red Rocks Campus, Lakewood, CO [Library symbol Library of Congress] (LCLS)
CoDCDH.......	Colorado State Department of Highways, Denver, CO [Library symbol Library of Congress] (LCLS)
CoDCH-M.....	Children's Hospital, Medical Library, Denver, CO [Library symbol Library of Congress] (LCLS)
CoDcL	Dolores County Public Library, Dove Creek, CO [Library symbol] [Library of Congress] (LCLS)
CoDCo	Cobe Laboratories, Denver, CO [Library symbol Library of Congress] (LCLS)
CoDCW	Colorado Women's College, Denver, CO [Library symbol Library of Congress] (LCLS)
CODD..........	Codices (ROG)
CoDDB	Denver Botanic Gardens, Inc., Denver, CO [Library symbol Library of Congress] (LCLS)
CoDDC	District Court Law Library, Second Judicial District, Denver, CO [Library symbol Library of Congress] (LCLS)
CoDDE	Colorado Department of Education, Resource Center, Denver, CO [Library symbol] [Library of Congress] (LCLS)
Cod Dip	Codex Diplomaticus [A publication] (ILCA)
Codd Lat Ant...	Codices Latini Antiquiores [A publication] (OCD)
CoDDP	Denver Post, Inc., Denver, CO [Library symbol Library of Congress] (LCLS)
Codd Tr M ...	Coddington's Digest of the Law of Trade Marks [A publication] (DLA)
CODE	Cable On-Line Data Exchange [Nielson Media Research] [Information service or system]
CODE	Canadian Organization for Development through Education
CODE	Citizens Organized to Defend the Environment
CODE	Client/Server Open Development Environment [Computer architecture] (PCM)
CODE	Coastal Ocean Dynamics Experiment [National Oceanic and Atmospheric Administration]
Code	Code of Justinian [A publication] (DLA)
Code	Codex Justinianus [Code of Justinian] [Latin A publication] (DLA)
CODE	Committee on Donor Enlistment [Later, OR] (EA)
CODE	Concord Energy [NASDAQ symbol] (TTSB)
CODE	Concord Energy, Inc. [NASDAQ symbol] (SAG)
CODE	Confederacion Democratica [Democratic Confederation] [Chile] [Political party]
CODE	Conference of Diocesan Executives [Episcopalian]
CODE	Continental Organization of Distributor Enterprises, Inc.
CODE	Controlled Object Deck Exploitation (PDAA)
CODE	Controller Decision Evaluation

CODE .... Cooperative Office Distributive Education (AEBS)
CODE .... Coordinators of Data Processing Education (HGAA)
CODE .... Council of Drama in Education (AC)
CoDE .... Education Commission of the States, Denver, CO [Library symbol Library of Congress] (LCLS)
CoDEA .... Colorado Center for Educational Assistance, Denver, CO [Library symbol] [Library of Congress] (LCLS)
CodeAl .... Code-Alarm, Inc. [Associated Press] (SAG)
Code Am ..... Code Amendments [A publication] (DLA)
CODEC .... Coder-Decoder [Telecommunications] (MCD)
CODEC .... Coding/Decoding Device
codec .... Compression/Decompression Standard [Computer science]
CODEC .... Compressor Decompressor [Computer science] (PCM)
Code Civ Pro... Code of Civil Procedure [A publication] (DLA)
Code Civ Proc... Code of Civil Procedure [A publication] (DLA)
Code Crim Proc... Code of Criminal Procedure [A publication] (DLA)
Code Cr Pro... Code of Criminal Procedure [A publication] (DLA)
Code Cr Proc... Code of Criminal Procedure [A publication] (DLA)
CODED .... Computer-Oriented Design of Electronic Devices
Code de Com... Code de Commerce [Commercial Code] (DLA)
Code de JM... Code de Justice Militaire [A publication] (DLA)
Code des F... Code des Faillites et Canqueroutes [A publication] (DLA)
CODEF .... Chairman of Defense Committee (NATG)
Code Fr An... Code Francais Annote [A publication] (DLA)
Code Gen Laws... Code of General Laws [A publication] (DLA)
CODEHUCA... Comision para la Defensa de los Derechos Humanos en Centroamerica [Commission for the Defense of Human Rights in Central America - CDHRCA] (EA)
CODEIN .... Codeine [Pharmacology] (DAVI)
CODEIN .... Computerized Drawing Electrical Information (NG)
CODEL .... Computer Developments Limited Automatic Coding System (IEEE)
CODEL .... Congressional Delegate [or Delegation] (CINC)
CODEL .... Coordination in Development (EA)
CoDel .... Delta Public Library, Delta, CO [Library symbol Library of Congress] (LCLS)
Code LA....... Civil Code of Louisiana [A publication] (DLA)
CODELAG..... Combined Diesel-Electric And Gas [Turbine] (DOMA)
CoDelC .... Delta Honor Camp, Delta, CO [Library symbol Library of Congress] (LCLS)
CoDelV .... Delta Vocational Technical Center, Delta, CO [Library symbol] [Library of Congress] (LCLS)
CODEM .... Coded Modulator-Demodulator (PDAA)
Code M .... Code Municipal [Quebec] [A publication] (DLA)
CODEM .... Computer-Graphics-Augmented Design and Manufacturing (IAA)
CODEM .... Computerized Design from Engineering Models (PDAA)
CODEMAC.... Comite des Demenageurs du Marche Commun
Code Me R... Code of Maine Rules [Also CMR] [A publication] (AAGC)
Code NY Rep... Code Reporter [New York] [A publication] (DLA)
Code of Civ Proc... Code of Civil Procedure [A publication] (DLA)
CODEP .... Council for a Department of Peace (EA)
CoDEPA .... United States Environmental Protection Agency, National Field Investigations Center Library, Denver, CO [Library symbol Library of Congress] (LCLS)
Code Prac.... Code of Practice [Legal term] (DLA)
Code Pro ..... Code of Procedure [Legal term] (DLA)
Code Proc.... Code of Procedure [Legal term] (DLA)
Code Pub Gen Laws... Code of Public General Laws [A publication] (DLA)
Code Pub Loc Laws... Code of Public Local Laws [A publication] (DLA)
Code R .... Code Reporter [New York] [A publication] (DLA)
Code Rep..... Code Reporter [New York] [A publication] (DLA)
Code Rep NS... New York Code Reports, New Series [A publication] (DLA)
Code RNS.... Code Reports, New Series [New York] [A publication] (DLA)
Code RNS (NY)... Code Reports, New Series [New York] [A publication] (DLA)
Code R (NY)... Code Reports [New York] [A publication] (DLA)
CO DERRY... County Londonderry [Northern Ireland]
CODES .... Collection Development and Evaluation Section [Reference and Adult Services Division] [American Library Association]
CODES .... Commutating Detection System
CODES .... Computer Design and Education System
CODES .... Computer Design and Evaluation System (IEEE)
CODES .... Computerized Deployment Execution System
CODES .... Crash Outcome Data Evaluation System [BTS] (TAG)
CODES .... Critical Outcome Data Evaluation System [Auto safety research]
CODES .... Critical Outcomes Data Evaluation System [Automobile accident reporting]
CODES .... National Centre for Ore Deposit and Exploration [University of Tasmania] [Australia]
CODESH .... Council for Democratic and Secular Humanism (EA)
CODESRIA ... Council for the Development of Economic and Social Research in Africa [Dakar, Senegal] (EAIO)
Code Supp... Supplement to the Code [A publication] (DLA)
Code Theod... Code of Theodosius [Roman law] [A publication] (DLA)
Code Theodos... Codex Theodosianus [Theodosian Code] [438AD] [Latin] [Legal term] (DLA)
CODEVER ..... Code Verification (IEEE)
CODEX .... Compiler of Differentiable Expressions (PDAA)
CODEX .... Exercise Code Word [NATO] (NATG)
CoDEx .... Exxon Corp., Exploration Library, Denver, CO [Library symbol Library of Congress] (LCLS)
CODEXAL..... Conseil Europeen du "Codex Alimentarius"
CODF .... Crystallite Orientation Distribution Function (MCD)
CoDF........... Fort Logan Mental Health Center, Denver, CO [Library symbol Library of Congress] (LCLS)
CoDFC .... Fort Logan Mental Health Center, Children's Library, Denver, CO [Library symbol Library of Congress] (LCLS)

CoDFG-M.... Fitzsimons General Hospital, Medical Technical Library, Denver, CO [Library symbol Library of Congress] (LCLS)
CODFIL .... Codification File (MCD)
CoDFM......... Masonic Grand Lodge, Denver, CO [Library symbol Library of Congress] (LCLS)
CoDFR .... Denver Federal Records Center, Denver, CO [Library symbol Library of Congress] (LCLS)
CoDFU .... National Farmers Union Library, Denver, CO [Library symbol Library of Congress Obsolete] (LCLS)
CoDGC .... Gilliam Center, Denver, CO [Library symbol Library of Congress] (LCLS)
CoDGH .... Colorado General Hospital, Residents' Library, Denver, CO [Library symbol Library of Congress] (LCLS)
CoDGL .... Church of Jesus Christ of Latter-Day Saints, Genealogical Society Library, Denver Branch, Stake Center, Denver, CO [Library symbol Library of Congress] (LCLS)
CoDGR .... Gates Rubber Co., Technical Library, Denver, CO [Library symbol Library of Congress] (LCLS)
CoDGRM-M... General Rose Memorial Hospital, Medical Library, Denver, CO [Library symbol Library of Congress] (LCLS)
CoDGS .... United States Geological Survey, Denver, CO [Library symbol Library of Congress] (LCLS)
CoDGS-R ..... United States Geological Survey, Resources/Appraisal Group, Denver, CO [Library symbol Library of Congress] (LCLS)
CoDGW........ Great Western Sugar Co., Technical Library, Denver, CO [Library symbol Library of Congress] (LCLS)
CODH.......... Carbon Monoxide Dehydrogenase [An enzyme]
CODH.......... Committee for Open Debate on the Holocaust [Defunct] (EA)
CoD-H.......... Denver Public Library, Denver General Hospital Library, Denver, CO [Library symbol Library of Congress] (LCLS)
CoDHO .... Humble Oil & Refining Co., Mineral Department Library, Denver, CO [Library symbol Library of Congress] (LCLS)
CoDHRI....... Committee for the Defense of Human Rights in India (EA)
CODI .... Codeine Tablet [Slang] (DSUE)
CODI .... Cornucopia of Disability Information [Internet] (PAZ)
CoDI............ Iliff School of Theology, Denver, CO [Library symbol Library of Congress] (LCLS)
CODIAC........ Centralized or Distributed Integrated Access Control [Computer science]
CODIAC........ Cooperative Distributed Interactive Atmospheric Catalog [Marine science] (OSRA)
CODIAC........ Cooperative Distributed Interactive Atmospheric Catolog (USDC)
CODIC .... Color Difference Computer (MUGU)
CODIC .... Computer-Directed Communication
CODICOM .... Computerized Distribution and Control of Microfilm [American Motors Corp.]
CODIL .... Content Dependent Information Language
CODIL .... Control Diagram Language [Computer science] (IEEE)
CODILS .... Commodity-Oriented Digital Label Input System
CoDIN .... International Nuclear Corp., Denver, CO [Library symbol Library of Congress] (LCLS)
CODIP.......... Conference de la Haye de Droit International Prive [Hague Conference on Private International Law] (EA)
CODIPHASE... Coherent Digital Phased Array System [ARPA]
CODIS .... Coded Discharge (DNAB)
CODIS .... Completed Discharge
CODIS .... Controlled Digital Simulator
CODIS .... Controlled Orbital Decay and Input System (DNAB)
CODIT .... Computer Direct to Telegraph
Cod Iust...... Codex Iustinianus [Classical studies] (OCD)
CoDJM .... Johns-Manville Sales Corp., Corporate Information Center, Denver, CO [Library symbol Library of Congress] (LCLS)
Cod Jur....... Gibson's Codex Ecclesiastia [1715] [A publication] (DLA)
Cod Jur Civ... Codex Juris Civilis [Latin A publication] (DLA)
CodJust....... Codex Justinianus (BJA)
CODL .... Code Alarm [NASDAQ symbol] (TTSB)
CODL .... Code-Alarm, Inc. [NASDAQ symbol] (NQ)
CODL .... Codicil
CoDL........... United States Lowry Air Force Base, Denver, CO [Library symbol Library of Congress] (LCLS)
CoDLC .... Legislative Council of Colorado, Denver, CO [Library symbol Library of Congress] (LCLS)
CoDLL......... Denver Law Libraries, Denver, CO [Library symbol] [Library of Congress] (LCLS)
CoDM......... Medical Society of the City and County of Denver, Denver, CO [Library symbol Library of Congress] (LCLS)
CODMAC...... Committee on Data Management and Computation [National Academy of Sciences]
COD MEMB... Codex Membranacius [A book written on vellum or skins] [Latin] (ROG)
CoDMG .... Medical Group Management Association, Information Reference Service, Denver, CO [Library symbol Library of Congress] (LCLS)
CoDMH .... Mercy Hospital, Library and Media Resources Center, Denver, CO [Library symbol Library of Congress] (LCLS)
CoDMH-M.... Mercy Hospital-School of Nursing, Library, Denver, CO [Library symbol Library of Congress] (LCLS)
CoDMM........ Martin Marietta Corp., Research Library, Denver, CO [Library symbol Library of Congress] (LCLS)
CoDMNH...... Denver Museum of Natural History, Denver, CO [Library symbol Library of Congress] (LCLS)
CoDMO .... Mobil Oil Corp., Exploration and Producing Division, Denver, CO [Library symbol Library of Congress] (LCLS)
CoDMSA ...... United States Department of Labor, Mine Safety and Health Administration, Denver, CO [Library symbol Library of Congress] (LCLS)

CoDMSE ...... Mountain States Employers Council, Information Center, Denver, CO [*Library symbol Library of Congress*] (LCLS)
CODN .... Component Operational Data Notice [*NASA*] (KSC)
CoDn .... King's Daughters Public Library, Del Norte, CO [*Library symbol Library of Congress*] (LCLS)
CoDNJ-M ..... National Jewish Hospital and Research Center, Medical Library, Denver, CO [*Library symbol Library of Congress*] (LCLS)
CoDNPS ...... United States National Park Service, Denver, CO [*Library symbol Library of Congress*] (LCLS)
CODOC .... Cooperation in Documentation and Communication [*An association*]
CODOC .... Cooperative Documents Network Project [*University of Guelph Library*] [*Information service or system*]
CODOC .... Cooperative Documents Project [*Ontario Universities Library Cooperative System*] [*Canada*] (NITA)
CoDoctor ..... Company Doctor (The) [*Associated Press*] (SAG)
CODOG .... Combined Diesel or Gas Turbine Propulsion
CoDol .... Dolores Public Library, Dolores, CO [*Library symbol Library of Congress*] (LCLS)
CODORAC .... Coded Doppler RADAR Command
CoDORN ...... Association of Operating Room Nurses, Denver, CO [*Library symbol*] [*Library of Congress*] (LCLS)
Codos .... Commandos Rouges [*Military group*] [*Chad*] (EY)
CODOT .... Classification of Occupations and Directory of Occupational Titles [*Formerly, MOLOC*] [*British*]
CoDP .... Public Service Co. of Colorado, Denver, CO [*Library symbol Library of Congress*] (LCLS)
CoDPH .... Colorado Psychiatric Hospital, Residents' Library, Denver, CO [*Library symbol Library of Congress*] (LCLS)
CoDPM-M ..... Presbyterian Medical Center, Doctors' Library, Denver, CO [*Library symbol Library of Congress*] (LCLS)
CoDPo-M ..... Porter Memorial Hospital, Physicians' Library, Denver, CO [*Library symbol Library of Congress*] (LCLS)
CoDPS .... Denver Public Schools, Professional Library, Denver, CO [*Library symbol Library of Congress*] (LCLS)
CoDR .... Regis College, Denver, CO [*Library symbol Library of Congress*] (LCLS)
CODRESS .... Coded Address [*NATO*]
CoDRN .... Rocky Mountain News, Denver, CO [*Library symbol*] [*Library of Congress*] (LCLS)
CoDRT .... Regional Transportation District, Technical Library, Denver, CO [*Library symbol Library of Congress*] (LCLS)
CODS .... Canadian Ocean Data System
CODS .... Charnes Organizational Diagnosis Survey [*Medicine*] (DMAA)
CoDS .... Sundstrand Corp., Denver Division, Engineering Department Library, Denver, CO [*Library symbol Library of Congress*] (LCLS)
CoDSC .... Shell Chemical Co., Denver, CO [*Library symbol Library of Congress*] (LCLS)
CODSIA .... Council of Defense and Space Industry Associations (EA)
CoDSM .... United States Department of Interior, Office of Surface Mining, Denver, CO [*Library symbol Library of Congress*] (LCLS)
CoDSMC ...... Swedish Medical Center, Denver, CO [*Library symbol Library of Congress*] (LCLS)
CoDSO .... Shell Oil Co., Denver, CO [*Library symbol Library of Congress*] (LCLS)
CoDSP .... Southeast Metropolitan Board of Cooperative Services, Professional Information Center, Denver, CO [*Library symbol Library of Congress*] (LCLS)
CoDSR .... Stearns-Roger Corp., Denver, CO [*Library symbol Library of Congress*] (LCLS)
CoDSS .... Colorado State Department of Social Services, Denver, CO [*Library symbol Library of Congress*] (LCLS)
Cod St .... Codified Statutes [*A publication*] (DLA)
CoDStA-M .... Saint Anthony Hospital, Memorial Medical Library, Denver, CO [*Library symbol Library of Congress*] (LCLS)
CoDStJ-M .... Saint Joseph Hospital, Denver, CO [*Library symbol Library of Congress*] (LCLS)
CoDStL-M .... Saint Luke's Hospital, Medical-Nursing Library, Denver, CO [*Library symbol Library of Congress*] (LCLS)
CoDStT .... Saint Thomas Seminary, Denver, CO [*Library symbol Library of Congress*] (LCLS)
CODSULI ...... Conference of Directors of State University Librarians of Illinois [*Library network*]
CODT .... Crane Oral Dominance Test [*English and Spanish test*]
Cod Theod ... Codex Theodosianus [*Theodosian Code*] [*438AD*] [*Latin*] [*Legal term*] (OCD)
Cod Theodos... Codex Theodosianus [*Theodosian Code*] [*438AD*] [*Latin*] [*Legal term*] [*A publication*] (DLA)
CoDu .... Durango Public Library, Durango, CO [*Library symbol Library of Congress*] (LCLS)
CoDU .... University of Denver, Denver, CO [*Library symbol Library of Congress*] (LCLS)
CODUA .... Collectif de Defense des Usagers de l'Acupuncture (AC)
CoDUCA .... United States Circuit Court of Appeals, Tenth Circuit, Denver, CO [*Library symbol Library of Congress*] (LCLS)
CoDuF .... Fort Lewis College, Durango, CO [*Library symbol Library of Congress*] (LCLS)
CoDuL .... Durango Public Library, Durango, CO [*Library symbol*] [*Library of Congress*] (LCLS)
CoDVA .... United States Veterans Administration Hospital, Denver, CO [*Library symbol Library of Congress*] (LCLS)
CoDVA-M ..... United States Veterans Administration Hospital, Medical Library, Denver, CO [*Library symbol Library of Congress*] (LCLS)
CODW .... Companions of Doctor Who Fan Club [*Defunct*] (EA)
CoDYC .... Colorado Youth Center, Denver, CO [*Library symbol Library of Congress*] (LCLS)

COE .... Army Corps of Engineers (AAGC)
COE .... Cab Over Engine [*Type of truck*]
COE .... Center for Optimum Environments (EA)
COE .... Centers of Excellence [*Army*] (RDA)
COE .... Central Office Equipment [*Bell System*]
COE .... Certificate of Eligibility [*Navy*]
COE .... Certification of Equivalency [*Air Force*]
COE .... Chamber Orchestra of Europe
CO(E) .... Change Order (Electronic)
COE .... Chief of Engineers [*Formerly, CE, C of E, C of ENGRS, COFENGS*] [*Army*] (AABC)
COE .... Church of England
COE .... Circles of Exchange (EA)
COE .... Coe Ranch [*California*] [*Seismograph station code, US Geological Survey*] (SEIS)
COE .... Coeur D'Alene [*Idaho*] [*Airport symbol*] (OAG)
COE .... Coeur D'Alene, ID [*Location identifier FAA*] (FAAL)
COE .... Cognizant Operations Engineer
COE .... Comite Europeen de l'Outillage [*European Tool Committee*] [*France*] (EAIO)
COE .... Comitel, Bedarfsfluge, KG [*Austria*] [*FAA designator*] (FAAC)
COE .... Commission on Education [*American Occupational Therapy Association*]
COE .... Committed out of Engineering
COE .... Committee on Education [*American Library Association*]
COE .... Common Operating Environment
COE .... Complete Operating Equipment
COE .... Cone Mills [*NYSE symbol*] (TTSB)
COE .... Cone Mills Corp. [*NYSE symbol*] (SPSG)
COE .... Conseil Oecumenique des Eglises [*World Council of Churches*]
COE .... Cooperative Energy Development Corp. [*Toronto Stock Exchange symbol*]
COE .... Corps of Engineers [*Army*] (AAG)
COE .... Cost of Electricity (MCD)
COE .... Council of Europe
COE .... Council on Optometric Education (EA)
COE .... Cross-Over Electrophoresis (PDAA)
COE .... Crude Oil Equivalent (PDAA)
COE .... Cube-On-Edge [*Metal grain structure*]
COE .... Current Operation Expenditure [*Business term*]
CoE .... Kiowa County Public Library, Eads, CO [*Library symbol Library of Congress*] (LCLS)
COE .... Pikes Peak Community College, Colorado Springs, CO [*OCLC symbol*] (OCLC)
COEA .... Chief Ordnance Electrical Artificer [*British military*] (DMA)
COEA .... Cost and Operational Effectiveness Analysis [*Military*] (AABC)
CoEa .... Eaton Public Library, Eaton, CO [*Library symbol Library of Congress*] (LCLS)
COE(ACE) .... Chief of Engineers (Assistant Chief of Engineers) [*Military*]
CoEag .... Eagle Public Library, Eagle, CO [*Library symbol Library of Congress*] (LCLS)
COEAMRA .... Council on Education of the American Medical Record Association (DAVI)
COEA/NPC.... Central Office Executives Association of National Panhellenic Conference (EA)
COEAO .... Coalition of Higher Education Assistance Organizations (EA)
COEBG .... Commission on Organization of the Executive Branch of the Government
COEBRA .... Computerized Optimization of Elastic Booster Autopilot
COEC .... CONAD [*Continental Air Defense Command*] Operational Employment Concept (AABC)
COEC .... Council Operations and Exercise Committee [*NATO*]
COECE .... Coordinacion de Organismos Empresariales de Comercio Exterior [*Mexican Business Coordinating Council for NAFTA*] (CROSS)
Coe Ch Pr.... Coe. Practice of the Judges' Chambers [*1876*] [*A publication*] (DLA)
CoEck .... Eckley Public Library, Eckley, CO [*Library symbol Library of Congress*] (LCLS)
COE(CW)...... Corps of Engineers (Civil Works) [*Army*]
COED .... Char-Oil-Energy-Development [*Process*] [*Project of Office of Coal Research*]
CO-ED .... Co-Editor
COED .... Coeducational
CoEd .... Co-Educational (AIE)
COED .... Composition and Editing Display [*Later, MRTT*] (MCD)
COED .... Computer-Operated [*or -Oriented*] Electronic Display
COED .... Computer Operated Electronics Display [*Program*] [*Computer science*] (ECII)
COED .... Concentration on Engineering Design (AAG)
COED .... Concise Oxford English Dictionary [*A publication*]
CoEdg .... Edgewater Public Library, Edgewater, CO [*Library symbol Library of Congress*] (LCLS)
COEES .... Central Office Equipment Estimation System [*Bell System*]
COEES .... Committee on Ocean Exploration and Environmental Services [*National Council on Marine Resources and Engineering Development*] (GFGA)
COEF .... Coefficient (KSC)
COEFF .... Coefficient
COEHS .... Church of England Historical Society [*Australia*]
COEI .... Carbon Monoxide Emission Index [*Automotive engineering*]
COEI .... Component of End Items (MCD)
COEI .... Composition of Ending Inventory
COEIL.......... Components of End Items List (MCD)
COEL .... Chain Overseas Extremely Low [*Aviation*]
COEL .... Chief Ordnance Electrician [*British military*] (DMA)
COEL .... Components of End Items [*Military*] (INF)

CoEli .... Elizabeth Public Library, Elizabeth, CO [*Library symbol Library of Congress*] (LCLS)

COELMN/PD... Corps of Engineers, Lower Mississippi Valley Division, New Orleans Planning Division [*Louisiana*]

COEMIS .... Corps of Engineers Management Information System [*DoD*] (GFGA)

COEMN .... Chief Ordnance Electrical Mechanician [*British military*] (DMA)

CoEn .... Englewood Public Library, Englewood, CO [*Library symbol Library of Congress*] (LCLS)

CoEnCA .... Colorado Academy, Englewood, CO [*Library symbol Library of Congress*] (LCLS)

CoEnCo .... Council for Environmental Conservation (EAIO)

COEnCS .... Cherry Creek Schools, Englewood, CO [*Library symbol*] [*Library of Congress*] (LCLS)

CoEnE .... Arapahoe County Evaluation Center, Englewood, CO [*Library symbol Library of Congress*] (LCLS)

CoEnS-M ...... Swedish Hospital, Medical Staff Library, Englewood, CO [*Library symbol Library of Congress*] (LCLS)

Co Ent .... Coke's Book of Entries [*1614*] [*England*] [*A publication*] (DLA)

COEO .... Council of Outdoor Educators of Ontario (AC)

COEP .... Central Office for Environmental Protection [*Basle, Switzerland*]

CoEp .... Estes Park Public Library, Estes Park, CO [*Library symbol Library of Congress*] (LCLS)

COEPL .... Cognizant Operations Engineer's Parts List

COEPS .... Cortically Originating Extra-Pyramidal System [*Physiology*]

COEPS .... Cortically Orignating Extrapyramidal Symptoms [*Neurology*] (DAVI)

CO-EQUAL .... Committee for Equality of Citizens Before the Courts (EA)

COER .... Crab Orchard & Egyptian Railroad [*American Rail Heritage Ltd.*] [*AAR code*]

CoEr .... Erie Public Library, Erie, CO [*Library symbol Library of Congress*] (LCLS)

COEs .... Centers of Excellence [*Marine science*] (OSRA)

COEs .... Centers of Excellence (USDC)

COESA .... Committee on Extension to the Standard Atmosphere

COET .... Crude Oil Equalization Tax [*Proposed, 1978*]

COEU .... Canadian Office Employees Union [*See also SCEB*]

COEU .... Confederation of Entertainment Unions [*British*] (DCTA)

Coeur .... Coeur D'Alene Mines Corp. [*Associated Press*] (SAG)

COEV .... Canadian Ocean Escort Vessel

COEV .... Comprehensive Envir'l Sys [*NASDAQ symbol*] (TTSB)

COEV .... Comprehensive Environmental Systems, Inc. [*NASDAQ symbol*] (SAG)

COEW .... Combined Operations Experimental Wing [*World War II*]

COF .... Canadian Order of Foresters [*Later, CFLIS*] (EA)

COF .... Canadian Orienteering Federation

COF .... Capital One Financial [*NYSE symbol*] (TTSB)

COF .... Capital One Financial Corp. [*NYSE symbol*] (SAG)

COF .... Captain of the Fleet [*Navy British*]

COF .... Caslon Old Face [*Typeface*] (DGA)

COF .... Catholic Order of Foresters (EA)

COF .... Cattle on Feed (GFGA)

COF .... Cause of Failure [*Telecommunications*] (TEL)

COF .... Center of Figure [*Topographical coordinate system*]

COF .... Central Okanagan Foundation (AC)

COF .... Chromatographic Optimization Function [*Analytical chemistry*]

CoF .... Cobra Factor

COF .... Cocoa, FL [*Location identifier FAA*] (FAAL)

COFi .... Coefficient of Friction [*Physics*]

CoF .... Cofactor [*Laboratory*] (DAVI)

COF .... Coffee

Cof .... Coffey's California Probate Decisions [*A publication*] (DLA)

COF .... Colorado State University, Fort Collins, CO [*OCLC symbol*] (OCLC)

COF .... Columbia Leisure [*Vancouver Stock Exchange symbol*]

COF .... Columbus Orbital Facility [*Space technology*]

COF .... Company Operating Facility

COF .... Computer Operations Facility

COF .... Computer Optimized Fabrication [*Sheet metal*] [*Raytheon Co.*]

COF .... Confortair, Inc. [*Canada ICAO designator*] (FAAC)

COF .... Conical Fin

COF .... Construction of Facilities [*NASA*] (KSC)

COF .... Contractor Overhaul Facility

COF .... Controlled Oxygen Fugacity [*Apparatus*]

COF .... Coordinadora de Organizaciones Feministas [*Coordination of Feminist Organizations*] [*Puerto Rico*] (EAIO)

COF .... Correct Operation Factor [*Telecommunications*] (OA)

COF .... Cost of Funds [*Business term*] (EMRF)

COF .... Council on Foundations [*Formerly the National Committee on Foundations and Trusts for Community Welfare*] (NFD)

COF .... Cutoff Frequency

CoF .... Fort Collins Public Library, Fort Collins, CO [*Library symbol Library of Congress*] (LCLS)

COFA .... Central Ohio Fibrositis Association (EA)

C of A .... Certificate of Airworthiness

C of A .... Certificate of Analysis

COFA .... Collocation Flutter Analysis

C of A .... Corps of Armourers [*British military*] (DMA)

C of AAF ...... Chief of the Army Air Forces [*World War II*]

C of AC .... Chief of Air Corps [*World War II*]

COFACE .... Comite des Organisations Familiales aupres des Communautes Europeennes [*Committee of Family Organizations in the European Communities*] [*Common Market*] [*Belgium*]

COFACE .... Compagnie Francaise pour l'Assurance du Commerce Exterieur

COFACTS ..... Cost-Factoring System for Force Readiness Projection (MCD)

COFAD .... Computerized Facilities Design (PDAA)

COFAF .... Committee on Food, Agriculture, and Forestry [*Association of South East Asian Nations*] [*Jakarta, Indonesia*] (EAIO)

COFAFCH ..... Chief of Air Force Chaplains

C of AFCH .... Chief of Air Force Chaplains

COFAG .... Comite des Fabricants d'Acide Glutamique de la CEE [*Committee of Glutamic Acid Manufacturers of the European Economic Community*] (EAIO)

COFAL .... Complement-Fixation for Avian Leucosis Virus [*Immunology*]

COFALEC .... Comite des Fabricants de Levure de Panification de la CEE [*Committee of Bread Yeast Manufacturers of the EEC*]

COFAQ .... Confederation des Organismes Familiaux du Quebec Inc. (AC)

C of AS .... Chief of Air Staff [*World War II*]

C of B .... Confirmation of Balance [*Banking*]

C of C .... Certificate of Competency [*Education*]

C of C .... Chamber of Commerce

C of C .... Children of the Confederacy (EA)

COFC .... Container on Flatcar [*Shipping*]

C of C .... Controller of Communications [*RAF*] [*British*]

C of C .... Course of Construction

COFC .... Court of Federal Claims [*Formerly Claims Court*] (AAGC)

C of CA .... Chief of Coast Artillery

C of CAV ...... Chief of Cavalry

COFCAW ..... Combination of Forward Combustion and Waterflooding [*Commercial oil production process*]

C of CE .... Cases of Contested Elections [*A publication*] (DLA)

C of CH .... Chief of Chaplains [*Later, CCH*] [*Army*]

COFCH .... Chief of Chaplains [*Later, CCH*] [*Army*]

COFCO .... China National Cereals Oils & Foodstuffs Import & Export Corp.

C of CWS .... Chief of the Chemical Warfare Service [*World War II*]

C of D .... Certificate of Deposit [*Banking*]

COFD .... Collective Bancorp, Inc. [*NASDAQ symbol*] (NQ)

C of D .... Convention of Dublin [*Freemasonry*] (ROG)

Cof Dig .... Cofer's Kentucky Digest [*A publication*] (DLA)

C of E .... Certificate of Exemption

C of E .... Certificate of Experience (DA)

C of E .... Chief of Engineers [*Later, COE*] [*Army*]

C of E .... Church of England

C of E .... [*The*] Comedy of Errors [*Shakespearean work*]

COFE .... Conditions of Execution (MCD)

C of E .... Convention of Edinburgh [*Freemasonry*] (ROG)

C of E .... Corps of Engineers [*Army*]

COFE .... Council on Forest Engineering (EA)

C of E Agr PI... General Agreement on Privileges and Immunities of the Council of Europe (DLA)

COFEB .... Confederation of European Bath Manufacturers (EAIO)

C of EE & W... Council of Emperor of East and West [*Freemasonry*] (ROG)

COFENAF .... Commission des Federations et Syndicats Nationaux des Entreprises de Recuperation de Ferrailles du Marche Commun [*Committee of the National Ferrous Scrap Federations and Associations of the Common Market - CNFSFACM*] (EAIO)

COFENGRS.. Chief of Engineers (MCD)

C of ENGRS... Chief of Engineers [*Later, COE*] [*Army*]

C of Engs..... Chief of Engineers [*Army*] (SAA)

COFENGS.... Chief of Engineers [*Later, COE*] [*Army*]

COFF .... Cause of Failure, Effect, and Correction (SAA)

C of F .... Chaplain of the Fleet [*Navy British*]

C of F .... Chief of Finance [*Army*]

COFF .... Chief of Finance [*Army*]

COFF .... Cofferdam [*Engineering*]

COFF .... Common-Object-File Format [*Computer science*]

COFF .... Consolidation of Functions and Facilities Cutoff (MCD)

C of F .... Construction of Facilities

C of F .... Cost of Facilities (NASA)

C/OFF .... Counteroffer [*Legal shorthand*] (LWAP)

C of F .... Custodian of Fund

COFF .... Cut Off [*Military*] (AABC)

C of F .... Cyclopaedia of Freemasonry [*A publication*] (ROG)

COFFEE ...... Community Organization for Full Employment Economy

Coffey .... Coffey's California Probate Decisions [*A publication*] (DLA)

Coffey Probate Dec... Coffey's California Probate Decisions [*A publication*] (DLA)

Coffey Prob Dec... Coffey's California Probate Decisions [*A publication*] (DLA)

Coffey's Prob Dec... Coffey's California Probate Decisions [*A publication*] (DLA)

COFFI .... Commission on Ore-Forming Fluid in Inclusions

COFFI .... Communications Frequency and Facility Information Systems [*ICAO databank*] (NITA)

COFFI .... Coupled Optics and Flow Field Integration (MCD)

CoffPeop ...... Coffee People, Inc. [*Associated Press*] (SAG)

Coff Prob ...... Coffey's California Probate Decisions [*A publication*] (DLA)

CoFFS .... United States Forest Service, Rocky Mountain Forest and Range Experiment Station, Fort Collins, CO [*Library symbol Library of Congress*] (LCLS)

COFFTI .... Contracting Operator Fast Fourier Transform Identification (PDAA)

C of G .... Carriage of Goods [*by sea*] [*Shipping*]

C of G .... Center of Gravity

C of G .... Convenience of the Government

C of GA .... Central of Georgia Railroad Co.

C of GH .... Cape of Good Hope [*South Africa*]

CoFGS .... Church of Jesus Christ of Latter-Day Saints, Genealogical Society Library, Fort Collins Branch, Fort Collins, CO [*Library symbol Library of Congress*] (LCLS)

C of H .... Circumference of Head [*Medicine*]

COFHE .... Consortium on Financing Higher Education (EA)

CoFHP .... Hewlett-Packard Co., Fort Collins Division, Fort Collins, CO [*Library symbol Library of Congress*] (LCLS)

C of I .... Ceremony of Installation [*Freemasonry*] (ROG)

COFI .... Charter One Financial, Inc. [*NASDAQ symbol*] (SAG)

COFI .... Charter One Finl [*NASDAQ symbol*] (TTSB)

COFI............	Checkout and Fault Isolation [*NASA*] (KSC)
C of I............	Church of Ireland
COFI............	Committee on Fisheries [*Food and Agriculture Organization*]
COFI............	Cost of Funds Index [*Banking*]
COFI............	Council of Forest Industries (AC)
CoFI............	Ideal Cement Co. Research Library, Fort Collins, CO [*Library symbol Library of Congress*] (LCLS)
COFIDS.......	Coherent Optical Fingerprint Identification System (MCD)
COFIL..........	Core File (IEEE)
C of IRE.......	Church of Ireland
COFIRS........	RPG System [*International Business Machines Corp.*] [*Report Program Generator*] (IAA)
C of L..........	Children of Light [*Freemasonry*] (ROG)
C of L..........	City of London [*British*]
COFL...........	Committee on Federal Laboratories [*Federal Council for Science and Technology*] [*Terminated, 1976*] (EGAO)
C of L..........	Convention of London [*Freemasonry*] (ROG)
C of L..........	Corporation of London [*The City of London as opposed to Greater London*]
C of L..........	Cost of Living [*Economics*] (AAG)
CoFla..........	Flagler Community Library, Flagler, CO [*Library symbol Library of Congress*] (LCLS)
CoFle..........	Fleming Community Library, Fleming, CO [*Library symbol Library of Congress*] (LCLS)
Coflexip......	Coflexip & Services, Inc. [*Associated Press*] (SAG)
CoFlo..........	Florence Public Library, Florence, CO [*Library symbol Library of Congress*] (LCLS)
CoFloV........	Colorado State Veterans Nursing Home, Florence, CO [*Library symbol Library of Congress*] (LCLS)
CoFlu..........	Fort Lupton Public Library, Fort Lupton, CO [*Library symbol Library of Congress*] (LCLS)
C of LY.......	City of London Yeomanry [*Military British*] (ROG)
C of M........	Center of Mass
C of M........	Certificate of Merit
COFML........	Coffee Mill
C of N.........	Certificate of Need
C of N.........	Controller of the Navy [*British*]
COFO..........	Committee on Forestry [*Food and Agricultural Organization*] [*United Nations*]
COFO..........	Council of Federated Organizations [*Also, CFO*] [*Defunct*]
COFOA........	Companions of the Forest of America [*New York, NY*] (EA)
COFOE........	Coalition for Free and Open Elections (EA)
COFOR........	Canadian Occupational Forecasting Program (EDAC)
COFORD......	Chief of Ordnance [*Army*]
C of ORD.....	Chief of Ordnance [*Army*]
CoFow........	Fowler Public Library, Fowler, CO [*Library symbol Library of Congress*] (LCLS)
Cof Pro.......	Coffey's California Probate Decisions [*A publication*] (DLA)
Cof Prob......	Coffey's California Probate Decisions [*A publication*] (DLA)
Cof Prob Dec (Cal)...	Coffey's California Probate Decisions [*A publication*] (DLA)
COFR..........	Certificate of Flight Readiness [*NASA*] (NASA)
C of R.........	Certificate of Registration (ADA)
CoFr...........	Summit County Public Library, Frisco, CO [*Library symbol Library of Congress*] (LCLS)
CoFra..........	Fraser Public Library, Fraser, CO [*Library symbol Library of Congress*] (LCLS)
COFRAM......	Control [*or Controlled*] Fragmentation Munitions (CINC)
COFRC........	Chevron Oil Field Research Co.
COFRON......	Coastal Frontier [*Coast Guard*]
COFRS........	Computerized Freight Remittance System [*Pronounced "coffers"*]
CoFru..........	Fruita Public Library, Fruita, CO [*Library symbol Library of Congress*] (LCLS)
CoFruFE......	Fruita Elementary School, Fruita, CO [*Library symbol Library of Congress*] (LCLS)
CoFruFJ......	Fruita Junior High School, Fruita, CO [*Library symbol Library of Congress*] (LCLS)
CoFruFM.....	Fruita Monument High School, Fruita, CO [*Library symbol Library of Congress*] (LCLS)
CoFruSE......	Shelledy Elementary School, Fruita, CO [*Library symbol Library of Congress*] (LCLS)
COFS..........	Cerebro-Oculo-Facial-Skeletal Syndrome [*Medicine*] (DMAA)
C of S.........	Chief of Section
C of S.........	Chief of Staff [*Military*]
COFS..........	Chief of Staff [*Military*]
C of S.........	Church of Scotland
C of S.........	Climates of the States [*A publication*]
CoFS...........	Colorado State University, Fort Collins, CO [*Library symbol Library of Congress*] (LCLS)
COFSA........	Chief of Staff, United States Army [*Later, CSA*]
C of SA.......	Chief of Staff, United States Army [*Later, CSA*]
COFSAF.......	Chief of Staff, United States Air Force (NATG)
C of S Ca.....	Court of Session Cases [*Scotland*] [*A publication*] (DLA)
C of S Ca 1st Series...	Court of Session Cases, First Series, by Shaw, Dunlop, and Bell [*Scotland*] [*A publication*] (DLA)
C of S Ca 2d Series...	Court of Session Cases, Second Series, by Dunlop, Bell, and Murray [*Scotland*] [*A publication*] (DLA)
C of S Ca 3rd Series...	Court of Session Cases, Third Series, by Macpherson, Lee, and Bell [*Scotland*] [*A publication*] (DLA)
C of S Ca 4th Series...	Court of Session Cases, Fourth Series, by Rettie, Crawford, and Melville [*Scotland*] [*A publication*] (DLA)
C of S Ca 5th Series...	Court of Session Cases, Fifth Series [*Scotland*] [*A publication*] (DLA)
C of S Ch.....	Church of Scotland Chaplain [*British military*] (DMA)
C of SCOT....	Church of Scotland
C of SptS.....	Chief of Support Services [*Army*] (AABC)

COFSPTS	Chief of Support Services [*Army*]
C of T	Chief of the Tabernacle [*Freemasonry*] (ROG)
C of T	Chief of Transportation [*Army*]
COFT...........	Chief of Transportation [*Army*]
COFT...........	Commander, Fleet Train
C of T	Commissioner of Taxation (ADA)
COFT...........	Conduct of Fire Trainer [*Army*]
COFTI.........	Conduct of Fire Trainer - Improved [*Army*] (MCD)
CoFtLVA......	United States Veterans Administration Hospital, Fort Lyon, CO [*Library symbol Library of Congress*] (LCLS)
COFTM........	Conseil des Organismes Francophones du Toronto Metropolitain (AC)
CoFtm........	Fort Morgan Carnegie Public Library, Fort Morgan, CO [*Library symbol Library of Congress*] (LCLS)
CoFtmM......	Morgan County Community College, Fort Morgan, CO [*Library symbol Library of Congress*] (LCLS)
COFW	Certificate of Flight Worthiness [*NASA*] (KSC)
COG	Cabot Oil & Gas [*NYSE symbol*] (SPSG)
COG	Cabot Oil & Gas 'A' [*NYSE symbol*] (TTSB)
COG	Canadian Organic Growers
COG	CANDU Owners Group (AC)
COG	Center of Gravity
COG	Central Oncology Group (DAVI)
COG	Chelsea GCA Realty [*NYSE symbol*] (SAG)
COG	Chief of Government
COG	Cleansing Officers' Guild [*British*] (BI)
COG	Closed Angle Glaucoma [*Ophthalmology*] (CPH)
COG	Coal-Oil-Gas [*Fuel mixture*]
COG	Cognac (ADA)
COG	Cognate (ROG)
COG	Cognitive [*Function tests*] [*Psychology*] (DAVI)
COG	Cognizant (NG)
COG	Coke Oven Gas
CoG	Colorado School of Mines, Golden, CO [*Library symbol Library of Congress*] (LCLS)
COG	Combat Operations Group (SAA)
COG	Commander of the Guard [*Military*]
COG	Commissural Ganglion [*Neurology*]
COG	Compact Orbital Gears Ltd.
COG	Compliance Order Guide
COG	Computer Operations Group
COG	Condoto [*Colombia*] [*Airport symbol*] (OAG)
COG	Congo [*ANSI three-letter standard code*] (CNC)
COG	Consultant Orthodontists Group [*British*] (DBA)
COG	Continuity of Government
COG	Control Orbitron Gauge
COG	Convenience of the Government
COG	Cooperative Oncology Group [*National Cancer Institute*]
COG	Coordinator General (ADA)
COG	Corresponding Objects Grid [*Computer science*]
COG	Council of Governments [*Voluntary organizations of municipalities and counties*]
COG	Course Made Good over the Ground [*Military*] (NVT)
COG	Covenant of the Goddess (EA)
COG	Crab-Oriented Gyro (SAA)
COG	Credit Officers Group (EA)
COG	Current Operational Group [*NATO*] (NATG)
COG	Customer-Owned Goods
COG	Customer's Own Goods (WDMC)
COG	Garfield County System, New Castle, CO [*OCLC symbol*] (OCLC)
Co G	Reports and Cases of Practice in Common Pleas Tempore Anne, George I, and Geor ge II, by Sir G. Coke [*Same as Cooke's Practice Reports*] [*1706-47 England*] [*A publication*] (DLA)
CoGA	AMAX, Inc., Golden, CO [*Library symbol Library of Congress*] (LCLS)
COGAG........	Combined Gas and Gas (PDAA)
COGAID.......	Coast Guard Assistance Instruction Data
COGAP........	Combustion Gas Analyzer Program [*Nuclear energy*] (NRCH)
COGAP........	Computer Graphics Arrangement Program (PDAA)
COGARD	Coast Guard
COGARDACFTPROGOFF...	Coast Guard Aircraft Program Office (DNAB)
COGARDANFAC...	Coast Guard Aids to Navigation Facility (DNAB)
COGARDANT...	Coast Guard Aids to Navigation Team (DNAB)
COGARDARSC...	Coast Guard Aircraft Repair and Supply Center (DNAB)
COGARDAVDET...	Coast Guard Aviation Detachment (DNAB)
COGARDAVTC...	Coast Guard Aviation Training Center (DNAB)
COGARDAVTECHTRACEN...	Coast Guard Aviation Technical Training Center (DNAB)
COGARDBST...	Coast Guard Boating Safety Team (DNAB)
COGARDCOMMSTA...	Coast Guard Communications Station (DNAB)
COGARDCOSARFAC...	Coast Guard Coastal Search and Rescue Facility (DNAB)
COGARDCOTP...	Coast Guard Captain of the Port Office (DNAB)
COGARDCRUITOFF...	Coast Guard Recruiting Office (DNAB)
COGARDEECEN...	Coast Guard Electronics Engineering Center (DNAB)
COGARDEP...	Coast Guard Depot (DNAB)
COGARDES...	Coast Guard Electronic Shop (DNAB)
COGARDESM...	Coast Guard Electronic Shop Minor (DNAB)
COGARDESMT...	Coast Guard Electronics Shop Minor Telephone and Teletype (DNAB)
COGARDEST...	Coast Guard Electronics Shop Major Telephone and Teletype (DNAB)
COGARDETNDBO...	Coast Guard Detachment National Data Buoy Office (DNAB)
COGARDFSTD...	Coast Guard Fire and Safety Test Detachment (DNAB)
COGARDINST...	Coast Guard Institute (DNAB)
COGARDLOCOMFLETRAGRU...	Coast Guard Liaison Officer, Commander Fleet Training Group (DNAB)

COGARDLOEPIC... Coast Guard Liaison Officer, Eastern Pacific Intelligence Center (DNAB)
COGARDLOREP... Coast Guard Liaison Officer Representative (DNAB)
COGARDLORMONSTA... Coast Guard LORAN [*Long-Range Aid to Navigation*] Monitor Station (DNAB)
COGARDLORSTA... Coast Guard LORAN [*Long-Range Aid to Navigation*] Station (DNAB)
COGARDLTSTA... Coast Guard Light Station (DNAB)
COGARDMID... Coast Guard Marine Inspection Detachment (DNAB)
COGARDMIO... Coast Guard Marine Inspection Office (DNAB)
COGARDMRDET... Coast Guard Maintenance Repair Detachment (DNAB)
COGARDMSD... Coast Guard Marine Safety Detachment (DNAB)
COGARDMSO... Coast Guard Marine Safety Office (DNAB)
COGARDNDBO... Coast Guard National Data Buoy Office (DNAB)
COGARDNMLBS... Coast Guard National Motor Lifeboat School (DNAB)
COGARDNSF... Coast Guard National Strike Force (DNAB)
COGARDNSFLANT... Coast Guard National Strike Force, Atlantic (DNAB)
COGARDNSFPAC... Coast Guard National Strike Force, Pacific (DNAB)
COGARDOCC... Coast Guard Operations Computer Center (DNAB)
COGARDOMSTA... Coast Guard Omega Station (DNAB)
COGARDONSOD... Coast Guard Omega Navigation Systems Office Detachment (DNAB)
COGARDOPDAC... Coast Guard Operations Data Analysis Center (DNAB)
COGARDORDSUPPFAC... Coast Guard Ordnance Support Facility (DNAB)
COGARDPSDET... Coast Guard Port Safety Detachment (DNAB)
COGARDPSSTA... Coast Guard Port Safety Station (DNAB)
COGARDRADSTA... Coast Guard Radio Station (DNAB)
COGARDRECDEP... Coast Guard Records Depot (DNAB)
COGARDREPNAVREGMEDCEN... Coast Guard Representative, Naval Regional Medical Center (DNAB)
COGARDREPSTUDREC... Coast Guard Representative, Student Records (DNAB)
COGARDREPTAMC... Coast Guard Representative, Tripler Army Medical Center (DNAB)
COGARDREPUSAFH... Coast Guard Representative, United States Air Force Hospital (DNAB)
COGARDREPUSPHS... Coast Guard Representative, United States Public Health Service Hospital (DNAB)
COGARDRESCEN... Coast Guard Reserve Center (DNAB)
COGARDRESTRACEN... Coast Guard Reserve Training Center (DNAB)
COGARDRIO... Coast Guard Resident Inspecting Officer (DNAB)
COGARDSICP... Coast Guard Stock Inventory Control Point (DNAB)
COGARDSIU... Coast Guard Ship Introduction Unit (DNAB)
COGARDSTA... Coast Guard Station (DNAB)
COGARDSUPCEN... Coast Guard Supply Center (DNAB)
COGARDSUPRTCEN... Coast Guard Support Center (DNAB)
COGARDSUPRTFAC... Coast Guard Support Facility (DNAB)
COGARDTRACEN... Coast Guard Training Center (DNAB)
COGARDVTS... Coast Guard Vessel Traffic System (DNAB)
COGAS......... Coal [*into*] Gas [*Process*]
COGAT......... Cognitive Abilities Test [*Academic achievement and aptitude test*]
COGB.......... Certified Official Government Business
COGD.......... Circulator Outlet Gas Duct (OA)
COGD.......... Cogdean [*England*]
CoGD.......... Dow Chemical Co., Rocky Flats Division, Golden, CO [*Library symbol Library of Congress*] (LCLS)
COGE .... Compare Generiks [*NASDAQ symbol*] (TTSB)
COGE .... Compare Generiks, Inc. [*NASDAQ symbol*] (SAG)
COGEAA...... Commercial Orchid Growers' and Exporters' Association [*Australia*]
COGECA...... Comite General de la Cooperation Agricole de la CE [*General Committee of Agricultural Cooperation in the EC*] (EAIO)
COGEL .... Council on Governmental Ethics Laws (EA)
COGENE...... Committee on Genetic Experimentation [*ICSU*]
COGENT...... Compiler and Generalized Translator [*Argonne National Laboratory*] [*List processor*] (IEEE)
COGENT...... Compiler Generator and Translator [*Computer science*] (NITA)
COGENT...... Cooperative Generic Technology [*Centers for cooperative government and industry work*]
CoGeo......... John Tomay Memorial Public Library, Georgetown, CO [*Library symbol Library of Congress*] (LCLS)
COGEODATA... Commission on Storage, Automatic Processing, and Retrieval of Geological Data (EAIO)
COGEP .... Confederation Generale de la Publicite (AC)
COGEU........ Compare Generiks Unit [*NASDAQ symbol*] (TTSB)
COGEW........ Compare Generiks Wrrt'A' [*NASDAQ symbol*] (TTSB)
COGG.......... Coggeshall [*England*]
CoGG .... Golden Gate Youth Camp, Residents' Library, Golden, CO [*Library symbol Library of Congress*] (LCLS)
Cogh Epit..... Coghlan's Epitome of Hindu Law Cases [*A publication*] (DLA)
COGI.......... Children's Own Garden International [*See also BjBI*] (EAIO)
COGI.......... Consolidated Graphics [*NASDAQ symbol*] (TTSB)
COGI.......... Consolidated Graphics, Inc. [*NASDAQ symbol*] (SAG)
CoGJ.......... Jefferson County Library, Golden, CO [*Library symbol Library of Congress*] (LCLS)
CoGj.......... Mesa County Public Library, Grand Junction, CO [*Library symbol Library of Congress*] (LCLS)
CoGjAE........ Appleton Elementary School, Grand Junction, CO [*Library symbol Library of Congress*] (LCLS)
CoGjBoJ....... Bookcliff Junior High School, Grand Junction, CO [*Library symbol Library of Congress*] (LCLS)
CoGjBrE....... Broadway Elementary School, Grand Junction, CO [*Library symbol Library of Congress*] (LCLS)
CoGjCeH...... Central High School, Grand Junction, CO [*Library symbol Library of Congress*] (LCLS)
CoGJCL........ Jefferson County Library, Golden, CO [*Library symbol*] [*Library of Congress*] (LCLS)

CoGjCoE ...... Columbine Elementary School, Grand Junction, CO [*Library symbol Library of Congress*] (LCLS)
CoGjCS .... Cornerstone Christian School Library, Grand Junction, CO [*Library symbol*] [*Library of Congress*] (LCLS)
CoGjCsE....... Columbus Elementary School, Grand Junction, CO [*Library symbol Library of Congress*] (LCLS)
CoGjEJ........ East Junior High School, Grand Junction, CO [*Library symbol Library of Congress*] (LCLS)
CoGjFE........ Fruitvale Elementary School, Grand Junction, CO [*Library symbol Library of Congress*] (LCLS)
CoGjFL........ Film Library of Mesa County, School, District 51, Grand Junction, CO [*Library symbol*] [*Library of Congress*] (LCLS)
CoGJ-G .... Golden Regional Library (J. Lester Trezise Regional Library), Golden, CO [*Library symbol Library of Congress*] (LCLS)
CoGjGH .... Grand Junction High School, Grand Junction, CO [*Library symbol Library of Congress*] (LCLS)
CoGjGS .... Church of Jesus Christ of Latter-Day Saints, Genealogical Society Library, GrandJunction Branch, Stake Center, Grand Junction, CO [*Library symbol Library of Congress*] (LCLS)
CoGjHF .... Holy Family School, Grand Junction, CO [*Library symbol*] [*Library of Congress*] (LCLS)
CoGjL.......... Lutheran School of Messiah Elementary Library, Grand Junction, CO [*Library symbol*] [*Library of Congress*] (LCLS)
CoGjLOE ...... Lincoln Orchard Mesa Elementary School, Grand Junction, CO [*Library symbol Library of Congress*] (LCLS)
CoGjLPE ...... Lincoln Park Elementary School, Grand Junction, CO [*Library symbol Library of Congress*] (LCLS)
CoGjM .... Mesa College, Grand Junction, CO [*Library symbol Library of Congress*] (LCLS)
CoGjME .... Mesa View Elementary School Library, Grand Junction, CO [*Library symbol Library of Congress*] (LCLS)
CoGjMW ...... Museum of Western Colorado, Grand Junction, CO [*Library symbol*] [*Library of Congress*] (LCLS)
CoGjNE .... Nisley Elementary School, Grand Junction, CO [*Library symbol Library of Congress*] (LCLS)
CoGjOAE ...... Orchard Avenue Elementary School, Grand Junction, CO [*Library symbol Library of Congress*] (LCLS)
CoGjOMJ ...... Orchard Mesa Junior High School, Grand Junction, CO [*Library symbol Library of Congress*] (LCLS)
CoGjPE .... Pomona Elementary School, Grand Junction, CO [*Library symbol Library of Congress*] (LCLS)
CoGjRE .... Riverside Elementary School, Grand Junction, CO [*Library symbol Library of Congress*] (LCLS)
CoGjSD .... School District No. 51, Special Services Media Materials, Grand Junction, CO [*Library symbol Library of Congress*] (LCLS)
CoGjSD-P .... School District No. 51, Professional Library, Grand Junction, CO [*Library symbol Library of Congress*] (LCLS)
CoGjSD-U .... Masa County School District 51, Union Catalog, Grand Junction, CO [*Library symbol*] [*Library of Congress*] (LCLS)
CoGjSD-V .... School District No. 51, Vocational Department, Grand Junction, CO [*Library symbol Library of Congress*] (LCLS)
CoGjSE .... Scenic Elementary School, Grand Junction, CO [*Library symbol Library of Congress*] (LCLS)
CoGjT.......... Colorado State Home and Training School, Grand Junction, CO [*Library symbol Library of Congress*] (LCLS)
CoGjTE........ Tope Elementary School, Grand Junction, CO [*Library symbol Library of Congress*] (LCLS)
CoGjThE....... Thunder Mountain Elementary School Library, Grand Junction, CO [*Library symbol Library of Congress*] (LCLS)
CoGjTS .... Colorado State Home and Training School, Staff Library, Grand Junction, CO [*Library symbol Library of Congress*] (LCLS)
CoGjUC .... Union Carbide Corp., Grand Junction, CO [*Library symbol Library of Congress*] (LCLS)
CoGjW .... Colorado State Library, Western Slope Clearinghouse, Grand Junction, CO [*Library symbol Library of Congress*] (LCLS)
CoGjWE .... Wingate Elementary School Library, Grand Junction, CO [*Library symbol Library of Congress*] (LCLS)
CoGjWJ........ West Junior High School, Grand Junction, CO [*Library symbol Library of Congress*] (LCLS)
CoGJY......... Jefferson County Youth Center, Golden, CO [*Library symbol Library of Congress*] (LCLS)
CoGl............ Grand Lake Public Library, Grand Lake, CO [*Library symbol Library of Congress*] (LCLS)
COGLA........ Canada Oil and Gas Lands Administration
CoGLM........ Lookout Mountain School for Boys, Golden, CO [*Library symbol Library of Congress*] (LCLS)
COGME .... Council for Opportunity in Graduate Management Education [*Defunct*] (EA)
COGME .... Council on Graduate Medical Education [*Department of Health and Human Services*]
COGME .... Council on Graduate Medical Education
COGN.......... Cognos, Inc. [*NASDAQ symbol*] (NQ)
COGNE........ Cognos Inc. [*NASDAQ symbol*] (TTSB)
Cognex........ Cognex Corp. [*Associated Press*] (SAG)
Cognitr........ Cognitronics Corp. [*Associated Press*] (SAG)
COGNN .... Canadian Obstetric, Gynecologic & Neonatal Nurses (AC)
Cognos........ Cognos, Inc. [*Associated Press*] (SAG)
COGNOSYS... Cognitive Operating System [*NASA*]
COGN W ...... Cognate With (ROG)
COGO.......... Commercially Owned, Government-Operated (AFIT)
COGO.......... Coordinated Geometry [*Programming language*] [*1957*] (CSR)
CoGO.......... Oil Shale Corp., Research Center Library, Golden, CO [*Library symbol Library of Congress*] (LCLS)
COGOG .... Combined Gas or Gas (PDAA)
COGOG .... Combined Gas Turbine or Gas Turbine Propulsion

COGP .... Commission on Government Procurement [*Terminated, 1973*]
COGR .... Council on Governmental Relations (EA)
CoGr .... Greeley Public Library, Greeley, CO [*Library symbol Library of Congress*] (LCLS)
CoGR .... Rockwell International Corp., Atomics International Division, Rocky Flats Plant, Golden, CO [*Library symbol Library of Congress*] (LCLS)
CoGrA .... Aims College, Greeley, CO [*Library symbol Library of Congress*] (LCLS)
CoGra .... Granada Public Library, Granada, CO [*Library symbol Library of Congress*] (LCLS)
CoGranG ...... Grand County Public Library, Granby Branch, Granby, CO [*Library symbol Library of Congress*] (LCLS)
CoGraP .... Granada Public Library, Granada, CO [*Library symbol*] [*Library of Congress*] (LCLS)
CoGrR .... Rocky Mountain Special Education Instructional Materials Center, Greeley, CO [*Library symbol Library of Congress*] (LCLS)
CoGrU .... University of Northern Colorado, Greeley, CO [*Library symbol Library of Congress*] (LCLS)
CoGrW .... Weld County Library, Greeley, CO [*Library symbol Library of Congress*] (LCLS)
COGS .... Church of Jesus Christ of Latter-Day Saints, Genealogical Society Library, Oakland Branch, Oakland, CA [*Library symbol Library of Congress*] (LCLS)
COGS .... Combat-Oriented General Support [*Army*]
COGS .... Commodity Oriented General Support
COGS .... Computer Oriented Geological Society [*Database producer*] (IID)
COGS .... Concordance Generation System [*A text editing system*] [*University of Toronto*] [*Canada*] (NITA)
COGS .... Consumer Goods System [*Computer science*]
COGS .... Continuous Orbital Guidance System
COGS .... Cost of Goods Sold
COGS .... Council of Graphological Societies (EA)
CoGs .... Glenwood Springs Public Library, Glenwood Springs, CO [*Library symbol Library of Congress*] (LCLS)
COGSA .... Carriage of Goods by Sea Act [*Shipping*]
CoGsC .... Colorado Mountain College, Western Campus, Glenwood Springs, CO [*Library symbol Library of Congress*] (LCLS)
COGSC .... Combat-Oriented General Support Center (MCD)
CoGSE .... Solar Energy Research Institute, Golden, CO [*Library symbol Library of Congress*] (LCLS)
CoGsP .... Glenwood Springs Public Library, Glenwood Springs, CO [*Library symbol*] [*Library of Congress*] (LCLS)
CoGT .... Tosco Corp., Technical Information Center, Golden, CO [*Library symbol Library of Congress*] (LCLS)
COGTT .... Cortisone [*Primed*] Oral Glucose Tolerance Test [*Medicine*]
CoGu .... Gunnison County Public Library, Gunnison, CO [*Library symbol Library of Congress*] (LCLS)
CoGuVS .... Gunnison Valley School, Gunnison, CO [*Library symbol*] [*Library of Congress*] (LCLS)
CoGuW .... Western State College of Colorado, Gunnison, CO [*Library symbol Library of Congress*] (LCLS)
CoGwGS ...... Gateway School, Gateway, CO [*Library symbol Library of Congress*] (LCLS)
CoGy .... Gypsum Community Library, Gypsum, CO [*Library symbol Library of Congress*] (LCLS)
CoGyS .... Sweetwater Library, Gypsum, CO [*Library symbol Library of Congress*] (LCLS)
COH .... Alameda County Health Department, Oakland, CA [*Library symbol Library of Congress*] (LCLS)
COH .... Carbohydrate
COH .... Carrier Overhaul (MCD)
COH .... Cash-on-Hand [*Banking*] (MHDW)
COH .... Center for Occupational Hazards (EA)
COH .... Cochiti [*New Mexico*] [*Seismograph station code, US Geological Survey*] (SEIS)
COH .... Coefficient of Haze [*Environment*]
COH .... Coheir [*Joint heir*] [*Genealogy*]
COH .... Coherence [*Statistics*]
COH .... Coherent (IAA)
COH .... Comite Olimpico Hondureno [*Honduran Olympic Committee*] (EAIO)
COH .... Comite Olympique Hongrois [*Hungarian Olympic Committee*] (EAIO)
COH .... Compensatory Ovarian Hypertrophy [*Endocrinology*]
COH .... Completion of Overhaul (DNAB)
COH .... Complex Overhaul (NVT)
COH .... Computer Operator Handbook
COH .... Control of Official Histories [*British*]
COH .... Cooch Behar [*India*] [*Airport symbol*] (AD)
COH .... Corporal of Horse [*British military*] (DMA)
COH .... United States Air Force Academy, USAF Academy, CO [*OCLC symbol*] (OCLC)
COHA .... Canadian Oldtimers Hockey Association
COHA .... Canadian Oral History Association [*See also SCHO*]
COHA .... Council on Hemispheric Affairs (EA)
CoHa .... Haxtun Public Library, Haxtun, CO [*Library symbol Library of Congress*] (LCLS)
COHART .... Costs of Hard Rock Tunnelling (PDAA)
CoHay .... Hayden Public Library, Hayden, CO [*Library symbol Library of Congress*] (LCLS)
COHB .... Carboxyhemoglobin [*Biochemistry*]
COHbA .... Carboxyhemoglobin A [*Biochemistry*]
COHC .... China Ocean Helicopter Corp. [*ICAO designator*] (FAAC)
Co Hd .... Coral Head [*Quality of the bottom*] [*Nautical charts*]
COHE .... College of Osteopathic Healthcare Executives (EA)

Cohen Adm Law... Cohen's Admiralty Jurisdiction, Law, and Practice [*A publication*] (DLA)
CohenST ...... Cohen & Steers Total Return Realty Fund [*Associated Press*] (SAG)
CohenStr ..... Cohen & Steers Realty Income Fund [*Associated Press*] (SAG)
CoherC .... Coherent Communications Systems Corp. [*Associated Press*] (SAG)
Cohernt .... Coherent, Inc. [*Associated Press*] (SAG)
Cohes .... Cohesant Technologies, Inc. [*Associated Press*] (SAG)
Cohesant ..... Cohesant Technologies, Inc. [*Associated Press*] (SAG)
COHETA ...... Conseil pour l'Homologation des Etablissements Theologiques en Afrique [*Accrediting Council for Theological Education in Africa - ACTEA*] (EAIO)
COHgB .... Carboxyhemoglobin [*Biochemistry*] (AAMN)
COHHV .... Cab Over [*Engine*] Heavy, High [*Mobility Multipurpose Wheeled*] Vehicle [*Army*]
CoHi .... Colorado State Historical Society, Denver, CO [*Library symbol Library of Congress*] (LCLS)
COHI .... Consumers Organization for the Hearing Impaired [*Defunct*] (EA)
COHI .... Crippled and Other Health Impaired [*Obsolete*]
CoHIV .... Colorado State Veterans Center, Homelake, CO [*Library symbol Library of Congress*] (LCLS)
COHMAP...... Cooperative Holocene Mapping Project [*Geology*]
COHMED...... Cooperative Hazardous Materials Enforcement Development Program [*RSPA*] (TAG)
COHNA ...... Canadian Occupational Health Nurses Association [*Formerly, National Association of Occupational Health Nurses*] (AC)
CO HO .... Coffee House (ROG)
COHO .... Coherent Oscillator [*RADAR*]
COHO .... Coho Energy [*NASDAQ symbol*] (TTSB)
COHO .... Coho Energy, Inc. [*NASDAQ symbol*] (SAG)
CO HO .... Copyhold [*British Legal term*] (ROG)
COHO .... Council of Health Organizations
CO HO .... Court House [*British*] (ROG)
CoHo .... Holyoke Public Library, Holyoke, CO [*Library symbol Library of Congress*] (LCLS)
CohoEn .... Coho Energy, Inc. [*Associated Press*] (SAG)
CoHol .... Women's Civic Club Library, Holly, CO [*Library symbol Library of Congress*] (LCLS)
COHORT ...... Cohesion, Operational Readiness, and Training [*Army*]
CoHotch....... Hotchkiss Public Library, Hotchkiss, CO [*Library symbol Library of Congress*] (LCLS)
COHQ .... Combined Operations Headquarters [*World War II*]
COHR .... Center for Oral Health Research [*University of Pennsylvania*] [*Research center*] (RCD)
COHR .... Coherent, Inc. [*NASDAQ symbol*] (NQ)
COHR .... COHR, Inc. [*Associated Press*] (SAG)
COHRED ...... Council on Health Research for Development [*Switzerland*] (ECON)
COHRIMS .... Committee on Human Rights in Malaysia and Singapore (EA)
COHS .... Center for Occupational Health and Safety [*University of Waterloo*] [*Research center*] (RCD)
COHS .... Chesapeake and Ohio Historical Society (EA)
COHSE .... Confederation of Health Service Employees [*Pronounced "cozy"*] [*A union*] [*British*] (DCTA)
Cohse .... Confederation of Health Service Employees [*British*] (ODBW)
CoHsp .... Grand County Public Library, Hot Sulphur Springs, CO [*Library symbol Library of Congress*] (LCLS)
COHT .... Cohesant Technologies [*NASDAQ symbol*] (TTSB)
COHT .... Cohesant Technologies, Inc. [*NASDAQ symbol*] (SAG)
COHT .... Cut-Out Halftone [*Graphic arts*] (DGA)
COHTW .... Cohesant Technologies Wrrt [*NASDAQ symbol*] (TTSB)
COHU .... Cohu, Inc. [*NASDAQ symbol*] (SAG)
CoHu .... Hugo Public Library, Hugo, CO [*Library symbol Library of Congress*] (LCLS)
CoHud .... Hudson Public Library, Hudson, CO [*Library symbol Library of Congress*] (LCLS)
COHVENT..... Coherent Event [*Trademark*]
COI............... Advisory Committee on the NAIC [*National Astronomy and Ionosphere Center*] Nation-Wide Marine Definition (EA)
COI.............. Called Output Image
COI.............. Camp of Israel [*Freemasonry*] (ROG)
COI.............. Center of Influence [*Military*]
COI.............. Central Obesity Index [*Medicine*] (DMAA)
COI.............. Central Office of Information [*London, England*]
COI.............. Certificate of Incorporation [*Business law*]
COI.............. Certificate of Indebtedness [*Finance*]
COI.............. Certificate of Insurance (HCT)
COI.............. Coast Orbital Insertion (MCD)
COI.............. Cocoa, FL [*Location identifier FAA*] (FAAL)
COI.............. Coimbra [*Portugal*] [*Seismograph station code, US Geological Survey*] (SEIS)
COI.............. Coin Lake Gold Mines Ltd. [*Toronto Stock Exchange symbol*]
Co-I.............. Coinvestigator
COI.............. Commission Oceanographique Intergouvernementale [*Intergovernmental Oceanographic Commission - IOC*] (EAIO)
COI.............. Communications Operations Instructions [*Air Force*]
COI.............. Community of Interest [*DoD*]
COI.............. Computer Operating Instruction
COI.............. Conflict of Interest [*Legal term*]
COI.............. Conjugi [*To My Spouse*] [*Latin*]
COI.............. Conseil Oleicole International [*International Olive Oil Council - IOOC*] (EAIO)
COI.............. Contingency Orbit Insertion [*NASA*] (KSC)
COI.............. Coordinator of Information
COI.............. Cost of Illness [*Environmental medicine*]
COI.............. Course of Instruction [*Military*]
COI.............. Critical Operational Issues Testing [*DoD*]

COI	Cube Order Index Rule
COI	Cytochrome Oxidase I [*An enzyme*]
COI	Iliff School of Theology, Denver, CO [*OCLC symbol*] (OCLC)
COIA	Conservative Orthopedics International Association (EA)
COIB	Correctional Officers' Interest Blank [*Screening and placement test*]
COIC	Canadian Oceanographic Identification Center (HGAA)
COIC	Careers and Occupational Information Centre (IID)
COIC	Combat Operations Intelligence Center (MCD)
COIC	Combined Operational Intelligence Center [*Navy*]
COID	Council of Industrial Design [*British*]
COIDIEA	Conseil des Organisations Internationales Directement Interessees a l'Enfance eta l'Adolescence [*Council of International Organizations Directly Interested in Children and Youth*] [*Geneva, Switzerland*] (EAIO)
COIE	Committee on Invisible Exports [*British*] (DS)
COIF	Charities Official Investment Fund [*Finance British*]
COIF	Control of Intensive Farming [*British*]
COIFF	Coiffure
Colg	Ignacio Public Library, Ignacio, CO [*Library symbol Library of Congress*] (LCLS)
COII	Canadian Occupational Interest Inventory [*Vocational test*]
COIK	Clear Only if Known [*Buzz words, acronyms, etc., that are clear in context only if already known to the reader*]
COIL	Central Oil Identification Laboratory [*Groton, CT*] [*Coast Guard*] (MSC)
COIL	Chemical Oxygen Iodine LASER (MCD)
COIL	Coast Guard Oil Identification Laboratory [*Groton, CT*]
COIL	Coiled [*Freight*]
COIL	Combat Illumination (MCD)
COIL	COMPAS [*Computer Acquisition System*] Online Interactive Language (PDAA)
COIL	Conference of Insurance Legislators [*Later, NCOIL*] (EA)
COIL	Crude Oil Analyses File [*Petroleum Information Corp.*] [*Information service or system*] (CRD)
COILS	CONUS [*Continental United States*] Installation Logistics Support (MCD)
COIM	Checkout Interpreter Module (MCD)
Co Imo	Come Primo [*As at First*] [*Music*]
COIMS	CONUS [*Continental United States*] Installation Maintenance Support (MCD)
COIN	California Olive Industry News
COIN	Central Ohio Interlibrary Network [*Library network*]
COIN	Coin Phone Operational and Information Network System [*Telecommunications*] (TEL)
COIN	Command Information (SAA)
COIN	Committee on Information Needs
COIN	Commodity-Embedded Insurance
COIN	Community Outreach Information Network
COIN	Complete Operating Information [*Computer science*]
COIN	Consumers Opposed to Inflation in the Necessities (EA)
COIN	Continuation Incentive Pay [*Proposed*] [*Army*]
COIN	Coordinated Occupational Information Network [*COIN Educational Products*] [*Information service or system*] (IID)
COIN	Council of Oil-Importing Nations
COIN	Counterinsurgency
CoinBill	Coin Bill Validator, Inc. [*Associated Press*] (SAG)
COINCNT	Coincidence Counts
CO IN HES	Communications and Information Handling Equipment and Services
COINIM	Centralny Osrodek Informacji Normalizacyjnej i Metrologicznej [*Center for Information on Standardization and Metrology*] [*Poland*] (EAIO)
Coinmch	Coinmach Laundry Corp. [*Associated Press*] (SAG)
COINOPS	Counterinsurgency Operations
COINS	Calspan On-Line Information Service [*Calspan Corp.*] [*Information service or system*] (IID)
COINS	Coinsurance
COINS	Committee on Improvement of National Statistics [*Inter-American*]
COINS	Community On-Line Intelligence Network System [*Computer network*] [*National Science Administration and Central Intelligence Agency*]
COINS	Computer and Information Sciences
COINS	Control in Information Systems
COINS	Cooperative Intelligence Network System [*Proposed*] [*Navy*]
Co Inst	Coke's Institutes [*England*] [*A publication*] (DLA)
Co Inst (Eng)	Coke's Institutes [*England*] [*A publication*] (DLA)
COINT	Commands Interested Have by Mail [*Military*] (DNAB)
COINTELPRO	Counterintelligence Program [*FBI program carried out against political activists from 1956 to 1971*]
Coin W	Coin World [*A publication*]
COIOEQ	Coal Operators' Industrial Organisation of Employers, Queensland [*Australia*]
COIP	Current Oil in Place [*Petroleum technology*]
COIR	Commanders Operational Intelligence Requirements (MCD)
COIS	Committee on International Standardization [*National Researh Council*] (NUCP)
Cols	Idaho Springs Public Library, Idaho Springs, CO [*Library symbol Library of Congress*] (LCLS)
COISS	CONUS [*Continental United States*] Installation Supply Support (MCD)
COIT	Central Office of the Industrial Tribunal [*Department of Employment*] [*British*]
COITS	CONUS [*Continental United States*] Installation Transportation System (MCD)
COITU	Confederation of Insurance Trade Unions [*British*] (DCTA)
COIU	Careers and Occupational Information Unit (AIE)
COIU	Congress of Independent Unions

COJ	Cogesco Mining Resources [*Toronto Stock Exchange symbol*]
COJ	Coonabarabran [*Australia Airport symbol*] (OAG)
COJ	Court of Justice
COJAC	Committee on Justice and the Constitution (EA)
COJAC	Congress of Joke-Abused Cities
COJE	Central Organization for Jewish Education (EA)
COJE	Conseil Oecumenique de Jeunesse en Europe [*Ecumenical Youth Council in Europe*] [*Northern Ireland*] (EAIO)
COJM	Concentrated Orange Juice for Manufacturing
COJO	Comite Organisateur de Jeux Olympiques [*Organizing Committee of the Olympic Games (1976)*] [*Canada*]
COJO	Conference of Jewish Organizations (BARN)
CoJo	Glenn A. Jones, MD, Memorial Library, Johnstown, CO [*Library symbol Library of Congress*] (LCLS)
COjOVM	Ojai Valley Museum, Ojia, CA [*Library symbol*] [*Library of Congress*] (LCLS)
CoJu	Julesburg Public Library, Julesburg, CO [*Library symbol Library of Congress*] (LCLS)
Co Jurid	Collectanea Juridica [*England*] [*A publication*] (DLA)
COK	Ciskei International Airways Corp. [*South Africa ICAO designator*] (FAAC)
COK	Cochin [*India*] [*Airport symbol*] (OAG)
COK	Cook Islands [*ANSI three-letter standard code*] (CNC)
CoK	Cost of Knowing
COK	Cous Creek Copper Mines [*Vancouver Stock Exchange symbol*]
CoK	Elbert County Public Library, Kiowa, CO [*Library symbol Library of Congress*] (LCLS)
COKE	Coca-Cola Bott Consol [*NASDAQ symbol*] (TTSB)
COKE	Coca-Cola Bottling Co. Consolidated [*NASDAQ symbol*] (NQ)
COKE	Cocaine [*Slang*] (DSUE)
Coke	Coke's English King's Bench Reports [*1572-1616*] [*A publication*] (DLA)
Coke (Eng)	Coke's English King's Bench Reports [*1572-1616*] [*A publication*] (DLA)
Coke Ent	Coke's Book of Entries [*1614*] [*England*] [*A publication*] (DLA)
Coke Inst	Coke's Institutes [*England*] [*A publication*] (DLA)
Coke Lit	Coke on Littleton [*England*] [*A publication*] (DLA)
COKER	Classroom Observations Keyed for Effectiveness Research (EDAC)
CoKr	Kremmling Public Library, Kremmling, CO [*Library symbol Library of Congress*] (LCLS)
COL	Capsule-Orbiting Bus Link [*NASA*]
COL	Carry-On Laboratory [*NASA*]
COL	Chain Overseas Low [*Aviation*]
COL	Checkout Language [*NASA*] (NASA)
COL	CircOlectric Bed [*A trademark*] [*Medicine*]
COL	Citizens for Ocean Law (EA)
COL	Coherent Optical LASER
COL	Cola [*or Colatus*] [*Strain See also COLAT*] [*Pharmacy*]
CO-L	Colatitude [*Navigation*]
col	Colbphon (BARN)
Col	Coldwell's Reports [*41-47 Tennessee*] [*A publication*] (DLA)
Col	Coleman's Reports [*99, 101-106, 110-129 Alabama*] [*A publication*] (DLA)
Col	Coleoptera [*Entomology*]
col	Collage (VRA)
COL	Collagen [*Biochemistry*]
COL	Collar
COL	Collate
COL	Collateral (WGA)
COL	Collation [*Library science*] (WDMC)
COL	Colleague (WGA)
COL	Collect
col	Collect (WDMC)
COL	Collection (WDAA)
COL	College
col	College (WDMC)
COL	College Outpost [*Alaska*] [*Seismograph station code, US Geological Survey*] (SEIS)
COL	Collegium (ROG)
Col	Collision (DS)
COL	Colloidal
COL	Colombia [*ANSI three-letter standard code*] (CNC)
COL	Colon (WDAA)
COL	Colonel [*Military*] (AABC)
Col	Colonel (DD)
COL	Colonel
COL	Colonial (ROG)
Col	Colonist
Col	Colony [*or Colonies*] [*Bacteriology*] (DAVI)
COL	Colony
COL	Color
col	Color (WDMC)
COL	Colorado
Col	Colorado Reports [*A publication*] (DLA)
COL	Colored
Col	Colossians [*New Testament book*]
COL	Colts Neck, NJ [*Location identifier FAA*] (FAAL)
Col	Columba [*Constellation*]
COL	Columbia Airlines Ltd. [*Canada ICAO designator*] (FAAC)
COL	Columbia HCA Healthcare Corp. [*NYSE symbol*] (SAG)
COL	Columbia/HCA Hlthcare [*NYSE symbol*] (TTSB)
COL	Columbia Healthcare [*NYSE symbol*] (SPSG)
COL	Columbus (ROG)
COL	Column (AAG)
col	Column (WDMC)

COL............ Commissioner of Official Languages [Canada]
COL............ Committee on Legislation [American Library Association]
COL............ [The] Commonwealth of Learning (AC)
COL............ Communications-Oriented Language
COL............ Computerized Office Layout (PDAA)
COL............ Computer Only Linofilm [Graphic arts] (DGA)
COL............ Computer-Oriented Language [Programming language] [Computer science]
COL............ Construction and Operating License
COL............ Control-Oriented Language [Computer science]
COL............ Corrida Oils Ltd. [Toronto Stock Exchange symbol]
COL............ Cost of Living [Economics]
COL............ Council on Occupational Licensing [Later, NCOL] (EA)
COL............ Council on Ocean Law (EA)
COL............ Counsel
COL............ Crisis on Location [Psychological test]
Col............. De Coloribus [of Aristotle] [Classical studies] (OCD)
COL............ Lansing Library Service, Oakland, CA [Library symbol Library of Congress] (LCLS)
COL............ Loretto Heights College, Denver, CO [OCLC symbol] (OCLC)
COLA.......... Camping and Outdoor Leisure Association [British] (DBA)
COLA.......... Center for Ocean-Land-Atmosphere Studies [Marine science] (OSRA)
COLA.......... Committee on Library Automation [American Library Association]
COLA.......... Constant-Output Level Adapter
COLA.......... Cooperation in Library Automation (NITA)
COLA.......... Cost of Living Adjustment
COLA.......... Cost of Living Allowance [Economics]
COLA.......... Cost of Living Award (PDAA)
COLA1D....... Coupled Ocean-Land-Atmosphere 1-Dimensional [Model] (USDC)
colab.......... Collaboration (VRA)
COLAC........ Central Organization of Liaison for Allocation of Circuit (NATG)
COLAC........ Confederacion Latinoamericana de Cooperativas de Ahorro y Credito [Latin American Confederation of Savings and Loan Cooperatives] (EAIO)
CoLaf.......... Lafayette Public Library, Lafayette, CO [Library symbol Library of Congress] (LCLS)
Colagen....... Collagen Corp. [Associated Press] (SAG)
CoLak.......... Lakewood Regional Library, Lakewood, CO [Library symbol Library of Congress] (LCLS)
CoLakJ........ Jefferson County School District R-1, Library Media Processing, Lakewood, CO [Library symbol Library of Congress] (LCLS)
CoLam........ Lamar Carnegie Public Library, Lamar, CO [Library symbol Library of Congress] (LCLS)
CoLamC....... Lamar Community College, Lamar, CO [Library symbol Library of Congress] (LCLS)
COL-AMCHAM... Colombian-American Chamber of Commerce (EA)
COLAN........ Central Office-based Local Area Network [Telecommunications] (ACRL)
CO-LAN....... Central Office - Local Area Network
CO-LAN....... Central Office Local Area Network (BTTJ)
Col & Cai..... Coleman and Caines' Cases [New York] [A publication] (DLA)
Col & Cai Cas... Coleman and Caines' Cases [New York] [A publication] (DLA)
Col & Caines Cas (NY)... Coleman and Caines' Cases [New York] [A publication] (DLA)
Col & C Cas... Coleman and Caines' Cases [New York] [A publication] (DLA)
COLANFORASCU... Commanding Officer, Landing Force Air Support Control Unit
CoLAPL....... County of Los Angeles Public Library
Col App........ Colorado Appeals Reports [A publication] (DLA)
CoLas.......... Las Animas Public Library, Las Animas, CO [Library symbol Library of Congress] (LCLS)
CoLasA........ Lower Arkansas Valley Regional Library, Las Animas, CO [Library symbol Library of Congress] (LCLS)
COLASL....... Compiler, Los Alamos Scientific Laboratories
COLAT........ Colatus [Strained] [See also COL] [Pharmacy]
COLAT........ Colectivo Latinoamericano de Trabajo Psico-Social [Belgium]
Co-Lat........ Complement of Latitude
CoLav.......... LaVeta Public Library, LaVeta, CO [Library symbol Library of Congress] (LCLS)
COLB.......... Columbia Banking System [NASDAQ symbol] (TTSB)
COLB.......... Columbia Banking Systems [NASDAQ symbol] (SAG)
COLB.......... Cost of Living Bonus (DGA)
ColBgp......... Colonial Bankgroup [Associated Press] (SAG)
ColBnk........ Columbia Banking Systems [Associated Press] (SAG)
Colb Pr........ Colby's Practice [A publication] (DLA)
COL C......... Col Canto [With the Melody] [Music]
COLC.......... Cost of Living Council [Also, CLC] [Terminated, 1974]
CoLc........... Lake City Public Library, Lake City, CO [Library symbol Library of Congress] (LCLS)
COLC.......... Laney College, Oakland, CA [Library symbol Library of Congress] (LCLS)
Col Cas........ Coleman's Cases of Practice [New York] [A publication] (DLA)
Col Cas (NY)... Coleman's Cases of Practice [New York] [A publication] (DLA)
COLCAT....... College Cataloguing (ADA)
Col CC........ Collyer's English Chancery Cases [1845-47] [A publication] (DLA)
COLCEL....... Columbia Cellulose [Company] [Canada]
COLCH........ Colchester [Municipal borough in England]
COLCIENCIAS... Fondo Colombiano de Investigaciones Cientificas y Proyectos Especiales [Colombian Fund for Scientific Research and Special Projects] [Colombia] [Information service or system] (IID)
ColCm......... Colonial Commercial Corp. [Associated Press] (SAG)
ColCmc........ Colonial Commercial Corp. [Associated Press] (SAG)
Col Comp..... College Composition and Communication [A publication] (BRI)
CoLcP.......... Lake City Public Library, Lake City, CO [Library symbol] [Library of Congress] (LCLS)

Col Crim Law... Colby's Criminal Law and Practice [New York] [A publication] (DLA)
ColctBcp...... Collective Bancorp, Inc. [Associated Press] (SAG)
COLD.......... Chronic Obstructive Lung Disease [Medicine]
COLD.......... Coherent Light Detector
Cold........... Coldwell's Tennessee Supreme Court Reports [1860-70] [A publication] (DLA)
COLD.......... Collated (ROG)
COLD.......... Colored (ROG)
COLD.......... Computer Output to LASER Disk (PCM)
COLD.......... Council on Oceanograhic Laboratory Directors [Marine science] (OSRA)
COLD.......... Council on Oceanographic Laboratory Directors (USDC)
ColData....... Colonial Data Technologies Corp. [Associated Press] (SAG)
ColdMtl....... Cold Metals Products [Associated Press] (SAG)
COLDS........ Common Optoelectronics LASER Detection System
Colds Pr ...... Coldstream's Scotch Court of Session Procedure [A publication] (DLA)
Cold (Tenn)... Coldwell's Reports [41-47 Tennessee] [A publication] (DLA)
Coldw......... Coldwell's Reports [41-47 Tennessee] [A publication] (DLA)
Coldwell ...... Coldwell's Reports [41-47 Tennessee] [A publication] (DLA)
Coldw (Tenn)... Coldwell's Reports [41-47 Tennessee] [A publication] (DLA)
COLE.......... Coefficient of Linear Extensibility
Cole........... Coleman's Reports [99, 101-106, 110-129 Alabama] [A publication] (DLA)
Cole........... Cole's Edition of Iowa Reports [A publication] (DLA)
COLE.......... College of Our Lady of the Elms [Chicopee, MA]
CoLe........... Lake County Public Library, Leadville, CO [Library symbol Library of Congress] (LCLS)
Cole & Cai Cas... Coleman and Caines' Cases [New York] [A publication] (DLA)
CoLeC......... Colorado Mountain College, Eastern Campus, Leadville, CO [Library symbol Library of Congress] (LCLS)
Cole Cas..... Coleman's Cases [New York] [A publication] (DLA)
Cole Cases... Coleman's Cases [New York] [A publication] (DLA)
Cole Cas Pr... Coleman's Cases [New York] [A publication] (DLA)
COLECO....... Connecticut Leather Co. [Original name of Coleco Industries]
Cole Cond... Cole. Particulars and Conditions of Sale [1879] [A publication] (DLA)
Cole Cr Inf... Cole. Criminal Informations [1843] [A publication] (DLA)
COLED........ Combat Loss and Expenditure Data (MCD)
Cole Dig ..... Colebrooke's Digest of Hindu Law [A publication] (DLA)
COLED-V...... Combat Loss and Expenditure Data - Vietnam
Cole Ejec.... Cole. Ejectment [1857] [A publication] (DLA)
Cole Eject.... Cole. Ejectment [1857] [A publication] (DLA)
Colem........ Coleman's Cases [New York] [A publication] (DLA)
Coleman..... Coleman's Cases [New York] [A publication] (DLA)
Colem & C Cas... Coleman and Caines' Cases [New York] [A publication] (DLA)
Colem Cas... Coleman's Cases [New York] [A publication] (DLA)
Colemn........ Coleman Co., Inc. [Associated Press] (SAG)
ColeMyr....... Coles Myer Ltd. [Associated Press] (SAG)
colen.......... Colentur [Let Them Be Strained] [Pharmacology] (DAVI)
ColeNatl ...... Cole National Corp. [Associated Press] (SAG)
COLENT....... Colentur [Let Them Be Strained] [Pharmacy] (ROG)
COLEPAC ..... Continuing Library Education Planning and Advisory Project
COLER......... Coleridge [England]
COLET......... Coletur [Let It Be Strained] [Pharmacy]
COLEX........ CIRC [Central Information Reference and Control] Online Experiment
COLEX........ Control of Logistics Expense [USAREUR] (MCD)
COLG .... Cold Leg [Nuclear energy]
Colg........... College [Army]
COLG .... College
COLG .... Commonwealth Office of Local Government [Australia]
Colgate U .... Colgate University (GAGS)
ColGenx....... CollaGenex Pharmaceuticals, Inc. [Associated Press] (SAG)
ColgP.......... Colgate-Palmolive Co. [Associated Press] (SAG)
ColgPal....... Colgate-Palmolive Co. [Associated Press] (SAG)
COLGT .... Collegiate
COLGTH ...... Cone Length [Botany]
CoLH.......... Loretto Heights College, Denver, CO [Library symbol Library of Congress] (LCLS)
ColHCA....... Columbia HCA Healthcare Corp. [Formerly, Columbia Healthcare] [Associated Press] (SAG)
ColHIn........ Colonial High Income Municipal Trust [Associated Press] (SAG)
COLI........... Collins Industries [NASDAQ symbol] (TTSB)
COLI........... Colloredo [Italy] [Seismograph station code, US Geological Survey] (SEIS)
COLI........... Colonel's Island [AAR code]
COLI........... Corporate-Owned Life Insurance (WYGK)
COLI........... Cost-of-Living Index [Economics]
CoLi........... Edwin A. Bemis Public Library, Littleton, CO [Library symbol Library of Congress] (LCLS)
CoLiA.......... Arapahoe Regional Library District, Littleton, CO [Library symbol Library of Congress] (LCLS)
CoLiAJ........ Arapahoe Community College, Littleton, CO [Library symbol Library of Congress] (LCLS)
COLIBI........ Comite de Liaison des Fabricants de Bicyclettes (EA)
COLIDAR...... Coherent Light Detecting and Ranging [RADAR] [Hughes Aircraft]
COLIDS........ Coherent Light Detector System (MCD)
CoLiGS .... Church of Jesus Christ of Latter-Day Saints, Genealogical Society Library, Littleton Branch, Littleton, CO [Library symbol Library of Congress] (LCLS)
CollHI .... Colonial Intermediate High Income Fund [Associated Press] (SAG)
COLIM .... Collimator (MSA)
CoLim.......... Limon Memorial Public Library, Limon, CO [Library symbol Library of Congress] (LCLS)

CoLiM.......... Marathon Oil Co., Technical Information Section, Littleton, CO [*Library symbol Library of Congress*] (LCLS)
COLIME....... Comite de Liaison des Industries Metalliques Europeennes
COLIMO ...... Comite de Liaison des Fabricants de Motocyclettes [*Liaison Committee of European Motorcycle Manufacturers*] [*Belgium*] (EAIO)
CoLimP........ Plains and Peaks Public Library System, Limon, CO [*Library symbol Library of Congress*] (LCLS)
COLINA....... Coalicion de Liberacion Nacional [*Panama*] [*Political party*] (EY)
COLINGO ..... Compile Online and Go [*Computer science*]
CoIIntln........ Colonial Intermarket Income Trust [*Associated Press*] (SAG)
Col Int'l Dr Comp... Colloque International de Droit Compare [*A publication*] (DLA)
CoInvG........ Colonial Investment Grade Municipal Trust [*Associated Press*] (SAG)
COLIPA........ Comite de Liaison des Associations Europeennes de l'Industrie de la Parfumerie, des Produits Cosmetiques, et de Toilette [*European Federation of the Perfume, Cosmetics, and Toiletries Industry*] (EAIO)
COLIPED...... Comite de Liaison des Fabricants de Pieces et Equipements de Deux Roues des Paysde la CEE [*Liaison Committee of Manufacturers of Parts and Equipment for Two-Wheeled Vehicles*] (EAIO)
CoLiSD .... Arapahoe County School District 6, Littleton, CO [*Library symbol Library of Congress*] (LCLS)
Co Lit.......... Coke on Littleton [*England*] [*A publication*] (DLA)
Co Litt .... Coke on Littleton [*England*] [*A publication*] (DLA)
Co Litt .... Commentaries upon Littleton, by Sir Edward Coke [*A publication*] (DLA)
Co Litt (Eng)... Coke on Littleton [*England*] [*A publication*] (DLA)
COLIWASA... Containerized Liquid Waste Sampler
Co LJ .... Cochin Law Journal [*A publication*] (DLA)
Co LJ .... Colonial Law Journal [*A publication*] (DLA)
CoLj............ Woodruff Memorial Library, La Junta, CO [*Library symbol Library of Congress*] (LCLS)
CoLja.......... Conejos County Public Library, La Jara, CO [*Library symbol*] [*Library of Congress*] (LCLS)
CoLjaGS ...... Church of Jesus Christ of Latter-Day Saints, Genealogical Society Library, LaJara Branch, Stake Center, LaJara, CO [*Library symbol Library of Congress*] (LCLS)
CoLjO.......... Otero Junior College, La Junta, CO [*Library symbol Library of Congress*] (LCLS)
COLL.......... Collagen [*Biochemistry*]
Coll............. Collarette [*Horticulture*]
COLL.......... Collate (WGA)
COLL.......... Collateral
coll............. Collateral (WDMC)
Coll............. Collatio [*Novels of Justinian*] [*A publication*] (DSA)
COLL.......... Collato [*Collated*] [*Latin*]
COLL.......... Collator
COLL.......... Colleague
COLL.......... Collect [*or Collection*] (AFM)
coll............. Collect (WDMC)
coll............. Collection (VRA)
Coll............. Collector (DLA)
COLL.......... Collector
COLL.......... College [*or Collegiate*]
coll............. College (WDMC)
Coll............. Colles' English Parliamentary Cases [*1697-1714*] [*A publication*] (DLA)
COLL.......... Colliery
COLL.......... Collins Industries, Inc. [*NASDAQ symbol*] (SAG)
COLL.......... Collision [*Insurance*]
COLL.......... Colloid
COLL.......... Colloquial
coll............. Colloquial (WDMC)
Coll............. Colloquium: The Australian and New Zealand Theological Review [*A publication*] (APTA)
Coll............. Collyer's English Chancery Cases [*1845-47*] [*A publication*] (DLA)
COLL.......... Collyrium [*Eye Wash*] [*Pharmacy*] (ROG)
coll............. Colorless [*Laboratory*] (DAVI)
COLL.......... Commanding Officer's Leave Listing (DNAB)
COLL.......... Cooper Cos. [*NYSE symbol*] (TTSB)
COLLAB ...... Collaborate [*or Collaborator*] (ROG)
CollAik........ Collins & Aikman Holdings Corp. [*Associated Press*] (SAG)
Coll Alex...... Collectanea Alexandrina [*A publication*] (OCD)
COLL & CR A... Collection and Credit Agency (DLA)
Coll & E Bank... Collier and Eaton's American Bankruptcy Reports [*A publication*] (DLA)
Coll & Mil BS... Collier and Miller on Bills of Sale [*A publication*] (DLA)
Coll & U ...... College and University [*A publication*] (DLA)
COLLAT........ Collateral [*Finance*]
Col Law Rep... Colorado Law Reporter [*A publication*] (DLA)
Col Law Rev... Columbia Law Review [*A publication*] (ILCA)
COILB.......... Columbia Laboratories, Inc. [*Associated Press*] (SAG)
Coll Bank...... Collier's Law of Bankruptcy [*A publication*] (DLA)
CollbClin...... Collaborative Clinical Research, Inc. [*Associated Press*] (SAG)
Coll CC .... Collyer's Chancery Cases Tempore Bruce, V-C [*63 English Reprint*] [*1844-45*] [*A publication*] (ILCA)
Coll Contr .... Collier's Law of Contribution [*1875*] [*A publication*] (DLA)
Coll CR........ Collyer's English Chancery Reports [*A publication*] (DLA)
COLLD .... Collated (ROG)
COLLD .... Collected (ROG)
ColldeClercq... Collection De Clercq. Catalogue Methodique et Raisonne: Antiquites Assyriens [*A publication*] (BJA)
COLLECT...... Collection
COLLECT...... Collectively (ROG)

COLLECT...... Connecticut On-Line Law-Enforcement Communications and Teleprocessing [*Computer law-enforcement system*]
COLLEG .... Collegiate (ROG)
Colles .... Colles' English Parliamentary Cases [*1697-1714*] [*A publication*] (DLA)
Colles (Eng)... Colles' English Parliamentary Cases [*1697-1714*] [*A publication*] (DLA)
Colles PC.... Colles' English Parliamentary Cases [*1697-1714*] [*A publication*] (DLA)
Coll Id .... Collinson on the Law of Idiots and Lunatics [*A publication*] (DLA)
Collier & E Am Bankr... Collier and Eaton's American Bankruptcy Reports [*A publication*] (DLA)
Collier Bank.... Collier and Eaton's American Bankruptcy Reports [*A publication*] (DLA)
Collier Bankr Cas... Collier's Bankruptcy Cases [*A publication*] (DLA)
Collins......... Collins Industries, Inc. [*Associated Press*] (SAG)
Col Lit .... College Literature [*A publication*] (BRI)
Col LJ .... Colonial Law Journal [*A publication*] (DLA)
Col LJNZ..... Colonial Law Journal (New Zealand) [*A publication*] (DLA)
Coll Jurid..... Collectanea Juridica [*England*] [*A publication*] (DLA)
Coll L .... Collection Letter [*Business term*] (MHDB)
Coll L Bull .... College Law Bulletin [*A publication*] (DLA)
Coll L Dig..... College Law Digest [*A publication*] (DLA)
Coll Lun....... Collinson on the Law of Idiots and Lunatics [*A publication*] (DLA)
Coll Min ...... Collier's Law of Mines [*A publication*] (DLA)
COLLN .... Collection
Coll NC........ Collyer's Chancery Cases Tempore Bruce, V-C [*63 English Reprint*] [*1844-45*] [*A publication*] (DLA)
COLLOQ....... Colloquial
Coll'Ott .... Coll'Ottava [*With the Octave*] [*Music*]
COLL'OTTA.... Coll'Ottava [*With the Octave*] [*Music*]
Coll Part .... Collyer's Law of Partnership [*A publication*] (DLA)
Coll Pat .... Collier on Patents [*A publication*] (DLA)
Coll PC .... Colles' English Parliamentary Cases [*1697-1714*] [*A publication*] (DLA)
COLLR .... Collector [*Business term*]
Col L Rep ..... Colorado Law Reporter [*A publication*] (DLA)
COLLS .... Collateral Branches [*Genealogy*] (ROG)
Coll St L ...... Collinson on the Stamp Laws [*A publication*] (DLA)
Coll Tor .... Collet on Torts and Measure of Damages [*A publication*] (DLA)
Coll Tr .... Collateral Trust (DLA)
COLLUN...... Collunarium [*Nose Wash*] [*Pharmacy*]
COLLUT ...... Collutorium [*Mouthwash*] [*Pharmacy*]
coll vol .... Collective Volume [*Medicine*] (DAVI)
COLLY .... Colliery (ROG)
Colly .... Collyer's English Vice Chancellors' Reports [*1845-47*] [*A publication*] (DLA)
Colly Ch Cas (Eng)... Collyer's English Chancery Cases [*1845-47*] [*A publication*] (DLA)
Colly Part .... Collyer's Law of Partnership [*A publication*] (DLA)
COLLYR ...... Collyrium [*Eye Wash*] [*Pharmacy*]
COLM.......... Colorado National Monument
Colm............ Columba [*Constellation*]
COLM.......... Column (AFM)
Col Mass Pr... Colby's Massachusetts Practice [*A publication*] (DLA)
COLM/ATC... Continental Land Masses Air Traffic Control [*NASA*] (MCD)
CoLmE........ Loma Elementary, Loma, CO [*Library symbol Library of Congress*] (LCLS)
COLMGP...... Column Gap [*Army*] (AABC)
Col Mines.... Collier's Law of Mines [*A publication*] (DLA)
col/ml .... Colonies per Milliliter [*Measurement*] (DAVI)
Col Mon....... Colonial Monthly [*A publication*]
Col Mort ...... Colby on Mortgage Foreclosures [*A publication*] (DLA)
ColMu......... Colonial Municipal Income Trust [*Associated Press*] (SAG)
Col Mun B ... Coler's Law of Municipal Bonds [*A publication*] (DLA)
COLN.......... Column
colnd .... Colonnade (VRA)
ColnlGas....... Colonial Gas Co. [*Associated Press*] (SAG)
Col NP .... Colorado Nisi Prius Decisions [*A publication*] (DLA)
COLO .... Colonels International, Inc. (The) [*NASDAQ symbol*] (SAG)
COLO .... Colonel's Intl. [*NASDAQ symbol*] (TTSB)
COLO .... Colonial National Historic Park
colo .... Colony (VRA)
COLO .... Colophon [*Publishing*] (WGA)
COLO .... Colorado (AFM)
Colo .... Colorado (ODBW)
Colo............ Colorado Reports [*A publication*] (DLA)
CoLo .... Longmont Public Library, Longmont, CO [*Library symbol Library of Congress*] (LCLS)
Colo Admin Code... Code of Colorado Regulations [*A publication*] (DLA)
Colo App...... Colorado Appellate Reports [*A publication*] (AAGC)
Colo App...... Colorado Court of Appeals Reports [*A publication*] (DLA)
ColoCas....... Colorado Casino Resorts, Inc. [*Associated Press*] (SAG)
Colo Const.... Colorado Constitution [*A publication*] (DLA)
COLOCYNTH... Colocynthus [*Bitter Apples*] [*Pharmacy*] (ROG)
COLOD........ Completed Loading [*Navy*]
Colo Dec...... Colorado Decisions [*A publication*] (DLA)
Colo Dec Fed... Colorado Decisions, Federal [*A publication*] (DLA)
Colo Dec Supp... Colorado Decisions Supplement [*A publication*] (DLA)
COLOG........ Cologarithm [*Mathematics*]
Colo IC .... Colorado Industrial Commission Report [*A publication*] (DLA)
Colo LR .... Colorado Law Reporter [*A publication*] (DLA)
Colo L Rep.... Colorado Law Reporter [*A publication*] (DLA)
Colom.......... Colombia
Colombo LJ... Colombo Law Journal [*A publication*] (DLA)

ColoMED...... Colorado MEDtech, Inc. [Associated Press] (SAG)
COLON......... Colonial
CoLoN......... Northern Colorado Educational Board of Cooperative Services, Longmont, CO [Library symbol Library of Congress] (LCLS)
Colonels....... Colonels International, Inc. (The) [Associated Press] (SAG)
COLONET..... Colorado Library Network [Colorado State Library] [Denver, CO] [Library network]
Colo NP Dec... Colorado Nisi Prius Decisions [A publication] (DLA)
ColonPT....... Colonial Properties Trust [Associated Press] (SAG)
COLOP........ Collection Opportunity (MCD)
COLOPH....... Colophon [Printing] (DGA)
Colo PUC...... Colorado Public Utilities Commission Decisions [A publication] (DLA)
Colo PUC Rep... Colorado Public Utilities Commission Report [A publication] (DLA)
COLOR........ Coloretur [Let It Be Colored] [Pharmacy] (ROG)
color........... Colorimetry [Biochemistry] (MAE)
COLOR........ Corporation for Laser Optics Research
Colo Rev Stat Ann... Colorado Revised Statutes Annotated [West] [A publication] (AAGC)
COLOS........ Command Off the Line of Sight [Military British]
Colo Sch Mines... Colorado School of Mines (GAGS)
Colo Sess Laws... Session Laws of Colorado [A publication] (DLA)
COLOSS....... Colossians [New Testament book] (ROG)
Colo St BA... Colorado State Bar Association Report [A publication] (DLA)
Colo St U... Colorado State University (GAGS)
COL OTTA.... Coll'Ottava [With the Octave] [Music] (ROG)
CoLou......... Louisville Public Library, Louisville, CO [Library symbol of Congress] (LCLS)
CoLov......... Loveland Public Library, Loveland, CO [Library symbol Library of Congress] (LCLS)
CoLovT....... Thompson R2-J School District, Loveland, CO [Library symbol] [Library of Congress] (LCLS)
COLP......... Center for Oceans Law and Policy (EA)
COL P......... Colla Parte [With the Solo Part] [Music] (ROG)
COL P......... Color Page [Printing] (DGA)
COLPA......... Commission on Law and Public Affairs
COLPA........ National Jewish Commission on Law and Public Affairs
Col Part....... Collyer's Law of Partnership [A publication] (DLA)
COL PL....... Colored Plate [Printing] (DGA)
colpo.......... Colposcopy [Gynecology] (DAVI)
COLPS......... Collapse
Colq........... Colquit's Reports [1 Modern] [England] [A publication] (DLA)
Colq Civ Law... Colquhoun on Roman Civil Law [A publication] (DLA)
Colq CL....... Colquhoun on Roman Civil Law [A publication] (DLA)
Colq Jud A... Colquhoun on the Judicature Acts [A publication] (DLA)
Colq Rom Civ Law... Colquhoun on Roman Civil Law [A publication] (DLA)
Colq Rom Law... Colquhoun on Roman Civil Law [A publication] (DLA)
COLQUAP.... Consumer Level Quality Audit Program [Military]
Colquit........ Colquit's Reports [1 Modern] [England] [A publication] (DLA)
COLR......... Circuit Order Layout Record [Telecommunications] (TEL)
COLRAD...... College on Research and Development (HGAA)
COLRAM...... Committee on Local Radio Audience Measurement [National Association of Broadcasters] (NTCM)
COLREGS.... International Regulations for Preventing Collisions at Sea [1972]
Col Rep....... Colorado Reports [A publication] (DLA)
Col Rev Stat... Colorado Revised Statutes [A publication] (DLA)
COLRIC....... Council for Learning Resources in Colleges [British]
COLS.......... Columns (ROG)
COLS.......... Communications for Online Systems [Computer science] (ODBW)
COLS.......... Coolant Level Sensor [Automotive engineering]
COLSEC....... Collective Security [Army] (MCD)
COLSED....... Collection Statute Expiration Date [IRS]
COL-SERGT... Colour-Sergeant [Army British]
Col-Sgt....... Colour-Sergeant [Army British] (DMA)
ColSP25....... Columbus Southern Power Co. [Associated Press] (SAG)
COLSS........ Core Operating Limit Supervisory System [Nuclear energy] (NRCH)
COLSS........ Core Operating Limit Support System [Nuclear energy] (NRCH)
COLT.......... Catalog Online Tool [DoD]
COLT.......... Central Office Line Tester (IAA)
COLT.......... CO₂ LASER Technology [Military]
Colt........... Coltman's Registration Appeal Cases [1879-85] [England] [A publication] (ILCA)
COLT.......... Combat Observation and Lasing Teams [Army] (INF)
COLT.......... Combined Operations Lasing Team [Army] (INF)
COLT.......... Communication Line Terminator [IBM Corp.]
COLT.......... Computerized Online Testing
COLT.......... Computer-Oriented Language Translator (IEEE)
COLT.......... Continuous Online Trading System [London Stock Exchange] (NITA)
COLT.......... Control Language Translator [Computer science] (IEEE)
COLT.......... Council on Library-Media Technical-Assistants (EA)
COLT.......... Council on Library Technology (NITA)
COLTAM...... Committee on Local Television Audience Measurement [National Association of Broadcasters] (NTCM)
CO LTD....... Closed Corporation [Business term] (MHDB)
Coltec........ Coltec Industries, Inc. [Associated Press] (SAG)
Coltm.......... Coltman's Registration Appeal Cases [1879-85] [England] [A publication] (DLA)
Colt (Reg Ca)... Coltman's Registration Appeal Cases [1879-85] [England] [A publication] (DLA)
Colt Reg Cas... Coltman's Registration Appeal Cases [1879-85] [England] [A publication] (DLA)
COLTS........ Communication Online Test System (IAA)
COLTS........ Continuously Offered Long-Term Securities [Merrill Lynch & Co.] [Finance]
COLTS........ Contractor Obligation and Liquidation Tracking System [Army]
COLTS........ Contrast Optical LASER Tracking Subsystem [Missile guidance]

COLTS........ Count on Losing this Sunday [Humorous interpretation of NFL team name]
COLTY........ Collotype (VRA)
COLUDE...... Committee for the Democratic Struggle [Mexico]
ColuEng....... Columbus Energy Corp. [Associated Press] (SAG)
COLUM....... Columbia (ROG)
COLUMB..... Columbia (ROG)
ColumBc...... Columbia Bancorp [Associated Press] (SAG)
Columbia U... Columbia University (GAGS)
Columbus C... Columbus College (GAGS)
Colum J Int'l Aff... Columbia Journal of International Affairs [A publication] (DLA)
Colum Jr...... Columbia Jurist [A publication] (DLA)
Colum Jur..... Columbia Jurist [A publication] (DLA)
Colum LT..... Columbia Law Times [A publication] (DLA)
ColumRT..... Columbus Realty Trust [Associated Press] (SAG)
Colum Soc'y Int'l L Bull... Columbia Society of International Law. Bulletin [A publication] (DLA)
Colum Survey Human Rights L... Columbia Survey of Human Rights Law [A publication] (DLA)
Colum Surv Hum Rts L... Columbia Survey of Human Rights Law [A publication] (DLA)
Colvil.......... Colvil's Manuscript Decisions, Scotch Court of Session [A publication] (DLA)
CoLvM........ Molybdenum Corp. of America, Louviers, CO [Library symbol Library of Congress] (LCLS)
COL VO....... Colla Voce [With the Voice] [Music]
COL VOCE.... Colla Voce [With the Voice] [Music] (ROG)
CoLw.......... Villa Regional Library, Lakewood, CO [Library symbol Library of Congress] (LCLS)
COLYAHAR... Columbia, Yale, Harvard [Used to refer to a project involving the medical libraries of these universities]
Coly Guar (De)... Colyar on Guarantees [A publication] (DLA)
Com........... Blackstone's Commentaries on the Laws of England [A publication] (DLA)
COM........... Candorado Mines Ltd. [Vancouver Stock Exchange symbol]
COM........... Carbon Monoxide Mass [Automotive engineering]
COM........... Cassette Operating Monitor
COM........... Catalogues on Microfiche (AIE)
COM........... Center for Optics Manufacturing (RDA)
COM........... Center of Mass [Coordinate system] (MCD)
COM........... Change Order Modification (KSC)
COM........... Character-Oriented Message (RDA)
COM........... Checkout Operations Manual (AAG)
COM........... Choice Old Marsala
COM........... Chronic Otitis Media [Medicine]
C/OM.......... Clothing and Organic Materials Laboratory [Army Natick Laboratories, MA]
COM........... Coal-Oil Mixture
COM........... Cockpit Operating Manual (GAVI)
COM........... Coefficient of Merit [Electronics] (IAA)
CoM........... Coenzyme M
COM........... Coleman, TX [Location identifier FAA] (FAAL)
COM........... College of Osteopathic Medicine (DAVI)
Com........... Coma Berenices [Berenice's Hair] [Constellation] [Latin] (BARN)
COM........... Comair, Inc. [ICAO designator] (FAAC)
Com........... Comberbach's English King's Bench Reports [1685-99] [A publication] (DLA)
COM........... Comedian [or Comedy] (ROG)
com........... Comedy (WDMC)
COM........... Comic
COM........... Comitan [Mexico] [Seismograph station code, US Geological Survey] (SEIS)
COM........... Comitatus [County] [Latin] (ROG)
COM........... Comiteco [Race of maize]
COM........... Comma (ROG)
com........... Comma (WDMC)
COM........... Command (AAG)
COM........... Commandant [Military]
COM........... Commander
COM........... Commemoration (ADA)
Com........... Comment [Legal term] (DLA)
COM........... Commentary
com........... Commentary (WDMC)
COM........... Commerce
COM........... Commercial (ROG)
com........... Commercial (WDMC)
COM........... Commissary
COM........... Commissary Operating Manual (AABC)
COM........... Commission [or Commissioner] (AABC)
COM........... Commissioned Officers Mess [Navy]
COM........... Committee (AABC)
com........... Committee (WDMC)
COM........... Committee on Mutagenicity [British]
COM........... Commode [Medicine]
COM........... Commodity
COM........... Commodo [In an Easy Style] [Music]
COM........... Commodore
COM........... Common
COM........... Common Object Model [Microsoft]
COM........... Commonwealth
COM........... Commune
COM........... Communicant [Religion] (ROG)
COM........... Communicate [or Communications]
COM........... Communications (DOMA)
COM........... Communications Port [Computer science]

COM............. Communications Processor
COM............. Communist
COM............. Communist Party of Australia [*Political party*]
COM............. Community (AABC)
COM............. Commutator [*Electromagnetism*] (IAA)
COM............. Commuter
COM............. Comoros [*ANSI three-letter standard code*] (CNC)
COM............. Companions
Com............. Compass: Theology Review [*A publication*] (APTA)
COM............. Compiler (IAA)
COM............. Complement (MUGU)
COM............. Completions
COM............. Component Object Model [*Computer science*]
COM............. Compromise (ROG)
COM............. Computer
COM............. Computer Output Microfilm [*or Microfiche or Microform*] (BUR)
Com............. Comstock's Reports [*1-4 New York Court of Appeals*] [*A publication*] (DLA)
Com............. Comyn's English King's Bench Reports [*1695-1741*] [*A publication*] (DLA)
COM............. Condition Monitoring (MCD)
COM............. Continuation of Message (ACRL)
COM............. Continuous Opacity Monitor [*Environmental Protection Agency*] (GFGA)
COM............. Copper Oxide Modulator
COM............. Cost of Money [*DoD*]
COM............. Council of Ministers [*European Economic Commission*] (DLA)
COM............. County Office Manager
COM............. Crowley, Milner & Co. [*AMEX symbol*] (SPSG)
COM............. Curve of Merit [*Electronics*] (IAA)
COM............. Customer's Own Material (WGA)
COM............. Customer's Own Merchandise (WDMC)
COM............. Cyclophosphamide, Oncovin [*Vincristine*], MeCCNU [*Semustine*] [*Antineoplastic drug regimen*]
COM............. Cyclophosphamide, Oncovin [*Vincristine*], Methotrexate [*Antineoplastic drug regimen*]
COM............. Merritt College, Oakland, CA [*Library symbol Library of Congress*] (LCLS)
COM............. Mesa College, Grand Junction, CO [*OCLC symbol*] (OCLC)
Com............. Plowden's English King's Bench Commentaries [*or Reports*] [*A publication*] (DSA)
Com............. United States Commerce Court Opinions [*A publication*] (DLA)
COM3........... Coma Level Greater than 400 Milligrams per Liter [*Medicine*] (DAVI)
COMA............ Coke Oven Managers' Association [*British*] (BI)
COMA......... Committee on Medical Aspects of Food Policy [*British*]
COMA......... Computer Operations Management Association
COMA......... Council on Mind Abuse [*Canada*]
COMA......... Court of Military Appeals
COMA......... Cyclophosphamide, Oncovin [*Vincristine*], Methotrexate, ara-C [*Antineoplastic drug regimen*]
CoMa........... Mancos Public Library, Mancos, CO [*Library symbol Library of Congress*] (LCLS)
COMA-A....... Cyclophosphamide, Oncovin [*Vincristine*], Methotrexate/citrovorum factor, Adriamycin, ara-C [*Cytarabine*] [*Antineoplastic drug regimen*]
COMAAC..... Commander, Alaskan Air Command (MCD)
COMAAFACE... Commander, Allied Air Force Central Europe
COMAAFCE... Commander Allied Air Forces Central Europe [*NATO*] (PDAA)
COMAC........ Commander, Military Airlift Command [*Formerly, COMATS*] (AFM)
COMAC........ Continuous Multiple Access Collator [*Proposed by Mortimer Taube, 1957*] [*Computer science*]
COMACA...... Committee for Medical Aid to Central America (EA)
COMAD........ Computer Methods for Automatic Diagnosis (PDAA)
COMADC...... Commander, Air Defense Command
COMAEGEANBASE... Commander, Aegean Defense Sector (NATG)
CoMaEL....... Mancos Elementary School, Mancos, CO [*Library symbol*] [*Library of Congress*] (LCLS)
COMAEWW... Commander, Airborne Early-Warning Wing (DNAB)
COMAF........ Comite des Constructeurs de Materiel Frigorifique de la CEE [*Committee of Manufacturers of Refrigeration Equipment of the EEC*]
COMAF........ Commodore, Amphibious Forces [*British military*] (DMA)
COMAFFOR... Commander, Air Force Forces (AABC)
Com Affrs ... Community Affairs (DLA)
comailing .... Combined Mailing [*Postal Service*] [*United States*] (WDMC)
COMAINT..... Command Maintenance [*Military*] (AABC)
Comair......... Comair, Inc. [*Associated Press*] (SAG)
COMAIR....... Commander, Air Forces [*Navy*]
COMAIR....... Commercial Air (NOAA)
COMAIRBALTAP... Commander, Allied Air Forces, Baltic Approaches (AABC)
COMAIRCANLANT... Air Commander, Canadian Atlantic Subarea
COMAIRCENT... Commander, Allied Air Forces, Central Europe
COMAIRCENTLANT... Air Commander, Central Atlantic Subarea
COMAIRLANT... Commander, Air Force, Atlantic Fleet
COMAIRNON... Commander, Allied Air Forces, North Norway (NATG)
COMAIRNORECHAN... Air Commander, Northeast Subarea Channel
COMAIRNORLANT... Air Commander, Northern Atlantic Subarea
COMAIRNORTH... Commander, Allied Air Forces, Northern Europe
COMAIRPAC... Commander, Air Force, Pacific Fleet
COMAIRPLYMCHAN... Air Commander, Plymouth Subarea Channel
COMAIRSHIPGR... Airship Group
COMAIRSOLS... Commander, Air Forces, Solomons
COMAIRSONOR... Commander, Allied Air Forces, South Norway (NATG)
COMAIRSOPAC... Commander, Air Forces, South Pacific Force
COMAIRSOUTH... Commander, Allied Air Forces, Southern Europe

COMAIRTRANS... Commander, Air Transport
COMAIRTRANSRON... Commander, Air Transport Squadron
COMAL .... Command Algorithmic Language [*Computer science*] (NITA)
COMAL .... Common Algorithmic Language [*Computer science*] (HGAA)
COMALAMGRU... Commander, Alameda Group
COMALF ...... Commander of Airlift Forces [*Air Force*] (DOMA)
COMALNAVNOREUR... Commander, Allied Naval Forces, Northern Europe
COMALSEAFRON... Commander, Alaskan Sea Frontier (MUGU)
COMALSEC... Commander, Alaskan Sector
COMAM ...... Continuous Motion Assembly Machine
CoManaES... Manassa Elementary School, Manassa, CO [*Library symbol*] [*Library of Congress*] (LCLS)
COMANBAT... Combat Maneuver Battalion [*Army*]
Com & Leg Rep... Commercial and Legal Reporter [*A publication*] (DLA)
Com & Mun L Rep... Commercial and Municipal Law Reporter [*A publication*] (DLA)
COMANDOS... Construction and Management of Distributed Office Systems [*ESPRIT*] (NITA)
COMANEX... Combat Analysis Extended
COMANTARCTICSUPPACT... Commander, Antarctic Support Activities
COMANTDEFCOM... Commander, Antilles Defense Command (AABC)
CoManz........ Manzanola Public Library, Manzanola, CO [*Library symbol Library of Congress*] (LCLS)
COMAO........ Combined Air Operations [*Air Force*] (DOMA)
COMAP .... Committee for the Alliance for Progress [*Department of Commerce*]
COMAP .... Conversational Macro Package (PDAA)
COM APP ... Commissioner of Appeals (DLA)
COMAQ........ Corporation des Officiers Municipaux Agrees du Quebec [*Corporation of Chartered Municipal Officers of Quebec*] (AC)
COMAR .... Coastal Marine Project (USDC)
COMAR .... Code of Maryland Regulations [*A publication*]
COMAR .... Committee on Man and Radiation [*National Research Council*] (NUCP)
COMAR .... Computer, Aerial Reconnaissance
COMAR .... Contour Mapping RADAR System (MCD)
COMARC..... Cooperative Machine-Readable Cataloging Program [*Library of Congress*]
COMARCARAREA... Commander, Marshalls-Carolines Area
COMARE...... Committee on Medical Aspects of Radiation in the Environment [*British*]
COMAREASWFOR... Commander, Area Antisubmarine Warfare Forces (DNAB)
COMAREGRU... Commander, Mare Island Group
COMARFOR... Commander, Army Forces
COMARRHIN... Commander, Maritime Rhine (NATG)
COMARSURV... Commander, Maritime Surveillance and Reconnaissance Force (DNAB)
COMARSURVRECFORDET... Commander, Maritime Surveillance and Reconnaissance Force Detachment (DNAB)
COMARSURVRECFORPASRAP... Commander, Maritime Surveillance and Reconnaissance Force, Passive ASRAP [*Acoustic Sensor Range Prediction*] Data (DNAB)
COMART ...... Commander, Marine Air Reserve Training
COMAS .... Combined Orbital Maneuvering and Abort System [*NASA*] (NASA)
COMAS .... Concentration-Modulated Absorption Spectrometry
COMASIII.... Computerized Maintenance and Administration Support III [*Telecommunications*] (TEL)
Co Mass Pr... Colby's Massachusetts Practice [*A publication*] (DLA)
COMASWFOR... Commander, Antisubmarine Warfare Force
COMASWFORLANT... Commander, Antisubmarine Warfare Forces, Atlantic (MUGU)
COMASWFORPAC... Commander, Antisubmarine Warfare Forces, Pacific (CINC)
COMASWGRU... Commander, Antisubmarine Warfare Group
COMASWSUPPTRADET... Commander, Antisubmarine Warfare Support Training Detachment (DNAB)
COMAT .... Characteristics of Materials (KSC)
COMAT .... Committee on Materials [*Federal Council for Science and Technology*]
COMAT .... Commodore Air Train [*Navy*]
COMAT .... Compatibility of Materials (MCD)
COMAT .... Computer-Assisted Training (IEEE)
COMATAFSONOR... Commander, Allied Tactical Air Forces, Southern Norway
COMATF ...... Commander, Amphibious Task Force (AABC)
COMATKCARAIRWING... Commander, Attack Carrier Air Wing
COMATKCARSTRIKEFOR... Commander, Attack Carrier Striking Force
COMATS ...... Commander, Military Air Transport Service [*Later, COMAC*]
COM/ATS ..... Communications / Air Traffic Service (SAA)
COMATS ...... Corporate Manufacturing Transfer System (IAA)
Com Att ...... Complete Attorney [*A publication*] (DLA)
COMAX .... Cotton Management Expert [*Computer program to improve crop production*]
CoMay .... Maybell Public Library, Maybell, CO [*Library symbol Library of Congress*] (LCLS)
COMB .... Canadian Outdoor Measurement Bureau
COMb.......... Carboxymyoglobin [*Biochemistry*]
COMB .... Center of Marine Biology [*University of Maryland*]
COMB .... Center of Marine Biotechnology [*Marine science*] (OSRA)
Comb .... Comberbach's English King's Bench Reports [*1685-99*] [*A publication*] (DLA)
COMB .... Combination [*or Combine*] (AFM)
comb .... Combination (VRA)
COMB .... Combined
COMB .... Combustion (AAG)
COMB .... Command Confirmation Buffer
Com B .... Common Bench Reports (Manning, Granger, and Scott) [*1846-65*] [*England*] [*A publication*] (DLA)
COMB .... Communications Buffer [*Air Force*]

COMB .... Console-Oriented Model Building [*Computer science*]
COMB .... Cyclophosphamide, Oncovin [*Vincristine*], MeCCNU , Bleomycin [*Semustine*] [*Antineoplastic drug regimen*]
COMB .... Cyclophosphamide, Oncovin [*Vincristine*], Methotrexate, Bleomycin [*Antineoplastic drug regimen*]
COMBALTAP... Allied Command Baltic Approaches [*NATO*]
COMBAP ...... Cytoxan [*Cyclophosphamide*], Oncovin , Methotrexate, Bleomycin, Adriamycin,Prednisone [*Vincristine*] [*Antineoplastic drug regimen*] (DAVI)
COMBARFORCLANT... Commander, Barrier Forces, Atlantic (NATG)
COMBARPAC... Commander, Barrier Pacific (CINC)
COMBASE .... Communications Data Base [*Canada*] [*Information service or system*] (IID)
COMBASFRANCE... Commander, [*US*] Ports and Bases, France
COMBAT ...... Coalition of Municipalities to Ban Animal Trafficking (EA)
COMBAT ...... Cost-Oriented Models Built to Analyze Tradeoffs (MCD)
COMBATCRULANT... Commander, Battleships-Cruisers, Atlantic Fleet (MUGU)
COMBATDIV... Commander, Battleship Division
COMBATEX... Combat Exercises [*Canadian Navy*]
COMBATLANT... Commander, Battleships, Atlantic Fleet
COMBATPAC... Commander, Battleships, Pacific Fleet
COMBAT-SIM... Computerized Battle Simulation
COMBAX...... Compact Blazing Combustion Axiom [*Auto engineering*]
COMB EFF .... Combustion Efficiency
COMBENECHAN... Commander, BENELUX Subarea Channel
COMBEX ...... Combined Exercise [*Military*] (NVT)
combi .... Combination (BARN)
ComBibSJeron... Commentario Biblico "San Jeronimo" [*A publication*] (BJA)
COMBIMAN... Computerized Biomechanical Man-Model [*Air Force*]
Combined Pension Ass Vic News... Combined Pensioners' Association of Victoria. News [*A publication*]
COMBISLANT... Commander, Bay of Biscay Atlantic Subarea [*NATO*]
COMBL .... Combustible (MSA)
Com Black ... A'Beckett's Comic Blackstone [*A publication*] (DLA)
COMBLACKBASE... Commander, Black Sea Defense Sector (NATG)
COMBLUE .... Commander Blue (Friendly) Force [*Navy*] (CAAL)
COMBN .... Combustion
comb nov... Combinatio Nova [*New Combination*] [*Biology, taxonomy*]
Com BNS .... English Common Bench Reports, New Series [*A publication*] (DLA)
COMBO .... Calculation of Miss Distance Between Objects [*Naval Research Laboratory*] (PS)
COMBO .... Computation of Miss Between Orbits [*Air Force*] (MCD)
COMBOIS..... Internationale Gemeinschaft fuer Holz-technologie-Transfer [*International Community for Wood-Technology Transfer*] (EAIO)
COMBOMRON... Commander, Bombing Squadron
COMBOSFORT... Commander, Bosphorus Fortifications (NATG)
COMBQUARFOR... Combined Quarantine Force [*US/Venezuela/Dominican Republic/Argentina*]
COMBRAX.... Commodore, Royal Canadian Navy Barracks at [*Place*]
COMBREMGRU... Commander, Bremerton Group
COMBRESTCHAN... Commander, Brest Subarea Channel
COMBRITELBE... Commander, British Naval Elbe Squadron (NATG)
COMBRITRHIN... Commander, British Naval Rhine Squadron (NATG)
COMBS .... Contractor-Managed Base Supply [*Facility*] (MCD)
COMBS .... Contractor Operated and Maintained Base Supply (MCD)
COMBSE ...... Confidential Measurement-Based Self-Evaluation [*Project*] (AIE)
COMBSNGRU... Commander, Boston Group
COMBSTN .... Combustion
COMBSVCSUPPSCOLANT... Combined Services Support Program School, Atlantic [*Navy*] (DNAB)
COMBSVCSUPPSCOLPAC... Combined Services Support Program School, Pacific [*Navy*] (DNAB)
COMBT .... Combat (CINC)
CoMBuen..... Compania de Minas Buenaventura SA [*Associated Press*] (SAG)
COMC .... Carboxymethylcellulose (DMAA)
COMC .... Chicago Osteopathic Medical Center
Co MC .... Coke's Magna Charta [*or Second Institute*] [*A publication*] (DLA)
Comc .... Comcast Corp. [*Associated Press*] (SAG)
Com C .... Commercial Code (DLA)
COMC .... Communications Controller (MCD)
COMC .... Comprehensive Organometallic Chemistry [*A Publication*]
COMC .... Mills College, Oakland, CA [*Library symbol Library of Congress*] (LCLS)
COMCABCO... Commercial Cable Co.
COMCAM ..... Compressible Cell and Maker
COMCAN..... Common Cause Analysis (PDAA)
COMCANLANT... Commander, Canadian Atlantic Subarea [*NATO*]
COMCAP...... Combat Capabilities (MCD)
COMCARANTISUBAIRGRU... Carrier Antisubmarine Air Group [*Navy*]
COMCARASWAIRGRU... Commander, Carrier Antisubmarine Air Group
COMCARDIV... Commander, Carrier Division
ComCare...... Community Care of America [*Associated Press*] (SAG)
COMCARGRU... Commander, Carrier Group (DNAB)
COMCARIBSEAFRON... Commander, Caribbean Sea Frontier (NATG)
COMCARIBSECASWGRU... Commander, Caribbean Sector Antisubmarine Warfare Group (DNAB)
COMCARSTRIKFOR... Commander, Carrier Striking Force (AFM)
COMCARSTRIKGRU... Commander, Carrier Striking Group
COMCARSTRIKGRUONE... Commander, Carrier Striking Group One (AFM)
COMCARSTRIKGRUTWO... Commander, Carrier Striking Group Two (AFM)
Com Cas ...... Commercial Cases [*1896-1941*] [*England*] [*A publication*] (DLA)
Com Cas...... Company Cases [*India*] [*A publication*] (DLA)
COMCAS ...... Computer-Oriented Modal Control and Appraisal System
Com Cas SCC... Commercial Cases, Small Cause Court [*1851-60*] [*Bengal, India*] [*A publication*] (DLA)

Comcast ...... Comcast Corp. [*Associated Press*] (SAG)
COMCASU.... Commander, Carrier Aircraft Service Unit
COMCAT ...... Computer Output Microform Catalog
COMCBLANT... Commander, Naval Construction Battalions, Atlantic Fleet
COMCBLANTDET... Commander, Naval Construction Battalions, Atlantic Detachment (DNAB)
COMCBLANT MLO... Commander, Naval Construction Battalions, Atlantic, Material Liaison Office (DNAB)
COMCBPAC... Commander, Naval Construction Battalions, Pacific Fleet
COMCEN ...... Communications Center [*NATO*] (NATG)
COMCENPAC... Commander, Central Pacific
COMCENTAG... Commander, Central Army Group, Central Europe
COMCENTLANT... Commander, Central Atlantic Subarea [*NATO*]
ComCentre... UK Centre for Communication Standards in the Manufacturing and Process Industries (ACII)
COMCERTS... Combat Systems Certification Site [*Navy*]
COMCG .... Communications Command Group [*Air Force*]
COMCHASNGRU... Commander, Charleston Group
COMCHERCHAN... Commander, Cherbourg Subarea Channel
COMCINCPACFLT... Commander-in-Chief, Pacific Fleet [*Navy*] (VNW)
COMCM .... Communication Countermeasures
COMCOGARD... Commander, Coast Guard District
COMCOGARDACTEUR... Commander, Coast Guard Activities, Europe (DNAB)
COMCOGARDEUR... Commander, Coast Guard Force, Europe (DNAB)
COMCOGARDFESEC... Commander, Coast Guard Section Office, Far East Section (DNAB)
COMCOGARDGANTSEC... Commander, Coast Guard Section Office, Guantanamo Section (DNAB)
COMCOGARDGRU... Commander, Coast Guard Group (DNAB)
COMCOGARDLANT... Commander, Coast Guard Force, Atlantic (DNAB)
COMCOGARDLANTWWMCCS... Commander, Coast Guard World-Wide Military Command and Control System, Atlantic (DNAB)
COMCOGARDMARSEC... Commander, Coast Guard, Maritime Section (DNAB)
COMCOGARDRON... Commander, Coast Guard Squadron (DNAB)
COMCOGARDSERON... Commander, Coast Guard Southeast Squadron (DNAB)
COMCOLUMGRU... Commander, Columbia River Group
COMCOMRON... Commander, Composite Squadron
COMCON...... Combat Control [*Army*]
Com Con...... Comyn's Law of Contracts [*A publication*] (DLA)
COMCONSUP... Combat, Control, Support [*Army*]
COMCORTDIV... Commander, Escort Division (DNAB)
COMCORTRON... Commander, Escort Squadron (DNAB)
COMCOSDIV... Commander, Coastal Division (DNAB)
COMCOSRON... Commander, Coastal Squadron (DNAB)
COMCOSURVFOR... Commander, Coastal Surveillance Force (DNAB)
ComCre...... Community Care of America [*Associated Press*] (SAG)
COMCRUDES... Commander, Cruiser-Destroyer Force
COMCRUDESFLOT... Commander, Cruiser-Destroyer Flotilla [*Acronym always followed by a number*] [*Navy*]
COMCRUDESGRU... Commander, Cruiser-Destroyer Group [*Navy*] (DNAB)
COMCRUDESLANT... Commander, Cruiser-Destroyer Forces, Atlantic [*Navy*] (DNAB)
COMCRUDESLANTSUPPGRU... Commander, Cruiser-Destroyer Forces, Atlantic Support Group [*Navy*] (DNAB)
COMCRUDESLANTSUPPGRUCHAR... Commander, Cruiser-Destroyer Forces, Atlantic Support Group, Charleston [*South Carolina*] [*Navy*] (DNAB)
COMCRUDESLANTSUPPGRUMPT... Commander, Cruiser-Destroyer Forces, Atlantic Support Group, Mayport [*Florida*] [*Navy*] (DNAB)
COMCRUDESLANTSUPPGRUNORVA... Commander, Cruiser-Destroyer Forces, Atlantic Support Group, Norfolk, Virginia [*Navy*] (DNAB)
COMCRUDESPAC... Command Cruiser-Destroyer Force, Pacific (DNAB)
COMCRUDESPAC... Commander, Cruiser-Destroyer Forces, Pacific [*Navy*] (MCD)
COMCRUDIV... Commander, Cruiser Division
COMCRULANT... Commander, Cruiser Forces, Atlantic Fleet (MCD)
COMCRUPAC... Commander, Cruiser Forces, Pacific Fleet
COMCRUSCORON... Commander, Cruiser Scouting Squadron
ComCtrl .... Communications Central [*Commercial firm Associated Press*] (SAG)
COMCVW ..... Commander, Carrier Air Wing [*Navy*] (NVT)
Comd .... Comdisco, Inc. [*Associated Press*] (SAG)
COMD .... Command (AFM)
COMD .... Commander (WGA)
COMD .... Commissioned (WGA)
COMD .... Commodore
COMD .... CompuRAD, Inc. [*NASDAQ symbol*] (SAG)
COMDA .... Canadian Office Machine Dealers Association (HGAA)
COMDAC ...... Comite d'Action en France
COMDAC ...... Component Design Augmented by Computer (PDAA)
COMDARFORT... Commander, Dardanelles Fortifications (NATG)
Comdata ...... Comdata Holding Corp. [*Associated Press*] (SAG)
COMDC .... Catalogue of Oriental Manuscripts in Danish Collections (BJA)
COMD DSR... Command Dental Service Report [*Air Force*]
COMDEC ...... Command Decision and Movement Control Charts
Com Dec...... Commissioners' Decisions [*US Patent and Trademark Office*] [*A publication*] (DLA)
COMDES ...... Commander, Destroyers
COMDESDEVGRU... Commander, Destroyer Development Group [*Navy*]
COMDESDIV... Commander, Destroyer Division
COMDESFLOT... Commander, Destroyer Flotilla
COMDESGRU... Commander, Destroyer Group
COMDESLANT... Commander, Destroyers, Atlantic Fleet
COMDESLANTDET... Commander, Destroyers, Atlantic Detachment (DNAB)
COMDESPAC... Commander, Destroyers, Pacific Fleet
COMDESPACDET... Commander, Destroyers, Pacific Detachment (DNAB)
COMDESRON... Commander, Destroyer Squadron

COMDEX...... Communications and Data Processing Exposition
COMDEX...... Computer Dealer's Exposition
COMDEX...... Computer Display and Exposition
COMDG....... Commanding (AFM)
COMDG....... Commanding
COMDG....... Commanding Officer [Military British] (ROG)
COMDGEN .... Commanding General
COMDG OF... Commanding Officer
COMDIEGOGRU... Commander, San Diego Group
Com Dig ...... Comyn's Digest of the Laws of England [1762-1882] [A publication] (DLA)
Comdis .... Comdisco, Inc. [Associated Press] (SAG)
Comdisco .... Comdisco, Inc. [Associated Press] (SAG)
COMDN........ Condemnation [Legal shorthand] (LWAP)
COMDO........ Commando (AFM)
COMDOC...... Combat Documentation (AFM)
Com Dow..... Comstock's Digest of the Law of Dower [A publication] (DLA)
COMDR........ Commander (AFM)
COMDRE...... Commodore (ADA)
COMDSGTMAJ... Command Sergeant Major [Army] (AABC)
COMDT........ Commandant [Air Force] (AFM)
COMDT .... Commandant
COMDTAFSC... Commandant, Armed Forces Staff College (DNAB)
COMDTCOGARD... Coast Guard Commandant
COMDTCOGARD... Commandant of the Coast Guard (DNAB)
COMDTINST... Commandant's Instruction
COMDTMARCORPS... Commandant of the Marine Corps
COMDTNOB.... Commandant, Naval Operating Base
COMDTNY.... Commandant, Navy Yard
COMDTUSCG... Commandant, United States Coast Guard
COMDTUSMC... Commandant, United States Marine Corps
COM(D) WA ... Commodore, (Destroyers) Western Approaches [British]
COMD WC ... Command Weapon Carrier (SAA)
COME.......... Chief Ordnance Mechanical Engineer [British] (ADA)
COME.......... Commentary (ROG)
COME.......... Committee (ROG)
COME.......... Committee on Missionary Evangelism (EA)
COME.......... Computer Output Microfilm Equipment
COMe.......... Cyclophosphamide, Oncovin [Vincristine], Methotrexate [Antineoplastic drug regimen]
CoMe .... Meeker Public Library, Meeker, CO [Library symbol Library of Congress] (LCLS)
COMEASTFRON... Commander, Eastern Sea Frontier [Navy] (MUGU)
COMEASTLANT... Commander, Eastern Atlantic Forces
COMEASTSEAFRON... Commander, Eastern Sea Frontier [Navy]
COMECE ...... Commission des Episcopats de la Communaute Europeenne [Association of Episcopacies of the European Community] (EA)
COMECON.... Council for Mutual Economic Assistance [Also known as CEMA, CMEA] [Communist-bloc nations: Poland, Russia, East Germany, Czechoslovakia, Romania, Bulgaria, Hungary Dissolved 1991]
COMED .... Combined Map and Electronic Display (MCD)
Comed .... Comed Financing I [Associated Press] (SAG)
COMED .... Communications Editing Unit (NOAA)
COMEDBASE... Commander, Mediterranean Defense Sector (NATG)
COMEDCENT... Commander, Central Mediterranean
COMEDEAST... Commander, Eastern Mediterranean (AFM)
COMEDNOREAST... Commander, Northeast Mediterranean (AABC)
COMEDOC.... Commander, Mediterranean Operations Center
COMEDS ...... CONUS [Continental United States] Meteorological Data System [or Distribution] (MCD)
COMEDSOUEAST... Commander, Southeast Mediterranean (AFM)
COMEINDORS... Composite Mechanized Information and Document Retrieval System
COMEL........ Comite de Coordination des Constructeurs des Machines Tournantes Electriques du Marche Commun [Coordinating Committee for Common Market Associations of Manufacturers of Rotating Electric Machinery] (EAIO)
COMELEC .... Commission on Elections [Philippines]
COMELEVEN... Commandant, Eleventh Naval District (MUGU)
COMENER.... Comision Centroamericana de Energia [Central American Energy Commission] (EAIO)
COMENT ...... Command Evaluation and Training (SAA)
ComEnt........ Communications & Entertainment Corp. [Associated Press] (SAG)
COMEODGRU... Commander, Explosive Ordnance Disposal Group (DNAB)
COMEPA ...... Comite European de Liaison du Commerce de Gros des Papiers et Cartons [European Liaison Committee of Wholesalers of Paper and Cardboard] (PDAA)
COMEPP ...... Cornell Manufacturing Engineering and Productivity Program [Cornell University] [Research center] (RCD)
COMER .... College of Mineral and Energy Resources [West Virginia University] (PDAA)
CoMeR........ Rio Blanco County Traveling Library, Meeker, CO [Library symbol Library of Congress Obsolete] (LCLS)
CoMERC ...... Colorado Migrant Education Resource Center (EDAC)
Comeric .... Comerica, Inc. [Associated Press] (SAG)
Com Err .... Comedy of Errors [Shakespearean drama] (BARN)
ComES........ Commonwealth Energy System [Associated Press] (SAG)
CoMes .... Mesa Verde Community Library, Mesa Verde National Park, CO [Library symbol Library of Congress] (LCLS)
COMESA ...... Committee on the Meteorological Effects of Stratospheric Aircraft
COMET........ Careers on the Move for Engineers of Tomorrow [An association]
COMET........ Child-Operated Mobile Electric Transport
COMET........ Coherent Electromagnetic Energy Transmission
COMET........ Collegium Medicorum Theatri (EA)
COMET........ Combined Organic Movement for Education and Training [British]

COMET........ Command Evaluation Teams (MCD)
COMET........ Commercial Experiment Transporter [BTS] (TAG)
COMET........ Committee of Middle East Trade [British Overseas Trade Board] (DS)
COMET........ Computerized Muscle Exerciser and Trainer [Bodylog, Inc.]
COMET........ Computer Message Transmission
COMET........ Computer-Operated Machine Evaluation Technique [Air Force] (MCD)
COMET........ Computer-Operated Management Evaluation Technique [AEC-Army]
COMET........ Consent to Medical Treatment [British Medical Association computer program]
COMET........ Continental [United States] Meteorological Teletype System [Navy]
COMET........ Controllability, Observability, and Maintenance Engineering Technique (PDAA)
COMET........ Cooperative Program for Operational Meteorology, Education and Training [Marine science] (OSRA)
COMET........ Cooperative Program for Operational Meteorology, Education and Training [National Center for Atmospheric Research] (USDC)
COMET........ Cost Measurement Technique (AAG)
COMET........ Meteorological Office Computer [British] (DEN)
COMETS ...... Career Oriented Modules to Explore Topics in Science (EDAC)
COMETS ...... Community Electronic Teller System
COMETS ...... Comprehensive Online Manufacturing and Engineering Tracking System (NITA)
COMETS ...... Computer-Operated Multifunction Electronic Test System (MCD)
COMETT....... Community Program for Education and Training in Technology [EC] (ECED)
COMETT....... Community Programme in Education and Training for Technology [British]
COMEX .... Commence Exercise [Military] (NVT)
COMEX .... Committee on Exchanges [Military]
COMEX .... Commodity Exchange (EA)
COMEX .... Commonwealth Expedition [British]
COMEX .... Communication Exercise [Military] (INF)
COMEX .... Communications Exhibition [Trade fair] [British]
COMEXDIV... Commander, Experimental Division [Navy]
COMEXO ...... Committee for Exploitation of the Oceans (BARN)
COMF.......... Cyclophosphamide, Oncovin [Vincristine], Methotrexate, Fluorouracil [Antineoplastic drug regimen]
CoMFA........ Comparative Molecular Field Analysis [Software]
COMFAIR...... Commander, Fleet Air
COMFAIRADAK... Commander, Fleet Air, Adak, Alaska
COMFAIRALAMEDA... Commander, Fleet Air, Alameda
COMFAIRBERMUDA... Commander, Fleet Air, Bermuda
COMFAIRBRUNSWICK... Commander, Fleet Air, Brunswick
COMFAIRELM... Commander, Fleet Air, Eastern Atlantic and Mediterranean (NATG)
COMFAIRHAWAII... Commander, Fleet Air, Hawaii (MUGU)
COMFAIRJAPAN... Commander, Fleet Air, Japan
COMFAIRJAX... Commander, Fleet Air, Jacksonville, Florida
COMFAIRKEFLAVIK... Commander, Fleet Air, Keflavik, Iceland
COMFAIRMED... Commander, Fleet Air, Mediterranean
COMFAIRNORFOLK... Commander, Fleet Air, Norfolk, Virginia
COMFAIRQUONSET... Commander, Fleet Air, Quonset Point, Rhode Island
COMFAIRSANDIEGO... Commander, Fleet Air, San Diego, California
COMFAIRSOWESTPAC... Commander, Fleet Air, Southwest Pacific (MUGU)
COMFAIRWESTPAC... Commander, Fleet Air, Western Pacific
COMFAIRWING... Commander, Fleet Air Wing
COMFAIRWINGLANT... Commander, Fleet Air Wing, Atlantic (NATG)
COMFAIRWINGNORLANT... Commander, Fleet Air Wing, Northern Atlantic (AABC)
COMFAR ...... Computer Model for Feasibility Analysis and Reporting [United Nations] (NITA)
COMFAX ...... Chip Operational Multifunction Auxiliary Computer (MCD)
COMFAX ...... Communications Facility [Control and Processing Co.]
ComFB .... Community First Bankshares [Associated Press] (SAG)
ComFed .... Community Federal Bancorp, Inc. [Associated Press] (SAG)
COMFET....... Conductivity-Modulated Field Effect Transistor (PDAA)
COMFEWSG... Commander, Fleet Electronic Warfare Support Group (DNAB)
COMFEWSGDET... Commander, Fleet Electronic Warfare Support Group Detachment (DNAB)
COMFIGHTRON... Commander, Fighting Squadron
COM file ...... Command File (CDE)
COMFIRSTFLEET... Commander, [US] First Fleet
COMFIRSTFLT... Commander, [US] First Fleet (MUGU)
COMFITWING... Commander Fighter Wing (MCD)
COMFIVE..... Commandant, Fifth Naval District (MUGU)
COMFIVEATAF... Commander, Fifth Allied Tactical Air Force (AFM)
com fix .... Complement Fixation [Immunology] (DAVI)
COMFLAGRU... Commander, Florida Group
COMFLDCOMDASA... Commander, Field Command, Defense Atomic Support Agency (AABC)
COMFLEACT... Commander, Fleet Activities (DNAB)
COMFLEACTDET... Commander, Fleet Activities Detachment (DNAB)
COMFLETRAGRU... Commander, Fleet Training Group
COMFLETRAGRULANT... Commander, Fleet Training Group, Atlantic (DNAB)
COMFLETRAGRUPAC... Commander, Fleet Training Group, Pacific (DNAB)
COMFLETRAGRUWATE... Commander, Fleet Training Group and Underway Training Element (MUGU)
COMFLETRAGRUWESPAC... Commander, Fleet Training Group, Western Pacific (DNAB)
COMFLOGWING... Commander, Fleet Logistic Air Wing
COMFLTBASTILLES... Commander, Atlantic Fleet Bases, Antilles
COMFOR ...... Commercial Wire Center Forecast Program [Telecommunications] (TEL)
COMFOR ...... International Computer Forum and Exposition (MHDB)
Comforce..... Comforce Corp. [Associated Press] (SAG)

Com Forms... Comer's Forms of Writs [*A publication*] (DLA)
COMFOURATAF... Commander, Fourth Allied Tactical Air Force, Central Europe
ComFtBk..... Community First Bankshares [*Associated Press*] (SAG)
COM'G........ Commencing
Com G & W... Comstock on Guardian and Ward [*A publication*] (DLA)
COMGAR...... Comando Geral do Ar [*Brazilian Air Force*]
COMGEN...... Command Generation Program [*Mariner*] [*NASA*]
COMGEN...... Commanding General
Com-Gen .... Commissary-General [*British military*] (DMA)
COMGEN...... Common Specifications Statements Generator (KSC)
COMGENAFMIDPAC... Commanding General, Army Forces, Mid-Pacific [*World War II*]
COMGENEUCOM... Commanding General, European Command (NATG)
COMGENMED... Commanding General, Mediterranean Theater of Operations [*World War II*]
COMGENPOA... Commanding General, Pacific Ocean Areas [*World War II*]
COMGENSOPAC... Commanding General, South Pacific Area [*World War II*]
COMGENTEN... Commanding General, Tenth Army
COMGENTHIRDAIR... Commanding General, Third Air Division (NATG)
COMGENUSAFE... Commanding General, United States Air Forces, Europe (NATG)
COMGENUSAREUR... Commanding General, United States Army, Europe (NATG)
COM-GEOM... Combinatorial Geometry
COMGERNORSEA... Commander, German North Sea Subarea (NATG)
COMGIB....... Commander, Gibraltar [*Navy*] (AABC)
COMGIBLANT... Commander, Atlantic Approaches Gibraltar (NATG)
COMGIBMED... Commander, Gibraltar-Mediterranean Command (AFM)
COMGREPAT... Commander, Greenland Patrol
COMGRU ..... Commander of a Numbered Group
COMGS........ Commissioner of the Great Seal [*British*] (ROG)
COMGTMOSECTASWU... Commander, Guantanamo Bay, Cuba Sector, Antisubmarine Warfare Unit (DNAB)
COMH .... Committee of the House [*British*] (ROG)
COMHAWSEAFRON... Commander, Hawaiian Sea Frontier [*Navy*]
COMHEDRON... Commander, Headquarters Squadron
ComHISy...... Community Health Systems, Inc. [*Associated Press*] (SAG)
COMHUKFORLAN... Commander, Hunter-Killer Force, Atlantic Fleet
Com/I......... Commercial Invoice (DS)
COMIBERLANT... Commander, Iberian Atlantic Area (NATG)
COMIC .... Colorant Mixture Computer [*Du Pont trademark*]
COMICEASWGRU... Commander, Iceland Antisubmarine Warfare Group
COMICEDEFOR... Commander, Iceland Defense Force
COMICEDEFOR/COMICEASWGRU... Commander, Iceland Defense Force/ Commander Iceland Antisubmarine Warfare Group (DNAB)
COMICPAC... Commander, Intelligence Center, Pacific (DNAB)
COMICS....... Computer-Oriented Managed Inventory Control System (MHDB)
COMIDEASTFOR... Commander, Middle East Force (AABC)
COMIDF ...... Commander, Iceland Defense Force (DNAB)
COMIFA ...... Commission Internationale pour l'Etude Scientifique de la Famille [*International Scientific Commission on the Family*]
COMIFSDIV... Commander, Inshore Fire Support Division (DNAB)
COM III ...... Communications III, Inc. [*Columbus, OH*] (TSSD)
COMIL .... Chairman of Military Committee (NATG)
COMIN .... Commander, Minecraft [*Navy*]
Cominc .... Cominco Ltd. [*Associated Press*] (SAG)
COMINCH .... Commander-in-Chief [*US fleet*]
COMINDIV .... Commander, Minecraft Division [*Navy*]
COMINE ...... Commander, Minecraft [*Navy*] (DNAB)
COMINEDIV... Commander, Minecraft Division [*Navy*] (DNAB)
COMINELANT... Commander, Mine Force, Atlantic Fleet [*Navy*]
COMINEPAC... Commander, Mine Force, Pacific Fleet [*Navy*]
COMINEWARFOR... Commander, Mine Warfare Forces
COMINFIL.... Communist Infiltration [*Name of 1960's FBI campaign against infiltrators*]
COMINFLOT... Commander, Mine Flotilla
COMINFORM... Communist Information
COMINGRP... Commander, Mine Group
COMINGRPOK... Commander, Mine Group, Okinawa
COMINLANT... Commander, Mine Force, Atlantic Fleet [*Navy*]
COMINPAC... Commander, Minecraft, Pacific Fleet [*Navy*]
COMINRON... Commander, Mine Squadron
COMINST..... Communications Instructions [*Navy*]
COMINT .... Communications Intelligence [*Military*]
Comintern.... Communist International (PPE)
COMIREX..... Committee on Imagery Requirements and Exploitation [*United States Intelligence Board*]
COMIS .... Collection Management Information System (MCD)
COMIS .... Command Management Information System [*Air Force*]
COMIS .... Committee Meeting Information System (MCD)
COMISH-US... Congo Military Mission - United States
COMISS .... Commission on Ministries in Specialized Settings [*Federal government*]
COMISS .... Commission on Pastoral Research (EA)
COMISS .... Computerized Medical Information Support System [*Veterans Administration*]
COMIT .... Compiler/Massachusetts Institute of Technology (IEEE)
COMIT CAUS... Comitatis Causa [*For the County's Sake*] [*Latin*] (ROG)
COMITEXTIL... Comite de Coordination des Industries Textiles de la Communaute Economique Europeenne [*Coordination Committee for the Textile Industries in the European Economic Community*] [*Brussels, Belgium*] (EAIO)
COMJAM...... Communications Jamming [*Military*]
COMJEF...... Commander, Joint Expeditionary Force
Com Jour.... Journals of the House of Commons [*A publication*] (DLA)
COMJTF...... Commander, Joint Task Force (AABC)
COMJUWATF... Commander, Joint Unconventional Warfare Task Force (AABC)

COMJUWTF... Commander, Joint Unconventional Warfare Task Force (DNAB)
COMKD....... Completely Knocked Down [*i.e., disassembled, as a toy or piece of furniture which must be assembled before use*] [*Freight*]
COML......... Columbia & Millstadt R. R. [*AAR code*]
COML......... Commercial (AFM)
COML......... Commercial Language (HGAA)
Com L........ Commercial Law [*Canada*] (DLA)
COML......... Committal (ROG)
Com LA...... Commercial Law Annual [*A publication*] (DLA)
COMLA .... Cyclophosphamide, Oncovin [*Vincristine*], Methotrexate with Leucovorin, araC [*Antineoplastic drug regimen*]
COMLAB ..... Commerce Laboratory [*NASA*]
COMLAIRDIR... Travel via Commercial Aircraft Is Directed [*Where Government Aircraft Is Not Available*] (MCD)
COMLANDCENT... Commander, Allied Land Forces, Central Europe
COMLANDENMARK... Commander, Allied Land Forces, Denmark (NATG)
COMLANDFOR... Commander, Land Forces [*Army*] (AABC)
COMLANDJUT... Commander, Allied Land Forces, Schleswig-Holstein and Jutland (AABC)
COMLANDMARK... Commander, Allied Land Forces, Denmark (AFM)
COMLANDNON... Commander, Land Forces, North Norway (NATG)
COMLANDNORWAY... Commander, Allied Land Forces, Norway
COMLANDSCHLESWIG... Commander, Allied Land Forces, Schleswig-Holstein
COMLANDSOUTH... Commander, Allied Land Forces, Southern Europe
COMLANDSOUTHEAST... Commander, Allied Land Forces, Southeastern Europe
Com L & T... Comyn on Landlord and Tenant [*A publication*] (DLA)
COMLANDZEALAND... Commander, Allied Land Forces, Zealand (AABC)
COMLANTFLTWPNRRAN... Commander, Atlantic Fleet Weapons Range (DNAB)
COMLANTFLTWPNRRNGE... Commander, Atlantic Fleet Weapons Range
Com Law..... Commercial Law (DLA)
Com Law Ann... Commercial Law Annual [*A publication*] (DLA)
Com Law R... English Common Law Reports [*A publication*] (DLA)
Com Law Rep... English Common Law Reports [*A publication*] (DLA)
COMLBEACHGRU... Commander, Long Beach Group
Com L League J... Commercial Law League. Journal [*A publication*] (DLA)
COMLO .... Combined Operations Material Liaison Officer
COMLO .... Compass Locator
COMLOG........ Communications Equipment Logistics (MCD)
COMLOGNET... Combat Logistics Network [*DoD*]
COMLOGNET... Communications Logistics Network (IEEE)
COMLOGSUPPFOR... Commander, Logistics Support Force (DNAB)
Com'l Ppr .... Commercial Paper [*Banking*] (MHDW)
Com LQ ...... Commercial Law Quarterly [*A publication*]
Com LR ...... Commonwealth Law Review [*A publication*]
Com LR ...... English Common Law Reports [*A publication*] (DLA)
Com L Rep... Common Law Reports [*1853-85*] [*A publication*] (DLA)
COMLSTDIV... Commander, Landing Ship Tank Division (DNAB)
COMLTRANSAUTH... Travel via Commercial Transportation Authorized [*Military*]
Comm.......... Blackstone's Commentaries on the Laws of England [*A publication*] (DLA)
COMM .... Cellular Communications, Inc. [*NASDAQ symbol*] (NQ)
COMM .... Command (WGA)
COMM .... Commander
COMM .... Commencement (ROG)
COMM .... Commentary
COMM .... Commerce [*or Commercial*]
Comm......... Commerce (AAGC)
Comm......... Commercial (AAGC)
COMM .... Commercial Mission [*NASA*]
COMM .... Commercial Operation and Maintenance Manual [*Military*]
COMM .... Commissary (ADA)
COMM .... Commission (KSC)
Comm......... Commission (AAGC)
comm......... Commission (DD)
COMM .... Commissioner (WGA)
COMM .... Commitment (MCD)
COMM .... Committee
COMM .... Commodore
Comm......... Commodus [*of Scriptores Historiae Augustae*] [*Classical studies*] (OCD)
COMM .... Common
COM-M .... Common Mode [*NASA*] (GFGA)
COMM .... Commonwealth
Comm......... Communal
COMM .... Communication (AFM)
COMM .... Communion [*Service*] (ROG)
COMM .... Communist Party [*Political party*]
COMM .... Community (WGA)
COMM .... Commutator
COMM .... Department of Commerce
Comm......... US Commissioner of Internal Revenue (AAGC)
COMMA ...... CellularCommunications'A' [*NASDAQ symbol*] (TTSB)
COMMA ...... Composite Maneuver Augmentation (MCD)
COMM/ADP... Communications/Automatic Data Processing Center [*Fort Monmouth, NJ*] [*Army*] (GRD)
COMMAGROCV... Commander, Military Assistance Group, Republic of China, Vietnam
COMMAIRCENTLANT... Commander, Maritime Air Central Subarea [*NATO*]
COMMAIRCHAN... Commander, Allied Maritime Air Force Channel [*NATO*]
COMMAIREASTLANT... Commander, Maritime Air Eastern Atlantic Area [*NATO*]
COMMAIRGIBLANT... Commander, Maritime Air Gibraltar Subarea [*NATO*] (NATG)
COMMAIRNORECHAN... Commander, Maritime Air Northeast Subarea Channel [*NATO*]
COMMAIRNORLANT... Commander, Maritime Air Northern Subarea [*NATO*]

COMMAIRPLYMCHAN... Commander, Maritime Air Plymouth Subarea Channel [NATO]
COMMAND... Command Model for Analysis and Design (MCD)
COMMANDS... Computer-Operated Marketing, Mailing and News Distribution System [Computer science] (MHDB)
COMMARFOR... Commander, Marine Forces
COMMARIANAS... Commander, Marianas
Comm B ..... Common Bench Reports (Manning, Granger, and Scott) [1846-65] [England] [A publication] (DLA)
COMMBCA... Department of Commerce Board of Contract Appeals
Comm BPL... Commercial Best Practices Laboratory [Army]
Comm C ...... Commercial Code (DLA)
COMMCE ..... Commence (ROG)
COMMCE ..... Commerce (ROG)
COMMCEN..... Communications Center
COMMCM..... Communications Countermeasures [Military] (NVT)
Comm Ct ..... Commerce Court (DLA)
COMMCTN..... Communication
COMMCTR..... Communications Center (SAA)
commd .... Commissioned (DLA)
COMMDAC... Communications Direction and Coordination
COMM DECK... Common Decking [Lumber]
Comm Del Order... Commissioner's Delegation Order (DLA)
COMMDET... Commissioning Detail
COMMDET ... Communications Detachment (MCD)
COMMDG..... Commanding
COMMDR..... Commander
COMMDT..... Commandant
COMMEL..... Communications-Electronics
COMMEM..... Commemorate
COMMEM..... Commemoration (DSUE)
COMMEMG... Commemorating
COMMEN..... Compiler Oriented for Multiprogramming and Multiprocessing Environments (IEEE)
COMMEND... Computer-Oriented Mechanical Design (MCD)
COMMEX ..... Communications Exploitation (MCD)
COMMFACMEDME... Communication Facilities Mediterranean and Middle East
COMMFEX... Communications Field Exercise [Military] (NVT)
Comm Fut L Rep... Commodity Futures Law Reporter [Commerce Clearing House] [A publication] (DLA)
commie .... Communist [Slang]
CommIn .... Communication Intelligence Corp. [Associated Press] (SAG)
COMMISR..... Commissioner (ROG)
Commiss ..... Commission (DLA)
COMMIT ...... Community Intervention Trial for Smoking Cessation [Department of Health and Human Services] (GFGA)
COMMITS .... Communications Integration Test Site [Military] (CAAL)
Comm Journ... House of Commons Journals [England] [A publication] (DLA)
Comm Jud J... Commonwealth Judicial Journal [A publication] (DLA)
COMML........ Commercial (ROG)
comml .... Commercial (WDMC)
COMMLOADEX... Communications Load Exercise [Military] (CAAL)
Comm LQ .... Commercial Law Quarterly [Australia A publication]
Comm LR .... Commercial Law Reports [Canada] [A publication] (DLA)
Comm Market L Rev... Common Market Law Review [A publication] (DLA)
COMM MGT SYS... Communications Management Systems [Military] (RDA)
Comm Mkt... Common Market (DLA)
Comm Mkt Rep... Common Market Reporter [Commerce Clearing House] [A publication] (DLA)
COMM MUX... Communications Multiplexer (NITA)
COMMN....... Commission
COMMN .... Commune
COMMNCMNT... Commencement
COMMND ...... Commissioned
Commnet..... CommNet Cellular, Inc. [Associated Press] (SAG)
COMMNQ..... Communique
COMMO .... Commodore
COMMO .... Communications Officer
COMMOBSUPPUDET... Commander, Mobile Support Unit Detachment (DNAB)
COMMOD..... Commodity
Commodity Futures L Rep... Commodity Futures Law Reporter [Commerce Clearing House] [A publication] (DLA)
COMMODORE... Command Modular Operation Room Equipment (PDAA)
COMMON..... Common [Commonly used] (OPSA)
Common Mkt L Rev... Common Market Law Review [A publication] (DLA)
Commonw ..... Commonwealth (DLA)
Commonw Act... Commonwealth Act (DLA)
Commonwealth Eng... Commonwealth Engineer [A publication]
Commonw L Rev... Commonwealth Law Review [A publication] (DLA)
Commonw Rec... Commonwealth Record [A publication]
COMMOPNSO... Communications Operations Officer [Air Force]
COMMOSCH... Communications Officer School [Air Force]
Comm Print... Congressional Committee Prints [A publication] (DLA)
COMMPUTE... Computer Oriented Music Materials Processed for User Transformation or Exchange (NITA)
COMMR .... Commissioner (EY)
COMMR .... Commissioner
commr .... Commissioner (DD)
COMMRCE... Commerce
Comm Rec... Commonwealth Record [Australia A publication]
COMMS ...... Central Office Maintenance Management System [Telecommunications] (TEL)
COMMS ...... Communications
COMMS ...... Communications Management Subsystem
COMMS ...... Customer Oriented Manufacturing Management Systems (ACII)

COMMSC ..... Commander, Military Sealift Command
Comm Sec... Commonwealth Secretariat (DLA)
COMMSECACT... Communication Security Activity
COMMSN...... Commission
COMMSNR..... Commissioner
COMMS-PM... Central Office Maintenance Management System - Preventive Maintenance [Telecommunications] (TEL)
COMMSq ..... Communications Squadron [Air Force]
COMMSR..... Commissioner (ROG)
COMMSTA ... Communications Station (MCD)
COMM-STOR... Communications Storage Unit
COMMSUPACT... Communication Supplementary Activity
COMMSUPDET... Communication Supplementary Detachment
CommSv...... Community Savings FA [Associated Press] (SAG)
COMMSWITCH... Communications-Failure Detecting and Switching Equipment (MDG)
COMMT........ Commencement (ROG)
Comm Tel Cas... Commission Telephone Cases Leaflets [New York] [A publication] (DLA)
commun ...... Communicable [Medicine]
COMMUN..... Communicate
commun ...... Communications (DD)
COMMUN..... Communications
COMMUN..... Community
commun dis... Communicable Disease (DAVI)
COMMUNICAT... Communications Satellite (MUGU)
Community Hlth Stud... Community Health Studies [A publication]
COMMUNV..... Communicative
Commw ...... Commonwealth (DLA)
Commw Ct... Commonwealth Court (DLA)
Commw Jud J... Commonwealth Judicial Journal [A publication] (DLA)
Commw Sec... Commonwealth Secretariat (DLA)
COMMY .... Commissary
COMMZ........ Communications Zone (MUGU)
COMN .... Commission
COMN .... Common
COMN .... Communication
COMNAB...... Commander, Naval Air Bases
COMNADEFLANT... Commander, North American Defense Force, Atlantic [NATO]
COMNAS(EA)... Commodore, Naval Air Stations, East Africa [British]
COMNATODEFCOL... Commandant, North Atlantic Treaty Organization Defense College (DNAB)
COMNAV...... Navy Command [Part of North American Air Defense Command]
COMNAVACT... Commander, Naval Activities (DNAB)
COMNAVACTS... Naval Activity
COMNAVACTUK... Commander, Naval Activities, United Kingdom (DNAB)
COMNAVAIR... Commander, Naval Air Force
COMNAVAIRLANT... Commander, Naval Air Force, Atlantic Fleet (MCD)
COMNAVAIRPAC... Commander, Naval Air Force, Pacific Fleet (MCD)
COMNAVAIRSYSCOM... Commander, Naval Air Systems Command (MCD)
COMNAVBALTAP... Commander, Allied Naval Forces, Baltic Approaches (AABC)
COMNAVBASE... Commander, Naval Base
COMNAVBASEDIEGO... Commandant, Naval Base, San Diego
COMNAVBREM... Commander, Bremerhaven Naval Group (NATG)
COMNAVCAG... Commander, Naval Forces, Central Army Group Area and Bremerhaven (NATG)
COMNAVCENT... Commander, Allied Naval Forces, Central Europe
COMNAVCOMM... Commander, Naval Communications (NVT)
COMNAVCRUITCOM... Commander, Navy Recruiting Command (DNAB)
COMNAVCRUITCOMINST... Navy Recruiting Command Instructions
COMNAVCRUITCOM QAT... Commander, Navy Recruiting Command, Quality Assurance Team (DNAB)
COMNAVDAC... Commander, Naval Data Automation Center (DNAB)
COMNAVDEFOREEASTPAC... Commander, Naval Defense Forces, Eastern Pacific (MUGU)
COMNAVDIST WASHDC... Commandant, Naval District, Washington, DC
COMNAVEASTLANTMED... Commander, [US] Naval Forces, Eastern Atlantic and Mediterranean
COMNAVELEXSYSCOM... Commander, Naval Electronic Systems Command (DNAB)
COMNAVELEXSYSCOM ALT... Commander, Naval Electronic Systems Command, Alternate Commander (DNAB)
COMNAVELEXSYSCOM ERS... Commander, Naval Electronic Systems Command, Emergency Relocation Site Commander (DNAB)
COMNAVELEXSYSCOMHQ... Commander, Naval Electronic Systems Command Headquarters (DNAB)
COMNAVEU... Commander, [US] Naval Forces, Europe
COMNAVFACENGCOM... Commander, Naval Facilities Engineering Command (DNAB)
COMNAVFACENGCOM ALT... Commander, Naval Facilities Engineering Command, Alternate Commander (DNAB)
COMNAVFACENGCOMDET... Commander, Naval Facilities Engineering Command Detachment (DNAB)
COMNAVFACENGCOM ERS... Commander, Naval Facilities Engineering Command, Emergency Relocation Site Commander (DNAB)
COMNAVFACENGCOMHQ... Commander, Naval Facilities Engineering Command Headquarters (DNAB)
COMNAVFE... Commander, [US] Naval Forces, Far East
COMNAVFMARIANAS... Commander, [US] Naval Forces, Marianas
COMNAVFOR... Commander, [US] Naval Forces
COMNAVFORCARIB... Commander, US Naval Forces, Caribbean (DNAB)
COMNAVFORCARIBDET... Commander, US Naval Forces, Caribbean Detachment (DNAB)
COMNAVFORCONAD... Commander, [US] Naval Forces, Continental Air Defense Command (MUGU)

COMNAVFORFE... Commander, US Naval Forces, Far East (DNAB)
COMNAVFORGER... Commander, [US] Naval Forces, Germany (MCD)
COMNAVFORICE... Commander, [US] Naval Forces, Iceland
COMNAVFORJAP... Commander, [US] Naval Forces, Japan (SAA)
COMNAVFORJAPAN... Commander, [US] Naval Forces, Japan (AFM)
COMNAVFORKOREA... Commander, [US] Naval Forces, Korea
COMNAVFORPHIL... Commander, [US] Naval Forces, Philippines
COMNAVFORV... Commander, [US] Naval Forces, Vietnam
COMNAVGER... Commander, [US] Naval Forces, Germany
COMNAVGERBALT... Commander, German Naval Forces, Baltic (NATG)
COMNAVICE... Commander, [US] Naval Forces, Iceland
COMNAVINSWARLANT... Commander, Naval Inshore Warfare Command, Atlantic
COMNAVINTCOM... Commander, Naval Intelligence Command (DNAB)
COMNAVJAP... Commander, Naval Activities, Japan
COMNAVLEGSVCCOM... Commander, Naval Legal Service Command (DNAB)
COMNAVLOGPAC... Commander, Naval Logistics Command, Pacific (DNAB)
COMNAVMAR... Commander, US Naval Forces, Marianas (DNAB)
COMNAVMARIANAS... Commander, [US] Naval Forces, Marianas (CINC)
COMNAVMILPERSCOM... Commander, Navy Military Personnel Command (NVT)
COMNAVNAW... Commander, [US] Naval Forces, Northwest African Waters
COMNAVNON... Commander, Allied Naval Forces, North Norway (AABC)
COMNAVNORCENT... Commander, Northern Area Forces, Central Europe (NATG)
COMNAVNORTH... Commander, Allied Naval Forces, Northern Europe
COMNAVOPSUPPGRU... Commander, Naval Operations Support Group (DNAB)
COMNAVOPSUPPGRULANT... Commander, Naval Operations Support Group, Atlantic (DNAB)
COMNAVORD... Commander Naval Ordnance [Military systems command]
COMNAVORDSYSCOM... Commander, Naval Ordnance Systems Command (MCD)
COMNAVOSUPPGRUPAC... Commander, Naval Operations Support Group, Pacific (DNAB)
COMNAVRESPERSCEN... Commander, Naval Reserve Personnel Center (DNAB)
COMNAVRESSECGRU... Commander, Naval Reserve Security Group (DNAB)
COMNAVSCAP... Commander, Allied Naval Forces, Scandinavian Approaches (AABC)
COMNAVSECGRU... Commander, Naval Security Group (DNAB)
COMNAVSONOR... Commander, Allied Naval Forces, South Norway (NATG)
COMNAVSOUTH... Commander, Naval Forces, Southern Europe (NATG)
COMNAVSPECWARGRU... Commander, Naval Special Warfare Group (DNAB)
COMNAVSPECWARGRUDET... Commander, Naval Special Warfare Group Detachment (DNAB)
COMNAVSUPPACT... Commander, Naval Support Activity (AFM)
COMNAVSUPPFOR... Commander, Naval Support Force
COMNAVSUPPFORANTARCTIC... Commander, Naval Support Force, Antarctic
COMNAVSUPSYSCOM... Commander, Naval Supply Systems Command (DNAB)
COMNAVSUPSYSCOM ERS... Commander, Naval Supply Systems Command, Emergency Relocation Site Commander (DNAB)
COMNAVSUPSYSCOMHQ... Commander, Naval Supply Systems Command Headquarters (DNAB)
COMNAVSURFGRUMED... Commander, Naval Surface Group, Mediterranean (DNAB)
COMNAVSURFGRUMIDPAC... Commander, Naval Surface Group, Mid-Pacific (DNAB)
COMNAVSURFGRUWESTPAC... Commander, Naval Surface Group, Western Pacific (DNAB)
COMNAVSURFGRUWESTPACDET... Commander, Naval Surface Group, Western Pacific Detachment (DNAB)
COMNAVSURFLA... Commander, Naval Surface Forces, Atlantic
COMNAVSURFLANT... Commander, Naval Surface Forces, Atlantic (DNAB)
COMNAVSURFLANTDET... Commander, Naval Surface Forces, Atlantic Detachment (DNAB)
COMNAVSURFLANTREP... Commander, Naval Surface Forces, Atlantic Representative (DNAB)
COMNAVSURFPAC... Commander, Naval Surface Forces, Pacific (DNAB)
COMNAVSURFPAC ADP... Commander, Naval Surface Forces, Pacific Automatic Data Processing (DNAB)
COMNAVSURFPAC DET... Commander, Naval Surface Forces, Pacific Detachment (DNAB)
COMNAVSURFPAC DISCUS... Commander, Naval Surface Forces, Pacific Distributed Information System for CASREP/UNIT Status (DNAB)
COMNAVSURFPAC ERS... Commander, Naval Surface Forces, Pacific, Emergency Relocation Site Commander (DNAB)
COMNAVSURFPACREP... Commander, Naval Surface Forces, Pacific Representative (DNAB)
COMNAVSURFRES... Commander, Naval Surface Reserve Force (DNAB)
COMNAVTELCOM... Commander, Naval Telecommunications Command (NVT)
COMNAVZOR... Commander, [US] Naval Forces, Azores
COMND... Commissioned
ComndAr... Commander Aircraft Co. [Associated Press] (SAG)
COMNDW... Commandant, Naval District, Washington, DC
COMNEATLANT... Commander, Northeast Atlantic (NATG)
COMNEED... Communications Need
COMNET... Communications Network (AFM)
Comnet... Comnet Corp. [Associated Press] (SAG)
COMNET... Computer Network Corp. [Information service or system] (IID)
COMNET... International Network of Centres for Documentation and Communication Research and Policies (EAIO)
COMNET... International Network of Communication Documentation Centres [Formerly, International Network of Centers for Documentation and Communication Research and Policies] [France] (EAIO)
COMNEWLONGRU... Commander, New London Group
COMNEWZEDV... Commander, New Zealand Assistance Detachment, Vietnam
COMNINE... Commandant, Ninth Naval District (MUGU)
COMNLONTEVDET... Commander, New London [Connecticut] Test and Evaluation Detachment (DNAB)
COMNMC... Commander, Naval Missile Center (MUGU)

COMNO... Combined Officer of Merchant Navy Operations [British]
COMNON... Commander, Allied Forces, North Norway (NATG)
COMNORASDEFLANT... Commander, North American Antisubmarine Defense Force, Atlantic [NATO]
COMNORECHAN... Commander, Northeast Subarea Channel
COMNORLANT... Commander, Northern Atlantic Subarea [NATO]
COMNORPAC... Commander, North Pacific Force
COMNORSEACENT... Commander, North Sea Subarea, Central Europe (NATG)
COMNORSECT... Commander, Northern Section (DNAB)
COMNORSTRIKFOR... Commander, Northern Striking Force (DNAB)
COMNORTHAG... Commander, Northern Army Group, Central Europe
COMNORVAGRU... Commander, Norfolk Group
COMNORVATEVDET... Commander, Norfolk, Virginia Test and Evaluation Detachment (DNAB)
COMNRCBPAC... Commander, Naval Reserve Construction Battalions, Pacific (DNAB)
COMNRCF... Commander, Naval Reserve Construction Force (DNAB)
COMNRCFREP... Commander, Naval Reserve Construction Force Representative (DNAB)
COMNRIUWGRU... Commander, Naval Reserve Inshore-Undersea Warfare Group (DNAB)
COMNRPC... Commander, Naval Reserve Personnel Center (DNAB)
COMNUPWRTRAGRULANT... Commander, Nuclear Power Training Group, Atlantic (DNAB)
COMNUPWRTRAGRUPAC... Commander, Nuclear Power Training Group, Pacific (DNAB)
COMNUWPNTRAGRULANT... Commander, Nuclear Weapons Training Group, Atlantic (DNAB)
COMNUWPNTRAGRUPAC... Commander, Nuclear Weapons Training Group, Pacific (DNAB)
COMNYKGRU... Commander, New York Group
COMNZAFFE... Commander, New Zealand Army Forces, Far East
COMO... Coherent Master Oscillator (NG)
COMO... Combat-Oriented Maintenance Organization [Army]
COMO... Commissioned Officers' Mess Open (DNAB)
COMO... Committee of Marketing Organizations [British]
COMO... Commodo [In an Easy Style] [Music] (ROG)
COMO... Commodore
COMO... Communications Officer
COMO... Compass Locator [Aviation] (DA)
COMO... Comprehensive Model
COMO... Computer Model (MCD)
COMO... Council of Military Organization
CoMo... Montrose County Regional District Library, Montrose, CO [Library symbol Library of Congress] (LCLS)
COMOA... Central Ontario Mopar Owners Association (AC)
COMOCEANLANT... Commander, Ocean Atlantic Subarea [NATO]
COMOCEANSUBAREA... Commander, Ocean Subarea
COMOCEANSYSLANT... Commander, Oceanographic Surveillance Systems, Atlantic (MUGU)
COMOCEANSYSPAC... Commander, Oceanographic Surveillance Systems, Pacific
Com Off... Commissioned Officer [Military]
COMOFORM... Cold Molded Thermoforming [Fiberglass production]
CoMoH... Montrose Memorial Hospital, Montrose, CO [Library symbol] [Library of Congress] (LCLS)
COMOI... Committee on Manpower Opportunities in Israel [Later, IAC]
COMOMAG... Commander, Mobile Mine Assembly Group (DNAB)
COMONE... Commandant, First Naval District (MUGU)
CoMoP... Pathfinder Regional Library Service System, Montrose, CO [Library symbol] [Library of Congress] (LCLS)
COMOPCONCEN... Commander, Operational Control Center
COMOPDEVFOR... Commander, Operational Development Force [Navy]
COMOPT... Combined Optical [Photography]
COMOPTEVFOR... Commander, Operational Test and Evaluation Force [Navy]
COMOPTEVFORLANT... Commander, Operational Test and Evaluation Force, Atlantic [Navy] (DNAB)
COMOPTEVFORPAC... Commander, Operational Test and Evaluation Force, Pacific [Navy] (DNAB)
COMOPTIONS... Commodity Options [I. P. Sharp Associates] [Database]
COMOR... Committee on Overhead Reconnaissance [Later, COMIREX]
COMORANGE... Commander Orange (Aggressor) Force [Navy] (CAAL)
CoMorM... Mount View School for Girls, Morrison, CO [Library symbol Library of Congress] (LCLS)
COMOROCLANT... Commander, Maritime Forces, Morocco
COMORSEAFRON... Commander, Moroccan Sea Frontier Forces
COMORTEXGRU... Commander, Orange, Texas, Group; Inactive Reserve Fleet, Atlantic
CoMos... Mosca Public Library, Mosca, CO [Library symbol Library of Congress] (LCLS)
ComOT... Commentaar op het Oude Testament [Kampen] [A publication] (BJA)
COMP... Cartilage Oligomeric Matrix Protein [Biology]
COMP... CCNU [Lomustine], Oncovin , Methotrexate, Procarbazine [Vincristine] [Antineoplastic drug regimen]
COMP... Charlotte Ordnance Missile Plant
COMP... Companion (MSA)
COMP... Company
COMP... Comparative
Comp... Comparative (AAGC)
COMP... Comparator (CET)
COMP... Compare
COMP... Comparison
comp... Comparison (VRA)
COMP... Compartment (MCD)
COMP... Compass
COMP... Compatible

COMP .... Compensate [or Compensating] (KSC)
Comp .... Competition
COMP .... Competitor (ADA)
COMP .... Compilation (ROG)
COMP .... Compiler
COMP .... Complaint
COMP .... Complement (AFM)
COMP .... Complete (ROG)
comp .... Complication [Medicine]
COMP .... Compliment (ROG)
comp .... Complimentary (WDMC)
COMP .... Complimentary Copy
COMP .... Component (AFM)
comp .... Compose [Typesetting] (WDMC)
COMP .... Composer (ROG)
COMP .... Composite (AFM)
COMP .... Composite Operational Mission Profiles (MCD)
COMP .... Composition
COMP .... Composition
COMP .... Compositor [Printers' term] (DSUE)
COMP .... Compositus [Compound] [Pharmacy]
COMP .... Compound
COMP .... Comprehensive
COMP .... Compressed
COMP .... Compression [Automotive engineering]
COMP .... Compressor [Automotive engineering]
COMP .... Comprising (WGA)
COMP .... Comptroller
COMP .... Computation (AFM)
COMP .... Computation Subsystem [Space Flight Operations Facility, NASA]
COMP .... Computer [or Computing] (AFM)
Comp .... Computer (DD)
COMP .... Computer-Oriented Microwaves Practices (PDAA)
COMP .... Council on Municipal Performance [Defunct] (EA)
COMP .... Cyclophosphamide, Oncovin [Vincristine], Methotrexate, Prednisone [Antineoplastic drug regimen]
Comp .... De Compositione Verborum [of Dionysius Halicarnassensis] [Classical studies] (OCD)
Compa .... Compania [Company] [Spanish] (BARN)
COMPA .... Compressed Air
COMPA .... Conference of Minority Public Administrators (EA)
COMPAC .... Commonwealth Transpacific [Submarine cable in Pacific]
COMPAC .... Computer Output Microfilm Package
COMPAC .... Computer Packages (MCD)
COMPAC .... Computer Program for Automatic Control
COMPACE .... Control of Material Planning Activities (PDAA)
COMPACELINTCEN... Commander, Pacific Electronic Intelligence Center (DNAB)
COMPACMISRAN... Commander, Pacific Missile Range (MUGU)
COMPACS .... Computer-Oriented Manufacturing Production and Control System (IAA)
COMPACS .... Computer Outputer Microforms Program and Concept Study (MCD)
COMPACT .... Combined Passive Active Detection [RADAR]
COMPACT .... Commercial Product Acquisition Team (EA)
COMPACT .... Committee to Preserve American Color Television (EA)
COMPACT .... Committee to Promote Action [Poverty program]
COMPACT .... Commodity Put and Call Trading Data [Database] [Chronometrics] [Information service or system] (CRD)
COMPACT .... Compatible Algebraic Compiler and Translator
COMPACT .... Computerization of World Facts [Stanford Research Institute] [Databank]
COMPACT .... Computer-Operated Micro-Program Automatic Commissioning Technique (PDAA)
COMPACT .... Computer Planning and Control Technique (BUR)
COMPACT .... Computer Predicting and Automatic Course Tracking (PDAA)
COMPACT .... Computer-Programmed Automatic Checkout and Test System
COMPACT .... Consolidation of Military Personnel Activities at Fixed Installations (AABC)
COMPAD .... Combined Office Material Procurement and Distribution
Comp Admin Sci Q... Comparative Administrative Science Quarterly [A publication] (DLA)
COMPAF .... Commander, Pacific Air Fleet
COMPAID .... Control of Materials Planning and Isometric Drawings
COMPANDER .... Compressor Expander [Telecommunications] (IEEE)
Companding... Compressing/Expanding [Electronics] (ACRL)
Comp & L .... Computers and Law [Australia A publication]
Comp & Law... Computers and Law [A publication] (DLA)
Companion IGasE... Companion of the Institution of Gas Engineers [British] (DBQ)
Compaq .... Compaq Computer Corp. [Associated Press] (SAG)
COMPAR .... Comparative
COMPARE .... Computerized Performance and Analysis Response Evaluator (IEEE)
COMPARE .... Computer-Oriented Method of Program Analysis, Review, and Evaluation [Computer science] (MHDB)
COMPARE .... Console for Optical Measurement and Precise Analysis of Radiation from Electronics
Comp Ar et Men... Comparatio Aristophanis et Menandri [of Plutarch] [Classical studies] (OCD)
Comparisons in L & Monet Com... Comparisons in Law and Monetary Comments [A publication] (DLA)
Comp Armed Forces... Compendium of Laws of Armed Forces [United States] [A publication] (DLA)
Compartr .... Comparator Systems Corp. [Associated Press] (SAG)
COMPAS .... Careers Office Management and Public Appraisal System (AIE)
COMPAS .... Committee on Physics and Society [of American Institute of Physics]
COMPAS .... Computer Acquisition System (PDAA)

COMPAS .... Computer-Oriented Metering Planning and Advisory System [Aviation] (DA)
COMPASEAFRON... Commander, Panama Sea Frontier
COMPASECT... Commander, Panama Section (DNAB)
COMPASECTASWGRU... Commander, Panama Section, Antisubmarine Warfare Group (DNAB)
COMPASS .... Automotive Competitive Assessment Data Bank [Ward's Research] [Database]
COMPASS .... Central Office Maintenance Printout Analysis and Suggestion System [Computer science] (MHDB)
COMPASS .... Competitive Aircraft Data Summary Sheets (MCD)
COMPASS .... Compiler-Assembler
COMPASS .... Complete Parallel Activity and Security System (IAA)
COMPASS .... Comprehensive Assembler System [Programming language] [1964 Control Data Corp.]
COMPASS .... Computer-Adjusted Spectrometry System
COMPASS .... Computer Assisted (IAA)
COMPASS .... Computer-Assisted Classification and Assignment System (IEEE)
COMPASS .... Computer-Assisted Paperless Automated Support System [USPS] (AAGC)
COMPASS .... Computer-Assisted Surveillance Subsystem (MCD)
COMPASS .... Computer-Assisted Yeast Identification System [AFRC Institute of Food Research] [Information service or system] (IID)
COMPASS .... Computer for Advanced Spare Systems (IAA)
COMPASS .... Computerized Movement Planning and Status System [Military] (AABC)
COMPASS .... Computer Optimal Media Planning and Selection System (PDAA)
COMPASS .... Controlled Overhead Management Performance and Standard System
COMPASU .... Commander, Patrol Aircraft Service Unit
COM PAT .... Commissioner of Patents [Legal term] (DLA)
COMPAT .... Compatibility (KSC)
COMPAT .... Computer-Aided Trade (DS)
COMPATASWDEVGRU... Commander, Patrol Antisubmarine Warfare Development Group (DNAB)
COMPATE .... Compassionate [Army] (AABC)
COMPATENFC... Compassionate Reassignment Not Favorably Considered [Army] (AABC)
COMPATFOR... Commander, Patrol Forces (NATG)
COMPATFORNORLANT... Commander, Patrol Forces, Northern Subarea, Atlantic (NATG)
COMPATPLANEREPRONSPAC... Command Patrol Plane Replacement Squadrons Pacific
COMPATRECONFOR... Commander, Patrol and Reconnaissance Force (DNAB)
COMPATRON... Commander, Patrol Squadron
COMPAY .... Computer Payroll (BUR)
COMPBAL .... Compensation Balance [Watchmaking] (ROG)
compbd .... Composition Board (VRA)
CompBnc .... Compass Bancshares, Inc. [Associated Press] (SAG)
Comp Cas .... Company Cases [India] [A publication] (DLA)
COMPCON .... Computer Conference
COMPCON .... Computer Convention (IAA)
COMPCOURDET... Upon Completion of Course of Instruction, Detach [Navy]
CompCre .... Comprehensive Care [Associated Press] (SAG)
Comp Cred... Composition with Creditors [A publication] (DLA)
COMPD .... Compound
compd .... Compound (VRA)
Comp Dec .... Decisions of the Comptroller of the Treasury [A publication] (AAGC)
Comp Dec... Decisions of the Comptroller of the United States Treasury [A publication] (DLA)
COMPDEP .... Complex Terrain Deposition [Model] [Marine science] (OSRA)
COMPDEP .... Complex Terrain Deposition [Model] (USDC)
COMPDES .... Compensator Design [Computer science]
COMPDESFLTSURG... Upon Completion of Duty, Hereby Designated Flight Surgeon [Navy]
Com P Div... Common Pleas Division, English Law Reports [1875-80] [A publication] (DLA)
CompDnt .... CompDent Corp. [Associated Press] (SAG)
Comp Dr .... Comparative Drama [A publication]
Comp Ed Rev... Comparative Education Review [A publication]
COMPEL .... Compute Parallel (IEEE)
COMPELS .... Computer Electrical System [Davy Computing Ltd.] [Software package] (NCC)
COMPELS .... Computerized Evaluation of the Logistics System [Army]
COMPEN .... Compensate [or Compensator] (AABC)
COMPENDEX... Computerized Engineering Index [Engineering Index, Inc.] [New York, NY Bibliographic database]
CompEng .... Computer Engineering (DD)
COMPENSON... Compensation (ROG)
COMPES .... Contingency Operation Mobility Planning and Execution System [Military]
COMPET .... Competition [or Competitive]
COMPETA .... Computer and Peripherals Equipment Trade Association (MHDB)
COMPETE .... Coalition for Manufacturing Performance through Technology
COMPEX .... Competition Evaluation Exercise
Comp Ex .... Comstock on Executors [A publication] (DLA)
COMPF .... Composition Floor
CompG .... Compare Generiks, Inc. [Associated Press] (SAG)
COMPG .... Composite Group [Air Force]
COMPG .... Comprehending (ROG)
COMPGEN .... Comptroller General
Comp Gen .... [The] Comptroller General of the United States (AAGC)
Comp Gen .... Decisions of the Comptroller General [A publication] (DLA)
COMPGENDEC... Comptroller General Decisions [Navy]
Comp Gen Dec... Decisions of the Comptroller General [A publication] (AAGC)

Comp Gen Op... Comptroller General Opinion [*A publication*] (DLA)
COMPHIB..... Commander, Amphibious Force
COMPHIBEU..... Commander, Amphibious Force, Europe
COMPHIBFOR... Commander, Amphibious Force
COMPHIBFORPAC... Commander, Amphibious Force, Pacific Fleet (MUGU)
COMPHIBGRU... Commander, Amphibious Group (CINC)
COMPHIBGRUDET... Commander, Amphibious Group Detachment (DNAB)
COMPHIBGRUEASTPAC... Commander, Amphibious Group, Eastern Pacific (DNAB)
COMPHIBLANT... Commander, Amphibious Force, Atlantic Fleet
COMPHIBNAW... Commander, Amphibious Force, Northwest African Waters
COMPHIBPAC... Commander, Amphibious Force, Pacific Fleet
COMPHIBRON... Commander, Amphibious Squadron
COMPHIBTRALANT... Commander, Amphibious Training Command, Atlantic
COMPHIBTRAPAC... Commander, Amphibious Training Command, Pacific
COMPHILAGRU... Commander, Philadelphia Group
COMPHILMAGV... Commander, Philippine Military Assistance Group, Vietnam
ComplEE..... Companion of the Institution of Electrical Engineers [*British*] (EY)
ComplERE.... Companion of the Institution of Electronic and Radio Engineers [*British*]
ComplP......... Companion of the Institute of Plumbing [*British*] (DBQ)
COMPIS...... Comprehensive Information Service
Compl.......... A Lover's Complaint [*Poem usually attributed to Shakespeare*] (BARN)
Com Pl .... Common Pleas [*Legal term*] (DAS)
Com Pl .... Common Pleas Division, English Law Reports [*1875-80*] [*A publication*] (DLA)
Comp L........ Comparative Literature [*A publication*] (BRI)
COMPL .... Complement
COMPL .... Complete (AAG)
compl .... Completed (VRA)
COMPL .... Compliance
COMPL .... Complication [*Medicine*]
COMPL .... Compliment
COMPLAINT... Complainant (ROG)
COMPLAN.... Communications Plan
Comp Laws... Compiled Laws [*A publication*] (DLA)
Com Pl Div... Common Pleas Division, English Law Reports [*1875-80*] [*A publication*] (DLA)
COMPLEX .... Committee on Planetary and Lunar Exploration [*National Research Council*]
Complex ...... Nuclear Weapons Complex
COMPLI .... Compliance (KSC)
complic........ Complication [*Medicine*] (AAMN)
COMPLIP ..... Computation of Manpower Programs Using Linear Programming (MCD)
Comp LJ .... Company Law Journal [*A publication*] (DLA)
Complnk...... Complink Ltd. [*Associated Press*] (SAG)
COMPLON.... Completion (ROG)
COMPLR ...... Compiler
Com Pl Reptr... Common Pleas Reporter [*Scranton, PA*] [*A publication*] (DLA)
Com Pl R (PA)... Common Pleas Reporter [*Scranton, PA*] [*A publication*] (DLA)
Comp LS...... Comparative Law Series. United States Bureau of Foreign and Domestic Commerce. General Legal Bulletin [*A publication*] (DLA)
COMPLT ...... Complainant
COMPLT ...... Complaint (ROG)
COMPLX ...... Complex
Comp L Yb... Comparative Law Yearbook [*A publication*] (DLA)
COMPLYMCHAN... Commander, Plymouth Subarea Channel
COMPMARK... Computer Marketing [*Standard & Poor's*]
COMPMR..... Commander, Pacific Missile Range (AAG)
COMPMRINST... Commander, Pacific Missile Range Instruction (MUGU)
COMPMRNOTE... Commander, Pacific Missile Range Notice (MUGU)
CompMS...... Computer Management Sciences, Inc. [*Associated Press*] (SAG)
COMPN........ Compensation (ADA)
COMPN .... Composition
COMPN .... Compression [*Automotive engineering*]
COMPNDNG... Compounding
COMPNNT.... Component
COMPO .... Composition (ROG)
COMPO .... Council of Motion Picture Organizations [*Defunct*] (EA)
COMPOOL.... Common Data Pool (MCD)
COMPOOL.... Communications Tag Pool
COMPORON... Composite Squadron
COMPOS ..... Composition
COMPOSE.... Computerized Production Operating System Extension (NITA)
COMPOST.... Computerized Principles of Structures (ADA)
CoMPP........ Coalition of Minority Policy Professionals (EA)
COMPR........ Commerce Department Procurement Regulations
COMPR .... Compare (FAAC)
COMPR .... Composition Roof
COMPR .... Compression (KSC)
COMPR .... Compressor (MSA)
compr.......... Computer (VRA)
COMPRD...... Comprised (ROG)
COMPREP..... Composite Reporting System (MCD)
Com P Reptr... Common Pleas Reporter [*Scranton, PA*] [*A publication*] (DLA)
COMPRESS... Commercial Production of Electronic Solid State Systems (MCD)
COMPRESS... Computer Research, Systems, and Software (IEEE)
COMPRET.... Upon Completion Return Duty Station and Resume Duties [*Navy*]
COMPRNC.... Commandant, Potomac River Naval Command (SAA)
COMPROC ... Command Processor [*Computer science*]
Com Prof..... Commonwealth Professional [*A publication*]
COMPROG ... Computer Program (IEEE)

COMPRSECTASWU... Commander, Puerto Rico Section Antisubmarine Warfare Unit (DNAB)
COMPRT..... Compartment (FAAC)
COMPRTV.... Comparative
COMPS .... Compose
COMPS .... Composite Squadron [*Air Force*]
comps.......... Composition (VRA)
COMPS .... Consolidation of Military Pay Services [*Strategic Air Command proposal*]
COMPS .... Contracted Out Money-Purchase Schemes [*Pension plan*] [*British*]
COMPS .... Council on Multiemployer Pension Security [*Defunct*] (EA)
COMPSAC.... Computer Software and Applications Conference
COMPSAP.... Computerized Static Automatic Restoring Equipment for Power System (PDAA)
CompSc...... Computer Science (DD)
CompSci...... Computer Sciences Corp. [*Database originator*] [*Associated Press*] (SAG)
COMPSERSq... Computer Service Squadron [*Air Force*]
COMPSG...... Compensating (MSA)
COMPSG...... Composite Support Group [*Air Force*]
CompSLEAT... Companion of the Society of Licensed Aircraft Engineers and Technologists [*British*] (DBQ)
COMPSN...... Composition
COMPSO...... Computer Software and Peripheral Show (IEEE)
Comp Sol..... Complete Solicitor [*A publication*] (DLA)
Comp St ...... Compiled Statutes [*A publication*] (DLA)
COMPST...... Composite
Comp Stat ... Compiled Statutes [*A publication*] (DLA)
COMPSY...... Computer Support in Military Psychiatry [*Project*] (RDA)
COMPSYSANLSTPGMR... Computer Systems Analyst and Programmer [*Air Force*]
COMPT .... Compartment (KSC)
COMPT .... Complainant (ROG)
COMPT .... Compliment (ROG)
Compt.......... Compositech Ltd. [*Associated Press*] (SAG)
Compt.......... Comptroller (AAGC)
COMPT .... Comptroller
compt .... Comptroller (DD)
COMPT .... Comptroller of the Navy
Compt & H... Computers and the Humanities [*A publication*] (BRI)
COMPTBL.... Compatible
COMPTBLE... Compatible
COMPT-CA... Comptroller of the Army Directorate of Cost Analysis [*Washington, DC*]
CompTch ..... Competitive Technologies, Inc. [*Formerly, University Patents*] [*Associated Press*] (SAG)
Comptch ...... Compositech Ltd. [*Associated Press*] (SAG)
Comptek ...... Comptek Research, Inc. [*Associated Press*] (SAG)
COMPTEL .... Competitive Telecommunications Association (EA)
COMPTEL .... Compton Telescope [*NASA*]
CompTI........ Companion of the Textile Institute [*British*]
CompTIA...... Computing Technology Industry Association [*Lombard, IL*] [*An association*] (CDE)
COMPTLR .... Comptroller
COMPTR...... Comparator [*Computer science*]
Comptr Treas Dec... Comptroller Treasury Decisions [*A publication*] (DLA)
COMPTRZD... Computerized
COMPTS...... Compliments (ROG)
COMPTU ..... Composite Training Unit [*Military*] (NVT)
COMPTU ..... New York Council of Motion Picture and Television Unions (EA)
COMPTUEX... Composite Training Unit Exercise [*Military*] (NVT)
COMPUL..... Compulsory (DSUE)
COMPUNET... Computer Networking Stand Alone Program
COMPUNICATIONS... Computers and Communications
CompUSA .... CompUSA, Inc. [*Associated Press*] (SAG)
CompuServe... CompuServe Information Service
Comput & Law... Computers and Law [*A publication*] (DLA)
Computat...... Computational Systems, Inc. [*Associated Press*] (SAG)
COMPUTEC... Computer Technology Division (ACII)
Computer L & Tax... Computer Law and Tax Report [*A publication*] (DLA)
Computer L & T Rep... Computer Law and Tax Report [*A publication*] (DLA)
Computer L Serv Rep... Computer Law Service Reporter [*A publication*] (DLA)
COMPUTEX... Irish Computer Exhibition [*SDL Exhibitions Ltd.*] (TSPED)
Computlg...... Computalog Ltd. [*Associated Press*] (SAG)
Computne..... Computone Corp. [*Associated Press*] (SAG)
Compuwr..... Compuware Corp. [*Associated Press*] (SAG)
COMPW ...... Composite Wing (MCD)
COMPWCS... Comprehensive Weight Control System
COMPY....... Company (ROG)
COMR......... Comair Holdings [*NASDAQ symbol*] (TTSB)
COMR......... Comair, Inc. [*NASDAQ symbol*] (SAG)
COMR .... Commissar
COMR .... Commissioner
COMR .... Court of Military Review (AFM)
COMRAC..... Combat Radius Capability [*Military*]
COMRADE.... Computer-Aided Design Environment [*Software system*] (IEEE)
COMRADEX... Containment and Meteorology for Radiation Exposure [*Nuclear energy*] (NRCH)
COMR & DSAT... Communication Research and Development Satellite [*NASA*] (NASA)
COMRAT...... Commuted Rations [*Acronym refers to married Marine living off base and receiving these special pay dispensations*]
COMRATE.... Committee on Mineral Resources and the Environment [*National Research Council*]
COMRATS PT... Commuted Rations, Proceed Time [*Marine Corps*] (DNAB)
COMRAZ...... Communication, Range, and Azimuth Unit [*Computer science*]

COMRCL...... Commercial
Comrco........ Comarco, Inc. [*Associated Press*] (SAG)
COMRDNAVFOR... Commander, Rapid Development Naval Force (DNAB)
COMREC...... Care-Oriented Medical Record [*University of Alabama*]
COMREC...... Component Reclamation (AFIT)
COMRECONATKRON... Reconnaissance Attack Squadron [*Navy*]
COMRECONATKWING... Reconnaissance Attack Wing [*Navy*]
COMREL...... Community Relations [*Military*] (NVT)
ComRelMiss... Commentarium pro Religionis et Missionariis [*Rome*]
　　　　　　　[*A publication*] (BJA)
Com Rep..... Comyn's English King's Bench Reports [*1695-1741*] [*A publication*]
　　　　　　　(DLA)
COMRESDESRON... Commander, Reserve Destroyer Squadron
COMRI...... Communications Routing Indicator
COMRIVDIV... Commander, River Division
COMRIVFLOT... Commander, River Flotilla
COMRIVFLOTONE... Commander, River Flotilla One
COMRIVPATFOR... Commander, River Patrol Force
COMRIVSUPPRON... Commander, River Support Squadron
COMRL........ Major Commands Material Readiness List (AFIT)
COMRNCBLANT... Commander, Reserve Naval Construction Battalions, Atlantic
　　　　　　　(DNAB)
COMRNCF... Commander, Reserve Naval Construction Force (DNAB)
COMRNDN... Commander, Riverine Division [*Navy*]
COMRNFLOT... Commander, Riverine Flotilla [*Navy*]
COMRNRON... Commander, Riverine Squadron [*Navy*]
COMROKFV... Commander, Republic of Korea Forces, Vietnam
COMROKMAGV... Commander, Republic of Korea Military Assistance Group,
　　　　　　　Vietnam
COMROUTE... Commander-in-Chief, [*US Fleet*], Convoy and Routing Section
COMRT...... Commissariat
COMRTMAGV... Commander, Royal Thai Military Assistance Group, Vietnam
COMS.......... 3Com Corp. [*NASDAQ symbol*] (TTSB)
COMS.......... Cerebrooculomuscular Syndrome [*Medicine*] (DMAA)
COMS.......... Collaborative Ocular Melanoma Study [*Medicine*]
COMS.......... College of Osteopathic Medicine and Surgery (OICC)
COMS.......... Commissioner
COMS.......... Communications (ROG)
COMS.......... Communications Support
COMS.......... Communication Subsystem (MCD)
COMS.......... Computer-Based Operations Management System (MHDI)
Coms.......... Comstock's Reports [*1-4 New York Court of Appeals*]
　　　　　　　[*A publication*] (DLA)
CoMs.......... Manitou Springs Public Library, Manitou Springs, CO [*Library symbol*
　　　　　　　Library of Congress] (LCLS)
COMS.......... Three Com Corp. [*NASDAQ symbol*] (SAG)
COMSAC...... Computerized Measurements for Safeguards and Accountability
　　　　　　　(PDAA)
COMSAMAR... Commander, Straits and Marmara Defense Sector (NATG)
COMSANFRANGRU... Commander, San Francisco Group
COMSAR...... Commander, Search and Rescue (DNAB)
COMSAT...... Communications Satellite (EECA)
COMSAT...... Communications Satellite (DOMA)
COMSAT...... Communications Satellite Corp. (DFIT)
COMSAT...... Communications Satellite Corporation [*Washington, D.C.*] (WDMC)
Comsat....... Comsat Corp. [*Associated Press*] (SAG)
COMSATCOM... Commercial Satellite Communications System
COMSATCORP... Communications Satellite Corp. [*See also COMSAT*]
COMSC........ Commander, Military Sealift Command
COMSCELM... Commander, Military Sealift Command, Eastern Atlantic and
　　　　　　　Mediterranean
COMSCEUR... Commander, Military Sealift Command, Europe (DNAB)
COMSCFE... Commander, Military Sealift Command, Far East
COMSCGULF... Commander, Military Sealift Command, Gulf Subarea
COMSCLANT... Commander, Military Sealift Command, Atlantic
COMSCMED... Commander, Military Sealift Command, Mediterranean
COMSCOR ... Consolidation and Management of Supply Consumption Rates (MCD)
COMSCORON... Commander, Scouting Squadron
COMSCPAC... Commander, Military Sealift Command, Pacific
COMSCSEA... Commander, Military Sealift Command, Southeast Asia (DNAB)
COMSE........ Committee on Marine Science and Engineering [*Federal Council for
　　　　　　　Science and Technology*] (NOAA)
COMSEAFRON... Commander, Sea Frontier
COMSEC...... Communications Security [*Military*]
COMSEC...... Communications Security Association (EA)
COMSEC...... Community Security (NVT)
COMSEC 1... Communications Security, Phase 1 [*Course*] [*Military*] (DNAB)
COMSECFLT... Commander, Second Fleet [*Atlantic*] (SAA)
COMSECFLTHQ... Commander, Second Fleet, Headquarters (MCD)
COMSECLOG... Communications Security Logistics (MCD)
COMSECONDFLT... Commander, Second Fleet (MUGU)
COMSED...... Continental Margin Sedimentology [*Oceanography*] (MSC)
COMSENEX... Combined Sensor Tracking Exercise [*Military*] (NVT)
COMSEQIN... Component Sequencing and Insertion (PDAA)
COMSEQUN... Component Sequencing and Insertion [*Computer science*] (MHDB)
COMSER...... Commission on Marine Science, Engineering and Research [*Stratton
　　　　　　　Commission*] [*Inactive*] [*Marine science*] (OSRA)
COMSER...... Commission on Marine Science, Engineering and Resources
　　　　　　　[*Stratton Commission*] [*Defunct*] (USDC)
ComSERC... Computational Science and Engineering Research Center (RDA)
COMSERFORLANT... Commander, Service Force, Atlantic (DNAB)
COMSERFORSOPACSUBCOM... Commander, Service Force, South Pacific
　　　　　　　Subordinate Command
Com Serj..... Common Serjeant [*British*] (ILCA)
COMSERPAC... Command Service Force, Pacific (MCD)

COMSERV...... Commander, Service Force
COMSERVFOR... Commander, Service Force (DNAB)
COMSERVGRU... Commander, Service Force Group (DNAB)
COMSERVGRUDET... Commander, Service Force Group Detachment (DNAB)
COMSERVLANT... Commander, Service Force, Atlantic (DNAB)
COMSERVLANT... Commander, Service Force, Atlantic Fleet
COMSERVPAC... Commander, Service Force, Pacific Fleet
COMSERVPACPETSCOL... Commander, Service Force, Pacific Petroleum School
　　　　　　　(DNAB)
COMSERVRON... Commander, Service Squadron
COMSERVSOWESPAC... Commander, Service Force, Southwest Pacific
COMSEVENTHFLT... Commander, Seventh Fleet (MUGU)
COMSFOR...... Combined Surveillance and Foliage Penetration RADAR (MCD)
Comshr........ Comshare, Inc. [*Associated Press*] (SAG)
COMSICL...... Common/See Individual Components List (MCD)
COMSIXATAF... Commander, Sixth Allied Tactical Air Force (AFM)
COMSIXFLT... Commander, Sixth Fleet (NATG)
COMSIXTHFLT... Commander, Sixth Fleet (NATG)
COMSL........ Communication System Simulation Language [*Computer science*]
　　　　　　　(IEEE)
COMSN...... Commission (AFM)
COMSND...... Commissioned (DA)
COMSNR...... Commissioner
COMSOAL.... Computer Method of Sequencing Operations for Assembly Lines
　　　　　　　(MCD)
COMSOC...... Communications Spacecraft Operation Center [*NASA*]
COMSOCCENT... Commander, Special Operating Forces Central Command
　　　　　　　[*Navy*] (ANA)
COMSOEASTPAC... Commander, Southeast Pacific Force
COMSOLANT... Commander, South Atlantic Force
COMSONOR... Commander, Allied Forces Southern Norway [*Navy*] (ANA)
COMSOPAC... Commander, South Pacific
COMSOS...... Common Supply Support Overseas [*Military*]
COMSOSECT... Commander, Southern Section (DNAB)
COMSOSECWESTSEAFRON... Commander, Southern Sector, Western Sea
　　　　　　　Frontier (MUGU)
COMSOTFE... Commander, Support Operations Task Force, Europe (AFM)
COMSOWESPAC... Commander, Southwest Pacific Force
ComSpirAT/NT... Commenti Spirituali dell'Antico Testamento/del Nuovo Testamento
　　　　　　　[*Rome*] [*A publication*] (BJA)
COMSPK...... Communications Speaker
COMSQN...... Communications Squadron [*Marine Corps*]
COMSR........ Communications Support Requirements (MCD)
COMSRNC ... Commandant, Severn River Naval Command (SAA)
COMSRY...... Commissary
COMSS........ Coastal/Oceans Monitoring Satellite System (PDAA)
COMSS........ Compare String with String [*Computer science*] (IAA)
COMSSIC..... Combat System Ship Interface Criteria [*Navy*] (CAAL)
Comst.......... Comstock's Reports [*1-4 New York Court of Appeals*]
　　　　　　　[*A publication*] (DLA)
COMSTA ...... Communication Station [*Military*] (CAAL)
COMSTAC.... Commercial Space Transportation Advisory Committee [*Department
　　　　　　　of Transportation*] [*Washington, DC*] (EGAO)
COMSTAC.... Commission on Standards and Accreditation of Services for the Blind
　　　　　　　[*Superseded by NAC*]
COMSTAT.... Communications Status Report (MCD)
COMSTAT.... Competitive Statistical Analysis (IAA)
COM-STAT.... Computer Stock Timing and Analysis Technique
COMSTATRPT... Communications Status Report [*Military*] (NVT)
ComstBk..... Comstock Bank [*Associated Press*] (SAG)
COMSTEEL.... Commonwealth Steel Company Ltd. [*Australia*]
COM-STEP.... Computerized Spot Television Evaluation and Processing
　　　　　　　[*Advertising*]
ComsthB..... Comsouth Bankshares, Inc. [*Associated Press*] (SAG)
ComstkRs.... Comstock Resources [*Associated Press*] (SAG)
COMSTOCKGRU... Commander, Stockton Group
COMSTRATRESCENT... Commander, Strategic Reserve, Allied Land Forces, Central
　　　　　　　Europe (NATG)
COMSTRATSUBFOR... Commander, Strategic Submarine Force (DNAB)
COMSTRIKFLANT... Commander, Striking Fleet, Atlantic (AABC)
COMSTRIKFLANTREPEUR... Commander, Striking Fleet, Atlantic Representative in
　　　　　　　Europe (NATG)
COMSTRIKFLTLANT... Commander, Striking Fleet, Atlantic (AFM)
COMSTRIKFORSOUTH... Commander, Striking and Support Forces, Southern
　　　　　　　Europe
COMSTS ...... Commander, Military Sea Transportation Service [*Obsolete*]
COMSTSELMAREA... Commander, Military Sea Transportation Service, Eastern
　　　　　　　Atlantic and Mediterranean Area
COMSTSFE... Commander, Military Sea Transportation Service, Far East (CINC)
COMSTSGULFSUBAREA... Commander, Military Sea Transportation Service, Gulf
　　　　　　　Subarea
COMSTSLANTAREA... Commander, Military Sea Transportation Service, Atlantic
　　　　　　　Area
COMSTSMIDPACSUBAREA... Commander, Military Sea Transportation Service, Mid-
　　　　　　　Pacific Subarea
COMSTS/MIS... Commander, Military Sea Transportation Service, Management
　　　　　　　Information System
COMSTSNORPACSUBAREA... Commander, Military Sea Transportation Service,
　　　　　　　Northern Pacific Subarea
COMSTSPACAREA... Commander, Military Sea Transportation Service, Pacific Area
COMSTSSEA... Commander, Military Sea Transportation Service, Southeast Asia
　　　　　　　(CINC)
COMSTSWESTPACAREA... Commander, Military Sea Transportation Service, West
　　　　　　　Pacific Area
Com Sub...... Commissary of Subsistence [*Military British*] (HGAA)

COMSUBACLANT... Commander, Submarine Allied Command, Atlantic (AABC)
COMSUBASE... Commander, Submarine Base
COMSUBCOMNELMCOMHEDSUPPACT... Commander, Subordinate Command, [US] Naval Forces Eastern Atlantic and Mediterranean, Commander Headquarters Support Activities [Said to be the longest English-language acronym]
COMSUBDEVGRU... Commander, Submarine Development Group
COMSUBDEVGRUDET... Commander, Submarine Development Group Detachment (DNAB)
COMSUBDEVGRU UMV... Commander, Submarine Development Group, Unmanned Vehicles (DNAB)
COMSUBDEVRON... Commander, Submarine Development Squadron (DNAB)
COMSUBDEVRONTRADET... Commander, Submarine Development Squadron Training Detachment (DNAB)
COMSUBDIV... Commander, Submarine Division
COMSUBEASTLANT... Commander, Submarine Force, Eastern Atlantic
COMSUBFLO... Commander, Submarine Flotilla
COMSUBFLOT... Commander, Submarine Flotilla (MUGU)
COMSUBFRONDEF... Commander, Sub-Frontier Defense (DNAB)
COMSUBFRONDEF/DELGRU... Commander, Sub-Frontier Defense/Delaware Group (DNAB)
COMSUBFRONDEF/SOGRU... Commander, Sub-Frontier Defense/Southern Group (DNAB)
COMSUBGRU 8... Commander Submarine Group 8
COMSUBGRUDET... Commander, Submarine Group Detachment (DNAB)
COMSUBLANT... Commander, Submarine Force, Atlantic
COMSUBLANTREP... Commander, Submarine Force, Atlantic Representative (DNAB)
COMSUBLEDNOREAST... Commander, Submarines, Northeast Mediterranean (NATG)
COMSUBMED... Commander, Submarine Force, Mediterranean (AABC)
COMSUBMEDNOREAST... Commander, Submarine Force, Northeast Mediterranean (AABC)
COMSUBPAC... Commander, Submarine Force, Pacific
COMSUBPAC CC... Commander, Submarine Force, Pacific Command Center (DNAB)
COMSUBPAC ECC... Commander, Submarine Force, Pacific Emergency Command Center (DNAB)
COMSUBPAC OTH... Commander, Submarine Force, Pacific, Over-the-Horizon Fleet Commander (DNAB)
COMSUBPACREP... Commander, Submarine Force, Pacific Representative (DNAB)
COMSUBRON... Commander, Submarine Squadron
COMSUBS... Commander, Submarines
COMSUBSSOWESPAC... Commander, Submarines, Southwest Pacific Force
COMSUBTRAFAC... Commander, Submarine Training Facilities
COMSUBTRAGRU... Commander, Submarine Training Group (DNAB)
COMSUBTRAGRUNORWEST... Commander, Submarine Training Group, Northwest Area (DNAB)
COMSUBTRAGRUWESCO... Commander, Submarine Training Group, West Coast Area (DNAB)
COMSUBWESTLANT... Commander, Submarine Force, Western Atlantic Area (AABC)
COMSUCOMLANTFLT... Commander, Subordinate Command, [US] Atlantic Fleet (NATG)
COMSUFRHIN... Commander, French Rhine River Squadron [NATO]
COMSUP... Combat Support Units [Army]
COMSUP... Communications Supervisor (PDAA)
COMSURFRON... Commander, Surface Squadron (DNAB)
COMSW... Compare String with Word [Computer science] (IAA)
COMSY... Commissary [Air Force] (AFM)
COMSY... Commissary
COMSYL... Communications System Language (NITA)
COMSYMP... Communist Sympathizer
ComSys... Communications Systems, Inc. [Associated Press] (SAG)
COMSYS... Communication Systems Ltd. [London, England] [Telecommunications] (TSSD)
COMSYSDISC... Communication System Discipline (IAA)
COMSYSTO... Commissary Store [Military] (DNAB)
COMSYSTOREG... Commissary Store Region [Military] (DNAB)
COMSYSTOREGDET... Commissary Store Region Detachment [Military] (DNAB)
COMSYSTR... Commissary Store [Army] (AABC)
COMT... Catechol-O-Methyltransferase [An enzyme]
COMT... Certified Ophthalmic Medical Assistant (DAVI)
COMT... Coda Music Tech [NASDAQ symbol] (TTSB)
COMT... Coda Music Technology, Inc. [NASDAQ symbol] (SAG)
COMT... Commandant
Comt... Commentary [A publication] (BRI)
COMT... Commit (AAG)
COMT... Communications Technician (MCD)
COMTAC... Commander, Tactical Air Command (AFM)
COMTAC... Command Tactical [Navy] (NVT)
COMTAC... Communications and Tactical [Publications] [Navy] (NVT)
COMTACGRU... Commander, Tactical Air Control Group
COMTACRON... Commander, Tactical Air Control Squadron
COMTAFDEN... Commander, Tactical Air Force, Denmark (NATG)
COMTAFNORNOR... Commander, Allied Tactical Air Force, North Norway (AABC)
COMTAFSONOR... Commander, Allied Tactical Air Force, South Norway (AABC)
COMTAIWANDEFCOMD... Commander, Taiwan Defense Command (MUGU)
COMTAIWANPATFOR... Taiwan Patrol Force (CINC)
COMTASKFORNON... Commander, Allied Task Forces, North Norway (AFM)
COMTBFLOT... Commander, Motor Torpedo Boat Flotilla
COMTBRON... Commander, Motor Torpedo Boat Squadron
COMTBRONTRACENT... Commander, Motor Torpedo Boat Squadron Training Center

ComTch... Com-Tech Communication Technologies, Inc. [Associated Press] (SAG)
Comtch... Comtech Telecommunications Corp. [Associated Press] (SAG)
COMTE... Committee
COMTEC... Computer Micrographics and Technology Group (NITA)
COMTec... Computer Micrographics Technology (EA)
COMTECHREP... Complementary Technical Report [Military] (AFM)
COMTEC/RAT... Comision Tecnica de la Red Andina Telecomunicaciones [Technical Commission for the Andean Telecommunication Network] (PDAA)
COMTEL... International Computer and Telecommunications Conference [International Conference Management, Inc.] [Dallas, TX] [Telecommunications] (TSSD)
COMTEMDET... Upon Completion of Temporary Duty, Detach [Navy]
COMTEMDIRDET... Upon Completion of Temporary Duty and When Directed, Detach [Navy]
COMTEMINS... Upon Completion of Temporary Duty under Instruction [Navy]
COMTEX... Communications-Oriented Multiple Terminal Executive (MHDI)
COMTEXGRU... Commander, Texas Group
COMTHIRTEEN... Commandant, Thirteenth Naval District (MUGU)
COMTHREE... Commandant, Third Naval District (MUGU)
Comtn... Commutation [Army]
COMTONGRU... Commander, Tongue Point Group, Inactive Reserve Fleet, Pacific
COMTORPRON... Commander, Torpedo Squadron
COMTR... Commutator [Automotive engineering]
COMTRAC... Computer-Based Case Tracing [Medicine]
COMTRADE... Compressed International Trade Database [United Nations]
COMTRAIN... Commodore Training [Computer science]
COMTRAINCARRONPAC... Commander, Carrier Training Squadron, Pacific Fleet
COMTRALANT... Commander, Training Command, Atlantic
COMTRAN... Commercial Translator
COMTRANSDIV... Commander, Transport Division
COMTRANSGR... Commander, Transport Group
COMTRANSGRSOPAC... Commander, Transport Group, South Pacific Force
COMTRANSPHIB... Commander, Transports, Amphibious Force
COMTRANSPHIBLANT... Commander, Transports, Amphibious Force, Atlantic Fleet
COMTRANSPHIBPAC... Commander, Transports, Amphibious Force, Pacific Fleet
COMTRAPAC... Commander, Training Command, Pacific
Comtrx... Comtrex Systems Corp. [Associated Press] (SAG)
COMTWELVE... Commandant, Twelfth Naval District (MUGU)
COMTWOATAF... Commandant, Second Allied Tactical Air Force
ComtyFin... Community Financial Corp. [Associated Press] (SAG)
COMUKADR... Commander, United Kingdom Air Defense Region (AFM)
COMUL... Complement-Fixation for Murine Leukemia [Test] [Immunology]
ComUnMil... Committee on the Unisex Military (EA)
COMUS... Commander, United States Forces (CINC)
Com Us... Comyn on the Law of Usury [A publication] (DLA)
COMus... Oakland Museum, Oakland, CA [Library symbol Library of Congress] (LCLS)
COMUSAFFOR... Commander, United States Air Force Forces
COMUSAFSO... Commander, United States Air Force Southern Command (AFM)
COMUSAFTF... Commander, United States Air Force Task Force (AABC)
COMUSARFOR... Commander, United States Army Forces
COMUSARJAPAN... Commander, United States Army, Japan (CINC)
COMUSARSO... Commander, United States Army Forces Southern Command (AABC)
COMUSARTF... Commander, United States Army Task Force
COMUSBASFRANCE... Commander, United States Ports and Bases, France
COMUSE... Conference on Computers in Undergraduate Science Education
COMUSFAC... Commander, United States Facility (DNAB)
COMUSFAIRWINGMED... Commander, United States Fleet Air Wing, Mediterranean (AABC)
COMUSFORAZ... Commander, United States Forces, Azores (AFM)
COMUSFORCARIB... Commander, United States Force, Caribbean (DNAB)
COMUSFORCARIBREP... Commander, United States Force, Caribbean Representative (DNAB)
COMUSFORICE... Commander, United States Force, Iceland (DNAB)
COMUSFORMAR... Commander, United States Force, Marianas (DNAB)
COMUSJ... Commander, United States Forces, Japan (MCD)
COMUSJAPAN... Commander, United States Forces, Japan (AFM)
COMUSJTF... Commander, United States Joint Task Force (AABC)
COMUSJUWTF... Commander, United States Joint Unconventional Warfare Task Force
COMUSK... Commander, United States Forces, Korea (MCD)
COMUSKOREA... Commander, United States Forces, Korea (AFM)
COMUSLANDFOR... Commander, United States Land Forces
COMUSLANT... Commander, United States Atlantic Subarea
COMUSMACTHAI... Commander, United States Military Assistance Command, Thailand (AFM)
COMUSMACV... Commander, United States Military Assistance Command, Vietnam
COMUSMARFOR... Commander, United States Marine Forces (AABC)
COMUSMARIANAS... Commander, United States Forces, Marianas
COMUSMARTF... Commander, United States Marine Task Force (AABC)
COMUSMILGP... Commander, United States Military Group
COMUSNAVCENT... Commander, US Naval Forces Central Command (ANA)
COMUSNAVFOR... Commander, United States Naval Forces (AABC)
COMUSNAVSO... Commander, United States Naval Forces, Southern Command (MUGU)
COMUSNAVTF... Commander, United States Naval Task Force (AABC)
COMUSRHIN... Commander, United States Rhine River Patrol (NATG)
COMUSSAG... Commander, United States Special Advisory Group (AFM)
COMUSSEASIA... Commander, United States Forces, Southeast Asia (CINC)
COMUSTDC... Commander, United States Taiwan Defense Command (AFM)
COMUT... CONUS [Continental United States] and Overseas Microfilm User Tests

COMUTRON... Commander, Utility Squadron
COMUTWING... Commander, Utility Wing
COMUTWINGSERVLANT... Commander, Utility Wing, Service Force, Atlantic
COMUTWINGSERVPAC... Commander, Utility Wing, Service Force, Pacific
COMV .... Cocksfoot Mottle Virus [Plant pathology]
CoMv .... Monte Vista Public Library, Monte Vista, CO [Library symbol Library of Congress] (LCLS)
Com Ver ..... Common Version of the Bible (BARN)
Comvers...... Comverse Technology [Associated Press] (SAG)
ComViat...... Communio Viatorum [Prague] [A publication] (BJA)
COMVX .... Commelina Virus X [Plant pathology]
Comw .... Commonweal [A publication] (BRI)
ComW .... Communications World International, Inc. [Associated Press] (SAG)
COMWESTAF... Commander, Western Transport Air Force [Travis AFB] (CINC)
COMWESTSEAFRON... Commander, Western Sea Frontier (MUGU)
ComWld ...... Communications World International, Inc. [Associated Press] (SAG)
Com'w'th ..... Commonwealth (DLA)
COMX .... Comtrex Systems [NASDAQ symbol] (TTSB)
COMX .... Comtrex Systems Corp. [NASDAQ symbol] (NQ)
COMYARD ... Commander of the Dockyard at [place]
ComYch ...... Com-Tech Communication Technologies, Inc. [Associated Press] (SAG)
Comyn .... Comyn's English King's Bench Reports [1695-1741] [A publication] (DLA)
Comyns....... Comyn's English King's Bench Reports [1695-1741] [A publication] (DLA)
Comyn's Dig... Comyn's Digest of the Laws of England [1762-1882] [A publication] (DLA)
COMZ.......... Communications Zone
COMZONE.... Communication Zone [British military] (DMA)
CON .... Cast-Out-Nines
CON .... Certificate of Need
CON .... Certificate of Need
CON .... Commander of the Order of the Niger [Nigeria]
Con .... Commission [French Business term]
CON .... Commission on the Nomenclature of Organic Chemistry [IUPAC]
CON .... Concanavalin [Biochemistry]
CON .... Concentration
CON .... Concepcion [Chile] [Seismograph station code, US Geological Survey] (SEIS)
CON .... Concerning (ADA)
CON .... Concerto [Music]
CON .... Concession (MSA)
CON .... Concisus [Cut] [Medicine] (ROG)
CON .... Conclusion
CON .... Concord [City in California, Massachusetts, New Hampshire, and North Carolina] (ROG)
CON .... Concord [New Hampshire] [Airport symbol] (AD)
CON .... Concord, NH [Location identifier FAA] (FAAL)
CON .... Concrete
CONAP .... Confidence (ADA)
CONAP .... Confluence (ROG)
CON .... Congo (WDAA)
CON .... Congress [or Congressman]
CON .... Conic (ADA)
CON .... Conico [Race of maize]
Con .... Coniunx [Wife] [Latin] (GPO)
CON .... Conjunction [Grammar] (ROG)
CON .... Conjux [Consort, Spouse] [Genealogy]
CON .... Connecticut (ROG)
CON .... Connection
Con .... Connolly's New York Surrogate Reports [A publication] (DLA)
Con .... Conover's Reports [Wisconsin] [A publication] (DLA)
CON .... Conrotatory [Chemistry]
CON .... Conscientious Objectors' News [British]
CON .... Consciousness
CON .... Consecrated (ROG)
Con .... Consensus
CON .... Conservation (AABC)
CON .... Conservatorium (ADA)
CON .... Consideration
CON .... Consol [Navigation] (AIA)
CON .... Console [Computer science] (IAA)
CON .... Consolidated
CON .... Consolidated Andex Resources Ltd. [Vancouver Stock Exchange symbol]
CON .... Constant (DNAB)
CON .... Constantinople [Later, Istanbul] [Turkey] (ROG)
CON .... Constructor (ADA)
CON .... Consul [or Consulate] (AABC)
CON .... Consult
CON .... Consultation (DSUE)
CON .... Continental (AFM)
CON .... Continental Homes Holding Corp. [NYSE symbol] (SPSG)
CON .... Continental Oil Co. [ICAO designator] (FAAC)
CON .... Contingency [Type classification] (MCD)
Con .... Continuation of Rolle's Reports [2 Rolle] [A publication] (DLA)
CON .... Continued
CON .... Continuous (GAVI)
CON .... Contl Homes Hldg [NYSE symbol] (TTSB)
CON .... Contra [Against] [Latin]
COMU........ Contract (ROG)
COMU........ Contralto [Music]
CON .... Control (AFM)
CON .... Controller (AFM)

CON .... Convenience (ADA)
CON .... Conversation (AABC)
CON .... Converter (IAA)
CON .... Convict (ADA)
CON .... Cross of the Order of the Niger
CON .... National Oceanic and Atmospheric Administration, Boulder, CO [OCLC symbol] (OCLC)
COn........... Ontario Public Library, Ontario, CA [Library symbol Library of Congress] (LCLS)
CON 8VA..... Con Ottava [With the Octave] [Music] (ROG)
CONA......... Canadian Orthopaedic Nurses' Association
CONA......... Comite Oceanografico Nacional [Chile] [Marine science] (OSRA)
conA .... Concanavalin A [Biology] (DOG)
Con A......... Concanavalin A [Biochemistry]
Con A......... Concanavalin A (DMAA)
CoNa......... Naturita Public Library, Naturita, CO [Library symbol Library of Congress] (LCLS)
CONAB....... Commanding Officer, Naval Advanced Base
CONAB....... Commanding Officer, Naval Air Base
CONAC....... Continental Air Command
CONACS...... Contractors Accounting System (PDAA)
CONAD....... Configuration Advisor (IAA)
CONAD....... Continental Advance Section [Originally called Coastal Base Section] [World War II]
CONAD....... Continental Air Defense Command [Discontinued, 1975]
CONAES...... Committee on Nuclear and Alternative Energy Systems [National Research Council] [Defunct]
CONAF....... Conceptual Design for the Army in the Field
CONAG....... Combined Nuclear Steam and Gas (PDAA)
ConAg....... ConAg, Inc. [Associated Press] (SAG)
CON/AGG ..... International Concrete and Aggregates Show (ITD)
ConAgr....... ConAgra, Inc. [Associated Press] (SAG)
Con A-HRP... Concanavilin A-Horse-Radish Peroxidas [Medicine] (DMAA)
CONAIR...... Commanding Officer, Naval Air Wing
CONALOG ... Contact Analog [Submarine instrumentation] (MCD)
CONALOG .... Continuity and Logic Unit
CONALT...... CONARC [Continental Army Command] Alternate Headquarters Plan [Obsolete]
CONALT...... Construction and Repair, Alteration [Coast Guard]
CONAME..... Committee on New Alternatives in the Middle East [Later, FOR] (EA)
CONAN........ Companhia de Navegacao do Norte [Shipping company] [Brazil] (EY)
CON AN ...... Con Anima [With a Soulful Feeling] [Music] (ROG)
Con & L...... Connor and Lawson's Irish Chancery Reports [1841-43] [A publication] (DLA)
Con & Law... Connor and Lawson's Irish Chancery Reports [1841-43] [A publication] (DLA)
Con & Sim... Connor and Simonton's South Carolina Equity Digest [A publication] (DLA)
CONAP........ Concurrent Admission Program [DoD]
CONAP........ Controlled Atmosphere Protected [Army] (MCD)
CONAPT...... Concrete Articulated Production Tower (PDAA)
CONAR....... Commanding Officer's Narrative Report
CONAR....... Continental Army
CONARC...... Continental Air Command (MCD)
CONARC...... Continental Army Command [Responsible for induction, processing, training of active duty personnel] [Superseded by FORSCOM]
CONARESTRAPROG... Connection Naval Air Reserve Training Program
CONAS........ Combined Nuclear and Steam [Propulsion] (DOMA)
CONAS........ Commanding Officer, Naval Air Station
CONASA...... Council of North Atlantic Shipping Associations [Also, CNASA]
CONATUR ... Comite Nacional de Turismo [National Committee on Tourism] [El Salvador] (EY)
CONBAT...... Converted Battalion Anti-Tank [Military] (PDAA)
ConBib........ Coniectanea Biblica [Lund] [A publication] (BJA)
CONC .... Concentrate [or Concentration] (AFM)
CONC .... Concentratus [Concentrated] [Pharmacy] (ROG)
CONC .... Concentric
CONC .... Concerning (ROG)
CONC .... Concerto [Music]
Conc .... Concession (DD)
CONC .... Concilium [Council] [Latin] (WGA)
CONC .... Concise (ROG)
conc.......... Conclusion
CONC .... Concordance (ROG)
CONC .... Concrete
CoNc.......... Garfield County Public Library, New Castle, CO [Library symbol Library of Congress] (LCLS)
CONCA........ Continue Calling Until (FAAC)
CONCACAF... Confederacion Norte, Centroamericana, y del Caribe de Futbol [North and Central American and Caribbean Football Confederation] (EAIO)
CONCAP...... Conversational Circuit Analysis Program [Computer science] (PDAA)
CONCAT...... Conventional Catamaran (PDAA)
CONCAWE.... Oil Companies' European Organization for Environmental and Health Protection (EA)
ConcCm...... Concurrent Computer [Associated Press] (SAG)
CONCD....... Concentrated
ConcdF .... Concord Fabrics, Inc. [Associated Press] (SAG)
CONCEET .... National Conference on Engineering and Training (ACII)
ConcEgy..... Concord Energy, Inc. [Associated Press] (SAG)
concentr ..... Concentrated (DAVI)
concep......... Conceptual (VRA)
CONCEPT.... Computation Online of Network Chemical Engineering Process Technology (IAA)

Concept ...... Conceptronic, Inc. [*Associated Press*] (SAG)
Concepts..... Conceptus, Inc. [*Associated Press*] (SAG)
ConcF .... Concord Fabrics, Inc. [*Associated Press*] (SAG)
CONCG .... Concerning [*Legal term*] (ROG)
CONCH .... Conchology
ConcH......... Concord Health Group, Inc. [*Associated Press*] (SAG)
ConcHlth...... Concore Health Group, Inc. [*Associated Press*] (SAG)
CONCHOL .... Conchology (WGA)
CONCIL....... Conciliation (ROG)
CONCIS....... Concisus [*Cut*] [*Medicine*]
CONCISE..... Computer-Oriented Notation Concerning Infrared Spectral Evaluation [*Programming language*] [*Analytical chemistry*]
CONCL .... Conclusion (MSA)
CONCLON ... Conclusion (ROG)
ConCMx...... Controladora Comercial Mexicana SA de CV [*Associated Press*] (SAG)
CONCN........ Concentration
Concntr....... Concentra Corp. [*Associated Press*] (SAG)
CONCNTRT... Concentrate
CONCOMO ... Convoy Commodore [*Navy*]
CONCON ..... Constellate Consultants (P) Ltd. [*Information service or system*] (IID)
CON-CON .... Constitutional Convention
CONCOR ..... Consistency and Correction Software [*Bureau of the Census*] (GFGA)
CONCOR ..... Construction Corps of the Philippines [*World War II*]
CONCORD.... Concordance [*Computer software*] (NITA)
CONCORD.... Connection Table to Coordinates [*Data analysis*]
Concordia C (III)... Concordia College (Illinois) (GAGS)
Concordia Teachers C (Nebr)... Concordia Teachers College (Nebraska) (GAGS)
CONCORP .... Construction Corp. [*Myanmar*] (DS)
ConcPap...... Concordia Paper Holding Ltd. [*Associated Press*] (SAG)
ConcpT .... Concept Tech Group [*Associated Press*] (SAG)
ConcptD...... Concepts Direct, Inc. [*Associated Press*] (SAG)
CONCR........ Concrete
concr .... Concrete (VRA)
Con Cr .... Contra Credit [*Banking*] (MHDW)
con cr .... Contra Credit [*Bookkeeping*] (ODBW)
CONCRS ..... Concourse
CONCRT ...... Concrete
CONCSSN .... Concession
ConcT .... Concept Tech Group [*Associated Press*] (SAG)
CONCTD...... Concentrated
CONCTG...... Concentrating
Con Cus...... Conroy's Custodian Reports [*1652-1788*] [*Ireland*] [*A publication*] (DLA)
CONCUSS .... Concussion (DSUE)
COND ..... Commanding Officer, Naval Divisions [*Canada*]
Cond .... Concentrated (BABM)
COND.......... Condensed
COND.......... Condenser [*Automotive engineering*]
COND.......... Condition (AFM)
COND.......... Conditional (Tense) [*Linguistics*]
COND.......... Conditioning
COND.......... Condominio
COND.......... Condor Services, Inc. [*NASDAQ symbol*] (NQ)
COND.......... Conduct [*or Conductivity*] (ROG)
cond........... Conductivity (MAE)
Cond........... Conductometric
COND.......... Conductor (KSC)
Cond Ch R ... Condensed English Chancery Reports [*A publication*] (DLA)
CONDEC ..... Consolidated Diesel Electric Co.
CONDECA .... Consejo de Defensa Centroamericana [*Central American Defense Council*] [*Guatemala, Guatemala*] (EAIO)
Cond Eccl .... Condensed Ecclesiastical Reports [*A publication*] (DLA)
Cond Ecc R... Condensed Ecclesiastical Reports [*A publication*] (DLA)
CONDEEP..... Concrete Deep Water Structure [*Oil platform*]
CONDEF....... Contract Definition
Condem .... Condemnation [*Legal term*] (DLA)
Cond Eng Ch... Condensed English Chancery Reports [*A publication*] (DLA)
Condensed Rep... Louisiana Supreme Court Condensed Reports [*A publication*] (DLA)
Condensed Rep... Peters' Condensed United States Reports [*A publication*] (DLA)
Condepa ...... Conciencia de Patria [*Bolivia*] [*Political party*] (EY)
CON DEVE ... Con Devotione [*With Devotion*] [*Music*] (ROG)
Cond Exch R... Condensed Exchequer Reports [*A publication*] (DLA)
Cond Ex R ... Condensed Exchequer Reports [*A publication*] (DLA)
CONDG .... Condensing
COND GEN.... Conductor Generalis (DLA)
Cond HC ...... Conders. Highway Cases [*A publication*] (DLA)
Con Dig .... Connor's Irish Digest [*A publication*] (DLA)
Con Dig Ind... Conover's Digested Index [*Ohio, Indiana, and Illinois*] [*A publication*] (DLA)
Condit Sale - Chat Mort Rep... Conditional Sale - Chattel Mortgage Reporter [*Commerce Clearing House*] [*A publication*] (DLA)
CONDL .... Conditional (ROG)
Cond Lou'a Reps... Louisiana Supreme Court Condensed Reports [*A publication*] (DLA)
Cond Marsh... Condy's Edition of Marshall on Insurance [*A publication*] (DLA)
condo.......... Condominium (VRA)
CONDO .... Condominium
CONDOC ...... Consortium to Develop an Online Catalog [*European Community*] (MHDB)
CON DOL ..... Con Dolore [*With Sadness*] [*Music*] (ROG)
CONDOMIN... Condominium [*Real estate*] (DLA)
CONDON ...... Condition [*Legal term*] (ROG)
CONDOP ...... Condominium/Cooperative [*Real estate*]

Condor........ Condor Services, Inc. [*Associated Press*] (SAG)
CONDR........ Condenser
CONDR .... Conditioner (NASA)
CONDR .... Conductor (AAG)
Cond R........ Peters' Condensed United States Reports [*A publication*] (DLA)
COND REF .... Conditioned Reflex (WGA)
Cond Rep.... Peters' Condensed United States Reports [*A publication*] (DLA)
Cond Rep US... Peters' Condensed United States Reports [*A publication*] (DLA)
COND RESP... Conditioned Response (WGA)
CONDT........ Conduit [*Automotive engineering*]
CONDTG ...... Conditioning [*Automotive engineering*]
CONDTN ...... Condition (MSA)
CONDTR ...... Conditioner
Conductu..... Conductus, Inc. [*Associated Press*] (SAG)
CONDUIT ..... Computers at Oregon State University, North Carolina Educational Computing Service, Dartmouth College, and the Universities of Iowa and Texas at Austin [*An educational consortium*]
CONE .... Collectors of Numismatic Errors
CONE .... Conestoga Bancorp [*NASDAQ symbol*] (TTSB)
CONE .... Conestoga Bancorp, Inc. [*NASDAQ symbol*] (SAG)
cone.......... Conization [*Of the cervix*] [*Gynecology*] (DAVI)
ConE .... Consolidated Edison Co. of New York, Inc. [*Associated Press*] (SAG)
CONE .... Controller Error (AFM)
CONE .... Creation of New Enterprises [*British*] (DI)
CONEA........ Confederation of National Educational Associations
CONEC .... Connection (AABC)
CONECA...... Combined Organizations of Numismatic Error Collectors of America (EA)
CONECS...... Connectorized Exchange Cable Splicing [*Telecommunications*] (TEL)
Con Ed .... Consolidated Edison (MHDW)
ConEd......... Consolidated Edison Co. of New York, Inc. [*Associated Press*] (SAG)
CONEDS...... CONARC [*Continental Army Command*] Education Data System [*Obsolete*] (AABC)
CONEFO...... Conference of New Emerging Forces [*Indonesia*] (CINC)
CONEG .... Coalition of Northeastern Governors
CONELA...... Confraternidad Evangelica Latinoamericana [*Confraternity of Evangelicals in Latin America*] [*Argentina*] (EAIO)
CONELL ...... Conference of New Law Librarians
CONELRAD... Control of Electromagnetic Radiations [*Purpose is to deny the enemy aircraft the use of electromagnetic radiations for navigation, while still providing essential services*]
ConEMA...... Conveyor Equipment Manufacturers Association
ConeMI....... Cone Mills Corp. [*Associated Press*] (SAG)
Conesco...... Conseco Industries Ltd. [*Associated Press*] (SAG)
CON ESP..... Con Espressione [*With Expression*] [*Music*]
CON ESPR ... Con Espressione [*With Expression*] [*Music*]
CONESTAB... Connection Establishment (MCD)
ConestEn.... Conestoga Enterprises, Inc. [*Associated Press*] (SAG)
Conestga .... Conestoga Bancorp, Inc. [*Associated Press*] (SAG)
CONEX .... Connecticut Construction Exposition [*Key Productions, Inc.*] (TSPED)
CONEX .... Container Express [*Army*] (AABC)
CONEX .... Container for Export (NATG)
CONEX .... Continental Exercise [*Military*]
Con Ex .... Controversiarum Excerpta [*of Seneca the Elder*] [*Classical studies*] (OCD)
CONEXION ... Contract Design Exposition [*Atlanta Market Center*] (TSPED)
CONF .... Add-On Conference Call [*Telecommunications*] (DOM)
CONF .... Confectio [*Confection*] [*Pharmacy*]
CONF .... Confectionery
CONF .... Confederation (WGA)
CONF .... Confer [*Compare*] [*Latin*]
CONF .... Conference (AFM)
CONF .... Conference Papers Index [*A database*] (NITA)
Conf .... Conference Reports, by Cameron and Norwood [*North Carolina*] [*A publication*] (DLA)
CONF .... Conferences in Energy, Physics, and Mathematics [*Fachinformationszentrum Karlsruhe GmbH*] [*Germany Information service or system*] (CRD)
CONF .... Confessor (ROG)
CONF .... Confidential (AFM)
CONF .... Configuration
CONF .... Confine [*or Confinement*] (AFM)
CONF .... Confirmation [*Purchasing*]
conf .... Confirmed (DAVI)
CONF .... Conformance
Conf........... De Confusione Linguarum [*Philo*] (BJA)
confab........ Confabulate [*An informal meeting*] [*Slang*] (WDMC)
CONFAC....... Consolidated Facilities Corp. [*Railroads*]
CONFAD...... Concept of a Family of Army Divisions (AABC)
CONFBUL..... Confidential Bulletin [*Navy*]
CONFCE....... Conference (ROG)
Conf Chart ... Confirmatio Chartarum [*Confirmation of the Charters*] [*Latin Legal term*] (DLA)
Conf Comm Uniformity Legis... Conference of Commissioners on Uniformity of Legislation in Canada (DLA)
CONFCTY..... Confectionary
CONFD........ Confederation (ADA)
CONFD........ Conferred (ROG)
CONFD........ Confidential [*Security classification*] [*Military*]
CONFDC....... Confidence (FAAC)
CONFEC....... Confectioner (ROG)
CONFED....... Confederation (EY)
CONFEMEN... Conference des Ministres de l'Education des Pays d'Expression Francaise
Conference (NC)... Conference Reports [*North Carolina*] [*A publication*] (DLA)

CONFG......... Conferring (ROG)
CONFG......... Configuration Process [*Telecommunications*] (TEL)
CONFI......... Confidential (DSUE)
CONFICS..... Cobra Night Fire Control System [*Military*]
CONFID....... Confidential (ADA)
CONFIDAL... Conjugate Filter Data Link
CONFIG....... Configuration (KSC)
CONFIGN.... Configuration (FAAC)
CONFIRM..... Conversational File Information Retrieval and Management System [*Computer science*] (MCD)
CONF L........ Conflict of Laws [*Legal term*] (DLA)
CONFLAG..... Conflagration Control (DNAB)
CONFLEX..... Conditioned Reflex [*Machine*] (IEEE)
CONFLOW... Controlled Flow
CONF-MH.... Confidential - Modified Handling [*Army*]
CONFMOD.... Confidential - Modified Handling Authorized [*Army*]
Conf on Char Found NYU Proc... Conference on Charitable Foundations. Proceedings. New York University [*A publication*] (DLA)
CONFORM ... Constrained Force Model (PDAA)
CONFORM ... Contract Formulation
CONFPONT... Confessor Pontifex [*Confessor and Bishop*] [*Latin*] (ADA)
Conf Proc Inter-Amer Bar Assoc... Conference Proceedings. Inter-American Bar Association [*A publication*] (DLA)
CONF R....... Confirmation Rolls (ROG)
Conf Rept .... Conference Report (DLA)
CONFU........ Conference on Fair Use
CON FUO ..... Con Fuoco [*With Force*] [*Music*] (ROG)
CON FUR ..... Con Furia [*With Fury*] [*Music*] (ROG)
CONG.......... Congenital [*Medicine*] (WGA)
CONG.......... Congestion [*Telecommunications*] (TEL)
CONG.......... Congius [*Gallon*] [*Pharmacy*]
Cong .... Congolese
Cong .... Congregation (BJA)
CONG.......... Congregational
CONG.......... Congress (AFM)
Cong .... Congress (AAGC)
Cong .... Congressional (AAGC)
CONG.......... Congressional (ROG)
Cong .... Congressman
CoNgA .... Adams County Public Library, Northglenn, CO [*Library symbol Library of Congress*] (LCLS)
CONGA........ Combat Operations, Naval Gunfire Activity
CONGA........ Concept Game [*A war game*]
Cong Deb.... Congressional Debates [*United States*] [*A publication*] (DLA)
Cong Dig .... Congdon's Digest [*Canada*] [*A publication*] (DLA)
Cong Dig .... Congressional Digest [*A publication*] (AAGC)
CONGDRTN... Confederation
Cong El Cas... Congressional Election Cases [*United States*] [*A publication*] (DLA)
CONGEN ...... Congenital [*Medicine*]
congen........ Congenital [*Medicine*] (DMAA)
CONGEN ...... Constrained Structure Generation
CONGEN ...... Consul General
Cong Gl ...... Congressional Globe [*A publication*] (DLA)
Cong Globe... Congressional Globe [*A publication*] (DLA)
CoNgGS .... Church of Jesus Christ of Latter-Day Saints, Genealogical Society Library, Denver North Branch, Northglenn, CO [*Library symbol Library of Congress*] (LCLS)
Conglm........ Congoleum Corp. [*Associated Press*] (SAG)
Cong Index (CCH)... Congressional Index (Commerce Clearing House) [*A publication*] (DLA)
CONGINT ..... Interest by Member of Congress
CONGL........ Conglomerate
CONGL........ Congregational
CONGL........ Congressional
CONG LIB .... Congressional Library (ROG)
Cong Min L... Congdon's Mining Laws of California [*A publication*] (DLA)
CONGN .... Congregation (ROG)
CONGO .... Conference on Non-Governmental Organizations in Consultative Status with the United Nations Economic and Social Council (EAIO)
CONGO .... Congregationalist [*Slang*] (DSUE)
CONGOOD.... Confederation of Non-Governmental Organizations for Overseas Development
CongOrat ..... Congregation of the Oratory [*Oratorians*] [*Roman Catholic men's religious order*]
CONGR .... Congregational
CONGR .... Congruent (MSA)
CON GRA .... Con Grazia [*With Grace*] [*Music*] (ROG)
CONGRATS... Congratulations (DSUE)
CONGRATS... Continuous Gradient Ray Tracing System
Cong Rec.... Congressional Record [*A publication*] (AAGC)
CONGREGTNL... Congregational
CONGRESS... Contiguous Node Group Restoral Supervision and Switching
CONGRIPS... Conference Group on Italian Politics and Society (EA)
CONGRSMAN... Congressman
CoNgSD .... Adams County School District No. 12, Northglenn, CO [*Library symbol Library of Congress*] (LCLS)
CON GUST... Con Gustoso [*With Taste*] [*Music*] (ROG)
CONH.......... United States Naval Hospital, Oakland, CA [*Library symbol Library of Congress*] (LCLS)
ConHCre ...... Consolidated Health Care Associates, Inc. [*Associated Press*] (SAG)
CONHYDROLANT... Confidential Hydrographic Office [*later, Naval Oceanographic Office*] Reports - Atlantic [*Navy*]
CONIN.......... Console Input (BTTJ)
ConiNT......... Coniectanea Neotestamentica [*Uppsala*] [*A publication*] (BJA)

con inv .... Consular Invoice (ODBW)
CONIO.......... Console Input/Output
CONIRIS ...... Calibrated Optical and Near Infrared Imaging System (MCD)
CONIT .... Connector for Networked Information Transfer [*Massachusetts Institute of Technology*] [*Information service or system*] (IID)
coniz.......... Conization [*Gynecology*] (DAVI)
CONJ .... Conjugation
CONJ .... Conjunction
conj .... Conjunction (VRA)
conj .... Conjunctiva [*Ophthalmology*] (DAVI)
CONJ .... Conjunctivitis [*Medicine*]
CONJ .... In Conjunction With (ADA)
CONJUG...... Conjugation (ADA)
conjunc........ Conjunctiva [*Ophthalmology*] (DAVI)
Conk Adm... Conkling's Admiralty [*A publication*] (DLA)
Conk Ex Pow... Conkling's Executive Powers [*A publication*] (DLA)
Conk JP...... Conkling's Iowa Justice of the Peace [*A publication*] (DLA)
Conk Treat... Conkling's Treatise on Jurisdiction and Practice of the United States Courts [*A publication*] (DLA)
Conk US Pr... Conkling's Treatise on Jurisdiction and Practice of the United States Courts [*A publication*] (DLA)
CONL .... Conical (MSA)
CONL .... Control
CONLIS........ Committee on National Library Information Systems
CONLOS........ CONARC [*Continental Army Command*] Logistics Operations - Streamline [*Obsolete*]
Conmed ...... Conmed Corp. [*Associated Press*] (SAG)
CONMET ...... Combined Operations Nuclear Medical Evaluation Team (MCD)
CON MO ...... Con Moto [*With the Movement*] [*Music*] (ROG)
CONN.......... Connected (ROG)
CONN.......... Connecticut
Conn .... Connecticut (ODBW)
CONN.......... Connector (KSC)
CONN.......... Connellan Airways Ltd.
Conn .... Connolly's New York Surrogate Reports [*A publication*] (DLA)
CONN.......... Connotation
Conn Acts... Connecticut Public and Special Acts (DLA)
Conn Agencies Reg... Regulations of Connecticut State Agencies [*A publication*] (DLA)
Conn App Proc... Maltbie's Appellate Procedure [*A publication*] (DLA)
Conn C....... Connecticut College (GAGS)
Conn Cir ...... Connecticut Circuit Court Reports [*A publication*] (DLA)
Conn Cir Ct... Connecticut Circuit Court Reports [*A publication*] (DLA)
Conn Comp Com... Connecticut Compensation Commissioners, Compendium of Awards [*A publication*] (DLA)
Conn Comp Dec... Connecticut Workmen's Compensation Decisions [*A publication*] (DLA)
Conn Const... Connecticut Constitution [*A publication*] (DLA)
Connct....... Connect, Inc. [*Associated Press*] (SAG)
Conn Dec.... Connecticut Decisions [*A publication*] (DLA)
CONNECT.... Connection
Connect ...... Connective Therapeutics, Inc. [*Associated Press*] (SAG)
Connecticut R... Connecticut Reports [*A publication*] (DLA)
Connecticut Rep... Connecticut Reports [*A publication*] (DLA)
Connect Rep... Connecticut Reports [*A publication*] (DLA)
ConnEn........ Connecticut Energy Corp. [*Associated Press*] (SAG)
ConNeot....... Coniectanea Neotestamentica [*Uppsala*] [*A publication*] (BJA)
Conn Gen Stat... General Statutes of Connecticut [*A publication*] (DLA)
Conn Gen Stat Ann... Connecticut General Statutes, Annotated [*A publication*] (DLA)
Conn Legis Serv... Connecticut Legislative Service (West) [*A publication*] (DLA)
Conn L J...... Connecticut Law Journal [*Administrative Rules*] (AAGC)
ConnNG....... Connecticut Natural Gas Corp. [*Associated Press*] (SAG)
Connolly ...... Connolly's New York Surrogate Reports [*A publication*] (DLA)
Connoly Sur Rep... Connolly's New York Surrogate Reports [*A publication*] (DLA)
Connoly Surr Rep... Connolly's New York Surrogate Reports [*A publication*] (DLA)
Connor & L... Connor and Lawson's Irish Chancery Reports [*1841-43*] [*A publication*] (DLA)
Conn Pub Acts... Connecticut Public Acts [*A publication*] (DLA)
Conn R .... Connaught Rangers [*Military British*] (DAS)
Conn R .... Connecticut Reports [*A publication*] (DLA)
CONN RANG... Connaught Rangers [*Military British*] (ROG)
Conn Rep.... Connecticut Reports [*A publication*] (DLA)
Conn Reports... Connecticut Reports [*A publication*] (DLA)
CONNROD.... Connecting-Rod
Conn S....... Connecticut Supplement [*A publication*] (DLA)
Conn Spec Acts... Connecticut Special Acts [*A publication*] (DLA)
Conn Sup.... Connecticut Supplement [*A publication*] (DLA)
Conn Supp... Connecticut Supplement [*A publication*] (DLA)
Conn Sur .... Connolly's New York Surrogate Reports [*A publication*] (DLA)
Conn Surr Rep... Connolly's New York Surrogate Reports [*A publication*] (DLA)
ConNT......... Coniectanea Neotestamentica [*Uppsala*] [*A publication*] (BJA)
CONNT........ Connaissance [*Bill of Lading*] [*Legal term French*]
ConnWt....... Connecticut Water Service, Inc. [*Associated Press*] (SAG)
CONO.......... Confirmation of Number of Order [*Purchasing*] (IAA)
CONO.......... Congou [*Tea trade*] (ROG)
CO/NO........ Current Operator - Next Operator [*Computer science*] (MDG)
CoNo.......... Norwood Public Library, Norwood, CO [*Library symbol Library of Congress*] (LCLS)
CONOBJTR... Conscientious Objector
CONOCO ...... Continental Oil Co.
CON OF....... Consisting Of [*Freight*]
CONOG .... Combined Nuclear Steam or Gas (PDAA)
Conolg .... Conolog Corp. [*Associated Press*] (SAG)
Conolog .... Conolog Corp. [*Associated Press*] (SAG)

CONOP........	Concept of Operations (DOMA)
CONOPPR....	CONARC [*Continental Army Command*] Operating Program [*Obsolete*] (AABC)
CONOPS	Concept of Operations (DOMA)
CONOPS	Continental United States Operations [*Army*]
CONOPS	Continuity of Operations (MCD)
CONOUT	Console Output (BTTJ)
Conover.......	Conover's Reports [*Wisconsin*] [*A publication*] (DLA)
CONP	Connection-Oriented Network Protocol [*Computer science*]
CONPADRI ...	Cyclophosphamide, Oncovin [*Vincristine*], L-PAM , Adriamycin [*Melphalan*] [*Antineoplastic drug regimen*]
ConPap	Consolidated Papers, Inc. [*Associated Press*] (SAG)
Con Par	Connell on Parishes [*A publication*] (DLA)
CONPASP	Construction Project Alternative Selection Program [*Bell System*]
CONPASS	Consortium of Professional Associations to Supervise Studies of Special Programsfor the Improvement of Instruction in American Education
ConPd	Consolidated Products, Inc. [*Associated Press*] (SAG)
CONPLAN ...	Concept Plan (NVT)
CONPLAN	Contingency Plan [*Military*]
CONPOR	Conference of Private Organizations (EA)
ConPort........	Consumer Portfolio Services [*Associated Press*] (SAG)
CONPR........	Contact Print (VRA)
CONPRESDU...	Continue Present Duty [*Military*]
CONPY	Contact Party [*Army*]
CONQ	Conquer [*or Conqueror*] (WDAA)
CONQ	Conquest (ROG)
ConqInd	Conquest Industries Corp. [*Associated Press*] (SAG)
CONQUISDR...	Conquistador
Conr............	Conroy's Custodian Reports [*1652-1788*] [*Ireland*] [*A publication*] (DLA)
CONR..........	Continental NORAD Region [*Aviation*] (FAAC)
CONRAD	Computerized National Range Documentation
CONRAD	Contour RADAR Data (PDAA)
CONRAD	Contraceptive Research and Development Program [*Research center*] (RCD)
CONRAD	Conversational On-Line Real-Time Algorithm Definition [*Computer science*] (MHDB)
Conrail.........	Conrail, Inc. [*Associated Press*] (SAG)
CONRAIL	Consolidated Rail Corp. [*Also, CR, CRC*]
Conrail........	Consolidated Rail Corporation (USGC)
ConRam.......	Consolidated Ramrod Gold Corp. [*Associated Press*] (SAG)
CONREC......	Conference for Reconciliation, Restitution Fund (EA)
CONREG	Congregation
CONREP......	CONARC [*Continental Army Command*] Emergency Relocation Plan [*Obsolete*]
CONREP......	Connected Replenishment [*Military*] (NVT)
CONROD	Connecting-Rod
CONROUTE...	Convoy and Routing [*Section*] [*US Fleet*]
ConrPr	Conner Peripherals, Inc. [*Associated Press*] (SAG)
CONS	Carrier-Operated Noise Suppression
CONS	Connection-Oriented Network Service [*Telecommunications*] (OSI)
Cons	Conscience [*A publication*]
CONS..........	Consecrated
Cons	Consecratione [*Decretum Gratiani*] [*A publication*] (DSA)
CONS..........	Consecutive (ADA)
Cons	Conseil [*Council*] [*French*] (DLA)
Cons	Conseiller [*Councillor, Judge*] [*French*] (ILCA)
CONS...........	Consequence
CONS...........	Conserva [*Conserve*] [*Pharmacy*]
CONS...........	Conservative
CONS...........	Conservative and Unionist Party [*British Political party*]
CONS...........	Conservative Savings Corp. [*NASDAQ symbol*] (NQ)
Cons	Conservatoire [*Conservatory*] [*French*]
Cons	Conservator (DLA)
CONS...........	Consider (AABC)
Cons	Considerant [*Whereas, In View*] [*French*] (ILCA)
CONS...........	Consign
CONS...........	Consignment [*Business term*]
Cons	Consist (AABC)
CONS...........	Console [*Computer science*]
CONS...........	Consolidate
CONS...........	Consolidated
cons............	Consonans [*Tinkling*] (DAVI)
CONS...........	Consonant
CONS...........	Constable
CONS...........	Constitution
CONS...........	Construction
CONS...........	Consul
CONS...........	Consult [*or Consultation, Consultant*] [*Medicine*]
Cons	Consultant (DAVI)
cons............	Consulting (DD)
CONS...........	Contracting Squadron [*Air Force*]
CONSA.........	Consular Shipping Adviser
CONSAL.......	Congress of Southeast Asian Librarians (EAIO)
Cons & Com Cred (P-H)...	Consumer and Commercial Credit (Prentice-Hall) [*A publication*] (DLA)
CONSAS.......	Constrado Structural Analysis System [*Structures & Computers Ltd.*] [*Software package*] (NCC)
Consc..........	Conseco, Inc. [*Associated Press*] (SAG)
CONSCAN	Conical Scan (NG)
CONSCE.......	Consequence (ROG)
CONSCIENCE...	Committee on National Student Citizenship in Every National Case of Emergency
CONSCO	Committee of National Security Companies [*Memphis, TN*] (EA)
Cons Const...	Conseil Constitutionnel [*Constitutional Council*] [*French*] (DLA)
Cons Cred Guide...	Consumer Credit Guide [*Commerce Clearing House*] [*A publication*] (DLA)
CONSD........	Commanding Officer, Naval Supply Depot (MCD)
CONSD........	Considered [*Legal*] [*British*] (ROG)
con sec........	Conic Section (BARN)
CONSEC.......	Consecutive (MSA)
Conseco	Conseco, Inc. [*Associated Press*] (SAG)
CONSED.......	Continental Shelf Sedimentology [*Oceanography*] (MSC)
CONSENSUS...	Cooperative North Scandinavian Enalapril Survival Study [*Medicine*]
Consep........	Consep, Inc. [*Associated Press*] (SAG)
CONSEQCE...	Consequence [*Legal*] [*British*] (ROG)
CONSEQT......	Consequent [*Legal*] [*British*] (ROG)
CONSER......	Conversion of Serials (MCD)
CONSER......	Conversion of Serials Project [*Database project*] (NITA)
CONSER......	Cooperative Online Serials [*Library of Congress*]
CONSERV ...	Conservation
CONSERV ...	Conservatory
CONSERVE....	Conservation
CONS et PRUD...	Consilio et Prudentia [*By Counsel and Prudence*] [*Latin*] (ADA)
ConsFn	Consumers Financial Corp. [*Associated Press*] (SAG)
CONSGEE......	Consignee [*Business term*] (ROG)
CONSGEN......	Consul General (EY)
CONSGOLD...	Consolidated Gold Fields [*British*]
ConsGph	Consolidated Graphics, Inc. [*Associated Press*] (SAG)
CONSGT......	Consignment [*Business term*]
CONSHELF....	Continental Shelf
CONSHIP	Control by Ship (NATG)
Cons Hon.....	De Consulatu Honorii [*of Claudianus*] [*Classical studies*] (OCD)
CONSHORE....	Control from Shore (NATG)
CONSID.......	Consider (ROG)
CONSIDO	Consolidated Special Information Dissemination Office [*Proposed for military intelligence gathering, late 1940's, but never activated*]
Consilm	Consilium, Inc. [*Associated Press*] (SAG)
CONSIM.......	Console Simulator [*Computer science*]
Consist	English Consistorial Reports, by Haggard [*1788-1821*] [*A publication*] (DLA)
Consist Rep...	English Consistorial Reports, by Haggard [*1788-1821*] [*A publication*] (DLA)
ConslDel	Consolidated Delivery & Logistis, Inc. [*Associated Press*] (SAG)
CONSLDTN...	Consolidation
CONSLDTR...	Consolidator
CONSLNT......	Consultant
CONSLTN......	Consolation
CONSLTNT...	Consultant (AABC)
CONSMR......	Consumer
CONSN.......	Consultation [*Legal*] [*British*] (ROG)
ConsNev	Consolidated Nevada Goldfields Corp. [*Associated Press*] (SAG)
ConsNG.......	Consolidated Natural Gas Co. [*Associated Press*] (SAG)
ConsNP.......	Conservative Nationalist Party [*Australia Political party*]
CONSO.......	Consolan Facility [*Aviation*]
CONSOB	Commissione Nazionale per le Societa e la Borsa
CONSOC	Conservative Society [*British*] (DI)
CONSOL......	Consolidate (AFM)
consol.........	Consolidated (DD)
CONSOL-BNR...	Consolidation Coal - Bethlehem Steel - National Steel - Republic Steel [*Coke pellet process developed by four-company group of steel and coke producers*]
CONSOLEX...	Consolidation Exercise [*Military*] (NVT)
Consolid Ord...	Consolidated General Orders in Chancery [*A publication*] (DLA)
CONSOLREC...	Consolidated Recreation (DNAB)
CONSOLS	Consolidated Annuities [*Insurance*] (DSUE)
CONSOLTD...	Consolidated (ADA)
CONSON	Consideration
ConsoPd	Conso Products Co. [*Associated Press*] (SAG)
Cons Ord in Ch...	Consolidated General Orders in Chancery [*A publication*] (DLA)
CONSORT	Conversational System with On-Line Remote Terminals [*Computer science*] (IEEE)
Consp	Conspiracy (ILCA)
ConsPdts	Consolidated Products, Inc. [*Associated Press*] (SAG)
Con Spec.....	Construction Specification (DAC)
CONSPERG...	Conspergere [*Dust or Sprinkle*] [*Pharmacy*]
conspic	Conspicuous
consr	Consecrated (VRA)
CONSRVTRY...	conservatory
Cons Stil......	De Consulatu Stilichonis [*of Claudianus*] [*Classical studies*] (OCD)
CONSSTOCS...	Contingency Support Stocks [*Military*] (AABC)
ConsSv	Conservative Savings Corp. [*Associated Press*] (SAG)
Const	Bott's Poor Laws, by Const [*1560-1833*] [*A publication*] (DLA)
CONST........	Consent (ROG)
CONST........	Consignment [*Business term*] (ROG)
Con St	Consolidated Statutes [*A publication*] (DLA)
CONST........	Constable
CONST........	Constant
const..........	Constant [*Medicine*] (DMAA)
CONST........	Constantine [*Roman emperor, 272-337AD*] (ROG)
CONST........	Constantinople [*Later, Istanbul*] [*Turkey*] (ROG)
CONST........	Constituency
CONST........	Constitutio [*Point at Issue, Regulation, Settlement*] [*Latin*] (OCD)
CONST........	Constitution [*or Constitutional*]
Const	Constitutional (AAGC)
Const	Constitutional Reports, Printed by Harper [*1 South Carolina*] [*A publication*] (DLA)
Const	Constitutional Reports, Printed by Mills [*South Carolina*] [*A publication*] (DLA)

Const .... Constitutional Reports, Printed by Treadway [*South Carolina*] [*A publication*] (DLA)
CONST .... Construct [*or Construction*] (AFM)
const........... Construction (DD)
Const .... Const's Edition of Bott's Poor Law Cases [*A publication*] (DSA)
CONSTAB..... Constabulary (AABC)
Const Afr States... Constitutions of African States [*A publication*] (DLA)
CONSTAL..... Constitutional [*Legal shorthand*] (LWAP)
Const Amend... Amendment to the Constitution (DLA)
Constan Copti... Constantinus Coptius [*Flourished, 16th century*] [*Authority cited in pre-1607 legal work*] (DSA)
Const & Parliam Inf... Constitutional and Parliamentary Information [*A publication*] (DLA)
Constan Roger... Constantius Rogerius [*Flourished, 16th century*] [*Authority cited in pre-1607 legal work*] (DSA)
CONSTANT... Constantinople [*Later, Istanbul*] [*Turkey*] (DSUE)
Constant ...... De Constantia Sapientis [*of Seneca the Younger*] [*Classical studies*] (OCD)
Con Stat ...... Consolidated Statutes [*A publication*] (DLA)
Const Bott.... Const's Edition of Bott's Poor Law Cases [*A publication*] (DLA)
Const Commentary... Constitutional Commentary [*A publication*] (DLA)
Const Dep & Sp Sov... Constitutions of Dependencies and Special Sovereignties [*A publication*] (DLA)
CONSTELEC... Construction Electrician [*Navy rating*] (DNAB)
ConstEng ..... Construction Engineering (DD)
CONSTENGR... Construction Engineer
Const Hist.... Hallam's Constitutional History of England [*A publication*] (DLA)
CONSTI........ Constipated (DSUE)
CONSTIT...... Constituency
constit .... Constituent (DAVI)
constit .... Constitution [*or Constitutional*] [*Medicine*] (DAVI)
CONSTL ...... Constitutional
ConstMgmt... Construction Management (DD)
CONSTN....... Constitution
Const Nations... Constitutions of Nations [*A publication*] (DLA)
Const NS ..... Constitutional Reports, New Series, Printed by Mills [*South Carolina*] [*A publication*] (DLA)
CONSTOCS... Contingency Support Stocks [*Military*] (NVT)
CONSTON .... Constitution (ROG)
Const Oth.... Constitutiones Othoni [*At the end of Lyndewood's Provinciale*] [*A publication*] (DLA)
CONSTR....... Constraint (KSC)
CONSTR....... Construction
constr .... Construction (VRA)
Constr .... Construction (AAGC)
CONSTR....... Constructor
Constr .... Construct State (BJA)
CONSTR....... Construe (ROG)
Constr Briefings... Construction Briefings [*A publication*] (AAGC)
CONSTRCT... Constructing
CONSTRCTN... Construction
Const Rep.... Constitutional Reports [*South Carolina*] [*A publication*] (DLA)
Const Rev.... Constitutional Review [*A publication*] (DLA)
Constr Law... Construction Lawyer [*ABA*] [*A publication*] (AAGC)
CONSTRN .... Construction
CONSTRON... Construction (ROG)
Const RSC ... Constitutional Reports, Printed by Treadway [*South Carolina*] [*A publication*] (DLA)
CONSTRUCTS... Control Data Structural System (DNAB)
Const SC...... Constitutional Reports, Printed by Treadway [*South Carolina*] [*A publication*] (DLA)
Const SCNS... Constitutional Reports, New Series, Printed by Mills [*South Carolina*] [*A publication*] (DLA)
Const US ..... Constitution of the United States [*A publication*] (DLA)
Const US Amend... Amendment to the Constitution of the United States (DLA)
CONSUB ...... Continental Shelf Submersible [*Undersea exploration vehicle*] (MCD)
CONSUB ...... Continuous Submarine Duty Incentive Pay (DNAB)
Consuet Feud... Consuetudines Feudorum [*The Book of Feuds*] [*Latin A publication*] (DLA)
CONSUL .... Consular Corps College and International Consular Academy (EA)
CONSUL....... Control Subroutine Language [*Computer science*] (IEEE)
Consulier..... Consulier Engineering [*Associated Press*] (SAG)
Consulr........ Consulier Engineering, Inc. [*Associated Press*] (SAG)
CONSULT..... Community, Industry, Accounting and Legal Consultants [*Database*] [*Australia*]
CONSULT..... Consultant
consult........ Consultant [*Medicine*] (DMAA)
CONSULTN... Consultation
CONSUM...... Consumer
Consumer Cred Guide (CCH)... Consumer Credit Guide (Commerce Clearing House) [*A publication*] (DLA)
Consumer Prod Safety Guide (CCH)... Consumer Product Safety Guide (Commerce Clearing House) [*A publication*] (DLA)
CONSUMP ... Consumption (ROG)
Con Sur ...... Connolly's New York Surrogate Reports [*A publication*] (DLA)
Consv........... Conservatorship (DLA)
CONSV......... Conservatory
CONSV......... Conserve (AABC)
ConsvSv....... Conservative Savings Corp. [*Associated Press*] (SAG)
CONT .... Contact (KSC)
CONT .... Contact
CONT .... Container (MCD)
CONT .... Containing
cont .... Containing (WDMC)
CONT .... Contamination Technology (SSD)

CONT .... Contano [*Parts so marked to rest*] [*Music*]
CONT .... Contemporary (ADA)
cont .... Contemporary (VRA)
CONT .... Contents
cont .... Contents (WDMC)
cont .... Contents (ODBW)
CONT .... Contested
CONT .... Continent
Cont.......... Continental
CONT .... Continental Airlines (MHDB)
CONT .... Continental Waste Industries [*NASDAQ symbol*] (SAG)
CONT .... Contingency (MCD)
CONT .... Continue [*or Continuing*] (AFM)
cont .... Continue[*d*] (WDMC)
cont .... Continued (ODBW)
CONT .... Continuentur [*Continue*] [*Pharmacy*] (ROG)
CONT .... Continuo [*Thorough Bass*] [*Music*]
CONT .... Continuous [*or Continuously*] (DAVI)
Cont.......... Continuum [*A publication*]
CONT .... Contra [*Against*] [*Latin*]
CONT .... Contract
cont .... Contract (WDMC)
Cont.......... Contract (AAGC)
cont .... Contract (ODBW)
cont .... Contracting (WDMC)
CONT .... Contrary (WGA)
CONT .... Control (MSA)
cont .... Control (WDMC)
CONT .... Controller (KSC)
cont .... Controller (DD)
CONT .... Contusus [*Bruised*] [*Medicine*]
Cont.......... De Vita Contemplativa [*Philo*] (BJA)
CONTA .... Conference on Conceptual and Terminological Analysis in the Social Sciences [*1981*]
CONTA .... Control Assembly
CONTAC....... Conference on the Atlantic Community (EA)
CONTAC....... Continuous Action [*Acronym is brand of decongestant capsule*]
CONTAC....... Coordinated Navy Total Acquisition Control [*System*]
CONTACA..... Conventional Tactical Air Model (MCD)
CONTACT.... Conformal Tactical Array (MCD)
CONTAD...... Concealed Target Detection (MCD)
contag .... Contagion [*Medicine*] (DMAA)
CONTAG....... Contagious
CONT (AH)... Continent, Antwerp-Hamburg Range [*Shipping*] (DS)
CONTAM...... Committee on Nationwide Television Audience Measurement (NTCM)
CONTAM...... Contaminated (KSC)
Cont App Dec (CCH)... Contract Appeals Decisions (Commerce Clearing House) [*A publication*] (DLA)
CONTAX....... Consumers and Taxpayers
CONTB........ Continuous Beam [*Camutek*] [*Software package*] (NCC)
CONTBD....... Contraband
CONTBG....... Contributing (ADA)
CONT (BH)... Continent, Bordeaux-Hamburg Range [*Shipping*] (DS)
CONTBN...... Contribution (WGA)
CONT BON MOR... Contra Bonos Mores [*Contrary to Good Manners*] [*Latin*]
CONTBR....... Contributor (WGA)
ContCan....... Continental Can Co., Inc. [*Associated Press*] (SAG)
Cont Cas Fed... Contract Cases, Federal [*A publication*] (DLA)
CONTCE....... Continuance
CONTD........ Contained
CONTD......... Continued
contd......... Continued (WDMC)
ContDev...... Control Devices, Inc. [*Associated Press*] (SAG)
CONTDVD ... Continental Divide (FAAC)
ConTech ...... Consolidated Technology [*Commercial firm Associated Press*] (SAG)
Cont Ed ...... Contemporary Education [*A publication*] (BRI)
Cont El........ Controverted Elections Judges [*England*] (DLA)
Cont Elect Case... Contested Election Cases [*United States*] [*A publication*] (DLA)
CONTEM ..... Contemplate (AABC)
CONTEMP .... Contemporary
CONTEMP .... Contemporary
CON TENA .. Con Tenerezza [*With Tenderness*] [*Music*] (ROG)
CONTER........ Contere [*Rub Together*] [*Pharmacy*]
CONTG........ Containing
CONTG........ Contingency (KSC)
CONTH........ Continue to Hold [*Aviation*] (FAAC)
CONT (HH)... Continent, Havre-Hamburg Range [*Shipping*] (DS)
CONTHP...... Continental Horsepower (IAA)
CONTIC....... CONARC [*Continental Army Command*] Intelligence Center [*Obsolete*] (AABC)
Contifin........ Contifinancial Corp. [*Associated Press*] (SAG)
CONTIG........ Contiguous (NASA)
CONTIN........ Continental (ROG)
CONTIN........ Continuance [*Legal term*] (DLA)
contin .... Continue (DAVI)
CONTIN........ Continuetur [*Let It Be Continued*] [*Pharmacy*]
Contin........ Continuum Co. [*Associated Press*] (SAG)
CONTIND ..... Continued (ROG)
CONTIN REM... Continuetur Remedium [*Let the Medicine Be Continued*] [*Pharmacy*] (ROG)
Continucre... Continucare [*Associated Press*] (SAG)
CONTL .... Continental (AABC)
CONTL .... Control
Cont L Rev... Contemporary Law Review [*India*] [*A publication*] (DLA)
ContMed ...... Contour Medical, Inc. [*Associated Press*] (SAG)

Cont Mgmt...	Contract Management [*NCMA*] [*A publication*] (AAGC)
ContMtl.......	Continental Materials Corp. [*Associated Press*] (SAG)
CONTN.........	Contain (ROG)
CONTN.........	Continuation
CONTNG	Continuing
CONTNR	Container
CONTNR	Container (KSC)
CONTNS......	Continuous
CONTNTL.....	Continental
Cont of Banking (P-H)...	Control of Banking (Prentice-Hall) [*A publication*] (DLA)
Cont Pac.....	Contemporary Pacific [*A publication*] (BRI)
CONTR.........	Container (KSC)
CONTR.........	Contra [*Against*] [*Latin*] (ROG)
CONTR.........	Contract [*or Contractor*] (AFM)
CONTR.........	Contraction (WGA)
CONTR.........	Contractor
CONTR.........	Contradiction (ADA)
CONTR.........	Contralto [*Music*]
CONTR.........	Contrary
CONTR.........	Contrast
CONTR.........	Contribution
CONTR.........	Control
CONTRA......	Contraindicated [*Medicine*]
CONTRA......	Contrario [*Opponent or Enemy*] [*Spanish*]
CONTRAIL...	Condensation Trail [*in the air*]
contralat	Contralateral [*Anatomy*] (MAE)
CONTRAN ...	Control Translator [*Honeywell, Inc.*] [*Computer science*]
CONTRANS...	Conceptual Thought, Random Net Simulation (MUGU)
Contr App Dec...	Contract Appeals Decisions [*CCH*] [*A publication*] (AAGC)
CONTRAST...	Condensed Strike Data Transmission System (MCD)
CONTR BON MOR...	Contra Bonos Mores [*Contrary to Good Manners*] [*Latin*] (ROG)
CONTRBTN...	Contribution
ContrCh........	Control Chief Holdings [*Associated Press*] (SAG)
CONTREAT...	Continue Treatment at Naval Hospital or Medical Facility Indicated
CONT REM...	Continuentur Remedia [*Continue the Medicines*] [*Pharmacy*]
CONTREQS...	Contingency Transportation Requirements System (MCD)
CONTRIB.....	Contribution (MSA)
contrib........	Contribution (WDMC)
contrib........	Contributor [*Publishing*] (WDMC)
CONTRIBOR...	Contributor (ROG)
contrit........	Contritus [*Broken, ground*] [*Pharmacy*] (DAVI)
CONTRL.......	Control (KSC)
CONTRLLD...	Controlled
CONTRLTR...	Contract Letter [*DLA*] (AAGC)
CONTRO	Contracting Officer [*Also, CO, KO*] (KSC)
CONTROL ...	Controller [*Computer hardware*] (NITA)
CONTROR...	Contractor (ROG)
Controv.......	Controversiae [*of Seneca the Elder*] [*Classical studies*] (OCD)
CONTROV ...	Controversy (ROG)
CONTRTN	Concentration
CONTRX......	Contraction (MEDA)
CONTRY......	Contrary (ROG)
CONTS........	Contains (ROG)
CONT/S........	Continuous Stationery [*Commercial firm*] [*British*] (DGA)
CONTT	Contract [*Legal term*]
CONTU........	National Commission on New Technological Uses of Copyrighted Works [*Terminated, 1978*] [*Library of Congress*]
CONTUND	Contundere [*To Be Bruised, Pounded*] [*Pharmacy*] (ROG)
CONTUS......	Contusus [*Bruised*] [*Medicine*]
ContW........	Continental Waste Industries [*Associated Press*] (SAG)
CONTW........	Continuous Window
CONTWR......	Conning Tower [*Naval architecture*]
ContWst.......	Continental Waste Industries [*Associated Press*] (SAG)
conu............	Conventual (TOCD)
CoNu............	Nucla Public Library, Nucla, CO [*Library symbol Library of Congress*] (LCLS)
CONUBS	Compact Nuclear Brayton System
CONUS........	Contiguous United States
CONUS........	Continental United States
Conus	Continental U.S. [*Television news company*] [*St. Paul, MN*] (WDMC)
CONUSA	CONUS [*Continental United States*] Army (MCD)
CONUSAMDW...	Continental United States and the Military District of Washington [*Refers to the numbered armies in that area*] (AABC)
CONUS INTEL...	Continental United States Intelligence [*Domestic intelligence project*] [*Army*]
CONUS OTH...	Continental United States Over-the-Horizon [*RADAR system*]
CONUS OTH-B...	Continental United States Over-the-Horizon-Backscatter [*RADAR system*]
conv............	Convalescence [*Medicine*] (DAVI)
CONV	Convalescent [*Medicine*] (AFM)
Conv	Convector (DAC)
CONV	Convenience
CONV	Convenient
CONV	Convent
CONV	Convention [*or Conventional*]
CONV	Convergence (IAA)
CONV	Conversation
CONV	Conversion
CONV	Converted (DCTA)
CONV	Converter (KSC)
CONV	Convertible
CONV	Conveyance [*Transportation*] (DCTA)
Conv	Conveyancer [*or Conveyancing*] [*Legal term*] (DLA)
CONV	Convict

CONV	Convocation
CONV	Convoy (NVT)
CONVAIR	Consolidated-Vultee Aircraft Corp. [*Later, General Dynamics Corp.*]
CONVAL	Convalescent [*Medicine*] (ROG)
CONVAL	Convalescent
CONVALESC...	Convalescent [*Medicine*] (ROG)
CONVATE	Connection Reactivation
CONVCE	Conveyance
CONVD........	Conveyed (ROG)
CONVDD	Converted Destroyer
CONVEL	Constant Velocity (SAA)
CONVEN	Convenience
converg........	Convergence [*Medicine*] (DMAA)
CONVERS ...	Connection Conversion
CONVERS ...	Conversation (ROG)
CONVERS ...	Conversazione [*Conversation*] [*Italian*] (ROG)
Converse	Converse, Inc. [*Associated Press*] (SAG)
Converse C...	Converse College (GAGS)
CONVERSIONEX...	Contact Conversion Exercise [*Military*] (NVT)
CONVERSN...	Conversion (ROG)
Conv Est	Convention of the Estates of Scotland [*A publication*] (DLA)
Convex.........	Convex Computer [*Associated Press*] (SAG)
CONVEX	Convoy Exercise [*Navy*] (NVT)
Convey.........	Conveyancer [*Legal term*] (DLA)
Conv FJ	European Community Convention on the Jurisdiction of the Courts and Enforcement of Judgments in Civil and Commercial Matters [*27 Sept. 1968*] (DLA)
CONVG........	Convergence (MSA)
ConvHld	Convertible Holdings [*Associated Press*] (SAG)
Conv Hosp ...	Convalescent Hospital (DAVI)
CON-VID	Concerned Broadcasters Using Inter-City Video Transmission Facilities (EA)
CONVL........	Conventional (AFM)
CONVN........	Convection (MSA)
CONVN........	Convenient (AABC)
CONVNT	Convenient
CONVO	Coalition of National Voluntary Organizations (DICI)
CONVOC	Convocation
CONVOLV JAP...	Convolvulus Jalapa [*Jalap Plant*] [*Pharmacology*] (ROG)
CONVR........	Convector (MSA)
Conv Rev	Conveyancing Review [*1957-63*] [*Scotland*] [*A publication*] (DLA)
CONVRS	Converse
CONVRTBL...	Convertible
CONVRTR ...	Converter
Conv Sept Sap...	Convivium Septem Sapientium [*of Plutarch*] [*Classical studies*] (OCD)
conv strab ...	Convergent Strabismus [*Ophthalmology*] (DAVI)
CONVT	Convenient (ROG)
ConvT	Conversion Technologies International, Inc. [*Associated Press*] (SAG)
CONVT	Convert (AABC)
ConvTch........	Conversion Technologies International, Inc. [*Associated Press*] (SAG)
CONVWEPS LOADEX...	Conventional Weapons Loading Exercise [*Navy*] (ANA)
Conv YB......	Conveyancers' Year Book [*1940-51*] [*A publication*] (DLA)
CONVYR	Conveyor
CONW.........	Consumers Water [*NASDAQ symbol*] (TTSB)
CONW.........	Consumers Water Co. [*NASDAQ symbol*] (SAG)
ConWat........	Consumers Water Co. [*Associated Press*] (SAG)
ConWPac......	Consolidated Western & Pacific Resources [*Associated Press*] (SAG)
Conwst........	Conwest Exploration Company Ltd. [*Associated Press*] (SAG)
CONZINE......	Convention Magazine [*Generic term for a publication covering science-fiction fans' conventions*]
COO	Cessna Owners Organization (EA)
COO	Chicago Operations Office [*Energy Research and Development Administration*]
COO	Chief of Outpost [*CIA officer in charge of a field office*]
COO	Chief Operating Officer
COO	Chief Ordnance Officer
COO	College of Optometry of Ontario
COO	Colonial Oil & Gas Ltd. [*Toronto Stock Exchange symbol*]
COO	Committee on Organization [*American Library Association*]
COO	Concept of Operations (MCD)
COO	Contract on Order (AFIT)
COO	Cooney Tunnel [*Armidale*] [*Australia Seismograph station code, US Geological Survey*] (SEIS)
COO	[*The*] Cooper Companies, Inc. [*NYSE symbol*] (SPSG)
COO	Cornell University, Ithaca, NY [*OCLC symbol*] (OCLC)
COO	Corporate Airlink [*Canada*] [*FAA designator*] (FAAC)
COO	Cost-of-Ownership
COO	Cotonou [*Benin*] [*Airport symbol*] (OAG)
COO	Cotonou [*Dahomey*] [*Airport symbol*] (AD)
COO	Council of Oriental Organizations
COO	Country of Origin [*International trade*] (DCTA)
COO	Covington, TN [*Location identifier FAA*] (FAAL)
Coo Agr T ...	Cooke. Agricultural Tenancies [*3rd ed.*] [*1882*] [*A publication*] (DLA)
COOAL	Coordinated Activity List [*Navy*] (NVT)
Coo & Al......	Cooke and Alcock's Irish King's Bench Reports [*1833-34*] [*A publication*] (DLA)
Coo & H Tr...	Cooke and Harwood's Charitable Trusts Acts [*A publication*] (DLA)
COOBA........	Chief Operating Officer of Business Affairs [*Proposed alternative to the hiring of a baseball commissioner*]
Coo Bankr....	Cooke's Bankrupt Laws [*A publication*] (DLA)
COOBSRON...	Commanding Officer, Observation Squadron
COOC	Calgary Olympic Organizing Committee [*Calgary, AB*] (EAIO)
CoOc............	Oak Creek Public Library, Oak Creek, CO [*Library symbol Library of Congress*] (LCLS)

Coo Cop ...... Cooke's Enfranchisement of Copyholds [2nd ed.] [1853] [A publication] (DLA)
COOD .... Chronic Obstructive Outflow Disease [Medicine]
Coo Def .... Cooke's Law of Defamation [A publication] (DLA)
Coode Leg Exp ... Coode's Legislative Expression [A publication] (DLA)
Coode Wr L ... Coode on the Written Law [A publication] (DLA)
Coo IA .... Cooke's Inclosure Acts [A publication] (DLA)
COOK .... Calif Culinary Academy [NASDAQ symbol] (TTSB)
COOK .... California Culinary Academy, Inc. [NASDAQ symbol] (SAG)
COOK .... Cookham [England]
COOK .... Cook Transit R. R. [AAR code]
Cook Adm .... Cooke's Admiralty Cases [Quebec] [A publication] (DLA)
Cook Adm .... Cook's Vice-Admiralty Reports [Canada] [A publication] (DLA)
Cook Corp .... Cook on Corporations [A publication] (DLA)
Cooke .... Cases under Sugden's Act [1838] [England] [A publication] (DLA)
Cooke .... Cooke. Act Book of the Ecclesiastical Court of Whalley [A publication] (DLA)
Cooke .... Cooke's Cases of Practice, English Common Pleas [A publication] (DLA)
Cooke .... Cooke's Tennessee Reports [A publication] (DLA)
Cooke Agr Hold ... Cooke on the Agricultural Holdings Act [A publication] (DLA)
Cooke Agr T ... Cooke. Agricultural Tenancies [3rd ed.] [A publication] (DLA)
Cooke & A ... Cooke and Alcock's Reports [Ireland] [A publication] (DLA)
Cooke & Al ... Cooke and Alcock's Reports [Ireland] [A publication] (DLA)
Cooke & Alc ... Cooke and Alcock's Reports [Ireland] [A publication] (DLA)
Cooke & Al (Ir) ... Cooke and Alcock's Irish King's Bench Reports [1833-34] [A publication] (DLA)
Cooke & H Ch Tr ... Cooke and Harwood's Charitable Trusts Acts [A publication] (DLA)
Cooke BL ..... Cooke's Bankrupt Laws [A publication] (DLA)
Cooke Cop ... Cooke's Enfranchisement of Copyholds [2nd ed.] [1853] [A publication] (DLA)
Cooke CP ..... Cooke's English Common Pleas Reports [1706-47] [A publication] (DLA)
Cooke Def .... Cooke's Law of Defamation [A publication] (DLA)
Cooke (Eng) ... Cooke's Cases of Practice [125 English Reprint] [A publication] (DLA)
Cooke High ... Cooke's New York Highway Laws [A publication] (DLA)
Cooke IA ...... Cooke's Inclosure Acts [A publication] (DLA)
Cooke Incl Acts ... Cooke's Inclosure Acts [A publication] (DLA)
Cooke Ins .... Cooke on Life Insurance [A publication] (DLA)
Cooke Pr Cas ... Cooke's Practice Reports, English Common Pleas [A publication] (DLA)
Cooke Pr Reg ... Cooke's Practical Register of the Common Pleas [A publication] (DLA)
Cooker .... Cooker Restaurant, Inc. [Associated Press] (SAG)
Cooke's Rep ... Cooke's Tennessee Reports [A publication] (DLA)
Cooke (Tenn) ... Cooke's Tennessee Reports [A publication] (DLA)
COOKI .... Coordinated Keysort Index (ADA)
Cook's Pen Code ... Cook's Penal Code [New York] [A publication] (DLA)
Cook Stock Stockh & Corp Law ... Cook on Stock, Stockholders, and General Corporation Law [A publication] (DLA)
Cook V Adm ... Cook's Vice-Admiralty Reports [Canada A publication] (DLA)
Cook Vice-Adm ... Cook's Vice-Admiralty Reports [Canada A publication] (DLA)
COOL .... Campus Outreach Opportunity League (EA)
COOL .... Checkout-Oriented Language [Computer science] (IEEE)
COOL .... Chorus Object-Oriented Layer [Computer science]
COOL .... Conservation OnLine [Database collection] [Internet]
COOL .... Control-Oriented Language [Computer science] (IEEE)
COOL .... Coolant (MSA)
COOL .... Cooling
COOL .... Cooper Development Co. [NASDAQ symbol] (NQ)
Cool Black ... Cooley's Edition of Blackstone's Commentaries [A publication] (DLA)
Cool Con Law ... Cooley's Constitutional Law [A publication] (DLA)
Cool Con Lim ... Cooley's Constitutional Limitations [A publication] (DLA)
Cooley .... Cooley's Reports [5-12 Michigan] [A publication] (DLA)
Cooley Bl Comm ... Cooley's Edition of Blackstone's Commentaries [A publication] (DLA)
Cooley Const Law ... Cooley's Constitutional Law [A publication] (DLA)
Cooley Const Lim ... Cooley on Constitutional Limitations [A publication] (DLA)
Cooley Const Limit ... Cooley on Constitutional Limitations [A publication] (DLA)
Cooley L Rev ... Cooley Law Review [A publication] (DLA)
Cooley Tax ... Cooley on Taxation [A publication] (DLA)
Cooley Tax'n ... Cooley on Taxation [A publication] (DLA)
COOLG .... Cooling
Cool Mich Dig ... Cooley's Michigan Digest [A publication] (DLA)
COOLS .... Concealed Original Optical Locating System (PDAA)
Cool Tax ...... Cooley on Taxation [A publication] (DLA)
Cool Torts ... Cooley on Torts [A publication] (DLA)
Coo Mort ..... Coote on Mortgages [A publication] (DLA)
Co on Courts ... Coke on Courts [or Fourth Institute] [England] [A publication] (DLA)
COOP .... Commander's Organization Orientation Program [Military] (INF)
COOP .... Communities Organization of People
COOP .... Contingency of Operations Planning (MCD)
COOP .... Continuity of Operations Plan [Army]
COOP .... Conventional Old Oil Prices
COOp .... Cooperate
COOP .... Cooperativa
COOP .... Cooperative (AABC)
co-op .... Cooperative Advertising (WDMC)
COOP .... Cooperative Bankshares [NASDAQ symbol] (SAG)
COOP .... Cooperative Degree Program [Army] (INF)
co-op .... Cooperative Program (WDMC)
Coop .... Cooper's Reports [21-24 Florida] [A publication] (DLA)

Coop .... Cooper's Tennessee Chancery Reports [A publication] (DLA)
COOP .... Craft of Opportunity Program [Minesweeper] (DOMA)
COOP .... Customer On-Line Order Processing System
CoOpBk .... Co-Operative Bank of Concord [Associated Press] (SAG)
CoopBk .... Cooperative Bankshares [Associated Press] (SAG)
Coop Ca .... Cooper Cameron Corp. [Associated Press] (SAG)
Coop C & PR ... Cooper's Chancery and Practice Reporter [Upper Canada] [A publication] (DLA)
Coop Ch .... Cooper's Tennessee Chancery Reports [A publication] (DLA)
CoopChy ...... Cooper & Chyan Technology, Inc. [Associated Press] (SAG)
Coop Chy ..... Tennessee Chancery Reports (Cooper) [A publication] (DLA)
CoopCo .... [The] Cooper Companies, Inc. [Associated Press] (SAG)
COOPCOMM ... Communications Facilities in Support of DA [Department of the Army] Continuity of Operations Plan (AABC)
Coop Corp ... Cooperative Corporations (DLA)
Co-Op Dig ... Co-Operative Digest, United States Reports [A publication] (DLA)
Coop Eq Dig ... Cooper's Equity Digest [A publication] (DLA)
Coop Eq Pl ... Cooper's Equity Pleading [A publication] (DLA)
Cooper .... Cooper Industries, Inc. [Formerly, Cooper-Bessemer Corp.] [Associated Press] (SAG)
Cooper .... Cooper's Florida Reports [21-24 Florida] [A publication] (DLA)
Cooper .... Cooper's Tennessee Chancery Reports [A publication] (DLA)
Cooper .... Upper Canada Chancery Chambers Reports [1857-72] [A publication] (DLA)
Cooper Ch ... Cooper's Tennessee Chancery Reports [A publication] (DLA)
Cooper Just Inst ... Cooper's Institutes of Justinian [A publication] (DLA)
COOPG .... Cooperage [Freight]
Coop Inst ..... Cooper's Institutes of Justinian [A publication] (DLA)
COOP-JCS ..... Continuity of Operations Plan of the Joint Chiefs of Staff
Coop Judg ... Cooper's Judgment [A publication] (DLA)
COOPLAN ... Continuity of Operations Plan [Navy]
COOPLEG ..... Co-Operative Legislation [ILO] [United Nations Information service or system] (DUND)
Coop Lib ...... Cooper's Law of Libel [A publication] (DLA)
Coop Med Jur ... Cooper's Medical Jurisprudence [A publication] (DLA)
CooprD .... Cooper Development Co. [Associated Press] (SAG)
Coop Rec ...... Cooper's Public Records of Great Britain [A publication] (DLA)
CooprL .... Cooper Life Sciences, Inc. [Associated Press] (SAG)
CooprTr .... Cooper Tire & Rubber Co. [Associated Press] (SAG)
COOPRTV ...... Cooperative
CO-OPS .... Carbon Dioxide Observational Platform System [NASA]
Coop Sel EC ... Cooper's Select Early Cases [Scotland] [A publication] (DLA)
Coop Ten Chy ... Cooper's Tennessee Chancery Reports [A publication] (DLA)
Coop Tenn Ch ... Cooper's Tennessee Chancery Reports [A publication] (DLA)
COOR .... Coordinate
COORAUTH ... Coordinating Authority (NATG)
COORD .... Coordinant
COORD .... Coordinate [or Coordination] (AFM)
CO-ORD .... Coordination [Channel] [Electronics] (ECII)
CoOrd .... Ordway Public Library, Ordway, CO [Library symbol Library of Congress] (LCLS)
COORDN ...... Coordination
COORDNTR ... Coordinator
COORI .... Cost-of-Ownership Reduction Investment (MCD)
COORS .... Communications Outage Reporting System
COORS .... Communications Outage Restoral Section [ADC]
Coors .... Coors [Adolph] Co. [Associated Press] (SAG)
COOS .... Chemical Orbit-to-Orbit Shuttle [NASA]
CoOs .... Olney Springs Public Library, Olney Springs, CO [Library symbol Library of Congress] (LCLS)
COOT .... Oakland Tribune, Oakland, CA [Library symbol Library of Congress] (LCLS)
CoOt .... Otis Public Library, Otis, CO [Library symbol Library of Congress] (LCLS)
Coote .... Coote on Mortgages [A publication] (DLA)
Coote Adm ... Coote's Admiralty Practice [A publication] (DLA)
Coote & Tr Pr Pr ... Coote. Practice of the Court of Probate, Edited by Tristram [A publication] (DLA)
Coote Ecc Pr ... Coote's Ecclesiastical Court Practice [A publication] (DLA)
Coote L & T ... Coote's Law of Landlord and Tenant [A publication] (DLA)
Coote Mor ... Coote on Mortgages [A publication] (DLA)
Coote Pro Pr ... Coote. Practice of the Court of Probate [9th ed.] [1883] [A publication] (DLA)
CoOu .... Ouray Public Library, Ouray, CO [Library symbol Library of Congress] (LCLS)
CoOv .... Ovid Public Library, Ovid, CO [Library symbol Library of Congress] (LCLS)
COP .... Calculator-Oriented Processor (MHDB)
COP .... Cam-Operated Plunger
COP .... Canada Olympic Park [Calgary, AB]
COP .... Canceled or Postponed
COP .... Capability Objective Package (MCD)
COP .... Capillary Osmotic Pressure [Physiology]
COP .... Capsule Observation Panel [Aerospace]
COP .... Career Opportunities Program [Office of Education] (EA)
COP .... Career Orientation Program [LIMRA]
COP .... Catalyst Oriented Packing [Chemical engineering]
COP .... Celescope Optical Package (KSC)
COP .... Central Operator Panel (IAA)
COP .... Central Ordering Point (IAA)
COP .... Certificate of Participation
COP .... Certificate of Posting [Post Office receipt] [British]
COP .... Change of Plaster [Medicine]
COP .... Changeover Panel (NATG)
COP .... Chief of Police

COP	....	Cicatricial Ocular Pemphigoid [*Ophthalmology*] (DAVI)
COP	....	City of Prineville Railway [*AAR code*]
COP	....	Coastal Ocean Program [*National Oceanic and Atmospheric Administration*] (USDC)
COP	....	Coast-Out Point (NVT)
COP	....	Coat Protein
COP	....	Coaxial Output Printer (IAA)
COP	....	Code of Practice [*Telecommunications*] (TEL)
COP	....	Coefficient of Performance
COP	....	Coherent Optical Processor
COP	....	Colloidal Osmotic Pressure [*Analytical biochemistry*]
COP	....	Colorado School of Mines, Golden, CO [*OCLC symbol*] (OCLC)
COP	....	Combat Organization Potential [*DoD*]
COP	....	Combat Outpost
COP	....	Combined Operations Personnel [*Navy British*]
COP	....	Combined Opposition Parties [*Politics*]
COP	....	Combined Opposition Party [*Pakistan*] [*Political party*] (FEA)
COP	....	Commanding Officer's Punishment (DNAB)
COP	....	Command Objective Plan [*Air Force*]
COP	....	Command Observation Post (AABC)
COP	....	Command Operating Program [*Army*] (AABC)
COP	....	Commissary Operating Program [*Air Force*] (AFM)
COP	....	Commission on Practice [*American Occupational Therapy Association*]
COP	....	Committee on Propagation (SAA)
COP	....	Common On-Line Package [*Fujitsu Ltd.*] [*Japan*]
COP	....	Communication Output Printer
COP	....	Communications On-Line Processor
COP	....	Community-Oriented Police
COP	....	Compact Periscope (MCD)
COP	....	Computerization of PAYE [*Pay as You Earn*] Taxation [*Inland Revenue*] [*British*]
COP	....	Computer Operating Properly
COP	....	Computer Optimization Package [*or Program*] [*General Electric Co.*]
COP	....	Computer Owner Protection [*IDX Technologies, Inc.*] (PCM)
COP	....	Concept Outline Plan (DOMA)
COP	....	Conditions of Participation [*Department of Health and Human Services*] (GFGA)
COP	....	Conference of the Parties [*Governments which have ratified UN climate change convention of 1992*]
COP	....	Conjugable Oxidation Product [*Fuel technology*]
COP	....	Consolidated Products, Inc. [*NYSE symbol*] (SAG)
COP	....	Consolidated Rio Plata Resources [*Vancouver Stock Exchange symbol*]
COP	....	Constable on Patrol
COP	....	Constant Offset Profile [*Seismology*]
COP	....	Constrained Optimization Procedure (MCD)
COPAS	....	Contingency Operations Plan (MCD)
COP	....	Continuation of Pay (DNAB)
COP	....	Continuity of Operations Plan [*Military*]
COP	....	Continuous Operation Program [*Computer science*] (MDG)
COP	....	Control of Operation Programs
COP	....	Control-Oriented Processor [*Computer science*] (PDAA)
COP	....	Co-Orbiting Platform (SSD)
Cop	....	Copacabana [*Record label*] [*Brazil*]
COP	....	Copenhagen [*Denmark*] [*Later, RSV*] [*Geomagnetic observatory code*]
COP	....	Copernicus (ROG)
COP	....	Copley Properties [*AMEX symbol*] (TTSB)
COP	....	Copley Properties, Inc. [*AMEX symbol*] (SPSG)
COP	....	Copper [*Chemical symbol is Cu*] (MSA)
COP	....	Copper
COP	....	Copper State Air Service, Inc. [*FAA designator*] (FAAC)
cop	....	Coptic [*MARC language code Library of Congress*] (LCCP)
COP	....	Coptic
COP	....	Copulative
COP	....	Copy (WGA)
COP	....	Copying of Parts (ADA)
cop	....	Copyright (WDMC)
COP	....	Copyrighted
COP	....	Costal Ocean Program [*Marine science*] (OSRA)
COP	....	Cost Operating Profits [*Accounting*]
COP	....	Crisis-Oriented Program
COP	....	Crude Oil Production [*Database*] [*Petroleum Intelligence Weekly*] [*Information service or system*] (CRD)
COP	....	Current Operating Procedure (MCD)
COP	....	Customer Order Processing (BUR)
COP	....	Customer-Orienting Program [*Computer science*]
COP	....	Customer-Owned Property
COP	....	Custom of the Port [*Shipping*]
COP	....	Cyclophosphamide, Oncovin [*Vincristine*], Prednisone [*Also, CVP*] [*Antineoplastic drug regimen*]
CoP	....	Pueblo Regional Library, Pueblo, CO [*Library symbol Library of Congress*] (LCLS)
COPA	....	Canadian Office Products Association
COPA	....	Canadian Owners and Pilots Association
COPA	....	Center for Overseas Program Analysis [*Department of State*]
COPA	....	Center Overage Pending Assignment (MCD)
COPA	....	Comite des Organisations Professionnelles Agricoles de la CEE [*Committee of Professional Agricultural Organizations in the EEC*]
COPA	....	Compania Panamena de Aviacion, SA [*Panamanian airline*]
COPA	....	Conditional Open Probability Analysis [*Mathematics*]
COPA	....	Control of Pollution Act [*1974*] [*British*] (DCTA)
Copa	....	Copacabana [*Record label*] [*Brazil*]

COPA	....	Corporate Purchasing Agreements (MCD)
COPA	....	Council on Postsecondary Accreditation (EA)
COPA	....	Cross-Organizational Program Analysis [*Department of Commerce*] (GFGA)
COPA	....	Cyclophosphamide, Oncovin [*Vincristine*], Prednisone, Adriamycin [*Antineoplastic drug regimen*]
COPAAC	......	Continuity of Operations, Alaskan Air Command
COPA-BLEO	......	Cyclophosphamide, Oncovin [*Vincristine*], Prednisone, Adriamycin, Bleomycin [*Antineoplastic drug regimen*]
COPAC	......	CCNU [*Lomustine*], Oncovin , Prednisone, Adriamycin, Cyclophosphamide [*Vincristine*] [*Antineoplastic drug regimen*]
COPAC	......	Comite Commun pour la Promotion de l'Aide aux Cooperatives [*Joint Committee for the Promotion of Aid to Cooperatives*] [*UN Food and Agriculture Organization*]
COPAC	......	Committee on Pollution Abatement and Control [*National Research Council*] (PDAA)
COPAC	......	Committee on Publications and Communications [*International Council of Scientific Unions*]
COPAC	......	Continuous Operation Production Allocation and Control [*Computer science*]
COPACE	......	Comite des Peches pour l'Atlantique Centre-Est [*Committee for the Eastern Central Atlantic Fisheries - CECAF*] [*Senegal*] (MSC)
COPAD	......	Cyclophosphamide, Oncovin [*Vincristine*], Prednisone, Doxorubicin [*Adriamycin*] [*Antineoplastic drug regimen*]
COPADOCI	......	Committee on Principals and Directors of Central Institutions (AIE)
COPAFS	......	Council of Professional Associations on Federal Statistics (EA)
COPAG	......	Collision Prevention Advisory Group [*US*]
COPAL	......	Cocoa Producers' Alliance
CO PAL	......	Counts Palatine [*Rulers of historical region now part of Germany*]
CoPal	......	Palisade Public Library, Palisade, CO [*Library symbol Library of Congress*] (LCLS)
CoPalJS	......	Palisade Junior-Senior High School, Palisade, CO [*Library symbol Library of Congress*] (LCLS)
CoPalTE	......	Taylor Elementary School, Palisade, CO [*Library symbol Library of Congress*] (LCLS)
COPAN	......	Command Post Alerting Network [*Military*]
COPANT	......	Comision Panamericana de Normas Tecnicas [*Pan American Standards Commission - PASC*] (EAIO)
CoPao	......	Paonia Public Library, Paonia, CO [*Library symbol Library of Congress*] (LCLS)
COPAR	......	Computerized Operational Audit Routine
COPAR	......	Cooperative Preservation of Architectural Records [*Defunct*] (EA)
CoParD	......	Douglas County Public Library, Parker Branch, Parker, CO [*Library symbol Library of Congress*] (LCLS)
COPARS	......	Contractor-Operated Parts Stores [*Military*]
Copart	......	Copart, Inc. [*Associated Press*] (SAG)
COPART	......	Counterpart
COPAS	......	Council of Petroleum Accountants Societies (EA)
COPAT	......	Cash Operating Profits after Tax (DICI)
COPB	......	Children's Organization for Peace and Brotherhood [*Defunct*] (EA)
COP/B	......	Command Operating Program/Budget [*DoD*] (MCD)
COPB	......	Cyclophosphamide, Oncovin [*Vincristine*], Prednisone, Bleomycin [*Antineoplastic drug regimen*]
COP-BLAM	......	Cyclophosphamide, Oncovin [*Vincristine*], Prednisone, Bleomycin, Adriamycin, Matulane [*Procarbazine*] [*Antineoplastic drug regimen*]
COP-BLEO	......	Cyclophosphamide [*or Chlorambucil*], Oncovin , Prednisone, Bleomycin [*Vincristine*] [*Antineoplastic drug regimen*]
Co PC	......	Coke's Pleas of the Crown [*or Third Institute*] [*A publication*] (DLA)
CoPC	......	Colorado Fuel & Iron Co., Pueblo, CO [*Library symbol Library of Congress*] (LCLS)
COPC	......	Combined Operational Planning Committee [*Royal Air Force and US 8th Air Force*] [*World War II*]
COPC	......	Commanding Officer, Pacific Coast [*Navy Canada*]
COPC	......	Community-Oriented Primary Care [*Medicine*]
CoPCC	......	Pueblo Community College, Pueblo, CO [*Library symbol*] [*Library of Congress*] (LCLS)
COPCOM	......	Controllers' Operations and Procedures Committee (FAAC)
COPCOM	......	Copernicus Common (DOMA)
COPCON	......	Comando de Operacoes do Continente [*Continental Operations Command*] [*Portugal*]
Cop Cop	......	Copinger. Copyright [*11th ed.*] [*1971*] [*A publication*] (DLA)
CoPCS	......	Colorado State Hospital, Hospital Community Library, Pueblo, CO [*Library symbol Library of Congress*] (LCLS)
CoPCS-C	......	Colorado State Hospital, Children's Center, Pueblo, CO [*Library symbol Library of Congress*] (LCLS)
CoPCS-M	......	Colorado State Hospital, Professional Library, Pueblo, CO [*Library symbol Library of Congress*] (LCLS)
COPD	......	Chronic Obstructive Pulmonary Disease [*Medicine*]
COPD	......	Coppered
COPDAB	......	Conflict and Peace Data Bank
COPDAF	......	Continuity of Operations Plan, Department of the Air Force (AFM)
COPE	......	CAMA [*Centralized Automatic Message Accounting*] Operator Position Exercise (PDAA)
COPE	......	Campership Outdoor Program of Education [*Federal antipoverty program*]
COPE	......	Canadian Organisation for the Promotion of Education Inc. [*Organization Canadienne pour la Promotion de l'Education Inc.*] (AC)
COPE	......	Carbon Monoxide Pollution Experiment [*NASA/General Electric*]
COPE	......	Career Opportunities and Planning for Employment Center [*Public library service*]
COPE	......	Career-Oriented Preparation for Employment [*Federal antipoverty program*]
COPE	......	Cassette Operating Executive (MHDI)

COPE .... Chronic Obstructive Pulmonary Emphysema [*Medicine*]
COPE .... Claus Oxygen-Based Process Expansion [*Petroleum technology*]
COPE .... Coastal Ocean Probing Experiment [*Marine science*] (OSRA)
COPE .... Coming Off Pills Entirely
COPE .... Commission on Public Ethics [*Australia*]
COPE .... Committee for Original People's Entitlement [*Eskimo claim to Canadian land*]
COPE .... Committee on Paperless Entries [*Atlanta*] (MHDB)
COPE .... Committee on Parenthood Education [*Defunct*] (EA)
COPE .... Committee on Political Education [*AFL-CIO*] (EA)
COPE .... Communications-Oriented Peripheral [*or Processing*] Equipment
COPE .... Community-Oriented Police Enforcement
COPE .... Comprehensive Offender Program Effort [*Department of Labor*]
COPE .... Computer Operating and Programming Environment (DNAB)
COPE .... Computer Operator Proficiency Examination (SAA)
COPE .... Concepts of Postal Economics [*A series of newsletters of Mail Advertising Corp.*]
COPE .... Conference of Podiatry Executives (EA)
Cope .... Congress of the People [*South Africa*] [*Political party*] (PPW)
COPE .... Console Operator Proficiency Examination [*Computer Usage Co.*]
COPE .... Consortium of Publishers for Employment
COPE .... Continuous Officer Professional Education (DNAB)
Cope .... Cope's Reports [*63-72 California*] [*A publication*] (DLA)
COPE .... Coping Operations Preference Enquiry [*Personality development test*] [*Psychology*]
COPE .... Copolyester Elastomer [*Plastics technology*]
COPE .... Corporate Organization and Procedures Economy (SAA)
COPE .... Cost Progress Evaluation (MCD)
COPE .... Council of Protocol Executives (EA)
COPE .... Council on Population and Environment (EA)
COPE .... Currency Overprinting and Processing Equipment [*Bureau of Printing and Engraving*]
COPE .... Custodian of Postal Effects [*Military*] (AFM)
COPE .... Cytoxan, Oncovin, Platinol, Etoposide [*Antineoplastic drug*] (CDI)
COPEC .... Conference on Christian Politics, Economics, and Citizenship (IIA)
COPECIAL .... Comite Permanent des Congres Internationaux pour l'Apostolat des Laics [*Permanent Committee of International Congresses for the Lay Apostolate*] [*Italy*]
COPED .... Cooperative Project for Educational Development [*Office of Education*]
COPEMCI ..... Conference Permanente Mediterraneenne pour la Cooperation Internationale [*Standing Mediterranean Conference for International Cooperation*] (EA)
COPEP .... Committee on Public Engineering Policy [*National Academy of Engineering*]
COPER .... Agencia Noticiosa Corporacion de Periodistas [*Press agency*] [*Chile*]
COPER .... Conference on Psychoanalytic Education and Research
COPERS .... Commission Preparatoire Europeenne de Recherches Spatiales [*European Preparatory Commission for Space Research*]
COPES .... Career Orientation Placement and Evaluation Survey [*Vocational guidance test*]
COPES .... Committee on Program Evaluation and Support [*American Library Association*]
COPES .... Community-Oriented Programs Environment Scale [*Psychosocial assessment test*]
COPES .... Computer-Oriented Purchasing and Engineering System (MHDB)
COPES .... Conceptually-Oriented Program in Elementary Science [*New York University*] (AEBS)
COPES .... Cost Planning and Evaluations System
COPESCAL .... Comision de Pesca Continental para America Latina [*Commission for Inland Fisheries of Latin America*] [*FAO*] [*Italy*] (ASF)
COPF .... Canadian Ornamental Plant Foundation [*Fondation Canadienne des Plantes Ornementales*] (AC)
CoPfAF .... United States Air Force, Base Library, Peterson Field, CO [*Library symbol Library of Congress*] (LCLS)
COPG .... Chairman, Operational Planners Group [*Military*]
COPH .... Congress of Organisms of the Physically Handicapped (EA)
COPHAN ...... Confederation des Organismes Provinciaux de Personnes Handicapees du Quebec (AC)
COPHL .... Conference of Public Health Laboratorians (EA)
COPHT .... Canadian Organization of Public Housing Tenants
COPHU .... Computer-Oriented Photo-Unit [*Linofilm*] (DGA)
COPI .... California Occupational Preference Inventory [*Psychology*] (DAVI)
COPI .... Committee on Policy Implementation [*American Library Association*]
COPI .... Computer-Oriented Programmed Instruction (IEEE)
COPI .... Consolidated Products [*NASDAQ symbol*] (TTSB)
COPI .... Consolidated Products, Inc. [*NASDAQ symbol*] (NQ)
COPI .... Cooperative Projects with Industry [*National Research Council, Canada*]
COPIC .... Computer Program Information Center (MCD)
COPICS .... Communications Oriented Product Information and Control System (NITA)
COPICS .... Communications-Oriented Production Information and Control System [*IBM Corp.*]
COPICS .... Copyright Office Publication and Interactive Cataloging System [*Library of Congress Washington, DC*]
COPICS EDL... Communications-Oriented Production Information and Control System Executive DataLink [*IBM Corp.*]
COPILOT ...... Cost-Oriented Production and Inventory Loading Operations Technique Works
Cop Ind Pr ... Copinger's Index to Precedents [*A publication*] (DLA)
COPIOR........ Committee of Professors in Operational Research (AIE)
COPL .... Center for Optics, Photonics, and LASERS [*Laval University*] [*Research center*] (RCD)

Co PI .... Coke's Pleadings [*Sometimes published separately*] [*A publication*] (DLA)
COPL .... Combat Outpost Line
COPL .... Committee for Oil Pipe Lines [*Later, AOPL*]
COPL .... Oakland Public Library, Oakland, CA [*Library symbol*] [*Library of Congress*] (LCLS)
CoPl .... Platteville Public Library, Platteville, CO [*Library symbol Library of Congress*] (LCLS)
CO PLAC..... County Placita [*British*] (ROG)
Copley .... Copley Properties, Inc. [*Associated Press*] (SAG)
CopleyPh...... Copley Pharmaceutical, Inc. [*Associated Press*] (SAG)
CoPIP.......... Platteville Public Library, Platteville, CO [*Library symbol*] [*Library of Congress*] (LCLS)
COPM .... Computer Operations Procedures Manual
COPMEC ...... Comite des Petites et Moyens Enterprises Commerciales [*Committee of Small and Medium Commercial Enterprises*] [*EEC*] (PDAA)
COPMV .... Cow Parsnip Mosaic Virus [*Plant pathology*]
COPO .... Catholic One Parent Organization (EA)
COPO .... Chief, Office of Personnel Operations [*Army*]
COPO .... Council of Philatelic Organizations (EA)
COPOC........ Committee of Publicly Owned Companies (EA)
COPOE........ Commanding Officer, Port of Embarkation
COPOL .... Council of Polytechnic Librarians [*British*] (NITA)
COPOLCO .... Committee on Consumer Policy [*ISO*] (DS)
COPP .... CCNU [*Lomustine*], Oncovin , Procarbazine, Prednisone [*Vincristine*] [*Antineoplastic drug regimen*]
COPP .... Change of Personal Particulars (ADA)
COPP .... Cobaltiprotoporphyrin [*Medicine*]
COPP .... Combined Operations Pilotage Party
COPP .... COSAL [*Coordinated Shipboard Allowance List*] Processing Point
COPP .... Crude Oil Processing Plant
COPP .... Cyclophosphamide, Oncovin [*Vincristine*], Procarbazine, Prednisone [*Antineoplastic drug regimen*]
COPPA .... Coordinated Procurement Program Appraisal [*DoD*]
Copp Ct Mar... Copp's Manual for Courts-Martial [*A publication*] (DLA)
COPPE .... Council on Plastics and Packaging in the Environment (EA)
CoPPE .... Parkview Episcopal Hospital, Pueblo, CO [*Library symbol Library of Congress*] (LCLS)
COPPER....... Consolidation of Pay and Personnel Functions [*Military*]
Copp Land.... Copp's Land Office Decisions [*A publication*] (DLA)
Copp LL....... Copp's Public Land Laws [*A publication*] (DLA)
Copp Min Dec... Copp's United States Mining Decision [*A publication*] (DLA)
Copp Pub Land Laws... Copp's Public Land Laws [*A publication*] (DLA)
Copp Pub LL... Copp's Public Land Laws [*A publication*] (DLA)
COPPS......... Committee on Power Plant Siting [*National Academy of Engineering*]
CO-PPT....... Coprecipitation
COPPUL....... Council of Prairie & Pacific University Libraries [*Formerly, Council of Prairie University Libraries*] (AC)
COPR .... Centre for Overseas Pest Research [*England*]
COPR .... Computerized Outside Plant Records [*Telecommunications*] (TEL)
COPR .... Control of Pesticides Regulations [*British*]
COPR .... Copier
COPR .... Copper [*Chemical symbol is Cu*]
COPR .... Copper Range R. R. [*AAR code*]
COPR .... Copyright (TEL)
copr .... Copyright (WDMC)
COPR .... Critical Officer Personnel Requirement [*Air Force*]
COPRA .... Comparative Postwar Recovery Analysis (MCD)
COPRA .... Cosmetic and Perfumery Retail Association [*British*]
COPRAQ ...... Cooperative Program of Research on Aquaculture [*UN Food and Agriculture Organization*]
COPREC ...... Command Post Record Capability [*Military*]
COPRED....... Consortium on Peace Research, Education, and Development (EA)
COPRED-SPN... COPRED Students Peace Network [*Later, COPRED-SPWG*] (EA)
COPRED-SPWG... COPRED [*Consortium on Peace Research, Education, and Development*] StudentsPeace Working Group (EA)
COPREX....... Coprecipitation X-Ray Fluorescence Spectroscopy
COPRL......... Command Operations Priority Requirements List [*Air Force*] (AFM)
COPRO........ Co-Production
COPRO........ Coproporphyrin [*Also, CP*] [*Clinical chemistry*]
CoPs........... Archuleta County Public Library, Pagosa Springs, CO [*Library symbol Library of Congress*] (LCLS)
COPS .... California Occupational Preference Survey
COPS .... Canadian Operating Statistics [*Database*] [*Statistics Canada*] [*Information service or system*] (CRD)
COPS .... Catalytic Optimum Profit-Sharing
COPS .... Chrysler Optical Processing Scanner
COPS .... Circuit Order Preparation [*or Processing*] System [*AT & T*]
COPS .... Coastal Ocean Prediction Systems Program [*Marine science*] (OSRA)
COPS .... Coherent Optical Processing System
COPS .... College of Osteopathic Physicians and Surgeons
COPS .... Communities Organized for Public Service (DICI)
COPS .... Community Oriented Policing Services
COPS .... Component Placement System [*Electronics*] (EECA)
COPS .... Computerized Officer Planning System [*Navy*] (NVT)
COPS .... Computerized Optimization Procedure for Stabilators (PDAA)
COPS .... Computer-Oriented Partial Sum (NVT)
COPS .... Concerns of Police Survivors [*An association*]
COPS .... Contingency Operations Plans Report (NVT)
COPS .... Contingency Operations Space [*Army*]
COPS PI .... Controller Oriented Processor Series [*Computer science*] (PDAA)
COPS .... Conversational Problem Solver (PDAA)
COPS .... Conversion of Production System [*Engineering Index, Inc.*]
COPS .... Costing Out Policy Systems (PDAA)

COPS	Council on Postal Suppression
COPS	Council on Professional Standards in Speech-Language Pathology and Audiology (EA)
COPS	Covered Option Securities (TDOB)
COPS	Current Operations
COPS	Customer Order Processing System
CoPS	Southern Colorado State College, Pueblo, CO [Library symbol Library of Congress] (LCLS)
COPS-91	Cooperative Oklahoma Profiler Studies-1991 [Marine science] (OSRA)
COPS-91	Cooperative Oklahoma Profiler Studies-1991 (USDC)
COPSAC	Computer Order Processing and Sales Accounting (IAA)
CoPsC	Archuleta County Public Library, Pagosa Springs, CO [Library symbol] [Library of Congress] (LCLS)
COPSCAULD	Council of Pennsylvania State College and University Library Directors [Library network]
COPSI	Council of Profit Sharing Industries [Later, PSCA] (EA)
COPSS	Committee of Presidents of Statistical Societies (EA)
CoPStMH	Saint Mary Corwin Hospital, Pueblo, CO [Library symbol Library of Congress] (LCLS)
COPT	Coke Oven Production Technology
CoPT	Colorado State Home and Training School, Residents' Library, Pueblo, CO [Library symbol Library of Congress] (LCLS)
COPT	Completed Procedure Turn [Aviation] (FAAC)
COPT	Constant Optimal Performance Theorem [Physics]
COPT	Coptic
Copt	Coptic (VRA)
COPT	Copyright
COPT	Counterpart (ROG)
COPT	Counterpoint [Music] (ROG)
COPTEC	Controller Overload Prediction Technique (PDAA)
Cop Tit D	Copinger on Title Deeds [A publication] (DLA)
CoPTP	Coalition of Publicly Traded Partnerships (EA)
CO-PTR	Co-Partner (ROG)
COPTRAN	Communication Optimization Program Translator [NASA]
CoPTS	Colorado State Home and Training School, Staff Library, Pueblo, CO [Library symbol Library of Congress] (LCLS)
COPUL	Copulative (ROG)
COPUOS	Committee on the Peaceful Uses of Outer Space [United Nations] (NITA)
COPUOS	United Nations Committee on the Peaceful Uses of Outer Space (EA)
COPUS	National Coalition of Independent College and University Students [Acronym represents organization's former name] [Defunct] (EA)
COPWE	Commission for Organizing the Party of the Working People of Ethiopia (PD)
Copx	Paradox, Paradox, CO [Library symbol] [Library of Congress] (LCLS)
COPY	Copyright (DLA)
copy	Copyright (WDMC)
COPY	Copytele, Inc. [NASDAQ symbol] (NQ)
COPY & LIT P	Copyright and Literary Property [Legal term] (DLA)
Copy Bull	Copyright Bulletin [A publication] (DLA)
Copy Dec	Copyright Decisions [A publication] (DLA)
COPYLIB	Copy Libraries
Copyright Bull	UNESCO Copyright Bulletin [A publication] (DLA)
Copyright L Rep (CCH)	Copyright Law Reporter (Commerce Clearing House) [A publication] (DLA)
Copyright L Symp(ASCAP)	Copyright Law Symposium. American Society of Composers, Authors, and Publishers [A publication] (DLA)
COPYS	Collection Operation Potential Yield System [IRS]
Copytel	CopyTele, Inc. [Associated Press] (SAG)
COQ	Certificate of Qualification (KSC)
COQ	Cloquet, MN [Location identifier FAA] (FAAL)
COQ	Club des Ornithologues de Quebec Inc. (AC)
COQ	Coastoro Resources [Vancouver Stock Exchange symbol]
CoQ	Coenzyme Q [Ubiquinone] [Also, Q, U, UQ] [Biochemistry]
COQ	Conquista [Brazil] [Airport symbol] (OAG)
COQ	Coque [Boil] [Pharmacy]
COQ	Cost of Quality [Engineering]
COQ	Southeast Metropolitan Board of Cooperative Services, Processing Center, Littleton, CO [OCLC symbol] (OCLC)
COQ ad MED CONSUMPT	Coque ad Medietatis Consumptionem [Boil to the Consumption of Half] [Pharmacy] (ROG)
COQ in SA	Coque in Sufficiente Aquae [Boil in Sufficient Water] [Pharmacy] (ROG)
Coq SA	Coque Secundum Artem [Boil According to Rule] [Pharmacy]
coq simul	Coque Simul [Boil at the Same Time] [Pharmacy] (DAVI)
COR	Cardiac Output Recorder [Physiology]
COR	Cargo Outturn Report (AABC)
COR	Carrier-Operated Relay
COR	Cash on Receipt
cor	Cash On Receipt (WDMC)
COR	Center for Operations Research [MIT] (MCD)
COR	Center of Rotation
COR	Central Office of Record [DoD]
COR	Change Order Request (DNAB)
COR	Chopper Mines Ltd. [Vancouver Stock Exchange symbol]
COR	Circular of Requirements
Co R	Code Reporter [New York] [A publication] (DLA)
COR	Coherent Optical Receiver
COR	Combat Operations Report
COR	Cominco Resources International Ltd. [Toronto Stock Exchange symbol Vancouver Stock Exchange symbol]
COR	Command Operationally Ready [Navy] (NVT)
COR	Committee of Responsibility

COR	Committee of the Regions [Belgium] (ECON)
COR	Communications Operations Report [Air Force]
COR	Comprehensive Outpatient Rehabilitation Facility (MEDA)
COR	Concentric-Orbit Rendezvous [NASA]
COR	Conditioned Orientation Reflex
COR	Conditioned Orienting Response [Neurology] (DAVI)
COR	Confederation of Regions [Canada Political party]
CoR	Congo Red [A dye]
COR	Contactor, Running
COR	Continental Operations Range (MCD)
COR	Contracting Officer's Representative (TEL)
COR	Contractor
COR	Contractors' Operational Representative
COR	Cooperative Research [in agriculture]
COR	Copper Oxide Rectifier
COR	Coral (ROG)
COR	Coram [Before] [Latin] (ROG)
COR	Corcoran, CA [Location identifier FAA] (FAAL)
COR	Cordoba [Argentina] [Airport symbol] (OAG)
Cor	Corinthians [New Testament book]
Cor	Coriolanus [Shakespearean work]
COR	Corner (KSC)
cor	Corner· (WDMC)
COR	Corner
COR	Cornet
cor	Cornish [MARC language code Library of Congress] (LCCP)
COR	Corno [Cornet or Horn] [Music] (ROG)
COR	Corona [A publication]
cor	Coronary [Cardiology] (DAVI)
COR	Coroner
COR	Coroners' Rolls [British]
COR	Coronet (ADA)
COR	Corporate Source [Online database field identifier]
COR	Corps [Army]
COR	Corpus [Body] [Latin]
COR	Correct (ROG)
COR	Correction
cor	Correction (WDMC)
COR	Correlative
COR	Correspond (ROG)
COR	Correspondence
cor	Correspondence (WDMC)
cor	Correspondent (WDMC)
COR	Corridor (AABC)
COR	Corrigendum [Publishing] (WGA)
COR	Corrosive
COR	Corrugated (WGA)
COR	Corrupt
COR	Corsica (ROG)
COR	Cortisone [Endocrinology]
COR	Corvallis [Oregon] [Seismograph station code, US Geological Survey] (SEIS)
Cor	Coryton's Reports [Bengal] [A publication] (DLA)
COR	Councillor (ROG)
COR	Crown Office Rules [A publication] (DLA)
COR	Crystal Oil [AMEX symbol] (TTSB)
COR	Crystal Oil Corp. [AMEX symbol] (SPSG)
COR	Custodian of Records (HGAA)
COr	Orange Free Public Library, Orange, CA [Library symbol Library of Congress] (LCLS)
COR	Regis College, Denver, CO [OCLC symbol] (OCLC)
CORA	Canadian Outrigger Racing Association (AC)
CORA	Code for One-Dimensional Reactor Analysis (PDAA)
CORA	Coherent RADAR Array
CORA	Commission on Religion in Appalachia (EA)
CORA	Computer Orientated Reproducer Assembly (DGA)
CORA	Conditional Response Analog Machine
CORA	Conditioned Orientation Reflex Audiometry [Medicine] (MAE)
CORA	Conditioned Reflex Analog (IEEE)
CorA	Corona Australis [Constellation]
CoRa	Rangely Public Library, Rangely, CO [Library symbol Library of Congress] (LCLS)
CoRaC	Colorado Northwestern Community College, Rangely, CO [Library symbol Library of Congress] (LCLS)
CORAD	Committee on Restrictions Against Disabled People (AIE)
CORAD	Correlation RADAR
CORADCOM	Communications Research and Development Command [Fort Monmouth, NJ] [Army]
CORAL	Class-Oriented Ring-Associative Language [Computer science]
CORAL	Coherent Optical RADAR Laboratory
CORAL	Command Radio Link
CORAL	Comparison of Recognition Algorithms [US Postal Service]
CORAL	Computer On-Line Real-Time Applications Language [Computer science] (IEEE)
CORAL	Coordinated Regional Allowance List (AFIT)
CORAL	Correlation Radio Link (MUGU)
CORAL	Council of Research and Academic Libraries [Library network]
CORAL	Council on Religion and Law [Defunct] (EA)
CoramH	Coram Healthcare Corp. [Associated Press] (SAG)
Coran N	Coran Nobis and Allied Statutory Remedies [A publication] (DLA)
CORAP	Configuration Report and Accounting Program [Military]
CORAPRAN	Cobelda RADAR Automatic Preflight Analyzer (IEEE)
CORAS	Corridor Assignment [Aviation] (FAAC)
CORAT	Christian Organisations Research and Advisory Trust [Church of England]

CORB	Chiropractors'and Osteopaths' Registration Board [*Victoria*] [*Australia*]
CorB	Corona Borealis [*Constellation*]
CORBA	Common Object Request Broken Architecture
CORBA	Common Object Request Broker Architecture [*Computer science*]
CORBA	Common-Object Request Broker Architecture [*Computer science*]
CORBA	Common Object Request Broker Architecture [*For computer databases*]
Corb & D	Corbett and Daniell's English Election Cases [*1819*] [*A publication*] (DLA)
Corb & Dan	Corbett and Daniell's English Election Cases [*1819*] [*A publication*] (DLA)
COR BD	Corner Bead [*Technical drawings*] (DAC)
CORBFUS	Copy of Reply Be Furnished This Office [*Army*] (AABC)
COrC	Chapman College, Orange, CA [*Library symbol Library of Congress*] (LCLS)
CORC	Chief, Office of Reserve Components [*Army*] (AABC)
CORC	Control-Oriented Computer (MCD)
CORC	Conventional Ordnance Release Computer (NG)
CORC	Corcom, Inc. [*NASDAQ symbol*] (NQ)
CORC	Cornell Computing Language [*Computer science*]
CORCAPS	Consolidated Reserve Components Reporting System (MCD)
Cor Cas	American and English Corporation Cases [*A publication*] (DLA)
CORCC	Canadian Overseas Military Railway Construction Corps [*World War I*]
COrCL	Orange County Public Library, Orange, CA [*Library symbol Library of Congress*] (LCLS)
CORCN	Coercion (MSA)
CORCN	Correction Control Number [*Army*]
CORCO	Commonwealth Refining Co. [*Puerto Rico*]
Corcom	Corcom, Inc. [*Associated Press*] (SAG)
CORCOM	Corps Communications (MCD)
CORCOM	Correcting Computer (MCD)
CORCOM	Corrupt Commissioners [*Federal operation investigating illegal practices by Oklahoma's county commissioners*]
CORCONU	Corrosion Control Unit (DNAB)
CorCp	Corrections Corp. of America [*Associated Press*] (SAG)
CorctCp	Corrections Corp. of America [*Associated Press*] (SAG)
CORCY	Corrected Copy (DNAB)
CORD	Canadian On-Line Record Database
CORD	Cascade Orificial Restrictive Device (MCD)
CORD	Center for Occupational Research and Development [*Research center*] (RCD)
CORD	Chief of Ordnance [*Army*]
CORD	Chronic Obstructive Respiratory Disease [*Medicine*]
CORD	Commanding Officer Reserve Divisions [*World War II Canada*]
CORD	Commercial Operational Requirements Document [*Military*]
CORD	Commissioned Officer Residency Deferment [*Program of Public Health Service*]
CORD	Computer-Reinforced Design (PDAA)
CORD	Computer with On-Line Remote Devices [*National Institute of Standards and Technology*]
CORD	Congress on Research in Dance (EA)
CORD	Consortium Research Development [*Office of Education*]
CORD	Coordinating of Research and Development [*Navy*]
CORD	Coordinator (DNAB)
Cord	Cordillera [*A mountain chain*] (BARN)
CORD	Cordis Corp. [*NASDAQ symbol*] (NQ)
CORDASF	Commissary Resale Division of the Army Stock Fund (AABC)
CORDAT	Coordinate Data Set
C or D by T or B	Collected or Delivered by Truck or Barge [*Shipping*]
Cordiant	Cordiant PLC [*Associated Press*] (SAG)
CORDIC	Coordinate Rotation Digital Computer
Cordis	Cordis Corp. [*Associated Press*] (SAG)
CORDIVEM	Corps Division Evaluation Model [*Army*] (RDA)
Cord Mar Wom	Cord on Legal and Equitable Rights of Married Women [*A publication*] (DLA)
CORDO	Chief Ordnance Officer
CORDP	Correlated RADAR Data Printout [*Electronics*] (SAA)
CORDPO	Correlated RADAR Data Printout [*Electronics*]
CORDPO-SORD	Correlated RADAR Data Printout - Separation of RADAR Data [*Electronics*]
CORDS	Civil Operations for Rural Development Support [*Army*]
CORDS	Civil Operations Revolutionary Development Support [*Army*] (AABC)
CORDS	Coherent-on-Receive Doppler System [*RADAR*]
CORDS	Coordination of Record and Data Base System [*Telecommunications*] (TEL)
CORDS	Corduroy Trousers [*Slang*] (DSUE)
Cord Sol	Cordery. Solicitors [*6th ed.*] [*1968*] [*A publication*] (DLA)
CORE	Canadian Offshore Resources Exposition (ITD)
CORE	Center for Organ Recovery and Education [*Medicine*]
CORE	Coherent-on-Receive
CORE	Cohesion, Organization, Resourcefulness and Energy Model (EDAC)
CORE	Collected Original Resources in Education [*Carfax Publishing*] (NITA)
CORE	Commission on Rehabilitation Education [*American Occupational Therapy Association*]
CORE	Committee on Research Evaluation [*US*]
CORE	Common Operational Research Equipment (NASA)
CORE	Common Register of Development Projects [*United Nations*]
CORE	Competitive Operational Readiness Evaluation [*Air Force*] (AFM)
CORE	Comprehensive Assessment and Referral Evaluation [*Medicine*] (DMAA)
CORE	Computer-Oriented Reporting Efficiency (AFM)
CORE	Computer-Related Equipment (IAA)
CORE	Congress of Racial Equality (EA)
CORE	[*The*] Consortium for Oceanographic Research and Education [*A lobby group*]
CORE	Contingency Response Program [*DoD*]
CORE	Cooperative Research Institute [*Defunct*] (EA)
CORE	Core, Inc. [*NASDAQ symbol*] (SAG)
CORE	CORE Inc. [*NASDAQ symbol*] (TTSB)
CO-RE	Co-Respondent (DSUE)
CORE	Cost-Oriented Resource Estimating Model [*Air Force*] (GFGA)
CORE	Council of Registrars [*Internet group*]
CORE	Council of Reprographics Executives [*Defunct*] (EA)
CORE	Council on Rehabilitation Education (PGP)
CoRe	Redcliff Public Library, Redcliff, CO [*Library symbol Library of Congress*] (LCLS)
CORECT	Citizens Organized to Restore an Effective Corporate Tax (EA)
CORECT	Committee on Renewable Energy Commerce and Trade (AAGC)
COREDITOR	Computer Retrieval Editor [*Used to manage CORKIPER file family*]
CoreIn	Core Industries, Inc. [*Associated Press*] (SAG)
Core Inc	Core, Inc. [*Associated Press*] (SAG)
CoreLab	Core Laboratories NV [*Associated Press*] (SAG)
CORELAP	Computerized Relationship Layout Planning
CorelCp	Corel Corp. [*Associated Press*] (SAG)
CoreMatl	Core Materials Corp. [*Associated Press*] (SAG)
COREN	Corps of Engineers [*Army*] (MUGU)
CORENG	Corps of Engineers [*Army*] (SAA)
Co Rep	Code Reporter [*New York*] [*A publication*] (DLA)
Co Rep	Coke's English King's Bench Reports [*1572-1616*] [*A publication*] (DLA)
COREP	Combined Operations Repair Organization [*For invasion of France*] [*World War II*]
COREP	Combined Overload Repair Control (MCD)
COREPER	Commission de Representants Permanents [*Committee of Permanent Representatives*] [*EEC*]
COREQ	Confirming Requisition Follows (FAAC)
CORES	Computer-Assisted Order Routing and Execution System [*Tokyo Stock Exchange*] [*Japan*] (ODBW)
CORES	Cooperative Radiation Effects Simulation Program [*Military*] (DNAB)
CORESCEL	Communications Requirements Systems Configuration and Equipment List (NVT)
CORESTA	Centre de Cooperation pour les Recherches Scientifiques Relatives au Tabac [*Cooperation Center for Scientific Research Relative to Tobacco*] [*Paris, France*] (EA)
CoreStF	Core States Financial [*Associated Press*] (SAG)
CORETECH	Council on Research and Technology (EA)
COREX	Coordinated Electronic Countermeasures Exercise [*Military*] (NVT)
CORF	Committee on Radio Frequencies [*National Academy of Sciences*]
CORF	Comprehensive Outpatient Rehabilitation Facility [*American Occupational Therapy Association*]
CoRf	Rocky Ford Public Library, Rocky Ford, CO [*Library symbol Library of Congress*] (LCLS)
CORG	Combat Operational Reserve Group (AAG)
CORG	Combat Operations Research Group [*Technical Operations, Inc.*] [*Fort Belvoir, VA*]
COrGH	Orange County General Hospital, Orange, CA [*Library symbol Library of Congress*] (LCLS)
CORGI	Confederation of Registered Gas Installers [*British*] (DI)
COrGS	Orange County California Genealogical Society, Orange, CA [*Library symbol Library of Congress*] (LCLS)
CORI	Community and Organization Research Institute [*Research center*] (RCD)
CoRi	Rifle Public Library, Rifle, CO [*Library symbol Library of Congress*] (LCLS)
CoRicD	Dolores County School District, Rico, CO [*Library symbol Library of Congress*] (LCLS)
COriK	John F. Kennedy University, Orinda, CA [*Library symbol Library of Congress*] (LCLS)
CorImag	Cornerstone Imaging, Inc. [*Associated Press*] (SAG)
Corimon	Corimon CA SACA [*Associated Press*] (SAG)
Corin	Corinthian (VRA)
Coriol	Coariolanus [*Shakespearean drama*] (BARN)
CORIS	Computerized Operating Room Information System
CORIS	Computerized Registry Information System [*UNIDO*] [*United Nations*] (DUND)
Cor Jud	Correspondances Judiciaires [*Canada*] [*A publication*] (DLA)
CORK	Canadian Olympic Regatta at Kingston
CORKIPER	Computer Retrieval of Kinetic Parameters of Electrode Reactions
CORKS	Computer Oriented Record Keeping System (NITA)
CORL	Collection Opportunity Requirements List (MCD)
COrL	Loyola Marymount University, Orange Campus, Orange, CA [*Library symbol Library of Congress*] (LCLS)
COrl	Orland Free Library, Orland, CA [*Library symbol Library of Congress*] (LCLS)
COriL	Orland Free Library, Orland, CA [*Library symbol*] [*Library of Congress*] (LCLS)
CORLQ	Conference des Organismes Regionaux de Loisirs du Quebec (AC)
CORM	Commission on Rules and Missions of the Armed Services (AAGC)
CORM	Council on Optical Radiation Measurement
CORMES	Communication Oriented Message System [*IBM Corp.*]
CORMOSEA	Committee on Research Materials on Southeast Asia (EA)
CORN	Canadian Clearinghouse for Ongoing Research in Nursing [*University of Alberta*] (IID)
CORN	Computer Resources Nucleus (AAGC)
CORN	Computer Resources Nucleus [*FAA*] (TAG)
CORN	Controlled Range Network (MCD)
CORN	Cornell (ROG)
Corn	Cornell University [*Record label*]

Corn............	Cornice (DAC)
CORN..........	Cornish (ROG)
CORN..........	Cornwall [County in England]
Corn............	Pro Cornelio de Maiestate [of Cicero] [Classical studies] (OCD)
CornCor.......	Cornell Corrections, Inc. [Associated Press] (SAG)
CornD.........	Corning Delaware Ltd. [Associated Press] (SAG)
Corn Deeds...	Cornish on Purchase Deeds [A publication] (DLA)
Corn Dig......	Cornwell's Digest [A publication] (DLA)
CORNEA......	Consortium of Registered Nurses for Eye Acquisition [Later, ANET] (EA)
Cornell LJ....	Cornell Law Journal [A publication] (DLA)
Cornell U.....	Cornell University (GAGS)
CORNER......	Corner [Commonly used] (OPSA)
CornerBk.....	Cornerstone Bank [Associated Press] (SAG)
CORNERS.....	Corners [Commonly used] (OPSA)
CORNET......	Construction Information Online Retrieval Network [Information service or system] (IID)
CORNET......	Corporation Network [Telephone communications]
CORNI.........	Columbus, Ohio Regional News Index [Grandview Heights Public Library] [Information service or system] (IID)
CorningIn.....	Corning, Inc. [Associated Press] (SAG)
Cornish Purch Deeds...	Cornish on Purchase Deeds [A publication] (DLA)
CORN NEP...	Cornelius Nepos [Historian, 31-14BC] (ROG)
CornNG........	Cornerstone Natural Gas [Associated Press] (SAG)
Corn Pr.......	Corner's Queen's Bench Practice [A publication] (DLA)
CornPrp.......	Cornerstone Propane Partners LP [Associated Press] (SAG)
Corn Pur D...	Cornish on Purchase Deeds [A publication] (DLA)
Corn Rem....	Cornish on Remainders [A publication] (DLA)
Co R NS	Code Reports, New Series [New York] [A publication] (DLA)
Cornucp......	Cornucopia Resources Ltd. [Associated Press] (SAG)
Corn Us......	Cornish on Uses [A publication] (DLA)
CORNW.......	Cornwall [County in England] (ROG)
Corn Wr......	Corner's Forms of Writs on the Crown Side [A publication] (DLA)
Cornw Tab...	Cornwall's Table of Precedents [A publication] (DLA)
Co R (NY)...	Code Reporter [New York] [A publication] (DLA)
CORO..........	Chicago Operations and Regional Office [Department of Energy] (GRD)
CORO..........	Coronado National Memorial
COro	Oroville Public Library, Oroville, CA [Library symbol Library of Congress] (LCLS)
COroB.........	Butte County Library, Oroville, CA [Library symbol Library of Congress] (LCLS)
COroBHi......	Butte County Historical Society, Oroville, CA [Library symbol] [Library of Congress] (LCLS)
CORODIM	Correlation of the Recognition of Degradation with Intelligibility Measurements [Telecommunications] (TEL)
COROIPAS ...	Conferences on Research on International Peace and Security [Founded International Peace Research Association]
COROL........	Corollary
COROLL.......	Corollary (ADA)
CORON	Coroner (DLA)
CORONA......	Control Rod Analysis [Nuclear energy]
COROS........	Collectors of Religion on Stamps (EA)
CO ROUTE ...	Company Route (GAVI)
CORP..........	Canadian Organization for the Rights of Prostitutes (AC)
CORP..........	Corporal
CORP..........	Corporate (ROG)
corp	Corporate (VRA)
CORP..........	Corporation (AFM)
CORP..........	Corporation
Corp...........	Corporation (DD)
CORP..........	Corpori [To the Body] [Pharmacy]
CORP..........	Corpse (DSUE)
Corp...........	Pennsylvania Corporation Reporter [A publication] (DLA)
CORPAL.......	Control Room Patching and Labeling
Corp & Ass'ns...	Corporations and Associations [A publication] (DLA)
Cor Pat......	Coryton on Patents [A publication] (DLA)
Corp C	Corporations Code [A publication] (DLA)
Corp Counsel Rev...	Corporate Counsel Review [A publication] (DLA)
Corp Dep.....	Corporate Depositary (DLA)
CorpEx........	Corporate Express, Inc. [Associated Press] (SAG)
CorpExp.......	Corporate Express, Inc. [Associated Press] (SAG)
Corp Guide...	Corporation Guide [Prentice-Hall, Inc.] [A publication] (DLA)
CorpHY.......	Corporate High Yield Fund, Inc. [Associated Press] (SAG)
CORPIQ.......	Corporation des Proprietaires Immobiliers du Quebec (AC)
CORP JUR ...	Corpus Juris [Body of Law] [Latin] (ROG)
Corp Jur Can...	Corpus Juris Canonici [The Body of the Canon Law] [Latin A publication] (DLA)
Corp Jur Civ...	Corpus Juris Civilis [The Body of the Civil Law] [Latin A publication] (DLA)
Corp Jus Canon...	Corpus Juris Canonici [The Body of the Canon Law] [Latin A publication] (DLA)
CORPL.........	Corporal
CORPL.........	Corporal
Corp Law.....	Journal of Comparative Corporate Law and Securities Regulation [A publication] (ILCA)
Cor-PLD......	Corynebacterium Pseudotuberculosis Phospholipase D [An enzyme]
Corp-Mgmt Ed (P-H)...	Corporation-Management Edition (Prentice-Hall, Inc.) [A publication] (DLA)
CORPN........	Corporation
CORPORAL...	Corporate Resource and Allocation (MHDB)
CORPPIN	Corporeal Pin [Method of tuberculin and histoplasmin testing] [Medicine]
Corp Prac Rev...	Corporate Practice Review [A publication] (DLA)
Corp Pract Rev...	Corporate Practice Review [A publication] (DLA)
CorpRen	Corporate Renaissance Group, Inc. [Associated Press] (SAG)
Corp Reorg..	Corporate Reorganizations [A publication] (DLA)
Corp Reorg & Am Bank Rev...	Corporate Reorganization and American Bankruptcy Review [A publication] (DLA)
Corp Rep	Pennsylvania Corporation Reporter [A publication] (DLA)
Corp Rep (PA)...	Pennsylvania Corporation Reporter [A publication] (DLA)
CORPRT......	Corporate
CORPS.........	Comprehensive Radiance Profile Synthesizer
CORPS.........	Customs Optical Reader Passport Systems [A scanning device capable of reading the latest US passports]
CORPSAM...	Corps Surface-to-Air Missile [Army] (DOMA)
CORPSE......	Coordination of Recent and Projected System Efforts [DoD]
CORPSMAN..	Children's Organ Replacement Program Special Medical Alert Network
CorpTann.....	Corpus Tannaiticum (BJA)
CorpTech	Corporate Technology Information Services, Inc. [Information service or system] (IID)
Corp Tr........	Corporate Trustee (DLA)
CORPUS	CORPUS [Corps of Reserve Priests United for Service] - National Association Resigned/Married Priests (EA)
CORR..........	Chemicals on Reporting Rules Database [Environmental Protection Agency]
CORR..........	Correct [or Corrected or Correction] (AFM)
corr............	Correction (WDMC)
CORR..........	Correct Report [Laboratory] (DAVI)
CORR..........	Correlation (KSC)
CORR..........	Correlative
corr............	Correspond (DLA)
CORR..........	Correspondence (AFM)
corr............	Correspondence (WDMC)
CORR..........	Correspondence
corr............	Correspondent (DLA)
CORR..........	Corresponding
corr............	Corresponding (VRA)
CORR..........	Corridor (DA)
corr............	Corrigenda (BJA)
COR R........	Corris Railway [Wales]
CORR..........	Corrosion (KSC)
CORR..........	Corrugated
CORR..........	Corrupt
CORR..........	Corruption (ROG)
CORR..........	Cor Therapeutics [NASDAQ symbol] (TTSB)
CORR..........	Cor Therapeutics, Inc. [NASDAQ symbol] (SAG)
Corr	Tribunal Correctionnel [Court of First Instance in Penal Matters] [Belgium] (ILCA)
CORRA........	Confederation of Resident & Ratepayer Associations (AC)
CORRA........	Council for Partnership on Rice Research in Asia [A consortium of agricultural research institutes]
CORRAL......	Computer-Oriented Retrieval of Auto Larcenists
CORRC.......	Coordinating Office for Regional Resource Centers
CORRE........	Coalition on Resource Recovery and the Environment (EA)
CORRE........	Correlate (MSA)
CORREC......	Corrective
CorrecSv.....	Correctional Services Corp. [Associated Press] (SAG)
CORREGATE...	Correctable Gate [Computer science] (MDG)
CORREL.......	Correlative
CORRES	Correspond (MSA)
corres	Correspondence (WDMC)
corres	Correspondent [Journalism] (WDMC)
CORRESP	Correspondence [or Corresponding]
Correspondances Jud...	Correspondances Judiciaires [Canada] [A publication] (DLA)
Corr Fell	Corresponding Fellow (WGA)
CORRGTD....	Corrugated
Corr Mem	Corresponding Member (BARN)
CORRO	Central Overseas Recruiting and Rotation Office [Military]
Corrpro........	Corrpro Companies [Associated Press] (SAG)
Corr Rom.....	Correctio Romana [Edition of the Decretals] [A publication] (DSA)
Corr Sec	Corresponding Secretary (BARN)
CORRSPNDNT...	Correspondent
CORRTEX.....	Continuous Reflectometry for Radius Versus Time Experiment [Nuclear testing verification]
CORRUP	Corrupted [or Corruption]
CORS	Canadian Operational Research Society
CORS	Cargo Outturn Reporting System
CORS	Committee on Research and Statistics [American Library Association]
CORS	Composite Operational Reporting System (CAAL)
CORS	Corners
CORS	Corners [Postal Service standard] (OPSA)
CORS	Corsica
Cors	Corsica (VRA)
CORS	Corus Bankshares, Inc. [NASDAQ symbol] (SAG)
CORS	Cronholm-Ottosson Rating Scale [Psychopathology]
COrS	Santiago Library System, Orange, CA [Library symbol Library of Congress] (LCLS)
CORSA........	Corvair Society of America (EA)
CORSA........	Cosmic Ray Satellite [Japan]
CORSAC.......	Council of Regional School Accrediting Commissions (EA)
CORSAIR	Computer-Oriented Reference System for Automatic Information Retrieval [Forsvarets Forskningsansalt] [Sweden]
CORSCHOPSDET...	Commanding Officer, Research Operations Detachment (DNAB)
COR SEC......	Corresponding Secretary (WDAA)
CORSI..........	Coherent RADAR Seeker Investigation (MCD)
CORSIM.......	Corps Battle Simulation

COrSJH	Saint Joseph Hospital, Orange, CA [*Library symbol Library of Congress*] (LCLS)
Cor Soc Cas	Coroner's Society Cases [*England*] [*A publication*] (DLA)
CORSPERS	Committee on Remote Sensing Programs for Earth Resource Survey [*Formerly, COSPEAR*] [*National Academy of Sciences*]
CORST	Council of Resident Summer Theatres [*Defunct*] (EA)
CORT	Certified Operating Room Technician
CORT	Cognitive Research Trust [*British*] (DI)
CORT	Cornet
CORT	Cort Business Services Corp. [*NASDAQ symbol*] (SAG)
CORT	Cortex [*Bark*] [*Pharmacy*]
cort	Cortical
CORT	Corticosterone [*A hormone*]
cort	Cortisone [*Endocrinology*]
CORT	Council of Repertory Theatres [*British*]
CortBus	Cort Business Services Corp. [*Associated Press*] (SAG)
CORT CINCHON	Cortex Cinchonae [*Bark of Cinchona or Peruvian Bark*] [*Pharmacy*] (ROG)
CORTDIV	Escort Division
Cortech	Cortech, Inc. [*Associated Press*] (SAG)
Cortecs	Cortecs International Ltd. [*Associated Press*] (SAG)
CORTEX	Communications-Oriented Real-Time Executive
CORTEX	Computer-Based Optimization Routines and Techniques for Effective X (DIT)
Cortex	Cortex Pharmaceuticals, Inc. [*Associated Press*] (SAG)
CorTher	Cor Therapeutics, Inc. [*Associated Press*] (SAG)
CORTIS	Cortisol [*Pharmacology*] (DAVI)
CORTRAIN	Corps and Division Training Coordination Program [*DoD*]
CORTRON	Escort Squadron
CORTS	Canada-Ontario Rideau-Trent-Severn Study Committee
CORTS	Component Overhaul/Repair Tracking Sheet (MCD)
CORTS	Conversion of Range Telemetry Systems (MCD)
CORTW	Cort Business Svcs Wrrt [*NASDAQ symbol*] (TTSB)
Cortx	Cortex Pharmaceuticals, Inc. [*Associated Press*] (SAG)
CORU	Corrugated
CorusBk	Corus Bankshares, Inc. [*Associated Press*] (SAG)
Corv	Corvus [*Constellation*]
Corvas	Corvas International, Inc. [*Associated Press*] (SAG)
Corvel	Corvel Corp. [*Associated Press*] (SAG)
Corvin El	Corvinus. Elementa Juris Civilis [*A publication*] (DLA)
Corvita	Corvita Corp. [*Associated Press*] (SAG)
Corv Jus	Corvinus' Jus Feodale [*A publication*] (DLA)
COR/WR	Corner Wear [*Deltiology*]
CORX	Cortex Pharmaceuticals [*NASDAQ symbol*] (TTSB)
CORX	Cortex Pharmaceuticals, Inc. [*NASDAQ symbol*] (NQ)
Cory	Coryton's Reports [*Calcutta*] [*A publication*] (DLA)
Cory Acc	Cory on Accounts [*A publication*] (DLA)
Cory Cop	Coryton on Copyrights [*A publication*] (DLA)
Cory Pat	Coryton on Patents [*A publication*] (DLA)
Cory St R	Coryton on Stage Rights [*A publication*] (DLA)
Coryton	Coryton's Reports, Calcutta High Court [*A publication*] (DLA)
COS	Calculator on Substrate (IAA)
COS	Call Originate Status [*Telecommunications*] (HGAA)
COS	Canadian Ophthalmological Society (DAVI)
COS	Canadian Otolaryngological Society (PDAA)
COS	Carbonyl Sulphide (PDAA)
COS	Card Operating System (IAA)
COS	Carry-On Oxygen System (MCD)
COS	Cash-on-Shipment
COS	Cassette-Operated System (MSA)
COS	Cassette Operating System (NITA)
COS	Centralized Operating System (IAA)
COS	Central Opera Service (EA)
COS	Central Operations System (PDAA)
COS	Central Orchid Society [*British*] (DBA)
COS	Certificate of Office Studies [*Academic degree*] (AIE)
COS	Chamber of Shipping (DAS)
COS	Change of Subscribers (TEL)
COS	Changeover Switch (NATG)
COS	Charity Organization Society [*British*]
COS	Chief of Section
COS	Chief of Staff [*Military*]
COS	Chief of Staff [*Medicine*] (DAVI)
COS	Chief of State
COS	Chief of Station [*CIA country team*]
CoS	Church of Scientology
COS	Cinema Organ Society [*British*]
COS	Civilian Occupational Specialty
COS	Class of Service [*Telecommunications*] (TEL)
COS	Clinical Orthopedic Society (EA)
COS	Colorado Springs [*Colorado*] [*Airport symbol*] (OAG)
COS	Colorado Springs, CO [*Location identifier FAA*] (FAAL)
COS	Commercial Office of Spain (EA)
COS	Commercial Operating System (IAA)
COS	Communication Operation Station
COS	Communications Operating System
COS	Communications Oriented Software
COS	Compact Operating System (IAA)
COS	Companies (ROG)
COS	Company Organization Survey [*Bureau of the Census*] (GFGA)
COS	Compatibility Operating System [*Computer science*]
COS	Complementary Switching (IAA)
COS	Complementary Symmetry (IAA)
COS	Complete Operational System (MCD)
COS	Conceptual Operational System

COS	Concors Latvian Air Service [*FAA designator*] (FAAC)
COS	Concurrent Operating System [*Sperry UNIVAC*] [*Computer science*] (IEEE)
COS	Condemned or Suppressed
COS	Conditions of Service [*Engineering*]
COS	Conservative Opportunity Society (EA)
COS	Console Operating System (NASA)
COS	Constant Optimum Separation Lane [*Aviation*] (DA)
COS	Consul [*Latin*] (OCD)
COS	Contactor, Starting
COS	Contaminated Oil Settling (PDAA)
COS	Cooper Ornithological Society (EA)
COS	Core Operating System [*Computer science*] (NITA)
COS	Corporation for Open Systems [*Telecommunications*] (EA)
COS	Cosiguina [*Nicaragua*] [*Seismograph station code, US Geological Survey*] (SEIS)
COS	Cosine [*Mathematics*] (MCD)
COS	Council of States [*An association*]
COS	Counseling-Orientation Preference Scale (EDAC)
COS	Cray Operating System [*Computer science*]
COS	Critical Occupational Specialty [*Military*] (INF)
COS	Customer's Other Service [*Telecommunications*] (TEL)
COS	Cutoff Signal (KSC)
COS	University of Southern Colorado, Pueblo, CO [*OCLC symbol*] (OCLC)
COSA	Car Wash Owners and Suppliers Association (EA)
COSA	Central Office Systems Analyst [*Computer science*]
COSA	Chairman of the Office of Savings Associations
COSA	Co-Dependents of Sexual Addicts [*Acronym is now organization's official name*] (EA)
COSA	Combat Operational Support Aircraft (NVT)
CO SA	Come Sopra [*As Above*] [*Music*] (ROG)
COSA	Completely Overlapped Subarray Antenna (MCD)
COSA	Corps Service Area [*Army*] (AABC)
COSA	Cost of Sales Adjustment [*Economics*] (DCTA)
CoSa	Salida Public Library, Salida, CO [*Library symbol Library of Congress*] (LCLS)
COSAC	Computer Operated Spectrophotometric Analysis of Cameras (NITA)
COSAC	Computing System for Air Cargo (DA)
COSADL	Configuration Status Accounting Data List (MCD)
COSAG	Combined Steam and Gas [*Propulsion*] (MCD)
COSAG	Concerned South Africans Group (ECON)
CoSag	Saguache County Public Library, Saguache, CO [*Library symbol Library of Congress*] (LCLS)
COSAGE	Combat Sample Generator [*Military*]
COSAL	Consolidated Ships Allowance List
COSAL	Coordinated Shipboard [*or Shorebased*] Allowance List [*Navy*]
COSAL	Council of Spokane Area Libraries [*Library network*]
COSALFA	Centro Panamericano de Fiebre Aftosa [*South American Commission for the Control of Foot-and-Mouth Disease*] (EAIO)
COSAM	COBOL Sampler EDP Program [*DCAA*] [*Also DCAM*] (AAGC)
COSAM	COBOL [*Common Business-Oriented Language*] Shared Access Method [*Pertec*]
COSAM	Computer Operated Spectrophotometric Analysis of Monitors (NITA)
COSAM	Cosite Analysis Model [*Computer science*]
CoSAMC	Commission for Special Applications of Meteorology and Climatology [*World Meteorological Organization*]
COSAMREG	Consolidation of Supply and Maintenance Regulations [*Military*] (AABC)
COSAN	Combined Steam and Nuclear [*Propulsion*] (DOMA)
COSAN	Conversational Statistical Analysis (MCD)
COSAP	Cooperative Online Serials Acquisition Project (NITA)
COSAR	Compression Scanning Array RADAR [*Raytheon*]
COSAT	Committee to Support the Antitrust Laws (EA)
COSATI	Committee on Scientific and Technical Information [*Federal Council for Science and Technology*] [*Defunct*] (DBA)
COSATU	Congress of South African Trade Unions
COSAW	Committee on South Asian Women (EA)
COSAWR	Committee on South African War Resistance [*Defunct*] (EAIO)
COSB	CSB Financial Corp. [*NASDAQ symbol*] (SAG)
COSBA	Computer Service and Bureaux Association [*British*]
COSBAL	Consolidated Shore-Based Allowance List (MCD)
COSBAL	Coordinated Shipboard [*or Shorebased*] Allowance List [*Navy*]
COSBE	Committee for Small Business Exports (EA)
COSBI	Canadian Organization of Small Business Inc. [*Also, The Voice of Business*] (AC)
COSC	Canadian Chiefs of Staff Committee
Co-SC	Colorado Supreme Court, Denver, CO [*Library symbol Library of Congress*] (LCLS)
COSC	Combat Operations Specialist Course [*Air Force*] (AFM)
COSC	Combined Operational Service Command
COSC	Cosmetic Center [*Formerly, Cosmetic & Fragrance Concept*] [*NASDAQ symbol*] (SPSG)
COSCA	Conference of State Court Administrators (EA)
COSCA	Cosmetic Center CI'A' [*NASDAQ symbol*] (TTSB)
COSCAA	Council of State Community Affairs Agencies (EA)
COSCB	Cosmetic Center CI'B'(vtg) [*NASDAQ symbol*] (TTSB)
COSCL	Common Operating System Control Language
COSCO	China Ocean Shipping Co.
COSCOM	Corps Support Command [*Army*] (AABC)
CosCtr	Cosmetic Center, Inc. [*Associated Press*] (SAG)
COSCTRACEN	Commanding Officer, Submarine Chaser Training Center
COSD	Combined Operations Supply Depot
COSD	Command Supply Depot [*British military*] (DMA)
COSD	Council of Organizations Serving the Deaf [*Defunct*] (EA)
COSDIF	Cost Differential (MCD)

COSDIV........ Coastal Division [*Navy*] (DNAB)
COSE .... Common Open Software Environment (PCM)
COSE .... Cooperative Operating System Environment [*Computer science*]
COSE .... Costilla Energy, Inc. [*NASDAQ symbol*] (SAG)
COSE .... Council Of Smaller Enterprises
CoSe .... Security Public Library, Security, CO [*Library symbol Library of Congress*] (LCLS)
COSEAL .... Compass System Extensively Altered (SAA)
COSEC .... Coordinating Secretariat of National Unions of Students [*in Africa*]
COSEC .... Cosecant
COSEC .... Culham On-Line Single Experimental Console [*Computer science*] (OA)
COSECH....... Cosecant, Hyperbolic [*Mathematics*] (ROG)
COSECTBASE... Commanding Officer, Section Base [*Navy*]
CoSed.......... Sedgwick Public Library, Sedgwick, CO [*Library symbol Library of Congress*] (LCLS)
COSEMCO.... Comite des Semences du Marche Commun [*Seed Committee of the Common Market*]
COSEP .... Committee on Special Educational Projects [*Cornell University*]
COSEPP .... Committee for Science, Engineering, and Public Policy
COSEPUP..... Committee for Science, Engineering, and Public Policy [*Formerly, COSPUP*] [*National Academy of Sciences*] [*Washington, DC*]
COSERV .... National Council for Community Services to International Visitors [*Later, NCIV*]
COSF .... Corel Corp. [*NASDAQ symbol*] (SAG)
COSF .... Cosmetic & Fragrance Concepts, Inc. (MHDW)
COSFAD ...... Computerized Safety and Facility Design (PDAA)
COSFF .... Corel Corp. [*NASDAQ symbol*] (TTSB)
COSFLOT ..... Coastal Flotilla [*Navy*] (DNAB)
COSFPS....... Commons, Open Spaces, and Footpaths Preservation Society [*British*] (BARN)
COSH .... Committee on Shipping Hydrography [*General Council of British Shipping*] (DS)
COSH .... Control Ordered SONAR Hardware (PDAA)
COSH .... Cosine, Hyperbolic [*Mathematics*]
COSHD........ Committee for Oil Shale Development [*Defunct*] (EA)
COSHEP....... Committee of Scottish Higher Education Principals (AIE)
CO/SHFT ..... Countershaft [*Automotive engineering*]
COSHH........ Control of Substances Hazardous to Health [*British*]
COSHI.......... Clearinghouse for Occupational Safety and Health Information [*HEW*] (IID)
COSHTI........ Council for Science and Technological Information (HGAA)
COSI .... Center of Science and Industry [*Ohio*] (AEBS)
COSI .... Closeout System Installation (NASA)
COSI .... Committee on Scientific Information [*Federal Council for Science and Technology*]
COSI .... Computer Outscoring Services [*NASDAQ symbol*] (SAG)
COSI .... Computer Outsourcing Svcs [*NASDAQ symbol*] (TTSB)
COSI .... Cost of Service Indexing
CoSi.......... Silverton Public Library, Silverton, CO [*Library symbol Library of Congress*] (LCLS)
CoSIDA ...... College Sports Information Directors of America (EA)
COSIE .... Commission on Software Issues in the 80s [*Defunct*] (EA)
COSIGN....... Coordination of Systems, Integrated Goals, and Networks [*DoD*]
COSI-KON .... Crimp-On Snap-In Contacts (MUGU)
COSIN......... Control Staff Instructions [*Army*] (MCD)
COSINE........ Committee on Computer Science in Electrical Engineering Education [*Military*]
COSINE........ Cooperation for Open Systems Interconnection Networking in Europe (OSI)
COSIP .... College Science Improvement Program [*National Science Foundation Defunct*]
COSIRA....... Council for Small Industries in Rural Areas [*British*]
COSIRS....... Case-Oriented Studies Information Retrieval System [*Later, TISCA*] [*Navy*]
COSIRS........ Covert Survivable in Weather Reconnaissance and Strike [*Military*] (DOMA)
COSIS .... Care of Supplies in Storage [*Military*] (AABC)
COSIT .... Computer Services Industry Training Council [*British*] (NITA)
COSL .... Commander Ocean Systems, Atlantic (DOMA)
CoSl.......... Costilla County Library, San Luis, CO [*Library symbol Library of Congress*] (LCLS)
COSLA .... Chief Officers of State Library Agencies (EA)
COSLA .... Convention of Scottish Local Authorities (EAIO)
COSM .... Checkout, Servicing, and Maintenance [*Airlock equipment*] (SSD)
COSMA .... Computer Services for Motor-Freight Activities (PDAA)
COSMAL ...... Consolidated Shorebase Material Allowance List (AAGC)
COSMAL ...... Coordinated Shorebased Material Allowance List [*Air Force*] (AFIT)
COSMAL ...... Coordinated Shore Maintenance Allowance List [*Navy*] (CAAL)
COSMAR ...... Committee on Surface Mining and Reclamation (DICI)
COSMAT ...... Committee on the Survey of Materials Science and Engineering [*National Ac ademy of Sciences*] [*Obsolete*]
COSMD........ Combined Operations Signal Maintenance Depot
COSMED ...... Chiefs of Staff, Mediterranean [*Military*]
COSMEP ...... Combined Stratospheric Measuring Program [*Army*]
COSMEP ...... Committee of Small Magazine Editors and Publishers [*In association name COSMEP, The International Association of Independent Publishers*] (EA)
Cosmetic ..... Cosmetic Group USA, Inc. [*Associated Press*] (SAG)
COSMIC .... Chief of Staff, Military Intelligence Committee (NATG)
COSMIC .... Coherent Optical System of Modular Imaging Collectors
COSMIC .... Coherent Space Mirror Complex
COSMIC .... Combination of Sequential Mutant Interaction Cycles [*Biochemistry*]
COSMIC .... Command Operations Simulation Model with Interrogation Control (SAA)

COSMIC .... Common Systems Main Interconnecting [*Frame system*] [*Bell System*]
COSMIC .... Commonwealth/State Migration Committee [*Australia*]
COSMIC .... Computer Software Management and Information Center [*University of Georgia*] [*NASA Research center*] (RCD)
COSMIC .... Computer Systems for Management Information and Control (PDAA)
COSMIS .... Computer System for Medical Information Services (DIT)
COSMMOS... Countersurge Missile Mortar System (MCD)
COSMO........ Combined Operations Signal Maintenance Officer
Cosmoceutical... Cosmetic Pharmaceutical
CosmoCm .... Cosmo Communictions [*Associated Press*] (SAG)
COSMOG...... Cosmography
COSMON...... Component Open/Short Monitor
COSMOS...... Centralization of Supply Management Operations [*DoD*]
COSMOS...... Coast Survey Marine Observation System
COSMOS...... Colorado Springs Maintenance and Operations System [*Space Defense Center*]
COSMOS...... Committee on SONAR Model Standards [*Navy*]
COS/MOS..... Complementary Symmetry/Metal Oxide Semiconductor
COSMOS...... Comprehensive Option Stiffness Method of Structural Analysis (PDAA)
COSMOS...... Computerized Online System for the Management of Spares [*Army*]
COSMOS...... Computer-Oriented System for Management Order Synthesis [*IBM Corp.*] (BUR)
COSMOS...... Computer System for Main Frame Operations [*Bell System*]
COSMOS...... Console-Oriented Statistical Matrix Operator System [*Computer science*]
COSMOS...... Countersurge Mortar System (MCD)
Cosmtc ...... Cosmetic Group USA, Inc. [*Associated Press*] (SAG)
COSMWST... Coal and Shale Mine Workers' Superannuation Tribunal [*Australia*]
CoSN .... Consortium for School Networking [*Internet*]
COSNOSTRA... Computer-Oriented System - Newly Organized Storage-to-Retrieval Apparatus (KSC)
COSO .... Combat-Oriented Supply Organization (MCD)
COSO .... Combined Operations Signal Officer
CO SO .... Come Sopra [*As Above*] [*Music*]
COSOD........ Conference on Scientific Ocean Drilling [*JOIDES*]
COSOFAM .... Comision de Solidaridad con las Familiares de Presos Politicos, Desaparecidos y Matados en Argentina
COSOS........ Conference on Self-Operating Systems [*Computer science*]
CoSp .... Baca County Public Library, Springfield, CO [*Library symbol Library of Congress*] (LCLS)
COSP .... Canada Oil Substitution Program
COSP .... Central Office Signaling Panel [*Telecommunications*] (TEL)
COSP .... Commander Ocean Systems Pacific (DOMA)
COSP .... Cosponsor
COSPA .... Comite de Solidaridad con el Pueblo Argentino [*Spain*]
COSPA .... Council of Student Personnel Associations in Higher Education [*Defunct*]
COSPAR ...... Committee on Space Research [*of the International Council of Scientific Unions*] [*French*]
COSPAS...... Cooperation in Space [*Former USSR*]
COSPEAR.... Committee on Space Programs for Earth Observations (EGAO)
COSPEC...... Correlation Spectrometer
COSPEN...... Committee on Special Educational Needs [*Scotland*] (AIE)
COSPIN....... Cosmic and Solar Particle Investigation [*Astronomy*]
COSPLUM.... Crystalline Overthrust Structures on the Platform Localizing Unconventional Me thane
COSPOIR ..... Conhairle Natsiunta Spoirt [*National Sports Council*] (EAIO)
COSPUP....... Committee on Science and Public Policy [*Later, COSEPUP*] [*National Academy of Sciences*]
COSQ .... Communications Operations Squadron [*Air Force*]
COSR .... Coastal Ocean Surface RADAR
COSR .... Cutoff Shear [*Tool*] (AAG)
COSRIMS...... Committee on Support of Research in the Mathematical Sciences [*National Academy of Sciences*]
COSRIVRON... Coastal River Squadron [*Navy*] (NVT)
COSRIVRON MST... Coastal River Squadron Mobile Support Team [*Navy*] (DNAB)
COSRO........ Conical Scan-on-Receive Only (NG)
COSRON ...... Coastal Squadron [*Navy*] (DNAB)
COSRRIB ..... Combat Support Rearm and Refuel in Battalions [*Study*] [*Army Logistics Center*]
COSS .... Commander's Operations Security Support System (MCD)
COSS .... Consules [*Consuls*] [*Latin*]
COSS .... Contractor-Operated Storage Site (MCD)
COSS .... Conventional Ordnance Status System (MCD)
COSS .... Co-Orbit Support System (SSD)
COSS .... Cost of Social Security [*International Labor Organization*] [*Information service or system United Nations*] (DUND)
CoSs .... Werner Memorial Public Library, Steamboat Springs, CO [*Library symbol Library of Congress*] (LCLS)
COSSA .... Consortium of Social Science Associations (EA)
COSSA .... Containerized Shipment and Storage of Ammunition (MCD)
COSSAC....... Chief of Staff to Supreme Allied Commander [*Europe*] [*World War II*]
COSSACT..... Command Systems Support Activity
COSSEC....... Cambridge, Oxford & Southern Secondary Examinations Council [*British*] (AIE)
COSSMHO..... Coalition of Spanish Speaking Mental Health Organizations [*Later, NCHHHSO*] (EA)
COSST .... Council of Social Service, Tasmania [*Australia*]
COSSTA....... Computer for Special Small Tactical Application
COSSU........ Coins on Stamps Unit [*American Topical Association*] (EA)
CoSsU.......... United States International University, Colorado Alpine Campus, Steamboat Springs, CO [*Library symbol Library of Congress*] (LCLS)

COS SUFF.... Consul Suffectus [*Latin*] (OCD)
COST .... Centre on Scientific and Technical Information [*Israel*] (NITA)
COST .... Coalition on Sensible Transport
COST .... Coalition Opposed to Signal Theft (EA)
COST .... Command Standard [*Program, Commissary*] (MCD)
COST .... Committee for Overseas Science and Technology [*British*] (PDAA)
COST .... Committee of Singled-Out Taxpayers [*Later, American Council of Taxpayers*] (EA)
COST .... Committee on Office Systems and Technology [*Stanford University*] [*Stanford, CA*] (CSR)
COST .... Committee on Scientific and Technical Information (NITA)
COST .... Computer Optimized Sheetmetal Technology [*Raytheon Co.*]
COST .... Congressional Office of Science and Technology
COST .... Contaminated Oil Settling Tank (AAG)
COST .... Continental Offshore Stratigraphic Test [*Offshore oil technology*]
COST .... Contingency Operations Selection Techniques (MCD)
COST .... Cooperation Europeene dans la Domaine de la Recherche Scientifique et Technique [*European Cooperation in the Field of Scientific and Technical Research*] (MSC)
COST .... Cost-Oriented Systems Technique
Cost .... Cost Reimbursement [*Type of contract*] (AAGC)
COST .... Costume (ROG)
COST .... Council of Stock Theatres
CoSt.......... Sterling Public Library, Sterling, CO [*Library symbol Library of Congress*] (LCLS)
COSTA .... Cost Accounting Code [*NASA*] (NASA)
COSTA .... Council of Subject Teaching Associations (AIE)
Cost Acc'g Stand Guide... Cost Accounting Standards Guide [*Commerce Clearing House*] [*A publication*] (DLA)
COSTALD .... Corresponding States Liquid Density [*Chemical engineering*]
CO-STAR...... Combat-Service to the Army (KSC)
COSTAR....... Combat Support of the Army (AFIT)
COSTAR....... Computer-Stored Ambulatory Record (MCD)
COSTAR....... Conversational On-Line Storage and Retrieval [*Computer science*] (MHDB)
COSTAR....... Corrective Optics Space Telescope Axial Replacement [*NASA*]
CO-STAR...... Covert Submarine Transmitter and Receiver (MCD)
CostaRica ... Costa Rica International, Inc. [*Associated Press*] (SAG)
CO-STAT...... County Statistics [*Bureau of the Census*] (GFGA)
Cost Bull...... Cost Bulletin [*A publication*]
COSTED .... Comite de la Science et de la Technologie dans les Pays en Voie de Developpement [*Committee on Science and Technology in Developing Countries*]
CostEner...... Costilla Energy, Inc. [*Associated Press*] (SAG)
COSTEP .... Commissioned Officer Student Training and Extern Program [*Public Health Service*]
COSTER....... Costermonger [*Fruit or vegetable seller*] [*British*] (DSUE)
COSTER....... Cost Optimizing System to Evaluate Reliability (MHDB)
COSTHA ...... Conference on Safe Transportation of Hazardous Articles (EA)
COSTI .... National Center of Scientific and Technological Information [*National Council for Research and Development*] [*Israel Also, CSTI*] (IID)
CoStN .... Northeastern Junior College of Colorado, Sterling, CO [*Library symbol Library of Congress*] (LCLS)
CostPlus...... Cost Plus, Inc. [*Associated Press*] (SAG)
COSTPRO ..... Canadian Organization for the Simplification of Trade Procedures
CoStr .... Stratton Public Library, Stratton, CO [*Library symbol Library of Congress*] (LCLS)
COSTS .... Committee on Sane Telephone Service
COSU .... Combined Operations Scout Unit
COSVN......... Central Office of South Vietnam [*North Vietnamese high command in the South*]
COS(W)....... Chiefs of Staff, Washington [*Military*]
COSW .... Citizens' Organisation for a Sane World [*British*] (DI)
CoSw .... Swink Public Library, Swink, CO [*Library symbol Library of Congress*] (LCLS)
COSWA....... Committee on the Status of Women in Anthropology (EA)
COSWA....... Conference on Science and World Affairs
COSWAP..... Coaxial Switch and Alternator Panel
COSWL .... Committee on the Status of Women in Librarianship [*American Library Association*]
COSY .... Checkout Operating System
COSY .... Compiler System
COSY .... Compressed Symbolic [*Programming language*] [*Control Data Corp.*]
COSY .... Correction System
COSY .... Correlated Spectroscopy
COT............. Cathodal Opening Tetanus [*Physiology*]
COT............. Center for Office Technology
COT............. Central Office Terminal [*Telecommunications*] (TEL)
COT............. Centre for Ocean Technology [*Canada*] (IRC)
COT............. Checkout Time
COT............. Cholesteryl Oleate-Triglyceride [*Biochemistry*]
COT............. Clutter on Target (MCD)
COT............. Cockpit Orientation Trainer [*Aviation*] (MCD)
COT............. Colony Overlay Test [*Microbiology*]
COT............. Coltec Industries [*NYSE symbol*] (TTSB)
COT............. Coltec Industries, Inc. [*NYSE symbol*] (SPSG)
COT............. Combined Oil and Tanker Group (NATG)
COT............. Commander of Troops [*for a parade or review*] [*Military*]
COT............. Commentaar op het Oude Testament [*A publication*] (BJA)
COT............. Commissioner of Taxes [*Northern Territory*] [*Australia*]
COT............. Committee on Toxicity [*British*]
COT............. Computer-Output-Typesetting (PDAA)
COT............. Conciliation Officer (Tribunal) [*British*]
COT............. Consecutive Oversea Tour [*Military*] (AFM)
COT............. Consolidated Operability Test [*or Trial*] (NG)

COT............. Consort Observation Time
COT............. Construction and Overhaul Testing
COT............. Content of Thought [*Medicine*] (DMAA)
COT............. Contingent
COT............. Continuity [*Telecommunications*] (TEL)
COT............. Continuity Signal [*Telecommunications*] (NITA)
COT............. Contralateral Optic Tectum [*Medicine*]
COT............. Coordinated Operability Test
COT............. Correct (ECII)
COT............. Coscan Development Corp. [*Toronto Stock Exchange symbol*]
COT............. Cotangent [*Mathematics*]
COT............. Cotquean (DSUE)
COT............. Cotter
COT............. Cottesmore TTTE [*British ICAO designator*] (FAAC)
COT............. Cotton (MSA)
cot............. Cotton (VRA)
COT............. Cotulla, TX [*Location identifier FAA*] (FAAL)
COT............. Counter-Obstacle Team [*Army*] (INF)
COT............. Course Ordered Transmitter
COT............. Court (DLA)
COT............. Create Occurrence Table [*University of Minnesota*] (NITA)
COT............. Critical Off-Time [*Medicine*] (MAE)
COT............. Cuneiform Inscriptions and the Old Testament (BJA)
COT............. Current Operating Time
COT............. Customer-Operated Terminal [*Computer science*]
COT............. Customer-Oriented Terminal [*Computer science*]
COT............. Customers Own Transport (DCTA)
COT............. Cyclooctatetraene [*or Cyclooctatetraenyl*] [*Organic chemistry*]
COT............. National Center for State Courts, Williamsburg, VA [*OCLC symbol*] (OCLC)
CoT............. Trinidad Carnegie Public Library, Trinidad, CO [*Library symbol Library of Congress*] (LCLS)
COTA .... Caribbean Organization of Tax Administrators (EAIO)
COTA .... Certified Occupational Therapy Assistant
COTA .... Children's Organ Transplant Association
COTA .... Cinetheodolite Orientation Target Array
CoTA .... Colorado State Home for the Aged, Trinidad, CO [*Library symbol Library of Congress*] (LCLS)
COTA .... Confirming Telephone [*or message*] Authority Of
COTA .... Cost and Training Effectiveness Analysis
COTA .... Council of Tourism Associations of British Columbia [*Formerly, Tourism Industry Association of BC*] (AC)
Cot Abr .... Cotton's Abridgment of the Records [*A publication*] (DLA)
COTAC........ Conference on Training Architects in Conservation [*London, England*]
COTAC........ Copilot/Tactical Coordinator [*In S-3 Viking*] [*Navy*] (DOMA)
Co-T/Agt ..... Co-Transfer Agent (DLA)
COTAL .... Confederacion de Organizaciones Turisticas de l' America Latina [*Confederation of Latin American Travel Organizations*] [*Spanish*] (BARN)
COTAM .... Military Air Transport Command [*France*]
COTANCE.... Confederation of Tanners' Associations in the European Community [*Brussels, Belgium*] (EAIO)
COTANSW.... Council on the Aging, New South Wales [*Australia*]
COTAR........ Contracting Officer's Technical Representative (DOMA)
COTAR........ Correction Tracking and Ranging Station
COTAR........ Correlated Orientation Tracking and Ranging (MSA)
COTAR........ Correlation Tracking and Ranging [*System*] [*Satellite and missile tracking term RADAR*]
COTAR........ Cosine Trajectory Angle and Range (IAA)
COTAR-AME... Correlation Tracking and Ranging Angle Measuring Equipment [*RADAR*]
COTAR-DAS... Correlation Tracking and Ranging Data Acquisition System [*RADAR*]
COTAR-DME... Correlation Tracking and Ranging Data Measuring Equipment [*RADAR*]
COTAT .... Correlation Tracking and Triangulation
COTAT .... Cosine Tracking and Triangulation (SAA)
COTAWS...... Collision and Obstacle/Terrain Avoidance Warning System
COTC .... Canadian Officers Training Corps
COTC .... Canadian Overseas Telecommunications Corp.
COTC .... Commander, Fleet Operational Training Command
COTCH........ Concorde out, Tourist Class Home
COTCLANT.... Commander, Fleet Operational Training Command, Atlantic Fleet
COTCO........ Consolidation of Telecommunications Center on Oahu (MCD)
COTCPAC..... Commander, Fleet Operational Training Command, Pacific Fleet
COTCPACSUBCOM... Commander, Fleet Operational Training Command, Pacific Subordinate Command
COTD .... Cardiac Output by Thermodilution [*Cardiology*] (DMAA)
COTDS .... Commanding Officer's Tactical Display System [*Navy*] (MCD)
COTe.......... Cathodal Opening Tetanus [*Physiology*]
COTE .... Comprehensive Occupational Therapy Evaluation [*Scale*]
CoTeE .... Telluride Elementary School, Telluride, CO [*Library symbol*] [*Library of Congress*] (LCLS)
CotellG .... Cotelligent Group, Inc. [*Associated Press*] (SAG)
COTEN & JT O... Cotenancy and Joint Ownership [*Legal term*] (DLA)
CoTeS .... Telluride High School, Telluride, CO [*Library symbol*] [*Library of Congress*] (LCLS)
COTF.......... Commander Operational Test and Evaluation Force [*Navy*] (CAAL)
COTFMA ...... Chippewa-Ottawa Treaty Fishery Management Authority
COTG .... Consolidated Technology [*NASDAQ symbol*] (SAG)
COTG .... Consolidated Technology Grp [*NASDAQ symbol*] (TTSB)
Cotg .... Cotgrave's Dictionary [*A publication*] (ROG)
COTH .... Cotangent, Hyperbolic [*Mathematics*]
COTH .... Council of Teaching Hospitals (EA)
COTH .... Council of Teaching Hospitals and Health Systems (DMAA)

Coth Stat	Cothran's Annotated Statutes of Illinois [*A publication*] (DLA)
CO-TIE	Cooperation via Televised Instruction in Education [*Colorado State University*]
CoTJ	Trinidad State Junior College, Trinidad, CO [*Library symbol Library of Congress*] (LCLS)
COTL	Cotelligent Group [*NASDAQ symbol*] (TTSB)
COTL	Cotelligent Group, Inc. [*NASDAQ symbol*] (SAG)
COTM	Committee of Ten Million (EA)
COTM	Customer Owned and Telephone Company Maintained [*Telecommunications*] (TEL)
COTMS	Computer-Operated Transmission Measuring Set (PDAA)
COTN	Delta & Pine Land Co. [*NASDAQ symbol*] (SAG)
COTNSD	Cottonseed [*Freight*]
COTP	Captain of the Port [*Coast Guard*]
COTP	Commanding Officer's Tactical Plan [*or Plot*] [*Navy*] (NG)
COTR	Cockpit Orientation Trainer [*Aviation*] (NG)
COTR	Contracting Officers' Technical Representative [*Army*]
Cotr	Cotgrave's Dictionary [*A publication*] (ROG)
Co-Tr	Co-Trustee (DLA)
CoTRA	Computer Threat Research Association [*British*] (DBA)
COTRAN	COBOL [*Common Business-Oriented Language*]-to-COBOL Translator (IEEE)
COTRAN	Conversational Traffic Analysis (MCD)
COTRANS	Coordinated Transfer Application System [*For medical students*]
COTS	Central Officers' Training School
COTS	Checkout Test Set (AAG)
COTS	Coalition on Temporary Shelter
COTS	Commercial Off-the-Shelf [*Software*]
COTS	Container Offloading and Transfer System (MCD)
COTS	Container Over-the-Shore
COTS	Council on Thai Studies
COTSW	Cotswold [*England*]
COTT	Cottage (ADA)
COTT	Cott Corp. [*NASDAQ symbol*] (SAG)
Cott	Cottenham. Reports, Chancery [*1846-48*] [*England*] [*A publication*] (DLA)
COTT	Cottesloe [*England*]
COTT	Cotton (ROG)
CottCp	Cott Corp. [*Associated Press*] (SAG)
COTTF	Cott Corp. [*NASDAQ symbol*] (TTSB)
Cott Mss	Cottonian Manuscripts [*British Museum*] [*A publication*] (DLA)
COTTS	Cottages
COTU	Central Organization of Trade Unions
COTUC	University of Toronto, Department of Chemistry, Toronto, ON, Canada [*Library symbol Library of Congress*] (LCLS)
COTUG	Combined Operations Tug Organization [*For invasion of France*] [*World War II*]
COTUNE	COBOL [*Common Business-Oriented Language*] Tuner
COTV	Cargo Orbit Transfer Vehicle (MCD)
COTX	Cast Off, to X-Ray [*Performed with the cast off*] [*Orthopedics*] (DAVI)
COTY	Car of the Year
COU	Cable Orderwire Unit (MCD)
COU	Cardiac Observation Unit [*Cardiology*] (DAVI)
COU	Clip-On Unit (DCTA)
CoU	Coalition Unity Party [*British*]
cou	Colorado [*MARC country of publication code Library of Congress*] (LCCP)
COU	Columbia [*Missouri*] [*Airport symbol*] (OAG)
COU	Columbia, MO [*Location identifier FAA*] (FAAL)
COU	Coralta Resources [*Vancouver Stock Exchange symbol*]
COU	Couch
COU	Council of Ontario Universities (EDAC)
COU	Country (ROG)
Cou	Couper's Justiciary Reports [*1868-85*] [*Scotland*] [*A publication*] (DLA)
COU	Courtaulds Ltd. [*AMEX symbol*] (SPSG)
COU	Courtaulds, plc ADR [*AMEX symbol*] (TTSB)
CoU	University of Colorado, Boulder, CO [*Library symbol Library of Congress*] (LCLS)
COU	University of Colorado, Medical Center, Denver, CO [*OCLC symbol*] (OCLC)
COUCH	Couchant [*Heraldry*] (ADA)
CoU-CS	University of Colorado at Colorado Springs, Colorado Springs, CO [*Library symbol Library of Congress*] (LCLS)
CoU-DA	University of Colorado at Denver, Auraria Libraries, Denver, CO [*Library symbol Library of Congress*] (LCLS)
COUD-I	Collectors of Unusual Data - International (EA)
CoU-G	University of Colorado, World Data Center A for Glaciology, Snow and Ice, Boulder, CO [*Library symbol*] [*Library of Congress*] (LCLS)
COUGH	Congregation Organized by United Genial Hackers
CoU-GH	University of Colorado, Colorado General Hospital, Denver, CO [*Library symbol Library of Congress*] (LCLS)
CoU-IA	University of Colorado, Institute of Arctic and Alpine Research, World Data Center A for Glaciology, Boulder, CO [*Library symbol Library of Congress*] (LCLS)
COUL	Coulomb [*Unit of electric charge*]
Coul	Coulometric
Coul & F Wat...	Coulston and Forbes on Waters [*6th ed.*] [*1952*] [*A publication*] (DLA)
CoU-M	University of Colorado, Medical Center, Denver, CO [*Library symbol Library of Congress*] (LCLS)
COUN	Council
COUN	Counsel
COUNC	Council (ROG)

COUNS	Counselor
Counsl	Counsel Corp. [*Associated Press*] (SAG)
Couns Mag...	Counsellors' Magazine [*1796-98*] [*A publication*] (DLA)
COUNT	Computer-Operated Universal Test
COUNTCL.....	Counterclaim [*Legal term*] (DLA)
Count Cts Ch...	County Courts Chronicle [*1847-1920*] [*England*] [*A publication*] (DLA)
Count Cts Chron...	County Courts Chronicle [*1847-1920*] [*England*] [*A publication*] (DLA)
COUNTERF...	Counterfeiting (DLA)
County Cc Cas...	County Council Cases [*Scotland*] [*A publication*] (DLA)
County Co Cas...	County Council Cases [*Scotland*] [*A publication*] (DLA)
County Court...	Pennsylvania County Court Reports [*A publication*] (DLA)
County Court R...	Pennsylvania County Court Reports [*A publication*] (DLA)
County Court Rep...	Pennsylvania County Court Reports [*A publication*] (DLA)
County Cts & Bankr Cas...	County Courts and Bankruptcy Cases [*A publication*] (DLA)
County Cts Chron...	County Courts Chronicle [*1847-1920*] [*England*] [*A publication*] (DLA)
County Cts Rep...	County Courts Reports [*1860-1920*] [*England*] [*A publication*] (DLA)
County R......	County Reports [*A publication*] (DLA)
COUP	Chicken Ovalbumin Upstream Promoter [*Genetics*]
COUP	Conference on University Purchasing (AIE)
COUP	Congress of Unrepresented People
Coup	Couper's Justiciary Reports [*1868-85*] [*Scotland*] [*A publication*] (DLA)
COUP	Coupon (ROG)
Couper.........	Couper's Justiciary Reports [*1868-85*] [*Scotland*] [*A publication*] (DLA)
Coup Just	Couper's Justiciary Reports [*1868-85*] [*Scotland*] [*A publication*] (DLA)
COUPLE	Communications-Oriented User Programming Language
COUP-TF......	Chicken Ovalbumin Upstream Promoter Transcription Factor [*Genetics*]
COUR	Courier
COUR	Courier
CoUr	Uravan Public Library, Uravan, CO [*Library symbol Library of Congress*] (LCLS)
Cour & Macl...	Courtnay and Maclean's Scotch Appeals [*6, 7 Wilson and Shaw*] [*A publication*] (DLA)
Courer	Courier Corp. [*Associated Press*] (SAG)
COURSE.......	Course [*Commonly used*] (OPSA)
Court...........	Bott's Poor Laws, by Court [*A publication*] (DLA)
COURT........	Cost Optimization Utilizing Reference Technique (PDAA)
COURT........	Court [*Commonly used*] (OPSA)
Court & Macl...	Courtnay and Maclean's Scotch Appeals [*6, 7 Wilson and Shaw*] [*A publication*] (DLA)
Court Appeals...	Texas Court of Appeals Reports [*A publication*] (DLA)
Court Cl.......	United States Court of Claims Reports [*A publication*] (DLA)
Court J & Dist Ct Rec...	Court Journal and District Court Record [*A publication*] (DLA)
Courtld.........	Courtaulds Ltd. [*Associated Press*] (SAG)
COURTS.......	Courts [*Commonly used*] (OPSA)
Court Sess Ca...	Court of Session Cases [*Scotland*] [*A publication*] (DLA)
COUS	Charitable Organizations of the US [*A publication*]
COUS	Cousin
COUSNAB ...	Commander, United States Naval Advanced Base [*Weser River, West Germany*]
CousPr.........	Cousins Properties, Inc. [*Associated Press*] (SAG)
COUSS	Commanding Officer, United States Ship
COUSSF(P)...	Commanding Officer, United States Special Forces (Provisional) (CINC)
COuT	Commentaar op het Oude Testament [*Kampen*] [*A publication*] (BJA)
Cout	Coutlee's Unreported Cases [*1875-1907*] [*Canada*] [*A publication*] (DLA)
Cout Dig	Coutlee's Digest, Canada Supreme Court [*A publication*] (DLA)
Coutlee........	Coutlee's Unreported Cases [*1875-1907*] [*Canada*] [*A publication*] (DLA)
Coutlee Unrep (Can)...	Coutlee's Unreported Cases [*1875-1907*] [*Canada*] [*A publication*] (DLA)
COUTS	Computer-Operated Universal Test System (IAA)
Cout SC	Notes of Unreported Cases, Supreme Court of Canada (Coutlee) [*A publication*] (DLA)
COV	Calculus of Variation [*NASA*]
COV	Checkout Valve
COV	Coefficient of Variation [*Mathematics*]
COV	Colchester [*Vermont*] [*Seismograph station code, US Geological Survey*] (SEIS)
COV	Concentrated Oil of Vitriol
COV	Connellsville, PA [*Location identifier FAA*] (FAAL)
COV	ConVest Energy Corp. [*AMEX symbol*] (SPSG)
COV	Coolant Override Valve [*Automotive engineering*]
COV	Corona Onset Voltage
COV	Counter-Obstacle Vehicle [*Military*] (RDA)
COV	Counter-Operating Voltage
COV	Covariance (DMAA)
COV	Covenant
COV	Coventry [*City in England*]
COV	Cover (MSA)
COV	Cove Resources [*Vancouver Stock Exchange symbol*]
COV	Covington [*Diocesan abbreviation*] [*Kentucky*] (TOCD)
COV	Crossover Value [*Genetics*]
COV	Cutoff Valve
COV	Cutoff Voltage

COV .... Cutout Valve
COV .... University of Northern Colorado, Greeley, CO [*OCLC symbol*] (OCLC)
CoV .... Victor Public Library, Victor, CO [*Library symbol Library of Congress*] (LCLS)
CoVa .... Vail Public Library, Vail, CO [*Library symbol Library of Congress*] (LCLS)
COVAM .... Capture Orbit Vehicle Assembly Mode
Cov & H Dig... Coventry and Hughes' Digest of the Common Law Reports [*A publication*] (DLA)
COVAR .... Consumption Variation (MCD)
COVART .... Computation of Vulnerable Area and Repair Time (MCD)
COVCE .... Conveyance [*Legal shorthand*] (LWAP)
Cov Conv Ev... Coventry. Conveyancers' Evidence [*1832*] [*A publication*] (DLA)
COVD .... College of Optometrists in Vision Development (EA)
COVD .... Covered
Covenant ...... Covenant Transport, Inc. [*Associated Press*] (SAG)
CoventBk ...... Covenant Bank for Savings [*Associated Press*] (SAG)
Coventry ...... Coventry Corp. [*Associated Press*] (SAG)
COVER .... Covering
COVER .... Cutoff Velocity and Range
CoverAll ...... Cover-All Technologies [*Associated Press*] (SAG)
COVERS .... Combat Vehicle Ram Simulation (MCD)
Covers .... Coversed Sine [*Mathematics*]
COVES .... Coves [*Commonly used*] (OPSA)
COVESA .... Collectors Vehicle Specialists Association [*British*] (DBA)
COVEX .... Coverage Exercise (MUGU)
CoVF .... Cobra Venom Factor [*Immunochemistry*]
COVFF .... Coverings, Facing, or Floor [*Freight*]
Cov Mort ..... Coventry. Mortgage Precedents [*1827*] [*A publication*] (DLA)
CoVnB .... Covenant Bank for Savings [*Associated Press*] (SAG)
COVNG .... Conveyancing [*Legal shorthand*] (LWAP)
COV PT .... Cover Point [*Cricket*] (ROG)
COVR .... Cover-All Technologies [*NASDAQ symbol*] (SAG)
Cov Rec ...... Coventry. Common Recoveries [*1820*] [*A publication*] (DLA)
CoVRT .... Commander and Staff Visualization Research Tool [*Army*] (RDA)
COVT .... Covenant (ROG)
COVTD .... Covenanted [*Legal term*] (ROG)
COVTEE .... Covenantee [*Legal term*] (ROG)
COVTOR .... Covenantor [*Legal term*] (ROG)
COVY .... Convey [*Legal shorthand*] (LWAP)
COW .... Chlorinated Organics in Wastewater
COW .... Coal-Oil-Water [*Fuel mixture*]
COW .... Collection on Wheels [*Shipping*] (DS)
COW .... Commanding Officer's Wife [*Slang*] (DNAB)
COW .... Committee of the Whole [*United Nations*]
COW .... Committee on Water [*National Academy of Science*] (MSC)
COW .... Cooperative Observational Week (MUGU)
COW .... Cornwall Petroleum [*Vancouver Stock Exchange symbol*]
COW .... Corowa [*New South Wales*] [*Airport symbol*] (AD)
COW .... Countries of the World and Their Leaders Yearbook [*A publication*]
COW .... Coventry Ordnance Works [*British military*] (DMA)
COW .... Cow Castle Creek [*South Carolina*] [*Seismograph station code, US Geological Survey*] (SEIS)
Cow .... Cowen's New York Reports [*A publication*] (DLA)
COW .... Cow Observers Worldwide [*An association*] (EA)
Cow .... Cowper's English King's Bench Reports [*1774-78*] [*A publication*] (DLA)
COW .... Crude Oil Washing [*of cargo tank*]
CoW .... Jackson County Public Library, Walden, CO [*Library symbol Library of Congress*] (LCLS)
COW .... Western State College of Colorado, Gunnison, CO [*OCLC symbol*] (OCLC)
COWA .... Council for Old World Archaeology [*Defunct*] (EA)
CoWa .... Huerfano County Public Library, Walsenburg, CO [*Library symbol Library of Congress*] (LCLS)
COWAC .... Council on Women and the Church [*Later, JFW*] (EA)
CoWaL .... Lathrop Park Youth Camp, Walsenburg, CO [*Library symbol Library of Congress*] (LCLS)
CoWals .... Walsh Public Library, Walsh, CO [*Library symbol Library of Congress*] (LCLS)
COWAR .... Joint ICSU-UATI Coordinating Committee on Water Research (EAIO)
COWAT .... Controlled Oral Word Association Test [*Speech and language pathology*] (DAVI)
Cow Att ...... Cowen on Warrants of Attachment [*A publication*] (DLA)
CoWc .... Custer County Public Library, Westcliffe, CO [*Library symbol Library of Congress*] (LCLS)
Cow Cr .... Cowen's Criminal Reports [*New York*] [*A publication*] (DLA)
Cow Cr Dig... Cowen's Criminal Digest [*A publication*] (DLA)
Cow Crim (NY)... Cowen's Criminal Reports [*New York*] [*A publication*] (DLA)
Cow Cr L ..... Cowen's Criminal Law [*New York*] [*A publication*] (DLA)
Cow Cr R ..... Cowen's Criminal Reports [*New York*] [*A publication*] (DLA)
Cow Cr Rep... Cowen's Criminal Reports [*New York*] [*A publication*] (DLA)
Cow Dic ...... Cowell's Law Dictionary [*A publication*] (DLA)
Cow Dict ..... Cowell's Law Dictionary [*A publication*] (DLA)
Cow Dig ...... Cowell's East India Digest [*A publication*] (DLA)
Cow Dig ...... Digest to Cowen's New York Reports [*A publication*] (DLA)
Cowd L Enc... Cowdery's Law Encyclopaedia [*California*] [*A publication*] (DLA)
COWEAEX ..... Cold Weather Exercise [*Military*] (NVT)
Cowell .... Cowell's Interpreter [*A publication*] (DLA)
Cowell .... Cowell's Law Dictionary [*A publication*] (DLA)
CoWeT .... Colorado State Home and Training School, Wheatridge, CO [*Library symbol Library of Congress*] (LCLS)
CoWeT-M ..... Colorado State Home and Training School, Medical Library, Wheatridge, CO [*Library symbol Library of Congress*] (LCLS)

CoWi .... Windsor Public Library, Windsor, CO [*Library symbol Library of Congress*] (LCLS)
Cow Inst ..... Cowell's Institutiones Juris Anglicani [*A publication*] (DLA)
Cow Int ...... Cowell's Interpreter [*A publication*] (DLA)
Cow JP .... Cowen's New York Treatise on Justices of the Peace [*A publication*] (DLA)
Cow Just ..... Cowen's New York Treatise on Justices of the Peace [*A publication*] (DLA)
COWL .... Cold Ocean-Warm Land [*Climatology*]
COWL .... Council of Wisconsin Libraries [*Information service or system*] (IID)
COWLEX ...... Cold Weather Landing Exercise [*Military*] (NVT)
COWLR .... Conference on Oriental-Western Literary Relations [*Later, ALD*] (EA)
Cow LR .... Cowan. Land Rights in Scotland [*A publication*] (ILCA)
COWM .... Coal-Oil-Water Mixture [*Fuel*]
CoWm .... Westminster Public Library, Westminster, CO [*Library symbol Library of Congress*] (LCLS)
Cow NY .... Cowen's New York Reports [*A publication*] (DLA)
COWP .... Contracting Officer's Warrant Program (AAGC)
COWP .... Cowpens National Battlefield Site
Cowp .... Cowper's English King's Bench Reports [*1774-78*] [*A publication*] (DLA)
CoWp .... Woodland Park Public Library, Woodland Park, CO [*Library symbol Library of Congress*] (LCLS)
Cowp Cas .... Cowper's Cases [*Third volume of Reports in Chancery*] [*A publication*] (DLA)
Cowp (Eng)... Cowper's English King's Bench Reports [*1774-78*] [*A publication*] (DLA)
COWPS .... Council on Wage and Price Stability [*Also, CWPS*] [*Abolished, 1981*]
Cow R .... Cowen's New York Reports [*A publication*] (DLA)
CoWr .... Wray Public Library, Wray, CO [*Library symbol Library of Congress*] (LCLS)
CoWrN .... Northeast Colorado Regional Library, Wray, CO [*Library symbol Library of Congress*] (LCLS)
COWRR .... Committee on Water Resources Research [*US*]
COWS .... Change Order Work Sheet (DNAB)
COWS .... Classification Order Watch Service [*Research Publications, Inc.*]
COWS .... Cold to the Opposite and Warm to the Same Side [*Audiometry*]
COWS .... Contracting Officer's Warrant System (AAGC)
Cow Tr .... Cowen's New York Treatise on Justices of the Peace [*A publication*] (DLA)
COX .... Calcium Oxalate [*Organic chemistry*]
COX .... Cast-Off X-Ray [*Performed with the cast off*] [*Orthopedics*] (DAVI)
COX .... Cox Communications'A' [*NYSE symbol*] (TTSB)
COX .... Cox Communications, Inc. [*NYSE symbol*] (SAG)
Cox .... Cox's English Chancery Reports [*1783-96*] [*A publication*] (DLA)
Cox .... Cox's English Criminal Cases [*A publication*] (DLA)
Cox .... Cox's Reports [*25-27 Arkansas*] [*A publication*] (DLA)
COX .... Coxswain
COX .... Cyclooxygenase [*An enzyme*]
COX .... Cytochrome C Oxidase (DMAA)
COx .... Oxnard Public Library, Oxnard, CA [*Library symbol Library of Congress*] (LCLS)
COX .... University of Colorado at Colorado Springs, Colorado Springs, CO [*OCLC symbol*] (OCLC)
Cox Adv ...... Cox. Advocate [*1852*] [*A publication*] (DLA)
Cox Am T Cas... Cox's American Trade-Mark Cases [*A publication*] (DLA)
Cox Am TM Cas... Cox's American Trade-Mark Cases [*A publication*] (DLA)
Cox Anc L .... Cox. Law and Science of Ancient Lights [*1871*] [*A publication*] (ILCA)
Cox & Atk .... Cox and Atkinson's Registration Appeal Cases [*1843-46*] [*England*] (DLA)
Cox & M'C ... Cox, Macrae, and Hertslet's English County Court Cases [*1847-58*] [*A publication*] (DLA)
Cox & S Cr L... Cox and Saunders' Criminal Law Consolidation Acts [*3rd ed.*] [*1870*] [*A publication*] (DLA)
COXCBS ...... Coxswain, Construction Battalion, Stevedore
Cox CC .... Cox's County Court Cases [*1860-1919*] [*England*] [*A publication*] (DLA)
Cox CC .... Cox's Crown Cases [*A publication*] (DLA)
Cox CC .... Cox's English Criminal Cases [*A publication*] (DLA)
Cox Ch .... Cox's English Chancery Cases [*A publication*] (DLA)
Cox Ch Cas (Eng)... Cox's English Chancery Cases [*A publication*] (DLA)
Cox Ch Pr .... Cox's Chancery Practice [*A publication*] (DLA)
Cox CL Pr .... Cox's Common Law Practice [*A publication*] (DLA)
CoxCm .... Cox Communications, Inc. [*Associated Press*] (SAG)
Cox Cr Ca ... Cox's English Criminal Cases [*A publication*] (DLA)
Cox Cr Cas... Cox's English Criminal Cases [*A publication*] (DLA)
Cox Cr Dig... Cox's Criminal Law Digest [*A publication*] (DLA)
Cox Crim Cas... Cox's English Criminal Cases [*A publication*] (DLA)
Cox Cty Ct Ca... Cox's County Court Cases [*1860-1919*] [*England*] [*A publication*] (DLA)
Cox Cty Ct Cas... Cox's County Court Cases [*1860-1919*] [*England*] [*A publication*] (DLA)
Coxe .... Coxe's Reports [*1 New Jersey Law*] [*A publication*] (DLA)
Coxe Bract... Coxe's Translation of Guterbach's Bracton [*A publication*] (DLA)
Cox Elect .... Cox's Registration and Elections [*14th ed.*] [*1885*] [*A publication*] (DLA)
Cox Eq .... Cox's Equity Cases [*England*] [*A publication*] (DLA)
Cox Eq Cas... Cox's Equity Cases [*England*] [*A publication*] (DLA)
Cox Gov ...... Cox's Institutions of the English Government [*A publication*] (DLA)
COXI .... Cytochrome Oxidase [*An enzyme*]
Cox Inst ..... Cox's Institutions of the English Government [*A publication*] (DLA)
Cox JS Cas... Cox's Joint Stock Company Cases [*1864-72*] [*England*] [*A publication*] (DLA)
Cox JS Comp... Cox's Joint Stock Company Cases [*1864-72*] [*England*] [*A publication*] (DLA)

Cox Jt Stk....	Cox's Joint Stock Company Cases [1864-72] [England] [A publication] (DLA)
Cox Mag Ca...	Cox's Magistrates' Cases [1859-1919] [England] [A publication] (DLA)
Cox Mag Cas...	Cox's Magistrates' Cases [1859-1919] [England] [A publication] (ILCA)
Cox M & H...	Cox, Macrae, and Hertslet's English County Court Reports [1847-58] [A publication] (DLA)
Cox Man Tr M...	Cox's Manual of Trade-Mark Cases [A publication] (DLA)
Cox MC........	Cox's Magistrates' Cases [1859-1919] [England] [A publication] (DLA)
Cox Mc & H...	Cox, Macrae, and Hertslet's English County Court Reports [1847-58] [A publication] (DLA)
Coxn	Coxswain [British military] (DMA)
Cox Pun........	Cox's Principles of Punishment [1877] [A publication] (DLA)
Cox PW.......	Cox's Edition of Peere Williams' Reports [England] [A publication] (DLA)
Cox Ques.....	Cox's Questions for the Use of Students [A publication] (DLA)
CoxRad........	Cox Radio, Inc. [Associated Press] (SAG)
COXRALM...	Composite Optical/X-Ray LASER Microscope
Cox Reg.......	Cox's Registration and Elections [14th ed.] [1885] [A publication] (DLA)
COXSRR	Coxswain, Ship Repair, Rigger
COXSRS......	Coxswain, Ship Repair, Canvasman
Cox Tr M	Cox's Manual of Trade-Mark Cases [A publication] (DLA)
Cox Tr M Ca...	Cox's American Trade-Mark Cases [A publication] (DLA)
Cox Tr M Cas...	Cox's American Trade-Mark Cases [A publication] (DLA)
COY	Career Opportunities for Youth (SAA)
COY	Car of the Year
COY	Colossal Energy, Inc. [Vancouver Stock Exchange symbol]
COY	Company
COY	Corporate High Yield Fund [NYSE symbol] (TTSB)
COY	Corporate High Yield Fund, Inc. [NYSE symbol] (SAG)
COY	Denver Law Librarians Group, Denver, CO [OCLC symbol] (OCLC)
COY	St. Croix, VI [Location identifier FAA] (FAAL)
COY	Transportes Aereos Coyhaique [Chile] [ICAO designator] (FAAC)
CoY	Yuma Public Library, Yuma, CO [Library symbol Library of Congress] (LCLS)
CoYa...........	Yampa Women's Club Library, Yampa, CO [Library symbol Library of Congress] (LCLS)
COYOTE	Come Off Your Old Tired Ethics [Prostitutes' lobbying group]
COZ.............	Calpetro Resources, Inc. [Vancouver Stock Exchange symbol]
COZ.............	Colorado State Library, Denver, CO [OCLC symbol] (OCLC)
COZ.............	Corair [France ICAO designator] (FAAC)
COZ.............	Cousin (ROG)
COZA	Combined Operations Headquarters, Zara [Former Yugoslavia] [World War II]
COZAC.......	Conservation Zone Advisory Committee [Australia]
COZI...........	Communications Zone Indicator [Air Force]
COZID	Cable Operated Zero Impedence Decoupler (MCD)
CP...............	Avions Mudry & Cie. [France], Lockheed Aircraft Corp. [ICAO aircraft manufacturer identifier] (ICAO)
CP...............	Calculator Printing (IAA)
CP...............	Calendar Process [Telecommunications] (TEL)
CP...............	Calibration Procedure
CP...............	Callaway Plant (NRCH)
CP...............	Callose Platelets [Botany]
CP...............	Call Paid [Telecommunications] (ADA)
CP...............	Call Process [Telecommunications] (NITA)
CP...............	Call Processor [Computer science]
CP...............	Calorific Power (IAA)
CP...............	Cambridge Pulsar (IIA)
CP...............	Caminhos de Ferro Portugueses [Railway] [Portugal] (EY)
CP...............	Camp
CP...............	Camp
CP...............	Campaign for Prosperity (EA)
CP...............	Canadian Pacific Ltd. [NYSE symbol Toronto Stock Exchange symbol Vancouver Stock Exchange symbol] (SPSG)
CP...............	Canadian Pacific, Ord [NYSE symbol] (TTSB)
CP...............	Canadian Press
CP...............	Candlepower [Physics]
cp	Candle Power (IDOE)
CP...............	Canister Purge [Automotive engineering]
CP...............	Cannibalization Point [Supply and Maintenance] [Military]
cp	Canton and Enderbury Islands [MARC country of publication code Library of Congress] (LCCP)
CP...............	Cape Province [of South Africa]
CP...............	Capillary Pressure [Physiology]
CP...............	Captain of the Parish [British] (ROG)
CP...............	Captopril [Also, CPT] [Antihypertensive drug]
CP...............	Carbamyl Phosphate [Also, CAP] [Organic chemistry]
CP...............	Carbonate Platform [Archaeology]
CP...............	Carbon Paste
C/P.............	Carbon/Phenolic
CP...............	Cardinal Point (ROG)
CP...............	Cardiopulmonary [Medicine]
CP...............	Card Punch [Computer science] (BUR)
CP...............	Card to Printer (IAA)
CP...............	Career Program [Army] (RDA)
CP...............	Cargo Program [or Projects] Office [NASA] (MCD)
CP...............	Car Park (ADA)
CP...............	Car Pricing
CP...............	Carriage Paid
CP...............	Cars of the Past [An association Defunct] (EA)
C-P.............	Cartesian to Polar

CP...............	Carto-Philatelists (EA)
Cp	Carya pecan [Pecan tree]
CP...............	Case Postale (DD)
CP...............	Case Preparation
C/P.............	Case Project [IRS]
Cp	Cassiopeium [An early name for the chemical element lutetium]
CP...............	Catch Phrase
CP...............	Cathodic Protection [Metallurgy]
CP...............	Cat Pack ["Women's Wear Daily" slang for jetsetters]
CP...............	Cattle-Plague (ROG)
CP...............	Caudate Putamen [Neuroanatomy]
CP...............	Cell Pack [Horticulture]
CP...............	Cellulose Paper
CP...............	Cellulose Propionate Plastic [Organic chemistry]
CP...............	Center of Pressure
CP...............	Centerpartiet [Center Party] [Sweden Political party] (PPE)
CP...............	Center Punch (MSA)
CP...............	Centipoise [Unit of viscosity]
CP...............	Central Point
CP...............	Central Press
CP...............	Central Problem [Psychometrics]
CP...............	Central Processor [Computer science]
cp	Central Processor (IDOE)
CP...............	Central Procurement [or Centrally Procured] (AFM)
CP...............	Central Provinces [Later, Madhya Pradesh, India]
C/P.............	Central to Peripheral Ratio [Anatomy]
CP...............	Centrifugal Photosedimentation
CP...............	Centrum Partii [Center Party] [Netherlands Political party] (EY)
CP...............	Cerebellopontine [Anatomy] (AAMN)
CP...............	Cerebral Palsy [Medicine]
CP...............	Cerebral Peduncle [Brain anatomy]
CP...............	Cerebropontine [Angle] [Neurosurgery] (DAVI)
CP...............	Certificate in Performance (PGP)
CP...............	Certification of Purchase
CP...............	Certified Patient [British]
CP...............	Certified Prosthetist
Cp	Ceruloplasmin [Biochemistry]
CP...............	Cesspits (ROG)
CP...............	Cesspool (AAG)
CP...............	Chain Procedure [Indexing] (NITA)
CP...............	Chamber Pressure
CP...............	Change Package (AAG)
CP...............	Change Pages (MCD)
CP...............	Change Point [Surveying]
CP...............	Change Proposal (KSC)
CP...............	Chappel-Perry Medium [Microbiology]
CP...............	Chapter
CP...............	Character Printer [Computer science]
CP...............	Charge Parity [Atomic physics]
CP...............	Charging Pump (NRCH)
CP...............	Charles Pfizer & Co. [Research code symbol]
CP...............	Charoen Pokphand [Thai business conglomerate] (ECON)
CP...............	Charter Party [Transportation]
CP...............	Check Parity (SAA)
CP...............	Checkpoint
CP...............	Chemically Pure [Chemistry]
CP...............	Chemical Polish
CP...............	Chemical Practitioner (DAS)
CP...............	Chemical Preparation (OA)
CP...............	Chemical Propulsion
CP...............	Chemical Pulp
CP...............	Chest Pain [Medicine] (MAE)
CP...............	Chicago Pile [Nuclear reactor]
Cp	Chickenpox [Also, CHPX] [Medicine]
CP...............	Chief of Police
CP...............	Chief Patriarch
CP...............	Chief Pilot
CP...............	Child Psychiatry
CP...............	Child Psychology
CP...............	Childsave Project [Defunct] (EA)
CP...............	Chirp Period [Entomology]
CP...............	Chlorinated Paraffin [Organic chemistry]
CP...............	Chloroprocaine [A local anesthetic]
CP...............	Chloropurine [Antineoplastic drug] (AAMN)
CP...............	Chloroquine and Primaquine [Antimalarial drugs] (AAMN)
C/P.............	Cholesterol/Phospholipid Ratio [Clinical chemistry]
CP...............	Chondritic Porous [Aggregate] [Inorganic chemistry]
CP...............	Chondromalacia Patella [Orthopedics] (DAVI)
CP...............	Christian Projects [Australia]
CP...............	Chromatin Protein [Biochemistry]
CP...............	Chrome Plated
CP...............	Chronic Pain (DAVI)
CP...............	Chronic Pancreatitis [Medicine] (PDAA)
CP...............	Chronic Progressive [Medicine]
CP...............	Chronic Pyelonephritis [Urology]
CP...............	Churchman Publishing [British]
CP...............	Cicatricial Pemphigoid [Medicine]
CP...............	Circadian Pacemaker [Neurophysiology]
CP...............	Circuit Package (MSA)
CP...............	Circular Pitch [Technical drawings]
CP...............	Circular Polarization [Optics]
CP...............	Circulation Pump
CP...............	Cisplatin [or Cis-platinum] [Antineoplastic drug] (DAVI)
CP...............	Cited Pages [Database terminology] (NITA)
CP...............	Citizen's Party [Defunct] (EA)

CP	Civilian Population (MCD)
CP	Civil Parish [*British*]
CP	Civil Power
CP	Civil Procedure [*Legal term*]
CP	Civil Procedure Reports [*New York*] [*A publication*] (DLA)
CP	Clarenden Press (DAS)
CP	Clarissima Puella [*Most Illustrious Maiden*] [*Latin*]
CP	Classical Philosophy
CP	Claw Plate [*Technical drawings*]
CP	Clay Pipe [*Technical drawings*]
CP	Cleft Palate [*Medicine*]
CP	Clerk of the Peace [*British*]
CP	Climate Pay [*British military*] (DMA)
CP	Clinical Pathology
CP	Clock Phase
CP	Clock Pulse
CP	Closed Position [*Dancing*]
CP	Close Packed (MSA)
CP	Closing Pressure [*Medicine*]
CP	Closing Price [*Business term*]
CP	Closing Purchase [*Business term*]
CP	Clottable Protein [*Medicine*] (MAE)
CP	Cloud Point [*Petroleum characteristic*]
CP	Coalicion Popular [*Popular Coalition*] [*Spain Political party*] (PPW)
CP	Coat [*or Capsid*] Protein [*Cytology*]
CP	Cochlear Potential [*Otolaryngology*]
CP	Code of Practice [*Legal term*]
CP	Code of Procedure [*Legal term*]
CP	Code Proficiency [*Amateur radio*]
CP	Codex Petropolitanus (BJA)
CP	Coefficient of Performance (IEEE)
CP	Coefficient of Protection [*Against insects*]
CP	Coherent Potential (OA)
CP	Cold Pack [*Medicine*]
CP	Cold Pipe [*Nuclear energy*] (NRCH)
CP	Coldplate (KSC)
CP	Cold Press [*Metallurgy*] (IAA)
CP	Cold-Punched [*Metal*]
CP	Colla Parte [*With the Solo Part*] [*Music*]
CP	Collar Pricing [*Investment term*]
CP	Collective Protection [*from NBC contaminants*] [*Military*] (RDA)
CP	College of Preceptors [*British*]
CP	Collision Probability (OA)
CP	Color Perception [*Medicine*]
CP	Color Printing [*Filter*] [*Photography*]
CP	Column Product [*Nuclear energy*] (NRCH)
CP	Combat Power [*DoD*]
CP	Combination Product [*Medicine*] (MAE)
CP	Combining Power
CP	Comedy Prescription [*An association*] (EA)
CP	Command Paymaster [*British military*] (DMA)
CP	Command Pilot (AFM)
CP	Command Point (AFIT)
CP	Command Post [*Military*]
CP	Command Pouch [*Air Force*] (AFM)
CP	Command Processor [*Computer science*] (BUR)
CP	Command Pulse (MSA)
CP	Commercial Paper [*Banking*]
CP	Commission de Paris [*Paris Commission - PARCOM*] (EAIO)
CP	Committee on Propagation [*National Defense Research Committee*]
CP	Commodity Prices [*A publication*]
CP	Common Pleas [*Legal term*]
CP	Common Prayer
CP	Common Process [*Telecommunications*] (TEL)
CP	Commonwealth Party [*Gibraltar*] [*Political party*] (PPE)
CP	Communication Personnel [*Marine Corps*]
CP	Communications Processor
CP	Communications Programs [*NASA*]
CP	Communications Project (EA)
CP	Communist Party [*Political party*]
CP	Community of the Presentation [*Anglican religious community*]
CP	Community Placement
CP	Company Policy (MCD)
CP	Compare
CP	Compensated Base [*Medicine*] (DAVI)
CP	Complete Physical [*Medicine*] (DAVI)
CP	Compline
CP	Component Parts (MCD)
CP	Compound [*Medicine*]
CP	Compressed Tablet [*Pharmacy*]
CP	Computed Point [*Navigation*]
CP	Computer (IAA)
CP	Computer Paragraph
CP	Computer Program (MCD)
CP	Computers [*JETDS nomenclature*] [*Military*] (CET)
CP	Concrete Piercing
CP	Concurrent Planometric [*A discrimination task*]
CP	Conditional Pardon (ADA)
CP	Conditional Proof [*Method in logic*]
CP	Conditional Purchase [*Business term*] (ADA)
CP	Condition Precedent [*Legal term*]
CP	Conductive Plastic
CP	Cone Point (MSA)
CP	Conference Paper
CP	Conference Proceedings (ADA)
CP	Confidence Probability [*Mathematics*]
CP	Congregation of the Passion (TOCD)
cp	Congregation of the Passion, Passionist Fathers (TOCD)
CP	Congregatio Passionis [*Congregation of the Passion*] [*Passionists*] [*Roman Catholic religious order*]
CP	Congregazione della Passione [*Congregation of the Passion*] (EAIO)
CP	Congress Party [*India*] [*Political party*]
CP	Conjugation-Parity [*Physics*]
CP	Connection Pending [*Telecommunications*] (TEL)
CP	Connection Point [*Computer science*] (IBMDP)
CP	Connector Panel
CP	Conservative Party [*South Africa*] [*Political party*]
CP	Console Processor (NASA)
CP	Constantinople Pentateuch (BJA)
CP	Constant Parity [*Physics*]
CP	Constant Potential (DEN)
CP	Constant Power (DA)
CP	Constant Pressure (MSA)
CP	Constant Property
CP	Constitutionalist Party [*Malta*] [*Political party*] (PPE)
CP	Constrained Procedure (AAG)
CP	Construction Apprentice (MUGU)
CP	Construction Permit [*FCC*]
CP	Construction Procedures [*Nuclear energy*] (NRCH)
CP	Constructive Placement [*Railcar*]
C/P	Consultation Paper (DCTA)
CP	Consulting Physician (ROG)
CP	Contact Party [*Army*]
CP	Contact Preclude (DNAB)
CP	Containerless Processing (SSD)
CP	Containment Purge [*Nuclear energy*] (NRCH)
CP	Contemporary Psychology [*A publication*] (BRI)
CP	Continental Pharma [*Belgium*] [*Research code symbol*]
CP	Continental Plan [*Hotel rate*]
CP	Continental Polar Air Mass
CP	Contingency Planning (MCD)
CP	Continuous Path [*Robotics*]
CP	Continuous Phase (OA)
CP	Contractile Pulse (PDAA)
CP	Contract Number Prefix [*Database terminology*] (NITA)
C/P	Contract Price
CP	Contrappunto [*Counterpoint*] [*Music*] (ROG)
CP	Contributory Place (ROG)
CP	Control Panel
CP	Control Pascal [*Compiler*] [*Computer science*]
CP	Control Point
CP	Control Post [*RADAR*]
CP	Control Procedures (MCD)
CP	Control Processor (IEEE)
CP	Control Program [*Computer science*]
C/P	Converter/Programmer (MCD)
CP	Convicted Poacher [*Legal*] [*British*] (ROG)
CP	Coolant Pump [*Nuclear energy*] (NRCH)
CP	Cooperative Power [*Later, SPG*] (EA)
CP	Coordinating Panel [*NATO*]
CP	Coordination Processor [*Telecommunications*]
CP	Copilot
CP	Copper Pair [*Telecommunications*]
CP	Coproporphyrin [*Also, COPRO*] [*Clinical chemistry*]
CP	Copula Pyramidna [*Neuroanatomy*]
CP	Copy (MCD)
CP	Coracoid Process [*Anatomy*]
CP	Core Prime (SAA)
CP	Coronagraph Polarimeter
CP	Cor Pulmonale [*Medicine*]
CP	Correction Processor
CP	Correlation Processor
CP	Correspondence Printer (MHDI)
CP	Corrosion Protection [*Telecommunications*] (TEL)
CP	Cortical Plate [*Neuroanatomy*]
CP	Cosmogenic (IAA)
CP	Cost and Performance
CP	Cost Plus [*Insurance*]
CP	Cost Price [*Business term*] (ADA)
CP	Cost Proposal
CP	Couch Potatoes [*Defunct*] (EA)
CP	Council for the Principality [*British*]
CP	Council of Presidents (EA)
CP	Council of Principals (AIE)
CP	Counterpoint [*Music*]
CP	Counterpoise [*Electricity*] (IAA)
CP	Countries and Peoples [*A publication*]
CP	Country Party [*Political party*] [*Australia*] (BARN)
CP	Country Profile (ADA)
CP	Coupe [*Automotive*]
CP	Coupe
CP	Coupling
CP	Coupon
CP	Court of Common Pleas (DLA)
CP	Court of Probate
CP	Court Physician (ROG)
CP	Couterpoise Procedure [*Physical chemistry*]
CP	Cover Point [*Lacrosse position*]
CP	Cowpea
CP	Crack Propagation (AAG)

CP .... Crankshaft Position [*Automotive engineering*]
CP .... Creatine Phosphate [*Phosphocreatine; see PC*] [*Biochemistry*]
CP .... Creatine Phosphokinase [*Biochemistry*] (DAVI)
CP .... Critical Path
CP .... Critical Period
CP .... Critical Power [*Nuclear energy*] (NRCH)
CP .... Cross Polarization [*Atomic physics*]
CP .... Cross Pollinated [*Genetics*]
CP .... Cross Products [*Statistics*]
CP .... Crown Pleas [*Legal term*] (DLA)
CP .... Crude Protein
CP .... Crystalline or Powdered
CP .... Crystal Palace, Sydenham [*British*]
CP .... Current Paper
CP .... Current Period
C/P .... Current/Pneumatic [*Nuclear energy*] (NRCH)
CP .... Current Practices
CP .... Cushioning Pads
CP .... Custodial Parent
C/P .... Custom and Port [*International trade*]
CP .... Customer Proven [*GMC truck marketing*]
CP .... Customized Processor [*IBM Corp.*] (IEEE)
CP .... Cuticular Plate [*Biology*]
CP .... Cyclic Permuted
Cp .... Cyclopentadienyl [*Also, cp*] [*Organic radical*]
CP .... Cyclophosphamide [*Cytoxan*] [*Antineoplastic drug*]
CP .... Cyclophosphamide, Prednisone [*Antineoplastic drug regimen*]
CP .... Cylindrical Perforated
CP .... Cyprus [*IYRU nationality code*] (IYR)
CP .... Law Reports, Common Pleas [*England*] [*A publication*] (DLA)
CP .... Pasadena Public Library, Pasadena, CA [*Library symbol Library of Congress*] (LCLS)
C$_P$ .... Phosphate Clearance [*Organic chemistry*] (DAVI)
C$_p$ .... Phosphate Clearance [*Medicine*] (MAE)
C$_p$ .... Prismatic Coefficient [*Boat design*]
CP .... Religious of the Passion of Jesus Christ (TOCD)
CP .... Sisters of the Cross and Passion [*Roman Catholic women's religious order*]
CP .... Station Open to Public Correspondence [*ITU designation*]
CP .... Upper Canada Common Pleas [*Legal term*] (DLA)
CP2 .... Contractor Performance Certification Program [*Army*] (RDA)
CP3 .... MIT [*Massachusetts Institute of Technology*]-Industry Composites and Polymer Processing Program [*Research center*] (RCD)
CP-5 .... Chicago Pile-5 [*Nuclear heavy-water-research reactor*]
CPA .... Ambassador College, Pasadena, CA [*Library symbol Library of Congress*] (LCLS)
CPA .... Cadmium Pigments Association (EAIO)
CPA .... Calcium-Binding Para-Albumin [*Biochemistry*]
CPA .... Calgary Police Association [*Association de la Police de Calgary*] (AC)
CPA .... Calico Printers' Association (DGA)
CPA .... California Pistachio Association (EA)
CPA .... Campaign Poster Award [*British*]
CPA .... Canadian Pacific Airlines Ltd. [*Facetious translations: Can't Possibly Arrive, Come Push Along*]
CPA .... Canadian Paraplegic Association [*Ontario*] (AC)
CPA .... Canadian Paraplegic Association (AC)
CPA .... Canadian Particleboard Association [*Canada*] (EAIO)
CPA .... Canadian Payments Association
CPA .... Canadian Payroll Association [*Association Canadienne de la Paie*] (AC)
CPA .... Canadian Peace Alliance [*Alliance Canadienne pour la Paix*] (AC)
CPA .... Canadian Petroleum Association
CPA .... Canadian Pharmaceutical Association (MCD)
CPA .... Canadian Philosophical Association
CPA .... Canadian Physiotherapy Association
CPA .... Canadian Pinzgauer Association (AC)
CPA .... Canadian Poetry Association [*Also, London Regional Literary Society*] (AC)
CPA .... Canadian Police Association
CPA .... Canadian Postmaster's Association
CPA .... Canadian Psychiatric Association
CPA .... Canadian Psychological Association (MCD)
CPA .... Cape Palmas [*Liberia*] [*Airport symbol*] (OAG)
CPA .... Carboxypeptidase A [*An enzyme*]
CPA .... Cardiopulmonary Arrest [*Medicine*] (CPH)
CPA .... Caribbean Press Association (NTCM)
CPA .... Carlisle Plastics CI'A' [*NYSE symbol*] (TTSB)
CPA .... Carlisle Plastics, Inc. [*NYSE symbol*] (SAG)
CPA .... Carotid Phonoangiography [*Medicine*]
CPA .... Carotid Photoangiography [*Cardiology*] (DAVI)
CPA .... Carry Propagate Adder [*Computer*]
CPA .... Cash Purchasing Agent (AFM)
CPA .... Cathay Pacific Airways Ltd. [*British ICAO designator*] (FAAC)
CPA .... Catholic Press Association (EA)
CPA .... Center for Policy Alternatives (EA)
CPA .... Center for Public Affairs [*Arizona State University*] [*Research center*] (RCD)
CPA .... Central Pacific Area [*Hawaiian area*] [*World War II*]
CPA .... Central Processing Area (ADA)
CPA .... Central Pulse Amplifier (MCD)
CPA .... Central Purchasing Authority [*Military*] (NVT)
CPA .... Centre for Policy on Ageing (EAIO)
CPA .... Cerebellopontine Angle [*Brain anatomy*]
CPA .... Certified Public Accountant

CPA .... Cessna Pilots Association (EA)
CPA .... Chairman's Program Assessment [*Joint Chiefs of Staff*] (DOMA)
CPA .... Change Process Authorization (MCD)
CPA .... Channel Program Area [*Computer science*] (IAA)
CPA .... Cha-Pa [*Vietnam*] [*Geomagnetic observatory code*]
CPA .... Charged Particle Activation
CPA .... Charged Particle Analyzer
CPA .... Chartered Patent Agent
CPA .... Chartered Public Accountant
CPA .... Chemical Propulsion Abstracts [*Database*] [*Chemical Propulsion Information Agency*] [*Information service or system*] (CRD)
CPA .... Cherokee Pilots Association [*Commercial firm*] (EA)
CPA .... Chicano Press Association (EA)
CPA .... Chief of Public Affairs (AABC)
CPA .... Children's Play Activities Ltd. [*British*] (BI)
CPA .... Chirped Pulse Amplification [*Physics*]
CPA .... Chlorobenzine Producers Association (EA)
CPA .... Chlorophenoxyacetic Acid [*Plant growth hormone*]
CPA .... Chlorophenylalanine [*Biochemistry*]
CPA .... Chloropicolinic Acid [*Organic chemistry*]
CPA .... Christian Palestinian Aramaic (BJA)
CPA .... Christian Patriot Association (EA)
CPA .... Christian Pilots Association (EA)
CPA .... Chronic Pain Anonymous [*Self-help program*]
CPA .... Church Penitentiary Association [*British*]
CPA .... Circularly Polarized Antenna [*or Array*]
CPA .... Circular Permutation Analysis [*Genetics*]
CPA .... Circulating Platelet Aggregate [*Hematology*]
CPA .... Civilian Personnel Advisor [*Military*]
CPA .... Civilian Production Administration [*Became part of Office of Temporary Controls, 1946*]
CPA .... Civilian Property Agent
CPA .... Civil Practice Act [*New York*] (DLA)
CPA .... Classroom Publishers Association (EA)
CPA .... Clay Products Association (EA)
CPA .... Closest Point of Approach [*Navigation*]
CPA .... Coast Protection Act [*Town planning*] [*British*]
CPA .... Cocoa Producers' Alliance (EAIO)
CPA .... Coherent Potential Approximation [*Physics*]
CPA .... Color Phase Alternation
CPA .... Combination Publication Authority
CPA .... Comite des Paysans Africains [*African Farmers Committee - AFC*] (EAIO)
CPA .... Commission on Preservation and Access
CPA .... Commonwealth Parliamentary Association [*British*] (EAIO)
CPA .... Commonwealth Pharmaceutical Association [*British*] (EAIO)
CPA .... Commonwealth Preference Area
CPA .... Communist Party of America [*Political party*] (CDAI)
CPA .... Communist Party of Arakan [*Myanmar*] [*Political party*]
CPA .... Communist Party of Argentina [*Political party*]
CPA .... Communist Party of Armenia [*Political party Defunct*]
CPA .... Communist Party of Australia [*Political party*] (PPW)
CPA .... Communist Party of Azerbaidzhan [*Political party*]
CPA .... Community Pride Association (EA)
CPA .... Commutative Principle for Addition [*Mathematics*]
CPA .... Compensated Pulsed Alternator (MCD)
CPA .... Compressed Pulse Altimeter
CPA .... Compulsory Purchase Act [*Town planning*] [*British*]
CPA .... Computer Performance Analysis [*Boole & Babbage, Inc.*]
CPA .... Computer Press Association (EA)
CPA .... Concrete Pipe Associations (EA)
CPA .... Concurrent Photon Amplification [*Air Force*]
CPA .... Conjugation-Parity Asymmetry [*Physics*]
CPA .... Connector Position Assurance [*Automotive electronics*]
CPA .... Conservative Party of Australia [*Political party*]
CPA .... Consolidated Property Account (MCD)
CPA .... Constantinopolitana (ROG)
CPA .... Constant Phase Angle [*Electronics*] (BARN)
CPA .... Constant Potential Accelerator
CPA .... Construction Plant-Hire Association [*British*] (DBA)
CPA .... Consumer Protection Act
CPA .... Consumer Protection Agency
CPA .... Contingency Planning Aid (NASA)
CPA .... Continuous Patrol Aircraft
CPA .... Controlled Products Area
CPA .... Control of Pollution Act [*1974*] [*British*]
CPA .... Control Program Assist [*IBM Corp.*]
CPA .... Control Purchasing Authority (NVT)
CPA .... Cooperative Power Association [*Nuclear energy*] (NRCH)
CPA .... Cooperative Publication Association (EA)
CPA .... Copolar Attenuation [*Telecommunications*] (TEL)
CPA .... Corporate Oil & Gas [*Vancouver Stock Exchange symbol*]
CPA .... Cost and Performance Analysis [*Air Force*] (AFIT)
CPA .... Costophrenic Angle [*Medicine*] (DMAA)
CPA .... Cost Planning and Appraisal [*Air Force Systems Command, Aeronautical Systems Division*]
CPA .... Cost Plus Award [*Military*]
CPA .... Cotswold Personality Assessment [*Psychology*]
CPA .... Coudersport & Port Allegany [*AAR code*]
CPA .... Council on Postsecondary Accreditation (DAVI)
CPA .... Country Press Association (DGA)
CPA .... Cour Permanente d'Arbitrage [*Permanent Court of Arbitration - PCA*] [*Hague, Netherlands*] (EAIO)
CPA .... Craftsmen Potters Association [*British*] (DBA)
CPA .... Crash Phone Activated [*Aviation*] (FAAC)

CPA............	Creative Printers of America
CPA............	Credit Populaire d'Algerie [*People's Credit Bank of Algeria*] (IMH)
CPA............	Credit Protection Association [*British*] (DBA)
CPA............	Critical Path Analysis
CPA............	Cross Program Auditor [*Applied Data Research, Inc.*]
CPA............	Cycle Parts and Accessories Association (EA)
CPA............	Cyclophosphamide [*Cytoxan*] [*Antineoplastic drug*]
CPA............	Cyproterone Acetate [*Endocrinology*]
CPa............	Palo Alto City Library, Palo Alto, CA [*Library symbol Library of Congress*] (LCLS)
CPA............	Pasadena City College, Pasadena, CA [*OCLC symbol*] (OCLC)
CPAA..........	Canadian Postmasters and Assistants Association
CPAA..........	Charged Particle Activation Analysis [*Analytical chemistry*]
CPAA..........	Colloquia for Presidents and Academic Administrators [*Formerly, ICUA*] (EA)
CPAA..........	Concrete Pipe Association of Australia
CPAA..........	CPA [*Certified Public Accountant*] Associates (EA)
CPAA..........	Cultured Pearl Association of America (EA)
CPAA..........	Cycle Parts and Accessories Association (EA)
CPAAQ........	[*La*] Corporation Professionnelle des Administrateurs Agrees du Quebec [*The Order of Chartered Administrators of Quebec*] (AC)
CPaB..........	Beckman Instruments, Inc., Technical Library, Palo Alto, CA [*Library symbol Library of Congress*] (LCLS)
CPAB..........	California Cling Peach Advisory Board (EA)
CPAB..........	California Prune Advisory Board [*Later, CPB*]
CPAB..........	Computer Programmer Aptitude Battery [*Test*]
CPAC..........	Ambassador College Library, Pasadena, CA [*Library symbol*] [*Library of Congress*] (LCLS)
CPAC..........	Center for Process Analytical Chemistry [*University of Washington*] [*Research center*] (RCD)
C-PAC.........	Clinical Probes of Articulation Consistency [*Speech evaluation test*]
CPAC..........	Coalition to Preserve the American Copyright [*Defunct*] (EA)
CPAC..........	Collaborative Pesticide Analytical Committee (DICI)
CPAC..........	Color Photographic Association of Canada
CPAC..........	Community Planning Association of Canada
CPAC..........	Computer Program Associated Contractor
CPAC..........	Concurrent Processor Architecture Control (MCD)
CPAC..........	Conservative Political Action Conference
CPAC..........	Consumer Protection Advisory Committee (ODBW)
CPAC..........	CPAC, Inc. [*Associated Press*] (SAG)
CPACC........	Caribbean Planning for Adaptation to Global Climate in the Caribbean
CPACS........	Coded Pulse Anticlutter System (CET)
CPACS........	Comprehensive Payroll Accounting System (MHDB)
CPAD..........	Central Pay Accounts Division [*Navy*]
CP Adm.......	Certificate in Public Administration
CPADN........	Career Planning and Adult Development Network (EA)
CPAE..........	Calf Pulmonary Artery Endthelial [*Cell line*]
CPAE..........	Coalition to Protect Animals in Entertainment (EA)
CPAE..........	Commission of Professors of Adult Education (EA)
CPaE..........	Electric Power Research Institute, Palo Alto, CA [*Library symbol Library of Congress*] (LCLS)
CPAF..........	Chlorpropamide-Alcohol Flushing [*Medicine*]
CPAF..........	Cost Plus Award Fee [*Business term*]
CPAG..........	Child Poverty Action Group [*British*] (BI)
CPAGA........	California Prune and Apricot Growers Association [*Later, Sunsweet Growers*]
CPaGE........	General Electric Co., Traveling Wave Tube Production Section, Palo Alto, CA [*Library symbol Library of Congress*] (LCLS)
Cpah..........	Para-Aminohippurate Clearance [*Chemical chemistry*] (AAMN)
CPaHP........	Hewlett-Packard Co., Corporate Library, Palo Alto, CA [*Library symbol Library of Congress*] (LCLS)
CPAI..........	Canvas Products Association International [*Later, IFAI*] (EA)
CPA-IGWAP...	Canadian Psychological Association - Interest Group on Women and Psychology
CP Air........	Canadian Pacific Airlines [*ICAO designator*] (AD)
CPAir.........	Canadian Pacific Airlines Ltd.
CPAK.........	CPAC, Inc. [*NASDAQ symbol*] (SAG)
CPAL.........	Canadian Pacific Airlines Ltd.
CPal..........	Codices Palatini (BJA)
CPAL.........	Computer Program Assistance Library (NITA)
CPAL.........	Containment Person Air Lock [*Nuclear energy*] (IEEE)
CPaL..........	Lockheed Missiles & Space Corp., Palo Alto, CA [*Library symbol Library of Congress*] (LCLS)
CPAM.........	Caisse Primaire d'Assurance Maladie [*French*] (DLA)
CPAM.........	Certified Patient Account Manager [*American Guild of Patient Account Mana gement*] [*Designation awarded by*]
CPAM.........	CNO [*Chief of Naval Operations*] Program Analysis Memorandum
CPAM.........	Continental Polar Air Mass (MSA)
CPAM.........	Countermeasures Penetrating Antiarmor Munitions (MCD)
CPAN.........	Certified Post-Anesthesia Nurse (MEDA)
CP&AR........	Government Contract Costs, Pricing and Accounting Report [*A publication*] (AAGC)
CP & B.......	Cover Paper and Board [*Printing*] (DGA)
CP & I........	Coastal Patrol and Interdiction [*Navy*] (DOMA)
CPA-NS.......	Canadian Paraplegic Association Nova Scotia (AC)
CPANSW.......	Concrete Paviors' Association of New South Wales [*Australia*]
CPANSW.......	Country Press Association of New South Wales [*Australia*]
CPANSW.......	Croquet Players' Association of New South Wales [*Australia*]
CPAO..........	Canoga Park Area Office [*AEC*] (MCD)
CPAP..........	Center for Public Administration and Policy [*Virginia Polytechnic Institute and State University*] [*Research center*] (RCD)
CPAP..........	Constant Positive Airway Pressure [*Medicine*]
CPAP..........	Continuous Positive Airway Pressure [*Resuscitation system*] [*Medicine*]

CPAP........	Control Parameter Assembly Program
CPAP........	Cyclopenta(alpha)phenanthrene [*Organic chemistry*]
CPaP........	Philco-Ford Corp., Western Development Laboratories, Palo Alto, CA [*Library symbol Library of Congress*] (LCLS)
CPA-PE......	Carbazopropionyl - Phosphatidyl Ethanolamine [*Organic chemistry*]
CPAPGPCA...	California Public Administrator, Public Guardian, and Public Conservator Association (SRA)
CPAPR......	Coalition to Protect Animals in Parks and Refuges (EA)
CPAR........	Canadian Physicians for Aid & Relif (AC)
CPAR........	Construction Productivity Advancement Research [*Military*] (RDA)
CPARS......	Compact Programmed Airline Reservation System [*Computer science*] (PDAA)
CPARS......	Contractor Performance Assessment Reporting System (AAGC)
CPAS........	Central Procurement Accounting System [*Air Force*] (GFGA)
CPAS........	Church Pastoral Aid Society [*British*]
CPAS........	Civilian Personnel Accounting System [*Military*] (MCD)
CPAS........	Conseil des Provinces Atlantiques pour les Sciences (AC)
CPAS........	Construction Program Administration System [*Telecommunications*] (TEL)
CPaS........	Syntex Corp., Research Library, Palo Alto, CA [*Library symbol Library of Congress*] (LCLS)
CPASA......	Country Press Association of South Australia
CPASC......	Canadian Permanent Army Service Corps (DMA)
CPASC......	Concrete Pipe Association of South Carolina (SRA)
CPASNSW....	Cancer Patients' Assistance Society of New South Wales [*Australia*]
CPASTATS...	Canadian Petroleum Association Statistics [*Information service or system*] (CRD)
CPaSy.......	SYVA Co., Palo Alto, CA [*Library symbol Library of Congress*] (LCLS)
CPAT........	Coalition to Promote America's Trade [*Washington, DC*] (EA)
CPAT........	Commercial Product Acquisition Team [*Later, COMPACT*] [*An association Defunct*]
CPAV........	Central Point Anti-Virus [*Central Point Software, Inc.*] [*Computer science*] (PCM)
CPAV........	Childbirth and Parenting Association of Victoria [*Australia*]
CPAV........	Cinque Ports Artillery Volunteers [*British military*] (DMA)
CPAV........	Council of Progress Associations of Victoria [*Australia*]
CPaVA......	United States Veterans Administration Hospital, Palo Alto, CA [*Library symbol Library of Congress*] (LCLS)
CPAVIH.....	Comite des Personnes Atteintes du VIH [*Committee of Persons Living with HIV*] (AC)
CPAWA......	Country Press Association of Western Australia
CPAWS......	Canadian Parks & Wilderness Society [*Societe pour la Protection des Parcs et des Sites Naturales du Canada*] (AC)
CPAWS......	Computer-Planning and Aircraft-Weighing Scales
CPaX........	Xerox Corp., Research Center, Palo Alto, CA [*Library symbol Library of Congress*] (LCLS)
CPB..........	California Prune Board (EA)
CPB..........	Campbell Soup [*NYSE symbol*] (TTSB)
CPB..........	Campbell Soup Co. [*NYSE symbol*] (SPSG)
CPB..........	Caneco Audio-Publishers, Inc. [*Vancouver Stock Exchange symbol*]
CPB..........	Carboxypeptidase B [*An enzyme*]
CPB..........	Cardiopulmonary Bypass [*Medicine*]
CPB..........	Career Planning Board [*Navy*] (NVT)
CPB..........	Casual Payments Book [*British*] (ADA)
CPB..........	Censorship of Publications Board [*Ireland*]
CPB..........	Censorship Policy Board [*World War II*]
CPB..........	Center of Pressure Back
CPB..........	Cetylpyridinium Bromide [*Medicine*] (DMAA)
CPB..........	Channel Program Block [*Computer science*]
CPB..........	Charged Particle Beam [*Weapon*] [*DoD*]
CPB..........	Civilian Personnel Branch [*BUPERS*]
CPB..........	Classification of Publications Board [*South Australia*]
CPB..........	Coast Protection Board [*South Australia*]
CPB..........	Colorado Potato Beetle
CP (B).......	Communist Party (Bolsheviks) [*Political party*]
CPB..........	Communist Party of Belgium [*Political party*]
CPB..........	Communist Party of Burma [*Political party*] (EY)
CPB..........	Communist Party of Byelorussia [*Political party*]
CPB..........	Community Programs Branch [*Australian Capital Territory*]
CPB..........	Companion to the Authorized Daily Prayer Book [*A publication*] (BJA)
CPB..........	Competitive Protein Binding [*Clinical chemistry*]
CPB..........	Computer Program Book
CPB..........	Confederacion Panamericana de Badminton [*Panamerican Badminton Conferation - PBC*] (EAIO)
CPB..........	Confederacion Panamericana de Basketball [*Pan American Basketball Confederation - PABC*] (EAIO)
CPB..........	Contractors Pump Bureau (EA)
CPB..........	Corporation for Public Broadcasting (EA)
CPB..........	CPB, Inc. [*Associated Press*] (SAG)
CPB..........	Critical Path Bar (PDAA)
CPB..........	Culver, IN [*Location identifier FAA*] (FAAL)
CPB..........	Current Physics Bibliographies [*A publication*] (MCD)
CPB..........	Cuyos Pies Beso [*Very Respectfully*] [*Formal correspondence*] [*Spanish*]
CPB..........	Cypher Policy Board [*British World War II*]
CPBA........	Chloroperbenzoic Acid [*Organic acid*]
CPBA........	(Chlorophenoxy)butanoic Acid [*Biochemistry*]
CPBA........	Competitive Protein-Binding Analysis [*or Assay*]
CPBC........	Canada-Pakistan Business Council [*Conseil de Commerce Canada Pakistan*] [*Formerly, Canada-Parkistan Trade & Economic Committee*] (AC)
CPBC........	Central Pacific Base Command [*Hawaiian Islands*] [*World War II*]
CPBD........	Cornell Parent Behavior Description (EDAC)

CPB-E .... Burroughs Corp., Western Region Central Technical Library, Pasadena, CA [*Library symbol Library of Congress*] (LCLS)

CPBE .... Certified Professional Bureau Executive [*Medical-Dental-Hospital Bureaus of America*] [*Designation awarded by*]

CPBF .... Campaign for Press and Broadcasting Freedom [*British*] (DI)

CPBH .... Bell & Howell Co., Research Laboratories, Pasadena, CA [*Library symbol Library of Congress*] (LCLS)

CPBI .... Cornell Parent Behavior Inventory (EDAC)

CPBI .... Counseling Practice Beliefs Inventory (EDAC)

CPBI .... CPB, Inc. [*NASDAQ symbol*] (NQ)

CPBL .... Capable [*or Capability*] (AFM)

CPBM .... Communist Party of Bohemia and Moravia [*Former Czechoslovakia*] [*Political party*] (EY)

CPBMA .... Canadian Paper Box Manufacturers' Association Inc. [*Association Canadienne des Fabricants de Boites en Cartons*] (AC)

CPBP .... Cancer Prevention Benefit Program [*National Cancer Institute*]

CPBRD........ Cupboard

CPBS .... Colorado Potato Beetle Spiroplasma [*Insect pathogen*]

CPBW .... Charged Particle Beam Weapon [*Computer science*] (PDAA)

CPBX .... Computerized Private Branch Exchange [*Telecommunications*]

CPC .... Aero Campeche SA de CV [*Mexico ICAO designator*] (FAAC)

CPC .... Cabin Pressure Controller [*Aviation*] (MCD)

CPC .... Calibration Procedure

CPC .... California Pistachio Commission (EA)

CPC .... Calling Party's Category [*Telecommunications*] (TEL)

CPC .... Cameroon Protestant College

CPC .... Canada Post Corporation Library [*UTLAS symbol*]

CPC .... Canadian Paralympic Committee [*Comite Paralympique du Canada*] [*Formerly, Canadian Federation of Sport Organizations for the Disabled*] (AC)

CPC .... Canadian Pension Commission

CPC .... Canadian Pork Council [*Formerly, Canadian Swine Council*] (AC)

CPC .... Canadian Postal Corps [*Later, RCPC*]

CPC .... Capital Press Club (EA)

CPC .... Capsular Polysaccharide Complex [*Biochemistry*]

CPC .... Capuchin Poor Clares (TOCD)

CPC .... Card Programmed Calculator [*IBM Corp. - late 1940's*] [*Computer science*]

CPC .... Card Programmed Computer (IAA)

CPC .... Cargo Processing Contract (MCD)

CPC .... Carolina Population Center [*University of North Carolina*] [*Research center*] (IID)

CPC .... Carotis Pulse Curve [*Cardiology*]

CPC .... Carroll Publishing Co. [*Information service or system*] (IID)

CPC .... Cartesian-to-Polar Converter (SAA)

CPC .... Cells per Colony [*Microbiology*]

CPC .... Cement-Plaster Ceiling [*Technical drawings*]

CPC .... Center for Plant Conservation (EA)

CPC .... Central Planning Center (NASA)

CPC .... Central Posterior Curve [*Ophthalmology*]

CPC .... Central Processing Console [*NBDS*]

CPC .... Central Property Control

CPC .... Centrifugal Partition Chromatography

CPC .... Century Publishing Co.

CPC .... Ceramic Printed Circuit (IAA)

CPC .... Ceramic-Wafer Printed Circuit

CPC .... Cerebellar Purkinje Cell [*Medicine*] (DMAA)

CPC .... Cerebral Palsy Clinic

CPC .... Cerebral Performance Category

CPC .... Cerebro-Pedal Commissure [*Medicine*]

CPC .... Certificate in Professional Counseling (PGP)

CPC .... Certificate in Publications and Communications (PGP)

CPC .... Certificate of Professional Competence [*British*] (DI)

CPC .... Certified Personnel Consultant [*Designation awarded by National Association of Personnel Consultants*]

CPC .... Certified Professional Chemist

CPC .... Cetylpyridinium Chloride [*Organic chemistry*]

CPC .... Channel Program Commands

CPC .... Chapelco [*Argentina*] [*Airport symbol*] (OAG)

CPC .... Characteristics Properties Code [*NASA*] (NASA)

CPC .... Characters per Column [*Typesetting*]

CPC .... Chemical Processing Cell [*Nuclear energy*] (NUCP)

CPC .... Chemical Protective Clothing

CPC .... Cherry Point [*North Carolina*] [*Seismograph station code, US Geological Survey Closed*] (SEIS)

CPC .... Cherry Processors' Cooperative [*Australia*]

CPC .... Chevrolet-Pontiac-Canada Group [*General Motors Corp.*]

CPC .... Chief Pay Clerk [*Navy rating Obsolete*]

CPC .... Chief Planning and Control Staff [*Coast Guard*]

CPC .... Child Protection Council [*New South Wales*] [*Australia*]

CPC .... Christian Peace Conference [*See also CCP*] [*Prague, Czechoslovakia*] (EAIO)

CPC .... Christian Preaching Conference [*Defunct*] (EA)

CPC .... Christmas Philatelic Club (EA)

CPC .... Chronic Passive Congestion [*Medicine*]

CPC .... Church Pensions Conference (EA)

CPC .... Church Periodical Club (EA)

CPC .... Circumferential Pneumatic Compression [*Medicine*]

CPC .... City Planning Commission (WDAA)

CPC .... City Police Commissioner (DAS)

CPC .... City Police Court [*British*] (DAS)

CPC .... Civilian Personnel Circular [*Army*]

CPC .... Clerk of the Privy Council [*British*]

CPC .... Climate Prediction Center

CPC .... Clinical Pathology Conference

CPC .... Clock Pulsed Control

C/PC........... Closure/Post-Closure

CPC .... Coastal Patrol Boat [*Navy symbol*]

CPC .... Coated Paper Copier [*Reprography*]

CPC .... Coated Powder Cathode

CPC .... Code of Civil Procedure [*Quebec*] [*A publication*] (DLA)

CPC .... Coldplate Clamp

CPC .... College Placement Council (EA)

CPC .... Collimated Proportional Counter (PDAA)

CPC .... Color Pack Camera

CPC .... Column Position Counter

CPC .... Combat Psychiatric Casualty [*Military*] (INF)

CPC .... Combined Policy Committee [*NATO*] (NATG)

CPC .... Command Point of Contact [*Navy*] (AFIT)

CPC .... Commerce Productivity Center

CPC .... Commercial Property Coverage [*Insurance*]

CPC .... Commissary Privilege Card [*DoD*]

CPC .... Committee for a Progressive Congress (EA)

CPC .... Common Peripheral Channel (NITA)

CPC .... Commonwealth Procurement Circular [*A publication*]

CPC .... Communication Planning Corp. [*Jacksonville, FL*] [*Telecommunications*] (TSSD)

CPC .... Communications Processing Center (CET)

CPC .... Communist Party of Canada [*Political party*]

CPC .... Communist Party of China [*Chung-Kuo Kung-Ch'an Tang*] [*Taiwan*] [*Political party*] (PPW)

CPC .... Communist Party of Colombia [*Political party*] (PPW)

CPC .... Community Patent Convention [*European Common Market*]

CPC .... Compact Personal Computer (HGAA)

CPC .... Component Parts Clause (AIA)

CPC .... Compound Parabolic Concentrator [*Solar energy research*]

CPC .... Computer Petroleum Corp. [*Information service or system*] (IID)

CPC .... Computer Power Center

CPC .... Computer Print Console

CPC .... Computer Process Control

CPC .... Computer Program Components (MCD)

CPC .... Computer Programming Concepts (BUR)

CPC .... Computing Centre [*University of East Anglia*] [*British*] (IRUK)

CPC .... Condensation Particle Counter [*Marine science*] (OSRA)

CPC .... Congres Panafricain du Cameroun [*Political party*] (EY)

CPC .... Conservative Political Centre [*British*]

CPC .... Consortium for Peaceful Coexistence (EA)

CPC .... Consortium Perfectae Caritatis [*Association of Perfect Love*] (EA)

CPC .... Constant Product Curve [*Economics*]

CPC .... Construction Project Control (IAA)

CPC .... Consultative Political Council [*Laos*]

CPC .... Consumer Protection Center (EA)

CPC .... Contact Process Cell [*Nuclear energy*] (GFGA)

CPC .... Continuous Process Control [*Design Software Ltd.*] [*Software package*] (NCC)

CPC .... Contract Progress Control (MCD)

CPC .... Control and Processing Center (MCD)

CPC .... Controlled-Pore Ceramic [*Organic chemistry*]

CPC .... Controlled-Potential Coulometer [*Nuclear energy*] (NRCH)

CPC .... Control Point Custodian [*Military*] (AFIT)

CPC .... Cooper Canada Ltd. [*Toronto Stock Exchange symbol*]

CPC .... Copper Phthalocyanine [*Colored pigment*]

CPC .... Copy Payments Center [*for copyrighted material*]

CPC .... Core Protection Calculator [*or Computer*] [*Nuclear energy*] (NRCH)

CPC .... Cost per Click [*Computer science*]

CPC .... Council on Professional Certification (EA)

CPC .... CPC International, Inc. [*Formerly, Corn Products Co.*] [*NYSE symbol*] (SPSG)

CPC .... CPC Intl. [*NYSE symbol*] (TTSB)

CPC .... Crafts, Protective and Custodial [*Military*] (DNAB)

C-P-C .... Craven-Pamlico-Carteret Regional Library [*Library network*]

CPC .... Cresolphthalein Complexone [*Analytical chemistry*]

CPC .... Crop Protection Chemical

CPC .... Custodial, Protective, and Crafts [*US government workers*]

CPC .... Cycle Program Control (MCD)

CPC .... Cycle Program Counter (IEEE)

CPC .... Cyclic Permutation Code

CPC .... Pacific Christian College, Fullerton, CA [*OCLC symbol*] (OCLC)

CPC .... St. Clare Capuchin Sisters (TOCD)

CPC .... Whiteville, NC [*Location identifier FAA*] (FAAL)

CPCA .... Camp Parks Communication Annex [*California*] (MCD)

CPCA .... Canadian Palliative Care Association (AC)

CPCA .... Canadian Portland Cement Association [*Association Canadienne du Ciment Portland*] (AC)

CPCA .... Cigarette Pack Collectors Association (EA)

CPCA .... Connecticut Primary Care Association (SRA)

CPCA .... Cyclopropanecarboxylic Acid [*Organic chemistry*]

CPC & N .... Certificate of Public Convenience and Necessity

CPCB .... Crew Procedures Control Board [*NASA*] (NASA)

CPCC .... Chicago Playing Card Collectors (EA)

CPCC .... Command Power Cruise Control [*Diesel engines*] [*Automotive engineering*]

CPCC .... Communications Processor Conversion Center

CPCCOQ..... Corporation Professionnelle des Conseilliers et Conseillieres d'Orientation du Quebec (AC)

CPCEAISD... Comite Permanent du CE de l'Association Internationale de la Savonnerie et de laDetergence [*Standing EEC Committee of the International Association of the Soap and Detergent Industry - SEECCIASDI*] [*Brussels, Belgium*] (EAIO)

CPCEI........... Computer Program Contract End Item

CPCEMR ...... Circum-Pacific Council for Energy and Mineral Resources (EA)
CPCFA .... Council of Pollution Control Financing Agencies [*Defunct*] (EA)
CPCGN .... Canadian Permanent Committee on Geographical Names
CPCH .... Calling Party Cannot Hear [*Telecommunications*] (TEL)
CPCH .... Collier de Perles, Carre de Hermes [*Pearl Necklace, Silk Scarf from the boutique Hermes*] [*French Yuppie garb*]
CPCI .... Canadian Prestressed Concrete Institute [*See also ICBP*]
CPCI .... Ciprico, Inc. [*NASDAQ symbol*] (NQ)
CPCI .... Computer Program Change Instruction (NASA)
CPCI .... Computer Program Configuration Identification
CPCI .... Computer Program Configured Item (MCD)
CPCI .... CPU Power Calibration Instrument
CPCI .... Cross-Pointer Course Indicator (MCD)
CPCI .... Cruise Passengers Club International (EA)
CPCiC .... Pasadena City College, Pasadena, CA [*Library symbol Library of Congress*] (LCLS)
CPCIP .... Commission Permanente de la Convention Internationale des Peches [*Permanent Commission of the International Fisheries Convention*] [*Political party*] (MSC)
CPCISF .... Conseil Permanent de la Convention Internationale de Stresa sur les Fromages (EAIO)
CPCIZ .... Comite Permanent des Congres Internationaux de Zoologie [*Permanent Committee of International Zoological Congresses*] [*France*]
CPcK .... Kaiser Permanente Medical Center, Health Science Library, Panorama City, CA [*Library symbol Library of Congress*] (LCLS)
CPCL .... Clare [*C.P.*] Corp. [*NASDAQ symbol*] (SAG)
CPCL .... Combined Passenger Check List (ADA)
CPCL .... Computer Program Change Library (NASA)
CPCL .... Computer Program Control Library (MCD)
CPCL .... Congenital Pulmonary Cystic Lymphangiectasis [*Medicine*]
CPCL .... C.P. Clare [*NASDAQ symbol*] (TTSB)
CPCM .... Certification as Professional Contract Manager (RDA)
CPCM .... Certified Professional Contracts Manager [*Exam*] (AAGC)
CPC(M-L) ..... Communist Party of Canada (Marxist-Leninist) [*Political party*]
CPcMn .... Central Pacific Minerals [*Associated Press*] (SAG)
CPCN .... Civilian Position Control Number
CPCNG .... Comite Permanent Canadien des Noms Geographiques [*Canadian Permanent Committee on Geographical Names - CPCGN*]
CPCO .... Central Port Call Office [*Army*] (AABC)
CPCO .... Chief Parliamentary Counsel's Office [*Victoria*] [*Australia*]
CpCo .... Clearwater Publishing Co., Inc., New York, NY [*Library symbol Library of Congress*] (LCLS)
CPCO .... Computer Pete [*NASDAQ symbol*] (TTSB)
CPCO .... Computer Petroleum Corp. [*NASDAQ symbol*] (SAG)
CPCOM .... Capsule Communications [*or Communicator*] [*NASA*] (IAA)
CPCP .... Cardiopulmonary Corp. [*NASDAQ symbol*] (SAG)
CPCP .... Chronic Progressive Coccidioidal Pneumonitis [*Medicine*]
CPCP .... Civilian Personnel Career Plan [*Air Force*]
CPCR .... Cardiopulmonary-Cerebral Resuscitation (DAVI)
CPCR .... Cardiopulmonary Cerebral Resuscitation [*Medicine*] (DMAA)
CPCR .... Computer Program Change Request (NASA)
CPCR .... Contractor Packaging Capability Review [*DoD*]
CPCR .... Crew Procedures Change Request (MCD)
CPCR .... Crop Protection Chemicals Reference
CPCRA .... Community Program for Clinical Research on AIDS [*FDA*]
CPCRIQ .... Corporation Professionnelle des Conseillers en Relations Industrielles du Quebec (AC)
CPCRS .... Canadian Physiotherapy Cardio-Respiratory Society (AC)
CPCS .... Cabin Pressure Control System [*Aviation*]
CPCS .... Caithness Paperweight Collectors Society [*Perth, Scotland*] (EAIO)
CPCS .... Central Property Control System (MCD)
CPCS .... Check Processing Control System [*IBM Corp.*] (BUR)
CPCS .... Christian Parent-Controlled Schools [*Australia*]
CPCS .... Circumferential Pneumatic Compression Suit [*Medicine*] (DMAA)
CPCS .... Coast Phase Control System [*Army*] (AABC)
CPCS .... Combat Personnel Control System [*Air Force*] (GFGA)
CPCS .... Common Part Convergence Sublayer [*Electronics*] (ACRL)
CPCS .... Common Program Control Station [*Emergency Broadcast System*]
C-PCS .... Congenital Portocaval Shunt [*Medicine*]
CPCS .... Conversion Process Controller System
CPCS .... Cost Planning and Control System (MCD)
CPCS .... Cyclic Pitch Control Stick
CPCSF .... Construction Permit Containment Support Fixture (NRCH)
CPC/SFA ...... Canadian Potato Chip/Snack Food Association [*Association Canadienne des Fabricants de Chips/Grignotines*] (AC)
CPCT .... Committee to Protect Our Children's Teeth [*Defunct*] (EA)
CPCU .... Chartered Property and Casualty Underwriter [*Designation awarded by American Institute for Property and Liability Underwriters*]
CPCU .... Council of Protestant Colleges and Universities [*Defunct*] (EA)
CPCU .... Custody Pending Completion of Use
CPCU .... Society of Chartered Property and Casualty Underwriters [*Malvern, PA*] (EA)
CPCUG .... Capital PC [*Personal Computer*] User Group (EA)
CPCZ .... Communist Party of Czechoslovakia [*Political party*] (EY)
CPD .... Calls per Day [*Telecommunications*] (IAA)
CPD .... Camping Products Division [*of Industrial Fabrics Association International*] (EA)
CPD .... Canadian Performance Distributors
CPD .... Cape Provincial Division Reports [*South Africa*] [*A publication*] (DLA)
CPD .... Cards per Day [*Computer science*] (BUR)
CPD .... Carolina Power & Light Co. [*NYSE symbol*] (SAG)
CPD .... Carolina Pwr & Lt 8.55%'QUICS' [*NYSE symbol*] (TTSB)
CPD .... Catalog of the Public Documents [*A bibliographic publication*]

CPD .... Center for Professional Development [*University of Kentucky*] [*Research center*] (RCD)
CPD .... Center for Public Dialogue (EA)
CPD .... Center Program Director [*NASA*] (KSC)
CPD .... Central Personnel Directorate [*British*]
CPD .... Central Postal Directory [*Army*] (AABC)
CPD .... Central Procurement Division [*Marine Corps*]
CPD .... Central Pulse Distributor [*Telecommunications*] (TEL)
CPD .... Cephalopelvic Disproportion [*Gynecology*]
CPD .... Cerro La Pandura [*Puerto Rico*] [*Seismograph station code, US Geological Survey*] (SEIS)
CPD .... Charge Priming Device [*Video technology*]
CPD .... Charterers Pay Dues (WGA)
CPD .... Chemical Propulsion Division [*NASA*] (KSC)
CPD .... Childhood Polycystic Disease (PAZ)
CPD .... Chorioretinopathy and Pituitary Dysfunction [*Medicine*]
CPD .... Chronic Pulmonary Disease (BARN)
CPD .... Circuit Protection Device
CPD .... Citrate-Phosphate-Dextrose [*Anticoagulant*] [*Hematology*]
CPD .... Civilian Personnel Directorate [*Military*] (GFGA)
CPD .... Clips per Day [*Photocopying, microfilming*]
CPD .... Coaxial Power Divider
CPD .... Coil Predriver (IAA)
CPD .... Combat Potential Display [*SAGE*] [*Air Force*]
CPD .... Command Processor Distributor (SAA)
CPD .... Commercial Product Development
CPD .... Commercial Program Development
CPD .... Commissioner of Public Debt
CPD .... Commission on Presidential Debates (EA)
CPD .... Committee for Presidents' Day [*Later, Presidents' Day National Committee*] (AEBS)
CPD .... Committee on Public Doublespeak (EA)
CPD .... Committee on the Present Danger (EA)
CPD .... Common Pleas Division [*Legal term*]
CPD .... Communications Planning and Development
CPD .... Communist Party of Denmark [*Political party*]
CPD .... Community Planning and Development [*HUD*] (OICC)
CPD .... Comparison Point Date [*Social Security Administration*]
CPD .... Compound
CPD .... Comptroller General's Procurement Decisions [*A publication*]
CPD .... Computer-Produced Drawing (IAA)
CPD .... Computer Products Directory [*Information service or system*] (IID)
CPD .... Concertacion de los Partidos de la Democracia [*Chile*] [*Political party*] (EY)
CPD .... Congressional Presentation Document
CPD .... Consolidated Programming Document
CPD .... Constant Pressure Date (DNAB)
CPD .... Constituency Proportion Distribution
CPD .... Contact Potential Difference
CPD .... Contagious Pustular Dermatitis [*Dermatology*]
CPD .... Continuing Professional Development (PDAA)
CPD .... Contract and Purchase Department [*British military*] (DMA)
CPD .... Contract Potential Difference (MCD)
CPD .... Controller of Projectile Development [*Ministry of Supply*] [*British World War II*]
CPD .... Converter, Pulse to DC [*Direct Current*] Voltage (NASA)
CPD .... Coober Pedy [*Australia Airport symbol*] (OAG)
C/PD .... Cost/Pricing Data [*Military*] (DOMA)
CPD .... Counter-Propaganda Directorate [*British*]
CPD .... Courier and Periodicals Division [*Later, UNESCO Publications and Periodicals*]
CPD .... Crew Passive Dosimeter [*NASA*] (KSC)
CPD .... Crew Procedures Division [*NASA*] (NASA)
CPD .... Crossing Protective Device
CPD .... Cumulative Population Doubling
CPD .... Cumulative Probability Distribution (IEEE)
CPD .... Cupboard
CPD .... Cycles per Day
CPD .... Cyclobutane Pyrimidine Dimer [*Organic chemistry*]
CPD .... Cyclopentadiene [*Organic chemistry*]
Cp D .... Doctor of Chiropody
CPD .... Falmouth, MA [*Location identifier FAA*] (FAAL)
CPD .... Law Reports, Common Pleas Division [*England*] [*A publication*] (DLA)
CPD .... Palomar College, San Marcos, CA [*OCLC symbol*] (OCLC)
CPD .... Popular Democratic Coalition [*Ecuador*] [*Political party*] (PPW)
CPD .... South African Law Reports, Cape Provincial Division [*South Africa*] [*A publication*] (DLA)
CPDA .... Chloramphenicol-Amended Potato Dextrose Agar [*Microbiology*]
CPDA .... Citrate-Phosphate-Dextrose-Adenine [*Anticoagulant*] [*Hematology*]
CPDA .... Clay Pipe Development Association [*British*] (DBA)
CPDA .... Copper Products Development Association [*Later, INCRA*]
CPDA .... Council for Periodical Distributors Associations (EA)
CPDAMS ...... Computer Program Development and Management System
CPDC .... Canadian People's [*Citizens and Residents*] Defence Committee
CPDC .... Command Processor Distributor Control (MCD)
CPDC .... Community Planning and Design Center [*Information service or system*] (IID)
CPDC .... Computer Program Development Center [*Air Force*] (MCD)
CPDC .... Conservative Party's Defense Committee [*British*]
CP/DC .... Corrosion Prevention/Deterioration Control
CPDD .... Calcium Pyrophosphate Deposition Disease [*Rheumatology*] (DAVI)
CPDD .... Calibrated Probability Density Distribution
cPDD .... cis-Platinum Diammine Dichloride [*Cisplatin*] [*Also, CDDP, cis-DDP, CPT, DDP, P*] [*Antineoplastic drug*]

CPDD .... Command Post Digital Display [SAGE] [Air Force]
CPDD .... Conceptual Project Design Description (NRCH)
CPDD .... Control Programs Development Division [Environmental Protection Agency] (GFGA)
CPDDS .... Computer Program Detail Design Specification (MCD)
CPD/EW .... Campaign for Peace and Democracy/East and West (EA)
CPDF .... Central Personnel Data File [Office of Personnel Management] [Washington, DC]
CPDF .... Centrifuge Plant Demonstration Facility [Department of Energy]
CP Div .... Common Pleas Division, English Law Reports [1875-80] [A publication] (DLA)
CP Div (Eng)... Common Pleas Division, English Law Reports [1875-80] [A publication] (DLA)
CPDL .... Canadian Patents and Developments Ltd.
CPDL .... Cumulative Population Doubling Level
CPDLC .... Bellefonte District Library Center [Library network]
CPDLC .... Controller Pilot Datalink Communications (GAVI)
CPDN .... CompDent Corp. [NASDAQ symbol] (SAG)
cpDNA .... Deoxyribonucleic Acid, Chloroplast [Biochemistry, genetics] [Also, Chl-DNA, ctDNA]
CPDP .... Computer Program Development Plan
CPDR .... Computer Program Deviation Request (MCD)
CPDR .... Contractor's Preliminary Design Review (MCD)
CPDS .... Carboxypyridine Disulfide [Biochemistry]
CPDS .... Commerce Procurement Data System [Marine science] (OSRA)
CPDS .... Commerce Procurement Data System (USDC)
CPDS .... Computer Program Design [or Development] Specification [NASA] (NASA)
CPDS .... Crew Procedures Documentation System (MCD)
CPDT .... Center for Professional Development and Training [University of Texas at Austin] (RDA)
CPDT .... Centre de Preparation Documentaire a la Traduction [Center for Translation Documentation] [Information service or system] (IID)
CPDU .... (Chloropropyl)deoxyuridine [Antiviral]
CPDW .... Circumpolar Deep Water [Also, CDW] [Oceanography]
CPDX .... Cefpodoxime (DMAA)
CPDYCONTR... Command Post Duty Controller [Air Force]
CPE .... Aerocomponentes Internacionales, SA de CV [Mexico] [FAA designator] (FAAC)
CPE .... Cable Pressurization Equipment
CPE .... Campeche [Mexico] [Airport symbol] (OAG)
CPE .... Campeche [Mexico] [Airport symbol] (AD)
CPE .... Camp Elliot [California] [Seismograph station code, US Geological Survey] (SEIS)
CPE .... Cape
CPE .... Cape
CPE .... Cape [Commonly used] (OPSA)
CPE .... Carbon Paste Electrode [Electrochemistry]
CPE .... Carboxypeptidase E [An enzyme]
CPE .... Cardiogenic Pulmonary Edema [Cardiology] (DAVI)
CPE .... Catch-per-Effort [Fishing]
CPE .... Cathodic Protection Equipment
CPE .... Cellulose Polyethylene [Organic chemistry]
CPE .... Center for Packaging Education (EA)
CPE .... Center for Popular Economics (EA)
CPE .... Centrally Planned Economy
CPE .... Central Processing Element [Computer science]
CPE .... Central Programmer and Evaluator
CPE .... Centrum voor Postoraal in Europa [Centre for Pastoral Work in Europe] (EAIO)
CPE .... Cercle Populaire Europeen [European Popular Circle - EPC] (EAIO)
CPE .... Certificate for Physical Education [British] (ROG)
CPE .... Certificate of Proficiency in English [Cambridge] [British] (AIE)
CPE .... Charged Particle Equilibrium (DEN)
CPE .... Chief Polaris Executive [Missiles]
CPE .... Chief Program Engineer [NASA] (NASA)
CPE .... Chlorinated Polyethylene [Organic chemistry]
CPE .... Chronic Pulmonary Emphysema [Medicine]
CPE .... Circadian Periodicity Experiment [Skylab] [NASA]
CPE .... Circular Probable Error
CPE .... Cis-Platinumdiamminedichloride [Also called Cisplatin and Platinol] [Antineoplastic drug] (DAVI)
CPE .... Clinical Pastoral Education
CPE .... Cloud Processing Equipment (AABC)
CPE .... Collective Protection Enclosure [NBC contamination] [Military] (RDA)
CPE .... Collective Protection Equipment
CPE .... College Proficiency Examination (WGA)
CPE .... Committee for Positive Education [Defunct] (EA)
CPE .... Common Professional Examination (DLA)
CPE .... Communications Program Element
CPE .... Communist Party of Ecuador [Political party]
CPE .... Communist Party of Estonia [Political party]
CPE .... Comparing Political Experiences [National Science Foundation project]
CPE .... Compass Resources Ltd. [Vancouver Stock Exchange symbol]
CPE .... Compensation, Pension, and Education (MAE)
CPE .... Computer Performance Evaluation
CPE .... Computer Peripheral Equipment (KSC)
CPE .... Congres du Peuple Europeen
CPE .... Consumer Premise Equipment (DOMA)
CPE .... Continuing Professional Education
CPE .... Continuous Particle Electrophoresis
CPE .... Contractor Performance Evaluation
CPE .... Controlled-Potential Electrolysis
CPE .... Control of Panel Emulator

CPE .... Conventional Polyethylene
CPE .... Corona-Penetrating Enzyme (MAE)
CPE .... Council of Public Education [Victoria] [Australia]
CPE .... Council on Podiatry Education [Later, CPME] (EA)
CPE .... Counter Position Exit (IAA)
CPE .... Coupe [Automotive] (WGA)
CPE .... Crew Personal Equipment
CPE .... Cryptopathic Effect
CPE .... Cumann Peile na Heireann [Football Association of Ireland] [Ireland] (EAIO)
CPE .... Current Product Engineering
CPE .... Customer Premises Equipment [Telecommunications]
CPE .... Customer Premises Equipment (ACRL)
CPE .... Customer Provided Equipment [Telecommunications]
CPE .... Cytopathogenic [or Cytopathic] Effect [Microbiology]
CPE .... Pepperdine University, Malibu, CA [OCLC symbol] (OCLC)
CPe .... Petaluma Free Public Library, Petaluma, CA [Library symbol Library of Congress] (LCLS)
CPE .... Society of Canadian Painter-Etchers and Engravers [1916-76] (NGC)
CPEA .... Chemically Pure Ethylamine (PDAA)
CPEA .... College Physical Education Association [Later, NAPEHE]
CPEA .... Concentrated Phosphate Export Association
CPEA .... Cooperative Program in Educational Administration
CPEB .... Central Physical Evaluation Board [Navy] (NVT)
CPEB .... Council for Professional Education for Business [Later, AACSB]
CPEB .... Cryogenic Positive Expulsion Bladder
CPEBS .... Central Processing Element BIT Slice [Computer science] (NITA)
CPEC .... Cranfield Product Engineering Centre [Cranfield Institute of Technology] [Research center British] (CB)
CPEC .... Cyclopentenylcytosine [Biochemistry]
CPed .... Certified Pedorthist
CPED .... Continuous Particle Electrophoresis Device (OA)
CPEFIBA ...... Conference Permanente de l'Europe de la Federation Internationale de Basketball [Standing Conference for Europe of the International Basketball Federation] (EAIO)
CPEG .... Contractor Performance Evaluation Group
CPEH .... Comhaltas Peil Eitleoiga na Heireann [Volleyball Association of Ireland] [See also VAI] [Ireland] (EAIO)
CPEHS .... Consumer Protection and Environmental Health Service [Later, Environmental Health Service] [US government]
CPEI .... Computer Program End Item (NASA)
CPEI .... Electro-Optical Systems, Inc., Pasadena, CA [Library symbol Library of Congress] (LCLS)
CPEIP .... Center for Training, Experimentation, and Research on Education (IID)
CPEJO .... Centre de Protection de l'Enfance et de la Jeunesse de l'Outaouais (AC)
CPEM .... Conference on Precision Electromagnetic Measurements (EA)
CPEMRC ...... Circum-Pacific Energy and Mineral Resources Conference
C Pen.......... Code Penal [Penal Code] [French] (BARN)
CPENC .... Canadian PEN Center (EAIO)
CP-ENDOR ... Circularly Polarized-Electron Nuclear Double Resonance [Spectroscopy]
CP (Eng) ..... Common Pleas Division, English Law Reports [1875-80] [A publication] (DLA)
CPEO .... Chronic Progressive External Ophthalmoplegia [Ophthalmology]
CPEO .... Coalition of Public Employee Organizations (EA)
CPEO .... Cooperative Program for Educational Opportunity (EA)
CPEP .... Committee on Public Engineering Policy [National Academy of Engineering]
CPEP........... Contractor Performance Evaluation Plan [or Program] [Military] (AABC)
CPEPC .... Canadian Poultry & Egg Processors Council [Formerly, Canadian Produce Council] (AC)
CPEQ .... Cente Patronal de l'Environnement du Quebec (AC)
CPEQ .... Corporation Professionnelle des Ergotherapeutes du Quebec (AC)
C-PER .... Calculated Protein Efficiency Ration [Nutrition]
CPER .... Central Plains Experimental Range (GNE)
CPER .... Chest Pain Emergency Room
CPER .... Contractor Personnel Employment Report (NG)
CPer........... Perris Public Library, Perris, CA [Library symbol Library of Congress] (LCLS)
CPERF .... Committee on Professional Ethics, Rights, and Freedom (EA)
CPERG .... Contractor Performance Evaluation Review Group (AAGC)
CPermK .... Kaiser Aluminum & Chemical Corp., Permanente, CA [Library symbol Library of Congress] (LCLS)
CPES .... Contractor Performance Evaluation System
CPES........... Crew Procedures Evaluation Simulator (MCD)
CPET .... Canadian Pacific Express and Transport
CPET .... Centre for Protein and Enzyme Technology [La Trobe University] [Australia]
CPET .... Charged Particle Electrostatic Thruster
CPET .... Crystallized Polyethylene Terephthalate [Plastics technology]
CPEUG .... Computer Performance Evaluation Users Group [Defunct] (EA)
CPEx .... Command Post Exercise [Military]
CPF .... Canadian Parents for French (AC)
CPF .... Canadian Patrol Frigate [Military]
CPF .... Canadian Psoriasis Foundation [Fondation Canadienne du Psoriasis] (AC)
CPF .... Cancer-Potency Factor [Environmental chemistry]
CPF .... Carcinogenic Potency Factor (FFDE)
CPF .... Cargo Processing Facility [Shipping] (NASA)
CPF .... Catalyst Pass Fraction
CPF .... Catholic Peace Fellowship (EA)
CPF............ Catholic Press Features

CPF............	Central Post Fund [*Army*]
CPF............	Central Processing Facility (MCD)
CPF............	Central Provident Fund [*Singapore*] (ECON)
CPF............	Chemical Processing Facility [*Nuclear energy*] (NUCP)
CPF............	Chlorine Pentafluoride [*Inorganic chemistry*]
CPF............	Church Pension Fund (EA)
CPF............	Circularly Polarized Fluorescence [*Physics*]
CPF............	Civilian Position File (MCD)
CPF............	Clot-Promoting Factor (MAE)
CPF............	Communist Party of Finland [*Political party*]
CPF............	Community Projects Foundation [*British*]
CPF............	Complete Power Failure [*Aviation*]
CPF............	Compromised Pulmonary Functions [*Medicine*]
CPF............	Conditional Peak Flow [*Biology*]
CPF............	Consolidated Professor Mines Ltd. [*Toronto Stock Exchange symbol*]
CPF............	Contraction Peak Force [*Medicine*] (DMAA)
CPF............	Contractor Performance Factor [*DoD*]
CPF............	Control Program Facility (MCD)
CPF............	Cost per Flight [*NASA*]
CPF............	Cotton Plant - Fargo Railway Co. [*AAR code*]
CPF............	Coupled-Pair Functional (MCD)
CPF............	Creative Playthings Foundation [*Defunct*]
CPF............	Cumulative Percentage Frequency
CPF............	Pepperdine University, Law Library, Malibu, CA [*OCLC symbol*] (OCLC)
CPFA...........	Concerned Persons for Adoption (EA)
CPFA...........	Custom Packages for Automation [*3D Digital Design & Development Ltd.*] [*Software package*] (NCC)
CPFA...........	Cyclopropenoid Fatty Acid [*Biochemistry*]
CPFC...........	Carl Perkins Fan Club [*Defunct*] (EA)
CPFC...........	Charley Pride Fan Club (EA)
CPFC...........	Comision de Proteccion Fitosanitaria para el Caribe [*Caribbean Plant Protection Commission - CPPC*] (EAIO)
CPFCS.........	Child Protection and Family Crisis Service [*New South Wales*] [*Australia*]
CPFE...........	COMSEC [*Communications Security*] Priorities Field Evaluation (MCD)
CPFF...........	Cost Plus Fixed Fee [*Business term*]
CPFF...........	Cost Plus Fixed Fee [*Investment term*] (DFIT)
CPFG...........	CNO [*Chief of Naval Operations*] Program Fiscal Guidance [*Navy*] (CAAL)
CPFH...........	Center for Population and Family Health [*Columbia University*] [*Research center*] (RCD)
CPFI...........	Christian Pharmacists Fellowship International (EA)
CPFL...........	Conference on Personal Finance Law [*Later, CCFL*] (EA)
CPFL...........	Contingency Planning Facilities Lists (CINC)
CPFMS........	COMRADE [*Computer-Aided Design Environment*] Permanent File Management System
CPFP...........	Canadian Patrol Frigates Program [*Canadian Navy*]
CPFP...........	Cancer Prevention Fellowship Program [*NCI*]
CPFR...........	Calling Party Forced Release [*Telecommunications*] (TEL)
CPFR...........	Continuous Page Facsimile Recorder
CPFR...........	Continuous Plug Flow Reactor [*Chemical engineering*]
CPFRC........	Central Pacific Fisheries Research Center [*National Oceanic and Atmospheric Administration*]
CPFSK........	Continuous Phase Frequency Shift Keying
CPFT...........	Contact Personality Factor Test [*Psychology*]
CPFT...........	Customer-Premises Facility Terminal [*Telecommunications*] (TEL)
CPFT...........	Fuller Theological Seminary, Pasadena, CA [*Library symbol Library of Congress*] (LCLS)
CPFV...........	Commercial Passenger Fishing Vessel
CPFV...........	Cucumber Pale Fruit Viroid
cpg..............	Calcified Pea Gravel [*Archeology*]
CPG.............	Candidate Pass Generator [*NASA*]
CPG.............	Capillary Blood Gases [*Medicine*] (DAVI)
CPG.............	Capitol Publishing Group [*Information service or system*] (IID)
CPG.............	Carmen de Patagones [*Argentina*] [*Airport symbol*] (AD)
CPG.............	Central Pattern Generator [*Neurochemistry*]
CPG.............	Certified Professional Geologist
CPG.............	Certified Program Generator (IAA)
CPG.............	Champagne Resources Ltd. [*Vancouver Stock Exchange symbol*]
CPG.............	Change Planning Group (NASA)
CPG.............	Chromatopyrography [*for polymer characterization*]
CPG.............	Civil Preparedness Guide [*Civil Defense*]
CPG.............	Clavis Patrum Graecorum (BJA)
CPG.............	Clinical Practice Guidelines
CPG.............	Clock Pulse Generator
CPG.............	Club for Philately in Gerontology [*Defunct*] (EA)
CPG.............	CMS Energy [*NYSE symbol*] (SAG)
CPG.............	CMS Energy Cl'G' [*NYSE symbol*] (TTSB)
CPG.............	COBOL Program Generator (NITA)
CPG.............	Collector Platemakers Guild (EA)
CPG.............	College Publishers Group [*Defunct*] (EA)
CPG.............	Communications Publishing Group, Inc. [*Boston, MA*] [*Information service or system Telecommunications*] (TSSD)
CPG.............	Communist Party of Georgia [*Political party*]
CPG.............	Communist Party of Germany [*Political party*] (EAIO)
CPG.............	Compliance Policy Guide [*Food and Drug Administration*]
CPG.............	Comprehensive Procurement Guidelines [*EPA*] (AAGC)
CPG.............	Constant Pattern Generator
CPG.............	Contingency Planning Guidance (DOMA)
CPG.............	Controlled Plasma Glassification [*Of solid waste*]
CPG.............	Controlled-Pore Glass [*Corning*]
CPG.............	Control Pattern Generator
CPG.............	Conversion Programmer's Guide

CPG.............	Copilot/Gunner (MCD)
CPG.............	Coronary Prevention Group [*British*]
CPG.............	Cotton Piece Goods
CPG.............	Current Pulse Generator [*Electronics*] (IAA)
CPg.............	Pacific Grove Public Library, Pacific Grove, CA [*Library symbol Library of Congress*] (LCLS)
CPG.............	Palm Springs Public Library, Palm Springs, CA [*OCLC symbol*] (OCLC)
CPGA..........	California Persimmon Growers Association (EA)
CPGA..........	China Pottery and Glassware Association (EA)
CP/GA.........	Contractor-Prepared, Government-Approved
CPGAF........	Commission on Population Growth and the American Future [*Presidential commission*]
CPGB..........	Communist Party of Great Britain [*Political party*] (DCTA)
CPGC..........	Course per Gyro Compass [*Navigation*]
CPgH..........	Hopkins Marine Station, Pacific Grove, CA [*Library symbol Library of Congress*] (LCLS)
CPGN..........	Chronic Proliferative Glomerulonephritis [*Immunology*]
CPGP..........	Copilot/Gunner Panel (MCD)
CPGRP........	Cost per Gross Rating Point [*Advertising*] (NTCM)
CpGV..........	Cydia Pomenella Granulosis Virus
CPH............	Candlepower Hour (IAA)
CPH............	Capital Pacific Hldgs [*AMEX symbol*] (TTSB)
CPH............	Capital Pacific Holdings [*AMEX symbol*] (SAG)
CPH............	Captain Cook [*Hawaii*] [*Seismograph station code, US Geological Survey*] (SEIS)
CPH............	Cards per Hour [*Computer science*]
CPH............	Catch per Hour [*Pisciculture*]
CPH............	Central Powerhouse
CPH............	Certificate in Public Health [*British*]
CPH............	Characters per Hour [*Computer science*]
cph..............	Characters Per Hour (WDMC)
CPH............	Chronic Persistent Hepatitis [*Medicine*]
CPH............	Clay Products Haulers Bureau, Inc., Worthington OH [*STAC*]
CPH............	Close-Packed Hexagonal [*Metallography*]
CPH............	Communistische Partij Holland [*Communist Party of Holland*] [*Netherlands*] (PPE)
CPH............	Compu-Home Systems International, Inc. [*Toronto Stock Exchange symbol*]
CPH............	Computer Polarization Holography
CPH............	Copenhagen [*Denmark*] [*Airport symbol*] (OAG)
cph..............	Copyright Holder [*MARC relator code*] [*Library of Congress*] (LCCP)
CPH............	Counts per Hour
CPH............	Huntington Memorial Hospital, Pasadena, CA [*Library symbol Library of Congress*] (LCLS)
CPH 5	Cutter Protein Hydrolysate Five Percent in Water [*Pharmacology*] (DAVI)
CPhA..........	Canadian Pharmaceutical Association (EAIO)
CPHA..........	Canadian Port & Harbour Association [*Association des Ports et Havres du Canada*] (AC)
CPHA..........	Canadian Public Health Association
CPHA..........	Commission on Professional and Hospital Activities (EA)
C/PHANE......	Cellophane (DGA)
CPHC..........	Central Pacific Hurricane Center [*Honolulu*] [*National Weather Service*] (NOAA)
CPhCE........	United States Naval Civil Engineering Laboratory, Port Hueneme, CA [*Library symbol Library of Congress*] (LCLS)
CPHD..........	Combined Pituitary Hormone Deficiency [*Medicine*]
CPHE..........	Common Personal Hygiene Equipment (KSC)
CPHE..........	Crew Personal Hygiene Equipment
CPHGM........	Conference of Prince Hall Grand Masters (EA)
CPHHC........	Card Programmable Hand-Held Calculator/Computer (MCD)
CPHI...........	Conference of Pharmaceutical Ingredients
CPHi...........	Pasadena Historical Society, Pasadena, CA [*Library symbol*] [*Library of Congress*] (LCLS)
CPhil..........	Classical Philology [*A publication*] (OCD)
CPHJ..........	Committee for Prisoner Humanity and Justice (EA)
CPHL..........	Central Professional Hockey League
CPHL..........	Central Public Health Laboratory [*British*] (IRUK)
CPHLD........	Conference of Public Health Laboratory Directors [*Later, COPHL*] (EA)
CPHM.........	Chief Pharmacist's Mate [*Navy rating Obsolete*]
CPHMDP......	Chief Pharmacist's Mate, Dental Prosthetic Technician [*Navy rating Obsolete*]
CPHM(RPA)...	Chief Pharmacist's Mate (Radium Plaque Adaptometer Operator) [*Navy rating Obsolete*]
CPHO.........	Chief Photographer [*Navy rating Obsolete*]
CPHOM........	Chief Photographer's Mate [*Navy rating Obsolete*]
CPHS..........	Calgary Photographic Historical Society (AC)
CPHS..........	Center for Public Health Studies [*Portland State University*] [*Research center*] (RCD)
CPHS..........	Containment Pressure High Signal [*Nuclear energy*] (IEEE)
CPHS..........	Cost per Hand Stitch [*Tailoring*]
CPHSLA.......	Central Pennsylvania Medical Librarians [*Library network*]
CPHV..........	Center to Prevent Handgun Violence (EA)
CPHV..........	Conference of Public Health Veterinarians (EA)
CpHYII........	Corporate High Yield II [*Associated Press*] (SAG)
CPI.............	Cable Pair Identification [*Telecommunications*] (TEL)
CPI.............	California Personality [*or Psychological*] Inventory
CPI.............	Call Progress Indicator [*Telecommunications*] (TEL)
CPI.............	Caltex Pacific Indonesia
CPI.............	Canadian Periodical Index [*The Globe and Mail*] [*Information service or system*] (CRD)
CPI.............	Canadian Plastics Institute [*Institut Canadien du Plastique*] (AC)
CPI.............	Cancer Potential Index

CPI	Capital Planning Information Ltd. [*Information service or system*] (IID)
CPI	Capitol Publications, Inc. [*Information service or system*] (IID)
CPI	Capri [*Italy*] [*Geomagnetic observatory code*]
CPI	Capri Resources Ltd. [*Vancouver Stock Exchange symbol*]
CPI	Carbon Preference Index [*Organic geochemistry*]
CPI	Carboxypeptidase Inhibitor [*in potatoes*]
CPI	Carded Packaging Institute (EA)
CPI	Cathedral Peace Institute (EA)
CPI	Cathodic Protection Index (PDAA)
CPI	Center for Public Integrity
CPI	Center of Programmed Instruction (DIT)
CPI	Center Pressure Index
CPI	Centrally Procured Items (MCD)
CPI	Central Patents Index [*A publication*]
CPI	Cerebral Palsy Ireland (EAIO)
CPI	Certificate in Planning Information (PGP)
CPI	Change Package Identification
CPI	Changes per Inch (IAA)
CPI	Channel Port Index
CPI	Characters per Inch [*Typesetting*]
cpi	Characters Per Inch [*Typesetting*] (WDMC)
CPI	Chemical Process Industry
CPI	Chief of Public Information [*Army*]
CPI	Chief Patrol Inspector [*Immigration and Naturalization Service*]
CPI	Chief Postal Inspector [*US Postal Service*]
CPI	Chip Performance Index [*Computer science*]
CPI	Chronic Pancreatic Insufficiency [*Medicine*]
CPI	Church Planting International (EA)
CPI	Clay Pipe Institute (EA)
CPI	Clergy Pensions Institution [*Church of England*]
CPI	Clock Pulse Interval
CPI	Closed Pore Insulation
CPI	Coalition for Public Information (AC)
CPI	Coherent Processing Interval [*Computer science*]
CPI	Cohort Production Intervals
CPI	Command Performance Indicator (MCD)
CPI	Commercial Performance Index (MHDW)
CPI	Commission on Personnel Interchange [*Presidential*]
CPI	Commission Permanente Internationale de l'Acetylene, de la Soudure Autogene, et des Industries qui S'y Rattachent [*Permanent International Committee on Acetylene, Oxy-Acetylene Welding, and Allied Industries*]
CPI	Commission Permanente Internationale Europeenne des Gaz Industriels et du Carbure de Calcium [*Permanent International European Commission on Industrial Gases and Calcium Carbide*] (EAIO)
CPI	Commission Phytosanitaire Interafricaine
CPI	Common Program Interface [*Computer science*]
CPI	Communications Processing Interface (MCD)
CPI	Communications Processor and Interface
CPI	Communist Party of India [*Political party*] (PPW)
CPI	Communist Party of Indonesia [*Political party*] (PD)
CPI	Communist Party of Ireland [*Political party*] (PPW)
CPI	Community Products, Inc.
CPI	Computer-Prescribed Instruction (IEEE)
CPI	Computer Projects, Inc. [*Greensboro, NC*] [*Telecommunications*] (TSSD)
CPI	Computer to PBX Interface [*Telecommunications*] (NITA)
CPI	Computing Power Index [*Computer science*] (PDAA)
CPI	Concert Productions International [*Canada*]
CPI	Confederation of Photographic Industries [*British*] (DBA)
CPI	Conference Proceedings Index [*Database*] [*British Library*] [*Information service or system*] (CRD)
CPI	Constitutional Psychopathic Inferior [*or Inferiority*]
CPI	Consumer Price Index [*Department of Labor*] [*Database*]
CPI	Continuous Process Improvement [*Chemical engineering*]
CPI	Contractor Preliminary Inspection
CPI	Control Position Indicator (IAA)
CPI	Coronary Prognostic Index [*Medicine*] (AAMN)
CPI	Corps of Permanent Instructors [*British military*] (DMA)
CPI	Corrugated Plate Inteceptor (PDAA)
CPI	Cost Performance Index (MCD)
CPI	Cost per Inquiry
cpi	Cost Per Inquiry (WDMC)
CPI	Cost per Instruction [*Computer science*]
CPI	Cost per Interview [*Marketing*] (WDMC)
cpi	Cost Per Interview (WDMC)
CPI	Cost Plus Incentive [*Business term*] (MSA)
CPI	Cottage Program International (EA)
CPI	Council of the Printing Industries of Canada (HGAA)
cpi	Counts Per Inch (CDE)
CPI	CPI Corp. [*Associated Press*] (SAG)
CPI	Crash Position Indicator [*Aviation*] (AFM)
CPI	Crating, Packaging Instructions
CPI	Credit Professionals International (EA)
CPI	Crop Protection Institute (EA)
CPI	Cross Pointer Indicator (MCD)
CPI	Cultural Pollution Index
CPI	Cumulative Paperback Index 1939-1959 [*A publication*]
CPI	Current Physics Information [*American Institute of Physics*] [*New York, NY Information service or system*]
CPI	Current Priority Indicator
CPI	Current Protocols in Immunology [*A publication*]
CPI	Customs Port Investigator [*US Customs Service*]

CPI	Cysteine Proteinase Inhibitor [*Biochemistry*]
CPI	Public Information Division [*Coast Guard symbol*]
CPIA	Canadian Printing Industries Association (EAIO)
CPIA	Cathodic Protection Industry Association (EA)
CPIA	Chemical Propulsion Information Agency [*Laurel, MD*] [*DoD*]
CPIA	Chlorinated Paraffins Industry Association (EA)
CPIA	Close-Pair Interstitial Atom
CPIA	Conservation Program Improvements Act
CPIA	CPI Aerostructures [*NASDAQ symbol*] (TTSB)
CPIA	CPI Aerostructures, Inc. [*NASDAQ symbol*] (SAG)
CPI Aero	CPI Aerostructures, Inc. [*Associated Press*] (SAG)
CPIAF	Cost-Plus-Incentive-Award Fee [*Business term*] (MCD)
CPIB	Chlorophenoxyisobutyrate [*Pharmacology*]
CPIC	Canadian Police Information Centre
CPIC	Charged Particles Information Center [*ORNL*]
CPIC	Coastal Patrol and Interdiction Craft [*Navy symbol*]
CPIC	Combined Photographic Interpretation Center
CPI/C	Common Programming Interface for Communication [*Telecommunications*] (ACRL)
CPI-C	Common Programming Interface for Communications (CDE)
CPIC	Communist Party of Indo-China [*Political party*] (PPW)
CPIC	Company Pensions Information Centre [*British*] (CB)
CPIC	Computer Program Integration Contractor
CPIC	Consumer Product Information Center
CPIC	Cost Price of the Items Canceled [*Business term*]
CPiC	Los Madonnas College, Pittsburg, CA [*Library symbol*] [*Library of Congress*] (LCLS)
CPID	Chronic Pelvic Inflammatory Disease [*Gynecology*] (DAVI)
CPID	Computer Program Integrated Document (OA)
CPIF	California Poultry Industry Federation (SRA)
CPIF	Character Position in Frame
CPIF	Cost-Plus-Incentive-Fee [*Business term*] (AFM)
CPI/FDR	Crash Position Indicator/Flight Data Recorder [*Aviation*] (MCD)
CPII	Consumer Products Information Index [*National Institute of Standards and Technology*]
CP-ILS	Correlation-Protected Instrument Landing System
CPI(M)	Communist Party of India (Marxist) [*Political party*] (PPW)
CPI(ML)	Communist Party of India (Marxist-Leninist) [*Political party*] (PD)
CPI M-L	Communist Party of Ireland (Marxist-Leninist) [*Political party*] (PPW)
CPIN	Canadian Press Information Network (IID)
CPIN	Change Package Identification Number
CPIN	Computer Program Identification Numbers (MCD)
CPIN	Concealed Product Identification Number [*Automotive*]
CPIN	Crankpin (MSA)
CP Ind	Central Provinces, India (DLA)
CPIOC	Communication Physical Input/Output Control System (IAA)
CPIP	Chronic Pulmonary Insufficiency of Prematurity [*Medicine*] (DMAA)
CPIP	Common Peak Developed Isovolumic Pressure [*Cardiology*] (DAVI)
CPIP	Computer Pneumatic Input Panel
CPIP	Computer Program Implementation Process
CPI/PPI	Consumer and Producer Price Indexes [*Department of Labor*] [*Database*]
CPIQ	Conseil Pedagogique Interdisciplinaire du Quebec (AC)
CPIR	Cephalic-Phase Insulin Release [*Medicine*] (DMAA)
CPIR	Command Performance Indicator Review (MCD)
CPIRA	Carbon Paper and Inked Ribbon Association [*Defunct*] (EA)
CPIRA	Copying Products and Inked Ribbon Association (EA)
CPIS	Center Pivot Irrigation System
CPIS	Computerised Personnel Information System [*British*]
CPIS	Consumer Price Index for Services
CPISRA	Cerebral Palsy International Sports and Recreation Association [*Arnhem, Netherlands*] (EAIO)
CPIT	Children's Picture Information Test [*Psychology*] (AEBS)
CPIT	Contract Price of Items Terminated [*Business term*]
CPITUS	Comite Permanent International des Techniques et de l'Urbanisme Souterrains [*Permanent and International Committee of Underground Town Planning and Construction*]
CPI-U	Consumer Price Index for All Urban Consumers (OICC)
CPIUS	Comite Permanent International d'Urbanisme Souterrain
CPIV	Comite Permanent des Industries du Verre de la CEE [*Brussels, Belgium*] (EAIO)
CPIV	Comite Permanent International du Vinaigre [*Permanent International Committee on Vinegar*] [*Common Market*]
CPIW	Certified Professional Insurance Woman [*National Association of Insurance Women*] [*Designation awarded by*]
CPIW	Certified Professional Insurance Women's Association [*Canada*] (DD)
CPI-W	Consumer Price Index for Urban Wage Earners and Clerical Workers (OICC)
CPIZ	Closed Pack Ice Zone [*Oceanography*]
CPJ	[*The*] Canadian Committee to Protect Journalists (AC)
CPJ	Care Point Medical Centres Ltd. [*Vancouver Stock Exchange symbol*]
CPJ	Center for Public Justice (EA)
CPJ	Chateau Properties [*NYSE symbol*] (SPSG)
CPJ	Citizens for Public Justice (AC)
CPJ	Collision Parts Journal [*A publication*] (EAAP)
CPJ	Committee for Public Justice (EA)
CPJ	Committee to Protect Journalists (EA)
CPJ	Conoseal Pipe Joint
CPJ	Cooperative Phantom Jamming (MCD)
CPJ	Corpus Papyrorum Judaicarum (BJA)
CPJI	Cour Permanente de Justice Internationale [*Permanent Court of International Justice*] [*Later, CIJ*]
CPJP	Jet Propulsion Laboratory, Pasadena, CA [*Library symbol Library of Congress*] (LCLS)
CPK	Cabbage Patch Kids

CPK............ Central Pastry Kitchen [Army] (AABC)
CPK............ Cents per Kilometer (ADA)
CPK............ Chesapeake Utilities [NYSE symbol] (SPSG)
CPK............ Communist Party of Kampuchea [Political party] (PD)
CPK............ Communist Party of Kazakhstan [Former USSR Political party]
CPK............ Cone Peak [Hawaii] [Seismograph station code, US Geological Survey] (SEIS)
cPk............ Continental Polar Cold Air Mass (BARN)
CPK............ Corey-Pauling-Koltun [Molecular models]
CPK............ Creatine Phosphokinase [Preferred form is CK] [An enzyme]
CPKD.......... Childhood Polycystic Kidney Disease [Medicine]
CPKD.......... Creatine Phosphokinase Depleted [Medicine]
CPKI........... Creatine Phosphokinase Isoenzyme [Biochemistry] (DAVI)
CPKISO....... Creatine Phosphokinase Isoenzyme [Biochemistry] (DAVI)
CPKO.......... Crude Palm Kernel Oil
CPL............ CAD [Computer-Aided-Design] Programming Language (PCM)
CPL............ Calgary Public Library [UTLAS symbol]
CPL............ Capability Password Level [Telecommunications] (TEL)
CPL............ Caprine Placental Lactogen [Medicine] (DMAA)
CPL............ Carnegie Library of Pittsburgh, Pittsburgh, PA [OCLC symbol] (OCLC)
CPL............ Carolina Power & Light Co. [NYSE symbol] (SPSG)
CPL............ Carolina Pwr & Lt [NYSE symbol] (TTSB)
cpl............ Carpel [Botany] (BARN)
CPL............ CAST [Computerized Automatic System Tester] Programming Language
CPL............ Cats Protection League [British] (DBA)
CPL............ Cement Plaster (AAG)
cpl............ Cents Per Litre
CPL............ Certified Professional Logistician (MCD)
CPL............ Chaparral [Colombia] [Airport symbol] (AD)
CPL............ Chaparral Airlines [ICAO designator] (FAAC)
cpl............ Chapel (VRA)
CPL............ Chapel
CPL............ Chapel Resources, Inc. [Vancouver Stock Exchange symbol]
CPL............ Chaplin [Connecticut] [Seismograph station code, US Geological Survey Closed] (SEIS)
CPL............ Characters per Line [Typesetting]
cpl............ Characters Per Line [Typesetting] (WDMC)
CPL............ Charge Pumping Logic (IAA)
CPL............ Chief of Personnel and Logistics [Navy British]
CPL............ Chord Plane Line (MCD)
CPL............ Circularly Polarized Luminescence [Spectroscopy]
CPL............ Circular Polarized Light [Physics]
CPL............ Civilian Personnel Letter
CPL............ Classification, Packaging and Labelling [Toxicology]
CPL............ Clavis Patrum Latinorum (BJA)
CPL............ Collective Pitch Lever
CPL............ Combined Programming Language [Computer science]
CPL............ Command Programming Language
CPL............ Commercial Pilot's Licence [British] (DBQ)
CPL............ Commercial Products List (AFIT)
CPL............ Common Program Language [Computer science] (AABC)
CPL............ Common Pulse Line
CPL............ Communist Party of Latvia [Political party]
CPL............ Communist Party of Lesotho [Political party] (PD)
CPL............ Communist Party of Lithuania [Political party]
CPL............ Communist Party of Luxembourg [Political party]
CPL............ Compartment for Peptide Loading [In antigen preventing cells] [Immunology]
CPL............ Complement
CPL............ Complete
CPL............ Compline (WGA)
CPL............ Component Preparation Laboratory [Oak Ridge] [Energy Research and Development Administration]
CPL............ Comprehensive Personal Liability [Insurance]
CPL............ Computer Program Library (BUR)
CPL............ Computer Projects Limited
CPL............ Congenital Pulmonary Lymphangiectasia [Medicine] (DMAA)
CPL............ Contractor Parts List
CPL............ Contractor Procurement List (NATG)
CPL............ Conversational Programming Language [High-level language] [Digital Equipment Corp.] [Computer science]
CPL............ Converted Prelease (ADA)
CPL............ Core Performance Log [Nuclear energy] (IEEE)
CPL............ Corporal [Military] (AABC)
CPL............ Corps Phase Line
CPL............ Corpus Poetarum Latinorum [A publication] (OCD)
CPL............ Council of Planning Librarians (EA)
CPL............ Couple (KSC)
CPL............ Criminal Procedure Law [New York, NY A publication]
CPL............ Critical Path Length
CPL............ Croatian Party of Law [Political party]
CPL............ Current Flight Plan [FAA] (TAG)
CPL............ Current Flight Plan Message [Aviation code]
CPL............ Current Privilege Level [Computer programs] (BYTE)
CPL............ Current Property Law [British]
CPL............ Current Property Lawyer [1852-53] [England] [A publication] (DLA)
CPL............ Cycle Proof Listing [IRS]
CPl............ Placentia District Library, Placentia, CA [Library symbol Library of Congress] (LCLS)
CPLA.......... Conference for Progressive Labor Action
CPLA.......... Cordillera People's Liberation Army [Philippines] [Political party] (EY)
CPla.......... El Dorado County Free Library, Placerville, CA [Library symbol Library of Congress] (LCLS)

CPlaHi........ El Dorado County Historical Museum, Placerville, CA [Library symbol] [Library of Congress] (LCLS)
CPL & D...... Civilian Personnel Letters and Dispatches
CPLANSW.... Country Public Libraries Association, New South Wales [Australia]
CPLC.......... Center for Philosophy, Law, Citizenship (EA)
CPLD.......... Coupled (MSA)
CPLE.......... Center for Policy and Law in Education [University of Miami] [Research center] (RCD)
CPLE.......... Constantinople [Later, Istanbul] [Province in Turkey]
CPLEE........ Charged Particle Lunar Environment Experiment [NASA]
CPLF.......... Congres des Psychanalystes de Langue Francaise [Congress of Romance Language Psychoanalysts] (EAIO)
CPLG.......... Coupling (KSC)
CPlhC......... Contra Costa County Library, Pleasant Hill, CA [Library symbol Library of Congress] (LCLS)
CPLI.......... Canadian Professional Logistics Institute [Institut Canadien Professionnel Logistique] [Formerly, Professional Logistics Institute of Canada] (AC)
CPLIA........ Contracting Plasterers' and Lathers' International Association [Later, IAWCC] (EA)
CPLJ.......... Camp Lejeune Railroad Co. [AAR code]
CPLK.......... Comite Permanent de Liaison des Kinesitherapeutes de la CEE [Standing Liaison Committee of Physiotherapists within the EEC - SLCP] [Copenhagen, Denmark] (EAIO)
CPLM.......... Cysteine-Peptone-Liver Infusion Media [Medicine] (MAE)
CPLMB........ Chief Plumber [British military] (DMA)
CPLMT........ Complement
CPLN.......... California Palace of the Legion of Honor [San Francisco]
CPLN.......... Concordia Paper Holding Ltd. [NASDAQ symbol] (SAG)
CPLNV........ Clover Primary Leaf Necrosis Virus [Plant pathology]
CPLNY........ Concordia Paper Holding ADS [NASDAQ symbol] (TTSB)
CPLPr........ Carol P&L $5 cm Pfd [AMEX symbol] (TTSB)
CPLQ.......... Centre de Promotion du Logiciel Quebecois (AC)
CPLR.......... Center of Pillar
CPLR.......... Central Provinces Law Reports [India] [A publication] (DLA)
CPLR.......... Civil Practice Law and Rules [New York, NY]
CPLR.......... Coupler (AAG)
CPLRY........ Capillary (MSA)
CPLS.......... Centre for Petrology and Lithospheric Studies [Macquarie University] [Australia]
CPLS.......... Cleft Palate and Lip Society [Australia]
CPLS.......... Cleft Palate-Lateral Synechia Syndrome [Medicine] (DMAA)
C/PLSEL..... Clothing and Personal Life Support Equipment Laboratory [Army Natick Laboratories, MA]
CPLT.......... Camino, Placerville & Lake Tahoe Railroad Co. [AAR code]
CPLT.......... Complete (ROG)
CPLT.......... Copilot
CPLX.......... Cerplex Group [NASDAQ symbol] (SAG)
CPLX.......... Complex
CPLY.......... Copley Pharmaceutical [NASDAQ symbol] (TTSB)
CPLY.......... Copley Pharmaceutical, Inc. [NASDAQ symbol] (SAG)
CPM........... Call Protocol Message [Telecommunications] (TEL)
CPM........... Calls per Minute [Telecommunications] (IAA) ·
CPM........... Capsule Positioning Mechanism [Aerospace]
CPM........... Cards per Minute [Computer science]
CPM........... Career Program Manager (MCD)
CPM........... Cargo Propulsion Module [NASA] (KSC)
CPM........... Catalogue of Printed Music [A publication]
CPM........... Cathode Pulse Modulation
CPM........... CCNU [Lomustine], Procarbazine, Methotrexate [Antineoplastic drug regimen]
CPM........... Center Program Manager [NASA] (KSC)
CPM........... Central Path Method [Computer science]
CPM........... Central Pontine Myelinolysis [Medicine]
CPM........... Central Processing Modules [Computer science] (MCD)
CPM........... Central Processor Molecules (NITA)
CPM........... Centre for Pest Management [Simon Fraser University] [Canada Research center] (RCD)
CPM........... Certificate in Public Management (PGP)
CPM........... Certified Property Manager [Institute of Real Estate Management] [Designation awarded by]
CPM........... Certified Purchasing Manager [National Association of Purchasing Manageme nt, Inc.] [Designation awarded by]
CPM........... Cesarean Prevention Movement (EA)
CPM........... Characters per Minute [Computer science]
cpm........... Characters Per Minute [Typesetting] (WDMC)
CPM........... Chief Patternmaker [Navy rating Obsolete]
CPM........... Chlorpheniramine Maleate [Antihistamine]
CPM........... Chosen People Ministries (EA)
CPM........... C L & P Capital Ltd. [NYSE symbol] (SAG)
CPM........... Coarse Particulate Matter [Pisciculture]
CPM........... COBOL [Common Business-Oriented Language] Performance Monitor [Computer science] (IAA)
CPM........... Collector of Public Moneys
CPM........... College of Petroleum and Minerals [Dhahran, Saudi Arabia]
CPM........... Colliding-Pulse-Mode [LASER]
CPM........... Colonial Police Medal [British]
CPM........... Coloured Progressive Matrices
CPM........... Combat Air Patrol Mission [Air Force]
CPM........... Comite du Patrimoine Mondial [World Heritage Committee - WHC] (EAIO)
CPMH.......... Comite pro Maria [An association Belgium] (EAIO)
CPM........... Command Processor Module
CPM........... Commissioner of Police for the Metropolis [British] (DI)
CPM........... Common Particular Meter [Music]

CPM .... Communist Party Marxist
CPM .... Communist Party of India - Marxist [*Political party*] (FEA)
CPM .... Communist Party of Malaya [*Political party*] (PD)
CPM .... Communist Party of Malta [*Political party*]
CPM .... Communist Party of Moldavia [*Political party*]
CPM .... Community Planning and Management [*HUD*]
CPM .... Commutative Principle for Multiplication [*Mathematics*]
CPM .... Company Program Manager (MCD)
CPM .... Component Parts manufacturer
CPM .... Compton, CA [*Location identifier FAA*] (FAAL)
CPM .... Computer Performance Management
CPM .... Computer Performance Monitor (PDAA)
CPM .... Computer Programmer's Manual (MCD)
CPM .... Computer Program Module (NASA)
CPM .... Conference Permanente d'Etudes sur les Civilisations du Monde Mediterraneen [*Standing Conference of Studies on the Civilisations of the Mediterranean World*] (EAIO)
CPM .... Conference Permanente Mediterraneenne pour la Cooperation Internationale [*Standing Mediterranean Conference for International Cooperation - COPEMCI*] (EAIO)
CPM .... Conference Preparatory Meeting [*ITU/WARC*]
CPM .... Congregation of Priests of Mercy [*Fathers of Mercy*] [*Roman Catholic religious order*]
CPM .... Congregation of the Fathers of Mercy (TOCD)
cpm .... Congregation of the Fathers of Mercy (TOCD)
CPM .... Continental Pharma Cryosan, Inc. [*Toronto Stock Exchange symbol*]
CPM .... Continue Present Management [*Medicine*] (DAVI)
CPM .... Continuous Particle Monitor [*Environmental Protection Agency*] (GFGA)
CPM .... Continuous Passive Motion [*Medicine*]
CPM .... Continuous Performance Measure (MCD)
CPM .... Continuous Processing Machine (PDAA)
CPM .... Contractor Performance Measurement (MCD)
CPM .... Contract Packager and/or Manufacturer [*Pharmaceutical distribution*]
CPM .... Contract Program Manager (MCD)
CP/M .... Control Program for Microcomputers [*Operating system*]
CP/M .... Control Program for Microcomputers (DOM)
CP/M .... Control Program for Microprocessors [*Computer science*]
CP/M .... Control Program/Monitor [*Computer science*]
CPM .... Conversational Program Module [*Fujitsu Ltd.*] [*Japan*]
CPM .... Cost Performance Management (MCD)
CPM .... Cost per Thousand [*Advertising*]
CPM .... Counts per Minute
CPM .... Critical-Path Management
CPM .... Critical Path Method [*Graph theory*] [*Telecommunications*] (TEL)
CPM .... Current Processor Mode
CPM .... Cycles per Minute
cpm .... Cycles Per Minute (WDMC)
CPM .... Cyclophosphamide [*Cytoxan*] [*Antineoplastic drug*]
CPMA .... California Podiatric Medical Association (SRA)
CPMA .... Canadian Print Marketers Association [*Association Canadienne des Courtiers en Imprimerie*] (AC)
CPMA .... Canadian Produce Marketing Association [*Association Canadienne de la Distribution de Fruite et Legumes*] [*Formerly, Canadian Fruit Wholesalers Association*] (AC)
CPMA .... Central Processor Memory Address [*Computer science*]
CPMA .... Chinchilla Pelt Marketing Association Ltd. [*British*] (BI)
CPMA .... Colorado Podiatric Medical Association (SRA)
CPMA .... Color Pigments Manufacturing Association
CPMA .... Common Price and Marketing Arrangement [*British*]
CPMA .... Computer Peripheral Manufacturers Association
CPMA .... Connecticut Podiatric Medical Association (SRA)
CPMAJO ...... Conference of Presidents of Major American Jewish Organizations (EA)
CPMAS .... Communications Performance Monitoring and Assessment [*Military*]
CPMAS .... Cross-Polarization Magic Angle Spinning [*Spectroscopy*]
CPmax .... Peak Serum Concentration [*Immunology*] (DAVI)
CPMB .... Centre for Plant Molecular Biology [*McGill University*] [*Canada*] (IRC)
CPMB .... Concrete Plant Manufacturers Bureau (EA)
CPMB .... Current Protocols in Molecular Biology [*A publication*]
CPMC .... Canadian Political Memorabilia Club (AC)
CPMC .... (Chlorophenyl)methylcarbamate [*Organic chemistry*]
CPMC .... Civilian Personnel Management Center [*Air Force*] (DOMA)
CPMC .... Columbia-Presbyterian Medical Center (DMAA)
CPMC .... Construction Products Manufacturers Council [*Defunct*] (EA)
CPMC .... Contractor Performance Measurement Course [*DSMC*] (AAGC)
CPmD .... Defense Language Institute, West Coast Branch, Presidio of Monterey, CA [*Library symbol Library of Congress*] (LCLS)
CPME .... Conseil Parlementaire du Mouvement Europeen
CPME .... Council for Postgraduate Medical Education [*British*] (DI)
CPME .... Council on Podiatric Medical Education (EA)
CPMF .... Case Project Master File [*IRS*]
CPMG .... Capital Media Group LLC [*NASDAQ symbol*] (SAG)
CPMG .... Carr-Purcell-Meiboom-Gill [*Radiologic instrumentation*]
CPMI .... Command Personnel Management Inspections (AABC)
CPmin .... Trough Serum Concentration [*Immunology*] (DAVI)
CPMINY .... Central Pac Minerals NL [*NASDAQ symbol*] (TTSB)
CPMIS .... Civilian Personnel Management Information System (MCD)
CPMIS .... Consolidated Personnel Management Information System [*OST*] (TAG)
CPMLS .... Centre for Petroleum and Mineral Law Studies [*University of Dundee*] [*British*] (CB)
CPMM .... Characters per Millimeter [*Typesetting*] (IAA)
CPMM .... Conseil des Premiers Ministres des Maritimes [*Council of Maritime Premiers - CMP*] [*Canada*]

CPM-ML .... Communist Party of Malaya - Marxist-Leninist [*Political party*] (PD)
CPMMV .... Cowpea Mild Mottle Virus [*Plant pathology*]
CPMN .... Central Pacific Minerals NL [*NASDAQ symbol*] (NQ)
CPMO .... Compendium of Plausible Materiel Options [*Army*]
CPMO .... Contract Parts Material Order
CPMO .... Control Processes in Multicellular Organisms
CPMOS .... Career Progression Military Occupational Specialty (MCD)
CPMOV .... Cowpea Mottle Virus [*Plant pathology*]
CPMP .... Civilian Personnel Modernization Project [*Military*]
CPMP .... Committee for Proprietary Medicinal Products [*European Directorate*]
CPMP .... Crew Procedures Management Plan [*NASA*] (NASA)
CPMPrA .... CL&P Capital LP.9.30%'MIPS' [*NYSE symbol*] (TTSB)
CPMQ .... Corporation Professionnelle des Medecins du Quebec [*Professional Corporation of Physicians of Quebec*] (AC)
CPMR .... Conference of Peripheral Maritime Regions of the EEC (EAIO)
CPM-RF .... Communist Party of Malaya - Revolutionary Faction [*Malaysia*] [*Political party*] (PD)
CPMS .... Cable Pressure Monitoring System [*Bell System*]
CPMS .... Canadian Paper Money Society
CPMS .... Canadian Pest Management Society [*Societe Canadienne de Lutte Contre les Organismes Nuisibles*] [*Formerly, Agricultural Pesticide Society*] (AC)
CPMS .... Check Plus Minus Subroutine
CPMS .... Chronic Progressive Multiple Sclerosis [*Medicine*] (DMAA)
CPMS .... College on the Practice of Management Science
CPMS .... Communications Procedures Management System (MCD)
CPMS .... Comprehensive Power Management System [*Military*] (CAAL)
CPMS .... Computerized Performance Monitoring System (DNAB)
CPMS .... Computer Plotting Matrix System (PDAA)
CPMS .... Constant Position Mounting System (PDAA)
CPMS .... Contractor Property Management System
CPmuN .... United States Navy, Naval Missile Center, Point Mugu, CA [*Library symbol Library of Congress*] (LCLS)
CPMV .... Cowpea Mosaic Virus [*Plant pathology*]
CPMVQ .... Corporation Professionnelle des Medecins Veterinaires du Quebec (AC)
CPN .... Butte, MT [*Location identifier FAA*] (FAAL)
CPN .... Calling Party Number [*Telecommunications*]
CPN .... Calpine Corp. [*NYSE symbol*] (SAG)
CPN .... Canadian Press Newstex [*The Canadian Press*] [*Information service or system*] (IID)
CPN .... Cape Rodney [*Papua New Guinea*] [*Airport symbol*] (OAG)
CPN .... Children's PKU [*Phenylketonuria*] Network (PAZ)
CPN .... Chronic Polyneuropathy [*Medicine*] (AAMN)
CPN .... Chronic Pyelonephritis [*Urology*]
CPN .... Commercial Paper Note [*Banking*]
CPN .... Communistische Partij van Nederland [*Communist Party of the Netherlands*] (PPE)
CPN .... Communist Party of Nepal [*Political party*] (FEA)
CPN .... Communist Party of Norway [*Political party*]
CPN .... Comp-Data International, Inc. [*Vancouver Stock Exchange symbol*]
CPN .... Computer Product News (MHDI)
Cpn .... Copenhagen (BARN)
CPN .... Corporation (ROG)
CPN .... Country Progressive National Party [*Australia Political party*]
CPN .... Coupon (ADA)
CPN .... CP-17 [*Nevada*] [*Seismograph station code, US Geological Survey Closed*] (SEIS)
CPN .... Critical Path Network
CPN .... Personal Names from Cuneiform Inscriptions of the Cassite Period (BJA)
CPNA .... Community Psychiatric Nursing Association [*British*]
CPNC .... Cameroon People's National Congress
CPNC .... Cherry Point, North Carolina [*Marine Corps Air Station*]
CPNE .... Combined Pulsed Neutron Experiment (MCD)
CPNF .... Cost Plus No Fee [*Business term*] (MCD)
CPNMR .... Cross-Polarization Nuclear Magnetic Resonance [*Physics*]
CPNP/A .... Certified Pediatric Nurse Practitioner/Associate (MEDA)
CPNS .... CP National Network Services [*Concord, CA*] [*Telecommunications*] (TSSD)
CPNSC .... Crystal Palace National Sports Centre [*British*]
CPNSW .... Council of Professions, New South Wales [*Australia*]
CPNTR .... Carpenter (MSA)
CPNZ .... Communist Party of New Zealand [*Political party*]
CPO .... California Polytechnic State University, Pomona, CA [*OCLC symbol*] (OCLC)
CPO .... Cancel Previous Order (DI)
CPO .... Cases per Officer [*Term used by crime laboratories*]
CPO .... Catholic Press Office [*British*]
CPO .... Census Promotion Office [*Bureau of the Census*] (GFGA)
CPO .... Center for Population Options (EA)
CPO .... Central Pay Office (AIE)
CPO .... Central Planning Office [*NASA*] (KSC)
CPO .... Central Procurement Office (AABC)
CPO .... Central Project Office [*of ARS, Department of Agriculture*]
CPO .... Central Provision Office [*World War II*]
CPO .... Central Purchasing Organization
CPO .... Centre for Chiropractic and Osteopathy [*Macquarie University*] [*Australia*]
CPO .... Certified Project Officer [*Environmental Protection Agency*] (GFGA)
CPO .... Certified Prosthetist and Orthotist
CPO .... Changing Path of Operation
CPO .... Chemical Protective Overgarment [*Army*] (DOMA)
CPO .... Chief of the Purchasing Office (AAGC)
CPO .... Chief Petty Officer [*Navy*]

CPO .... Chief Political Officer [*British Military Administration*]
CPO .... Chief Post Office [*British*] (ADA)
CPO .... Chief Preventive Officer [*Customs*] [*British*] (ROG)
CPO .... Chief Procurement Officer (AAGC)
CPO .... Christian Publicity Organisation [*British*]
CPO .... Circular Parking Orbit [*Aerospace*] (AAG)
CPO .... Civilian Personnel Office [*or Officer*]
CPO .... Civil Post Office (AFM)
CPO .... Cloud Physics Observatory [*University of Hawaii*]
CPO .... Code Practice Oscillator
CPO .... Command Post Officer [*Military*]
CPO .... Command Pulse Output
CPO .... Committee on Period One [*US committee concerned with the period between the end of the German War and the end of the Japanese War*] [*World War II*]
CPO .... Commodity Pool Operator
CPO .... Community Post Office
CPO .... Complete Provisions Only
CPO .... Component Pilot Overhaul [*Navy*] (NG)
CPO .... Compulsory Purchase Order [*British*]
CPO .... Computer Printout (ADA)
CPO .... Concurrent Peripheral Operations (BUR)
CPO .... Conference of Private Organizations [*Defunct*] (EA)
CPO .... Contract Provider Organization [*Information service or system*] (HCT)
CPO .... Controlled Precision Oscillator
CPO .... Copaipo [*Chile*] [*Airport symbol*] (AD)
CPO .... Coproporphyrinogen Oxidase (DMAA)
CPO .... Corporate Aircraft Co. [*ICAO designator*] (FAAC)
CPO .... Cost per Order [*Advertising*] (WDMC)
CPO .... Cost Proposal Outline (AAG)
CPO .... Cumberland Plateau [*Tennessee*] [*Seismograph station code, US Geological Survey*] (SEIS)
CPO .... Custom Patrol Officer [*British*]
CPO .... Mount Wilson Observatory, Pasadena, CA [*Library symbol Library of Congress*] (LCLS)
CPOA .... Completion of Post Overhaul Availability (DNAB)
CPOA .... Concerned Pet Owners' Association (EA)
CPOA .... United States Coast Guard Chief Petty Officer Association (EA)
CPOACMN.... Chief Petty Officer, Aircrewman [*British military*] (DMA)
CPOAQ .... Corporation Professionnelle des Orthophonistes et Audiologistes du Quebec (AC)
CPO ATA...... Chief Petty Officer Air Technical Aircraft [*Military Australia*]
CPO ATC...... Chief Petty Officer Air Technical Communication [*Military Australia*]
CPOB .... Carcinogenic Potency Database [*Toxicology*]
CPOB .... Cyclophosphamide, Prednisone, Oncovin [*Vincristine*], Bleomycin [*Antineoplastic drug regimen*]
CPOC .... Calculated Particulate Organic Carbon [*Oceanography*]
CPOC .... Chief Petty Officer of the Command [*Navy*] (DNAB)
CPOC .... Chrysler Product Owners Club (EA)
CPOC .... Clay Pigmented Organic Coating
CPOC .... Corps Personnel Operations Center [*Army*]
CPOCA .... Chief Petty Officer, Caterer [*British military*] (DMA)
CPO CD........ Chief Petty Officer Clearance Diver [*Military Australia*]
CPOCK.......... Chief Petty Officer, Cook [*British military*] (DMA)
CPO COX ..... Chief Petty Officer Coxswain [*Military Australia*]
CPODA......... Contention Priority Oriented Demand Assignment [*Protocol*] [*Computer science*]
CPO DEN ..... Chief Petty Officer Dental [*Military Australia*]
CPO ETC ...... Chief Petty Officer Electronic Technical Communications [*Military Australia*]
CPO ETP ...... Chief Petty Officer Electrical Technical Power [*Military Australia*]
CPO ETW..... Chief Petty Officer Electrical Technical Weapons [*Military Australia*]
CPO EW .... Chief Petty Officer Electronic Warfare [*Military Australia*]
CPO FC .... Chief Petty Officer Fire Control [*Military Australia*]
CPO FF .... Chief Petty Officer Firefighter [*Military Australia*]
CPOFP .... Computer Program Operational Flight Program (MCD)
CPOG .... Chemical Protective Overgarment [*Military*] (INF)
CPOIC .... Chief Petty Officer-in-Charge [*Navy*] (DNAB)
CPOL .... Communications Procedure-Oriented Language [*Computer science*]
CPOM .... Chief Petty Officer, Master [*Navy*] (WGA)
CPOM .... Coarse Particulate Organic Matter
CPom........... Pomona Public Library, Pomona, CA [*Library symbol Library of Congress*] (LCLS)
CPOMA .... Chief Petty Officer, Medical Assistant [*British military*] (DMA)
CPomCP ...... California Polytechnic State University, Pomona, CA [*Library symbol Library of Congress*] (LCLS)
CPO MED..... Chief Petty Officer Medical [*Military Australia*]
CPO MET ..... Chief Petty Officer Meteorology [*Military Australia*]
CPomG .... General Dynamics Corp., Pomona Division Library, Pomona, CA [*Library symbol Library of Congress*] (LCLS)
CPOMP........ Center for Population Options' Media Project (EA)
CPomP......... Pacific State Hospital, Pomona, CA [*Library symbol Library of Congress*] (LCLS)
CPO MTD..... Chief Petty Officer Motor Transport Driver [*Military Australia*]
CPO MTH..... Chief Petty Officer Marine Technical Hull [*Military Australia*]
CPO MTP..... Chief Petty Officer Marine Technical Propulsion [*Military Australia*]
CPO MUSN... Chief Petty Officer Musician [*Military Australia*]
CPO MW...... Chief Petty Officer Mine Warfare [*Military Australia*]
CPOP .... Certified Park Operators Program (EA)
CPOP .... Community Patrol Officer Program [*Police work*]
CPO PH........ Chief Petty Officer Photography [*Military Australia*]
CPOPT .... Chief Petty Officer, Physical Trainer [*British military*] (DMA)
CPO QMG .... Chief Petty Officer Quartermaster Gunner [*Military Australia*]
CPor............. Porterville Public Library, Porterville, CA [*Library symbol Library of Congress*] (LCLS)
CPorH .... Porterville State Hospital, Porterville, CA [*Library symbol Library of Congress*] (LCLS)
CPO RO .... Chief Petty Officer Radio Operator [*Military Australia*]
CPO RP........ Chief Petty Officer Radio Plotter [*Military Australia*]
C-PORT........ Committee for Private Offshore Rescue and Towing (EA)
CPOS .... Chief Petty Officer, Senior [*Navy*] (WGA)
CPOS .... Civilian Personnel Occupational Standards [*Military*] (AABC)
CPOS .... Continuous Production Operation Sheet
CPOS .... Cursor Position (MCD)
CPOSA......... Chief Petty Officer, Stores Accountant [*British military*] (DMA)
CPO SE........ Chief Petty Officer Survival Equipment [*Military Australia*]
CPO SIG ...... Chief Petty Officer Signalman [*Military Australia*]
CPOSMA...... Conference of Presidents and Officers of State Medical Associations [*Later, FMA*] (EA)
CPO SN........ Chief Petty Officer Stores Naval [*Military Australia*]
CPO SR........ Chief Petty Officer Survey Recorder [*Military Australia*]
CPOSTD....... Chief Petty Officer, Steward [*British military*] (DMA)
CPO SV........ Chief Petty Officer Stores Victualling [*Military Australia*]
CPO UC........ Chief Petty Officer Underwater Control [*Military Australia*]
CPOW .... Chief Petty Officer of the Watch [*Navy*]
CPO WS....... Chief Petty Officer Work Study [*Military Australia*]
CPOWTR...... Chief Petty Officer, Writer [*British military*] (DMA)
CPP............. Calprop Corp. [*AMEX symbol*] (SPSG)
CPP............. Caltech Population Program [*Agency for International Development*] (IID)
CPP............. Cambodian People's Party [*Political party*] (ECON)
CPP............. Canada Pension Plan
CPP............. Canadian Parks Partnership [*Partenaires des Parcs Canadiens*] (AC)
CPP............. Canadian Picture Pioneers (AC)
CPP............. Cancer Proneness Phenotype [*Medicine*] (DMAA)
CPP............. Capital Punishment Project (EA)
CPP............. Captive Power Plant
CPP............. Carboxy Terminus of Propressophysin [*Laboratory*] (DAVI)
CPP............. Card Print Processor [*Computer science*] (IAA)
CPP............. Card Punching Printer [*Computer output device*] [*Computer science*] (BUR)
CPP............. Career Planning Program [*Vocational guidance test*]
CPP............. Center for Plutonium Production [*France*] (NRCH)
CPP............. Center for Policy Process [*Defunct*]
CPP............. Center for the Progress of Peoples (EAIO)
CPP............. Central Perfusion Pressure [*Medicine*]
CPP............. Central Processing Point [*Computer science*]
CPP............. Cerebral Perfusion Pressure [*Medicine*]
CPP............. Certified Professional Purchaser [*Canada*] (DD)
CPP............. Certified Protection Professional [*American Society for Industrial Securi ty*] [*Designation awarded by*]
CPP............. Characters Per Pica [*Typesetting*] (WDMC)
CPP............. Children's Plea for Peace [*Later, World Pen Pals*]
CPP............. Chondrosoma Permeation Pattern [*Oncology*]
CPP............. Choroid Plexus Papilloma [*Medicine*]
CPP............. Civilian Personnel Pamphlet [*Military*]
CPP............. Coal and Petroleum Products [*Department of Employment*] [*British*]
CPP............. Coalition for Prompt Pay (EA)
CPP............. Coil Power Programmer [*Nuclear energy*] (NRCH)
CPP............. Collaborative Perinatal Project
CPP............. Commercial Practices Program [*Air Force*]
CPP............. Commercial Property Products
CPP............. Committee on Persistent Pesticides (EA)
CPP............. Committee on Political Parties
CPP............. Communications Patching Panel
CPP............. Communist Party of the Philippines [*Political party*]
CPP............. Competitive Prototype Phase (MCD)
CPP............. Compliance Policy and Planning [*Environmental Protection Agency*] (GFGA)
CPP............. Computer Position Profile (PDAA)
CPP............. Computer Printout Processing (PDAA)
CPP............. Computer Program Package (CAAL)
CPP............. Conditioned Place Preference [*Psychophysiology*]
CPP............. Conductive Plastic Potentiometer
CPP............. Consolidated Pipe Lines Co. [*Toronto Stock Exchange symbol*]
CPP............. Constant Purchasing Power
CPP............. Consumer Pesticide Project (EA)
CPP............. Containment Pressure Protection [*Nuclear energy*] (IEEE)
CPP............. Contract Pricing Proposal (MCD)
CPP............. Control and Protection Panel
CPP............. Controllable Pitch Propeller [*For ships*] (MCD)
CPP............. Convention People's Party [*1949-1966*] [*Ghana*]
CPP............. Cooperative Planting Program (GNE)
CPP............. Copiapo [*Chile*] [*Seismograph station code, US Geological Survey*] (SEIS)
CPP............. Coronary Perfusion Pressure [*Cardiology*]
CPP............. Corpus of Dated Palestinian Pottery (BJA)
CPP............. Corpus of Palestinian Pottery (BJA)
CPP............. Corrosion Prevention Panel
CPP............. Cost per Point [*Advertising*] (WDMC)
CPP............. Council of Psychoanalytic Psychotherapists (EA)
CPP............. Country Policy Programme [*Foreign trade*] [*British*]
CPP............. Critical Path Planning
CPP............. Croatian Peasant Party (EA)
CPP............. Croatian Peasants Party [*Political party*] (EY)
CPP............. Cryoprecipitate [*Laboratory*] (DAVI)
CPP............. Cullman, AL [*Location identifier FAA*] (FAAL)
CPP............. Curie Point Pyrolysis (PDAA)
CPP............. Current Purchasing Power
CPP............. Cyclopentenophenanthrene [*Organic chemistry*] (AAMN)

CPP............. Cyclopyrophosphoglycerate [Biochemistry]
CPP............. Pasadena Public Library, Pasadena, CA [OCLC symbol] (OCLC)
CPPA .... Canadian Pacific Police Association [Association des Policiers du Canadien Pacifique] (AC)
CPPA .... Canadian Periodical Publishers Association
CPPA .... Canadian Potash Producers Association
CPPA .... Canadian Pulp and Paper Association [See also ACPPP]
CPPA .... Center for Prevention of Premature Arterial Sclerosis
CPPA .... (Chlorophenoxy)propionic Acid [Biochemistry]
CPPA .... Chrysler Performance Parts Association (EA)
CPPA .... Classroom Periodical Publishers Association [Later, CPA] (EA)
CPPA .... Coal Preparation Plant Association [British] (EAIO)
CPPA .... Coated and Processed Paper Association [Defunct]
CPPA .... Conference for Progressive Political Action
CPPA .... Crusher and Portable Plant Association
CPPB .... Certified Professional Public Buyer (AAGC)
CPPB .... Comite de Problemas de Productos Basicos [Committee on Commodity Problems] [Italy] (ASF)
CPPB .... Constant [or Continuous] Positive-Pressure Breathing [Medicine] (DAVI)
CPPB .... Continuous Positive Pressure Breathing [Physiology]
CPPC .... Caribbean Plant Protection Commission [Trinidad and Tobago] (EAIO)
CPPC .... Collatis Pecuniis Poni Curaverunt [They Collected the Money and Had Put in Position] [Latin]
CPPC .... Cost Plus a Percentage of Cost
CPPCA .... California Probation, Parole, and Correctional Association
CPPCA .... Colour Printed Pottery Collectors Association (EA)
CPPCC .... Chinese People's Political Consultative Conference
CP-PCO .... Cargo Projects - Program Control Office [NASA] (NASA)
CPPD .... Calcium Pyrophosphate Deposition [Medicine]
CPPD .... Calcium Pyrophosphate Dihydrate [Inorganic chemistry]
CPPD .... Capped (MSA)
CPPD .... Chest Physiotherapy and Physical Drainage [Medicine]
CPPD .... Consumers Public Power District
CPPER .... Commonwealth Program for the Promotion of Excellence in Research [Australia]
CPPG .... Cable Program Providers Group [British] (DBA)
CPPG .... CNO [Chief of Naval Operations] Policy and Planning Guidance
CPPI............ Canadian Petroleum Products Institute [Institut Canadien des Produits Petroliers] [Formerly, Petroleum Association for Conservation of the Canadian Environment] (AC)
CPPI............ Competitive Pipeline Price Index
CPPI............ Coolant Pump Power Inverters (MCD)
CPPL........... Civilian Personnel and Payroll Letter [Military]
CPPM.......... Civilian Personnel Procedures Manual [Military]
CPPM.......... Communication Prediction Program [NASA] (KSC)
CPPMA .... Canadian Public Personnel Management Association
CPPME........ Canadian Professors for Peace in The Middle East (AC)
CPP/ML....... Communist Party of the Philippines/Marxist-Leninist [Political party]
CPP-MR....... Current Perpendicular to Plane Magnetoresistance [Physics]
CPPN.......... Children's Public Policy Network [Later, CAN] (EA)
CPPO .... Certified Public Purchasing Officer [Canadian]
CPPO .... Claimant Procurement Planning Officer
CPPO .... Controlled Production Planning Officer
CPPP .... Center for Philosophy and Public Policy [Later, IPPP] (EA)
CPPP .... Computerized Production Process Planning (MCD)
CPP-PFIP ..... [The] Christian People's Party - Progressive and Fishing Industry Party [Kristiligi Folkaflokkurin, Foroya Framburds- og Fiskivinnuflokkurin] [The Faroe Islands] [Political party] (EY)
CPPPN........ Commission on Private Philanthropy and Public Needs [Defunct] (EA)
CPPQ .... Corporation Professionnelle des Physiotherapeutes du Quebec (AC)
CPPQ .... Corporation Professionnelle des Psychologues du Quebec (AC)
CPPR .... Cassel Psychotherapy Progress Record [Psychology]
CPPR .... Construction Permit Power Reactor (NRCH)
CPpR .... Will Rogers State Historic Park, Pacific Palisades, CA [Library symbol Library of Congress] (LCLS)
CPPS .... Combined Procurement Processing Series (MCD)
CPPS .... Comision Permanente del Pacifico Sur [Permanent Commission for the South Pacific - PCSP] (EAIO)
CPPS .... Commission Permanente du Pacifique Sud [Permanent Commission for the South Pacific]
CPPS .... Composite Professional Performance Score
CPPS .... Computer Programming Performance Specification (MCD)
CPPS .... Computer Program Product Specification (MCD)
CPPS .... Congregatio Pretiosissimi Sanguinis [Society of the Most Precious Blood] [Roman Catholic religious order]
CPPS .... Critical Path Planning and Scheduling
CPPS .... Cyclohexylphenyl(piperidinylethyl)silanol [Organic chemistry]
CPPS .... Sisters of the Most Precious Blood (O'Fallon, MO) (TOCD)
CPPS .... Sisters of the Precious Blood (Dayton, Ohio) (TOCD)
CPPS .... Society of the Most Precious Blood (TOCD)
cpps............ Society of the Precious Blood (TOCD)
CPPSBOSH... Committee for Purchase of Products and Services of the Blind and Other Severely Handicapped [Later, Committee for Purchase from the Blind and Other Severely Handicapped]
CPPSO .... Consolidated Personal Property Shipping Office [Military] (DNAB)
CPPT........... Coronary Primary Prevention Trial [National Heart, Lung, and Blood Institute]
CPPT........... Cost per Positive Termination [Job Training and Partnership Act] (OICC)
CPP/TMH ..... Citizens Participation Project/the Missing Half [Defunct] (EA)
CPPUI .... Center for Public Policy, Union Institute (EA)
CPPV .... Continuous Positive Pressure Ventilation [Medicine]

CPQ .... Campinas [Brazil] [Airport symbol] (OAG)
CPQ .... Center for Produce Quality
CPQ .... Children's Personality Questionnaire [Psychology]
CPQ .... Civil Procedures, Quebec
CPQ .... Compaq Computer [NYSE symbol] (TTSB)
CPQ .... Compaq Computer Corp. [NYSE symbol] (SPSG)
CPQ .... Conpac Resources Ltd. [Vancouver Stock Exchange symbol]
CPQ .... Conpak Seafoods, Inc. [Toronto Stock Exchange symbol]
CPQ .... Conseil de la Peinture du Quebec (AC)
CPQ .... Conseil de la Peinture du Quebec [1978, founded 1966 as SAPQ, SAVVQ from 1980, CAPQ from 1982] [Canada] (NGC)
CPQ .... Conseil de Presse du Quebec (AC)
CPQ .... Conseil du Patronat du Quebec (AC)
CPQ .... Lansing, MI [Location identifier FAA] (FAAL)
CPQA .... Certified Professional in Quality Assurance (HCT)
CPQMC .... Conseil Provincial du Quebec des Metiers de la Construction (AC)
CPQRA........ Chemical Process Quantitative Risk Assessment [Chemical engineering]
CPR .... Calendar of Patent Rolls [British]
CPR .... Campaign for Pesticide Reform [Environmental Protection Agency] (GFGA)
CPR .... Campaign for Political Rights [Defunct] (EA)
CPR .... Cam Plate Readout
CPR .... Canadian Pacific Railway [Facetious translations: Can't Pay Rent, Can't Promise Returns]
CPR .... Canadian Philosophical Reviews [A publication] (BRI)
CPR .... Cape Peninsular Rifles [British military] (DMA)
CPR .... Cape Romanzof [Alaska] [Seismograph station code, US Geological Survey Closed] (SEIS)
CPR .... Cardiac Pulmonary Reserve [Physiology]
CPR .... Cardiopulmonary Resuscitation [Medicine]
CP/R .... Card Punch and Reader [Computer science]
CPR .... Career Placement Registry, Inc. [Database producer] [Information service or system] (IID)
CPR .... Carrier Performance Rating (AABC)
CPR .... Casper [Wyoming] [Airport symbol] (OAG)
CPR .... Casper, WY [Location identifier FAA] (FAAL)
CPR .... Caudal Photoreceptor [Biology]
CPR .... Ceiling Price Regulation (DLA)
CPR .... Center for Parapsychological Research [Defunct] (EA)
CPR .... Center for Policy Research (EA)
CPR .... Center for Political Research [Later, Government Research Corp.]
CPR .... Center for Preservation Research
CPR .... Center for Public Representation (EA)
CPR .... Center for Public Resources (EA)
CPR .... Central Point Recuperator [Computer program] (PCM)
CPR .... Central Premonitions Registry (EA)
CPR .... Centre of Polish Research [Institute of Comparative Civilizations] [Canada] (IRC)
CPR .... Centripetal Rub [Medicine]
CPR .... Cerebral Cortex Perfusion Rate [Medicine] (MAE)
CPR .... Cerebral-Pedal Regulator [Neurobiology]
CPR .... Chemically Perturbed Region [Meteorology]
CPR .... Chemicals, Plastic Research
CPR .... Chicken Progesterone Receptor [Genetics]
CPR .... Chief Parachute Rigger [Navy]
CPR .... Child Protection Report [A publication]
CPR .... Chinese People's Republic
CPR .... Chlorophenyl Red [A dye]
CPR .... Chromacom Proof Recorder (DGA)
CPR .... Circular Polarization Ratio [Physics]
CPR .... Citizens for Proportional Representation (EA)
CPR .... Civilian Personnel Records [Military]
CPR .... Civilian Personnel Regulation [Military]
CPR .... Clearport Petroleum Ltd. [Vancouver Stock Exchange symbol]
CPR .... Clerk (Pay and Records) [British military] (DMA)
CPR .... Clock Pulse Repeater
CPR .... Clothing Pattern Repository [DoD]
CPR .... Cloud Physics Radiometer
C Pr .... Code of Procedure [Legal term] (DLA)
CPR .... Code of Professional Responsibility [American Bar Association]
CPR .... Cold Pressor Response Test [Medicine]
CPR .... Cold Protective Response [Physiology]
CPR .... Combined Processor and RAM Module [Computer science] (NITA)
CPR .... Command Performance Review
CPR .... Committee on Polar Research [Later, PRB] [US]
CPR .... Commodity Policy and Relief [British]
CPR .... Company Persistency Rater [LIMRA]
CPR .... Component Pilot Rework [Navy] (NG)
CPR .... Component to Part Record
CPR .... Computerized Patient Record
CPR .... Computerized Performance Rating [of a horse]
CPR .... Conditional Prepayment Rate [for mortgages]
CPR .... Conserve, Preserve, and Restore (GNE)
CPR .... Consistent Payment Rate [Finance] (EMRF)
CPR .... Consolidated Progress Report
CPR .... Constant Prepayment Rate [Mortgage-backed securities]
CPR .... Construction Period Recapture [Nuclear power plant licensing]
CPR .... Consumer Product and Manufacturer Ratings [A publication]
CPR .... Consumer Product Safety Commission, Washington, DC [OCLC symbol] (OCLC)
CPR .... Continuing Property Records
CPR .... Continuing Property Records
CPR .... Continuous Plankton Recorder [Oceanography] (MSC)
CPR .... Continuous Progress Indicator [Telecommunications] (TEL)

CPR .... Contractor Performance Record [*DoD*]
CPR .... Contractor Performance Report
CPR .... Contract Pricing Report
CPR .... Contract Procurement Request (MUGU)
CP-R .... Control Program - Real-Time [*Xerox Corp.*]
CPR .... Copper [*Chemical symbol is Cu*]
CPR .... Corporate Air, Inc. [*ICAO designator*] (FAAC)
CPR .... Correct, Pause, Recovery [*Automobile driving*]
CPR .... Cortisol Production Rate [*Medicine*] (MAE)
CPR .... Cost Performance Report (MCD)
CPR .... Cost Proposal Requirement (MCD)
CPR .... Counsel for Procurement Reform (AAGC)
CPR .... Coupon Preparation Requirement (MCD)
CPR .... Crater Production Rate [*Geology*]
CPR .... Crew Provisioning Report
CPR .... Critical Power Ratio [*Nuclear energy*] (NRCH)
CPR .... Critical Problem Report [*NASA*] (NASA)
CPR .... Croatian Party of Rights [*Political party*]
CPR .... Customary, Prevailing, and Reasonable Charges [*Department of Health and Human Services*] (GFGA)
CPR .... Cut Paraboloidal Reflector
CPR .... Cycle Pressure Ratio (MCD)
CPr .... Paso Robles Public Library, Paso Robles, CA [*Library symbol Library of Congress*] (LCLS)
CPR (2d) ..... Canadian Patent Report, Second Series [*A publication*] (DLA)
CP/RA .... Canadian Parks/Recreation Association [*Association Canadienne des Loisirs/Parcs*] (AC)
CPRA .... Canadian Polystyrene Recycling Association (AC)
CPRA .... Chemical Public Relations Association [*Later, CCA*] (EA)
CPRA .... Communications Processor Assembly [*Ground Control Facility, NASA*]
CPRA .... Compressed Pulse RADAR Altimeter
CPRA .... Congo Protestant Relief Agency [*Defunct*]
CP Rail .... Canadian Pacific Railroad (MHDB)
CPRB .... Combined Production and Resources Board [*World War II*]
CPRC .... California Primate Research Center [*Research center*] (RCD)
CPRC .... Canadian Plains Research Center [*University of Regina*] [*Information service or system*] (IID)
CPRC .... Caribbean Primate Research Center [*University of Puerto Rico*] [*Research center*] (RCD)
CPRC .... Center for Population Research and Census [*Portland State University*] [*Oregon*] [*Information service or system*] (IID)
CPRC .... Chrysler Products Restorers Club [*Later, CRC*] (EA)
CPRC .... Civilian Payroll Circular
CPRC .... Combined Personnel Recovery Center (CINC)
CPRC .... Committee Program Review Council (AAGC)
CPRCA .... Constitutional Pure Red Cell Aplasia [*Medicine*] (DMAA)
CPRCASC .... Cytotechnology Programs Review Committee of the American Society of Cytology (DAVI)
CPRC (NS) ... Civil Procedure Reports, New Series [*1908-13*] [*New York*] [*A publication*] (DLA)
CPRD .... Cable Programming Resource Directory [*A publication*] (TSSD)
CPRD .... Chronic Progressive Renal Disease [*Medicine*] (CPH)
CPRD .... Committee on Prosthetics Research and Development [*National Research Council*]
CPRD .... Computer Products [*NASDAQ symbol*] (TTSB)
CPRD .... Computer Products, Inc. [*NASDAQ symbol*] (NQ)
CPRD .... Consumer and Professional Relations Division [*of HIAA*] [*Washington, DC*] (EA)
CPRDC .... Coordinated Program of Research in Distributed Computing [*British*] (NITA)
CPRDM .... Committee on the Acquisition and Use of Scientific and Technical Information in Pesticide Regulatory Decision Making at the Federal and State Levels [*National Research Council*]
CPRE .... Center for Policy Research in Education [*New Brunswick, NJ*] [*Department of Education*] (GRD)
CPRE .... Council for the Protection of Rural England (EAIO)
CPREA .... Canadian Peace Research and Education Association [*See also ACREP*]
CPREF .... Candelabra Prefocused
CP Rep .... Common Pleas Reporter [*Scranton, PA*] [*A publication*] (DLA)
CP Rept ...... Common Pleas Reporter [*Scranton, PA*] [*A publication*] (DLA)
CPRESS ...... Compound Pressure
CPRF .... Confinement Physics Research Facility
CPRG .... Computer Personnel Research Group [*Later, Special Interest Group for Computer Personnel Research*]
CPRH .... Council on Peace Research in History (EA)
CPRI .... Canadian Peace Research Institute
CPRI .... Central Psi Research Institute (EA)
CPRI .... Cold Pressor Recovery Index (PDAA)
CPRI .... Computer-Based Patient Record Institute [*Medicine*]
C (Print) ...... Color Print [*Publishing*]
C Priv .... Committee for Privileges, House of Commons/Lords (DLA)
CPRM .... Companhia Portuguesa Radio Marconi [*Portuguese Radio Marconi Co.*] [*Lisbon*] [*Information service or system*] (IID)
CPR-NICHD... Center for Population Research - National Institute of Child Health and Human Development [*Bethesda, MD*] [*Department of Health and Human Services*] (GRD)
CPR (NS) ..... Civil Procedure Reports, New Series [*1908-13*] [*New York*] [*A publication*] (DLA)
CPRO .... CellPro, Inc. [*NASDAQ symbol*] (SPSG)
CPRP .... Ciskei People's Rights Protection Party [*South Africa*] [*Political party*] (EY)
CPRP .... Civilian Personnel Reduction Plan (MCD)
cPRP .... Platelet-Rich Plasma, citrated [*Hematology*]

CPRP .... Ralph M. Parsons, Electronics Division, Pasadena, CA [*Library symbol Library of Congress*] (LCLS)
CPRR .... Civil Pilots for Regulatory Reform (EA)
CPR/R .... Component Pilot Rework/Repair [*Navy*] (MCD)
CPRR .... Construction Permit Research Reactor (NRCH)
CPRR .... Cost per Reportable Result
CPRR-NEA .. Commission on Professional Rights and Responsibilities of the NEA [*Defunct*] (EA)
CPRS .... Canadian Public Relations Society
CPRS .... Canadian Public Relations Society
CPRS .... Centralized Personnel Record System [*Telecommunications*] (TEL)
CPRS .... Central Policy Review Staff [*British*]
CPRS .... CINCPAC [*Commander-in-Chief, Pacific*] Route Slip (CINC)
CPRS .... Comprehensive Psychopathological Rating Scale
CPRS .... Compress (MSA)
CPRS .... Construction Progress Reporting Survey [*Bureau of the Census*] (GFGA)
CPRS .... Contractor Performance Review System (AAGC)
CPRSD .... Controller of Physical Research and Signals Development [*Ministry of Supply*] [*British*]
CPRSN .... Compression (MSA)
CPRSR .... Compressor (MSA)
CPRSV .... Cowpea Ringspot Virus [*Plant pathology*]
CPRT .... Cold Pressor Response Test [*Medicine*]
CPRT .... College de la Prevention des Risques Technologiques [*College for the Prevention of Technological Risks*] [*France*]
CPRT .... Copart, Inc. [*NASDAQ symbol*] (SAG)
CPRTR .... Chief Printer [*Navy rating Obsolete*]
CPRTRL .... Chief Printer, Lithographer [*Navy rating Obsolete*]
CPRTRM ...... Chief Printer, Offset Process [*Navy rating Obsolete*]
CPRV .... Cabin Pressure Relief Valve [*Aviation*] (KSC)
CPRV .... Canister Purge Regulator Valve [*Automotive engineering*]
CPRV .... Cinque Ports Rifle Volunteers [*British military*] (DMA)
CPRW .... Campaign for the Protection of Rural Wales [*See also YDCW*] (EAIO)
CPRW .... Council for the Protection of Rural Wales (EAIO)
CPRX .... CompScript
CPRX .... CompScript, Inc. [*NASDAQ symbol*] (SAG)
CPS .... Cabinet Pressurization System
CPS .... California Polytechnic State University, San Luis Obispo, CA [*OCLC symbol*] (OCLC)
CPS .... Calling Processing Subsystem [*Telecommunications*] (TEL)
CPS .... Cambridge Physical Series [*A publication*]
CPS .... Camshaft Profile Switching [*Automotive engine design*]
CPS .... Canada Plan Service
CPS .... Canadian Institute for International Peace and Security [*UTLAS symbol*]
CPS .... Canadian Paediatric Society (EAIO)
CPS .... Canadian Penitentiary Service
CPS .... Canadian Physiological Society [*Societe Canadienne de Physiologie*] (AC)
CPS .... Canadian Phytopathological Society Inc. [*Societe Canadienne de Phytopathologie*] (AC)
CPS .... Canadian Population Society [*See also SCP*]
CPS .... Canadian Power Squadrons [*Boating*]
CPS .... Canadian Programming Service [*Service Canadien de Programmation*] (AC)
CPS .... Canberra Philharmonic Society [*Australia*]
CPS .... Capacitance Proximity Sensor (PDAA)
CPS .... Capacity Planning System (IAA)
CPS .... Capsular Polysaccharide [*Biochemistry*]
CPS .... Carbamyl-Phosphate Synthetase [*An enzyme*]
CPS .... Card Programming System [*Computer science*] (CMD)
CPS .... Cards per Second [*Computer science*]
CPS .... Cargo & Passenger Air Services Ltd. [*Switzerland ICAO designator*] (FAAC)
CPS .... Carlson Psychological Survey [*Test*]
CPS .... Cataloging and Provisioning System (MCD)
CPS .... Cathode Potential Stabilized
CPS .... Catholic Pamphlet Society of the United States (EA)
CPS .... Cell Processor System (MCD)
CPS .... Cente de Prevention du Suicide (AC)
CPS .... Center for Peace Studies (EA)
CPS .... Center for Philosophy of Science [*University of Pittsburgh*] [*Research center*] (RCD)
CPS .... Center for Prevention Services [*Department of Health and Human Services*] (GFGA)
CPS .... Center for Process Studies (EA)
CPS .... Centipoise [*Unit of viscosity*]
CPS .... Centrale des Professionnelles et Professionnels de la Sante (AC)
CPS .... Centralized Payroll System (ADA)
CPS .... Central Pain Syndrome [*Medicine*]
CPS .... Central Plasma Sheet
CPS .... Central Power Supply
CPS .... Central Power System
CPS .... Central Processing System [*Computer science*]
CPS .... Central Processor System (NITA)
CPS .... Centre for Policy Studies [*Monash University*] [*Australia*]
CPS .... Centre for Policy Studies [*British*]
CPS .... Cents per Share (ODBW)
CPS .... Cephalo Pedal Sinus
CPS .... Certificate of Prior Submission [*Navy*]
CPS .... Certificate of Professional Studies (PGP)
CPS .... Certified Professional Secretary [*Institute for Certifying Secretaries*] [*Designation awarded by*]

CPS............	Certified Public Secretary
CPS............	Chairmakers' Protection Society [*A union*] [*British*]
CPS............	Change Processing Station (AAG)
CPS............	Characters per Second [*Computer science*]
cps............	Characters Per Second [*Computer science*] (WDMC)
cps............	Characters Per Second [*Computer science*]
CPS............	Charles S. Peirce Society (EA)
CPS............	Chemical Process Synthesis [*Chemical engineering*]
CPS............	Chloroquine, Pyrimethamine, Sulfisoxazole (MAE)
CPS............	Christian Psychological Services [*Australia*]
CPS............	Circuit Package Schematic (MSA)
CPS............	Circuit Provision System [*AT & T*]
CPS............	Citizens Protection Society [*British*]
CPS............	Civilian Public Service
CPS............	Clerk of Petty Sessions [*British*] (ADA)
CPS............	Clinical Performance Score [*Medicine*] (MAE)
CPS............	Clinton Power Station [*Nuclear energy*] (GFGA)
CPS............	Clock Pulse (IAA)
CPS............	Close-Packed Structure
CPS............	Cloth Pressers' Society [*A union*] [*British*] (DCTA)
CPS............	Coarse Pointing System (SSD)
CPS............	Coastal Plains Sands
CPS............	Coils per Slot [*Technical drawings*]
CPS............	Collective Protective System [*Navy*]
CPS............	College of Petroleum and Energy Studies [*British*]
CPS............	College of Psychic Studies [*London*]
CPS............	College Placement Services [*Later, CCDM*] (EA)
CPS............	College Press Service (EA)
CPS............	Collimated Photon Scattering (MCD)
CPS............	Colorado Psychiatric Society (SRA)
CPS............	Color Picture Signal
CPS............	Combined Planning Staff [*Military British*]
CPS............	Combined Principles Simulator [*Nuclear engine*]
CPS............	Command Personnel Summary (AABC)
CPS............	Commission du Pacifique Sud [*South Pacific Commission - SPC*] (EAIO)
CPS............	Commission on the Patent System
CPS............	Committee for Production Sharing [*Defunct*] (EA)
CPS............	Communications Processing System
CPS............	Communist Party of Slovakia [*Political party*]
CPS............	Company [*or Corporate*] Policy Statement
CPS............	Compass Aviation [*British ICAO designator*] (FAAC)
CPS............	Compendium of Pharmaceuticals and Specialities [*A publication*]
CPS............	Compensation and Pension Service [*Veterans Administration*]
CPS............	Competitive Prototyping Strategy (DOMA)
CPS............	Complex Partial Seizures [*Medicine*] (DMAA)
CPS............	Compliance Program and Schedule [*Environmental Protection Agency*] (GFGA)
CPS............	Composite Primary Structures (MCD)
CPS............	Computer Power Supply
CPS............	Computer Programming Service
CPS............	Computer Program Specification (AFM)
CPS............	Computer Program System [*Boeing Co.*]
CPS............	Comrey Personality Scale
CPS............	Condensate Polishing System [*Nuclear energy*] (NRCH)
CPS............	Condensation Pressure Spread
CPS............	Conference of Philosophical Societies (EA)
CPS............	Conference on the Public Service
CPS............	Congregational Publishing Society
CPS............	Connecticut Psychiatric Society (SRA)
CPS............	Console Programming System (IAA)
CPS............	Consolidated Package Store [*Military*] (DNAB)
CPS............	Constant Problem Size
CPS............	Constitutional Psychopathic State
CPS............	Consumer Purchasing Service
CPS............	Containment Purge System [*Nuclear energy*] (NRCH)
CPS............	Contingency Planning System (MHDB)
CPS............	Contour Plotting System
CPS............	Contractor Performance Summary (AAGC)
CPS............	Contractor's Profile System [*Department of Health and Human Services*] (GFGA)
CPS............	Contract Pilot School
CPS............	Contract [*or Contractor*] Plant Services (NG)
CPS............	Contracts Processing System (MCD)
CPS............	Controlled Path System [*Computer science*]
CPS............	Controller Processor Signal (CAAL)
CPS............	Control Panel Subassembly
CPS............	Control Power Supply
CPS............	Control Pressure System (AAG)
CPS............	Control Program Services (IAA)
CPS............	Control Programs Support (IEEE)
CPS............	Conversational Programming System [*Computer science*]
CPS............	Conversion Program System (NRCH)
CPS............	Convertible Preferred Stock [*Investment term*]
CPS............	Copy Processing System [*Photocomposition*]
CPS............	Corporate Payment System
CPS............	Corporate Planning System (IAA)
CPS............	Council for Philosophical Studies (EA)
CPS............	Counts per Second (DEN)
CPS............	Court of Petty Sessions [*Australia*]
CPS............	Covered Pedestrian Space
CPS............	C-Polysaccharide [*Clinical chemistry*]
CPS............	Crankshaft Position Sensor [*Automotive engineering*]
CPS............	Creative Problem-Solving (PDAA)
CPS............	Crew Procedures Simulator

CPS............	Critical Path Scheduling [*or System*]
CPS............	Croatian Philatelic Society (EA)
CPS............	Crown Prosecution Service [*British*] (ECON)
CPS............	Cumulative Preferred Stock [*Investment term*]
CPS............	Cumulative Probability of Success (MAE)
CPS............	Current Population Survey [*Census Bureau*]
CPS............	Customer Premises System [*Bell System*]
CPS............	Custos Privati Sigilli [*Keeper of the Privy Seal*] [*Latin*]
CPS............	Cycles per Second [*See also Hz*]
cps............	Cycles Per Second [*Telecommunications*] (WDMC)
CPS............	East St. Louis, IL [*Location identifier FAA*] (FAAL)
CPS............	Missionary Sisters of the Precious Blood [*Italy*]
CPS............	Missionary Sisters of the Precious Blood (TOCD)
CPs............	Palm Springs Public Library, Palm Springs, CA [*Library symbol Library of Congress*] (LCLS)
CPS............	Stuart Co., Pasadena, CA [*Library symbol Library of Congress*] (LCLS)
CPSA	Canadian Political Science Association
CPSA	Canadian Professional Sales Association [*Association Canadienne des Professionnels de la Vente*] [*Formerly, Commercial Travellers Association of Canada*] (AC)
CPSA	Canine Pulmonary Surfactant
CPSA	Caribbean Public Services Association [*Barbados*] (EAIO)
CPSA	Catholic Poetry Society of America [*Defunct*] (EA)
CPSA	Chronopotentiometric Stripping Analysis [*Analytical electrochemistry*]
CPSA	Civil and Public Services Association [*British*]
CPSA	Clay Pigeon Shooting Association [*British*]
CPSA	Commonwealth Preference Standstill Area (PDAA)
CPSA	Communist Party of South Africa [*Political party*] (PD)
CPSA	Conservative Party of South Africa [*Konserwatiewe Party van Suid-Afrika*] [*Political party*] (PPW)
CPSA	Consumer Product Safety Act [*1972*]
CPSA	Cuban Philatelic Society of America (EA)
CPSA	Current Physics Selected Articles [*A publication*] (MCD)
CPSA-BC	Cerebral Palsy Sports Association of British Columbia (AC)
CPSAC	Cycles per Second Alternating Current (AAG)
CPS Act	Consumer Product Safety Act [*1972*] (DLA)
CPSAH	Committee to Promote the Study of Austrian History (EA)
CPSase	Carbamyl Phosphate Synthetase (PDAA)
CPSB	Compulsorily Preserved Superannuation Benefit
CPSC	Canadian Permanent Signal Corps [*British military*] (DMA)
CPSC	Canadian Posture and Seating Centre [*Research center*] (RCD)
CPSC	Consumer Product Safety Commission [*Federal agency*]
CPSC	Contingency Planning Support Capability (AFM)
CPSC	Stuart Co., Pasadena, CA [*Library symbol*] [*Library of Congress*] (LCLS)
CPSCI	Central Personnel Security Clearance Index [*Nuclear energy*] (NRCH)
CPSCS	Children's Perceived Self-Control Scale
CPSCS-UTM...	Children's Perceived Self-Control Scale - Usually That's Me
CPSD	Cross-Power Spectral Density
CPSDAA......	Compliance and Program Staff to the Deputy Assistant Administrator [*Environmental Protection Agency*] (GFGA)
CPSDF	Catch per Standard Day of Fishing [*Fishery management*] (MSC)
CPSE...........	Carr-Purcell Spin-Echo
cpse...........	Centipoise (BARN)
CPSE...........	Common Payload Support Equipment [*NASA*] (NASA)
CPSE...........	Complementary Pair Switch Element
CPSE...........	Complex Problem-Solving Environment
CPSE...........	Counterpoise (MSA)
CPSE...........	Crew and Passenger Support Equipment [*Military*] (AFIT)
CPSEAQ	Community Pre-School Employers' Association of Queensland [*Australia*]
CPSES	Commanche Peak Steam Electric Station (NRCH)
CPSF...........	Candle Power/Square Foot (KSC)
CPSF...........	Cleavage and Polyadenylation Specificity Factor [*Biochemistry*]
CPSF...........	Color Purple Educational Fund Foundation (EA)
CPSG	Children of Prisoners Support Group [*Australia*]
CPSG	China Philatelic Study Group [*Defunct*] (EA)
CPSG	China Policy Study Group [*British*]
CPSG	Chronic Pain Support Group (EA)
CPSG	Common Power Supply Group
CP Ships.....	Canadian Pacific Steamships (MHDB)
CPSI	Creative Problem-Solving Institute (EDAC)
CPSK	Cathodic Protection Survey Kit
CPSK	Coherent Phase Shift Keyed [*System*] [*Computer science*]
CPSK	Coherent Phase Shift Keying (NITA)
CPSL...........	Canadian Professional Soccer League
CPSL...........	Capsule (MSA)
CPSL...........	Communist Party of Slovakia [*Former Czechoslovakia*] [*Political party*] (EY)
CPSL...........	Communist Party of Sri Lanka [*Political party*] (FEA)
CPSL...........	Communist Party of Syria and the Lebanon [*Political party*] (BJA)
CPSM..........	Comite Permanent des Sous-Ministres [*Continuing Committee of Deputy Ministers - CCDM*] [*Canada*]
CPSM..........	Computer Program Submodule (MCD)
CPSM..........	Continuous Phase Shift Modulation [*Army*]
CPSM..........	Critical Path Scheduling Method [*Management*]
CPSMA	Canadian Podiatric Sports Medicine Academy
CPSMV	Cowpea Severe Mosaic Virus [*Plant pathology*]
CPSN	Capstan
CPSNSW	Cat Protection Society of New South Wales [*Australia*]
CPSO	Cumberland Plateau Seismological Observatory
CPSP	Central Poststroke Pain [*Medicine*] (DMAA)
CPSPA	Common Pleas Subpoena [*Legal*] [*British*] (ROG)

CPSPB .... Current Population Survey Processing Branch [*Bureau of the Census*] (GFGA)

CPSR .... Calibration Procedure Status Report [*Polaris missile*]

CPSR .... Centre for Public Sector Research [*University of Canberra*] [*Australia*]

CPSR .... Computer Professionals for Social Responsibility (EA)

CPSR .... Contractor Procurement System Review [*DoD*]

CPSR .... Contract Purchasing System Review (DOMA)

CPSR .... Controlled Process Serum Replacements [*Cell culture*]

CPSR .... Cost and Performance Summary Report [*Army*]

CPSS .... Central Processing Subsystem [*Computer science*]

CPSS .... Certified Professional Soil Scientist [*Environmental science*]

CPSS .... Chemist's Personal Software Series

CPSS .... Cold Plate Support Structure (MCD)

CPSS .... College of Phsicians & Surgeons of Saskatchewan (AC)

CPSS .... Committee of Presidents of Statistical Societies (EA)

CPSS .... Common Program Support System

CPSS .... Compagnie des Pretres de St. Sulpice [*Society of the Priests of St. Sulpice - SPSS*] [*France*] (EAIO)

CPSS .... Component Percentage Shipment Schedule (NG)

CPSS .... Computerized Parcel Shipping System

CPSS .... Computer Power Support System

CPSS .... Consumer Portfolio Services [*NASDAQ symbol*] (SAG)

CPSS .... Consumer Portfolio Svcs [*NASDAQ symbol*] (TTSB)

CPSS .... Critical Phase System Software [*NASA*] (NASA)

CPSSC .... California Preschool Scale of Social Competence (EDAC)

CPST........... Capacitive Position Sensing Transducer (PDAA)

CPST........... Commission on Professionals in Science and Technology (EA)

CPST........... Committee to Promote Science and Technology

CPSU .... Calcutta Port Shramik Union [*India*]

CPSU .... California Polytechnic State University (PDAA)

CPSU .... Central Processor Subunit [*Computer science*]

CPSU .... Chemistry and Physics Study Unit (EA)

CPSU .... Communist Party of the Soviet Union [*Political party*] (PPW)

CPSU .... Community and Public Sector Union [*Australia*]

CPSU .... Cooperative National Park Resources Studies Unit [*Research center*] (RCD)

CPSUG......... CPS [*Itek Copy Processing System*] User Group [*Defunct*] (EA)

CPSU/UH ..... Cooperative National Park Resource Studies Unit, University of Hawaii [*Research center*] (RCD)

CPSV .... Cat Protection Society of Victoria [*Australia*]

CPSVN .... Comprehensive Plan, South Vietnam (CINC)

CPsyc.......... Community Psychiatric Centers [*Associated Press*] (SAG)

CPsych......... Certified Psychologist [*Canada*] (DD)

CPT............. California Institute of Technology, Pasadena, CA [*Library symbol Library of Congress*] (LCLS)

CPT............. Camden Property Trust [*NYSE symbol*] (SPSG)

CPT............. Camp Pendleton [*California*] [*Seismograph station code, US Geological Survey*] (SEIS)

CPT............. Camptothecin [*Antineoplastic drug*] (CDI)

CPT............. Canstat Petroleum Corp. [*Vancouver Stock Exchange symbol*]

CPT............. Capacitive Pressure Transducer [*Engineering*] (IAA)

CPT............. Cape Town [*South Africa*] [*Airport symbol*] (OAG)

CPT............. Capiat [*Let the Patient Take*] [*Pharmacy*] (ROG)

CPT............. Captain [*Military*]

CPT............. Captopril [*Antihypertensive drug*]

CPT............. Cargo Processing Technician (NASA)

CPT............. Caribou Performance Test

CPT............. Carotid Pulse Tracing [*Cardiology*] (DAVI)

CPT............. Carpet [*Classified advertising*] (ADA)

cpt .... Carpet (VRA)

CPT............. Carpet

CPT............. Casement Projected Transom [*Technical drawings*]

CPT............. Centennial Park Trust [*Australia*]

CPT............. Center for Particle Theory [*University of Texas at Austin*] [*Research center*] (RCD)

CPT............. Central Planning Team (NATG)

CPT............. Centre for Precision Technology [*Australia*]

CPT............. Ceramic Planar Tube

CPT............. Charge Conjugation - Parity - Time-Reversal [*Theorem*] [*Atomic physics*]

CPT............. Charged Particle Telescope

CPT............. Charge, Parity, and Time Coordinates [*Physics*]

CPT............. Chest Physiotherapy [*Medicine*]

CPT............. Chicago Produce Terminal Co. [*Later, CPTC*] [*AAR code*]

CPT............. Chief Programmer Team [*Computer science*]

CPT............. Cisplatin [*Also, cis-DDP, CDDP, CPDD, DDP, P*] [*Antineoplastic drug*]

CPT............. Civilian Pilot Training [*Became War Training Service*] [*World War II*]

CPT............. Clinical Pharmacokinetics Team [*Pharmacology*] (DAVI)

CPT............. Clock, Programming, and Timing [*NASA*] (KSC)

CPT............. Cockpit Procedures Trainer [*Air Force*] (AFM)

CPT............. Cold Presors [*or Pressure*] Test [*Cardiology*] (DAVI)

CPT............. Colored People's Time [*Slang*]

CPT............. Color Picture Tube [*Electronics*] (EECA)

CPT............. Color Pyramid Test [*Psychology*]

CPT............. Combining Power Test (AAMN)

CPT............. Committee for Pedestrian Tolls [*Defunct*] (EA)

CPT............. Common Procedural Terminology [*Human resources*] (WYGK)

CPT............. Communist Party of Tadzhikistan [*Political party*]

CPT............. Communist Party of Thailand [*Political party*] (PD)

CPTB .... Communist Party of Turkey [*Political party*] (PD)

CPT............. Communist Party of Turkmenistan [*Political party*]

CPT............. Comparison Test (MCD)

cpt .... Compartment (NITA)

CPT............. Compatibility

CPT............. Computer Program Tapes (MCD)

CPT............. Cone Penetrometer Tests [*Computer science*]

CPT............. Consolidated Pilot Training Program [*Air Force*]

CPT............. Continuous Performance Test [*Psychology*]

CPT............. Continuous Primary Test [*Psychiatry*] (DAVI)

CPT............. Contractor Provided Training

CPT............. Contralateral Pyramidal Tract (PDAA)

Cpt............. Contrepoint [*Record label*] [*France*]

CPT............. Control Power Transformer (MSA)

CPT............. Copilot Time (DNAB)

cpt .... Corel Photopaint [*Computer science*]

CPT............. Corporate Air [*ICAO designator*] (FAAC)

CPT............. Cost per Thousand (ODBW)

CPT............. Counterpoint [*Music*]

CPT............. Crew Procedures Trainer

CPT............. Critical Path Technique

CPT............. Critical Pitting Temperature [*Metallurgy*]

CPT............. Critical Process Team (AAGC)

CPT............. Cryogenic Pressure Transducer

CPT............. Crystal Pressure Transducer

CPT............. Current Physics Titles [*A publication*]

CPT............. Current Procedural Technology [*Department of Health and Human Services*] (GFGA)

CPT............. Current Procedural Terminology [*American Medical Association*]

CPT............. Customer Provided Terminal [*Telecommunications*] (IAA)

CPT............. Cyclopentyltheophylline [*Organic chemistry*]

CPT............. Physician's Current Procedural Terminology

CPT............. Point Loma College, San Diego, CA [*OCLC symbol*] (OCLC)

CPTA .... Canadian Paper Trade Association (AC)

CPTA .... Canadian Play Therapy Association (AC)

CPTA .... Central Paying and Transfer Agent [*Business term*] (EMRF)

CPTA .... Ciliary Particle Transport Activity

CPTA .... College of Physical Therapists of Alberta (AC)

CPTA .... Computer Programming and Testing Activity (IEEE)

CPTAL .... Capital

CPT & E....... Computer Program Test and Evaluation

CPTB .... Clay Products Technical Bureau [*British*]

CPTC .... Canadian Passenger Transportation Corp. [*Proposed*]

CPTC .... Central Processor Test Console [*Computer science*]

CPTC .... Chicago Produce Terminal Co. [*Formerly, CPT*] [*AAR code*]

CptConc ...... Computer Concepts Corp. [*Associated Press*] (SAG)

CPT/CTL...... Crew Procedures Trainer / Combat Training Launch (SAA)

CPTD .... Cumulative Pulmonary Toxicity Dose [*Deep-sea diving*]

CPTE .... Committee for the Preservation of the Tule Elk (EA)

CPTF .... Central Plains Turfgrass Foundation [*Later, KTF*] (EA)

CPTH .... Chronic Post-Traumatic Headache [*Neurology*] (DAVI)

CPTH .... C-Terminal Parathyroid Hormone [*Endocrinology*] (DAVI)

CPTI .... Computer Telephone CI'1 [*NASDAQ symbol*] (TTSB)

CpTI .... Cowpea Trypsin Inhibitor [*Biochemistry*]

CPTL .... Computer Telephone Corp. [*NASDAQ symbol*] (NQ)

CPTL .... Cutaneous Peripheral T-Cell-Derived Lymphomas

CPTLP......... Coalition of Publicly Traded Limited Partnerships [*Later, CoPTP*] (EA)

CptM.......... Computer Marketplace, Inc. [*Associated Press*] (SAG)

CptMk........ Computer Marketplace, Inc. [*Associated Press*] (SAG)

CPTMQ .... Corporation Professionnelle des Technologistes Medicaux du Quebec (AC)

CPTN .... Culture-Postive Toxin-Negative [*Medicine*] (DMAA)

CPTNG MATS RGS... Carpeting Mats or Rugs [*Freight*]

CptNwk....... Computer Network Technology Corp. [*Associated Press*] (SAG)

CPTO .... Chief Programmer Team Organization [*Computer science*] (MHDI)

CPTOL .... Capitol

CptOuts....... Computer Outscoring Services [*Associated Press*] (SAG)

CPTP .... Computer Program Test Plan

CPTP .... Computer Program Test Procedure

CPTP .... Culture-Positive Toxin-Positive [*Medicine*] (DMAA)

CPTPL .... Computer Program Test Plan (CAAL)

CPTPQ .... Corporation Professionnelle des Technologues Professionnelles du Quebec (AC)

CPTPR .... Computer Program Test Procedures (CAAL)

CPTR .... Capture (AABC)

CPTR .... Carpenter (AABC)

CPTR .... Chemical Propulsion Technology Reviews [*Chemical Propulsion Information Agency*] (MCD)

CPTR .... Chief Painter [*Navy rating Obsolete*]

CPTR .... Computer Program Test Report (MCD)

CptrLrn .... Computer Learning Centers, Inc. [*Associated Press*] (SAG)

CptrMkt....... Computer Marketplace, Inc. [*Associated Press*] (SAG)

CptrPtl .... Computer Petroleum Corp. [*Associated Press*] (SAG)

CPTRV .... Chief Painter, Aircraft [*Navy rating Obsolete*]

CPTS .... Coalition for Peace through Strength [*Later, CCNS*] (EA)

CPTS .... Comptroller Squadron [*Air Force*]

CPTS .... Computer Product Testing Service

CPTS .... Conceptus, Inc. [*NASDAQ symbol*] (SAG)

CPTS .... Conceptus Inc. [*NASDAQ symbol*] (TTSB)

CPtSH .... Patton State Hospital, Patton, CA [*Library symbol Library of Congress*] (LCLS)

CPTSq......... Comptroller Service Squadron [*Air Force*]

CPTSQ .... Corporation Professionnelle des Travailleurs Sociaux du Quebec (AC)

CPTSS .... Comptroller Service Squadron [*Air Force*]

CPTST......... Contrapuntist [*Music*]

CPTV .... Creative Progm Tech Venture [*NASDAQ symbol*] (TTSB)

CPTV .... Creative Programming & Technology [*NASDAQ symbol*] (SAG)

CPTY	Capacity (FAAC)
CPU	Canadian Paperworkers Union
CPU	Card Pick Up (DCTA)
CPU	Caudate Putamen (DMAA)
CPU	Caudate-Putamen Complex [Anatomy]
CPU	Central Processing Unit [Computer science]
CPU	Central Processing Unit (DMAA)
CPU	Central Production Unit [Publishing services] [American Library Association]
CPU	Children's Peace Union [Defunct] (EA)
CPU	Church Peace Union [Later, CRIA]
CPU	Collective Protection Unit (IEEE)
CPU	Command Programmer Unit (DWSG)
CPU	Commercial Property Underwriting [Insurance]
CPU	Commonwealth Press Union [London, England] (EAIO)
CPU	Communications Processing Unit (CET)
CPU	Communications Processor Utility [Telecommunications] (TEL)
CPU	Communist Party of Ukraine [Political party]
CPU	CompUSA, Inc. [NYSE symbol] (SPSG)
CPU	Computer Peripheral Unit (IEEE)
CPU	Computer Printer Unit (MCD)
CPU	Computer Processor Unit
CPU	Computer Program Update
CPU	Controlled Production Unit [Project sponsored by the Elder Craftsmen]
CPU	Control Phasing Unit [for aircraft] (RDA)
CPU	Control Processing Unit (MCD)
CPU	Coon Peak [Utah] [Seismograph station code, US Geological Survey] (SEIS)
CPU	Cost per Unit
CPU	Crime Prevention Unit [British]
CPU	Critical Processing Unit
CPU	ME Compu Software, Inc. [Vancouver Stock Exchange symbol]
CPU	Pacific Union College, Angwin, CA [OCLC symbol] (OCLC)
CPUBINFO	Chief of Public Information Division [NATO] (NATG)
CPUC	Common Pleas Reports [Upper Canada] [A publication] (DLA)
CPUD	Central Processing Unit Diagnostic Program
CPUE	Catch per Unit Effort [Pisciculture] (MSC)
CPUE	Chest Pain of Unknown Etiology [Medicine]
CPUID	Central Processing Unit Identification Number [Computer science]
CPUN	United States Naval Ordnance Test Station, Pasadena, CA [Library symbol Library of Congress] (LCLS)
CPUNCH	Counterpunch (KSC)
CPUOS	Committee on the Peaceful Uses of Outer Space [United Nations] (BARN)
CPUP	Catalogo Colectivo de Publicaciones Periodicas [Database] [Ministerio de Cultura] [Spanish] [Information service or system] (CRD)
CPUQ	Corporation Professionnelle des Urbanistes du Quebec (AC)
CPURMC	Committee to Promote Uniformity in the Regulation of Motor Carriers
CPUS	Coalition for the Peaceful Uses of Space (EA)
CPUS	Constitution Parties of the United States [An association] (EA)
CPUSA	Communist Party of the United States of America [Political party] (EA)
CPUSAC	Crafted with Pride in USA Council (EA)
CPUSA/ML	Communist Party of the USA/Marxist Leninist [Political party] (EA)
CPUSOFBLNJ	Committee on Peaceful Uses of the Sea-Bed and Ocean Floor Beyond Limits of National Jurisdiction [United Nations] (EA)
CPUSS	Computer Services Squadron [Air Force]
CPUz	Communist Party of Uzbekistan [Political party]
CPV	Camera Processor Viewer (NITA)
CPV	Campina Grande [Brazil] [Airport symbol] (OAG)
CPV	Canine Parovirus
CPV	Canopus Probe near Limb of Venus Angle [NASA]
CPV	Capacity Planning Volume
CPV	Cape Verde [ANSI three-letter standard code] (CNC)
CPV	Circulating Plasma Volume [Hematology]
CPV	Coated Polycarbonate Visor
CPV	Command Post Vehicle [British military] (DMA)
CPV	Communist Party of Venezuela [Political party]
CPV	Compania Peruana de Vapores [Peruvian airline]
CPV	Concrete Pressure Vehicle (PDAA)
CP-V	Control Program-Five [Operating system] [Xerox Corp.]
CPV	Cytoplasmic Polyhedrosis Virus [Medicine] (PDAA)
CPv	Palos Verdes Library District, Palos Verdes Estates, CA [Library symbol Library of Congress] (LCLS)
CPVC	Chlorinated Poly(vinyl Chloride) [Organic chemistry]
CPVC	Critical Pigment Volume Concentration [Paint technology]
CPVD	Congenital Polyvalvular Disease [Medicine] (DMAA)
CPVE	Certificate of Pre-Vocational Education [Academic degree] (AIE)
CPVE	Certificate of Professional and Vocational Education [British]
CPVEA	Carl Perkins Vocational Education Act [1984] (OICC)
CP/VM	Call Processing/Voice Messaging (BTTJ)
CPvMC	Marymount College, Palos Verdes Estates, CA [Library symbol Library of Congress Obsolete] (LCLS)
CPVR	Committee on Procedure and Valuation of Reparations [Allied German Occupation Forces]
CPVTA	Canadian Photo Video Trade Association [Formerly, Canadian Photographic Trade Association] (AC)
CPW	Canadian Pawnee Oil [Vancouver Stock Exchange symbol]
CPW	Capitol Peak [Washington] [Seismograph station code, US Geological Survey] (SEIS)
CPW	Certified Pediatric Worker (BARN)
CPW	Chippewa Air Commuter, Inc. [ICAO designator] (FAAC)
CPW	Circumpolar Water [Oceanography]

CPW	Club of Printing Women of New York (EA)
CPW	Commercial Projected Window [Technical drawings]
CPW	Cooked Potato Weight [Food technology] (OA)
CPW	Coplanar Waveguide
CPW	Critical Performance Weight (SAA)
CPW	Western Personnel Institute, Pasadena, CA [Library symbol Library of Congress] (LCLS)
CPWA	Canadian Petroleum Writers Association (AC)
CPWD	Caucus for Producers, Writers, and Directors (EA)
CPWDA	Canadian Paint and Wallpaper Dealers' Association
CPWE	Centre for Pastoral Work in Europe [See also CPE] (EAIO)
CPWi	Wuanco Engineering Technical Library, Pasadena, CA [Library symbol Library of Congress] (LCLS)
CPWM	Cost Plus [NASDAQ symbol] (TTSB)
CPWM	Cost Plus, Inc. [NASDAQ symbol] (SAG)
CPWR	Compuware Corp. [NASDAQ symbol] (SAG)
CPWU	Ceylon Plantation Workers' Union [Obsolete]
CPWY	Cardiac Pathways Corp. [NASDAQ symbol] (SAG)
CPX	Capital Air Service, Inc. [ICAO designator] (FAAC)
CPX	Cardiopulmonary Exercise Testing [Medicine]
CPX	Charged Pigment Xerography (IEEE)
CPX	Cineplex Odeon [NYSE symbol] (TTSB)
CPX	Cineplex Odeon Corp. [NYSE symbol Toronto Stock Exchange symbol]
CPX	Clinopyroxene [A mineral]
CPX	Command Post Exercise [Military]
CPX	Command Post Experience [Army British]
CPX	Complete Physical Examination [Medicine] (DAVI)
CPX	CP1 [Nevada] [Seismograph station code, US Geological Survey] (SEIS)
CPX	Culebra [Puerto Rico] [Airport symbol] (OAG)
CPX	Isla De Culebra, PR [Location identifier FAA] (FAAL)
CPXD	Chondrodysplasia Punctata, X-Linked Dominant [Medicine] (DMAA)
CPXR	Chondrodysplasia Punctata, X-Linked Recessive [Medicine] (DMAA)
CPY	Carboxypeptidase Y [An enzyme]
CPY	Cargo Preference Year [MARAD] (TAG)
CPY	Clips per Year [Photocopying, microfilming]
CPY	Consolidated Paymaster [Vancouver Stock Exchange symbol]
CPY	Copy (BUR)
CPY	Copyright [Deltiology]
CPY	CPI Corp. [NYSE symbol] (SPSG)
CPYB	Central Pennsylvania Youth Ballet
CPZ	Cargo & Passenger Air Services Ltd. [Switzerland ICAO designator] (FAAC)
CPZ	Chlorpromazine [Sedative]
CPZ	Compazine [Tranquilizer] [Trademark of Smith, Kline, & French Co.]
CPZ	La Pryor, TX [Location identifier FAA] (FAAL)
CQ	Aero-Chaco [ICAO designator] (AD)
CQ	Aerolinea Federal Argentina [ICAO designator] (AD)
cq	Call To Quarter [Wire-service jargon for correction] (WDMC)
CQ	Call to Quarters [General call preceding transmission of radio signals]
CQ	Camera Quality (MUGU)
CQ	Canine Quarterly: a Parody of the World's Most Elegant Magazine for Men [A publication]
CQ	Carbazilquinone [Antineoplastic drug]
CQ	Carolina Quarterly [A publication] (BRI)
CQ	Carrier Qualification [Navy] (CAAL)
C/Q	Certificate of Assignment of Quarters [Navy]
CQ	Change of Quarters (DNAB)
CQ	Charge of Quarters [Army]
CQ	Checklist Question (CAAL)
CQ	Chloroquine [Antimalarial drug]
CQ	Chloroquine-Quinine [Antimalarial drug] [Pharmacology] (DAVI)
CQ	Circadian Quotient (MAE)
CQ	Command of Quarters [Army] (VNW)
CQ	Commercial Quality
CQ	Committed Quitters
cq	Comoro Islands [MARC country of publication code Library of Congress] (LCCP)
CQ	Comsat Corp. [See also COMSAT] [NYSE symbol] (SPSG)
CQ	Conceptual Quotient [Psychology]
CQ	Conditionally Qualified (AFM)
CQ	Congressional Quarterly (AAGC)
CQ	Congressional Quarterly, Inc. [Washington, DC]
CQ	Congressional Quarterly Service [A publisher] [Washington, D.C.] (WDMC)
CQ	Constraint Qualification (DNAB)
CQ	Correct
CQ	Correspondence Quality (IAA)
CQ	Creativity Quotient [Testing term]
CQ	Cree Questionnaire [Psychology]
CQ	Crew Quarters (KSC)
CQA	Canadian Quilters Association (AC)
CQA	Celina, OH [Location identifier FAA] (FAAL)
CQA	Chalk Quarrying Association [British] (BI)
CQA	Coast Air Ltd. [Kenya] [ICAO designator] (FAAC)
CQA	Component Quality Assurance
CQA	Computer-Aided Question Answering [Computer science] (MHDB)
CQA	Construction Quality Assurance [Environmental science]
CQALCA	Central Queensland Articled Law Clerks' Association [Australia]
CQAR	Corporate Quality Assurance Regulations (MCD)
CQB	Chandler, OK [Location identifier FAA] (FAAL)
CQB	Chiquita Brands International [NYSE symbol] (SPSG)
CQB	Chiquita Brands Intl. [NYSE symbol] (TTSB)

CQB	Close-Quarter Battle [*British military*] (DMA)
CQBPrA	Chiquita Br Intl $2.875 Cv'A'Pfd [*NYSE symbol*] (TTSB)
CQC	Citizens for a Quieter City [*New York City*] [*Defunct*] (EA)
CQC	Complete Quadratic Combination [*Computer science*]
CQC	Construction Quality Control [*Environmental science*]
CQC	Continental Quilting Congress (EA)
CQC	Contractor Quality Control (DNAB)
CQC	Crop Quality Council (EA)
CQC	Cusac Industries Ltd. [*Toronto Stock Exchange symbol Vancouver Stock Exchange symbol*]
CQCA	Central Queensland Consumers Association [*Australia*]
CQCC	Citroen Quarterly Car Club (EA)
CQCD	Conseil Quebecois du Commerce de Detail (AC)
CQCF	CICS [*Customer Information Control System*] Queue Command Facility [*Computer science*] (HGAA)
CQCH	Confederation Quebecoise des Cooperatives d'Habitation (AC)
CQCHR	Confederation Quebecoise des Centres d'Hebergement et de Readaptation (AC)
CQCL	Plumas County Free Library, Quincy, CA [*Library symbol Library of Congress*] (LCLS)
CQCM	Cryogenic Quartz Crystal Microbalance
CQCP	Correspondence Quality Control Program (MCD)
CQD	Call Quickly Distress [*International telegrapher's signal for an emergency*] (WDMC)
CQD	Canacord Resources, Inc. [*Toronto Stock Exchange symbol*]
CQD	Come Quick - Danger [*International distress signal, used before SOS*]
CQD	Customary Quick Dispatch
CQD	Erie, PA [*Location identifier FAA*] (FAAL)
CQDE	Centre Quebecois du Droit de l'Environnement [*Quebec Environmental Law Centre*] (AC)
CQDR	Critical Qualification Design Review (NASA)
CQE	Cognizant Quality Engineer (NRCH)
CQE	Command Qualification Examination (MCD)
CQE	Conseil Quebecois de l'Estampe [*1984, founded 1971 as AGQ, CGQ from 1978*] [*Canada*] (NGC)
CQE	Conseil Quebecois de l'Estampe Inc. (AC)
CQE	Critical Quality Element (NRCH)
CQEMB	Central Queensland Egg Marketing Board [*Australia*]
CQF	Calais [*France*] [*Airport symbol*] (AD)
CQF	Canada Lease Financing Ltd. [*Toronto Stock Exchange symbol*]
CQG	Carson Gold Corp. [*Vancouver Stock Exchange symbol*]
CQGSMB	Central Queensland Grain Sorghum Marketing Board [*Australia*]
CQH	Philadelphia, PA [*Location identifier FAA*] (FAAL)
CQI	Commodity Quotations, Inc. (IID)
CQI	Continuous Quality Improvement [*Quality control*]
CQI	Council, ID [*Location identifier FAA*] (FAAL)
CQJ	Asheboro, NC [*Location identifier FAA*] (FAAL)
CQL	Carbondale, CO [*Location identifier FAA*] (FAAL)
CQL	Consolidated Lone Star Resource Corp. [*Vancouver Stock Exchange symbol*]
CQM	Chief Quartermaster [*Navy rating Obsolete*]
CQM	Chloroquine Mustard (MAE)
CQM	Class Queue Management (IAA)
CQM	Constructing Quartermaster [*Army*]
CQM	Control Quality Monitor
CQM	Crystal Quartz Modern
CQMC	Chief Quartermaster Clerk [*Navy rating Obsolete*]
CQMS	Camp Quartermasters Store [*British military*] (DMA)
CQMS	Circuit Quality Monitoring System
CQMS	Company Quartermaster-Sergeant
CQMS	Cost Quality Management System [*for hospitals*]
CQN	Chattanooga, TN [*Location identifier FAA*] (FAAL)
CQO	Canadian Microcool Corp. [*Vancouver Stock Exchange symbol*]
CQO	Chief Quality Officer [*Business term*] (ECON)
CQ/P	Carbon and Quartz/Phenolic
CQPC	Conseil Quebecois des professionnels et Cadres (AC)
CQPEN	Centre Quebecois du PEN [*Poets, Playwrights, Editors, and Novelists*] International [*Canada*] (EAIO)
CQPR	Cumulative Quality Point Ratio
CQPrA	COMSAT Capital 1 8.125%'MIPS' [*NYSE symbol*] (TTSB)
CQQ	Crato [*Brazil*] [*Airport symbol*] (AD)
CQR	Chandalar Lake, AK [*Location identifier FAA*] (FAAL)
CQR	Chloroquine Resistance [*Chemoprophylaxis*]
CQR	Chloroquine-Resistant [*Genetics*]
CQR	Complete Controlled Quick Release
CQR	Controlled Quick Release
CQR	Cost Quote Request
CQR	Crest Resources Ltd. [*Vancouver Stock Exchange symbol*]
CQR	Secure (Anchor Type) [*Navy symbol*]
CQRI	Centre Quebecois de Relations Internationales [*Quebec Center for International Relations*] [*Canada*] (IRC)
CQS	California Q-Set [*Psychology*]
CQS	Chase Resources [*Vancouver Stock Exchange symbol*]
CQS	Chloroquine-Susceptible [*Genetics*]
CQS	Chloroquinoxaline Sulfonamide [*Antineoplastic drug*]
CQS	Common Query System [*Navy*] (DNAB)
CQS	Composite Quotation System (DICI)
CQS	Court of Quarter Sessions [*Legal*] [*British*] (ROG)
CQS	Custom Quality Studio [*Photography*]
CQSS	Central Queensland Speleological Society [*Australia*]
CQSW	Certificate as a Qualified Social Worker [*British*]
CQT	Capacitor Qualification Test
CQT	Caquetania [*Colombia*] [*Airport symbol*] (OAG)
CQT	Carburized, Quenched, and Tempered [*Steel heat treatment*] (IIA)

CQT	College Qualification Test (WGA)
CQT	Command Quality Team (DOMA)
CQT	Conseil Quebecois du Theatre (AC)
CQT	Control Question Test [*For lie detectors*]
CQT	Correct [*Computer science British*]
CQTU	Carrier Qualification Training Unit
CQU	Central Queensland University [*Australia*]
CQU	College Qualification Test
C-Quam	Compatible Quadrature Amplitude Modulation [*Radio design*] [*Motorola, Inc.*]
CQUCC	Commission on Quantities and Units in Clinical Chemistry (DAVI)
CQV	Consolidated Suntec Ventures [*Vancouver Stock Exchange symbol*]
CQW	Cheraw, SC [*Location identifier FAA*] (FAAL)
CR	Cable Rack (KSC)
CR	Calculus Removal (MAE)
CR	Caledonian Railway [*Scotland*]
CR	Calendrier Republicain [*Republican Calendar*] [*French*]
CR	Call Request [*Telecommunications*]
CR	Caloric Restriction
CR	Cambrian Railway [*British*] (ROG)
CR	Camera Ready [*Publishing*] (WDMC)
CR	Camera Rehearsal
CR	Camera Repairman [*Navy rating*]
CR	Canadian Reports, Appeal Cases [*1828-1913*] [*A publication*] (DLA)
CR	Canadian Restricted [*Broadcasting term*]
CR	Cardiac Rehabilitation (DAVI)
CR	Cardiorespiratory [*Medicine*]
CR	Card Reader [*Computer science*] (NVT)
CR	Card Ready [*Computer science*] (SAA)
CR	Card Reproducer [*Computer science*] (IAA)
CR	Carolina Regina [*Queen Caroline*] [*Latin*]
CR	Carolus Rex [*King Charles*] [*Latin*]
CR	Car Return (ECII)
CR	Carriage Reset (WDMC)
CR	Carriage Return
CR	Carrier's Risk [*Shipping*]
CR	Carry Register (NITA)
CR	Cartercar Registry (EA)
CR	Cartilage Residue [*Orthopedics*] (DAVI)
CR	Cash Reserve [*Business term*]
CR	Catalytic Reforming (IAA)
CR	Cathode Ray
CR	Cathode Reaction
CR	Ceiling Register (OA)
CR	Cellular Radio
CR	Cement Render
CR	Center (DS)
CR	Center of Resistance
CR	Center Right [*Theatrical term*] (WDMC)
CR	Center Right [*Theater*] (WDMC)
CR	Central Railway [*British*] (ROG)
CR	Central Recorder Subsystem [*NASA*]
CR	Central Registry [*of the Ordnance Survey*] [*British*]
CR	Central Reporter [*A publication*] (DLA)
CR	Centric Relation [*Dentistry*]
CR	Cerebral Ridge [*Medicine*]
C/R	Certificate of Retirement (MUGU)
CR	Certification Requirement (MCD)
CR	Certified Remodeller
CR	Chancery Reports Tempore Car. I to Queen Anne [*A publication*] (DLA)
C/R	Change of Rating
CR	Change Recommendation (AFM)
CR	Change Release [*Military*]
CR	Change Request
CR	Channels Ratio
CR	Characteristic Relief
CR	Character Reader [*Computer science*] (IAA)
CR	Charge-Recombination [*Physical chemistry*]
CR	Chemical Abstracts Reference (NITA)
CR	Chemical Report
CR	Chest and Right Arm [*Cardiology*]
CR	Chest Roentgenogram [*Radiology*]
CR	Chicago Reactor (NRCH)
CR	Chief Ranger
CR	Child Resistant
CR	Chimeric Receptor
CR	ChiroClec Resolves
CR	Chirp Rate [*Entomology*]
CR	Chloroprene Rubber
CR	Christiana [*City in South Africa*] (ROG)
CR	Christian Research (EA)
Cr	Chromium [*Chemical element*]
CR	Chronic Rejection [*Medicine*]
CR	Church Record [*Genealogy*]
CR	Chylomicron Remnant [*Physiology*]
CR	Circle (ROG)
CR	Circulating Reflux [*Chemical engineering*]
cr----	Circumcaribbean [*MARC geographic area code Library of Congress*] (LCCP)
CR	Cited Reference [*Online database field identifier*]
CR	Citizen Radio [*Telecommunications*] (IAA)
CR	Civil Rights
CR	Civis Romanus [*Roman Citizen*] [*Latin*]
CR	Clarification Request (AAGC)

CR............... Classification Research
CR............... Classified Register (AAG)
CR............... Class Rate [Business term]
CR............... Class Room
CR............... Clearance Required [Civil Service]
CR............... Clear Record [Telecommunications] (TEL)
CR............... Clear Round [Show jumping] (ADA)
CR............... Clinical Record [Medicine]
CR............... Clinical Research [Medicine] (DAVI)
CR............... Closed Reduction [Osteology] (AAMN)
CR............... Closed Routine (SAA)
CR............... Close Ratio [Automotive engineering]
CR............... Clot Retraction [Medicine]
CR............... Cockroach Antigen [Immunology]
C-R............... Codd-Rennie [Boundary condition] [Nuclear energy] (NRCH)
CR............... Code Receiver [Computer science] (IAA)
CR............... Code Reporter [New York] [A publication] (DLA)
CR............... Codex Reuchlinianus (BJA)
CR............... Coefficient of Fat Retention (AAMN)
CR............... Coefficient of Retraction
CR............... Cold-Rolled [Metal]
CR............... Collaborative Research, Inc.
C/R............... Collection/Requirements
CR............... Collins Resources Ltd. [Vancouver Stock Exchange symbol]
CR............... Colon Resection [Medicine]
CR............... Colorado Register [A publication] (AAGC)
CR............... Color Response [Psychology] (BARN)
CR............... Combat Reaction
CR............... Combat Ready (AFM)
CR............... Combat Reserve [Military]
Cr............... Commander [Navy British]
C/R............... Command Receiver (KSC)
CR............... Command Register
CR............... Command Representative (CINC)
CR............... Command/Response [Computer science]
C/R............... Command/Response [Computer science] (ACRL)
CR............... Command Review
CR............... Commencement of Rifling (NATG)
CR............... Commendation Ribbon [Military decoration]
CR............... Commercial Radio
CR............... Commodity Rate
CR............... Common Return [Electronics] (IAA)
CR............... Commonwealth Record [Australia A publication]
CR............... Communication Representative
CR............... Communication Resources [Haddonfield, NJ] [Telecommunications] (TSSD)
CR............... Communications Register
CR............... Community of the Resurrection [Anglican religious community]
CR............... Community Regeneration [Defunct] (EA)
CR............... Community Relations (AABC)
C/R............... Commutation Rate (MCD)
CR............... Company's Risk [Insurance]
CR............... Competing Risks
CR............... Complement Receptor [Immunology]
CR............... Complete Remission [Medicine]
CR............... Complete Response [Medicine]
CR............... Complete Round [Technical drawings]
CR............... Component Repair (MSA)
CR............... Compression Ratio
CR............... Computer Repair, Parts, and Tools (SAA)
CR............... Computer Resource
CR............... Concentric Rings [Botany]
CR............... Concept Requirement [Automotive project management]
CR............... Condemnation Rate
CR............... Conditional Release [Nuclear energy] (NRCH)
CR............... Conditioned Reflex [or Response] [Psychometrics]
CR............... Conference Report
CR............... Conference Room (DNAB)
CR............... Confidence Range [Statistics]
CR............... Configuration Review (MCD)
CR............... Conflict Resolution
CR............... Congregation of Clerics Regular [Theatine Fathers] [Roman Catholic religious order]
cr............... Congregation of the Resurrection, Resurrectionist Fathers (TOCD)
CR............... Congregation of the Resurrection Theatine Fathers (TOCD)
CR............... Congregatio Resurrectionis [Congregation of the Resurrection] [Roman Catholic religious order]
CR............... Connaught Rangers [Military British]
CR............... Connection Request [Computer science] (TNIG)
CR............... Connector Replacement (MCD)
CR............... Connect Request (ACRL)
CR............... Consciousness-Raising
CR............... Conseil de la Reine [Canada] (DD)
CR............... Conseiller de la Reine [Queen's Counsel] [Canada]
C-R............... Conservatism-Radicalism Opinionaire [Student attitude test]
CR............... Consolidated Rail Corp. [Also, CONRAIL, CRC] [AAR code]
CR............... Consolidated Report
CR............... Consolidated Revenue
CR............... Constant Rate (OA)
CR............... Constant Routine
CR............... Constitutional Revival (EA)
CR............... Constructionman Recruit [Navy]
CR............... Construction Recruit [Navy]
CR............... Consultant Report (NATG)
CR............... Consumers' Research (EA)

CR............... Contact Resistance [Electricity] (IAA)
CR............... Containment Rupture [Nuclear energy] (NRCH)
CR............... Contemporary Review [A publication] (BRI)
CR............... Contemporary Rock (LAIN)
CR............... Continence Restored (EA)
CR............... Contingency Reserve (MCD)
CR............... Continuing Resolution
CR............... Continuing Revolution
CR............... Continuous-Release [Pharmacy]
CR............... Continuous Rod (NG)
CR............... Contract-Relax Method [Medicine]
CR............... Contract [or Contractor] Report
C/R............... Contract Requirement
CR............... Contributions Record [Database terminology] (NITA)
CR............... Controlled Rectifier
CR............... Controlled Reflex [Neurology and psychiatry] (DAVI)
CR............... Controlled Release [Neurology and psychiatry] (DAVI)
CR............... Controlled Response [Neurology and psychiatry] (DAVI)
CR............... Controlled Rheology [Plastics technology]
CR............... Control Rating [British military] (DMA)
CR............... Control Register [Computer science] (IAA)
CR............... Control Relay
CR............... Control Rod [Nuclear energy] (NRCH)
CR............... Control Room (MSA)
CR............... Control Routine
CR............... Conversion Ratio [Endocrinology] (DAVI)
CR............... Convertible Report (PDAA)
CR............... Conveyancing Review [1957-63] [Scotland] [A publication] (DLA)
CR............... Copper Range Railroad (IIA)
CR............... Corbin Research [An association] (EA)
CR............... Core
CR............... Co-Responsibility Levy [Cereal production tax] [British]
CR............... Coronary Reserve [Cardiology]
CR............... Coronation (ROG)
CR............... Corotation Resonance [Planetary science]
CR............... Corpus Reformatorum (BJA)
CR............... Correlation Radiometer (MCD)
CR............... Corrosion Resistant [Material] [Manufacturing] (DCTA)
CR............... Cosmic Ray
CR............... Cosmis Rays
CR............... Costa Rica [ANSI two-letter standard code] (CNC)
cr............... Costa Rica [MARC country of publication code Library of Congress] (LCCP)
CR............... Cost per Region [Agricultural economics]
CR............... Cost Reimbursement
CR............... Councillor (ADA)
CR............... Counter Register
CR............... Counter Rotation (PDAA)
CR............... Count Reverse [Computer science]
CR............... Country Representative
CR............... Coupled Range-Finders
CR............... Court Reporting Program [Association of Independent Colleges and Schools specialization code]
Cr............... Cranch. Circuit Court Reports [United States] [A publication] (DLA)
CR............... Crane [Shipping] (DS)
CR............... Crane Co. [NYSE symbol] (TTSB)
CR............... Cranial [Anatomy]
CR............... Cras [Tomorrow] [Pharmacy]
CR............... Crate
CR............... Cream [Pharmacy] (DAVI)
cr............... Cream [Philately]
CR............... Crease [Deltiology]
CR............... Created [or Creation]
Cr............... Creatinine [Biochemistry]
CR............... Creation Research
CR............... Credit (AFM)
CR............... Creditable Record
CR............... Creditor (ROG)
CR............... Credit Rating [Business term] (ADA)
CR............... Credit Report [Business term]
CR............... Credit Requisition (MCD)
CR............... Credo [Creed] [Latin]
CR............... Creek [Maps and charts]
CR............... Creek [Commonly used] (OPSA)
CR............... Creeping [Horticulture]
CR............... Crescendo [Music] (ROG)
CR............... Crescentic
CR............... Cresol Red [Acid-base indicator] (AAMN)
CR............... Cresyl Red [Chemistry] (DAVI)
CR............... Crew (MSA)
CR............... Crew Rest [Military] (AFM)
Cr............... Criminal (DLA)
CR............... Crimson (ROG)
CR............... Crisis Relocation (MCD)
CR............... Crisis Response [A publication]
CR............... Cristobalite [A mineral]
CR............... Critical Ratio
CR............... Crochet
CR............... Crookston [Diocesan abbreviation] [Minnesota] (TOCD)
CR............... Crops Research Division [of ARS, Department of Agriculture]
Cr............... Cross (DAC)
CR............... Cross
CR............... Cross Angle
CR............... Crossroads [Maps and charts]
CR............... Crown [Paper size]

CR............ Crown [Dentistry] (DAVI)
CR............ Crown-Rump Length [of fetus] [Medicine]
CR............ Cruise (WDAA)
CR............ Cruiser
CR............ Cruiser Flag [Navy British]
CR............ Cruzeiro [Monetary unit] [Brazil]
CR............ Cryptographer [Navy rating]
CR............ Crystal [or Crystallize] (IAA)
CR............ Crystallography (IAA)
CR............ Crystal Rectifier (AAG)
CR............ Crystals [JETDS nomenclature] [Military] (CET)
C/R........... Cuenta y Riesgo [For Account and Risk Of] [Spanish Business term]
CR............ Cultwatch Response [An association] (EA)
CR............ Cum Rights [With Rights] (ADA)
CR............ Curia Regis [King's Court] [Latin Legal term] (DLA)
CR............ Currency Regulation
CR............ Current Rate [Business term]
CR............ Current Relay (MSA)
CR............ Customer's Report [Telecommunications] (TEL)
CR............ Customer's Request (SAA)
CR............ Custos Rotulorum [Keeper of the Rolls] [Latin]
CR............ Cutter [Ship] (ROG)
CR............ Cylinder Rate (NVT)
Cr............. La Sainte Bible (1923) [A. Crampon] [A publication] (BJA)
CR............ Right Center (WDMC)
CR............ Sisters of the Resurrection (TOCD)
CR............ Station Open to Limited Public Correspondence [ITU designation]
Cr............. Texas Court of Appeals Reports (Criminal Cases) [A publication] (DLA)
Cr............. Texas Criminal Reports [A publication] (DLA)
CR............ Theatine Fathers (TOCD)
cr............. Theatine Fathers (TOCD)
CR0........... Control Register Zero [Computer science] (PCM)
CR1........... Complement Receptor Type 1 [Medicine] (DMAA)
Cr 8vo........ Crown Octavo [Book size]
CRA .... California Redwood Association (EA)
CRA .... Camera-Ready Art [Publishing]
CRA .... Canadian Racquetball Association
CRA .... Canadian Restaurant Association
CRA .... Canadian Rheumatism Association (HGAA)
CRA .... Canonesses Regular of St. Augustine [Roman Catholic women's religious order]
CRA .... Capital Realty Investment Tax Exempt Fund Ltd. [AMEX symbol] (SPSG)
CRA .... Cap Rlty Inv TaxExFdL P1 [AMEX symbol] (TTSB)
CRA .... Carbon Rod Atomizer [Spectroscopy]
CRA .... Cargo Reinsurance Association [New York, NY] (EA)
CRA .... Carry Ripple Adder [Computer science] (IAA)
CRA .... Cassegrain Reflector Antenna
CRA .... Catalog Recovery Area [Computer science]
CRA .... Cave Research Associates (EA)
CRA .... Center for Rural Affairs (EA)
CRA .... Centralized Referral Activity [Military] (AFM)
CRA .... Centralized Repair Activity [Air Force] (AFIT)
CRA .... Central Research Agency [Cuc Nghien-Chu Trung-Uong] [North Vietnamese intelligence agency]
CRA .... Central Retinal Artery [Ophthalmology]
CRA .... Cereal Ryegrowers' Association [Australia]
CRA .... Certified Retinal Angiographer
CRA .... Certified Review Appraiser [Finance] (EMRF)
CRA .... Charles River Associates Library, Boston, MA [OCLC symbol] (OCLC)
CRA .... Chemical Recovery Association [British] (DBA)
CRA .... Chernovtsy [Former USSR Seismograph station code, US Geological Survey Closed] (SEIS)
CRA .... Children's Rights of America (EA)
CRA .... China Research Associates
CRA .... Chinese Restaurant Asthma [Medicine]
CRA .... Christian Restoration Association (EA)
CRA .... Chromium Release Assay [Clinical chemistry]
CRA .... Civil Rights Act [1957, 1964, 1968]
CRA .... Classification Review Area [Environmental Protection Agency] (GFGA)
CRA .... Clydesdale Runner's Association [Defunct] (EA)
CRA .... Colorado River Association (EA)
CRA .... Coma Recovery Association (EA)
CRA .... Commander, Royal Artillery [Division level] [British]
CRA .... Command Relationship Agreements [Army] (AABC)
CRA .... Commercial Rabbit Association [British] (BI)
CRA .... Committee for Real Ale (EA)
CRA .... Committee to Resist Abortion (EA)
CRA .... Commons Registration Act [Town planning] [British]
CRA .... Community Radio Association [British]
CRA .... Community Redevelopment Agency
CRA .... Community Reinvestment Act [1977] [Requires banks to list credit facilities available to the communities they serve]
CRA .... Community Research Associates (EA)
CRA .... Component Reword Analyst (MCD)
CRA .... Composite Research Aircraft
CRA .... Computer Retailers Association [British] (NITA)
CRA .... Concrete Repair Association [British] (DBA)
CRA .... Conditional Release Authorization (SAA)
CRA .... Conflict Resolution Advisory [FAA] (TAG)
CRA .... Congress of Russian Americans (EA)
CRA .... Contemporaneous Reserve Accounting [Banking]

CRA .... Continuing Resolution Authority [Military] (AFM)
CRA .... Controlled Rupture Accuracy (MUGU)
CRA .... Control Relay Automatic
CRA .... Control Repeater Amplifier
CRA .... Control Rod Absorber [Nuclear energy] (NUCP)
CRA .... Control Rod Assembly [Nuclear energy] (NRCH)
CRA .... Cooperative Research Act
CRA .... Corn Refiners Association (EA)
CRA .... Corolla Resources Ltd. [Vancouver Stock Exchange symbol]
CrA .... Corona Australis [Constellation]
CRA .... Coronado Aerolineas Ltda. [Colombia] [ICAO designator] (FAAC)
CRA .... Corrosion Resistant Alloy [Metallurgy]
CRA .... Cosmic Ray Altimeter
CRA .... Craddock [City in South Africa] (ROG)
CRA .... Craft (DNAB)
CRA .... Craiova [Romania] [Airport symbol] (OAG)
CRA .... CRA Managed Care, Inc. [Associated Press] (SAG)
Cra .... Cranch. Circuit Court Reports [United States] [A publication] (DLA)
CRA .... Crater (ROG)
Cra .... Cratylus [of Plato] [Classical studies] (OCD)
CRA .... Crease Recovery Angle [Textile technology]
CRA .... Crew Reception Area [Apollo] [NASA]
CRA .... Crime Reporters Association [British] (DBA)
CRA .... Sandoz Pharmaceuticals [Research code symbol]
CrAA .... Commander at Arms [Navy British]
CRAA .... Committee of Religion and Art of America [Later, FAAR] (EA)
CRAA .... CRA Managed Care [NASDAQ symbol] (TTSB)
CRAA .... CRA Managed Care, Inc. [NASDAQ symbol] (SAG)
CRAA .... Credit Reference Association of Australia
CRAA .... Critical Reflection Activation Analysis
CRAB .... Caging Retainer and Boresight [Air Force]
CRAB0 .... California Raisin Advisory Board (EA)
CRAB .... Cement Riverine Assault Boat [Navy] (MCD)
CRAB .... Centralized Requisitioning Accounting and Billing
CRAB .... Coastal Research Amphibious Buggy [Army] (MSC)
CRAB .... Combined Resources Allocation Board [World War II]
CRAB .... Communications Research Advisory Board [Canada]
CRAB .... Controlled Range Air Burst Fuze (RDA)
Crab .... Crabbe's United States District Court Reports [A publication] (DLA)
CRABB .... Cellular Remote Access Bulletin Board [Cellular Communications Industry Association] [Information service or system] (IID)
Crabb CL .... Crabb on the Common Law [A publication] (DLA)
Crabb Com Law... Crabb on the Common Law [A publication] (DLA)
Crabb Conv.... Crabb's Treatise on Conveyancing [A publication] (DLA)
Crabb Dig Stat... Crabb's Digest of Statutes [A publication] (DLA)
Crabbe........ Crabbe's United States District Court Reports [A publication] (DLA)
Crabb Eng.... Crabb's English Synonyms [A publication] (DLA)
Crabb Eng L... Crabb's History of the English Law [A publication] (DLA)
Crabb Eng Law... Crabb's History of the English Law [A publication] (ILCA)
Crabb Hist Eng Law... Crabb's History of the English Law [A publication] (DLA)
Crabb Prec... Crabb's Precedents in Conveyancing [A publication] (DLA)
Crabb Real Prop.... Crabb on the Law of Real Property [A publication] (DLA)
Crabb RP .... Crabb on the Law of Real Property [A publication] (DLA)
Crabb Technol Dict... Crabb's Technological Dictionary [A publication] (DLA)
CRABI .... Child Restraint and Air Bag Information [Automotive safety]
CRABP .... Cellular Retinoic Acid-Binding Protein [Biochemistry]
CRABP .... Cytoplasmic Retinoic Acid-Binding Protein [Biochemistry]
CRABS .... Close Range Analytical Bundle System (PDAA)
CRABS .... Computerized Reference and Bibliographic Services [University of Maryland at Baltimore] (OLDSS)
CRAC .... Calculations of Reactor Accident Consequences (NRCH)
CRAC .... Canadian Reports, Appeal Cases [1828-1913] [A publication] (DLA)
CRAC .... Careers Research and Advisory Centre [British]
CRAC .... Central Religious Advisory Committee [British]
CRAC .... Club Royale d'Automobile du Canada [Royal Automobile Club of Canada]
CRAC .... Commander, Royal Armoured Corps [British military] (DMA)
CRAC .... Community Relations Advisory Council [Military]
CRAC .... Conseil de Recherche Agricole du Canada [Canadian Agricultural Research Council]
CRAC .... Contract-Relax, Antagonistic-Contract Method [Medicine]
CRACA .... Council on Roentgenology of the American Chiropractic Association (EA)
CRAcad Inscr... Comptes Rendus. Academie des Inscriptions et Belles-Lettres [A publication] (OCD)
CRACC .... Communication and RADAR Assignment Coordinating Committee
Cra CC .... Cranch. Circuit Court Reports [United States] [A publication] (DLA)
CRACCA .... Canadian Refrigeration & Air Conditioning Contractors Association (AC)
CRACCUS .... Comite Regional d'Afrique Centrale pour la Conservation et l'Utilisation du Sol
CRACH........ Central Register and Clearing House [British]
CRAC-KIT..... Croft Readiness Assessment in Comprehension Kit [Child development test]
CRACL .... Civil Rights Act Compliance Log (OICC)
CRACS .... Control Room Air Conditioning System [Nuclear energy] (NRCH)
Cr Act .... Criminal Act (DLA)
CRAD .... Centre de Recherches en Amenagement et en Developpement [Laval University] [Canada Research center] (RCD)
CRAD .... Chief, Research and Development [Department of National Defence] [Canada]
CRAD .... Composite RADAR Data Processing (FAAC)
CRAD .... Contract Research and Development
CRADA .... Collaborative Research and Development Agreement

CRADA......... Cooperative Research and Development Agreement [*Department of Energy National Laboratories*]

CRADA......... Cooperative Research and Development Agreement [*Government-industry programs*]

CRADS......... Contraves/Raytheon Air Defense System

CRAE .... Combat Readiness Assessment Exercise [*Obsolete Navy*] (NG)

CRAE .... Combined Readiness Air Exercise (MCD)

CRAE .... Committee for the Reform of Animal Experimentation [*British*]

CRAE .... CRA [*Conzinc Riotinto of Australia*] Exploration Ltd.

CRAF .... Central Reserve Air Fleet

CRAF .... Certified Round Assembly Facility [*Military*]

CRAF .... Civil Reserve Aircraft Fleet [*OST*] (TAG)

CRAF .... Civil Reserve Air Field [*Department of Commerce*] (MCD)

CRAF .... Civil Reserve Air Fleet [*Department of Commerce*]

CRAF .... Civil Reserve Airlift Fleet (DOMA)

CRAF .... Comet Rendezvous and Asteroid Flyby [*Proposed NASA mission*]

CRAFREP.... Civil Reserve Air Fleet Summary Report [*Department of Commerce*]

CRAFT .... Centre Regional Africain de Conception et de Fabrication Techniques [*African Regional Centre for Engineering Design and Manufacturing - ARCEDEM*] (EAIO)

CRAFT .... Changing Radio Automatic Frequency Transmission

CRAFT .... Combat Reserve Air Fleet [*Military*]

CRAFT .... Comparing Reading Approaches in First Grade Teaching

CRAFT .... Computerized Relative Allocation of Facilities Technique [*IBM Corp.*]

CRAFT .... Continuous Random Analog to Frequency Transmission

CRAFT .... Cooperative Research Action for Technology

CRAFTS ...... Central Regional Automated Funds Transfer System

CRAFTS ...... Civil Reserve Auxiliary Fleet Ships (DOMA)

CRAFTS ...... Credit Card Authorisation and Fund Transfer System [*British*]

CRAG .... Carrier Replacement Air Group [*Navy*]

CRAG .... Combat Readiness Air Group (DNAB)

CRAG .... Contractor Risk Assessment Guide [*Military*]

CRAG .... Cranfield Robotics and Automation Group [*British*]

CRAG .... Cyclists' Rights Action Group [*Australia*]

CragrInd ...... Cragar Industries, Inc. [*Associated Press*] (SAG)

CRAGS......... Chemistry Records and Grading System [*Computer science*]

CRAHCA...... Center for Research in Ambulatory Health Care Administration (EA)

CRAI .... Computer Resident Automatic Instruction (MCD)

Craig........... Craig Corp. [*Associated Press*] (SAG)

Craig & P ... Craig and Phillips' English Chancery Reports [*1840-41*] [*A publication*] (DLA)

Craig & Ph... Craig and Phillips' English Chancery Reports [*1840-41*] [*A publication*] (DLA)

Craig & Ph (Eng)... Craig and Phillips' English Chancery Reports [*1840-41*] [*A publication*] (DLA)

Craig & St ... Craigie, Stewart, and Paton's Scotch Appeal Cases [*1726-1821*] [*A publication*] (DLA)

CraigCE....... Craig Consumer Electronics [*Associated Press*] (SAG)

Craig Dict.... Craig's Etymological, Technological, and Pronouncing Dictionary [*A publication*] (DLA)

Craigius Jus Feud... Craigius Jus Feudale [*A publication*] (DLA)

Craig Jus Feud... Craigius Jus Feudale [*A publication*] (DLA)

Craig Pr....... Craig's Practice [*A publication*] (DLA)

Craig S & P... Craigie, Stewart, and Paton's Scotch Appeal Cases [*1726-1821*] [*A publication*] (DLA)

Craig St & Pat... Craigie, Stewart, and Paton's Scotch Appeal Cases [*1726-1821*] [*A publication*] (DLA)

Craik CC ..... Craik's English Causes Celebres [*A publication*] (DLA)

CRALC........ Cedar Rapids Area Library Consortium [*Library network*]

CRALOG...... Council of Relief Agencies Licensed for Operation in Germany [*Post-World War II*]

CRAM .... Campaign Against Racism in the Media [*British*] (DI)

CRAM .... Card Random-Access Memory [*NCR Corp.*] [*Computer science*]

CRAM .... Centre de Recherches sur l'Afrique Mediterraneenne

CRAM .... Centre for Research on Atoms and Molecules [*Laval University*] [*Canada Research center*] (RCD)

CRAM .... Collapsible Rollup Antenna Mast

CRAM .... Combat Resource Allocation Model (MCD)

CRAM .... Common RADAR Antenna Mount (DWSG)

CRAM .... Compression, Retrieval, and Maintenance [*of data*] (DNAB)

CRAM .... Computerized Reliability Analysis Method

CRAM .... Conditional Relaxation Analysis Method

CRAM .... CONRAIL [*Consolidated Rail Corp.*] Analysis Model [*Computer science*]

CRAM .... Contractual Requirements, Recording, Analysis, and Management [*Air Force*]

CRAM .... Core and Random Access Manager [*General Automation, Inc.*]

CRAM .... Critical Resource Allocation Method (PDAA)

CRAM .... Cumulative Radio Audience Method (NTCM)

CRAMD .... Cosmic Ray Anti-Matter Detector (PDAA)

CRAMM ...... Coupon Reading and Marking Machine (MHDI)

CRAMMM .... Chain Store Renovation and Maintenance, Materials, Modernization

CRAMP .... Comprehending Reflex Development, Attitude Formation, Memorizing, Procedural Learing (PDAA)

CRAMPS ..... Combined Rotation and Multiple-Pulse Spectroscopy [*Physics*]

CRAMRA..... Convention on the Regulation of Antarctic Mineral Resource Activities (GNE)

CRAMSHIP... Complete Round Ammunition Shipment

cran .... Cranial [*Anatomy*]

CRAN .... Craniology

CRAN .... Cross-Scan Terrain-Avoidance Displays

CRAN .... Crown-Andersen [*NASDAQ symbol*] (TTSB)

CRAN .... Crown Andersen, Inc. [*NASDAQ symbol*] (NQ)

CRANB .... Cranborne [*England*]

Cranbrook Acad Art... Cranbrook Academy of Art (GAGS)

Cranch .... Cranch's District of Columbia Reports [*1-5 District of Columbia*] [*1801-40*] [*A publication*] (DLA)

Cranch CC ... Cranch. Circuit Court Reports [*United States*] [*A publication*] (DLA)

Cranch CC ... District of Columbia Appeals Cases Reports [*1-5 United States*] [*A publication*] (DLA)

Cranch CC ... District of Columbia Supreme Court Reports [*1-5 District of Columbia*] [*1801-40*] [*A publication*] (DLA)

Cranch Pat Dec... Cranch's Patent Decisions [*United States*] [*A publication*] (DLA)

CRAND........ Cosmic Ray Albedo Neutron Decay [*Geophysics*]

Cr & Br........ Crown and Bridge [*Dentistry*] (DAVI)

CR & D........ Chief of Research and Development [*Army*]

CR & D........ Contract Research and Development (SSD)

CR & D........ Contractual Research and Development (MCD)

Cr & Dix ..... Crawford and Dix's Irish Circuit Court Cases [*A publication*] (DLA)

Cr & Dix Ab Ca... Crawford and Dix's Irish Abridged Cases [*A publication*] (DLA)

Cr & Dix Ab Cas... Crawford and Dix's Irish Abridged Cases [*A publication*] (DLA)

Cr & Dix CC... Crawford and Dix's Irish Circuit Court Cases [*A publication*] (DLA)

CR & DO..... Commanders Research and Development Objective

CR & FA ..... Canadian Restaurant and Foodservices Association

CR & I .... [*The*] Chicago River & Indiana Railway Co. [*Absorbed into Consolidated Rail Corp.*]

CRANDIC .... Cedar Rapids & Iowa City [*Railway*] (MHDB)

Cr & M .... Crompton and Meeson's English Exchequer Reports [*1832-34*] [*A publication*] (DLA)

Cr & Ph ...... Craig and Phillips' English Chancery Reports [*1840-41*] [*A publication*] (DLA)

CR & R .... Calibration, Repair, and Return

Cr & St .... Craigie, Stewart, and Paton's Scotch Appeal Cases [*1726-1821*] [*A publication*] (DLA)

CR & T .... Columbia River and Tributaries Study (NOAA)

CRANE .... Cosmic Ray Nuclear [*or Nuclei*] Experiment (MCD)

Crane.......... Crane Co. [*Associated Press*] (SAG)

Crane.......... Crane's Reports [*22-29 Montana*] [*A publication*] (DLA)

Crane CC ..... Cranenburgh's Criminal Cases [*India*] [*A publication*] (DLA)

CRANIOL..... Craniology (ROG)

CRANIOM .... Craniometry (ROG)

CRANIOT .... Craniotomy (ROG)

Cra NY Pr .. Crary's New York Practice, Special Pleading [*A publication*] (DLA)

CRAO .... Central Retinal Artery Occlusion [*Ophthalmology*]

CRAOC........ Commander, Royal Army Ordnance Corps [*Military British*]

CRAP .... Calorific Recovery Anaerobic Process [*Inc*]

CRAP .... Canfield, Rodeman, Adams, and Preller [*Philadelphia law firm in Spiro Agnew's book, "The Canfield Decision"*]

CRAP .... Committee on Rhetoric, Administration, and Perspicacity [*Satirical bureaucracy term*]

CRAP .... Committee to Resist Acronym Proliferation

CRAP .... Constructive Republican Alternative Programs [*Position papers on legislative issues prepared for Republican House leaders during Lyndon Johnson administration*]

CRAPE .... Committee for the Restructuring and Progress of Equity [*Actors' Trade Union*] [*British*] (DI)

Cr App .... Criminal Appeals (DLA)

Cr App R...... Criminal Appeal Reports [*England*] [*A publication*] (DLA)

Cr App Rep... Criminal Appeal Reports [*England*] [*A publication*] (DLA)

Cr App R(S)... Criminal Appeal Reports (Sentencing) [*England*] [*A publication*] (DLA)

CRAR .... Center for Research Animal Resources [*Cornell University*] [*Research center*] (RCD)

CRAR .... Committee for the Recovery of Archaeological Remains

CRAR .... Control ROM [*Read-Only Memory*] Address Register [*Computer science*]

CRAR .... Critical Reliability Action Report (AAG)

CRARA........ Canadian Rock Art Research Associates

CR ARM...... Crusader Armaments [*Army*] (RDA)

Crar Pr....... Crary's New York Practice, Special Pleading [*A publication*] (DLA)

CRARR........ Cente for Research-Action on Race Relations (AC)

CR-ARRV .... Challenger Armored Repair and Recovery Vehicle [*British*]

CR-ARS....... Crops Research Division Agricultural Research Service [*Washington, DC*] [*Department of Agriculture*]

CRAS .... Coder and Random Access Switch (AAG)

CRAS .... Composite RADAR Absorbing Structure (MCD)

CRAS .... Cost Reduction Alternative Study [*Economics*] (NASA)

CRASC......... Commander, Royal Army Service Corps [*British*]

CRASH........ Center for Reproductive and Sexual Health [*Defunct*] (EA)

CRASH........ Citizens Responsible Action for Safety on the Highways

CRASH........ Citizens to Reduce Airline Smoking Hazards [*Student legal action organization*]

CRASH........ Cornell Reconstruction of Accident Speeds on the Highway

CRASH........ Creep in Axisymmetric Shells

CRASS......... Convoy, Routing, and Scheduling System [*USAREUR*]

Crass.......... Crassus [*of Plutarch*] [*Classical studies*] (OCD)

CRAST .... Crastinus [*Of Tomorrow*] [*Pharmacy*]

CRAT .... Centre Regional Africain de Technologie [*African Regional Centre for Technology - ARCT*] (EA)

CRAT .... Charitable Remainder Annuity Trust (NFD)

CRAT .... Civil Reserve Air Tanker [*Department of Commerce*] (MCD)

CRAT .... Colonel, Royal Artillery Training [*British*]

Crat............. Crater [*Constellation*]

CRATT .... Covered Radio Teletype (NVT)

CRATTZ...... Communication Radio and Teletype (Secure) System

CRAVE .... Cancer Risk-Assessment Verification Endeavor

CRAVS .... Control Room Area Ventilation System [*Nuclear energy*] (NRCH)

CR/AVTC .... Conflict Resolution/Alternatives to Violence Training Center (EA)

CRAW .... Carrier Replacement Air Wing [*Navy*]

CRAW .... Combat Readiness Air Wing

CRAW .... Crawford & Co. (MHDW)
Craw .... Crawford's Reports [53-69, 72-101 Arkansas] [A publication] (DLA)
Craw & D.... Crawford and Dix's Irish Circuit Court Cases [A publication] (DLA)
Craw & D Ab Cas... Crawford and Dix's Irish Abridged Cases [A publication] (DLA)
Craw & D Abr Cas... Crawford and Dix's Irish Abridged Cases [A publication] (DLA)
Craw & DCC (Ir)... Crawford and Dix's Irish Circuit Court Cases [A publication] (DLA)
Craw & D (Ir)... Crawford and Dix's Irish Abridged Cases [A publication] (DLA)
Craw & Dix... Crawford and Dix's Irish Circuit Court Cases [A publication] (DLA)
Craw (Ark)... Crawford's Reports [53-69, 72-101 Arkansas] [A publication] (DLA)
Craw Co Leg J (PA)... Crawford County Legal Journal [Pennsylvania] [A publication] (DLA)
Crawf & D ... Crawford and Dix's Irish Circuit Court Cases [A publication] (DLA)
Crawf & D Abr Cas... Crawford and Dix's Irish Abridged Cases [A publication] (DLA)
Crawf & Dix... Crawford and Dix's Irish Circuit Court Cases [A publication] (DLA)
Crawf & Dix... Crawford and Dix's Irish Criminal Cases [A publication] (DLA)
Crawford Co Leg Jour... Crawford County Legal Journal [Pennsylvania] [A publication] (DLA)
CRAY .... Crayfish (DSUE)
cray .... Crayon (VRA)
CrayRs......... Cray Research, Inc. [Associated Press] (SAG)
CRAZI .... Count Routine Applied to Zero Input [Computer program]
CrazyW .... Crazy Woman Creek Bancorp, Inc. [Associated Press] (SAG)
CRB .... Cab Research Bureau [Later, ITA] (EA)
CRB .... Cambridge Research Biochemicals [British]
CRB .... Cam Ranh Bay [Vietnam]
CRB .... Capital Realty Investment Tax Exempt Fund Ltd. [AMEX symbol] (SPSG)
CRB .... Cap Rlty Inv TaxExFdLP II [AMEX symbol] (TTSB)
CRB .... Certified Residential Broker [Realtors National Marketing Institute of th e National Association of Realtors] [Designation awarded by]
CRB .... Change Review Board [NASA] (KSC)
CRB .... Chemical, Radiological, Biological Warfare [NATO] (NATG)
CRB .... Chernovtsy [Former USSR Seismograph station code, US Geological Survey Closed] (SEIS)
CRB .... Chiropractors' Registration Board [Australia]
CRB .... Clemency Review Board [for Vietnam War draft dodgers and defectors]
CRB .... Clutch Release Bearing
CRB .... Clutter Reject Band (MCD)
CRB .... Columbia River Basalts [Geology]
CRB .... Command Review Board [Aerospace]
CRB .... Commodity Research Bureau
CRB .... Community Reference Bureau Databank [European Atomic Energy Community] (NITA)
CRB .... Community Research Bureau
CRB .... Composite Razor Blade (MCD)
CRB .... Container Repair Building
CRB .... Contingency Reference Book (MCD)
CRB .... Contractor Review Board (AAGC)
CRB .... Corbit-Calloway Memorial Library, Odessa, DE [OCLC symbol] (OCLC)
CrB............. Corona Borealis [Constellation]
CrB............. Coronae Borealis [Astronomy]
CRB .... Council of Review Board [Army]
CRB .... Council on Research in Bibliography, Inc. (DIT)
CRB .... Country Radio Broadcasters (EA)
CRB .... Course Record Book [Education] (AIE)
CRB .... Crop Reporting Board
CRB .... Current Research in Britain [A publication]
CRB .... Curriculum Review Board of the American Association of Medical Assistants (DAVI)
CRB .... Customer Records and Billing [Bell System]
CRBA .... Christian Record Benevolent Association [Later, CRBF]
CRBA .... Cinnamon Rabbit Breeders Association (EA)
CRBAL .... Carpatho-Russian Benevolent Association Liberty (EA)
CRBBB........ Complete Right Bundle Branch Block [Cardiology]
CRBBN....... Caribbean
CRBC .... Canada-Russia Business Council (AC)
CRBC .... Canadian Radio Broadcasting Commission [Later, Canadian Broadcasting Corp.]
CRBC .... Chick Red Blood Cells
CRbCL........ Tehama County Free Library, Red Bluff, CA [Library symbol Library of Congress] (LCLS)
CRBD .... Configuration Review Board Directive [Military]
CRBE .... Conversational Remote Batch Entry [Computer science]
CRBF .... Christian Record Braille Foundation [Later, CRS] (EA)
CRBG .... Columbia River Basalt Group [Geology]
CRBIF .... Crisis Basic Imagery File (MCD)
CrBioMol .... Creative BioMolecules, Inc. [Associated Press] (SAG)
CRBL .... Charles River Breeding Laboratories
CRBM .... Centre de Recherche en Biologie Marine [Marine Biology Research Center] [Research center] (RCD)
CRBN .... Calgon Carbon Corp. (MHDW)
CRBNATD .... Carbonated
CRBNT........ Carbonate (MSA)
CRBO .... Carbo Ceramics [NASDAQ symbol] (TTSB)
CRBO .... Carbo Ceramics, Inc. [NASDAQ symbol] (SAG)
CRBO .... Centralized Records Business Office [Telecommunications] (TEL)
CRBP .... Carboxyribitol Bisphosphate [Biochemistry]
CRBP .... Cellular Retinol-Binding Protein [Biochemistry]
CRBP .... Colorado River Basin Project
CRBP .... Construction Report, Building Permits [A publication]

CRBR .... Clinch River Breeder Reactor
CRBR .... Controlled Recirculation Boiling Water Reactor
CRBRP .... Clinch River Breeder Reactor Plant [Department of Energy]
CRBRP .... Clinch River Breeder Reactor Project [Department of Energy] (NUCP)
CRBRPO ...... Clinch River Breeder Reactor Program Office [Nuclear Regulatory Commission] (GFGA)
CRBSD .... Curbside (MSA)
CRBT .... Columbia River Basin Treaty (NOAA)
CRBV .... Chiropodists' Registration Board of Victoria [Australia]
CRBW .... Carson's Rule Bandwidth
CRC .... Cable Communications Resource Center (EA)
CRC .... Calibration and Repair Center
CRC .... California Railroad Commission Digest of Decisions [A publication] (DLA)
CRC .... Calomel, Rhubarb, Colocynth [Medicine]
CRC .... Cambridge Research Center [Air Force]
CRC .... Camera-Ready Copy [Publishing]
CRC .... Canadian Railway Cases [A publication] (DLA)
CRC .... Canadian Railway Commission
CRC .... Canadian Religious Conference
CRC .... Canadian Reprography Collective
CRC .... Canadian Retransmission Collective (AC)
CRC .... Cancer Research Campaign [British]
CRC .... Cancer Research Center [Research center] (RCD)
CRC .... Capital Research Center
CRC .... Cardiac Reconditioning Center [Rehabilitation] (DAVI)
CRC .... Cardiology Research Center [Russian]
CRC .... Cardiovascular Reflex Conditioning [Medicine]
CRC .... Carlow College, Pittsburgh, PA [OCLC symbol] (OCLC)
CRC .... Carriage Return Contact
CRC .... Carrier Return Character [Computer science]
CRC .... Cartago [Colombia] [Airport symbol] (OAG)
CRC .... Castle Rock [California] [Seismograph station code, US Geological Survey] (SEIS)
CRC .... Cataloging Responsibility Code
CRC .... Cavity Rim Cup [A contraceptive device]
CRC .... Central Registry of Charities [British]
CRC .... Central Requirements Committee
CRC .... Central Rhine Commission [Post-World War II]
CRC .... Century Research Center Corp. [Information service or system] (IID)
CRC .... Ceramic Refraction Coating
CRC .... Certified Rehabilitation Counselor
CRC .... Chapter Relations Committee [American Library Association]
CRC .... Character Recognition Circuit (IAA)
CRC .... Chatterbox Recording Club [British] (EAIO)
CRC .... Chemical Referral Center (EA)
CRC .... Chemical Research Consultants, Inc.
CRC .... Chemical Resistant Coating
CRC .... Chemical Rubber Co.
CRC .... Chesapeake Research Consortium
CRC .... Chief of Reserve Components [Army]
CRC .... Child-Resistant Closure [Medicine containers, etc.]
CRC .... Christian Reformed Church
CRC .... Chromcraft Revington [NYSE symbol] (TTSB)
CRC .... Chromcraft Revington, Inc. [NYSE symbol] (SAG)
CRC .... Chrysler Restorers Club [Formerly, CPRC] (EA)
CRC .... Circle, AK [Location identifier FAA] (FAAL)
CRC .... Civil Rights Commission [Federal government]
CRC .... Clinical Research Center [University of Utah] [Research center] (RCD)
CRC .... Clinical Research Center [University of Rochester] [Research center] (RCD)
CRC .... Clinical Research Center [Case Western Reserve University] [Research center] (RCD)
CRC .... Clinical Research Center [Massachusetts Institute of Technology] [Research center] (RCD)
CRC .... Clinical Research Center [Medical Research Institute of Delaware] [Research center]
CRC .... Clinical Research Center [UCLA] [Research center]
CRC .... Clinical Research Center [University of Tennessee] [Research center] (RCD)
CRC .... Clinical Research Centre [British] (CB)
CRC .... Closed Roller Chock [Shipfitting]
CRC .... Coastal Research Center (GNE)
CRC .... Coke on Regenerated Catalyst [Chemical engineering]
CRC .... Collectors Record Club (EA)
CRC .... Collins Radio Co. (KSC)
CRC .... Colorado Research Corp. (AAG)
CRC .... Colorectal Cancer [Oncology] (DAVI)
CRC .... Colorectal Carcinoma [Oncology]
CRC .... Column Research Council [Later, SSRC] (EA)
CRC .... Combat Reporting Center (AFM)
CRC .... Command Reporting Center
CRC .... Committee to Restore the Constitution (EA)
CRC .... Commonwealth Research Centre
CRC .... Communication Research Center [Florida State University] [Research center] (RCD)
CRC .... Communication Research Center [Boston University] [Research center] (RCD)
CRC .... Communication Research Center [University of Florida] [Research center] (RCD)
CRC .... Communications Regulatory Commission
CRC .... Communications Relay Center [Air Force]
CRC .... Communications Research Center [University of Tennessee at Knoxville] [Research center] (RCD)

CRC .... Communications Research Centre [*Defunct Canada*]
CRC .... Community Rating by Class
CRC .... Community Recreation Council [*Victoria*] [*Australia*]
CRC .... Community Relations Commission [*British*]
CRC .... Community Research Center [*University of Illinois*] [*Research center*] (RCD)
CRC .... Community Residential Care [*Veterans Administration*] (GFGA)
CRC .... Complete Round Chart
CRC .... Composing Reducing Camera [*Microfilm*] (NITA)
CRC .... Composing Room Chapel [*Unions*] [*British*] (DGA)
CRC .... Computer Response Corp.
CRC .... Computer Results Corp. [*Information service or system*] (IID)
CRC .... COMSEC [*Communications Security*] Repair Center [*Army*] (NG)
CRC .... Conair Aviation Ltd. [*Canada ICAO designator*] (FAAC)
CRC .... Condition Reservation Code [*Army*] (AABC)
CRC .... Confederation of Roofing Contractors [*British*] (DBA)
CRC .... Conflict Resolution Center (EA)
CRC .... Congressional Report on Communications [*Arlington, VA*] [*A publication*] (TSSD)
CRC .... Congressional Rural Caucus (EA)
CRC .... Consistency Recording Controller
CRC .... Consolidated Rail Corp. [*Also, CR, CONRAIL*]
CRC .... Consolidated Reactor Uranium [*Vancouver Stock Exchange symbol*]
CRC .... Constitutional Reform Centre [*British*] (CB)
CRC .... Contractor-Recommended Coding (MCD)
CRC .... Contract Requirement Card
CRC .... Contre-Reforme Catholique [*In association name CRC Canada*] [*Catholic Counter-Reform Canada*]
CRC .... Control and Reporting Center [*Air Force*]
CRC .... Control Recognition Character [*Computer science*] (ECII)
CRC .... CONUS [*Continental United States*] Replacement Center [*Military*] (GFGA)
CRC .... Conventionally Refined Carrageenan [*Food grade*]
CRC .... Cooperative Research Council
CRC .... Coordinating Research Council (EA)
CRC .... Copper Recovery Corp.
CRC .... Copy Research Council (EA)
CRC .... Core Removal Coding (DNAB)
CRC .... Corrosion of Reinforcing Steel in Concrete [*Rilem Technical Committee*] [*British*]
CRC .... Corrosion-Resistant Cladding [*Nuclear energy equipment*]
CRC .... Cost Realism Committee (AAGC)
CRC .... Cost Reduction Curve [*Economics*] (NASA)
CRC .... Cost Reimbursement Contract [*Government contracting*]
CRC .... Cost-Reimbursement Contracting (AAGC)
CRC .... Cotton Research Corp.
CRC .... CRC Press [*Boca Raton, FL*]
CRC .... Credit Research Center [*Purdue University*] [*Research center*] (RCD)
CRC .... Crew Chief
CRC .... Criminology Research Council [*Australia*]
CRC .... Crisis Resolution Center [*Psychiatry*] (DAVI)
CRC .... Critical Reactor Component (NRCH)
CRC .... Critical Rule Curve (NOAA)
CRC .... Cuba Resource Center [*Defunct*] (EA)
CRC .... Cumulative Results Criterion (IEEE)
CRC .... Current Replacement Cost [*Accounting*]
CRC .... Custom Refresh Controller
CRC .... Cybernetics Research Consultants [*British*] (NITA)
CRC .... Cyclic Redundancy Character (PDAA)
CRC .... Cyclic Redundancy Check [*Computer science*]
CRC .... Cyclic Redundancy Code (PDAA)
CRC .... Czechoslovak Red Cross
CRC .... General Clinical Research Center [*University of Vermont*] [*Research center*] (RCD)
CRc .... Redwood City Public Library, Redwood City, CA [*Library symbol Library of Congress*] (LCLS)
CRCA .... Canadian Recreational Canoeing Association
CRCA .... Canadian Roofing Contractors' Association
CRCA .... Cellular Radio Communications Association [*Later, CCIA*] (EA)
CRCA .... Central Records Control Area (SAA)
CRCA .... Central Region Cultural Authority [*South Australia*]
CRCA .... Cold-Rolled Close-Annealed [*Metal*]
CRCA .... Construction Report, Construction Activity [*A publication*]
CRCA .... Crown Circuit Assistant [*Legal term*] (DLA)
CRcAm .... Ampex Corp., Redwood City, CA [*Library symbol Library of Congress*] (LCLS)
CRC/AODA ... Certification Reciprocity Consortium/Alcoholism and Other Drug Abuse [*Later, NCRC/AODA*] (EA)
Cr Cas Res... Crown Cases Reserved (DLA)
CRCAT .... Combat Readiness Categories [*Navy*] (NG)
CRCAWA ...... Country Regional Councils' Association of Western Australia
CRCC .... Canadian Red Cross Committee (HGAA)
CRCC .... Central Rural Construction Command [*Military*] (CINC)
CRCC .... Commission on Rehabilitation Counselor Certification (EA)
CRCC .... Communist Rebel Combat Captives (CINC)
CRCC .... Consolidated Record Communications Center [*Army*] (AABC)
CRCC .... Cooperative Research Centres Committee [*Australia*]
Cr CC .... Cranch. Circuit Court Reports [*United States*] [*A publication*] (DLA)
CRCC .... Cyclic Redundancy Check Character [*Computer science*] (IEEE)
CRC card .... Class Responsibility Collaboration Card (CDE)
CRCCC .... Canton Island Range Communications Control Center [*Military*] (MCD)
CRCCF .... Centre de Recherche en Civilisation Canadienne-Francaise [*Center for Research in French Canadian Civilisation*]
CRCCH .... Chile Resource Center and Clearinghouse (EA)

CRCCYP ...... Certificate in the Residential Care of Children and Young People [*British*] (DI)
CRCD .... Canadian Rehabilitation Council for the Disabled
CRCE .... Centre for Research into Communist Economies [*Research center British*] (IRC)
CRCE .... Chicago Rice and Cotton Exchange (EA)
CRCE .... Chief Railway Construction Engineer [*British military*] (DMA)
CRCGR .... Cyclic Redundancy Check Generator/Checker [*Microprocessing*] (NITA)
CRCH .... Centre de Recherche sur la Croissance Humaine [*University of Montreal*] [*Research center*] (RCD)
CRCH .... Crew Chief
CRCHF .... Crew Chief (FAAC)
CRCHI .... Capital Region Centre for the Hearing Impaired [*Centre de la Region de la Capitale pour les Personnes a Deficience Auditive*] (AC)
Cr Cir Comp... Crown Circuit Companion [*Ireland*] [*A publication*] (DLA)
CRCJ .... Center for the Rights of Campus Journalists (EA)
CRcK .... Kaiser-Permanente Medical Center, Medical Library, Redwood City, CA [*Library symbol Library of Congress*] (LCLS)
CrckrRT....... Crocker Realty Trust, Inc. [*Associated Press*] (SAG)
CRCL .... Centre de Readaptation Constance-Lethbridge [*Constance Lethbridge Rehabilitation Centre*] (AC)
CRCL .... Circle [*Commonly used*] (OPSA)
CRCL .... Circle Financial Corp. [*NASDAQ symbol*] (SAG)
CRCL .... Circle Finl [*NASDAQ symbol*] (TTSB)
CR-CL .... Civil Rights-Civil Liberties (DLA)
CRCL .... Clearinghouse for Research in Child Life [*Federal Security Administration*]
CRCL .... Columbia River Conservation League (EA)
CRCL .... Contractor-Recommended Change List
CrCl .... Creatinine Clearance [*Biochemistry*] (DAVI)
CRCLE .... Circle [*Commonly used*] (OPSA)
CRCLR .... Circular
CRCLT .... Circulate (MSA)
CRCM .... Centre for Research in Comparative Medicine [*Canada*] (IRC)
CRCM .... Commission on Recent Crustal Movements [*Oceanography*] (MSC)
CRCMF .... Circumference (MSA)
CRCN .... Counterreconnaissance [*Army*] (IAA)
CRCNA........ Christian Reformed Church in North America (AC)
Cr Code ...... Criminal Code [*A publication*] (DLA)
Cr Code Prac... Criminal Code of Practice [*A publication*] (DLA)
CRCOM........ Change Review Committee [*Military*] (AABC)
CRCP .... Certificate of the Royal College of Physicians [*British*]
CRCP .... Committee of Religious Concern for Peace (EA)
CRCP .... Continuously Reinforced Concrete Pavement (OA)
CRC/P .... Control and Reporting Center/Post [*Air Force*] (MCD)
CRCPD........ Clinical Research Center for Periodontal Disease [*University of Minnesota*]
CRCPD........ Conference of Radiation Control Program Directors (EA)
CRCPI .... Coordinating Research Council of the Petroleum Industry
CRCR .... Center for Rate Controlled Recordings [*Defunct*] (EA)
CRCS .... Cardiovascular Reflex Conditioning System [*Medicine*]
CRCS .... Center Range Control Station [*NASA*] (KSC)
CRCS .... Centre de Recherches sur les Communications [*Sherbrooke University*] [*Canada Research center*] (RCD)
CRCS .... Certificate of the Royal College of Surgeons [*British*]
CRCS .... Circus
CRCS .... Clerici Regulares Congregationis Somaschae [*Somaschi Fathers*] [*Roman Catholic religious order*]
CRCS .... Clinical Record Cover Sheet [*Army medical*]
CRCS .... CR [*Christian Rovsing*] Computer Systems, Inc. [*Los Angeles, CA*] [*Telecommunications*] (TSSD)
CRCSU .... Ceylon Railway Clerical Service Union [*Obsolete*]
CRCT .... Center for Research in Computing Technology [*Harvard University*] [*Research center*] (RCD)
CRCT .... Circuit (KSC)
CRCT .... Circuit
CRCT .... Commander, Royal Corps of Transport [*Military British*]
CRCTA .... Composite Reactor Components Test Activity (NRCH)
CRCTD .... Corrected (MSA)
CRCV .... Cooperative Research Centre for Viticulture [*Australia*]
CRCWLM .... Christian Reformed Church World Literature Ministries (EA)
CRD .... Aerolineas Cordillera Ltda. [*Chile*] [*ICAO designator*] (FAAC)
CRD .... Capacitor-Resistor Diode
CRD .... Carbohydrate-Recognition Domain [*Cytology*]
CRD .... Carbohydrate Recognition Domain [*Biochemistry*]
CRD .... Card Reader [*Computer science*]
CRD .... Cavedale Road [*California*] [*Seismograph station code, US Geological Survey*] (SEIS)
CRD .... Center for Resource Development in Adult Education [*University of Missouri - Kansas City*] [*Research center*] (RCD)
CRD .... Center for Responsive Design [*Defunct*] (EA)
CRD .... Central Records Depository
CRD .... Central Recruiting Division [*Military*]
CRD .... Central Registration Depository [*Investment term*]
CRD .... Central Repair Depot (NATG)
CRD .... Change Request Disposition (MCD)
CRD .... Chief of Research and Development [*Army*]
CRD .... Chronic Renal Disease [*Medicine*]
CRD .... Chronic Respiratory Disease [*Medicine*]
CRD .... Civil Rights Division [*Department of Justice*]
CRD .... Classified Restricted Data (DNAB)
CRD .... College Recruitment Database [*Executive Telecom System, Inc.*] [*Information service or system*] (CRD)
CRD .... Columbia River Datum

CRD	Committee on Reciprocal Deliveries [*Allied German Occupation Forces*]
CRD	Community Relations Director
CRD	Community Relations Division [*Environmental Protection Agency*] (GFGA)
CRD	Comodoro Rivadavia [*Argentina*] [*Airport symbol*] (OAG)
CRD	Complete Reaction of Degeneration [*Physiology*]
CRD	Complex Repetitive Discharge [*Neurophysiology*]
CRD	Computer-Readable Databases [*A publication*]
CRD	Confidential Restricted Data
CRD	Conrad, MT [*Location identifier FAA*] (FAAL)
CRD	Constant Ringing Drop [*Alarm system*]
CRD	Continuous Ream Discharge [*Papermaking*]
CRD	Controlled Release Device (KSC)
CRD	Controller of Research and Development [*Ministry of Aircraft Production*] [*British*]
CRD	Control Rod Drive [*or Driveline*] [*Nuclear energy*] (NRCH)
Crd	Cordierite [*A mineral*]
CRD	Coronado Resources, Inc. [*Vancouver Stock Exchange symbol*]
CRD	Corporate Research and Development
CRD	Cosmic Ray Detector [*NASA*]
CRD	Criminal Records Directorate [*Army*] (ADDR)
CRD	Critical Ratio of the Difference
CRD	Cross-Reacting Determinant [*Immunochemistry*]
CRD	Crown-Rump Distance [*Of fetus*] [*Medicine*] (DAVI)
crd	Crude (BARN)
CRD	Customs Rules Decisions [*A publication*] (DLA)
CRD	Cysteine-Rich Domain [*Genetics*]
CRD	Monsanto Chemical Co. [*Research code symbol*]
CRD	Southern California Rapid Transit District, Los Angeles, CA [*OCLC symbol*] (OCLC)
CRD	Tanabe Seiyaku Co. Ltd. [*Japan*] [*Research code symbol*]
CRDA	Canadian Resort Development [*Formerly, Canadian Resort & Recreational Development Association*] (AC)
CRDA	Candidates Reply Date Agreement [*Education*]
CRDA	Chief of Research, Development, and Acquisition [*Army*] (RDA)
CRDA	Control Rod Drive Assembly [*Nuclear energy*] (IEEE)
CRDA	Converging Runway Display Aid [*FAA*] (TAG)
CRDA	Cooperative Research and Development Agreement [*Department of Energy National Laboratories*]
CRD.A	Crawford&Co. Cl'A'non-vtg [*NYSE symbol*] (TTSB)
CrdAcp	Credit Acceptance Corp. [*Associated Press*] (SAG)
CRDB	Committee for Restoration of Democracy in Burma (EA)
CRDB	Computer-Readable Databases: a Directory and Data Sourcebook [*A publication*]
CRD.B	Crawford & Co. Cl'B' [*NYSE symbol*] (TTSB)
CRdb	Redondo Beach Public Library, Redondo Beach, CA [*Library symbol Library of Congress*] (LCLS)
CRdbT	TRW Systems Group, Redondo Beach, CA [*Library symbol Library of Congress*] (LCLS)
CRDC	Cardiac
CRDC	Centre de Reperage des Debouches du Canada [*Canada Business Opportunity Centre - CBOC*]
CRDC	Chemical Research and Development Center [*Aberdeen Proving Ground, MD*] [*Army*] (RDA)
CRDC	Climate Research Data Center [*Project*] [*Marine science*] (OSRA)
CRDC	Climate Research Data Center [*Project*] (USDC)
CRDC	Columbia Research and Development Corp. (MCD)
CRDCS	Contingency Rerouting of Communications [*NATO*] (NATG)
CRDCS	Control Rod Drive Control System [*Nuclear energy*] (NRCH)
CRDD	Control Rod Disconnect Driveline [*Nuclear energy*] (NRCH)
CrdDept	Credit Depot Corp. [*Associated Press*] (SAG)
CRDE	Centre de Recherche et Developpement en Economique (AC)
CRDE	Certified Rooms Division Executive [*Educational Institute of the American Hotel and Motel Association*] [*Designation awarded by*]
CRDEC	Center for Research and Documentation on the European Community [*American University*] [*Research center*]
CRDEC	Chemical Research, Development, and Engineering Center [*Aberdeen Proving Ground, MD*] [*Army*] (RDA)
CRDES	Chemical-Related Data Estimation Subroutines [*Environmental science*]
CRDF	Canadian Radio-Direction Finder (MCD)
CRDF	Cathode-Ray Direction Finder [*RADAR*]
CRDF	Civilian Research and Development Foundation [*An organization formed to retain former FSU scientists in civilian research*]
CRDF	Civilian Research and Development Foundation for the Independent States of the FSU [*former Soviet Union*]
CRDF	Colorado River Dam Fund [*Department of the Interior*] (GFGA)
CRDG	Curriculum Research and Development Group [*University of Hawaii*] [*Research center*] (RCD)
CRDGRPHC	Cardiographic
CRDH	Centre de Recherche en Developpement Humain [*Centre for Research in Human Development*] [*Concordia University*] [*Canada*] [*Research center*] (RCD)
CRDHS	Control Rod Drive Hydraulic System [*Nuclear energy*] (NRCH)
CR/DIR	Change Request Directive (MCD)
CRDL	Chemical Research and Development Laboratories [*Edgewood Arsenal, MD*] [*Army*]
CRDL	Collateral Recurring Document Listing [*Defense Intelligence Agency*] (DNAB)
CRDL	Contract Required Detection Limits
CRDL	Cradle (MSA)
CRDLGY	Cardiology
CRDM	Chief RADARman [*Navy rating Obsolete*]
CRDM	Control Rod Drive Mechanism [*Nuclear energy*] (GFGA)
CRDM	Control Rod Drive Motor [*Nuclear energy*] (IEEE)
CRDMS	Control Rod Drive Mechanism Shroud [*Nuclear energy*] (NRCH)
CRDN	Ceradyne, Inc. [*NASDAQ symbol*] (NQ)
CRDP	Centre de Recherche en Droit Public [*Center for Research in Public Law*] [*Canada*] (IRC)
CRDP	Computer Resources Development Plan [*NASA*] (NASA)
CRDR	Corridor [*Board on Geographic Names*]
CRDR/A	Control Room Design Review/Audit [*Nuclear energy*] (NRCH)
CRDS	Certified Reliability Data Shell [*Computer science*] (PDAA)
CRDS	Charles River Data Systems, Inc. (NITA)
CRDS	Chemical Reactions Documentation Service [*Derwent Publications Ltd.*] [*Bibliographic database*] (IID)
CRDS	Colgate-Rochester Divinity School [*Rochester, NY*]
CRDS	Component Repair Data Sheets (NG)
CRDS	Control Rod Drive System [*Nuclear energy*] (NRCH)
CRDS	Customer Requirements Data Set (SSD)
CRDSD	Current Research and Development in Scientific Documentation [*A publication*]
CRDT	Credit
CRDTools	Climate Research Data Tools [*Marine science*] (OSRA)
CRDtools	Climate Research Data Tools (USDC)
CRDU	Command Relay Driver Unit (MCD)
CRDVF	Control Rod Drive Ventilating Fan [*Nuclear energy*] (NRCH)
CRDVSCLR	Cardiovascular
CRDWA	Canal, River, and Dock Watchmen's Association [*A union*] [*British*]
CRE	Cadena Radial Ecuatoriana (EY)
CRE	CarrAmerica Realty [*NYSE symbol*] (TTSB)
CRE	Carr America Realty Corp. [*NYSE symbol*] (SAG)
CRE	Carr Realty Corp. [*NYSE symbol*] (SPSG)
CRE	Cation-Responsive Electrode
CRE	Cauchy-Riemann Equation [*Mathematics*]
CRE	Centrally Reportable Equipment (AAGC)
CRE	Central Reconnaissance Establishment [*British military*] (DMA)
CRE	Central Research Establishment [*Home Office Forensic Science Service*] [*British Information service or system*] (IID)
CRE	Chemical Reaction Engineering
CRE	Chief Radio Electrician [*Navy rating Obsolete*]
CRE	Coal Research Establishment [*British*] (IRUK)
CRE	Collection, Repair, Evacuation (MCD)
CRE	Combat Readiness Evaluation [*Army*]
CRE	Commander, Royal Engineers [*British*]
CRE	Command Receiver Equipment (KSC)
CRE	Commercial Relations and Exports (DS)
CRE	Commission for Racial Equality [*British*]
CRE	Communications Research Establishment (NATG)
CRE	Compton Recoil Electron
CRE	Conference Permanente des Recteurs, Presidents, et Vice Chanceliers des Universites Europeennes (EAIO)
CRE	Conference Permanente des Recteurs, Presidents et Vice Chancellors (AIE)
CRE	Conseil des Regions d'Europe [*Council of European Regions - CER*] (EAIO)
CRE	Conservation and Renewable Energy
CRE	Console Remote Equipment (MCD)
CRE	Consolidated Rail Corp. (Eastern District) [*AAR code*]
CRE	Controlled Residual Element [*Nuclear energy*]
CRE	Control of Recombination [*Genetics*]
CRE	Corrosion Resistant (AAG)
CRE	Cosmic Ray Exposure [*Geophysics*]
CRE	Council on Rehabilitation Education (EA)
CRE	Courtesy Return Envelope (NFD)
cre	Cree [*MARC language code Library of Congress*] (LCCP)
CRE	Cree Airways Corp. [*Canada ICAO designator*] (FAAC)
CRE	Creosote
CRE	Cross-Range Error
CRE	Cumulative Radiation Effect
CRE	Cyclic-AMP [*Adenosine Monophosphate*] Response Element [*Genetics*]
CRE	Cyclic-AMP [*Adenosine Monophosphate*]-Responsive Transcriptional Enhancer [*Genetics*]
CRE	North Myrtle Beach, SC [*Location identifier FAA*] (FAAL)
CREA	Canadian Real Estate Association
CREA	Centre for Regional Economic Analysis [*Australia*]
CREA	Certified Real Estate Appraiser [*National Association of Real Estate Appr aisers*] [*Designation awarded by*]
CREA	Chief Radio Electrical Artificer [*British military*] (DMA)
CREA	Congressional Reports Elimination Act
CREA	Conversion for Reclaiming Earth in the Americas [*An association*]
CREA	Creatinine [*Biochemistry*] (DAVI)
CREA	Creative Technology Ltd. [*NASDAQ symbol*] (SAG)
CreaCpt	Creative Computers, Inc. [*Associated Press*] (SAG)
CREAF	Creative Technology [*NASDAQ symbol*] (TTSB)
CREALR	Computerized Real Estate Assessment and Land Records (MCD)
CREAM	Combat Readiness Electromagnetic Analysis and Measurement (MCD)
CREAM	Computer Realtime Access Method (IAA)
CREAMS	Chemicals, Runoff, and Erosion from Agricultural Management Systems [*Agricultural Research Service*]
CREA-S	Creatinine Urine Spot [*Test*] [*Biochemistry*] (DAVI)
Creas Col Const	Creasy's Colonial Constitutions [*A publication*] (DLA)
Creas Eng Cons	Creasy's Rise and Progress of the English Constitution [*A publication*] (DLA)
Creas Int L	Creasy on International Law [*A publication*] (DLA)
Creasy	Creasy's Ceylon Reports [*A publication*] (DLA)
creat	Creatine [*Biochemistry*]

creat	Creatinine [*Biochemistry*]
CREAT	Creation
CreatC	Creative Computer Applications, Inc. [*Associated Press*] (SAG)
CREATE	Center for Research and Evaluation in Applications of Technology in Education [*Palo Alto, CA*]
CREATE	Center for Research on Educational Accountability and Teacher Evaluation [*Western Michigan University*] [*Research center*] (RCD)
CREATE	Computational Requirements for Engineering and Simulation, Training and Education [*Time-sharing computer complex*] [*Air Force*]
CREATION	Cultural and Recreational Education Achieved through Investigations Ordinarily Neglected [*University course*]
CreatLrn	Creative Learnings Products [*Associated Press*] (SAG)
CREATV	Creative
CREA-U	Creatinine Urine [*Test*] [*Biochemistry*] (DAVI)
CREB	Champion Parts [*NASDAQ symbol*] (TTSB)
CREB	Champion Parts Rebuilders, Inc. [*NASDAQ symbol*] (NQ)
CREB	Cyclic AMP [*Adenasine Monophosphate*] Responsive Element-Binding Protein [*Biochemistry*]
CREBs	Cyclic AMP [*Adenosine Monophosphate*] Response Element Binding Proteins [*Genetics*] (DOG)
CREC	Combat Readiness Evaluation Criteria [*Navy*] (NG)
CREC	COMSEC [*Communications Security*] Research and Engineering Coordinating Group [*Army*] (AABC)
CRECENT	Crescent [*Commonly used*] (OPSA)
CRECON	Counterreconnaissance [*Army*]
CRECORD	Congressional Record On-Line [*Capitol Services, Inc.*] [*Washington, DC Bibliographic database*]
CRED	Center for Research on Economic Development [*University of Michigan*] [*Research center*] (RCD)
CRED	Credit (AABC)
CRED	Crediton [*England*]
CRED	Credo Pete [*NASDAQ symbol*] (TTSB)
CRED	Credo Petroleum Corp. [*NASDAQ symbol*] (NQ)
CREDATA	Communications Resources Data System [*Defense Communications Agency*] (MCD)
CRED B	Creditors' Bill [*Legal term*] (DLA)
CRedCL	Shasta County Free Library, Redding, CA [*Library symbol Library of Congress*] (LCLS)
CREDD	Customer-Requested Earlier Due Date [*Business term*] (MHDB)
CRedE	Shasta County Office of Education, Redding, CA [*Library symbol*] [*Library of Congress*] (LCLS)
CRedGS	Church of Jesus Christ of Latter-Day Saints, Genealogical Society Library, Redding Branch, Redding, CA [*Library symbol Library of Congress*] (LCLS)
Credicp	Credicorp Ltd. [*Associated Press*] (SAG)
CREDIL	Comite Regional d'Education pour le Developpement International de la Region de Lanaudiere (AC)
CREDIT	Cost Reduction Early Decision Information Techniques [*Hughes Aircraft Co.*]
CREDITEL	Canadian Credit Management Association [*Formerly, Creditel of Canada Ltd.*]
CRedI	A. K. Smiley Public Library, Redlands, CA [*Library symbol Library of Congress*] (LCLS)
CRedIG	Grand Central Rocket Co., Redlands, CA [*Library symbol Library of Congress*] (LCLS)
CRedII	Inland Library System, Redlands, CA [*Library symbol Library of Congress*] (LCLS)
CRedIL	Latin American Bibliographic Foundation, Redlands, CA [*Library symbol*] [*Library of Congress*] (LCLS)
CRedIU	University of Redlands, Redlands, CA [*Library symbol Library of Congress*] (LCLS)
CREDO	Canadian Resources for Enterprise Development Organization (AC)
CREDO	Centralized Reliability Data Organization [*Nuclear Regulatory Commission*] (GFGA)
CREDO	Centre for Curriculum Renewal and Educational Development Overseas
CREDO	Chaplains' Relevance to the Emerging Drug Order [*Navy*]
CREDOC	Centre de Recherche Documentaire [*Documentary Research Center*] [*Information service or system*] (IID)
CredoPt	Credo Petroleum Corp. [*Associated Press*] (SAG)
CredSys	Credence Systems Corp. [*Associated Press*] (SAG)
CREE	Cree Research [*NASDAQ symbol*] (TTSB)
CREE	Cree Research, Inc. [*NASDAQ symbol*] (SAG)
CREEC	Consortium of Regional Environmental Education Councils
CREED	Christian Rescue Effort for the Emancipation of Dissidents [*Acronym now used as organization name*] (EA)
CREEJ	Center for Russian and East European Jewry (EA)
CREEK	Creek [*Commonly used*] (OPSA)
CReeK	Kings View Hospital, Reedley, CA [*Library symbol Library of Congress*] (LCLS)
CREEP	Committee to Re-Elect the President [*Also, CRP*] [*1972*]
CREEP	Committee to Resist the Efforts of the Ex-President [*Opposed Richard Nixon's visit to Oxford University, 1978*]
CREEP	Container, Restrainer, Environment, Energy Absorption, Post-Crash Failure [*Aviation*] (PDAA)
CreeRsh	Cree Research, Inc. [*Associated Press*] (SAG)
CREES	Center for Russian and East European Studies [*University of Michigan*] [*Research center*] (RCD)
CREES	Centre for Russian and East European Studies [*University of Birmingham*] [*British*] (CB)
CREES	Centre for Russian and East European Studies [*University of Toronto*] [*Canada*] (IRC)
CREET	Campaign to Re-Elect Mrs. [*Margaret*] Thatcher [*British Obsolete*]

CREF	Cardiothoracic Research and Education Foundation (EA)
CREF	Centre de Recherche sur l'Enseignement du Francais [*St. Anne University*] [*Canada Research center*] (RCD)
CREF	College Retirement Equities Fund [*New York, NY*] (EA)
CREF	Commingled Real Estate Funds (MHDW)
CREF	Cross Reference (AFM)
CREFAL	Centro Regional de Educacion de Adultos y Alfabetizacion Funcional para America Latina [*Regional Center for Adult Education and Functional Literacy for Latin America*] [*Mexico*] (EAIO)
CREFSA	Centre for Research Into Economics and Finance in South Africa [*London School of Economic and Political Science*] (ECON)
CREG	Cancer Research Emphasis Grants
CREG	Centre for Research and Education on Gender [*University of London*] [*British*] (AIE)
CREG	Concentrated Range Extension with Gain [*Telecommunications*] (TEL)
CREG	Controlled Reluctance Eddy Current Generator (PDAA)
CREG	Craig Consumer Electronics [*NASDAQ symbol*] (SAG)
CREG	Craig Consumers Electronics [*NASDAQ symbol*] (TTSB)
CREGO	Chief Regulating Officer [*Southwest Pacific Area, World War II*] [*Army*]
CREI	Capitol Radio Engineering Institute [*Now known only by initialism*]
Creighton U	[*The*] Creighton University (GAGS)
CREIPAC	Centre de Rencontres et d'Echanges Internationaux du Pacifique [*Center of International Cultural and Linguistic Exchanges in the Pacific*] [*Noumea, New Caledonia*] (EAIO)
CREL	Chief Radio Electrician [*British military*] (DMA)
CREL	Cold Regions Engineering Laboratory
CRELIQ	Centre de Recherche en Litterature Quebecoise [*Universite Laval, Quebec*] [*Canada*]
CREM	Cremate [*or Crematorium*] (DSUE)
CREM	Cyclic-Adenosine Monophosphate-Responsive Element Modulator [*Genetics*]
CREM	Cyclic AMP [*Adenosine Monophosphate*] Responsive Element Modulator [*Genetics*]
CREME	Commander, Royal Electrical and Mechanical Engineers [*Military British*]
CREMN	Chief Radio Electrical Mechanician [*British military*] (DMA)
CREN	Corporate Renaissance Group [*NASDAQ symbol*] (TTSB)
CREN	Corporate Renaissance Group, Inc. [*NASDAQ symbol*] (SAG)
CREN	Corporation for Research and Educational Networking [*Internet*]
CREN	Crenated [*Red blood cells*] [*Hematology*] (DAVI)
CREN	Crendon [*England*]
CRENA%	Percent of Crenated Red Blood Cells on Differential Count [*Hematology*] (DAVI)
CREN/BITNET	Corporation for Research and Educational Networking [*Computer science*] (TNIG)
CREO	Career Reenlistment Objectives [*Navy*]
CREO	Central Real Estate Office [*Military*]
CREO	Conservation and Renewable Energy Office [*Canada*]
CREO	Counter-Racism, Equal Opportunity [*Military*] (NVT)
CREOG	Council on Resident Education in Obstetrics and Gynecology (EA)
CREOL	Center for Research in Electro-Optics and Lasers [*University of Central Florida*] [*Research center*] (RCD)
CREP	Crepitus [*Crepitation*] [*Medicine*]
CREPE	Cosmic Ray Emulsion Plastic Equipment [*NASA*] (MCD)
CrePrg	Creative Programing & Technology [*Associated Press*] (SAG)
CREPUQ	Conference des Recteurs et des Principaux des Universites du Quebec
CREPUQ	Conference des Recteurs et des Principaux des Universites du Quebec [*Conference of Rectors & Principals of Quebec Universities*] (AC)
CRER	Centre for Research in Ethnic Relations [*University of Warwick*] [*British*] (CB)
CRES	Center for Research in Engineering Science [*University of Kansas*]
CRES	Centre for Resource and Environmental Studies
CRES	Command Readiness Exercise System [*Air Force*] (GFGA)
CRES	Computer Readability Editing System (MCD)
CRES	Condominium Research and Education Society
CRES	Conservation Reporting and Evaluation System [*Department of Agriculture*]
CRES	Constant Ratio Elasticity of Substitution (PDAA)
CRES	Corrosion Resistant (MCD)
CRES	Corrosion-Resistant Steel [*Manufacturing*]
CRES	Crescendo [*Music*]
CRES	Crescent (MCD)
CRES	Crescent [*Commonly used*] (OPSA)
CRES	Crescent
Cres	Crescent (DD)
Cres	Cressent [*A publication*] (BRI)
CRESALC	Centro Regional para la Educacion Superior en America Latina y el Caribe [*Regional Center for Higher Education in Latin America and the Caribbean-Venezuela*] [*United Nations*] (IID)
CRESC	Crescendo [*Music*]
cresc	Crescendo [*Music*] (ODBW)
CRESC	Crescent
CRESCENT	Crescent [*Commonly used*] (OPSA)
CRESENT	Crescent [*Commonly used*] (OPSA)
CRESH	Constant Ratios of Elasticities of Substitution-Homothetic [*Statistics*]
CRESM	Centre de Recherche et d'Etudes sur les Societes Mediterraneennes [*Center forResearch and Studies on Mediterranean Societies*] [*Information service or system*] (IID)
CRESO	Crescendo [*Music*]

CRESP .... Center for Religion, Ethics, and Social Policy [Cornell University] [Research center] (RCD)

CresRE .... Crescent Real Estate Equities [Associated Press] (SAG)

CRESS .... Center for Research in Social Systems [American University] (MCD)

CRESS .... Central Regulatory Electronic Stenographic System (NRCH)

CRESS .... Centre for Research in Experimental Space Science [York University] [Canada Research center] (RCD)

CRESS .... Claims Representative Exam for Social Security [Federal job exam]

CRESS .... Clearinghouse on Rural Education and Small Schools [ERIC]

CRESS .... Combined Reentry Effort in Small Systems

CRESS .... Computerized Reader Enquiry Service System (IEEE)

CRESS .... Computer Reader Enquiry Service System [Automated library system] (NITA)

Cress .... Cresswell's Insolvency Cases [1827-29] [England] [A publication] (DLA)

CRESS/AU .... Center for Research in Social Systems of the American University (IEEE)

Cress Ins Ca ... Cresswell's Insolvency Cases [1827-29] [England] [A publication] (ILCA)

Cress Ins Cas ... Cresswell's Insolvency Cases [1827-29] [England] [A publication] (DLA)

Cress Insolv Cas ... Cresswell's Insolvency Cases [1827-29] [England] [A publication] (DLA)

CRESST .... Center for Research on Evaluation, Standards, and Student Testing [Los Angeles, CA] [Department of Education] (GRD)

CRESST .... Cryogenic Rare Event Search with Superconducting Thermometers [Astrophysics]

Cres sub Pond Virt ... Crescit sub Pondere Virtus [Virtue Increases under a Burden] [Latin]

CREST .... Calcinosis, Raynaud's Phenomenon, Esophageal Dysfunction, Sclerodactyly, and Telangiectasia [A medical syndrome]

CREST .... Calcinosis, Raynaud's Phenomenon, Esophageal Dysmotility [or Dysfunction],Sclerodactyly, and Telangiectasia [Syndrome] [Rheumatology] (DAVI)

CREST .... Center for Cold Regions Engineering, Science, and Technology [State University of New York at Buffalo] [Research center] (RCD)

CREST .... Combat Readiness by Electronic Service Testing [Army] (AABC)

CREST .... Combat Reporting System [Air Force] (MCD)

CREST .... Committee on Reactor Safety Technology

CREST .... Committee on Rural Economic and Social Trends

CREST .... Computer Routine for Evaluation of Submarine Threats (MCD)

CREST .... Consolidated Reporting and Evaluating System, Tactical [Computer program] [Air Force]

CREST .... Core Research for Evolutional Science and Technology [Japan]

CREST .... Crest [Commonly used] (OPSA)

CREST .... Crew Escape Technologies [Air Force]

CREST .... Crewstation Evaluation Facility [Warminster, PA] [Naval Air Development Center] (GRD)

CREST .... Criterion-Referenced English Syntax Test (EDAC)

CREST .... Crown Estate Commissioner [British]

CreStaff ...... CoreStaff, Inc. [Associated Press] (SAG)

Crestar .... Crestar Financial Corp. [Associated Press] (SAG)

CRESTS ...... Courtauld's Rapid Extract, Sort, and Tabulate System (IEEE)

CRET .... Cathode-Ray Electron Tube

CRET .... Commission Regionale Europeenne du Tourisme

CRET .... Cretaceous [Geology]

CRETC .... Combined Radiation Effects Test Chamber (OA)

CreTch .... Creative Technologies Corp. [Associated Press] (SAG)

CreTcLtd ...... Creative Technology Ltd. [Associated Press] (SAG)

CRETE .... Common Radio and Electronic Test Equipment [Navy British] (DEN)

CRET PP ...... Creta Praeparata [Prepared Chalk] [Pharmacy] (ROG)

CREVO .... Creation-Evolution

CREVS .... Control Room Emergency Ventilation System (IEEE)

CREW .... Center for Reproduction of Endangered Wildlife [Research center] (RCD)

CREW .... Centre for Research in Education and Work [Macquarie University] [Australia]

CREW .... Centre for Research on European Women [Belgium] (EAIO)

CREWTAF ..... Crew Training Air Force

CRF .... Calendar Reform Foundation [Defunct] (EA)

CRF .... Capacitor Resonance Frequency

CRF .... Capital Recovery Factor

CRF .... Career Recruiter Force (DNAB)

CRF .... Carnot [Central African Republic] [Airport symbol] (AD)

CRF .... Carrier Frequency Telephone Repeater [Telecommunications]

CRF .... Cathode-Ray Furnace

CRF .... Cave Research Foundation (EA)

CRF .... Central Repair Facility (MCD)

CRF .... Central Retransmission Facility (IAA)

CRF .... Change Request Forms

CRF .... Christian Revival Fellowship [Australia]

CRF .... Christian Rural Fellowship [Defunct] (EA)

CRF .... Chromatofocusing [Analytical biochemistry]

CRF .... Chromatographic Response Factor

CRF .... Chronic Renal Failure [Medicine]

CRF .... Chronic Respiratory Failure [Medicine] (DAVI)

CRF .... Citizens' Research Foundation (EA)

CRF .... Citrovorum Rescue Factor [Medicine] (MEDA)

CRF .... City Reference File [Bureau of the Census] (GFGA)

CRF .... Classical Receptive Field [Biochemistry]

CRF .... Clean Report of Findings [Societe Generale de Surveillance SA] (DS)

CRF .... Cloud Radiation Feedback [Marine science] (OSRA)

CRF .... Cloud Radiation Feedback (USDC)

CRF .... Cloud Radiative Forcing [Climatology]

CRF .... Coagulase-Reacting Factor [Biochemistry] (MAE)

CRF .... Coalition for Religious Freedom (EA)

CRF .... Combustion Research Facility [Department of Energy] [Livermore, CA]

CRF .... Comicorum Romanum Fragmenta [A publication] (OCD)

CRF .... Committee for Religious Freedom

CRF .... Community Residential Facility [For the handicapped]

CRF .... Complement Restriction Factors [Biochemistry]

CRF .... Composite Rear Fuselage

CRF .... Compressor Research Facility (IAA)

CRF .... Computer Dealers Forum [Acronym represents organization's former name] [Later, NCDF] (EA)

CRF .... Connection-Related Function [Telecommunications]

CRF .... Conservation and Research Foundation (EA)

CRF .... Constitutional Rights Foundation (EA)

CRF .... Contingency Relief Force [Military]

CRF .... Continuous Reinforcement [Psychometrics]

CRF .... Contrast Rendering Factor (PDAA)

CRF .... Control Relay Forward

CRF .... Corfu [Washington] [Seismograph station code, US Geological Survey] (SEIS)

CRF .... Correspondence Routing Form (NRCH)

CRF .... Corticotrophin-Releasing Factor [Also, CRH] [Endocrinology]

CRF .... Corticotropin Releasing Factor [Neurochemistry]

CRF .... Cosmic Ray Flux

CRF .... Credit Research Foundation [Lake Success, NY] (EA)

CRF .... Crimea Air [Ukraine] [FAA designator] (FAAC)

CRF .... Cross-Reference File

CRF .... Crown Forest Industries Ltd. [Toronto Stock Exchange symbol] [Vancouver Stock Exchange symbol]

CRF .... Cryptographic Repair Facilities

CRF .... Current Requisition File [DoD]

CRF .... Current Research File [NIOSH] [Database]

CRF .... Czech Republic Fund [NYSE symbol] (TTSB)

CRF .... [The] Czech Republic Fund, Inc. [NYSE symbol] (SAG)

CRFA .... Canadian Renewable Fuels Association (AC)

CRFA .... Canadian Restaurant & Foodservices Association [Association Canadienne des Restaurateurs et des Services Alimentaires] (AC)

CRFA .... Czechoslovak Rationalist Federation of America (EA)

CRFB .... Committee for a Responsible Federal Budget (EA)

CRFC .... Charlie Rich Fan Club (EA)

CRFC .... Cost-Reimbursement Facilities Contract (AAGC)

CRFCA .... Cliff Richard Fan Club of America (EA)

CRFDP .... Columbia River Fisheries Development Program

CR/FF .... Country Representative/Freight Forwarder (AAGC)

CRFG .... California Rare Fruit Growers (EA)

CRFI .... Custom Roll Forming Institute (EA)

CRFK .... Crandell Feline Kidney [Cytology]

CRFL .... Centre de Recherches Forestieres des Laurentides [Laurentian Forest Research Center] [Canada] (ARC)

CRF-LI .... Corticotropin-Releasing Factor-Like Immunoreactivity [Medicine]

CRFM .... Condenser-Radiator Fan Module [Automotive cooling systems]

CRFMD .... Center for Research in Faith and Moral Development (EA)

CRFNN .... Cassandra: Radical Feminist Nurses Network (EA)

CRFR .... Corticotropin-Releaseing Factor Receptor [Medicine] (DMAA)

CRFS .... Combined Reference Frequency System

CRFS .... Copper Reverbatory Furnace Slag (PDAA)

CRFS .... Crash-Resistant Fuel System (RDA)

CRFT .... Craft

CRFT .... Craftmade International, Inc. [NASDAQ symbol] (SAG)

CRFT .... Craftmade Intl. [NASDAQ symbol] (TTSB)

CRFT .... Crowfoot (MSA)

CRFTLA .... Centre Regional de Formation aux Techniques des Leves Aeriens [Regional Center for Training in Aerial Surveys - RECTAS] (EAIO)

Crftmde .... Craftmade International, Inc. [Associated Press] (SAG)

CRFUSAIC .... Central Records Facility, United States Army Intelligence Center

CRFW .... Catalyst Resources for Women [A database] [Bibliographic Retrieval Service] (NITA)

CRG .... Cardiorespirogram [Medicine] (DAVI)

CRG .... Cargo

CRG .... Carriage (MSA)

CRG .... Catalytic Rich Gas

CRG .... Cave Research Group of Great Britain (BI)

CRG .... Center for Responsive Governance (EA)

CRG .... Change Review Group [NASA] (GFGA)

CRG .... Chessminster Group Ltd. [Vancouver Stock Exchange symbol]

CRG .... Children's Record Guild [Record label]

CRG .... Children's Rights Group [Defunct] (EA)

CRG .... City-Link Airlines Ltd. [Nigeria] [ICAO designator] (FAAC)

CRG .... Classification Research Group [British]

CRG .... Coast Community College District, Orange Coast College, Costa Mesa, CA [OCLC symbol] (OCLC)

CRG .... Collaborative Research Group [Of scientific institute]

CRG .... Communications Relay Group (MCD)

CRG .... Computer Research Group, Inc. [Information service or system] (IID)

CRG .... Control Rate Gyro [Aerospace] (KSC)

CRG .... Correction and Rehabilitation Group [Air Force]

CRG .... Correspondence Review Group [NASA] (NASA)

CRG .... Cosmic Ray Gas

CRG .... Council for Responsible Genetics (EA)

CRG .... Council of Regional Groups [Association for Library Collections and Technical Services]

CRG	Counterfire Reference Grid (AABC)	CRI	Costa Rica [ANSI three-letter standard code] (CNC)
CRG	Craig Corp. [NYSE symbol] (SAG)	CRI	Craigmont Mines [Toronto Stock Exchange symbol Vancouver Stock Exchange symbol]
CRG	Creative Resources Guild (EA)	CRI	Cray Research, Inc.
CRG	Cross Grain [Technical drawings]	CRI	Crikey [An exclamation] [British] (DSUE)
CRG	Cryptologic Readiness Group [Military] (DOMA)	CRI	Crime
CRG	Jacksonville, FL [Location identifier FAA] (FAAL)	CRI	Crimean
CRGO	Competitive Research Grants Office [for federal research in agriculture]	CRI	Criterion [Theatre and restaurant at Piccadilly Circus] [London] (DSUE)
CRGP	Caseless Round Gun Program [Military] (MCD)	CRI	Criterion-Referenced Instruction
CRGPr	Craig Corp. CI'A' [NYSE symbol] (TTSB)	Cri	Crito [of Plato] [Classical studies] (OCD)
CRGR	Coalition for Responsible Genetic Research (HGAA)	CRI	Croce Rossa Italiana [Italian Red Cross]
CRGR	Committee to Review Generic Requirements [Nuclear Regulatory Commission]	CRI	Crooked Island [Bahamas] [Airport symbol] (OAG)
CRGR	Cragar Industries, Inc. [NASDAQ symbol] (SAG)	CRI	Cross-Reactive Idiotype [Genetics]
Crgrlnd	Cragar Industries, Inc. [Associated Press] (SAG)	CRI	Crown Research Institute [New Zealand]
CRGS	Chemical Regulations and Guidelines System [CRC Systems, Inc.] [Information service or system] (IID)	CRI	Cure Rate Index [Rubber technology]
		CRI	Cybernetics Research Institute
CRGT	Control Rod Guide Tube [Nuclear energy] (NRCH)	CRIA	Canadian Recording Industry Association
CRH	Calibre-Radius Head [of projectile] [British]	CRIA	Committee to Rescue Italian Art
CRH	Carson Hill [California] [Seismograph station code, US Geological Survey] (SEIS)	CRIA	Council on Religion and International Affairs [Later, CCEIA] (EA)
CRH	Casualty Receiving Hospital [British]	CRIAC	Centre de Recherches Industrielles en Afrique Centrale
CRH	Constant Rate of Heating	CRI & P	Chicago, Rock Island & Pacific Railroad Co. [Nickname: The Baby Road]
CRH	Control Relay Hand	CRIARL	Consortium of Rhode Island Academic and Research Libraries [Library network]
CRH	Coram Healthcare [NYSE symbol] (TTSB)		
CRH	Coram Healthcare Corp. [NYSE symbol] (SAG)	CRIAW	Canadian Research Institute for the Advancement of Women [Research center] (RCD)
CRH	Corticotrophin-Releasing Hormone [Also, CRF] [Endocrinology]	CRIB	Carolina Record of Individual Behavior (EDAC)
CRH	Council on Religion and the Homosexual [Defunct] (EA)	CRIB	Chemotherapy Research Bulletin
CRH	CRH PLC [Associated Press] (SAG)	CRIB	Computerized Resources Information Bank [United States Geological Survey] [Later, MRDS] (IID)
CRH	Critical Relative Humidity		
CRH	Rio Hondo Junior College Library, Whittier, CA [OCLC symbol] (OCLC)	CribCig	Caribbean Cigar Co. [Associated Press] (SAG)
		CRIBS	Charter, Rural, and Intercity Bus Survey [Bureau of the Census] (GFGA)
CRHA	Canadian Railroad Historical Association		
CRHA	Canadian Retail Hardware Association (PDAA)	CRIC	Canonici Regulares Immaculate Conceptionis [Canons Regular of the Immaculate Conception] [Roman Catholic men's religious order]
CRHA	Colorado Ranger Horse Association (EA)		
CRHC	Controlled-Release Hydrocodone [An analgesic] [Pennwalt Corp.]	CRIC	Canons Regular of the Immaculate Conception (TOCD)
CRHC	CRH, Ltd. [NASDAQ symbol] (NQ)	CRIC	Citizens Research and Investigative Committee [California]
CRHCY	CRH plc [NASDAQ symbol] (TTSB)	CRIC	Components Response Information Center (MCD)
CRHD	Council for Rural Housing and Development (EA)	CRIC	Cost Reimbursement Incentive Contracting [Government contracting]
CRHH	Cold-Rolled Half Hard [Metal]	CRic	Richmond Public Library, Richmond, CA [Library symbol Library of Congress] (LCLS)
CR-HI	Channel Request-High Priority (MHDB)		
CRHIFC	Carla Riggs-Hall International Fan Club (EA)	C Rica	Costa Rica (VRA)
CRHL	Collaborative Radiological Health Laboratory [Colorado State University] [Department of Health and Human Services Research center] (RCD)	CRICAP	Carpet and Rug Industry Consumer Action Panel [Defunct]
		CRicC	Chevron Research Co., Technical Information Center, Richmond, CA [Library symbol Library of Congress] (LCLS)
CRHS	Commonwealth Regional Health Secretariat (EA)	CRicCR	California Research Corp., Richmond, CA [Library symbol Library of Congress] (LCLS)
CRHS	Competent Reliability History Survey [Navy]		
CRHS	Construction Report, Housing Starts [A publication]	CRICISAM	Center for Research in College Instruction of Science and Mathematics (EA)
CRHSI	Center for Research in the Hospitality Service Industries (EA)	CRICKET	Cold Rocket Instrument Carrying Kit
CRHSWW	Committee for the Reexamination of the History of the Second World War (EA)	CRICO	Committee for the Revision of the Criminal Code [Allied German Occupation Forces]
CRI	Cambridge Reports, Inc. [Database producer] (IID)	CRICON	Crisis Confrontation
CRI	Canari Airlines [Israel] [ICAO designator] (FAAC)	CRicRM	Richmond Museum Association, Richmond, CA [Library symbol Library of Congress] (LCLS)
CRI	Canarsie, NY [Location identifier FAA] (FAAL)		
CRI	Carbohydrate Research Institute [Queen's University at Kingston] [Canada Research center] (RCD)	CRicS	Stauffer Chemical Co., Richmond, CA [Library symbol Library of Congress] (LCLS)
		CRID	Capital ROK [Republic of Korea] Infantry Division
CRI	Career Resources Information [JA Micropublishing, Inc.] [Information service or system] (IID)	CRID	Centro di Riferimento Italiano DIANE [Italian Reference Center for EURONET DIANE] [National Research Council] [Information service or system] (IID)
CRI	Caribbean Research Institute [College of the Virgin Islands]		
CRI	Caring Relationship Inventory [Psychology]	CRIDEV	Centre Rennais d'Information pour le Developpement et la Liberation des Peuples [France]
CRI	Carpet and Rug Institute (EA)		
CRI	Catheter-Related Infection [Medicine]	CRidGS	Church of Jesus Christ of Latter-Day-Saints, Genealogical Society Library, Ridgecrest [Library symbol] [Library of Congress] (LCLS)
CRI	Cell Research Institute [University of Texas at Austin] [Research center] (RCD)		
CRI	Cellulose Research Institute [Syracuse University]	CRIDP	Centre for Research in Industrial Democracy and Participation [University of Glasgow] [British] (CB)
CRI	CHAMPUS [Civilian Health and Medical Program of the Uniformed Services] Reform Initiative (GFGA)	CRIE	Cosmic Ray Isotope Experiment (MCD)
		CRIE	Crossed Radioimmunoelectrophoresis [Analytical biochemistry]
CRI	Change Routing Indicator (MCD)	CRIET	Comites Reunis de l'Industrie de l'Ennoblissement Textile dans le CE [EC] (ECED)
CRI	Chemical Rust-Inhibiting		
CRI	[The] Chicago River & Indiana Railway Co. [Absorbed into Consolidated Rail Corp.] [AAR code]	CRIF	Centre de Recherches Scientifiques et Techniques de l'Industrie des Fabrications Metalliques [Center for Scientific and Technical Research for the Metal Manufacturing Industry] [Information service or system] (IID)
CRI	Children in Residential Institutions Program [Australia]		
CRI	Children's Relief International [British] (BI)		
CRI	Children's Rights, Inc. [CFC] [Superseded by] (EA)	CRIF	Centre for Research in Finance [University of New South Wales] [Information service or system] (IID)
CRI	Christian Research Institute (EA)		
CRI	Christian Response International (EA)	CRIFC	Cheryl Roth International Fan Club (EA)
CRI	Circuit Reliability Improvement	CRIFO	Civilian Research, Interplanetary Flying Objects
CRI	Classroom Reading Inventory (EDAC)	CRIG	Capacitor Rate-Integrating Gyroscope
CRI	Code Relations Index	Criimi	Criimi Mae, Inc. [Associated Press] (SAG)
CRI	Cold Running Intelligibility [Test for hearing continuous speech] (BABM)	CriimiMa	Criimi Mae, Inc. [Associated Press] (SAG)
		CRIL	Consolidated Repairable Item List
CRI	Color Rendition [or Rendering] Index [Measure of Color distortion]	CRILA	Credit Insurance Logistics Automated (PDAA)
CRI	Color Reversal Intermediate [Photography] (NTCM)	CRI Liq	CRI Liquidating Real Estate Investment Trust [Associated Press] (SAG)
CRI	Commission on Research Integrity [Congressional group]		
CRI	Committee for Reciprocity Information [A federal government body]	Crim	Arret de la Chambre Criminelle de la Cour de Cassation [Decision of the Court of Appeal, Criminal Division] [French] (ILCA)
CRI	Communications Research Institute (MCD)		
CRI	Complex Refraction Index	CRIM	Center for Research in Integrated Manufacturing [University of Michigan] [Research center] (RCD)
CRI	Composer Recordings, Inc. [Recording label]		
CRI	Concentrated Rust-Inhibiting [or Inhibitor] [Chemistry]	CRIM	Clinical Research Institute of Montreal [University of Montreal] [Research center] (RCD)
CRI	Conflict Resolution Inventory [Psychology]		
CRI	Constant Rate Injector [Instrumentation]	CRIM	Comite Regional Intersyndical de Montreal [Montreal Regional Inter-Trade Union Committee] [Canada]
CRI	Control Room Isolation [Nuclear energy] (NRCH)		
CRI	Co-Payment Requirement Rider [Health insurance] (GHCT)		
CRI	Core Indus [NYSE symbol] (TTSB)		
CRI	Core Industries, Inc. [NYSE symbol] (SPSG)		

CRIM .... Component Record Intensive Management
CRIM .... Component Requiring Intensive Management
CRIM .... Criminal (AFM)
CRIM .... Criminologist (WDAA)
CRIM .... Crimson (ROG)
Crim App .... Court of Criminal Appeals [England] (DLA)
Crim App .... Criminal Appeal Reports [England] [A publication] (DLA)
Crim App (Eng)... Criminal Appeal Reports [England] [A publication] (DLA)
Crim App R... Criminal Appeal Reports [England] [A publication] (DLA)
Crim App Rep... Cohen's Criminal Appeals Reports [England] [A publication] (DLA)
Crim Case & Com... Criminal Case and Comment [A publication] (DLA)
Crim Code ... Criminal Code [A publication] (DLA)
CRIM CON ... Criminal Conversation [Adultery] [Slang] (DSUE)
CRIME .... Censorship Records and Information Middle East [Military]
CRIME .... Controlled Response in Maitland Emergencies
Crime & Del... Crime and Delinquency [A publication] (DLA)
Crime & Delin'cy Abst... Crime and Delinquency Abstracts [A publication] (DLA)
Crime & Delin'cy Lit... Crime and Delinquency Literature [A publication] (DLA)
Criminal L Mag & Rep... Criminal Law Magazine and Reporter [A publication] (DLA)
Crim Inj Comp Bd... Criminal Injuries Compensation Board [British] (DLA)
Criminol ..... Criminologica [A publication] (DLA)
Criminol ..... Criminologie [Criminology] [French] (DLA)
Criminol ..... Criminologist (DLA)
CRIMINOL.... Criminology (ADA)
Crim J & B... Criminal Justice and Behavior [A publication] (BRI)
Crim JJ .... Criminal Justice Journal [A publication] (DLA)
Crim Just Q... Criminal Justice Quarterly [A publication] (DLA)
Crim Just Rev... Criminal Justice Review [A publication] (DLA)
CRIML .... Criminal (ROG)
Crim Law..... Criminal Law (DLA)
Crim Law J... Criminal Law Journal [A publication]
Crim Law Reps (Green)... Criminal Law Reports, by Green [United States] [A publication]
Crim L Mag... Criminal Law Magazine [A publication] (DLA)
CRIM LR ..... Criminal Law Reports [A publication]
Crim L Rec... Criminal Law Recorder [A publication] (DLA)
CRIMP .... Composite Resin Infusion Molding Process
CRIMP .... Computer Report on Importance (PDAA)
CRIMP .... Consolidated RVNAF [Republic of Vietnam Armed Forces] Improvement and Modernization Program (AABC)
CRIMP .... Crisis Management Plan (MCD)
Crim Pro ..... Criminal Procedure [Legal term] (DLA)
Crim Proc .... Criminal Procedure [Legal term] (DLA)
Crim Rec .... Criminal Recorder [A publication] (DLA)
CRIMREP .... Crisis Management Information Report
CRIMS .... Chemical Reaction Interface Mass Spectrometry
CRINC .... University of Kansas Center for Research, Inc. [Research center] (RCD)
CRIO .... COMSEC [Communications Security] Regional Issuing Office [or Officer] [Army] (AABC)
CRIP .... Combined Reconnaissance and Intelligence Platoon [Military] (VNW)
CRIP .... Controlled Retracting Injection Port [System for underground coal burning]
CRIP .... Cysteine-Rich Intestinal Protein [Medicine] (DMAA)
CRIP .... International Center for Research on Language Planning (AC)
CRIPA .... Civil Rights of Institutionalized Persons Act of 1980 (EDAC)
CRIPL .... Consolidated Remain-in-Place List
Cripp Ch Cas... Cripp's Church and Clergy Cases [1847-50] [England] [A publication] (DLA)
Cripp Ch L... Cripp's Law Relating to Church and Clergy [8th ed.] [1937] [A publication] (DLA)
Cripp Comp... Cripp's Compulsory Acquisition of Land [11th ed.] [1962] [A publication] (DLA)
Cripps.......... Cripp's Church and Clergy Cases [1847-50] [England] [A publication] (DLA)
Cripps Cas... Cripp's Church and Clergy Cases [1847-50] [England] [A publication] (DLA)
Cripp's Ch Cas... Cripp's Church and Clergy Cases [1847-50] [England] [A publication] (DLA)
Cripps Church Cas... Cripp's Church and Clergy Cases [1847-50] [England] [A publication] (DLA)
CRIPS .... Church Research and Information Projects
CRIPT .... Curriculum Review Integrated Product Team [Army]
CRIQ .... Centre de Recherche Industrielle du Quebec [Industrial Research Center of Quebec] [Information service or system] (IID)
CRIR .... Code of Rhode Island Rules [A publication] (AAGC)
CRIS .... Calibration Recall Information Systems (KSC)
CRIS .... Carrier Route Information System [Postal Service] [United States] (WDMC)
CRIS .... Centro Ricerche Interdisciplinari sul Suicidio [Interdisciplinary Research Center on Suicide] [Italy] (EAIO)
CRIS .... Coalition for Retirement Income Security (EA)
CRIS .... Coastal RADAR Integration System (MCD)
CRIS .... Collectif de Recherche et d'Information Sociales [Collective of Research and Social Information] [Canada]
CRIS .... Combined Retrospective Index Sets [Information service or system] (IID)
CRIS .... Command Retrieval Information System
CRI's.......... Community Research Initiatives [Community-based AIDS treatment organizations]
CRIS .... Community Resources Information Service, Inc. [Information service or system] (IID)
CRIS .... Compliance Review Information System [Office of Federal Contract Compliance] (GFGA)

CRIS .... Comprehensive Research Injury Scale (PDAA)
CRIS .... Computerized Recall Identification System [Automobile industry]
CRIS .... Computerized Research Information Service [Colorado School of Mines] (OLDSS)
CRIS .... Concentric Research Information Service (IID)
CRIS .... Control Risks Information Services [British Information service or system] (IID)
CRIS .... Corporate Research Information Service [Frederick Research]
CRIS .... Council for Religion in Independent Schools (EA)
CRIS .... Counterintelligence Records Information System [Army]
CRIS .... Crime Report Information System [Metropolitan Police database] [British]
CRIS .... Crime Reporting Information System [British] (NITA)
CRIS .... Current Research Information System [Department of Agriculture Information service or system]
CRIS .... Curriculum and Resource Information Service (AIE)
CRISC .... Complex Reduced-Instruction-Set Architecture [Intel Corp.]
CRISCI........ Center for Research in Innovative Services for the Communicatively Impaired [Memphis State University] [Research center] (RCD)
CRISCI........ Center for Research Initiatives and Strategies for the Communicatively Impaired [Memphis State University] [Research center] (RCD)
CRISCO....... Cream Received in Separating Cottonseed Oil
CRISCON .... Crisis Condition (MCD)
CRISD .... Computer Resources Integrated Support Data (MCD)
CRISD .... Computer Resources Integrated Support Document [Military]
CRISL .... Contract Repair Initial Support List (AFIT)
CRISP .... Center for Research on Industrial Strategy and Policy [Illinois Institute of Technology] [Research center] (RCD)
CRISP .... Child's Report of the Impact of Separation by Parents (EDAC)
CRISP .... Computer Resources Integrated Support Plan [Military] (AFIT)
CRISP .... Computer Retrieval of Information on Scientific Projects [National Institutes of Health Information service or system] (IID)
CRISP .... Control Restrictive Instruction for Structural Programming (MCD)
CRISP .... Cosmic Ray Ionization Program [NASA]
CRISP .... Creep Isostatic Pressing
CRISPE .... Computerised Retrieval Information Service on Precision Engineering [Cranfield Institute of Technology] [A database] [British] (NITA)
CRISS .... Center for Research in Surface Science and Submicron Analysis [Montana State University] [Research center] (RCD)
CRISTAL ...... Contract Regarding an Interim Supplement to Tanker Liability for Oil Pollution [Oil industry]
CristChile .... Cristalerias de Chile SA [Associated Press] (SAG)
CristChle .... Cristalerias de Chile SA [Associated Press] (SAG)
CRISTIG....... Chemically Recuperated Intercooled Steam-Injected Gas Turbine
CRIT............ Community Research Initiative of Toronto [Initiative de Recherche Communautaire de Toronto] (AC)
CRIT............ Criterion (AABC)
CRIT............ Critical [Telecommunications] (TEL)
CRIT............ Criticism
crit............. Hematocrit [Hematology] (DAVI)
Critch.......... Critchfield's Reports [5-21 Ohio State] [A publication] (DLA)
Critch (Ohio St)... Critchfield's Reports [5-21 Ohio State] [A publication] (DLA)
CRITCOM..... Critical Communications System [Military] (AABC)
CRITE .... Committee for Research into Teacher Education (AIE)
CRITF.......... Critical Frequency (MSA)
CRITHOUSA.. Critical Housing Shortage At [named place] [Army]
Criti .... Critias [of Plato] [Classical studies] (OCD)
CRITIC .... Critical Intelligence Report (CINC)
CRITICOM.... Critical Intelligence Communications System [DIN/DSSCS]
CRITICOMM.. Critical Intelligence Communication
Criticre .... Criticare Systems, Inc. [Associated Press] (SAG)
Critiq .... Critique [A publication] (BRI)
Critm .... Criticism [A publication] (BRI)
Crit Q .... Critical Quarterly [A publication] (BRI)
Crit R......... Critical Review [A publication] (BRI)
CRITTER ...... Civil Rotorcraft IFR [Instrument Flight Rules] Terminal-Area Technology Enhancement Research (GAVI)
CRiv.......... Riverside Public Library and Riverside County Free Library, Riverside, CA [Library symbol Library of Congress] (LCLS)
CRivGS .... Church of Jesus Christ of Latter-Day Saints, Genealogical Society Library, Riverside Branch, Riverside, CA [Library symbol Library of Congress] (LCLS)
CRivGS-W.... Church of Jesus Christ of Latter-Day Saints, Genealogical Society Library, Riverside West Branch, Riverside, CA [Library symbol Library of Congress] (LCLS)
CRivL.......... Loma Linda University, Riverside Campus, Riverside, CA [Library symbol Library of Congress] (LCLS)
CRivLM........ United States Bureau of Land Management, California Desert District, Riverside District Office, Riverside, CA [Library symbol] [Library of Congress] (LCLS)
CRIWG........ Central Region Interface Working Group [NATO] (NATG)
CRJ............. Canadair Regional Jet
CRJ............. Cargojet [Formerly, Yugoslav Republic] [FAA designator] (FAAC)
CRJ............. Cash Receipts Journal [Accounting]
CRJ............. Claude Resources, Inc. [Toronto Stock Exchange symbol]
CRJ............. Commission for Racial Justice (EA)
CRJBS .... Community of Reparation to Jesus in the Blessed Sacrament [Anglican religious community]
CRJE .... Conversational Remote Job Entry [Computer science]
CRJO .... Centre de Readaptation le Jeunes de l'Outaouais (AC)
CRJO .... Commission on Reform Jewish Outreach (EA)
CRJO .... Cost Reduction Journal
CRJP.......... Center for Research on Judgment and Policy [University of Colorado - Boulder] [Research center] (RCD)

CRJWA ...... Council of Religious Jewish Workers of America [Defunct] (EA)
CRK .... Air Pacific Crake [Philippines] [ICAO designator] (FAAC)
CRK .... Circle K Corp. [NYSE symbol] (SAG)
CRK .... Clean Room Kit
CRK .... Comstock Resources [NYSE symbol] (SAG)
CRK .... Cork
CRK .... Crank (KSC)
CRK .... Crankcase
CRK .... Creek (MCD)
CRK .... Creek
CRKC .... Crankcase (KSC)
CrkrBrl .... Cracker Barrel Old Country Store, Inc. [Associated Press] (SAG)
CRKSFT ...... Crankshaft
CRKSHV ..... Cranksheave (MSA)
CRKT .... CPG Rocket Selection (MCD)
CRL .... Cadmium Red Line
CRL .... Calibration Requirements List (MCD)
CRL .... Cambridge Research Laboratory
CRL .... Candida Rugosa Lipase [An enzyme]
CRL .... Canonici Regulares Lateranenses [Canons Regular of the Lateran]
CRL .... Canons Regular of the Lateran (TOCD)
crl .... Canons Regular of the Lateran (TOCD)
CRL .... Capital Realty Investment Tax Exempt Fund Ltd. [AMEX symbol] (SPSG)
CRL .... Cap Rlty Inv TaxExFdLP III [AMEX symbol] (TTSB)
CRL .... Carleton, MI [Location identifier FAA] (FAAL)
CRL .... Carloforte [Sardinia] [Seismograph station code, US Geological Survey Closed] (SEIS)
CRL .... Cathode-Ray Lamp
CRL .... Cellular Radio Ltd. [British] (NITA)
CRL .... Center for Research Libraries [Library network] (EA)
CRL .... Center for Research Libraries, Chicago, IL [Inactive] [OCLC symbol] (OCLC)
CRL .... Central Reference Library [British] (DIT)
CRL .... Central Regional Laboratory [Environmental Protection Agency] (GFGA)
CRL .... Centre for Research in Librarianship [University of Toronto] [Research center] (RCD)
CRL .... Cereal Rust Laboratory [Department of Agriculture] (GRD)
CRL .... Certificate Revocation List (ACRL)
CRL .... Certified Record Librarian
CRL .... Certified Reference Librarian (BARN)
CRL .... Cerulein [Biochemistry]
CRL .... Choctawhatchee Regional Library [Library network]
CRL .... Cholera Research Laboratory [Bangladesh]
CRL .... Clonal Apple Rootstock Liner
CRL .... College & Research Libraries [A publication] (BRI)
CRL .... Communications Research Laboratories [Information service or system] (IID)
CRL .... Communications Research Laboratory [McMaster University] [Canada Research center] (RCD)
CRL .... Complement Receptor Lymphocyte [Immunology]
CRL .... Compound Refractive Lens [Optics]
CRL .... Computing Research Laboratory [New Mexico State University] [Research center] (RCD)
CRL .... Control Record Listing [IRS]
CRL .... Control Relay Latch
CRL .... Copper Refineries Ltd. [Australia]
Crl. .... Coral [Record label] [USA, Europe]
CRL .... Cornell University Research Laboratory
CRL .... Corse Air International [France ICAO designator] (FAAC)
CRL .... Crain, Inc. [Toronto Stock Exchange symbol]
CRL .... Crew Research Laboratory [Randolph Air Force Base, TX]
Cr L .... Criminal Lawyer [India] [A publication] (DLA)
CRL .... Cross Reference Listing
CRL .... Crown-Rump Length [of fetus] [Medicine]
CRL .... Customer Requirements List (MCD)
CRLA .... California Rural Legal Assistance (BARN)
CRLA .... Canadian Railway Labour Association
CRLA .... Crater Lake National Park
CRLAS .... Cavity Ringdown LASER Absorption Spectroscopy
Cr Law Mag.. Criminal Law Magazine [A publication] (DLA)
Cr Law Rec... Criminal Law Recorder [A publication] (DLA)
CRLB .... Core Laboratories NV [NASDAQ symbol] (SAG)
CRLB .... Cosmic Ray Logic Box (IAA)
CRLBF .... Core Laboratories N.V. [NASDAQ symbol] (TTSB)
crlc .... Cannons Regular of the Immaculate Conception (TOCD)
CRLC .... Capitol Region Library Council [Library network]
CRLC .... Central Reserve Life [NASDAQ symbol] (SAG)
CRLC .... Chicana Research and Learning Center (EA)
CRLC .... Circulate (FAAC)
CRLCMP ..... Computer Resources Life-Cycle Management Plan
CRLDD .... Cornell University Research Laboratory for Diseases of Dogs
CRLDNG ..... Carloading
CRLE .... Center for Respect of Life and Environment (GNE)
CRLEA .... Canadian Railway Labour Executives' Association
CR/LF......... Carriage Return/Line Feed [Computer science]
CRLG .... Carlyle Golf, Inc. [NASDAQ symbol] (SAG)
CRLGW ...... Carlyle Golf Wrrt [NASDAQ symbol] (TTSB)
CRLI .... Circuit Research Laboratories, Inc. [NASDAQ symbol] (NQ)
CRLI .... Circuit Resh Labs [NASDAQ symbol] (TTSB)
CRLIND........ Civil Rail Lines Important to National Defense [BTS] (TAG)
CRLL .... Conclusions, Recommendations, and Lessons Learned
CRLLB .... Center for Research on Language and Language Behavior [University of Michigan]

Cr L Mag .... Criminal Law Magazine [A publication] (DLA)
CR-LO......... Channel Request-Low Priority (MHDB)
CRLP .... Center for Reproductive Law and Policy (EA)
CRLR .... Chemical and Radiological Laboratories [Army]
CRLR .... Civil Rights and Law Reform [Australia]
CRLS .... Chronic Reactive Lymphadenopathy Syndrome [Medicine]
CRLS .... Coast Guard Radio Liaison Station
CRLT.......... Center for Research on Learning and Teaching [University of Michigan] [Research center] (RCD)
CRLT.......... Central Research Laboratory of Tashiba
CRLV .... Cherry Rasp Leaf Virus [Plant pathology]
CrlyGl .... Carlyle Golf, Inc. [Associated Press] (SAG)
CrlyleGlf ..... Carlyle Golf, Inc. [Associated Press] (SAG)
CRM............ Adorno Fathers (TOCD)
crm............. Adorno Fathers (TOCD)
CRM............ Camera-Ready Mechanical
CRM............ Canadian Risk Manager (DD)
CRM............ Cash by Return Mail [Business term]
CRM............ Catarman [Philippines] [Airport symbol] (OAG)
CRM............ Cause-Related Marketing [Finance]
CRM............ Centre de Reflexion sur le Monde Non Occidental [Center for the Study of the Non-Occidental World] (EA)
CRM............ Certified Raw Milk (MEDA)
CRM............ Certified Records Manager [Institute of Certified Records Managers] [Designation awarded by] (MCD)
CRM............ Certified Reference Materials
CRM............ Change Request Material (AAG)
CRM............ Chemical Release Module (MCD)
CRM............ Chemical Remanent Magnetization [Geophysics]
CRM............ Chief Radioman [Navy rating Obsolete]
CRM............ Christian Renewal Ministry (EA)
CRM............ Chrome (MSA)
CRM............ Cisco Router Module [Cisco Systems, Inc.] [Computer science]
CRM............ Citizens' Rights Movement [Israel] [Political party] (ECON)
CRM............ Clerici Regulares Minores [Clerics Regular Minor] [Adorno Fathers] [Roman Catholic religious order]
CRM............ Clinch River Mile [Energy Research and Development Administration]
CRM............ Cloud-Croft Radiation Measurement
CRM............ Cockpit Resource Management (MCD)
CRM............ Collision Risk Model [Aviation] (DA)
CRM............ Combat Readiness Medal [Military decoration] (AFM)
CRM............ Comet Rendezvous Mission
CRM............ Commander Mexicana SA de CV [Mexico ICAO designator] (FAAC)
CRM............ Command Receiver Monitor (AAG)
CRM............ Communications/Research/Machines, Inc. [Publisher]
CRM............ Computer Resource Management [Army] (IAA)
CRM............ Conceptual Reference Mission [NASA]
CRM............ Confusion Reflector Material
CRM............ Conseil de Recherches Medicales [Medical Research Council] [Canada]
CRM............ Consolidated Rexspar Minerals & Chemicals Ltd. [Toronto Stock Exchange symbol]
CRM............ Construction Risk Management [International Risk Management Institute] [A publication]
CRM............ Containment Radiation Monitor [Nuclear energy] (IEEE)
CRM............ Control and Reproducibility Monitor (IEEE)
CRM............ Control Relay Master
CRM............ Control Rod Mechanism [Nuclear energy] (NUCP)
CRM............ Coordinacion Revolucionaria de las Masas [Revolutionary Coordination of the Masses] [El Salvador] (PD)
CRM............ Core Restraint Mechanism [Nuclear energy] (NRCH)
CRM............ Corimon ADS [NYSE symbol] (TTSB)
CRM............ Corimon CA [NYSE symbol] (SPSG)
CRM............ CounterRADAR Measures
CRM............ CounterRADAR Missile
CRM............ Count Rate Meter
CRM............ Cream (ADA)
CRM............ Cream
CR/M............ Crew Member
CRM............ Crew Research Management (GAVI)
CRM............ Crew Resource Management [FAA] (TAG)
CRM............ Criterion-Referenced Measurement [Education]
CRM............ Cross-Reacting Material [Immunology]
CRM............ Cruise Missile (BARN)
CRM............ Cultural Resource Management [Archaeology]
CRM............ Curriculum Resource Materials
CRM............ Customer Relations Manager (DCTA)
CRM............ Cyber Record Manager [Computer science]
CRMA .... Centre de Recherche de Mathematiques Appliquees [University of Montreal] [Research center] (RCD)
CRMA .... City and Regional Magazine Association (EA)
CRMA .... Commercial Refrigerator Manufacturers Association (EA)
CRMA .... Cotton and Rayon Merchants Association [British] (BI)
Cr M & R.... Crompton, Meeson, and Roscoe's English Exchequer Reports [1834-36] [A publication] (DLA)
CRMB .... Combined Raw Materials Board [US and Britain] [World War II]
CRM/BAM ... CYBER Record Manager Basic Access Method [Computer science] (NITA)
CRMC .... Center for Research for Mothers and Children [National Institutes of Health] (GRD)
CRMC .... Ceramic
CRMC .... Certified Radio Marketing Consultant (NTCM)
CRMC .... Classic Racing Motorcycle Club [Defunct] (EA)
CRMC .... Coastal Resources Management Council [United Nations]
CRMD .... Class for Retarded in Mental Development

CRMD .... Clerici Regulares Matris Dei [*Clerics Regular of the Mother of God*] [*Roman Catholic religious order*]
CRMD .... Computer Resources Management Data (MCD)
CRME .... Center for Research on Multi-Ethnic Education [*University of Oklahoma*] [*Research center*] (RCD)
CRME .... Council for Research in Music Education (EA)
CR-MED ..... Channel Request-Medium Priority (MHDB)
CRMF .... Cancer Relief Macmillan Fund [*British*] (DBA)
CRMF .... Congo-Red Millipore Filter
CrMg .... Cro-Magnon (VRA)
CRMI .... Clerici Regulares Ministrantes Infirmis [*Clerics Regular Attendant on the Sick, Camillini, Camilliani*] [*Roman Catholic religious order*]
CRML .... Champion Road Machinery Ltd. [*NASDAQ symbol*] (SAG)
CRML .... Coalition for Responsible Mining Law [*Defunct*] (EA)
CRMLE .... Champion Road Machinery [*NASDAQ symbol*] (TTSB)
CRMN .... Crewman (AABC)
CRMNL .... Criminal
CRMNY .... Ceremony
CRMO .... Craters of the Moon National Monument
CR MOB ...... Crusader Mobility [*Army*] (RDA)
CRMP .... Coastal Resources Management Programme [*Canada*] (EAIO)
CRMP .... Computer Resource Management Plan [*Army*] (RDA)
CrmpKnl ..... Crompton & Knowles Corp. [*Associated Press*] (SAG)
CRMPT .... Commendation Ribbon with Metal Pendant [*Military decoration*]
CRMR .... Continuous-Reading Meter Relay
CRMR .... Contract Requirements Master Record [*Military*]
CRMRY .... Creamery
CRMS .... Center for Research in Management Science [*University of California*] (MCD)
CRMS .... Charles Rennie Mackintosh Society (EAIO)
CRMS .... Clerks Regular, Ministers of the Sick [*Rome, Italy*] (EAIO)
CRMS .... Close Range Missile System (PDAA)
CRMS .... Communications Resource Management System [*CHI/COR Information Management, Inc.*]
CRMSS .... Central Registry of Magazine Subscription Solicitors [*Defunct*] (EA)
CRMT .... Chromate (MSA)
CRMTRY ..... Crematory
CR MUN/RES... Crusader Munitions/Resupply [*Army*] (RDA)
CRM-USA .... Cliff Richard Movement - USA [*Later, CRFCA*] (EA)
CRMWD ...... Colorado River Municipal Water District
crmwr .... Creamware (VRA)
CRN .... Cable Routing Rotation (MCD)
CRN .... Cardiac-Recurrent Nerve [*Medicine*] (PDAA)
CRN .... Carolina & Northwestern Railway Co. [*AAR code*]
CRN .... Carrigan Industries Ltd. [*Vancouver Stock Exchange symbol*]
CRN .... CERMET [*Ceramic Metal Element*] Resistor Network
CRN .... Charge Routing Network (IAA)
CRN .... Children's Radio Network (NTCM)
CRN .... Common Random Number [*Mathematics*] (IAA)
CRN .... Complement Requiring Neutralizing
CRN .... Continuous-Random-Network [*Noncrystalline structure*]
CRN .... Contract Revision Number (NASA)
CRN .... Corinaldo [*Italy*] [*Seismograph station code, US Geological Survey*] (SEIS)
CRN .... Cornell Corrections, Inc. [*AMEX symbol*] (SAG)
Crn .... Corrin [*Biochemistry*]
CRN .... Corrosion-Resistant Nebulizer
CRN .... Council for Responsible Nutrition (EA)
CRN .... Crane (MSA)
CRN .... Crane
CrN .... Cranial Nerves [*Neurology*] (DAVI)
CRN .... Cross Lake Minerals [*Vancouver Stock Exchange symbol*]
CRN .... Crown (MSA)
CRN .... Customs Registered Number [*British*] (DS)
CRN .... Empresa Aerocaribbean SA [*Cuba*] [*ICAO designator*] (FAAC)
CRN .... Sparrevohn, AK [*Location identifier FAA*] (FAAL)
CRN .... United States Commission on Civil Rights, Washington, DC [*OCLC symbol*] (OCLC)
CRNA .... Certified Registered Nurse Anesthetist
cRNA .... Ribonucleic Acid, Chromosomal [*Biochemistry, genetics*]
cRNA .... Ribonucleic Acid, Complementary [*Biochemistry, genetics*]
CRNAF .... Campaign for the Restoration of the National Anthem and Flag [*British*] (DBA)
CRNBRRY ... Cranberry
CRNC .... College Republican National Committee (EA)
CrnCP .... Crown Central Petroleum Corp. [*Associated Press*] (SAG)
CRNE .... Cosmic Ray Nuclei [*or Nuclear*] Experiment (SSD)
CRNF .... Cysteine Rich Neurotrophic Factor [*Neurochemistry*]
CRN-FAN .... Combine Regency Network - Flaming Arrow Network [*Military*]
CRNHP .... Concerned Relatives of Nursing Home Patients (EA)
crnhs .... Cornhusks (VRA)
CRNI .... Certified Registered Nurse of Infusion
CRNKSHFT... Crankshaft
CRNL .... Chalk River Nuclear Laboratories [*Atomic Energy of Canada Ltd.*] [*Information service or system Research center*] (IID)
crnltn .... Crenellation (VRA)
CRNMTC ..... Chronometric
CRNMTR ..... Chronometer
cr nn .... Cranial Nerves [*Neurology*] (DAVI)
CRNO .... Cold-Rolled Non-Oriented [*Metallurgy*]
CRNP .... Certified Registered Nurse Practioner (DAVI)
CRNPR .... Corrected Relative Net Protein Ratio [*Nutrition*]
crnr .... Corner (VRA)
CRNR .... Cornerstone Imaging [*NASDAQ symbol*] (TTSB)
CRNR .... Cornerstone Imaging, Inc. [*NASDAQ symbol*] (SAG)

CrnrB .... Cornerstone Bank [*Associated Press*] (SAG)
CrnrFn .... Cornerstone Financial Corp. [*Associated Press*] (SAG)
CRNS .... Code Reports, New Series [*New York*] [*A publication*] (DLA)
cr ns .... Cranial Nerves [*Anatomy*] (MAE)
CRNS .... Cronus Industries, Inc. (MHDW)
CRNSF .... Cronos Group [*NASDAQ symbol*] (TTSB)
CRNWL ...... Cornwall [*County in England*]
CRO .... Carded for Record Only
CRO .... Carnarvon Tracking Station [*NASA*]
CRO .... Carnasaw Mountain - Lookout Tower [*Oklahoma*] [*Seismograph station code, US Geological Survey*] (SEIS)
CRO .... Cathode-Ray Oscilloscope [*or Oscillograph*]
CRO .... Cave Rescue Organization [*British*] (PDAA)
CRO .... Central Radio Office [*Telecommunications*] (TEL)
CRO .... Central Records Office
CRO .... Centric Relation Occlusion [*Dentistry*]
CRO .... Chief Recruiting Officer [*British military*] (DMA)
CRO .... Chief Resource Officer
CRO .... Christian Renewal Outreach [*Australia*]
CRO .... Civilian Repair Organization [*Aircraft*]
CRO .... Civil Readjustment Officer [*Military*]
CRO .... Commonwealth Relations Office [*Later, CO*] [*British*]
CRO .... Companies Registration Office [*British*] (DS)
CRO .... Complete with Related Order [*Telecommunications*] (TEL)
CRO .... Computer Readable Output [*Computer science*] (PCM)
CRO .... Continuous Receiver On [*Electronic device*]
CRO .... Contractor Resident Office (AAG)
CRO .... Contract-Research Organization (ECON)
CRO .... Control Room Operator [*Nuclear energy*] (NRCH)
CRO .... Copyright Receipt Office [*British Library Automated Information Service*] (NITA)
CRO .... Corcoran, CA [*Location identifier FAA*] (FAAL)
CRO .... Cosmic Ray Observatory
CRO .... County Registrars Office (BARN)
CRO .... Criminal Record Office [*Scotland Yard*]
CRO .... Croatia (ECON)
Cro .... Croke's English King's Bench Reports [*1582-1641*] [*A publication*] (DLA)
CRO .... Crown Airways, Inc. [*ICAO designator*] (FAAC)
CRO .... Crown Pacific Partners Ltd. [*NYSE symbol*] (SAG)
CRO .... Crown Pac Partners L.P. [*NYSE symbol*] (TTSB)
CRO .... CRT [*Cathode-Ray Tube*] Readout (CAAL)
Cro .... Keilway's English King's Bench Reports [*72 English Reprint*] [*A publication*] (DLA)
CRo .... Roseville Public Library, Roseville, CA [*Library symbol Library of Congress*] (LCLS)
CROACUS .... Comite Regional Ouest-Africain pour la Conservation et l'Utilisation du Sol
C(RO & H)... Center (Regional Office and Hospital) [*Veterans Administration*]
C(RO & INS)... Center (Regional Office and Insurance) [*Veterans Administration*]
Croat .... Croatia
CROB .... Center for Research in Oral Biology [*University of Washington*] [*Research center*] (RCD)
C Rob .... Christopher Robinson's English Admiralty Reports [*165 English Reprint*] [*A publication*] (DLA)
C Rob Adm... Christopher Robinson's English Admiralty Reports [*165 English Reprint*] [*A publication*] (DLA)
C Rob (Eng)... Christopher Robinson's English Admiralty Reports [*165 English Reprint*] [*A publication*] (DLA)
CROC .... Combat Required Operational Capability (AFIT)
CROC .... Committee for Rejection of Obnoxious Commercials
CROC .... Computer Review and Orientation Course
CROC .... Crocodile (DSUE)
CROC .... Crocus Saffron [*Pharmacy*] (ROG)
Cro Car ..... Croke's English King's Bench Reports Tempore Charles I [*1625-41*] [*A publication*] (DLA)
Cro Car (Eng)... Croke's English King's Bench Reports Tempore Charles I [*1625-41*] [*A publication*] (DLA)
Cro Cas........ Croke's English King's Bench Reports Tempore Charles I [*1625-41*] [*A publication*] (DLA)
Crock Cor..... Crocker on the Duties of Coroners in New York [*A publication*] (DLA)
Crockford..... English Maritime Law Reports, Published by Crockford [*1860-71*] [*A publication*] (DLA)
Crock Forms... Crocker's Notes on Common Forms [*Massachusetts*] [*A publication*] (DLA)
Crock Notes... Crocker's Notes on the Public Statutes of Massachusetts [*A publication*] (DLA)
Crockr .... Crocker Realty Investors, Inc. [*Associated Press*] (SAG)
Crock Sh...... Crocker on Sheriffs and Constables [*A publication*] (DLA)
CROCP .... Committee for Review of Our China Policy [*Defunct*]
CRocS .... Sierra College, Rocklin, CA [*Library symbol Library of Congress*] (LCLS)
CROED .... Civil Rights Office, Education Department (OICC)
Cro Eliz....... Croke's English King's Bench Reports Tempore Elizabeth [*1582-1603*] [*A publication*] (DLA)
Cro Eliz (Eng)... Croke's English King's Bench Reports Tempore Elizabeth [*1582-1603*] [*A publication*] (DLA)
CROET .... Center for Research on Occupational and Environmental Toxicology [*Oregon Health Sciences University*] [*Research center*] (RCD)
CROF .... Controllerate Royal Ordnance Factories (PDAA)
CROFC .... Clint Ritchie Official Fan Club [*Defunct*] (EA)
CROG .... Croghan [*New York*] [*Seismograph station code, US Geological Survey*] (SEIS)
CROHMS...... Columbia River Operational Hydromet Management System (NOAA)
crois .... Croissant (DD)

Cro Jac........	Croke's English King's Bench Reports Tempore James (Jacobus) I [*A publication*] (DLA)
Cro Jac (Eng)...	Croke's English King's Bench Reports Tempore James (Jacobus) I [*A publication*] (DLA)
Croke..........	Croke's English King's Bench Reports [*1582-1641*] [*A publication*] (DLA)
Croke..........	Keilway's English King's Bench Reports [*72 English Reprint*] [*A publication*] (DLA)
CROM.........	Capacitive Read-Only Memory [*Computer science*] (IEEE)
CROM.........	Cervical Range of Motion [*Medicine*] (DMAA)
CROM.........	Control Read-Only Memory [*Computer science*]
Crom...........	Crompton's Office of a Justice of the Peace [*1637*] [*A publication*] (DLA)
CroMo.........	Chromemoly
Cromp.........	Star Chamber Cases, by Crompton [*A publication*] (DLA)
Cromp & F...	Fitzherbert's Justice, Enlarged by Crompton [*A publication*] (DLA)
Cromp & J...	Crompton and Jervis' English Exchequer Reports [*1830-32*] [*A publication*] (DLA)
Cromp & J (Eng)...	Crompton and Jervis' English Exchequer Reports [*1830-32*] [*A publication*] (DLA)
Cromp & Jer...	Crompton and Jervis' English Exchequer Reports [*1830-32*] [*A publication*] (DLA)
Cromp & Jerv...	Crompton and Jervis' English Exchequer Reports [*1830-32*] [*A publication*] (DLA)
Cromp & M...	Crompton and Meeson's English Exchequer Reports [*1832-34*] [*A publication*] (DLA)
Cromp & Mees...	Crompton and Meeson's English Exchequer Reports [*1832-34*] [*A publication*] (DLA)
Cromp & M (Eng)...	Crompton and Meeson's English Exchequer Reports [*1832-34*] [*A publication*] (DLA)
Cromp Cts ...	Crompton's Jurisdiction of Courts [*A publication*] (DLA)
Cromp Exch R...	Crompton's English Exchequer Reports [*A publication*] (DLA)
Cromp Ex R...	Crompton's English Exchequer Reports [*A publication*] (DLA)
Cromp JC.....	Crompton's Jurisdiction of Courts [*A publication*] (DLA)
Cromp Jur ...	Crompton's Jurisdiction of Courts [*A publication*] (DLA)
Cromp Just...	Crompton's Office of a Justice of the Peace [*1637*] [*A publication*] (DLA)
Cromp M & R...	Crompton, Meeson, and Roscoe's English Exchequer Reports [*1834-36*] [*A publication*] (DLA)
Cromp M & R (Eng)...	Crompton, Meeson, and Roscoe's English Exchequer Reports [*1834-36*] [*A publication*] (DLA)
Cromp R & C Pr...	Crompton's Rules and Cases of Practice [*A publication*] (DLA)
Crompt.........	Star Chamber Cases, by Crompton [*A publication*] (DLA)
CRomR........	Rosemead Graduate School of Psychology, Rosemead, CA [*Library symbol Library of Congress*] (LCLS)
CronosG.......	Cronos Group [*Associated Press*] (SAG)
CROP.........	Centre de Recherches sur l'Opinion Publique [*Research Centre on Public Opinion*] [*Canada*]
CROP..........	Christian Rural Overseas Program [*Acronym is now the official name of organization*] (EA)
CROP.........	Compliance Registered Options Principal (MHDB)
CROP..........	Consolidated Rules of Practice [*Environmental Protection Agency*] (GFGA)
CROP..........	Cyclophosphamide, Rubidazone [*Zorubicin*], Oncovin , Prednisone [*Vincristine*] [*Antineoplastic drug regimen*]
CROPAM......	Cyclophosphamide, Rubidazone, Oncovin [*Vincristine*], Prednisone, L-Asparaginase, Methotrexate [*Antineoplastic drug regimen*] (DAVI)
CropGrw	Crop Growers Corp. [*Associated Press*] (SAG)
CROR..........	Creditor [*Legal shorthand*] (LWAP)
CROS..........	Capacitor Read-Only Storage [*Computer science*]
CROS..........	Committee on Radiation Oncology Studies [*National Cancer Institute*]
CROS..........	Common Real-Time Operating System (CAAL)
CROS..........	Computerized Reliability Organization System
CROS..........	Contralateral Routing of Signal [*Audiometry*]
CROS..........	Cross File Search Database [*Information service or system*] (IID)
CROS..........	Crossman Communities, Inc. [*NASDAQ symbol*] (SAG)
CROS..........	Crossmann Communities [*NASDAQ symbol*] (TTSB)
CrosCAu......	Cross-Continent Auto Retailers, Inc. [*Associated Press*] (SAG)
CrosCom......	CrossCom Corp. [*Associated Press*] (SAG)
CROSH........	Changing Role of the Secondary Head [*Project*] (AIE)
CROSS........	Committee to Retain Our Segregated Schools [*Group in Arkansas, organized to oppose STOP*]
CROSS........	Computerized Rearrangements of Special Subjects [*or Subject Specialties*]
Cross	Cross, [*A. T.*] Co. [*Associated Press*] (SAG)
CROSSBOW...	Computer Retrieval of Organic Structures Based on Wiswesser
CROSSING...	Crossing [*Commonly used*] (OPSA)
Cross Lien...	Cross. Lien and Stoppage in Transitu [*1840*] [*A publication*] (DLA)
Crossman ...	Crossman Communities, Inc. [*Associated Press*] (SAG)
CROSSPATE...	Coordinative Retrieval of Selectively Sorted Permuted Analogue-Title Entries [*Computer science*]
CROSSROAD...	Crossroad [*Commonly used*] (OPSA)
CrosTim.......	Cross Timbers Royalty Trust [*Associated Press*] (SAG)
CrosTmb......	Cross Timbers Oil Co. [*Associated Press*] (SAG)
Cros Wills ...	Crosley on Wills [*1828*] [*A publication*] (DLA)
Crosw Pat Ca...	Croswell's Collection of Patent Cases [*United States*] [*A publication*] (DLA)
Crosw Pat Cas...	Croswell's Collection of Patent Cases [*United States*] [*A publication*] (DLA)
CROTCE.......	Crotonyloxymethyl(trihydroxy)cyclohexene [*Antineoplastic drug*]
Crounse.......	Crounse's Reports [*3 Nebraska*] [*A publication*] (DLA)
CROVL........	C-Rating Overall [*Military*] (CAAL)
CROW.........	Center for Research on Women [*Duke University*] [*Research center*] (RCD)
CROW.........	Center for Research on Women [*Stanford University*] (RCD)
CROW.........	Combined Rocket Warhead (KSC)
CROW.........	Counter Recoil-Operated Weapon Launcher [*Military*] (VNW)
CROW.........	Counter-Rotating Optical Wedge
Crow	Crowther's Ceylon Reports [*A publication*] (DLA)
CROWCASS...	Central Registry of War Criminals and Security Suspects [*World War II*]
CROWD........	Central Registry of World Dancers (EA)
CrowlMil......	Crowley, Milner & Co. [*Associated Press*] (SAG)
CROWT & MIN...	Crowthorne and Minety [*England*]
Crowth........	Crowther's Ceylon Reports [*A publication*] (DLA)
Crowther......	Crowther's Ceylon Reports [*A publication*] (DLA)
CROX..........	Chromium Oxalate [*Organic chemistry*]
CROYD........	Croydon [*Borough of London*]
CRP	Aerotaxis Corporativo SA de CV [*Mexico ICAO designator*] (FAAC)
CRP	Calendarium Rotulorum Patentum [*Calendar of the Patent Rolls*] [*Latin*]
CRP	Capacity Requirements Planning (MCD)
CRP	CAPE [*Capability and Proficiency Evaluation*] Review Period
CRP	Carbinol Reduction Potential [*Chemistry*]
CRP	Card Reader/Punch [*Computer science*]
CRP	Carson Pirie Scott [*NYSE symbol*] (TTSB)
CRP	Carson Pirie Scott & Co. [*NYSE symbol*] (SAG)
CRP	Center for Responsive Politics (EA)
CRP	Center for Responsive Psychology (EA)
CRP	Centers for Radiological Physics
CRP	Centralized Receiving Point
CRP	Central R. R. of Pennsylvania [*AAR code*]
CRP	Cercle pour le Renoveau et le Progres [*Gabon*] [*Political party*] (EY)
CRP	Chemical Research Project [*Military*]
CRP	Chicago Review Press [*Publisher*]
CRP	Chicana Rights Project [*Defunct*] (EA)
CRP	Chinese Republican Party [*Political party*] (EY)
CRP	Chopp Computer Corp. [*Vancouver Stock Exchange symbol*]
CRP	Christian Republican Party [*Bulgaria*] [*Political party*]
CRP	Civil Rights Party [*South Korea Political party*] (PPW)
CRP	Clauson Rolling Platform
CRP	Climate Research Project [*Boulder, CO*] [*Department of Commerce*] (GRD)
CRP	Comando de Resistencia Popular Javier Carrera [*Javier Carrera Popular Resistance Commando*] [*Chile*] (PD)
CRP	Comandos Revolucionarios del Pueblo [*Peru*] [*Political party*] (EY)
CRP	Combat Reconnaissance Platoon
CRP	Combat Reporting Post
CRP	Combined Refining Process (PDAA)
CRP	Command Read Pulse (KSC)
CRP	Committee to Re-Elect the President [*Also, CREEP*] [*1972*]
CRP	Common Reference Point [*Navigation*] (IAA)
CRP	Community Relations Plan
CRP	Community Release Program [*Australia*]
CRP	Community Renewal Program
CRP	Complement Regulatory Protein [*Genetics*]
CRP	Component Reliability Prediction
CRP	Composition Reduction Printing
CRP	Compton Recoil Particle
CRP	Computer Reset Pulse (KSC)
CRP	Computer Resident Planning (MCD)
CRP	COMSEC [*Communications Security*] Resources Program [*Army*] (AABC)
CRP	Configuration Requirements Processing (MCD)
CRP	Congregatio Reformatorium Praemonstratensium [*Premonstratensians*] [*Roman Catholic men's religious order*]
CRP	Conservation Reserve Program [*Department of Agriculture Department of Energy*]
CRP	Constant Rate of Penetration (OA)
CRP	Continuous Record of Personnel (ADA)
CRP	Control and Reporting Post [*RADAR*] [*Air Force*]
CRP	Controllable and Reversible Pitch Propeller [*For ships*] (MCD)
CRP	Controlled Referral Plan
CRP	Cooperative Research Program [*Military and Office of Education*]
CRP	Coordinated Reconnaissance Plan (CINC)
CRP	Coordinated Resources Plan
CRP	Corpus Christi [*Texas*] [*Airport symbol*] (OAG)
CRP	Cosmic Ray Particle
CRP	Cost Reduction Program [*Economics*] (AFM)
CRP	Counter-Rotation [*or Rotating*] Platform (MHDB)
CRP	C-Reactive Protein [*Clinical chemistry*]
CrP.............	Creatine Phosphate [*or Phosphocreatine*] [*Biochemistry*] (DAVI)
Cr P	Creatinine Phosphate [*Biochemistry*] (AAMN)
crp	Creoles and Pidgins [*MARC language code Library of Congress*] (LCCP)
CRP	Crepe
Cr P	Criminal Procedure [*Legal term*] (DLA)
CRP	Crimp [*Engineering*]
CRP	Crisis Relocation Plans [*Federal Emergency Management Agency*]
CRP	Cross-Reference Project
CRP	Crystal River Plant (NRCH)
CRP	Cuban Refugee Program [*HEW*]
CRP	Cyclic-AMP [*Adenosine Monophosphate*] Receptor Protein [*Also, CAP*] [*Genetics*]
CRP	Riverside City and County Public Library, Riverside, CA [*OCLC symbol*] (OCLC)
CRPA	Controlled Radiation [*or Reception*] Pattern Antenna
CRPA	C-Reactive Protein Antiserum [*Clinical chemistry*]
CRPAG........	Calendar Reform Political Action Group [*Defunct*] (EA)

Cr Pat Dec...	Cranch's Decisions on Patent Appeals [*A publication*] (DLA)
CRPB	Cerprobe Corp. [*NASDAQ symbol*] (NQ)
CRPBI	Child Report of Parent Behavior Inventory (EDAC)
CRPC	Centre for Research on Perception and Cognition [*University of Sussex*] [*British*] (CB)
CRPD	Chronic Restrictive Pulmonary Disease [*Medicine*] (DMAA)
CRPF	Chloroquine-Resistant Plasmodium Falciparum [*Chemoprophylaxis*]
CRPH	Conference on Research in Peace History (EA)
CRPHN	Centre for Research into Public Health and Nursing [*La Trobe University*] [*Australia*]
CRPI	Card Reader-Punch Interpreter [*Computer science*] (DNAB)
CRPI	Control Rod Position Indication [*Nuclear energy*] (NRCH)
CRPL	Central Radio Propagation Laboratory [*Later, ITS*]
CRPL	Centre for Research in Philosophy and Literature [*University of Warwick*] [*British*] (CB)
CRPL	Chromium Plate [*Metallurgy*]
CRPL	Consolidated Repair Parts List (MCD)
CRPL	Cosmic Ray Physics Laboratory (NASA)
CRPLF	Communaute des Radios Publiques de Langue Francaise (EAIO)
CRPM	Cholorquinine-Resistant Malaria
CRPM	Combined Registered Publication Memoranda
CRPM	Communication Registered Publication Memoranda
CRPNTRY	Carpentry
CRPO	Consolidated Reserve Personnel Office [*Air Force*] (AFM)
CRPO	Continuous Rating Permitting Over-Load
CRPOCS	Cultural Resources Protection on the Outer Continental Shelf [*Oceanography*] (MSC)
CRPPH	Committee for Radiation Protection and Public Health [*EURATOM*] (NUCP)
CRPRR	Candidate Repair Parts Redistribution Report
CRpS	California State College, Sonoma, Rohnert Park, CA [*Library symbol Library of Congress*] (LCLS)
CRPS	Cuban Refugee Program Staff [*HEW*]
CRPT	Carpet [*Classified advertising*] (ADA)
CRPV	Canister Return Purge Valve [*Automotive engineering*]
CRPV	Cottontail Rabbit Papillomavirus
CRQ	Air Creebec [*Canada ICAO designator*] (FAAC)
CRQ	Call Request [*Telecommunications*] (TEL)
CRQ	Carlsbad, CA [*Location identifier FAA*] (FAAL)
CRQ	Cirque
CRQ	Commutation of Rations and Quarters [*Military*]
CRQ	Console Reply Queuing
CRQ	Current Requirements
CRR	Canadian Regulatory Reporter [*Database*] [*Canadian Law Information Council*] [*Information service or system*] (CRD)
CRR	Carrier Removal Rate (PDAA)
CRR	Carrizo [*California*] [*Seismograph station code, US Geological Survey*] (SEIS)
CRR	Center for Radiation Research [*National Institute of Standards and Technology*]
CRR	Center for Reformation Research (EA)
CRR	Center for Renewable Resources (EA)
CRR	Chief Registrar's Reports [*England*] [*A publication*] (DLA)
CRR	Chinese Refugee Relief [*Defunct*] (EA)
CRR	Churchill Research Range [*Air Force*]
CRR	Circle, MT [*Location identifier FAA*] (FAAL)
CRR	Clutter Rejection RADAR
CRR	[*The*] Coinage of the Roman Republic [*A publication*] (OCD)
CRR	Combat Readiness Requirements [*Canadian Navy*]
CRR	Combat Ready Rate (MCD)
CRR	Committee for the Restoration of the Republic [*Defunct*] (EA)
CRR	Complete Remission Rate [*Oncology*]
CRR	Computer Run Report (NASA)
CRR	Conrail, Inc. [*NYSE symbol*] (SPSG)
CRR	Conservation Research Report [*A publication*]
CRR	Consolidated Rambler Mines Ltd. [*Toronto Stock Exchange symbol*]
CRR	Constant Ratio Rule (PDAA)
CRR	Constant Ringing Relay [*Alarm system*]
CRR	Consumer's Reliability Risk
CRR	Contemporaneous Reserve Requirements [*Banking*]
CRR	Contractor Reports Register
CRR	Conversion Result Register (IAA)
crr	Corrector [*MARC relator code*] [*Library of Congress*] (LCCP)
CRR	Cost Reduction Report [*Economics*]
CRR	Cost Reporting Requirements
CRR	Council Recycling Debate [*Australia*]
CRR	Critical Requirements Review (NASA)
Cr R	Curia Regis Rolls [*British Legal term*] (DLA)
CRRA	Canadian Retransmission Right Association (AC)
CRRAG	Countryside Recreation Research Advisory Group [*British*]
CRRB	Carrollton Bancorp [*NASDAQ symbol*] (SAG)
CRRB	Central Reference Room Bulletin (SAA)
CRRB	Change Request Review Board [*Marine science*] (OSRA)
CRRB	Change Request Review Board (USDC)
CRRC	Cold Regions Research Co. (MCD)
CRRC	Combat Rubber Raiding Craft (DOMA)
CRRC	Community Resource and Research Center [*University of Nebraska - Lincoln*] [*Research center*] (RCD)
CRRC	Construction Requirements Review Committee [*Military*] (AABC)
CRRC	Courier Corp. [*NASDAQ symbol*] (NQ)
CRRC	Cream Ridge Fruit Research Center [*Rutgers University*] [*Research center*] (RCD)
CrrcS	Correctional Services Corp. [*Associated Press*] (SAG)
CRRCT	Correction
CRRCTNL	Correctional

CRRE	Community for Religious Research and Education (EA)
CRRE	Cross-Leveling, Redistribution, Replenishment, and Excessing (MCD)
CRREF	Cross Reference
CRREL	Cold Regions Research and Engineering Laboratory [*Hanover, NH*] [*Army Also, an information service or system*] (IID)
CRRERIS	Commonwealth Regional Renewable Energy Resources Information Service (IID)
CRRES	Chemical Release and Radiation Effects Satellite [*NASA*]
CRRES	Combined Release and Radiation Effects Satellite [*NASA*]
Cr Rg	Criminal Rulings [*Bombay, India*] [*A publication*] (DLA)
CRRI	Central Rice Research Institute (GNE)
CRRL	Canadian Radio Relay League (PDAA)
CRRL	Contour Rolls (AAG)
CRRM	Centre for Rural Research Management [*University of New England*] [*Australia*]
CRRN	Certified Rehabilitation Registered Nurse
CRR of NJ	Central Railroad Co. of New Jersey [*Absorbed into Consolidated Rail Corp.*]
CRRS	CHAMPUS [*Civilian Health and Medical of the Uniformed Services*] Regional Review System
CRRS	Combat Readiness Rating System [*Air Force*]
CRRS	Crown Resources Corp. [*NASDAQ symbol*] (NQ)
CRRT	Certified Respiratory Therapy Technician (DAVI)
CRRT	Children's Reading Round Table
CR-RT SORT	Carrier Route Sort [*Postal Service*] [*United States*] (WDMC)
CRS	Cable Reinforcement Set (MCD)
CRS	Cable Running Sheets
CRS	Calibration Recall System [*Army*]
CRS	Calibration Requirements Summary
CRS	Camp Reception Station [*A kind of field hospital*] [*British*]
CRS	Camp Sentinel RADAR [*Military*] (RDA)
CRS	Canada Remote Systems Ltd. [*Information service or system*] (IID)
CRS	Canadian Rose Society [*Formerly, Rose Society of Ontario*] (AC)
CRS	Cancer Research Society Inc. [*Societe de Recherche sur le Cancer Inc.*] (AC)
CRS	Canopy Removal System [*for helicopters*] (RDA)
CRS	Capital Recovery Schedule
CRS	Carbon Dioxide Reduction Subsystem (NASA)
CRS	Career Reserve Status [*Air Force*]
CRS	Carolina Southern Railway Co. [*AAR code*]
CRS	Carpenter Technology [*NYSE symbol*] (TTSB)
CRS	Carpenter Technology Corp. [*Formerly, Carpenter Steel Co.*] [*NYSE symbol*] (SPSG)
CRS	Case Review Section [*Social Security Administration*] (OICC)
CRS	Cash by Return Steamer [*Business term*]
CRS	Cathode Ray Setter (DGA)
CRS	Catholic Record Society (EA)
CRS	Catholic Relief Services [*Later, CRS-USCC*]
CRS	Catholic Renascence Society [*Defunct*] (EA)
CRS	Caudill, Rowlett & Scott [*Architectural firm*]
CRS	Center for Rural Studies [*University of Vermont*] [*Research center*] (RCD)
CRS	Center on Religion and Society (EA)
CRS	Centralized Referral System [*Military*] (AFM)
CRS	Centralized Results System [*Telecommunications*] (TEL)
CRS	Central Recorder Subsystem [*NASA*]
CRS	Central Reference Supply
CRS	Central Repeater System (MCD)
CRS	Centre for Remote Sensing [*Imperial College of Science and Technology*] [*British*] (CB)
CRS	Centre for Remote Sensing [*James Cook University*] [*Australia*]
CRS	Centre for Resource Studies [*Queen's University at Kingston*] [*Canada Research center*] (RCD)
CRS	Certified Residential Specialist [*Realtors National Marketing Institute o f the National Association of Realtors*] [*Designation awarded by*]
CRS	Chain RADAR System
CRS	Change Record Sheet (MCD)
CRS	Charismatic Renewal Services (EA)
CRS	Check Reporting Service
CRS	Children's Reading Service (AEBS)
CRS	Chinese Restaurant Syndrome [*Monosodium glutamate sensitivity*] [*Medicine*]
CRS	Christian Record Services (EA)
CRS	Cis Repressor Sequence [*Genetics*]
CRS	Citizen Radio Service [*Telecommunications*] (IAA)
CRS	Clericorum Regularium Somaschensium [*Clerics Regular of Somasca*] [*Somascan Fathers*] [*Roman Catholic religious order*]
CRS	Coarse (AAG)
CRS	Coelliptic Rendezvous Sequence [*Aerospace*]
CRS	Coherent Raman Spectroscopy (MCD)
CRS	Cold-Rolled Steel
CRS	Collectors Record Society [*Record label*]
CRS	Colon and Rectal [*or Colorectal*] Surgery [*Medicine*]
CRS	Comercial Aerea SA de CV [*Mexico ICAO designator*] (FAAC)
CRS	Command Readout Station [*Military*]
CRS	Command Relationship Study
CRS	Command Retrieval System (DEN)
CRS	Communications Relay Set (MCD)
CRS	Communications Research Center (HGAA)
CRS	Community Rating System [*National Flood Insurance Program*]
CRS	Community Relations Service [*Department of Justice*] [*Terminated*]
CRS	Community Research Services [*Illinois State University*] [*Normal*] [*Information service or system*] (IID)
CR's	Complete Responders [*to medication*]

CRS .... Component Repair Squadron (MCD)
CRS .... Computerized Radiology Society [*Later, CMIS*] (EA)
CRS .... Computerized Reference Service [*William Paterson College of New Jersey*] (OLDSS)
CRS .... Computerized Reservation Systems (BTTJ)
CRS .... Computerized Retrieval Service
CRS .... Computer Readable System
CRS .... Computer Recognition Systems [*Commercial firm*] [*British*] (NITA)
CRS .... Computer Reservation System
CRS .... Conductivity Recording Switch [*Nuclear energy*] (NRCH)
CRS .... Configuration Report Server (ACRL)
CRS .... Congenital Rubella Syndrome [*Medicine*]
CRS .... Congressional Research Service [*Formerly, Legislative Reference Service*] [*Washington, DC*] [*Library of Congress OCLC symbol*]
CRS .... Containment Recirculation Spray System [*Nuclear energy*] (NRCH)
CRS .... Containment Rupture Signal [*Nuclear energy*] (IEEE)
CRS .... Content Replication Service [*Microsoft Corp.*] [*Computer science*]
CRS .... Contingency Remoting System [*Military*] (RDA)
CRS .... Contingency Retention Stock [*Military*] (AFIT)
CRS .... Contractor Registration System (AAGC)
CRS .... Contractor Relations Specialist [*DoD*]
CRS .... Contract Repair Service (MCD)
CRS .... Control and Reporting System (NATG)
CRS .... Controlled Radial Steering (PDAA)
CRS .... Controlled Release Society (EA)
CRS .... Control Reconfiguration Strategy (MCD)
CRS .... Coolant Recovery System [*Automotive engineering*]
CRS .... Coolant Reserve System [*Automotive engineering*]
CRS .... Cooperative Recreation Service [*Later, World Around Songs*] (EA)
CRS .... Cooperative Research Service [*Kentucky State University*] [*Research center*] (RCD)
CRS .... Co-Operative Retail Services [*British*]
CRS .... Cooperative Retail Society (ODBW)
CRS .... Coreceptor Skewed [*Immunology*]
CRS .... Correctional Reporting System [*Army*]
CRS .... Correction and Rehabilitation Squadron [*Air Force*]
CRS .... Corsicana, TX [*Location identifier FAA*] (FAAL)
CRS .... Cosmic Ray Shower
CRS .... Cosmic-Ray Subsystem [*Astrophysics*]
CRS .... Council of Rehabilitation Specialists (EA)
CRS .... Countermeasures Receiving Set
CRS .... Course (AABC)
CRS .... Course
CRS .... Creation Research Society (EA)
CRS .... Creative Research Systems [*Information service or system*] (IID)
CRS .... Crescent (ADA)
CRS .... Crescent Mines Ltd. [*Vancouver Stock Exchange symbol*]
CRS .... Crew Reserve Status [*Military*] (AFM)
CRS .... Cross (ADA)
CRS .... Cross-Section
CRS .... Crypto Radio Service
CRS .... Cubic Spline Regression [*Statistics*]
CRS .... Customer Reaction Survey
CRS .... Customer Reservations System [*Airlines*]
CRS .... Somascan Fathers (TOCD)
crs .... Somascan Fathers, Order of St. Jerome Aemilian (TOCD)
CRSA .... Administration Sciences Research Centre [*University of Moncton*] [*Canada Research center*] (RCD)
CRSA .... Canadian Regional Science Association [*See also ACSR*]
CRSA .... Center of Research in Administrative Sciences [*University of Moncton*] [*Research center*] (RCD)
CRSA .... Centralized Repair Service Attendants [*Telecommunications*] (TEL)
CRSA .... Cold Rolled Sections Association [*British*] (DBA)
CRSA .... Control Rod Scram Accumulator [*Nuclear energy*] (IEEE)
Cr S & P ..... Craigie, Stewart, and Paton's Scotch Appeal Cases [*1726-1821*] [*A publication*] (DLA)
CRSAS .... Centro Regional de Sismologia para America del Sur [*Regional Center for Seismology for South America - RCSSA*] (EAIO)
CRSB .... Center for Research in Social Behavior [*University of Missouri - Columbia*] [*Research center*] (RCD)
CRSC .... Californian Rabbit Specialty Club (EA)
CRSC .... Center for Remote Sensing and Cartography [*University of Utah Research Institute*] [*Research center*] (RCD)
CRSC .... Center for Research in Scientific Communication [*Johns Hopkins University*] (IID)
CRSC .... Center for Research in Social Change [*Emory University, Atlanta, GA*]
CRSC .... Contract Review and Selection Criteria [*DoD*]
CRSCNT ...... Crescent [*Commonly used*] (OPSA)
CRSCT .... Crescent (ROG)
CRSD .... Contractor Required Shipment Date
CRSD .... Crusade
CRSDA .... Community Recreation and Skill Development Activities (AABC)
CRSDR .... Crusader
CRSE .... Central Research and Support Establishment [*Information service or system*] (IID)
CRSE .... Course
CRSE .... Course
CRSE .... Course [*Postal Service standard*] (OPSA)
CRSENT .... Crescent [*Commonly used*] (OPSA)
CRSF .... CUNA [*Credit Union National Association*] Retirement Savings Fund
CRSFD .... Cross Feed
CRSFF .... Central Region SEATO [*Southeast Asia Treaty Organization*] Field Forces (CINC)
CRSG .... Contractor Risk Assessment Guide (DOMA)

crsg .... Crossing (VRA)
CRSGF .... Canadian Rhythmic Sportive Gymnastic Federation [*Federation Canadienne de Gymnastique Rythmique Sportive*] [*Formerly, Canadian Modern Rhythmic Gymnastic Federation*] (AC)
CRSHC .... Conseil de Recherches en Sciences Humaines du Canada [*Social Sciences and Humanities Research Council of Canada - SSHRCC*]
CRSHD .... Crosshead (MSA)
CRSI .... Cardinal Realty Services, Inc. [*NASDAQ symbol*] (SAG)
CRSI .... Cardinal Realty Svcs [*NASDAQ symbol*] (TTSB)
CRSI .... Ceramic Reusable Surface Insulation (NASA)
CRSI .... Concrete Reinforcing Steel Institute (EA)
CRSIS .... Centre for Research into Strategic Information Systems [*University of Bath*] [*British*]
CRSL .... Christian Road Safety League [*British*] (BI)
CRSL .... Computer Recognition Systems Ltd. [*British*]
CRsLfe .... Central Reserve Life Corp. [*Associated Press*] (SAG)
CRSM .... Calcium-Reduced Skim Milk
CRSM .... Center for Robotic Systems in Microelectronics [*Research center*] (RCD)
CRSM .... Certified Real Estate Securities Member [*Real Estate Securities and Syndi cation Institute of the National Association of Realtors*] [*Designation awarded by*]
CRSM .... Cherry Red Spot Myoclonus [*Medicine*] (DMAA)
CRSMP .... Calcium-Reduced Skim Milk Powder (OA)
CRSN .... Centre de Recherche en Sciences Neurologiques [*Center for Research in Neurological Sciences*] [*Canada*] (IRC)
CRSN .... Corrosion (MSA)
CRS-NCWC ... Catholic Relief Services - National Catholic Welfare Conference [*Later, CRS-USCC*] (EA)
CRSNT .... Crescent [*Commonly used*] (OPSA)
CRSO .... Cellular Radio Switching Office [*Telecommunications*]
CRSO .... Center for Research on Social Organization [*University of Michigan*] [*Research center*] (RCD)
CRSOA .... County Road Safety Officers' Association [*British*] (DBA)
CRSP .... Center for Research in Security Prices [*University of Chicago*] [*Chicago, IL Information service or system*] (IID)
CRSP .... Clerici Regulares Pauperum Matris Dei Scholarum Piarum [*Clerics Regular of the Poor Men of the Mother of God for Pious Schools*] [*Piarists*] [*Roman Catholic religious order*]
CRSP .... Clerici Regulares Sancti Pauli [*Clerics Regular of St. Paul*] [*Barnabites Also, Barn*] [*Roman Catholic men's religious order*]
CRSP .... Clerics Regular of St. Paul (TOCD)
crsp .... Clerics Regular of St. Paul, Barnabite Fathers (TOCD)
CRSP .... Collaborative Research Support Program [*Agency for International Development*]
CRSP .... Colorado River Storage Project [*Department of the Interior*]
CRSP .... Combat Ready Storage Program (DOMA)
CRSP .... Comprehensive Renal Scintillation Procedure [*Medicine*] (DMAA)
CRSP .... Contractor Recommend Support Plan [*Military*]
CrSp .... Craniospinal [*Anatomy*] (AAMN)
CRSP .... Criminally Receiving Stolen Property
CRSPPA ...... International Pen-Pals Association [*Cross River State Pen-Pals Associatio n*] [*Acronym is based on former name,*] (EAIO)
CRSR .... Center for Radiophysics and Space Research [*Cornell University*] [*Research center*]
CRSR .... Centre for Rural Social Research [*Charles Sturt University*] [*Australia*]
CRSS .... California Rug Study Society (EA)
CRSS .... Canadian Remote Sensing Society (EAIO)
CRSS .... Certified Real Estate Securities Sponsor [*Real Estate Securities and Synd ication Institute of the National Association of Realtors*] [*Designation awarded by*]
CRSS .... Chemically Rigidized Space Structure
CRS(S) .... Chief Radio Supervisor (Special) [*British military*] (DMA)
CRSS .... Children's Reinforcement Survey Schedule
CRSS .... College Reading and Study Skills Inventory (EDAC)
CRSS .... Colo-Rectal Surgical Society
CRSS .... Community Refugee Settlement Scheme [*Australia*]
CRSS .... Critical Resolved Shear Stress
CRSSING ..... Crossing [*Commonly used*] (OPSA)
CRSSNG ...... Crossing [*Commonly used*] (OPSA)
CRST .... Calcinosis Cutis, Raynaud's Phenomenon, Sclerodactyly, and Telangiectasia [*A medical syndrome*]
CRST .... [*The*] Claremont Ras Shamra Tablets [*A publication*] (BJA)
CRST .... Cold-Rolled Steel (IAA)
CRST .... Crest [*Postal Service standard*] (OPSA)
CRST .... Crest
crst .... Crushed Stone (BARN)
CRST .... Crystallographic [*Origin*] [*Of precious stones*]
CrstCp .... Crested Corp. [*Associated Press*] (SAG)
CRSTIAC ...... Cold Regions Science and Technology Information Analysis Center [*DoD*] (MSC)
CRSTPA .... Columbia River Salmon and Tuna Packers Association (EA)
CRS-USCC ... Catholic Relief Services - US Catholic Conference (EA)
CRSV .... Carnation Ringspot Virus
CRSV .... Carriage Services, Inc. [*NASDAQ symbol*] (SAG)
CRSV .... Computer-Related Systems Validation [*Engineering*]
CRSV .... Corrosive (MSA)
CRSVI .... Conference Regionale du Service Volontaire International [*Regional Conference on International Voluntary Service*] (EAIO)
CRSVR .... Crossover [*Technical drawings*] (MSA)
CRSW .... Certificate in Residential Social Work [*British*] (DI)
CRS(W) .... Chief Radio Supervisor (Warfare) [*British military*] (DMA)
CRT .... Canadian Railway Troops [*World War I*]

CRT	Cardiac Resuscitation Team [*Medicine*]
CRT	Caribintair SA [*Haiti*] [*ICAO designator*] (FAAC)
CRT	Cartuja [*Granada*] [*Spain*] [*Seismograph station code, US Geological Survey*] (SEIS)
CRT	Cash Register Tape
CRT	Cathode-Ray Terminal
CRT	Cathode-Ray Tube
crt	Cathode-Ray Tube (IDOE)
CRT	Cathode-Ray Typesetting
CRT	C-Band RADAR Transponder
CRT	Center for Rehabilitation Technology [*Georgia Institute of Technology*] [*Research center*] (RCD)
CRT	Centre de Recherche sur les Transports [*Center for Transport Research*] [*University of Montreal*] [*Research center*] (RCD)
CRT	Centre for Rural Transport [*St. David's University College*] [*British*] (CB)
CRT	Channel Reference Tone (MCD)
CRT	Channel Response Time (IAA)
CRT	Charactron Tube [*Electronics*]
CRT	Charitable Remainder Trust
CRT	Chicago Research & Trading Bank (ECON)
CRT	Chief Radio Technician [*Navy rating Obsolete*]
CRT	Choice Reaction Time (PDAA)
CRT	Circuit Requirement Table (MSA)
CRT	Classroom Trainer (MCD)
CRT	Clerici Regulares Theatini [*Theatines*] [*Roman Catholic religious order*]
CRT	Cold-Rolled and Tempered [*Metal*]
CRT	Columbus Research Tool [*Control Data Corp.*]
CRT	Combat Rated Thrust [*Navy*] (NG)
CRT	Combat Reaction Time
CRT	Combat Readiness Trainer [*or Training*]
CRT	Combined Radiation Test
CRT	Combined Radiation Treatment [*Oncology*]
CRT	Complex Reaction Time [*or Timer*] [*Neurology*] (AAMN)
CRT	Composite-Rate Tax [*British*]
CRT	Composite Readiness Test
CRT	Computer Remote Terminal (MCD)
CRT	Continuous Ring Tone [*Telecommunications*] (TEL)
CRT	Contract Regulation Tribunal [*New South Wales*] [*Australia*]
CRT	Control of Radio Transmission [*British World War II*]
CRT	Control Relay Translator (IAA)
CRT	Control Route Tag (IAA)
CRT	Copper Reduction Test [*Chemistry*] (DAVI)
CRT	Copyright Royalty Tribunal [*Library of Congress*]
CRT	Correct (MUGU)
CRT	Corrected Retention Time [*Medicine*] (DAVI)
CRT	CorRecTerm [*Mergenthaler typesetting*]
CRT	Cortisone-Resistant Thymocyte [*Biochemistry*]
CRT	Cosmic Ray Telescope
CRT	Counter Recovery Time
CRT	Count Reduction Technique [*Food bacteriology*]
CRT	Court
Crt	Court (DD)
CRT	Court Reporting Typist
CRT	Cranial Radiotherapy
CRT	Crate
Crt	Crater [*Constellation*]
CRT	Criterion-Referenced Test [*or Testing*] [*Education*]
CRT	Crossett, AR [*Location identifier FAA*] (FAAL)
CRT	Cross Timbers Royalty Tr [*NYSE symbol*] (TTSB)
CRT	Cross Timbers Royalty Trust [*NYSE symbol*] (SAG)
CRT	Crown Trust Co. [*Toronto Stock Exchange symbol*]
CRT	Current Transformer
Crt	With Certificate [*Philately*]
CRTA	Chief of Rocket Troops and Artillery (MCD)
CRTB	Critical Reasoning Test Battery
CRTC	Canadian Radio-Television and Telecommunications Commission [*Conseil de la Radiodiffusion et des Telecommunications Canadiennes*] [*Ottawa, ON*] [*Telecommunications*]
CRTC	Canadian Railway and Transport Cases [*A publication*] (DLA)
CRTC	Cathode-Ray Tube Controller
CRTC	Cathode Ray Tube Controller (NITA)
CRTC	Cavalry Replacement Training Center
CRTC	Circle Repertory Theater Company
CRTC	Clay Roofing Tile Council [*British*] (DBA)
CRTC	Cold Regions Test Center [*Seattle, WA*] [*Army*] (RDA)
crtch	Cartouche (VRA)
CRTCQ	Conseil Regional des Travailleuses et Travailleuses Centre du Quebec (AC)
CRTF	Central Receiver Test Facility [*Department of Energy*]
CRTF	Core Restraint Test Facility [*Nuclear energy*] (NRCH)
CRTF	Corporate Responsibility Task Force of the Business Roundtable (EA)
CRTF	Create Test File (IAA)
CRTFCA	Chicago Religious Task Force on Central America (EA)
CRTFP	Commission des Relations de Travail dans la Fonction Publique [*Public Service Staff Relations Board - PSSRB*] [*Canada*]
CRTFY	Certify (FAAC)
CRTG	Cartridge (MSA)
CRTH	Council for Research on Turkish History [*Defunct*] (EA)
CRTI	Center for the Rights of the Terminally Ill (EA)
CRTIS	Chicago Railroad Terminal Information System [*Pronounced "Curtis"*]
CRTL	Criticality
CRTM	Cartilage Matrix Protein [*Medicine*] (DMAA)

CRTM	Curtis Mathes Hldg [*NASDAQ symbol*] (TTSB)
CRTM	Curtis Mathes Holding Corp. [*NASDAQ symbol*] (SAG)
CRTN	Carton [*Packaging*]
crtn	Cartoon (VRA)
CRTN	Certron Corp. [*NASDAQ symbol*] (NQ)
CRTN	Correction (MUGU)
CRTN	Curtain
crtnstl	Corten Steel (VRA)
CRTO	Cathode-Ray Tube Oscillograph
CRTOG	Cartographer [*or Cartography*] (AFM)
CRTOS	Cathode Ray Tube Operating System (NITA)
CRTP	Commercial Receiver Test Program
CRTP	Consciousness Research and Training Project (EA)
CRTPB	Canadian Radio Technical Planning Board (NTCM)
CRTQ	Cortech, Inc. [*NASDAQ symbol*] (SAG)
CRTR	Courtier
CrTr	Crutch Training [*Orthopedics*] (DAVI)
CRTR	Current Retail Trade Reports [*A publication*]
CRTS	Cathode-Ray Tube Shield
CRTS	COMINT [*Communications Intelligence*] Receiver Test System (MCD)
CRTS	Constant Returns to Scale [*Econometrics*]
CRTS	Controllable RADAR Target Simulator
CRTSY	Courtesy
CRTT	Cathode-Ray Tube Tester
CRTT	Certified Respiratory Therapy Technician
CRTU	Combined Receiving and Transmitting Unit
CRTV	Composite Reentry Test Vehicle (MCD)
CRTV	Creative Technologies [*NASDAQ symbol*] (TTSB)
CRTV	Creative Technologies Corp. [*NASDAQ symbol*] (SAG)
CRTX	Cast Removed, Take to X-Ray [*Orthopedics*] (DAVI)
CRU	Cancer Research Unit [*Flinders University*] [*Australia*]
CRU	Cardiac Rehabilitation Unit [*Cardiology*] (DMAA)
CRU	Card Reader Unit [*Computer science*]
CRU	Carriacou [*Windward Islands*] [*Airport symbol*] (OAG)
CRU	Catalytic Reforming Unit [*Petroleum refining*]
CRU	Catalytic Research Unit (SSD)
CRU	Children's Research Unit [*Market research company*] [*British*]
CRU	Civilian Repair Unit [*British military*] (DMA)
CRU	Civil Resettlement Unit [*British*] (DAS)
CRU	Climatic Research Unit
CRU	Clinical Research Unit
CRU	Collective Reserve Unit [*International finance*]
CRU	Combined Rotating Unit [*Nuclear energy*]
CRU	Command and Response Unit
CRU	Commodities Research Unit Ltd. [*Originator and Databank*] [*Information service or system*] (IID)
CRU	Communications Register Unit (IAA)
CRU	Community Residential Unit [*Victoria*] [*Australia*]
CRU	Compass Re-Transmission Unit (PDAA)
CRU	Compliance Review Unit (OICC)
CRU	Computer Resource Unit
CRU	Constitutional Repeating Unit [*Organic chemistry*]
CRU	Consultancy and Research Unit [*Department of Information Studies, University of Sheffield*] [*British*] (AIE)
CRU	Control and Reporting Unit
CRU	Control Relay Unlatch
CRU	Converter Regulator Unit (MCD)
CRU	Cooperatives Research Unit [*British*]
CRU	Corps Reinforcement Unit [*British military*] (DMA)
CRU	Crated - Rocket Unit [*Military*]
CRU	Credit Union
CRU	Criminology Research Unit [*Australia*]
CRU	Crisan Resources Ltd. [*Vancouver Stock Exchange symbol*]
CRU	Crisis Resolution Center [*Psychiatry*] (DAVI)
CRU	Cruiser [*Navy*]
Cru	Cruise's Digest of the Law of Real Property [*1804-35*] [*England*] [*A publication*] (DLA)
CRU	Crutchfield [*Kentucky*] [*Seismograph station code, US Geological Survey*] (SEIS)
Cru	Crux [*Constellation*]
CRU	Customer Replaceable Unit (IAA)
CrU	Universidad de Costa Rica, San Jose, Costa Rica [*Library symbol Library of Congress*] (LCLS)
CRU	University of California, Riverside, Riverside, CA [*OCLC symbol*] (OCLC)
CRUB	Calgary Round-Up Band Association (AC)
CRUBATFOR	Cruisers, Battle Force [*Navy*]
CRUD	Carbon, Rust, and Undesirable Dirt [*Facetious interpretation of what collects on objects left unprotected*] [*Automotive engineering*]
CRUD	Chalk River Unidentified Deposit [*Nuclear energy*] (GFGA)
CRUDE	Committee to Remove Unnatural Deposits from the Environment [*Student legal action organization*]
CRUDESFLOT	Cruiser-Destroyer Flotilla [*Navy symbol*]
CRUDESLANT	Cruiser-Destroyer Force, Atlantic Fleet [*Navy symbol*]
CRUDESPAC	Cruiser-Destroyer Force, Pacific Fleet [*Navy symbol*]
Cru Dig	Cruise's Digest of the Law of Real Property [*1804-35*] [*England*] [*A publication*] (DLA)
Cru Dign	Cruise on Dignities [*A publication*] (DLA)
CRUDIV	Cruiser Division [*Navy*]
CRUDZINE	Crude Magazine [*Generic term for a one-person science-fiction fan magazine, produced by an inexperienced publisher*]
CRUEL	Commission on Reform of Undergraduate Education and Living [*University of Illinois*]
Cru Fin	Cruise's Fines and Recoveries [*A publication*] (DLA)
CRUFON	Citizens Radio UFO [*Unidentified Flying Object*] Network

CRUIS.........	Cruising (KSC)
CruisAm......	Cruise America, Inc. [Associated Press] (SAG)
Cruise Dig ...	Cruise's Digest of the Law of Real Property [1804-35] [England] [A publication] (DLA)
Cruise's Dig...	Cruise's Digest of the Law of Real Property [1804-35] [England] [A publication] (DLA)
CRUIT.........	Recruiting Office [or Officer] [Navy]
CRUITNOP ...	Recruiting Station and Office of Naval Officer Procurement
CRUITSTA....	Recruiting Station
CRULANT.....	Cruisers, Atlantic Fleet [Navy]
CRULANTFLT...	Cruisers, Atlantic Fleet [Navy]
CRUMBS......	Continuous, Remote, Unobstructive Monitoring of Biobehavioral Systems
Crump Ins....	Crump on Marine Insurance [A publication] (DLA)
Crump Jud Pr...	Crump. Practice under the Judicature Acts [A publication] (DLA)
Crump Mar Ins...	Crump on Marine Insurance [A publication] (DLA)
Crump S & Pl...	Crump. Sale and Pledge [A publication] (DLA)
Crumrine.....	Crumrine's Reports [116-146 Pennsylvania] [A publication] (DLA)
Crumrine	Pittsburgh Reports, Edited by Crumrine [A publication] (DLA)
CRUNCH......	Consolidated Record of Uncontrolled Naval Calamitious Happenings
CRUPAC......	Cruisers, Pacific Fleet [Navy]
CRUPACFLT..	Cruisers, Pacific Fleet [Navy]
CRUS.........	Centre for Research on User Studies [University of Sheffield] [England] [Information service or system] (IID)
CRUS..........	Cirrus Logic [NASDAQ symbol] (TTSB)
CRUS..........	Cirrus Logic, Inc. [NASDAQ symbol] (NQ)
CRUS..........	[The] Consultancy and Research Unit, University of Sheffield [England] [Information service or system] (IID)
CRUS..........	Cruise
CRUS..........	Customs Regulations of the United States
CRUSBP......	Campaign to Remove US Bases from the Philippines [Later, CAB] (EA)
CRUSCOFOR...	Cruiser-Scouting Force [Navy]
CRUSCORON...	Cruiser-Scouting Squadron [Navy]
CRUSK........	Center for Research on Utilization of Scientific Knowledge [University of Michigan]
CRUST........	Consolidated Residual Undeleted Subordinated Tranches [Finance]
CRUT	Charitable Remainder Unitrust (NFD)
CRUTEPO.....	Commission Regionale de l'Utilisation des Terres et des Eaux au Proche-Orient [Regional Commission on Land and Water Use in the Near East - RCLWUNE] (EAIO)
Cru Titl	Cruise on Titles of Honor [A publication] (DLA)
Cru Us	Cruise on Uses [A publication] (DLA)
CRUZ..........	Cruise [Automotive advertising]
Cruz...........	Cruzeiro [Monetary unit] [Brazil]
CRUZEIRO ..	Servicos Aereos Cruzeiro do Sul SA [Brazilian airline]
CRV	Call Reference Value [Telecommunications] (ACRL)
CRV	Caravelas [Brazil] [Airport symbol] (AD)
CRV	Caraveli [Peru] [Seismograph station code, US Geological Survey Closed] (SEIS)
crv	Carved (VRA)
CRV	Central Retinal Vein [Ophthalmology]
CRV	Certificate of Reasonable Value [Veterans Administration]
CRV	Chrome Vanadium
CRV	Cloth, Rollers, and Varnished [Maps] (ROG)
CRV	Coast Distribution Sys [AMEX symbol] (TTSB)
CRV	Coast Distribution Systems [AMEX symbol] (SPSG)
CRV	Coffee Ringspot Virus [Plant pathology]
CRV	Comfortable Recreation Vehicle
CRV	Comment Recevez-Vous [French]
CRV	Committee of Returned Volunteers [Defunct] (EA)
CRV	Conditional Release Violator [FBI standardized term]
CRV	Cone Resistance Value [Civil engineering] (IAA)
CRV	Constant Reflector Voltage (IAA)
CRV	Contact Resistance Variation [Telecommunications] (TEL)
CRV	Controlled Rotary Vane [Compressor] [Automotive engineering]
CRV	Corvette Petroleum Corp. [Vancouver Stock Exchange symbol]
Crv............	Corvus [Constellation]
CRV	Curve (MSA)
CRV	How Do You Receive [International telex abbreviation] (WDMC)
CRVA	Canadian Recreational Vehicle Association (EAIO)
CRVAN........	Chrome Vanadium
CRVC	Cambridgeshire Rifle Volunteer Corps [British military] (DMA)
CRVC	Cross-Range Velocity Correlator (MUGU)
CR VESP....	Cras Vespere [Tomorrow Evening] [Pharmacy]
CRVF	Congestive Right Ventricular Failure [Medicine] (DMAA)
CRVICS.......	Containment and Reactor Vessel Isolation Control System (NRCH)
CRVL	CorVel Corp. [NASDAQ symbol] (SPSG)
CRVO	Central Retinal Vein Occlusion [Ophthalmology]
CRVR	Computerized Register of Voice Research [No longer maintained] [Southern Illinois University at Carbondale] [Information service or system] (IID)
CRVS	California Relative Value Studies [Medicine] (DHSM)
CRW	Carrier Wave [A form of radio transmission in code] (KSC)
CRW	Charleston [West Virginia] [Airport symbol] (OAG)
CRW	Charleston, WV [Location identifier FAA] (FAAL)
CRW	Cinram Ltd. [Toronto Stock Exchange symbol]
CRW	Clean RADWASTE [Radioactive waste] [Nuclear energy] (NRCH)
CRW	Commission on Rural Water [Defunct] (EA)
CRW	Community Radio Watch
CRW	Conceptual Recoilless Weapons (MCD)
CRW	Continuous Rod Warhead (MCD)
CRW	Control Read/Write (MCD)
CRW	Counter-Revolutionary Warfare [British military] (DMA)
CRW	Counter-Revolutionary Wing [Special Air Service] [Military British]

CRW	Crownair [Canada ICAO designator] (FAAC)
CRW	Crown Crafts [NYSE symbol] (TTSB)
CRW	Crown Crafts, Inc. [NYSE symbol] (SAG)
CRWA	Community Resources Workshop Association [Later, NAIEC] (EA)
CRWAD........	Conference of Research Workers in Animal Diseases (EA)
CRWC	Connecticut River Watershed Council (EA)
CRWCS........	Canning Rvier Wetlands Conservation Society [Australia]
CRWF	Catalyst Resource on the Work Force and Women [Catalyst Information Center] [Information service or system] (IID)
CRWF	CRW Financial [NASDAQ symbol] (TTSB)
CRWF	CRW Financial, Inc. [NASDAQ symbol] (SAG)
Crwfd.........	Crawford & Co. [Associated Press] (SAG)
CRW Fn	CRW Financial, Inc. [Associated Press] (SAG)
CRWG	Computer Resources Working Group [Military] (AFIT)
CRWI	Coalition for Responsible Waste Incineration (EA)
CRWLRA.......	Commission on Research of the World Leisure and Recreation Association (EA)
CRWM	Civilian Radioactive Waste Management [Department of Energy] (NUCP)
CRWM	Committee on Radioactive Waste Management [Later, BRWM] (EA)
CRWMP	Commendation Ribbon with Medal Pendant [Military decoration]
CRWMS-M&O...	Civilian Radioactive Waste Management System--Management and Operating [Contractor] (GAAI)
CRWN	Crown
CRWN	Crown Books [NASDAQ symbol] (TTSB)
CRWN	Crown Books Corp. [NASDAQ symbol] (NQ)
CrwnAm.......	Crown American Realty Trust [Associated Press] (SAG)
CrwnAn	Crown Andersen, Inc. [Associated Press] (SAG)
CrwnL........	Crown Laboratories, Inc. [Associated Press] (SAG)
CrwnRs	Crown Resource Corp. [Associated Press] (SAG)
CrwnVn	Crown Vantage, Inc. [Associated Press] (SAG)
CRWO	Coding Room Watch Officer [Navy]
CRWP	Census Registration Working Party [US Military Government, Germany]
CRWR	Center for Research in Water Resources [University of Texas at Austin] [Research center] (RCD)
CRWRC........	Christian Reformed World Relief Committee (EA)
CRWSS........	Condensate and Refueling Water Storage System [Nuclear energy] (NRCH)
CRX	Corinth, MS [Location identifier FAA] (FAAL)
CRX	Cross Air AG [Switzerland ICAO designator] (FAAC)
CRX	Crownx, Inc. [Toronto Stock Exchange symbol]
CRY	Chrysolite [Jewelry] (ROG)
CRY	Clovis, NM [Location identifier FAA] (FAAL)
CRY	Cryogenics (SSD)
CRY	Crystal [or Crystallography]
CRY-AB.......	Cryptococcal Antibody [Immunology] (DAVI)
CRY-AG.......	Cryptococcal Antigen [Immunology] (DAVI)
Cryenco	Cryenco Sciences, Inc. [Associated Press] (SAG)
CRYG	Carrying (MSA)
CRYGNC	Cryogenic
CRYL	Cryolife, Inc. [NASDAQ symbol] (SAG)
CRY N.........	Crystal Number [On urinalysis] [Biochemistry] (DAVI)
CRYNG........	Carrying [Freight]
CRYO	Cryogenic
CRYO	Cryoglobulin [Biochemistry] (DAVI)
cryo	Cryosurgery [Medicine] (DAVI)
cryo	Cryotherapy [Medicine] (DAVI)
CRYOG........	Cryogenic (KSC)
Cryolife........	Cryolife, Inc. [Associated Press] (SAG)
Cryomed.......	Cryomedical Sciences, Inc. [Associated Press] (SAG)
CRYOSAR	Cryostatic Switching-Avalanche and Recombination (MCD)
CRYPTA.......	Cryptanalysis [Air Force] (AFM)
CRYPTO	Cryptococcus [Immunology] (DAVI)
CRYPTO	Cryptographic [or Cryptography] (AFM)
CRYPTONET...	Crypto-Communication Network (MDG)
CRYS	Crystal
crys...........	Crystal (VRA)
CRYS	Crystallume Inc. [NASDAQ symbol] (TTSB)
CRYSNET......	Crystallographic Computing Network [AEC] (IID)
CRYST	Crystal [or Crystalline or Crystallize or Crystallography]
CRYST	Crystal Examination Screen [Medicine] (DAVI)
CRYSTAL	Crystallography (ROG)
CRYSTALLOG...	Crystallography (ROG)
CRYSTD.......	Crystallized
CRYSTL	Crystal
CRYSTMET...	Metals Crystallographic Data File [Canada Institute for Scientific and Technical Information] [Information service or system] (CRD)
CRYSTN.......	Crystallization
CrystOil.......	Crystal Oil Co. [Associated Press] (SAG)
crytd	Caryatid (VRA)
CRZ.............	Cape Reinga [New Zealand] [Seismograph station code, US Geological Survey] (SEIS)
CRZ.............	Close Reconnaissance Zone [Army] (AABC)
CRZ.............	Corning, IA [Location identifier FAA] (FAAL)
CRZ.............	Cruise (GAVI)
CRZ.............	Cruise [ICAO] (FAAC)
CRZ.............	Servicios Aereos Cruzeiro do Sul SA [Brazil] [ICAO designator] (FAAC)
CRZAM	Cruise and Maintain [Aviation] (FAAC)
CRZWTR	Cruise Well to Right [Aviation] (FAAC)
CRZY	Crazy
CRZY	Crazy Woman Creek Bancorp, Inc. [NASDAQ symbol] (SAG)
CRZY	Crazy Woman Creek Bncp [NASDAQ symbol] (TTSB)
CS	Adventist Community Services (EA)

CS	Air Toronto [*ICAO designator*] (AD)
CS	Beta, Beta-Dicyano-O-Chlorostyrene [*Organic chemistry*] (DAVI)
CS	Cable Ship [*Followed by name of cable-laying ship*]
CS	Cabletron Systems [*NYSE symbol*] (TTSB)
CS	Cabletron Systems, Inc. [*NYSE symbol*] (SPSG)
CS	Caesarean Section [*Medicine*]
CS	Calcium Intake Score [*Medicine*]
CS	Caledonian Society [*Australia*]
CS	Calf Serum [*Biochemistry*] (DAVI)
C-S	California State Library, Sutro Branch, San Francisco, CA [*Library symbol Library of Congress*] (LCLS)
CS	Calix Society (EA)
CS	Call Sign [*or Signal*] [*Radio*]
CS	Calls per Second [*Telecommunications*] (TEL)
CS	Call Store [*Telecommunications*] (TEL)
CS	Camera Site [*NASA*] (KSC)
CS	Camillus Salernus [*Flourished, 16th century*] [*Authority cited in pre-1607 legal work*] (DSA)
CS	Camouflage-Sensitive [*Designation*] [*Army*] (RDA)
CS	Camptothecin Sodium [*Biochemistry*] (AAMN)
CS	Canberra Skeptics [*Australia*]
CS	Candidate Selection [*Army*]
CS	CanSurmount (EA)
CS	Canvasback Society (EA)
CS	Capital Secure [*Finance*]
CS	Capital Ship [*Bomb*]
CS	Capital Stock
CS	Carbon Steel
CS	Carcinoid Syndrome [*Oncology*] (DAVI)
CS	Cardiogenic Shock
CS	Card Service [*Computer science*] (PCM)
CS	Card Socket [*Electronics*] (IAA)
CS	Card Station [*Computer science*] (BUR)
CS	Careers Services [*Navy British*]
CS	Carolina Southern Railway Co. (IIA)
CS	Carotid Sheath [*Cardiology*] (DAVI)
CS	Carotid Sinus [*Cardiology*] (DAVI)
CS	Carrier Stability
CS	Carrier Suitability (DNAB)
CS	Carrier Supply (MSA)
CS	Car Service [*Railroads*]
CS	Carson and Staughton [*Inventors of a teargas*] (BARN)
CS	Case
cs	Case (WDMC)
CS	Casein Plastic [*Organic chemistry*]
CS	Case Supervisor [*Red Cross*] [*Services to the Armed Forces; Disaster Services*]
C/S	Cash Sale [*Business term*] (ADA)
CS	Cassenne [*France*] [*Research code symbol*]
CS	Cast Steel
CS	Cast Stone (AAG)
CS	Category Stimulus [*To light*]
CS	Cathedral Series [*A publication*]
CS	Cat Scratch [*Medicine*] (AAMN)
CS	Caught Stealing [*Baseball*]
CS	Caulking Seam (DAC)
CS	Cechoslovakische Statistik [*Czechoslovakia*]
CS	Cedars-Sinai Medical Center [*Los Angeles, CA*]
CS	Celiac Sprue [*Medicine*] (DAVI)
CS	Census
CS	Center for Cybernetic Studies [*University of Texas*] (PDAA)
CS	Center for Statistics [*Later, CES*] [*Department of Education*] (IID)
CS	Center Section
CS	Center Stage [*A stage direction*]
CS	Centistere [*Metric*]
cs	Centistoke [*Also, cSt*] [*Unit of kinematic viscosity*]
CS	Central School (ADA)
CS	Central Service [*Medicine*] (DHSM)
C/S	Central Site
CS	Central States [*An association*] (EA)
C/S	Central Station [*NASA*]
CS	Central Supply (KSC)
CS	Centrifugal Spraying
CS	Cephalic Sinus
Cs	Cephalosporium Stripe [*of wheat*] [*Plant pathology*]
CS	Cerebrospinal [*Medicine*]
CS	Certificate of Service [*Military*] (MCD)
CS	Cerulein and Secretin (Test) [*Clinical chemistry*]
CS	Cervical Spine [*Neurology and orthopedics*] (DAVI)
CS	Cervical Stimulation [*Neurology and orthopedics*] (DAVI)
Cs	Cesium [*Chemical element*]
CS	Champlain Society (EA)
C/S	Change of Speed (DNAB)
CS	Change of Status (NASA)
CS	Change Sheet [*Marine Corps*]
CS	Channel Status
CS	Characteristic Slope
CS	Characteristic Standard
CS	Charge for Service
CS	Charge-Separation [*Physical chemistry*]
CS	Chartered Surveyor (ODBW)
CS	Checkout Station (MCD)
CS	Check Sorter
CS	Checksum Error (MCD)
CS	Check Surface (IAA)

CS	Chemical Shift [*Physical chemistry*]
CS	Chemical Society [*Later, RSC*] [*British*]
CS	Chemical Sympathectomy [*Neurology*] (DAVI)
CS	Chest Strap [*Medicine*]
CS	Chief of Section
CS	Chief of Staff [*Military*]
CS	Chief Scientist [*Marine science*] (OSRA)
CS	Chief Scientist [*National Oceanic and Atmospheric Administration*] (USDC)
CS	Chief Secretary (ADA)
CS	Chief Superintendent (ADA)
CS	Child Support Rulings [*Australian Taxation Office*] [*A publication*]
CS	China Spring (EA)
CS	Chinese Alliance for Democracy (EA)
CS	Chip Select Input [*Computer science*]
CS	Chip Selection [*Electronics*] (ECII)
CS	Chi Square
CS	Chlorobenzalmalononitrile [*Tear gas*] [*Army symbol*]
CS	Chondroitin Sulfate [*Biochemistry*]
CS	Chorionic Somatomammotrophin [*Endocrinology*]
CS	Christian Science
CS	[*The*] Christian Sisters (Pious Union) (TOCD)
CS	Chromate Sensitivity [*Immunology*]
CS	Chronic Schizophrenia (AAMN)
CS	Chrysoberyl [*Jewelry*] (ROG)
CS	Churches Speak [*A publication*]
CS	Church Scene [*A publication*] (APTA)
CS	Cigarette Smoke [*or Smoker*] (DAVI)
CS	Cincinnatus Society [*Defunct*] (EA)
CS	Cinemascope
CS	Circuit Switching [*Telecommunications*]
CS	Circumsporozoite [*Protozoology*]
CS	Cirrostratus [*Meteorology*]
CS	Cities in Schools [*An association*] (EA)
CS	Citizen Soldier (EA)
CS	Citrate Synthase [*An enzyme*]
CS	Civil Servant (DLA)
CS	Civil Service
CS	Civil Society (EA)
CS	Civil Surgeon (DAS)
CS	Clarsach Society (EAIO)
CS	Class of Service [*Telecommunications*] (TEL)
CS	Class of Supply [*Military*]
CS	Clear and Subtract
CS	Clear Status (MCD)
CS	Clerk of Sessions [*British*] (ROG)
CS	Clerk to the Signet [*British*]
CS	Clinical Specialist (PGP)
CS	Clinical Staging [*Oncology*]
CS	Clinical State
CS	Clock Synchronization
CS	Closed Shell
CS	Close Shot [*Photography*]
CS	Close Support [*Army*]
CS	Closing Sale [*Business term*]
CS	Cloth Sides [*Bookbinding*]
CS	Cloud Shadow (DNAB)
CS	Clymer System
CS	Coal and Steel (NATG)
CS	Coaling Station [*As part of a symbol*]
CS	Coal Store (OA)
CS	[*The*] Coastal Society (EA)
CS	Coblentz Society (EA)
CS	Cockayne's Syndrome [*Medicine*]
CS	Coco Solo, Canal Zone
CS	Code Segment [*Computer science*]
CS	Coding Specification
CS	Cogitive Style (EDAC)
CS	Cognitive Stimulation [*Experimental psychology*]
CS	Cognizance Symbol
CS	Coil Sketch (MSA)
CS	COINTELPRO [*FBI Counterintelligence Program*] Survivors [*Defunct*] (EA)
CS	Cold Stabilized [*Automotive engineering*]
CS	Cold Storage
CS	Coleopterists' Society (EA)
CS	Colla Sinistra [*With the Left Hand*] [*Music*]
CS	Collet-Sicard [*Syndrome*] [*Otorhinolaryngology and neurology*] (DAVI)
C/S	Colliery Screened (ROG)
CS	Colonial Secretary [*British*] (ADA)
CS	Colophon Society [*Australia*]
CS	[*The*] Colorado & Southern Railway Co. [*AAR code*]
CS	Colorimetric Solution
CS	Color Specification
CS	Color Strength [*Dye technology*]
CS	Columbian Squires (EA)
CS	Column Split [*Computer science*] (IAA)
Cs	Combat Rations [*Military*] (VNW)
CS	Combat Support
CS	Combat System [*Military*] (CAAL)
CS	Comedy Store [*Nightclub in which inexperienced comedians appear free in return for exposure to an audience*]
CS	Come Sopra [*As Above*] [*Music*]
CS	Command Selector
CS	Command System (NATG)

CS	Commercial Standard [*A publication*]
CS	Commercial System [*Data General Corp.*]
C/S	Commercial Vehicle Substitute
CS	Commissaryman [*Navy rating*]
CS	Commissary of Subsistence [*Military British*] (ROG)
CS	Commissary Store [*Navy*]
CS	Commissioners of Sewers [*British*] (ROG)
CS	Commit Stop (AAG)
CS	Committee of Seismology [*National Academy of Sciences*] (USDC)
CS	Committee on Seismology [*Marine science*] (OSRA)
CS	Common and Standard [*Items*] (AAG)
CS	Common Serjeant [*British*] (ROG)
CS	Common Set (MCD)
CS	Common Slavic [*Language, etc.*]
CS	Common Steel [*Projectile*]
CS	Common Stock [*Investment term*]
CS	Commonwealth Secretariat [*Australia*]
CS	Commonwealth Secretariat [*British*] (EAIO)
CS	Communication Segment (MCD)
CS	Communications Satellite [*Japan*]
CS	Communications Services (NITA)
CS	Communications Simulator [*Sperry UNIVAC*]
CS	Communications Squadron [*Air Force*]
CS	Communications Switcher
CS	Communications System
CS	Communication Station
CS	Communication Studies (AIE)
CS	Communis [*Common*] [*Latin*]
CS	Community Service [*An association*] (EA)
CS	Company of the Savior [*Roman Catholic women's religious order*]
CS	Company Secretary
CS	Competitive Sensitive (MCD)
CS	Competitive Strategies [*NATO*]
CS	Compiled Statutes [*A publication*] (DLA)
CS	Complementary Symmetry [*Electronics*] (ECII)
CS	Completed Stroke [*Neurology*] (DAVI)
CS	Completed Suicide [*Psychiatry*] (DAVI)
CS	Complex Spikes
CS	Compliance and Security (SAA)
CS	Component Specification (AAG)
CS	Component Supports (NRCH)
CS	Composite Service [*Army*] (AABC)
CS	Comprehensive System (SAA)
CS	Comptroller and Surveyor [*British*] (ROG)
C/S	COMPUSTAT Services, Inc. [*Information service or system*] (IID)
CS	Computers and Systems (MCD)
CS	Computer Science (BUR)
CS	Computer Simulation (RDA)
CS	Computer Slave [*Computer science*] (DGA)
CS	Computer Software (MCD)
CS	Concentrated Strength [*of solutions*] [*Pharmacy*]
CS	Concrete Slab (OA)
CS	Concrete Society [*British*] (EAIO)
CS	Concurrent Stereometric [*A discrimination task*]
CS	Conditional Sale [*Legal shorthand*] (LWAP)
CS	Conditioned Stimulus [*Psychometrics*]
CS	Condition Status [*Computer science*]
CS	Condition Subsequent [*Legal term*]
CS	Conducted Susceptibility (IEEE)
CS	Conestoga Society (EA)
CS	Confederate States (HGAA)
CS	Congenital Syphilis [*Medicine*]
CS	Congregatio Missionariorum a Sancto Carlo [*Congregation of the Missionary Fathers of St. Charles*] [*Formerly, PSSC*] [*Roman Catholic religious order*]
CS	Congregation of Salesians [*Australia*]
CS	Congress and Session Number (NITA)
CS	Congressional Session [*Online database field identifier*]
CS	Conjunctival Secretion [*Ophthalmology*] (DAVI)
CS	Conjunctival Secretions [*Medicine*] (MEDA)
CS	Connecticut Supplement [*A publication*] (DLA)
CS	Consciousness [*Neurology and psychiatry*] (DAVI)
CS	Conseil de Securite [*United Nations*]
CS	Conservation Society [*British*] (DCTA)
CS	Consolidated Statutes [*A publication*] (DLA)
CS	Con Sordino [*With Mute*] [*Music*]
CS	Constantian Society (EA)
CS	Construcciones Aeronauticas SA [*Spain ICAO aircraft manufacturer identifier*] (ICAO)
CS	Constructor Syntax (MHDI)
CS	Consul
CS	Consulting Surgeon [*British*] (ROG)
CS	Consumables Status (MCD)
CS	Consumer Sourcebook [*A publication*]
CS	Contact Sensitivity [*Allergy and dermatology*] (DAVI)
CS	Containment Safety [*Nuclear energy*] (NRCH)
CS	Containment Spray [*Nuclear energy*] (NRCH)
CS	Contemporary Sociology [*A publication*] (BRI)
CS	Continental Sediment [*Geology*]
CS	Contingency Sample [*NASA*] (KSC)
CS	Continue Same [*Treatment*] [*Medicine*] (DAVI)
CS	Continue-Specific [*Mode*] [*Computer science*] (IBMDP)
CS	Continuing Smoker (DAVI)
CS	Continuous Scan [*Computer science*] (IAA)
CS	Continuous Service [*British military*] (DMA)
CS	Continuous Stationery [*Commercial firm British*]
CS	Continuous Strip Film (DNAB)
CS	Continuous Stripping [*Surgery*] (DAVI)
CS	Continuous Survey (DS)
CS	Contractor Sensitization (DNAB)
CS	Contractor State Code [*Database terminology*] (NITA)
CS	Contractor Support
CS	Contract Specialist (GFGA)
CS	Contracts Station (AAG)
CS	Contract Surgeon [*Military*]
CS	Controlled Stock (SAA)
CS	Controlled Stress [*Physiology*]
CS	Control Scanner
CS	Control Section (IAA)
CS	Control Segment (MCD)
CS	Control Set
CS	Control Signal
CS	Control Slip (CINC)
CS	Control Station (MCD)
CS	Control Store
CS	Control Switch (MSA)
CS	Control Systems (MCD)
CS	Convalescent Status [*Medicine*]
CS	Conventional System [*Indexing*] (NITA)
CS	Convergence Sublayer [*Electronics*] (ACRL)
CS	Convergent Stereoscopic [*Photography*]
CS	Conveyor Section of the Material Handling Institute (EA)
CS	Coolant Sampling (DNAB)
CS	Cooperative Society
CS	Copper or Steel [*Freight*]
CS	Coppersmith [*British*]
CS	Coppersmiths Society [*A union*] [*British*]
CS	Core Segment (NASA)
CS	Core Sharing [*Computer science*] (IAA)
CS	Core Shift
CS	Core Spray [*Nuclear energy*] (NRCH)
CS	Corn Stunt [*Plant pathology*]
CS	Coronary Sclerosis [*Medicine*]
CS	Coronary Sinus [*Cardiology*]
CS	Coronary Status [*Cardiology*]
CS	Corporate Source [*Online database field identifier*]
CS	Corps of Signals [*British*] (DAS)
CS	Corpus Striatum (MAE)
CS	Correct Selection [*Statistics*]
CS	Corresponding Secretary (IIA)
CS	Corse Air International [*France ICAO designator*] (ICDA)
CS	Cortical Spoking [*Ophthalmology*] (DAVI)
CS	Corticoid Sensitive [*Laboratory*] (DAVI)
CS	Corticosteroid [*Endocrinology*]
CS	Cosmetology Program [*Association of Independent Colleges and Schools specialization code*]
CS	Costing System (DGA)
C/S	Cost of Sale [*Accounting*]
C/S	Cost/Schedule
CS	Cost Sharing
C/S	Cost-Stirling [*Antibodies*] [*Immunology*] (DAVI)
CS	Cotton Seed
CS	Cotton Silk [*Wire insulation*] (IAA)
CS	Counselor Structured
CS	Counter-Sabotage (AABC)
CS	Countershocks
CS	Countersink [*Technical drawings*]
CS	Counterstamped [*Numismatics*]
CS	Counting Switch
C/S	Counts per Second (NASA)
CS	Coupe Sport [*Automotive*]
CS	Coupled States [*Physics*]
CS	Court of Session [*Scotland*]
CS	Cousteau Society [*Established to Fund Marine Research*] (GNE)
CS	Cover Screen [*Medicine*] (DAVI)
C/S	Crankshaft [*Automotive engineering*]
CS	Cream Shade [*Paper*]
CS	Creation Sheet (SAA)
CS	Credit Suisse [*Bank*]
CS	Creo Society [*Defunct*] (EA)
C/S	Crew-Served Weapon
CS	Crew Station [*NASA*] (KSC)
CS	Crew Systems
CS	Crime Stoppers USA [*Later, CSI*] (EA)
CS	Critical Sensitive
CS	Cromolyn Sodium [*Pharmacology*]
CS	Cross Section
CS	Crown Side [*Records*] [*British*] (ROG)
CS	Crown Solicitor [*Australia*]
CS	Cruiser, Scout
CS	Cruiser Squadron [*Navy*]
CS	Crustacean Society (EA)
CS	Crystallographic Shear [*Crystallography*]
CS	Ctenidial Sinus [*Biology*]
CS	Cultural Survival (EA)
CS	Culture Supernatant [*Microbiology*]
CS	Currency Sign [*Telecommunications*] (TEL)
CS	Current Series [*Army*]
CS	Current Smoker (DAVI)
CS	Current Source

CS.............. Current Strength
CS.............. Current Switch (IAA)
CS.............. Curschmann-Steinert [*Syndrome*] [*Medicine*] (DAVI)
CS.............. Curtain Sided Trailer [*Shipping*] (DCTA)
CS.............. Cushing's Syndrome [*Endocrinology*] (DAVI)
CS.............. Customer Service (BUR)
CS.............. Customer Support (BUR)
CS.............. Custos Sigilli [*Keeper of the Seal*] [*Latin*]
CS.............. Cutaneous Stimulation [*Psychometric test*]
CS.............. Cut Sizes [*Paper*] (DGA)
CS.............. Cutting Specification (AAG)
CS.............. Cycad Society (EA)
CS.............. Cycle Sequence
CS.............. Cycle Shift
C/S............. Cycles per Second [*See also Hz*]
CS.............. Cycle Stealing [*Computer science*] (IAA)
CS.............. Cycloserine [*Antibacterial*] (AAMN)
cs.............. Czechoslovakia [*MARC country of publication code Library of Congress*] (LCCP)
CS.............. Czechoslovakia [*ANSI two-letter standard code*] (CNC)
CS.............. IEEE Communications Society (EA)
CS.............. IEEE Computer Society (EA)
CS.............. Missionaries of St. Charles-Scalabrinians (TOCD)
cs.............. Missionaries of St. Charles-Scalabrinians (TOCD)
CS.............. Quebec Supreme Court Reports [*A publication*] (DLA)
CS.............. Reading, English, and Communications [*Educational Resources Information Center (ERIC) Clearinghouse*] [*Indiana University*] (PAZ)
CS.............. Sacramento City-County Library System, Sacramento, CA [*Library symbol Library of Congress*] (LCLS)
CS.............. Scout Cruiser [*Navy symbol Obsolete*]
C$............. Source Capacitance (IDOE)
C$............. Standard Capacitance (IDOE)
CS.............. St. Clair Resources Ltd. [*Vancouver Stock Exchange symbol*]
CS.............. STS [*Space Transportation System*] Cargo Operations [*Kennedy Space Center Directorate*] [*NASA*] (NASA)
CS.............. Sumitomo Chemical Co. [*Japan*] [*Research code symbol*]
CS.............. Tear Gas [*US Chemical Corps symbol*]
CS1............. Commissaryman, First Class [*Navy rating*]
CS².............. Combat Service Support Level [*Military*] (INF)
CS2............. Commissaryman, Second Class [*Navy rating*]
CS2............. Cost Schedule Control System (MCD)
CS3............. Combat Service Support System [*Army*]
CS3............. Commissaryman, Third Class [*Navy rating*]
CS³............. Conceptual Satellite Surveillance System
CS3............. Critically Sensitive Level 3 [*Information*]
CS4............. Critically Sensitive Level 4 [*Information*]
Cs-137....... Cesium-137
CSA............. Albertine Sisters (Krakow, Poland) (TOCD)
CSA............. Army Chief of Staff (AAGC)
CSA............. Assistant Chief of Staff for Studies and Analysis [*Air Force*]
CSA............. California State University, Sacramento, Sacramento, CA [*OCLC symbol*] (OCLC)
CSA............. Called Subscriber Answer [*Telecommunications*] (TEL)
CSA............. CallPath Services Architecture (CDE)
CSA............. Cambridge Scientific Abstracts [*Information service or system*] (IID)
CSA............. Camphorsulfonic Acid [*Organic chemistry*]
CSA............. Campus Safety Association [*of the National Safety Council*] (EA)
CSA............. Canadian Semiotic Association [*See also ACS*]
CSA............. Canadian Shipowners Association (EAIO)
CSA............. Canadian Shipping Act [*1970*] (MSC)
CSA............. Canadian Ski Association
CSA............. Canadian Snowbird Association (AC)
CSA............. Canadian Soccer Association
CSA............. Canadian Society for Aesthetics (AC)
CSA............. Canadian Society of Agronomy
CSA............. Canadian Space Agency
CSA............. Canadian Speech Association
CSA............. Canadian Spice Association (AC)
CSA............. Canadian Standards Approval
CSA............. Canadian Standards Association
CSA............. Canavaninosuccinic Acid [*Organic chemistry*] (MAH)
CSA............. Canoe South Australia
CSA............. Cape Sarichef [*Alaska*] [*Seismograph station code, US Geological Survey Closed*] (SEIS)
CSA............. Caravan Sites Act [*Town planning*] [*British*]
CSA............. Caribbean Studies Association (EA)
CSA............. Caricaturists Society of America (EA)
CSA............. Carrier Serving Area [*Telecommunications*] (ACRL)
CSA............. Carry-Save Adder [*Computer science*] (IAA)
CSA............. Casting Society of America (WDMC)
CSA............. Casualty Surgeons Association [*British*]
CSA............. Catalog Services Association [*Defunct*] (EA)
CSA............. Catalysed Signal Amplification [*Analytical biochemistry*]
CSA............. Catch Society of America [*Defunct*] (EA)
CSA............. Cebu Stevedores Association [*Philippines*]
CSA............. Cell Surface Antigens [*Immunology*]
CSA............. Cellular Surface Area [*Cytology*]
CSA............. Cellulose Synthase Activator [*Biochemistry*]
CSA............. Cemetery Supply Association [*Later, ICSA*] (EA)
CSA............. Center for Safety in the Arts (PAZ)
CSA............. Center for Social Analysis [*State University of New York at Binghamton*] [*Research center*] (RCD)
CSA............. Center for Sustainable Agriculture (EA)
CSA............. Center for the Study of Aging (EA)

CSA............. Central & Southern Motor Freight Tariff Association, Inc., Louisville KY [*STAC*]
CSA............. Central South Africa Railway (ROG)
CSA............. Central Supplies Agency (NATG)
CSA............. Central Supply Association [*Later, ASA*] (EA)
CSA............. Certificate in Systems Analysis (IAA)
CSA............. Ceskoslovenske Aerolinie [*Czechoslovakia*] [*ICAO designator*] (FAAC)
CSA............. Channel Swimming Association [*British*] (EAIO)
CSA............. Character Scan or Alternate [*Computer science*]
CSA............. Charolais Society of Australia
CSA............. Chemical Shielding Anisotropy [*Physics*]
CSA............. Chemical Shift Anisotropy [*Physical chemistry*]
CSA............. Chemical Sources Association (EA)
CSA............. Chemical Storage Area (NRCH)
CSA............. Chemical Structure Association (EAIO)
CSA............. Chief of Staff, United States Army [*Formerly, COFSA, C of SA*]
CSA............. Chief Scientific Adviser [*British*] (RDA)
CSA............. Chief Special Artificer [*Navy rating Obsolete*]
CSA............. Child Study Association of America (BARN)
CSA............. Child Support Agency [*British*] (ECON)
CSA............. China Society of America (EA)
CSA............. Chios Societies of America (EA)
CSA............. Chlorosulfonic Acid [*Organic chemistry*]
CSA............. Chondroitin Sulfate A [*Biochemistry*]
CSA............. Chopper Stabilized Amplifier
CSA............. Christian Schools' Association [*Australia*]
CSA............. Christliche-Sozialistische Arbeitsgemeinschaft [*Christian Social-Workers' Community*] [*Lithuania*] [*Political party*] (PPE)
CSA............. Chromogenic Systems Analyzer
CSA............. Cigar Smokers of America [*Defunct*] (EA)
CSA............. Clean Shelter Area [*Army*] (ADDR)
CSA............. Client Server Architecture (CDE)
CSA............. Client Service Agent (OSI)
CSA............. Clinical Sociology Association [*Later, SPA*] (EA)
CSA............. Close Support Area [*Military*] (CAAL)
CSA............. Cluster Significance Analysis [*Data Analysis*]
CSA............. Coalition on Southern Africa (EA)
CSA............. Coast Savings Financial, Inc. [*NYSE symbol*] (SPSG)
CSA............. Coast Svgs Finl [*NYSE symbol*] (TTSB)
CSA............. Coeliac Society of Australia
CSA............. Cognizant Security Authority [*Military*]
CSA............. College Stores Association
CSA............. Collegiate Soaring Association (EA)
CSA............. Colon-Specific Antigen [*Biochemistry*] (DAVI)
CSA............. Colony-Stimulating Activity [*Genetics*]
CSA............. Combat Surveillance Agency [*Signal Corps*]
CSA............. Combat System Architecture [*Military*]
CSA............. Combat Systems Assessment [*Navy*] (DOMA)
CSA............. Command Session Abort [*Computer science*] (IAA)
CSA............. Commercial Service Area [*Military*] (AFM)
CSA............. Commercial Service Authorization [*Military*]
CSA............. Committee for Sustainable Agriculture (EA)
CSA............. Common Sense Algorithm (MCD)
CSA............. Common Service Area [*Computer science*] (BUR)
CSA............. Common Services Agency [*Scottish Health Service*] [*Research center*]
CSA............. Common System Area (IAA)
CSA............. Communal Studies Association (EA)
CSA............. Communications Service Authorization [*Obsolete*]
CSA............. Communications Support Area
CSA............. Communications Systems Agency [*Fort Monmouth, NJ*] [*Army*] (RDA)
CSA............. Community Service Activities [*AFL-CIO*]
CSA............. Community Service Announcement
CSA............. Community Services Administration [*Superseded Office of Economic Opportunity*] [*HEW*]
CSA............. Community Standards Association [*British*] (DI)
CSA............. Community-Supported Agriculture
CSA............. Compensation System Analyst
CSA............. Compliance Schedule Approval (DOMA)
CSA............. Compound Spectral Array
CSA............. Compressed Spectral Assay (MAE)
CSA............. Compromise Sales Agreement [*Business term*] (EMRF)
CSA............. Compulsive Stutterers Anonymous (EA)
CSA............. Computer Security Act [*1987*]
CSA............. Computer Services Association [*British*]
CSA............. Computer System Analyst (BUR)
CSA............. Computer Systems Association
CSA............. Computing Services Association [*British*]
CSA............. Concerned Senators for the Arts (EA)
CSA............. Confederacion Sudamericana de Atletismo [*South American Athletic Confederation - SAAC*] (EAIO)
CSA............. Confederate Stamp Alliance (EA)
CSA............. Confederate States Army
CSA............. Confederate States of America
CSA............. Conference Society of Alberta (AC)
CSA............. Configuration Status Accounting
CSA............. Conical Scan Antenna
CSA............. Conseil Scientifique pour l'Afrique au Sud de Sahara [*Scientific Council for Africa South of the Sahara*]
CSA............. Conseil Superieur de l'Audioviseul [*France*] (EY)
CSA............. Conservative Society of America
CSA............. Consular Shipping Adviser
CSA............. Consumer Savings Alliance (EA)

CSA............	Contractor Support Area (KSC)
CSA............	Contract Services Association (AAGC)
CSA............	Contract Services Association of America (EA)
CSA............	Controlled Substances Act [1970] (GFGA)
CSA............	Control Stick Assembly (MCD)
CSA............	Control Switching Assembly
CSA............	Core Special Assembly [Nuclear energy] (NRCH)
CSA............	Core Structure Accident [Nuclear energy] (NRCH)
CSA............	Cornish Scottish Australia [Mine]
CSA............	Corps Service Area
CSA............	Corps Storage Area [Military] (AABC)
CSA............	Correctional Service Associates
CSA............	Costume Society of America (EA)
CSA............	Council for a Secure America (EA)
CSA............	Council on School Administration [Canada] (AEBS)
CSA............	Council on Southern Africa (EA)
CSA............	Countermeasures Set, Acoustic (NVT)
CSA............	Creative Services Association [British] (DBA)
CSA............	Criminology Series [A publication]
CSA............	Cross-Sectional Area
CSA............	Cross Sectional Area
CSA............	Cross-Service Agreement [Obsolete Military]
CSA............	Cryogenic Society of America (EA)
CSA............	CSA Fraternal Life [Acronym represents organization's former name] (EA)
CSA............	CSA Management Ltd. [Toronto Stock Exchange symbol]
CSA............	Current Source Amplifier
CSA............	Customer Supply Assistance [Military]
CSA............	Cyclic Strain Attenuator (NASA)
CSA............	Cyclosporin A [See CYA] [An immunosuppressant drug]
CSA............	Cymbidium Society of America (EA)
CSA............	Cysteine Sulphinic Acid (PDAA)
CSA............	Czech Airlines JSC [FAA designator] (FAAC)
CSA............	Czechoslovak Society of America [Later, CSA Fraternal Life]
CSa............	San Anselmo Public Library, San Anselmo, CA [Library symbol Library of Congress] (LCLS)
CSA............	Sisters of Charity (of St. Augustine) [Roman Catholic religious order]
CSA............	Sisters of the Congregation of St. Agnes [Roman Catholic religious order]
CSAA	California State Automobile Association (ACRL)
CSAA	Canadian Sociology and Anthropology Association [See also ACSA]
CSAA	Central Station Alarm Association (EA)
CSAA	Child Study Association of America [Defunct] (EA)
CSAA	Civil Service Arbitration Awards (DLA)
CSAA	Composite Structures for Advanced Aircraft (MCD)
CSAA	Coopworth Sheep Society of Australia
CSAA	Council of Specialized Accrediting Agencies [Defunct] (EA)
CSAAS	Child Sexual Abuse Accommodation Syndrome
CSA-AZA-P...	Cyclosporin A, Azathioprine, Prednisone [Antineoplastic drug regimen]
CSAB	California Strawberry Advisory Board (EA)
CSAB	Civil Service Arbitration Awards (DLA)
CSAB	Cognitive Skills Assessment Battery (EDAC)
CSAB	Combat Support Aviation Battalion [Army]
CSAB	Combined Shipping Adjustment Board [World War II]
CSAB	Contract Settlement Appeal Board [United States] (DLA)
CSAB	Counseling Services Assessment Blank [Test for counseling centers]
CSABE	Central and South African Basic Encyclopedia [A publication]
CSABGC......	Cymdeithas Swyddogion Addysg Bellach a Gwasanaeth Leuctid Cymru [Welsh Association of Further Education and Youth Service Offices]
CSAC	Cameron State Agricultural College [Oklahoma]
CSAC	Canadian Society for Aesthetics
CSAC	Central Ships Alignment Console [Navy] (NG)
CSAC	Citizens' Stamp Advisory Committee [US Postal Service] (EA)
CSAC	Civil Service Association of Canada
CSAC	Coalition for Safety of Abortion Clinics [Defunct] (EA)
CSAC	Combat Support Aviation Company [Army]
CSAC	Command Study Advisory Committee [TRADOC] (MCD)
CSAC	Congregatio Sororum Apostolatus Catholici [Pallottine Sisters of the Catholic Apostolate] [Roman Catholic religious order]
CSAC	Connors State Agricultural College [Oklahoma]
CSAC	Correctional Services Advisory Council [South Australia]
CSAC	Council on Superconductivity for American Competitiveness
CSAC	Sisters of the Catholic Apostolate (Pallottine) (TOCD)
CSACCS	Customer Service Administration Control Center System [Telecommunications] (TEL)
CSACI	Canadian Society of Allergy & Clinical Immunology [Societe Canadienne d'Allergie et d'Immunologie Clinique] (AC)
CSACIS	Centre for the Study of Arms Control and International Security [University of Lancaster, Fylde College] [British] (CB)
CSACPS......	Canadian Society for Aesthetic (Cosmetic) Plastic Surgery (EAIO)
CSACS	Centralized Status, Alarm, and Control System [Bell System]
CSAD	Capsule Systems Advanced Development [Aerospace] (MCD)
CSAD	Center for Soviet-American Dialogue (EA)
CSAD	Chief Special Artificer, Synthetic Training Devices [Navy rating Obsolete]
CSAD	Combat System Alignment Document (NVT)
CSAD	Configuration Status Accounting Document (MCD)
CSAD	Corporate Services Administration Department [Medicine] (DMAA)
CSadC.........	Calaveras County Free Library, San Andreas, CA [Library symbol Library of Congress] (LCLS)
CSadM.........	Calaveras County Museum & Archives Library, San Andreas, CA [Library symbol] [Library of Congress] (LCLS)
CSADR........	Configuration Status Accounting Data Requirements (MCD)
CSAE.........	Canadian Society of Agricultural Engineering
CSAE.........	Canadian Society of Association Executives [Formerly, Institute of Canadian Trade Association Executives] (AC)
CSAE.........	Canadian Society of Association Executives (NFD)
CSAE.........	Canadian Society of Association Executives
CSAE.........	Committee for the Study of the American Electorate (EA)
CSAES	Centre for South Australian Economic Studies [Flinders University] [Australia]
CSAF.........	Chief of Staff, United States Air Force
CSAF.........	Course Severity Adjustment Factor [Tire testing]
CSAFF.......	Center for the Study of the American Family Farm (EA)
CSAFM.......	Chief of Staff Air Force Memorandum (AFM)
CSAG........	Combat Systems Advisory Group [NMC] (DNAB)
CSAG........	Commonwealth-State Advisory Group [Australia]
CSAG........	Philips Roxane Laboratories [Research code symbol]
CSAGI.......	Comite Special de l'Annee Geophysique Internationale [Special Committee for the International Geophysical Year] [Superseded by CIG]
CSAGM......	Committee for the Suit Against Government Misconduct (EA)
CSah........	St. Helena Public Library, St. Helena, CA [Library symbol Library of Congress] (LCLS)
CSAI.........	Chief Special Artificer, Instruments [Navy rating Obsolete]
CSAI.........	Competitive State Anxiety Inventory (EDAC)
CSAID.......	Cytokine-Suppressive Antiinflammatory Drug [Biochemistry]
CSAITR	Chief Special Artificer, Instruments, Typewriter and Office Equipment Repairman [Navy rating Obsolete]
CSAIWR......	Chief Special Artificer, Instruments, Watch Repairman [Navy rating Obsolete]
CSAJ.........	Cartel Suisse des Associations de Jeunesse [Switzerland]
CSal.........	Salinas Public Library, Salinas, CA [Library symbol Library of Congress] (LCLS)
CSalCL........	Monterey County Library, Salinas, CA [Library symbol Library of Congress] (LCLS)
CSalH........	Hartnell College, Salinas, CA [Library symbol Library of Congress] (LCLS)
CSalJS........	John Steinbeck House, Salinas, CA [Library symbol Library of Congress] (LCLS)
CSalM........	Monterey Bay Area Cooperative System, Salinas, CA [Library symbol Library of Congress] (LCLS)
CSALT........	Canadian Society for the Advancement of Legal Technology [Association Canadienne pour l'Advancement de l'Informatique Juridique] (AC)
CSALU	Connecticut State Association of Life Underwriters (SRA)
CSAM........	California Society of Addiction Medicine (SRA)
CSAM........	Canadian Society of Aerospace Medicine [Societe Medicale Aeronautique du Canada] (AC)
CSAM........	Chief of Staff, Army Memorandum [Air Force]
CSAM........	Circular Sequential Access Memory
CSAM........	Coalition to Save America's Music (EA)
CSAM........	Comite Sida Aide Montreal (AC)
CSAM........	Computer Support Applications Manager [Computer Support Corp.] [Computer science]
C-SAM........	Contingency Special Airlift Mission [Air Force]
CSAM........	Convenience Store Association of Michigan (SRA)
CSAM........	Crinkled Single Aluminized Mylar (NASA)
CSAM/MEADS...	Corps Surface-to-Air Missile/Medium Extended Air Defense System [Military] (RDA)
CSAMT.......	Controlled-Source Audiofrequency Megnetotelllurics [Geophysics]
CS & CSS....	Christmas Seal and Charity Stamp Society (EA)
CS & J.......	Cushing, Storey, and Joselyn's Election Cases [Massachusetts] [A publication] (DLA)
CS & M.......	Cellular Sales & Marketing [Creative Communications] [Information service or system] (IID)
CS & P	Craigie, Stewart, and Paton's Scotch Appeal Cases [1726-1821] [A publication] (DLA)
CS & TAE....	Combat Surveillance and Target Acquisition Equipment [Army]
CSANSC......	Campus Safety Association of the National Safety Council (EA)
CSANT	Cold Storage Association of the Northern Territory [Australia]
CSAO	Chief Special Artificer, Optical [Navy rating Obsolete]
CSAO	Customer Supply Assistance Office [Military]
CSAP	Canadian Society of Applied Art [1905, founded 1903 as Society of Arts and Crafts of Canada] (NGC)
CSAP	Center for Substance Abuse Prevention [Department of Health and Human Services]
CSAP	Child Sexual Assault Program [Australia]
CSAP	Child Survival Assistance Program [Agency for International Development]
CSAP	Colon-Specific Antigen Protein [Biochemistry] (DAVI)
CSAP	Comedian Society for Amateurs and Professionals [Defunct] (EA)
CSAP	Committee for Single Adoptive Parents (EA)
CSAP	Control Systems Analysis Program (MCD)
CSAQ	Cold Storage Association of Queensland [Australia]
CSAR	American River College, Sacramento, CA [Library symbol Library of Congress] (LCLS)
CSAR	Caraustar Industries [NASDAQ symbol] (TTSB)
CSAR	Carauster Industries, Inc. [NASDAQ symbol] (SAG)
CSAR	Center for Scientific Anomalies Research [Ann Arbor, MI]
CSAR	Characteristic Storage and Retrieval (EDAC)
CSAR	Coherent Synthetic Aperture RADAR (MCD)
CSAR	Combat Search and Rescue [Aviation]
CSAR	Communications Satellite Advanced Research [AFSC]
CSAR	Computer System Acceptance Review
CSAR	Configuration Status Accounting Report (KSC)
CSAR	Control Store Address Register
CSARJ	Commission on Social Action of Reform Judaism (EA)

CSARS .... Close Support Artillery Rocket System (MCD)
CSARS .... Coastal Structure Acoustic Raster Scanner (RDA)
CSarW .... West Valley College, Saratoga, CA [Library symbol] [Library of Congress] (LCLS)
CSAS .... Canadian Society for Asian Studies
CSAS .... Canadian Society of Animal Science
CSAS .... Cargo Security Advisory Standards [Department of Transportation]
CSAS .... Central States Anthropological Society (EA)
CSAS .... Centre for Southeast Asian Studies [Monash University] [Australia]
CSAS .... Centre for Southern African Studies [University of York] [British] (CB)
CSAS .... Children's Strategies Assessment System (EDAC)
CSAS .... Command and Stability Augmentation System (MCD)
CSAS .... Computerized Status Accounting System (MCD)
CSAS .... Configuration Status Accounting System
CSAS .... Containment Spray Actuating Signal [Nuclear energy] (NRCH)
CSAS .... Czechoslovak Society of Arts and Sciences (EA)
CSASA .... Czechoslovak Society of Arts and Sciences in America [Later, CSAS] (EA)
CSASP .... Classical Scattering Aerosol Spectrometer [Aerosol measurement device]
CSAT .... Cell-Substrate Attachment [Immunology]
CSAT .... Center for Substance Abuse Treatment [Department of Health and Human Services]
CSAT .... Center Science Assessment Team [NASA]
CSAT .... Civil Service Arbitration Tribunal [British]
CSAT .... Cold Storage Association of Tasmania [Australia]
CSAT .... Combat System Alignment Test
CSAT .... Combat Systems Assessment [Navy] (DOMA)
CSAT .... Combined Systems Acceptance Test (MCD)
CSaT .... San Francisco Theological Seminary, San Anselmo, CA [Library symbol Library of Congress] (LCLS)
CsatCap ...... Comsat Corp. Capital [Associated Press] (SAG)
CSATMS ...... Combat Support Air Traffic Management System (MCD)
CSATR .... Climb So as to Reach [Aviation] (FAAC)
CSATX .... Climb So as to Cross [Aviation] (FAAC)
CSau .... Sausalito Free Public Library, Sausalito, CA [Library symbol Library of Congress] (LCLS)
CSA/USA ..... Celiac Sprue Association/United States of America (EA)
CSAUSA ...... Clan Sinclair Association (USA) (EA)
CSAV .... Compania Sud America de Vapores [Chilean airline]
CSAVP .... Cerebral Subarachnoid Venous Pressure [Medicine] (DMAA)
CSAVR .... Council of State Administrators of Vocational Rehabilitation (EA)
CSAW .... Circumferential Selectable Aim Warhead
CSAW .... Close Support Assault Weapon [Obsolete Navy] (MCD)
CSAWA ...... Cold Storage Association of Western Australia
CSAWA ...... Country Shires Association of Western Australia
CSAWS ...... Close Support Artillery Weapon System (MCD)
CSB .... Bachelor of Christian Science
CSB .... Basilian Fathers (TOCD)
csb .... Basilian Fathers (TOCD)
CSB .... Caffeine Sodium Benzoate [Chemistry] (DAVI)
CSB .... California State College, San Bernardino, San Bernardino, CA [OCLC symbol] (OCLC)
CSB .... Called Subscriber Busy [Telecommunications] (NITA)
CSB .... Cambridge, NE [Location identifier FAA] (FAAL)
CSB .... Canada Savings Bond [Investment term]
CSB .... Careers Service Branch [Department of Employment] [British] (AIE)
CSB .... Carrier and Sideband (DA)
CSB .... Catholic Slovak Brotherhood
CSB .... Center for the Study of Beadwork [An association] (EA)
CSB .... Center Stage Back [A stage direction]
CSB .... Centralized Support Base [Military]
CSB .... Central Statistical Board [Functions taken over by Bureau of the Budget, 1940]
CSB .... Central Statistics Bureau [British Columbia Ministry of Industry and Small Business Development] [Information service or system] (IID)
CSB .... Chemical Screening Battery (DAVI)
CSB .... Chemical Species Balance (GFGA)
CSB .... Chemical Stimulation of the Brain (WGA)
CSB .... Christian Service Brigade (EA)
CSB .... Christian Services for the Blind [Australia]
CSB .... Civilian Supply Branch [Army Service Forces] [World War II]
CSB .... Civil Service Board (AAG)
CSB .... Closely Spaced Basing [Proposed plan for protecting MX missiles from enemy attack]
CSB .... Coalition for Scenic Beauty [Later, SA] (EA)
CSB .... Collectors Service Bureau (EA)
CSB .... College of St. Benedict [St. Joseph, MN]
CSB .... College Service Bureau (EA)
CSB .... Colonia Sabana [Puerto Rico] [Seismograph station code, US Geological Survey] (SEIS)
CSB .... Combined S-Band
CSB .... Combined Signal Board [North Africa] [World War II]
CSB .... Combustible Storage Building (AAG)
CSB .... Committee for Safe Bicycling [Defunct] (EA)
CSB .... Communication Scanner Base (IBMDP)
CSB .... Complementary Straight Binary [Computer science] (HGAA)
CSB .... Computer Support Base (AFIT)
CSB .... ComSouth Bankshares [AMEX symbol] (TTSB)
CSB .... Comsouth Bankshares, Inc. [AMEX symbol] (SAG)
CSB .... Concrete Splash Block [Technical drawings]
CSB .... Congregation of St. Brigid [Roman Catholic women's religious order]
CSB .... Congregatio Sancti Basilii [Congregation of the Priests of St. Basil] [Basilians] [Roman Catholic men's religious order]

CSB .... Consolidated Silver Butte Mines [Vancouver Stock Exchange symbol]
CSB .... Consolidated Spot Buying [Radio and TV advertising]
CSB .... Consumer Sounding-Board (IEEE)
CSB .... Consumer Sourcebook [A publication]
CSB .... Contaminated Small Bowel [Medicine] (DMAA)
CSB .... Continuous Subcarrier Barrage (MCD)
CSB .... Contract Settlement Board [Canada] (AAGC)
CSB .... Copper Shielding Braid
CSB .... Core Support Barrel [Nuclear energy] (NRCH)
CSB .... Corps Support Brigade
CSB .... Craniosynostosis, Boston Type [Medicine] (DMAA)
CSB .... Customer Support Branch (AFIT)
CSb .... San Bernardino Public Library, San Bernardino, CA [Library symbol Library of Congress] (LCLS)
CSBA .... California School Boards Association (SRA)
CSBA .... Canadian School Boards Association [Association Canadienne des Commissions/Conseils Scolaires] [Formerly, Canadian School Trustees' Association] (AC)
CSBA .... Char-Swiss Breeders Association (EA)
CSBA .... Chief Sick Berth Attendant [British military] (DMA)
CSBA .... Columbia Sheep Breeders Association of America (EA)
CSBA .... Commonwealth Savings Bank of Australia
CSBA .... Community and Special Broadcasting Agency [British]
CSBA .... Cookie and Snack Bakers Association (EA)
CSbC .... California State College, San Bernardino, San Bernardino, CA [Library symbol Library of Congress] (LCLS)
CSBC .... Central & Southern Holding [NASDAQ symbol] (TTSB)
CSBC .... Central & Southern Holding Co. [NASDAQ symbol] (NQ)
CSBC .... China Shipbuilding Corp.
CSBC .... Comite des Services Bibliographiques pour le Canada [Committee on Bibliographical Services for Canada]
CSBC .... Consolidated Statutes of British Columbia [A publication] (DLA)
CSbCL .... San Bernardino County Free Library, San Bernardino, CA [Library symbol Library of Congress] (LCLS)
CSBE .... Committee for Small Business Exports (EA)
CSBF .... Civil Service Benevolent Fund [British]
CSBF .... Coronary Sinus Blood Flow [Cardiology]
CSBF .... CSB Financial [NASDAQ symbol] (TTSB)
CSBF .... CSB Financial Group, Inc. [NASDAQ symbol] (SAG)
CSBFin .... CSB Financial Group, Inc. [Associated Press] (SAG)
CSB Fn .... CSB Financial Corp. [Associated Press] (SAG)
CSBG .... Community Services Block Grant
CSBG .... Concerned Seniors for Better Government (EA)
CSbGS .... Church of Jesus Christ of Latter-Day Saints, Genealogical Society Library, San Bernardino Branch, San Bernardino, CA [Library symbol Library of Congress] (LCLS)
CSBI .... Century South Banks [NASDAQ symbol] (TTSB)
CSBI .... Century South Banks, Inc. [NASDAQ symbol] (SAG)
CSbIC .... International Christian Graduate University, San Bernardino, CA [Library symbol] [Library of Congress] (LCLS)
CSBISSS ...... Commission on Soil Biology of the International Society of Soil Science (EAIO)
CSBK .... Carolina Southern Bank [NASDAQ symbol] (NQ)
CSBK .... Carolina Sthrn Bk Spartn SC [NASDAQ symbol] (TTSB)
CSBkS .... Ceskoslovenska Bioklimatologicka Spolecnost [Czechoslovak Bioclimatological Society] [Multinational association] (EAIO)
CSBL .... Consolidated Site Base Loading
CSBM .... Confidence and Security-Building Measures
CSBN .... Captured Steam Bubble Nuclear
CSBP .... Committee for Solidarity with the Bolivian People [Defunct] (EA)
CSBP .... CSAID Binding Protein [Biochemistry]
CSBPA .... Canadian Sugar Beet Producers' Association (AC)
CSBPC .... Control Stick Boost and Pitch Compensator (MCD)
CSBPD .... CINCPAC [Commander-in-Chief, Pacific] Supplement to DoD Basic Planning [Department of Defense] (CINC)
CSBR .... Coil Spring-loaded Beveled-edge Ring [Automotive engineering]
CSbr .... San Bruno Free Public Library, San Bruno, CA [Library symbol Library of Congress] (LCLS)
CSBR .... United States Bureau of Reclamation, Sacramento, CA [Library symbol Library of Congress] (LCLS)
CSbrP .... San Bruno Free Public Library, San Bruno, CA [Library symbol] [Library of Congress] (LCLS)
CSbrS .... Skyline College, San Bruno, CA [Library symbol Library of Congress] (LCLS)
CSBS .... Canadian Society of Biblical Studies [See also SCEB]
CSBS .... Civil Service Building Society [British]
CSBS .... Combat to Support Balance Study
CSBS .... Commander's Statement and Budget Summary (AFIT)
CSBS .... Conference of State Bank Supervisors [Washington, DC] (EA)
CSBS .... Contaminated Small Bowel Syndrome [Medicine] (DMAA)
CSBS .... Course Setting Bombsight
CSBSR .... Center for Social and Behavior Science Research [Research center] (RCD)
CSbUSAF ..... United States Air Force, Norton Air Force Base, San Bernardino, CA [Library symbol Library of Congress] (LCLS)
CSBUSSS ..... Commission on Soil Biology of the International Society of Soil Science [Netherlands] (EAIO)
CSBV .... Cucumber Soilborne Virus
CSC .... Brothers of the Congregation of Holy Cross (TOCD)
CSC .... Cable/Show Cause [FCC] (NTCM)
CSC .... Cadmium-Sulfide Cell
CSC .... California State College, California, PA [OCLC symbol] (OCLC)
C-SC .... California Supreme Court, San Francisco, CA [Library symbol Library of Congress] (LCLS)
CSC .... Campbell Soup Co. Ltd. [Toronto Stock Exchange symbol]

CSC............ Canada Safety Council (AC)
CSC............ Canada Supreme Court (DLA)
CSC............ Canadian Society for Chemistry (EAIO)
CSC............ Canadian Society for Colour in Art, Industry, and Science (EAIO)
CSC............ Canadian Society of Cinematographers
CSC............ Canadian Society of Cytology
CSc............ Candidate of Historical Sciences
C Sc........... Candidate of Science
CSC............ Cape Support Coordinator [*NASA*] (KSC)
CSC............ Capital Speakers Club (EA)
CSC............ Cardinal Stritch College [*Wisconsin*]
CSC............ Card Store Control [*Computer science*] (IAA)
CSC............ Cargo Services Conference [*IATA*] (DS)
CSC............ Cartridge Storage Case
CSC............ Center for the Study of Commercialism (EA)
CSC............ Centralized Supervisory and Control (BUR)
CSC............ Central Security Control [*Military*] (AFM)
CSC............ Central Serous Chorioretinopathy [*or Choroidopathy*] [*Ophthalmology*]
CSC............ Central State College [*Ohio, Oklahoma*]
CSC............ Central Switching Center [*Telecommunications*] (TEL)
CSC............ Central Switching Concept (KSC)
CSC............ Certificate of Security Clearance (NATG)
CSC............ Change Schedule Chart
CSC............ Charles Stuart Calverley [*19th-century British parodist*]
CSC............ Chief Commissaryman [*Later, MSC*] [*Navy rating*]
CSC............ Chief Sector Control [*Aviation*] (OA)
CSC............ Chiefs of Staff Committee [*Australia*]
CSC............ Childhood Sensuality Circle (EA)
CSC............ Children's Self-Conceptions Test
CSC............ Children's Service Council [*Australian Capital Territory*]
CSC............ Child Safety Council [*Later, NCSC*] (EA)
CSC............ Child Study Center [*Brown University*] [*Research center*] (RCD)
CSC............ Chile Solidarity Campaign (EAIO)
CSC............ China Solidarity Committee [*An association Defunct*] (EA)
CSC............ Christian Service Club (EA)
CSC............ Christian Service Corps [*Defunct*] (EA)
CSC............ Church of Scientology of California (EA)
CSC............ Church Schools Company Ltd. [*British*] (BI)
CSC............ Cigarette Smoke Condensate
CSC............ Cincinnati Service Center [*IRS*]
CSC............ Circuit Switching Center [*Telecommunications*] (TEL)
CSC............ Citizens' Service Corps
CSC............ Civilian Screening Center
CSC............ Civilian Skill Code (MCD)
CSC............ Civil Service Club [*British*]
CSC............ Civil Service College [*British*]
CSC............ Civil Service Commission [*Later, MSPB*]
CSC............ Classic Stage Company
CSC............ Clock Start Command
CSC............ Clothing and Survival Equipment Change [*Naval Air Systems Command*] (NG)
CSC............ Clyde Shipping Co. (MHDW)
CSC............ Cntrolled Slip Clutch
CSC............ Coastal Surveillance Center
CSC............ Coil Stock Cradle
CSC............ Colby-Sawyer College [*Formerly, CJCW*] [*New London, NH*]
CSC............ Collagen Sponge Contraceptive
CSC............ College of St. Catherine [*St. Paul, MN*]
CSC............ Colorado State College [*Later, University of Northern Colorado*]
CSC............ Colour Sub Carrier [*Telecommunications*] (NITA)
CSC............ Columbia [*South Carolina*] [*Seismograph station code, US Geological Survey Closed*] (SEIS)
CSC............ Combat Support Center [*Army*]
CSC............ Combat Support Company [*Army*]
CSC............ Combat System Coordinator [*Military*] (CAAL)
CSC............ Combined Service Command (DOMA)
CSC............ Combined Shipbuilding Committee [*World War II*]
CSC............ Command and Staff College [*Air Force*]
CSC............ Commander of Service Cross [*British*] (ROG)
CSC............ Command Scheduling Chain [*Computer science*] (IAA)
CSC............ Command Selector Control
CSC............ Command Senior Chief [*Navy*] (DOMA)
CSC............ Command Support Center (MCD)
CSC............ Commemorative Stamp Club [*US Postal Service*]
CSC............ Commercial Solvents Corp.
CSC............ Commercial Steamship Company
CSC............ Commissariat Staff Corps [*British military*] (DMA)
CSC............ Commissioner of Soil Conservation [*Western Australia*]
CSC............ Committed Stem Cell [*Hematology*]
CSC............ Committee for the Survey of Chemistry [*National Academy of Sciences*]
CSC............ Committee of Southern Churchmen (EA)
CSC............ Common Signaling Channel (IEEE)
CSC............ Commonwealth Science Council [*London, England*] (EAIO)
CSC............ Commonwealth Scientific Committee [*British*]
CSC............ Commonwealth Service Corps [*British*]
CSC............ Commonwealth Supply Council [*British World War II*]
CSC............ Communication Skills Corp. [*British*]
CSC............ Communications Satellite Corp. [*See also COMSAT*]
CSC............ Communications Simulator Console (IAA)
CSC............ Communications Subcommittee [*Allied German Occupation Forces*]
CSC............ Communications Switchboard Console
CSC............ Communications Systems Center

CSC............ Community of the Servants of the Cross [*Anglican religious community*]
CSC............ Community of the Sisters of the Church [*Anglican religious community*]
CSC............ Community Service Council of Central Indiana [*United Way of Central Indiana*] [*Also, an information service or system*] (IID)
CSC............ Commuter Services Corp. [*Formerly, ACSC*]
CSC............ Compass System Controller (MCD)
CSC............ Complex Support Controller [*NASA*] (KSC)
CSC............ Comprehensive Self-Check [*Computer*]
CSC............ Computer Science Center [*University of Maryland*] [*Research center*] (RCD)
CSC............ Computer Science Center [*North Carolina A & T State University*] [*Research center*] (RCD)
CSC............ Computer Sciences [*NYSE symbol*] (TTSB)
CSC............ Computer Sciences Corp. [*El Segunda, CA*] [*Database originator*] [*NYSE symbol*] (SPSG)
CSC............ Computer Search Center [*Illinois Institute of Technology Research Center*] [*Chicago, IL*] [*Defunct*]
CSC............ Computer Service Center
CSC............ Computer Services Co. [*British*] (NITA)
CSC............ Computer Set Control (CAAL)
CSC............ Computer Society of Canada
CSC............ Computer Software Component (SSD)
CSC............ Computer Subsystem Controller
CSC............ Computer Systems Command [*Also, ACSC*] [*Army*]
CSC............ Computing Services Center [*Texas A & M University*] [*Research center*] (RCD)
CSC............ Confederation des Syndicats Canadiens [*Confederation of Canadian Unions - CCU*]
CSC............ Configuration Switch Controller (CET)
CSC............ Congregatio a Sancta Cruce [*Congregation of Holy Cross*] [*Roman Catholic religious order*]
CSC............ Congressional Space Caucus (EA)
CSC............ Congressional Staff Club (EA)
CSC............ Congressional Steel Caucus (EA)
CSC............ Conical Shaped Charge (NASA)
CSC............ Consolidated Statutes of Canada [*A publication*] (DLA)
CSC............ Consolidated Supply Contract [*Department of Housing and Urban Development*] (GFGA)
CSC............ Conspicuous Service Cross [*Later, DSC*] [*British*]
CSC............ Construction Scheduling and Coordination [*AT & T*]
CSC............ Construction Specifications Canada [*Toronto, ON*]
CSC............ Consumer Safety Committee [*Queensland*] [*Australia*]
CSC............ Container Safety Convention [*ISO*] (DS)
CSC............ Containment Spray Cooling [*Nuclear energy*] (NRCH)
CSC............ Continental Service Corps (EA)
CSC............ Continental Shelf Crawler
CSC............ Contingency Support Center (MCD)
CSC............ Continuous Service Certificate [*Navy*]
CSC............ Contractor Supply Center [*Army*]
CSC............ Conventional Systems Committee [*DoD*] (DOMA)
CSC............ Convention for Safe Containers (MCD)
CSC............ Convention-Seminar Cassettes [*Commercial firm*]
CSC............ Cooking for Survival Consciousness (EA)
CSC............ Coolant Spark Control [*Automotive engineering*]
CSC............ Core Standby Cooling [*Nuclear energy*] (IEEE)
CSC............ Core Support Cylinder [*Nuclear energy*] (NRCH)
CSC............ Cornea, Sclera, Conjuctiva [*Ophthalmology*] (DAVI)
CSC............ Corresponding Studies Course [*DoD*]
CSC............ Corsica/Sardinia/Calabria Microplate [*Geology*]
CSC............ Cosecant [*Mathematics*] (GPO)
C/SC.......... Cost/Schedule Control (MCD)
CSC............ Cotton Stabilization Corp. [*New Deal*]
CSC............ Coup sur Coup [*In Small Doses at Short Intervals*] [*French*]
CSC............ Course and Speed Calculator [*or Computer*]
CSC............ Court of Session Cases [*Scotland*] [*A publication*] (DLA)
CSC............ Criminal Sexual Conduct
CSC............ Crown and Sleeve Coping Prosthesis [*Dentistry*]
CSC............ Cryogenic Storage Container
CSC............ Cryptologic Support Center [*Military*]
CSC............ Cued Speech Center (EA)
CSC............ Culver-Stockton College [*Canton, MO*]
CSC............ Customer Service Center
CSC............ Cycle-Speedway Council [*British*] (DBA)
CSC............ Cyclosporin C [*An immunosuppressant drug*]
CSC............ Cylinder Stroke Control
CSC............ Cypher Security Committee [*British World War II*]
CSC............ International Convention for Safe Containers
csc............ Large and Small Capital Letters (WDMC)
csc............ Priests and Brothers of the Congretation of Holy Cross (TOCD)
csc............ Priests of the Congregation of Holy Cross (TOCD)
CSC............ Sichuan Airlines [*China*] [*ICAO designator*] (FAAC)
CSC............ Sisters of Holy Cross (TOCD)
C/SC2........ Cost/Schedule Control System Criteria
CSCA .... Central States College Association [*Defunct*]
CSCA .... Civil Service Clerical Association [*Later, CPSA*] [*British*] (DI)
CSCA .... Clumber Spaniel Club of America (EA)
CSCA .... Combined Setter Clubs of America (EA)
CSCA .... Committee to Stop Chemical Atrocities (EA)
CSCA .... Conference of State Cable Agencies
CSCA .... Council of Scottish Clan Associations [*Later, COSCA*] (EA)
CSCAA .... College Swimming Coaches Association of America (EA)
C-SCAN....... Carrier System for Control Approach of Naval Aircraft
CSCAR .... Citizens for Sensible Control of Acid Rain [*Defunct*] (EA)

CSCAS .... Conference of State Cemetery Association Secretaries (EA)
C-SCAT .... C-band Scatterometer [*Marine science*] (OSRA)
C-SCAT .... C-Band Scatterometer (USDC)
CSCB .... Canadien Society of Customs Brokers [*Societe Canadienne des Coutiers en Douane*] (AC)
CSCB .... Civil Service Cadet Battalion [*British military*] (DMA)
CSCB .... Command Scheduling Control Block [*Computer science*] (BUR)
CSCB .... Contractor's Summary Cost Breakdown (MCD)
CSCBS .... Commodore Superintendent Contract Built Ships [*Navy British*]
CSCC .... Canadian Society of Clinical Chemists [*Societe Canadienne des Clinico-Chimistes*] (AC)
CSCC .... Canadian Society of Copyright Consumers [*Societe Canadienne des Consommaters Copyright*] [*Formerly, Musical Protective Society of Canada*] (AC)
CSCC .... Canadian Steel Construction Council
CSCC .... Cascade Communications [*NASDAQ symbol*] (SAG)
CSCC .... Centre for the Study of Communication and Culture [*British*] (CB)
CSCC .... City of Sydney Cultural Centre [*Australia*]
CSCC .... Civil Service Commission of Canada (BARN)
CSCC .... Cockburn Sound Conservation Council [*Western Australia*]
CSCC .... Combat Support Coordination Center
CSCC .... Command Session Change Control (IAA)
CSCC .... Command Support Control Console
CSCC .... Communications System Category Code [*Air Force*] (AFIT)
CSCC .... Communications System Control Console
CSCC .... Comprehensive Sickle Cell Center [*Terminated, 1977*] [*HEW*]
CSCC .... Council of State Chambers of Commerce (EA)
CSCC .... Cumulative Sum Control Charts [*Statistics*]
CSCC .... Cutaneous Squamous Cell Carcinoma [*Medicine*] (DMAA)
CSCCC .... CSC Clearing Corp. (EA)
CSCCL .... Center for Studies in Criminology and Criminal Law [*Later, SCSCCL*] (EA)
CSCCU .... Computer Select and Cross Connect Unit (MCD)
CSCD .... Carrier Sense Collision Detection (SSD)
CSCD .... Center for Sickle Cell Disease (EA)
CSCD .... Character Set Computer Development
CSCD .... Coalition to Support Cuban Detainees [*Defunct*] (EA)
CSCD .... Committee on Sugar Cane Diseases (EA)
CSCE .... Canadian Society for Chemical Engineers [*Also, CSChe*]
CSCE .... Canadian Society for Civil Engineering
CSCE .... Coffee, Sugar, and Cocoa Exchange (EA)
CSCE .... Commission on Security and Cooperation in Europe [*Washington, DC*] (EGAO)
CSCE .... Communications Support Control Element (MCD)
CSCE .... Communications System Control Equipment
CSCE .... Communication System Control Element [*of TCCF*] (MCD)
CSCE .... Conference on Security and Cooperation in Europe (PD)
CScE .... Eimac, Division of Varian Associates, Technical Library, San Carlos, CA [*Library symbol*] [*Library of Congress*] (LCLS)
CSCF .... California State College at Fresno
CSCF .... Center for the Study of the College Fraternity (EA)
CSCFC .... Conference of Scottish Centrally Funded Colleges (AIE)
CSCFE .... Civil Service Council for Further Education [*British*]
CSCG .... Communications Security Control Group [*Navy*] (MCD)
CSCH .... Canadian Society of Church History [*See also SCHE*]
CSCH .... Cosecant, Hyperbolic [*Mathematics*] (GPO)
CSChE .... Canadian Society for Chemical Engineering
CsChrO .... Corpus Scriptorum Christianorum Orientalium [*Louvain*] (BJA)
CSCI .... Canadian Society for Clinical Investigation [*Societe Canadienne de Recherches Cliniques*] (AC)
CSCI .... Canadian Society of Computational Studies of Intelligence (IAA)
CSC-I .... Civil Service Commission - Investigations
CSCI .... Computer Software Configuration Item [*Computer science*]
CSCI .... Corticosterone Side-Chain Isomerase (DMAA)
CSCI .... Cryenco Sciences [*NASDAQ symbol*] (TTSB)
CSCI .... Cryenco Sciences, Inc. [*NASDAQ symbol*] (SAG)
CSCIH .... Canadian Society for Cultural and Intellectual History
CSCJ .... Center for Studies in Criminal Justice (EA)
CSCL .... Care of Ship Checkoff List (DNAB)
CsCl .... Cesium Chloride
CSCL .... Close Surveillance Contractor List [*DoD*]
CSCL .... Community of St. Clare [*Anglican religious community*]
CSCL .... Contractor Supply Center List
CScL .... Lenkurt Electric Co., San Carlos, CA [*Library symbol Library of Congress*] (LCLS)
CSCLK .... Chief Ship's Clerk [*Navy rating Obsolete*]
CSCM .... Combat System Configuration Matrix [*Military*] (CAAL)
CSCM .... Commissaryman, Master Chief [*Navy rating*]
CSCM .... Committee to Stop Children's Murder [*Defunct*] (EA)
CSCMS .... Combat Support Capability Management System (MCD)
CSCMV .... Cassava Common Mosaic Virus [*Plant pathology*]
CSCN .... Canadian Society of Clinical Neurophysiologists [*Societe Canadienne de Neurophsiologistes Cliniques*] (AC)
CSCN .... Character Scan Command [*Computer science*]
CSCN/CHSA... Commander, Subordinate Command, [*US*] Naval Forces Eastern Atlantic and Mediterranean, Commander Headquarters Support Activities
CScO .... Chief Scientific Officer [*Also, CSO*] [*Ministry of Agriculture, Fisheries, and Food*] [*British*]
CSCO .... Cisco Systems [*NASDAQ symbol*] (SAG)
C-SCOPE ...... Cathode-Ray Screen [*Air Force*]
CSCP .... Canadian Society for Clinical Pharmacology [*Societe Canadienne de Pharmacologie Clinique*] (AC)
CSCPA .... California Society of Certified Public Accountants (SRA)
CSCPA .... Colorado Society of Certified Public Accountants (SRA)

CSCPA .... Connecticut Society of Certified Public Accountants (SRA)
CSCPB .... Central Sugar Cane Prices Board [*Queensland*] [*Australia*]
CSCPCA .... Comite Scientifique Consultatif des Peches Canadiennes dans l'Atlantique [*Canadian Atlantic Fisheries Scientific Advisory Committee - CAFSAC*] (ASF)
CSCPRC .... Committee on Scholarly Communications with the People's Republic of China
CSCQ .... Correctional Services Corp. [*NASDAQ symbol*] (SAG)
CSCR .... Center for Surface Coatings Research [*Lehigh University*]
CSCR .... Central Society for Clinical Research (EA)
CSCR .... Cincinnati Superior Court Reporter [*Ohio*] [*A publication*] (DLA)
CSCR .... Complementary Semiconductor
CSCR .... Complementary Semiconductor Controlled Rectifier (MSA)
CSCR .... Consumnes River College, Sacramento, CA [*Library symbol Library of Congress*] (LCLS)
CSCRC .... Canadian Steel Can Recycling Council (AC)
CSCRF .... Computer System for Crop Response to Fertilizers [*United Nations*] (NITA)
CSCRR .... Centre for the Study of Community and Race Relations [*Brunel University*] [*British*] (CB)
CSCS .... Canadian Society of Corporate Secretaries (AC)
CSCS .... Centre for the Study of Comprehensive Schools [*Wentworth College, University of York*] [*British*] (CB)
CSCS .... Chukchi Sea Circulation Study [*Marine science*] (OSRA)
CSCS .... Chukchi Sea Circulation Study (USDC)
CSCS .... Civil Service Cooperative Society [*British*]
CSCS .... Consolidated Scientific Computing System [*Marine science*] (OSRA)
CSCS .... Consolidated Scientific Computing System (USDC)
CSCS .... Core Standby Cooling System [*Nuclear energy*] (NRCH)
CSCS .... Cost/Schedule Control System (MCD)
CSCS .... Senior Chief Commissaryman [*Later, MSCS*] [*Navy rating*]
CSCSAT .... Commercial Synchronous Communication Satellite (NASA)
CSCSB .... California State College, San Bernardino (PDAA)
CSCSC .... Canadian Society for the Comparative Study of Civilizations [*See also SCECC*]
C/SCSC .... Cost/Schedule Control System Criteria
CSCSGL .... Computer Systems Command Support Group, Fort Lee (MCD)
CSCSI .... Canadian Society of Computational Studies of Intelligence
CSCT .... Canadian Society for Chemical Technology (EAIO)
CSCT .... Communications Security Control Terminal (MCD)
CSCU .... Countersink Cutter
CSCUC .... Community Service Credit Union Council [*Defunct*] (EA)
CSCV .... Critical Serum Chemistry Value (DMAA)
CSCW .... Church Society for College Work (EA)
CSCW .... Computer-Supported Cooperative Work [*Computer science*]
CSCWO .... Command Support Center Watch Officer (MCD)
CSD .... Cadbury Schweppes Delaware LP [*NYSE symbol*] (SAG)
CSD .... Calibrated Sweep Delay
CSD .... Cambridge Structural Database [*Genetics*]
CSD .... Car Service Department
CSD .... Cat Scratch Disease [*Medicine*]
CSD .... Centrale des Syndicats Democratiques [*Congress of Democratic Unions*]
CSD .... Centrifugal Spray Deposition [*Steelmaking*]
CSD .... Certificate in Spiritual Direction (PGP)
CSD .... Character Sequence Detector (MCD)
CSD .... Chartered Society of Designers [*British England*] (EAIO)
CSD .... Chemical Spray Deposition (PDAA)
CSD .... Chemical Stockpile Disposal [*Military*] (RDA)
CSD .... Chemical Systems Division [*NASA*] (NASA)
CSD .... Chief Scientist's Directorate [*Nature Conservancy Council*] [*British*]
CSD .... Children's Services Division [*American Library Association*] [*Later, ALSC*] (EA)
CSD .... (Chlorosulfonyl)dicyclohexylamine [*Antineoplastic drug*]
CSD .... Church of Spiritual Discovery (EA)
CSD .... Circuit Switched Data [*Telecommunications*]
CSD .... Circular Standard Deviation [*Statistics*]
CSD .... Citizens for Safe Drivers [*Formerly, CBDR*] (EA)
CSD .... Civilian Supply Division [*Allied Military Government*] [*World War II*]
CSD .... Civil Service Department [*British*]
CSD .... Closed Shelter Deck [*Shipping*] (DS)
CSD .... Coalition on Sexuality and Disability (EA)
CSD .... Cold-Shock Domain [*Genetics*]
CSD .... Cold Shutdown [*Nuclear energy*] (NRCH)
CSD .... Cold Side
CSD .... Combat System Detection [*Military*] (CAAL)
CSD .... Combined Support Division [*Canadian Navy*]
CSD .... Command Signal Decoder
CSD .... Commission on Sustainable Development
CSD .... Committee for Stable Deterrence (EA)
CSD .... Committee on Statistics of Drilling [*American Association of Petroleum Geologists*] (IID)
CSD .... Common Strategic Doppler (MCD)
CSD .... Commonwealth Society for the Deaf [*British*] (ADA)
CSD .... Communication System Development (IAA)
CSD .... Community of St. Denys [*Anglican religious community*]
CSD .... Computer Science Division
CSD .... Computer Services Division [*University of South Carolina at Columbia*] [*Research center*] (RCD)
CSD .... Computer Simulated Design (DGA)
CSD .... Computer Software Documentation
CSD .... Computer System Design (IAA)
CSD .... Computer Systems Development Ltd. [*Software supplier*] [*London, England*] (NCC)
CSD .... Computer Systems Director (KSC)

CSD .... Computing Services Division [*Seton Hall University*] [*Research center*] (RCD)
CSD .... Concise Scots Dictionary [*Aberdeen University Press*] [*A publication*]
CSD .... Conditionally Streptomycin Dependent [*Pharmacology*] (DAVI)
CSD .... Configuration Standardization Document [*Deep Space Instrumentation Facility, NASA*]
CSD .... Constant-Speed Drive
CSD .... Constant Stimulus Difference [*Pair comparison*] [*Aircraft noise*]
CSD .... Construction Statistics Division [*Washington, DC Department of Commerce*] (OICC)
CSD .... Continental Shelf Discus [*Buoy system*] (MSC)
CSD .... Contract Start Date (SSD)
CSD .... Contract Support Detachment
CSD .... Controlled-Slip Differentials (IEEE)
CSD .... Control System Document (MCD)
CSD .... Convection Suppression Device [*for energy collectors*]
CSD .... Convective Storms Division [*National Center for Atmospheric Research*]
CSD .... Convex Set Stochastic Dominance [*Statistics*]
CSD .... Core Shift Driver (CET)
CSD .... Cortical Spreading Depression [*Medicine*]
CSD .... Courier Services, Inc. [*ICAO designator*] (FAAC)
CSD .... Court Services Department [*South Australia*]
CSD .... Crack Surface Displacement (PDAA)
CSD .... Crew Systems Division [*NASA*]
CSD .... Criteria and Standards Division [*Environmental Protection Agency*] (GFGA)
CSD .... Critical Sector Detector [*FAA*] (TAG)
CSD .... Critical-Size Defect [*Medicine*]
CSD .... Critical Solvent De-Ashing [*Coal processing*]
CSD .... Critical Subsystems Development (MCD)
CSD .... Cross-Strike Discontinuity [*Tectonics*]
CSD .... Crystallographic Structural Database [*University of Cambridge*] [*British Information service or system*] (CRD)
CSD .... Crystal Size Distribution
CSD .... C. S. Draper Laboratory, Inc. Cambridge, MA [*OCLC symbol*] (OCLC)
CSD .... Cumulative Sum Diagram [*Statistics*]
CSD .... Current Source-Density [*Neuroelectricity*]
CSD .... Current System Description (SSD)
CSD .... Cyclosporin D [*An immunosuppressant drug*]
CSD .... Doctor of Christian Science [*Used by teachers who received instruction directly from Mary Baker Eddy*]
CSd .... San Diego Public Library, San Diego, CA [*Library symbol Library of Congress*] (LCLS)
CSDA .... California Special Districts Association (SRA)
CSDA .... Canadian Society of Decorative Arts [*Cercle Canadien des Arts Decoratifs*] (AC)
CSDA .... Canadian Soft Drink Association [*Association Canadeinne de l'Industrie des Boissons Gazeuses*] [*Formerly, Canadian Association of Carbonated Beverages*] (AC)
CSDA .... Canadian Stamp Dealers' Association
CSDA .... Center for the Study of Development and Aging [*University of Detroit*] [*Research center*] (RCD)
CSDA .... Central Systems Design Agency
CSDA .... Concrete Sawing and Drilling Association (EA)
CSDA .... Connecticut State Dental Association (SRA)
CSdA .... Fine Arts Gallery of San Diego, San Diego, CA [*Library symbol Library of Congress*] (LCLS)
CSDB .... Cat Scratch Disease Bacillus [*Medicine*] (DMAA)
CSDB .... Continuous Seam Diffusion Bonding
CSDC .... Child Service Demonstration Center [*Department of Education*]
CSDC .... Circuit Switched Digital Capability [*AT & T*]
CSDC .... Continental Scientific Drilling Committee [*National Academy of Science*]
CSdCiC .... San Diego City College, San Diego, CA [*Library symbol Library of Congress*] (LCLS)
CSdCL .... San Diego County Library, San Diego, CA [*Library symbol Library of Congress*] (LCLS)
CSdCu .... Cubic Corp., San Diego, CA [*Library symbol Library of Congress*] (LCLS)
CSdCWL ...... California Western School of Law, San Diego, CA [*Library symbol*] [*Library of Congress*] (LCLS)
CSDD .... Center for the Study of Drug Development [*Tufts University*] [*Research center*] (RCD)
CSDD .... Cluster Systems Description Document (KSC)
CSDD .... Computer Subprogram Design Document (MHDI)
CSDD .... Conceptual System Design Description
CSDD .... Control Systems Development Division [*NASA*] (NASA)
CSDE .... Center for Studies in Demography and Ecology [*University of Washington*] [*Research center*] (RCD)
CSDE .... Central Servicing Development Establishment (MCD)
CSDE .... Ceskoslovenska Socialni Demokracie v Exilu [*Czechoslovak Social Democratic Party*] (EAIO)
CSDE .... Communications Systems Developing Element
CSDF .... Canadian Student Debating Federation
CSDF .... Central Source Data File (MCD)
CSDF .... Computer System Development Facility (MHDI)
CSDF .... Core Segment Development Facility [*Nuclear energy*] (NRCH)
CSDF .... Crew Station Design Facility (MCD)
CSdG .... General Dynamics/Convair Aerospace Division, San Diego, CA [*Library symbol Library of Congress*] (LCLS)
CSdGA .... General Atomic Co., San Diego, CA [*Library symbol Library of Congress*] (LCLS)

CSdGS .... Church of Jesus Christ of Latter-Day Saints, Genealogical Society Library, San Diego Branch, San Diego, CA [*Library symbol Library of Congress*] (LCLS)
CSDH .... Coalition to Save Our Documentary Heritage [*Defunct*] (EA)
CSDH .... Council of Societies in Dental Hypnosis [*Defunct*] (EA)
CSDHA .... Centre for Social Development and Humanitarian Affairs [*United Nations*] (EAIO)
CSdHi .... San Diego Historical Society, Junipero Serra Museum Library, San Diego, CA [*Library symbol Library of Congress*] (LCLS)
CSDI .... Center for the Study of Democratic Institutions [*Later, Robert Maynard HutchinsCenter for the Study of Democratic Institutions*] (EA)
CSDI .... Centre de Sensibilisation au Developpement International (AC)
CSDI .... Coalition for the Strategic Defense Initiative (EA)
CSdI .... United States International University, San Diego, CA [*Library symbol Library of Congress*] (LCLS)
CSDIC .... Combined Services Detailed Interrogation Center [*World War II*]
CSDICNOI .... Combined Services Detailed Interrogation Center - Nonoperational Intelligence [*World War II*]
CSDIP .... City and State Directories in Print [*A publication*]
CSdJ .... Jewish Community Center, Samuel and Rebecca Astor Judaica Library, San Diego, CA [*Library symbol Library of Congress*] (LCLS)
CSDL .... Charles Stark Draper Laboratory, Inc. [*MIT*] [*Research center*] (NASA)
CSDL .... Conceptual Schema Definition Language [*Computer science*] (MHDI)
CSDL .... Current Switching Diode Logic (IAA)
CSDM .... Computer Software Diagnostic Manual
CSDM .... Continuous Slope Delta Modulation [*Telecommunications*]
CSDMS .... Canadian Society of Diagnostic Medical Sonographers (AC)
CSDN .... Circuit Switched Data Network (NITA)
CSDN .... Circuit-Switched Digital [*or Data*] Network [*Telecommunications*] (IAA)
CSdN .... San Diego Society of Natural History, Natural History Museum, Balboa Park, San Diego, CA [*Library symbol Library of Congress*] (LCLS)
CSdNEL...... United States Navy, Electronics Laboratory, San Diego, CA [*Library symbol Library of Congress*] (LCLS)
CSdNH .... United States Naval Hospital, San Diego, CA [*Library symbol Library of Congress*] (LCLS)
CSdNPS ...... United States National Park Service, Cabrillo National Monument, San Diego, CA [*Library symbol Library of Congress*] (LCLS)
CSdNUC...... United States Navy, Naval Undersea Center, San Diego, CA [*Library symbol Library of Congress*] (LCLS)
CSDP .... Center for the Study of Data Processing [*Washington University*] [*Research center*] (RCD)
CSDP .... Center for the Study of Drug Policy [*NORML*] [*Absorbed by*] (EA)
CSDP .... Chemical Stockpile Disposal Program [*Military*] (DOMA)
CSDP .... Command Supply Discipline Program [*Army*]
CSDP .... Continental Scientific Drilling Program [*National Science Foundation, USGS, and Department of Energy*]
CSDP .... Control System Design Program
CSDP .... Coordinated Ship Development Plan [*Navy*]
CSDP .... Customer Service Department Procedure
CSdP........... Point Loma College, San Diego, CA [*Library symbol Library of Congress*] (LCLS)
CSDPrA........ Cadbury Schwep LP 8.625%'QUIPS' [*NYSE symbol*] (TTSB)
CSDR .... Combat System Design Requirement [*Military*] (CAAL)
CSDR .... Computed Slant Detection Range
CSDR .... Consider (FAAC)
CSDR .... Control Store Data Register
CSDR .... Cross-Section Data Reduction
CSdRA .... Ryan Aeronautical Co., Lindbergh Field, San Diego, CA [*Library symbol Library of Congress*] (LCLS)
CSDRBL...... Considerable (FAAC)
CSDRBT...... Coalition to Stop Draize Rabbit Blinding Tests [*Later, CADRBT*] (EA)
CSdRS .... Rees-Stealy Medical Clinic, San Diego, CA [*Library symbol Library of Congress*] (LCLS)
CSDS .... Casino Data Systems [*NASDAQ symbol*] (SAG)
CSDS .... Center for Control Science and Dynamical Systems [*University of Minnesota*] [*Research center*] (RCD)
CSDS .... Center for the Study of Democratic Societies (EA)
CSDS .... Centre for the Study of Developing Societies [*Information service or system*] (IID)
CSDS .... Circuit-Switched Digital Services [*Telecommunications*] (HGAA)
CSDS .... Command Ship Data System [*Navy*] (MUGU)
CSDS .... Communication Signal Distribution System
CSDS .... Constant-Speed Drive/Starter (NG)
CSdSC .... Stromberg-Datagraphix, San Diego, CA [*Library symbol Library of Congress*] (LCLS)
CSdSer .... Serra Cooperative Library System, San Diego, CA [*Library symbol Library of Congress*] (LCLS)
CSdS-IV ...... San Diego State University, Imperial Valley Campus, Imperial, CA [*Library symbol Library of Congress*] (LCLS)
CSDT .... Computer Software Data Tapes (MCD)
CSDT .... Continuous Space-Discrete Time (PDAA)
CSDT .... Control for Submarine Discharge Torpedo (MCD)
CSdU .... University of San Diego, San Diego, CA [*Library symbol Library of Congress*] (LCLS)
CSdU-L .... University of San Diego Law School, San Diego, CA [*Library symbol Library of Congress*] (LCLS)
CSdUT .... San Diego Union-Tribune Publishing Co., San Diego, CA [*Library symbol Library of Congress*] (LCLS)
CSdV........... United States Veterans Administration Hospital, San Diego, CA [*Library symbol Library of Congress*] (LCLS)

CSDWPUSCC... Committee on Social Development and World Peace of the US Catholic Conference (EA)
CSE............. Canadian Society of Extension
CSE............. Carmelite Sisters of the Eucharist (TOCD)
CSE............. Case Corp. [Formerly, Case Equipment] [NYSE symbol] (SAG)
CSE............. Center for Scholarly Editions [Formerly, CEAA] (EA)
CSE............. Center for Software Engineering [Army]
CSE............. Center for the Study of Economics [Columbia, MD] (EA)
CSE............. Center for the Study of Evaluation [Department of Education] (GRD)
CSE............. Central Signals Establishment [Military British]
CSE............. Centre for Software Engineering Ltd. [British] (CB)
CSE............. Certificate of Secondary Education [British]
CSE............. Certificate of Secondary Education (BARN)
CSE............. Certified Systems Engineer (CDE)
CSE............. Chargeable to Support Equipment (MCD)
CSE............. Chief Systems Engineer (SSD)
CSE............. Childress [Texas] [Seismograph station code, US Geological Survey] (SEIS)
CSE............. Child Support Enforcement [Department of Health and Human Services]
CSE............. Chip Select
CSE............. Cincinnati Stock Exchange [Ohio]
CSE............. Circuit-Switched Exchange [Telecommunications] (IAA)
CSE............. Citizens for a Safe Environment (AC)
CSE............. Citizens for a Sound Economy [Washington, DC] (EA)
CSE............. Civil and Sanitary Engineering (MCD)
CSE............. Cognizant Sustaining Engineer
CSE............. Cold Start Entry [Computer science]
CSE............. College of Saint Elizabeth, Convent Station, NJ [OCLC symbol] (OCLC)
CSE............. Combat System Engineer [Military] (CAAL)
CSE............. Combined Services Entertainment [British military] (DMA)
CSE............. Command Session End [Computer science] (IAA)
CSE............. Commission on Science Education
CSE............. Commission Seismologique Europeenne [European Seismological Commission - ESC] (EAIO)
CSE............. Committee of Security Experts [Military] (CINC)
CSE............. Committee on Scholarly Editions (EA)
CSE............. Common Support Equipment (NASA)
CSE............. Communications Satellite for Experimental Purposes [Japan Telecommunications]
CSE............. Communications Support Element [Military] (AFM)
CSE............. Communications Systems Engineer (KSC)
CSE............. Competitive Study Engineer
CSE............. Computer Science and Engineering
CSE............. Computer Support Equipment (MCD)
CSE............. Computer Systems Engineer (PGP)
CSE............. Conference Spatiale Europeenne [European Space Conference]
CSE............. Conference sur la Securite Europeene [Conference on Security in Europe] (NATG)
CSE............. Configuration Switching Equipment (MCD)
CSE............. Connaught Biosciences, Inc. [Toronto Stock Exchange symbol]
CSE............. Consortium for Superconducting Electronics
CSE............. Containment Steam Explosion [Nuclear energy] (IEEE)
CSE............. Containment Systems Experiment [Nuclear energy]
CSE............. Control and Switching Equipment [RADAR]
CSE............. Control Systems Engineering
CSE............. Core Storage Element
CSE............. Corresponding States Equation [Physics]
CSE............. Costs of the Soviet Empire [International economics]
CSE............. Course
CSE............. Critical Specifications Element (DNAB)
CSE............. Cross-Section Echocardiography (DAVI)
CSE............. Cruise
CSE............. CSE Aviation Ltd. [British] [FAA designator] (FAAC)
CSE............. Steam Explosion in Containment [Nuclear energy] (NRCH)
CSEA........... California School Employees Association (SRA)
CSEA........... California Society of Enrolled Agents (SRA)
CSEA........... California State Employee's Association (SRA)
CSEA........... Canadian Society for Education through Art [1951] (NGC)
CSEA........... Canadian Society for Education through Art (AC)
CSEA........... Canadian Steel Environmental Association [Association Environnemental de la Siderurgie Canadienne] (AC)
CSEA........... Civil Service Employees Association (EA)
CSEA........... Combat System Engineering Authorization
CSeaGS ...... Church of Jesus Christ of Latter-Day Saints, Genealogical Society Library, Monterey Branch, Seaside, CA [Library symbol Library of Congress] (LCLS)
CSEB........... Canadian Society of Environmental Biologists [La Societe Canadienne des Biologistes de l'Environnement] (AC)
CSEB........... Clothing and Survival Equipment Bulletin (MCD)
CSeb........... Sebastopol Public Library, Sebastopol, CA [Library symbol Library of Congress] (LCLS)
C/SEC.......... Cesareans/Support, Education, and Concern [An association] (EA)
CSEC........... Clothing and Survival Equipment Change [Naval Air Systems Command]
CSEC........... Compliance Schedule for Existing Sources [Environmental Protection Agency]
CSEC........... Computer Security Evaluation Center
CSECE......... Canadian Society for Electrical and Computer Engineering (EAIO)
CSECS......... Canadian Society for Eighteenth-Century Studies (AC)
C Sect......... Caesarean [or Cesarean] Section [Obstetrics] (DAVI)
CSECT......... Control Section (MCD)
C (Section).. Caesarean Section [Medicine]
CSED .... Collection Statute Expiration Date [IRS]

CSED .... Combat System Engineering Development [Military] (CAAL)
CSED .... Consolidated Ships Electronic Design [Navy] (NG)
CSED .... Coordinated Ship Electronics Device [Navy]
CSEDC .... Centre for Study of Education in Developing Countries [Netherlands] (EAIO)
CSEDS .... Combat System Engineering Development Site
CSEE .... Canadian Society for Electrical Engineers (MCD)
CSEE .... Comite Syndical Europeen des Personnels de l'Education [European Teachers Trade Union Committee] [EC] (ECED)
CSEE .... Committee of Stock Exchanges in the European Community [See also CBCE] (EAIO)
CSEEB .... Communications Security Equipment Engineering Bulletin (MCD)
CSEES .... Center for Slavic and East European Studies [University of Connecticut] [Research center] (RCD)
CSEES .... Center for Soviet and East European Studies [University of Connecticut] [Research center] (RCD)
CSEF .... Canadian Siberian Expeditionary Force
CSEF .... Current Switch Emitter/Follower (OA)
CSEG .... Canadian Society of Exploration Geophysicists (AC)
CSEHD .... Center for Studies in Education and Human Development [Gallaudet College] [Research center] (RCD)
CSEI........... Concentrated Solar Energy Imitator (PDAA)
CSEI........... Coopersmith Self-Esteem Inventory [Psychometrics]
CSEIP .... Center for the Study of the Evaluation of Instructional Programs
CSEL.......... Communication Systems Engineering Laboratory [NASA] (MCD)
CSEL.......... Consolidated Support Equipment List (MCD)
CSEM.......... Canadian Society for Engineering Management [Societe Canadienne de Gestion en Ingenierie] [Formerly, EIC General Members Society] (AC)
CSEM.......... Committee for the Study of Environmental Manpower [National Research Council]
CS En.......... Certificate in Sales Engineering
CSEOA .... Community Service Employment for Older Americans [Department of Labor]
CSEOL .... Center for the Study of Evolution and the Origin of Life [University of California at Los Angeles] [Research center] (RCD)
CSEP.......... Canadian Society for Exercise Physiology [Formerly, Canadian Association of Sport Sciences] (AC)
CSEP.......... Center for the Study of Ethics in the Professions [Illinois Institute of Technology] [Research center] (RCD)
CSEP.......... Chemical Stockpile Emergency Preparedness [Military] (RDA)
CSEP.......... College Senior Engineering Program [Air Force]
CSEP.......... Communications Systems Engineering Program [Army] (RDA)
CSEP.......... Connecticut Society of Eye Physicians (SRA)
CSEP.......... Consep, Inc. [NASDAQ symbol] (SAG)
CSEP.......... Corticosomatosensory Evoked Potential [Electrophysiology]
CSEPA .... Central Station Electrical Protection Association [Later, CSAA] (EA)
CSEPA .... Comite de Surveillance Ecologique des Pulverisations Seriennes [Canada]
CSepVA....... United States Veterans Administration Hospital, Sepulveda, CA [Library symbol Library of Congress] (LCLS)
CSER .... Centre for the Study of Economics and Religion [Fraser Institute] [Canada] (IRC)
CSER .... Committee on Solar Electromagnetic Radiation [British] (NUCP)
CSERA .... Center for Studies of Ethnicity and Race in America [University of Colorado at Boulder] [Research center] (RCD)
CSERB .... Computer Systems and Electronics Requirements Board [British]
CSERD .... Contractor Support Equipment Recommendation Data (MCD)
CSERIAC ..... Crew System Ergonomics Information Analysis Center [DoD] (IID)
CSES.......... Center for the Study of Earth from Space [University of Colorado] [National Oceanic and Atmospheric Administration Research center] (GRD)
CSES.......... College Self-Expression Scale
CSES.......... Configuration and Switching Equipment Subsystem (MCD)
CSES.......... Council for Social and Economic Studies (EA)
CSESAS .... Center for State Employment Security Automated Systems
CSESD .... Communications Security Equipment Systems Document [National Security Agency] (MCD)
C Sess .... Court of Session [Scotland] [A publication] (DLA)
CSET.......... Coalition for Safe and Efficient Transportation [MTMC] (TAG)
CSET.......... Combat Systems Equipment Training (MCD)
CSETQ .... Corporation des Services aux Etablissements Touristiques Quebecois (AC)
CSEU .... Combined Services Entertainment Unit [British military] (DMA)
CSEU .... Confederation of Shipbuilding and Engineering Unions [British]
CSF............. Camp Strike Force [Military] (VNW)
CSF............. Canada Studies Foundation [See also FEC]
CSF............. Canadian-Scandinavian Foundation (AC)
CSF............. Canadian Schizophrenia Foundation (AC)
CSF............. Canadian Spooner Resources, Inc. [Toronto Stock Exchange symbol]
CSF............. Canadian Standard Freeness [Drainage rate of synthetic pulps]
CSF............. Canadian Sugar Factories Ltd.
CSF............. Caribbean Sea Frontier [Navy]
CSF............. Carrier Striking Force [Tactical Air Command]
CSF............. Carrier Suppression Filter (IAA)
CSF............. Casualty Staging Facility [Military] (AFM)
CSF............. Center for Southern Folklore (EA)
CSF............. Center for Study of Federalism [Temple University] [Research center] (RCD)
CSF............. Center for the Study of the Future (EA)
CSF............. Center Stage Front [A stage direction]
CSF............. Central Service Facility (NRCH)
CSF............. Central Supply Facility (MCD)
CSF............. Central Switching Facility
CSF............. Centrifugation-Sugar Flotation [Soil testing]

CSF............ Ceramic Silicone Foam [Chemistry]
CSF............ Cerebrospinal Fluid [Medicine]
CSF............ Channel Status Field [Electronics] (ECII)
CSF............ Character Scan or Fail [Computer science]
CSF............ Chief Shipfitter [Navy rating Obsolete]
CSF............ Chi-Squared Function
CSF............ Civil Service Forum (EA)
CSF............ Coalition for Safe Food [Defunct] (EA)
CSF............ College of Saint Francis [Joliet, IL]
CSF............ Colony-Stimulating Factor [Hematology]
CSF............ Combat Support Force
CSF............ Communication Service Facility (IAA)
CSF............ Community of St. Francis [Anglican religious community]
CSF............ Community Support Framework [EC] (ECED)
CSF............ Community Systems Foundation (EA)
CSF............ Completely Symmetric Function (PDAA)
CSF............ Condensate Storage Facility [Nuclear energy] (NRCH)
CSF............ Configuration State Function (MCD)
CSF............ Congregation of the Sacerdotal Fraternity [Canada] (EAIO)
CSF............ Consol Synthetic Fuel [Coal liquefaction process]
CSF............ Containment Support Fixture [Nuclear energy] (NRCH)
CSF............ Contingency Support Force [Air Force] (DOMA)
CSF............ Contractor Support Facility (MCD)
CSF............ Contract Stationers Forum (EA)
CSF............ Contract Status File [Military] (AFIT)
CSF............ Contract Supply Facility
CSF............ Contrast Sensitivity Function [of the retina]
CSF............ Contrast Spatial Frequency [Vision research]
CSF............ Control and Simulation Facility (MCD)
CSF............ Cost Sensitivity Factor (NASA)
CSF............ Council on Synthetic Fuels (EA)
CSF............ Critical Speed Formula
CSF............ Critical Success Factor [Management tool]
CSF............ Cylindrically Symmetrical Field
CSF............ Cytostatic Factor [Cytology]
CSf............ San Francisco Public Library, San Francisco, CA [Library symbol Library of Congress] (LCLS)
CSF............ San Francisco State University, San Francisco, CA [OCLC symbol] (OCLC)
CSfA............ California Academy of Sciences, San Francisco, CA [Library symbol Library of Congress] (LCLS)
CSFA............ California School of Fine Arts
CSFA............ California State Firefighters Association (SRA)
CSFA............ Canadian Science Film Association
CSFA............ Center for the Study of Foreign Affairs (EA)
CSFA............ Citizens' Scholarship Foundation of America (EA)
CSF(A)........ Community Systems Foundation (Australia)
CSFAC........ Canadian Sport & Fitness Administration Centre [Centre Canadien d'Administration du Sport et de la Condition Physique] (AC)
CSfAR........ American Russian Institute, San Francisco, CA [Library symbol Library of Congress] (LCLS)
CSfB............ Bank of California, San Francisco, CA [Library symbol Library of Congress] (LCLS)
CSFB............ Channel State Feedback (PDAA)
CSFB............ Credit Suisse First Boston [Banking] (ECON)
CSFBA........ Bancroft, Avery & McAlister, San Francisco, CA [Library symbol] [Library of Congress] (LCLS)
CSfBe........ Bechtel Group, Inc., San Francisco, CA [Library symbol Library of Congress] (LCLS)
CSfBk........ Book Club of California, San Francisco, CA [Library symbol Library of Congress] (LCLS)
CSfBo........ Bohemian Club, San Francisco, CA [Library symbol Library of Congress] (LCLS)
CSfBPH........ Brobeck, Phleger, and Harrison, San Francisco, CA [Library symbol Library of Congress] (LCLS)
CSfBPH........ Brobeck, Phleger & Harrison, San Francisco, CA [Library symbol] [Library of Congress] (LCLS)
CSFC............ Canadian Sailfish Corp. [See also OCPS]
CSFC............ Chicago Standbys Fan Club (EA)
CSFC............ Church of Scotland and Free Churches [British military] (DMA)
CSFC............ Committee for the Survival of a Free Congress
CSFC............ Connie Stevens Fan Club (EA)
CSFC............ CSF Holdings, Inc. [NASDAQ symbol] (SAG)
CSfCAB........ Crocker National Bank, San Francisco, CA [Library symbol Library of Congress] (LCLS)
CSFCBM...... Chief Shipfitter, Construction Battalion, Mechanical Draftsman [Navy rating Obsolete]
CSFCBP........ Chief Shipfitter, Construction Battalion, Pipe Fitter and Plumber [Navy rating Obsolete]
CSFCBR........ Chief Shipfitter, Construction Battalion, Rigger [Navy rating Obsolete]
CSFCBS........ Chief Shipfitter, Construction Battalion, Steel Worker [Navy rating Obsolete]
CSFCBW...... Chief Shipfitter, Construction Battalion, Welder [Navy rating Obsolete]
CSfCC........ San Francisco Chamber of Commerce, Research Department Library, San Francisco, CA [Library symbol Library of Congress] (LCLS)
CSfCCL........ Commonwealth Club of California, San Francisco, CA [Library symbol Library of Congress] (LCLS)
CSFCh........ Church of Scotland and Free Churches Chaplain [Navy British]
CSfCI........ California Institute of Asian Studies, San Francisco, CA [Library symbol Library of Congress] (LCLS)
CSfCiC........ City College of San Francisco, San Francisco, CA [Library symbol Library of Congress] (LCLS)
CSfCP........ Society of California Pioneers, San Francisco, CA [Library symbol Library of Congress] (LCLS)

CSfCPS........ College of Physicians and Surgeons, and School of Dentistry, San Francisco, CA [Library symbol Library of Congress] (LCLS)
CSfCR........ Catholic Russian Center, San Francisco, CA [Library symbol Library of Congress] (LCLS)
CSfCSM...... California State Division of Mines, San Francisco, CA [Library symbol Library of Congress] (LCLS)
CSfCW........ San Francisco College for Women, San Francisco, CA [Library symbol Library of Congress] (LCLS)
CSfCWL...... Chinese World, San Francisco, CA [Library symbol Library of Congress] (LCLS)
CSfCZ........ Crown Zellerbach Corp., San Francisco, CA [Library symbol Library of Congress] (LCLS)
CSfD........ Donahue Library [Catholic Library of San Francisco], San Francisco, CA [Library symbol Library of Congress] (LCLS)
CSfDeY........ M. H. de Young Memorial Museum, San Francisco, CA [Library symbol Library of Congress] (LCLS)
CSFDR........ Crash-Survivable Flight Data Recorder (MCD)
CSFE............ Canadian Society of Forest Engineers (HGAA)
CSfeQ........ Queen of the Angels Seminary, San Fernando, CA [Library symbol Library of Congress] (LCLS)
CSfeVA........ United States Veterans Administration Hospital, San Fernando, CA [Library symbol Library of Congress] (LCLS)
CSFF............ Commander, SEATO [Southeast Asia Treaty Organization] Field Forces (CINC)
CSfFB........ Federal Reserve Bank of San Francisco, San Francisco, CA [Library symbol Library of Congress] (LCLS)
CSfFD........ Foremost Dairies, Inc., San Francisco, CA [Library symbol Library of Congress] (LCLS)
CSfFDM...... Fedgwick, Dettret, Moran & Arnold, San Francisco, CA [Library symbol] [Library of Congress] (LCLS)
CSfFL........ French Library [L'Alliance Francaise], San Francisco, CA [Library symbol Library of Congress] (LCLS)
CSfFRC........ Federal Records Center, San Francisco, CA [Library symbol Library of Congress] (LCLS)
CSfFU........ Insurance Underwriters Association of the Pacific, San Francisco, CA [Library symbol Library of Congress] (LCLS)
CSfGB........ Grizzly Bear Club, San Francisco, CA [Library symbol Library of Congress] (LCLS)
CSfGG........ Golden Gate College, San Francisco, CA [Library symbol Library of Congress] (LCLS)
CSfGG-L........ Golden Gate University, School of Law, San Francisco, CA [Library symbol Library of Congress] (LCLS)
CSfH........... University of California, San Francisco, Hastings College of the Law, San Francisco, CA [Library symbol Library of Congress] (LCLS)
CSF Hd........ CSF Holdings, Inc. [Associated Press] (SAG)
CSfHE........ Heller, Ehrman, White & McCauliffe, San Francisco, CA [Library symbol] [Library of Congress] (LCLS)
CSfHP........ Howard, Prim, Rice, Nemerovski, Canady & Pollak, San Francisco, CA [Library symbol Library of Congress] (LCLS)
CSFI............ Coalition to Stop Food Irradiation [Later, NCSFWI] (EA)
CSFI............ Company Standard Form Instruction
CSFII............ Continuing Survey of Food Intakes by Individuals [Department of Agriculture] (GFGA)
CSfII............ Industrial Indemnity Co., San Francisco, CA [Library symbol Library of Congress] (LCLS)
CSfIL............ International Longshoremen's and Warehousemen's Union, San Francisco, CA [Library symbol Library of Congress] (LCLS)
CSfK............ Kaiser-Permanente Medical Center, San Francisco, CA [Library symbol Library of Congress] (LCLS)
CSFL............ Central States Football League
CSfL............. San Francisco Law Library, San Francisco, CA [Library symbol Library of Congress] (LCLS)
CSfLH........ California Palace of the Legion of Honor, San Francisco, CA [Library symbol Library of Congress] (LCLS)
CSfLM........ Lone Mountain College, San Francisco, CA [Library symbol Library of Congress] (LCLS)
CSfLMC........ Lillick, Mchose & Charles, San Francisco, CA [Library symbol] [Library of Congress] (LCLS)
CSfLP........ Langley-Porter Neuropsychiatric Institute, San Francisco, CA [Library symbol Library of Congress] (LCLS)
CSFLpc........ Cerebrospinal Fluid Leukocyte Particle Counter [Instrumentation]
CSFM........ Canadian Sports & Fitness Marketing Inc. [Le Marketing Canadien du Sport et de la Condition Physique] (AC)
CSfMetL........ Metropolitan Life Insurance Co., San Francisco, CA [Library symbol Library of Congress] (LCLS)
CSfMI........ Mechanics Institute, San Francisco, CA [Library symbol Library of Congress] (LCLS)
CSfMM........ San Francisco Maritime Museum, San Francisco, CA [Library symbol Library of Congress] (LCLS)
CSFMS........ Centralized Ships Force Management System
CSfMus........ San Francisco Museum of Art, San Francisco, CA [Library symbol Library of Congress] (LCLS)
CSFN........ Cell Surface Fibronectin [Biochemistry]
CSFN........ Congregation of the Sisters of the Holy Family of Nazareth [Australia]
CSFN........ Congregatio Sororum Sacrae Familiae de Nazareth [Sisters of the Holy Family of Nazareth] [Roman Catholic religious order]
CSFO........ Copeland/Sewell Family Organization (EA)
CSFOD........ Combined Special Forces Operational Detachment (CINC)
CSFP........ Cerebrospinal Fluid Pressure [Medicine] (AAMN)
CSFP........... Commodity Supplemental Food Program [Food and Nutrition Service]
CSFP........... Credit Suisse Financial Products [British] (ECON)
CSfPaul........ Paulist Library, San Francisco, CA [Library symbol Library of Congress] (LCLS)
CSFPCPM.... Chambre Syndicale des Fabricants de Papiers a Cigarettes et Autres Papiers Minces (EAIO)

CSfPG .... Pacific Gas & Electric Co., San Francisco, CA [*Library symbol Library of Congress*] (LCLS)

CSFPN .... Commission on Soil Fertility and Plant Nutrition [*of the International Society of Soil Science*] (EA)

CSfPP .... Planned Parenthood of Alameda, San Francisco, San Francisco, CA [*Library symbol Library of Congress*] (LCLS)

CSfPr .... Press and Union League Club of San Francisco, San Francisco, CA [*Library symbol Library of Congress*] (LCLS)

CSFPSC ...... Commander, Subordinate Command, Service Force Pacific Fleet [*Navy*]

CSfPUC .... Pacific Union Club, San Francisco, CA [*Library symbol Library of Congress*] (LCLS)

CSFR .... Czech and Slovak Federal Republic (RDA)

CSFRE .... Canadian Society of Fund Raising Executives (NFD)

CSFRE .... Canadian Society of Fund Raising Executives

CSFS .... Canadian Society of Forensic Science (AC)

CSfSA .... Strybing Arboretum Society of Golden Gate Park, San Francisco, CA [*Library symbol Library of Congress*] (LCLS)

CSFSAC .... Civil Service Foreign Service Allowances Committee [*British*]

CSfSC .... Sierra Club, San Francisco, CA [*Library symbol Library of Congress*] (LCLS)

CSfSFL .... California Labor Federation AFL-CIO Library, San Francisco, CA [*Library symbol Library of Congress*] (LCLS)

CSfSM .... Saint Mary's Hospital, San Francisco, CA [*Library symbol Library of Congress*] (LCLS)

CSfSO .... Standard Oil Co. of California, San Francisco, CA [*Library symbol Library of Congress*] (LCLS)

CSfSP .... Southern Pacific Co., San Francisco, CA [*Library symbol Library of Congress*] (LCLS)

CSfSPA .... Saint Peter's Academy, San Francisco, CA [*Library symbol Library of Congress*] (LCLS)

CSFSR .... Chief Shipfitter, Ship Repair [*Navy rating Obsolete*]

CSfSRA .... Saint Rose Academy, San Francisco, CA [*Library symbol Library of Congress*] (LCLS)

CSFSRP ...... Chief Shipfitter, Ship Repair, Pipe Fitter and Plumber [*Navy rating Obsolete*]

CSFSRW ..... Chief Shipfitter, Ship Repair, Welder [*Navy rating Obsolete*]

CSfSt .... San Francisco State University, San Francisco, CA [*Library symbol Library of Congress*] (LCLS)

CSfTheo ...... Theosophical Society, San Francisco, CA [*Library symbol Library of Congress*] (LCLS)

CSfU .... University of San Francisco, San Francisco, CA [*Library symbol Library of Congress*] (LCLS)

CSfUM .... United States Bureau of Mines, Fuels Technology Library, San Francisco, CA [*Library symbol Library of Congress*] (LCLS)

CSF/USA ...... Correctional Service Federation - USA (EA)

CSfUSA .... United States Army, Sixth Army Command, Reference Center Library and Library Depot, San Francisco, CA [*Library symbol Library of Congress*] (LCLS)

CSfUSA-L ..... United States Army, Sixth Army Command, Letterman General Hospital Libraries, San Francisco, CA [*Library symbol Library of Congress*] (LCLS)

CSFV .... Classical Swine Fever Virus

CSfV .... United States Veterans Administration Hospital, San Francisco, CA [*Library symbol Library of Congress*] (LCLS)

CSfW .... Wine Institute, San Francisco, CA [*Library symbol Library of Congress*] (LCLS)

CSfWA .... World Affairs Council of Northern California, San Francisco, CA [*Library symbol Library of Congress*] (LCLS)

CSfWF .... Wells Fargo Bank, San Francisco, CA [*Library symbol Library of Congress*] (LCLS)

CSfWF-H ...... Wells Fargo Bank, History Room Library, San Francisco, CA [*Library symbol Library of Congress*] (LCLS)

CSF-WR .... Cerebrospinal Fluid-Wassermann Reaction [*Medicine*] (AAMN)

CSfWT .... World Trade Center Libraries, San Francisco, CA [*Library symbol Library of Congress*] (LCLS)

CSG .... Cadbury Schweppes ADS [*NYSE symbol*] (TTSB)

CSG .... Cadbury Schwepps PLC [*NYSE symbol*] (SAG)

CSG .... Calibration Signal Generator

CSG .... Canada Systems Group [*Database producer*] [*Ottawa, ON*] [*Information service or system*]

CSG .... Canopy Smoke Grenade (DWSG)

CSG .... Can't Say Good-By

CSG .... Capital Systems Group, Inc. [*Information service or system*] (IID)

CSG .... Career-Shortening Gesture

CSG .... Casing (KSC)

CSG .... Chairman's Staff Group [*DoD*]

CSG .... Chimney Sweep Guild [*Later, NCSG*] (EA)

CSG .... Chronic Simple Glaucoma [*Ophthalmology*] (CPH)

CSG .... Clean Sweep Generator (NVT)

CSG .... Close Support Gun (DNAB)

CSG .... Coast Range Resources Ltd. [*Vancouver Stock Exchange symbol*]

CSG .... Collective Stick Grip (MCD)

CSG .... Columbus [*Georgia*] [*Airport symbol*] (OAG)

CSG .... Combat Service Group [*Army*]

CSG .... Combat Support Group [*Army*]

CSG .... Combined Studies Group [*Central Intelligence Agency operation in Southeast Asia*]

CSG .... Comite Permanent des Secretaires Generaux [*Standing Committee of Secretaries General*] [*NATO*] (NATG)

CSG .... Command Signal Generator

CSG .... Command Subsystem Group (MCD)

CSG .... Community Service Grant [*Corporation for Public Broadcasting*]

CSG .... Computer Support Group [*Marine science*] (OSRA)

CSG .... Computer Support Group (USDC)

CSG .... Console Set Group

CSG .... Consolidated Steam Generator (PDAA)

CSG .... Constructive Solid Geometry

CSG .... Context Sensitive Grammar [*Computer science*] (IAA)

CSG .... Control Synthetic Gas [*Process*]

CSG .... Council of State Governments (EA)

CSG .... Course and Speed Made Good over the Ground [*Military*] (NATG)

CSG .... Cryptologic Support Group [*Military*] (NVT)

CSG .... Guided Missile Strike Cruiser [*Navy symbol*] (NVT)

CSG .... Sacramento City College Library, Sacramento, CA [*OCLC symbol*] (OCLC)

CSG2 .... Commander, Service Group Two [*Navy*]

CSGA .... Canadian Seed Growers Association (HGAA)

CSGA .... Canadian Society of Graphic Art [*1923-76, founded c.1903 as GAC, SGA from 1912*] (NGC)

CSGA .... Canadian Sporting Goods Association [*Association Canadienne d'Article Sport*] (AC)

CSGB .... Cartophilic Society of Great Britain

CSGB .... Cremation Society of Great Britain

CSGBI .... Cardiac Society of Great Britain and Ireland (DAVI)

CSGC .... Consumer Safety Glazing Committee

CSGCC .... Commission on Soil Genesis, Classification, and Cartography [*of the International Society of Soil Science*] (EA)

CSGI .... Citizens Security Group, Inc. [*NASDAQ symbol*] (NQ)

CSGI .... Citizens Security Grp [*NASDAQ symbol*] (TTSB)

CSGMP .... Cross-Scan Ground Map Pencil (DNAB)

CSGN .... Nuclear-Powered Strike Cruiser

CSGNSW ...... Commercial Services Group, New South Wales [*Australia*]

CSGp .... Combat Support Group [*Air Force*] (AFM)

CSGP .... Community Services Grants Program [*Australia*]

CSGS .... Campaign to Stop Government Spying [*Later, CPR*] (EA)

CSGS .... Church of Jesus Christ of Latter-Day Saints, Genealogical Society Library, Sacramento Branch, Sacramento, CA [*Library symbol Library of Congress*] (LCLS)

CSGS .... Combat Center Simulation Generation System [*Military*] (SAA)

CSGS .... CSG Systems International, Inc. [*NASDAQ symbol*] (SAG)

CSGS .... CSG Systems Intl. [*NASDAQ symbol*] (TTSB)

CSGSys .... CSG Systems International, Inc. [*Associated Press*] (SAG)

C/Sgt .... Colour-Sergeant [*Army British*] (DMA)

CSGUS .... Clinical Society of Genito-Urinary Surgeons (EA)

CSGV .... Coalition to Stop Gun Violence (EA)

CSGW .... Coalition to Stop Government Waste (EA)

CSGWPP ...... Comprehensive State Ground Water Protection Program [*Environmental science*]

CSH .... Cableshare, Inc. [*Toronto Stock Exchange symbol*]

CSH .... Calcium Silicate Hydrate [*Inorganic chemistry*]

CSH .... California State [*University*], Hayward [*California*] [*Seismograph station code, US Geological Survey*] (SEIS)

CSH .... California State University, Hayward, Hayward, CA [*OCLC symbol*] (OCLC)

CSH .... Called Subscriber Held [*Telecommunications*] (TEL)

CSH .... Capsure Holdings [*NYSE symbol*] (SPSG)

CSH .... Carotid Sinus Hypersensitivity [*Cardiology*] (DAVI)

CSH .... Cash (DCTA)

CSH .... Center for Socialist History (EA)

C-Sh .... Chair Shower [*Medical rehabilitation*] (DAVI)

CSH .... Chronic Subdural Hematoma [*Medicine*]

CSH .... Coalition on Smoking or Health (EA)

CSH .... Cold Spring Harbor Laboratory [*Cold Spring Harbor, NY*]

CSH .... College of the Sacred Heart [*Puerto Rico*]

CSH .... Combat Support Hospital (AABC)

CSH .... Communications Soft Hat [*NASA*] (KSC)

CSH .... Conventional Spin Hamiltonian (PDAA)

CSH .... Cortical Stromal Hyperplasia [*Medicine*] (MAE)

CSH .... Shanghai Airlines [*China*] [*ICAO designator*] (FAAC)

CSh .... Signal Hill Public Library, Signal Hill, CA [*Library symbol Library of Congress*] (LCLS)

CSHA .... California Society for Healthcare Attorneys (SRA)

CSHA .... California State Horseman's Association (SRA)

CSHA .... Civil Service Housing Association [*British*]

CSHA .... Colorado Speech-Language-Hearing Association (SRA)

CSHA .... Council of State Housing Agencies (EA)

CSHAFT .... Crankshaft

CShaHi .... Shafter Historical Society, Shafter, CA [*Library symbol*] [*Library of Congress*] (LCLS)

CSHA(SP) .... Commonwealth-State Housing Agreement (Service Personnel) [*Australia*]

CSHCN .... Children's Special Health Care Needs Program [*Social Security Administration (SSA)*] (PAZ)

CSHCN .... Children with Special Health Care Needs

CSHEP .... Constriction, Sclerosis, Hemorrhage, Exudate, Papilledema [*Ophthalmology*]

C/SHFT .... Cross Shaft [*Automotive engineering*]

CSHG .... Collective of Self Help Groups [*Australia*]

CSHG .... Committee on the Standardization of Hospital Graphics [*Defunct*]

CSHH .... Congenital Self-Healing Histiocytosis [*Medicine*] (DMAA)

CSHI .... Christian Services for the Hearing Impaired [*Australia*]

CSHIB .... Chemical Safety and Hazardous Investigation Board [*Environmental Protection Agency*]

CSHL .... Centre for the Study of Human Learning [*Brunel University*] [*British*] (CB)

CSHM .... Canadian Society for the History of Medicine [*See also SCHM*]

CSHM .... Committee for the Study of Handgun Misuse (EA)

CSHM .... Conseil des Syndicats Hospitaliers de Montreal Inc. [*Montreal Council of Hospital Syndicates Inc.*] (AC)

CSHN	Cushion
CSHO	Compliance Safety and Health Officer [Occupational Safety and Health Administration]
CSHP	Canadian Society of Hospital Pharmacists
CSHP	Conference of Societies for the History of Pharmacy [Madrid, Spain] (EAIO)
CSHPE	Center for Study of Higher and Postsecondary Education [University of Michigan] [Research center] (RCD)
CSHPM	Canadian Society for the History and Philosophy of Mathematics [See also SCHPM]
CSHPS	Canadian Society for the History and Philosophy of Science [See also SCHPS]
CSHPSS	Central Solar Heating Plant with Seasonal Storage [Pronounced "chips"] [Thermal technology] (PS)
CSHR	Canadian Society for the History of Rhetoric [See also SCHR]
CSHR	Center for the Study of Human Rights (EA)
CSHS	Canadian Society for Horticultural Science (AC)
CSHS	Canadian Standardbred Horse Society
CSHS	Chief Superintendent of Hydrographic Supplies
CSHSE	Council for Standards in Human Service Education
CSHX	Containment Spray Heat Exchange [Nuclear energy] (NRCH)
CSI	Cable Systems International
CSI	Cable Systems International
CSI	Cable Systems International
CSI	Campus Studies Institute (EA)
CSI	[The] Canadian Securities [Institut Canadien des Valeurs Mobilieres] (AC)
CSI	Canadian Sugar Institute [Institut Canadien du Sucre] (AC)
CSI	Cancer Serum Index
CSI	Canned Salmon Institute [Later, SI] (EA)
CSI	Cannon Street Investments [Finance British]
CSI	Capitol Services, Inc. [Database producer] [Information service or system] (IID)
CSI	Casino [Australia Airport symbol] (OAG)
CSI	C-Band Sensitivity Improvement [Navy] (MCD)
CSI	Cellulose Sponge Institute [Defunct] (EA)
CSI	Center for Science Information (EA)
CSI	Center for the Study of Instruction [of NEA]
CSI	Center Point, TX [Location identifier FAA] (FAAL)
CSI	Central Skyport, Inc. [ICAO designator] (FAAC)
CSI	Cesium Iodide
CSI	Cetacean Society International (EA)
CSI	Change Seeker Index
CSI	Chartered Surveyors' Institution [British] (DAS)
CSI	Chase Brass Indus [NYSE symbol] (TTSB)
CSI	Chase Brass Industries, Inc. [NYSE symbol] (SAG)
CSI	Chemical Substances Inventory [Environmental Protection Agency] (GFGA)
CSI	Chemical Substructure Index [Trademark]
CSI	Chlorosulfonyl Isocyanate [Organic chemistry]
CSI	Cholesterol Saturation Index [Clinical chemistry]
CSI	Christian Schools International (EA)
CSI	Christian Solidarity International [Zurich, Switzerland] (EAIO)
CSI	Chromatography Signal Interface
CSI	Church of South India
CSI	Cinematheque Scientifique Internationale [International Scientific Film Library]
CSI	Clarion State College, School of Library Media, Clarion, PA [OCLC symbol] (OCLC)
CSI	Clean Sites, Inc. (EA)
CSI	Coalition of Service Industries [Washington, DC] (EA)
CSI	Coastal Studies Institute [Louisiana State University] [Research center]
CSI	Coelliptic Sequence Initiation [Aerospace]
CSI	Cold Start Injector [Automotive engineering]
CSI	College of Staten Island [New York]
CSI	Colloquium Spectroscopicum Internationale
CSI	Combat Studies Institute [Command and General Staff College, Fort Leavenworth] [Army] (INF)
CSI	Combat System Integration (MCD)
CSI	Command String Interpreter [Digital Equipment Corp.]
CSI	Commissioners Standard Industrial Mortality Table [Insurance]
CSI	Commission Sericicole Internationale [International Sericultural Commission - ISC] (EAIO)
CSI	Commission Sportive Internationale [Auto racing]
CSI	Commodity Systems, Inc. [Information service or system] (IID)
CSI	Communications Services, Inc. [Junction City, KS]
CSI	Communications Solutions, Inc. [San Jose, CA] [Information service or system Telecommunications] (TSSD)
CSI	Communications Systems, Inc.
CSI	Compact Source Iodide (WDMC)
CSI	Companion of the [Order of the] Star of India [British]
CSI	Company Source Inspection
CSI	Competition-Sensitive Information [Military]
CSI	Competitive Strategies Initiative [Military] (DOMA)
CSI	Compliance Sampling Inspection [Environmental Protection Agency] (GFGA)
CSI	Compressive Safety Index [Engineering design]
CSI	CompuServe, Inc. [Commercial firm]
CSI	Computerized Stress Inventory [Personality development test] [Psychology]
CSI	Computer Search International Corp. [Database producer]
CSI	Computer Security Institute (EA)
CSI	Computer Synthesized Imagery (MCD)
CSI	Computer Systems Institute

CSI	Computer Systems International
CSI	Concentric Sequence Initiation [Aerospace]
CSI	Conditional Symmetric Instability [Marine science] (OSRA)
CSI	Conditional Symmetric Instability (USDC)
CSI	Consortium for the Study of Intelligence (EA)
CSI	Consorzio per il Sistema Informativo Piemonte [Piedmont Consortium for Information Systems] [Information service or system] (IID)
CSI	Construction Specifications Institute
CSI	Construction Surveyors Institute [Later, Architects and Surveyors Institute] (EA)
CSI	Consumer Satisfaction Index
CSI	Contractor Source Inspection [Military]
CSI	Contractor Standard Item (AAG)
CSI	Control Servo Input (NASA)
CSI	Control Software, Inc.
CSI	CONUS [Continental United States] Sustaining Increment [Army] (AABC)
CSI	Correct Seating Institute
CSI	Corrosion Status Index [Military] (RDA)
CSI	Cost System Indicator (AFIT)
CSI	Council for the Securities Industry [Stock exchange] [London, England]
CSI	Counseling Satisfaction Inventory [Education]
CSI	Coupe Sport Injection [Automobile designation]
CSI	Creative Strategies International (HGAA)
CSI	Credit Systems Inc.
CSI	Crew Software Interface (MCD)
CSI	Crime Stoppers International (EA)
CSI	Critical Safety Item [Military]
CSI	CSI Computer Specialists [Associated Press] (SAG)
CSI	Culture Shock Inventory [Interpersonal skills and attitudes test]
CSI	Customer Satisfaction Index [Automotive retailing]
CSI	Cycle-Significant Items (MCD)
CSI	Decisions of the Commissioners under the National Insurance (Industrial Injuries) Acts Relating to Scotland [A publication] (DLA)
CSIA	California Self-Insurers Association (SRA)
CSIA	Canadian Ski Instructors' Alliance
CSIA	Canadian Solar Industries Association
CSIA	Center for Science and International Affairs [Harvard University] [Research center]
CSIA	Chimney Safety Institute of America (EA)
CSIA	Coupe Sport Injection Automatic [Automobile designation]
CSIAPL	Canadian Section International Association of Penal Law (EAIO)
CSIAV	Cold Storage and Ice Association of Victoria [Australia]
CSIC	Computer Stock Inventory Control (MCD)
CSIC	Computer System Interface Circuits (IEEE)
CSIC	Customer Specific Integrated Circuit [Electronics]
CSICC	Canadian Steel Industries Construction Council (HGAA)
CSICOP	Committee for the Scientific Investigation of Claims of the Paranormal (EA)
CSICU	Cardiac Surgical Intensive Care Unit [Medicine]
CSID	Convergence Source-Image Distortion [Crystal]
CSID	Correct Calling Station Identifier [Telecommunications] (PCM)
CSID	Customer Subscriber Identification [Telecommunications] (PCM)
CSIE	Center for the Study of Information and Education [Syracuse University] (IID)
CSIE	Centre for Studies on Integration in Education [British] (CB)
CSIE	Council for Sex Information and Education (EA)
CSie	Sierra Madre Free Public Library, Sierra Madre, CA [Library symbol Library of Congress] (LCLS)
CSIER	Centre for the Study of International Economic Relations [University of Western Ontario] [Canada] (IRC)
CSIET	Council on Standards for International Educational Travel (EA)
CSIF	Collagen Synthesis Inhibitory Factor [Biochemistry]
CSIF	Communications Systems Industrial Funds (MCD)
CSIF	Cytokine Synthesis Inhibitory Factor [Immunology]
CSIG	Control Systems Integration Group (SAA)
CSIGC	Chief, Signal Corps [Army]
CSIGO	Chief Signal Officer [Army]
CSIH	Canadian Society for Industrial Heritage (AC)
CSIH	Canadian Society for International Health [Societe Canadienne pour la Sante Internationale] [Formerly, Canadian Society for Tropical Medicine & International Health] (AC)
CSII	Communications Systems, Inc. [NASDAQ symbol] (NQ)
CSII	Communic Sys [NASDAQ symbol] (TTSB)
CSII	Continuous Subcutaneous Insulin Infusion [Medicine]
CSIICG	Combat System Integration and Interface Control Group [Military] (CAAL)
CSIIP	Continuous Subcutaneous Insulin Infusion Pump [Medicine] (DMAA)
CSIM	Canadian Society of Internal Medicine [Societe Canadienne de Medecine Interne] (AC)
CSIM	Combat System Integration Manager [Military] (CAAL)
CSIM	Consilium, Inc. [NASDAQ symbol] (NQ)
CSIM	Consortium for Sharing Instructional Materials [Library network]
CSIN	Chemical Substances Information Network [No longer exists] [Environmental Protection Agency Information service or system]
CSIN	Computational Systems [NASDAQ symbol] (TTSB)
CSIN	Computational Systems, Inc. [NASDAQ symbol] (SAG)
CSINK	Countersink [Engineering] (IAA)
CSIO	Centre for Study of Insurance Operations (AC)
CS:IP	Code Segment:Instruction Pointer [Computer science]
CSIP	Combat System Initialization Procedure [Military] (CAAL)
CSIP	Combat Systems Improvement Program [Navy] (PDAA)
CSIP	Critical Safety Item Program [Army]

CSIPP .... Committee to Support Irish Political Prisoners (EA)
CSIR .... Computer Systems Integration Review (NASA)
CSIR .... Council of Scientific and Industrial Research [*Information service or system South Africa*] (IID)
CSIRA .... Canadian Steel Industry Research Association
CSIRAC .... Commonwealth Scientific and Industrial Research Automatic Computer [*British*] (IAA)
CSIR Bull.... Council for Scientific and Industrial Research. Bulletin [*A publication*]
CSIRO .... Commonwealth Scientific and Industrial Research Organisation [*Australia*] [*Information service or system*] (NITA)
CSIRONET.... [*The*] Commonwealth Scientific and Industrial Research Organization Network [*Australia*] [*Computer science*] (TNIG)
CSIRONET.... Commonwealth Scientific and Research Organisation Network [*Australia*] [*Information service or system*] (NITA)
CSIRT .... Comite Scientifique International de Recherches sur les Trypanosomiases
CSIS............ Canadian Security and Intelligence Service
CSIS............ Canadian Society for Industrial Security
CSIS............ Canadian Society for Italian Studies
CSIS............ Center for Strategic and International Studies [*Georgetown University*]
CSIS............ Central Secondary Item Stratification [*Military*] (AFIT)
CSIS............ Civil Service Insurance Society [*British*]
CSIS............ Clinical Supplies and Inventory System [*Medicine*] (DMAA)
CSIS............ Containment Spray Injection System [*Nuclear energy*] (NRCH)
CSIS............ Core Spray Injection System [*Nuclear energy*] (IAA)
CSIS............ CSI Computer Specialists [*NASDAQ symbol*] (SAG)
CSISAS .... Cross Section Information Storage and Retrieval System [*National Neutron Cross Section Center*] (NITA)
CSISM .... Cryptographic Supplement to the Industrial Security Manual [*DoD*]
CSISRS .... Cross-Section Information Storage and Retrieval System [*Brookhaven National Laboratory*] [*Information service or system*] (NITA)
CSISW .... CSI Computer Specialists Wrrt'A' [*NASDAQ symbol*] (TTSB)
CSIT............ Chapin Social Insight Test [*Psychology*]
CSIT............ Combat System Integration Test [*Military*] (CAAL)
CSIT............ Combat System Interface Test [*Military*] (CAAL)
CSIT............ Comite Sportif International du Travail [*International Workers Sport Committee*] [*Brussels, Belgium*] (EAIO)
CSITSL........ Comite Syndical International du Tourisme Social et des Loisirs [*International Trade Unions Committee of Social Tourism and Leisure - ITUCSTL*] (EA)
CSITT .... Combat System Interface Test Tool (NVT)
CSIU .... Core Segment Interface Unit (NASA)
CSJ .... Cape San Juan [*Puerto Rico*] [*Seismograph station code, US Geological Survey*] (SEIS)
CSJ .... Cape St. Jacques [*South Vietnam*] [*Airport symbol*] (AD)
CSJ .... Carolian Systems International, Inc. [*Toronto Stock Exchange symbol*]
CSJ .... Castle Aviation, Inc. [*ICAO designator*] (FAAC)
CSJ .... Chemical Society of Japan
CSJ .... Citizens for Social Justice (EA)
CSJ .... Columbus SoPwr 8.375% Sub Db [*NYSE symbol*] (TTSB)
CSJ .... Columbus Southern Power Co. [*NYSE symbol*] (SAG)
CSJ .... Commission for Social Justice (EA)
CSJ .... Congregation of St. Joseph (TOCD)
csj .... Congregation of St. Joseph (TOCD)
CSJ .... Congregatio Sancti Joseph [*Congregation of St. Joseph*] [*Roman Catholic religious order*]
CSJ .... Control System Jet
CSJ .... Court of Summary Jurisdiction [*British*] (ROG)
CSJ .... Crime and Social Justice [*Australia A publication*]
CSj .... San Jose Public Library, San Jose, CA [*Library symbol Library of Congress*] (LCLS)
CSJ .... San Jose State University, San Jose, CA [*OCLC symbol*] (OCLC)
CSJ .... Sisters of St. Joseph (Boston, Brighton) (TOCD)
CSJ .... Sisters of St. Joseph (Chicago, Lagrange Park) (TOCD)
CSJ .... Sisters of St. Joseph (Cleveland) (TOCD)
CSJ .... Sisters of St. Joseph (Lafayette, IN) (TOCD)
CSJ .... Sisters of St. Joseph (Lyons, MI) (TOCD)
CSJ .... Sisters of St. Joseph of Carondelet (TOCD)
CSJ .... Sisters of St. Joseph of Chambery (TOCD)
CSJ .... Sisters of St. Joseph of Medaille (TOCD)
CSJ .... Sisters of St. Joseph (Orange) (TOCD)
CSJ .... Sisters of St. Joseph (Pittsburgh, Baden) (TOCD)
CSJ .... Sisters of St. Joseph (Rockville Centre, Brentwood) (TOCD)
CSJ .... Sisters of St. Joseph (Salina, Concordia) (TOCD)
CSJ .... Sisters of St. Joseph (Wichita) (TOCD)
CSjac .... San Jacinto Public Library, San Jacinto, CA [*Library symbol Library of Congress*] (LCLS)
CSJAGA ...... Military Affairs Division, Office of Judge Advocate General, United States Army (DLA)
CSjB............ Berliner, Cohen & Biogini, Law Library, San Jose, CA [*Library symbol Library of Congress*] (LCLS)
CSJB .... Community of St. John the Baptist [*Anglican religious community*]
CSJB .... Congregation of St. John the Baptist (TOCD)
CSjb .... San Juan Bautista City Library, San Juan Bautista, CA [*Library symbol Library of Congress*] (LCLS)
CSJB .... Sisters of St. John the Baptist (TOCD)
CSjBC .... Berliner, Coher & Biogini, Law Library, San Jose, CA [*Library symbol*] [*Library of Congress*] (LCLS)
CSJCA......... Central Sephardic Jewish Community of America (EA)
CSjCiC .... San Jose City College, San Jose, CA [*Library symbol Library of Congress*] (LCLS)
CSjCL.......... Santa Clara County Free Library, San Jose, CA [*Library symbol Library of Congress*] (LCLS)

CSjCLA .... Cooperative Library Agency for Systems and Services, San Jose, CA [*Library symbol Library of Congress*] (LCLS)
CSJE .... Community of St. John the Evangelist [*Anglican religious community*]
CSjE .... Evergreen Valley College, San Jose, CA [*Library symbol Library of Congress*] (LCLS)
CSJF .... Case Study and Justification Folder
CSJFET .... Charge Storage Junction Field Effect Transistor (IAA)
CSjGS .... Church of Jesus Christ of Latter-Day Saints, Genealogical Society Library, San Jose Branch, San Jose, CA [*Library symbol Library of Congress*] (LCLS)
CSjHi .... San Jose Historical Society, San Jose, CA [*Library symbol*] [*Library of Congress*] (LCLS)
CSjHMC ...... Hopkins, Mitchell & Carley, Law Library, San Jose, CA [*Library symbol*] [*Library of Congress*] (LCLS)
CSjIBM .... International Business Machines Corp., San Jose, CA [*Library symbol Library of Congress*] (LCLS)
CSjL............ Santa Clara County Law Library, San Jose, CA [*Library symbol*] [*Library of Congress*] (LCLS)
CSJMENA .... Community for Social Justice in the Middle East and North Africa (EA)
CSJP .... Sisters of St. Joseph of Peace (TOCD)
CSjSV .... Silicon Valley Information Center, San Jose, CA [*Library symbol*] [*Library of Congress*] (LCLS)
CSjU .... San Jose State University, San Jose, CA [*Library symbol Library of Congress*] (LCLS)
CSJWOE ..... Commission on the Status of Jewish War Orphans in Europe, American Section [*Defunct*] (EA)
CSK............ Cable Splicing Kit
CSK............ Cap Skirring [*Senegal*] [*Airport symbol*] (OAG)
CSK............ Carnes Creek Explorations [*Vancouver Stock Exchange symbol*]
CSK............ Cask
CSK............ Cathodic Survey Kit
CSK............ Chesapeake Corp. [*NYSE symbol*] (SPSG)
CSK............ Chief Storekeeper [*Navy rating Obsolete*]
CSK............ Community of St. Katharine of Egypt [*Anglican religious community*]
CSK............ Consumer Survival Kit [*Program on public TV*]
CSK............ Cooperative Study of the Kuroshio [*UNESCO*]
CSK............ Cooperative Study of the Kuroshio [*UNESCO*]
CSK............ Cooperative Study of the Kuroshio and Adjacent Regions [*Marine science*] (OSRA)
CSK............ Cooperative Study of the Kuroshio and Adjacent Regions [*Intergovernmental Oceanographic Commission Coordination Group*] (USDC)
CSK............ Countersink (KSC)
CSK............ CSK Corp. [*Associated Press*] (SAG)
CSK............ Cytoskeleton [*Cytology*]
CSK............ Czechoslovakia [*ANSI three-letter standard code*] (CNC)
CSKCB .... Chief Storekeeper, Construction Battalion, Stevedore [*Navy rating Obsolete*]
CSKD .... Chief Storekeeper, Disbursing [*Navy rating Obsolete*]
CSKH .... Countersunk Head
CSKK .... CSK Corp. [*NASDAQ symbol*] (NQ)
CSKKY .... CSK Corp. ADS [*NASDAQ symbol*] (TTSB)
CSKO .... Countersink Other Side
Csk-OS......... Countersink Other Side
CSKS .... Casks
CSKT........... Casket
CSKT........... Chief Storekeeper, Technical [*Navy rating Obsolete*]
CSKV .... Chief Storekeeper, Aviation [*Navy rating Obsolete*]
CSL............ Canada Steamship Lines
CSL............ Canadian Slovak League
CSL............ Canreos Minerals [*Vancouver Stock Exchange symbol*]
CSL............ Cardiolipin Synthetic Lecithin [*Biochemistry*] (MAE)
CSL............ Carlisle Companies [*NYSE symbol*] (SPSG)
CSL............ Casual
CSL............ Center for the Study of Learning [*Pittsburgh, PA*] [*Department of Education*] (GRD)
CSL............ Ceskoslovenska Strana Lidova [*Czechoslovak People's Party*] (PPE)
CSL............ Chemical Systems Laboratory [*Later, CRDC*] [*Army*] (RDA)
CSL............ Chicago Short Line Railway Co. [*AAR code*]
CSL............ Cinderella Softball Leagues (EA)
CSL............ Circle of State Librarians [*British*]
CSL............ Circuit Switched Line [*Telecommunications*] (MCD)
CSL............ Coaxial Slotted Line
CSL............ Code Selection Language [*Computer science*] (BUR)
CSL............ Coincidence Site Lattice (MCD)
CSL............ Coles Signal Laboratory [*Army*] (MCD)
CSL............ Combat Support Liaison (CINC)
CSL............ Combat Surveillance Laboratory
CSL............ Combined Single Limit [*Insurance*]
CSL............ Commander Service Force, Atlantic (MCD)
CSL............ Command Signal Limiter (MCD)
CSL............ Common Specification Language (NATG)
CSL............ Communication Sciences Laboratory [*University of Florida*]
CSL............ Communication Services Ltd. [*Hong Kong*] [*Telecommunications*]
CSL............ Community of St. Laurence [*Anglican religious community*]
CSL............ Comparative Systems Laboratory
CSL............ Complete Service Life
CSL............ Component Save List [*Military*] (AFIT)
CSL............ Component Source List (IAA)
CSL............ Computer Science Laboratory [*Sony*] [*Japan*] (ECON)
CSL............ Computer Sensitive Language [*Programming language*]
CSL............ Computer Simulation Language (BUR)
CSL............ Computer Status Lights (MCD)
CSL............ Computer Structure Language [*1974*] [*Computer science*] (CSR)

CSL............	Computer System Language
CSL............	Computer Systems Laboratory [Bethesda, MD] [Department of Health and Human Services] (GRD)
CSL............	Conseil Superieur de Livre [Canada]
CSL............	Console (AAG)
CSL............	Constant Scattering Length (OA)
CSL............	Context-Sensitive Language [Computer science] (IAA)
CSL............	Control and Simulation Language [Computer science]
CSL............	Control and Status Logic (KSC)
CSL............	Controlled Saturation Logic (IAA)
CSL............	Control Systems Laboratory [University of Illinois] (MCD)
CSL............	Coordinated Science Laboratory [University of Illinois] [Research center]
CSL............	Cosmopolitan Soccer League (EA)
CSL............	Counsel (ROG)
CSL............	Coupe Sport Leicht [Automobile model designation] [German]
CSL............	Crew Systems Laboratory [NASA] (NASA)
CSL............	Current Sink Logic (IAA)
CSL............	Current Source Logic (IAA)
CSL............	Current Switch Logic (IEEE)
CSL............	Minson Aviation, Inc. [ICAO designator] (FAAC)
CSl............	San Leandro Community Library Center, San Leandro, CA [Library symbol Library of Congress] (LCLS)
CSL............	San Luis Obispo, CA [Location identifier FAA] (FAAL)
CSL............	University of Southern California, Los Angeles, CA [OCLC symbol] (OCLC)
CSLA..........	Canadian School Library Association
CSLA..........	Canadian Society of Landscape Architects
CSLA..........	Church and Synagogue Library Association (EA)
CSLA..........	Commercial Space Launch Act
CSLA..........	Communications Security Logistics Agency (MCD)
CSLA..........	Computer Science Lecturers' Association [British]
CSLATP.......	Canadian Society of Landscape Architects and Town Planners (HGAA)
CSLB..........	Computer Services - Long Beach (MCD)
CSLBTS......	Combat System Land-Based Test Site (CAAL)
CSLC..........	Center for Studies in Language and Communication [Gallaudet College] [Research center] (RCD)
CSLC..........	Coherent Side-Lobe Cancellation
CSLC..........	Consolidated Statutes of Lower Canada [A publication] (DLA)
CSLDB........	California Spanish Language Data Base [Information service or system] (IID)
CSLDF........	Creation Science Legal Defense Fund (EA)
CSLDT........	Consolidate (FAAC)
CSLEA........	Center for the Study of Liberal Education for Adults (EA)
CSLES........	Children's Stressful Life Events Scale
CSLFC........	Council of Savings and Loan Financial Corporations (EA)
CSLGC........	Committee on State and Local Government Cooperation
CSLI...........	Center for the Study of Language and Information [Stanford University] [Research center] (RCD)
CSLI...........	Cotton States Life Ins [NASDAQ symbol] (TTSB)
CSLI...........	Cotton States Life Insurance [NASDAQ symbol] (SAG)
CSLIN.........	Contract Subline Item Number (MCD)
CSLIP.........	Compressed SLIP [Serial Line Internet Protocol] (CDE)
CSLL..........	Sacramento County Law Library, Sacramento, CA [Library symbol Library of Congress] (LCLS)
CSL Lgt.......	CSL Lighting Manufacturing [Associated Press] (SAG)
CSLM..........	Confocal Scanning LASER Microscope [or Microscopy]
CSLM..........	Consolidated Mercantile Corp. [NASDAQ symbol] (NQ)
CSLMF........	Consolidated Mercantile [NASDAQ symbol] (TTSB)
CSLMR.......	Chief Sailmaker [British military] (DMA)
CSLO..........	Canadian Scientific Liaison Office (HGAA)
CSLP..........	Canada Student Loans Program
CSLP..........	Center for Short-Lived Phenomena (EA)
CSLP..........	Center for the Study of Law and Politics (EA)
CSLP..........	Croatian Social-Liberal Party [Political party]
CSLR..........	City and South London Railway ["The Tube"] (ROG)
CSLR..........	Consulier Engineering, Inc. [NASDAQ symbol] (NQ)
CSLR..........	Consulier Engr [NASDAQ symbol] (TTSB)
CSLS..........	Center for the Study of Law and Society [University of California, Berkeley] [Research center] (RCD)
CSLS..........	Centre for Socio-Legal Studies [British] (CB)
CSLS..........	Civil Service Legal Society [British]
CSLS..........	Cost Schedule, Logistics, and NATO Standardization (MCD)
CSLT..........	Canadian Society of Laboratory Technologists (EAIO)
CSLT..........	Control for Surface-Launched Torpedoes (MCD)
CSLTY........	Casualty
CSLU..........	Chronic Stasis Leg Ulcer [Medicine] (AAMN)
CSlu...........	San Luis Obispo Public Library, San Luis Obispo, CA [Library symbol Library of Congress] (LCLS)
CSluCL........	San Luis Obispo County Free Library, San Luis Obispo, CA [Library symbol Library of Congress] (LCLS)
CSluCu........	Cuesta College, San Luis Obispo, CA [Library symbol Library of Congress] (LCLS)
CSluGS	Church of Jesus Christ of Latter-Day Saints, Genealogical Society Library, San Luis Obispo Branch, San Luis Obispo, CA [Library symbol Library of Congress] (LCLS)
CSluHi.........	San Luis Obispo Historical Society, San Luis Obispo, CA [Library symbol] [Library of Congress] (LCLS)
CSluSP........	California Polytechnic State University, San Luis Obispo, CA [Library symbol Library of Congress] (LCLS)
CSLV..........	Council of the State Library of Victoria [Australia]
CSLX..........	CSL Lighting Manufacturing [NASDAQ symbol] (SAG)
CSLX..........	CSL Lighting Mfg [NASDAQ symbol] (TTSB)
CSM............	Call Supervision Module [Telecommunications] (TEL)

CSM............	Camborne School of Mines [British] (IRUK)
CSM............	Camouflage Signature Measurement [Army] (RDA)
CSM............	Canadian Ski Marathon [Marathon Canadien de Ski] (AC)
CSM............	Canadian Society of Microbiologists (EAIO)
CSM............	Capital Stock Model [Congressional Budget Office] (GFGA)
CSM............	Carotid Sinus Massage [Cardiology]
CSM............	Carrier Sense Multiple Access [Telecommunications service] (BARN)
CSM............	Casamicciolo [Isola D'Ischia] [Italy] [Seismograph station code, US Geological Survey] [Closed] (SEIS)
CSM............	Cellular Slime Mold [Biology]
CSM............	Cement-Sand-Molasses (PDAA)
CSM............	Cerebrospinal Meningitis [Medicine]
CSM............	Certified Shopping Center Manager [International Council of Shopping Cent ers] [Designation awarded by]
CSM............	Chaparral Steel Co. [NYSE symbol] (SPSG)
CSM............	Chemical Surety Material (MCD)
CSM............	Chief of Staff Memorandum [Military] (AABC)
CSM............	Chief Signalman [Navy rating Obsolete]
CSM............	Chopped Strand Mat (PDAA)
CSM............	Chopped Strand Mat
CSM............	Christian Science Monitor [A publication] (BRI)
CSM............	Circulation, Sensation [or Sensory], Movement [or Motion] [Neurology and orthopedics] (DAVI)
CSM............	Circumstellar Matter [Astrophysics]
CSM............	Climate System Monitoring [Marine science] (OSRA)
CSM............	Clinton, OK [Location identifier FAA] (FAAL)
CSM............	Close Support Missile [Air Force] (MCD)
CSM............	Coalition for Sound Money (EA)
CSM............	Coaxial Switching Matrix
CSM............	Coffin Strategic Missile
CSM............	Cold Splice Miter-Joint
CSM............	College of Saint Mary [Omaha, NE]
CSM............	College of San Mateo [California]
CSM............	Colonial Society of Massachusetts (EA)
CSM............	Colorado School of Mines [Golden, CO]
CSM............	Color Shadow Mask [Type of cathode ray tube] (NITA)
Csm............	Colosseum [Record label]
CSM............	Combat System Manager [Military] (CAAL)
CSM............	Combined Symbol Matching [Fax compression technology] [Compression Labs, Inc.] (PCM)
CSM............	Combustion Stability Monitor
CSM............	Command and Service Module [NASA] (MCD)
CSM............	Command Sergeant Major [Army]
CSM............	Commission for Synoptic Meteorology
CSM............	Committee of Special Means [British military] (DMA)
CSM............	Committee on Safety of Medicines [British]
CSM............	Committee on the Safety of Machines [British]
CSM............	Common Support Module [NASA] (NASA)
CSM............	Communication Services Manager [Novell, Inc.]
CSM............	Company Sergeant-Major [Army British]
CSM............	Composite Signal Mixer
CSM............	Computer Simulation Model (MCD)
CSM............	Computer Status Matrix (MCD)
CSM............	Computer System Manual
CSM............	Conditional Select Multiplexer
CSM............	Confessing Synod Ministries (EA)
CSM............	Consolidated Manitou Resources [Vancouver Stock Exchange symbol]
CSM............	Consolidated Statutes of Manitoba [A publication] (DLA)
CSM............	Consolidated Support Model (MCD)
CSM............	Continental Shelf Mining
CSM............	Continuous Sampler Monitor [Radioactivity]
CSM............	Continuous Sheet Memory [Computer science] (BUR)
CSM............	Continuous Sheet Music (MCD)
CSM............	Continuous Slowing Down Models [Physics]
CSM............	Continuous Survey of Machinery
CSM............	Continuous Symmetry Measure [Physical chemistry]
CSM............	Contractor Support Milestone (DNAB)
CSM............	Control Stick Maneuver (MCD)
CSM............	Control Switching Module [Electronics] (ECII)
CSM............	Convention Services Manager
CSM............	Convexity, Symmetry, Maximum [Statistics]
CSM............	Cooperative Study in the Mediterranean (OSRA)
CSM............	Cooperative Study in the Mediterranean [Intergovernmental Oceanographic Commission Coordination Group] (USDC)
CSM............	Corn, Soybean, and Milk Products [Main ingredients of a formulated food]
CSM............	Cost Savings Model (MCD)
CSM............	Cost-Schedule-Milestone [Chart]
CSM............	Cottonseed Meal
CSM............	Council for the Study of Mankind [Defunct] (EA)
CSM............	Council of the Southern Mountains [Defunct] (EA)
CSM............	Creation Science Movement [British]
CSM............	Crosspoint Switching Matrix (IAA)
CSM............	Cross-Species Mapping [Zoology]
CSM............	Current Switching Mode (IAA)
CSM............	Master of Christian Science
CSM............	McGeorge School of Law, University of the Pacific, Sacramento, CA [Library symbol Library of Congress] (LCLS)
CSm............	San Marino Public Library, San Marino, CA [Library symbol Library of Congress] (LCLS)
CSM............	Sisters of St. Martha of Antigonish N.S. (TOCD)
CSM............	Sisters of St. Martha of Prince Edward Island [Roman Catholic religious order]

CSM .... Southern California College, Costa Mesa, CA [*OCLC symbol*] (OCLC)

CSMA .... Canadian Society of Marine Artists

CSMA .... Carrier Sense Multiple Access [*Telecommunications*]

CSMA .... Celiac, Superior Mesenteric Artery [*Anatomy*]

CSMA .... Chain Saw Manufacturers Association [*Later, PPEMA*] (EA)

CSMA .... Chemical Specialties Manufacturers Association (EA)

CSMA .... Chronic Spinal Muscular Atrophy [*Medicine*] (DMAA)

CSMA .... Civil Service Motoring Association [*British*] (BI)

CSMA .... Communications Systems Management Association (MCD)

CSMA/CA ... Carrier Sense Multiple Access with Collision Avoidance [*Networking technique*]

CSMA/CD ... Carrier Sense Multiple Access with Collision Detection [*Networking technique*]

CSMA/CP .... Carrier Sense Multiple Access with Collision Prevention [*Telecommunications*] (OSI)

CSMAM .... CINCPAC [*Commander-in-Chief, Pacific*] Supplement to the Military Assistance Manual (CINC)

CSM and AA... Community of St. Michael and All Angels [*Anglican religious community*]

CSmarP .... Palomar College, San Marcos, CA [*Library symbol Library of Congress*] (LCLS)

CSmat .... San Mateo Public Library, San Mateo, CA [*Library symbol Library of Congress*] (LCLS)

CSmatC .... College of San Mateo, San Mateo, CA [*Library symbol Library of Congress*] (LCLS)

CSmatHi ...... San Mateo County Historical Association, San Mateo, CA [*Library symbol Library of Congress*] (LCLS)

CSmatT .... San Mateo Times, San Mateo, CA [*Library symbol Library of Congress*] (LCLS)

CSMB .... Center for Study of Multiple Birth (EA)

CSMBF .... Centre for Studies in Money, Banking, and Finance [*Macquarie University*] [*Australia*]

CSMC .... Catholic Students' Mission Crusade [*Defunct*]

CSMC .... Combat System Maintenance Central [*Navy*] (DOMA)

CSMC .... Confederation des Sourds et des Malentendants du Canada (AC)

CSMCC .... Charles Stewart Mott Community College [*Formerly, Genesee Community College*] [*Flint, MI*]

CSMD .... Combat System Mission Demonstration [*Military*] (CAAL)

CSME .... Canadian Society for Mechanical Engineering

CSME .... Canadian Society of Magazine Editors (AC)

CSME .... Centre for Science and Mathematics Education [*British*] (AIE)

CSME .... Confederation Syndicale Mondiale des Enseignants [*World Confederation of Teachers - WCT*] [*Brussels, Belgium*] (EAIO)

CSMed .... Sacramento County Medical Society, Sacramento, CA [*Library symbol Library of Congress*] (LCLS)

CSMF .... Carl Schurz Memorial Foundation [*Later, NCSA*] (EA)

CSMFB .... Central States Motor Freight Bureau

CSMFTA....... Central & Southern Motor Freight Tariff Association, Inc.

CSMG .... Castable Smoke Mix Grenade (MCD)

CSMG .... Center for the Study of Multiple Gestation [*Later, CSMB*] (EA)

CSmH .... Henry E. Huntington Library, San Marino, CA [*Library symbol Library of Congress*] (LCLS)

CSMHA .... Center for Studies of Mental Health of the Aging [*National Institute of Mental Health*] (GRD)

CSMHC .... Council for the Single Mother and Her Child [*Australia*]

CSMI .... Cognitive Style Mapping Inventory (EDAC)

CSMI .... Company Sergeant-Major Instructor [*Army British*]

CSmi .... Smith River Library, Smith River, CA [*Library symbol Library of Congress*] (LCLS)

CSMITH ...... Coppersmith (KSC)

CSML .... Continuous Self Mode Locking [*Electronics*] (OA)

CSML .... Contractor Support Material List (MCD)

CSMM .... Camborne School of Metalliferous Mining [*British*]

CSMM .... Canadian Society for Medical Mycology [*Societe Canadienne de Mycologie Medicale*] (AC)

CSMM .... Crew Station Maintenance Manual [*Navy*] (CAAL)

CSMMG ...... Chartered Society of Massage and Medical Gymnastics (DAVI)

CSMMG ...... Conjoint Society of Massage and Medical Gymnastics [*British*]

CSMMI .... Canadian Society of Military Medals and Insignia

CSMNS .... Combat Swimmer Mine Neutralization System (DOMA)

CSMO .... Close Station March Order

CSMO .... Cosmo Communications Corp. [*NASDAQ symbol*] (NQ)

CSMOL .... Control Station Manual Operating Level (AAG)

CSMP .... Chloramphenicol-Sensitive Microsomal Protein (DMAA)

CSMP .... Combat System Management Plan [*Military*] (CAAL)

CSMP .... Comprehensive School Mathematics Program (EDAC)

CSMP .... Continuous System Modeling Program [*Computer science*]

CSMP .... Current Ship's Maintenance Project

CSMPS .... Computerized Scientific Management Planning System (AAG)

CSMQ .... Corporation des Secretaires Municipaux du Quebec Inc. (AC)

CSMR .... Center for Survey Methods Research [*Bureau of the Census*] (GFGA)

CSMR .... Centre for the Study of Mental Retardation [*Canada*]

CSMS .... Cabin Service/Management System [*Aviation*]

CSMS .... Canadian Society for Mesopotamian Studies [*Societe Canadienne des Etudes Mesopotamiens*] [*Formerly, Society for Mesopotamian Studies*] (AC)

CSMS .... Central System Maintenance Support (NATG)

CSMS .... Challenger Society for Marine Science [*British*] (EAIO)

CSMS .... College of Saint Mary of the Springs [*Ohio*]

CSMS .... Combined Support Maintenance Shop [*USNG*] (MCD)

CSMS .... Communications Security Material System (MCD)

CSMS .... Computerized Specifications Management System (DNAB)

CSMS .... Consolidated State Maintenance Shop [*USNB*] (MCD)

CSMS .... Corps Support Missile System (MCD)

CSMSA .... California State Managers and Supervisors (SRA)

CSMT .... Canadian Society for Musical Traditions (EAIO)

CSMT .... Casement [*Technical drawings*]

CSMT .... Center for Studies in Music Technology [*Yale University*] [*Research center*] (RCD)

CSMT .... Circuit Switching Magnetic Tape [*Telecommunications*] (AFM)

CSMT .... Clearing-House for Specialized Media and Technology

CSMTC .... Cosmetic

CSMTLGST... Cosmetologist

CSMTS .... Card Setting Machine Tenters' Society [*A union*] [*British*] (DCTA)

CSMTT .... Combat Systems Mobile Training Team [*Navy*] (ANA)

CS-MUX ...... Circuit Switched Multiplexer [*Telecommunications*]

CSMV .... Celiac, Superior Mesenteric Vein [*Anatomy*]

CSMV .... Chloris Striate Mosaic Virus [*Plant pathology*]

CSMV .... Community of St. Mary the Virgin [*Anglican religious community*]

CSMV .... Mountain Valley Library System, Sacramento, CA [*Library symbol Library of Congress*] (LCLS)

CSmyS .... St. Mary's College of California, St. Mary's College, CA [*Library symbol Library of Congress*] (LCLS)

CSN .... Caesarean Support Network [*British*] (DBA)

CSN .... Campana de Solidaridad con Nicaragua [*Nicaragua Solidarity Campaign*] (EAIO)

CSN .... Canadian Saturday Night [*A publication*]

CSN .... Canadian Switched Network

CSN .... Card Security Number [*Banking*]

CSN .... Card-Select Number [*Computer science*] (PCM)

CSN .... Carotid Sinus Nerve [*Cardiology*] (AAMN)

CSN .... Casanova, VA [*Location identifier FAA*] (FAAL)

CSN .... Catholic Scholarships for Negroes [*Defunct*] (EA)

CSN .... Century Sports Network

CSN .... Certified School Nurse (MEDA)

CSN .... Child Support Network [*Defunct*] (EA)

CSN .... China Southern Airlines [*FAA designator*] (FAAC)

CSN .... Cincinnati Bell [*NYSE symbol*] (TTSB)

CSN .... Cincinnati Bell, Inc. [*NYSE symbol*] (SPSG)

CSN .... Circuit Switching Network [*Telecommunications*]

CSN .... Cognos, Inc. [*Toronto Stock Exchange symbol*]

CSN .... Comhairle Sabhailteacht Naisiunta [*National Safety Council*] [*Ireland*] (EAIO)

CSN .... Committee to Support Nicaragua [*Defunct*] (EA)

CSN .... Common Services Network [*Telecommunications*] (TEL)

CSN .... Common Subnet Node [*Telecommunications*] (OSI)

CSN .... Computer Sequence Number

CSN .... Computer Service Network (IAA)

CSN .... Concession

CSN .... Confederate States Navy

CSN .... Confederation des Syndicats Nationaux [*Confederation of National Trade Unions - CNTU*] [*Canada*]

CSN .... Congregation of Sisters of Nazareth (TOCD)

CSN .... Contract Serial Number (AFM)

CSN .... Contract Student Numbers (AIE)

CSN .... Contract Surgeon [*Military*] (AABC)

CSN .... Control Symbol Number (AFM)

CSN .... Courage Stroke Network (EA)

CSN .... Cousin [*Genealogy*]

CSN .... Crosby, Stills, and Nash [*Rock music group*] [*Later, CSN & Y*]

CSN .... Cuisine

CSN .... Guangzhou Regional Administration of CAA of China [*ICAO designator*] (FAAC)

CSNA .... Canadian Sewing & Needlecraft Association [*Association Canadienne des Travaux d'Aiguilles*] [*Formerly, Canadian Home Sewing & Needlecraft Association*] (AC)

CSNA .... Classification Society of North America (EA)

CSN & Y ..... Crosby, Stills, Nash, and Young [*Rock music group*] [*Formerly, CSN*]

CSNav .... CompuServe Navigator [*CompuServe, Inc.*] [*Telecommunications*] (PCM)

CSNB .... Congenital Stationary Night Blindness

CSNB .... Consolidated Statutes of New Brunswick [*A publication*] (DLA)

CSNC .... Chemical Societies of the Nordic Countries (EAIO)

CSND .... Center for Studies of Nonlinear Dynamics [*Research center*] (RCD)

CSNDT .... Canadian Society for Non-Destructive Testing

CSNE .... College Stores of New England (SRA)

CSNET .... Computer Science Network [*University Corp. for Atmospheric Research*]

CSNF .... Common Source Noise Figure

CSNFWA ...... Campaign to Save Native Forests, Western Australia

CSNI .... Committee on the Safety of Nuclear Installation [*Nuclear Regulatory Commission*] (NRCH)

CSNK .... Casein Kinase (DMAA)

CSNM .... Chief Superintendent of Naval Meteorology [*British*]

CSNMDU..... Center for the Study of Non-Medical Drug Use [*Later, CSDP*] (EA)

CSNO .... Casino America [*NASDAQ symbol*] (TTSB)

CSNO .... Casino America, Inc. [*NASDAQ symbol*] (SAG)

CSNP .... Causeway Section, Nonpowered [*Navy*] (ANA)

CSNP .... Communication Subnet Processor (OSI)

CSNP .... Complete Sequence Number Packet [*Computer science*] (ACRL)

CSNR .... Casino Resource [*NASDAQ symbol*] (TTSB)

CSNR .... Casino Resource Corp. [*NASDAQ symbol*] (SAG)

CSNRT .... Corrected Sinus Node Recovery Time [*Medicine*]

CSNRW .... Casino Resource Wrrt 'A' [*NASDAQ symbol*] (TTSB)

CSNS .... Carotid Sinus Nerve Stimulation [*or Stimulator*] [*Cardiology*] (AAMN)

CSNS .... Cartoid Sinus Nerve Stimulation [*Medicine*] (DMAA)

CSNS .... Chemical Structure and Nomenclature System [*Environmental Protection Agency*]

CSNVTAL ..... Combat Surveillance Night Vision and Target Acquisition Laboratories [*Army*] (RDA)
CSNWC .... Civil Service National Whitley Council [*British*]
CSNY .... Canadian Society of New York (EA)
CSNYS .... Canal Society of New York State (EA)
CSO .... Carrasco [*Montevideo, Uruguay*] [*Airport symbol*] (AD)
CSO .... Car Service Order
CSO .... Catholic Schools Office [*Australia*]
CSO .... Catholics Speak Out [*Quixote Center*] (EA)
CSO .... Center Standards Officer [*Job Corps*]
CSO .... Centralized Service Observation [*Telecommunications*] (TEL)
CSO .... Central Selling Organization [*London diamond exchange*]
CSO .... Central Services Organization
CSO .... Central Sign Off (AAG)
CSO .... Central Standards Office (OICC)
CSO .... Central Statistical Office [*British Information service or system*] (IID)
CSO .... Chained Sequential Operation
CSO .... Chemically Stable Oxide
CSO .... Chicago Symphony Orchestra
CSO .... Chief Scientific Officer [*Also, CScO*] [*Ministry of Agriculture, Fisheries, and Food*] [*British*]
CSO .... Chief Signal Officer [*Army*]
CSO .... Chief Staff Officer
CSO .... Cincinnati Symphony Orchestra (BARN)
CSO .... Civilian Support Operation [*Military*] (INF)
CSO .... Clonal Seed Orchard
CSO .... Clothing Supply Office [*Military*]
CSO .... Club Safety Officer (DNAB)
CSO .... Coastal States Organization (EA)
CSO .... Cognizant Security Office [*Controls industrial security at government facilities*] [*Military*]
CSO .... Cognizant Security Officer (AAGC)
CSO .... Color Separation Overlay
CSO .... Combined Sewer Overflow
CSO .... Commissioners Standard Ordinary Table [*Insurance*]
CSO .... Communication Standing Order
CSO .... Community Service Obligation
CSO .... Complex Safety Officer [*Air Force*] (AFM)
CSO .... Complex Support Office [*NASA*] (KSC)
CSO .... Computer Service Office (IAA)
CSO .... Computer Systems Officer (ADA)
CSO .... Computing Services Office [*Telecommunications*]
CSO .... Conference Services Office [*American Library Association*]
CSO .... Consular Security Officer
CSO .... Consumer Services Organization (EA)
CSO .... Corn Stunt Organism [*Plant pathology*]
CSO .... Correspondence Survey Officer (MCD)
CSO .... Cottonseed Oil (OA)
CSO .... Counterinsurgency Support Office [*Army*] (VNW)
CSO .... Cross-Service Order [*Military*] (AFM)
CSO .... Crown Solicitor's Office [*British*] (ADA)
CSO .... Customer Service Officer
CSO .... Customer Support Operation
CSO .... Sonoma State College, Rohnert Park, CA [*OCLC symbol*] (OCLC)
CSo .... Sonora Public Library, Sonora, CA [*Library symbol Library of Congress*] (LCLS)
CSOA .... Combined Special Operations Area [*Military*] (DOMA)
CSOA .... Commonwealth Steamship Owners' Association [*Australia*]
CSOA .... CS Owner's Association (EA)
CSOB .... Clothing Store Operating Budgets [*Air Force*] (AFIT)
CSOC .... Communist Suppression Operations Command [*Thailand*]
CSOC .... Consolidated Security Operations Center [*Military*]
CSOC .... Consolidated Space Operations Center [*Colorado Springs, CO*] [*Military*]
CSOC .... Construction Special Operations Center
CSOC .... Current SIGINT [*Signal Intelligence*] Operations Center [*National Security Agency*] (MCD)
CSoCL .... Tuolumne County Free Public Library, Sonora, CA [*Library symbol Library of Congress*] (LCLS)
CSOCR .... Code Sort Optical Character Recognition [*Computer science*]
CSOD .... Combat System Operational Design [*Military*] (CAAL)
CSOD .... Crack Surface Opening Displacement
CSOF .... Chief Superintendent of Ordnance Factories [*British World War II*]
CS of JT ..... Chief Superintendent of Juvenile Templars [*Order of Good Templars*] [*Freemasonry*] (ROG)
CSO-HNS .... Canadian Society of Otolaryngology - Head and Neck Surgery (EAIO)
C Sol .... Complete Solicitor [*A publication*] (DLA)
CSOM .... Chief SONARman [*Navy rating Obsolete*]
CSOM .... Chronic Serous Otitis Media [*Otorhinolaryngology*] (DAVI)
CSOM .... Chronic Suppurative Otitus Media [*Otolaryngology*]
CSOM .... Colorado Society of Osteopathic Medicine (SRA)
CSOM .... Combat System Operability Monitor [*Military*] (CAAL)
CSOM .... Computer Software Operator's Manual
CSOM .... Computer System Operators Manual
CSOM .... Conical Scanning Optical Microscope
CSom .... Sonoma Public Library, Sonoma, CA [*Library symbol Library of Congress*] (LCLS)
CSoM .... Toulomne County Museum, Sonora, CA [*Library symbol*] [*Library of Congress*] (LCLS)
CSOMH .... Chief SONARman, Harbor Defense [*Navy rating Obsolete*]
CSomL .... Sonoma Public Library, Sonoma, CA [*Library symbol*] [*Library of Congress*] (LCLS)
CSOP .... Clothing Store Operating Programs [*Air Force*] (AFIT)
CSOP .... Coastal Shelf Oceanography Program [*Marine science*] (MSC)

CSOP .... Commission to Study the Organization of Peace (EA)
CSOP .... Crew Systems Operating Procedures (MCD)
CSORO .... Conical Scan-on-Receive Only (CET)
CSOS .... Center for Social Organization of Schools [*Department of Education*] [*Research center*] (GRD)
CSOS .... Center for Social Organization Studies [*University of Chicago*] [*Research center*] (RCD)
CSOs .... Civil-Society Organizations
CSOS .... Communications Switch Operating System (MCD)
CSOS .... Complementary Silicon on Sapphire (MHDI)
CSOS .... Connecticut Society of Oral Surgeons (SRA)
CSOSS .... Combat System Operational Sequencing System [*Navy*] (DOMA)
CSOST .... Canadian Service for Overseas Students and Trainees
CSOT .... Canadian Society of Orthopaedic Technologists (EAIO)
CSOT .... Combat Systems Operability Test (NVT)
CSP .... American Strategic Income Portfolio [*NYSE symbol*] (SPSG)
CSP .... American Strategic Income Portfolio III [*NYSE symbol*] (SAG)
CSP .... Amer Strategic Inc. Portfol III [*NYSE symbol*] (TTSB)
CSP .... Calendar of State Papers [*British*] (ROG)
CSP .... California Society of Pathologists (SRA)
CSP .... California Society of Periodontists (SRA)
CSP .... Camas Prairie Railroad Co. [*AAR code*]
CSP .... Canadian Student Pugwash
CSP .... Cape Spencer, AK [*Location identifier FAA*] (FAAL)
CSP .... Carotid Sinus Pressure [*Cardiology*] (CPH)
CSP .... Casper Air Service, Inc. [*ICAO designator*] (FAAC)
CSP .... Catholic Solo Parents [*Australia*]
CSP .... Cavum Septum Pellucidum (DAVI)
CSP .... Cedar Springs [*California*] [*Seismograph station code, US Geological Survey*] (SEIS)
CSP .... Cell Surface Protein [*Also known as LETS protein*] [*Cytochemistry*]
CSP .... Cellulose Sodium Phosphate [*Organic chemistry*]
CSP .... Center for Security Policy (EA)
CSP .... Center for Space Policy, Inc. [*Cambridge, MA*] [*Telecommunications*] (TSSD)
CSP .... Center for Surrogate Parenting (EA)
CSP .... Center for the Study of Power [*Later, SPI*] (EA)
CSP .... Center for the Study of the Presidency (EA)
CSP .... Central Serous Retinopathy [*Medicine*] (CPH)
CSP .... Central Service Point [*DoD*] (AFIT)
CSP .... Central Signal Processor
CSP .... Certified Safety Professional [*Designation awarded by Board of Certified Safety Professionals*]
CSP .... Certified Speaking Professional
CSP .... Certified Systems Professional [*Institute for Certification of Computer P rofessionals*] [*Designation awarded by*]
CSP .... Certified Systems Professional (CDE)
CSP .... Change Status Page (MCD)
CSP .... Channeled-Substrate-Planar [*Materials science*]
CSP .... Chaplain Service Personnel [*Air Force*]
CSP .... Character Shape Player (PCM)
CSP .... Chartered Society of Physiotherapy [*British*]
CSP .... Chief Specialist [*Navy rating Obsolete*]
CSP .... Chiral Stationary Phase [*Chemical separation technique*]
CSP .... Chlorosulphonated Polyethylene
CSP .... Christlich Soziale Partei [*Christian Social Party*] [*Liechtenstein*] [*Political party*] (PPW)
CSP .... Circumsporozoite Precipitation [*Clinical chemistry*]
CSP .... Clerk of State Papers [*British*] (ROG)
CSP .... Coder Sequential Pulse
CSP .... Coherent Signal Processor
CSP .... Cold-Shock Protein [*Biochemistry*]
CSP .... Colonial Society of Pennsylvania (EA)
CSP .... Column Shock Protection [*Chromatography*]
CSP .... Combat Security Police [*Air Force*] (VNW)
CSP .... Combined Staff Planners
CSP .... Commander Service Force, Pacific (MCD)
CSP .... Command Selector Panel (DNAB)
CSP .... Commemorative Stamp Posters
CSP .... Commercial Space Package
CSP .... Commercial Subroutine Package [*IBM Corp.*] (BUR)
CSP .... Commission on the Study of Peace (EA)
CSP .... Committed to Scheduled Programs [*Military*] (CINC)
CSP .... Common Signal Processor [*Military*] (DOMA)
CSP .... Communications and Signal Processing [*British*]
CSP .... Communication Sequential Process [*Computer science*]
CSP .... Communications Satellite Program [*NASA*]
CSP .... Communications Security Publication
C/SP .... Communications/Symbiont Processor [*Sperry UNIVAC*]
CSP .... Community of St. Peter [*Anglican religious community*]
CSP .... Community Services Program [*Canada*]
CSP .... Community Shelter Plan [*Civil Defense*]
CSP .... Community Support Program [*National Institute of Mental Health*]
CSP .... Company of Saint Paul (EA)
CSP .... Company Standard Practice
CSP .... Component Scheduling Procedure
CSP .... Computer Simulation Program
CSP .... Computer Supported Purchasing
CSP .... Computer Support Program [*NASA*] (NASA)
CSP .... Concentrated Super-Phosphate (OA)
CSP .... Concurrent Spare Parts (AFM)
CSP .... Congregatio Sancti Pauli [*Paulists*] [*Roman Catholic men's religious order*]
CSP .... Conseil du Salut du Peuple [*People's Salvation Council*] [*Burkina Faso*] (PD)

CSP............ Consolidated Ascot Petroleum [*Toronto Stock Exchange symbol Vancouver Stock Exchange symbol*]
CSP............ Consolidated Supply Program [*Department of Housing and Urban Development*] (GFGA)
CSP............ Conspecific Sperm Precedence [*Entomology*]
CSP............ Constraint Satisfaction Problem [*Computer science*]
CSp............ Containment Spray Pump [*Nuclear energy*] (NRCH)
CSP............ Contingency Support Package (MCD)
CSP............ Continuous Sampling Plan (IEEE)
CSP............ Continuous Seismic Profiling (NUCP)
CSP............ Continuous Stratification Profiler
CSP............ Contractor Standard Parts
CSP............ Contractor Support Plan
CSP............ Contract Services Program [*General Services Administration*] (GFGA)
CSP............ Contract Strategy Paper
CSP............ Controlled Surface Porosity
CSP............ Controlled Surface Process
CSP............ Control Setting Panel (IAA)
CSP............ Control Signal Processor [*for spacecraft*]
CSP............ Control Switching Point (BUR)
CSP............ Control System Program [*Manufacturing engineering*] [*Computer science*]
CSP............ Cooperative School Program [*US Employment Service*] [*Department of Labor*]
CSP............ Cooperative Statistical Program [*For IUD data*]
CSP............ Coproduction for Security Program [*US and Italy*]
CSP............ Corporation Standard Practice (AAG)
CSP............ Corrugated Steel Pipe (DICI)
CSP............ Council for Scientific Policy
CSP............ Council to Save the Postcard [*Defunct*] (EA)
CSP............ Count Strength Product
CSP............ Criminal Sexual Psychopath
CSP............ Crisis Staffing Procedures (MCD)
CSP............ Cross System Product (BTTJ)
CSP............ Crystallographic Shear Plane
CSP............ CSP, Inc. [*Associated Press*] (SAG)
CSP............ Cumulative Sporulation [*of fungal colonies*]
CSP............ Cysteine String Protein [*Biochemistry*]
CSP............ Paulist Fathers (TOCD)
csp............ Paulist Fathers (TOCD)
CSp............ South Pasadena Public Library, South Pasadena, CA [*Library symbol Library of Congress*] (LCLS)
CSP............ Stockton and San Joaquin County Public Library, Stockton, CA [*OCLC symbol*] (OCLC)
CSPA .... California State Psychological Association
CSPA .... Canadian Sport Parachuting Association (EA)
CSPA .... Canadian Steel Producers Association (AC)
CSPA .... Catholic School Press Association [*Defunct*] (EA)
CSPA .... Chesapeake Seafood Packers Association (EA)
CSPA .... Chief Specialist, Physical Training Instructor [*Navy rating Obsolete*]
CSPA .... CINC's [*Commander in Chief's*] Strategic Priorities Assessment (DOMA)
CSPA .... Civil Service Pensioners Alliance [*British*]
CSPA .... Clay Sewer Pipe Association (EA)
CSPA .... Columbia Scholastic Press Association (EA)
CSPA .... Committee for a Strong Peaceful America [*Defunct*] (EA)
CSPA .... Council of Sales Promotion Agencies [*New York, NY*] (EA)
CSPA .... Council of State Policy and Planning Agencies [*Later, CGPA*] (EA)
CSPAA .... Columbia Scholastic Press Advisers Association (EA)
CSPAA .... Conference de Solidarite des Pays Afro-Asiatiques
CSPAC .... Campaign for Space Political Action Committee [*Defunct*] (EA)
C-SPAN........ Cable Satellite Public Affairs Network [*Cable-television system*]
C-Span........ Cable-Satellite Public Affairs Network [*Washington, D.C.*] (WDMC)
CSPAQ........ Crushed Stone Producers' Association of Queensland [*Australia*]
CSPAR .... Center for the Study of Parental Acceptance and Rejection [*University of Connecticut*] [*Research center*] (RCD)
CSPAR .... CINC [*Commander in Chief*] Strategic Preparedness Assessment Report (DOMA)
CSpaW........ Contra Costa College, San Pablo, CA [*Library symbol Library of Congress*] (LCLS)
CSPBI .... Comite Special du Programme Biologique International [*Special Committee for the International Biological Program*]
CSPC .... California State Polytechnic College [*Later, California Polytechnic State University*]
CSPC .... Cargo Systems and Procedures Committee [*IATA*] (DS)
CSPC .... Children's Services Planning Committee [*Australia*]
CSPC .... Coal and Steel Planning Committee [*NATO*] (NATG)
CSPC .... Communication Satellite Planning Center [*Stanford University*] [*Research center*] (RCD)
CSPC .... Conference of Small Private Colleges [*Defunct Defunct*] (EA)
CSPC .... Cost and Schedule Planning and Control
CSPCA .... Canadian Society for the Prevention of Cruelty to Animals (BARN)
CSPCA .... Chinese Shar-Pei Club of America (EA)
CSPCC .... Canadian Society for the Prevention of Cruelty to Children
C/SPCS .... Cost/Schedule Planning and Control Specification [*Air Force*]
CSPD .... Central Still-Photo Depository (DNAB)
CSPD .... Chemical and Statistical Policy Division [*Environmental Protection Agency*] (GFGA)
CSPD .... Comprehensive System of Personnel Development [*Education*]
CSPD .... Cruising Speed
CSPDN .... Circuit Switched Public Data Network [*Telecommunications*]
CSPDT .... Crawford Small Parts Dexterity Test [*Education*]
CSPE .... California Society of Professional Engineers (SRA)
CSPE .... Canadian Society for Professional Engineers (AC)
CSPE............ Chlorosulphonated Polyethylene

CSPE .... Communications System Planning Element
CSPE .... Connecticut Society of Professional Engineers (SRA)
CSPEC .... Confederation of Socialist Parties of the European Community [*Belgium Political party*] (EAIO)
C SPEC .... Product Specification (AAGC)
CSPF .... Central States Pension Fund
CSPG .... California Sweet Potato Growers (SRA)
CSPG .... Canadian Society of Petroleum Geologists (DD)
CSPG .... Canadian Society of Petroleum Geologists [*Formerly, Alberta Society of Petroleum Geologists*] (AC)
CSPG .... Center for the Study of Political Graphics [*An association*]
CSPG .... Chrondroitin Sulfate Proteoglycans [*Biochemistry*]
CSPG .... Code Sequential Pulse Generator (IAA)
CSPG .... Committee in Solidarity with the People of Guatemala (EA)
CSPG .... Common Source Power Gain
CSPHA .... Conference of State and Provincial Health Authorities of North America [*Defunct*] (EA)
CSPHD........ Canadian Society of Public Health Dentists [*Association Canadienne des Dentistes en Sante Publique*] (AC)
CSPI .... Center for Science in the Public Interest (EA)
CSPI .... Center for Science in the Public Interest (GNE)
CSPI .... Center for the Study of Parent Involvement (EA)
CSPI .... College Student Personnel Institute [*Defunct*]
CSPI .... Committee in Solidarity with the People of Iran (EA)
CSPI .... CSP Inc. [*NASDAQ symbol*] (NQ)
CSPL .... Canada Southern Petroleum Ltd. [*NASDAQ symbol*] (SAG)
CSPLF .... Canada South'n Petrol [*NASDAQ symbol*] (TTSB)
CSPLSP ...... Canadian Society for Psychomotor Learning and Sport Psychology (EDAC)
CSPM .... Code Ship Parametric Model (MCD)
CSPM .... Communication Security Publication Memorandum [*Army*]
CSPM .... Computer Services Procedures Manual
CSPMP .... Chief Specialist, Motion Picture Production [*Navy rating Obsolete*]
CSPO .... Chief Specialist, Petroleum Inspector [*Navy rating Obsolete*]
CSPO .... Communications Satellite Project Office
CSPO .... Control Systems Procurement Office (SAA)
CSPOCP........ Conference of Speakers and Presiding Officers of Commonwealth Parliaments [*Canada*] (EAIO)
CSPOE .... Combat Systems Post-Overhaul Examination [*Navy*] (ANA)
CSPOS .... Community Shelter Planning Officer, State [*Civil Defense*]
CSPP .... California School of Professional Psychology
CSPP .... Campaign to Save the People of Palestine (EA)
CSPP .... Canadian Society of Plant Physiologists (AC)
CSPP .... Centre for the Study of Public Policy [*University of Strathclyde*] [*British*] (CB)
CSPP .... Coalition for State Prompt Pay (EA)
CSPP .... Computer Systems Policy Project (BTTJ)
CSPPA .... Comite de Solidarite avec les Prisonniers Politiques Arabes et du Proche Orient [*Solidarity Committee for Arab and Near-Eastern Political Prisoners*]
CSPPHLD.... Conference of State and Provincial Public Health Laboratory Directors (EA)
CSPPLB ...... Chief Specialist, Laboratory [*Navy rating Obsolete*]
CSPPPG ...... Chief Specialist, Photogrammetry [*Navy rating Obsolete*]
CSPPVM ..... Chief Specialist, V-Mail [*Navy rating Obsolete*]
CSPR .... California Department of Parks and Recreation, Sacramento Area State Parks, Sacramento, CA [*Library symbol Library of Congress*] (LCLS)
CSPR .... Chief Specialist, Identification [*Navy rating Obsolete*]
CSPR .... Chief Specialist, Recruiter [*Navy rating Obsolete*]
CSPR .... Conference on Science, Philosophy, and Religion (EA)
CSPRT .... Compound Sequential Probability Ratio Test
CSPRU .... Civil Service Pay Research Unit (DLA)
CSPS .... Canadian Ski Patrol System [*Organisation de la Patrouille Canadienne de Ski*] (AC)
CSPS .... Canadian Society of Patristic Studies [*See also ACEP*]
CSPS .... Canadian Society of Plastic Surgeons [*Societe Canadienne des Chirurgiens Plasticiens*] (AC)
CSPS .... Chief Specialist, Personnel Supervisor [*Navy rating Obsolete*]
CSPS .... Chief Specialist, Shore Patrol and Security [*Navy rating Obsolete*]
CSPS .... Christian Science Publishing Society (EA)
CSPS .... Coherent Signal Processing System [*Army*] (AABC)
CSPS .... Committee to Save the Peace Symbol [*Student legal action organization*]
CSPS .... Continued Skin Peeling Syndrome [*Dermatology*]
CSPS .... C. S. [*Charles Sanders*] Peirce Society (EA)
CSpSR .... Stanford Research Institute, South Pasadena, CA [*Library symbol Library of Congress*] (LCLS)
CSPT .... Chief Specialist, Teacher [*Navy rating Obsolete*]
CSPT .... Command Start Point [*Military*]
CSPT .... Conference for the Study of Political Thought (EA)
CSPTE......... Center for the Study of Pharmacy and Therapeutics for the Elderly (EA)
CSPTLT........ Chief Specialist, Link Trainer Instructor [*Navy rating Obsolete*]
CSPU .... Core Segment Processing Unit (NASA)
CSPUP .... California State Polytechnic University of Pomona (MCD)
CSPV .... Chief Specialist, Transport Airman [*Navy rating Obsolete*]
CSPW .... Chief Specialist, Chaplain's Assistant [*Navy rating Obsolete*]
CSPWC ...... Canadian Society of Painters in Water Color (AC)
CSPWC ...... Canadian Society of Painters in Water Colour [*1925*] (NGC)
cspx.......... Brothers of Saint Pius X (TOCD)
CSPX .... Brothers of St. Pius X [*Roman Catholic religious order*]
CSPX .... Chief Specialist, All Designators [*Navy rating Obsolete*]
CSPY .... Chief Specialist, Control Tower Operator [*Navy rating Obsolete*]
CSQ .... Cassiar Mining Corp. [*Toronto Stock Exchange symbol*]

CSQ .... Coastal Sentry Quebec
CSQ .... Collecte Selective Quebec (AC)
CSQ .... College Student Questionnaires [*Psychology*]
CSQ .... Conseil de la Sculpture du Quebec (AC)
CSQ .... Conseil de la Sculpture du Quebec [*1978, founded 1961 as ASQ*] [*Canada*] (NGC)
CSQ .... Creston, IA [*Location identifier FAA*] (FAAL)
CSQ .... Cryptofacility Security Questionnaire [*Army*]
CSQ .... Genus Equity Corp. [*Toronto Stock Exchange symbol*]
CSR .... Anchorage/Ft. Richardson, AK [*Location identifier FAA*] (FAAL)
CSR .... Cable/Special Relief [*FCC*] (NTCM)
CSR .... Cable Spreading Room [*Nuclear energy*] (NRCH)
CSR .... Campaign for Surplus Rosaries [*Defunct*] (EA)
CSR .... Career Structure Review [*Australia*]
CSR .... Center for Seafarers' Rights (EA)
CSR .... Center for Social Research [*Stanford University*] [*Research center*] (RCD)
CSR .... Center for Social Research [*City University of New York*] [*Research center*] (RCD)
CSR .... Center for Space Research [*Massachusetts Institute of Technology*] [*Research center*] (RCD)
CSR .... Center for Space Research and Applications [*University of Texas at Austin*] [*Research center*] (RCD)
CSR .... Center for Strategy Research, Inc. [*Information service or system*] (IID)
CSR .... Center for Survey Research [*University of Massachusetts*] [*Research center*] (RCD)
CSR .... Center for the Study of Reading [*Later, RREC*] [*Department of Education*] (GRD)
CSR .... Central & South West Corp. [*NYSE symbol*] (SPSG)
CSR .... Central & So. West [*NYSE symbol*] (TTSB)
CSR .... Central Supply Room
CSR .... Centre for Software Reliability [*City University*] [*British*] (IRUK)
CSR .... Certification Status Report (NASA)
CSR .... Certified Shorthand Reporter
CSR .... Change Status Report (MCD)
CSR .... Channel Select Register [*Telecommunications*] (NITA)
CSR .... Chartered Stenographic Reporter
CSR .... Chase Ranch [*California*] [*Seismograph station code, US Geological Survey*] (SEIS)
CSR .... Check Signal Return (NASA)
CSR .... Check Status Reply (KSC)
CSR .... Chemically-Stimulated Rubber (PDAA)
CSR .... Cheyne-Stokes Respiration [*Medicine*]
CSR .... Chief of Staff Regulations
CSR .... Child Support Resistance (EA)
CSR .... Chlorinated Synthetic Rubber
CSR .... Circulating Shift Register (IAA)
CSR .... Cis-Air [*Czechoslovakia*] [*ICAO designator*] (FAAC)
CSR .... Civil Service Reserve [*British*] (ROG)
CSR .... Civil Service Retirement
CSR .... Civil Service Rule
CSR .... Clamped Speed Regulator
CSR .... Client Services Review [*Australia*]
CSR .... Clock-Sync Receiver Assembly [*Deep Space Instrumentation Facility, NASA*]
CSR .... Coastal Surveillance RADAR (MCD)
CSR .... Coaxial Single-Pole Relay
CSR .... College of Saint Rose [*Albany, NY*]
CSR .... Collimated Slit Radiography (MCD)
CSR .... Combat Search and Rescue [*Aviation*] (MCD)
CSR .... Combat Service Readiness (DWSG)
CSR .... Combat Stress Reaction [*Army*] (ADDR)
CSR .... Combat Surveillance RADAR
CSR .... Commando Shackle Relay [*Intelligence gathering*] [*Vietnam*] (MCD)
CSR .... Commercial Spares Release
CSR .... Common Services Rack [*Telecommunications*] (TEL)
CSR .... Communication Service Request
CSR .... Communications Satellite Relay (NG)
CSR .... Communications System Replacement [*Military*] (GFGA)
CSR .... Communication Systems Research Ltd. [*Ilkley, W. Yorkshire, England*] (TSSD)
CSR .... Compensation System Review
CSR .... Component Selection Record
CSR .... Composite Station Rate
CSR .... Comstate Resources Ltd. [*Toronto Stock Exchange symbol*]
CSR .... Conference on Science and Religion [*Later, UDC*] (EA)
CSR .... Configuration Selection Register
CSR .... Connected Speech Recognition (MCD)
CSR .... Console Send/Receive [*Computer science*] (IAA)
CSR .... Constant Stress Rate (IAA)
CSR .... Continuous Sampling Run (DNAB)
CSR .... Continuous Service Rating [*Engine technology*]
CSR .... Continuous Speech Recognizer [*ITT Corp.*] (NITA)
CSR .... Contract Status Report
CSR .... Controlled Silicon Rectifier [*Electronics*] (IAA)
CSR .... Controlled Supply Rate (AABC)
CSR .... Controller Supply Rate (DOMA)
CSR .... Control Section Report [*NATO*]
CSR .... Control Shift Register (CET)
CSR .... Control Status Register
CSR .... Copper Sulfide Rectifier
CSR .... Corps Specifications Revision (AAG)
CSR .... Corrected Sedimentation Rate [*Medicine*]
CSR .... Corrective Septorhinoplasty [*Otorhinolaryngology*] (DAVI)

CSR .... Cortisol [*or Cortical*] Secretion Rate [*Medicine*] (MAE)
CSR .... Cost, Scheduling, Reporting
CSR .... Council on the Study of Religion (EA)
CSR .... Council Situation Room [*NATO*] (NATG)
CSR .... Counter Shift Register [*Computer science*] (IAA)
CSR .... Course Status Report
CSR .... Crankshaft Rate (NVT)
CSR .... Crew Station Review [*NASA*] (NASA)
CSR .... Critical Shortage Report (AAG)
CSR .... Culture Supply Room [*Microbiology*]
CSR .... Current Sensitive Relay (DNAB)
CSR .... Current Situation Room (MCD)
CSR .... Customer Service Representative
CSR .... Customer Signature Required (MSA)
CSR .... Custom Spherical Resins
CSr .... San Rafael Public Library, San Rafael, CA [*Library symbol Library of Congress*] (LCLS)
CSR .... Sisters of Holy Redeemer (TOCD)
CSRA .... Canadian Street Rod Association
CSRA .... Civil Service Reform Act [*1978*] (RDA)
CSRA .... Comite Scientifique pour les Recherches Antarctiques [*Scientific Committee on Antarctic Research*] (MSC)
CSRA .... Compound-Specific Radiocarbon Analyses
CSRA .... Consolidated States Racing Association [*Auto racing sanctioning organization*]
CSRA .... Copper Smelters and Refiners Association [*British*] (DBA)
CSRA .... Corporate Security Regulation Appendices
CS(RAF) .... Chief Scientist (Royal Air Force) [*British*]
CSRAO .... Chartered Shorthand Reporters' Association of Ontario (AC)
CSraS .... Shell Chemical Co., Information Services Library, San Ramon, CA [*Library symbol Library of Congress*] (LCLS)
CSRC .... Chicano Studies Research Center [*University of California, Los Angeles*] [*Research center*] (RCD)
CSRC .... China Securities Regulatory Commission (ECON)
CSRC .... Communication Science Research Center [*Battelle Memorial Institute*] (MCD)
CSRC .... Complex Systems Research Center [*University of New Hampshire*] [*Research center*] (RCD)
CSRCBA .... Central States Roller Canary Breeders Association (EA)
CSrCL .... Marin County Free Library, San Rafael, CA [*Library symbol Library of Congress*] (LCLS)
CSRCO .... Communications Status and Restoration Coordination Office
CSRCSP .... Center for the Study of Race, Crime, and Social Policy [*Cornell University*] [*Research center*] (RCD)
CSRD .... Center for Supercomputing Research and Development [*University of Illinois*] [*Urbana*] [*Information service or system*] (IID)
CSRD .... Chief Superintendent, Research Department [*British military*] (DMA)
CSrD .... Dominican College of San Rafael, San Rafael, CA [*Library symbol Library of Congress*] (LCLS)
CSRDF .... Civil Service Retirement and Disability Fund
CSRDF .... Crew Station Research and Development Facility [*Ames Research Center*]
CSRE .... Canadian Society of Rural Extension
CSRE .... Center for Social Research and Education (EA)
CSRE .... Closed System Respirator Evaluator (KSC)
CSRE .... Comshare, Inc. [*NASDAQ symbol*] (NQ)
CSREES .... Cooperative State Research, Education, and Extension Service [*US Department of Agriculture*]
CSRes .... California Resources Agency, Sacramento, CA [*Library symbol Library of Congress*] (LCLS)
CSRF .... Civil Service Retirement Fellowship [*British*]
CSRF .... Commissary Store Reserve Fund [*Military*] (DNAB)
CSRFG .... Commissary Store Reserve Fund Grant [*Military*] (DNAB)
CSRHFA .... Charles Simkins and Rachel Hawthorne Family Association (EA)
CSRI .... Centre for the Study of Regulated Industries [*McGill University*] [*Canada Research center*] (RCD)
CSRI .... Computer Systems Research Institute [*University of Toronto*] [*Research center*] (RCD)
CSRI .... Creative Strategies Research International [*Information service or system*] (IID)
CSRI .... Customer Satisfaction Research Institute [*Lenexa, KS*] [*Telecommunications*] (TSSD)
CSRIPPED .... China Society for International Professionals Exchange and Development (EAIO)
CSRL .... Center for Study of Responsive Law (EA)
CSRL .... Center for the Study of Responsive Law (GNE)
CSRL .... Common Strategic Rotary Launcher
CSRL .... Communications Strategic Rotary Launcher [*Military*]
CSRM .... Controlled Solid Rocket Motors (KSC)
CSRO .... Chemical Short-Range Order (MCD)
CSRO .... Chief, Superintendent Range Operations [*NASA*] (KSC)
CSRO .... Comite Scientifique pour les Recherches Oceaniques [*Scientific Committee on Oceanic Research - SCOR*] [*France*] (MSC)
CSRO .... Consolidated Standing Route Order [*Army*] (AABC)
CSRO .... Contract Service Rework Orders (NG)
CSROEPM ..... Communication, System, Results, Objectives, Exception, Participation, Motivation [*Business term*] (MHDB)
CSRP .... Canadian Sprinkler Risk Pool
CSRP .... Computers and Software Review Panel [*NASA*] (NASA)
CSRR .... Combat Systems Readiness Review [*Navy*] (MCD)
CSRS .... Canadian Society for Renaissance Studies [*See also SCER*]
CSRS .... Civil Service Retirement System (MCD)
CSRS .... Coherent Stokes Raman Spectroscopy
CSRS .... Composite Standard Reference Section
CSRS .... Constant-Switch-Pace Symmetric Random Signal (PDAA)

CSRS	Containment Spray Recirculation System [*Nuclear energy*] (NRCH)
CSRS	Cooperative State Research Service [*Department of Agriculture Washington, DC*]
C/SRS	Cost/Schedule Reporting System (SSD)
CSRT	California Society of Radiologic Technologists (SRA)
CSRT	Canadian Society of Radiological Technicians
CSRT	Canadian Society of Respiratory Therapists (AC)
CSRT	Combat Systems Readiness Test (NVT)
CSRT	Combined Stress Reliability Test (MCD)
CSRT	Comprehensive System Readiness Tests (MCD)
CSRUIDR	Chemical Society Research Unit in Information Dissemination and Retrieval [*British*] (DIT)
CSRV	Civil Service Rifle Volunteers [*British*]
CSRV	CompuServe Corp. [*NASDAQ symbol*] (SAG)
CSRV	CompuServe Corp. [*NASDAQ symbol*] (TTSB)
CSRW	Commission of the Status and Role of Women (EA)
CSS	California State Supervisors (SRA)
CSS	California State University, Sacramento, Sacramento, CA [*Library symbol Library of Congress*] (LCLS)
CSS	Canada Standard Size [*Of Clothing*] (BARN)
CSS	Canadian Scientific Ship (BARN)
CSS	Canadian Sleep Society (AC)
CSS	Canadian Statistical Society
CSS	Carbon Shell System
CSS	Caribbean Super Station [*Satellite television system*]
CSS	Carotid Sinus Stimulation [*Cardiology*]
CSS	Car Service Section [*Railroads*]
CSS	Cascading Style Sheets [*Computer science*]
CSS	Cascading Stylesheets [*Computer science*]
CSS	Cask Support Structure [*Nuclear energy*] (NRCH)
CSS	Cassilandia [*Brazil*] [*Airport symbol*] (OAG)
CSS	CBPO [*Consolidated Base Personnel Office*] Strength Summary Card (AFM)
CSS	Cement Squeeze Simulator [*For testing well drilling material*]
CSS	Centaur Standard Shroud [*NASA*]
CSS	Center for Self-Sufficiency (EA)
CSS	Center for Separation Science [*University of Arizona*]
CSS	Center for Sports Sponsorship (EA)
CSS	Center for the Social Sciences [*Columbia University*] [*Research center*] (RCD)
CSS	Central Security Service [*National Security Agency*] [*Obsolete*] (AABC)
CSS	Central Sterile Supply [*Medicine*] (CPH)
CSS	Central Structure Storage [*Computer science*] (BYTE)
CSS	Central Support Services [*Marine science*] (OSRA)
CSS	Central Support Services [*National Weather Service*] (USDC)
CSS	Certificate in Social Service [*British*] (DBQ)
CSS	Certificate of Sanitary Science [*British*]
CSS	Certificate of Special Studies (PGP)
CSS	Ceskoslovenska Strana Socialisticka [*Czechoslovak Socialist Party*] (PPE)
CSS	Character Start-Stop
CSS	Character String Scanner [*Computer program*]
CSS	Chewing, Sucking, Swallowing [*Medicine*]
CSS	Chicago South Shore & South Bend Railroad [*AAR code*]
CSS	Chief of Support Services [*Army*]
CSS	China Stamp Society (EA)
CSS	Chronic Subclinical Scurvy [*Medicine*]
CSS	Cinegraphic Scoring System (MCD)
CSS	Circuit Switching Station [*Telecommunications*] (CET)
CSS	Clock Subsystem (CET)
CSS	Clothing Sales Store (AABC)
CSS	Coastal Survey Ship [*Marine science*] (MSC)
CSS	Cockpit Systems Simulator [*Aviation*]
CSS	Coded Switch System [*To permit or deny the ability to arm nuclear weapons in strategic aircraft*]
CSS	Cognitive Science Society (EA)
CSS	College of Saint Scholastica [*Duluth, MN*]
CSS	College Scholarship Service [*Service mark of the College Entrance Examination Board*]
CSS	College Selection Service [*Peterson's Guides*] [*Information service or system*] (IID)
CSS	Color Sync Signal
CSS	Columbus City School, Columbus, OH [*OCLC symbol*] (OCLC)
CSS	Combat Service Support [*DoD*] (AABC)
CSS	Combat Support Squadron [*Air Force*]
CSS	Combat Systems Support [*Military*] (DNAB)
CSS	Command Security Service (MCD)
CSS	Command Session Start [*Computer science*] (IAA)
CSS	Command Substitution System (NITA)
CSS	Command Supply System (MCD)
CSS	Command Synchronizer Slave (MCD)
CSS	Commercial Satellite Systems [*Berkeley, CA*] [*Telecommunications*] (TSSD)
CSS	Commit Sequence Summary (AAG)
CSS	Committee in Support of Solidarity (EA)
CSS	Committee on State Sovereignty [*Defunct*] (EA)
CSS	Commodity Stabilization Service [*Name changed to Agricultural Stabilization and Conservation Service, 1961*]
CSS	Common Services Subsystem [*Telecommunications*] (TEL)
CSS	Common Skills Shop [*Military*] (DNAB)
CSS	Commonwealth Scholarship Scheme [*Australia*]
CSS	Communications Security System (MCD)
CSS	Communications Subsystem
CSS	Communication Support System (MCD)

CSS	Complete Service Supplier [*Vendor operations*]
CSS	Complete Statistical System
CSS	Comprehensive Support Software [*Computer science*] (NITA)
CSS	Computer Scheduling System (IAA)
CSS	Computer Search Services
CSS	Computer Sentry Software
CSS	Computer Sharing Services, Inc. [*Information service or system*] (IID)
CSS	Computer Subsystem (NASA)
CSS	Computer System Simulator [*Programming language*] [*1969*]
CSS	Computing Support Services [*California Institute of Technology*] [*Research center*] (RCD)
CSS	Conceptual Signaling and Status Store [*Telecommunications*] (OSI)
CSS	Condensate Storage System [*Nuclear energy*] (NRCH)
CSS	Confederated Spanish Societies [*Defunct*] (EA)
CSS	Confederate States Ship
CSS	Conference of State Societies [*Later, National Conference of State Societies*] (EA)
CSS	Congregation of the Sacred Stigmata [*Stigmatine Fathers and Brothers*] [*Roman Catholic religious order*]
CSS	Consolidated Supply Support Activity (MCD)
CSS	Consolidated Support System
CSS	Consort Speed Servo
CSS	Constant Security Surveillance [*Shipping*]
CSS	Constituted Soil Columns [*Agronomy*]
CSS	Containment Spray System [*Nuclear energy*] (NRCH)
CSS	Contemporary Science Series [*A publication*]
CSS	Contemporary Specialty Services [*Merchandiser*] [*Chicago, IL*]
CSS	Content Scramble System [*Computer science*]
CSS	Contingency Support Staff (MCD)
CSS	Continuity of Service Set (MCD)
CSS	Continuous Surveillance Service (MCD)
CSS	Contractor Storage Site (AFM)
CSS	Contractor Support Service (MCD)
CSS	Contrans Corp. [*Toronto Stock Exchange symbol*]
CSS	Control and Status System [*NASCOM*] (MCD)
CSS	Controlled Swirl Scavenging [*Automotive engine design*]
CSS	Control Signaling Subsystem [*Telecommunications*] (TEL)
CSS	Control Stick Steering [*Aviation*] (NG)
CSS	Control Subsystem
CSS	Control Systems Society (EA)
CSS	Conversational Software System [*National CSS, Inc.*]
CSS	Coordinated Situation System
CSS	Cordless Switchboard Section [*Telecommunications*] (NITA)
CSS	Cordless Switchboard System
CSS	Core Segment Simulator (NASA)
CSS	Core Support Structure [*Nuclear energy*] (NRCH)
CSS	Corn Stunt Spiroplasma [*Plant pathology*]
CSS	Corn Syrup Solids
CSS	Corporate Shareholder System (IAA)
CSS	Corps Support Services [*Military*]
CSS	Corse Aero Service [*France ICAO designator*] (FAAC)
CSS	Council for Science and Society [*British*]
CSS	Council of Social Service [*British*]
CSS	County Surveyors Society [*British*] (DCTA)
CSS	Crew Safety System
CSS	Critical Shear Stress
CSS	Cryogenic Storage System [*Apollo project*] [*NASA*]
CSS	CSS Industries [*Associated Press*] (SAG)
CSS	CSS Industries [*NYSE symbol*] (TTSB)
CSS	CSS Industries, Inc. [*NYSE symbol*] (SPSG)
CSS	Current Steering Switch (KSC)
CSS	Cursus Sacrae Scripturae [*Paris*] (BJA)
CSS	Customer Service System [*Computer surveillance*] [*British*]
CSS	Customer Switching System [*Telecommunications*] (TEL)
CSS	IEEE Circuits and Systems Society (EA)
CSS	IEEE Control Systems Society (EA)
CSS	Ontario Ministry of Community and Social Services Library [*UTLAS symbol*]
CSS	Stigmatine Fathers and Brothers (TOCD)
css	Stigmatine Fathers and Brothers, Congregation of the Sacred Stigmata (TOCD)
CSS	Washington Court House, OH [*Location identifier FAA*] (FAAL)
CSS7	Channel Signaling System No. 7 [*Computer science*] (TNIG)
CSSA	Cactus and Succulent Society of America (EA)
CSSA	Canadian Sanitation Standards Association
CSSA	Canadian Sanitation Supply Association [*Association Canadienne des Fournisseurs de Produits Sanitaires*] [*Formerly, Canadian Sanitation Standards Association*] (AC)
CSSA	Canadian Social Science Abstracts [*York University*] [*Canada*] [*A database*] (NITA)
CSSA	Central States Speech Association (AEBS)
CSSA	Central Supply Support Activity
CSSA	Civilian Science Systems Administration [*Proposed for National Science Foundation*]
CSSA	Civil Service Supply Association [*British*]
CSSA	Cleaning and Support Services Association [*British*] (EAIO)
CSSA	Clothing and Small Stores Account [*Military*]
CSSA	Cold Start Spark Advance [*Automotive engineering*]
CSSA	Combat Service Support Area [*Army*]
CSSA	Communications Supply Service Association (EA)
CSSA	Conseil Superieur du Sport en Afrique [*Supreme Council for Sport in Africa - SCSA*] [*Yaounde, Cameroon*] (EAIO)
CSSA	Control Stick Sensor Assembly (MCD)
CSSA	Crop Science Society of America (EA)
CSSA	Seaman Apprentice, Commissaryman, Striker [*Navy rating*]

CSSAA .... Computer Systems Selection and Acquisition Agency [Army] (MCD)
CSSACT ...... Cactus and Succulent Society of the Australian Capital Territory
CSSAD .... Committee for the Scientific Survey of Air Defence [British World War II]
CSSAE .... Communication Skills Self-Assessment Exam (DMAA)
CSSAO .... Committee for the Scientific Survey of Air Offence [British World War II]
CSSARA ...... California Service Station and Automotive Repair Association (SRA)
CSSAS .... Campaign for State-Supported Alternative Schools (AIE)
CSSAW .... Committee for the Scientific Survey of Air Warfare [British World War II]
CSSB .... Cedar Shake and Shingle Bureau (EA)
CSSB .... Civilian Supervisory Selection Battery [Military] (AFM)
CSSB .... Civil Service Selection Board [Pronounced "sissby"] [British]
CSSB .... Compatible Single Sideband
CSSB .... Cross-Sectional and Special Studies Branch [Department of Education] (GFGA)
CSSBI .... Canadian Sheet Steel Building Institute [Institut Canadien de la tole d'Acier pour le Batiment] (AC)
CSSC .... CBPO [Consolidated Base Personnel Office] Strength Summary Card (AFM)
CSSC .... Center for Space Structures and Controls [University of Colorado at Boulder] [Research center] (RCD)
CSSC .... Center Special Slotted Container [Packaging]
CSSC .... Civil Service Sports Council [British] (DI)
CSSC .... Clans and Scottish Societies of Canada
CSSC .... Classification of Secondary School Courses [National Center for Education Statistics] (EDAC)
CSSCA .... Circus Saints and Sinners Club of America (EA)
CSSCC .... Congregatio Sacratissimorum Cordium [Missionaries of the Sacred Hearts of Jesus and Mary] [Roman Catholic religious order]
CSS/CG .... Container Systems Standardization/Coordination Group
CSSCiC .... Sacramento City College, Sacramento, CA [Library symbol Library of Congress] (LCLS)
CSSCO .... Cunard Steamship Co. (MHDB)
CSSCO .... Staff Communications Office, Office of the Chief of Staff [Army]
CSSCS .... Combat Service Support Control System [Army]
CSSD .... Central Sterile Supply Department [Medicine] (DAVI)
CSSD .... Ceskoslovenska Socialnedemokraticka Strana Delnicka [Czechoslovak Social Democratic Workers' Party] (PPE)
CSSD .... Chemically Sensitive Semiconductor Devices
CSSD .... Coated Solid-State Device [Sensor]
CSSD .... Combat Service Support Detachment [Marine Corps] (DOMA)
CSSD .... Communications System Status Display (KSC)
CSSD .... Computer Services and Systems Division [Environmental Protection Agency] (GFGA)
CSSD .... Contact Soil Sampling Device [Aerospace]
CSSD .... Controlled Substance Sensing Device (AAGC)
CSSDA .... Council of Social Science Data Archives [Defunct]
CSSDCA ...... Conference on Security, Stability, Development, and Cooperation in Africa
CSSE .... Canadian Society for the Study of Education [See also SCEE] [University of Ottawa] [Research center] (RCD)
CSSE .... Canadian Society of Safety Engineering
CSSE .... Center for Social Studies Education (EA)
CSSE .... Combat Service Support Element [Marine Corps] (DOMA)
CSSE .... Combat System Support Equipment [Military] (CAAL)
CSSE .... Conference of State Health and Environmental Managers [Conference of Stat e Sanitary Engineers] [Acronym is based on former name, Defunct] (EA)
CSSE .... Conference of State Sanitary Engineers
CSSE .... Control System Simulation Equipment (MCD)
CSSEA .... Computer Services Support and Evaluation Agency
CSSEAS ...... Center for South and Southeast Asian Studies [University of Michigan] [Research center] (RCD)
CSSEC .... Computer Systems Support and Evaluation Command
CSSEDC ...... Conference for Secondary School English Department Chairpersons (EA)
CSSER .... Center for Solid State Electronics [Arizona State University] [Research center] (RCD)
CSSF .... Canadian Shooting Sports Foundation [La Fondation des Sports de Tir] (AC)
CSSF .... Clothing and Small Stores Fund [Military]
CSSF .... Congregation of the Sisters of St. Felix [Felician Sisters] [Roman Catholic religious order]
CSSf .... Felician Sisters (TOCD)
CSsf .... South San Francisco Free Public Library, South San Francisco, CA [Library symbol Library of Congress] (LCLS)
CSSF .... Sutter's Fort State Monument, Sacramento, CA [Library symbol Library of Congress] (LCLS)
CSSG .... Chairman, Special Studies Group [Joint Chiefs of Staff]
CSSG .... Combat Service Support Group [Army]
CSSG .... Combat System Steering Group [Military] (CAAL)
CSSG .... Computer Software and Services Group (IAA)
CSSGS .... Croatian Serbian Slovene Genealogical Society (EA)
CSSH .... Chief of Staff Supreme Headquarters [British]
CSSH .... Cold Start Spark Hold [Automotive engineering]
CSSH .... Society for the Comparative Study of Society and History (EA)
CSSHE .... Canadian Society for the Study of Higher Education [See also SCEES]
CSSHS .... Creation Social Science and Humanities Society (EA)
CSSI .... Computer Software and Services Industry (HGAA)
CSSI .... Coriolis Sickness Susceptibility Index [Orientation]
CSSIA .... Computer Software and Services Industry Association [Formerly, ADAPSO] (NITA)

CSSID .... Center for the Study of Sensory Integrative Dysfunction [American Occupational Therapy Association]
CSS Inds. .... CSS Industries [Associated Press] (SAG)
CSSL .... Canada Steamship Lines [AAR code]
CSSL .... Central Sierra Snow Laboratory [Norden, CA]
CSSL .... Continuous Systems Simulation Language [Computer science]
CSSL .... Cyclical Stress Sensitivity Limit
CSSM .... Chief Ship's Service Man [Navy rating Obsolete]
CSSM .... Children's Special Service Mission [British]
CSSM .... Computer System Security Manager (DNAB)
CSSM .... Coso Springs South [California] [Seismograph station code, US Geological Survey] (SEIS)
CSSMB .... Chief Ship's Service Man, Barber [Navy rating Obsolete]
CSSMC .... Chief Ship's Service Man, Cobbler [Navy rating Obsolete]
CSSME .... Centre for Studies in Science and Mathematical Education [University of Leeds] [British] (CB)
CSSME .... Coalition for Strategic Stability in the Middle East (EA)
CSSML .... Chief Ship's Service Man, Laundryman [Navy rating Obsolete]
CSSMT .... Chief Ship's Service Man, Tailor [Navy rating Obsolete]
CSSN .... Canadian Society for the Study of Names [See also SCEN]
CSSN .... Common Source Spot Noise
CSSN .... Seaman, Commissaryman, Striker [Navy rating]
CSSNF .... Common Source Spot Noise Figure
CSSNSW ..... Combined Scottish Society of New South Wales [Australia]
CSSO .... Canadian Society of Surgical Oncology [Societe Canadienne d'Oncologie Chirurgicale] (AC)
CSSO .... Chief State School Officer (AEE)
CSSO .... Computer System Security Officer (DNAB)
CSSO .... Consolidated Surplus Sales Office [Military - Merged with Defense Supply Agency]
CSSP .... Canadian Society of Scientific Photography [Societe Canadienne de la Photographie Scientifique] (AC)
CSSP .... Center for Studies of Suicide Prevention [National Institute of Mental Health]
CSSP .... Center for the Study of Social Policy (EA)
CSSP .... Certified Security and Safety Professional [Environmental science]
CSSP .... Classical Scattering Spectrometer Probe [Aerosol measurement device]
CSSP .... Combined Services Support Program [Navy] (NG)
CSSP .... Congregatio Sancti Spiritus [Congregation of the Holy Ghost] [Holy Ghost Fathers] [Roman Catholic religious order]
CSSP .... Council of Scientific Society Presidents (EA)
CSSp .... Holy Ghost Fathers (TOCD)
cssp .... Holy Ghost Fathers, Congregation of the Holy Ghost (TOCD)
CSSp .... Sisters of Holy Spirit (TOCD)
CSS PCC ..... Combat Service Support Precommand Course
CSSPT .... Common Supply Support [Military] (AABC)
CSSQ .... Child Safety Seat Questionnaire [Auto safety research]
CSSQ .... Coalition Sida des Sourds du Quebec (AC)
CSSQ .... Computer Systems Squadron
CSSQT .... Combat System Ship Qualification Trial [Military] (CAAL)
CSSR .... Canadian Society for the Study of Religion [See also SCER]
CSSR .... Communication Systems Sector [or Segment] Replacement [Military]
CSSR .... Congregatio Sanctissimi Redemptoris [Congregation of the Most Holy Redeemer] [Redemptionists] [Roman Catholic men's religious order]
CSSR .... Consolidated Stock Status Report
CSSR .... Cost Schedule Status Report [Military]
CSSR .... Council of Societies for the Study of Religion (EA)
CSSR .... Czechoslovak Socialist Republic
CSSR .... Redemptorist Fathers (TOCD)
cssr .... Redemptorist Fathers (TOCD)
CSSRA .... Canadian Shipbuilding and Ship Repairing Association
CSSRNA ...... Center for Supplying Services by Redemptorists for North America
CSSS .... Canadian Society of Soil Science [Societe Canadienne de la Science du Sol] (AC)
CSSS .... Canadian Soil Science Society (MCD)
CS/SS .... Card Service/Socket Service [Computer science] (PCM)
CSSS .... Civil Service and Post Office Sanitorium Society [British] (DI)
CSSS .... Combat Service Support System [Army]
CSSS .... Commonwealth Secondary Scholarship Scheme [Australia]
CSSS .... Conceptual Satellite Surveillance System
CSSS .... Council of State Science Supervisors (EA)
CSSS .... Cross-Spin Stabilization Systems
CSSSA .... Crop Science Society of South Australia
CSST .... Carmelite Sisters of St. Teresa (TOCD)
CSST .... Central Standard Summer Time
CSST .... Commission de la Sante et de la Securite du Travail du Quebec [Quebec Workers Health and Security Commission] [Montreal] [Information service or system] (IID)
CSST .... Compatible Sidelobe Suppression Technique (AAG)
CSST .... Computer System Science Training [IBM Corp.]
CSST .... Corrugated Stainless-Steel Tubing
CSSTC .... Cambridge Series for Schools and Training Colleges [A publication]
CSSTPB .... Cap Screw and Special Threaded Products Bureau [Defunct] (EA)
CSSTR .... Continuous Segregated Stirred Tank Reactor [Chemical engineering]
CSSTSS .... Combat Service Support Training Simulator System [Army]
CSSU .... Cats on Stamps Study Unit [American Topical Association] (EA)
CSSU .... Central Sterile Supply Unit [Medicine] (DMAA)
CSSU .... Church Sunday School Union [British]
CSSU .... Converter Simulator Signal Unit (MCD)
CS Supp ...... Supplement to the Compiled Statutes [A publication] (DLA)
CSSUWA ...... Children's Services Support Unit of Western Australia
CSSV .... Cacao Swollen Shoot Virus [Plant pathology]
CSSV .... Combat Support Smoke Vehicle [Army]

CSS-X-4............ China Surface-to-Surface Experimental Number 4 [*Rocket*]
CSSYPT .... Committee for Single Six-Year Presidential Term (EA)
CSSYS .... Composition Support System (DGA)
CST............. Canadian Scholarship Trust Foundation [*Fondation Fiduciaire Canadienne de Bourses d'Etudes*] [*Formerly, CST Foundation*] (AC)
CST............. Capillary Suction Times
CST............. Capital Stock Tax Ruling, Internal Revenue Bureau [*United States*] [*A publication*] (DLA)
CST............. Capsule Systems Test [*NASA*]
CST............. Cardiac Stress Test [*Medicine*] (MAE)
CST............. Carmelite Sisters of St. Therese of the Infant Jesus [*Roman Catholic religious order*]
CST............. Carrier Power Supply, Transistorized [*Telecommunications*] (TEL)
cst............. Cast (VRA)
CST............. Castanospermine [*Biochemistry*]
CST............. Castaway [*Fiji*] [*Airport symbol*] (OAG)
CST............. Castrovirreyna [*Peru*] [*Seismograph station code, US Geological Survey*] (SEIS)
CST............. Cast Stone [*Technical drawings*]
CST............. Cavernous Sinus Thrombosis [*Medicine*]
CST............. Celeste Resources [*Vancouver Stock Exchange symbol*]
CST............. Center for Sustainable Transportation (EA)
cSt............. Centistoke [*Also, cs*] [*Unit of kinematic viscosity*]
CST............. Central Standard Time
CST............. Certification Short Test [*Exhaust emissions testing*] [*Automotive engineering*]
CST............. Certified Surgical Technologist (HCT)
CST............. Channel Status Indicator [*Computer science*] (MDG)
CST............. Channel Status Table [*Computer science*] (IAA)
CST............. Chief of Supplies and Transport [*Navy British*]
CST............. Chief Steward [*Later, MSC*] [*Navy rating*]
CST............. Child Study Team [*Education*]
CST............. [*The*] Christiana Companies, Inc. [*NYSE symbol*] (SPSG)
CST............. Classification on Science and Technology
CST............. Coast [*Board on Geographic Names*]
CST............. Coast
CST............. Coast Air KS [*Norway ICAO designator*] (FAAC)
CST............. Code Segment Table [*Computer science*]
CST............. Coding Speed Test (DNAB)
CST............. College of Saint Teresa [*Winona, MN*]
CST............. College of Speech Therapists [*British*]
CST............. College of St. Thomas [*St. Paul, MN*]
CST............. Colloidal System Test
CST............. Combat Support Training [*Military*] (AABC)
CST............. Combat Systems Training (NVT)
CST............. Combined Service Territory [*Red Cross*]
CS/T............. Combined Station/Tower [*Aviation*]
CST............. Combined Systems Test
CST............. Commander Sea Training [*Canadian Navy*]
CST............. Commerce, Science, and Transportation (DLA)
CST............. Commercial Subsurface Transformer (IAA)
CST............. Commit Start (AAG)
CST............. Common Specialist Training
CST............. Communications Surveillance Transistor
CST............. Communications Systems Technician (MCD)
CST............. Competency Screening Test (EDAC)
CST............. Complex Safety Technician [*Air Force*] (AFM)
CST............. Compound Series Test [*Intelligence test*]
CST............. Comprehensive Screening Tool for Determining Optimal Communication Mode [*Speech evaluation test*]
CST............. Concentration Stress Test [*Psychical stress*]
CST............. Conceptual Systems Test
CST............. Condensate Storage Tank [*Nuclear energy*] (NRCH)
CST............. Conformal Solution Theory (MCD)
CST............. Conical Shock Tube
CST............. Consolidated Schedule Technique
CST............. Consortium on Soils of the Tropics
CST............. Container Service Tariff [*Shipping*] (DS)
CST............. Continuously Stirred Tank
CST............. Contraction Stress Test [*Obstetrics*]
CST............. Contract Supplemental Tooling (NASA)
CST............. Control System Test (AAG)
CST............. Conventional Stability Talks [*Arms control*]
CST............. Convulsive Shock Therapy [*Medicine*]
CST............. Cortico-Spinal Tract [*Anatomy*]
CST............. Council on Student Travel [*Later, CIEE*] (EA)
CST............. Countdown Sequence Timer [*Aerospace*] (IAA)
CST............. Countersniper Team [*Army*] (INF)
CST............. Country Support Team [*United Nations*]
CST............. Crew Station Trainer [*NASA*]
CST............. Crew Systems Trainer [*NASA*] (NASA)
CST............. Critical Solution Temperature
CST............. Critical Surface Tension [*Physical chemistry*]
CST............. Crude Sulfate Turpentine
CST............. Crystalline Style
CST............. Cumulative Sum Techniques (MHDB)
CST............. Current Summary of Threat (MCD)
CST............. Cycling Strength Test
CST............. School of Theology at Claremont Library, Claremont, CA [*OCLC symbol*] (OCLC)
CSt.............. Stanford University, Stanford, CA [*Library symbol Library of Congress*] (LCLS)
Cst............. Static Compliance (MAE)
CSTA............. Cable/Special Temporary Authority [*FCC*] (NTCM)

CSTA.............. Canadian Seed Trade Association (AC)
CSTA.............. Canadian String Teachers' Association
CSTA.............. Civil Service Typists' Association [*A union*] [*British*]
CSTA.............. Cloak and Suit Trucking Association (EA)
CSTA.............. Combat Surveillance and Target Acquisition [*Army*]
CSTA.............. Combat Systems Test Activity [*Aberdeen Proving Ground, MD*] [*Army*] (RDA)
CSTA.............. Combat Systems Text Agency [*Military*]
CSTA.............. Computer-Supported Telecommunications Applications
CSTA.............. Consolidating Station
CSTA.............. Council of Subject Teaching Associations (AIE)
CSTA.............. Crew Software Training Aid (MCD)
CSTA.............. Cross-Scan Terrain Avoidance (DNAB)
CSta............. Santa Ana Public Library, Santa Ana, CA [*Library symbol Library of Congress*] (LCLS)
CStaB-E ...... Borg-Warner Corp., B-J Electronics Division, Santa Ana, CA [*Library symbol Library of Congress*] (LCLS)
CStaC.......... Santa Ana College, Santa Ana, CA [*Library symbol Library of Congress*] (LCLS)
CStaE.......... Electron Engineering Co. of California, Santa Ana, CA [*Library symbol Library of Congress*] (LCLS)
CStaHi .... Orange County Historical Society, Santa Ana, CA [*Library symbol*] [*Library of Congress*] (LCLS)
CSTAIN .... Commander's Surveillance and Target Acquisition Information Needs (MCD)
CSTAL.......... Combat Surveillance and Target Acquisition Laboratory [*Army*] (RDA)
C-stand .... Century Stand [*Filmmaking*] (WDMC)
CStaOL .... Orange County Law Library, Santa Ana, CA [*Library symbol Library of Congress*] (LCLS)
CSTAR .... Classified Scientific and Technical Aerospace Reports [*NASA*]
CSTAR .... Combat Surveillance Target Acquisition RADAR
CSTAR .... Combat Systems Technical Aerospace Report
C Stat .... Static Lund Compliance [*Medicine*] (DAVI)
CSTATC....... Combat Surveillance and Target Acquisition Training Command [*Army*]
C Staten Island (CUNY)... [*The*] College of Staten Island of The City University of New York (GAGS)
CSTB............. California State Bank [*NASDAQ symbol*] (NQ)
CStb............. Santa Barbara Public Library, Santa Barbara, CA [*Library symbol Library of Congress*] (LCLS)
CSt-B .... Stanford University, Graduate School of Business, Stanford, CA [*Library symbol Library of Congress*] (LCLS)
CStbCiC ...... Santa Barbara City College, Santa Barbara, CA [*Library symbol Library of Congress*] (LCLS)
CStbF.......... Fielding Institute, Santa Barbara, CA [*Library symbol Library of Congress*] (LCLS)
CStbGE .... General Electric Co., Santa Barbara, CA [*Library symbol Library of Congress*] (LCLS)
CStbGR .... General Research Corp., Effects Technology, Inc., Santa Barbara, CA [*Library symbol Library of Congress*] (LCLS)
CStbHi .... Santa Barbara Historical Society, Santa Barbara, CA [*Library symbol*] [*Library of Congress*] (LCLS)
CStbK.......... Karpeles Manuscript Library, Santa Barbara, CA [*Library symbol*] [*Library of Congress*] (LCLS)
CStbM.......... Santa Barbara Museum of Natural History, Santa Barbara, CA [*Library symbol Library of Congress*] (LCLS)
CStbMHi ...... Montecito History Association, Santa Barbara, CA [*Library symbol*] [*Library of Congress*] (LCLS)
CstBn.......... Coastal Bancorp [*Associated Press*] (SAG)
CstBncp....... Coastal Bancorp [*Associated Press*] (SAG)
CStbOL .... Our Lady of Light Catholic Library, Santa Barbara, CA [*Library symbol Library of Congress*] (LCLS)
CStbOM .... Old Mission Santa Barbara Seminary, Santa Barbara, CA [*Library symbol Library of Congress*] (LCLS)
CSTBR .... Continuous Stirred Tank Biological Reactor [*Chemical engineering*]
CStbW .... Westmont College, Santa Barbara, CA [*Library symbol*] [*Library of Congress*] (LCLS)
CStC............. Center for Advanced Study in the Behavioral Sciences, Stanford, CA [*Library symbol Library of Congress*] (LCLS)
CSTC............. Charleston Submarine Training Center [*South Carolina*]
CSTC............. Combined Strategic Targets Committee [*World War II*]
CStCC .... Stanford Center for Chicano Research, Stanford, CA [*Library symbol Library of Congress*] (LCLS)
CStcl........... Santa Clara Public Library, Santa Clara, CA [*Library symbol Library of Congress*] (LCLS)
CStclF.......... FMC Corp., Santa Clara, CA [*Library symbol Library of Congress*] (LCLS)
CStclGS ...... Church of Jesus Christ of Latter-Day Saints, Genealogical Society Library, SantaClara Branch, Santa Clara, CA [*Library symbol Library of Congress*] (LCLS)
CStclHi .... Santa Clara County Historical and Genealogical Society, Santa Clara, CA [*Library symbol*] [*Library of Congress*] (LCLS)
CStcll........... Intel Corp., Santa Clara, CA [*Library symbol Library of Congress*] (LCLS)
CStclM......... Memorex Corp., Santa Clara, CA [*Library symbol Library of Congress*] (LCLS)
CStclR .... Rolm Corp. Library, Santa Clara, CA [*Library symbol Library of Congress*] (LCLS)
CStclU .... University of Santa Clara, Santa Clara, CA [*Library symbol Library of Congress*] (LCLS)
CStclU-L ...... University of Santa Clara, Law Library, Santa Clara, CA [*Library symbol Library of Congress*] (LCLS)
CStcrCL........ Santa Cruz Public Library [*Santa Cruz City and County Library*], Santa Cruz, CA [*Library symbol Library of Congress*] (LCLS)

CStcrF......... Forest History Society, Santa Cruz, CA [*Library symbol Library of Congress*] (LCLS)

CStcrGS....... Genealogical Society of Santa Cruz County, Santa Cruz, CA [*Library symbol*] [*Library of Congress*] (LCLS)

CSTCS......... Combat Systems Technical School Command

CSTCS......... Cost Schedule Technical Control System

CSTD............ Commonwealth Society of Teachers of Dancing [*Australia*]

C/STD.......... Conductivity (Salinity)-Temperature-Depth [*Oceanography*]

CSTD............ United Nations Center for Science and Technology for Development (EA)

CSTDD.......... Combat Systems Test Development Director (DNAB)

CSTDPHE..... Conference of State and Territorial Directors of Public Health Education (EA)

CSTDSS........ Consolidated Short-Term Demand Simulation System [*Department of Energy*] (GFGA)

CSTE............ Council of State and Territorial Epidemiologists (EA)

CstEngy........ Coastwide Energy Services [*Associated Press*] (SAG)

CSTEnt......... CST Entertainment Imaging, Inc. [*Associated Press*] (SAG)

CSTES.......... Center for Student Testing, Evaluation, and Standards [*Later, CRESST*] [*Department of Education*] (GRD)

CSt-ES.......... Stanford University, Branner Earth Sciences Library, Systems Office, Stanford, CA [*Library symbol*] [*Library of Congress*] (LCLS)

CSTEX.......... Combat Systems Training Exercise (DNAB)

CSTF............ Canadian Standardized Test of Fitness

CSTF............ Continuous Stirred Tank Fermentator (OA)

CSTF............ CoreStaff, Inc. [*NASDAQ symbol*] (SAG)

CsTFA........... Cesium Trifluoroacetate [*Reagent*]

CSTG............ Casting (KSC)

CSt-H............ Stanford University, Hoover Institution on War, Revolution, and Peace, Stanford,CA [*Library symbol Library of Congress*] (LCLS)

CSTHA.......... Canadian Science & Technology Historical Association (AC)

CSTHOPHS... Conference of State and Territorial Health Officers with Public Health Service (EA)

CSTI.............. Centre for Scientific and Technological Information [*Council for Scientific and Industrial Research*] [*Pretoria, South Africa*]

CSTI.............. Chattanooga State Technical Institute [*Tennessee*]

CSTI.............. Civil Space Technology Initiative [*NASA*] (GFGA)

CSTI.............. Clearinghouse for Scientific and Technical Information [*Later, NTIS*] [*National Institute of Standards and Technology*]

CSTI.............. Committee on Scientific and Technical Information [*Federal Council for Sc ience and Technology*] [*Defunct*] (IEEE)

CSTI.............. Control Stick Tie-In [*Aviation*] (MUGU)

CSTIP........... Combat System Test Implementation Plan [*Military*] (CAAL)

CStJ.............. Commander, Order of St. John of Jerusalem [*British*]

CSTL............ Castellate

CSTL............ Castelle [*NASDAQ symbol*] (TTSB)

CSTL............ Chemical Science and Technology Laboratory [*National Institute of Standards and Technology*]

CSTL............ Coastal

CSTL............ Coastal

CstI.............. [*The*] Coastal Corp. [*Formerly, Coastal State Gas Producing Co.*] [*Associated Press*] (SAG)

CSt-L........... Stanford University, Lane Medical Library, Stanford, CA [*Library symbol Library of Congress*] (LCLS)

CSt-Law....... Stanford University, Law Library, Stanford, CA [*Library symbol Library of Congress*] (LCLS)

CstIFncl....... Coastal Financial Corp. [*Associated Press*] (SAG)

CstIPhys...... Coastal Physician Group [*Associated Press*] (SAG)

CSTM........... Canadian Society for Musical Traditions [*Societe Canadienne pour les Traditions Musicales*] [*Formerly, Canadian Folk Music Society*] (AC)

CSTM........... Canadian Society for Transfusion Medicine [*Societe Canadienne de Medecine Transfusionnelle*] [*Formerly, Canadian Association of Immunohematologists*] (AC)

CSTM........... Centro Studi Terzo Mondo [*Study Center for the Third World*] [*Italy*] (EAIO)

CSTM........... Cervical Prevertebral Soft Tissue Measurement [*Medicine*] (DMAA)

CSTM........... Coal Supply and Transportation Model [*Department of Energy*] (GFGA)

CSTM........... Custom

CSTM........... Custom Chrome [*NASDAQ symbol*] (TTSB)

CSTM........... Custom Chrome, Inc. [*NASDAQ symbol*] (SPSG)

CStma.......... Santa Maria Public Library, Santa Maria, CA [*Library symbol Library of Congress*] (LCLS)

CStmaAH..... Allan Hancock College, Santa Maria, CA [*Library symbol Library of Congress*] (LCLS)

CStMLK........ Martin Luther King Junior Papers Project, Stanford University Libraries, Stanford, CA [*Library symbol*] [*Library of Congress*] (LCLS)

CStmo.......... Santa Monica Public Library, Santa Monica, CA [*Library symbol Library of Congress*] (LCLS)

CStmoCiC.... Santa Monica City College, Santa Monica, CA [*Library symbol Library of Congress*] (LCLS)

CStmoD....... Douglas Aircraft Co., Santa Monica Division, Santa Monica, CA [*Library symbol Library of Congress*] (LCLS)

CStmoI......... INTREC, Inc., Santa Monica, CA [*Library symbol Library of Congress*] (LCLS)

CStmoR....... Rand Corp., Santa Monica, CA [*Library symbol Library of Congress*] (LCLS)

CStmoR-W... Rand Corp., Washington, DC [*Library symbol Library of Congress*] (LCLS)

CStmoS........ System Development Corp., Technical Information Center Library, Santa Monica, CA [*Library symbol Library of Congress*] (LCLS)

CSTMP.......... Carotid Sinus Transmural Pressure [*Cardiology*]

CSTMR........ Continuous Stirred Tank Membrane Reactor [*Chemical engineering*]

CSTMS......... Customs

CSTM-TR..... Comite de Solidarite Tiers-Monde/Trois-Rivieres [*Third World Solidarity Committee/Trois-Rivieres*] (AC)

CSt-Mus...... Stanford University, Music Library, Stanford, CA [*Library symbol Library of Congress*] (LCLS)

CSTN.......... Cokesbury Satellite Television Network [*United Methodist Publishing House*] [*Telecommunications service*] (TSSD)

CSTN.......... Cornerstone Financial Corp. [*NASDAQ symbol*] (NQ)

CSTO.......... Country Standard Technical Order (MCD)

CSto............ Stockton and San Joaquin County Public Library, Stockton, CA [*Library symbol Library of Congress*] (LCLS)

CStoC.......... University of the Pacific, Stockton, CA [*Library symbol Library of Congress*] (LCLS)

CStoC-M...... University of the Pacific, Pacific Medical Center, Health Sciences Library, San Francisco, CA [*Library symbol*] [*Library of Congress*] (LCLS)

CStoC-PM.... University of the Pacific, Pacific Marine Station, Dillon Beach, CA [*Library symbol Library of Congress*] (LCLS)

CStoC-S...... University of the Pacific, Science Library, Stockton, CA [*Library symbol Library of Congress*] (LCLS)

CStoF.......... [*The*] 49-99 Cooperative Library System, Stockton, CA [*Library symbol*] [*Library of Congress*] (LCLS)

CStoGH....... San Joaquin County General Hospital, Stockton, CA [*Library symbol Library of Congress*] (LCLS)

CStoGS....... Church of Jesus Christ of Latter-Day Saints, Genealogical Society Library, Stockton Branch, Stockton, CA [*Library symbol Library of Congress*] (LCLS)

CStoH.......... Humphreys College, Stockton, CA [*Library symbol Library of Congress*] (LCLS)

CStoHD....... San Joaquin County Local Health District, Stockton, CA [*Library symbol Library of Congress*] (LCLS)

CStoHi........ San Joaquin County Historical Society, Stockton, CA [*Library symbol*] [*Library of Congress*] (LCLS)

CStoHM....... [*The*] Haggin Museum, Stockton, CA [*Library symbol*] [*Library of Congress*] (LCLS)

C-STOL....... Controlled Short Takeoff and Landing [*Acronym used for a type of aircraft*]

CSTOM......... Combat System Tactical Operation Manual [*Navy*] (NVT)

CStoPM........ San Joaquin Pioneer Museum and Haggin Art Galleries Library, Stockton, CA [*Library symbol Library of Congress*] (LCLS)

C-STORE...... Convenience Store

c-store........ Convenience Store (WDMC)

CStoSC........ San Joaquin Delta College, Stockton, CA [*Library symbol Library of Congress*] (LCLS)

CStoSH........ Stockton State Hospital, Stockton, CA [*Library symbol Library of Congress*] (LCLS)

CStoSJ........ Saint Joseph Hospital, Stockton, CA [*Library symbol Library of Congress*] (LCLS)

CStoSL........ San Joaquin County Law Library, Stockton, CA [*Library symbol Library of Congress*] (LCLS)

CSTOT......... Combat System Team Operational Trainer [*Military*] (CAAL)

CStoTP........ San Joaquin County Teachers' Professional Library, Stockton, CA [*Library symbol Library of Congress*] (LCLS)

CStp............ Blanchard Community Library, Santa Paula, CA [*Library symbol Library of Congress*] (LCLS)

CSTP.......... Committee for Scientific and Technological Policy (DMAA)

CSTP.......... Conceptual Site Treatment Plan (DOGT)

CSTP.......... Conceptual Site Treatment Plan [*Department of Energy*]

CSTP.......... Crew Scheduling and Training Plan (NVT)

CSTP.......... Cubic Centimeters at Standard Temperature and Pressure [*Also, CCSTP*]

CSTPA......... Council on Soil Testing and Plant Analysis (EA)

CStP & KC... Chicago, St. Paul & Kansas City Railway

CStPM & O... Chicago, St. Paul, Minneapolis & Omaha Railway

CSTR.......... Canister (KSC)

CSTR.......... Centre for Speech Technology Research [*British*] (CB)

CSTR.......... Committee on Solar-Terrestrial Research [*National Academy of Sciences*]

CSTR.......... Computer Software Trouble Report (MCD)

CSTR.......... Continuously Stirred Tank Reactor [*Chemical engineering*]

CSTR.......... Continuous Stirred Tank Reactor [*Chemical engineering*]

CStr............ Santa Rosa-Sonoma County Free Public Library, Santa Rosa, CA [*Library symbol Library of Congress*] (LCLS)

CStrJC........ Santa Rosa Junior College, Santa Rosa, CA [*Library symbol Library of Congress*] (LCLS)

CStRLIN...... Research Libraries Information Network, Stanford, CA [*Library symbol Library of Congress*] (LCLS)

CStrNB....... North Bay Cooperative Library System, Santa Rosa, CA [*Library symbol*] [*Library of Congress*] (LCLS)

C St Rose..... [*The*] College of Saint Rose (GAGS)

CSTR/UF..... Continuous Stirred Tank Reactor with an Ultrafiltration Membrane [*Chemical en gineering*]

CSTS........... Combat Support Training System [*Military*]

CSTS........... Combined System Test Stand (IEEE)

CSTS........... Computer Sciences Teleprocessing System (PDAA)

CSTS........... Computer Science Teleprocessing System (IAA)

CSTS........... Computer Science Time-Sharing System (IAA)

CSTS........... Condensate Storage and Transfer System [*Nuclear energy*] (NRCH)

CSTS........... Construction and Startup/Turnover Surveillance Group [*Nuclear energy*] (NRCH)

CSTS........... Copper Sulfate Treated Sorbeads

CSTS........... Cryogenic Storage and Transfer System (MCD)

C St Scholastica... College of St. Scholastica (GAGS)

CSTSF......... Combat Systems Test and Support Facility [*Canadian Navy*]

CSTT........... Catastrophic Sexual Transmutation Theory [*Plant genetics*]

CSTT .... Chinese School of Table Tennis [*France*] (EAIO)
CSTT .... Core Storage Terminal Table [*Computer science*]
CSTU .... Combat System Training Unit (NVT)
CSTU .... Combined Systems Test Unit (MCD)
CSTU .... Composite Standard Time Units
cstu .... Costume (VRA)
CSTV .... Cable Subscription Television
CSTV .... Control System Test Vehicle (DNAB)
CSt-V .... Stanford University, Nathan Van Patten Library, Stanford, CA [*Library symbol Library of Congress*] (LCLS)
CSTVRP .... Computer Security Technical Vulnerability Reporting Program [*Army*] (ADDR)
CSU .... California State University [*Formerly, San Francisco State College*]
CSU .... Canadian Seamen's Union
CSU .... Canadian Shopcraft Union
CSU .... Cardiac Surveillance Unit (DAVI)
CSU .... Cardiovascular Surgery Unit (DAVI)
CSU .... Casualty Staging Unit [*Military*] (AFM)
CSU .... Catheter Specimen of Urine [*Medicine*]
CSU .... Central Services Unit for University Careers and Appointments Services [*British*]
CSU .... Central State University [*Wilberforce, OH*]
CSU .... Central Statistical Unit [*of VLRL*]
CSU .... Central Switching Unit
CSU .... Certificate Signing Unit (ACRL)
CSU .... Channel Service Unit [*Telecommunications*] (TEL)
CSU .... Channel Synchronizer Unit [*Computer science*]
CSU .... Check Signal Unit [*Telecommunications*] (TEL)
CSU .... Chemistry Study Unit [*Later, CPSU*] (EA)
CSU .... Chess on Stamps Unit [*Defunct*] (EA)
CSU .... Christian Social Union [*Germany*]
CSU .... Christlich-Soziale Union [*Political party in Bavaria connected with the CDU*] [*West Germany*]
CSU .... Christmas Study Unit [*American Topical Association*] (EA)
CSU .... Circuit Switching Unit [*Telecommunications*] (CET)
CSU .... Civilian Service Unit (AFM)
CSU .... Civil Service Union [*British*]
CSU .... Clear and Subtract (IAA)
CSU .... Cleveland State University, Cleveland, OH [*OCLC symbol*] (OCLC)
CSU .... Code Storage Unit
CSU .... Colorado State University [*Fort Collins*]
CSU .... Columbus Southern Power Co. [*NYSE symbol*] (SAG)
CSU .... Combat Support Units [*Army*]
CSU .... Combined Shaft Unit
CSU .... Common Services Unit [*Telecommunications*] (TEL)
CSU .... Communications Switching Unit (CAAL)
CSU .... Community Skills Unit (AIE)
CSU .... Computer Software Unit
CSU .... Consolidated Cisco Resources [*Vancouver Stock Exchange symbol*]
CSU .... Constant Speed Unit [*Aviation*] (ADA)
CSU .... Crime Scene Unit (LAIN)
CSU .... Crystalline Sucrose Unit [*i.e., sugar cube*] [*Slang*]
CSU .... Current Sensor Unit [*American Solenoid Co.*] [*Somerset, NJ*]
CSU .... Customer Service Unit (IAA)
CSU .... Customer Set-Up [*Computer science*]
CSU .... Customer Support Unit (AFIT)
CSU .... Cycle Stealing Unit [*Computer science*] (IAA)
CSUC .... California State University and Colleges [*System*]
CSUC .... California State University, Chico
CSUC .... Consolidated Statutes of Upper Canada [*A publication*] (DLA)
CSuc .... Sun City Branch Library, Sun City, CA [*Library symbol Library of Congress*] (LCLS)
CSUCA .... Confederacion Universitaria Centroamericana [*Confederation of Central American Universities*] (EAIO)
CSUCE .... Conference of State Utility Commission Engineers [*Later, NCRUCE*] (EA)
CSU/DSU ..... Channel Service Unit/Data Service Unit
CSUF .... California State University, Fresno (PDAA)
CSUF .... Continuous Slow Ultrafiltration [*Medicine*] (DMAA)
CSUI .... Command Session User Information (IAA)
CSUK .... Coeliac Society of the United Kingdom (EAIO)
CSuLas .... Lassen County Free Library, Susanville, CA [*Library symbol Library of Congress*] (LCLS)
CSULB .... California State University, Long Beach
CSU-MAW .... Charles Sturt University - Murray, at Albury Wodonga [*Australia*]
CSU-MB ...... Charles Sturt University - Mitchell at Bathurst [*Australia*]
CSUN .... California State University, Northridge
CSUnet .... [*The*] California State University Network [*Computer science*] (TNIG)
CSUPS .... Combat Supplies [*British*]
CSU-RAMS... CSU Regional Atmospheric Modeling System (USDC)
CSURF .... Colorado State University Research Foundation [*Research center*] (RCD)
CSUS .... California State University, Sacramento
CSUSA .... Copyright Society of the USA (EA)
CSV .... Calligraphy Society of Victoria [*Australia*]
CSV .... Cambrian Society of Victoria [*Australia*]
CSV .... Cammed-Gear Speed Variator
CSV .... Capacity Selector Valve (MCD)
Csv .... Cash Surrender Value [*Insurance*]
CSV .... Casino Silver Mines [*Vancouver Stock Exchange symbol*]
CSV .... Cathodic Stripping Voltammetry [*Analytical chemistry*]
CSV .... Cellular Size Volume
CSV .... Characteristic Statistical Value
CSV .... Chreschtlech-Sozial Vollekspartei [*Christian Social Party*] [*Luxembourg*] [*Political party*] (PPW)

CSV .... Chrysanthemum Stunt Viroid
CSV .... Circuit Switched Voice [*Telecommunications*]
CSV .... Citicorp Scrimgeour Vickers [*Commercial firm British*] (ECON)
CSV .... Clerici Sancti Viatoris [*Clerics of St. Viator*] [*Viatorian Fathers*] [*Roman Catholic religious order*]
CSV .... Clerics of St. Viator (TOCD)
csv .... Clerics of St. Vistor, Viatorian Fathers (TOCD)
CSV .... Cocksfoot Streak Virus [*Plant pathology*]
CSv .... Combat Support Vehicle (MCD)
CSV .... Command Selector Value (DNAB)
CSV .... Comma Separated Values File [*Computer science*]
CSV .... Community Service Volunteers [*British*]
CSV .... Conical Shell Vibration
CSV .... Corona Starting Voltage
CSV .... Critical Sliding Velocity [*Automotive safety, vehicle rollover*]
CSV .... Crossville, TN [*Location identifier FAA*] (FAAL)
CSv .... Sunnyvale Public Library, Sunnyvale, CA [*Library symbol Library of Congress*] (LCLS)
CSVC .... Core Sample Vacuum Container [*NASA*]
CSvE .... ESL, Inc., Sunnyvale, CA [*Library symbol Library of Congress*] (LCLS)
CSVLI .... Cash Surrender Value of Life Insurance
CSVNSNSW... Christian Science Visiting Nurse Service New South Wales [*Australia*]
CSVP .... Sisters of Charity of St. Vincent de Paul [*Roman Catholic religious order*]
CSVT .... Close Space Vapor Transport [*Photovoltaic energy systems*]
CSvUT .... United Technology Center, Sunnyvale, CA [*Library symbol Library of Congress*] (LCLS)
CSW .... Canada Southern Petroleum Ltd. [*Toronto Stock Exchange symbol*]
CSW .... Center for Signals Warfare [*Warrenton, VA*] [*Army*] (GRD)
CSW .... Center for the Study of Writing [*Berkeley, CA*] [*Department of Education*] (GRD)
CSW .... Certified Social Worker
CSW .... Channel Status Word [*Computer science*] (BUR)
CSW .... Childress [*Texas*] [*Seismograph station code, US Geological Survey*] (SEIS)
CSW .... Chilled Sea Water [*Pisciculture*]
CSW .... Combat Support Wing
CSW .... Command Surveillance and Weather
CSW .... Commercial Sex Worker [*Social science terminology for a prostitute*]
CSW .... Commission on the Status of Women [*Economic and Social Council of the UN*] [*Vienna, Austria*] (EAIO)
CSW .... Communications Switching System [*Army*] (RDA)
CSW .... Community of St. Wilfrid [*Anglican religious community*]
CSW .... Compression Switch
CSW .... Computer Sports World [*Information service or system*] (IID)
CSW .... Concentrated Sea Water
CSW .... Continental Shelf Wave
CSW .... Continuous Seismic Wave [*Radio transmission*] (IAA)
CSW .... Control Switch (MSA)
CSW .... Conventional Standoff Weapon
CSW .... Course and Speed Made Good through the Water [*Military*] (NATG)
CSW .... Current Sleep Walker [*Medicine*] (DMAA)
CSW .... Worldwide Air Charter Systems [*Canada ICAO designator*] (FAAC)
CSWA .... Canadian Science Writers' Association [*Association Canadienne des Redacteurs Sceintifiques*] (AC)
CSWA .... Captain, Surface Weapons Acceptance [*British military*] (DMA)
CSWAE .... Commission on the Status of Women in Adult Education [*Later, WISE*] (EA)
CSWAP .... Committee on the Status of Women in the Archival Profession (EA)
CSWAY .... Causeway
CSWC .... Capital Southwest [*NASDAQ symbol*] (TTSB)
CSWC .... Capital Southwest Corp. [*NASDAQ symbol*] (NQ)
CSWC .... Crew-Served Weapons Captured
CSWD .... Center for the Survival of Western Democracies (EA)
CSWD .... Council on Size and Weight Discrimination (EA)
CSWE .... Council on Social Work Education (EA)
CSWEP .... Committee on the Status of Women in the Economics Profession (EA)
CSWFB .... Canadian Society of Wildlife and Fishery Biologists
CSWG .... Chemical Selection Working Group [*National Cancer Institute*]
CSWG .... Combat System Working Group [*Military*] (CAAL)
CSWG .... COMSEC [*Communications Security*] Wargaming [*Simulation*] (MCD)
CSWG .... CROSSBOW [*Computer Retrieval of Organic Structures Based on Wiswesser*] Subcommittee Working Group
CSWL .... Committee on the Status of Women in Linguistics (EA)
CSWM .... Committee on the Status of Women in Microbiology (EA)
CSWMNS ..... Council of Social Welfare Ministers, National Secretariat [*Australia*]
CSWP .... Civil Service Working Party [*US Military Government, Germany*]
CSWP .... Committee for the Status of Women in Philosophy (EA)
CSWPL .... Center on Social Welfare Policy and Law (EA)
CSWR .... Conversation Specifications and Work Requirements (DNAB)
CSWS .... Committee on the Status of Women in Sociology (EA)
CSWS .... Corps Support Weapon System
CSWS .... Crew-Served Weapon Sight
CSWTS .... Crew-Served Weapon Thermal Sight [*Army*] (INF)
CSWU .... Christlich-Soziale Waehler Union im Saarland [*Christian Social Voters' Union in Saarland*] [*Germany Political party*] (PPW)
CSWY .... Causeway (KSC)
CSWY .... Causeway
CSX .... Carroll Shelby Experimental [*Automobile model*]
CSX .... Changsha [*China*] [*Airport symbol*] (OAG)
CSX .... Coastair [*Denmark ICAO designator*] (FAAC)
CSX .... Conventional Solvent Extraction [*Separation science and technology*]

CSX	CSX Corp. [*Formed by merger of Chessie System, Inc. and Seaboard Coast Line Railroad*] [*Formerly, CO*] [*NYSE symbol*] (SPSG)
CSY	Casey [*Australia Geomagnetic observatory code*]
CSY	Coastline Resources [*Vancouver Stock Exchange symbol*]
CSY	San Francisco, CA [*Location identifier FAA*] (FAAL)
CSY	Shuangyang General Aviation Co. [*China*] [*FAA designator*] (FAAC)
CSY	Skyline College Library, San Bruno, CA [*OCLC symbol*] (OCLC)
CSY	Sulphocynogen [*Pharmacy*] (ROG)
CSYI	Circuit Systems [*NASDAQ symbol*] (TTSB)
CSYI	Circuit Systems, Inc. [*NASDAQ symbol*] (NQ)
CSYS	Certificate of Sixth Year Studies [*Scotland*] (DBQ)
CSZ	Athens, TX [*Location identifier FAA*] (FAAL)
CSZ	Capital Special Zone [*Saigon, Vietnam*] (VNW)
CSZ	Coastal Security Zone (MCD)
CSZ	Copper, Steel, or Zinc [*Freight*]
CSZ	Cubic Stabilized Zirconia
CSZ	Shenzhen Airlines [*China*] [*FAA designator*] (FAAC)
CSZ	University of Southern California, Norris Medical Library, Los Angeles, CA [*OCLC symbol*] (OCLC)
CT	Cable, Test
C/T	Cable Transfer [*of funds*]
C/T	Cable Tray (KSC)
CT	Cable Twist
CT	Calcitonin [*Also, TCA, TCT*] [*Endocrinology*]
CT	Calendar Time
CT	Calibration Team
CT	Calibration Technician (KSC)
CT	California Real Estate Investment Trust SBI [*NYSE symbol*] (SPSG)
CT	California Terms [*Grain shipping*]
CT	California Tomorrow [*An association*] (EA)
CT	Calif REIT SBI [*NYSE symbol*] (TTSB)
CT	Cameroon Tribune [*A publication*]
CT	Canada Trustco Mortgage Co. [*Toronto Stock Exchange symbol*]
CT	Candidate of Theology (IIA)
Ct	Canticles [*Song of Solomon*] [*Old Testament book*] (BJA)
CT	Canton and Enderbury Islands [*ANSI two-letter standard code*] (CNC)
CT	Cape Times [*A publication*] (DLA)
CT	Captive Test
CT	Captive Trainer
CT	Carat [*Unit of measure for precious stones or gold*]
CT	Carbon Tetrachloride [*Also, CTC*] [*Organic chemistry*]
Ct	Carboxyl Terminal (DMAA)
CT	Cardiac Type
CT	Cardiothoracic Ratio [*Medicine*]
CT	Cardiovascular Technologist (DAVI)
CT	Card Type (DNAB)
ct	Career Trainee (BARN)
CT	Cargo Tank [*Shipping*] (DS)
CT	Carotid Tracing [*Medicine*]
CT	Carpal Tunnel [*Medicine*]
CT	Carrier's Tax (DLA)
CT	Carrier's Tax Ruling [*IR Bulletin*] [*A publication*] (DLA)
CT	Carrier Telephone Channel
CT	Cartographer [*Navy rating*]
CT	Carton (MCD)
CT	Cartridge Tape (NTCM)
CT	Cased Telescoped [*Type of ammunition*] (DOMA)
CT	Cash Trade [*Investment term*]
CT	Cassette Tape
CT	Casters and Towbar
Ct	Cataphyll [*Botany*]
CT	Cattle Containers (DCTA)
CT	Caught
CT	Cellular Therapy [*Medicine*]
CT	Cement Tile [*Classified advertising*] (ADA)
C/T	Cenomanian/Turonian [*Geological boundary zone*]
CT	Cent [*Monetary unit*]
CT	Cental [*Short hundredweight*] [*British*] (ROG)
CT	Center Tap [*Technical drawings*]
CT	Center Thickness [*Optics*]
CT	Central Tap [*Electronics*] (ECII)
CT	Central Time (GPO)
CT	Centre de Transit [*International routing term*] [*Telecommunications*] (NITA)
C/T	Centrifugal Throwout [*Automotive engineering*]
CT	Centum [*Hundred*]
CT	Ceramic Tile [*Technical drawings*]
CT	Cerebral Thrombosis [*Medicine*]
CT	Cerebral Tumor [*Medicine*]
CT	Certificate [*Stock exchange term*] (SPSG)
CT	Certificated Teacher [*British*]
CT	Certificate of Title
CT	Cervical Traction [*Neurology, orthopedics, and physical therapy*] (DAVI)
CT	Champion Tracker
CT	Channel Terminator (HGAA)
CT	Charcoal Treated
CT	Chargeable Time (DGA)
CT	Charge-Transfer [*Intermolecular electron transfer*]
CT	Chart
CT	Checkout Tape [*Computer science*] (IAA)
CT	Check Template (MCD)
CT	Check Test (MCD)
CT	Chemical Test (MCD)
CT	Chemical Transfer (MCD)
CT	Chemische Technik [*A database*] (NITA)
CT	Chemotherapy [*Medicine*]
CT	Chest, Training [*Parachute*]
CT	Chest Tube [*Medicine*]
CT	Chicago Tribune [*A publication*]
CT	Chief of Transportation [*Army*]
CT	Chief Telegrapher [*Navy rating Obsolete*]
CT	Children Today [*A publication*] (BRI)
CT	Child Trends (EA)
CT	China Theater [*World War II*]
CT	Chlorothiazide [*Diuretic*]
CT	Cholera Toxin [*Medicine*]
CT	Chorda Tympani [*Neuroanatomy*]
CT	Choreographers Theatre (EA)
CT	Chronometer Time [*Navigation*] (IAA)
CT	Chymotrypsin [*An enzyme*]
CT	Ciguatoxin
CT	Cipher Text [*Telecommunications*] (MCD)
CT	Circadian Time [*Physiology*]
CT	Circle Card Test [*For syphilis*]
CT	Circle Track [*A publication*]
CT	Circuit
CT	Circuit Technology (IAA)
CT	Circuit Theory [*Electricity*] (MCD)
CT	Circular Tank System [*Pisciculture*]
CT	Circulation Time [*Cardiology*]
CT	Civic Trust (DCTA)
CT	Classic Technique [*Surgery*] (DAVI)
C/T	Classroom Teaching (OICC)
CT	Classroom Trainer (MCD)
C/T	Clean and Tight [*Publishing*]
CT	CLEM [*Closed-Loop Ex-Vessel Machine*] Transporter [*Nuclear energy*] (NRCH)
CT	Clipped, Torched [*Ecology*]
CT	Clock Time
CT	Closed Throttle [*Automotive engineering*]
CT	Close Tolerance
CT	Close Triplet (SAA)
CT	Clotrimazole [*Antifungal agent*]
CT	Clotting [*or Coagulation*] Time [*Hematology*]
C-T	Cloudiness-Temperature [*Hypothesis*] [*Meteorology*]
CT	Coastal Telegraph Station [*ITU designation*] (CET)
CT	Coated Tablet [*Pharmacy*]
CT	Code Table (IAA)
CT	Code Telegram
CT	Codex Theodosianus [*Theodosian Code*] [*438AD*] [*Latin*] [*Legal term*] (BJA)
CT	Coffin Texts (BJA)
CT	Cold Transient [*Automotive engineering*]
CT	Collar Tie
CT	Collateral Trust [*Bond*]
CT	Collecting Tubule (MAE)
CT	Collective Training [*Army*]
CT	Collimator Target (MCD)
CT	Colloidal Thorium (OA)
CT	Color Temperature (NTCM)
C/T	Color Transparency (WDMC)
CT	Combat Team
CT	Combined Transport [*Shipping*]
CT	Combined Trials [*Shipbuilding*]
CT	Combustion Turbine [*Type of cogenerator*]
CT	Command Airways [*ICAO designator*] (AD)
C/T	Command Transmitter (KSC)
CT	Commercial Television [*FCC*] (NTCM)
CT	Commercial Translator (IEEE)
CT	Commercial Traveler
CT	Commercial Tribunal [*South Australia*]
CT	Committee of Transylvania (EA)
CT	Communications Technician [*Navy rating*]
CT	Communications Technology
CT	Communications Technology (NITA)
CT	Communications Terminal [*Computer science*]
CT	Communication Trench [*Military*]
CT	Communist Terrorist
CT	Community Transit [*System*] [*Shipping EEC*] (DS)
CT	Compact Toroid (MCD)
CT	Company Team [*Combat Electronic Warfare Intelligence*] [*Army*]
CT	Comparative Testing
CT	Compartment Testing (NITA)
CT	Compatibility Test (MCD)
CT	Complete Translation [*Telecommunications*] (TEL)
CT	Component Test (KSC)
CT	Composers Theatre (EA)
CT	Compressed Tablet [*Pharmacy*]
CT	Computed Tomography [*Also, CAAT, CAT*] [*Roentgenography*]
CT	Computerized Tomography (ECON)
CT	Computer Technology (IEEE)
CT	Computer Transformer
CT	Computer Transponder (MCD)
CT	Condensed Tannin [*Botany*]
CT	Conductivity Transmitter (IAA)
CT	Conduit [*Electronics*] (IAA)
CT	Conference Terms (DS)

CT .... Conference Title [Database terminology] (NITA)
CT .... Confirmatory Test [Army] (AABC)
CT .... Connecticut [Postal code]
CT .... Connecticut Reports [A publication] (DLA)
Ct .... Connecticut State Library, Hartford, CT [Library symbol Library of Congress] (LCLS)
CT .... Connective Tissue
CT .... Connectivity Table [Computer science]
CT .... Conservation Trust [British] (EAIO)
CT .... Console Typewriter (IAA)
CT .... Constitutiones Tiberii [A publication] (DLA)
CT .... Constitutive Transcript [Genetics]
CT .... Consulting Teacher
CT .... Contact Team
CT .... Contact Tension
CT .... Container Tariff
CT .... Container Terminal [Shipping]
CT .... Contemporary Theatre [A publication]
CT .... Continental Tropical Air [Meteorology] (DA)
CT .... Continue Treatment [Medicine]
CT .... Continuity Transceiver [Telecommunications] (TEL)
CT .... Continuous-Flow Tub
CT .... Continuous Tone [Color printing]
CT .... Contour Template
CT .... Contraceptive Technique [Gynecology]
CT .... Contraction Time (MAE)
CT .... Contractor's Training (MCD)
CT .... Contrast
CT .... Contraterrene [Anti-matter in science fiction] (BARN)
CT .... Controlled Temperature
CT .... Controlled Term [Online database field identifier]
CT .... Control Tag (MCD)
CT .... Control Tower [For chart use only] [Aviation]
CT .... Control Transformer
CT .... Conventional Therapy [Medicine]
CT .... Conventional Tillage [Agroecosystem]
CT .... Convergent Technologies Expo [Publications and Communications, Inc.] (TSPED)
CT .... Cooling Tower [Nuclear energy] (NRCH)
CT .... Coombs' Test [for the presence of globulin on the surface of red cells] [Hematology]
CT .... Cordless Telephone
CT .... Corneal Thickness [Ophthalmology] (DAVI)
CT .... Corneal Transplant [Medicine]
CT .... Coronary Thrombosis [Medicine]
CT .... Corporation Tax [British]
CT .... Corps of Transportation [Army]
CT .... Corrected Transposition (MAE)
CT .... Corrective Therapist [or Therapy]
CT .... Correct Time (IAA)
CT .... Correlation Track
CT .... Cortical Plate Thickness [Anatomy]
CT .... Corticosterone [A hormone]
Ct .... Cotyledon [Botany]
CT .... Count
CT .... Counter
CT .... Countertenor [Music]
CT .... Counterterrorist (ADA)
CT .... Counter Timer
CT .... Countertrade [Economics] (IMH)
CT .... Counter Tube [Electronics] (IAA)
CT .... Country Team [Military] (CINC)
CT .... County
CT .... Courant [Of the Current Month] [French]
CT .... Court
ct .... Court (VRA)
CT .... Court
CT .... Court Rolls [British]
CT .... Court Trust [Includes executor, administrator, guardian] [Legal term] (DLA)
CT .... Cover Test [Ophthalmology]
C/T .... Crawler/Transporter [Aerospace] (KSC)
CT .... Creative Time (EA)
CT .... Creativity Tests for Children [Child development test series]
CT .... Credit [or Creditor] (ROG)
CT .... Credit Transfer
CT .... Credit Tribunal [Victoria] [Australia]
CT .... Crest Time (MAE)
C-T .... Cretaceous and Tertiary [Geology]
CT .... Crista Terminalis [Cardiology]
CT .... Cristobalite-Tridymite [A form of silica]
CT .... Critical Temperature
CT .... Crossmatch: Transfusion
CT .... Crosstrail [Military]
Ct .... Ctenocephalides [A genus of fleas] [Entomology] (DAVI)
CT .... CT Financial Services [Formerly, Canada Trustco Mortgage Co.] [Vancouver Stock Exchange symbol]
CT .... Cubic Tonnage [Shipping]
CT .... Cuneiform Texts from Babylonian Tablets in the British Museum (BJA)
CT .... Current
CT .... Current Transactions (NATG)
CT .... Current Transformer
CT .... Current Transformer [Instrumentation]
CT .... Customer Test [Army]

CT .... Cycle Time (NVT)
CT .... Cystine-Tellurite [Medium] [Microbiology]
CT .... Cytarabine, Thioguanine [Antineoplastic drug] (CDI)
CT .... Cytotechnologist
CT .... Torrance Public Library, Torrance, CA [Library symbol Library of Congress] (LCLS)
CT .... Training Cruiser (MCD)
CT .... Transit Switching Center [Telecommunications] (TEL)
CT1 .... Communications Technician, First Class [Navy rating]
CT2 .... Communications Technician, Second Class [Navy rating]
CT3 .... Communications Technician, Third Class [Navy rating]
CTA .... Association of Civilian Technicians
CTA .... Cable Television Association [British] (NITA)
CTA .... Cable Twist Angle
CTA .... Calculated Time of Arrival (DA)
CTA .... Call Time Adjustor [Military communications]
CTA .... Call to Australia [Political party]
CTA .... Camping Trade Association of Great Britain Ltd. (BI)
CTA .... Canadian Telebook Agency [ACCORD] [Source file] [UTLAS symbol]
CTA .... Canadian Testing Association
CTA .... Canadian Trotting Association
CTA1 .... Canadian Trucking Association (AC)
CTA .... Canadian Trucking Association
CTA .... Canadian Tuberculosis Association (DAVI)
CTA .... Cargo Traffic Analysis (MCD)
CTA .... Caribbean Tourism Association [Later, Caribbean Tourism Organization] (EA)
CTA .... Cariboo Tourist Association (AC)
CTA .... Carpenter Lake Resources [Vancouver Stock Exchange symbol]
CTA .... CasTech Aluminum Group [NYSE symbol] (TTSB)
CTA .... Castech Aluminum Group, Inc. [NYSE symbol] (SAG)
cta .... Catamenia [Menstruation] (CPH)
CTA .... Catania [Italy] [Airport symbol] (OAG)
CTA .... Catering Teachers Association [British]
CTA .... Cellulose Triacetate [Organic chemistry]
CTA .... Center for Technology and Administration [American University] [Research center] (RCD)
CTA .... Center for Total Access [Army]
CTA .... Center for Tropical Agriculture [University of Florida] [Research center] (RCD)
CTA .... Central Technical Authority (MCD)
CTA .... Central TMDE [Test, Measuring, and Diagnostic Equipment] Activity [Army] (MCD)
CTA1 .... Central Transport Authority (ADA)
CTA .... Centre Technique de Cooperation Agricole et Rural [Technical Centre for Agricultural and Rural Cooperation] (EAIO)
CTA .... Cetyltrimethylammonium [Organic chemistry]
CTA .... Ceylon Tamil Association [Victoria] [Australia]
CTA .... Chain Testers Association of Great Britain (BI)
CTA .... Chain-Transfer Agent [Organic chemistry]
CTA .... [The] Channel Tunnel Association [British]
CTA .... Chaplain of the Territorial Army [British]
CTA .... Charters Towers [Australia Seismograph station code, US Geological Survey] (SEIS)
CTA .... Chemical Toilet Association (EA)
CTA .... Chicago Transit Authority
CTA .... Children's Theatre Association of America [Formerly, CTC] (EA)
CTA .... Children's Transplant Association (EA)
CTA .... Chromotropic Acid (MAE)
CTA .... Cinema Theatre Association [British]
CTA .... Circuit Terminating Arrangement
CTA .... Citraconic Anhydride [Organic chemistry]
CTA .... Classic Thunderbird Association (EA)
CTA .... Clear to Auscultation [Medicine] (DAVI)
CTA1 .... College of Technology and Art (AIE)
CTA .... Collision Threat Assessment
CTA .... Combined Target Area
CTA .... Commercial Trailer Association [British]
CTA .... Committee on Thrombolytic Agents
CTA .... Commodity Trading Advisor
CTA .... Common Table of Allowances [Army] (AABC)
CTA .... Communiquer a Toutes Adresses [To Be Circulated to All Addresses] [Telecommunications French]
CTA .... Compagnie de Transport Aerien [Switzerland ICAO designator] (FAAC)
CTA .... Compagnie de Transports Aeriens [Airline] [Switzerland]
CTA .... Companion Trainer Aircraft
CTA .... Compatibility Test Area [NASA] (KSC)
CTA .... Component Test Area
CTA .... Computational Transonic Aerodynamics (MCD)
CTA .... Computer and Telecommunications Acronyms [A publication]
CTA .... Computerized Tomoangiography [Radiology] (DAVI)
CTA .... Computerized Travel Aid [Mobility device for the blind]
CTA .... Computer Technology Associates [Goddard Spaceflight Center - Greenbelt, MD] [NASA] (NASA)
CTA .... Computer Traders Association [British] (NITA)
CTA .... Consolidated Tape Association (EA)
CTA .... Continental Transportation Association [Defunct] (EA)
CTA .... Contractor Technical Assistance (MCD)
CTA .... Control Area [ICAO International Civil Aviation Organization=>> Term] (GAVI)
CTA .... Controlled Airspace (IAA)
CTA .... Controlled Thrust Assembly (NASA)
CTA .... Controlled-Time of Arrival (GAVI)
CTA .... Controlled Time of Arrival [FAA] (TAG)

CTA	Control Technology and Application Training Series (ACII)
CTA	Conurbation Transport Authority
CTA	Copper Trade Association
CTA	Corporate Tax Association [Australia]
CTA	Corpus des Tablettes en Cuneiformes Alphabetiques Decouvertes a Ras Shamra-Ugarit de 1929 a 1939 (BJA)
CTA	Council for Technological Advancement (EA)
CTA	Counter-Target-Acquisition (MCD)
CTA	Covered Threads Association [Defunct] (EA)
CTA	Cum Testamento Annexo [With the Will Annexed] [Latin]
CTA	Customer Technical Assistance
CTA	Customs Tariff Act [Canada]
CTA	Cyanoacrylate Tissue Adhesive [Medicine]
CTA	Cyanotrimethyl-Androsterone [Endocrinology] (DAVI)
CTA	Cyproterone Acetate [Endocrinology] (MAE)
CTA	Cystine Trypticase Agar [Microbiology]
CTA	Cytotoxic Assay (MAE)
CTA1	Cryptologic Technician, Administrative, First Class [Navy rating] (DNAB)
CTA2	Cryptologic Technician, Administrative, Second Class [Navy rating] (DNAB)
CTA3	Cryptologic Technician, Administrative, Third Class [Navy rating] (DNAB)
CTAA	Canadian Technical Asphalt Association (EAIO)
CTAA	Children's Theatre Association of America [Formerly, CTC] (EA)
CTAA	Community Transportation Association of America [ENO] (TAG)
CTAA	Corporate Tax Association of Australia
CTAA	Corporate Transfer Agents Association [New York, NY] (EA)
CTAB	Cetyltrimethylammonium Bromide [Also, CETAB, CTBM] [Antiseptic]
CTAB	Commerce Technical Advisory Board [Terminated, 1981] [Department of Commerce] (EGAO)
CTAB	Cross Tabulation of Frequencies
CTABC	Cardiology Technologists' Association of British Columbia (AC)
CTAC	Cable Television Technical Advisory Committee [FCC] (NTCM)
CTAC	Cancer Treatment Advisory Committee [HEW] (EGAO)
CTAC	Carrow Test for Auditory Comprehension [Speech and language pathology] (DAVI)
CTAC	Center for Teaching about China (EA)
CTAC	Creative Tourist Agents' Conference [British] (BI)
CTAC	Cryptologic Technician, Administrative, Chief [Navy rating] (DNAB)
CTAC	Portable Word Processor
CTACl	Cetyltrimethylammonium Chloride [Organic chemistry]
CTACM	Cryptologic Technician, Administrative, Master Chief [Navy rating] (DNAB)
CTACN	Cetyltrimethylammonium Cyanide [Organic chemistry]
CTACS	Cryptologic Technician, Administrative, Senior Chief [Navy rating] (DNAB)
CTAD	Cambridge Training and Development [British] (AIE)
CTA-DLP	Call to Australia - Democratic Labor Party Coalition [Political party]
CTAF	Committee to Abolish the Fed (EA)
CTAF	Common Traffic Advisory Frequency [FAA] (TAG)
CTAF	Common Traffic Advisory Frequency (FAAC)
CTAF	Crew Training Air Force
CTaf	Taft College, Taft, CA [Library symbol Library of Congress] (LCLS)
CTAG	Cultural Tourism Advisory Group [Australia]
CTAH	Center for Tropical Animal Health [Texas A & M University] [Research center] (RCD)
CTAK	Cipher Text Auto Key [Computer science]
CTAL	Catalytica, Inc. [NASDAQ symbol] (SAG)
CTAL	Crystal
CTAM	Cable Television Administration and Marketing Society (EA)
CTAM	Climb to and Maintain [Aviation] (FAAC)
CTAM	Continental Tropical Air Mass (MSA)
CTAN	CINCPAC [Commander-in-Chief, Pacific] Teletype Automated Net (NVT)
CT & DB	Cough, Turn, and Deep Breathe [Medicine]
CT & DDS	Central Timing and Data Distribution System (SAA)
C TANT	Cum Tanto [With the Same Amount Of] [Pharmacy]
CTAO	Charters Towers [Australia Seismograph station code, US Geological Survey] (SEIS)
CTAP	Circuit Transient Analysis Program (IAA)
CTAP	Connective Tissue Activating Peptide [Medicine] (DMAA)
CTAP	Contact Approach [Aviation] (IAA)
CTAPCJS	Commodore Thomas ap Catesby Jones Society [Defunct] (EA)
C-TAPE	Committee for Thorough Agricultural Political Education [Associated Milk Producers, Inc.]
Ct App CC	Texas Civil Cases [A publication] (DLA)
Ct App CC	Texas Court of Appeals Reports [A publication] (DLA)
Ct App NZ	Court of Appeals Reports [New Zealand] [A publication] (DLA)
Ct Apps	Texas Court of Appeals Reports [A publication] (DLA)
CTAPS	Contingency TAC Automated Planning System (MCD)
CTAQ	Commercial Travellers' Association of Queensland [Australia]
CTAQ	Cooperating Teachers' Attitude Questionnaire
CTarA	American Astronomical Society, Tarzana, CA [Library symbol Library of Congress] (LCLS)
CTarB	Edgar Rice Burroughs, Inc., Tarzana, CA [Library symbol Library of Congress] (LCLS)
CTARC	Chemical Testing and Assessment Research Commission (GNE)
CTAS	Center Tracon Automation System [FAA] (PS)
CTAS	Centralized Transient Accounting System (MCD)
CTAS	Cintas Corp. [NASDAQ symbol] (NQ)
CTAS	Cobalt Thiocyanate Active Substance [Organic analysis]
CTAS	Commonwealth Trans-Antarctic Expedition [1955-58]
CTAS	Constant Temperature Anemometer System
CTAS	Controlled Airspace [ICAO designator] (FAAC)

CTASA	Christian Television Association of South Australia
CTASC	Corps/Theater Automatic Data Processing Service Center [Military]
CT(ASCP)	Cytotechnologist (American Society of Clinical Pathologists) (DAVI)
CTAT	Cetyl Trimethylammonium Tosylate [Organic chemistry]
CTAT	Colloque sur le Traitement Automatique des Textes [Colloquium on the Computer Processing of Textual Data - CCPTD]
CTAT	Computerized Transaxial Tomography
CTAT	Conseil du Travails de l'Abitibi-Temiscaminque (AC)
CTAT	Contractor Turnaround Time
CTAU	Catholic Total Abstinence Union
CTAUA	Catholic Total Abstinence Union of America (EA)
CTAV	Cold-Temperature-Actuated Vacuum [Automotive engineering]
CTAWA	Commercial Travellers' Association of Western Australia
CTAX	Climb to and Cross [Aviation] (FAAC)
C Tax C	Canadian Tax Cases [A publication] (DLA)
CTaylor	Cole Taylor Financial Group, Inc. [Associated Press] (SAG)
CtB	Bridgeport Public Library, Bridgeport, CT [Library symbol Library of Congress] (LCLS)
CTB	Calibration Test Box
CTB	California Test Bureau [McGraw Hill, Inc.] [Psychology]
C/TB	Cargo/Tanker Branch (DNAB)
CTB	Ceased to Breathe [Medicine]
CTB	Cement-Treated Base
CTB	Central Tracing Bureau [Post-World War II]
CTB	Ceramic-Tile Base [Technical drawings]
CTB	Ceylon Tourist Board (EAIO)
CTB	Chief of Tariff Bureau
CTB	Cholera Toxin B [Medicine]
CTB	Classification Test Battery [Aptitude and skills test]
CTB	Coast Torpedo Boat [Navy symbol Obsolete]
CTB	Code Table Buffer
CTB	Coffee Table Book [Large, extensively illustrated book designed for display and browsing]
CTB	Collateral Trust Bond [Investment term]
CTB	Combined Travel Board [Allied German Occupation Forces]
CTB	Command Telemetry Buoy
CTB	Commercial Text-Books [A publication]
CTB	Commercial Traffic Bulletin
CTB	Commonwealth Telecommunications Board [Later, CTO] [British]
CTB	Companies and Their Brands [Formerly, TND:CI] [A publication]
CTB	Comprehensive Test Ban [Nuclear weapons]
CTB	Computer Time Bookers
CTB	Concentrator Terminal Buffer [Computer science] (IBMDP)
CTB	Constant Tension Band [Mechanical clamping device]
CTB	Consulting Traffic Bureau
CTB	Controlled Temperature Bath
CTB	Control Test Bed
CTB	Cooper Tire & Rubber [NYSE symbol] (TTSB)
CTB	Cooper Tire & Rubber Co. [NYSE symbol] (SPSG)
CTB	Curacao Tourist Board (EA)
CTB	Cut Bank, MT [Location identifier FAA] (FAAL)
CTBA	Canada-Taiwan Business Association (AC)
CTBA	Cetrimonium Bromide [Organic chemistry] (DAVI)
CTBA	Commonwealth Trading Bank of Australia
CTBF	Cinema and Television Benevolent Fund [British]
CtBFAST	Fannie Smith School, Bridgeport, CT [Library symbol Library of Congress] (LCLS)
CTBI	Community Trust Bancorp, Inc. [NASDAQ symbol] (SAG)
CTBK	Center Banks [NASDAQ symbol] (SAG)
CTBL	Calyx Tube Length [Botany]
CTBL	Cloud-Topped Boundary Layer [Meterology]
CtBl	Prosser Public Library, Bloomfield, CT [Library symbol Library of Congress] (LCLS)
CtBIE	Emhart Manufacturing Co. [Later, Emhart Corp.], Bloomfield, CT [Library symbol Library of Congress] (LCLS)
CtBIST	Saint Thomas Seminary, Bloomfield, CT [Library symbol Library of Congress] (LCLS)
CTBM	Cetyltrimethylammonium Bromide [Also, CETAB, CTAB] [Antiseptic] (AAMN)
CTBM	Chief Testboard Man [Telecommunications] (TEL)
CtBN	Bridgeport City Normal School, Bridgeport, CT [Library symbol Library of Congress Obsolete] (LCLS)
CTBN	Carboxyl-Terminated Butadiene-Acrylonitrile [Organic chemistry]
CTBP	Cytotactin-Binding Proteoglycan
Ct-BPH	Regional Library for the Blind and Physically Handicapped, Hartford, CT [Library symbol Library of Congress] (LCLS)
CTBR	Commonwealth Taxation Board of Review [Australia]
CtBrJ	James Blackstone Memorial Library, Branford, CT [Library symbol Library of Congress] (LCLS)
CTBS	California Test of Basic Skills [Education]
CTBS	Canadian Test of Basic Skills [Education]
CTBS	Comprehensive Tests of Basic Skills [Education]
CTBSH	Cenomanian Turonian Black Shale Horizon [Nuclear energy] (NUCP)
CtBSH	Sacred Heart University, Bridgeport, CT [Library symbol Library of Congress] (LCLS)
CTBT	Comprehensive Test Ban Treaty
CtBU	University of Bridgeport, Bridgeport, CT [Library symbol Library of Congress] (LCLS)
CTBUH	Council on Tall Buildings and Urban Habitat (EA)
CTC	Cab Trade Council [A union] [British]
CTC	Camera, Timing, and Control (NASA)
CTC	Cam Timing Contact
CTC	Canada Tax Cases [A publication] (DLA)
CTC	Canadian Test Centre Inc. (AC)
CTC	Canadian Theological College

CTC............	Canadian Transport Commission
CTC............	Canister Treatment Cell [*Nuclear energy*] (NUCP)
CTC............	Cape Town Cavalry [*British military*] (DMA)
CTC............	Capsule Test Conductor [*NASA*] (KSC)
CTC............	Captain Consolidated Resources [*Vancouver Stock Exchange symbol*]
CTC............	Carbon Tetrachloride [*Also, CT*] [*Organic chemistry*]
CTC............	Card-to-Tape Converter [*Computer science*] (IAA)
CTC............	Career Technologies Corp. [*Database producer*] (IID)
CTC............	Cargo Tank Center (DS)
CTC............	Cassette Tape Controller (IAA)
CTC............	Catamarca [*Argentina*] [*Airport symbol*] (OAG)
CTC............	Catholic Teachers College [*Rhode Island*]
CTC............	CCATS [*Communications, Command, and Telemetry Systems*] Telemetry Controller [*NASA*]
CTC............	Center for Trace Characterization [*Texas A & M University*] [*Research center*] (RCD)
CTC............	Center on Transnational Corporations [*United Nations*]
CTC............	Centralized Traffic Control [*TRB*] (TAG)
CTC............	Centralized Train Central (GAVI)
CTC............	Central Tracking Center (IAA)
CTC............	Central Traffic Control
CTC............	Central Train Control (IAA)
CTC............	Central Training Council [*Department of Employment*] [*British*]
CTC............	Central Trust of China
CTC............	Certified Travel Counselor [*Institute of Certified Travel Agents*] [*Designation awarded by*]
CTC............	Channel-to-Channel (MCD)
CTC............	Channel Traffic Control (IAA)
CTC............	Chargeable Time Clock [*Telecommunications*] (NITA)
CTC............	Charleston Training Center [*South Carolina*]
CTC............	Chetwynd [*British Columbia*] [*Seismograph station code, US Geological Survey Closed*] (SEIS)
CTC............	Chicago Teachers College [*Later, Chicago State University*]
CTC............	Chicago Technical College
CTC............	Chicano Training Center (EA)
CTC............	Chief Test Conductor (NASA)
CTC............	Chief Turret Captain [*Obsolete Navy*]
CTC............	Children's Theatre Conference (EA)
CTC............	Chlortetracycline [*Antibiotic*]
CTC............	Circuit Trial Counsel
CTC............	Citizens' Training Corps
CTC............	City Technology Colleges [*British*]
CTC............	Civilian Technology Corporation (AAGC)
CTC............	Cleveland Trust Co.
CTC............	Climate Test Chamber
CTC............	Clinical Trial Certificate [*Medicine*] (DMAA)
CTC............	Closed Timelike Curve [*Time travel*]
CTC............	Coaxial Thermal Converter (IAA)
CTC............	Cold Type Composition [*Selection of Printing Industries of America*]
CTC............	Combat Training Center [*Army*] (INF)
CTC............	Combined Training Center
CTC............	Commanders' Target Criteria [*Army*] (ADDR)
CTC............	Commando Training Centre [*British*]
CTC............	Commissariat and Transport Corps [*British military*] (DMA)
CTC............	Commission on Transnational Corporations [*United Nations*]
CTC............	Communications Technician, Chief [*Navy rating*]
CTC............	Communication Training Consultants, Inc. [*New York, NY*] [*Telecommunications*] (TSSD)
CTC............	Community Transportation Coordinator [*MOCD*] (TAG)
CTC............	Compact Transpiration Cooling
CTC............	Compania de Telecom Chile ADS [*NYSE symbol*] (TTSB)
CTC............	Compania de Telecomunicaciones de Chile SA [*NYSE symbol*] (SAG)
CTC............	Compania de Telefonos de Chile SA [*NYSE symbol*] (SAG)
CTC............	Compania de Telefonos de Chile SA [*Santiago*] [*Telecommunications service*]
CTC............	Compaq Telecommunications Corp. [*Dallas, TX*]
CTC............	Compatibility Test Capsule
CTC............	Computer Technology Center
CTC............	Concept to Customer
CTC............	Concordia Teachers College [*Illinois, Nebraska*]
CTC............	Conditional Transfer of Control
CTC............	Congres du Travail du Canada [*Canadian Labour Congress - CLC*]
CTC............	Congressional Textile Caucus (EA)
CTC............	Constant Temperature Circulator [*Instrumentation*]
CTC............	Constant Torque Compensation
CTC............	Contact
CTC............	Continuity Test Current
CTC............	Continuous Thymus-Cell [*Cell line*]
CTC............	Contract Target Cost (MCD)
CTC............	Contract Task Charge (DNAB)
CTC............	Contract Technical Compliance (MUGU)
CTC............	Contract Termination and Completion (MCD)
CTC............	Control and Traffic Center
CTC............	Corn Trade Clauses [*Shipping*]
CTC............	Counter/Timer Circuit [*Computer science*]
CTC............	Counter-Timer Control
CTC............	Critical Trauma Care [*Medicine*] (BARN)
CTC............	Cross-Track Contiguous
CTC............	Crush, Tear, Curl [*Tea processing*]
CTC............	CTC Air, SA [*Spain*] [*FAA designator*] (FAAC)
CTC............	Customs Transaction Code (DS)
CTC............	Cut, Tear, and Curl [*Tea*]
CTC............	Cyclists' Touring Club

CTC............	Manual Communications Unit
CTC............	Treasury Department, Comptroller of the Currency, Washington, DC [*OCLC symbol*] (OCLC)
CTCA.........	Cairn Terrier Club of America (EA)
CTCA.........	Canadian Telecommunications Carriers Association
CTCA.........	Canadian Telecommunications Consultants Association (AC)
CTCA.........	Canadian Theatre Critics Association [*Association des Critiques de Theatre du Canada*]
CTCA.........	Canadian Theatre Critics Association [*Canada*] (WWLA)
CTCA.........	Channel and Traffic Control Agency [*of AACS*]
CTCA.........	Channel to Channel Adapter [*Computer science*] (IBMDP)
CTCA.........	Commission for Technical Cooperation in Africa
CTCA.........	Corpus des Tablettes en Cuneiformes Alphabetiques Decouvertes a Ras Shamra-Ugarit de 1929 a 1939 (BJA)
CTCC.........	Central Transport Consultative Committee [*British*]
CTCC.........	Confederation des Travailleurs Catholiques du Canada [*Catholic Federation of Labour, 1922-1960*]
CTCC.........	Contact Center Control (FAAC)
CTCC.........	Continental Division, Transport Control Center [*Military*]
CTCCC........	Canadian Tire Coupon Collectors Club [*Club de Collectionneurs de Coupons Canadian Tire*] (AC)
CTCCC........	Close Type Control Circuit Contact (MSA)
CTCEEH.......	Chronology of Twentieth-Century Eastern European History [*A publication*]
CTCEN........	Contact Center (FAAC)
CTCF.........	Channel and Technical Control Facility [*In a tape-relay station in the AIRCOMNET*]
CTcHi.........	North Lake Tahoe Historical Society, Tahoe City, CA [*Library symbol*] [*Library of Congress*] (LCLS)
CTCI.........	China Technical Consultants, Inc.
CTCI.........	Classic Thunderbird Club International (EA)
CTCI.........	Classification Type pour le Commerce International [*Standard International Trade Classification*] [*French*]
CTCIA........	Contract Technical Compliance Inspection
CTCIA........	Ceramic Tile Contractors & Industry Association of British Columbia (AC)
CTCL.........	Characters in Twentieth-Century Literature [*A publication*]
CTCL.........	Community and Technical College Libraries
CTCL.........	Count Clock [*NASA*] (KSC)
Ct Cl	Court of Claims [*Renamed CAFC in 1992*] (AAGC)
CTCL.........	Cutaneous T-Cell Lymphoma [*Medicine*]
Ct Cl	Official Reports of the Court of Claims [*GPO*] (AAGC)
Ct Cl	United States Court of Claims Reports [*A publication*] (DLA)
Ct Cl Act.....	Court of Claims Act (DLA)
Ct Cl NY	Court of Claims Reports [*New York*] [*A publication*] (DLA)
CTCLR	Cape Times Common Law Reports [*South Africa*] [*A publication*] (DLA)
Ct Cl R........	Court of Claims Rules [*A publication*] (DLA)
CTCLS........	Court of Claims
Ct Cls.........	United States Court of Claims (DLA)
Ct Cl TJ Op...	Court of Claims Trial Judge Opinion (AAGC)
Ct Cl Trial Div...	Court of Claims Trial Division [*Defunct*] (AAGC)
CTCM.........	Chroma Time Compressed Multiplex (NTCM)
CTCM.........	Communications Technician, Master Chief [*Navy rating*]
CTCM.........	Computer Timing and Costing Model (MHDB)
CTCM and H...	Certificate in Tropical Community Medicine and Health [*British*] (DI)
CTCNC........	Christian Temperance Council for the Nordic Countries (EA)
CTCO	Check Technology [*NASDAQ symbol*] (TTSB)
ctCO$_2$	Concentration of Total Carbon Dioxide [*Medicine*] (DAVI)
Ct Com Pl	Court of Common Pleas (DLA)
CTCOR........	Chrysler Town and Country Owners Registry (EA)
CTCOTP	Cold Temperature Carbon Monoxide Test Procedure [*Exhaust emissions testing*] [*Automotive engineering*]
CTCP..........	Combat Theater Communications Program [*Air Force*] (MCD)
CTCP..........	Combat Trains Command Post [*Army*] (INF)
CTCP..........	Contract Task Change Proposal (AAG)
CTCQ	Check Technology Corp. [*NASDAQ symbol*] (NQ)
CTCR	Chrysler Town and Country Owners Registry (EA)
CTCRI	Central Tuber Crops Research Institute
CTCRM	Commando Training Centre, Royal Marines [*British military*] (DMA)
CTCS.........	Cabin/Cockpit Temperature Control Systems [*Aviation*]
CTCS.........	Communications Technician, Senior Chief [*Navy rating*]
CTCS.........	Consolidated Telecommunications Center System (MCD)
CTCS.........	Consolidated Telemetry Checkout System [*Air Force*]
CTCSS	Code Tone Call Selective Signalling [*Telecommunications*] (PDAA)
CTCSS	Continuous Tone-Coded Squelch System [*Telecommunications*] (PDAA)
CTC/TES......	Combat Training Centers / Tactical Engagement Simulation
CTCU	Canadian Textile and Chemical Union
CTCU	Channel and Traffic Control Unit [*Subordinate unit of the Channel and Traffic Control Agency*]
Ct Cust & Pat App...	Court of Customs and Patent Appeals (DLA)
Ct Cust App...	Court of Customs Appeals (DLA)
Ct Cust App...	Court of Customs Appeals Reports [*1919-29*] [*A publication*] (DLA)
CTCZ.........	Carrier Tactical Control Zone [*Military*] (NVT)
CTD............	Carboxyl-Terminal Domain [*Genetics*]
CTD............	Carpal Tunnel Decompression [*Medicine*]
C/T/d.........	Carrier-to-Noise Temperature, Downlink
CTD............	Catalogue des Theses de Doctorat [*A bibliographic publication*] [*France*]
CTD............	Celestial Training Device (MCD)
CTD............	Central Target Director [*Military*] (CAAL)
CTD............	Centre for Telecommunications Development [*ITU*] [*United Nations*] (DUND)
CTD............	Certificate of Tax Deposit [*British*]

CTD............	Certified Test Data
CTD............	Change Transfer Device (MCD)
CTD............	Charged Tape Detection [*Fuel-failure monitor*] [*Nuclear energy*] (NRCH)
CTD............	Charge-Transfer Device [*Electronics*]
CTD............	Chemical Transport and Deposition (MCD)
CTD............	Chest Tube Drainage [*Medicine*] (DAVI)
CTD............	Circulation Time Distribution [*Chemical engineering*]
CTD............	Clutter Threshold Detector (CET)
CTD............	Coated (KSC)
CTD............	Coated
CTD............	College Training Detachment
CTD............	Combined Transport Document [*Shipping*]
CTD............	Commander, Transportation Division
CTD............	Commercial Training Device
CTD............	Communications Trade Division (EA)
CTD............	Communicative Technology Directorate [*Army Training Support Center*] [*Fort Eustis, VA*]
CTD............	Community Training and Development [*An association*] (EA)
CTD............	Completion Tour of Duty
CTD............	Conductivity, Temperature, and Depth [*Oceanography*]
CTD............	Conductivity-Temperature-Depth Probe [*Marine science*] (OSRA)
CTD............	Conductivity-Temperature-Depth Profiler [*Marine science*] (OSRA)
CTD............	Congenital Thymic Dysplasia [*Medicine*] (MAE)
CTD............	Connective-Tissue Disease [*Medicine*]
CTD............	Continuity Tone Detector [*Telecommunications*] (TEL)
CTD............	Control Data Corp. [*Toronto Stock Exchange symbol*]
CTD............	Controlled Thermolytic Dissociation
CTD............	Control Technology Document [*Environmental Protection Agency*] (GFGA)
CTD............	Convalescent Training Depot (NATG)
CTD............	Corporate Technology Database [*Corporate Technology Information Services, Inc.*] (CRD)
CTD............	Corrective Therapy Department [*Medical rehabilitation*] (DAVI)
CTD............	Council for Television Development [*Defunct*]
Ct D	Court Decisions, National Labor Relations Act [*A publication*] (DLA)
CTD............	Crew Task Demand
CTD............	Crew Task Detail
CTD............	Cross-Track Distance [*Aerospace*]
CTD............	Cumulative Trauma Disorder [*Medicine*]
CTD............	Current, Temperature, Density
CtD............	Darien Library, Darien, CT [*Library symbol Library of Congress*] (LCLS)
CTD............	Western Connecticut State College, Haas Library, Danbury, CT [*OCLC symbol*] (OCLC)
CTDA	Ceramic Tile Distributors Association (EA)
CTDA	Critical Turning Distance Add (SAA)
CTDA	Custom Tailors and Designers Association of America (EA)
CtDab..........	Danbury Public Library, Danbury, CT [*Library symbol Library of Congress*] (LCLS)
CtDabN	Western Connecticut State College, Danbury, CT [*Library symbol Library of Congress*] (LCLS)
CTDC	Chemical Thermodynamics Data Center [*National Institute of Standards and Technology*]
CTDC	Company Technical Document Center
CTDC	Control Track Direction Computer (AABC)
CTDC	Copper Technical Data Centre [*Australia*]
CTDCS	Common Test Data Collection System (MCD)
CtDe...........	Derby Public Library, Derby, CT [*Library symbol Library of Congress*] (LCLS)
Ct Dec NLRA...	Court Decisions, National Labor Relations Act [*A publication*] (DLA)
CTDEP	Connecticut Department of Environmental Protection (DOGT)
CTDEP	Connecticut Department of Environmental Protection
CTDF...........	Community Telecommunications Development Foundation [*Washington, DC*] (TSSD)
CTDF...........	Contract Technical Data File (AAGC)
CTDH	Command and Telemetry Data Handling (IEEE)
CTDMIS	Combat and Training Development Management Information System
CTDMPLUS...	Improved Complex Terrain Dispersion Model (USDC)
CTDN	Countdown [*NASA*] (KSC)
ctDNA	Deoxyribonucleic Acid, Chloroplast [*Biochemistry, genetics*] [*Also, Chl-DNA, cpDNA*]
CTDO	Central Technical Doctrine Officer (DNAB)
CTDO	Central Technical Documents Office [*Naval Ordnance Systems Command*] [*Information service or system*] (IID)
CTDR	Commercial Training Device Requirement
CTDS	Canadian Transportation Documentation System [*Database*] [*Transport Canada Library and Information Center*] [*Information service or system*] (CRD)
CTDS	Code Translation Data System [*Air Force*]
CTDS	Consolidated Test Data System [*Military*]
C/TDS	Count/Time Data System (IEEE)
CTDT...........	Conductivity Temperature Depth Transmissometer [*Oceanography*]
CTDV	Cereal Tillering Disease Virus [*Plant pathology*]
CTE............	Air Tenglong [*China*] [*ICAO designator*] (FAAC)
CTE............	Cable Termination Equipment (CET)
CTE............	Calf Thymus Extract [*Medicine*] (DMAA)
CTE............	Canton and Enderbury Islands [*ANSI three-letter standard code*] (CNC)
CTE............	Cardiotech International, Inc. [*AMEX symbol*] (SAG)
CTE............	Carti [*Panama*] [*Airport locator*] (OAG)
CTE............	Cartier Resources, Inc. [*Toronto Stock Exchange symbol*]
CTE............	Car-Tours in Europe, Inc.
CTE............	Center for Teaching Effectiveness [*University of Texas at Austin*] [*Research center*] (RCD)

CTE............	Central Telegraph Exchange [*British*]
CTE............	Central Timing Equipment
CTE............	Central Translation Evidence
CTE............	Certificati del Tesoro in Euroscudi [*Italy*] (ECON)
CTE............	Channel Translating Equipment [*Telecommunications*] (TEL)
CTE............	Charge Transfer Efficiency [*In photodetectors*]
CTE............	Coefficient of Thermal Expansion
CTE............	Commander, Task Element
CTE............	Commercial Test Equipment (MCD)
CTE............	Committee on Trade & the Environment [*World Trade Organization*]
CTE............	Component Test Equipment (KSC)
CTE............	Compte [*Account*] [*French Business term*] (ROG)
CTE............	Computer TELEX Exchange [*RCA Corp.*]
CTE............	Conditioning Thio Emulsion [*Roux Laboratories, Inc.*]
CTE............	Constitutive Transport Element [*Biochemistry*]
CTE............	Contractor Technical Evaluation (CAAL)
CTE............	Contractor Test and Evaluation (MCD)
CTE............	Contractor Training Equipment (SAA)
CTE............	Cross-Track Error
CTE............	Cultured Thymic Epithelium [*Immunochemistry*]
CTE............	Customer's Terminal Equipment [*Telecommunications British*]
CTEA	Canadian Telephone Employees' Association [*See also ACET*]
CTEA	Canadian Transportation Equipment Association
CTEA	Celestial Seasonings [*NASDAQ symbol*] (TTSB)
CTEA	Celestial Seasonings, Inc. [*NASDAQ symbol*] (SAG)
CTEA	Channel Transmission and Engineering Activation
CTEA	Cost and Training Effectiveness Analysis
CTEA	Council for Technology Education Associations (EA)
CtEahav	Hagaman Memorial Library, East Haven, CT [*Library symbol Library of Congress*] (LCLS)
CTEB	Council of Technical Examining Bodies [*British*]
CTEC	Cholestech Corp. [*NASDAQ symbol*] (SAG)
CTEC	Combined Transportation Equipment Committee [*Combined Production and Resources Board*] [*World War II*]
CTEC	Communication Technical Evaluation Console (KSC)
CTEC	CTEC Corp. [*Associated Press*] (SAG)
CTED	Civilian Training, Education, and Development (MCD)
CTEE	Committee
CtEh	East Hartford Public Library, East Hartford, CT [*Library symbol Library of Congress*] (LCLS)
CtEhad	Rathbun Memorial Library, East Haddam, CT [*Library symbol Library of Congress*] (LCLS)
CtEham	East Hampton Public Library, East Hampton, CT [*Library symbol*] [*Library of Congress*] (LCLS)
CtEhUA	United Aircraft Corp., East Hartford, CT [*Library symbol Library of Congress*] (LCLS)
CTEI............	Contract Trainer End Item (SAA)
CTEK	Compositech Ltd. [*NASDAQ symbol*] (SAG)
CTEM	Complex Targets Evaluation Model (MCD)
CTEM	Conventional-Transmission Electron Microscope
CTEM	Cryogenic Transmission Electron Microscopy
CTEN	Counter Tenor [*Music*]
CtEnA	Asnuntuck Community College, Learning Resources Center, Enfield, CT [*Library symbol Library of Congress*] (LCLS)
CTEOC	Caterpillar Truck Engine Owners Club
CTEP	Cancer Therapy Evaluation Program [*Bethesda, MD*] [*National Cancer Institute*] [*Department of Health and Human Services*] (GRD)
CTEP	Centre for Transport Engineering Practice [*Loughborough University of Technology*] [*British*] (CB)
CTEP	Coal and Technology Export Program (AAGC)
CT ERR	Court of Error [*Legal term*] (DLA)
Ct Err & App...	Court of Errors and Appeals [*New Jersey*] (DLA)
Ct Errors and App...	Court of Errors and Appeals [*New Jersey*] (DLA)
CTES	Cool Thermal Energy Storage [*Air-conditioning*] (PS)
CTES	Council for Tertiary Education in Scotland (AIE)
CTETF	Cargo Technical Evaluation Task Force [*IATA*] (DS)
CTETOC.......	Council for Technical Education and Training for Overseas Countries (BARN)
CTEX	C-TEC Corp. [*NASDAQ symbol*] (NQ)
CTEXB	C-TEC Corp.'B' [*NASDAQ symbol*] (TTSB)
CTF............	Canadian Tax Foundation (AC)
CTF............	Canadian Taxpayers Federation (AC)
CTF............	Canadian Teachers Federation
CTF............	Cancer Therapy Facility
CTF............	Career Training Foundation (EA)
CTF............	Cask Tilting Fixture [*Nuclear energy*] (NRCH)
CTF............	Catholic Teachers Federation [*British*] (DBA)
CTF............	Cavity Turnable Filter
CTF............	C-Band Temperature
CTF............	Central Task Force
CTF............	Central Training Facility (MCD)
CTF............	Ceramic-Tile Floor [*Technical drawings*]
CTF............	Ceramic Tube Fabrication
CTF............	Certificate
CTF............	Cetfa SA [*Spain ICAO designator*] (FAAC)
CTF............	Chaplain to the Territorial Forces [*British*]
CTF............	Chesterfield, SC [*Location identifier FAA*] (FAAL)
CTF............	Chlorine Trifluoride [*Inorganic chemistry*]
CTF............	Chlorotrifluroethane [*Organic chemistry*]
CTF............	Clinical Treatment Failure
CTF............	Coffee Trade Federation [*British*] (DBA)
CTF............	Collective Training Facility [*Army*] (INF)
CTF............	Colorado Tick Fever [*Hematology*] (DAVI)
CTF............	Combat Training Facilities [*DoD*]

CTF .... Combined Task Force [*NATO*] (NATG)
CTF .... Combined Test Force [*Military*]
CTF .... Commander, Task Force
CTF .... Common Test Facility
CTF .... Common Transmission Format (MCD)
CTF .... Communications Test Facility [*Fort Huachuca, AZ*] [*United States Army Electronic Proving Ground*] (GRD)
CTF .... Community Task Force [*British*]
CTF .... Congress Task Force (EA)
CTF .... Consolidated Training Facility [*Army*]
CTF .... Contrast Transfer Function [*Video technology*]
CTF .... Controlled Temperature Furnace
CTF .... Controlled Thermonuclear Fusion
CTF .... Core Test Facility
CTF .... Correctional Training Facility [*Army*] (AABC)
CTF .... Correction to Follow
CTF .... Counsellors Tandem [*NYSE symbol*] (SPSG)
CTF .... Counsellors Tandem [*NYSE symbol*] (TTSB)
CTF .... Counsellors Tandem Securities Fund [*Associated Press*] (SAG)
CTF .... Credit Transfer Fee [*Business term*]
CTF .... Crisis Task Force (MCD)
CTF .... Critical Tolerance Factor (MCD)
CTF .... Cytotoxic Factor
CtF .... Farmington Village Library, Farmington, CT [*Library symbol Library of Congress*] (LCLS)
CTFA .... Canada-Taiwan Friendship Association (AC)
CTFA .... Cosmetic, Toiletry, and Fragrance Association (EA)
CtFa .... Fairfield Public Library, Fairfield, CT [*Library symbol Library of Congress*] (LCLS)
CtFaU .... Fairfield University, Fairfield, CT [*Library symbol Library of Congress*] (LCLS)
CTFC .... Central Time and Frequency Control
CTFC .... Central Tractor Farm & Country [*NASDAQ symbol*] (TTSB)
CTFC .... Central Tractor Farm & Country, Inc. [*NASDAQ symbol*] (SAG)
CTFC .... Conway Twitty Fan Club [*Defunct*] (EA)
CTFE .... Chlorotrifluoroethylene [*Organic chemistry*]
CTFG .... Cole Taylor Financial Group, Inc. [*NASDAQ symbol*] (SAG)
CTFG .... Cole Taylor Financial Grp [*NASDAQ symbol*] (TTSB)
CTFG .... Counterfeiting [*FBI standardized term*]
CTFJC .... Centre Terry Fox de la Jeunesse Canadienne [*Terry Fox Canadian Youth Centre*]
CTFM .... Continuous-Transmission Frequency-Modulated [*SONAR*]
CTFO .... Controlled Tuning Fork Oscillator
CTFO .... Council for a Tobacco-Free Ontario (AC)
CtFP .... Miss Porter's School, Farmington, CT [*Library symbol*] [*Library of Congress*] (LCLS)
CTFPHE .... Canadian Task Force on the Periodic Health Examination
CTFR .... Lawson's Classroom Test of Formal Reasoning (EDAC)
CTFSH .... Catfish
CTFT .... Contemporary Theatre, Film, and Television [*A publication*]
CTFT .... Counterfeit [*FBI standardized term*]
CTG .... Canadian Coast Guard [*ICAO designator*] (FAAC)
CTG .... Cardiotocography [*Gynecology*]
CTG .... Cartage
CTG .... Cartagena [*Colombia*] [*Airport symbol*] (OAG)
ctg .... Cartographer [*MARC relator code*] [*Library of Congress*] (LCCP)
CTG .... Cartridge (AABC)
CTG .... Channel Tunnel Group [*British*]
C/TG .... Cholesterol/Triglyceride Ratio [*Clinical chemistry*] (AAMN)
CTG .... Closing the Gap [*An association*] (PAZ)
CTG .... Coating (MSA)
CTG .... Combined Task Group [*NATO*] (NATG)
CTG .... Commander, Task Group
CTG .... Communications Task Group [*CODASYL*]
CTG .... Computer Task Group (HGAA)
CTG .... Comtech Group International Ltd. [*Toronto Stock Exchange symbol*]
CTG .... Connecticut Nat Gas [*NYSE symbol*] (TTSB)
CTG .... Connecticut Natural Gas Corp. [*NYSE symbol*] (SPSG)
CTG .... Containing
CTG .... Contributing (ADA)
CTG .... Control Techniques Guidelines [*Environmental Protection Agency*]
CTG .... Copy to Go (NTCM)
CTG .... Corporate Technology Group [*British*]
CTG .... Cotangent [*Mathematics*] (IAA)
CTG .... Cottage
CTG .... Counting (KSC)
CTG .... Crating (MSA)
CTG .... Cutting (MSA)
CTG .... Cyclodextrin Transglycosylase [*An enzyme*]
CTGA .... Complete Transposition of Great Arteries [*Medicine*] (DMAA)
CTGC .... California Table Grape Commission (EA)
CTGE .... Cartage [*Shipping*]
CTGE .... Cottage (ADA)
CTGF .... Clean Tanks, Gas Free (NVT)
CTGF .... Connective-Tissue Growth Factor [*Biochemistry*]
CTGH .... Cotangent, Hyperbolic [*Mathematics*]
CTGH .... Cryptograph (MSA)
CTGI .... Canadian Test of General Information [*Education*] (AEBS)
CtGr .... Groton Public Library, Groton, CT [*Library symbol Library of Congress*] (LCLS)
CtGre .... Greenwich Library, Greenwich, CT [*Library symbol Library of Congress*] (LCLS)
CtGreN .... News Bank, Inc., Greenwich, CT [*Library symbol Library of Congress*] (LCLS)

CtGrN-M ...... United States Navy Submarine Base, Naval Submarine Medical Research Laboratory, Groton, CT [*Library symbol Library of Congress*] (LCLS)
CtGroN-M .... United States Navy Submarine Base, Naval Submarine Medical Research Laboratory, Groton, CT [*Library symbol Library of Congress Obsolete*] (LCLS)
CtGrU .... University of Connecticut, Southeastern Branch, Groton, CT [*Library symbol Library of Congress*] (LCLS)
CTGY .... Category (FAAC)
CTH .... Cancer Treatment Holdings, Inc. [*AMEX symbol*] (SAG)
C Th .... Candidate of Theology
CTh .... Carrier-Specific T-Helper [*Cell*] [*Medicine*] (DMAA)
CTH .... Catalogue des Textes Hittites [*Paris*] (BJA)
CTH .... Catalytic Transfer Hydrogenation
CTH .... Ceramide Trihexosides [*Biochemistry*]
CTH .... China General Aviation Corp. [*ICAO designator*] (FAAC)
cth .... Cloth (VRA)
C Th .... Code of Theodosius [*Roman law*] [*A publication*] (DSA)
CTH .... Committee on Tidal Hydraulics [*Army*]
CTH .... Commonwealth (ADA)
Ct-H .... Connecticut State Department of Health, Hartford, CT [*Library symbol Library of Congress*] (LCLS)
CTH .... Contractions Handbook
CTH .... Corinth Resources Ltd. [*Vancouver Stock Exchange symbol*]
CTH .... Craftech Manufacturing, Inc. [*Toronto Stock Exchange symbol*]
CTH .... Crateus [*Brazil*] [*Airport symbol*] (AD)
CTH .... Cure to Handling
CTH .... Cycle Test Hours
CtH .... Hartford Public Library, Hartford, CT [*Library symbol Library of Congress*] (LCLS)
CTh .... Theodosian Code (BJA)
CTHA .... China Tourist Hotel Association (EAIO)
CTHA .... Colonial Treasure Hunters Association (EA)
CtHa .... Theodore A. Hungerford Memorial Library, Harwinton, CT [*Library symbol Library of Congress*] (LCLS)
CtHamQ .... Quinnipiac College, Hamden, CT [*Library symbol Library of Congress*] (LCLS)
CTHB .... Cruise, Transition, Hover, Bob-Up (MCD)
CtHB .... Hartford Bar Library Association, Hartford, CT [*Library symbol Library of Congress*] (LCLS)
CTHBP .... Citizens for the Treatment of High Blood Pressure (EA)
CTHC .... Certificate in the Teaching of Handicapped Children (ADA)
CtHC .... Hartford Seminary Foundation, Hartford, CT [*Library symbol Library of Congress*] (LCLS)
CTHD .... Chlorthalidone (DMAA)
CTHDL .... Cathedral
CTHEC .... Cancer Treatment Hldgs [*ECM symbol*] (TTSB)
C the K .... Cyrus the King [*Freemasonry*] (ROG)
C Theod .... Codex Theodosianus [*Theodosian Code*] [*438AD*] [*Latin*] [*A publication*] (DLA)
CTHF .... Canadian Team Handball Federation
CtHHC .... Hartford Conservatory, Hartford, CT [*Library symbol Library of Congress*] (LCLS)
CtHHy .... Hillyer College, Hartford, CT [*Library symbol Library of Congress*] (LCLS)
CtHi .... Connecticut Historical Society, Hartford, CT [*Library symbol Library of Congress*] (LCLS)
CtHJH .... Julius Hartt Musical Foundation, Hartford, CT [*Library symbol Library of Congress*] (LCLS)
CtHM .... Hartford Medical Society, Hartford, CT [*Library symbol Library of Congress*] (LCLS)
CtHMTH .... Mark Twain Memorial, Hartford, CT [*Library symbol Library of Congress*] (LCLS)
Ct Ho .... Courthouse
CTHS .... Canadian Thoroughbred Horse Society [*Societe Canadienne du Cheval Thoroughbred*] (AC)
CTHS .... Canadian Trakehner Horse Society (AC)
CTHS .... Comite des Travaux Historiques et Scientifiques [*Ministere de l'Education Nationale*] [*Database*]
cths............ Courthouse (VRA)
CtHSD .... Stowe-Day Memorial Library and Historical Foundation, Hartford, CT [*Library symbol Library of Congress*] (LCLS)
CtHT .... Trinity College, Hartford, CT [*Library symbol Library of Congress*] (LCLS)
CtHT-W .... Trinity College, Watkinson Library, Hartford, CT [*Library symbol Library of Congress*] (LCLS)
CtHU .... University of Connecticut, MBA Library, Hartford, CT [*Library symbol Library of Congress*] (LCLS)
CtHWa .... Wadsworth Atheneum, Hartford, CT [*Library symbol Library of Congress*] (LCLS)
CTI .... Cambridge Technology, Inc.
CTI .... Camera Timing Indicator
CTI .... Canadian Textiles Institute (EAIO)
CTI .... CCD [*Charge-Coupled Device*] Transit Instrument [*Telescope*]
CTI .... Center for Telephone Information [*Laguna Hills, CA*] [*Telecommunications*] (TSSD)
CTI .... Centralized Ticket Investigation [*Telecommunications*]
CTI .... Central Technical Institute [*Netherlands*]
CTI .... Centre de Traitement de l'Information [*Data Processing Center*] [*Ministry of Economic Affairs*] [*Belgium*] [*Information service or system*] (IID)
CTI .... Charge Transfer Inefficiency [*in Photodetectors*] (IAA)
CTI .... Chart Industries [*NYSE symbol*] (SPSG)
CTI .... Cheap Trick International (EA)
CTI .... Citicorp [*Toronto Stock Exchange symbol*]

CTI	Coaxial Transceiver Interface
CTI	Columbus Technical Institute, Columbus, OH [*OCLC symbol*] (OCLC)
CTI	Command Technical Inspection [*Army*] (AABC)
CTI	Communications Technician Intercept [*Navy rating*] (IAA)
CTI	Comparative Tracking Index [*Electronics*] (EECA)
CTI	Competent to Instruct [*British military*] (DMA)
CTI	Complaint Type Investigation [*Army*] (AABC)
CTI	Composition Technology, Inc.
CTI	Computers in Teaching Initiative (AIE)
CTI	Computer Technology Innovations (HGAA)
CTI	Computer Telephony Integration [*Telecommunications*]
CTI	Computer Translation, Inc. [*Information service or system*] (IID)
CTI	Conrad Technologies, Inc.
CTI	Consumable Toroidal Igniter (MCD)
CTI	Consumer Technology Index [*Computer Intelligence InfoCorp*] (PCM)
CTI	Contractor Training Instruction (DNAB)
CTI	Contract Technical Instructor [*Army*] (AABC)
CTI	Contract Termination Inventory [*DoD*]
CTI	Cooling Tower Institute (EA)
CTI	Corporate Travel Index [*A publication*]
CTI	Course Technology, Inc. [*Publishing*]
CTI	Creed Taylor, Inc. [*Recording label*]
CTI	Critical Technologies Institute [*Federally funded research and development center*]
CTI	Critical Transportation Item (MCD)
CTI	Crossroads Technical Instrumentation [*Atomic weapons testing*]
CTI1	Cryptologic Technician, Interpretative, First Class [*Navy rating*] (DNAB)
CTI2	Cryptologic Technician, Interpretative, Second Class [*Navy rating*] (DNAB)
CTI3	Cryptologic Technician, Interpretative, Third Class [*Navy rating*] (DNAB)
CTIA	Cellular Telecommunications Industry Association (EA)
CTIA	Committee to Investigate Assassinations
CTIA	Counter Technical Intelligence Activities (MCD)
CTIAC	Chemical Transportation Industry Advisory Committee
CTIAC	Concrete Technology Information Analysis Center [*Army Corps of Engineers*] [*Vicksburg, MS*] (IID)
CTIAQ	Caravan Trade and Industries Association of Queensland [*Australia*]
CTIB	Commercial Technology and Industrial Base (AAGC)
CTibF	United States National Marine Fisheries Service, Southwest Fisheries Center, Tiburon Laboratory, Tiburon, CA [*Library symbol Library of Congress*] (LCLS)
CTIC	Cable Television Information Center [*Defunct*] (EA)
CTIC	Coal Technology Information Centre [*Alberta Research Council*] [*Information service or system*] (IID)
CTIC	Conservation Tillage Information Center
CTIC	Corporate Technical Information Center (DIT)
CTIC	Cryptologic Technician, Interpretative, Chief [*Navy rating*] (DNAB)
CTICM	Cryptologic Technician, Interpretative, Master Chief [*Navy rating*] (DNAB)
CTICS	Cryptologic Technician, Interpretative, Senior Chief [*Navy rating*] (DNAB)
CTICU	Cardiothoracic Intensive Care Unit
CTIDB	China's Travel Information Database [*Information service or system*] (IID)
CTIDP	Common Technical Interface Design Plan [*Joint technical document developed by the US, UK, and Germany*] [*Military*] (RDA)
CTIF	Centre Technique des Industries de la Fonderie [*Database producer*]
CTIF	Comite Technique International de Prevention et d'Extinction du Feu [*International Technical Committee for the Prevention and Extinction of Fire*] (EAIO)
CTIF	Commercial Travelers Insurance Federation [*Defunct*]
CTII	Cytotherapeutics, Inc. [*NASDAQ symbol*] (SAG)
CTIL	Capsule Technology International Ltd.
C/T/im	Carrier-to-Noise Temperature, Intermodulation
CTIM	Childtime Learning Centers [*NASDAQ symbol*] (TTSB)
CTIM	Childtime Learning Centers, Inc. [*NASDAQ symbol*] (SAG)
CTIM	Cooked Therapeutic Inflight Meal (DNAB)
CTINB	Corporation des Traducteurs, Traductrices, Terminologues et Interpretes du Nouveau-Brunswick [*Corporation of Translators, Terminologists & Interpreters of New Brunswick*] (AC)
CTIO	Cerro-Tololo Inter-American Observatory [*Chile*] [*National Science Foundation*]
CTIO	Cerro Tololo Interamerican Observatory [*Astronomy*]
CTIOA	Ceramic Tile Institute of America (EA)
CTIP	Committee for Truth in Psychiatry (EA)
CTIP	Coordinated Federal Lands Highways Technial Information Program [*MTMC*] (TAG)
CTIP	Coupled Chermosphere-Ionosphere-Plasmasphere [*Model*] (USDC)
CTIPS	Comprehensive Transportation Information & Planning System [*MTMC*] (TAG)
CTIR	Center for Teaching International Relations
CTIS	Carrier Terminal Information Services (DNAB)
CTIS	Central Tire Inflation System [*Automotive engineering*]
CTIS	Combat Terrain Information System [*Military*]
CTIS	Crawler/Transporter Intercom System [*Aerospace*] (KSC)
CTISS	Computers in Teaching Initiative Support Service (AIE)
CTIU	Cardiac/Thoracic Intensive Care Unit [*Medicine*] (DAVI)
CTIX	Canadian Trade Index [*Canada Systems Group*] [*Information service or system*]
CTIX	Conversion Tech Intl. [*NASDAQ symbol*] (TTSB)
CTIX	Conversion Technologies International, Inc. [*NASDAQ symbol*] (SAG)
CTIXW	Conversion Tech Intl.Wrrt'A' [*NASDAQ symbol*] (TTSB)
CTIXZ	Conversion Tech Intl.Wrrt'B' [*NASDAQ symbol*] (TTSB)

CTJ	Canadian Trace Minerals Ltd. [*Vancouver Stock Exchange symbol*]
CTJ	Carrollton, GA [*Location identifier FAA*] (FAAL)
CTJ	Citizens for Tax Justice (EA)
CTJC	Centralia Township Junior College [*Illinois*]
CTJTF	Counterterrorist Joint Task Force [*Military*]
Ct Just	Court of Justiciary (DLA)
CTK	Canton, IL [*Location identifier FAA*] (FAAL)
CTK	Cases Tempore King, Chancery [*A publication*] (DLA)
CTK	Ceskoslovenska Tiskova Kancelar [*Czechoslovak News Agency*]
CTK	Composite Tool Kit [*Military*] (AFIT)
CTK	Comptek Research, Inc. [*AMEX symbol*] (SPSG)
cTk	[*Tropical*] Continental Cold Air Mass (BARN)
CTK	Copper Stack Resources Ltd. [*Vancouver Stock Exchange symbol*]
CTK	Crimping Tool Kit
CTK	East Midlands Helicopters [*British*] [*FAA designator*] (FAAC)
CTL	CAGE [*Computerized Aerospace Ground Equipment*] Test Language [*Computer science*] (KSC)
CTL	Canadian Talent Library
CTL	Canoga Test Laboratory [*NASA*] (NASA)
CTL	Carrier Tracking Loop
CTL	Cassette Tape Loader
CTL	Cattle
CTL	Cental [*Short hundredweight*] [*British*] (ROG)
CTL	Central (MSA)
CTL	Central Airlines, Inc. [*ICAO designator*] (FAAC)
CTL	Century Tel Enterp [*NYSE symbol*] (TTSB)
CTL	Century Telephone Enterprises, Inc. [*NYSE symbol*] (SPSG)
CTL	Certified Tool List (AAG)
CTL	Charge Transport Layer (MCD)
CTL	Charleville [*Australia Airport symbol*] (OAG)
CTL	Checkout Test Language [*Computer science*]
CTL	Chilworth Technology Ltd. [*British*] (IRUK)
CTL	Coastal Transport Ltd. [*Steamship*] (MHDW)
CTL	Code Transfer Logic
CTL	Combat Training Launch (AFM)
CTL	Communications Test Lab (SSD)
CTL	Compass Test Language
CTL	Compiler Target Language [*Computer science*] (MHDB)
CTL	Complementary Transistor Logic [*Computer science*]
CTL	Component Test Laboratory (KSC)
CTL	Composite Tape Lay-Up [*Engineering*]
CTL	Computer Technology Limited [*British*] (NITA)
CTL	Condensed Tannin Leucoanthocyanin
CTL	Confidence Training Launch
CTL	Connecticut College, New London, CT [*OCLC symbol*] (OCLC)
CTL	Consolidated Tenants League (EA)
CTL	Constant Time Loci
CTL	Constructive Total Loss [*Insurance*]
ctl	Contact Lens [*Ophthalmology*] (DAVI)
CTL	Continental Bank of Canada [*Toronto Stock Exchange symbol*]
CTL	Control (AAG)
CTL	Core Transistor Logic [*Computer science*]
CTL	Crown Theological Library [*A publication*]
CTL	Cut to Length
CTL	Cytologic Thymus-Dependent Lymphocyte [*Endocrinology*] (DAVI)
CTL	Cytolytic Thymus-Dependent Lymphocyte [*Cell biology*]
CTL	Cytotoxic T Lymphocyte [*Hematology*]
CTLA	Control Area (FAAC)
CTLA	Council of Tree and Landscape Appraisers (EA)
CTLA	Cytotoxic T Lymphocyte Antigen [*Immuno chemistry*]
CtlAir	Continental Airlines, Inc. [*Associated Press*] (SAG)
CTLB	Control Boundary (FAAC)
CtlCC	Continental Choice Care, Inc. [*Associated Press*] (SAG)
CtlCCare	Continental Choice Care, Inc. [*Associated Press*] (SAG)
CTL Cr	CTL Credit, Inc. [*Associated Press*] (SAG)
CTLD	Controlled (IAA)
CTLG	Catalogue
CTLG	Specialty Catalog Corp. [*NASDAQ symbol*] (SAG)
CtlHi	Litchfield Historical Society, Litchfield, CT [*Library symbol Library of Congress*] (LCLS)
CtlHme	Continental Homes Holding Corp. [*Associated Press*] (SAG)
CTLI	Combat Training Launch Instrumentation [*Minuteman*]
CTLI	CTL Credit [*NASDAQ symbol*] (TTSB)
CTLI	CTL Credit, Inc. [*NASDAQ symbol*] (SAG)
CTLJ	California Trial Lawyers Journal [*A publication*] (DLA)
CTLL	Conseil des Travailleurs et Travailleuses des Laurentides-Lanaudiere (AC)
CTLL	Cytolytic T-Lymphocyte Line [*Cell line*]
CTLM	Charge Transfer Light Modulator [*Instrumentation*]
CtlMtg	Continental Mortgage & Equity Trust [*Associated Press*] (SAG)
CTLN	Cut to Length and Notch
CTLO	Cattlemans, Inc. [*NASDAQ symbol*] (SAG)
CTLO	Cattlemans Inc. [*NASDAQ symbol*] (TTSB)
CTLO	Cervicothoracolumbar Orthosis [*Medicine*]
CTLO	Constructive Total Loss Only [*Insurance*]
CTLP	Cytolytic T-Lymphocyte Precursor [*Immunochemistry*]
CTLPL	Control Panel [*Electronics*] (ECII)
CTLRY	Cutlery (MSA)
CTLS	Central Texas Library System [*Library network*]
CTLS	Centre for Teaching and Learning Services [*McGill University*] [*Canada Research center*] (RCD)
CTLS	Cumberland Trail Library System [*Library network*]
CTLSO	Cervicothoracolumbosacral Orthosis [*Medicine*]
CtlSou	Central & Southern Holding Co. [*Associated Press*] (SAG)
CTLST	Catalyst (MSA)

CTLT .... Cadet Troop Leader Training (MCD)

CTLV .... Carrot Thin Leaf Virus [*Plant pathology*]

CTLVR .... Combined Total Loan-to-Value Ratio [*Business term*] (EMRF)

CTLZ .... Control Zone [*Aviation*]

CTM .... Cable Testing Meter

CTM .... Cable Transfer Machine [*Nuclear energy*] (NRCH)

CTM .... Canada Tungsten Mining Corp. Ltd. [*Toronto Stock Exchange symbol*]

CTM .... Cardiotachometer [*Medicine*]

CTM .... Castle Mountain [*California*] [*Seismograph station code, US Geological Survey*] (SEIS)

CTM .... Catholic Traditionalist Movement (EA)

CTM .... Causal Tree Method [*Engineering*]

CTM .... Cavity Transfer Mixer [*Chemical engineering*]

CTM .... Center for Telecommunications Management [*UCLA*] (TSSD)

CTM .... Certified Traffic Manager

CTM .... Chetumal [*Mexico*] [*Airport symbol*] (OAG)

CTM .... Chief Torpedoman's Mate [*Navy rating Obsolete*]

CTM .... Chlortrimeton [*Antihistamine*] [*Trademark of Schering-Plough Corp.*]

CTM .... Christian Television Mission (EA)

CTM .... Christ Truth Ministries (EA)

CTM .... Close Talking Microphone

CTM .... Coal Traffic Manager

CTM .... Cognizant Technical Manager

CTM .... Collective Trademark (MCD)

CTM .... Collimation Test Module [*Nuclear energy*] (GFGA)

CTM .... Commandement du Transport Aerien Militaire Francais [*France ICAO designator*] (FAAC)

CTM .... Communications Technology Management, Inc. [*McLean, VA*] [*Telecommunications*] (TSSD)

CTM .... Communications Terminal Module [*Computer science*]

CTM .... Complete Treatment Module [*Telecommunications*] (TEL)

CTM .... Complimentary Technical Manual

CTM .... Concordia Tract Mission (EA)

CTM .... Configuration and Tuning Module [*Computer science*]

CTM .... Connective Tissue Massage [*Medicine*]

CTM .... Conseil des Travailleurs et Travailleuses du Montreal Metropolitain (AC)

CTM .... Consulting Traffic Manager

CTM .... Continuity Transceiver Module [*Telecommunications*] (TEL)

CTM .... Contractor Technical Meeting (AAG)

CTM .... Contract Technical Manager

CTM .... Contract Termination Manual (AAG)

CTM .... Coolimation Test Module [*Nuclear energy*] (NRCH)

CTM .... Cost to Manuacture

CT/M .... Count per Minute (MSA)

CTM .... Critical Thermal Maximum

CTM .... Crystalline Transitional Material (NASA)

CTM .... Cutaneous Trunci Muscle [*Anatomy*]

CtM .... Russell Public Library, Middletown, CT [*Library symbol Library of Congress*] (LCLS)

CTM1 .... Cryptologic Technician, Maintenance, First Class [*Navy rating*] (DNAB)

CTM2 .... Cryptologic Technician, Maintenance, Second Class [*Navy rating*] (DNAB)

CTM3 .... Cryptologic Technician, Maintenance, Third Class [*Navy rating*] (DNAB)

CTMA .... Camping Trailer Manufacturers Association [*Later, RVIA*]

CTMA .... Canadian Tooling Manufacturers' Association [*Association Canadienne des Fabricants d'Outillage*] (AC)

CTMA .... Canadian Turkey Marketing Agency [*Office Canadien de Commercialisation du Dindon*] (AC)

CTMA .... Canadian Turnaround Management Association [*Association Canadienne de Restructuration d'Entreprises*] (AC)

CTMA .... Center Traffic Management Advisor [*FAA*] (TAG)

CTMA .... Collapsible Tube Manufacturers' Association [*British*] (BI)

CTMA .... Commercial Truck Maintenance Association (MHDB)

CTMA .... Cutting Tool Manufacturers Association [*Later, Cutting Tool Manufacturers of America*] (EA)

CTMA .... Cutting Tool Manufacturers of America (EA)

CtMaHi .... Mansfield Historical Society, Mansfield Center, CT [*Library symbol Library of Congress*] (LCLS)

CtMan .... Mary Cheney Library, Manchester, CT [*Library symbol Library of Congress*] (LCLS)

CtManC .... Manchester Community College, Manchester, CT [*Library symbol Library of Congress*] (LCLS)

CtManGS ..... Church of Jesus Christ of Latter-Day Saints, Genealogical Society Library, Hartford Branch, Manchester, CT [*Library symbol Library of Congress*] (LCLS)

CTMB .... Canal Transport Marketing Board [*British*] (BI)

ctmb .... Catacomb (VRA)

CTMBL .... Cloud-Topped Marine Boundary Layer [*Marine science*] (OSRA)

CTMBL .... Cloud-Topped Marine Boundary Layer (USDC)

CTMC .... Canadian Tobacco Manufacturers' Council

CTMC .... Centurion Mines [*NASDAQ symbol*] (SAG)

CTMC .... Communications Terminal Module Controller [*Computer science*]

CTMC .... Connective-Tissue-Type Mast Cell [*Cytology*]

CTMC .... Cryptologic Technician, Maintenance, Chief [*Navy rating*] (DNAB)

CTMCM .... Cryptologic Technician, Maintenance, Master Chief [*Navy rating*] (DNAB)

CTMCS .... Cryptologic Technician, Maintenance, Senior Chief [*Navy rating*] (DNAB)

CTME .... Chief Torpedoman's Mate, Electrical [*Navy rating Obsolete*]

CTME .... Clothestime, Inc. [*NASDAQ symbol*] (NQ)

CTMEO .... Clothes Time Inc. [*NASDAQ symbol*] (TTSB)

CtMer .... Curtis Memorial Public Library, Meriden, CT [*Library symbol Library of Congress*] (LCLS)

CTMF .... Ceramic Tile Marketing Federation [*Defunct*] (EA)

CtMG .... Godfrey Memorial Library, Middletown, CT [*Library symbol Library of Congress*] (LCLS)

Ct Mgmt J ... Court Management Journal [*A publication*] (DLA)

CTMGSA .... Commercial Trailer-Mounted Generator Set Assembly

CTMI .... Celltech Media, Inc. [*NASDAQ symbol*] (SAG)

CTMI .... Contour Medical [*NASDAQ symbol*] (TTSB)

CTMI .... Contour Medical, Inc. [*NASDAQ symbol*] (SAG)

CTMM .... California Test of Mental Maturity

CTMM .... Computed Tomographic Metrizamide Myelography

CTMMA .... Central Technical Manual Management Activity [*Navy*] (NVT)

CTMO .... Centesimo [*or Centimo*] [*Monetary unit in many Spanish-American countries*]

CTMO .... Community Trade Mark Office [*EC*] (ECED)

CtMor .... Morris Public Library, Morris, CT [*Library symbol Library of Congress*] (LCLS)

CTMP .... Chemithermomechanical Pulp [*Papermaking*]

CTMP .... Comprehensive Treatment and Management Plan (DOGT)

CTMP .... Comprehensive Treatment and Management Plan [*Department of Energy*]

CTMP .... Contractor Technical Manual Plan [*DoD*]

CTMP .... CONUS [*Continental United States*] Telephone Modernization Program

CTMPP .... Committee of Tin Mill Products Producers (EA)

CT/MPR .... Computed Tomography with Multiplanar Reconstructions [*Radiology*] (DAVI)

CTMS .... Carrier Transmission Maintenance System [*Bell System*]

CTMS .... Ceramic-to-Metal Seal

CTMS .... Clinical Trials Monitoring System

CTMS .... Commanders Training Management System [*DoD*]

CTMS .... Commercial Teleoperator Maneuvering System (SSD)

CTMS .... Computer-Controlled Test Management System [*Environmental science*]

CTMS .... Countermeasures (AABC)

CTMSOA .... Central Telegraph Male Superintending Officers' Association [*A union*] [*British*]

CT/MSS .... Crawler/Transporter/Mobile Service Structure [*Aerospace*] (KSC)

CTMT .... Combined Thermomechanical Treatment

CTMT .... Containment (IEEE)

CTMV .... Chief Torpedoman's Mate, Aviation [*Navy rating Obsolete*]

CtMyMHi ..... Mystic Seaport, Inc., Mystic, CT [*Library symbol Library of Congress*] (LCLS)

CTN .... Cable Termination Network

CTN .... CANCOM [*Canadian Satellite Communications, Inc.*] Teleconference Network, Inc. [*Telecommunications service*] (TSSD)

CTN .... Canton Railroad Co. [*AAR code*]

CTN .... Carleton University Library [*UTLAS symbol*]

CTN .... Carton

ctn .... Carton (WDMC)

CTN .... Cases Tempore Northington [*Eden's English Chancery Reports*] [*A publication*] (DLA)

CTN .... Catholic Television Network [*Cable-television system*]

CTN .... Caution

CTN .... Cellulose Trinitrate [*Organic chemistry*]

CTN .... Centennial Minerals [*Toronto Stock Exchange symbol Vancouver Stock Exchange symbol*]

CTN .... Centennial Technologies [*AMEX symbol*] (TTSB)

CTN .... Centennial Technologies, Inc. [*AMEX symbol*] (SAG)

CTN .... Centre d'Etudes des Consequences Generales des Grands Techniques Nouvelles [*Center for the Study of the General Results of New Technologies*] (EA)

CTN .... Certification Test Network [*NASA*] (KSC)

CTN .... Command Trust Network (EA)

CTN .... Confectioner, Tobacconist, and Newsagent [*British*] (DI)

CTN .... Confectionery, Tobacco, and Newsagent [*British*]

CTN .... Cooktown [*Australia Airport symbol*] (OAG)

CTN .... Cotangent [*Mathematics*]

CTN .... Cotton

CTN .... [*New York*] Cotton Exchange (BARN)

CT/N .... Counter, n Stages [*Electronics*] (DEN)

CTN .... Cowboy Television Network

CTN .... Croatia Airlines [*ICAO designator*] (FAAC)

CTN .... Ctenidial Nerve [*Biology*]

CTNA .... Catalina 25 National Association (EA)

CTNA .... Catholic Telecommunications Network of America [*Staten Island, NY*] (TSSD)

CTNA .... Committee on Societal Consequences of Transportation Noise Abatement [*National Research Council*]

CtNaUSR ...... Uniroyal, Inc., Chemical Division, Information Center Library, Naugatuck, CT [*Library symbol Library of Congress*] (LCLS)

CtNb .... New Britain Public Library, New Britain, CT [*Library symbol Library of Congress*] (LCLS)

CtNbT .... Central Connecticut State College, New Britain, CT [*Library symbol Library of Congress*] (LCLS)

CTnC .... Cardiac Troponin C [*Biochemistry*]

CTNC .... Commission on Transnational Corporations [*United Nations*]

CTNC .... Cross-Track Noncontiguous

CtNc .... New Canaan Library, New Canaan, CT [*Library symbol Library of Congress*] (LCLS)

CtNcHi .... New Canaan Historical Society, New Canaan, CT [*Library symbol Library of Congress*] (LCLS)

CTND .... Caretenders Healthcorp. [*NASDAQ symbol*] (SPSG)

CTNDS .... Commercial Transport Navigation Display System

CTNE — Compania Telefonica Nacional de Espana [*National Telephone Co. of Spain*] [*Telecommunications*]

CtNeV — United States Veterans Administration Hospital, Newington, CT [*Library symbol Library of Congress*] (LCLS)

CTNF — Computerized Telephone Number File [*FBI listing, begun in 1970, of political activists' telephone numbers*] [*Obsolete*]

CTNF — Controlled Thermonuclear Fusion

ctnh — [*Hyperbolic*] Contangent [*Mathematics*] (BARN)

CtNh — New Haven Free Public Library, New Haven, CT [*Library symbol Library of Congress*] (LCLS)

CtNhA — Albertus Magnus College, New Haven, CT [*Library symbol Library of Congress*] (LCLS)

CtNhAS — Connecticut Agricultural Experiment Station, New Haven, CT [*Library symbol Library of Congress*] (LCLS)

CtNhH — Human Relations Area Files, New Haven, CT [*Library symbol Library of Congress*] (LCLS)

CtNhHi — New Haven Colony Historical Society, New Haven, CT [*Library symbol Library of Congress*] (LCLS)

CtNhMH — Connecticut Mental Health Center, New Haven, CT [*Library symbol Library of Congress*] (LCLS)

CtNhN — Southern Connecticut State College, New Haven, CT [*Library symbol Library of Congress*] (LCLS)

CtNhO — Olin Corp., New Haven, CT [*Library symbol Library of Congress*] (LCLS)

CtNhU — University of New Haven, New Haven, CT [*Library symbol Library of Congress*] (LCLS)

CtNhW — Winchester-Western Co., New Haven, CT [*Library symbol Library of Congress*] (LCLS)

CTNL — Center for the New Leadership (EA)

CtNl — New London Public Library, New London, CT [*Library symbol Library of Congress*] (LCLS)

CtNlC — Connecticut College, New London, CT [*Library symbol Library of Congress*] (LCLS)

CtNlCG — United States Coast Guard Academy, New London, CT [*Library symbol Library of Congress*] (LCLS)

CtNlHi — New London County Historical Society, New London, CT [*Library symbol Library of Congress*] (LCLS)

cTNM — Clinical-Diagnostic Staging of Cancer [*Oncology*] (DAVI)

CtNowa — Norwalk Public Library, Norwalk, CT [*Library symbol Library of Congress*] (LCLS)

CtNowaB — Burndy Corp., Technical Library, Norwalk, CT [*Library symbol Library of Congress*] (LCLS)

CtNowaS — Saint Mary's Seminary, Ferndale, Norwalk, CT [*Library symbol Library of Congress*] (LCLS)

CtNowaT — Technoserve, Norwalk, CT [*Library symbol Library of Congress*] (LCLS)

CTNSA — Catalina 22 National Sailing Association (EA)

CtnSLf — Cotton States Life Insurance [*Associated Press*] (SAG)

CTNSW — Commercial Tribunal, New South Wales [*Australia*]

CtNwch — Otis Library, Norwich, CT [*Library symbol*] [*Library of Congress*] (LCLS)

CtNwchA — Norwich Free Academy, Norwich, CT [*Library symbol Library of Congress*] (LCLS)

CTO — Aerotaxis del Centro SA [*Mexico ICAO designator*] (FAAC)

CTO — Calverton, NY [*Location identifier FAA*] (FAAL)

CTO — Canceled to Order [*Philately*]

CTO — Cape Town [*South Africa*] [*Later, HER*] [*Geomagnetic observatory code*]

CTO — Caribbean Tourism Organization (EAIO)

CTO — Carmelite Third Order [*Rome, Italy*] (EAIO)

CT O — Catering Officer [*British military*] (DMA)

CTO — Cavity Tuned Oscillator

CTO — Central Telegraph Office [*British*] (ROG)

CTO — Central Telephone Operator [*British*] (ROG)

CTO — Central Torpedo Office

CTO — Central Treaty Organization [*Also, CENTO*] [*Formerly, Baghdad Pact*]

CTO — Cervicothoracic Orthosis [*Also, CER*] [*Medicine*]

CTO — Charge Transforming Operator (IEEE)

CTO — Chest Tube Out [*Medicine*]

CTO — Chief Technical Officer [*British*] (ADA)

CTO — China Theater of Operations [*World War II*]

CTO — Circular Terminal Orbit [*Aerospace*] (AAG)

CTO — Cognizant Transportation Office [*or Officer*] [*Air Force*] (AFM)

CTO — Combined Transport Operator [*Shipping*]

CTO — Commerce Total Return Fund, Inc. (MHDW)

CTO — Commercial Transportation Officer

CTO — Commonwealth Telecommunications Organization [*England*]

CTO — Concerto [*Music*]

CTO — Consolidated Tomoka Land [*AMEX symbol*] (SPSG)

CTO — Container Terminal Operator [*Shipping*] (DS)

CTO — Control Technology Office [*Environmental Protection Agency*] (GFGA)

CTO — Control Tower Operator [*Army*] (AABC)

CTO — Conventional Takeoff [*Aviation*] (NATG)

CTO — Coolant Temperature Override [*Automotive engineering*]

CTO — Courier Transfer Office [*or Officer*]

Ct/O — Court Order (DLA)

CTO — Crew Training Officer (SAA)

CTO — Crude Tall Oil [*Industrial chemistry*]

CTO — Cutoff [*Telecommunications*] (TEL)

CTO — Cut-Through Operate (IAA)

CTO — Cyprus Tourism Organization (EA)

CTO — San Joaquin Delta College, Stockton, CA [*OCLC symbol*] (OCLC)

CTO1 — Cryptologic Technician O (Communications), First Class [*Navy rating*] (DNAB)

CTO2 — Cryptologic Technician O (Communications), Second Class [*Navy rating*] (DNAB)

CTO3 — Cryptologic Technician O (Communications), Third Class [*Navy rating*] (DNAB)

CTOA — Cable and Telegraph Operators' Association [*A union*] [*British*]

CTOA — Crack Tip-Opening Angle (MCD)

CTOA — Creative Tour Operators Association

C to C — Center to Center [*Technical drawings*]

CTOC — Central Technical Order Coordination Unit

CTOC — Communications Technical Operations Center [*Air Force*]

C-to-C — Computer-to-Computer (NASA)

C-to-C — Computer-to-Computer

CTOC — Corps Tactical Operations Center

CTOC — Cryptologic Technician O (Communications), Chief [*Navy rating*] (DNAB)

CTOCM — Cryptologic Technician O (Communications), Master Chief [*Navy rating*] (DNAB)

CTOCS — Cryptologic Technician O (Communications), Senior Chief [*Navy rating*] (DNAB)

CTOCU — Central Technical Order Control [*or Coordination*] Unit (MCD)

CTOD — Character-to-Date [*Microsoft Corp. FoxPro function*] (PCM)

CTOD — Crack Tip-Opening Displacement (MCD)

C to D of M — Contributing to Delinquency of Minor [*FBI standardized term*]

C to E — Center to End

Ct of Cls — United States Court of Claims (DLA)

Ct of Er and Appeals — Court of Errors and Appeals [*New Jersey*] (DLA)

C to G — Clerk to Guardians [*British*] (ROG)

CtOg — Perrot Memorial Library, Old Greenwich, CT [*Library symbol Library of Congress*] (LCLS)

CTOI — Cultural Travel Organizations International (EA)

C to K — Curious to Know [*An inquisitive customer*] [*Merchandising slang*]

CToL — California Lutheran College, Thousand Oaks, CA [*Library symbol Library of Congress*] (LCLS)

CTOL — Controlled Takeoff and Landing (MCD)

CTOL — Conventional Take-off and Landing [*Aircraft*]

C to P — Confined to Post

CTOQ — Conseil des Travailleurs et Travailleuses de l'Outaouais Quebecois (AC)

CToR — Rockwell International, Science Center, Thousand Oaks, CA [*Library symbol Library of Congress*] (LCLS)

CTORP — Chief Torpedoman [*Navy rating Obsolete*]

CTorr — Torrance Public Library, Torrance, CA [*Library symbol*] [*Library of Congress*] (LCLS)

C to S — Carting to Shipside [*Shipping*]

CTOS — Cassette Tape Operating System (IEEE)

CTOS — Convergent Technologies Operating System [*Computer science*]

CTOS — Corps Tactical Operations System (MCD)

CTOS — Council of the Thirteen Original States (EA)

CTP — California Test of Personality [*Psychology*]

CTP — Canada Taxation Publications [*Database*] (IID)

CTP — Capacitor Test Program

CTP — Catapilco [*Chile*] [*Seismograph station code, US Geological Survey*] (SEIS)

CTP — Celltropin [*Biochemistry*]

CTP — Central Maine Power [*NYSE symbol*] (TTSB)

CTP — Central Maine Power Co. [*AMEX symbol*] (SAG)

CTP — Central Maine Power Co. [*NYSE symbol*] (SPSG)

CTP — Central Transfer Point

CTP — Challenge Test Plan

CTP — Charge-Transfer Photography

CTP — Charge Transforming Parameter (IEEE)

CTP — Chemical Treatment Pond (IEEE)

CTP — Chicago Technology Park

CTP — Children as the Peacemakers (EA)

CTP — Christmas Tree Pattern

CTP — Coded Telemetry Processor

CTP — Collective Training Plan [*Army*]

CTP — Command Translator and Programmer

CTP — Commercial Type Property

CTP — Communications Timing Procedure (NASA)

CTP — Community Telephone Plan (ADA)

CTP — Comprehensive Testing Program [*Academic achievement and aptitude test*]

CTP — Comprehensive Treatment Plan [*Medicine*] (DAVI)

CTP — Compulsory Third Party [*Australia*]

CTP — Computer-to-Plate [*Printing*] (DGA)

CTP — Condensed Tannin Proanthocyanidin

CTP — Confidence Test Program [*NASA*] (KSC)

CTP — Conservez Taxe Payee [*Retain Charge Paid*] [*French Business term*]

CTP — Consolidated Telecommunications Program [*Military*] (GFGA)

CTP — Construction Test Procedure (NRCH)

CTP — Contractor Transition Plan

CTP — Controlled Temperature Profile [*Vapor trap*] [*Nuclear energy*] (NRCH)

CTP — Coordinated Test Plan [*Obsolete*]

CTP — Coordinated Test Program [*Military*] (AABC)

CTP — Corpo de Tropas Paraquedistas [*Paratroopers Corps*] [*Air Force Portugal*]

CTP — Corporate Trade Payment [*Automated Clearing House*]

CTP — Creative Times Project [*Later, CT*] (EA)

CTP — Critical Technical Parameters (RDA)

CTP — Cumhuriyetci Turk Partisi [*Republican Turkish Party*] [*Turkish Cyprus*] [*Political party*] (PPE)

CTP — Cyclic Time Processor (MCD)

CTP............ Cyclohexylthiophthalimide [Organic chemistry]
CTP............ Cytidine Triphosphate [Biochemistry]
CTP............ Cytosine Triphosphate [Biochemistry]
ctpa .... Coaxial to Twisted Pair Adapter (HGAA)
CTPA .... Cosmetic, Toiletry, and Perfumery Association [British] (DBA)
CTPB........... Carboxyl-Terminated Polybutadiene Binder [Organic chemistry]
CTPB........... Central Tracing Policy Board [Post-World War II]
CTPC .... Cargo Traffic Procedures Committee [IATA] (DS)
CTPD .... Crew Training and Procedures Division [Johnson Space Center] [NASA] (NASA)
CTPDA .... Canadian Television Producers and Directors Association
CTPE .... Carboxyl-Terminated Polyester Propellant (MCD)
CTPEC......... Coal Tar Pitch Emulsion Council [Defunct] (EA)
CTP H .... Cytidine Triphosphate Tritium-Labeled [Chemistry] (DAVI)
CTPI........... Canadian Textbook Publishers' Institute
CTPI........... Conventional Weapon Technical Proficiency Inspection [Military] (CAAL)
CTPL........... Centre for Trade Policy and Law [Established to promote greater public understanding of trade policies] [Canada] (CROSS)
CTPL........... Commission for Teacher Preparation and Licensing
CTPP.......... Census Transportation Planning Package [BTS] (TAG)
CTPP.......... Cerebral Tissue Perfusion Pressure [Medicine] (DMAA)
CTPPr......... Central Maine Pwr,3 1/2% Pfd [AMEX symbol] (TTSB)
CTPPrA .... Central Maine Pwr 7.875% Pfd [NYSE symbol] (TTSB)
CT-PS .... Changeable Type-Plate Style
CTPV.......... Coal Tar Pitch Volatile [Organic chemistry]
CTQ............ Conseil des Travailleurs et Travailleuses de Quebec (AC)
CTQ............ Consolidated PCR Industries Ltd. [Vancouver Stock Exchange symbol]
CTQ............ Corporation des Thanatologues du Quebec (AC)
CTQ............ Santa Vitoria [Brazil] [Airport symbol] (AD)
CTR............ Calcitonin Receptor [Endocrinology]
CTR............ California Tumor Registry
CTR............ Canadian Tire Corp. Ltd. [Toronto Stock Exchange symbol]
CTR............ Canaveral Test Report
CTR............ Cape Times Supreme Court Reports, Cape Of Good Hope [South Africa] [A publication] (DLA)
CTR............ Capital Type Rehabilitation Facility (MCD)
CTR............ Cardiothoracic Ratio [Medicine]
CTR............ Carpal Tunnel Release [Medicine] (DMAA)
CTR............ Carrier Telegraph Receiver
CTR............ Cash Transaction Report [Finance]
CTR............ Castle Rock [New York] [Seismograph station code, US Geological Survey] (SEIS)
CTR............ Caterpillar Tractor Co. [NYSE symbol; later, CAT] [Wall Street slang name: "Cat"] (SPSG)
CTR............ Cavitation Tendency Ratio
CTR............ C-Band Tracking RADAR
CTR............ Center (AAG)
ctr .... Center (WDMC)
CTR............ Center
CTR............ Center for Telecommunications Research [Columbia University] [New York, NY Telecommunications service] (TSSD)
CTR............ Center for Transportation Research [University of Texas at Austin] [Research center] (RCD)
CTR............ Central Territory Railroad Tariff Bureau
CTR............ Central Tool Room
CTR............ Central Tumor Registry [Medicine] (BARN)
CTR............ Certification Test Requirement [NASA]
CTR............ Certified Test Record (IAA)
CTR............ Certified Test Results (NRCH)
CTR............ Certified Tumor Registrar [Medicine] (BARN)
CTR............ Chemical Temperature Resistant [Automotive engineering]
CTR............ Chemical Transport Reaction
CTR............ Chester, MA [Location identifier FAA] (FAAL)
CTR............ Civil Tilt Rotor [Aviation] (DA)
CTR............ Collective Television Reception (OA)
CTR............ Collective Training Range (MCD)
CTR............ Committed to Ride (SAA)
CTR............ Commuter Trip Reduction [MOCD] (TAG)
CTR............ Complementary Transistor Register [Computer science] (IAA)
CTR............ Composite Teacher Rating
CTR............ Computer Tape Recorder
CTR............ Computer Technology Research Corp. (IID)
CTR............ Consolidated Training Request [Military]
CTR............ Consolidate Time Rate
CTR............ Continuous-Flow Tank Reactor [Chemical engineering]
CTR............ Continuous Tubular Reactor [Chemical engineering]
CTR............ Contour (MSA)
CTR............ Contract Technical Representative (NASA)
CTR............ Contractual Technical Report (AAG)
CTR............ Contributor
CTR............ Controllable Twist Rotor [Aviation]
CTR............ Controlled Thermonuclear Reaction [or Reactor] [National Institute of Standards and Technology]
CTR............ Controlled Thermonuclear Research
CTR............ Controlled Tornado Research (MCD)
CTR............ Control Zone [Aviation]
CTR............ Cooperative Threat Reduction [Military] (RDA)
CTR............ Core Transistor Register
C Tr............ Corporate Trust [Legal term] (DLA)
CTR............ Council for Textile Recycling (EA)
CTR............ Council for Tobacco Research
CTR............ Counter (KSC)
ctr.............. Counter (WDMC)

CT R .... Court Rolls [British] (ROG)
CTR............ Currency Transaction Report [IRS]
CTR............ Current Transfer Ratio [Bell System]
CTR............ Cutter (MSA)
CTR............ Standing Committee for Controlled Thermonuclear Research [AEC]
CTR............ Transaction Technology, Inc., Technical Library, Los Angeles, CA [OCLC symbol] (OCLC)
CTR............ Transport Air Centre [France ICAO designator] (FAAC)
CTr............. Truckee Public Library, Truckee, CA [Library symbol] [Library of Congress] (LCLS)
CTR1.......... Cryptologic Technician R (Collection), First Class [Navy rating] (DNAB)
CTR2.......... Cryptologic Technician R (Collection), Second Class [Navy rating] (DNAB)
CTR3.......... Cryptologic Technician R (Collection), Third Class [Navy rating] (DNAB)
CTRA .... Coal Tar Research Association [British] (BI)
CTRA .... Concentra Corp. [NASDAQ symbol] (SAG)
CTRAC........ Common Terminal RADAR Approach Control [Aviation] (FAAC)
CTRAP .... Customer Trouble Report Analysis Plan [Telecommunications] (TEL)
C Trav........ Code du Travail [Labor Code] [A publication] (ILCA)
CTRB.......... Chymotrypsinogen B [Biochemistry]
CtrBnk........ Center Banks [Associated Press] (SAG)
CTRC .... Caribbean Tourism Research and Development Centre [Later, Caribbean Tourism Organization] (EAIO)
CTRC .... Colorado Technical Reference Center [University of Colorado - Boulder] [Information service or system] (IID)
CTRC .... Cryptologic Technician R (Collection), Chief [Navy rating] (DNAB)
CTRCLM ...... Counterclaim [Legal term] (ROG)
CTRCM .... Cryptologic Technician R (Collection), Master Chief [Navy rating] (DNAB)
CtrCOp........ Central Cooperative Bank [Associated Press] (SAG)
CTRCS .... Cryptologic Technician R (Collection), Senior Chief [Navy rating] (DNAB)
CTRDA .... Canadian Tuberculosis and Respiratory Disease Association
CtRe........... Mark Twain Library Association, Redding, CT [Library symbol] [Library of Congress] (LCLS)
Ct Rep NZ .... Court of Appeals Reports [New Zealand] [A publication] (DLA)
CTREPTR .... Court Reporter (AABC)
CTRF.......... Canadian Transportation Research Forum
CTRF.......... Center Frequency (MSA)
CTRFCTN..... Certification
CTRG .... Centering
CTRI.......... Catholic Tape Recorders, International (EA)
CTRI.......... Clevetrust Realty [NASDAQ symbol] (SAG)
CTRIPS .... Concepts, Trends, Relationships, Issues, Problems, Solutions
CTRIS .... Canadian Transportation Research Information Service
CTRIS .... Cleve Trust Realty SBI [NASDAQ symbol] (TTSB)
CTRL.......... Central
CTRL.......... Central
CTRL.......... Chemi Trol Chem [NASDAQ symbol] (TTSB)
CTRL.......... Chemi-Trol Chemical Co. [NASDAQ symbol] (SAG)
CTRL.......... Chymotrypsin-Like [Protease] (DMAA)
CTRL.......... Control (WGA)
CTRL.......... Control Character [Keyboard] (CINC)
CtrlDt......... Control Data Systems, Inc. [Associated Press] (SAG)
CtrlTrac...... Central Tractor Farm & Country, Inc. [Associated Press] (SAG)
CtrlVA........ Central Virginia Bankshares [Associated Press] (SAG)
CTRM......... Control Room [Nuclear energy] (NRCH)
CTRN .... Computron Software [NASDAQ symbol] (TTSB)
CTRN .... Computron Software, Inc. [NASDAQ symbol] (SAG)
CtRogR .... Rogers Corp., Lurie Research and Development Center, Rogers, CT [Library symbol Library of Congress] (LCLS)
CTRPT .... Counterpart [Legal term] (ROG)
CTRQ .... Crown/Treasury of Relevant Quotations [A publication]
CTRS .... Centers [Postal Service standard] (OPSA)
CTRS .... Centers
CTRS .... Citrus
CTRS .... Component Test Requirements Specifications (MCD)
CTRS .... Conners Teaching Rating Scale
CTRS .... Contrast (MSA)
CTR-USA...... Council for Tobacco Research - USA (EA)
CTRX .... Ceftriaxone (DMAA)
CTRX .... Celtrix Pharmaceuticals [NASDAQ symbol] (SAG)
ctry........... Country (VRA)
CtrySo........ Century South Banks, Inc. [Associated Press] (SAG)
CtryStr....... Country Star Restaurants, Inc. [Associated Press] (SAG)
CtryWTr ...... Country Wide Transport Services, Inc. [Associated Press] (SAG)
CTS............ Cable Telemetry System
CTS............ Cable Terminal Section [Telecommunications] (TEL)
CTS............ Cable Test Set (MCD)
CTS............ Cable Turning Section [Telecommunications] (TEL)
CTS............ Cable Turning System [Telecommunications] (NITA)
CTS............ Cab Tyred Sheathed (PDAA)
CTS............ Canadian Technology Satellite (MCD)
CTS............ Canadian Theological Seminary
CTS............ Canadian Theological Society [See also SCT]
CTS............ Canadian Thoracic Society [Societe Canadienne de Thoracologie] (AC)
CTS............ Capistrano Test Site
CTS............ Captive Trajectory System [Air Force]
CTS............ Card-to-Magnetic Tape Conversion System [Computer science] (DIT)
CTS............ Cargill Technical Services, Ltd. [British] [Commercial firm]
CTS............ Carpal Tunnel Syndrome [Medicine]
CTS............ Carriage Tape Simulator [Computer science] (IAA)

CTS............. Carrier Test Switch (IEEE)
CTS............. Carrier Transfer Station
CTS............. Cartographic Test Standard [Air Force]
CTS............. Cash Terminals Systems [Commercial firm] (NITA)
CTS............. Cassette Transport System
CTS............. Castel Tesino [Italy] [Geomagnetic observatory code]
CTS............. Catalase [An enzyme]
CTS............. Catholic Truth Society [British] (BI)
CTS............. Cellular Telephone Service (HGAA)
CTS............. Center for Technical Services [Air Force]
CTS............. Center for Telecommunications Studies [Formerly, Broadcast Research Center] [Ohio University] [Research center] (RCD)
CTS............. Center for Theoretical Studies [University of Miami] [Research center] (RCD)
CTS............. Center for Transportation Studies [Morgan State University] [Research center] (RCD)
CTS............. Center on Technology and Society, Inc. [Research center] (RCD)
CTS............. Centralized Translation System [Communications]
CTS............. Central Tactical System [RAF] (MCD)
CTS............. Central Target Simulator [Navy] (MCD)
CTS............. Central Timing System
CTS............. Central Training Section [Air Force] (AFM)
CTS............. Centre for Transportation Studies [University of British Columbia] [Canada] (IRC)
CTS............. Certificate of Theological Studies (PGP)
CTS............. Certification Test Specification [NASA] (KSC)
CTS............. Certified Tax Specialist (PGP)
CTS............. Cesium Time Standard
CTS............. Charge-Transfer Spectrum
CTS............. Chemically Treated Steel (DICI)
CTS............. Chicago Theological Seminary
CTS............. Chief, Technical Services
CTS............. China Travel Service (ECON)
CTS............. Chinese Television System (EY)
CTS............. Circuit Test Set [Electricity]
CTS............. Circuit-to-Specification (IAA)
CTS............. Clear to Send [Telecommunications]
CTS............. Clear To Stand [Telecommunications] (EECA)
CTS............. Close to Shoulder (MSA)
CTS............. Cloud Top Scanner (MCD)
CTS............. Coded Time Sequence (MCD)
CTS............. Coherent Transient Spectroscopy (MCD)
CTS............. College Theology Society (EA)
CTS............. Command and Telemetry System (AAG)
CTS............. Commandant's Training Strategy [Military]
CTS............. Commercial Transaction System [Business term] (MHDB)
CTS............. Committee on the Teaching of Science [ICSU] (IRUK)
CTS............. Commodity Transportation Survey [Census Bureau]
CTS............. Common Terminating System (MCD)
CTS............. Common Test Subroutine [Computer science]
CTS............. Communication and Tracking Subsystem [Military] (IAA)
CTS............. Communications and Tracking System [or Subsystem]
CTS............. Communications Technology Satellite
CTS............. Communications Technology Specialist [International Communications Industries Association] [Designation awarded by] (TSSD)
CTS............. Communications Terminal, Synchronous [Computer science]
CTS............. Communications Test Station [NASA]
CTS............. Compass Tilt Signal
CTS............. Component Test Set (MCD)
CTS............. Component Test Stand [Nuclear energy] (NUCP)
CTS............. Component Test System (IAA)
CTS............. Component Transaction Service [Computer science]
CTS............. Composite Tail Section [Aviation] (MCD)
CTS............. Composite Training School [British military] (DMA)
CTS............. Composite Treatment Score [Medicine] (MEDA)
CTS............. Computed Thermography System [Computer science]
CTS............. Computerized Tomography Society [Later, Computerized Radiology Society - CRS] (EA)
CTS............. Computerized Topographic Scanner [Medicine]
CTS............. Computerized Training System [Army Signal Center and School] [Fort Monmouth, NJ] (RDA)
CTS............. Computer Telewriter Systems (MCD)
CTS............. Computer Test Set
CTS............. Computer Training System
CTS............. Computer Typing System
CTS............. Concentrate Transfer System [Nuclear energy] (NRCH)
CTS............. Concise Tax Service [Australia A publication]
CTS............. Concordia Theological Seminary [Later, Concordia Seminary] [Missouri]
CTS............. Condensate Transfer and Storage [Nuclear energy] (NRCH)
CTS............. Configuration and Trace System [Military]
CTS............. Conflict Tactics Scale (EDAC)
CTS............. Conformance Testing Service [Computer science] (TNIG)
CTS............. Consolidated Tape System [Preferred name is Consolidated Transaction Reporting System] [Investment term]
CTS............. Consolidated Translation Survey [CIA]
CTS............. Consolidated Treaty Series [A publication] (DLA)
CTS............. Constant Temperature Sampling [Automotive engineering]
CTS............. Contact Test Set [Military]
CTS............. Continental Tire System
CTS............. Contingency Transfer System [Aerospace]
CTS............. ContiTire System [German]
CTS............. Contractor Technical Support (MCD)
CTS............. Contract [or Contractor] Technical Services [Air Force]

CTS............. Contract Termination Settlement
CTS............. Contralateral Threshold Shift (OA)
CTS............. Controlled Thermal Severity (OA)
CTS............. Conversational Terminal System [Computer science] (BUR)
CTS............. Conversational Time-Sharing [Computer science] (IEEE)
CTS............. Coolant Temperature Sensor [Automotive engineering]
CTS............. Cooperative Tracking System (MCD)
CTS............. Coordinate Transformation System (MCD)
CTS............. Cosmic Top Secret (NATG)
CTS............. Counseling and Testing Site
CTS............. Countess
CT/S............ Count per Second (MSA)
CTS............. Courier Transfer Station
CTS............. Course Training Standard [Air Force] (AFM)
CTS............. Courts [Postal Service standard] (OPSA)
CTS............. Courts
CTS............. Crates
CTS............. Cream of Tartar Substitute
CTS............. Crescomm Transmission Services, Inc. [Fairfield, NJ] [Telecommunications] (TSSD)
CTS............. Critical Tool Service
CTS............. Crosier Theological Seminary [Onamia, MN]
CTS............. Cryogenic Temperature Sensor [or Source]
CTS............. CTS Corp. [NYSE symbol] (SPSG)
CTS............. Current Time Sensing (CAAL)
CTS............. Sapporo/Chitose [Japan] [Airport symbol] (OAG)
CTS............. Shell Chemical Co., Torrance, CA [Library symbol Library of Congress Obsolete] (LCLS)
CtS............. Stamford Public Library, Stamford, CT [Library symbol Library of Congress] (LCLS)
CTSA........... Advanced Composite Wing Cover-to-Substructure Attachment (MCD)
CtSA........... American Cyanamid Co., Stamford, CT [Library symbol Library of Congress] (LCLS)
CTSA........... Catholic Theological Society of America (EA)
CTSA........... Counted Thread Society of America (EA)
CTSA........... Crucible and Tool Steel Association [British] (BI)
CTSA........... Cryptologic Technician, Seaman Apprentice [Navy] (DNAB)
CTSA........... Seaman Apprentice, Communications Technician, Striker [Navy rating]
CtSal........... Scoville Memorial Library, Salisbury, CT [Library symbol] [Library of Congress] (LCLS)
CTSB........... Combined Travel Security Board [Allied German Occupation Forces]
CTSC........... Cellular Technical Services [NASDAQ symbol] (SAG)
CTSC........... Cellular Technical Svcs [NASDAQ symbol] (TTSB)
CT scan........ Computerized Tomography [Also, CATSCAN] [Medical test] (PAZ)
CTSCREEN... Complex Terrain Screening [Model] [Marine science] (OSRA)
CTSCREEN... Complex Terrain Screening [Model] (USDC)
CTSD .... Computerized Training Systems Directorate [Army Training Support Activity] [Fort Gordon, GA]
CTSD .... Computer Test Sequences Document (MCD)
CTSDB........ Centralized Theater Surveillance Database (MCD)
CTSE........... Chicago, Terre Haute & Southeastern R. R. [AAR code]
CTSE........... Common Test/Support Equipment (MCD)
CTSE........... Conceptual Test of Spelling Errors (EDAC)
CTS-EOA ..... Contact Test Set - Electro Optical Augmentation [Military] (DWSG)
Ct Sess Cas... Court of Session Cases [Scotland] [A publication] (DLA)
Ct Sess Ist Ser... Scotch Court of Session Cases, First Series [A publication] (DLA)
CTSF........... California Traffic Safety Foundation [Defunct] (EA)
CTSF........... Central Technical Support Facility [Army]
CTSF........... Conservation Treaty Support Fund [An association] (EA)
CTSG........... Central Timing Signal Generator [Air Force] (MCD)
CTSHFT....... Countershaft (MSA)
CTSI........... Cardiothoracic Systems [NASDAQ symbol] (TTSB)
CTSI........... CardioThoracic Systems, Inc. [NASDAQ symbol] (SAG)
CTSI........... Central Terminal Signaling Interface [Telecommunications] (TEL)
CTSI........... Common Track Stores Indicator (CAAL)
CTSI........... Computer Transceiver Systems, Inc.
CTSK........... Countersunk
CTSKLS....... Catskills (FAAC)
CTSL........... Central Track Store Locator (MCD)
CTSL........... Coherent Tilted Superlattice [Solid state physics]
CTSN........... Seaman, Communications Technician, Striker [Navy rating]
CTSOA .... Central Telegraph Superintending Officers' Association [A union] [British]
CtSoP.......... Pequot Library Association, Southport, CT [Library symbol Library of Congress] (LCLS)
CTSP........... Called to See Patient [Medicine] (CPH)
CTSP........... Contract Services Personnel (AFM)
CT SPEC SESS.... Court of Special Sessions [Legal term] (DLA)
CTSPTEP...... Central Test Site for Personnel and Training Evaluation Program [Military] (DNAB)
CTSPTEPDET... Central Test Site for Personnel and Training Evaluation Program Detachment [Military] (DNAB)
CTSRGWA.... Commercial Travellers and Sales Representatives' Guild of Western Australia
CTSRTS ...... Clear to Send/Request to Send
CTS/RTS ...... Clear to Send/Request to Send [Telecommunications] (NITA)
CTSS........... Cathepsin S (DMAA)
CTSS........... Closed Tracheal Suction System [Medicine] (DMAA)
CTSS........... Communication and Tracking Subsystem (MCD)
CTSS........... Compatible Time-Shared System
CTSS........... Compatible Time-Sharing System [Massachusetts Institute of Technology] [Computer science]
CTSS........... Computer Time Sharing Service (MHDI)

CTSS............	Countess
CT/ST..........	Cassette Tape / Selectric Typewriter (HGAA)
CTST...........	Coaxial Triple-Stud Tuner
CtStr...........	Stratford Library Association, Stratford, CT [*Library symbol Library of Congress*] (LCLS)
CtSU...........	University of Connecticut, Stamford Branch, Stamford, CT [*Library symbol Library of Congress*] (LCLS)
CtSuL..........	Kent Memorial Library, Suffield, CT [*Library symbol*] [*Library of Congress*] (LCLS)
CTSWG........	Consolidated Training Support Work Group [*DoD*]
CTSX...........	Central Track Stores Index (MCD)
CTT.............	Cable Trouble Ticket [*Telecommunications*] (TEL)
CTT.............	Capital Transfer Tax [*British*]
CTT.............	Card-to-Tape Tape [*Computer science*]
CTT.............	Carousel Transfer Tube
C/T/t...........	Carrier-to-Noise Temperature, Total
C T T...........	Cases Tempore Talbot, English Chancery [*1734-38*] [*A publication*] (DLA)
CTT.............	Cask Transfer Tunnels [*Nuclear energy*] (NRCH)
CTT.............	Central Trunk Terminal
CTT.............	Centre des Technologies Textiles (AC)
CTT.............	Challenger International Ltd. [*Formerly, Coastal International Ltd.*] [*Toronto Stock Exchange symbol*]
CTT.............	College of Trades and Technology [*St. John's, NF*]
CTT.............	Color Trace Tube (IAA)
CTT.............	Combat Targeting Team [*Military*]
CTT.............	Combat Tracking [*or Tracker*] Team
CTT.............	Combat Training Theater
CTT.............	Combined Test Team (MCD)
CTT.............	Command Training Team (DNAB)
CTT.............	Common Task Test [*Army*] (INF)
CTT.............	Common Task Training [*Military*] (ADDR)
CTT.............	Competitive Technologies [*AMEX symbol*] (TTSB)
CTT.............	Competitive Technologies, Inc. [*Formerly, University Patents*] [*AMEX symbol*] (SAG)
CTT.............	Compressed Tablet Triturate [*Pharmacology*]
CTT.............	Computed Transaxial Tomography [*Later, CT*]
CTT.............	Coordination and Training Team [*Special Operations Force*] [*Military*] (DOMA)
CTT.............	Corrugated TEFLON Tubing
CTT.............	Council of Travel and Tourism [*British*] (DBA)
CTT.............	Crew Transfer Tunnel [*NASA*]
CTT.............	Critical Temperature Threshold [*Chemical technology*]
CTT.............	Critical Tracking Task [*System for preventing drunken driver from starting car*]
CTT.............	Crosstelling Technician (SAA)
CTT1...........	Cryptologic Technician, Technical, First Class [*Navy rating*] (DNAB)
CTT2...........	Cryptologic Technician, Technical, Second Class [*Navy rating*] (DNAB)
CTT3...........	Cryptologic Technician, Technical, Third Class [*Navy rating*] (DNAB)
CTTA...........	Canadian Table Tennis [*Association Canadienne de Tennis de Table*] (AC)
CTTAC........	Clinical Trials and Treatments Advisory Committee [*Australia*]
CTTB...........	Central Trade Test Board [*British*]
CTTB...........	Checkout Techniques Test Bed (NASA)
CTTBA.........	Canadian Transport Tariff Bureau Association
CTTC...........	Canadian Toy Testing Council
CTTC...........	Canadian Trade and Tariffs Committee
CTTC...........	Chanute Technical Training Center [*Air Force*]
CTTC...........	Congressional Travel and Tourism Caucus (EA)
CTTC...........	Cryptologic Technician, Technical, Chief [*Navy rating*] (DNAB)
CTTCM.........	Cryptologic Technician, Technical, Master Chief [*Navy rating*] (DNAB)
CTTCO........	Central Test Technology Coordinating Office [*Army*] (RDA)
CTTCS.........	Cryptologic Technician, Technical, Senior Chief [*Navy rating*] (DNAB)
CTTE...........	Conseil des Travailleurs et Travailleuses de l'Estrie (AC)
CTTE...........	Council on Technology Teacher Education (EA)
CTTE...........	Cyprus Turkish Tourist Enterprises Ltd. (EY)
CTTEE.........	Committee (EY)
CTTG...........	Counter-Targeting [*Navy*] (DOMA)
CTTL...........	Cattle
CTTL...........	Complementary Transistor-Transistor Logic
CTTR...........	Center for Transportation Training and Research [*Texas Southern University*] [*Research center*] (RCD)
CTTRE.........	Center for Tissue Trauma Research and Education (EA)
CTTS...........	Change-Transfer-to-Solvent [*Physical chemistry*]
CTTS...........	Classical T Tauri Stars [*Astronomy*]
CTTS...........	Closed Transition Transfer Switch
CTTS...........	Computer Technology and Telecommunications Staff [*Department of Justice*] (GFGA)
CTU.............	Cabin Telecommunications Unit [*Telecommunications*] (PCM)
CTU.............	California State College, Stanislaus, Turlock, CA [*OCLC symbol*] (OCLC)
CTU.............	Capsule Test Unit [*Aerospace*]
CTU.............	Captive Test Unit (MCD)
CTU.............	Cardiac/Thoracic Unit [*Medicine*]
CTU.............	Cardiology Transcription Unit [*Medicine*]
C/T/u..........	Carrier-to-Noise Temperature, Uplink
CTU.............	Cartridge Tape Unit [*Telecommunications*] (TEL)
CTU.............	Catholic Theological Union [*Australia*]
CTU.............	Centigrade Thermal Unit
CTU.............	Central Telephone and Utilities Corp. (NITA)
CTU.............	Central Terminal Unit [*Telecommunications*]
CTU.............	Central Timing Unit (KSC)
CTU.............	Central Trades' Union [*British*]
CTU.............	Chad Therapeutics [*AMEX symbol*] (TTSB)

CTU.............	Chad Therapeutics, Inc. [*AMEX symbol*] (SAG)
CTU.............	Channel Testing Unit [*Telecommunications*] (OA)
CTU.............	Chateau Stores of Canada Ltd. [*Toronto Stock Exchange symbol*]
CTU.............	Chengdu [*China*] [*Airport symbol*] (OAG)
CTU.............	CIE [*Communications Interface Equipment*] Test Unit
CTU.............	Circuit Terminal Unit [*Mercury Communications Ltd.*] [*British*]
CTU.............	Combat Training Unit
CTU.............	Commander, Task Unit
CTU.............	Commercial Telegraphers' Union [*Later, C/UBC*] (EA)
CTU.............	Committee for Time Uniformity [*Defunct*]
CTU.............	Compatibility Test Unit
CTU.............	Components Test Unit (AAG)
CTU.............	Computer Test Unit (MCD)
CTU.............	Conference on Transportation Unity [*Defunct*] (EA)
ctu.............	Connecticut [*MARC country of publication code Library of Congress*] (LCCP)
CTU.............	Conservative Trade Unionists [*British*]
CTU.............	Consolidated TOE Update [*DoD*]
CTU.............	Constitutive Transcription Unit [*Genetics*]
CTU.............	Construction Training Unit
CTU.............	Control and Timing Unit [*Computer science*]
CTU.............	Custom, Tradition, and Usage (MCD)
CtU.............	University of Connecticut, Storrs, CT [*Library symbol Library of Congress*] (LCLS)
CTUC...........	Committee on Tunneling and Underground Construction (EA)
CTUC...........	Commonwealth Trade Union Council [*British*] (EAIO)
CTUF...........	Ceylon Trade Union Federation [*Sri Lanka*] (FEA)
CtU-H..........	University of Connecticut, Health Center Library, Hartford, CT [*Library symbol Library of Congress*] (LCLS)
CTUK..........	Computer Town United Kingdom [*Computer literacy project*] (NITA)
CTul...........	Tulare Free Public Library, Tulare, CA [*Library symbol Library of Congress*] (LCLS)
CtU-L..........	University of Connecticut, School of Law, West Hartford, CT [*Library symbol Library of Congress*] (LCLS)
CTUNA.........	Commercial Telegraphers Union (HGAA)
CTur...........	Turlock City Library, Turlock, CA [*Library symbol Library of Congress*] (LCLS)
CTurS..........	California State College, Stanislaus, Turlock, CA [*Library symbol Library of Congress*] (LCLS)
CTUSA........	ComputerTown, United States of America [*Defunct*] (EA)
CTUSA........	Contact Teleministries USA (EA)
CtU-SW........	University of Connecticut, School of Social Work, West Hartford, CT [*Library symbol Library of Congress*] (LCLS)
CTUT...........	Committee on the Training of University Teachers (AIE)
CTUWSD......	Chest Tube Under Water-Seal Drainage [*Medicine*] (MEDA)
CTV.............	Cable Television [*Formerly, CATV*]
CTV.............	Canadian Television Network
CTV.............	Canarctic Ventures [*Vancouver Stock Exchange symbol*]
CTV.............	Captive Test Vehicle
CTV.............	Centro Televisivo Vaticano [*Vatican Television Center*] [*1984*]
CTV.............	Cervical and Thoracic Vertebrae [*Medicine*] (DMAA)
CTV.............	Channel Television [*Channel Islands network*]
CTV.............	Charlottesville [*Virginia*] [*Seismograph station code, US Geological Survey Closed*] (SEIS)
CTV.............	China Television Co. (EY)
CTV.............	Citrus Tristeza Virus
CTV.............	Clinical Target Volume [*Medicine*] (DMAA)
CTV.............	Coaxial Thermal Voltmeter
CTV.............	Cockpit Television Sensor (MCD)
CTV.............	Color Television (DEN)
CTV.............	Comedy Television [*Cable-television system*]
CTV.............	Command Test Vehicle (IAA)
CTV.............	Commercial Television
CTV.............	Community Television (NITA)
CTV.............	Community Television Sydney [*Australia*]
CTV.............	Compatibility Test Van [*Military*]
CTV.............	Computer Trade Video [*British*] [*A publication*] (NITA)
CTV.............	Constant Tangential Velocity
CTV.............	Control Test Vehicles
CTV.............	Crown Television Productions [*Commercial firm*] [*British*]
CTV.............	Curly Top Virus
CTVANSW....	Christian Television Association of New South Wales [*Australia*]
CTVC..........	Cable Television Construction Ltd. [*British*] (NITA)
CTVC..........	Cable Trays Vertical Chase [*Nuclear energy*] (NRCH)
CTVD..........	Cinema Television Digest
CTVI...........	Capsid-Targeted Viral Inactivation [*Immunlogy*]
CTVM..........	Centre for Tropical Veterinary Medicine [*Overseas Development Administration*] [*British*] (DS)
CTVO..........	Centavo [*Cent*] [*Monetary unit in many Spanish-American countries*]
CTVS..........	Calibration and Tracking Visible Sensor (MCD)
CTVS..........	Cockpit Television Sensor
CTVWA.......	Charitable Trust for Vietnam War Art (EA)
CTW............	Can't Tell What [*Accounting slang*]
CTW............	Cargo Tank Wing [*of a ship*] (DS)
CTW............	Cargo Three, Inc. [*Panama*] [*FAA designator*] (FAAC)
CTW............	Catlow Resources Ltd. [*Vancouver Stock Exchange symbol*]
CTW............	Central Terminal of Wilson (DAVI)
CTW............	Children's Television Workshop (EA)
CTW............	Console Typewriter (IAA)
cTw............	[*Tropical*] Continental Warm Air Mass (BARN)
CTW............	Cottonwood Mountains [*California*] [*Seismograph station code, US Geological Survey*] (SEIS)
CTW............	Counter-Terrorist Warfare (LAIN)
CTW............	Counterweight (AAG)
CTW............	Course Made Good through the Water [*Military*] (NATG)

CTW............. Crotone [Italy] [Airport symbol] (AD)
CTW............. Eastern Connecticut State College, J. Eugene Smith Library, Willimantic, CT [OCLC symbol] (OCLC)
CTW............. Newcomerstown, OH [Location identifier FAA] (FAAL)
CtW............. Wesleyan University, Middletown, CT [Library symbol Library of Congress] (LCLS)
CTWA.......... Commercial Tribunal of Western Australia
CtWAB .... Anaconda American Brass Co., Waterbury, CT [Library symbol Library of Congress] (LCLS)
CTWALK ..... Catwalk
CtWat.......... Watertown Library, Watertown, CT [Library symbol Library of Congress] (LCLS)
CtWatU....... University of Connecticut, Waterbury Branch, Waterbury, CT [Library symbol Library of Congress] (LCLS)
CtWB .... Silas Bronson Public Library, Waterbury, CT [Library symbol Library of Congress] (LCLS)
CtWehar ...... West Hartford Public Library, West Hartford, CT [Library symbol Library of Congress] (LCLS)
CtWeharS .... Saint Joseph College, West Hartford, CT [Library symbol Library of Congress] (LCLS)
CtWeharU.... University of Hartford, West Hartford, CT [Library symbol Library of Congress] (LCLS)
CtWehavM... Miles Laboratories, Inc., Miles Pharmaceutical, West Haven, CT [Library symbol Library of Congress] (LCLS)
CtWehavV.... United States Veterans Administration Hospital, West Haven, CT [Library symbol Library of Congress] (LCLS)
CtWep.......... Westport Public Library, Westport, CT [Library symbol Library of Congress] (LCLS)
CtWepSC .... Save the Children, Westport, CT [Library symbol Library of Congress] (LCLS)
CtWetHi ...... Wethersfield Historical Society, Wethersfield, CT [Library symbol Library of Congress] (LCLS)
CtWhvM...... Miles Laboratories, Inc., Miles Pharmaceutical, West Haven, CT [Library symbol] [Library of Congress] (LCLS)
CtWhvV....... United States Veterans Administration Medical Center, West Haven, CT [Library symbol] [Library of Congress] (LCLS)
CtWih.......... Windham Free Public Library, Windham, CT [Library symbol] [Library of Congress] (LCLS)
CtWillN....... Eastern Connecticut State College, Willimantic, CT [Library symbol Library of Congress] (LCLS)
CtWisHi ...... Windsor Historical Society, Fyler House, Windsor, CT [Library symbol] [Library of Congress] (LCLS)
CtWMHi ...... Mattatuck Museum of the Mattatuck Historical Society, Waterbury, CT [Library symbol] [Library of Congress] (LCLS)
CTWO .... Center for Third World Organizing (EA)
CTWS.......... Connecticut Water Service, Inc. [NASDAQ symbol] (NQ)
CTWS.......... Connecticut Wtr Svc [NASDAQ symbol] (TTSB)
CTWT.......... Counterweight (KSC)
CTWU .... Canadian Transport Workers Union [Syndicat Canadien des Travailleurs du Transport] (AC)
CTX............. Cargo Tank Common [of a ship] (DS)
CTX............. Carolina Air Transit, Inc. [ICAO designator] (FAAC)
CTX............. Cefotaxime [An antibiotic]
CTX............. Center of Technical Excellence [Army] (RDA)
CTX............. Centex Corp. [NYSE symbol] (SPSG)
CTX............. Centex Corp. [NYSE symbol] (TTSB)
CTX............. Centrex System Number [Bell System] [Telecommunications] (TEL)
CTX............. Cerebrotendinous Xanthomatosis [Medicine]
CTX............. Charybdotoxin [Biochemistry]
ctx............. Cholera Toxin [Medicine]
CTX............. Ciguatoxin [Agent in fish poisoning]
CTX............. Clear-Type Exterior Trim [Weyerhaeuser Co.]
CTX............. Cobra Toxin
CTX............. Combined Training Exercise [Military] (ADDR)
CTX............. Consoltex Canada, Inc. [Toronto Stock Exchange symbol]
CTX............. Continuously Variable Transaxle [Automotive engineering]
CTX............. Corporate Trade Exchange [Automated Clearing House]
CTX............. Corrosion Center of Excellence [US Army Materials Technology Laboratory]
CTX............. Cytoxan [Cyclophosphamide] [Also, C, CP, CPA, CPM, CY, CYC, CYP, CYT] [Antineoplastic drug]
CTX............. Xanthomatosis [Medicine] (DAVI)
CTXCO .... Centrex Central Office [Telecommunications] (TEL)
CTXCU .... Centrex Customer [Telecommunications] (TEL)
CTXN .... Contraction [Obstetrics and orthopedics] (DAVI)
CTX-PLAT .... Cyclophosphamide, Platinol [Cisplatin] [Antineoplastic drug regimen]
CTXR .... Core Technologies [NASDAQ symbol] (TTSB)
CTXS.......... Citrix Systems [NASDAQ symbol] (TTSB)
CTY............. Center for Talented Youth [Johns Hopkins University] (PAZ)
CTY............. City
CTY............. Community
CTY............. Community Banks, Inc. [AMEX symbol] (SAG)
CTY............. Community Banks (PA) [AMEX symbol] (TTSB)
Cty .... Contemporary Records [Los Angeles] [Record label]
CTY............. Control Energy [Vancouver Stock Exchange symbol]
CTY............. County [Board on Geographic Names]
CTY............. Cross City, FL [Location identifier FAA] (FAAL)
CTY............. Cryderman Air Service [ICAO designator] (FAAC)
CtY............. Yale University, New Haven, CT [Library symbol Library of Congress] (LCLS)
CTYA.......... Century Communic'ns'A' [NASDAQ symbol] (TTSB)
CTYA.......... Century Telecommunications [NASDAQ symbol] (SAG)
CtY-A .... Yale University, School of Fine Arts, New Haven, CT [Library symbol Library of Congress] (LCLS)

CtY-B .... Yale University, Osborn Memorial Laboratories of Biological Sciences, New Haven, CT [Library symbol Library of Congress] (LCLS)
CtY-BA .... Yale University, Yale Center for British Art, New Haven, CT [Library symbol Library of Congress] (LCLS)
CtY-BR........ Yale University, Beinecke Rare Book and Manuscript Library, New Haven, CT [Library symbol Library of Congress] (LCLS)
CtY-BS .... Yale University, Babylonian Seminary, New Haven, CT [Library symbol Library of Congress] (LCLS)
CtY-C .... Yale University, Sterling Chemistry Laboratories, New Haven, CT [Library symbol Library of Congress] (LCLS)
Cty Ct Chron... County Courts Chronicle [1847-1920] [England] [A publication] (DLA)
Cty Ct R ...... County Courts Reports [1860-1920] [England] [A publication] (DLA)
ctyd............. Courtyard (VRA)
CtY-D .... Yale University, Divinity School, New Haven, CT [Library symbol Library of Congress] (LCLS)
CtY-E .... Yale University, Department of Economics, Economic Growth Center, New Haven, CT [Library symbol Library of Congress] (LCLS)
CtY-EC .... Yale University, Elizabethan Club, New Haven, CT [Library symbol Library of Congress] (LCLS)
CtY-EP .... Yale University, Department of Epidemiology and Public Health, New Haven, CT [Library symbol Library of Congress] (LCLS)
CtY-FE .... Yale University, Far Eastern Library, New Haven, CT [Library symbol Library of Congress] (LCLS)
CtY-FS .... Yale University, School of Forestry, New Haven, CT [Library symbol Library of Congress] (LCLS)
CtY-H .... Yale University, Hammond Metallurgical Laboratories, New Haven, CT [Library symbol Library of Congress] (LCLS)
CtyHld.......... City Holding Co. [Associated Press] (SAG)
CtY-K .... Yale University, Kirkland Hall, New Haven, CT [Library symbol Library of Congress] (LCLS)
CtY-KS .... Yale University, Kline Science Library, New Haven, CT [Library symbol Library of Congress] (LCLS)
CtY-L .... Yale University, Law Library, New Haven, CT [Library symbol Library of Congress] (LCLS)
CtyLTr .... City Investing Co. Liquidating Trust [Associated Press] (SAG)
CtY-M .... Yale University, Medical School, New Haven, CT [Library symbol Library of Congress] (LCLS)
CtyMT.......... Community Medical Transport, Inc. [Associated Press] (SAG)
CtY-Mus....... Yale University, School of Music, New Haven, CT [Library symbol Library of Congress] (LCLS)
CtyNY.......... Contemporary Records (New York) [Record label]
CTYP........... Cyanotype (VRA)
CtY-P .... Yale University, Peabody Museum of Natural History, New Haven, CT [Library symbol Library of Congress] (LCLS)
CTYS.......... Cityscape Financial [NASDAQ symbol] (TTSB)
CTYS.......... Cityscape Financial Corp. [NASDAQ symbol] (SAG)
Ctyscape...... Cityscape Financial Corp. [Associated Press] (SAG)
CtY-SSE ...... Yale University, Social Sciences and Economic Growth Center, New Haven, CT [Library symbol Library of Congress] (LCLS)
CtY-T .... Yale University, Transportation Library, New Haven, CT [Library symbol Library of Congress] (LCLS)
CTZ............. Cata SACIFI [Argentina ICAO designator] (FAAC)
CTZ............. Chemoreceptor Trigger Zone
CTZ............. Chlorothiazide [Diuretic] (MAE)
CTZ............. Clinton, NC [Location identifier FAA] (FAAL)
CTZ............. Control Zone [Aviation]
CTZ............. Corps Tactical Zone [Military]
CTZ............. Corpus Christi Bancshares [AMEX symbol] (SPSG)
CtzBcp .... Citizens Bancorp [Associated Press] (SAG)
CtzBnch....... Citizens Bancshares, Inc. [Associated Press] (SAG)
CtzFBk .... Citizens Federal Bank, FSB [Associated Press] (SAG)
CTZN.......... Citfed Bancorp [NASDAQ symbol] (TTSB)
CTZN.......... CitFed Bancorp, Inc. [NASDAQ symbol] (SAG)
CtznCp .... Citizens Corp. [Associated Press] (SAG)
CtzSec .... Citizens Security Group, Inc. [Associated Press] (SAG)
CU............... Cable Untwist
CU............... California Unreported Cases [1855-1910] [A publication] (DLA)
CU............... Call-Us, Inc.
CU............... Cambridge University [England]
CU............... Camouflage Unit [Military]
CU............... Canadian Utilities Ltd. [Toronto Stock Exchange symbol]
CU............... Casting Up [Printing] (DGA)
CU............... Casualties Union (EA)
CU............... Catholic University
CU............... Cause Unknown [Medicine] (DAVI)
CU............... Central Unit [Computer science] (IAA)
CU............... Certification Unit
CU............... Children of the Universe [Defunct] (EA)
CU............... Christian Union [University student group] [British]
CU............... Chronic Urticaria [Immunology]
CU............... Church Union [British] (DAS)
CU............... Chymotrypsin Unit
CU............... Clavieruebung [Music]
CU............... Clinical Unit
CU............... Close-Up [A photograph or motion picture sequence taken from a short distance]
cu............... Close-Up (WDMC)
CU............... Coefficient of Utilization
CU............... Colorado University (PDAA)
CU............... Color Unit (MAE)
CU............... Columbia University [New York, NY]
C/U............. Come-Up
CU............... Commercial Union Assurance Co. Ltd. [British] (ECON)

CU............ Common Use (ROG)
CU............ Communications Unlimited [*Charlotte, NC*] [*Telecommunications*] (TSSD)
CU............ Compensation Unit
CU............ Composite Utility
CU............ Computer Unit (EA)
CU............ Congregational Union
CU............ Congressional Union (EA)
CU............ Construction Unit [*Computer science*]
CU............ Consumers Union of United States (EA)
CU............ Control Unit [*Computer science*]
CU............ Convalescent Unit [*of a hospital*]
CU............ Conversion Unit [*British military*] (DMA)
cu............ Copper (VRA)
Cu............ Copper (GNE)
CU............ Cornell University [*Ithaca, NY*]
CU............ Coronary Unit (IIA)
CU............ Corrected Unpostable [*IRS*]
CU............ Couplers [*JETDS nomenclature*] [*Military*] (CET)
CU............ Credit Union
CU............ Cross-Talk Unit
CU............ Crystal Unit [*Piezoelectricity*]
CU............ Cuba [*ANSI two-letter standard code*] (CNC)
cu............ Cuba [*MARC country of publication code Library of Congress*] (LCCP)
CU............ Cubana Airlines [*ICAO designator*] (AD)
CU............ Cubana Airways (DS)
CU............ Cube
CU............ Cubic (EY)
CU............ Cubitainer (MCD)
CU............ CUC International, Inc. [*Formerly, Comp-U-Card International*] [*NYSE symbol*] (SPSG)
CU............ CUC Intl. [*NYSE symbol*] (TTSB)
CU............ Cucumber [*Slang*] (DSUE)
CU............ Culinary Arts Program [*Association of Independent Colleges and Schools specialization code*]
CU............ Cumulative List Indicator [*IRS*]
CU............ Cumulus [*Cloud*] [*Meteorology*]
Cu............ Cuprum [*Copper*] [*Chemical element*]
CU............ Curacao [*Netherlands Antilles*]
Cu............ Curie [*Unit of radioactivity*] [*See Ci*] (AAMN)
CU............ Customer Premise (NRCH)
CU............ Customer Utilization (SSD)
CU............ Customs Union [*British*] (DAS)
CU............ Movimiento Colombia Unida [*United Colombian Movement*] [*Political party*] (EY)
CU............ Piezoelectric-Crystal Unit (IEEE)
CU............ University of California, Berkeley, Main Library, Berkeley, CA [*Library symbol Library of Congress*] (LCLS)
C$_u$............ Urea Clearance [*Biochemistry*] (DAVI)
Cu-7............ Copper-7 [*A contraceptive device*] [*Gynecology*] (DAVI)
CUA .... Canadian Underwriters Association
CUA .... Canadian Urological Surgeons
CUA .... Catholic University of America [*Washington, DC*]
CUA .... Catholic University of America, Washington, DC [*OCLC symbol*] (OCLC)
CUA .... China United Airlines [*ICAO designator*] (FAAC)
CUA .... Circuit Unit Assembly
CUA .... Colour Users' Association [*British*] (BI)
CUA .... Commercial Union Assurance Company of Australia Ltd.
CUA .... Commercial Utilisation Area
CUA .... Committee for University Assistance [*Military British*]
CUA .... Commonly Used Acronym
CUA .... Common User Access [*Computer science*] (BYTE)
CUA .... Communication International [*Vancouver Stock Exchange symbol*]
CUA .... Compliant Utilities and Applications [*Computer science*] (PCM)
CUA .... Compugraphics Users Association [*Bend, OR*] (EA)
CUA .... Computer Users Association
CUA .... Confederated Unions of America [*Later, NFIU*]
CUA .... Conference of University Administrators [*British*] [*An association*] (DBA)
CUA .... Cooperative Upper-Air Unit [*National Weather Service*]
CUA .... Council for Urban Affairs [*Terminated, 1970*]
CUA .... Credit Union Australia Ltd.
CUA .... Cuajimalpa [*Mexico*] [*Later, TEO*] [*Geomagnetic observatory code*]
CU-A............ University of California, Davis, Main Library, Davis, CA [*Library symbol Library of Congress*] (LCLS)
CUA Architecture... Common User Access Architecture [*Computer science*] (DOM)
CUAC............ Cartographic Users Advisory Council [*American Library Association*]
CUACS......... Center for Urban Affairs and Community Services [*North Carolina State University*] [*Research center*] (RCD)
CUAG.......... Computer Users Associations Group (MHDB)
CU-AGRI ..... University of California, Berkeley, Agriculture Library, Berkeley, CA [*Library symbol Library of Congress*] (LCLS)
CU-AL.......... University of California, Davis, Law Library, Davis, CA [*Library symbol Library of Congress*] (LCLS)
CUALS .... Catholic University of America Law School (DLA)
CU-AM........ University of California, Davis, Health Sciences Library, Davis, CA [*Library symbol Library of Congress*] (LCLS)
CU & PFC .... Criminally Uttering and Publishing False [*or Forged*] Check [*Legal term*]
CU-ANTH ..... University of California, Berkeley, Anthropology Library, Berkeley, CA [*Library symbol Library of Congress*] (LCLS)
CUAP .... Active Pass, BC [*ICAO location identifier*] (ICLI)

CUARO......... California Undersea Aqueduct Reconnaissance-Oceanography Study [*Department of the Interior*] (GFGA)
CUAS .... Cambridge University Air Squadron [*British*] (DI)
CUAS .... Computer Utilization Accounting System (IEEE)
CUAS .... Cooperative Upper-Air Station [*National Weather Service*] (NOAA)
CUASA......... Carleton University Academic Staff Association [*Association du Personnel Enseignant de l'Universite Carleton*] (AC)
CU-ASTR...... University of California, Berkeley, Astronomy Library, Berkeley, CA [*Library symbol Library of Congress*] (LCLS)
CUB .... Carlton and United Breweries [*Australia*]
CUB .... Central Unit-Buffer (IAA)
CUB .... Citizens United for Bear
CUB .... Citizens Utility Board
CUB .... Clean Up Buck (MCD)
CUB .... Coalition United for Bear
CUB .... Columbia, SC [*Location identifier FAA*] (FAAL)
CUB .... Commonality Usage Board (NASA)
CUB .... Companies Update Bulletin [*National Companies and Securities Commission*] [*A publication*]
CUB .... Concerned United Birthparents (EA)
CUB .... Control Unit Busy (CMD)
CuB .... Copper Band [*Dentistry*]
CUB .... Council for UHF Broadcasting (EA)
CUB .... Cuba [*ANSI three-letter standard code*] (CNC)
CUB .... Cube Resources [*Vancouver Stock Exchange symbol*]
CUB .... Cubic
CUB .... Cubic Corp. [*AMEX symbol*] (SPSG)
CUB .... Cubicle (MSA)
cub. .... Cubicle (VRA)
CUB .... Customary Behavior [*Psychology*]
CUB .... Empresa Cubana de Aviacion [*Cuba*] [*ICAO designator*] (FAAC)
CUBA .... College and University Business Administration, Administrative Service [*National Association of College and University Business Officers*] [*A publication*]
CUBA .... Herzfeld Caribbean Basin Fund [*NASDAQ symbol*] (SAG)
CU-BANC .... University of California, Berkeley, Bancroft Library, Berkeley, CA [*Library symbol Library of Congress*] (LCLS)
CUBC .... Citizen Utility Board Campaign [*Defunct*] (EA)
C/UBC .... CWA/UTW Bargaining Council (EA)
CUBE .... C-CUBE Microsystems [*NASDAQ symbol*] (SAG)
CUBE .... Conceptual Understanding through Blind Evaluation [*Educational test*]
CUBE .... Concertation Unit for Biotechnology in Europe
CUBE .... Cooperating Users of Burroughs Equipment (EA)
CUBE .... Cubicle
CUBG .... College and University Booksellers' Group [*British*]
CUBIC .... Common User Baseline for the Intelligence Community (MCD)
Cubic .... Cubic Corp. [*Associated Press*]
CU-BIOC ..... University of California, Berkeley, Biochemistry Library, Berkeley, CA [*Library symbol Library of Congress*] (LCLS)
CU-BIOL...... University of California, Berkeley, Biology Library, Berkeley, CA [*Library symbol Library of Congress*] (LCLS)
CubistPh ..... Cubist Pharmaceuticals, Inc. [*Associated Press*] (SAG)
CUBMW ...... Canadian Union of Base Metal Workers
CUBN .... CU Bancorp [*NASDAQ symbol*] (SPSG)
CU Bnc ...... CU Bancorp. [*Associated Press*] (SAG)
CUBOL .... Computer Usage's Business-Oriented Language [*Computer science*]
CUBS .... Calls Underwritten by Swanbrook [*Investment term*] (DFIT)
CUBS .... Center for Urban Black Studies (EA)
CUBS .... City University Business School [*London, England*]
CUBS .... Congress for the Unity of Black Students
CubV .... Cuban Victor [*Record label*]
CUC .... Cameroon United Congress [*Political party*]
CUC .... Canadian Union College
CUC .... Canadian Unitarian Council
CUC .... Cask Unloading Cell [*Nuclear energy*] (NRCH)
CUC .... Chronic Ulcerative Colitis [*Medicine*]
CUC .... Clinical Unit Coordinator
CUC .... Coal Utilisation Council [*British*]
CUC .... Columbia Union College, Takoma Park, MD [*OCLC symbol*] (OCLC)
CUC .... Comite de Unidad Campesina [*Committee of Peasant Unity*] [*Guatemala*] [*Political party*] (PD)
CUC .... Communications Union Canada
CUC .... Computers Users' Committee [*United Nations Development Program*]
CUC .... Computer Usage Control (NASA)
CUC .... [*Le*] Conseil pour l'Unite Canadienne [*The Council for Canadian Unity*] (AC)
CUC .... Continuous until Cancelled [*Insurance*]
CUC .... Cooperative Union of Canada
CUC .... Crystal Unit Cell
CUC .... Cucuta [*Colombia*] [*Airport symbol*] (OAG)
CUC .... Culbro Corp. [*NYSE symbol*] (SPSG)
CUC .... Cutlass Industries Corp. [*Vancouver Stock Exchange symbol*]
CUC .... Cyrillic Union Catalog [*Library of Congress*]
CUCA .... Cambridge University Conservative Association (ECON)
CUCA .... Carpet and Upholstery Cleaning Association [*Australia*]
CUCB .... Control Unit / Control Block [*Computer science*] (IAA)
CUCB .... Cumulus and Cumulonimbus [*Clouds*] [*Meteorology*]
CUCCA........ Canadian University & College Counselling Association [*Association Canadienne de Counselling Universitaire et Collegial*] [*Formerly, University Counselling & Placement Association*] (AC)
CUCCOA...... Canadian University & College Conference Officers Association (AC)
CUCD .... Council for University Classics Departments (AIE)
CU-CHEM.... University of California, Berkeley, Chemistry Library, Berkeley, CA [*Library symbol Library of Congress*] (LCLS)

CUC Intl CUC International [*Associated Press*] (SAG)
CUCM Cubic Centimeter
CUCM Master Chief Constructionman [*Navy rating*]
CUCND Combined Universities Campaign for Nuclear Disarmament [*Canada*]
CUCO Conservative and Unionist Central Office [*British*] (DAS)
CUCO Cucos, Inc. [*NASDAQ symbol*] (NQ)
Cucos Cucos, Inc. [*Associated Press*] (SAG)
CUCOSS California Universities Council on Space Sciences
CUCR Complementary Under-Color Removal [*Printing technology*]
CUCS Centre for Urban and Community Studies [*University of Toronto*] [*Research center*] (RCD)
CUCS Computation-Universal Cellular Space (PDAA)
CU-CS University of California, Berkeley, Center for Chinese Studies, Berkeley, CA [*Library symbol Library of Congress*] (LCLS)
Cu Ct Customs Court Reports [*A publication*] (DLA)
CUCUC College and University Computer Users Conference (EA)
CUCURB CRUENT Cucurbitula Cruenta [*Cupping Glass with Scarificator*] [*Pharmacy*] (ROG)
CUCV Commercial Utility Cargo Vehicle [*Army*] (RDA)
CUCW Central Union for Child Welfare [*Finland*] (EAIO)
CUD Caloundra [*Australia Airport symbol*] (OAG)
CUD Cause Undetermined [*Medicine*] (DAVI)
CUD Congenital Urinary Tract Deformity [*Medicine*] (AAMN)
CUD Craft Union Department [*AFL-CIO*]
CUDAMN Common User, Dynamic Allocation Multi-Media Network (MCD)
CUDAT Common User Data [*Telecommunications*] (TEL)
CUDAT Common User Data Terminal [*Military*] (AABC)
CUDBC Conseil Universitaire des Directeurs de Biologie du Canada (AC)
CUDD Cuddesdon Theological College [*Later, Rippon College, Cuddesdon*] [*Oxford*] [*British*] (ROG)
Cudd Copyh Cuddon. Copyhold Acts [*1865*] [*A publication*] (ILCA)
CUDE Cambridge University Department of Education [*British*] (AIE)
CUDIX Common User Digital Information Exchange [*Satellite communication*] (NVT)
CUDIXS Common User Digital Information Exchange System [*or Subsystem*] [*Satellite communication*] (MCD)
CUDM Cubic Decimeter (IAA)
CUDN Common User Data Network (ADA)
CU-DOCU University of California, Berkeley, Documents Department, Berkeley, CA [*Library symbol Library of Congress*] (LCLS)
CUDOS Continuously Updated Dynamic Optimizing Systems (IEEE)
CUDS Common User Data Services (NITA)
CUDS Cumulative Data Statistics (NASA)
CUDWR Columbia University, Division of War Research
CUE Catch per Unit Effort [*Pisciculture*]
CUE Center for Urban Education [*Research center*] (RCD)
CUE Chemical Underwater Explosive (PDAA)
CUE Coastal Upwelling Experiment [*Marine science*] (MSC)
CUE Cognizant User Engineer [*Deep Space Network, NASA*]
CUE Common Usage Equipment (NASA)
CUE Communications Unit Executor
CUE Component Utilization Effectiveness
CUE Computer Update Equipment
CUE Computer User Education [*An association*]
CUE Computer Utilization Efficiency (IAA)
CUE Concentrated Urban Enforcement [*Bureau of Alcohol, Tobacco, and Firearms*]
CUE Configuration Utilization Efficiency (BUR)
CUE Configuration Utilization Evaluator (IAA)
CUE Control Unit End (CMD)
CUE Cooperating Users' Exchange
CUE Correction, Update, and Extension Software Program [*Department of Commerce*] (GFGA)
CUE Correlating Users Exchange (SAA)
CUE Cruiser Minerals [*Vancouver Stock Exchange symbol*]
CUE Cucumber [*Slang*] (DSUE)
CUE Cuenca [*Ecuador*] [*Airport symbol*] (OAG)
CUE IUME/ERIC [*Institute for Urban and Minority Education/Educational Resources Information Center*] Clearinghouse on Urban Education [*Columbia University*] [*Research center*] (RCD)
CUEA Coastal Upwelling Ecosystems Analysis [*Marine science*] (MSC)
CU-EART University of California, Berkeley, Earth Sciences Library, Berkeley, CA [*Library symbol Library of Congress*] (LCLS)
CU-EAST University of California, Berkeley, East Asiatic Library, Berkeley, CA [*Library symbol Library of Congress*] (LCLS)
CUEBS Commission on Undergraduate Education in the Biological Sciences
CUEC Congressional Underwater Explorers Club (EA)
CUECOS University College Cardiff English Centre for Overseas Students [*British*] (CB)
CUED Center for Urban Economics Development [*University of Illinois at Chicago*] [*Research center*] (RCD)
CUED National Council for Urban Economic Development (EA)
CUE/DSO Configuration Usage Evaluator / Data Set Optimizer (PDAA)
CU-EDUC University of California, Berkeley, Education-Psychology Library, Berkeley, CA [*Library symbol Library of Congress*] (LCLS)
CU-EERC University of California, Berkeley, Earthquake Engineering Research Center, Richmond, CA [*Library symbol*] [*Library of Congress*] (LCLS)
CUEFL Communicative Use of English as a Foreign Language (AIE)
CUEFS Cooperative Users of Equimatics Financial Systems (CSR)
CUE-KY Computer-Using Educators of Kentucky (EDAC)
CU-ENGI University of California, Berkeley, Engineering Library, Berkeley, CA [*Library symbol Library of Congress*] (LCLS)
CU-ENTO University of California, Berkeley, Entomology Library, Berkeley, CA [*Library symbol Library of Congress*] (LCLS)

CU-ENVI University of California, Berkeley, Environmental Design Library, Berkeley, CA [*Library symbol Library of Congress*] (LCLS)
CUEP Central Unit on Environmental Pollution [*British*]
CUEPACS Congress of Unions of Employees in the Public and Civil Services [*Malaya*]
CUERL Columbia University Electronic Research Laboratory (SAA)
CUERL Columbia University Electronics Research Laboratories
CUES Center for Urban Environmental Studies (EA)
CUES College and University Environment Scales [*Psychology*]
CUES Computer Utility Educational System (MCD)
CUES Credit Union Executives Society
CUESG Curtin University Environmental Studies Group [*Australia*]
CUESTA Communications User Emulated System for Traffic Analysis (MHDI)
CUEW Canadian Union of Educational Workers
CUEW Congregational Union of England and Wales (BARN)
CUF Canada Income Plus Fund 1987 Trust Units [*Toronto Stock Exchange symbol*]
CUF Catholicarum Universitatum Federatio [*Federation of Catholic Universities*]
CUF Catholics United for the Faith (EA)
CUF Civic United Front [*Tanzania*] [*Political party*]
CUF Columbia, CA [*Location identifier FAA*] (FAAL)
CUF Common University Fund [*British*]
CUF Cross Utilization File (MCD)
CUF University of San Francisco, Gleeson Library, San Francisco, CA [*OCLC symbol*] (OCLC)
CUFA Concordia University Faculty Association [*Association des Professeurs de l'Universite Concordia*] (AC)
CUFA/BC Confederation of University Faculty/Associations of British Columbia (AC)
CUFAM Cooperative Users of FICS and MARS [*Atlanta, GA*] (CSR)
CUFC Consortium of University Film Centers [*Library network*] (EA)
CU-FORE University of California, Berkeley, Forestry Library, Berkeley, CA [*Library symbol Library of Congress*] (LCLS)
CUFOS Center for UFO [*Unidentified Flying Object*] Studies [*Information service or system*] (IID)
CU-FPRO University of California, Berkeley, Forest Products Laboratory, Berkeley, CA [*Library symbol Library of Congress*] (LCLS)
CUFRA Cumulus Fractus [*NWS*] (FAAC)
CUFT Center for the Utilization of Federal Technology [*National Technical Information Service*] [*Springfield, VA*]
CUFT Cubic Feet [*or Foot*] (MSA)
cu ft Cubic Feet (IDOE)
cu ft Cubic Foot (IDOE)
CUG Census User Guide
CUG Closed User Group [*Communications*]
CUG Common User Group [*SAGE*]
CUG Concurrency Update Group
CUG Continental Gold Corp. [*Vancouver Stock Exchange symbol*]
CUG Contol Unit Group [*Computer science*]
CUG Crosfield Users Group (EA)
CUG Cuglieri [*Italy*] [*Seismograph station code, US Geological Survey*] (SEIS)
CUG Cystidine-Uridine-Guanidine [*Organic chemistry*] (DAVI)
CUG Cystourethrogram [*Medicine*]
CUG Orange-Cudal [*Australia Airport symbol*] (OAG)
CUG University of California, Los Angeles, Graduate School of Library and Information Science, Los Angeles, CA [*OCLC symbol*] (OCLC)
CUGA Cumberland Gap National Historical Park [*National Park Service designation*]
CUG IOC Control Unit Group Input/Output Control Unit [*Computer science*]
CUGS Community United Group Services [*British*]
CUH Control Users Handbook
CUH Cumulus Technology Ltd. [*Vancouver Stock Exchange symbol Toronto Stock Exchange symbol*]
Cu H Current History [*A publication*] (BRI)
CUH Cushing, OK [*Location identifier FAA*] (FAAL)
CUH University of California, San Francisco, Hastings College of the Law, Library, San Francisco, CA [*OCLC symbol*] (OCLC)
CUHA Quaqtaq, PQ [*ICAO location identifier*] (ICLI)
CUHL Columbia University Hudson Laboratory
CUHP Council of Urban Health Providers [*Defunct*] (EA)
CUHS Computer Use in the Health Service [*British*]
CU-HUMA University of California, Berkeley, Humanities Graduate Service, Berkeley, CA [*Library symbol Library of Congress*] (LCLS)
CUI Canadian Urban Institute [*Institut Urbain du Canada*] (AC)
CUI Character-Based User Interface [*Computer science*]
CUI Childhelp USA, Inc. (EA)
CUI Chronic Uterine Inflammation [*Medicine*]
CUI Chymotrypsin Units Inhibited
CUI Cincinnati Uplink, Inc. [*Cincinnati, OH*] [*Telecommunications*] (TSSD)
CUI Common User Interface [*Computer science*]
CUI Control Unit Interface [*Computer science*] (IAA)
CUI Currie Rose Resources, Inc. [*Vancouver Stock Exchange symbol*]
CU-I University of California, Irvine, General Library, Irvine, CA [*Library symbol Library of Congress*] (LCLS)
CUI University of California, Irvine, Irvine, CA [*OCLC symbol*] (OCLC)
CUIC Cardiff University Industry Centre [*British*] (IRUK)
CUIDES Consejo Universitario Inter-Americana para el Desarrollo Economico y Social [*Inter-American University Council for Economic and Social Development - IUCESD*] (EA)
CU-IG University of California, Berkeley, Institute of Governmental Studies, Berkeley,CA [*Library symbol Library of Congress*] (LCLS)
CUIL Common Usage Item List (NASA)

CU-I-M .... University of California, Irvine, College of Medicine, Irvine, CA [*Library symbol Library of Congress*] (LCLS)

CUIN .... Common User Interoffice Network [*Telecommunications*] (ECII)

CUIN .... Cubic Inch

cu in .... Cubic Inch (IDOE)

cu in .... Cubic Inches (IDOE)

CUIR .... Cuirassed [*Numismatics*]

CUIRL .... Committee of University Industrial Relations Librarians

CU-IS .... University of California, Berkeley, Institute of International Studies, Berkeley, CA [*Library symbol Library of Congress*] (LCLS)

CU-IT .... University of California, Berkeley, Institute of Transportation Studies, Berkeley, CA [*Library symbol Library of Congress*] (LCLS)

CUIUA .... Council of University Institutes for Urban Affairs [*Later, UAA*] (EA)

CUJ .... Canutama [*Brazil*] [*Airport symbol*] (AD)

CUJ .... Cujus [*Of Which*] [*Latin*]

CUJ LIB .... Cujus Libet [*Of Any You Please*] [*Pharmacy*]

CUJS .... Canadian Union of Jewish Students

CUJT .... Complementary Unijunction Transistor (IEEE)

CUJUSL .... Cujus Libet [*Of Any You Please*] [*Pharmacy*] (ROG)

CUK .... Combika [*Sao Paulo, Brazil*] [*Airport symbol*] (AD)

CUK .... Polo Aviation Ltd. [*British*] [*FAA designator*] (FAAC)

CUk .... Ukiah Public Library, Ukiah, CA [*Library symbol Library of Congress*] (LCLS)

CUKAC .... Combined United Kingdom / Australian Long Range Weapons Committee

CUKC .... Citizens of the United Kingdom and Commonwealth

CUKCC .... Canada-United Kingdom Chamber of Commerce (DS)

CUKE .... Cucumber [*Slang*] (DSUE)

CUkHi .... Mendocino County Historical Society, Held-Poage Memorial Home and Research Library, Ukiah, CA [*Library symbol*] [*Library of Congress*] (LCLS)

CUKT .... Carnegie United Kingdom Trust (BARN)

CUKUA .... Compugraphic United Kingdom Users' Association (DGA)

CUL .... Cambridge University Library [*British*] (DLA)

CUL .... Canonical Unit of Length

CUL .... Carmi, IL [*Location identifier FAA*] (FAAL)

CUL .... Catholics United for Life (EA)

CUL .... Chukyo University [*UTLAS symbol*]

CUL .... Command Uplink [*NASA*] (KSC)

CUL .... Communist University of London [*England*] (AIE)

Cul .... Culex [*Classical studies*] (OCD)

CUL .... Culiacan [*Mexico*] [*Airport symbol*] (OAG)

CUL .... Culiacan [*Mexico*] [*Seismograph station code, US Geological Survey Closed*] (SEIS)

CUL .... Culinary (ADA)

CUL .... Culligan Water Tech [*NYSE symbol*] (TTSB)

CUL .... Cuyahoga Community College, Learning Resource Center, Cleveland, OH [*OCLC symbol*] (OCLC)

CUL .... See You Later [*Telegrapher's slang*]

CU-L .... University of California, Berkeley, Law Library, Berkeley, CA [*Library symbol Library of Congress*] (LCLS)

CUL8R .... See You Later [*Computer science*] (DOM)

CU-Lbl .... University of California, Lawrence Berkeley Laboratory, Berkeley, CA [*Library symbol Library of Congress*] (LCLS)

Culbro .... Culbro Corp. [*Associated Press*] (SAG)

CULER .... Cryogenic Upper Atmosphere Limb Emission Radiometer (MCD)

CULGB .... Credit Union League of Great Britain (DI)

CU-LIBR ...... University of California, Berkeley, Library School Library, Berkeley, CA [*Library symbol Library of Congress*] (LCLS)

CULL .... Corning Uniformity Limit Level

CULL .... Cross-Reference Utility [*Computer science*]

CULL .... Cullompton [*England*]

Cull BL .... Cullen's Bankrupt Law [*A publication*] (DLA)

CullnFr .... Cullen-Frost Bankers, Inc. [*Associated Press*] (SAG)

CULO .... Cornell University Laboratory of Ornithology (EA)

CULP .... California Union List of Periodicals [*Cooperative Library Agency for Systems and Services*] [*Database*]

CULP .... Computer Usage List Processor (IEEE)

CULP .... Culp, Inc. [*NASDAQ symbol*] (NQ)

Culp Inc ...... Culp, Inc. [*Associated Press*] (SAG)

CU-Lrl .... University of California, Lawrence Livermore Laboratory, Livermore, CA [*Library symbol Library of Congress*] (LCLS)

CULS .... Convertible Unsecured Loan Stock [*Finance*]

CULT .... Central Off-Equatorial Pacific Upper Layer Temperature [*Oceanography*]

CULT .... Chinese University Language Translation [*Human-aided machine translation*] [*Hong Kong*] (NITA)

CULT .... Common User Land Transportation [*Military*] (NVT)

cult .... Cultivated [*Botany*]

CULT .... Cultural

CULT .... Culture [*Microbiology*]

CULTER .... University of Colorado at Boulder Long-Term Ecological Research Project [*Research center*] (RCD)

CULTIVON .... Cultivation (ROG)

CULTURE ..... Creative Use of Leisure Time under Restrictive Environments [*Federally funded prison program*]

CULTUREX .... Association for Cultural Exchange (EA)

CULTVR .... Cultivator

CULV .... Culvert

CUM .... Cambridge University Mission

CUM .... Casualty Underwriting Manual [*Insurance*]

CUM .... Central Unit-Memory (MCD)

CUM .... Committee on the Unisex Military [*Defunct*] (EA)

CUM .... Computer Utilization Monitor (IAA)

Cum .... Concerteum [*Record label*] [*France*]

CUM .... Cubic Meter

CUM .... Cumana [*Venezuela*] [*Airport symbol*] (OAG)

CUM .... Cumana [*Venezuela*] [*Seismograph station code, US Geological Survey*] (SEIS)

CUM .... Cummins Engine [*NYSE symbol*] (TTSB)

CUM .... Cummins Engine Co., Inc. [*NYSE symbol*] (SPSG)

CUM .... Cumulative (KSC)

CUM .... Curry College, Milton, MA [*OCLC symbol*] (OCLC)

CU-M .... University of California, San Francisco, Medical Center, San Francisco, CA [*Library symbol Library of Congress*] (LCLS)

CUMA .... Canadian Urethane Manufacturers Association (HGAA)

Cum & Dun Rem Tr... Cummins and Dunphy's Remarkable Trials [*A publication*] (DLA)

CU-MAPS ..... University of California, Berkeley, Maps Collection, Berkeley, CA [*Library symbol Library of Congress*] (LCLS)

CUMARC ...... Cumulated Machine-Readable Cataloging [*Computer science*]

CU-MARK .... University of California, Berkeley, Mark Twain Collection, Berkeley, CA [*Library symbol Library of Congress*] (LCLS)

CU-MATH..... University of California, Berkeley, Mathematics/Statistics Library, Berkeley, CA [*Library symbol Library of Congress*] (LCLS)

CUMB .... Cumberland [*County in England*]

CUMB .... Cumberland Holdings, Inc. [*NASDAQ symbol*] (SAG)

Cumb .... Cumberland Law Journal [*Pennsylvania*] [*A publication*] (DLA)

CUMB .... Cumbria [*County in England*] (WGA)

Cumberland LJ (PA)... Cumberland Law Journal [*Pennsylvania*] [*A publication*] (DLA)

Cumb Law Jrnl... Cumberland Law Journal [*Pennsylvania*] [*A publication*] (DLA)

Cumbld .... Cumberland [*England*] (BARN)

Cumb Nat ..... Cumberland's Law of Nature [*A publication*] (DLA)

Cumb-Sam L Rev... Cumberland-Samford Law Review [*A publication*] (DLA)

Cum Civ L ..... Cummins' Manual of Civil Law [*A publication*] (DLA)

cum cp .... [*With*] Coupon [*Commerce*] (BARN)

CUMD .... Continuous Update Memory Display

Cum Div ...... Cum Dividend [*With Dividend*] [*Latin Stock exchange term*]

CUME .... Cumulative Audience [*Telecommunications*]

CUMECS ...... Cubic Meters per Second

CumEng .... Cummins Engine Co., Inc. [*Associated Press*] (SAG)

CUMFU .... Complete Utter Monumental Foul-Up [*Military slang*] [*Bowdlerized version*]

CUMI .... Council for Understanding Mental Illness [*Defunct Defunct*] (EA)

CUMI .... Cubic Mile (HGAA)

cum int........ [*With*] Interest [*Commerce*] (BARN)

CUMITECH ... Cumulative Techniques and Procedures in Clinical Microbiology [*Medicine*] (DMAA)

CUM LAUDE... Computerized Understanding of Morphology-Language Acquisition Under Development in Education (PDAA)

CUMM .... Council of Underground Machinery Manufacturers [*British*]

CUMM .... Cubic Millimeter

CUMMFU .... Complete Utter Monumental Military Foul-Up [*Slang*] [*Bowdlerized version*]

Cummins ..... Cummins' Reports [*1866-67*] [*Idaho*] [*A publication*] (DLA)

CUMN .... Cubic Micron (IAA)

CU-MODE .... University of California, Berkeley, Modern Authors Collection, Berkeley, CA [*Library symbol Library of Congress*] (LCLS)

CU-MORR .... University of California, Berkeley, Morrison Collection, Berkeley, CA [*Library symbol Library of Congress*] (LCLS)

CUMP .... Central Unit-Memory Programmer (MCD)

Cum PP .... Cumulative Pocket Parts (DLA)

cum pref...... Cumulative Preference [*Commerce*] (BARN)

CUMREC ...... College and University Machine Records Conference [*Later, CUCUC*] (EA)

CUMS .... Canadian University Music Society [*See also SMUC*]

CUMS .... Cumulated Summaries

CUMSAD ...... Current Meter Speed and Detection

Cum Sam L Rev... Cumberland-Samford Law Review [*A publication*] (DLA)

Cum Supp..... Cumulative Supplement (DLA)

CUMU .... Cubic Micron

CU-MUSI..... University of California, Berkeley, Music Library, Berkeley, CA [*Library symbol Library of Congress*] (LCLS)

CUMWA ...... Consortium of Universities of the Metropolitan Washington Area

CUN .... Canadian United Minerals [*Vancouver Stock Exchange symbol*]

CUN .... Cancun [*Mexico*] [*Airport symbol*] (OAG)

CUN .... Cumulonimbus [*Cloud*] [*Meteorology*]

Cun .... Cunningham's English King's Bench Reports [*A publication*] (DLA)

CUN .... Fairbanks, AK [*Location identifier FAA*] (FAAL)

CUN .... Nanzan University Library [*UTLAS symbol*]

CUN .... University of California, San Francisco, CA [*OCLC symbol*] (OCLC)

CUNA .... Credit Union National Association (EA)

CUNB .... Cupertino National Bank [*NASDAQ symbol*] (SAG)

CUNB .... Cupertino Natl Bancorp [*NASDAQ symbol*] (TTSB)

Cun Bill Exch... Cunningham's Law of Notes and Bills of Exchange [*A publication*] (DLA)

Cun Bills..... Cunningham's Bills, Notes, and Insurances [*A publication*] (DLA)

Cun Dict ..... Cunningham's Dictionary [*A publication*] (DLA)

CUNE .... Clandestine Underwater Nuclear Explosion

CU-NEWS ... University of California, Berkeley, Newspaper and Microcopy Division, Berkeley, CA [*Library symbol Library of Congress*] (LCLS)

Cun Hind L... Cunningham on Hindu Law [*A publication*] (DLA)

cunif .... Cuneiform (VRA)

Cu Nim .... Cumulonimbus [*Cloud*] [*Meteorology*] (AIA)

CU-NL .... University of California, Northern Regional Library Facility, Richmond, CA [*Library symbol*] [*Library of Congress*] (LCLS)

Cun LD .... Cunningham's Law Dictionary [*A publication*] (DLA)

Cunn .... Cunningham's English King's Bench Reports [*A publication*] (DLA)

Cunningham... Cunningham's English King's Bench Reports [*A publication*] (DLA)

Cunningham (Eng)... Cunningham's English King's Bench Reports [*A publication*] (DLA)
Cun Pl .... Cunningham's Maxims and Rules of Pleading [*A publication*] (DLA)
CUNR.......... Campaign for UN Reform (EA)
CUNR.......... Conference of UN Representatives, UNA [*United Nations Association*]-USA (EA)
CUNRE........ Center for UN Reform Education (EA)
CUNS.......... Center for UN Studies (EAIO)
Cun Sim ..... Cunningham on Simony [*A publication*] (DLA)
CUNY.......... City University of New York (CDAI)
CUNY (Grad Cent)... City University of New York (Graduate Center) (GAGS)
CUO .... C.C. Enrique Cuahonte Delgado, Marta Amezcua de Cuahonte [*Mexico*] [*FAA designator*] (FAAC)
CUO .... Continental Materials Corp. [*AMEX symbol*] (SPSG)
CUO .... Contl Materials [*AMEX symbol*] (TTSB)
CUO .... Copper Oxide (KSC)
CUO .... Credit Union Office (DNAB)
CUOE .... Canadian Union of Operating Engineers and General Workers
CU-OPTO ..... University of California, Berkeley, Optometry Library, Berkeley, CA [*Library symbol Library of Congress*] (LCLS)
CUOTC .... Cambridge University Officer Training Corps [*British military*] (DMA)
CUP .... Cambridge University Press
CUP .... Canadian University Press (DGA)
CUP .... Carcinoma of Undetermined Primary [*A cancer condition*] (CDI)
CUP .... Care Unit Program [*Chemical dependency*] (DAVI)
CUP .... Carupano [*Venezuela*] [*Airport symbol*] (OAG)
CUP .... Cascade Uprating Program [*AEC*]
CUP .... Cask Unloading Pool [*Nuclear energy*] (NRCH)
CUP .... Center for Urban Policy [*Loyola University of Chicago*] [*Research center*] (RCD)
CUP .... Center for Urban Programs [*St. Louis University*] [*Research center*] (RCD)
CUP .... Central Utah Project [*Federal aqueduct-and-reservoir plan*]
CUP .... Code Universel de Produit [*Universal Product Code*] [*French*]
CUP .... Cohesive Unit Program [*Army*]
CUP .... Columbia Computing Services Ltd. [*Toronto Stock Exchange symbol*]
CUP .... Columbia University Press
CUP .... Commonality Usage Proposal (NASA)
CUP .... Communications User Program [*Sperry UNIVAC*]
CUP .... Conditional Use Permit (GNE)
CUP .... Copper Unit of Pressure (WGA)
CUP .... Cuban Peso [*Monetary unit*] (ODBW)
CUP .... Culebra [*Puerto Rico*] [*Seismograph station code, US Geological Survey*] (SEIS)
CUP .... Cupboard
Cup .... Cupol [*Record label*] [*Sweden*]
CUP .... Cupola
CUPA .... College and University Personnel Association (EA)
CUPE .... Canadian Union of Public Employees
CUPE .... Cranfield Unit for Precision Engineering [*British*]
CU-PHIL....... University of California, Berkeley, Philosophy Library, Berkeley, CA [*Library symbol Library of Congress*] (LCLS)
CU-PHYS ..... University of California, Berkeley, Physics Library, Berkeley, CA [*Library symbol Library of Congress*] (LCLS)
CUPID......... Combat Using Price Incentives Doctrine
CUPID......... Commercial Users Program for Index Data (PDAA)
CUPID......... Completely Universal Processor and I/O [*Input/Output*] Design [*Computer science*]
CUPID .... Computer for Uprange Point-of-Impact Determination [*NASA*] (KSC)
CUPID......... Contractor Using Price Incentive Doctrine (SAA)
CUPID......... Conversational Utility Program for Information Display (PDAA)
CUPID......... Create, Update, Interrogate, and Display [*Computer science*] (MHDI)
CUpl............ Upland Public Library, Upland, CA [*Library symbol Library of Congress*] (LCLS)
CUPLE .... Cambridge University Press Limited Editions
CUPLL .... Coalition for Uniform Product Liability Law (EA)
cuplt .... Copperplate (VRA)
CUPM .... Clinically Undetectable Primary Malignancy [*Oncology*]
CupNBk....... Cupertino National Bank [*Associated Press*] (SAG)
CUpp........... Upper Lake Library District, Upper Lake, CA [*Library symbol Library of Congress*] (LCLS)
CUPPI .... Circumstances Undetermined Pending Police Investigation
CUPR .... Catholic University of Puerto Rico
CUPR.......... Center for Urban Programs and Research [*St. Louis University*] [*Research center*] (RCD)
CUPRFOR .... Centro de Utilizacion y Promocion de Productos Forestales [*Forestry project*] [*Honduras*]
CUPS .... Concentrated Urban Placement Service [*Department of Labor*]
CUPS .... Consolidated Unit Personnel Section
CUPTE .... Canadian Union of Professional and Technical Employees
CUPU .... Committee of Urban Program Universities
CU-PUBL..... University of California, Berkeley, Public Health Library, Berkeley, CA [*Library symbol Library of Congress*] (LCLS)
CU-PU-FU ... National Clean Up - Paint Up - Fix Up Bureau [*Defunct*] (EA)
CUPUOS ...... Committee on the Peaceful Uses of Outer Space [*United Nations*] (NTCM)
CUPW .... Canadian Union of Postal Workers
CUQ .... Coen [*Australia Airport symbol*] (OAG)
CUQC.......... Stirling, ON [*ICAO location identifier*] (ICLI)
CUR .... Cambridge University Rifles [*British military*] (DMA)
CUR .... Carbon Usage Rate [*Environmental Protection Agency*]
CUR .... Chagan-Uzun [*Former USSR Seismograph station code, US Geological Survey*] (SEIS)
CUR .... Comando Urbano Revolucionario [*Guatemala*] [*Political party*] (EY)
CUR .... Command Uplink Request [*NASA*] (KSC)

CUR .... Complex Utility Routine
CUR .... Cost per Unit Requirement (MCD)
CUR .... Council on Undergraduate Research (EA)
CUR .... Curacao [*Netherlands Antilles*] [*Airport symbol*] (OAG)
CUR .... Curate (ROG)
CUR .... Curative [*Medicine*]
CUR .... Curator
CUR .... Curator Resources [*Vancouver Stock Exchange symbol*]
CUR .... Curia [*Court*] [*Latin*] (DLA)
CUR .... Curia Regis Rolls [*British*]
CUR .... Curious (ROG)
CUR .... Currency
CUR .... Current (AAG)
cur .... Current (IDOE)
CUR .... Current Income Shares, Inc. [*NYSE symbol*] (SPSG)
CUR .... Current Inc. Shares [*NYSE symbol*] (TTSB)
CUR .... Currentis [*Of the Current Month or Year*] [*Latin*]
Cur............. Curtis' United States Circuit Court Reports [*A publication*] (DLA)
CUR .... University of Redlands, Redlands, CA [*OCLC symbol*] (OCLC)
CURA .... Center for Urban and Regional Affairs [*University of Minnesota*] [*Research center*] (RCD)
Cur Ab Tit.... Curwen's Abstract of Titles [*A publication*] (DLA)
CUR ADV VULT... Curia Advisari Vult [*The Court Wishes to Consider*] [*Latin Legal term*] (ROG)
CURAGI....... Comite pour l'Utilisation des Resultats de l'Annee Geophysique Internationale [*IGY completion committee*]
CU-RARE ..... University of California, Berkeley, Rare Books and Special Collections Department, Berkeley, CA [*Library symbol Library of Congress*] (LCLS)
CURAT .... Curatio [*A Dressing*] [*Pharmacy*]
CURB .... Campaign on Use and Restriction of Barbiturates [*British*] (DI)
CURB .... Curtis Bay Railroad Co. [*AAR code*]
Cur Bl .... Curry's Abridgment of Blackstone [*A publication*] (DLA)
Curc........... Curculio [*of Plautus*] [*Classical studies*] (OCD)
Cur Com ..... Current Comment and Legal Miscellany [*A publication*] (DLA)
Cur Cr Proc.. Indian Code of Criminal Procedure, Curries' Edition [*A publication*] (DLA)
Cur Dec ...... Curtis' Decisions of the United States Supreme Court [*A publication*] (DLA)
CURDS........ Centre for Urban and Regional Development Studies [*University of Newcastle upon Tyne*] [*British*] (CB)
CURE .... Center for Ulcer Research and Education [*University of California, Los Angeles*] [*Research center*] (RCD)
CURE .... Center for UN Reform Education (EA)
CURE .... Christians United for Responsible Entertainment (EA)
CURE .... Citizens United for Racial Equality
CURE .... Citizens United for Rehabilitation of Errants (EA)
CURE .... Citizens United for Research and Education (EA)
CURE .... Citizens United for Responsible Energy (EA)
CURE .... Clean Urban River Environments [*Project*]
CURE .... Color Uniformity Recognition Equipment [*Quality control*]
CURE .... Conference for Universal Reason and Ethics [*Founded by motion picture actor Lew Ayres*]
CURE .... Conference Upon Research and Education in World Government (EA)
CURE .... Consumers United for Rail Equity (EA)
CURE .... Control of Unwanted Radiated Energy
CURE .... Council for Unified Research and Education [*Defunct*] (EA)
CURE .... Council of Urban Rebuilding Enterprises
CURE .... Curative Health Services, Inc. [*NASDAQ symbol*] (SAG)
CURE .... Curative Technologies [*NASDAQ symbol*] (SPSG)
CURE .... Curative Technology [*NASDAQ symbol*] (TTSB)
CURE .... Curecanti Recreation Area [*National Park Service designation*]
CURE .... CURE [*Citizens United to Reduce Emmissions*] Formaldehyde Poisoning Association (EA)
CU-REFE ..... University of California, Berkeley, Reference and Bibliography Collection, Berkeley, CA [*Library symbol Library of Congress*] (LCLS)
CURES .... Computer Utilization Reporting System (IEEE)
CURFCOE.... Common Usage Radio Frequency Checkout Equipment (KSC)
CurHlth .... Curative Health Services, Inc. [*Associated Press*] (SAG)
CURI .... College - University Resource Institute (EA)
Cur IC .... Current Indian Cases [*1912-15*] [*A publication*] (DLA)
CURIE .... Canadian Universities' Reciprocal Insurance Exchange
CurInc......... Current Income Shares, Inc. [*Associated Press*] (SAG)
CUR-in-CH ... Curate-in-Charge [*Church of England*] (ROG)
Cur Ind Cas... Current Indian Cases [*1912-15*] [*A publication*] (DLA)
CURIO......... Curiosity (DSUE)
CU-Riv........ University of California, Riverside, Main Library, Riverside, CA [*Library symbol Library of Congress*] (LCLS)
CU-RivA....... University of California, Riverside, Bioagriculture Library, Riverside, CA [*Library symbol Library of Congress*] (LCLS)
CU-RivP....... University of California, Riverside, Physical Sciences Library, Riverside, CA [*Library symbol Library of Congress*] (LCLS)
CURL .... Compartment of Uncoupling Receptor and Ligand [*Cytology*]
CURL .... Consortium of University Research Libraries [*British*] (IID)
Cur LR .... Current Law Reports [*Ceylon*] [*A publication*] (DLA)
CURMCO...... City Urban Renewal Management Corp. [*New York City*]
CURN.......... Certified Urological Registered Nurse (MEDA)
CURN.......... Conduct and Utilization of Research in Nursing
Cur Ov Ca ... Curwen's Overruled Cases [*Ohio*] [*A publication*] (DLA)
CURP.......... Certificate in Urban and Regional Planning (PGP)
CUR PHIL .... Curia Phillippica [*Latin*] (DLA)
Cur Prop L ... Current Property Law [*British A publication*] (DLA)
CURR.......... Currency (AFM)

CURR.......... Current (EY)
CURR.......... Curriculum
CURR.......... Curriculum
Cur R.......... Curriculum Review [*A publication*] (BRI)
CUR REG.... Curia Regis [*King's Court*] [*Latin Legal term*] (ROG)
Cur Reg R... Curia Regis Rolls [*British Legal term*] (DLA)
CURRENT ... Committee Urging Regulatory Reform for Efficient National Trucking [*Later, BCIPT*] (EA)
Current Com & Leg Mis... Current Comment and Legal Miscellany [*A publication*] (DLA)
Current LY... Current Law Year Book [*A publication*] (DLA)
Current Med for Att'ys... Current Medicine for Attorneys [*A publication*] (DLA)
Current Prop L... Current Property Law [*British A publication*] (DLA)
CURRIC....... Curriculum
Curric P...... Curriculum Perspective [*A publication*]
Curr Legal Prob... Current Legal Problems [*A publication*] (DLA)
Curr No Int Aff... Current Notes on International Affairs [*A publication*]
CURRT........ Current (ROG)
Curry.......... Curry's Reports [*6-19 Louisiana*] [*A publication*] (DLA)
CURS.......... Center for Urban and Regional Studies (EA)
curs.......... Cursive (BJA)
CURS BE...... Cursitor Baron of the Exchequer [*British*] (ROG)
CUR SCACC... Cursus Scaccarii [*Latin*] (DLA)
CURS CAN... Cursus Cancellariae [*Latin*] (DLA)
Cur Stat...... Curwen's Statutes of Ohio [*A publication*] (DLA)
CURT.......... Cubic Root (IAA)
CURT.......... Current
CURT.......... Curtain (MSA)
Curt.......... Curteis' English Ecclesiastical Reports [*A publication*] (DLA)
Curt.......... Curtis' Circuit Court Reports [*United States*] [*A publication*] (DLA)
Curt.......... Curtis' Edition, United States Supreme Court Reports [*A publication*] (DLA)
Curt Adm Dig... Curtis' Admiralty Digest [*A publication*] (DLA)
CURTAGE..... Current or Voltage
Curt CC....... Curtis' United States Circuit Court Decisions [*A publication*] (DLA)
CurTch........ Curative Technologies, Inc. [*Associated Press*] (SAG)
Curt Cond ... Curtis' Edition, United States Supreme Court Reports [*A publication*] (DLA)
Curt Cond Rep... Curtis' Decisions of the United States Supreme Court [*A publication*] (DLA)
Curt Conv.... Curtis' American Conveyancer [*A publication*] (DLA)
Curt Cop ..... Curtis' Copyright [*1847*] [*A publication*] (DLA)
Curt Dec ..... Curtis' Decisions of the United States Supreme Court [*A publication*] (DLA)
Curt Dig....... Curtis' Digest [*United States*] [*A publication*] (DLA)
Curt Ecc...... Curteis' English Ecclesiastical Reports [*A publication*] (DLA)
Curt Eccl..... Curteis' English Ecclesiastical Reports [*A publication*] (DLA)
Curt Eccl (Eng)... Curteis' English Ecclesiastical Reports [*A publication*] (DLA)
Curt Eq Pr.... Curtis' Equity Precedents [*A publication*] (DLA)
Curtis.......... Curtis' Circuit Court Reports [*United States*] [*A publication*] (DLA)
Curtis.......... Curtis' Edition, United States Supreme Court Reports [*A publication*] (DLA)
Curtis CC ..... Curtis' United States Circuit Court Reports [*A publication*] (DLA)
Curtis SC Reports... Curtis' Decisions of the United States Supreme Court [*A publication*] (DLA)
Curtis US Sup Ct R... Curtis' Decisions of the United States Supreme Court [*A publication*] (DLA)
Curt Jur ...... Curtis on the Jurisdiction of United States Courts [*A publication*] (DLA)
Curt Pat .... Curtis on Patents [*A publication*] (DLA)
CURTS......... Common User Radio Transmission System (IAA)
CURTS......... Communications User Radio Transmission Sounding [*Navy*]
Curt US Const... Curtis' History of the Constitution of the United States Courts [*A publication*] (DLA)
Curt US Courts... Curtis' Commentaries on the United States Courts [*A publication*] (DLA)
CurtWr......... Curtiss-Wright Corp. [*Associated Press*] (SAG)
CURV.......... Cable-Controlled Underwater Research Vehicle
CURV.......... Cable-Controlled Unmanned Recovery Vehicle (MCD)
CURV.......... Curve
CURV.......... Curve [*Postal Service standards*] (OPSA)
CURVE........ Curve [*Commonly used*] (OPSA)
Curw.......... Curwen's Overruled Cases [*Ohio*] [*A publication*] (DLA)
Curw.......... Curwen's Statutes of Ohio [*A publication*] (DLA)
Curw LO ...... Curwen's Laws of Ohio [*1 vol.*] [*1854*] [*A publication*] (DLA)
Curw Ov Cas... Curwen's Overruled Cases [*Ohio*] [*A publication*] (DLA)
Curw RS ...... Curwen's Revised Statutes of Ohio [*A publication*] (DLA)
CUS.......... Canadian Union of Students
Cus.......... Cantus [*Record label*] [*Sweden*]
CUS.......... Cartoid Ultrasound [*Neurology*] (CPH)
CUS.......... Center for Urban Studies [*University of Chicago*] [*Research center*] (RCD)
CUS.......... Center for Urban Studies [*Wayne State University*] [*Research center*] (RCD)
CUS.......... Chronic Undifferentiated Schizophrenia [*Psychiatry*] (DAVI)
CUS.......... Cities of the United States [*A publication*]
CUS.......... Clean-Up System (IEEE)
CUS.......... Columbus, NM [*Location identifier FAA*] (FAAL)
CUS.......... Common User System [*Telecommunications*] (TEL)
CUS.......... Continental United States
CUS.......... Control, Utility, and Support (IAA)
CUS.......... Course [*Ships*] (CINC)
CUS.......... Cronus Airlines [*Greece*] [*FAA designator*] (FAAC)
CUS.......... Cusco [*Peru*] [*Seismograph station code, US Geological Survey*] (SEIS)

cus.......... Cushitic [*MARC language code Library of Congress*] (LCCP)
CUS.......... Customedix Corp. [*AMEX symbol*] (SPSG)
CUS.......... Customer Code [*Telecommunications*] (TEL)
CUS.......... Customs Available [*Aviation*] (DA)
CUS.......... University of California, San Diego, La Jolla, CA [*OCLC symbol*] (OCLC)
CU-S.......... University of California, San Diego, Main Library, La Jolla, CA [*Library symbol Library of Congress*] (LCLS)
CUSA.......... Catholics United for Spiritual Action (EA)
CUSA.......... Cavitron Ultrasonic Surgical Aspirator [*Medicine*]
CUSA.......... Centrifugal Urine Separator Assembly [*Aerospace*] (MCD)
CUSA.......... Congress of Unions of South Africa
CUSA.......... Cosmetic Group USA [*NASDAQ symbol*] (TTSB)
CUSA.......... Cosmetic Group USA, Inc. [*NASDAQ symbol*] (SAG)
Cusac.......... Cusac Gold Mines Ltd. [*Associated Press*] (SAG)
Cusac.......... Cusac Industries Ltd. [*Associated Press*] (SAG)
CUS & US... Customs and Usages (DLA)
CUSAR......... Commission on US-African Relations (EA)
CUSARROTC... Chief, United States Army Reserve and Reserve Officers Training Corps Affairs
CUSAT......... Customer Satisfaction
CUSAW........ Cosmetic Group USA Wrrt [*NASDAQ symbol*] (TTSB)
CUSB.......... Credit Union Stabilisation Board [*South Australia*]
CU-SB.......... University of California, Santa Barbara, Main Library, Santa Barbara, CA [*Library symbol Library of Congress*] (LCLS)
CUSC.......... Channel Unit Signal Controller (IAA)
CUSC.......... Combined Union and Shop Committee [*Australia*]
CU-SC.......... University of California, Santa Cruz, Main Library, Santa Cruz, CA [*Library symbol Library of Congress*] (LCLS)
CUSCLN....... Committee of United States Citizens Living in Nicaragua (EA)
CUSCM........ Center for US Capital Markets (EA)
CUSD.......... Credit Union Share Draft
CUSEC......... Canada-United States Environmental Council (EA)
CUSEC......... Cubic Feet per Second
CUSEC......... Czechoslovak-US Economic Council (EA)
CUSEM........ Computer Users Survival Electronic Magazine [*Information service or system*] (IID)
CUSFI.......... Consumers United to Stop Food Irradiation (AC)
CUSH.......... Computer Users in Speech and Hearing (EA)
Cush.......... Cushing's Massachusetts Supreme Judicial Court Reports [*1848-53*] [*A publication*] (DLA)
CUSH.......... Cushion (MSA)
Cush.......... Cushman's Reports [*23-29 Mississippi*] [*A publication*] (DLA)
Cush Elec Cas... Cushing's Election Cases in Massachusetts [*A publication*] (DLA)
Cushing...... Cushing's Reports [*1848-53*] [*A publication*] (DLA)
Cush Law & Prac Leg Assem... Cushing's Law and Practice of Legislative Assemblies [*A publication*] (DLA)
Cush Leg Ass... Cushing's Law and Practice of Legislative Assemblies [*A publication*] (DLA)
Cushm .... Cushman's Reports [*23-29 Mississippi*] [*A publication*] (DLA)
Cush Man ... Cushing's Manual of Parliamentary Law [*A publication*] (DLA)
Cush (Mass)... Cushing's Reports [*1848-53*] [*A publication*] (DLA)
Cus Ho........ Customhouse
Cush Parl Law... Cushing's Law and Practice of Legislative Assemblies [*A publication*] (DLA)
Cush Rom Law... Cushing's Study of the Roman Law [*A publication*] (DLA)
Cush Trust Pr... Cushing on Trustee Process [*A publication*] (DLA)
CUSI.......... Configurable Unified Search Engine [*Internet*] (DAVI)
CUSI.......... Coordinamento Uruguaiano di Solidarieta in Italia
CUSI.......... Cusac Gold Mines Ltd. [*NASDAQ symbol*] (SAG)
CUSIE......... Cusp Injection Experiment [*Nuclear energy British*] (NUCP)
CUSIF......... Cusac Gold Mines [*NASDAQ symbol*] (TTSB)
CUSIP......... Committee on Uniform Securities Identification Procedures (MHDB)
CUSJ.......... Citizens United for Safety and Justice [*Canada*]
CUSLAR....... Commission of United States Latin American Relations (EA)
CusM.......... Custom Microfilm Systems, Inc., Riverside, CA [*Library symbol Library of Congress*] (LCLS)
CU-SM........ University of California, San Diego, Biomedical Library, San Diego, CA [*Library symbol Library of Congress*] (LCLS)
CUSMAP...... Conterminous United States Mineral Resource Assessment Program [*Department of the Interior*]
CUSNO........ Customs Has Been Notified [*Aviation*] (FAAC)
CUSO.......... Canadian University Service Overseas
CU-SOCS....... University of California, Berkeley, Graduate Social Science Library, Berkeley, CA [*Library symbol Library of Congress*] (LCLS)
CU-SOCW...... University of California, Berkeley, Social Welfare Library, Berkeley, CA [*Library symbol Library of Congress*] (LCLS)
CUSP.......... Central Unit for Scientific Photography [*Royal Aircraft Establishment*] [*British*]
CUSP.......... Commonly Used System Programs [*Digital Equipment Corp.*]
cusp.......... Cuspid [*Dentistry*] (DAVI)
CUSPAR....... Cusparia [*Angustura Bark*] [*Pharmacology*] (ROG)
CUSPEA....... China-United States Physics Examination and Application Program
CUSR.......... Canada/United States Region (NATG)
CUSR.......... Central United States Registry [*Army*]
CUSR.......... Computer Users for Social Responsibility (EA)
CUSRPG ..... Canada-United States Regional Planning Group [*NATO*]
CUSS.......... Computerized Ultrasonic Scan System (MCD)
CUSS.......... Computerized Uniterm Search System (NITA)
CUSS.......... Continental, Union, Shell, and Superior [*In CUSS I, ocean drilling barge named after oil companies that financed its development*]
CUSS.......... Cooperative Union Serials System
CU-SSe........ University of California, San Diego, Science and Engineering Library, San Diego,CA [*Library symbol Library of Congress*] (LCLS)

CU-SSh........ University of California, San Diego, Society-University Hospital, San Diego, CA [*Library symbol Library of Congress*] (LCLS)
CU-SSi........ University of California, San Diego, Scripps Institute of Oceanography, San Diego, CA [*Library symbol Library of Congress*] (LCLS)
CUSSN........ Computer Use in Social Services Network (EA)
CUSSR........ Commission on US-Soviet Relations (EA)
CUST.......... Chicago Union Station Co. [*AAR code*]
CUST.......... Custer Battlefield National Monument [*National Park Service designation*]
CUST.......... Custodian [*Banking*] (AFM)
CUST.......... Custody (AFM)
CUST.......... Custom [*Automotive engineering*]
CUST.......... Customer (MSA)
CUST.......... Customer
CUST.......... Customized
CUST.......... Customs
Cust A........ United States Customs Appeals (DLA)
Cust & Pat App (Cust) (F)... Customs and Patent Appeals Reports (Customs) [*A publication*] (DLA)
Cust & Pat App (Pat) (F)... Customs and Patent Appeals Reports (Patents) [*A publication*] (DLA)
Cust App...... United States Customs Appeals (DLA)
Cust B & Dec... Customs Bulletin and Decisions [*A publication*] (DLA)
Cust Bull..... Customs Bulletin [*A publication*] (DLA)
CustCh........ Custom Chrome, Inc. [*Associated Press*] (SAG)
CUSTCT .... Customs Court
Cust Ct....... Customs Court Reports [*United States*] [*A publication*] (DLA)
Cust Ct R.... Customs Court Rules [*A publication*] (DLA)
Cust D .... Customs Duties and Import Regulations [*A publication*] (DLA)
CUSTDN....... Custodian
Custmd....... Customedix Corp. [*Associated Press*] (SAG)
CUSTMY...... Customary (ROG)
CUSTOD...... Custodian (ADA)
Customs ..... United States Customs Service [*A publication*] (DLA)
Cust Pen Dec... Customs Penalty Decisions [*A publication*] (DLA)
CUSTR........ Customer
Cust Rep..... Custer's Ecclesiastical Reports [*A publication*] (DLA)
CUSUM....... Cumulative Sum
CUSURDI..... Council of United States Universities for Rural Development in India
CUSUSSRI... Center for US-USSR Initiatives (EA)
CUSUSWASH... Council of United States Universities for Soil and Water Development in Arid andSub-Humid Areas
CUSW .... Cusac Gold Mines Ltd. [*NASDAQ symbol*] (SAG)
CUSWF .... Cusac Inds Ltd Wrrt [*NASDAQ symbol*] (TTSB)
CUT............ Canonical Unit of Time
CUT............ Church Universal and Triumphant (EA)
CUT............ Circuit under Test [*Electricity*] (IEEE)
CUT............ Code and Unit Test
CUT............ Come-Up Time [*Time required for a retort to reach operating conditions*]
CUT............ Component Under Test (NITA)
CUT............ Control Unit Terminal [*Computer science*]
CUT............ Control Unit Tester [*Sperry UNIVAC*] (BUR)
CUT............ Coordinated Universal Time (NASA)
CUT............ Cross Utilization Training
CUT............ Custom Petroleum [*Vancouver Stock Exchange symbol*]
CUT............ Cutral-Co [*Argentina*] [*Airport symbol*] (OAG)
CUT............ Cutter [*Ship*]
CUT............ Cutting
CUT............ Hancock, MI [*Location identifier FAA*] (FAAL)
Cut............ Indian Law Reports, Orissa Series [*A publication*] (DLA)
CUT............ University of California, Santa Barbara, Santa Barbara, CA [*OCLC symbol*] (OCLC)
CUTA .... Canadian Urban Transit Association
CUTAS .... Committee on Uniform Traffic Accident Statistics [*Later, Traffic Records Committee*] (EA)
CUTC .... Combat Unit Training Center [*Army*] (MCD)
CUTC .... CutCo Indus [*NASDAQ symbol*] (TTSB)
CUTC .... Cutco Industries, Inc. [*NASDAQ symbol*] (NQ)
Cutco .... Cutco Industries, Inc. [*Associated Press*] (SAG)
CUTD .... Characteristics of Urban Transportation Demand (MCD)
CUTE.......... Canadian Union of Transportation Employees
CUTE.......... Common Use Terminal Equipment [*Travel industry*]
CUTE.......... Computer User Terminal Equipment [*Airport computer system*]
CUTG .... Cutting
CUTH .... Council of University Teaching Hospitals [*Defunct*] (EA)
CUTHB........ Cuthbert College (ROG)
CUTHE .... Canadian University Teachers of Home Economics [*See also PEDUC*]
CUTI........... Complicated Urinary Tract Infection [*Medicine*]
CUTIE.......... Coolest Ultra Tiny Individuals on Earth [*Toy figures*] [*Mattel, Inc.*]
Cut Ins L..... Cutler's Insolvent Laws of Massachusetts [*A publication*] (DLA)
CUTLASS ..... Collaborative UK Twin Location Auroral Sounding System [*A radar interferometer with antennae in Finland and Iceland*]
Cut Leg Sys... Cutler's Legal System of the English, the Hindoos, Etc. [*A publication*] (DLA)
Cutler......... Reports of English Patent Cases [*1884*] [*A publication*] (DLA)
Cut LT........ Cuttack Law Times [*India*] [*A publication*] (DLA)
CUTLY .... Cutlery
CUT mode ... Control Unit Terminal Mode (CDE)
Cut Nat ...... Cutler on Naturalization Laws [*A publication*] (DLA)
Cut Pat Cas... Cutler's Trademark and Patent Cases [*A publication*] (DLA)
CUTS .... Cassette User Tape System
CUTS .... Computer Users' Tape System (ODBW)

CUTS .... Computer Utilized Turning System [*Warner & Swasey*]
CuTS .... Cubital Tunnel Syndrome [*Medicine*] (DMAA)
CUTS .... Cut Stone
CUTS .... Supercuts, Inc. [*NASDAQ symbol*] (SPSG)
CutterB ...... Cutter & Buck, Inc. [*Associated Press*] (SAG)
Cutt LT....... Cuttack Law Times [*India*] [*A publication*] (DLA)
CUTVC .... Clean Up TV Campaign [*Defunct*] (EA)
CUU .... Calnor Resources Ltd. [*Vancouver Stock Exchange symbol*]
CUU .... Chihuahua [*Mexico*] [*Airport symbol*] (OAG)
CU-UARC ..... University of California, Berkeley, Archives Collection, Berkeley, CA [*Library symbol Library of Congress*] (LCLS)
CU-UC........ University of California, Union Catalog, Berkeley, CA [*Library symbol Library of Congress*] (LCLS)
CUUI .... Center for US-USSR Initiatives (EAIO)
CU-UNDE ..... University of California, Berkeley, Moffitt Undergraduate Library, Berkeley, CA [*Library symbol Library of Congress*] (LCLS)
CUUP .... Ottawa/Uplands, Canadian Forces Base ON [*ICAO location identifier*] (ICLI)
CUV .... Casigua [*Venezuela*] [*Airport symbol*] (AD)
CUV .... Clean Urban Vehicle
CUV .... Commercial Utility Vehicle
CUV .... Construction Unit Value (DCTA)
CUV .... Cricket Union of Victoria [*Australia*]
CUV .... Current Use Value (MHDB)
CUV .... Cuvier Mines, Inc. [*Toronto Stock Exchange symbol*]
CUV .... University of California, Davis, Shields Library, Davis, CA [*OCLC symbol*] (OCLC)
CUVA .... [*The*] Cuyahoga Valley Railway Co. [*AAR code*]
CUW .... CNI-Computer Networks International Ltd. [*Vancouver Stock Exchange symbol*]
CUW .... Colorado-Utah-Wyoming Committee, Chicago IL [*STAC*]
CUW .... Committee on Undersea Warfare
CU-WR........ University of California, Berkeley, Water Resources Center Archives, Berkeley, CA [*Library symbol Library of Congress*] (LCLS)
CUWS .... Cask Unloading Warm Shop [*Nuclear energy*] (NRCH)
CUWTF .... Combined Unconventional Warfare Task Force (CINC)
CUWU .... Claimants and Unemployed Workers' Union (AIE)
CUX .... Casau Explorations Ltd. [*Vancouver Stock Exchange symbol*]
CUX .... Checkup X-Ray [*Radiology*] (DAVI)
CUX .... Corpus Christi, TX [*Location identifier FAA*] (FAAL)
CUX .... University of California, Davis, Health Sciences Library, Davis, CA [*OCLC symbol*] (OCLC)
CUY .... Cutty Resources, Inc. [*Vancouver Stock Exchange symbol*]
CUY .... University of California, Berkeley, Berkeley, CA [*OCLC symbol*] (OCLC)
CUYD .... Cubic Yard
CUYV .... Cucumber Yellows Virus [*Plant pathology*]
CUZ........... Broken Bow, NE [*Location identifier FAA*] (FAAL)
CUZ........... Capilano Resources, Inc. [*Vancouver Stock Exchange symbol*]
CUZ........... Cousins Properties [*NYSE symbol*] (TTSB)
CUZ........... Cousins Properties, Inc. [*NYSE symbol*] (SPSG)
CUZ........... Cuzco [*Peru*] [*Airport symbol*] (OAG)
CUZ........... University of California, Santa Cruz, Santa Cruz, CA [*OCLC symbol*] (OCLC)
CV.............. Air Chathams [*Airline code*] [*Australia*]
CV.............. Aircraft Carrier [*Navy symbol*]
CV.............. Associated Airlines [*ICAO designator*] (AD)
CV.............. Callisthenics Victoria [*Australia*]
CV.............. Calorific Value [*of a fuel*]
C(V)........... Capacitance as a Function of Voltage (IEEE)
CV.............. Cape Verde [*ANSI two-letter standard code*] (CNC)
cv.............. Cape Verde [*Islands*] [*MARC country of publication code Library of Congress*] (LCCP)
CV.............. Carbonyl Value [*Food science*]
CV.............. Cardiff Valleys [*Welsh depot code*]
CV.............. Cardinal Virtues [*Freemasonry*] (ROG)
CV.............. Cardiovascular [*Medicine*]
CV.............. Career Vitae [*Job applications*] (DCTA)
CV.............. Cargo Variant [*LSD 41 variant*] (DOMA)
CV.............. Carrier Vehicle [*Military*]
CV.............. Cataclysmic Variable [*Astronomy, physics*]
CV.............. Cave (ROG)
CV.............. Cellular Ventures, Inc. [*Atlanta, GA*] [*Telecommunications*] (TSSD)
CV.............. Cell Volume [*Hematology*]
CV.............. Central Vein [*or Venous*] [*Anatomy*]
CV.............. Central Vermont Public Service Corp. [*NYSE symbol*] (SPSG)
CV.............. Central Vermont Railway, Inc. [*AAR code*]
CV.............. Central VT Pub Svc [*NYSE symbol*] (TTSB)
CV.............. Cerebrovascular [*Medicine*]
C/V............ Certificate of Value [*DS*]
CV.............. Cervical Vertebra [*Medicine*]
CV.............. Cervico [*Vertical*] [*Medicine*] (ROG)
CV.............. Chairman of Volunteers [*Red Cross*]
CV.............. Chaparral Vulcan [*Army*]
CV.............. Check Valve
CV.............. Cheval-Vapeur [*Horsepower*] [*French*]
CV.............. Chief Value
CV.............. Chikungunya Virus
CV.............. Christian Voice (EA)
CV.............. Circular Vection [*Optics*]
CV.............. Cisplatin, VePesid [*Antineoplastic drug*] (CDI)
CV.............. Cited Volume [*Database terminology*] (NITA)
CV.............. Closed Vitrectomy [*Ophthalmology*] (DAVI)
CV.............. Closing Volume [*Physiology*]
CV.............. Code Variante [*Codification*] (NATG)

CV	Code-View [*Computer software*] (PCM)
CV	Coefficient of Variation [*Mathematics*]
CV	Colla Voce [*With the Voice*] [*Music*]
CV	Collection Voucher
CV	Color Vision [*Ophthalmology*]
CV	Combat Vehicle [*Army*]
CV	Command Vehicle
CV	Command Verification [*NASA*]
CV	Commercial Value
CV	Commercial Vehicle [*Automotive engineering*]
CV	Common Version [*Bible*]
CV	Compact Video
CV	Computervision [*Commercial firm British*]
CV	Computer Vision
CV	Concentrated Volume [*of solutions*] (AAMN)
CV	Condensing Vacuole (OA)
CV	Conduction Velocity [*Neurology*]
CV	Confraternity Version (BJA)
CV	Conjugata Vera [*Conjugate diameter of pelvic inlet*] [*Anatomy*]
CV	Connersville, IN [*Location identifier FAA*] (FAAL)
CV	Consonant-Vowel
CV	Constant Value
CV	Constant Velocity
CV	Constant-Viscosity [*Rubber*]
CV	Constant Voltage (IAA)
CV	Constant Volume
CV	Constitution of Virginia [*A publication*] (DLA)
CV	Consumer Video (NITA)
CV	Contingent Valuation [*Environmental medicine*]
CV	Continuously Variable
CV	Continuous Vulcanization
CV	Contrast Value
CV	Contributing Value [*Shipping*]
CV	Controlled Variable [*Psychology*] (BARN)
CV	Controlled Ventilation [*Automotive engineering*]
CV	Controlled Ventilation
CV	Control Valve
CV	Control Valve [*Computer science*] (ECII)
CV	Control Van [*Diving apparatus*]
CV	Conventional
CV	Conventional Vehicle [*Environmental science*]
CV	Conventional Ventilation [*Medicine*]
CV	Conversational Voice [*Medicine*]
CV	Converters [*Electronic*] [*JETDS nomenclature*] [*Military*] (CET)
CV	Convertible [*Automotive engineering*]
CV	Convertible [*Stock exchange term*] (SPSG)
CV	Convertible Security [*Investment term*] (DFIT)
CV	Coronavirus
CV	Corpuscular Volume [*Hematology*]
CV	Costovertebral [*Angle*] [*Anatomy*] (DAVI)
CV	Cost Variance (MCD)
C/V	Coulombs per Volt
CV	Counter Voltage
CV	Cove
CV	Cove
CV	Cras Vespere [*Tomorrow Evening*] [*Pharmacy*]
CV	Cresyl Violet [*Biological stain*]
CV	Cross of Valour [*Military award*] [*Canada*]
CV	Cruise Vehicle [*Military*] (AFM)
CV	Crystal Violet [*An indicator*] [*Chemistry*]
cv	Cultivar [*Cultural Variety*] [*Biology*]
CV	Cult of the Virgin (EA)
CV	Curriculum Vitae [*Job applications*]
CV	Cyclic Voltammetry [*Analytical electrochemistry*]
CV	Cyclophosphamide and VP-16 [*Antineoplastic drug*] (DAVI)
cv	Cylindrical Vertical Tank [*Liquid gas carriers*]
CV	Cynara Virus [*Plant pathology*]
CV	General Dynamics Corp. [*ICAO aircraft manufacturer identifier*] (ICAO)
CV	Gingivectomy [*Dentistry*] (DAVI)
CV	Single Cotton Varnish [*Wire insulation*] (AAG)
Cv	Specific Heat at Constant Volume [*Chemistry*] (DAVI)
CV	Station Open Exclusively to the Correspondence of a Private Agency [*ITU designation*] (CET)
CV	Vallejo Public Library, Vallejo, CA [*Library symbol Library of Congress*] (LCLS)
CV1S	Center Vee One Side [*Lumber*] (DAC)
CV2	Cactus Virus 2 [*Plant pathology*]
CV2S	Center Vee Two Sides [*Lumber*] (DAC)
CV4	Cucumber Virus 4 [*Plant pathology*]
CV-8A	Cleared V-8 Juice Agar [*Microbiology*]
CV-8B	Cleared V-8 Juice Broth [*Microbiology*]
CVA	Air Transport (Chatham Island) Ltd. [*New Zealand*] [*ICAO designator*] (FAAC)
CVA	Attack Aircraft Carrier [*Navy symbol*]
CVA	Calendar Variations Analysis
CVA	Canadian Vocational Association (AC)
CVA	Canonical Variates Analysis [*Mathematics*]
CVA	Cardiovascular Accident [*Medicine*] (DMAA)
CVA	Centre for Visual Arts [*University of New England*] [*Australia*]
CVA	Cerebrovascular Accident [*Medicine*]
CVA	Chance Vought Aircraft, Inc. [*Obsolete*]
CVA	Chronic Villous Arthritis [*Medicine*] (DMAA)
CVA	Columbia Valley Authority
CVA	Committee for the Visual Arts [*Later, CVAAS*] (EA)

CVA	Commonwealth Veterinary Association
CVA	Company Voluntary Arrangement [*Business term*] (ECON)
CVA	Consecutive-Valve Actuation [*Nuclear energy*] (NRCH)
CVA	Constant Velocity Alignment [*Drive system coupling*]
CVA	CONVAIR [*Consolidated-Vultee Aircraft Corp.*] Astronautics Corp. Astronautics Corp. [*Later, General Dynamics Corp.*] (AAG)
CVA	Cordova [*Alaska*] [*Seismograph station code, US Geological Survey*] (SEIS)
CVA	Corporate Value Associates [*Commercial firm British*]
CVA	Costovertebral Angle [*Medicine*]
CVA	Crown Victoria Association (EA)
CVA	Cumulative Volcano Amplitude [*Volcanology*]
CVA	Current Value Accounting
CVA	Current Variable Attenuator
CVA	Cyclophosphamide, Vincristine, Adriamycin [*Antineoplastic drug regimen*]
CVA	Davenport, IA [*Location identifier FAA*] (FAAL)
CVa	Vacaville District Library, Vacaville, CA [*Library symbol Library of Congress*] (LCLS)
CVAA	Cold Vapor Atomic Absorption Spectrometry [*Also, CVAAS*]
CVAAS	Cold Vapor Atomic Absorption Spectrometry [*Also, CVAA*]
CVAAS	Committee for the Visual Arts/Artists Space (EA)
CVA-BMP	Cyclophosphamide, Vincristine, Adriamycin, BCNU [*Carmustine*], Methotrexate, Procarbazine [*Antineoplastic drug regimen*]
CVAC	Consolidated-Vultee Aircraft Corp. [*Later, General Dynamics Corp.*]
CVACL	Cowichan Valley Association for Community Living [*Formerly, Duncan & District Association for the Mentally Handicapped*] (AC)
CVAD	Continuously Variable Accessory Drive
CVAD	Converter, Voltage, AC [*Alternating Current*] to DC [*Direct Current*] (MCD)
CVAE	Coordinated Vocational-Academic Education
CVAL	Chester Valley Bancorp [*NASDAQ symbol*] (TTSB)
CVAL	Chester Valley Bancorp, Inc. [*NASDAQ symbol*] (SAG)
C/VAL	Control Valve [*Automotive engineering*]
CValA	California Institute of the Arts, Valencia, CA [*Library symbol Library of Congress*] (LCLS)
C/VAM	Compass Vertical Angular Measurement (RDA)
CVAN	Attack Aircraft Carrier (Nuclear Propulsion) [*Navy symbol*]
CVAN	CINCPAC [*Commander-in-Chief, Pacific*] Voice Automated Net (NVT)
CVAN	Crown Vantage [*NASDAQ symbol*] (TTSB)
CVAN	Crown Vantage, Inc. [*NASDAQ symbol*] (SAG)
CVanA	United States Air Force, Base Library, Vandenberg Air Force Base, CA [*Library symbol Library of Congress*] (LCLS)
C-VAR	Canadian Vegans for Animal Rights (AC)
CVAS	Configuration Verification and Accounting System
CVAS	Corvas International [*NASDAQ symbol*] (TTSB)
CVAS	Corvas International, Inc. [*NASDAQ symbol*] (SAG)
C-Vasc	Cerebral Vascular Profile Study [*Cardiology*] (DAVI)
CVaSGS	Solano County Genealogical Society, Vacaville, CA [*Library symbol*] [*Library of Congress*] (LCLS)
CVAST	Combat Vehicle Armament System Technology [*Army*]
CV-ASWM	Carrier-Based Antisubmarine Warfare Module [*Navy*] (CAAL)
CVAT	Costovertebral Angle Tenderness [*Medicine*] (MAE)
CVB	Canadian Vent Corp. [*Vancouver Stock Exchange symbol*]
CVB	Castroville, TX [*Location identifier FAA*] (FAAL)
CVB	CCNU [*Lomustine*], Vinblastine, Bleomycin [*Antineoplastic drug regimen*]
CVB	Chorionic Villi Biopsy [*Medicine*]
CVB	Chrysanthemum Virus B [*Plant pathology*]
CVB	Combined VHF [*Very-High-Frequency*]-Band
CVB	Convert to Binary (IAA)
CVB	CVB Financial [*AMEX symbol*] (TTSB)
CVB	CVB Financial Corp. [*AMEX symbol*] (SPSG)
CVB	Large Aircraft Carrier [*Navy symbol Obsolete*]
CVBC	Cape Volunteer Bearer Corps [*British military*] (DMA)
CVBEM	Complex Variable Boundary Element Method (IAA)
CVB Fn	CVB Financial Corp. [*Associated Press*] (SAG)
CVBG	Carrier Battle Group [*Navy*]
CVBK	Central Virginia Bankshares [*NASDAQ symbol*] (SAG)
CVC	Cablevision Sys'A' [*AMEX symbol*] (TTSB)
CVC	Cablevision Systems Corp. [*AMEX symbol*] (SPSG)
CVC	Canadian Overseas Exploration [*Vancouver Stock Exchange symbol*]
CVC	Carrier Virtual Circuit [*Telecommunications*]
CVC	Central Venous Catheter [*Medicine*]
CVC	Cesium Vapor Cathode
CVC	Chemical and Volume Control [*Nuclear energy*] (NRCH)
CVC	Cholame Valley [*California*] [*Seismograph station code, US Geological Survey*] (SEIS)
CVC	Civic
CVC	Clovis-Carver Public Library, Clovis, NM [*OCLC symbol*] (OCLC)
CVC	Combat Vehicle Crewmen (MCD)
CVC	Committee for a Voluntary Census (EA)
CVC	Compact Video Cassette Recorder
CVC	Consecutive Voyage Charter (DNAB)
CVC	Conservative Victory Committee [*An association*] (EA)
CVC	Conserved Vector Current
CVC	Consonant-Vowel-Consonant [*Cuneiform sign*] (BJA)
CVC	Constant Vacuum Control [*Automotive emissions*]
CVC	Contactless Vacuum Controller
CVC	Convalescent Camp [*Military*]
CVC	Convertible Security [*Business term*] (MHDW)
CVC	Crime Victims Research and Treatment Center [*Medical University of South Carolina*] [*Research center*] (RCD)
CVC	Crying Vital Capacity [*Medicine*] (AAMN)

CVC............ Cryogenic Vacuum Calorimeter
CVC............ Current Voltage Characteristic (OA)
CVC............ Current Voltage Converter (IAA)
CVC2.......... Combat Vehicle Command and Control [Army] (RDA)
CVCC .... Classic Vehicle Club's Committee [British] (DBA)
CVCC .... Combat Vehicle Command and Control (RDA)
CVCC .... Compound Vortex Combustion Chamber [Auto engine]
CV/CC .... Constant Voltage/Constant Current (IEEE)
CVCC .... Continuously Varying Cell Constant [Electrochemical instrumentation]
CVCF.......... Citicorp Venture Capital Fund [Investment term]
CVCF.......... Constant Voltage and Constant Frequency (BUR)
CVCHP........ Cascade Variable Conductance Heat Pipe (PDAA)
CVCL.......... Constant Voltage Current Limiting (IAA)
CVCO .... Cavco Indus [NASDAQ symbol] (TTSB)
CVCO .... Cavco Industries, Inc. [NASDAQ symbol] (NQ)
CVCP .... Committee of Vice-Chancellors and Principals of the Universities of
             the United Kingdom [British]
CVCPE .... Combat Vehicle Crewman's Protective Ensemble [Army] (RDA)
CV/CPP .... Current Value/Constant Purchasing Power [Accounting]
CVCPr......... CablevisionSys 8.50% Dep Cv Ex Pfd [AMEX symbol] (TTSB)
CVCR .... Control Van Connecting Room (NATG)
CVCS .... Cardiovascular Conditioning Suit [Medicine]
CVCS .... Chemical and Volume Control System [Nuclear energy] (NRCH)
CVCT.......... Cardiovascular Computerized Tomography [Scanner] [Cardiology]
             (DAVI)
CVCUS .... Combat Vehicle Crewman Uniform System [Army] (INF)
CVD .... Canova Resources Ltd. [Vancouver Stock Exchange symbol]
CVD .... Capacitive Voltage Divider
CVD .... Carbon Vacuum Deoxidized
CVD .... Cardiovascular Disease [Medicine]
CVD .... Cash Versus Documents
CVD .... Cerebrovascular Disease [Neurology and psychiatry] (DAVI)
CVD .... Chemical Vapor Deposition [Coating technology]
CVD .... Christelijke Vervoerarbeiders en Diamantbewerkers [Christian Trade
             Union of Transport and Diamond Workers] [Belgium] (EAIO)
CVD .... Collagen Vascular Disease [Medicine]
CVD .... Color Vision Deviate [Ophthalmology]
CVD .... Column Valve Diaphragm
CVD .... Communication Valve Development [British]
CVD .... Continuous Variable Damper [Automotive suspensions]
CVD .... Conversion Industries, Inc. [AMEX symbol] (SPSG)
CVD .... Convert to Decimal (IAA)
CVD .... Countervailing Duty [Customs] (FEA)
CVD .... Coupled Vibration Dissociation (IEEE)
CVD .... Creative Visual Dynamics (OA)
CVD .... Current-Voltage Diagram
cvd............ Curved
CVD .... Sisters of Bethany [Roman Catholic religious order]
CVDA .... Converter, Voltage Discrete, AC [Alternating Current] (NASA)
CVDS .... Cardiovascular Diagnostics [NASDAQ symbol] (TTSB)
CVDI .... Cardiovascular Diagnostics, Inc. [NASDAQ symbol] (SAG)
CVDLS .... California Veterinary Diagnostic Laboratory System
CVDP .... Coupled Vibration Dissociation Process
CVDS .... Cardiovascular Disease Study [British]
CVDT .... Constant Volume Drop Time
CVDV .... Coupled Vibration Dissociation Vibration (IEEE)
CVE .... Calibration Vibration Exciter
CVE .... Central Pulmonary Vessels Enlargement [Medicine]
CVE .... Cerebrovascular Episode [Medicine] (CPH)
CVE2 .... Coatesville, PA [Location identifier FAA] (FAAL)
CVE .... Complete Vehicle Erector (SAA)
CVE .... Complete Verification Record (MCD)
CVE .... Complex Vehicle Erector (KSC)
CVE............ COMSAT [Communications Satellite Corp.] Video Enterprises
             [Washington, DC] (TSSD)
CVE............ Continuously Variable, for Emergency
CVE............ Converse, Inc. [NYSE symbol] (SAG)
CVE............ Conversion Industries, Inc. [Vancouver Stock Exchange symbol]
CVE............ Customer-Vended Equipment (AAG)
CVE............ Escort Aircraft Carrier [Navy symbol]
CVEB.......... Cisplatin, Vinblastine, Etoposide, Bleomycin [Antineoplastic drug]
             (CDI)
CVEH.......... Combat Vehicle [Army] (AABC)
CVen........... Canes Venatici [Constellation]
CVer........... Vernon Public Library, Vernon, CA [Library symbol Library of
             Congress]
C Verd Isls... Cape Verde Islands
CV Esc........ Cape Verde Escudo (ODBW)
CVESPA .... Chateauguay Valley English-Speaking Peoples' Association (AC)
CVF............ Calvi [Corsica] [Seismograph station code, US Geological Survey]
             (SEIS)
CVF............ Castle Convert Fund [AMEX symbol] (TTSB)
CVF............ Castle Convertible Fund, Inc. [AMEX symbol] (SPSG)
CVF............ Central Visual Field [Optics]
CVF............ Circular Variable Filter [Instrumentation]
CVF............ Cobra Venom Factor [Immunochemistry]
CVF............ Compressed Volume File [Computer science]
CVF............ Constant-Volume Feeder [Nuclear energy] (NUCP)
CVF............ Continuously Variable Filter [Spectrometry]
CVF............ Controlled Visual Flight
CvF............ Conversion Factor
CVF............ Correspondent Validity File [IRS]
CVF............ Courchevel [France] [Airport symbol] (OAG)
CVFA.......... Conseil de la Vie Francaise en Amerique (AC)
CVFC.......... Concord Video and Film Council (EAIO)

CV/FES........ Children's Version/Family Environment Scale [Child development
             test] [Psychology]
CVFM.......... Cyclophosphamide, Vincristine, Fluorouracil, Methotrexate
             [Antineoplastic drug regimen]
CVFP.......... Charted Visual Flight Procedure Approach [FAA] (TAG)
CVFR .... Controlled Visual Flight Rules [Military]
CVFS.......... Cesium Vapor Feed System
CVFS.......... Circular Variable Filter Spectrometer
CVG .... Carrier Air Group [Navy] (MUGU)
CVG .... Cincinnati [Ohio] [Airport symbol] (OAG)
CVG .... Cincinnati [Ohio] - Covington [Kentucky] [Airport symbol]
CVG .... Constructive Variational Geometry [Computer science]
CVG .... Continuously Variable Gearbox (PDAA)
CVG .... Coronary Vein Graft [Medicine]
CVG .... Covington, KY/Cincinnati, OH [Location identifier FAA] (FAAL)
CVG .... Guided Missile Aircraft Carrier [Navy symbol]
CVGE .... Coverage
CVGH.......... Guided Missile Aircraft Carrier [Navy symbol]
CVGIP......... Computer Vision Graphics and Image Processing [A publication]
CVGK.......... Customs Value per Gross Kilogram (DS)
CVGN.......... Nuclear-Powered Guided Missile Aircraft Carrier [Navy symbol]
CVGP.......... Customs Value per Gross Pound (DS)
CVH .... Aircraft Carrier, Helicopter [NATO]
CVH .... Calvada Resources [Vancouver Stock Exchange symbol]
CVH .... Combined Ventricular Hypertrophy (MAE)
CVH .... Common Variable Hypogammaglobulinemia [Medicine] (MAE)
CVH .... Compound Valve Hemispherical Head [Engine]
CVHA.......... Containment Vent Header [Nuclear energy] (NRCH)
CVHA.......... Assault Helicopter Aircraft Carrier [Navy symbol Obsolete]
CVHC.......... Coastal Helicopter Aircraft Carrier [Ship symbol] (NATG)
CvHd.......... Convertible Holdings [Associated Press] (SAG)
CVHE.......... Escort Helicopter Aircraft Carrier [Navy symbol]
CVHEE......... Coalition for Vocational Home Economics Education (EA)
CVHGN........ Guided Missile Aircraft Carrier [Navy symbol]
CVHN.......... Nuclear-Powered V/STOL [Vertical / Short Take-off and Landing]
             Aircraft Carrier [Navy symbol]
CVHQ.......... Central Volunteer Headquarters [Military British]
CV-HRU........ Combat Vehicle - Heading Reference Unit
CVHT.......... Continuously Variable Hydromechanical Transmission [Engineering]
CVI............ Cape Verde Islands
CVI............ Cardiovascular Institute [Boston University] [Research center] (RCD)
CVI............ Cassovia Air [Slovakia] [ICAO designator] (FAAC)
CVI............ Central Vehicle Index [Record of cars lost or stolen in London]
CVI............ Cerebrovascular Insufficiency [Medicine]
CVI............ Certified Vendor Information (NRCH)
CVI............ Chemical Vapor Infiltration [Materials science]
CVI............ Children's Vaccine Initiative [Coalition of international donors]
CVI............ Cholera Vaccine Immunization [Medicine]
CVI............ Cisplatis, VePesid, Ifosfamide [Antineoplastic drug] (CDI)
CVI............ Cofield, NC [Location identifier FAA] (FAAL)
CVI............ College of the Virgin Islands
CVI............ Colorado Video, Inc.
CVI............ Common Variable Immunodeficiency [Medicine]
CVI............ Competitive Voluntary Indefinite [Status] [Army] (INF)
CVI............ Computer Video Instrument (NITA)
CVI............ Conditional Voluntary Indefinite [Status] [Army] (INF)
CVI............ Configuration Verification Index
CVI............ Congregation of Incarnate Word and Blessed Sacrament (TOCD)
CVI............ Containment Ventilation Isolation [Nuclear energy] (NRCH)
CVI............ Continuous Venous Infusion [Chemotherapy] (DAVI)
CVI............ Counterflow Virtual Impactor [Instrumentation]
CVI............ Current Variable Inductor
CVI............ CV REIT, Inc. [NYSE symbol] (SPSG)
CVI............ Religious of the Incarnate Word (TOCD)
CVi............ Visalia Public Library, Visalia, CA [Library symbol Library of
             Congress] (LCLS)
CVIA.......... Computer Virus Industry Association (EA)
CVIASA .... Commercial Vehicle Industry Association of South Australia
CVIAV .... Commercial Vehicle Industry Association of Victoria [Australia]
CVIC.......... Aircraft Carrier Intelligence Center (NVT)
CVIC.......... Conditional Variable Incremental Computer (IEEE)
CViCL......... Tulare County Free Library, Visalia, CA [Library symbol Library of
             Congress] (LCLS)
CViCS .... College of the Sequoias, Visalia, CA [Library symbol Library of
             Congress] (LCLS)
C Vict........ Dominion of Canada Statutes in the Reign of Victoria
             [A publication] (DLA)
CVID .... Common Variable Immune Deficiency [Immunology] (DAVI)
CVIIAS .... Cowichan Valley Intercultural & Immigrant Society (AC)
CViKD .... Kaweah Delta District Hospital, Visalia, CA [Library symbol Library of
             Congress] (LCLS)
CVIMS .... Central Vancouver Island Multicultural Society (AC)
C VINAR ...... Cyathus Vinarius [Wineglassful] [Pharmacy] (ROG)
CVINO......... Clearance Void if Not Off [Aviation] (FAAC)
CVIP.......... Computer Vision and Image Processing
CVIS.......... Computerized Vocational Information System [Guidance program]
CVISC......... Combat Visual Information Support Center [DoD]
CVISN......... Commercial Vehicle Information System and Network
cVit............ Chicken Vitellogenin
CVIU.......... Computer Vision and Understanding
CViVC......... Visalia Community Counseling Center, Visalia, CA [Library symbol
             Library of Congress] (LCLS)
CVJ............ Continuous Velocity Joint [Automotive engineering]
CVJB.......... Cryptologic Van Junction Box [Navy] (ANA)
CVK............ Centerline Vertical Keel

CVK............ Cherokee Village, AR [*Location identifier FAA*] (FAAL)
CVK............ Consolidated Amhawk Enterprise [*Vancouver Stock Exchange symbol*]
CVKI............ Combat Vehicle Kill Indicator (MCD)
CVKI-PD...... Combat Vehicle Kill Indicator Pyrotechnic Device (MCD)
CVL............ Calcutta Volunteer Lancers [*British military*] (DMA)
CVL............ Cape Vogel [*Papua New Guinea*] [*Airport symbol*] (OAG)
CVL............ Central Veterinary Laboratory [*Research center British*] (IRC)
CVL............ Civil (MSA)
CVL............ Civil
CVL............ Colville River, AK [*Location identifier FAA*] (FAAL)
CVL............ Computer Vision Laboratory [*University of Maryland*] [*Research center*] (RCD)
CVL............ Configuration Verification List (MCD)
CVL............ Coval Air Ltd. [*Canada ICAO designator*] (FAAC)
CVL............ Crystal Violet Lactone [*Organic chemistry*]
CVL............ Small Aircraft Carrier [*Navy symbol*]
C/VL............ Specific Compliance [*Laboratory terminology*] (DAVI)
CVLA............ Coosa Valley Librarians Association [*Library network*]
CVL/CVE ..... Light/Escort Carrier [*Ship symbol*] (NATG)
CVLD .... Combat Vehicle LASER Detector Assembly (MCD)
CVLFE......... Compact Very-Low-Frequency Equipment (DWSG)
CVLG .... Guided Missile Light Aircraft Carrier (MCD)
CVLGN........ Nuclear-Powered Guided Missile Light Aircraft Carrier (MCD)
CVLI............ Cash Value Life Insurance
CVLI............ Commissioned Vessel Liaison Inquiry (DNAB)
CVLN .... Nuclear-Powered Light Aircraft Carrier (MCD)
CVLS .... Central Vacuum Loading System
CVM............ Alton, IL [*Location identifier FAA*] (FAAL)
CVM............ California Maritime Academy, Vallejo, CA [*Library symbol Library of Congress*] (LCLS)
CVM............ Capacitance Voltage Measurements (MCD)
CVM............ Cardiovascular Monitor [*Medicine*]
CVM............ Center for Veterinary Medicine [*Food and Drug Administration*]
CVM............ Central Vehicle Monitoring [*Automotive engineering*]
CVM............ Christian Volunteer Ministries (EA)
CVM............ Ciudad Victoria [*Mexico*] [*Airport symbol*] (OAG)
CVM............ Cluster Variation Method [*Physics*]
CVM............ COBOL [*Common Business-Oriented Language*] Virtual Machine
CVM............ College of Veterinary Medicine [*University of Florida*] [*Research center*] (RCD)
CVM............ Community Voice Mail [*Program providing the homeless with voice mail*] [*Telecommunications*] (ECON)
CVM............ Consumable Vacuum Melt [*Steel*]
CVM............ Contingent Value Method [*Pisciculture*]
CVM............ Control Valve Module (NASA)
CVM............ Council for a Volunteer Military [*Defunct*] (EA)
CVM............ Cramer - von Mises Test [*Statistics*]
CVM............ Cyclophosphamide, Vincristine, Methotrexate [*Antineoplastic drug regimen*]
CVM............ Cylindrical Vibration Mount
CVMA.......... Canadian Veterinary Medical Association (EAIO)
CVMA.......... Commercial Vehicle Manufacturers' Association [*Australia*]
CVMAS .... Continuously Variable Mechanical Advantage Shifter
CVMI........... Commercial Vehicle Maintenance Implications (MCD)
CVMISS ...... Comox Valley Multicultural & Immigrant Support Society (AC)
CVMO .... Commercial Value Movement Order (DCTA)
CVMP......... Combat Vehicle Maintenance Policy Study
CVMP......... Committee for Veterinary Medicinal Products [*European Community*]
CVMP......... Committee on Veterans Medical Problems [*US*]
CVMUG .... Canada VM Users Group (EAIO)
CVMV......... Carnation Vein Mottle Virus [*Plant pathology*]
CVN............ Aircraft Carrier, Nuclear Propulsion [*Navy symbol*] (NVT)
CVN............ Bromma Flygskola/Cabair [*Sweden ICAO designator*] (FAAC)
CVN............ Cable Value Network [*Television*]
CVn............ Canes Venatici [*Constellation*]
CVN............ Carl Vinson Nuclear Powered Carrier [*DoD*]
CVN............ Casualty Vulnerability Number
CVN............ Change Verification Notice
CVN .... Charpy V-Notch [*Nuclear energy*] (NRCH)
CVN .... CINCPAC Voice Alert Net (MCD)
CVN............ Clovis [*New Mexico*] [*Airport symbol*] (OAG)
CVN............ Clovis, NM [*Location identifier FAA*] (FAAL)
CVN............ Computervision Corp. [*NYSE symbol*] (SPSG)
CVN............ Construction Verification Notification [*Nuclear energy*] (NRCH)
CVN............ Convene (AABC)
CVN............ Courvan Mining Co. Ltd. [*Toronto Stock Exchange symbol*]
CVnCR .... Carnation Research Laboratories, Van Nuys, CA [*Library symbol Library of Congress*] (LCLS)
CVnITT......... International Telephone & Telegraph Corp., Gilfillan Division, Engineering Library, Van Nuys, CA [*Library symbol Library of Congress*] (LCLS)
CVnL........... Los Angeles Valley College, Van Nuys, CA [*Library symbol Library of Congress*] (LCLS)
CVNM .... Vallejo Naval and Historical Museum, Vallejo, CA [*Library symbol*] [*Library of Congress*] (LCLS)
CVNNT........ Covenant
CVNPA........ Carolinas-Virginia Nuclear Power Associates, Inc.
Cvnr............ Convenor
CVnRCAM .... Radio Corp. of America, West Coast Missile & Surface RADAR Division, Van Nuys, CA [*Library symbol Library of Congress*] (LCLS)
CVNS .... Combat Vehicle Night Sight
CVNT .... Convertible Note
CVNTL .... Conventional (MSA)

CVO .... Albany-Corvallis [*Oregon*] [*Airport symbol*] (AD)
CVO .... Cascades Volcano Observatory [*US Geological Survey*]
CVO .... Central Vein Occlusion [*Medicine*] (DMAA)
CVO .... Certificate of Value and Origin (DS)
CVO .... Chevy Oil Corp. [*Vancouver Stock Exchange symbol*]
CVO .... Chief Veterinary Officer [*Ministry of Agriculture, Fisheries, and Food*] [*British*]
CVO .... College of Veterinarians of Ontario (AC)
CVO .... Commander of the Royal Victorian Order [*British*]
CVO .... Commercial Vehicle Operations [*Highway safety*]
CVO .... Commercial Vehicle Operations
CVO .... Communications Validating Office (CET)
CVO .... Conjugata Vera Obstetrica [*Conjugate diameter of pelvic inlet*] [*Anatomy*]
CVO .... Corvallis, OR [*Location identifier FAA*] (FAAL)
CVOA .... Cosworth Vega Owner's Association [*Defunct*] (EA)
C VOC .... Colla Voce [*With the Voice*] [*Music*]
CVOD .... Cerebrovascular Obstructive Disease (MAE)
CVP............ Callao Caves [*Philippines*] [*Seismograph station code, US Geological Survey*] (SEIS)
CVP............ Carma Ltd. [*Toronto Stock Exchange symbol*]
CVP............ Cell Volume Profile [*Hematology*]
CVP............ Central Valley Project [*California*] (ECON)
CVP............ Central Venous Pressure [*Medicine*]
CVP............ Cerebrovascular Profile [*Cardiology*] (DAVI)
CVP............ Chemical Vapor Plating
CVP............ Chimaeric Virus Particles [*Biochemistry*]
CVP............ Christelijke Volkspartij [*Christian Social Party*] [*Also, PSC*] [*Belgium*] [*Political party*] (PPW)
CVP............ Christlichdemokratische Volkspartei der Schweiz [*Christian Democratic Party of Switzerland*] [*Political party*] (PPE)
CVP............ Christliche Volkspartei [*Christian People's Party*] [*Pre-1945 Germany*] [*Political party*] (PPE)
CVP............ Climate, Vegetation, Productivity
CVP............ Computer Validation Program (DNAB)
CVP............ Conservative Party of Australia [*Political party*]
CVP............ Consolidated Carma Corp. [*Toronto Stock Exchange symbol*]
CVP............ Containment Vacuum Pump [*Nuclear energy*] (IEEE)
CVP............ Content Vectoring Protocol [*Computer science*]
CVP............ Content Vectoring Protocol [*Computer science*]
CVP............ Cost-Volume-Power
CVP-........... Cost-Volume-Profit [*Analysis*] (MCD)
C-V-P......... Cost-Volume-Profit (AAGC)
CVP............ Covina Public Library, Covina, CA [*OCLC symbol*] (OCLC)
CVP............ Crystal Violet-Pectate [*Microbiological medium*]
CVP............ Cyclophosphamide, Vincristine, Prednisone [*Also, COP*] [*Antineoplastic drug regimen*]
CVP + Bleo... Cyclophosphamide [*Cytoxan*], Vincristine, Predinisone, Bleomycin [*Antineoplastic drug regimen*] (DAVI)
CVPC .... Control Valve Primary Coolant (MCD)
CVPDS .... Command Video Prelaunch Distribution System (IAA)
CVPETS....... Condenser Vacuum Pump Effluent Treatment System [*Nuclear energy*] (NRCH)
CVPlab........ Cardiovascular Pulmonary Laboratory [*Medicine*] (MAE)
CVPO .... Chemical Vapor Phase Oxidization (EECA)
CVPP .... CCNU [*Lomustine*], Vinblastine, Prednisone, Procarbazine [*Antineoplastic drug regimen*]
CVPP .... Cyclophosphamide, Vinblastine, Procarbazine, Prednisone [*Antineoplastic drug regimen*]
CVPP-CCNU... Cyclophosphamide, Vinblastine, Procarbazine, Prednisone, CCNU [*Lomustine*] [*Antineoplastic drug regimen*]
CVPR .... Combat Vehicle Program Review
CVPT........... Certificate for Vocational Preparation Tutors (AIE)
CVPV .... Centre de Valorisation du Patrimoine Vivant (AC)
CVPV .... Containment Vacuum Pump Valve [*Nuclear energy*] (NRCH)
CVQ .... Carnarvon [*Australia Airport symbol*] (OAG)
CVQ .... Carnarvon [*Western Australia*] [*Airport symbol*] (AD)
CVQ .... Coventry Ventures [*Vancouver Stock Exchange symbol*]
CVR .... Calaveras Reservoir [*California*] [*Seismograph station code, US Geological Survey*] (SEIS)
CVR .... Cardiovascular-Renal [*Medicine*]
CVR .... Cardiovascular Respiratory System [*Medicine*]
CVR .... Carrier Vessel Reactor
CVR .... Center for Venture Research (EA)
CVR .... Cephalic Vasomotor Response [*Medicine*] (DMAA)
CVR .... Ceramic Vacuum Relay
CVR .... Cerebrovascular Resistance [*Medicine*]
CVR .... Change Verification Record
CVR .... Chicago Rivet & Mach [*AMEX symbol*] (TTSB)
CVR .... Chicago Rivet & Machine Co. [*AMEX symbol*] (SPSG)
CVR .... Cockpit Voice Recorder
CVR .... Command Verification
CVR .... Command Voltage Regulator
CVR .... Computer Voice Response
CVR .... Configuration Verification Review (MCD)
CVR .... Conservation Voltage Reduction [*Public Utilities Commission*]
CVR .... Constant Velocity Recording
CVR .... Constant Voltage Reference
CVR .... Continental Silver [*Vancouver Stock Exchange symbol*]
CVR .... Contingent Value Right [*Finance*]
CVR .... Continuous Vertical Retort [*Metallurgy*] [*Fuel technology*]
CVR .... Continuous Video Recorder (IAA)
CVR .... Contraceptive Vaginal Ring [*Gynecology*]
CVR .... Controlled Visual Rules [*FAA*]
CVR .... Coronary Vascular Resistance [*Medicine*]

CVR	Cover
CVR	Crystal Video Receiver
CVR	Culver City, CA [*Location identifier FAA*] (FAAL)
CVR	Current Viewing Resistor
CVR	Current Voltage Regulator (IAA)
CVRC	Consensus Voluntary Reference Compound [*Environmental science*]
CVRD	Cardiovascular Renal Disease [*Medicine*]
CVRD	Cardiovascular Respiratory Disease [*Medicine*]
CVR/D	Command Verification/Drop
CVRD	Companhia Vale do Rio Doce
CVRD	Converter, Variable Resistance, to DC [*Direct Current*] Voltage (NASA)
CVRD HPR	Covered Hopper [*Freight*]
CV REI	CV REIT [*Real Estate Investment Trust*], Inc. [*Associated Press*] (SAG)
CVRI	Cardiovascular Research Institute [*University of California, San Francisco*] [*Research center*] (RCD)
CVRI	Coronary Vascular Resistance Index [*Cardiology*] (DAVI)
CVRM	Chemico-Viscous Remanent Magnetization [*Geophysics*]
CVROS	Compact Video-Rate Optical Scanner [*Instrumentation*]
CVRP	Commercial Vehicle Repair Parts (MCD)
CVRSN	Conversion (MSA)
CVR(T)	Combat Vehicle, Reconnaissance (Tracked) [*British military*] (MCD)
CVR(T)(APC)	Combat Vehicle, Reconnaissance (Tracked) (Armoured Personnel Carrier) [*British military*]
CVRTC	Cardiovascular Research and Training Center [*University of Alabama in Birmingham*] [*Research center*] (RCD)
CVRTC	Commercial Vehicle and Road Transport Club [*British*] (BI)
CVRTC	Nora Eccles Harrison Cardiovascular Research and Training Center [*University of Utah*] [*Research center*] (RCD)
CVR(T)(GW)	Combat Vehicle, Reconnaissance (Tracked)(Guided Weapon Carrier) [*British military*]
CVR(T)(REC)	Combat Vehicle, Reconnaissance (Tracked) (Recovery) [*British military*]
CVR(W)	Combat Vehicle, Reconnaissance (Wheeled) [*British military*] (DMA)
CVS	ASW [*Antisubmarine Warfare*] Support Aircraft Carrier [*Navy symbol*]
CVS	CAD [*Computer-Aided Design*] for VLSI [*Very Large Scale Integration*] System [*Electronics*] (NITA)
CVS	Calibration Verification Sample [*Spectroscopy*]
CVS	Cardiovascular Surgery [*Medicine*]
CVS	Cardiovascular System [*Medicine*]
CVS	Cathodic Voltammetry Stripping [*Marine science*] (OSRA)
CVS	Cathodic Voltametry Stripping (USDC)
CVS	Center for a Voluntary Society [*Defunct*] (EA)
CVS	Center for Vietnamese Studies [*Southern Illinois University at Carbondale*] [*Research center*] (RCD)
CVS	Center for Visual Science [*University of Rochester*] [*Research center*] (RCD)
CVS	Challenge Virus Strain
CVS	Chorionic Biopsy [*Also, Chorionic Villus Sampling*] [*Medicine*] (PAZ)
CVS	Chorionic Villi Sampling [*Medicine*]
CVS	Clean Voided Specimen [*Medicine*]
CVS	Clovis, NM [*Location identifier FAA*] (FAAL)
CVS	Combat Vehicle Simulator (MCD)
CVS	Committee on Valuation of Securities
CVS	Common Video System
CVS	Community Volunteer Services Commission of B'nai B'rith International (EAIO)
CVS	Computer-Controlled Vehicle System (IAA)
CVS	Computer Vision Syndrome
CVS	Constant Voltage Source
CVS	Constant Volume Sampling [*ACF Industries*]
CVS	Consumer Value Stores
CVS	Continuously Variable Stroke [*Automotive engineering*]
CVS	Continuous Vent System (KSC)
CVS	Convenience, Value, Service
CVS	Covert Viewing System
CVS	Coves
CVS	Crash Vehicle Simulator
CVS	Current Vital Signs [*Medicine*]
CVS	CVS Corp. [*NYSE symbol*] (SAG)
CVS	Cyclic Voltametric Stripping [*Electrochemistry*]
CVS	Seaplane Carrier [*Navy symbol Obsolete*]
CVSA	Commercial Vehicle Safety Alliance [*FHWA*] [*RSPA*] (TAG)
CVSA	Commission on Voluntary Service and Action (EA)
CVSA	Cyclic Vomiting Syndrome Association
CVSC	Community Volunteer Services Commission of B'nai B'rith International (EA)
CVSC	Control Valve Secondary Coolant (MCD)
CVSCC	Coolant Vacuum Switch Cold Closed [*Automotive engineering*]
CVS Corp	CVS Corp. [*Associated Press*] (SAG)
CVSD	Coded Voice System Digitization (NITA)
CVSD	Continuously Variable Slope Delta Modulation [*Telecommunications*]
CVSDM	Continuously Variable Slope Delta Modulation [*Telecommunications*] (TEL)
CVSF	Conduction Velocity of Slower Fibers (PDAA)
CVSG	Carrier Antisubmarine Air Group [*Navy*] (NVT)
CVSG	Channel Verification Signal Generator
CVSI	Conditional Value of Sample Information [*Statistics*]
CVSMP	Combat Vehicle Signature Management Plan [*Army*] (RDA)
CVSN	Conversion [*Legal shorthand*] (LWAP)
CVSRF	Crew-Vehicle Simulation Research Facility [*National Aeronautics and Space Administration Ames*] (GAVI)
CVSSUS	Central Verband der Siebenburger Sachsen of the United States [*Later, Alliance of Transylvanian Saxons*] (EA)

CVST	Cerebral Venous Sinus Thrombosis [*Medicine*]
CVSU	Cardiovascular Studies Unit [*University of Pennsylvania*] [*Research center*] (RCD)
CVT	Calvert Gas & Oils Ltd. [*Toronto Stock Exchange symbol*]
CVT	Cardiovascular Technologist (HCT)
CVT	Cavernous Sinus Thrombosis [*Medicine*]
CVT	Center for Vocational and Technical Education, Ohio State University, Columbus, OH [*Inactive*] [*OCLC symbol*] (OCLC)
CVT	Central Vermont Railway, Inc.
CVT	Chemical Vapor Transport
CVT	Color Video Tape (MCD)
CVT	Command Verify/Transmit
CVT	Commissioner for Vocational Training [*New South Wales*] [*Australia*]
CVT	Communication Vector Table (BUR)
CVT	Concept Verification Test (NASA)
CVT	Configuration Verification Test
CVT	Constant Velocity Transmission
CVT	Constant Voltage Transformer
CVT	Continuously Variable Transmission [*Of engines*]
CVT	Controlled Variable Time [*Fuze*] (NVT)
CVT	Convert
CVT	Convertible [*Stock exchange term*]
CVT	Coventry [*England*] [*Airport symbol*] (OAG)
CVT	Crystal Violet Tetrazolium (OA)
CVT	Current Values Table
CVT	TCW Convertible Security Fund [*NYSE symbol*] (SPSG)
CVT	TCW Conv Sec Fund [*NYSE symbol*] (TTSB)
CVT	Training Aircraft Carrier [*Navy symbol*]
CVt	Ventura County-City Free Library, Ventura, CA [*Library symbol Library of Congress*] (LCLS)
CVTA	Corvita Corp. [*NASDAQ symbol*] (SAG)
CVTAC	Corvita Corp. [*NASDAQ symbol*] (TTSB)
CVTAE	Center for Vocational, Technical, and Adult Education [*University of Wisconsin - Stout*] [*Research center*] (RCD)
CVtB	Black Gold Cooperative Library System, Ventura, CA [*Library symbol Library of Congress*] (LCLS)
CVtGS	Church of Jesus Christ of Latter-Day Saints, Genealogical Society Library, Ventura Branch, Ventura, CA [*Library symbol Library of Congress*] (LCLS)
CV Ther	CV Therapeutics, Inc. [*Associated Press*] (SAG)
CVTI	Covenant Transport'A' [*NASDAQ symbol*] (TTSB)
CVTI	Covenant Transport, Inc. [*NASDAQ symbol*] (SAG)
CVT-ICU	Cardiovascular Thoracic Intensive Care Unit (DAVI)
CVtMHA	Ventura County Museum of History and Art, Ventura, CA [*Library symbol*] [*Library of Congress*] (LCLS)
CVTP-ICU	Cardiovascular Thoracic Post-Intensive Care Unit (DAVI)
CVtPS	Central Vermont Public Service Corp. [*Associated Press*] (SAG)
CVTR	Carolinas-Virginia Tube Reactor
CVTR	Charcoal Viral Transport [*Medium*] [*Microbiology*]
CVT S	Cardiovascular-Thoracic Surgery (DAVI)
CVTSC	Carrier-Based Tactical Support Center [*Navy*] (NVT)
CVtV	Ventura College, Ventura, CA [*Library symbol Library of Congress*] (LCLS)
CVTX	CV Therapeutics, Inc. [*NASDAQ symbol*] (SAG)
CVTY	Coventry Corp. [*NASDAQ symbol*] (SPSG)
CVU	Calibration Validation Unit [*Instrumentation*]
CVU	Constant Voltage Unit
CVU	Contact Ventures [*Vancouver Stock Exchange symbol*]
CVU	Control Vision Unit [*Automotive engineering*]
CVU	Grand Canyon Airlines, Inc. [*FAA designator*] (FAAC)
CVU	Utility Aircraft Carrier [*Navy symbol Obsolete*]
CVUG	Cystoscopy and Voiding Urethrogram [*Radiology and urology*] (DAVI)
CVUS	CellularVision USA [*NASDAQ symbol*] (TTSB)
CVUS	CellularVision USA, Inc. [*NASDAQ symbol*] (SAG)
CVUSA	Children's Village, USA [*of International Orphans Inc.*] [*Later, CVC*] (EA)
CVV	Aircraft Carrier, Medium Sized [*Navy symbol*] (MCD)
CVV	Charlottesville [*Virginia*] [*Seismograph station code, US Geological Survey*] (SEIS)
CVV	Citrus Variegation Virus [*Plant pathology*]
CVV	Control Variable Valve
CVVTMC	Council of Veteran, Vintage and Thoroughbred Motor Clubs [*Australia*]
CVW	Attack Carrier Air Wing [*Navy symbol*]
CVW	CodeView for Windows [*Program debugger*] [*Computer science*] (PCM)
CVW	Computer Virus as a Weapon [*DoD*]
CVW	Consolidated General Western Industries Ltd. [*Vancouver Stock Exchange symbol Toronto Stock Exchange symbol*]
CVWA	Canadian Vintage Wireless Association [*Defunct*] (EA)
CVWM	Combined Volume-Weighted Mean [*Statistics*]
CVWS	Combat Vehicle Weapons System [*Army*]
CVWS(LR)	Combat Vehicle Weapons System (Long-Range) [*Army*]
CVX	Cactus Virus X [*Plant pathology*]
CVX	Charlevoix, MI [*Location identifier FAA*] (FAAL)
CVX	Cleveland Electric Illuminating Co. [*NYSE symbol*] (SAG)
CVX	Communaute Mondiale de Vie Chretienne [*World Christian Life Community*] [*Italy*] (EAIO)
CVX	Consolidated TVX Mining Corp. [*Toronto Stock Exchange symbol*]
CVX	Convex (MSA)
CVXPr	ClevelandElec $7.40 cm A Pfd [*NYSE symbol*] (TTSB)
CVXPrB	Cleveland Elec III $7.56 Pfd [*NYSE symbol*] (TTSB)
CVXPrL	Cleveland Elec III Adj L Pfd [*NYSE symbol*] (TTSB)
CVXPrT	Cleveland Elec III'93 Sr'A'Dep Pfd [*NYSE symbol*] (TTSB)
CVY	Charlie/Victor/Yankee [*Military*] (CAAL)

CVY	Conventures Ltd. [*Toronto Stock Exchange symbol*]
CVY	Fort Riley, KS [*Location identifier FAA*] (FAAL)
CVYS	Council for Voluntary Youth Service (AIE)
CVZ	Caara Ventures, Inc. [*Vancouver Stock Exchange symbol*]
CVZ	Centralverein-Zeitung [*A publication*] (BJA)
CW	Air Marshall Islands [*Airline code*] [*Australia*]
CW	Call Waiting [*Telephone communication*]
CW	Camping Women (EA)
CW	Canada West
CW	Carapace Width
CW	Carcass Weight [*Animal husbandry*]
CW	Cardiac Work [*Physiology*]
CW	Care for the Wild [*An association British*] (EAIO)
CW	Carrier Wave [*A form of radio transmission in code*]
C/W	Carter-Wallace, Inc.
CW	Casework [*or Caseworker*]
CW	Catholic Workman (EA)
CW	Cavity Wall
CW	Cedar Waxwing [*Ornithology*]
CW	Cell Wall
CW	Cement Water Ratio (IAA)
CW	Channel Word (IAA)
CW	Chemical Warfare
CW	Chemical Weapons
CW	Chemical Wood [*Paper*] (DGA)
CW	Chesapeake Western Railway (IIA)
CW	Chest Wall [*Medicine*]
CW	Chief Warrant Officer [*Military rank*]
CW	Children of War [*An association*] (EA)
CW	Children's Ward [*of a hospital*]
CW	Child Welfare
CW	Chilled Water [*Aerospace*] (DNAB)
C-W	Chronometer Time Minus Watch Time [*Navigation*]
CW	Churchwarden
CW	Circulating Water [*Nuclear energy*] (NRCH)
CW	Cities of the World [*A publication*]
CW	Civil Works [*Assistant Secretary of the Army*]
CW	Classical World [*A publication*] (BRI)
CW	Classical Writers [*A publication*]
CW	Clean Water (IEEE)
C/W	Clerk of the Works (DAC)
CW	Clifford & Wills [*Commercial firm*]
CW	Clockwise
CW	Clothes Washer
CW	Coal-Water [*Fuel mixture*]
CW	Coast Waiter [*Coast Guard British*] (ROG)
CW	Code Wave (BARN)
CW	Code Word (IAA)
CW	Cold Wall
CW	Cold War (CINC)
CW	Cold Water [*Technical drawings*]
CW	Cold Weld [*Mechanics*] (BARN)
CW	Cold Welding
CW	Cold-Worked [*Nuclear energy*] (NRCH)
CW	Colonial Williamsburg, Inc. (CDAI)
CW	[*The*] Colorado & Wyoming Railway Co. [*AAR code*]
CW	Column Waste [*Nuclear energy*] (NRCH)
CW	Comfortably Weird [*In the record business, refers to a successful performer who has retained his individuality*]
CW	Commander's Office Writer [*British military*] (DMA)
CW	Command Word [*Computer science*] (MCD)
CW	Commercial Weight
CW	Commission and Warrant [*British military*] (DMA)
Cw	Commonwealth
CW	Communications Wing [*Air Force*]
C/W	Compatible With (DAVI)
C/W	Complete With (MSA)
CW	Complied With (AFIT)
CW	Composite Wave (IEEE)
CW	Computer Weekly [*British*] [*A publication*] (NITA)
CW	Computer Wizard [*Information service or system*] (IID)
CW	Concealed Weapons
C/W	Concurrent With
CW	Congress Watch (EA)
CW	Connected With (IAA)
C/W	Consistent With (DAVI)
CW	Constant Wear (KSC)
CW	Continuous Wave [*A form of radio transmission*]
CW	Continuous-Wound (DEN)
CW	Control Word (MCD)
CW	Conventional Wisdom [*Professional political opinion*]
CW	Conventional Wisdom Watch [*Newsweek Magazine*]
cw	Cook Islands [*MARC country of publication code Library of Congress*] (LCCP)
CW	Cooling Water [*Nuclear energy*] (NRCH)
CW	Cool White (DAC)
CW	Copper Weld
CW	Copywriting
CW	Corporate Word [*Database terminology*] (NITA)
CW	Cotton or Wool [*Freight*]
C/W	Counterweight (AAG)
CW	Counties (Wales)
CW	Countries of the World [*A publication*]
CW	Coursewriter [*IBM Corp. programming language*]
CW	Covers [*JETDS nomenclature*] [*Military*] (CET)

CW	Crawlerway [*NASA*] (KSC)
CW	Cream Wove [*Paper*] (DGA)
CW	Crutch Walking [*Medicine*]
CW	Cubic Weight
CW	Curb Weight [*Automotive engineering*]
CW	Curtiss-Wright [*NYSE symbol*] (TTSB)
CW	Curtiss-Wright Corp. [*ICAO aircraft manufacturer identifier*] (ICAO)
CW	Curtiss-Wright Corp. [*NYSE symbol*] (SPSG)
CW	Cypher Writing [*Freemasonry*] (ROG)
CW	St. Andrews Airways [*ICAO designator*] (AD)
CW2	Chief Warrant Officer 2 [*Army*]
CW3	Chief Warrant Officer 3 [*Army*]
CW4	Chief Warrant Officer 4 [*Army*]
CWA	California Warehouse Association (SRA)
CWA	California Water Association (SRA)
CWA	California Wheelchair Aviators (EA)
CWA	Canada Water [*Canada*] [*A database*] (NITA)
CWA	Canada West Air Ltd. [*ICAO designator*] (FAAC)
CWA	Canadian Western Approaches
CWA	Caution and Warning Annunciator (MCD)
CWA	Center Weather Advisory [*FAA*] (TAG)
CWA	Central Wholesalers Association (EA)
CWA	Children's Wear Association (EA)
CWA	Chinese Women's Association (EA)
CWA	Chung Wah Association [*Australia*]
CWA	Civil Works Administration [*1933-1934*]
CWA	Clean Water Act [*Environmental Protection Agency*]
CWA	Clean Water Action [*An association*] (EA)
CWA	Clean Work Area [*NASA*] (NASA)
CWA	Coalition for Women's Appointments (EA)
CWA	Cockcroft-Walton Accelerator [*Physics*]
CWA	Comedy Writers Association (EA)
CWA	Communications Workers of America (EA)
CWA	Communication Workers Alliance [*Philippines*]
CWA	Concerned Women for America (EA)
CWA	Congregationalist Witchcraft Association Corporation (AC)
CWA	Construction Writers Association (EA)
CWA	Contractor Work Authorization (KSC)
CWA	Controlled Work Area (MCD)
CWA	Control Word Address
CWA	Country Women's Association
CWA	Crime Writers' Association (EAIO)
CWA	Curtiss-Wright of Canada [*Toronto Stock Exchange symbol*]
CWA	Customer Work Authorization (AAG)
CWA	C. W. - Tariff Agency, Inc., Lansing MI [*STAC*]
CWA	Mosinee, WI [*Location identifier FAA*] (FAAL)
CWA	Wausau [*Wisconsin*] Central Wisconsin [*Airport symbol*] (OAG)
CWAA	Cotton Warehouse Association of America (EA)
CWAA	Croatian Workers Association of America (EA)
CWABBA	Canadian Western Amateur Bodybuilding Association
CWAC	Canadian Women's Army Corps
CWAC	Clean Waters Advisory Committee [*New South Wales*] [*Australia*]
CWAC	Community Welfare Advisory Council [*New South Wales*] [*Australia*]
CWAD	Concurrent with Aircraft Delivery (MCD)
CWAE	Channel Work Area Expansion [*Computer science*] (ECII)
CWAF	Combined Welfare Administration Fund
CWAG	Cold War Activities Group [*Military*] (CINC)
CWAI	Confederation of Western Australian Industry, Inc. [*Australia*]
Cwal	Cwaliton [*Qualiton*], Swansea [*Record label*] [*Wales*]
CW & B	Cincinnati, Washington & Baltimore Railroad
CW & WOA	Chief Warrant and Warrant Officers Association, United States Coast Guard (EA)
CWANSW	Cambodian Women's Association of New South Wales [*Australia*]
CWAO	Coalition of Women's Art Organizations (EA)
CWAO	Montreal, PQ [*ICAO location identifier*] (ICLI)
CWAP	Caution and Warning Advisory Panel (MCD)
CWAP	Clean Water Action Project [*Later, CWA*] (EA)
CWAPI	Caution and Warning Advisory Panel Indicators (MCD)
CWAR	Continuous Wave Acquisition RADAR [*Military*]
CWARC	Canadian Workplace Automation Research Centre [*Department of Communications*] (IRC)
CWAS	Caution and Warning Advisory Signals (MCD)
CWAS	Centre of West African Studies [*University of Birmingham*] [*British*] (CB)
CWAS	College Women's Assertion Sample (EDAC)
CWAS	Committee on Women in Asian Studies (EA)
CWAS	Contractor's Weighted Average Share in Cost Risk [*Accounting*]
CWAS	Contractor Weighted Average Share (AAGC)
CWAS	Cryogenic Whole Air Sampler [*Instrumentation*]
CWasB	Bioferm Corp., Research Library, Wasco, CA [*Library symbol Library of Congress*] (LCLS)
CWAS-NA	Contractor Weighted Average Share-Not Applicable (AAGC)
CWASP	Catholic White Anglo-Saxon Protestant
CWASRO	Christian Welfare and Social Relief Organization [*Sierra Leone*] (EAIO)
CWAT	Continuous Wave Acquisition and Track (MCD)
CWats	Watsonville Public Library, Watsonville, CA [*Library symbol Library of Congress*] (LCLS)
CWatsHi	Pajaro Valley Historical Association, Watsonville, CA [*Library symbol*] [*Library of Congress*] (LCLS)
CWB	Canadian Western Bank [*Toronto Stock Exchange symbol*]
CWB	Canadian Wheat Board
CWB	Canadian Wheat Board Library [*UTLAS symbol*]
CWB	Center for Wooden Boats (EA)
CWB	Central Weather Bureau [*Taiwan*] [*Marine science*] (OSRA)

CWB............	Central Weather Bureau [*Taiwan*] (USDC)
CWB............	Central Welsh Board
CWB............	Coalition on Women and the Budget [*Defunct*] (EA)
CWB............	Commonwealth Writers of Britain (BI)
CWB............	Curitiba [*Brazil*] [*Airport symbol*] (OAG)
CWBA.........	Chinese Women's Benevolent Association (EA)
CWBAD......	Clockwise Bottom Angular Down (OA)
CWBAU......	Clockwise Bottom Angular Up (OA)
CWBCNA.....	Credit Women's Breakfast Clubs of North America [*Later, CPI*] (EA)
CWBF.........	Battle Harbour, NF [*ICAO location identifier*]
CWBH........	Continuous Wage and Benefit History [*Unemployment insurance*]
CWBHP.......	Center for the Well-Being of Health Professionals (EA)
CWBL.........	Catholic Women's Benevolent Legion (EA)
CWBS.........	Contract Work Breakdown Structure
CWbT.........	Chaldaeisches Woerterbuch ueber die Targumim [*A publication*] (BJA)
CWBTS.......	Capillary Whole Blood True Sugar [*Medicine*] (AAMN)
CWBW.......	Chemical Warfare - Bacteriological Warfare
CWBY.........	Cowboy
CWC...........	Calibrating Work Center (AFIT)
CWC...........	Cam Wedge Clamp
CWC...........	Canadian Wood Council
CWC...........	Caribiner International [*NYSE symbol*] (TTSB)
CWC...........	Caribiner Intl., Inc. [*NYSE symbol*] (SAG)
CWC...........	Carpet Wool Council [*Defunct*]
CWC...........	Catering Wages Commission [*British*] (DAS)
CWC...........	Cell Wall Constituent (OA)
CWC...........	Center on War and the Child (EA)
CWC...........	Challenge Air Cargo, Inc. [*ICAO designator*] (FAAC)
CWC...........	Charleston & Western Carolina Railway Co. [*Seaboard Coast Line Railroad*] [*AAR code*]
CWC...........	Chemical Weapons Convention [*Proposed treaty*]
CWC...........	Child Welfare Center [*British*] (DAS)
CWC...........	Civilian War Casualties (VNW)
CWC...........	Clear Write Condition
CWC...........	Cold War Council
CWC...........	Colorado Women's College [*Formerly, Temple Buell College*]
CWC...........	Combined Wage Claim [*Unemployment insurance*]
CWC...........	Comenius World Council (EA)
CWC...........	Committee for Western Civilization (EA)
CWC...........	Commonwealth Gold [*Vancouver Stock Exchange symbol*]
CWC...........	Commonwealth of World Citizens
CWC...........	Communications, Electronic, Technical, and Salaried Workers of Canada
CWC...........	Communication Workers of Canada
CWC...........	Competition with Confidence (AFIT)
CWC...........	Composite Warfare Commander [*Military*] (NVT)
CWC...........	Conventional [*Non-Nuclear*] War Capability (AAG)
CWC...........	Cottonwood [*California*] [*Seismograph station code, US Geological Survey*] (SEIS)
CWC...........	Council of Women Chiropractors [*Defunct*] (EA)
CWC...........	Council of Women Citizens
CWC...........	Country Whence Consigned [*Shipping*] (DS)
CWC...........	Country Women's Council USA (EA)
CWC...........	Cuban Women's Club (EA)
CWC...........	Curtiss-Wright Corp.
CWC...........	National Committee for a Confrontation with Congress (EA)
CWC...........	Whittier College, Whittier, CA [*OCLC symbol*] (OCLC)
CWCA.........	Civil War Centennial Association
CWCA.........	Commission for World Christian Action
CW/CBD.....	Chemical Warfare/Chemical Biological Defense (RDA)
CWCC........	Civil War Centennial Commission [*Terminated, 1966*]
CWCCA......	Cardigan Welsh Corgi Club of America (EA)
CWCCI.......	Crayon, Water Color, and Craft Institute (EA)
CWcD.........	Dow Chemical USA, Western Division Library, Walnut Creek, CA [*Library symbol Library of Congress*] (LCLS)
CWCE........	Cold Weather Clothing and Individual Equipment [*Military*]
CWCG........	Cool Water Coal Gasification [*Fuel technology*]
CWCI.........	Center for World Christian Interaction (EA)
CWCI.........	CW Communications, Inc. [*Publisher*]
CWCL........	Conspectus of Workers' Compensation Legislation [*Australia A publication*]
CWCMF......	Professor Chen Wen-Chen Memorial Foundation (EA)
CW/CMG.....	CW Conference Management Group [*Framingham, MA*] [*Telecommunications service*] (TSSD)
CWCO........	Cayman Water Co. Ltd. [*NASDAQ symbol*] (SAG)
CWCOF.......	Cayman Water Co. Ltd [*NASDAQ symbol*] (TTSB)
CWCP........	Combat Wing Command Post
CWCS........	Combined Wheat Control Section [*Allied German Occupation Forces*]
CWCS........	Common Weapon Control System [*Military*]
CWCT........	[*A*] Child's Wish Come True (EA)
CWCV........	Catholic Walking Club of Victoria [*Australia*]
CWD..........	Casualty Weapon Director
CWD..........	Catchword
CWD..........	Cell Wall Defective [*Microbiology*]
CWD..........	Chemical Warfare Defense
CWD..........	Civilian War Dead
CWD..........	Clerical Work Data (MHDI)
CWD..........	Cold-Water Detergent
CWD..........	Concealed Weapon Detector
CWD..........	Consecutive-Weeks Discount [*Marketng*] (DOAD)
CWD..........	Continuous Wave Detector (IAA)
CWD..........	Continuous-Wave Doppler [*Radiology*] (DAVI)
CWD..........	Cooperative Weapon Delivery (MCD)
CWD..........	Cotswold Executive Aviation [*British ICAO designator*] (FAAC)
CWD..........	Creosoted Wood Duct [*Telecommunications*] (TEL)
CWD..........	Crowder Communications Corp. [*Vancouver Stock Exchange symbol*]
CWD..........	Current Wage Developments [*A publication*]
CWD..........	Cyclotron Wave Device
CWDA.........	Canadian Wholesale Drug Association [*Association des Grossistes en Medicaments du Canada*] (AC)
CWDB........	Clockwise Down Blast (OA)
CWDD........	Chemical Warfare Directional Detector [*Military*] (CAAL)
CWDE.........	Centre for World Development Education [*Regent's College*] [*British*] (CB)
CWDE.........	Chemical Warfare Defense Equipment
CWDF.........	Cell Wall-Deficient Bacterial Form [*Microbiology*] (MAE)
CWDF.........	Central Waste Disposal Facility [*Oak Ridge National Laboratory*]
CWDF.........	Continuous Wave Deuterium Fluoride
CWDIC........	Cooperative Weapons Data Indexing Committee [*AEC and DoD*]
CWDMA......	Canadian Window and Door Manufacturers Association
CWDP.........	Casualty Weapon Director Panel
CWDR.........	Concurrent with Design Release (MCD)
CWDS.........	Centre for Women's Development Studies [*India*] (EAIO)
CWDWD......	Committee for World Development and World Disarmament [*Defunct*] (EA)
CWE...........	Cactus West Explorations Ltd. [*Vancouver Stock Exchange symbol*]
CWE...........	California Western School of Law Library, San Diego, CA [*OCLC symbol*] (OCLC)
CWE...........	Caution and Warning Electronics (NASA)
CWE...........	Caution and Warning Equipment [*NASA*] (KSC)
CWE...........	Center for Water and Environment [*University of Minnesota*]
CWE...........	Cleared without Examination [*Business term*]
CWE...........	Clerical Work Evaluation [*British*]
CWE...........	Coated Wire Electrode [*Sensor*]
CWE...........	Cockcroft-Walton Experiment [*Physics*]
CWE...........	Coil Winding Equipment
CWE...........	Comed Financial I [*NYSE symbol*] (SAG)
CwE...........	Commonwealth Edison Co. [*Associated Press*] (SAG)
CWE...........	Contractor's Work Estimate [*Military*]
CWE...........	Cotton-Wool Exudate [*Ophthalmology*] (DAVI)
CWE...........	Cromwell [*New Zealand*] [*Airport symbol*] (AD)
CWE...........	Current Working Estimate [*Military*]
CWE...........	CWE, Inc. [*Associated Press*] (SAG)
CWE...........	National Commission for Women's Equality (EA)
CWE...........	Welen [*Former USSR Geomagnetic observatory code*]
CWEA........	Canadian Wind Engineering Association
CWEA........	Caution and Warning Electronics Assembly [*Apollo*] [*NASA*]
CWED	Cold Weld Evaluation Device (OA)
CWEEA........	Cooperative Work Experience Education Association (EA)
CWeeC........	College of the Siskoyous, Weed, CA [*Library symbol Library of Congress*] (LCLS)
CWEG	Edmonton, AB [*ICAO location identifier*] (ICLI)
CWEI..........	Canadian Wood Energy Institute
CWEI..........	Clayton Williams Energy [*NASDAQ symbol*] (TTSB)
CWEI..........	Clayton Williams Energy, Inc. [*NASDAQ symbol*] (SAG)
CWEPrC......	Commonwealth Ed, $1.90 Pref [*NYSE symbol*] (TTSB)
CWEPrD......	Commonwealth Ed, $2.00 Pref [*NYSE symbol*] (TTSB)
CWEPrE......	Commonwealth Ed,$7.24 Pref [*NYSE symbol*] (TTSB)
CWEPrF......	Commonwealth Ed,$8.40 Pref [*NYSE symbol*] (TTSB)
CWEPrI.......	Commonwealth Ed,$8.38 Pref [*NYSE symbol*] (TTSB)
CWEPrJ.......	Commonwealth Ed $8.40 Pvet [*NYSE symbol*] (TTSB)
CWEPrK......	Commonwealth Ed,$2.425 Pref [*NYSE symbol*] (TTSB)
CWEPrT......	ComEd Financing 1 8.48% 'TOPrS' [*NYSE symbol*] (TTSB)
CWEPT.......	Cockpit Weapons Emergency Procedural Trainer [*Military*]
CWERA........	Catholic Women for the ERA (EA)
CWERSI.......	Committee on Women's Employment and Related Social Issues (EA)
CWeT..........	Trinity County Free Library, Weaverville, CA [*Library symbol Library of Congress*] (LCLS)
CWEU	Caution and Warning Electronics Unit (MCD)
CWEU	Council of Western European Union (IIA)
CWEX.........	CWE, Inc. [*NASDAQ symbol*] (SAG)
CWF...........	Canadian Wildlife Federation [*Federation Canadienne de la Fuane*] (AC)
CWF...........	Career Women's Forum (EAIO)
CWF...........	Charnwood Forest [*England*] [*Seismograph station code, US Geological Survey*] (SEIS)
CWF...........	China First Capital [*Vancouver Stock Exchange symbol*]
CWF...........	Christian Women's Fellowship (EA)
CWF...........	Christian Workers Fellowship [*Sri Lanka*] (EAIO)
CWF...........	Civilian Welfare Fund (AABC)
CWF...........	Clean Water Fund [*An association*] (EA)
CWF...........	Coal-Water Mixture Fuel
CWF...........	Commonwealth Weightlifting Federation [*Ammanford, Dyfed, Wales*] (EAIO)
CWF...........	Composite Wave Filter
CWF...........	Conservative Way Forward [*British Political party*]
CWF...........	Consolidated Working Fund (OICC)
CWF...........	Construction Workers Federation [*San Marino*] (EAIO)
CWF...........	Cornwell-Weisskopf Formula
CWF...........	Crosswind Force
CWF2.........	Cornell Word Form 2 [*Psychology*]
CWFF.........	Closed, Well-Formed Formula [*Logic*]
CWFFEMM...	Continuous Wave Fixed Frequency Electromechanical Modulation (IAA)
CWFHC.......	Canadian Weightlifting Federation/Halterophile Canadienne
CWFI..........	Children's Wish Foundation International (EA)
CWFM.........	Continuous Wave Frequency-Modulated (MSA)
CWFO.........	Catlow/Whitney Family Organization (EA)
CWFO	Commercial Warehouse Field Officer [*Military*]

CWFS......... Crashworthy Fuel Systems [*Aviation*]
CWFSP....... Caution and Warning/Fire Suppression Panel (MCD)
CWG........... Campaign for World Government
CWG........... Canwest Global Communications Corp. [*NYSE symbol*] (SAG)
CWG........... Clayton, W. G., III, Buffalo NY [*STAC*]
CWG........... Closed Waveguide
CWG........... Colonial Waterbird Group [*Later, CWS*] (EA)
CWG........... Colostomy Welfare Group [*British*]
CWG........... Committee for Women in Geophysics [*Defunct*] (EA)
CWG........... Community of the Will of God [*Anglican religious community*]
CWG........... Conformal Wire Grating
CWG........... Consolidated Wellington Resources [*Vancouver Stock Exchange symbol*]
CWG........... Constant-Wear Garment [*Apollo*] [*NASA*]
CWG........... Continuous Wave Gas
CWG........... Corrugated Wire Glass [*Technical drawings*]
CWGA......... Catholic Writers Guild of America (EA)
CWGC......... Commonwealth War Graves Commission [*Maidenhead, Berkshire, England*] (EAIO)
CWGEA....... Cooperative Whole Grain Education Association (EA)
CWH........... Canadian Warplane Heritage, Inc.
CWH........... Canadian Warplane Heritage Museum [*ICAO designator*] (FAAC)
CWH........... Chronology of Womens's History [*A publication*]
CWH........... Clarke, W. H., New York NY [*STAC*]
CWH........... Committee of the Whole House, House of Lords [*British*] (DLA)
CWH........... Huntsville, AL [*Location identifier FAA*] (FAAL)
CWh........... Whittier Public Library, Whittier, CA [*Library symbol Library of Congress*] (LCLS)
CWhA......... American Potash & Chemical Corp., Whittier, CA [*Library symbol Library of Congress*] (LCLS)
CWhC......... Whittier College, Whittier, CA [*Library symbol Library of Congress*] (LCLS)
CWhC-L...... Whittier College, School of Law, Whittier, CA [*Library symbol Library of Congress*] (LCLS)
CWhHi........ Whittier Historical Society, Whittier, CA [*Library symbol*] [*Library of Congress*] (LCLS)
CWHJ......... Holberg, BC [*ICAO location identifier*] (ICLI)
CWHN........ Church of What's Happening Now (EA)
CWhR......... Rio Hondo Junior College, Whittier, CA [*Library symbol Library of Congress*] (LCLS)
CWHS........ Centre for Women's Health Studies [*Cumberland College of Health Sciences*] [*Australia*]
CWHS........ Continuous Work History Sample [*Department of Labor*]
CWHSS....... Coalition for Women in the Humanities and Social Sciences [*Defunct*] (EA)
CWHSSA..... Contract Work Hours and Safety Standards Act
CWHX........ Bedford, NS [*ICAO location identifier*] (ICLI)
CWI........... Call Waiting Indication [*Telecommunications*] (TEL)
CWI........... Cardiac Work Index [*Physiology*]
CWI........... CCW System Ltd. [*Vancouver Stock Exchange symbol*]
CWI........... Chicago & Western Indiana Railroad Co. [*AAR code*]
CWI........... Child Welfare Institute (EA)
CWI........... Christian Witness International [*British*]
CWI........... Clean World International [*Brighton, East Sussex, England*] (EAIO)
CWI........... Clearinghouse on Women's Issues (EA)
CWI........... Clinton [*Iowa*] [*Airport symbol*] (OAG)
CWI........... Clinton, IA [*Location identifier FAA*] (FAAL)
CWI........... Coil Winding International Exhibition [*British*] (ITD)
CWI........... Continuous Wave Illuminator (NG)
CWI........... Continuous Wave Indicator (DWSG)
CWI........... Conventional Weapon Index (MCD)
CWI........... Country Workshops, Inc. [*An association*] (EA)
CW-I.......... Credit Women - International [*Later, CPI*] (EA)
CWI........... Cultural Work, Inc. [*An association*] (EA)
CWI........... Decisions of the Commissioners under the National Insurance (Industrial Injuries) Acts Relating to Wales [*A publication*] (DLA)
CWIAU....... Canadian Women's Intercollegiate Athletic Union
CWIC........ Chase World Information Corp. [*Information service or system*] (IID)
CWIC........ Children's Wonderland [*NASDAQ symbol*] (TTSB)
CWIC........ Childrens Wonderland, Inc. [*NASDAQ symbol*] (SAG)
CWIC........ Clearinghouse on Women's Issues in Congress [*Later, CWI*] (EA)
CWIC........ Competition with Industrial Cooperation
CWIC........ Compiler for Writing and Implementing Compilers
CWICU....... Childrens Wonderland Unit [*NASDAQ symbol*] (TTSB)
CWICW...... Children's Wonderland Wrrt [*NASDAQ symbol*] (TTSB)
CWID........ Call-Waiting Identification [*Telecommunications service*]
CWID........ Coalition for Women in International Development (EA)
CWIE........ Container, Weapon, Individual Equipment [*Army*] (ADDR)
CWIED....... Command Wire Improvised Explosive Device [*Military*] (LAIN)
CWIF......... Continuous Wave Intermediate Frequency
CWII......... Communications World International, Inc. [*NASDAQ symbol*] (NQ)
CWII......... Communications World Intl. [*NASDAQ symbol*] (TTSB)
CWIIW...... Communications Wrld Intl. Wrrt [*NASDAQ symbol*] (TTSB)
CWIK........ Chemical World Index Key
CWIK........ Cutting with Intent to Kill
CWILLBC.... Canadian Writers and Illustrators of British Columbia [*Canada*] (WWLA)
CWiN........ North State Cooperative Library System, Willows, CA [*Library symbol Library of Congress*] (LCLS)
CWine....... Canandaigua Wine Co., Inc. [*Associated Press*] (SAG)
CWINJ....... Cold Weather Injury [*Military*]
CWIP........ Clerical Work Improvement Program [*British*]
CWIP........ Construction Work in Progress
CWIR........ Continuous Wave Illuminator RADAR [*Military*]
CWIR........ Victoria Marine Radio, BC [*ICAO location identifier*] (ICLI)

CWIS......... Campus-Wide Information Systems [*Internet*]
CWIS......... Cotton Warehouse Inspection Service [*Defunct*] (EA)
CWIS......... Council for Women in Independent Schools (EA)
CWIS/NPC... Child Welfare Information Services/Non-Profit Computer Services [*Information service or system*] (IID)
CWIT........ Color-Word Interference Test
CWIT........ Concordance Words in Titles [*Indexing*]
CWit......... Willits Public Library, Willits, CA [*Library symbol Library of Congress*] (LCLS)
CWiW........ Willows Public Library, Willows, CA [*Library symbol Library of Congress*] (LCLS)
CWiWCL..... Glen County Library, Willows, CA [*Library symbol Library of Congress*] (LCLS)
CWJ......... Comparative Wage Justice (ADA)
CWJ......... Continuous Wave Jammer (MCD)
CWK......... Cam-Net Communications Network, Inc. [*Vancouver Stock Exchange symbol*]
CWKT........ Cam-Net Communications Network, Inc. [*NASDAQ symbol*] (NQ)
CWKTF...... Cam-Net Communic Ntwk [*NASDAQ symbol*] (TTSB)
CWL......... Calm Water Line
CWL......... Cancer Patients, Weight Losing
CWL......... Cardiff [*Wales*] [*Airport symbol*] (OAG)
CWL......... Carney, William L., Bresman IN [*STAC*]
CWL......... Case Western Reserve University Law Library, Cleveland, OH [*OCLC symbol*] (OCLC)
CWL......... Catholic Women's League (BARN)
CWL......... Chartwell Re Corp. [*NYSE symbol*] (SAG)
CWL......... Chemical Warfare Laboratories [*Army Chemical Center, MD*] (MCD)
CWL......... Child Welfare League (BARN)
CWL......... Continuous Wave LASER
CWL......... Cornwall R. R. [*AAR code*]
CWL......... Cranwell FTU [*British ICAO designator*] (FAAC)
CWL......... Cutaneous Water Loss
CWLA........ Catholic Women's League of Australia [*An association*]
CWLA........ Child Welfare League of America (EA)
CWLC........ Child Welfare League of Canada [*La Ligue pour la Protection de l'Enfance du Canada*] (AC)
CWLM........ Caution and Warning Limit Module [*NASA*] (NASA)
CWLM........ Continuous Working Level Monitor (GNE)
CWLM........ Cumulative Working Level Months [*Radon exposure measure*] (ERG)
CWLR........ Chartwell Re Corp. [*NASDAQ symbol*] (TTSB)
CWLS........ Canadian Well Logging Society
CWLS........ Central Western Law Society [*Australia*]
CWLS........ Conventional Weighted Least Square
CWLTH...... Commonwealth
CwltSav..... Commonwealth Savings Bank [*Associated Press*] (SAG)
CWlvC....... Canyon Research Group, Inc., Westlake Village, CA [*Library symbol Library of Congress*] (LCLS)
CWM......... Camino Resources Ltd. [*Vancouver Stock Exchange symbol*]
CWM......... Catholic Worker Movement (EA)
CWM......... Cell Wall Material [*Biochemistry*]
CWM......... Change Weight Manifest [*Aviation*] (FAAC)
CWM......... Christian Women's Movement [*Bulgaria*] [*Political party*]
CWM......... Clerical Work Measurement (MHDI)
CWM......... Coal-Water Mixture Fuel
CWM......... Coil Winding Machine
CWM......... Cold Weather Modulator [*Automotive engineering*]
CWM......... Commercial Water Movement Number
CWM......... Communist Workers' Movement [*British*] (PPW)
CWM......... Conference for World Mission [*British Council of Churches*]
CWM......... Continuous Water Movement (SAA)
CWM......... Convertible Wraparound Mortgage [*Banking*]
CWM......... Cruciform Wing Module (MCD)
CWM......... CWM Mortgage Hldgs [*NYSE symbol*] (TTSB)
CWM......... CWM Mortgage Holdings, Inc. [*NYSE symbol*] (SAG)
CWMA........ Church Women's Missionary Association [*Episcopalian*]
CWMA........ Country Wool Merchants Association [*British*] (BI)
CWMAA...... Clock and Watch Manufacturers Association of America [*Defunct*]
C Wm & Mary... College of William and Mary (GAGS)
CWME........ Commission on World Mission and Evangelism (EAIO)
CWMEWCC... Commission on World Mission and Evangelism of the World Council of Churches [*Later, CWME*] (EA)
CWMK........ Simcoe, ON [*ICAO location identifier*] (ICLI)
CWML........ Colorado Weights and Measures Laboratory [*National Institute of Standards and Technology*]
CWM Mt..... CWM Mortgage Holdings, Inc. [*Associated Press*] (SAG)
CWMN....... Mount Forest, ON [*ICAO location identifier*] (ICLI)
CWMS........ Color, Warmth, Movement Sensation [*Medicine*] (DMAA)
CWMTU...... Cold Weather Materiel Test Unit [*Military*]
CWN......... Calcutta Weekly Notes [*A publication*] (DLA)
CWN......... Canadian Western Natural Gas Co. Ltd. [*Toronto Stock Exchange symbol*]
CWN......... Certificate of War Necessity [*World War II*]
CWN......... CircuitWriter Network [*Information service or system*] (IID)
CWN......... Commodity World News Network [*Later, Futures World News*] [*Information service or system*] (IID)
CWN......... Contract Work Notification (KSC)
CWN......... Crown American Realty Trust [*NYSE symbol*] (SPSG)
CWN......... Crown Amer Realty Tr [*NYSE symbol*] (TTSB)
CWN......... North Conway, NH [*Location identifier FAA*] (FAAL)
CWNA........ Canadian Weekly Newspapers Association (DGA)
CW/NBC...... Chemical Warfare/Nuclear, Biological, and Chemical (RDA)
CwnBk....... Crown Books Corp. [*Associated Press*] (SAG)
CWNC........ Christian Women's National Concerns [*Defunct*] (EA)
CwnCas...... Crown Casino Corp. [*Associated Press*] (SAG)

CwnCork ...... Crown Cork & Seal Co., Inc. [*Associated Press*] (SAG)
CwnCr .... Crown Crafts, Inc. [*Associated Press*] (SAG)
CwnCrk .... Crown Cork & Seal Co., Inc. [*Associated Press*] (SAG)
CWNIB .... Coalition of Women in National and International Business [*Boston, MA*] (EA)
CWNMR .... Continuous Wave Nuclear Magnetic Resonance
CWNP .... Consolidated Western & Pacific Resources [*NASDAQ symbol*] (SAG)
CwnPac .... Crown Pacific Partners Ltd. [*Associated Press*] (SAG)
CWNPF .... Cons Westn & Pac Res [*NASDAQ symbol*] (TTSB)
CWNS .... Canadian War Narrative Section [*World War I*]
CWNS .... C & W [*Cable & Wireless North America, Inc.*] Network Services [*Dallas, TX*] [*Telecommunications*] (TSSD)
CWO .... Canadian War Office (DMA)
CWO .... Capital Work Order (NRCH)
CWO .... Carrier Wave Oscillator [*Radio transmission device*] (IAA)
CWO .... Cash with Order [*Business term*]
CWO .... Ceylonese Welfare Organisation [*Australia*]
CWO .... Chief Warrant Officer [*Army*] (GPO)
CWO .... Chief Watch Officer [*Navy*]
CWO .... Command Works Office [*British military*] (DMA)
CWO .... Commissioned Warrant Officer
CWO .... Communication Watch Officer
CWO .... Continuous Wave Oscillator
CWO .... Corvallis Workstation Operation (HGAA)
CWO .... Council of Writers Organizations (EA)
CWO .... Custom Work Order [*Telecommunications*] (TEL)
CWo .... Woodland Free Public Library, Woodland, CA [*Library symbol Library of Congress*] (LCLS)
CWO-2 .... Chief Warrant Officer, W-2 [*Army*] (AABC)
CWO-3 .... Chief Warrant Officer, W-3 [*Army*] (AABC)
CWO-4 .... Chief Warrant Officer, W-4 [*Army*] (AABC)
CWOA .... Chief Warrant and Warrant Officers Association, United States Coast Guard
CWOH .... Ste. Agathe Des Monts, PQ [*ICAO location identifier*] (ICLI)
CWOHC .... Commissioned Warrant Officer Hospital Corps
CWohL .... Litton Industries, Inc., Guidance and Central Systems Division, Engineering Library, Woodland Hills, CA [*Library symbol Library of Congress*] (LCLS)
CWOIH .... Council of World Organizations Interested in the Handicapped [*Later, ICOD*] (EA)
CWON .... Canadian Women of Note [*Database*] [*York University*] [*Defunct*] [*Information service or system*] (CRD)
CWON .... Center for a Woman's Own Name [*An association Defunct*] (EA)
CWOP .... Childbirth without Pain
CWOP .... Cold Weather Operations [*Military*]
CWORF .... Customer Work Order File (MCD)
CWOSM .... Composite Warfare Oceanographic Support Module [*Navy*] (DOMA)
CWoY .... Yolo County Free Library, Woodland, CA [*Library symbol Library of Congress*] (LCLS)
CWP .... Cable & Wireless AD [*NYSE symbol*] (TTSB)
CWP .... Cable & Wireless Ltd. ADS [*NYSE symbol*] (SPSG)
CWP .... Campbellpore [*Pakistan*] [*Airport symbol*] (AD)
CWP .... Center for Water Policy [*International Ground Water Modeling Center*]
CWP .... Centimeters of Water Pressure [*Measurement*] (DAVI)
CWP .... Central Weather Processor [*FAA*] (TAG)
CWP .... Cheese Whey Powder
CWP .... Chemical Waste Program [*Stanford University*]
CWP .... Chicago, West Pullman & Southern Railroad Co. [*AAR code*]
CWP .... Childbirth without Pain (MAE)
CWP .... Christian Workers Party [*Malta*] [*Political party*] (PPE)
CWP .... Circulating Water Pump
CWP .... Civil Works Program
CWP .... Cloud Water Project [*A cooperative ecosystem study*]
CWP .... Coal Workers' Pneumoconiosis [*Black lung*] [*Medicine*]
CWP .... Communicating Word Processor
CWP .... Communist Workers Party [*Political party*]
CWP .... Community of the Whole Person (EA)
CWP .... Comparable Worth Project (EA)
CWP .... Computer Word Processing (IAA)
CWP .... Consolidated WWMCCS [*Worldwide Military Command and Control System*] Program [*DoD*]
CWP .... Contractor Work Plan (NRCH)
CWP .... Control Withdrawal Prohibit [*Nuclear energy*] (NRCH)
CWP .... Coordinating Working Party on Atlantic Fishery Statistics
CWP .... Council of the World Poultry [*British*]
CWP .... Cream Wove Large Post [*Paper*] (DGA)
CWP .... Cumulative Weight Percent
CWP .... Current Word Pointer
CWP .... Cutting and Welding Permit
CWPA .... Committee for Women in Public Administration (EA)
CWPB .... Canadian Wood Preservers Bureau [*Bureau Canadien de la Preservation du Bois*] (AC)
CWPC .... Calcined Waste Packaging Cell [*Nuclear energy*] (NRCH)
CWPC .... Cam Wedge Power Clamp
CWPC .... Canadian Women's Press Club [*Later, Media Club of Canada*]
CWPC .... Civil War Press Corps (EA)
CWPC .... Pincher Creek, AB [*ICAO location identifier*] (ICLI)
CWPCA .... Canadian Wood Pallet and Container Association (EAIO)
CWPD .... Class Work Planning Document [*Navy ship overhauls*]
CWPEA .... Childbirth without Pain Education Association [*Also known as Lamaze Birth without Pain Education Association*] (EA)
CWPH .... Circulating Water Pumphouse [*Nuclear energy*] (NRCH)
CWPI .... Configuration Work Package Item [*Army*] (AABC)
CWPM .... Correct Words per Minute [*Typewriting, etc.*]

CWPNM .... Center for War, Peace, and the News Media (EA)
CWPO .... Pilot Mount, MB [*ICAO location identifier*] (ICLI)
CWPOS .... Cane, Wicker, and Perambucot Operatives' Society [*A union*] [*British*]
C W Post (LIU)... C. W. Post Campus of Long Island University (GAGS)
CWPR .... Centre for Water Policy Research [*University of New England*] [*Australia*]
CWPR .... Committee on Women in Public Relations (NTCM)
CW/PS .... Center for War/Peace Studies (EA)
CWPS .... Center for Women Policy Studies (EA)
CWPS .... Civil War Philatelic Society [*Later, AHPS*] (EA)
CWPS .... Communicating Word Processing System
CWPS .... Council on Wage and Price Stability [*Also, COWPS*] [*Abolished, 1981*]
CWQ .... Curlew Lake [*Vancouver Stock Exchange symbol*]
CWQA .... Canadian Water Quality Association [*Association Canadienne pour la Qualite de l'Eau*] (AC)
CWR .... Cabinet War Room
CWR .... Calculated Weight Report
CWR .... California Western Railroad [*AAR code*]
CWR .... Case Western Reserve University, Cleveland, OH [*OCLC symbol*] (OCLC)
CWR .... Center for Welding Research [*Ohio State University*] [*Research center*] (RCD)
CWR .... Central Western Region
CWR .... Ceylon Weekly Reporter [*A publication*] (ILCA)
CWR .... Checkwriting Redemptions [*Business term*]
CWR .... Coalition on Women and Religion (EA)
CWR .... Coastal Watching RADAR (NATG)
CWR .... Compliance with Requirements (MCD)
CWR .... Continuously Welded Rail (ADA)
CWR .... Cooling Water Return [*Nuclear energy*] (NRCH)
CWRA .... Canadian Water Resources Association (EAIO)
CWRA .... Conditioned Wrinkle Recovery Angle [*Textile technology*]
CWRC .... Civilian Welfare and Recreation Committee (MUGU)
CWRC .... Climb Well to Right of Course [*Aviation*] (FAAC)
CWRENAF ..... Chief WREN [*Women's Royal Naval Service*] Air Fitter [*British military*] (DMA)
CWRENCINE... Chief WREN [*Women's Royal Naval Service*] Cinema Operator [*British military*] (DMA)
CWRENCK.... Chief WREN [*Women's Royal Naval Service*] Cook [*British military*] (DMA)
CWRENDHYG... Chief WREN [*Women's Royal Naval Service*] Dental Hygienist [*British military*] (DMA)
CWRENDSA.... Chief WREN [*Women's Royal Naval Service*] Dental Surgery Assistant [*British military*] (DMA)
CWRENEDUC... Chief WREN [*Women's Royal Naval Service*] Education Assistant [*British military*] (DMA)
CWRENMET.... Chief WREN [*Women's Royal Naval Service*] Meteorological Observer [*British military*] (DMA)
CWRENPHOT... Chief WREN [*Women's Royal Naval Service*] Photographer [*British military*] (DMA)
CWRENQA .... Chief WREN [*Women's Royal Naval Service*] Quarters Assistant [*British military*] (DMA)
CWREN(R)... Chief WREN [*Women's Royal Naval Service*] (RADAR) [*British military*] (DMA)
CWRENREG... Chief WREN [*Women's Royal Naval Service*] Regulating [*British military*] (DMA)
CWRENREL... Chief WREN [*Women's Royal Naval Service*] Radio Electrician [*British military*] (DMA)
CWRENRS(M)... Chief WREN [*Women's Royal Naval Service*] Radio Supervisor (Morse) [*British military*] (DMA)
CWRENSA... Chief WREN [*Women's Royal Naval Service*] Stores Accountant [*British military*] (DMA)
CWRENS(C)... Chief WREN [*Women's Royal Naval Service*] Stores Assistant (Clothes) [*British military*] (DMA)
CWRENSTD... Chief WREN [*Women's Royal Naval Service*] Steward [*British military*] (DMA)
CWRENS(V)... Chief WREN [*Women's Royal Naval Service*] Stores Assistant (Victualling) [*British military*] (DMA)
CWRENTEL... Chief WREN [*Women's Royal Naval Service*] Telephonist [*British military*] (DMA)
CWRENTSA... Chief WREN [*Women's Royal Naval Service*] Training Support Assistant [*British military*] (DMA)
CWRENWA... Chief WREN [*Women's Royal Naval Service*] Weapon Analyst [*British military*] (DMA)
CWRENWTR(G)... Chief WREN [*Women's Royal Naval Service*] Writer (General) [*British military*] (DMA)
CWRENWTR(P)... Chief WREN [*Women's Royal Naval Service*] Writer (Pay) [*British military*] (DMA)
CWRENWW... Chief WREN [*Women's Royal Naval Service*] Welfare Worker [*British military*] (DMA)
CWRL .... Cooperative Wildlife Research Laboratory [*Southern Illinois University at Carbondale*] [*Research center*] (RCD)
CWRM .... Cell Water Removal Mechanism
CWRO .... Canadian War Records Office [*World War I*]
CWRR .... Center for Water Resources Research [*University of Nevada*]
CWRR .... Curtiss-Wright Research Reactor
CWRT .... Canadian Women in Radio & Television (AC)
CWRT .... Center for Waste Reduction Technologies (EA)
CWRTA .... Civil War Round Table Associates (EA)
CWRU .... Case Western Reserve University [*Cleveland, OH*]
CWS .... Air Swazi Cargo (Pty) Ltd. [*Swaziland*] [*ICAO designator*] (FAAC)
CWS .... Canadian Home Shopping Network Ltd. [*Toronto Stock Exchange symbol*]

CWS............	Canadian Wildlife Service, Quebec Region [*Environment Canada*] [*Research center*]
CWS............	Cancer Patients, Weight Stable
CWS............	Caribbean Writers Series [*Heinemann Educational Books Ltd.*] [*British*]
CWS............	Casework Supervisor [*Red Cross*]
CWS............	Catalog Typing Worksheet [*for MT/ST typist*]
CWS............	Caucus for Women in Statistics (EA)
CWS............	Caution and Warning Status (MCD)
CWS............	Cell Wall Skeleton [*Cytology*]
CWS............	Center for Women and Sport [*Defunct*] (EA)
CWS............	Center Work System [*NASA*] (KSC)
CWS............	Central Wireless Station [*Air Force British*]
CWS............	Charles Williams Society [*British*] (EAIO)
CWS............	Chemical Warfare Service [*Army*]
CWS............	Chest Wall Stimulation [*Medicine*]
CWS............	Child Welfare Service
CWS............	Chilled Water Supply [*Aerospace*] (AAG)
CWS............	Chung Wah Society [*Northern Territory*] [*Australia*]
CWS............	Church World Service [*Later, CWSW*] (EA)
CWS............	Circulating Water System [*Nuclear energy*] (NRCH)
CWS............	Civil War Society
CWS............	Clearinghouse on Women's Studies (EA)
CWS............	Clockwise (AAG)
CWS............	Coal-Water Slurry [*Fuel*]
CWS............	Coast and Wetlands Society [*New South Wales*] [*Australia*]
CWS............	Cold-Water Soluble
CW-S..........	College Work-Study [*Program*]
CWS............	College Work-Study [*Financial aid*] (PAZ)
CWS............	Collision Warning System (MCD)
CWS............	Collision Warning System [*Automotive safety*]
CWS............	Colonial Waterbird Society (EA)
Cwth..........	Commander's Weapons Station (MCD)
CWS............	Community War Services [*of FSA*] [*World War II*]
CWS............	Community Water System [*Environmental Protection Agency*]
CWS............	Compiler Writing System (MCD)
CWS............	Complex Wiring System
CWS............	Consolidated Western Steel (AAG)
CWS............	Container Weapon System (MCD)
CWS............	Continental Wage Schedule [*Military*] (AABC)
CWS............	Contract War Service
CWS............	Contract Work Statement (MCD)
CWS............	Control Wheel Steering (NG)
CWS............	Conway, AR [*Location identifier FAA*] (FAAL)
CWS............	Cooling Water System [*Nuclear energy*] (NRCH)
CWS............	Cooperative Wholesale Society [*British*]
CWS............	Co-Operative Wholesale Society [*British*]
CWS............	Copper Weld Steel [*Telecommunications*] (TEL)
CWS............	Cotton-Wool Spot [*Ophthalomology*] (DAVI)
CWS............	Crew Weapons Sight
CWS............	Westmont College, Santa Barbara, CA [*OCLC symbol*] (OCLC)
CWSA..........	Canadian Water Ski Association
CWSA..........	Canadian Wheelchair Sports Association
CWSA..........	Canadian Women's Studies Association [*See also ACEF*]
CWSA..........	Contract Work Study Association (MHDB)
CWSAB........	Canadian War Supplies Assignment Board [*World War II*]
CWSAHA.....	Church World Service Aids for the Horn of Africa (EA)
CWSAM.......	Continuous Wave Surface-to-Air Missile (MCD)
CWSD..........	Continuous Wave Space Duplexed
CWSDSC.....	Citizens Welfare Service, Drummond Street Centre [*Australia*]
CWSF..........	Catholic Women's Seminary Fund [*Defunct*] (EA)
CWSF..........	Coal-Water Slurry Fuel
CWSF..........	Commander, Western Sea Frontier
CWSI..........	Crop Water Stress Index [*Agronomy*]
CWSIGGEN..	Continuous Wave Signal Generator (IAA)
CWSIRP......	Church World Service, Immigration and Refugee Program (EA)
CWSJ..........	Congressional Wives for Soviet Jewry (EA)
CWSL..........	California Wilderness Survival League (EA)
CWSO..........	Chemical Warfare Service Officer [*Army*]
CWSP..........	College Work-Study Program
CWSP..........	Communications with and Service to the Public [*Army*] (AABC)
CWSRA........	Canadian Women's Sailboat Racing Association
CWSRA........	Chester White Swine Record Association (EA)
CWSS..........	Center for Women's Studies and Services (EA)
CWST..........	Combat Water Survival Test [*Army*] (INF)
CWSU..........	Caution and Warning Status Unit [*NASA*] (NASA)
CWSU..........	Center Weather Service Unit [*FAA*] (TAG)
CWSU..........	Central Weather Service Unit [*Marine science*] (OSRA)
CWSU..........	Central Weather Service Unit (FAAC)
CWSU..........	Central Weather Service Unit [*FAA*] (USDC)
CWSU..........	Condensate Water Servicing Unit
CWSV..........	Citizens Welfare Service of Victoria [*Australia*]
CWSW........	Church World Service and Witness (EA)
CWT............	Cadre Weather Team (MCD)
CWT............	California Water Service Co. [*NYSE symbol*] (SAG)
CWT............	Calif Water Svc [*NYSE symbol*] (TTSB)
CWT............	Carrier Wave Telegraphy (IAA)
CWT............	Carrier Wave Transmission (IAA)
CWT............	Center for World Thanksgiving (EA)
CWT............	Central Winter Time
CWT............	Centum Weight [*Hundredweight*] [*Latin*] (GPO)
CWT............	Chemical Warfare Specialist, Medical [*Navy rating*]
CWT............	Chief Water Tender [*Navy rating Obsolete*]
CWT............	Childress [*Texas*] [*Seismograph station code, US Geological Survey*] (SEIS)

CWT............	Climatic Wind Tunnel [*Automotive testing*]
CWT............	Coalition for Workplace Technology [*Defunct*] (EA)
CWT............	Coded Wire Tagging [*Pisciculture*]
CWT............	Cold Water Tank
CWT............	Cold Water Temperature
CWT............	Cold Water Treatment [*Medicine*]
CWT............	Color Word Test
CWT............	Command Word Trap [*Computer science*] (IAA)
CWT............	Compensated Work Therapy
CWT............	Constant Wall Temperature [*Engineering*]
CWT............	Consumers for World Trade (EA)
CWT............	Continuous Wave Tunable (IAA)
CWT............	Conventional Weapons Technology (MCD)
CWT............	Cooperative Wind Tunnel
CWT............	Council on World Tensions [*Later, Institute on Man and Science*] (EA)
C/WT..........	Counterweight [*Automotive engineering*]
CWT............	Cowra [*Australia Airport symbol*] (OAG)
CWT............	Crew Natural Resources [*Vancouver Stock Exchange symbol*]
CWT............	Critical Water Temperature (OA)
CWT............	Hundredweight (AFM)
CWTA..........	Cold Water Reactor Test Assembly
CWTAD........	Clockwise Top Angular Down (OA)
CWTAU........	Clockwise Top Angular Up (OA)
CWTB..........	Cylindrical Water Tube Boiler [*of a ship*] (DS)
CWTBS........	Cylindrical Water Tube Boiler Survey [*of a ship*] (DS)
CWTC..........	Chemical Warfare Technical Committee
CWTC..........	Chemical Waste Transportation Council [*Washington, DC*] (EA)
CWTD..........	Continuous Wave Target Detection (NATG)
CWTDC........	Continuous Wave Tactical Detection Console (NATG)
CWTG..........	Computer World Trade Group [*British*]
CWTH..........	Clockwise Top Horizontal (OA)
Cwth..........	Commonwealth
CWTI..........	Chemical Waste Transportation Institute
CWTI..........	Civilian Wartime Injuries
CWTI..........	Civil War Times Illustrated [*A publication*]
CWTO..........	Toronto, ON [*ICAO location identifier*] (ICLI)
CWTP..........	Community Work and Training Program [*Department of Labor*]
CWTP..........	Comprehensive Work Training Program [*Employment and Training Administration*] [*Department of Labor*]
CWTPI........	Conventional Weapons Tactical Proficiency Inspection [*Navy*] (DOMA)
CWTR..........	Climb Well to Right [*Aviation*] (FAAC)
CWTS..........	Civil War Token Society (EA)
CWTS..........	Country Wide Transport Services, Inc. [*NASDAQ symbol*] (SAG)
CWTS..........	Country Wide Trans Svcs [*NASDAQ symbol*] (TTSB)
CWTWT........	Continuous Wave Traveling Wave Tube (MCD)
CWU............	Camp Williams [*Utah*] [*Seismograph station code, US Geological Survey*] (SEIS)
CWU............	Caution and Warning Unit (MCD)
CWU............	Chemical Workers' Union
CWU............	Christliche Waehlerunion Bayern [*Christian Voters' Union of Bavaria*] [*Germany Political party*] (PPW)
CWU............	Church Women United (EA)
CWU............	Colonial Warriors United (EA)
CWU............	Composite Weighted Work Unit (AFM)
CWU............	Congress of World Unity (EA)
CWU............	Czech World Union (EA)
CWU............	Wuhan Airlines [*China*] [*ICAO designator*] (FAAC)
CWUA..........	Confectionery Workers' Union of Australia
CWUAA........	Canada West Universities Athletic Association [*Association Sportive Universitaire de l'Ouest Canadien*] [*Formerly, Western Canadian Intercollegiate Athletic Union*] (AC)
CWUB..........	Clockwise Up Blast (OA)
CWUL..........	Montreal, PQ [*ICAO location identifier*] (ICLI)
CWV............	Catholic War Veterans of the USA (EA)
CWV............	Commercial Bancshares, Inc. [*AMEX symbol*] (SAG)
CWV............	Continuous Wave Video
CWV............	Crest Working Voltage [*Electronics*] (IAA)
CWV............	Croesus Resources, Inc. [*Vancouver Stock Exchange symbol*]
CWVA..........	Bonavista, NF [*ICAO location identifier*] (ICLI)
CWVA..........	Catholic War Veterans of the USA Ladies Auxiliary [*Later, CWVUSAA*] (EA)
CWVM........	Compiler Writer's Virtual Machine
CWVR..........	Vancouver, BC [*ICAO location identifier*] (ICLI)
CWVS..........	College Women's Volunteer Service [*World War II*]
CWVUSAA....	Catholic War Veterans of the USA Auxiliary (EA)
CWW............	California's Wine Wonderland [*A publication*] (EAAP)
CWW............	Canadian Woodmen of the World (EA)
CWW............	Canadian Worldwide Energy Ltd. [*Toronto Stock Exchange symbol*]
CWW............	CanAir [*Canada*] [*FAA designator*] (FAAC)
CWW............	Chrome Wire Wheels [*Automotive accessory*]
CWW............	Contemporary World Writers [*A publication*]
CWW............	Continuous Weather Watch (MCD)
CWW............	Cruciform Wing Weapon (MCD)
CWWA..........	Canadian Water & Wastewater Association (AC)
CWWA..........	Capricornia Wildlife Welfare Association [*Australia*]
CWWA..........	Coloured Workers' Welfare Association [*British*] (BI)
CWWF..........	Churches Committee for Work Among Women Serving with HM Forces [*British military*] (DMA)
CWWG..........	Chemical Weapons Working Group [*A coalition of groups living near chemical weapons incinerators*]
CWWG..........	Winnipeg, MB [*ICAO location identifier*] (ICLI)
CWX............	Canwest Trustco [*Vancouver Stock Exchange symbol*]
CWX............	Continuous Wave Transmitter (CAAL)

CWX............	Cool White Deluxe (DAC)
CWY............	Canada World Youth (AC)
CWY............	Clackamas, OR [*Location identifier FAA*] (FAAL)
CWY............	Clearway [*Aviation code*]
CX............	Blister Gas [*US Chemical Corps symbol*]
CX............	Cancel [*or Cancelled*] (CINC)
CX............	Cargo/Transport Aircraft - Experimental
CX............	Carrier [*Telecommunications*] (CET)
CX............	Cathay Pacific Airways [*ICAO designator*] (AD)
CX............	Centerior Energy [*NYSE symbol*] (SAG)
cx............	Central African Republic [*MARC country of publication code Library of Congress*] (LCCP)
CX............	Central Exchange
CX............	Cervix [*Anatomy*]
CX............	Charing Cross Station [*England*] (ROG)
CX............	Chest X-Ray [*Medicine*]
Cx............	Clearance [*Physiology*]
CX............	Coinbox Set [*Telecommunications*] (TEL)
CX............	Coin Collecting Box, Pay Station [*Telecommunications*] (TEL)
CX............	Color Exterior Film (MCD)
CX............	Column Extractant [*Nuclear energy*] (NRCH)
CX............	Compatible Expansion [*Noise-reduction system for manufacturing phonograph records*] [*CBS*]
CX............	Complex (KSC)
CX............	Composite
CX............	Composite Signaling [*Telecommunications*] (TEL)
CX............	Connection [*Technical drawings*]
CX............	Control Transmitter (MUGU)
CX............	Convex
CX............	Correct Copy [*A printing direction*]
CX............	Count Register [*Computer science*]
CX............	Criticality Experiment [*Nuclear energy*] (NRCH)
Cx............	Culture [*Biochemistry*] (DAVI)
CX............	Cyclophosphamide [*or Cytoxan*] [*Antineoplastic drug*] (DAVI)
CX............	Cylinder Axis [*Optometry*]
CX............	Nonradio Frequency Cable Assemblies [*JETDS nomenclature*] [*Military*] (CET)
CX............	Uruguay [*International civil aircraft marking*] (ODBW)
CXA............	Caicara [*Venezuela*] [*Airport symbol*] (OAG)
CXA............	Caicara de Orinoco [*Venezuela*] [*Airport symbol*] (AD)
CXA............	Cancel Approved Arrival [*Aviation*] (FAAC)
CXA............	Central Exchange Area [*Telecommunications*] (NITA)
CXA............	Consolidated HCI Holdings Corp. [*Toronto Stock Exchange symbol*]
CXA............	Xiamen Airlines [*China*] [*ICAO designator*] (FAAC)
CXB............	Can-Mac Exploration Ltd. [*Vancouver Stock Exchange symbol*]
CXB............	Cosmic X-Ray Background
CXB............	Cox's Bazar [*Bangladesh*] [*Airport symbol*] (OAG)
CXB............	Salomon, Inc. [*NYSE symbol*] (SAG)
CXBG	Comprehensive Extended Term Banker's Guarantee (DS)
CXC............	Caribbean Examinations Council [*St. Michael, Barbados*] (EAIO)
CXC............	Chitina, AK [*Location identifier FAA*] (FAAL)
Cxc............	Clavibacter Xyli Cynodontis [*Microbiology*]
CXC............	Computrex Centres [*Vancouver Stock Exchange symbol*]
CXC............	Corrections Corp. Amer [*NYSE symbol*] (TTSB)
CXC............	Corrections Corp. of America [*NYSE symbol*] (SAG)
CXCS	Center for Cross-Cultural Studies [*University of Alaska, Fairbanks*] [*Research center*] (RCD)
cxCu............	Cold-Extractable Copper
CXC.WS......	Corrections Cp Amer Wrrt [*NYSE symbol*] (TTSB)
CXD	Cancel Approved Departure [*Aviation*] (FAAC)
CXD	Custom Xpress Delivery
CXE............	Charge Exchange Excitations [*Physics*]
CXE............	Chase City, VA [*Location identifier FAA*] (FAAL)
CXE............	Colonial High Income Municipal Trust [*NYSE symbol*] (SPSG)
CXE............	Xerox Corp., El Segundo, CA [*OCLC symbol*] (OCLC)
CXF............	Coldfoot, AK [*Location identifier FAA*] (FAAL)
CXF............	Colonial High Income Muni [*NYSE symbol*] (TTSB)
CXF............	Continental Pacific [*Vancouver Stock Exchange symbol*]
CXG	Coxheath Gold Holdings Ltd. [*Toronto Stock Exchange symbol*]
CXGLN	Glands on Calyx Margin [*Botany*]
CXH	China Xinhua Airlines [*FAA designator*] (FAAC)
CXH	Colonial Investment Grade Municipal [*NYSE symbol*] (SPSG)
CXH	Colonial Inv Grade Muni [*NYSE symbol*] (TTSB)
CXH	Vancouver-Harbour Seaport [*Canada*] [*Airport symbol*] (OAG)
CX-HLS........	Cargo/Transport Aircraft Experimental - Heavy Logistics System (KSC)
cxHM............	Citrate-Extractable Heavy Metal
CXI............	Caulfield Resources Ltd. [*Vancouver Stock Exchange symbol*]
CXI............	Christmas Island [*Kiribati*] [*Airport symbol*] (OAG)
CXI............	Commodore Applied Technologies, Inc. [*AMEX symbol*] (SAG)
CXI............	Common X Interface [*Computer science*]
CXI............	Crosstell Input
CXI............	Shanxi Airlines [*China*] [*FAA designator*] (FAAC)
CXIL............	Chem International, Inc. [*NASDAQ symbol*] (SAG)
CXIM............	Criticare Systems [*NASDAQ symbol*] (TTSB)
CXIM............	Criticare Systems, Inc. [*NASDAQ symbol*] (NQ)
CXIP............	Coflexip [*NASDAQ symbol*] (SAG)
CXIPY............	Coflexip ADS [*NASDAQ symbol*] (TTSB)
CXJ	Caxias do Sul [*Brazil*] [*Airport symbol*] (AD)
CXK	Bellaire, MI [*Location identifier FAA*] (FAAL)
CXK............	Consolidated Norex Resources Corp. [*Toronto Stock Exchange symbol Vancouver Stock Exchange symbol*]
CXL............	Calexico, CA [*Location identifier FAA*] (FAAL)
CXL............	Cancelled

CXM............	Camindex Mines Ltd. [*Toronto Stock Exchange symbol*]
CXM............	Cefuroxime [*Antibacterial drug*]
CXM............	Cycloheximide [*Also, CH, CHX, Cyh*] [*Fungicide*]
CXM............	Traverse City, MI [*Location identifier FAA*] (FAAL)
CXMD............	Canine X-Linked Muscular Dystrophy
CxMT	Cervical Motion Tenderness [*Gynecology*] (DAVI)
CXN	China Southwest Airlines [*ICAO designator*] (FAAC)
CXN	Chromex Nickel Mines Ltd. [*Vancouver Stock Exchange symbol*]
CXO	Comox Resources Ltd. [*Vancouver Stock Exchange symbol*]
CXO	Conroe Aviation Services, Inc. [*ICAO designator*] (FAAC)
CXO	Conroe, TX [*Location identifier FAA*] (FAAL)
CXO	Crosstell Output
CxP	Celery and Parsley Cross [*Genetics*]
CXP............	Centex Construction Prod [*NYSE symbol*] (TTSB)
CXP............	Centex Construction Products [*NYSE symbol*] (SAG)
CXP............	Cilicap [*Indonesia*] [*Airport symbol*] (OAG)
CXP............	Cuyahoga County Public Library, Cleveland, OH [*OCLC symbol*] (OCLC)
CXP............	TEM Enterprises [*ICAO designator*] (FAAC)
CXR	Carrier [*Telecommunications*]
CXR	Chardon, OH [*Location identifier FAA*] (FAAL)
CXR	Chest X-Ray [*Medicine*]
CXR	Christmas Island [*ANSI three-letter standard code*] (CNC)
CXR	Comaplex Resources International Ltd. [*Toronto Stock Exchange symbol*]
CXR	Cox Radio, Inc. [*NYSE symbol*] (SAG)
CXS	Caxias [*Brazil*] [*Airport symbol*] (AD)
CXS	Consort Parallax Servo
CXS	Counsel Corp. [*Toronto Stock Exchange symbol*]
CXSN	Counsel Corp. [*NASDAQ symbol*] (SAG)
CXSNF	Counsel Corp. [*NASDAQ symbol*] (TTSB)
CXT............	American Municipal Term Trust III [*NYSE symbol*] (SPSG)
CXT............	Canamera Explorations, Inc. [*Vancouver Stock Exchange symbol*]
CXT............	Charters Towers [*Australia Airport symbol*] (OAG)
CXT............	Coastal Air Transport [*St. Croix*] [*ICAO designator*] (FAAC)
CXT............	Common External Tariff [*EEC*] [*Also, CET*]
CXU	Camilla, GA [*Location identifier FAA*] (FAAL)
CXU	Charge Spotting Bomb Unit
CXW	Cooper Ind 6.00%'DECS'1998 [*NYSE symbol*] (TTSB)
CXW	Cooper Industries [*NYSE symbol*] (SAG)
CXX............	Callex Mineral Exploration [*Vancouver Stock Exchange symbol*]
CXY............	Canadian Occidental Petrol [*AMEX symbol*] (TTSB)
CXY............	Canadian Occidental Petroleum Ltd. [*AMEX symbol*] (SPSG)
CXY............	Cat Cay [*Bahamas*] [*Airport symbol*] (OAG)
CXY............	Harrisburg, PA [*Location identifier FAA*] (FAAL)
CXZ............	Can-Ex Resources Ltd. [*Vancouver Stock Exchange symbol*]
CY............	Calendar Year (TEL)
CY............	Capacity (ADA)
CY............	Carry
CY............	Case Copy [*Computer science*]
CY............	Cases and Cabinets [*JETDS nomenclature*] [*Military*] (CET)
CY............	Central Yiddish (BJA)
CY............	Ceylon [*Sri Lanka*] (ROG)
CY............	Chief Yeoman [*Navy rating Obsolete*]
CY............	Choay [*France*] [*Research code symbol*]
CY............	Chun-ying [*Leung*] [*Hong Kong politician*]
CY............	City (MCD)
CY............	Colby Resources Corp. [*Vancouver Stock Exchange symbol*]
CY............	Communication Yeoman [*Navy rating British*]
CY............	Conference Year [*Database terminology*] (NITA)
CY............	Connecticut Yankee Station [*Nuclear energy*] (NUCP)
Cy............	Connolly's New York Surrogate Reports [*A publication*] (DLA)
CY............	Container Yard [*Shipping*] (DCTA)
CY............	Convention of York [*Freemasonry*] (ROG)
CY............	Copy (AABC)
CY............	Country [*Online database field identifier*]
CY............	County
CY............	Cubic Yard (KSC)
CY............	Currency
CY............	Current Year (DOMA)
CY............	Current Yield [*Banking*]
CY............	Cyanide (WDAA)
CY............	Cyanogen [*Toxic compound*]
CY............	Cybernetics (IAA)
CY............	Cycle (AAG)
CY............	Cycling [*Chemical engineering*] (IAA)
Cy............	Cyclonium (MAE)
CY............	Cyclophosphamide [*Cytoxan*] [*Antineoplastic drug*]
CY............	Cyclosporine [*An immunosuppressant drug*]
CY............	Cylinder
CY............	Cypress Semiconductor [*NYSE symbol*] (TTSB)
CY............	Cypress Semiconductor Corp. [*NYSE symbol*] (SPSG)
Cy	Cyprianus Florentinus [*Flourished, 12th century*] [*Authority cited in pre-1607 legal work*] (DSA)
Cy............	Cypriote (BJA)
CY............	Cyprus [*ANSI two-letter standard code*] (CNC)
cy............	Cyprus [*MARC country of publication code Library of Congress*] (LCCP)
CY............	Cyprus Airways [*ICAO designator*] (AD)
CY............	People's Republic of China [*License plate code assigned to foreign diplomats in the US*]
CY............	Sri Lanka [*IYRU nationality code*] (IYR)
CYA............	Canadian Yachting Association
CYA............	Carded Yarn Association [*Later, AYSA*] (EA)
CYA............	Catholic Youth Adoration Society [*Defunct*] (EA)

CYA............ Catholic Youth Association [*Lithuania*] (EAIO)
CYA............ Cheyenne Airways, Inc. [*ICAO designator*] (FAAC)
CYA............ Choya [*Argentina*] [*Seismograph station code, US Geological Survey*] (SEIS)
CYA............ Classic Yacht Association (EA)
CYA............ Claymore Resources [*Vancouver Stock Exchange symbol*]
CYA............ Covenant Young Adults [*Defunct*] (EA)
CYA............ Cover Your Anatomy [*Military, government slang*] [*Bowdlerized version*]
CYA............ Cyclosporin A [*See CSA*] [*An immunosuppressant drug*]
Cya .... Cysteic Acid [*An amino acid*]
CYAA.......... Ottawa, ON [*ICAO location identifier*] (ICLI)
CYAB.......... Arctic Bay, NT [*ICAO location identifier*] (ICLI)
CYAD.......... Cytoplasm Average Optical Density [*Microscopy*]
CyADIC....... Cyclophosphamide, Adriamycin, DIC [*Dacarbazine*] [*Antineoplastic drug regimen*]
CYAJ........... Komakuk, YT [*ICAO location identifier*] (ICLI)
CYAL.......... Alert Bay, BC [*ICAO location identifier*] (ICLI)
CYAM......... Sault Ste. Marie, ON [*ICAO location identifier*] (ICLI)
CYAMEX ...... Cyana-Mexique (MSC)
CYAN......... Cyanosis [*Medicine*]
CYAN......... Cyanotech Corp. [*NASDAQ symbol*] (NQ)
Cyanotc....... Cyanotech Corp. [*Associated Press*] (SAG)
CYATH .... Cyathus [*Glassful*] [*Pharmacy*]
CYATH AMP... Cyathus Amplus [*Tumblerful*] [*Pharmacy*]
CYATH THEAE... Cyatho Theae [*In a Cup of Tea*] [*Pharmacy*] (ROG)
CYATH VIN... Cyathus Vinosus [*Wineglassful*] [*Pharmacy*]
CYATH VINOS... Cyathus Vinosus [*Wineglassful*] [*Pharmacy*] (ROG)
CYAV .... Winnipeg/St. Andrews, MB [*ICAO location identifier*] (ICLI)
CYAW .... Halifax/Shearwater Canadian Forces Base, NS [*ICAO location identifier*] (ICLI)
CYAWP .... Cover Your Anatomy with Paper [*Military, government slang*] [*Bowdlerized version*]
CYAY .... St. Anthony, NF [*ICAO location identifier*] (ICLI)
CYAZ........... Tofino, BC [*ICAO location identifier*] (ICLI)
CYB............. Cayman Brac [*West Indies*] [*Airport symbol*] (OAG)
CYB............. City Air Bus Ltd. [*British*] [*FAA designator*] (FAAC)
CYB............. Commonwealth Year Book [*A publication*]
CYB............. Cybermedix, Inc. [*Toronto Stock Exchange symbol*]
CYB............. Cybex International [*AMEX symbol*] (SAG)
CYBA .... Banff, AB [*ICAO location identifier*] (ICLI)
CYBB .... Pelly Bay, NT [*ICAO location identifier*] (ICLI)
CYBC .... Baie Comeau, PQ [*ICAO location identifier*] (ICLI)
CyBC........... Cyprus Broadcasting Corp.
CYBE .... CyberOptics Corp. [*NASDAQ symbol*] (NQ)
CYBER .... Cybernetics (ADA)
CYBERLOG... Cybernetic Logistics Planning, Control, and Management Information System [*Military*] (AABC)
CyberMd ...... CyberMedia, Inc. [*Associated Press*] (SAG)
Cyberonic .... Cyberonics, Inc. [*Associated Press*] (SAG)
Cybex.......... Cybex Corp. [*Associated Press*] (SAG)
CybexIntl ..... Cybex International [*Associated Press*] (SAG)
CYBG .... Bagotville Canadian Forces Base, PQ [*ICAO location identifier*] (ICLI)
CYBG .... CyberGuard Corp. [*NASDAQ symbol*] (SAG)
CybGrd........ CyberGuard Corp. [*Associated Press*] (SAG)
CYBK .... Baker Lake, NT [*ICAO location identifier*] (ICLI)
CYBL........... Campbell River, BC [*ICAO location identifier*] (ICLI)
Cybm .... Cubic Yard Bank Measurement (DAC)
CYBMV........ Cymbidium Mosaic Virus [*Plant pathology*]
CYBORG ...... Cybernetic Organism [*Concept of machine to alter man's bodily functions for space environment*]
CYBR .... Brandon, MB [*ICAO location identifier*] (ICLI)
CYBR .... CyberMedia, Inc. [*NASDAQ symbol*] (SAG)
CYBR .... Cybernetics Products, Inc. [*NASDAQ symbol*] (NQ)
CybrCsh....... CyberCash, Inc. [*Associated Press*] (SAG)
Cybrnet........ Cybernetics Products, Inc. [*Associated Press*] (SAG)
CYBRNTC.... Cybernetic
CybrOpt........ Cyber Optics Corp. [*Associated Press*] (SAG)
CybrOpt........ Cyber Optics Corp. [*Associated Press*] (SAG)
CYBT........... Brochet, MB [*ICAO location identifier*] (ICLI)
CYBX .... Cyberonics, Inc. [*NASDAQ symbol*] (SAG)
CYC............. Canterbury Yeomanry Cavalry [*British military*] (DMA)
CYC............. Catholic Youth Council [*Belgium*] (EAIO)
CYC............. Chinese Youth Council [*Later, CDC*] (EA)
CYC............. Colby Junior College for Women [*Later, CSC*], New London, NH [*Inactive*] [*OCLC symbol*] (OCLC)
CYC............. Company of Young Canadians [*Federal crown corporation to employ young people, 1966-75*]
CYC............. Crow Canyon [*California*] [*Seismograph station code, US Geological Survey*] (SEIS)
Cyc............. Cyclazocine [*Morphine antagonist*]
CYC............. Cycle
CYC............. Cyclone
CYC............. Cyclopedia
CYC............. Cyclopedia of Law and Procedure [*New York*] [*A publication*] (DLA)
CYC............. Cyclophosphamide [*Cytoxan*] [*Antineoplastic drug*]
Cyc............. Cyclops [*of Euripides*] [*Classical studies*] (OCD)
CYC............. Cyclorama [*Staging and scenery*]
cyc............. Cyclotron [*Physics*] (DAVI)
CYC............. Cypair Tours Ltd. [*Cyprus*] [*ICAO designator*] (FAAC)
CYCA .... Cartwright, NF [*ICAO location identifier*] (ICLI)
CYCA .... Clyde Yacht Clubs Association [*British*] (DBA)
CYCA .... Craft Yarn Council of America (EA)
Cyc Ann .... Cyclopedia of Law and Procedure Annotations [*A publication*] (DLA)
Cycare .... CyCare Systems, Inc. [*Associated Press*] (SAG)

CYCB .... Cambridge Bay, NT [*ICAO location identifier*] (ICLI)
CYcCL......... Sutter County Free Library, Yuba City, CA [*Library symbol Library of Congress*] (LCLS)
Cyc Corp...... Fletcher's Cyclopedia of Corporations [*A publication*] (DLA)
CYCD.......... Nanaimo, BC [*ICAO location identifier*] (ICLI)
Cyc Dict...... Cyclopedia Law Dictionary [*A publication*] (DLA)
CYCG.......... Castlegar, BC [*ICAO location identifier*] (ICLI)
CYCH.......... Chatham Canadian Forces Base, NB [*ICAO location identifier*] (ICLI)
CYCH.......... CyberCash, Inc. [*NASDAQ symbol*] (SAG)
CYCH.......... Cyber Cash Inc. [*NASDAQ symbol*] (TTSB)
CYCIS .... Child and Youth Centered Information Systems
CYCL.......... Centennial Cellular 'A' [*NASDAQ symbol*] (TTSB)
CYCL.......... Centennial Cellular Corp. [*NASDAQ symbol*] (SAG)
CYCL.......... Charlo, NB [*ICAO location identifier*] (ICLI)
CYCL.......... Cycle
CYCL.......... Cycle
CYCL.......... Cyclopedia
Cyc Law & Proc... Cyclopedia of Law and Procedure [*A publication*] (DLA)
Cyclc3pss..... Cyclc3PSS Corp. [*Associated Press*] (SAG)
CYCLD........ Cycloidal Propeller [*on a ship*] (DS)
CYCLES........ Cyclonic Extratropical Storms [*National Oceanic and Atmospheric Administration*]
CYCLGN...... Cyclogenesis [*NWS*] (FAAC)
CYCLO .... Cyclopedia
Cyclo .... Cyclophosphamide [*Cytoxan*] [*Antineoplastic drug*] (MAE)
cyclo .... Cyclopropane (Anesthetic) [*Organic chemistry*]
CYCLO .... Cyclotron (IAA)
Cyclo C .... Cyclocytidine Hydrochloric Acid [*Organic chemistry*] (DAVI)
Cyclop Dict... Shumaker and Longsdorf's Cyclopedic Dictionary [*A publication*] (DLA)
CYcM.......... Community Memorial Museum of Sutter County, Yuba City, CA [*Library symbol*] [*Library of Congress*] (LCLS)
CYCM.......... Cubic Yard Compacted Measurement (DAC)
CYCO.......... Central Yiddish Culture Organization (EA)
CYCO.......... Coppermine, NT [*ICAO location identifier*] (ICLI)
Cycom........ Cycomm International, Inc. [*Associated Press*] (SAG)
Cycomm....... Cycomm International, Inc. [*Associated Press*] (SAG)
CYCS .... Chesterfield Inlet, NT [*ICAO location identifier*] (ICLI)
CYCT.......... Coronation, AB [*ICAO location identifier*] (ICLI)
CYCV.......... Montreal/Cartierville, PQ [*ICAO location identifier*] (ICLI)
CYCW .... Chilliwack, BC [*ICAO location identifier*] (ICLI)
CYCX .... Camp Gagetown Canadian Forces Base, NB [*ICAO location identifier*] (ICLI)
CYCY .... Clyde River, NT [*ICAO location identifier*] (ICLI)
CYD............. Carlyle Energy Ltd. [*Toronto Stock Exchange symbol*]
CYD............. China Yuchai International Ltd. [*NYSE symbol*] (SAG)
CYD............. China Yuchai Intl. [*NYSE symbol*] (TTSB)
CYD............. College Young Democrats of America (EA)
CYD............. Cubic Yard (ADA)
Cyd............. Cytidine [*Also, C*] [*A nucleoside*]
CYDA .... Dawson, YT [*ICAO location identifier*] (ICLI)
CYDAC .... Cytophotometric Data Converter [*Instrumentation*]
CYDB .... Burwash, YT [*ICAO location identifier*] (ICLI)
CYDC .... Princeton, BC [*ICAO location identifier*] (ICLI)
CYDEF .... Cyrenaica Defence Force [*British military*] (DMA)
CYDF .... Deer Lake, NF [*ICAO location identifier*] (ICLI)
CYDL .... Dease Lake, BC [*ICAO location identifier*] (ICLI)
CYDN .... Dauphin, MB [*ICAO location identifier*] (ICLI)
CYDQ .... Dawson Creek, BC [*ICAO location identifier*] (ICLI)
CYDR .... Broadview, SK [*ICAO location identifier*] (ICLI)
CYDS .... Cygne Designes [*NASDAQ symbol*] (TTSB)
CYDS .... Cygne Designs, Inc. [*NASDAQ symbol*] (SAG)
CYE............. Cal Dynamics Corp. [*Vancouver Stock Exchange symbol*]
CYE............. Charcoal Yeast Extract [*Agar medium*] [*Microbiology*]
CYE............. Cheyenne Software [*AMEX symbol*] (TTSB)
CYE............. Cheyenne Software, Inc. [*AMEX symbol*] (SPSG)
CYE............. Wilkes-Barre, PA [*Location identifier FAA*] (FAAL)
CYEC.......... Commonwealth Youth Exchange Council [*British*]
CYED.......... Edmonton/Namao Canadian Forces Base, AB [*ICAO location identifier*] (ICLI)
CYEE........... Central Youth Employment Executive [*Department of Employment*] [*British*]
CYEG.......... Edmonton International, AB [*ICAO location identifier*] (ICLI)
CYEK.......... Eskimo Point, NT [*ICAO location identifier*] (ICLI)
CYEN .... Estevan, SK [*ICAO location identifier*] (ICLI)
CYEP.......... Estevan Point, BC [*ICAO location identifier*] (ICLI)
CYET.......... Edson, AB [*ICAO location identifier*] (ICLI)
CYEU.......... Eureka, NT [*ICAO location identifier*] (ICLI)
CYEV.......... Inuvik, NT [*ICAO location identifier*] (ICLI)
CYF............. Canadian Youth Foundation (AC)
CYF............. Chefornak [*Alaska*] [*Airport symbol*] (OAG)
CYF............. Chefornak, AK [*Location identifier FAA*] (FAAL)
CYF............. Conservative Youth Federation [*Defunct*] (EA)
CYFB........... Frobisher, NT [*ICAO location identifier*] (ICLI)
CYFC.......... Fredericton, NB [*ICAO location identifier*] (ICLI)
CYFE.......... Forestville, PQ [*ICAO location identifier*] (ICLI)
CYFERNET ... Child, Youth, and Family Education Network [*Online resource*] (PAZ)
CYFL........... Cyst Fluid [*Biochemistry*] (DAVI)
CYFL........... Fort Reliance, NT [*ICAO location identifier*] (ICLI)
CYFN .... Century Financial Corp. [*NASDAQ symbol*] (SAG)
CYFO .... Flin Flon, MB [*ICAO location identifier*] (ICLI)
CYFR .... Fort Resolution, NT [*ICAO location identifier*] (ICLI)
CYFS........... Fort Simpson, NT [*ICAO location identifier*] (ICLI)
CYG .... Caprock Energy Ltd. [*Vancouver Stock Exchange symbol*]
CYG .... Captain of the Yeoman of the Guard [*British*] (ROG)

Cyg	Cygnus [*Constellation*]
CYGA	Gagnon, PQ [*ICAO location identifier*] (ICLI)
CYGK	Kingston, ON [*ICAO location identifier*] (ICLI)
CYGL	La Grande Riviere, PQ [*ICAO location identifier*] (ICLI)
CYGM	Gimli, MB [*ICAO location identifier*] (ICLI)
Cygn	Cygnus [*Constellation*]
CYGN	Cygnus Therapeutic Systems [*NASDAQ symbol*] (SPSG)
CYGN	Cygrus Inc. [*NASDAQ symbol*] (TTSB)
CygneD	Cygne Designs, Inc. [*Associated Press*] (SAG)
Cygnus	Cygnus Therapeutic Systems [*Associated Press*] (SAG)
CYGP	Gaspe, PQ [*ICAO location identifier*] (ICLI)
CYGQ	Geraldton (North), ON [*ICAO location identifier*] (ICLI)
CYGR	Iles De La Madeleine, PQ [*ICAO location identifier*] (ICLI)
CYGT	Iglooklik, NT [*ICAO location identifier*] (ICLI)
CYGW	Kuujjuarapik, PQ [*ICAO location identifier*] (ICLI)
CYGX	Gillam, MB [*ICAO location identifier*] (ICLI)
CYGY	Deception, PQ [*ICAO location identifier*] (ICLI)
CYGZ	Grise Fiord, NT [*ICAO location identifier*] (ICLI)
CYH	Community Health Systems, Inc. [*NYSE symbol*] (SAG)
CYH	Community Hlth Sys [*NYSE symbol*] (TTSB)
CYH	Continental Tyre Ltd. [*Vancouver Stock Exchange symbol*]
CYH	Coyote Hills [*California*] [*Seismograph station code, US Geological Survey*] (SEIS)
Cyh	Cycloheximide [*Also, CH, CHX, CXM*] [*Fungicide*]
CYH	Springerville, AZ [*Location identifier FAA*] (FAAL)
CYH	Yunnan Airlines [*China*] [*ICAO designator*] (FAAC)
CYHA	Canadian Youth Hostels Association
CYHB	Hudson Bay, SK [*ICAO location identifier*] (ICLI)
CYHD	Dryden, ON [*ICAO location identifier*] (ICLI)
CYHE	Hope, BC [*ICAO location identifier*] (ICLI)
CYHI	Holman/Holman Island, NT [*ICAO location identifier*] (ICLI)
CYHK	Gjoa Haven, NT [*ICAO location identifier*] (ICLI)
CYHM	Hamilton, ON [*ICAO location identifier*] (ICLI)
CYHO	Hopedale, NF [*ICAO location identifier*] (ICLI)
CYHONC	Committee of Youth Hostel Organizations in the Nordic Countries (EA)
CYHQ	Ottawa, ON [*ICAO location identifier*] (ICLI)
CYHU	Montreal/St. Hubert, PQ [*ICAO location identifier*] (ICLI)
CYHY	Hay River, NT [*ICAO location identifier*] (ICLI)
CYHZ	Halifax/International, NS [*ICAO location identifier*] (ICLI)
CYI	Canary Islands (KSC)
CYI	Chiayi [*Taiwan*] [*Airport symbol*] (OAG)
CYI	Cooperative Youth Initiative [*British*]
CYI	Cycomm International, Inc. [*AMEX symbol*] (SPSG)
CYI	Cycomm Int(New) [*AMEX symbol*] (TTSB)
CYI	Cymric Resources Ltd. [*Toronto Stock Exchange symbol*]
CYIB	Atikokan, ON [*ICAO location identifier*] (ICLI)
CYIO	Pond Inlet, NT [*ICAO location identifier*] (ICLI)
CYIR	Council of Young Israel Rabbis (EA)
CYIV	Island Lake/Garden Hill, MB [*ICAO location identifier*] (ICLI)
CYJ	Chandeleur Bay [*Vancouver Stock Exchange symbol*]
CYJA	Jasper, AB [*ICAO location identifier*] (ICLI)
CYJN	Saint-Jean, PQ [*ICAO location identifier*] (ICLI)
CYJT	Stephenville, NF [*ICAO location identifier*] (ICLI)
CYK	Consider Yourself Kissed [*Correspondence*]
CYK	Copconda-York [*Vancouver Stock Exchange symbol*]
CYKA	Kamloops, BC [*ICAO location identifier*] (ICLI)
CYKF	Waterloo-Wellington/Kitchener, ON [*ICAO location identifier*] (ICLI)
CYKL	Schefferville, PQ [*ICAO location identifier*] (ICLI)
CYKY	Kindersley, SK [*ICAO location identifier*] (ICLI)
CYKZ	Toronto/Buttonville, ON [*ICAO location identifier*] (ICLI)
CYL	Casein Yeast Lactate [*Media*] [*Biochemistry*] (DAVI)
CYL	Cassidy's Ltd. [*Toronto Stock Exchange symbol*]
CYL	Communist Youth League
CYL	Controlled Yeast Lysate
CYL	Cycle
CYL	Cylinder (AAG)
cyl	Cylindrical (VRA)
CYL	Cylindrical Lens [*Ophthalmology*]
CYI	Yorba Linda District Library, Yorba Linda, CA [*Library symbol Library of Congress*] (LCLS)
CYLA	Langara, BC [*ICAO location identifier*] (ICLI)
CYLC	Lake Harbour, NT [*ICAO location identifier*] (ICLI)
CYLD	Chapleau, ON [*ICAO location identifier*] (ICLI)
CYLDET	Cylinder-Pressure Monitoring and Conditioning Detection System
CYL DRM	Cylinder or Drum [*Freight*]
CYLH	Lansdowne House, ON [*ICAO location identifier*] (ICLI)
CYLJ	Meadow Lake, SK [*ICAO location identifier*] (ICLI)
CYLK	Cylink Corp. [*NASDAQ symbol*] (TTSB)
CYLL	Cylinder Lock
CYLL	Cylindrical (ROG)
CYLL	Cylindric Lens (ROG)
CYLL	Lloydminster, AB [*ICAO location identifier*] (ICLI)
CYLNDL	Cylindrical
CYLO	Shilo Canadian Forces Base, MB [*ICAO location identifier*] (ICLI)
CYLS	Cylindrical Surface (MSA)
CYLT	Alert, NT [*ICAO location identifier*] (ICLI)
CYLV	Carrot Yellow Leaf Virus [*Plant pathology*]
CYLW	Kelowna, BC [*ICAO location identifier*] (ICLI)
CYLY	Lytton, BC [*ICAO location identifier*] (ICLI)
CYM	Cayman Islands [*ANSI three-letter standard code*] (CNC)
CYM	Chatham, AK [*Location identifier FAA*] (FAAL)
CYM	Compass Airlines of Australia [*ICAO designator*] (FAAC)
CYM	Crystal Mountain [*Vancouver Stock Exchange symbol*]
Cym	Cymbeline [*Shakespearean work*]
CYM	Cymric [*Language, etc.*] (ROG)
CYM	Cyprus Amax Minerals [*NYSE symbol*] (SPSG)
CYMA	Mayo, YT [*ICAO location identifier*] (ICLI)
CYMD	Mould Bay, NT [*ICAO location identifier*] (ICLI)
CYMJ	Moose Jaw Canadian Forces Base, SK [*ICAO location identifier*] (ICLI)
CYMK	Canadian Ukrainian Youth Association
CYMK	Cyan, Yellow, Magenta, Black [*Color model*] (PCM)
CYMM	Fort McMurray, AB [*ICAO location identifier*] (ICLI)
CYMO	Moosonee, ON [*ICAO location identifier*] (ICLI)
CYMOV	Cynosurus Mottle Virus [*Plant pathology*]
CYMR	Merry Island, BC [*ICAO location identifier*] (ICLI)
CYMS	Catholic Young Men's Society [*Ireland*] (BI)
CYMV	Cacao Yellow Mosaic Virus [*Plant pathology*]
CYMV	Clover Yellow Mosaic Virus
CYMW	Maniwaki, PQ [*ICAO location identifier*] (ICLI)
CYMX	Montreal/Mirabel International, PQ [*ICAO location identifier*] (ICLI)
CYN	Canyon
CYN	Canyon
CYN	Canyon [*Commonly used*] (OPSA)
CYN	City National [*NYSE symbol*] (TTSB)
CYN	City National Corp. [*NYSE symbol*] (SPSG)
CYN	Communications Yeoman [*Navy rating*]
CYN	Consolidated Ramrod Gold Corp. [*Vancouver Stock Exchange symbol*]
CYN	Coyle, NJ [*Location identifier FAA*] (FAAL)
CYN	Coyotepe [*Nicaragua*] [*Seismograph station code, US Geological Survey*] (SEIS)
Cyn	Cyanide (KSC)
Cyn	Cynegeticus [*of Xenophon*] [*Classical studies*] (OCD)
Cyn	Cynipidae [*Entomology*]
CYN	Zhongyuan Aviation Co. [*China*] [*ICAO designator*] (FAAC)
CYNA	Natashquan, PQ [*ICAO location identifier*] (ICLI)
CYNAP	Cytotoxicity Negative - Absorption Positive [*Immunology*]
CYND	Gatineau, PQ [*ICAO location identifier*] (ICLI)
CYNI	Nitchequon, PQ [*ICAO location identifier*] (ICLI)
CYNM	Matagami, PQ [*ICAO location identifier*] (ICLI)
CYNR	Canyon Resources [*NASDAQ symbol*] (TTSB)
CYNR	Canyon Resources Corp. [*NASDAQ symbol*] (NQ)
CYNX	Consolidated Ramrod Gold Corp. [*NASDAQ symbol*] (SAG)
CYNY	Enderby, BC [*ICAO location identifier*] (ICLI)
CYO	Catholic Youth Organization
CYO	Circleville, OH [*Location identifier FAA*] (FAAL)
CYO	Council on Youth Opportunity [*Disbanded 1971; functions taken over by Domestic Council and OMB*]
CYO	Cyrano Resources, Inc. [*Vancouver Stock Exchange symbol*]
CYOC	Old Crow, YT [*ICAO location identifier*] (ICLI)
CYOD	Cold Lake Canadian Forces Base, AB [*ICAO location identifier*] (ICLI)
CYOJ	High Level, AB [*ICAO location identifier*] (ICLI)
CYoM	Yosemite Museum, Nature Library, Yosemite, CA [*Library symbol Library of Congress*] (LCLS)
CYOW	Ottawa/International, ON [*ICAO location identifier*] (ICLI)
CYP	Calbayog [*Philippines*] [*Airport symbol*] (OAG)
CYP	Canadian Youth for Peace
CYP	Cheyenne Petroleums [*Vancouver Stock Exchange symbol*]
CYP	Christian Yellow Pages [*A publication*]
CYP	Commonwealth Youth Programme [*British*]
CYP	Cyanopindolol [*Organic chemistry*]
CYP	Cyclopedia of Portraits
CYP	Cyclophilin [*Biochemistry*]
CYP	Cyclophosphamide [*Cytoxan*] [*Antineoplastic drug*]
CYP	Cypress [*Botany*] (ROG)
cyp	Cypress (VRA)
Cyp	Cyprianus Florentinus [*Flourished, 12th century*] [*Authority cited in pre-1607 legal work*] (DSA)
CYP	Cyproheptadine [*Antihistaminic and antipruritic*]
CYP	Cyprus [*ANSI three-letter standard code*] (CNC)
Cyp	Cyprus (ROG)
CYP	Cyprus Airways Ltd. [*ICAO designator*] (FAAC)
CYP	Cytoproct [*Protozoology*]
CYPA	Children and Young Persons Act [*British*]
CYPA	Prince Albert, SK [*ICAO location identifier*] (ICLI)
CYPB	Cypress Bioscience [*NASDAQ symbol*] (TTSB)
CYPB	Cypress Bioscience, Inc. [*NASDAQ symbol*] (SAG)
CypBio	Cypress Bioscience, Inc. [*Associated Press*] (SAG)
CYPBW	Cypress Bioscience Wrrt [*NASDAQ symbol*] (TTSB)
CYPE	Peace River, AB [*ICAO location identifier*] (ICLI)
CYPF	Esquimalt, BC [*ICAO location identifier*] (ICLI)
CYPG	Portage La Prairie, MB [*ICAO location identifier*] (ICLI)
CYPH	Cytoclonal Pharmaceuticals [*NASDAQ symbol*] (TTSB)
CYPH	Cytoclonal Pharmaceuticals, Inc. [*NASDAQ symbol*] (SAG)
CYPH	Inukjuak, PQ [*ICAO location identifier*] (ICLI)
CYPHERTEXT	Cyphernetics Text Processing Language [*1970*] [*Computer science*] (CSR)
CYPHW	Cytoclonal Pharm Wrrt'C' [*NASDAQ symbol*] (TTSB)
CYPHZ	Cytoclonal Pharm Wrrt'D' [*NASDAQ symbol*] (TTSB)
CYPK	Pitt Meadows, BC [*ICAO location identifier*] (ICLI)
CYPL	Pickle Lake, ON [*ICAO location identifier*] (ICLI)
CYPM	Cyprus Minerals Co. (MHDW)
CYPN	Port Menier, PQ [*ICAO location identifier*] (ICLI)
CYPR	Cypress Semiconductor Corp. (MHDW)
CYPR	Cypros Pharmaceutical [*NASDAQ symbol*] (TTSB)
CYPR	Cypros Pharmaceutical Corp. [*NASDAQ symbol*] (SAG)
CYPR	Cyprus

CYPR	Prince Rupert, BC [*ICAO location identifier*] (ICLI)
CyprB	Cypress Bioscience, Inc. [*Associated Press*] (SAG)
CyprBio	Cypress Bioscience, Inc. [*Associated Press*] (SAG)
Cypros	Cypros Pharmaceutical Corp. [*Associated Press*] (SAG)
Cyprus	Cyprus Amax Minerals Co. [*Associated Press*] (SAG)
Cyprus LR	Cyprus Law Reports [*A publication*] (DLA)
CYPRZ	Cypros Pharmaceutical Wrrt'B' [*NASDAQ symbol*] (TTSB)
CypSem	Cypress Semiconductor [*Associated Press*] (SAG)
CYPY	Fort Chipewyan, AB [*ICAO location identifier*] (ICLI)
CYQA	Muskoka, ON [*ICAO location identifier*] (ICLI)
CYQB	Quebec, PQ [*ICAO location identifier*] (ICLI)
CYQD	The Pas, MB [*ICAO location identifier*] (ICLI)
CYQF	Red Deer Industrial, AB [*ICAO location identifier*] (ICLI)
CYQG	Windsor, ON [*ICAO location identifier*] (ICLI)
CYQH	Watson Lake, YT [*ICAO location identifier*] (ICLI)
CYQI	Yarmouth, NS [*ICAO location identifier*] (ICLI)
CYQK	Kenora, ON [*ICAO location identifier*] (ICLI)
CYQL	Lethbridge, AB [*ICAO location identifier*] (ICLI)
CYQM	Moncton, NB [*ICAO location identifier*] (ICLI)
CYQN	Nakina, ON [*ICAO location identifier*] (ICLI)
CYQQ	Comox Canadian Forces Base, BC [*ICAO location identifier*] (ICLI)
CYQR	Regina, SK [*ICAO location identifier*] (ICLI)
CYQT	Thunder Bay, ON [*ICAO location identifier*] (ICLI)
CYQU	Grande Prairie, AB [*ICAO location identifier*] (ICLI)
CYQV	Yorkton, SK [*ICAO location identifier*] (ICLI)
CYQW	North Battleford, SK [*ICAO location identifier*] (ICLI)
CYQX	Gander/International, NF [*ICAO location identifier*] (ICLI)
CYQY	Sydney, NS [*ICAO location identifier*] (ICLI)
CYQZ	Quesnel, BC [*ICAO location identifier*] (ICLI)
CYR	Cairo, GA [*Location identifier FAA*] (FAAL)
CYR	Carleton and Regiment [*British military*] (DMA)
CYR	Colonia [*Uruguay*] [*Airport symbol*]
CYR	Core Ventures [*Vancouver Stock Exchange symbol*]
CYR	Cray Research [*NYSE symbol*] (TTSB)
CYR	Cray Research, Inc. [*NYSE symbol*] (SPSG)
Cyr	Cyropaedia [*of Xenophon*] [*Classical studies*] (OCD)
CYR	Cyrus [*Persian emperor, d. 529BC*] (ROG)
Cyr	Die Inschriften von Cyros, Koenig von Babylon [*A publication*] (BJA)
CYRA	Commission's Yellowfin Regulatory Area [*Inter-American Tropical Tuna Commission*] (MSC)
CYRB	Resolute, NT [*ICAO location identifier*] (ICLI)
CYRI	Riviere Du Loup, PQ [*ICAO location identifier*] (ICLI)
Cyrix Cp	Cyrix Corp. [*Associated Press*] (SAG)
CYRJ	Roberval, PQ [*ICAO location identifier*] (ICLI)
CYRK	Cyrk, Inc. [*NASDAQ symbol*] (SAG)
CYRM	Rocky Mountain House, AB [*ICAO location identifier*] (ICLI)
CYRQ	Trois-Rivieres, PQ [*ICAO location identifier*] (ICLI)
CYrS	Siskiyou County Public Library, Yreka, CA [*Library symbol Library of Congress*] (LCLS)
CYRSV	Cymbidium Ringspot Virus [*Plant pathology*]
CYRT	Rankin Inlet, NT [*ICAO location identifier*] (ICLI)
CYRX	Cyrix Corp. [*NASDAQ symbol*] (SAG)
CYS	Board of Education for the City of York Library [*UTLAS symbol*]
CYS	Calypso Development Ltd. [*Vancouver Stock Exchange symbol*]
CYS	Cathays [*Cardiff*] [*Welsh depot code*]
CYS	Cheyenne [*Wyoming*] [*Airport symbol*] (OAG)
CYS	Cheyenne, WY [*Location identifier FAA*] (FAAL)
CYS	Compression Yield Strength [*Engineering*] (BARN)
CYS	CyCare Systems [*NYSE symbol*] (TTSB)
CYS	CyCare Systems, Inc. [*NYSE symbol*] (SPSG)
Cys	Cysteine [*Also, C, CySH*] [*An amino acid*]
cys	Cysteine [*Also, C*] [*An amino acid*] (DOG)
Cys	Cystine [*Also, CyS*] [*An amino acid*]
CYS	Cystoscopy [*Medicine*]
CYSA	Combed Yarn Spinners Association [*Later, AYSA*] (EA)
CYSA	Community and Youth Service Association (AIE)
CYSA	Sable Island, NS [*ICAO location identifier*] (ICLI)
CYSB	Sudbury, ON [*ICAO location identifier*] (ICLI)
CYSC	Sherbrooke, PQ [*ICAO location identifier*] (ICLI)
Cys-Cys	Cystine [*An amino acid*] [*Also, CYS, CYSTIN*] (DAVI)
CYSD	Center for Youth and Social Development [*India*] (EAIO)
CYSD	Cytoplasm Sum Optical Density [*Microscopy*]
CYSD	Suffield, AB [*ICAO location identifier*] (ICLI)
CY/SEC	Cycles per Second [*See also Hz*]
CYSF	Stony Rapids, SK [*ICAO location identifier*] (ICLI)
CySH	Cysteine [*Also, C, Cys*] [*An amino acid*]
CYSH	Cytoplasmic Shape [*Microscopy*]
CYSIWIG	Color You See Is What You Get [*Computer science*]
CYSJ	Saint John, NB [*ICAO location identifier*] (ICLI)
CYSK	Sanikiluaq/Belcher Island, NT [*ICAO location identifier*] (ICLI)
CYSM	Fort Smith, NT [*ICAO location identifier*] (ICLI)
CYSR	Nanisivik/Strathcona Sound, NT [*ICAO location identifier*] (ICLI)
CYSS	Slate Island, ON [*ICAO location identifier*] (ICLI)
CYSTEX	Combat System Exercise (MCD)
CYSTO	Cystogram [*Urology*] (DAVI)
cysto	Cystoscopic Examination [*Medicine*] (MAE)
Cysto	Cystoscopy [*Medicine*]
CYSU	Summerside Canadian Forces Base, PE [*ICAO location identifier*] (ICLI)
CYSV	Carnation Yellow Stripe Virus [*Plant pathology*]
CYSV	Concordia - Youth Service Volunteers (EAIO)
CYSY	Sachs Harbour, NT [*ICAO location identifier*] (ICLI)
CYSYS	Center for Cybernetics Systems Synergism
CYSZ	Cytoplasmic Size [*Microscopy*]
CYT	Cassidy Resources Ltd. [*Vancouver Stock Exchange symbol*]

CYT	Crystal Shamrock [*ICAO designator*] (FAAC)
CYT	Cyclophosphamide [*Antineoplastic drug*] (DAVI)
CYT	Cytec Industries [*NYSE symbol*] (TTSB)
CYT	Cytec Industries, Inc. [*NYSE symbol*] (SPSG)
Cyt	Cytochrome [*Biochemistry*]
CYT	Cytology
Cyt	Cytosine [*Also, C*] [*Biochemistry*]
CYT	Cytoxan [*Cyclophosphamide*] [*Antineoplastic drug*]
CYT	Yakataga, AK [*Location identifier FAA*] (FAAL)
CYTA	California Yoga Teachers Association (EA)
CYTA	Christian Youth Travel Association [*Australia*]
CytaBOM	Cytarabine [*ara C*], Bleomycin, Oncovin , Methotrexate with Leucovorin [*Vincristine*] [*Antineoplastic drug regimen*]
CYTC	Cytyc Corp. [*NASDAQ symbol*] (TTSB)
CYTC	Ethelda Bay, BC [*ICAO location identifier*] (ICLI)
CYTD	Cytochalasin D [*Biochemistry*]
CYTE	Cape Dorset, NT [*Canada*] [*ICAO location identifier*] (ICLI)
Cytec	Cytec Industries, Inc. [*Associated Press*] (SAG)
CYTECH	Cytotechnology
Cytel	Cytel Corp. [*Associated Press*] (SAG)
CYTH	Thompson, MB [*ICAO location identifier*] (ICLI)
CYTL	Big Trout Lake, ON [*ICAO location identifier*] (ICLI)
CYTL	Cytel Corp. [*NASDAQ symbol*] (SAG)
CYTO	Cytogen Corp. [*NASDAQ symbol*] (NQ)
CYTO	Cytotechnologist (HCT)
Cytocre	Cytocare, Inc. [*Associated Press*] (SAG)
CYTOGENET	Cytogenetics
Cytogn	Cytogen Corp. [*Associated Press*] (SAG)
CYTOL	Cytology
CYTOMG	Cytomegalovirus [*Immunology*] (DAVI)
CytoPh	Cytoclonal Pharmaceuticals, Inc. [*Associated Press*] (SAG)
Cytothr	Cytotherapeutics, Inc. [*Associated Press*] (SAG)
CYTOW	Cytogen Corp. Wrrt [*NASDAQ symbol*] (TTSB)
CYTR	Cytrax Corp. [*NASDAQ symbol*] (SAG)
CYTR	CytRx Corp. [*NASDAQ symbol*] (TTSB)
CYTR	Trenton Canadian Forces Base, ON [*ICAO location identifier*] (ICLI)
CytRx	Cytrax Corp. [*Associated Press*] (SAG)
CYTS	Timmins, ON [*ICAO location identifier*] (ICLI)
Cyt Sys	Cytochrome System [*Laboratory*] (DAVI)
CYTZ	Toronto Island, ON [*ICAO location identifier*] (ICLI)
CYU	Cheryl Resources, Inc. [*Vancouver Stock Exchange symbol*]
CYUA	Shingle Point, YT [*ICAO location identifier*] (ICLI)
CYUB	Tuktoyaktuk, NT [*ICAO location identifier*] (ICLI)
CYUC	Nicholson Peninsula, NT [*ICAO location identifier*] (ICLI)
CYUC (M-L)	Communist Youth Union of Canada (Marxist-Leninist)
CYUF	Pelly Bay, NT [*ICAO location identifier*] (ICLI)
CYUH	Clinton Point, NT [*ICAO location identifier*] (ICLI)
CYUI	Cape Young, NT [*ICAO location identifier*] (ICLI)
CYUJ	Lady Franklin Point, NT [*ICAO location identifier*] (ICLI)
CYUK	Byron Bay, NT [*ICAO location identifier*] (ICLI)
CYUL	Montreal/Dorval International, PQ [*ICAO location identifier*] (ICLI)
CYUQ	Jenny Lind Island, NT [*ICAO location identifier*] (ICLI)
CYUR	Gladman Point, NT [*ICAO location identifier*] (ICLI)
CYUS	Shepherd Bay, NT [*ICAO location identifier*] (ICLI)
CYUT	Repulse Bay, NT [*ICAO location identifier*] (ICLI)
CYUV	Longstaff Bluff, NT [*ICAO location identifier*] (ICLI)
CYUX	Hall Beach, NT [*ICAO location identifier*] (ICLI)
CYUY	Rouyn, PQ [*ICAO location identifier*] (ICLI)
CYV	Clover Yellows Virus [*Plant pathology*]
CYVADACT	Cyclophosphamide, Vincristine, Adriamycin, Dactinomycin [*Actinomycin D*] [*Antineoplastic drug regimen*]
CYVADIC	Cyclophosphamide, Vincristine, Adriamycin, Dacarbazine [*Antineoplastic drug regimen*]
CYVC	La Ronge, SK [*ICAO location identifier*] (ICLI)
CYVG	Vermilion, AB [*ICAO location identifier*] (ICLI)
CYVM	Broughton Island, NT [*ICAO location identifier*] (ICLI)
CYVMAD	Cyclophosphamide, Vincristine, Methotrexate, Adriamycin, Dacarbazine [*Antineoplastic drug regimen*]
CYVN	Cape Dyer, NT [*ICAO location identifier*] (ICLI)
CYVO	Val D'Or, PQ [*ICAO location identifier*] (ICLI)
CYVP	Quujjuaq, PQ [*ICAO location identifier*] (ICLI)
CYVQ	Norman Wells, NT [*ICAO location identifier*] (ICLI)
CYVR	Vancouver/International, BC [*ICAO location identifier*] (ICLI)
CYVT	Buffalo Narrows, SK [*ICAO location identifier*] (ICLI)
CYVV	Clitoria Yellow Vein Virus [*Plant pathology*]
CYVV	Clover Yellow Vein Virus
CYVV	Wiarton, ON [*ICAO location identifier*] (ICLI)
CYW	Clay Center, KS [*Location identifier FAA*] (FAAL)
CYW	Color Your World, Inc. [*Toronto Stock Exchange symbol*]
CYWA	Petawawa Canadian Forces Base, ON [*ICAO location identifier*] (ICLI)
CYWG	Winnipeg/International, MB [*ICAO location identifier*] (ICLI)
CYWK	Wabush, NF [*ICAO location identifier*] (ICLI)
CYWL	Williams Lake, BC [*ICAO location identifier*] (ICLI)
CYWO	Lupin, NT [*ICAO location identifier*] (ICLI)
CYWR	White River, ON [*ICAO location identifier*] (ICLI)
CYWY	Wrigley, NT [*ICAO location identifier*] (ICLI)
CYX	Colony Pacific Explorations Ltd. [*Toronto Stock Exchange symbol Vancouver Stock Exchange symbol*]
CYXC	Cranbrook, BC [*ICAO location identifier*] (ICLI)
CYXD	Edmonton/Municipal, AB [*ICAO location identifier*] (ICLI)
CYXE	Saskatoon, SK [*ICAO location identifier*] (ICLI)
CYXH	Medicine Hat, AB [*ICAO location identifier*] (ICLI)
CYXI	Killaloe/Bonnechere, ON [*ICAO location identifier*] (ICLI)
CYXJ	Fort St. John, BC [*ICAO location identifier*] (ICLI)

CYXL............ Sioux Lookout, ON [*ICAO location identifier*] (ICLI)
CYXN .... Whale Cove, NT [*ICAO location identifier*] (ICLI)
CYXP .... Pangnirtung, NT [*ICAO location identifier*] (ICLI)
CYXR .... Earlton, ON [*ICAO location identifier*] (ICLI)
CYXS .... Prince George, BC [*ICAO location identifier*] (ICLI)
CYXT .... Terrace, BC [*ICAO location identifier*] (ICLI)
CYXU .... London, ON [*ICAO location identifier*] (ICLI)
CYXX .... Abbotsford, BC [*ICAO location identifier*] (ICLI)
CYXY .... Whitehorse, YT [*ICAO location identifier*] (ICLI)
CYY .... Carpita Corp. [*Toronto Stock Exchange symbol*]
CYYB .... North Bay, ON [*ICAO location identifier*] (ICLI)
CYYC .... Calgary/International, AB [*ICAO location identifier*] (ICLI)
CYYD .... Smithers, BC [*ICAO location identifier*] (ICLI)
CYYE .... Fort Nelson, BC [*ICAO location identifier*] (ICLI)
CYYF .... Penticton, BC [*ICAO location identifier*] (ICLI)
CYYG .... Charlottetown, PE [*ICAO location identifier*] (ICLI)
CYYH .... Spence Bay, NT [*ICAO location identifier*] (ICLI)
CYYJ .... Victoria/International, BC [*ICAO location identifier*] (ICLI)
CYYL .... Lynn Lake, MB [*ICAO location identifier*] (ICLI)
CYYN .... Swift Current, SK [*ICAO location identifier*] (ICLI)
CYYO .... Wynyard, SK [*ICAO location identifier*] (ICLI)
CYYQ .... Churchill, MB [*ICAO location identifier*] (ICLI)
CYYR .... Goose Bay, NF [*ICAO location identifier*] (ICLI)
CYYT .... St. John's, NF [*ICAO location identifier*] (ICLI)
CYYU .... Kapuskasing, ON [*ICAO location identifier*] (ICLI)
CYYW .... Armstrong, ON [*ICAO location identifier*] (ICLI)
CYYY .... Mont-Joli, PQ [*ICAO location identifier*] (ICLI)
CYYZ .... Toronto/International, ON [*ICAO location identifier*] (ICLI)
CYZ .... Canterbury Resources, Inc. [*Vancouver Stock Exchange symbol*]
CYZ .... Cauayan [*Philippines*] [*Airport symbol*] (OAG)
CYZ .... Grand Rapids, MI [*Location identifier FAA*] (FAAL)
CYZA .... Ashcroft, BC [*ICAO location identifier*] (ICLI)
CYZD .... Toronto/Downsview, ON [*ICAO location identifier*] (ICLI)
CYZE .... Gore Bay, ON [*ICAO location identifier*] (ICLI)
CYZF .... Yellowknife, NT [*ICAO location identifier*] (ICLI)
CYZH .... Slave Lake, AB [*ICAO location identifier*] (ICLI)
CYZP .... Sandspit, BC [*ICAO location identifier*] (ICLI)
CYZR .... Sarnia, ON [*ICAO location identifier*] (ICLI)
CYZS .... Coral Harbour, NT [*ICAO location identifier*] (ICLI)
CYZT .... Port Hardy, BC [*ICAO location identifier*] (ICLI)
CYZU .... Whitecourt, AB [*ICAO location identifier*] (ICLI)
CYZV .... Sept-Iles, PQ [*ICAO location identifier*] (ICLI)
CYZW .... Teslin, YT [*ICAO location identifier*] (ICLI)
CYZX .... Greenwood Canadian Forces Base, NS [*ICAO location identifier*] (ICLI)
cz .... Canal Zone [*MARC country of publication code Library of Congress*] (LCCP)
CZ .... Canal Zone [*Postal code*] (AFM)
CZ .... Cane-Zebiak [*Marine science*] (OSRA)
CZ .... Carzinophilin [*Antineoplastic drug*] (DAVI)
CZ .... Cascade Airways [*ICAO designator*] (AD)
CZ .... Cefazolin [*An antibiotic*]
CZ .... Coahuila & Zacatecas Railway [*AAR code*]
CZ .... Coefficient Z-Axis [*Downforce on a racing car*] [*Aerodynamics*]
CZ .... Combat Zone
CZ .... Communications Zone (MCD)
CZ .... Control Zone [*For chart use only*] [*Aviation*]
CZ .... Convergence Zone [*Military*] (NVT)
CZ .... Coryza [*Medicine*]
CZ .... Crown Zellerbach Corp.
CZ .... Cubic Zirconia [*Simulated diamonds*]
CZ .... Czechoslovakia [*IYRU nationality code*]
CZ .... Czochralski Crystal Growth [*Crystallization process*]
CZA .... Chichen Itza [*Mexico*] [*Airport symbol*] (OAG)
CZA .... Coari [*Brazil*] [*Airport symbol*] (AD)
CZA .... San Mateo County Free Library, Belmont, CA [*OCLC symbol*] (OCLC)
CZAG .... Committee for Zero Automobile Growth (EA)
CZARA .... Coastal Zone Act Reauthorization Amendments [*1990*]
CZARTAC .... CZ [*Convergence Zone*] Area Reduction Tactic [*Military*] (CAAL)
CZB .... Carbon Zinc Battery
CZB .... Casey, IL [*Location identifier FAA*] (FAAL)
CZB .... Cruz Alta [*Brazil*] [*Airport symbol*] (OAG)
CZBA .... Canal Zone Biological Area [*A preserve administered by the Smithsonian Institution*] [*Later, Smithsonian Tropical Research Institute*]
CzBrS .... Statni Vedecka Knihova [*State Scientific Library*], Brno, Czechoslovakia [*Library symbol Library of Congress*] (LCLS)
CzBrU .... Universita J. E. Purkyne [*Purkyne University*], Brno, Czechoslovakia [*Library symbol Library of Congress*] (LCLS)
CzBU .... Univerzita Komenskeho Bratislava [*Comenius University of Bratislava*], Bratislava, Czechoslovakia [*Library symbol Library of Congress*] (LCLS)
CzBUK .... Ustredna Kniznica Slovenskej Akademie Vied [*Central Library of the Slovak Academy of Science*], Bratislava, Czechoslovakia [*Library symbol Library of Congress*] (LCLS)
CZC .... Canal Zone Code [*A publication*] (DLA)
CZC .... Chromated Zinc Chloride [*Wood preservative*]
CZC .... Citizens Corp. [*NYSE symbol*] (SPSG)
CZC .... Copper Center, AK [*Location identifier FAA*] (FAAL)
CZCH .... Czech Industries [*NASDAQ symbol*] (TTSB)
CZCH .... Czech Industries, Inc. [*NASDAQ symbol*] (SAG)
CZCHW .... Czech Inds Wrrt'A' [*NASDAQ symbol*] (TTSB)
CZ Code ...... Canal Zone Code [*A publication*] (DLA)
CZCP .... CZ [*Convergence Zone*] Confirmation Pattern [*Military*] (CAAL)

CZCS .... Coastal Zone Color Scanner
CZD .... Calculated Zenith Distance
CZD .... Cozad, NE [*Location identifier FAA*] (FAAL)
CZE .... Capillary Zone Electrophoresis [*Physical chemistry*]
CZE .... Clarksville, AR [*Location identifier FAA*] (FAAL)
CZE .... Compare Zone Equal [*Computer science*]
CZE .... Coro [*Venezuela*] [*Airport symbol*] (OAG)
CZE .... Czech [*Language, etc.*]
cze .... Czech [*MARC language code Library of Congress*] (LCCP)
Czech .... Czech Industries, Inc. [*Associated Press*] (SAG)
CZECH .... Czechoslovakia
CzechFd ...... [*The*] Czech Republic Fund, Inc. [*Associated Press*] (SAG)
Czech J Int'l L... Czechoslovak Journal of International Law [*A publication*] (DLA)
Czech YB Int'l L... Czechoslovak Yearbook of International Law [*A publication*] (DLA)
CZEG .... Edmonton, AB [*ICAO location identifier*] (ICLI)
CZE-MS .... Capillary Zone Electrophoresis - Mass Spectrometry [*Analytical chemistry*]
CZF .... Canadian Zionist Federation [*La Federation Sioniste Canadienne*] (AC)
CZF .... Canusa Financial Corp. [*Vancouver Stock Exchange symbol*]
CZF .... Cape Romanzof [*Alaska*] [*Airport symbol*] (OAG)
CZF .... Cape Romanzof, AK [*Location identifier FAA*] (FAAL)
CZF .... CitiSave Financial [*AMEX symbol*] (TTSB)
CZF .... Citisave Financial Corp. [*AMEX symbol*] (SAG)
CZFA .... Faro, YT [*ICAO location identifier*] (ICLI)
CZFM .... Fort McPherson, NT [*ICAO location identifier*] (ICLI)
CZG .... Canal Zone Government [*Superseded by Panama Canal Commission*]
CZG .... Casa Grande, AZ [*Location identifier FAA*] (FAAL)
CZG .... Cheni Gold Mines, Inc. [*Toronto Stock Exchange symbol Vancouver Stock Exchange symbol*]
CZH .... Castello Resources Ltd. [*Vancouver Stock Exchange symbol*]
CZH .... Corozal [*Belize*] [*Airport symbol*] (OAG)
CZH .... Jacksonville, FL [*Location identifier FAA*] (FAAL)
CZI .... Crazy Woman, WY [*Location identifier FAA*] (FAAL)
CZI .... Crystalline Zinc Insulin [*Medicine*]
CZIC .... Coastal Zone Information Center (GNE)
CZINVEST .... CZ [*Convergence Zone*] Investigation [*Military*] (CAAL)
CZIP .... CZ [*Convergence Zone*] Investigation Pattern [*Military*] (CAAL)
CZJ .... Center, TX [*Location identifier FAA*] (FAAL)
CZJ .... Citadel Capital Corp. [*Toronto Stock Exchange symbol*]
CZJ .... Corazon De Jesus [*Panama*] [*Airport symbol*] (OAG)
CZJC .... Canal Zone Junior College
CZK .... Cascade Locks, OR [*Location identifier FAA*] (FAAL)
CZK .... Colossus Resources [*Vancouver Stock Exchange symbol*]
CZKR .... Czechoslovakian Kronen [*Monetary unit*]
CZL .... Calhoun, GA [*Location identifier FAA*] (FAAL)
CZL .... Canus Laboratories Ltd. [*Vancouver Stock Exchange symbol*]
CZL .... Connecticut State Library, Hartford, CT [*OCLC symbol*] (OCLC)
CZL .... Constantine [*Algeria*] [*Airport symbol*] (OAG)
CZM .... CalMat Co. [*NYSE symbol*] (SPSG)
CZM .... Coastal Zone Management
CZM .... Cozumel [*Mexico*] [*Airport symbol*] (OAG)
CZMA .... Coastal Zone Management Act [*1972*]
CZMAC .... Coastal Zone Management Advisory Committee [*Department of Commerce*] (MSC)
CZMP .... Coastal Zone Management Program (GNE)
CZMS .... Canal Zone Merit System (MHDB)
CZN .... Chisana [*Alaska*] [*Airport symbol*] (OAG)
CZN .... Chisana, AK [*Location identifier FAA*] (FAAL)
CZN .... Chlorzotocin [*Organic chemistry*] (DAVI)
CZN .... Citizens Utilities Co. [*NYSE symbol*] (SAG)
CZN.A .... Citizens Util'A' [*NYSE symbol*] (TTSB)
CZN.B .... Citizens Util 'B' [*NYSE symbol*] (TTSB)
CZNB .... North Bay Canadian Forces Base, ON [*ICAO location identifier*] (ICLI)
CznBh .... Panama Canal Zone Library-Museum, Balboa Heights, CZ [*Library symbol Library of Congress*] (LCLS)
CZNPr .... Citiz Util Tr 5%'EPPICS' [*NYSE symbol*] (TTSB)
CZO .... Chistochina, AK [*Location identifier FAA*] (FAAL)
CZON .... Cefuzonam [*Antibacterial*]
CZP .... Clonazepam [*Antiepileptic drug*]
CZP .... Convergence Zone Propagation [*Military*]
CZP .... Peninsula Library System, Belmont, CA [*OCLC symbol*] (OCLC)
CzP .... Statni Knihovna Ceske Socialisticke Republiky [*State Library of the Czech Socialist Republic*], Klementinum, Czechoslovakia [*Library symbol*] [*Library of Congress*] (LCLS)
CZPS .... Czechoslovak Philatelic Society [*Later, SCP*]
CzPS .... Statni Technicka Knihova, Ustredi Vedeckych, Technickych a Ekonomickych Informaci, Prague, Czechoslovakia [*Library symbol Library of Congress*] (LCLS)
CZQM .... Moncton, NB [*ICAO location identifier*] (ICLI)
CZQX .... Gander, NF [*ICAO location identifier*] (ICLI)
CZR .... Center for Zoroastrian Research (EA)
CZR .... Convergence Zone Range [*Military*] (CAAL)
CZR .... Czar Resources Ltd. [*Toronto Stock Exchange symbol*]
CZ Rep .... Canal Zone Reports, Supreme and District Courts [*A publication*] (DLA)
CZRP .... Convergence Zone Resolution Pattern [*Military*] (CAAL)
CZ-RSV .... Rous Sarcoma Virus, Carr-Zilber Strain
CZS .... Cruzeiro Do Sul [*Brazil*] [*Airport symbol*] (OAG)
CZS .... Czechoslovakia
CZSG .... Canal Zone Study Group (EA)
CZ-SLOV ...... Czechoslovakia

CZT .... Cadmium, Zinc, and Telluride
CZT .... Carrizo Springs, TX [*Location identifier FAA*] (FAAL)
CZT .... Chirp-Z-Transform
CZT .... Chlorozotocin [*Antineoplastic drug*]
CZT .... Combustion Zone Temperature [*Fuel technology*]
CZT .... Port Alfred [*Formerly, Crozet*] [*South Africa*] [*Geomagnetic observatory code*]
CZU .... Compare Zone Unequal [*Computer science*]
CZU .... Corozal [*Colombia*] [*Airport symbol*] (AD)
CZU .... South Portland, ME [*Location identifier FAA*] (FAAL)
CZUE .... Cape Parry, NT [*ICAO location identifier*] (ICLI)

CZUL .... Montreal, PQ [*ICAO location identifier*] (ICLI)
CZVR .... Vancouver, BC [*ICAO location identifier*] (ICLI)
CZW .... Convergence Zone Width [*Military*] (CAAL)
CZWG .... Winnipeg, MB [*ICAO location identifier*] (ICLI)
CZX .... Canaustra Gold Explorations [*Vancouver Stock Exchange symbol*]
CZX .... Crosyton, TX [*Location identifier FAA*] (FAAL)
CZY .... Canadian Estate Land Corp. [*Vancouver Stock Exchange symbol*]
CZY .... Cluny [*Queensland*] [*Airport symbol*] (AD)
CZYZ .... Toronto, ON [*ICAO location identifier*] (ICLI)
CZZ .... Campo, CA [*Location identifier FAA*] (FAAL)
CZZ .... Consolidated Talcorp Ltd. [*Toronto Stock Exchange symbol*]

D
By Acronym

D............... Air-Cushion Vehicle built by Denny Brothers [*England*] [*Usually used in combination with numerals*]

D............... Air Force Training Category [*Inactive duty training periods and 15 days active duty training per year*]

D............... Application for Writ of Error Dismissed for Want of Jurisdiction [*Legal term*] (DLA)

D............... Arithmetic Factor Register [*Computer science*]

D............... Aspartic Acid [*One-letter symbol; see Asp*]

d............... British Penny [*Derived from Latin "denarius"*]

D............... Chemiewerke Homburg [*Germany*] [*Research code symbol*]

D............... Cholecalciferol [*Organic chemistry*] (DAVI)

D............... Cleveland [*Branch in the Federal Reserve regional banking system*] (BARN)

D............... Codex Bezae (BJA)

d............... Collision Diameter of a Molecule [*Symbol*] [*IUPAC*]

D............... Combustible Metals [*Fire classification*]

D............... Court of Divorce and Matrimonial Causes [*England*] (DLA)

D............... Da [*Give*] [*Pharmacy*]

D............... Dahlonega [*Georgia*] [*Mint mark, when appearing on US coins*]

D............... Daily

d............... Daily (WDMC)

D............... Daler [*Numismatics*]

D............... Dallas' Pennsylvania and United States Reports [*A publication*] (DLA)

D............... Dallas' United States Supreme Court Reports [*A publication*] (DLA)

D............... Dam

D............... Damasus [*Flourished, 13th century*] [*Authority cited in pre-1607 legal work*] (DSA)

D............... Dame

D............... Damn

D............... Dance Halls (Commercial) [*Public-performance tariff class*] [*British*]

D............... Danger Area [*ICAO*] (FAAC)

d............... Dangling, at Bedside [*Medicine*]

D............... Darcy [*Physics*]

d............... Dare [*To Give*] [*Latin*] (MAE)

D............... Darkness [*or Darktime*] [*Endocrinology*]

D............... Data

d............... Data (WDMC)

D............... Date

D............... Dative (ROG)

D............... Datum

D............... Daughter

D............... Daunorubicin [*Daunomycin, Rubidomycin*] [*Also, DNR, DRB, R*] [*Antineoplastic drug*]

D............... Day [*Broadcasting term*]

d............... Day [*SI symbol*]

D............... Day [*Approach and landing charts*] [*Aviation*]

d............... Day (WDMC)

D............... Day Return [*Round trip fare within one calendar day*] [*British*]

D............... Daytime (NTCM)

D............... Deacon

D............... Dead [*or Deceased*]

D............... Dead Air Space

D............... Dead Space [*Medicine*] (DAVI)

D............... Dean

D............... Dear (ROG)

D............... Death

D............... Debenture [*Type of bond*] [*Investment term*]

D............... Debye [*Unit of electric moment or movement*]

D............... Decalin [*A trademark*]

D............... Decca [*Record label*] [*Great Britain, Europe, Australia, etc.*]

D............... Deceased

D............... December

D............... Decessit [*Died*] [*Latin*]

d............... Deci [*A prefix meaning divided by ten*] [*SI symbol*]

D............... Deciduous

D............... Decimal (BUR)

D............... Decimal Reduction Time (DAVI)

D............... Decision (ADA)

D............... Decision Table Language [*Ace Microsystems*] [*A programming language*] (NITA)

D............... Deck (NASA)

D............... Declination

D............... Decoy [*Missile mission symbol*]

D............... Decree (ADA)

D............... Decret [*Decree*] [*French*] (ILCA)

D............... Decreto [*Decree*] [*Italian*] (ILCA)

D............... Decretum [*Decree*] [*Latin*]

D............... Deed (ROG)

D............... Deep (MSA)

d............... Deepwell Pump [*Liquid gas carriers*]

D............... Defeated

D............... Defendant

D............... Defendant [*Legal shorthand*] (LWAP)

D............... Defense [*Basketball; lacrosse*]

D............... Defense Department [*US government*]

D............... Defense Notice [*Classification given to British news items which are considered harmful to national security and which are voluntarily censored by the press*]

D............... Deferred [*Finance*]

D............... Deflection (IAA)

D............... Degree

d............... Degree (IDOE)

d............... Deictic [*Linguistics*]

D............... Delaware Reports [*A publication*] (DLA)

D............... Delay [*Electronics*]

D............... Deleted

D............... Delivery [*or Delivered*]

D............... Delta [*Phonetic alphabet*] [*International*] (DSUE)

D............... Demand Curve [*Economics*]

D............... Democrat [*or Democratic*]

D............... Demy [*Half*] [*Size of paper*] (ADA)

D............... Denarii [*Pence*] [*Monetary unit*] [*British*]

D............... Denarius [*or Denarii*] [*Silver coin in Ancient Rome; gold coin in Roman Empire*]

D............... Denied [*Legal term*] (DLA)

D............... Denio's New York Reports [*A publication*] (DLA)

D............... Denison's English Crown Cases [*1844-52*] [*A publication*] (DLA)

D............... Denmark [*IYRU nationality code*]

D............... Denominator [*In formulas for life annuities and life insurance premiums*]

D............... Density

d............... Density (IDOE)

D............... Dental

D............... Dental Surgery Attendant [*Ranking title*] [*British Royal Navy*]

D............... Dentes [*Applied to Teeth*] (ROG)

D............... Dentur [*Give*] [*Pharmacy*]

D............... Denver [*Colorado*] [*Mint mark, when appearing on US coins*]

d............... Deoxy [*or Desoxy*] [*Biochemistry*]

d............... Deoxyribose [*Biochemistry*] (MAE)

D............... Depart

D............... Department

D............... Depositus [*Laid to Rest*] [*Latin*]

D............... Depot [*DoD*]

D............... Depreciation

D............... Depression

D............... Depth

D............... Depth of Ship

D............... Deputy

D............... Derated (GAVI)

D............... Derivation [*or Derivative*] (IAA)

D............... Derivative (WGA)

D............... Dermatologist [*or Dermatology*]

D............... Deserter [*Military*]

D............... Design (AAG)

D............... Destination

D............... Destra [*Right*] [*Italian*]

D............... Destroyed

D............... Destroyer [*Navy British*]

D............... Detail (AAG)

D............... Detective

D............... Detector (NFPA)

D............... Deterministic (IAA)

d............... Detur [*Give*] [*Pharmacy*] (MAE)

D............... Deus [*God*] [*Latin*] (GPO)

D............... Deuterium [*Also, H²*] [*Radioisotope of hydrogen*]

D............... Deuteron [*Nuclear physics*] (WGA)

D............... Deuteronomist Source of the Pentateuch (BJA)

D............... Deutschland [*Germany*] [*German*]

D............... Developed [*Medicine*] (DAVI)

D............... Developer [*Photography*] (DGA)

D............... Development

D............... Deviation

D................ Devonian Period [Geology]
d................ Devteron [A nuclear particle]
D................ Dewoitine [French aircraft type] [World War II]
D................ Dexamethasone [Also, DEX, DXM] [Antineoplastic drug]
D................ Dexter [Right] [Latin]
D................ Dextro [Configuration in chemical structure]
d................ Dextro(rotatory) [Chemistry]
D................ Dextrose [Medicine] (MAE)
D................ Diagnosis
D................ Diagonal Engines (DS)
D................ Diagonal Polarization [Physics] (ECON)
D................ Diagram
D................ Diameter
d................ Diameter [Symbol] [IUPAC]
D................ Diamond (ADA)
D................ Diaphragm
D................ Diarrhea [Medicine]
D................ Diathermy [Medicine]
D................ Diazepam [Also, DAP, DZ] [A sedative]
D................ Dicta (DLA)
D................ Dictum (DLA)
D................ Didymium [Mixture of rare-earth elements] [Chemistry] (ROG)
D................ Died
d................ Died (VRA)
D................ Dielectric
D................ Dies [Day] [Latin]
D................ Diesel [British Waterways Board sign]
D................ Diesel Oil
D................ Dietitian
D................ Difference
d................ Differential (IDOE)
D................ Differential Coefficient
D................ Differential (of)
D................ Differentiation
D................ Diffuse [Immunology]
D................ Diffusing Capacity
D................ Diffusion Coefficient [Symbol] [IUPAC]
D................ Diffusion Constant [Medicine] (DAVI)
D................ Digest
D................ Digest of Justinian [A publication] (DLA)
D................ Digest of Public General Bills [Library of Congress A publication]
D................ Digit [or Digital] (MDG)
D................ Dihydrotestosterone [Also, DHT] [Endocrinology]
D................ Dihydrouridine [One-letter symbol; see H₂Urd]
D................ Dime [Monetry unit]
D................ Dimensional
D................ Dinar [Monetary unit] [Tunisia]
D................ Diode (MDG)
D................ Diopter [Also, DIOPT] [Optics]
D................ Dip
D................ Diplomat [License plate code assigned to foreign diplomats in the US]
D................ Diplomate (MAE)
D................ Direction [Computer science]
D................ Director [Films, television, etc.]
D................ Director aircraft capable of controlling drones or missiles [Designation for all US military aircraft]
D................ Dirt [Gossip] [Slang]
D................ Discharged
D................ Disc Issuer and Assistant [Sports]
D................ Discount
D................ Disease
D................ Dismissed [Legal term] (DLA)
D................ Disney's Ohio Superior Court Reports [A publication] (DLA)
D................ Dispenser (MCD)
D................ Displacement
D................ Display (MDG)
D................ Dispose [or Destroy] [Routing slip]
D................ Disqualified [Horse racing]
D................ Dissertation (BJA)
D................ Dissipation (IAA)
d................ Dissipation (IDOE)
D................ Dissolve (NTCM)
D................ Distal [Medicine]
D................ Distance
d................ Distance (IDOE)
D................ Distance Winner [Horse racing]
D................ Distinctio [Decretum Gratiani] [A publication] (DSA)
D................ Distinction
D................ Distinguished (ADA)
d................ Distinguished [Case at bar different either in law or fact from case cited for reasons given] [Used in Shepard's Citations] [Legal term] (DLA)
D................ Distortion (IAA)
D................ District
D................ District Court [Federal] (DLA)
d................ Diurnal (MAE)
D................ Diver [British military] (DMA)
D................ Diversity [Genetics]
D................ Diverticulum [Anatomy] (AAMN)
D................ Dividend [Investment term]
D................ Division
D................ Divorced
D................ Divus [The Late] [Latin]
D................ Doctor

D................ Document
D................ Dog [Veterinary science] (DAVI)
D................ Dog [Phonetic alphabet] [World War II] (DSUE)
D................ Dollar [Monetary unit]
D................ Dom [Port] [Latin] (ROG)
D................ Domain [Telecommunications]
D................ Dome
D................ Domestic
D................ Dominant [Applied to a species]
D................ Dominion Resources [NYSE symbol] (TTSB)
D................ Dominion Resources, Inc. [NYSE symbol] (SPSG)
D................ Dominion Rubber Co. [Canada] [Research code symbol]
D................ Dominus [The Lord] [Latin] (GPO)
D................ Don [Phonetic alphabet] [Pre-World War II] (DSUE)
D................ Don [Sir] [Spanish]
D................ Donative (ROG)
D................ Dong [Monetary unit] [Vietnam] (BARN)
D................ Donor
D................ Dopamine [Pharmacology] (DAVI)
D................ Doriden [Glutethimide] [Sedative]
D................ Dorsal
D................ Dorsal Spine [Anatomy] (DAVI)
D................ Dorsal Vertebra [Anatomy] (DAVI)
D................ Dosis [Dose] [Pharmacy]
D................ Douane [Customs] [French]
D................ Double
D................ Doublet
D................ Doubtful
D................ Dowager
D................ Download [Computer science] [Telecommunications]
d................ Down (Quark) [Atomic physics]
D................ Downrange Distance during Launch [NASA]
D................ Doxorubicin [Also, DOX, DXR] [Formerly, ADR, Adriamycin] [Antineoplastic drug]
D................ Drachma [Monetary unit in Greece]
D................ Draft [or Drafting] (ROG)
D................ Drafting Program [Association of Independent Colleges and Schools specialization code]
D................ Drag (MCD)
D................ Dragoons [Military unit] [British]
D................ Drain [Electron device] (MSA)
d................ Drain (IDOE)
D................ Drama
D................ Draperies [Astronomy] (BARN)
D................ Draw
D................ Dream Time [Neurology and psychiatry] (DAVI)
D................ Dressing [Medicine]
D................ Drive [State] [Psychology]
d................ Drive (IDOE)
D................ Driver [British military] (DMA)
D................ Driving
D................ Drizzling [Meteorology]
D................ Droit [Right] [French]
D................ Drone Plane [Navy symbol]
D................ Drop
D................ Droppable Fuel Tank [Suffix to plane designation]
D................ Drug
D................ Druids [Freemasonry]
D................ Drum (MDG)
D................ Dry (NFPA)
D................ Dry-Bulk Container [Packaging] (DCTA)
D................ Dual Capacity [London Stock Exchange]
D................ Duchess
D................ Duchy
D................ Duct (NFPA)
D................ Dues
D................ Duff [Phonetic alphabet] [Royal Navy World War I] (DSUE)
D................ Duke
D................ Dulcis [Dear One] [Latin]
D................ Dull
D................ Dummy [in game of bridge]
D................ Dump
D................ Dun [Thoroughbred racing]
D................ Dunlop, Bell, and Murray's Scotch Court of Session Cases, Second Series [1838-62] [A publication] (DLA)
D................ Duodecimo [Book up to 20 centimeters in height]
D................ Duodenum [Anatomy]
D................ Duplex
D................ Duration
D................ Dusio [In Cisitalia car model "D46"]
D................ Dust [Meteorology]
D................ Dutch
D................ Duty [Navy]
D................ Duxbury's High Court Reports [South African Republic] [A publication] (DLA)
D................ Dwarf
D................ Dye [Classification key in textile printing]
D................ Dyer's Edition of Valiant's English King's Bench Reports [1513-82] [A publication] (DLA)
D................ Dynamic Capital Corp. [Toronto Stock Exchange symbol]
D................ Dynamotor (IAA)
D................ Dyne [Unit of force] [Also, Dy, dyn Preferred unit is N, Newton]
D................ Electric Displacement [Symbol]
D................ Faulty Diction [Used in correcting manuscripts, etc.]
D................ Five Hundred [Roman numeral]

D	Intermediate Dialing Center on a Toll Ticket [Telecommunications] (TEL)
D	Knoll AG [Germany] [Research code symbol]
D	Labs. Dr. J. Auclair [France] [Research code symbol]
D	Mean Dose [Pharmacology] (DAVI)
D	Medium [Men's shoe width]
D	Morison's Dictionary of Scotch Session Cases [A publication] (DLA)
D	Naturally Aspirated [Automotive engineering]
D	Penny [Nail size]
d	Relative Density [Symbol] [IUPAC]
D	Response to Detail [Rorschach] [Psychology]
d	Response to Small Detail [Rorschach] [Psychology]
D	Shoe Width Greater than C and Less than E (BARN)
D	Siegfried AG [Switzerland] [Research code symbol]
D	Troponwerke Dinklage & Co. [Germany] [Research code symbol]
D	United States District Court [Used citation] (AAGC)
D	Usually Reliable Source of Intelligence [Military]
D	Wide [Women's shoe width]
D1	Double First Class
D1	First Coast Guard District [Boston, MA] [USCG] (TAG)
D_1	First Dorsal Nerve [Second dorsal nerve is D_2, etc., through $D12$] [Medicine] (DAVI)
D_1	First Dorsal Vertebra [Second dorsal vertebra is D_2, etc.] [Medicine]
D1A	Dickey [Maine] [Seismograph station code, US Geological Survey] (SEIS)
D1S	Dressed One Side [Lumber] (DAC)
D2	Angola [Aircraft nationality and registration mark] (FAAC)
D2	Angola [International civil aircraft marking] (ODBW)
D2	Second Coast Guard District [St. Louis, MO] [USCG] (TAG)
D2A	Dickey [Maine] [Seismograph station code, US Geological Survey] (SEIS)
D2B	Deceptive Deployment Basing [Military]
D2B	Digital Data Base [Computer science] (PDAA)
D2S	Dressed Two Sides [Lumber] (DAC)
D2S & CM	Dressed Two Sides and Center Matched [Lumber] (DAC)
D2S & M	Dressed Two Sides and Matched [Lumber] (DAC)
D2S & SM	Dressed Two Sides and Standard Matched [Lumber] (DAC)
D2T2	Dye Diffusion Thermal Transfer [Printer technology] (PCM)
D^3	Detection, Discrimination, and Designation
D3A	Dickey [Maine] [Seismograph station code, US Geological Survey] (SEIS)
D3WCA	Davis 3-Wheel Club of America (EA)
D4	Cape Verde [Aircraft nationality and registration mark] (FAAC)
D4	Cape Verde Islands [International civil aircraft marking] (ODBW)
D4S	Dressed Four Sides [Lumber] (DAC)
D5	Dextrose Five Percent [Pharmacology] (DAVI)
D5	Fifth Coast Guard District [Portsmouth, VA] [USCG] (TAG)
D/5HS	Dextrose (5%) in Hartman's Solution [Medicine]
D5LR	Dextrose (5%) in Lactated Ringer's Solution [Medicine]
D5/NS	Dextrose 5% in Normal Saline [Pharmacology] (DAVI)
D5/NSS	Dextrose (5%) in Normal Saline Solution [Medicine]
D5/S	Dextrose (5%) in Saline [Medicine]
D5/W	Dextrose (5%) in Water [Medicine]
D6	Comoros [International civil aircraft marking] (ODBW)
D7	Seventh Coast Guard District [Miami, FL] [USCG] (TAG)
D8	Eighth Coast Guard District [New Orleans, LA] [USCG] (TAG)
D9	Ninth Coast Guard District [Cleveland, OH] [USCG] (TAG)
D11	Eleventh Coast Guard District [Los Angeles, CA] [USCG] (TAG)
D13	Thirteenth Coast Guard District [Seattle, WA] [USCG] (TAG)
D14	Fourteenth Coast Guard District [Honolulu, HI] [USCG] (TAG)
D17	Seventeenth Coast Guard District [Juneau, AK] [USCG] (TAG)
D-66	Democraten '66 [Democrats '66] [Netherlands] (PPW)
D 860	Tolbutamide [Pharmacology] (DAVI)
DA	Daily (AFIT)
DA	Daily Abstract [Tea trade] (ROG)
DA	Daily Allowance
Da	Dakota Territory Reports [A publication] (DLA)
Da	Dalton [Physics] [Chemistry] (DOG)
DA	Damaged (CINC)
Da	Damasus [Flourished, 13th century] [Authority cited in pre-1607 legal work] (DSA)
DA	Dan-Air Services [ICAO designator] (AD)
DA	Danger Area (DA)
DA	Danish
DA	Danish Army (NATG)
DA	Dansylaspartate [Biochemistry]
DA	Dark Agouti [Rat strain]
DA	Dassault-Breguet [Avions Marcel Dassault] [France ICAO aircraft manufacturer identifier] (ICAO)
DA	Data Acquisition (MDG)
DA	Data Adapter (MCD)
DA	Data Administrator
DA	Data Analysis (AFM)
DA	Data Assembler
DA	Data Automation (AFM)
DA	Data Available
DA	Date [Online database field identifier]
D/A	Date of Admission [Medicine] (AAMN)
DA	Daughter
DA	Daunomycin and Cytosine Arabinoside [Antineoplastic drug regimen] (DAVI)
DA	Daunorubicin, ara-C [Cytarabine] [Antineoplastic drug regimen]
DA	Day
d/A	Day of Admission [Medicine] (DAVI)
DA	Days after Acceptance [Business term]
DA	Deacon-Arrow (SAA)
DA	Deaerator (NRCH)
DA	Dealers Alliance (EA)
DA	Debtors Anonymous (EA)
D/A	Debt to Asset Ratio [Economics]
da	Deca [A prefix meaning multiplied by 10] [SI symbol]
DA	Decimal Add
DA	Decimal-to-Analog (CET)
DA	Decision Altitude [Aviation] (DA)
DA	Decision Analysis [Military] (DOMA)
DA	Decision Area (MCD)
DA	Decubitus Angina [Cardiology] (DAVI)
D/A	Deductible Average [Business term]
DA	Defence Act (DLA)
DA	Defence Adviser [British]
DA	Defence Attache [British] (DS)
DA	Defence of Airfields [British World War II]
DA	Defense Aid [Lend-Lease] [World War II]
DA	Deferred Annuity [Insurance] (ADA)
DA	Define Area
DA	Degenerative Arthritis
da	Deka (IDOE)
DA	Delay Amplifier [Electronics] (OA)
DA	Delayed Action [Pharmacy]
DA	Delayed Arming [of explosive device]
DA	Delta Air Lines, Inc. (AAG)
DA	Delta Amplitude (AAG)
DA	Deluxe Paint Animation [Electronic art]
DA	Demand Assignment [Telecommunications] (TEL)
DA	Democratic Agenda (EA)
DA	Democratic Alliance [Philippines] [Political party] (FEA)
DA	Democrats Abroad (EA)
DA	Demokratischer Aufbruch [Democratic Awakening] [Later, Christian Democratic Union] [Germany] (EAIO)
DA	Denmark [Message traffic] [Military] (DNAB)
DA	Density Altitude [Navigation]
DA	Dental Anesthetic [Medicine]
DA	Dental Apprentice
DA	Dental Assistant
DA	Department of Agriculture
DA	Department of the Army
DA	Departure Approved [Aviation] (FAAC)
DA	Depletion Allowance [Business term]
DA	Deployment Assembly [Skylab] [NASA]
DA	Deposit Account [Banking]
DA	Deposit Administration
DA	Depth Appearing [Typography] (DGA)
DA	Deputy Advocate [Legal term] (DLA)
DA	Deputy Assistant (DAS)
DA	Descending Aorta [Anatomy]
DA	Descent Advisor (GAVI)
DA	Descent Advisor [FAA] (TAG)
DA	Design Agent (CAAL)
DA	Designated Adult [Most serious person in a group of flippant people]
DA	Design Authorization
DA	Design Automation (BUR)
DA	Desk Accessory [Computer science] (BYTE)
da	Desk Assistant [Broadcasting] (WDMC)
DA	Destination Address
DA	Detector Amplifier (IAA)
DA	Detector Assembly
DA	Detergent Aid
DA	Detroit Arsenal [Michigan] [Army] (MCD)
DA	Developing Activity [Military] (DOMA)
DA	Developing Agency (CAAL)
DA	Developmental Age
DA	Development Assistance
DA	Deviation Authorization
DA	Device Adapter (IAA)
DA	Device Address (ACRL)
DA	Devil's Advocate
DA	Dextrose Agar [Microbiology]
DA	Diabetes Australia
DA	Diagnostic Aid
DA	Diagnostic Analyzer
DA	Dicti Anni [Of the Said Year] [Latin]
DA	Dictionary of Americanisms [A publication]
DA	Did Not Answer (IIA)
DA	Differential Amplifier
DA	Differential Analyzer (IEEE)
DA	Diffused Base Alloy (IAA)
DA	Digestive Anlage
DA	Digital Alternator
D-A	Digital-to-Analog [Converter] [Computer science]
D/A	Digital-to-Analog (ACRL)
d/a	Digital-to-Analog (IDOE)
DA	Digital-to-Analog (IDOE)
D/A	Digital-to-Analog (IDOE)
DA	Dinar [Monetary unit] [Algeria]
DA	Dinner Ale [British] (ADA)
DA	Diphenylchloroarsine [Tear gas] [Army symbol]
DA	Diploma in Anaesthetics [British]
DA	Diploma in Art
DA	Direct Access (BUR)
DA	Direct Action [Bomb or shell fuze]

DA	Direct Address [*Telecommunications*] (NITA)
DA	Direct Admission [*Medicine*] (DAVI)
DA	Direct Agglutination [*Clinical chemistry*]
DA	Direct Answer (HGAA)
DA	Direct Ascent (AAG)
DA	Direction Action [*Bomb fuze*]
DA	Directional Antenna
da	Directional Antenna (WDMC)
DA	Direction Finding [*JETDS nomenclature*]
DA	Director of Aircraft (MUGU)
da	Director's Assistant (WDMC)
DA	Directory Assistance [*Telecommunications*] (TEL)
DA	Disability Assistance
DA	Disaggregated (MAE)
DA	Disassemble
DA	Discharge Afloat
D/A	Discharge and Advise [*Medicine*]
DA	Discrete Address
DA	Discretionary Account [*Investment term*]
DA	Discrimination Acuity
DA	Discrimination Analysis [*Agronomy*]
DA	Dislocation Allowance [*Military*] (AFM)
DA	Dispense as Directed [*Medicine*] (MEDA)
DA	Dispensing Allowance [*British military*] (DMA)
DA	Display Adapter
D/A	Dissemin/Action [*Defunct*] (EA)
DA	Dissolved Acetylene
DA	Distributed Application [*Automotive engineering*]
DA	Distribution-Abundance [*Ecology*]
DA	Distribution Amplifier
DA	Distribution Assembly [*Ground Communications Facility, NASA*]
DA	Distribution Automation (ACII)
DA	District Administrator
DA	District Agent [*Insurance*]
DA	District Assembly [*British*]
DA	District Attorney
DA	District Authorities [*British*]
DA	Division Artillery [*Army*]
DA	Divorce Anonymous [*Defunct*] (EA)
DA	Docking Adapter [*Aerospace*] (MCD)
DA	Doctor of Accounting (PGP)
DA	Doctor of Archaeology
DA	Doctor of Arts
DA	Documentary Bill for Acceptance
DA	Documentation Associates Information Services, Inc. (IID)
D/A	Documenti Contro Accettazione [*Documents Against Acceptance*] [*Italian Business term*]
D/A	Documentos Contra Aceptacion [*Documents Against Acceptance*] [*Spanish Business term*]
D/A	Documents Against Acceptance [*Banking*]
DA	Documents against Acceptance [*Investment term*] (DFIT)
DA	Documents Attached
D/A	Documents Contre Acceptation [*Documents Against Acceptance*] [*French Banking*]
D/A	Documents for Acceptance [*Banking*] (ROG)
DA	Doesn't Answer (ADA)
da	Doesn't Answer [*Telephone marketing*] (WDMC)
D/A	Dokumente Gegen Akzept [*Documents Against Acceptance*] [*German Banking*]
DA	Dollar Averaging Cost [*Investment term*]
DA	Domestic Android [*Quasar Industries*]
DA	Dominion Arsenal [*World War I*] [*Canada*]
DA	Dominion Atlantic Railway Co. [*Absorbed into CP Rail*] [*AAR code*]
DA	Donor-Acceptor
DA	Do Not Answer
DA	Dopamine [*Biochemistry*]
DA	Dormant Account [*Banking*]
DAF	Dorsal Aorta [*Anatomy*]
DA	Dorsal Area [*Anatomy*]
DA	Dose Assessment [*Nuclear energy*] (NRCH)
DA	Double-Acting
DA	Double Aged [*Metals*]
DA	Double Amplitude (KSC)
DA	Double Armor [*Telecommunications*] (TEL)
DA	Draft Action [*Defunct*] (EA)
DA	Dragon Airways Ltd.
DA	Drift Angle [*Navigation*]
DA	Drug Addict
DA	Drugs Anonymous (EA)
DA	Dual Action
DA	Ducktail [*Hair style*] [*Bowdlerized version*]
DA	Ductus Arteriosus [*Anatomy*]
DA	Dummy Antenna
DA	Dummy Load [*JETDS nomenclature*] [*Military*] (CET)
DA	Dunlap & Associates, Inc. (MCD)
DA	DUSTOFF [*Dedicated Unhesitating Service to Our Fighting Forces*] Association (EA)
DA	Dynamic Analysis Branch [*Redstone Arsenal*]
Da	[*The*] "Holy Scriptures" (1881) [*J. N. Darby*] [*A publication*] (BJA)
DA	Istituto de Angeli [*Italy*] [*Research code symbol*]
DA	National Council, Daughters of America [*Harrisburg, OH*] (EA)
DA-1	Directional Antenna Day and Night [*Broadcasting term*]
DA-2	Directional Antenna with Changing Patterns, Day and Night [*Broadcasting term*]

DA-3	Directional Antenna with Changing Patterns, Day and Night with Additional Pattern Change [*Broadcasting term*]
DA '91	Democratisch Alternatief 1991 [*Democratic Alternative 1991*] [*Suriname*] [*Political party*] (EY)
DAA	Data Access Arrangement [*Telecommunications Obsolete*]
DAA	Data Authentication Algorithm (HGAA)
DAA	Data Automation Activity (AFM)
DAA	Days after Anthesis [*Botany*]
DAA	Deaf Artists of America (EA)
DAA	Decatur Aviation, Inc. [*ICAO designator*] (FAAC)
DAA	Decimal Adjust Accumulator
DAA	Dehydroascorbic Acid [*Also, DHA*] [*Oxidized form of Vitamin C*] [*Biochemistry*]
DAA-3	Department of Aeronautics and Astronautics [*MIT*] (MCD)
DAA	Dependents Assistance Act
DAA	Deposit Administration Arrangement (WYGK)
DAA	Deputy Assistant Adjutant [*Military British*] (ROG)
DAA	Deputy Assistant Administrator (GFGA)
DAA	Derivative Activation Analysis [*Analytical chemistry*]
DAA	Desaparagine Insulin [*Pharmacology*]
DAA	Designated Approval Authority (MCD)
DAA	Diacetone Acrylamide [*Organic chemistry*]
DAA	Diacetone Alcohol [*Organic chemistry*]
DAA	Diaminoacetanilide [*Organic chemistry*]
DAA	Diaminoanisole [*A dye*] [*Organic chemistry*]
DAA	Diesel Automobile Association [*Defunct*] (EA)
DAA	Digital Automatic Acquisition (MCD)
DAA	Diploma of the Advertising Association (DGA)
DAA	Direct Access Arrangement [*Telecommunications*]
DAA	Director of Army Automation
DAA	Distributed Applications Architecture [*Computer science*] (BTTJ)
DAA	Division Administrative Assistant
DAA	Divisional Administrative Area [*Military British*]
DAA	DNA Amplification Assay
DAA	Doctor of Applied Arts
DAA	Documents Against Acceptance [*Banking*]
DAA	Doubly Asymptotic Approximation (MCD)
DAA	Drug Amendments Act (BARN)
DAA	Drug and Alcohol Abuse (OICC)
DAA	Drugs Available Abroad [*A publication*]
DAA	Dual Access Array (MCD)
DAA	Durene Association of America (EA)
DAA	Fort Belvoir, VA [*Location identifier FAA*] (FAAL)
DAAA	Alger [*Algeria*] [*ICAO location identifier*] (ICLI)
DAAA	Department of the Army Administrative Area
DAA & AM	Defense Aid [*Lend-Lease*] Aircraft and Aeronautical Material [*World War II*]
DAA & QMG	Deputy Assistant-Adjutant and Quartermaster-General [*British*]
DAAAS	American Association for the Advancement of Science, Washington, DC [*Library symbol*] [*Library of Congress*] (LCLS)
DAAB	Blida [*Algeria*] [*ICAO location identifier*] (ICLI)
DAAC	Digital Adaptive Area Correlation
DAAC	Director of Allied Air Cooperation [*World War II*]
DAAC	Distributed Active Archive Center [*NASA*]
DAACA	Delegation for Afro-American and Caribbean Cultural Affairs
DAACA	Department of the Army Allocation Committee, Ammunition (AABC)
DAACCE	Department of the Army Alternate Command and Control Element (AABC)
DAACM	Direct Airfield Attack Combined Munition [*Air Force*] (DOMA)
DAACT	Diabetes Association of the Australian Capital Territory
DAAD	Bou Saada [*Algeria*] [*ICAO location identifier*] (ICLI)
DAAD	Deutscher Akademischer Austauschdienst [*German Academic Exchange Service*] (EA)
DAAD	Diazaanthracenedione [*Organic chemistry*]
DAADB	Department of the Army Active Duty Board
DAAE	Bejaia/Soummam [*Algeria*] [*ICAO location identifier*] (ICLI)
DAAE	Defense Aid [*Lend-Lease*] Administration Expenses [*World War II*]
DAAE	Diethylamine Analog of Ethmozine [*Biochemistry*]
DAAF	Aoulef [*Algeria*] [*ICAO location identifier*] (ICLI)
DAAG	Alger/Houari Boumediene [*Algeria*] [*ICAO location identifier*] (ICLI)
DAAG	Deputy Assistant Adjutant-General [*British*]
DAAG	Dose Assessment Advisory Group [*Department of Energy*] [*Las Vegas, NV*] (EGAO)
DA-AHEW	Department of the Army Plan for Assistance in Department of Health, Education, and Welfare (AABC)
DAAI & OC	Defense Aid [*Lend-Lease*] Agricultural, Industrial, and Other Commodities [*World War II*]
DAAIUGM	Disaster Aid Association of the International Union of Gospel Missions (EA)
DAAJ	Djanet [*Algeria*] [*ICAO location identifier*] (ICLI)
DAAK	Boufarik [*Algeria*] [*ICAO location identifier*] (ICLI)
DAAL	Alger [*Algeria*] [*ICAO location identifier*] (ICLI)
DAAM	Telergma [*Algeria*] [*ICAO location identifier*] (ICLI)
DAAMP	Department of the Army Avionics Master Plan (AABC)
DAAMRA	Department of the Army Acquisition Management Review Agency (MCD)
DAAN	Reggan [*Algeria*] [*ICAO location identifier*] (ICLI)
DA & A	Drug Addiction and Alcoholism [*Title XVI*] [*Social Security Administration*] (OICC)
Da & Bos	Darby and Bosanquet's Statutes of Limitation [*2nd ed.*] [*1893*] [*A publication*] (DLA)
DA & D	Data Acquisition and Distribution
DA & M	Director of Administration and Management [*DoD*] (DOMA)
DA & P	Data Acquisition and Processing
DA & P	Data Analysis and Processing (SAA)

DA & QMG... Deputy Adjutant and Quartermaster General [*British*]
DAAO D-Amino Acid Oxidase [*An enzyme*]
DAAP Department of the Army Audiovisual Program
DAAP Illizi [*Algeria*] [*ICAO location identifier*] (ICLI)
DAAPP Department of the Army Audiovisual Production Program (MCD)
DAAPPP Data Archive on Adolescent Pregnancy and Pregnancy Prevention [*Sociometrics Corp.*] [*Information service or system*] (IID)
DAAPS Division of Advanced Automotive Power Systems [*Energy Research and Development Administration*]
DAAQ Ain Oussera [*Algeria*] [*ICAO location identifier*] (ICLI)
DAAR Daily Air Activity Report (CINC)
DAAR Department of the Army, Office of the Chief, Army Reserve
DAAR Deviation Approved as Requested [*Aviation*] (FAAC)
DAARL Directory of Australian Academic and Research Libraries [*Australia A publication*]
DAARP American Association of Retired Persons, Washington, DC [*Library symbol*] [*Library of Congress*] (LCLS)
DAAS Defense Activity Address System (MCD)
DAAS Defense Automated Addressing System (AAGC)
DAAS Defense Automatic Addressing System (AFIT)
DAAS Demonstration Advanced Avionics System (MCD)
DAAS Diamineanisole Sulfate [*Organic chemistry*]
DAAS Discrete Automatic Address System
DAAS DoD [*Department of Defense*] Automatic Addressing System (NG)
DAAS Drilling Activity Analysis System [*Petroleum Information Corp.*] [*Information service or system*] (NITA)
DAAS Setif/Ain-Arnat [*Algeria*] [*ICAO location identifier*] (ICLI)
DAASM Doppler Arrival Angle Spectral Measurement System [*Geophysics*]
DAASO Defense Automatic Addressing System Office (NATG)
DAAT Tamanrasset [*Algeria*] [*ICAO location identifier*] (ICLI)
DAATCO Department of the Army Air Traffic Coordinating Officer
DAAUW American Association of University Women Educational Foundation, Washington, DC [*Library symbol Library of Congress*] (LCLS)
DAAV Jijell/Taher [*Algeria*] [*ICAO location identifier*] (ICLI)
DAAVMPP Department of the Army Audiovisual Media Production Program
DAAW Bordj Omar Driss [*Algeria*] [*ICAO location identifier*] (ICLI)
DAAWA Dental Assistants' Association of Western Australia
DAA w/o OP... Driving Away Auto without Owner's Permission [*FBI standardized term*]
DAAX Cheragas [*Algeria*] [*ICAO location identifier*] (ICLI)
DAAY Mecheria [*Algeria*] [*ICAO location identifier*] (ICLI)
DAAZ Relizane [*Algeria*] [*ICAO location identifier*] (ICLI)
DAB Daily Audience Barometer [*British*] (ADA)
DAB Data Acquisition Bus (NASA)
DAB Daytona Beach [*Florida*] [*Airport symbol*] (OAG)
DAB Deacon Air Ballistic (MUGU)
DAB Defense Acquisition Board [*DoD*]
DAB Delayed Accessory Bus [*Automotive engineering*]
DAB Delayed Action Bomb
DAB Democratic Alliance of Burma [*Myanmar*] [*Political party*] (EY)
DAB Destroyer Advisory Board [*Navy*]
DAB Deutsches Arzneibuch [*German Medical Book*] [*Medicine*]
DAB Devereux Adolescent Behavior [*Rating scale*] [*Also, ABRS*] [*Psychology*]
DAB Diabrasive International Ltd. [*Toronto Stock Exchange symbol*]
DAB Diagnostic Achievement Battery
DAB Dial-a-Bus [*TRB*] (TAG)
DAB Diaminobenzene [*Organic chemistry*]
DAB Diaminobenzidine [*Organic chemistry*]
DAB Diaminobutanoic Acid [*An amino acid*]
DAB Diazabutadiene [*Organic chemistry*]
DAB Dictionary of Assyrian Botany [*A publication*] (BJA)
DAB Digital Audio Broadcast [*or Broadcasting*] (IAA)
DAB Dimethylaminoazobenzene [*Organic chemistry*]
DAB Directly Authorised Body [*Securities and Investments Board*] [*British*]
DAB Director of the Army Budget
DAB Display Arrangement Bits (NITA)
DAB Display Assignment BITS [*Binary Digits*]
DAB Display Attention BITS [*Binary Digits*] [*Computer science*]
DAB Dysrhythmic Aggressive Behavior
DABA Diaminobenzanilide [*Organic chemistry*]
DABA Diaminobenzoic Acid [*Organic chemistry*]
DABAWAS Datenbank fuer Wassergefahrdende Stoffe [*Data Bank on Substances Harmful to Water*] [*Information service or system Germany*] (IID)
DABB Annaba/El Mellah [*Algeria*] [*ICAO location identifier*] (ICLI)
DABC African Bibliographic Center, Washington, DC [*Library symbol Library of Congress*] (LCLS)
DABC Constantine/Ain El Bey [*Algeria*] [*ICAO location identifier*] (ICLI)
DABCO Diazabicyclooctane [*Organic chemistry*]
DABI Del Greco Assertive Behavior Inventory [*Psychology*] (EDAC)
DABIA (Dimethylaminoazobenzene)iodoacetamide [*Organic chemistry*]
DABITC (Dimethylaminoazobenzene)isothiocyanate [*Organic chemistry*]
DABL Daisy Behavioural Language [*Computer science*] (NITA)
DABLC Director, Advanced Base Logistics Control [*Navy*]
DABOA Director, Advanced Base Office, Atlantic [*Navy*]
DABOP Director, Advanced Base Office, Pacific [*Navy*]
DABP Skikda [*Algeria*] [*ICAO location identifier*] (ICLI)
D Abr D'Anvers' General Abridgment of the Common Law [*A publication*] (DLA)
DABRK Daybreak
DABS Direct Access Beacon System (MCD)
DABS Discrete Address Beacon System
DABS Dynamic Air Blast Simulator (MCD)
DABS Tebessa [*Algeria*] [*ICAO location identifier*] (ICLI)

DABSCI Dimethylamino Azobenzene Sulfonyl Chloride [*Organic chemistry*]
DABS-IPC Discrete Address Beacon System with Intermittent Positive Control (PDAA)
DABT Batna [*Algeria*] [*ICAO location identifier*] (ICLI)
DABT Diamino(tribromopropyl)triazine [*Flame retardant*] [*Organic chemistry*]
DABTH Dimethylaminobenzenethiohydantoin [*Organic chemistry*]
DABW Directory of American Book Workers [*A publication*]
DAC Dacca [*Bangladesh*] [*Airport symbol*]
DAC Dachiardite [*A zeolite*]
DAC Dalby Agricultural College [*Australia*]
DAC Darwin [*California*] [*Seismograph station code, US Geological Survey*] (SEIS)
DAC Data Acceptance Check [*Bureau of the Census*] (GFGA)
DAC Data Acquisition and Control (NASA)
DAC Data Acquisition and Control
DAC Data Acquisition Camera
DAC Data Acquisition Chassis (AAG)
DAC Data Acquisition Computer
DAC Data Acquisition Controller
DAC Data Analysis Computer
DAC Data Analysis Console (AFM)
DAC Data Analysis Control (MCD)
DAC Data and Computation Center [*University of Wisconsin, Madison*] [*Research center*] (RCD)
DAC Data Assembly Centers [*Marine science*] (OSRA)
DAC Data Authentication Code [*Telecommunications*] (OSI)
DAC Day Activity Center
DAC Days after Contact
DAC Days after Contract [*Business term*] (MCD)
DAC Decrement Accumulator
DAC Deductible Average Clause [*Insurance*]
DAC Defect Action Sheet [*A publication*]
DAC Defenders of the American Constitution (EA)
DAC Defense Acquisition Circular [*DoD*] (RDA)
DAC Delayed Atomization Cuvette [*Laboratory analysis*]
DAC Delivery Against Cost [*Business term*]
DAC Demand Assignment Controller
DAC Democratic Action Committee [*Pakistan*] [*Political party*]
DAC Democratic Action Congress [*Trinidad and Tobago*] [*Political party*] (PPW)
DAC Department of the Army Civilian
DAC Derived Air Concentration (MCD)
DAC Design Augmented by Computer [*General Motors Corp.*]
DAC Developmental Activity Center
DAC Development Assistance Committee [*Organization for Economic Cooperation and Development*] [*Paris, France*] (EAIO)
DAC Diallyl Chlorendate [*Fire retardant*]
DAC Diamond Anvil Cell [*Spectrometry*]
DAC Dictionary of the Apostolic Church [*A publication*] (BJA)
DAC Digital Analysis Converter (NITA)
DAC Digital Area Correlator
DAC Digital Arithmetic Center
DAC Digital Azimuth Control
DAC Digital-to-Analog Circuit [*Computer science*] (IAA)
DAC Digital-to-Analog Control [*Computer science*] (IAA)
DAC Digital-to-Analog Converter [*Computer science*]
DAC Diocesan Advisory Committee [*Church of England*]
DAC Diode-Assisted Commutation (PDAA)
DAC Direct Access Capability (MCD)
DAC Direct Access Communications (MCD)
DAC Direct Access Computing (MCD)
DAC Direct Access Control (MCD)
DAC Direct Air Cycle
DAC Director Assignment Console (NVT)
DAC Directors Advisory Committee [*National Institutes of Health*]
DAC Directory of Associations in Canada [*Micromedia, Ltd.*] [*Information service or system A publication*] (IID)
DAC Disabilities Aids Collective [*Australia*]
DAC Disabled Adult Child [*Social Security Administration*] (OICC)
DAC Disablement Advisory Committee [*Department of Employment*] [*British*]
DAC Disaster Assistance Center [*Federal Emergency Management Agency*]
DAC Discretionary Access Control (CDE)
DAC Discriminative Avoidance Conditioning [*Biochemistry*]
DAC Display Analysis Console
DAC Distance Amplitude Correction (OA)
DAC Distribution Automation and Control (MCD)
DAC Divisional Ammunition Column (ADA)
DAC Division of Adult Corrections (OICC)
DAC Division of Ambulatory Care [*Later, DACHP*] (EA)
D Ac Doctor of Accounts
DAC Document Availability Code (MCD)
DAC Domestic Affairs Council [*Replaced Urban Affairs Council, Rural Affairs Council, and Cabinet Committee on Environment*] [*White House*]
DAC Domestic Annual Fishing Capacity [*Fishery management*] (MSC)
DAC Double-Action Cylinder
DAC Douglas Aircraft Co. [*of McDonnell Douglas Corp.*]
DAC Douglas Aircraft Corporation (AAGC)
DAC Downed Aircraft (NVT)
DAC Drug Abuse Council [*Defunct*]
DAC Drugs Advisory Committee [*Australian Capital Territory, South Australia*]
DAC Dual Attachment Concentrator [*Telecommunications*] (ACRL)

DAC	Duplicate Aperture Card
DAC	Durex Abrasives Corp. [*Defunct*] (EA)
DAC	Dynamic Accelerated Cooling [*Sumitomo Metals*]
DAC	McDonnell Douglas Corp. [*ICAO designator*] (FAAC)
DAC	National Society, Daughters of the American Colonists (EA)
DAC	Yuma, AZ [*Location identifier FAA*] (FAAL)
DACA	Days after Contract Award [*Business term*] (MCD)
DACA	Department of the Army Certificate of Achievement
DACA	Department of the Army Corps of Engineers [*Military Project*] (AAGC)
DACA	Design Accreditation and Certification Advisers (AIE)
DACA	Digital-to-Analog Control Apparatus [*Computer science*] (IAA)
DACA	Drug Abuse Control Amendment (DAVI)
DACAB	Dutch-Australian Community Assistance Bureau
DACAC	Digital-to-Analog Converter, Alternating Current [*Computer science*] (IAA)
DACAD	Dansylcadaverine [*Biochemistry*]
DACAN	Data Acquisition and Analysis (NOAA)
DACAN	Douglas Aircraft Co. of Canada [*of McDonnell Douglas Corp.*] (MCD)
DACAN	Military Committee Standing Group Distribution and Accounting Agency, NATO
DACAPS	Data Collection and Processing System (IAA)
DACAR	Damage Assessment and Casualty Report [*Military*]
DACARY	Decoustics/ACS Centre for Acoustical Research [*York University*] [*Research center*] (RCD)
DACAS	Damage Assessment and Casualty Report [*Military*] (AFM)
DACB	Data Acquisition and Control Buffer (MCD)
DACB	Diaminochlorobenzene [*Organic chemistry*]
DACBU	Data Acquisition and Control Buffer Unit (NASA)
DACC	Danish American Chamber of Commerce (EA)
DACC	De Havilland Aircraft Co., Canada
DACC	Department of the Army Communications Center (AABC)
DACC	Direct Access Communications Channels
D Acc	Doctor of Accountancy [*or Accounting*]
Dacca	All India Reporter, Dacca Series [*1949-50*] [*A publication*] (DLA)
DACCA	Deflect Amplifier Circuit Card (DWSG)
Dacca	Pakistan Law Reports, Dacca Series [*A publication*] (DLA)
DACCC	Defense Area Communications Control Center
DACCC	Detroit Area Consortium of Catholic Colleges [*Library network*]
DACCC-AL	Defense Area Communications Control Center, Alaska
DACCC-CON	Defense Area Communications Control Center, CONUS
DACCEUR	Defense Area Communications Control Center, Europe (NATG)
DACCP	Diaminocyclohexane(carboxyphthalato)platinum [*Antineoplastic drug*]
DACCS	Department of the Army Command and Control System (AABC)
DACD	Delaware Association of Conservation Districts (SRA)
DACDIC	Digital-to-Analog Converter, Direct Current [*Computer science*] (IAA)
DACE	Data Acquisition and Control Executive [*Hewlett-Packard Co.*]
DACE	Data Administration Center Equipment [*Telecommunications*] (TEL)
DACE	Department of the Army Alternate Command and Control Element (AABC)
DACE	Design and Computational Experiments
DACE	Doctor of Air Conditioning Engineering
DACE	United States Army, Corps of Engineers, Office of the Chief of Engineers Library, Washington, DC [*Library symbol Library of Congress*] (LCLS)
DACEC	Digital Azimuth Control / Environmental Control
DACEMS	Data Communications Equipment Monitoring and Switching (MCD)
DAC Eng	Doctor of Air Conditioning Engineering
DACFC	David Allan Coe Fan Club (EA)
DACG	Departure Airfield Control Group [*Military*] (AABC)
DACG	Deputy Assistant Chaplain-General [*British*]
DACG	Deputy Assistant Commissary-General [*Military British*] (ROG)
DACH	Department of Arts and Cultural Heritage [*Australia*]
DACH	Diaminocyclohexane [*Organic chemistry*]
DA Chem	Doctor of Applied Chemistry
DACHP	Division of Ambulatory Care and Health Promotion [*of the American Hospital Association*] (EA)
DACI	Direct Adjacent Channel Interference
DACI	Dual Audio Cassette Interface
DACIL	Department of the Army Critical Items List
DACL	Depression Adjective Check Lists [*Psychology*]
DACL	Diablo Application Compiler Language [*Computer science*] (MHDI)
DACL	Dynamic Analysis and Control Laboratory [*MIT*] (MCD)
DACM	Defensive Air Combat Maneuvering [*Military*]
DACM	(Dimethylamino(methyl)coumarinyl)maleimide [*Organic chemistry*]
DACM	Director of Acquisition Career Mangement [*DoD*]
DACM	Dissimilar Air Combat Maneuvers
DACMIS	Development and Configuration Management Information System (MCD)
DACO	Data Consistency Orbit
DACO	Departure Airfield Group [*Army*] (ADDR)
DACO	Divisional Administrative Contracting Officer [*Military*]
DACO	Douglas Aircraft Co. Overseas [*Obsolete*]
DACOM	Data Communications Corp. of Korea [*Seoul, South Korea*] [*Telecommunications service*] (TSSD)
Da-Com	Data Communications, Inc. [*Information service or system*] (IID)
DACOM	Datascope Computer Output Microfilmer [*Eastman Kodak Co.*]
DACOM	Differential-Absorption Carbon Monoxide Monitor (MCD)
DACOMP	Damage Assessment Computer Program [*Military*]
DACOMP	Data Compressor (MCD)
DACON	Dac Cong [*North Vietnamese combat engineers*] (VNW)
DACON	Data Controller
DACON	Digital-to-Analog Converter [*Computer science*]
DACOR	Data Correction [*IBM Corp.*]
DACOR	Data Correlator
DACOR	Diplomatic and Consular Officers, Retired (EA)

DACOS	Data Communication Operating System
DACOS	Deputy Assistant Chief of Staff (NATG)
DACOWITS	Defense Advisory Committee on Women in the Services [*DoD Washington, DC*]
DA/CP	Data Acquisition and Control Processor [*Computer science*] (NITA)
DACP	Deserving Airman Commissioning Program [*Military*]
DACPO	Data Count Printout [*Computer science*]
DACQ	Data Acquisition (IAA)
DACR	Director of Airfield and Carrier Requirements [*British*]
DACRB	Department of the Army Compassionate Review Board
DACRP	Department of the Army Communication Resources Plan (AABC)
DACRS	Department of the Army Classification Review Committee (MCD)
DACRYLON	Dacron and Nylon
DACS	American Chemical Society, Washington, DC [*Library symbol Library of Congress*] (LCLS)
DACS	Data Acquisition, Control, and Simulation Centre [*University of Alberta*] [*Research center*] (RCD)
DACS	Data Acquisition Control System (IEEE)
DACS	Data and Analysis Center for Software [*Air Force Information service or system*] (IID)
DACS	DCSOPS [*Deputy Chief of Staff for Operations and Plans*]/ACSI Computer System [*Assistant Chief of Staff for Intelligence*] [*Army*]
DACS	De La Rue Automatic Cash System [*Banknote-disbursing equipment*] [*British*]
DACS	Design and Artists Copyright Society Ltd. [*British*]
DACS	Digital Access and Crossconnect System [*Telecommunications*] (TEL)
DACS	Digital Access Cross-Current System [*Telecommunications*] (NITA)
DACS	Digital Acquisition and Control System (MCD)
DACS	Digital Animated Control System
DACS	Digital Avionics Control System (MCD)
DACS	Digital-to-Analog Converter [*Electronics*] (ECII)
DACS	Discrete Address Communications System
DACST	Department of Arts, Culture, Science, and Technology [*South Africa*] [*Research center*]
DACT	Dactinomycin (Actinomycin-D) [*Also, act-D, AMD*] [*Antineoplastic drug*]
DACT	Deactivate (KSC)
DACT	Direct Acting
DACT	Disposable Absorption Collection Trunk (MCD)
DACT	Dissimilar Air Combat Tactics [*Navy*] (MCD)
DACT	Dissimilar Air Combat Training (MCD)
DACT	United States ACTION Library, Washington, DC [*Library symbol Library of Congress*] (LCLS)
DACTL	Declarative Alvey Compiler Target Language [*Computer science*] (NITA)
DACTS	Dispersion Against Concealed Targets [*Experiment*] [*Army*] (RDA)
DACU	Data Acquisition and Control Unit
DACU	Device Attachment Control Unit [*IBM Corp.*]
DACU	Digital Azimuth Control Unit
DACU	Digital-to-Analog Converter Unit [*Computer science*]
DACU	Digitizing and Control Unit
DACVR	Digital Analog Convertera (NITA)
DACW	Department of the Army Corps of Engineers (Civil Works Project) (AAGC)
DAD	Dads Against Discrimination [*An association*] (EA)
DAD	Damage Assessment Department (SAA)
DAD	Danang [*Vietnam*] [*Airport symbol*] (OAG)
DAD	Danang [*South Vietnam*] [*Airport symbol*] (AD)
DAD	Database Action Diagram (CDE)
DAD	Data Description Language [*Computer science*]
DAD	Davis Distributing Ltd. [*Toronto Stock Exchange symbol*]
DAD	Days after Deployment
DAD	Depression after Delivery (EA)
DAD	Deputy Assistant Director
DAD	Design and Development (ADA)
DAD	Design Approval Data
DAD	Designated Alert Detachment [*Military*] (MCD)
DAD	Desktop Application Director [*Computer science*] (PCM)
DAD	Dial-a-Design [*Computer-based design service*]
DAD	Differential Amplitude Discriminator (PDAA)
DAD	Diffuse Alveolar Damage [*Medicine*]
DAD	Digital Address
DAD	Digital Angle Data
DAD	Digital Audio Disc [*Audio/video technology*]
DAD	Dignity after Death (EA)
DAD	Direct Access Desktop [*Fifth Generation Systems*] (PCM)
DAD	Directional Aerial Disposal [*Insecticide spray*]
DA-D	Directional Antenna Daytime Only [*Broadcasting term*]
DAD	Directorate of Armament Development [*British*] (MCD)
DAD	Directory of Australian Directories [*A publication*]
DAD	Dispense as Directed [*Pharmacy*]
DAD	Documents Against Discretion [*Banking*]
DAD	Donor-Acceptor-Donor [*Physiology*]
DAD	Doppler Azimuth Discrimination (MCD)
DAD	Dorado Air [*Dominican Republic*] [*ICAO designator*] (FAAC)
DAD	Double-Acting Door [*Technical drawings*]
DAD	Double-Amplitude Displacement (MCD)
DAD	Douglas County Public Library, Castle Rock, CO [*OCLC symbol*] (OCLC)
DAD	Draft Addendum (OSI)
DAD	Drug Administration Device [*Pharmacology*] (DAVI)
DAD	Drug and Alcohol Directorate [*New South Wales*] [*Australia*]
DAD	Drum and Display [*Computer science*] (ADA)

DAD	Dual Air Density [*Explorer satellite*] [*NASA*]
DADA	Deputy Assistant Director of Artillery [*British*]
DADA	Designers and Art Directors Association [*British*] (BI)
DADA	Diisopropylamine [*or Diisopropylammonium*] Dichloroacetate [*Pharmacology*]
DADAC	Department of the Army Distribution/Allocation Committee (AABC)
DADAC	Digital-to-Analog Deck Angle Converter [*Computer science Navy*]
DADADS	Deputy Assistant Director of Army Dental Services [*British*]
DADAG	Diacetyldianhydrogalacitol [*Antineoplastic drug*]
DADAH	Deputy Assistant Director of Army Health [*British*]
DADAVS	Deputy Assistant Director, Army Veterinary Services
DADB	Data Analysis Database
DADC	Digital Air Data Computer
DADC	Digital Audio Disc Corp. [*Sony Corp.*]
DADC	Direct Access Data Channel (IAA)
DAD-C2	Division Air Defense Command and Control (MCD)
DAD-C3	Division Air Defense Command, Control, and Communications [*Study*] (MCD)
DADCAP	Dawn and Dusk Combat Air Patrol
DADCMI	Department of the Army Policy for Disclosure of Classified Military Information [*to foreign government*] (AABC)
DADCOK	Digital Air Data Computer Status
DADCSLOG	Department of the Army, Deputy Chief of Staff for Logistics
DADCTS	Digital Air Data Computer Test Set
DADDS	Diacetyldiaminodiphenylsulfone [*Antibacterial compound*]
DADDTC	Diethylammonium Diethyldithiocarbamate [*Organic chemistry*]
DADE	Data Acquisition and Decommutation Equipment
DADE	Department of Army Directed Effort
DADE	Digital Acquisition and Documentation Equipment (KSC)
DADE	Dual Air Density Explorer [*Satellite*] [*NASA*]
DADEAC	Diallyldiethylammonium Chloride [*Organic chemistry*]
DADEC	Design and Demonstration Electronic Computer (MHDB)
DADEE	Dynamic Analog Differential Equation Equalizer
DADEMS	Department of the Army Data Elements Management System (MCD)
DADF	Diacetyldihydrofluorescein [*Organic chemistry*]
DADGMS	Deputy Assistant Director-General of Medical Services [*British*] (ADA)
DADHT	Diacetyldioxohexahydrotriazine [*Laundry bleach activator*]
DAdI	Adas Israel Congregation, Washington, DC [*Library symbol Library of Congress*] (LCLS)
DADI	Dianisidine Diisocyanate (DICI)
DADIC	Data Dictionary [*Computer science*]
DADIOS	Direct Analog-to-Digital Input-Output System [*Computer science*] (MHDB)
DADiSP	Data Acquisition and Digital Signal Processing
DADISP	Data Analysis and Display [*Computer science*]
DADIT	Daystrom Analog-to-Digital Integrating Translator
DADIWT	Deputy Assistant Director of Inland Water Transport [*British military*] (DMA)
DADL	(D-Ala, D-Leu) Enkephalin [*Biochemistry*]
DADL	Deputy Assistant Director of Labor [*Allied Control Commission*] [*World War II*]
DADLE	(D-Ala, D-Leu) Enkephalin [*Biochemistry*]
DADM	Data Acquisition and Data Management
DADM	Decision Authority, Decision Memorandum [*Military*] (MCD)
DADM	Deductively Augmented Data Management [*Computer science*]
D Adm	Doctor of Administration
DADMAC	Diallyldimethylammonium Chloride [*Organic chemistry*]
DADMC	Defense Advanced Disposal Management Course [*Army*]
DADMCS	Department of the Army Decoration for Meritorious Civilian Service
DADME	Deputy Assistant Director of Mechanical Engineering [*British military*] (DMA)
D Adm Eng	Doctor of Administrative Engineering
DADMS	Defense Automated Document Management System (MCD)
DADMS	Defense Mapping Agency Automated Distribution Management System (DNAB)
DADMS	Deputy Assistant Director of Medical Services [*Military*]
DAD/MSD	Deputy Assistant Director for Management Support Division [*Vietnam*]
DADO	Data Automation Design Office [*Air Force*] (AFM)
DADOS	Deputy Assistant Director of Ordnance Stores [*Military*]
DADOS(E)	Deputy Assistant Director of Ordnance Services (Engineering) [*British*]
DADOTA	Drug and Alcohol Dependent Offenders' Treatment Act of 1986
dADP	Deoxyadenosine Diphosphate [*Biochemistry*]
DAD/PE	Deputy Assistant Director for Plans and Evaluation [*Vietnam*]
DADPE	Diaminodiphenyl Ether [*Organic chemistry*]
DADPM	Diaminodiphenylmethane [*Organic chemistry*]
DAD/POD	Deputy Assistant Director for the Psychological Operations Division [*Vietnam*]
DADPR	Deputy Assistant Director of Public Relations [*British military*] (DMA)
DADPS	Diaminodiphenyl Sulfone [*Also, DAPSONE, DDS*] [*Pharmacology*]
DADPTC	Defence Automatic Data Processing Training Centre [*British military*] (DMA)
DADQ	Deputy Assistant Director of Quartering [*British*]
DADR	Deputy Assistant Director of Remounts [*British*]
DADR	Digital Angle Data Recorder
DADRT	Deputy Assistant Director of Railway Transport [*British military*] (DMA)
DADS	Dads Advising Dads
DADS	DARCOM [*Development and Readiness Command, Army*] Announcement DistributionSystem (RDA)
DADS	Data Access and Dissemination System (AAGC)
DADS	Data Acquisition and Display System [*or Subsystem*]
DADS	Defense Acquisition and Display System (AAGC)
DADS	Defense Acquisition Data System (AAGC)

DADS	Defense Audiovisual Depository System
DADS	Defense Automated Depot System (MCD)
DADS	Deficiency Analysis Data System (DNAB)
DADS	Digital Air Data System
DADS	Digital Analog Data System (CAAL)
DADS	Digital Audio Distribution System
DADS	Director of Army Dental Services [*British*]
DADS	Dittler Airline Data Systems [*Information service or system*] (IID)
DADS	Division Air Defense System [*Military*]
DADS	Dosimetry Acquisition and Display System
DADS	Dual Air Density Satellite [*NASA*] (NASA)
DADS	Dynamic Analysis and Design of Systems (RDA)
DADS	Dynamic Analysis and Design Software
DADSM	Direct Access Device Space Management (MCD)
DADSOT	Digital/Analog Daily System Operability Tests (MCD)
DADST	Deputy Assistant Director of Supplies and Transport [*British*]
DADT	Deputy Assistant Director of Transportation [*British*]
DADTA	Durability and Damage Tolerance Analysis [*Air Force*]
DADU	Data Accumulation and Distribution Units [*Navy*] (MCD)
DADVRS	Deputy Assistant Director of Veterinary and Remount Services [*British military*] (DMA)
DADVS	Deputy Assistant Director of Veterinary Services (DMA)
Dady	Dadyburjar. Small Court Appeals [*India*] [*A publication*] (DLA)
DAE	Danish Air Force [*ICAO designator*] (FAAC)
DAE	Data Acquisition Equipment (KSC)
DAE	Data Automatión Equipment
DAE	Days after Emergence [*Botany*]
DAE	Dealers Art Exchange (EA)
DAE	Defense Acquisition Executive (MCD)
DAE	Defense Acquisition Executive (AAGC)
DAE	Department of Atomic Energy [*India*]
DAE	Differential-Algebraic Equations [*Mathematics*]
DAE	Diphenylanthracene Endoperoxide [*Organic chemistry*]
DAE	Diploma in Advanced Education (ADA)
DAE	Diploma in Advanced Engineering [*British*]
DAE	Director of Aircraft Equipment [*Ministry of Aircraft Production*] [*British*]
DAE	Director of Army Education [*British*]
DAE	Distributed Automation Edition [*Computer science*] (BTTJ)
DAE	District Airport Engineer
DAE	Diving Air Embolism [*Medicine*] (DAVI)
DAE	Division of Adult Education [*Office of Education*]
D Ae	Doctor of Aeronautics
DAE	Doctor of Art Education
DAE	Dry Air Equivalent [*Engineering*]
DAE	DSA [*Defense Supply Agency*] Augmentation Element
DAE	Dynamics Augmentation Experiment (MCD)
DAEA	Dimethyl Aminoethyl Acetate [*Organic chemistry*]
DAEA	Drug Abuse Education Act (OICC)
DAEC	Danish Atomic Energy Commission
DAEC	Duane Arnold Energy Center (NRCH)
DA Ed	Doctor of Arts in Education (PGP)
DAEDAC	Drug Abuse Epidemiology Data Center [*Ceased operation*] [*Texas Christian University*] (IID)
DAEDARC	Department of the Army Equipment Data Review Committee (AABC)
D Ae E	Doctor of Aeronautical Engineering
D Ae Eng	Doctor of Aeronautical Engineering
DAEEP	Division of Applied Experimental and Engineering Psychologists (EA)
DAEM	Digital Acoustic Emission Monitor (PDAA)
DAEM	Directorate of Aircraft Engineering and Maintenance (MCD)
DAEM	Draper Aden Environmental Modeling
DAEMON	Data Adaptive Evaluator and Monitor
DAEO	Designated Agency Ethics Official (AAGC)
DAEP	Department of the Army Equipment Publication
DAEP	Diamino(adamantyl)ethylpyrimidine [*Biochemistry*]
DAE/PE	Defense Acquisition Executive/Procurement Executive (AAGC)
DAERA	Disability Alliance Educational and Research Association [*British*]
D Aero E	Doctor of Aeronautical Engineering
DAES	Defense Acquisition Executive Summary
DAES	Diploma in Advanced Educational Studies, University of Newcastle [*British*] (DBQ)
DAES	Direct Access Education System (AEBS)
DAES	Division of Adult Education Service [*of NEA*]
D Ae S	Doctor of Aeronautical Science
DAES	Drug Abuse Education Specialist (DNAB)
D Ae Sc	Doctor of Aeronautical Science
DAF	Dafare [*Djibouti*] [*Seismograph station code, US Geological Survey*] (SEIS)
DAF	Danish Air Force [*Denmark*] [*FAA designator*] (FAAC)
DAF	Data Acquisition Facility [*of STADAN*]
DAF	Data Analysis Facility
DAF	Days after Flowering [*Botany*]
DAF	Decay-Accelerating Factor [*Biochemistry*]
DAF	Dedicated Access Facility [*Library science*]
DAF	Deferred Annuity Fund
DAF	Delay Amplification Factor (IAA)
DAF	Delayed Action Fuse
DAF	Delayed Auditory Feedback [*Audiology*]
DAF	Delivered at Frontier [*Seller's responsibility is fulfilled when goods have arrived at frontier, but before "customs border," of country named*] [*"INCOTERM," International Chamber of Commerce official code*]
DAF	Demographic Adjustment Factor (NTCM)
DAF	Demonstration Air Force
DAF	Denmark-America Foundation (EA)

DAF .... Department of Agriculture and Fisheries [*New South Wales*] [*Australia*]
DAF .... Department of Agriculture and Fisheries [*Scotland*]
DAF .... Department of the Air Force
DAF .... Departure Airfield (AABC)
DAF .... Desalkylflurazepam [*Sedative*]
DAF .... Desert Air Force [*British*]
DAF .... Design Action to Follow
DAF .... Destination Address Field [*Computer science*] (IBMDP)
DAF .... Deutsche Arbeitsfront [*German Workers Front*] [*Post-World War II*]
DAF .... Device Assembly Facility
DAF .... Diacetylferrocene [*Organic chemistry*]
DAF .... Diacetylfluorescein [*Organic chemistry*]
DAF .... Dilutin Attenuation Factor [*Metallurgy*]
DAF .... Discard at Failure (MCD)
DAF .... Dissolved Air Flotation
DAF .... Distributed Acquisition Facility (NITA)
DAF .... Document Acquisition File (DNAB)
DAF .... Draw-a-Family [*Test*] [*Psychology*] (DAVI)
DAF .... Dressing after Finish [*Manufacturing term*]
DAF .... Dry and Ash-Free [*Coal*]
DAF .... Dual Access Feature (IAA)
DAF .... Due and Ancient Form [*Freemasonry*]
DAF .... Dynamic Axial Fatigue (PDAA)
DAF .... Framework for Distributed Application [*Telecommunications*] (OSI)
DAF .... Van Doorn's Automobile Fabrieken [*Dutch automobile manufacturer; acronym used as name of its cars*]
DAFA .... American Forestry Association, Washington, DC [*Library symbol Library of Congress*] (LCLS)
DAFA .... Data Accounting Flow Assessment (MHDB)
DAF & E ...... Defense Aid [*Lend-Lease*] Facilities and Equipment [*World War II*]
DAFB .... Dyess Air Force Base [*Texas*] (AAG)
DAFC .... Departure Airfield Control (AABC)
DAFC .... Dictionnaire Apologetique de la Foi Catholique [*A publication*] (BJA)
DAFC .... Digital Automatic Frequency Control
DAFCCS ...... Department of the Air Force Command and Control System
DAFCG .... Departure Airfield Control Group [*Military*] (AABC)
DAFCS .... Digital Automatic Flight Control System
DAFD .... Dayton Air Force Depot
DAFD .... Department of the Army Forward Depot (AABC)
DAFDS .... Digital Autopilot Flight Director System (MCD)
DAFDTA .... Dipole Antenna with Feed-Points Displaced Transverse to Its Axis (PDAA)
DAFF .... Daffodil (DSUE)
DAFFA .... Delicatessen and Fine Food Association [*British*] (DBA)
DAFFD .... Department of the Army Forward-Floating Depot (AABC)
DAFFS .... Design of Advanced Fossil Fuel System
DAFFY .... Direct Aid for Full Value
DAFG .... Deutsch-Albanische Freundschaftsgesellschaft EV [*German Albanian Friendship Society*] [*Germany*] (EAIO)
DAFH .... Tilrempt/Hassi R'Mel [*Algeria*] [*ICAO location identifier*] (ICLI)
DAFH .... United States Air Force, Headquarters U.S. Air Force, Office of Air Force History, Bolling Air Force Base, Washington, DC [*Library symbol*] [*Library of Congress*] (LCLS)
DAFI .... Djelfa/Tletsi [*Algeria*] [*ICAO location identifier*] (ICLI)
DAFICCS ...... Department of the Air Force Integrated Command and Control Systems (MCD)
DAFIE .... Directorate for Armed Forces Information and Education [*Military*]
DAFL .... American Federation of Labor and Congress of Industrial Organizations Library, Washington, DC [*Library symbol Library of Congress*] (LCLS)
DAFL .... Differential Area Force Law (MCD)
DAFM .... Department of the Army Field Manuals
DAFM .... Direct Access File Manager
DAFM .... Discard-at-Failure Maintenance (IEEE)
DAFM .... Distal Accessory Flexor Muscle [*of a lobster*]
DAFO .... Division Accounting and Finance Office [*Air Force*] (AFIT)
DAFOSR .... United States Air Force, Office of Scientific Research, Washington, DC [*Library symbol Library of Congress*] (LCLS)
DAFS .... Damage Analysis and Fundamental Studies (MCD)
DAFS .... Department of Agriculture and Fisheries for Scotland
DAFS .... Direct Aerial Fire Support [*Military*] (AABC)
DAFS .... Director of Army Fire Services [*British*]
DAFS .... Duty Air Force Specialty
DAFSC .... Duty Air Force Specialty Code
DAFSO .... Department of the Air Force Special Order (AFM)
DAFT .... Data Acquisition Frequency Table (MCD)
DAFT .... Digital Analogic Function Table [*Electronics*] (ECII)
DAFT .... Digital-to-Analog Function Table [*Packard Bell Computer Corp.*]
DAFT .... Draw-A-Family Test (MEDA)
DAFW .... Directorate of Air Force Welfare [*British*]
DAG .... Agriculture Canada Library [*UTLAS symbol*]
DAG .... Aquadag [*Graphite coating*] (NTCM)
DAG .... Daggett, CA [*Location identifier FAA*] (FAAL)
DAG .... Danmarkshavn [*Greenland*] [*Seismograph station code, US Geological Survey*] (SEIS)
DAG .... Data Analysis Group [*Military*]
DAG .... Debendox Action Group [*British*] (DBA)
DAG .... Defense Aerial Gunner
DAG .... Defense Special Security Communications System Address Group (MCD)
DAG .... Dekagram [*Unit of measure*]
DAG .... Department of the Attorney-General [*Commonwealth, Queensland*] [*Australia*]
DAG .... Deputy Adjutant-General [*Military*]

DAG .... Deputy Advocate-General [*Military British*] (ROG)
DAG .... Design Advisory Group (IAA)
DAG .... Development Assistance Group
DAG .... Diacylglycerol [*Organic chemistry*]
DAG .... Dianhydrogalacitol [*Antineoplastic drug*] (DAVI)
DAG .... Dianilinogossypol [*Organic chemistry*]
DAG .... Directed Acyclic Graph (MCD)
DAG .... Division Advisory Group (MCD)
DAG .... Division Artillery Group [*Military*] (AABC)
D Ag .... Doctor of Agriculture
DAG .... Doll Artisan Guild (EA)
DAG .... Dystrophin-Associated Glycoprotein [*Biochemistry*]
DAGAS .... Dangerous Goods Advisory Service [*British*] (NITA)
DAGC .... Delayed Automatic Gain Control (MSA)
DAGC .... Digital Automatic Gain Control (MCD)
Dag Cr L .... Dagge's Criminal Law [*A publication*] (DLA)
Dag Ct M .... D'Aguilar on Courts-Martial [*A publication*] (DLA)
DAGDL .... Diacetyl(glucarodilactone) [*Biochemistry*]
DAGMAR ..... Defining Advertising Goals for Measured Advertising Results [*Title of book written by Russell Colley and published by the Association of National Advertisers*]
DAGMAR ..... Drift and Ground-Speed Measuring Airborne RADAR
DAGN .... Diaminoguanidine Nitrate [*Organic chemistry*]
DAGNA .... Association of the German Nobility in North America (EA)
DAGNA .... Deutsche Adels-Gesellschaft in Nord Amerika [*Association of the German Nobility in North America*] (EA)
DAGO .... District Aviation Gas Office [*Navy*]
DAGR .... Dictionnaire des Antiquites Grecques et Romaines d'Appres les Textes et les Monuments [*A publication*] (BJA)
D Agr .... Doctor of Agriculture
DAGR .... Green [*Daniel*] Co. [*NASDAQ symbol*] (NQ)
DAGRA .... Deputy Adjutant-General, Royal Artillery [*British military*] (DMA)
D Agr E ...... Doctor of Agricultural Engineering
D Agr Eng .... Doctor of Agricultural Engineering
D Agric .... Doctor of Agriculture
D Agr S .... Doctor of Agricultural Science
D Agr Sc ...... Doctor of Agricultural Science
DAgSc .... Doctor of Agricultural Science (ADA)
DAGT .... Direct Antiglobulin Test [*Clinical chemistry*] (MAE)
DAGUERR .... Daguerrotype [*Photography*] (ROG)
D'Agu Oeuv .. D'Aguesseau. Oeuvres [*A publication*] (DLA)
DAH .... Air Algerie [*Algeria*] [*ICAO designator*] (FAAC)
DAH .... Dahomey (ROG)
Dah .... Dahomy (VRA)
DAH .... Dathina [*Yemen*] [*Airport symbol*] (AD)
DAH .... Dictionary of American History [*A publication*]
DAH .... Dictionary of American Hymnology [*Database*] [*Hymn Society of America, Inc.*] [*Information service or system*] (IID)
DAH .... Disordered Action of the Heart [*Medicine*]
DAH .... Domestic Annual Harvest
DAH .... National Society Women Descendants of the Ancient and Honorable Artillery Company (EA)
DAHAC .... Department of the Army Historical Advisory Committee [*Washington, DC*] (EGAO)
DAHC .... Dutch-American Historical Commission (EA)
DAHE .... Department of Allied Health Evaluation [*AMA*]
DAHEA .... Department of Allied Health Education and Accreditation [*AMA*] (DAVI)
DAHL .... Dahlen [*Saxony*] (ROG)
Dahl Mar Int L.. Dahlgren's Maritime International Law [*A publication*] (DLA)
DAHM .... Division of Allied Health Manpower [*Bureau of Health Professions Education and Manpower Training, HEW*]
DAHP .... Division of Associated Health Professions [*DHHS*]
DAHQ .... Di-tert-amylhydroquinone [*Organic chemistry*]
DAHRS .... Doppler Attitude Heading Reference System (MCD)
DAHRT .... Dual-Axis Radiographic Hydrotest [*For evaluating nuclear weapons*]
DAHRT .... Dual-Axis Radiographic Hydrotest Facility [*For simulation of nuclear weapons*]
DAHS .... Danish American Heritage Society (EA)
DAI .... Daimler-Benz AG [*NYSE symbol*] (SPSG)
DAI .... Daimler-Benz Aktieng ADS [*NYSE symbol*] (TTSB)
DAI .... Dairen [*Republic of China*] [*Seismograph station code, US Geological Survey Closed*] (SEIS)
DAI .... Dan' Air [*Benin*] [*FAA designator*] (FAAC)
DAI .... Death Attitude Indicator
DAI .... Death from Accidental Injuries [*Military*]
DAI .... Demonstrators Association of Illinois (EA)
DAI .... Detroit Adjustment Inventory [*Psychology*]
DAI .... Development Alternatives, Inc.
DAI .... Diamidinoindole [*Organic chemistry*]
DAI .... Diffues Axonal Injury [*Neurology*] (DAVI)
DAI .... Digital Applications International [*Commercial firm*] [*British*] (NITA)
D-AI .... Diplomate, American Board of Allergy and Immunology (DHSM)
DAI .... Direct Access Information
DAI .... Director of Aeronautical Inspection [*British*]
DAI .... Director of Army Instruction
DAI .... Discrete Activity Indicator [*NASA*] (KSC)
DAI .... Disease Activity Index [*Medicine*]
DAI .... Distributed Artificial Intelligence [*Computer science*]
DAI .... Dittberner Associates, Inc. [*Bethesda, MD*] [*Information service or system Telecommunications*] (TSSD)
DAI .... Doubly Auto-Ionizing (PDAA)
DAI .... Drift Angle Indicator [*Navigation*]
DAI .... Dynamic Application Integration [*Computer science*] (PCM)

DAIA .... American Institute of Architects, Washington, DC [*Library symbol Library of Congress*] (LCLS)
D/AIA .... DoD [*Department of Defense*]/Army Information Architecture (RDA)
DAIB .... (Dimethylamino)isoborneol [*Organic chemistry*]
DAIC .... United States Industrial College of the Armed Forces [*Fort McNair*], Washington, DC [*Library symbol Library of Congress*] (LCLS)
DAICS .... Data Inventory Control System (MCD)
DAID .... Delayed Action Incendiary Device
DAID .... United States Agency for International Development, Office of Population, Washington, DC [*Library symbol Library of Congress*] (LCLS)
DAIDS .... Division of the AIDS [*Acquired Immune Deficiency Syndrome*] [*National Institutes of Health*] (EGAO)
DAIE .... Dai'ei, Inc. [*NASDAQ symbol*] (NQ)
Dai Ei .... Dai'ei, Inc. [*Associated Press*] (SAG)
DAIEY .... Daiei Inc.ADS [*NASDAQ symbol*] (TTSB)
DAIG .... Daig Corp. [*NASDAQ symbol*] (SAG)
DAIG .... Department of the Army Inspector General
DAIG .... Deputy Assistant Inspector General (GFGA)
DaigCp .... Daig Corp. [*Associated Press*] (SAG)
Daily Leg News (PA)... Daily Legal News (Pennsylvania) [*A publication*] (DLA)
Daily Leg (PA)... Daily Legal Record [*Pennsylvania*] [*A publication*] (DLA)
Daily L N ..... Daily Legal News [*Pennsylvania*] [*A publication*] (DLA)
Daily L R ..... Daily Legal Record [*Pennsylvania*] [*A publication*] (DLA)
Daily Trans... New York Daily Transcript, Old and New Series [*A publication*] (DLA)
Daily Transc... New York Daily Transcript [*A publication*] (DLA)
DAIM .... Data Analysis Information Memorandum
DAIM .... Dynamic Active Index Matrix (BUR)
DAIMC .... Defense Advanced Inventory Management Course [*Army*]
DAIMS .... Department of the Army Integrated Materiel Support
DAIO .... Data I/O [*NASDAQ symbol*] (TTSB)
DAIO .... Data I/O Corp. [*NASDAQ symbol*] (NQ)
DAIO .... Divisional Artillery Intelligence Officer [*British*]
DAIP .... Defense Acquisition Improvement Program [*DoD*]
DAIP .... Deliquency Account Inventory Profile [*IRS*]
DAIP .... Department of the Army Intelligence Plan
DAIP .... Diallyl Isophthalate [*Organic chemistry*]
DAIPR .... Department of the Army in Process Review (MCD)
DAIR .... Debit Accounting Information Retrieval
DAIR .... Direct Altitude and Identification Readout [*Aviation*] (MCD)
DAIR .... Driver Aid, Information, and Routing [*Computer science*]
DAIR .... Dynamic Allocation Interface Routine [*Computer science*] (BUR)
DAIR .... Dynamic Assignation Interface Routine [*Electronics*] (ECII)
DAIRE .... Direct Altitude and Identification Readout Equipment [*Aviation*] (FAAC)
Dai Reg .... New York Daily Register [*A publication*] (DLA)
DAIRO .... Department of the Army International Rationalization Office (RDA)
DAIRS .... Dial Access Information Retrieval System [*Shippensburg State College, Shippensburg, PA*]
Dairy .... Dairy Mart Convenience Stores, Inc. [*Associated Press*] (SAG)
DAIS .... Data Acquisition and Information System [*Telecommunications*] (NITA)
DAIS .... Data Avionics Information System (MCD)
DAIS .... Dealer Association Information Service [*Association of Free Newspapers*] [*British*]
DAIS .... Defense Automatic Integrated Switching [*Army communications system*]
DAIS .... Digital Avionics Information System [*Air Force*]
DAIS .... Digital Avionics Integration System
DAIS .... Direct Access Intelligence System (PDAA)
DAIS .... Directorate of Aeronautical Inspection Services [*British*]
DAIS .... Directory of Automated Information Systems (MCD)
DAIS .... Distributed Ada Interface Set (SSD)
DAIS .... Doctor of Arts in Information Science (GAGS)
DAISEY .... Development Assessment and Instruction for Success in the Early Years [*Education*] (AIE)
DAISY .... Daily Summary (MCD)
DAISY .... Dairy Information System [*British*] (NITA)
DAISY .... Data Acquisition and Interpretation System
DAISY .... Data Analysis of the Interpreter System (IAA)
DAISY .... Decision Aiding Information System
DAISY .... Double-Precision Automatic Interpretive System
Daisytk .... Daisytek International Corp. [*Associated Press*] (SAG)
DAITA .... Database of Antiviral and Immunomodulatory Therapies for AIDS [*Acquired Immune Deficiency Syndrome*]
DAITDM .... Department of the Army Integrated Technical Document Manual (MCD)
DAIU .... Digital-to-Analog Interface Unit [*Computer science*]
DAIV .... Data Area Initializer and Verifier [*Telecommunications*] (TEL)
DAJ .... Direct Air [*British ICAO designator*] (FAAC)
DAJAG .... Deputy Assistant Judge Advocate General [*Legal term*] (DLA)
DAJS .... Distributed Area Jamming System [*Air Force*]
DAK .... Dakair [*France ICAO designator*] (FAAC)
DAK .... Dakar [*Senegal*] [*Seismograph station code, US Geological Survey Closed*] (SEIS)
dak .... Dakota [*MARC language code Library of Congress*] (LCCP)
Dak .... Dakota (ODBW)
Dak .... Dakota Territory Reports [*A publication*] (DLA)
DAK .... Decision Acknowledge (BUR)
DAK .... Deny All Knowledge [*Telecommunications*] (TEL)
DAK .... Deutsches Afrika Korps [*World War II*]
DAK .... Fayetteville, AR [*Location identifier FAA*] (FAAL)
Daka .... Daka International, Inc. [*Associated Press*] (SAG)
Dakota .... Dakota Reports [*A publication*] (DLA)
Dakotah .... Dakotah, Inc. [*Associated Press*] (SAG)
DakotaM .... Dakota Mining Corp. [*Associated Press*] (SAG)
DAKT .... Daktronics, Inc. [*NASDAQ symbol*] (SAG)
Daktron .... Daktronics, Inc. [*Associated Press*] (SAG)
Dal .... Benloe and Dalison's English Common Pleas Reports [*A publication*] (DLA)
DAL .... Dalhousie University Library [*UTLAS symbol*]
Dal .... Dalison's English Common Pleas Reports [*A publication*] (DLA)
DAL .... Dallas [*Texas*] [*Seismograph station code, US Geological Survey*] (SEIS)
DAL .... Dallas [*Texas*] Love Field [*Airport symbol*]
Dal .... Dallas' Pennsylvania Reports [*A publication*] (DLA)
Dal .... Dallas' United States Reports [*A publication*] (DLA)
Dal .... Dalrymple. Scotch Court of Session Cases [*A publication*] (DLA)
Dal .... Daly's New York Common Pleas Reports [*A publication*] (DLA)
DAL .... Dash Lake Resources [*Vancouver Stock Exchange symbol*]
DAL .... Data Accession List (NASA)
DAL .... Data Access Language [*Apple, Inc.*] (PCM)
DAL .... Data Access Line
DAL .... Data Acquisition Language [*Computer science*] (CSR)
DAL .... Data Acquisition List (MCD)
DAL .... Data Address Line
DAL .... Data-Aided Loop [*NASA*]
DAL .... Data Analysis Laboratory [*Temple University*] [*Research center*]
DAL .... Defect Action Level [*FDA*]
DAL .... Defence Analysts Ltd. [*British*]
DAL .... Defender Australia Ltd.
DAL .... Dekaliter [*Unit of measure*]
DAL .... Delta Air Lines [*NYSE symbol*] (TTSB)
DAL .... Delta Air Lines, Inc. [*NYSE symbol Air carrier designation symbol*] (SPSG)
DAL .... Design Analysis Language [*Programming language*]
DAL .... Design Approval Layout (SAA)
DAL .... Destructive Action Link (ECON)
DAL .... Digital Access Line (IAA)
DAL .... Digital Analysis Library [*Computer Design*] [*Software package*] (NCC)
DAL .... Direct Address Line [*Telecommunications*] (NITA)
DAL .... Directional Arm Lock
DAL .... Distribution Authority List (MCD)
DAL .... Dog at Large [*Humorous notation put on letters that cannot be delivered*] [*British postmen's slang*]
DAL .... Downed Aircraft Locator [*Military*] (PDAA)
DAL .... Drawing Assembly List (MCD)
DAL .... Drug Analysis Laboratory (DAVI)
DAL .... United States Army Library, Pentagon Building, Arlington, VA [*Library symbol Library of Congress*] (LCLS)
DALA .... (D-Ala^2)-Met-enkephalinamide [*Analgesic peptide*]
DALA .... Delta-Aminolevulinic Acid [*Biochemistry*]
D Alaska ...... United States District Court for the District of Alaska (DLA)
DALATS .... Data Logging and Transmission System (MCD)
DALB .... Dictionary of American Literary Biography [*A publication*]
DALC .... Danquah. Akan Laws and Customs [*Ghana*] [*A publication*] (DLA)
DALC .... Deployment Area Location Code [*Army*] (AABC)
DALC .... Divided Access Line Circuit
DALC .... Dubuque Area Library Consortium [*Library network*]
DALC .... Dynamic Asynchronous Logic Circuit
Dal Coop ..... Dallas' Report of Cooper's Opinion on the Sentence of a Foreign Court of Admiralty [*A publication*] (DLA)
DALCOS .... Digital Advanced Lead-Computing Optical Signature (MCD)
Dal C P .... Dalison's English Common Pleas Reports [*A publication*] (DLA)
DALDO .... Disposite d'Aide a la Designation d'Objectif [*Target Designation Aid System*] [*French*]
DALE .... Dale [*Commonly used*] (OPSA)
Dale .... Dale's Judgments [*1868-71*] [*England*] [*A publication*] (DLA)
Dale .... Dale's Reports [*2-4 Oklahoma*] [*A publication*] (DLA)
DALE .... Developmental Assessment of Life Experiences [*Test*]
DALE .... Drug Abuse Law Enforcement [*Department of Justice*]
Dale Cl HB... Dale's Clergyman's Legal Handbook [*A publication*] (DLA)
Daleco .... Daleco Resources Corp. [*Associated Press*] (SAG)
Dale Ecc ...... Dale's Ecclesiastical Reports [*England*] [*A publication*] (DLA)
Dale Eccl ..... Dale's Ecclesiastical Reports [*England*] [*A publication*] (DLA)
Dale Leg Rit... Dale's Legal Ritual [*Ecclesiastical Reports*] [*1868-71 England*] [*A publication*] (DLA)
Dale Par Ch... Dale's Law of the Parish Church [*5th ed.*] [*1975*] [*A publication*] (DLA)
DALGT .... Daylight (FAAC)
DALI .... Digitally Archived Library Images
Dal in Keil... Dalison's Reports in Keilway [*1533-64*] [*England*] [*A publication*] (DLA)
Dalison .... Dalison's English Common Pleas Reports [*Bound with Benloe*] [*123 English Reprint*] [*A publication*] (DLA)
DALK .... Data Link Controller [*Computer science*] (NITA)
Dall .... Dallam's Texas Supreme Court Decisions [*A publication*] (DLA)
Dall .... Dallas' Laws of Pennsylvania [*A publication*] (DLA)
Dall .... Dallas' Pennsylvania and United States Reports [*A publication*] (DLA)
Dall .... Dallas' Styles of Writs [*Scotland*] [*A publication*] (DLA)
Dallam Dig (Tex)... Dallam's Digest [*Texas*] [*A publication*] (DLA)
Dallas .... Dallas' Pennsylvania and United States Reports [*A publication*] (DLA)
Dall Coop .... Dallas' Report of Cooper's Opinion on the Sentence of a Foreign Court of Admiralty [*A publication*] (DLA)
Dall Dec ...... Dallam's Texas Decisions, from Dallam's Digest [*A publication*] (DLA)
Dall Dig .... Dallam's Digest and Opinions [*Texas*] [*A publication*] (DLA)
DallG .... Dallas Gold & Silver Exchange, Inc. [*Associated Press*] (SAG)
Dall in Keil... Dallison [*or Dalison*] in Keilway's Reports, English King's Bench [*A publication*] (DLA)

Dall L .... Dallas' Laws of Pennsylvania [*A publication*] (DLA)
Dall Laws .... Dallas' Laws of Pennsylvania [*A publication*] (DLA)
Dall (PA) ..... Dallas' Pennsylvania Reports [*4*] [*A publication*] (DLA)
Dall S C ...... Dallas' United States Supreme Court Reports [*A publication*] (DLA)
Dall Sty ...... Dallas' Styles of Writs [*Scotland*] [*A publication*] (DLA)
Dall Tex..... Dallas' Supreme Court Decisions [*Texas*] [*A publication*] (DLA)
DALM.......... Dysplasia-Associated Lesion or Mass [*Medicine*]
DALO .... Defense Attache Liaison Officer (AFM)
DALO .... Disconnect at Lift-Off [*NASA*] (KSC)
DALPrC........ Delta Air Lines Cv Dep Pfd [*NYSE symbol*] (TTSB)
Dal R .... Dalhousie Review [*A publication*] (BRI)
Dalr .... Dalrymple. Decisions of the Scotch Court of Session [*A publication*] (DLA)
Dalr .... (Dalrymple of) Stair's Decisions of the Scotch Court of Session [*A publication*] (DLA)
DALR .... Dry Adiabatic Lapse Rate [*Heat transfer*]
Dalr Dec...... Dalrymple. Decisions of the Scotch Court of Session [*A publication*] (DLA)
Dalr Ent ...... Dalrymple on the Polity of Entails [*A publication*] (DLA)
Dalr Feud Prop... Dalrymple on Feudal Property [*A publication*] (DLA)
Dalr Feu Pr... Dalrymple on Feudal Property [*A publication*] (DLA)
DALRLV ...... Department of the Army Logistics Readiness Liaison Visits (AABC)
DALRO .... Dramatic, Artistic, and Literary Rights Organization (DGA)
Dalr Ten ...... Dalrymple on Tenures [*A publication*] (DLA)
DALRTF ...... Department of the Army Long-Range Technological Forecast
DAL S .... Dal Segno [*Repeat from the Sign*] [*Music*]
DALS .... Data Acquisition Logging System
DALS .... Digital Approach and Landing System [*Aviation*] (IAA)
DALS .... Director [*or Directorate*] of Army Legal Services [*British*]
DALS .... Distress Alerting and Locating System
DALS .... Dive Auditory Location System (MCD)
DALS .... Double-Acting Limit Switch
DALSCOM.... DoD [*Department of Defense*] ATE Language Standardization Committee
DAL SEG...... Dal Segno [*Repeat from the Sign*] [*Music*]
DalSem........ Dallas Semiconductor [*Associated Press*] (SAG)
Dal Sh .... Dalton on Sheriffs [*A publication*] (DLA)
DALSO .... Department of Army Logistics Support Officer
Dalt............. Dalton's Justices of the Peace [*Many eds.*] [*1618-1746*] [*A publication*] (DLA)
DALT .... Department of the Army Liaison Team (AABC)
DALT .... Drop Altitude
DALTA .... Dramatic and Lyric Theatres Association [*British*] (BI)
Dalt Just..... Dalton's Justices of the Peace [*Many eds.*] [*1618-1746*] [*A publication*] (DLA)
DALTS .... Data Link Test Set
Dalt Sh .... Dalton's Sheriff [*A publication*] (DLA)
DALVP .... Delay Enroute Authorized as Ordinary Leave Provided It Does Not Interfere with Reporting Date [*Military*]
Daly............ Daly's New York Common Pleas Reports [*A publication*] (DLA)
DALY .... Disability-Adjusted Life Year [*Public health*] (ECON)
Daly May Ct... Daly's Hand-Book on Practice in the Lord Mayor's Court [*A publication*] (DLA)
Daly's R ...... Daly's New York Common Pleas Reports [*A publication*] (DLA)
Daly Sur ...... Daly's Nature of Surrogate's Courts [*New York*] [*A publication*] (DLA)
DAM............ Dam [*Commonly used*] (OPSA)
DAM............ Damage (AABC)
DAM............ Damascus [*Syria*] [*Airport symbol*] (OAG)
DAM............ Damocles [*Greek courtier, c.300BC*] (ROG)
DAM............ Data Addressed Memory [*Computer science*]
DAM............ Data Association Message
DAM............ Database Access Manager [*Computer science*] (BTTJ)
DAM............ Decametric Radio Emission
DAM............ Decontaminating Agent, Multipurpose [*Military*] (DOMA)
DAM............ Defended Area Model [*Army*] (AABC)
DAM............ Definition, Analysis, and Mechanization
DAM............ Degraded Amyloid [*Medicine*]
DAM............ Dekameter
DAM............ Descriptor Attribute Matrix
DAM............ Detection and Mapping [*Package*] [*NASA*]
DAM............ Diacetyl Monooxine [*Organic chemistry*]
DAM............ Diacetylmorphine [*Pharmacology*]
DAM............ Diagnostic Abilities in Math [*Educational test*]
DAM............ Diagnostic Acceptability Measure (PDAA)
DAM............ Diallyl Maleate [*Organic chemistry*]
DAM............ Diallylmelamine [*Organic chemistry*]
DAM............ Dictionary of Abbreviations in Medicine [*A publication*]
DAM............ Digital-to-Analog Multiplier (IEEE)
DAM............ Direct Access Memory [*Computer science*] (BUR)
DAM............ Direct Access Method [*Sperry UNIVAC*] [*Computer science*]
DAM............ Direction des Applications Militaries [*France*]
DAM............ Director Attack Mine [*Air Force*] (MCD)
DAM............ Director of Air Material [*Navy British*]
DAM............ Display Aided Maintenance [*Army*]
DAM............ DNA [*Deoxyribonucleic Acid*] Adenine Methylation [*Biochemistry*]
DAM............ Double Aluminized Mylar (NASA)
DAM............ Downrange Antimissile Program [*Army*]
DAM............ Draft Amendment (OSI)
DAM............ Driver Amplifier Module (NASA)
DAM............ Dual Absorption Model [*Nuclear physics*] (OA)
DAM............ United States Army Topographic Command, Washington, DC [*Library symbol Library of Congress*] (LCLS)
DAM² .... Square Dekameter
DAM³ .... Cubic Dekameter
DAM³/D....... Cubic Decameters per Day

DAMA .... American Medical Association, Washington Office, Washington, DC [*Library symbol Library of Congress*] (LCLS)
DAMA .... Data Administration Management Association International (EA)
DAMA .... Demand Assignment Multiple Access [*Telecommunications*]
DAMA .... Department of the Army Materiel Annex (AABC)
DAMA .... Diode Array Multichannel Analyzer [*Instrumentation*]
Damark....... Damark International, Inc. [*Associated Press*] (SAG)
Damas .... Damasus [*Flourished, 13th century*] [*Authority cited in pre-1607 legal work*] (DSA)
DAMC .... Dimethylaminomethylcoumarin [*Organic chemistry*]
DAMCONTRACEN... Damage Control Training Center [*Military*] (DNAB)
DAMCS .... Display Aided Maintenance Control System [*Army*]
DAMDA .... Dairy Appliance Manufacturers' and Distributors' Association Ltd. (BI)
DAMDF .... Durham Air Monitoring Demonstration Facility [*Environmental Protection Agency*] (GFGA)
DAME.......... Dark Avenger Mutation Engine [*A polymorphic encryption engine*] (PCM)
DAME.......... Data Acquisition and Monitoring Equipment [*Electronics*]
DAME..... Defense Against Methods of Entry [*Military intelligence*]
DAME..... Determination of Air-Launched Missile Environment (MCD)
DAME..... Dictionary of American English [*A publication*]
DAME..... Digital Automatic Measuring Equipment (MHDB)
DAME..... Distance and Angularity Measurement Equipment [*Navy*] (MCD)
DAME..... Distance Azimuth Measuring Equipment [*Navy*] (MCD)
DAME..... Division Airspace Management Element [*Military*] (INF)
DAMEC .... Drug and Alcohol Multicultural Education Centre [*Medicine Australia*]
DameMr .... Dames & Moore, Inc. [*Associated Press*] (SAG)
Damen........ Damen Financial Corp. [*Associated Press*] (SAG)
DAMF.......... Director of Air Ministry Factories [*British World War II*]
DAMG .... Damages [*Legal term*] (DLA)
DAM-Geog ... United States Army Topographic Command, Office of Geography, Washington, DC [*Library symbol Library of Congress*] (LCLS)
DAMGO....... Deputy Assistant Master-General of Ordnance [*British*]
DAMH .... United States Army, U.S. Army Center for Military History, Washington, DC [*Library symbol*] [*Library of Congress*] (LCLS)
DAMHB........ Directorate of Ancient Monuments and Historic Buildings [*Department of the Environment*] [*British*] (DI)
DAMI........... Designated Aircraft Maintenance Inspector
DAMID......... Discounting Analysis Model for Investment Decisions (PDAA)
DAM II-EE.... Defended Area Model II Engagement Evaluation [*Army*] (AABC)
DAM II-EP.... Defended Area Model II Engagement Planning [*Army*] (AABC)
DAMIS .... Department of the Army Management Information System (AABC)
DAMIT .... Data Analysis [*Program*] of Massachusetts Institute of Technology
DAmL.......... AMTRAK Library, Washington, DC [*Library symbol Library of Congress*] (LCLS)
DAML .... Directorate, Army MAP [*Military Assistance Program*] Logistics
DAMLG .... Dental Amalgamator
DAMM .... Alger [*Algeria*] [*ICAO location identifier*] (ICLI)
DAMM .... Drinkers Against Mad Mothers (EA)
DAMMO .... Directorate of Ammunition [*Canada*] [*Military*]
DAMMS .... Department of the Army Movements Management System (MCD)
DAMMS-R.... Department of the Army Movements Management System-Redesign (GFGA)
DAMN .... Diaminomaleonitrile [*Organic chemistry*]
DAMN .... Dynamic Analysis of Mechanical Networks (PDAA)
DA MOB C2S... Department of the Army Mobilization Command and Control System (MCD)
DA-MON-YR.. Day-Month-Year (DNAB)
DAMOS .... Data Moving System (PDAA)
DAMOS .... Disposal Area Monitoring System
DAMP .... Dallas Area Media Project [*Library network*]
DAMP .... Databank of Atomic and Molecular Physics [*Queen's University Belfast*] [*British*] (NITA)
dAMP .... Deoxyadenosine Monophosphate [*Biochemistry*]
DAMP .... Department of the Air Member for Personnel [*British*]
DAMP .... Department of the Army Materiel Program
DAMP .... Diacetoxydiphenylmethylpyridine [*Pharmacology*]
DAMP .... Dibutyryl CAMP [*Cyclic Adenosine Monophosphate*] [*Biochemistry*]
DAMP .... Dinitroanilino Amino-Methylpropylamine
DAMP .... Distribution Amplifier (MSA)
DAMP .... Downrange Antimissile Measurement Program [*RADAR*]
Dampier MSS... Dampier's Paper Book, Lincoln's Inn Library [*A publication*] (DLA)
DAMPIP ...... Department of the Army Productivity Improvement Program
DAMPL .... Department of the Army Master Priority List (AABC)
DAMPL .... Department of the Army Material Priority List
DAMPMT .... Department of the Army Military Personnel Management Team (AABC)
DAMPR .... Digital Automatic Multiple Pressure Recorder [*Lewis Research Center*]
DAMPRE...... Drill Attendance Monitoring Procedure and Report [*National Guard*]
DAMPS .... Data Acquisition Multiprogramming System [*IBM Corp.*] [*Computer science*]
DAMP/TVPB... Department of the Army Motion Picture/Television Production Board (AABC)
DAMP/TVPP... Department of the Army Motion Picture/Television Production Program
DAMQAM ..... Dynamically Adaptive Multicarrier Quadrative Amplitude Modulation [*Computer science*]
DAMR .... Director of Aircraft Maintenance and Repair [*Navy British*]
DAMR .... Division of Adult and Management Review [*United Nations*] (ECON)
DAMRC .... Department of the Army Material Readiness Command (MCD)
DAMRIP....... Department of the Army Management Review and Improvement Program (AABC)
DAMR(N) .... Director of Aircraft Maintenance and Repair (Naval) [*British*]
DAMR(W) .... Director of Aircraft Maintenance and Repair (Washington) [*Navy*]

DAMS	Deductive Analysis of Missile Systems (MCD)	
DAMS	Defencively Armed Merchant Ship [*World War I*] [*British*]	
DAMS	Defense Against Missiles Systems	
DAMS	Deputy Assistant Military Secretary [*British*]	
DAMS	Direct Access Management System	
DAMS	Disposal Accounting Management System [*DoD*]	
DAMSO	Department of the Air Member for Supply and Organization [*British*]	
DAMSO	Deputy of the Air Member for Supply and Organization [*British*]	
DAMSU	Digital Automanual Switching Unit [*Telecommunications*] (TEL)	
DAMT	Department of the Air Member for Training [*British*]	
DAMUS	Data Management and User Services System [*National Oceanic and Atmospheric Administration*] (GFGA)	
DAMUSC	Direct Access, Multi-User, Synchrocyclotron Computer (PDAA)	
DAMUT	Ducted-Air Medium Underground Transmission (PDAA)	
DAMV	Dasheen Mosaic Virus [*Plant pathology*]	
DAMV	Destruction of Aircraft or Motor Vehicles	
DAMV	Double-Air Movement Valve	
DAMWO	Department of the Army Modification Work Order	
DAN	Army and Navy Club, Washington, DC [*Library symbol Library of Congress*] (LCLS)	
DAN	Dana College, C. A. Dana-Life Library, Blair, NE [*OCLC symbol*] (OCLC)	
DAN	Danair AS [*Denmark ICAO designator*] (FAAC)	
Dan	Dana's Reports [*31-39 Kentucky*] [*A publication*] (DLA)	
DAN	Dane [*Ontario*] [*Seismograph station code, US Geological Survey Closed*] (SEIS)	
Dan	Daniel [*Old Testament book*]	
DAN	Daniel Indus [*NYSE symbol*] (TTSB)	
DAN	Daniel Industries, Inc. [*NYSE symbol*] (SPSG)	
Dan	Daniell's Exchequer and Equity Reports [*159 English Reprint*] [*1817-23*] [*A publication*] (DLA)	
Dan	Daniels' Compendium Compensation Cases [*England*] [*A publication*] (DLA)	
DAN	Danish	
dan	Danish [*MARC language code Library of Congress*] (LCCP)	
Dan	Danner's Reports [*42 Alabama*] [*A publication*] (DLA)	
DAN	Danube [*River in central Europe*]	
D'An	D'Anvers' General Abridgment of the Common Law [*A publication*] (DLA)	
DAN	Danville [*Virginia*] [*Airport symbol*] (OAG)	
DAN	Danville, VA [*Location identifier FAA*] (FAAL)	
DAN	Deacon and Nike [*Research rocket*]	
DAN	Defense Activity North Carolina (MCD)	
daN	Dekanewton [*Unit of force*]	
DAN	Deployment Adjustment Notification [*Military*] (CINC)	
DAN	Deposit Account Number (NG)	
D-AN	Diplomate, American Board of Anesthesiology (DHSM)	
DA-N	Directional Antenna Nighttime Only [*Broadcasting term*]	
DAN	Disciplinary Action Notice (DNAB)	
DAN	Distributed Audio Network [*Sound Apprentice*]	
DAN	Divers Alert Network [*Marine science*] (OSRA)	
DAN	Diver's Alert Network	
DAN	Divers Alert Network (USDC)	
DAN	Document Accession Number (IAA)	
DAN	Dual Area Nozzle (KSC)	
DAN	Duration Mines Ltd. [*Toronto Stock Exchange symbol Vancouver Stock Exchange symbol*]	
Dana	Dana's Kentucky Supreme Court Reports [*1833-40*] [*A publication*] (DLA)	
DANA	Delaware Association of Nonprofit Agencies (SRA)	
DANA	Deutsche Allgemeine Nachrichten Agentur [*German general news agency, sponsored by US newspapermen as a successor to the NAZI-controlled DNB*] [*Post-World War II*]	
DANA	Drug and Alcohol Nursing Association (EA)	
DANA	Drug-Induced Antinuclear Antibodies [*Immunology*] (DAVI)	
Dan Abr	Dane's Abridgment of American Law [*A publication*] (DLA)	
DanaCp	Dana Corp. [*Associated Press*] (SAG)	
DANAGRO	Danish Agricultural Organizations (ECON)	
Dana (KY)	Dana's Reports [*31-39 Kentucky*] [*A publication*] (DLA)	
Dan & L	Danson and Lloyd's English Mercantile Cases [*A publication*] (DLA)	
Dan & Ll	Danson and Lloyd's English Mercantile Cases [*A publication*] (DLA)	
Dan & Lld	Danson and Lloyd's English Mercantile Cases [*A publication*] (DLA)	
Dan Att	Daniel's Law of Attachment [*A publication*] (DLA)	
Dana Wh	Dana's Edition of Wheaton's International Law [*A publication*] (DLA)	
DANB	Danbury [*England*]	
DANB	Dave & Buster's [*NASDAQ symbol*] (TTSB)	
DANB	Dave & Busters, Inc. [*NASDAQ symbol*] (SAG)	
DANB	Dental Assisting National Board (EA)	
DANC	Decontaminating Agent, Noncorrosive	
DANCA	Dimethylamino(naphthoyl)cyclohexanoic Acid [*Organic chemistry*]	
Dance	Dance Magazine [*A publication*] (BRI)	
Dance RJ	Dance Research Journal [*A publication*] (BRI)	
Dan Ch	Daniell's Chancery Practice [*A publication*] (DLA)	
Dan Ch Pr	Daniell's Chancery Practice [*A publication*] (DLA)	
DANCOM	Danube Commission (BARN)	
DAND	Dandus [*To Be Given*] [*Pharmacy*]	
D & A	Dear and Anderson's Scotch Session Cases [*1829-32*] [*A publication*] (DLA)	
D & A	International Defense and Aid Fund for Southern Africa, US Committee (EA)	
D & B	Deals and Boards [*Business term*] (ROG)	
D & B	Dearsley and Bell's English Crown Cases [*1856-58*] [*A publication*] (DLA)	
D & B	Design-and-Build (ECON)	

D & B	Devereux and Battle's North Carolina Equity Reports [*A publication*] (DLA)	
D & B	Devereux and Battle's North Carolina Law Reports [*A publication*] (DLA)	
D & B	Docking and Berthing (SSD)	
D&B	Dun & Bradstreet (AAGC)	
D & B	Dun & Bradstreet, Inc.	
D & B CC	Dearsley and Bell's English Crown Cases [*1856-58*] [*A publication*] (DLA)	
D & BCS	D & B Computing Services [*Information service or system*] (IID)	
D & B Pr Pr	Dodd and Brook. Probate Practice [*A publication*] (ILCA)	
D & C	David & Charles [*Commercial firm British*]	
D & C	Deacon and Chitty's English Bankruptcy Reports [*1832-35*] [*A publication*] (DLA)	
D & C	Dean and Chapter [*Anglican Church*]	
D & C	Development & Commercial Bank [*Malaysia*]	
D & C	Dilation [*or Dilatation*] and Curettage [*of the uterus*] [*Obstetrics*]	
D & C	Display and Control (KSC)	
D & C	District and County Reports [*Pennsylvania*] [*A publication*] (DLA)	
D & C	Dow and Clark's English House of Lords Cases [*A publication*] (DLA)	
D & C	Drill and Ceremony [*Military*] (ADDR)	
D & C	Drug and Cosmetic Colors	
D & C	Drugs and Cosmetics [*Pharmacology*] (DAVI)	
D & C2d	District and County, Second Series [*A publication*] (DLA)	
D & CB	Debt and Correspondence Branch [*BUPERS*]	
D & CC	Pennsylvania District and County Reports [*A publication*] (DLA)	
D & Ch	Deacon and Chitty's English Bankruptcy Reports [*1832-35*] [*A publication*] (DLA)	
D & Chit	Deacon and Chitty's English Bankruptcy Reports [*1832-35*] [*A publication*] (DLA)	
D & Cl	Dow and Clark's Reports [*A publication*] (DLA)	
D & CM	Dressed and Center Matched [*Lumber*] (DAC)	
D & COH	Daughter and Co-Heiress [*Genealogy*]	
D & CS	Display and Control Subsystem (NASA)	
D & CT	Docking and Crew Transfer [*Aerospace*]	
D & D	Death and Dying [*Medical course*]	
D & D	Decontaminate and Decommission [*Nuclear energy*]	
D&D	Decontamination and Decommissioning (DOGT)	
D & D	Decoration and Design [*Building*] [*New York City*]	
D & D	Degaussing and Deperming [*Navy*]	
D & D	Deposit and Difference [*Tea trade*] (ROG)	
D & D	Design and Development (SSD)	
D & D	Desk and Derrick [*Oil industry*]	
D & D	Detection and Discrimination	
D & D	Devonshire and Dorset Regiment [*British military*] (DMA)	
D & D	Diarrhea and Dehydration [*Gastroenterology*] (DAVI)	
D & D	Direct and Distribution [*Postal Service*]	
D & D	Drunk and Dirty [*Military*]	
D & D	Drunk and Disorderly	
D & D	Dungeons and Dragons [*Game*]	
D & DC	Drunk and Disorderly Conduct	
D & DS	Dictatorships and Double Standards [*Title of an article written by Jeane Kirkpatrick in 1979 that became basis of conservative foreign policy*]	
D & E	Diet and Elimination [*Gastroenterology*] (DAVI)	
D & E	Diet and Excretion [*Gastroenterology*] (DAVI)	
D & E	Dilatation and Evacuation [*Medicine*]	
D & E	Durnford and East's (Term) Reports, English King's Bench [*1785-1800*] [*A publication*] (DLA)	
D & E Cm	D & E Communications [*Associated Press*] (SAG)	
D & F	Determination and Findings	
D & F	Disposition and Findings (AAG)	
D & F	Judgments of Divisional and Full Courts, Gold Coast [*A publication*] (DLA)	
D & F 11-16	Divisional and Full Court Judgments [*1911-1916*] [*A publication*] (DLA)	
D & G	Diprose and Gammon's Reports of Law Affecting Friendly Societies [*1801-97*] [*England*] [*A publication*] (DLA)	
D & G	Doom and Gloom	
D&H	Dangerous and Hazardous [*MARAD*] (TAG)	
D & H	Daughter and Heiress [*Genealogy*]	
D & H	Delaware & Hudson Railway Co. [*Nickname: Delay and Hesitate*]	
D & H	Dressed and Headed [*Lumber*]	
D & HAA	Dock and Harbour Authorities' Association [*British*] (ODBW)	
D & I	Disassembly and Inspection (DNAB)	
D & I	Drawn and Ironed	
D & IC	Dependency and Indemnity Compensation [*Military*] (AFM)	
D & IR	Duluth & Iron Range Railway Co.	
D & J	December and June [*Denotes semiannual payment of interest or dividends in these months*] [*Business term*]	
D & J	De Gex and Jones' English Chancery Reports [*A publication*] (DLA)	
D & JB	De Gex and Jones' English Bankruptcy Reports [*1857-59*] [*A publication*] (DLA)	
D & K Int Rev	Davidge and Kimball's Internal Revenue Laws [*A publication*] (DLA)	
D & K Whl	D & K Wholesale Drug, Inc. [*Associated Press*] (SAG)	
D & L	Distillate plus Loss	
D & L	Dowling and Lowndes' English Bail Court Reports [*A publication*] (DLA)	
D & M	Davison and Merivale's English Queen's Bench Reports [*A publication*] (DLA)	
D & M	Deep and Meaningful	
D & M	Detroit & Mackinac Railway Co.	
D & M	Doctor and Martyr (ROG)	
D & M	Dressed and Matched [*Technical drawings*]	

D & Mer ...... Davison and Merivale's English Queen's Bench Reports [*A publication*] (DLA)

D & MRR ..... Detroit & Mackinac Railway Co.

D & N .... Dekker & Nordemann [*Publisher*]

D & NF .... D & N Financial Corp. [*Associated Press*] (SAG)

D & N Fn ...... D & N Financial Corp. [*Associated Press*] (SAG)

D & O .... Description and Operations (NASA)

D & O .... Description and Operations

D & O .... Directors' and Officers' [*Liability insurance*]

DANDOK ...... Danish Committee for Scientific and Technical Information and Documentation [*Information service or system*] (IID)

D & P .... Damon and Pythias [*Fourth-century BC Greek philosophers renowned for their loyalty to one another*]

D & P .... Deberny and Peignot (DGA)

D & P .... Denison and Pearce's English Crown Cases [*1844-52*] [*A publication*] (DLA)

D & P .... Design and Production

D & P .... Developing and Printing

D & P .... Drain and Purge (NASA)

D & P .... Drunk and Proud

D & PD .... Definition and Preliminary Design (SSD)

D & PS .... Design and Performance Specification (MCD)

D & PS .... Dog and Pony Show

D & R .... Distiller and Rectifier

D & R .... Dowling and Ryland's English King's Bench Reports [*A publication*] (DLA)

D & RG .... Denver & Rio Grande Railroad

D & RGW ..... [*The*] Denver & Rio Grande Western Railroad Co.

D & R Mag Cas... Dowling and Ryland's English Magistrates' Cases [*A publication*] (DLA)

D & RMC ..... Dowling and Ryland's English Magistrates' Cases [*A publication*] (DLA)

D & RNP ..... Dowling and Ryland's English Nisi Prius Cases [*A publication*] (DLA)

D & RNPC ... Dowling and Ryland's English Nisi Prius Cases [*A publication*] (DLA)

D & S .... Dangerous and Suspicious

D & S .... Deane and Swabey's English Ecclesiastical Reports [*A publication*] (DLA)

D & S .... De Gex and Smale's English Chancery Reports [*63-64 English Reprint*] [*1846-52*] [*A publication*] (DLA)

D & S .... Demand and Supply (WDAA)

D & S .... Deployment and Support [*Military*]

D & S .... Dermatology and Syphilology [*Medicine*] (MAE)

D & S .... Display and Storage (MSA)

D & S .... Doctor and Student [*A publication*] (DLA)

D & S .... Documentation and Status (AAG)

D & S .... Dollars & Sense [*Economic Affairs Bureau*] [*A publication*]

D & S .... Dominance and Submission

D & S .... Drewry and Smale's English Chancery Reports [*A publication*] (DLA)

D & SF .... Denver & Santa Fe Railway

D & SL .... Denver & Salt Lake Railroad

D & Sm .... De Gex and Smale's Reports Tempore Knight-Bruce and Parker, Vice-Chancellor's Court [*1846-52*] [*England*] [*A publication*] (DLA)

D & SM .... Dressed and Standard Matched [*Lumber*] (DAC)

D & Sm .... Drewry and Smale's English Chancery Reports [*A publication*] (DLA)

D & SU .... Daughters and Sons United (EA)

D & Sw .... Deane and Swabey's English Ecclesiastical Reports [*A publication*] (DLA)

D & T .... Demonstration and Training

D & T .... Development and Technology

D & TSL ...... [*The*] Detroit & Toledo Shore Line Railroad Co.

D & V .... Diarrhea and Vomiting [*Medicine*]

D & W .... Danville & Western Railroad (IIA)

D & W .... Detection and Warning

D & W .... Drury and Walsh's Irish Chancery Reports [*1837-40*] [*A publication*] (DLA)

D & W .... Drury and Warren's Irish Chancery Reports [*1841-43*] [*A publication*] (DLA)

D & Wal ...... Drury and Walsh's Irish Chancery Reports [*1837-40*] [*A publication*] (DLA)

D & War ...... Drury and Warren's Irish Chancery Reports [*1841-43*] [*A publication*] (DLA)

D & WTF ..... Daily and Weekly till Forbidden [*Advertising*]

D & YE .... Diabetes and Your Eyes [*National Eye Institute*] [*A publication*]

DANE .... Defense Activity for Nontraditional Education Support [*Military*] (MCD)

Dane Abr ..... Dane's Abridgment of American Law [*A publication*] (DLA)

Dane's Abr... Dane's Abridgment of American Law [*A publication*] (DLA)

Dan Exch ..... Daniell's Exchequer and Equity Reports [*159 English Reprint*] [*1817-23*] [*A publication*] (DLA)

Dan Exch (Eng)... Daniell's Exchequer and Equity Reports [*159 English Reprint*] [*1817-23*] [*A publication*] (DLA)

Dan Forms... Daniell. Forms and Precedents in Chancery [*7th ed.*] [*1932*] [*A publication*] (DLA)

DANFS .... Dictionary of American Naval Fighting Ships [*A publication*] (DLA)

DANG .... Dangerous [*FBI standardized term*]

DANG .... Director of the Army National Guard

DANGER ...... Divisionalized Analytical Ground Rule Exception Report

Danher .... Danaher Corp. [*Associated Press*] (SAG)

Dani .... Daniel [*Old Testament book*] (DSA)

DANI .... Department of Agriculture for Northern Ireland [*British*] (IRUK)

DANIDA .... Danish International Development Agency

Daniel .... Daniel Industries, Inc. [*Associated Press*] (SAG)

Daniell Ch Pl & Prac... Daniell's Chancery Pleading and Practice [*A publication*] (DLA)

Daniell Ch Pr... Daniell's Chancery Pleading and Practice [*A publication*] (DLA)

Daniell Ch Prac... Daniell's Chancery Pleading and Practice [*A publication*] (DLA)

Daniel Neg Inst... Daniel's Negotiable Instruments [*A publication*] (DLA)

DANIS .... Datennachweis Informationssystem [*Arbeitsgemeinschaft Sozialwissenschaftlicher Institut*] [*Germany Information service or system Defunct*] (CRD)

DANK .... Danka Business Systems [*NASDAQ symbol*] (SAG)

DANK .... Deutsch-Amerikanischer National-Kongress [*German-American National Congress*] (EA)

Danka .... Danka Business Systems [*Associated Press*] (SAG)

DANKY .... Danka Business Systems ADR [*NASDAQ symbol*] (TTSB)

Danl .... Daniel [*Old Testament book*]

DanlHd .... Danielson Holding Corp. [*Associated Press*] (SAG)

DANMARC... Danish Machine-Readable Catalogue (NITA)

Dan Moll ...... Daniel Moller [*Deceased, 1600*] [*Authority cited in pre-1607 legal work*] (DSA)

Dann .... Danner's Reports [*42 Alabama*] [*A publication*] (DLA)

DANN .... Danninger Medical Technology [*NASDAQ symbol*] (SAG)

DANN .... Danninger Med Tech [*NASDAQ symbol*] (TTSB)

Dann .... Dann's Reports [*1 Arizona*] [*A publication*] (DLA)

Dann .... Dann's Reports [*22 California*] [*2nd ed. 1871*] [*A publication*] (DLA)

Dan Neg Ins... Daniel's Negotiable Instruments [*A publication*] (DLA)

Danner .... Danner's Reports [*42 Alabama*] [*A publication*] (DLA)

Danngr .... Danninger Medical Technology, Inc. [*Associated Press*] (SAG)

DAN-NY ...... Disposal Analysis Network for New York [*U.S. Army Corps of Engineers*]

Dan Ord .... Danish Ordinances [*A publication*] (DLA)

Danquah ...... Cases in Gold Coast Law [*A publication*] (DLA)

DANS .... Danskin, Inc. [*NASDAQ symbol*] (SAG)

DANS .... Dimethylaminonaphthalenesulfonyl Chloride [*Also, DNSC*] [*Fluorescent reagent*]

DANS .... Director of Army Nursing Services [*British military*] (DMA)

Dans & L ...... Danson and Lloyd's English Mercantile Cases [*A publication*] (DLA)

Dans & LL ..... Danson and Lloyd's English Mercantile Cases [*A publication*] (DLA)

DANSE .... Dance Artists' Nationwide Space Emergency [*In association name, DANSE Coalition*] (EA)

DaNSHC ...... Cambridge Military Library, Halifax, NS, Canada [*Library symbol Library of Congress*] (LCLS)

Danskin .... Danskin, Inc. [*Associated Press*] (SAG)

DANSW .... Diabetes Australia - New South Wales [*Medicine Australia*]

Dansyl .... Dimethylaminonaphthalenesulfonyl [*Also, Dns, DNS*] [*Biochemical analysis*]

DANTE .... Delivery of Advanced Network Technology for Europe (ECON)

DANTES .... Defense Activity for Nontraditional Education Support [*Military*]

DANTISC ...... Dantiscum [*Dantzig*] (ROG)

Dan T M .... Daniel. Trade Marks [*1876*] [*A publication*] (DLA)

DANTS .... Day and Night Television System [*Army*] (MCD)

Danv .... D'Anvers' General Abridgment of the Common Law [*A publication*] (DLA)

Danv Abr ..... D'Anvers' General Abridgment of the Common Law [*A publication*] (DLA)

DANY .... Dannemora [*New York*] [*Seismograph station code, US Geological Survey*] (SEIS)

DAO .... Daallo Airlines [*Djibouti*] [*FAA designator*] (FAAC)

DAO .... Data Access Objects [*Microsoft Corp.*] (PCM)

DAO .... Data Automation Officer [*Air Force*]

DAO .... Dayton Area Office [*Energy Research and Development Administration*]

DAO .... Deasphalted Oil [*Petroleum refining*]

DAO .... Defense Attache Office (AFM)

DAO .... Department Administrative Order [*Department of Commerce*] (NOAA)

DAO .... Dial Assist Operator (CET)

DAO .... Diamine Oxidase [*Also, DO*] [*An enzyme*]

DAO .... Disability Adviser's Officer (South Australia) [*Medicine*]

DAO .... District Accounting Office [*or Officer*] [*Navy*]

DAO .... District Aviation Office [*or Officer*] [*Navy*]

DAO .... Division Air Officer

DAO .... Divisional Agricultural Officer [*Ministry of Agriculture, Fisheries, and Food*] [*British*]

DAO .... Division Ammunition Office [*or Officer*] [*Army*]

DAO .... Doctor of Art of Oratory

DAO .... Dorsal Accessory Olive [*Neuroanatomy*]

DAO .... Duly Authorized Officer

DAO .... Fort Huachuca, AZ [*Location identifier FAA*] (FAAL)

DAO & OS ... Defense Aid [*Lend-Lease*] Ordnance and Ordnance Stores [*World War II*]

DAOB .... Daily Average Occupied Beds [*Medicine*]

DAOB .... Tiaret [*Algeria*] [*ICAO location identifier*] (ICLI)

DAOC .... Bechar/Ouakda [*Algeria*] [*ICAO location identifier*] (ICLI)

DAOC .... Deputy Air Officer Commanding [*British military*] (DMA)

DAOC-in-C ... Deputy Air Officer Commanding-in-Chief [*British military*] (DMA)

DAOE .... Bou Sfer [*Algeria*] [*ICAO location identifier*] (ICLI)

DAOF .... Tindouf [*Algeria*] [*ICAO location identifier*] (ICLI)

DAOI .... Ech-Cheliff [*Algeria*] [*ICAO location identifier*] (ICLI)

DAOL .... Oran/Tafaroui [*Algeria*] [*ICAO location identifier*] (ICLI)

DAON .... Tlemcen/Zenata [*Algeria*] [*ICAO location identifier*] (ICLI)

DAOO .... Oran/Es Senia [*Algeria*] [*ICAO location identifier*] (ICLI)

DA-OPRR .... Department of the Army Plan for [*Possession, Control, and*] Operation of Railroads (AABC)

DAOR .... Bechar/Ouakda [*Algeria*] [*ICAO location identifier*] (ICLI)

DAOS .... Sidi Bel Abbes [*Algeria*] [*ICAO location identifier*] (ICLI)

DAOT .... Director of Air Organisation and Training [*British military*] (DMA)

DAOV .... Ghriss [*Algeria*] [*ICAO location identifier*] (ICLI)

DAP .... Aerovias Dap [*Chile*] [*ICAO designator*] (FAAC)

DAP .... Application for Writ of Error Dismissed by Agreement of Parties [*Legal term*] (DLA)

DAP	Data Access Protocol [*Telecommunications*]
DAP	Data Acquisition Package (IAA)
DAP	Data Acquisition Plan (MCD)
DAP	Data Analysis Program
DAP	Data Automation Panel (MCD)
DAP	Data Automation Proposal (AFM)
DAP	Days after Pollination [*Botany*]
DAP	Declines Appointment [NOAA]
DAP	Decontamination Apparatus, Portable
DAP	Defense Acquisition Package [*DoD*]
DAP	Defense Acquisition Program
DAP	Deformation of Aligned Phase (MCD)
DAP	Delayed Alpha Particle
DAP	Democratic Action Party [*Malaysia*] [*Political party*] (PPW)
DAP	Democratic Action Party [*Malta*] [*Political party*] (PPE)
DAP	Department of the Army Pamphlet
DAP	Department of the Army Publication (DOMA)
DAP	Depolarizing After-Potential [*Neurochemistry*]
DAP	Depot Acceptance Procedures
DAP	Derived Attainable Performance [*Industrial engineering*]
DAP	Designated Acquisition Program
DAP	Detail Assembly Panel
DAP	Developmental Articulation Profile [*Speech evaluation test*]
DAP	Diabetes-Associated Peptide [*Biochemistry*]
DAP	Diallyl Phthalate [*Organic chemistry*]
DAP	Diaminopimelic Acid [*Also, DAPA, DPM*] [*An amino acid*]
DAP	Diaminopurine [*Biochemistry*]
DAP	Diaminopyridine [*Organic chemistry*]
DAP	Diammonium Phosphate [*Inorganic chemistry*]
DAP	Diazepam [*Also, D, DZ*] [*A sedative*]
DAP	Diffused Alloy Power
DAP	Digital Assembly Program (MCD)
DAP	Digital Autopilot (MCD)
DAP	Digital Avionics Processor [*Northrop Corp.*]
DAP	Dihydroxyacetone Phosphate [*Also, DHAP*] [*Organic chemistry*]
DAP	Dipeptidyl Aminopeptidase [*An enzyme*]
DAP	Direct Aid Program
DAP	Directed Audit Program (AFM)
DAP	Direct Latex Agglutination Pregnancy [*Test*] [*Medicine*]
DAP	Director Assign Panel (MCD)
DAP	Directorate of Accident Prevention [*RAF*] [*British*]
DAP	Director of Aeroplane Production [*Air Ministry*] [*British World War II*]
DAP	Director of Air Personnel [*Air Force British*]
DAP	Director of Ammunition Production [*Ministry of Supply*] [*British World War II*]
DAP	Director of Army Programs (AABC)
DAP	Director of Army Psychiatry [*British*]
DAP	Directory Access Protocol [*Telecommunications*] (OSI)
DAP	Discount Auto Parts [*NYSE symbol*] (SPSG)
DAP	Display Adjust Panel (MCD)
DAP	Distant Aiming Point
DAP	Distributed Analysis Program (MCD)
DAP	Distributed Array Processor [*Sperry UNIVAC*] [*Telecommunications*]
DAP	Division of Air Pollution [*Public Health Service*] [*Obsolete*]
DAP	Do All Possible
DAP	Documents Against Payment [*Banking*] (ADA)
DAP	Dodecylammonium Propionate [*Organic chemistry*]
DAP	Domestic Action Program [*Army*] (INF)
DAP	Domestic Annual Processing
DAP	Double-Amplitude Peak (DEN)
DAP	Double Antiparallel [*Molecular biology*]
D-A-P	Draw-a-Person [*Psychology*]
DAP	Dynamic Assertion Processor [*Computer science*]
DAP	Dystrophin-Associated Protein [*Biochemistry*]
DAPA	Diaminopimelic Acid [*Also, DAP, DPM*] [*An amino acid*]
DAPA	Drug and Alcohol Abuse Program Advisor [*Navy*] (NVT)
DAPAC	Danger Areas in the Pacific
DA PAM	Department of the Army Pamphlet
DAP & E	Diploma in Applied Parasitology and Entomology [*British*]
DAPATF	Department of the Army Property Accountability Task Force (MCD)
DAPB	Diallylpentobarbital [*Sedative*]
DAPC	Diarachidoylphosphatidylcholine [*Biochemistry*]
DAPCA	Development and Procurement Costs of Aircraft (MCD)
DAPCA	Development and Production Costs for Aircraft (SAA)
DAPD	Descend at Pilot's Discretion [*Aviation*] (FAAC)
DAPD	Directorate of Aircraft Production Development [*British*] (DEN)
DAPE	Developed Armament Probable Error (SAA)
DAPEP	Department of the Army Panel on Environmental Physiology
DAPF	Data Analysis and Processing Facility
DAPFS	Direct-Ascent Powered-Flight Simulation [*NASA*]
DAPG	Deutsch-Amerikanische Petroleum Gesellschaft [*German-American Petroleum Society*]
DAPG	Drug and Allied Products Guild [*Later, NAPM*]
DAPGIR	Defense Advisory Panel on Government Industry Relations [*DoD*]
DAPh	American Pharmaceutical Association, Washington, DC [*Library symbol Library of Congress*] (LCLS)
DAPHNE	Dido and Pluto Handmaiden for Nuclear Experiments [*Nuclear reactor at Harwell, England*]
DAPI	American Petroleum Institute, Washington, DC [*Library symbol Library of Congress*] (LCLS)
DAP I	Diahydrogalactitol, Adriamycin, Cisplatin [*Antineoplastic drug regimen*] (DAVI)
DAPI	Diamidinophenylindole [*A dye*] [*Organic chemistry*]
DAPIA	Design Approval Primary Inspection Agency [*Department of Housing and Urban Development*] (GFGA)

DAP-II	Dianhydrogalactitol, Adriamycin, Platinol [*Cisplatin*] [*Antineoplastic drug regimen*]
DAPL	Directory of Australian Public Libraries [*Australia A publication*]
DAPM	Deputy Assistant Provost-Marshall [*British*]
DAPM	Diaminodiphenylmethane [*Organic chemistry*]
DAPMC	Defense Advanced Procurement Management Course [*Army*]
DAP/MIS	Deficiency Abatement Program/Management Information System [*Navy*]
DAPN	Dauphin Deposit [*NASDAQ symbol*] (TTSB)
DAPN	Dauphin Deposit Corp. [*NASDAQ symbol*] (NQ)
DAPN	Directional Antenna Phasing Network
DAPO	Deep Attack Programs Office [*Army*]
DAPO	Digital Advance Production Order [*Telecommunications*] (TEL)
DAPP	Daily Ambient Photophase [*Biochronometry*]
DAPP	Data Acquisition and Processing Program [*Later, DMSP*] [*Air Force*]
DAPP	Defense Acquisition Pilot Program [*Army*] (RDA)
DAPP	Department of Army Productivity (Improvement) Program
DAPP	Design Aid for Post-Processors [*IBM Corp.*]
DAPP	Development Aid from People to People (EAIO)
DAPPER	Distribution Analysis for Power Planning, Evaluation, and Reporting [*Computer science*]
DAPPL	Department of the Army Programming Priority List
DAppSc	Doctor of Applied Science (ADA)
DAPR	Department of the Army Program Report
DAPR	Department of the Army Program Review (RDA)
DAPR	Digital Automatic Pattern Recognition (IEEE)
DAPRE	Daily Adjustable Progressive Resistance Exercise
DAPRU	Drug Abuse Prevention Resource Unit [*National Institute on Drug Abuse*] [*Databank*]
DAPS	Data Acquisition and Processing System
DAPS	Data Processing Automatic Publication Service
DAPS	Direct Access Performance Software (IAA)
DAPS	Direct Access Programming System [*Computer science*]
DAPS	Director of Army Postal Services [*British*]
DAPS	Distributed Application Processing System
DAPS	Double Absorption Photofragment Spectroscopy
DAPS	Downed Airman Power Source [*Navy*]
DAPSONE	Diaminodiphenyl Sulfone [*Also, DADPS, DDS*] [*Pharmacology*]
DAPSRB	Department of the Army Physical Security Review Board (MCD)
DAPST	Denver Auditory Phoneme Sequencing Test [*Speech and language therapy*] (DAVI)
Dapt	Daptazole (MAE)
DAPT	Diamino(diethoxyphosphinyl)triazine [*Organic chemistry*]
DAPT	Diaminophenylthiazole [*Pharmacology*]
DAPT	Direct Agglutination Pregnancy Test [*Clinical chemistry*]
DAPT	Draw-A-Person Test (MEDA)
DAPTRA	Drug Abuse Prevention, Treatment, and Rehabilitation Act [*1972*]
DAPU	Data Acquisition and Processing Unit [*Viking orbiter system*] [*NASA*]
D-APV	D-Amino Phosphonovaleric Acid
DAQ	Data Acquisition
DAQ	Develop and Qualify
DAQ	Diabetes Association of Queensland [*Medicine Australia*]
DAQC	Data Acquisition Center (KSC)
DAQMG	Deputy Assistant Quartermaster General
DAR	Daily Activity Report [*Military*]
DAR	Damage Assessment Routines (MDG)
DAR	Damned Average Raiser [*A diligent student*] [*Slang*]
DAR	Danish Army [*ICAO designator*] (FAAC)
DAR	Dar Es Salaam [*Tanzania*] [*Airport symbol*] (OAG)
DAR	Darien Library [*UTLAS symbol*]
DAR	Darwin [*Australia Seismograph station code, US Geological Survey Closed*] (SEIS)
DAR	Data Access Register [*Computer science*] (MDG)
DAR	Data Acquisition Recorder
DAR	Data-Aided Receiver [*NASA*]
DAR	Data Article Requirements (AAG)
DAR	Data Automation Requirement
DAR	Day-After Recall [*Advertising*]
DAR	Debrett Ancestry Research [*British*]
DAR	Defense Acquisition RADAR
DAR	Defense Acquisition Regulation [*or Requirement*]
DAR	Defense Aid Report (IIA)
DAR	Deficiency Action Report (NATG)
DAR	Delaware Association of Realtors (SRA)
DAR	Delayed Allergic Response [*Medicine*] (BARN)
DAR	Delayed Automatic Reclose (IAA)
DAR	Delayed Auto-Reclose (PDAA)
DAR	Delinquent Accounts and Returns [*IRS*]
DAR	Departure Approval Request [*Aviation*] (DNAB)
DAR	Depletion-Approximation Replacement (MCD)
DAR	Deployment Adjustment Request [*Military*] (CINC)
DAR	Design Action Request (MCD)
DAR	Design Assessment Report [*Nuclear energy*] (NRCH)
DAR	Destination Access Register [*Computer science*] (NITA)
DAR	Detroit Arsenal [*Michigan*] [*Army*] (NATG)
DAR	Developed Area Ratio [*Propellers*] (DNAB)
DAR	Development-Accelerator-Releasing Couplers [*Photography*]
DAR	Deviation Approval Request [*NASA*] (KSC)
DAR	Dial-a-Ride [*TRB*] (TAG)
DAR	Differential Absorption Ratio (IAA)
DAR	Differentiation with Asymmetrical Reinforcement
DAR-II	Digital Angle Recorder
DAR	Digital Autopilot Requirements (NASA)
DAR	Directorate of Armament Requirements [*RAF*] [*British*]
DAR	Directorate of Army Research (GRD)

DAR .... Directorate of Atomic Research [*Canada*] (BARN)
DAR .... Director of Army Requirements [*British*]
DAR .... Distributed Array RADAR (MCD)
DAr .... District of Columbia Archives, Washington, DC [*Library symbol*] [*Library of Congress*] (LCLS)
DAR .... Drawing Analysis Record (MCD)
DAR .... Driver Augmented Readout [*Computer science*]
DAR .... Drone Anti-RADAR [*German military - World War II*]
DAR .... Drug-Appropriate Responding [*Biochemistry*]
DARA .... Deputy Associate Regional Administrator
DARA .... Deutsche Arbeitsgemeinschaft fuer Rechen-Anlagen [*German Working Committee for Computing Machines*]
DARAC .... Damped Aerodynamic Righting Attitude Control
DARACS .... Damped Aerodynamic Righting Attitude Control System
DARAS .... Direction and Range Acquisition System (MCD)
DARB .... Distressed Airman Recovery Beacon (IAA)
Darb & B Lim... Darby and Bosanquet's Statutes of Limitations [*2nd ed.*] [*1893*] [*A publication*] (DLA)
DARC .... American National Red Cross, Washington, DC [*Library symbol Library of Congress*] (LCLS)
DARC .... Data Acquisition and Reduction Center (IAA)
DARC .... Data Acquisition and Reports Control [*Army*] (AABC)
DARC .... Data Radio Channel
DARC .... Defense Acquisition Regulatory Council (MCD)
DARC .... Device for Automatic Remote Data Collection [*Marine science*] (OSRA)
DARC .... Device for Automatic Remote Data Collection (USDC)
DARC .... Direct-Access RADAR Channel [*System*] [*Aviation*]
DARC .... Documentation and Automatization of Researches for Correlations [*For molecular structure*] [*Chemical physics*]
DARCEE .... Demonstration and Research Center for Early Education [*George Peabody College, Nashville*]
D Arch .... Diploma in Architecture [*British*]
D Arch .... Doctor of Architecture
D Arch Des... Doctor of Architectural Design
D Arch E.... Doctor of Architectural Engineering
D Arch Eng... Doctor of Architectural Engineering
DARCIMC ..... Development and Readiness Command Installation Management Course [*Military*]
DARCOM ...... Army Materiel Development and Readiness Command [*Now AMC*] (AAGC)
DARCOM ...... Development and Readiness Command [*Formerly, AMC*] [*See also MDRC Alexandria, VA*] [*Army*]
DARCOMALMSA... Development and Readiness Command Automated Logistics Management Systems Agency [*Army*] (AABC)
DARCOM-C... Development and Readiness Command Circular [*Army*]
DARCOMFASC... Development and Readiness Command Facilities and Services Center [*Army*] (AABC)
DARCOMFSA... Development and Readiness Command Field Safety Agency [*Army*] (AABC)
DARCOMI & SA... Development and Readiness Command Installations and Service Agency [*Army*] (AABC)
DARCOMLDC... Development and Readiness Command Logistics Data Center [*Army*] (AABC)
DARCOMLSSA... Development and Readiness Command Logistics Systems Support Agency [*Army*] (AABC)
DARCOMPI... Development and Readiness Command Procurement Instruction [*Army*] (MCD)
DAR Council... Defense Acquisition Regulatory Council [*Also DARC*] (AAGC)
DARD .... Data Acquisition Requirements Document (KSC)
DARD .... Depressives Anonymous: Recovery from Depression (EA)
DARDC .... Device for Automatic Remote Data Collection [*National Weather Service*]
Darden .... Darden Restaurants, Inc. [*Associated Press*] (SAG)
DARDO .... Direct Access to Remote Data Bases Overseas [*Italy Telecommunications*]
DARE .... Damage Assessment Reduction and Evaluation (SAA)
DARE .... Data Automatic Reduction Equipment (CET)
DARE .... Data Automation Research and Experimentation (CET)
DARE .... Data Retrieval Area (MCD)
DARE .... Decision Aids for Resource Expenditure (MCD)
DARE .... Delay Asymptotic Relative Efficiency (IAA)
DARE .... Demand and Resource Evaluation (ODBW)
DARE .... Denver AWIPS [*Advanced Weather Interactive Processing System*] Risk Reduction and Requirements Evaluation [*Workstation*] [*Marine science*] (OSRA)
DARE .... Denver AWIPS Risk Reduction and Requirements Evaluation [*Workstation*] (USDC)
DARE .... Diagnostic Analysis of Reading Errors [*Educational test*]
DARE .... Diagnostic and Repair Expert [*Computer-aided tank maintenance program*] [*Army*] (RDA)
DARE .... Dictionary of American Regional English [*A publication*]
DARE .... Dictionary of American Regional English Project [*University of Wisconsin - Madison*] [*Research center*] (RCD)
DARE .... Differential Analyzer Replacement [*Programming language*] [*1967*] (CSR)
DARE .... Digital Avionics Research System (MCD)
DARE .... Director Action for Rehabilitation and Employment [*Ex-offenders*] (OICC)
DARE .... Disabled Adults Residential Establishments [*Australian Capital Territory*]
DARE .... Document Abstract Retrieval Equipment (IEEE)
DARE .... Documentation Automated Retrieval Equipment [*System*] [*Army*]
DARE .... Doppler and Range Evaluation
DARE .... Doppler Automatic Reduction Equipment (MCD)

DARE .... DOVAP [*Doppler Velocity and Position*] Automatic Reduction Equipment (AAG)
DARE .... Drug Abuse Resistance Education
DARE .... Drug Addiction Rehabilitation Enterprise (EA)
DARES .... Data Analysis and Reduction System
DARF .... Defense Atomic Research Facility (MCD)
DARFAX .... Department of the Army Secure Facsimile (AABC)
DARFD .... Depressives Anonymous: Recovery from Depression (EA)
DARFIS .... Department of Army Financial Information System
DARG .... Discourse Analysis Research Group [*University of Calgary*] [*Research center*] (RCD)
DArI .... Arab Information Center, Arab League Office, Washington, DC [*Library symbol*] [*Library of Congress*] (LCLS)
DARI .... Center for Applied Research in the Apostolate [*CARA*], African Research andInformation Center, Washington, DC [*Library symbol Library of Congress*] (LCLS)
DARI .... Digital Angular Readout by LASER Interferometry (MCD)
DARIAS .... Digico Automated Radio-Immunoassay Analytical System (PDAA)
DARIS .... Detroit Art Registration Information System [*Detroit Institute of Arts*] [*Information service or system*] (IID)
D Ariz .... United States District Court for the District of Arizona (DLA)
DARK .... Discrimination Analysis Technique Adapted and Refined at Kwajalein [*Army*] (AABC)
D Ark .... Doctor of Archaeology
DARL .... Darling [*Correspondence*] (DSUE)
DARL .... Darling International [*NASDAQ symbol*] (TTSB)
DARL .... Darling International, Inc. [*NASDAQ symbol*] (SAG)
DARL .... Douglas Advanced Research Laboratories [*Obsolete*] (KSC)
DARLI .... Digital Angular Readout by LASER Interferometry (MCD)
Darling .... Darling International, Inc. [*Associated Press*] (SAG)
Darl Pr Ct Sess... Darling. Practice of the Scotch Court of Session [*A publication*] (DLA)
DARMA .... Defense against Rocket and Mortar Attack Fires [*Military*] (VNW)
DARMA .... Discrete Autoregressive-Moving Average Model [*Statistics*]
DArmD .... Directorate of Armament Development [*Ministry of Aircraft Production*] [*British World War II*]
DARME .... Director, Armament Engineering [*Canada*] [*Military*]
DARMS .... Developmental Army Mobilization System (DOMA)
DARMS .... Digital Alternate Representation of Musical Symbols
DARMS .... Drifting Automatic Radiometeorological Station
DARNG .... Director of the Army National Guard
DARO .... Days after Receipt of Order (MCD)
DARO .... Defense ADPE [*Automatic Data Processing Equipment*] Reutilization Office
DARO .... Defense Airborne Reconnaissance Office
DARP .... Drug Abuse Reporting Program (EDAC)
DARPA .... Defense Advanced Research Projects Agency [*Arlington, VA*] [*DoD*]
DARPP .... Dopamine- and Cyclic AMP-Regulated Phosphoprotein [*Biochemistry*]
DARR .... Delft Atmospheric Research RADAR (MCD)
DARR .... Department of the Army Regional Representative (AABC)
DARR .... Drawing and Assembly Release Record (AAG)
DARRIS .... Department of the Army Requisitioning, Receipt, and Issue System
DARS .... Daily Aerial Reconnaissance and Surveillance [*Military*] (DOMA)
DARS .... Data Accumulating and Reporting Sheet
DARS .... Data Acquisition and Reduction System
DARS .... Data Acquisition and Reporting System [*Data processing*]
DARS .... Data Acquisition Recording System
DARS .... Decommutation and Readout System [*Computer science*]
DARS .... Defense Acquisition Regulatory System [*DoD*] (RDA)
DARS .... Department of the Army Relocation Sites (AABC)
DARS .... Differential-Absorption Remote Sensing [*LASER*]
DARS .... Digital Adaptive Recording System
DARS .... Digital Attitude and Rate System (IEEE)
DARS .... Digital Attitude Reference System
DARS .... Digital Audio Radio Service
D Ar Sc .... Doctor of Arts and Sciences
DARSS .... Diode Array Rapid Scan Spectrometer
DART .... Daily Automatic Rescheduling Technique [*Computer science*]
DART .... Dallas Area Rapid Transit [*FHWA*] (TAG)
DART .... Damage Analysis in Rapid Time (MCD)
DART .... Dart Drug Corp. [*NASDAQ symbol*] (SAG)
Dart .... Dart on Vendors and Purchasers [*A publication*] (DLA)
DART .... Data Analysis Real-Time [*Southwest Research Institute*]
DART .... Data Analysis Recording Tape
DART .... Data Analysis Reduction Tape (SAA)
DART .... Data Reduction Translator
DART .... Decentralized Advanced Replenishment Technique (AFIT)
DART .... Decomposed Ammonia Radioisotope Thruster [*Aerospace*]
DART .... Delay and Retransmit
DART .... Demand Actuated Road Transit
DART .... Deployable Automatic Relay Terminal [*Air Force*]
DART .... Depot Automatic Rescheduling Technique
DART .... Depression: Awareness, Recognition, and Treatment [*National Institute of Mental Health program*]
DART .... Design Automation Routing Tool (IAA)
DART .... Detection, Action, and Response Technique
DART .... Development and Reproductive Toxicology [*Database*] [*Environmental Protection Agency*]
DART .... Development of Advanced Rate Techniques
DART .... Diagnostic-Assistance Reference Tool
DART .... Dial-a-Ride Transportation
DART .... Digital Automatic Readout Tracker [*Computer science*] (IAA)
DART .... Diode Automatic Reliability Tester (IAA)
DART .... Direct Advisory of Recorded Transactions (AABC)

DART	Direct Airline Reservations Ticketing
DART	Directional Automatic Realignment of Trajectory (NG)
DART	Director and Response Tester (KSC)
DART	Directorate of Ranges and Targets [Army]
DART	Director of Army Research and Technology [Washington, DC] (GRD)
DART	Directory of American Research and Technology [R. R. Bowker Co.] [Information service or system A publication]
DART	Disappearing Automatic Retaliatory Target [Military] (RDA)
DART	Disaster Assistance Recovery Teams [Military]
DART	Discovery Activities Related to Science
DART	Distant Area Reduced Toll [Telecommunications] (TSSD)
DART	Dive and Release Trajectory (MCD)
DART	Downed Aircraft Recovery Team [Army] (DOMA)
DART	Drill Attendance Reporting Test [National Guard]
DART	Dual Axis Rate Transducer [A gyroscope]
DART	Dublin Area Rapid Transit [Ireland]
DART	Dynamic Acoustic Response Trigger (IEEE)
DART	Dynamically Adaptive Receiver Transmitter (CAAL)
DART	Dynamic Analysis and Replanning Tool
DART	Dynamic Automatic RADAR Tester (SAA)
DART	Dynamic Simulation of Auto and Passenger Rail Transports
DARTA	Dart Group CI'A' [NASDAQ symbol] (TTSB)
Dart Col Ca...	Dartmouth College Case [A publication] (DLA)
Dart Coll......	Dartmouth College [Hanover, NH]
DartGp	Dart Drug Corp. [Associated Press] (SAG)
DARTM	Dartmouth [Municipal borough in England]
DARTM	Defeat Armor Road Target Mine
Dartmouth C...	Dartmouth College (GAGS)
DARTS	Data Analysis, Recovery, and Training Systems (MCD)
DARTS	Deployable Acoustic Readiness Training System (MCD)
DARTS	Design Aids for Real-Time Systems [Computer science] (MCD)
DARTS	Digital Antijam Radio Teletype System (MCD)
DARTS	Digital Automated RADAR Tracking System (MCD)
DARTS	Digital Azimuth Range Tracking System
DARTS	Drug and Alcohol Rehabilitation Testing System [Navy] (NVT)
DARTS	Dutch-Auction-Rate Transferable Securities [Investment term]
DARTS	Dynamic Analytic Replanning Tools [DoD]
Dart Vend	Dart on Vendors and Purchasers [A publication] (DLA)
Darw Cr L	Darwin's Criminal Law [A publication] (DLA)
DARYL	Data Analysing Robot Youth Lifeform [From the movie entitled "D.A.R.Y.L."]
Das	Common Law Reports, Volume 3 [England] [A publication] (DLA)
DAS	Daisetta, TX [Location identifier FAA] (FAAL)
DAS	Dante Alighieri Society [Australia]
Das	Dasent's Bankruptcy and Insolvency Reports [1853-55] [England] [A publication] (DLA)
DAS	Dassen Gold Resources Ltd. [Vancouver Stock Exchange symbol]
DAS	Data Access Security
DAS	Data Accountability System
DAS	Data Acquisition Station
DAS	Data Acquisition System
DAS	Data Administration Section (MCD)
DAS	Data Administrative Services
DAS	Data Amplification Sheet (KSC)
DAS	Data Analysis Software [Telecommunications] (TEL)
DAS	Data Analysis Station (NASA)
DAS	Data Analysis System [Computer science] (NITA)
DAS	Data Automation System [or Subsystem] [NASA]
DAS	Data Auxiliary Set [Telecommunications] (TEL)
DAS	Datatron Assembly System [Burroughs Corp.]
DAS	Date Arrived Station [Military] (AFM)
DAS	Days At Sea [Marine science] (OSRA)
DAS	Days at Sea (USDC)
DAS	Death Anxiety Scale
DAS	Decision Assist System (SAA)
DAS	Defense Against Self-Defense [Suggested program against falling missiles]
DAS	Defense Analysis Seminar [Military]
DAS	Defense Attache System [Department of State]
DAS	Defense Audit Service [Abolished 1982, functions transferred to Office of the Inspector General (DoD)]
DAS	Deficiency Analysis Summary
DAS	Delayed Anovulatory Syndrome [Medicine] (DMAA)
DAS	Delivered Alongside Ship
DAS	Demand-Assignment Signaling (MCD)
DAS	Dendrite Arm Spacing (RDA)
DAS	Department of Aboriginal Sites [Australia]
DAS	Design Analysis System (MCD)
DAS	Detector Angular Subtense [Instrumentation]
DAS	Development Advisory Service (ODBW)
DAS	Dextroamphetamine Sulfate [CNS stimulant]
DAS	Diacetoxyscirpenol [Fungal toxin]
DAS	Dial Assistance Switchboard (CET)
DAS	Dialdehyde Starch [Wet-strength agent]
DAS	Diallyl Sulfide
DAS	Diaminostilbenedisulfonic Acid [Also, DASD, DASDS] [Organic chemistry]
DAS	Dictionary of American Slang [A publication]
DAS	Differential-Absorption and Scattering [Remote sensing technique]
DAS	Digital Address System (MCD)
DAS	Digital Aircraft Simulator (MCD)
DAS	Digital Altimeter Scanner
DAS	Digital Analog Simulator [Computer science]
DAS	Digital Analog System [Computer science] (IAA)
DAS	Digital Attenuator System

DAS	Digital Avionics System (MCD)
DAS	Dimer-Adatom-Stacking [Fault model]
DAS	Dimethoxyanthracene Sulfonate [Organic chemistry]
DAS	Dipole Antenna System
DAS	Direct Access Store [Computer science] (IAA)
DAS	Direct Acting Steam (MSA)
DAS	Direct Air Support [Military] (AFM)
DAS	Direct Automotive Support
DAS	Directorate for Advanced Systems [Army] (RDA)
DAS	Directorate of Aerospace Studies [Kirtland Air Force Base, NM]
DAS	Director of Administrative Services [US Military Government, Germany]
DAS	Director of Armament Supplies [British World War II]
DAS	Director of the Army Staff
DAS	Directory Assistance System [Telecommunications] (TEL)
DAS	Disk Auxiliary Storage [Computer science] (ECII)
DAS	Distance Aids School (SAA)
DAS	Disturbance Analysis System [Nuclear energy] (NRCH)
DAS	Division of Applied Sciences [Harvard University] [Research center] (RCD)
DAS	Division of Assistance to States [Department of Education]
DAS	Division of Atmospheric Surveillance [Environmental Protection Agency]
DAS	Doctor of Applied Science
D As	Doctor of Astronomy
DAS	Document Analysis Sheet (MCD)
DAS	Documentation Accountability Sheet (MCD)
DAS	Documentation Aid System (IAA)
DAS	Dollar Air Services Ltd. [British ICAO designator] (FAAC)
DA's	Domestic Afflictions [Menstruation] [Slang] (DSUE)
DAS	Dramatic Authors' Society [British]
DAS	Dual Attached Station [Computer science] (TNIG)
DAS	Dutch Australian Society
DAS	Dyadic Adjustment Scale [Psychology] (EDAC)
DAS	Dynamic Angle Spinning [Spectroscopy]
DAS	Dynamiclly Alterable System (PDAA)
DAS	Dynamo Alert System (AAG)
DAS	United States Department of Commerce, National Oceanic and Atmospheric Administration, Atmospheric Sciences Library, Silver Spring, MD [Library symbol Library of Congress] (LCLS)
DAS3	Decentralize ADP [Automatic Data Processing] Service Support System
DAS3	Decentralized Automated Service Support System [Army] (RDA)
DASA	Data Acquisition Signal Analysis [Computer science] (NITA)
DASA	Defense Atomic Support Agency [Later, DNA]
DASA-A	Delaware Association of School Administrators (SRA)
DASA	Department of the Army Security Agency (MCD)
DASA	Deutsche Aerospace (ECON)
DASA	Distal Articular Set Angle [Orthopedics] (DAVI)
DASA	Domestic Appliance Service Association [British] (DBA)
DASA	Dual Aerospace Servo Amplifier (NASA)
DASA	Dumping at Sea Act [1974]
DASA-DC	Defense Atomic Support Agency Data Center
DASADD	Defense Atomic Support Agency Data Division (SAA)
DAS & E	Defense Aid [Lend-Lease] Services and Expenses [World War II]
DASA(P)	Deputy Assistant Secretary, Army (Procurement) (AAGC)
DASAT	Data Selector and Tagger (MUGU)
DASA-TP.....	Defense Atomic Support Agency Technical Publications
DASC	DA System Coordination (MCD)
DASC	Defence Aid Supply Committee [Later, ISC] [World War II]
DASC	Defense Automotive Supply Center
DASC	Department of the Army System Coordinator (RDA)
DASC	Direct Air Support Center [Later, ASOC]
DASC	District Air Support Center (MCD)
DASc...........	Doctor in Agricultural Sciences
DA Sc	Doctor of Applied Science
DASC	Double-Aperture Speckle Camera
DASC-A.......	Direct Air Support Center-Airborne (DOMA)
DASCAR......	Data Acquisition System for Crash Avoidance Research [NHTSA] (TAG)
DASCH........	Disk Automation Storage Control Hardware [Macintosh computer]
DAS/CM	Directory Assistance Systems / Computer and Microfilm [Bell System]
DASCO........	Digital-to-Analog Synchro Converter (DNAB)
DASCO........	Discriminant Analysis with Shrunken Coveriances [Mathematics]
DASCOTAR...	Data Acquisition System, Correlation Tracking and Ranging [Air Force]
DASCS	Direct Air Support Center Squadron [Air Force]
DASD	Data Acquisition Support Document (KSC)
DASD	Department of the Army Shipping Document
DASD	Deputy Assistant Secretary of Defense
DASD	Diaminostilbenedisulfonic Acid [Also, DAS, DASDS] [Organic chemistry]
DASD	Direct Access Storage Device [Pronounced "daz-dee"] [Computer science]
DASD	Direct Access Storage Drive [Computer science] (NITA)
DASD	Director, Anti-Submarine Division [British military] (DMA)
DASD	Director of Army Staff Duties [British] (RDA)
DASD(CP)...	Deputy Assistant Secretary of Defense (Civilian Personnel) (DNAB)
DASD(EO)...	Deputy Assistant Secretary of Defense (Equal Opportunity) (DNAB)
DASDI.........	Direct Access Storage Device Initialization Program [Computer science] (IAA)
DASDL........	Data and Structure Definition Language [Computer science] (BUR)
DASD(MP)...	Deputy Assistant Secretary of Defense (Military Personnel Policy) (DNAB)

DASDR........ Direct Access Storage Dump Restore
DASDS........ Diaminostilbenedisulfonic Acid [*Also, DAS, DASD*] [*Organic chemistry*]
DASE.......... Data Adaptive Signal Estimator (MCD)
DASE.......... Defense Against Sound Equipment [*Military intelligence*]
DASE.......... Denver Articulation Screening Exam [*Speech evaluation test*]
DASE.......... Digital Automatic Stabilization Equipment (MCD)
DASE.......... Diploma in Advanced Studies in Education [*British*] (DI)
DASE.......... Directory Access Service Element [*Telecommunications*] (OSI)
DASEB........ Department of the Army Suitability Evaluation Board (AABC)
DASEC........ Digital Automatic Stabilization Equipment Computer (MCD)
DASEL........ Data Analysis and Statistical Experimental Language [*Computer science*] (MHDI)
Dasent........ Acts of the Privy Council (Dasent) [*England*] [*A publication*] (DLA)
Dasent........ Dasent's Bankruptcy and Insolvency Reports [*1853-55*] [*England*] [*A publication*] (DLA)
DASES........ Digital Automatic Stabilization Equipment System [*or Subsystem*] (MCD)
DASET........ Deputy Assistant Secretary for Employment and Training [*Department of Labor*]
DASF.......... Defense Aid [*Lend-Lease*] Special Fund [*World War II*]
DASF.......... Direct Access Storage Facility [*Computer science*]
DASF.......... Direct Air Support Flight [*Military*] (AFM)
DASG.......... Developmental Assessment of Spanish Grammar (EDAC)
DASH.......... Database Acquisition for Student Health
DASH.......... Destroyer, Antisubmarine Helicopter
DASH.......... Developmental Assessment for the Severely Handicapped [*Test*]
DASH.......... Differential Air-Speed Hold (PDAA)
DASH.......... Digital Audio Stationary Head [*Recording*] (NTCM)
DASH.......... Direct Access Storage Handler [*Telecommunications*] (TEL)
DASH.......... Display and Sight Helmet System (MCD)
DASH.......... Distress Alarm for Severely Handicapped [*British*]
DASH.......... Downtown Area Short Hops [*Battery-powered bus service in Long Beach, California*]
DASH.......... Drishat Shalom [*Best Regards*] [*Hebrew*]
DASH.......... Drone Antisubmarine Helicopter [*Air Force, Navy*]
DASH.......... Dual Access Storage Handling
DASH.......... Dynamic ALGOL [*Algorithmic Language*] String Handling [*Computer science*] (IAA)
DASHO........ Designed Agency Safety and Health Official (ERG)
DASI.......... Developing Anti-Sexist Innovations (AIE)
DASI.......... Developmental Activities Screening Inventory [*Psychology*]
DASI.......... Diffusion of Arsenic in Silicon (PDAA)
DASI.......... Digital Altimeter Setting Indicator [*FAA*] (TAG)
DASI.......... Digital Altimeter Setting Indicator [*Aviation*] (FAAC)
DASIAC....... DoD [*Department of Defense*] Nuclear Information and Analysis Center [*Defense Atomic Support Agency Information and Analysis Center*] [*Kaman Tempo*] [*Acronym is based on former name,*] [*Information service or system*] (IID)
DASL.......... Data Access System Language
DASL.......... Department of the Army Strategic Logistics [*Study*]
DASL.......... Digital Adapter for Subscriber Loops [*Telecommunications*] (NITA)
DASL.......... Directory of Special Libraries in Australia [*A publication*]
DASM.......... Direct Access Storage Media [*Computer science*]
DASM.......... Director of Advanced Systems Management
DA/SM........ Director of Antisubmarine Material [*British*]
DAS/M........ Directory Assistance System/Microfilm [*Bell System*]
DASO.......... Demonstration and Shakedown Operations [*Military*] (AFM)
DASO.......... Department of the Army Special Order
DASO.......... District Armament Supply Officer [*British*]
DASOC........ Disturbance Accommodation Standard-Deviation Optimal Controller [*Space telescope*] [*NASA*]
DASOP........ Demonstration and Shakedown Operation Piggyback [*Kit*] [*Military*]
DASP.......... Defense Acquisition Scholarship Program [*DoD*] (RDA)
DASP.......... Director of Advanced Systems Planning
DASP.......... Discrete Analog Signal Processing
DASP.......... Double Antibody Solid-Phase [*Clinical chemistry*] (AAMN)
DASP.......... Double Antibody Solid-Phase Radioimmunoassay [*Clinical chemistry*]
DASP.......... Double Arm Magnetic Spectrometer
DASPA........ Defense Attache System Property Accounting (MCD)
DASPAC....... Defense Audit Service, Pacific (DNAB)
DASPAN....... Data Spanning (IAA)
DASPO........ Department of the Army Special Photographic Office (AABC)
DASPS........ Department of the Army Standard Port System
DASPS-E...... Department of the Army Standard Port System - Enhanced (MCD)
DASPS-E-SDG... Department of the Army Standard Port System - Enhanced - System Development Group (MCD)
DAS-PSG..... Department of Administrative Services - Purchasing and Sales Group [*Australia*]
DASq.......... Direct Air Support Squadron [*Military*] (AFM)
DASR.......... Data Acquisition Statistical Recorder
DASR.......... Defense Analysis Special Report (MCD)
DASR.......... Directorate of Aviation Safety Regulation [*Australia*]
DASS.......... Data Access Security System (IAA)
DASS.......... Defined Antigen Substrate Sphere [*Medicine*] (PDAA)
DASS.......... Demand-Assignment Signaling and Switching Unit
DASS.......... Diesel Air Start System (IEEE)
DASS.......... Digital Access Signaling System [*Telecommunications*] (OSI)
DASS.......... Digital Access Signalling System
DASS.......... Digital Access Signalling System (NITA)
DASS.......... Digital Acoustic Sensor Simulation (MCD)
DASS.......... Digital Acoustic Simulation System (MCD)
DASS.......... Digital-Analog Servo System [*Computer science*] (SAA)
DASS.......... Direct Access Signalling System
DASS.......... Direct Air Support Squadron [*Air Force*]
DASS.......... Disturbance Analysis and Surveillance System [*NRC*]
D As S........ Doctor of Association Science
DASSC........ Dante Alighieri Society of Southern California [*Defunct*] (EA)
D As Sc....... Doctor of Association Science
DASSC........ Double-Aperture Speckle Shearing Camera (PDAA)
Dass Dig...... Dassler's Kansas Digest [*A publication*] (DLA)
Dass Ed....... Dassler's Edition, Kansas Reports [*A publication*] (DLA)
Dass Ed (Kan)... Dassler's Edition, Kansas Reports [*A publication*] (DLA)
DASSH........ Dean of Arts, Social Sciences and Humanities
DASSO........ Data Systems Support Office (MCD)
DASSO........ Department of the Army Systems Staff Officer (AABC)
DASSq........ Direct Air Support Squadron [*Air Force*]
DASSS........ Demand-Assignment Signaling and Switching Subsystem [*Telecommunications*] (IAA)
Dass Stat..... Dassler's Kansas Statutes [*A publication*] (DLA)
DAST.......... Denver Audiometric Screening Test
DAST.......... Design, Architecture, Software, and Testing (MCD)
DAST.......... Detective - Agents - Science Fiction - Thriller [*Acronym used as title of magazine*]
DAST.......... Device Assignment Table
DAST.......... Diethylaminosulfur Trifluoride [*Organic chemistry*]
DAST.......... Diploma of Advanced Studies in Teaching (PGP)
DAST.......... Direct Air Support Team [*Military*] (CINC)
DAST.......... Directorate of Advanced Systems Technology
DAST.......... Division for Advanced Systems Technology (SAA)
DAST.......... Drones for Aerodynamic and Structural Testing (MCD)
DASTARD.... Destroyer Antisubmarine Transportable Array Detector
DASTL........ Defense Atomic Support Agency Technical Letters
DASTM........ Double-Acting Steam
DASTY........ Dassault Systemes
DASV.......... Differential Anodic Stripping Voltammetry [*Electronics*]
DASVA........ Defense Attache System Vehicle Accounting (MCD)
DA/SW........ Director of Antisubmarine Warfare [*British*]
DASWE........ Director, Admiralty Surface Weapons Establishment [*Navy British*]
DASWZ........ Data Switch Wrrt [*NASDAQ symbol*] (TTSB)
DASY.......... Data Analysis System
DAT............ Dangerous Articles Tariff
DAT............ Data Abstract Tape [*Computer science*]
DAT............ Data Acceptance Tests
DAT............ Data Acquisition Test [*Later, DST*]
DAT............ Data File [*Computer science*]
DAT............ Data General Corp., Westboro, MA [*OCLC symbol*] (OCLC)
DAT............ Dative
DAT............ Datum (MSA)
DAT............ Datumone Petroleum [*Vancouver Stock Exchange symbol*]
DAT............ Daunomycin, ara-C [*Cytarabine*], Thioguanine [*Antineoplastic drug regimen*]
DAT............ Days after Treatment [*Agriculture*]
DAT............ Decorative Arts Trust (EA)
DAT............ Defense Attache
DAT............ Delayed Action Tablet [*Pharmacy*]
DAT............ Delta Air Transport [*Belgium ICAO designator*] (FAAC)
DAT............ Dementia Alzheimer Type [*Medicine*]
DAT............ Den, Aoyama, and Takemake [*Early investors in automobile manufacturer Nissan*] [*Initials used in creating automobile name DATSUN*] [*Japan*]
DAT............ Dental Admission Test [*Education*]
DAT............ Dental Aptitude Test [*Education*] (AEE)
DAT............ Dental Aptitude Test (GAGS)
DAT............ Deoxyaconitine [*Biochemistry*]
DAT............ Department Approved Training (OICC)
DAT............ Dependents Assistance Team [*Military*] (DNAB)
DAT............ Deployment Action Team [*Army*] (DOMA)
DAT............ Design Acceptance [*or Approval*] Test
DAT............ Design Approval Test (DNAB)
DAT............ Designation Acquisition Track (IAA)
DAT............ Desktop Analysis Tool [*A publication*]
DAT............ Detail Assembly Template
DAT............ Development Acceptance Test [*Army*]
DAT............ Development Assist Test
DAT............ Device Assignment Table (MCD)
DAT............ Diaminotropolone [*Biochemistry*]
DAT............ Diet as Tolerated [*Medicine*]
DAT............ Differential Agglutination Titer [*Hematology*]
DAT............ Differential Antibody Titer [*Immunology*] (DAVI)
DAT............ Differential Aptitude Test [*Psychology*]
DAT............ Diffused-Alloy Transistor [*Electronics*] (ECII)
DAT............ Digital Acoustic Target
DAT............ Digital Audio Tape [*Also facetiously translated as Damn the Artist and Talent*]
DAT............ Di(isoamyloxy)thiocarbanilide [*Pharmacology*]
DAT............ Diphtheria Antitoxin [*Immunology*]
DAT............ Direct Action Team (MCD)
DAT............ Direct Agglutination Test [*Clinical chemistry*] (MAE)
DAT............ Direct Amylase Test [*Clinical chemistry*]
DAT............ Direct Antiglobulin Test [*Clinical chemistry*]
DAT............ Director [*or Directorate*] of Advanced Technology [*Air Force*]
DAT............ Director of Army Training [*British*]
DAT............ Director of Army Transportation
DAT............ Disaster Action Team [*Red Cross*]
DAT............ Disconnect Actuating Tools [*Nuclear energy*] (NRCH)
DAT............ Disk Allocation Table [*Computer science*] (IBMDP)
DAT............ Distillate Assistance/Advisory Team [*Military*] (DNAB)
DAT............ District Advisory Team [*Military*] (VNW)
DAT............ Division of Applied Technology [*Coast Guard*]

DAT	Docking Alignment Target [*NASA*] (MCD)
DAT	Dopamine Transporter [*Biochemistry*]
DAT	Drone Assisted Torpedo
DAT	Drug Abuse Team [*Military*] (DNAB)
DAT	Duration Adjusting Type
DAT	Dynamic Address Table [*Computer science*] (IAA)
DAT	Dynamic Address Translation [*Computer science*]
DAT	Dynamic Allocation Translator [*Computer science*] (IAA)
DATA	Babystar, Inc. [*NASDAQ symbol*] (SAG)
DATA	Datatrend Services [*NASDAQ symbol*] (TTSB)
DATA	Decision Aids for Target Aggregation (MCD)
DATA	Defense Air Transportation Administration [*Abolished 1962, functions transferred to Office of the Under Secretary of Commerce for Transportation*]
DATA	Derivation & Tabulation Associates, Inc. [*Information service or system*] (IID)
DATA	Design and Technology Association (AIE)
DATA	Development and Technical Assistance
DATA	Dial a Teacher Assistance [*Telephone service*]
DATA	Direct Access Terminal Application [*Computer science*] (BUR)
DATA	Display Automated Telemetry Analyzer (MCD)
DATA	Draughtsmen's and Allied Technicians' Association [*British*] (DI)
DATA	Drawing for Army Training Aids
DATAC	Data Acquisition Division [*National Weather Service*]
DATAC	Data Analog Computer
DATAC	Defense and Tactical Armament Control
DATAC	Digital Automatic Tester and Classifier
DATAC	Digital Autonomous Terminal Access Communication [*Data Bus*]
DATACOL	Data Collection
DATACOM	Data Communications
DATACOM	Data Communication Service (NITA)
DATACOM	Data Communications Network [*Air Force*] (NITA)
DATACORTS	Data Correlation and Transfer System
DATA/DAT	Data Digital Audio Tape (CDE)
DATAGEN	Data File Generator (MCD)
DataGn	Data General Corp. [*Associated Press*] (SAG)
Data IO	Data I-O [*Associated Press*] (SAG)
Datalgx	Datalogix International, Inc. [*Associated Press*] (SAG)
DATALINK	Digitized Information Transfer [*Air/ground*] (GAVI)
DATAMAN	Data Management System [*Computer science*] (MCD)
DATAMAP	Data from Aeromechanics' Test and Analytics-Management and Analysis Package (RDA)
Datamet	Datametrics Corp. [*Associated Press*] (SAG)
DATAN	Data Analysis (IEEE)
DAT & OV	Defense Aid [*Lend-Lease*] Tanks and Other Vehicles [*World War II*]
DATANET	Data Network (CET)
DATAP	Data Transmission and Processing (NATG)
Datapt	Datapoint Corp. [*Associated Press*] (SAG)
DATAR	Digital Automatic Tracking and Ranging [*or Remoting*] [*Air Force*]
DATAR	Digital Autotransducer and Recorder (IEEE)
Dataram	Dataram Corp. [*Associated Press*] (SAG)
DataRce	Date Race, Inc. [*Associated Press*] (SAG)
DATAS	Data in Associative Storage [*Computer science*] (MHDB)
DATAS	Data Link and Transponder Analysis System (DA)
Datascpe	Dastascope Corp. [*Associated Press*] (SAG)
Datastr	Datastream Systems, Inc. [*Associated Press*] (SAG)
DataSysN	Data Systems Network Corp. [*Associated Press*] (SAG)
DataSyst	Data Systems & Software, Inc. [*Associated Press*] (SAG)
DATAW	Datatrend Svcs Wrrt [*NASDAQ symbol*] (TTSB)
Dataware	Dataware Technologies, Inc. [*Associated Press*] (SAG)
DATB	Department of the Army Technical Bulletin (MCD)
DATB	Diaminotrinitrobenzene [*An explosive*]
DATBP	Diallyl Tetrabromophthalate [*Organic chemistry*]
DATC	Development and Training Center [*Navy*] (NVT)
DATC	Dichloroallyl Diisopropylthiocarbamate [*Di-allate*] [*Herbicide*]
DATC	Direct Assistance and Training Command [*Navy*] (NVT)
DATC	Director of Air Training Corps [*British*]
DATCIG	Deferred Adverse Tax Consequences Implementation Group [*IRS*]
DATCO	Duty Air Traffic Control Officer (DA)
DATCOL	Data Collection (IAA)
DATCOM	Data Compendium (MCD)
DATCOM	Data Support Command [*Army*]
DATD	Diallyltartardiamide [*Also, DATDA*] [*Organic chemistry*]
DATDA	Diallyltartardiamide [*Also, DATD*] [*Organic chemistry*]
DATDC	Data Analysis and Technique Development Center
DA/TDMA	Demand Assigned/Time Division Multiple Access
DATE	Dash Automatic Test Equipment
DATE	Data Exchange Service (IAA)
DATE	Data for Allotments Transmitted Electronically (MCD)
DATE	DATICO [*Digital Automatic Tape Intelligence Checkout*] Acceptance Test Evaluation (MCD)
DATE	Dental Auxiliary Teacher Education [*Medicine*] (DMAA)
DATE	Designation Accuracy Test Equipment
DATE	Dial Access Technical Education [*Telecommunications*] (PDAA)
DATE	Digital Angular Torquing Equipment
DATE	Digital Audio for Television [*System to improve sound*] [*Public Broadcasting Service*]
DATE	Dynamic, Acoustic, Thermal Environment (MCD)
DATE	Dynamics, Acoustics, and Thermal Environment (NASA)
DATEC	Data and Telecommunications
DATEC	Data Technical Support Group [*Telecommunications*] (TEL)
DATEC	Design and Art Technician Education Council (AIE)
DATEC	Differential and Alignment Unit and Total Error Corrector (PDAA)
DATEC	Digital Adaptive Technique for Efficient Communications

DATEL	Data Telecommunications [*RCA Global Communications Data Transmission Service over Telephone Circuits*] [*Telecommunications*] (TEL)
DATEP	Department of the Army Telecommunications Plan (MCD)
DATEPLAN	Data Tabulation and Editing Program Language (IAA)
DATEX	Data Exchange (IAA)
Datflx	Dataflex Corp. [*Associated Press*] (SAG)
DATHF	Dideazatetrahydrofolic Acid [*Antineoplastic drug*]
DATI	Director of Army Technical Information (AABC)
DATICO	Data Analysis and Technique Development Center [*Alexandria, VA*]
DATICO	Digital Automatic Tape Intelligence Checkout
DATICS	Data Inventory Control System
DATIMTEX	Data, Images, and Text [*European Patent Office*]
DATIN	Data Inserter
Datkey	Datakey, Inc. [*Associated Press*] (SAG)
DATL	Doctor of Arts in Training and Learning (GAGS)
DATM	Bordj Mokhtar [*Algeria*] [*ICAO location identifier*] (ICLI)
DATM	Datum, Inc. [*NASDAQ symbol*] (NQ)
DATM	Department of the Army Technical Manual (NATG)
DATM	Dual Approach Temperatures Method [*Heat exchange design*]
Datmar	Datamarine International, Inc. [*Associated Press*] (SAG)
DATMOBAS	David W. Taylor Model Basin [*Also, DTMB, TMB*] [*Later, DTNSRDC, NSRDC*] (MUGU)
DATMP	Diethylaluminum Tetramethylpiperidide [*Organic chemistry*]
DATMRPSTL	Department of the Army Technical Manual Repair Parts Special Tool List
DATO	Disbursing and Transportation Office
DATO	Discover America Travel Organizations, Inc. [*Later, TIA*]
DATOC	Division Artillery Tactical Operations Center (MCD)
DATOM	Data Aids for Training, Operations, and Maintenance
DATOM	Direct Access to Members [*Trade union membership database*] [*British*]
DATOR	Data Operational Requirements Board [*NATO Military Committee*] (NATG)
DATOR	Digital Data, Auxiliary Storage, Track Display, Outputs, and RADAR Display
DATOS	Detection and Tracking of Satellites (CINC)
DATOS	Drug Abuse Treatment Outcome Study [*National Institute on Drug Abuse*]
dATP	Deoxyadenosine Triphosphate [*Biochemistry*]
DATP	Detailed Acceptance Test Procedure (KSC)
DATP	Detroit Arsenal Tank Plant [*Army*]
DATP	Dissolved Adenosine Triphosphate [*Oceanography*]
Datpt	Datapoint Corp. [*Associated Press*] (SAG)
DATR	Design Acceptance [*or Approval*] Test Report
DATRDA	Defense Aid [*Lend-Lease*] Testing, Reconditioning, etc., of Defense Articles [*World War II*]
DATREC	Data Recording (CET)
DATRIX	Direct Access to Reference Information [*Xerox Corp.*]
Datron	Datron Systems, Inc. [*Associated Press*] (SAG)
DAtS	Atonement Seminary of the Holy Ghost, Washington, DC [*Library symbol Library of Congress*] (LCLS)
DATS	Data Accumulation and Transfer Sheet
DATS	Data Acquisition and Transmission System (MCD)
DA/TS	Data Acquisition/Transmittal Sheet
DATS	Data Automated Tower Simulator [*Army, Air Force*]
DATS	Data Transmission System
DATS	Despun Antenna Test Satellite [*Air Force*]
DATS	Detailed Acceptance Test Specification (KSC)
DATS	Digital Access Timeslot Selector (MCD)
DATS	Digital Avionic Transmission System (IAA)
DATS	Director, Auxiliary Territorial Service [*British military*] (DMA)
DATS	Drill and Transfer System
DATS	Dynamic Accuracy Test Set [*or System*]
DATSA	Depot Automatic Test System for Avionics (DWSG)
DATSC	Department of the Army Training and Support Committee (AABC)
Datscp	Datascope Corp. [*Associated Press*] (SAG)
DatSN	Data Systems Network Corp. [*Associated Press*] (SAG)
DATST	Datura stramonium [*Jimsonweed*]
DATT	Defense Attache (AFM)
DATTA	Diagnostic and Therapeutic Technology Assessment [*Medicine*]
DATU	Direct-Access Test Unit [*Computer science*]
Datum	Datum, Inc. [*Associated Press*] (SAG)
DATUM	Dokumentations- und Ausbildungszentrum fuer Theorie und Methode der Regionalforschung [*Documentation and Training Center for Theory and Methods of Regional Research*] [*Germany*]
DAT-VR	Differential Aptitude Test-Verbal Reasoning [*Psychology*] (EDAC)
DATX	Data Translation [*NASDAQ symbol*] (TTSB)
DATX	Data Translation, Inc. [*NASDAQ symbol*] (NQ)
DAU	American University, Washington, DC [*Library symbol Library of Congress*] (LCLS)
DAU	Daniels Canyon [*Utah*] [*Seismograph station code, US Geological Survey*] (SEIS)
DAU	Daru [*Papua New Guinea*] [*Airport symbol*] (OAG)
DAU	Data Acquisition Unit
DAU	Data Adapter Unit
DAU	Data Arithmetic Unit [*Computer science*]
DAU	Daughter
DAU	Declaration of Atlantic Unity [*Defunct*]
DAU	Defense Acquisition University [*DoD*] (RDA)
DAU	Dental Auxiliary Utilization
DAU	Digital Adapter Unit (MCD)
DAU	Digital Amplifier Unit (DWSG)
DAU	Digital Applique Unit (MCD)
DAU	Display Assembly Unit (MCD)

DAU .... Distributed Access Unit [*Computer science*]

DAU .... Drugs of Abuse in Urine [*Toxicology*]

DAUA .... Adrar/Touat [*Algeria*] [*ICAO location identifier*] (ICLI)

DAU & COH... Daughter and Co-Heir [*Genealogy*] (ROG)

DAU & H ...... Daughter and Heir [*Genealogy*] (ROG)

DAUB .... Biskra [*Algeria*] [*ICAO location identifier*] (ICLI)

Dau Co Rep... Dauphin County Reports [*Pennsylvania*] [*A publication*] (DLA)

DAUD .... Director of Anti-U-Boat Division [*British World War II*]

D Au E .... Diploma in Automobile Engineering [*British*]

D Au E .... Doctor of Automobile Engineering

DAUE .... El Golea [*Algeria*] [*ICAO location identifier*] (ICLI)

D Au Eng .... Doctor of Automobile Engineering

DAUG .... Ghardaia/Noumerate [*Algeria*] [*ICAO location identifier*] (ICLI)

DAUGR .... Daughter

DAUH .... Hassi-Messaoud/Oued Irara [*Algeria*] [*ICAO location identifier*] (ICLI)

DAUHS........ Daughters (ROG)

DAUI .... In Salah [*Algeria*] [*ICAO location identifier*] (ICLI)

DAUK .... Touggourt/Sidi Mahdi [*Algeria*] [*ICAO location identifier*] (ICLI)

DAU-L .... American University, Washington College of Law, Washington, DC [*Library symbol Library of Congress*] (LCLS)

DAUL .... Laghouat [*Algeria*] [*ICAO location identifier*] (ICLI)

Daun .... Daunorubicin [*Antineoplastic drug*] (DAVI)

DAUO .... El Oued/Guemar [*Algeria*] [*ICAO location identifier*] (ICLI)

Dauph........ Dauphin County Reporter [*Pennsylvania*] [*A publication*] (DLA)

Dauph Co Rep... Dauphin County Reporter [*Pennsylvania*] [*A publication*] (DLA)

Dauphn........ Dauphin Deposit Corp. [*Associated Press*] (SAG)

DAUS .... Defense Against Underwater Swimmers [*Military*] (MCD)

DAusE......... Australian Embassy, Washington, DC [*Library symbol Library of Congress*] (LCLS)

DAUT .... Timimoun [*Algeria*] [*ICAO location identifier*] (ICLI)

DAUU .... Ouargla [*Algeria*] [*ICAO location identifier*] (ICLI)

DAUWE........ Director, Admiralty Underwater Weapons Establishment [*Navy British*]

DAUZ .... Zarzaitine/In Amenas [*Algeria*] [*ICAO location identifier*] (ICLI)

DAV .... Data above Voice [*Telecommunications*] (TEL)

DAV .... Data Available (MCD)

DAV .... Data Valid (IEEE)

DAV .... Davao [*Philippines*] [*Seismograph station code, US Geological Survey*] (SEIS)

DAV .... Davenport [*Diocesan abbreviation*] [*Iowa*] (TOCD)

DAV .... David [*Panama*] [*Airport symbol*] (OAG)

DAV .... David Minerals Ltd. [*Vancouver Stock Exchange symbol*]

Dav .... Davies' English Patent Cases [*1785-1816*] [*A publication*] (DLA)

Dav .... Davies' Irish King's Bench and Exchequer Reports [*1604-12*] [*A publication*] (DLA)

Dav .... Davies' United States District Court Reports [*Republished as 2 Ware*] [*A publication*] (DLA)

Dav .... Davis' Hawaiian Reports [*A publication*] (DLA)

Dav .... Davis' Reports [*Abridgment of Sir Edward Coke's Reports*] [*A publication*] (DLA)

Dav .... Davis' United States Supreme Court Reports [*A publication*] (DLA)

DAV .... Delayed Automatic Volume (IAA)

DAV .... Delta-Aminovaleric Acid [*Organic chemistry*]

DAV .... Diaminovaleric Acid [*Biochemistry*]

DAV .... Digital Analyzing Voltmeter [*Electricity*] (NITA)

DAV .... Dirac Aviation [*France ICAO designator*] (FAAC)

DAV .... Disabled American Veterans (EA)

Dav .... Reports of Irish Cases, by Sir John Davis [*1604-11*] [*A publication*] (DLA)

DAVA .... Defense Audiovisual Agency [*DoD*]

DAVA .... Diaminovaleric Acid

DAVA .... Director [*or Directorate*] of Audiovisual Activities [*Army*]

DAVA .... Disabled American Veterans Auxiliary (EA)

DAVA .... DoD [*Department of Defense*] Audiovisual Activities

Dav & Dic Pr... Davidson and Dicey's Concise Precedents in Conveyancing [*A publication*] (DLA)

Dav & Kim IRL... Davidge and Kimball's Internal Revenue Laws [*A publication*] (DLA)

Dav & M...... Davison and Merivale's English Queen's Bench Reports [*A publication*] (DLA)

Dav & M (Eng)... Davison and Merivale's English Queen's Bench Reports [*A publication*] (DLA)

Dav & Mer... Davison and Merivale's English Queen's Bench Reports [*A publication*] (DLA)

DAV & OW... Defense Aid [*Lend-Lease*] Vessels and Other Watercraft [*World War II*]

Dav Ann...... Davies on Annuities [*A publication*] (DLA)

DAVAR........ Dealer-Authorized Value-Added Retailer (HGAA)

DAVBADS..... Defense Audiovisual Booking and Distribution System

Dav B & B... Davidson on Banks and Banking [*Canada A publication*] (DLA)

Dav Bdg Soc... David on Building Societies [*A publication*] (DLA)

DAVC .... Delayed Automatic Volume Control

Dav Can...... Davis' English Church Canons [*A publication*] (DLA)

Davco........ Davco Restaurants, Inc. [*Associated Press*] (SAG)

Dav Coke..... Davis' Abridgment of Coke's Reports [*A publication*] (DLA)

Dav Conv..... Davidson's Conveyancing [*A publication*] (DLA)

Dav Cr Cons... Davis' Criminal Law Consolidation Acts [*A publication*] (DLA)

Dav Cr Law... Davis' Criminal Law [*A publication*] (DLA)

DAVD .... Davidson & Associates, Inc. [*NASDAQ symbol*] (SAG)

Dav Dig ...... Davis' Indiana Digest [*A publication*] (DLA)

DAVDS........ Data Acquisition and Visual Display System (NRCH)

Davdsn ...... Davidson & Associates, Inc. [*Associated Press*] (SAG)

DAVE .... Data Addition, Verification, and Editing [*Lotus 1-2-3*]

DAVE .... Do Anything Very Easily [*Computer science*] (PCM)

DAVE .... Famous Daves of America, Inc. [*NASDAQ symbol*] (SAG)

Dave&B ...... Dave & Busters, Inc. [*Associated Press*] (SAG)

Davel .... Davel Communications Corp. [*Associated Press*] (SAG)

Dav Elec..... Davis' Law of Registration and Election [*A publication*] (DLA)

Dav Eng Ch Can... Davis' English Church Canons [*A publication*] (DLA)

Dav Fr Merc Law... Davies on French Mercantile Law [*A publication*] (DLA)

Dav Fr Soc... Davis on Friendly Societies and Trade Unions [*A publication*] (DLA)

DAVH .... Dibromodulcitol, Adriamycin, Vincristine, Halotestin [*Fluoxymesterone*] [*Antineoplastic drug regimen*]

DAVI .... Department of Audiovisual Instruction [*of NEA*] [*Later, AECT*] (EA)

DAVI .... Dynamic Antiresonant Vibration Isolator

DAVIC .... Digital Audio Visual Council (DOM)

DAVID .... Data Above Video System (NITA)

DAVID .... Defense of Airborne Vehicles in Depth

DAVID .... Digital and Video Interactive Device (EDAC)

DAVID .... Digital Audio/Video Interactive Decoder [*Computer science*]

DAVID .... Dynamic Audio Video Interactive Device [*Hearing aid*]

Davidson .... Davidson's Reports [*92-111 North Carolina*] [*A publication*] (DLA)

DAVIE .... Department of the Army Vocabulary of Information Elements (AABC)

DAVIE .... Digital Alphanumeric Video Insertion Equipment [*Aviation*] (OA)

Davies .... Davies' Patent Cases [*1785-1816*] [*A publication*] (DLA)

Davies .... Davies' United States District Court Reports [*Republished as 2 Ware*] [*A publication*] (DLA)

Davies (Eng)... Davies' English Patent Cases [*1785-1816*] [*A publication*] (DLA)

Davies (US)... Davies' District Court Reports [*2 Ware*] [*United States*] [*A publication*] (DLA)

Dav Ind Dig... Davis' Indiana Digest [*A publication*] (DLA)

Dav Ind Soc... Davis on Industrial and Provident Societies [*A publication*] (DLA)

DAVIPP........ Department of the Army Visual Information Production Program

Davis .... Davis' Hawaiian Reports [*A publication*] (DLA)

Davis .... Davis' United States Supreme Court Reports [*A publication*] (DLA)

DAVIS .... Defense Audiovisual Information System [*DoD*]

DAVIS .... Defense Automated Visual Information System [*Database*] (IID)

Davis Admin Law... Davis' Administrative Law Treatise [*A publication*] (DLA)

Davis Bdg ... Davis' Law of Building Societies [*A publication*] (DLA)

Davis Bldg Soc... Davis' Law of Building Societies [*A publication*] (DLA)

Davis Cr Law... Davis' Criminal Law [*A publication*] (DLA)

Davis (JCB)... Davis' United States Supreme Court Reports [*A publication*] (DLA)

Davis Land Ct Dec (Mass)... Davis' Land Court Decisions (Massachusetts) [*1898-1908*] [*A publication*] (ILCA)

Davis L Ct Cas... Davis' Land Court Decisions [*1898-1908*] [*A publication*] (DLA)

Davis Mass Convey Hdbk... Davis' Massachusetts Conveyancer's Handbook [*A publication*] (DLA)

Davis Rep... Davis' Hawaiian Reports [*A publication*] (DLA)

Dav Jus ...... Davis' Justice of the Peace [*A publication*] (DLA)

DAVL .... Data Available - Low (MCD)

DAVL .... Davel Communications Corp. [*NASDAQ symbol*] (SAG)

DAVL .... Davel Communications Grp [*NASDAQ symbol*] (TTSB)

Dav Lab L... Davis on the Labor Laws [*A publication*] (DLA)

Dav Land Ct Cas... Davis' Land Court Decisions [*1898-1908*] [*A publication*] (DLA)

DAVLB .... Desacetylvincaleukoblastine

Dav M & S... Davis' Law of Master and Servant [*A publication*] (DLA)

D Av Med ... Diploma in Aviation Medicine [*British*]

DAVNO........ Division Aviation Officer

DAVO .... Daylight Visual Observation (MCD)

DAVO .... Dynamic Analog of Vocal Tract

DAVOR........ Datenbank fuer Forderungsvorhaben [*Ongoing Research Project Data Bank*] [*Ministry for Research and Technology*] [*Information service or system*] (IID)

Davox .... Davox Corp. [*Associated Press*] (SAG)

DAVP .... Deamino-Agrinine Vasopressin [*Medicine*] (DMAA)

DAVP .... Doctrinal Audio-Visual Program [*Military*]

Dav Pat Cas... Davies' English Patent Cases [*1785-1816*] [*A publication*] (DLA)

Dav P C...... Davies' English Patent Cases [*1785-1816*] [*A publication*] (DLA)

Dav Prec Conv... Davidson's Precedents in Conveyancing [*A publication*] (DLA)

Dav Prec Ind... Davis' Precedents of Indictment [*A publication*] (DLA)

DAVR .... Division of Adult and Vocational Research [*Office of Education*]

Dav Reg ..... Davison on Registration and Elections [*A publication*] (DLA)

DAVRS........ Director of Army Veterinary and Remount Services [*British*]

DAVSA........ Defense Audiovisual Support Activity

DAVSS........ Doppler Acoustic Vortec Sensing System [*FAA*] (MCD)

DAVSS........ Doppler Acoustic Vortex Sensing Equipment [*Meteorology*] (DA)

Dav Tr Un... Davis' Trade Unions [*A publication*] (DLA)

Dav (US)...... Davies' District Court Reports [*2 Ware*] [*United States*] [*A publication*] (DLA)

DavWht........ David White, Inc. [*Associated Press*] (SAG)

DavWtr .... Davis Water & Waste Industries, Inc. [*Associated Press*] (SAG)

DAVX .... Davox Corp. [*NASDAQ symbol*] (NQ)

Davys......... Davys' English King's Bench Reports [*A publication*] (DLA)

Davys (Eng)... Davys' English King's Bench Reports [*A publication*] (DLA)

DAW .... Daw [*New Britain*] [*Seismograph station code, US Geological Survey Closed*] (SEIS)

DAW .... Dawson College Library [*UTLAS symbol*]

DAW .... Days a Week [*Classified advertising*]

DAW .... Dienstanweisung [*Service regulations*] [*German military - World War II*]

DAW .... Directorate of Atomic Warfare

DAW .... Director of Naval Air Warfare [*British military*] (DMA)

DAW .... Dispense as Written [*Prescription cannot be filled using a generic equivalent*] [*Pharmacy*]

DAW .... Dry Active Waste [*Nuclear energy*] (NUCP)

DAWA .... Danish American Women's Association [*Defunct*] (EA)

DAWA .... Diabetes Association of Western Australia

DAWA .... Divinatory Arts World Association [*See also AMAD*] [*Rillieux-La-Pape, France*] (EAIO)

Daw Ar ...... Dawe on Arrest in Civil Cases [*A publication*] (DLA)

Daw Att.......	Dawson's Attorney's [*A publication*] (DLA)	DB...............	Day Book [*Accounting*]
Daw Cr & Pun...	Dawe on Crimes and Punishments [*A publication*] (DLA)	DB...............	Dead Band
DAWG..........	Deployable Array Working Group (DWSG)	DB...............	Dead Body (IIA)
DAWG..........	Dynamic Air War Game [*Military*]	DB...............	Deaf/Blind
DAWH..........	White [*David*], Inc. [*NASDAQ symbol*] (SAG)	DB...............	Deals and Battens [*Business term*]
DAWIA.........	Defense Acquisition Workforce Improvement Act (RDA)	DB...............	Debenture [*Type of bond*] [*Investment term*]
DAWID.........	Device for Automatic Word Identification and Discrimination [*Computer science*]	DB...............	Debit
		dB...............	Decibel [*Symbol*] [*SI unit of sound level*]
DAWK..........	Daw Technologies [*NASDAQ symbol*] (TTSB)	db...............	Decibel (WDMC)
DAWK..........	Daw Technologies, Inc. [*NASDAQ symbol*] (SAG)	D/B.............	Decimal to Binary [*Computer science*] (KSC)
DAWK..........	Dove and Hawk [*One who took a moderate position on the Vietnam War*]	DB...............	Deep Basing [*Underground placement of missiles*]
		DB...............	Deep Breath [*or Breathe*] [*Medicine*]
Daw Land Pr...	Dawe's Epitome of the Law of Landed Property [*A publication*] (DLA)	DB...............	Defensive Back [*Football*]
		DB...............	Deficit Budget
DAWN..........	Digital Access to Wide Area Network [*Telemax Corp.*]	DB...............	Define Byte [*Computer science*] (PCM)
DAWN..........	Digital Automatic Weather Network	DB...............	Delayed Broadcast [*Television*]
DAWN..........	Drug Abuse Warning Network [*Public Health Service*] [*Rockville, MD*]	DB...............	Demand Base (DNAB)
DAWNS........	Design of Aircraft Wing Structures [*Computer program*]	DB...............	Dental Branch [*British military*] (DMA)
Daw Or Leg...	Dawson's Origo Legum [*A publication*] (DLA)	DB...............	Departmentalized Billing
Daw Real Pr...	Dawe's Real Estate Law [*A publication*] (DLA)	D/B.............	Deposit Book
DAWS.........	Director of Army Welfare Services [*British*]	DB...............	Depth Bomb [*Military*]
DAWS.........	Diver Alternative Work System	DB...............	Der Betrieb-Data Bank [*Handelsblatt GmbH*] [*Germany Information service or system*] (IID)
DawsnP.......	Dawson Production Services, Inc. [*Associated Press*] (SAG)	DB...............	Desert Biome [*Ecological biogeographic study*]
Dawson.......	Dawson Geophysical Co. [*Associated Press*] (SAG)	DB...............	Design Baseline (NASA)
Dawson's Code...	Dawson's Code of Civil Procedure [*Colorado*] [*A publication*] (DLA)	DB...............	Design Burst (KSC)
		DB...............	Deutsche Bibliothek [*Database producer*]
DAWT	Director of Naval Air Warfare and Flying Training [*British*]	DB...............	Deutsche Bundesbahn [*German Federal Railway*] [*Since 1949*] [*Germany*]
Daw Tch	Daw Technologies, Inc. [*Associated Press*] (SAG)		
DAX	Aalborg Airtaxi [*Denmark ICAO designator*] (FAAC)	DB...............	Developmental Bulletin (MCD)
DAX	Data Acquisition and Control	DB...............	Dextran Blue [*Organic chemistry*] (MAE)
DAX	Data Exchange	Db...............	Diabetic [*Medicine*] (DAVI)
DAX	Deutscher Aktien Index [*German Index of Stock Prices*] [*A publication*] (BARN)	DB...............	Dibromodifluoromethane [*Fire extinguishing agent*] [*Organic chemistry*] (ADA)
DAXBT	Deep Airborne Expendable Bathythermograph [*Naval Oceanographic Office*]	DB...............	Diconjugate Bilirubin [*Biochemistry*]
		DB...............	Dictionary of the Bible [*A publication*] (BJA)
Dax Exch Pr...	Dax's Exchequer Precedents [*A publication*] (DLA)	DB...............	Dictionnaire de la Bible [*A publication*] (BJA)
DAXI..........	Digital Auxiliary Information Code [*Computer science*]	DB...............	Die Bahn [*Tourist card for rail travel*] [*Germany*]
Dax Mast Pr...	Dax's Practice in the Offices of the Masters [*A publication*] (DLA)	DB...............	Diet Beverage
Daxor..........	Daxor Corp. [*Associated Press*] (SAG)	DB...............	Diffused Base
DAXREP.......	Department of the Army Command and Control Reporting System (AABC)	DB...............	Diffusion Bonding
		DB...............	Digital Block [*Computer science*]
DAY	Benday [*Engraving*] (NTCM)	D/B.............	Digital-to-Binary (NTCM)
DAY	Daylight (NTCM)	DB...............	Dignity Battalion [*Paramilitary group formed to bolster the regime of Panamanian strongman, Manuel Noriega*]
Day	Day's Connecticut Reports [*A publication*] (DLA)		
Day	Day's Election Cases [*1892-93*] [*England*] [*A publication*] (DLA)	DB...............	Dip Brazing
DAY	Dayton [*Ohio*] [*Airport symbol*] (OAG)	DB...............	Direct Bilirubin [*Medicine*] (DMAA)
DAY	Dayton Mining [*AMEX symbol*] (TTSB)	DB...............	Direct Billing
DAY	Dayton Mining Corp. [*AMEX symbol*] (SAG)	DB...............	Director Bomber [*Air Force*]
DAY	Dayton, OH [*Location identifier FAA*] (FAAL)	DB...............	Dirty Book
DAY	Dialysis and You [*of the DAY Association*] [*Defunct*] (EA)	DB...............	Disability (MAE)
DAY	Dwarf Aster Yellows [*Plant pathology*]	DB...............	Disc Brakes [*Automotive engineering*]
DAY	University of Dayton, Dayton, OH [*OCLC symbol*] (OCLC)	DB...............	Disciplinary Barracks
Day(Conn) ...	Connecticut Reports, by Day [*1802-13*] [*A publication*] (DLA)	DB...............	Dispersal Base [*Military*] (AFM)
Day Elect Cas...	Day's Election Cases [*1892-93*] [*England*] [*A publication*] (DLA)	DB...............	Display Buffer [*Computer science*]
DAyM..........	Doctor of Ayurvedic Medicine	DB...............	Distobuccal [*Dentistry*]
DAYR..........	Day Runner [*NASDAQ symbol*] (TTSB)	DB...............	Distribution Box [*Technical drawings*]
DAYR..........	Day Runner, Inc. [*NASDAQ symbol*] (SAG)	DB...............	Dive Bank
DayRun........	Day Runner, Inc. [*Associated Press*] (SAG)	DB...............	Dive Bomb
Day's Ca......	Day's Connecticut Reports [*A publication*] (DLA)	DB...............	Dive Bomber Aircraft
Day's Ca Er..	Day's Connecticut Reports [*A publication*] (DLA)	DB...............	Division Base [*Army*]
Day's Cases...	Day's Connecticut Reports [*A publication*] (DLA)	Db...............	Dobra [*Monetary unit*] (ODBW)
Day's Conn Rep...	Day's Connecticut Reports [*A publication*] (DLA)	DB...............	Dock Brief [*British*] (ADA)
Day Sur	Dayton's Law of Surrogates [*A publication*] (DLA)	D/B.............	Documentary Bill (ADA)
DaytHd........	Dayton-Hudson Corp. [*Associated Press*] (SAG)	DB...............	Dolly Back [*Films, television, etc.*]
DaytMn........	Dayton Mining Group [*Associated Press*] (SAG)	DB...............	Domesday Book [*Census-like record of the lands of England, 1085-86*]
Dayton	Dayton Superior and Common Pleas Reports [*Ohio*] [*A publication*] (DLA)		
Dayton	University of Dayton. Intramural Law Review [*A publication*] (DLA)	DB...............	Double-Barreled (ADA)
DaytonMn	Dayton Mining Group [*Associated Press*] (SAG)	DB...............	Double Bass [*Music*]
Dayton (Ohio)...	Dayton Reports (Ohio) [*A publication*] (DLA)	DB...............	Double Bayonet Base [*Electronics*] (IAA)
Dayton Rep...	Dayton Reports [*Ohio*] [*A publication*] (DLA)	db...............	Double Bed
DAYTOP.......	Drug Addicts Yield to Persuasion [*of Daytop Village, Inc., a narcotics-addiction rehabilitation facility*]	DB...............	Double Biased (CET)
		DB...............	Double Blind Study [*Medicine*] (DMAA)
Dayt Sur	Dayton's Law of Surrogates [*A publication*] (DLA)	DB...............	Double Bottom (MSA)
Dayt Term Rep...	Dayton Term Reports [*Ohio*] [*A publication*] (DLA)	DB...............	Double Bounce [*Electronics*] (IAA)
DAZ............	Deleted in Azoospermia [*Genetics*]	DB...............	Double Braid (AAG)
DAZD	Double Anode Zener Diode	DB...............	Double Break
DAZZ..........	Danceable Jazz [*In music group name Dazz Band*]	DB...............	Double Breasted [*Clothing industry*]
DB..............	Bachelor of Divinity	DB...............	Double-Ended Boiler [*Shipping*] (DS)
Db.............	Base Diameter [*Manufacturing term*]	db...............	Drab [*Philately*]
DB.............	Baudeloeque's Diameter [*External conjugate diameter of pelvis*] [*Obstetrics*] (DAVI)	DB...............	Draw Bar (ADA)
		DB...............	Drop Box (LAIN)
DB..............	Bomber [*Russian aircraft symbol*]	DB...............	Drop-By [*Brief social appearance*]
DB..............	Brittany Air International [*ICAO designator*] (AD)	DB...............	Dry Basis
DB..............	Daily Bulletin [*Military*] (AABC)	DB...............	Dry Bath [*Instrumentation*]
DB..............	Daimler-Benz [*Name of German engine factory*] [*World War II*]	DB...............	Dry Bulb [*Thermometer, of a psychrometer*] [*Meteorology*]
DB..............	Damned Bad	DB...............	Duke of Buccleuch [*British*] (ROG)
DB..............	Data Bank	DB...............	Dunnage Board
DB..............	Database [*Computer science*]	DB...............	Duplex Bearing [*Military*]
DB..............	Database	DB...............	Dutch Belted [*Rabbits*]
DB..............	Data Bus [*Computer science*] (MCD)	DB...............	Dynamic Braking
DB..............	Datebook (WDMC)	DB2..............	Database Two [*Computer science*] (HGAA)
DB..............	Date of Birth	DBA	Air Alpha, Inc. [*ICAO designator*] (FAAC)
DB..............	David Brown [*Prefix designation on Aston-Martin cars*] [*British*]	DBA	Bar Association of the District of Columbia, Washington, DC [*Library symbol Library of Congress*] (LCLS)
DB..............	Davis-Bacon Act Decision [*DOL*] (AAGC)		

DBA .... Danish Brotherhood in America (EA)
DBA .... Database Administration [*or Administrator*] [*Computer science*] (BUR)
DBA .... Davis-Bacon Act [*1921*]
DBA .... Days before Anthesis [*Botany*]
DBA .... Daytime Broadcasters Association [*Defunct*] (EA)
DBA .... DBA Systems, Inc. [*Associated Press*] (SAG)
DBA .... Dead before Arrival [*Term used by some members of Congress to describe 1986 federal budget proposals*]
DBA .... Dealer Bank Association [*Washington, DC*] (EA)
DBA .... De Bonis Asportatis [*Trespass to Personalty*] [*Latin Legal term*] (DLA)
dB(A) .... Decibel A-Weighted
dBA .... Decibel A-Weighted
dBA .... Decibels, Adjusted
dba .... Decibels on the A Scale
DBA .... Deep Battle Area (INF)
DBA .... Defense Base Act
DBA .... Dense Blasting Agent (MCD)
DBA .... Design Basis Accident [*Nuclear energy*]
DBA .... Dibasic Acid [*Waste from adipic acid production*]
DBA .... Dibenzanthracene [*Carcinogen*]
DBA .... Dibenzoylacetylene [*Organic chemistry*]
DBA .... Dibenzylamine [*Organic chemistry*]
DBA .... Dihydro-Dimethyl-Benzopyranbutyric Acid
DBA .... Directory of British Associations [*A publication*]
DBA .... Disabled Businesspersons Association (EA)
DBA .... Doctor of Business Administration
DBA .... Doing Business As [*Followed by company name*]
dba .... Doing Business As (AAGC)
DBA .... Dolichos biflorus Agglutinin [*Immunology*]
DBA .... Duct Burner Augmentation
DBA .... Dynamic Bandwidth Allocation [*Computer science*]
DBAAM .... Disk Buffer Area Access Method
DBAC .... Distributed Budget at Completion
DBACS .... Database Administrator Control System
DBACS .... Drawback Accounting and Computing System [*Australia*]
DBACT .... Dental Board of the Australian Capital Territory
DB Ad .... Doctor of Business Administration
DB Adm .... Doctor of Business Administration
DBAE .... Dihydroxyborylaminoethyl [*Organic chemistry*]
DBAF .... Database Access Facility
DBAG .... Daimler-Benz AG [*Manufacturer of Mercedes-Benz cars and trucks*] [*German*]
DBAH .... Diisobutylaluminum Hydride [*Also, DIBAH*] [*Organic chemistry*]
DBAM .... Database Access Method
DBAM .... Database Access Module (NITA)
DBA/M .... Data Base Administrator/Manager [*Army*]
DB & C .... Deep Breathing and Coughing [*Medicine*] (DAVI)
DB & M .... Dunlop, Bell, and Murray's Scotch Court of Session Cases, Second Series [*1838-62*] [*A publication*] (DLA)
D (Bank) .... Data Bank
DBAO .... Digital Block And-Or Gate [*Computer science*] (IEEE)
DBAS .... DBA Systems [*NASDAQ symbol*] (TTSB)
DBAS .... DBA Systems, Inc. [*NASDAQ symbol*] (NQ)
DBAS .... Division of Biometry and Applied Sciences [*Department of Health and Human Services*] (GFGA)
DBASI .... Digital Bar and Altitude Setting Indicator (DWSG)
DBASI .... Digital Barometer Altimeter Setting Indicator [*Aviation*] (FAAC)
DBATS .... Dynamic Balancing and Tracking System (MCD)
DBAWG .... Database Administration Working Group [*CODASYL*]
DBB .... Bethune-Cookman College, Daytona Beach, FL [*OCLC symbol*] (OCLC)
DBB .... Deals, Battens, and Boards [*Business term*]
DBB .... Detector Back Bias
DBB .... Detector Balanced Bias
DBB .... Deutsche Bundesbahn [*German Federal Railway*] [*Since 1949*] [*Germany*]
DBB .... Dibenzoylbenzene [*Organic chemistry*]
DBB .... Dinner, Bed, and Breakfast
DBB .... United States Office of Management and Budget, Washington, DC [*Library symbol Library of Congress*] (LCLS)
DBBA .... Danny Boy Breeders Association (EA)
DBBB .... Cotonou/Cadjehoun [*Benin*] [*ICAO location identifier*] (ICLI)
DBBC .... Cana/Bohicon [*Benin*] [*ICAO location identifier*] (ICLI)
DBBD .... Djougou [*Benin*] [*ICAO location identifier*] (ICLI)
DBBK .... Kandi [*Benin*] [*ICAO location identifier*] (ICLI)
DBBL .... Dismounted Battlespace Battle Lab [*Army*] (INF)
DBBN .... Natitingou [*Benin*] [*ICAO location identifier*] (ICLI)
DBBO .... Porga [*Benin*] [*ICAO location identifier*] (ICLI)
DBBP .... Dibutyl Butylphosphonate [*Organic chemistry*]
DBBP .... Parakou [*Benin*] [*ICAO location identifier*] (ICLI)
DBBR .... Bimbereke [*Benin*] [*ICAO location identifier*] (ICLI)
DBBS .... Save [*Benin*] [*ICAO location identifier*] (ICLI)
DBBV .... Cotonou [*Benin*] [*ICAO location identifier*] (ICLI)
DBC .... Darwin Bushwalking Club [*Australia*]
DBC .... Database Computer (MCD)
DBC .... Data Base Configuration [*Computer science*] (ECII)
DBC .... Data Bibliography Card
DBC .... Data Bus Control [*Computer science*] (MCD)
DBC .... Data Bus Coupler [*Computer science*] (MCD)
DBC .... D. B. Communications, Inc. [*Bethesda, MD*] [*Telecommunications service*] (TSSD)
DBC .... Deaf Broadcasting Campaign [*British*]
DBC .... Decatur Baptist College [*Iowa*]

dBc .... Decibels above One Carrier
dBc .... Decibels Referred to Carrier (IDOE)
DBC .... Decimal to Binary Conversion [*Computer science*] (IAA)
DBC .... Decomposed Block Code (IAA)
DBC .... Delamination, Bond, Crack [*Plastics technology*]
DBC .... Delaware Business Connection
DBC .... Democratic Business Council (EA)
DBC .... Denied-Boarding Compensation [*Airlines*]
DBC .... Deputy Brigade Commander [*Army*]
DBC .... Desert Bighorn Council (EA)
DBC .... Developmental Biology Center [*Case Western Reserve University*] [*Research center*] (RCD)
DBC .... Diameter Bolt Circle [*Technical drawings*]
DBC .... Dictionnaire Biographique du Canada [*A publication*]
DBC .... Digital-to-Binary Converter [*Computer science*]
DBC .... Dimethylbenzimidazolylcobamide [*Biochemistry*]
DBC .... Director of Barrack Construction [*British military*] (DMA)
DBC .... Display Blocks Configuration [*Computer science*] (ECII)
DBC .... Disturbing Behavior Checklist [*Psychology*] (EDAC)
DBC .... Doctor of Beauty Culture
DBC .... Dodge Brothers Club (EA)
DBC .... Don Bosco College [*Newton, NJ*]
DBC .... Double Bottom Center [*of a ship*] (DS)
DBC .... Dries Below a Century [*Ink*] (DGA)
DBC .... Duck Book Communications Ltd. [*Vancouver Stock Exchange symbol*]
DBC .... Dye-Binding Capacity
DBC .... United States Bureau of the Census, Suitland, MD [*Library symbol Library of Congress*] (LCLS)
DBCA .... Deaf-Blind Care Association [*Australia*]
DBCAA .... Dutch Belted Cattle Association of America (EA)
DBCATA .... Disposable Barrel Cartridge Area Target Ammunition [*Weapon launcher*]
DBCB .... Database Control Block
DBCC .... Data Broadcasting [*NASDAQ symbol*] (TTSB)
DBCC .... Data Broadcasting Corp. [*NASDAQ symbol*] (SAG)
DBCC .... Decrement, Test, Branch if Condition True [*Computer science*]
DBCC .... District Business Conduct Committee [*of the National Association of Securities Dealers*]
DBCD .... Differential Base Current Drift
DBCI .... DB with Respect to a Circular Polarized Antenna (GFGA)
DBCL .... Database Command Language
DBCL .... Dilute Blood Clot Lysis Method [*Hematology*] (MAE)
DB Clg .... Double-Headed Ceiling (DAC)
DBCO .... Digital Block Clock Oscillator [*Computer science*]
DBCP .... Data Buoy Cooperation Council [*Marine science*] (OSRA)
DBCP .... Dibromochloropropane [*Pesticide*]
DBCP .... Double Bounce, Circularly Polarized
DBCS .... Database Control System
DBCS .... Deterministic Bounded Cellular Space (PDAA)
DBCS .... Double-Byte Character Set [*Computer science*] (PCM)
DBCU .... Data Bus Control Unit [*Computer science*] (KSC)
DBD .... Air Niagara Express, Inc. [*Canada ICAO designator*] (FAAC)
DBD .... Dashboard
DBD .... Database Definition (BYTE)
DBD .... Database Description [*Computer science*] (BUR)
DBD .... Database Design Document
DBD .... Database Diagnostics (NITA)
DBD .... Database Directory (IAA)
DBD .... Demokratische Bauernpartei Deutschlands [*Democratic Farmers' Party of Germany*] (PPW)
DBD .... Detailed Budget Decision (AFM)
DBD .... Dibromodulcitol [*Mitolactol*] [*Antineoplastic drug*]
DBD .... Diebold, Inc. [*NYSE symbol*] (SPSG)
DBD .... Diesel Belt Drive (MSA)
DBD .... Digital Bargraph Display
DBD .... Digoxigenin Bisdigitoxoside [*Biochemistry*]
DBD .... DNA [*Deoxyribonucleic Acid*] Binding Domain [*Genetics*]
DBD .... Double-Base Diode
DBD .... Double Beta Decay
DBDA .... Database Design Aid [*Computer science*] (BUR)
DBDA .... Design Basis Depressurization Accident [*Nuclear energy*] (NRCH)
DB/DC .... Database/Data Communications [*IBM Corp.*]
DBDC .... Dennis Brutus Defense Committee (EA)
DBDD .... Database Design Document (MCD)
DBDG .... Distobuccal Developmental Groove [*Medicine*] (DMAA)
DBDL .... Database Definition Language
DBDPO .... Decabromodiphenyl Oxide [*Flame retardant*] [*Organic chemistry*]
DBDS .... Data Base Directory Service [*Formerly, Data Base User Service*] [*Knowledge Industry Publications, Inc. Database*]
DBDS .... Duffel Bag Delivery System [*Military*] (INF)
DBDU .... Desert Battle Dress Uniform [*Military*] (INF)
DBDU .... Digital Bargraph Display Unit
DBE .... British Embassy, Washington, DC [*Library symbol Library of Congress*] (LCLS)
DBE .... Dame Commander of the [*Order of the*] British Empire
DBE .... Danube-Air Ltd. [*Hungary ICAO designator*] (FAAC)
DBE .... Data Bus Element [*Computer science*]
DBE .... Data Bus Enable [*Computer science*]
DBE .... De Bene Esse [*Conditionally*] [*Latin Legal term*] (DLA)
DBE .... Deep Breathing Exercise [*Medicine*] (DAVI)
DBE .... Design Basis Earthquake [*Nuclear energy*] (NRCH)
DBE .... Design Basis Event [*Nuclear energy*] (NRCH)
DBE .... Dibasic Ester [*DuPont organic solvent*]
DBE .... Dibenzyl Ether [*Organic chemistry*]

DBE............	Dibromoethane [*Same as EB, EDB*] [*Organic chemistry*]
DBE............	Disadvantaged Business Enterprise [*Business term*]
DBE............	Dispatch Payable Both Ends [*Shipping*] (DS)
DBE............	Division of Biological Effects [*Bureau of Radiological Effects*]
DBE............	Division of Biometry and Epidemiology [*Department of Health and Human Services*] (GFGA)
DBE............	Double Bond Equivalent [*Analytical chemistry*]
DBE............	Dynamic Balancing Equipment
DBE............	National Society, Daughters of the British Empire in the United States of America (EA)
DBEATS.......	Dispatch Payable Both Ends All Time Saved [*Shipping*] (DS)
DBED.........	Dibenzylethylenediamine [*Organic chemistry*]
DB Ed.........	Doctor of Business Education
DBED.........	Penicillin G Benzathine [*Pharmacology*] (DAVI)
DBeer.........	DeBeers Consolidated Mines [*Associated Press*] (SAG)
DBeer.........	DeBeers Consolidated Mines Ltd. [*Associated Press*] (SAG)
DBELTS.......	Dispatch Payable Both Ends on Laytime Saved [*Shipping*] (DS)
DBenz........	Daimler-Benz AG [*Associated Press*] (SAG)
DBER.........	Division of Biomedical and Environmental Research [*Later, Office of Health and Environmental Research*] [*Department of Energy*]
dBEST........	Database of Expressed Sequence Tags [*Genetics*]
DBF............	Data Base File [*Military*] (AABC)
DBF............	Demodulator Band Filter (MSA)
DBF............	Design Basis Fault [*Nuclear energy*] (NRCH)
DBF............	Digital Beam-Forming (PDAA)
DBF............	Digital Block Flop [*Computer science*] (IAA)
DBF............	Disturbed Bowel Function [*Medicine*] (MEDA)
DBF............	Divorced Black Female [*Classified advertising*] (CDAI)
DBF............	Dominant Bubble Frequency [*Nuclear energy*] (NRCH)
DBF............	Double Book Form [*Photography*] (ROG)
DBF............	Dressing before Finish [*Manufacturing term*]
DBF............	Dual Bowl Feeder
DBFB..........	Deep-Bed Filter and Blower Building [*Nuclear energy*] (NRCH)
DBFC..........	David Birney Fan Club (EA)
DBFC..........	Debby Boone Fan Club [*Defunct*] (EA)
DBFF..........	Digital Block Flip-Flop [*Computer science*]
DBFL..........	Design Basis Flooding Level [*Nuclear energy*] (NRCH)
DBFM.........	Dun & Bradstreet France Marketing [*Dun & Bradstreet France*] [*Database*]
DBFN.........	Database File Numbers (MCD)
DBFN.........	Data Bus File Number (NASA)
DBFR.........	Domestic Base Factor Report [*Army*]
DBFS.........	Deep Bed Farming Society (EA)
DBFS.........	Department of Bush Fire Services [*New South Wales*] [*Australia*]
DBFS.........	Dull Black Finish Slate (KSC)
DBG...........	Database Generator
DBG...........	Data Bus Group [*Computer science*] (MCD)
DBG...........	David Ben-Gurion (BJA)
DBG...........	Desert Botanical Garden [*An association*] (EA)
DBG...........	Design Business Group [*British*] (DBA)
DBG...........	Division of Basic Grants [*Office of Education*]
DBG...........	Dyersburg Corp. [*NYSE symbol*] (SPSG)
DBGCM.......	Dun & Bradstreet Guide to Canadian Manufacturers [*Information service or system*] (IID)
DBGEN.......	Database Generation [*Computer science*]
DBGLS.......	Development Bank of the Great Lake States [*Zaire*] (EAIO)
DBGMP.......	Data Bus Generation and Maintenance Package [*Computer science*] (MCD)
DBGS.........	Database Generation System (MCD)
DBH...........	Development Big Hydrofoil [*Also, DEH*] (MCD)
DBH...........	Diameter at Breast Height [*Of trees*]
DBH...........	Diazabicycloheptene [*Organic chemistry*]
DBH...........	Division Beachhead [*Army*]
DBH...........	Dopamine Beta-Hydroxylase [*An enzyme*]
DBH...........	DTIC [*Dacarbazine*], BCNU , and Hydroxyurea [*Carmustine*] [*Antineoplastic drug regimen*] (DAVI)
DBHI..........	DBH [*Dopamine Beta-Hydroxylase*] Index
DBHN.........	Dibutyl Hyponitrite [*Organic chemistry*]
DBHP.........	Drawbar Horsepower
DBHR.........	Debrett's Business History Research [*British*]
DBHS.........	Database Handling System
DBI............	Brookings Institution, Washington, DC [*Library symbol Library of Congress*] (LCLS)
DBI............	Data Base Index [*SDC Information Services*]
DBI............	Data Bus Interface Unit-Launch [*Computer science*] (MCD)
DBI............	Decibels (Isotropic) (MCD)
DBI............	Design Basis Incident [*Nuclear energy*] (NRCH)
DBI............	Deutsches Bibliotheksinstitut [*German Library Institute*] [*Information service or system*] (IID)
DBI............	Development at Birth Index [*Medicine*]
DBI............	Diazepam Binding Inhibitor [*Biochemistry*]
DBI............	Dibi Resources, Inc. [*Vancouver Stock Exchange symbol*]
DBI............	Dictionary of the Bible [*A publication*] (BJA)
DBI............	Differential Bearing Indicator
DBI............	Dittler Brothers, Inc [*Printer of U.S. postage stamps*] (BARN)
DBI............	Diver Biographical Inventory [*Navy*]
DBI............	Double Byte Interleaved
DBI............	Dull but Important [*Wall Street Journal slang*] (WDMC)
DBI............	Phenethylbiguanide [*or Phenformin*] [*Pharmacology*] (DAVI)
DBIA..........	Danish Brotherhood in America (EA)
DBIA..........	Data Bus Interface Adapter [*Computer science*] (MCD)
DBIA..........	Data Bus Isolation Amplifier [*Computer science*] (MCD)
DBIA..........	Digital Block Inverter Amplifier [*Computer science*]
D Bib........	Douay Bible
DBIC...........	Dibutylindolocarbazole [*Organic chemistry*]
D Bi Ch.......	Doctor of Biochemistry
D Bi Chem...	Doctor of Biochemistry
DBiChem.....	Doctor of Biological Chemistry (NADA)
DBIDI..........	Database Imagery Derived Information (MCD)
D Bi E........	Doctor of Biological Engineering
D Bi Eng.....	Doctor of Biological Engineering
DBII...........	Digital Biometrics [*NASDAQ symbol*] (TTSB)
DBII...........	Digital Biometrics, Inc. [*NASDAQ symbol*] (SAG)
DBII...........	Dunserve II [*Canada Systems Group*] [*Information service or system*] (IID)
DBIL..........	Database Input Languages [*Computer science*]
DBIL..........	Direct Bilirubin [*Also, DBili*] [*Clinical chemistry*]
DBili..........	Direct Bilirubin [*Also, DBIL*] [*Clinical chemistry*]
DBIN..........	Data Bus In [*Computer science*]
DBIOC........	Database Input/Output Control
DBIP..........	Discrimination by Identification of Pictures [*Psychiatry*] (DAVI)
D Bi Phy.....	Doctor of Biological Physics
DBIR..........	Directory of Biotechnology Information/Resources [*American Type Culture Collection*] [*Information service or system*] (CRD)
DBIRD........	Department of Business, Industry, and Regional Development [*Queensland*] [*Australia*]
D Bi S........	Doctor of Biological Sciences
DBIS..........	Document-Based Indexing System (ADA)
D Bi Sc.......	Doctor of Biological Sciences
DBIU..........	Data Bus Interface Unit [*Computer science*] (MCD)
DBIU..........	Dominion Board of Insurance Underwriters [*Canada*] (ODBW)
DBJ...........	Duchess of Brittany (Jersey) Ltd. [*British ICAO designator*] (FAAC)
DBK...........	Data Bank (AABC)
DBK...........	Decarboxylase Base Moeller [*Biochemistry*] (DAVI)
dBK...........	Decibels above One Kilowatt (DEN)
DBK...........	Diabetic Management [*Medicine*] (DAVI)
DBK...........	Dibromomannitol [*or Mitobronitol*] [*Antineoplastic drug*] (DAVI)
DBK...........	Drawback [*Business term*]
DBK...........	N.B. MacDonald Services Ltd. [*New Zealand*] [*FAA designator*] (FAAC)
DBL............	Damage before Launch (CINC)
DBL............	Dantrolene Blood Level [*Clinical chemistry*]
DBL............	Database Language [*Computer science*]
DBL............	Database List (CINC)
DBL............	Database Load [*Computer science*]
DBL............	Debarred Bidder's List
DBL............	Desbromoleptophos [*Insecticide*]
DBL............	Deutsche Biologische Literatur [*German Biological Literature*] [*Also, DT BIOL Database Forschungsinstitut Senckenberg*] [*Information service or system*] (CRD)
DBL............	Diffusive Boundary Layer [*Physical chemistry*]
DBL............	Direct Broadcasting Ltd. [*British*]
DBL............	Direct Business Lines [*Telecom Canada*] [*Telecommunications service*] (TSSD)
DBL............	Disability Benefit Law [*Insurance*]
DBL............	Displaced Business Loan [*Small Business Administration*]
DBL............	Double (AAG)
dbl............	Double (VRA)
dbl............	Double (WDMC)
DBL............	Double
DBL............	Drawing Breakdown List
DBLACT.......	Double-Acting (IAA)
DBLCN........	Double Contact Switch (IAA)
DBLE..........	Double (ROG)
DBLE..........	Double Eagle Pete & Mng [*NASDAQ symbol*] (TTSB)
DBLE..........	Double Eagle Petroleum & Mining Co. [*NASDAQ symbol*] (NQ)
DblEgl........	Double Eagle Petroleum & Mining Co. [*Associated Press*] (SAG)
Dbletree......	Doubletree Corp. [*Associated Press*] (SAG)
DBLF..........	Double Face
DBLR..........	Doubler (KSC)
DBLS..........	Debarred Bidders List System [*GSA bulletin board*] [*Now EPL*] (AAGC)
DBLSA........	Defense Basic Logistics Support Analysis [*DoD*] (RDA)
DBLTG........	Database Language Task Group [*CODASYL*]
DBLW.........	Double Wall
DBM...........	Database Machines (AAGC)
DBM...........	Database Management [*or Manager*] [*Computer science*] (NVT)
DBM...........	Data Buffer Module (IEEE)
DBM...........	Data Bus Monitor [*Computer science*]
DBM...........	Debra Markos [*Ethiopia*] [*Airport symbol*] (AD)
DBM...........	Decarboxylase Base Moeller [*Medium*] [*Microbiology*]
DBM...........	Decibel Meter (KSC)
dBM...........	Decibels above One Milliwatt
DBM...........	Decibels below One Milliwatt
DBM...........	Decibels to One Milliwatt [*Unit of signal strength*] [*Telecommunications*] (NITA)
DBM...........	Demineralized Bone Matrix [*Substance which, when surgically implanted, stimulates development of new bone*]
DBM...........	Dense-Branching Morphology [*Physical chemistry*]
DBM...........	Deputy Base Manager (MUGU)
DBM...........	Diabetic Management [*Medicine*]
DBM...........	Diazobenzyloxymethol [*Organic chemistry*]
DBM...........	Dibromomannitol [*Mitobronitol*] [*Antineoplastic drug*]
DBM...........	Dibutylmagnesium [*Organic chemistry*]
DBM...........	Dibutyl Maleate [*Organic chemistry*]
DBM...........	Dielectric Breakdown Model [*Physics*]
DBM...........	Diploma in Business Management (NADA)
DBM...........	Direct Branch Mode
D/BM.........	Directorate of Ballistic Missiles
DBM...........	Division Battle Model (MCD)

DBM............ Divorced Black Male [*Classified advertising*] (CDAI)
DBM............ Doctor of Business Management
DBM............ Double Balanced Mixer
DBM............ Drake Beam Morin, Inc.
DBM............ Dry Bulk Material
DBM............ Dual-Bed Monolith [*Automotive engineering*]
dBmOp........ Decibels above One Milliwatt, Referred to or Measured at a Point of Zero Transmission Level, Psophometrically Weighted
DB/M² .... Decibels above Milliwatt per Square Meter (MCD)
DBMA......... Dibenzylmethylamine [*Organic chemistry*]
DBMA......... Dibutylmalonic Acid [*Organic chemistry*]
DBMA......... Distillate Burner Manufacturers Association (EA)
DBMC......... Di-tert-butyl-m-cresol [*Organic chemistry*]
DBMCS....... Database Management and Control System (MCD)
DBME......... Data Base Management Element (SSD)
DBMIB........ Dibromomethyl(isopropyl)benzoquinone [*Organic chemistry*]
DBMOP....... DBMO and Psophometrically Weighted for Telephony [*Telecommunications*] (NITA)
DBMOPS..... DBMO and Psophometrically Weighted for Sound Programme Transmission [*Telecommunications*] (NITA)
DBM paper... Diazobenzyloxymethyl Paper [*Genetics*] (DOG)
DBMS......... Database Management Software [*Computer science*]
DBMS......... Database Management System [*or Subsystem*] [*Computer science*] (BUR)
DBMS......... Director of Base Medical Services
DBMSPSM.. Database Management System Problem Specification Model
DBMV......... Digital Block Multivibrator [*Computer science*]
DBMW........ Decibels above One Milliwatt (IAA)
DBN............ Database Network
DBN............ Data Bus Network [*Computer science*] (MCD)
DBN............ Day Beacon [*USCG*] (TAG)
DBN............ De Bilt [*Netherlands*] [*Later, WIT*] [*Geomagnetic observatory code*]
DBN............ De Bonis Non [*Of the Goods Not Yet Administered*]
DBN............ Diazobicyclononene [*Organic chemistry*]
DBN............ Dibutylnitrosamine [*Also, DBNA*] [*Organic chemistry*]
DBN............ Double Bassoon [*Music*]
DBN............ Dublin, GA [*Location identifier FAA*] (FAAL)
Dbn............ Durban [*South Africa*] (ILCA)
DBNA......... Dibutylnitrosamine [*Also, DBN*] [*Organic chemistry*]
DBNA......... Digital Block Noninverting Amplifier [*Computer science*]
DBNK......... Data Bank
DBNMA....... Disposable Baby Napkin Manufacturers Association [*British*] (DBA)
DBNPA....... Dibromonitrilopropionamide [*Organic chemistry*]
DBNPG....... Dibromoneopentyl Glycol [*Flame retardant*] [*Organic chemistry*]
DBNPS....... Davis-Besse Nuclear Power Station (NRCH)
DBNS......... Digital Bombing-Navigation System
DBNSW....... Dental Board of New South Wales [*Australia*]
DBNUSSE .... Dual Binary Non-Uniform Simple Surface Evaporation Model [*US Army Chemical Research, Development, and Engineering Center*] (RDA)
DBO .... Data Buoy Office [*National Oceanic and Atmospheric Administration*] (DNAB)
DBO .... Dawn Battle Order [*British military*] (DMA)
DBO .... Dead Blackout (IIA)
DBO .... Design-Build-Operate (AAGC)
DBO .... Diploma of British Orthoptics
DBO .... Directorate of Biological Operations [*Pine Bluff Arsenal, AR*]
DBO .... Distobucco-Occlusal [*Dentistry*]
DBO .... District Barrack Officer [*British military*] (DMA)
DBO .... District Building Officer [*National Health Service*] [*British*] (DI)
DBO .... Drop Build-Out Capacitor [*Telecommunications*] (TEL)
DBO .... Dual Beam Oscilloscope
DBO .... Dubbo [*Australia Airport symbol*] (OAG)
DBO .... Dubbo [*New South Wales*] [*Airport symbol*] (AD)
DBO .... Royal Phoenix Airlines [*Nigeria*] [*ICAO designator*] (FAAC)
DBOA.......... Delayed Breeder or Alternative [*Nuclear energy*] (NRCH)
DBOEP........ Di(butoxyethyl) Phthalate [*Organic chemistry*]
DBOF .... Defense Business Operating Fund [*Military*] (DOMA)
DBOI .... Developmental Basis of Issue [*Military*] (AABC)
DBOM .... Design, Build, Operate, Maintain
DBOMP....... Database Organization and Maintenance [*or Management*] Processor
DBOO .... Design-Build-Own-Operate (AAGC)
DBOps........ Director of Bombing Operations [*Air Ministry*] [*British World War II*]
DBOS.......... Database Operating System (IAA)
DBOS.......... Disk-Based Operating System [*Computer science*] (IEEE)
DBOT .... Design-Build-Operate-Transfer (AAGC)
DBP .... Darband [*Pakistan*] [*Seismograph station code, US Geological Survey*] (SEIS)
DBP .... Database Processor
DBP .... Data Buoy Project [*Navy Coast Guard*] (DNAB)
dBP............. Decibels above One Picowatt (DEN)
DBP .... Defense Budget Project (EA)
DBP .... Defined Benefit Plan [*Human resources*] (WYGK)
DBP .... Demineralized Bone Powder [*Medicine*]
DBP .... Descent Battery Pack (KSC)
DBP .... Design Baseline Program
DbP............. Dewan Bahasa Dan Pustaka, Kuala Lumpur, Malaysia [*Library symbol Library of Congress*] (LCLS)
DBP .... Diastolic Blood Pressure [*Medicine*]
DBP .... Dibromophenol
DBP .... Dibutyl Phosphate [*Organic chemistry*] (NUCP)
DBP .... Dibutylphosphoric Acid [*Organic chemistry*]
DBP .... Dibutyl Phthalate [*Also, DBPh*] [*Organic chemistry*]
DBP .... Dichlorobenzophenone [*Also, DCBP*] [*Organic chemistry*]

DBP .... Dicionario Bibliografico Portugues [*A bibliographical publication*] [*Portugal*]
DBP .... Disinfection By-Product [*Enviromental chemistry*]
DBP .... Distobuccopulpal [*Dentistry*]
DBP .... DNA [*Deoxyribonucleic Acid*]-Binding Protein [*Genetics*]
DBP .... Dohle Body Panmyelopathy [*Medicine*] (DMAA)
DBP .... Double-Base Propellant (AAG)
DBP .... Drawbar Pull
DBP .... Dried Bakery Products [*An animal feed*]
DBPA .... Decanediylbis(phosphonic acid) [*Organic chemistry*]
DBPA .... Decanediylbis-phosphonic Acid [*Organic chemistry*]
DBPB .... Design Basis Pipe Break [*Nuclear energy*] (NRCH)
DBPC .... Di-tert-butyl-p-cresol [*Also, BHT*] [*Antioxidant*]
DBPCI .... Dibenzylphosphoryl Chloride [*Organic chemistry*]
DBPh .... Dibutyl Phthalate [*Also, DBP*] [*Organic chemistry*]
DBPH .... Division for the Blind and Physically Handicapped [*Later, NLS*] [*Library of Congress*]
DBPO .... Data Buoy Project Office [*Later, NDBC*] [*National Oceanic and Atmospheric Administration*]
DBPR .... DB - Panhard Registry (EA)
DBPW .... Decibels above One Picowatt (IAA)
DBQ .... Database Query (MCD)
DBQ .... Debrisoquin [*Pharmacology*] (DAVI)
DBQ .... Dental Board of Queensland [*Australia*]
DBQ .... [*The*] Dictionary of Biographical Quotation [*A publication*]
DBQ .... Dubuque [*Iowa*] [*Airport symbol*] (OAG)
DBQ .... Dubuque [*Iowa*] [*Seismograph station code, US Geological Survey*] (SEIS)
DBR .... Database Retrieval
DBR .... Data Block Reader [*Computer science*] (SAA)
DBR .... David Brown Racing [*Prefix designation on Aston-Martin racing cars*] [*British*]
DBR .... Descriptor Base Register [*Computer science*] (IAA)
DBR .... Direct Bilirubin [*Also, DBIL, DBili*] [*Clinical chemistry*] (DAVI)
DBR .... Director of Biological Research [*Military British*]
DBR .... Disk, Balls, and Roller
DBR .... Distributed Bragg Reflector [*LASER*]
DBR .... Doppler Beam Rider (MCD)
DBR .... Doubly Buffered Ringer [*Physiology*]
DBR .... Dubrovnik [*Yugoslavia*] [*Seismograph station code, US Geological Survey Closed*] (SEIS)
DBR .... National Society, Daughters of the Barons of Runnemede (EA)
dBRAP .... Decibels above Reference Acoustic Power (DEN)
DBRC .... Dairy Breeding Research Center [*Pennsylvania State University*] [*Research center*] (RCD)
DBRC .... Database Recovery Control [*Computer science*] (HGAA)
DBRE .... Association of American Railroads, Economics and Finance Department Library, Washington, DC [*Library symbol Library of Congress*] (LCLS)
DBRF .... Dog Bite-Related Fatality
DBRI .... Danish Building Research Institute
DBRITE .... Digital Bright RADAR Indicator Tower Equipment [*Air traffic control*]
DBRL .... Dibrell Brothers, Inc. [*NASDAQ symbol*] (NQ)
DBRN .... Data Bank Release Notice (NASA)
dBRN .... Decibels above Reference Noise
DBRN .... Dress Barn [*NASDAQ symbol*] (SAG)
dBRNC .... Decibels above Reference Noise, C-Message Weighted (IEEE)
DBRS .... De Beers Consolidated Mines [*NASDAQ symbol*] (NQ)
dbrs .... Debris (VRA)
DBRSY .... DeBeers Cons Mns ADR [*NASDAQ symbol*] (TTSB)
DB RTS....... Debenture Rights [*Investment term*] (MHDW)
DBRTS .... Double-Barrier Resonant Tunneling Structure [*Physics*]
DBS .... Danbus Resources, Inc. [*Vancouver Stock Exchange symbol*]
DBS .... Database Access Service [*Eastern Telecommunications Philippines, Inc.*] [*Information service or system*] (IID)
DBS .... Database Software (IAA)
DBS .... Data Base Supplier (NITA)
DBS .... Database System (MCD)
DBS .... Deep Brain Stimulation [*Neurology*] (DAVI)
DBS .... Demodulator BIT [*Binary Digit*] Synchronizer (MCD)
DBS .... Denis Browne Splint [*Orthopedics*] (DAVI)
DBS .... Despeciated Bovine Serum
DBS .... Dibromosalicil [*Germicide*]
DBS .... Dibromostyrene [*Organic chemistry*]
DBS .... Dibutyl Sebacate [*Organic chemistry*]
DBS .... Dibutyl Sulfate [*Organic chemistry*]
DBS .... Dictionnaire de la Bible. Supplement [*A publication*] (BJA)
DBS .... Digital Beacon Simulator (MCD)
DBS .... Diminshed Breath Sound [*Medicine*] (DAVI)
DBS .... Diploma in Buddhist Studies
DBS .... Direct Broadcast Satellite [*Television transmission system in which signals are transmitted by satellite directly to individual locations*] (MCD)
DBS .... Direct Broadcast System
DBS .... Distressed British Seaman [*Granted a free passage home*]
DBS .... Division Battle Simulation
DBS .... Division of Biologics Standards [*FDA*]
DBS .... Doctor of Business Science
DBS .... Dodecyl Benzenesulfonate [*Organic chemistry*]
DBS .... Dominion Bureau of Statistics [*Canada*]
DBS .... Donkey Breed Society [*British*] (DBA)
DBS .... Doppler Beam Sampling [*Air navigation*]
DBS .... Doppler Beam Shaping
DBS .... Doppler Beam Sharpener
DBS .... Doppler Broadening Spectroscopy

DBS	Double Bass [*Music*]
DBS	Double Beam Spectrophotometer
DBS	Double Blind Study
DBS	Drama Book Specialists
DBS	Drinking Behavior Scale [*Test*]
DBS	Dual-Beam-Sputtering [*Coating technology*]
DBS	Dubois, ID [*Location identifier FAA*] (FAAL)
DBS	United States National Bureau of Standards, Gaithersburg, MD [*Library symbol Library of Congress*] (LCLS)
DBSA	Dawn Bible Students Association (EA)
DBSA	Dental Board of South Australia
DBSA	Direct Broadcast Satellite Association [*Later, SBCA*] (EA)
DBSC	(Dibutylaminosulfenyl)methylcarbamate [*Insecticide*]
DBSC	Digital Block Slave Clock [*Computer science*]
DBSC	Direct Broadcast Satellite Corp. [*Bethesda, MD*] [*Telecommunications*] (TSSD)
DB Sc	Doctor of Business Science
DBSE	Distance between Shaft Ends [*Mechanical engineering*]
DBSM	Decibels per Square Meter
DBSO	District Base Service Office
DBSP	Double-Base Solid Propellant (MSA)
DBSR/SQL ...	Database System Relational/Structured Query Language [*NCR Corp.*]
DBSSS	Double Bowl Stainless Steel Sink [*Classified advertising*] (ADA)
DBST	Digital Block Schmitt Trigger [*Computer science*]
DBST	Double Bituminous Surface Treatment
DBST	Double British Standard Time (IAA)
DBST	Double British Summer Time
DBT	Deballasted Test Vehicle
DBT	Debit (ROG)
DBT	Debra Tabor [*Ethiopia*] [*Airport symbol*] (AD)
DBT	Deck Board Tie Connector [*Simpson Strong-Tie*] [*Construction*]
DBT	Department of Biotechnology [*Medicine*]
DBT	Depleted Base Transistor (IAA)
DBT	Design Basis Tornado [*Nuclear energy*] (NRCH)
DBT	Dibenzothiophene [*Organic chemistry*]
DBT	Dibutyltin [*Organic chemistry*]
DBT	Dictionary of Biblical Theology [*A publication*] (BJA)
DBT	(Dodecylbenzyl)trimethylammonium Chloride [*Organic chemistry*]
DBT	Doppler Bearing Tracker [*Military*] (CAAL)
DBT	Double-Base Transistor
Dbt	Downbeat [*A publication*] (BRI)
DBT	Dry Bed Training [*Medicine*]
DBT	Dry Blood Temperature (MAE)
DBT	Dry Bulb Temperature
DBTC	Department of Business, Technology, and Communications [*Northern Territory*] [*Australia*]
DBTDL	Dibutyltin Dilaurate [*Organic chemistry*]
DBTF	Doubtful (FAAC)
DBTG	Database Task Group [*CODASYL*]
DBTL	Dibutyltin Dilaurate [*Organic chemistry*]
DBTO	DBT Online, Inc. [*NASDAQ symbol*] (SAG)
DBTO	Di(benzotriazolyl)oxalate [*Organic chemistry*]
DBT Onl	DBT Online, Inc. [*Associated Press*] (SAG)
DBTT	Ductile to Brittle Transition Temperature
dBU	Decibel Unit
DBU	Diazabicycloundecene [*Biochemistry*]
DBU	Diazobicycloundecane [*Organic chemistry*]
DBU	Digital Buffer Unit
DBU	Disadvantaged Business Utilization (MCD)
DBUR	Databank Update Request (NASA)
DBus	Doctor of Business (ADA)
DBUS	Dun & Bradstreet United States [*STM Systems Corp.*] [*Canada Information service or system*] (CRD)
DBUT	Database Update Time
DBV	De Badande Vannerna [*Sweden*]
dBV	Decibels above One Volt
DBV	Dental Board of Victoria [*Australia*]
DBV	Deutsches Bucherverzeichnis [*A bibliographic publication*] [*German*]
DBV	Diagonal Braked Vehicle [*FAA*]
DBV	Dieticians' Board of Victoria [*Australia*]
DBV	Distributed Budget Variance (MCD)
DBV	Doppler Broadening Velocity [*Spectroscopy*] (OA)
DBV	DTIC [*Dacarbazine*], BCNU , and Vincristine [*Carmustine*] [*Antineoplastic drug regimen*] (DAVI)
DBV	Dubrovnik [*Former Yugoslavia*] [*Airport symbol*] (OAG)
DBVF	Dual Bowl Vibratory Feeder
DBW	Data Bus Wire [*Computer science*] (MCD)
dBW	Decibels above One Watt
DBW	Design Bandwidth
DBW	Desirable Body Weight [*Medicine*]
DBW	Differential Ballistic Wind
DBW	Drive by Wire [*Electronics Automotive engineering*]
DBWC	Differential Ballistic Wind Computer
DBWI	Disc Brake Wear Indicator [*Automotive engineering*]
DBWO	Differential Ballistic Wind Offset
DBWP	Double Braid Weatherproof [*Wire insulation*] (IAA)
DBX	Decibel Above the Reference Coupling (MCD)
dbx	Decibels Expanded [*Initialism is name of electronics company and brand name of its products*]
DBY	Dalby [*Australia Airport symbol*] (OAG)
DBZ	Dibenzamine [*Pharmacology*] (DAVI)
DC	Complete Depolarization
DC	Cuba [*License plate code assigned to foreign diplomats in the US*]
DC	Da Capo [*Return to Beginning*] [*Music*]

DC	Daily Census [*Medicine*]
DC	Dairylea Cooperative (EA)
DC	Daisy Chains [*Oil industry term*]
DC	"Daisy Cutter" [*A type of World War II bomb*]
DC	Damage Control [*or Controlman*] [*Navy*]
DC	DANSE Coalition (EA)
DC	Danube Commission (EA)
DC	Data Call
DC	Data Camera
DC	Data Cartridge
DC	Data Cell [*Computer science*]
DC	Data Center (EA)
DC	Data Channel [*Computer science*]
DC	Data Check (BUR)
DC	Data Classifier (IEEE)
DC	Data Code
DC	Data Collection
DC	Data Communication [*Computer science*] (BUR)
DC	Data Concentrator [*Computer science*] (BUR)
DC	Data Control (AFM)
DC	Data Controller
D/C	Data Conversion [*Computer science*] (KSC)
DC	Data Coordinator (MCD)
DC	Data Counter [*Computer science*] (IAA)
DC	Datametrics Corp. [*AMEX symbol*] (SPSG)
DC	Daughters of Charity [*Australia*]
DC	Daughters of Charity of St. Vincent de Paul [*Roman Catholic religious order*]
DC	Daughters of the Cincinnati (EA)
DC	Daughters of the Cross [*Roman Catholic religious order*]
DC	Daunomycin, Cytarabine [*Antineoplastic drug*] (CDI)
DC	Davy Crockett [*A tactical atomic weapon*] [*Army*]
DC	Dead Center
DC	Death Certificate
DC	Debit Collection
DC	Decade Counter
DC	Decagram [*Unit of issue*] [*Military*] (DNAB)
DC	De Candolle [*Botanist, 1778-1841*] (ROG)
DC	Decertify
DC	Decimal Classification
DC	Deck Cargo
DC	Deck Count
DC	Deck Court
DC	Decoder Connector
DC	Decontamination
DC	Decorators Club (EA)
DC	Decrease
DC	Deep Discount Issue [*In bond listings of newspapers*] [*Investment term*]
DC	Defense Committee (NATG)
DC	Defense Counsel
DC	Define Constant (MDG)
DC	Definitive Contract
DC	Degree of Conjugation [*Analytical biochemistry*]
DC	Degrees Celsius (KSC)
DC	Deiters' Cell [*Anatomy*]
DC	Delay Code
DC	Delayed Coker [*Chemical engineering*]
DC	Deleted Unpostable from Cards [*IRS*]
DC	Delivered Capacity
DC	Delray Connecting Railroad Co. [*AAR code*]
DC	Democracia Cristiana [*Christian Democratic Party*] [*Colorado Political party*] (PPW)
DC	Democracia Cristiana [*Christian Democratic Party*] [*Paraguay*] [*Political party*] (PD)
DC	Dendritic Cell [*Cytology*]
DC	Density Controller
DC	Dental Corps [*Navy*]
DC	Deoxycholate [*Biochemistry*] (MAE)
dC	Deoxycytidylate [*Biochemistry*]
DC	Departmental Circulars
DC	Departmental Computing
DC	Department of Commerce
DC	Dependent Coverage Rider [*Health insurance*] (GHCT)
DC	Deposited Carbon
DC	Depth Charge [*Aerial*] [*Navy*]
DC	Deputy Captain [*Military British*] (ROG)
DC	Deputy Chief
DC	Deputy Commandant
DC	Deputy Commissioner [*British*] (ADA)
DC	Deputy [*Police*] Commissioner (LAIN)
DC	Deputy Consul
DC	Deputy Counsel [*British*] (ADA)
DC	Descriptor Code [*Database terminology*] (NITA)
DC	Design Change (AAG)
DC	Design Concept
DC	Design Contractor (NRCH)
DC	Design Cooperative [*British*]
DC	Design Council [*British*] (DI)
DC	Designs for Change [*An association*] (EA)
DC	Desk Checking (IAA)
DC	Destruct Charge
DC	Detail Condition (MDG)
DC	Detection Coil [*Magneto-encephalography*]
DC	Detective Constable [*Scotland Yard*]

D/C............	Detention Clause [*Insurance*]
DC............	Deterioration Control
DC............	Deuterocanonicals
DC............	Developed Country
DC............	Developing Country
DC............	Development Center (MCD)
DC............	Development Characteristic
DC............	Development Commission [*British*]
DC............	Development Committee
DC............	Development Costs
DC............	Deviation Clause [*Business term*]
DC............	Device Context (PCM)
DC............	Device Control
DC............	Device Coordinate
DC............	Dewey Decimal Classification [*Also, DDC*]
DC............	Diagnostic Center
DC............	Diagnostic Code [*Medicine*]
DC............	Diagonal Conjugate [*Medicine*]
D/C............	Diarrhea/Constipation (MEDA)
DC............	Dielectric Constant
DC............	Difference, Center
DC............	Different Coupling [*Music*]
DC............	Differential Calculus (AAG)
DC............	Differential Correction
DC............	Differential Cross Talk (IAA)
DC............	Difficult Communication
DC............	Digestibility Coefficient (OA)
DC............	Digital Clock
DC............	Digital Code (AAG)
DC............	Digital Comparator
DC............	Digital Computer
DC............	Digital Control (IAA)
DC............	Digit Copying [*Psychiatry*]
DC............	Dihydrocodeine [*An analgesic*]
DC............	Dilated Cardiomyopathy [*Cardiology*]
DC............	Dinero Contante [*Cash*] [*Spanish Business term*]
DC............	Diners Club, Inc. (ADA)
DC............	Diode Cathode (IAA)
DC............	Dip Coating
DC............	Diphenylarsine Cyanide
DC............	Diphenylcyanoarsine [*A war gas*]
DC............	Diplomatic Corps
DC............	Direct and Consensual [*Neurology and ophthalmology*] (DAVI)
DC............	Direct Command
DC............	Direct Connection [*Telecommunications*] (OA)
DC............	Direct Control (IAA)
DC............	Direct Coupled
DC............	Direct Current
dc............	Direct Current (IDOE)
DC............	Direct Cycle
DC............	Directed Change (MCD)
DC............	Directional Control [*Rocket*] (RDA)
DC............	Directional Coupler
DC............	Direction Center [*SAGE*] [*RADAR*]
DC............	Direction Cosine (KSC)
DC............	Direction Cycle (MDG)
DC............	Directives Control [*Employment and Training Administration*] [*Department of Labor*]
DC............	Direct Operating Cost (DA)
DC............	Director Deputy of Communications-Electronics (AFIT)
DC............	Director of Ceremonies [*Freemasonry*] (ROG)
DC............	Directory Clearinghouse [*Defunct*] (EA)
DC............	Dirt [*or Dust*] Collector (AAG)
DC............	Disabled Child [*Title XVI*] [*Social Security Administration*] (OICC)
DC............	Disarmament Commission [*Also, DC (UN), UNDC*]
DC............	Disaster Control (AAG)
DC............	Disc Controller [*Computer science*] (HGAA)
DC............	Discharge [*or Discharged*]
DC1............	Disciples of Christ
DC............	Discommensurate Model [*Physics*]
DC............	Disconnect (NTCM)
DC............	Discontinue
DC............	Discrepancy Check (KSC)
DC............	Discrete (IAA)
DC............	Discrete Command
DC............	Dishonored Check [*IRS*]
DC............	Disk Controller [*Computer science*] (IEEE)
DC............	Disk to Card [*Computer science*] (IAA)
DC............	Disorderly Conduct
DC............	Dispersion Coefficient
DC............	Displaced Civilian [*Military*] (INF)
DC............	Display Code
DC............	Display Compartments [*Freight*]
DC............	Display Computer
DC............	Display Console (KSC)
DC............	Display Coupler (MCD)
D/C............	Disseminated Intravascular Coagulation [*Hematology*] (DAVI)
D/C............	Dissimilarity Coefficient [*Numerical taxonomy*]
DC............	Distance (IAA)
DC............	Distocervical [*Dentistry*]
DC............	Distorted Communication (IAA)
D/C............	Distribution Centers
DC............	Distribution Code
DC............	Distribution Coefficient
DC............	District Commissioner [*British government*]
DC............	District Council [*British*]
DC............	District Court
DC............	District of Columbia [*Postal code*]
DC............	District of Columbia Reports [*A publication*] (DLA)
DC............	Divisional Court [*Legal term*] (DLA)
DC............	Division of Classification [*Energy Research and Development Administration*]
DC............	Division of Contracts
DC............	Doctor of Chiropractic
DC............	Doctor of Chiropraxis
DC............	Document Code [*Computer science*]
DC............	Document Control
DC............	Domestic Council [*Executive Office of the President*] [*Abolished 1978, functions transferred to the President*]
DC............	Donor's Cells [*Medicine*]
DC............	Door Closer (AAG)
DC............	Dopo Cristo [*After Christ*] [*Italian*]
DC............	Dorsal Cortex [*Neuroanatomy*]
DC............	Dot Cycle [*Telecommunications*] (IAA)
DC............	Double Cap [*or Crown*] [*Paper size*]
DC............	Double Column [*Publishing*] (NTCM)
DC............	Double-Concentric
DC............	Double Conductor
DC............	Double Contact [*Switch*]
DC............	Double Contact [*Lamp base type*] (NTCM)
DC............	Double Cotton [*Wire insulation*] (AAG)
DC............	Double Crochet
DC............	Double Cropped [*Agriculture*]
DC............	Double Crown [*Paper*] (DGA)
DC............	Double Crown [*Monetary unit*] [*British*]
DC............	Double-Crucible [*Optics*] (EECA)
DC............	Double Current (IAA)
dc............	Double-Cylinder Tank [*Liquid gas carriers*]
DC............	Douglas Commercial [*Airplane*] (IIA)
DC............	Down Center [*Theater*] (WDMC)
DC............	Downconverter [*Satellite communications*]
DC............	Downtime Costs [*Quality control*]
DC............	Dracula and Co. [*An association*] (EA)
DC............	Drag Coefficient
DC............	Drain Channel (NRCH)
DC............	Drama Criticism [*A publication*]
DC............	Drawing Center (EA)
DC............	Drawing Change (AAG)
DC............	Drift Chamber (MCD)
D/C............	Drift Correction
DC............	Driver Cell (IAA)
DC............	Dry Chemical System [*NFPA pre-fire planning symbol*] (NFPA)
DC............	Dual Capable (NATG)
DC............	Dual Channel
DC............	Dublin Castle
DC............	Duchy of Cornwall [*British*] (ROG)
dc............	Duck (VRA)
DC............	Duct Carcinoma [*Oncology*]
DC............	Duplicate Copy
DC............	Duty Controller [*Tactical Air Command*]
DC............	Duty Cycle [*Engineering*]
DC............	Dyskeratosis Congenita [*Medicine*] (DMAA)
DC............	I/S Datacentralen [*Information service or system*] (IID)
DC............	McDonnell-Douglas Aircraft Co., Inc. [*ICAO aircraft manufacturer identifier*] (ICAO)
DC............	Partito della Democrazia Cristiana [*Christian Democrat Party*] [*Italy Political party*] (EY)
DC............	Pennsylvania District and County Reports [*A publication*] (DLA)
DC............	Trans Catalina Airlines [*ICAO designator*] (AD)
DC............	Treasury Department Circular [*United States*] [*A publication*] (DLA)
DC............	United States Department of Commerce, Washington, DC [*Library symbol Library of Congress*] (LCLS)
DC1............	United States District Court (DLA)
DC1............	Damage Controlman, First Class [*Navy*] (DNAB)
DC2............	Damage Controlman, Second Class [*Navy*] (DNAB)
DC 2d	Pennsylvania District and County Reports, Second Series [*A publication*] (DLA)
DC3............	Damage Controlman, Third Class [*Navy*] (DNAB)
DC³............	Distributed Command, Control, and Communications [*Army*]
DC³I............	Distributed Command, Control, Communications, and Intelligence [*Army*] (RDA)
DC63............	Darvon Compound 63 [*Eli Lilly & Co.*] (DAVI)
DCA	Corcoran Art Gallery, Washington, DC [*Library symbol Library of Congress*] (LCLS)
DCA	Dachshund Club of America (EA)
DCA	Dacono-Air [*Former USSR*] [*FAA designator*] (FAAC)
DCA	Dalmatian Club of America (EA)
DCA	Damage Control Assessment (MCD)
DCA	Damage Control Assistant [*Military*] (NVT)
DCA	Dance Critics Association (EA)
DCA	Data Communications Administrator
DCA	Data Correction Amplifier
DCA	Debt Collection Agency (DCTA)
DCA	Decade Counting Assembly (IEEE)
DCA	Defense Communications Agency [*Arlington, VA*] [*DoD*]
DCA	Defense Contract Administrator (MCD)
DCA	Defense Contre Aeronefs [*Antiaircraft Defense*] [*French*]
DCA	Defense Control Administration
DCA	Defense Cooperation Agreement (MCD)
DCA	Defensive Counterair [*Army*] (ADDR)

DCA .... Deferred Commercial Annuity [*Insurance*]
DCA .... Deferred Compensation Administrator
DCA .... Deflection Coil Amplifier
DCA .... Delahaye Club of America (EA)
DCA .... Democratic Congress Alliance [*Gambia*]
DCA .... Denmark Cheese Association [*Defunct*] (EA)
DCA .... Deoxycholate-Citrate Agar [*Microbiology*]
DCA .... Deoxycholic Acid [*Biochemistry*]
DCA .... Deoxycorticosterone [*or Desoxycorticosterone*] Acetate [*Also, DOCA*] [*Endocrinology*]
DCA .... Department of Courts Administration [*New South Wales*] [*Australia*]
DCA .... Deputy Chief Architect [*British*]
DCA .... Deputy Chief of Staff for Administration
DCA .... Deputy County Architect [*British*]
DCA .... Design Change Authorization (KSC)
DCA .... DeSoto Club of America (EA)
DCA .... Desoxycorticosterone Acetate [*Endocrinology*] (MAH)
DCA .... Detachable Container Association [*Defunct*] (EA)
DCA .... Detrended Correspondence Analysis [*Mathematics*]
DCA .... Device Control Area (IAA)
DCA .... Devon Cattle Association (EA)
DCA .... Diagnostic Connector Assembly (RDA)
DCA .... Diamond Council of America (EA)
DCA .... Diastematic Club of America [*Later, IDC*] (EA)
DCA .... Dicarboxylic Aciduria [*Medicine*]
DCA .... Dichloroacetate [*Organic chemistry*]
DCA .... Dichloroacetic Acid [*Pharmacology*] (DAVI)
DCA .... Dichloroaniline [*Dye intermediate*]
DCA .... Dictionary of Christian Antiquities [*A publication*] (BJA)
DCA .... Dicyanoanthracene [*Organic chemistry*]
DCA .... Digital Command Assembly [*NASA*] (KSC)
DCA .... Digital Communications Associates, Inc. [*Alpharetta, GA*] (CDE)
DCA .... Digital Computer Association (MUGU)
DCA .... DiLucia Chinese Alphabet [*57-character Chinese type font created for typewriter keyboards*]
DCA .... Direct Calorimetric Analysis (OA)
DCA .... Direct-Contact Aftercooler [*Engineering*]
DCA .... Direct-Current Amplifier
DCA .... Direct-Current Arc
DCA .... Direction Center Active [*SAGE*] [*RADAR*]
DCA .... Directorate of Civil Aviation
DCA .... Director of Civil Affairs [*Military British*]
DCA .... Discrepancy Control Area (SAA)
DCA .... Displacement Contour Analyzer (MCD)
DCA .... Distributed Communications Architecture (BUR)
DCA .... Distribution Contractors Association [*Tulsa, OK*] (EA)
DCA .... Distribution Control Assembly (MCD)
DCA .... Divisional Court of Appeal [*Legal term*] (ILCA)
DCA .... Doctor of Commercial Arts
DCA .... Doctor of Creative Arts
DCA .... Document Change Analysis (SAA)
DCA .... Document Change Authorization (SAA)
DCA .... Document Content Architecture [*IBM Corp.*]
DCA .... Document Control Assistant [*Environmental Protection Agency*] (EPA)
DCA .... Doll Collectors of America (EA)
DCA .... Doppler Count Accumulator (IAA)
DCA .... Dorion's Queen's Bench Reports [*Canada*] [*A publication*] (DLA)
DCA .... Dosimeter Corp. of America [*Nuclear energy*] (NRCH)
DCA .... Double Conversion Adapter
DCA .... Downlink Channel Assignment (CAAL)
DCA .... Drift Correction Angle
DCA .... Driver Control Area [*Computer science*] (BUR)
DCA .... Dual-Capable Aircraft (MCD)
DCA .... Dynamic Channel Allocation (PDAA)
DCA .... Washington [*DC*] National Airport [*Airport symbol*]
DCAA .... Defense Contract Audit Agency [*DoD*]
DCAA .... Dichloroacetic Acid [*Organic chemistry*]
DCAA .... Dissolved Combined Amino Acid [*Marine biology*]
DCAA .... Dual-Call Auto Answer (HGAA)
DCAA CAM... Defense Contract Audit Agency Contract Audit Manual [*A publication*] (AAGC)
DCAAI .... Defense Contract Audit Agency Instruction (AAGC)
DCAAM .... Defense Contract Audit Agency Manual [*A publication*] (AAGC)
DCAAP .... Defense Contract Audit Agency Pamphlets [*DoD*]
DCAAR .... Defense Contract Audit Agency Regulation [*A publication*] (AAGC)
DCAB .... Defense Contract Adjustment Board (AAGC)
DCAB .... Department of Commerce Appeals Board (AAGC)
DCAB .... United States Civil Aeronautics Board, Washington, DC [*Library symbol Library of Congress*] (LCLS)
DCABG........ Double Coronary Artery Bypass Graft [*Medicine*]
DCAC .... Defense Communications Agency Circular
DCAC .... Design Change Approval Committee (SAA)
DCAC .... Dichloroacetyl Chloride [*Organic chemistry*]
DCAC .... Direct-Current / Alternating-Current (IAA)
DCACA .... Data Collection, Analysis, and Corrective Action (CAAL)
DCA/CCCS... Defense Communications Agency Center for Command, Control, and Communications Systems [*Arlington, VA*]
DCA/CCSO ... Defense Communications Agency Command and Control Systems Organization [*Washington, DC*]
DCADS........ Defense Contract Action Data System (AAGC)
DCaE........... Canadian Embassy, Washington, DC [*Library symbol Library of Congress*] (LCLS)
DCAe .... Diploma of the College of Aeronautics [*British*]
DCAEUR....... Defense Communications Agency, Europe (NATG)

DCAF .... Design Corrective Action Form
DCAG .... Deputy Air Wing Commander [*No longer used*] [*Navy*] (DOMA)
DCAI .... Defense Communications Agency Instruction
DCAI .... Defense Contract Audit Institute (AAGC)
DCAI .... Dialysis Corp. Amer [*NASDAQ symbol*] (TTSB)
DCAI .... Dialysis Corp. of America [*NASDAQ symbol*] (SAG)
DCAI .... Digital Consulting Associates, Inc. [*Andover, MA*] [*Later, DCI*] [*Telecommunications*] (TSSD)
DCAI .... Direct-Current Analog Input (MCD)
DCAIU .... Dialysis Corp. Amer Unit [*NASDAQ symbol*] (TTSB)
DCAIW .... Dialysis Corp. Amer Wrrt [*NASDAQ symbol*] (TTSB)
DCAJ .... Dixie Council of Authors and Journalists (EAJ)
DCA/JDSSC... Defense Communications Agency Joint Data Systems Support Center [*Washington, DC*]
DCAL .... Center for Applied Linguistics, Washington, DC [*Library symbol Library of Congress*] (LCLS)
DCAL .... Danquah. Cases in Akan Law [*Ghana*] [*A publication*] (DLA)
DCAM .... Data Collection Access Method
DCAM .... Data Communication Access Method (IAA)
DCAM .... Defense Contract Audit Agency Manual [*A publication*] (AAGC)
DCAM .... Director of Craft and Amphibious Material [*British military*] (DMA)
DCAMIP ...... Data Center for Atomic and Molecular Ionization Processes
DCAMP ...... Dibutyryl Cyclic Adenosine Monophosphate [*Organic chemistry*] (DAVI)
DCA/MSO.... Defense Communications Agency/MILSATCOM [*Military Satellite Communications*] Systems Office [*Arlington, VA*]
DCAN .... Defense Communications Agency Note [*or Notice*]
DC & B .... Dilation, Curettage, and Biopsy [*Gynecology*] (DAVI)
DC & C .... Diabetes Control and Complications [*Medicine*]
DC & S .... Detroit, Caro & Sandusky Railroad (IIA)
DC & T .... Detection, Classification, and Targeting [*or Tracking*]
DC & TSC ... Defense Clothing and Textile Supply Center [*Later, Defense Personnel Support Center*] [*DoD*]
D Can L ...... Doctor of Canon Law
DCAO .... Digital Card and-or Gate [*Computer science*]
DCAOC .... Defense Communications Agency Operations Center
DCap........... Capitol [*Record label*] [*Great Britain*]
DCAP .... Decompression Computation and Analysis Program
DCAP .... Deficiency Corrective Action Program [*Surface missile systems*]
DCAP .... Dependent Care Assistance Plan [*Insurance*] (WYGK)
DCAP .... Dihydrocapaicin [*Biochemistry*]
DCAP .... Double Foolscap [*Paper*] (ADA)
DC App .... District of Columbia Appeals Reports [*A publication*] (DLA)
DCAR .... Design Corrective Action Report (NASA)
DCAR .... Discrepancy and Corrective Action Report
DCARE .... Driver Control Area Region Extension [*Computer science*] (BUR)
DCART .... Disease-Controlling Antirheumatic Therapy [*Medicine*]
DCAS .... Corcoran School of Art, Washington, DC [*Library symbol Library of Congress*] (LCLS)
D/CAS .... Data Cassette (CDE)
DCAS .... Data Collection and Analysis System [*NASA*]
DCAS .... Defense Contract Administration Services [*DoD*]
DCAS .... Deputy Chief of the Air Staff [*British*]
DCAS .... Deputy Commander of Aerospace Systems [*Inglewood, CA*] [*Air Force*]
DCAS .... Digital Control and Automation System (NITA)
DCAS .... Distribution Cost Analysis System (MCD)
DCASA .... Defense Contract Administration Services Agency (AAGC)
DCASD .... Defense Contract Administration Services District [*DoD*] (AABC)
DCASEF .... Defense Communications Agency Systems Engineering Facility [*Reston, VA*]
DCASMA ..... Defense Contract Administration Services Management Area [*DoD*] (MCD)
DCASMARO... Defense Contract Administration Services Management Area Regional Office (AAGC)
DCASO .... Defense Contract Administration Services Office [*DoD*] (AABC)
DCASPO....... Defense Contract Administration Services Plant Office [*DoD*] (DNAB)
DCASPRO ... Defense Contract Administration Services Plant Representative Office [*DoD*] (AABC)
DCASR .... Defense Contract Administration Services Region [*DoD*]
DCASR .... Defense Contract Administration Services Region (USGC)
DCASS .... Defense Communications and Army Switched System (RDA)
DCAT .... Developing Cognitive Abilities Test [*Canadian Comprehensive Assessment Program*]
DCAT .... Directional Control Antitank [*Missile*]
DCAT .... Discourse Comprehension Abilities Test (EDAC)
DCAT .... Drug, Chemical, and Allied Trades Association (EA)
DCAT .... Dry Contact Acoustic Transmission [*Automotive engineering*]
DCATS .... Defense Communications and Army Transmissions System [*DoD*]
DC-AUTOMET... Directional Controlled-Automatic Meteorological Compensation (DNAB)
DCAVU........ Clear or Scattered Clouds and Visibility Greater than Ten, Remainder of Report Missing [*NWS*] (FAAC)
DCB .... Damage Control Booklet (DNAB)
DCB .... Dame Commander of the Order of the Bath [*British*] (ADA)
DCB .... Data Control Block [*Computer science*]
DCB .... Data Control Bus [*Computer science*] (NITA)
Dcb .... December (CDAI)
DCB .... Decimal Code Binaire [*Binary Coded Decimal*] [*French Computer science*]
DCB .... Defense Communications Board
DCB .... Define Control Block [*Computer science*] (OA)
DCB .... Design Certificate Board
DCB .... Destination Code Base
DCB .... Devereux Child Behavior [*Rating scale*] [*Psychology*]

DCB	Device Control Block [*Computer science*] (PCM)
DCB	Dichlorobenzidine [*Organic chemistry*]
DCB	Dichlorobenzoate [*Organic chemistry*]
DCB	Dichlorobiphenyl [*Organic chemistry*]
DCB	Dictionary of Canadian Biography [*A publication*]
DCB	Dictionary of Christian Biography and Literature [*A publication*] (OCD)
DCB	Dicyanobenzene [*Also, DCNB*] [*Organic chemistry*]
DCB	Dilutional Cardiopulmonary Bypass [*Cardiology*] (AAMN)
DCB	Disciplinary Control Board [*Air Force*]
DCB	Distant-Control Boat
DCB	District Contracts Board [*Australia*]
DCB	Dithionite-Citrate-Bicarbonate [*Extractive chemistry*]
DCB	Division Crime Buffer
DCB	Document Control Book (MCD)
DCB	Double Cantilever Beam [*Stress condition of aluminum alloy*]
DCB	Drawout Circuit Breaker [*Electronics*] (OA)
DCB	United States Bureau of Customs, Washington, DC [*Library symbol Library of Congress*] (LCLS)
DCBA	Damage Control Breathing Apparatus (PDAA)
DCBA	Deer Breeders' Co-operative Association [*Australia*]
DCBC	Daily Child Behavior Checklist [*Psychology*] (EDAC)
DCBC	Dichlorobenzyl Chloride [*Organic chemistry*]
DCBD	Define Control Block Dummy [*Computer science*] (OA)
DCBD	Division for Children with Behavioral Disorders [*of Council for Exceptional Children*] (EA)
DCBD	Division of Cancer Biology and Diagnosis [*National Cancer Institute*]
DCBE	Double Contrast Barium Enema [*X-ray procedure*] (CPH)
DCBI	Delphos Citizens Bancorp, Inc. [*NASDAQ symbol*] (SAG)
DCBK	Desert Community Bank [*NASDAQ symbol*] (SAG)
DCBP	Dichlorobenzophenone [*Also, DBP*] [*Organic chemistry*]
DCBP	Dissemination Capacity Building Project (EDAC)
DCBRE	Defence Chemical, Biological, and Radiation Establishment [*Canada*]
DCBRL	Defence Chemical, Biological, and Radiation Laboratories [*Canada*]
DCBS	Dual Combined Brake System [*Motorcycle engineering*]
DCBTF	Dichlorobenzotrifluoride [*Organic chemistry*]
DCC	Caribbean Air Cargo [*Barbados*] [*ICAO designator*] (FAAC)
DCC	Chamber of Commerce of the United States, Washington, DC [*Library symbol Library of Congress*] (LCLS)
DCC	Chief Damage Controlman [*Navy*]
DCC	Dairy Council of California (SRA)
DCC	Dale Carnegie Course
DCC	Dallas Cowboys Cheerleaders
DCC	Damage Control Center (NATG)
DCC	Damage Controlman, Chief [*Navy*] (DNAB)
DCC	Data Channel Converter (NITA)
DCC	Data Circuit Concentration
DCC	Data Collection Center [*Army Infantry Board*] (RDA)
DCC	Data Communication Channel (DOM)
DCC	Data Communications Channel
DCC	Data Communications Controller [*Computer science*]
DCC	Data Communications Corp. [*Information service or system*] (IID)
DCC	Data Computation Complex [*NASA*] (NASA)
DCC	Data Condition Code
DCC	Data Control Characters (CMD)
DCC	Data Country Code [*Telecommunications*] (OSI)
DCC	Day Care Center
DCC	Dean and Chapter of Canterbury [*Anglican Church*] (ROG)
DCC	Debarkation Control Center [*Navy*] (CAAL)
DCC	Deck Compression Chamber (PDAA)
DCC	Deep Catalytic Crack [*Chemical engineering*]
DCC	Defence Construction Canada
DCC	Defense Concessions Committee
DCC	Defense Control Center (AABC)
DCC	Delayed Contact Closure
DCC	Delcommune [*Zaire*] [*Seismograph station code, US Geological Survey*] (SEIS)
DCC	Delegation Catholique pour la Cooperation (EA)
DCC	Deleted in Colon Cancer [*Gene*]
DCC	Deleted in Colorectal Carcinomas [*A gene*]
DCC	Deputy Chief Constable
DCC	Design Change Control
DCC	Design Concept Change (AAG)
DCC	Development Capital Corp. [*British*]
DCC	Development Control Center
DCC	Device Cluster Controller
DCC	Device Control Character [*Computer science*] (IEEE)
DCC	Devis de Construction Canada [*Construction Specifications Canada*] [*Formerly, Association des Redacteurs de Devis du Canada - ARDC*]
DCC	Dextran-Coated Charcoal
DCC	Dick Clark Companies
DCC	Dicyclohexylcarbodiimide [*Also, DCCD, DCCI*] [*Organic chemistry*]
DCC	Dielectric Constant Change [*Analytical chemistry*]
DCC	Digital Communication Console (IAA)
DCC	Digital Compact Cassette [*Audio technology*]
DCC	Digital Control Computer
DCC	Digital Cross Current
DCC	Diocesan Consistory Court [*Legal term*] (DLA)
DCC	Diploma of Chelsea College [*British*] (DI)
DCC	Direct Cable Connection [*Computer science*]
DCC	Direct Commercial Contracts (AAGC)
DCC	Direct Computer Control
DCC	Direct Conductor-to-Circuit [*Advanced Circuit Technology, Inc.*] [*Electronics*]
DCC	Direct Control Channel
DCC	Direct Current Clamp (IAA)
DCC	Directorate of Covert Collection [*South African secret military-intelligence unit*] (ECON)
DCC	Disaster Control Center (AAG)
DCC	Discrimination and Control Computer (MUGU)
DCC	Display Channel Complex [*FAA*] (TAG)
DCC	Display Control Console (KSC)
DCC	Distributed Call Center [*Telecommunications*]
DCC	Distribution Control Center (AAG)
DCC	District Communications Center [*Navy*]
DCC	Division of Cataloging and Classification [*Later, CCS, RTSD*] [*American Library Association*]
DCC	Division of Consumer Credit [*Federal Trade Commission*]
DCC	Document Control Center
DCC	Document Control Chief [*NASA*]
DCC	Dodge City College [*Kansas*]
DCc	Double Concave [*Medicine*]
DCC	Double Cotton Covered [*Wire insulation*]
DCC	Dow Chemical Co.
DCC	Downtown Copy Center [*Washington, DC*] [*Telecommunications*] (TSSD)
DCC	Drill, Command, and Ceremony [*Military*] (DNAB)
DCC	Drone Control Center [*Military*] (MCD)
DCC	Dry-Column Chromatography
DCC	Dual Cam Clutch
DCC	Dynamic Component Change (MCD)
DCCA	Department of Commerce and Community Affairs
DCCA	Design Change Cost Analysis (PDAA)
DCCA	Dextran-Coated Charcoal Analysis [*Analytical biochemistry*]
DCCA	Dichloroisocyanuric Acid [*Organic chemistry*]
DCCA	District of Columbia Compensation Act (DLA)
DCCA	Drying Control Chemical Additive [*Ceramic technology*]
DCCAB	District of Columbia Contract Appeals Board (AAGC)
DCCAO	Deputy Chief Civil Affairs Officer [*US and Britain*]
DCCB	Defense Center Control Building [*Army*] (AABC)
DCCC	Data Communication Control Character (IEEE)
DCCC	Defense Communications Control Center
DCCC	Defense Communications Control Complex (IAA)
DCCC	Democratic Congressional Campaign Committee (EA)
DCCC	Design Change Coordination Committee (SAA)
DCCC	Domestic Coal Consumers' Council [*British*] (DI)
DCCC	Double Current Cable Code [*Telecommunications*]
DCCC	Droplet Countercurrent Chromatography
DCCD	Dicyclohexylcarbodiimide [*Also, DCC, DCCI*] [*Organic chemistry*]
DCCD	Division for Children with Communication Disorders [*Council for Exceptional Children*]
DCCE	District of Columbia Code Encyclopedia [*A publication*] (DLA)
DCCEAS	District of Columbia Council of Engineering and Architecture (SRA)
DCCG	Digital Check Character Generator (PDAA)
DCCH	Commerce Clearing House, Washington, DC [*Library symbol Library of Congress*] (LCLS)
DCCI	Data Converter-Control Indicator (DNAB)
DCCI	Dicyclohexylcarbodiimide [*Also, DCC, DCCD*] [*Organic chemistry*]
DC Cir	[*Court of Appeals for the*] District of Columbia Circuit (AAGC)
DC Cir.........	District of Columbia Court of Appeals Cases [*A publication*] (DLA)
DC Cir R	District of Columbia Circuit Court Rules [*A publication*] (DLA)
DCCL	Digital Charge-Coupled Logic (MCD)
DCCM	Master Chief Damage Controlman [*Navy rating*]
DCCMP	Daunorubicin, Cyclocytidine [*Ancitabine*], Mercaptopurine, Prednisone [*Antineoplastic drug regimen*]
DC$_{CO}$	Diffusing Capacity for Carbon Dioxide [*Medicine*] (DAVI)
DCCO	Digital Card Clock Oscillator [*Computer science*]
DC Code	District of Columbia Code [*A publication*] (DLA)
DC Code Ann...	District of Columbia Code, Annotated [*A publication*] (DLA)
DC Code Encycl...	District of Columbia Code Encyclopedia [*A publication*] (DLA)
DC Code Legis & Admin Serv...	District of Columbia Code Legislative and Administrative Service (West) [*A publication*] (DLA)
DCCP	Design Change Control Program
DCCP	Digital Computer Control Panel
DCCR	Documentation Change Control Report
DCCRM	Center for Chinese Research Materials, Washington, DC [*Library symbol Library of Congress*] (LCLS)
DCCS	Defense Case Control System (DNAB)
DCCS	Defense Communications Control System [*Air Force*]
DCCS	Design Change Clearance Sheet (MCD)
DCCS	Digital Camera Control System
DCCS	Digital Command Communications System (MCD)
DCCS	Distributed Capacity Computing System (NITA)
DCCS	Distributed Command and Control System
DCCS	Senior Chief Damage Controlman [*Navy rating*]
DCCSA	Dictionary of Computer and Control Systems Abbreviations, Signs, and Symbols [*New York: Odyssey Press, 1965*] [*A publication*]
DCCT	Design Center of Connecticut Technology
DCCT	Diabetes Control and Complications Trial
DCCT	Direct Current-Current Transformer (IAA)
DCCTC	United States Department of Defense, Command and Control Technical Center, the Pentagon, Washington, DC [*Library symbol Library of Congress*] (LCLS)
DCCU	Data Communications Control Unit (DEN)
DCCU	Data Correlation Control Unit
DCCU	Decommutator Conditioning Unit (KSC)
DCCU	Digital Command and Control Unit (NASA)
DCCU	Digital Communications and Control Unit (MCD)
DCCU	Digital Television Equipment Cluster Control Unit (MCD)
DCCU	Display Computer Control Unit (MCD)

DCCVS	Domestic Council Committee on Veterans Services [*Veterans Administration*]
DCCWS	Deputy Chief, Chemical Warfare Service [*Army*]
DCD	Congressional Digest, Washington, DC [*Library symbol Library of Congress*] (LCLS)
DCD	Damage Control Diagrams [*Naval Ship Systems Command*]
DCD	Data Carrier Detect [*or Detector*] [*Data communication signal*] [*Telecommunications*] (TEL)
DCD	Data Collecting Device (IAA)
DCD	Data Correlation and Documentation System (IAA)
DCD	Deceased (ADA)
DCD	Decennial Census Division [*Census*] (OICC)
DCD	Decode (MSA)
DCD	Decomposition Diagramer [*Computer science*]
DCD	Defecation-Collection Device [*Apollo*] [*NASA*]
DCD	Defense Communications Department (IAA)
DCD	Deflection Coil Drive
DCD	Delco Chassis Division [*General Motors Corp.*]
DCD	Department of Community Development [*Proposed government department*]
DCD	Design Change Document
DCD	Design Control Drawing
DCD	Dicyandiamide [*or Dicyanodiamide*] [*Also, DICY*] [*Organic chemistry*]
DCD	Differential Current Density
DCD	Digital Coherent Detector (OA)
DCD	Digital Compact Disk
DCD	Digital Countdown Display [*Computer science*]
DCD	Dimensional Control Drawing
DCD	Diode-Capacitor-Diode
DCD	Diploma in Chest Diseases [*British*]
DCD	Direct Contact Desulfation
DCD	Direct-Current Dialing (IAA)
DCD	Direct-Current Dump
DCD	Directorate of Combat Developments [*Army*]
DCD	Director of Combat Development [*British*] (RDA)
DCD	Director of Communications Development [*Ministry of Aircraft Production*] [*British*]
DCD	Director of Compass Department [*British military*] (DMA)
DCD	Don't-Care-a-Damn [*British naval slang term for torpedo-boat destroyer*] [*World War I*]
DCD	Double Channel Duplex
DCD	Dynamically-Correlated Domain [*Physics*]
DCD	Dynamic Computer Display (IEEE)
DCD	NAVSHIPS [*Naval Ship Systems Command*] Damage Control Diagrams
DCDA	Data Communication Dealers Association (EA)
DCDA	Delyn Cooperative Development Agency [*British*]
DCDB	Digital Cartographic Database [*Computer science*]
DC/DC	Data Communication to Disk Control
DC/DC	Direct Current to Direct Current [*Telecommunications*]
DCDCEC	Division on Career Development of the Council for Exceptional Children (EA)
DCDCR	Definition of Control, Display, and Communications Requirement (DNAB)
DCDD	Dichlorodibenzodioxin [*Also, DDD*] [*Organic chemistry*]
DCDFL	Defense Civil Disturbance Facility List
DCDG	Diode-Capacitor-Diode Gate
DCDH	Diploma in Child Dental Health [*British*] (DBQ)
DC Dist Col	United States District Court for the District of Columbia (DLA)
DCDL	Digital Control Design Language [*1968*] [*Computer science*] (CSR)
DCDL	Double Cylinder Deadlock
DCD-LPR	Digital Clock Distribution - Local Primary Reference [*Navigation systems*]
DCDM	Digitally Controlled Delta Modulator (MCD)
DCDMA	Diamond Core Drill Manufacturers Association (EA)
DCDP	Defense Center Data Processing [*Army*] (AABC)
dCDP	Deoxycytidine Diphosphate [*Biochemistry*]
DCDPO	Directorate for Civil Disturbance Planning and Operations [*Army*] (AABC)
DCDPS	Dichlorodiphenylsulfone [*Organic chemistry*]
DCDR	Data Collection and Data Relay [*Telecommunications*] (TEL)
DCDR	Decoder (AAG)
D-CDR	Deputy Commander (DNAB)
DCDR	Direct Cycle Diphenyl Reactor
DCDRS	Drone Control and Data Retrieval System [*Later, CDRS*] [*Air Force*] (MCD)
DCDS	Deceased Confirmed Dead at Scene [*Criminology*] (LAIN)
DCDS	Deputy Chief of Defence Staff [*British*]
DCDS	Digital Control Design System (IEEE)
DCDS	Digital Countdown Display System [*Computer science*]
DCDS	Distributed Computer Design System (SDI)
DCDS	Double Cotton Double Silk [*Wire insulation*]
DCDS	Dual Channel Dual Speed
DCDS(OR)	Deputy Chief of Defence Staff (Operational Requirements) [*British*]
DCDT	Decedent [*Legal shorthand*] (LWAP)
DCDT	Direct-Current Differential Transformer
DCDT	Direct-Current Displacement Transducer (IAA)
DCDT	Division on Career Development and Transition [*Council for Exceptional Children*] (PAZ)
DCDU	Data Collection and Distribution Units [*Military*] (AABC)
DCE	Dallas Cotton Exchange (EA)
DCE	Data Circuit-Terminating Equipment [*Computer science*] (BUR)
DCE	Data Communication Equipment
DCE	Data Communications Equipment (DOM)
DCE	Data Concentrating Equipment [*Computer science*] (DGA)
DCE	Data Consultants of Europe (NITA)
DCE	Data Control Equipment (IAA)
DCE	Data Conversion Equipment [*Computer science*]
DCE	Defense Combat Evaluation (AABC)
DCE	Department of Conservation and Environment [*Proposed name for US Department of the Interior*]
DCE	Department of Continuing Education (AIE)
DCE	Despin Control Electronics [*Aerospace*]
DCE	Device Control Entry [*Computer science*]
DCE	Dichloroethane [*Organic chemistry*]
DCE	Dicyanoethylene [*Organic chemistry*]
DCE	Differential Compound Engine (PDAA)
DCE	Digital Control Element (NITA)
DCE	Diploma of Curative Education [*British*]
DCE	Direct Contact Evaporator [*Chemical engineering*]
DCE	Director [*or Directorate*] of Civil Engineering [*Air Force*]
DCE	Director [*or Directorate*] of Communications - Electronics [*ADC*]
DCE	Discounted Cash Equivalent (ADA)
DCE	Distributed Computing Environment
DCE	Division of Career Education [*Office of Education*]
DCE	Dnepropetrovsk Commodity Exchange [*Ukraine*] (EY)
DCE	Doctor of Civil Engineering
DCE	Domestic Credit Expansion
DCE	Drive Control Equipment
DCEA	Democratic Council on Ethnic Americans [*Defunct*] (EA)
DCEC	Defense Communications Engineering Center [*Reston, VA*] [*DoD*] (GRD)
DC Ed	Doctor of Commercial Education
DCEE	Defence Components and Equipment Exhibition [*British*] (ITD)
DCEE	Defense Components and Equipment Exposition
DCEE	Dichloroethyl Ether [*Organic chemistry*]
D Ce Eng	Doctor of Cement Engineering
DCEF	Discounted Cash Equivalent Flow (ADA)
DCEL	Direct-Current Electroluminescence
DCEM	Drilling Cost Estimates Model [*Department of Energy*] (GFGA)
DCEO	Defense Communications Engineering Office [*Army*]
DCEO	Division Communications-Electronics Officer [*Military*] (AABC)
DCEP	Diploma of Child and Educational Psychology (ADA)
DCER	Data Circuit-Terminating Equipment Ready [*Computer science*] (ACRL)
DCER	United States Army, Corps of Engineers, Coastal Engineering Research Center, Fort Belvoir, VA [*Library symbol Library of Congress*] (LCLS)
D Cer E	Doctor of Ceramic Engineering
D Cer Eng	Doctor of Ceramic Engineering
DCERR	Depot Component/Equipment Rework Report [*Navy*] (NG)
DCES	Data Collection and Evaluation System (NVT)
DCES	Dermal Clinical Evaluation Society
DCES	Discretionary Capital Expenditure System [*Bell System*]
DCES	DSS [*Deep Space Station*] Communications Equipment Subsystem
DCET	Dicarbethoxythiamine [*Pharmacology*]
DCEU	Dictionary of Carribean English Usage [*A publication*]
DCEV	Diabetes Center of Eastern Virginia [*Eastern Virginia Medical School*]
DCF	Claretian Fathers Library, Washington, DC [*Library symbol Library of Congress*] (LCLS)
DCF	Daniell. Forms and Precedents in Chancery [*7th ed.*] [*1932*] [*A publication*] (ILCA)
DCF	Data Channel Filter [*Computer science*]
DCF	Data Collection Form [*Civil Defense*]
DCF	Data Communications Formatter (IAA)
DCF	Data Control Facility (MCD)
DCF	Data Conversion File [*Bureau of the Census*] (GFGA)
DCF	Data Correlation Facility
DCF	Data Count Field [*Computer science*] (ACRL)
DCF	Deal-Cased Frame [*Carpentry*]
DCF	Defenders of the Christian Faith [*Later, CCI*] (EA)
DCF	Degradation Conversion Factor (MCD)
DCF	Democratic Candidate Fund (EA)
DCF	Democratie Chretienne Francaise [*French Christian Democracy*] [*Political party*] (PPE)
DCF	Deoxycoformycin [*Also, dCF*] [*Antileukemia drug*]
DCF	Dependency Certificate Filed
DCF	Deputy for Contract Financing [*Air Force*]
DCF	Developing Countries Foundation of 1962 [*Denmark*] (EAIO)
DCF	Dicarboxyfluorescein [*A biological stain*]
DCF	Die Casting Federation [*Defunct*] (EA)
DCF	Direct Centrifugal Flotation [*Parasitology*]
DCF	Direct Control Feature (CMD)
DCF	Directed Chopped Fiber [*Plastics technology*]
DCF	Disaster Control Force
DCF	Discounted Cash Flow
DCF	Discrete Correlation Function [*Mathematics*]
DCF	Dishonored Check File [*IRS*]
DCF	Disk Controller/Formatter [*Computer science*]
DCF	Dispersion Coated Fabric [*Plastics technology*]
DCF	Distribution Chart File
DCF	Doctor of City Forestry
DCF	Document Composition Facility [*IBM Corp.*]
DCF	Document Control File
DCF	Dominica-Cane [*West Indies*] [*Airport symbol*] (OAG)
DCF	Dopachrome Conversion Factor [*Medicine*] (DMAA)
DCF	Dose Commitment Factor [*Radioactivity calculations*]
DCF	Dose Conversion Factor [*Radioactivity calculations*] (NRCH)
DCF	Droplet Combustion Facility
DCF	Dry Cubic Feet (ERG)

DCF............	Dynamic Coercive Force
DCFA..........	Damage Controlman, Fireman Apprentice [*Navy*]
DCFB..........	Dichlorotetrafluorobenzene [*Organic chemistry*]
DCFC..........	Dale Chapp Fan Club [*Defunct*] (EA)
DCFC..........	Danny Cooksey Fan Club (EA)
DCFC..........	David Copperfield Fan Club (EA)
DCFC..........	Dehydrated and Convenience Foods Council [*Defunct*] (EA)
DCFC..........	Desiree Coleman Fan Club (EA)
DCFC..........	Dick Curless Fan Club (EA)
DCFEM........	Dynamic Crossed-Field Electron Multiplication
DCFF..........	Digital Card Flip-Flop [*Computer science*]
DCFF..........	Direct-Current Flip-Flop [*Electronics*] (IAA)
DCFG..........	Direct-Current Free Gyro
DCFL..........	Department of Conservation, Forests, and Lands [*Victoria*] [*Australia*]
DCFL..........	Direct-Coupled FET [*Field Effect Transistor*] Logic [*Integrated circuitry*]
DCFLOS......	Dynamic Cloud Free Line of Sight (MCD)
DCFM..........	Discounted Cash Flow Method
DCFM..........	Doppler Color Flow Mapping [*Cardiology*] (DAVI)
DCFMD........	Director of Coastal Forces Material Department [*British*]
DCFN..........	Damage Controlman, Fireman [*Navy*]
DCFP..........	Dynamic Crossed-Field Photomultiplier
DCFRN........	Developing Countries Farm Radio Network (EAIO)
DCFRR........	Discounted Cash Flow Rate of Return [*Business term*]
DCFT..........	Commodity Futures Trading Commission, Washington, DC [*Library symbol Library of Congress*] (LCLS)
DCFT..........	Double-Coated Foam Tape
DCG	Dacryocystography [*Ophthalmology*] (CPH)
DCG	Damage Control Group [*Military*] (DNAB)
DCG	Dancing (ADA)
DCG	Data Control Group (MCD)
DCG	Decigram [*Unit of measure*]
DCG	Decisions of the Comptroller General
DCG	Decoupled Gun (MCD)
DCG	Definite Clause Grammar [*Computer programming*] (BYTE)
DCG	Deoxycorticosterone Glucoside [*Also, DOCG*] [*Endocrinology*]
DCG	Dependent Charge Group [*Telecommunications*] (TEL)
DCG	Deputy Chaplain-General [*British*]
DCG	Deputy Commanding General
DCG	Deputy Commissary-General
DCG	Derived Concentration Guide
DCG	Designs Coordination Group [*Telecommunications*] (TEL)
DCG	Diagnostic Cost Group
DCG	Diagonostic Cost Group [*Medicine*] (HCT)
DCG	Dichromated Gelatin
DCG	Dictionary of Christ and the Gospels [*A publication*] (BJA)
DCG	Diode-Capacitor Gate
DCG	Diploma in Careers Guidance [*British*] (DI)
DCG	Direct-Current Generator
DCG	Disaster Control Group
DCG	Disodium Cromoglycate [*Pharmacology*] (MAE)
DCG	Displacement Cardiograph [*Medicine*]
DCG	Divisional Controls Group [*British*] (NITA)
DCG	Doppler Control Gain (IAA)
DCG	Double Current Generator
DCG	Dynamic Cardiogram
DCG	Hereditary Order of the Descendants of Colonial Governors (EA)
DCG	San Diego, CA [*Location identifier FAA*] (FAAL)
DC/GCI........	Direction Center - Ground Controlled Intercept [*SAGE*] [*RADAR*] (CINC)
DCG/CONARC...	Deputy Commanding General, Continental Army Command [*Later, DCG/T*] [*Army*]
DCGFF........	Diode-Coupled Gate Flip-Flop
DCGICP........	Deputy Commanding General for International Cooperative Programs [*Army*]
DCGMD........	Deputy Commanding General for Materiel Development [*Army*]
DCGMR........	Deputy Commanding General for Materiel Readiness [*Army*]
DCGO..........	District Coast Guard Officer
DCGRDA......	Deputy Commanding General for Research, Development, and Acquisition [*Army*]
DCGS..........	Deputy Chief of the General Staff in the Field [*Military British*]
DCG/T	Deputy Commanding General, Training [*Formerly, DCG/CONARC*] [*Army*]
D Ch	Chirurgiae Doctor [*Doctor of Surgery*]
DCH	Damage Control Hulk (DNAB)
DCH	Data Channel [*Computer science*]
DCH	Data Chief
DCH	Data Communications Handler (DNAB)
DCH	Deep Case Hardened
D Ch	Delaware Chancery Reports [*A publication*] (DLA)
DCH	Delayed Cutaneous Hypersensitivity [*Medicine*] (AAMN)
DCH	Denote Chassis
DCH	Department of Community Health [*Australia*]
DCH	Dicyclohexyl [*Organic chemistry*]
DCH	Diploma in Child Health [*British*]
DCH	District Chaplain [*Navy*]
DCH	Drain Collection Header [*Nuclear energy*] (NRCH)
DCH	Reports of the United States District Court of Hawaii [*A publication*] (DLA)
DCHA..........	Dicyclohexylamine [*Organic chemistry*]
DCHAN........	Difference Channel (MSA)
D-channel....	Data Channel (PCM)
D-channel....	Delta Channel [*Used for communicating between the phone company switch and an ISDN adapter*] [*Computer science*]
DCHBH.........	Dicyclohexylborane [*Organic chemistry*]

DCHC..........	Dunbarton College of Holy Cross [*Closed, 1973*] [*Washington, DC*]
DCHD..........	Di(N-carbazoly)hexadiyne [*Organic chemistry*]
DChD	Doctor Chirurgiae Dentalis [*Doctor of Dental Surgery*] [*British*]
D Ch E	Doctor of Chemical Engineering
D Che E	Doctor of Chemical Engineering
DChem........	Doctor of Chemistry (GAGS)
D Chem	Doctor of Chemistry (PGP)
DCHEM........	Dry Chemical
D Chem E ...	Doctor of Chemical Engineering
D Ch Eng	Doctor of Chemical Engineering
DCHFB........	Dichlorohexafluorobutane [*Organic chemistry*] (MAE)
DCHi	Columbia Historical Society, Washington, DC [*Library symbol Library of Congress*] (LCLS)
DCHN..........	Dicyclohexylamine Nitrite [*Organic chemistry*] (MAE)
D Ch O	Diploma in Opthalmic Surgery [*British*]
DCHP..........	Dicyclohexyl Phthalate [*Organic chemistry*]
DCHQ..........	Damage Control Headquarters [*Military British*]
D Chr Ed	Doctor of Christian Education
DCHS	Center for Hellenic Studies, Harvard University, Washington, DC [*Library symbol Library of Congress*] (LCLS)
DCHS	Disciples of Christ Historical Society (EA)
DCHSS.........	Duchess
DCHT	Diploma in Community Health in Tropical Countries [*British*] (DBQ)
DCHT	Direct-Contact Heat Transfer [*Chemical engineering*]
DCHV..........	Domiciliary Care for Homeless Veterans [*Department of Veterans Affairs*]
DCI.............	Carnegie Institution of Washington, Washington, DC [*Library symbol Library of Congress*] (LCLS)
DCI.............	Daily Call-In
DCI.............	Damage Control Instructor [*Navy*] (DNAB)
DCI.............	DARCOM [*Development and Readiness Command, Army*] Career/ Control Inventory (MCD)
DCI.............	Data Communication Interrogate (OA)
DCI.............	Data Communications, Inc.
DCI.............	Data Communications Interface
DCI.............	Data Communications Interrogate (HGAA)
DCI.............	Data Composition, Inc. [*Information service or system*] (IID)
DCI.............	Data Courier, Inc. (IID)
DCI.............	Deaf Communications Institute [*Defunct*] (EA)
DCI.............	Decompression Illness
DCI.............	Defence Council Instructions [*Military British*]
DCI.............	Defence Counter-Proliferation Initiative (ECON)
DCI.............	Defence for Children International Movement [*See also DEI*] [*Database producer*] (EAIO)
DCI.............	Defense Computer Institute
DCI.............	Deliverable Contract Item (KSC)
DCI.............	DeLorean Club International (EA)
DCI.............	Department of Central Index [*Computer center*] [*Department of Health and Social Security*] [*British*]
DCI.............	Department of Central Intelligence [*Thailand*] (CINC)
DCI.............	Deputy Chief for Intelligence (AAG)
DCI.............	Design Change Information (SAA)
DCI.............	Des Moines & Central Iowa Railway Co. [*AAR code*]
DCI.............	Desorption Chemical Ionization
DCI.............	Dialing Code Information [*Telecommunications British*]
DCI.............	Dichloroisocoumarin [*Organic chemistry*]
DCI.............	Dichloroisoprenaline
DCI.............	Dichloroisoproterenol [*Pharmacology*]
DCI.............	Dielectric Constant Indicator
DCI.............	Differential Current Integrator (IAA)
DCI.............	Digital Clock Indicator
DCI.............	Digital Consulting, Inc. [*Andover, MA*] (TSSD)
DCI.............	Digital Control Interface [*Computer science*] (PCM)
DCI.............	Direct Carrier Injection
DCI.............	Direct Channel Interface
DCI.............	Direct Computer Input (MCD)
DCI.............	Direct-Coupled Inverter (IAA)
DCI.............	Direct Cylinder Injection [*Engine design*]
DCI.............	Director of Central Intelligence
DCI.............	Director of Combat Intelligence (MCD)
DCI.............	Director of Corporate Information
DCI.............	Disk Core Image (CMD)
DCI.............	Display Control Interface [*Computer science*] (PCM)
DCI.............	Disseminated Cryptococcus Neoformans Infection [*Medicine*]
DCI.............	Distribution Codes Institute [*Defunct*] (EA)
DCI.............	Division of Chemical Information [*American Chemical Society*] [*Information service or system*] (IID)
DCI.............	Documentation Change Instruction (KSC)
DCI.............	Donaldson Co. [*NYSE symbol*] (TTSB)
DCI.............	Donaldson Co., Inc. [*NYSE symbol*] (SPSG)
DCI.............	Double Column Inch [*Typography*] (DGA)
DCI.............	Dramatic Criticism Index [*A publication*]
DCI.............	Driving Car Intoxicated
DCI.............	Driving Control Indicator
DCI.............	Drum Corps International (EA)
DCI.............	Dry Creek [*Idaho*] [*Seismograph station code, US Geological Survey*] (SEIS)
DCI.............	Ductile Cast Iron
DCIA	Digital Card Inverting Amplifier [*Computer science*]
DCIA	Direction Center Initial Appearance (SAA)
DCIB	Data Communication Input Buffer
DCIB	Defense Counterintelligence Board (MCD)
DCIC	Defense Ceramic Information Center [*Later, MCIC*] [*Battelle Memorial Institute*] (MCD)
DCIC	Double Column Ion Chromotography

DCID	Director of Central Intelligence Directive
DCID	Director of Central Intelligence Document
DCIEM	Defence and Civil Institute of Environmental Medicine [*Canada*]
DCI-G	Carnegie Institution of Washington, Geophysical Laboratory, Washington, DC [*Library symbol Library of Congress*] (LCLS)
DCIGS	Deputy Chief of the Imperial General Staff [*Military British*]
DCII	Defense Central Index of Investigations (AFM)
DCILM	Direct Computer Input Load Module (MCD)
DCIM	Display System Computer Input Multiplexer (MCD)
DCIMI	Defense Council of Integrity in Management and Improvement [*DoD*]
DCIO	Direct Channel Interface Option
DCIP	Data Correction Indicator Panel (MUGU)
DCIP	Dichlorophenolindophenol [*Also, DCPI, DCPIP, DPIP*] [*Analytical reagent*]
DCIP	Disk Cartridge Initialization Program (CMD)
DCIP	Display and Controls Input Processor
DCIPT	Damage Control In-Port Training (NVT)
DCIR	Daily Cadweld Inspection Report [*Nuclear energy*] (NRCH)
DCIRC	Defense Contracting for Information Resources Course [*DoD*] (RDA)
DCIS	Dartmouth College Information System [*Library network*] (IT)
DCIS	Defense Criminal Investigation Service
DCIS	Delta Computec [*NASDAQ symbol*] (TTSB)
DCIS	Digital Computer Interface System (MCD)
DCIS	Distribution Construction Information System [*IBM Corp.*]
DCIS	Downrange Computer Input System (MUGU)
DCIS	Duct Carcinoma In Situ [*Oncology*]
DCIST	Directory of Computerized Information in Science and Technology [*Leonard Cohen, ed., New York: Science Associates International, 1968*] [*A publication*]
DCI-T	Carnegie Institution of Washington, Department of Terrestrial Magnetism, Washington, DC [*Library symbol Library of Congress*] (LCLS)
DCIU	Digital Control and Interface Unit (MCD)
DCI-USA	Defense for Children International - United States of America (EA)
DCivL	Doctor of Civil Law (NADA)
DCJ	Carmelitae Divini Cordis Jesu [*Carmelite Sisters of the Divine Heart of Jesus*] [*Roman Catholic religious order*]
DCJ	DISCovering Careers and Jobs [*Database*]
DCJ	District Court Judge
DCJ	Doctor of Criminal Jurisprudence
DCJC	Dawson County Junior College [*Montana*]
DCK	Dahl Creek, AK [*Location identifier FAA*] (FAAL)
DCKG	Docking (MSA)
DCKNG	Docking [*Aerospace*] (NASA)
DCKP	Direct-Current Key Pulsing (IEEE)
DCL	Data Checklist
DCL	Data Compression Library (CDE)
DCL	Data Control Language [*NCR Corp.*]
DCL	Data Control List (IAA)
DCL	Decalitre
DCL	Declaration (ADA)
DCL	Decline (WDAA)
DCL	Defence Construction [*1951*] Ltd. [*Canada*]
DCL	Delayed Call Limited [*Telecommunications*] (TEL)
DCL	Demountable Cathode Lamp
DCL	Depth of Cut Line (MCD)
DCL	Deputy Commander for Logistics (MCD)
DCL	Designate Command Line [*Computer science*]
DCL	Design Capability Line [*Army*] (AABC)
DCL	Design Change Listing
DCL	Designer Choice Logic
DCL	Detailed Checklist
DCL	Detailed Configuration List (MCD)
DCL	Detroit College of Law [*Michigan*]
DCL	Diagnostic Chemicals Ltd.
DCL	Diamond Cut Lug (DICI)
DCL	Diffuse [*or Disseminated*] Cutaneous Leishmaniasis [*Medicine*] (DMAA)
DCL	Digital Channel Link
DCL	Digital Command Language [*Digital Equipment Corp.*] (NITA)
DCL	Digital Computer Laboratory [*Massachusetts Institute of Technology*] (MCD)
DCL	Digital Control Loading [*System*] (MCD)
DCL	Digital Counter/Locator [*Medical dictation and transcription equipment*] (DAVI)
DCL	Direct Coal Liquefaction [*Fuel science*]
DCL	Direct Communications Link [*US/USSR*]
DCL	Direct-Coupled Logic
DCL	Director of Contract Labour [*Admiralty*] [*British*]
DCL	Discretionary Credit Limit [*Business term*] (MHDB)
DCL	Division of Chemical Literature [*ACS*]
DCL	Doctor of Canon Law
DCL	Doctor of Civil Law
DCL	Doctor of Classical Literature
DCL	Doctor of Commercial Law
DCL	Doctor of Comparative Law (DLA)
DCL	Document Change List (MCD)
DCL	Door Closer
DCL	Drawing Change List
DCL	Dual Current Layer (OA)
DCL	Dynamic Characteristic Load
DCL	United States Department of Commerce, Washington, DC [*OCLC symbol*] (OCLC)
DCLA	Deputy Chief of Staff, Logistics and Administration [*NATO*] (NATG)

DC Lab S	Dominion of Canada Labour Service [*Commerce Clearing House*] [*A publication*] (DLA)
DClark	Dick Clark Productions, Inc. [*Associated Press*] (SAG)
DCLC	Drift Cyclotron Loss Cone [*Plasma physics*]
DCLC	RLIN [*Research Libraries Information Netword*] code for the Library of Congress
DCLCS	Data Conversion and Limit Check Submodule [*Computer science*] (IAA)
DCLF	Diploma in Contact Lens Fitting [*British*] (DBQ)
DCLI	Duke of Cornwall's Light Infantry [*Military unit*] [*British*]
DCLIR	Dead Cat Lying in the Road [*Traffic report*]
DCLM	Department of Command, Leadership, and Management [*DoD*]
DCLN	Direct Coupled Loop Network [*Computer science*]
DCLP	Diploma in Contact Lens Practice [*British*] (DBQ)
DCLPT	In-Port Damage Control Training [*Navy*] (NVT)
DCLR	Decelerate (MSA)
DCLR	Defense Contract Litigation Reporter [*Shepard's McGraw-Hill*] [*A publication*]
DCLR	District Court Law Reports [*Hong Kong*] [*A publication*] (ILCA)
DCLR(Can)	Dominion Companies Law Reports [*Canada*] [*A publication*] (DLA)
DCLRT	Decelerate [*Aviation*] (FAAC)
DCLS	Data Collection and Location System [*Telecommunications*]
DCLS	Deoxycholate-Citrate-Lactose-Sucrose [*Agar*] [*Microbiology*]
DCISc	Doctor of Clinical Science (ADA)
DCISci	Doctor of Clinical Science (NADA)
DCLTC	Dry Cargo Loading Technical Committee [*NATO*] (NATG)
DCLTR	Decline Transfer (NOAA)
DCLU	Declutch
DCM	Chester, SC [*Location identifier FAA*] (FAAL)
DCM	Dangerous Cargo Manifest [*RSPA*] (TAG)
DCM	Data Channel Module [*Computer science*] (NOAA)
DCM	Data Communications Multiplexer
DCM	Data Conversion Machine (MCD)
DCM	Day Care Mother (ADA)
DCM	DC Noise Margin (MCD)
DCM	Decameter
DCM	Decommutator Control Memory (MCD)
DCM	Deep Chlorophyll Maximum [*Oceanography*]
DCM	Defense Common Market (MCD)
DCM	Defensive Countermaneuvering
DCM	Defined Culture Medium [*For blastoderms*]
DCM	Department of the Chief Minister [*Northern Territory*] [*Australia*]
DCM	Deputy Chief of Maintenance (MCD)
DCM	Deputy Chief of Mission [*Diplomatic corps*]
DCM	Diagnostic Controlled MODEM [*Computer science*] (BUR)
DCM	Dichloromaleic Acid [*Organic chemistry*]
DCM	Dichloromethane [*Anesthetic*] [*Organic chemistry*]
DCM	Dichloromethotrexate [*Also, DCMTX*] [*Antineoplastic drug*]
DCM	Die Casting Mold (MCD)
DCM	Digital Capacitance Meter (IDOE)
DCM	Digital Circuit Module [*Computer science*]
DCM	Digital Circuit Multiplication [*Computer science*] (ACRL)
DCM	Digital Conference Module [*Telecommunications*] (NITA)
DCM	Dilated Cardiomyopathy [*Cardiology*]
DCM	Dimension Control Memory
DCM	Diocesan Carmelites of Maine (TOCD)
DCM	Direct Connection Module [*Computer science*]
DCM	Direct-Current, Main (IAA)
DCM	Direction Cosine Matrix (MCD)
DCM	Directorate for Classification Management [*DoD*]
DCM	Director of Civilian Marksmanship [*Army*]
DCM	Directory Control Module [*Computer science*] (HGAA)
DCM	Disability Case Management [*Insurance*] (WYGK)
DCM	Display and Control Module (MCD)
DCM	Distinguished Conduct Medal [*British*]
DCM	District Court-Martial [*Facetious translation: "Don't Come Monday," in reference to a one-day suspension*] [*British*]
DCM	District Cub Master [*Scouting*]
DCM	Diversified Composite Material (PDAA)
DCM	Division of Civilian Marksmanship [*Army*]
DCM	Doctor of Church Music (PGP)
DCM	Doctor of Comparative Medicine
DCM	Dominican Campaign Medal
DCM	Double Common Meter [*Music*]
DCM	Double Common Multiple [*Mathematics*] (ROG)
DCM	Double Crystal Monochromator
DCM	Drawing Control Manual (MCD)
DCM	Dreyfus California Municipal Income, Inc. [*AMEX symbol*] (CTT)
DCM	Dreyfus Cal Muni Income [*AMEX symbol*] (TTSB)
DCM	Dry Cell Mass
DCM	Dry Cubic Meter (EG)
DCM	Dyssynergia Cerebellaris Myoclonica [*Medicine*] (DMAA)
DCMA	Defense Contract Management Agency
DCMA	Dichloromaleic Acid [*Organic chemistry*]
DCMA	Direct-Current Milliamp (IAA)
DCMA	District of Columbia Manpower Administration
DCMA	Dry Color Manufacturers Association (EA)
DCMA	Duty Cycle Modulation Alternator
DCMAILSUB	Discharge Certificate Mailed Subsequent to Separation [*Navy*] (DNAB)
DCM & G	Direct Current Motor and Generator Facility [*General Electric Co.*]
DCMAO	Defense Contract Management Area Operation (DOMA)
DCMAO	Defense Contract Management Area Operations (RDA)
DCMAS	Debt Collection and Management Assistance Service [*Department of Education*] (GFGA)

DC-MAW ..... Directionally-Controlled-Medium Anti-Tank Assault Weapon (SAA)
DCMB .... Development Configuration Management Board (MCD)
DCMC .... Defense Contract Management Command [*DoD*]
DCMD .... Defense Contract Management District [*Replaced DCASR*] (AAGC)
DCMD .... District of Columbia Military District (AABC)
DCMDA .... Demonstration Cities and Metropolitan Development Act
DCME .... Dichloromethyl Methyl Ether [*Organic chemistry*]
DCME .... Digital Circuit Multiplication Equipment [*Telecommunications*]
DCMG .... Dame Commander of the Order of St. Michael and St. George
                     [*British*]
DCMH .... Data Collection Module, High Speed
DCMI .... Disclosure of Classified Military Information [*to foreign
                     governments*] (AFM)
DCML .... Data Collection Module, Low Speed
DCML .... Differential Current Mode Logic [*Computer science*] (NITA)
DCML .... Diplomatic Conference of International Maritime Law
DCMNTN ..... Documentation
DCMO .... Dairy, Cowshed, and Milk Shop Order [*1885-1886*] [*Legal*] [*British*]
                     (ROG)
DCMO .... Documentation and Configuration Management Office (SSD)
DCMP .... Daunorubicin, Cytarabine, Mercaptopurine, Prednisone
                     [*Antineoplastic drug regimen*]
dCMP .... Deoxycytidine Monophosphate [*Biochemistry*]
dCMP .... Deoxycytidine-Phosphate [*Biochemistry*] (DAVI)
DCMPO .... Deputy Chief of the Military Planning Office
DCMPS .... Degaussing Compass
DCMPTR ..... Degaussing Computer
DCMR .... Defense Contract Management Regions (DOMA)
DCMR .... District Of Columbia Municipal Regulations [*A publication*]
DCMS .... Data Capture and Management System (IAA)
DCMS .... Data Control Multiplex System
DCMS .... Dedicated Computer Message Switching
DCMS .... Depot Command Management System
DCMS .... Deputy Commissioner Medical Services [*British*] (DAS)
DCMS .... Digital Capacitance Measuring System (MCD)
DCMS .... Digital Communications Management System [*Navy*]
DCMS .... Director Communications Material Security (MCD)
DCMSN .... Decommission (FAAC)
DCMSND ..... Decommissioned
DCMT .... Decrement (EECA)
DCMT .... Diploma in Clinical Medicine of the Tropics [*British*]
DCMT .... Doctor of Clinical Medicine of the Tropics [*British*] (DAVI)
DCMTX .... Dichloromethotrexate [*Also, DCM*] [*Antineoplastic drug*]
DCMU .... (Dichlorophenyl)dimethylurea [*Herbicide*]
DC Mun App ... Municipal Court of Appeals for the District of Columbia (DLA)
DCMV .... Digital Card Multivibrator [*Computer science*]
DCMX .... Dichloro-meta-Xylenol [*Organic chemistry*]
DCMXT .... Dichloromethotrexate [*Antineoplastic drug*] (DAVI)
DCN .... Daily Consumer News [*Consumers' Association*] [*Information service
                     or system*] (IID)
DCN .... Dana Corp. [*NYSE symbol*] (SAG)
DCN .... Data Change Notice (KSC)
DCN .... Data Communications Network [*Computer science*] (ACRL)
DCN .... Deacon
DCN .... Debt Crisis Network [*Defunct*] (EA)
DCN .... Deep Cerebellar Nuclei [*Brain anatomy*]
DCN .... Defence Communication Network [*British*] (NATG)
DCN .... Delayed Conditional Necrosis (MAE)
DCN .... Dental Care Network [*Blue Cross and Blue Shield*] [*Insurance*]
DCN .... Depot Control Number
DCN .... Design Change Notice
DCN .... Development Change Notice [*Aerospace*]
DCN .... Dichloronitrosalicylanilide [*Economic poison*] [*Organic chemistry*]
DCN .... Dicyanonaphthalene [*Organic chemistry*]
DCN .... Digital Computer Newsletter [*A publication*] (DNAB)
DCN .... Discalced Carmelite Nuns [*Italy*] (EAIO)
DCN .... Disconnect
DCN .... Distributed Computer Network
DCN .... Documentation Change Notice
DCN .... Document Change Notice
DCN .... Document Control Number (AFM)
DCN .... Dorsal Cardiac Nerve [*Anatomy*]
DCN .... Dorsal Cutaneous Nerve
DCN .... Double Crown [*Monetary unit*] [*British*] (ADA)
DCN .... Draft Change Notice (MCD)
DCN .... Drawing Change Notice
DCN .... Federal Armed Forces of Germany [*ICAO designator*] (FAAC)
DCNA .... Data Communication Network Architecture (BUR)
DCNA .... Deputy Chief Naval Adviser [*British*]
DCNA .... Dichloronitroaniline [*Also, DICHLORAN*] [*Fungicide*]
DCNA .... Digital Card Noninverting Amplifier [*Computer science*]
DCNB .... Dicyanobenzene [*Also, DCB*] [*Organic chemistry*]
DCNEO .... Deputy Chief Naval Engineering Officer [*British*]
DCNET .... Direct Current Network [*Solutions for resistive components and
                     voltage sources*]
DCNF .... Dishonored Check Name File [*IRS*]
DCNG .... District of Columbia National Guard (AABC)
DCNI .... Department of the Chief of Naval Information [*British military*] (DMA)
D Cn L .... Doctor of Canon Law
DCNM .... Deputy Chief of Naval Material
DCNM(A) ..... Deputy Chief of Naval Material (Acquisition) (MCD)
DCNM(D) ..... Deputy Chief of Naval Material, Development
DCNM(L) ..... Deputy Chief of Naval Material (Logistics) (MCD)
DCNM(M & F) ... Deputy Chief of Naval Material, Material and Facilities
DCNM(M & O) ... Deputy Chief of Naval Material, Management and Organization

DCNM(P & FM) ... Deputy Chief of Naval Material, Programs and Financial
                     Management
DCNO .... Deputy Chief of Naval Operations
DCNOA .... Deputy Chief of Naval Operations, Administration
DCNO(AIR) ... Deputy Chief of Naval Operations (Air)
DCNO(D) ..... Deputy Chief of Naval Operations (Development)
DCNOFOR ... Deputy Chief of Naval Operations, Fleet Operations and Readiness
DCNO(L) ..... Deputy Chief of Naval Operations (Logistics)
DCNO(M & NR) ... Deputy Chief of Naval Operations (Manpower and Naval
                     Reserve)
DCNO(MPT) ... Deputy Chief of Naval Operations (Manpower, Personnel, and
                     Training) (DNAB)
DCNO(P & P) ... Deputy Chief of Naval Operations (Plans and Policies)
DCNO(P & R) ... Deputy Chief of Naval Operations (Personnel and Naval Reserve)
DCNO(R) ..... Deputy Chief of Naval Operations (Readiness) [*British*]
DCNO(SW) ... Deputy Chief of Naval Operations (Submarine Warfare) (DNAB)
DCNOTEMAILSUB ... Discharge Certificate/Notification Mailed Subsequent to
                     Separation [*Navy*] (DNAB)
DCNP .... Document Change Notice Proposal (MCD)
DCNP .... Donald C. Cook Nuclear Power Plant (NRCH)
DCNPP .... Diablo Canyon Nuclear Power Plant (NRCH)
DCNR .... Department of Conservation and Natural Resources [*Victoria*]
                     [*Australia*]
DCNS .... Deputy Chief of Naval Staff [*Marine Corps; also, British Navy*]
DCNSW .... Disability Council of New South Wales [*Australia*]
DCNSW .... District Court of New South Wales [*Australia*]
DCNU .... Chlorozotocin [*Organic chemistry*] (DAVI)
DCO .... Covington & Burling, Washington, DC [*OCLC symbol*] (OCLC)
DCO .... Data Center Operations [*Social Security Administration*]
DCO .... Data Collection Order (MCD)
DCO .... Data Control Office (AAG)
DCO .... Debt Collection Order (DCTA)
DCO .... Deco Plantminder [*Vancouver Stock Exchange symbol*]
DCO .... Dehydrated Castor Oil [*Organic chemistry*]
DCO .... Delayed Compliance Order [*Compliance Assurance Agreement*]
                     [*Environmental Protection Agency*] (EPA)
DCO .... Depth Cut Out [*Navy*] (NG)
DCO .... Deputy Censorship Office [*London*] [*World War II*]
DCO .... Deputy Chief of Staff, Operations [*NATO*] (NATG)
DCO .... Deputy Commander of Operations
DCO .... Deputy Commanding Officer
DCO .... Detailed Checkout
DCO .... Development Contract Officer (MUGU)
DCO .... Dial Central Office (MCD)
Dco .... Diffusing Capacity for Carbon Monoxide (MAE)
DCO .... Digital Central Office [*Trademark of the Stromberg-Carlson Corp.*]
                     [*Telecommunications*]
DCO .... Digitally-Controlled Oscillator [*Electronics*]
DCO .... Diploma of the College of Optics [*British*] (EY)
DCO .... Direct Clinical Observation [*Psychology*]
DCO .... Directional Coupler Oscillator (IAA)
DCO .... Director of Combat Operations
DCO .... Director of Combined Operations [*British Army*] [*World War II*]
DCO .... Disaster Control Officer (AAG)
DCO .... District Camouflage Office [*or Officer*]
DCO .... District Clothing Office [*or Officer*]
DCO .... District Communication Officer
DCO .... District Council Office [*British*] (ROG)
DCO .... Division Classification Officer
D Co .... Doctor of Cosmology
DCO .... Document Control Officer [*Environmental Protection Agency*] (EPA)
DCO .... Dominions, Colonies, and Overseas [*British*] (DI)
DCO .... Draft Collection Only [*Business term*]
DCO .... Drawing Change Order (MUGU)
DCO .... Dry Carbon Monoxide
DCO .... Ducommun, Inc. [*AMEX symbol*] (SPSG)
DCO .... Duke of Cambridge's Own [*Military unit*] [*British*]
DCO .... Duke of Connaught's Own [*Military unit*] [*British*]
DCO .... Duty Cypher Officer [*Military British*]
DCO .... Dynamic Checkout [*Aerospace*] (IAA)
Dco .... Pulmonary Diffusion Capacity for Carbon Monoxide [*Medicine*]
                     (DAVI)
DCO2 .... Dry Carbon Dioxide
DCOA .... Direct-Current Operational Amplifier [*Electronics*]
DCOC .... Drain Cutoff Current
DCOFS .... Deputy Chief of Staff
DC of S .... Deputy Chief of Staff
DC of SA ..... Deputy Chief of Staff, Army
DCOG .... Diploma of College of Obstetricians and Gynecologists
DCO(I) .... Director of Combined Operations (India)
DCOL .... Direct Control Oriented Language [*Computer science*]
DCOL .... Discovery Channel Online [*Computer science*]
d col .... Double Column [*Advertising*] (ODBW)
D-COL .... Double Column (ADA)
D Colo .... United States District Court for the District of Colorado (DLA)
DCoIU .... Columbia Union College, Takoma Park, MD [*Library symbol Library
                     of Congress*] (LCLS)
DCOM .... Departmental Coordinating Committee on Ocean Minings [*Canada*]
DCOM .... Disk Communications Area (CMD)
DCOM .... Distributed Component Object Model [*Computer science*]
D Com .... Doctor of Commerce
D Com Adm ... Doctor of Commercial Administration
DCO(ME) ..... Director of Combined Operations (Middle East)
DCOME .... Dworkin/Culatta Oral Mechanism Examination [*Speech and language
                     therapy*] (DAVI)

DComL........	Doctor of Commercial Law (ADA)
DComm........	Doctor of Commerce
DCOMP....	Data Center Operations Management Plan [*Social Security Administration*]
D Comp L	Doctor of Comparative Law
D Com Sc	Doctor of Commercial Science
D Conn	United States District Court for the District of Connecticut (DLA)
DCOP........	Detailed Checkout Procedures (MCD)
DCOP........	Displays, Controls, and Operation Procedures (NASA)
DCOPA........	Dichloropropyl Acrylate [*Organic chemistry*]
DCOPO........	Deputy Chief of Personnel Operations (AABC)
DCOR........	Defense Committee on Research [*Air Force*]
DCos...........	Cosmos Club, Washington, DC [*Library symbol Library of Congress*] (LCLS)
DCOS........	Data Collection Operating System
DCOS........	Data Communication Output Selector (KSC)
DCOS........	Deputy Chief of Staff (NATG)
DCOS........	Direct Couple Operating System
DCOS........	Downrange Computer Output System (MUGU)
DC/OSx.......	DataCenter/OSx (CDE)
DCOT........	Distant Central Office Transceivers
DCOTFP.......	Deputy Commander, Operational Test and Evaluation Force, Pacific [*Navy*]
DCov...........	Covington & Burling, Washington, DC [*Library symbol Library of Congress*] (LCLS)
DCP	Daily Cumulative Persistence [*Environmental science*]
DCP	Daniell's Chancery Practice [*A publication*] (DLA)
DCP	Data Change Proposal
DCP	Data Collection Plan (MCD)
DCP	Data Collection Platform [*National Weather Service*] [*Weather satellite system*]
DCP	Data Communication Processor [*Computer science*] (BUR)
DCP	Data Control Processor (IAA)
DCP	Dean and Chapter of St. Paul's [*Anglican Church*] (ROG)
DCP	Decentralized Pharmacy (DAVI)
DCP	Decision Coordinating Paper
DCP	Defense Concept Paper [*Military*] (RDA)
DCP	Defined Contribution Plan [*Insurance*] (WYGK)
DCP	Degree Completion Program [*Army*] (INF)
DCP	Dental Capitation Plan [*Insurance*] (WYGK)
DCP	Dental Care Plan [*Insurance*] (WYGK)
DCP	Dental Continuation Pay [*Military*] (AABC)
DCP	Dependent Care Program [*Insurance*] (WYGK)
DCP	Depot Condemnation Percent (NASA)
DCP	Depth-Charge Projector
DCP	Deputy Controller of Property [*World War II*]
DC(P)	Deputy Controller (Polaris) [*Navy British*]
DCP	Desen Computer Industries, Inc. [*Vancouver Stock Exchange symbol*]
DCP	Design Change Package (IEEE)
DCP	Design Change Proposal
DCP	Design Competition Phase (AAGC)
DCP	Design Criteria Plan (IEEE)
DCP	DEU [*Display Electronics Unit*] Control Program [*NASA*] (NASA)
DCP	Development Concept Paper (MCD)
DCP	Development Control Program (SAA)
DCP	Development Cost Plan (NASA)
DCP	Diagnostic Control Program (IAA)
DCP	Dicalcium Phosphate [*Inorganic chemistry*]
DCP	Dicapryl Phthalate [*Organic chemistry*]
DCP	Dicetyl Phosphate [*Organic chemistry*]
DCP	Dichlorophenol [*Organic chemistry*]
DCP	Dichloropropane [*Pesticide*]
DCP	Dicumyl Peroxide [*Organic chemistry*]
DCP	Dicyclopentadiene [*Also, DCPD*] [*Organic chemistry*]
DCP	Differential Computing Potentiometer
DCP	Digital Clock Pulse
DCP	Digital Communications Protocol [*Computer science*] (NITA)
DCP	Digital Computer Processor (IEEE)
DCP	Digital Computer Programming [*Computer science*] (BUR)
DCP	Dipeptidyl Carboxypeptidase [*An enzyme*]
DCP	Diploma in Clinical Pathology [*British*]
DCP	Diploma in Clinical Psychology [*British*]
DCP	Direct Current Panel
DCP	Direct-Current Plasma [*Spectrometry*]
DCP	Director of [*Air*] Campaign Plans [*Central Command*] [*Military*] (DOMA)
DCP	Director of Civilian Personnel [*Navy*]
DCP	Disaster Control Plan (AFM)
DCP	Discharge Plan (MEDA)
DCP	Discrete Component Part
DCP	Display Control Panel
DCP	Display Control Program (NTCM)
DCP	Distributed Communications Processor [*Sperry UNIVAC*]
DCP	Distribution Common Point [*Telecommunications*] (TEL)
DCP	District Community Physician
DCP	Division de Chimie Physique [*Division of Physical Chemistry - DPC*] (EAIO)
DCP	Doctor in Clinical Pathology
DCP	Doctor of City Planning
DCP	Donald C. Cook Plant [*Nuclear energy*] (NRCH)
DCP	Draft Concept Paper
DCP	Drill Cluster Plate (MCD)
DCP	Dry Chemical Powder (PDAA)
DCP	Dynamic Compression-Plate

DCP	Freight or Carriage Paid To _____ [*"INCOTERM," International Chamber of Commerce official code*]
DCP	United States Patent Office, Washington, DC [*OCLC symbol*] (OCLC)
DCPA	Defense Civil Preparedness Agency [*FEMA*] [*Washington, DC*]
DCPA	DEU [*Display Electronics Unit*] Control Program [*End Item*]
DCPA	Dichloropropionanilide [*Also, DPA*] [*Herbicide*]
DCPA	Dimethyl Tetrachloroterephthalate [*Herbicide*]
DCPANDP ...	Deputy Chief of Staff, Plans and Policy [*NATO*] (NATG)
DC Path	Diploma of the College of Pathologists [*British*]
DCPB	Daughters of Charity of Most Precious Blood (TOCD)
DCPB	Departmental Civilian Personnel Branch
DC-PBH	Double-Channel Planar Buried Heterostructure
DCPC	Dichlorodiphenylmethylcarbinol [*Also, DMC*] [*Insecticide*]
DCPC	Division of Cancer Prevention and Control [*National Cancer Institute*]
DCPC	Dual Channel Port Controller (MHDI)
DCPC	Dual Channel Port Controller [*Computer science*] (NITA)
DCPCD	Dicyclopentadine
DCPCM	Differentially Coherent Pulse Code Modulation
DCPD	Defense Contract Property Disposition [*DoD*] (RDA)
DCPD	Dicalcium Phosphate Dihydrate [*Inorganic chemistry*]
DCPD	Dicyclopentadiene [*Also, DCP*] [*Organic chemistry*]
DCPD	Direct-Current Potential Drop (MCD)
DCPDC	Dual Chamber Preliminary Design Code (MCD)
DCPE	Documentacion y Comunicacion Publicitaria Espanola [*Database*] [*Universidad Complutense de Madrid*] [*Spanish*] [*Information service or system*] (CRD)
DCPEI	DEU [*Display Electronics Unit*] Control Program End Item [*NASA*] (NASA)
DCPF	Displaced Cosine Pulse Function (IAA)
DCPG	Defense Communications Planning Group (KSC)
DCPG	Digital Clock Pulse Generator
DCPG	Direction Center Programming Group [*Semiautomatic Ground Environment*] (IAA)
DCPI	Deputy Chief Patrol Inspector [*Immigration and Naturalization Service*]
DCPI	Deputy Police Commissioner for Public Information (LAIN)
DCPI	Dichlorophenolindophenol [*Also, DCIP, DCPIP, DPIP*] [*Analytical reagent*]
DCPI	dick clark productions [*NASDAQ symbol*] (TTSB)
DCPI	Dick Clark Productions, Inc. [*NASDAQ symbol*] (NQ)
DCPIP	Dichlorophenolindophenol [*Also, DCIP, DCPI, DPIP*] [*Analytical reagent*]
DCPL	Demonstrated Compliance Parameter Limits [*Environmental science*] [*Environmental Protection Agency*]
DCPL	Distributed Control Programming Language [*Computer science*] (CSR)
DCPL	District of Columbia Public Library
DCP-LA	Direct-Current Plasma-LASER Ablation
DCPLS	Data Collection and Platform Location System [*National Weather Service*] [*Weather satellite system*] (NOAA)
DCPM	Daunomycin Cytarabine, Prednisolone, Mercaptopurine [*Antineoplastic drug*] (CDI)
DCPM	Decision Critical Path Method
DCPM	Di(chlorophenoxy)methane (IIA)
DCPMAS	Double Cross-Polarization, Magic Angle Spinning [*Spectroscopy*]
DCPMU	(Dichlorophenyl)methylurea [*Organic chemistry*]
DCPO	Damage Control Petty Officer [*Navy*] (DNAB)
DCPO	Deputy Chief of Staff, Personnel and Organization [*NATO*] (NATG)
DCPO	Deputy Chief of Staff, Plans and Operations (MCD)
DCPO	Deputy Chief Political Officer [*British Military Administration*]
DCPO	District Civilian Personnel Office [*or Officer*]
DCPO	DSA [*Defense Supply Agency*] Civil Preparedness Office
DCPOC	Document Center of the Patent Office of China [*Library*]
DCPolaris	Deputy Controller (Polaris) [*Navy British*]
DCPP	Data Communication Preprocessor
DCPR	Defense Contractor Planning Report
DCPR	Deputy Chief of Staff for Plans and Research
DCPR	Direction Center Processor for Remote Combat Center (SAA)
DCPRS	Data Collection Platform Radio Sets [*National Weather Service*] [*Weather satellite system*] (NOAA)
DCPS	Data Communication Processing System
DCPS	Data Control Panel Submodule
DC/PS	Digital Computer / Power Supply
DCPS	Digitally Controlled Power Source (IEEE)
DCPS	Dynamic Crew Procedures Simulator
DCPSK	Differential [*or Differentially*] Coherent Phase Shift Keyed [*or Keying*] [*System*] [*Computer science*]
DCPSP	Direct-Current Power Supply Panel (AAG)
DCPT	Direct-Current Plasma Torch
DCPT	Doctor of Chiropractic and Physiological Therapeutics
DCPTA	(Dichlorophenoxy)triethylamine [*Herbicide*]
DCPV	Direct-Current Peak Voltage (IAA)
DCQM	Deputy Chief Quartermaster
DCQM	Digital Circuit Quality Monitor [*Computer science*]
DCR	Dacro-Cysto-Rhinostomy [*Medicine*]
DCR	Daily Communication Report
DC/R	Data Collection/Relay (MCD)
DCR	Data Communication Read (OA)
DCR	Data Conversion Receiver [*Computer science*]
DCR	Data Coordinator and Retriever [*Computer science*]
DCR	Decatur, IN [*Location identifier FAA*] (FAAL)
DCR	Decision Circuit Reception
DCR	Decor
DCR	Decoration (AABC)
DCR	Decrease (KSC)

DCR .... Degree of Cell Rupture
DCR .... Delayed Cutaneous Reaction [*Dermatology*] (DAVI)
DCR .... Delray Connecting Railroad (MHDB)
DCR .... Democratic Constitutional Rally [*Tunisia*] [*Political party*] (BARN)
DCR .... Dental Corps, General Service [*USNR officer designation*]
DCR .... Dependent-Care Reimbursement [*Insurance*] (WYGK)
DCR .... Deputy Commander for Resources [*Air Force*] (DOMA)
DCR .... Design Certification Review [*NASA*] (KSC)
DCR .... Design Change Recommendation [*or Request*]
DCR .... Design Characteristic Review (AAG)
DCR .... Design Concern Report (NASA)
DCR .... Destruct Command Receiver (KSC)
DCR .... Detail Condition Register
DCR .... Development Council for Research (MUGU)
DCR .... Dewar Cryogenic Refrigerator
DCR .... Differential Correlation Radiometer (MCD)
DCR .... Digital Cassette Recorder
DCR .... Digital Coded RADAR
DCR .... Digital Concentration Readout [*Computer science*]
DCR .... Digital Condition Register (NITA)
DCR .... Digital Conversion Receiver
DCR .... Direct Conversion Reactor
DCR .... Direct Cortical Response
DCR .... Direct Critical Response (MEDA)
DCR .... Direct-Current Restorer
DCR .... Disposition of Contract Request (SAA)
DCR .... District Chief Ranger [*Ancient Order of Foresters*]
DCR .... Division of Computer Research [*Formerly, OCA*] [*National Science Foundation*]
DCR .... Doctor of Comparative Religion
D Cr .... Doctor of Criminology
DCR .... Document Change Record (NASA)
DCR .... Document Change Release
DCR .... Dominant Control Region [*Genetics*]
DCR .... Downstream Control Region [*Biochemistry*]
DCR .... Drawing Change Request
DCR .... Drawing Copy Request (MCD)
DCR .... Drayage Carriers Inc., Fort Wayne IN [*STAC*]
DCR .... Dried Coffee Residue
DCR .... Dual Channel Radiometer
DCR .... Dual Channel Receiver (MCD)
DCR .... Dual Combustor Ramjet (MCD)
DCR .... Dual Cycle Rifle
DCR .... Duff and Phelps Credit Rating [*NYSE symbol*] (TTSB)
DCR .... Duff & Phelps Credit Rating Co. [*NYSE symbol*] (SAG)
DCR .... Dynamic Color Rendition [*Computer science*]
DCRA .... DCASR [*Defense Contract Administration Services Region*], Atlanta
DCRA .... Dominion of Canada Rifle Association
DCRA .... Dry Crease Recovery Angle [*Textile technology*]
DCRA .... Dyers' and Cleaners' Research Association (BI)
DCRABS ...... Disk Copy Restore and Backup System
DCR & Regs... District of Columbia Rules and Regulations [*A publication*] (DLA)
DCRB .... DCASR [*Defense Contract Administration Services Region*], Boston
DCRB .... Descriptive Cataloging of Rare Books [*American Library Association*]
DCRB .... Design Change Review Board
DCRB .... Drawn Cup Roller Bearing
DCRC .... DCASR [*Defense Contract Administration Services Region*], San Francisco
DCRCH........ Duke of Connaught's Royal Canadian Hussars [*British military*] (DMA)
DCRD .... DCASR [*Defense Contract Administration Services Region*], Detroit
DCRDR .... Detailed Control Room Design Review [*Nuclear energy*] (NRCH)
DCRE .... Decree [*Legal shorthand*] (LWAP)
DCRE .... Deputy Commandant Royal Engineers [*British*]
DCREO......... Design Change Request Engineering Order
DCRESMAILSUB... Discharge Certificate/Naval Reserve Appointment Mailed Subsequent to Separation [*Navy*] (DNAB)
DCRF .... Die Casting Research Foundation (EA)
DCRI .... DCASR [*Defense Contract Administration Services Region*], Chicago
DCrim .... Doctor of Criminology (GAGS)
DCRK .... Democratic Confederate Republic of Koryo [*Reunified Korean state*] [*Proposed*]
DCRL .... DCASR [*Defense Contract Administration Services Region*], Los Angeles
DCRM .... Discrepancy Check Request Memorandum (SAA)
DCR MU ...... Diploma of the College of Radiographers in Medical Ultra Sound [*British*] (DBQ)
DCRN .... Dashpot Cup Retention Nut [*Nuclear energy*] (NRCH)
DCRN.......... DCASR [*Defense Contract Administration Services Region*], New York
DCRNM....... Diploma of the College of Radiographers in Nuclear Medicine [*British*] (DI)
DCRNZ........ Diacrin Inc. Unit [*NASDAQ symbol*] (TTSB)
DCRO .... DCASR [*Defense Contract Administration Services Region*], Cleveland
DCRO .... District Civil Readjustment Office [*or Officer*]
DCRP .... DCASR [*Defense Contract Administration Services Region*], Philadelphia
DCRP .... Department of City and Regional Planning [*MIT*] (MCD)
DCRP .... Design Controlled Repair Parts (MCD)
DCRP .... Developmental Cycle Research Plan
DCRP .... Direct-Current Reverse Polarity [*Electronics*]
DCRP .... Disaster Control Recovery Plan
DCRR.......... District of Colu8mbia Rules and Regulations [*A publication*] (AAGC)

DCR RNI ...... Diploma of the College of Radiographers in Radionuclide Imaging [*British*] (DBQ)
DCRS .... Data Collection and Reduction System
DCRS .... DCASR [*Defense Contract Administration Services Region*], St. Louis
D-CRS......... Diplomate, American Board of Colon and Rectal Surgery (DHSM)
DCRS .... Document Control Remote Station
DCRSEO....... Design Change Request Serial Engineering Order (MCD)
DCRT .... DCASR [*Defense Contract Administration Services Region*], Dallas
DCRT .... Division of Computer Research and Technology [*Bethesda, MD*] [*National Institutes of Health*]
DCRTO........ DSA [*Defense Supply Agency*] Central Regional Telecommunications Office
DCRTR........ Decorator
DCRZ.......... Descend to and Cruise [*Aviation*] (FAAC)
DCS .... Dalton Computer Services, Inc. [*Information service or system*] (IID)
DCS .... Damage Control School [*Navy*]
DCS .... Damage Control Suit [*Navy*]
DCS .... Damage Control System (KSC)
DCS .... Dartmouth Computing Services
DCS .... Data Capture Subsystem (MCD)
DCS .... Data Carrier System [*Teltone Corp.*] [*Kirkland, WA*] (TSSD)
DCS .... Data Classification System (IAA)
DCS .... Data Collection System [*or Subsystem*] [*Computer science*]
DCS .... Data Communication Services [*Regie des Telegraphes et des Telephones*] [*Brussels, Belgium*]
DCS .... Data Communication System [*or Subsystem*]
DCS .... Data Conditioning System [*NASA*]
DCS .... Data Control Services (BUR)
DCS .... Data Control System [*Burroughs Corp.*] (AAG)
DCS .... Data Conversion System [*Computer science*]
DCS .... Davis Computer Systems, Inc.
DCS .... Deck Cooling System (MCD)
DCS .... Decompression Sickness [*Deep-sea diving*]
DCS .... Defect Control System [*The Software Edge, Inc.*] [*Computer science*] (PCM)
DCS .... Defense Communications System [*DoD*]
DCS .... Defense Construction Service (NATG)
DCS .... Defense Courier Service [*DoD*]
DCS .... Defined Context Set [*Telecommunications*] (OSI)
DCS .... Deflection Coil Set
DCS .... Delayed Coincidence Spectroscopy
DCS .... Dense Canalicular System [*Medicine*] (DMAA)
DCS .... Department of Computer Science [*University of Illinois*] [*Research center*] (RCD)
DCS .... Department of Computing Service [*University of Waterloo*] [*Research center*] (RCD)
DCS .... Department of Correctional Services [*Northern Territory, South Australia*]
DCS .... Department of Corrective Services [*New South Wales, Western Australia*]
DCS .... Departure Control System [*IATA*] (DS)
DCS .... Deputy Chief of Staff
DCS .... Deputy Clerk of Session [*British*]
DCS .... Deputy Crown Solicitor (ADA)
DCS .... Design Change Schedule
DCS .... Design Change Summary (AAG)
DCS .... Design Communication System (MCD)
DCS .... Design Control Specification (KSC)
DCS .... Design Criteria Specification (NASA)
DCS .... Desktop Color Separation [*Quark, Inc.*] (PCM)
DCS .... Despin Control Subsystem [*Aerospace*]
DCS .... Destruct Command System (MUGU)
DCS .... Detail Checkout Specifications (MCD)
DCS .... Diagnostic Control Software
DCS .... Diagnostic Control Store
DCS .... Dichlorosilane [*Photovoltaic energy systems*]
DCS .... Diecasting Society [*British*] (DBA)
DCS .... Differential Cross Section [*Chemistry*]
DCS .... Diffuse Cortical Sclerosis [*Medicine*] (DMAA)
DCS .... Digital Camera System [*Eastman Kodak Co.*]
DCS .... Digital Classified Software (NITA)
DCS .... Digital Command Signal [*Telecommunications*] (OSI)
DCS .... Digital Command System [*or Subsystem*]
DCS .... Digital Communication System [*Computer science*]
DCS .... Digital Computer System [*Vancouver Stock Exchange symbol*]
DCS .... Digital Control Station [*Computer science*]
DCS .... Digital Control System
DCS .... Digital Cordless Standard [*Telecommunications*] (ACRL)
DCS .... Digital Countdown System [*Computer science*]
DCS .... Digital Cross-Connect System [*Telecommunications*]
DCS .... Dimensional Control Standard (MCD)
DCS .... Direct-Coupled System (IAA)
DCS .... Direct Couple System
DCS .... Direct-Current Sensor
DCS .... Direction Center Standby [*SAGE*] [*RADAR*]
DCS .... Director Comptroller Systems (AABC)
DCS .... Director of Clothing and Stores [*Military British*]
DCS .... Disadvantaged Children Series [*A publication*]
DCS .... Discount Communications Services [*Telecommunications service*] (TSSD)
DCS .... Dispatch Critical System (MCD)
DCS .... Display and Control Station
DCS .... Distributed Commercial System (IAA)
DCS .... Distributed Communications System [*Telecommunications*] (CDE)
DCS .... Distributed Computer Systems (MDG)

DCS	Distributed Computing Services
DCS	Distributed Control System [*Engineering*]
DCS	Diversity Combiner System
DCS	Divisional Chief Superintendent [*British police*]
DCS	Division Clearing Station [*Medicine Army*]
DCS	Doctor of Christian Science
DCS	Doctor of Christian Service
DCS	Doctor of Commercial Science
DCS	Doctor of Computer Science (PGP)
DCS	Doctrine and Command Systems [*Army*] (RDA)
DCS	Document Control Services
DCS	Document Control Software (CDE)
DCS	Document Control System [*Computer science*]
DCS	Dorsal Column Stimulator [*Pain killer*]
DCS	Double Channel Simplex
DCS	Double Compton Scattering
DCS	Double Cotton Single Silk [*Wire insulation*] (AAG)
DCS	Drawing Change Summary
DCS	Drone Control System [*Military*]
DCS	Dual Catalyst System [*Automotive engineering*]
DCS	Dual Checkout Station (MCD)
DCS	United States Civil Service Commission, Washington, DC [*Library symbol Library of Congress*] (LCLS)
DCS	University of South Carolina, College of Librarianship, Columbia, SC [*OCLC symbol*] (OCLC)
DCSA	Direct-Current Servo Amplifier
DCSA	Double Contrast Shoulder Arthrography [*Radiology*] (DAVI)
DCSA	Dual Chamber Shock Absorbers (MCD)
DCSADN	Defense Communications System Automatic Digital Network [*DoD*]
DC/SAF	Deputy Chief of Staff, Air Force
DCSAIROPNET	Defense Communications System Air Operational Network (AFM)
DCSAO	Defense Customer Supply Assistance Office [*DoD*]
DCSAR	Defense Contract Services Administration Region
DCS/AUTODIN	Defense Communications System Automatic Digital Information Network [*DoD*]
DCSC	Defense Construction Supply Center [*Defense Supply Agency*]
DCS/C	Deputy Chief of Staff, Comptroller
DCSC	Digital Card Slave Clock [*Computer science*]
DC Sc	Doctor of Commercial Science
DCSCD	Deputy Chief of Staff for Combat Developments (AABC)
DCSC-E	Deputy Chief of Staff, Communications-Electronics [*Army*] (AABC)
DCSCI	Defense Communications Systems Configuration Items (MCD)
DCSCOMPT	Deputy Chief of Staff, Comptroller (AABC)
DCSCS	Data Code and Speed Conversion Subsystem [*Computer science*] (NITA)
DCS/D	Deputy Chief of Staff, Development
DCSD	Doctrine and Command Systems Directorate [*Army*] (RDA)
DCSDATANET	Defense Communications System Data Network (NG)
DCSDOC	Deputy Chief of Staff for Doctrine
DC Se	Doctor of Commercial Service
DCSF	Digital Cockpit Simulation Facility (MCD)
DCSF	Downton Castle Sandstone Formation [*England*] [*Geology*]
DCS/FF	Deputy Chief of Staff / Flight Facilities (SAA)
DCSFOR	Deputy Chief of Staff, Force Development (AABC)
DCSG	Data Computation Subsystem Group
DCSG	David Cassidy Support Group (EA)
DCSHG	DC-Induced Second Harmonic Generation (MCD)
DCSI	Data and Control Signal Interface (NASA)
DCSI	Defense Satellite Communication Systems Installation (RDA)
DCSI	Deputy Chief of Staff for Intelligence [*Army*] (AABC)
DC/S(I & L)	Deputy Chief of Staff, Installations and Logistics [*Marine Corps*] (DOMA)
DCSIM	Deputy Chief of Staff for Information Management [*Army*]
DCSIM	District of Columbia Society of Internal Medicine (SRA)
DCS/INT	Deputy Chief of Staff, Intelligence [*Air Force*] (MCD)
DCSL	Deputy Chief of Staff, Logistics [*Army*] (KSC)
DCSL	Deterministic Context Sensitive Language [*Computer science*] (MHDI)
DCSLAM	Development of a Corps Logistics Analysis Methodology
DCS/LE	Deputy Chief of Staff for Logistics and Engineering [*See also AF/LE*] [*Air Force*] (DOMA)
DCSLOG	Deputy Chief of Staff, Logistics [*Army*]
DCSM	Deputy Chief of Staff, Materiel
DCSM	Deterministic Complete Sequential Machine (PDAA)
DCS(M & RA)	Deputy Chief of Staff (for Manpower and Reserve Affairs) (RDA)
DCSMG	Deputy Chief of Staff for Military Government [*World War II*]
DCSMIS	Deputy Chief of Staff, Management Information Systems (AABC)
DC/SMO	Deputy Chief of Staff, Military Operations [*Army*]
DCSN	Decision
DCSO	Defense Communications System Organization
DCSO	Deputy Chief of Staff, Operations
DCSO	Deputy Chief Scientific Officer [*British*]
DCSO	Deputy Chief Signal Officer [*British military*] (DMA)
DCSO	DSA [*Defense Supply Agency*] Command Security Support Office
DCSOA	Deputy Chief of Staff, Operations and Administration
DCSO & T	Deputy Chief of Staff, Operations and Training (AABC)
DCSOC	Defense Communications System Operations Center (RDA)
DCSOI	Deputy Chief of Staff for Operations and Intelligence (AABC)
DCSOPS	Deputy Chief of Staff for Operations [*Army*]
DCSOPS	Deputy Chief of Staff for Operations and Plans [*Army*]
DCSOPS-FD	Deputy Chief of Staff for Operations - Force Development [*Army*]
DCSOR	Deputy Chief-of-Staff Operational Requirements [*Army*]
DCSOT	Deputy Chief of Staff for Operations and Intelligence [*Army*]
DCSP	Defense Communications Satellite Project [*or Program*]
DCS/P	Deputy Chief of Staff, Personnel

DCSP	Digital Control Signal Processor (NASA)
DCSP	Direct-Current Straight Polarity (MCD)
DCSPA	Deputy Chief of Staff, Personnel and Administration (AABC)
DCSPAL	Deputy Chief of Staff for Personnel, Administration, and Logistics
DCS/P & O	Deputy Chief of Staff for Plans and Operations (AFM)
DCS/P & P	Deputy Chief of Staff for Plans and Programs
DCS/P & R	Deputy Chief of Staff for Programs and Resources (AFM)
DCS/PEAB	Defense Communications System - Personnel Emergency Actions Book
DCSPER	Deputy Chief of Staff, Personnel [*Army*]
DCSPR	Deputy Chief of Staff for Plans and Research [*Army*]
DCSR	Da Capo Senza Replica [*From the Beginning, Playing Only Once the Parts Marked with Repeats*] [*Music*]
DCSR	DISC Inc. [*NASDAQ symbol*] (TTSB)
DC/SR	Display and Control/Storage and Retrieval
DCSR	Document Imaging Systems Corp. [*NASDAQ symbol*] (SAG)
DCSR	Dominican College of San Rafael [*California*]
DCSR & D	Deputy Chief of Staff, Research and Development [*Army*]
DCS/R & T	Deputy Chief of Staff, Research and Technology
DCS/RC	Deputy Chief of Staff, Reserve Components [*Army*]
DCSRDA	Deputy Chief of Staff for Research, Development, and Acquisition [*Army*]
DCS RD & S	Deputy Chief of Staff for Research, Development, and Studies [*Marine Corps*] (DOMA)
DCS(RDL)	Deputy Chief-of-Staff (Research Development and Logistics) [*Air Force*]
DCSRM	Deputy Chief of Staff for Resource Management (AABC)
DCSROTC	Deputy Chief of Staff for Reserve Officers' Training Corps (AABC)
DCSRW	DISC Inc. Wrrt [*NASDAQ symbol*] (TTSB)
DCSS	Damage Control Suit System [*Navy*]
DCSS	Defense Communications Satellite System [*Telecommunications*] (TEL)
DCSS	Digital Communications Satellite Subsystem (MCD)
DCS/S & L	Deputy Chief of Staff, Systems and Logistics
DCST	Deputy Chief of Staff for Training [*Army*]
DCST	Digital Card Schmitt Trigger [*Computer science*]
DCST	Dynamic Combat System Test [*Military*] (CAAL)
DCSTC	Defense Communications Station Technical Control (DNAB)
DCSTE	Deputy Chief of Staff for Test and Evaluation [*Army*]
DCSTS	Deputy Chief of Staff for Training and Schools (AABC)
DCSTTYNET	Defense Communications System Teletype Network (AFM)
DCSU	Differential Corrected Spectral Unit [*Spectrometry*]
DCSU	Digital Computer Switching Unit (MCD)
DCT	Damage Control Texts [*Naval Ship Systems Command*]
DCT	Data Communications Terminal
DCT	Data Conversion Transmitter [*Computer science*]
DCT	Daunomycin Cytarabine, Thioguanine [*Antineoplastic drug*] (CDI)
DCT	Deaf Communicating Terminal [*Telephone for the deaf*]
DCT	Decceleration Time
DCT	Decimal Code Translator
DCT	Decoding Part (IAA)
DCT	Deep Chest Therapy [*Medicine*] (DAVI)
DCT	Department of Classroom Teachers [*of NEA*] (EA)
DCT	Depth-Charges Track
DCT	Depth-Charge Thrower
DCT	Depth Control Tank
DCT	Destination Control Table [*Computer science*] (IAA)
DCT	Detection, Classification, and Targeting [*or Tracking*] (MCD)
DCT	Device Characteristics Table [*Computer science*] (IBMDP)
DCT	Diastolic Control Team [*Cardiology*] (DAVI)
DCT	Dichlorotoluene [*Organic chemistry*]
DCT	Digital Comm Tech [*AMEX symbol*] (TTSB)
DCT	Digital Communications Technology Corp. [*AMEX symbol*] (SAG)
DCT	Digital Communications Terminal (MCD)
DCT	Digital Computer Trainer (IAA)
DCT	Digital Curve Tracer (IAA)
DCT	Dihydrotestosterone, Corticosterone, and Thyroxine [*Endocrinology*]
DCT	Diode Curve Tracer
DCT	Direct [*In relation to flight plan clearances and type of approach*] [*Aviation*]
DCT	Direct Antiglobulin Coombs' Test [*Medicine*]
DCT	Direct Carbon Transfer
DCT	Direct Cosine Transform (SSD)
DCT	Direct-Coupled Transistor (IAA)
DCT	Direct Flight Ltd. [*British ICAO designator*] (FAAC)
DCT	Director, Control Tower [*British military*] (DMA)
DCT	Disaster Control Team (AFM)
DCT	Discrete Cosine Transform [*Telecommunications*]
DCT	Dissector Camera Tube
DCT	Distal Convoluted Tubule [*Nephrology*]
DCT	Distributed Computer Telephony
D Ct	District Court [*Usually federal*] (DLA)
DCT	Diversified Computer Technology, Inc. (MCD)
DCT	Divide Check Test [*Computer science*] (IAA)
DCT	Division of Cancer Treatment [*Department of Health and Human Services*] (GFGA)
DCT	Docked Configuration Transfer (MCD)
DCT	Doctor of Christian Theology
DCT	Doctor of Christian Training
DCT	Document (ADA)
DCT	Dodrill, Charles T., Hurricane WV [*STAC*]
DCT	Doklady Chemical Technology
DCT	DSS [*Deep Space Station*] Communications Terminal Subsystem
DCT	NAVSHIPS [*Naval Ship Systems Command*] Damage Control Texts

D Ct	Selected Judgments of the Divisional Courts [*Ghana*] [*A publication*] (DLA)
DCTA	Diaminocyclohexanetetraacetic Acid [*Also, OCTA*] [*Organic chemistry*]
DCTAF	(Dichlorotriazinyl)aminofluorescein [*Also, DTAF*] [*Analytical biochemistry*]
DCTB	Data Communications Testing Branch [*Social Security Administration*]
DCTC	Dependent Care Tax Credit
DCTC	Digital Centroid Terminal Correlation
DCTC	District of Columbia Teachers College [*Later, University of the District of Columbia*]
DCTG	Dihydrotestosterone, Corticosterone, Thyroxine, and Growth Hormone [*Endocrinology*]
DCTL	Diode-Capacitor-Transistor Logic [*Electronics*] (ECII)
DCTL	Direct-Coupled Transistor Logic
DCTLC	Direct-Coupling Transistor Logic Circuit
DCTM	DC Technology Missile (MCD)
DCTM	Delay Computer Tomographic Myelography [*Radiology*] (DAVI)
DCTM	Direct-Current Torque Motor
DCTM	Documentum, Inc. [*NASDAQ symbol*] (SAG)
DCTM	Documentum Inc. [*NASDAQ symbol*] (TTSB)
DCTMA	Desoxycorticosterone Trimethylacetate [*Endocrinology*]
DCTN	Decoration
DCTN	Defense Commercial Telecommunications Network (DOMA)
DCTP	Deoxycytidinetriphosphate [*Organic chemistry*]
DCTP	Duct Type
DCTPA	Desoxycorticosterone Triphenylacetate [*Endocrinology*] (AAMN)
dCTPase	Deoxycytidinetriphosphatase [*An enzyme*]
DCTR	Division of Controlled Thermonuclear Research [*Energy Research and Development Administration*]
DCTS	Data Communication Terminal System [*Computer science*] (DA)
DCTS	Digital Coordinate Transformation System
DCTS	Double-Charge-Transfer Spectroscopy (MCD)
DCTSC	Defense Clothing and Textile Supply Center [*Later, Defense Personnel Support Center*] [*DoD*]
DCTT	Division Contract Termination Team (AAG)
DCTV	Digital Color Television
DCU	Catholic University of America, Washington, DC [*Library symbol Library of Congress*] (LCLS)
DCU	Data-Cache Unit [*Computer science*]
DCU	Data Capture Unit (AIE)
DCU	Data Collection Unit
DCU	Data Command Unit (MCD)
DCU	Data Communications Unit
DCU	Data Communications Utility [*Social Security Administration*]
DCU	Data Control Unit
DCU	Decade Counting Unit
DCU	Decatur, AL [*Location identifier FAA*] (FAAL)
DCU	Decimal Counting Unit
dcu	Decimal Counting Unit (IDOE)
DCU	Dedicated Control Unit (SSD)
DCU	Deer Creek Reservoir [*Utah*] [*Seismograph station code, US Geological Survey*] (SEIS)
DCU	Deployment Control Unit [*Army*] (DOMA)
DCU	Desert Camouflage Uniform [*Military*]
DCU	Detection and Control Unit (MCD)
DCU	Device Control Unit
DCU	Dichloral Urea [*Medicine*] (MAE)
DCU	Digital Coefficient Unit [*Computer science*] (RDA)
DCU	Digital Computer Unit (MCD)
DCU	Digital Control Unit (KSC)
DCU	Digital Counting Unit
DCU	Disbandment Control Unit [*Allied Military Government of Occupied Territory*] [*Post-World War II*]
DCU	Discrete Control Unit [*American Solenoid Co.*] [*Somerset, NJ*]
DCU	Disk Cartridge Unit [*Computer science*] (ECII)
DCU	Disk Control Unit [*Computer science*] (IAA)
DCU	Dispenser Control Unit (RDA)
DCU	Display and Command Unit [*Military*]
DCU	Display and Control Unit (CET)
DCU	Distribution Control Unit
dcu	District of Columbia [*MARC country of publication code Library of Congress*] (LCCP)
DCU	Drum Control Unit (AABC)
DCU	Dublin City University (ACII)
DCU	Dynamic Checkout Unit [*Aerospace*] (AAG)
DCUA	Division of College and University Assistance [*HEW*]
DCU-C	Catholic University of America, Clementine Library, Washington, DC [*Library symbol Library of Congress*] (LCLS)
DCUC	Defense Credit Union Council (EA)
DCUG	Datamac Computer Users Group (HGAA)
DCU-H	Catholic University of America, Hyvernat Collection, Washington, DC [*Library symbol Library of Congress*] (LCLS)
DCU-IA	Catholic University of America, Ibero-American Collection, Washington, DC [*Library symbol Library of Congress*] (LCLS)
DCUL	Delaware Credit Union League (SRA)
DC (UN)	Disarmament Commission of the United Nations [*Also, DC, UNDC*]
DCU-R	Data Control Unit-Receiver (MCD)
DCUTL	Direct-Coupled Unipolar Transistor Logic
DCV	Dacarbazine, CCNU [*Lomustine*], Vincristine [*Antineoplastic drug regimen*]
dcv	DC Voltage (IDOE)
dcv	DC Volts (IDOE)
DCV	Dense-Cored Vesicles [*Anatomy*]

DCV	Derivative Cyclic Voltammetry [*Analytical electrochemistry*]
DCV	Design Change Verification
DCV	Digital Coded Voice (IAA)
DCV	Direct-Current Volts
DCV	Directional Control Valve
DCV	Double-Check Valve
DCV	Double Cotton Varnish [*Wire insulation*] (AAG)
DCV	DTIC [*Dacarbazine*], CCNU , Vincristine [*Lomustine*] [*Antineoplastic drug regimen*] (DAVI)
DCVC	Dichlorovinylcysteine [*Biochemistry*]
DCVG	Dichlorovinylglutathione [*Biochemistry*]
DCVG	Digital Control and Vector Generator
DCVGLA	Digital Control Variable Gain Linear Amplifier (IAA)
DCVH	Democratic Community of Vojvodina Hungarians [*Former Yugoslavia*] [*Political party*]
DCVO	Dame Commander of the Royal Victorian Order [*British*]
DCVO	Deputy Chief Veterinary Officer (DAVI)
DCVO	Deputy Chief Veterinary Officr (BABM)
DCVR	Direct-Current Voltage Reference
DCVR	Direct-Current Voltage Regulator
D/CVR	Dust Cover [*Automotive engineering*]
DCW	Data Communication Write [*Computer science*] (HGAA)
DCW	Data Control Word (CMD)
DCW	Dean and Chapter of Westminster [*Anglican Church*] (ROG)
DCW	Define Constant with Wordmark
DCW	Dependent Coverage Waiver [*Insurance*] (WYGK)
DCW	Diagonal Conducting Wall (MCD)
DCW	Digital Chart of the World [*Database*] [*Army*]
DCW	Dynamic Channel Exchange (NITA)
DCW	National Society, Daughters of Colonial Wars
DCWCS	Directional Control and Warning Communications System (MCD)
DCWO	Design Change Work Order
DCWOS	Deaerating Cold Weather Oil System
DCWS	Division of Church World Service [*Later, CWSW*] (EA)
DCWV	Direct-Current Working Volts
DCX	DCX, Inc. [*Associated Press*] (SAG)
DCX	Device Control Character [*Computer science*] (CMD)
DCX	Digital Equipment Corp., Colorado Springs, Colorado Springs, CO [*OCLC symbol*] (OCLC)
DCX	Direct-Current Experiments [*Nuclear energy*] (NRCH)
DCX	Double-Charge Exchange
DCx	Double Convex
DCX	Miami, FL [*Location identifier FAA*] (FAAL)
DC-XA	Delta Clipper Experimental Advanced [*Rocket*] [*An experimental rocket that takes off and lands on its tail*] [*NASA*]
DCXI	DCX, Inc. [*NASDAQ symbol*] (NQ)
DCY	Dicon Systems Ltd. [*Toronto Stock Exchange symbol*]
DCY	Washington, IN [*Location identifier FAA*] (FAAL)
DCYRA	Duster Class Yacht Racing Association (EA)
DCZ	Dichloro Analog of Zomepirac [*Biochemistry*]
DCZ	Die Cast Zinc
DD	Associate Directorate for Design [*Kennedy Space Center*] [*NASA*] (NASA)
DD	Association Internationale: Donnees pour le Developpement [*Data for Development International Association - DFD*] (EA)
DD	Command Airways [*ICAO designator*] (AD)
DD	Daily Docket [*Costing*] (DGA)
DD	Daily Double [*Horse racing*]
DD	Damage Done [*Insurance*] (ODBW)
DD	Dangerous Defective [*British*]
DD	Dangerous Drug
DD	Database Description (ACRL)
DD	Data Definition [*Computer science*] (BUR)
DD	Data Definition Statement (NITA)
DD	Data Demand
DD	Data Depository (MCD)
DD	Data Description (MCD)
DD	Data Dictionary [*Computer science*]
DD	Data Directory [*Computer science*] (IAA)
DD	Data Display (NASA)
DD	Data Division [*Computer science*]
D/D	Dated
D/D	Date of Draft [*Business term*]
d/D	Day of Discharge (DAVI)
DD	Days after Date [*Business term*]
DD	Days after Delivery
DD	Day's Date
DD	Dayton Development Corp. [*Vancouver Stock Exchange symbol*]
DD	Deadline Data [*Computer science*] [*Database terminology*] (NITA)
DD	Deadline Date
DD	Deaf and Dumb (IIA)
DD	Death from Disease [*Military*]
DD	Decimal Device (ECII)
DD	Decimal Display
DD	Decimal Divide
DD	Decision Data [*Computer science*] (NITA)
DD	Declaration Date [*of dividend payment*] [*Investment term*]
DD	Decoder Driver (MCD)
DD	De Dato [*Of Today's Date*] [*Latin*]
DD	Dederunt [*They Gave*] [*Latin*]
DD	Dedicated Displays (MCD)
DD	De Die [*Daily*] [*Pharmacy*]
DD	Dedit [*or Dedicavit*] [*Gave, Dedicated*] [*Latin*]
DD	Deep-Drawn [*Metals*]
DD	Defense Department [*US government*] (MCD)

DD	Defense Depot [*DoD*]
DD	Deferred Delivery [*Especially, of securities*]
DD	Deferred Development
DD	Define Double-Word [*Computer science*] (PCM)
DD	Definite Decoding
DD	Definitely Dull [*Medicine*]
DD	Degenerative Disease (DAVI)
DD	Degree Days
DD	Degree of Difficulty [*Diving*]
DD	Delay Driver (MCD)
DD	Delayed Delivery [*Especially, of Securities*]
D/D	Deletions/Deferments [*Military*]
DD	Delivered
dd	Delivered (WDMC)
DD	Delivered at Docks
DD	Demand Deposits
DD	Demand Draft [*Business term*]
DD	Demonstration Division [*Marine science*] (OSRA)
DD	Demonstration Division [*Forecast Systems Laboratory*] (USDC)
DD	Density Dependent (OA)
DD	Deo Dedit [*He Gave to God*] [*Latin*]
DD	Department of Defense
DD	Departure Date
DD	Dependent Drainage [*Medicine*]
DD	Deputy Director
DD	Designator Detector (MCD)
DD	Design Deviation [*Aerospace*] (AAG)
DD	Desmethyldiazepam [*Biochemistry*]
DD	Destination/Destination [*Inspection/Acceptance point*] (MCD)
DD	Destroyer [*Navy symbol*]
DD	Destructive Dilemma [*Rule of inference*] [*Logic*]
DD	Detailed Design [*Phase*]
DD	Determination of Dependency
DD	Detur Ad [*Let It Be Given To*] [*Pharmacy*]
D-D	Deuterium-Deuterium Reaction [*Nuclear energy*] (NRCH)
DD	Developer Demonstrator
DD	Developer's Digest [*Australia A publication*]
DD	Developmental Disability [*Medicine*]
DD	Developmentally Delayed
DD	Development Decade [*Ten-year plan designed to bring about self-sufficiency in developing countries*] [*United Nations*]
DD	Development Directive
DD	Deviation Difficulty [*Aerospace*] (AAG)
DD	Deviation Drawing (MCD)
DD	Device Description (ACII)
DD	Dewey Decimal Number [*Online database field identifier*]
DD	Dichloropropene-Dichloropropane [*Pesticide*]
DD	Died of Disease (MAE)
DD	Diesel Direct (MSA)
DD	Differential Diagnosis [*Medicine*]
DD	Differential Doppler
DD	Diffusion Destainer [*Electrophoresis*]
DD	Digital Data (CET)
DD	Digital Differential Analyzer [*Algorithm*] [*Computer science*] (IAA)
DD	Digital Display
DD	DiGuglielmo's Disease [*Medicine*] (AAMN)
DD	Diploma in Dermatology [*British*] (DI)
D-D	Diplomate, American Board of Dermatology (DHSM)
DD	Direct Debit [*Banking*]
DD	Direct Development [*Phylogeny*]
DD	Directed Dialing [*or Dialed*] [*Telecommunications*] (TEL)
DD	Direct Drive
DD	Directives Documentation [*NASA*] (NASA)
DD	Disability Determination [*Social Security Administration*] (OICC)
DD	Disc Diameter (BABM)
DD	Discharged Dead [*On a serviceman's papers*]
DD	Disconnecting Device (MSA)
DD	Discriminating Digit [*Telecommunications*] (TEL)
DD	Discrimination Difficulty [*Psychometrics*]
DD	Dishonorable Discharge
dd	Disk Diameter [*Ophthalmology*]
DD	Disk-to-Disk (IAA)
DD	Display Driver
DD	District Director
DD	Dividend [*Investment term*] (IAA)
DD	Divinitatis Doctor [*Doctor of Divinity*] [*Latin*]
DD	Dockyard Department [*Navy British*]
DD	Doctor Divinitatis [*Doctor of Divinity*] [*Latin*]
DD	Doctor of Divinity (DD)
DD	Doctor of Divinity in Metaphysics
D/D	Documentary Draft (ADA)
DD	Document Delivery [*Computer science*] (NITA)
DD	Document Distribution (SAA)
DD	Dogs for the Deaf (EA)
DD	Domain Directory (ACRL)
DD	Domestic Duties (ADA)
D/D	Donation on Discharge
DD	Donum Dedit [*Gave, Dedicated*] [*Latin*]
DD	Dot and Dash (IAA)
DDL	Doubled
DD	Double Dacron Braid Lacquered (MDG)
DD	Double Dark [*Photography*] (ROG)
DD	Double Deck
DD	Double Demy [*Paper*] (DGA)
DD	Double Density

DD	Double Diamond (MSA)
DD	Double Diffusion [*Test*]
DD	Double Diode
DD	Double-Dipper [*Retired military-government employee*]
DD	Double Dominance [*Ethology*]
DD	Double Draft [*Banking*] (ROG)
DD	Double Drift [*As used in a navigator's log*]
DD	Down Drain [*Medicine*] (DAVI)
DD	Draft for Development (OSI)
DD	Drama Desk (EA)
DD	Drawing Deviation (MCD)
D/D	Drift Down (GAVI)
DD	Drilled (WDAA)
DD	Drop Dead
DD	Drug Discrimination [*Psychopharmacology*]
DD	Drum Demand
DD	Dry Days [*Ecology*]
DD	Drydock
DD	Dry Dressing [*Medicine*]
DD	Dual Diaphragm [*Automotive engineering*]
DD	Duct Detector [*NFPA pre-fire planning symbol*] (NFPA)
DD	Due Date
DD	Dumb Driver [*Auto-racing*]
DD	Duplex-Drive [*Amphibious tank*]
DD	Du Pont [*E. I.*] De Nemours & Co., Inc. [*NYSE symbol*] (SPSG)
DD	duPont(EI)deNemours [*NYSE symbol*] (TTSB)
DD	Dutch Door [*Technical drawings*]
DD	Duty Driver [*Military*]
DD	Dynein Defective Cilia [*Medicine*]
DD	German Democratic Republic [*ANSI two-letter standard code*] (CNC)
Dd	Response to Very Small Detail [*Rorschach*] [*Also written dd*] [*Psychology*]
DDA	Dallas, TX [*Location identifier FAA*] (FAAL)
DDA	Dangerous Drugs Act [*British*]
DDA	Data Differential Analyzer (OA)
DDA	Dell Drive Array [*Computer science*]
DDA	Demand Deposit Account (TDOB)
DDA	Demand Deposit Accounting [*Banking*] (MDG)
DDA	Dental Dealers of America (EA)
DDA	Depth-Duration-Area
DDA	Deputy Director for Administration [*National Security Agency*]
DDA	Deputy Director of Armaments [*British*]
DDA	Designated Deployment Area
DDA	Designated Development Agency (MCD)
DDA	Design Direction Approval [*Automotive project management*]
DDA	Detroit Diesel Allison Division [*of General Motors Corp.*]
DDA	Development Display Assembly
ddA	Dideoxyadenosine [*Biochemistry Medicine*]
DDA	Diemakers and Diecutters Association [*Later, NADD*] (EA)
DDA	Digital Dealers Association (EA)
DDA	Digital Differential Analyzer [*Algorithm*] [*Computer science*]
DDA	Digital Differential Analyzer [*Computer science*] (BARN)
DDA	Digital Directory Assistance, Inc. [*Information service or system*] (IID)
DDA	Digital Display Alarm
DDA	Digital Drive Amplifier (AABC)
DDA	Digitally Directed Analog (MSA)
DDA	Direct Data Attachment
DDA	Direct Device Attachment (NITA)
DDA	Direct Digital Analysis (IAA)
DDA	Direct Disk Attachment
DDA	Directed Duty Assignment [*Military*] (AFM)
DDA	Disabled Drivers' Association [*British*]
DDA	Discrete Dipole Approximation [*Physics*]
DDA	Display and Decision Area
DDA	Dividend Disbursing Agent [*DLA*]
DDA	Division of Drug Advertising [*FDA*]
DDA	Doctor of Dramatic Art
DDA	Dodecenyl Acetate [*Pheromone*] [*Organic chemistry*]
DDA	Dodecylamine [*Organic chemistry*]
DDA	Dodecyldimethylamine [*or Dimethyldodecylamine*] [*Organic chemistry*]
DDA	Dominica Democratic Alliance [*Political party*] (PPW)
DDA	Drawing Departure Authorization (KSC)
DDA	Dr. Dvorkovitz & Associates [*Information service or system*] (IID)
DDA	Duty Deferment Account [*Customs*] (DS)
DDA	Duty Deposit Account [*Customs*] (DS)
DDA	Dynamic Demand Assignment [*Army*] (MCD)
DDA	Dynamics Differential Analyzer (IEEE)
DDA	ICD [*Interface Control Document*] Departure Authorization [*NASA*] (NASA)
DD(A & HR)	Deputy Director (Attaches and Human Resources) [*Defense Intelligence Agency*] (DNAB)
DDAB	Didodecyldimethyl Ammonium Bromide [*Inorganic chemistry*]
DDAB	Didodecyldimethyl Ammonium Bromide [*Organic chemistry*]
DDACM	Deputy Director for Acquisition Career Management [*Army*] (RDA)
DDACS	Dandenong and District Aborigines Cooperative Society [*Australia*]
DDAD	Detroit Diesel Allison Division [*of General Motors Corp.*]
DDAFP	Diesel-Driven Auxiliary Feed Water Pump (IEEE)
DDAG	Disabled Drivers' Action Group [*British*] (DI)
DDAL	Doris Day Animal League (EA)
DDALV	Days Delay Enroute Authorized Chargeable as Leave [*Military*]
DDALVAHP	Days Delay at Address within CONUS [*Continental United States*] Authorized Chargeable as Leave [*Military*]
DDAM	Dynamic Design Analysis Method [*Navy*]
DDAMP	Dideoxyadenosine Monophosphate [*Biochemistry*]

DDAMS .... Dynamic Design Analysis Method System [*Navy*]
DD & A .... Depreciation, Depletion, and Amortization
DD & CS ..... Dedicated Display and Control Subsystem (NASA)
DD & RB ..... Document Distribution and Reproduction Branch [*NTIS*]
DD & Shpg... Dock Dues and Shipping (DLA)
DD & T .... Detection, Discrimination, and Tracking
DDANS .... Deputy Director of Army Nursing Services [*British military*] (DMA)
DDAP .... Deutsche Demokratische Arbeiterpartei [*German Democratic Workers' Party*] [*Germany Political party*] (PPW)
DDAPS .... Digital Data Acquisition and Processing System
DDAR .... Department of Disarmament and Arms Regulation [*United Nations*]
DDAR .... Division of Defense Aid Reports [*Abolished, 1941*] [*Military*]
DDARS .... Digital Data Acquisition and Reduction System (MCD)
DDAS .... Dedicated Demand Assignment Signaling (MCD)
DDAS .... Design of Data Acquisition Subsystem (NOAA)
DDAS .... Digital Data Acquisition System
DDAS .... Digital Data Archives System
DDAS (ET) ... Deputy Director of Armament Supply (Eastern Theater)
DDATS .... Deputy Director, Auxiliary Territorial Service [*British military*] (DMA)
DDAU .... Doctoral Dissertations Accepted by American Universities [*A bibliographic publication*]
DDAVP .... Deamino-D-arginine Vasopressin [*Antidiuretic*]
D (Day) .... Decimalisation Day [*February 15, 1971, day English money was decimalized*]
DDB .... Colorado State Publications Depository and Distribution Center, Denver, CO [*OCLC symbol*] (OCLC)
DDB .... Data Display Board
DDB .... Data Display Buffer
DDB .... Dead Band Setting [*Electronics*] (ECII)
DDB .... De Dion-Bouton [*Automobile*] [*French*]
DDB .... Design Data Book
DDB .... Device-Dependent Bitmap [*Computer science*] (PCM)
DDB .... Diagnostic Development Branch [*National Institutes of Health*]
DDB .... Dial Drive Belt
DDB .... Digital Database (MCD)
DDB .... Digital Data Buffer
DDB .... Distributed Database
DDB .... Distribution Disk Builder [*Computer science*]
DDB .... Division of Drug Biology [*Department of Health and Human Services*] (GRD)
DDB .... Dodecylbenzene [*Organic chemistry*]
DDB .... Don't Ditch a Buddy [*Promise made by members of the Junior Woodchucks, organization to which comic strip character Donald Duck's nephews belonged*]
DDB .... Dortmund Data Bank [*University of Dortmund*] [*Germany Information service or system*] (IID)
DDB .... Double Declining Balance [*Depreciation method*] [*Accounting*]
DDB .... Double-Declining-Balance Depreciation Method [*Finance*] (DFIT)
DDB .... Doyle Dane Bernbach, Inc. [*Advertising agency*]
DDB .... Dutch Dairy Bureau (EA)
DDBA .... Digioxigenin(dibromoacetate) [*Biochemistry*]
DDBDBFC .... Dave Durham and the Bull Durham Band Fan Club (EA)
DDBF .... Damaged DNA [*Deoxyribonucleic Acid*] Binding Factor [*Biochemistry*]
DDBG .... DIMDI [*Deutsches Institut fuer Medizinische Dokumentation und Information*] Database Generator [*Index to Scientific Reviews*] (NITA)
DDBJ .... DNA [*Deoxyribonucleic Acid*] Data Bank of Japan
DDBMS .... Distributed Database Management System [*Computer science*]
DDBOps .... Deputy Director of Bomber Operations [*Air Ministry*] [*British World War II*]
DDBP .... Dance Data Bank Project [*University of California*] [*Los Angeles*] [*Information service or system*] (IID)
D/DBP .... Disinfectants & Disinfection By-Products Rule (ACII)
DDB-P .... Distinguished Pistol Shot Badge [*Military decoration*] (GFGA)
DDB-R .... Distinguished Rifleman Badge [*Military decoration*] (GFGA)
DDBS .... Descriptor Database System
DDBS .... Dodecyl Benzenesulfonate [*Organic chemistry*]
DDBSA .... Dodecylbenzenesulfonic Acid [*Organic chemistry*]
DDBTP .... Digital Database Transformation Program (MCD)
DDC .... Corvette [*Navy symbol Obsolete*]
DDC .... Dangerous Drug Cabinet [*Lockable auxiliary to bathroom medicine chest*]
DDC .... Data Display Central
DDC .... Data Display Controller
DDC .... Data Distribution Center
DDC .... Data Documentation Costs
DDC .... Date Due Calibration [*Military*] (AFIT)
DDC .... Decision, Design, and the Computer [*Symposium*]
DDC .... Deck Decompression Chamber [*Undersea technology*]
DDC .... Defense Documentation Center [*for Scientific and Technical Information*] [*Later, DTIC Alexandria, VA*]
DDC .... Defensive Driving Course [*National Safety Council*]
DDC .... Departmental Data Coordinator (MCD)
DD(C) .... Deputy Director for Collection [*Defense Intelligence Agency*] (DNAB)
DDC .... Designed Data [*Vancouver Stock Exchange symbol*]
DDC .... Detroit Data Center [*IRS*]
DDC .... Detroit Diesel [*NYSE symbol*] (SPSG)
DDC .... Detroit Diesel Corp. [*Automotive industry supplier*]
DDC .... Developmental Disability Center [*Columbia University*] [*Research center*] (RCD)
DDC .... Dewey Decimal Classification [*Also, DC*]
DDC .... Diamond Dealers Club (EA)
DDC .... Dicarbethoxydihydrocollidine [*Biochemistry*]
DDC .... Diccionario de Citas [*A publication*]
DDC .... Dideoxycytidine [*Biochemistry*]

DDC .... Diecasting Development Council (EA)
DDC .... Diethyldithiocarbamate [*Also, DDTC, DEDC*] [*Organic chemistry*]
DDC .... Diethyldithiocarbamic Acid [*Organic chemistry*] (AAMN)
DDC .... Digital Data Cell (NASA)
DDC .... Digital Data Conversion [*Computer science*] (NITA)
DDC .... Digital Data Converter
DDC .... Digital Display Conversion [*Computer science*] (NITA)
DDC .... Digital Display Converter (BUR)
DDC .... Digitally Directed Control (MSA)
DDC .... Digital-to-Digital Converter [*Electronics*] (IAA)
DDC .... Dihydrocollidine [*Organic chemistry*] (DAVI)
DDC .... Direct Data Channel
DDC .... Direct Digital Computer (IAA)
DDC .... Direct Digital Control
DDC .... Direct Display Console (MAE)
DDC .... Direct Drawing Change (AAG)
DDC .... Display Data Channel [*Computer science*] (PCM)
DDC .... Display Data Controller (IAA)
DDC .... Distributed Digital Control [*Computer science*]
DDC .... District Court, District of Columbia (DLA)
DDC .... Diverticular Disease of the Colon [*Medicine*] (DMAA)
DDC .... Division Data Center [*Army*] (RDA)
DDC .... Division of Drug Chemistry [*Department of Health and Human Services*] (GRD)
DDC .... Docteur en Droit Canonique [*Doctor of Canon Law*] [*French*] (ILCA)
DDC .... Dodge City [*Kansas*] [*Airport symbol*] (OAG)
DDC .... Dominican House of Studies, Immaculate Conception Convent Library, Washington, DC [*Library symbol Library of Congress OCLC symbol*] (LCLS)
DDC .... Dopa Decarboxylase [*An enzyme*]
DDC .... Doris Day Collectors (EA)
DDC .... Double-Doped Crystal
DDC .... Driver Development Centre [*South Australia*]
DDC .... Dual Diversity Comparator
DDC .... Duration of Disease Control
DDC1 .... Display Data Channel (PCM)
DDCA .... Defense Communications Agency, Technical Library, Washington, DC [*Library symbol Library of Congress*] (LCLS)
DDCA .... Deputy Director of Civil Affairs [*War Office*] [*British World War II*]
DDCA .... Diethyldithio Carbamic Acid [*Organic chemistry*]
DDCA .... Director, Defense Communications Agency (CINC)
DDCAS .... Deputy Director, Contract Administration Services [*DoD*]
DDCASM ..... Deputy Director, Contract Administration Services Memorandum [*DoD*]
DDCC .... Developmental Disability Center for Children [*Louisiana State University*] [*Research center*] (RCD)
DDCDM .... Didemethylchlordimeform [*A pesticide*]
DDCE .... Digital Data Conversion Equipment
DDCI .... Deputy Director of Central Intelligence [*CIA*] (ECON)
DDCI .... Douglas Development Co. - Irvine [*California*]
DDCMP .... Digital Data Communications Message Protocol [*Digital Equipment Corp.*]
DDCO (I) ...... Deputy Director of Combined Operations (India)
DDCONUS ... Date Departed Continental United States [*Military*] (AFM)
DDCP .... Department of Defense Claimant Program
DDCP .... Direct Digital Color Proofing [*Graphic arts*] (DGA)
DDCP .... Draft Development Concept Paper (RDA)
DDCPO .... Division Damage Control Petty Officer [*Navy*] (DNAB)
DDCS .... Data Definition Control System
DDCS .... Dedicated Data Calibration System
DDCS .... Digital Data Calibration System (KSC)
DDCS .... Digital Display and Control Set (MCD)
DDCS .... Direct Digital Control System
DDCS .... Distributed Database Connection Service [*IBM Corp.*] (PCM)
DDCS .... Double Differential Cross Section
DDCSTI .... Defense Documentation Center for Scientific and Technical Information [*DoD*] (DNAB)
ddCTP .... Dideoxycytidine Triphosphate [*Biochemistry*]
DDD .... Comprehensive Dishonesty, Disappearance, and Destruction Policy [*Insurance*]
DD/D .... Data Dictionary/Directory [*Computer science*]
DDD .... Dat, Dicat, Dedicat [*He Gives, Devotes, and Dedicates*] [*Latin*]
DDD .... Date Deficiency [*or Discrepancy*] Discovered (MCD)
DDD .... Deadline Delivery Date
DDD .... Debility, Dependency, and Dread [*Factors producing compliance in hostages, prisoners, etc.*]
DDD .... Dedicated Display Device (MCD)
DDD .... Degenerative Disc Disease [*Medicine*]
DDD .... Dense Deposit Disease (MAE)
DDD .... Deputy Director of Design [*British*]
DDD .... Design Definition Document [*NASA*] (NASA)
DDD .... Design Disclosure Data
DDD .... Desired Delivery Date (AFM)
DDD .... Desired Deposit of Dividends [*Investment term*] (MHDW)
DDD .... Detailed Data Display
DDD .... Deutscher Depeschen-Dienst [*Press agency*] [*Germany*]
DDD .... Dichlorodibenzodioxin [*Also, DCDD*] [*Organic chemistry*]
DDD .... Dichlorodiphenyldichloroethane [*Also, TDE*] [*Insecticide*]
DDD .... Diesel Direct Drive
DDD .... Digital Data Distributor (CET)
DDD .... Digital Depth Detector (DNAB)
DDD .... Digital Diagnostic Diskette [*Computer science*] (NITA)
DDD .... Digital Display Driver (KSC)
DDD .... Dihydroxydinaphthyl Disulfide [*Analytical chemistry*]
DDD .... Direct Deposit of Dividends

DDD .... Direct Distance Dialing [*of telephone numbers for toll calls*]
DDD .... Display Decoder Drive (MCD)
DDD .... Domestic Door-to-Door [*Personal property*]
DDD .... Dono Dedit Dedicavit [*He Gave and Dedicated as a Gift*] [*Latin*]
DDD .... Drug Detection Dog (DNAB)
DDD .... Dual Diaphragm Distributor [*Automotive engineering*]
DDD .... Duplexed Display Distributor
DDD .... Dynamic Dummy Director
DDD .... Three Dimensional [*Also, 3D*] (DAVI)
DDDA .... Decimal Digital Differential Analyzer
DDDA .... Dodecadienyl Acetate [*Pheromone*] [*Organic chemistry*]
DDDA .... Dodecanedioic Acid [*Organic chemistry*]
DDDC .... Didehydrodideoxycytidine [*Antiviral*]
DDDC .... Disk Drive Dry Cleaner (NITA)
DDDD .... Dignum Deo Donum Dedit [*Latin*] (DLA)
DDDD .... Fourth Dimension Software [*NASDAQ symbol*] (SAG)
DDDDF .... New Dimension Software [*NASDAQ symbol*] (TTSB)
DDDEP .... Defense Development Data Exchange Program (MCD)
DDDL .... Digital Data Down Link [*Computer science*] (MCD)
DDDM .... Dihydroxydichlorodiphenylmethane [*Fungicide*]
DDDOL .... Dodecandienol [*Pheromone*] [*Organic chemistry*]
DDDP .... Discrete Differential Dynamic Programming [*Computer science*]
DDDR & E (T & E)... Deputy Director, Defense Research and Engineering (Test and Evaluation) [*DoD*] (DOMA)
DDDRE .... Deputy Director, Defense Research and Engineering [*Army*]
DD/DS .... Data Dictionary/Directory System [*Computer science*]
DDDS .... Deputy Director of Dental Services [*Military British*]
DDDS .... Dichlorodiphenyl Disulfide [*Insecticide*]
DDDS .... Digital Data Display System
DDDS .... Directorate of Documentation and Drawing Services (MCD)
DDDT .... Didehydrodideoxythymidine [*Antiviral*]
DDDU .... Digital Decoder Driver Unit (MCD)
DDDU .... Drug Detector Dog Unit
DDE .... Decentralized Data Entry (IEEE)
DDE .... Deputy Director of Equipment [*Air Force British*]
DDE .... Dichlorodiphenyldichloroethylene [*Pesticide residue*]
DDE .... Differential Difference Equation [*Mathematics*] (IAA)
DDE .... Diospyrin Dimethyl Ether [*Biochemistry*]
DDE .... Direct Data Entry [*Computer science*] (BUR)
DDE .... Direct Digital Encoder
DDE .... Director Design Engineering (KSC)
DDE .... Distributed Data Entry
DDE .... Diversified Entertainment [*Vancouver Stock Exchange symbol*]
DDE .... Double Diffusion Epitaxial Process (IAA)
DDE .... Dual Displacement Engine
DDE .... Dwight David Eisenhower [*US general and president, 1890-1969*]
DDE .... Dynamic Data Exchange [*Message protocol*] [*Computer science*] (BYTE)
DDE .... Escort Destroyer [*Navy symbol*]
DDEAMC ..... Dwight D. Eisenhower Army Medical Center [*Fort Gordon, GA*]
DDEC .... Detroit Diesel Electronic [*or Engine*] Control [*Automotive engineering*]
D Dec .... Dix's School Law Decisions [*New York*] [*A publication*] (DLA)
DDEDS .... Defense Disposal Executive Development Seminar [*DoD*]
DD/EFT .... Direct Deposit / Electronic Fund Transfer
d de JC .... Despues de Jesucristo [*After Jesus Christ*] [*Spanish*] (GPO)
DDEL .... Defense Development and Engineering Laboratories [*Military*]
DDEL .... Dwight D. Eisenhower Library
D Del .... United States District Court for the District of Delaware (DLA)
DDEML .... Dynamic Data Exchange Management Library [*Microsoft, Inc.*] (PCM)
DDEOC .... Destroyer Engineered Operating Cycle (MCD)
DDEP .... Defense Development Data Exchange Program (AAGC)
DDEP .... Defense Development Exchange Program (AFM)
DDEP .... Dicarbethoxy(dimethyl)(ethyl)dihydropyridine [*Biochemistry*]
DDEP .... Double Diffusion Epitaxial Plane
DDEPHS ...... Dwight D. Eisenhower Philatelic and Historical Society (EA)
DDERS .... Direct Data Entry Replacement System
DDES .... Digital Data Exchange Standards [*Telecommunications*] (DGA)
DDES .... Direct Data Entry Station (NITA)
DDES .... Direct Data Entry System
D Des .... Doctor of Design
DDESB .... Department of Defense Explosives Safety Board [*Alexandria, VA*]
DDF .... Database Definition File (NITA)
DDF .... Data Description Facility (PDAA)
DDF .... Data Dictionary File [*Computer science*] (PCM)
DDF .... Defense Department Form (AAG)
DDF .... Delaware Group Dividend Income [*NYSE symbol*] (SPSG)
DDF .... Delaware Grp Dividend Income [*NYSE symbol*] (TTSB)
DDF .... Dental Documentary Foundation
DDF .... Deputy Director for Field Management and Evaluation [*National Security Agency*]
DDF .... Design Discharge Format
DDF .... Design Disclosure Formats [*Naval Applied Science Laboratory*]
DDF .... Dielectric Dissipation Factor
DDF .... Digital Distribution Frame [*Telecommunications*] (TEL)
DDF .... Director's Discretionary Fund
DDF .... Discontinued Depreciation Function
DDF .... Dominion Drama Festival [*Canada*]
DDF .... Downtown Development Foundation [*Washington, DC Defunct*] (EA)
DDF .... Dual Doctor Families (EA)
DDF .... Due-In - Due-Out File (AFIT)
DDF .... Food and Drug Administration Medical Library, Rockville, MD [*OCLC symbol*] (OCLC)
DDF .... Military Order, Devil Dog Fleas (EA)
DDFC .... Deoxydifluorocytidine [*Antineoplastic drug*]
DDFT .... Design, Development, Fabrication, Testing

DDG .... Data Display Generator
DDG .... Decoy Discrimination Group (AAG)
DDG .... Deer Lodge, MT [*Location identifier FAA*] (FAAL)
DDG .... Deoxy-D-Glucose [*Also, DG, DOG*] [*Biochemistry*]
DDG .... Deputy Director-General [*British*]
DDG .... Deutsche Dermatologische Gesellschaft [*German Dermatological Society*] (EAIO)
DDG .... Dial Depth Gauge
DDG .... Didecyl Glutarate [*Organic chemistry*]
DDG .... Dideoxyguanosine [*Antiviral*]
DDG .... Digital Data Generator (IEEE)
DDG .... Digital Data Group
DDG .... Digital Display Generator
DDG .... Distillers Dried Grain
DDG .... Dodge
DDG .... Double Derivatized Guar [*Chemical technology*]
DDG .... Guided Missile Destroyer [*Navy symbol*]
DDGB .... Double-Dose Gallbladder [*Medicine*] (MEDA)
DDGC .... Dishonorable Discharge, General Court-Martial, after Confinement in Prison [*Navy*]
DDGE .... Digital Display Generator Element
DDGI .... Dishonorable Discharge, General Court-Martial, Immediate [*Navy*]
DDGM .... District Deputy Grand Master [*Freemasonry*] (ROG)
DDGMR ...... Deputy Director-General of Military Railways [*British military*] (DMA)
DDGN .... Nuclear Powered Guided Missile Destroyer [*Navy symbol*]
DDGOF .... Deputy Director-General of Ordnance Factories [*Ministry of Supply*] [*British World War II*]
DDGOF(E) ... Deputy Director-General of Ordnance Factories, Engineering Factories [*Ministry of Supply*] [*British World War II*]
DDGOF(F) .... Deputy Director-General of Ordnance Factories, Filling Factories [*Ministry of Supply*] [*British World War II*]
DDGOS .... Deep-Diving Submarines, General Overhaul Specifications (DNAB)
DDGP .... Deputy Director-General of Production [*Ministry of Aircraft Production*] [*British World War II*]
DDGP .... Dishonorable Discharge, General Court-Martial, after Violation of Probation [*Navy*]
DDGS .... Distillers' Dried Grain with Solubles [*Feedstuff*]
DDGT .... Deputy Director-General of Transportation [*British military*] (DMA)
DDGTP .... Dideoxyguanosine Triphosphate [*Biochemistry*]
DDGX .... Guided Missile Destroyer
DDH .... Destroyer, Antisubmarine Helicopter [*NATO*]
DDH .... Dichlorodimethylhydantoin [*Organic chemistry*]
DDH .... Digital Data Handling
DDH .... Diploma in Dental Health [*British*]
DDH .... Director, Division of Health [*New Zealand*]
DDH .... Dissociated Double Hypertropia [*Ophthalmology*]
DDH .... Division of Dental Health [*Bureau of Health Professions Education and Manpower Training, HEW*]
DDH .... Dodecahedron [*Golf ball design*]
DDHA .... Digital Data Handling Assembly (MCD)
DDH & DS ... Digital Data Handling and Display System (NRCH)
DDHBirm ..... Diploma in Dental Health, University of Birmingham [*British*] (DI)
DDHEALTH... Health Issues for People with Developmental Disabilities
DDHG .... Deputy Director, Home Guard [*British military*] (DMA)
DDHG .... Guided Missile Aviation Destroyer [*Navy symbol*]
DDHGN ...... Nuclear-Powered Guided Aviation Destroyer [*Navy symbol*]
DD/HH:MM:SS... Day/Hour:Minute:Second (NASA)
DDHO .... Deputy Director of Home Operations [*Air Ministry*] [*British World War II*]
DDHP .... Deputy Director of Hygiene and Pathology [*Military British*]
DDHP .... Deringer Duell Head Process
DDHS .... Decimp Data Line Switch [*Computer science*]
DDHS .... Digital Data Handling System (NOAA)
DDHSF .... Darling Downs Health Services Foundation [*Australia*]
DDI .... Data and Dimensions Interface
DDI .... Data Development, Inc. [*Database producer*] (IID)
DDI .... Data Display Indicator
DDI .... Daydream Island [*Australia Airport symbol*] (OAG)
DDI .... Dedicated Display Indicator (NASA)
DDI .... Dehra Dun [*India*] [*Later, SAB*] [*Geomagnetic observatory code*]
DDI .... Delivery Distribution Indicator (MCD)
DDI .... Demand Development Interval (MCD)
DDI .... Demographic Data for Development, International Statistical Program Center [*Bureau of the Census*] (GFGA)
DDI .... Density Dependent Inhibition [*of cell growth*]
DDI .... Depression Deviation Indicator
DDI .... Depth Deviation Indicator
DDI .... Deputy Director for Intelligence [*CIA*] (DOMA)
DDI .... Deputy Director of Intelligence [*Air Ministry*] [*British World War II*]
DDI .... Device-Driver Interface [*Computer science*]
DDI .... Diazodicyanoimidazole [*Organic chemistry*]
DDI .... Didanosine [*Drug used in the treatment of AIDS*]
ddI .... Dideoxyinosine [*Medicine*]
DDI .... Dideoxyinosine Videx [*An AIDS treatment drug*] (CDI)
DDI .... Diethyl Dicarbocyanine Iodide [*Organic chemistry*]
DDI .... Digital Data Indicator (MCD)
DDI .... Digital Display Indicator (MCD)
DDI .... Direct Dial In (BUR)
DDI .... Direct Digital Interface
DDI .... Directed Drawing Instrument
DDI .... Director of Defense Information (DNAB)
DDI .... Director of Defense Information (DOMA)
DDI .... Discrete Data Input (MCD)
DDI .... Discrete Digital Input (NASA)
DDI .... Distilled Deionized [*Chemistry*]

DDI .... Divisional Detective Inspector [*British police*]
DDI .... Document Disposal Indicator
DDI .... Dodecylimidazole [*Antifungal*]
DDI .... Dressing Dry and Intact [*Medicine*] (DAVI)
DDI .... Drug Dynamics Institute [*University of Texas at Austin*] [*Research center*] (RCD)
D(DIA) .... Director (Defense Intelligence Agency) [*DoD*]
DDIB .... Disease Detection Information Bureau [*Medicine*] (DMAA)
DDIC .... Department of Defense Disease and Injury Codes (DNAB)
D Did .... Doctor of Didactics
DDIE .... Direct Digital Interface Equipment [*Telecommunications*] (TEL)
D Di E .... Doctor of Diesel Engineering
D Di Eng ..... Doctor of Diesel Engineering
DDIF .... Digital Document Interchange Format
DDIFC .... Dick Damron International Fan Club [*Defunct Defunct*] (EA)
DDII .... Data Documents [*NASDAQ symbol*] (TTSB)
DDII .... Data Documents, Inc. [*NASDAQ symbol*] (SAG)
DDIM .... Data Dimensions [*NASDAQ symbol*] (TTSB)
DDIM .... Data Dimensions, Inc. [*NASDAQ symbol*] (SAG)
DDIM .... Dry Deposition Inferential Method [*Marine science*] (OSRA)
DDIM .... Dry Deposition Inferential Method (USDC)
DDIMP .... Dideoxyinosine Monophosphate [*Biochemistry*]
DD in D .... De Die in Diem [*From Day to Day*] [*Latin*]
DDIP .... Darling Downs Institute Press (DGA)
D Dipl .... Doctor of Diplomacy
DDIR .... District Directors of Internal Revenue [*IRS*]
DDIR .... Division of Drug Information Resources [*Public Health Service*] [*Information service or system*] (IID)
D/DIRNSA .... Deputy Director, National Security Agency
DDIS .... Data Display
DD(IS) .... Deputy Director (Information Systems) [*Defense Intelligence Agency*] (DNAB)
DDIS .... Document Data Indexing Set
DDIS .... Document Depository Index System (MCD)
DDIS .... Dover Downs International Speedway [*Auto racing facility*]
DDiv .... Doctor of Divinity
DDIWT .... Deputy Director of Inland Water Transport [*British military*] (DMA)
DDJ .... Digital Differencing Junction
DDJ .... Dr. Dobb's Journal [*M & T Publishing, Inc.*] [*Information service or system*] (CRD)
DDK .... Daini Denden Kikaku
DDK .... Device Development Kit [*Microsoft Corp.*]
DDK .... Device Driver Kit [*Computer science*] (PCM)
DDK .... Dunsink Observatory [*Ireland*] [*Seismograph station code, US Geological Survey*] (SEIS)
DDK .... Hunter-Killer Destroyer [*Navy ship symbol*] [*Navy Obsolete*]
DDL .... Data Definition Language [*NCR Corp.*]
DDL .... Data Description Language [*Computer science*]
DDL .... Data Dialog
DDL .... Data Distribution List
DDL .... Data Down Link [*Computer science*] (MCD)
DDL .... Data Drawing List
DDL .... Dated Drawing List (MCD)
DDL .... DDL Electronics [*Formerly, Data-Design Laboratories*] [*NYSE symbol*] (SPSG)
DDL .... DDL Foodshow [*Food emporium which derives its name from its creator, movie producer Dino DeLaurentiis*]
DDL .... Delegation of Disclosure Authority Letters [*Military*] (AFIT)
DDL .... Deputy Director of Labour [*British*]
DDL .... Detailed Data List (MCD)
DDL .... Device Description Language (ACII)
DDL .... Differential Distribution Law [*Meteorology*]
DDL .... Digital Data Link
DDL .... Digital Data Logger
DDL .... Digital Delay Line [*Electronic musical instruments*]
DDL .... Digital Design Language [*Air Force Computer science*]
DDL .... Diode-Diode Logic [*Physics*]
DDL .... Direct Data Link (CDE)
DDL .... Dispersive Delay Line
DDL .... Doctor of Divine Literature
DDL .... Documentation Distribution List (KSC)
DDL .... Document Description Language [*Computer science*]
DDL .... Dodollo [*Ethiopia*] [*Airport symbol*] (AD)
DDL .... Light Destroyer (ADA)
DDLC .... Data Description Language Committee [*CODASYL*]
DDLC .... Data Description Language Computer (IAA)
DDLCN .... Distributed Double Loop Computer Network (MCD)
DDLDS .... Date Departed Last Duty Station [*Military*] (AFM)
DDL Elc .... DDL Electronics [*Associated Press*] (SAG)
DDLM .... Digital Data Link Monitor
DDLP .... Database Definition Language Processor (BYTE)
DDL-P .... Digital Design Language-PASCAL (MCD)
DDLS .... Dump Data Line Switch (MCD)
DDLT .... Diagnostic Decision Logic Table [*Computer science*]
DDM .... Data Demand Module (IEEE)
DDM .... Data Diffusion Machine [*Computer science*]
DDM .... Data Display Module (MCD)
DDM .... Data Display Monitoring (MCD)
DDM .... Decision Direct Measurement (IAA)
DDM .... Defense Disposal Manual [*DoD*] (AFIT)
DDM .... Department of Data Management [*Veterans Administration*]
DDM .... Derived Delta Modulation
DDM .... Design Decision Memo (MCD)
DDM .... Dialkyl Dihexadecylmalonate [*Organic chemistry*]
DDM .... Diaminodiphenylmethane [*Organic chemistry*]

DDM .... Dichlorodiphenylmethane [*Organic chemistry*]
DDM .... Difference in Depth of Modulation (IEEE)
DDM .... Digital Database Maps (MCD)
DDM .... Digital Data Multiplexer [*Telecommunications*] (ACRL)
DDM .... Digital Display Machine
DDM .... Digital Display Makeup
DDM .... Diphenyldiazomethane [*Organic chemistry*]
DDM .... Diploma in Dermatological Medicine [*British*]
DDM .... Discrete Data Management (MCD)
DDM .... Distributed Data Manager
DDM .... Doctor of Dental Medicine
DDM .... Dodecylmorpholine [*Antifungal*]
DDM .... Donnely Dome [*Alaska*] [*Seismograph station code, US Geological Survey*] (SEIS)
DDM .... Double Diffused Mesa
DDM .... Drop Dynamics Module (MCD)
DDM .... Dynamic Depletion Mode (IAA)
DDM .... Master of Dental Medicine
DDMA .... Disk Direct Memory Access
DDMAC .... Division of Drug Marketing, Advertising, and Communications [*Food and Drug Administration*]
DDMC .... Design and Drafting Management Council [*Defunct*] (EA)
DDMC .... Directed Deployable Maintenance Concept (MCD)
DDMC .... Disabled Drivers' Motor Club [*British*]
DDME .... Deputy Director of Mechanical Engineering [*British*]
DDMI .... Deputy Director of Military Intelligence [*British*]
DDMIIS .... David Davies Memorial Institute of International Studies (MSC)
DDMOI .... Deputy Director of Military Operations and Intelligence [*British*]
DDMOW .... Deputy Director of Medical Organization for War [*Military British*]
DDMP .... Deep-Drawn Metal Part
DDMP .... Defense Depot - Mechanicsburg, Pennsylvania [*DoD*]
DDMP .... Deputy Director of Manpower Planning [*Military British*]
DDMQ .... Deputy Director of Movements and Quartering [*Military British*]
DDMS .... Department of Defense Manned Space Flight
DDMS .... Deputy Director of Medical Services [*Military British*]
DDMS .... Digital Data Measuring System
DDMS .... DoD [*Department of Defense*] Manager for Space Shuttle Support (MCD)
DDMT .... Defense Depot - Memphis, Tennessee [*DoD*]
DDMT .... Deputy Director of Military Training [*British*]
DDMTMA .... Department of Defense Military Traffic Management Agency (AAG)
DDN .... Deep Draft Navigation [*Type of water project*]
DDN .... Defense Data Network
DDN .... Delta Downs [*Australia Airport symbol Obsolete*] (OAG)
DDN .... Design Decision Notice (MCD)
DDN .... Design-Drafting-Numerical Control [*Automotive engineering*]
DDN .... Devis Directeurs Nationaux [*Canada*] (DD)
DDN .... Digital Data Network
DDN .... Diploma de Droit Notarial [*Canada*] (DD)
D Dn .... Doctor of Design
DDN .... Documentation Development Notification (KSC)
DDN .... Documented Discount Notes [*Banking*]
D(DNA) .... Director (Defense Nuclear Agency) [*DoD*]
DDNAME ...... Data Definition Name (ECII)
DDNC .... Deputy Director of Naval Construction [*British*]
DDNC .... Digestive Disease National Coalition (EA)
DDNC .... Direct Digital Numerical Controller
DDNI .... Deputy Director of Naval Intelligence [*British*]
DDNJ FDC ... Food and Drug Administration, Notices of Judgment [*A publication*] (DLA)
DDNN .... Dominis Nostris [*To Our Lords*] [*Latin*]
DDNO .... Dodecyldimethylamine [*or Dimethyldodecylamine*] N-Oxide [*Organic chemistry*]
DDNP .... Diazodinitrophenol [*Organic chemistry*]
ddNTP .... Dideoxyribonucleotide Triphosphate [*Organic chemistry*]
DDNTP .... Didicyclohexylammonium Naphthylthiolphosphate [*Organic chemistry*]
DDO .... Dansyl Derivative of Oligothymidilate [*Biochemistry*]
DDO .... Deputy Director of Operations [*Air Force*]
DDO .... Deputy Director of Organisation [*Air Ministry*] [*British*]
DDO .... Deputy Disbursing Officer (DNAB)
DDO .... Destroyers, Disbursing Office [*Navy*]
DDO .... Developmental Disabilities Office [*Department of Health and Human Services*]
DDO .... Diocesan Director of Ordinands [*Church of England*]
DDO .... Diploma in Dental Orthopaedics [*British*]
DDO .... Director, Development and Operations (MUGU)
DDO .... Discrete Data Output (MCD)
DDO .... Discrete Digital Output (MCD)
DDO .... Dispatch Discharging Only [*Shipping*] (DS)
DDO .... District Dental Office [*or Officer*] [*Navy*]
DDO .... Double Draw-Off [*Crystallizer*] [*Chemical engineering*]
DDO .... Dumbarton Oaks Research Library of Harvard University, Washington, DC [*Library symbol Library of Congress OCLC symbol*] (LCLS)
DDO .... Dummy Delivery Order (DNAB)
DDOA .... Deputy Director of Operations and Administration (DNAB)
DDOATS .... Deputy Director of Organisation, Auxiliary Territorial Service [*British military*] (DMA)
DDOCE .... Digital Data Output Conversion Element [*or Equipment*]
DDOD .... Deputy Director of Operations Division [*Air Ministry*] [*British*]
DDOE .... United States Department of Energy, Washington, DC [*Library symbol Library of Congress*] (LCLS)
DD of T .... Director, Division of Traffic
DDOF(X) ...... Deputy Director of Ordnance Factories, Explosives Factories [*Ministry of Supply*] [*British World War II*]

DDOI	Deputy Director of Operations and Intelligence [*Air Ministry*] [*British*]
DDOMC	Defense Depot Operations Management Course [*DoD*]
DDOP	DSA [*Defense Supply Agency*] Disposal Operating Procedures
DDORCPS Glas	Diplomate in Dental Orthoptics of the Royal College of Physicians and Surgeons of Glasgow [*British*]
DDOrthRCPS(Glas)	Diploma in Dental Orthopaedics of the Royal College of Physicians and Surgeons (Glasgow) (DI)
DDOS	Deputy Director of Ordnance Services [*British*]
DDOT	United States Department of Transportation, Washington, DC [*Library symbol Library of Congress*] (LCLS)
DDOU	Defense Depot - Ogden, Utah [*DoD*]
DDP	Cisplatin [*Antineoplastic drug*] (DAVI)
DDP	Daily Delinquency Penalty [*IRS*]
DDP	Data Display Parameter
DDP	Data Distribution Panel (KSC)
DDP	Data Distribution Point [*NATO*] (NATG)
DDP	Datagram Delivery Protocol
DDP	Debriefing Display Program (SAA)
DDP	Declaration of Design Performance [*British*]
DDP	Defense Dissemination Program (MCD)
DDP	Deferred Development Program [*Military*]
DDP	Deliverable Data Package (SSD)
DDP	Delivered Duty Paid [*"INCOTERM," International Chamber of Commerce official code*]
DDP	Delivery Distribution Point (MCD)
DDP	Delta Dental Plan
DDP	Demand Development Period (MCD)
DDP	Density-Dependent Phosphoprotein [*Medicine*] (DMAA)
DDP	Department of Defense Production
DDP	Dependents' Dental Plan [*DoD*]
DDP	Deputy Director of Plans [*CIA*]
DDP	Derecha Democratica Espanola [*Spanish Right-Wing Democratic Party*] (PPW)
DDP	Design Data Package
DDP	Design Development Plan (NASA)
DDP	Deutsche Demokratische Partei [*German Democratic Party*] [*Political party*] (PPE)
DDP	Diamminodichloroplatinum [*Cisplatin*] [*Also, CDDP, cis-DDP, CPDD, CPT, P*] [*Antineoplastic drug*]
DDP	Dichlorodiammineplatinum [*Organic chemistry*]
DDP	Didecyl Phthalate [*Organic chemistry*]
DDP	Differential Dynamic Programming (MCD)
DDP	Digital Data Processor
DDP	Digital Display Processor (CMD)
DDP	Direct Deposit of Payroll
DDP	Director [*or Directorate*] of Development Planning [*Air Force*]
DDP	Distributed Data Processing [*Computer science Telecommunications*]
DDP	Distribution Drop Point (AABC)
DDP	Doctors for Disaster Preparedness (EA)
DDP	Dodecylpyrene [*Organic chemistry*]
DDP	Dorado [*Puerto Rico*] [*Airport symbol*] (OAG)
DDP	Double Diode-Pentode
DDP	Dry Discharge Pump
DDP	Erato (Discophiles de Paris Series) [*Record label*] [*France*]
DDP	San Juan, PR [*Location identifier FAA*] (FAAL)
DDPA	Delta Dental Plans Association (EA)
DDPC	DCSLOG [*Deputy Chief of Staff for Logistics*] Data Processing Center [*Military*] (AABC)
DDPC	Departmental Data Processing Center [*Department of Labor*]
DDPC	Digital Data Processing Center [*or Complex*] (MCD)
DD(PCD & T)	Deputy Director (Personnel, Career Development, and Training) [*Defense Intelligence Agency*] (DNAB)
DDPE	Digital Data Processing Equipment
DDPF	Dedicated Display Processing Function (NASA)
DDPH	Diploma in Dental Public Health [*British*]
DDPHP	Deputy Director of Post-Hostilities Plans [*Military British*]
DDPHRCS Eng	Diploma in Dental Public Health, Royal College of Surgeons of England
DDPL	Data Drawing and Parts List
DDPL	Demand Deposit Program Library [*Computer science*] (OA)
DDPLO	Designated Disabled Persons Liaison Officer (AIE)
DDPM	Distributed Data Processing Model (MCD)
DDPOW	Deputy Director of Prisoners of War [*British*]
DDPP	Deputy Director for Plans and Policy [*National Security Agency*]
DDPR	Deputy Director for Programs and Resources [*National Security Agency*]
DDPR	Deputy Director of Public Relations [*Military British*]
DDPrA	du Pont(E.I.),\$3.50 Pfd [*NYSE symbol*] (TTSB)
DDPrB	du Pont(E.I.),\$4.50 Pfd [*NYSE symbol*] (TTSB)
DDPS	Data Directed Programming System [*British*] (DIT)
DDPS	Department of Defense Project Specification (MCD)
DDPS	Deputy Director of Personal Services [*Navy British*]
DDPS	Digital Data Processing System
DDPS	Discrete Depth Plankton Sampler
DDPS	Discrimination Data Processing System (AABC)
DDPS	Dual Driver Protective Service [*MTMC*] (TAG)
DDPU	Digital Data Processing Unit (IEEE)
DDQ	Deputy Director of Quartering [*Military British*]
DDQ	Dichlorodicyanobenzoquinone [*Organic chemistry*]
DDQ	Dimensions Description Questionnaire
DDQ	Minot, ND [*Location identifier FAA*] (FAAL)
DDR	Daily Demand Rate
DDR	DASD [*Direct Access Storage Device*] Dump Restore [*Computer science*] (IBMDP)
DDR	Data Direction Register [*Microcomputer*]
DDR	Data Discrepancy Report (MCD)
DDR	Daughters of the Defenders of the Republic, USA (EA)
DDR	Daughters of the Divine Redeemer [*Roman Catholic religious order*]
DDR	Decoy Discrimination RADAR
DDR	Deficiency and Disposition Report [*Nuclear energy*] (NRCH)
DDR	Delayed Disposition Record (MCD)
DDR	Delinquency Delivery Report (MCD)
DDR	Density Dependent Recruitment [*Pisciculture*]
DDR	Design Development Record (MCD)
DDR	Detail Design Review (MCD)
DDR	Detector Dependent Response [*Measurement*]
DDR	Deutsche Demokratische Republik [*German Democratic Republic (East Germany)*]
DDR	Developers Diversified Realty [*NYSE symbol*] (SPSG)
DDR	Developers Diversified Rlty [*NYSE symbol*] (TTSB)
DDR	Development Discrepancy Report
DDR	Device Dependent Routine
DDR	Dialed Digit Receiver [*Telecommunications*] (TEL)
DDR	Dial-on-Demand Routing [*Telecommunications*] (PCM)
DDR	Digital Data Receiver
DDR	Digital Data Recorder (MCD)
DDR	Digital Demand Recorder (IAA)
DDR	Digital Disk Recorder (DOM)
DDR	Digroup Data Reduction [*Telecommunications*] (MCD)
DDR	Diploma in Diagnostic Radiology [*British*]
DDR	Direct Debit [*Banking*] (DCTA)
DDR	Direct Drive
DDR	Discharged During Referral [*Medicine*] (MEDA)
DDr	Doctor of Divinity (EY)
DDR	Dodaira [*Japan*] [*Seismograph station code, US Geological Survey*] (SEIS)
DDR	Double Drift Region (IEEE)
DDR	Downrange Data Report
DDR	Drawing Data Requirement (IAA)
DDR	Drunk Driving Defense (LAIN)
DDR	Dual Discrimination Ratio (IAA)
DDR	Dynamic Device Reconfiguration [*IBM Corp.*] [*Computer science*] (MDG)
DDR	RADAR Picket Destroyer [*Navy symbol Navy*]
DDRA	Dead Despite Resuscitation Attempt [*Medicine*] (CPH)
DDRA	Deputy Director of Royal Artillery [*Military British*]
DDRA	Didehydroretinoic Acid [*Biochemistry*]
DDR & E	Defense Development Research and Engineering (MCD)
DDR&E	Deputy Director, Defense Research and Engineering [*OSD*] (AAGC)
DDR & E	Detailed Design Review and Evaluation (MCD)
DDR & E	Director [*or Directorate*] of Defense Research and Engineering [*DoD*]
DDRB	Danish Defense Research Board
DDRB	Doctors' and Dentists' Review Body [*British*] (DI)
DDRC	Drawing Data Required for Change (KSC)
DDRD	Deputy Director of Recruiting and Demobilization [*Military British*]
DDRE	Danish Defense Research Establishment (NATG)
DDRE	Director [*or Directorate*] of Defense Research and Engineering [*DoD*]
DDRF	Degenerative Diseases Research Foundation (EA)
DDRH	Digital Data Recording Head
DDRI	Design Drafting Reference Information
DDRI	Diversified Data Resources, Inc. [*Information service or system*] (IID)
DDRM	Data, Document, and Records Management (SSD)
DDRM	Direct Dial Response Marketing, Inc. [*Information service or system*] (IID)
DDRP	Dial Dictation Relay Panel (HGAA)
DDRPrA	Developers Div Rlty 9.50% Pfd [*NYSE symbol*] (TTSB)
DDRPrB	Developers Div Rlty 9.44% Pfd [*NYSE symbol*] (TTSB)
DDRR	Digital Data Recorder Reproducer (DWSG)
DDRR	Digital Data Regenerative Repeater (DNAB)
DDRR	Directional Discontinuity Ring Radiator
DDRS	Declassified Documents Reference System [*Research Publications, Inc.*] [*Woodbridge, CT*]
DDRS	Defense Data Repository System [*DoD*]
DDRS	Demographic Data Retrieval System [*Census Bureau*] [*Information service or system*] (IID)
DDRS	Digital Data Recording System
DDS	Damaged Disc Syndrome [*Medicine*] (DMAA)
DDS	Damien Dutton Society for Leprosy Aid (EA)
DDS	Dapsone [*Antimalarial medication*] (VNW)
DDS	Data Dialog System (MCD)
DDS	Data Dictionary System [*Computer science*]
DDS	Data Display Set (MCD)
DDS	Data Display System [*or Subsystem*]
DDS	Data Display System
DDS	Data Dissemination System [*European Space Agency - Information Retrieval Service*] [*Rome, Italy*]
DDS	Data Distribution System [*or Subsystem*]
DDS	Data-Phone Digital Service [*Trademark of the American Telephone & Telegraph Co.*]
DDS	Dataphone Digital System [*AT&T*] (NITA)
DDS	Decoy Dispensing Set (MCD)
DDS	Deep-Diving System
DDS	Defense Dissemination System (MCD)
DD/S	Delivered Sound [*Shipping*]
DDS	Demos D Scale [*Psychology*]
DDS	Dendrodendritic Synaptosome [*Medicine*] (DMAA)
DDS	Dental Distress Syndrome [*Medicine*] (DMAA)
DDS	Dentist
DDS	Denys-Drash Syndrome [*Medicine*]
DDS	Deployable Defense System (IEEE)

DDS .... Depressed DNA Synthesis [*Medicine*] (DMAA)
DD(S) .... Deputy Director for Support [*Defense Intelligence Agency*] (DNAB)
DDS .... Deputy Director of Science [*Military British*]
DDS .... Designator Detection System (MCD)
DDS .... Design Data Sheet [*Naval Ship Engineering Center*]
DDS .... Design Disclosure Standard
DDS .... Detailed Design Specification (MCD)
DDS .... Developmental Disabilities Service
DDS .... Development Data Sheet (MCD)
DDS .... Deviation Dependent Sensitivity [*Navigation*] (IAA)
DDS .... Dialysis Disequilibrium Syndrome
DDS .... Diaminodiphenyl Sulfone [*Also, DADPS, DAPSONE*] [*Pharmacology*]
DDS .... Digital Dataphone Service [*Telecommunications*] (DOM)
DDS .... Digital Data Secure (DWSG)
DDS .... Digital Data Service [*Telecommunications*] (ADA)
DDS .... Digital Data Service (CDE)
DDS .... Digital Data Servo
DDS .... Digital Data Storage [*Computer science*]
DDS .... Digital Data System
DDS .... Digital Display Scope
DDS .... Digital Drafting System
DDS .... Digital Dynamics Simulator (IEEE)
DDS .... Dillard Department Stores, Inc. Class A [*NYSE symbol*] (SPSG)
DDS .... Dillard Dept Str'A' [*NYSE symbol*] (TTSB)
DDS .... Direct Dial Service [*Telecommunications*] (HGAA)
DDS .... Direct Digital Synthesizer (MCD)
DDS .... Direct Distance Service
DDS .... Directional Doppler Sonography [*Medicine*] (DMAA)
D/DS .... Director of Dental Services [*British*]
DDS .... Directory Development Study
DDS .... Disability Determination Service [*Social Security Administration*] (GFGA)
DDS .... Discrete Depth Sampler
DDS .... Display and Debriefing Subsystem (MCD)
DDS .... Distillation Desalination System
DDS .... Distillers Dried Solubles (OA)
DDS .... Distributed Defense Study [*DoD*]
DDS .... Diving Dentists Society (EA)
DDS .... Doctor of Dental Science
DDS .... Doctor of Dental Surgery
DDS .... Documentation Distribution System (NASA)
DDS .... Dodecyl Sulfate [*Medicine*] (DMAA)
DDS .... Donovan Data Systems [*A company*] [*New York, NY*] (WDMC)
DDS .... Doped Deposited Silical [*Corning process*]
DDS .... Doppler Detection Station [*Detection station on the Mid-Canada Line*]
DDS .... Doppler Detection System
DDS .... Dose Detector System
DDS .... Double Decidual Sac [*Medicine*] (DMAA)
DDS .... Dow Dividend Strategy
DDS .... Drug Delivery System [*Pharmacy*]
DDS .... Drug Development (Scotland) Ltd. [*British*] (IRUK)
DDS .... Dry Deck Shelter [*Navy*] (DOMA)
DDS .... Dummy Director Set
DDS .... Dynamically Decoupled Steering [*Automotive engineering*]
DDS .... Dynamic Diagnostic System (MCD)
DDS .... Dystrophy-Dystocia Syndrome [*Medicine*] (MAE)
DDSA .... Dodecenylsuccinic Anhydride [*Organic chemistry*]
DD:S & T .... Diamond Depositions: Science and Technology [*A publication*]
DDS&T .... Directorate of Science and Technology [*CIA*] (LAIN)
DD Sc .... Doctor of Dental Science
DDSD .... Deputy Director of Staff Duties [*Military British*]
DDSE .... Design Disclosure for Systems and Equipment
DDSG .... Digital Data Switching Group (CAAL)
DDSI .... Digital Descriptor Systems [*NASDAQ symbol*] (SAG)
DDSIU .... Digital Descriptor Sys Unit [*NASDAQ symbol*] (TTSB)
DDSIW .... Digital Descriptor Sys Wrrt'A' [*NASDAQ symbol*] (TTSB)
DDSIZ .... Digital Descriptor Sys Wrrt'B' [*NASDAQ symbol*] (TTSB)
DDSLA .... Damien Dutton Society for Leprosy Aid (EA)
DDSM .... Decontrolled Defense Supply Material
DDSM .... Defense Distinguished Service Medal [*Military decoration*]
DDSM .... Digital Data Switching Matrix
DDSN .... Parkfield Downhole Digital Seismic Network [*Seismology*]
DDSO .... Diaminodiphenyl Sulfoxide [*Pharmacology*] (MAE)
DDSOT .... Digital Daily System Operability Test
DDSP .... Defense Development Sharing Program [*US and Canada*] (RDA)
DDSP .... Deputy Director of Selection of Personnel [*Military British*]
DDSS .... Developmental Disabilities Special Interest Section [*American Occupational Therapy Association*]
DDSSJ .... Drone Deceptive Self-Screening Jammer [*Military*] (MCD)
DDST .... Denver Developmental Screening Test [*For mental development of infants*]
DDST .... Deputy Director of Supply and Transport [*British*]
DDSU .... Digital Data Storage Unit
DD Sur .... Doctor of Dental Surgery
DDT .... Data Debugging Tool
DDT .... Data Description Table (BUR)
DDT .... Davidson Tisdale Mines Ltd. [*Toronto Stock Exchange symbol*]
DDT .... Debye Dipole Theory [*Physics*]
DDT .... Deduct
DDT .... Define Device Table (MCD)
DDT .... Deflagration to Detonation Transition (IEEE)
DDT .... Delayed Dialing Tone [*Telecommunications*] (TEL)
DD(S) .... Design and Drafting Techniques
DDT .... Design Data Transmittal (NRCH)
DDT .... Design Development Test

DDT .... Diagnostic Decision Table [*Computer science*]
DDT .... DIBOL Debugging Technique [*Digital Equipment Corp.*]
DDT .... Dichlorodiphenyltrichloroethane [*Insecticide*]
DDT .... Dideoxythymidine [*Biochemistry*]
DDT .... Digital Data Terminal (MCD)
DDT .... Digital Data Transceiver
DDT .... Digital Data Transmitter
DDT .... Digital Debugging Tape
DDT .... Digital Demodulation Technique
DDT .... Digital Diagnostic Tool [*Automotive engineering*]
DDT .... Doctor of Drugless Therapy
DDT .... Dodecanethiolate [*Organic chemistry*]
DDT .... Doppler Data Translator
DDT .... Double Deflection Tube (BUR)
DDT .... Double Diode-Triode
DDT .... Double Dual Tandem [*Aviation*] (DA)
DDT .... Dual Deflection Tube (IAA)
DDT .... Ductus Deferens Tumor [*Type of cell line*]
DDT .... Duplex-Drive Tank
DDT .... Dynamic Debugging Tape (IAA)
DDT .... Dynamic Debugging Technique (DEN)
DDT .... Dynamic Display Tester
DDT .... Dyslexia Determination Test [*Educational test*]
DDT .... Training Destroyer [*Navy symbol*]
DDTA .... Deputy Director of Technical Administration [*Ministry of Supply*] [*British*]
DDTA .... Derivative Differential Thermal Analysis (PDAA)
DDTA .... Displayed Data Video Recorder
D/DTA .... Durability/Damage Tolerance Analysis [*Air Force*]
DD-T & E ..... Deputy Director for Test and Evaluation [*NASA*]
DDT & E ...... Design, Development, Test, and Evaluation
DDT & E ...... Director, Defense Test and Evaluation (DOMA)
DDTC .... Defense Depot - Tracy, California [*DoD*]
DDTC .... Diethyldithiocarbamate [*Also, DDC, DEDC*] [*Organic chemistry*]
DDTCA .... Dandie Dinmont Terrier Club of America (EA)
DDTE .... Digital Data Terminal Equipment
DDTE .... Director, Defense Test and Evaluation [*Army*] (RDA)
DDTE .... OSD [*Office of the Secretary of Defense*] Developmental Test and Evaluation (RDA)
DDTESM ...... Digital Data Terminal Equipment Service Module
DDTESS ...... Digital Data Terminal Equipment Service Submodule (IAA)
DDTF .... Dynamic Docking Test Facility [*NASA*] (NASA)
DDTI .... Deputy Director of Tactical Investigation [*Military British*]
DDTL .... Diode-Diode Transistor Logic [*Electronics*] (IAA)
DDTL .... Double Diffused Transistor Logic [*Electronics*] (IAA)
DDTO .... Demonstration Detail Test Objectives (AAG)
DDTO .... District Domestic Transportation Office [*or Officer*]
DDTS .... Digital Data Test Set (MCD)
DDTS .... Digital Data Transmission System (KSC)
DDTS .... Direct Dial Telephone System
DDTS .... Distributed Database Testbed System (MCD)
DDTS .... Dynamic Docking Test System [*NASA*] (NASA)
ddTTP .... Dideoxythymidine Triphosphate [*Biochemistry*]
DDTV .... Dry Diver Transport Vehicle [*Navy*]
DDU .... Dadu [*Pakistan*] [*Airport symbol*] (AD)
DDU .... Data Display Unit (NASA)
DDU .... Decommutator Distribution Unit (MCD)
DDU .... Delivered Duty Unpaid
DDU .... Diagnostic Display Unit (MCD)
DDU .... Digital Data Unit (MUGU)
DDU .... Digital Display Unit
DDU .... Digital Distributing Unit
DDU .... Diploma in Diagnostic Ultrasound
DDU .... Disk Data Unit
DDU .... Display and Debug Unit [*Computer science*] (MDG)
DDU .... Display Driver Unit (NASA)
DDU .... Dual Diversity Unit
DDU .... University of District of Columbia, Van Ness Campus, Washington, DC [*OCLC symbol*] (OCLC)
DDUS .... Date Departed United States [*Military*]
DDV .... Columbus, OH [*Location identifier FAA*] (FAAL)
DDV .... Deck Drain Valve
DDV .... Deep-Diving Vehicle [*Navy*]
DDV .... Destroyer Variant [*Surface warfare study*] [*Navy*] (DOMA)
DDV .... Displacement Ducted Vessel [*Marine architecture*]
DDVP .... Dichlorvos (GNE)
DDVP .... Dimethyl Dichlorovinyl Phosphate [*An insecticide*]
DDVRS .... Deputy Director, Veterinary Remount Service [*British military*] (DMA)
DDVS .... Deputy Director of Veterinary Services [*British military*] (DMA)
DDW .... Deionized-Distilled Water
DDW .... Direct Digital Writer
DDWE & M... Deputy Director of Works, Electrical and Mechanical [*British*]
DDWP .... Deputy Directorate of Weapons, Polaris [*Navy British*]
DDx .... Differential Diagnosis [*Medicine*] (CPH)
DDX .... Digital Data Exchange [*Telecommunications*] (TEL)
DDX .... Goldsboro, NC [*Location identifier FAA*] (FAAL)
DDXF .... DISSOS [*Distributed Office Support System*] Document Exchange Facility [*IBM Corp.*] (NITA)
DDX-P .... Digital Data Exchange-Packet [*Telecommunications*] (TSSD)
DDY .... Dynayoke Deflection Yoke
DDZ .... Dedza [*Malawi*] [*Airport symbol*] (AD)
DE .... Assistant Vice Director for Estimates (MCD)
DE .... Dail Eireann [*House of Representatives*] [*Ireland*] (ILCA)
DE .... Damage Equivalent
DE .... Damage Expectancy (NATG)

DE...............	Data Element [*Computer science*]
DE...............	Data Encoder
DE...............	Data Entry
D/E.............	Data of Establishment (WDAA)
DE...............	Date of Entry [*Military*]
DE...............	Date of Extension [*Military*]
DE...............	Daughters of Evrytania (EA)
DE...............	Deceleration Enleanment [*Automotive fuel systems*]
DE...............	December (ADA)
DE...............	Decimeter [*Unit of measure*]
DE...............	Decision Element
DE...............	Decision Error
DE...............	Deck and Engineering Duties, General Service [*USNR officer designation*]
DE...............	Deckle-Edged [*Paper*]
DE...............	Declared Excess [*Military*]
DE...............	Deemphasis
DE...............	Deep Etch [*Lithography term*]
DE...............	Deere & Co. [*NYSE symbol*] (SPSG)
DE...............	Defense Electronics [*A publication*] (DOMA)
DE...............	Defense Emergency (AABC)
DE...............	Defensive End [*Football*]
DE...............	Deflection Error [*Military*]
DE...............	Degree of Elasticity (IAA)
DE...............	Delaware [*Postal code*]
De...............	Delaware. Department of Community Affairs and Economic Development, Division of Libraries, Dover, DE [*Library symbol Library of Congress*] (LCLS)
DE...............	Delivered Energy
DE...............	Demokratiki Enosis [*Democratic Union*] [*Greek*] (PPE)
DE...............	Denmark (NATG)
DE...............	Densimeter (DNAB)
DE...............	Dentistry (DAVI)
DE...............	Departmental Estimate (AAG)
DE...............	Department of Education [*Generic*]
DE...............	Department of Employment [*Formerly, DEP, MOL*] [*British*]
DE...............	Department of Energy (ILCA)
D/E.............	Depression/Elevation (CAAL)
DE...............	Deprived Eye [*Optics*]
DE...............	Descent Engine [*NASA*] (KSC)
DE...............	Descriptor [*Online database field identifier*]
DE...............	Descriptor Entry Version [*Database terminology*] (NITA)
DE...............	Designation Equipment
DE...............	Design Engineering (KSC)
DE...............	Design Evaluation
DE...............	Desktop Engineering
DE...............	Destroyer Escort [*Navy symbol*]
DE...............	Detector (NFPA)
DE...............	Deterministic Equivalent (PDAA)
DE...............	Developer Evaluation
DE...............	Development Engineering
DE...............	Development Ephemeris
DE...............	Development Estimate
DE...............	Device End
DE...............	Dextrose Equivalent [*Food technology*]
DE...............	Diatomaceous Earth (PDAA)
DE...............	Dictation Equipment
DE...............	Die Deborah (BJA)
DE...............	Diesel Electric
DE...............	Differential Equation
de...............	Digestible Energy (OA)
DE...............	Digestive Energy [*Medicine*] (MAE)
DE...............	Digital Element (IEEE)
DE...............	Digital Encoder (MSA)
DE...............	Digital Equipment [*Electronics*] (IAA)
DE...............	Directed Energy [*Weaponry*] (INF)
DE...............	Direct Encounter (KSC)
DE...............	Directorate of Design Engineering [*NASA*] (KSC)
DE...............	Director Error [*Military*] (AFM)
DE...............	Director of Engineering [*Navy British*]
DE...............	Discard-Eligibility [*Computer science*]
DE...............	Disk Electrophoresis
DE...............	Dispersed Emission [*Spectroscopy*]
DE...............	Display Electronics (KSC)
DE...............	Display Element
DE...............	Display Equipment
DE...............	Distant Element (MDG)
DE...............	Distributed Executive (SSD)
DE...............	Distributive Education
DE...............	District Engineer [*Army*]
DE...............	District of Europe [*Proposed location of an EEC federal capital*]
DE...............	Division Entry (BUR)
DE...............	Division Equivalent (MCD)
DE...............	Doctor of Economics (NADA)
DE...............	Doctor of Engineering
DE...............	Doctor of Entomology
DE...............	Doppler Extractor (MCD)
DE...............	Dose Equivalent [*Radioactivity calculations*]
DE...............	Double Elephant [*Paper*] (ADA)
DE...............	Double Enamel [*Insulation*] (MSA)
DE...............	Double End [*Technical drawings*]
DE...............	Double Entry [*Bookkeeping*]
de...............	Double Entry [*Bookkeeping*] (ODBW)
DE...............	Double Extension [*Camera stand*] (ROG)
DE...............	Downeast Airlines [*ICAO designator*] (AD)

DE...............	Dream Element [*Psychology*] (MAE)
DE...............	Drive End (MSA)
DE...............	Drug Evaluation
DE...............	Dual Camshafts and Electronic Management [*Automotive engineering*]
DE...............	Duke of Edinburgh's Wiltshire Regiment [*Military unit*] [*British*] (ROG)
DE...............	Duration of Ejection (MAE)
DE...............	Dynamic Energy [*Foglight*] [*Hella, Inc.*] [*Automotive engineering*]
DE...............	Dynamic Engineer
DE...............	Dynamics Explorer [*NASA*]
DE...............	Escort Ship [*Destroyer Escort*] [*Navy symbol*]
DE...............	Federal Republic of Germany [*ANSI two-letter standard code*] (CNC)
DEA............	ANSA [*Agenzia Nazionale Stampa Associata*]'s Electronic Documentation Service [*ANSA Agency*] (IID)
DEA............	Dairy Engineers' Association [*British*] (BI)
DEA............	Dance Educators of America (EA)
DEA............	Data Encryption Algorithm
DEA............	Data Exchange Agreement
DEA............	Data Exchange Annex (AABC)
DEA............	Davis Escape Apparatus [*British military*] (DMA)
DEA............	Deacon
Dea............	Deady's United States Circuit and District Court Reports [*A publication*] (DLA)
DEA............	Deak International Resources Corp. [*Toronto Stock Exchange symbol*]
DEA............	Dean (ROG)
DEA............	Defense Exchange Agreement (MCD)
DEA............	Deflection Error Average [*Military*] (MUGU)
DEA............	Dehydroepiandrosterone [*Also, DHA, DHEA, DHIA*] [*Endocrinology*] (AAMN)
DEA............	Delta Aerotaxi [*Italy ICAO designator*] (FAAC)
DEA............	Department of Economic Affairs [*Department of Agriculture*]
DEA............	Deployed Electronics Assembly (MCD)
DEA............	Desethylamiodarone [*Biochemistry*]
DEA............	Design Engineering Analysis [*Army*]
DEA............	Development, Engineering, and Acquisition [*Directorate*] [*Army*] (RDA)
DEA............	Dictionary of Electronics Abbreviations, Signs, and Symbols [*A publication*]
DEA............	Dielectric Analyzer
DEA............	Diethanolamine [*Also, DIOLAMINE*] [*Organic chemistry*]
DEA............	Diethoxyanthracene [*Organic chemistry*]
DEA............	Diethylamine [*Organic chemistry*]
DEA............	Dimethylaniline [*Organic chemistry*]
DEA............	Directory of European Associations [*A publication*]
DEA............	Display Electronics Assemblies (KSC)
DEA............	Division of Ecumenical Affairs [*Church of England*]
DEA............	Dominican Educational Association [*Defunct*] (EA)
DEA............	Driver Evaluation Assembly [*Nuclear energy*] (NRCH)
DEA............	Drug Enforcement Administration [*Formerly, Bureau of Narcotics and Dangerous Drugs*]
DEA............	Dynamo Electric Amplifier
DEAA	Diethylacetoacetamide [*Organic chemistry*]
Dea & Ch....	Deacon and Chitty's English Bankruptcy Reports [*1832-35*] [*A publication*] (DLA)
Dea & Chit..	Deacon and Chitty's English Bankruptcy Reports [*1832-35*] [*A publication*] (DLA)
Dea & Sw....	Deane and Swabey's English Ecclesiastical Reports [*A publication*] (DLA)
DEAC	Data Exchange Auxiliary Console (CAAL)
deac...........	Deaccentuator (IDOE)
DEAC	Deacon
Deac	Deacon's English Bankruptcy Reports [*1835-40*] [*A publication*] (DLA)
DEAC	Dealer Election Action Committee [*Campaign funding*]
DEAC	Defense Economic Analysis Council (MCD)
DEAC	Diethylaluminum Chloride [*Organic chemistry*]
Deac & C....	Deacon and Chitty's English Bankruptcy Reports [*1832-35*] [*A publication*] (DLA)
Deac & Ch...	Deacon and Chitty's English Bankruptcy Reports [*1832-35*] [*A publication*] (DLA)
Deac & Chit...	Deacon and Chitty's English Bankruptcy Reports [*1832-35*] [*A publication*] (DLA)
Deac Bank Pr...	Deacon's Bankruptcy Law and Practice [*3rd ed.*] [*1864*] [*A publication*] (DLA)
Deac Cr Law...	Deacon on Criminal Law of England [*A publication*] (DLA)
Deac Dig	Deacon's Digest of the Criminal Law [*A publication*] (DLA)
DEACON......	Defense Estimates Analytical Computer On-Line Network (MCD)
DEACON......	Definitions Abbreviations and Conventions [*Handbook*]
DEACON......	Direct English Access and Control [*Computer science*]
Deacon & C...	Deacon and Chitty's English Bankruptcy Reports [*1832-35*] [*A publication*] (DLA)
Deacon & C Bankr Cas...	Deacon and Chitty's English Bankruptcy Records [*1832-35*] [*A publication*] (DLA)
Deacon & C Bankr Cas (Eng)...	Deacon and Chitty's English Bankruptcy Cases [*A publication*] (DLA)
Deacon Bankr Cas...	Deacon's English Bankruptcy Cases [*A publication*] (DLA)
Deacon Bankr (Eng)...	Deacon's English Bankruptcy Cases [*A publication*] (DLA)
DEACT	Deactivation (KSC)
DEAD	Dallas Encephalopathic and Abortifactive Disease [*Acronym used as title of novel*]
DEAD	Dedicated to Eliminating Acronymic Designations [*An association*]
DEAD	Diethyl Azodicarboxylate [*Organic chemistry*]
DEAD	Doppler Evaluated Attack Depth [*Navy*] (CAAL)
Dead Or Laws...	Deady and Lane's Oregon General Laws [*A publication*] (DLA)

DEADS........	Detroit Air Defense Sector [*ADS*]
Deady........	Deady's United States Circuit and District Court Reports [*A publication*] (DLA)
DEAE...........	Diethylaminoethanol [*Organic chemistry*]
DEAE...........	Diethylaminoethyl [*Organic radical*]
DEAE...........	Diethylaminoethyl Cellulose [*Organic chemistry*] (MAE)
DEAE...........	Division of Eligibility and Agency Evaluation [*OE*]
DEAE-cellulose...	Diethylaminoethyl-Cellulose (DOG)
DEAE-D........	Diethylaminoethyl Dextran [*Organic chemistry*]
DEAEM........	Diethylaminoethyl Mercaptan [*Organic chemistry*]
DEAEMA........	Diethylaminoethyl Methacrylate [*Organic chemistry*]
DEAFWATCH...	Demanding Equal Access to Facts and Warnings Aired on TV for Citizens Who are Hearing-Impaired [*Student legal action organization*] (EA)
DEAH	Diethylaluminum Hydride [*Organic chemistry*]
DEAI...........	Diethylaluminum Iodide [*Organic chemistry*]
DEAL...........	Data Entry Application Language
DEAL...........	Decision Evaluation and Logic
DEAL...........	Detachment Equipment Authorization List [*Military*]
De Alex Fort...	De Fortuna Alexandri [*of Plutarch*] [*Classical studies*] (OCD)
DEALS........	Demountable Externally Anchored Low-Stress Magnet (MCD)
De An	De Anima [*of Aristotle*] [*Classical studies*] (OCD)
DEAN........	Deputy Educators Against Narcotics [*Defunct*]
Deane..........	Deane and Swabey's English Ecclesiastical Reports [*A publication*] (DLA)
Deane..........	Deane and Swabey's English Probate and Divorce Reports [*A publication*] (DLA)
Deane..........	Deane's English Blockade Cases [*A publication*] (DLA)
Deane..........	Deane's Reports [*24-26 Vermont*] [*A publication*] (DLA)
Deane & S Eccl...	Deane and Swabey's English Ecclesiastical Reports [*A publication*] (DLA)
Deane & S Eccl (Eng)...	Deane and Swabey's English Ecclesiastical Reports [*A publication*] (DLA)
Deane & S Eccl Rep...	Deane and Swabey's English Ecclesiastical Reports [*A publication*] (DLA)
Deane & Sw...	Deane and Swabey's English Ecclesiastical Reports [*A publication*] (DLA)
Deane Bl	Deane's English Blockade Cases [*A publication*] (DLA)
Deane Ecc ...	Deane and Swabey's English Ecclesiastical Reports [*A publication*] (DLA)
Deane Ecc Rep...	Deane and Swabey's English Ecclesiastical Reports [*A publication*] (DLA)
Deane Ecc Rep B...	Deane and Swabey's English Ecclesiastical Reports [*A publication*] (DLA)
Deane Neut...	Deane on the Effect of War as to Neutrals [*A publication*] (DLA)
DeanFd........	Dean Foods Co. [*Associated Press*] (SAG)
De Anim	De Testimonio Animae [*of Tertullian*] [*Classical studies*] (OCD)
Dean Med Jur...	Dean's Medical Jurisprudence [*A publication*] (DLA)
De Antr Nymph...	De Antro Nympharum [*of Porphyry*] [*Classical studies*] (OCD)
DEAP...........	Diethoxyacetophenone [*Organic chemistry*]
DEAP...........	Differential Equation Analyzer Program (MCD)
DEAP...........	Diffused Eutectic Aluminum Process (IEEE)
DEAP...........	Division of Engineering and Applied Physics [*Harvard University*] (MCD)
DEAPA........	Diethylaminopropylamine [*Organic chemistry*]
DEAPA........	Downeast Association of Physician Assistants (SRA)
DEAPSIE......	Department of Economic, Administrative, and Policy Studies (AIE)
De-Ar...........	Delaware Department of State, Division of Historical and Cultural Affairs, Hall of Records, Dover, DE [*Library symbol Library of Congress*] (LCLS)
DEAR	Department of Energy Acquisition Regulation [*A publication*] (AAGC)
DEAR	Diamonds, Emeralds, Amethysts, and Rubies
DEAR	Disease and Environmental Alert Report [*Army*] [*A publication*] (INF)
DEAR	Drop Everything and Read
De Arch	De Architectura [*of Vitruvius*] [*Classical studies*] (OCD)
DEARG PIL...	Deargentur Pilulae [*Let The Pills Be Silverized*] [*Pharmacy*]
Dears..........	Dearsley's English Crown Cases Reserved [*169 English Reprint*] [*1852-56*] [*A publication*] (DLA)
Dears & B ...	Dearsley and Bell's English Crown Cases [*1856-58*] [*A publication*] (DLA)
Dears & BCC...	Dearsley and Bell's English Crown Cases [*1856-58*] [*A publication*] (DLA)
Dears & B Crown Cas...	Dearsley and Bell's English Crown Cases [*1856-58*] [*A publication*] (DLA)
Dears C C ...	Dearsley's English Crown Cases [*1852-56*] [*A publication*] (DLA)
Dears Cr Pr...	Dearsley's Criminal Process [*1853*] [*A publication*] (DLA)
Dearsl Cr Pr...	Dearsley's Criminal Process [*1853*] [*A publication*] (ILCA)
DEARTG.......	Deaerating
DEAS	Data Entry Aboard Ship [*Navy*] (NVT)
DEAS	Delaware Education Accountability System (EDAC)
DEAS	Directorate of Engineering, Aeronautical Systems (SAA)
DEAS	Duke of Edinburgh Award Scheme [*Australia*]
DEASA........	Diethylanilinesulfonic Acid [*Organic chemistry*]
Deas & A.....	Deas and Anderson's Decisions [*1829-33*] [*Scotland*] [*A publication*] (DLA)
Deas & And...	Deas and Anderson's Decisions [*1829-33*] [*Scotland*] [*A publication*] (DLA)
DEA-SOG	Drug Enforcement Administration - Special Operations Group
Deas Ry.......	Deas on the Law of Railways in Scotland [*A publication*] (DLA)
Deaug Pil ...	Deaurentur Pilulae [*Let the Pills Be Gilded*] [*Pharmacology*] (DAVI)
DEAUR.........	Deauretur [*Let It Be Gilded*] [*Pharmacy*]
DEAUR PIL...	Deaurentur Pilulae [*Let The Pills Be Gilded*] [*Pharmacy*]
DEB............	Data Event Block [*Computer science*] (EECA)
DEB............	Data Extent Block (MCD)
DEB............	De Baca Resources, Inc. [*Vancouver Stock Exchange symbol*]

DEB............	Debate [*Legal shorthand*] (LWAP)
DEB............	Debenture [*Type of bond*] [*Investment term*]
deb............	Debenture [*Investment term*] (ODBW)
DEB............	Debit
DEB............	Debrecen [*Hungary*] [*Seismograph station code, US Geological Survey Closed*] (SEIS)
deb	Debridement [*Medicine*] (DAVI)
DEB	Debut (WDAA)
DEB............	Debutante
DEB............	Decaying Extrastellar Body [*Astronomy*]
DEB............	Defense Estimative Brief (MCD)
DEB............	Dental Estimates Board [*British*] (DI)
DEB............	Dental Examining Board
DEB............	Diethylbutanediol [*Organic chemistry*] (AAMN)
DEB............	Digital European Backbone [*System*] (MCD)
DEB............	Division of Environmental Biology [*National Science Foundation*]
DEB............	Downward Ejection Bomblet (MCD)
DEB............	Drug Evaluation Branch [*Therapeutic Goods Administration*] [*Australia*]
DEB............	Dynamic Ephemeral Bodies [*Planetary science*]
DEB............	Dystrophic Epidermolysis Bullosa [*Medicine*]
DEBA.........	Diethylbarbituric Acid (MAE)
DEBA.........	Dynamically-Loaded Engineering Bearing Analysis (PDAA)
De Bapt	De Baptismo [*of Tertullian*] [*Classical studies*] (OCD)
DEBE..........	Does Everything but Eat [*Superseded by DITTO*] [*Computer science*]
DEBHS........	Dr. Edward Bach Healing Society [*Defunct*] (EA)
Debil..........	Debility (AAMN)
Deb Jud......	Debates on the Judiciary [*A publication*] (DLA)
DEBK.........	Debark (AABC)
DEBM.........	Directorate of Engineering, Ballistic Missiles (SAA)
DeB Mar Int L...	DeBurgh's Maritime International Laws [*A publication*] (DLA)
DEBR	Division of Economic and Business Research [*University of Arizona*] [*Tucson*] [*Information service or system*] (IID)
DEBRA........	Dystrophic Epidermolysis Bullosa Research Association of America (EA)
DEBRE	Debenture [*Investment term*] (ROG)
DEBS	Deb Shops [*NASDAQ symbol*] (TTSB)
DEBS	Deb Shops, Inc. [*NASDAQ symbol*] (NQ)
DEBS	Deoxyerythronolide B Synthase [*An enzyme*]
DEBS	Digital Electron Beam Scanner
DEBS	Display Exercise for Battle Staff (SAA)
DEBSA........	Doctor Edward Bach Society of Australia
DebShp.......	Deb Shops, Inc. [*Associated Press*] (SAG)
DEB SPIS....	Debita Spissitudo [*Proper Consistency*] [*Pharmacy*] (MAH)
DEB SPISS...	Debita Spissitudo [*Proper Consistence*] [*Pharmacy*]
Debt & Cred...	Debtor and Creditor (DLA)
DEBUT	Daughters of the Elderly Bridging the Unknown Together (EA)
DeC............	Claymont Public Library, Claymont, DE [*Library symbol Library of Congress*] (LCLS)
DEC............	Control Escort Vessel [*Navy symbol*]
DEC............	Daily Effective Circulation [*Advertising*] (WDMC)
DEC............	Daily Effective Circulation [*Advertising*] (WDMC)
DEC............	Date of Estimated Closing (AAGC)
DEC............	Davis and Elkins College [*West Virginia*]
DEC............	Deaf Broadcasting Campaign [*England*]
DEC............	Decade (WGA)
DEC............	Decal
DEC............	Decani [*Of the Dean*] [*Music*]
DEC............	Decanta [*Pour Off*] [*Pharmacy*]
Dec............	Decanus [*Dean*] [*Latin*] (ILCA)
DEC............	Decatur [*Illinois*] [*Airport symbol*] (OAG)
dec............	Decayed [*Quality of the bottom*] [*Nautical charts*]
DEC............	Decca
DEC............	Deceased
dec............	Deceased (WDMC)
DEC............	December (EY)
Dec............	December (ODBW)
DEC............	Deception Island [*Antarctica*] [*Seismograph station code, US Geological Survey Closed*] (SEIS)
dec............	Deciduous (MAE)
Dec............	Decile [*Statistics*] (BARN)
DEC............	Decimal (KSC)
DEC............	Decimal Equivalent Chart
DEC............	Decimate (ROG)
DEC............	Decimeter [*Unit of measure*] (ROG)
DEC............	Decision
DEC............	Declaration
DEC............	Declared [*Cricket*] (ROG)
DEC............	Declension (ROG)
DEC............	Declination
DEC............	Declination
DEC............	Decoder
DEC............	Decompose
DEC............	Decorated [*or Decoration*] (ROG)
DEC............	Decorative
dec............	Decorative (VRA)
DEC............	Decrease (AAG)
dec............	Decrease (WDMC)
DEC............	Decrement
DEC............	Decrescendo [*Decreasing in Loudness*] [*Music*] (ROG)
DEC............	Deductible Employee Contribution [*IRS*]
DEC............	Deltec Resources Ltd. [*Vancouver Stock Exchange symbol*]
DEC............	Dendritic Epidermal Cell [*Cytology*]
DEC............	Dental Education Center [*Veterans Administration*] (GFGA)
DEC............	Detached Experiment Carrier (MCD)

DEC............	Developing Economies [*A publication*]
DEC............	Development and Education Command
DEC............	Diecast Exchange Club (EA)
DEC............	Diethanol Cocoamide [*Surfactants*]
DEC............	Diethylaminoethyl Chloride [*Organic chemistry*]
DEC............	Diethylcarbamazine [*Anthelmintic drug*]
DEC............	Digital Equipment [*NYSE symbol*] (TTSB)
DEC............	Digital Equipment Corp. [*Maynard, MA*] [*NYSE symbol*] (SPSG)
DEC............	Digital Equipment Corp. Australia Proprietary Ltd.
DEC............	Digital Equipment Corp., Corporate Library, Maynard, MA [*OCLC symbol*] (OCLC)
DEC............	Digital Evaluation Computer
DEC............	Diplome d'Etudes Collegiales [*Canada*]
DEC............	Direct Energy Conversion
DEC............	Disposable Extraction Column
DEC............	Distant Electric Control (IAA)
DEC............	Distributor Electronic Control
DEC............	Diver Escape Capsule (MCD)
DEC............	Division for Early Childhood (EA)
D Ec............	Doctor of Economics
DEC............	Document Effected Code (IAA)
DEC............	Document Evaluation Center (IAA)
DEC............	Drug Evaluation and Classification [*NHTSA*] (TAG)
DEC............	Drug Evaluation Center
DEC............	Dry Electrolytic Capacitor
DEC............	Dynamic Energy Conversion
DEC............	Dynamic Environmental Conditioning [*Cycling*] [*Medicine*] (DAVI)
DEC............	Dynamic Equilibrium Cycling (IAA)
DECA..........	Decathalon Association [*Acronym is used as name of association*] (EA)
DeCA..........	Defense Commissary Agency [*DoD*]
DECA..........	Descent Engine Control Assembly [*Apollo*] [*NASA*]
DECA..........	Digital Electronic Countermeasures Analyzer (MCD)
DE(CA)........	Director of Economics, Civil Affairs [*War Office*] [*British World War II*]
DECA..........	Display/AGAP [*Attitude Gyro Accelerometer Package*] Electronic Control Assembly (KSC)
DECA..........	Distributive Education Clubs of America (EA)
DECADE......	DEC [*Digital Equipment Corp.*] Automatic Design (NITA)
DECAF........	Decaffeinated (WDAA)
DECAF........	Distribution Control Analysis File [*NASA*] (MCD)
DECAL........	Decalcomania
decal..........	Decalcomania [*An adhesive paper*] (WDMC)
Decal..........	De Decalogo [*Philo*] (BJA)
DECAL........	Design Communication Algorithm (MCD)
DECAL........	Desk Calculator (IAA)
DECAL........	Detailed Experimental Computer-Assisted Language
DECAL........	Detection and Classification of Acoustic Lens (IAA)
DECAL........	Digital Equipment Corporation Author Language [*Computer science*] (CSR)
DECAN........	Distance Measuring Equipment Command and Navigation
DE C Ann.....	Delaware Code, Annotated [*A publication*] (DLA)
DECAP-CHUTE...	Decontamination Capabilities - Chemical Units and Teams (MCD)
DECARB......	Decarburization (MSA)
DECAT........	Driver Energy Conservation Awareness Training [*US government program*]
DECB..........	Data Event Control Block [*Computer science*] (BUR)
DECC..........	D & E Communications [*NASDAQ symbol*] (SAG)
DECC..........	Diethylcarbamazine Citrate [*Biochemistry*]
DECC..........	Diethylcarbamoyl Chloride [*Organic chemistry*]
DECC..........	Diethylcarbamoyl Chloride (GNE)
DECC..........	Disciples Ecumenical Consultative Council (EA)
DECCA........	Defense Commercial Communications Activity [*Military*]
DECCC........	Defense Commercial Communications Center [*Military*]
DecCen........	Decadal-to-Centennial [*Marine science*] (OSRA)
Dec Ch.........	Decisions from the Chair (Parliamentary) [*England*] [*A publication*] (DLA)
DECCO........	Defense Commercial Communications Office [*Military*]
DECCO........	Defense Commercial Contracting Office (DOMA)
Dec Comm'r Pat...	Patents, Decisions of the Commissioner and of United States Courts [*A publication*] (DLA)
Dec Com Pat...	Decisions of the Commissioner of Patents [*A publication*] (DLA)
DECD..........	Deceased (AFM)
DECD..........	Declared
DECD..........	Decreased (MUGU)
Dec Dig.......	American Digest System, Decennial Digests [*A publication*] (DLA)
DECDR........	Decoder (NITA)
DECE..........	Decease (ROG)
DECE..........	Denominational Executives of Christian Education (EA)
DECEA........	Defense Communication Engineering Agency (AABC)
DECED........	Deceased (ROG)
DECEL........	Deceleration (NVT)
DECELERON...	Decelerator and Aileron [*NASA*]
Decen Dig ...	American Digest (Decennial Edition) [*A publication*] (ILCA)
DECENT	Distribution of Exact Classical Energy Transfer [*Physics*]
DECEO........	Defense Communications Engineering Office [*Army*] (AABC)
DECFA........	Distributed Emission Crossed Field Amplifier (IAA)
Dec-FB........	Decrease Feedback
Dec Fed Mar Comm'n...	Decisions of the Federal Maritime Commission [*United States*] [*A publication*] (DLA)
DE CH........	Delaware Chancery Reports [*A publication*] (DLA)
DECH..........	Diethylcyclohexane [*Organic chemistry*]
DE Ch E	Doctor of Electro-Chemical Engineering
DECHEMA....	Deutsche Gesellschaft fuer Chemisches Apparatewesen, Chemische Technik, und Biotechnologie eV [*Database producer*] (IID)
DE Ch Eng ...	Doctor of Electro-Chemical Engineering

DECI..........	Defense Employment Cost Index [*DoD*]
DECID.........	Deciduous
DECIM........	Decimeter [*Unit of measure*]
DECIM........	Defense Environmental Corporate Information Management [*DoD*]
DECIS........	Decision
DECIT..........	Decimal Digit (DIT)
De Civ D......	De Civitate Dei [*of Augustine*] [*Classical studies*] (OCD)
Dec Jt Com...	Decisions of Joint Commission [*A publication*] (DLA)
DECK..........	Deckers Outdoor [*NASDAQ symbol*] (TTSB)
DECK..........	Deckers Outdoor Corp. [*NASDAQ symbol*] (SAG)
DeckOut......	Deckers Outdoor Corp. [*Associated Press*] (SAG)
DECL..........	Declaration (ROG)
DECL..........	Declare
DECL..........	Declassify [*Military*] (NVT)
DECL..........	Declension
DECL..........	Decline
DECL..........	Diode-Emitter-Coupled Logic
DECL..........	Direct Energy Conversion Laboratory [*Johnson Space Center*] [*NASA*] (NASA)
DECLAB	Digital Equipment Corp. Laboratory
DECLAN	Declaration (ROG)
DECLG	Double-Ended Cold Leg Guillotine [*Nuclear energy*] (NRCH)
Decl J	Declaratory Judgements [*A publication*] (DLA)
DECLN	Declaration [*Legal shorthand*] (LWAP)
DECLON	Declaration (ROG)
DECM........	Deceptive Electronic Countermeasure [*Military*] (CAAL)
DECM........	Defense Electronic Countermeasure
DECM........	Digital Electronic Countermeasure (LAIN)
DECmcc	DEC [*Digital Equipment Corporation*] Managment Control Center (CDE)
DECMSN	Decommission (DNAB)
DECMSND...	Decommissioned (DNAB)
DECN..........	Decision (AFM)
DECN..........	Declaration (ADA)
DECN..........	Declension
DECN..........	Decontamination
DECNET	DEC [*Digital Equipment Corp.*] Network (NITA)
DECNET	Digital Equipment Corporation Telecommunications Network
DECO..........	Deconvolution [*Computer program*] (MCD)
DECO..........	Decora Industries [*NASDAQ symbol*] (TTSB)
DECO..........	Decora Industries, Inc. [*NASDAQ symbol*] (SAG)
DECO..........	Decreasing Consumption of Oxygen [*Endocrinology*]
DECO..........	Direct Energy Conversion Operation
DECO..........	Document Engineering Co., Inc. [*Information service or system*] (IID)
Dec O	Ohio Decisions [*A publication*] (DLA)
DECOCT.......	Decoctum [*Decoction*] [*Pharmacy*]
Dec of Ind Acc Com...	Decisions of the Industrial Accident Commission of California [*A publication*] (DLA)
De Col	De Colyar's English County Court Cases [*1867-82*] [*A publication*] (DLA)
De Col Guar...	De Colyar's Law of Guaranty [*A publication*] (DLA)
De Coly........	De Colyar's English County Court Cases [*1867-82*] [*A publication*] (DLA)
DECOM	Decommissioned (AFM)
DECOM	Decommutator
DECOM	Delay Cost Model
DECOM	Low-Rate Engineering Decommutator Executive [*Computer program*] [*NASA Viking Mission*]
DECOMD.......	Decommissioned (DNAB)
DECOMG.......	Decommissioning [*Date*] [*Navy*] (NVT)
DECOMM	Decommissioning [*Date*] [*Navy*] (NVT)
DECOMM	Decommutation
DECOMNET...	Dedicated Communications Network (MCD)
decomp.......	Decompensation [*Cardiology*]
DECOMP......	Decompose [*or Decomposition*]
DECOMP......	Decomposition Mathematical Programming System
DECOMPN......	Decompression (MSA)
DECOMPR......	Decompression
DECON	Decontaminate (AABC)
DECON	Decontamination
D Econ........	Doctor of Economics (EY)
D Econ Sc....	Doctor of Economic Science
DECONTN	Decontamination (KSC)
DECOR........	DECHEMA [*Deutsche Gesellschaft fuer Chemisches Apparatewesen, Chemische Technik, und Biotechnologie eV*] Corrosion Data Base [*Germany Information service or system*] (CRD)
DECOR........	Decorating
DECOR........	Decorative (ROG)
De Cor	De Corona [*of Demosthenes*] [*Classical studies*] (OCD)
DECOR........	Digital Electronic Continuous Ranging
Decora........	Decora Industries, Inc. [*Associated Press*] (SAG)
Decorat........	Decorator Industries, Inc. [*Associated Press*] (SAG)
DECPrA........	Digital Equip 8.875% Dep'A'Pfd [*NYSE symbol*] (TTSB)
DECPSK.......	Differentially Encoded Coherent Phase Shift Keying [*Telecommunications*] (TEL)
DECPT MAN...	Deceptive Maneuver (MCD)
DECR..........	December (ROG)
DECR..........	Decrease [*or Decrement*] (MSA)
dec (R)........	Decrease, Relative (DAVI)
DECR..........	Decrement (GAVI)
DECR..........	Document Error/Clarification Request (SAA)
Dec R	Ohio Decisions Reprint [*A publication*] (DLA)
Dec Re	Ohio Decisions Reprint [*A publication*] (DLA)
Dec Rep	Ohio Decisions Reprint [*A publication*] (DLA)
Dec Repr......	Ohio Decisions Reprint [*A publication*] (DLA)

DECRES....... Decrescendo [*Decreasing in Loudness*] [*Music*]
DECRESC..... Decrescendo [*Decreasing in Loudness*] [*Music*]
Decretal...... Decretalia of the Canon Law [*A publication*] (DLA)
Decret Greg IX... Decretales Gregorii IX [*A publication*] (DSA)
DECRT........ Decrement (MSA)
DECRTN...... Decoration
DECS.......... Data Entry Control System
DECS.......... Deceased (DAVI)
DECS.......... Decoration for Exceptional Civilian Service [*Army civilian employee award*]
DECS.......... Dual Employed Coping Scale [*Psychology*] (EDAC)
Dec SDA...... Bengal Sadr Diwani Adalat Decisions [*A publication*] (DLA)
DECT.......... Digital European Cordless Telecommunications [*or Telephone*]
DECT.......... Digital European Cordless Telephone (ACRL)
Dec T H & M... Admiralty Decisions Tempore Hay and Marriott [*England*] [*A publication*] (DLA)
DECTP........ Diethylchlorothiophosphate [*Ethyl Chemical Co.*] [*Organic chemistry*]
DECTRA....... Decca Tracking and Ranging [*MCD*]
DECU.......... Data Exchange Control Unit (NASA)
DECU.......... Digital Engine Control Unit (MCD)
DECUB........ Decubitus [*Lying Down*] [*By extension, the medical term for bedsores*]
DECUF........ Defense Capability Under Fallout (SAA)
DECUK........ Duane Eddy Circle, United Kingdom (EAIO)
DECUS........ Digital Equipment Computer Users Society (EA)
DECUS........ Duane Eddy Circle, USA (EA)
Dec US Comp Gen... Decisions of the Comptroller General of the United States [*A publication*] (DLA)
Dec US Compt Gen... Decisions of the United States Comptroller General [*A publication*] (DLA)
Dec US Mar Comm'n... Decisions of the United States Maritime Commission [*A publication*] (DLA)
DED .... Data Element Definition [*DoD*]
DED .... Data Element Descriptor [*Computer science*] (IAA)
DED .... Data Element Dictionary [*A publication Army*]
DED .... Date Expected Delivery [*Medicine*]
DED .... Declared Dead [*Military*]
DED .... Dedendum [*Design engineering*]
DED .... Dedicated [*or Dedication*] (ROG)
ded .... Dedicated (VRA)
DED .... Deduct [*or Deductible*] (AABC)
DED .... Defense Electronics Division (SAA)
DED .... Deland, FL [*Location identifier FAA*] (FAAL)
DED .... Delayed Erythema Dose [*Medicine*] (DMAA)
DED .... Dell Embedded Diagnostics [*Computer science*] (PCM)
DED .... Design Engineering Directorate (KSC)
DED .... Development Engineering Division (SAA)
DED .... Diesel Engine Driven (NATG)
DED .... Director of Engine Development [*Ministry of Aircraft Production*] [*British*]
DED .... Director of the Education Department [*Navy British*]
DED .... Distant End Disconnect [*Telecommunications*] (TEL)
D Ed .... Doctor of Education
DEd .... Doctor of Education (AIE)
DED .... Doctor of English Divinity
DED .... Doctor of Environmental Design (GAGS)
DED .... Double Error Detection
DED .... Dutch Elm Disease
DEDA .... Data Entry and Display Assembly [*Apollo*] [*NASA*]
DEDAAS....... Digital Electrophysiological Data Acquisition and Analysis System [*Neurometrics*]
D Ed AS....... Diploma in Education Administration and Supervision
DEDB .... Digital Elevation Database (RDA)
DEDC .... Diethyl Dicarbonate [*Fungistatic agent*]
DEDC .... Diethyldithiocarbamate [*Also, DDC, DDTC*] [*Organic chemistry*]
DED/D......... Data Element Dictionary/Directory [*A publication*]
DEDD.......... Diesel-Electric Direct Drive
DEDE.......... Density-Depth
DEDEC .... Detroit Deere Corp. [*Proposed trademark*]
De Def Or .... De Defectu Oraculorum [*of Plutarch*] [*Classical studies*] (OCD)
De Deo Soc... De Deo Socratico [*of Apuleius*] [*Classical studies*] (OCD)
DEDIC .... Dedication
DE D in D .... De Die in Diem [*From Day to Day*] [*Latin*]
DEDIP .... Department of Environmental and Drug-Induced Pathology [*Later, DETP*] (EA)
DEDL .... Data Element Description List [*Computer science*]
DEDM .... Diethyl Diazomalonate [*Organic chemistry*]
DEDO.......... Defense Engineering Data Office
De Dog Plat... De Dogmate Platonis [*of Apuleius*] [*Classical studies*] (OCD)
DEDP .... Data Entry and Display Panel (MCD)
DEDS .... Data Entry and Display Subsystem
DeDS .... Delaware State College, Dover, DE [*Library symbol Library of Congress*] (LCLS)
DEDS .... Digital Error Detection Subsystem [*Computer science*] (AABC)
DEDS .... Directory of Engineering Document Services [*A publication*]
DEDS .... Dual Exchangeable Disc Storage (NITA)
DEdStudies... Doctor of Educational Studies
DeDT .... Delaware Technical and Community College, Dover, DE [*Library symbol Library of Congress*] (LCLS)
DEduc .... Doctor of Education (ADA)
DEDUCOM ... Deductive Communicator (IEEE)
DEE............ Data Encryption Equipment [*Telecommunications*] (OSI)
DEE............ Del Norte Chrome [*Vancouver Stock Exchange symbol*]
DEE............ Diethoxyethylene [*Organic chemistry*]
DEE............ Diethyl Ether (PDAA)

DEE............ Digital Evaluation Equipment
DEE............ Digital Events Evaluator (MCD)
DEE............ Diploma in Electrical Engineering (ADA)
DEE............ Direct Engineering Estimate (MCD)
DEE............ Discrete Event Evaluator (KSC)
DEE............ Doctor of Electrical Engineering
DEE............ Transportation America Corp. [*ICAO designator*] (FAAC)
DEEC.......... Digital Electronic Engine Control (MCD)
DEEDS .... Documents of Essex England Data Set [*System for the analysis of medieval charters*] [*Canada*] (NITA)
DEEG .... Depth Electroencephalogram [*or Electroencephalography*] [*Neurology*] (DAVI)
DEEG .... Depth Electrography [*Neurology*] (DAVI)
DE Eng .... Doctor of Electrical Engineering
DEEO .... Director of Equal Employment Opportunity [*Department of Labor*]
DEEP .... Dairy Export Enhancement Program [*Department of Agriculture*]
DEEP .... Data Exception Error Protection
DEEP .... Deep Tech International [*NASDAQ symbol*] (TTSB)
DEEP .... DeepTech International, Inc. [*NASDAQ symbol*] (SAG)
DEEP .... Describe Each Element in the Procedure (PDAA)
DEEP .... Developmental Economic Education Program
DEEP .... Development Education Exchange Papers [*FAO*] [*Information service or system United Nations*] (DUND)
DEEP.......... Diffusion of Exemplary Educational Practices (EDAC)
DEEPDET ..... Double Exposure Endpoint Detection Technique (IAA)
DEEPSEAT ... Deep-Sea System for Evaluating Acoustic Transducers [*Navy*] (MCD)
DEEPSUBSYS... Deep Submergence Systems [*Navy*]
DEEPSUBSYSPROJO... Deep Submergence Systems Project Office [*Navy*]
DeepTech .... DeepTech International, Inc. [*Associated Press*] (SAG)
DEER .... Deer Environment Ecology and Resources [*An association*]
DEER .... Directional Explosive Echo Ranging
Deere.......... Deere & Co. [*Associated Press*] (SAG)
Deering's Cal Adv Legis Serv... Deering's California Advance Legislative Service [*A publication*] (DLA)
Deering's Cal Code Ann... Deering's Annotated California Code [*A publication*] (DLA)
Deering's Cal Gen Laws Ann... Deering's California General Laws, Annotated [*A publication*] (DLA)
DEERS .... Defense Enrollment Eligibility Reporting System [*DoD*]
DEES .... Dynamic Electromagnetic Environment Simulator
DEESC .... Deescalate (ABBR)
DEESCD ...... Deescalated (ABBR)
DEESCG ...... Deescalating (ABBR)
DEESCN ...... Deescalation (ABBR)
Dees Ins...... Dees on the Law of Insolvent Debtors [*A publication*] (DLA)
DEET.......... Diethyl-m-toluamide [*Insect repellent*]
DEEVAL....... Detailed European Evaluation (MCD)
DEEVE .... Dynamically Equivalent Equal-Volume Ellipsoid
De Exil........ De Exilio [*of Plutarch*] [*Classical studies*] (OCD)
DEF........... Daily Electronic Feed [*ABC news service*] (WDMC)
DEF........... Data Entry Facility
DEF........... Data Extension Frame [*Computer science*] (NITA)
DEF........... Decayed, Extracted, or Filled [*Dentistry*]
DEF........... Default [*Business term*]
DEF........... Defeated
DEF........... Defecation
DEF........... Defection [*or Defector*] (ABBR)
DEF........... Defective (MSA)
DEF........... Defendant
DEF........... Defense (AFM)
DEF........... Defensor [*Defender*] [*Coin inscription*] [*Latin*] (ROG)
DEF........... Deferred
DEF........... Defiance College, Defiance, OH [*OCLC symbol*] (OCLC)
def .... Deficiency [*or Deficient*]
DEF........... Deficit
DEF........... Define [*or Definite*] (KSC)
DEF........... Definition
DEF........... Definitive (ROG)
DEF........... Deflagrate (ABBR)
DEF........... Deflect (ABBR)
DEF........... Defoliation
DEF........... Defrost
DEF........... Defunctus [*Deceased*] [*Latin*] (ADA)
DEF........... Delay Equalizer, Fixed Set (IAA)
DEF........... Development Evaluation Facility (LAIN)
DEF........... Dielectric Foil (IAA)
DEF........... Disarm Education Fund (EA)
DEF........... Duck Embryo Fibroblasts (PDAA)
DEFA.......... Daily Express Film Award [*British*]
De Fac........ De Facie in Orbe Lunae [*of Plutarch*] [*Classical studies*] (OCD)
DEFAIR .... Defense Air (MCD)
DEFAR .... Department of Defence, Army [*Australia*]
DEF ART ..... Definite Article (WDAA)
DEFBA .... Domestic European Ferret Breeders Association (EA)
DEFCE......... Defence (ROG)
DEFCLOTH & TEXSUPCEN... Defense Clothing and Textile Supply Center [*Later, Defense Personnel Support Center*] [*DoD*]
DEFCOM ...... Defense Command
DEFCOMARS... Defence Communications Automatic Relay Station
DEFCOMMNET... Defence Force Communications Network [*Australia*]
DEFCOMMSYS... Defense Communications System [*DoD*] (DNAB)
DEFCON...... Defense Condition [*The higher number indicates a higher state of military readiness*] [*Numbered from 1 through 5*] [*Military*] (DOMA)
DEFCON...... Defense Readiness Condition [*Army*]

DEFCON.......	Defensive Concentration
DEFCON.......	Defensive Contact [*Artillery fire*] [*Military*] (VNW)
DEFCONTRSUPCEN...	Defense Construction Supply Center [*Defense Supply Agency*]
DEFCS	Digital Electronic Flight Control System (MCD)
DEFEC.........	Defective (IAA)
DEFECT.......	Defective Verb [*Grammar*] (ROG)
DEFEL........	Deferred Delivery
DEFELECSUPCEN...	Defense Electric Supply Center
DEFEWS	Design Engineers Field Experience with Soldiers [*Army*] (RDA)
DEFFC........	Defence Forces Charter [*Australia*]
DEFGAN.......	Desensitized Fertilizer-Grade Ammonium Nitrate [*Nonexplosive*]
DEFGENSUPCEN...	Defense General Supply Center
DEFGR	Defogger [*Automotive engineering*]
DEFI............	Defiance Inc. [*NASDAQ symbol*] (TTSB)
DEFI............	Defiance Precision Products [*NASDAQ symbol*] (NQ)
DEFI............	Deficiency (ABBR)
DEFI............	Digital Electronic Fuel Injection [*Automotive engineering*]
DEFIB..........	Defibrillate [*Cardiology*]
DEFIC..........	Deficiency (ROG)
defic............	Deficit (CPH)
DEFINDPLANTEQUIPCEN...	Defense Industrial Plant Equipment Center [*DoD*]
DEFINDSUPCEN...	Defense Industrial Supply Center
DEFINDSUPDEP...	Defense Industrial Supply Depot
DEFINTELAGCY...	Defense Intelligence Agency [*Formerly, JJ-2*]
DEFL..........	Deflate (ABBR)
DEFL..........	Deflect [*or Deflection*] (MSA)
DEFL..........	Deflector [*Automotive engineering*]
DEFL..........	Diode Emitter Follower Logic
DEFL..........	Direct Effective Fire Line [*Military*] (INF)
DeflcShd......	Deflecta Shield Corp. [*Associated Press*] (SAG)
DEFLOR.......	Defloration (ABBR)
DEFLOWH....	Defense Liaison Officer to the White House (AABC)
DEFLT.........	Deflect (AAG)
DEFLTN.......	Deflection (AAG)
DEFLTR.......	Deflector (AAG)
DeF Min	De Fooz on Mines [*A publication*] (DLA)
DEFMT........	Deafmute (ABBR)
DEFN	Deafen (ABBR)
DEFN	Deficiency (AABC)
DEFNAV.......	Department of Defence, Navy [*Australia*]
DEFNC.........	Defence
DEFND........	Deafened (ABBR)
DEFNG........	Deafening (ABBR)
DEFNGY.......	Deafeningly (ABBR)
DefnInc.......	Defiance Precision Products [*Associated Press*] (SAG)
DEFNS	Deafness (ABBR)
DEFNS	Defense
DEFOL	Defoliation (CINC)
deform.........	Deformity
De Fort Rom...	De Fortuna Romanorum [*of Plutarch*] [*Classical studies*] (OCD)
DEFPERSUPPCEN...	Defense Personnel Support Center
DEFR	Deafer (ABBR)
DEFR	Defrauding [*FBI standardized term*]
DEFR	Defroster [*Automotive engineering*]
DEFRA	Deficit Reduction Act [*1984*]
De Frat Amor...	De Fraterno Amore [*of Plutarch*] [*Classical studies*] (OCD)
DEFREP	Defense Readiness Posture [*Army*] (AABC)
DEFREPNAMA...	Defense Representative, North Atlantic and Mediterranean Area
DEFREPNAMA/USRO...	Defense Representative North Atlantic and Mediterranean Areas / United States Regional Office (SAA)
DEFSATCOM...	Defense Satellite Communications System [*Military*]
DEFSCAP	Defense Standard Contract Administration Procedure
DEFSCE.......	Defeasance (ROG)
DEFSEC.......	Defense Sector [*Navy*]
DEFSIP	Defense Scientists Immigration Program (AFM)
DEFSMAC	Defense Special Missile and Astronautics Center [*Pronounced "deff-smack"*] [*National Security Agency*]
DEFST.........	Deafest (ABBR)
DEFSUBSUPCEN...	Defense Subsistence Supply Center [*Later, Defense Personnel Support Center*]
DEFT...........	Defendant
DEFT...........	Definite-Time [*Relay*]
DEFT...........	Deflection (ADA)
DEFT...........	Design Effect [*Ratio used in statistics*]
DEFT...........	Development and Evaluation of a Firearms Training Facility
DEFT...........	Diagnostic Expert-Final Test [*IBM Corp.*]
DEFT...........	Direct Electronic Fourier Transform [*Camera*]
DEFT...........	Direct Epifluorescence Filter Technique [*Microbiology*]
DEFT...........	Director Evaluation Feasibility [*or Flight*] Test (MCD)
DEFT...........	Display Evaluation Flight Testing (MCD)
DEFT...........	Driven Equilibrium Fourier Transform [*Mathematics*]
DEFT...........	Dynamic Error-Free Transmission
DEFTNS	Deftness (ABBR)
DEFUNCT.....	Desirability Function
DEFWEAPSYSMGTCEN...	Defense Weapons System Management Center
DEFY...........	Deafly (ABBR)
DEG	Dawson Eldorado Gold [*Vancouver Stock Exchange symbol*]
DEG	Degaussing Calibration (NVT)
DEG	Degenerate Electron Gas
DEG	Degeneration
De G	De Gex's English Bankruptcy Reports [*A publication*] (DLA)
DEG	Degrade
DEG	Degree (AFM)
deg	Degree (IDOE)

deg	Degrees (IDOE)
Deg	DeGroot, Dr. A. T., Texas Christian University, Fort Worth, TX [*Library symbol Library of Congress*] (LCLS)
DEG	Destroyer Escort, Guided Missile [*British military*] (DMA)
DEG	Development Economics Group
DEG	Diagnostic Educational Grouping
DEG	Diethylene Glycol [*Organic chemistry*]
DEG	Diethylglycine [*Biochemistry*]
DEG	Double-Ended Guillotine [*Nuclear energy*] (NRCH)
DEG	Guided Missile Escort Ship [*Navy symbol*]
DEGA	Depth Gauge
DEGA	Diethylene Glycol Adipate [*Organic chemistry*]
DEGA	Diethylene Glycolamine [*Organic chemistry*]
DEGADIS.....	Dense Gas Dispersion [*Computer model*]
DEG & DEP...	Degaussing and Deperming [*Navy*]
De G & J	De Gex and Jones' English Chancery Reports [*A publication*] (ILCA)
De G & JB...	De Gex and Jones' English Bankruptcy Appeals [*1857-59*] [*A publication*] (DLA)
De G & J By...	De Gex and Jones' English Bankruptcy Appeals [*1857-59*] [*A publication*] (ILCA)
De G & S...	De Gex and Smale's English Chancery Reports [*63-64 English Reprint*] [*1846-52*] [*A publication*] (DLA)
De G & Sm...	De Gex and Smale's English Chancery Reports [*63-64 English Reprint*] [*1846-52*] [*A publication*] (ILCA)
De Garr.......	De Garrulitate [*of Plutarch*] [*Classical studies*] (OCD)
DEGB	Double-Ended Guillotine Break [*Nuclear energy*] (NRCH)
De G Bankr...	De Gex's English Bankruptcy Reports [*A publication*] (DLA)
De G Bankr (Eng)...	De Gex's English Bankruptcy Reports [*A publication*] (DLA)
degC..........	Degree Celsius [*British Standards Institution*]
DEGCALB.....	Degaussing Calibration (NVT)
DEGCENT.....	Degree Centigrade (IAA)
DEGE	DeGeorge Financial Corp. [*NASDAQ symbol*] (SAG)
DeGE	Eleutherian Mills Historical Library, Greenville, DE [*Library symbol Library of Congress*] (LCLS)
degen	Degeneration
De Gen	De Genio Socratis [*of Plutarch*] [*Classical studies*] (OCD)
DeGeT	Delaware Technical and Community College, Southern Campus, Georgetown, DE [*Library symbol Library of Congress*] (LCLS)
De Gex	De Gex's English Bankruptcy Reports [*A publication*] (DLA)
De Gex F & J...	De Gex, Fisher, and Jones' English Chancery Reports [*A publication*] (DLA)
De Gex J & S...	De Gex, Jones, and Smith's English Chancery Reports [*A publication*] (DLA)
De Gex M & G...	De Gex, Macnaghten, and Gordon's English Reports [*A publication*] (DLA)
De Gex M & GB...	De Gex, Macnaghten, and Gordon's English Bankruptcy Reports [*A publication*] (DLA)
degF	Degree Fahrenheit [*British Standards Institution*]
De G F & J...	De Gex, Fisher, and Jones' English Chancery Reports [*A publication*] (DLA)
Degge	Degge's Parson's Counsellor and Law of Tithes [*A publication*] (DLA)
DeGH	Hagley Museum and Library, Greenville, DE [*Library symbol*] [*Library of Congress*] (LCLS)
De G J & S...	De Gex, Jones, and Smith's English Chancery Reports [*A publication*] (DLA)
De G J & S By...	De Gex, Jones, and Smith's English Bankruptcy Appeals [*1862-65*] [*A publication*] (DLA)
De G J & S (Eng)...	De Gex, Jones, and Smith's English Chancery Reports [*A publication*] (DLA)
De G J & Sm...	De Gex, Jones, and Smith's English Chancery Reports [*A publication*] (DLA)
degK..........	Degree Kelvin [*British Standards Institution*]
De Glor Ath...	De Gloria Atheniensium [*of Plutarch*] [*Classical studies*] (OCD)
DEGLUT	Deglutiatur [*Swallow*] [*Pharmacy*]
DEGLUTIEND...	Deglutiendus [*To be Taken or Swallowed*] [*Pharmacy*] (ROG)
De G M & G...	De Gex, Macnaghten, and Gordon's English Bankruptcy Reports [*A publication*] (DLA)
De G M & G...	De Gex, Macnaghten, and Gordon's English Chancery Reports [*A publication*] (DLA)
De G M & G By...	De Gex, Macnaghten, and Gordon's English Bankruptcy Appeals [*1837-55*] [*A publication*] (DLA)
DEGN	Diethylene Glycol Dinitrate [*Explosive*]
DEGpGl	Delaware Group Global Dividend Fund [*Associated Press*] (SAG)
DEGpGlb......	Delaware Group Global Dividend Fund [*Associated Press*] (SAG)
degR..........	Degree Rankine [*British Standards Institution*]
DEGRA	Degradation (DSUE)
DEGRAD	Degradable (ABBR)
DeGrgeFnl...	DeGeorge Financial Corp. [*Associated Press*] (SAG)
DEGS..........	Diethylene Glycol Succinate [*Organic chemistry*]
DEG/SEC.....	Degrees per Second
DEGSVC......	Degaussing Services [*Navy*] (NVT)
DEGUSG	Degaussing
DEH	Dallas Enviro-Health Systems Ltd. [*Vancouver Stock Exchange symbol*]
DEH	Decorah, IA [*Location identifier FAA*] (FAAL)
DEH	Deepwater Escort Hydrofoil [*Also, DBH*] (MCD)
DEH	Department of Environment and Heritage [*Queensland*]
DEH	Diethylhydroxylamine [*Also, DEHA*] [*Organic chemistry*]
DEH	Digital Electrohydraulic (NRCH)
DEH	Digital Encoder Handbook
DEH	Direct Electrical Heating (PDAA)
DEH	Direct Engineering Hours (MCD)
DEH	Directorate of Engineering and Housing [*Army*] (RDA)
DEH	Drifting Electron Hole
DEH	Dysplasia Epiphysealis Hemimelica [*Medicine*] (DMAA)

DEHA .... Di(ethylhexyl) Adipate [*Also, DOA*] [*Organic chemistry*]
DEHA .... Diethylhydroxylamine [*Also, DEH*] [*Organic chemistry*]
DeHa .... Harrington Public Library, Harrington, DE [*Library symbol*] [*Library of Congress*] (LCLS)
De Hart Mil Law... DeHart on Military Law [*A publication*] (DLA)
DEHB .... Digital Encoder Handbook
DEHB .... Double Extra Hard Black [*Pencil leads*] (ROG)
DEHFT .... Developmental Hand Function Test
DeHi .... Historical Society of Delaware, Wilmington, DE [*Library symbol Library of Congress*] (LCLS)
DeH ML .... DeHart on Military Law [*A publication*] (DLA)
DEHP .... Di(ethylhexyl)phthalate [*Also, DOP, DHP*] [*Organic chemistry*]
DEHP .... Diethyl Hydrogen Phosphite [*Organic chemistry*]
DEHPA .... Di(ethylhexyl)phosphoric Acid [*Organic chemistry*]
DEHT .... Deep-Etched Halftone [*Engraving*] (DGA)
DEHYD .... Dehydrated
DEI .... Defense des Enfants - International [*Defence for Children International Movement - DCI*] (EAIO)
DEI .... Defense Electronics, Inc.
DEI .... Denis Island [*Seychelles Islands*] [*Airport symbol*] (OAG)
DEI .... Dent [*Idaho*] [*Seismograph station code, US Geological Survey Closed*] (SEIS)
DEI .... Design Engineering Identification (NASA)
DEI .... Design Engine Inspection (AFM)
DEI .... Development Engineering Inspection (MCD)
DEI .... Display Evaluation Index
DEI .... Dose Equivalent Iodine [*Nuclear energy*] (NRCH)
DEI .... Dutch East Indies
DEI .... Dynamic Effect Induction [*Automotive engineering*]
DEI .... Export-Import Bank of the United States, Washington, DC [*Library symbol Library of Congress*] (LCLS)
DEIB .... Developmental Engineering Inspection Board (AAG)
DEIC .... Diver Equipment Information Center [*Battelle Memorial Institute*] [*Information service or system*] (IID)
DEIFCN .... Deification (ABBR)
DEIFD .... Deified (ABBR)
DEIFG .... Deifying (ABBR)
DEIFR .... Deifier (ABBR)
De Imit .... De Imitatione [*of Dionysius Halicarnassensis*] [*Classical studies*] (OCD)
DEIMOS .... Development Investigations in Military Orbiting Systems
DEIMOS .... Diesel Engine Intelligent Monitoring System [*Automotive engineering*]
DEIMS .... Defense Economic Impact Modeling System
Deiot........... Pro Rege Deiotaro [*of Cicero*] [*Classical studies*] (OCD)
DEIP .... Dairy Export Incentive Program
DEIS............ Defense Energy Information System [*DoD Washington, DC*] (AFM)
DEIS............ Design Engineering Inspection Simulation (NASA)
DEIS............ Design Evaluation Inspection Simulator (NASA)
DEIS............ Digital Electronic Image Stabilization (PS)
DEIS............ Director of Engineering and Industrial Services [*Edgewood Arsenal, MD*]
DEIS............ DoD [*Department of Defense*] Worldwide Energy Information System (MCD)
DEIS............ Draft Environmental Impact Statement [*NRC*] (MSC)
DEIS............ Dual Electron Injector Structure (MCD)
DEIS............ IEEE Dielectrics and Electrical Insulation Society (EA)
De Is et Os... De Iside et Osiride [*of Plutarch*] [*Classical studies*] (OCD)
DEJ .... Albany, NY [*Location identifier FAA*] (FAAL)
DEJ .... David Ezekiel Joshua [*Shanghai*] (BJA)
DEJ .... Dejour Mines Ltd. [*Toronto Stock Exchange symbol*]
DEJ .... Delta Jet SA [*Spain ICAO designator*] (FAAC)
DEJ .... Dento-Enamel Junction [*Dentistry*]
DEJ .... Dermoepidermal Junction [*Anatomy*]
DEJ ALVI ..... Dejectiones Alvi [*Discharge from the Bowels*] [*Pharmacy*] (ROG)
De Jure Mar... Hale's De Jure Maris, Appendix to Hall on the Sea Shore [*A publication*] (DLA)
DEK............. Data Entry Keyboard [*Computer science*] (MCD)
DEK............. Dekeleia [*Greece*] [*Later, PEN*] [*Geomagnetic observatory code*]
DEK............. Demokratiki Enosis Kyprou [*Democratic Union of Cyprus*] [*Political party*] (PPE)
DEK............. Devtek Corp. [*Toronto Stock Exchange symbol*]
DEK............. Diethyl Ketone [*Organic chemistry*]
DEKAG .... Dekagram [*Unit of measure*]
DEKAL .... Dekaliter [*Unit of measure*] (ROG)
DEKAM .... Dekameter [*Unit of measure*] (ROG)
DEKE........... Doppler Ekelund Ranging [*Navy*] (CAAL)
DEKO .... Demokratiko Komma [*Democratic Party*] [*Greek Cyprus*] [*Political party*] (PPE)
De Krets ..... DeKretser's Matara Appeals [*Ceylon*] [*A publication*] (DLA)
DEL............. Carib Aviation Ltd. [*Antigua and Barbuda*] [*FAA designator*] (FAAC)
DEL............. Data Entry Language
DEL............. Defence Electric Light [*British military*] (DMA)
Del............. Delane's English Revision Cases [*1832-35*] [*A publication*] (DLA)
DEL............. Delary [*Sweden*] [*Seismograph station code, US Geological Survey*] (SEIS)
DEL............. Delaware (AFM)
del............. Delaware [*MARC language code Library of Congress*] (LCCP)
Del............. Delaware (ODBW)
Del............. Delaware County Reports [*Pennsylvania*] [*A publication*] (DLA)
Del............. Delaware Reports [*A publication*] (DLA)
Del............. Delaware Supreme Court Reports [*1832-*] [*A publication*] (ILCA)
DEL............. Delay
del............. Delay (WDMC)
DELE........... Delegacy (ROG)
DEL............. Delegate [*or Delegation*] (ADA)

DEL............. Del Electronics Corp. [*AMEX symbol*] (SPSG)
DEL............. Delete (OSI)
del............. Delete (WDMC)
DEL............. Delete [*Computer science*] (ECII)
DEL............. Delete Character [*Keyboard*] (CMD)
DEL............. Del Global Technologies [*AMEX symbol*] (TTSB)
DEL............. Delhi [*India*] [*Airport symbol*] (OAG)
DEL............. Deliberate (ABBR)
DEL............. Delineation (MSA)
DEL............. Delineavit [*He (or She) Drew It*] [*Latin*] (ROG)
DEL............. Delinquent
Del............. Delitzsch (BJA)
DEL............. Deliver [*or Delivery*] (KSC)
DEL............. Dellaterra Resources Ltd. [*Vancouver Stock Exchange symbol*]
Del............. Delphinus [*Constellation*]
DEL............. Delusion
DEL............. Deorbit, Entry, and Landing [*Aerospace*] (MCD)
DEL............. Direct Electrical Linkage
DEL............. Direct Exchange Line [*Telecommunications*]
DEL............. Directly Employed Labour [*British*]
DEL............. Directly Executable Language (MCD)
D El .... Doctor of Elements
D EL .... Doctor of English Literature
DEL............. Dollar Error Limit (DICI)
DEL............. Donor Energy Level
DEL............. Duck Egg Lysozyme [*Biochemistry*]
Del............. Hymnus in Delum [*of Callimachus*] [*Classical studies*] (OCD)
DELA........... Delactonized Ascorbate [*Biochemistry*]
DEIA........... Dictionary of Electrical Abbreviations, Signs, and Symbols [*A publication*]
DELACCT ..... Delinquent Account
DelaGP .... Delaware Group Dividend & Income Fund [*Associated Press*] (SAG)
Delane........ Delane's Revision Courts Decisions [*England*] [*A publication*] (DLA)
DelaOts....... Delaware Ostego Corp. [*Associated Press*] (SAG)
DELARF .... Delaware Association of Rehabilitation Facilities (SRA)
DELASEM ... Delegation for Assistance to Jewish Emigrants [*World War II organization*]
De Lat Viv ... De Latenter Vivendo [*of Plutarch*] [*Classical studies*] (OCD)
Delaware Co Reps... Delaware County Reports [*Pennsylvania*] [*A publication*] (DLA)
Delaware J Corp L... Delaware Journal of Corporate Law [*A publication*] (DLA)
Del C Ann.... Delaware Code, Annotated [*A publication*] (ILCA)
DELCAP .... Delay/Capacity [*Airport terminal*] [*FAA*]
Del Cas....... Delaware Cases [*1792-1830*] [*A publication*] (DLA)
DELCD .... Declared (ROG)
Del Ch .... Delaware Chancery Reports [*A publication*] (DLA)
Delchm....... Delchamps, Inc. [*Associated Press*] (SAG)
Del Civ Dec... Delaware Chancery Reports [*A publication*] (DLA)
Del Civ Dec... Delhi Civil Decisions [*India*] [*A publication*] (DLA)
DELCO .... Dayton Engineering Laboratories Co.
Del Co .... Delaware County Reports [*Pennsylvania*] [*A publication*] (DLA)
Del Code ..... Delaware Code (DLA)
Del Code Ann... Delaware Code, Annotated [*A publication*] (DLA)
Del Co L J (PA)... Delaware County Law Journal [*Pennsylvania*] [*A publication*] (DLA)
DELCOMBI... Command Delivering Orders Initiate Background Investigation [*Military*] (DNAB)
Del Const..... Delaware Constitution [*A publication*] (DLA)
Del Co (PA)... Delaware County Reports [*Pennsylvania*] [*A publication*] (DLA)
Del Co R...... Delaware County Reports [*Pennsylvania*] [*A publication*] (DLA)
Del Co Reps... Delaware County Reports [*Pennsylvania*] [*A publication*] (DLA)
Del County... Delaware County Reports [*Pennsylvania*] [*A publication*] (DLA)
Del County Rep... Delaware County Reports [*Pennsylvania*] [*A publication*] (DLA)
Del Cr Cas ... Delaware Criminal Cases [*A publication*] (DLA)
Del Ct M...... Delafon on Naval Courts Martial [*A publication*] (DLA)
DELCY .... Delinquency (ABBR)
DELD .... Delivered
Dele............ Deleatur [*Delete*] [*Latin*] (DLA)
DELE........... Delete (ABBR)
dele .... Delete (WDMC)
D El Ed .... Diploma in Elementary Education
DELEG .... Delegate
DELEG .... Delegation (ROG)
Delehanty ... New York Miscellaneous Reports [*A publication*] (DLA)
DelElc......... Del Electronics Corp. [*Associated Press*] (SAG)
Del El Cas ... Delane's Election Revision Cases [*England*] [*A publication*] (DLA)
DELENT .... Delete in Its Entirety (AAG)
DELEX......... Destroyer Life Extension [*Canadian Navy program*]
DELFIA........ Dissociation Enhanced Lanthanide Fluoroimmunoassay [*Clinical chemistry*]
DELFIC........ Defense Land Fallout Interpretive Code (MCD)
delfwr......... Delftware (VRA)
DELG .... Dealing (ABBR)
DELG .... Delgratia Mining Corp. [*NASDAQ symbol*] (SAG)
Del GCL ...... Delaware General Corporation Law [*A publication*] (DLA)
DELGF .... Delgratia Mining [*NASDAQ symbol*] (TTSB)
DelGlobal ... Del Global Technologies Corp. [*Associated Press*] (SAG)
Delgn.......... Delegation
Delgrt......... Delgratia Mining Corp. [*Associated Press*] (SAG)
DELI............ Delicatessen
DELI............ Delicatessen
DELI............ Desertification Library [*Database*] [*UNEP*] [*United Nations*] (DUND)
DELI............ Jerry's Famous Deli [*NASDAQ symbol*] (TTSB)
DELI............ Jerry's Famous Deli, Inc. [*NASDAQ symbol*] (SAG)
DELIB.......... Deliberation (ROG)

DELIC..........	Delicatamente [*Delicately*] [*Music*]
DELICAT.......	Delicatamente [*Delicately*] [*Music*] (ROG)
DELICATISS...	Delicatissimo [*Very Delicately*] [*Music*] (ROG)
DELILAH......	Duck Experiment on Low-Frequency and Incident-Band Longshore and Across-Shore Hydrodynamics [*Coastal Engineering Research Center*]
DELIN..........	Delineavit [*He (or She) Drew It*] [*Latin*] (WGA)
DELIN..........	Delinquency (ABBR)
DELIND........	Delineated (ROG)
DELINQ........	Delinquent (MUGU)
DELINUS......	Authorized to Delay [*Number of Days*], Any Portion of Which May Be Taken inCONUS [*Navy*]
DELIQ..........	Deliquescent
DEL key.......	Delete Key (CDE)
DELL...........	Dell Computer Corp. [*NASDAQ symbol*] (NQ)
DelLabs.......	Del Laboratories, Inc. [*Associated Press*] (SAG)
Del Law.......	Delaware Lawyer [*A publication*] (DLA)
Del Laws.....	Laws of Delaware [*A publication*] (DLA)
DellCpt.......	Dell Computer Corp. [*Associated Press*] (SAG)
DELMAR......	Data Element Management Accounting and Reporting
DELMARVA...	Delaware, Maryland, Virginia [*Peninsula*]
DelmPL........	Delmarva Power & Light Co. [*Associated Press*] (SAG)
Delmrv........	Delmarva Power Financing I [*Associated Press*] (SAG)
DELNQY.......	Delinquency
DELO..........	Delicato [*Delicately*] [*Music*] (ROG)
D Elo	Doctor of Elocution
De Lolme Eng Const...	De Lolme on the English Constitution [*A publication*] (DLA)
Del Order.....	Delegation Order (DLA)
DELP...........	Department of Environment, Lands, and Planning [*Australian Capital Territory*]
DELPARTURE...	Authorized to Delay [*Number of Days*], Any Portion of Which May Be Taken Prior to or after Departure [*Navy*]
DelpFin........	Delphi Financial Group, Inc. [*Associated Press*] (SAG)
Delph..........	Delphinus [*Constellation*]
DelphCt.......	Delphos Citizens Bancorp, Inc. [*Associated Press*] (SAG)
DELPHO......	Deliver by Telephone [*Message handling*]
DelpInf........	Delphi Information Systems [*Associated Press*] (SAG)
Del PM Ex ..	Delafield on Post Mortem Examinations [*A publication*] (DLA)
DELPRO.......	Delegated Procurement System [*Science*]
DELQ..........	Delinquent
DELR	Dealer (ABBR)
DELR	Deliver (ROG)
DELRAC......	DECCA Long-Range Area Coverage (MCD)
Del Reg of Regs...	Delaware Register of Regulations [*A publication*] (DLA)
DELREP.......	Authorized to Delay [*Number of Days*], in Reporting [*Navy*]
DELREPANY...	Authorized to Delay [*Number of Days*], in Reporting, Any Portion of Which May Be Taken Prior to or after Reporting at Temporary Duty Station [*Navy*]
DELREPARUS...	Authorized to Delay [*Number of Days*], Any Portion of Which May Be Taken Prior to or after Arrival in United States [*Navy*]
DELREPGRAD...	Authorized to Delay [*Number of Days*], in Reporting, to Count as GraduationLeave [*Navy*]
DELREPVAN...	Authorized to Delay [*Number of Days*], in Reporting, Keep New Station Advised Address [*Navy*]
DELRIBACO...	Delaware River Basin Commission [*Successor to INCODEL*]
Delrina	Delrina Corp. [*Associated Press*] (SAG)
DELRIVEPOE...	Delay in Arriving at Port of Embarkation [*Navy*]
DELS...........	Direct Electrical Linkage System (MCD)
DELSA	Doppler Electrophoretic Light Scanning Analyzer
DELT...........	Deck Edge Light (AAG)
DELT...........	Delete (AAG)
DELT...........	Delineavit [*He (or She) Drew It*] [*Latin*]
DELT...........	Dynamic Environmental Laboratory Test
DELTA..........	Decision Box, Event Box, Logic Box, Time Arrow, and Activity Box (PDAA)
DELTA..........	Dedication & Everlasting Love to Animals [*Rescue*]
DELTA..........	Dedication and Everlasting Love to Animals [*An association*]
DELTA..........	Detailed Labor and Time Analysis [*PERT*]
DELTA..........	Determination Effective Levels of Task Automation [*Computer science*]
DELTA..........	Developing European Learning through Technological Advance [*EC*] (ECED)
DELTA..........	Development of European Learning through Technological Advance [*British*]
DELTA..........	Development of Learning and Teaching in the Arts (AIE)
DELTA..........	Development of Learning through Technological Advance [*European Community*] (MHDB)
DELTA..........	Differential Electronically-Locking Test Accessory
DELTA..........	Distributed Electronic Test and Analysis
DeltaA.........	Delta Air Lines, Inc. [*Associated Press*] (SAG)
DeltaAir	Delta Air Lines, Inc. [*Associated Press*] (SAG)
DELTABANK...	Drug Effects on Laboratory Tests: Attention [*Worldwide Medical Information Ltd.*] [*Database*]
Delta St U ...	Delta State University (GAGS)
DeltaW	Delta Woodside Industries, Inc. [*Associated Press*] (SAG)
Del Term R...	Delaware Term Reports [*A publication*] (DLA)
DELTIC........	Delay Line Time Compression
DeltNG........	Delta Natural Gas Co. [*Associated Press*] (SAG)
DeltPine	Delta & Pine Land Co. [*Associated Press*] (SAG)
DeltPnt	DeltaPoint, Inc. [*Associated Press*] (SAG)
DELU..........	Delusion (ABBR)
DELURN.......	Delay in Returning to Duty Station [*Military*] (DNAB)
Deluxe	Deluxe Corp. [*Associated Press*] (SAG)
DELV..........	Deliver (ADA)
Delv...........	Delivered (DLA)

DEL V	Deluge Valve (DAC)
DELV'D	Delivered
DELVRNC......	Deliverance
DELWU	Delegate [*or Delegation*] to Western Union [*NATO*] (NATG)
DELXO	Delivery Ex Option [*Shares*]
DELY	Delivery
Dely	Delyse [*Record label*] [*Great Britain*]
DEM...........	Data Entry Mode (MCD)
DEM...........	Decoy Ejection Mechanism
Dem...........	De Demosthene [*of Dionysius Halicarnassensis*] [*Classical studies*] (OCD)
DEM...........	Delta Modulation [*Telecommunications*] (TEL)
DEM...........	Demagogue (ROG)
Dem...........	Dema'i (BJA)
DEM...........	Demand
Dem...........	Demarest's New York Surrogate's Court Reports [*A publication*] (DLA)
DEM...........	Dembidollo [*Ethiopia*] [*Airport symbol*] (OAG)
De M	De Mello's Extradition Cases [*1877-1913*] [*Malaya*] [*A publication*] (DLA)
Dem...........	Demerol [*Meperidine hydrochloride*] [*Analgesic compound Trademark*]
DEM...........	Demijohn [*Freight*]
DEM...........	Democrat [*or Democratic*] (EY)
DEM...........	Democratic
DEM...........	Demodulator [*Telecommunications*] (KSC)
DEM...........	Demolish [*Technical drawings*]
DEM...........	Demonstration
DEM...........	Demonstration Account [*For messages to and from UTLAS*]
Dem...........	Demonstrative (BJA)
DeM...........	DeMorgans Theorems [*Rules of replacement*] [*Logic*]
Dem...........	Demosthenes [*of Plutarch*] [*Classical studies*] (OCD)
Dem...........	Demosthenes [*Greek orator, 384-322BC*] [*Classical studies*] (OCD)
DEM...........	Demote (AABC)
DEM...........	Demulcent [*Softening, Lubricating*] [*Pharmacy*] (ROG)
DEM...........	Demur (ABBR)
DEM...........	Demurrage [*Shipping*]
DEM...........	Demy [*Half*] [*Size of paper*]
DEM...........	Department of Emergency Medicine (MEDA)
DEM...........	Detective, Enigma, and Mystery [*Publisher*] [*Former USSR*] (ECON)
DeM...........	Deus Misereatur [*67th Psalm*] [*Music*]
DEM...........	Diethyl Maleate [*Biochemistry*]
DEM...........	Diethyl Malonate [*Organic chemistry*]
DEM...........	Diethylmandelamide [*Organic chemistry*]
DEM...........	Digital Elevation Model [*For study of topography*]
DEM...........	Digital Elevation Model
DEM...........	Directional Emittance Measurement
DEM...........	Distribution, Excretion, and Metabolism [*Environmental chemistry*]
DEMA.........	Data Entry Management Association (EA)
DEMA.........	Diesel Engine Manufacturers Association [*Defunct*] (EA)
DEMA.........	Distributed Emission Magnetron Amplifier (MSA)
DEMA.........	Diving Equipment Manufacturers Association (EA)
DEMAC	Diesel Engine Monitoring and Control [*ASMAP Electronics Ltd.*] [*Software package*] (NCC)
DEMAND	Digitalized Electronics MARC [*Machine-Readable Cataloging*] and Non-MARC Display [*Machine-Readable Cataloging*] [*Library of Congress*]
DEMAR	Data Element Management Accounting and Reporting (MCD)
Demarest.....	Demarest's New York Surrogate's Court Reports [*A publication*] (DLA)
DEMATRON...	Distributed Emission Magnetron Amplifier
DEMBOMB...	Demolition Bomb
DEMC........	Defense Electronics Management Center (DNAB)
DEMD	Demised (ROG)
DEMD	Digital Engine Monitor Display (PDAA)
DEME	Director of Electrical and Mechanical Engineering [*Military British*]
DE-ME-DRIVE...	Decoding Memory Drive [*Computer science*] (MDG)
DEMERIL	Demerol [*Trademark of Winthrop Pharmaceuticals*] [*Analgesic compound*] (DAVI)
DEMETER ...	Digital Electronic Mapping of European Territory
Demetr	Demetrius [*of Plutarch*] [*Classical studies*] (OCD)
DEMI..........	Deliverable, Executable Machine Instructions
DEMI..........	DEM Inc. [*NASDAQ symbol*] (TTSB)
DEMIL.........	Demilitarize (AABC)
DEMIS	Defense Environmental Management Information System [*Navy*]
DEMIZ	DEW [*Distant Early Warning*] East Military Identification Zone
DEMJ..........	Demijohn [*Freight*] (WGA)
DEML..........	Detached Enlisted Men's List [*Army*]
DEM/LAB	Demographics Laboratory [*Information service or system*] (IID)
DEML(CIC)....	Enlisted Men on Duty with the Counter Intelligence Corps [*Army*]
DEML(NG)....	Enlisted Men on Duty with the National Guard [*Army*]
DEML(OR)....	Enlisted Men on Duty with the Organized Reserves [*Army*]
DEML(ROTC)...	Enlisted Men on Duty with the Reserve Officers' Training Corps [*Army*]
DEMLTN	Demolition
DEMMA.......	Direct Electronic Mail Marketing Association
DemNPN......	Democratic Non-Party Nationalist Party [*British*]
DEMNS	Distributed Explosive Mine Neutralization System (DOMA)
Dem (NY)	Demarest's New York Surrogate's Court Reports [*A publication*] (DLA)
DEMO	Demolition
DEMO	Demonstration (WDAA)
DEMO'D	Demonstrator (KSC)
DEMOB.......	Demobilize (AABC)
DEMOBED....	Demobilized (ABBR)

DEMOC....... Democracy (ABBR)
Democr....... Democritus [*Fifth century BC*] [*Classical studies*] (OCD)
DEMOD....... Demodulator [*Telecommunications*] (AAG)
DEMOD....... Depletion Etch Method (IAA)
DEMOD....... Deployment Model [*Army*] (AABC)
DEMOG....... Demography
DEMOL....... Demolition
Demol....... Demolombe's Code Napoleon [*A publication*] (DLA)
Demol C N.. Demolombe's Code Napoleon [*A publication*] (DLA)
DEMON....... Decision Mapping via Optimum Go-No Networks
DEMON....... Demodulated Noise (CAAL)
Demon....... Demonax [*of Lucian*] [*Classical studies*] (OCD)
DEMON....... Demonology (ABBR)
DEMON....... Demonstrative
DEMON....... Digital Electric Monitor
DEMON....... Diminishing Error Method of Optimization for Networks [*Computer science*] (RDA)
De Monog.... De Monogamia [*of Tertullian*] [*Classical studies*] (OCD)
DEMONOL..... Demonologic (ABBR)
DEMONS...... Demonstrative (ROG)
DEMONST.... Demonstrator
DEMONSTR.. Demonstrative (Pronoun) [*Linguistics*]
DEMOS....... Democratic Opposition of Slovenia [*Political party*] (EY)
demos........ Demographics [*The external characteristics of a population*] (WDMC)
DEMP........ Democratic Party [*Slang*]
DEMP........ Dispersed Electro-Magnetic Pulse (PDAA)
DEMP........ Drug Emporium [*NASDAQ symbol*] (TTSB)
DEMP........ Drug Emporium, Inc. [*NASDAQ symbol*] (NQ)
DEMR........ Department of Energy, Mines, and Resources [*Canada*]
DEMS........ Defensively-Equipped Merchant Ship
DEMS......... Development Engineering Management System [*Air Force*]
DEMS......... Differential Electrochemistry/Mass Spectrometry
DEMS......... Digital Electronic Message Systems
DEMS......... Digital Error Monitoring System (MCD)
DEMS......... Diver Equivalent Manipulator System [*General Electric*]
DEMS......... Dormant Equipping of Merchant Ships [*Organization*] (MCD)
DEMSS...... Defensively-Equipped Merchant Ship School
DEMSTAT.... Deployment/Employment/Mobilization Status System [*MTMC*] (TAG)
Dem Surr..... Demarest's New York Surrogate's Court Reports [*A publication*] (DLA)
DEMU .... Diesel Electric Multiple Unit (ADA)
De Mul Vir... De Mulierum Virtutibus [*of Plutarch*] [*Classical studies*] (OCD)
DEMUR....... Demurrer (ROG)
DEMUR....... Double Electron Muon Resonance (MCD)
De Mus....... De Musica [*of Plutarch*] [*Classical studies*] (OCD)
DEMUX....... Demultiplexer [*Computer science*]
DEM/VAL .... Demonstration/Validation (MCD)
DEM/VAL .... Demonstration/Validation Phase (AAGC)
DEMYC .... Democrat Youth Community of Europe [*Formerly, Conservative and Christian Democrat Youth Community of Europe*] (EA)
DEN .... Data Element Number (MCD)
DEN .... DenAmerica Corp. [*AMEX symbol*] (SAG)
DEN .... DenAmerica Corp. [*AMEX symbol*] (TTSB)
DEN .... Denbighshire [*County in Wales*] (ROG)
DEN .... Dengue [*Virus*]
Den .... Denied [*Legal term*] (DLA)
den .... Denied (AAGC)
den .... Denier [*Later, tex*]
Den............. Denio's New York Reports [*A publication*] (DLA)
Den............. Denison and Pearce's English Crown Cases Reserved [*169 English Reprint*] [*1844-52*] [*A publication*] (DLA)
DEN .... Denison Mines Ltd. [*Toronto Stock Exchange symbol Vancouver Stock Exchange symbol*]
Den............. Denis' Reports [*32-46 Louisiana*] [*A publication*] (DLA)
DEN............. Denmark
Den............. Denmark (VRA)
Den............. Denmark (ODBW)
DEN............. Denote (MSA)
DEN .... Denouement (ROG)
DEN .... Density
DEN .... Dental (AABC)
DEN .... Dentist (WDAA)
DEN .... Denver [*Colorado*] [*Seismograph station code, US Geological Survey*] (SEIS)
DEN .... Denver [*Colorado*] [*Airport symbol*]
DEn .... Department of Energy [*British*]
DEN .... Device Evaluation Network [*FDA*] [*Information service or system*]
DEN .... Diethylnitrosamine [*Also, DENA*] [*Carcinogen*]
DE(N)......... Director of Engineering (Naval) [*British military*] (DMA)
DEN .... District Enrolled Nurse [*British*]
D En............ Doctor of English
DEN .... Document Enabled Networking [*Computer science*]
DEN .... Dow Epoxy Novolac
DeN .... Newark Free Library, Newark, DE [*Library symbol Library of Congress*] (LCLS)
DEN .... Stapleton International Airport [*FAA*] (TAG)
DENA .... Delrina Corp. [*NASDAQ symbol*] (SAG)
DENA .... Diethylnitrosamine [*Also, DEN*] [*Carcinogen*]
DENALT ...... Density Altitude [*Computer*]
DenAmer..... DenAmerica Corp. [*Associated Press*] (SAG)
Den & P ...... Denison and Pearce's English Crown Cases [*1844-52*] [*A publication*] (DLA)
Den & PCC... Denison and Pearce's English Crown Cases [*1844-52*] [*A publication*] (DLA)

Den & Sc Pr... Denison and Scott's House of Lords Appeal Practice [*A publication*] (DLA)
Den App ...... Denying Appeal (DLA)
DENAS .... Daily European Naval Activity Summary (MCD)
DENAT .... Denatured
DENB .... Denbighshire [*County in Wales*]
Den BA Rec.. Denver Bar Association. Record [*A publication*] (DLA)
DENBIGHS ... Denbighshire [*County in Wales*]
DENBN .... Dental Battalion (DNAB)
DENBS .... Denbighshire [*County in Wales*]
DENC .... Divergent Exhaust Nozzle Control (MCD)
Den C C ...... Denison's English Crown Cases [*1844-52*] [*A publication*] (DLA)
DeNcD........ Delaware State Hospital, New Castle, DE [*Library symbol Library of Congress*] (LCLS)
DENCO........ Dental Co. [*Marine Corps*]
DEND .... Dendrology (ABBR)
D en D .... Docteur en Droit [*Doctor of Law*] [*French*]
DeND.......... E. I. Du Pont de Nemours & Co., Stine Laboratory, Newark, DE [*Library symbol Library of Congress*] (LCLS)
DENDRAL .... Dendritic Algorithm [*Organic molecules*]
DENDRO ..... Dendrometer (ABBR)
DENDROL .... Dendrology (ABBR)
Dendrte....... Dendrite International, Inc. [*Associated Press*] (SAG)
DENet .... [*The*] Danish Ethernet Network [*Computer science*] (TNIG)
D Eng.......... Doctor of Engineering
DEngg......... Doctor of Engineering
D Eng P .... Doctor of Engineering Physics
D Eng Sc ..... Doctor of Engineering Science
DENI .... Damage Equivalent of Normally Incident (IAA)
DENI .... Department of Education of Northern Ireland [*British*]
Denio .... Denio's New York Supreme Court Reports [*1845-48*] [*A publication*] (DLA)
Denio R .... Denio's New York Reports [*A publication*] (DLA)
Denis .... Denis' Reports [*32-46 Louisiana*] [*A publication*] (DLA)
Denison Cr Cas... Denison's English Crown Cases [*1844-52*] [*A publication*] (DLA)
DENK .... Dual Employed, No Kids [*Lifestyle classification*]
Den L N .... Denver Legal News [*A publication*] (DLA)
DENM .... Denmark
DENN .... Denomination (ROG)
DENOM .... Denomination
denom .... Denominative [*or Denominator*] (BJA)
DENOT .... Denotation (ABBR)
DENPA........ Density Phenomena [*Japan*]
DENPAY....... Dental Pay
DENPRE ...... Density Probe (MUGU)
DENR .... Denominator (ROG)
DENR .... Department of Energy and Natural Resources
Den Rearg ... Denying Reargument [*Legal term*] (DLA)
Den Reh ...... Denying Rehearing [*Legal term*] (DLA)
DENRF .... Denbury Resources [*NASDAQ symbol*] (TTSB)
DENS .... Density (AFM)
dens........... Density (IDOE)
Dens .... Denslow's Notes to Second Edition [*1-3 Michigan*] [*A publication*] (DLA)
DENS .... Diffuse Elastic Neutron Scattering (MCD)
DENS .... Directory and Equipment Number Status System (MCD)
DENSP .... Deanship (ABBR)
DENT .... Dental (ROG)
DENT .... Dental Exposure Normalization Technique [*Medicine*] (DMAA)
DENT .... Dentistry
DENT .... Dentition [*Medicine*]
DENT .... Dentur [*Give*] [*Pharmacy*]
DENT .... Denture (ABBR)
DENT .... Directions for Education in Nursing via Technology
D Ent .... Doctor of Entomology
DENTAC....... Dental Activity (AABC)
DENTCAP..... Dental Civic Action Program [*Vietnam*]
DENTCORPS... Dental Corps [*Air Force*]
DENTL .... Dental
DENTR .... Denture
DENTS .... Director of Naval Education and Training Support
Dentsply ..... Dentsply International [*Associated Press*] (SAG)
DENT TAL DOS... Dentur Tales Doses [*Give in Such Doses*] [*Pharmacy*]
DE-NUM...... Data Element Dictionary Number
DENV .... Denver [*Colorado*] (ROG)
D Env.......... Doctor of Environment (PGP)
DEnvDes...... Doctor of Environmental Design (GAGS)
Denver J Int L & Policy... Denver Journal of International Law and Policy [*A publication*] (DLA)
Denver J Int'l L... Denver Journal of International Law [*A publication*] (DLA)
Denver L N... Denver Legal News [*A publication*] (DLA)
DeNvo......... DeNovo [*Associated Press*] (SAG)
DENYG........ Denying
DEO .... Deck Edge Outlet [*Navy*]
Deo .... De Deo [*Philo*] (BJA)
DEO .... Deobstruent [*Removing Obstructions*] [*Pharmacy*] (ROG)
DEO .... Department of Executive Officer
DEO .... Diesel Engine Oil
DEO .... Digital End Office [*Telecommunications*]
DEO .... District Engineer Officer [*Army*]
DEO .... Divisional Education Officer [*British*]
DEO .... Divisional Entertainments Officer [*British*]
DEO .... Divisional Executive Officer [*British*]
DEO .... Doped Erbium Oxide
DEO .... Duke of Edinburgh's Own [*Military unit*] [*British*]

DEOA	Department of Education Organization Act (GFGA)
DEO(A)	Dependents' Education Office (Atlantic) (DNAB)
DEOB	Dental Explanation of Benefits [Army]
DEOC	District Emergency Operations Controller [Australia]
DEOD	Deodorant (ABBR)
DEODZ	Deodorize (ABBR)
DEODZD	Deodorized (ABBR)
DEODZG	Deodorizing (ABBR)
DEODZN	Deodorization (ABBR)
DEODZR	Deodorizer (ABBR)
DEOMI	Defense Equal Opportunity Management Institute
DEO(P)	Dependents' Education Office (Pacific) (DNAB)
De Or	De Oratore [of Cicero] [Classical studies] (OCD)
De Orat	Cicero's De Oratore [A publication] (DLA)
DEORB	Deorbit (NASA)
DEOS	Data Exchange Optimization Study [DoD] (MCD)
DEOS	Director of Equipment and Ordnance Stores [British military] (DMA)
DEOT	Disconnect, End of Transmission
DEOVR	Duke of Edinburgh's Own Volunteer Rifles [Military unit] [British]
DEOWRB	Dictionaries, Encyclopedias, and Other Word-Related Books [A publication]
DEP	Data Entry Panel (MCD)
DEP	Data Exchange Program
DEP	Decorated End-Papers [Publishing]
DEP	Dedicated Experiment Processor [Spacelab mission]
DEP	Deep External Pudendal Artery [Anatomy]
DEP	Defence and Ex-Services Party of Australia [Political party]
DEP	Defense Electronic Products
DEP	Defense Enterprise Program [DoD]
DEP	Defense Estimate for Production (MCD)
DEP	Deflection Error Probable [Military] (AFM)
DEP	Degradation Effects Program
DEP	Delayed Enlistment [or Entry] Program [Military] (AFM)
DEP	Dense Electronic Population
Dep	Density Dependent [Biology]
DEP	Depart (AFM)
DEP	Department
dep	Department [Also dept or dpt] (WDMC)
DEP	Department of Employment and Productivity [Later, DE] [British]
DEP	Departure Message [Aviation code]
DEP	DEP Corp. [Associated Press] (SAG)
DEP	Dependencies (ROG)
DEP	Dependent
DEP	Depilate (ABBR)
DEP	Depilatory (ABBR)
DEP	Deployment
DEP	Deponent
DEP	Deport (ROG)
DEP	Deportation [FBI standardized term]
DEP	Deposed
DEP	Deposit [or Depositor] (EY)
dep	Deposit (WDMC)
DEP	Depositary [Banking]
DEP	Deposit Guaranty Corp. [NYSE symbol] (SAG)
DEP	Deposition (ADA)
DEP	Depository
DEP	Depot (AFM)
DEP	Depressed [Technical drawings]
DEP	Depth
DEP	Depuratus [Purified] [Pharmacy]
DEP	Deputy (AFM)
dep	Deputy (WDMC)
DEP	Design Engineering Program [Military]
DEP	Design External Pressure (NRCH)
DEP	Design Eye Point [Cockpit visibility]
DEP	Detailed Experiment Plan (MCD)
DEP	Diagnostic Execution Program (NOAA)
DEP	Diagnostic Executive Program (NITA)
DEP	Dielectrophoresis
DEP	Diethyl Phthalate [Organic chemistry]
DEP	Diethylpropanediol [Biochemistry]
DEP	Diethyl Pyrocarbonate [Chemical preservative] [Also, DEPC] [Organic chemistry]
DEP	Displaced Employee Program [Department of Labor]
DEP	Domestic Emergency Plan (AAG)
DEP	Double-Ended Pivot
DEP	Double-Exposure Prevention [Advanced photo system]
DEP	Draft Experiment Publication (MCD)
DEP	Dual Element Pump
DEPA	Defense Electric Power Administration [Terminated, 1977] [Department of the Interior]
DEPA	Defense Entry and Departure Act [1918]
DEPA	Diethylene Phosphoramide [Organic chemistry] (BABM)
DEPA	Diversified Economic and Planning Associates
DEPA	United States Environmental Protection Agency, Headquarters Library, Washington, DC [Library symbol Library of Congress] (LCLS)
DEPACTV	Depot Activity
DEPAIR	Air Deputy [NATO] (NATG)
DEPA-NA	United States Environmental Protection Agency, Office of Noise Abatement and Control, Washington, DC [Library symbol Library of Congress] (LCLS)
DEPART	Department
DePaul U	DePaul University (GAGS)
DEPC	Defence Equipment Policy Committee [British] (RDA)

DEPC	Defence Equipment Procurement Council [British]
DEPC	DEP Corp. [NASDAQ symbol] (NQ)
DEPC	Diethyl Pyrocarbonate [Chemical preservative] [Also, DEP] [Organic chemistry]
DEPCA	Digital Ethernet Personal Computer Adapter
DEPCDR(R & D)	Deputy Commander for Research and Development [Navy]
DEPCDR(SA)	Deputy Commander for Ship Acquisitions [Navy]
DEPCH	Deputy Chief (CINC)
DEPCHNAVMAT	Deputy Chief of Naval Material (DNAB)
DEPCHNAVMAT(MAT & FAC)	Deputy Chief of Naval Material (Material and Facilities) (DNAB)
DEPCOM	Deputy Commander (DNAB)
DEPCOMFEWSG	Deputy Commander, Fleet Electronic Warfare Support Group [Navy] (DNAB)
DEPCOMLANTNAVFACENGCOM	Deputy Commander, Atlantic Naval Facilities Engineering Command (DNAB)
DEPCOMOPTEVFORLANT	Deputy Commander, Operational Test and Evaluation Force, Atlantic [Navy] (DNAB)
DEPCOMOPTEVFORPAC	Deputy Commander, Operational Test and Evaluation Force, Pacific [Navy]
DEPCOMPACNAVFACENGCOM	Deputy Commander, Pacific Naval Facilities Engineering Command (DNAB)
DEPCOMPT	Deputy Comptroller (DNAB)
DEPCOMSTRIKFORSOUTH	Deputy Commander, Naval Striking and Support Forces, Southern Europe (NATG)
DEPCOMSTS	Deputy Commander, Military Sea Transport Service [Obsolete Navy]
DEPCOMUSMACTHAI	Deputy Commander, United States Military Assistance Command, Thailand
DEPCOMUSMACV	Deputy Commander, United States Military Assistance Command, Vietnam
DEPCON	Departure Control
DEPCOS	Deputy Chief of Staff [Military] (CAAL)
DEPCRU	Dependents' Daylight Cruise [Navy] (NVT)
Dep Ctf	Deposit Certificate [Banking] (MHDW)
DEPD	Departed (ABBR)
DEPD	Division Engineering Planning Document
DEPDA	Deployment Data File
DEPDIR	Deputy Director
DEPDIRPACDOCKS	Deputy Director Pacific Division, Bureau of Yards and Docks [Later, NFEC] [Navy]
DEPE	Double Escape Peak Efficiency [Nuclear science] (OA)
DEPEND	Dependency (ABBR)
DEPERM	Deperming [Navy] (ANA)
DEPERMSTA	Deperming and Flashing Station [Navy]
DEPES	Development Environment for Pronunciation Expert Systems [Computer science]
DEPEVACPAY	Dependents' Evacuation Pay [Military]
DEPEX	Deployment Exercise [Military] (ADDR)
DEPEX	Deployment on NIKE/X Study [Military]
DEPG	Departing (ABBR)
DepGty	Deposit Guaranty Corp. [Associated Press] (SAG)
DE Phy	Doctor of Engineering Physics
DEPI	Differential Equations Pseudocode Interpreter [Jet Propulsion Laboratory, NASA]
DEPIC	Dual-Expanded Plastic-Insulated Conductor [Telecommunications] (TEL)
DEPICT	Defense Electronics Products Integrated Control Technique (PDAA)
depict	Depicting (VRA)
DEPID	Deployment Indicator Code
DEPILAT	Depilatorium [Depilatory] [Pharmacy]
DEP in CT	Deposits in Court [Legal term] (DLA)
DEP INST	Depot Installed (SAA)
DEPL	Depilation (ABBR)
DEPL	Depletion (KSC)
DEPL	Deploy (KSC)
DEPL-MAN	Deployment Manifest [Army]
DEPLOC	Daily Estimated Position Location [Navy] (NVT)
DEPMED	Deployable Medical [Equipment] [Military]
DEPMEDS	Deployable Medical System [Military]
DEPMIS	Depot Management Information System [Army]
DEPN	Dependent (AFM)
DEPNAV	Naval Deputy [NATO] (NATG)
DEPNAVSCI	Department of Naval Science (DNAB)
DEPNOTAUTH	Dependents Not Authorized Overseas Duty Station [Military]
depo	Deposit
DEPO	Deposition [Legal shorthand] (LWAP)
DEPO	DepoTech Corp. [NASDAQ symbol] (SAG)
DEPO	Depo Tech Inc. [NASDAQ symbol] (TTSB)
DEPO	Devils Postpile National Monument
DEPOL	Depolarization
DEPON	Deponent (ABBR)
DEPOPSDEP	Deputy Operations Deputy [In JCS system] [Military]
DEPOS	Depositary [Banking] (EY)
DEPOS & D	Deposition and Discovery [Legal term] (DLA)
DEPOSN	Deposition
DEPOT	Desktop and Electronic Publishing Online Terminal
DEPP	Daily Encephalic Photophase [Biochronometry]
DEPP	Deep Earth Penetrating Projectile (MCD)
DEPPC	Declared Excess Personal Property Catalog [Military]
DEPR	Depreciation [Accounting, Economics]
depr	Depressed [Psychiatry] (DAVI)
DEPR	Depression [Board on Geographic Names] (MSA)
DEPRA	Defense European and Pacific Redistribution Activity [DoD] (AFIT)

De Praescr Haeret... De Praescriptione Haereticorum [*of Tertullian*] [*Classical studies*] (OCD)
DEPREC....... Depreciation
DEPREP....... Deployment Reporting System
DEPRESS.... Depressurize (NASA)
depr neur..... Depressive Neurosis [*Psychiatry*] (DAVI)
De Prof Virt... De Profectu in Virtute [*of Plutarch*] [*Classical studies*] (OCD)
DEPS .... Departmental Entry Processing Systems [*Customs processing for sea and airports*] [*October, 1981*] [*British*] (DCTA)
DEPS .... Deposit Guaranty [*NASDAQ symbol*] (TTSB)
DEPS .... Deposit Guaranty Corp. [*NASDAQ symbol*] (NQ)
DEPS .... Distal Effective Potassium Secretion [*Medicine*] (DMAA)
DEPS .... Double-Ended Pump Suction [*Nuclear energy*] (NRCH)
DEPSACLANT... Deputy Supreme Allied Commander, Atlantic (NATG)
DEPSCoR.... Defense Experimental Program to Stimulate Competitive Research (RDA)
DEPSEC .... Deputy Secretary (ADA)
DEPSECDEF... Deputy Secretary of Defense (AABC)
DEPSK........ Differential Encoding Phase Shift Keying (MCD)
DEPSO........ Department Standardization Office [*Navy*]
DEPSTAR..... Deployment Status of Army Units (AABC)
DEPSUM...... Daily Estimated Position Summary [*Navy*]
DEPSUM...... Deployment Summary Report [*Air Force*]
DEPT........... Depart
DEPT........... Department (EY)
dept .... Department (DD)
Dept........... Department (ODBW)
DEPT........... Department
DEPT........... Departure (ABBR)
DEPT........... Deponent [*Legal term*] (ROG)
DEPT........... Deposit (ROG)
DEPT........... Deputy
DEPT........... Distortionless Enhancement by Polarization Transfer [*Spectroscopy*]
Dept56........ Department 56, Inc. [*Associated Press*] (SAG)
DEPTAR....... Department of the Army
DEPTAR/MAIN... Department of the Army/Main (AABC)
DEPTD .... Division of Electric Power Transmission and Distribution [*Energy Research and Development Administration*]
DEPTEL........ State Department Telegram (NATG)
DEPTL......... Departmental (ABBR)
DEPTM........ Draft Equipment Publication Technical Manual (MCD)
DEPTNAVINSTR... Department of Naval Instruction (DNAB)
Dept R .... Department Reports, State Department [*New York*] [*A publication*] (DLA)
Dept R Un ... New York State Department Reports, Unofficial [*A publication*] (DLA)
DEPU .... Departure (ABBR)
DEPU .... De Paul University [*Chicago, IL*]
DEPUTN....... Deputation
Depuy .... Depuy, Inc. [*Associated Press*] (SAG)
DEPV .... Air-Cushion Vehicle built by Research Vehicle Department [*Brazil*] [*Usually used in combination with numerals*]
DEPY .... Deputy
De Pyth Or... De Pythiae Oraculis [*of Plutarch*] [*Classical studies*] (OCD)
DEQ .... Daydream Island [*Queensland*] [*Airport symbol*] (AD)
DEQ .... Department of Environment Quality
DEQ .... DeQueen, AR [*Location identifier FAA*] (FAAL)
DEQ .... Dequeue [*Computer science*]
DE/Q .... Design Evaluation/Qualification (KSC)
DEQ .... Dose Equivalent [*Radioactivity calculations*] (IEEE)
DEQ .... Idaho Department of Health and Welfare [*Division of Environmental Quality*] (DOGT)
DEQMAR...... Determining Economic Quantities of Maintenance Resources (PDAA)
DEQUIP........ DECHEMA [*Deutsche Gesellschaft fuer Chemisches Apparatewesen, Chemische Technik, und Biotechnologie eV*] Equipment Suppliers Databank [*Database*]
DEQUISA...... Desarrollo Quimico Industrial, SA [*Spain*]
DER .... Declining Error Rate
DER .... Defective Equipment Review (MCD)
DER .... Delegated Engineering Representative
DER .... Demonstration and Evaluation Report (MCD)
DER .... Denar Mines Ltd. [*Vancouver Stock Exchange symbol*]
DER .... Departure End of Runway [*Aviation*] (DA)
DER .... Derby [*Colorado*] [*Seismograph station code, US Geological Survey Closed*] (SEIS)
DER .... Derekh Erets Rabbah [*or Derek Erez Rabbah*] (BJA)
DER .... De Rigo ADS [*NYSE symbol*] (TTSB)
DER .... DeRigo SPA [*NYSE symbol*] (SAG)
DER .... Derim [*Papua New Guinea*] [*Airport symbol*] (OAG)
DER .... Derivation [*or Derivative*]
der............ Derivative of Chromosome [*Genetics*] (DAVI)
DER .... Derived (ROG)
DER .... Dermatine
DER .... Dermatology (DAVI)
DER .... Derricks (DS)
DER .... Designated Engineer Representative [*FAA title*] (AFM)
DER .... Design Electrical Rating [*Nuclear energy*] (NRCH)
DER .... Destroyer Escort RADAR (IAA)
DER .... Development Engineering Review (AAG)
DER .... Diesel Engine, Reduction Drive
DER .... Directly Executable Representation
DER .... Distributed Energy Release [*Computer program*]
DER .... Disulfiram-Ethanol Reaction [*Medicine*] (DMAA)
DER .... Division of Economic Research [*Social Security Administration*] [*Washington, DC*] (GRD)

DER .... Division of Engineering Research [*Michigan State University*] [*Research center*] (RCD)
DER .... Division of Evaluation and Research [*Department of Labor*] (GRD)
DER .... Document Error Report
DER .... Double Edge Receiver (MCD)
DER .... Double-Ended Rupture [*Nuclear energy*] (NRCH)
DER .... Drawing Error Report (NASA)
DER .... Out of Order [*International telex abbreviation*] (WDMC)
DER .... RADAR Picket Escort Ship [*Navy symbol*]
DeR .... Reaction of Degeneration [*Physiology*]
DER .... United States Army Engineer Research and Development Laboratory, Technical Documents Center, Fort Belvoir, VA [*Library symbol Library of Congress*] (LCLS)
DERA .... Defense Eastern Regional Audit Office [*DoD*]
DERA .... Defense Environmental Restoration Account [*DoD*]
DERA .... Defense European Redistribution Activity [*DoD*] (MCD)
DERA .... Direction de l'Analyse Economique et Regionale [*Economic and Regional Analysis Branch*] [*Transport Canada*]
DERA .... Directory of Education Research and Researchers in Australia (NITA)
DERAX .... Detection and Range [*Early name for RADAR*]
DERB .... Derby (ROG)
DERB .... Derbyshire [*County in England*]
Derbs .... Derbyshire [*County in England*] (DAS)
DERBSH....... Derbyshire [*County in England*] (ROG)
DERBY .... Derbyshire [*County in England*]
Derby .... Derbyshire [*County in England*] (ODBW)
DERBYS....... Derbyshire [*County in England*]
DERC .... Development Economics Research Centre [*University of Warwick*] [*British*] (CB)
DERC .... Directory of Executive Recruitment Consultants [*A publication*]
DERCCA....... Derbyshire England Red Cap Club of America (EA)
DERD .... Diesel Electric Reduction Drive
DERD .... Display of Extracted RADAR Data (DA)
DERDA .... United States Energy Research and Development Administration, Washington, DC [*Library symbol Library of Congress*] (LCLS)
DERE .... Dounreay Experimental Reactor Establishment [*British*]
DEREC .... Definitive Election Results Evaluation Computer (DI)
DEREK .... Deductive Estimation of Risk from Existing Knowledge [*Data analysis*]
DERES .... DECHEMA [*Deutsche Gesellschaft fuer Chemisches Apparatewesen, Chemische Technik, und Biotechnologie eV*] Research and Education Databank [*Frankfurt Am Main, Federal Republic of Germany*] [*Information service or system*] (IID)
DERF .... Division of Educational and Research Facilities [*Bureau of Health Professions Education and Manpower Training, HEW*]
DERF .... Dynamical Extended Range Forecasting [*Meteorology*]
DERG .... Deferred Exchange-Rate Guarantee [*Investment term*] (ECON)
DERI .... Deep Electric Research Investigation [*Navy*]
DERI .... Diethyl(ribityl)isoalloxazine [*Biochemistry*]
DERIC .... De Ea Re Ita Censuere [*Concerning That Matter Have So Decreed*] [*Latin Legal term*] (DLA)
DERIGID ..... Derigidize (NASA)
DeRigo .... DeRigo SPA [*Associated Press*] (SAG)
DERIPS........ Doppler-Enhanced RADAR Intensity Profiling System (MCD)
DERIV .... Derivation [*or Derivative*]
DERIV .... Derived (ROG)
DERIVB........ Derivable (ABBR)
DERIVD........ Derived (ABBR)
DERIVG........ Deriving (ABBR)
DERIVN........ Derivation (ABBR)
DERIVP........ Derivative Program (MCD)
DERIVV........ Derivative (ABBR)
DERL .... Derived Emergency Reference Level [*of radiation*]
DERM .... Delayed Echo RADAR Marker
DERM .... Derma [*Skin*] [*Medicine*] (ROG)
DERM .... Derma-Lock Medical Corp. [*Norway*] (NQ)
DERM .... Dermatitis [*Medicine*]
DERM .... Dermatology [*or Dermatologist*]
DERM .... Dermatophyte (ABBR)
DERM .... Diagnostic Energy Reserve Module [*Airbags and safety systems*]
DERM .... Dynamic Econometric Retention Model (MCD)
DERM .... Penederm, Inc. [*NASDAQ symbol*] (SAG)
DermaSci .... Derma Sciences, Inc. [*Associated Press*] (SAG)
DERMAT ...... Dermatology (ABBR)
DERMATOL... Dermatology
DERMTLGST... Dermatologist
DERN .... Dermatology
DERNS......... Dearness (ABBR)
DEROG........ Derogatory (DCTA)
DEROS......... Date Eligible for Return from Overseas [*Military*]
DEROS......... Date of Estimated Return from Overseas [*Military*]
DEROS......... Departing Roster (DNAB)
DERP .... Defective Equipment Repair Program [*Telephone company*]
DERP .... Defense Environmental Restoration Program [*DoD*]
DERP .... Deficient Equippage Reporting Procedures
DERR .... Daily Effective Repair Rate (MCD)
DERR .... Duke of Edinburgh's Royal Regiment [*Military unit*] [*British*]
DERRY .... Londonderry [*County in Ireland*] (ROG)
DERS .... Data Entry Reporting System
DERS .... Division of Educational Research Services [*University of Alberta*] [*Research center*] (RCD)
DERTO .... DSA [*Defense Supply Agency*] Eastern Regional Telecommunications Office
DERV .... Diesel Engined Road Vehicle
DES............. Chilcotin Caribou Aviation [*Canada ICAO designator*] (FAAC)

DES............	Data Elements Standardization Requirements (MCD)
DES............	Data Encryption Standard [*National Institute of Standards and Technology*]
DES............	Data Engineering Section
DE/S...........	Data Entry/Separation (MCD)
DES............	Data Entry System
DES............	Data Exchange System (NASA)
DES............	Dead-End Shaft
DES............	Department of Education and Science [*British*]
Des............	Desaussure. South Carolina Equity Reports [*1784-1816*] [*A publication*] (DLA)
DES............	Descend To [*Aviation*]
DES............	Descent (KSC)
DES............	Descriptor (NITA)
DES............	Desc S.A. ADS [*NYSE symbol*] (TTSB)
DES............	Desc SA de CV [*NYSE symbol*] (SAG)
DES............	Desert [*Hawaii*] [*Seismograph station code, US Geological Survey*] (SEIS)
DES............	Desert Botanical Garden [*An association*] (EA)
DES............	Desertion
DES............	Desferrioxamine [*Also, Deferoxamine*] [*A chelating agent*]
DES............	Design (NASA)
des............	Design (VRA)
DES............	Designator (KSC)
DES............	Designatus [*Named*] [*Latin*]
DES............	Designavit [*He, or She, Drew It*] [*Latin*] (ROG)
DES............	Design Engineering Show and Conference (ITD)
DES............	Design Engineering Support (MCD)
DES............	Designer (WDAA)
DES............	Design Expansion System
DES............	Desire (AABC)
DES............	Dessert (WDAA)
DES............	Destroyer [*Navy*]
DES............	Dialysis Encephalopathy Syndrome [*Medicine*] (DMAA)
DES............	Diccionario Enciclopedico Salvat [*A publication*]
DES............	Diesel Electric Ship (IAA)
DES............	Diesel Electronic Submarine (MCD)
DES............	Diethylstilbestrol [*Endocrinology*]
DESgnF........	Diethyl Succinate [*Organic chemistry*]
DES............	Diethyl Sulfate [*Organic chemistry*]
DES............	Differential Energy Spectrum
DES............	Differential Equation Solver
DES............	Diffuse Esophageal Spasm [*Medicine*]
DES............	Digital Echo Suppressor (NITA)
DES............	Digital Encryption Standard [*Computer science*] (PCM)
DES............	Digital Exchange System (MCD)
DES............	Digital Expansion System
DES............	Diplome d'Etudes Superieures [*Canada*] (DD)
DES............	Director of Educational Services [*Air Force British*]
DES............	Director of Engineer Stores Service [*British*]
DES............	Discrete Elastic System
DES............	Disequilibrium Syndrome [*Medicine*]
DES............	Dispersed Emergency Station (NATG)
DES............	Division of Earth Sciences [*Marine science*] (OSRA)
DES............	Division of Earth Sciences [*National Research Council*] (USDC)
DES............	Division of Educational Services [*Department of Education*]
DES............	Division of Energy Storage [*Energy Research and Development Administration*]
DES............	Division of Environmental Science [*Marine science*] (OSRA)
DES............	Division of Environmental Sciences [*National Science Foundation*] (USDC)
DES............	Doctor of Engineering Science
DES............	Doctor of Environmental Studies (DD)
DES............	Doctors Emergency Service [*New York City*]
DES............	Douglas Equipment Specification
DES............	Dow Education Systems [*Dow Chemical Corp.*]
DES............	Draft Environmental Statement [*Bureau of Outdoor Recreation*]
DES............	Drug Education Specialist [*Military*] (AABC)
DES............	Dual Exciter System
DES............	Ducosyn Excitation Switch
DES............	Dynamic Electrospeaker
DES............	Dynamic Environment Simulator [*Air Force*]
DES............	Office of Economic Security, Department of Economic Security, St. Paul, MN [*OCLC symbol*] (OCLC)
DESA..........	Division of Epidemiology and Statistical Analysis [*Department of Health and Human Services*] (GFGA)
DESAC........	Destroyer SONAR Analysis Center [*Navy*] (NVT)
DESAD........	Diethylstilbestrol Adenosis [*Oncology*]
DESAF........	Destroyers, Asiatic Fleet [*Navy*]
Desai.........	Handbook of Criminal Cases [*India*] [*A publication*] (DLA)
DESAL........	Desalinization (ABBR)
De Sanctis Stor Rom...	De Sanctis, Storia dei Romani [*1907-1966*] [*A publication*] (OCD)
DESAT........	Defense Small Business Advanced Technology Program
DESAT........	Desaturated (NASA)
Desaus........	Desaussure. South Carolina Equity Reports [*A publication*] (DLA)
Desaus Eq...	Desaussure. South Carolina Equity Reports [*A publication*] (DLA)
DESB..........	Desborough [*England*]
DESB..........	Devereux Elementary School Behavior [*Rating scale*] [*Psychology*]
DESBATFOR...	Destroyer Battle Force [*Navy*]
DESC..........	Data Entry System Controller
DESC..........	Defense Electronics Supply [*or Support*] Center [*DSA*]
DESC..........	Descend
DESC..........	Descendant (WDAA)
DESC..........	Descent (NASA)

DESC..........	Description (MCD)
DESC..........	Digital Equation-Solving Computer (IEEE)
DESc..........	Doctor of Economic Science (DD)
DE Sc.........	Doctor of Engineering Science
DESC..........	Dry Etching Station Computerized [*Graphic arts*] (DGA)
DESC & D....	Descent and Distribution [*Legal term*] (DLA)
DESCDT......	Descendant
DESCHA......	Destination Change [*Military*] (NVT)
DESCNET....	Data Network on Environmentally Significant Chemicals (DCTA)
DESCOFOR...	Destroyer Scouting Force [*Navy*]
DESCOM......	Depot Systems Command [*Army*] (RDA)
DESCP........	Description (MSA)
DESCR........	Describe (KSC)
DESCR........	Other Abnormal Morphology [*On differential*] [*Biochemistry*] (DAVI)
DESCRD......	Described (ROG)
De Script Eccles Proleg...	De Scriptoribus Ecclesiasticis Prolegomena [*of St. Jerome*] [*Classical studies*] (OCD)
DESCRON....	Description
DESCRPN....	Description (ABBR)
DESCRUPAC...	Destroyers/Cruisers, Pacific Fleet [*Navy*]
DescSA.......	Desc SA de CV [*Associated Press*] (SAG)
DESCSD......	Directorate of Evaluation, Standardization, Concepts, Studies and Doctrine [*Army*]
DESDEVDIV...	Destroyer Development Division [*Navy*] (DNAB)
DESDEVGRU...	Destroyer Development Group [*Navy*]
DESDEVRON...	Destroyer Development Squadron [*Navy*] (DNAB)
DESDIV.......	Destroyer Division [*Navy*]
DESEFF.......	Deserter's Effects [*Military*]
De Sera......	De Sera Numinis Vindicta [*of Plutarch*] [*Classical studies*] (OCD)
Desert........	Desert Community Bank [*Associated Press*] (SAG)
DESEX........	Deployment Staff Exercise (MCD)
DESFEX.......	Desert Field Exercise [*Military*] (NVT)
DESFIREX....	Desert Firing Exercise [*Military*] (NVT)
DESFLOT.....	Destroyer Flotilla [*Navy*]
DESFLTSURG...	Designated Student and Naval Flight Surgeon (DNAB)
DESFTD.......	Department of Employment, Small Firms and Tourism Division [*British*]
DESG..........	Designate (AFM)
DesgnF........	Designer Finance Trust [*Associated Press*] (SAG)
DESI...........	Designated Hitter [*Formerly, DPH*] [*Also, DH Baseball*]
DESI...........	Designs, Inc. [*NASDAQ symbol*] (NQ)
DESI...........	Drug Efficacy Study Implementation Notice [*Food and Drug Administration*]
DESID........	Desiderata (ABBR)
DESID........	Desideratum [*Wanted*] [*Latin*] (ADA)
DESID........	Desired (ABBR)
DESIDER......	Desiderative (ABBR)
DESIG........	Designate [*or Designation*] (KSC)
DESIG........	Designer (ABBR)
DESIGDISBAGENT...	Designated Special Disbursing Agent
DESIGNAP...	Designated as Naval Aviation Pilot [*Marine Corps*]
DesignH.......	Designer Holdings Ltd. [*Associated Press*] (SAG)
Designs......	Designs, Inc. [*Associated Press*] (SAG)
DESILU.......	Desi-Lucille Arnaz Co.
DESIR........	Direct English Statement Information Retrieval [*Military*]
DESIS........	Desertification Information System [*UNEP*] [*United Nations*] (DUND)
DeskTopDt...	Desktop Data, Inc. [*Associated Press*] (SAG)
DESL..........	Diesel (ABBR)
DESL..........	Double-Ended Suction Leg Slot [*Nuclear energy*] (NRCH)
DESLANT....	Destroyer Force, Atlantic Fleet [*Navy symbol*]
DESMC.......	Department of Defense Systems Management Center (MCD)
DESMO.......	DoD [*Department of Defense*] Logistics Data Element Standardization and Management Office
DESNAVAV...	Designated Student Naval Aviator
DESO..........	De Soto National Memorial
DESO..........	District Educational Services Officer [*Navy*]
DESOIL.......	Diesel Oil
De Soll An...	De Sollertia Animalium [*of Plutarch*] [*Classical studies*] (OCD)
DESOMS......	Deaf Sons of Master Masons
DeSoto........	DeSoto, Inc. [*Associated Press*] (SAG)
DESP..........	Department of Elementary School Principals [*of NEA*] (EA)
DESP..........	Despatch
DESP..........	Primeros Puestos del Deporte Espanol [*Ministerio de Cultura*] [*Spain Information service or system*] (CRD)
DESPAC......	Destroyer Force, Pacific Fleet [*Navy symbol*]
De Spect.....	De Spectaculis [*of Tertullian*] [*Classical studies*] (OCD)
DESPORT....	Daily Equipment Status Report [*Army*] (AABC)
DESPOT......	Design Performance Optimization (NASA)
DESR..........	Daily Effective Supply Rate (MCD)
DESRAD......	Desiccant-Enhanced Radiative Cooling [*Solar-cooling concept*]
Des RCA......	Diploma of Designer, Royal College of Art [*British*]
DESREP......	Destroyer Repair [*Navy*]
DESREP......	Destroyer Representative [*Navy*]
DESROC......	Destroyer Rocket
DESRON......	Destroyer Squadron [*Navy*]
DESRT........	Demonstration of Site Remediation Technology [*Environmental science*]
DESS..........	Department of Economics and Social Science [*MIT*] (MCD)
Dess..........	Dessaussure's Equity [*South Carolina*] [*A publication*] (DLA)
DESS..........	Destroyer Schoolship [*Navy*]
Dessaus......	Dessaussure's Equity [*South Carolina*] [*A publication*] (DLA)
DesScEco....	Docteur es Sciences Economiques (DD)
DESSIM.......	Defense System Simulator
DESSIM.......	Design Simulator
D Es S LJ....	Dar Es Salaam Law Journal [*A publication*] (DLA)

DESSOWESPAC... Destroyers, Southwest Pacific Fleet [Navy]
D Es S ULJ... Dar Es Salaam University. Law Journal [A publication] (DLA)
DeST........... Delaware Technical and Community College, Stanton Campus, Newark, DE [Library symbol Library of Congress] (LCLS)
DEST........... Denver Eye Screening Test
DEST........... Destillata [Distilled] [Pharmacy]
DEST........... Destination (AABC)
DEST........... Destra [Right] [Italian]
DEST........... Destroy (AABC)
DEST........... Destroyer [Navy British]
DEST........... Destruct (KSC)
DEST........... Dichotic Environmental Sounds Test [Medicine] (DMAA)
Dest Cal Dig... Desty's California Digest [A publication] (DLA)
Dest Com & Nav... Desty on Commerce and Navigation [A publication] (DLA)
DEST-DIST... Destructively Distilled
Destec........ Destec Energy [Associated Press] (SAG)
DESTECH..... Design and Technology in Education (AIE)
Dest Fed Cit... Desty's Federal Citations [A publication] (DLA)
Dest Fed Cons... Desty on the Federal Constitution [A publication] (DLA)
Dest Fed Proc... Desty's Federal Procedure [A publication] (DLA)
DESTIL........ Destilla [Distill] [Pharmacy] (ROG)
DESTIN .... Destination (DNAB)
DESTN .... Destination
DESTR .... Desires to Transfer (NOAA)
DESTR .... Destroyed [or Destructor] (AAG)
destr .... Destroyed (VRA)
DESTR FIR... Destructive Firing (SAA)
Dest Sh & Adm... Desty on Shipping and Admiralty [A publication] (DLA)
Desty Tax'n... Desty on Taxation [A publication] (DLA)
DESUBEX..... Destroyer/Submarine Antisubmarine Warfare Exercise [Military] (NVT)
De Superst... De Superstitione [of Plutarch] [Classical studies] (OCD)
Deswell....... Deswell Industries, Inc. [Associated Press] (SAG)
Deswll........ Deswell Industries, Inc. [Associated Press] (SAG)
DET............. Damage Evaluation Team (SAA)
DET............. Delta Aviation SA [Spain ICAO designator] (FAAC)
DET............. Department of Employment and Training [Victoria] [Australia]
DET............. Design Evaluation Test
DET............. Detach
Det............. Detachable (DLA)
DET............. Detachment
DET............. Detail
det............. Detail (VRA)
DET............. Detainee
DET............. Detection [or Detector] (AFM)
DET............. Detective
DET............. Determine
DET............. Detent [Mechanical Engineering] (NASA)
DET............. Detergent (ROG)
DET............. Determination [or Determine] (KSC)
DET............. Determinative (ROG)
DET............. Determiner [Linguistics]
DET............. Detonator (MSA)
DET............. Detroit [City in Michigan] (ROG)
DET............. Detroit [Michigan] City Airport [Airport symbol] (OAG)
DET............. Detur [Give] [Pharmacy]
DET............. Device Error Tabulation [Computer science] (IAA)
DET............. Diesel Electric Tandem Motor Drive
DET............. Diesel Electric Trawler (IAA)
DET............. Diethyltartarate [Organic chemistry]
DET............. Diethyltoluamide [Also, DETA] [Insect repellant] [Organic chemistry]
DET............. Diffusive Equilibration in a Thin-Film [Physical chemistry]
DET............. Digital Event Timer (KSC)
DET............. Dimethyltryptamine [A hallucinogenic drug]
DET............. Direct Energy Transfer
DET............. Displaced Equipment Training [DoD]
DET............. Distributed Explosive Technologies [Military] (DOMA)
DET............. Domestic Escorted Tour [Travel]
DET............. Double Eagle Energy [Vancouver Stock Exchange symbol]
DET............. Double Electron Transfer (MCD)
DET............. Double End Trimmed (DAC)
DET............. Dust Erosion Tunnel (MCD)
Det............. Quod Deterius Potiori Insidiari Soleat [Philo] (BJA)
DE/TA.......... Department of Employment / Training Agency [British]
DETA.......... Dielectric Thermal Analysis
DETA.......... Diethylenetriamine [Also, DTA] [Organic chemistry]
DETA.......... Diethyltoluamide [Also, DET] [Insect repellant] [Organic chemistry]
DETA.......... Divisao de Exploracao dos Transportes Aereos [Angolan airline]
DETAB........ Decision Table [Computer science]
DETABGT.... Decision Table General Translator [Computer science] (IAA)
DETAB-X..... Decision Table, Experimental [Computer science]
DETAC........ Digital Equipment Technology Analysis Center (MCD)
DETALL....... Detached from Duty Indicated and from All Other Duty Assigned
DETAP........ Decision Table Processor [IBM Corp.]
Det BJ........ Detroit Bar Journal [A publication] (DLA)
DETC.......... Dendritic Epidermal T Cell [Biochemistry]
DETC.......... Detection Systems [NASDAQ symbol] (TTSB)
DETC.......... Detection Systems, Inc. [NASDAQ symbol] (NQ)
DETC.......... Diethylthiacarbocyanine [Organic chemistry]
DETC.......... Digital Element Tester Console (MCD)
DETC.......... Distance Education and Training Counsel [Formerly National Home Study Council (NHSC)] (PAZ)
DetCan....... Detroit & Canada Tunnel Corp. [Associated Press] (SAG)
detch .... Detached (VRA)
DET CON..... Detective Constable [Scotland Yard] [British] (ADA)

DETD .... Detached Duty (DNAB)
DETD .... Determined
DetDiesl ..... Detroit Diesel Corp. [Associated Press] (SAG)
DetE........... Detroit Edison Co. [Associated Press] (SAG)
DETe.......... Diethyltelluride
DETE.......... Distributed Electronic Telephone Exchange [Telecommunications] (PDAA)
DetE25........ Detroit Edison Co. [Associated Press] (SAG)
DetE26........ Detroit Edison Co. [Associated Press] (SAG)
DETEC....... Detection (KSC)
DETED .... Determined (ROG)
DetEd......... Detroit Edison Co. [Associated Press] (SAG)
DETEN .... Detention (DSUE)
DETEQ....... DECHEMA [Deutsche Gesellschaft fuer Chemisches Apparatewesen, Chemische Technik, und Biotechnologie eV] Environmental Technology Equipment Databank [Information service or system Germany] (IID)
DETER........ Determination (KSC)
DETERMD.... Determined (ROG)
DETERME ... Determine (ROG)
determin..... Determination
DETERMN ... Determination [Legal term] (ROG)
DETERS...... Damage Tolerant/Easy Repair Structures (MCD)
DETES........ Deep-Towed Explosive Source [Seismology]
DETEST...... Demystify the Established Standardized Tests [Project]
DETF.......... Data Exchange Test Facility (DA)
DETG .... Defense Energy Task Group (DNAB)
DETHERM.... DECHEMA [Deutsche Gesellschaft fuer Chemisches Apparatewesen, Chemische Technik, und Biotechnologie eV] Thermophysical Property Data Bank [Germany Information service or system] (CRD)
DETHERM-SDC... DECHEMA [Deutsche Gesellschaft fuer Chemisches Apparatewesen, Chemische Technik, und Biotechnologie eV] Thermophysical Property Data Bank - Data Evaluation System [Database]
DETHERM-SDR... DECHEMA [Deutsche Gesellschaft fuer Chemisches Apparatewesen, Chemische Technik, und Biotechnologie eV] Thermophysical Property Data Bank - Data RetrievalSystem [Database]
Det in 2 Plo... Detur in Duplo [Let Twice as Much Be Given] [Pharmacy] (DAVI)
Det in Dup... Detur in Duplo [Let Twice as Much Be Given] [Pharmacy] (DAVI)
DET INSP..... Detective Inspector [Scotland Yard] [British] (ADA)
DETIR......... Defense Technology Information Repository (MCD)
Det Leg N ... Detroit Legal News [A publication] (DLA)
Det LJ........ Detroit Law Journal [A publication] (DLA)
Det L Rev ... Detroit Law Review [A publication] (DLA)
DETM......... Determine (AABC)
Detmt......... Detachment [British military] (DMA)
DETN .... Detection (NASA)
DETN .... Detention (MSA)
DETN .... Determination
DETO .... Devils Tower National Monument
DETO .... Dyestuffs Environmental and Toxicology Organization
DETOC....... Decision Table to COBOL [Common Business-Oriented Language] Processor [Computer science]
DETOL....... Directly Executable Test-Oriented Language [1968] [Computer science] (CSR)
DE-TO PR .... Derated Takeoff Engine Pressure Ratio (GAVI)
DETOX....... Detoxification (DSUE)
DETOX....... Wet Oxidation Waste Treatment Technology (DOGT)
DETP......... Department of Environmental and Toxicologic Pathology [An association] (EA)
DETP.......... Diethylenetriaminepentaacetic Acid [Also, DETPA, DTPA] [Chelating agent]
DETP.......... Displaced Equipment Training Plan [DoD]
DETPA .... Diethylenetriaminepentaacetic Acid [Also, DETP, DTPA] [Chelating agent]
DETR .... Detector
DETR .... Detrimental (AABC)
DETRAH....... Detrahatur [Let It, or Them, Be Drawn] [Pharmacy] (ROG)
DETRAHAT... Detrahatur [Let It, or Them, Be Drawn] [Pharmacy] (ROG)
DETRAN...... Decision Table Translator [Computer science]
DETRAN...... Decision Translator (NITA)
De Tranq Anim... De Tranquillitate Animi [of Plutarch] [Classical studies] (OCD)
DETRESFA.... Distress Phase [Aviation]
DETRINS..... Detailed Routing Instructions (NATG)
Detroit BQ ... Detroit Bar Quarterly [A publication] (DLA)
Detroit C Law... Detroit College of Law (GAGS)
Detroit Coll L... Detroit College of Law [Michigan] (DLA)
Detroit L..... Detroit Lawyer [A publication] (DLA)
Detroit Leg N... Detroit Legal News [A publication] (DLA)
Detroit L J... Detroit Law Journal [A publication] (DLA)
Detroit L Rev... Detroit Law Review [A publication] (DLA)
DetrxC........ Detrex Corp. [Associated Press] (SAG)
D et S.......... Detur et Signatur [Let It Be Given and Labeled] [Pharmacy]
D et S.......... Detur et Signatur [Let It Be Given and Labeled] [Pharmacy] (DAVI)
DETS.......... Digital Element Test Set
DET SGT...... Detective Sergeant [Scotland Yard] [British] (ADA)
DetSys........ Detection Systems, Inc. [Associated Press] (SAG)
D'ETTE........ Dinette [Classified advertising] (ADA)
DETU.......... Diethylthiourea [Organic chemistry]
DETW......... Detroit & Western [Later, DW] [AAR code]
DEU .... Data Encoder Unit
DEU .... Data Encryption Unit
DEU .... Data Entry Unit

DEU .... Data Exchange Unit
deu .... Delaware [*MARC country of publication code Library of Congress*] (LCCP)
DEU .... Digital Evaluation Unit
DEU .... Display Electronics Unit (NASA)
DEU .... Duplicates Exchange Union (EA)
DEU .... Federal Republic of Germany [*ANSI three-letter standard code*] (CNC)
DeU .... University of Delaware, Newark, DE [*Library symbol Library of Congress*] (LCLS)
DEUA .... Digitronics Equipment Users Association
DeU-Ag .... University of Delaware, Agricultural Experiment Station, Newark, DE [*Library symbol Library of Congress*] (LCLS)
DEUC .... Division of End Use Conservation [*Energy Research and Development Administration*]
DEUCE .... Deployable Universal Combat Earthmover (RDA)
DEUCE .... Digital Electronic Universal Calculating [*or Computing*] Engine
DEurL .... Doctor of European Law (DD)
DEUS .... Dual Energy Use System
Deus .... Quod Deus Immutabilis Sit [*Philo*] (BJA)
DEUT .... Data Encoder Unit Transmitter
Deut .... Deuteronomy [*Old Testament book*]
DeutR .... Deuteronomy Rabba (BJA)
Deut Tel ...... Deutsche Telekom AG [*Associated Press*] (SAG)
DEV .... Delay Equalizer, Variable (IAA)
DEV............ Denver Silver [*Vancouver Stock Exchange symbol*]
DEV............ Derecha Emergente de Venezuela [*Political party*] (EY)
DEV............ Design Evaluation Vehicle
DEV............ Deva [*Romania*] [*Seismograph station code, US Geological Survey*] (SEIS)
dev............ Devant [*Front*] (BARN)
DEV .... Develop [*or Development*] (AFM)
Dev .... Development (AAGC)
DEV .... Development
Dev .... Devereux's North Carolina Law Reports [*A publication*] (DLA)
Dev .... Devereux's Reports, United States Court of Claims [*A publication*] (DLA)
DEV............ Deviation (AAG)
DEV............ Device (KSC)
DEV............ Devjo Industries, Inc. [*Toronto Stock Exchange symbol*]
DEV............ Devonian [*Geology*]
Dev .... Devonshire County [*England*] (BARN)
DEV............ Director [*or Directorate*] of Evaluation [*Army*]
DEV............ Duck Egg Virus [*or Duck Embryo Vaccine*] [*Immunology*]
DEV............ Red Devils Parachute Display Team [*British ICAO designator*] (FAAC)
DEVA .... Death Valley National Monument
DEVA .... Development Acceptance (AABC)
DEVA .... Development Validation Acceptance
DEVA .... Drone Employment Value Analysis (MCD)
DEVA IPR ...... Demonstration and Validation In-Process Review
DEVAIPR ...... Development Acceptance in Process Review (RDA)
Dev & B ...... Devereux and Battle's North Carolina Equity Reports [*A publication*] (DLA)
Dev & B ...... Devereux and Battle's North Carolina Law Reports [*A publication*] (DLA)
Dev & Bat.... Devereux and Battle's North Carolina Law Reports [*A publication*] (DLA)
Dev & Bat Eq... Devereux and Battle's North Carolina Equity Reports [*A publication*] (DLA)
Dev & B Eq... Devereux and Battle's North Carolina Equity Reports [*A publication*] (DLA)
Dev & BL (NC)... Devereux and Battle's North Carolina Law Reports [*A publication*] (DLA)
DEVAT .... Depot Vehicle Automatic Tester
DeVBul .... DeVlieg Bullard, Inc. [*Associated Press*] (SAG)
DeVBul .... DeVlieg Bullard, Inc. [*Associated Press*] (SAG)
DEVC .... Devcon International [*NASDAQ symbol*] (TTSB)
DEVC .... Devcon International Corp. [*NASDAQ symbol*] (NQ)
DEVC .... Development Change [*Aerospace*] (AAG)
Dev CC .... Devereux's Reports, United States Court of Claims [*A publication*] (DLA)
DEVCO .... Development Committee [*ISO*] (DS)
DEVCOM ...... Device Communications [*Computer science*]
Devcon .... Devcon International Corp. [*Associated Press*] (SAG)
Dev Ct Cl .... Devereux's Reports, United States Court of Claims [*A publication*] (DLA)
DEVCTR ...... Development Center (MCD)
DevD.......... Developers Diversified Realty Corp. [*Associated Press*] (SAG)
DEVD .... Devilled [*Culinary*] (ROG)
DEVD .... Devised (ROG)
Dev Deeds... Devlin on Deeds and Real Estate [*A publication*] (DLA)
DEVE.......... Devise (ROG)
DEVEL .... Development
devel .... Development (DD)
Developing Ed... Developing Education [*A publication*]
Dev Eq........ Devereux's North Carolina Equity Reports [*A publication*] (DLA)
DevG.......... Devisengesetz [*Law on Exchange Control*] [*German*] (DLA)
DEV GENC ... Federation of Turkish Revolutionary Youth
DEV HGT...... Developed Height (MSA)
DEVIL .... Development of Integrated Logistics (NATG)
DEVIL .... Direct Evaluation of Indexed Language (IAA)
De Vir III .... De Viris Illustribus [*of St. Jerome*] [*Classical studies*] (OCD)
Dev Kin Bl.... Devereux's Kinne's Blackstone [*A publication*] (DLA)
Dev Kin Kent... Devereux's Kinne's Kent [*A publication*] (DLA)

Dev L .... Devereux's North Carolina Law Reports [*A publication*] (DLA)
Devl Deeds... Devlin on Deeds [*A publication*] (DLA)
DevlDv........ Developers Diversified Realty Corp. [*Associated Press*] (SAG)
DEVLPMNTL... Developmental
DEVLPMT...... Development
DEVLPMTL.... Developmental
DEVN .... Deviation (MSA)
DEVN .... Devon Group [*NASDAQ symbol*] (TTSB)
DEVN .... Devon Group, Inc. [*NASDAQ symbol*] (NQ)
DevnE........ Devon Energy Corp. [*Associated Press*] (SAG)
DEVNET ...... Development Information Network [*United Nations*] (NITA)
DEVNO........ Deviation Request Number (DNAB)
DEVO .... De-Evolution [*Acronym is name of musical group*]
Devon .... Devon Group, Inc. [*Associated Press*] (SAG)
DEVON .... Devonshire [*County in England*]
Devons .... Devonshire [*County in England*]
Devpt .... Development
DEVR .... Distortion-Eliminating Voltage Regulator
DEVR .... Dominant Exudative Vitreoretinopathy [*Ophthalmology*] (DAVI)
DeVry .... DeVry, Inc. [*Associated Press*] (SAG)
DEVS .... Devotions
DEVS .... DODAAC [*Department of Defense Activity Address Code*] Edit/Validation System [*Military*]
DEVSIS .... Development Sciences Information System [*Information service or system Canada*] (IID)
DEVT.......... Data-Entry Virtual Terminal [*Computer science*]
DEVT.......... Developed Technology Resource [*NASDAQ symbol*] (TTSB)
DEVT.......... Development
Devt Assoc Bull... Development Association. Bulletin [*A publication*]
DEVTOS ...... Developmental Tactical Operations Systems (MCD)
Devts Mfuring Ind... Developments in Manufacturing Industry [*A publication*]
DEV WD...... Developed Width (MSA)
DEW.......... Delmarva Power & Light Co. [*NYSE symbol*] (SPSG)
DEW.......... Delmarva Power Financing I [*NYSE symbol*] (SAG)
DEW.......... Delmarva Pwr & Lt [*NYSE symbol*] (TTSB)
Dew .... Dewey's Kansas Court of Appeals Reports [*A publication*] (DLA)
Dew .... Dewey's Reports [*60-70 Kansas*] [*A publication*] (DLA)
DEW.......... Digital Encyclopedia Workstation [*Medinfo 86*]
DEW.......... Directed Energy Warfare [*Army*] (INF)
DEW.......... Directed Energy Weapon
DEW.......... Distant Early Warning [*North American RADAR system*] [*Obsolete*]
DEW.......... Division Early Warning [*Army*] (INF)
DEWA .... Delaware Water Gap National Recreation Area
DeWAt .... Atlas Chemical Industries, Inc., Wilmington, DE [*Library symbol Library of Congress*] (LCLS)
DEWAT .... Deactivated War Trophy (DICI)
DeWB .... Brandywine College, Wilmington, DE [*Library symbol Library of Congress*] (LCLS)
DEWCOM..... Divisional Electronic Warfare Combat (MCD)
DEWCOM T & E... Divisional Electronic Warfare Combat Model Test and Evaluation
DEWD .... Detailed Elementary Wiring Diagrams
Dew Div...... Dewey on Divorce Law [*A publication*] (DLA)
DeWDJ .... E. I. Du Pont de Nemours & Co., Jackson Laboratory, Wilmington, DE [*Library symbol Library of Congress*] (LCLS)
DeWDL .... E. I. Du Pont de Nemours & Co., Lavoisier Library, Wilmington, DE [*Library symbol Library of Congress*] (LCLS)
DeWDT .... E. I. Du Pont de Nemours & Co., Technical Library, Wilmington, DE [*Library symbol Library of Congress*] (LCLS)
D'Ewes J .... D'Ewes' Journal and Parliamentary Collection [*A publication*] (DLA)
DeWH.......... Hercules Powder Co. [*Later, Hercules, Inc.*], Experiment Station, Wilmington,DE [*Library symbol Library of Congress*] (LCLS)
DeWHI .... Hercules, Inc., Wilmington, DE [*Library symbol Library of Congress*] (LCLS)
DEWI .... Direct Environmental Warming Impact
DeWI .... Wilmington Institute Free Library and the New Castle County Free Library, Wilmington, DE [*Library symbol Library of Congress*] (LCLS)
DEWIFAS ..... Divisional Electronic Warfare Intelligence Functional Analysis (MCD)
DeWint .... Henry Francis DuPont Winterthur Museum, Winterthur, DE [*Library symbol Library of Congress*] (LCLS)
DeWint-M.... Henry Francis DuPont Winterthur Museum, Joseph Downs Manuscript and Microfilm Collection, Winterthur, DE [*Library symbol Library of Congress*] (LCLS)
DeWitt .... DeWitt's Reports [*24-42 Ohio State*] [*A publication*] (DLA)
DEWIZ .... Distant Early Warning Identification Zone [*North American RADAR system*] [*Obsolete*]
DEWK .... Dual Employed, with Kids [*Lifestyle classification*]
DEWKS .... Dual Employed With Kids (DFIT)
DEW LINE.... Distant Early Warning Line [*North American RADAR system*] [*Obsolete*]
DeWolfe ...... [*The*] DeWolfe Cos., Inc. [*Associated Press*] (SAG)
DEWPO........ Distant Early Warning Project Office [*North American RADAR System*] [*Obsolete*] (IAA)
Dew St........ Dewey's Compiled Statutes of Michigan [*A publication*] (DLA)
DEWSUM.... Distant Early Warning Summary (MCD)
DeWT.......... Delaware Technical and Community College, Northern Campus, Wilmington, DE [*Library symbol Library of Congress*] (LCLS)
DeWTC .... Third Circuit Court of Appeals, Wilmington, DE [*Library symbol Library of Congress*] (LCLS)
DEWTRG...... Dewatering (MSA)
DEW-V .... Directed Energy Weapons - Vehicle [*Army*]
DeWV .... United States Veterans Administration Center, Wilmington, DE [*Library symbol Library of Congress*] (LCLS)
DEX............ Data Exchange
DEX............ Decision Expediting [*Graphic Sciences, Inc., copying machine*]

DEX............	Deferred Execution
DEX............	Destroyer Escort Experimental (MCD)
DEX............	Dexamethasone [*Also, D, DXM*] [*Antineoplastic drug*]
DEX............	Dexamphetamine Sulfate Tablet [*Slang*] (DSUE)
DEX............	Dexedrine
DEX............	Dexter [*Right*] [*Latin*] (ROG)
DEX............	[*The*] Dexter Corp. [*NYSE symbol*] (SPSG)
DEX............	Dextran [*Organic chemistry*]
dex.............	Dextrorotatory (DOG)
dex.............	Dextrose [*Pharmacology*] (DAVI)
dex.............	Dextro-Stix [*Pharmacology*] (DAVI)
D Ex............	Doctor of Expression
DEX............	Double Exposure
DEX............	Interflight, Inc. [*ICAO designator*] (FAAC)
DEXA...........	Dual Energy X-Ray Absorptiometry [*Analytical chemistry*]
DEXAN........	Digital Experimental Airborne Navigator
DEXGAL.......	Dexamethasonyl Galactoside [*Biochemistry*]
DEXGLU......	Dexamthasonyl Glucopyranoside [*Biochemistry*]
D/EXH........	Dual Exhaust [*Automotive engineering*]
DEXIE.........	Dexedrine
DEXT...........	Dexter [*Right*] [*Latin*]
DEXT...........	Distant End Cross-Talk [*Telecommunications*] (NITA)
DEXTER.......	Dental X-Ray Teaching and Training Replica
Dexter.........	[*The*] Dexter Corp. [*Associated Press*] (SAG)
DEXTOR......	Deep Experimental Torpedo [*Also, DSWS*] [*Later, EXTOR*] (MCD)
DEZ............	Deir Ez Zor [*Syria*] [*Airport symbol*] (OAG)
DEZ............	Derekh 'Erets Zuta [*or Derek Erez Zuta*] (BJA)
DEZ............	Diethyl Zinc [*Used for deacidification of paper to arrest book decay*]
DEZ............	Docklands Enterprise Zone [*British*]
DF..............	Air Nebraska [*ICAO designator*] (AD)
DF..............	Associate Directorate for Facilities and Systems Management [*Kennedy Space Center*] [*NASA*] (NASA)
DF..............	Daedalian Foundation (EA)
DF..............	Damage Free [*Business term*]
DF..............	Damping Factor
DF..............	Danny Foundation (EA)
DF..............	Data Field [*Computer science*]
DF..............	Data Folder
DF..............	Date Filed [*IRS*]
DF..............	Day Frequency (IAA)
DF..............	Daylight Factor (DAC)
DF..............	Dead Freight [*Shipping*]
DF..............	Dean Foods [*NYSE symbol*] (TTSB)
DF..............	Dean Foods Co. [*NYSE symbol*] (SPSG)
DF..............	Dean of the Faculty
DF..............	Decapacitation Factor [*with reference to sperm*] [*Medicine*]
DF..............	Decayed and Filled [*Dentistry*] (DAVI)
DF..............	Decimal Factor (MCD)
DF..............	Decimal Fraction (MDG)
DF..............	Decontamination Facility
DF..............	Decontamination Factor
DF..............	Deere Funk [*Automotive industry supplier*]
DF..............	Defence Fellowship [*British*]
DF..............	Defensive Fire
DF..............	Defensor Fidei [*Defender of the Faith*] [*Latin*]
DF..............	Deferoxamine [*Also, Desferrioxamine*] [*Chelating agent*]
DF..............	Deficiency Factor (MAE)
DF..............	Defined Flora Animal [*Medicine*] (DMAA)
DF..............	Definition
DF..............	Deflection Factor (IEEE)
DF..............	Defogging (AAG)
DF..............	Degrees Fahrenheit (KSC)
DF..............	Degrees of Freedom [*of movement*]
D/F.............	Degrees of Freedom (DOG)
DF..............	Deionization-Filtration
DF..............	Delay Fuse
DF..............	Democracy Fund [*Defunct*] (EA)
DF..............	Dense Flint (AAG)
DF..............	Deposition Form [*Army*] (ADDR)
DF..............	Depot Fixed (AAG)
DF..............	Depreciation Factor (IAA)
DF..............	Depth of Field [*or Focus*] [*Photography*]
DF..............	Derating Factor
DF..............	Derivation of Frequency with Respect to Time (IAA)
DF..............	Dermatology Foundation (EA)
DF..............	Describing Function
DF..............	Desferrioxamine [*Deferoxamine*] [*Pharmacology*] (DAVI)
DF..............	Design Formula
DF..............	Destination Field
DF..............	Destroyer Flotilla [*Navy*]
DF..............	Detailed Forecast (MCD)
DF..............	Deterioration Factor [*Automotive engineering*]
DF..............	Deutereium Fluoride (IEEE)
DF..............	Development Fixture (MCD)
DF..............	Development Flight (NASA)
DF..............	Development-Forward (MCD)
DF..............	Development Fund
DF..............	Device Flag [*Computer science*]
DF..............	Device Function [*Computer science*] (IAA)
DF..............	Diabetic Father [*Medicine*]
DF..............	Dialogue Foundation (EA)
DF..............	Dialysis Fluid [*Physiology*]
DF..............	Dialyzable Fraction
DF..............	Diamond Flap [*Envelopes*]
DF..............	Dicke-Fix [*Electronics*]
DF..............	Diesel Fuel [*or Fueled*] (CINC)
DF..............	Dietary Fiber [*Nutrition*]
DF..............	Differential Frequency (IAA)
DF..............	Differentiation Factor [*Biochemistry*]
DF..............	Dilution Factor [*Also, Fd*] [*Nuclear energy*] (NRCH)
DF..............	Dimensional Flowcharting [*Computer science*]
DF..............	Dirac-Fock Theory [*Electrodynamics*]
DF..............	Direct Flight (MCD)
DF..............	Direct Flow
DF..............	Direct Fluorescence
DF..............	Direction Finder [*or Finding*] [*Radio aid to navigation*]
df...............	Direction Finding (IDOE)
DF..............	Disaccommodation Factor
DF..............	Disassembly Facility [*NASA*] (NASA)
DF..............	Discharge Flow [*Chemical kinetics*]
DF..............	Discriminant Function [*Physiology*]
DF..............	Discrimination Filter (AAG)
DF..............	Disk File [*Computer science*] (BUR)
DF..............	Dislocated Farmer [*Job Training and Partnership Act*] (OICC)
DF..............	Disposition Form [*Army*]
DF..............	Disseminated Foci [*Medicine*]
DF..............	Dissipation Factor
DF..............	Distortion Factor [*Telecommunications*] (IAA)
DF..............	Distribution Factor
DF..............	Distribution Feeder [*Telecommunications*] (OA)
DF..............	Distribution Frame (KSC)
DF..............	Distribution Function [*Statistics*]
DF..............	Ditchley Foundation (EA)
DF..............	Diva Foundation (EA)
DF..............	Diversity Factor
DF..............	Diverted Force (CINC)
DF..............	Doctor of Forestry
DF..............	Dong Feng [*East Wind*] [*Chinese missile*]
DF..............	Don't Fragment [*Telecommunications jargon*] (ACRL)
DF..............	Door in Flat [*Theater*]
DF..............	Dorsal Fold
DF..............	Dorsiflexion [*Medicine*]
DF..............	Dose Factor [*Radioactivity calculations*]
DF..............	Double Feeder [*Line*] [*Technical drawings*]
DF..............	Double Foolscap [*Paper*] (ADA)
DF..............	Double Frequency
D-F.............	Double-Fronted
DF..............	Douglas Fir (MSA)
DF..............	Draft (ADA)
DF..............	Drag Friction
DF..............	Dream Factory (EA)
DF..............	Drinking Fountain (AAG)
DF..............	Drive Fit [*Technical drawings*]
DF..............	Drop Forge (KSC)
DF..............	Dual Facility
DF..............	Duty Factor [*Military*] (CAAL)
DF..............	Duty Free [*Customs*]
DF..............	Dye-Free [*Pharmacy*]
DF..............	Dynamic Fermenter [*Microbiology*]
DF..............	Dysautonomia Foundation (EA)
DF..............	Fallout Forecast Data [*Civil Defense*]
DFA............	Aero Coach Aviation International, Inc. [*ICAO designator*] (FAAC)
DFA............	Dance Films Association (EA)
DFA............	Defense Fisheries Administration [*Abolished, 1953*]
DFA............	Department for the Arts [*Western Australia*] [*Australia*]
DFA............	Department of Food and Agriculture [*Victoria*] [*Australia*]
DFA............	Department of Foreign Affairs (CINC)
DFA............	Deposit Fund Account
DFA............	Describing Function Analyzer [*NASA*]
DFA............	Designated Field Activity [*DoD*]
DFA............	Design Fabrication Assembly
DFA............	Design for Assembly [*Automotive engineering*]
DFA............	Design for Automation [*Manufacturing technology*]
DFA............	Deterministic Finite Automation (MCD)
DFA............	Detonation Fragmentation and Air Blast (SAA)
DFA............	Diamonds Fields Artillery [*British military*] (DMA)
DFA............	Dick Family Association (EA)
DFA............	Die Forged Aluminum
DFA............	Diesel Fuel with an Antarctic Additive
DFA............	Diet for Age [*Medicine*] (DAVI)
DFA............	Digital Fault Analysis
DFA............	Digital Frequency Analyzer
DFA............	Dimensional Fund Advisors [*Fund-management firm*] (ECON)
DFA............	Diploma in Foreign Affairs (ADA)
DFA............	Diploma of Fine Art [*British*]
DFA............	Direct Fluorescent Antibody (Stain) [*Clinical medicine*]
DFA............	Direct Immunofluorescent Assay [*Analytical biochemistry*]
DFA............	Direction Finding Antenna
DFA............	Distributed Function Architecture
DFA............	Dividend Franking Account
DFA............	Division Final Appearance (SAA)
DFA............	Division Freight Agent
DFA............	Doctor of Fine Arts
DFA............	Doctors for Artists (EA)
DFA............	Dominant Feature Analysis
DFA............	Dried Fruit Association of California [*Later, DFA of California*] (EA)
DFA............	Drive Front Axle
DFA............	Driver Fuel Assembly [*Nuclear energy*] (NRCH)
DFA............	Drop Forging Association [*Later, FIA*] (EA)
DFA............	Dummy Fuel Assembly [*Nuclear energy*] (NRCH)

DFA............	Dynamic Force Analysis
DFA............	Partnership for a Drug Free America (EA)
DFAA..........	Dissolved Free Amino Acids
DFAA..........	United States Federal Aviation Administration, Washington, DC [*Library symbol Library of Congress*] (LCLS)
DFAC..........	Dining Facilities Administration Center (MCD)
DFAC..........	Dried Fruit Association of California [*Later, DFA of California*]
DFAD..........	Digital Feature Analysis Data
DFAE..........	Director of Facilities and Engineering [*Military*] (AABC)
DFAED........	Dated Forecast Authorization Equipment Data (MCD)
DFAI...........	Department of Foreign Affairs and Information [*South Africa*]
DFAIR........	Defense Financial and Investment Review [*Pronounced "dee-fair"*] [*DoD*]
DFAM.........	Derived File Access Method [*Computer science*] (PDAA)
DFAMS........	Defense Fuels Automated Management System [*DoD*]
DFAN.........	Dean of the Faculty, Aeronautics [*Air Force Academy*]
DFAn...........	Discriminate Function Analysis
DF & J........	De Gex, Fisher, and Jones' English Chancery Reports [*A publication*] (DLA)
DF & JB.......	De Gex, Fisher, and Jones' English Bankruptcy Reports [*A publication*] (DLA)
DFAO..........	Food and Agricultural Organization of the United Nations, North American Regional Office, Washington, DC [*Library symbol Library of Congress*] (LCLS)
DFAR..........	Daily Field Activity Report
DFARS........	Defense Federal Acquisition Regulation Supplement (RDA)
DFARS........	Department of Defense FAR Supplement [*A publication*] (AAGC)
DFAS..........	Defense Finance and Accounting Service [*DoD*]
DFAST........	Dynamic File Allocation System
DFAT..........	Destination Final Acceptance Test (LAIN)
DFAT..........	Direct Fluorescent Antibody Technique [*Clinical chemistry*]
DFAW.........	Direct Fire Antitank Weapon
DFAWS........	Direct Fire Antitank Weapon System (SAA)
DFAX..........	Diversifax, Inc. [*NASDAQ symbol*] (SAG)
DFB............	Data Flag Branch [*Computer science*] (NITA)
DFB............	Deutsche Frauenbewegung [*German Women's Movement*] [*Germany*] (PPW)
DFB............	Diffusion Brazing
DFB............	Dinitrofluorobenzene [*Also, DNFB, FDNB*] [*Organic chemistry*]
DFB............	Distributed Feedback
DFB............	Distribution Fuse Board (IEEE)
DFB............	Dried Fruits Board [*New South Wales, South Australia, Western Australia*]
DFB............	Dry Film Binder
DFB............	Dysfunctional Uterine Bleeding [*Gynecology*] (DAVI)
DFB-LD.......	Distributed Feedback LASER Diode
DFBM.........	Data Flag Branch Manager [*Computer science*] (NITA)
DFBPT........	Digital Force Balance Pressure Transducer
DFBR..........	Data Flag Branch Register [*Computer science*] (NITA)
DFBW.........	Digital Fly by Wire [*Aviation*]
DFC............	Data Flow Control [*Computer science Telecommunications*] (IBMDP)
DFC............	Data Format Converter
DFC............	De Facto Cases [*Australia A publication*]
DFC............	Desert Fishes Council (EA)
DFC............	Design Field Change (NRCH)
DFC............	Designs for Change (EA)
DFC............	Development Finance Company [*Generic term*] [*Banking*]
DFC............	Devo Fan Club (EA)
DFC............	Diagnostic Flow Chart [*Computer science*] (IEEE)
DFC............	Di'anno Fan Club (EA)
DFC............	Diesel Fuel and Coolant [*Nuclear energy*]
DFC............	Diffusion Formed Coating
DFC............	Digital Fire Control [*Military*] (CAAL)
DFC............	Digital Flight Controller (AAG)
DFC............	Digital Future Coalition
DFC............	Disc File Controller [*Computer science*] (NITA)
DFC............	Disk File Check [*Computer science*]
DFC............	Disk File Control [*Computer science*]
DFC............	Distinguished Flying Cross [*US and British*] [*Military decoration*]
DFC............	Division Forms Control (AAG)
DFC............	Document Flow Component [*Computer science*] (IAA)
DFC............	Dondino Fan Club (EA)
DFC............	Doppler Frequency Converter (MCD)
DFC............	Double Frequency Change (IAA)
DFC............	Double Front Contact [*Photovoltaic energy systems*]
DFC............	Drop Forged Clamp
DFC............	Dry-Filled Capsules [*Pharmacy*]
DFC............	Dual-Feed Carriage (IAA)
DFC............	Dual-Feed Channel (IAA)
DFC............	Dual-Feed Coupler
DFC............	Dust-Free Chamber
DFC............	Dynasty Fan Club (EA)
DFC............	Federal City College [*Later, UDC*], Washington, DC [*Library symbol Library of Congress Obsolete*] (LCLS)
DFC............	Headquarters Defense Communications Agency, Washington, DC [*OCLC symbol*] (OCLC)
DFCA..........	Dual Fault Correction Actuator
DFCA..........	National Fire Prevention and Control Administration, Washington, DC [*Library symbol Library of Congress*] (LCLS)
DFCC..........	Digital Fire Control Computer [*Military*] (MCD)
DFCC..........	United States Federal Communications Commission, Washington, DC [*Library symbol Library of Congress*] (LCLS)
DFCI...........	Dana-Farber Cancer Institute [*Harvard Medical School*] [*Research center*] (RCD)
DFCLS........	Digital Flight Control and Landing System
DFCLT........	Difficult (FAAC)
DFCNV........	Disk Data File Conversion Program [*IBM Corp.*]
DFCO..........	Destron Fearing [*NASDAQ symbol*] (TTSB)
DFCO..........	Destron Fearing Corp. [*NASDAQ symbol*] (SAG)
DFCO..........	Duty Flying Control Officer [*Navy*]
DFCOFP......	Digital Flight Control Operational Flight Program (MCD)
DFCP..........	Division Funding Control Point
DFCS..........	Department of Family and Community Services [*South Australia*]
dFCS..........	Dialyzed Fetal Calf Serum
DFCS..........	Digital Fire Control System [*Military*] (CAAL)
DFCS..........	Digital Flight Control Software [*NASA*] (NASA)
DFCS..........	Digital Flight Control System
DF/CS.........	Direction Finding Control Station (MCD)
DFCS..........	Director Fire Control System [*Air Force*] (MCD)
DFCS..........	Distinguished Federal Civilian Service [*Award*] (RDA)
DFCS..........	Drone Formation Control System [*Military*]
DFCU..........	Disk File Control Unit [*Computer science*]
DFCU..........	Dynamic Flow Control Unit [*Chromatography*]
DFD............	Dancers for Disarmament [*Defunct*] (EA)
DFD............	Data Flow Diagram
DFD............	Data for Development International Association [*See also DD*] [*Marseille, France*] (EAIO)
DFD............	Data Functional Diagram (MCD)
DFD............	Defined Formula Diets [*Dietetics*] (DAVI)
DFD............	Demolition Firing Device
DFD............	Designed for Disassembly [*Product design*]
DFD............	Design-for-Discard [*Engineering*]
DFD............	Digital Flight Display
DFD............	Digital Frequency Discrimination [*Military*] (CAAL)
DFD............	Digital Frequency Display
DFD............	Di-Isopropyl Phosphorofluoridate [*Organic chemistry*] (DAVI)
DFD............	Dogs for Defense [*Organization which trained dogs for armed services*] [*World War II*]
DFDA..........	United States Food and Drug Administration, Bureau of Food, Washington, DC [*Library symbol Library of Congress*] (LCLS)
DFDAT........	Defence Force Discipline Appeal Tribunal [*Australia*]
DFDAU........	Digital Flight Data Acquisition Unit [*Aviation*]
DFDC..........	Defence Force Development Committee [*Australia*]
DFDC..........	Difluorodeoxycytidine [*Biochemistry*]
DFDC..........	Disk File Descriptor Control [*Computer science*]
DFDD..........	Difluoro-Diphenyl-Dichloroethane [*Organic chemistry*] (DAVI)
DFDEL........	Deferred Delivery
DFDHIDWA...	Die Furcht des Herrn Ist der Weisheit Anfang [*Fear of the Lord Is the Beginning of Wisdom*] [(*Ps., CXI. 10) Motto of Dorothee Hedwig, Princess of Anhalt (1587-1608); Johann Sigismund, Elector of Brandenburg (1572-1619)*]
DFDL..........	Dorsal Fin, Depressed Length [*Pisciculture*]
DFDNB........	Difluoro(dinitro)benzene [*Organic chemistry*]
DFDP..........	Distribution-Free Doppler Processor (PDAA)
DFDR..........	Digital Flight-Data Recorder (MCD)
DFDRS........	Digital Flight Data Recording System (MCD)
DFDSS........	Data Facility Data Set Services
DFDT..........	Difluorodiphenyltrichloroethane [*Insecticide*]
DFDT..........	Dynamic Fault Diagnosis Technique (MCD)
DFE............	Data Facility Extended
DFE............	Data Flow Engineer (MCD)
DFE............	Debye-Falkenhagen Effect [*Physics*]
DFE............	Decision Feedback Equalizer (IAA)
DFE............	Department for Education [*British*]
DFE............	Derivative Fighter Engine
DFE............	Desktop Functional Equivalent [*Computer science*]
DFE............	Directed Fan Engine
DFE............	Direction Finding Equipment
DFE............	Directorate of Facilities Engineering [*Military*]
DFE............	Distal Femoral Epiphysis [*Orthopedics*] (DAVI)
DFE............	Division Force Equivalents [*Army*] (AABC)
DFE............	Doctor of Forest Engineering
DFEC..........	Defense Finance Economic Committee (NATG)
DFEC..........	Douglas Fir Export Co. [*Defunct*] (EA)
DF Eng.......	Doctor of Forest Engineering
DFES..........	Doctor of Forestry and Environmental Studies (PGP)
DFES..........	Doctor of Forestry and Environmental Systems (GAGS)
D-FET.........	Depletion (NITA)
DFET..........	Drift Field-Effect Transistor [*Electronics*]
DFEU..........	Disk File Electronics Unit [*Computer science*]
DFF............	Debbie Foe Foundation [*Later, NACH*] (EA)
DFF............	Delay Flip-Flop [*Computer science*] (IAA)
DFF............	Display Format Facility
DFF............	Division Final Fade
DFFC..........	David Frizzell Fan Club (EA)
DFFC..........	Donna Fargo Fan Club [*Later, DFIFC*] (EA)
DFFF..........	Demokratiska Foerbundet av Finlands Folk [*Finnish People's Democratic League*] (PPE)
DFFME........	Direction Finding Frequency Measuring Equipment (IAA)
DFFR..........	Dynamic Forcing Function [*Information*] Report [*Nuclear energy*] (NRCH)
DFG............	Data Flow Graph
DFG............	Difference Frequency Generator (MCD)
DFG............	Digital Function Generator
DFG............	Diode Function Generator
DFG............	Discrete Frequency Generator
DFG............	Display Format Generator (MCD)
DFG............	Freer Gallery of Art, Washington, DC [*Library symbol Library of Congress*] (LCLS)
DF/GA........	Day Fighter/Ground Attack [*British military*] (DMA)

DFGA .... Distributed Floating Gate Amplifier (MCD)
DFGO .... Damn Fool Ground Officer [*Military slang*] (DNAB)
DFGR .... Dual Frequency GPS Receiver
DFGS .... Digital Flight Guidance System (IEEE)
DFGS/C .... Digital Flight Guidance System/Computer (GAVI)
DFH .... Defense Family Housing [*Army*] (AABC)
DFH .... Deployable Field Headquarters
DFH .... Developmental Fast Hydrofoil (MCD)
DFH .... Dollars per Flight Hour (MCD)
DFH .... Dual Filter Hybrid
DFHL .... United States Federal Home Loan Bank Board, Research Library, Washington, DC [*Library symbol Library of Congress*] (LCLS)
DFHMA .... Defense Family-Housing Management Account (DNAB)
DF Hom ...... Diploma of the Faculty of Homoeopathy [*British*]
DFHS .... Dutch Family Heritage Society (EA)
DFHSM .... Data Facility Hierarchical Storage Manager [*IBM Corp.*] (NITA)
DFI .... Dark Field Illumination
DFI .... Decorative Fabrics Institute [*Defunct*] (EA)
DFI .... Decreased Fuel Ingestion
DFI .... Deep Foundations Institute (EA)
DFI .... Defiance, OH [*Location identifier FAA*] (FAAL)
DFI .... Delegationen for Vetenskaplig och Teknisk Informationsforsorjning [*Swedish Delegation for Scientific and Technical Information*] [*Information service or system Defunct*] (IID)
DFI .... Designs for Information
DFI .... Developmental Flight Instrumentation [*NASA*]
DFI .... Diabetes Foundation, Inc. [*Later, JDC*]
DFI .... Dialogue with People of Living Faith and Ideologies [*A publication*] (BJA)
DFI .... Differential Fluorescence Induction [*Analytic biochemistry*]
DFI .... Digitally Fuel-Injected [*Automotive engineering*]
DFI .... Direct Foreign Investment
DFI .... Direct Fourier Inversion [*Mathematics*]
DFI .... Direct Fuel Injection [*Automotive engineering*]
DF I .... Direction Finding, Phase I [*Course*] [*Military*] (DNAB)
DFI .... Directorate for the Freedom of Information [*Formerly, Directorate for Security Review*] [*DoD*]
DFI .... Directory of Foreign Investors in the US [*A publication*]
DFI .... Disease-Free Intervals
DFI .... Disk File Interrogate [*Computer science*]
DFI .... Domain Specific Part Format Identifier [*Telecommunications*] (ACRL)
DFI .... Duty Free International, Inc. [*NYSE symbol*] (SPSG)
DFI .... Duty Free Intl. [*NYSE symbol*] (TTSB)
DFI .... Dynamic Functional Interaction (EDAC)
DFIB .... Data Function Information Book
DFIC .... Dehydrated Foods Industry Council [*Later, DCFC*]
DFIFC .... Donna Fargo International Fan Club (EA)
DF II .... Direction Finding, Phase II [*Course*] [*Military*] (DNAB)
DFIN .... Damen Financial [*NASDAQ symbol*] (TTSB)
DFIN .... Damen Financial Corp. [*NASDAQ symbol*] (SAG)
DFING .... Direction Finding [*Radio*] [*Military*]
DFIS .... Digital Facsimile Interface System
DFIS .... Dual Filament Ion Source
DFISA .... Dairy and Food Industries Supply Association (EA)
DFIST .... Duty-Free Into-Store Cost
DFJ .... Dual Function Jammer
DFJ .... New Bedford, MA [*Location identifier FAA*] (FAAL)
DFL .... Daily Flight Log [*Aviation*] (FAAC)
DFL .... Deflating (MSA)
DFL .... Deflect (KSC)
DFL .... Degree of Financial Leverage
DFL .... Democrat-Farmer-Labor [*Party*] [*Minnesota*]
DFL .... Department of Family Life [*Later, Commission on Marriage and Family Life*] [*of NCC*] (EA)
DFL .... Department of Foreign Languages [*National Education Association*] (AEBS)
DFL .... Deviation for Failure Location
DFL .... Display Formatting Language
DFL .... Doctor of Family Life
DFL .... Donauflug Bedarfsfluggesellschaft GmbH [*Austria ICAO designator*] (FAAC)
DFL .... Double Four-Valve Long Distance [*Cosworth racing engines*]
DFL .... Dry Film Lubricant
Dfl .... Dutch Florin [*Monetary unit*] (IMH)
DFLC .... Division of Foreign Labor Conditions [*Department of Labor*]
Dflct .... Deflection (DAC)
DFLD .... Distribution-Free Logic Design
DFLP .... Democratic Front for the Liberation of Palestine (PD)
DFLS .... Day Fighter Leaders School [*British military*] (DMA)
DFLX .... Dataflex Corp. [*NASDAQ symbol*] (NQ)
DFM .... Decorative Furniture Manufacturers Association [*Defunct*] (EA)
DFM .... Defiant Minerals [*Vancouver Stock Exchange symbol*]
DFM .... Design for Maintainability (RDA)
DFM .... Design for Manufacturing
DFM .... Diesel Fuel, Marine (NVT)
DFM .... Dietary Food Management
DFM .... Digital Frequency Meter [*or Monitor*]
DFM .... Diploma in Forensic Medicine (ADA)
DFM .... Direct Flight Mode
DFM .... Director, Food Management [*Army*] (AABC)
DFM .... Director of Fleet Maintenance [*Navy British*]
DFM .... Distinguished Flying Medal [*British*]
DFM .... Distortion Factor Meter [*Telecommunications*] (IAA)
DFM .... Double Failure Matrix [*Hazard quantification method*]
DFM .... Douglas Furnished Material [*DAC*]

DFM .... Dual-Frequency Method
DFM .... Franciscan Monastery, Washington, DC [*Library symbol Library of Congress*] (LCLS)
DFMA .... Design Failure-Mode Analysis
DFMA .... Design for Manufacture and Assembly (RDA)
DFMA .... Design for Manufacturing and Assembly
DFMA .... Difluoromethylarginine [*Organic chemistry*]
DFMA .... Director for Military Assistance (NATG)
DFMACH ... Drafting Machine
DFManS ..... Director of Fleet Management Services [*Navy British*]
DFMC .... Daily Fetal Movement Count [*Obstetrics*] (DAVI)
DFMEA .... Design Failure-Mode Effects Analysis [*Automotive engineering*]
DFML .... Dictionary of Folklore, Mythology, and Legend [*A publication*]
DFMMS ...... Data File/Media Management System
DFMO .... Difluoromethylornithine [*Organic chemistry*]
DFMO .... Doppler Filter Mixer-Oscillator [*Electronics*] (AABC)
DFMR .... Daily Fetal Movements Record
DFMS .... Domestic and Foreign Missionary Society [*British*]
DFMSR .... Directorate of Flight and Missile Safety Research [*Air Force*]
DFN .... Data File Number
DFN .... Deutsches Foerschungsnetz [*German*] [*Computer science*] (TNIG)
DFNJ .... Descendants of Founders of New Jersey (EA)
DFNT .... Definite (FAAC)
DFNTN .... Definition
DFO .... Decade Frequency Oscillator (IAA)
DFO .... Defense Food Order [*Production and Marketing Administration*] [*Department of Agriculture*] (DLA)
DFO .... Deferoxamine [*Pharmacology*] (DAVI)
DFO .... Department of Fisheries and Oceans [*Canada*] (OSRA)
DFO .... Deputy for Flight Operations [*NASA*] (KSC)
DFO .... Desferrioxamine [*Also, Deferoxamine*] [*A chelating agent*] (AAMN)
DFO .... Diazafluorenone [*Organic chemistry*]
DFO .... Directed Format Option [*Rapid access management information system*]
DFO .... Director, Flight Operations [*NASA*] (KSC)
DFO .... Disaster Field Office [*Federal Emergency Management Agency*] (GFGA)
DFO .... Disk File Optimizer [*Computer science*] (BUR)
DFO .... Distilled Fuel Oil
DFO .... District Finance Officer
DFO .... Division Follow-On
DFO .... Dorsal Fold (Oesophagus)
DFo .... Folger Shakespeare Library, Washington, DC [*Library symbol Library of Congress*] (LCLS)
DFOA .... Deferoxamine [*Also, Desferrioxamine*] [*Chelating agent*]
DFOD .... Defense Field Operations Department (SAA)
DF-ODMR ... Delayed-Fluorescence Optically Detected Magnetic Resonance [*Physics*]
DFOLS .... Depth of Flash Optical Landing System [*Navy*]
DFOM .... Deferoxamine Methanesulfonate [*or Desferrioxamine Mesylate*] [*Pharmacology*]
DFOM .... Difference Figure of Merit (MCD)
DFOP .... Direction Finder Operator (IAA)
DForSc .... Doctor of Forest Science (ADA)
DFOS .... Diesel Fuel Oil System [*Nuclear energy*] (NRCH)
DFOV .... Dual Field-of-View
DFP .... Data Facility Product
DFP .... Davidon-Fletcher-Powell [*Method*]
DFP .... Dedicated Function Pushbutton
DFP .... Define File Processor [*Computer science*]
DFP .... Demand Forecasting Program (BUR)
DFP .... Demokratische Fortschrittliche Partei [*Democratic Progressive Party*] [*Austria*] (PPE)
DFP .... Designated Force Potential [*Military*]
DFP .... Detroit Free Press [*A publication*]
DFP .... Deviant Flight Plan
DFP .... Diastolic Filling Period [*Medicine*]
DFP .... Diesel Fire Pump [*Nuclear energy*] (NRCH)
DFP .... Difluorophosphate [*Inorganic chemistry*]
DFP .... Diisopropyl Fluorophosphate [*or Diisopropyl Fluorophosphonate*] [*Also, DIFP Ophthalmic drug*]
DFP .... Diode Flat Pack
DFP .... Diploma of Financial Planning
D-FP .... Diplomate, American Board of Family Practice (DHSM)
DFP .... Dipole Flat Plate
DFP .... Direct Fire Plan [*Army*] (INF)
DFP .... Distribution Fuse Panel
DFP .... Dominica Freedom Party [*Political party*] (PPW)
DFP .... Drawing File Processor (MCD)
DFP .... Dry Film Processor
DFP .... Dry Filter Processing
DFP .... Ductile Fracture Propagation [*Engineering*]
DFP .... Dun's Financial Profiles Report [*Dun & Bradstreet Credit Services*] [*Information service or system*] (CRD)
DFP .... Dynamic Flow Parameter
DFPA .... Douglas Fir Plywood Association [*Later, APA*] (EA)
DFPA .... National Society, Daughters of Founders and Patriots of America (EA)
DFPase .... Di-isopropyl Phosphorofluoridase [*An enzyme*]
DFPC .... United States Federal Power Commission, Washington, DC [*Library symbol Library of Congress*] (LCLS)
DFPE .... Deflection Probable Errors (MCD)
DFPL .... Data Flow Programming Language
DFPS .... Digital Ferrite Phase Shifter
DFPT .... Disk File Protection Table [*Computer science*] (IAA)

DFQAO........	Defense Fuel Quality Assurance Office [DoD]
DFQAR........	Defense Fuel Quality Assurance Residency [DoD] (DNAB)
DFQIS.........	Dual Fuel Quantity Indicating System (MCD)
DFR	Board of Governors, Federal Reserve System, Washington, DC [Library symbol Library of Congress] (LCLS)
DFR	Decreasing Failure Rate
DFR	Defence Force Reserves [Australia]
DFR	Defense Fuel Region [DoD]
DFR	Defer (AABC)
DFR	Defrost (MSA)
DFR	Degradation Failure Rate
DFR	Delayed Free Recall
DFR	Design for Reliability (RDA)
DFR	Diabetic Floor Routine [Medicine] (DMAA)
DFR	Dihydroflavonol Reductase [An enzyme]
DFR	Direction Finding Receiver
DFr.............	Discophiles Francais [Record label] [France]
DFR	Disk File Read [Computer science] (OA)
DFR	Distance - Force - Resistance [Instrumentation]
DFR	Dofor Inc. [Toronto Stock Exchange symbol]
DFR	Doppler Frequency Rate (MCD)
DFR	Double Frequency Recording (HGAA)
DFR	Dounreay Fast Reactor [British]
DFR	Dropped from Rolls
DFR	Dual-Frequency Receiver
DFR	Dun's Financial Records [Dun's Marketing Services] [Parsippany, NJ] [Information service or system] (IID)
DFR+	Dun's Financial Records Plus [Dun's Marketing Services] [Information service or system] (IID)
DFR	Durant Family Registry (EA)
DFR	Dust-Free Room
DFRA	Decreasing Failure Rate Average
DFRA	Drop Forging Research Association [British]
DFRC	Dairy Forage Research Center [Department of Agriculture] [Madison, WI] (GRD)
DFRC	Distillers Feed Research Council (EA)
DFRC	Dryden Flight Research Center [NASA]
DFRDBS......	Defence Force Retirement and Death Benefits Scheme [Australia]
DFRDC........	Dried Fruits Research and Development Council [Australia]
DFRDP........	Dairy Farmers for Responsible Dairy Policy (EA)
DFR/E.........	Defense Fuel Region/Europe [Military] (DOMA)
DFRIF	Defense Freight Railway Interchange Fleet [Army] (AABC)
DFRL	Differential Relay (KSC)
DFR/ME	Defense Fuel Region/Middle East [Military] (DOMA)
DFRN	Differential
DFRN	Differential Velocity (NASA)
DFRP	Deficiency and Replacement
DFRP	Downcomer Flow Resistance Plate [Nuclear energy] (NRCH)
DFRR	Detailed Functional Requirements Review (SSD)
DFRS	Differs (FAAC)
DFRT	Demonstration Flight Rating Test (MCD)
DFS.............	Daisy Fault Simulator [On Daisy CAD work station] (NITA)
DFS.............	Dancer-Fitzgerald-Sample [Advertising agency]
DfS..............	Dataflow Systems, Inc. [Information service or system] (IID)
DFS.............	Defense Facsimile System (MCD)
DFS.............	Defense Fuel Support [DoD] (DNAB)
DFS.............	Demonstration Flight Satellite (MCD)
DFS.............	Denali Fault System [Geology]
DFS.............	Dental Fear Syndrome
DFS.............	Deoxyfructoserotonin [Antibacterial]
DFS.............	Department 56 [NYSE symbol] (TTSB)
DFS.............	Department 56, Inc. [NYSE symbol] (SPSG)
DFS.............	Departure from Specifications (DNAB)
DFS.............	Depth-First Search
DFS.............	Detailed Functional Specification (DA)
DFS.............	Detail Finish Specification (MCD)
DFS.............	[A] Dictionary of Forces' Slang [A publication]
DFS.............	Digital Fascimile System (MCD)
DFS.............	Digital Field System
DFS.............	Digital Frequency Synthesizer
DFS.............	Direct Fire Simulator
DFS.............	Direct Fire System
DFS.............	Direct Flow Sampler [Meteorology]
DFS.............	Direct Forces Support [Military]
DFS.............	Direct Function Search (PDAA)
DFS.............	Direction Finding Set [or System]
DFS.............	Director of Flight Safety [Air Force]
DFS.............	Disease-Free Survival (MEDA)
DFS.............	Dispersive Fourier Spectroscopy (PDAA)
DFS.............	Display Formatting System
DFS.............	Distance Finding Station
DFS.............	Distributed File System
DFS.............	Dividends from Space [Defunct] (EA)
DFS.............	Doctor of Foreign Science
DFS.............	Doctor of Foreign Service
DFS.............	Doctor of Forest Science
DFS.............	Dofasco, Inc. [Toronto Stock Exchange symbol]
DFS.............	Down Feeding Spindle
DFS.............	Dragon Flight Simulator [Military] (MCD)
DFS.............	Dwyer Aircraft Sales, Inc. [ICAO designator] (FAAC)
DFS.............	Dynamic Flight Simulator
DFSB	Defense Force Section Base [Navy]
DFSC	Defense Fuel Supply Center [Alexandria, VA] (MCD)
DFSc	Doctor of Financial Science
DFSD	Directorate of Fleet Supply Duties [Navy British]

DFSG	Direct Formed Supergroup [Telecommunications] (TEL)
DFSHW	Department of Family Services and Housing Welfare [Queensland] [Australia]
DFSI............	Dice Fanual Similarity and Index [Ecology]
DFSK	Double Frequency Shift Keying [Radio]
DFSM	Deterministic Finite-State Machine (PDAA)
DFSM	Dispersion Flattened Single Mode (IAA)
DFSP	Data Flow Signal Processor (MCD)
DFSP	Defense Fuel Support Point [DoD]
DFSP	Dermatofibrosarcoma Protuberans [Oncology]
DFSR	Detailed Function System Requirement
DFSR	Diffuser (AAG)
DFSR	Director [or Directorate] of Flight Safety Research [Air Force]
DFSS	Democratic Front for the Salvation of Somalia (PD)
DFSTN	Direction Finding Station [Aviation] (FAAC)
DFSU	Disk File Storage Unit [Computer science]
DFSU	Dual Frequency Signaling Units (MCD)
DFSWO........	Department of the Financial Secretary of the War Office [British]
DFT.............	Air Direct Ltd. [British ICAO designator] (FAAC)
DFT.............	Deaerating Feed Tank
DFT.............	Defendant
DFT.............	Density Functional Theory [Quantum chemistry]
DFT.............	Deployment for Training
DFT.............	Design Feasibility Test
DFT.............	Design for Testability [Military]
DFT.............	Development Flight Test [Military] (CAAL)
DFT.............	Diagnostic Function Test [Computer science]
DFT.............	Digital Facility Terminal [Telecommunications] (TEL)
DFT.............	Digital Filtering Technique
DFT.............	Digital Fourier Transform [or Transformation] [Computer science]
DFT.............	Direct Flight Test (KSC)
DFT.............	Director, Fleet Training
DFT.............	Discrete Fourier Transform
DFT.............	Distributed Function Terminal (ACRL)
DFT.............	Distribution Function Terminal [Computer science]
DFT.............	Document File Transfer [Computer science]
DFT.............	Downdraft (DA)
DFT.............	Draft
dft..............	Draft (WDMC)
DFT.............	Drift (MSA)
DFT.............	United States Federal Trade Commission, Washington, DC [Library symbol Library of Congress] (LCLS)
DFT/A..........	Draft Attached [Business term]
DFTA...........	Dwarf Fruit Trees Association [Later, International Dwarf Fruit Trees Association] (EA)
DFT/C..........	Clean Draft [Business term]
DFTFACE......	Direction Finding and Tracking of Frequency Agile Communications Emitter (MCD)
DFTG	Drafting (KSC)
DFTI...........	Dansk Fiskeriteknologisk Institut [Danish Fisheries Technology Institute] [Also, an information service or system] (IID)
DFTI...........	Distance from Threshold Indicator (PDAA)
DFTI...........	Distance from Touchdown Indicator [Aviation] (DA)
DFTM	Direction Finder Team (IAA)
DFTM	Douglas-Fir Tussock Moth
DFTMN	Draftsman (AFM)
DFTPP	Decaflucrotriphenylphosphine
DFTR	Deflector (MSA)
DFTS	Dispersive Fourier Transform Spectroscopy (MCD)
DFTSMN	Draftsman (KSC)
DFTSMN	Draftsman
DFU	Data File Utility [Computer science] (IBMDP)
DFU	Dead Fetus in Uterus
DFU	Dideoxyfluorouridine [Medicine] (DMAA)
DFU	Difluorourea [Organic chemistry]
DFU	Directions For Use [Packaging]
DFU	Drainage Fixture Unit (DNAB)
DFU	Dummy Firing Unit
DFUS	Diffuse (FAAC)
DF(V)...........	Deafness Foundation [Victoria] [Australia]
DFV.............	Designed for Victory [Auto racing engine designation]
DFV.............	Diarrhea with Fever and Vomiting [Medicine] (DMAA)
DFV.............	Double Four Valve [Cosworth racing engines]
DFV.............	Dual Camshaft Four-Valve [Engine] [Automotive engineering]
DFVLR	Deutsche Forschungs und Versuchsanstalt fuer Luft und Raumfahrt [German Research Institute for Air and Space Travel] [An association]
DFVR	Defense Visual Flight Rule [Military] (DA)
DFW............	Dallas/Fort Worth [Texas] [Airport symbol]
DFW............	Delegation for Friendship among Women (EA)
DFW............	Diesel Fuel Waiver (DNAB)
DFW............	Diffusion Welding
DFW............	Director of Fortifications and Works [British]
DFW............	Disk File Write [Computer science] (OA)
DFWA	Drug-Free Workplace Act of 1988 (WYGK)
DFWES	Direct Fire Weapons Effect Simulator [Military] (PDAA)
DFWM	Degenerate Four-Wave Mixing [Optical reflection]
DFWMAC	Distributed Foundation Wireless Media Access Control [Computer science]
DFWT..........	Dallas Fort Worth Teleport Ltd. [Irving, TX] [Telecommunications] (TSSD)
DFWU	Detroit Fast Food Workers' Union [Defunct] (EA)
DFX.............	Dicke-Fix [Electronics] (CET)
DFX.............	Dylan Flight Service SA [Switzerland ICAO designator] (FAAC)
DFY.............	Dafrey Resources, Inc. [Vancouver Stock Exchange symbol]

DG	Daily Guardian [*A publication*]
DG	Damaged Goods
DG	Damianus Gulianus [*Authority cited in pre-1607 legal work*] (DSA)
DG	Dangerous Goods [*Shipping*]
DG	Dansyl Glutamate [*Biochemistry*]
DG	Danygraig [*Welsh depot code*]
DG	Darien Airlines [*ICAO designator*] (AD)
DG	Dark Green
DG	Data General Corp. [*Computer manufacturer*]
DG	Data Generator (MCD)
DG	Datagram [*Telecommunications*]
DG	Decigram [*Unit of measure*] (GPO)
dg	Decigram (IDOE)
DG	Declaration de Guerre [*Declaration of War*] [*French*] (ILCA)
DG	Decreto Governatoriale [*Governor's Decree*] [*Italian*] (ILCA)
DG	Defense Grouping (DNAB)
DG	Defense Guidance
DG	Defensive Guard [*Football*]
DG	Degaussing
DG	De Gex's English Bankruptcy Reports [*A publication*] (DLA)
DG	Degree (IAA)
DG	Degree Year [*Database terminology*] (NITA)
DG	Dei Gratia [*By the Grace of God*] [*Latin*] (GPO)
DG	Dekagram [*Unit of measure*] (ROG)
DG	Density Gradient
DG	Dentate Granule Cell
DG	Dentate Gyrus [*Neuroanatomy*]
DG	Deo Gratias [*Thanks Be to God*] [*Latin*] (GPO)
DG	Deoxy-D-glucose [*Also, DDG, DOG*] [*Biochemistry*]
DG	Deoxyglucose [*Biochemistry*] (DAVI)
DG	Deoxyguanosine [*Biochemistry*]
dG	Deoxyguanylate [*Biochemistry*]
DG	Dependency Graph and Control [*Computer science*]
DG	Design Guide [*Army Corps of Engineers*] (AAGC)
DG	Destroyer, Guided Missile [*Surface-to-air*] [*NATO*]
DG	Deutsche Genossenschaftsbank [*Germany*]
DG	Diagnosis (AABC)
DG	Diastolic Gallop [*Medicine*]
DG	Diesel General [*Service*] [*Automotive engineering*]
DG	Diesel Generator (NRCH)
DG	Differential Gain
DG	Differential Generator
DG	Differentially (Expressed) Gastrula [*Genetics*]
DG	Digestive Gland
DG	Digital Group (NITA)
DG	Diglyceride [*Clinical chemistry*]
DG	Digoxigenin [*Biochemistry*]
DG	Diode Gate
DG	Direct Grant
DG	Directional Grid (IAA)
DG	Directional Gyro
DG	Director-General
DG	Disc Grind [*Technical drawings*]
DG	Displacement Gyro [*Aerospace*]
DG	Display Generator (MCD)
DG	Distinguished Graduate [*Military*]
DG	Distinguished Guest [*Hotel term*]
DG	Distogingival [*Dentistry*]
DG	District Guard [*British military*] (DMA)
DG	Disturbed Gum [*Philately*]
Dg	Diving [*British military*] (DMA)
D-G	Divisional-General [*British*]
DG	Documentation Group [*Range Commanders Council*] [*NASA*]
DG	Dogged
DG	Dollar General [*NYSE symbol*] (TTSB)
DG	Dollar General Corp. [*NYSE symbol*] (SAG)
DG	Double Gear [*Engineering*] (ROG)
DG	Double Glass (AAG)
DG	Double Groove [*Insulators*]
DG	Double-Gummed [*Envelopes*]
DG	Downgrade (NVT)
DG	Dragoon Guards [*Military unit*] [*British*]
DG	Dramatists Guild (EA)
DG	Dutch Guilder [*Monetary unit*] (NATG)
DG	Dynamogram
DG	General Aviation Services Ltd. [*British ICAO designator*] (ICDA)
DGA	Damned Good Airplane
DGA	Dangriga [*Belize*] [*Airport symbol*] (OAG)
DGA	Delegation General pour l'Armament [*General Armaments Delegation*] [*France*]
DGA	Democratic Governors Association (EA)
DGA	Dense Grade Aggregate
DGA	Deutsche Gesellschaft fuer Amerikastudien [*German Association for American Studies*] (EA)
DGA	Diglycolamine [*Organic chemistry*]
DGA	Diploma in Government Administration [*British*]
DGA	Directors Guild of America (EA)
DGA	Dummy Guide Assembly [*Nuclear energy*] (NRCH)
DGA	Durum Growers Association of the United States (EA)
DGAA	Accra/Kotoka International [*Ghana*] [*ICAO location identifier*] (ICLI)
DGAA	Distressed Gentlefolks' Aid Association [*British*] (DI)
DGAC	Accra [*Ghana*] [*ICAO location identifier*] (ICLI)
DGAD	Ada [*Ghana*] [*ICAO location identifier*] (ICLI)
DGAE	Director-General of Aircraft Equipment [*Ministry of Aircraft Production*] [*British*]

DGAE	Director-General of Army Education [*British*]
DGAE	Kete-Krachi [*Ghana*] [*ICAO location identifier*] (ICLI)
DGAEM	Director-General of Aerospace and Engineering Maintenance (MCD)
DGAH	Ho [*Ghana*] [*ICAO location identifier*] (ICLI)
DGAK	Akuse [*Ghana*] [*ICAO location identifier*] (ICLI)
DGAMS	Director-General of Army Medical Services [*British*]
DGA(N)	Director-General of Aircraft (Naval) [*British military*] (DMA)
DG & J	De Gex and Jones' English Chancery Reports [*A publication*] (DLA)
DG & JB	De Gex and Jones' English Bankruptcy Reports [*1857-59*] [*A publication*] (DLA)
DGANL	Digital to Analog (MCD)
DGAO	United States General Accounting Office, Washington, DC [*Library symbol Library of Congress*] (LCLS)
DGAP	Akatsi [*Ghana*] [*ICAO location identifier*] (ICLI)
DGAP	Development Group for Alternative Policies (EA)
DGAR	Director-General of Army Requirements [*British*]
DGAS	Delta Natural Gas [*NASDAQ symbol*] (TTSB)
DGAS	Delta Natural Gas Co., Inc. [*NASDAQ symbol*] (NQ)
DGAS	Diesel Generator Auxiliary System [*Nuclear energy*] (NRCH)
DGAS	Saltpond [*Ghana*] [*ICAO location identifier*] (ICLI)
DGAT	Tema [*Ghana*] [*ICAO location identifier*] (ICLI)
DGAV	Director-General of Armoured Vehicles [*British*]
DGAVP	Desglycinamide-Arginine-Vasopressin [*Antidiuretic*]
DGAVS	Director-General of the Army Veterinary Service [*British military*] (DMA)
DGB	Dangerous Goods Board [*IATA*] (DS)
DGB	Deutscher Gewerkschaftsbund [*Confederation of German Trade Unions*] [*Germany*] (DCTA)
DGB	Diesel Generator Building [*Nuclear energy*] (NRCH)
DGB	Disk Gap Band [*Parachute*]
DGBA	Diethylene Glycol Butyl Acetate [*Organic chemistry*]
DGBAW	Der Grosse Baumeister aller Welten [*The Grand Architect of the Universe*] [*Freemasonry*] [*German*]
DGBC	Digital Geoballistic Computer
DGBC	Digital Geoballistic Computer System (NITA)
DGBE	Diethylene Glycol Butyl Ether [*Organic chemistry*]
DG BRIT REG FD	Dei Gratia Britanniarum Regina, Fidei Defensor [*By the Grace of God, Queen of England, Defender of the Faith*] [*Latin*] (ROG)
DGBUS	Digital Ground Bus
DGC	Data General Corp. [*Computer manufacturer*]
DGC	Data Graphics Corp.
DGC	Democratic Governors Conference (EA)
DGC	Diamond Grain Configuration
DGC	Digicon, Inc. [*AMEX symbol*] (SPSG)
DGC	Digital Geoballistic Computer
DGC	Diploma in Guidance and Counselling (ADA)
DGC	Directors Guild of Canada
DGC	Durango [*Colorado*] [*Seismograph station code, US Geological Survey Closed*] (SEIS)
DGC	Dystrophin-Glycoprotein Complex [*Biochemistry*]
DGC	Gallaudet College, Washington, DC [*Library symbol Library of Congress*] (LCLS)
DGCA	Director-General of Civil Aviation [*British*]
DGCAIES	Diesel Generator Combustion Air Intake and Exhaust System [*Nuclear energy*] (NRCH)
DGCC	Director-General of Civilian Clothing [*British*]
DGCCP	Dental Guidance Council for Cerebral Palsy (EA)
DGCGO	Dangerous Cargo (FAAC)
DGC-K	Gallaudet College, Kendall Demonstration School, Washington, DC [*Library symbol Library of Congress*] (LCLS)
DGC-M	Gallaudet College, Model Secondary School for the Deaf, Washington, DC [*Library symbol Library of Congress*] (LCLS)
DG/CS	Data General/Communications System [*Data General Corp.*] (NITA)
DGCStJ	Dame Grand Cross of the Order of Saint John of Jerusalem [*British*] (ADA)
DGCWS	Diesel Generator Cooling Water System [*Nuclear energy*] (NRCH)
DGCWS	Digicon Inc. Wrrt [*AMEX symbol*] (TTSB)
DGD	Deutsche Gesellschaft fuer Dokumentation [*German Society for Documentation*] [*Information service or system*] (IID)
DGD	Dialkylglycine Decarboxylase [*An enzyme*]
DGD	Diesel Geared Drive
DGD	Director, Gunnery Division [*British military*] (DMA)
DGD	Director of Ground Defence [*Military British*]
DGD	Dogwood, MO [*Location identifier FAA*] (FAAL)
DGD	Double Glass Door [*Classified advertising*] (ADA)
DGD	Dynamic Gas Disengagement [*Chemical engineering*]
DGD	Dynamic Gravity Detector
DGDB	Dipropylene Glycol Dibenzoate [*Organic chemistry*]
DG/DBMS	Data General/Data Base Management System [*Data General Corp.*] (NITA)
DGDC	Deputy Grand Director of Ceremonies [*Freemasonry*]
DGDG	Digalactosyl Diacyl Glycerol [*Organic chemistry*]
DGDG	Distributor-to-Group Display Generator
DGDGE	Distributor-to-Group Display Generator Electronics (IAA)
dGDP	Deoxyguanosine Diphosphate [*Biochemistry*]
DGDP	Double Groove, Double Petticoat [*Insulators*]
DGE	Davisson-Germer Experiment [*Physics*]
DGE	Density Gradient Electrophoresis
DGE	Design Engineer
DGE	Director-General of Equipment [*Air Force British*]
DGE	Dual Gauge Expander
DGE	Dusty Gas Enveloped [*Astronomy*]
DGE	Mudgee [*Australia Airport symbol*] (OAG)
DGEBA	Diglycidyl Ether of Bisphenol A [*Monomer*] [*Organic chemistry*]
D Ge E	Doctor of Geological Engineering

D Ge Eng ..... Doctor of Geological Engineering
DGEL .... Director-General Engineering, Land [*Canada*]
DGEMER ...... Diglycidyl Ether of Methylolresorcinol [*Organic chemistry*] (MCD)
DGEN .... Data Generation
DGEP .... Director-General of Engine Production [*British*]
DGES .... Division of Graduate Education in Science [*National Science Foundation*]
DGF .... Degrees Fahrenheit (AAG)
DGF .... Delaware Group Global Dividend Fund [*NYSE symbol*] (SAG)
DGF .... Delaware Grp Global Div & Inc. [*NYSE symbol*] (TTSB)
DGF .... Dragonfly Distillers [*Vancouver Stock Exchange symbol*]
DG F & J ..... De Gex, Fisher, and Jones' English Chancery Reports [*A publication*] (DLA)
DG F & JB... De Gex, Fisher, and Jones' English Bankruptcy Reports [*A publication*] (DLA)
DGFC .... Accra [*Ghana*] [*ICAO location identifier*] (ICLI)
DGFC .... Del Gray Fan Club (EA)
DGFF .... Director-General of Filling Factories [*Formerly, DGOF(F)*] [*Ministry of Supply*] [*British*] [*World War II*]
DGFOSTS ..... Diesel Generator Fuel Oil Storage and Transfer System [*Nuclear energy*] (NRCH)
DGFV .... Director-General of Fighting Vehicles [*British military*] (DMA)
DGFVE .... Director-General of Fighting Vehicles and Engineer Equipment [*British*] (RDA)
DGG .... Department of Geology and Geophysics [*MIT*] (MCD)
DGG .... Deutsche Grammophon Gesellschaft [*Phonograph recording company*]
DGG .... D-Glutamylglycine [*Biochemistry*]
DGG .... Dynamic Gravity Generator
DGGB .... Directors Guild of Great Britain
DGGD .... Director-General of Ground Defence [*Military British*]
DGGE .... Denaturing Gradient-Gel Electrophoresis [*Analytical Biochemistry*]
DGGHP .... Deputy General Grand High Priest [*Freemasonry*]
DGGWL .... Director-General of Guided Weapons and Electronics [*British*] (RDA)
DGH .... Diameter at Ground Height [*Botany*]
DGH .... District General Hospital
DGHe .... Embassy of Ghana, Washington, DC [*Library symbol Library of Congress*] (LCLS)
DGHG .... Director-General, Home Guard [*British military*] (DMA)
DGHP .... Deputy Grand High Priest [*Freemasonry*]
DGHP .... Drive-Gearhead Package
Dghtie .... Doughtie's Foods, Inc. [*Associated Press*] (SAG)
DGHTR .... Daughter
DGI .... Date Growers' Institute [*Defunct*] (EA)
DGI .... Decision Graphics, Inc.
DGI .... Dental Gold Institute (EA)
DGI .... Deoxyglucose Imaging [*Medicine*] (CPH)
DGI .... Direccion General de la Inteligencia [*Intelligence agency*] [*Cuba*]
DGI .... Disc Graphics, Inc. [*AMEX symbol*] (SAG)
DGI .... Disseminated Gonococcal Infection [*Clinical chemistry*]
DGI .... Duncan Gold Resources [*Vancouver Stock Exchange symbol*]
DGIA .... Director-General of Internal Audit [*British*] (RDA)
DGIAB .... Durable Goods Industries Advisory Board [*New Deal*]
DGIC .... Donegal Group [*NASDAQ symbol*] (TTSB)
DGIC .... Donegal Group, Inc. [*NASDAQ symbol*] (NQ)
DGII .... Digi International [*NASDAQ symbol*] (TTSB)
DGII .... Digi International, Inc. [*NASDAQ symbol*] (NQ)
DGILLO .... Downgrade in Lieu of Layoff
DGIS .... Direct Graphics Interface Specification
DGIS .... Direct Graphics Interface Standard (CDE)
DGIS .... Director-General of Intelligence and Security (MCD)
DGIS .... DoD [*Department of Defense*] Gateway Information System [*Defense Technical Information Center*] (TSSD)
DGIT .... Digital Generation Systems [*NASDAQ symbol*] (TTSB)
DGIX .... Dyna Group International, Inc. [*NASDAQ symbol*] (NQ)
DGIX .... Dyna Group Intl. [*NASDAQ symbol*] (TTSB)
DGJ .... Donovan, Gerard J., Co., Inc., North Attleboro MA [*STAC*]
DG J & S ..... De Gex, Jones, and Smith's English Chancery Reports [*A publication*] (DLA)
DG J & SB... De Gex, Jones, and Smith's English Bankruptcy Reports [*A publication*] (DLA)
DGK .... Diacylglycerol Kinase [*An enzyme*]
DGKA .... Akim Oda [*Ghana*] [*ICAO location identifier*] (ICLI)
DGKK .... Koforidua [*Ghana*] [*ICAO location identifier*] (ICLI)
DGL .... Dangling Construction [*Used in correcting manuscripts, etc.*]
DG/L .... Data General's System Programming Language
DGL .... Diagonal European Airways Link [*France*] [*FAA designator*] (FAAC)
DGL .... Diffuse Galactic Light
DGL .... Distinguished Guest Lecturer (DOMA)
DGL .... Doped Glass LASER
DGL .... Douglas, AZ [*Location identifier FAA*] (FAAL)
DGL .... Douglas [*Arizona*] Municipal [*Airport symbol*] (OAG)
DGLB .... Bole [*Ghana*] [*ICAO location identifier*] (ICLI)
DGLD .... Diaphragm Gland
DGLE .... Tamale [*Ghana*] [*ICAO location identifier*] (ICLI)
DGLF .... Dark Green Leafy Vegetable (DI)
DGLN .... Navrongo [*Ghana*] [*ICAO location identifier*] (ICLI)
DGLS .... Diesel Generator Lubrication System [*Nuclear energy*] (NRCH)
DGLS .... Missouri Division of Geology and Land Survey [*State of Missouri Department of Natural Resources*] [*Research center*] (RCD)
DglsLom ...... Douglas & Lomason Co. [*Associated Press*] (SAG)
DGLW .... Wa [*Ghana*] [*ICAO location identifier*] (ICLI)
DGLY .... Yendi [*Ghana*] [*ICAO location identifier*] (ICLI)
DGM .... Data Gathering Monitoring [*System*]
dgm .... Decigram [*Unit of measure*]

DGM .... Defense Guidance Memorandum
DGM .... Deputy General Manager [*AEC*]
DGM .... Deputy Grand Marshal (ROG)
DGM .... Deputy Grand Master [*Freemasonry*]
DGM .... Destroyer, Guided Missile [*Surface-to-air/Surface-to-surface*] [*NATO*]
DGM .... Digital Group Multiplexer (MCD)
DGM .... Directional Gyro Mode
DGM .... Director-General of Manpower [*Ministry of Labour*] [*British*]
DGM .... Dissolved Gaseous Mercury [*Environmental chemistry*]
DGM .... Draco Gold Mines [*Vancouver Stock Exchange symbol*]
DGM .... Ductal Glandular Mastectomy [*Medicine*] (DAVI)
DGM .... Dummy Guided Missile
DGM .... Durable Goods Manufacturer [*DoD*]
DGMA .... Dental Group Management Association (EA)
DG M & G .... De Gex, Macnaghten, and Gordon's English Chancery Reports [*A publication*] (DLA)
DG M & GB... De Gex, Macnaghten, and Gordon's English Bankruptcy Reports [*A publication*] (DLA)
DGMechE(S)... Director-General of Mechanical Engineering, Supply [*Ministry of Supply*] [*British*]
DG-MG........ Diesel Geared - Motor Geared
dGMP.......... Deoxyguanosine Monophosphate [*Biochemistry*]
DGMP.......... Director-General of Munitions Production [*Ministry of Supply*] [*British World War II*]
DGMR.......... Director-General of Military Railways [*British military*] (DMA)
DGMS.......... Director-General of Medical Services [*British*]
DGMS.......... Division of General Medical Sciences [*National Institutes of Health*]
DGMT.......... Director-General of Military Training [*British*]
DGMW.......... Director-General of Military Works [*British military*] (DMA)
DGMW.......... Double-Gimbaled Momentum Wheel
DGN .... Dangerous Goods Note [*Shipping*] (DCTA)
DGN .... Data General [*NYSE symbol*] (TTSB)
DGN .... Data General Corp. [*NYSE symbol*] (SPSG)
DGN .... Design
DGN .... Direccion General de Normas [*National Standards Organization*] [*Mexico*]
DGN .... Dragoon Resources Ltd. [*Vancouver Stock Exchange symbol*]
DGNL .... Diagonal (FAAC)
DGNMT......... Director-General of Naval Manpower and Training [*British*]
DGNPS........ Director-General of Naval Personnel Services [*British*]
DGNSTC....... Diagnostic
DGNSTC....... Diagnostic
DGO .... Degaussing Officer [*Navy*]
DGO .... Diploma in Gynecology and Obstetrics [*British*]
DGO .... Directional Gyro Operation
DGO .... Director-General of Organization [*RAF*] [*British*]
DGO .... Domego Resources Ltd. [*Toronto Stock Exchange symbol*]
DGO .... Durango [*Mexico*] [*Airport symbol*] (OAG)
DGOA .... Director-General of [*Quality*] Assurance
DGOF .... Director-General of Ordnance Factories [*Ministry of Supply*] [*British World War II*]
DGOF(F) ..... Director-General of Ordnance Factories (Filling) [*Later, DGFF*] [*Ministry of Supply*] [*British*] [*World War II*]
DGOH.......... Directorate General of Highways [*Vietnam*]
DGOR.......... Deutsche Gesellschaft fuer Operations Research [*German Society for Operational Research*] [*Germany*]
DGOS........... Director-General, Ordnance Systems [*Canada*]
DGP .... Dabrowa Gornicza [*Poland*] [*Seismograph station code, US Geological Survey*] (SEIS)
DGP .... Dangerous Goods Panel [*ICAO*] (DA)
DGP .... Data Generating Program
DGP .... Dean's Grant Project (EDAC)
DGP .... Deoxyglucose-Phosphate [*Biochemistry*]
DGP .... Design Guidance Package [*Military*] (CAAL)
DGP .... Destruction of Government Property
DGP .... Diploma in Graduate and Professional Studies (PGP)
DGP .... Director-General of Personnel [*British*]
DGP .... Director-General of Production [*British Air Ministry*]
DGP .... Drive-Gearhead Package
DGP .... Dry Gas Pump
DGP .... USX-Delhi Group [*NYSE symbol*] (SPSG)
DGP .... USX Delhi Group [*NYSE symbol*] (SAG)
DGPA .... Deputy General Purchasing Agent [*Military*]
DGPL .... Downers Grove Public Library [*Illinois*]
DGPO.......... United States Government Printing Office, Washington, DC [*Library symbol Library of Congress*] (LCLS)
DGPO-S ...... United States Government Printing Office, Serials Library, Alexandria, VA [*Library symbol Library of Congress*] (LCLS)
DGPS .... Differential Global Positioning System
DGPS(N)...... Director-General, Personal Services (Naval) [*British military*] (DMA)
DGQA.......... Director-General of Quality Assurance [*British*]
DGR .... Danger
DGR .... Degrease
DGR .... Directorate of Geophysics Research [*Air Research and Development Command*] (AAG)
DGR .... Director of Graves Registration [*British*]
DGR .... Division of Geothermal Research [*Energy Research and Development Administration*]
DGR .... Division of Government Research [*University of New Mexico*] [*Research center*] (RCD)
DGR .... Door Gunner [*Military*]
DGRA.......... Diamond and Gemstone Remarketing Association [*Defunct*] (EA)
DGRAFMS.... Director-General of Royal Air Force Medical Services [*British*]
DGRD.......... Director-General, Research and Development Policy [*Military Canada*]

DGRDS .... Director-General, Research and Development Services [*Military Canada*]
DGRM.......... Director-General of Raw Materials [*Ministry of Supply*] [*British*]
DGRO........... Degaussing Range Officer [*Navy*]
DGRTP......... Death Gratuity Payment [*Army*] (AABC)
DGS .... Data Gathering System (MCD)
DGS .... Data Ground Station [*NASA*] (KSC)
DGS .... Degaussing System
DGS .... Density Gradient Sedimentation [*Analytical biochemistry*]
DGS .... Deputy General Secretary (DCTA)
DGS .... Destroyer, Guided Missile (Surface-to-Surface) [*NATO*]
DGS .... Diabetic Glomerulosclerosis [*Endocrinology*] (DAVI)
DGS .... DiGeorge Syndrome [*Medicine*]
DGS .... Digital Ground System
DGS .... Diploma in Graduate Studies [*British*]
DGS .... Director of Ground Safety [*Air Force*]
DGS .... Display Generation System
DGS .... Distributed Graphics System (MCD)
DGS .... Dominion Government Survey [*Canada*]
DGS .... Don't Give a Spit [*Slang*] [*Bowdlerized version*]
DGS .... Double Green Silk Covered [*Wire insulation*]
DGS .... Drill Guidance System
DGS .... Drone Generation Squadron
DGS .... University of Denver, Graduate School of Librarianship, Denver, CO [*OCLC symbol*] (OCLC)
DGSA.......... Dairy Goat Society of Australia
DGSAA........ Director-General of Small Arms Ammunition Production [*Ministry of Supply*] [*British World War II*]
DGSB .... Sefwi-Bekwai [*Ghana*] [*ICAO location identifier*] (ICLI)
DGSC........... Defense General Supply Center
DGSD .... Digital Sound Corp. [*NASDAQ symbol*] (SAG)
DGSD .... Double Glass Sliding Doors [*Classified advertising*] (ADA)
DGSE .... Developmental Ground Support Equipment (DNAB)
DGSE .... Direction Generale de la Securite Exterieure [*Formerly, SDECE*] [*French intelligence agency*]
DGSFR......... Degasifier
DGShips ...... Director-General, Ships [*Navy British*]
DGSI .... Digital Solutions [*NASDAQ symbol*] (TTSB)
DGSI .... Digital Solutions, Inc. [*NASDAQ symbol*] (NQ)
DGSI .... Don't Get Sucked In
DGSI .... Kumasi [*Ghana*] [*ICAO location identifier*] (ICLI)
DGSJ .... Druggist's Guild of St. James [*Defunct*] (EA)
DGSM .... Director-General of Servicing and Maintenance [*RAF*] [*British*]
DGSN .... Sunyani [*Ghana*] [*ICAO location identifier*] (ICLI)
DGSP .... Director-General of Statistics and Planning [*Ministry of Supply*] [*British*]
DGSR .... Director-General, Ship Refitting [*Ministry of Defence*] [*British*]
DGSRD .... Director-General of Scientific Research and Development [*Ministry of Supply*] [*British*]
DGSS .... Diesel Generator Starting System [*Nuclear energy*] (NRCH)
DGSS .... Distributed Graphics Support Subroutines [*Tektronix, Inc.*] (NITA)
DGST .... Digest
DGST .... Director-General, Supply and Transport [*British military*] (DMA)
DG/STAGE... Data General's Standard Applications and Graphics Environment [*Engineering software*]
DGStJ .... Dame of Grace, Order of St. John of Jerusalem [*Later, D St J*] [*British*]
DGST(N) ...... Director-General of Supplies and Transport (Naval) [*British*]
DGSW .... Wenchi [*Ghana*] [*ICAO location identifier*] (ICLI)
DGT .... Database Graphics Toolkit [*Blackhawk Data Corp.*]
DGT .... Daughter (WGA)
DGT .... Digit
DGT .... Digital Equipment Corp. [*ICAO designator*] (FAAC)
DGT .... Digitech Ltd. [*Toronto Stock Exchange symbol*]
DGT .... Direction Generale des Telecommunications [*Telecommunications administration*] [*France*]
DGT .... Direction Generale des Telecommunications [*Government of Quebec*] [*Canada*] (TSSD)
DGT .... Directorate General of Telecommunications [*Taipei, Taiwan*]
DGT .... Director-General of Training [*British military*] (DMA)
DGT .... Director-General of Transportation [*British military*] (DMA)
DGT .... Dumaguete [*Philippines*] [*Airport symbol*] (OAG)
DGT .... Large German Telescope [*Acronym is based on German phrase*]
DGTA .... Director-General of the Territorial Army [*British*]
DGTC .... Del Global Technologies Corp. [*NASDAQ symbol*] (SAG)
DGTF .... Director-General of the Territorial Force [*British military*] (DMA)
DGTK .... Takoradi [*Ghana*] [*ICAO location identifier*] (ICLI)
DGTL .... Digital (MSA)
DGTL .... Digital
DGTL .... Digital Systems International, Inc. [*NASDAQ symbol*] (SAG)
DGTL .... Digital Systems Intl. [*NASDAQ symbol*] (TTSB)
DgtlLnk....... Digital Link Corp. [*Associated Press*] (SAG)
DG Tn .... Director-General of Transportation Services [*British*]
DGTO .... Degaussing Technical Officer [*Navy*]
DGTP .... Deoxyguanosine Triphosphate [*Biochemistry*]
DG/TPMS.... Data General/Transaction Processing Management System [*Data General Corp.*] (NITA)
DgTrns........ Digital Transmission Systems, Inc. [*Associated Press*] (SAG)
DGTX .... Axim [*Ghana*] [*ICAO location identifier*] (ICLI)
DGTZR .... Digitizer (MSA)
DGU .... Boston, MA [*Location identifier FAA*] (FAAL)
DGU .... Dedougu [*Upper Volta*] [*Airport symbol*] (AD)
DGU .... Directional Gyro Unit
DGU .... Display Generator Unit (DNAB)
DGU .... Downgrade to Unclassified [*Military*] (MCD)

DGU............ Georgetown University, Washington, DC [*Library symbol Library of Congress OCLC symbol*] (LCLS)
D Guam ...... United States District Court for the District of Guam (DLA)
DGU-KIE ..... Georgetown University, Kennedy Institute, Center for Bioethics, Washington, DC [*Library symbol Library of Congress*] (LCLS)
DGU-L.......... Georgetown University, Law Library, Washington, DC [*Library symbol Library of Congress*] (LCLS)
DGU-M........ Georgetown University, Medical, Dental, and Nursing Library, Washington, DC [*Library symbol Library of Congress*] (LCLS)
DGU-Pop..... Georgetown University, Kennedy Institute, Center for Population Research, Washington, DC [*Library symbol Library of Congress*] (LCLS)
DGU-S .... Georgetown University, Science Library, Washington, DC [*Library symbol Library of Congress*] (LCLS)
DGU-W .... Georgetown University, Woodstock Theological Center, Washington, DC [*Library symbol Library of Congress*] (LCLS)
DG/UX......... Data General UNIX (CDE)
DGV .... Degaussing Vessel [*British military*] (DMA)
DGV .... Dextrose-Gelatin-Veronal [*Solution*] [*Microbiology*]
DGV .... Dienst Grondwaterverkenning [*TNO Institute of Applied Geoscience*] [*Information service or system Netherlands*] (IID)
DGV .... Digital Generator Video (DNAB)
DGVA .... Delta-Guanidinovaleric Acid [*Biochemistry*]
DGVB .... Dextrose-Gelatin-Veronal Buffer [*Microbiology*] (MAE)
DGVC .... Georgetown Visitation Preparatory School, Washington, DC [*Library symbol Library of Congress*] (LCLS)
DGVT .... Director General for Vocational Training (AIE)
DGW .... Director-General of Weapons [*British military*] (DMA)
DGW .... Director-General of Works [*RAF*] [*British*]
DGW .... Double Gypsy Winch
DGW .... Douglas, WY [*Location identifier FAA*] (FAAL)
DGW .... George Washington University, Washington, DC [*Library symbol Library of Congress OCLC symbol*] (LCLS)
DGW(A) ...... Director-General of Weapons (Army) [*British military*] (RDA)
DGW-C........ George Washington University, Carnegie Endowment for International Peace Collection, Washington, DC [*Library symbol Library of Congress*] (LCLS)
DGWE .... Director General of Water Engineering (DCTA)
DGWIP......... Director-General of Weapons and Instruments Production [*Military British*]
DGW-L........ George Washington University, Law Library, Washington, DC [*Library symbol Library of Congress*] (LCLS)
DGW-M....... George Washington University, Medical Library, Washington, DC [*Library symbol Library of Congress*] (LCLS)
DGW(N)...... Director-General of Weapons Department (Naval) [*British*]
DGWO......... Degaussing Wiping Officer [*Navy*]
DGW-PIP..... George Washington University, Medical Center, Population Information Program, Washington, DC [*Library symbol Library of Congress*] (LCLS)
DGWS .... Division for Girls' and Women's Sports [*of American Association for Health, Physical Education, and Recreation; also used in a book title*] [*Later, NAGUS*]
DGWT .... Digital Guided Weapon Technology (MCD)
DGX .... Director-General of Explosives Production [*Ministry of Supply*] [*British World War II*]
DGX .... Dungannon Explorations Ltd. [*Vancouver Stock Exchange symbol*]
DGX .... Quest Diagnostics, Inc. [*NYSE symbol*] (SAG)
DG XIII........ Directorate-General (Section XIII) [*Council of European Communities*] (NITA)
DGZ .... Designated Ground Zero (MSA)
DGZ .... Desired Ground Zero [*Bombing*]
DGZ .... Deutsche Girozentrale - Deutsche Kommunalbank [*West German bank*]
DGZPRO ...... Desired Ground Zero Program [*Military*] (IAA)
DGZPRO ...... Desired Ground Zero Tape Prepare Program [*Bombing*] (SAA)
DH .... Das Heisst [*That Is*] [*German*]
DH .... Data Handbook (MCD)
DH .... Day Hospital
DH .... Dayton Hudson [*NYSE symbol*] (TTSB)
DH .... Dayton Hudson Corp. [*NYSE symbol*] (SAG)
DH .... Deadhead [*Freight*]
DH .... Dead Heat
DH .... Decay Heat [*Nuclear energy*] (NRCH)
DH .... Deccan Horse [*British military*] (DMA)
D-H .... Decimal to Hexadecimal (IEEE)
DH .... Decision Height [*Aviation*]
DH .... De Havilland Aircraft Co.
DH .... De Havilland Aircraft of Canada Ltd. [*ICAO aircraft manufacturer identifier*] (ICAO)
DH .... Dehydratase [*An enzyme*]
DH .... Dehydrocholic Acid [*Organic chemistry*] (MAE)
DH .... Dehydrogenase [*An enzyme*]
DH .... Delayed Hypersensitivity [*Immunology*]
DH .... Deliquescence Humidity
DH .... Demeure Historique [*An association France*] (EAIO)
DH .... Dental Hygienist [*British military*] (DMA)
DH .... Dermatitis Herpetiformis [*Medicine*]
DH .... Designated Hitter [*Formerly, DPH*] [*Also, DESI Baseball*]
DH .... Design Handbook
DH .... Destination Hospital [*Aeromedical evacuation*]
D/H .... Deuterium/Hydrogen Ratio
DH .... Developmental History [*Medicine*] (DMAA)
DH .... Device Handler
DH .... Diapause Hormone [*In insects*] [*Endocrinology*]
DH .... Diaphragmatic Hernia [*Gastroenterology*] (DAVI)

DH	Difference in Height
DH	Diffuse Histiocytic [*Lymphoma*] [*Oncology*] (DAVI)
DH	Dignitatis Humanae [*Declaration on Religious Freedom*] [*Vatican II document*]
D/H	Direct Hit
DH	Directly Heated (DEN)
DH	Director of Hygiene [*British military*] (DMA)
DH	Dirham [*Monetary unit*] [*Morocco*]
DH	Disc Harrowing [*Agriculture*]
DH	Discovery Airlines [*ICAO designator*] (AD)
DH	Dislocated Homemaker [*Job Training and Partnership Act*] (OICC)
DH	Disorderly House
DH	Display Hold
DH	Disseminated Histoplasmosis [*Medicine*]
DH	Diuretic Hormone [*Endocrinology*]
DH	Doctor of Humanics
DH	Doctor of Humanities
DH	Document Handling (IAA)
DH	Dominant Hand [*Psychometrics*]
DH	Doors of Hope [*An association*] (EA)
DH	Double Helix [*Cytology, genetics*]
DH	Double Heterostructure [*Physics*]
DH	Double Homology [*Biochemistry*]
DH	Double-Hung [*Construction*]
DH	Double Hydrant [*On fire insurance maps*]
DH	Dow Chemical Co. [*Research code symbol*]
DH	Downhill [*Bicycle handlebars*]
DH	Drug Hypersensitivity [*Medicine*] (DAVI)
DH	Ductal Hyperplasia [*Medicine*] (DMAA)
DH	Tonga Air Service [*ICAO designator*] (AD)
Dh8	Boeing Canada Dash-8 [*Airplane code*]
DHA	Dairy Husbandry Adviser [*Ministry of Agriculture, Fisheries, and Food*] [*British*]
DHA	Dehydrated Humulinic Acid (OA)
DHA	Dehydroacetic Acid [*Pharmacology*]
DHA	Dehydroascorbic Acid [*Also, DAA*] [*Oxidized form of Vitamin C*] [*Biochemistry*]
DHA	Dehydroepiandrosterone [*Also, DEA, DHEA, DHIA*] [*Endocrinology*]
DHA	Denver Handwriting Analysis [*Educational test*]
DHA	Department of Humanitarian Affairs [*United Nations*]
DHA	Dependent Housing Area [*Army*] (AABC)
DHA	Design Hazard Analysis (MCD)
DHA	Dhahran [*Saudi Arabia*] [*Airport symbol*] (OAG)
DHA	Dihydroactinidiolide [*Organic chemistry*]
DHA	Dihydroalprenolol [*Pharmacochemistry*]
DHA	Dihydroanthracene [*Organic chemistry*]
DHA	Dihydroxyacetone [*Organic chemistry*]
DHA	District Health Authority [*British*]
DHA	District Heating Association [*British*]
DHA	Docosahexaenoic Acid [*Organic chemistry*]
DHA	Doctor of Hospital Administration
DHA	Double Heave Amplitude
DHA	Dutch Harbor [*Alaska*] [*Seismograph station code, US Geological Survey Closed*] (SEIS)
DHAA	Dehydroabietic Acid [*Organic chemistry*]
DHAD	Dihydroxyanthracenedione [*Quinazarin*] [*Organic chemistry*]
DH Adm	Doctor of Hospital Administration
DHAEMAE	Disposable Hypodermic and Allied Equipment Manufacturers Association of Europe (EAIO)
DHAN	Dihaloacetonitrile [*Organic chemistry*]
DHANP	Diplomate of Homeopathic Academy of Naturopathic Physicians [*Medicine*]
DHAP	Dihydroxyacetone Phosphate [*Also, DAP*] [*Organic chemistry*]
DHAS	Deborah Harry Appreciation Society (EA)
DHAS	Dehydroepiandrosterone Sulfate [*Biochemistry*]
DHAS	Doctors Health Advisory Service [*Australia*]
DHAT	Dental Hygiene Aptitude Test (EDAC)
DHA(T)	District Health Authority (Teaching) [*National Health Service*] [*British*] (DI)
D Hawaii	United States District Court, District of Hawaii (DLA)
DHB	Daniel Hudson Burnham [*Architect and urban planner, 1846-1912*]
DHB	Dihydroxybenzoic Acid [*Organic chemistry*]
DHBA	Dihydroxybenzylamine [*Organic chemistry*]
DHBD	Dihydroxybiphenyl Dioxygenase [*An enzyme*]
DHBG	(Dihydroxybutyl)guanine [*Biochemistry*]
DHBP	Dihydroxybenzophenone [*Organic chemistry*]
DHBS	Dihydroxybenzoylserine [*Organic chemistry*]
DHBV	Duck Hepatic B Virus
DHC	Air-Cushion Vehicle built by DeHavilland Aircraft Co. of Canada [*Usual ly used in combination with numerals*] [*Canada*]
DHC	Boeing Dehavilland Canada [*ICAO designator*] (FAAC)
DHC	Danielson Holding [*AMEX symbol*] (TTSB)
DHC	Danielson Holding Corp. [*AMEX symbol*] (SPSG)
DHC	Data Handling Center (KSC)
DHC	Defence Housing Committee [*Australia*]
DHC	Defense Homes Corp. [*World War II*]
DHC	De Havilland, Inc. [*Canada*] [*FAA designator*] (FAAC)
DHC	Dehydrocholesterol [*Organic chemistry*]
DHC	Dehydrocholic Acid [*Organic chemistry*]
DHC	Dihydrochalcone [*Sweetening agent*]
DHC	Dihydrocodeine [*An analgesic*] [*Pharmacology*]
DHC	Dilute Homogeneous Charge
DHC	District Health Council [*Australia*]
DHC	Doctorat Honoris Causa [*Canada*] (DD)
DHC	Donohue, Inc. [*Toronto Stock Exchange symbol*]
DHC	Drop Head Coupe [*Convertible automobile*] [*British*]
DHC	Dry Hydrocarbon
DHCA	Deep Hypothermia and Circulatory Arrest [*Medicine*] (DMAA)
DHCA	Dihydroxycholestanoic Acid [*Biochemistry*]
DHCA	Kaya [*Burkina Faso*] [*ICAO location identifier*] (ICLI)
DHCB	Barsalogho [*Burkina Faso*] [*ICAO location identifier*] (ICLI)
DHCC	Decay Heat Closed Cooling [*Nuclear energy*] (IEEE)
DHCC	Dihydroxycholecalciferol [*Vitamin D_3*]
DHCC	Ouahigouya [*Burkina Faso*] [*ICAO location identifier*] (ICLI)
DHCD	Department of Housing and Community Development (OICC)
DHCD	Didyr [*Burkina Faso*] [*ICAO location identifier*] (ICLI)
DHCE	Batie [*Burkina Faso*] [*ICAO location identifier*] (ICLI)
DHCF	Distributed Host Command Facility (NITA)
DHCF	Holy Cross Foreign Mission Seminary, Washington, DC [*Library symbol Library of Congress*] (LCLS)
DHCG	Kongoussi [*Burkina Faso*] [*ICAO location identifier*] (ICLI)
DHCHST	Downey Hand Center Hand Sensitivity Test
DHCI	Titao [*Burkina Faso*] [*ICAO location identifier*] (ICLI)
DHCJ	Djibo [*Burkina Faso*] [*ICAO location identifier*] (ICLI)
DHCK	Koudougou [*Burkina Faso*] [*ICAO location identifier*] (ICLI)
DHCL	Leo [*Burkina Faso*] [*ICAO location identifier*] (ICLI)
DHCM	Manga [*Burkina Faso*] [*ICAO location identifier*] (ICLI)
DHCO	Boromo [*Burkina Faso*] [*ICAO location identifier*] (ICLI)
DHCP	Decentralized Hospital Computer Program [*Veterans Administration*]
DHCP	Double Hexagonal Close-Packed [*Metallography*]
DHCP	Dynamic Host Configuration Program [*Computer science*]
DHCP	Dynamic Host Configuration Protocol [*Computer science*]
DHCP	Dynamic Host Control Protocol [*Computer science*]
DHCP	Po [*Burkina Faso*] [*ICAO location identifier*] (ICLI)
DHCR	Poura [*Burkina Faso*] [*ICAO location identifier*] (ICLI)
DHCS	Debbie Harry Collector's Society (EA)
DHCS	Seguenega [*Burkina Faso*] [*ICAO location identifier*] (ICLI)
DHCT	Tenado [*Burkina Faso*] [*ICAO location identifier*] (ICLI)
DHCU	Data Handling and Control Unit
DHCU	Gourcy [*Burkina Faso*] [*ICAO location identifier*] (ICLI)
DHCY	Division of Handicapped Children and Youth [*HEW*]
DHCY	Yako [*Burkina Faso*] [*ICAO location identifier*] (ICLI)
DHD	Dihydrodigoxin [*Biochemistry*]
DHD	Double Heat-Sink Diode (CET)
DHD	Drop-Hammer Die (MSA)
DHD	Durham Downs [*Australia Airport symbol*] (OAG)
DHDAA	Dihexadecyldimethylammonium Acetate [*Organic chemistry*]
DHDD	Digital High-Definition Display (KSC)
DHDI	Drop-Hammer Die
DHDMI	Dihydroxy(dimethyl)imidazolidinone [*Organic chemistry*]
DH-DOC	Dihydrodeoxycorticosterone [*Endocrinology*]
DHDS	Data Handling and Display Subsystem
DHDSC	Dayton Hudson Department Store Co. [*Division of Dayton-Hudson Corp.*]
DHE	Data Handling Equipment
DHE	Debye-Hueckel Equation [*Physics*]
DHE	Department of Home Economics [*of NEA*] [*Later, HEEA*] (EA)
DHE	Dielectric Heating Equipment
DHE	Dihematoporphirin Ether [*Pharmacology*]
DHE	Dihydroergocornine [*Endocrinology*]
DHE	Dihydroergotamine [*Pharmacology*]
DHE	Diploma in Horticulture, Royal Botanic Garden, Edinburgh [*British*] (DBQ)
DHE	Doctor of Church History
DHE	Dump Heat Exchanger [*Nuclear energy*] (OA)
DHEA	Boulsa [*Burkina Faso*] [*ICAO location identifier*] (ICLI)
DHEA	Dehydroepiandrosterone [*Also, DEA, DHA, DHIA*] [*Endocrinology*]
DHEAS	Dehydroepiandrosterone Sulfate [*Biochemistry*]
DHEB	Bogande [*Burkina Faso*] [*ICAO location identifier*] (ICLI)
DHEBA	(Dihydroxyethylene)bisacrylamide [*Organic chemistry*]
DHEC	Dihydroergocryptine [*Organic chemistry*]
DH Ec	Doctor of Home Economics
DH Ec	Doctor of Household Economy
DHEC	Komin-Yanga [*Burkina Faso*] [*ICAO location identifier*] (ICLI)
DHED	Diapaga [*Burkina Faso*] [*ICAO location identifier*] (ICLI)
DHEE	Dori [*Burkina Faso*] [*ICAO location identifier*] (ICLI)
DHEF	Fada N'Gourma [*Burkina Faso*] [*ICAO location identifier*] (ICLI)
DHEG	Di(hydroxyethyl)glycine [*Organic chemistry*]
DHEG	Gorom-Gorom [*Burkina Faso*] [*ICAO location identifier*] (ICLI)
DHEK	Koupela [*Burkina Faso*] [*ICAO location identifier*] (ICLI)
DHEL	Kantchari [*Burkina Faso*] [*ICAO location identifier*] (ICLI)
DHEM	Tambao [*Burkina Faso*] [*ICAO location identifier*] (ICLI)
DHEN	Garango [*Burkina Faso*] [*ICAO location identifier*] (ICLI)
DHEO	Zorgo [*Burkina Faso*] [*ICAO location identifier*] (ICLI)
DHEP	Detailed Human Engineering Plan
DHEP	Pama [*Burkina Faso*] [*ICAO location identifier*] (ICLI)
DHER	Arli [*Burkina Faso*] [*ICAO location identifier*] (ICLI)
DHERF	Dental Health Education and Research Foundation [*Australia*]
DHES	Division of Health Examination Statistics [*HEW*]
DHES	Sebba [*Burkina Faso*] [*ICAO location identifier*] (ICLI)
DHESN	Dihydroergosine [*Biochemistry*]
DHET	Dihydroergotoxine [*Organic chemistry*]
DHET	Tenkodogo [*Burkina Faso*] [*ICAO location identifier*] (ICLI)
DHEW	Department of Health, Education, and Welfare [*Later, DHHS*]
DHEW	United States Department of Health, Education, and Welfare, Washington, DC [*Library symbol Library of Congress*] (LCLS)
DHEY	Ouargaye [*Burkina Faso*] [*ICAO location identifier*] (ICLI)
DHEZ	Zabre [*Burkina Faso*] [*ICAO location identifier*] (ICLI)
DHF	Dag Hammarskjold Foundation [*Sweden*] (EAIO)
DHF	Data Handling Function (SSD)

DHF .... Demand History File [*DoD*]
DHF .... Dengue Hemorrhagic Fever [*Medicine*]
DHF .... Dihydrofolate [*Biochemistry*]
DHF .... Dihydroxyflavone [*Organic chemistry*]
DHF .... Document History File (MCD)
DHF .... Double Hollow Fork [*Bicycle part or a fool*] [*Slang British*] (DSUE)
DHFA .... Double-Conductor, Heat and Flame-Resistant, Armored [*Cable*]
DHFC .... David Hasselhoff Fan Club (EA)
DHFC .... David Heavener Fan Club (EA)
DHFC .... David Hedison Fan Club [*Defunct*] (EA)
DHFC .... Deidre Hall Fan Club (EA)
DHFR .... Dihydrofolate Reductase [*An enzyme*]
DHFS .... Dengue Hemorrhagic Fever Syndrome [*Medicine*]
DHG .... Di(hydroxyethyl)glycinate [*Organic chemistry*]
DHg .... Doctor of Hygiene
DHGE .... Dictionnaire d'Histoire et de Geographie Ecclesiastique [*A publication*] (BJA)
DHGG .... Deaggregated Human Gammaglobulin [*Medicine*] (DMAA)
DHH .... Deaf and Hard of Hearing
DHH .... Doctor of Honorary Humanities
DHHEC .... Deaf and Hard of Hearing Entrepreneurs Council (EA)
DHHH .... Ouagadougou (Airport) [*Burkina Faso*] [*ICAO location identifier*] (ICLI)
DHHS .... Department of Health and Human Services
DHHS .... United States Department of Health and Human Services, Washington, DC [*Library symbol Library of Congress*] (LCLS)
DHHV .... Ouagadougou [*Burkina Faso*] [*ICAO location identifier*] (ICLI)
DHI .... Dairy Herd Improvement (OA)
DHI .... Dental Health International (EA)
DHI .... Department Head Instruction (NRCH)
DHI .... Dhangarhi [*Nepal*] [*Airport symbol*] (OAG)
DHI .... Dictionary of the History of Ideas [*A publication*]
DHI .... Dihydroxyindol
DHI .... Directional Horizon Indicator
DHI .... Door and Hardware Institute (EA)
DHI .... D.R.Horton [*NYSE symbol*] (TTSB)
DHI .... DR Horton, Inc. [*NYSE symbol*] (SAG)
DHIA .... Dairy Herd Improvement Association [*Later, AIPL*] (EA)
DHIA .... Dehydroisoandrosterone [*Also, DEA, DHA, DHEA*] [*Endocrinology*]
DHIC .... Dihydroisocodeine [*Pharmacology*]
DHIFC .... Doyle Holly International Fan Club [*Defunct*] (EA)
DHIR .... Dairy Herd Improvement Registry
DHIRS .... District Headquarters Induction and Recruiting Station [*Marine Corps*]
DHIS .... Division of Health Interview Statistics [*Department of Health and Human Services*] (GFGA)
DHISF .... Document Handling and Information Services Facility [*General Accounting Office*] (IID)
DHIY .... Devonshire Hussar Imperial Yeomanry [*Military British*] (ROG)
DHK .... Diet/Health Knowledge Survey [*Department of Agriculture*] (GFGA)
DHK .... Dihydrokaempferol [*Botany*]
DHL .... Dag Hammarskjold Library [*United Nations*] (DUND)
DHL .... David Herbert Lawrence [*British novelist, 1885-1930*]
DHL .... Davies Herbarium, University of Louisville [*Kentucky*]
DHL .... Dhala [*Aden*] [*Airport symbol*] (AD)
DHL .... DHL Airways, Inc. [*FAA designator*] (FAAC)
DHL .... Diffuse Histiocytic Lyphoma [*Medicine*]
DHL .... Digital Equipment Corp., Hudson, Westboro, MA [*OCLC symbol*] (OCLC)
DHL .... Doctor of Hebrew Letters
DHL .... Doctor of Hebrew Literature
DHL .... Doctor of Humane Letters
DHL .... House of Lords Appeals, in Dunlop's Court of Session Cases, from Vol. 13 [*1851-62*] [*A publication*] (DLA)
DHLB .... Dihydrolevobunolol [*Biochemistry*]
DHLG .... Department of Housing and Local Government [*Queensland*] [*Australia*]
DH Lit .... Doctor of Hebrew Literature
DH Litt .... Doctor of Hebrew Letters [*or Literature*]
DHLLP .... Direct High-Level Language Processor
DHLNL .... Dihydroxylysinonorleucine [*Biochemistry*]
DHlthSc ...... Diploma in Health Science
DHLW .... Defense High-Level Radioactive Waste [*Nuclear energy*]
DHM .... Daughters of the Heart of Mary [*Roman Catholic religious order*]
DHM .... Debye-Huckel-Manning [*Theory*] [*Physical chemistry*]
DHM .... Dexterous Hand Master [*Robotics*]
DHM .... Dihydromorphine [*Analgesic compound*] [*Organic chemistry*]
DHM .... Dihydromuscimol [*Biochemistry*]
DHM .... Diocesan Home Missionary
DHM .... Dry Honing Machine
DHM .... Mokuleia, Oahu, HI [*Location identifier FAA*] (FAAL)
DHMA .... Dihydroxymandelic Acid [*Also, DMA, DOMA*] [*Organic chemistry*]
DHMA .... Drapery Hardware Manufacturers Association [*Defunct*] (EA)
DHMAA .... Draft Horse and Mule Association of America (EA)
DHMPA .... Dihydromycoplanecin A [*Biochemistry*]
DHMPA .... Dihydroxymethoxyphenylalanine [*Biochemistry*]
DHMS .... Dense Hydrous Magnesium Silicate [*Geochemistry*]
DHMSA .... Diploma in the History of Medicine, Society of Apothecaries of London [*British*] (DBQ)
DHMY .... Dehumidify (MSA)
DHN .... Dihydronaphthacene [*Organic chemistry*]
DHN .... Displaced Homemakers Network (EA)
DHN .... Dothan [*Alabama*] [*Airport symbol*] (OAG)
DHN .... Dynamic Hardness Number
DHO .... Deuterium Hydrogen [*Protium*] Oxide [*Organic chemistry*] (DAVI)
DHO .... Dihydroouabain [*Biochemistry*]

DHO .... Director of Home Operations [*Air Ministry*] [*British World War II*]
DHO .... District Historical Office [*or Officer*] [*Navy*]
DHOA .... Dano [*Burkina Faso*] [*ICAO location identifier*] (ICLI)
DHOB .... Banfora [*Burkina Faso*] [*ICAO location identifier*] (ICLI)
DHOD .... Dedougou [*Burkina Faso*] [*ICAO location identifier*] (ICLI)
DHOF .... Safane [*Burkina Faso*] [*ICAO location identifier*] (ICLI)
DHOG .... Gaoua [*Burkina Faso*] [*ICAO location identifier*] (ICLI)
DH/OH .... Down Hours to Operating Hours Ratio [*Quality control*]
DHOH .... Hounde [*Burkina Faso*] [*ICAO location identifier*] (ICLI)
DHOL .... Loumana [*Burkina Faso*] [*ICAO location identifier*] (ICLI)
DHON .... Nouna [*Burkina Faso*] [*ICAO location identifier*] (ICLI)
DHOO .... Bobo-Dioulasso [*Burkina Faso*] [*ICAO location identifier*] (ICLI)
D Hor .... Doctor of Horticulture
DHOR .... Orodara [*Burkina Faso*] [*ICAO location identifier*] (ICLI)
DHOS .... Sideradougou [*Burkina Faso*] [*ICAO location identifier*] (ICLI)
D Ho Sc ...... Doctor of Household Science
DHOT .... Tougan [*Burkina Faso*] [*ICAO location identifier*] (ICLI)
DHOU .... Diebougou [*Burkina Faso*] [*ICAO location identifier*] (ICLI)
DHOY .... Aribinda [*Burkina Faso*] [*ICAO location identifier*] (ICLI)
DHP .... Dehydrogenative Polymerization [*Biology*]
DHP .... Dehydroproline [*Biochemistry*]
DHP .... Delivered Horsepower to Propeller (IAA)
DHP .... Demokratik Halk Partisi [*Democratic People's Party*] [*Turkish Cyprus*] [*Political party*] (PPE)
DHP .... Deoxidized High-Residual Phosphorus [*Copper*]
DHP .... Department Head Procedures (NRCH)
DHP .... Designed Horsepower (IAA)
DHP .... Deutsche Hannover Partei [*German Hanover Party*] (PPE)
DHP .... Developed Horsepower
DHP .... Diheptyl Phthalate [*Organic chemistry*]
DHP .... Dihexadecyl Phosphate [*Organic chemistry*]
DHP .... Dihydroheptaprenol [*Biochemistry*]
DHP .... Dihydropyrane [*Organic chemistry*]
DHP .... Dihydropyridine [*Organic chemistry*]
DHP .... Dihydroxyphenol [*Organic chemistry*]
DHP .... Diploma in Hypnosis and Psychotherapy [*British*] (DBQ)
DHP .... Document Handler Processor
DHP .... Drawbar Horsepower
DHPA .... Degree of Honor Protective Association [*St. Paul, MN*] (EA)
DHPA .... Dihydroxypropyladenine [*Biochemistry*]
DHPC .... Dorsal Hippocampus [*Neuroanatomy*]
DHPE .... Data Hardware Project Engineer [*NASA*]
DHPE .... Dihydroxyphenylethanol [*Organic chemistry*]
DHPG .... Dehydroxyphenylglycol [*Also, DOPEG*] [*Organic chemistry*]
DHPG .... Dihydroxyphenethyleneglycol [*Organic chemistry*]
DHPG .... (Dihydroxypropoxymethyl)guanine [*Biochemistry*]
DHPGTP ...... (Dihydroxypropoxymethyl)guanine Triphosphate [*Antiviral compound*]
DHPMA .... Dihydroxypropyl Methacrylate [*Organic chemistry*]
DHPR .... Dihydropteridine Reductase [*An enzyme*]
DHPR .... Dihydropyridine Receptor [*Biochemistry*]
dhPRL .... Decidual Proclactin (BABM)
dhPRL .... Decidual Prolactin [*Medicine*] (DAVI)
DHPTA .... Diaminohydroxypropanetetraacetic Acid [*Also, DTA, DPTA*] [*Organic chemistry*]
dHpuA .... Deoxyheptulosonic Acid [*Biochemistry*]
DHQ .... Dihydroquercetin [*Botany*]
DHQ .... Dihydroquinidine [*Organic chemistry*]
DHQ .... District Headquarters
DHQ .... Division Headquarters [*Military*]
DHQ .... Mean Diurnal High-Water Inequality
DHQHS .... Dihydroqinghaosu [*Organic chemistry*]
DHR .... Danaher Corp. [*NYSE symbol*] (SPSG)
DHR .... Decay Heat Removal [*Nuclear energy*] (NRCH)
DHR .... Delayed Hypersensitivity Reaction [*Medicine*]
DHR .... Delivery History Report (AFIT)
DHR .... Department of Human Resources (IAA)
DHR .... Double High-Resolution File [*Computer science*]
DHR .... Holy Redeemer College, Washington, DC [*Library symbol Library of Congress*] (LCLS)
DHRA .... Delta Houseboat Rental Association (EA)
DHRC .... Douglas Hospital Research Centre [*McGill University, Douglas Hospital*] [*Canada Research center*] (RCD)
DHRS .... Data Handling Recording System [*Computer science*] (PDAA)
DHRS .... Decay Heat Removal Service [*or System*] [*Nuclear energy*] (NRCH)
DHRS .... Direct Heat Removal Service [*or System*] [*Nuclear energy*] (IEEE)
DHS .... Dance History Scholars (EA)
DHS .... Data Handling System
DHS .... Daughters of the Holy Spirit [*Roman Catholic religious order*]
DHS .... Decontamination Hot Shop [*Nuclear energy*] (NRCH)
DHS .... Demographic and Health Survey [*Agency for International Development*]
DHS .... Department of Health Services (DOGT)
DHS .... Desert Hot Springs [*California*] [*Seismograph station code, US Geological Survey Closed*] (SEIS)
DHS .... Design History Society [*British*] (DBA)
DHS .... Despun Heat Shield
DHS .... Destroyer Helicopter System (MCD)
DHS .... Dihydrostreptomycin [*Also, DHSM, DST*] [*Antimicrobial agent*]
DHS .... Dinshah Health Society (EA)
DHS .... Diploma in Horticultural Science (ADA)
DHS .... Director Historical Section [*World War I*] [*Canada*]
DHS .... Director of Health Services [*Army*] (AABC)
DHS .... Discrete Horizon Sensor (MCD)
DHS .... Divorce Help Sourcebook [*A publication*]
DHS .... Doctor of Health Science

DHS	Doctor of Hebrew Studies (BJA)
DHS	Doctor of Humanitarian Service
DHS	Doctor of Human Services (GAGS)
DHS	Domestic Heating Society [British] (DBA)
DHS	Donor Horse Serum [Pharmaceutical manufacture]
DHS	Doppler Hover System (MCD)
DHS	Dry Heat Sterilization
DHS	Dual-Hardness Steel
DHS	Duration of Hospital Stay
DHS	Dynamic Hip Screw [System] [Orthopedics] (DAVI)
DHSFT	Dynamic High-Speed Functional Tester (MCD)
DHSH	Department of Human Services and Health [Australia]
DHSM	Diagnostic Health Services, Inc. [NASDAQ symbol] (SAG)
DHSM	Diagnostic Health Svcs [NASDAQ symbol] (TTSB)
DHSM	Dihydrostreptomycin [Also, DHS, DST] [Antimicrobial agent]
DHSS	Data Handling Subsystem (NATG)
DHSS	Department of Health and Social Security [British]
DHSS	Dihydrostreptomycin Sulfate [Antimicrobial agent]
DHSV	Down-Hole Safety Valve
DHT	Dalhart, TX [Location identifier FAA] (FAAL)
DHT	Dehydrotestosterone [A banned performance-enhancng drug] (ECON)
DHT	Delayed Hypersensitivity to Tuberculin [Medicine]
DHT	Dihydrotachysterol [Same as ATL-IO] [Biochemistry]
DHT	Dihydrotestosterone [Also, D] [Endocrinology]
DHT	Dihydrothymine (MAE)
DHT	Dihydroxytryptamine [Biochemistry]
DHT	Discrete Hartley Transform (BYTE)
DHT	Discrete Hilbert Transform (IEEE)
Dht	Twin Otter [Airplane code]
DHTB	Dihydroteleocidin B [Biochemistry]
DH Tch	DH Technology, Inc. [Associated Press] (SAG)
DHTDMAC...	Dihydrogenated Tallow Dimethylammonium Chloride [Fabric softener] [Organic chemistry]
DHTI	Dynamic Healthcare Tech [NASDAQ symbol] (TTSB)
DHTI	Dynamic Healthcare Technologies, Inc. [NASDAQ symbol] (SAG)
DHTK	DH Technology [NASDAQ symbol] (TTSB)
DHTK	DH Technology, Inc. [NASDAQ symbol] (NQ)
dHTML........	Dynamic HTML [HyperText Markup Language] [Computer science]
DHTML	Dynamic HTML [Hyper Text Markup Language] [Computer science]
DHTP	Dihydrotestosterone Propionate [Endocrinology]
DHTR	Delayed Hemolytic Transfusion Reaction [Medicine]
DHU	Deck Hand Uncertified [Shipping] (DS)
DHU	Disability Hearings Unit [Social Security Administration] (OICC)
D Hu	Doctor of Humanities
DHU	Document Handler Unit
DHU	Howard University, Washington, DC [Library symbol Library of Congress OCLC symbol] (LCLS)
DHUD..........	Department of Housing and Urban Development
DHUD..........	United States Department of Housing and Urban Development, Washington, DC [Library symbol Library of Congress] (LCLS)
D Hu L	Doctor of Humane Letters
DHUL	Dorchester Hugoton Ltd. [NASDAQ symbol] (NQ)
DHU-L.........	Howard University, School of Law, Washington, DC [Library symbol] [Library of Congress] (LCLS)
DHULZ	Dorchester Hugoton [NASDAQ symbol] (TTSB)
D Hum	Doctor of Humanities
DHumL	Doctor of Humane Letters (NADA)
DHumLitt	Doctor of Humane Letters
DHV	Design Hourly Volume [Transportation]
DHV	Duck Hepatitis Virus
DHVA	De Haas-van Alphen [Effect]
DHVM	Digital Hardware Voter Monitor (MCD)
DHW	Domestic Hot Water
DHW	Double-Hung Windows [Technical drawings]
DHW	Dyer Hill [Washington] [Seismograph station code, US Geological Survey] (SEIS)
DHX	Dump Heat Exchanger [Nuclear energy] (NRCH)
DHXCS	Dump Heat Exchanger Control System [Nuclear energy] (NRCH)
DHY	Deuterated Hydrogen Y [Type of zeolite]
DHY	Develet Hava Yollari [Airline]
DHY	Dhoney [Ship's rigging] (ROG)
D Hy	Doctor of Hygiene
D Hyg	Doctor of Hygiene
DHZ	Dihydralazine [Antihypertensive agent]
DI	Argo, SA [Dominican Republic] [ICAO designator] (ICDA)
DI	Daily Inspection [Military] (MCD)
DI	Dark Ignition
DI	Das Ist [That Is] [German]
DI	Data Input [Computer science] (IEEE)
DI	Data Integrator (MCD)
DI	Data Interchange
DI	Data Interface
DI	Data Item
DI	Date of Injury [Medicine] (HGAA)
DI	Daylight Impression [Psychical research]
DI	Dead Indian [Careless man] [Army slang]
DI	Deciliter [NHTSA] (TAG)
DI	Deep Interdiction
DI	Defective-Interfering [Virology]
DI	Defence Intelligence [British]
DI	Defense Industry
DI	Defense Information (AFM)
DI	Defense Instruction (ADA)
DI	Deformability Index

DI................	Deicing
DI................	Deionization
DI................	Delay Indefinite (FAAC)
DI................	Delta Air [ICAO designator] (AD)
DI................	Demand Indicator (KSC)
DI................	[The] Democracy International (EA)
DI................	Density Indicator
DI................	Dental Information (EA)
DI................	Dentinogenesis Imperfecta [Medicine] (DMAA)
DI................	Departmental Instruction (AAG)
DI................	Department of Industry [British] (DCTA)
DI................	Department of the Interior (MCD)
DI................	Deputy for Intelligence
DI................	Deputy Inspector [British] (ROG)
DI................	Description and Instructions
DI................	Designation Indicator
DI................	Design Integration (DNAB)
DI................	Design International (EA)
DI................	Desorption Ionization
DI................	Destination Index [Computer science]
DI................	Detective Inspector [Scotland Yard]
DI................	Detergent Inhibitor [Lubricants]
DI................	Deterioration Index [Index of intellectual impairment on intelligence test]
DI................	Detrusor Instability [Urology] (DAVI)
DI................	Development Integrated (MCD)
DI................	Development International [Defunct] (EA)
DI................	Deviation Indicator
DI................	Device Independence
DI................	Device Interface [Electronics] (ECII)
DI................	Diabetes Insipidus
DI................	Diagnostic Imaging [Radiology] (DAVI)
DI................	Diagnostic Inspection [Clean Water Act] [Environmental Protection Agency] (EPA)
DI................	Diameter
Di................	Diatoms [Quality of the bottom] [Nautical charts]
Di................	Didymium [Mixture of rare-earth elements] [Chemistry] (ROG)
Di................	Diego [Blood group]
DI................	Dielectric Isolation
DI................	Difference Index [Protein calculation] [Biochemistry]
DI................	Differentiated Infiltrating Tumor [Oncology]
DI................	Difficulty Index (AEE)
DI................	Diffusion Index [Economics]
DI................	Digital Input [Computer science]
Di................	Dinus de Mugello [Flourished, 1278-98] [Authority cited in pre-1607 legal work] (DSA)
DI................	Diode (IAA)
di................	Diopside [CIPW classification] [Geology]
DI................	Diplomatic Immunity (ADA)
DI................	Direct Impulse (DNAB)
DI................	Direct-Indirect
DI................	Direct Injection [Automotive engineering]
DI................	Direct Investor
DI................	Direction Indicator
DI................	Directivity Index
D/I...............	Director/Illuminator (CAAL)
DI................	Director of Infantry [Military British]
DI................	Director [or Directorate] of Installations [Abolished 1953, functions transferred to Department of Defense] [Air Force]
DI................	Directory Information [Newsletter]
DI................	Disability Income [Insurance]
DI................	Disability Insurance (AAG)
DI................	Disabled Individual [Title XVI] [Social Security Administration] (OICC)
DI................	Disc Harrowing and Ridging [Agriculture]
DI................	Discomfiture Index [Weather]
DI................	Discrete Input [Computer science] (KSC)
DI................	Disease Index [Botany]
DI................	Dispenser [Unit of issue] [Military] (DNAB)
DI................	Display Interface (NASA)
DI................	Disposition Instructions
DI................	Distal [Medicine]
DI................	Distillation [Calorimetry]
DI................	Distinctio [Decretum Gratiani] [A publication] (DSA)
DI................	Distinctive Insignia [Military]
DI................	Distoincisal [Dentistry]
DI................	Distribution Intsruction
DI................	Distribution of Industry [British]
DI................	District Inspector [Navy]
DI................	Diverting Ileostomy [Medicine]
DI................	Divisional Inspector [Education] (AIE)
DI................	Division Increment [DoD]
DI................	DOCARE International (EA)
DI................	Document Identifier [Military] (AFM)
DI................	Dolly In [Films, television, etc.]
DI................	Dominance Index [Neurology]
DI................	Donor Insemination [Medicine]
DI................	Doppler Inertial
DI................	Double Imperial [Paper] (ADA)
DI................	Double Indemnity [Insurance]
DI................	Double Injection
DI................	Dresser Industries [NYSE symbol] (TTSB)
DI................	Dresser Industries, Inc. [NYSE symbol] (SPSG)
DI................	Drifters, Inc. (EA)
DI................	Drill Instructor [Marine Corps]
DI................	Drug Information

DI...............	Drug Interactions
DI...............	Due In
DI...............	Dvorak International (EAIO)
DI...............	Dyskaryosis, Index of [*Cytopathology*]
DI...............	Dyspnea Index [*Medicine*] (DAVI)
DI...............	Fighter [*Russian aircraft symbol*]
DI...............	Flight Path Deviation Indicator [*Navigation*]
D$_I$...............	Insulin Dialysance [*Endocrinology*] (DAVI)
Di...............	Inulin Dialysance [*Medicine*] (MAE)
DI...............	United States Department of the Interior, Washington, DC [*Library symbol Library of Congress*] (LCLS)
DIA.............	Date of Initial Appointment
DIA.............	Defense Intelligence Agency [*Formerly, JJ-2*] [*DoD Washington, DC*]
DIA.............	Defense Intelligence Agency, Washington, DC [*OCLC symbol*] (OCLC)
DIA.............	Deficiency in Allowance [*Military*] (MSA)
DIA.............	Denver International Airport [*Facetious translation: Delay It Again*] (ECON)
DIA.............	Design and Industries Association [*British*]
DIA.............	Design Institute of Australia
DIA.............	Diabetes [*Medicine*] (DHSM)
DIA.............	Diagram (ADA)
DIA.............	Dialect (ADA)
DIA.............	Dialectic (WDAA)
DIA.............	Dialogue (NTCM)
DIA.............	Diameter
dia	Diameter (VRA)
dia	Diameter (IDOE)
DIA.............	Diamond
Dia.............	Diaphon [*Record label*] [*Australia*]
DIA.............	Diaphone [*Fog signal*]
DIA.............	Diaphoretic [*Inducing Perspiration*] [*Pharmacy*] (ROG)
DIA.............	Diaphragm (NTCM)
DIA.............	Diathermy [*Medicine*]
DIA.............	Differentiation Inhibitory Activity [*Cytology*]
DIA.............	Dig-In Angle
DIA.............	Digital Input Adaptor [*Computer science*] (NITA)
DIA.............	Digital Interface Adapter [*Computer science*] (MCD)
DIA.............	Digital Isolation Amplifier
DIA.............	Dimethylindoaniline [*Organic chemistry*]
DIA.............	Diploma in International Affairs (ADA)
DIA.............	Direct Air, Inc. [*Germany ICAO designator*] (FAAC)
DIA.............	Direct Interface Adapter
DIA.............	Disabled in Action National [*Defunct*] (EA)
DIA.............	Division of International Affairs [*An association*] (EA)
DIA.............	Doctor of Industrial Arts
DIA.............	Documentation et Information Africaines [*African Documentation and Information*] [*Catholic News Agency*]
DIA.............	Document Filing and Retrieval [*Telecommunications*] (OSI)
DIA.............	Document Interchange Architecture [*Telecommunications*] (OSI)
DIA.............	Documents Information Accessing (BUR)
DIA.............	Driving Instructors Association [*British*] (DBA)
DIA.............	Drug Induced Agranulocytosis [*Medicine*]
DIA.............	Drug Information Association (EA)
DIA.............	Dual Interface Adapter
DIA.............	Dubai International Airport
DIA.............	Due in Assets
DIA.............	Dulles International Airport [*FAA*]
DIA.............	Dutch Interchurch Aid and Service to Refugees [*Netherlands*]
DIA.............	Dyadic Interaction Analysis
DIAA	Dairy Industry Association of Australia
DIAB	Diabetes [*or Diabetic*]
DIAC	Dairy Industry Advisory Committee [*Australia*]
DIAC	Data Interpretation and Analysis Center [*Canadian Navy*]
DIAC	Defense Industry Advisory Council [*Later, IAC*] (AFM)
DIAC	Defense Information Analysis Center [*DoD*]
DIAC	Diiodothyroacetic Acid [*Biochemistry*]
DIAC	Diode, Alternating Current (IAA)
DIAC	Directorate of Internal Affairs and Communications [*Allied German Occupation Forces*]
DIAC	Distributed Intelligence Acquisition and Control (PDAA)
DIACS	Documentation Information and Control System [*Military*]
DIAD	Adiake [*Ivory Coast*] [*ICAO location identifier*] (ICLI)
DIAD	Data Immediate Access Diagram
DIAD	Diademed [*Numismatics*]
DIAD	Digital Image Analysis and Display [*Computer science*] (NITA)
DIAD	Digital Interferometric Analyzer and Display (MCD)
DIAD	Donor-Insulator-Acceptor Device [*Electronics*]
DIAD	Drum Information Assembler and Dispatcher
DIAD	Inter-American Defense College, Fort McNair, Washington, DC [*Library symbol Library of Congress*] (LCLS)
DIADEM	Dynamic International Access to Databases and Economic Models [*Economic Models Ltd.*] [*British*] (NITA)
DIADS	Digital Image Analysis and Display System [*Computer science*]
DIAE	Agboville [*Ivory Coast*] [*ICAO location identifier*] (ICLI)
DIA-FS	Design Institute of Australia Federal Secretariat
DIAG	Diagnosis
Diag	Diagnostic/Retrieval Systems, Inc. [*Associated Press*] (SAG)
DIAG	Diagonal
diag	Diagonal (WDMC)
Diag	Diagonal Bands [*Navigation markers*]
DIAG	Diagram (KSC)
diag	Diagram (VRA)
diag	Diagram (WDMC)
DIAG	Spectral Diagnostics, Inc. [*NASDAQ symbol*] (SAG)
DIAGE	Defense Industry Advisory Group Europe [*Terminated, 1977*]
DIAGF	Spectral Diagnostics [*NASDAQ symbol*] (TTSB)
DiagH	Diagnostic Health Services, Inc. [*Associated Press*] (SAG)
DiagHlt	Diagnostic Health Services, Inc. [*Associated Press*] (SAG)
DIAGL	Defense Intelligence Agency Guidance Letter (MCD)
DIAGN	Diagnose (NASA)
diagn	Diagnostic (BJA)
DiagPd	Diagnostic Products Corp. [*Associated Press*] (SAG)
DIAGR	Diagrammatic
DiagRet	Diagnostic Retrieval Systems [*Associated Press*] (SAG)
Diags	Diagnostics
DIAI	Defense Intelligence Agency Instruction (MCD)
DIAKONIA ...	World Federation of Diaconal Associations and Sisterhoods [*Germany*] (EAIO)
DIAL	Data Independent Analysis Library (CAAL)
DIAL	Data Information Accession List (MCD)
DIAL	Data Information Access Link [*Computer science*]
DIAL	Decimal Index of Art in the Lowlands [*A publication*]
DIAL	Deficiencies in Allowance List [*Military*] (NVT)
DIAL	Developmental Indicators for the Assessment of Learning [*Education*]
DIAL	Device Independent Access Level [*Telecommunications*] (OSI)
DIAL	Dialect [*or Dialectal*]
dial	Dialect (WDMC)
Dial	Dialogi [*of Seneca the Younger*] [*Classical studies*] (OCD)
DIAL	Dialogue
dial	Dialogue (WDMC)
Dial	Dialogus de Oratoribus [*of Tacitus*] [*Classical studies*] (OCD)
DIAL	Differential-Absorption LIDAR [*Spectroscopy*]
DIAL	Digital Image Analysis Laboratory [*University of Arizona*] [*Research center*] (RCD)
DIAL	Direct Information Access Link [*Computer science*]
DIAL	Disablement Information Advice Lines [*British*]
DIAL	Disk Interrogation Alternation and Loading (IAA)
DIAL	Display Interactive Assembly Language [*Computer science*] (IEEE)
DIAL	Distance Instruction for Adult Learning [*New School for Social Research, New York*]
DIAL	Documentacion Iglesial America Latina [*France*]
DIAL	Draper Industrial Assembly Language [*Computer science*]
DIAL	Drum Interrogation, Alteration, and Loading System [*Honeywell, Inc.*] (IEEE)
DialCp	Dial Corp. [*Associated Press*] (SAG)
DialCp	Dialysis Corp. of America [*Associated Press*] (SAG)
DialCpA	Dialysis Corp. of America [*Associated Press*] (SAG)
Dial D	Dialogi Deorum [*of Lucian*] [*Classical studies*] (OCD)
DIALGOL	Dialect of Algorithmic Language
Dial Meret ...	Dialogi Meretricii [*of Lucian*] [*Classical studies*] (OCD)
Dial Mort	Dialogi Mortuorum [*of Lucian*] [*Classical studies*] (OCD)
DIALOG	Direction for Army Logistic (MCD)
DIALOG	On-Line Search Service [*Lockheed*] (DLA)
Dialogic	Dialogic Corp. [*Associated Press*] (SAG)
DIA-LOGICS...	Document Indexing and Listing of Graphic Information Codes System [*Jet Propulsion Laboratory, NASA*]
Dialogue......	Dialogue: Canadian Philosophical Review [*A publication*] (BRI)
DialPge.......	Dial Page, Inc. [*Associated Press*] (SAG)
DIAL-R	Developmental Indicators for the Assessment of Learning - Revised [*Child development test*]
DIALS	Defense Information Automated Locator System (AABC)
DIALS	Digital Integrated Automatic Landing System [*Aviation*]
DIAM	Data Independent Architecture Model
DIAM	Defense Intelligence Acquisition Manual (MCD)
DIAM	Defense Intelligence Agency Manual (MCD)
DIAM	Defense Intelligence Agency Memorandum (MCD)
DIAM	Diameter
diam	Diameter (IDOE)
DIAMAT	Dialektischer Materialismus
DiaMet.......	Dia Met Minerals Ltd. [*Associated Press*] (SAG)
Diametrc......	Diametrics Medical, Inc. [*Associated Press*] (SAG)
DiamM........	Diamond Multimedia Systems, Inc. [*Associated Press*] (SAG)
DIAMON	Diagnostic Monitor [*Computer science*]
DIAMOND	Dielectrically Isolated Arrays of Monolithic Devices (MCD)
DIAN	DECCA Integrated Airborne Navigator
DIAN	Dianon Systems [*NASDAQ symbol*] (TTSB)
DIAN	Dianon Systems, Inc. [*NASDAQ symbol*] (SPSG)
DIAN	Digital Analog [*Computer science*] (IEEE)
DIAN	Digital Analog Simulator (NITA)
Dian	Hymmus in Dianam [*of Callimachus*] [*Classical studies*] (OCD)
DIANA	Descriptive Intermediate Attributed Notation for ADA [*Computer science*] (NITA)
DIANA	Dimokratiki Ananeossi [*Greece*] [*Political party*] (ECED)
DIANA	Dusseldorf's Institution Art Network Application (IID)
DianaCp......	Diana Corp. [*Associated Press*] (SAG)
DIAND	Department of Indian Affairs and Northern Development [*Canada*]
DIANE	Digital Integrated Attack and Navigation Equipment
DIANE	Direct Information Access Network for Europe [*Commission of the European Communities*] [*Information service or system Defunct*] (IID)
DIANE	Disque pour l'Analyse Economique (IID)
DIANE	Distance Indicating Automatic Navigation Equipment
DIANE	Duct Integrity and Nozzle Efficiency (MCD)
DIANM........	Defense Intelligence Analytical Memorandum (MCD)
Dianon........	Dianon Systems, Inc. [*Associated Press*] (SAG)
DIAO	Aboisso [*Ivory Coast*] [*ICAO location identifier*] (ICLI)
DIAOB.........	Defense Intelligence Air Order of Battle (MCD)
DiaOff........	Diamond Offshore Drilling, Inc. [*Associated Press*] (SAG)
DIAOLS	Defense Intelligence Agency On-Line Information System (MCD)

DIAP	Abidjan/Port Bouet [Ivory Coast] [ICAO location identifier] (ICLI)
DIAP	Diapason [Octave] [Music]
DIAP	Digitally-Implemented Analogue Processing (IAA)
DIAP	Drug Interdiction Assistance Program [FHWA] (TAG)
DIAPAS	Diabetes Personalized Alerting Service
DIAPER	Division Adaptation Personnel (SAA)
DIAPH	Diaphragm (MSA)
diaph	Diaphragmatic (MAE)
DIAR	Defense Intelligence Agency Regulation
DIAR	Department of the Interior Acquisition Regulation [A publication] (AAGC)
DIAR	Development-Inhibitor Anchimeric Releasing [Photography]
DIAR	Drew Institute for Archaeological Research [Drew University] [Research center] (RCD)
DI Arch	Doctor of Interior Architecture
DI Arch E	Doctor of Interior Architectural Engineering
DI Arch Eng	Doctor of Interior Architectural Engineering
DIAS	Delivery and Impact Analysis System (MCD)
DIAS	Diastolic [Medicine]
DIAS	Digital Integrated Avionics System (MCD)
DIAS	DIMDI's [Deutsches Institut fuer Medizinische Dokumentation und Information] Administration System
DIAS	Distributed Intelligent Actuators and Sensors (ACII)
DIAS	Double Isobaric Analogue State [Physics]
DIAS	Dublin Institute for Advanced Studies
DIAS	DUNS [Data Universal Numbering System] Industrial Affiliations Service (IID)
DIAS	Dynamic Inventory Analysis System [Computer science]
DiaShm	Diamond Shamrock R & M, Inc. [Associated Press] (SAG)
DIAST	Diastolic [Medicine] (WDAA)
DiaSys	DiaSys Corp. [Associated Press] (SAG)
DIAT	Dairy Industry Appeals Tribunal [Queensland] [Australia]
DIATH	Diathermy [Medicine]
Diath SW	Diathermy Short Wave [Physical therapy] (DAVI)
DIAU	Abengourou [Ivory Coast] [ICAO location identifier] (ICLI)
DIAV	Abidjan [Ivory Coast] [ICAO location identifier] (ICLI)
DIAWA	Dairy Industry Authority of Western Australia
DIB	Butyl Di-Iodohydroxybenzoate [Organic chemistry] (DAVI)
DIB	Daily Intelligence Bulletin [British] [A publication] (NITA)
DIB	Data Input Bus [Computer science] (MDG)
DIB	Decency in Broadcasting (NTCM)
DIB	Defence Information Bulletin [A publication]
DIB	Defense Industrial Base [DoD]
DIB	Defense Intelligence Board (MCD)
DIB	Department Information Bulletin
DIB	Department of Information and Broadcasting
DIB	Design Information Bulletin
DIB	Device-Independent Bitmap [Microsoft, Inc.] (PCM)
DIB	Device Independent Bitmap (CDE)
DIB	Dibrugarh [India] [Airport symbol] (OAG)
DIB	Dictionary of International Biography [A publication]
DIB	Dielectric Infrared Beamsplitter
DIB	Diffuse Interstellar Band [Astrophysics]
DIB	Digital Interconnecting Box (DWSG)
DIB	Diphenylisobenzofuran [Organic chemistry]
DIB	Directory Information Base (CDE)
DIB	Directory Information Base [Computer science] (TNIG)
DIB	Disability Insurance Benefits [Social Security Administration] (OICC)
DIB	Domestic and International Business (MCD)
DIB	Dot Immunobinding Assay [Immunology]
DIB	Dry Cleaning Information Bureau [British] (CB)
DIBA	Digital Integral Ballistic Analyzer (NG)
DIBA	Diisobutyl Adipate [Organic chemistry]
DIBA	Diisobutylamine [Organic chemistry]
DIBA	Doctor of International Business Administration (GAGS)
DIBA	Domestic and International Business Administration [Terminated 1977, functions assumed by Industry and Trade Administration] [Department of Commerce]
DIBAC	Diisobutylaluminum Chloride [Organic chemistry]
DIBAH	Diisobutylaluminum Hydride [Also, DBAH] [Organic chemistry]
DIBBL	Dismounted Infantry Battle Space Battle Lab [Army] (RDA)
DIBC	Bocanda [Ivory Coast] [ICAO location identifier] (ICLI)
DIBHP	Diisopropylbenzene Hydroperoxide [Organic chemistry]
DIBI	Boundiali [Ivory Coast] [ICAO location identifier] (ICLI)
DIBIT	Di-Binary Digit [Two consecutive binary digits] (TEL)
DIBK	Bouake [Ivory Coast] [ICAO location identifier] (ICLI)
DIBK	Diisobutyl Ketone [Organic chemistry]
DIBK	Dime Financial Corp. [NASDAQ symbol] (NQ)
DIBK	Dime Finl (CT) [NASDAQ symbol] (TTSB)
DIBL	Drain-Induced Barrier Lowering (IAA)
DIBN	Bouna/Tehini [Ivory Coast] [ICAO location identifier] (ICLI)
DIBOA	Dihydroxy Benoxazin One [Organic chemistry]
DIBOL	Digital Business Oriented Language [Digital Equipment Corp.] (NITA)
DIBOL	Digital Equipment's Business-Oriented Language [Computer science]
DIBP	Diisobutyl Phthalate
DIBRAC	Direct Broadcast Access (MCD)
DIBS	Digital Integrated Business System [Digital Equipment Corp.]
DIBU	Bondoukou/Soko [Ivory Coast] [ICAO location identifier] (ICLI)
DIC	Automatic Door Isolating Cock [British railroad term]
DIC	Dairy Industry Committee (EA)
DIC	Dairy Institute of California (SRA)
DIC	Data Input Check (HGAA)
DIC	Data Input Clerk [Computer science]
DIC	Data Input Consoles [Computer science] (NVT)
DIC	Data Insertion Converter

DIC	Data Interchange Code (IAA)
DIC	Data Item Catalog (IAA)
DIC	Data Item Category
DIC	Days in Culture [of cells]
DIC	Death and Indemnity Compensation [Veterans Administration] (GFGA)
DIC	Defense Identification Code (NATG)
DIC	Defense Intelligence Commentary (MCD)
DIC	Demand-Increasing Costs [Economics]
DIC	Democratie Integrale au Cameroun [Political party] (EY)
DIC	Department of Industrial Cooperation [University of Maine] [Research center] (RCD)
DIC	Dependency and Indemnity Compensation [Military]
DIC	Designers d'Interieur du Canada [Interior Designers of Canada - IDC]
DIC	Detailed Interrogation Center [Navy]
DIC	Detroit Institute for Children
DIC	Deviation Indicating Controller (IAA)
dic	Dicentric (MAE)
Dic	Dicta (DLA)
DIC	Dictionary
DIC	Difference in Conditions
DIC	Differential Interference Contrast [Microscope]
DIC	Diffuse Intravascular Coagulation [or Coagulopathy] [Hematology]
DIC	Digital Input [or Integrating] Computer [Computer science]
DIC	Digital Input Control [Computer science] (IAA)
DIC	Digital Integrated Circuit [Computer science]
DIC	Digital Interchange Code (NITA)
DIC	Digital Interface Component (MCD)
DIC	Diisopropylaminoethyl Chloride [Organic chemistry]
DIC	Dili [Zaire] [Airport symbol] (AD)
DIC	Dimethylamino Isopropyl Chloride [Organic chemistry]
DIC	(Dimethyltriazenyl)imidazolecarboxamide [Dacarbazine] [Also, DTIC Antineoplastic drug]
DIC	Diploma in Industrial Chemistry
DIC	Diploma of Membership of Imperial College of Science and Technology, University of London [British]
DIC	Diploma of the Imperial College of Science, Technology, and Medicine [Canada] (DD)
DIC	Discrete Integrated Circuit (IAA)
DIC	Disseminated Intravascular Coagulation [Hematology]
DIC	Dissolved Inorganic Carbon [Also, DIOC]
DIC	Divestiture Implementation Committee [Ghana]
DIC	Diving Information Center [Navy]
DIC	Division of Industrial Cooperation [MIT] (MCD)
DIC	Documentacion Internacional de Carreteras [International Road Research Documentation] [Database Ministerio de Obras Publicas y Urbanismo] [Spanish] [Information service or system] (CRD)
DIC	Document Identifier Code [Military] (AFM)
DIC	Driver Information Center [Automotive engineering]
DIC	Drunk in Charge
DIC	Dual In-Line Case [Computer science] (IAA)
DIC	United States Interstate Commerce Commission, Washington, DC [Library symbol Library of Congress] (LCLS)
DICA	Dance in Canada Association
DICA	Defense Industry Cooperation Agreement [Military]
DICA	Derecho de Importacion Centroamericano [Central American Import Right] [Central American Common Market] (EY)
DICA	Diagnostic Interview for Children and Adolescents
DICAB	Directive Coordinated and Approved by Budget Director [Air Force]
DICAM	Datasystem Interactive Communications Access Method [Digital Equipment Corp.]
DICAP	Direct-Current Circuit Analysis Program [Computer science]
DICAS	Directional Command Activated Sonobuoy [System] [Navy] (NVT)
DICASS	Directional Command Activated Sonobuoy System [Navy]
DICBM	Defense Intercontinental Ballistic Missile
DICBM	Depressed-Trajectory Intercontinental Ballistic Missile (MCD)
DICBM	Detection of Intercontinental Ballistic Missile (IAA)
DICC	Digital Interface Code Converter [Computer science]
DICCAP	Distributed Impressed Current Cathodic Protection [Anticorrosion system]
DICCASS	Document and Information Center of the Chinese Academy of Social Sciences
Dic Dom	Dicey. Law of Domicil [A publication] (DLA)
DICE	Crown Casino [NASDAQ symbol] (TTSB)
DICE	Crown Casino Corp. [NASDAQ symbol] (SAG)
DICE	DARPA [Defense Advanced Research Projects Agency] Initiatives in Concurrent Engineering [DoD]
DICE	Development Interim Control Equipment (IAA)
Dice	Dice's Reports [79-91 Indiana] [A publication] (DLA)
DICE	Digital Integrated Circuit Element [Computer science]
DICE	Digital Intercontinental Conversion Equipment (MCD)
DICE	Digital Interface Countermeasures Equipment [Air Force]
DICE	Digitally Implemented Communications Experiment (MCD)
DICE	Division of Improved Conversion Efficiency [Energy Research and Development Administration]
Dice	Double [or Dual] Income, Children, and Everything [Term coined by William F. Doescher, publisher of "D & B Reports"] [Lifestyle classification]
DICE	Dynamic Input to Control Center Equipment (IAA)
DICEF	Digital Communications Experimental Facility [Air Force]
Dicey & Morris	Dicey. Conflict of Laws [A publication] (DLA)
Dicey Confl Laws	Dicey. Conflict of Laws [A publication] (DLA)
Dicey Const	Dicey's Lectures Introductory to the Study of the Law of the English Constitution [A publication] (DLA)

Dicey Dom... Dicey. Law of Domicil [*A publication*] (DLA)
Dicey Domicil... Dicey. Law of Domicil [*A publication*] (DLA)
DIChem........ Diploma of Industrial Chemistry (ADA)
DICHLORAN... Dichloronitroaniline [*Also, DCNA*] [*Fungicide*]
DICIFER....... Digital Image Complex for Image Feature Extraction and Recognition System (MCD)
DICIFER....... Digital Interactive Complex for Image Feature Extraction and Recognition [*Air Force*]
DICIS .... Duane Information Center Indexing Service [*Database compilers*] (NITA)
Dick .... Dickens' English Chancery Reports [*A publication*] (DLA)
Dick .... Dickinson's New Jersey Equity Precedents [*A publication*] (DLA)
dick............ Ethyldichloroarsine [*Organic chemistry*] (DAVI)
Dick Black ... Dickson's Analysis of Blackstone's Commentaries [*A publication*] (DLA)
Dick Ch........ Dickens' English Chancery Reports [*A publication*] (DLA)
Dick Ch (Eng)... Dickens' English Chancery Reports [*A publication*] (DLA)
Dickens....... Dickens' English Chancery Reports [*A publication*] (DLA)
Dick Eq Pr ... Dickinson's New Jersey Equity Precedents [*A publication*] (DLA)
Dick Ev .... Dickson's Law of Evidence in Scotland [*A publication*] (DLA)
Dickinson Sch Law... [*The*] Dickinson School of Law (GAGS)
Dick Int'l L Ann... Dickinson's International Law Annual [*A publication*] (DLA)
Dick Just ..... Dickinson's Justice [*A publication*] (DLA)
Dick Kent..... Dickson's Analysis of Kent's Commentaries [*A publication*] (DLA)
Dick (NJ) ..... Dickinson's New Jersey Equity Precedents [*A publication*] (DLA)
Dick Quar Ses... Dickinson's Practical Guide to the Quarter Sessions [*A publication*] (DLA)
DICM .... Differential Interference Contrast Microscope
DICNAVAB .... Dictionary of Naval Abbreviations [*A publication*]
DICO .... Discovery [*or Dissemination*] of Information through Cooperative Organization
DICODE....... Digital Correlation Demonstrator
DICOM......... Digital Imaging and Communications in Medicine
DICOMSS...... Direct Commissary Support System [*DoD*]
DICOMTA.... Documentation Informatisee pour les Comptables [*CEDIC*] [*Database*]
DICON......... Digital Communication through Orbiting Needle (IAA)
DICORAP ..... Directional Controlled Rocket-Assisted Projectile (MCD)
DICORS....... Diver Communication Research System (PDAA)
DICOS .... Digital Communications System Evaluator (MCD)
DICOSE .... Digital Communications System Evaluator (MCD)
DICOSY....... Directional Coupler Synthesis (MCD)
DICP .... Drop-In Care Partners (EA)
Dic Par .... Dicey on Parties to Actions [*A publication*] (DLA)
DICR .... Daily Inspection Call Record (MCD)
DICS .... Digital Channel Selection (IAA)
DICS .... Display Interface Computer System (MCD)
DICS .... Down-Island Communication System [*Taiwan*] (CINC)
DICT........... Dictaphone
DICT........... Dictation
DICT........... Dictator
DICT........... Dictator
dict .... Diction (WDMC)
dict .... Dictionary (WDMC)
DICT........... Dictionary
Dicta........... Dicta of Denver Bar Association [*A publication*] (DLA)
DICTA .... Dictaphone (IAA)
DICTA .... Digital Integrated Circuit Training Aid [*Computer science*] (IAA)
DICU .... Digital Interface and Control Unit
DICWA........ Defence Industries Council of Western Australia
DICY .... Dicyanodiamide [*Also, DCD*] [*Organic chemistry*]
DID .... Daily Intelligence Digest
DID .... Dangerous Infectious Disease [*British*] (ROG)
DID .... Data Identification [*or Identifier*]
DID .... Data Input Display [*Computer science*]
DID .... Data Item Description
DID .... Datamation Industry Directory (MCD)
DID .... Dead of Intercurrent Disease [*Medicine*] (MAE)
DID .... Delayed Ischemic Deficit [*Medicine*]
DID .... Department of Industries and Development [*Northern Territory*] [*Australia*]
DID .... Destron/Idi, Inc. [*Vancouver Stock Exchange symbol*]
DID .... Detailed Issue Depot [*Military supply organization for Allied armies in Europe*] [*World War II*]
DID .... Device Identifier
Did............ Didache (BJA)
DID .... Didactic
did .... Didactic (VRA)
DID .... Didcot [*British depot code*]
DID .... Digital Information Detection [*Computer science*] (IAA)
DID .... Digital Information Display [*Computer science*]
DID .... Dimethylphthalate Indalone Dimethylcarbonate [*Insect repellant*] (IIA)
DID .... Direct Injection Diesel [*Automotive engineering*]
DID .... Direct Inward Dialing [*Telecommunications*]
DID .... Direct Inward Dialling
DID .... Director of the Intelligence Division [*British military*] (DMA)
DID .... Discharge Ionization Detector
DID .... Disodium Iminodiacetate [*Organic chemistry*]
DID .... Display Interface Device [*Telecommunications*] (TEL)
DID .... Division of Innovation and Development [*Department of Education*]
DID .... Division of Institutional Development [*Office of Education*]
DID .... Division of Isotopes Development [*AEC*]
DID .... Double Isotope Derivative
DID .... Drivers Integrated Display [*Military*] (RDA)
DID .... Drum Information Display

DID .... Dust Impact Detection System [*Astrophysics*]
DIDA........... Defense Industry Development and Support Administration [*Turkey*]
DIDA........... Depository Institutions Deregulation and Monetary Control Act of 1980
DIDA .... Differential In-Depth Analysis (PDAA)
DIDA .... Digital Data Network [*NASDAQ symbol*] (TTSB)
DIDA .... Dignity in Death Alliance [*British*]
DIDA .... Diisodecyl Adipate [*Organic chemistry*]
DIDA .... Director of Intelligence, Division of the Admiralty [*British*]
DIDA .... Dynamic Instrumentation Digital Analyzer
DIDAC......... Defense Intelligence Agency Dissemination Center (DNAB)
DIDAC......... Digital Data Communication (IAA)
DIDAC......... Digital Data Computer
DIDACS.... Digital Data Communications System (MCD)
DIDAD......... Digital Data Display
Dida de Segu... Didacus de Segura [*Flourished, 16th century*] [*Authority cited in pre-1607 legal work*] (DSA)
D Idaho....... United States District Court for the District of Idaho (DLA)
DIDAP......... Digital Data Processor
DIDAS......... Digital Data System (IAA)
DIDAS......... Dynamic Instrumentation Data Automobile System [*Telemetering system for auto test tracks*]
DIDAW........ Digital Data Network Wrrt [*NASDAQ symbol*] (TTSB)
DIDB .... Dabou [*Ivory Coast*] [*ICAO location identifier*] (ICLI)
DIDB .... Inter-American Development Bank, Washington, DC [*Library symbol Library of Congress*] (LCLS)
DIDC .... Data Input Display Console [*Computer science*]
DIDC .... Depository Institutions Deregulation Committee [*Department of the Treasury*] [*Terminated, 1986*]
DIDD .... Dense Intramembranous Deposit Disease [*Medicine*] (DMAA)
DIDD .... Dynamic Integrated Data Display
DIDDF .... Dual Input Discrete Describing Function [*Computer science*] (IAA)
DIDDS .... Dynamic Integrated Data Display System
DI/DES .... Vessels Disposed of by Sinking, Burning, Abandoning, or Other Means of Destruction [*Navy*]
DIDF .... Dual Input Describing Function [*Computer science*]
DIDG .... Diisodecyl Glutarate [*Organic chemistry*]
Did Iul .... Didius Iulianus [*of Scriptores Historiae Augustae*] [*Classical studies*] (OCD)
DIDK .... Dimbokro [*Ivory Coast*] [*ICAO location identifier*] (ICLI)
DIDL .... Daloa [*Ivory Coast*] [*ICAO location identifier*] (ICLI)
DIDL .... Digital Integrated Design Language [*Computer science*] (CSR)
DIDM .... Document Identification and Description Macros [*IBM Corp.*]
DIDMCA....... Depository Institutions Deregulation and Monetary Decontrol Act [*1980*]
DIDMOAD .... Diabetes Insipidus, Diabetes Mellitus, Optic Atrophy, Deafness Syndrome [*Medicine*] (DMAA)
DI/DO.......... Data Input/Data Output [*Computer science*]
DIDO........... Device Independent Disk Operation [*Computer science*] (IAA)
DIDO........... Digital Input/Digital Output [*Computer science*]
DIDO........... Directional Doppler (MCD)
DIDOC......... Desired Image Distribution Using Orthogonal Constraints [*Illinois Institute of Technology*]
DIDOCS....... Device-Independent Display Operator Console Support (BUR)
dIDP........... Deoxyinosine Diphosphate [*Biochemistry*]
DIDP........... Diisodecyl Phthalate [*Organic chemistry*]
DIDS .... Data Item Description System (MCD)
DIDS .... Defense Information Distribution System [*Proposed in-home disaster warning system*]
DIDS .... Defense Integrated Data System (AFM)
DIDS .... Digital Information Display System [*Computer science*]
DIDS .... Diisothiocyano (Disulfonic Acid) Stilbene [*Organic chemistry*]
DIDS .... DLSC [*Defense Logistics Services Center*] Integrated Data System [*Military*]
DIDS .... Document Information Directory System [*NIOSH*] [*Database*]
DIDS .... Domestic Information Display System [*Computer graphics*]
DIDS-CD ...... Decision Information Distribution System - Civil Defense [*Military*] (AABC)
DIDSIM........ Defense In-Depth Simulation
DIDSO......... Defense Integrated Data System Program Management Office [*DoD*]
DIDSRS........ Defense Intelligence Dissemination, Storage, and Retrieval System (MCD)
DIDSY......... Dust Impact Detection System [*Astrophysics*]
DIDU .... Defense Item Data Utilization
DIDV .... Divo [*Ivory Coast*] [*ICAO location identifier*] (ICLI)
DIE .... Defense Intelligence Estimate (MCD)
DIE .... Deuterium Isotope Effect (MCD)
DIE .... Developmental Independent Evaluator [*Army*]
DIE .... Died in Emergency Room (MAE)
DIE .... Diego Suarez [*Madagascar*] [*Airport symbol*] (OAG)
DIE .... Digital Image Enhancement [*Microscopy*]
DIE .... Diploma in Industrial Engineering (ADA)
DIE .... Diploma of the Institute of Engineering [*British*]
DIE .... Direct Injection Enthalpimetry
DIE .... Directors-in-Exile [*British*]
DIE .... Distance in Error
DIE .... Division of International Education [*Office of Education*]
DIE .... Doctor of Industrial Engineering
DIE .... Document of Industrial Engineering (KSC)
DIE .... Double Injection Effect
DIEA........... Dictionary of Industrial Engineering Abbreviations [*A publication*] (KSC)
DIEA........... (Diisopropyl)ethylamine [*Organic chemistry*]
DIE (ACE).... Division of International Education (of the American Council on Education) (EA)

DIEAG .... Defense Industry Export Advisory Group
DIEB .... Department of the Interior Energy Board [*Marine science*] (OSRA)
DIEB .... Department of the Interior Energy Board (USDC)
DIEB ALT ..... Diebus Alternis [*Every Other Day*] [*Pharmacy*]
Diebold .... Diebold, Inc. [*Associated Press*] (SAG)
DIEB SECUND... Diebus Secundis [*Every Second Day*] [*Pharmacy*]
DIEB TERT ... Diebus Tertiis [*Every Third Day*] [*Pharmacy*]
DIEC .... Defense Item Entry Control (AFIT)
DIECA .... Diethyldithiocarbonate [*Analytical chemistry*]
DIECAST ...... Display Interaction Enhancing Computer-Aided Shape Technique
 (PDAA)
DIECO .... Defense Item Entry Control Office [*Military*]
DIECP .... Defense Item Entry Control Program [*Military*] (AABC)
DIED .... Department of Industrial and Economic Development
DIEDA .... Diethyl-Iminodiacetic Acid [*Biochemistry*] (DAVI)
DIEG .... Diehl Graphsoft [*NASDAQ symbol*] (TTSB)
DIEG .... Diehl Graphsoft, Inc. [*NASDAQ symbol*] (SAG)
Diehl .... Diehl Graphsoft, Inc. [*Associated Press*] (SAG)
DiehlG .... Diehl Graphsoft, Inc. [*Associated Press*] (SAG)
DIEL .... Dielectric (IAA)
DIEL .... Diesel Electric
DIELEC .... Dielectric
DIELGUIDE... Dielectric Waveguide (MCD)
DIEM .... Control Chief Hldgs [*NASDAQ symbol*] (TTSB)
DIEMN .... Dust-Induced Electromagnetic Noise
DIEN .... Data Input Ensemble (NITA)
dien .... Diethylenediamine [*Organic chemistry*]
DI Eng .... Doctor of Industrial Engineering
DIEO .... Decennie Internationale d'Exploration des Oceans [*International
 Decade of Ocean Exploration*] (MSC)
DIEOB .... Defense Intelligence Electronic Order of Battle (MCD)
DIEP .... Department of Industry and Economic Planning
DIEP .... Diabetes in Early Pregnancy [*Medicine*]
DIER .... Departmental Industrial Equipment Reserve (AAGC)
DIER .... Department Instrument Equipment Reserve
DIES .... Diesel
DIES .... Distributed Illuminated Electronic System (DWSG)
DIESA .... Department of International Economic and Social Affairs [*United
 Nations Information service or system*] (IID)
DIET .... Desorption Induced by Electronic Transition [*Physics*]
DIET .... Dietary (WDAA)
DIET .... Dietetics
DIET .... Dietician (WDAA)
DIET .... Division of Integration and Environmental Testing [*Social Security
 Administration*]
DIETC .... Dietetic
Diet Tech..... Dietetic Technician (DAVI)
DIF .... Dakota Indian Foundation
DIF .... Data Interchange Format
DIF .... Data Interface Facility (SSD)
DIF .... Decay in Flight [*Nuclear physics*]
DIF .... Defense Industrial Fund
DIF .... Deposit Insurance Fund [*Pronounced "diff"*]
DIF .... Descriptive Item File
DIF .... Device Input Format
DIF .... Difference (AFM)
dif .... Different (VRA)
DIF .... Differential (AFM)
DIF .... Differentiation Inducting Factor [*Immunology*]
DIF .... Difficulty-Importance-Frequency
DIF .... Diffuse
DIF .... Diffuse Interstitial Fibrosis [*Medicine*] (AAMN)
DIF .... Diffuser [*Freight*] [*Microbiology*]
DIF .... Diiodofluorescein [*Organic chemistry*]
DIF .... Direct Immunofluorescence [*Analytical biochemistry*] (CPH)
DIF .... Direction Finder [*or Finding*] [*Radio aid to navigation*]
DIF .... Discrete Increment Filter (NASA)
DIF .... Discriminate Function [*Physiology*]
DIF .... Display Information Facility (CDE)
DIF .... Division of International Finance [*of FRS*]
DIF .... Document Interchange Facility (IAA)
DIF .... Document Interchange Format
DIF .... DOMSAT [*Domestic Satellite*] Interface Facility (MCD)
DIF .... Drug Information Fulltext [*American Society of Hospital Pharmacists*]
 [*Bethesda, MD Database*]
DIF .... Dual In-Line Flatpack (CDE)
DIF .... Duty Involving Flying [*Military*]
DIF .... Dvorak International Federation (EA)
DIFA .... Deposit Insurance Flexibility Act [*1982*]
DIFA .... Differential Amplifier (MSA)
DIFA .... Difurfurylideneacetone [*Organic chemistry*]
DIFAD .... Digitally Integrated Fleet Air Defense
DIFAR .... Directional Frequency Analysis and Recording System (MCD)
DIFAR .... Direction-Finding and Ranging
DIFC .... Decommutator Interface Controller (MCD)
DIFCE .... Difference
DIFCLT .... Difficult
DIFCLTY ...... Difficulty
DIFCREW ..... Duty Involving Flying Crewman [*Military*] (NVT)
DIFCT .... Difficult (ROG)
DIFCTY .... Difficulty (ROG)
DIFDEN .... Duty in a Flying Status Not Involving Flying [*Air Force*] (NVT)
DIFDENIS..... Duty under Instruction in a Flying Status Not Involving Flying
 [*Military*] (DNAB)

DIFDENRELAS... Duty in a Flying Status Not Involving Flying as His Relief
 [*Military*] (DNAB)
DIFDENREPT... Detailed to Duty in a Flying Status Not Involving Flying Effective
 upon Reporting [*Military*] (DNAB)
DIFET .... Double Injection Field Effect Transistor [*Electronics*]
DIFF .... Development Import Finance Facility [*Australia*] [*Defunct*]
DIFF .... Difference (KSC)
DIFF .... Different
DIFF .... Differential (AABC)
DIFF .... Differential Blood Count
diff .... Difficult (DAVI)
DIFFA .... Design Industries Foundation for AIDS [*Acquired Immune Deficiency
 Syndrome*] (EA)
DIFFAMP ..... Differential Amplifier (IAA)
DIFFCALC ..... Differential Calculus (IAA)
DIFFCE .... Difference (ROG)
Diff Diag..... Differential Diagnosis (AAMN)
DIFFER .... Difference (DSUE)
DIFFFWR ..... Differential and Full Wave Rectifier (IAA)
DIFFR .... Diffraction (MSA)
DIFF SENS ... Differential Sense [*Computer science*]
DIFFSN .... Diffusion
DIFFTR .... Differential Time Relay (IEEE)
DIFFTRAP ..... Digital Fast Fourier Transform Processor (PDAA)
DIFFU .... Diffusion (WDAA)
DIFFUS .... Diffusing
DIFID .... Disposal from an Instantaneous Dump [*US Army Corps of
 Engineers*]
DIFINSOPS... Duty under Instruction in a Flying Status Involving Operational or
 Training Flights [*Military*] (DNAB)
DIFINSPRO... Duty under Instruction in a Flying Status Involving Proficiency Flying
 [*Military*] (DNAB)
DIFK .... Ferkessedougou [*Ivory Coast*] [*ICAO location identifier*] (ICLI)
DI/FLC .... Vessels in Forward Areas Transferred to State Department Foreign
 Liquidation Corporation [*Navy*]
DIFM .... Due-In from Maintenance [*Military*] (AFM)
DIFMA .... Dresdner International Financial Markets (Australia) Ltd.
DIFMOS .... Dual-Injection Floating-Gate Metal Oxide Semiconductor (PDAA)
DIFO .... Due-In from Overhaul [*Military*] (MCD)
DIFOPS .... Duty in a Flying Status Involving Operational or Training Flights [*Air
 Force*] (NVT)
DIFOPSDORSE... Duty in a Flying Status Involving Operational or Training Flights
 Effective SuchDate as Endorsed [*Military*] (DNAB)
DIFOT .... Duty Involving Operational or Training Flights [*Air Force*]
DIFOTDORSE... Duty in a Flying Status Involving Operational or Training Flights
 Effective Such Date as Endorsed [*Military*] (DNAB)
DIFOTECH.... Duty in a Flying Status Involving Operational or Training Flights as a
 TechnicalObserver [*Air Force*]
DIFOTINS.... Duty in a Flying Status Involving Operational or Training Flights
 under Instruction [*Air Force*]
DIFOTRELAS... Duty in a Flying Status Involving Operational or Training Flights as
 His Relief [*Air Force*]
DIFOTRVK.... Duty in a Flying Status Involving Operational or Training Flights
 Revoked [*Air Force*]
DIFP .... Diisopropyl Fluorophosphonate [*Also, DFP*] [*Toxic compound*]
DIFP .... Diphenyliodonium Hexafluorophosphate [*Biochemistry*]
DIFP .... International Food Policy Research Institute, Washington, DC [*Library
 symbol Library of Congress*] (LCLS)
DIFPP .... Defense Industrial Facilities Protection Program [*DoD*]
DIFPRO .... Duty in a Flying Status Involving Proficiency Flying [*Air Force*] (NVT)
DIFS .... Defense Integrated Financial System (AAGC)
DIFSD .... Diversified Foods, Inc. (MHDW)
DIFT .... Dartford International Freight Terminal [*British*] (DS)
DIFT .... Different
DIFTECH ..... Duty as Technical Observer in a Flying Status Involving Operational
 or Training Flights [*Military*] (DNAB)
DI-FTMS ..... Desorption Ionization Fourier Transform Mass Spectrometry
DIFU .... Deutsches Institut fuer Urbanistik [*Vereins fuer
 Kommunalwissenschaften eV*] [*Database producer*]
DIG .... Delivery Indicator Group (NATG)
DIG .... Delphi International Group (EA)
DIG .... Departement Documentation et Information Geologique [*Geological
 Information and Documentation Department*] [*Bureau of
 Geological and Mining Research*] [*Information service or
 system*] (IID)
DIG .... Deputy Inspector-General
DIG .... Designated Industry Group (AAGC)
DIG .... Design Implementation Guide [*Telecommunications*] (TEL)
DIG .... Detonator Inspection Gauge
DIG .... Diffuse Ionized Gas [*Astrophysics*]
Dig. .... Digeratur [*Let It Be Digested*] [*Pharmacy*]
Dig. .... Digest [*1901-06*] [*Lahore, India*] [*A publication*] (DLA)
DIG .... Digest
Dig. .... Digesta [*Latin*] (OCD)
Dig. .... Digest of Justinian [*A publication*] (DLA)
Dig. .... Digest of Writs [*A publication*] (DLA)
DIG .... Digital (AFM)
DIG .... Digital-Image-Generated [*Computer science*] (IEEE)
DIG .... Digital Input Gate
DIG .... Digitalis [*Foxglove*] [*Pharmacy*]
DIG .... Digitoxin
DIG .... Digoxin
DIG .... Disablement Income Group [*British*]
DIG .... Discussion in Groups
DIG .... Doppler-Inertial Gyrocompass (PDAA)

DIG .... Justinian Digesta [*Libri Pandectarum*] [*Legal*] (ROG)
DIGA .... Department of Infrastructure and Government Assets [*Western Australia*]
DIGA .... Dynamics International Gardening Association (EA)
DIGA .... Gagnoa [*Ivory Coast*] [*ICAO location identifier*] (ICLI)
DIGAC .... Digital Avionics Control
DIGACC .... Digital Guidance and Control Computer
DIGACE .... Digital Guidance and Control Equipment (IAA)
DIGAP .... Direct Investigation Group on Aerial Phenomena [*British*] (DBA)
DIGATEC ...... Digital Gas Turbine Engine Control (MCD)
Digby RP ...... Digby's History of the Law of Real Property [*A publication*] (DLA)
DIGCIRENGR... Digital Circuit Engineer (IAA)
Dig CLW ...... Digest of Commercial Law of the World [*A publication*] (DLA)
DIGCOM .... Digital Computer (IEEE)
DIGCOMP .... Digital Computer (IAA)
Dig Crim Proc... Stephen's Digest of Criminal Procedure [*9th ed.*] [*1950*] [*A publication*] (DLA)
DigDs......... Digital Descriptor Systems [*Associated Press*] (SAG)
DigDsc....... Digital Descriptor Systems [*Associated Press*] (SAG)
DIGE .... Digene Corp. [*NASDAQ symbol*] (TTSB)
DIGEST .... Diebold Generator for Statistical Tabulation (MUGU)
Digest......... Digest of Justinian [*A publication*] (DLA)
Digex .... Digex Incorp. [*Associated Press*] (SAG)
DIGEX .... Disabled Interest Group Electronic Exchange (HGAA)
Dig Fla .... Thompson's Digest of Laws [*Florida*] [*A publication*] (DLA)
DIGI .... Digital
DIGI .... DSC Communications [*NASDAQ symbol*] (TTSB)
DIGI .... DSC Communications Corp. [*NASDAQ symbol*] (NQ)
Digic .... Digicon, Inc. [*Associated Press*] (SAG)
DIGICOM ...... Digital Communications
DIGICOM ...... Digital Communications System (NITA)
Digicon....... Digicon, Inc. [*Associated Press*] (SAG)
DIGIDOPS .... Digital Doppler System (MCD)
DigiIntl .... Digi International, Inc. [*Associated Press*] (SAG)
DIGILIN....... Digital Linear (IAA)
Digimet....... Digimetrics, Inc. [*Associated Press*] (SAG)
DIGINESS ..... Digital Network Simulation System (MCD)
DIGIRAD ...... Digital RADIAC
DIGIRALT...... Digital RADAR Altimeter (MUGU)
DIGISAT....... Digital Data Satellite Service [*Communications Satellite Corp.*]
DIGISMAC.... Digital Scene Matching Area Correlator [*Military*] (MCD)
DIGISPLAY... Digitally Scanned Image Display (MCD)
DIGIT .... Digitalis [*Foxglove*] [*Pharmacy*] (ROG)
DIG-IT......... Dramatic Interpretation of the Ghetto through Improvisational Theater [*Washington, DC*]
DIGITAC....... Digital Tactical Automatic Control (IEEE)
Digital .... Digital Equipment Corp. [*Associated Press*] (SAG)
DIGITAL .... Digitalis [*Foxglove*] [*Pharmacy*] (ROG)
DIGITALIS .... Discussion Group on Information Technology in Library and Information Studies Schools (AIE)
DIGITAR....... Digital Airborne Computer (IEEE)
DigitBio ...... Digital Biometrics, Inc. [*Associated Press*] (SAG)
DigitCT .... Digital Communications Technology Corp. [*Associated Press*] (SAG)
DigitR......... Digital Recorders, Inc. [*Associated Press*] (SAG)
DigitRec...... Digital Recorders, Inc. [*Associated Press*] (SAG)
DigitTel....... Digitale Telekable AG [*Associated Press*] (SAG)
DIGIVISION... Digital Television (NITA)
DIGL .... Guiglo [*Ivory Coast*] [*ICAO location identifier*] (ICLI)
Dig LL .... Digest Law of Libels [*A publication*] (DLA)
DIGLYME...... Diethylene Glycol Dimethyl Ether [*Organic chemistry*]
DIGM .... Control Chief Holdings [*NASDAQ symbol*] (SAG)
DIGM .... Digimetrics, Inc. [*NASDAQ symbol*] (NQ)
DigMic....... Digital Microwave Corp. [*Associated Press*] (SAG)
DIGN .... Diagnostic (MSA)
DIGN .... Grand Bereby/Nero Mer [*Ivory Coast*] [*ICAO location identifier*] (ICLI)
Dignity........ Dignity Partners, Inc. [*Associated Press*] (SAG)
DIGOPS....... Digest of Operations (DNAB)
Dig Ops JAG... Digest of Opinions of Judge Advocate General, United States [*A publication*] (DLA)
DIGOXN ...... Digoxin [*Pharmacology*] (DAVI)
Dig Proem ... Digest of Justinian, Proem [*A publication*] (DLA)
DIGRM .... Digit/Record Mark [*Computer science*] (MDG)
DIGRMGM..... Digit/Record Mark Group/Mark [*Computer science*] (MDG)
DIGRO .... Digital Readout [*Computer science*] (AAG)
Dig R Pr ...... Digby's Introduction to the History of Real Property [*A publication*] (DLA)
DIGS .... Defense Information Guidance Series [*A publication*] (DNAB)
DIGS .... Delta [*or Digital*] Inertial Guidance System [*NASA*]
DIGS .... Deputy Inspector-General for Safety [*Air Force*]
DIGS .... Diagnostic Interview for Genetic Studies
DIGS .... Diggings [*i.e., Lodgings*] [*British*] (ROG)
DIGS .... Digital Inertial Guidance System
DI-GS .... United States Geological Survey, Reston, VA [*Library symbol Library of Congress*] (LCLS)
Dig Shares... Digby's Sales and Transfer of Shares [*A publication*] (DLA)
DIGSIGPROC... Digital Signal Processor [*Computer science*] (IAA)
Dig St .... English's Digest of the Statutes [*Arkansas*] [*A publication*] (DLA)
DIGTL .... Digital (KSC)
DigtlSol ...... Digital Solutions, Inc. [*Associated Press*] (SAG)
DigtlSy....... Digital Systems International, Inc. [*Associated Press*] (SAG)
Dig Tox .... Digitalis Toxicity [*Medicine*] (DAVI)
DigtsSd ...... Digital Sound Corp. [*Associated Press*] (SAG)
DigVd......... Digital Video Systems, Inc. [*Associated Press*] (SAG)
Dig Vet .... Digestum Vetus [*A publication*] (DSA)
DigVid .... Digital Video Systems, Inc. [*Associated Press*] (SAG)

DigVideo...... Digital Video Systems, Inc. [*Associated Press*] (SAG)
DIGX .... Digex Incorp. [*NASDAQ symbol*] (SAG)
DIH .... Deputy Inspector-General of Hospitals and Fleet [*Navy British*] (ROG)
DIH .... Diploma in Industrial Health [*British*]
DIH .... Discrete Input High (MCD)
DIHEST .... Direct-Induced High-Explosive Simulation Technique (MCD)
DIHL .... Declaration of Independence House and Library [*An association*] (EA)
DIHP .... Diisoheptyl Phthalate
DIHPPA....... Diiodo(Hydroxyphenyl)pyruvic Acid [*Organic chemistry*]
DIHY .... Dihydrate
DII .... Decorator Indus [*AMEX symbol*] (TTSB)
DII .... Decorator Industries, Inc. [*AMEX symbol*] (SPSG)
DII .... Defense Industry Initiative (AAGC)
DII .... Defense Information Infrastructure [*Military*]
DII .... Diode Ion Injector
DIIA .... Daily Industrial Index Analyzer [*News-a-tron Corp.*] [*Information service or system*] (CRD)
DIIC .... Daughters of Isabella, International Circle (EA)
DIIC .... Dielectrically Isolated Integration Circuit
DIIG .... DII Group [*NASDAQ symbol*] (TTSB)
DIII........... Abidjan [*Ivory Coast*] [*ICAO location identifier*] (ICLI)
DI Ind .... DI Industries [*Associated Press*] (SAG)
DI/INT .... Disposition of Vessel by Department of the Interior (DNAB)
DIIO .... District Industrial Incentive Office [*or Officer*] [*Navy*]
DIIP .... Defense Inactive Item Program (NG)
DIIP .... Defense Intelligence Interoperability Panel
DIIP .... Delinquency Investigation Inventory Profile [*IRS*]
DIIR .... Digital Infared Image Reformatter
DIIS .... DCAA [*Defense Contract Audit Agency*] Integrated Information System [*DoD*] (GFGA)
DIIS .... DIA [*Defense Intelligence Agency*] Integrated Intelligence System
DIIVS .... Defense Intransit Item Visibility System (MCD)
DIJ .... Dijon [*France*] [*Airport symbol*] (AD)
DIJOA .... Dominantly Inherited Juvenile Optic Atrophy [*Ophthalmology*] (DAVI)
DIK........... Dickinson [*North Dakota*] [*Airport symbol Obsolete*] (OAG)
DIK........... Dixon [*Former USSR Geomagnetic observatory code*]
Dik .... Double [*or Dual*] Income, Kids [*Lifestyle classification*]
DIK........... Drug Identification Kit
DIKO .... Demokratiko Komma [*Democratic Party*] [*Cyprus*] [*Political party*] (EY)
DIKO .... Korhogo [*Ivory Coast*] [*ICAO location identifier*] (ICLI)
DIL .... Data In-Line [*Computer science*] (IAA)
DIL .... Deliverable Items List (NASA)
Dil .... Dilantin [*Diphenylhydantoin*] [*Anticonvulsant*]
DIL .... Dilatus [*Dissolve*] [*Pharmacy*] (DHSM)
DIL .... Dili [*Indonesia*] [*Airport symbol*] (OAG)
DIL .... Dillard University, New Orleans, LA [*OCLC symbol*] (OCLC)
DIL .... Dillon (ROG)
DIL............ Dillon Ranch [*California*] [*Seismograph station code, US Geological Survey*] (SEIS)
Dil .... Dillon's United States Circuit Court Reports [*A publication*] (DLA)
DIL .... Dilloway (ROG)
DIL .... Dilly [*Portuguese Timor*] [*Airport symbol*] (AD)
DIL .... Diltiazem [*Pharmacology*]
DIL .... Dilute
DIL .... Director of International Logistics [*Military*]
DIL .... Disability Insurance Letter [*Social Security Administration*] (OICC)
DIL .... Discrete Input Low (MCD)
DIL .... Dispatch Inoperative List (MCD)
DIL .... Displayed Impact Line (MCD)
DIL .... Diversity Interfacility Link (LAIN)
DIL .... Division of Insured Loans [*Office of Education*]
DIL .... Doctor of International Law
DIL .... Doppler Inertial LORAN
DIL .... Double Injection Luminescence
DIL .... Dual In-Line [*Electronic components*]
DILAG .... Differential LASER Gyro (MCD)
DILAN .... Dilantin [*Parke, Davis & Co.*] [*Pharmacology*] (DAVI)
DILAPD .... Dilapidated (ROG)
DILAPIDN .... Dilapidation (ROG)
DILAT......... Dilation [*Medicine*]
Dil Cir Court Rep... Dillon's United States Circuit Court Reports [*A publication*] (DLA)
DILD .... Diffuse Infiltrative Lung Disease [*Medicine*]
DILD .... Diluted
DILE.......... Drug-Induced Lupus Erythematosus [*Rheumatology*] (DAVI)
DILEP......... Digital Line Engineering Program [*Telecommunications*] (TEL)
DILET......... Dilettante (ROG)
DIL (Hack)... Digest of International Law (Hackworth) [*A publication*] (DLA)
DILIC......... Dual In-Line Integrated Circuit [*Electronics*] (IAA)
DILK.......... Double [*or Dual*] Income, Lots of Kids [*Lifestyle classification*]
Dill........... Dillon's United States Circuit Court Reports [*A publication*] (DLA)
Dillard .... Dillard Department Stores [*Associated Press*] (SAG)
Dill Ir Jud A... Dillon on the Irish Judicature Act [*A publication*] (DLA)
Dill Laws Eng & Am... Dillon's Laws and Jurisprudence of England and America [*A publication*] (DLA)
Dill Mun Bonds... Dillon on Municipal Bonds [*A publication*] (DLA)
Dill Mun Cor... Dillon on Municipal Corporations [*A publication*] (DLA)
Dill Mun Corp... Dillon on Municipal Corporations [*A publication*] (DLA)
Dillon....... Dillon's United States Circuit Court Reports [*A publication*] (DLA)
Dillon CC..... Dillon's United States Circuit Court Reports [*A publication*] (DLA)
Dillon Cir Court Rep... Dillon's United States Circuit Court Reports [*A publication*] (DLA)

Dillon Mun Corp... Dillon on Municipal Corporations [*A publication*] (DLA)
Dill Rem Caus... Dillon on the Removal of Causes [*A publication*] (DLA)
Dill Rep....... Dillon's United States Circuit Court Reports [*A publication*] (DLA)
DILM.......... Dartmouth Intensive Language Model (EDAC)
DILMC....... Defense International Logistics Management Course [*DoD*]
DIL (Moore)... Digest of International Law (Moore) [*A publication*] (DLA)
DILN .... Dilution
DILOT .... [*An*] Introduction to the Literature of the Old Testament [*S. R. Driver*] [*A publication*] (BJA)
DILP........... Dual In-Line Package [*Computer science*]
DILS........... Dataskil Integrated Library System [*International Computers Ltd.*] [*British*] (NITA)
DILS........... Departmental Information Locator System [*Department of Agriculture*] (GFGA)
DILS........... Doppler Inertial LORAN System
DILSUP....... Disposal List Ship Unit Portsmouth [*Navy British*]
DILUC .... Diluculo [*At Daybreak*] [*Pharmacy*]
DILUT .... Dilutus [*Dilute*] [*Pharmacy*]
DIL (White)... Digest of International Law (Whiteman) [*A publication*] (DLA)
DIM............ Data and Instruction Management Machine (NITA)
DIM............ Data Interpretation Module
DIM............ Defense Information Memorandum (NATG)
DIM............ Dense Ionized Medium [*Astrophysics*]
DIM............ Description, Installation, and Maintenance
DIM............ Design Information Manual (KSC)
DIM............ Design Interface Meeting (NASA)
DIM............ Device Interface Module
DIM............ Differential Interference Microscopy (PDAA)
DIM............ Digital Ignorant Mechanism [*Pocket calculator facetiously described by T. R. Reid in his book, "The Chip"*]
DIM............ Digital Imaging Microscope
DIM............ Digital Input Module [*Computer science*]
DIM............ Digital Input Multiplexer (CAAL)
DIM............ Dimension (KSC)
dim .... Dimension (VRA)
dim .... Dimension (WDMC)
DIM............ Dimension
DIM............ Dimidius [*One-Half*] [*Pharmacy*]
DIM............ Diminished
dim .... Diminished (WDMC)
DIM............ Diminuendo [*Getting Softer*] [*Music*]
DIM............ Diminutive
DIM............ Dimissory [*Ecclesiastical*] (ROG)
DIM............ Dimitrovgrad [*Bulgaria*] [*Seismograph station code, US Geological Survey*] (SEIS)
DIM............ Dimmer
DIM............ Diploma in Industrial Management (ADA)
DIM............ Directory of International Mail [*A publication*]
DIM............ Display Image Manipulation (IAA)
DIM............ District Industrial Manager [*Navy*]
DIM............ District Inspector of Musketry [*Military British*] (ROG)
DIM............ Divalent Ion Metabolism (MAE)
DIM............ Dorsal Intersegmental Muscles [*Anatomy*]
DIM............ Drop-In-Maintenance (MCD)
DIM............ Dynamic Impedance Measurement
DIMA .... Direct Imaging Mass Analyzer
DIMA .... Drilling Individual Mobilization Augmentation [*Army*] (DOMA)
DIMAC .... DIMAC Corp. [*Associated Press*] (SAG)
DIMACS ...... Center for Discrete Mathematics and Theoretical Computer Science [*Rutgers University*] [*Research center*] (RCD)
DIMADC...... Diffusion in Metals and Alloys Data Center [*National Institute of Standards and Technology*]
DIMAP .... Digital/Modular Avionics Program [*Aerospace*] (MCD)
DIMAPA...... Dimethylaminopropylamine [*Also, DMAPA*] [*Organic chemistry*]
Dimark........ DiMark, Inc. [*Associated Press*] (SAG)
DIMATE...... Depot-Installed Maintenance Automatic Test Equipment
DIMBOA...... Dihydroxymethoxybenzoxazinone [*Organic chemistry*]
DIMC .... Defense Inventory Management Course [*DoD*]
DIMC .... Division of Information Management and Compliance [*Department of Education*] (GFGA)
DIMD .... Diamond Multimedia Systems [*NASDAQ symbol*] (TTSB)
DIMD .... Diamond Multimedia Systems, Inc. [*NASDAQ symbol*] (SAG)
DIMDI .... Deutsches Institut fuer Medizinische Dokumentation und Information [*German Institute for Medical Documentation and Information*] [*Ministry for Youth, Family, and Health Affairs Database producer*] [*Information service or system*] (IID)
DIME.......... Development of Integrated Monetary Electronics [*EC*] (ECED)
DIME.......... Dime Community Bancorp, Inc. [*NASDAQ symbol*] (SAG)
DIME.......... Division of International Medical Education [*Association of American Medical Colleges*]
DIME.......... Dual Independent Map Encoding [*Transportation*]
DimeBcp...... Dime Bancorp, Inc. [*Formerly, Dime Savings Bank NY*] [*Associated Press*] (SAG)
DimeCo....... Dime Community Bancorp, Inc. [*Associated Press*] (SAG)
DIMECO ...... Dual Independent Map Encoding File of Countries [*Harvard University*] [*A databank*] (NITA)
DIMEDONE... Dimethylcyclohexanedione [*Analytical chemistry*]
DimeFn........ Dime Financial Corp. [*Associated Press*] (SAG)
DIMEN .... Dimension
DIMEO .... Defense Industrial and Management Engineering Office [*DoD*]
DIMES .... Defense Improved Management Engineering System [*Military*]
DIMES .... Defense Integrated Management Engineering System [*Military*] (AFM)
DIMES .... Development of Improved Management Engineering Systems [*Military*] (AABC)

DIMES .... Development of Integrated Management Engineering Systems [*Military*]
DIMES .... Digital Image Manipulation and Enhancement Systems
DIMIA .... Depository Institution Management Interlocks Act [*1978*]
DIMID .... Dimidius [*One-Half*] [*Pharmacy*]
DIMIN .... Diminuendo [*Getting Softer*] [*Music*] (WGA)
DIMIN .... Diminutive (WDAA)
DIMIS .... Depot Installation Management Information System [*Army*]
DIML .... Dimensional
DIMM .... Defense Integrated Material Management (MCD)
DIMM .... Dual In-Line Memory Module [*Computer science*] (DOM)
DIMM .... Dual In-Line Memory Module [*Computer science*]
DIMN .... Man [*Ivory Coast*] [*ICAO location identifier*] (ICLI)
DIMOAD...... Diabetes Insipidus, Diabetes Mellitus, Optic Atrophy, and Deafness [*Medicine*]
DIMOB .... Defense Intelligence Missile Order of Battle (MCD)
DIMON........ Dimension (ROG)
Dimon........ Dimon, Inc. [*Associated Press*] (SAG)
dIMP.......... Deoxyinosine Monophosphate [*Biochemistry*]
DIMP .... Diisopropyl Methylphosphonate [*Organic chemistry*]
DIMPC .... Defense Item Management Coding Program [*DoD*] (AFIT)
DIMPEA ...... (Dimethoxyphenyl)ethylamine [*Also, DMPE, DMPEA*] [*Psychomimetic compound*]
DIMPLE....... Deuterium Moderated Pile Low Energy [*Reactor*]
Dimps......... Dual Income, Money Problems [*Lifestyle Classification*]
DIMS .... Data and Information Management System [*Computer science*] (ODBW)
DIMS .... Data Information and Manufacturing System (PDAA)
DIMS .... Digital Imaging Medical System
DIMS .... Director, International Military Staff Memorandum [*NATO*] (NATG)
DIMS .... Disorder of Initiating and Maintaining Sleep [*Medicine*]
DIMS .... Distributed Intelligence Microcomputer System
DIMS .... Document-and-Image Management System [*Computer science*] (PCM)
DIMSA .... Depot Integrated Maintenance Support Agreement [*Air Force*]
DIMSA .... Distribuidora de Impresos, Sociedad Anonima [*Mexico*]
DIMUS .... Digital Multibeam Steering
DIMUS .... Directional Multibeam Steering
DIN .... Aerodin SA de CV [*Mexico ICAO designator*] (FAAC)
DIN .... Consorcio G. Grupo Dina [*NYSE symbol*] (SPSG)
DIN .... Consorcio G Grupo Dina ADS [*NYSE symbol*] (TTSB)
DIN .... Data Identification Number (AFM)
DIN .... Dedicated Intelligence Network (MCD)
DIN .... Defense Intelligence Notice (MCD)
DIN .... Deutsches Institut fuer Normung [*German Institute for Standardization*] (IID)
DIN .... Device Initialize [*Computer science*] (IAA)
DIN .... Digital Input [*Computer science*] (KSC)
DIN .... Dinar [*Monetary unit*] [*Former Yugoslavia*]
DIN .... Dinghy [*Coast Guard*] (DNAB)
din .... Dinka [*MARC language code Library of Congress*] (LCCP)
DIN .... Dinner (ADA)
DIN .... Dinuclear (IAA)
DIN .... Direct Injection Nebulization [*For spectrometry*]
DIN .... Dissolved Inorganic Nitrogen [*Chemistry*]
DIN .... Document Identification Number (NG)
DIN .... Do It Now [*Category of service call for maintenance or repair work*] [*Air Force*]
DIN .... Do It Now Foundation [*An association*]
D in 2PLO... Detur in Duplo [*Let Twice as Much Be Given*] [*Pharmacy*] (ROG)
DINA .... Departamento de Inteligencia Nacional [*National Intelligence Department*] [*Chilean secret police Superseded by CNI*]
DINA .... Digital Network Analyzer
DINA .... Diisononyl Adipate
DINA .... Direct Internal Noise Amplification (NG)
DINA .... Distributed Information Processing Network Architecture
DINA .... Japan Database Industry Association [*Tokyo*] [*Information service or system*] (IID)
DINADE ...... Diode Interrogation, Navigation, and Detection (IAA)
DINATUR ..... Direccion Nacional de Turismo [*National Direction of Tourism*] [*Bolivia*] (EAIO)
Dinc............ Double [*or Dual*] Income, No Children [*Lifestyle classification*]
DInd........... Doctor of Industrial Engineering
D Ind .... Doctor of Industry
DIN/DCSS .... Digital Network-Defense Special Security Communications System [*National Security Agency*]
D in DUP ..... Detur in Duplo [*Let Twice as Much Be Given*] [*Pharmacy*]
DINET .... Defense Industrial Network [*DoD*]
DINET .... Defense Information Network [*DoD*]
D-INF .... Director of Infantry [*Military British*]
DINF .... Do It Now Foundation (EA)
DINFOS....... Defense Information School
DING .... Directory of Item Names for the Gas Industry [*A publication*]
D Ing .... Doctor of Engineering
Dink .... Double [*or Dual*] Income, No Kids [*Lifestyle classification*]
DINK .... Dual Income, No Kids (TAG)
DINKS .... Dual-Income, No Kids (DFIT)
Dinky......... Double [*or Dual*] Income, No Kids Yet [*Lifestyle classification*]
DIN.L .... Consorcio G Grupo Dina'L'ADS [*NYSE symbol*] (TTSB)
DINN.......... Dual Input Null Network
DINO .... Deputy Inspector of Naval Ordnance
DINO .... Dinosaur National Monument
DINOB........ Defense Intelligence Naval Order of Battle (MCD)
DINOS........ Distributed Interactive Operating System (IAA)
DINP .... Diisononyl Phthalate [*Organic chemistry*]

D in P AEQ...	Dividatur in Partes Aequales [*Divide into Equal Parts*] [*Pharmacy*]
DINS	Directorate for Inspection Services [*Assistant Secretary of Defense for Administration*] (CINC)
DINS	Dormant Inertial Navigation System (MCD)
DINSA	Disability Information Network of South Australia
DINUPS.......	DIMDI's [*Deutsches Institut fuer Medizinische Dokumentation und Information*] Input and Updata System (NITA)
DIO	Data Input/Output [*Computer science*]
DIO	Defence Arrangements for Indian Ocean [*British World War II*]
DIO	Defense Intelligence Officer [*Defense Intelligence Agency*] (MCD)
DIO	Diet-Induced Obese [*Mice*]
DIO	Digital Input/Output [*Computer science*]
DIO	Diocese
DIO	Diocese
DIO	Diode (KSC)
DIO	Diodes, Inc. [*AMEX symbol*] (SPSG)
Dio	Dionysius [*Authority cited in pre-1607 legal work*] (DSA)
DIO	Direct Input/Output [*Telecommunications*] (TEL)
DI(O)	Directorate of Intelligence (Operations) [*RAF*] [*British*]
DIO	Director of Industrial Operations [*Military*] (AABC)
DIO	District Intelligence Officer
DIO	Doppler Inertial Omega (IAA)
DIO	Duty Intelligence Officer [*Air Force*]
DIOA	Differential Input Operational Amplifier [*Electronics*]
DIOA	Diisooctyl Adipate [*Organic chemistry*]
DIOA	Dynamic Input-Output Analysis [*Economics*]
DIOB	Digital Input/Output Buffer [*Computer science*]
DIOBS	Defense Intelligence Order of Battle Systems (MCD)
DIOC	Digital Input/Output Control [*Computer science*]
DIOC	Dimethyloxacarbocyanine [*Organic chemistry*]
DIOC	Diocese [*or Diocesean*]
DIOC	Dissolved Inorganic Carbon [*Also, DIC*]
DIOC	District Intelligence Operations Centers [*Vietnam*]
DIOC	Ducati International Owners Club (EA)
Dio Cass	Dio Cassius [*Third century AD*] [*Classical studies*] (OCD)
DIOCC	District Intelligence and Operations Coordination Center [*Vietnam*] (VNW)
Dio Chrys	Dio Chrysostomus [*First century AD*] [*Classical studies*] (OCD)
DIOCN	Diocesan (ROG)
DIOD	Diode
Diod	Diodorus Siculus [*First century BC*] [*Classical studies*] (OCD)
DIOD	Odienne [*Ivory Coast*] [*ICAO location identifier*] (ICLI)
DIODE	Digital Input/Output Display Equipment
Diodes	Diodes, Inc. [*Associated Press*] (SAG)
Diod Sic	Diodorus Siculus [*First century BC*] [*Classical studies*] (OCD)
DIOF	Ouango Fitini [*Ivory Coast*] [*ICAO location identifier*] (ICLI)
DIOG	Decylidenimino(octyl)guanidine [*Organic chemistry*]
Diog Laert	Diogenes Laertius [*Third century AD*] [*Classical studies*] (OCD)
DIOH	Due in from Overhaul (AFIT)
DIOI	Digital Input/Output Interface [*Computer science*] (KSC)
DIOLAMINE...	Diethanolamine [*Also, DEA*] [*USAN*] [*Organic chemistry*]
Diomed Mari...	Diomedes Mariconda [*Deceased, 1511*] [*Authority cited in pre-1607 legal work*] (DSA)
Dionex	Dionex Corp. [*Associated Press*] (SAG)
Dion Hal	Dionysius Halicarnassensis [*First century BC*] [*Classical studies*] (OCD)
DIOP	Defense Intelligence Objectives and Priorities (MCD)
DIOP	Digital Input/Output Package [*Computer science*]
DIOP	Diisooctyl Phthalate [*Organic chemistry*]
DIOP	Directorate for Information, Operation, and Patents (AAGC)
DIOP	Double-Density Disk Drive Input/Output Processor [*Computer science*] (NITA)
DIOPT	Diopter [*Also, D*] [*Optics*]
DIOR	Directorate for Information Operations and Reports [*Washington, DC*] [*DoD*]
DIOS	Diisooctyl Sebacate [*Organic chemistry*]
Dios	Dionysius [*Authority cited in pre-1607 legal work*] (DSA)
DIOS	Direct Memory Access Input/Output Subsystem (MCD)
DIOS	Direct Memory Access Input/Output System [*Computer science*] (NITA)
DIOS	Distributed Input/Output System
DIOS	Distribution, Information, and Optimizing System (OA)
DIOX	Dioxide [*Freight*]
DIP	Data Input Processor [*Computer science*]
DIP	Dead Item Purge [*Military*] (AFIT)
DIP	Debtor-in-Possession (TDOB)
DIP	Defamation, Identification, and Publication
DIP	Defense Intelligence Plan (MCD)
DIP	De-Inking Pulp [*Process*] [*Paper recycling*]
DIP	Designated Inspection Points (MCD)
DIP	Design Improvement Program
DIP	Design Internal Pressure [*Nuclear energy*] (NRCH)
DIP	Desquamative Interstitial Pneumonia [*Medicine*]
DIP	Destruction of Interstate Property
DIP	Detailed Inspection Procedure (MCD)
DIP	Diapaga [*Burkina Faso*] [*Airport symbol*] (OAG)
DIP	Diapaga [*Upper Volta*] [*Airport symbol*] (AD)
DIP	Digital Image Processing (LAIN)
DIP	Digital Impact Predictor
DIP	Digital Incremental Plotter
DIP	Digital Instrumentation Programmer
DIP	Diisopropylphenol [*Anesthetic*]
DIP	Di-Isopropyl Phosphate [*Organic chemistry*] (DAVI)
DIP	Diphtheria [*Medicine*]
DIP	Diploma
Dip	Diploma (DD)
DIP	Diplomat (WDAA)
DIP	Diplomat Resources [*Vancouver Stock Exchange symbol*]
Dip	Diptera [*Entomology*]
DIP	Dipyridyl [*Also, DIPY*] [*Organic chemistry*]
DIP	Direct Immunoperoxidase [*Clinical medicine*]
DIP	Direct Insertion Probe
DIP	Direct Intraperitoneal Insemination [*Alternative to traditional in-vitro fertilization (IVF)*] (PAZ)
DIP	Directories in Print [*Formerly, DOD*] [*A publication*]
DIP	Director of Industrial Planning [*War Office*] [*British World War II*]
DIP	Displayed Impact Point (MCD)
DIP	Display Information Processor [*Air Force*]
DIP	Display Input Processor (NASA)
DIP	Display Interface Processing (MCD)
DIP	Disposition of Inactive Parts List
DIP	Dissolved Inorganic Phosphorus [*Chemistry*]
DIP	Distal Interphalangeal [*Joint*] [*Anatomy*]
DIP	Distributed Information Processing
DIP	Dividend Investment Plan [*Stock purchase*] [*Investment term*]
DIP	Division of Industrial Participation [*AEC*]
DIP	Doctrine Improvement Program
DIP	Document Image Processing [*Computer science*]
DIP	Dokumentations- und Informationssystem fuer Parlamentsmaterial [*Documentation and Information System for Parliamentary Materials*] [*German Federal Diet Division of Scientific Documentation*] [*Information service or system*] (IID)
DIP	Dormit in Pace [*Sleeps in Peace*] [*Latin*]
DIP	Double In-Line Package [*Computer science*]
DIP	Drip Infusion Pyelography [*Radiography*]
DIP	Driver Improvement Program [*American Automobile Association*]
DIP	Droit International Prive [*Private International Law*] [*French*] (DLA)
DIP	Drug-Induced Pneumonitis [*Medicine*]
DIP	Dual In-Line Package [*Computer science*]
DIP	Dual In-Line Pin
DIP	Ductile Iron Pipe (PDAA)
DIP	Dust Infall Predominant (AAG)
DIP	Dynamic Inclined Plane (PDAA)
DIPA	Diamond Industrial Products Association [*British*] (DBA)
DIPA	Diisopropanolamine [*Organic chemistry*]
DIPA	Diisopropylamine [*Also, DIPAM*] [*Organic chemistry*]
DipA	Diploma in Analytical Chemistry
DIPA	Interacting Protein A [*Biochemistry*]
DipAc	Diplomate of Acupuncture [*Medicine*]
DipAcc	Diploma in Accounting
DipAcctgFin...	Diploma in Accounting and Finance
Dip AD	Diploma in Art and Design
DipAdmin(Nursing)...	Diploma in Administration (Nursing)
DipAdminSc...	Diploma in Administrative Science (ADA)
DipAdStudEd...	Diploma in Advanced Studies in Education
DipAdvAcc	Diploma in Advanced Accounting (ADA)
DipAdvEd	Diploma of Advanced Education (ADA)
DipAE	Diploma in Adult Education [*British*] (DI)
DipAg	Diploma in Agriculture (ADA)
DipAgE	Diploma in Agricultural Economics
DipAgEc	Diploma in Agricultural Economics (ADA)
DipAgExt	Diploma in Agricultural Extension
DipAgr	Diploma in Agriculture
DipAgrChem...	Diploma in Agricultural Chemistry (ADA)
DipAgrEc	Diploma in Agricultural Economics (ADA)
DipAgrEnt	Diploma in Agricultural Entomology (ADA)
DipAgrExt	Diploma in Agricultural Extension (ADA)
DipAgrExtn...	Diploma in Agricultural Extension (ADA)
DipAgrGen ...	Diploma in Agricultural Genetics (ADA)
DipAgrMicro...	Diploma in Agricultural Microbiology (ADA)
DipAgrSc	Diploma in Agricultural Science (ADA)
DipAK	Diploma in Applied Kinesiology
DipALing	Diploma in Applied Linguistics (ADA)
DIPAM	Diisopropylamine [*Also, DIPA*] [*Organic chemistry*]
Dip AM	Diploma in Applied Mechanics [*British*]
DipAmerBdP & N...	Diplomate, American Board of Psychiatry and Neurology (DAVI)
DipAnat	Diploma in Anatomy
DipAnHus	Diploma in Animal Husbandry (ADA)
DipAnth	Diploma in Anthropology (ADA)
DipAnthr	Diploma in Anthropology
DipAnthrop...	Diploma in Anthropology (ADA)
DipAppChem...	Diploma in Applied Chemistry
DipAppChildPsych...	Diploma in Applied Child Psychology
DipAppFarmMgmt...	Diploma in Applied Farm Management
DipAppLing...	Diploma in Applied Linguistics
DipAppMath...	Diploma in Applicable Mathematics
DipAppPhys...	Diploma of Applied Physics
DipAppPsych...	Diploma in Applied Psychology (ADA)
DipAppSc	Diploma of Applied Science (ADA)
DipAppSci	Diploma in Applied Science (NADA)
DipAppSc(Nursing)...	Diploma in Applied Science (Nursing)
DipAppSt	Diploma in Applied Statistics
Dip Arch	Diploma in Architecture [*British*]
DipArchAdm...	Diploma in Architectural Administration
DipArchComp...	Diploma in Architectural Computing
DipArchDes...	Diploma in Architectural Design (ADA)
DipArchivAdmin...	Diploma in Archives Administration (ADA)
Dip ARM	Diploma, Australian Risk Management
DipArs	Diploma in Arts (NADA)

DipArt..........	Diploma in Art
DipArtEd.........	Diploma in Art Education
DipArtFilmTV...	Diploma in Art Film and Television
DipArts..........	Diploma in Arts (ADA)
DIPAS..........	Defence Institute of Physiology and Allied Sciences [*New Delhi, India*]
DipAse(CofP)...	Graduate Level Specialist Diplomas in Advanced Study in Education, College of Preceptors [*British*] (DBQ)
DipAst..........	Diploma in Astrology
DipAud.........	Diploma in Audiology
DipAvMed.......	Diploma in Avian Medicine
DipAvMed.......	Diploma in Aviation Medicine (ADA)
DIPB...........	Diisopropylbenzene [*Organic chemistry*]
DipBac.........	Diploma in Bacteriology (NADA)
Dip Bact	Diploma in Bacteriology [*British*]
DipBdgSc......	Diploma in Building Science
DipBdgSc(ECD)...	Diploma in Building Science (Energy-Conservative Design) (ADA)
DipBiom......	Diploma in Biometry (ADA)
DipBM	Diploma in Business Management (ADA)
DipBMS	Diploma in Basic Medical Sciences (ADA)
DipBuildSc...	Diploma in Building Science
DipBus.........	Diploma in Business (ADA)
DipBusAdmin...	Diploma in Business Administration
DipBusMangt...	Diploma in Business Management (ADA)
DipBusStud...	Diploma in Business Studies (ADA)
DipBusStudies...	Diploma in Business Studies (ADA)
DIPC	Diffuse Interstitial Pulmonary Calcification [*Medicine*] (AAMN)
DIPC	Diisopropyl Carbodiimide [*Organic chemistry*]
DipCAM	Diploma of the Communication Advertising and Marketing Education Foundation [*British*] (DBQ)
DipCard	Diploma in Cardiology (ADA)
DipCareers...	Diploma in Careers
DipCD.........	Diploma in Civic Design [*British*]
DipCE..........	Diploma of Civil Engineering (ADA)
DipCEpi......	Diploma in Clinical Epidemiology
DipCH........	Diploma in Clinical Hypnotherapy (ADA)
DipChD........	Diploma in Chest Diseases
Dip Chem	Diploma in Chemistry [*Medicine*] (DMAA)
DipChemE......	Diploma of Chemical Engineering
DipChemInd...	Diploma of Chemistry in Industry
DipChiLit	Diploma in Children's Literature
DipClinHyp...	Diploma in Clinical Hypnosis
DipClinHypno...	Diploma in Clinical Hypnotherapy
DipClinNut...	Diploma in Clinical Nutrition
Dip Clin Path...	Diploma in Clinical Pathology [*British*]
DipClinPharm...	Diploma in Clinical Pharmacology
DipClinPsych...	Diploma in Clinical Psychology
DipClinSc	Diploma in Clinical Science (ADA)
DipCM	Diploma in Community Medicine
DipCoalGeol...	Diploma in Coal Geology
DipCom........	Diploma of Commerce (ADA)
DipCom & Con...	Diploma in Computers and Control
DipComDP...	Diploma in Commercial Data Processing
DipComm ...	Diploma in Commerce (ADA)
DipComm(Acc)...	Diploma in Commerce (Accounting)
DipCommArt...	Diploma in Commercial Art
DipCommChildHealth...	Diploma in Community Child Health
DipCommSc...	Diploma in Community Science
DipCommun...	Diploma in Communications
DipCommunityMgmt...	Diploma of Community Management
DipComp...	Diploma in Computer Studies
DipCompEd...	Diploma in Computer Education
DipCompSc...	Diploma in Computer Science (ADA)
DipCompSt...	Diploma in Computer Studies
DipConsStud...	Diploma in Conservation Studies
DipContEd...	Diploma in Continuing Education (ADA)
Dip Cor........	Diplomatic Correspondence of the United States [*A publication*] (DLA)
DipCOT	Diploma of the College of Occupational Therapists [*British*] (DBQ)
DipCoun......	Diploma in Counselling
DipCPsy......	Diploma in Child Psychiatry
DipCrim	Diploma in Criminology (ADA)
Dip CS.........	Diploma in Christian Studies (PGP)
DipCS	Diploma of the Chamber of Shipping [*Australia*]
DipCultSt	Diploma in Cultural Studies
DipCVD.......	Diploma in Cardiovascular Disease
DIPD...........	Double Inverse Pinch Device [*Physics*] (OA)
DipDDCP......	Diploma in Drug Development and Clinical Pharmacology
DipDentTherapy...	Diploma in Dental Therapy
DipDermat...	Diploma in Dermatology
DipDes.........	Diploma in Design
DipDesCra ...	Diploma in Design and Crafts
DipDevDis ...	Diploma in Developmental Disabilities
DipDHus	Diploma in Dairy Husbandry (ADA)
DipDiet	Diploma in Dietetics (ADA)
DipDistEd	Diploma in Distance Education
DipDiv	Diploma in Divinity
DipDN.........	Diplome en Droit Civil (DD)
DipDomArts...	Diploma in Domestic Arts
DipDomSc ...	Diploma in Domestic Science
DIPDOP........	Disc and Drum Input/Output Routines [*Honeywell, Inc.*]
DipDP	Diploma in Drawing and Painting (NADA)
DipDramArt...	Diploma in Dramatic Art
DipDramEd...	Diploma in Drama Education

DipDS	Diploma in Dental Surgery (NADA)
DIPE...........	Diisopropyl Ether [*Gasoline*] [*Organic chemistry*]
DIPE...........	Diisopropyl Ether [*Organic chemistry*]
DIPEC.........	Defense Industrial Plant (USGC)
DIPEC	Defense Industrial Plant Equipment Center [*DoD*] (AFM)
DIPEC	Defense Industrial Production Equipment Center
DipEc.........	Diploma in Economics (ADA)
DipEco.........	Diploma in Economics (NADA)
Dip Econ	Diploma of Economics (ADA)
DipEconGeog...	Diploma of Economic Geography (ADA)
DipEconStats...	Diploma in Economic Statistics (ADA)
DipEcStud	Diploma in Economic Studies
DIPED	Diisopropylethanediol [*Organic chemistry*]
DipEd	Diploma of Education [*British*] (EY)
DipEdAdm ...	Diploma in Education Administration
DipEdAdmin...	Diploma in Educational Administration (ADA)
DipEdMan ...	Diploma in Educational Management
DipEdPsych...	Diploma in Educational Psychology (ADA)
DipEdRes...	Diploma in Education Research
DipEdSt	Diploma in Education Studies
DipEdStud...	Diploma in Education Studies
DipEdTech ...	Diploma in Education Technology
DipEEng ...	Diploma of Electrical Engineering (ADA)
DIPEF..........	Defense Industrial Plant Equipment Facility [*DoD*]
DipEF.........	Diploma in Executive Finance [*British*] (DBQ)
DipEH.........	Diploma in Environmental Health [*British*] (DBQ)
DipElecEng...	Diploma of Electrical Engineering (ADA)
DipEMA.......	Diploma in Executive Finance for Non-Accountants [*British*] (DBQ)
Dip Eng.......	Diploma in Engineering [*British*]
DipEngGeol...	Diploma in Engineering Geology
DipEngMgt...	Diploma in Engineering Management (ADA)
DipEnvHlth...	Diploma in Environmental Health
DipEnvIA....	Diploma in Environmental Impact Assessment
DipEnvironEng...	Diploma in Environmental Engineering
DipEnvironStud...	Diploma in Environmental Studies (ADA)
DipEnvSc...	Diploma in Environmental Science
DipEnvSt...	Diploma in Environmental Studies
DipEnvStud...	Diploma in Environmental Studies
DipEpid........	Diploma in Epidemiology
DipFA..........	Diploma in Fine Arts (ADA)
DipFamMed...	Diploma in Family Medicine
DipFamT...	Diploma in Family Therapy
DipFashArt...	Diploma in Fashion Art
DipFD	Diploma in Funeral Directing, National Association of Funeral Directors [*British*] (DBQ)
DipFDA	Diploma in Food and Drug Analysis (ADA)
DipFIA	Diploma in Furniture and Interior Architecture
DipFinMan ...	Diploma in Financial Management
DipFinMangt...	Diploma in Financial Management (ADA)
DipFM	Diploma in Financial Management
DipFor	Diploma of Forestry (ADA)
DipFP	Diploma in Family Planning
DipFP	Diploma in Financial Planning
DipFrenchStud...	Diploma in French Studies
DipFSt	Diploma in Film Studies
DipFTV........	Diploma in Film and Television
DIPG	Port Gauthier [*Ivory Coast*] [*ICAO location identifier*] (ICLI)
DipGA	Diploma in Graphic Arts
DipG&O	Diploma in Gynaecology and Obstetrics (NADA)
DipGD	Diploma in Graphic Design
DipGem	Diploma in Gemmology
DipGenLing...	Diploma in General Linguistics
DipGeog...	Diploma in Geography
DipGeotEng...	Diploma in Geotechnical Engineering
DipGerm ...	Diploma in German
DipGraphicDes...	Diploma of Graphic Design
DipGT	Diploma in Glass Technology (ADA)
DipGUM	Diploma in Genito-Urinary Medicine
DIPH	Diphtheria [*Medicine*]
DIPH	Diphthong [*Linguistics*]
DipHA	Diploma in Health Administration (ADA)
DipHCM	Diploma in Hotel and Catering Management
DipHE	Diploma in Highway Engineering (ADA)
DipHE	Diploma in Hydraulic Engineering
DipHE	Diploma of Higher Education
DipHealthSc...	Diploma in Health Science
DipHEd	Diploma in Higher Education
DipHHRE......	Diploma in Health and Human Relations Education
DipHigherEd...	Diploma in Higher Education (ADA)
DipHistStud...	Diploma in History Studies
DipHlthE	Diploma in Health Education
DipHlthSc ...	Diploma in Health Science
DipHMS	Diploma in Human Movement Studies
DipHom	Diploma in Homeopathy
DipHomEc...	Diploma in Home Economics
DipHortSc ...	Diploma in Horticultural Science (ADA)
DipHospAdm...	Diploma in Hospital Administration
DipHospAdmin...	Diploma in Hospital Administration (ADA)
DipHPharm...	Diploma in Hospital Pharmacy (ADA)
DipHS	Diploma in Health Sciences
DipHSc	Diploma in Home Science (ADA)
DIPH/TET ...	Diphtheria/Tetanus [*Immunology*]
DIPHTH........	Diphthong (WDAA)
DIPH TOX	Diphtheria Toxoid [*Immunology*]
DIPH TOX AP...	Diphtheria Toxoid, Alum Precipitated [*Immunology*]

DipHum....... Diploma in Humanities
DipHumBiol... Diploma in Human Biology
DipHumNut... Diploma in Human Nutrition
DipHumRelEd... Diploma in Human Relations Education
DipHus........ Diploma in Husbandry (NADA)
DipH-WU ..... Diploma of Heriot-Watt University [British] (DI)
DipHyp........ Diploma in Hypnosis
DIPI........... Diimidazolinophenylindole [Biochemistry]
DipIB(Scot).... Diplomate of the Institute of Bankers in Scotland [British] (DBQ)
DipIllumDes... Diploma in Illumination Design
DipIllus........ Diploma in Illustration
DipIM-ArchivAd... Diploma in Information Management - Archives Administration (ADA)
DipIM-Lib .... Diploma in Information Management - Librarianship (ADA)
DipImm........ Diploma in Immunology
Dip Ind Chem... Diploma in Industrial Chemistry [British]
DipInfMan.... Diploma in Information Management
DipInfmProcessing... Diploma in Information Processing (ADA)
DipIntAffs..... Diploma in International Affairs
DipIntDes ..... Diploma of Interior Design (ADA)
DipIntMed.... Diploma in Internal Medicine
DipIPharm.... Diploma in Industrial Pharmacy (ADA)
DipJ .... Diploma of Journalism (ADA)
DipJ .... Diploma of Jurisprudence
DIPJ........... Distal Interphalangeal Joint [Anatomy]
DipJewDes.... Diploma of Jewellery Design
DipJour........ Diploma in Journalism (ADA)
DipJourn...... Diploma in Journalism (ADA)
DipJur......... Diploma in Jurisprudence
DipJuris....... Diploma of Jurisprudence (ADA)
DipKindT...... Diploma in Kindergarten Teaching
DIPL........... Diploma (EY)
Dipl........... Diploma (PGP)
DipL........... Diploma in Language (NADA)
DipL........... Diploma of Law
dipl........... Diplomat [or Diplomacy]
DIPL........... Diplomat Corp. [NASDAQ symbol] (SAG)
DIPL........... Diplomatic (ADA)
DIPL........... Diplomatist (WDAA)
DIPL........... Display Initial Program Load (MCD)
DipLA.......... Diploma in Landscape Architecture
DipLabAnimSc... Diploma in Laboratory Animal Science
DipLabRel ... Diploma in Labour Relations
DipLabRelations and the Law... Diploma in Labour Relations and the Law
DipLaw .... Diploma in Law
DipL(BAB).... Diploma of Law (Barristers' Admission Board)
Dipl Chem ... Diploma in Chemistry [British]
DipLD.......... Diploma of Landscape Design (ADA)
DipLDes....... Diploma in Landscape Design
DipLE.......... Diploma in Land Economy
DipLegStud... Diploma in Legal Studies
Dipl Eng ..... Diploma in Engineering [British]
DipLib......... Diploma in Librarianship (ADA)
DipLibSc...... Diploma in Library Science
DipLibSci..... Diploma in Library Science (NADA)
DipLibStud... Diploma in Library Studies (ADA)
DipLing........ Diploma in Linguistics
DipLIS......... Diploma in Library and Information Studies
DipLitLangEd... Diploma in Literacy and Language Education
Dipl Kaufm... Diploma in Commerce [German]
Dipl Kfm ..... Diploma in Commerce [German]
DipLLIRel .... Diploma in Labor Law and Industrial Relations
Diplm.......... Diplomat Corp. [Associated Press] (SAG)
Dipl Math ... Diploma in Mathematics [British]
DipLocGovt... Diploma in Local Government
DipLocGovtAdmin... Diploma in Local Government Administration
DIPLOM....... Diploma (ROG)
Diplomat...... Diplomat Corp. [Associated Press] (SAG)
Dipl PA .... Diploma in Public Administration [British]
Dipl Phys..... Diploma in Physics [British]
DipLS.......... Diploma of Legal Studies
DipL(SAB).... Diploma of Law (Solicitors' Admission Board)
DipLSc........ Diploma in Library Science (ADA)
DIPLW........ Diplomat Corp. Wrrt [NASDAQ symbol] (TTSB)
DIPLXR....... Diplexer [Electronics]
DipM.......... Diploma in Marketing, Institute of Marketing [British] (DBQ)
DipMan....... Diploma in Management
DipManTech... Diploma in Manufacturing Technology
DipMark...... Diploma in Marketing
DipMatEng... Diploma in Materials Engineering
DipMathsEd... Diploma in Mathematics Education
DipMathStud... Diploma in Mathematical Studies
DipME......... Diploma in Mechanical Engineering (NADA)
DipMechE .... Diploma of Mechanical Engineering (ADA)
DipMed....... Diploma in Medicine
DipMedAc.... Diploma in Medical Acupuncture
DipMedHyp... Diploma in Medical Hypnosis
DipMedia..... Diploma in Media
DipMedRad... Diploma in Medical Radiography
DipMedSurg... Diploma in Medical Surgery (ADA)
DipMEE....... Diploma in Mechanical and Electrical Engineering
DipMet........ Diploma in Metallurgy
DipMFOS .... Diploma in Maxial, Facial, and Oral Surgery (ADA)
DipMgmt...... Diploma in Management (NADA)
DipMH .... Diploma in Mental Health

DipMic........ Diploma in Microbiology
DipMicro...... Diploma in Microbiology
Dip Microbiol... Diploma in Microbiology [British]
DipMid........ Diploma in Midwifery
DipMigStud... Diploma in Migrant Studies
DipMigTeach... Diploma in Migrant Teaching
DipMilStudies... Diploma in Military Studies
DipMinSc..... Diploma in Mineral Science
DipMJ(Clin)... Diploma in Medical Jurisprudence (Clinical)
DipMLT....... Diploma in Medical Laboratory Technology
DipMRT ...... Diploma in Medical Radiation Therapy
DipMS .... Diploma in Museum Studies
DipMT........ Diploma of Medical Technology (ADA)
DipMus ...... Diploma in Music (ADA)
DipMusComp... Diploma in Musical Composition
Dip (Mus Ed) RSAM... Diploma in Musical Education, Royal Scottish Academy of Music and Drama
DipMusEdu... Diploma in Musical Education (NADA)
DipMuseumStud... Diploma in Museum Studies
DIPN .... Diisopropylnaphthalene [Organic chemistry]
DipNA .... Diploma in Nursing Administration
DipNA & AC... Diploma in Numerical Analysis and Automatic Computing (ADA)
DipNAdmin... Diploma of Nursing Administration (ADA)
DipNatRes ... Diploma in Natural Resources (ADA)
DipNatTh .... Diploma in Natural Therapies
DipND......... Diploma in Nutrition and Dietetics (ADA)
DipNE......... Diploma in Nursing Education
DipNEd .... Diploma in Nursery School Education (ADA)
DipNEd .... Diploma in Nursing Education
DipNSEdu.... Diploma in Nursery School Education (NADA)
DipNSTC..... Diploma of the Nursery School Teachers' College [Australia]
DipNucEng... Diploma in Nuclear Engineering (ADA)
DipNucSc.... Diploma in Nuclear Science (ADA)
DipNurs ...... Diploma in Nursing
DipNut & Diet... Diploma in Nutrition and Dietetics
DipNutrDiet... Diploma in Nutrition and Dietetics
Dip O & G ... Diploma in Obstetrics and Gynaecology (ADA)
DipOccHazMan... Diploma in Occupational Hazard Management
DipOccHlth... Diploma in Occupational Health
DipOccHyg... Diploma of Professional Competence in Comprehensive Ocupational Hygiene [British] (DBQ)
DipOccMed... Diploma in Occupational Medicine
DipOccThy ... Diploma in Occupational Therapy (ADA)
Dip of N ..... Diploma of Nursing (ADA)
DipOHS........ Diploma in Occupational Health and Safety
DipOL .... Diploma in Oriental Learning (ADA)
DIPOLES...... Defense Intelligence Photoreconnaissance On-Line Exploitation System (MCD)
DipOpArt..... Diploma in Operatic Art
DipOpsRes... Diploma in Operations Research
DipOrth .... Diploma in Orthodontics (ADA)
DipOS .... Diploma in Operational Salesmanship [British] (DI)
DipOS .... Diploma in Oral Surgery
DipOsteo..... Diploma in Osteopathy
DipOT .... Diploma in Occupational Therapy
DipOutEd..... Diploma in Outdoor Education
DIPP .... Dairy Indemnity Payment Program [Department of Agriculture]
DIPP .... Defence Industry Productivity Program [Canada]
DIPP .... Defense Industrial Procurement Program [Canada]
DIPP .... Defense Intelligence Projection for Planning (MCD)
DIPP .... Diisopropyl Percarbonate [Organic chemistry]
DIPPA .... Digital Parallel Processing Array
DipPA .... Diploma of Practitioners in Advertising [British]
DipPaed....... Diploma in Paediatrics
DipPall .... Diploma in Palliative Care
DipP&OT..... Diploma in Physical and Occupational Therapy (NADA)
Dip PE .... Diploma in Physical Education [British]
DipPerfArt.... Diploma in Performing Arts
DipPersMan... Diploma in Personnel Management
DipPetResEng... Diploma in Petroleum and Reservoir Engineering
DipPH .... Diploma in Public Health
DipPhar ...... Diploma in Pharmacology (NADA)
DipPharm .... Diploma in Pharmacy (ADA)
DipPharmMed... Diploma in Pharmaceutical Medicine [British] (DBQ)
DipPhilMed... Diploma in Philosophy of Medicine
DipPhot....... Diploma in Photogrammetry (ADA)
DipPhty....... Diploma in Physiotherapy (ADA)
DipPHus ..... Diploma in Poultry Husbandry (ADA)
DipPhysAnth... Diploma in Physical Anthropology
DipPhysEd ... Diploma in Physical Education (ADA)
DipPhysEdu... Diploma in Physical Education (NADA)
DipPhysio ... Diploma of Physiotherapy (ADA)
DipPlPath .... Diploma in Plant Pathology (ADA)
DipPM .... Diploma in Medical Practice Management
DipPM .... Diploma in Professional Management
DipPowEng... Diploma in Power Engineering
DipPPS .... Diploma in Public Policy Studies
DIPPR......... Design Institute for Physical Property Data [AIChE]
DipPrDerm... Diploma in Practical Dermatology
DipPrehistArch... Diploma of Prehistoric Archaeology (ADA)
DipPrimEd ... Diploma in Primary Education
DipPrimT..... Diploma in Primary Teaching
DipPrivSec... Diploma of the Institute of Private Secretaries [Australia]
DipProArtS... Diploma in Professional Art Studies
DipProcessSystemsEng... Diploma in Process Systems Engineering

DipProd	Diploma in Production
DipPSA	Diploma in Public and Social Administration
DipPsy	Diploma in Psychiatry
DipPsy	Diploma in Psychotherapy
DipPsych	Diploma in Psychiatry
Dip Psych ...	Diploma in Psychology [British]
DipPsychol...	Diploma in Psychology
DipPsyMed...	Diploma in Psychological Medicine (ADA)
DipPT	Diploma in Psychotherapy
DipPubAd	Diploma in Public Administration (ADA)
DipPubAdm...	Diploma in Public Administration (NADA)
DipPubAdmin...	Diploma in Public Administration (ADA)
DipPubPol	Diploma in Public Policy
DipQS	Diploma in Quantity Surveying (ADA)
DIPR	Departmental Industrial Plant Reserve [DoD] (AFIT)
DIPR	Detailed In-Process Review (MCD)
DIPR	Direct Interaction with Product Repulsion [Chemical kinetics]
DIPRA	Ductile Iron Pipe Research Association (EA)
DipRADA......	Diploma of Royal Academy of Dramatic Art [British] (EY)
DipRadDiagnostic...	Diploma in Diagnostic Radiography
DipRadEng...	Diploma in Radio Engineering
DipRadTVProd...	Diploma in Radio and Television Production
DipRAM	Diploma of the Royal Academy of Music [British] (DBQ)
DipRCM	Diploma of the Royal College of Music [British] (DBQ)
DipRE	Diploma in Religious Education
DipRectMan...	Diploma in Recreation Management
DipREd	Diploma of Religious Education
DipRehabStud...	Diploma in Rehabilitation Studies
DipRelStud...	Diploma in Religious Studies
DipRemEd	Diploma of Remedial Education
DipResGeol...	Diploma in Resource Geology
DipRMS	Diploma of the Royal Microscopical Society [British] (DBQ)
DIPROG	Request Diagnosis, Prognosis, Present Condition [Army] (AABC)
DipRTP	Diploma in Regional and Town Planning (ADA)
DipRurAcc ...	Diploma in Rural Accounting (ADA)
DIPS	Defection, Intercept-Passive Submarine (MCD)
DIPS	Defense Intelligence Production Schedule (MCD)
DIPS	Development Information Processing System
DIPS	Diagnostic Inventory of Personality and Symptoms [Personality development test] [Psychology]
DIPS	Dietary Information Processing System (SAA)
DIPS	Digital Imagery Processing System (MCD)
DIPS	Digital Program Selection (IAA)
DIPS	Dual Impact Prediction System [Aerospace] (IAA)
DIPS	Dynamic Isotope Power System
DipS & PA...	Diploma in Social and Public Administration (ADA)
DipScAg.......	Diploma in Science in Agriculture (ADA)
DIPSCAM.....	Diploma Scam [FBI investigation of mail-order colleges]
DipSchoolAdmin...	Diploma in School Administration
DipSecEd.....	Diploma in Secondary Education (ADA)
DipSecStud...	Diploma in Secretarial Studies
DipSKTC	Diploma of the Sydney Kindergarten Teachers' College [Australia]
DipSM	Diploma in Sports Medicine
DipSObC.....	Diploma in Shared Obstetric Care
DipSoc........	Diploma in Sociology (ADA)
Dip Soc Ad...	Diploma in Social Administration [British]
DipSocAdmin...	Diploma of Social Administration (ADA)
DipSocCommun...	Diploma in Social Communication
DipSociol.....	Diploma in Sociology
Dip Soc Med...	Diploma in Social Medicine [British]
DipSocSc....	Diploma in Social Science
DipSocSci....	Diploma in Social Science (ADA)
DipSocStud...	Diploma in Social Studies (ADA)
Dip Soc Studies...	Diploma in Social Studies [British]
DipSocWk....	Diploma of Social Work
DipSoilSc	Diploma in Soil Science
DipSP	Diploma in Sound Preservation
DipSpecEd ...	Diploma in Special Education
DipSpecSubjTeach...	Diploma of Special Subject Teaching
DipSpEd......	Diploma of Special Education
DipSpSc.......	Diploma in Sport Science
DipSpSci.....	Diploma in Sports Science
DipSpThy	Diploma in Speech Therapy (ADA)
DipSS	Diploma in Social Studies (ADA)
DipStats.......	Diploma in Statistics
DipStructEng...	Diploma in Structural Engineering
DipStructFoundEng...	Diploma in Structural and Foundation Engineering
DipSurvSc....	Diploma in Surveying Science (ADA)
DipSW	Diploma in Social Work (ADA)
DIP switch ...	Dual In-Line Package Switch [Electronics] (DOM)
DIP switch ...	Dual In-Line Package Switch (CDE)
DIPT............	Diisopropyl Tartrate [Organic chemistry]
DipT............	Diploma in Teaching (ADA)
DIPT............	Diplomate
DIPTAC	DIFAR [Directional Frequency Analyzing and Recording] Pointing Tactic [Military] (CAAL)
DipT & CP ...	Diploma of Town and Country Planning (ADA)
DipTaxLaw...	Diploma in Tax Law
DipTCD	Diploma in Tuberculosis and Chest Diseases
DipTchg.......	Diploma of Teaching
DipTChM......	Diploma in Traditional Chinese Medicine
DipTchrLib...	Diploma in Teacher Librarianship (ADA)
DipTCP	Diploma in Town and Country Planning (ADA)
DipTE	Diploma in Transportation Engineering [British] (DBQ)
DipTeach	Diploma in Teaching
DipTeach(ECE)...	Diploma in Teaching (Early Childhood Education)
DipTeachLib...	Diploma in Teacher Librarianship
DipTeach(Nursing)...	Diploma in Teaching (Nursing)
DipTeach(Primary)...	Diploma in Teaching (Primary)
DipTeach(Tert)...	Diploma of Teaching (Tertiary)
DipTec	Diploma in Technology (NADA)
Dip Tech	Diploma in Technology [British]
DipTech(Arch)...	Diploma in Technology (Architecture) (ADA)
DipTech(Buil)...	Diploma in Technology (Building) (ADA)
DipTechBusAdmin...	Diploma in Technical Business Administration
DipTech(Comm)...	Diploma in Technology (Commerce) (ADA)
Dip Tech (Eng)...	Diploma of Technology (Engineering) [British]
DipTech(InfProc)...	Diploma in Technology (Information Processing) (ADA)
DipTech(Mgt)...	Diploma in Technology (Management) (ADA)
DipTech(PubAdm)...	Diploma in Technology (Public Administration) (ADA)
DipTech(PubRel)...	Diploma in Technology (Public Relations) (ADA)
DipTech(Sci)...	Diploma in Technology (Science) (ADA)
DipTechT	Diploma in Technical Teaching
DipTEFL	Diploma in Teaching of English as a Foreign Language (ADA)
DipTelecomm...	Diploma in Telecommunications
DipTEM	Diploma in Teaching English to the Migrant (ADA)
DipTertEd	Diploma in Tertiary Education
DipTertiary Ed...	Diploma in Tertiary Education (ADA)
DipTertStud...	Diploma in Tertiary Studies
DipTESL......	Diploma of Teaching English as a Second Language (ADA)
DipTexInd....	Diploma of Textile Industry
DipTG	Diploma of the Teachers Guild (ADA)
DipTh	Diploma in Theology (ADA)
DipThe	Diploma in Theology (NADA)
Dip Theol	Diploma of Theology
DipTLiB........	Diploma in Teachers Librarianship (ADA)
DipTM.........	Diploma in Training Management, the Institute of Training and Development [British] (DBQ)
DipTP	Diploma in Town Planning [British]
DipTP	Diploma of Teacher of Physiotherapy
DipTPT.........	Diploma in Theory and Practice of Teaching [British]
DipTropAgron...	Diploma in Tropical Agronomy (ADA)
DipTRP	Diploma in Town and Regional Planning (ADA)
DipUEMan ...	Diploma in Urban Estate Management
DipUrbDes(Arch)...	Diploma in Urban Design
DipUrbRegSt...	Diploma in Urban and Regional Studies
DipUrbSoc ...	Diploma in Urban Sociology
DipUrbStud...	Diploma in Urban Studies
DipUSP	Diploma in Urban and Social Planning
DipVA	Diploma of Visual Arts
Dip Ven	Diploma in Venereology [British]
DipVetAn	Diploma in Veterinary Anaesthesia
DipVetClinStud...	Diploma in Veterinary Clinical Studies
DipVetPath...	Diploma in Veterinary Pathology (ADA)
DipVetRad...	Diploma in Veterinary Radiology
DipVFM.......	Diploma in Valuation and Farm Management (ADA)
DipVisArts ...	Diploma in Visual Arts
DipWCF	Diploma of the Worshipful Company of Farriers [British] (DI)
DipWildlifeMed & Hus...	Diploma in Wildlife Medicine and Husbandry
DipWomSt ...	Diploma in Women's Studies
DIPX	Diplex [Electronics] (MSA)
DIPY	Dipyridyl [Also, DIP] [Organic chemistry]
DIQ	Deviation Intelligence Quotient [Education]
DIQ	Due-In Quantity
DIQ	Las Vegas, NV [Location identifier FAA] (FAAL)
DIQD...........	Disk-Insulated Quad [Telecommunications] (TEL)
DIR	Daiwa Institute of Research Ltd. [Database producer] (IID)
DIR	Darlington International Raceway [Auto racing]
DIR	Data Input Register [Computer science]
DIR	Data Item Requirement
DIR	Defect Introduction Rate
DIR	Defense Industrial Reserve [DoD]
DIR	Defense Intelligence Report (MCD)
DIR	Delivered in Room [Obstetrics] (CPH)
DIR	Departmentally-Initiated Review
DIR	Depot Inspection and Repair
DIR	Design Information Release
DIR	Development-Inhibitor-Releasing [Photography]
DIR	Diamond Ranch [California] [Seismograph station code, US Geological Survey] (SEIS)
DIR	Digital Instrumentation RADAR
DIR	Direct
dir..............	Directione [Directions] [Latin] (DAVI)
DIR	Directive
DIR	Director [or Directorate] (AFM)
dir..............	Director (WDMC)
DIR	Director
dir..............	Director (DD)
DI(R)...........	Directorate of Intelligence (Research) [RAF] [British]
DIR	Directory
DIR	Dire Dawa [Ethiopia] [Airport symbol] (OAG)
DIR	Dirgantara Air Service PT [Indonesia] [ICAO designator] (FAAC)
DIR	Dirigo [I Guide] [Latin] (ROG)
DIR	Disassembly Inspection Report
DIR	Discipline Oriented Information Retrieval (NITA)
DIR	Dispersive Infrared [Automotive engineering]
DIR	Doctrine of Incremental Reduction
DIR	Document Information Record (KSC)
DIR	Document Information Retrieval (NITA)
DIR	Double Isomorphous Replacement [Medicine] (DMAA)

DIR .... Dynamic Inducer Rotor (MCD)
DIRAC .... Direct Access [*Computer science*] (MHDB)
DIRAFIED.... Director, Armed Forces Information and Education Division (DNAB)
DIRAM .... Digital Range Machine
DIRARFCOS... Director, Armed Forces Courier Service (DNAB)
DIRBE .... Diffuse Infrared Background Experiment [*Spectral instrumentation*]
DIRBY .... When Directed By
DIRC .... Defense Intelligence Relay Center (MCD)
DIRC .... Defense Investigative Review Council
DIRC .... Dithered Infrared Configuration
DIRCARIBDOCKS... Caribbean Division Naval Facilities Engineering Command
DIRCHESDOCKS... Chesapeake Division Naval Facilities Engineering Command
DIRCOL........ Direction Cosine Linkage
DIRCONN..... Direct-Connected [*Mechanical engineering*] (IAA)
DIRCOUP ..... Directional Coupler (IAA)
DIRCTN........ Direction
DIRCTNL...... Directional
DIRCTRT...... Directorate
DIRCTRY..... Directory
DIRD .... Data and Information Resource Directory [*Navy*] (GFGA)
DIRD .... Director, International Research and Development [*Military Canada*]
DIRDET .... When Directed, Detach Duty Indicated
D Ir E .... Doctor of Irrigation Engineering
DIREC .... Direct Instant Response Electronic Composition
DIREC .... Director (ROG)
DIR/ECT .... Directory Project [*Bell Laboratories*]
DIRECT .... Driver Information Experimenting with Communication Technology [*FHWA*] (TAG)
D Ir Eng....... Doctor of Irrigation Engineering
DIREP .... Difficulty Report (AFIT)
DIREURDOCKS... European Division Naval Facilities Engineering Command
DIRF .... Delinquent Investigation Research File [*IRS*]
DIRFLDSUPPACT... Director, Field Summary Activity
DIRFM .... Director Field Maintenance [*Army*] (AABC)
DIR-GEN ...... Director-General (WDAA)
DIRGULFDOCKS... Gulf Division Naval Facilities Engineering Command
DIRH............ Dirham [*Monetary unit*] [*Iraq*]
DIRID .... Directional Infrared Intrusion Detector (MCD)
DIR/INTC...... Direct Intercept (GAVI)
DIRJOAP...... Director, Joint Oil Analysis Program [*Military*] (DNAB)
DIRJOAPTSC... Director, Joint Oil Analysis Program Technical Support Center [*Military*] (DNAB)
DIRK .... Dosemeter Issue and Record Keeping
Dirl .... Dirleton's Decisions, Court of Sessions [*Scotland*] [*A publication*] (DLA)
DIRLANTDOCKS... Director, Atlantic Division, Bureau of Yards and Docks [*Obsolete*]
DIRLAUTH ... Direct Liaison Authorized [*Military*] (NVT)
Dirl D.......... Dirleton's Doubts and Questions in the Law [*A publication*] (DLA)
Dirl Dec....... Dirleton's Decisions, Court of Sessions [*Scotland*] [*A publication*] (DLA)
DIRLINE ...... Directory of Information Sources Online [*National Library of Medicine*] [*Database*]
DirLt .... Direction Light [*Navigation*]
DIRM .... Defense Intelligence Requirement Manual (AFM)
DIRMIDWESTDOCKS... Midwest Division Naval Facilities Engineering Command
DIRNAVCURSERV... Director, Naval Courier Service (DNAB)
DIRNAVHIS... Director of Naval History (DNAB)
DIRNAVHIST... Director of Naval History
DIRNAVINSERV... Director, Naval Investigative Service (DNAB)
DIRNAVMARCORMARS... Director, Navy-Marine Corps Military Affiliate Radio Service (DNAB)
DIRNAVPUBPRINTSERV... Director, Navy Publication and Printing Service
DIRNAVRESINTPRO... Director, Naval Reserve Intelligence Program (DNAB)
DIRNAVSECGRUEUR... Director, Naval Security Group, Europe (DNAB)
DIRNAVSECGRULANT... Director, Naval Security Group, Atlantic (DNAB)
DIRNAVSECGRUPAC... Director, Naval Security Group, Pacific (DNAB)
DIRNCPB ..... Director, Naval Council of Personnel Boards (DNAB)
DIRNCPBDET... Director, Naval Council of Personnel Boards Detachment (DNAB)
DIRNRL........ Director, Naval Research Laboratory (SAA)
DIRNSA....... Director, National Security Agency [*Pronounced "dern-za"*]
DIRNSA/CHCSS... Director National Security Agency / Chief Central Security Service
DIRNSCPO ... Director, Navy Secretariat Civilian Personnel Office (DNAB)
DIRO .... Deionization Reverse Osmosis [*Water treatment*]
DIRO .... District Industrial Relations Officer [*Navy*]
DIROCD .... Director, Office of Civil Defense (AABC)
DIRON .... Direction
DIR OP .... Directie Overheids-Personeelsbeleid [*Netherlands*]
DIROR .... Director (ROG)
DIRPA.......... Director of Personnel and Administration [*Army*] (AABC)
DIRPACALDOCKS... Director, Pacific and Alaskan Divisions, Bureau of Yards and Docks [*Obsolete*]
DIRPACDOCKS... Director, Pacific Division, Bureau of Yards and Docks [*Obsolete*]
DIRPRO........ When Directed Proceed
DIR PROP.... Directione Propria [*With Proper Direction*] [*Pharmacy*]
DIRS .... Damage Information Reporting System [*Military*] (MCD)
DIRS .... Data Information Requirements System [*Military*]
DIRS .... Departmental Industrial Reserve System
DIRS .... Digital Image Rectification System (MCD)
DIRS .... DIMDI Information Retrieval System (NITA)
DIRS .... Division Integrated Record System (SAA)
DIRSDIMA ... Director, San Diego [*California*] Intermediate Maintenance Activity [*Military*] (DNAB)
DIRSOEASTDOCKS... Southeast Division Naval Facilities Engineering Command

DIRSOWESTDOCKS... Southwest Division Naval Facilities Engineering Command
DIRSP/PROJMGRFBM... Director, Special Projects/Project Manager, Fleet Ballistic Missile
DIRSSP........ Director, Strategic Systems Project Office [*Navy*]
DIRT .... Data in Real Time
DIRT .... Defense Infrared Test (MCD)
DIRT .... Deposit Interest Retention Tax [*Ireland*]
DIRT .... Director's Instant Reversible Talkback [*Device enabling contact between director in control room and crew in studio*]
DIRT .... Drivers' Independent Race Tracks [*An association*]
DIRT .... Dust Infrared Test (MCD)
DIRTY .... Darned Insulting, Rotten, Terrible Yarns [*Book title*]
DIRVIR........ Directory Verification Processor [*Computer science*]
DIRW .... Director of Women Marines
DIRWESTDOCKS... Western Division Naval Facilities Engineering Command
DIRWSEG ... Director, Weapons Systems Evaluation Group (CINC)
DIS .... Daily Issue Store [*British military*] (DMA)
DIS .... Database Information Services (NITA)
DIS .... Database Information System
DIS .... Data Input Supervisor [*Computer science*] (IAA)
DIS .... Data Input System [*Computer science*]
DIS .... Data Inspection Station
DIS .... Data Interpretation System (BTTJ)
DIS .... Daytona International Speedway [*Auto racing*]
DIS .... Decision Information Services Ltd. [*Information service or system*] (IID)
DIS .... Deep Inelastic Scattering [*Particle physics*]
DIS .... Defence Intelligence Staff [*British*]
DIS .... Defense Institute of Security Assistance Management, Wright-Patterson AFB, OH [*OCLC symbol*] (OCLC)
DIS .... Defense Intelligence School
DIS .... Defense Intelligence Staff (MCD)
DIS .... Defense Intelligence Summary (MCD)
DIS .... Defense Investigative Service [*DoD*]
DIS .... Department of Defense Index of Specifications and Standards
DIS .... Department of Internal Security
DIS .... Design Improvement Study
DIS .... Design Integration Sheet (MCD)
DIS .... Design Integration Subsystem
DIS .... Development Information System [*United Nations Information service or system*] (IID)
DIS .... Diagnostic Interview Schedule [*Psychology*]
DIS .... Dialectic Information System (PDAA)
DIS .... Dialog Terminal System (IAA)
DIS .... Digalactosyl Diglycerideafta [*Organic chemistry*]
DIS .... Digital Identification Signal [*Computer science*]
DIS .... Digital Imaging Spectrophotometer [*or Spectroscopy*]
DIS .... Digital Instrumentation Subsystem
DIS .... Digital Integration System (IEEE)
DIS .... Diploma in Industrial Studies, Loughborough University of Technology [*British*] (DBQ)
DIS .... Direct Ignition System [*Automotive engineering*]
DIS .... Directorate of Installation Services (MCD)
DI(S)........... Directorate of Intelligence (Security) [*RAF*] [*British*]
DIS .... Directory Information Service [*A publication*]
DIS .... Disability
DIS .... Disabled (ECII)
DIS .... Disagree (NASA)
DIS .... Discharge
DIS .... Disciple
DIS .... Discipline
DIS .... Disconnect (DEN)
DIS .... Discontinued
dis .... Discontinuity [*Geology*] (BARN)
DIS .... Discount
DIS .... Discrete (AAG)
DIS .... Discutient [*Dissolving*] [*Pharmacy*] (ROG)
DIS .... Disease
DIS .... Disease Intervention Specialist [*Medicine*]
DIS .... Disintegration
dis .... Dislocation (DAVI)
DIS .... [*The*] Disney [*Walt*] Co. [*Wall Street slang name: "Mickey Mouse"*] [*NYSE symbol*] (SPSG)
Dis .... Disney's Ohio Superior Court Reports [*A publication*] (DLA)
DIS .... Disorderly [*FBI standardized term*]
DIS .... Dispensed (ADA)
DIS .... Display (KSC)
DIS .... Disrotatory [*Chemistry*]
dis .... Dissaying [*Slang*] (WDMC)
DIS .... Disseminated Intravascular Coagulation [*Medicine*] (BARN)
Dis .... Dissent [*A publication*] (BRI)
DIS .... Dissertation Inquiry Service [*Xerox Corp.*]
Dis .... Dissolve [*Optical technique*] [*Filmmaking*] (WDMC)
Dis .... Dissolved
DIS .... Distance (MUGU)
DIS .... Distanced [*Horse racing*]
DIS .... Distant
Dis .... Distinctio [*Decretum Gratiani*] [*A publication*] (DSA)
DIS .... Distribute (ROG)
DIS .... Distributed Information System [*Computer science*]
DIS .... Distributed Instructional System [*Military*]
DIS .... Distributed Interactive Simulation [*Army*] (RDA)
DIS .... Distribution Information System
DIS .... Distributor Gasket [*Automotive engineering*]
DIS .... Distributorless Ignition System [*Automotive engineering*]

DIS.............. District
DIS.............. Division of Information Services [*Council for Scientific and Industrial Research*] [*South Africa*] (IID)
DIS.............. Division of Information Services [*Council of State Governments*] [*Information service or system*] (IID)
DIS.............. Documentation Index System (MCD)
DIS.............. Doppler Imaging System [*Physics*]
DIS.............. Doppler Inertial System (AAG)
DIS.............. Douglas Inspection Standard (SAA)
DIS.............. Draft International Standard [*International Standards Organization*]
DIS.............. Drilling Information Services [*Adams Engineering, Inc.*] [*Information service or system*] (IID)
DIS.............. Drosophila Information Service [*Genetics*]
DIS.............. Drug Information Service [*Memorial Medical Center of Long Beach*] [*Information service or system*] (IID)
DIS.............. Drug Information Services [*University of Minnesota, Minneapolis*] (IID)
DIS.............. Dual Image System
DIS.............. Ductile Iron Society (EA)
DIS.............. Loubomo [*Congo*] [*Airport symbol*] (OAG)
DISA........... Dairy Industries Supply Association [*Later, DFISA*]
DISA........... Dansk Industri Syndikat A/S [*Danish manufacturer of a machine gun mount being tested by US Army*] (RDA)
DISA........... Data Interchange Standards Association (AAGC)
DISA........... Data Interchange Standards Association
DISA........... Defense Information Services Activity (USGC)
DISA........... Defense Information Services Agency (DOMA)
DISA........... Defense Information Systems Agency [*Formerly, DCA*] (DOMA)
DISA........... Defense Information Systems Agency [*Formerly, DSA*] [*DoD*]
DISA........... Defense Institute of Security Assistance (MCD)
DISA........... Direct Inward System Access (HGAA)
DISA........... Division of International Security Affairs [*Energy Research and Development Administration*]
DISA........... Division of Security Affairs [*ERDA*] (AAGC)
DISA........... Dwarf Iris Society of America (EA)
DISAB......... Disability (ADA)
DISAB......... DoD [*Department of Defense*] Information Security Advisory Board
DISABLD...... Disabled (FAAC)
DISAC......... Digital Simulator and Computer (IEEE)
DISACET...... Dissolution of Acetaminophen [*Clinical chemistry*]
DISAF......... Delinquency Item Summary and Forecast (MCD)
DI/SAL........ Vessels Disposed of by Sale through Navy Material Redistribution Agency [*Navy*]
DISALLCE.... Disallowance [*Legal*] [*British*] (ROG)
DISALLD...... Disallowed [*Legal*] [*British*] (ROG)
DISAM......... Defense Institute of Security Assistance Management [*Air Force*]
DISAO......... Designated Independent Senior Acquisition Official (AAGC)
DISAP......... Disapprove (AABC)
DISAPG....... Disappearing
Disappr........ Disapproved In [*or Disapproving*] [*Legal term*] (DLA)
DISASSM..... Disassemble
DISASSY...... Disassembly (KSC)
DISB........... Disburse (AABC)
DISBMT....... Disbursement (AFM)
DISBMT....... Disbursement
DISBN......... Distribution (DCTA)
DISBO......... Disbursing Officer [*Military*] (DNAB)
DISBOFF...... Disbursing Officer
DISBOFFCOP... Disbursing Officer Making Payment on These Orders Forward Copy [*Military*] (DNAB)
DISBS......... Disbursements [*Business term*]
DISBSUBREPT... Disbursing Officer Making Payment Submit Monthly Letter Reports [*Military*] (DNAB)
DISC........... Daily Intelligence Summary Cable (MCD)
DISC........... Dakota Information Service to the Community (IID)
DISC........... Data Index for Software Configuration (MCD)
DISC........... Data Index for Software Control (MCD)
DISC........... Data, Information, and System Control
DISC........... Data Information System for Management Control [*Military*]
DISC........... Data Processing and Information Science Contents [*BRS Information Technologies*] [*Online database Discontinued*]
DISC........... Decision Information Screening Center (MCD)
DISC........... Defect Information and Servicing Control [*Aviation*]
DISC........... Defense Industrial Supply Center
DISC........... Defense Industrial Support Center (MCD)
DISC........... Delay in Separation Code [*Military*] (AABC)
DISC........... Delivering Information Solutions to Customers [*British*]
DISC........... Diagnostic Interview Schedule for Children [*Psychology*]
DISC........... Differential Scatter [*Remote sensing technique*]
DISC........... Digital International Switching Center [*Telecommunications*] (TEL)
DISC........... Digital Simulation Computer System (SAA)
DISC........... Direct-Injected Stratified Charge [*Engine*] (RDA)
DISC........... Disability Insurance Sales Course [*LUTC*]
DISC........... Discharged [*Military*]
DISC........... Disciple (ADA)
DISC........... Discipline (WDAA)
DISC........... Discone (NASA)
DISC........... Disconnect (KSC)
DISC........... Discontinue (AFM)
DISC........... Discount
disc............ Discount (WDMC)
DISC........... Discount
DISC........... Discourse (ROG)
DISC........... Discover [*or Discoverer*]
DISC........... Discovery Channel [*Cable television channel*]

DISC........... Discrepancy Identification and System Checkout (DNAB)
DISC........... Discrete (KSC)
DISC........... Discriminator (IAA)
DISC........... Distribution Stock Control System (MHDB)
DISC........... District
DISC........... Divisional Interests Special Committee [*American Library Association*]
DISC........... Documentation and Integration of Software into the Classroom Project (EDAC)
DISC........... Domestic International Sales Corp. [*See also Foreign Sales Corp. - FSC*]
DISC........... Drilling Information Service Co. [*Houston, TX*] [*Telecommunications*] (TSSD)
DISC........... Drop-In Skills Centre [*British*] (AIE)
DISC........... Dynamic Intelligent Scheduling [*Computer science*]
DISC4......... Director of Information Systems for Command, Control, Communications, and Computers [*DoD*]
DISCA......... Dissolution Inhibitor Solubilizable by Chemical Amplification [*Chemistry*]
DISCAN....... Christian Church (Disciples of Christ) in Canada [*Formerly, All-Canada Committee of the Christian Church (Disciples of Christ)*] (AC)
DISCAS....... Defense Intelligence Special Career Automated System (MCD)
DiscAut....... Discount Auto Parts Co. [*Associated Press*] (SAG)
DISCCNC..... Declaration of Independence Second Centennial Commemorative National Committee (EA)
DiscGph...... Disc Graphics, Inc. [*Associated Press*] (SAG)
DISCH......... Defense Intelligence School [*Air Force*]
DISCH......... Discharge (AFM)
DISCHE....... Discharge (ROG)
DISCIP........ Disciplinary (DSUE)
DISCO......... Defense Industrial Security Clearance Office
DISCO......... Discotheque (DSUE)
DISCO......... Dissertations on Chemical Oceanography
DISCOID...... Direct Scan Operating with Integrated Delay (MCD)
Discol......... Discolored
DISCOLA..... Digital Integrated Solid-State Controller for Low-Cost Automation (PDAA)
DISCOM...... Digital Selective Communications
DISCOM...... Division Support Command [*Army*] (AABC)
DISCON...... Disconnect (KSC)
DISCON...... Discontinue
DISCON...... Discrepancy in Shipment Confirmation [*DoD*]
discontd...... Discontinued
DISCOP....... Digital Simulation of Continuous Processes
DISCORAP... Directionally-Controlled Rocket-Assisted Projectile
DISCORS..... Discrepancy-in-Shipment Cargo Outturn Reporting System [*DoD*] (DNAB)
discort........ Disconnect [*Disorderly Conduct*] (BARN)
DISCOS....... Disturbance Compensation System [*Navy satellite navigation*]
DISCOVD..... Discovered (ROG)
DISCOVY..... Discovery (ROG)
DISCOY....... Discovery (ROG)
DISC-P........ Diagnostic Interview Schedule for Children - Parents Form [*Psychology*]
DI/SCP....... Disposition of Vessel by Scrapping (DNAB)
DI/SCP....... Vessels Disposed of by Scrapping [*Navy*]
DISCR........ Directorate of Industrial Security Clearance Review [*DoD*]
DISCR........ Discrepancy (GAVI)
DISCR........ Discriminate (AABC)
Discreet...... Discreet Logic, Inc. [*Associated Press*] (SAG)
DISCREP..... Discrepancy Report
DISCRM...... Discriminate (MUGU)
DISCRON..... Discretion
DISCRP....... Discrepancy (AABC)
DISCR Review... Directorate for Industrial Security Clearance (AAGC)
DISCT......... Discount
DISCT......... District
Discur......... Discuriosities [*Record label*]
DISCUS....... Dealer Information System for Customer Satisfaction [*Automotive retailing*]
DISCUS....... Disposal and Collection User Simulation (PDAA)
DISCUS....... Distilled Spirits Council of the United States (EA)
DiscZone..... Discovery Zone, Inc. [*Associated Press*] (SAG)
DISD.......... Data and Information Systems Division [*IT & T*]
DISD.......... Defense Industrial Supply Depot
DISDEP....... Distant Deployment (DNAB)
DisDGM...... District Deputy Grand Master [*Freemasonry*]
DISDKB....... Descendants of the Illegitimate Sons and Daughters of the Kings of Britain (EA)
DISE.......... Development in Science Education [*National Science Foundation*] (GRD)
DISE.......... Distribution and Illumination System, Electrical [*Army*] (INF)
DISECS....... Defense Intelligence Space Exploitation and Correlation System (MCD)
DISEM........ Disseminate (AABC)
DISEMB...... Disembark (AABC)
DISENG....... Disengage
DISESTAB.... Disestablish
DISFP......... Disc-Indexed Sequential File Package [*Computer science*] (PDAA)
DISFREE..... Distribution-Free Statistics
DISG.......... Seguela [*Ivory Coast*] [*ICAO location identifier*] (ICLI)
DIS GOSC.... Distributed Interactive Simulation General Officer Steering Committee [*Army*] (RDA)
DISGRAT..... Discharge Gratuity [*Military*]
DISH.......... Data Interchange in the Shipping Industry

DISH	Diffuse Idiopathic Skeletal Hyperostosis [*Medicine*]
DISH	Disseminated Idiopathic Skeletal Hyperostosis [*Medicine*] (DAVI)
Dish	Double [*or Dual*] Income, Separate Homes [*Lifestyle classification*]
DISH	EchoStar Communications'A' [*NASDAQ symbol*] (TTSB)
DISH	EchoStar Communications Corp. [*NASDAQ symbol*] (SAG)
DISHES	Determined Involved Supermodels Helping to End Suffering [*An association*]
DISHON	Dishonorable (ADA)
DISHOND	Dishonored (ROG)
DISI	Defense Industrial Security Institute [*DoD*]
DISI	Diode Ion Source Injector
DISI	Door Insulating Systems Index
DISI	Dorsal Intercalary Segment Instability [*Medicine*]
DISIDS	Display and Information Distribution System [*or Subsystem*] (MCD)
DISIM	Digital Input Simulator [*Computer science*]
DISINT	Discrete Integrator (IAA)
DISJ	Disjunctive (ROG)
DISJUNCT....	Disjunctive [*Linguistics*]
DISK	Image Entertainment [*NASDAQ symbol*] (TTSB)
DISK	Image Entertainment, Inc. [*NASDAQ symbol*] (NQ)
DISKCOMP...	Disk Compare [*Computer science*]
Disl	Dislocation (DAVI)
DISLAN	Display Language [*Computer science*] (MHDB)
DISLOC	Dislocation [*Medicine*]
DISLVD	Dissolved
DISM	Delayed Impact Space Missile (IAA)
DISM	Dismantle (MSA)
DISM	Dismiss (AABC)
DISMD	Dismissed [*Legal shorthand*] (LWAP)
DisMD	Distal Muscular Dystrophy [*Medicine*]
DIS/MIN......	Disintegrations per Minute
DISN	Defense Information System Network
DISN	Diiminosuccinonitrile [*Organic chemistry*]
Disn	Disney's Superior Court of Cincinnati Reports [*Ohio*] [*A publication*] (DLA)
DISNET	Defense Integrated Secure Network (DOMA)
DISNET	Drug Information Systems Network
Disney	[*The*] Disney [*Walt*] Co. [*Wall Street slang name: "Mickey Mouse"*] [*Associated Press*] (SAG)
Disn Gam	Disney. Gaming [*1806*] [*A publication*] (DLA)
Disn (Ohio)...	Disney's Ohio Superior Court Reports [*A publication*] (DLA)
DISO	Dictionnaire des Inscriptions Semitiques de l'Ouest [*A publication*] (BJA)
DISOD..........	Disodium
DISOP..........	Discharge by Operator (DNAB)
Dis Op	Dissenting Opinion [*Legal term*] (DLA)
DISORD H....	Disorderly House [*Legal term*] (DLA)
DISOSS........	Distributed Office Support System [*IBM Corp.*]
DISP	Defense Industrial Security Program [*DoD*]
DISP	Defense Industry Studies Program (NG)
DISP	Dispatch
DISP	Dispatcher (MSA)
DISP	Dispensary (AFM)
DISP	Dispensation
disp	Dispensatory (DAVI)
DISP	Dispenser
DISP	Dispensetur [*Dispense*] [*Pharmacy*]
DISP	Disperse
DISP	Dispersion (WDAA)
disp	Dispersion (VRA)
DISP	Displacement
DISP	Display (KSC)
DISP	Displayed Composition [*Graphic arts*] (DGA)
DISP	Disposal
DISP	Disproportionation
DISP	DoD [*Department of Defense*] Industrial Security Program (AABC)
DISP	Draft International Standardized Profile [*OSI*] (OSI)
DISP	San Pedro [*Ivory Coast*] [*ICAO location identifier*] (ICLI)
DISPAC........	Domestic and International Scientific Planning and Cooperation
DISPENS......	Dispensary (ADA)
DISPERSE....	Discretionary Population Effects for Riot and Stability Employment [*Crowd control*]
DISPL	Displacement (AAG)
DISPLAN	Disaster Plan [*Australia*]
DISPLAY	Digital Service Planning Analysis [*Telecommunications*] (TEL)
DISPN..........	Disposition (MSA)
DISPNSG	Dispensing
dispo	Disposition (DAVI)
DISPOSAL....	Developing Improved Sizing Procedures Over Sanitary Area Landfills
DISPOSN.....	Disposition (ROG)
DISPR..........	Dispatcher
DISQ	Disquisition (ROG)
DISQUAL.....	Disqualify (AABC)
DISR	Daily Indicator Status Report (MCD)
DISR	Defense Indications Status Report (MCD)
DISR	Discrepant Item - Ships Record
Dis R	Disney's Superior Court of Cincinnati Reports [*Ohio*] [*A publication*] (DLA)
DISRE..........	Disregard (AABC)
DISREP........	Discrepancy in Shipment Report [*DoD*] (AABC)
DIS RET......	Disability Retirement [*Military*] (DNAB)
DISS	Data Input Subsystem [*Computer science*] (SAA)
DISS	Digest of Intelligence and Security Services (MCD)
DISS	Digital Interface Switching System
DIS/S	Disintegrations per Second

DISS	Dissenter
DISS	Dissertation
DISS	Dissolve
DISS	Distributed Information Processing Service System (NITA)
DISS	Sassandra [*Ivory Coast*] [*ICAO location identifier*] (ICLI)
DissadHRP...	Dissertationes ad Historiam Religionum Pertinentes [*A publication*] (BJA)
DISSC	Dredging Industry Size Standard Committee (EA)
DISSCO........	User Community [*Programming language*] [*Argonne National Laboratory Argonne, IL*] (CSR)
dissd...........	Dissolved
DIS/SEC	Disintegrations per Second
DISSEM	Disseminated
DISSERT......	Dissertation
DISSIG	Distress Signal (IAA)
DISSIP	Dissipation
DISSOC........	Dissociate
DISSP	Defense Information Systems Security Program [*Military*] (DOMA)
DISSPLA	Display Integrated Software System and Plotting Language [*Computer science*]
DISSYS	Distribution System (IAA)
DIST.............	AMCON Distributing [*NASDAQ symbol*] (SAG)
DIST.............	AMCON Distributing [*NASDAQ symbol*] (TTSB)
DIST.............	AMOON Distributing [*NASDAQ symbol*] (SAG)
DIST.............	Data Input Strobe (NITA)
DIST.............	Delegation for Scientific and Technical Information (IID)
DIST.............	Department of Industry, Science, and Technology [*Australia*]
DIST.............	Discount
DIST.............	Distal [*Medicine*]
DIST.............	Distance [*or Distant*] (AFM)
dist	Distance (WDMC)
DIST.............	Distanced [*Horse racing*]
dist	Distant (VRA)
dist	Distant (WDMC)
DIST.............	Distilla [*Distill*] [*Pharmacy*] (ROG)
Dist.............	Distillate
DIST.............	Distilled [*or Distillery*]
Dist.............	Distinctio [*Decretum Gratiani*] [*A publication*] (DSA)
DIST.............	Distinction (ROG)
DIST.............	Distinguish
DIST.............	Distort (IAA)
DIST.............	Distribute
DIST.............	Distributed Time (KSC)
dist	Distribution (IEEE)
DIST.............	Distributor (KSC)
DIST.............	District (AFM)
dist	District (WDMC)
DIST.............	District
DIST.............	Disturbance [*FBI standardized term*]
DIST.............	Division of Information Science and Technology [*National Science Foundation*]
DISTAB	Disestablish (NVT)
DISTAD	District Administrator (CINC)
DISTAFF	Directing Staff (NATG)
DISTAN........	Distributed Interactive Secure Telecommunications Area Network (MCD)
Dist & Co Rep...	Pennsylvania District and County Reports [*A publication*] (DLA)
DISTAR	Direct Instructional System for Teaching Arithmetic and Reading
DISTAR	Direct Instructional Systems to Arithmetic and Reading (AIE)
Dist Atty	District Attorney (WGA)
Dist C	District Court (DLA)
Dist Col App...	District of Columbia Court of Appeals (DLA)
Dist Ct	District Court [*State*] (DLA)
Dist Ct App...	District Court of Appeal (DLA)
DISTD..........	Distilled
DISTENGR ...	District Engineer [*Army*] (AABC)
DISTEX	District Relief Exercise [*Military*] (DNAB)
Dist F	Distinguished From [*Medicine*] (DAVI)
DISTING......	Distinguish
DISTING......	Distinguished (ROG)
DISTLLRY	Distillery
DISTLR	Distiller
DISTMEDO...	District Medical Officer [*Military*] (DNAB)
DISTN	Distillation
DISTN	Distortion (MSA)
DISTN	Distribution (AAG)
DISTNCTV ...	Distinctive
DISTO	Defense Industrial Security Education and Training Office (AABC)
DISTR	Distracted
DISTR	Distribution [*or Distributor*] (AFM)
DISTR	Distributor
DISTR	District (ROG)
distr	District (VRA)
Dist R	Pennsylvania District Reports [*A publication*] (DLA)
DISTRA........	Distribution Authority [*Army*] (AABC)
DISTRAM.....	Digital Space Trajectory Measurement System [*Raytheon Co.*]
DISTRAN.....	Diagnostic FORTRAN [*Formula Translating System*] (IAA)
distrb	Distribute (VRA)
DISTRB	Distributes
DISTRB	Distribution
Distr Col BAJ...	District of Columbia Bar Association. Journal [*A publication*] (DLA)
DISTREAT....	Upon Discharge Treatment [*Military*]
Dist Rep	District Reports [*A publication*] (DLA)
Dist Reports...	Pennsylvania District Reports [*A publication*] (DLA)
Dist Reps.....	Pennsylvania District Reports [*A publication*] (DLA)

DISTRG....... Distributing
DISTRIB...... Distribution
District........ Pennsylvania District Reports [*A publication*] (DLA)
District Court LR... District Court Law Reports [*Hong Kong*] [*A publication*] (DLA)
District Reps... Pennsylvania District Reports [*A publication*] (DLA)
DISTRIPRESS... Federation Internationale des Distributeurs de Presse [*International Federation of Wholesale Newspaper, Periodical, and Book Distributors*]
DIS TX........ Disable Transmit (NITA)
DISU.......... Digital International Switching Unit [*Telecommunications*] (TEL)
DISUB........ Duty Involving Underway Operations in Submarines
DISUM........ Daily Intelligence Summary [*Air Force*]
DISUS........ Disused (ROG)
DISY.......... Dimokratikos Synagermos [*Democratic Rally*] [*Political party*] (EAIO)
DISY.......... Disyllable
DISYLL....... Disyllable (ROG)
DISYNDA..... Display of Synoptic Data
DIT........... Data Identification Table (MCD)
DIT........... Data Inquiry Terminal
DIT........... Defense Intelligence Thesaurus (MCD)
DIT........... Defining Issues Test (EDAC)
DIT........... Delay Ignition [*or Igniting*] Tracer [*Military*] (MCD)
DIT........... Delivery Issue Team (MCD)
DIT........... Department of Information Technology [*Commonwealth of Virginia*] [*Telecommunications service*] (TSSD)
DIT........... Detroit Institute of Technology
DIT........... Digital Instrumentation Technology, Inc. (PCM)
DIT........... Diiodotyrosine [*Biochemistry*]
DIT........... Director for Individual Training (MCD)
DIT........... Directory Information Tree (TNIG)
DIT........... Dithiothreitol [*Organic chemistry*]
DIT........... Diversified Techs Inc. [*Vancouver Stock Exchange symbol*]
DIT........... Doctor of Industrial Technology (GAGS)
DIT........... Documentation Implementation Team [*Deep Space Network, NASA*]
DIT........... Documentation Information Transmittal (NVT)
DIT........... Domestic Independent Tour [*or Travel*]
DIT........... Dorsal Intermediate Tract [*Anatomy*]
DIT........... Double Incidence Technique
DIT........... Double Income Tax (ODBW)
DIT........... Drexel Institute of Technology [*Pennsylvania*] (MCD)
DIT........... Dual Input Transponder
DIT........... Dublin Institute of Technology (ACII)
DIT........... Dynamic Integrated Test (MCD)
DITA.......... Diesel Tank Vessel
DITAC........ DIFAR [*Directional Frequency Analyzing and Recording*] Tactic [*Military*] (CAAL)
DITACS....... Digital Tactical System (PDAA)
DITAR........ Digital Telemetry Analog Recording
DITB.......... Digital Imagery Test Bed
DITB.......... Distribution Industry Training Board [*Terminated British*]
DITB.......... Tabou [*Ivory Coast*] [*ICAO location identifier*] (ICLI)
DITC.......... Disability Insurance Training Council [*Washington, DC*] (EA)
DITE.......... Diverter Injection Tokamak [*Toroidal Kamera Magnetic*] Experiment (MCD)
DITEC........ Digital Television Camera (MCD)
DITEC........ Digital Television Encoding
DI/TES....... Vessels Disposed of by Using as Targets and Tests [*Navy*]
DITL.......... [*A*] Day in the Life [*Series*] [*Photojournalism project*]
DITLA........ [*A*] Day in the Life of America [*Photojournalism project*]
DITLOHA..... [*A*] Day in the Life of Hawaii [*Photojournalism project*]
DITM.......... Touba/Mahana [*Ivory Coast*] [*ICAO location identifier*] (ICLI)
DITMCO...... Data Information Test Material Checkout
dITP.......... Deoxyinosine Triphosphate [*Biochemistry*]
DITP.......... Detailed Individual Test Plan (MCD)
DITR.......... Deutsches Informationszentrum fuer Technische Regeln [*German Information Center for Technical Rules*] [*German Institute for Standardization*] [*Information service or system*] (IID)
DITRAN...... Diagnostic FORTRAN [*Computer science*] (IEEE)
DI/TRN....... Vessels Transferred to Other Government Agencies and Miscellaneous Activities [*Navy*]
DITROFF..... Device Independent Typesetting Run Off [*Typography*] (DGA)
DITS.......... Dancing in the Streets
DITS.......... Digital Information Transfer Set (CAAL)
DITS.......... Digital Information Transfer System
DITS.......... Digital Television Spectrometer (NG)
DITT.......... Department of Industry, Trade and Technology [*South Australia*]
DITTO........ Data Interfile Transfer, Testing, and Operations Utility [*IBM program product*]
DITTO........ Directory of Independent Training and Tutorial Organisations (AIE)
DITU.......... Digital Interface Test Unit [*Computer science*] (KSC)
DITY.......... Committee for Do-It-Yourself Household Moving (EA)
DITY.......... Do-It-Yourself (MCD)
DIU........... Data Information Unit [*Marine science*] (OSRA)
DIU........... Data Interchange Utility (IAA)
DIU........... Data Interface Unit
DIU........... Dedicated Interface Unit
DIU........... Destratification Impeller Unit
DIU........... Destruction Initiation Unit (CAAL)
DIU........... Digital Input Unit [*Computer science*]
DIU........... Digital Insertion Unit [*Computer science*]
DIU........... Digital Interchange Utility (NITA)
DIU........... Digital Interface Unit [*Computer science*] (KSC)
DIU........... Diuretic [*Increasing Discharge of Urine*] [*Pharmacy*] (ROG)
DIU........... Diversion Investigative Unit [*Drug Enforcement Administration*]

DIU........... Office of Development Information and Utilization [*Agency for International Development*] [*Information service or system*] (IID)
Diu........... Sanol Arzneimittel Dr. Schwarz [*Germany*] [*Research code symbol*]
DIUP.......... Diisoundecyl Phthalate
DIUP.......... Director, Industry and University Programs [*Military Canada*]
DIV........... Data in Voice [*Telecommunications*]
DIV........... Days in Vitro [*Cell culture*]
Div........... De Divinatione [*of Cicero*] [*Classical studies*] (OCD)
DIV........... Defense Intelligence Videocassettes (MCD)
DIV........... Desired Intermediate Vertex (IAA)
DIV........... Devon Industries [*Vancouver Stock Exchange symbol*]
DIV........... Differential Interface Velocity [*Engineering*]
DIV........... Digital Input Group Voltage (IAA)
DIV........... Direction de l'Information de la Valorisation [*Information and Valorization Directorate*] [*National Institute of Agronomic Research*] [*Information service or system*] (IID)
DIV........... Divergence
DIV........... Diverse (ROG)
DIV........... Diverter (KSC)
DIV........... Divide (MSA)
DIV........... Dividend [*Investment term*]
div........... Dividend (ODBW)
DIV........... Divine [*or Divinity*]
DIV........... Diving
Div........... Divinity (BARN)
DIV........... Divisi [*Divide*] [*Music*]
DIV........... Division (EY)
DIV........... Division
div........... Division (DD)
DIV........... Divisor [*Mathematics*] (ROG)
DIV........... Divorced
Div........... Divorce Proceedings [*Legal term*] (DLA)
DIV........... Double-Inlet Ventricle [*Cardiology*] (DAVI)
DIV........... Dynamic Imagery Viewer
DIV........... Hancock [*John*] Patriot Select Dividend Trust [*NYSE symbol*] (SPSG)
DIV........... John Hancock Patr Sel Div Tr [*NYSE symbol*] (TTSB)
DIVA.......... Data Input-Voice Answerback [*Telecommunications*] (EECA)
DIVA.......... Digital Input Voice Answerback [*Telecommunications*] (NITA)
DIVA.......... Digital Inquiry - Voice Answerback [*Touch-tone*] [*Bell System*] [*Telecommunications*]
DIVA.......... Digital Intravenous Angiography [*Cardiology*] (DAVI)
DIVAD........ Division Air Defense
DIVADA...... Division Air Defense Artillery (MCD)
DIVADS...... Division Air Defense Study
DIVADS...... Divisional Air Defense System (AAGC)
Div & Mat Ct.. Divorce and Matrimonial Causes Court (DLA)
DIV & S...... Divorce and Separation (DLA)
DIVAR........ Diving Instrumentation Vehicle for Environmental and Acoustic Research (MCD)
DIVART....... Division Artillery [*Army*]
DIVARTY..... Division Artillery [*Army*] (INF)
DIVBASE..... Division Base [*Army*]
DIVBC........ Disseminated Intravascular Blood Coagulation [*Medicine*] (DMAA)
Div C......... Division Court [*Canada*] (DLA)
Div Caec..... Divinatio in Caecilium [*of Cicero*] [*Classical studies*] (OCD)
DIV CF....... Divinity Calf [*Bookbinding*] (DGA)
DIV CIRC.... Divinity Circuit Edges [*Bookbinding*] (DGA)
DIVCOM...... Division Commander [*Navy*]
Div Ct........ Divisional Court Selected Judgments, Divisional Courts of the Gold Coast Colony [*A publication*] (DLA)
DIVD.......... Dividend [*Investment term*]
Divde......... Dividende [*Dividend*] [*French Business term*] (ILCA)
DIVE.......... American Oilfield Divers, Inc. [*NASDAQ symbol*] (SAG)
DIVE.......... Amer Oilfield Divers [*NASDAQ symbol*] (TTSB)
DIV E........ Divinity Edges [*Bookbinding*] (DGA)
DIVE.......... Division Engineer (MCD)
DIVEMA...... Divinyl Ether-Maleic Anhydride [*Organic chemistry*]
DIVENGR.... Division Engineer [*Army*] (AABC)
divers....... Diversion (DD)
divertic...... Diverticulum [*Medicine*] (DAVI)
DIVERTORD... Diversion Order [*Military*] (NVT)
DIVHED....... Division Headquarters [*Army*]
DIVIC........ Digital Variable Increment Computer
divid......... Dividatur [*Let It Be Divided*] [*Latin*] [*Pharmacy*] (BARN)
DIVIDE....... Divide [*Commonly used*] (OPSA)
DIVINFO..... Division of Information [*Marine Corps*]
DIV in PAR AEQ... Dividatur in Partes Aequales [*Divide into Equal Parts*] [*Pharmacy*]
DIV in PT AEQ... Dividatur in Partes Aequales [*Divide into Equal Parts*] [*Pharmacy*]
DIVLEV....... Division Level [*Combat model*] (MCD)
DIVLOGMOD... Division Logistics Model (MCD)
DIVN.......... Division
DIVNL........ Divisional (ADA)
DIVOO........ Division Ordnance Officer
DIVOT........ Digital-to-Voice Translator
DIVOTS...... Data Input Voice Output Telephone System
DIVPAY...... Diving Pay [*Navy*]
Divrs......... Diversifax, Inc. [*Associated Press*] (SAG)
Divrsfax..... Diversifax, Inc. [*Associated Press*] (SAG)
DIVS.......... Signed Division [*Computer science*]
DIVSNL....... Divisional
Div Somn..... De Divinatione per Somnia [*of Aristotle*] [*Classical studies*] (OCD)
DIVSP........ Division Supply Point
DIVTAG....... Division through Army Group
DIVTOS...... Division Tactical Operations System (MCD)

DIVU .... Unsigned Division [*Computer science*]
DIVWAG .... Division War Game (MCD)
Divx .... Digital Video Express [*Computer science*]
DIVYEO .... Diving Yeoman [*British military*] (DMA)
DIW .... Dead in the Water [*Navy*] (NVT)
DIW .... Design Information Worksheet
DIW .... Deutsches Institut fuer Wirtschaftsforschung [*Data Resources, Inc.*] [*Database*]
DIWAC .... Digital Interface Weapon Aiming Computer (MCD)
DI/WSA .... Vessels Transferred to War Shipping Administration - Maritime Commission for Disposition [*Navy*]
DIWT .... Director of Inland Water Transport Service [*British*]
DIWT .... Dokumentations - und Informationsgesellschaft fuer Wirtschaft und Touristik mbH [*Database producer*]
DIWTM .... Dictionary of Initials - What They Mean [*A publication*]
DIX .... Digital, Intel, and Xerox [*Telecommunications*] (ACRL)
DIX .... Discount [*Stock exchange*] [*British*] (ROG)
DIX .... Dixieline Products, Inc. (MHDW)
DIX .... Dixon, CA [*Location identifier FAA*] (FAAL)
DIX .... Grand Dixence [*Switzerland*] [*Seismograph station code, US Geological Survey*] (SEIS)
Dix Av .... Dixon on General Average [*A publication*] (DLA)
DIXBI .... Diaminotriazine Xanthene Biphenyl Imide [*Biochemistry*]
Dix Dec .... Dix's School Law Decisions [*New York*] [*A publication*] (DLA)
Dix Dec (NY)... Dix's School Law Decisions [*New York*] [*A publication*] (DLA)
Dix Farm ..... Dixon's Law of the Farm [*6th ed.*] [*1904*] [*A publication*] (DLA)
DixieN .... Dixie National Corp. [*Associated Press*] (SAG)
DixieYr .... Dixie Yarns, Inc. [*Associated Press*] (SAG)
DIXIT .... Delegation for Scientific and Technical Information, Communication, and Culture [*Information service or system*] (IID)
Dix Mar Ins... Dixon's Marine Insurance and Average [*A publication*] (DLA)
Dix Mar Law... Dixon's Abridgment of the Maritime Law [*A publication*] (DLA)
DixnTic .... Dixon Ticonderoga Co. [*Associated Press*] (SAG)
Dix Part ...... Dixon on Partnership [*1866*] [*A publication*] (DLA)
Dix Pr .... Dixon's Probate and Administration Law and Practice [*3rd ed.*] [*1912*] [*A publication*] (DLA)
Dix Ship ...... Dixon's Law of Shipping [*A publication*] (DLA)
DIX standard... DEC-[*Digital Equipment Corp.*] Intel-Xerox Standard (CDE)
Dix Subr ...... Dixon's Law of Subrogation [*A publication*] (DLA)
DIXT .... Diaminotriazine Xanthene Thymine [*Biochemistry*]
Dix Tit D ...... Dixon on Title Deeds [*A publication*] (DLA)
DIXY .... Dipole Xerography
DIY .... Derbyshire Imperial Yeomanry [*British military*] (DMA)
DIY .... Diyarbakir [*Turkey*] [*Airport symbol*] (OAG)
DIY .... Do-It-Yourself
DIYE .... Do-It-Yourself Economics
DIYH .... DIY Home Warehouse [*NASDAQ symbol*] (SAG)
DIYH .... D.I.Y. Home Warehouse [*NASDAQ symbol*] (TTSB)
DIY Hme ...... DIY Home Warehouse Co [*Associated Press*] (SAG)
DIYO .... Yamoussoukro [*Ivory Coast*] [*ICAO location identifier*] (ICLI)
DIYRI .... Do-It-Yourself Research Institute [*Later, HIRI*] (EA)
DIYS .... DiaSys Corp. [*NASDAQ symbol*] (SAG)
DIYSW .... DiaSys Corp. Wrrt [*NASDAQ symbol*] (TTSB)
DIZ .... Defense Identification Zone
DIZ .... Dissolve (NTCM)
Diz Epigr ...... Dizionario Epigrafico di Antichita Romana [*A publication*] (OCD)
DJ .... Air Djibouti [*ICAO designator*] (AD)
DJ .... Daiichi Seiyaku Co. Ltd. [*Japan*] [*Research code symbol*]
DJ .... Dark-Eyed Junco [*Ornithology*]
DJ .... Dieses Jahres [*Of This Year*] [*German*] (ROG)
DJ .... Diffused Junction
dj .... Diffused Junction (IDOE)
DJ .... Digital Junction [*Telecommunications*] (TEL)
DJ .... Dinner Jacket (ADA)
DJ .... Diploma in Journalism (ADA)
DJ .... Disc Jockey
dj .... Disc Jockey (WDMC)
DJ .... Disc Jockeys (Mobile) [*Public-performance tariff class*] [*British*]
DJ .... Dishonest John [*In TV series "Time for Beany"*]
DJ .... Distributed Jamming (MCD)
DJ .... District Judge
DJ .... District Office of Jurisdiction [*IRS*]
DJ .... Diversity-Joining [*Genetics*]
DJ .... Divorce Judge (DAS)
DJ .... Djibouti [*IYRU nationality code*] [*ANSI two-letter standard code*] (CNC)
DJ .... Doctor Juris [*Doctor of Law*]
DJ .... Double Jeopardy
DJ .... Dow Jones & Co. [*NYSE symbol*] (TTSB)
DJ .... Dow Jones & Co., Inc. [*Also, the stock market averages compiled by this company*] [*NYSE symbol*] (SPSG)
DJ .... Dragon Jump [*Pack*] [*Military*] (MCD)
DJ .... Drill Jig (MSA)
DJ .... Dust Jacket [*Paper cover for a hardbound book*]
dj .... Dust Jacket (WDMC)
DJ .... United States Department of Justice, Washington, DC [*Library symbol Library of Congress*] (LCLS)
DJA .... Disabled Journalists of America (EA)
DJA .... Disc Jockey Association (NTCM)
DJA .... Djakarta [*Batavia*] [*Java*] [*Seismograph station code, US Geological Survey*] (SEIS)
DJA .... Dow Jones Averages [*Information retrieval*]
DJAA .... Dog Judges Association of America [*Defunct*] (EA)
DJAG .... Deputy Judge Advocate General

DJ & S .... De Gex, Jones, and Smith's English Chancery Reports [*A publication*] (DLA)
DJ & SB ..... De Gex, Jones, and Smith's English Bankruptcy Reports [*A publication*] (DLA)
DJB .... Air Djibouti [*ICAO designator*] (FAAC)
DJB .... Cleveland, OH [*Location identifier FAA*] (FAAL)
DJB .... Djambi [*Indonesia*] [*Airport symbol*] (AD)
DjB .... Dow Jones Books, Princeton, NJ [*Library symbol Library of Congress*] (LCLS)
DJB .... Drill Jig Bushing
DJB .... Jambi [*Indonesia*] [*Airport symbol*] (OAG)
DJB .... Joint Bank-Fund Library, Washington, DC [*OCLC symbol*] (OCLC)
DJBF .... International Monetary Fund and International Bank for Reconstruction and Development, Joint Bank-Fund Library, Washington, DC [*Library symbol*] [*Library of Congress*] (LCLS)
DJC .... Application for Writ of Error Dismissed, Judgment Correct [*Legal term*] (DLA)
DJC .... Danville Junior College [*Illinois*]
DJC .... Detroit Jazz Center [*Defunct*] (EA)
DJCB .... Dominican Junior College of Blauvelt [*Later, Dominican College*] [*New York*]
DJC/JRI .... Detroit Jazz Center/Jazz Research Institute [*Later, DJC*] (EA)
DJCN .... Dow Jones Cable News [*Cable-television system*]
DJCO .... Daily Journal [*NASDAQ symbol*] (TTSB)
DJCO .... Daily Journal Corp. South Carolina [*NASDAQ symbol*] (NQ)
DJD .... Degenerative Joint Disease
DJDE .... Dynamic Job Description Entity [*For Xerox printer*] (NITA)
DJDR .... Jones, Day, Reavis and Pogue, Law Library, Washington, DC [*Library symbol*] [*Library of Congress*] (LCLS)
DJDS .... Division of Juvenile Delinquency Service [*of SSA*]
DJE .... Deflected Jet Exhaust
DJE .... Demokratischer Jugendverband Europas [*Democrat Youth Community of Europe*] [*Political party*] (EAIO)
DJE .... Dictionary of Jamaican English [*A publication*]
DJE .... Djerba [*Tunisia*] [*Airport symbol*] (OAG)
DJ Ed .... Doctor of Jewish Education (PGP)
DJF .... December-January-February [*Marine science*] (OSRA)
DJF .... Descriptor Justification Form [*ERIC*]
DJF .... Divorced Jewish Female [*Classified advertising*]
DJG .... Djanet [*Algeria*] [*Airport symbol*] (OAG)
DJHi .... Jewish Historical Society of Greater Washington, Washington, DC [*Library symbol*] [*Library of Congress*] (LCLS)
DJI .... Dow Jones Index [*Stock market*] [*Investment term*]
DJIA .... Dow Jones Industrial Average [*Stock market*] [*Investment term*]
DJIC .... Dow Jones Index - Composite [*Stock market*] [*Investment term*]
DJII .... Dow Jones Index - Industrials [*Stock market*] [*Investment term*]
DJIN .... Dow Jones Investor Network
DJIRS .... Dow Jones Information Retrieval System (HGAA)
DJIT .... Dow Jones Index - Transport [*Stock market*] [*Investment term*]
DJIU .... Dow Jones Index - Utilities [*Stock market*] [*Investment term*]
DJJ .... Djajapura [*West Irian, Indonesia*] [*Airport symbol*] (AD)
DJJ .... Jayapura [*Indonesia*] [*Airport symbol*] (OAG)
DJK .... Daughters of Jesus of Kermaria [*See also FJ*] [*Paris, France*] (EAIO)
DJL .... Doctor of Jewish Literature (BJA)
DJM .... Director, Joint Staff Memorandum [*Military*]
DJM .... Divorced Jewish Male [*Classified advertising*]
DJM .... Djambala [*Congo*] [*Airport symbol*] (AD)
DJN .... Delta Junction, AK [*Location identifier FAA*] (FAAL)
DJN .... Demijohn [*Freight*]
DJN .... Dow Jones News [*Dow Jones & Co., Inc.*] [*Information service or system*] (CRD)
DJNF .... Dow Jones Newspaper Fund (EA)
DJNR .... Dow Jones News/Retrieval [*Princeton, NJ*] [*Bibliographic database*] [*Information service or system*]
DJO .... Daloa [*Ivory Coast*] [*Airport symbol*] (OAG)
DJOEO .... Development Job Outline Engineering Order [*DAC*]
DJOT .... Delayed Jam on Target
DJOWT .... District of Columbia Teachers College [*Later, University of the District of Columbia*], Washington, DC [*Library symbol Library of Congress Obsolete*] (LCLS)
DJP .... Democratic Justice Party [*Mauritania*] [*Political party*] (EY)
DJP .... Democratic Justice Party [*South Korea Political party*] (PPW)
DJP .... Doctor of Jewish Pedagogy
DJP .... Dragon Jump Pack [*Military*] (MCD)
DJPC .... Deputy Justice of Peace Clerk [*British*] (ROG)
DJR .... Dajarra [*Queensland*] [*Airport symbol*] (AD)
DJR .... Marietta, GA [*Location identifier FAA*] (FAAL)
DJS .... David Jones Society [*British England*] (EAIO)
DJS .... Deception Jamming System
DJS .... Director, Joint Staff [*Military*] (AABC)
DJS .... Doctor of Jewish Studies (PGP)
DJS .... Doctor of Judicial Science
DJS .... Doctor of Juridical Science
DJS .... Dubin-Johnson Syndrome [*Medicine*] (CPH)
DJSC .... Daily Journal of the Supreme Court
DJ Sc .... Doctor of Judicial Science
DJSM .... Director, Joint Staff Memorandum [*Military*] (AABC)
DJStJ .... Dame of Justice of St. John of Jerusalem [*Later, D St J*] [*British*]
DJSU .... Digital Junction Switching Unit (IAA)
DJT .... Denver Jet, Inc. [*ICAO designator*] (FAAC)
DJT .... Doctor of Jewish Theology
DJT .... Trump Hotels & Casino Resorts [*NYSE symbol*] (TTSB)
DJT .... Trump Hotels & Casino Resorts, Inc. [*NYSE symbol*] (SAG)
DJTA .... Dow Jones Transportation Average [*Information retrieval*]
DJ Th .... Doctor of Jewish Theology

DJUA .... Dow Jones Utility Average [*Information retrieval*]

DJUOL .... Daily JUMPS [*Joint Uniform Military Pay System*] Update Output Listing (AABC)

D Jur .... Doctor of Jurisprudence

D Jur et Rer Pol... Doctor Juris et Rerum Politicarum [*Doctor of Law and Politics*] [*Latin*]

DJuris......... Doctor of Jurisprudence

D Jur Sc ..... Doctor of Juridical Science

DJV............ Dabajuro [*Venezuela*] [*Airport symbol*] (AD)

DJV............ Deshapremi Janatha Viyaparaya [*Patriotic People's Organisation*] [*Sri Lanka*] [*Political party*]

DK.............. Dance Kaleidoscope [*Indiana*]

DK.............. Danish Krone [*Monetary unit*] (NATG)

DK.............. Dark

dk............... Dark (VRA)

DK.............. Daughters of the King (EA)

DK.............. David Kaufmann Collection. Hungarian Academy of Sciences [*Budapest*] (BJA)

DK.............. Deca [*or Deka*] [*A prefix meaning multiplied by 10*] (KSC)

DK.............. Decatur [*ICAO designator*] (AD)

DK.............. Decay (MAE)

DK.............. Deck

DK.............. Degrees Kelvin (KSC)

DK.............. Democratic Kampuchea [*Pol Pot's regime in Cambodia*]

DK.............. Democratic People's Republic of Korea [*IYRU nationality code*] (IYR)

DK.............. Denmark [*ANSI two-letter standard code*] (CNC)

dk............... Denmark [*MARC country of publication code Library of Congress*] (LCCP)

DK.............. Deutscher Kulturbund [*German Cultural Federation*] [*Germany*] (PPE)

DK.............. Dezimal Klassifikation [*Netherlands*]

DK.............. Diet Kitchen

Dk.............. Diffusion Coefficient [*or Permeability constant as described by Krogh*] [*Medicine*] (DAVI)

DK.............. Disbursing Clerk [*Navy rating*]

DK.............. Diseased Kidney [*Medicine*] (MAE)

DK.............. Disk [*Computer science*] (IAA)

DK.............. Display/Keyboard [*Computer science*] (MCD)

DK.............. Dock

DK.............. Docking

DK.............. Dog Kidney (MAE)

DK.............. Don't Know

DK.............. Dorling Kindersley, Ltd. [*British*]

DK.............. Dorsal Kidney

D/K............. Downlink

DK.............. Duck

DK.............. Duct Keel [*of a ship*] (DS)

DK.............. Duke (ROG)

DK1............ Disbursing Clerk, First Class [*Navy rating*]

DK2............ Disbursing Clerk, Second Class [*Navy rating*]

DK3............ Disbursing Clerk, Third Class [*Navy rating*]

DKA .... Daka [*Kazakhstan*] [*ICAO designator*] (FAAC)

DKA .... Deutscher Koordinierungsausschuss [*Coordinating European Council*]

DKA .... Diabetic Ketoacidosis [*Medicine*]

DKA .... Diketogulonic Acid [*Organic chemistry*]

DKAI .... Daka International, Inc. [*NASDAQ symbol*] (CTT)

DKAI .... DAKA Intl. [*NASDAQ symbol*] (TTSB)

DKAM......... Double Known Addition Method [*Analytical electrochemistry*]

D Kan .... United States District Court for the District of Kansas (DLA)

DKB .... Dai-Ichi Kangyo Bank [*Japan*]

DKB .... Decimal Keyboard [*Computer science*]

DKB .... Deep Knee Bends (DAVI)

DKB .... DeKalb, IL [*Location identifier FAA*] (FAAL)

DKB .... Distributed Knowledge Base [*Computer science*] (ODBW)

DKBS .... Deep Knowledge Based Systems [*Computer science*]

DKC .... Dickinson College, Carlisle, PA [*OCLC symbol*] (OCLC)

DKC .... Disbursing Clerk, Chief [*Navy rating*]

DKCM .... Disbursing Clerk, Master Chief [*Navy rating*]

DKCS .... Disbursing Clerk, Senior Chief [*Navy rating*]

DKDI .... Dinking Die [*Tool*] (AAG)

DKDP .... Deuterated Potassium Dihydrogen Phosphate [*Electronics*] (BARN)

DKE............ Deck Edge

DKE............ Delta Kappa Epsilon [*Society*]

DKE............ Jubilee Airways Ltd. [*British ICAO designator*] (FAAC)

DKEL.......... Demokratikon Komma Ergazomenou Laou [*Democratic Party of Working People*] [*Greek*] (PPE)

DKEY .... Datakey, Inc. [*NASDAQ symbol*] (NQ)

DKF............ Dokumentation Kraftfahrwesen [*Motor Vehicle Documentation*] [*Germany Information service or system*] (IID)

DKF............ Dudley, Kenneth F., Ottumwa IA [*STAC*]

DKFC.......... David Kirchner Fan Club [*Defunct*] (EA)

DKFC .... Dena Kaye Fan Club (EA)

Dkfm.......... Diploma in Commerce [*German*]

DKG .... Columbus, OH [*Location identifier FAA*] (FAAL)

Dkg............ Decking (DAC)

DKG .... Dekagram [*Unit of measure*] (GPO)

DKG .... Delta Kappa Gamma Society, International (AEBS)

DKG .... Diketogluconic Acid [*Organic chemistry*]

DKG .... Docking [*Aerospace*] (KSC)

DKGM......... Dekagram [*Unit of measure*] (ROG)

DKI............. Daniel K. Inouye [*US Senator from Hawaii*]

DKI............. Dart & Kraft, Inc. [*Toronto Stock Exchange symbol*] (SPSG)

DKI............. Data Key Idle

DKI............. Docking Initiate

DKI............. Don't Knock It [*Slang*]

DKI............. Dunk Island [*Australia Airport symbol*] (OAG)

DKIE........... Decontamination Kit Individual Equipment [*Army*] (DOMA)

DKK .... Dunkirk, NY [*Location identifier FAA*] (FAAL)

DKL .... Dekaliter [*Unit of measure*] (GPO)

DKL .... Dickinson School of Law, Sheeley-Lee Law Library, Carlisle, PA [*OCLC symbol*] (OCLC)

DKL .... Dielectro-Kinetic Laboratories, LLC

DklbGn........ DeKalb Genetics [*Associated Press*] (SAG)

DklbGn........ DeKalb Genetics [*Associated Press*] (SAG)

Dk LR .... Dickinson Law Review [*A publication*] (DLA)

DKM........... Dakomat [*Poland ICAO designator*] (FAAC)

DKM........... Dekameter [*Unit of measure*] (GPO)

DKM........... Duke Minerals Ltd. [*Vancouver Stock Exchange symbol*]

Dkm² .... Square Dekameter

Dkm³ .... Cubic Dekameter

DKN .... Dakon Metals, Inc. [*Vancouver Stock Exchange symbol*]

DKNY .... Donna Karan New York [*Sportswear*]

DKO .... Ayer, Ft. Devens, MA [*Location identifier FAA*] (FAAL)

DKO .... Dankoe Mines Ltd. [*Vancouver Stock Exchange symbol*]

DKO .... Delay Key On

DKO .... Die Deutsche Kirche im Orient [*Cairo*] [*A publication*] (BJA)

DKO .... Double Knockout [*Genetics*]

DKP .... Dania Kommunista Partja [*Communist Party of Denmark*] [*Political party*]

DKP .... Danmarks Kommunistiske Parti [*Communist Party of Denmark*] [*Political Party*] (PPW)

DKP .... Democratic Korea Party [*South Korea Political party*] (PPW)

DKP .... Deutsche Kommunistische Partei [*German Communist Party*] [*Political party*] (PPE)

DKP .... Dikalium Phosphate [*Pharmacology*]

DKP .... Diketopiperazine [*Organic chemistry*]

DKP .... DK Platinum Corp. [*Vancouver Stock Exchange symbol*]

DKPG .... Depth Keeping

DKR .... Dakar [*Senegal*] [*Airport symbol*] (OAG)

D KR .... Danish Krone [*Monetary unit*]

Dkr............. Dan Korona [*Danish Crown*] [*Monetary unit*]

DKR .... Decker Resources Ltd. [*Vancouver Stock Exchange symbol*]

DKS .... Dekastere [*Unit of measure*]

DKS .... Deoxyketosteroids (MEDA)

DKS .... Deputy Keeper of the Signet (DLA)

DKS .... Direct Keying System

DKS .... Doniphan, Kensett & Searcy Railway [*AAR code*]

DKSA .... Seaman Apprentice, Disbursing Clerk, Striker [*Navy rating*]

DKSEN .... Don King Sports and Entertainment Network [*Cable-television system*]

DKSN .... Seaman, Disbursing Clerk, Striker [*Navy rating*]

DKT............ Dahl-Kirkam Telescope

DKT............ Dakota Energy Corp. [*Vancouver Stock Exchange symbol*]

DKT............ Dakota Mining [*Formerly, MinVen Gold Corp.*] [*AMEX symbol*] (SPSG)

Dkt............. Docket [*Law, Packaging*]

Dkt............. West Publishing Company's Docket [*1909-41*] [*A publication*] (DLA)

DKTC .... Dog Kidney Tissue Culture

DKTH .... Dakotah, Inc. [*NASDAQ symbol*] (SAG)

DKTS .... Dakotas (FAAC)

DKV............ Deer Kidney Virus

DKW .... Dampf-Kraft-Wagen [*Steam-Powered Vehicle*] [*German*]

DKW .... Das Kleine Wunder [*The Little Wonder*] [*Initialism used as name of German automobile, manufactured by Auto Union*]

DKWD .... D & K Wholesale Drug [*NASDAQ symbol*] (SAG)

DKWT .... De Kalb & Western Transportation R. R. [*AAR code*]

DKX............ Knoxville, TN [*Location identifier FAA*] (FAAL)

DKY .... Donkey Boiler [*of a ship*] (DS)

DL.............. Associate Directorate for LPS [*Launch Processing System*] Development [*Kennedy Space Center*] [*NASA*] (NASA)

DL.............. Dacron Braid Lacquered (MDG)

DL.............. Dale

DL.............. Dale

DL.............. Damage Limitation [*Strategy*] [*Military*]

DL.............. Danger List [*Medicine*]

DL.............. Danske Lov [*Laws in Force*] [*Denmark*] (ILCA)

DL.............. Dark on Light

DL.............. Data Language

DL.............. Data Length (IAA)

DL.............. Data Link

DL.............. Data List [*DoD*]

DL.............. Datum Level

DL.............. Davidson Laboratory [*Stevens Institute of Technology*]

DL.............. Day Letter [*Telegraphy*]

DL.............. Daylight (MSA)

DL.............. Days Lost [*Military*]

DL.............. Dead Light (AAG)

DL.............. Deadline (AABC)

DL.............. Dead Load

DL.............. Deadweight Loss [*of grain*] [*Agriculture*]

dl............... Decaliter (AAMN)

DL.............. Deciliter [*Unit of measure*] (GPO)

DL.............. Decision Leaflets [*US Patent Office*]

DL.............. Decret-Loi [*Decree-Law*] [*French*] (ILCA)

DL.............. Decreto Legge [*Decree-Law*] [*Italian*] (ILCA)

DL.............. Dedicated Landline

DL.............. Defence Light [*British military*] (DMA)

DL.............. Dekaliter [*Unit of measure*] (ROG)

DL.............. Delay Line

DL.............. D'Eldona Resources Ltd. [*Toronto Stock Exchange symbol*]

DL .... Delta Air Lines, Inc. [*ICAO designator*]
D/L .... Demand Loan
DL .... Dentate Line [*Anatomy*]
D/L .... Deorbit/Landing [*Aerospace*] (MCD)
DL .... Departmental Letter [*Air Force*] (AAGC)
DL .... Department of Labor
DL .... Departure Locator
DL .... Deputy Lieutenant [*British*]
DL .... Derived Limit (PDAA)
DL .... Description of Leaf (ROG)
DL .... Destroyer Leader [*Navy*]
DL .... Detection Limit [*Analytical chemistry*]
DL .... Developed Length (AAG)
DL .... Development-Left (MCD)
dl .... Dextro-Levo(rotary) [*Also, r, rac*] [*Chemistry*]
DL .... Diagnostic Laparoscopy [*or Laparotomy*] (DAVI)
DL .... Dial Corp. [*NYSE symbol*] (SPSG)
DL .... Dielectric Loading Factor [*Electronics*] (MDG)
DL .... Difference Limen [*Physiology, psychology*]
DL .... Difference of Latitude [*Navigation*] (MUGU)
DL .... Diffraction Limited (MCD)
DL .... Diffuse Leiomyomatosis [*Medicine*]
DL .... Diffuse Lymphoma [*Oncology*] (DAVI)
DL .... Diffusing Capacity of the Lung (AAMN)
DL .... Digital Stimulation [*Of rectal sphincter*] [*Gastroenterology*] (DAVI)
DL .... Diode Logic
DL .... Diogenes Laertius [*Third century AD*] [*Classical studies*] (OCD)
DL .... Direct Labor
DL .... Direct Laryngoscopy [*Otorhinolaryngology*] (DAVI)
DL .... Direct Line [*Followed by telephone number*]
DL .... Direct Listening (CAAL)
DL .... Direct Load
DL .... Director Layer [*British military*] (DMA)
DL .... Director of Laboratories [*AFSC*]
DL .... Director of Labour [*Military British*]
DL .... Disabled List [*Athletics*]
DL .... Disjunctively Linear
D/L .... Displacement to Length [*Ratio*]
DL .... Distolingual [*Dentistry*]
DL .... Distributed Lab (MDG)
DL .... Distribution List
DL .... District Office of Location [*IRS*]
DL .... Disturbance Lines [*Marine science*] (OSRA)
DL .... Disturbance Lines (USDC)
DL .... Doctor of Laws
DL .... Doctor of Letters
DL .... Doctor of Literature
DL .... Document Log (AABC)
DL .... Dominical Letter
D-L .... Donath-Landsteiner [*Hemolysin*] [*Hematology*]
DL .... Doppellafette [*Two-barreled mount*] [*German military - World War II*]
DL .... Dorsal Lip
DL .... Dorsal Longitudinal
DL .... Double Ledger [*Accounting*]
DL .... Dow-Lepetit [*Research code symbol*]
DL .... Down Left [*The front left portion of a stage*] [*A stage direction*]
DL .... Down Link [*Computer science*]
D/L .... Downlist (NASA)
DL .... Draft Legislation
DL .... Drawing List [*Engineering*]
DL .... Drill Leader [*British military*] (DMA)
DL .... Driving Licence [*British*] (ADA)
DL .... Dual Language
dl .... Dull [*Philately*]
DL .... Dummy Load [*Military*] (MCD)
DL .... Duolateral
DL .... Dynamic Load Characteristic (MDG)
DL .... Frigate [*Navy symbol*]
DL .... General Counsel (AAGC)
DL .... Most Distal Leaf [*Botany*]
DL .... United States Department of Labor Library, Washington, DC [*Library symbol Library of Congress*] (LCLS)
DL/1 .... Data Language Version 1 [*Computer science*]
DLA .... Air Dolomiti [*Italy ICAO designator*] (FAAC)
DLA .... Damaged Lyman-Alpha [*Galaxy*]
DLA .... Data Link Acquisition (MCD)
DLA .... Data Link Adapter
DLA .... Data Link Address
DLA .... Declination of Launch Asymptote [*NASA*] (KSC)
DLA .... Decorative Lighting Association [*British*] (DBA)
DLA .... Defense Logistics Agency [*Alexandria, VA*]
DLA .... Defense Logistics Area (MCD)
DLA .... Delaware [*Ontario*] [*Seismograph station code, US Geological Survey*] (SEIS)
DLA .... Delaware Law School of Widener College, Wilmington, DE [*OCLC symbol*] (OCLC)
DLA .... Delay Line Assembly
DLA .... Delay Message [*Aviation code*]
DLA .... Democratic Labor Association [*Philippines*]
DLA .... Dental Laboratories Association [*British*] (DBA)
DLA .... Department of Land Administration [*Western Australia*]
DLA .... Depot Level Activity (NATG)
DLA .... Diffusion-Limited Aggregation [*Physical chemistry*]
DLA .... Dislocation Allowance [*Military*]
DLA .... Distolabial [*Dentistry*]

DLA .... Distributed Lumped Active [*Electronics*] (OA)
DLA .... Divisional Land Agent [*Ministry of Agriculture, Fisheries, and Food*] [*British*]
DLA .... Division of Library Automation [*University of California, Berkeley*] [*Information service or system*] (IID)
DLA .... Doctor of Liberal Arts
DLA .... Dog Lymphocytotoxicity
DLA .... Dole Food Co. [*AMEX symbol*] (SAG)
DLA .... Douala [*Cameroon*] [*Airport symbol*] (OAG)
DLA .... Dual Launching Adaptor (DNAB)
DLAA .... DARCOM [*Development and Readiness Command, Army*] Logistics Assistance Activity (MCD)
DLAB .... Defense Language Aptitude Battery [*Army*] (INF)
DLAB .... Divisor Latch Access BIT [*Computer science*]
D-L Ab .... Donath-Landsteiner Antibody [*Immunology*] (MAE)
DLAC .... Delay Account Of (FAAC)
DLAH .... Defense Logistics Agency Handbook [*A publication*] (AAGC)
DLA-HSI .... Defense Logistics Agency-Headquarters Staff Instructor (AAGC)
DLAI .... Distolabioincisal [*Dentistry*]
D La L .... Doctor of Latin Letters
DLAM .... Defense Logistics Agency Manual [*A publication*] (AAGC)
DL & B .... Direct Laryngoscopy and Bronchoscopy [*Medicine*] (DAVI)
DL & E. .... Design Limit and Endurance
DL & W .... Delaware, Lackawanna & Western Railroad [*Nicknames: Delay, Linger & Wait; Darn Long & Winding; Dirty, Long & Weary*]
DL & WRR .... Delaware, Lackawanna & Western Railroad
D Lang .... Doctor of Languages
DLANT .... Department of the Legislative Assembly of the Northern Territory [*Australia*]
DLAO .... Defense Logistics Analysis Office (MCD)
DLAP .... Defense Logistics Agency Pamphlet (AAGC)
DLaP .... Distolabiopulpal [*Dentistry*]
DLAPS .... Defense Logistics Agency Publishing System [*CD-ROM*] (AAGC)
DLAR .... Defense Logistics Acquisition Regulation (AAGC)
DLAR .... Defense Logistics Agency Regulation [*DoD*] (GFGA)
DL Arch .... Doctor of Landscape Architecture
DLAS .... Damped Lyman-Alpha System [*Galactic science*]
DLAS .... Department of Labour and Administrative Services [*Northern Territory*] [*Australia*]
DLAT .... Defense Language Aptitude Test [*Army*] (AABC)
DLAT .... Delay Time [*Aviation*] (FAAC)
DLAT .... Destructive Lot Acceptance Testing (NASA)
DLAT .... Difference of Latitude [*Navigation*]
DLAT .... Discharge-Line Air Temperature [*Nuclear energy*] (NRCH)
D Law .... Doctor of Law (PGP)
DLB .... Brandywine College of Widener University, Wilmington, DE [*OCLC symbol*] (OCLC)
DLB .... d'Albertis [*Australia*] [*Airport symbol*] (AD)
DLB .... Dannemiller, Lawrence B., Columbus OH [*STAC*]
DLB .... Dead Letter Box (BARN)
DLB .... Dead-Letter Box (LAIN)
DLB .... Delbancor Industry [*Vancouver Stock Exchange symbol*]
DLB .... Dementia with Lewy Bodies [*Nerve cell pathology*]
DLB .... Deposit Liquidation Board
DLB .... Dictionary of Literary Biography [*A publication*]
DLB .... DLB Oil & Gas, Inc. [*NYSE symbol*] (SAG)
DLBI .... Differential Long-Baseline Interferometer [*Radio interferometry*]
DLBI .... DLB Oil & Gas [*NASDAQ symbol*] (TTSB)
DLBI .... DLB Oil & Gas, Inc. [*NASDAQ symbol*] (SAG)
DLB OG .... DLB Oil & Gas, Inc. [*Associated Press*] (SAG)
DLC .... Dalien [*China*] [*Airport symbol*] (OAG)
DLC .... Data Link Connector [*Electronics*]
DLC .... Data Link Control [*Computer science*] (BUR)
DLC .... David Lipscomb College [*Tennessee*]
DLC .... Dealy Clearance [*Aviation*] (FAAC)
DLC .... Delay Line Case
DLC .... Democratic Leadership Council (EA)
DLC .... Dental Laboratory Conference [*Defunct*] (EA)
DLC .... Develcon Electronics Ltd. [*Toronto Stock Exchange symbol*]
DLC .... Development Loan Committee [*Department of State*]
DLC .... Diamondlike Carbon [*Materials science*]
DLC .... Differential Leukocyte Count [*Hematology*]
DLC .... Digital Light and Color [*Computer science*] (PCM)
DLC .... Digital Logic Circuit
DLC .... Digital Loop Carrier [*Telecommunications*] (OSI)
DLC .... Dillon, SC [*Location identifier FAA*] (FAAL)
DLC .... Diploma of Loughborough College [*British*]
DLC .... Direct Lift Control
DLC .... Disaster Loan Corp. [*Dissolved 1945, functions transferred to Reconstructi on Finance Corp.*]
DLC .... Doctor of Celtic Literature
DLC .... Donation Land Claim [*Legal term*] (DLA)
DLC .... Down Left Center (IAA)
DLC .... Drummond Lighterage [*AAR code*]
DLC .... Duolateral Coil [*Electromagnetism*] (IAA)
DLC .... Duplex Line Control (BUR)
DLC .... Dymo LASER Composer (DGA)
DLC .... Dynamic Load Characteristic
DLC .... Library of Congress, Washington, DC [*Library symbol Library of Congress OCLC symbol*] (OCLC)
DLC .... Osterhout Free Library [*Library network*]
DLC .... United States Library of Congress, Washington, DC [*Library symbol*] [*Library of Congress*] (LCLS)
DLCA .... Dairymen's League Cooperative Association [*Later, DC*] (EA)
DLCA .... Diffusion-Limited Cluster Aggregation [*Physical chemistry*]

DLCA	Driver Leasing Council of America (EA)
DLCA	Dynamic Logic Chassis Analyzer
DLCB	Drifting Low-Capability Buoys [*National Oceanic and Atmospheric Administration*] (MCD)
DLC-B	Library of Congress, National Library Service for the Blind and Physically Handicapped, Washington, DC [*Library symbol Library of Congress*] (LCLS)
DLC-BM	Library of Congress, National Library Service for the Blind and Physically Handicapped, Music Library, Washington, DC [*Library symbol Library of Congress*] (LCLS)
DLCC	Data Link Control Chip [*Computer science*] (HGAA)
DLCC	Desert Locust Control Committee [*Food and Agriculture Organization*] [*United Nations*] (EA)
DLCC	Division Logistics Control Center
DLC(ESR)	United States Library of Congress, Early State Records Collection, Washington, DC [*Library symbol Library of Congress*] (LCLS)
DLCF..........	Data Link Control Field [*Computer science*]
DLC-GB	United States Library of Congress, Generalized Bibliography System, Washington, DC [*Library symbol*] [*Library of Congress*] (LCLS)
DLCH	Delchamps, Inc. [*NASDAQ symbol*] (NQ)
DLCI...........	Data Link Connection Identifier [*Computer science*]
DLCL	Diffuse Large-Cell Lymphoma [*Oncology*]
DLCM	Drinker Library of Choral Music (EA)
DLCN	Distributed Loop Computer Network (PDAA)
DLC-N	United States Library of Congress, National Serials Data Program, Washington, DC [*Library symbol Library of Congress*] (LCLS)
DLC-NR........	United States Library of Congress, National Resources Program, Washington, DC [*Library symbol*] [*Library of Congress*] (LCLS)
DLC-NTC......	United States Library of Congress, National Translations Center, Washington, DC [*Library symbol*] [*Library of Congress*] (LCLS)
DLCO	Deck Landing Control Officer [*British*]
DLCO	Diffusing Capacity of the Lungs for Carbon Monoxide
DLCO	Direct Labor Charges by Organization (MCD)
DLCO$_2$	Diffusing Capacity for Lung Carbon Dioxide [*Medicine*] (DAVI)
D$_L$CO/M²	Diffusing Capacity of the Lungs for Carbon Monoxide per Square Meter of Body Surface [*Medicine*] (DAVI)
DLCO-SB.....	Single-Breath Diffusing Capacity of the Lung for Carbon Monoxide [*Medicine*] (MEDA)
D$_{LCOSB}$..........	Single Breath Diffusing Capacity of the Lungs for Carbon Monoxide [*Medicine*] (DAVI)
DLCO-SS.....	Steady State Diffusing Lung Capacity for Carbon Monoxide (MAE)
DLCP	Data Link Controller-Processor [*Automotive engineering Electronics*]
DLCP	Data Link Control Panel [*Computer science*] (MCD)
DLC-P4	United States Library of Congress, Priority Four Collection, Washington, DC [*Library symbol Library of Congress*] (LCLS)
DLCPP	Depository Library Council to the Public Printer (EA)
DLC-R.........	United States Library of Congress, Regional and Cooperative Cataloging Division, Washington, DC [*Library symbol*] [*Library of Congress*] (LCLS)
DLCS	Data-Line Concentration System [*Bell System*]
DLCS	Data Link Controller Series [*or Serial*] [*Electronics*]
DLC-S	United States Library of Congress, Serial Record Division, Washington, DC [*Library symbol*] [*Library of Congress*] (LCLS)
DLCTRC	Dielectric
DLD	Dark Line Defect (PDAA)
DLD	Data Link Decoder (MCD)
DLD	Deadline Date [*Air Force*] (AFM)
DLD	Delaware Technical and Community College, Wilmington, DE [*OCLC symbol*] (OCLC)
DLD	Delivered
DLD	Destruct Logic Decoder
DLD	Digital Light Deflector
DLD	Diploma of Landscape Design (ADA)
DLD	Direction Level Detector (IAA)
DLD	Discount Long Distance [*Larose, LA*] [*Telecommunications*] (TSSD)
DLD	Display List Driver [*Computer science*] (PCM)
DLD	Division of Learning Disabilities [*Council for Exceptional Children*]
DLD	Dromoland Development [*Vancouver Stock Exchange symbol*]
DLDBS	Distributed-Loop Database System (PDAA)
DLDED	Division Level Data Entry Device (MCD)
DL Des	Doctor of Landscape Design
DLDPANSW...	Dental Laboratories and Dental Prosthetists' Association of New South Wales [*Australia*]
DLDR..........	Differential Line Driver Receiver (IAA)
DLDV	Differential LASER Doppler Velocimeter (PDAA)
DLE.............	Data Link Equipment
DLE.............	Data Link Escape [*Computer science*] (NITA)
DLE.............	Data Link Escape Character [*Keyboard*] (CMD)
DLE.............	Deflected Lamine Electrophoresis
DLE.............	Delaware Technical and Community College, Stanton Campus, Newark, DE [*OCLC symbol*] (OCLC)
DLE.............	Delayed Light Emission [*Green plant phenomenon*]
DLE.............	Detailed Labor Estimate (MCD)
DLE.............	Dialyzable Leukocyte Extract [*Hematology*]
DLE.............	Digital Local Exchange (PDAA)
DLE.............	Direct Laboratories Estimate (MCD)
DLE.............	Discoid Lupus Erythematosus [*Medicine*]
DLE.............	Disseminated Lupus Erythematosus [*Hematology*]
DLE.............	Dole [*France*] [*Airport symbol Obsolete*] (OAG)
DLE.............	Dreaded Lake Effect [*Weather condition, resulting in increased precipitation, produced by Utah's Great Salt Lake*]
DLE.............	Drooped Leading Edge
DLEA..........	Double Leg Elbow Amplifier
DLEC..........	Data Link Escape Character [*Computer science*] (EECA)
DL Ec..........	Doctor of Library Economics

DLEED	Diffuse Low-Energy Electron Diffraction [*Microscopy*]
DL Eng........	Doctor of Landscape Engineering
DLES..........	Division of Law Enforcement Sciences [*Bureau of Indian Affairs*] (BARN)
DLES..........	Doctor of Letters in Economic Studies
D Let	Doctor of Letters
D Level.......	Depot Level of Maintenance (AAGC)
DLF.............	Data List File
DLF.............	Daughters of Our Lady of Fatima (TOCD)
DLF.............	Delaware Academy of Medicine, Wilmington, DE [*OCLC symbol*] (OCLC)
DLF.............	Del Rio, TX [*Location identifier FAA*] (FAAL)
DLF.............	Designers Lighting Forum
DLF.............	Deutschlandfunk [*Radio network*] [*Germany*]
DLF.............	Development Loan Fund [*Abolished 1961, functions redelegated to Agency for International Development*]
DLF.............	Dielectric Loading Factor [*Electronics*] (IAA)
DLF.............	Diffraction Limited Focusing
DLF.............	Digitalis-Like Factor [*Biochemistry*]
DLF.............	Digoxin-Like Factor [*Biochemistry*]
DLF.............	Direct Lytic Factor [*Polypeptide from cobra venom*]
DLF.............	Disabled [*or Disability*] Living Foundation [*British*] (DI)
DLF.............	Document Library Facility [*Computer science*]
DLF.............	Dorsolateral Fascicle [*Muscular anatomy, neuroanatomy*]
DLF.............	Dorsolateral Funiculus [*Neuroanatomy*]
DLF.............	Downlink Frequency
DLF.............	Drydock Launch Facility
DLFDU	Data Line Flight Direction Unit (MCD)
DLFI...........	Delphi Financial Group, Inc. [*NASDAQ symbol*] (SAG)
DLFI...........	Delphi Fin'l Group'A' [*NASDAQ symbol*] (TTSB)
DLFM..........	Division Level Financial Management [*System*] (MCD)
DLG	Daddy's Little Girl
DLG	Dealing
D Lg...........	Decreto Legislativo [*Legislative Decree*] [*Italian*] (ILCA)
DLG	Defense Liaison Group (CINC)
DLG	Destroyer Leader, Guided Missile (MCD)
DLG	Digital Line Graph
DLG	Dillingham [*Alaska*] [*Airport symbol*] (OAG)
DLG	Distolingual Groove [*Medicine*] (DMAA)
DLG	Dynamic Lead Guidance (PDAA)
DLG	Guided Missile Frigate [*Navy symbol*]
DLG	Wilmington Medical Center, Wilmington, DE [*OCLC symbol*] (OCLC)
DLGC..........	Dialogic Corp. [*NASDAQ symbol*] (SAG)
DLGHT........	Delight
dLGN	Dorsal Lateral Geniculate Nucleus [*Also, LGd*] [*Anatomy*]
DLGN	Guided Missile Frigate (Nuclear Propulsion) [*Navy symbol*]
DLGNC........	Diligence
DLGS	Doppler Landing Guidance System
DLGX	Datalogix International, Inc. [*NASDAQ symbol*] (SAG)
DLGX	Datalogix Intl. [*NASDAQ symbol*] (TTSB)
DLH	Dalhousie [*India*] [*Seismograph station code, US Geological Survey Closed*] (SEIS)
DLH	Data Link Hardware (IAA)
DLH	Data Link Layer Header [*Telecommunications*] (ACRL)
DLH	Data Lower Half Byte (IAA)
DLH	Department of Lands and Housing [*Northern Territory*] [*Australia*]
DLH	Deutsche Lufthansa AG [*German Lufthansa*] [*Airline*] (EG)
DLH	Direct Labor Hours (DNAB)
DLH	Docking Lock Handle
DLH	Duluth [*Minnesota*] [*Airport symbol*] (OAG)
DLH	Duluth [*Minnesota-Superior, Wisconsin*] [*Airport symbol*] (AD)
DLH	Henry Francis DuPont Winterthur Museum, Winterthur, DE [*OCLC symbol*] (OCLC)
DLHC..........	Diamondlike Hydrocarbon [*Coating material*]
DLI.............	Dalat [*South Vietnam*] [*Airport symbol*] (AD)
DLI.............	Deck-Launched Intercept (MCD)
DLI.............	Defense Language Institute [*DoD Washington, DC*]
DLI.............	Delay Indefinite (DA)
DLI.............	Del Laboratories [*AMEX symbol*] (TTSB)
DLI.............	Del Laboratories, Inc. [*AMEX symbol*] (SPSG)
DLI.............	Depolarized Light Intensity
DLI.............	Digital Line Interface [*Computer science*] (NITA)
DLI.............	Direct Liquid Inlet [*Interface*] [*Analytical instrumentation*]
DLI.............	Distolinguoincisal [*Dentistry*]
DLI.............	Distributorless Ignition [*Automotive engineering*]
DLI.............	Doctor of Literary Interpretation
DLI.............	Do-List Item [*Military*]
DLI.............	Double Label Index [*Medicine*] (DMAA)
DLI.............	Durham Light Infantry [*Military unit*] [*British*]
DLI.............	E. I. Du Pont de Nemours & Co., Haskell Laboratory, Newark, DE [*OCLC symbol*] (OCLC)
DLIC...........	Detachments Left in Contact [*Military*]
DLIC...........	Digital Line Interface Controller [*Telecommunications*] (NITA)
DLIDC.........	Defense Logistics Instructor Development Course [*Army*]
DLIEC.........	Defense Language Institute, East Coast Center (AABC)
DLIEL.........	Defense Language Institute, English Language Center (AABC)
DLIELC.......	Defense Language Institute, English Language Center [*Military*]
DLIF..........	Design Limit Load Factor
DLIF..........	Digoxin-Like Immunoreactive Factor [*Laboratory analysis*]
DLIFLC.......	Defense Language Institute, Foreign Language Center (AABC)
DLILMN	Dial Illumination
DLIMP	Descriptive Language Implemented by Macroprocessors
DLINDG.......	Dial Indicating
DLIP...........	Directory of Library and Information Professionals [*Gale Research, Inc.*] [*Information service or system*] (CRD)

DLIR	Depot Level Inspection Auto Repair (MCD)
DLIR	Downward-Looking Infrared [*Air Force*]
DLIS	Digoxin-Like Immunoreactive Substance [*Biochemistry*]
DLIS	Diploma in Library Information Services
DLIS	Doctor of Library and Information Sciences (GAGS)
DLIS	Dowlais Central [*Cardiff*] [*Welsh depot code*]
DLIS	Downward-Looking Infrared System [*Air Force*] (MCD)
DLISC-EP	Defense Language Institute, Support Command - El Paso (AABC)
DLISDA	Defense Language Institute, Systems Development Agency (AABC)
DLISW	Defense Language Institute, Southwest Branch (AABC)
D Lit	Doctor of Letters
D Lit	Doctor of Literature
DLitt	Doctor of Letters
DLitt	Doctor of Literature
DLittS	Doctor of Sacred Letters
DLIWC	Defense Language Institute, West Coast Branch (AABC)
DLJ	DLJ Capital Trust I [*NYSE symbol*] (SAG)
DLJ	Donaldson Lufkin & Jenrette [*NYSE symbol*] (SAG)
DLJC	Disciples of the Lord Jesus Christ (TOCD)
DLJ Ca	DLJ Capital Trust I [*Associated Press*] (SAG)
DLK	Data Link (KSC)
DLK	Democratic League of Kosovo [*Albania*] [*Political party*] (ECON)
DLK	Diamond Locking Knurl
DLK	ICI Americas, Inc., Wilmington, DE [*OCLC symbol*] (OCLC)
DLK	Salomon, Inc. [*AMEX symbol*] (SAG)
DLK	Salomon Inc. 6.75% DEC'ELKS' [*AMEX symbol*] (TTSB)
DLL	Dalhousie University Law Library [*UTLAS symbol*]
DLL	Dames of the Loyal Legion of the United States of America (EA)
DLL	Damietta-Latakia Line [*Nile river delta*] [*Geology*]
DLL	Delay Locked Loop [*Computer science*] (IAA)
DLL	Dells, WI [*Location identifier FAA*] (FAAL)
DLL	Design Load Limit (MSA)
DLL	Dial Long Line [*Bell System*]
DLL	Dihomo-Gammalinoleic Acid [*Biochemistry*] (DAVI)
DLL	Discharge-Line Length [*Nuclear energy*] (NRCH)
DLL	Doctor of Late Laws
DLL	Double Length Line
DLL	Downline Loading
DLL	Dynamic Link Library [*Software*] [*Computer science*] (BYTE)
DLLD	Direct Linear Loop Detector [*Computer science*] (IAA)
DLLE	Decoy Low-Level Electronics
DL-LEA	Directed Listening-Language Experience Approach (EDAC)
DLLF	Design Limit Load Factor (MCD)
DLLI	Dulcitol Lysine Lactose Iron [*Agar*] [*Microbiology*]
DLLR	Dollar
DLLRS	Dollars [*Monetary unit*] (ROG)
DllrTree	Dollar Tree Stores, Inc. [*Associated Press*] (SAG)
DLLs	Deleting Important Program Files [*Computer science*]
DLM	Daily List of Mail (IAA)
DLM	Dalaman [*Turkey*] [*Airport symbol*] (OAG)
DLM	Dalhousie University Health Sciences Library [*UTLAS symbol*]
DLM	Data Line Monitor
DLM	Delay Line Memory
DLM	Democratic Labour Movement [*Guyana*] [*Political party*] (PPW)
DLM	Depolarized Light Mixing (PDAA)
DLM	Depot Level Maintenance [*Air Force*] (AFM)
DLM	Deputy Lord Mayor [*British*] (ADA)
DLM	Des Laufenden Monats [*Of the Current Month*] [*German*]
DLM	Destination Load Model (SAA)
DLM	Digital Linking Module (NITA)
DLM	Digital Logic Module
DLM	Director of Liaison and Munitions [*Military British*]
DLM	Distributed Lock Manager (ACRL)
DLM	Divine Light Mission [*A cult*]
DLM	Doctor of Landscape Management
DLM	Dominica Liberation Movement [*Political party*] (EY)
DLM	Dorsal Longitudinal Muscle [*Anatomy*]
DLM	Double Long Meter [*Music*]
DLM	University of Delaware, Newark, DE [*OCLC symbol*] (OCLC)
DLMA	Department of Labor, Manpower Administration
DLMA	Diocesan Lay Ministry Adviser [*Church of England*]
DLMCP	Distributed Loop Message Communication Protocol
DLMF	Depot Level Maintenance Facility (MCD)
DLMF	Drug Literature Microfilm File (NITA)
DLMH	Direct Labor Man-Hours (RDA)
DLMP	Date of Last Menstrual Period [*Medicine*] (DMAA)
DLMP	Depot Level Maintenance Plant
DLMP	Down-Link Multipath (MCD)
DLMPS	Division of Logic, Methodology, and Philosophy of Science [*International Council of Scientific Unions*]
DLMRR	Depot Level Maintenance Requirement Review (AFIT)
DLMS	Digital Land Mass Simulation (MCD)
DLMS	Digital Land Mass System [*Directorate of Military Survey*] [*British*]
DLMTB	Defense Logistics Management Training Board (AFM)
DLN	Daily Legal News [*Pennsylvania*] [*A publication*] (DLA)
DLN	Dalton [*Australia Seismograph station code, US Geological Survey Closed*] (SEIS)
DLN	Digital Ladder Network (IAA)
DLN	Dillon, MT [*Location identifier FAA*] (FAAL)
DLN	Document Locator Number [*Computer science*]
DLN	Dorsolateral Nucleus [*Neuroanatomy*]
DLN	Double Length Number
DLNC	Deputy Local Naval Commander
DLNC	Document Locator Number Counter File [*IRS*]
DLNK	Digital Link [*NASDAQ symbol*] (TTSB)

DLNK	Digital Link Corp. [*NASDAQ symbol*] (SAG)
DLNMP	Date of Last Normal Menstrual Period [*Medicine*] (DMAA)
DLO	Daleco Resources Corp. [*Vancouver Stock Exchange symbol*]
DLO	Data Link Occupied [*Computer science*] (HGAA)
DLO	Daylight Opening
DLO	Dead Letter Office [*US Postal Service*]
DLO	Decisions de l'Orateur (NITA)
DLO	Defense Liaison Office
DLO	Defense Logistics Agency, Alexandria, VA [*OCLC symbol*] (OCLC)
DLO	Delano, CA [*Location identifier FAA*] (FAAL)
DLO	Delayed Output [*Computer science*]
DLO	Deputy for Launch Operations [*NASA*] (KSC)
DLO	Desired Learner Outcomes [*Education*]
DLO	Difference of Longitude [*Navigation*]
DLO	Diploma in Laryngology and Otolaryngology [*British*]
DLO	Direct Labor Organization
DLO	Director, Launch Operations [*NASA*] (KSC)
DLO	Dirty Lubricating Oil (AAG)
DLO	Dispatch Loading Only
DLO	Distolinguo-Occlusal [*Dentistry*]
DLO	District Legal Office [*or Officer*] [*Navy*]
DLO	Division Liaison Officer
DLO	Double Local Oscillator
DLO	Dual Loop Oscillator
DLO	Duke of Lancaster's Own [*British military*] (DMA)
D$_{LO2}$	Diffusing Capacity of the Lungs for Oxygen [*Medicine*] (DAVI)
DLOA	Draft Letter of Agreement (MCD)
DLOC	Daimler and Lanchester Owners' Club (EA)
DLOC	Division Logistical Operation Center
DLOCK	Dial Lock
DLOC of NA	Daimler and Lanchester Owners Club of North America (EA)
DLOGS	Division Logistics System (MCD)
DLONG	Difference of Longitude [*Navigation*]
D loop	Displacement Loop [*Genetics*] (DOG)
DLOR	Downward Light Output Ratio (PDAA)
DLOS	Distributed Loop Operating System
DLOS	Division Logistics Organization Structure (MCD)
DLOV	Daleco Resources Corp. [*NASDAQ symbol*] (NQ)
DLOVF	Daleco Res [*NASDAQ symbol*] (TTSB)
DLOY	Duke of Lancaster's Own Yeomanry [*Military unit*] [*British*]
DLP	Damage Limiting Program
DLP	Data Link Processor [*Burroughs Corp.*] [*Computer science*] (BUR)
DLP	Data Link Programs (MCD)
DLP	Data Listing Programs (IEEE)
DLP	Date of Last Payment [*Insurance*]
DLP	Defense Language Program (AFM)
DLP	Delcorp Resources, Inc. [*Vancouver Stock Exchange symbol*]
DLP	Delta and Pine Land [*NYSE symbol*] (TTSB)
DLP	Democratic Labor Party [*Trinidad and Tobago*] [*Political party*] (PPW)
DLP	Democratic Labor Party [*Australia Political party*]
DLP	Democratic Labor Party [*Barbados*] [*Political party*] (PPW)
DLP	Democratic Left Party [*Turkey Political party*] (MENA)
DLP	Democratic Liberal Party [*Taiwan*] [*Political party*] (EY)
DLP	Democratic Liberal Party [*South Korea Political party*]
DLP	Deoxidized Low-Residual Phosphorus [*Copper*]
DLP	Digital LASER Printer (PDAA)
DLP	Digital Library Project
DLP	Digital Light Processing
DLP	Digital Light Processing [*Texas Instruments*] (PCM)
DLP	Digital Light Processing [*A projection system*] (PCM)
DLP	Diocesan Labor Priests (TOCD)
dlp	Diocesan Labor Priests (TOCD)
DLP	Direct Letter Perfect [*Actors' slang*]
DLP	Director of Laboratory Programs [*Navy*]
DLP	Display-List Processor [*Computer science*]
DLP	Distance Learning Project [*Joint program of the Center for Talented Youth (Johns Hopkins University) and the Education Program for Gifted Youth (Stanford University)*] (PAZ)
DLP	Distolinguopulpal [*Dentistry*]
DLP	Doctrinal Literature Program [*Military*]
D/LP	Dome Lamp [*Automotive engineering*]
DLP	Dominica Labor Party [*Political party*] (PPW)
DLP	Double Large Post (ADA)
DLP	Double Layer Polysilicon (IAA)
DLP	Drone Launch Platform [*Navy*] (CAAL)
DLP	Dynamic Limit Programming (MHDB)
DLP	Graf und Maresch GmbH, Augsburg [*Germany*] [*FAA designator*] (FAAC)
DLPA	Decorative Laminate Products Association (EA)
DLPA	dl-Phenylalanine [*Biochemistry*]
DLPA	Dry Lining and Partition Association [*British*] (DBA)
DLPC	Dilauroylphosphatidylcholine [*Biochemistry*]
DLPE	Dilaurylphosphatidylethanolamine [*Biochemistry*]
dlPFC	Dorsolateral Prefrontal Cortex [*Brain anatomy*]
DLPFC	Dorsolateral Prefrontal Cortex [*Brain anatomy*]
DLPG	DIMDI [*Deutsches Institut fuer Medizinische Dokumentation und Information*] List Program Generator (NITA)
DLPH	Delphi Information Sys [*NASDAQ symbol*] (TTSB)
DLPH	Delphi Information Systems, Inc. [*NASDAQ symbol*] (NQ)
DLPP	Data Link Pre-Processor [*Ferranti Ltd.*]
DLPR	Defense Logistics Procurement Regulation (MCD)
DLPr	Dial Corp. $4.75cmPfd [*NYSE symbol*] (TTSB)
DLPS	Deck Landing Projector Sight [*British military*] (DMA)
DLPT	Defense Language Proficiency Tests [*Military*]
DLPU	Data Link Processor Unit (DA)

DLQ	Deck Landing Qualification [*Navy*] (DOMA)	
DLQ	Mean Diurnal Low-Water Inequality	
DLR	Data Link Receiver [*Computer science*] (MCD)	
DLR	Dealer (MSA)	
DLR	Delay Line Register	
DLR	Depot Level Repairable (NVT)	
DLR	Depot Logistics Report (MCD)	
DLR	Deutsche Forschungsanstalt fuer Luft-und Raumfahrt [*Germany*]	
DLR	Developing Learning Readiness	
DLR	Dickinson Law Review [*A publication*] (DLA)	
DLR	Direct Labor Rate	
DLR	Division of Labor Relations [*Energy Research and Development Administration*]	
DLR	Docklands Light Railway [*British*] (ECON)	
DLR	Dollar [*Monetary unit*]	
DLR	Dominion Law Reporter [*India*] [*Usually with a province abbreviation, as DLR (AM), Ajmer-Merwara*] [*A publication*] (DLA)	
DLR	Doppler LASER RADAR	
DLR	DOS LAN Requester [*Computer science*]	
DLR	Draft Letter Requirement (MCD)	
DLR	Driving after License Revoked	
DLR	Driving Licences Regulations [*British*] (ILCA)	
DLR	Dynamic Line Regulation	
DLR	Dynamic Load Regulation	
DLR	German Aerospace Research Establishment (GAVI)	
DLRA	Department of Labor Recreation Association	
DLRA	Divorce Law Reform Association [*British*] (DBA)	
DLRA	Door Lock Rotary Actuator	
DLRD	Design Layout Report Date [*Telecommunications*] (TEL)	
DLRF	Direct Loan Revolving Fund [*Department of Veterans Affairs*]	
DLRL	Diffraction Limited Raman LASER	
DLRO	District Labor Relations Office [*or Officer*] [*Navy*]	
DLRP	Data Link Reference Point (NVT)	
DLRTD	Dollar Time Group(New) [*NASDAQ symbol*] (TTSB)	
DLRU	Dryland Research Unit [*Washington State University*] [*Research center*] (RCD)	
DLRV	Dual Mode Lunar Roving Vehicle [*NASA*]	
DLRWS	Dirty Liquid Radioactive Waste System [*Nuclear energy*] (NRCH)	
DLS	Dallas [*Texas*] [*Seismograph station code, US Geological Survey Closed*] (SEIS)	
DLS	Dallas Gold & Silver Exchange, Inc. [*AMEX symbol*] (SAG)	
DLS	[*The*] Dalles [*Oregon*] [*Airport symbol*] (AD)	
DLS	Damped Least Square [*Mathematics*]	
DLS	Data Librarian System (PDAA)	
DLS	Data Link Set	
DLS	Data Link Simulator	
DLS	Data Link Software (IAA)	
DLS	Data Link Splitter (DA)	
DLS	Data Link Support	
DLS	Data Link Switching [*Computer science*] (PCM)	
DLS	Data Logging System	
DLS	Debt Liquidation Schedule	
DLS	Decoy Launching System [*Navy*] (CAAL)	
DLS	Deep Look Surveillance (MCD)	
DLS	Defence Light Section [*British military*] (DMA)	
DLS	Defense Legal Services Agency [*DoD*]	
DLS	Delay Line Synthesizer	
DLS	Differential Light Scattering	
DLS	Differential Load Sensing [*Hydraulics*]	
DLS	Digital Library Systems, Inc. [*Database producer*] (IID)	
DLS	Digital Line System [*Telecommunications*] (TEL)	
DLS	Digital Logic System	
dL'S	Dilaudid [*or Hydromorphone*] [*Knoll Pharmaceutical Co. Chemical dependency Slang*] (DAVI)	
DLS	Direct Least Squares [*Econometrics*]	
DLS	Direct Logistical Support (RDA)	
DLS	Director of Legal Services [*British military*] (DMA)	
DLS	Distance Least-Squares [*Mathematics*]	
DLS	Divergent Lobed Suppressor [*NASA*]	
DLS	Division of Labor Studies [*Indiana University*] [*Research center*] (RCD)	
DLS	Doctor of Library Science	
DLS	Doctor of Library Science (GAGS)	
DLS	Documents of Limited Significance (MCD)	
DLS	Dogwood Library System [*Library network*]	
dls	Dolares [*Dollars*] [*Monetary unit*] [*Spanish*]	
DLS	Dollars [*Monetary unit*]	
DLS	Dominion Land Surveyor [*Canada*]	
DLS	Double Left Shift	
DLS	Downloadable Sample [*Computer science*]	
DLS	Driving after License Suspended	
DLS	DuPage Library System [*Library network*]	
DLS	Dynamic Light Scattering	
DLS	Dynamic Light Scattering [*Physics*]	
DLS	Dynamic Load Simulator (NASA)	
DLS	The Dalles, OR [*Location identifier FAA*] (FAAL)	
DLS	University of Pittsburgh, School of Librarianship and Information Science, Pittsburgh, PA [*OCLC symbol*] (OCLC)	
DLSA	Defense Legal Services Agency [*DoD*]	
DLSA	Digital Linear Slide Switch Assembly	
DLSAP	Data Link Service Access Point (TNIG)	
DLSC	Defense Logistics Service Center [*Military*] (AFIT)	
DLSC	Defense Logistics Support Center [*Military*]	
DLSC	Defense Logistics System Center	
DLSC	Differential Logistics Services Center [*AEC*]	

DL Sc	Doctor of Library Science
DLSEF	Division of Library Services and Educational Facilities [*Office of Education*]
DLSF	Dog-Leg Severity Factor [*Well drilling technology*]
DLSHLS	Dorothy L. Sayers Historical and Literary Society [*British*]
DLSI	Detectable Least Signal Increment [*Instrumentation*]
DLSIE	Defense Logistics Studies Information Exchange [*Army*]
DLSLD	Documents of Limited Significance - Limited Distribution (MCD)
DLSM	Data Link Summary Message (MCD)
D/LSM	Directorate of Logistic Support Management [*or Manager*] (AAG)
DLSN	Dorsolateral Septal Nucleus [*Neuroanatomy*]
DLSO	Dial Line Service Observing [*Telecommunications*] (TEL)
DLSS	Digital Linear Slide Switch (MCD)
DLSS	Direct Logistic Support System (MCD)
DLSSA	Digital Linear Slide Switch Assembly (MCD)
DLS/SHR	Dollars per Share [*Investment term*] (MHDW)
DLSSO	Defense Logistics Standards Systems Office
DLS Soc	Dorothy L. Sayers Society (EAIO)
DLST	Division Logistics System Test [*Army*] (AABC)
DLST/SEACAPS	Division Logistics System Test/Seventh Army Card Processor System
DLSw	Data Link Switching [*IBM Co.*] (ACRL)
DLT	Daily Letter Telegram (IAA)
DLT	Dalton [*California*] [*Seismograph station code, US Geological Survey Closed*] (SEIS)
DLT	Darton, Longman & Todd [*Publisher*] [*British*]
DLT	Data Line Terminal (IAA)
DLT	Data Line Translator (IAA)
DLT	Data Link Layer Trailer [*Telecommunications*] (ACRL)
DLT	Data Link Terminal
DLT	Data Link Translator
DLT	Data Loop Transceiver [*Computer science*]
dlt	Daylight (WDMC)
DLT	Decision Logic Table [*DoD*]
DLT	Decision Logic Translator
DLT	Deck Landing Training
DLT	Delete (FAAC)
DLT	Delivery Lead Time [*Army*]
DLT	Delivery Term [*Military*]
DLT	Delta
DLT	Delta Air Lines, Inc. (MCD)
DLT	Depletion-Layer Transistor (IEEE)
DLT	Developed Layout Template (MCD)
DLT	Development Land Tax [*British*]
DLT	Digital Linear Tape [*Computer science*] (PCM)
DLT	Digital Line Termination [*Telecommunications*] (TEL)
DLT	Dihydroepiandrosterone Loading Test [*Endocrinology*]
DLT	Dilauryl Thiodipropionate [*Also, DLTDP, DLTP*] [*Food preservative*]
DLT	Direct Labor Time
DLT	Direct Linear Transformation (PDAA)
DLT	Direct Lunar Transport (IIA)
DLT	Distributed Language Translation [*Project being developed by BSO, a Dutch computer company*]
DLT	Double Reduction-Locked Train
DLT	Dual Language Translation [*Chinese University of Hong Kong*] (NITA)
DltaPtr	Delta Petroleum Corp. [*Associated Press*] (SAG)
DLTDP	Dilauryl Thiodipropionate [*Also, DLT, DLTP*] [*Food preservative*]
DLTM	Data Line Terminal Module [*Military*] (RDA)
DLTM	Data Link Test Message
DLTMA	Dynamic Load Thermo-Mechanical Analysis [*Thermal analysis*]
DLTO	Dog-Leg-to-Orbit (SAA)
DLTOE	Draft Living Table of Organization and Equipment [*Military*] (INF)
DLT/P	Deck-Landing Training/Practice [*Navy British*]
DLTP	Dilauryl Thiodipropionate [*Also, DLT, DLTDP*] [*Food preservative*]
DLTR	Data Link Terminal Repeater (NASA)
DLTR	Data Link Transmission Repeater (NASA)
dltr	Dollar Tree Stores [*NASDAQ symbol*] (TTSB)
DLTR	Dollar Tree Stores, Inc. [*NASDAQ symbol*] (SAG)
DLTS	Deck Landing Training School
DLTS	Deep Level Transient Spectroscopy
DLTS	Defraction Limited Thermograph System (MCD)
DLTT	Down-Link Television Terminal
DLU	Data Line Unit
DLU	Development Laboratory Unit (MCD)
DLU	Digital Line Unit [*Telecommunications*]
DLU	Digitizer Logic Unit
DLU	Display Logic Unit
DLUG	Double Lock Up Garage
DLUR/DLUS	Dependent Lu [*Logical Unit*] Requester/Server (CDE)
DLV	Dandelion Latent Virus [*Plant pathology*]
DLV	Defective Leukemia Virus [*Medicine*] (DMAA)
DLV	Differential Lung Ventilation
DLV	Direct LASER Vaporization
DLV	Discharge-Line Volume [*Nuclear energy*] (NRCH)
DLV	Montgomery, AL [*Location identifier FAA*] (FAAL)
DLV	US Delivery Systems, Inc. [*NYSE symbol*] (SAG)
DLVD	Delivered (NATG)
DLVL	Diverted into Low-Velocity Layer (OA)
DLVO	Derjaguin-Landau-Verwey-Overbeek [*Colloid science*]
DLVO Theory	Derjaguin-Landau-Verwey-Overbeek Theory [*Stability of colloidal dispersions*]
DLVR	Cortecs International Ltd. [*NASDAQ symbol*] (SAG)
DLVR	Deliver (AABC)
DLVRY	Contecs Intl Ltd ADS [*NASDAQ symbol*] (TTSB)

DLVRY........	Delivery
DLVY..........	Delivery (MSA)
DLW...........	Delaware, Lackawanna & Western Railroad [*AAR code*]
DLW...........	Delaware Resources Corp. [*Vancouver Stock Exchange symbol*]
DLW...........	Delta Woodside Ind. [*NYSE symbol*] (TTSB)
DLW...........	Delta Woodside Industries, Inc. [*NYSE symbol*] (CTT)
DLW...........	Doubly-Labelled Water [*Analytical chemistry*]
DLWD.........	Delta Woodside Industries, Inc. (MHDW)
DLWL.........	Designed Load Waterline [*Technical drawings*] (IAA)
DLWL.........	Discharge-Line Water-Leg Length [*Nuclear energy*] (NRCH)
DLX............	Deluxe (MSA)
DLX............	DeLuxe Corp. [*NYSE symbol*] (SPSG)
DLX............	Die Lock
DLX............	Dylex Ltd. [*Toronto Stock Exchange symbol*]
DLX............	Washington, DC [*Location identifier FAA*] (FAAL)
DLY............	Daily
DLY............	Daily
DLY............	Delay (KSC)
DLY............	Delivery (ROG)
DLY............	Dillon Bay [*Vanuatu*] [*Airport symbol*] (OAG)
DLY............	Dolly (MSA)
DLY............	Paine Webber Group [*AMEX symbol*] (SAG)
DlyJour......	Daily Journal Corp. [*Associated Press*] (SAG)
DLZ............	Delaware, OH [*Location identifier FAA*] (FAAL)
DLZ............	Drop Landing Zone [*Air Force*] (AFM)
dm..............	Dahomey [*Benin*] [*MARC country of publication code Library of Congress*] (LCCP)
DM.............	Daily Mirror [*A publication*]
DM.............	Dam
DM.............	Dam
DM.............	Dame
DM.............	Dames & Moore, Inc. [*NYSE symbol*] (SPSG)
DM.............	Damien Ministries (EA)
D/M............	Dance/Movement Therapy
DM.............	Dark Matter [*Astrophysics*]
DM.............	Data Management (KSC)
DM.............	Data Manager
DM.............	Data Master
DM.............	Data Memory
DM.............	Daughters of Mary of the Immaculate Conception [*Roman Catholic religious order*]
DM.............	Daughters of Our Lady of Mercy [*Roman Catholic religious order*]
DM.............	Daunomycin [*Antineoplastic drug*]
DM.............	Davison and Merivale's King's Bench Reports [*64 RR*] [*1843-44*] [*A publication*] (DLA)
DM.............	Deacon and Martyr [*Church calendars*]
DM.............	Deaf Missions (EA)
DM.............	Debit Memorandum (MCD)
DM.............	Debugging Mode
DM.............	Decameter
DM.............	Decamired
DM.............	Deciduous (Primary) Molar [*Dentistry*]
DM.............	Decimal Multiply
DM.............	Decimeter [*Unit of measure*]
DM.............	Decision Maker
DM.............	Decreto Ministeriale [*Ministerial Decree*] [*Italian*] (ILCA)
DM.............	Deflection Modulation (IAA)
DM.............	Dekameter [*Unit of measure*]
DM.............	Delay Modulation (NITA)
DM.............	Deletion Mutant [*Genetics*]
DM.............	Delta Ministry [*Later, DMM*] (EA)
DM.............	Delta Modulation
DM.............	Demand Meter
DM.............	Demineralized [*Water*] (NRCH)
D/M............	Demodulate/Modulate
DM.............	Density Meter [*Instrumentation*]
DM.............	Dental Mechanic [*Ranking title*] [*British Royal Navy*]
DM.............	Depot Maintenance (AAGC)
DM.............	Depot Manufacture (MCD)
DM.............	Deputy for Materiel
DM.............	Deputy Master [*Freemasonry*] (ROG)
DM.............	Dermatomyositis [*Medicine*]
DM.............	Dermorphin [*Biochemistry*]
DM.............	Descriptive Method
DM.............	Design Manual
DM.............	Design Memorandum
DM.............	Design Modified
DM.............	Des Moines [*Diocesan abbreviation*] [*Iowa*] (TOCD)
DM.............	Destra Mano [*Right Hand*] [*Music*] [*Italian*]
DM.............	Destroyer Minelayer [*Navy symbol*] (MCD)
DM.............	Detecting Magnetometer (IAA)
DM.............	Detecting Mechanism (IAA)
DM.............	Detector Mosaic
DM.............	Detroit & Mackinac Railway Co. [*AAR code*]
DM.............	Deutsche Mark [*Monetary unit*] [*Germany*]
DM.............	Development Manager
DM.............	Development Milestone [*Aerospace*] (AAG)
DM.............	Development Motor (MCD)
DM.............	Devon Militia [*British military*] (DMA)
DM.............	Dextromethorphan [*Antitussive*] [*Pharmacy*]
DM.............	Diabetes Mellitus [*Medicine*]
DM.............	Diabetic Mother [*Medicine*]
DM.............	Diagnostic Monitor [*Computer science*] (IAA)
DM.............	Diastolic Murmur [*Medicine*]
DM.............	Dichroic Mirror

DM.............	Die Musik [*A publication*]
DM.............	Diesel Mechanic [*or Mechanical*]
DM.............	Diesel Moderate [*Service*] [*Automotive engineering*]
DM.............	Dieses Monats [*Of This Month*] [*German*] (ROG)
DM.............	Differential Mechanism
DM.............	Differential Mode [*Electronics*] (OA)
DM.............	Diffused Mesa
DM.............	Diffuse Mixed [*Lymphoma*] [*Oncology*] (DAVI)
Dm.............	Diffusing Capacity of the Alveolar Capillary Membrane [*Medicine*] (DAVI)
DM.............	Digital Module [*Telecommunications*] (TEL)
DM.............	Digital Monolithic [*Electronics*] (OA)
DM.............	Digital Multimeter (IAA)
DM.............	Digital Multiplex (LAIN)
DM.............	Digital Music Tuner [*Cable television*]
DM.............	Diis Manibus [*To the Manes, i.e., Departed Souls*] [*Latin*]
DM.............	Dioxane-Methanol [*Scintillation solvent*] [*Bray solution*]
DM.............	Diphenylaminechloroarsine [*Tear gas*] [*Military*]
DM.............	Diploma in Dermatological Medicine (DAVI)
D-M............	Diplomate, American Board of Internal Medicine (DHSM)
DM.............	Direct Mail
DM.............	Direct Marketing
DM.............	Directorate of Maintenance (AFIT)
DM.............	Director of Management [*Military*]
DM.............	Director of Mobilization [*British military*] (DMA)
DM.............	Director of Music [*British military*] (DMA)
DM.............	Disassembly Manual (MCD)
DM.............	Disassembly Manual [*NASA*]
DM.............	Discard Message (CET)
DM.............	Disconnected Mode [*Telecommunications*]
DM.............	Disconnecting Manhole
DM.............	Diseased Mucosa [*Oncology*]
DM.............	Disease Management
D/M............	Disintegrations per Minute
DM.............	Disk Monitor [*Computer science*] (IAA)
DM.............	Dispersion Measure [*Astronomy*]
DM.............	Distribution Module [*Telecommunications*]
DM.............	District Manager
DM.............	District Members [*Also, EN for secrecy*] [*Fenian Brotherhood*] (ROG)
DM.............	Ditch Mile [*Newmarket Racecourse*] [*Horseracing*] [*British*]
DM.............	Docking Mechanism (MCD)
DM.............	Docking Module [*NASA*]
DM.............	Doctor Martens [*Footwear*]
DM.............	Doctor of Dental Medicine (DAVI)
DM.............	Doctor of Management (PGP)
DM.............	Doctor of Mathematics
DM.............	Doctor of Medicine
DM.............	Doctor of Music
DM.............	Doctor of Musicology (NADA)
DM.............	Documenta et Monumenta [*A publication*] (BJA)
DM.............	Documentation
DM.............	Documentation Manager [*Air Force*] (AFM)
DM.............	DodecylMaltoside [*Organic chemistry*]
DM.............	Dominica [*ANSI two-letter standard code*] (CNC)
DM.............	Dopamine [*Biochemistry*] (AAMN)
DM.............	Doppler Missile (MUGU)
DM.............	Dot Matrix
DM.............	Double Make (IAA)
DM.............	Double Master [*LORAN stations*]
DM.............	Double Medium (ADA)
DM.............	Double Minute [*Cytology*]
DM.............	Douglas Model (SAA)
DM.............	Drafting Manual (AABC)
DM.............	Dram (MCD)
D/M............	Dr. & Mrs. (VRA)
DM.............	Drive Magnet
DM.............	Driver, Master
DM.............	Driver Mechanic [*British military*] (DMA)
DM.............	Driving and Maintenance (IAA)
DM.............	Drum
DM.............	Drum Module [*Computer science*] (IAA)
DM.............	Dry Mass
DM.............	Dry Matter
DM.............	Dummy Round (MCD)
DM.............	Dungeon Master [*In game Dungeons and Dragons*]
DM.............	Dynamic Melting [*Chemistry*]
DM.............	Dynamo (IAA)
DM.............	Dynamotor (IAA)
DM.............	Illustrator Draftsman [*Navy rating*]
DM.............	Iran [*License plate code assigned to foreign diplomats in the US*]
DM.............	Light Minelayer [*Later, MMD*] [*Navy symbol*]
DM.............	Magnetic Drum Module [*Computer science*]
DM.............	Master Diver [*Navy*]
DM.............	Master of Divinity
DM.............	Meersk Air [*ICAO designator*] (AD)
Dm.............	Membrane Component of Diffusion [*Cytology*] (MAE)
DM.............	Vomiting Gas [*US Chemical Corps symbol*]
DM1............	Draftsman, First Class, Illustrator [*Navy*] (DNAB)
DM2............	Draftsman, Second Class, Illustrator [*Navy*] (DNAB)
Dm^2.........	Square Decimeter (ROG)
Dm^3.........	Cubic Decimeter (ROG)
DM3............	Draftsman, Third Class, Illustrator [*Navy*] (DNAB)
DMA...........	Dance Masters of America (EA)
DMA...........	Data Management Agent (MCD)
DMA...........	Data Management Analysis

DMA............ Data-Matching Agency
DMA............ Data Memory Access
DMA............ Dealer Management Association [*Exeter, NH*] [*Commercial firm*] (EA)
DMA............ Dean Martin Association (EAIO)
DMA............ Debt Market Analysis [*MMS International*] [*Information service or system*] (CRD)
DMA............ Defence Manufacturers Association [*British*] (DS)
DMA............ Defense Manpower Administration [*Superseded by Office of Manpower Administration, 1953*] [*Department of Labor*]
DMA............ Defense Mapping Agency [*Washington, DC*]
DMA............ Degraded Mission Assessment
DMA............ Dental Manufacturers of America (EA)
DMA............ Department of Memorial Affairs [*Veterans Administration*]
DMA............ Deployed Mechanical Assembly (MCD)
DMA............ Depot Maintenance Activity (MCD)
DMA............ Designated Maintenance Activity (MCD)
DMA............ Designated Market Area [*Advertising*]
DMA............ Design Management Award [*Financial Times and London Business School*] [*British*]
DMA............ Devil Mountain [*Alaska*] [*Seismograph station code, US Geological Survey*] (SEIS)
DMA............ Dietary Managers Association (EA)
DMA............ Differential Mobility Analyzer [*Marine science*] (OSRA)
DMA............ Digital Major Alarm (MCD)
DMA............ Digital Map Analyzer
DMA............ Dihydroxymandelic Acid [*Also, DHMA, DOMA*] [*Organic chemistry*]
DMA............ Dimethylacetamide [*Also, DMAC*] [*Organic chemistry*]
DMA............ Dimethyladenosine [*Organic chemistry*] (MAE)
DMA............ Dimethyl Adipimidate [*Biochemistry*]
DMA............ Dimethylamine [*Organic chemistry*]
DMA............ Dimethylaniline [*Organic chemistry*]
DMA............ Dimethylanisole [*Organic chemistry*]
DMA............ Dimethylarginine [*Biochemistry*]
DMA............ Dimethyl Arsonic Acid [*Organic chemistry*]
DMA............ Diploma in Municipal Accounting (ADA)
DMA............ Diploma in Municipal Administration [*British*]
DMA............ Direct Marketing Association [*New York, NY*] (EA)
DMA............ Direct Memory Access [*Computing method*]
DMA............ Direct Memory Address [*Computer science*]
DMA............ Director of Medical Affairs (HCT)
DMA............ Director of Military Assistance
DMA............ District Manager's Assistant [*British*] (DCTA)
DMA............ Divisional Maintenance Area [*Military British*]
DMA............ Division of Military Application [*Energy Research and Development Administration*]
DMA............ Doctor of Municipal Administration
DMA............ Doctor of Musical Arts
DMA............ Doctor of Musical Arts (GAGS)
DMA............ Dominica [*ANSI three-letter standard code*] (CNC)
DMA............ Double Motor Alternator
DMA............ Drive Motor Assembly (MCD)
DMA............ Drum Memory Assembly [*Computer science*]
DMA............ Dry Matter Accumulation (OA)
DMA............ Dynamic Mechanical Analysis
DMA............ Dynamic Microprocessor Associates (PCM)
DMA............ Maersk Air IS [*Denmark ICAO designator*] (FAAC)
DMA............ Tucson, AZ [*Location identifier FAA*] (FAAL)
DMA............ United States Maritime Administration, Washington, DC [*Library symbol Library of Congress*] (LCLS)
DMAA .... Dimethylacetoacetamide [*Organic chemistry*]
DMAA .... Dimethylarsenonic Acid [*Organic chemistry*]
DMAA .... Direct Mail Advertising Association [*Later, DMMA*]
DMAAC .... Defense Mapping Agency Aerospace Center [*Formerly, ACIC*]
DMAAC-ST... Defense Mapping Agency Aerospace Center Directorate of Systems and Techniques
DMAAC-TC... Defense Mapping Agency Aerospace Center Technical Library/ Translation Section
DMAB .... Defended Modular Array Basing [*Military*]
DMAB .... Dimethylaminobenzaldehyde [*Ehrlich's reagent*] [*Analytical chemistry*]
DMAB .... Dimethylaminoborane [*Organic chemistry*]
DMABA .... Dimethylaminobenzaldehyde [*Analytical chemistry*] (AAMN)
DMABO .... Defense Mapping Agency Branch Office (DNAB)
DMABODET... Defense Mapping Agency Branch Office Detachment (DNAB)
DMAC .... Dimethylacetamide [*Also, DMA*] [*Organic chemistry*]
DMAC .... Direct Memory Access Channel [*Pronounced "DEEmack"*] [*Computer science*]
DMAC .... Direct Memory Access Control [*Computer science*]
DMAC .... Disseminated Mycobacterium Avium Complex [*Medicine*]
DMAC .... Dusty Mac Oil & Gas Ltd. [*NASDAQ symbol*] (SAG)
DMACC .... Direct Marketing Association Catalog Council [*New York, NY*] (EA)
DMACP .... Direct Memory Access Communications Processor
DMACS .... Descriptive Macro Code Generation System [*Computer science*]
DMAD .... Diagnostic Machine Aids/Digital [*Raytheon Co.*] [*Programming language*] (CSR)
DMAD .... Dimethylacetylenedicarboxylate [*Organic chemistry*]
DMADISTRCEN... Defense Mapping Agency Distribution Center (DNAB)
DM Adm ...... Doctor of Municipal Administration
DMAE .... Dimethylaminoethanol [*Antidepressant*]
D Ma E .... Doctor of Marine Engineering
DMAEMA ..... Dimethylaminoethyl Methacrylate [*Organic chemistry*]
D Ma Eng ... Doctor of Marine Engineering
DMAHC .... Defense Mapping Agency Hydrographic Center [*Later, DMAHTC*]
DMAHP .... Dystrophia Myotonica-Associated Homeodomain Protein [*Biochemistry*]

DMAHTC ...... Defense Mapping Agency Hydrographic/Topographic Center [*Washington, DC Also, an information service or system*] (IID)
DMAI .... Direct Memory Access Interface
D/Maj.......... Drum-Major [*British military*] (DMA)
DMALO .... Defense Mapping Agency Liaison Office (DNAB)
DMAM .... Dimethyl Aminoethyl Methacrylate [*Organic chemistry*]
DMAM .... Di(methylamyl) Maleate [*Organic chemistry*]
DMaM.......... United States Marine Corps Museum, Washington, DC [*Library symbol Library of Congress*] (LCLS)
DMAMP .... (Dimethylaminomethyl)phenol [*Organic chemistry*]
DMAMP .... Dimethylamino(methyl)propanol [*Organic chemistry*]
DMAN .... Data Manager (KSC)
DM & CW .... Diploma in Maternity and Child Welfare
DM & E........ Dakota, Minnesota & Eastern Railroad
D M & G....... De Gex, Macnaghten, and Gordon's English Chancery Reports [*A publication*] (DLA)
D M & GB.... De Gex, Macnaghten, and Gordon's English Bankruptcy Reports [*A publication*] (DLA)
DM & IR ...... Duluth, Missabe & Iron Range Railway Co.
DM & IRR..... Duluth, Missabe & Iron Range Railroad (MHDB)
DM & M....... D'Arcy-MacManus & Masius [*Advertising agency*]
DM & N....... Duluth, Missabe & Northern Railway
DM & O .... Data Management and Operations (SSD)
DM & S .... Department of Medicare and Surgery [*Veterans Administration*] (GFGA)
DM & T....... Defense Markets & Technology [*Predicasts, Inc.*] [*Database*]
DM & TS ..... Department of Mines and Technical Survey [*Canada*] (DNAB)
DM & V .... Delaware, Maryland & Virginia Railroad
DMANS .... Dimethylamino(nitro)stilbene [*Organic chemistry*]
DManSc ...... Doctor of Management Sciences
DMAO .... Directorate of Military Aid Overseas [*British*]
DMAODS...... Defense Mapping Agency Office of Distribution Services (DNAB)
DMAP .... DARCOM [*Development and Readiness Command, Army*] Modification Application Plan (MCD)
DMAP .... Digital Missile Autopilot (MCD)
DMAP .... Dimethylaminopurine [*Organic chemistry*]
DMAP .... Dimethylaminopyridine [*Organic chemistry*]
DMAP .... Direct Matrix Abstraction Process
DMAPA .... Dimethylaminopropylamine [*Also, DIMAPA*] [*Organic chemistry*]
DMAPMA .... Dimethylaminopropyl Methacrylamide [*Organic chemistry*]
DMAPN .... (Dimethylaminophenyl)phenylnitrone [*Organic chemistry*]
DMAPN .... Dimethylaminopropionitrile [*Organic chemistry*]
DMAPP .... Dimethylallyl Pyrophosphate [*Organic chemistry*]
DMAR .... Datamarine International, Inc. [*NASDAQ symbol*] (NQ)
DMAR .... Datamarine Int'l [*NASDAQ symbol*] (TTSB)
DMAR .... Deferred Maintenance and Repair [*DoD*]
DMarC .... Marist College, Washington, DC [*Library symbol Library of Congress*] (LCLS)
DMARD........ Disease-Modifying Antirheumatic Drug [*Medicine*]
DMarS .... Marist Seminary, Washington, DC [*Library symbol Library of Congress*] (LCLS)
DMAS .... Defense Manufacturers and Supplies Association of America (AAGC)
DMAS .... Defense Material Allotment System (AFIT)
DMAS .... Digital Modular Avionics System
DMAS .... Distribution Management Accounting System (IEEE)
D Mass .... United States District Court for the District of Massachusetts (DLA)
DMAT.......... Decision-Making Ability Test [*Psychology*] (BARN)
DMAT.......... Digital Module Automatic Tester
D-MAT .... Directorate of Materials Research and Development [*Aviation British*]
DMATC .... Defense Mapping Agency Topographic Center [*Later, DMAHTC*]
DMath.......... Doctor of Mathematics (NADA)
DMATS .... Defense Metropolitan Area Telephone Service [*or System*] (MCD)
D-MAT/S...... Directorate of Materials and Structures Research and Development [*British*]
DMB............ Daily Maximum Benefit [*Insurance*]
DMB............ Data Management Block
DMB............ Defense Manufacturing Board [*DoD*]
DMB............ Defense Mobilization Board [*Terminated, 1958*]
DMB............ Demineralized Bone [*Medicine*]
DMB............ Dibutanoylmorphine [*An analgesic*]
DMB............ Dichloro (Methyl) Benzhydrol [*Organic chemistry*]
DMB............ Dihydro(methyl)benzodiazepinone [*Biochemistry*]
DMB............ Dimethoxybenzene [*Organic chemistry*]
DMB............ Dimethylbenzamil [*Organic chemistry*]
DMB............ Dimethylbusulfan [*Organic chemistry*]
DMB............ Dimethylmethylene Blue [*Organic chemistry*]
DMB............ Disconnect and Make Busy [*Telecommunications*] (TEL)
DMB............ Distinguished Marksmanship Badge
DMB............ Division Maintenance Battalion (MCD)
DMB............ Double Mouldboard [*Ploughing*]
DMB............ Dynamic Multipoint Bridging [*Computer science*] (ACRL)
DMBA .... Dimethylbarbituric Acid [*Organic chemistry*]
DMBA .... Dimethylbenzanthracene [*Carcinogen*]
DMBA .... Dimethyl(butyl)amine [*Organic chemistry*]
DMBAO .... Dimethylbenzanthraceneoxide [*Organic chemistry*]
DMBAS .... Dimethoxy(amino)stilbene [*Organic chemistry*]
DMBC .... Dimethylbenzylcarbinol [*Organic chemistry*]
DMBC .... Direct Material Balance Control
DMBC .... Double Mark Blank Column (BUR)
DMBCA .... Dimethylbenzylcarbinol Acetate [*Organic chemistry*]
DMBE .... Double Many-Body Expansion [*Kinetics*]
DMBS .... Defense Material Billing System (AFIT)
DMBZ .... Dimethylbenzimidazole [*Organic chemistry*]
DMC............ Chief Illustrator Draftsman [*Navy rating*]
DMC............ Dactinomycin, Methotrexate, Cytoxan [*Antineoplastic drug*] (CDI)

DMC............ Darryl McDaniels [*A rap recording artist whose initials appear in the album title, "Run-D.M.C."*]
DMC............ Data Management Center   (CAAL)
DMC............ Data Management Channel
DMC............ Data Management Computer   (KSC)
DmC............ Data Microfilming Corp., Whittier, CA [*Library symbol Library of Congress*]   (LCLS)
DMC............ Dead Man Controls   (SAA)
DMC............ Decision Module Compiler   (DNAB)
DMC............ Deck Motion Compensator   (MCD)
DMC............ Defence Movement Coordination Committee [*Australia*]
DMC............ Defense Manpower Commission
DMC............ Defense Materiel Council [*DoD*]
DMC............ Degraded Mission Capability
DMC............ DeLorean Motor Co. [*Initials used as name of its cars*]
DMC............ Demeclocycline [*Also, DMCT*] [*Antimicrobial compound*]
DMC............ Democratic Movement for Change [*Political party*] [*Israel*]
DMC............ Deputy Marshal of Ceremonies   (ROG)
DMC............ Design, Manage, Construct
DMC............ Destination Digital Media Computers
DMC............ Destination Digital Media Computers [*Computer science*]
DMC............ Destination Management Company [*Generic term*]
DMC............ Detroit Medical Center
DMC............ Dichlorodiphenylmethylcarbinol [*Also, DCPC*] [*Insecticide*]
DMC............ Dichloromethotrexate [*Antineoplastic drug*]   (CDI)
DMC............ Dielectric, Magnetic and Capacitor   (IAA)
DMC............ Diffusion Monte Carlo [*Mathematics*]
DMC............ Digital Microcircuit
DMC............ Digital Monitor Computer
DMC............ Digital Multiplex Control   (IAA)
DMC............ DIMAC Corp. [*AMEX symbol*]   (SAG)
DMC............ Dimethoxychalcone [*Organic chemistry*]
DMC............ Dimethylaminoethyl Chloride [*Organic chemistry*]
DMC............ Dimethyl Carbinol [*Organic chemistry*]
DMC............ Dimethyl Carbonate [*Organic chemistry*]
DMC............ Dimethylcysteine (Penicillamine) [*Pharmacology*]
DMC............ Direct Maintenance Cost   (NASA)
DMC............ Direct Manufacturing Cost [*Marketing*]
DMC............ Direct Memory Channel
DMC............ Direct Microscopic Count [*Biochemistry*]   (DAVI)
DMC............ Direct Multiplexed Control
DMC............ Direct Multiplexor Channel
DMC............ Discrete Memoryless Channel [*Computer science*]
DMC............ Disk Memory Controller [*Computer science*]
DMC............ Dough-Molding Compound [*Plastics technology*]
DMC............ DSIF [*Deep Space Instrumentation Facility*] Monitor and Control Subsystem [*NASA*]
DMC............ Dull Men's Club   (EA)
DMC............ Dynamic Matrix Control [*Chemical engineering*] [*Computer science*]
DMC............ Dynamic Memory Control [*Computer science*]
DMC............ Metropolitan Club, Washington, DC [*Library symbol Library of Congress*]   (LCLS)
DMCA......... DeLorean Motor Club of America [*Defunct*]   (EA)
DMCA......... Dependents' Medical Care Act [*HEW*]
DMCA......... Direct Marketing Computer Association [*Defunct*]   (EA)
DMCA......... Direct Marketing Credit Association [*Defunct*]   (EA)
DMCB......... Data Measurement Corp. [*NASDAQ symbol*]   (NQ)
DMCBAC...... Dimethylcetylbenzylammonium Chloride [*Antiseptic*] [*Organic chemistry*]
DMCC......... Dean Martin Collector's Club [*Defunct*]   (EA)
DMCC......... Depot Maintenance Control [*or Coordinator*] Center [*Army*]   (AABC)
DMCC......... Dimethylcarbamoyl Chloride [*Organic chemistry*]
DMCC......... Direct Microscopic Clump Count
DMCCC....... Deputy Missile Combat Crew Commander
DMCd......... Dimethylcadmium
DMCE......... Division of Medicaid Cost Estimates [*Department of Health and Human Services*]   (GFGA)
DMCF......... Deservicing, Maintenance, and Checkout Facility [*NASA*]   (NASA)
DMCG......... Direct Marketing Creative Guild [*New York, NY*]   (EA)
DMCGS...... Descriptive Macro-Code Generation System   (DNAB)
DMCHA...... Dimethylcyclohexamine [*Organic chemistry*]
DMCL......... Device Media Control Language [*CODASYL/Honeywell, Inc.*]
DMCL......... Digital MODEM Command Language [*Computer science*]   (BYTE)
DMCM........ Dimethoxyethylcarboline Carboxylate [*Organic chemistry*]   (DAVI)
DMCM........ Double Density Modular Core Memory   (MCD)
DMCM........ Master Chief Illustrator Draftsman [*Navy rating*]
DMCOD...... Dimethylcyclooctadiene [*Organic chemistry*]
DMC/PC...... Drives, Motors, Controls, and Programmable Controllers Exhibition [*British*]   (ITD)
DMCR......... Director, Marine Corps Reserve
DMC's........ Dialysis-Related Muscle Cramps [*Medicine*]
DMCS......... Digital Missile Controller Set
DMCS......... Dimethyldichlorosilane [*Organic chemistry*]
DMCS......... Senior Chief Illustrator Draftsman [*Navy rating*]
DMCT......... Demethylchlortetracycline [*Obsolete name*] [*Antimicrobial compound See DMC*]
DMCTC....... Directorate of Missile Captive Test   (AAG)
DMCTC....... Dimethylchlortetracycline [*Antimicrobial compound*]   (DAVI)
DMCU........ Display Monitor and Control Unit
DMCu......... Metropolitan Club, Washington, DC [*Library symbol*] [*Library of Congress*]   (LCLS)
DMCV........ Dairy Mart Convenience Stores [*NASDAQ symbol*]   (SAG)
DMCVA...... Dairy Mart Conven Str'A' [*NASDAQ symbol*]   (TTSB)
DMCVB...... Dairy Mart Conven Str'B' [*NASDAQ symbol*]   (TTSB)
DMD.......... Carrizo Springs, TX [*Location identifier FAA*]   (FAAL)

DMD............ Dark Mantle Deposit [*Lunar surface*]
DMD............ Data Model Diagramer [*Computer science*]
DMD............ Defense Manufacturing Board [*DoD*]   (EGAO)
DMD............ Deformable Device [*Texas Instruments, Inc.*] [*Computer science*]
DMD............ Deployment Manning Document   (MCD)
Dm/d............ Depth Molded   (DS)
DMD............ Deputy Managing Director
DMD............ Devices Management Directorate [*Army*]
DMD............ Diamond   (MSA)
dmd............ Diamond   (VRA)
DMD............ Diamond Resources [*Vancouver Stock Exchange symbol*]
DMD............ Digital Map Display
DMD............ Digital Message Device   (AABC)
DMD............ Digital Micromirror Device [*Silicon chip*] [*Telecommunications*]   (PCM)
DMD............ Digital Micromirror Display [*Electronics*]   (PS)
DMD............ Digital Missile Device   (MCD)
DMD............ Digital Muirhead Display   (NOAA)
DMD............ Digoxigenin Monodigitoxoside [*Biochemistry*]
DMD............ Dimethadione [*Biochemistry*]
DMD............ Doctor of Dental Medicine
DMD............ Doctor of Mathematics and Didactics
DMD............ Doctor of Medical Dentistry
DMD............ Domodossola [*Italy*] [*Seismograph station code, US Geological Survey Closed*]   (SEIS)
DMD............ Doomadgee Mission [*Australia Airport symbol*]   (OAG)
DMD............ Double Meridian Distance   (PDAA)
DMD............ Dry Matter Disappearance   (OA)
DMD............ Dual Mode Display
DMD............ Duchenne Muscular Dystrophy
DMD............ Dynamic Map Display
DMD............ Dystonia Musculorum Deformans [*Medicine*]
DM D.......... RST Aviation, NV [*Belgium ICAO designator*]   (FAAC)
D MD.......... United States District Court for the District of Maryland   (DLA)
DMDAAC..... Dimethyldiallylammonium Chloride [*Organic chemistry*]
DMDB........ Depot Maintenance Data Bank [*DARCOM*]   (MCD)
DMDC......... Defense Manpower Data Center [*Alexandria, VA*]
DMDC......... Diffusion in Metals and Alloys Data Center [*National Institute of Standards and Technology*]   (IID)
DMDC......... Dimethyl Dicarbonate [*Fungistatic agent*]
DMDC......... Dimethyldithiocarbamate [*Organic chemistry*]
DMDC/MRB.. Defense Manpower Data Center Management [*or Market*] Research Branch [*Arlington, VA*]
DMDCS....... Depot Management Data Collection System   (MCD)
DMDC/SMAD.. Defense Manpower Data Center Survey and Market Analysis Division [*Arlington, VA*]
DMDEL....... Dimethyldiethyllead [*Organic chemistry*]
DMDG........ Department of the Medical Director-General [*Navy British*]
DMDG........ Digital Message Device Group [*Later, SOICS*] [*Army*]   (INF)
DMDHEU..... Dimethylol Dihydroxyethyleneurea [*Used to provide durable press finish in fabrics*]
DMDMH..... Dimethylol dimethylhydantoin [*Organic chemistry*]
DMDP........ Data Maintenance Diagnostic Program
DMD/PACT... Digital Message Device/Processing and Communication Terminal   (MCD)
DMDR........ (Demethoxy)daunorubicin [*Antineoplastic drug*]
DMDS........ Dimethyl Disulfide [*Organic chemistry*]
DMDT......... Dimethoxydiphenyl Trichloroethane [*Organic chemistry*]   (DMAA)
DMDT......... Methoxychlor [*An insecticide*]   (DAVI)
DME........... Defense Microelectronics   (IIA)
DME........... Department of Mechanics [*JHU*]
DME........... Depot Maintenance Equipment   (SAA)
DME........... Designated Mechanic Examiners
DME........... Design Margin Evaluation   (NG)
DME........... Design Mission Effect
DME........... Design Mission Evaluation
DME........... Dextromethorphan [*Pharmacology*]   (DAVI)
DME........... Diagnostic Monitor Executive [*Computer science*]
D-M-E........ Dialogue, Music, and Effects [*Film*]   (WDMC)
DME........... Digital Motor Electronics
DME........... Digital Multiplex Equipment [*Telecommunications*]
DME........... Dime Bancorp [*NYSE symbol*]   (TTSB)
DME........... Dime Savings Bank of New York [*NYSE symbol*]   (SPSG)
DME........... Dimethoxyethane [*Also known as GLYME*] [*Organic chemistry*]
DME........... Dimethylethanolamine [*Organic chemistry*]
DME........... Dimethyl Ether [*Organic chemistry*]
DME........... Dimethyl Ether
DME........... Dimethyl ether [*Gasoline*] [*Organic chemistry*]
DME........... Diploma in Mechanical Engineering   (ADA)
DME........... Direct Machine Environment
DME........... Direct Measurements Explorer [*Satellite*]
DME........... Director of Mechanical Engineering [*War Office*] [*British World War II*]
DME........... Director of Medical Education
DME........... Distance Measuring Equipment [*Navigation*]
DME........... Distance Measuring Equipment [*Ground navigational aid that can provide display of distance to selected ground navigational radio transmitter*]   (GAVI)
DME........... Distance Monitoring Equipment [*Military*]
DME........... Distributed Management Environment
DME........... Division of Mechanical Engineering [*National Research Council of Canada*]
DME........... Doctor of Mechanical Engineering
D Me.......... Doctor of Metaphysics
DME........... Doctor of Music Education   (PGP)
DME........... Draftsman, Electrical   (IAA)

DME	Drilling Mud Emulsifier (BARN)
DME	Dropping Mercury Electrode [*Electrochemistry*]
DME	Dulbecco's Modified Eagle's Medium [*Also, DMEM, DMM*] [*Medium for cell growth*]
DME	Durable Medical Equipment
DME	Dynamic Mission Equivalent (IAA)
DME	Moscow [*Former USSR Airport symbol*]
DME	Moscow Domodedovo Airport [*Former USSR Airport symbol*] (OAG)
DME	United States Department of Commerce, National Oceanic and Atmospheric Administration, Marine and Earth Sciences Library, Rockville, MD [*Library symbol Library of Congress*] (LCLS)
D ME	United States District Court for the District of Maine (DLA)
DMEA	Damage Modes and Effects Analysis (MCD)
DMEA	Defense Minerals Exploration Administration [*Department of the Interior*]
DME-A	Direct Measurements Explorer A [*Satellite*]
DMEC	Defense Metals Equipment Center (DNAB)
DMecE	Doctor of Mechanical Engineering (NADA)
D Mech	Doctor of Mechanics
DME/COTAR	Distance Measuring Equipment/Correlation Tracking and Ranging
DMeCP	Dimethylcarboxypsoralen [*Metabolite of TMeP*]
DMECS	Dimethl(ethyl)chlorosilane [*Organic chemistry*]
DMED	Diametrics Medical [*NASDAQ symbol*] (TTSB)
DMED	Diametrics Medical, Inc. [*NASDAQ symbol*] (SAG)
DMED	Digital Message Entry Device [*Computer science*]
D Med	Doctor of Medicine
DM Ed	Doctor of Musical Education
DMEDA	Director of Medical Activities (AABC)
DMedRehab	Diploma in Medical Rehabilitation [*British*] (DBQ)
D Med Sc	Doctor of Medical Science (PGP)
DMedVer	Doctor Medicinae Veterinariae [*Doctor of Veterinary Medicine*] [*Latin*]
DMEF	Dannemiller Memorial Educational Foundation (EA)
DMEF	Direct Marketing Educational Foundation [*New York, NY*] (EA)
DMEG	Discharge Multimedia Environmental Goals [*Environmental Protection Agency*]
DMEG	Distance Measuring Equipment Collocated With Glide Slope [*Aviation*] (FAAC)
DMEL	Distance Measuring Equipment Collocated With Localizer [*Aviation*] (FAAC)
DMEM	Dulbecco's Minimum Essential Medium
DMEM	Dulbecco's Modified Eagle's Medium [*Also, DME, DMM*] [*Medium for cell growth*]
DM Eng	Doctor of Mechanical Engineering
DMEP	Data Network Modified Emulator Program [*Telecommunications*] (TEL)
DME/P	Precision Distance Measuring Equipment [*FAA*] (TAG)
DMER	Distance Measuring Equipment Tactical Air Navigation With DME Only Commissioned [*Aviation*] (FAAC)
DMES	Digital Message Entry System
DMESFET	Depletion-Mode Metal Semiconductor Field Effect Transistor (IAA)
DMET	Defense Management Educating and Training [*DoD*] (AFM)
DMET	Distance Measuring Equipment TACAN [*Tactical Air Navigation*] (NG)
DMET	Distance Measuring Equipment Terminal (CET)
D Met	Doctor of Metallurgy
DMet	Doctor of Meteorology (ADA)
DMETB	Defense Management Education and Training Board [*DoD*]
D Met E	Doctor of Metallurgical Engineering
DMETEG	Dimethyl Ether of Tetraethylene Glycol [*Organic chemistry*]
D Met Eng	Doctor of Metallurgical Engineering
DMeteor	Doctor of Meterology (NADA)
DMEU	Dimethylolethyleneurea [*Organic chemistry*]
DMEW	Deterministic Mix Evaluation Worldwide (MCD)
DMF	Dance Magazine Foundation (EA)
DMF	Data Management Facility
DMF	Data Migration Facility [*Computer science*]
DMF	Decayed, Missing, Filled [*Dentistry*]
DMF	Deoxymorpholinofructose [*Biochemistry*]
DMF	Depot Maintenance Facility (SAA)
DMF	Detail Matching Figures Test [*Psychology*] (EDAC)
DMF	Digital Matched Filter
DMF	Digital Multiplexing and Formatting [*Computer science*] (MCD)
DMF	Dimethylformamide [*Also, DMFA*] [*Organic chemistry*]
DMF	Disabled Motorists Federation [*British*] (DBA)
DMF	Disk Management Facility [*Computer science*]
DMF	Distribution Media Format (CDE)
DMF	Dominican Mission Foundation (EA)
DMF	Dose Modifying Factor [*Medicine*]
DMF	Dreyfus Municipal Income Fund [*AMEX symbol*] (CTT)
DMF	Dreyfus Muni Income [*AMEX symbol*] (TTSB)
DMF	Drug Master File
DMF	DSIF [*Deep Space Instrumentation Facility*] Maintenance Facility [*NASA*]
DMF	Dummy Missile Firing
DMF	Dyers of Man-Made Fibre Fabrics Federation [*British*] (BI)
DMFA	Dimethylformamide [*Also, DMF*] [*Organic chemistry*]
DMFA	Direct Mail Fundraisers Association (EA)
DMFC	Daniel McVicar Fan Club (EA)
DMFC	Debbie Myers Fan Club (EA)
DMFC	Direct Methanol Fuel Cell
DMFL	Dimethylformal [*Organic chemistry*]
DMFO	Defense Medical Facilities Office [*DoD*] (GFGA)
DMFP	Draft Materiel Fielding Plan [*Army*]
DMF-R	Depot Maintenance Facility - Recycle (SAA)
DMFS	Decayed, Missing, or Filled Surfaces [*Dentistry*]

DMFT	Decayed, Missing, and Filled Teeth [*Dentistry*]
DMFT	Doctor of Marriage and Family Therapy (PGP)
DMG	Damage (AFM)
DMG	Data Management Group (MCD)
DMG	Davis Medical Group [*Commercial firm*]
DMG	Defense Marketing Group [*AMA*]
DMG	Deputy Master-General [*Military British*]
DMG	Deputy Military Governor [*US Military Government, Germany*]
DMG	Deterministic Microgrinding [*Optics manufacturing*] (RDA)
DMG	Deutsche Morgan Grenfell [*Germany*] [*Banking*]
DMG	Deutsche Morgan Grenfell [*Germany*]
DMG	Digital Map Generator (MCD)
DMG	Dimethylglycine [*Biochemistry*]
DMG	Dimethylglyoxime [*Organic chemistry*]
DMG	Directed Metalation Group [*Organic chemistry*]
DMG	Distinguished Military Graduate
DMGBL	Dimethyl-gamma-butyrolactone [*Biochemistry*]
DMGO	Department of the Master General of the Ordnance [*British*]
DMGO	Divisional Machine Gun Officer [*British military*] (DMA)
DMGT	Data Management (MSA)
DMGZ	Demagnetize
DMH	Decimeter Height-Finder [*RADAR*]
DMH	Department of Marine and Harbours [*South Australia, Western Australia*]
DMH	Department of Mental Health [*or Hygiene*]
DMH	Device Message Handler [*IBM Corp.*] (NITA)
DMH	Dextromethorphan [*Antitussive*] [*Pharmacy*]
DMH	Dimension House [*Vancouver Stock Exchange symbol*]
DMH	Dimethylhexane [*Organic chemistry*]
DMH	Dimethylhydrazine [*Rocket fuel base, convulsant poison*]
DMH	Direct Man-Hours
DMH	Donald Mitchell Healey [*Designer of Healey sports cars*] [*British*]
DMH	Drop Manhole [*Technical drawings*]
DMH	Dual Mode Hydrazine
DMHF	Dimethylhydantoin Formaldehyde [*Organic chemistry*]
DMHR	Daughters of the Most Holy Redeemer [*Roman Catholic religious order*]
DMHS	Director of Medical and Health Services [*British*]
DMI	Danish Meteorological Institute
DMI	Daughters of Mary Immaculate (Chaldean) (TOCD)
D/M/I	Decision/Making/Information [*Information service or system*] (IID)
DMI	Defense Material Item
DMI	Defense Mechanisms Inventory [*Psychology*]
DMI	Depot Maintenance Interservice
DMI	Design Management Institute (EA)
DMI	Desipramine [*Antidepressant*] (DAVI)
DMI	Desktop Management Interface [*Computer science*] (PCM)
DMI	Desmethylimipramine [*Antidepressant*]
DMI	Des Moines [*Iowa*] [*Seismograph station code, US Geological Survey Closed*] (SEIS)
DMI	Destratification Motor Impeller
DMI	Detroit, MI [*Location identifier FAA*] (FAAL)
DMI	Diagnostic Mathematics Inventory
DMI	Diagnostic Medical Instruments [*Commercial firm*] (DAVI)
DMI	Diamond Manufacturers and Importers Association of America
DMI	Diaphragmatic Myocardial Infarct [*Cardiology*] (MAE)
DMI	Digital Master Imager (DGA)
DMI	Digital Multiplexed Interface (HGAA)
DMI	Dimethylimidazolidinone [*Organic chemistry*]
DMI	Dimethyl Isosorbide [*Organic chemistry*]
DMI	Direct Material Inventory (DNAB)
DMI	Direct Memory Interface
DMI	Direct Memory Interface [*Computer science*] (NITA)
DMI	Director of Military Intelligence [*US, British*]
DMI	Distance Measuring Instrument
DMI	DiTomasso Methodology Inventory (EDAC)
DMI	DMI International Airlines [*Ukraine*] [*FAA designator*] (FAAC)
DMI	Dumagami Mines Ltd. [*Toronto Stock Exchange symbol*]
DMI	Dun's Market Identifiers [*Dun's Marketing Services*] [*Information service or system*] (CRD)
DMI	Dynamic Memory Interface [*Computer science*] (NITA)
DMIA	Dual Multiplexer Interface Adapter (NASA)
DMIAA	Diamond Manufacturers and Importers Association of America (EA)
DMIC	Defense Metals Information Center [*Later, MCIC*] [*Battelle Memorial Institute*] (MCD)
DMIC	Digital Microwave [*NASDAQ symbol*] (TTSB)
DMIC	Digital Microwave Corp. [*NASDAQ symbol*] (NQ)
DMIC	Direct Marketing Insurance Council [*New York, NY*] (EA)
D Mic	Doctor of Microbiology
DMID	Department of Manufacturing and Industry Development [*Victoria*] [*Australia*]
DMIDF	Depot Master Item Data File [*Army*]
D Mi E	Doctor of Mining Engineering
D Mi Eng	Doctor of Mining Engineering
DMIF	Depot Maintenance Industrial Fund (MCD)
DMIF	DMI Furniture [*NASDAQ symbol*] (TTSB)
DMIF	DMI Furniture, Inc. [*NASDAQ symbol*] (NQ)
DMIFCUS	Depot Maintenance Industrial Funding Customer (MCD)
DMI Frn	DMI Furniture, Inc. [*Associated Press*] (SAG)
DMII	Descriptive Method Item Identification [*DoD*]
DMIL	Demilitarization
DMIL/EOD	Demilitarization / Explosive Ordnance Demolition
D Mil S	Doctor of Military Science
DMil Sc	Doctorate of Military Science (DD)
DMIM	Double Mannitol Isolation Method [*Microscopy*]

DMIM............ Dual Mode Imbedded Munitions (MCD)
D/MIN........... Disintegrations per Minute
DMin............ Doctor of Ministry
DMIN............ United States Bureau of Marine Inspection and Navigation, Washington, DC [Library symbol Library of Congress Obsolete] (LCLS)
D Minn .... United States District Court for the District of Minnesota (DLA)
DMINS.......... Distributed Minicomputer Systems (AAGC)
DMINS.......... Dual Miniature Inertial Navigation Systems (MCD)
DMIP .... Defense Materiel Interservicing Program [DoD]
DMIP .... Democratic Malaysia Indian Party [Political party] (FEA)
DMIP .... Dimethyl Isophthalate [Organic chemistry]
DMIR........... Designated Manufacturing Inspection Representative (MCD)
DMIR........... Duluth, Missabe & Iron Range Railway Co. [AAR code]
DMIRR.......... Demand Mode Integral Rocket Ramjet (MCD)
DMIS........... Data Management Information System [DoD]
DMIS........... DATICO [Digital Automatic Tape Intelligence Checkout] Missile Interface Simulator
DMIS .... Defense Medical Information System (DOMA)
DMIS .... Director, Management Information Systems [Later, ADD] [Army] (AABC)
DMIS .... Distribution/Transportation Management Information System [Computer science] (PDAA)
DMIS .... Donnelley Marketing Information Services [Database producer] (IID)
DMISA.......... Depot Maintenance Interservice Support Agreement [Military]
D Miss .... Doctor of Missiology (PGP)
DMIU .... Destratification Motor Impeller Unit
DMJ............. Daughters of Mary and Joseph [Roman Catholic religious order]
DMJ............. Deus Meumque Jus [God and My Right] [Freemasonry] [Latin]
DMJ............. Diploma in Medical Jurisprudence [British]
DMJ (Clin)... Diploma in Medical Jurisprudence (Clinical) [British]
DMJM........... Daniel, Mann, Johnson, & Mendenhall [A major contributor to architecture in Jakarta, Sidney, Manila, and Seoul]
DMJO........... Defense Management Journal Office [DoD]
DMJP........... Door Mounted Junction Panel
DMJP........... Dragon Missile Jump Pack [Military] (MCD)
DMJ (Path).. Diploma in Medical Jurisprudence (Pathological) [British]
DMJS........... December, March, June, September [Denotes quarterly payments of interest or dividends in these months] [Business term]
DMJTC......... Differential Multi-Junction Thermal Converter (PDAA)
DMK............. Demirkoy [Turkey] [Seismograph station code, US Geological Survey] (SEIS)
DMK............. Dial Marking Kit
DMK............. Digital Equipment Corp., Merrimack, Merrimack, NH [OCLC symbol] (OCLC)
DMK............. Dimark, Inc. [Formerly, Mars Graphic Services, Inc.] [AMEX symbol] (SPSG)
DMK............. Dravida Munnetra Kazhagam [India] [Political party] (PPW)
DMKA .... Diabetes Mellitus Ketoacidosis [Endocrinology] (DAVI)
DML............. Data Management Language [Digital Equipment Corp.]
DML............. Data Manipulation Language [Digital Equipment Corp.] [Computer science]
DML............. Demolition
DML............. Depot Maintenance Level
DML............. Depot Maintenance Literature (MCD)
DML............. Describe Macro Language [Computer science]
DML............. Developmental Instrumentation Medium-Left
DML............. Developmental [Instrumentation] MDM [Manipulator Deployment Mech anism] Left
DML............. Diffuse Mixed Lymphoma [Oncology]
DML............. Digitized Message Link
DML............. Dimyristoyl-Lecithin [Biochemistry]
DML............. Direct Memory Line (IAA)
DML............. Dock Mounted Loader (RDA)
DML............. Doctor Martin Luther College, New Ulm, MN [OCLC symbol] (OCLC)
DML............. Doctor of Modern Languages
DML............. Double Mars Loiter
DML............. Dry Matter Loss
DML............. Dual Mode LASER
DML DY...... Demolition Duty (DNAB)
DMLF.......... Descending Medial Longitudinal Fasciculus
DMLIA .... Double-Modified Lysine Iron Agar [Microorganism medium]
DMLS.......... Doppler Microwave Landing System
DMLT.......... Diploma in Medical Laboratory Technology (ADA)
DMM............ [The] Dansville & Mount Morris Railroad Co. [AAR code]
DMM............ Dark Mantling Material [Lunar surface]
DMM............ Data Management Module [Aviation]
DMM............ Data Manipulation Mode
DMM............ Dayton and Montgomery County Public Library, Dayton, OH [OCLC symbol] (OCLC)
DMM............ Dedicated Man/Months [Jet Propulsion Laboratory, NASA]
DMM............ Defense Market Measures [Database on Department of Defense contracts] (NITA)
DMM............ Delta Ministry of Mississippi [Defunct] (EA)
dMM............ Deoxymannojirimycin [Biochemistry]
DMM............ Depleted MORB [Mid-Ocean Ridge Basalt] Mantle [Geology]
DMM............ Desmethylmetoxuron [Organic chemistry]
DMM............ Dia Met Minerals Ltd. [Vancouver Stock Exchange symbol]
DMM............ Dia Met Minerals Ltd. [AMEX symbol] (SAG)
DMM............ Digital Multimeter
dmm............ Digital Multimeter (IDOE)
DMM............ Digital Multiservice Module [Telecommunications]
DMM............ Dimethoxymethane [Organic chemistry]
DMM............ Dimethylmercury [Toxicology]
DMM............ Dimethylmyleran [Organic chemistry] (DAVI)

DMM............ Diploma in Manufacturing Management [British]
DMM............ Direct Mail Manager [Software package]
DMM............ Direct Memory Management [Computer science] (NITA)
DMM............ Direct Metal Mastering [System for manufacturing phonograph records]
DMM............ Directorate of Materiel Management (MCD)
DMM............ Director of Mechanical Maintenance [British military] (DMA)
DMM............ Doctor of Music Ministry (PGP)
DMM............ Domestic Mail Manual [US Postal Service] [A publication]
DMM............ Dulbecco's Modified Eagle's Medium [Also, DME, DMEM] [Medium for cell growth]
DMMA .... Dimethylmuconic Acid [Organic chemistry]
DMMA .... Direct Mail/Marketing Association (EA)
DMM & SA... Depot Materiel Maintenance and Support Activities [Army]
DMMB .... Defense Medical Material Board (AFM)
DMMC .... Digital Multimeter Control
DMMC .... Division Materiel Management Center [Military] (AABC)
DMMC .... DM Management [NASDAQ symbol] (TTSB)
DMMC .... DM Management Co. [NASDAQ symbol] (SAG)
DMMCS .... Dimethylmonochlorosilane [Organic chemistry]
DMMEF....... Direct Mail/Marketing Educational Foundation (EA)
DMMF......... Dry and Mineral Matter Free [Coal]
DMMG......... Displacement Method Matrix Generator
DM Mgt ...... DM Management Co. [Associated Press] (SAG)
DMMH/FH... Direct Maintenance Man-Hours per Flight Hour [Navy] (NG)
DMMH/MA... Direct Maintenance Man-Hours per Maintenance Action
DMMH/ME ... Direct Maintenance Man-Hours per Maintenance Event
DMMIS .... Depot Maintenance Management Information System [Air Force] (GFGA)
DMMM........ Direct Maintenance Man-Minutes (MCD)
DMMnom..... Development Manmouths Nominal
DMMO........ Direct Marketing Minorities Opportunities [Defunct] (EA)
DMMP........ Dimethyl Methylphosphonate [Organic chemistry]
DMMP........ Direct Marketing Market Place [A publication]
DMMS........ Depot Maintenance Management Subsystem (DNAB)
DMMU........ Discrete Main Memory Unit [Computer bus]
DMN........... Data Model Normalizer [Computer science]
DMN........... Data Multiplexing Network [FAA] (TAG)
DMN........... Defective Material Notice (KSC)
DMN........... Deming, NM [Location identifier FAA] (FAAL)
DMN........... Differential-Mode Noise [Electronics] (IAA)
DMN........... Dimension (AABC)
DMN........... Dimethylnaphthalene [Organic chemistry]
DMN........... Dimethylnitrosamine [Also, DMNA, NDMA] [Organic chemistry]
DMN........... Dimethylnaphthidine [An indicator] [Chemistry]
DMN........... Dimon, Inc. [NYSE symbol] (SAG)
DMn........... Dissolved Manganese [Chemistry]
DMN........... Dominion Explorers, Inc. [Toronto Stock Exchange symbol]
DMN........... Dominion Explorers, Inc. [Vancouver Stock Exchange symbol]
DMN........... Dorsal Motor Nucleus [of the vagus]
DMN........... Dorsomedial Nucleus [Brain anatomy]
DMNA......... Dimethylnitrosamine [Also, DMN, NDMA] [Organic chemistry]
DMNA......... Distributed Microcomputer Network for Avionics (MCD)
DMND......... Diamon
DMNFA....... Daily Mail National Film Award [British]
DMNI .... Device Multiplexing Nonsynchronized Inputs [Computer science]
DMNO......... Device Multiplexing Nonsynchronized Outputs [Computer science] (CET)
DMNPAA..... Dimethyl(nitrophenylazo)anisole [Organic chemistry]
DMNRLZR.... Demineralizer
DMNSTR...... Demonstrator (IAA)
DMNT .... Dominant (FAAC)
DMO .... Data Management Office [or Officer] [Air Force] (AFM)
DMO .... Decision Making Organizer [Test]
DMO .... Defense Mobilization Order
DMO .... Demineralized Oil [Petroleum Refining]
DMO .... Dental Maintenance Organization
DMO .... Dependent Meteorological Office
DMO .... Dimethadone [Pharmacology] (DAVI)
DMO .... Dimethyloxazolidinedione [Pharmacology]
DMO .... Diode Microwave Oscillator
DMO .... Directed Military Overstrength (GFGA)
DMO .... Director Meteorological Officer, Ministry of Defence, London [British] (NATG)
DMO .... Director of Manpower and Organization [Air Force]
DMO .... Director of Maritime Operations [RAF] [British]
DMO .... Director [or Directorate] of Military Operations
DMO .... Directory of Mortuary Operations [Army] (AABC)
DMO .... District Management Office
DMO .... District Marine Officer [Navy]
DMO .... District Material Officer [Navy]
DMO .... District Medical Officer [Navy]
DMO .... Divisional Medical Officer [British]
DMO .... Documentation Management Officer [Air Force] (AFM)
DMO .... Domodedovo Civil Air Production Association [Former USSR] [FAA designator] (FAAC)
DMO .... Sedalia [Missouri] [Airport symbol Obsolete] (OAG)
DMOB......... Defensive Missile Order of Battle (MCD)
DMOC......... Diabetes Mellitus Out of Control [Medicine] (MEDA)
DMOC......... Distinguished Members of the Corps [Army]
DMOD......... Delta Modulation (NITA)
DMOD......... Dimethyloctadiene [Organic chemistry]
DMOI .... Director of Military Operations and Intelligence
DMON.......... Discrete Monitoring (MCD)

DMon............	Montessori School, Washington, DC [*Library symbol Library of Congress*] (LCLS)
D Mont	United States District Court for the District of Montana (DLA)
DMOOC........	Diabetes Mellitus Out of Control [*Medicine*] (DMAA)
DMOR...........	Distinguished Member of the Regiment
DMOS	Data Management Operating System
DMOS	Depletion Metal-Oxide Semiconductor (BUR)
DMOS	Diffusion Metal-Oxide Semiconductor [*Telecommunications*] (TEL)
DMOS	Diffusive Mixing of Organic Solutions [*Materials processing*]
DMOS	Discrete Metal-Oxide Semiconductor (HGAA)
DMOS	Double-Diffused Metal-Oxide Semiconductor [*Microelectronics*] (MCD)
DMOS	Duty Military Occupational Specialty
DMOS	Dynamic Model Operations Section
DMOS(N)	Director of Meteorological and Oceanographical Services (Naval) [*British*]
DMOST	Double-Diffused Medal Oxide Semiconductor Technology [*Microelectronics*] (PDAA)
DMOT	Dimethyloctatriene [*Organic chemistry*]
DMP............	Data Management Plan [*Jet Propulsion Laboratory, NASA*]
DMP............	Data Management Program
DMP............	Defecation Motor Program [*Physiology*]
DMP............	Defense Manpower Policy
DMP............	Defense Materials Procurement Agency [*Abolished 1953, functions transferred to General Services Administration*] (DLA)
DMP............	Delayed Merge Package (MCD)
DMP............	Demokratik Merkez Partisi [*Democratic Centre Party*] [*Turkey Political party*] (EY)
DMP............	Demokratik Mucadele Partisi [*Democratic Struggle Party*] [*Turkish Cyprus*] [*Political party*] (EY)
DMP............	De Mortibus Persecutorum (BJA)
DMP............	Deployable Maintenance Platform (MCD)
DMP............	Dermatopathology [*Medical specialty*] (DHSM)
DMP............	DEU [*Display Electronics Unit*] Message Processor (NASA)
DMP............	Deutsche Mittelstandspartei [*German Middle Class Party*] (PPW)
DMP............	Digital Map Processor
DMP............	Dimercaptopropanol [*Also, BAL: British Anti-Lewisite*] [*Detoxicant*] [*Organic chemistry*]
DMP............	Dimethoxypropane [*Organic chemistry*]
DMP............	Dimethylphenol [*Organic chemistry*]
DMP............	Dimethyl Phthalate [*Organic chemistry*]
DMP............	Dimethylpiperazine [*Also, DMPP*] [*Organic chemistry*]
DMP............	Dimethylpropanediol [*Organic chemistry*]
DMP............	Dimethyl Pyrocarbonate [*Organic chemistry*]
DMP............	Dimethylpyrrole [*Organic chemistry*]
DMP............	Diploma in Medical Psychology (ADA)
DMP............	Direct Maximum Principle (IAA)
DMP............	Direct Memory Processor
DMP............	Director of Manpower Planning [*British*]
DMP............	Director of Military Personnel [*Air Force*]
DMP............	Disarmed Military Personnel
DMP............	Display Maintenance Program
DMP............	Display Makeup (IAA)
DMP............	Documented Material Processed
DMP............	Dorsal Median Pallium [*Neuroanatomy*]
dMP............	Dorsal Midline Precursor [*Neuroanatomy*]
DMP............	Dump [*Computer science*]
DMP............	Pathfinder Regional Library Service System, Montrose, CO [*OCLC symbol*] (OCLC)
DMPA	Defense Materials Procurement Agency [*Abolished 1953, functions transferred to General Services Administration*]
DMPA	Depomedroxyprogesterone Acetate [*Contraceptive*]
DMPA	(Dichlorophenyl) Methyl Isopropylphosphoramidothioate [*Herbicide*]
DMPA	Dimethoxyphenylacetophenone [*Organic chemistry*]
DMPA	Dimethylolpropionic Acid [*Organic chemistry*]
DMPA	Dimyristoyl Phosphatidic Acid [*Biochemistry*]
DMPA	Direct Mail Producers Association [*British*] (DBA)
DMPA	Distal Main Pulmonary Artery [*Anatomy*]
DMPC	Dimethylaminopropyl Chloride [*Organic chemistry*]
DMPC	Dimyristoyl Phosphatidylcholine [*Biochemistry*]
DMPD	Defense Medical Purchase Description [*Defense Supply Agency*]
DMPD	Dimethylphenylenediamine [*Organic chemistry*]
DMPD	Director of Dockyard Manpower and Productivity [*Navy British*]
DMPDT	Dimethylphosphorodithioate [*Organic chemistry*]
DMPE	Depot Maintenance Plant Equipment (MCD)
DMPE	(Dimethoxyphenyl)ethylamine [*Also, DIMPEA, DMPEA*] [*Psychomimetic compound*]
DMPE	Dimyristoyl Phosphatidylethanolamine
DMPEA	(Dimethoxyphenyl)ethylamine [*Also, DIMPEA, DMPE*] [*Psychomimetic compound*]
DMPG	Dimyristoylphosphatidylglycerol [*Biochemistry*]
DMPG	Dumping (MSA)
DMPI	Desired Mean Point of Impact [*Military*]
DMPI	Dimyristoyl Phosphatidylinositol
DMPIA	Dimethoxyphenylisopropylamine [*Organic chemistry*]
DMPK	Dystrophia Myotonica Protein Kinase [*An enzyme*]
DMPL	Digital Microprocessor Plotter Language (CDE)
DMPO	Data Management Policy Office [*Army*]
DMPO	Dimethylpyrrolineoxide [*Organic chemistry*]
DMPP	Dimethyl(phenyl)piperazinium [*Organic chemistry*]
DMPP	Dimethylpiperazine [*Also, DMP*] [*Organic chemistry*]
DMPP	Display and Multi-Purpose Processor [*Computer science*]
DMPPD	Dimethyl-para-phenylenediamine [*Organic chemistry*]
DMPR	Damper (KSC)
DMPR	Depot Maintenance Production Report
DMPRL	Defense Master Priority Requirements List
DMPS	Deepwater Motion Picture System
DMPS	Dimercaptopropanesulfonate [*Salt*] [*Organic chemistry*]
DMPS	Dimethylpolysiloxane [*Organic chemistry*]
DMPU	Dimethylolpropyleneurea [*Organic chemistry*]
DMQ	Dimethylquinoline [*Organic chemistry*]
DMQ	Direct Memory Queue [*Computer science*]
DMQ	Director of Movements and Quartering [*British*]
DMQ	Dominco Industry Corp. [*Vancouver Stock Exchange symbol*]
DMQR	Douglas Material Qualification Report [*DAC*]
DMR	DAC Maintainability Representative (MCD)
DMR	Daily Market Report [*Coffee, Sugar, and Cocoa Exchange*] [*A publication*]
DMR	Daily Mechanical Report
DMR	Data Management Routine
DMR	Date Material Required
DMR	Defective Materiel Report [*Air Force*]
DMR	Defense Management Report [*DoD*]
DMR	Defense Management Review [*Army*] (RDA)
DMR	Demultiplexing/Mixing/Remultiplexing [*Device*] [*Telecommunications*] (TEL)
DMR	Departmental Materiel Requisition
DMR	Department of Mineral Resources [*New South Wales*] [*Australia*]
DMR	Deutsche Motorrad Register [*German Motorcycle Register*] [*Defunct*] (EA)
DMR	Developmental Instrumentation Medium-Right (NASA)
DMR	Diagnostic Reading Scales [*Diagnostic assessment test*] (PAZ)
DMR	Differential Microwave Radiometer [*Cosmic Background Explorer*] [*NASA*]
DMR	Digital Equipment Corp., Marlboro, Marlboro, MA [*OCLC symbol*] (OCLC)
DMR	Digital Meter Reader (IAA)
DMR	Digital Mobilized Radio (BARN)
DMR	Dimmer (MSA)
DMR	Diploma in Medical Radiology [*British*]
DMR	Diploma in Medical Rehabilitation
DMR	Direct Magnification Radiography
DMR	Direct Metal Reaction [*Soap making*]
DMR	Directorate of Medical Research [*Army*]
DMR	Director of Materiel Readiness [*Army*]
DMR	Discharge Monitoring Report [*Environmental Protection Agency*] (EG)
DMR	Distributed Message Router (NITA)
DMR	Distributor-Manufacturer-Representative
DMR	Division of Materials Research [*National Science Foundation*]
DMR	Downy Mildew Resistant (GNE)
DMR	Drummer [*Military British*]
DMR	Dual Mode Recognizer (MCD)
DMR	Dynamic Module Replacement
DMRA	DSA [*Defense Supply Agency*] Central Regional Audit Office
DMRC	Dynamic Mid-Ride Controls [*Truck seating*]
DMRD	Davy McKee Research & Development [*British*] (IRUK)
DMRD	Defense Management Review Decision [*Army*] (RDA)
DMRD	Defense Management Review Directive (AAGC)
DMRD	Diploma in Medical Radio-Diagnosis [*British*]
DMRE	Diploma in Medical Radiology and Electrology [*British*]
DMRE	Division of Medical Radiation Exposure [*Bureau of Radiological Health*]
DMRF	Dystonia Medical Research Foundation (EA)
DMRI	Data Material Required, Increasing Urgency [*Navy*] (NG)
DMRI	Dynamic Magnetic Resonant Imaging [*Medicine*]
DMRIS	Defense Medical Regulating Information System (DOMA)
DMRK	Damark International'A' [*NASDAQ symbol*] (TTSB)
DMRK	Damark International, Inc. [*NASDAQ symbol*] (SAG)
DMRL	Decreasing Mean Residual Life
DMRLS	Data Management and Research Liaison Staff [*Environmental Protection Agency*] (GFGA)
DMR(N)	Director of Materials Research (Naval) [*British*]
DMRP	Dredged Material Research Program [*Waterways Experiment Station*] [*Army*] (RDA)
DMRR	Defense Manpower Requirements Report (DNAB)
DMRS	Data Management and Retrieval System
DMRsBW	Dominion Resources Black Warrior Trust [*Associated Press*] (SAG)
DMRsEW	Dominion Resources Black Warrior Trust [*Associated Press*] (SAG)
DMRT	Diploma in Medical Radio-Therapy [*British*]
DmS............	Dakota Microfilm Service, Inc., Denver, CO [*Library symbol Library of Congress*] (LCLS)
DMS............	Database Management System [*Computer science*]
DMS............	Data Management Service (IEEE)
DMS............	Data Management System [*Computer science*]
DMS............	Data Measuring System
DMS............	Data Monitoring System
DMS............	Data Multiplex System [*Computer science*]
DMS............	Decision Making System
DMS............	Defense Management Simulation (OA)
DMS............	Defense Management System (NATG)
DMS............	Defense Mapping School [*Army*] (AABC)
DMS............	Defense Marketing Survey (MCD)
DMS............	Defense Materials Service [*of GSA*]
DMS............	Defense Materials System
DMS............	Defense Messaging System (DOMA)
DMS............	Defense Missile Systems (KSC)
DMS............	Delayed Matching-to-Sample [*Psychology*]
DMS............	Delayed Muscle Soreness
DMS............	Delta Milliohm Sensor
DMS............	Delta Modulation System

DMS............	Demarcation Membrane System [*Medicine*] (DMAA)	
DMS Sc........	Denominational Ministry Strategy [*Later, CSM*] (EA)	
DMS............	Dense Media Separation (PDAA)	
DMS............	Dense Medium Separating [*Chemical engineering*]	
DMS............	Density Manipulation Subsystem (MCD)	
DMS............	Departmental Management System [*Department of Labor*]	
DMS............	Depot Maintenance Service (AFIT)	
DMS............	Depot Maintenance Study [*Army*]	
DMS............	Depot Maintenance Support (AAG)	
DMS............	Deputy Military Secretary [*British*]	
DMS............	Dermatomyositis [*Medicine*]	
DMS............	[*The*] Designer Menswear Show [*British*] (ITD)	
DMS............	Desktop Management Suite [*Computer science*]	
DMS............	Desktop Mapping System	
DMS............	Destroyer Minesweeper [*Navy symbol Obsolete*]	
DMS............	Development Management System [*IBM Corp.*]	
DMS............	Deviation from Mean Standard (MUGU)	
DMS............	Diagnostic Medical Sonographer (DAVI)	
DMS............	Diagnostic Methodology Section [*National Institute of Dental Research*]	
DMS............	Diagonostic Medical Sonographer (HCT)	
DMS............	Difference of Messing Subscription [*British military*] (DMA)	
DMS............	Differential Maneuvering Simulator [*Aviation*]	
DMS............	Differential Multiple Simulator (MCD)	
DMS............	Digital Matrix Switch (MCD)	
DMS............	Digital Microsystems [*Digital Microsystems Ltd.*] [*Software package*] (NCC)	
DMS............	Digital Motion System	
DMS............	Digital Multiplexing Synchronizer [*Computer science*]	
DMS............	Digital Multiplex Switch [*Trademark of Northern Telecom Ltd.*]	
DMS............	Diis Manibus Sacrum [*Sacred to the Manes, i.e., Departed Souls*] [*Latin*]	
DMS............	Dimercaptosuccinic Acid [*Organic chemistry*]	
DMS............	Dimethyl Silicone [*Organic chemistry*]	
DMS............	Dimethylstilbestrol [*Biochemistry*]	
DMS............	Dimethylsuberimidate [*Organic chemistry*]	
DMS............	Dimethyl Sulfide [*Organic chemistry*]	
DMS............	Dimethyl Sulfoxide [*Also, DMSO*] [*Organic chemistry*]	
DMS............	Diminishing Manufacturing Service (MCD)	
DMS............	Diminishing Manufacturing Sources	
DMS............	Diploma in Management Studies [*British*]	
DMS............	Direct Match Screening	
DMS............	Direct Molded Sole [*Boot*] [*Military*]	
DMS............	Directorate of Microgram Services [*RAF*] [*British*]	
DMS............	Director for Mutual Security	
DMS............	Director of Medical Services [*British*]	
DMS............	Discrete Memoryless Source [*Computer science*] (HGAA)	
DMS............	Disk Monitor System [*Computer science*]	
DMS............	Display Management System [*IBM Corp.*]	
DMS............	Distance Measuring System	
DMS............	Distinguished Military Students	
DMS............	Distributed Maintenance Services (NITA)	
DMS............	Distributed Models and Simulation [*Army*]	
DMS............	Distributed Monitoring System (ACII)	
DMS............	Distributor Modulator System [*Automotive engineering*]	
DMS............	Docking Mechanism System [*or Subsystem*] [*NASA*] (NASA)	
DMS............	Docking Module Subsystem (MCD)	
DMS............	Doctor in Missionology	
DMS............	Doctor of Mechanical Science	
DMS............	Doctor of Medical Science [*or Sciences*]	
DMS............	Doctor of Military Science	
DMS............	Documentary Management System [*for citations*]	
DMS............	Documentation of Molecular Spectroscopy	
DMS............	Document Management Software [*Computer science*]	
DMS............	Document Management System	
DMS............	Domini Sportswear [*Vancouver Stock Exchange symbol*]	
DMS............	Doppler Measurement System	
DMS............	Dragon [*Missile*] Maintenance Set [*Military*]	
DMS............	Drilling Mud Surfactant (BARN)	
DMS............	Drone Maintenance Squadron	
DMS............	Drum Memory System [*Computer science*]	
DMS............	Dual Maneuvering Simulator (MCD)	
DMS............	Dual Mechanical Seal [*Engineering*]	
DMS............	Dun's Marketing Services [*Dun & Bradstreet, Inc.*] [*Parsippany, NJ*] [*Information service or system*] (IID)	
DMS............	Dynamic Mapping System [*Hewlett-Packard Co.*]	
DMS............	Dynamic Missile Simulator	
DMS............	Dynamic Modelling System (AIE)	
DMS............	Dynamic Motion Simulator (MCD)	
DMS............	Dynamo Management System (AAG)	
DMS............	High-Speed Minesweeper [*Navy symbol Obsolete*]	
DMSA.........	Defense Medical Activity SL (USGC)	
DMSA.........	Defense Medical Support Activity (DOMA)	
DMSA.........	Dimercaptosuccinic Acid [*Organic chemistry*]	
DMSA.........	Diploma in Medical Services Administration [*British*]	
DMSA.........	Illustrator Draftsman, Seaman Apprentice [*Navy rating*]	
DMSAFIF.....	Depot Maintenance Service Air Force Industrial Fund (AFIT)	
DMSC.........	Defence Material Standardization Committee [*British military*] (DMA)	
DMSC.........	Defense Medical Supply Center [*Later, Defense Personnel Support Center*]	
DMSC.........	Direct Simulation Monte Carlo Technique [*Statistics*]	
DMSC.........	Disinfected Mail Study Circle (EA)	
DM Sc	Doctor of Medical Science	
DMSc..........	Doctor of Missionary Science	
DMSCC.......	Direct Microscopic Somatic Cell Count (OA)	

DMS/CS	Data Management System/Computer Subsystem [*Computer science*]
DMSD	Digital Multistandard Decoding [*Computer science*]
DMSDS	Direct Mail Shelter Development System [*Civil Defense*]
DMSE	Direct Mission Support Equipment (MCD)
DMSELC	Diatomic Molecule Spectra and Energy Levels Center
DMSes	Document-Management Systems
DMSH	Diminish (FAAC)
DMS-HZ	Dimethyl Sulfate-Hydrazine [*Organic chemistry*]
dmsk..........	Damask (VRA)
DMSL..........	Descriptive Macro Simulation Language [*Computer science*] (PDAA)
DMSLT........	Daytime Multiple Sleep Latency Test [*Neurology*] (DAVI)
DMSM	Defense Manpower Static Model
DMSM	Defense Meritorious Service Medal [*Military decoration*]
DMSM	Diminishing Manufacturing Sources and Material Shortages (MCD)
DMSMART ...	Dredged Material Spatial Management Analysis Resolution Tool [*U.S. Army Corps of Engineers*]
DMS/MS	Diminishing Manufacturing Sources/Material Shortages (MCD)
DMS(N).......	Director of Marine Services (Naval) [*British*]
DMSN	Illustrator Draftsman, Seaman [*Navy rating*]
DmS-O........	Dakota Microfilm Service, Inc., Orlando, FL [*Library symbol Library of Congress*] (LCLS)
DMSO	Defense Materials Systems Office
DMSO	Defense Modeling and Simulation Office [*Military*]
DMSO	Dimethyl Sulfoxide [*Also, DMS*] [*Organic chemistry*]
DMSO	Director Major Staff Office (MCD)
DMSOG.......	Diploma in Medicine, Surgery, Obstetrics and Gynecology
DMSP	Data Management Summary Processor (KSC)
DMSP	Defense Meteorological Satellite Program [*Formerly, DAPP*] [*Air Force*]
DMSP	Depot Maintenance Support Plan [*Air Force*] (AFM)
DMSP	Dichroic Microspectrophotometer
DMSP	Dimethylsulfoniopropionate [*Organic chemistry*]
DMSP	Dimethyl Sulfoniopropionate [*Organic chemistry*]
DMSP	Dragon Missile Special Jump Pack [*Military*] (MCD)
DMSPSM	Data Management System Problem Specification Model [*Air Force*]
DMSQ	Duty Military Occupational Specialty Qualified [*Army*] (DOMA)
DMSR	Director of Missile Safety Research [*Air Force*]
DMSR	Director of Mission Safety Research [*Air Force*]
DMSRD.......	Directorate of Materials and Structures Research and Development [*British*]
DMSS	Data Management System Simulator [*NASA*] (NASA)
DMSS	Data Multiplex Subsystem [*Computer science*]
DMSS	Defense Meteorological Satellite System [*Air Force*]
DMSS	Digital Multibeam Steering System
DMSS	Directorate of Military Satellite Systems (AAG)
DMSS	Director of Medical and Sanitary Services [*British*]
DMSSB	Defense Material Specifications and Standards Board (DNAB)
DMSSB	Direct Mail Services Standards Board [*British*]
DMSSC	Defense Medical Systems Support Center [*DoD*] (GFGA)
DmS-SP	Dakota Microfilm Service, Inc., Saint Paul, MN [*Library symbol Library of Congress*] (LCLS)
DMST.........	Demonstrate (AFM)
DMSTN	Demonstration (AFM)
DMSU	Digital Main Network Switching Unit (NITA)
DMT...........	Air Dan [*Nigeria*] [*FAA designator*] (FAAC)
DMT...........	Daily Metabolic Turnover (SAA)
DMT...........	Deep Mobile Target
DMT...........	Defense Mechanism Test [*Psychometrics*]
DMT...........	Demountable [*Technical drawings*]
DMT...........	Demycinosyltylosin [*Antibacterial*]
DMT...........	Detailed Maneuver Table
DMT...........	Diamantina [*Brazil*] [*Airport symbol*] (AD)
DMT...........	Dictaphone Machine Transcriber
DMT...........	Digital Message Terminal (MCD)
DMT...........	Dimensional Motion Time
dmt	Dimethoxytrityl [*As substituent on nucleoside*] [*Biochemistry*]
DMT...........	Dimethoxytryptamine [*Possible central nervous system neuroregulator*]
DMT...........	Dimethyl Terephthalate [*Organic chemistry*]
DMT...........	Dimethyltryptamine [*Hallucinogenic agent*]
DMT...........	Direct Memory Transfer [*Computer science*]
DMT...........	Direct Modulation Technique
DMT...........	Director of Machine Tools [*Ministry of Aircraft Production and Ministry of Supply*] [*British*]
DMT...........	Director of Military Training
DMT...........	Disk Operating System - Module Tester [*Computer science*] (IAA)
DMT...........	Dismounted Marksmanship Test [*Military*] (INF)
DMT...........	Dispersive Mechanism Test (NRCH)
DMT...........	Doctor of Medical Technology
DMT...........	Dorsal Median Tract [*Anatomy*]
DMT...........	Dual Mode Tracker (MCD)
DMT...........	Dynamic Mechanical Testing
DMTA.........	Dynamic Mechanical Thermal Analysis
DMTB.........	Deployment Mobilization Troop Basis (AABC)
DMTC.........	Digital Magnetic Tape Controller (CAAL)
DMTC.........	Digital Message Terminal Computer (IEEE)
DMTCNQ....	Dimethyl(Tetracyano)Quinodimethane
DMTD.........	Dimercaptothiadiazole [*Organic chemistry*]
DMTF.........	Desktop Management Task Force (PCM)
DMTF.........	Diffraction Limited Modulation Transfer Function (MCD)
DMTI..........	Digitized Moving Target Indicator (CET)
DMTI..........	Doppler Moving Target Indicator (IAA)
DMTIK	Dimethyl Terephthalate [*Organic chemistry*] (NUCP)
DMTM........	Detailed Monthly Trade Monitor [*Database*] [*Data Resources, Inc.*] [*Information service or system*] (CRD)

DMTPS	Digital Magnetic Tape Plotting System
DMTR	Dounreay Materials Testing Reactor [*British*]
DMTS..........	Delayed Matching to Sample [*Psychology*]
DMTS... ..	Department of Mines and Technical Survey [*Canada*]
DMTS... ..	Digital Magnetic Tape System (CAAL)
DMTS..........	Digital Module Test Set
DMTS..........	Dimethyl Trisulfide [*Organic chemistry*]
DMTS..........	Dynamic Multi-Tasking System (DNAB)
DMTSF.........	Dimethyl(methylthio)sulfonium Fluoroborate [*Organic chemistry*]
DMTT	Dimethyltetrahydrothiadiazinethione [*Pesticide*] [*Organic chemistry*]
DMTU	Digital Magnetic Tape Controller Unit
DMTU	Digital Magnetic Tape Unit (MCD)
DMTU	Dimethylthiourea [*Organic chemistry*]
DMTU	Dual Modular Magnetic Tape Unit (CAAL)
DMTZR	Demagnetizer
DMU	Data Management Unit [*Computer science*]
DMU	Data Measurement Unit (SAA)
DMU	Decision-Making Unit (WDMC)
DMU	Des Moines Union Railway Co. [*AAR code*]
DMU	Destratification Motor Unit
DMU	Device Mount Unit (MCD)
DMU	Diesel Multiple Unit
DMU	Digital Management Unit (MCD)
DMU	Digital Message Unit (MCD)
DMU	Digital Microfilm Unit (NITA)
DMU	Digital Monitor Unit
DMU	Digital Multiplexer Unit [*Electronics*] (ECII)
DMU	Dimapur [*India*] [*Airport symbol*] (OAG)
DMU	Dimethylolurea [*Organic chemistry*]
DMU	Dimethyluracil [*Biochemistry*]
DMU	Diploma in Medical Ultrasound
DMU	Directly Managed Unit [*Hospital administration*]
DMU	Distance-Measuring Unit (IAA)
DMU	Distributed Microprocessor Unit
DMU	Dual Maneuvering Unit [*A spacecraft*]
DMU	Dynamic Mockup
DMUP	Defense Materiel Utilization Program [*DoD*]
DMUS	Data Management Utility System
D Mus.........	Doctor of Music
D Mus A	Doctor of Musical Arts
DMusCantuar...	Archbishop of Canterbury's Doctorate in Music [*British*] (DBQ)
D Mus Ed	Doctor of Musical Education
DMusEd	Doctor of Music Education (GAGS)
DMUX	Demultiplexer [*Computer science*]
DMV..........	Dahlia Mosaic Virus [*Plant pathology*]
DMV..........	Daisy Mentor Valid (NITA)
DMV..........	Delay Multivibrator
DMV..........	Delta Multivibrator
DMV..........	Department of Motor Vehicles
DMV..........	Deserted Medieval Village [*British*]
DMV..........	Digital Message Voice [*Device*] (MCD)
DMV..........	Division of Motor Vehicles (MCD)
DMV..........	Doctorat en Medecin Veterinaire (DD)
DMV..........	Doctor of Veterinary Medicine (NADA)
DMV..........	Dolphin Morbillivirus
DMV..........	Dual-Mode Vehicle (PDAA)
DMV..........	Mount Vernon College, Washington, DC [*Library symbol Library of Congress*] (LCLS)
DMVC	Dayton-Miami Valley Library Consortium - Library Division [*Library network*]
DMVS	Desert Mobility Vehicle System [*Army*]
DMVS	Deutz Magnetic Valve System [*Diesel engines*]
DMW	Decimetric Wave [*Electromagnetism*] (IAA)
DMW	Demineralized Makeup Water [*Nuclear energy*] (NRCH)
DMW	Demineralized Water
DMW	Digital Milliwatt [*Telecommunications*] (TEL)
DMW	Dissimilar-Metal Weld
DMWG	Direct Marketing Writers Guild [*Later, DMCG*] (EA)
DMWP	Depot Maintenance Workload Plan (MCD)
DMWR	Depot Maintenance Work Request [*or Requirement*] [*Army*] (AABC)
DMWS	Direct Mineral Water Supply (ROG)
DMWV	Descendants of Mexican War Veterans [*An association*] (EA)
DMX..........	Data Multiplex [*Computer*]
DMX..........	Data Multiplexer (NITA)
DMX..........	Diathermy, Massage, and Exercise [*Physical therapy*] (DAVI)
DMX..........	Digital Musical Express (ECON)
DMX..........	Direct Memory Exchange
DMX Inc	DMX, Inc. [*Associated Press*] (SAG)
DM-XX	Douglas Missile - Model XX (MCD)
DMY..........	Dummy (KSC)
DMY..........	Merrill Lynch & Co. [*AMEX symbol*] (SAG)
DMZ..........	Declared Management Zone
DMZ..........	Demilitarized Zone
DMZ..........	Dorsal-Axial [*Embryology*]
DMZ..........	Drug Mending Zone [*Drug abuse center*]
DMZn.........	Dimethylzinc
Dn............	Daniel [*Old Testament book*]
DN	Data Name
DN	Data Net (MCD)
DN	Data Number
DN	Date Number
DN	Day and Night [*Approach and landing charts*] [*Aviation*]
D/N	Day-for-Night (WDMC)
DN	Day Number (SSD)
DN	Deacon (ROG)

DN	Debit Note [*Business term*]
DN	Decimal Number
dn	DeciNEM [*One-tenth of a NEM*] [*See NEM*]
dN	Decineper [*Physics*] (DEN)
DN	Decineper [*Reference unit*] (NITA)
DN	Deficiency Notice [*Government contracting*]
DN	DekaNEM [*Ten NEM*] [*See NEM*]
DN	Delayed Neutron
D/N	Delivery Note (ADA)
D/N	Demand Note [*Banking*]
DN	Democrazia Nazionale - Constituente di Destra [*National Democracy - Right Constituent*] [*Italy Political party*] (PPE)
Dn............	Denial [*Psychology*]
DN	Dentalman [*Nonrated enlisted man*] [*Navy*]
DN	Departmental Notice (AAG)
DN	Department of the Navy
DN	Descending Neuron [*Neurology*]
DN	Destra Nazionale [*National Right*] [*Italy Political party*] (PPE)
DN	Detail Networks (MCD)
D:N	Dextrose:Nitrogen Ratio
DN	Dialect Notes [*A publication*]
DN	Dibucaine Number [*Anesthesiology*]
DN	Dicrotic Notch [*Cardiology*]
DN	Dinitro-ortho-Cresol [*Also, DNOC*] [*Herbicide*]
DN	Diploma in Nursing
DN	Diploma in Nutrition [*British*]
DN	Direct Normalized [*Steel*]
DN	Directorate Notice (AAG)
DN	Directory Number [*Computer science*]
DN	Discrepancy Notice [*NASA*] (NASA)
D/N	Dispatch Note [*Shipping*]
DN	Disposition Pennant [*Navy British*]
DN	District Nurse [*British*]
DN	Divine Name (BJA)
DN	Division Notice (AAG)
DN	Doctor of Nursing
DN	Document Number (NITA)
Dn............	Dolphin [*Mooring post*] [*British*]
DN	Domino Nostro [*Our Lord*] [*Latin*]
DN	Dominus [*The Lord*] [*Latin*]
DN	Dominus Noster [*Our Lord*] [*Latin*]
DN	Dore-Norbaska Resources, Inc. [*Toronto Stock Exchange symbol*]
DN	Dorsal Nerve [*Anatomy*]
DN	Double Negation [*Rule of replacement*] [*Logic*]
DN	Down
dn	Down (WDMC)
DN	Dozen (ROG)
Dn............	Dragoon [*British military*] (DMA)
DN	Dublin [*City and county in Ireland*] (ROG)
DN	Duke of Northumberland [*British*] (ROG)
DN	Dun (WGA)
DN	Duplicate Negative (MCD)
Dn............	Kongelige Bibliotek [*Royal Library*], Kobenhavn, Denmark [*Library symbol Library of Congress*] (LCLS)
DN	Skystream Airlines [*ICAO designator*] (AD)
DN	United States Department of the Navy, Department Library, Washington, DC [*Library symbol Library of Congress*] (LCLS)
DNA	Aerodespachos de El Salvador [*ICAO designator*] (FAAC)
DNA	Dance Network Australia
DNA	Data Network Architecture (IAA)
DNA	Defense Nuclear Agency [*DoD Washington, DC*]
DNA	Del Norske Arbeiderparti [*Norwegian Labor Party*] (BARN)
DNA	Delta Nu Alpha Transportation Fraternity (EA)
DNA	Deoxyribonucleic Acid [*Biochemistry, genetics*]
DNA	Deputy for Nuclear Affairs (NATG)
DNA	Dermatology Nurses' Association (EA)
DNA	Designated National Agency [*for exchange of oceanographic data*] (MSC)
DNA	Det Norske Arbeiderparti [*Norwegian Labor Party*] (PPE)
DNA	Deutscher Normenausschuss [*German Standards Committee*] [*Later, DIN*] (EG)
DNA	Diana Corp. [*NYSE symbol*] (SPSG)
DNA	Did Not Arrive [*For no-show hotel reservation*]
DNA	Did Not Attend
DNA	Digital Network Architecture [*Digital Equipment Corp.*] [*Computer science*]
DNA	DIMUS [*Digital Multibeam Steering*] Narrow-Band Accelerated (NVT)
DNA	Director of Naval Accounts [*Obsolete British*]
DNA	Disposal Notification Area [*Community Land Act*] [*British*] (DI)
DNA	Distributed Network Architecture (IAA)
DNA	District Nursing Association [*British*] (DBA)
DNA	DNA Plant Technology Corp. [*Associated Press*] (SAG)
D Na	Doctor of Navigation
DNA	Does Not Answer [*Telephone operator's designation*]
DNA	Does Not Apply (MSA)
Dna...........	Dona [*Mrs.*] [*Spanish*] (BARN)
DNA	Dynamar Energy Ltd. [*Toronto Stock Exchange symbol*]
DNA	United States National Archives and Records Service, National Archives Library, Washington, DC [*Library symbol Library of Congress*] (LCLS)
DNAA	Abuja/International [*Nigeria*] [*ICAO location identifier*] (ICLI)
DNAA	Delayed Neutron Activation Analysis (PDAA)
DNA-AEC....	Defense Nuclear Agency-Atomic Energy Commission (DNAB)
DNAase........	Deoxyribonuclease [*Preferred form, DNase*] [*An enzyme*]
DNACC........	Defense National Agency Check Center [*DoD*]

DNAD..........	Director of Naval Air Division
DNADA........	Division of Narcotic Addiction and Drug Abuse [*National Institute of Mental Health*]
DNAE..........	Dissemination Network for Adult Educators (EDAC)
DN-Aer........	United States Department of the Navy, Naval Air Systems Command, Arlington, VA [*Library symbol Library of Congress*] (LCLS)
DNAG..........	Decade of North American Geology [*Geological Society of America*]
DNAL..........	United States National Agricultural Library, Beltsville, MD [*Library symbol Library of Congress*] (LCLS)
DNAM..........	Data Network Access Method
DNAME........	Department of Naval Architecture and Marine Engineering [*MIT*] (MCD)
DNAO..........	Director of Naval Air Organization [*British*]
DNA-P..........	Deoxyribonucleic Acid-Phosphorus [*Biochemistry*] (DAVI)
DNAp..........	Deoxyribonucleic Acid Polymerase [*An enzyme*]
DNAP..........	(Dinitrophenylazo)phenol [*Organic chemistry*]
DNAP..........	Directorate of Naval Administration Planning [*British*]
DNAP..........	DNA [*Deoxyribonucleic Acid*] Affinity Precipitation [*Analytical biochemistry*]
DNAP..........	DNA Plant Technology [*NASDAQ symbol*] (TTSB)
DNAP..........	DNA Plant Technology Corp. [*NASDAQ symbol*] (NQ)
DNAPL........	Dense Non-Aqueous Phase Liquid [*Chemical engineering*]
DNA PI.......	DNA Plant Technology Corp. [*Associated Press*] (SAG)
DNAPP........	DNA Plant Tech $2.25 Cv Ex Pfd [*NASDAQ symbol*] (TTSB)
DNAR..........	Do Not Attempt Resuscitation [*Medicine*] (HCT)
DNAr..........	United States National Arboretum, Washington, DC [*Library symbol Library of Congress*] (LCLS)
DN Arch	Doctor of Naval Architecture
D Na S........	Doctor of Naval Science
DNASA........	United States National Aeronautics and Space Administration, Washington, DC [*Library symbol Library of Congress*] (LCLS)
DNASA-G	United States National Aeronautics and Space Administration, Goddard Space Flight Center, Greenbelt, MD [*Library symbol Library of Congress*] (LCLS)
D Na Sc.......	Doctor of Naval Science
DNase.........	Deoxyribonuclease [*An enzyme*]
DNAS-HRB...	National Academy of Sciences, Highway Research Board Library, Washington, DC [*Library symbol Library of Congress*] (LCLS)
DNAS-NAE ...	National Academy of Sciences, National Academy of Engineering Library, Washington, DC [*Library symbol Library of Congress*] (LCLS)
D Nat..........	Doctor of Naturopathy
DNA-TP.......	Defense Nuclear Agency Technical Publications [*DoD*]
DNAU..........	Digital Network Access Unit [*Bytex Corp.*]
DnAu..........	Statsbiblioteket i Arhus Universitetsbiblioteket [*State and Arhus University Library*], Arhus, Denmark [*Library symbol Library of Congress*] (LCLS)
DNAW..........	Directorate of Naval Air Warfare [*British*]
DNB	Dance Notation Bureau (EA)
DNB	Departure from Nucleate Boiling (NRCH)
DNB	Deutsche Nachrichtenburo [*German News Bureau*]
DNB	Did Not Bat [*Cricket*]
DNB	Dinitrobenzene [*Organic chemistry*]
DNB	Dinitrobenzidine [*Organic chemistry*]
DNB	Dinitrochlorobenzene [*Organic chemistry*] (DAVI)
DNB	Diplomate of the National Board of Medical Examiners (AAMN)
DNB	Distribution Number Bank
DNB	Dun & Bradstreet [*NYSE symbol*] (TTSB)
DNB	Dun & Bradstreet, Inc. [*NYSE symbol*] (SPSG)
DNB	Dunbar [*Australia Airport symbol Obsolete*] (OAG)
DNBA..........	Dinitrobenzoic Acid [*Organic chemistry*]
DNBA..........	Di-normal-butylamine [*Organic chemistry*]
DNBC..........	Dinitrobenzoyl Chloride [*Organic chemistry*]
DNBE..........	Benin [*Nigeria*] [*ICAO location identifier*] (ICLI)
DNBI..........	Bida [*Nigeria*] [*ICAO location identifier*] (ICLI)
DNBI..........	Disease and Nonbattle Injury [*Military*] (NVT)
DNBJ..........	Abuja [*Nigeria*] [*ICAO location identifier*] (ICLI)
DNBM..........	Di-normal-Butylmagnesium [*Organic chemistry*]
DNBP..........	Dinitrobutyphenol [*Biochemistry*] (DAVI)
DNBP..........	Dinitro-ortho-secondary-butylphenol [*Also, DNOSBP, DNSBP*] [*Herbicide*]
DNBPG.........	Dinitrobenzoylphenylglycine [*Biochemistry*]
DNBR..........	Departure from Nucleate Boiling Ratio (NRCH)
DNBS..........	Dinitrobenzenesulfonic [*Organic chemistry*]
DNBSC........	Dinitrobenzenesulfenyl Chloride [*Organic chemistry*]
DNC	Dance
DNC	Daon Centre Ltd. [*Partnership units*] [*Vancouver Stock Exchange symbol*]
DNC	Data Name Card
DNC	Day-Night Capability [*Aerospace*] (AAG)
DNC	Delayed Neutron Counting
DNC	Democratic National Committee (EA)
DNC	Department of the Navy Civilian (DNAB)
DNC	Did Not Come
DNC	Did Not Compete [*Yacht racing*] (IYR)
DNC	Dinitrocarbanilide [*Organic chemistry*]
DNC	Dinitrocellulose [*Organic chemistry*]
DNC	Direct Notice of Cancellation [*Insurance*]
DNC	Direct Numerical Control [*Automation method*] [*Computer science*]
DNC	Directorate of National Coordination (CINC)
DNC	Director of Naval Construction [*British*]
DNC	Director of Navy Communications
DNC	Disaster Nursing Chairman [*Red Cross*]
DNC	Distributed Numerical Control [*Computer science*] (ODBW)

DNC	Washington Cathedral, Washington, DC [*Library symbol Library of Congress*] (LCLS)
DNCA..........	Calabar [*Nigeria*] [*ICAO location identifier*] (ICLI)
DNCB..........	Dinitrochlorobenzene [*Organic chemistry*]
DNCC..........	Data Network Control Centre (NITA)
DNCCC........	Defense National Communications Control Center
DNCCC........	Directorate of Naval Command, Control and Communications
DNCCCS......	Defense National Communications Control Center System (IAA)
DNCD..........	National Society of Colonial Dames of America, Washington, DC [*Library symbol Library of Congress*] (LCLS)
DNCDCC	Democratic National Committee - Department of Constituent Coordination [*Defunct*] (EA)
DNCE..........	Directorate of Naval Communications Engineering
DNCG..........	Digital Null Command Generator
DNCIAWPRC...	Danish National Committee of the International Association on Water Pollution Research and Control (EAIO)
D/NCIG........	Day/Night Approach Computer Image Generator [*Aviation*]
DNCINST......	Director, Naval Communications Instruction
DNCNOTE	Director, Naval Communications Notice
DNCS	Day/Night Camera System (MCD)
DNCS	Distributed Network Control System
DNCSS........	Director, Navy Configuration Survival and Safety
DNCT..........	National Cable Television Association, Washington, DC [*Library symbol Library of Congress*] (LCLS)
DNCTL	Down Control (IAA)
DNCU..........	Data Net Control Unit (NVT)
DNCW..........	United States Catholic Conference, Washington, DC [*Library symbol Library of Congress*] (LCLS)
DNCWAD	Democratic National Committee - Women's Affairs Division [*Later, DNCWD*] (EA)
DNCWD........	Democratic National Committee - Women's Division [*Formerly, DNCWAD*] (EA)
DND	Danra Resources Ltd. [*Vancouver Stock Exchange symbol*]
DND	Demodulator Neon Driver
DND	Department of National Defence [*Canada*]
DND	Deutscher Nachrichten Dienst [*German News Service*] (BARN)
DND	Died a Natural Death
DND	Director of Navigation and Direction [*British military*] (DMA)
DND	Directory of Numerical Databases [*Database*] [*NASA Information service or system*] (CRD)
DND	Disqualification Not Discardable [*Yacht racing*] (IYR)
DND	Do Not Duplicate
DND	Dundee [*Scotland*] [*Airport symbol*] (OAG)
DND	Eldinder Aviation [*Sudan*] [*ICAO designator*] (FAAC)
D ND	United States District Court for the District of North Dakota (DLA)
DNDAR	Daughters of the American Revolution, Washington, DC [*Library symbol Library of Congress*] (LCLS)
DNDFT........	Downdraft
DNDS..........	Dinitrodiphenyl Disulfide [*Organic chemistry*]
DNDS..........	Dinitrostilbenedisulfonic Acid [*Antimalarial*]
DNDS..........	Director, Naval Dental Services [*British*]
DNDT..........	Department of the Navy Declassification Team (DNAB)
DNDU..........	National Defense University, Fort Lesley J. McNair, Washington, DC [*Library symbol*] [*Library of Congress*] (LCLS)
DNE	Department of Nuclear Engineering [*MIT*] (MCD)
DNE	Diffuse Neuroendocrine System [*Also, DNS*]
DNE	Diploma in Nursing Education (ADA)
DNE	Director of Naval Equipment
DNE	Director of Nursing Education
DNE	Dnepa-Air [*Ukraine*] [*FAA designator*] (FAAC)
DNE	Doctor of Naval Engineering
DNE	Doctor of Nursing Education (DAVI)
DNE	Doron Exploration, Inc. [*Vancouver Stock Exchange symbol*]
DNE	Duluth & Northeastern Railroad Co. [*AAR code*]
DNE	Group D Nonenterococcal Streptococcus [*Bacteriology*] (DAVI)
DNEA	National Education Association, Washington, DC [*Library symbol Library of Congress*] (LCLS)
DNEC	Distribution Navy Enlisted Classification (DNAB)
DNED	Deputy, Naval Education Development (MCD)
DN Ed	Doctor of Nursing Education
DNEDS........	Director of Naval Education Service [*British*]
DNEN	Enugu [*Nigeria*] [*ICAO location identifier*] (ICLI)
DN Eng	Doctor of Naval Engineering
DNES	Director of Naval Education Service [*British*] (DMA)
DNET	Data-Net [*Data-Net, Inc.*] [*Rochester, NY*] [*Telecommunications*] (TSSD)
DNET	Director of Naval Engineering Training [*British military*] (DMA)
DNET	Division of Nuclear Education and Training [*AEC*]
D Nev	United States District Court for the District of Nevada (DLA)
DNEX	Dionex Corp. [*NASDAQ symbol*] (NQ)
DNEY	Da Nang East Yard [*Vietnam*] [*Navy*]
DNF	Defenders of Nature Foundation [*Guatemala*] (EAIO)
DNF	Det Nye Folkepartiet [*New People's Party*] [*Norway*] (PPE)
DNF	Did Not Finish
DNF	Disjunctive Normal Formula
DNF	Dominion Naval Forces
DNFA	Dinitrofluoroaniline [*Organic chemistry*]
DNFB	Dinitrofluorobenzene [*Also, DFB, FDNB*] [*Organic chemistry*]
DNFC	D & N Financial Corp. [*NASDAQ symbol*] (SPSG)
DNFC	D&N Finl Corp. [*NASDAQ symbol*] (TTSB)
DNFCT	Director of Naval Foreign and Commonwealth Training [*British*]
DNFCW	D&N Financial Wrrt [*NASDAQ symbol*] (TTSB)
DNFPS........	Director, Naval Future Policy Staff [*British*]
DNFSB........	Defense Nuclear Facilities Safety Board [*Military*] (DOMA)
DNFST	Department of Nutrition, Food Science, and Technology [*MIT*] (MCD)

DNFYP......... Department of the Navy Five-Year Program
DNG............ Da Nang [*Vietnam*] (VNW)
DNG............ Danger
DNG............ Danghila [*Ethiopia*] [*Airport symbol*] (AD)
DNG............ Daru [*Papua New Guinea*] [*Seismograph station code, US Geological Survey Closed*] (SEIS)
DNG............ Dining
DNG............ Distinguished Naval Graduate
DNG............ Dorsal (Nephridial Gland)
DNG............ Dutch New Guinea [*Later, Irian Barat*]
DNG............ National Geographic Society, Washington, DC [*Library symbol Library of Congress*] (LCLS)
DNGA.......... National Gallery of Art, Washington, DC [*Library symbol Library of Congress*] (LCLS)
DN-GF......... United States Department of the Navy, Naval Gun Factory, Washington, DC [*Library symbol Library of Congress Obsolete*] (LCLS)
DNGS.......... National Genealogical Society, Washington, DC [*Library symbol Library of Congress*] (LCLS)
DNGU.......... Gusau [*Nigeria*] [*ICAO location identifier*] (ICLI)
DNGuA......... National Guard Association of the United States, Washington, DC [*Library symbol*] [*Library of Congress*] (LCLS)
DNGV.......... Dedicated Natural Gas Vehicle [*Automotive engineering*]
DNGW......... Director of Naval Guided Weapons [*British*]
DNH............ Dunhuang [*China*] [*Airport symbol*] (OAG)
D NH........... United States District Court for the District of New Hampshire (DLA)
DN-HC .... United States Department of the Navy, Naval Historical Center, Operational Archives, Washington, DC [*Library symbol Library of Congress*] (LCLS)
DNHM.......... Di-normal-Hexylmagnesium [*Organic chemistry*]
DN-HO .... United States Department of the Navy, Naval Oceanographic Office, Washington, DC [*Library symbol Library of Congress*] (LCLS)
DNHS.......... Di-Normal-Hexyl Sulfide [*Organic chemistry*]
DNI .... Desktop Network Interface [*Cabletron Systems, Inc.*] [*Computer science*]
DNI .... Digital Equipment Corp., Salem, Salem, NH [*OCLC symbol*] (OCLC)
DNI .... Digital Non-Interpolated (LAIN)
DNI .... Director of Naval Intelligence [*US, British*]
DNI .... Distributable Net Income
DNI .... Division of Naval Intelligence
DNI .... DNI Holdings, Inc. [*Vancouver Stock Exchange symbol*]
DNI .... Do Not Intubate [*Medicine*] (DAVI)
DNI .... Do Not Invite
DNI .... Sherman-Denison, TX [*Location identifier FAA*] (FAAL)
DNI .... Wad Medani [*Sudan*] [*Airport symbol*] (AD)
DNIAS......... Day-Night Indirect Attack Seeker (DNAB)
DNIB........... Ibadan [*Nigeria*] [*ICAO location identifier*] (ICLI)
DNIC........... Data Net Identification Code (NITA)
DNIC........... Data Network Identification Code [*Telecommunications*] (TEL)
DNIC........... Diffuse Noxious Inhibitory Control (PDAA)
DNIC........... Digital Network Interface Circuit [*Telecommunications*]
DNIE........... National Institute of Education, Washington, DC [*Library symbol Library of Congress*] (LCLS)
DNIF........... Duty Not Involving Flying
DNigE.......... Nigerian Embassy, Washington, DC [*Library symbol Library of Congress*] (LCLS)
DNIH........... United States National Institutes of Health, Bethesda, MD [*Library symbol Library of Congress*] (LCLS)
DNIH-HM ..... United States National Institutes of Health, Bureau of Health Manpower, Bethesda, MD [*Library symbol Library of Congress*] (LCLS)
DNIL........... Ilorin [*Nigeria*] [*ICAO location identifier*] (ICLI)
DNIS........... Dataport Network Information System [*California*] [*Bulletin board system*]
DN-IS.......... Defense Intelligence School, Washington, DC [*Library symbol Library of Congress*] (LCLS)
DNIS........... Dialed Number Identification Service [*Telecommunications*] (ACRL)
DNJ............. Drone Noise Jammers [*Military*]
D NJ .... United States District Court for the District of New Jersey (DLA)
DN-JAG........ United States Department of the Navy, Office of the Judge Advocate General, Law Library, Washington, DC [*Library symbol Library of Congress*] (LCLS)
DNJC .... Dominus Noster Jesus Christus [*Our Lord Jesus Christ*] [*Latin*]
DNJO .... Jos [*Nigeria*] [*ICAO location identifier*] (ICLI)
DNJS .... Descendants of the New Jersey Settlers (EA)
DNK .... Denmark [*ANSI three-letter standard code*] (CNC)
DNK .... Did Not Keep Appointment [*Medicine*] (CPH)
DNKA.......... Did Not Keep Appointment [*Medicine*]
DNKA.......... Kaduna [*Nigeria*] [*ICAO location identifier*] (ICLI)
DnKBO........ Bibliotekernes Oplysningskontor, Centre de Pret International, Kobenhavn, Denmark [*Library symbol Library of Congress*] (LCLS)
DnKDR........ Center for Development Research, Koobenhavn, Denmark [*Library symbol Library of Congress*] (LCLS)
DNKK.......... Kano [*Nigeria*] [*ICAO location identifier*] (ICLI)
DnKL.......... Danmarks Laererhojskole [*Royal Danish School of Educational Studies*], Kobenhavn, Denmark [*Library symbol Library of Congress*] (LCLS)
DNKN.......... Kano/Mallam Aminu International [*Nigeria*] [*ICAO location identifier*] (ICLI)
DnKP .... Danmarks Paedagogiske Bibliotek [*Danish National Library of Education*], Kobenhavn, Denmark [*Library symbol Library of Congress*] (LCLS)

DnKU .... Kobenhavns Universitetsbibliotekets [*University of Copenhagen*], Afdeling, Norre Alle, Kobenhavn, Denmark [*Library symbol Library of Congress*] (LCLS)
DnKU-S........ Kobenhavns Universitetsbibliotekets [*University of Copenhagen*], Afdeling, Fiolstraede, Kobenhavn, Denmark [*Library symbol Library of Congress*] (LCLS)
DNKY .... Donnkenny, Inc. [*NASDAQ symbol*] (SAG)
DNL .... Augusta, GA [*Location identifier FAA*] (FAAL)
DNL .... Day and Night Average Sound Levels
DNL .... Det Norske Luftfartselskap AS [*Norwegian Airlines Ltd.*] (EY)
DNL .... Diack Newsletter [*Database*] [*Diack, Inc.*] [*Information service or system*] (CRD)
DNL .... Differential Non-Linearity (OA)
DNL .... Director of Naval Laboratories
DNL .... Do Not Like
DNL .... Do Not List
DNL .... Do Not Load [*Instruction re a freight car*]
DNL .... Dune Resources Ltd. [*Toronto Stock Exchange symbol*]
DNL .... Dynamic Noise Limiter [*Electronics*] (IAA)
DNLC .... Dixie National Corp. [*NASDAQ symbol*] (NQ)
DNLC .... Dixie Natl [*NASDAQ symbol*] (TTSB)
DNLCA........ Deoxynorlaudanosolinecarboxylic Acid [*Biochemistry*]
DNLK .... Downlink (MCD)
DNLL .... Lagos App [*Nigeria*] [*ICAO location identifier*] (ICLI)
DNLM .... United States National Library of Medicine, Bethesda, MD [*Library symbol Library of Congress*] (LCLS)
DNLR .... National Labor Relations Board, Washington, DC [*Library symbol Library of Congress*] (LCLS)
DNLT .... Downlist (NASA)
DNM .... Delayed Neutron Monitor [*Nuclear energy*] (NRCH)
DNM .... Denham [*Australia Airport symbol*] (OAG)
dNM .... Deoxynojirimycin [*Biochemistry*]
DNM .... Director of Naval Manning [*British military*] (DMA)
DNM .... Distance to Nearest Male Plant [*Botany*]
DNM .... Dreyfus New York Municipal Income Fund [*AMEX symbol*] (CTT)
DNM .... Dreyfus N.Y. Muni Income [*AMEX symbol*] (TTSB)
DNM .... Dulce [*New Mexico*] [*Seismograph station code, US Geological Survey Closed*] (SEIS)
D NM .... United States District Court for the District of New Mexico (DLA)
DNMA.......... Maiduguri [*Nigeria*] [*ICAO location identifier*] (ICLI)
DNMC .... United States Naval Medical Center, Bethesda, MD [*Library symbol Library of Congress*] (LCLS)
DN-MHi....... United States Department of the Navy, United States Marine Corps Historical Library, Washington, DC [*Library symbol Library of Congress*] (LCLS)
DNMK.......... Makurdi [*Nigeria*] [*ICAO location identifier*] (ICLI)
DNMM.......... Division of Nuclear Materials Management [*AEC*]
DNMM.......... Lagos/Murtala Muhammed [*Nigeria*] [*ICAO location identifier*] (ICLI)
DNMO.......... Director of Naval Management and Organization [*British military*] (DMA)
DNMO.......... District Naval Material Office
DNMP .... Deoxynucleoside Monophosphate [*Biochemistry*]
DNMP .... Director of Naval Manpower Planning [*British*]
DNMR .... Director of Naval Manpower Requirements [*or Resources*] [*British*]
DNMR .... Dynamic Nuclear Magnetic Resonance
DN-MRC ...... United States Department of the Navy, Naval Regional Medical Center, San Francisco, CA [*Library symbol Library of Congress*] (LCLS)
DN-MRI........ United States Department of the Navy, Naval Medical Research Institute, Bethesda, MD [*Library symbol Library of Congress*] (LCLS)
DNMRT........ Duncan's New Multiple Range Test (OA)
DNMS .... Delayed Neutron Monitoring Subsystem [*Nuclear energy*] (NRCH)
DNMS .... Delayed Nonmatch to Sample [*Test design*]
DNMS .... Dial Network Management System [*Telecommunications*]
DNMS .... Division of Nuclear Materials Safeguards [*AEC*]
DN-MS......... United States Department of the Navy, Naval Medical School, Bethesda, MD [*Library symbol Library of Congress*] (LCLS)
DNMSP........ Director of Naval Manpower Structure Planning [*British military*] (DMA)
DNMT .... Director of Naval Manning and Training [*British*]
DNN .... Dalton, GA [*Location identifier FAA*] (FAAL)
DNN .... Dannevirke [*New Zealand*] [*Seismograph station code, US Geological Survey Closed*] (SEIS)
DNN .... Dansk Normal Nul [*Oceanography*]
DN-NPG .... United States Department of the Navy, Naval Weapons Laboratory, Technical Library, Dahlgreen, VA [*Library symbol Library of Congress*] (LCLS)
DNNS.......... Dinitronaphtholsulfonic Acid [*Organic chemistry*]
DNO .... Alinord [*Italy ICAO designator*] (FAAC)
DNO .... Debit Note Only
DNO .... Descending Node Orbit (MCD)
DNO .... Director of Naval Operations
DNO .... Director of Naval Ordnance [*Admiralty*] [*Obsolete British*]
DNO .... District Naval Officer [*British*] (ADA)
DNO .... District Nursing Officer
DNO .... United States Naval Observatory, Washington, DC [*OCLC symbol*] (OCLC)
DNOA.......... Director of Naval Officer Appointments [*British*]
DN-Ob.......... United States Department of the Navy, Naval Observatory, Washington, DC [*Library symbol Library of Congress*] (LCLS)
DNOC.......... Dinitro-ortho-Cresol [*Also, DN*] [*Herbicide*]
DNOCHP ...... Dinitrocyclohexylphenol [*Insecticide*]

DN-OGC...... United States Department of the Navy, Office of the General Counsel, Arlington, VA [Library symbol Library of Congress] (LCLS)

DN-OL........ United States Department of the Navy, Naval Ordnance Laboratory, White Oak, MD [Library symbol Library of Congress] (LCLS)

DNOM......... Director of Naval Oceanography and Meteorology [British]

DN-ONR...... United States Department of the Navy, Office of Naval Research, Arlington, VA [Library symbol Library of Congress] (LCLS)

DNOP.......... Director of Naval Officer Procurement

DNOR.......... Directorate of Naval Operational Requirements [British]

DN-Ord........ United States Department of the Navy, Naval Ordnance Systems Command, Arlington, VA [Library symbol Library of Congress] (LCLS)

DNOS.......... Director of Naval Operational Studies [British]

DNOS.......... Oshogbo [Nigeria] [ICAO location identifier] (ICLI)

DNOSBP ...... Dinitro-ortho-secondary-butylphenol [Also, DNBP, DNSBP] [Herbicide]

DNOT.......... Directorate of Naval Operations and Trade [British]

DnOU.......... Odense Universitet [Odense University], Odense, Denmark [Library symbol Library of Congress] (LCLS)

DNOX.......... Dry Oxides of Nitrogen

DNP............ Dai Nippon Printing Co. Ltd. [Publisher] [Japan]

DNP............ Dang [Nepal] [Airport symbol] (OAG)

DNP............ Declared National Program [to share oceanographic data with other nations]

DNP............ Deferred Nesting Program (MCD)

DNP............ Democratic Nationalist Party [1959-1966] [Malta] [Political party] (PPE)

DNP............ Denpasar [Indonesia] [Seismograph station code, US Geological Survey] (SEIS)

DNP............ Deoxyribonucleoprotamine [Biochemistry]

DNP............ Deoxyribonucleoprotein [Biochemistry]

DNP............ Did Not Play

DNP............ Diiodonitrophenol [Pharmacology]

DNP............ Dinitrophenol [Organic chemistry]

Dnp............ Dinitrophenyl [Biochemistry]

DNP............ Dinitrophenylhydrazine [Also, DNPH] [Organic chemistry]

DNP............ Dinonyl Phthalate [Organic chemistry]

DNP............ Do Not Publish

DNP............ Drill Nonpay Status [Naval Reserve]

DNP............ Dry Non-Polish

DNP............ Duff/Phelps Util Income [NYSE symbol] (TTSB)

DNP............ Duff/Phelps Utilities Income [NYSE symbol] (SPSG)

DNP............ Dummy Nose Plug

DNP............ Dynamic Nuclear Polarization

DNPA.......... Dinitropropyl Acrylate [An explosive]

DNPA.......... Di-normal-propylamine [Organic chemistry]

DNPBA........ Dinitroperoxybenzoic Acid [Organic chemistry]

DNPC.......... Dinitro-p-cresol [Organic chemistry]

DN-PC.......... United States Department of the Navy, Naval Photographic Center, Washington, DC [Library symbol Library of Congress] (LCLS)

DNPD.......... Di(naphthyl)phenylenediamine [Organic chemistry]

DN-Pers...... United States Department of the Navy, Bureau of Naval Personnel, Washington, DC [Library symbol Library of Congress] (LCLS)

DNPG.......... Defense Navigation Planning Group [DoD]

DNPH.......... Dinitrophenylhydrazine [Also, DNP] [Organic chemistry]

DN-PIC........ United States Department of the Navy, Naval Intelligence Support Center, Washington, DC [Library symbol Library of Congress] (LCLS)

DNP-KLK..... Dinitrophenylated Keyhole Limpet Hemocyanin [Immunology]

DNPlans ...... Directorate of Naval Plans [British]

DNPM.......... Dinitrophenylmorphine [Biochemistry] (AAMN)

DNPO.......... Port Harcourt [Nigeria] [ICAO location identifier] (ICLI)

DNPP.......... Dinitrophenyl Phosphate [Organic chemistry]

DNPP.......... Director, Navy Program Planning

DNPP.......... Dominus Noster Papa Pontifex [Our Lord the Pope] [Latin]

DN-PP.......... United States Department of the Navy, Naval Ordnance Station, Indian Head, MD [Library symbol Library of Congress] (LCLS)

DNPPG......... Department of the Navy Policy and Planning Guidance (MCD)

DNPR.......... Director, Navy Petroleum Reserves

DNPr.......... National Press Club, Washington, DC [Library symbol Library of Congress] (LCLS)

DNPS.......... Dresden Nuclear Power Station (NRCH)

DNPS.......... United States National Park Service, National Capital Park Library, Washington, DC [Library symbol Library of Congress] (LCLS)

DNPS-NR.... United States National Park Service, National Register Division, Washington, DC [Library symbol Library of Congress] (LCLS)

DNPT.......... Dinitrosopentamethylenetetramine [Organic chemistry]

DNPTS........ Director of Naval Physical Training and Sport [British]

DNPV.......... National Paint, Varnish, and Lacquer Association, Inc., Washington, DC [Library symbol Library of Congress] (LCLS)

DNPZ.......... Dinitrosopiperazine [Animal carcinogen]

DNQ............ Deniliquin [Australia Airport symbol] (OAG)

DNQ............ Diazonaphthoquinone [Organic chemistry]

DNQ............ Did Not Qualify [Automobile racing]

DNQX.......... Dinitroquinoxalinedione [Organic chemistry]

DNR............ Daily News Record [A publication] [New York, NY] (WDMC)

DNR............ Daunorubicin [Daunomycin] [Also, D, DRB, R] [Antineoplastic drug]

DNR............ Department of Natural Resources [Department of Agriculture] [Sometimes facetiously referred to as Department of Nuts with Rifles]

D/NR.......... Dextrose to Nitrogen Ratio (AAMN)

DNR............ Diana Resources Ltd. [Vancouver Stock Exchange symbol]

DNR............ Did Not Report (OICC)

DNR............ Did Not Respond

DNR............ Digital Noise Reduction [Television]

DNR............ Dinard [France] [Airport symbol] (OAG)

DNR............ Diner

DNR............ Director of Naval Recruiting [British]

DNR............ Director of the Naval Reserve (DOMA)

DNR............ Division of Naval Reactors [Energy Research and Development Administration]

DNR............ Does Not Run

dnr............ Donor [MARC relator code] [Library of Congress] (LCCP)

DNR............ Do Not Reduce

DNR............ Do Not Renew [A policy] [Insurance]

DNR............ Do Not Report [Medicine] (DAVI)

DNR............ Do Not Resuscitate [Medicine]

DNR............ Dovas Nordiske Rad [Nordic Council for the Deaf - NCD] (EAIO)

DNR............ Downrange [NASA] (KSC)

DNR............ Dynamair Aviation, Inc. [Canada ICAO designator] (FAAC)

DNR............ Dynamic Noise Reduction [Video technology]

DNRC.......... Democritus Nuclear Research Center [Greece]

DNRC.......... United States Nuclear Regulatory Commission, Washington, DC [Library symbol Library of Congress] (LCLS)

DNRH.......... Director of Naval Records and History

DNRIU.......... Digital Net Radio Interface Unit (MCD)

DN-RL.......... United States Department of the Navy, Naval Research Library, Arlington, VA [Library symbol Library of Congress] (LCLS)

DnRoU.......... Roskilde Universitet [Roskilde University], Roskilde, Denmark [Library symbol Library of Congress] (LCLS)

DNRQ.......... Did Not Receive Questionnaire

DNRS.......... Day/Night Reflex Sight [Military] (INF)

DN-RTPC .... United States Department of the Navy, Navy Training Publication Center, Pensacola, FL [Library symbol Library of Congress] (LCLS)

DNS............ DACOM-Net Service [A packet-switching public data network]

dns............ Dansyl [As substituent on nucleoside] [Biochemistry]

DNS............ Decentralized Data Processing Network System (BUR)

DNS............ Decimal Number System (AAG)

DNS............ Deflected Nasal Septum [Medicine]

DNS............ Denison, IA [Location identifier FAA] (FAAL)

DNS............ Denniston [New Zealand] [Seismograph station code, US Geological Survey Closed] (SEIS)

DNS............ Dense (FAAC)

DNS............ Department of National Savings [British]

DNS............ Development Needs Analysis

DNS............ Deviated Nasal Septum [Otorhinolaryngology] (DAVI)

D/NS.......... Dextrose in Normal Saline [Pharmacology] (DAVI)

DNS............ Diaphragm Nerve Stimulation

DNS............ Did Not Show [Medicine]

DNS............ Did Not Start [Racing] (IYR)

DNS............ Did Not Suit

DNS............ Diffuse Neuroendocrine System [Also, DNE]

DNS............ Dimethylaminonaphthalenesulfonyl [Also, Dansyl, dns] [Biochemical analysis]

DNS............ Dinitrosalicylic [Organic chemistry]

DNS............ Dinonyl Sebacate [Organic chemistry]

D-NS.......... Diplomate, American Board of Neurological Surgery (DHSM)

DNS............ Directorate of Naval Signals [British]

DNS............ Director of Naval Signals [British military] (DMA)

DNS............ Director of Nuclear Safety [Air Force]

DNS............ Director of the Naval Service [Canada, 1910-1926]

DNS............ Discrete Network Simulation

DNS............ Dispatch News Service (IIA)

DNS............ Distributed Nesting System (MCD)

DNS............ Distributed Network System

DNS............ Distributor Nesting System [Military]

DNS............ Doctor of Nursing Science

DNS............ Domain Name Service

DNS............ Domain Name System [or Service] [Computer science]

DNS............ Domain Naming System

DNS............ Do Not Set [Printing] (DICI)

DNS............ Doppler Navigation Sensor

DNS............ Doppler Navigation System

DNS............ Dowling's English Bail Court Reports, New Series [1841-43] [A publication] (DLA)

DNS............ Dow. New Series [Dow and Clark, English House of Lords Cases] [A publication] (DLA)

DNS............ Downs [Maps and charts] (ROG)

DNS............ Dynamic Noise Suppression [Electronics]

DNS............ Dysplastic Nevus Syndrome [Medicine]

DNSA.......... Dimethylaminonaphthalenesulfonamide [Organic chemistry]

DNSA.......... Dinitrosalicylate [Organic chemistry]

DNSA.......... Diploma in Nursing Administration (ADA)

DN-SA.......... United States Department of the Navy, Naval Supply Systems Command, Alexandria, VA [Library symbol Library of Congress] (LCLS)

DNSAP........ Danmarks Nationalsocialistisk Arbejderparti [National Socialist Worker's Party of Denmark (or Danish NAZI Party)] (PPE)

DNSAR........ Sons of the American Revolution, National Society Library, Washington, DC [Library symbol Library of Congress] (LCLS)

DNSARC...... Department of the Navy System Acquisition Review Council (MCD)

DNSBP.......... Dinitro-ortho-secondary-butylphenol [Also, DNBP, DNOSBP] [Herbicide]

DNSC.......... Data Network Service Centre (NITA)

DNSC.......... Democratic National Strategy Council (EA)

DNSC.......... Digital Network Service Centre (NITA)

DNSC.......... Dimethylaminonaphthalenesulfonyl Chloride [Also, DANS] [Fluorescent reagent]

DNSC	Director of Naval Service Conditions [*British*]
DN Sc	Doctor of Nursing Science
DNSc	Doctor of Nursing Science (GAGS)
DNSDC	Defence National Storage and Distribution Centre [*Australia*]
DNSDP	Defense Navigation Satellite Development Program (MCD)
DnsePc	Dense Pac Microsystems, Inc. [*Associated Press*] (SAG)
DNSF	Democratic National Salvation Front [*Romania*] [*Political party*] (ECON)
DNSF	National Science Foundation, Washington, DC [*Library symbol Library of Congress*] (LCLS)
DN-Sh	United States Department of the Navy, Naval Ship Systems Command, Washington, DC [*Library symbol Library of Congress*] (LCLS)
DNSLP	Downslope (FAAC)
DNS-MIM	Distributed Network Server - Media Interface Module [*Cabletron Systems, Inc.*]
DNSO	Sokoto [*Nigeria*] [*ICAO location identifier*] (ICLI)
DNSPD	Divisions of Naval Staff Plans Division [*British*]
DNSPRB	DOC [*Department of Commerce*]/NASA Satellite Program Review Board (NOAA)
DNS-PS	Dimethylaminonaphthalenesulfonyl Phosphatidylserine [*Biochemistry*]
DNSR	Director of Nuclear Safety Research [*Air Force*]
DNSS	Defense Navigation Satellite System [*Formerly, SSPN*] (MCD)
DNSS	Doppler Navigation Satellite System (PDAA)
DNST	Daughters of the Nile, Supreme Temple (EA)
DNSTRM	Downstream (FAAC)
DNSW	Day Night Switching Equipment [*Telecommunications*]
DNSy	Directorate of Naval Security [*British*]
DNT	Denton [*Texas*] [*Seismograph station code, US Geological Survey Closed*] (SEIS)
DNT	Dermonecrotic Toxin [*Immunology*]
DNT	Developing Nations Tractor [*Ford Motor Co.*]
DNT	Device Name Table (IAA)
DNT	Did Not Test [*Medicine*]
DNT	Digital Network Terminator
DNT	Dinitrotoluene [*Organic chemistry*]
DNT	Dinitrotrifluoromethyl [*Organic chemistry*]
DNT	Director of Naval Telecommunications
DNT	Director of Naval Training [*British military*] (DMA)
DNT	Downtime [*Computer science Telecommunications*]
DNT	Dragon Night Tracker [*Military*] (MCD)
DNT	National Trust for Historic Preservation, Washington, DC [*Library symbol Library of Congress*] (LCLS)
DNT	Natitingou [*Dahomey*] [*Airport symbol*] (AD)
DNTA	Dinitrosoterephthalamide [*Organic chemistry*]
DNTh	Diploma in Natural Therapeutics [*British*]
DNTKFX	DownTrack Fix (GAVI)
DNTL	Dental (MSA)
DNTL	Dental
DNTM	Disseminated Nontuberculous Mycobacterial Infection
DN-TMB	United States Department of the Navy, Naval Ship Research and Development Center, Carderock, MD [*Library symbol Library of Congress*] (LCLS)
DNTO	Divisional Naval Transport Officer [*British military*] (DMA)
DNTP	Deoxynucleoside Triphosphate [*Biochemistry*]
DNTP	Diethyl Nitrophenyl Phosphorothioate [*Insecticide*]
DNTP	Parathion (GNE)
DNTRD	Denatured
DNTS	Director, Naval Transportation Service [*Later, CNTS*]
DNTSTRY	Dentistry
DNU	Democracy Now in Ulster [*Northern Ireland*] [*An association*]
DNU	Denison University, Granville, OH [*OCLC symbol*] (OCLC)
DNU	Digital Networking Unit [*Telecommunications*] (ACRL)
DNU	Directorio Nacional Unido [*Guerrilla forces*] [*Honduras*] (EY)
DNU	Do Not Use
DNU	Dundee Resources [*Vancouver Stock Exchange symbol*]
D-NuM	Diplomate, American Board of Nuclear Medicine (DHSM)
DNV	Danville [*Illinois*] [*Airport symbol*] (OAG)
DNV	Don Airlines [*Former USSR*] [*FAA designator*] (FAAC)
DNVO	DeNovo [*NASDAQ symbol*] (SAG)
DNVOF	De Novo Corp. [*NASDAQ symbol*] (TTSB)
DNVP	Deutschnationale Volkspartei [*German National People's Party*]
DNVT	Digital Nonsecure Voice Telephone (DWSG)
DNVT	Digital Nonsecure Voice Terminal (MCD)
DNW	Directorate of Naval Warfare [*British*]
DNW	Dunoir, WY [*Location identifier FAA*] (FAAL)
DNW	United States National War College, Fort McNair, Washington, DC [*Library symbol Library of Congress*] (LCLS)
DNWC	Director of Naval Weapons Contracts [*British*]
DNWM	National Museum of Women in the Arts, Washington, DC [*Library symbol*] [*Library of Congress*] (LCLS)
DNWND	Downwind [*Aviation*] (FAAC)
DNWR	Desert National Wildlife Range
DNWS	Director of Naval Weather Service, Ministry of Defence [*British*] (NATG)
DNWS	Discrete Network Simulation
DNX	DNX Corp. [*Associated Press*] (SAG)
DNXX	DNX Corp. [*NASDAQ symbol*] (SPSG)
DNY	Danish Navy [*ICAO designator*] (FAAC)
DNY	Delancey, NY [*Location identifier FAA*] (FAAL)
DNY	Dersam [*New York*] [*Seismograph station code, US Geological Survey*] (SEIS)
DNY	Destiny Resources Ltd. [*Vancouver Stock Exchange symbol*]
DNY	Donnelley [*R. R.*] & Sons Co. [*NYSE symbol*] (SPSG)
DNY	Donnelley(RR)& Sons [*NYSE symbol*] (TTSB)

DN-YD	United States Department of the Navy, Naval Facilities Engineering Command, Washington, DC [*Library symbol Library of Congress*] (LCLS)
DNYO	Yola [*Nigeria*] [*ICAO location identifier*] (ICLI)
DNZA	Zaria [*Nigeria*] [*ICAO location identifier*] (ICLI)
Do	Byk-Gulden Lomberg [*Germany*] [*Research code symbol*]
DO	Compania Dominicana de Aviacion SA [*ICAO designator*] (OAG)
D-O	Dansgaard-Oeschger [*Climatic cycles*]
DO	Data Output [*Computer science*] (IEEE)
D/O	Daughter Of [*Genealogy*]
DO	Day-Old
DO	Day Order [*Investment term*]
DO	Decanter Oil [*Petroleum technology*]
D-O	Decimal to Octal [*Computer science*] (IEEE)
DO	Defence Operations [*British World War II*]
DO	Defense Order
DO	Deferred Ordinary (ADA)
DO	Delegation Order [*Legal term*] (DLA)
D/O	Delivery Order [*Business term*]
D/O	Delivery Order (DFIT)
DO	Demi Official [*Military British*]
DO	Demolition Order (ROG)
DO	Dental Officer
D/O	Depot Overhaul (MCD)
DO	Depression Obvious [*Psychology*]
DO	Deputy for Operations
DO	Derived Operand (MCD)
DO	Designated Official (NRCH)
DO	Design Objective (IEEE)
DO	Desirable Objective (KSC)
DO	Deviating Oscillator
DO	Diamine Oxidase [*Also, DAO*] [*An enzyme*]
DO	Diamond Offshore Drilling [*NYSE symbol*] (TTSB)
DO	Diamond Offshore Drillings, Inc. [*NYSE symbol*] (SAG)
do	Dictum [*As Before*] [*Latin*] (DAVI)
d/o	Died Of (DAVI)
DO	Diesel Oil
DO	Digital Output [*Computer science*]
DO	Diode Outline (IAA)
DO	Diploma in Ophthalmology
DO	Diploma in Osteopathy [*British*]
D-O	Directive-Organic [*Designation for biologically oriented, authoritarian psychiatrists*]
DO	Direct Obligation
DO	Direct Order
DO	Director of Operations
DO	Director's Office
DO	Disability Officer
DO	Disbursing Officer
DO	Disbursing Order
DO	Discrete Output [*Computer science*] (KSC)
D/O	Disorder (DAVI)
DO	Dissolved Oxygen
DO	Disto-Occlusal [*Dentistry*]
DO	Distribution Office (DCTA)
DO	District Office [*or Officer*]
DO	Ditto (AFM)
do	Ditto (WDMC)
DO	Diving Officer
DO	Divisional Officer [*Agricultural Development and Advisory Service*] [*British*]
DO	Divisional Orders
DO	Dock Office (ROG)
DO	Dock Operations (DS)
DO	Doctor of Ophthalmology
DO	Doctor of Optometry
DO	Doctor of Oratory
DO	Doctor of Osteopathy
DO	Doctor's Orders
DO	Dollar [*Monetary unit*]
DO	Dolly Out [*Cinematography*] (NTCM)
Do	Dominance [*Psychology*]
DO	Dominicana de Aviacion [*ICAO designator*] (AD)
DO	Dominican Republic [*ANSI two-letter standard code*] (CNC)
Do	Dominicus de Sancto Geminiano [*Flourished, 1407-09*] [*Authority cited in pre-1607 legal work*] (DSA)
DO	Dominions Office [*British*]
DO	Donor [*Searchable field, Dialog*] [*Information service or system*] (NITA)
DO	Donors' Offspring [*An association*] (EA)
DO	Doppler (IAA)
DO	Dora Explorations Ltd. [*Vancouver Stock Exchange symbol*]
DO	Dornier [*German airplane type*]
DO	Dornier-Werke GmbH [*Germany ICAO aircraft manufacturer identifier*] (ICAO)
DO	Double Offset [*Engineering*]
DO	Draw Out (KSC)
D/O	Drop Off
DO	Dropout (AAG)
DO	Due Out [*Army*]
DO-YD	Duty Officer [*Military*]
DO	Oiselet [*Record label*] [*France*]
DO	Oligophranic Detail [*Psychology*]
Do8	Dornier 228 [*Airplane code*]

DOA	Compania Dominicana de Aviacion SA [*Dominican Republic*] [*ICAO designator*] (FAAC)
DOA	Dasher Owners of America (EA)
DOA	Date of Admission [*Medicine*]
DOA	Date of Availability [*Military*] (AFM)
DOA	Date of Contract Award (DNAB)
DOA	Day of Ammunition
DOA	Dead on Arrival [*Medicine*]
DOA	Dead on Arrival [*Rock music group*]
DOA	Defeat Opiate Addiction [*An association*]
DOA	Degree Of Anoxicity [*Biology*]
DOA	Delegation of Authority (MCD)
DOA	Department of Agriculture
DOA	Department of the Army
DOA	Dicks of America [*An association*] (EA)
DOA	Differential Operational Amplifier [*Electronics*] (OA)
DOA	Digital Output Adapter
DOA	Dioctyl Adipate [*Also, DEHA*] [*Organic chemistry*]
DOA	Direction of Arrival
DOA	Director of Officer Appointments [*British military*] (DMA)
DOA	Disabled Officers Association (EA)
DOA	Dissolved Oxygen Analyzer (DNAB)
DOA	Doany [*Madagascar*] [*Airport symbol*] (OAG)
DOA	Documents on Acceptance [*Banking*]
DOA	Dominant Obstacle Allowance (MCD)
DOA	Driver of Automobile (MAE)
DOA	Duty Orbital Analyst (IAA)
DOA	Organization of American States, Washington, DC [*OCLC symbol*] (OCLC)
DOAC	Dubois Oleic Albumin Complex [*Microbiology*]
DOA-DRA	Dead On Arrival Despite Resuscitative Attempts [*Emergency medicine*] (DAVI)
DOAE	Defence Operational Analysis Establishment [*British*]
DOAL	Directorate of Airlift [*Air Force*] (MCD)
DOALOS	Division for Ocean Affairs and the Law of the Sea [*United Nations*] (OSRA)
DOAM	Distributed Office Application Model [*Telecommunications*] (OSI)
DOAMS	Distant Object Attitude Measuring System (MCD)
DO/AO	District Office/Area Office [*IRS*]
DOAO(FE)	Defence Operational Analysis Organisation [*Far East*]
DOAP	Daunorubicin, Oncovin [*Vincristine*], ara-C, Prednisone [*Antineoplastic drug regimen*]
DOARS	Donnelly Official Airline Reservation Service (SAA)
DOAS	Diesel Odor Analysis System
DOAS	Differential Optical Absorption Spectrometer
DOAS	Organization of American States, Washington, DC [*Library symbol*] [*Library of Congress*] (LCLS)
DOA/TOA	Direction of Arrival/Time of Arrival (MCD)
DOB	Data Output Bus [*Computer science*]
DOB	Date of Birth
DOB	Daughters of Bilitis [*Superseded by United Sisters*] (EA)
DOB	Daughters of Bosses
DOB	Decent Old Buffer [*British Slang*]
DOB	Defense Office Building [*Pentagon*] (DNAB)
DOB	Department of Energy, Bartlesville Energy Technology Center, Bartlesville, OK [*OCLC symbol*] (OCLC)
DOB	Deployed Operating Base (MCD)
DOB	Depth of Burial [*of explosives*]
DOB	Depth of Burst (NATG)
DOB	Detained on Board [*Referring to seamen*]
DOB	Discrete Out Blockhouse [*NASA*] (KSC)
DOB	Dispersed Operating Base [*Air Force*] (AFM)
DOB	Dobrolet Airlines [*Russian Federation*] [*ICAO designator*] (FAAC)
DOB	Dobutamine [*Pharmacology*] (DAVI)
DOB	Doctor's Order Book
DOB	Dombas [*Norway*] [*Geomagnetic observatory code*]
DOB	Marietta, GA [*Location identifier FAA*] (FAAL)
DOBA	Diploma of the Orthoptic Board of Australia
DOBANIAN	Descendants of Black African Natives in the American North [*Proposed appellation*]
DOBC	Diesel Oil, Bentonite, Cement [*Oil well drilling technology*]
DOBETA	Domestic Oil Burning Equipment Testing Association [*British*] (DI)
DOBG	Doughtie's Foods [*NASDAQ symbol*] (TTSB)
DOBIS	Dortmunder Bibliothekssystem [*Dortmund Bibliographic Information System*] [*Cataloguing system developed in Germany*]
DOBP	Dodecyloxyhydroxybenzophenone [*Organic chemistry*]
DOBQ	Doughtie's Foods, Inc. [*NASDAQ symbol*] (NQ)
DOBRO	Dopyera Brothers [*Guitar*] (IIA)
DObst	Diploma in Obstetrics
D Obst RCOG	Diploma in Obstetrics, Royal College of Obstetricians and Gynaecologists [*British*]
DOC	DARCOM [*Development and Readiness Command, Army*] Operations Center (MCD)
DOC	Data Operating Control
DOC	Data Operation Center (IAA)
DOC	Data, Operations, and Control
DOC	Data Optimizing Computer
DOC	Data Output Channel (MSA)
DOC	Date of Change
DOC	Date of Commencement
DOC	Datsun Owners Club [*Defunct*] (EA)
DOC	Decimal to Octal Conversion
DOC	Deck of Cards (MCD)
DOC	Defense Operations Center
DOC	Degree of Control (MCD)

DOC	Degree of Cooperation [*Military*] (NVT)
DOC	Delayed Opening Chaff
DOC	Denominazione di Origine Controllata [*Italian wine designation*]
DOC	Deoxycholate [*Biochemistry*]
DOC	Deoxycorticoid (MAE)
DOC	Deoxycorticosterone [*Endocrinology*]
DOC	Department of Commerce
DOC	Department of Communications [*Canada*]
DOC	Descend on Course [*Aviation*]
DOC	Designated Operational Coverage (DA)
DOC	Design Operation Capability (MCD)
DOC	Developmental Optical Correlator (PDAA)
DOC	Diabetes Out of Control [*Endocrinology*] (DAVI)
DOC	Died of Other Causes [*Medicine*]
DOC	Digital Optical Cassette [*Information retrieval*]
DOC	Digital Oscillator Chip [*Apple Computer, Inc.*]
DOC	Digital Output Channel (MCD)
DOC	Digital Output Control
DOC	Direct Operating Cost [*Accounting*]
DOC	Directorate of Contracting [*Military*] (RDA)
DOC	Director of Camouflage [*British*]
DOC	Director of Contracts [*Military British*]
DOC	Disaster Operations Center (GNE)
DOC	Dissolved Organic Carbon
DOC	Distributed Operator Console [*Environmental science*]
DOC	District Officer Commanding
DOC	Divested Operating Company
DOC	DOC (Doctors Ought to Care) (EA)
Doc	Docent
DOC	Docket
DOC	Doctor (EY)
DOC	Doctor Blade [*Photogravure*] (DGA)
Doc	Doctores Bononienses [*Latin*] (DSA)
DOC	Document [*or Documentation*] (AFM)
doc	Document (WDMC)
doc	Document [*Computer science*]
doc	Documentary (WDMC)
DOC	Douglas College Learning Resources Centre [*UTLAS symbol*]
DOC	Drawn-on-Cover [*Graphic arts*] (DGA)
DOC	Drive Other Cars [*Insurance*]
DOC	Dropout Compensator (NTCM)
DOC	Dropout Connector
DOC	Dr. Pepper Co. (IIA)
DOC	Due-Out Cancellation [*Military*] (AFM)
DOC	Dynamic Overload Controls [*Telecommunications*]
DOC	Norsk Luftambulanse AS [*Norway ICAO designator*] (FAAC)
DOC	Oblate College, Washington, DC [*Library symbol Library of Congress*] (LCLS)
DOCA	Date of Change of Accountability [*Military*]
DOCA	Date of Current Appointment [*Military*]
DOCA	Defense Orientation Conference Association (EA)
DOCA	Deoxycorticosterone [*or Desoxycorticosterone*] Acetate [*Also, DCA*] [*Endocrinology*]
DoCA	Department of Communications and the Arts [*Australia*]
DOCA	Director of Overseas Civil Aviation [*British*]
DOCB	Deep Ocean Cable Burial
Doc Bon	Doctores Bononienses [*Latin*] (DSA)
DOCC	Defense Communications Agency Operations Center Complex
DOCC	Ducati Owners' Club of Canada (EA)
DOCC	Office of the Comptroller of the Currency, Washington, DC [*Library symbol Library of Congress*] (LCLS)
DOCDEL	Document Delivery [*Information service or system*]
DOCE	Date of Current Enlistment [*Military*]
Doc Eng	Doctor of Engineering
DOCEX	Document Exploitation
DOCFAX	Document Facsimile Transmission (NITA)
DOCG	Denominazione di Origine Controllata e Garantita [*Italian wine designation*]
DOCG	Deoxycorticosterone Glucoside [*Also, DCG*] [*Endocrinology*]
DOCGEN	Document Generator
DOCHSIN	District of Columbia Health Sciences Information Network [*Library network*]
DOCI	DecisionOne Holdings [*NASDAQ symbol*] (TTSB)
DOCID	Document Identifier [*Military*] (MCD)
DocIm	Document Imaging Systems Corp. [*Associated Press*] (SAG)
DocImg	Document Imaging Systems Corp. [*Associated Press*] (SAG)
DOCK	[*The*] Chicago Dock & Canal Trust [*NASDAQ symbol*] (NQ)
DOCK	Docket (DLA)
Docket	Docket and the Barrister [*1889-98*] [*Canada*] [*A publication*] (DLA)
Docket	West Publishing Company's Docket [*1909-41*] [*A publication*] (DLA)
DOCKS	Chicago Dock & Canal Trust [*NASDAQ symbol*] (TTSB)
DOCL	Department of Commerce Library (IID)
DOCLINE	Document Ordering Online [*Document delivery system, MEDLARS*] (NITA)
DOCLINE	Documents On-Line [*Medicine*] (DMAA)
DOCMOD	Documentation Modernization [*Program*] [*Army*] (INF)
DOCO	Director to Commissary Operations [*Military*] (AABC)
DOCP	Delaware Otsego Corp. [*NASDAQ symbol*] (NQ)
DOCPAL	Sistema de Documentacion sobre Poblacion en America Latina [*Latin American Population Documentation System*] [*Economic Commission for Latin America and the Caribbean*] [*United Nations*] [*Information service or system*] (IID)
Doc Parl	Documents Parlementaires [*A publication*] (DLA)
DOCPR	Department of Commerce Procurement Regulation [*A publication*] (AAGC)

DocRerPol ... Doctor Rerum Politicarum [*Doctor of Political Science*] [*Latin*]
DOCS .... Design Optimization Codes for Structures (MCD)
DOCS .... Dictionary of Organic Compounds [*A publication*]
DOCS .... Disk-Oriented Computer System (IEEE)
Docs .... Doctores Bononienses [*Latin*] (DSA)
D Oc S .... Doctor of Ocular Science
DOCS .... Document Organization and Control System [*Telecommunications*] (TEL)
DOCS .... Documents
DOCS .... DSCS [*Defense Satellite Communication System*] Operations Control System [*DoD*]
DOCS .... PC DOCS Group International [*NASDAQ symbol*] (SAG)
D Oc Sc ..... Doctor of Ocular Science
DOCSF .... PC DOCS Gp Intl. [*NASDAQ symbol*] (TTSB)
DOC-SR ...... Desoxycorticosterone Secretion Rate [*Endocrinology*] (MAE)
DOCSV .... Data over Circuit-Switched Voice [*Computer science*] (PCM)
DOCSYS .... Display of Chromosome Statistics System
Doct .... Doctor
Doct .... Doctores Bononienses [*Latin*] (DSA)
DOCT .... Doctrine (ROG)
DOCT .... Document
DoctArch ..... Doctor of Christian Archeology
Doct Dem ..... Doctrine of Demurrers [*A publication*] (DLA)
Doc To ...... Doctores Tholosani [*Latin*] (DSA)
DOCTOR ...... Dictionary Operation and Control for Thesaurus Organization (PDAA)
Doct Pl ...... Doctrina Placitandi [*A publication*] (DLA)
DOCTRN ...... Doctrine
DOCU .... DocuCon, Inc. [*NASDAQ symbol*] (NQ)
DOCU .... Document (AABC)
DocuCn .... DocuCon, Inc. [*Associated Press*] (SAG)
docum .... Documentary (BARN)
Documnt ...... Documentum, Inc. [*Associated Press*] (SAG)
DOCUS .... Display-Oriented Computer Usage System
DocuSci ...... Document Sciences Corp. [*Associated Press*] (SAG)
Doc Ve ...... Doctores Veteres [*Latin*] (DSA)
DOCX .... Document Sciences Corp. [*NASDAQ symbol*] (SAG)
DOD .... Date of Death
DOD .... Dead [*or Died*] of Disease (DAVI)
DOD .... Dear Old Dad (DICI)
DOD .... Degree of Disorder [*Coatings*]
DoD .... Department of Defense [*Washington, DC*]
DOD .... Department of Defense (AAGC)
DOD .... Department of Defense (USGC)
DOD .... Department of Defense (USDC)
DOD .... Depth of Discharge [*Electric vehicles*]
DOD .... Depth of Discharge
DOD .... Detroit Ordnance District [*Army*]
DOD .... Development Operations Division [*NASA*] (KSC)
DOD .... Died of Disease
DOD .... Dielectric Outer Diameter (IAA)
DOD .... Digital Optical Disc [*Storage medium*] (NITA)
DOD .... Dihydroxydiphenyl [*Antioxidant*] [*Organic chemistry*]
DOD .... Director of Dockyards [*Admiralty*] [*British*]
DOD .... Director of Operations Division [*Navy British*]
DOD .... Directory of Directories [*Later, DIP*] [*A publication*]
DOD .... Directory of Online Databases [*A publication*]
DOD .... Directory on Disk [*Information service or system*] (IID)
DOD .... Direct Outward Dialing [*Telecommunications*]
DOD .... Dissolved Oxygen Deficit [*Water pollution*]
DOD .... Dodge City [*Diocesan*] [*Kansas*] (TOCD)
DOD .... Dodoma [*Tanzania*] [*Airport symbol*] (OAG)
DOD .... Dodoma [*Tanzania*] [*Seismograph station code, US Geological Survey Closed*] (SEIS)
Dod .... Dodson's English Admiralty Reports [*A publication*] (DLA)
Dod .... Dod's Parliamentary Companion. Annual [*A publication*] (DLA)
DOD .... Draft on Demand [*Banking*] (ROG)
DOD .... Drop-on-Demand [*Computer printer*]
DOD .... United States Department of Energy, Regional Energy Information Center, Dallas, TX [*OCLC symbol*] (OCLC)
DODA .... Department of Defence, Australia
DODA .... Door and Operator Dealers Association (EA)
DODAAC ..... Department of Defense Activity Address Code (AABC)
DODAAD ..... Department of Defense Activity Address Designer (MCD)
DODAAD ..... Department of Defense Activity Address Directory (AFM)
DODAAF ...... Department of Defense Activity Address File
DODAAS ..... Department of Defense Automatic Address System (MCD)
DODAC .... Department of Defense Ammunition Code (AFM)
DODAC .... Dioctadecyldimethylammonium Chloride [*Organic chemistry*]
DODADL ..... Department of Defense Authorized Data List
Dod Adm ..... Dodson's English Admiralty Reports [*A publication*] (DLA)
DOD-AGFSRS... Department of Defense Aircraft Ground Fire Suppression and Rescue Office
Dod Ant Parl... Doderidge on the Antiquity and Power of Parliaments [*A publication*] (DLA)
DODAQAC .... Department of Defense Acquisition Quality Assurance Course (RDA)
DODAQAMC... Department of Defense Acquisition Quality Assurance Management Course (RDA)
DODAR .... Determination of Direction and Range (IAA)
DODAR .... Director of Drafting and Records [*British military*] (DMA)
DODAS .... Digital Oceanographic Data Acquisition System (MCD)
DOD C & T... Department of Defense Clothing and Textile Load (EGAO)
DODCAPS .... Department of Defense Central Automated Personnel System (AFM)
DODCCP ...... Department of Defense Central Control Point (AAGC)
DODCI .... Department of Defense Computer Institute
DODCI .... Diethyloxadicarbocyanine Iodide [*A dye*]

DODCLIPMI... Department of Defense Consolidated List of Principal Military Items
DODCLPMI... Department of Defense Consolidated List of Principal Military Items
DODCPM...... Department of Defense Civilian Personnel Manual (MCD)
DODCSC .... Department of Defense Computer Security Center (GFGA)
DODD.......... Department of Defense Directive
DODD.......... DOD [*Department of Defense*] Document (DOMA)
DODDAC...... Department of Defense Damage Assessment Center
Dodd & Br Pr Pr... Dodd and Brooks' Probate Court Practice [*A publication*] (DLA)
Dodd Bur Fees... Dodd on Burial and Other Church Fees [*A publication*] (DLA)
DODDS........ Department of Defense Dependents Schools
DODDSLANT... Department of Defense Dependents Schools, Atlantic (DNAB)
DODE.......... Development Optical Diagnostic Equipment [*Military*]
DODEA........ Department of Defense Education Education Activity [*DoD*]
Dod Eng Law... Doderidge's English Lawyer [*A publication*] (DLA)
DODEP........ Department of Defense Emergency Plans (AABC)
DODEP........ Department of Defense Exercise Planning (AFM)
Do de Ro..... Domini de Rota [*Authority cited in pre-1607 legal work*] (DSA)
Do de San Gemi... Dominicus de Sancto Geminiano [*Flourished, 1407-09*] [*Authority cited in pre-1607 legal work*] (DSA)
DODEX........ DOD [*Department of Defense*] [*Intelligence Information System*] Extension (DOMA)
DOD(F) .... Director of Operations Division (Foreign) [*Navy British*]
DODFCI........ Department of Defense Foreign Counterintelligence Program
DODFDCO .... Department of Defense Foreign Disclosure Coordinating Office (AABC)
DODGAR ..... Department of Defense Grant and Agreement Regulation [*A publication*] (AAGC)
DODGE........ Department of Defense Gravity Experiment [*Satellite*]
DODGE-M..... Department of Defense Gravity Experiment, Multipurpose [*Satellite*]
DODH.......... Department of Defense Handbook
DOD(H)........ Director of Operations Division (Home) [*Navy British*]
DoD/HA....... Department of Defense for Health Affairs
DODHBK .... Department of Defense Handbook
DODHGCSO... Department of Defense Household Goods Commercial Storage Office
DODHGFO ... Department of Defense Household Goods Field Office
DODHSNS..... Department of Defense High School Newspaper Service
DODI.......... Department of Defense Instruction
DODI.......... District Office Direct Input [*Social Security computerized system*]
DODIC........ Department of Defense Identification Code (AFM)
DODIC........ Department of Defense Item Code
DODIDENTBAD... Department of Defense Identification Badge
DODIEC .... Department of Defense Item Entry Control
DODIER........ Department of Defense Industrial Equipment Reserve (AABC)
DODIG .... Department of Defense Inspector General
DOD IGARTS... Department of Defense Inspector General Audit Report Tracking System (AAGC)
DODIIS........ Department of Defense Intelligence Information System (MCD)
DODIM........ Department of Defense Inventory Manager
DODINST .... Department of Defense Instruction
DODIPP....... Department of Defense Intelligence Production Program [*CIA terminology*]
DOD-IR .... Department of Defense Intelligence Reports (DNAB)
DODIS........ Distribution of Oceanographic Data at Isentropic Levels System
DODISB........ Department of Defense Industrial Security Bulletin
DODISC....... Department of Defense Item Standardization Code
DODISL........ Department of Defense Industrial Security Letter
DODISM...... Department of Defense Industrial Security Manual
DODISPR ..... Department of Defense Information Security Program Regulation (MCD)
DODISR ...... Department of Defense Industrial Security Regulation
DODISS........ Department of Defense Index of Specifications and Standards
DODJET........ Drop on Demand Jet Printing [*Carpet manufacturing*] (ECON)
DOD-JIC...... DOD [*Department of Defense*] Joint Intelligence Center (DOMA)
Dod Law L... Doderidge's The Lawyer's Light [*A publication*] (DLA)
DODLOGPLAN... Department of Defense Logistics Systems Plan (MCD)
DODM.......... Department of Defense Manual
DODMAM...... Department of Defense Military Assistance Manual
DODMDS...... Department of Defense Material Distribution System (MCD)
DODMERB .... Department of Defense Medical Examination Review Board
DOD/MIS...... Department of Defense Management Information System
DODMNL...... Department of Defense Manual
DODMPAC.... Department of Defense Military Pay and Allowance Committee
DODMPRC.... Department of Defense Military Personnel Records Center
DODMUL...... Department of Defense Master Urgency List (AFM)
DODNACC.... Department of Defense National Agency Check Center (AABC)
Dod Nobility... Doderidge's Nobility [*A publication*] (DLA)
DODO.......... Drain on Day One [*Classification for new newspaper*]
DOD-PEC ..... Department of Defense Program Element Code (AFIT)
DODPM........ Department of Defense Military Pay and Allowance Entitlements Manual (AABC)
DODPMRP .... Department of Defense Precious Metals Recovery Program
DOD/POPHM... Department of Defense Performance-Oriented Packaging of Hazardous Materials [*Washington, DC*]
DODPRO...... Department of Defense, Pacific Research Office (CINC)
DODPRT ...... Date of Departure [*Military*] (AABC)
DODPSTR .... Department of Defense Poster
DODR.......... Department of Defense Regulation
DODRE........ Department of Defense Research and Engineering
DODS.......... Definitive Orbit Determination System [*NASA*]
DODS.......... Different Orbitals for Different Spins [*Atomic physics*]
Dods .... Dodson's English Admiralty Reports [*A publication*] (DLA)
DODSASP .... Department of Defense Small Arms Serialization Program
DodSO4........ Dodecyl Sulfate [*Organic chemistry*]
Dodson Adm (Eng)... Dodson's English Admiralty Reports [*A publication*] (DLA)

DODSPBL .... Department of Defense Surplus Property Bidders List
DOD-SSP .... Department of Defense Single Stock Point (MCD)
DODT .... Design Option Decision Tree
DODT .... Display Octal Debugging Technique
DODX .... Department of Defense Oversized Flatcar (INF)
DODX .... Department of Defense-Owned Rail Cars [*MTMC*] (TAG)
DOE .... Date of Enlistment [*Military*]
DOE .... Date of Examination [*Medicine*] (DAVI)
DOE .... Deep Ocean Environment
D-O-E .... Deoxyephedrine [*or Desoxyephedrine*] [*Pharmacology*]
DOE .... Department of Education [*Cabinet department*] (CDAI)
DOE .... Department of Energy [*Washington, DC*]
DoE .... Department of Energy
DOE .... Department of the Environment [*Formerly, MPBW, MT*] [*British*]
DOE .... Depends on Experience [*Employment*] (ODBW)
doe .... Depends on Experience [*Employment*] (ODBW)
DOE .... Design of Experiments [*Army*] (RDA)
DOE .... Desoxyephedrine Hydrochloride [*Pharmacy*] (AAMN)
DOE .... Device-Oriented Electronic (IAA)
DOE .... Dictionary of Old English [*University of Toronto*] [*Canada Information service or system*] (IID)
DOE .... Direct Observation Evaluation [*Medicine*] (DMAA)
DOE .... Dissolved Oxygen Electrode
DOE .... Distributed Objects Everywhere [*Computer science*]
DOE .... Djoemoe [*Surinam*] [*Airport symbol*] (OAG)
DOE .... Doctor of Oral English
DOE .... Dyspnea on Exercise [*or Exertion*] [*Medicine*]
DOE .... Dyspnea on Exertion [*Medicine*] (DMAA)
DOE .... United States Department of Energy Library, Washington, DC [*OCLC symbol*] (OCLC)
DOE/AL .... DOE [*Department of Engery*] Albuquerque Operations Office, Albuquerque, NM (GAAI)
DOEBCA ...... Department of Energy Board of Contract Appeals (AAGC)
D Oec .... Doctor Oeconomiae [*Doctor of Economics*]
DOE/CAO ..... DOE [*Department of Energy*] Carlsbad Area Office, Carlsbad, NM (GAAI)
DOE/CH .... DOE [*Department of Energy*] Chicago Operations Office [*Illinois*] (GAAI)
DoEd .... Department of Education
DOE/DP .... DOE [*Department of Energy*] Office of Defense Programs (GAAI)
DOE/EIA ...... DOE [*Department of Energy*] Energy Information Administration (GAAI)
DOE/EM .... DOE [*Department of Energy*] Office of Environmental Management (GAAI)
DOE/ER .... Department of Energy, Office of Energy Research [*Washington, DC*]
DOE/ET .... Department of Energy/Assistant Secretary for Energy Technology [*Washington, DC*]
DOE/FN .... DOE [*Department of Energy*] Fernald Area Office [*Ohio*] (GAAI)
DOE/HQ .... DOE [*Department of Energy*] Headquarters (GAAI)
DOE/ID .... DOE [*Department of Energy*] Idaho Operations Office (GAAI)
DOEM .... Designated Official for Environmental Matters (GNE)
DOEN .... Department of Energy (WDAA)
DOE/NV .... Department of Energy Nevada Operations Office [*Marine science*] (OSRA)
DOE/NV .... DOE [*Department of Energy*] Nevada Operations Office (USDC)
DOEO .... Darwin Office of Equal Opportunity [*Australia*]
DOE/OAK ..... DOE [*Department of Energy*] Oakland Operations Office [*Oakland, CA*] (GAAI)
DOE/OH .... DOE [*Department of Energy*] Ohio Field Office (GAAI)
DOE/OR .... DOE [*Department of Energy*] Oak Ridge Operations Office [*Oak Park Ridge, TN*] (GAAI)
DOE/OSTI .... DOE [*Department of Energy*] Office of Scientific and Technical Information [*Tennessee*] (GAAI)
DOE-PMR .... Department of Energy Property Management Regulations [*A publication*] (AAGC)
DOE-PR .... Department of Energy Procurement Regulation [*A publication*] (AAGC)
DOER .... Dredging Operations and Environmental Research [*U.S. Army Corps of Engineers*]
DOER .... Dredging Operations and Environmental Research [*US Army Corps of Engineers*]
DOE/RECON... Department of Energy's Remote Console Information System [*Department of Energy*] [*Database*]
DOE/RF .... DOE [*Department of Energy*] Rocky Flats Office [*Colorado*] (GAAI)
DOE/RI .... DOE [*Department of Energy*] Richland Operations Office [*Richland, WA*] (GAAI)
DOES .... Decision-Oriented Evaluation System
DOES .... Defense Organization Entity Standards [*DoD*]
DOES .... Defense Organization Entity System [*DoD*] (MCD)
DOES .... Direct Order Entry System [*Computer science*] (MHDB)
DOES .... Directory of Educational Software [*British*] (NITA)
DOES .... Disk-Oriented Engineering System [*Computer science*]
DOES .... Disorders of Excessive Somnolence [*Medicine*] (MEDA)
DOES .... Distribution Order Entry System (IAA)
DOE/SR .... DOE [*Department of Energy*] Savannah River Operations Office [*Aiken, South Carolina*] (GAAI)
DOET .... Dimethoxyethyl Amphetamine [*A hallucinogenic drug, more commonly known as STP*] (MAH)
DOE-TIC...... Department of Energy Technical Information Center [*Oak Ridge, TN*] [*Database producer*]
DOETS .... Dual-Object Electronic Tracking System
DOE/WIPP.... DOE [*Department of Energy*] WIPP [*Waste Isolation Pilot Plant*] Project Office [*Carlsbad, NM*] (GAAI)
DOE/WVAO... DOE [*Department of Energy*] West Valley Area Office [*West Valley, NY*] (GAAI)

DOF .... Deep Ocean Floor
DOF .... Defenders of Furbearers [*Later, Defenders of Wildlife*]
DOF .... Degree of Freedom
DOF .... Delivery on Field
DOF .... Demonstration of Operational Feasibility
DOF .... Department of Fisheries [*South Australia*]
DOF .... Department of Forestry [*Queensland*] [*Australia*]
DOF .... Depot Overhaul Factor
DOF .... Depth of Field (MCD)
DOF .... Depth of Focus [*Optics*]
DOF .... Device Output Format
DOF .... Dioctyl Fumarate [*Organic chemistry*]
DOF .... Direction of Fire [*Weaponry*] (INF)
DOF .... Direction of Flight (KSC)
DOF .... Director of Ordnance Factories [*Ministry of Supply*] [*British World War II*]
DOF .... United States Department of Energy NEICA, Albuquerque, NM [*OCLC symbol*] (OCLC)
DOFA .... Date of Full Availability
D of A......... Deltiologists of America (EA)
D of A......... Department of Agriculture
DOFA .... Details of Agreement [*NATO*] (NATG)
D of A......... Director of Artillery [*British*]
D of A......... National Council, Daughters of America
DOFAB .... Damned Old Fool About Books [*Acronym created by Eugene Field*]
D of C .... Daughters of the Confederacy
DOFC .... Defense Orthopedic Footwear Clinic [*Military*] (AABC)
DOFC .... Donny Osmond Fan Club (EA)
D of CORN LI... Duke of Cornwall's Light Infantry [*Military unit*] [*British*] (ROG)
DOFD .... Date of First Demand [*Military*] (AFIT)
D of D .... Director of Dockyards [*Admiralty*] [*British*]
DOF(E)........ Director of Ordnance Factories, Engineering Factories [*Ministry of Supply*] [*British World War II*]
D of F .... Department of Finance (ADA)
D of I .... Department of the Interior
D of I .... Director of Intelligence [*RAF*] [*British*]
DOFIC .... Domain-Originated Functional Integrated Circuit (IEEE)
D of J .... Department of Justice
D of L .... Department of Labor
DOFL .... Diamond Ordnance Fuze Laboratory [*Later, Harry Diamond Laboratories*] [*AMC Washington, DC*]
D of L .... Duchy of Lancaster [*British*] (ILCA)
D of M .... Dames of Malta (EA)
D of M .... Director of Manning [*British military*] (DMA)
D of M .... Supreme Caldron, Daughters of Mokanna (EA)
D of NR ...... Director of Naval Recruiting [*British*]
D of P .... Degree of Pocahontas
D of P .... Director of Planes [*Admiralty*] [*British*]
D of PD(Q)... Director of Plans Division (Quartering) [*Navy British*]
D of PS .... Director of Public Service
D of Q .... Director of Quartering [*British military*] (DMA)
D of Q(N) .... Directorate of Quartering (Navy) [*British*]
D of R .... Director of Remounts [*Military British*]
D of S .... Daughters of Scotia [*Bayonne, NJ*]
D of S .... Day of Supply [*Military*]
DOFS .... Day of Supply [*Military*]
DOFS .... Department of Organization and Field Services, AFL-CIO (EA)
D of S .... Department of State
D of S .... Depot of Supplies [*Marine Corps*]
DOFS .... Depot of Supplies [*Marine Corps*]
DOFS(W) .... Director of Stores (Washington) [*Navy*] (DNAB)
D of S (W)... Director of Stores (Washington) [*Navy*]
D of T .... Department of the Treasury [*Commonly TD, Treasury Department*]
D of T .... Director of Traffic
D of TD...... Director of Tactical Division [*Navy British*]
D of V .... Director of Victualling [*British military*] (DMA)
D of W .... Department of Works [*Military British*]
DOF(X)........ Director of Ordnance Factories, Explosives Factories [*Ministry of Supply*] [*British World War II*]
DOG .... Days of Grace [*for payment*] [*Business term*]
DOG .... Deoxy-D-glucose [*Also, DDG, DG*] [*Biochemistry*]
DOG .... Difference of Gaussians [*Image processing*]
DOG .... Dioctanoylglycerol [*Organic chemistry*]
D-OG .... Diplomate, American Board of Obstetrics and Gynecology (DHSM)
DOG .... Directory of Opportunities for Graduates [*A publication*]
DOG .... Disgruntled Old Graduate [*West Point*]
DOG .... Dissolver Off-Gas [*Nuclear energy*] (NRCH)
DOG .... Division Officer's Guide [*A publication*] (DNAB)
DOG .... Dog Owners' Guild
DOG .... Dongola [*Sudan*] [*Airport symbol*] (OAG)
DOG .... Double Chain Branch-Oblong Master Link-Grab Hook
DOG .... Drop Out Generator (NG)
DOG .... Due-Out of Group [*Military*] (MCD)
Dog Fan...... Dog Fancy [*A publication*] (BRI)
DOGI .... Dottrina Giuridica [*Consiglio Nazionale delle Ricerche*] [*Italy Information service or system*] (CRD)
DOGIT .... Deed of Grant in Trust
DOGM .... Dogmatic
DOGS......... Drawing Office Graphics System [*Deltacam Systems Ltd.*] [*Software package*] (NCC)
DOGS......... Dwingeloo Obscured Galaxy Survey
DOH .... Department of Health [*British*] (ECON)
DoH .... Department of Health (AIE)
DOH .... Deutscher Orden der Harugari [*German Order of Harugari*] (EA)
DOH .... Diploma in Occupational Health

DOH............	Discrete Output High (MCD)
DOH............	Doha [*Qatar*] [*Airport symbol*] (OAG)
DOH............	Dorchester Hotels, Inc. [*Vancouver Stock Exchange symbol*]
DOH............	Fort Bragg, NC [*Location identifier FAA*] (FAAL)
DOHA..........	Daughters of Hirsutism Association of America (EA)
DOHC..........	Double Overhead Camshaft [*Automotive term*]
DOHL..........	Dohle Bodies [*Biochemistry*] (DAVI)
DOHS..........	Diploma of Occupational Health and Safety
DOHSA........	Death on the High Seas Act
DOHSW.......	Department of Health, Safety, and Welfare [*Western Australia*]
DO Hyg.......	Diploma in Occupational Hygiene [*British*]
DOI	Date of Information (MCD)
DOI	Date of Injury [*Medicine*]
DOI	Date of Introduction (ADDR)
DOI	Dead of Injuries [*Medicine*] (BARN)
DOI	Deep Ocean Installation
DOI	Defence Oceanology International Exhibition [*British*] (ITD)
DOI	Department of Industry [*British*] (DS)
DOI	Department of the Interior (AABC)
DoI	Department of the Interior
DOI	Department Operating Instruction
DOI	Descent Orbit Insertion [*Aerospace*]
DOI	Died of Injuries [*Military*] (AABC)
DOI	Differential Orbit Improvement
DOI	Digital Object Identifier [*Computer science*]
DOI	Digital Object Identifier [*Computer science*]
DOI	Directorate Office Instruction
DOI	Distinctness of Image [*Mobay Corp.*]
DOI	Division Operating Instruction [*Air Force*]
DOI	Document-Oriented Interface [*Computer science*]
doi	Dogri [*MARC language code Library of Congress*] (LCCP)
DOI	Wing Director of Intelligence
DOIC..........	Defence Operations and Intelligence Centre [*Australia*]
DOIM..........	Delivery Order Initiating Meeting Procurement
DOIM..........	Director [*or Directorate*] of Information Management [*DoD*]
DOIM..........	Directory of International Mail [*A publication*]
DOIO..........	Directly Operable Input/Output
DOIP..........	Dioctyl Isophthalate [*Organic chemistry*]
DOIT...........	Database Oriented Interrogation Technique [*Comserv Corp.*]
DO/IT..........	Digital Output/Input Translator [*Computer science*]
DO-IT.........	Disabilities, Opportunities, Internetworking, and Technology
DOJ.............	Department of Justice (AABC)
DOJ.............	Department of Justice [*Queensland, Tasmania*] [*Australia*]
DOJ.............	Dominican Oblates of Jesus [*Roman Catholic women's religious order*]
DOJ.............	United States Department of Justice Library, Washington, DC [*OCLC symbol*] (OCLC)
DOK	De Odeon Kring [*The Odeon Club, for homosexuals*] [*Holland*]
DOK	Donetsk [*Former USSR Airport symbol Obsolete*] (OAG)
DOKDI.........	Documentation Service [*Swiss Academy of Medical Sciences*] [*Information service or system*] (IID)
DOKK..........	Dramatic Order Knights of Khorassan (EA)
DOL	Daily Official List [*London Stock Exchange prices*]
DOL	Daily Operating Log
DOL	Deauville [*France*] [*Airport symbol*] (AD)
DOL	Degree of Operating Leverage [*Finance*]
DOL	Department of Labor
DOL	Department of Labour [*South Australia, Victoria*]
DOL	Department of Lands [*Queensland*] [*Australia*]
DOL	Department of Law [*Northern Territory*] [*Australia*]
DOL	Detached Officer's List [*Army*]
DOL	Directorate of Licensing [*AEC*] (NUCP)
DOL	Director of Laboratories (MCD)
DOL	Director [*or Directorate*] of Logistics [*DoD*]
DOL	Discrete Output Low (MCD)
DOL	Display-Oriented Language [*Computer science*] (IEEE)
DOL	Doctor of Oriental Languages
DOL	Doctor of Oriental Learning
dol	Dolar [*Dollar*] [*Monetary unit*] [*Portugal*]
dol	Dolar [*Dollar*] [*Monetary unit*] [*Poland*]
DOL	Dolce [*Sweet*] [*Music*]
DOL	Dole Food Co. [*NYSE symbol*] (SAG)
DOL	Dolichol [*Biochemistry*]
dol	Dollar [*Monetary unit*] [*French*]
DOL	Dolomite [*Lithology*]
dol	Dolor [*Unit of Pain*] [*Medicine*] (BARN)
Dol	Dolphin
DOL	Dynamic Octal Load
DOL	Dynamic Oil Ltd. [*Vancouver Stock Exchange symbol*]
DOL	Ebsco, Inc. [*ICAO designator*] (FAAC)
DOLA..........	Dog Owners League of America [*Defunct*] (EA)
DOLA/DOLD..	Date of Last Adjustment/Date of Last Demand [*Military*] (AFIT)
DOLAN........	Design Office Language [*Computer science*]
DOLAR........	Department of Labor Acquisition Regulation [*A publication*] (AAGC)
DOLARS.......	Departmental On-Line Reporting System [*Military*]
DOLARS.......	Digital Offline Automatic Recording System
DOLARS.......	Disk On-Line Accounts Receivable System [*Computer science*] (MHDB)
DOLARS.......	Doppler Location and Ranging System
DolAutEx.....	Dole Food Co. [*Associated Press*] (SAG)
DOLCE........	Digital On-Line Cryptographic Equipment (NATG)
DOLCEM......	Dolcemente [*Sweetly, Softly*] [*Music*] (ROG)
DOLCIS.......	Dolcissimo [*Very Sweetly*] [*Music*]
DOLCISS......	Dolcissimo [*Very Sweetly*] [*Music*] (ROG)
Dolco..........	Dolco Packaging Corp. [*Associated Press*] (SAG)

DOLCO........	Down-Link Communications [*Antisubmarine warfare*] (MCD)
DOLDIS........	Directory of Online Databases Produced in Sweden [*Database*] [*Royal Institute of Technology Library*] [*Information service or system*] (CRD)
DOLE	Designing Out Labour Electronically (NITA)
Dole............	Dole Food Co. [*Associated Press*] (SAG)
DOLENT PART...	Dolenti Parti [*To the Afflicted Part*] [*Pharmacy*]
DOLF	Date of Last Follow-Up (AFIT)
DOLI	Date of Last Inventory (AFIT)
DOLICH.......	Dolichos [*Plant commonly known as Cowitch*] [*Pharmacology*] (ROG)
DOLITAC......	Department of Labor International Technical Assistance Corps
DOLL	Dollar [*Monetary unit*] (ROG)
DollrGn.......	Dollar General Corp. [*Associated Press*] (SAG)
DOLLS	Delayed Opening Leaflet System [*Military propaganda*]
DOLLY	Data Link (FAAC)
DOLM	College of Our Lady of Mount Carmel, Washington, DC [*Library symbol Library of Congress*] (LCLS)
DOLO	Disbursing Officers Liaison Office
DOLO	Doloroso [*Mournfully*] [*Music*] (ROG)
DOLPHIN	Deep Ocean Long Path Hydrographic Instrument (ECON)
DOLPR.........	Department of Labor Procurement Regulation [*A publication*] (AAGC)
DOLPS	Dual Output Linear Power Supply (DWSG)
DolrTr	Dollar Tree Stores, Inc. [*Associated Press*] (SAG)
DOLT	Date of Last Transaction (AFIT)
DOL URG.....	Dolore Urgente [*When the Pain Is Severe*] [*Pharmacy*]
DOLV	Double Outlet Left Ventricle [*Cardiology*] (DAVI)
DOM	Database Options Menu
DOM	Data Output Multiplexer [*Computer science*] (KSC)
DOM	Datur Omnibus Mori [*It Is Allotted unto All to Die*] [*Latin*]
DOM	Daughters of Mercy (Croatian) (TOCD)
DOM	Dealer Operations Manager [*Automotive retailing*]
DOM	Dealer Operations Manager [*Automobile sales*]
DOM	Deaminated-O-Methyl Metabolite [*Biochemistry*] (MAE)
Dom...........	De Domo Sua [*of Cicero*] [*Classical studies*] (OCD)
DOM	Delivery Order Manager [*Army*]
DOM	Deo Optimo Maximo [*To God, Most Good, Most Great*] [*Latin*]
DOM	Department of Medicine
DOM	Department of Mines [*Tasmania*] [*Australia*]
DOM	Depth of Modulation
DOM	Description, Operation, and Maintenance
DOM	Designing Out Maintenance
DOM	Digital Ohmmeter
DOM	Digital Output Multiplexer (CAAL)
DOM	Dimethoxymethylamphetamine [*A hallucinogenic drug, more commonly known as STP*]
DOM	Diploma in Ophthalmic Medicine
DOM	Dirty Old Man [*Slang*]
DOM	Disk Operating Monitor [*Computer science*]
DOM	Dispersed Organic Matter [*Chemistry*]
DOM	Dissolved Organic Matter
DOM	Distributed Object Management [*Computer science*]
DOM	Division of Overseas Ministries [*National Council of Churches*]
DOM	Document Object Model [*Computer science*]
DOM	Doman Industries Ltd. [*Toronto Stock Exchange symbol Vancouver Stock Exchange symbol*]
DOM	Domesday [*British*] (ROG)
DOM	Domestic (AFM)
DOM	Domestic
DOM	Domicile
DOM	Dominance [*Psychology*]
DOM	Dominant
Dom...........	Domingo [*Sunday*] [*Spanish*]
DOM	Dominica [*West Indies*] [*Airport symbol*] (OAG)
DOM	Dominica [*West Indies*] [*Seismograph station code, US Geological Survey*] (SEIS)
DOM	Dominica [*Leeward Islands*] [*Airport symbol*] (AD)
DOM	Dominican Republic [*ANSI three-letter standard code*] (CNC)
DOM	Dominion
DOM	Dominion Res Black Warrior Tr [*NYSE symbol*] (TTSB)
DOM	Dominion Resources Black Warrior Trust [*NYSE symbol*] (SAG)
DOM	Dominus [*The Lord*] [*Latin*]
DOM	Dominus Omnium Magister [*God the Master, or Lord, of All*] [*Motto of the Benedictine Order*] [*Latin*]
Dom...........	Domitianus [*of Suetonius*] [*Classical studies*] (OCD)
DOM	Dos Mundos [*Dominican Republic*] [*ICAO designator*] (FAAC)
DOM	Drawn over Mandrel [*Tubes*]
DOM	Quit for Domestic Reasons [*Unemployment insurance*] (OICC)
DOMA..........	Dihydroxymandelic Acid [*Also, DHMA, DMA*] [*Organic chemistry*]
DOMA.........	Director, Operation and Maintenance, Army
DOMA.........	Dokumentation Maschinenbau [*Mechanical Engineering Documentation*] [*Technical Information Center*] [*Information service or system*]
DOMAC.......	Drug Marketing, Advertising, and Communications [*FDA*]
DOMAIN......	Distributed Operating Multi-Access Interactive Network [*Apollo Computer, Inc.*] [*Chelmsford, MA*] [*Telecommunications*] (TSSD)
DOMAINS	Deep Ocean Instrumented Station (SAA)
DOMAINS	Deep Ocean Manned Instrumented Station [*National Oceanic and Atmospheric Administration*] (PDAA)
DOMAPP......	Domestic Appliance (IAA)
DOMAR.......	Doppler Martin RADAR [*Air Force*]
Domat Civ Law...	Domat's Civil Law [*A publication*] (DLA)
DOMB	Dead Old Martian Bacterium [*Humorous biology terminology*]
DOMB	Deep Ocean Moored Buoy [*Marine science*] (MSC)
Dom Book....	Domesday Book [*Census-like record of the lands of England, 1085-86*] [*A publication*] (DLA)

Dom Civ Law... Domat's Civil Law [*A publication*] (DLA)
DOMD........ Digestible Organic Matter in Dry (OA)
DOMD........ Digital Oxygen Metering Device [*Aerospace*]
DOME......... Development of Opportunities through Meaningful Education [*Project*]
DOME......... Diagnosis, Objectives, Method, Evaluation [*Formula*] [*LIMRA*]
DOME......... Distributed Object Management Environment [*Computer science*] (BTTJ)
DOMES...... Deep Ocean Mining Environmental Study [*National Oceanic and Atmospheric Administration*]
DOMES...... Digest of Middle East Studies [*A publication*] (BRI)
Domes........ Domesday Book [*Census-like record of the lands of England, 1085-86*] [*A publication*] (DLA)
DOMESA..... Don't Overlook Mature Expertise, South Australia
DOMESD..... Domesday Book [*Census-like record of the lands of England, 1085-86*] (ROG)
Domesday ... Domesday Book [*Census-like record of the lands of England, 1085-86*] [*A publication*] (DLA)
DOMESTIC ... Development of Minicomputers in an Environment of Scientific and Technological Information Centers [*Computer science*]
DOMEV....... Don't Overlook Mature Expertise, Victoria [*Australia*]
DOMEX....... Display Oriented Macro Expander [*Computer science*] (PDAA)
Dom Ex....... Domestic Exchange (MHDW)
DOMF......... Dibromohydroxymercurifluorescein [*Antiseptic*]
DOMF......... Distributed Object-Management Facility
Domi.......... Dominicus de Sancto Geminiano [*Flourished, 1407-09*] [*Authority cited in pre-1607 legal work*] (DSA)
DOM ICE..... Domestic Icebreaking [*USCG*] (TAG)
Domi de San Gemi... Dominicus de Sancto Geminiano [*Flourished, 1407-09*] [*Authority cited in pre-1607 legal work*] (DSA)
DOMINA....... Distribution-Oriented Management Information Analyzer [*Computer science*] (MHDI)
Dominican C San Rafael... [*The*] Dominican College of San Rafael (GAGS)
DOMLIB...... Domestic Library Automation Functions [*Computer science*]
DOMMDA..... Drawing Office Material Manufacturers' and Dealers' Association [*British*] (BI)
Domng........ Dominguez Services Corp. [*Associated Press*] (SAG)
DOMNN....... Dominion
DOMO......... Deep Ocean Mining Operations [*Marine science*] (MSC)
DOMO......... Dispensing Opticians Manufacturing Organisation [*British*] (BI)
domo .... Domingo [*Sunday*] [*Spanish*]
DOMO......... Downwardly Mobile [*Lifestyle classification*]
DOMP......... Dope and Wimp [*Term used by Ross Thomas in his book, "Briarpatch"*]
DOMPRINT... DOMESTIC [*Development of Microcomputers in an Environment of Scientific and Technological Information Centers*] Print Generator [*Computer science*]
DOM PROC... Domus Procerum [*The House of Lords*] [*Latin*] (ROG)
DOMREP..... Dominican Republic (AFM)
Dom Rep..... Dominican Republic (VRA)
DomRes...... Dominion Resources, Inc. [*Associated Press*] (SAG)
DOMS......... Delayed-Onset Muscle Soreness
DOMS......... Depot Operation Management System [*Army*]
DOMS......... Diploma in Ophthalmic Medicine and Surgery [*British*]
DOMS......... Directorate of Military Support (AABC)
DOMS......... Doctor of Orthopaedic Medicine and Surgery
DOMSAT...... Domestic Communications Satellite (DOAD)
DOMSAT...... Domestic Satellite [*Australia*] (NITA)
DOM SC...... Domestic Science [*Freight*]
Domtar .... Domtar Ltd. [*Associated Press*] (SAG)
DOMZ.......... Dominguez Services Corp. [*NASDAQ symbol*] (NQ)
DOMZ.......... Dominquez Services [*NASDAQ symbol*] (TTSB)
DON............ Delayed Order Notice [*Telecommunications*] (TEL)
DON............ Demand Order Number [*Army*] (AABC)
DON............ Deoxynivalenol [*A mycotoxin*]
DON............ Department of the Navy
DON............ Diazooxo-L-norleucine [*Antineoplastic drug*]
DON............ Dimensionality of Nations Project [*Hawaii*]
DON............ Director of Nursing
DON............ Dissolved Organic Nitrogen [*Analytical chemistry*]
DON............ Distribution Octane Number [*Engineering*] (IAA)
DON............ Donair Flying Club Ltd. [*British ICAO designator*] (FAAC)
DON............ Donative
DON............ Donec [*Until*] [*Pharmacy*] (ROG)
DON............ Donegal [*County in Ireland*]
DON............ Dongola [*Missouri*] [*Seismograph station code, US Geological Survey*] (SEIS)
DON............ Donnelly Corp. [*AMEX symbol*] (SPSG)
DON............ Donnelly Corp. Cl'A' [*AMEX symbol*] (TTSB)
DON............ Doppler Optical Navigation
DON............ Dysbaric Osteonecrosis [*Scuba diving disorder*]
DONA.......... Decentralized Open Network Architecture (BUR)
DONA.......... Doulas of North America [*An association*] (PAZ)
DONADPM ... Department of the Navy Automatic Data Processing Management (DNAB)
Donaker...... Donaker's Reports [*165 Indiana*] [*A publication*] (DLA)
DONAL........ Department of the Navy Occupational Level (DNAB)
Donaldsn ..... Donaldon Co., Inc. [*Associated Press*] (SAG)
don alv sol fuerit... Donec Alvus Soluta Fuerit [*Until the Bowels Are Opened*] [*Latin Medicine*] (DAVI)
Donat.......... Aelius Donatus [*Fourth century AD*] [*Classical studies*] (OCD)
DONCS........ Director of Operations Narcotics Control Reports [*CIA*]
DONEC ALV BIS DEJ... Donec Alvus Bis Dejiciatur [*Until the Bowels Have Been Twice Evacuated*] [*Pharmacy*] (ROG)
DONEC ALV SOL FUER... Donec Alvus Soluta Fuerit [*Until the Bowels Are Opened*] [*Pharmacy*] (ROG)

DONEC ALV SOL FUERIT... Donec Alvus Soluta Fuerit [*Until the Bowels Are Opened*] [*Pharmacy*]
DONEC DOL NEPH EXULAV... Donec Dolor Nephriticus Exulaverit [*Until the Nephritic Pain Is Removed*] [*Pharmacy*] (ROG)
DONEG........ Donegal [*County in Ireland*] (ROG)
Donegal....... Donegal Group, Inc. [*Associated Press*] (SAG)
Donelly....... Donnelley Corp. [*Associated Press*] (SAG)
DON FEORP... Department of the Navy Federal Equal Opportunity Recruitment Program (DNAB)
Donkeny...... Donnkenny, Inc. [*Associated Press*] (SAG)
DonLJ.......... Donaldson Lufkin & Jenrette [*Associated Press*] (SAG)
Donlley........ Donnelley [*R.R.*] & Sons Co. [*Associated Press*] (SAG)
DONMICS..... Department of the Navy Management Information Control System
Donn........... Donnell's Irish Land Cases [*1871-76*] [*A publication*] (DLA)
Donn........... Donnelly's English Chancery Reports [*A publication*] (DLA)
Donnelly...... Donnelly's English Chancery Reports [*A publication*] (DLA)
Donnelly (Eng)... Donnelly's English Chancery Reports [*A publication*] (DLA)
Donn Eq...... Donnelly's English Chancery Reports [*A publication*] (DLA)
Donn Ir Land Cas.. Donnell's Irish Land Cases [*1871-76*] [*A publication*] (DLA)
DONO.......... Dimethyloctadecanamine N-Oxide [*Organic chemistry*]
DONOACS.... Department of the Navy Office Automation and Communication Systems (GFGA)
DONPIC....... Department of the Navy Program Information Center
DonSoc....... Donizetti Society (EA)
DONSS........ Directorate of Naval Survival and Safety
Don Tr......... Donovan's Modern Jury Trials [*A publication*] (DLA)
DONUT........ Doughnut
DONUTS ..... Driver Oriented New Ultimate Tire Science
DOO............ Deep Ocean Ordnance
DOO............ Departmental Organization Order [*Marine science*] (OSRA)
DOO............ Department Organization Order [*Department of Commerce*] (NOAA)
DOO............ Directing Ordnance Officer [*Military British*]
DOO............ Director, Office of Oceanography [*UNESCO*]
DOO............ Disposition One Only (MCD)
DOO............ District Operations Office [*or Officer*] [*Navy*]
DOO............ District Ordnance Office [*or Officer*] [*Navy*]
DOO............ Division Ordnance Officer
DOO............ Doolan Road [*California*] [*Seismograph station code, US Geological Survey*] (SEIS)
DOO............ Dorobisoro [*Papua New Guinea*] [*Airport symbol*] (OAG)
DOO............ Driver-Only Operation [*Railroad*] [*British*]
DOOBE........ Disillusioned, Overcharged, Outraged Buyers Explode [*Computer hacker's terminology*] (PCM)
DOOC.......... Diabetes Out of Control [*Medicine*] (MEDA)
DOOD.......... De Olympiade Onder Dectatuur [*The Olympics Under Dictatorship*] [*An exhibition in 1936 by 150 artists protesting Nazi repression*] [*Reconstructed in 1996 by the Amsterdam Municipal Archives*]
DOODY .... Do-Object-Oriented-Development-Yourself [*Computer science*]
DOOF.......... Driver-Only Operation, Freight [*Railroad*] [*British*]
DOOL.......... Days of Our Lives [*NBC-TV daytime serial*]
DOOLAR ..... Deep Ocean Object Location and Recovery [*Navy*]
DOOM......... Deep Ocean Optical Measurement
DOOP.......... Driver-Only Operation, Passenger [*Railroad*] [*British*]
DOOPO........ Director of Operations, Operational Plans Officer (MUGU)
DOOR.......... Deafness, Onycho-Osteodystrophy, Mental Retardation Syndrome [*Medicine*] (DMAA)
DOORS .... Data on Occupations Retrieval System [*Great Britain Manpower Services Commission*] [*Information service or system*] (CRD)
DOORS .... Development of Operational Reasoning Skills
DOORS .... Directory of Outpatient Ostomy Resources and Services [*International Association for Enterostomal Therapy*]
DOOW......... Diving Officer-of-the-Watch [*Navy*] (DNAB)
DOP............ Degree of Protection
DOP............ Degree of Pyritization [*Geology*]
DOP............ Dermo-Optical Perception [*Parapsychology*]
DOP............ Designated Overhaul Point
DOP............ Desoctapeptide Insulin [*Medicine*]
DOP............ Detachment of Patients
DOP............ Detailed Operating Procedure
DOP............ Detection Operational Program [*Military*] (CAAL)
DOP............ Developer Oxidation Product [*Photography*]
DOP............ Developing-Out Paper
DOP............ Dilution of Precision
DOP............ Dioctyl Phosphate [*Organic chemistry*]
DOP............ Dioctyl Phthalate [*Also, DEHP*] [*Organic chemistry*]
D-OP........... Diplomate, American Board of Ophthalmology (DHSM)
DOP............ Director of Office of Programming [*Military*]
DOP............ Disaster Operations Plan [*Nuclear energy*] (NRCH)
DOP............ Di-Secondary Octyl Phthalate (GFGA)
DOP............ Dissolved Organic Phosphorus
DOP............ Diver Operated Plug (MCD)
DOP............ Documents on Payment [*Banking*]
DOP............ Dolpa [*Nepal*] [*Airport symbol*] (OAG)
DOP............ Dopamine [*Pharmacology*] (DAVI)
DOP............ Doppler (KSC)
DOPA.......... Dihydroxyphenylalanine [*Biochemistry*]
DOPA.......... Dopamine [*Pharmacology*] (DAVI)
DOPA.......... Dynamic Output Printer Analyzer (IAA)
DOPAA........ Description of Proposed Actions and Alternatives [*Military*]
DOPAC........ Dihydroxyphenylacetic Acid [*Biochemistry*]
DOPACK...... Doppler Software Package (ADA)
DOPASE...... Dihydroxyphenylalanine Oxidase [*Organic chemistry*] (DMAA)
DOPC.......... Dioleoylphosphatidylcholine [*Organic chemistry*]
DOPE.......... Databank of Program Evaluations [*University of California, Los Angeles*] (IID)

DOPE	Dioleylphosphatidylethanolamine [*Organic chemistry*]
DOPE	Display, Oral, Printed, and Electronic [*Media*]
DOPE	Double Odd Pass Even [*System in game of bridge*]
DOPEG	Dihydroxyphenylglycol [*Also, DHPG*] [*Organic chemistry*]
DOPET	Dihydroxyphenylethanol [*Organic chemistry*]
DOPF	Duty Directed in Order Is Being Performed For
D OPH	Doctor of Ophthalmology (WDAA)
DOPHHH	Division on Physically Handicapped, Homebound, and Hospitalized [*Later, DPH*] (EA)
DOphth	Doctor of Ophthalmology (NADA)
DOPI	Overseas Private Investment Corp., Washington, DC [*Library symbol Library of Congress*] (LCLS)
DOPIC	Documentation of Programs in Core [*Computer science*] (IEEE)
DOPLIGHT	Doppler-Balloon [*Marine science*] (OSRA)
DOPLIGHT	Doppler-Lighting (USDC)
DOPLOC	Doppler Location (IAA)
DOPLOC	Doppler Phase Lock
DOPLOON	Doppler-Balloon (USDC)
DOPMA	Defense Officer Personnel Management Act [*1980*] (MCD)
DOPMS	Defense Officer Personnel Management Study (NVT)
DOPODT	Doped Polysilicon Diffusion Technology [*Electronics*] (IAA)
DOPOS	Doped Polysilicon Diffusion Source [*Electronics*] (IAA)
DOPP	Dioctylphenyl Phosphonate [*Organic chemistry*]
DOPP	Doppler (MUGU)
DOPP PED	Doppio Pedale [*Double Pedal*] [*Music*]
DOPR	Defense Order Priority Rating [*DoD*] (GFGA)
DOPRT	Date of Departure [*Army*]
DOPS	DIA [*Defense Intelligence Agency*] Outline Plotting System
DOPS	Diffuse Obstructive Pulmonary Syndrome [*Medicine*] (MAE)
DOPS	Digital Optical Projection System [*IEEE*]
DOPS	Dihydroxyphenylserine [*Biochemistry*]
DOPS	Dioleoylphosphatidylserine [*Biochemistry*]
DOPS	Direct Optical Position Sensor [*Instrumentation*]
DOpt	Diploma in Ophthalmics (ADA)
D OPT	Doctor of Optometry (WDAA)
DOPTAR	Doppler Tracking and Ranging [*Military*] (CAAL)
D Opth	Doctor of Ophthalmology
DOQ	Dynamic Order Quantity
DOR	Daily Operational Report
DOR	Daily Outage Report (SSD)
DOR	Dance-Oriented Rock [*Music*] (BARN)
DOR	Data Output Register [*Computer science*]
DOR	Date of Rank [*Air Force*]
DOR	Date of Request (AFM)
DOR	Design Objective Reliability
DOR	Digital Optical Record (IAA)
DOR	Digital Output Relay
DOR	Director of Operational Requirements [*Air Ministry*] [*British*]
DOR	Disaster Operations Room [*Public safety*]
DOR	Discharged on Own Recognizance (IIA)
DOR	Division of Research [*Indiana University*] [*Research center*] (RCD)
D Or	Doctor of Oratory
DOR	Document Ordres et Reglements Statutaires [*Statutory Orders and Regulations - SOR*] [*Database Federal Department of Justice*] [*Canada*] [*Information service or system*] (CRD)
Dor	Dorado [*Constellation*]
DOR	Dori [*Burkina Faso*] [*Airport symbol*] (OAG)
DOR	Dori [*Upper Volta*] [*Airport symbol*] (AD)
DOR	Doric
Dor	Dorion's Quebec Reports [*A publication*] (DLA)
DOR	Dormitory
DOR	Dornier Reparaturwerft GmbH [*Germany ICAO designator*] (FAAC)
DOR	Double Rotation [*Spectroscopy*]
DOR	Dropout Rate (DNAB)
DOR	Dropped Own Request [*Navy*]
DOR	Dundarave Resources [*Vancouver Stock Exchange symbol*]
DOR	Graduate School of Business Administration, Division of Research [*University of Michigan*] [*Research center*] (RCD)
D OR	United States District Court for the District of Oregon (DLA)
DORA	Defence of the Realm Act [*World War I*] [*British*]
DORA	Directory of Rare Analyses [*A publication*]
DORA	Disbursing Officers' Relief Act [*1982*]
Dora	Dorado [*Constellation*]
DORA	Double Roll Out Arrays (MCD)
DORA	Dynamic Operator Response Apparatus
DORACE	Design Organization, Record, Analyze, Charge, Estimate (MHDB)
DORAN	Doppler Range and Navigation [*Electronics*]
Dor Bank	Doria's Law and Practice in Bankruptcy [*2nd ed.*] [*1873*] [*A publication*] (DLA)
DORCA	Dynamic Operational Requirements and Cost Analysis [*Computer program*] [*NASA*]
DORCG	Date of Rank, Current Grade [*Air Force*] (AFM)
DORCH	Dorchester [*City in England*] (ROG)
DORCMA	Door Operator and Remote Controls Manufacturers Association (EA)
DORCSA	District Officer for Reserve Communication Supplementary Activities
DORDEC	Domestic Refrigeration Development Committee [*British*] (BI)
DORE	DoD [*Department of Defense*] Officer Record Examination
DORF	Diamond Ordnance Radiation Facility [*Nuclear reactor*]
DORFA	Subcommittee on Department Operations, Research, and Foreign Agriculture [*Congress*]
DORIDN	Doriden [*Rhone-Poulenc Rorer Consumer Pharmaceuticals*] [*Pharmacology*] (DAVI)
Dor Ins	Dorsay's Law of Insolvency [*A publication*] (DLA)
Dorion	Dorion's Quebec Queen's Bench Reports [*A publication*] (DLA)

Dorion (Can)	Dorion's Quebec Queen's Bench Reports (Canada) [*A publication*] (DLA)
Dorion QB	Dorion's Quebec Queen's Bench Reports [*A publication*] (DLA)
DORIS	Dealers' Office Realtime Information System [*London Stock Exchange*] (NITA)
DORIS	Deck-Operated Remote Inspection Submersible
DORIS	Demographic Online Retrieval Information System [*CACI, Inc.*]
DORIS	Development of Reasoning in Science
DORIS	Direct Order Recording and Invoicing System [*A computer-based system of British petroleum companies*]
DORIS	Division of Research Information System (SAA)
DORIS	Doppler Orbitography and Radiopositioning Integrated by Satellite [*Marine science*] (OSRA)
DORIS	Doppler Orbitography Integrated by Satellite
DORIS	Doppler Ranging and Information System [*Navy*] (MCD)
DORIS	Dornier Recoverable Instrument Sonde (MCD)
DORIS	Double-Ring Storage [*Particle accelerator*]
DORK	Diagnostically Optimizable Recursive Keyword [*Program generator*] (NITA)
DORL	Diploma in Otorhinolaryngology
DORM	Dormitory
dorm	Dormitory (VRA)
Dor MD Laws	Dorsey's Maryland Laws [*A publication*] (DLA)
DORPG	Date of Rank, Permanent Grade [*Air Force*] (AFM)
Dor QB	Dorion's Quebec Queen's Bench Reports [*A publication*] (DLA)
DORS	Davis Online Reference Services [*University of California, Davis*] (OLDSS)
DORS	Defence Operational Requirements [*British military*] (DMA)
DORS	Defense Outplacement Referral System [*DoD*]
Dors	Dorset [*County in England*] (ODBW)
DORS	Dorsetshire [*County in England*] (ROG)
DORS	Dynamic Operator Response System
D Or Sc	Doctor of the Science of Oratory
DORSET	Dorsetshire [*County in England*]
DorseyTr	Dorsey Trailers, Inc. [*Associated Press*] (SAG)
DOrth	Diploma in Orthodontics [*British*]
DOrth	Diploma in Orthopedics
D Orth	Diploma in Orthoptics [*British*]
D Orth RCS Eng	Diplomate in Orthodontics, Royal College of Surgeons of England
DORTS	Department of Rapid Transit Systems [*Taipei*] (ECON)
DORV	Deep Ocean Research Vehicle (IEEE)
DORV	Double Outlet Right Ventricle [*Cardiology*]
DORx	Date of Treatment [*Medicine*] (DAVI)
DOS	Data Organization Service (IAA)
DOS	Date of Separation [*Military*]
DOS	Date of Service
DOS	Date of Surgery (DAVI)
DOS	Day of Sale [*Business term*] (ADA)
DOS	Days of Supply [*Rations*]
DOS	Decision Outstanding [*Computer science*] (BUR)
DOS	Defense Occupational Specialties [*Army*]
DOS	Deferred Organic Supply (MCD)
DOS	Degenerate Oscillating System
DOS	Deliverer of Services (OICC)
DOS	Densities of States [*Photovoltaic energy systems*]
DOS	Density of States [*Physics*]
DOS	Deoxystreptamine [*Organic chemistry*]
DOS	Department of State
DOS	Department of State, Washington, DC [*OCLC symbol*] (OCLC)
DOS	Department of Surgery
DOS	Dependents Overseas [*Military*]
DOS	Diabetes Opinion Survey [*Child development test*] [*Psychology*]
DOS	Digital Operation System (IEEE)
DOS	Dioctyl Sebacate [*Organic chemistry*]
DOS	Diploma in Orthopaedic Surgery (ADA)
D-OS	Diplomate, American Board of Orthopaedic Surgery (DHSM)
DOS	Direct Operating System [*Computer technology*]
DOS	Directorate of Overseas Surveys [*Overseas Development Administration*] [*British*] (DS)
DOS	Director of Ordnance Services [*Military British*]
DOS	Director of Sales
DOS	Director of Stores [*Navy British*]
DOS	Director [*or Directorate*] of Support [*Army*]
DOS	Discrete Orthonormal Sequence
DOS	Disk Operating System [*Computer science*] (IID)
DOS	Distributed Operation System [*Computer science*] (IAA)
DOS	Division of Operational Safety [*Energy Research and Development Administration*] (MCD)
DOS	Doctor of Ocular Science
DOS	Doctor of Optical Science
DOS	Doctor of Optometric Science
DOS	Dosage [*Medicine*]
DOS	Dos Bocas Dam [*Puerto Rico*] [*Seismograph station code, US Geological Survey*] (SEIS)
DOS	Dosis [*Dose*] [*Pharmacy*] (ROG)
DOS	Drum Out of Service (CET)
DOSAAF	Dobrovol'noe Obshchestvo Sodeistviia Armii, Aviatsii, i Flotu [*Voluntary Society for Cooperation with the Army, Aviation, and the Fleet*] [*Former USSR*]
DOSAR	Department of State Acquisition Regulation [*A publication*] (AAGC)
DOSAR	Dosimetry Applications Research Facility [*AEC*]
DOSC	Dimensions of Self-Concept [*Personality test*]
DO Sc	Doctor of Optometric Science
DOSC	Dubois Oleic Serum Complex [*Bacteriology*]

DOSCA.........	Department of State Correspondents Association (EA)
DOSE...........	Capstone Pharmacy Services, Inc. [NASDAQ symbol] (SAG)
DOSE...........	Capstone Pharmacy Svc [NASDAQ symbol] (TTSB)
DOSE...........	Choice Drug Systems, Inc. [NASDAQ symbol] (NQ)
DOSE...........	Disk Operating System - Enhanced [Computer science] (MCD)
DOSE...........	Distributed Office Support Executive [IBM Corp.] (IAA)
DOSECC.......	Deep Observation and Sampling of the Earth's Continental Crust [National Science Foundation]
DOSEW........	Capstone Pharmacy Svcs Wrrt [NASDAQ symbol] (TTSB)
DOSF...........	Deep Ocean Simulation Facility (SAA)
Doshisha LJ...	Doshisha Law Journal. International Edition [A publication] (DLA)
Doshisha L Rev...	Doshisha Law Review [A publication] (DLA)
DOSIM.........	Dosimeter (NASA)
DOSK..........	Distributed Operating System Kernel [Computer science]
Dos Let.......	Dosis Letalis [Lethal Dose] [Latin]
DOS-LV.......	Disk Operating System - Large Volumes [Computer science]
DOSM..........	Desialylated Ovine Submaxillary Mucin [Biochemistry]
DOSN..........	Disbursing Office Serial Number
DOSP..........	Dalhousie Ocean Studies Programme [Dalhousie University] [Canada Research center] (RCD)
DOSP..........	Deep Ocean Sediment Probe [Marine science] (MSC)
Dos Passos Stock-Brok...	Dos Passos on Stock-Brokers and Stock Exchanges [A publication] (DLA)
DOSPR........	Department of State Procurement Regulations
DOSS..........	Decision-Oriented Scheduling System (MCD)
DOSS..........	Deep Ocean Search System [Marine science]
DOSS..........	Dioctyl Sodium Sulfosuccinate [Organic chemistry]
DOSS..........	Disk-Oriented Supply System [Computer science] (DNAB)
DOSS..........	Distal Over-Shoulder Strap
DOSS..........	Documentation on Social Security [ILO] [Information service or system United Nations] (DUND)
DOSS..........	Docusate Sodium [Medicine] (DMAA)
DOSS..........	Doppler Optical Surveillance System
DOSS..........	DSCS [Defense Satellite Communication System] Operational Support System [DoD]
DOSS-AF.....	Directorate of Operational Support Services - Air Force
DOSSU........	Dogs on Stamps Study Unit (EA)
DOS-SV.......	Disk Operating System - Small Volumes [Computer science]
DOST..........	Data Output Strobe (NITA)
DOST..........	Department of Science and Technology [Science and Technology Information Institute] [Philippines] (IID)
DOST..........	Dictionary of the Older Scottish Tongue [A publication]
DOst...........	Diploma in Osteopathy [Australia]
DOSV..........	Deep Oceanographic Survey Vehicle [Naval Oceanographic Office]
DOS/VS.......	Disk Operating System/Virtual Storage [IBM Corp.] [Computer science] (MCD)
DOSY..........	Digiset Oriented Setting System [Siemens-Hell] (NITA)
DOT...........	Daily Operability Test [Military] (CAAL)
DOT...........	Date of Trade [Investment term]
DOT...........	Deep Oceanic Turbulence
DOT...........	Deep Ocean Technology
DOT...........	Deep Ocean Transponder
DOT...........	Deep-Operating Torpedo (MCD)
DOT...........	Delayed on Target
DOT...........	Department of Overseas Trade [British]
DOT...........	Department of the Treasury (AFM)
DoT...........	Department of Trade [British]
DOT...........	Department of Transport [Canada]
DOT...........	Department of Transportation
DOT...........	Department of Treasury [Victoria] [Australia]
DOT...........	Dependent Overseas Territory
DOT...........	Deployment Operations Team
DOT...........	Designated Order Turnaround [NYSE term]
DOT...........	Designating Optical Tracker [Telescope]
DOT...........	Dictionary of Occupational Titles [Department of Labor] [A publication]
DOT...........	Died on [Operating] Table [Medicine] (DAVI)
DOT...........	Differential Oil Temperature [Automotive engineering]
DOT...........	Digital Optical Technology System [Computer science]
DOT...........	Digital Optical Transceiver [Citifax Corp.]
DOT...........	Digital Output Timer [Computer science]
DOT...........	Dioctyltin [Organic chemistry]
DOT...........	Diploma of Occupational Therapy
D-OT..........	Diplomate, American Board of Otolaryngology (DHSM)
DOT...........	Direction of Trade (NITA)
DOT...........	Directly-Observed Therapy
DOT...........	Director of Operational Training [RAF] [British]
DOT...........	Director [or Directorate] of Training [Army]
DOT...........	Director on Target [Military] (CAAL)
DOT...........	Directory of Occupational Titles (DNAB)
DOT...........	Discrete Ordinate Transport
DOT...........	Displacement-Oriented Transducer
DOT...........	Dissolved Oxygen Tension [Chemistry]
DOT...........	Division of Organ Transplantation [Department of Health and Human Services] (PAZ)
DOT...........	Domain Tip (PDAA)
DOT...........	Doppler Ophthalmic Test (CPH)
DOT...........	Dorset Resources Ltd. [Toronto Stock Exchange symbol]
DOT...........	Double Offset Tactic (SAA)
DOT...........	Duplex One-Tape System
DOT...........	Dynamic Operation Test
DOT...........	Kansas City, MO [Location identifier FAA] (FAAL)
DOTA..........	Diakonia of the Americas (EA)
DOT&E........	Director, Operational Test and Evaluation [OSD] (AAGC)
DOTAP........	Dioleoyl Trimethylammonium Propane [Organic chemistry]
DOT BCA.....	Department of Transportation Board of Contract Appeals (AAGC)
DOTC..........	Data Observing Testing Console
DOTC..........	Director, Office of Transport and Communications [Department of State] (AAG)
DOTCAB......	Department of Transportation Contract Adjustment Board (AAGC)
DOTCAB......	Department of Transportation Contract Appeals Board
DOTCAP......	Department of Transportation Contract Assistance Program (AAGC)
DOT-CG-N...	Department of Transportation Coast Guard Office of Navigation [Washington, DC]
DOT/CIAP....	Department of Transportation/Climatic Impact Assessment Program (NASA)
DOTCOOP ...	Department of Transportation Continuity of Operations Plan [Federal emergency plan]
DOTD..........	Directorate of Training and Development [Army]
DOTE..........	OSD [Office of the Secretary of Defense] Operational Test and Evaluation (RDA)
DOTEO........	Department of Transportation's Emergency Organization
DOT/FAA/AM...	Department of Transportation Federal Aviation Administration Office of Aviation Medicine [Washington, DC]
DOT/FAA/AP...	Department of Transportation Federal Aviation Administration Office of Airports Programs [Washington, DC]
DOT/FAA/ASF...	Department of Transportation Federal Aviation Administration Office of Aviation Safety [Washington, DC]
DOT/FAA/AT...	Department of Transportation Federal Aviation Administration Air Traffic Service [Washington, DC]
DOT/FAA/CP...	Department of Transportation Federal Aviation Administration Airport Capacity Program Office [Washington, DC]
DOT/FAA/EE...	Department of Transportation Federal Aviation Administration Office of Environment and Energy [Washington, DC]
DOT/FAA/EM...	Department of Transportation Federal Aviation Administration Office of Systems Engineering Management [Washington, DC]
DOT/FAA/ES...	Department of Transportation Federal Aviation Administration Systems EngineeringService [Washington, DC]
DOT/FAA/PM...	Department of Transportation Federal Aviation Administration Program Engineeringand Maintenance Service [Washington, DC]
DOT/FAA/PP...	Department of Transportation Federal Aviation Administration Office of Airport Planning and Programming [Washington, DC]
DOT/FAA/PS...	Department of Transportation Federal Aviation Administration Program EngineeringService [Washington, DC]
DOT/FAA/RD...	Department of Transportation Federal Aviation Administration Systems Research and Development Service [Washington, DC]
DOTFAP.......	Department of Transportation Financial Assistance Program (AAGC)
DOTG..........	Di-ortho-toylguanidine [Organic chemistry]
DOT-HS.......	Department of Transportation National Highway Traffic Safety Administration [Washington, DC]
DOTI..........	Department of Trade and Industry [British] (NITA)
DOTI..........	Director of Operations, Training and Intelligence [Army] (AABC)
DOTIC.........	Directory of Title Pages Indexes and Contents Pages [UK Serials Group] (NITA)
DOTIG.........	Department of Transportation Inspector General
DOTIPOS.....	Deep Ocean Test-in-Place and Observation System [Navy]
DOTLMS	Doctrine, Organizations, Training, Leaders, Material, and Soldiers [Military] (RDA)
DOTM.........	Due-Out to Maintenance [Military] (MCD)
DOT-OS.......	Department of Transportation Office of Assistant Secretary for Systems Development and Technology [Washington, DC]
DOTP..........	Deep Ocean Technology Project
DOTP..........	Dental Officer Training Plan [Canada]
DOTp..........	Department of Transport [British] (DA)
DOTP..........	Dioctyl Terephthalate [Organic chemistry]
DOTP..........	Duty Operational Test Director
DOTPR........	Department of Transportation Procurement Regulations (AAGC)
DotR..........	Dramatists of the Restoration [British] (ROG)
DOTRAM.....	Domain Tip Random Access Memory [Computer science]
DOTREX......	Deep Ocean Tracer Experiment [Marine science] (OSRA)
Dotrnix.......	Dotronics, Inc. [Associated Press] (SAG)
DOTS..........	Deviation of Temperature and Salinity
DOTS..........	Digital Optical Technology System [3-D television system]
DOTS..........	Diploma of Tertiary Studies
DOTS..........	Direction of Trade Statistics [International Monetary Fund] [Information service or system] (CRD)
DOTS..........	Directly Observed Treatment Short-Course [Therapy regime]
DOTS..........	Division On-Line Tool System [Allan Collautt Associates, Inc.] [Automotive engineering]
DOTS..........	Dredging Operations Technical Support (RDA)
DOTS..........	Dynamic Ocean Track System (DA)
DOTSP........	Distinctive Ovarian Tumor with Sexual Precocity
DOTSP........	Doctrinal and Organization Test Support Package [Army]
DOT-SST......	Department of Transportation Office of Supersonic Transportation [Washington, DC]
DOTSYS......	Dot System [Mitre Corp.] [Braille translation system] (NITA)
DOTT..........	Decision-Oriented Templating Techniques
DOTT..........	Di-o-tolylthiourea [Organic chemistry]
DOTT..........	Doctrinal and Organizational Training Team [Army]
DOTT..........	Documents from Old Testament Times [A publication] (BJA)
DOTT..........	Duties Other than Teaching (ADA)
Dott Ing......	Dottore Ingenieur [Doctor of Engineering] [Italian]
DOTX.........	Dotronics, Inc. [NASDAQ symbol] (SAG)
DOTX.........	Dotronix, Inc. [NASDAQ symbol] (NQ)
DOU..........	Definitive Observation Unit [Medicine] (MEDA)
DOU..........	Dourados [Brazil] [Airport symbol] (OAG)
DOU..........	Dourbes [Belgium] [Seismograph station code, US Geological Survey] (SEIS)
DOUDDAS....	Deep Ocean Untended Digital Data Acquisition System [Marine science] (MSC)

DOUG..........	Douglas & Lomason [*NASDAQ symbol*] (TTSB)
DOUG..........	Douglas & Lomason Co. [*NASDAQ symbol*] (NQ)
Doug...........	Douglas' English Election Cases [*A publication*] (DLA)
Doug...........	Douglas' English King's Bench Reports [*A publication*] (DLA)
Doug...........	Douglas' Michigan Supreme Court Reports [*A publication*] (DLA)
Doug...........	Douglas' Reports [*A publication*] (DLA)
Doug El Ca...	Douglas' English Election Cases [*A publication*] (DLA)
Doug El Cas...	Douglas' English Election Cases [*A publication*] (DLA)
DOUG FIR-L...	Douglas Fir Larch [*Lumber*]
Doug KB	Douglas' English King's Bench Reports [*A publication*] (DLA)
Dougl El Cas...	Douglas' English Election Cases [*A publication*] (DLA)
Dougl KB	Douglas' English King's Bench Reports [*A publication*] (DLA)
Dougl KB (Eng)...	Douglas' English King's Bench Reports [*A publication*] (DLA)
Dougl (Mich)...	Douglas' Michigan Supreme Court Reports [*A publication*] (DLA)
Doug (Mich)...	Douglas' Michigan Supreme Court Reports [*A publication*] (DLA)
DOULT	Doulton Ware [*Ceramics*] (ROG)
DOUSER	Doppler Unbeamed Search RADAR
Dout Pr........	Doutre. Procedure Civile de Bas Canada [*A publication*] (DLA)
DOV	Data over Voice [*Telecommunications*] (TEL)
DOV	Diaphragm Operated Valve
DOV	Disbursing Officer's Voucher
DOV	Discharged on Visit [*Psychiatry*]
DOV	Discreet Operations Vehicle [*Military*] (LAIN)
DOV	Discrete Out Vehicle [*NASA*] (KSC)
DOV	Distilled Oil of Vitriol
DOV	Double Oil of Vitriol
DOV	Dover [*Delaware*] [*Airport symbol*] (AD)
DOV	Dover Corp. [*NYSE symbol*] (SPSG)
DOV	Dover, DE [*Location identifier FAA*] (FAAL)
DOV	Dover Public Library, Dover, DE [*OCLC symbol*] (OCLC)
DOV	Doverton Oils Ltd. [*Vancouver Stock Exchange symbol*]
DOVACK......	Differential, Oral, Visual, Aural, Computerized Kinesthetic
DOVAP........	Doppler, Velocity and Position [*NASA*]
Dovatrn........	DOVatron International [*Associated Press*] (SAG)
DOVE	Data on Vocational Education [*Department of Education*] (GFGA)
DOVE	Dove Audio [*NASDAQ symbol*] (TTSB)
DOVE	Dove Audio, Inc. [*NASDAQ symbol*] (SAG)
DoveAud	Dove Audio, Inc. [*Associated Press*] (SAG)
Dover..........	Dover Corp. [*Associated Press*] (SAG)
DoverD	Dover Downs Entertainment, Inc. [*Associated Press*] (SAG)
DOVETT	Double Velocity Transit Time [*Physics*]
DOV PULV ...	Doveri Pulvis [*Dover's Powder*] [*Pharmacy*] (ROG)
DOVT	Dovatron International [*NASDAQ symbol*] (SAG)
DOW	Defenders of Wildlife
DOW	Delivery on Wheels [*Shipping*] (DS)
DOW	Density of Water
DOW	Department of Wildlife (GNE)
DOW	Died of Wounds [*Military*]
DOW	Direct Overwrite [*Computer science*]
DOW	Doppler on Wheels [*Instrumentation*]
DOW	Dow Chemical [*NYSE symbol*] (TTSB)
DOW	Dow Chemical Co. [*NYSE symbol Toronto Stock Exchange symbol*]
DOW	Dow Chemical Co., Granville Research Center, Granville, OH [*OCLC symbol*] (OCLC)
DOW	Dower [*or Dowager*]
Dow	Dowling's English Practice Cases [*A publication*] (DLA)
DOW	Downeast Flying Service, Inc. [*FAA designator*] (FAAC)
Dow	Dow's House of Lords (Parliamentary) Cases [*Same as Dow's Reports*] [*3 English Reprint*] [*A publication*] (DLA)
DOW	Duration of War
Dow & C......	Dow and Clark's English House of Lords Cases [*A publication*] (DLA)
Dow & C (Eng)...	Dow and Clark's English House of Lords Cases [*A publication*] (DLA)
Dow & Cl....	Dow and Clark's English House of Lords Cases [*A publication*] (DLA)
Dow & L......	Dowling and Lowndes' English Bail Court Reports [*A publication*] (DLA)
Dow & Lownd...	Dowling and Lowndes' English Practice Cases [*A publication*] (DLA)
Dow & Ry....	Dowling and Ryland's English King's Bench Reports [*A publication*] (DLA)
Dow & Ry....	Dowling and Ryland's English Nisi Prius Cases [*A publication*] (DLA)
Dow & Ry KB...	Dowling and Ryland's English King's Bench Reports [*A publication*] (DLA)
Dow & Ry KB...	Dowling and Ryland's English Nisi Prius Cases [*A publication*] (DLA)
Dow & Ry MC...	Dowling and Ryland's English Magistrates' Cases [*A publication*] (DLA)
Dow & Ry NP...	Dowling and Ryland's English Nisi Prius Cases [*A publication*] (DLA)
DOWB..........	Deep Ocean Work Boat [*Marine science*] (MSC)
DOWB..........	Deep Operating Work Board [*IEEE*]
DOWB..........	Director of Works and Buildings [*British*]
DowCh........	Dow Chemical Co. [*Associated Press*] (SAG)
Dowd Ins	Dowdeswell on Life and Fire Insurance [*A publication*] (DLA)
Dow Inc	Dowell's Income Tax Acts [*9th ed.*] [*1934*] [*A publication*] (DLA)
DowJns........	Dow Jones & Co., Inc. [*Associated Press*] (SAG)
Dowl	Dowling's English Bail Court (Practice) Cases [*A publication*] (DLA)
Dowl & L.....	Dowling and Lowndes' English Bail Court Reports [*A publication*] (DLA)
Dowl & Lownd...	Dowling and Lowndes' English Bail Court Reports [*A publication*] (DLA)
Dowl & R.....	Dowling and Ryland's English King's Bench Reports [*A publication*] (DLA)
Dowl & R (Eng)...	Dowling and Ryland's English King's Bench Reports [*A publication*] (DLA)

Dowl & R Mag Cas (Eng)...	Dowling and Ryland's English Magistrates' Cases [*A publication*] (DLA)
Dowl & R NP...	Dowling and Ryland's English Nisi Prius Cases [*A publication*] (DLA)
Dowl & R NP (Eng)...	Dowling and Ryland's English Nisi Prius Cases [*A publication*] (DLA)
Dowl & Ryl...	Dowling and Ryland's English King's Bench Reports [*A publication*] (DLA)
Dowl & Ryl MC...	Dowling and Ryland's English Magistrates' Cases [*A publication*] (DLA)
Dowl & Ryl NP...	Dowling and Ryland's English Nisi Prius Cases [*A publication*] (DLA)
Dowl (Eng)...	Dowling's English Bail Court (Practice) Cases [*A publication*] (DLA)
Dowl NS	Dowling's English Bail Court Reports, New Series [*1841-43*] [*A publication*] (DLA)
Dowl NS (Eng)...	Dowling's English Bail Court Reports, New Series [*1841-43*] [*A publication*] (DLA)
Dowl PC	Dowling's English Bail Court (Practice) Cases [*A publication*] (DLA)
Dowl PC (Eng)...	Dowling's English Bail Court (Practice) Cases [*A publication*] (DLA)
Dowl PC NS...	Dowling's English Practice Cases, New Series [*A publication*] (DLA)
Dowl Pr	Dowling's Common Law Practice [*A publication*] (DLA)
Dowl PR	Dowling's Practice Reports [*A publication*] (DLA)
Dowl Pr Cas...	Dowling's English Practice Cases [*A publication*] (DLA)
Dowl Pr C NS...	Dowling's English Practice Cases, New Series [*A publication*] (DLA)
DOWM........	Database of Off-Site Waste Management [*Public Data Access, Inc.*] [*No longer available online*] [*Information service or system*]
DOWN..........	Downing College [*Cambridge University*] (ROG)
Down & Lud...	Downton and Luder's English Election Cases [*A publication*] (DLA)
DowneyF......	Downey Financial Corp. [*Formerly, Downey S & L Association*] [*Associated Press*] (SAG)
Dow NS	Dow and Clark's English House of Lords Cases [*A publication*] (DLA)
Dow NS	Dowling's English Bail Court Reports, New Series [*1841-43*] [*A publication*] (DLA)
Dow PC.......	Dowling's English Practice Cases [*A publication*] (DLA)
Dow PC.......	Dow's House of Lords (Parliamentary) Cases [*Same as Dow's Reports*] [*3 English Reprint*] [*A publication*] (DLA)
Dow PC (Eng)...	Dowling's English Practice Cases [*A publication*] (DLA)
Dow PC (Eng)...	Dow's House of Lords (Parliamentary) Cases [*Same as Dow's Reports*] [*3 English Reprint*] [*A publication*] (DLA)
Dow Pr	Dowling's English Practice Cases [*A publication*] (DLA)
Dow St........	Dowell's Stamp Duties [*1873*] [*A publication*] (DLA)
DOX	Dolphin Explorations Ltd. [*Vancouver Stock Exchange symbol Toronto Stock Exchange symbol*]
DOX	Dongara [*Australia Airport symbol*] (OAG)
DOX	Doxology (ROG)
DOX	Doxorubicin [*Also, D, DXR*] [*Formerly, ADR, Adriamycin*] [*Antineoplastic drug*]
Dox Graec ...	Doxographi Graeci [*A publication*] (OCD)
DOXOL........	Doxorubicinol [*Antineoplastic drug*]
DOY	Day of Year
DOY	Deboyne [*Louisiade Archipelago, Papua*] [*Airport symbol*] (AD)
DOZ	Dioctyl Azelate [*Organic chemistry*]
DOZ	Dozen (AFM)
DP................	By Direction of the President
DP................	Cochise Airlines [*ICAO designator*] (AD)
DP................	Daily Penalty (ROG)
DP................	Damp-Proofing (AAG)
DP................	Dash Pot [*Relay*]
DP................	Data Acquisition Package (IAA)
D/P..............	Database Size/Program Size
DP................	Data Package (SSD)
DP................	Data Path
DP................	Data Pointer [*Computer memory*]
DP................	Data Printer
DP................	Data Processing
DP................	Data Processing and/or Computer Programming Programs [*Association of Independent Colleges and Schools specialization code*]
DP................	Data Processing Technician [*Navy rating*]
DP................	Data Protection Act [*1980's*] [*British*]
DP................	Data Pulse (IAA)
DP................	Date of Publication [*Online database field identifier*]
DP................	Datum Point
DP................	Daughters of Penelope (EA)
DP................	Days' Purposes [*Shipping*]
DP................	Dead Point
DP................	Decimal Place [*Mathematics*] (IAA)
DP................	Decision Package [*Military*]
DP................	Decision Point (CAAL)
DP................	Deck Piercing
DP................	Deed Poll
DP................	Deep (FAAC)
DP................	Deep Penetration [*Air Force*]
DP................	Deep Pulse [*Medicine*]
DP................	Defense Point
D/P..............	Deferred Payment [*Business term*] (ADA)
DP................	Deflection Plate [*Technical drawings*]
DP................	Degradation Products [*Hematology*]
DP................	Degree of Polymerization
DP................	Delacorte Press [*Publisher*]
DP................	Delayed Procurement (NASA)
D/P..............	Delivery Against Payment [*Business term*] (ADA)
DP................	Delivery Point

DP............... Deltopectoral [*Anatomy*] (DAVI)
DP............... Demand Meter, Printing
DP............... Dementia Praecox [*or a patient with this condition*] [*Medical slang*]
DP............... Demi-Pension [*Hotel rate*]
DP............... Democracy Project (EA)
DP............... Democratic Party [*Kenya*] [*Political party*] (EY)
DP............... Democratic Party [*Lithuania*] [*Political party*] (EAIO)
DP............... Democratic Party [*Thailand*] [*Political party*] (PPW)
DP............... Democratic Party [*Poland Political party*] (PPW)
DP............... Democratic Party [*Cook Island*] [*Political party*] (PPW)
DP............... Democratic Party [*Uganda*] [*Political party*] (PD)
DP............... Democratische Partij - Bovenwinden [*Democratic Party - Windward Islands*] [*Netherlands Antilles*] [*Political party*] (PPW)
DP............... Democratische Partij van Curacao [*Democratic Party - Curacao*] [*Netherlands Antilles*] [*Political party*] (PPW)
DP............... Democrazia Proletaria [*Proletarian Democracy*] [*Italy Political party*] (PPE)
DP............... Demokratesch Partei [*Democratic Party*] [*Luxembourg*] [*Political party*] (PPE)
DP............... Demokraticheska Partiia [*Democratic Party*] [*Bulgaria*] [*Political party*] (PPE)
DP............... Demokratiki Parataksis [*Democratic Front*] [*Greek*] (PPE)
DP............... Dental Prosthetics [*Dentistry*] (DAVI)
DP............... Dental Prosthetic Technician
DP............... Depart (DA)
DP............... Department (IAA)
DP............... Department of the Pacific [*Marine Corps*]
DP............... Departure Point (AFM)
DP............... Deployment Payload (MCD)
DP............... Deployment Pennant [*Navy British*]
D-P............... Depo-Provera [*Contraceptive*] [*The Upjohn Co.*]
DP............... Deposit
DP............... Deposited Plan (ADA)
DP............... Depreciation Percentage [*Finance*] (WDAA)
DP............... De Profundis
DP............... Depth (MSA)
dp............... Depth (VRA)
DP............... Depth Perception (PAZ)
DP............... Der Deutsche Pionier [*A publication*] (BJA)
Dp............... Dermatophagoides pteronyssinus [*House dust*]
DP............... Description Pattern
DP............... Desiderius Pastor [*Pseudonym used by Gerard Moultree*]
DP............... Design Proof (NASA)
DP............... Design Proposal
DP............... Desktop Publishing [*Computer science*]
D/P............... Detained Pay
DP............... Detention of Pay (DNAB)
DP............... Detrucking Point
DP............... Deutsche Partei [*German Party*] [*Political party*] (PPE)
DP............... Developed Pressure [*Cardiology*]
DP............... Developing Proboscis
DP............... Development Phase (NASA)
DP............... Development Plan
DP............... Development Play (EDAC)
DP............... Development Program [*Military*]
DP............... Development Proposal (NVT)
DP............... Development Prototype
DP............... Devil Pups (EA)
DP............... Dew Point
DP............... Diabetes-Prone [*Medicine*]
DP............... Diagnostic Products [*NYSE symbol*] (TTSB)
DP............... Diagnostic Products Corp. [*NYSE symbol*] (SPSG)
DP............... Dial Pulse [*Telecommunications*]
DP............... Diametrical Pitch
DP............... Diaphosgene [*A choking agent*] (ADDR)
DP............... Diaphragm (IAA)
DP............... Diastatic Power
DP............... Diastolic Pressure [*Medicine*]
DP............... Diesel Particulate
DP............... Difference in Pressure
DP............... Difference of Potential
DP............... Difference, Port [*Navigation*]
DP............... Differential Phase [*Telecommunications*]
DP............... Differential Pressure
DP............... Differential Pulse
DP............... Diffused Planar
DP............... Diffusion Pressure
DP............... Diffusion Pump
DP............... Digestible Protein [*Medicine*] (MAE)
DP............... Digitally Programmed (IAA)
DP............... Digital Plotter
DP............... Digital Processor (MCD)
DP............... Digit Present
DP............... Dining Permit [*Slang*]
DP............... Diode Plate (IAA)
DP............... Diphenyl [*Organic chemistry*]
DP............... Diphosgene [*Poison gas*] [*Army symbol*]
DP............... Diphosphate [*Biochemistry*]
DP............... Diploma in Pediatrics
D-P............... Diplomate, American Board of Pathology (DHSM)
DP............... Dipole (DEN)
DP............... Dipropionate [*Pharmacology*] (MAE)
DP............... Directed Proliferation
DP............... Directing Point
DP............... Directional Preponderance (MAE)

DP............... Directione Propria [*With Proper Direction*] [*Pharmacy*]
DP............... Direction of President
DP............... Director of Pathology
DP............... Director of Personnel (MCD)
DP............... Director of Photography [*Cinematography*] (WDMC)
DP............... Director of Postings [*RAF*] [*British*]
DP............... Director of Programs [*Air Force, Army*]
DP............... Direct Participation (ADA)
DP............... Direct Path (NVT)
DP............... Direct Port [*Transportation*]
DP............... Direct Positive [*Photography*] (WDMC)
DP............... Direct Price
DP............... Disability Pension (MAE)
DP............... Disabled Person (ADA)
DP............... Disadvantaged Person
DP............... Disaster Preparedness (NVT)
DP............... Discharged Patient [*British*]
DP............... Disciple
DP............... Disconnection Pending [*Telecommunications*] (TEL)
DP............... Disc Plowing [*Agriculture*]
DP............... Discretionary Program (OICC)
DP............... Discussion Paper
DP............... Disk Pack [*Computer science*] (IEEE)
DP............... Disk to Printer (IAA)
DP............... Disopyramide Phosphate [*Cardiac depressant*] (AAMN)
DP............... Disorderly Person
DP............... Dispatch Point
DP............... Dispensing Precaution
DP............... Dispersal Point
DP............... Dispersed Phase (OA)
DP............... Displaced Person [*Post-World War II*]
DP............... Displaced Personnel [*Military*]
DP............... Displacement
DP............... Display Package
DP............... Display Panel
DP............... Display Processor
DP............... Dissolution Patterns [*Physics*]
D/P............... Distal Interphalangeal [*Joints*] [*Anatomy*] (DAVI)
DP............... Distal Pancreatectomy [*Medicine*] (AAMN)
DP............... Distending Pressure
DP............... Distopulpal [*Dentistry*]
DP............... Distribution Plan (AFIT)
DP............... Distribution Point
DP............... Distribution Programmer (IAA)
DP............... Docking Protein [*Biochemistry*]
DP............... Doctor of Pharmacy
DP............... Doctor of Philosophy
DP............... Doctor of Podiatry (WGA)
D/P............... Documenti Contro Pagamento [*Documents Against Payment*] [*Italian Business term*]
D/P............... Documentos Contra Pago [*Documents Against Payment*] [*Spanish Business term*]
DP............... Document Publishing (IAA)
D/P............... Documents Against Payment [*Banking*]
DP............... Documents against Payment (DFIT)
D/P............... Documents Contre Paiement [*Documents Against Payment*] [*French Banking*]
DP............... Documents Presargoniques [*A publication*] (BJA)
D-P............... Dog Pound [*Multistory parking lot*] [*Slang British*]
DP............... Domestic Prelate
DP............... Dom Perignon [*Champagne*]
DP............... Domus Procerum [*The House of Lords*] [*Latin*]
DP............... Donor's Plasma [*Medicine*]
DP............... Doppelposten [*Double Sentry*] [*German military - World War II*]
DP............... Dorsalis Pedis [*Pulse*] [*Medicine*]
DP............... Dorsal Pallium [*Neuroanatomy*]
DP............... Dorsal Pioneer Cell [*Cytology*]
DP............... Dorsal Pitt
DP............... Dot Pitch (CDE)
DP............... Double Paper [*Wire insulation*] (AAG)
DP............... Double Parallel [*Molecular biology*]
DP............... Double Petticoat [*Insulators*]
DP............... Double Plasma
DP............... Double Play [*Baseball*]
DP............... Double Pole [*Switch*]
DP............... Double Precision (NASA)
DP............... Double-Purpose Gun
DP............... Draft Proposal
DP............... Drain Panel (AAG)
DP............... Drill Pay
DP............... Drill Plate [*Tool*] (MSA)
DP............... Drill Purposes [*British military*] (DMA)
DP............... Drip-Proof (AAG)
DP............... Driving Power
DP............... Drop Point [*Air Force*] (AFM)
DP............... Drum Processor [*Computer science*] (IEEE)
DP............... Dry Point
DP............... Dual Phase (MCD)
DP............... Dual Pilot (MUGU)
DP............... Dual Purpose (NG)
DP............... Dual Purpose (DOMA)
DP............... Ducted Propellers [*Aviation*] (AAG)
DP............... Due Process
DP............... Dummy Part (MCD)
DP............... Dungpit (ROG)

DP.............. Duplicate Positive (MCD)
DP.............. Durable Press [Textile technology]
DP.............. Duty Paid [International trade]
DP.............. Duty Pay
DP.............. Dynamically Positioned
DP.............. Dynamic Programming [Computer science]
DP.............. Dynorphin [Biochemistry]
DP.............. Potential Difference [Electricity] (ROG)
DP.............. Two Pole (MSA)
DP.............. United States Patent Office, Arlington, VA [Library symbol Library of Congress] (LCLS)
DP1............. Data Processing Technician, First Class [Navy rating]
DP2............. Data Processing Technician, Second Class [Navy rating]
DP3............. Data Processing Technician, Third Class [Navy rating]
DPA............ Black Data Processing Associates (EA)
DPA............ Chicago/West Chicago, IL [Location identifier FAA] (FAAL)
DPA............ Dampier Port Authority [Australia]
DPA............ Darwin Port Authority [Australia]
DPA............ Data Processing Activities
DPA............ Data Processing Agency
DPA............ Data Processing Algorithm
DPA............ Data Processing Area
DPA............ Data Processing Assembly (MCD)
DPA............ Data Protection Act [British] (NITA)
DPA............ Data Protection Agency [British]
DPA............ Deep Water Ports Act [1974] [Environmental Protection Agency] (EPA)
DPA............ Deepwater Ports Act (GNE)
DPA............ Defense Production Act [Obsolete] (NG)
DPA............ Defense Production Administration [Functions transferred to Office of Defense Mobilization]
DPA............ Deferred Payment Account [Business term] (WDAA)
DPA............ Delegation of Procurement Authority
DPA............ Demand Protocol Architecture [Computer science] (PCM)
DPA............ Democratic Party of Albania [Political party] (EY)
DPA............ Demonstration Programs Administration [HUD]
DPA............ Designated Processing Agency (MCD)
DPA............ Designated Procuring Activity (MCD)
DPA............ Desktop Publishing Association (EA)
DPA............ Destructive Part Analysis
DPA............ Destructive Physical Analysis
DPA............ Detailed Performance Analysis [Bell System]
DPA............ Deutsche Presse Agentur [German Press Agency]
DPA............ Dextroposition of Aorta [Cardiology] (DAVI)
DPA............ Diagnostic Prescriptive Arithmetic (EDAC)
DPA............ Dial Pulse Access [Telecommunications] (TEL)
DPA............ Diary Publishers' Association [British] (BI)
DPA............ Dichloropropionanilide [Also, DCPA] [Herbicide]
DPA............ Different Premises Address [Telecommunications] (TEL)
DPA............ Digital Processor Assembly (MCD)
DPA............ Diphenolic Acid [Organic chemistry]
DPA............ Diphenylamine [Organic chemistry]
DPA............ Diphenylanthracene [Organic chemistry]
DPA............ Dipicolinic Acid [Organic chemistry]
DPA............ Diploma in Public Administration [British]
DPA............ Dipropylacetate (MAE)
DPA............ Dipropylacetic Acid [Also, VPA] [Valproic acid Anticonvulsant compound]
DPA............ Dipropylamine [Organic chemistry]
DPA............ Directorate of Policy [Air Ministry] [British]
DPA............ Directory Publishers Alliance (EA)
DPA............ Directory Publishers Association [British England] (EAIO)
DPA............ Direct Provider Agreement
DPA............ Disabled Peoples' Association [Singapore] (EAIO)
DPA............ Discharged Prisoners' Aid [British]
DPA............ Displacements per Atom (MCD)
DPA............ Distribution Plan Authorization [Military] (AFIT)
DPA............ Diversion Path Analysis (PDAA)
D Pa........... Doctor of Painting
DPA............ Doctor of Public Administration
DPA............ Document Printing Network Signaling System [Telecommunications] (OSI)
DPA............ Domestic Policy Association [Later, NIF] (EA)
DPA............ Double-Precision Arithmetic (AAG)
DPA............ D-Pantothenyl Alcohol [Biochemistry]
DPA............ Driving Point Admittance
DPA............ Dual Photon Absorptiometry [Analytical chemistry]
DPA............ Duck Producers Association [British] (DBA)
DPAA.......... Data Processing, Analysis, and Archiving (NOAA)
DPAA.......... Desktop Publishing Applications Association (EA)
DPAA.......... Draught Proofing Advisory Association [British] (DBA)
DPAC.......... Data Processing and Control (Unit) (CAAL)
DPAC.......... Defense Policy Advisory Committee [DoD]
DPAC.......... Dense-Pac Microsystems [NASDAQ symbol] (TTSB)
DPAC.......... Dense-Pac Microsystems, Inc. [NASDAQ symbol] (NQ)
DPACCS...... Displaced Persons Assembly Center Camp Staffs [Allied Military Government of Occupied Territory] [Post-World War II]
DPACT........ Defense Policy Advisory Committee on Trade [DoD]
DP Adm...... Doctor of Public Administration
DPAE.......... Data Processing Automatic Equipment
DPAE.......... Director of Program Analysis and Evaluation (RDA)
DPaed......... Doctor of Paediatrics [Medicine]
DPaed......... Doctor of Pedagogy
DPAH.......... Direct Product Actual Hours (MCD)
DPAHC........ Durable Power of Attorney for Health Care

DPAHO........ Pan American Health Organization, Pan American Sanitary Bureau, Washington, DC [Library symbol Library of Congress] (LCLS)
DPAHO-FH... Pan American Health Organization, Documentation Center, Division of Family Health, Washington, DC [Library symbol Library of Congress] (LCLS)
DPAI .... (Dipropylaminoethyl)indole [Organic chemistry]
DPAIAI........ Disregard Previous Assignment Instructions and Assign as Indicated [Army] (AABC)
DPAMMH.... Direct Productive Annual Maintenance Manhours (MCD)
DP & L .... Dallas Power & Light Co.
DP & P .... Director of Plans and Programs [Army] (RDA)
DP & S .... Data Processing and Software (NASA)
DP & S .... Data Processing and Software
DP & SPA.... Display Producers' and Screen Printers' Association (DGA)
DP & SS..... Data Processing and Software Subsystem (NASA)
D/P & T ...... Director of Personnel and Training [Army]
DPANZ........ Decorator and Painter for Australia and New Zealand [A publication]
DPAO.......... Deputy Public Affairs Officer [United States Information Service]
DPAO.......... District Public Affairs Officer [Military]
DPAP.......... Dipeptidyl Aminopeptidase [An enzyme]
D-PARC....... Daigo Proving Ground and Research Centre [Japan]
DPARS........ Data Processing Automatic Record Standardization
DPAS.......... Defense Priorities and Allocations System [DoD] (GFGA)
DPAS.......... Discharged Prisoners' Aid Society [British]
DPASV........ Differential Pulse Anodic Stripping Voltammetry [Electrochemistry]
D-PAT......... Drum-Programmed Automatic Tester
D Path .... Diploma in Pathology [British]
DPB .... Bucks County Free Library, Doylestown, PA [OCLC symbol] (OCLC)
DPB .... Dampier's Paper Book, Lincoln's Inn Library [A publication] (DLA)
DPB .... Data Path Bus
DPB .... Data Plotting Board
DPB .... Data Processing Branch (IEEE)
DPB .... Defence Production Board [NATO] (NATG)
DPB .... Defence-Protected Build-Down [Nuclear arms reduction strategy] [British]
DP-B .... Democratische Partij - Bonaire [Democratic Party - Bonaire] [Netherlands Antilles] [Political party] (EY)
DPB .... Dental Practice Board of England and Wales [British]
DPB .... Department of Plant Biology [Carnegie Institution of Washington] [Research center] (RCD)
DPB .... Deposit Byte [Computer science] (NHD)
DPB .... Deposit Passbook [Banking]
DPB .... Destruct Package Building (SAA)
DPB .... Dibutyl Phosphate [Organic chemistry] (NUCP)
DPB .... Diphenylbutadiene [Organic chemistry]
DPB .... Disability Policy Board [Veterans Administration]
DPB .... Disabled Persons Bureau [Northern Territory] [Australia]
DPB .... Disaster Preparedness Bill (DNAB)
DPB .... Distinguished Pistol Badge
DPB .... Doctor of Physical Biology
DPB .... Document Processing Branch [NTIS]
DPB .... Dodecylpyridinium Bromide [Organic chemistry]
DPB .... Drive Parameter Block [Computer science] (PCM)
Dp BA........ Diploma in Business Administration [British]
DPBA .... Dr. Pepper Bottlers Association (EA)
DpBact .... Diploma in Bacteriology [British] (DBQ)
DPBC .... Depolarizing Bipolar Cell [In the retina]
DPBC .... Double-Pole, Back Connected [Switch] (MCD)
DPBC .... Double-Pole, Both Connected [Switch]
DPBG .... Democratic Party for British Gibraltar (PPW)
DPBO .... Division Property Book Officer [Military] (AABC)
DPBSP........ Drowning Prevention and Beach Safety Program (EA)
DPC .... Chief Data Processing Technician [Formerly, MAC] [Navy rating]
DPC .... Damp-Proof Course [Civil engineering] (IAA)
DPC .... Database Promotion Center, Japan [Information service or system] (IID)
DPC .... Data Path Control [Computer science] (IAA)
DPC .... Data Processing Center
DPC .... Data Processing Central
DPC .... Data Processing Computer (CAAL)
DPC .... Data Processing Control (AFM)
DPC .... Date Physically Completed (AAGC)
DPC .... Dating Problems Checklist [Psychology]
DPC .... Defence Planning Committee [NATO] (NATG)
DPC .... Defence Production Chief [British]
DPC .... Defence Production Committee [NATO] (NATG)
DPC .... Defense Planning Council
DPC .... Defense Plant Corp. [Subsidiary of Reconstruction Finance Corp.] [Obsolete]
DPC .... Defense Procurement Circular [DoD]
DPC .... Delayed Primary Closure [Medicine]
DPC .... Democratic Policy Commission [Defunct] (EA)
DP-C .... Democratische Partij - Curacao [Democratic Party - Curacao] [Netherlands Antilles] [Political party] (EY)
DPC .... Department of the Premier and Cabinet [South Australia, Tasmania, Victoria] [Australia]
DPC .... Departure Control (DA)
DPC .... Desaturated Phosphatidylcholine [Biochemistry]
DPC .... Desert Protective Council (EA)
DPC .... Destination Point Code [Telecommunications] (TEL)
DPC .... Devotional and Practical Commentary [A publication]
DPC .... Diagnostic Products Corp.
DPC .... Differential Photocalorimetry [Analytical technique]
DPC .... Differential Pressure Control
DPC .... Digital Phase Comparator

DPC	Digital Planimetric Compiler [Computer science] (PDAA)
DPC	Digital Pressure Converter
DPC	Digital Process Controller
DPC	Diphenylaminecarboxylate [Organic chemistry]
DPC	Diphenylcarbazide [Organic chemistry]
DPC	Diphenylcarbene [Organic chemistry]
DPC	Diphenyl Carbonate [Organic chemistry]
DPC	Directive Parental Counseling
DPC	Direct Patient Care [Medicine]
DPC	Direct Power Conversion [Nuclear energy] (AAG)
DPC	Direct Program Control (BUR)
DPC	Discharge Planning Coordinator [Medicine] (DMAA)
DPC	Disk Pack Controller [Computer science] (IAA)
DPC	Displaced Persons' Camps
DPC	Displaced Persons Commission [Terminated, 1952]
DPC	Display Power Control
DPC	Display Processor Code
DPC	Distal Palmar Crease [Anatomy]
DPC	Distribution Processing Center (MCD)
DPC	Division of Physical Chemistry (EA)
DPC	Doctor of Pastoral Counseling (PGP)
DPC	Documentation Processing Center [British]
DPC	Dodecylpyridinium Chloride [Also, LPC] [Organic chemistry]
DPC	Doklady Physical Chemistry
DPC	Dollar Penny Coalition (EA)
DPC	Domestic Policy Council [Executive Office of the President] (GFGA)
DPC	Double Paper-Covered [Wire insulation] (DEN)
DPC	Dowling's English Practice Cases [A publication] (DLA)
DPC	Duke Primate Center [North Carolina]
DPC	Duty Preference Card (DNAB)
DPC	Dystrophin Protein Complex [Biochemistry]
DPC	Peace Corps, Information Services Division, Washington, DC [Library symbol] [Library of Congress] (LCLS)
DPCA	Data Processing Control Area [Space Flight Operations Facility, NASA]
DPCA	Department of Public and Consumer Affairs
DPCA	Diphenylcyclopentylamine [Organic chemistry]
DPCA	Director of Personnel and Community Activities [Army] (AABC)
DPCA	Displaced Phase Center Antenna
DPCA	Doberman Pinscher Club of America (EA)
DPCAQ	DEP Corp. 'A' [NASDAQ symbol] (TTSB)
DPCBQ	DEP Corp.'B' [NASDAQ symbol] (TTSB)
DPCC	Data Processing Control Center [or Console] [Space Flight Operations Facility, NASA]
DPCC	Director of Postal and Courier Communications [British military] (DMA)
DPCC	Duneland Post Card Club [Defunct] (EA)
DPCCP	Defective Parts and Components Control Program
DPCE	Data Processing Customer Engineering (ADA)
DPCF	Dorsal Peristomial Collar Fold
DPCI	Distributed Processing Contractual Input [Computer science]
DPCM	Delta Pulse Code Modulation [Electronics] (IAA)
DPCM	Differential Pulse Code Modulation [Transmission technique]
DPCM	Distributed Processing Communications Module
DPCM	Master Chief Data Processing Technician [Formerly, MACM] [Navy rating]
DPCN	D-Penicillamine [Pharmacology]
DPCP	Department of Prices and Consumer Protection [British]
DPCR	Departure Procedure [Aviation] (FAAC)
DPCS	Desktop Page Composition System [Vision Research]
DPCS	Difference Pressure Control Switch
DPCS	Senior Chief Data Processing Technician [Formerly, MACS] [Navy rating]
DPCSMA	Dry Process Ceramic and Steatite Manufacturers Association [Later, TECMA] (EA)
DPCT	Differential Protection Current Transformer
DPCTE	Data Processor and Computer Test Equipment
DPCTG	Database Program Conversion Task Group [CODASYL]
DPCU	Digital Processing and Control Unit
DPCX	Distributed Processing Control Executive [IBM Corp.]
DPD	Data Processing Department
DPD	Data Processing Detachment
DPD	Data Processing Directive (ODBW)
DPD	Data Processing Division [IBM Corp.]
DPD	Data Procurement Document (SSD)
DPD	Data Project Directive (AFM)
DPD	Deaminophenylalaninedehydroproline [Biochemistry]
DPD	Decontamination as Precursor to Decommissioning [Nuclear energy] (NRCH)
DPD	Depression Pure Disease [Medicine] (DMAA)
DPD	Desoxypyridoxine [or Deoxypyridoxine] Hydrochloride [Pharmacology] (DAVI)
DPD	(Diethyl)phenylenediamine [Organic chemistry]
DPD	Diffuse Pulmonary Disease [Medicine]
DPD	Diffusion Pressure Deficit
DPD	Digital Phase Difference
DPD	Digit Plane Driver [Computer science] (IEEE)
DPD	Dignitary Protective Division [US Secret Service]
DPD	Diphenamid [or Diphenyl-dimethylacetamide] [Organic chemistry] (DAVI)
DPD	Diploma in Public Dentistry [British]
D-Pd	Diplomate, American Board of Pediatrics (DHSM)
DPD	Director of Plans Division [Navy British]
DPD	Director, Personnel Department [Marine Corps]
DPD	Directory of Portable Databases [A publication]

DPD	Direct Payroll Deposit
DPD	District Port Director [Navy]
D Pd	Doctor of Pedagogy
DPD	Domestic Presidential Directive [Jimmy Carter Administration]
DPD	Double Plug Diode (IAA)
DPDA	Deterministic Pushdown Automata (PDAA)
DPDA	Phosphorodiamidic Anhydride [Organic chemistry] (DAVI)
DPDC	Double Paper, Double Cotton [Wire insulation]
DPDD	Defense Property Disposal Detachment (AFIT)
DPDI	Dimple Die
DPDL	Diffuse Poorly Differentiated Lymphocytic (Lymphoma) [Oncology]
DPDL	Distributed Program Design Language
DPDLL	Diffuse, Poorly Differentiated, Lymphocytic Lymphoma [Oncology] (DAVI)
DPDM	Diphenyl Diazomalonate [Organic chemistry]
DPDM	Diphenyldiazomethane [Organic chemistry]
DPDM	Double Pulse Duration Modulation (KSC)
DPDM-R	Defense Property Disposal Precious Metals Recovery [DoD] (AFIT)
DPDO	Defense Property Disposal Office [DoD]
DPDP	Defense Property Disposal Program [DoD] (DNAB)
DPDPMRO-E	Defense Property Disposal Precious Metals Recovery Office - Earle [New Jersey] [DoD]
DPDR	Defense Property Disposal Region [DoD]
DPDRAM	Dual-Ported Dynamic Random Access Memory [Computer science]
DPDREG	Defense Property Disposal Region [DoD] (DNAB)
DPDRPACDET	Defense Property Disposal Region, Pacific Detachment [DoD] (DNAB)
DPDRPACSO	Defense Property Disposal Region, Pacific Sales Office [DoD] (DNAB)
DPDS	DARC [Description, Acquisition, Retrieval, and Conception] Pluridata System [Association for Research and Development of Chemical Informatics] [Information service or system] (IID)
DPDS	Defense Property Disposal Service [DoD]
DP/DT	Delta Pressure/Delta Time (MCD)
DPDT	Double Pole, Double Throw [Switch]
dpdt	Double-Pole, Double-Throw (IDOE)
DPDTSW	Double-Pole, Double-Throw Switch
DPDU Dund	Diploma in Public Dentistry, University of Dundee [British]
DPDZ	Destor-Porcupine Deformation Zone [Geology]
DPE	Data Processing Equipment
DPE	Delta Pi Epsilon [Fraternity] (AEE)
DPE	Demilitarization Protective Ensemble (RDA)
DPE	Department for Professional Employees [AFL-CIO]
DPE	Desktop Publishing Editor [Computer program]
DPE	Detailed Plan Execution (MCD)
DPE	Deuterated Polyethylene [Organic chemistry]
DPE	Development Project Engineer (NRCH)
DPE	Dieppe [France] [Airport symbol Obsolete] (OAG)
DPE	Differential Paramagnetic Effect [Low-temperature physics]
DPE	Diphenylethylene [Organic chemistry]
DPE	Diphenyltrichloroethane [Also, DPT] [Organic chemistry]
DPE	Diploma in Physical Education [British]
DPE	Director Program Evaluation [Navy] (CAAL)
DPE	Direct Plate Exposer [Printing] (NITA)
DPE	Direct Plate Exposure (DGA)
DPE	Distributed Processing Environment
DPE	Distributor-to-Printer Electronics
DPE	District Power Equalizer [Formula for school grants]
DPE	Doctor of Physical Education
DPE	Doctor of Physical Education (GAGS)
DPE	Duration of the Present Emergency [British World War II]
DPE	Dynamic Phase Error
DPEC	Diploma in Parent Education and Counselling
DPEc	Doctor of Political Economy
D Ped	Doctor of Pedagogy
D Pe E	Doctor of Petroleum Engineering
D Pe Eng	Doctor of Petroleum Engineering
DPEK	Differential Phase Exchange Keying (IEEE)
DPEM	Depot Purchased Equipment Management [DoD]
DPEP	Deoxophylloerythroetioporphyrin [Biochemistry]
DPER	Donor Procurement Efficiency Rating [Medicine]
DPERPLA	Delegacion del Parlamento Europeo para las Relaciones con los Paises de Latinoamerica [Europe-Latin America Interparliamentary Assembly - ELAIA] [Luxembourg, Luxembourg] (EAIO)
DPESE	Densely Packaged Encased Standard Element (AAG)
DPESO	Department of Defense Product Engineering Services Office (MCD)
DPETD	Department of the Premier, Economic and Trade Development [Queensland] [Australia]
DPEWS	Design-to-Price Electronics Warfare System [Military]
DPEX	Distributed Processing Executive Program
DPF	Data Processing Facility
DPF	Data Processing Federation [France] (NITA)
DPF	Defatted Peanut Flour [Food industry]
DPF	Deferred Pay Fund
DPF	Denier per Filament [Textile technology]
DPF	Dense Plasma Focus
DPF	Dental Practitioner's Formulary
DPF	Depression Position-Finder
DPF	Diesel Particulate Filter [Automotive emissions]
DPF	Diesel Particulate Filter
DPF	Differential Pressure Feedback (KSC)
DPF	Differential Procedure Feedback [Military]
DPF	Disciples Peace Fellowship (EA)
DPF	Diversified Processed Foods [Vancouver Stock Exchange symbol]

DPF..........	Drill Press Feed
DPF..........	Driving Point Function [*Control system*] (IAA)
DPF..........	Drug Policy Foundation (EA)
DPF..........	Dual Program Feature
DPF..........	Dynamic Pressure Feedback
DPFAG......	Data Processing, Financial and General (IAA)
dPFC........	Direct Plaque-Forming Cell [*Immunology*]
DPFC........	Dolly Parton Fan Club (EA)
DPFC........	Double Pole, Front Connected [*Switch*]
DPFD........	Deptford [*Region of London*]
DPFLP......	Democratic Popular Front for the Liberation of Palestine (BJA)
DPFM........	Discrete Time Pulse Frequency Modulation (IAA)
DPFO........	Data Processing Field Office (MCD)
DPFP........	Double-Precision Floating Point [*Computer science*]
DPFT........	Desk, Double-Pedestal Flat-Top
DPG..........	Damping (MSA)
DPG..........	Data Processing Group [*Army*] (AABC)
DPG..........	Date of Permanent Grade
DPG..........	Debutanized Pyrolysis Gasoline
DPG..........	Dedicated Packet Group
DPG..........	Defense Planning Guidance [*Formerly, Defense Guidance*] (DOMA)
DPG..........	Defense Policy Guidance [*Military*]
DPG..........	Defense Production Guarantees, Army
DPG..........	Desulfurize Pyrolysis Gasoline [*Petroleum refining*]
DPG..........	Development Program Grant (MHDB)
DPG..........	Digital Pattern Generator
DPG..........	Diphenylguanidine [*Organic chemistry*]
DPG..........	Diphosphoglycerate [*Also, DPGA*] [*Biochemistry*]
DPG..........	Disodium Phosphoglycerate [*Organic chemistry*]
DPG..........	Displacement Placentogram [*Medicine*] (MAE)
DPG..........	Dripolene Pyrolysis Gasoline [*Lummus Crest, Inc. process*]
DPG..........	Dugway Proving Ground [*Dugway, UT*] [*Army*] (AABC)
DPG..........	Dugway/Tooele, UT [*Location identifier FAA*] (FAAL)
DPG..........	Dumping
DPGA........	Diphosphoglycerate [*Also, DPG*] [*Biochemistry*]
DPGE........	Dial Page, Inc. [*NASDAQ symbol*] (SAG)
DPGM........	Deputy Provincial Grand Master [*Freemasonry*] (ROG)
DPGM........	Diphosphoglyceromutase [*An enzyme*]
DPGN........	Diffuse Proliferative Glomerulonephritis [*Medicine*]
DPGp........	Data Processing Group [*Air Force*] (AFM)
DPGP........	Diphosphoglycerate Phosphatase [*An enzyme*] (DAVI)
DPGR........	Dugway Proving Ground [*Utah*] [*Army*]
DPG-S........	Dugway Proving Ground Studies Branch [*Utah*] [*Army*]
DPG/TA......	Dugway Proving Ground Technical Analysis and Information Office [*Utah*] [*Army*]
DPH..........	Department of Planning and Housing [*Victoria*] [*Australia*]
DPH..........	Department of Public Health
DPH..........	Depth of Hold
DPH..........	Designated Pinch Hitter [*Later, DH*] [*Baseball*]
DPH..........	Diamond Penetrator Hardness
DPH..........	Diamond Pyramid Hardness (MSA)
DPH..........	Diphenhydramine [*Organic chemistry*] (DAVI)
DPH..........	Diphenylhexatriene [*A fluorophore*] [*Organic chemistry*]
DPH..........	Diphenylhydantoin [*Anticonvulsant*]
DPH..........	Diploma in Public Health [*British*]
DPH..........	Disintegrations per Hour
DPH..........	Disk Pack Handler [*Computer science*] (IAA)
DPH..........	Division for Physically Handicapped (EA)
D Ph........	Doctor of Philosophy
DPH..........	Doctor of Public Health
DPH..........	Doctor of Public Hygiene
DPH..........	Double-Phase Hologram
DPHA........	Descripcion del Patrimonio Historico-Artistico Espanol [*Database*] [*Ministerio de Cultura*] [*Spanish*] [*Information service or system*] (CRD)
D Phar........	Doctor of Pharmacy
D Phar C.....	Doctor of Pharmaceutical Chemistry
DPharm.......	Doctor of Pharmacy (ADA)
D Ph C........	Doctor of Pharmaceutical Chemistry
D Phc........	Doctor of Pharmacology
DPHDent.....	Diploma in Public Health Dentistry (ADA)
DPHE........	Doctor of Public Health Engineering
DPH Ed.......	Doctor of Public Health Education
DPH Eng......	Doctor of Public Health Engineering
DPHGM.......	Diaphragm (IAA)
D Phil........	Doctor of Philanthropy
D Phil........	Doctor of Philosophy
D Ph M........	Doctor of Philosophy in Metaphysics
DPHN........	Diploma in Public Health Nursing (ADA)
DPHN........	Doctor of Public Health Nursing
D Pho........	Doctor of Photography
DPHRCSEng...	Diploma in Dental Public Health, Royal College of Surgeons of England [*British*] (DBQ)
D Ph S........	Doctor of Physical Science
D Ph Sc.......	Doctor of Physical Science
DPHU........	Dispersed Phase Hold Up [*Chemical engineering*]
DPhy..........	Doctor of Philosophy
D Phy........	Doctor of Physics
DPHy........	Doctor of Public Hygiene
DPhys........	Diploma of Physiotherapy [*British*]
DPhysiol......	Diploma in Physiology
D Phys Med...	Diploma in Physical Medicine [*British*]
DPI..........	Data Processing Installation
DPI..........	Data Publishing International [*Netherlands*] [*Information service or system*] (IID)

DPI..........	Days Post Inoculation [*Medicine*] (DMAA)
DPI..........	Deal Proneness Index [*Marketing*]
DPI..........	Defense Plant Installation
DPI..........	Delayed Procurement Item
DPI..........	Departmental Personnel Instruction
DPI..........	Department of Public Information [*United Nations*]
DPI..........	Desired Point of Impact [*Military*]
DPI..........	Detail Program Interrelationships (NASA)
DPI..........	Detected Pulse Interference (CET)
DPI..........	Device Programmer Interface [*Computer science*] (EECA)
dPI..........	Difference Pressure Indicating [*Engineering*]
DPI..........	Differential Pressure Indicator [*Automotive engineering*]
DPI..........	Different Premises Information [*Telecommunications*] (TEL)
DPI..........	Digital Process Instrument [*Computer science*] (IEEE)
DPI..........	Digital Pseudorandom Inspection (IEEE)
DPI..........	(Dihydroxyphenylimino)imidazolidine [*Biochemistry*]
DPI..........	Diphosphoinositide [*Biochemistry*]
DPI..........	Diploma of the Plastics Institute [*British*] (DI)
DPI..........	Director of Public Instruction
DPI..........	Disabled Peoples' International (EAIO)
DPI..........	Disposable Personal Income
DPI..........	Domestic Product of Industry (MHDB)
dpi..........	Dots-per-Inch [*Printing technology*]
DPI..........	Dots Per Inch (WDMC)
DPI..........	Dry Powder Inhaler [*Pharmacy*]
DPI..........	Duoplasmation Ion
DPI..........	Dynamic Personality Inventory [*Psychology*]
DPIA........	Diethylenetriamine Producers Importers Alliance (EA)
DPIA........	Disabled Peoples' International [*Australia*]
DPIBF........	Diphenylisobenzofuran [*Organic chemistry*]
DPIC........	Death Penalty Information Center (EA)
DPIC........	Deputy Paymaster in Chief
DPIC........	Drug and Poison Information Centre [*University of British Columbia*] [*Information service or system*] (IID)
DPICM........	Dual-Purpose Improved Conventional Munition (AABC)
DPICS........	Dyadic Parent-Child Interaction Coding System [*Psychology*]
DPIF........	Destruct Package Installation Facility (SAA)
DPIF........	Drug Product Information File [*American Society of Hospital Pharmacists*] [*Information service or system*] (IID)
DPIFE........	Department of Primary Industry, Fisheries, and Energy
DPII........	Dairy Products Improvement Institute (EA)
DPIL........	Democracy and Peace (Iterim) League [*Myanmar*] [*Political party*]
DPIO........	District Public Information Office [*or Officer*] [*Navy*]
DPIP........	Dichlorophenolindophenol [*Also, DCIP, DCPI, DCPIP*] [*Analytical reagent*]
DPIR........	Data Processing and Information Retrieval (DIT)
DPIR........	Detailed Photo Interpretation Report (DNAB)
DPIS........	Differential Pressure Isolation Switch (IEEE)
DPIS........	Duoplasmation Ion Source
DPIUSA........	Disabled Peoples' International USA (EA)
DPJ..........	Ohio Power Co. [*NYSE symbol*] (SAG)
DPK..........	Deer Park, NY [*Location identifier FAA*] (FAAL)
DPK..........	Delta Psi Kappa [*Society*]
DPK..........	Democratic Party of Kurdistan [*Iraq*] [*Political party*] (PPW)
DPK..........	Driscoll Play Kit [*Psychological testing*]
DPKC........	Diagnostic Problem-Knowledge Coupler
DPKG........	Dolco Packaging Corp. [*NASDAQ symbol*] (SAG)
DPL..........	Data Processing Language
DPL..........	Denver Public Library, Denver, CO [*OCLC symbol*] (OCLC)
DPL..........	Deploy (AABC)
DPL..........	Descriptor Privilege Level [*Computer science*] (BYTE)
DPL..........	Design and Programming Language (IAA)
DPL..........	Detroit Public Library
DPL..........	Development Prototype Launcher
DPL..........	Diagonal Proof Line [*Technical drawings*]
DPL..........	Dipalmitoyl Lecithin [*Biochemistry*]
DPL..........	Diploma (ROG)
DPL..........	Diplomat (WGA)
DPL..........	Dipole (KSC)
DPL..........	Dipolog [*Philippines*] [*Airport symbol*] (OAG)
DPL..........	Discrete Phase Loop (IAA)
DPL..........	Distopulpolingual [*Dentistry*]
DPL..........	Distribution Plot List
DPL..........	Doctor of Patent Law
DPL..........	Document Processing Language (IAA)
DPL..........	Dome Petroleum Ltd. [*Canada ICAO designator*] (FAAC)
DPL..........	Double [*or Dual*] Propellant Loading (AFM)
DPL..........	DPL, Inc. [*Formerly, Dayton Power & Light Co.*] [*NYSE symbol*] (SPSG)
DPL..........	Dual Propellant Loading
DPL..........	Due Process of Law [*Legal shorthand*] (LWAP)
DPL..........	Dunlop's Parochial Law [*A publication*] (DLA)
DPL..........	Duplex (IAA)
DPL..........	Dynex Petroleum Ltd. [*Toronto Stock Exchange symbol*]
DPL..........	Kenansville, NC [*Location identifier FAA*] (FAAL)
DPLa........	Distopulpolabial [*Dentistry*]
DPLCS........	Digital Propellant Level Control System (KSC)
DPLE........	Digital Principal Local Exchange
DPLF........	Data [*or Digital*] Phone Line Formatter
DPLG........	Day Plane Guard [*Military*] (NVT)
DPLL........	Digital Phase-Locked Loop [*Space communication*]
DPLL........	Digital Phase Lock Loop (NITA)
DPLM........	Domestic Public Land Mobile [*Telecommunications*] (TEL)
DPLM........	Dual Pulse LASER Microwelder
DPLN........	Diffuse Proliferative Lupus Nephritis [*Medicine*]

DPLO .... District Postal Liaison Officer [*Navy*]
DPLOA .... Draft Proposed Letter of Agreement
DPLR .... Department of Productivity and Labour Relations [*Western Australia*]
DPLR .... Doppler (MCD)
D-PIS .... Diplomate, American Board of Plastic Surgery (DHSM)
dplx .... Duplex (BARN)
DPLXR .... Duplexer (MSA)
DPLY .... Deploy (KSC)
Dpm .... Dampproof Membrane (DAC)
DPM .... Data Preparation and Maintenance (CAAL)
DPM .... Data Processing Machine (AAG)
DPM .... Data Processing Manager
DPM .... Decays per Minute [*Radiochemistry*]
DPM .... Decomposable Plant Material [*Soil science*]
DPM .... Defense Program Memorandum (AABC)
DPM .... Deflectable Photomultiplier
DPM .... Delhi Pacific Resources Ltd. [*Toronto Stock Exchange symbol*]
DPM .... Department Personnel Manual
DPM .... Depot Paymaster [*Military British*] (ROG)
DPM .... Deputy Prime Minister [*British*]
DPM .... Deputy Program Management [*DoD*]
DPM .... Deputy Program Manager (DOMA)
DPM .... Deputy Project Manager
DPM .... Deputy Provost Marshal [*British*]
DPM .... Designated for Prompt Mobilization
DPM .... Designated Project Manager
DPM .... Development Planning Memo (MCD)
DPM .... Development Program Manuals (AFIT)
DPM .... Development Proposal Manager (MCD)
DPM .... Diaminopimelic Acid [*Also, DAP, DAPA*] [*An amino acid*]
DPM .... Dichroic Parametric Mirror
DPM .... Diesel Particulate Matter [*Environmental chemistry*]
DPM .... Digital Panel Meter [*Computer science*]
dpm .... Digital Panel Meter (IDOE)
DPM .... Digital Plotter Map [*Military British*]
DPM .... Digital Power Meter (IAA)
dpm .... Digital Power Meter (IDOE)
DPM .... Diphenylmethane [*Organic chemistry*]
DPM .... Dipivaloylmethanate [*Organic chemistry*]
DPM .... Diploma in Psychological Medicine [*British*]
DPM .... Directional Policty Matrix
DPM .... Directory of Paper Makers [*A publication*] (DGA)
DPM .... Direct Procurement Method [*Personal property*]
DPM .... Discontinue Previous Medication [*Pharmacology*]
DPM .... Disintegrations per Minute
dpm .... Disintegrations per Minute (IDOE)
DPM .... Disruptive Pattern Material [*British military*] (DMA)
DPM .... Doctor of Pediatric Medicine (NADA)
DPM .... Doctor of Physical Medicine
DPM .... Doctor of Podiatric Medicine
DPM .... Doctor of Preventative Medicine
DPM .... Doctor of Psychiatric Medicine
DPM .... Documents per Minute [*Computer science*] (BUR)
DPM .... Downtown People Mover
DPM .... Drafting Practice Manual
DPM .... Draft Presidential Memorandum [*DoD*]
DPM .... Dried Poultry Manure
DPM .... Dual Point Memorandum
DPM .... Dual-Port Memory [*Computer science*] (MCD)
DPM .... Dual Purpose Missile (KSC)
DPM .... Dynamic Pressure Measurements
DPMA .... Data Processing Management Association (EA)
DPMA .... Dictionary of Physics and Mathematics Abbreviations, Signs, and Symbols [*A publication*]
DPMA .... Distributive Principle of Multiplication over Addition [*Mathematics*]
DPMA .... Dummy Part Master (MCD)
DPMAS .... Driver Performance Measurement and Analysis System (MCD)
DPMAWA ..... Dairy Products Manufacturers' Association of Western Australia
DPMB-AF ..... Directorate of Project Management B - Air Force
DPMC .... Defense Procurement Management Course [*DoD*]
DPMC .... Deli/Prepared Meats Committee (EA)
DPMC .... Department of the Prime Minister and Cabinet [*Australia*]
DPMC .... Director of Personnel, Marine Corps
DPMC .... Dual-Port Memory Control [*Computer science*]
DPMH .... Direct Productive Man-Hours (AFIT)
DPMI .... DOS [*Disk Operating System*] Protected Mode Interface [*Computer science*] (PCM)
DPMI .... DuPont Photomasks, Inc. [*NASDAQ symbol*] (SAG)
DPMIAC .... Defense Pest Management Information Analysis Center [*Database*] [*DoD Washington, DC*]
DPML .... Deputy Program Manager for Logistics (AFIT)
DPMM .... Dew Point Moisture Monitors [*Nuclear energy*] (NRCH)
DPMM .... Division of Production and Materials Management [*Energy Research and Development Administration*]
DPMO .... Defense Program Management Office [*DoD*]
DPMOAP ...... [*Society of*] Data Processing Machine Operators and Programmers (NITA)
DPMOAP ...... National Society of Electronic Data Processing Machine Operators and Programmers [*Inactive*]
DPMP .... Depot Plant Modernization Plan [*Army*]
D-PMR .... Diplomate, American Board of Physical Medicine and Rehabilitation (DHSM)
DPMR .... District Postmaster [*British*] (DCTA)
DPMS .... Data Project Management System (IEEE)
DPMS .... Departmental Property Management System

DPM/S .... Disintegrations per Minute/Second (DEN)
DPMS .... Display Power Management Signaling [*Computer science*] (PCM)
DPMS .... Display Power Management Support [*Computer science*] (PCM)
DPMS .... DOS [*Disk Operating System*] Protected Mode Service (PCM)
DPN .... Data Processing Network [*Trademark of Northern Telecom Ltd.*] (IAA)
DPN .... Diabetic Polyneuropathy [*Medicine*] (DMAA)
DPN .... Diamond Pyramid Hardness Number
DPN .... Diphosphopyridine Nucleotide [*Also, ARPPRN, NAD*] [*Biochemistry*]
D-PN .... Diplomate, American Board of Psychiatry and Neurology (DHSM)
DPN .... Dipropylnitrosamine [*Also, DPNA, NDPA*] [*Organic chemistry*]
DPNA .... Dipropylnitrosamine [*Also, DPN, NDPA*] [*Organic chemistry*]
DPNA .... Dual-Port Network Adapter [*Telecommunications*] (PCM)
DPNase .... Diphosphopyridine Nucleotide Glycohydrolase [*Also, NaDase*] [*An enzyme*]
DPNC .... Democratic Party of Nigeria and the Cameroons
DPNDBL .... Dependable
DPNE .... Division of Peaceful Nuclear Explosives [*AEC*]
DPNG .... Deepening (FAAC)
DPNH .... Diphosphopyridine Nucleotide, Reduced Form [*Biochemistry*]
DPNL .... Distribution Panel
DPNR .... Deproteinized Natural Rubber
DPNR .... Dignity Partners [*NASDAQ symbol*] (TTSB)
DPNR .... Dignity Partners, Inc. [*NASDAQ symbol*] (SAG)
DPNS .... Douglas Point Nuclear Station (GFGA)
DPNSS .... Digital Private Network Signalling System (NITA)
DPO .... Data Processing Officer (AIE)
DPO .... Data Processing Operation
DPO .... Defense Program Operation (AAG)
DPO .... Delayed Pulse Oscillator
DPO .... Demokratische Partei Oesterreichs [*Democratic Party of Austria*] (PPE)
DPO .... Deployable Payloads Projects Office [*Kennedy Space Center*] [*NASA*] (NASA)
DPO .... Depot (MCD)
DPO .... Depot Property Officer
DPO .... Deputy Principal Officer [*Foreign Service*]
DPO .... Development Planning Objective
DPO .... Development Planning Officer [*Military*]
DPO .... Development Project Officer (MCD)
DPO .... Devonport [*Tasmania*] [*Australia Airport symbol*] (OAG)
DPO .... Dial Pulse Originating [*Telecommunications*] (TEL)
DPO .... Digital Processing Oscilloscope (MCD)
DPO .... Diphenyloxazole [*Organic chemistry*]
DPO .... Diphenyl Oxide [*Organic chemistry*]
DPO .... Director, Planning and Operations (MCD)
DPO .... Directory of Post Office (AFM)
DPO .... Direct Purchasing Organisation [*Commercial firm British*]
DPO .... Disabled Persons Organization [*Bahamas*] (EAIO)
DPO .... Discontinued Post Office [*Deltiology*]
DPO .... Distributing Post Office
DPO .... District Personnel Office [*or Officer*] [*Navy*]
DPO .... District Postal Office [*or Officer*] [*Navy*]
dpo .... Dividend Payout Ratio [*Stock exchange term*]
DPO .... Divisional Pests Officer [*Ministry of Agriculture, Fisheries, and Food*] [*British*]
DPO .... Double Pulse Operation
DPO .... Dripproof Open
DPO .... Drop Out (KSC)
DPO .... DSA [*Defense Supply Agency*] Planning Objective
DPO .... Duty Petty Officer [*Navy*] (DNAB)
DPO .... Placid Oil Co., Exploration Library, Dallas, TX [*OCLC symbol*] (OCLC)
DPO .... United States Postal Service, Washington, DC [*Library symbol Library of Congress*] (LCLS)
DPOA .... Dissatisfied Peugeot Owners of America (EA)
DPOB .... Date and Place of Birth
DPOC .... Base de Documentos en Politica Criminal [*Criminal Law Documents Data Base*] [*United Nations Latin American Institute for Crime Prevention and Treatment of Offenders*] (IID)
DPOC .... Dynamic Processor Overload Control [*Telephone technology*]
DPOD .... DSA [*Defense Supply Agency*] Objective Document
DPODP .... Double-Precision Orbit Determination Program [*NASA*]
DPOI .... Delay-On-Pull-In
DPOIR .... Dial Pulse Originating Incoming Register [*Telecommunications*]
DPOL .... Political Directorate [*Allied German Occupation Forces*]
DPolEco ...... Doctor of Political Economy (NADA)
D Pol Sc ..... Doctor of Political Science
DPolSci .... Doctor of Political Science (NADA)
DPopC .... Population Crisis Committee, Washington, DC [*Library symbol Library of Congress*] (LCLS)
DPopI .... Population Institute, Washington, DC [*Library symbol Library of Congress*] (LCLS)
DPopR .... Population Reference Bureau, Washington, DC [*Library symbol Library of Congress*] (LCLS)
DPOS .... District Planning Officers Society [*British*]
DPO-SA .... Development Project Office for Selected Ammunition [*Army*] (RDA)
DpoTch .... DepoTech Corp. [*Associated Press*] (SAG)
DPOW .... Prisoners of War and Displaced Persons Directorate [*Allied German Occupation Forces*]
DPOWA .... Distributive, Processing, and Office Workers Union of America
DPP .... Dairy Produce Packers Ltd. [*British*]
DPP .... Data Project Plan (AFIT)
DPP .... Date of Prescribed Period [*Social Security Administration*] (OICC)
DPP .... Days Postpollination [*Botany*]

DPP	Decentralized Printing Program [*Army*]
DPP	Decision Process Pattern (RDA)
DPP	Deep Pseudopupil [*Optical effect*]
DPP	Defense Procurement Program [*DoD*]
DPP	Deferred Payment Plan [*Banking, finance*]
DPP	Delayed Procurement Program
DPP	Delegate Production Policy (MCD)
DPP	Democratic People's Party [*Taiwan*] [*Political party*] (ECON)
DPP	Democratic Progressive Party [*Transkei*] [*Political party*] (PPW)
DPP	Democratic Progressive Party [*Taiwan*] [*Political party*]
DPP	Deployment Pointing Panels (NASA)
DPP	Detailed Pass Plan (SAA)
DPP	Detailed Project Plan
DPP	Development Program Plan
DPP	Diepdaume Mines [*Vancouver Stock Exchange symbol*]
DPP	Differential Pulse Polarography [*Analytical chemistry*]
DPP	Digital Parallel Processor
DPP	Diketopyrrolopyrrole [*Organic chemistry*]
DPP	Dimethoxyphenyl Penicillin [*Medicine*] (MAE)
DPP	Dipeptidyl Peptidase [*An enzyme*]
DPP	Diphenyl Phthalate [*Organic chemistry*]
DPP	Diphloretin Phosphate [*Biochemistry*]
DPP	Diphtheria Pertussis Prophylactic [*Medicine*]
DPP	Diploma in Plant Pathology (ADA)
DPP	Director of Personnel Planning [*Air Force*]
DPP	Director of Procurement and Production [*Army*]
DPP	Director of Public Prosecutions [*British*]
DPP	Direct Product Profitability [*Analysis*]
DPP	Disaster Preparedness Plan (DNAB)
DPP	Disaster Prevention and Preparedness [*Marine science*] (OSRA)
DPP	Display Processor Program (MCD)
DPP	Disposable Plotter Pen [*Koh-I-Noor Rapidograph, Inc.*]
DPP	Distributed Parallel Processing [*Computer science*]
DPP	Distributed Phase Plate [*LASER technology*]
DPP	Division of Personnel Preparation [*Department of Education*]
DPP	Division of Polar Programs [*National Science Foundation Information service or system*] (IID)
DPP	Drip Pan Pot [*of closed-loop ex-vessel machine*] [*Nuclear energy*] (NRCH)
DPP	Dripproof Protected
DPP	Dry Photo Process
DPP	Dual Progress Plan [*Education*] (AEE)
DPP	Duplicating Pattern Production (MCD)
DPP	Political Party Democrats 66 [*Netherlands*] [*Political party*] (EAIO)
DPPA	Diphenylphosphoryl Azide [*Organic chemistry*]
DPPA	Double Pumped Parametric Amplifier
DPPB	Disaster Preparedness Planning Board (AFM)
DPPC	Data Processing Products Contract
DPPC	Defense Planning and Programming Catalog (MCD)
DPPC	Defense Planning Programming Category
DPPC	Developmental Potential of Preschool Children [*Psychology*]
DPPC	Development and Project Planning Centre [*University of Bradford*] [*British*] (IRC)
DPPC	Dipalmitoyl Phosphatidylcholine [*Biochemistry*]
DPPC	Diphenyl Phosphorochloridate [*or Diphenylphosphoric Acid Monochloride*] [*Organic chemistry*]
DPPD	Diphenylphenylenediamine [*Organic chemistry*]
DPPE	Data Processing Project Engineer
DPPE	Dipalmitoyl Phosphatidylethanolamine [*Biochemistry*]
DPPG	Defense Planning and Programming Guidance
DPPG	Defense Policy Planning Guidance (NVT)
DPPH	Diphenylpicrylhydrazyl [*Analytical chemistry*]
DPPM	Dynamic Pulse Position Modulation [*LASER technology*]
DPPNGS	Douglas Point Project Nuclear Generating Station (NRCH)
DPPO	Deepwater Ports Project Office [*Marine science*] (MSC)
DPPO	Dental Preferred Provider Organization [*Insurance*] (WYGK)
DPPO	Development Production Prove Out [*Army*] (RDA)
DPPO	Direct Procurement Petty Officer
DPPO	District Publications and Printing Office
DPPO	Division Police Petty Officer [*Navy*] (DNAB)
DPPP	Deferred Premium Payment Plan [*Business term*] (IIA)
DPPSO	Data Processing Programming Support Office [*Military*]
DPPT	Director of Personnel Procurement and Training [*Air Force*]
DPPWA	Director of Public Prosecutions for Western Australia
DPPX	Distributed Processing Programming Executive [*IBM*] (NITA)
DPPX	Distributed Processing Programming Executive Base [*IBM Corp.*]
DPQ	Defense Planning Questionnaire (MCD)
DPQ	Defense Position Questionnaire (MCD)
DPQ	Double-Precision Quantity
DPQCA	Dairy Products Quality Checked Association (EA)
DPQMR	Draft Proposal Qualitative Materiel Requirement
DPQS	Draw-a-Person Quality Scale [*Psychology*]
DPR	Daily Production Report
D Pr	Darling. Practice of the Scotch Court of Session [*A publication*] (DLA)
DPR	Data Processing Request
DPR	Data Protection Register (NITA)
DPR	Data Protection Registrar [*British*]
DPR	Day Press Rate [*Telegraph rate*] (NTCM)
DPR	Defect Prevention Reports
DPR	Definition Phase Review (NASA)
DPR	Degrees per Revolution
DPR	Demonstration Power Reactor (NRCH)
DPR	Department of Physical Research [*British*]
DPR	Department Performance Rating
DPR	Deployment Position RADAR (MCD)

DPR	Depolymerized Rubber
DPR	Development Planning Reports (MCD)
DPR	Dial Pulse Receiver [*Telecommunications*] (PDAA)
DPR	Dial Pulse Repeater [*Telecommunications*] (IAA)
DPR	Diaminopropanoic Acid [*An amino acid*]
DPR	Diaper
DPR	Diazo Print
DPR	Dihydropyridine [*Organic chemistry*]
DPR	Directions and Program Review [*American Library Association*]
DPR	Director of Public Relations
DPR	Direct Particle Rolling (PDAA)
DPR	Disabled Persons Railcard [*British*]
DPR	Dispenser [*Technical drawings*]
DPR	District Probate Registry
DPR	Division of Physical Research [*Energy Research and Development Administration*]
DPR	Domestic Policy Review
DPR	Double Pulse Ranging (NG)
DPR	Double Pure Rubber (IAA)
DPR	Drogue Parachute Deployment
DPR	Drug Price Review
DPR	Dual Pen Recorder
DPR	Dundee-Palliser Resources, Inc. [*Toronto Stock Exchange symbol*]
DPR	Dupree, SD [*Location identifier FAA*] (FAAL)
DPR	Puerto Rico Reports, Spanish Edition [*A publication*] (DLA)
D PR	United States District Court for the District of Puerto Rico (DLA)
DPRB	Defense Planning and Resources Board [*Formerly, Defense Resources Board*] (DOMA)
DPRC	Data Processing Resources [*NASDAQ symbol*] (TTSB)
DPRC	Data Processing Resources Corp. [*NASDAQ symbol*] (SAG)
DPRC	Defence Policy and Requirements Committee [*British military*] (DMA)
DPRC	Defense Program Review Committee [*Military*] (CAAL)
DPREP	Disk Preparation Processor [*Computer science*]
DPRF	Drug Product Reference File [*US Public Health Service*] [*Information service or system*] (IID)
DPRF	Dual Pulse Ranging Fuse
DPRK	Democratic People's Republic of Korea [*Also known as North Korea*]
DPRM	Diploma of Physical and Rehabilitation Medicine (ADA)
D-PrM	Diplomate, American Board of Preventive Medicine (DHSM)
DPR(N)	Directorate of Public Relations (Naval) [*British*]
DPRO	Defense Plant Representative Officer (RDA)
DPRO	Defense Plant Representative Offices [*or Officers*] (RDA)
DPRO	Defense Plant Representatives Office (DOMA)
DPRO	Digital Projection Readout (CAAL)
DPRO	District Public Relations Office [*or Officer*] [*Navy*]
DPROC	Draft Proposed Required Operational Capability (MCD)
DProGM	Deputy Provincial Grand Master [*Freemasonry*]
DPRORM	Drafting, Pay and Records Office, Royal Marines [*British*]
D PROV GM	Deputy Provincial Grand Master [*Freemasonry*] (ROG)
DPRP	Dripproof and Ratproof
DPRS	Data Processing Requirements Summary
DPRS	Dynamic Preferential Runway System [*Aviation*]
DPRSD	Depressed
DPRT	Depart (AABC)
DPRT	Drawing Parts Release Ticket (MCD)
DPRTF	Drought Policy Review Task Force [*Australia*]
DPS	Dales Pony Society [*British*] (BI)
DPS	Data Package Set (CAAL)
DP(S)	Data Packet (Subsystem) [*Telecommunications*] (TEL)
DPS	Data Presentation System (IAA)
DPS	Data Present Signal
DPS	Data Processing and Software (NASA)
DPS	Data Processing Service (NASA)
DPS	Data Processing Services Co. [*Information service or system*] (IID)
DPS	Data Processing Software System (NASA)
DPS	Data Processing Standards [*NASA*] (KSC)
DPS	Data-Processing Station
DPS	Data Processing System [*or Subsystem*]
DPS	Decision Package Sets
DPS	Decision Program Set
DPS	Dedicated Printer Share [*AC DataLink*] [*Computer science*]
DPS	Deep Passive Sensors (MCD)
DPS	Defence Policy Staff [*British*]
DPS	Defense Planning Staff [*Military*] (AABC)
DPS	Defense Printing Service
DPS	Defense Priorities System [*DoD*]
DPS	Defense Protective Service (DOMA)
DPS	Degrees per Second
DPS	Delayed Printer Simulator
DPS	Delegate Production System (MCD)
DPS	Demokratische Partei Saar [*Democratic Party of the Saar*] [*Germany Political party*] (PPE)
DPS	Demokratska Partija Socijalista [*Democratic Party of Socialists*] [*Montenegro*] [*Political party*] (EY)
DPS	Denison & Pacific Suburban Railway Co. [*AAR code*]
DPS	Denpasar [*Indonesia*] [*Airport symbol*] (OAG)
DPS	Descent Power System [*NASA*]
DPS	Descent Propulsion System
DPS	Design and Procedure Standard [*NASA*]
DPS	Destainer Power Supply [*Electrophoresis*]
DPS	Detail Process Standard (MCD)
DPS	Development and Proof Services [*Aberdeen Proving Ground, MD*] (MCD)
DPS	Dewan Pengurus Sementara [*Provisional Management Board Section*] [*Indonesia*]

DPS	Diagnostic Problem Solver [*Computer science*]
DPS	Dialectic Problem Solver
DPS	Dial Pulse Sender [*Telecommunications*] (PDAA)
DPS	Differential Phase Shift (PDAA)
DPS	Differential Power Switch
DPS	Different Premises Subscriber [*Telecommunications*] (TEL)
DPS	Digital Panel Meter [*Electronics*] (ECII)
DPS	Digital Phase Shifter
DPS	Digital Plotter System
DPS	Digital Power Supply
DPS	Dimethylpolysiloxane [*Organic chemistry*] (MAE)
DPS	Diode Phase Shifter
DPS	Diphenylstilbene [*Organic chemistry*]
DPS	Diphenyl Sulfone [*Organic chemistry*]
D Ps	Diploma of Psychology (PGP)
DPS	Director of Personal Services [*Navy British*]
DPS	Director of Postal Services [*British*]
DPS	Disintegrations per Second
DPS	Disk Processing System (IAA)
DPS	Disk Programming System [*IBM Corp.*] (IEEE)
DPS	Display Power Supply
DPS	Distributed Presentation Services [*IBM Corp.*]
DPS	Distributed Present Services [*IBM*] (NITA)
DPS	Distributed Processing System [*Honeywell, Inc.*]
DPS	Distributed Programming System (IAA)
DPS	Diversified Pharmaceutical Services [*ECON*]
DPS	Dividend per Share [*Investment term*] (ADA)
DPS	Division Primary Standards (AAG)
DPS	Doctor of Political Science
DPS	Doctor of Professional Studies (PGP)
D Ps	Doctor of Psychology
DPS	Doctor of Public Service
DPS	Document Processing System [*IBM Corp.*] [*Computer science*]
DPS	Double-Pole, Snap Switch (IAA)
DPS	Dripproof Semienclosed
DPS	Drogue Parachute System (SAA)
DPS	Drought Preparedness [*US Army Corps of Engineers*]
DPS	Dry Peridotite Solidus [*Geochemistry*]
DPS	Dual Porosity Sinter
DPS	Dynamic Philatelic Society
DPS	Dynamic Processing System [*Mitsubishi*] (NITA)
DPSA	Dartmoor Pony Society of America (EA)
DPSA	Data Processing Supplies Association [*Later, IOSA*] (MCD)
DPSA	Deep Penetration Strike Aircraft
DPSA	Diploma in Public and Social Administration (ADA)
DPSA	Distinguished Public Service Award (MUGU)
DPSA	Doctor of Public School Art
DPSA	Seaman Apprentice, Data Processing Technician, Striker [*Navy rating*]
DPSB	Defence Production Supply Board [*NATO*] (NATG)
DPSBad	Distinguished Pistol Shot Badge [*Military decoration*] (AABC)
DPSC	Data Processing Service Center
DPSC	Defense Personnel Support Center (AFM)
DPSC	Defense Petroleum Supply Center
DP Sc	Doctor of Political Science
DPSC	Double Paper, Single Cotton [*Wire insulation*] (AAG)
DPSCA	Darwin Pensioners and Senior Citizens' Association [*Australia*]
DPSCPAC....	Data Processing Service Center, Pacific (DNAB)
DPSD	Dew Point Sensing Device
DPSD	Dimensionless Power Spectral Density
DPSDR........	Douglas Process Standard Development Record [*DAC*]
DPSH	Direct Product Standard Hours (AFIT)
DPSI	Dawson Production Services, Inc. [*NASDAQ symbol*] (SAG)
DPSI	Dawson Production Svcs [*NASDAQ symbol*] (TTSB)
DPSK	Differential Phase Shift Keying [*Telecommunications*]
DPSM	Diode Phase Shifter Module
DpSM	Diploma in Surgery Medicine
DPSM	Doctor of Public School Music
DPSM	Dual-Purpose Submunitions [*Military*] (INF)
DPSN	Seaman, Data Processing Technician, Striker [*Navy rating*]
DPSO	Data Processing Systems Office [*Picatinny Arsenal, NJ*]
DPSO	Defense Projects Support Office [*NASA*]
DPSP	Diffuse Process Such as Pericarditis [*Cardiology*]
DPSPT	Combat Consumption Support from D-Day to P-Day [*Military*] (AABC)
DPSR	Daily Problem Status Report
DPSR	Data Processing Service Request (NVT)
DPSR	Data Processing System Requirements
DPSS	Data Processing and Services Subsystem (NOAA)
DPSS	Data Processing Subsystem
DPSS	Data Processing Switching System [*Space Flight Operations Facility, NASA*]
DPSS	Data Processing System Simulator (IEEE)
DPSS	Deep Passive Sonobuoy System (MCD)
DPSS	Department of Public Social Services
DPSS	Director of Printing and Stationery Services [*Military British*]
DPSS	Direct Program Search System (IAA)
DPSS	Display Presentation Subsystem (IAA)
DPSS	Double-Pole Snap Switch (IAA)
DPsSc	Doctor of Psychological Science (ADA)
DPSSO........	DSA [*Defense Supply Agency*] Performance Standards Support Office
DPST	Deposit
DPST	Deposit
dpst	Double-Pole, Single-Throw (IDOE)
DPST	Double Pole, Single Throw [*Switch*]

DP-StE.........	Democratic Party - Statia [*Netherlands Antilles*] [*Political party*] (EY)
D Ps Th	Doctor of Psycho-Therapy
DPSTK	Dipstick
DP-StM	Democratic Party - St. Maarten [*Netherlands Antilles*] [*Political party*] (EY)
DPSTNC......	Double-Pole, Single-Throw, Normally Closed Switch (IAA)
DPSTNO......	Double-Pole, Single-Throw, Normally Open Switch (IAA)
DPSTSW......	Double-Pole, Single-Throw Switch
DPSW	Differential Pressure Seawater
DPSW	Double-Pole Switch
DPSX	Dipropyl(sulphophenyl)xanthine [*Organic chemistry*]
D Psych	Diploma in Psychiatry [*British*]
D PSYCH	Doctor of Psychology (WDAA)
DPsychol	Doctor of Psychology
DPsyMedNeuro...	Diploma in Psychiatric Medicine and Neurology
DPSySci	Doctor of Psychological Science (NADA)
DPT.............	Datapoint Corp. [*NYSE symbol*] (SPSG)
DPT.............	Days per Thousand
DPT.............	Dedicated Planning Terminal (CAAL)
DPT.............	Deep Pressure Touch
DPT.............	Demerol-Phenergan-Thorazine [*Drug regime*]
DPT.............	Democratic Party of Tadzhikistan [*Political party*]
DPT.............	Depart
DPT.............	Department
DPT.............	Departure Control (MUGU)
DPT.............	Depletion Perturbation Theory (PDAA)
DPT.............	Deponent
DPT.............	Deposit (ADA)
DPT.............	Depot
DPT.............	Depth
Dpt.............	Dermatophagoides pteronyssinus [*House dust*]
DPT.............	Descent Performance Test
DPT.............	Design Proof Tests
DPT.............	Development Project Team (MCD)
DPT.............	Development Prototype (NG)
DPT.............	Dew-Point Temperature [*Measure of humidity*]
DPT.............	Dew Point Tester
DPT.............	Diagnostic Prescriptive Teacher [*or Teaching*]
DPT.............	Dial Pulse Terminating [*Telecommunications*] (TEL)
DPT.............	Dichotic Pitch Discrimination Test [*Medicine*] (DMAA)
DPT.............	Diesel Particulate Trap [*Automotive engineering*]
DPT.............	Differential Pressure Transducer
DPT.............	Different Premises Telephone Number [*Telecommunications*] (TEL)
DPT.............	Digital Picture Terminal (NOAA)
DPT.............	Digital Piezoelectric Translator [*Instrumentation*]
DPT.............	Digital Pressure Transducer
DPT.............	Dimethyltryptamine [*Hallucinogenic agent*] (DAVI)
DPT.............	Diphenyltrichloroethane [*Also, DPE*] [*Organic chemistry*]
DPT.............	Diphosphothiamine [*Also, TDP, TPP*] [*Biochemistry*]
DPT.............	Diphtheria, Pertussis, and Tetanus [*Also, DTP*] [*Immunology*]
DPT.............	Diploma of Physio-Therapy [*British*]
DPT.............	Dipropyltryptamine [*Hallucinogenic agent*]
DPT.............	Director of Plans and Training [*Military*] (AABC)
DPT.............	Director, Polaris Technical [*Missiles*]
DPT.............	Dissatisfied Parents Together (EA)
DPT.............	Distributed Processing Technology [*Computer science*]
DPT.............	Doctor of Physical Therapy (PGP)
DPT.............	Dripproof Totally Enclosed
DPT.............	Drive Parameter Tracking [*Computer science*] (PCM)
DPT.............	Dummy Part (MCD)
DPT.............	Duplicating Pattern Tooling (MCD)
DPT.............	Dynamic Plume Test
DPTA	Diaminopropanoltetraacetic Acid [*Also, DTA, DHPTA*] [*Organic chemistry*]
DPTA	Diethylenetriamine Penta-Acetic Acid [*Organic chemistry*] (DAVI)
dPTC..........	Dispersed Human Parathyroid Cell [*Clinical chemistry*]
DPTDR	Draft Proposed Training Device Requirement (MCD)
DPTH	Depth (FAAC)
DPTH	Dipentamethylenethiuram Hexasulfide [*Organic chemistry*]
DPTH	Diphenylthiohydantoin [*Organic chemistry*]
DPTI...........	Diastolic Pressure Time Index (AAMN)
DPTM..........	Director of Plans, Training, and Mobilization [*DoD*]
DPTNAVSCI...	Department of Naval Science (DNAB)
DPTO	District Property Transportation Office [*or Officer*] [*Navy*]
DPTOE.........	Draft Plan Table of Organization and Equipment (MCD)
DPTPrA........	Datapoint $1 cm Pfd [*NYSE symbol*] (TTSB)
DPTR	Data Pointer [*Computer memory*] (BYTE)
DPTR	Delta Petroleum [*NASDAQ symbol*] (SAG)
DPTRAJ	Double-Precision Trajectory Program [*NASA*]
DPTRK	Dumptruck (AABC)
DPTS	Digital Programming Test Set (SAA)
DPTS	Dimethylamino Pyridiniumtoluenesulfonic Acid [*Organic chemistry*]
DPTS	Director of Physical Training and Sports [*Navy British*]
DPTSI	Design Professions Technical Specialty Index [*National Society of Professional Engineers*] [*Information service or system*] (IID)
DPTT...........	Double Pole, Triple Throw [*Switch*]
DPT vaccine...	Diptheria, Pertussis [*Whooping Cough*], and Tetanus Vaccine [*Also, called DTP vaccine*] (PAZ)
DPTW	Desk, Double-Pedestal Typewriter
DPTX	Distributed Processing Terminal Exchange [*Prime Computers*] (NITA)
DPTY	Deputy
DPTY	Deputy
dpty	Diptych (VRA)
DPU	Data Path Unit [*Computer science*]
DPU	Data Processing Unit

DPU	Delayed Pressure Urticaria [*Dermatology*] (DAVI)
DPU	Demand Processing Unit [*Military*]
DPU	Depuy, Inc. [*NYSE symbol*] (SAG)
DPU	Design Proof Unit (KSC)
DPU	Differential Pressure Unit (DNAB)
DPU	Digital Patch Unit
DPU	Digital Processing Unit
DPU	Diphenylhydantoin [*Also, DPH*] [*Anticonvulsant*] (DAVI)
DPU	Disabled Persons Unit [*United Nations*] (DUND)
DPU	Disk Pack Unit [*Computer science*]
DPU	Display Processor Unit (IAA)
DPU	Document Processing Unit [*Computer science*] (IAA)
DPU	Driver Propulsion Unit
DPU	Dual Processing Unit [*Computer science*] (WGA)
DPU	Dumpu [*New Guinea*] [*Airport symbol*] (AD)
DPU	Organization of American States, Washington, DC [*Library symbol Library of Congress Obsolete*] (LCLS)
D Pub Adm...	Doctor of Public Administration
DPUD............	Department of Planning and Urban Development [*Western Australia*] [*Australia*]
DP-UDC	Democracia Popular - Union Democrata Cristiana [*People's Democracy - Christian Democratic Union*] [*Ecuador*] [*Political party*] (PPW)
DPUO............	Duty Directed Is Being Performed for Unit Issuing Order
DPV	Design Point Vehicle
DPV	Deutscher Verein zur Erforschung Palaestinas [*A publication*] (BJA)
DPV	Differential Pulse Voltammetry [*Analytical chemistry*]
DPV	Diffuse and Perivascular [*Medicine*]
DPV	Diver Propulsion Vehicle (DNAB)
DPV	Dockside Proofing Vehicle
DPV	Doppler Predict Voltage
DPV	Dry Pipe Valve
DPV	Duty Paid Value [*Business term*]
DPVM............	Demand-Page Virtual Memory [*Computer science*] (PDAA)
DPVM............	Discrete Process Variable Measurement [*Process control*]
DPVS	Digitally-Programmed Voltage Source (IAA)
DPW	Davis Polk & Wardwell, Library, New York, NY [*OCLC symbol*] (OCLC)
DPW	Dealer Proceeds Withheld [*Automobile sales*]
DPW	Department of Public Welfare
DPW	Department of Public Works
DPW	Director of Prisoners of War [*British World War II*]
DPWG............	Defence Planning Working Group [*of Defense Ministers*] [*NATO*] (NATG)
DPWH............	Department of Parks, Wildlife, and Heritage [*Tasmania*] [*Australia*]
DPWM............	Double-Sided Pulse-Width Modulation [*Telecommunications*]
DPWO............	District Public Works Office
DPWP............	Director of Planning of War Production [*Air Ministry*] [*British World War II*]
DPWR............	Data Process Work Request (AAG)
DPWS	Dual Purpose Weapon System
DPX	Diethyl(phenyl)xanthine [*Organic chemistry*]
DPX	Displaced Persons Executive [*Allied Military Government detachments, Red Cross teams, and UN Relief and Rehabilitation Administration Corps*] [*Post-World War II*]
DPX	Duplex (ADA)
DPX	Duplex Products, Inc. [*AMEX symbol*] (SPSG)
DPY	Deploy (NASA)
DPZ...............	Dale-Parizeau, Inc. [*Toronto Stock Exchange symbol*]
DQ	Coastal Air Transport [*ICAO designator*] (AD)
DQ	Dairy Queen [*Commercial firm*]
DQ	Deep Quest
DQ	Definite Quantity (AFM)
DQ	Deleted Quality Review Transaction [*IRS*]
DQ	Design Qualification (MCD)
DQ	Destination Queues [*Computer science*] (MDG)
DQ	Detention Quarters [*British*]
DQ	Deterioration Quotient [*Medicine*]
DQ	Development Quotient
DQ	Directory Enquiry Service [*Telecommunications*] (TEL)
DQ	Direct Question [*Legal testimony*]
DQ	Disqualified
dq	Dominica [*MARC country of publication code Library of Congress*] (LCCP)
DQ	Drawing Quality (DNAB)
D-Q	Drocourt-Queant Line [*World War I*] [*Canada*]
DQ	Duquesne Capital [*NYSE symbol*] (SAG)
DQ	Fiji [*Aircraft nationality and registration mark*] (FAAC)
DQA	Defence Quality Assurance
DQA	Design Quality Assurance [*Telecommunications*] (TEL)
DQA	Division of Quality Assurance [*Department of Education*] (GFGA)
DQA	D'Or Val Mines Ltd. [*Toronto Stock Exchange symbol Vancouver Stock Exchange symbol*]
DQA	Drawing Quality Audit (MCD)
DQAB	Defence Quality Assurance Board [*British*] (RDA)
DQADO	DCAS [*Defense Contract Administration Services*] Quality Assurance Staff Development Office
DQC	Data Quality Control
DQC	Definite Quantity Control
DQC	Delayed Quick Cure (MCD)
D-QC	Drug-Quaternary Carrier [*Biochemistry*]
DQC	Dynamic Quality Control
DQCIR..........	Directory Enquiry Computerized Information Retrieval System [*BT*] (NITA)
DQCM...........	Data Quality Control Monitor

DQD	Digital Quadrature Detection [*Instrumentation*]
DQDB	Distributed Queue Dual Bus [*Telecommunications*] (PCM)
DQE	De Queen & Eastern Railroad Co. [*AAR code*]
DQE	Descriptor Queue Element [*Computer science*] (IAA)
DQE	Detective Quantum Efficiency [*Photon device*]
DQE	DQE [*NYSE symbol*] (TTSB)
DQE	DQE Co. [*Associated Press*] (SAG)
DQE	DQE, Inc. [*NYSE symbol*] (SPSG)
DQF	Division of Quality Enhancement (AIE)
DQG	Charlotte, NC [*Location identifier FAA*] (FAAL)
DQH	Douglas, GA [*Location identifier FAA*] (FAAL)
DQI	Cimber Air, Sonderjyllands Flyveselskab [*Denmark ICAO designator*] (FAAC)
DQI	Distributor Quality rating Index [*Chemical engineering*]
DQL	DataEase Query Language [*Search method*] [*Computer science*] (PCM)
DQM	Data Quality Monitors (MDG)
DQM	Depot Quartermaster [*Marine Corps*]
DQM	Digital Quality Monitor
DQM	Division Quartermaster
DQMG	Deputy Quartermaster General
DQMS	Deputy Quartermaster-Sergeant [*British*]
DQN	Depot Quartermaster, Norfolk, Virginia [*Marine Corps*]
DQN	Diazonaphthoquinone-Sensitized Novolac [*Photoresist resin system*]
DQO	Data Quality Objective
DQO	Wilmington, DE [*Location identifier FAA*] (FAAL)
DQP	Depot Quartermaster, Philadelphia, Pennsylvania [*Marine Corps*]
DQP	Designated Qualified Person [*Department of Agriculture*]
DQP	Diode Qualification Program
DQPH	Depot Quartermaster, Pearl Harbor, Hawaii [*Marine Corps*]
DQ/PL	Definite-Quantity Price List [*Type of contract*] (AAGC)
DQPrA..........	Duqesne Cap L.P.8.375%'MIPS' [*NYSE symbol*] (TTSB)
DQQ	Depot Quartermaster, Quantico, Virginia [*Marine Corps*]
DQR	Depot Quartermaster, Richmond, Virginia [*Marine Corps*]
DQR	Design Qualification Requirement
DQR	Design, Quality, Reliabilty
DQR	Dihydroquercetin Reductase [*An enzyme*]
DQRS	Distributed Query and Retrieval System [*Telecommunications*] (PS)
DQS	Digital Quartz Servo [*Thomson video control system*] (NITA)
DQS	Drawing Quality Steel
DQS	Index-Digest Quarterly System
DQSF	Depot Quartermaster, San Francisco, California [*Marine Corps*]
DQSK...........	Drawing Quality, Special-Killed [*Metallurgy*]
DQT	Diode Qualification Test
DQT	Division Quality Team [*DOMA*]
DQTP	Design Qualification Test Plan (MCD)
DQTP	Diode Qualification Test Program
DQU	Deganawidah-Quetzalcoatl University [*Initials preferred to spelled-out name*] [*California*]
DQU	Dequincy, LA [*Location identifier FAA*] (FAAL)
DQU	Duquesne Light Co. [*Later, DQE*] [*NYSE symbol*] (SPSG)
DQUPrA.........	Dunquesne Lt cm$2.10 Pfd [*NYSE symbol*] (TTSB)
DQUPrB.........	Duquesne Lt 3.75% Pfd [*NYSE symbol*] (TTSB)
DQUPrC	Duquesne Lt 4% Pfd [*NYSE symbol*] (TTSB)
DQUPrD.........	Duquesne Lt4.10% Pfd [*NYSE symbol*] (TTSB)
DQUPrE.........	Duquesne Lt 4.15% Pfd [*NYSE symbol*] (TTSB)
DQUPrG.........	Duquesne Lt 4.20% Pfd [*NYSE symbol*] (TTSB)
DQV	Deckerville, MI [*Location identifier FAA*] (FAAL)
DR	Advance Airlines [*ICAO designator*] (AD)
DR	Coastal Healthcare Group, Inc. [*NYSE symbol*] (SAG)
DR	Coastal Physican Grp [*NYSE symbol*] (TTSB)
DR	Dacca Reports [*India*] [*A publication*] (DLA)
DR	Dahlgren Rifle
DR	Daily Record [*Penny newspaper in "He Knew He Was Right" by Anthony Trollope*]
DR	Daily Report
DR	Daily Review
DR	Damping Ratio (IAA)
D-R	Damp Rag [*Decontamination method*] [*Nuclear energy*] (NRCH)
DR	Danish Reactor (NRCH)
DR	Danmarks Retsforbund [*Justice Party of Denmark*] (PPE)
DR	Dardanelle & Russellville Railroad Co. [*AAR code*]
DR	Dark Red [*Philately*]
DR	Darkroom [*Photography*]
D/R	Database Reference [*A publication*]
DR	Data Rate [*Telecommunications*] (TEL)
DR	Data Receiver [*or Recorder*]
DR	Data Recorder (MCD)
DR	Data Recovery [*Computer science*] (ECII)
DR	Data Reduction (KSC)
DR	Data Register
DR	Data Reorganizer (IAA)
DR	Data Report
DR	Data Request
DR	Data Requirements [*NASA*]
DR	Date of Rank [*Air Force*]
DR	Daughter (ROG)
DR	Daughters of the Revolution
DR	Daunorubicin [*Antineoplastic drug*] (DAVI)
DR	Dead Reckoning [*Navigation*]
DR	Dead Reckoning [*Plot*] [*Navy*] (DOMA)
DR	Dead Rise (DS)
DR	Dealer [*Automotive sales*]
DR	Dear (ROG)
DR	Death Rate

DR .... Death Row
DR .... Debit
DR .... Debit Request
DR .... Debtor
DR .... Decanus Ruralis [*Rural Dean*]
DR .... Decorator Remodeling [*A publication*]
DR .... Deduced Reckoning [*Navigation*] (OA)
DR .... Defence Regulation (DAS)
DR .... Defense [*or Disaster*] Readiness (OICC)
DR .... Defensive Response [*Psychology*]
DR .... Deficiency Report [*Air Force*] (AFM)
DR .... Defined Readout [*Telecommunications*] (OA)
DR .... Degeneration Reaction
DR .... Degrees Rankine (KSC)
DR .... Deliquency Report [*Military*] (VNW)
DR .... Delivery Rate [*DoD*]
DR .... Delivery Room [*Medicine*]
DR .... Demodulation/Remodulation (IAA)
DR .... Demolition Rocket (NATG)
DR .... Density Report [*Army*]
DR .... Dental Recruit
DR .... Dependents Rate [*Air Force*] (AFM)
DR .... Deposition Rate [*Electrochemistry*]
DR .... Deposit Receipt [*Banking*]
DR .... Deputy Remembrancer [*A publication*] (DLA)
DR .... De-Rating and Rating Appeals [*England and Scotland*] [*A publication*] (DLA)
DR .... Derrick (DS)
DR .... Designator Register [*Computer science*]
DR .... Design Requirement
DR .... Design Review (AAG)
DR .... Despatch Rider [*Military British*]
DR .... Destroyer Flag [*Navy British*]
DR .... Detailed Report
DR .... Detection RADAR
DR .... Deuteronomy Rabba (BJA)
DR .... Deutsche Reichsbahn [*German Democratic Republic Railway*] (DCTA)
DR .... Deutsche Reichspartei [*German National Party*] [*Political party*] (PPE)
DR .... Deutsches Recht [*German Law*] (ILCA)
DR .... Deutsches Reich [*German Empire*]
DR .... Development Report
DR .... Development-Right (MCD)
DR .... Deviation Range
DR .... Deviation Ratio
DR .... Deviation Report
DR .... Devin Register [*An association*] (EA)
DR .... Diabetes-Resistant [*Medicine*]
DR .... Diabetic Retinopathy [*Medicine*]
DR .... Diagnostic Radiology [*Medicine*]
DR .... Diesel Radial [*Aircraft engine*]
DR .... Dietary Restriction [*Medicine*]
DR .... Differential Rate
DR .... Differential Relay
DR .... Digital Radiography
DR .... Digital Rectal [*Proctoscopy*]
DR .... Digital Resolver
DR .... Digit Receiver
DR .... Dihydrotestosterone Receptor [*Endocrinology*]
DR .... Dining Room
DR .... Diploma in Radiology [*British*]
D-R .... Diplomate, American Board of Radiology (DHSM)
D/R .... Directional Radio
DR .... Directive Antenna with Reflector
DR .... Director (ADA)
DR .... Direct Reading [*Spectroscopy*]
DR .... Direct Recording (IAA)
DR .... Direct Reduction [*Ironmaking process*]
DR .... Direct Repeat [*Genetics*]
D/R .... Direct/Reverse
DR .... Direct Route
DR .... Disaster Recovery (DA)
DR .... Disaster Representative [*Red Cross*]
DR .... Discharging Resistor
DR .... Discount Rate [*Banking*]
DR .... Discrepancy Record [*or Report*] (KSC)
DR .... Discrete Register (MCD)
DR .... Disc Ridge Splitting [*Agriculture*]
DR .... Discrimination RADAR
DR .... Discrimination Reversal [*Neurophysiology*]
DR .... Disk Recorder (DEN)
DR .... Dispatch Reliability (NASA)
D/R .... Dispatch Rider [*Marine Corps*]
DR .... Display Racks [*Freight*]
DR .... Display Result
DR .... Disposal Rate [*Of hormone metabolism*]
DR .... Disposition Record (NASA)
DR .... Dissociative Recombination [*Chemistry*]
DR .... Distant Range
DR .... Distant Reading (IAA)
DR .... Distant Reception (IAA)
DR .... Distribution Regulation [*Office of Price Stabilization*] (DLA)
DR .... Distribution Request
DR .... Distributor

DR .... District Railway [*London*]
DR .... District Registry
DR .... Diurnal Rhythm [*Medicine*] (MEDA)
DR .... Divided Ringing (IAA)
DR .... Division of Research [*Navy*]
DR .... Division Register (IAA)
DR .... Divisor [*Mathematics*]
DR .... DMR Group, Inc. [*Toronto Stock Exchange symbol*]
DR .... Dock Receipt
DR .... Doctor (EY)
Dr .... Doctor (DD)
DR .... Doctor
DR .... Doctor of Religion
DR .... Document Register (MCD)
DR .... Document Report
DR .... Dogger [*Ship's rigging*] (ROG)
DR .... Dollar [*Monetary unit*] (ROG)
dr .... Dominican Republic [*IYRU nationality code*] [*MARC country of publication code Library of Congress*] (LCCP)
DR .... Door
dr .... Door (VRA)
DR .... Dorsal Raphe [*Brain anatomy*]
DR .... Dorsal Root [*of spinal nerve*] [*Anatomy*]
DR .... Dose Ratio [*Medicine*]
DR .... Double Reduced [*Tinplate*]
Dr .... Double Reduction Gearing (DS)
DR .... Double Royal [*Paper*] (ADA)
D/R .... Downrange
DR .... Down Right [*The front right portion of a stage*] [*A stage direction*]
dr .... Drachm [*Unit of weight*] [*German*]
DR .... Drachma [*Monetary unit*] [*Greece*] (EY)
DR .... Draft
DR .... Drafting Request (MSA)
DR .... Draft Recommendation [*International Standards Organization*]
DR .... Draft Release (MCD)
DR .... Dragoon (ROG)
DR .... Drain (MSA)
DR .... Dram
dr .... Dram (IDOE)
DR .... Drama (ADA)
DR .... Draped [*Numismatics*]
DR .... Draw (WDAA)
DR .... Drawer
DR .... Drawn (AABC)
DR .... Draw Ratio [*Plastics technology*]
DR .... D-Related [*Antigen*] [*Immunology*]
DR .... Dressed [*Fish processing*]
DR .... Dresser
DR .... Dressing [*Medicine*]
DR .... Dressing Room (DAC)
DR .... Dress Rehearsal (MUGU)
Dr .... Drewry's English Vice Chancellors' Reports [*A publication*] (DLA)
Dr .... Dries [*Maps and charts*] [*British*]
DR .... Drift Rate
DR .... Drill (MSA)
DR .... Drill Regulations
DR .... Drill Rod
DR .... Drive [*or Driver*] (AFM)
DR .... Drive
Dr .... Drive (DD)
DR .... Drug Rehabilitation
DR .... Drum (MUGU)
DR .... Drummer (WDAA)
Dr .... Drury's Irish Chancery Reports Tempore Napier [*1858-59*] [*A publication*] (DLA)
Dr .... Drury's Irish Chancery Reports Tempore Sugden [*A publication*] (DLA)
DR .... Ducted Rocket (MCD)
DR .... Dump Revenues [*Solid waste management*]
DR .... Duplicating Requisition (MCD)
DR .... Dutch Reformed Church (IIA)
DR .... Dynamic Radius [*Tires*]
DR .... Dynamic Range
DR .... Dynamic Reprocessing (NITA)
DR .... European Right [*European Parliament*] (ECED)
DR .... Increment of Response [*Psychology*]
Dr .... La Sainte Bible (1884) (Drioux) [*A publication*] (BJA)
DR .... Reaction of Degeneration [*Physiology*]
DR .... Robin Avions [*Pierre Robin*] [*France ICAO aircraft manufacturer identifier*] (ICAO)
DRA .... Dancers Responding to AIDS [*An association*]
DRA .... Data Reformatter Assembly
DRA .... Data Research Associates, Inc. [*Information service or system*] (IID)
DRA .... Data Resource Administrator
DRA .... Dead Reckoning Analyzer
DRA .... Decision Risk Analysis [*Army*]
DRA .... Defence Research Agency [*British*]
DRA .... Defense [*or Disaster*] Relief Act (OICC)
DRA .... Defense Reorganization Act
DRA .... Delco Remy America
DRA .... Dependent Relative Allowance (DLA)
DRA .... Deputy Regional Administrator
DRA .... De-Rating Appeals [*England*] [*A publication*] (DLA)
DRA .... Designated Responsible Activity (MCD)
DRA .... Design Review Agreement (MCD)

DRA	Despite Resuscitation Attempts [*Medicine*] (MEDA)
DRA	Diagnosis-Rework Action (AAG)
DRA	Dielectric Rod Antenna
DRA	Diffuse Reflection Attachment [*Spectroscopy*]
DRA	Digital Read-In Assembly [*Computer science*]
DRA	Digital Recorder Analyzer [*Computer science*]
DRA	Directed Reading Activity [*Education*]
DRA	Director of Royal Artillery [*British*]
DRA	Direct Reckoning Analyzer (MUGU)
DRA	Discrete Recovery Area (KSC)
DRA	Divorce Registration Area [*Department of Health and Human Services*] (GFGA)
DRA	DMR Group, Inc. Class A SV [*Toronto Stock Exchange symbol*]
DRA	Document Release Authorization (KSC)
DRA	Doppler RADAR
Dra.	Draco [*Constellation*]
DRA	Drag Reducing Agent [*Petroleum pipeline transport*]
Dra.	Draper's Upper Canada King's Bench Reports [*A publication*] (DLA)
dra	Dravidian [*MARC language code Library of Congress*] (LCCP)
DRA	Dravidian Air Services Ltd. [*British ICAO designator*] (FAAC)
DRA	Drawing Release Authorization
DRA	Draw International Resources Corp. [*Formerly, Draw Resources Corp.*] [*Vancouver Stock Exchange symbol*]
DRA	Drum-Read Amplifier [*Computer science*] (CET)
DRA	Dude Ranchers' Association (EA)
DRA	Mercury, NV [*Location identifier FAA*] (FAAL)
DRA	Sandoz AG [*Germany*] [*Research code symbol*]
DRAAG	Design Review and Acceptance Group [*Reviews nuclear weapon designs for DoD*]
DRA (BB & S)	Decisions in Review and Appeal Cases (Basutoland, Bechuanaland, and Swaziland) [*A publication*] (ILCA)
DRAC	Defense Research Advisory Committee (NATG)
DRAC	Delta Region Aviation Command [*Military*] (VNW)
DRAC	Director of the Royal Armoured Corps [*British*]
DRAC	Distributed Read Address Counter
DrAc	Doctor of Acupuncture [*British*] (DBQ)
Drac	Draco [*Constellation*]
DRACO	Dead Reckoning Automatic Computer [*Obsolete*]
DRACOG	Diploma of Royal Australian College of Obstetricians and Gynaecologists (BABM)
DRACR	Diploma of Royal Australasian [*Medicine*] (DMAA)
DRACULA	Data Repository for Addressing Combat Unified Logistics Analysis
DRAD	Digital Remote Antenna Driver [*Telecommunications*] (ACRL)
DRAD	Drill Adapter
DRADA	Depression and Related Affective Disorders Association (EA)
D/RADEX	Digitized RADAR Experiment
Dra Dow	Draper on Dower [*A publication*] (DLA)
DRADS	Degradation of RADAR Defense System
DRAE	Defence Research Analysis Establishment [*Canada*]
Dr Ae	Doctor of Aviation
D Ra E	Doctor of Radio Engineering
D Ra Eng	Doctor of Radio Engineering
Dr Ae S	Doctor of Aeronautical Science
Dr Ae Sc	Doctor of Aeronautical Science
DRAFT	Display Retrieval and Formatting Technique (MCD)
DRAFT	Document Read and Format Translator
Dragns	Dragoons [*Military unit*] [*British*] (DMA)
DRAGONAIR	Hong Kong Dragon Airlines (FEA)
Dr Agr	Doctor of Agriculture
DRAI	Data Research Associates [*NASDAQ symbol*] (TTSB)
DRAI	Data Research Associates, Inc. [*NASDAQ symbol*] (SAG)
DRAI	Dead Reckoning Analog [*or Analyzer*] Indicator
DRA/INED	Development Research Associates, Inc., Institute for New Enterprise Development
Drake Att	Drake on Attachment [*A publication*] (DLA)
Drake Attachm	Drake on Attachment [*A publication*] (DLA)
Drake U	Drake University (GAGS)
DRAM	Detection RADAR Automatic Monitoring (CET)
DRAM	Display Random Access Memory [*Computer science*] (IAA)
DRAM	Drama (ADA)
DRAM	Dramatic
DRAM	Dramatist (WDAA)
DRAM	Dynamic Memory [*Computer science*]
DRAM	Dynamic RAM [*Random Access Memory*] (NITA)
DRAM	Dynamic Random Access Mechanization
d-RAM	Dynamic Random Access Memory [*Computer science*]
DRAM	Dynamic Random Access Memory [*Computer science*] (ACRL)
DRAM	Dynamic Reliability, Availability, and Maintainability
DRAM	Dynamic Response of Articulate Machinery [*MDI*] (NITA)
DRAMA	Digital Radio and Multiplexer Acquisition (MCD)
DRAMD	Demand Return Disposal Average Monthly Demand
DRAMEDY	Drama and Comedy [*Slice-of-life television show*]
DRAM PERS	Dramatis Personae [*Characters of the Play*] [*Latin*]
DRAMS	Digital Recording and Measuring System
DR & A	Data Reduction and Analysis
DR & A	Data Reporting and Accounting (AFM)
DR & A	Data Requirements and Analysis (MCD)
DR & E	Defense Research and Engineering [*DoD*]
Dr & Nap	Drury's Irish Chancery Reports Tempore Napier [*1858-59*] [*A publication*] (DLA)
Dr & S	Doctor and Student [*A publication*] (DSA)
Dr & Sm	Drewry and Smale's English Vice Chancellors' Reports [*1860-65*] [*A publication*] (DLA)
Dr & Sug	Drury's Irish Chancery Reports Tempore Sugden [*A publication*] (DLA)

Dr & Wal	Drury and Walsh's Irish Chancery Reports [*1837-40*] [*A publication*] (DLA)
Dr & War	Drury and Warren's Irish Chancery Reports [*1841-43*] [*A publication*] (DLA)
DRANS	Data Reduction and Analysis System
DRAO	Dominion Radio Astrophysical Observatory [*Herzberg Institute of Astrophysics, National Research Council of Canada*] [*Research center*] (RCD)
DRAP	Deployment Readiness Assistance Program [*Military*]
DRAP	Direct Reading Azimuth Protractor [*Bureau of Mines*]
dr ap	Drachm Apothecaries' Weight [*Pharmacology*] (DAVI)
DRAP	Dram, Apothecary
DRAP	Drapery
DRAPE	Data Recording and Processing Equipment
DRAPE	Digital Recording and Playback Equipment (MCD)
Draper	Draper's Upper Canada King's Bench Reports [*A publication*] (DLA)
Draper (Can)	Draper's Upper Canada King's Bench Reports [*A publication*] (DLA)
Draper (Ont)	Draper's Upper Canada King's Bench Reports [*A publication*] (DLA)
DRAPF	Data Reduction and Processing Facility (IAA)
DRAS	Defense Retiree and Annuitant Pay System [*DoD*]
DRAS	Django Reinhardt Appreciation Society [*Inactive*] (EA)
DRASER	Doppler RADAR and Storm Electricity Research Group [*Norman, OK*] [*Department of Commerce*] (GRD)
DRAT	Data Reduction Analysis Tape
DRAT	Demonstration Reliability Acceptance Test
DRAT	Differential Rheumatoid Agglutination Test [*Medicine*] (DMAA)
DRATE	Difference of Rate
Dr Att	Drake on Attachment [*A publication*] (DLA)
DRAV	Dram, Avoirdupois
Drav	Dravidian [*Family of languages from southern India and Sri Lanka*] (BARN)
Dravo	Dravo Corp. [*Associated Press*] (SAG)
DRAW	Direct Read after Write [*Computer science*]
DRAW	Drag Racing Association of Women
DRAX	Draxis Health, Inc. [*NASDAQ symbol*] (SAG)
DRAXF	Draxis Health [*NASDAQ symbol*] (TTSB)
Draxis	Draxis Health, Inc. [*Associated Press*] (SAG)
DRB	Dartmouth College, Hanover, NH [*OCLC symbol*] (OCLC)
DRB	Data Review Board [*Military*] (AFIT)
DRB	Daunorubicin [*Daunomycin*] [*Also, D, DNR, R*] [*Antineoplastic drug*]
DRB	Decade Resolver Bridge
DRB	Decimal Register Binary
DRB	Defence Research Board [*Canada*]
DRB	Defense Resources Board
DRB	Defense Review Board [*Aerospace*]
DRB	Deficiency Review Board (AFIT)
DRB	Departmental Records Branch [*Military*]
DRB	Derby [*Australia Airport symbol*] (OAG)
DRB	Design Requirements Baseline (NASA)
DRB	Design Review Board
DRB	Deutsche Reichsbahn [*German State Railways*] [*Pre-1945*]
DRB	Dichlororibofuranosylbenzimidazole [*Biochemistry*]
DRB	Digital Readout Box [*Computer science*]
DRB	Disability Retirement Branch [*BUPERS*]
DRB	Discarding Rotating Band [*Military*] (CAAL)
DRB	Drainboard [*Technical drawings*]
DRB	Dursunbey [*Turkey*] [*Seismograph station code, US Geological Survey Closed*] (SEIS)
DRBA	Dharma Realm Buddhist Association (EA)
DRBC	Delaware River Basin Commission [*Successor to INCODEL*]
DRBG	Drill Bushing
Dr Bi Ch	Doctor of Biological Chemistry
DrBiChem	Doctor of Biological Chemistry (NADA)
Dr Bi Phy	Doctor of Biophysics
DrBl	Dark Blend [*Philately*]
DRBL	Design Requirements Baseline
DrBusAdm	Doctor of Business Administration (NADA)
DrBusAdmin	Doctor of Business Administration
DRC	Damage Risk Contours
DRC	Damage-Risk Criteria [*Tolerable limits for noise exposure*]
DRC	Data Rate Changer
DRC	Data Recording Camera
DRC	Data Recording Control (NITA)
DRC	Data Recording Controller [*Computer science*] (BUR)
DRC	Data Reduction Center [*or Complex*]
DRC	Data Reduction Compiler [*or Computer*] (MCD)
DRC	Data Resource Center [*Bureau of the Census*] (GFGA)
DRC	Data Return Capsule [*or Container*]
DRC	Daylight Rapid Contacting (DGA)
DRC	Defence Requirements Committee [*British military*] (DMA)
DRC	Defence Research Committee [*British*]
DRC	Defence Review Committee [*NATO*] (NATG)
DRC	Deficit Reduction Coalition [*Defunct*] (EA)
DRC	Democratiaid Rhyddfrydol Cymru [*Welsh Liberal Democrats*] [*Political party Wales*] (EAIO)
DRC	Democratic Republic of China (CINC)
DRC	Democratic Republic of the Congo [*Later, Zaire*]
DRC	Demographic Research Co., Inc. [*Information service or system*] (IID)
DRC	Deployment Readiness Condition [*Army*] (AABC)
DRC	Depot Repair Cycle (MCD)
DRC	Deputy Regional Commander
DRC	Deputy Regional Counsel (GFGA)

DRC .... Design Research Center [*Carnegie-Mellon University*] [*Research center*] (RCD)
DRC .... Design Rule Checker [*For integrated circuitry*]
DRC .... Dictionary Research Centre [*University of Exeter*] [*British*] (IRC)
DRC .... Dictionary Research Centre [*Macquarie University*] [*Australia*]
DRC .... Dielectric Relaxation Current (PDAA)
DRC .... Diminished Radix Complementation (DICI)
DRC .... Diploma of the Royal College of Science and Technology, Glasgow [*British*]
DRC .... Direct-Reaction Calculation
DRC .... Disability Review Council [*Military*] (AABC)
DRC .... Disability Rights Center (EA)
DRC .... Disappearing RADAR Contact (MCD)
DRC .... Disarmament Resource Center [*Defunct*] (EA)
DRC .... Disaster Research Center [*Ohio*] (AEBS)
DRC .... Discoverer Recovery Capsule [*NASA*]
DRC .... Discrete Rate Command (MCD)
DRC .... Distant Reading Compass
DRC .... District Recruiting Command [*Army*] (AABC)
DRC .... Division of Rehabilitation Counseling [*of the APGA*]
DRC .... Document Record Card
DRC .... Documents Review Committee [*American Occupational Therapy Association*]
DRC .... Dolphin Research Center (EA)
DRC .... Domaine de la Romanee-Conti [*French vintner*]
DRC .... Domestic Revenue Cost Coefficient [*Economics*]
DRC .... Donkey Red Cell [*s*]
DRC .... Dose Response Curve [*Medicine*]
DRC .... Drawing Record Card (MCD)
DRC .... DRCA Medical Corp. [*AMEX symbol*] (SPSG)
DRC .... DRC Resources Corp. [*Vancouver Stock Exchange symbol*]
DRC .... Dropped Rod Control [*Nuclear energy*] (NRCH)
DRC .... Dry Rubber Content
DRC .... Dutch Reformed Church
DRC .... Dynamic Research Console
DRC .... Dynamics Research Corp.
DRC .... Triton Airlines, Inc. [*Canada ICAO designator*] (FAAC)
DRCA .... DRCA Medical Corp. [*Associated Press*] (SAG)
Dr Can L ...... Doctor of Canon Law
DRCCA .... Division of Resources, Centers, and Community Activities [*National Cancer Institute*]
DRCCC .... Defense Regional Communications Control Center
DRCCC-FE..... Defense Regional Communications Control Center, Far East (CINC)
DRCCC-SEA... Defense Regional Communications Control Center, Southeast Asia (CINC)
DRCDE .... Development and Engineering Directorate [*Army*] (RDA)
DRCDG .... Data Recording (MSA)
Dr C Ec .... Droit Civil Ecclesiastique [*A publication*] (DLA)
DR-CG .... Data Reduction and Computing Group [*Range Commanders Council*] [*NASA*]
DRCG .... Discrimination RADAR Control Group (AAG)
DR CHEM ..... Doctor of Chemistry (WDAA)
DrchHu .... Dorchester Hugoton Ltd. [*Associated Press*] (SAG)
DRCL .... Defence Research Chemical Laboratories [*Canada*]
DRCM .... Differential Reinforced Clostridial Medium (PDAA)
DRCO .... Dynamics Research [*NASDAQ symbol*] (TTSB)
DRCO .... Dynamics Research Corp. [*NASDAQ symbol*] (NQ)
DRCOG .... Diploma of the Royal College of Obstetricians and Gynaecologists [*Australia*]
DRCOG .... Diploma of the Royal College of Obstetrics and Gynaecology [*British*]
Dr Com .... Doctor of Commerce
Dr Com .... Droit Commercial [*Commercial Law*] [*French*] (DLA)
DrComSc ...... Doctor of Commercial Science
DRCP .... Dummy Rip Cord Pulls (DICI)
DRC Path..... Diploma of the Royal College of Pathologists [*British*]
DRCPM-NUC... Development Readiness Command Program Manager - Nuclear [*Army*]
DRCPR......... Differential Reactive Current Project Relay
DR/CR......... Data Requirements/Change Request (MCD)
Dr Cr Jus ..... Doctor of Criminal Jurisprudence
DRCS .... Directorate of Reserve Component Support [*DoD*]
DRCS .... Distress Radio Call System [*Telecommunications*] (TEL)
Dr CS .... Doctor of Commercial Science
DRCS .... Dynamically Redefinable Character Set [*Computer science*]
DRCSA .... Distance Runners Club of South Australia
DRCT .... Depot Repair Cycle Time
DRCT .... Direct (AFM)
DRCT .... Dry Rod Consolidation Technology (GAAI)
DRCT .... Dynamic Recipe Control Table
DRCTN......... Direction (FAAC)
DRCTY .... Directly (MSA)
DRCTY .... Directory (AFM)
Dr Cul S ...... Doctor of Cultural Science
Dr Cul Sc ..... Doctor of Cultural Science
DRCV .... Distributor Retard Control Valve [*Automotive engineering*]
DR-CWG ...... Data Reduction and Computing Working Group [*Range Commanders Council*] [*NASA*]
DRD .... Data Recording Device [*Computer science*] (BUR)
DRD .... Data Requirement Description [*NASA*] (MCD)
DRD .... Data Requirements Document [*NASA*] (NASA)
DRD .... Data Resources Directory Publications Subsystem [*Department of Energy*] [*Database*]
DRD .... Defence Research Directors [*NATO*] (NATG)
DRD .... Demand Return Disposal
DRD .... Depressed Reticle Dive [*Military*]

DRD .... Design Requirement Drawing (MCD)
DRD .... Detailed Requirements Document (MCD)
DRD .... Diesel Reduction Drive
DRD .... Differenced-Range Doppler
DRD .... Director [*or Directorate*] of Research and Development [*Air Force*]
DRD .... Dividend Received Deduction [*Finance*]
DRD .... Division of Reactor Development [*AEC*]
Dr D .... Doctor of Divinity
DRD .... Documentary Research Division [*Air Force*]
DRD .... Document Requirement Description (KSC)
DRD .... Dorunda Station [*Australia Airport symbol Obsolete*] (OAG)
DRD .... Draw and Re-Draw [*Tin can manufacturing*]
DRD .... Draw Die [*Tool*] (MCD)
DRD .... Drum-Read Driver [*Computer science*]
DRD .... Dual Readout Devices (MCD)
DRDA .... Director, Research and Development, Air [*Military Canada*]
DRDA .... Distributed Relational Database Access [*Computer science*] (TNIG)
DRDA .... Distributed Relational Database Architecture [*IBM Corp.*] [*Computer protocol*] [*Computer science*] (PCM)
DRDA .... Division of Research Development and Administration [*University of Michigan*] [*Information service or system*] (IID)
DRDBMS..... Distributed Relational DBMS [*Database Management System*] (CDE)
DRDC........... Dairy Research and Development Corp. [*Australia*]
DRDCN .... Data Reduction (MSA)
DRDCS......... Director, Research and Development, Communications and Space [*Military Canada*]
DRDE .... Differential Read Data Enhancement [*Computer science*]
Dr DES........ Doctor of Design (PGP)
DRDF........... Densified Refuse-Derived Fuel (RDA)
DRDG RGE ... Dredging Range [*Nautical charts*]
DRDHP .... Director, Research and Development, Human Performance [*Military Canada*]
DRDL........... Data Requirements and Distribution List [*Navy*]
DRDL........... Defense Research and Development Laboratory [*India*]
DRDL........... Director, Research and Development, Land [*Military Canada*]
DRDM........... Director, Research and Development, Maritime [*Military Canada*]
DRDP........... Detection RADAR Data Processing (CET)
DRDP........... Digital Range Data Processor (MCD)
DRDP........... Director, Research and Development, Program Control [*Military Canada*]
DRDRCSEd... Diploma in Restorative Dentistry, Royal College of Surgeons of Edinburgh [*British*] (DBQ)
DRDRM....... Director, Research and Development, Resource Management [*Military Canada*]
DRDS........... Degradation of RADAR Defense System
DRDSS......... Division of Research and Demonstrations Systems Support [*Department of Health and Human Services*] (GFGA)
DRDT........... Differential Range Delay Time
DRDT........... Division of Reactor Development and Technology [*AEC*]
DRDT & E... Director, Research, Development, Test, and Evaluation [*Military*] (DNAB)
DRDTO......... Detection RADAR Data Takeoff [*Air Force*]
DRE .... Data Recording Equipment (OA)
DRE .... Data Reduction Equipment
DRE .... Dead Reckoning Equipment (MSA)
DRE .... Defence Research Establishment [*Atlantic Canada*] [*UTLAS symbol*]
DRE .... Defense Research Establishment [*Israel*]
DRE .... Department of Rural Education [*of NEA*] [*Later, REA*] (EA)
DRE .... Destruction and Removal Efficiency [*Of waste incinerators*]
DRE .... Digital Rectal Examination [*Medicine*]
DRE .... Diploma in Remedial Electrolysis, Institute of Electrolysis [*British*] (DBQ)
DRE .... Directional Reservation Equipment [*Telecommunications*] (TEL)
DRE .... Director of Radio Equipment [*Navy British*]
DRE .... Director of Religious Education
DRE .... Director [*or Directorate*] of Research and Engineering [*Military*]
DRE .... Direct Reading Encoder
DRE .... Direct-Recording Electronic [*Technology*]
D/RE .... Disassembly/Reassembly Equipment [*Nuclear energy*] (NRCH)
DRE .... District Reserve Equipment [*Army*] (AABC)
DRE .... Diversity Reception Equipment
DRE .... Doctor of Recreation Education (GAGS)
D Re .... Doctor of Religion
DRE .... Doctor of Religious Education
DRE .... Dokumentationsring Elektrotechnik [*Database*]
DRE .... Doppler RADAR Equipment
DRE .... Downrange Error [*NASA*]
DRE .... Drachma [*Monetary unit in Greece*] (EY)
DRE .... Duke Realty Investments, Inc. [*NYSE symbol*] (SPSG)
DRE .... Michigan Airways, Inc. [*ICAO designator*] (FAAC)
DREA .... Defence Research Establishment, Atlantic [*Canada*]
DREA .... Dreco Energy Services Ltd. [*NASDAQ symbol*] (SAG)
DREAC......... Drum Experimental Automatic Computer (IAA)
DREAF......... Dreco Energy Svcs 'A' [*NASDAQ symbol*] (TTSB)
DREAM .... Data Retrieval, Entry, and Management
DREAM .... Design Realization, Evaluation, and Modelling (MHDI)
DREAM .... Development Rehabilitation of the Environment through Arts and Media [*Philippines Earth Savers movement*]
DREAM .... Digital Recording and Measurement [*Computer science*] (MHDI)
DREAM .... Distributed Real-Time Ever Available Microcomputing Laboratory [*University of California, Irvine*] [*Research center*] (RCD)
DREAMS...... Data Retrieval, Entry, and Management Systems (DGA)
DREC .... Detection RADAR Electronic Component
Dr Ec .... Doctor of Economics
DrecoE......... Dreco Energy Services Ltd. [*Associated Press*] (SAG)

DRECP .... Design Release Engineering Change Proposal (MCD)
DRED .... Daily Readiness [*Testing*] (MCD)
DRED .... Data Routing and Error Detecting
DRED .... Detection RADAR Environmental Display [*Air Force*]
DRED .... Directed Rocket Engine Demonstrator
DR Ed .... Doctor of Religious Education
DRED .... Ducted Rocket Engine Development (MCD)
DREDF .... Disability Rights Education and Defense Fund (EA)
DREE .... Department of Regional Economic Expansion [*Canada*]
D Re E .... Doctor of Refrigeration Engineering
D Re Eng ..... Doctor of Refrigeration Engineering
D-REF .... Data Reference [*Environment Canada*] [*Information service or system Information service or system*] (CRD)
DREF .... Distribution Research and Education Foundation (EA)
DREF .... Dose Rate Effectiveness Factor [*Toxicology of radiation*]
DREG .... Data Regulations (KSC)
DREG .... Dressing (MSA)
DREGE .... Diabetes Retrieval Element Generator and Executor
DRelEd .... Doctor of Religious Education
DREME .... Division of Research and Evaluation in Medical Education [*Ohio State University*] [*Research center*] (RCD)
DREN .... Defense Research and Engineering Network [*DoD*]
Dr En .... Doctor of English
Dr Eng .... Doctor of Engineering
Dr Ent .... Doctor of Entomology
DREO .... Defence Research Establishment, Ottawa [*Canada*]
DREO .... Defense Research and Engineering Office [*DoD*]
DREP .... Defence Research Establishment, Pacific [*Canada*]
DRep .... Ohio Decisions Reprint [*A publication*] (DLA)
DREPO .... District Reserve Electronics Program Officer
DRepr .... Ohio Decisions Reprint [*A publication*] (DLA)
DRES .... DARCOM [*Development and Readiness Command, Army*] Readiness Evaluation System (MCD)
DRES .... Defence Research Establishment, Suffield [*Canada*] (MCD)
DRES .... Direct Reading Emission Spectrograph (NRCH)
DRES .... Dresden [*City in East Germany*] (ROG)
DresB .... Dress Barn, Inc. [*Associated Press*] (SAG)
Dres Int Rev... Dresse on Internal Revenue Laws [*A publication*] (DLA)
DRESS .... Depth Resolved Surface Coil Spectroscopy
Dressr .... Dresser Industries, Inc. [*Associated Press*] (SAG)
DRESTC .... Defence Research Establishment, Suffield, Test Centre [*British*] (NATG)
DRET .... Defence Research Establishment, Toronto [*Canada*]
DRET .... Direct Reentry Telemetry [*Air Force*] (MCD)
DRET .... Dissociative Return Electron Transfer
DRETS .... Direct Reentry Telemetry System [*Air Force*]
DREV .... Defence Research Establishment, Valcartier [*Canada*]
Drew .... Drewry's English Vice Chancellors' Reports [*A publication*] (DLA)
Drew .... Drew's Reports [*13 Florida*] [*A publication*] (DLA)
Drew & S.... Drewry and Smale's English Chancery Reports [*A publication*] (DLA)
Drew & S (Eng)... Drewry and Smale's English Chancery Reports [*A publication*]
Drew & Sm... Drewry and Smale's English Chancery Reports [*A publication*] (DLA)
Drew Ch F... Drewry's Chancery Forms [*1876*] [*A publication*] (DLA)
Drew (Eng)... Drewry's English Chancery Reports [*A publication*] (DLA)
Drew Eq Pl... Drewry's Equity Pleading [*A publication*] (DLA)
DrewInd .... Drew Industries, Inc. [*Associated Press*] (SAG)
Drew Inj ...... Drewry on Injunctions [*1841*] [*A publication*] (DLA)
Drew Pat .... Drewry's Patent Law Amendment Act [*1838*] [*A publication*] (DLA)
DREWS .... Direct Readout Equatorial Weather Satellite
Drew Tr M... Drewry's Trade Marks [*1878*] [*A publication*] (DLA)
Drew U .... Drew University (GAGS)
Drexel U ...... Drexel University (GAGS)
Drexlr .... Drexler Technology Corp. [*Associated Press*] (SAG)
DreyerG .... Dreyer's Grand Ice Cream, Inc. [*Associated Press*] (SAG)
DREZ .... Dorsal Root Entry Zone [*Medicine*]
DRF .... Daily Replacement Factor [*Of lymphocytes*] [*Medicine*]
DRF .... Dairy Remembrance Fund (EA)
DRF .... Dance Research Foundation (EA)
DRF .... Data Reporting Form
DRF .... Data Request Form [*NASA*] (NASA)
DRF .... Data Requirement Form (KSC)
DRF .... Deafness Research Foundation (EA)
DRF .... Depot Recovery Factor (MCD)
DRF .... Depression Range Finder [*British military*] (DMA)
DRF .... Destiny Research Foundation (EA)
DRF .... Diamond Radiation Facility
DRF .... Differential Reinforcement [*Psychometrics*]
DRF .... Differentiation Retarding Factor [*Cytology*]
DRF .... Digital, Radio Frequency (MCD)
DRF .... Direct Radiative Forcing [*Atmospheric science*]
DRF .... Direct Relief Foundation [*Later, DRI*]
DRF .... Dirty Rotten Form [*Slang*] (ADA)
DRF .... Disaster Response Force [*Military*]
DRF .... Discharge Ringing Frequency
DRF .... Division Ready Force [*Army*] (MCD)
DRF .... Doctorate Records File [*National Research Council*] [*Information service or system*] (CRD)
Dr F .... Doctor of Forestry
DRF .... Documentation Request Form (MCD)
DRF .... Dose Reduction Factor (DEN)
DRF .... Dry Rectifier
DRF .... Dual Role Fighter (MCD)
DRF .... Duke Realty Inv [*NYSE symbol*] (TTSB)
DRF .... Kenai, AK [*Location identifier FAA*] (FAAL)

DRFB .... Doubly Refractile Fat Bodies [*Biochemistry*] (DAVI)
DRFC .... David Rappaport Fan Club (EA)
DRFC .... Del Reeves Fan Club (EA)
Dr Fi .... Doctor of Finance
DRFL .... Drainage Fluid [*Medicine*] (DAVI)
DRflmnBad... Distinguished Rifleman Badge [*Military decoration*] (AABC)
DRFN .... Driefontein Consolidated [*NASDAQ symbol*] (NQ)
DRFNY .... Dviefontein Consol ADR [*NASDAQ symbol*] (TTSB)
DRFO .... Danube River Field Organization [*Allied German Occupation Forces*]
DRFP .... Design-Rated Full Power (DNAB)
DRFP .... Division of Retail Food Protection [*Food and Drug Administration*]
DRFP .... Draft Request for Proposal (MCD)
DRFR .... Division of Research Facilities and Resources [*National Institutes of Health*]
DRFS .... Destination Rail Station [*MARAD*] (TAG)
DRFT .... Drift [*NWS*] (FAAC)
DRFTNG .... Drafting
DRFX .... Drill Fixture
DRG .... Data Reporting Guideline [*Environmental Protection Agency*]
DRG .... Deering [*Alaska*] [*Airport symbol*] (OAG)
DRG .... Defense Research Group [*NATO*]
DR-G .... Deputy Registrar-General [*British*]
DRG .... Diagnosis-Related Group (ECON)
DRG .... Diagnosis-Related Group [*Insurance*] (WYGK)
DRG .... Diagnostic Related Group [*Medicine*]
DRG .... Dickinson Robinson Group Ltd. [*British*]
DRG .... Digital Ranging Generator [*Apollo*] [*NASA*]
DRG .... Disaster Research Group [*National Academy of Sciences*]
DRG .... Division of Research Grants [*National Institutes of Health*]
DRG .... Dorsal Respiratory Group [*Medicine*]
DRG .... Dorsal Root Ganglion [*Neuroanatomy*]
DRG .... Drag
DRG .... Drawing
DRG .... DRG, Inc. [*Toronto Stock Exchange symbol*]
DRG .... Drogue (KSC)
DRG .... During
Dr Ge .... Doctor of Geology
Dr Geo .... Doctor of Geography
DRGN .... Distributed Real-Time Groove Network [*Computer science*]
DRGN .... Dragon
Dr GP .... Doctor of Geopolitics
DRGR .... Dredger (MSA)
DRGS .... Direct Readout Ground Station
DRGW .... [*The*] Denver & Rio Grande Western Railroad Co. [*AAR code*]
DRH .... Digital Readout Head [*Computer science*]
DRH .... DriverHarris [*AMEX symbol*] (TTSB)
DRH .... Driver-Harris Co. [*AMEX symbol*] (SPSG)
Drhc .... Doctor Honoris Causa [*Honorary Doctor*] [*Latin*] (BARN)
DRHD .... Drill Head
DRHI .... Horton [*D.R.*], Inc. [*NASDAQ symbol*] (SAG)
Dr HL .... Doctor of Humanities of Learning
DRHLA .... Double-Conductor, Radio, High-Tension, Lead-Armored [*Cable*] (IAA)
DRHM .... Durham [*City and county in England*]
Dr Hor .... Doctor of Horticulture
DR Hort ...... DR Horton, Inc. [*Associated Press*] (SAG)
DR Horton ... DR Horton, Inc. [*Associated Press*] (SAG)
DRHP .... Diagnosis and Remediation of Handwriting Problems [*Educational test*]
Dr HS .... Doctor of Humanitarian Service
Dr Hy .... Doctor of Hygiene
DrHyg .... Doctor of Hygiene (DAVI)
DRI .... Darden Restaurants [*NYSE symbol*] (TTSB)
DRI .... Darden Restaurants, Inc. [*NYSE symbol*] (SAG)
DRI .... Data Rate Indicator (NASA)
DRI .... Data Recording Instrument (IAA)
DRI .... Data Recording Interface (MCD)
DRI .... Data Reduction Interpreter
DRI .... Data Resources, Inc. [*Database originator and operator*] [*Information service or system*] (IID)
DRI .... Data Routing Indicator
DRI .... Davenport, Rock Island & North Western Railway Co. [*AAR code*]
DRI .... Dead Reckoning Indicator (MSA)
DRI .... Deductible Requirement Rider [*Health insurance*] (GHCT)
DRI .... Defense Research Institute [*Later, DRI - Defense Research and Trial Lawyers Association*] (EA)
DRI .... Dental Research Institute [*University of California, Los Angeles*] [*Research center*] (RCD)
DRI .... Denver Research Institute [*University of Denver*] [*Research center*]
DRI .... Department of Resource Industries [*Queensland*] [*Australia*]
DRI .... De Ridder, LA [*Location identifier FAA*] (FAAL)
DRI .... Descent Rate Indicator [*Aviation*]
DRI .... Desert Research Institute [*University of Nevada*] [*Research center*]
DRI .... Development of Regional Impact [*Land use*]
DRI .... Diabetes Research Institute [*University of Miami*] [*Research center*] (RCD)
DRI .... Dietary Reference Intakes
DRI .... Differential Refractive Index Detector (MCD)
DRI .... Digital Research, Inc.
DRI .... Direct Read-Out Infrared (PDAA)
DRI .... Direct Reduction Iron [*Ironmaking process*]
DRI .... Direct Relief International (EA)
DRI .... Direct Rooming In [*Medicine*] (DAVI)
DRI .... Disaster Research Institute (EAIO)
DRI .... Discharge Readiness Inventory (MAE)
DRI .... Document Retrieval Index

DRI	Dose Rate Instrumentation
DRI	Drive
DRI	Dual Roll Idler
DRI	Dynamic Response Index
D RI	United States District Court for the District of Rhode Island (DLA)
dRib	Deoxyribose [Genetics] and Laboratory (DAVI)
DRI-BAS	DRI [Data Resources, Inc.] Bank Analysis Service [Information service or system] (CRD)
DRIC	Defence Research Information Centre [Research center British]
DRIC	Dental Research Information Center (DIT)
DRI-CEI	DRI [Data Resources, Inc.] Current Economic Indicators Data Bank [Information service or system] (CRD)
DRICOM	DRI [Data Resources, Inc.] Commodities [Information service or system] (CRD)
DRID	Deflection Refractive Index Detector
DRID	Direct Readout Image Dissector [Camera system]
DRID	Double Radial Immunodiffusion [Medicine] (DMAA)
DRIDAC	Drum Input to Digital Automatic Computer
DRIE	Department of Regional Industrial Expansion [Canada]
DriefC	Driefontein Consolidated Ltd. [Associated Press] (SAG)
DRIF	Defense Freight Railway Interchange Fleet [Army] (DNAB)
DRIF	Diabetes Research Institute Fund
DRIF	Disposal Regional Inventory File [Military] (AFIT)
DRI-FACS	DRI [Data Resources, Inc.] Financial and Credit Statistics [Information service or system] (CRD)
DRIFT	Diffuse Reflectance Infrared Fourier Transform [Spectrometry]
DRIFT	Diversity Receiving Instrumentation for Telemetry
DRIFT	Dynamic Reliability Instantaneous Forecasting Technique
DRIFTS	Diffuse Reflectance Infrared Fourier Transform Spectroscopy
DRIG	Digital Rate-Integrating Gyro (MCD)
DRIL	Detect, Recognize, Identify, and Locate [Military]
DRIL	Directorio Revolucionario Iberico de Liberta [Revolutionary Directorate for Iberian Liberation]
DRILL	Delaware Rapid Interlibrary Loan Project [Library network]
DRILL	Drilling
DRILS	Defense Retail Interservice Logistic Support [Military]
DRIMS	Diagnostic Rifle Marksmanship Simulator (MCD)
DRINC	Dairy Research, Inc. (EA)
Dr Ind	Doctor of Industry
Dr Ing	Doctor Ingeniariae [Doctor of Engineering]
Drink	Drinkwater's English Common Pleas Reports [1840-41] [A publication] (DLA)
Drinkw	Drinkwater's English Common Pleas Reports [1840-41] [A publication] (DLA)
Drinkwater	Drinkwater's English Common Pleas Reports [1840-41] [A publication] (DLA)
Drinkw (Eng)	Drinkwater's English Common Pleas Reports [1840-41] [A publication] (DLA)
DRIP	Data Reduction Input Program [Computer science]
DRIP	Digital Ray and Intensity Projector
DRIP	Dividend Reinvestment Plan [Also, DRP]
DRIP	Downspout Rechargement Infusion Program [Energy development program]
DRIPS	Dynamic Real-Time Information Processing System (MCD)
DRIR	Direct Readout Infrared Radiometer
DRIRU	Dry Rotor Inertial Reference Unit [NASA] (NASA)
DRIS	Defense Retail Interservice Support [Military] (MCD)
DRIS	Diagnosis and Recommended Integrated System [Plant pathology]
DRIS	Diffuse Reflectance Infrared Spectroscopy [Physics]
DRIS	Digital Read-In System [Computer science] (DNAB)
DRI-SEC	DRI [Data Resources, Inc.] US Equity and Debt Securities [Information service or system] (CRD)
DRISS	Digital Read-In Subsystem [Computer science]
DRIT	DTIC Retrieval and Indexing Terminology [DoD]
Dr Iur	Doctor of Laws
DRIV	Drive [Automotive engineering]
DRIVE	Dedicated Road Infrastructure for Vehicle Safety in Europe [British]
DRIVE	Dedicated Road Infrastructure for Vehicle safety in Europe [Automotive navigation systems]
DRIVE	Dedicated Road Infrastructure of Vehicle Safety [European Community] (MHDB)
DRIVE	Democratic Republican Independent Voter Education Committee [Political Action Committee]
DRIVE	Document Read, Information Verify, and Edit
DRIVE	Drive [Commonly used] (OPSA)
DRIVE	Driving
DRIVER	Division of Research and Improvement, Vocational Education, and Rehabilitation [Department of Education]
DRIVES	Drives [Commonly used] (OPSA)
DrivHar	Driver-Harris Co. [Associated Press] (SAG)
DRJ	Data Requirements Justification [Military]
DrJ	Doctor Juris [Doctor of Law]
DRJG	Drill Jig
DRJI	Drill Jig (AAG)
Dr JS	Doctor of Judicial Science
Dr J Sc	Doctor of Judicial Science
DrJU	Doctor Juris Utriusque [Doctor of Both Laws]
Dr Jur	Doctor Juris [Doctor of Law] (EY)
Dr Jur Can	Doctor Juris Canonici [Doctor of Canon Law] [Latin]
Dr Jur et Rer Pol	Doctor of Laws and Political Science
DRK	Dark
DRK	Data Request Keyboard
DRK	Democratic People's Republic of Korea
DRK	Derrick (MSA)
DRK	Display Request Keyboard (KSC)

DRK	Druk Air [Bhutan] [ICAO designator] (FAAC)
DRK	Drunk [FBI standardized term]
DRKL	Defence Research Kingston Laboratory [Canada] (MCD)
DRKN	Durakon Industries [NASDAQ symbol] (TTSB)
DRKN	Durakon Industries, Inc. [NASDAQ symbol] (NQ)
DRL	Data Reduction Laboratory
DRL	Data Requirement List (KSC)
DRL	Data Requirements Language
DRL	Data Retrieval Language [National Institute of Standards and Technology]
DRL	Date Required to Load (AABC)
DRL	Daytime Running Lights [Automotive engineering]
DRL	Defense Research Laboratory
DRL	Derlan Industries Ltd. [Toronto Stock Exchange symbol]
DRL	Design Review List (MCD)
DRL	Differential Reinforcement of Low Rate [Psychometrics]
DRL	Digital Readout Light [Computer science]
DRL	DI Industries [Formerly, Drillers, Inc.] [AMEX symbol] (SPSG)
DRL	Diode Resistor Logic (IAA)
DRL	Directional Reference Locator
DRL	Direct Retrieval Language (NITA)
DRL	Division of Reactor Licensing [AEC]
DRL	Document Requirement List (KSC)
DRLI	Data Requirements List Item (SSD)
Dr Lit	Doctor of Literature
Dr Litt	Doctor of Letters
Dr LL	Doctor of Laws
DRLL	Drill
DRLMS	Digital RADAR Landmass Simulator
DRL/S	Data Requirements List/Schedule
DRLS	Del Rio Language Screening [Speech and language therapy] (DAVI)
DRLS	Despatch-Rider Letter-Service [Military British]
Dr LS	Doctor of Library Science
DRLS	Dragon Remote Launch System [Military] (MCD)
DRL/UT	Defense Research Laboratory/University of Texas (MUGU)
DRM	Data Records Management (MCD)
DRM	Data Resource Management (NITA)
DRM	Data Retrieval Mode
DRM	Dead Reckoning Module
DRM	Decay Rate Meter
DRM	Decimal Rate Multiplier (IAA)
DRM	Defense Research Member (AAGC)
DRM	Defense Resource Management (AAGC)
DRM	Defense Resources Model [Congressional Budget Office] (GFGA)
DRM	Dental Repair Technician [Navy]
DRM	Depositional Remanent Magnetization (IAA)
DRM	Design Reference Mission [NASA]
DRM	Design Reference Model (KSC)
DRM	Destructive Readout Memory (DNAB)
DRM	Detrital Remanent Magnetization [Geophysics]
DRM	Development Reactor Mock-Up
DRM	Diamond Shamrock [NYSE symbol] (TTSB)
DRM	Diamond Shamrock Co. [NYSE symbol] (SPSG)
DRM	Digital Radiometer
DRM	Digital Range Machine
DRM	Digital Road Map [Digital Equipment Corp.] (PCM)
DRM	Digital Road Map
DRM	Diploma in Resource Management (ADA)
DRM	Direction of Relative Movement [Navigation]
DRM	Directorate for Resource Management [CIA]
DRM	Direct Reduction Mortgage [Banking]
DRM	Drafting [or Drawing] Room Manual
DRM	Drama [Greece] [Airport symbol] (AD)
DRM	Drawing Requirements Manual [NASA] (NASA)
DRM	Dream
DRM	Drum [Shipping]
DRM	Drummond Island, MI [Location identifier FAA] (FAAL)
DRM	Ducted Rocket Motor
DRM	Dunraine Mines Ltd. [Toronto Stock Exchange symbol]
DRMA	Drama
DRMAJ	Drum Major [Marine Corps]
DRMD	Duramed Phamaceutical [NASDAQ symbol] (TTSB)
DRMD	Duramed Pharmaceuticals, Inc. [NASDAQ symbol] (SAG)
Dr Med	Doctor of Medicine
DrMedUniv	Doctor Medicinae Universae [Latin]
Dr Med Vet	Doctor Medicinae Veterinariae [Doctor of Veterinary Medicine] [Latin]
DRMF	Damon Runyon Memorial Fund for Cancer Research [Later, DRWWCF] (EA)
DRMI	Dual Radio Magnetic Indicator (MCD)
DRML	Defence Research Medical Laboratory [Canada]
DRMO	Defense Reutilization and Marketing Office [DoD]
DRMO	Defense Reutilization and Materials Organization (DOMA)
DRMO	District Records Management Office [or Officer]
Dr Mont	Doctor Rerum Montanarum [Latin]
DRMP	Design Reference Mission Profile [DoD]
DRMS	Data Resources Management System
DRMS	Defense Reutilization and Marketing Service [DoD]
DRMS	Department of Defense Resource Management System (NG)
DRMS	Design Rock-Mass Strength [Mining technology]
DRMS	Distance Root Mean Square (FAAC)
Dr MT	Doctor of Mechanotherapy
Dr Mus	Doctor of Music
DRN	Daily Reports Notice [Air Force] (AFM)
DRN	Data Record Number (MCD)

DRN	Data Reference Number
DRN	Data Release Notice (DNAB)
DRN	Dirranbandi [Australia Airport symbol Obsolete] (OAG)
DRN	Document Release Notice [Jet Propulsion Laboratory, NASA]
DRN	Document Revision Notice (MCD)
DRN	Dorsal Raphe Nucleus [Brain anatomy]
DRN	Dorsal Root Neurons [Neuroanatomy]
DRN	Double-Round Nose
DRN	Drain (NASA)
DRN	Drain
DRN	Drawn [Cricket] (ROG)
dRNA	DNA[Deoxyribonucleic Acid]-like RNA[Ribonucleic Acid] [Genetics] (DOG)
dRNA	Ribonucleic Acid, Diverse [Biochemistry, genetics]
DrNatSc	Doctor of Natural Science
DrNatSci	Doctor of Natural Science (NADA)
DrNatTechn	Doctor Rerum Naturalium Technicarum [Latin]
drng	Drainage [Medicine] (DAVI)
DRNG	Drainage
DRNK	Cable Car Beverage [NASDAQ symbol] (TTSB)
DRNK	Cable Car Beverage Corp. [NASDAQ symbol] (NQ)
DRNL	Defence Research Northern Laboratory [Canada]
Dr N Ph	Doctor of Natural Philosophy
Dr N Sc	Doctor of Natural Sciences
DRnt	Diagnostic Roentgenology [Radiology] (DAVI)
DRO	Daily Receipt of Obligation [Military]
DRO	Daily Report of Obligation [Navy] (NG)
DRO	Daily Routine Order
DRO	Dancing Room Only
DRO	Data Readout [Navy] (NVT)
DRO	Day Room Orderly [Army]
DRO	Desert Rose Resources [Vancouver Stock Exchange symbol]
DRO	Destructive Readout
DRO	Development Release Order
DRO	Differential Reinforcement of Other Behavior [Psychometrics]
DRO	Digital Readout [Computer science]
DRO	Digital Readout Oscilloscope [Computer science]
dro	Dinheiro [Monetary unit] [Portugal]
DRO	Dining Room Orderly [Military] (VNW)
DRO	Director of Recruiting and Organization [Military British]
DRO	Directory of Religious Organizations [A publication]
DRO	Direct Readout [Computer science]
DRO	Direct Recording Oscillograph
DRO	Disablement Resettlement Office [or Officer] [British]
DRO	Disposal Release Order [DoD]
DRO	Divisional Records Office [British military] (DMA)
DRO	Divisional Routine Order
DRO	Division of Regional Operations (AAGC)
DRO	Document Release Order (NASA)
DRO	Domestic Route Order
DRO	Doubly Resonant Oscillator (IEEE)
DRO	Drawing Requirement Outline
DRO	Durango [Colorado] [Airport symbol] (OAG)
DRO	Dynamic Runout [Automotive engineering]
DRO	House Democratic Research Organization (EA)
DROD	Delayed Readout Detector [Satellite instrument]
Dr of Eng	Doctor of Engineering
Dr of PE	Doctor of Physical Education
Dr of Rec	Doctor of Recreation
DROG	Drogue
Droit CC	Droit Civil Canadien [A publication] (DLA)
DROL	Defense RDT & E [Research, Development, Test, and Evaluation] Online System [DTIC] (MCD)
DRO-LA	Defense Research Office, Latin America [Army] (AABC)
DROLLS	Defense RDT&E On-Line System (AAGC)
DROLS	Defense RDT & E [Research, Development, Test, and Evaluation] Online System [DTIC]
DROM	Decoder Read-Only Memory
DROM	Dromore [District in Northern Ireland] (ROG)
DROMDI	Direct Readout Miss Distance Indicator
DRON	Data Reduction (MCD)
Drone Cop	Drone on Copyrights [A publication] (DLA)
DROO	Digital Readout Oscilloscope [Computer science]
DROO	Durban Roodepoort Deep Ltd. [NASDAQ symbol] (SAG)
DROP	Data Printout Program
DROP	Distribution Register of Organic Pollutants [In Water] [Environmental Protection Agency]
DROPS	Demountable, Rack, Off-Loading, and Pick-Up System [British Army]
DRORM	Drafting and Records Office, Royal Marines [British military] (DMA)
DROS	Date Returned from Overseas [Military]
DROS	Dead Reckoning Own Ship
DROS	Direct Readout Satellite
DROS	Disk Resident Operating System [Computer science] (IEEE)
Dr O Sc	Doctor of the Science of Oratory
DROT	Delayed Range on Target [Air Force]
Dr OT	Doctor of Occupational Therapy (PGP)
droupie	Data groupie [Person who likes to spend time in the company of programmers and data processing professionals.] (CDE)
DROWS	Direct Readout Weather Satellite
DRP	Data Reception Process [Telecommunications] (TEL)
DRP	Data Reduction Procedure [or Program]
DRP	Data Retrieval Program (CAAL)
DRP	Dead Reckoning Plotter
DRP	Degree of Reading Power [Test]
DRP	Delayed Reenlistment Program [Air Force]
DRP	Democratic Reform Party [South Africa Political party] (EY)
DRP	Democratic Republican Party [South Korea Political party] (PPW)
DRP	Demonstration Reprocessing Plant [Nuclear energy] (NUCP)
DRP	Densest Random Packing [Solid state physics]
DRP	Designated Repair [or Rework] Point [Military] (CAAL)
DRP	Detected Radiant Power
DRP	Deutsche Rechtspartei [German Party of the Right] [Political party] (PPE)
DRP	Deutsches Reichspatent [German State Patent]
DRP	Development Resources Panel [United Nations Development Program]
DRP	Digital Recording Process
DRP	Digoxin Reduction Products [Clinical chemistry]
DRP	Directional Radiated Power [Telecommunications] (TEL)
DRP	Director of Radio Production [Air Ministry] [British World War II]
DRP	Direct Repair Program [Automotive collision repairs]
DRP	Direct Requisitioning Procedure (DNAB)
DRP	Disaster Recovery Plan [Computer systems]
DRP	Discontinuously Reinforced Plastic
DRP	Discoverer Research Program [NASA] (IAA)
DRP	Dissolved Reactive Phosphorus [Environmental science]
DRP	Distribution Reinvestment Program [Stock exchange term]
DRP	Distribution Resource Planning
DRP	Dividend Reinvestment Plan [Also, DRIP]
DRP	Doctor of Regional Planning
DRP	Documentation Research Project [American Institute of Physics]
DRP	Dorsal Root Potential [Anatomy]
DRP	Draft Requirements Package (MCD)
DRP	Dredging Research Program [U.S. Army Corps of Engineers]
DRP	Drill Plate [Tool] (MCD)
DRP	Drone Recovery Platform (NVT)
DRP	During Reporting Period
DRP	Dystrophin-Related Protein [Biochemistry]
DRPA	Delaware River Port Authority
Dr Pa	Doctor of Painting
Dr PA	Doctor of Public Administration
DRPC	Defence Research Policy Committee [British]
DRPC	Direct Reading Pocket Chamber
DRPC	Division Reliability Policy Committee (AAG)
Drpd	Dropped [Army]
DRPE	Drill Plate [Tool] (AAG)
Dr PH	Doctor of Public Health
DrPH	Doctor of Public Health (GAGS)
Dr PH	Doctor of Public Hygiene
Dr Pharm	Doctor Pharmaciae [Latin]
Dr PH Hy	Doctor of Public Health and Hygiene
Dr Phi	Doctor of Philanthropy
Dr Phil	Doctor Philosophiae [Doctor of Philosophy]
Dr Phil Fac Theol	Doctor Philosophiae Facultatis Theologicae [Latin]
Dr Phil Nat	Doctor of Natural Philosophy
Dr Philos	Doctor of Philosophy
Dr Pho	Doctor of Photography
DRPHS	Dense Random Packing of Hard Spheres (MCD)
Dr Phy	Doctor of Physics
DRPI	Digital Rod Position Indication [Nuclear energy] (NRCH)
DRPL	Drill Plate [Tool]
DRPLA	Dentatorubral Pallidoluysian Atrophy [Medicine]
DRPM	Direct Reporting Program Manager [Navy] (DOMA)
DRPO	Defense Resources Planning Operation (AAG)
DrPolSc	Doctor of Political Science (NADA)
Dr Pol Sci	Doctor of Political Science
DRPP	Data Routing Patch Panel (MCD)
DRPR	Drawing Practice (NG)
Dr Pr M	Doctor of Preventative Medicine
DRPS	Disk Real-Time and Programming System [Computer science]
DRPS	Dry Reed Pushbutton Switch
DRPS	Dynamic Memory Relocation and Protection System (NITA)
Dr P Sc	Doctor of Physical Science
D RPT	Dead Reprint (DGA)
DRPTV	Ducted Rocket Propulsion Test Vehicle (MCD)
DRQ	Data Ready Queue [IBM Corp.] (IBMDP)
DRQ	Data Request
DRQ	Discomfort Relief Quotient [Medicine] (AAMN)
DRR	Daily Regulatory Reporter
DRR	Data Recorder/Reproducer (MCD)
DRR	Data Redundancy Reduction [or Removal] (KSC)
DRR	Deployment Readiness Review [Aviation] (FAAC)
DRR	Descent Rate RADAR
DRR	Design Release [or Request] Review
DRR	Design Requirements Review [NASA] (NASA)
DRR	Development Revision Record (KSC)
DRR	Digital RADAR Relay
DRR	Direct Reading Receiver
DRR	Discounted Rate of Return [Marketing] (PDAA)
DRR	Disparity Reduction Rate [Measures progress a country has made toward reconciling its current Physical Quality of Life Index with its optimum projected PQLI for the year 2000] [Overseas Development Council]
DRR	Diversity Reception Receiver
DRR	Division of Research Resources [Bethesda, MD] [National Institutes of Health]
DRR	Document Release Record (NRCH)
DRR	Dorado Resources Ltd. [Vancouver Stock Exchange symbol]
DRR	Dough Rate of Reaction [Food science]
DRR	Durrie [Australia Airport symbol Obsolete] (OAG)

DRRA.......... Direct Reading Range Assessor (DNAB)
DRRA.......... Tessaoua [*Niger*] [*ICAO location identifier*] (ICLI)
DrRaEng...... Doctor of Radio Engineering (NADA)
DRRB.......... Data Requirements Review Board [*DoD*]
DRRC.......... Dogondoutchi [*Niger*] [*ICAO location identifier*] (ICLI)
Dr RCA........ Doctor of the Royal College of Art
DRRD.......... Division of Reactor Research and Development [*Energy Research and Development Administration*]
DRRD.......... Dosso [*Niger*] [*ICAO location identifier*] (ICLI)
DRRE.......... Tera [*Niger*] [*ICAO location identifier*] (ICLI)
DrRec......... Doctor of Recreation (NADA)
DrReEng...... Doctor of Refrigeration Engineering (NADA)
Dr Rer Comm... Doctor Rerum Commercialium [*Latin*]
Dr Rer Nat.... Doctor Rerum Naturalium [*Doctor of Natural Science*] [*Latin*]
Dr Rer Pol.... Doctor Rerum Politicarum [*Doctor of Political Science*] [*Latin*]
Dr Rer Soc Oec... Doctor Rerum Socialium Oeconomicarumque [*Latin*]
Dr Rer Tech... Doctor of Technical Science
DRRF.......... Division Rapid Reaction Force [*Army*] (AABC)
DRRG.......... Gaya [*Niger*] [*ICAO location identifier*] (ICLI)
DRRI.......... Bilma [*Niger*] [*ICAO location identifier*] (ICLI)
DRRI.......... Defense Race Relations Institute [*Air Force*]
DRRL.......... Digital RADAR Relay Link
DRRL.......... Tilabery [*Niger*] [*ICAO location identifier*] (ICLI)
DRRM.......... Maradi [*Niger*] [*ICAO location identifier*] (ICLI)
DRRN.......... Niamey Airport [*Niger*] [*ICAO location identifier*] (ICLI)
DRRP.......... La Tapoa [*Niger*] [*ICAO location identifier*] (ICLI)
DRRR.......... Niamey [*Niger*] [*ICAO location identifier*] (ICLI)
DRRT.......... Data Reception, Recording, and Transmission (MCD)
DRRT.......... Tahoua [*Niger*] [*ICAO location identifier*] (ICLI)
Dr R T Nap... Drury's Irish Chancery Reports Tempore Napier [*1858-59*] [*A publication*] (DLA)
Dr R T Sug... Drury's Irish Chancery Reports Tempore Sugden [*A publication*] (DLA)
DRRU.......... Ouallam [*Niger*] [*ICAO location identifier*] (ICLI)
DRRV.......... Niamey [*Niger*] [*ICAO location identifier*] (ICLI)
DRS............ Clarepine Industries, Inc. [*Toronto Stock Exchange symbol*]
DRS............ Daily River Stages (NOAA)
DRS............ Dar Es Salaam [*Tanzania*] [*Geomagnetic observatory code*]
DRS............ Data Rate Selector
DRS............ Data Reaction System (AAG)
DRS............ Data Receiving Station (KSC)
DRS............ Data Recording Set
DRS............ Data Recording System (MUGU)
DRS............ Data Reduction Software (IAA)
DRS............ Data Reduction System [*Computer science*]
DRS............ Data Relay Satellite [*NASA*]
DRS............ Data Relay Station (NASA)
DRS............ Data Relay System (CAAL)
DRS............ Data Requirements Specification (KSC)
DRS............ Data Retrieval and Storage
DRS............ Data Retrieval System [*Computer science*] (BUR)
DRS............ Debtor Reporting System [*World Bank*]
DRS............ Defense Research Sciences
DRS............ Deficiency Reporting System [*Military*]
DRS............ Dementia Rating Scale [*Psychometric testing*]
DRS............ Design Requirement Sheet [*Military*]
DRS............ Detection and Ranging Set (CAAL)
DRS............ Development Reference Service [*Society for International Development*] (IID)
DRS............ Development Requirements Specification [*Nuclear energy*] (NRCH)
DRS............ Diabetic Retinopathic Study [*National Eye Institute*]
DRS............ Diagnostic Reading Scales [*Education*]
DRS............ Diagnostic/Retrieval Sys [*AMEX symbol*] (TTSB)
DRS............ Diagnostic/Retrieval Systems, Inc. [*AMEX symbol*] (SPSG)
DRS............ Diagnostic Rework Sheets (AAG)
DRS............ Diffuse Reflection Spectroscopy
DRS............ Digital RADAR Simulator
DRS............ Digital RADAR System
DRS............ Digital Range Safety (NASA)
DRS............ Digital Readout System [*Computer science*]
DRS............ Digital Receiver Station [*Computer science*]
DRS............ Digital Recording System
DRS............ Dipping-Reflector Sequence [*Geology*]
DRS............ Director of Repair and Service [*British military*] (DMA)
D/RS.......... Disassembly/Reassembly Station [*Nuclear energy*] (NRCH)
DRS............ Discrepancy Reporting System [*NASA*]
DRS............ Discrepancy Report Squawk [*NASA*] (SAA)
DRS............ Disk Resident System [*Computer science*] (IAA)
DRS............ Dissolved Reactive Silica [*Environmental science*]
DRS............ Distributed Resource System (IAA)
DRS............ Division of Research Services [*Bethesda, MD*] [*National Institutes of Health*]
DRS............ Division Reference Standards (AAG)
DRS............ Division Restructuring Study [*TRADOC*] [*Army*] (INF)
DRS............ Django Reinhardt Society (EA)
DRS............ Document Retrieval Services [*Information service or system*] (IID)
DRS............ Document Retrieval System
DRS............ Doppler RADAR Set (DNAB)
DRS............ Double Right Shift
DRS............ Downrange Ship (SAA)
DRS............ Drenair [*Spain ICAO designator*] (FAAC)
DRS............ Dresden [*Germany Airport symbol*] (OAG)
DRS............ Dress
DRS............ Dressed [*Lumber*]
DRS............ Drives

DRS............ Drives [*Postal Service standard*] (OPSA)
DRS............ Drowsiness (KSC)
DRS............ Dry Reed Switch
DRS............ Dynamic Reflectance Spectroscopy
DRSA......... Data Recording System Analyst (MUGU)
DRSAM....... Diploma of the Royal Scottish Academy of Music and Drama
DRSAMD..... Diploma of the Royal Scottish Academy of Music and Dance (BARN)
DRSC......... Defence Required Strategic Capability
DRSC......... Direct RADAR Scope Camera
DRSC......... Direct Reading Scope Camera
Dr Sc........ Doctor of Science
Dr Sci....... Doctor of Science
Dr Sci Nat... Doctor of Natural Sciences
Dr Sc Jur.... Doctor of the Science of Jurisprudence
DRSCPO...... District Reserve Supply Corps Program Officer (DNAB)
Dr Sc Pol.... Doctor of Political Sciences (EY)
DRSCR........ Digital Range Safety Command Receiver [*NASA*] (KSC)
DRSCS........ Digital Range Safety Command System [*NASA*] (MCD)
Dr Sc Techn... Doctor of Technical Science
DRSEM....... Deployable Receive Segment Engineering Model (MCD)
DRSG......... Digital Recorder Signal Generator [*Computer science*]
DRSG......... Division Restructuring Study Group [*TRADOC*] [*Army*] (RDA)
DRSG......... Dominican Republic Study Group [*Defunct*] (EA)
DRSG......... Dressing [*Medicine*]
DRSH......... Drill Shell
DRSHC........ Deletion Reason/Supply History Code
DRSN......... Drifting Snow [*Meteorology*]
DRSNSW..... Doctors' Reform Society of New South Wales [*Australia*]
Dr So........ Doctor of Sociology
Dr So Sc..... Doctor of Social Science
DRSP......... Death Row Support Project (EA)
DRSP......... Defense Reconnaissance Support Program
DRSP......... Digital RADAR Signal Processor (MCD)
DRSR......... Direct RADAR Scope Recorder (MCD)
DRSR......... Dresser (MSA)
DRSS......... Data Relay Satellite System [*NASA*]
DRSS......... Discrepancy Report Squawk Sheet [*NASA*] (NASA)
DRSS......... Division of Retirement and Survivors Studies [*Social Security Administration*] (GRD)
DRSS......... Downrange Support Ship
DRSW......... Documentary Relations of the South West [*Arizona State Museum*] [*Tucson*] [*Information service or system*] (IID)
DRT........... Darta [*France ICAO designator*] (FAAC)
Drt........... Dartmouth (BARN)
DRT........... Data Reckoning Tracer (MSA)
DRT........... Data Recovery Tester [*Computer science*] (HGAA)
DRT........... Data Review Technician
DRT........... Daughters of the Republic of Texas (EA)
DRT........... Dead Reckoning Tracer [*RADAR*]
DRT........... Dead Reckoning Trainer
DRT........... Decade Ratio Transformer
DRT........... Decision Response Time
DRT........... Del Rio [*Texas*] [*Airport symbol Obsolete*] (OAG)
DRT........... Department of Roads and Transport [*Tasmania*] [*Australia*]
DRT........... Department of Road Transport [*South Australia*] [*Australia*]
DRT........... Design Reference Timeline (MCD)
DRT........... Deviation for Replacement Time
DRT........... Device Reference Table
DRT........... Device Rise Time [*Photomultipliers for scintillation counting*] (IEEE)
DRT........... Diagnostic Rhyme Test
DRT........... Digital Readout Timer [*Computer science*]
DRT........... Digital Rotary Transducer
DRT........... Diode Recovery Tester
drt........... Director [*MARC relator code*] [*Library of Congress*] (LCCP)
DRT........... Director of Railway Transport [*British military*] (DMA)
DRT........... Direct Reading Telemeter (IAA)
DRT........... Direct Reading Totalizer
DRT........... Disaster Recovery Training (DNAB)
DRT........... Discrimination RADAR Transmitter (IAA)
DRT........... Dismounted Reconnaissance Team [*Army*] (INF)
DRT........... Distant Remote Transceiver (IAA)
DRT........... Distribution Requirement Table (MCD)
DRT........... Division Reconnaissance Team [*Warsaw Pact forces*]
DRT........... Domain-Referenced Test [*Education*] (AEE)
DRT........... Dome Removal Tool
DRT........... Drawing Release Ticket (MCD)
DRT........... Drill Template (MCD)
DRT........... Driver Reaction Time
DRTA......... Darwin Region Tourism Association [*Australia*]
DR-TA........ Directed Reading-Thinking Activity (EDAC)
DRTA......... Direct Reading Thinking Activity [*Education*] (AEE)
DRTA......... Driptank
DRTC......... Diabetes Research and Training Center [*Washington University*] [*Research center*] (RCD)
DRTC......... Diabetes Research and Training Center [*Yeshiva University*] [*Research center*] (RCD)
DRTC......... Diabetes Research and Training Center [*University of Chicago*] [*Research center*] (RCD)
DRTC......... Diploma of the Royal Technical College [*British*]
DRTC......... Documentation Research and Training Centre
DRTE......... Defence Research Telecommunication Establishment [*Canada*]
DRTE......... Dendrite International [*NASDAQ symbol*] (TTSB)
DRTE......... Dendrite International, Inc. [*NASDAQ symbol*] (SAG)
DRTE......... Doctor of Radio and Television Engineering
Dr Tech....... Doctor of Technology

Dr Techn	Doctor of Technology
DRT Eng	Doctor of Radio and Television Engineering
Dr Theol	Doctor of Theology
DRTI	Dual Roll Trough Idler
DRTK	GTS Duratek [*NASDAQ symbol*] (TTSB)
DRTK	GTS Duratek Corp. [*NASDAQ symbol*] (NQ)
DRTL	Diode Resistor Transistor Logic (MSA)
DRTM	Disk Real-Time Monitor [*Computer science*]
Dr T Med	Doctor of Tropical Medicine
Dr T Nap	Drury's Irish Chancery Reports Tempore Napier [*1858-59*] [*A publication*] (DLA)
DRTP	Drill Template
DRTR	Dead Reckoning Trainer
Dr Trav	Droit du Travail: Revue Mensuelle [*French A publication*] (DLA)
DRTS	Detecting, Ranging, and Tracking System (MCD)
DRTSA	Defense Reconnaissance Tactical Support Activity (MCD)
Dr T Sug	Drury's Irish Chancery Reports Tempore Sugden [*A publication*] (DLA)
DRU	Data Reference Unit
DRU	Data Reorganization Utility [*Computer science*]
DRU	Data Retrival Unit (GAVI)
DRU	Demolition Research Unit
DRU	Digital Range Unit
DRU	Digital Register Unit
DRU	Digital Remote Unit [*Computer science*] (MCD)
DRU	Direct Reporting Unit
DRU	Disaccharide Repeating Unit [*Biochemistry*]
DRU	Document Reproduction Unit
DRU	Document Retention Unit [*IRS*]
DRU	Drew University, Madison, NJ [*OCLC symbol*] (OCLC)
DRU	Drive Unit
DRU	Drummond, MT [*Location identifier FAA*] (FAAL)
DRU	Drummond Petroleum Ltd. [*Toronto Stock Exchange symbol*]
Dru	Drury's Irish Chancery Reports Tempore Sugden [*A publication*] (DLA)
Dru & Nap	Drury's Irish Chancery Reports Tempore Napier [*1858-59*] [*A publication*] (DLA)
Dru & Sug	Drury's Irish Chancery Reports Tempore Sugden [*A publication*] (DLA)
Dru & Wal	Drury and Walsh's Irish Chancery Reports [*1837-40*] [*A publication*] (DLA)
Dru & War	Drury and Warren's Irish Chancery Reports [*1841-43*] [*A publication*] (DLA)
DRUB	Digital Remote Unit Buffer [*Computer science*] (MCD)
DRUC	Disposition Record Unsatisfactory Condition (MCD)
D Ru E	Doctor of Rural Engineering
D Ru Eng	Doctor of Rural Engineering
Drug Abuse LR	Drug Abuse Law Review [*A publication*] (DLA)
Drug Abuse L Rev	Drug Abuse Law Review [*A publication*] (DLA)
DrugE	Drug Emporium, Inc. [*Associated Press*] (SAG)
DRUID	Digital Readout Unit and Interactive Displays (MCD)
DRUIDS	Diffuse Reflectance Using Infrared Dispersive Spectrophotometry
DRUJ	Distal Radioulnar Joint [*Anatomy*]
DRUL	Downrange Up Link [*Apollo*] [*NASA*]
DRUM	Deep Reflections from the Upper Mantle [*Geology*]
DRUM	Dodge Revolutionary Union Movement
DR UNIV PAR	Doctor of the University of Paris (ROG)
DRurSc	Doctor of Rural Science (ADA)
DRurSci	Doctor of Rural Science (NADA)
Drury	Drury's Irish Chancery Reports [*A publication*] (DLA)
Drury & Wal	Drury and Walsh's Irish Chancery Reports [*1837-40*] [*A publication*] (DLA)
Drury & Wal (Ir)	Drury and Walsh's Irish Chancery Reports [*1837-40*] [*A publication*] (DLA)
Drury & War	Drury and Warren's Irish Chancery Reports [*1841-43*] [*A publication*] (DLA)
Drury & War (Ir)	Drury and Warren's Irish Chancery Reports [*1841-43*] [*A publication*] (DLA)
Drury C	Drury College (GAGS)
Drury (Ir)	Drury's Irish Chancery Reports [*A publication*] (DLA)
Drury T Nap	Drury's Irish Chancery Reports Tempore Napier [*1858-59*] [*A publication*] (DLA)
Drury T Sug	Drury's Irish Chancery Reports Tempore Sugden [*A publication*] (DLA)
Dru T Nap	Drury's Irish Chancery Reports Tempore Napier [*1858-59*] [*A publication*] (DLA)
Dru T Sug	Drury's Irish Chancery Reports Tempore Sugden [*A publication*] (DLA)
Dru T Sugden	Drury's Irish Chancery Reports Tempore Sugden [*A publication*] (DLA)
DRUV	Diffuse-Reflectance Ultraviolet-Visible [*Spectra*]
DRV	Data Recovery Vehicle
DRV	Deep-Diving Research Vehicles (KSC)
DRV	Deep Research Vehicle [*or Vessel*] [*NOO*]
DRV	Democratic Republic of Vietnam [*North Vietnam*]
DRV	Development Reentry Vehicle [*Aerospace*] (IAA)
DRV	Dravo Corp. [*NYSE symbol*] (SPSG)
DRV	Drive [*Commonly used*] (OPSA)
DRV	Dumont D'Urville [*Pointe Geologie, Adelie*] [*Antarctica*] [*Seismograph station code, US Geological Survey*] (SEIS)
DRVID	Differenced-Range Versus Integrated Doppler [*Charged particle measurement*]
DRVN	Democratic Republic of Vietnam [*North Vietnam*]
DRVN	Driven [*Automotive engineering*]
DRVR	Driver (MSA)
DRVS	Diabetic Retinopathy Vitrectomy Study [*National Eye Institute*]
DRVS	Doppler RADAR Velocity Sensor
DRVS	Drill Vise
DRW	Darwin [*Australia Airport symbol*] (OAG)
DRW	Defensive Radio Warfare (NATG)
DRW	Dennis R. Williams [*Designer's mark on US bicentennial dollar*]
DRW	Dirty RADWASTE [*Nuclear energy*] (NRCH)
DRWAW	Distillery, Rectifying, Wine, and Allied Workers International Union of America [*Later, DWAW*] (EA)
DRWG	Data Reduction Working Group (SAA)
DRWG	Drawing (NATG)
DRWI	Drew Industries, Inc. (MHDW)
DR WIND	Door or Window [*Freight*]
Drwl	Dry Wall (DAC)
DRWWCF	Damon Runyon-Walter Winchell Cancer Fund (EA)
DRX	Drachma [*Monetary unit*] [*Greece*]
DRX	Drexel University, School of Library and Information Science, Philadelphia, PA [*OCLC symbol*] (OCLC)
DRX	Drucox Petroleum [*Vancouver Stock Exchange symbol*]
DRXR	Drexler Technology [*NASDAQ symbol*] (TTSB)
DRXR	Drexler Technology Corp. [*NASDAQ symbol*] (NQ)
DRY	Dairy
DRY	Deraya Air Taxi PT [*Indonesia*] [*ICAO designator*] (FAAC)
DRY	Dryden Resources Corp. [*Vancouver Stock Exchange symbol*]
DRY	Manchester, NH [*Location identifier FAA*] (FAAL)
DryCal	Dreyfus California Municipal Income Fund [*Associated Press*] (SAG)
DryfMu	Dreyfus Municipal Income Fund [*Associated Press*] (SAG)
DryfNY	Dreyfus New York Municipal Income Fund [*Associated Press*] (SAG)
dryp	Drypoint (VRA)
Drypers	Drypers Corp. [*Associated Press*] (SAG)
DRYR	Dreyer's Grand Ice Cream, Inc. [*NASDAQ symbol*] (NQ)
DRYR	Dreyer's Gr Ice Cr [*NASDAQ symbol*] (TTSB)
DrySM	Dreyfus Strategic Municipal Bond Fund, Inc. [*Associated Press*] (SAG)
DryStG	Dreyfus Strategic Government Income Fund [*Associated Press*] (SAG)
DryStrt	Dreyfus Strategic Municipals [*Associated Press*] (SAG)
DRYWL	Drywall
DRZ	Deep Reconnaissance Zone [*Army*] (AABC)
DRZ	Disturbed-Rock Zone [*Geology*]
DRZA	Agades-Sud [*Niger*] [*ICAO location identifier*] (ICLI)
DRZD	Dirkou [*Niger*] [*ICAO location identifier*] (ICLI)
DRZG	Goure [*Niger*] [*ICAO location identifier*] (ICLI)
DRZI	Iferouane [*Niger*] [*ICAO location identifier*] (ICLI)
DRZL	Arlit [*Niger*] [*ICAO location identifier*] (ICLI)
DRZM	Maine-Soroa [*Niger*] [*ICAO location identifier*] (ICLI)
DRZN	N'Guigmi [*Niger*] [*ICAO location identifier*] (ICLI)
DRZR	Zinder [*Niger*] [*ICAO location identifier*] (ICLI)
DRZT	Tanout [*Niger*] [*ICAO location identifier*] (ICLI)
DS	Air Senegal [*ICAO designator*] (AD)
DS	Compagnie Senegalaise de Transports Aeriens [*Senegal*] [*ICAO designator*] (ICDA)
D-S	Dada-Surrealism
DS	Dairy Shrine (EA)
DS	Dajnavna Sigurnost [*Bulgarian Secret Police affiliated with the KGB*]
DS	Dallas Semiconductor [*NYSE symbol*] (TTSB)
DS	Dal Segno [*Repeat from the Sign*] [*Music*]
DS	Dalton on Sheriffs [*A publication*] (DLA)
DS	Dance Tuition Schools [*Public-performance tariff class*] [*British*]
DS	Danmarks Statistik [*Denmark*]
DS	Dansk Samling [*Danish Union*] (PPE)
DS	Dantrolene Sodium [*Muscle relaxant*]
DS	Daoist Sanctuary (EA)
DS	Dark Shadows [*Television program*]
DS	Data Scanning (BUR)
DS	Data Security (IAA)
DS	Data Segment
DS	Data Series (IAA)
DS	Data Set [*Computer science*]
DS	Data Sheet (NATG)
DS	Data Station [*Spectroscopy*]
DS	Data Storage [*Computer science*] (NASA)
DS	Data Synchronization (DEN)
DS	Data System
DS	Data Systems Technician [*Navy rating*]
DS	Date of Service [*Military*]
DS	Daughters of Scotia (EA)
D/S	Day of Surgery (DAVI)
DS	Days after Sight [*Business term*]
DS	Dead Air Space [*Physiology*]
DS	Debenture Stock [*Investment term*] (ADA)
DS	Debugging System
DS	Decade Scaler (MSA)
DS	Decanning Scuttle
DS	Decimal Subtract
DS	Decision and Switching
DS	Decision Sheet (NATG)
DS	Decistere [*Unit of measure*] (ROG)
DS	Decoder Simulator (IAA)
DS	Decomposition Sintering (RDA)
DS	Decontamination Shop [*Nuclear energy*] (NRCH)
DS	Deepstar [*A manned, self-propelled submersible vehicle built by Western Electric Corp.*]
DS	Defence Secretariat [*Ministry of Defence*] [*British*]
DS	Defense Support (CINC)

DS	Defense Suppression
DS	Defined Substrate [*Medicine*] (MAE)
DS	Define Storage
DS	Define Symbol
DS	Degree of Substitution
DS	Dehydroepiandrosterone Sulfate [*Biochemistry*] (AAMN)
DS	Dekastere [*Unit of measure*] (ROG)
DS	Delayed Sensitivity [*Medicine*] (DMAA)
DS	Delius Society (EA)
DS	Delivery Schedule
DS	Delphian Society
DS	Delphinium Society (EA)
DS	Delta Society (EA)
DS	Democracia Socialista [*Spain Political party*] (EY)
DS	Demokraticheska Sgovor [*Democratic Alliance*] [*Bulgaria*] [*Political party*] (PPE)
DS	Demokraticka Strana [*Democratic Party*] [*Former Czechoslovakia*] [*Political party*] (PPE)
DS	Demokratikos Sinaspismos [*Democratic Coalition*] [*Greece*] [*Political party*] (PPE)
DS	Demokratikos Synagermos [*Democratic Rally*] [*Greek Cyprus*] [*Political party*] (PPE)
DS	Density Standard [*Medicine*] (MAE)
DS	Dental Surgery [*or Surgeon*] [*Medical Officer designation*] [*British*]
DS	Departed Station (SAA)
DS	Department of State
DS	Depolarization Shift [*Electrophysiology*]
DS	Depression Subtle [*Psychology*]
DS	Depth Sounder
DS	Deputy-Secretary [*British*]
DS	Deputy Sheriff (DLA)
DS	Dermatan Sulfate [*Biochemistry*]
DS	Descent Stage [*NASA*] (KSC)
D/S	Descent State [*NASA*] (KSC)
DS	Descent System
DS	Designer Software [*Computer science*]
DS	Design Sheet
DS	Design Specification (MCD)
DS	Design Standards
DS	Desk Stand (IAA)
DS	Destroyer Surface-Effect Ship (MCD)
DS	Desynchronized Sleep [*Medicine*] (MEDA)
DS	Detached Service [*Army*]
DS	Detail Specification (MCD)
DS	Detective Sergeant [*Scotland Yard*]
DS	Development System
DS	Device Selector
D/S	Dextrose and Saline [*Medicine*]
D/S	Dextrose and Sodium Chloride [*Injection*] [*Pharmacology*] (DAVI)
DS	Dextrose Stick (DAVI)
DS	Dial System
D/S	Diastolic/Systolic [*Ratio*] [*Cardiology*]
DS	Dickens Society (EA)
DS	Dictionnaire de Spiritualite Ascetique et Mystique, Doctrine et Histoire [*Paris*] [*A publication*] (BJA)
DS	Dielectric Spectroscopy
DS	Diesel Severe [*Service*] [*Automotive engineering*]
DS	Difference Sensation [*Psychology*]
DS	Difference Spectroscopy
DS	Difference, Starboard [*Navigation*]
DS	Differential Spacing [*Typography*]
DS	Differentiated Staffing [*Education*] (AEE)
ds	Digital Science [*Kodak*] [*Computer science*]
DS	Digital Signal
DS	Digital Switching [*Telecommunications*] (IAA)
DS	Digital System
DS	Digit Select (BUR)
DS	Digit Symbol [*Psychometrics*]
DS	Dilute Strength [*Chemistry*]
DS	Dinosaur Society (EA)
DS	Diode Switch
DS	Dioptric Strength
D-S	Diplomate, American Board of Surgery (DHSM)
DS	Diplomatic Security [*U.S. Department of State*] (BARN)
DS	Diplomatic Service [*or Servant*] [*British*]
DS	Dip Soldering
DS	Directing Staff
DS	Directing Station (IAA)
DS	Directionally Solidified [*Metallurgy*]
DS	Direction Sports (EA)
DS	Director of Services [*Air Force*]
DS	Director of Signals [*British military*] (DMA)
DS	Directory Synchronization (ACRL)
DS	Direct Sequence [*Telecommunications*] (TEL)
D/S	Direct Ship (MCD)
DS	Direct Steamer
DS	Direct Support [*Army*]
DS	Disabled Spouse [*Title XVI*] [*Social Security Administration*] (OICC)
DS	Disaster Services [*Red Cross*]
DS	Discarding Sabot [*Navy*]
DS	Disclosure Statement (AAGC)
DS	Disconnect Switch (MSA)
DS	Discontinue (BUR)
DS	Discriminating Stimulus [*Psychology*] (AEE)
D/S	Disintegrations per Second

DS	Disjunctive Syllogism [*Rule of inference*] [*Logic*]
DS1	Disk Storage [*Computer science*] (NASA)
DS	Disk System
DS	Dispersion Staining [*Analytical chemistry*]
DS	Dispersion Strengthened [*Metallurgy*]
DS	Display Screen
DS	Display Section
DS	Display Started (IAA)
DS	Display Station (IAA)
DS	Display Subsystem (MCD)
DS	Disseminated Sclerosis [*Medicine*]
Ds	Dissimulation [*Psychology*]
DS	Dissociator [*Genetics*]
DS	Dissolved Solids
DS	Distant (IAA)
DS	Distant Surveillance
D/S	Distributed/Stand-Alone [*Pricing*]
DS	Distributed System
DS	Distribution Space
DS	District Secretary [*British*]
D-S	Ditley-Simonsen, Halfdan & Co. [*Steamship*] (MHDB)
DS	Diver, Salvage [*Navy rating*]
DS	Diving Saucer
DS	Divisional Superintendent [*British police*]
DS	Division/Station Code [*Searchable field*] [*Dialog*] (NITA)
DS	Divorce Support [*An association*] (EA)
DS	Docking Survey
DS	Docking System
DS	Dock Service
DS	Doctor of Science
DS	Doctor of Surgery
DS	Documented Sample (KSC)
DS	Document Signed
D-S	Doerfler-Stewart [*Test*] [*Medicine*] (MEDA)
DS	Dokumentation Schweisstechnik [*Welding Documentation*] [*Federal Institute for Materials Testing*] [*Information service or system*] (IID)
DS	Dolly Shot [*Cinematography*] (NTCM)
DS	Dolphin Society (EA)
DS	Domesday Survey [*Census-like record of the lands of England, 1085-86*]
DS	Domestic Service [*Equipment specification*]
DS	Dominion Securities Ltd. [*Toronto Stock Exchange symbol Vancouver Stock Exchange symbol*]
DS	Dominus [*The Lord*] [*Latin*]
DS	Donor's Serum [*Medicine*]
DS	Doppler Shift [*Physics*]
DS	Doppler SONAR (IAA)
DS	Double Sandwich
D/S	Double-Screened [*Coal*]
DS	Double-Sided [*Disks*] [*Computer science*]
DS	Double Silk [*Wire insulation*] (AAG)
DS	Double Slave [*LORAN stations*]
DS	Double Stitch [*Bookbinding*]
DS	Double Stout [*Brewing*] (ROG)
DS	Double Stranded (OA)
DS	Double Strength [*Medicine*]
DS	Double Subdominance [*Ethology*]
DS	Downspout (AAG)
DS	Down's Syndrome [*Medicine*]
DS	Downstage [*Toward audience*] [*A stage direction*]
DS	Downstream (AAG)
DS	Downtime between Sorties [*Military*] (AFIT)
DS	Dracula Society (EA)
DS	Drafting Site [*NFPA pre-fire planning symbol*] (NFPA)
DS	Draft Stop [*Technical drawings*]
DS	Drawing Society (EA)
DS	Drawing Summary (AAG)
DS	Dressed Sides [*of lumber*] (BARN)
DS	Drill Sergeant [*Army*]
DS	Drive System
DS	Drone Squadron
D/S	Dropped Shipped (DNAB)
DS	Drop Siding
DS	Drugstore [*US maps*]
DS	Drum Storage [*Computer science*] (IEEE)
DS	Drum Switch
DS	Dry Sunk (ROG)
DS	Dry Swallow [*Medicine*]
DS	Dudley Herbarium of Stanford University [*San Francisco, CA*]
DS	Duration of Systole (MAE)
DS	Durham & Southern Railway Co. [*AAR code*]
DS	Dust Storm [*Astronomy*]
DS	Duty Section [*Air Force*] (AFM)
DS	Duty Status [*Air Force*] (AFM)
DS	Dwarf Shoot [*Botany*]
DS	Dyestuffs
D/S	Dynamic to Static
DS	United States Department of State Library [*Division of Library and Reference Services*], Washington, DC [*Library symbol Library of Congress*] (LCLS)
DS1	Data Systems Technician, First Class [*Navy rating*]
DS1	Digital Signal 1 [*Telecommunications*]
DS2	Data Systems Technician, Second Class [*Navy rating*]

DS-2	Decontaminating Solution Number Two [Chemical defense] [Army] (RDA)
DS3	Data Systems Technician, Third Class [Navy rating]
DS4	Direct Support Unit Standard Supply System [Army] (AABC)
DSA	Dairy Science Abstracts [Database] [Commonwealth Bureau of Dairy Science and Technology] [Information service or system] (CRD)
DSA	Dalcroze Society of America (EA)
DSA	Danbury Airways, Inc. [ICAO designator] (FAAC)
DSA	Dante Society of America (EA)
DSA	Dataroute Serving Area [TransCanada Telephone System/Computer Communications Group]
DSA	Data Set Adapter [Computer science]
DSA	Data Systems Administration (NVT)
DSA	Data Systems Architecture (SSD)
DSA	Day Sailer Association (EA)
DSA	Deadly Serious Party of Australia [Political party]
DSA	Deep Space Antenna [Aerospace] (IAA)
DSA	Defense Shipping Authority
DSA	Defense Special Assessment [Defense Intelligence Agency] (DOMA)
DSA	Defense Supply Advisor (DOMA)
DSA	Defense Supply Agency [Later, Defense Logistics Agency] [Alexandria, VA]
DSA	Defense Supply Association [Later, ALA] (EA)
DSA	Defense Support Agency
DSA	Defense Systems Analysis [DoD]
DSA	Define Symbol Address [Computer science] (IAA)
DSA	Delay Study Analysis
DSA	Dell SCSI Array [Computer science]
DSA	Democratic Socialists of America [Political party] (EA)
DSA	Dental Surgery Assistant [British]
DSA	Deployable Solar Array
DSA	Deputy Scientific Adviser [British]
DSA	Deputy-Secretary to the Admiralty [British]
DSA	Deputy Sector Advisor
DSA	Deputy Senior Advisor
DSA	Designated Security Agency (NATG)
DSA	Design Schedule Analysis
DSA	Design Services Allocation (DNAB)
DSA	Developmental Sentence Analysis [Education]
DSA	Development Signature Approval
DSA	Dial Service Analysis [Telecommunications] (TEL)
DSA	Dial Service Assistance [Telecommunications] (CET)
DSA	Dial Service Auxiliary [Telecommunications] (IAA)
DSA	Dielectric Stimulated Arcing (PDAA)
DSA	Diffusion Self-Alignment
DSA	Digital Serving Area [Telecommunications] (TEL)
DSA	Digital Signal Analyzer (IEEE)
DSA	Digital Signature Algorithm [Telecommunications]
DSA	Digital Spectrum Analyzer (NVT)
DSA	Digital Storage Architecture
DSA	Digital Subtraction Angiography [or Angiogram] [Medicine]
DSA	Dimensionally Stabilized Anode
DSA	Diploma in Social Administration
DSA	Diplome en Sciences Administratives (DD)
DSA	Directory Service Agent (OSI)
DSA	Directory System Agent (ACRL)
DSA	Direct Selling Association (EA)
DSA	Direct Service Activities (MCD)
DSA	Direct Storage Access
DSA	Disaster Support Area (GNE)
DSA	Discrete Sample Analyzer
DSA	Dispersal Anchorage [Navy] (NVT)
DSA	Distributed Systems Architecture [Computer science] (HGAA)
DSA	District Senior Advisory (MCD)
DSA	Division Senior Advisor [US advisor to the Army of the Republic of Vietnam] (VNW)
DSA	Division Service Area [Army]
DSA	Division Support Area (AABC)
DSA	Docteur es Sciences Agricole [Doctor of Agricultural Sciences] (DD)
DSA	Doctor of Agricultural Sciences (DD)
DSA	Documentation Staging Area [Military]
DSA	Dodecylsuccinic Anhydride [Organic chemistry]
DSA	Donkey Society of Australia
DSA	Doppler Spectrum Analyzer
DSA	Double-Submerged Arc (PDAA)
D Sa A	Down Sensor Assembly (PDAA)
DSA	Down's Syndrome Association [British]
DSA	Dozenal Society of America (EA)
DSA	Dragonfly Society of America (EA)
DSA	Drilling and Sawing Association [British] (DBA)
DSA	Drillsite Supervisors Association (EA)
DSA	Drum Seiners Association [Defunct] (EA)
DSA	Duluth, South Shore & Atlantic Railroad [AAR code Obsolete]
DSA	Duodecimal Society of America (AEBS)
DSA	Dynamic Safety Suspension [Automotive engineering]
DSA	Dynamic Shear Adhesion (PDAA)
DSA	Dynamic Signal Analyzer
DSA	Dynamic Spring Analysis
DSA	Dynamic Storage Area (CMD)
DSA	Sidley & Austin, Washington, DC [Library symbol] [Library of Congress] (LCLS)
DSA	Spectro-Angular Density Method of Forecasting Ocean Waves [Marine science] (MSC)
DSA	Supreme Lodge of the Danish Sisterhood of America (EA)
DSAA	Dairy Shorthorn Association of Australia
DSAA	Defense Security Assistance Agency
DSAA	Direct Selling Association of Australia
DSAA	Driving School Association of America (EA)
DSA/AAO	Development Signature Approval - Advanced Assembly Outline
DSAB	Dictionary of South African Biography [A publication]
DSABL	Disable (AABC)
DSABLSEVP	Disability Severance Pay
DSAC	Deceleration Spark Advance Control [Automotive engineering]
DSAC	Deputy Supreme Allied Commander (AABC)
DSAC	Diaper Service Accreditation Council (EA)
DSAC	Dixon Springs Agricultural Center [University of Illinois] [Research center] (RCD)
DSACAS	Defense Supply Agency Contract Administration Services [DoD]
DSACEL	Defense Supply Agency Contractor Experience List [DoD]
DSACEUR	Deputy Supreme Allied Commander, Europe (NATG)
DSACS	Defense Standard Ammunition Computer System [DoD] (GFGA)
DSACT	Direct Sinoatrial Conduction Time [Medicine] (DMAA)
DSAD	Data Systems and Analysis Directorate (MCD)
DSAD	Data Systems Application Division [Agricultural Research Service]
DSAD	Data Systems Authorization Directory (AFIT)
DSAD	Destruct Safe Arm Device
D-SAFE	Depot System Support Activity Far East [US Army Materiel Command]
DSA/FO	Development Signature Approval - Fabrication Order
DSAFSM	Deputy Safeguard [Missile defense] System Manager (AABC)
DSAFSM	Deputy System Manager [Army] (AABC)
DSAG	Defence Systems Analysis Group [Canada]
DSAH	Defense Supply Agency Handbook [DoD]
DSAHBK	Defense Supply Agency Handbook [DoD]
DSAI	Digital Solar Aspect Indicator (IIA)
DSAIER	Defense Supply Agency Industrial Equipment Reserve [DoD]
DS-AIK	Demokratiske Sosialister - Arbeidernes Informasjon Kommitte [Democratic Socialists - Workers' Information Committee] [Norway Political party] (PPE)
DSAM	Defense Supply Agency Manual [DoD]
DSAM	Defense Systems Acquisition Management [DoD]
DSAM	Dual-Surface Attenuation Module (MCD)
DSAMOS	Diffusion Self-Aligned Metal-Oxide Semiconductor (BUR)
DSAMOSFET	Diffusion Self-Aligned Metal-Oxide Semiconductor Field Effect Transistor [Electronics] (IAA)
DSAMOST	Diffusion Self-Aligned Metal-Oxide Semiconductor Transistor [Electronics] (IAA)
DSAMT	Down Syndrome Association of Metropolitan Toronto
DSAN	Debug Syntax Analysis [Telecommunications] (TEL)
DS & DH	Data Switching and Data Handling (AFM)
DS & R	Data Storage and Retrieval (MSA)
DS & S	Data Systems and Statistics (AFM)
DS & SO	Data Systems and Statistics Officer [Air Force]
DSANSW	Down Syndrome Association of New South Wales [Australia]
DSAO	Data Systems Automation Office [Columbus, Ohio] [Military]
DSAO	Diplomatic Service Administration Office [British]
DSAP	Data Self-Auditing Program [Environmental Protection Agency] (EPA)
DSAP	Data Systems Automation Program
DSAP	Dee Scofield Awareness Program [Defunct] (EA)
DSAP	Defense Security Assistance Program (NVT)
DSAP	Defense Supply Agency Poster [DoD] (MCD)
DSAP	Defense Systems Application Program [DoD]
DSAP	Designated Security-Assessed Position
DSAP	Destination Service Access Point
DSAP	Directory Scope Analysis Program [Bell System]
DSAP	Disseminated Superficial Actinic Porokeratosis [Medicine] (MAE)
DSAQ	[The] Down Syndrome Association of Queensland
DSAR	Daily Subsistence Allowance Rates [Business travel] (BARN)
DSAR	Data-Sampling Automatic Receiver (MCD)
DSAR	Defense Supply Agency Regulation [DoD]
DSARC	Defense Systems Acquisition Review Council [Pentagon board] (MCD)
DSARMNT	Disarmament
DSAS	Data Set Analysis System [Computer science] (HGAA)
DSAS	Del Shannon Appreciation Society (EAIO)
DSAS	Dial Service Assistance Switchboard [Telecommunications] (CET)
DSAS	Direct Support Aviation Section [Army]
DSAS	Discrete Subaortic Stenosis [Medicine]
DSASBL	Disassemble (IAA)
DSASC	Defense Supply Agency Administrative Support Center [DoD]
D Sa Sc	Doctor of Sacred Sciences
DSASO	Deputy Senior Air Staff Officer [British military] (DMA)
DSAT	Defensive Satellite (MCD)
DSAT	Disk Storage Allocation Table (MCD)
DSATR	Descend So as to Reach [Aviation] (FAAC)
DSATX	Descend So as to Cross [Aviation] (FAAC)
DSAV	Dr Solomon's Anti-Virus [Software]
DSAW	Dispersive Surface Acoustic Wave (MCD)
DSA-WRAO	Defense Supply Agency - Western Regional Audit Office [DoD]
DSB	Air Senegal, Societe Nationaloal de Transport Aerien [ICAO designator] (FAAC)
DSB	Dahlgren Smoothbore
DSB	Danske Statsbaner [Danish State Railways]
DSB	Data Set Block
DSB	Debit sans Brene [Charge without Abatement] [French Business term]
DSB	Debit sans Brevet [Debt without Writ] [French Legal term] (DLA)
DSB	Debitum Sine Brevi [Debt without Writ] [Latin Legal term] (DLA)
DSB	Decade Synchronic Bridge
DSB	Defence Signal Board [British]

DSB	Defense Science Board [*DoD*]
DSB	Demand Scheduled Bus (OA)
DSB	Department of Small Business [*Australia*]
DSB	Department of State. Bulletin [*A publication*]
DSB	Device Status Byte [*Computer science*] (BUR)
DSB	Diagnostic Skills Battery [*Educational test*]
DSB	Dictionary of Scientific Biography [*A publication*]
DSB	Digital Storage Buffer (IAA)
DSB	Diplomatic Services Bureau
DSB	Direct Sound Broadcast
DSB	Direct Support Battery [*Army*] (ADDR)
DSB	Disbursement
DSB	Distribution Switchboard
DSB	Divine Science Bachelor
DSB	Documentation Standards Committee (ECII)
DSB	Document Status Bulletin (MCD)
DSB	Double Sideband
DSB	Double Strand Break [*Genetics*]
DSB	Drill Spacer Block (MCD)
DSB	Drug Supervisory Body
DSB	Duty Steam Boat [*British military*] (DMA)
DSBAM	Double-Sideband Amplitude Modulation [*Telecommunications*] (TEL)
DSBAMRC....	Double-Sideband Amplitude Modulation Reduced Carrier [*Telecommunications*] (IEEE)
DSBB	Double Sheath Bronchial Brushing [*Medicine*] (DAVI)
DSBC	DS Bancor [*NASDAQ symbol*] (TTSB)
DSBC	DS Bancor, Inc. [*NASDAQ symbol*] (NQ)
DSBCO........	Defense Surplus Bidders Control Office
DSBE	Di-secondary-butyl Ether [*Organic chemistry*]
DSBEC	Double-Sideband Emitted Carrier [*Telecommunications*] (TEL)
DSBG	Disbursing (AFM)
DSBK	Data Set by Key [*Computer science*] (IAA)
DSBL	Disable (MSA)
DSBLTY	Disability
DSBLTY	Disability
DS Bnc	DS Bancor, Inc. [*Associated Press*] (SAG)
DSBR	Double-Strand Break Repair [*Genetics*]
DSBRC	Double-Sideband Reduced Carrier [*Telecommunications*] (TEL)
DSBS	Defense Science Board Subcommittee [*DoD*]
DSBS	Droughtmaster Stud Breeders' Society [*Australia*]
DSBSC	Double-Sideband Suppressed Carrier [*Modulation*]
DSBTC	Double-Sideband Transmitted Carrier [*Telecommunications*]
DSB (UN)....	Drug Supervisory Body of the United Nations
DSBV	Double-Sealed Ball Valve
DSBWC	Double Sideband with Carrier [*Modulation*] (IAA)
DSC	Data Separator Card (MCD)
DSC	Data Services Center [*International City Management Association*] [*Information service or system*] (IID)
DSC	Data Set Controller
DSC	Data Statistics Comparison Software [*Computer science*]
DSC	Data Stream Compatability (IAA)
DSC	Data Synchronizer Channel
DSC	Data System Console (CAAL)
DSC	Data Systems Controller (MCD)
DSC	Data Systems Technician, Chief [*Navy rating*]
DSC	Debye-Sears Cell [*Physics*]
DSC	[*A*] Decade of Study of the Constitution [*Defunct*] (EA)
DSC	Decent Suit of Civvies [*British slang military decoration*] [*World War I*]
DSC	Decision Sciences Corp. (IID)
DSC	Dedicated Signal Conditioner (MCD)
DSC	Defense Shipping Council [*NATO*]
DSC	Defense Supply Center (AABC)
DSC	Defense Supply Corp. [*World War II*]
DSC	Defensiveness Scale for Children [*Psychology*]
DSC	Delaware State College [*Dover*]
DSC	Delivered System Capability
DSC	Depot Supply Center
DSC	Deputy Sheriff Clerk (ROG)
DSC	Design Safety Criteria [*Nuclear energy*] (NRCH)
DSC	Detroit Stock Exchange (MHDB)
DSC	Differential Scanning Calorimeter [*or Calorimetry*] [*Instrumentation*]
DSC	Differential Signal Control
DSC	Digital Scan Converter (MCD)
DSC	Digital Selective Calling
DSC	Digital Set Point Control (IAA)
DSC	Digital Signal Conditioner (MCD)
DSC	Digital Sound Corp. [*Telecommunications service*] (TSSD)
DSC	Digital Spectrum Compatible (PS)
DSC	Digital Stabilization Console
DSC	Digital Subscriber Controller [*Telecommunications*]
DSC	Diploma of the Sydney Conservatorium of Music [*Australia*]
DSC	Directional Solidification Crystal (SSD)
DSC	Direct Satellite Communications
DSC	Disappearance of Single Cell [*Assay*] [*Cytology*]
DSC	Discone Antenna
DSC	Discrete System Concept
DSC	Discrete Timesystems, Inc. [*Toronto Stock Exchange symbol*]
DSC	Disk Storage Controller [*Computer science*] (CMD)
DSC	Disodium Cromoglycate [*Pharmacology*]
DSC	Distant Station Connected [*Computer science*] (BUR)
DSC	Distinguished Service Cross [*US and British*] [*Military decoration*]
DSC	Distribution of Stockage Code (AABC)
DSC	District Switching Center [*Telecommunications*]
DSC	District Switching Centre [*Telecommunications network*] (NITA)

DSC	DIVAD Systems Controller (MCD)
DSC	Divided Spouses Coalition [*Defunct*] (EA)
DSC	Doctor of Christian Science
DSC	Doctor of Commercial Science
D Sc	Doctor of Science
DSc	Doctor of Science (GAGS)
DSC	Doctor of Surgical Chiropody
D Sc	Doctor Scientiae [*Doctor of Science*] [*Latin*]
DSC	Documentation Standards Committee [*British*] (DIT)
DSC	Document Service Center
DSC	Domestic Satellite Carrier [*Computer science*] (TNIG)
DSC	Dominant-Subordinate Conflict [*Biology*]
DSC	Doppler Shift Compensation [*Physics*]
DSC	Double Silk Covered [*Wire insulation*]
dsc..............	Double Silk Covered (IDOE)
DSC	Down's Syndrome Congress [*Later, NDSC*] (EA)
DSC	Downstage Center [*Toward audience*] [*A stage direction*]
DSC	Drain Saturation Current
DSC	DSC Communications Corp. [*Associated Press*] (SAG)
DSC	Duns Scotus College [*Detroit, MI*]
DSC	Dynamic Sequential Control (AAG)
DSC	Dynamic Slide Compensator
DSC	Dynamic Stability Control [*Automotive*]
DSC	Dynamic Standby Computer (KSC)
DSC	International Die Sinkers' Conference
DSC	Scottish Rite of Freemasonry, Southern Jurisdiction USA, Supreme Council Library, Washington, DC [*Library symbol Library of Congress*] (LCLS)
DSC	South Carolina State Library, Columbia, SC [*OCLC symbol*] (OCLC)
D SC	United States District Court for the District of South Carolina (DLA)
DSCA	Data Systems Coordinating Activity [*DoD*] (DNAB)
DSCA	Department of State Correspondents Association (EA)
DScA	Doctor of Science in Agriculture
DSCAB	Department of State Contract Appeals Board (AAGC)
DScAdm......	Doctor in Administrative Sciences
DSCAEF	Deputy Supreme Commander, Allied Expeditionary Force
DScAg	Doctor of Science in Agriculture (ADA)
D Sc Agr	Doctor of Science in Agriculture
DSc(Agric) ..	Doctor of Science in Agriculture (ADA)
DSCAPRS	Dental Suction Apparatus
DSCAT	Data Set Catalog [*Computer science*] (IAA)
DSCB	Data Set Control Block [*Computer science*]
DSCC	Deep Space Communications Complex (MCD)
DSCC	Deferred Specification Compliance Change (MCD)
DSCC	Democratic Senatorial Campaign Committee [*Commercial firm*] (EA)
DSCC	Desiccant [*Chemistry*]
DSCC	Division Support Control Center [*Army*]
DSCC	Double Silk, Cotton Covered [*Wire insulation*] (IAA)
D Sc Com ..	Doctor of Science in Commerce
DSCD	Directorate of Stores and Clothing Development [*British*]
DScD	Doctor of Science and Didactics (ADA)
DScD	Doctor of Science in Dentistry (WGA)
DScD	Doctor of Science in Dentistry (GAGS)
DScE	Doctor of Science in Engineering
DScEco	Doctor of Science in Economics (NADA)
D Sc Econ....	Doctor of Science in Economics
DSCEMS	Depth-Selective Conversion Electron Mossbauer Spectroscopy
D Sc (Eng)..	Doctor of Science (Engineering) (EY)
DSCF	Doppler-Shifted Constant Frequency [*Biosonar research*]
DSCF	Dry Standard Cubic Feet (GFGA)
DScFin........	Doctor of Financial Science
DScFor........	Doctor of Science in Forestry (ADA)
DSCG	Digital Sine/Cosine Generator (IAA)
DSCG	Directional Solidification Crystal Growth (SSD)
DSCG	Disodium Cromoglycate [*Pharmacology*]
DscGph........	Disc Graphics, Inc. [*Associated Press*] (SAG)
DSCH	Dark Skies for Comet Halley [*Defunct*] (EA)
D Sch Mus...	Doctor of School Music
D Sc Hyg	Doctor of Science in Hygiene
DSCI	Derma Sciences [*NASDAQ symbol*] (TTSB)
DSCI	Derma Sciences, Inc. [*NASDAQ symbol*] (SAG)
D Sci	Doctor of Science
DScI	Doctor of Science in Industry (NADA)
D Sci H	Doctor of Science and Hygiene
DSCIL	Defense Supply Center Indication List (DNAB)
DSCIM	Display Select Computer Input Multiplexer (MCD)
DSCIM	Display System Computer Input Multiplexer [*NASA*] (NASA)
D Sc in VM...	Doctor of Science in Veterinary Medicine
DScJur........	Doctor of Science of Jurisprudence (NADA)
D Sc L	Doctor of the Science of Law
DSCI	Durable Sprayed Cladding (PDAA)
DSCLO	Disclosure-Online [*Information service or system*]
DSCM	Data Systems Technician, Master Chief [*Navy rating*]
DSCM	Dry Standard Cubic Meter (EG)
DScMil........	Doctor of Military Science (ADA)
D Scn..........	Doctor of Scientology
DSCNT	Descent [*Aviation*] (FAAC)
D Sc O	Doctor of the Science of Oratory
DSCONT......	Discontinue (MSA)
D Sc Os	Doctor of the Science of Osteopathy
DSCP	Datascope Corp. [*NASDAQ symbol*] (NQ)
DSCP	Defense Satellite Communications Program (MCD)
DSCP	Defense Suppression Concept Plan (MCD)
DSCP	Division Supply Control Point
DScP..........	Doctor of Political Science

DScPol........	Doctor of Political Science (NADA)
DSCR..........	District Sub-Chief Ranger [Ancient Order of Foresters]
DSCRM.......	Discriminator (MSA)
DSCRP........	Descriptor [Computer science]
DSCS..........	Data Systems Technician, Senior Chief [Navy rating]
DSCS..........	Defense Satellite Communications System [DoD]
DSCS..........	Defense Space Communications Squadron
DSCS..........	Desk Side Computer System [General Electric Co.]
DSCS..........	Digital Simulator Computer System
DScS..........	Doctor of Social Science
DSCS NCF ...	Defense Satellite Communications System Network Control Facility (MCD)
DSCSOC......	Defense Satellite Communications Systems Operations Center (DOMA)
DScSoc........	Doctor of Social Science
DSCS OCE ...	Defense Satellite Communications System Operations Control Element (MCD)
DSc(Social Sciences)...	Doctor of Science in the Social Sciences, University of Southampton [British] (DBQ)
DSCS PO	Defense Satellite Communications System Program Office (MCD)
DSCS-TD.....	Defense Satellite Communications Support Training Device
DSCT..........	Double Secondary Current Transformer (MSA)
D Sc Tech....	Doctor of Technical Science
DScVM........	Doctor of Science in Veterinary Medicine (GAGS)
DSD	Daily Staff Digest (SAA)
DSD	Data-Scanner Distributor
DSD	Data Set Definition [Computer science] (IBMDP)
DSD	Data Status Display
DSD	Data Storage Device
DSD	Data Stream Direct [Computer science]
DSD	Data Structure Diagram
DSD	Data Systems Designator (AFM)
DSD	Dead Sea Scrolls: Manual of Discipline (BJA)
DSD	DECHEMA [Deutsche Gesellschaft fuer Chemisches Appartewesen, Chemische Technik, und Biotechnologie eV] Stoffdaten Dienst [DECHEMA Physical Property Data Service] [Information service or system] (IID)
DSD	Deep Submergence Device (NVT)
DSD	Deep Suspended DIFAR [Military] (CAAL)
DSD	Demographic Surveys Division [Census] (OICC)
DSD	Departmental Science Development [National Science Foundation]
DSD	Depression Sine Depression [Psychology]
DSD	Deputy Secretary of Defense
DSD	Detailed System Design [Computer science]
dsd.............	Diamond-Square-Diamond [Lipscomb polyhedral rearrangement in borane anion and carborane series]
DSD	Digital System Design (IEEE)
DSD	Digital System Diagram
DSD	Diode Semiconductor Device
DSD	Director of Signal Department [Obsolete Navy British]
DSD	Director of Staff Duties [Military British]
DSD	Direct-Search Discretized [Computer science]
DSD	Discharge Summary Dictated [Medicine] (DMAA)
DSD	Disk Storage Device [Computer science]
DSD	Divine Science Doctor
DSD	Doctrine and Systems Directorate [Army] (RDA)
DSD	Double-Single-Dummy [in game of bridge]
DSD	Dry Sterile Dressing [Medicine]
DSD	DSIF [Deep Space Instrumentation Facility] Supply Depot [NASA]
DSD	Duales System Deutschland [German recycling organization]
DSD	Dual-Speed Drive
DSD	La Desirade [Guadeloupe] [Airport symbol] (OAG)
D SD	United States District Court for the District of South Dakota (DLA)
DSD	United States Superintendent of Documents, Washington, DC [Library symbol Library of Congress] (LCLS)
DSDA.........	Dedicated and Switched Digital Access [Tylink Corp.]
DSDAR........	Deputy and Scientific Director of Army Research
DSDC.........	Data Systems Design Center [Air Force]
DSDC.........	Direct Services Dialing Capability [Telecommunications] (OSI)
DSDD.........	Defense Subsystem Development and Demonstration (MCD)
DSDD.........	Double Sided Double Density [Magnetic disc format] (NITA)
DSDD.........	Double-Sided, Double-Density Disk [Computer science]
DSDI..........	Descendants of the Signers of the Declaration of Independence (EA)
DS Di..........	Doctor of Scientific Didactics
DSDIO.........	Director, Strategic Defense Initiative Organization [Military] (SDI)
DSDL..........	Data Storage Description Language
dsDNA........	Deoxyribonucleic Acid, Double-Stranded [Genetics] [Biochemistry]
DSDP.........	Data System Development Plan
DSDP.........	Deep-Sea Drilling Project [Later, IPOD] [National Science Foundation]
DSDR.........	Design Section Drawing Record (MCD)
DSDRS........	DoD [Department of Defense] Standard Data Repository System
DSDS.........	Dataphone Switched Digital Service [AT & T]
DSDS.........	Digital Synchro Data Source
DSDS.........	Document Survey Data Sheet (KSC)
DSDS.........	Dual-Source Dynamic Synchronous (DNAB)
DSDS.........	Dynamic Synchro Data Service [or Source] (MCD)
DSDS.........	Naval School Deep Sea Divers
DSDT.........	Data-Set Definition Table [Computer science]
DSDT.........	Deformographic Storage Display Tube [IBM Corp.]
DSDT.........	Discrete Space and Discrete Time
DSDTR........	Delinquent Supplier Data Transmittal (MCD)
DSDU.........	Data Storage Distribution Unit (MCD)
DSDVOR	Double-Sideband Doppler Very-High-Frequency Omnidirectional Range [FAA]

DSE...........	Dacca Stock Exchange [Bangladesh]
DSE...........	Data Set Extension [IBM Corp.] [Computer science] (BUR)
DSE...........	Data Storage Equipment
DSE...........	Data Support Element (MCD)
DSE...........	Data Switching Equipment [Computer science] (ACRL)
DSE...........	Data Switching Exchange [Telecommunications]
DSE...........	Data Systems Engineering
DSE...........	Debye-Sears Effect [Physics]
DSE...........	Department of School Education [New South Wales, Victoria] [Australia]
DSE...........	Designated Spouse Equivalent
DSE...........	Dessie [Ethiopia] [Airport symbol] (OAG)
DSE...........	Detector, Selector, and Effector [Social science]
DSE...........	Development Student Engineer (MCD)
DSE...........	Development Support Equipment
DS/E..........	Digital Scrambler/Encoder [NITA]
DSE...........	Digital Select Emitter (IAA)
DSE...........	Digital Shaft Encoder
DSE...........	Digital Subtraction Echocardiogram [Cardiology] (DAVI)
DSE...........	Dimensionally Stabilized Electrode [Electrochemistry]
DSE...........	Directorate of Systems Engineering (AAG)
DSE...........	Direct Sequence Encoding [Telecommunications]
DSE...........	Direct Support Element [Military] (NVT)
DSE...........	Direct Switching Equipment (NITA)
DSE...........	Direct Switching Exchange [Telecommunications] (NITA)
DSE...........	Distal Sequence Element [Genetics]
DSE...........	Distributed Systems Environment [Honeywell, Inc.] (BUR)
DSE...........	Doctor of Sanitary Engineering
DSE...........	Doctor of Science in Economics
DSE...........	Domestic Sewage Exclusion
DSE...........	Draft Safety Evaluation (NRCH)
DSE...........	Driver Screening Evaluator
DSE...........	Dual System Estimator [Demography]
DSE...........	Dyad Symmetry Element [Genetics]
DSE...........	Dynamic System Electronics
DSEA..........	Data Storage Electronics Assembly [Apollo] [NASA]
DSEA..........	Davis Submerged Escape Apparatus [British military] (DMA)
D Se A........	Doctor of Secretarial Arts
DSEB..........	Defense Shipping Executive Board [NATO]
DSEB..........	Discharged Servicemen's Employment Board [Victoria] [Australia]
DSEC..........	Director of Security (AABC)
DSECT.........	Dummy Control Section [Computer science]
DSED..........	Defense Suppression Expendable Drone (MCD)
DSEDM........	Departure Sequencing Engineering Development Model [FAA] (TAG)
DSEE..........	Designated Special Emphasis Engineering (KSC)
DSEE..........	Domain Software Engineering Environment
DSEF..........	Direct Selling Education Foundation (EA)
DSE/FAD......	Data Systems Environment Functions and Application Design [Course] [Computer science]
DSEG..........	Data Systems Engineering Group (MCD)
DSEG..........	Defense Systems Evaluation Group [Air Force]
DSEG..........	Design Studies Evaluation Group [NATO]
DSEI..........	Daily Summary of Enemy Intelligence [World War II]
DSEL..........	Doctor of Science and English Literature
DS Eng	Doctor of Sanitary Engineering
DSENGA......	Disengaging
DSENGR	Data Systems Engineer
DSEP..........	Data Services Educational Profile
DSEP..........	Defense Science and Engineering Program (MCD)
DSES..........	Defense Systems Evaluation Squadron [Air Force] (AFM)
D Se Sc	Doctor of Secretarial Science
DSESq........	Defense System Evaluation Squadron [Air Force]
D Se St........	Doctor of Secretarial Studies
DSF............	Dairy Suppliers Foundation [Defunct] (EA)
DSF............	Data Scanning and Formatting
DSF............	Daughters of St. Francis of Assisi [Roman Catholic religious order]
DSF............	David See Flying Services [British] [FAA designator] (FAAC)
DSF............	Day-Second-Foot [Measurement]
DSF............	Defatted Soy Flour (OA)
DSF............	Defense Stock Fund [DoD]
DSF............	Delancey Street Foundation (EA)
DSF/...........	Departmental Square Feet (MCD)
DSF............	Design Safety Factor
DSF............	Deutsch-Sowjetische-Freundschaft [German-Soviet Friendship] [Common street name in East Germany]
DSF............	Development Stimulating Factor [Biochemistry]
DSF............	Directional Solidification Furnace
DSF............	Disc Storage Facility (NITA)
DSF............	Disk Storage Facility [Computer science]
DSF............	Disulfiram [Organic chemistry]
DSF............	Doctor of the Science of Forestry
DSFA..........	Defense Solid Fuels Administration [Terminated, 1954]
DSFAAS	Domestic Solid Fuel Appliances Approval Scheme (PDAA)
DSFB..........	David Syme Faculty of Business [Chisholm Institute of Technology] [Australia]
DSFC..........	Dark Shadows Fan Club (EA)
DSFC..........	Dinah Shore Fan Club (EA)
DSFC..........	Direct Side Force Control [Aviation]
DSFC..........	Dogman and the Shepherds Fan Club (EA)
DSFF..........	Downflow Stationary Fixed-Film [Chemical engineering]
DSFG..........	Diamond Setters Fraternal Guild [Defunct] (EA)
DSFI..........	Derogatis Sexual Functioning Inventory [Psychology]
DSFI..........	Divine Science Federation International (EA)
DSFR..........	Detailed System Functional Requirements
DSFS..........	Doppler Shift Frequency Spectrum

DSFT............	Detection Scheme with Fixed Thresholds [*Communication signal*]
DSFT............	Discrete Sliding Fourier Transform (PDAA)
DSFU	Danish Sailors' and Firemen's Union (EA)
DSG	Danzig Study Group [*German Philatelic Society*] (EA)
DSG	Dataset Generator (SAA)
DSG	Data Systems Group [*Computer science*] (ACRL)
DSG	Decision Support Graphics [*Hewlett-Packard Co.*]
DSG	Deep Submergence Group
DSG	Defense Steering Group [*Military*]
DSG	Defense Suppression Group [*DoD*] (MCD)
DSG	Defense Systems Group
DSG	Democratic Study Group (EA)
DSG	Deoxyspergualin [*Antineoplastic drug*]
DSG	Deputy Secretary General (NATG)
DSG	Desaguadero [*Bolivia*] [*Seismograph station code, US Geological Survey Closed*] (SEIS)
DSG	Designate (AABC)
DSG	Designer Shoe Guild (EA)
DSG	Design Systems Group (HGAA)
DSG	Desktop Systems Group [*Novell, Inc.*] (PCM)
DSG	Digital Signal Generator
DSG	Digital Symbology Generator (MCD)
DSG	Directed Studies Group [*Air Force*] (AFM)
DSG	Direct Support Group [*Army*] (AABC)
DSG	Disuccinimidyl Glutarate [*Organic chemistry*]
dsg............	Dressing [*Medicine*]
DSGA	Double Conductor, Shipboard General Use, Armor [*Cable*] (IAA)
DSGI	DSG International Ltd. [*NASDAQ symbol*] (SAG)
DSGIF	DSG International Ltd [*NASDAQ symbol*] (TTSB)
DSG Int.......	DSG International Ltd. [*Associated Press*] (SAG)
DSGM	Director Standing Group Memorandum [*NATO*] (NATG)
DSGN	Design (AFM)
DSGN	Design
DSGN	Designate (AFM)
DSGN	Designer (WDAA)
DSGND	Designated (FAAC)
DSGNG	Designing
dsgnr	Designator
DSGNR	Designer
DSGp	Directed Studies Group [*Air Force*] (AFM)
DSGR	Disc Graphics [*NASDAQ symbol*] (TTSB)
DSGR	Disc Graphics, Inc. [*NASDAQ symbol*] (SAG)
DSGRW	Disc Graphics Wrrt [*NASDAQ symbol*] (TTSB)
DS/GS	Direct Support/General Support (MCD)
DSGS(CAR)...	Deputy Secretary of the General Staff (Coordination and Reports) [*Army*] (AABC)
D/Sgt	Drill Sergeant [*British military*] (DMA)
DSH	Deactivated Shutdown Hours [*Electronics*] (IEEE)
DSH	Deafness, Speech, & Hearing Publications, Inc. (AEBS)
DSH	Deliberate Self-Harm Syndrome
DSH	Designer Finance Trust [*NYSE symbol*] (SAG)
DSH	Designer Holdings [*NYSE symbol*] (TTSB)
DSH	Designer Holdings Ltd. [*NYSE symbol*] (SAG)
DSH	Dushanbe [*Stalinabad*] [*Former USSR Seismograph station code, US Geological Survey*] (SEIS)
DSH	Northeast Management, Inc. [*ICAO designator*] (FAAC)
DS/HD..........	Double Sided High-Density Disk [*Computer software*] (PCM)
DSHE	Downstream Heat Exchanger (AAG)
DSHEA	Dietary Supplement Health and Education Act of 1994
D/SHLD.......	Dust Shield [*Automotive engineering*]
DSHMRA.......	Deep Seabed Hard Mineral Resources Act
DSHP..........	Disodium Hydrophosphate [*Inorganic chemistry*] [*Also, DSP*]
DSHR	Dish-Rinsing
DSI............	Dairy Society International [*Australia*]
DSI............	Data Set Identifier
DSI............	Data Submitted Information (KSC)
DSI............	Data System Integration [*NASA*]
DSI............	Data Systems Inquiry (AABC)
DSI............	Dead Sea Isaiah Scroll (BJA)
DSI............	Decision Sciences Institute (EA)
DSI............	Deep Shock Insulin [*Endocrinology*] (DAVI)
DSI............	Defense Simulation Internet [*Computer science*] (RDA)
DSI............	Defense Simulation Internet [*Army*] (RDA)
DSI............	Delivered Source Instructions
DSI............	Delivery to Surgery Interval [*Gynecology*]
DSI............	DeSales Secular Institute (EA)
DSI............	Design Science Institute
DSI............	Desktalk Systems, Inc.
DSI............	Digitally Sensed Image (DGA)
DSI............	Digital Speech Interpolation [*Telephone channels*]
DSI............	Digital Speech Interpretation
DSI............	Digital Strain Indicator
DSI............	Digital Subtraction Imaging [*Cardiology*] (DAVI)
DSI............	Directorate of Scientific Intelligence (SAA)
DSI............	Direct Support Item [*Army*]
DSI............	Dissociative Surface Ionization [*Organic chemistry*]
DSI............	Distilled Spirits Institute [*Later, DISCUS*] (EA)
DSI............	Distribution Sciences, Inc. [*Information service or system*] (IID)
DSI............	Divisional Safety Inspector [*Ministry of Agriculture, Fisheries, and Food*] [*British*]
DSI............	Division of Science Information [*National Science Foundation*] (IID)
DSI............	Dominion-Scottish Investments Ltd. [*Toronto Stock Exchange symbol*]
DSI............	Domini Social Index [*Stock exchange term*]
DSI............	Double Sandwich Indirect

DSI	Downey Financial [*NYSE symbol*] (TTSB)
DSI	Down's Syndrome International (EA)
DSI	Dreyfus Strategic Government [*NYSE symbol*] (SPSG)
DSI	Dreyfus Strategic Gvts [*NYSE symbol*] (TTSB)
DSI	Drinking Straw Institute [*Defunct*] (EA)
DSI	Drug-Seeking Index (MEDA)
DSI	Dwelling Sculpture Institute [*Defunct*] (EA)
DSI	Smithsonian Institution, Washington, DC [*Library symbol Library of Congress*] (LCLS)
DSIA	Defense Suppression Integration Analysis (MCD)
DSIA	Diaper Service Industry Association [*Later, NADS*] (EA)
DSI-AAA	Smithsonian Institution, Archives of American Art, Washington, DC [*Library symbol Library of Congress*] (LCLS)
DSIATP	Defense Sensor Interpretation and Application Training Program (AFM)
DSIC	DSI Industries [*NASDAQ symbol*] (SAG)
DSICA	Distilled Spirits Industry Council of Australia
DSID	Data Set Identification [*Computer science*] (IBMDP)
DSID	Disposable Seismic Intrusion Detector (MCD)
DSID	Divergence Source-Image Distortion [*Crystal*]
DSIDA	Disodium Iminodiacetate [*Organic chemistry*]
DSIDBAD	Drill Sergeant Identification Badge [*Military decoration*] (GFGA)
DSIdentBad...	Drill Sergeant Identification Badge [*Military decoration*] (AABC)
DSIE	Deutsche Stiftung fur Internationale Entwicklung [*German Foundation for International Development*] (EAIO)
DSIF..........	Deep Space Instrumentation Facility
DSig..........	Digital Signature Initiative [*Computer science*]
DSI-HMS	Smithsonian Institution, Hirshhorn Museum and Sculpture Garden, Washington, DC [*Library symbol Library of Congress*] (LCLS)
DSI Ind	DSI Industries [*Associated Press*] (SAG)
DSIIR	Direct Support Imagery Interpretation Report (MCD)
DSIM	Doctor of Science in Industrial Medicine
DSI-MAA......	Smithsonian Institution, Museum of African Art, Washington, DC [*Library symbol Library of Congress*] (LCLS)
DSI-MHT......	Smithsonian Institution, National Museum of History and Technology, Washington, DC [*Library symbol Library of Congress*] (LCLS)
DSI-Mus	Smithsonian Institution, Museum Reference Center, Washington, DC [*Library symbol Library of Congress*] (LCLS)
DSI-NAS	Smithsonian Institution, National Space and Air Museum, Washington, DC [*Library symbol Library of Congress*] (LCLS)
DS in BA.....	Doctor of Science in Business Administration
DSI-NCF.......	Smithsonian Institution, National Collection of Fine Arts, Washington, DC [*Library symbol Library of Congress*] (LCLS)
DS in Ge Engr...	Doctor of Science in Geological Engineering
DS in Gp Engr...	Doctor of Science in Geophysical Engineering
DS in Met Engr...	Doctor of Science in Metallurgical Engineering
DS in PE.....	Doctor of Science in Petroleum Engineering
DSI-NPG	Smithsonian Institution, National Portrait Gallery, Washington, DC [*Library symbol Library of Congress*] (LCLS)
DS in PRE ...	Doctor of Science in Petroleum Refining Engineering
DSIP	Delta-Sleep-Inducing Peptide
DSIPS	Digital Satellite Image Processing System (MCD)
DSIPT	Dissipate [*NWS*] (FAAC)
DSIR	Department of Scientific and Industrial Research [*of the Privy Council for Scientific and Industrial Research*] [*Later, SRC*] [*British*]
DSIS	Defence Scientific Information Service [*Canada Information service or system*] (IID)
DSIS	Defense Communications System SCF [*Satellite Control Facility*] Interface System (MCD)
DSIS	Director [*or Directorate*] of Scientific Information Service [*Canada*]
DSIS	Distributed Support Information Standard (PCM)
DSISI	Double-Sided Inter-Symbol Interference (PDAA)
DSI-SOA	Smithsonian Institution, National Museum of Natural History, Office of Anthropology, Washington, DC [*Library symbol Library of Congress*] (LCLS)
DSIU	Discrete Signal Interface Unit (DWSG)
DSJ............	Differential Spacing Justifying [*Typography*] (SAA)
DSJ............	Discrete Sonic Jet
DSJ............	Doctor of the Science of Jurisprudence
DSK	Aero Algarve Lda. [*Portugal*] [*FAA designator*] (FAAC)
DSK	Delay Shift Keying (IAA)
DSK	Demokratikon Sosialistikon Komma [*Democratic Socialist Party*] [*Greece*] [*Political party*] (PPE)
DSK	Demokratski Savez Kosovo [*Democratic Alliance of Kosovo*] [*Serbia*] [*Political party*] (EY)
DSK	Deputy Seal Keeper [*British*] (ROG)
DSK	Dera Ismail Khan [*Pakistan*] [*Airport symbol*] (OAG)
DSK	Disk [*Computer science*]
DSK	Disk Island [*Alaska*] [*Seismograph station code, US Geological Survey*] (SEIS)
DSK	Dvorak Simplified Keyboard [*Typewriter keyboard developed by August Dvorak in the 1920's*]
DskDt..........	Desktop Data, Inc. [*Associated Press*] (SAG)
DSKY	Display and Keyboard [*Computer science*]
DSL............	Daru [*Sierra Leone*] [*Airport symbol*] (AD)
DSL............	Data Set Label [*Computer science*]
DSL............	Data Simulation Language
DSL............	Data Structures Language [*Computer science*] (BUR)
DSL............	Decalogue Society of Lawyers (EA)
DSL............	Deep Scattering Layer [*Undersea populations*]
DSL............	Defence Standards Laboratories [*British*]
DSL............	Delivered Source Lines [*of Code*]
DSL............	Denver & Salt Lake Railroad [*AAR code*]
DSL............	Depot Stockage List [*Army*]
DSL............	Depressed Sight Line (MCD)

DSL............ Detailed Ship Loading
DSL............ Detroit Signal Laboratory [*Army*]
DSL............ Development Support Library (IAA)
DSL............ Diamond Sakha Airlines [*Former USSR*] [*FAA designator*] (FAAC)
DSL............ Dickinson School of Law [*Pennsylvania*]
DSL............ Diesel (MSA)
DSL............ Diesel
DSL............ Digital Simulation Language [*Computer science*] (CSR)
DSL............ Digital Subscriber Line [*Telecommunications*] (PCM)
DSL............ Digital Subscriber Line [*Telecommunications*] (ACRL)
DSL............ Directory of Special Libraries and Information Centers [*A publication*]
DSL............ Direct Static Logic (SAA)
DSL............ Doctor of Sacred Literature
DSL............ Document Summary List
DSL............ Domestic Substances List [*Canada*]
DSL............ Downey Financial Corp. [*NYSE symbol*] (SAG)
DSL............ Downstage Left [*Toward audience*] [*A stage direction*]
DSL............ Downwind Safety Limit
DSL............ Drawing and Specification Listing (NRCH)
DSL............ Dual Shift Left (SAA)
DSL............ Dynamic Simulation Language [*Computer science*]
DSLA .... Directory of Special Libraries in Australia [*A publication*]
DSLC .... Data Subscriber Line Carrier [*Computer science*] (HGAA)
DSLC .... Digital Synchronizing Load Sensing Control [*Electronic controls*] [*Diesel engines*]
DSLD .... Digital Seismic Listing Device (DWSG)
DSLE......... Directorate of Security and Law Enforcement [*Military*] (DNAB)
DSLG .... Discreet Logic, Inc. [*NASDAQ symbol*] (SAG)
DSLGF .... Discreet Logic [*NASDAQ symbol*] (TTSB)
DSLIM ......, Double-Sided Linear Induction Motor (PDAA)
DSLO .... Disaster Services Liaison Officer
DSLO .... Distributed Systems Licensing Option [*IBM Corp.*]
DSLP .... Danish Social-Liberal Party [*Political party*] (EAIO)
DSLP .... Diary of Social Legislation and Policy [*Australia A publication*]
DSLT........... Deck Surface Light (AAG)
DSLT........... Detection Scheme with Learning of Thresholds [*Communication signal*]
DSLTR .... Desalter (MSA)
DSLV .... Dissolved (NVT)
DSM............ Danziger Statistische Mitteilungen [*Danzig*] [*A publication*]
DSM............ Data Set Manager (MCD)
DSM............ Data Status Messages (KSC)
DSM............ Data Storage Memory
DSM............ Data Systems Modernization
DSM............ Deep Space Measurement (KSC)
DSM............ Defence Studies Methodology [*British*]
DSM............ Defense Standardization Manual [*DoD*]
DSM............ Defense Subcontract Model (AAGC)
DSM............ Defense Suppression Missile
DSM............ Delta Sigma Modulator (IAA)
DSM............ Demand-Side Management
DSM............ Dense-Staining Material [*Cytology*]
DSM............ Design Standards Manual (AAG)
DSM............ Des Moines [*Iowa*] [*Airport symbol*] (OAG)
DSM............ Detonation Sensing Module [*Automotive electronics*]
DSM............ Development of Substitute Materials
DSM............ Device Strategy Module (IAA)
DSM............ Dextrose Solution Mixture [*Medicine*] (MAE)
DSM............ Diagnostic and Statistical Manual of Mental Disorders [*A publication*]
DSM............ Digital Scanning Electron Microscope
DSM............ Digital Select Matrix
DSM............ Digital Select Module (KSC)
DSM............ Digital Simulation Model (KSC)
DSM............ Digital Storage Media [*Computer science*]
DSM............ Digital Subscriber Modem [*Telecommunications*] (NITA)
DSM............ Diploma in Social Medicine [*British*]
DSM............ Diploma in State Medicine (ROG)
DSM............ Direction of Systems Management
DSM............ Director of Supply and Maintenance [*Army*]
DSM............ Direct Signal Monitoring [*Telecommunications*] (TEL)
DSM............ Direct Support Maintenance [*Army*]
DSM............ Discovery Mines Ltd. [*Toronto Stock Exchange symbol*]
DSM............ Discrete Source with Memory [*Computer science*] (HGAA)
DSM............ Disk Space Management [*Computer science*]
DSM............ Distinguished Service Medal [*US and British*] [*Military decoration*]
DSM............ Distributed Shared Memory [*Computer science*]
DSM............ Distributed Systems Management [*Computer science*]
DSM............ District Sales Manager
DSM............ District Scout Master [*Scouting*]
DSM............ Divisional Sergeant-Major [*British military*] (DMA)
DSM............ Doctor of Sacred Music
DSM............ Double Short Meter [*Music*]
DSM............ Dreyfus Strategic.Muni Bd Fd [*NYSE symbol*] (TTSB)
DSM............ Dreyfus Strategic Municipals, Inc. [*NYSE symbol*] (SPSG)
DSM............ Dried Skim Milk
DSM............ Drink Skim Milk [*Dietetics*] (DAVI)
DSM............ Dutch State Mines
DSM............ Dynamic Scattering Mode (IEEE)
DSM............ Dynamic Stiffness Modulus (PDAA)
DSM............ United States Department of the Interior, Office of Surface Mining, Washington, DC [*Library symbol Library of Congress*] (LCLS)
DSMA .... Defense Supply Management Agency
DSMA .... Digital Sense Multiple Access [*Telecommunications*] (ACRL)
DSMA .... Direct Support Maintenance Activity [*Army*] (MCD)
DSMA .... Disodium Methyl Arsonate [*Herbicide*]

DSMA .... Distributed Scheduling Multiple Access [*Telecommunications*] (OSI)
DSMA .... Divine Science Ministers Organization (EA)
DSMA .... Division of Small Manufacturers Assistance [*FDA*]
DSMA .... Doll Supply Manufacturers Association (EA)
DSMA .... Door and Shutter Manufacturers' Association [*British*]
DSMAC .... Digital Scene Matching Area Correlator [*Navy*]
DSMB .... Data Safety Monitoring Board [*Generic term*]
DSMC .... Dealers Safety and Mobility Council (EA)
DSMC .... Defense Specification Management Course [*Army*]
DSMC .... Defense Systems Management College [*Fort Belvoir, VA*] [*Army*] (RDA)
DSMC .... Defense Systems Management Course [*Air Force*]
DSMC-PMC... Defense Systems Management College - Program Management Course [*DoD*]
DSMD .... Discount Schedule and Marketing Data
dsmd .... Dismissed (MHDB)
DSMD .... Draft Ships Manpower Document [*Navy*] (CAAL)
DSMetEng... Doctor of Science in Metallurgical Engineering (NADA)
DSMG .... Designated Systems Management Group [*Military*]
DSMGP........ Designated Systems Management Group [*Military*]
DSM-III ...... Diagnostic and Statistical Manual [*of Mental Disorders, Third Edition*]
DSM-III-R ... Diagnostic and Statistical Manual of Mental Disorders [*A publication*]
DSMO .... Dimethyl Sulfoxide [*Topical anti-inflammatory*] [*Medicine*] (DAVI)
DSMP .... Daughters of St. Mary of Providence [*Roman Catholic religious order*]
DSMP .... Defense Satellite Meteorological Program (LAIN)
DSMPW .... Director, Submarine Policy and Warfare [*Military*]
DSMS .... Data Systems and Mathematics Staff [*Bureau of Radiological Health*] (IID)
DSMS .... Defense Systems Management School [*Fort Belvoir, VA*] (AABC)
DSMS .... Document Service Management System (NITA)
DSMS .... Drawing Submittal Monitoring System [*MAC*]
DSMSB .... Die Set Manufacturers Service Bureau (EA)
DSMT .... Dual-Speed Magnetic Transducer
DSMTD .... Dismounted
DSMTI .... Discrete Signal Moving Target Indicator
DSN .... Dance Services Network
DSN .... Data Set Name
DSN .... Data Smoothing Network [*Telecommunications*]
DSN .... Data Source Name [*Computer science*]
DSN .... Deep Space Network [*NASA*]
DSN .... Defence Stock Number
DSN .... Defense Secure Network [*Military*]
DSN .... Defense Switched [*or Switchboard*] Network
DSN .... Derived Services Network [*Telecommunications*] (NITA)
DSN .... Detroit Suburban Network [*Radio*]
DSN .... Digital Switching Network [*Telecommunications*]
DSN .... Distributed Sensor Network (MCD)
DSN .... Distributed Systems Network [*Hewlett-Packard Co.*]
DSN .... Doctor of Science in Nursing (PGP)
DSN .... Dusing [*New York*] [*Seismograph station code, US Geological Survey Closed*] (SEIS)
DSN .... Marquette, MI [*Location identifier FAA*] (FAAL)
DSNA .... Dictionary Society of North America (EA)
DSNADNS .... Dihydroxy(hydroxydisulfonaphthylazo)naphthalenedisulfonic Acid [*An indicator*] [*Chemistry*]
DSND.......... Descend [*Aviation*] (FAAC)
DSNDI......... Descend Immediately [*Aviation*] (FAAC)
DSNET .... Defense Secure Network (DOMA)
DSNET .... Defense Secure Network [*Computer science*] (RDA)
DSNI .... [*The*] DocketSearch Network, Inc. [*Information service or system*] (IID)
DSNS .... Division of Space Nuclear Systems [*Energy Research and Development Administration*]
DSNSW........ Deaf Society of New South Wales [*Australia*]
DSNT.......... Descent (KSC)
DSNTZ .... Desensitize (MSA)
DSO .... Companion of the Distinguished Service Order [*Canada*] (DD)
DSO .... Dallas Symphony Orchestra (BARN)
DSO .... Data Security Officer (HGAA)
DSO .... Data Services Operations [*Informatics, Inc.*] (IID)
DSO .... Data Set Optimizer [*Boole & Babbage, Inc.*]
DSO .... Data Systems Office
DSO .... Days Sales Outstanding [*Business term*] (MHDB)
DSO .... Deck Stowage Only [*Shipping*]
DSO .... Defence Sales Organisation [*Ministry of Defence*] [*British*]
DSO .... Defense Sciences Office [*Arlington, VA*] [*DoD*] (GRD)
DSO .... Defense Security Officer [*Military*]
DSO .... Defense Subsistence Office [*DoD*]
DSO .... Defense System Operator [*ECM operator*]
DSO .... Dependents Schooling Office [*Military*]
DSO .... Designate Senior Official (AAGC)
DSO .... Design Stop Order
DSO .... DeSoto, Inc. [*NYSE symbol*] (SAG)
DSO .... De Soto, Inc. [*NYSE symbol*] (SPSG)
DSO .... Detailed Secondary Objective (MCD)
DSO .... Detailed Supplementary Objective (MCD)
DSO .... Digital Storage Oscilloscope [*Gould, Inc.*]
DSO .... Digital Storage Oscilloscope
DSO .... Directorate of Supply Operations (AFIT)
DSO .... Director of Site Operations [*Nuclear energy*] (NRCH)
DSO .... Direct Shipment Order (AAG)
DSO .... Direct System Output [*Computer science*] (MCD)
DSO .... Display Switching Oscilloscope
DSO .... Distal Subungual Onychomycosis

DSO	Distinguished Service Order [*British*]
DSO	District Sales Office
DSO	District Security Office [*or Officer*] [*Navy*]
DSO	District Service Office [*or Officer*] [*Navy*]
DSO	District Signal Officer [*Navy*] (IAA)
DSO	District Sorting Office [*British*] (ROG)
DSO	District Staff Officer [*British*] (ROG)
DSO	District Supply Office [*or Officer*] [*Navy*]
DSO	Division Signal Officer [*Army*]
DSo	Division Supply Officer [*Army*]
D So	Doctor of Sociology
DSO	Doctor of the Science of Oratory
DSO	Donora Southern R. R. [*AAR code*]
DSO	Drawing Sign Out (MCD)
DSO	Evansville, IN [*Location identifier FAA*] (FAAL)
DSOAG	Deputy Senior Officer, Assault Group [*British military*] (DMA)
DSOB	Dirksen Senate Office Building [*Washington, DC*] (DLA)
DSOC	Democratic Socialist Organizing Committee [*Later, DSA*] (EA)
DSOC	Division Support Operations Center (MCD)
DSOC	Dynamic Simulated Optimized Contact
DSoC	Society of the Cincinnati, Washington, DC [*Library symbol*] [*Library of Congress*] (LCLS)
DSocS	Doctor of Social Science
D Soc Sc	Doctor of Social Science
DSocSci	Doctor of Social Science
DSODS	Drug Specific Oral Delivery System [*Pharmacy*]
DSOFC	David Selby Official Fan Club (EA)
DSOM	Digital Systems Operations Panel (MCD)
DSOM	Distributed System Object Model [*Computer science*] (PCM)
DSOPS	Direct Support Operations (NVT)
DSORDRS....	Disorders
DSORG	Data Set Organization (IAA)
DSOS	Data Switch Operating System
D So Sc	Doctor of Social Science
D So Se	Doctor of Social Service
DSOT	Daily Systems Operability Test [*for surface-to-air missiles*]
DSOTS	Demonstration Site Operational Test Series
DSOW	Denmark Strait Overflow Water [*Oceanography*]
DSP	Dataset Printer (SAA)
DSP	Data Source Panel (MCD)
DSP	Data Standardization Project [*DoD*]
DSP	Daughters of St. Paul, Missionary Sisters of the Catholic Editions [*Roman Catholic religious order*]
DSP	Days since Planting [*Botany*]
DSP	Decessit sine Prole [*Died without Issue*] [*Latin*]
DSP	Deep-Sea Particles
DSP	Deep South Petroleum [*Vancouver Stock Exchange symbol*]
DSP	Deep Space Probe
DSP	Deep Submergence Program (MCD)
DSP	Defense Development Sharing Program [*US and Canada*] (RDA)
DSP	Defense Satellite Platform [*Strategic Defense Initiative*]
DSP	Defense Satellite Program (MCD)
DSP	Defense Science Program
DSP	Defense Standardization Program [*DoD*]
DSP	Defense Support Program
DSP	Demisit-Sene-Prole [*Died without issue*] [*Latin*]
DSP	Democratic Socialist Party [*Japan Political party*] (PPW)
DSP	Democratic Socialist Party [*South Korea Political party*] (PPW)
DSP	Democratic Socialist Party [*Ireland*] [*Political party*] (PPW)
DSP	Democratic Socialist Party [*Australia Political party*]
DSP	Democratic Socialist Party [*India*] [*Political party*] (PPW)
DSP	Departure Sequencing Program [*FAA*] (TAG)
DSP	Deployable Solar Panel
DSP	Derogatis Stress Profile [*Personality development test*] [*Psychology*]
DSP	Designated Stock Point
Dsp	Dessertspoon (ADA)
DSP	Detachment Support Package (MCD)
DSP	Deutsche Sex Partei [*German Political party*]
DSP	Dextran Sulphate Precipitable (OA)
DSP	Diarrhetic Shellfish Poisoning [*Medicine*]
DSP	Digital Signal Processing [*Telecommunications*] (ACRL)
DSP	Digital Signal Processing Chip [*Computer science*] (MHDB)
DSP	Digital Signal Processor [*Computer science*]
DSP	Digital Strip Printer
DSP	Digital Subtraction Phlebography [*Medicine*] (DMAA)
DSP	Dimensionally-Stable Polyester [*Tire manufacturing*]
DSP	Director of Selection and Personnel [*British*]
DSP	Director Selector Panel
DSP	Directory Service Protocol [*Telecommunications*] (OSI)
DSP	Direct Support Plan (MCD)
DSP	Direct Support Platoon
DSP	Direct System Platemaker
DSP	Disassemble Sequence Parameter (IAA)
DSP	Disodium Phosphate [*or Dibasic Sodium Phosphate*] [*Also, DSHP Inorganic chemistry*]
DSP	Dispensary (DNAB)
DSP	Display Simulation Program
DSP	Display System Protocol [*Telecommunications*] (ACRL)
DSP	Distilled Spirits Plant
DSP	Distributed System Program [*Computer science*]
DSP	Distribution Point
DSP	Dithiobis(succinimidylpropionate) [*Organic chemistry*]
DSP	Division Standard Practice (AAG)
D Sp	Doctor of Speech
DSP	Doctor of Surgical Podiatry (WGA)

DSP	Document Services for Printing [*Xerox Co.*] (PCM)
DSP	Domain Specific Part [*Telecommunications*] (OSI)
DSP	Doppler Spectrum Processor
DSP	Double Silver Plate
DSP	Drain Source Protected (IAA)
DSP	DSP Technology, Inc. [*Associated Press*] (SAG)
DSP	Dual Speed
DSP	Dynamic Sequence Parameters (SAA)
DSP	Dynamic Speaker
DSP	Dynamic Subscription Promotion
DSP	Dynamic Support Program [*Computer science*]
DSPA	Data Systems Participating Agency (DNAB)
DSPC	Defense Small Purchase Course [*DoD*] (RDA)
DSPC	Disaturated Phosphatidylcholine [*Biochemistry*]
DSPC	Distearoyl Phosphatidylcholine [*Biochemistry*]
DSPC	DSP Communications [*NASDAQ symbol*] (SAG)
DSPCH	Dispatch (AABC)
DSPCm	DSP Communications [*Associated Press*] (SAG)
DSPD	Disalicylidenepropanediamine [*Organic chemistry*]
DSP-E	Defense Satellite Platform-East [*Strategic Defense Initiative*]
DSPE	Division of Scientific Personnel and Education [*National Science Foundation*]
DSPEC	Design Specification
D SPEC	Process Specification (AAGC)
DSPF	Data Services Planning Form
DSPG	Defense Special Projects Group (MCD)
DSPG	Drill Service in Paygrade [*Military*] (DNAB)
DSPG	DSP Group [*NASDAQ symbol*] (TTSB)
DSPG	DSP Group, Inc. [*NASDAQ symbol*] (SAG)
DSP Gp	DSP Group, Inc. [*Associated Press*] (SAG)
DSPH	Diopter Spherical
DSPL	Decessit sine Prole Legitima [*Died without Legitimate Issue*] [*Latin*]
DSPL	Definitized Spare Parts List (AAG)
DSPL	Disciplinary
DSPL	Display
DSPL	Disposal
DSPL	Douglas Space Physics Laboratory (MUGU)
DSPLC	Displace (FAAC)
DSPLCD	Displaced
DSPLN	Discipline (AFM)
DSPLY	Display (IAA)
DSPLY	Display
DSPM	Decessit sine Prole Mascula [*Died without Male Issue*] [*Latin*]
DSPM	Designated Subsystems Project Manager [*NASA*] (NASA)
DSPM	Double Strokes per Minute (MSA)
DSPMO	Defense SAAMS [*Special Airlift Assignment Missions*] Program Management Office [*DoD*]
DSPMS	Decessit sine Prole Mascula Superstita [*Died without Surviving Male Issue*] [*Latin*]
DSPN	Dispensary
DSPN	Disposition (AFM)
DSPNSG	Dispensing
DSPO	Dispose (AABC)
DSPO	Duty Security Petty Officer [*Navy*] (DNAB)
DSPR	Defense Supply Procurement Regulation [*Military*]
DSPRL	Dispersal (FAAC)
DSPRM	Digital Signal Processor Resource Manager [*Computer science*]
DSPS	Decessit sine Prole Superstita [*Died without Surviving Issue*] [*Latin*]
DSPS	Delayed Sleep Phase Syndrome
DSPS	Digital Signal Processing System
DSPS	Digital Signal Processors [*Computer science*]
DSPS	Disabled Students' Programs and Services
DSPSL	Disposal
DSPT	Diagnostic Spelling Potential Test [*Educational test*]
DSPT	DSP Technology [*NASDAQ symbol*] (TTSB)
DSPT	DSP Technology, Inc. [*NASDAQ symbol*] (NQ)
DSPU	Downstream Physical Unit [*Computer science*]
DSPV	Decessit sine Prole Virile [*Died without Male Issue*] [*Latin*] (ADA)
DSP-W	Defense Satellite Platform-West [*Strategic Defense Initiative*]
DSPY	Display (GAVI)
DSQ	Deaf Society, Queensland [*Australia*]
DSQ	Director of Supplies and Quartering [*British military*] (DMA)
DSQ	Discharged to Sick Quarters
DSQ	Disqualified [*Racing*] (IYR)
DSQD	Double-Sided Quad-Density [*Disk drive*] [*Scottsdale Systems*] [*Computer science*]
DSR	Daily Service Report
DSR	Daily Status Report (AAG)
DSR	Dairo Air Services Ltd. [*Uganda*] [*ICAO designator*] (FAAC)
DSR	Danmarks Radio (EY)
DSR	Dasher Resources [*Vancouver Stock Exchange symbol*]
DSR	Data Scanning and Routing
DSR	Data Set Ready [*Model signal*]
DSR	Data Set Ready (NITA)
DSR	Data Specification Request
DSR	Data Storage and Retrieval (MCD)
DSR	Data Survey Report (AAG)
DSR	Daughters of St. Rita of the Immaculate Heart [*Roman Catholic religious order*]
DSR	Debt Service Ratio (ODBW)
DSR	Defense Source Register (MCD)
DSR	Defense Subsistence Region [*DoD*]
DSR	Defense Suppression Rocket
DSR	Delayed Sound Reinforcement
DSR	Departmental Staff Records (AIE)

DSR .... Depolymerized Scrap Rubber [*Waste recycling*]
DSR .... De Ridder, LA [*Location identifier FAA*] (FAAL)
DSR .... Desire (FAAC)
DSR .... Device State Register (NITA)
DSR .... Differentiation with Symmetrical Reinforcement
DSR .... Digital Satellite Radio (PS)
DSR .... Digital Shift Register
DSR .... Digital Stepping Recorder
DSR .... Digit Storage Relay
DSR .... Director of Scientific Research [*British*]
DSR .... Director of Surveillance and Reconnaissance [*Army*]
DSR .... Direct Ship Release (MCD)
DSR .... Direct Ship Requirements (MCD)
DSR .... Direct Space Refinement
DSR .... Direct Stage Recorder (MCD)
DSR .... Direct Storage Recorder
DSR .... Discriminating Selector Repeater (DEN)
DSR .... Display System Replacement [*FAA*] (TAG)
DSR .... Distributed State Response
DSR .... Division of Solar Research [*Energy Research and Development Administration*]
DSR .... Division of Sponsored Research [*Massachusetts Institute of Technology*] (MCD)
DSR .... Division of Sponsored Research [*University of South Florida*] [*Research center*] (RCD)
DSR .... Document Search and Research [*Xerox Corp.*]
DSR .... Document Status Report [*Military*]
DSR .... Downstage Right [*Toward audience*] [*A stage direction*]
DSR .... Dual Shift Right (IAA)
DSR .... Dummy Stowage Receptacle
DSR .... Dynamic Shift Register
DSR .... Dynamic Sideband Regulator
DSR .... Dynamic Spatial Reconstructor [*X-ray scanning machine*]
DSRA .... Dockyard Ship Riggers' Association [*A union*] [*British*]
DSRC .... David Sarnoff Research Center [*RCA*] (MCD)
DSRC .... Dedicated Short-Range Communications
DSRC .... Distant Space Radio Center (IAA)
DSRC .... Double Sideband Reduced Carrier [*Telecommunications*] (IAA)
DSRD .... Data Systems Research and Development [*Oak Ridge National Laboratory*]
DSRE .... Defense Subsistence Region - Europe (AABC)
DSREDS ...... Digital Storage and Retrieval of Engineering Data System [*Army*] (MCD)
DSRF .... Debt Service Reserve Fund [*Information service or system*] (HCT)
DSRGD ...... Disregard (FAAC)
DSRI .... Danish Space Research Institute
DSRK .... Deutsche Schiffs Revision und Klassifikation [*German ship classification society*] (DS)
DSR/LOC..... Debt Service Reserve/Letter of Credit Program [*Investment term*]
dsRNA .... Double-Stranded Ribonucleic Acid [*Biochemistry, genetics*]
dsRNase..... Double-Stranded Ribonuclease
DSRO .... Designated Self-Regulatory Organization (MHDB)
DSRP .... Democratic and Social Republican Party [*Mauritania*] [*Political party*] (EY)
DSRPAC...... Defense Subsistence Region, Pacific [*DoD*] (DNAB)
DS/RPIE ..... Direct Support Real Property Installed Equipment (AFIT)
DSRS .... Data Signalling Rate Select (IAA)
DSRS .... Deep Submergence Rescue System [*Navy*] (NVT)
DSRS .... Direct Scope Recording System (MCD)
DSRS .... Distal Splenorenal Shunt [*Medicine*]
DSRT .... Desert [*Board on Geographic Names*]
DSRT .... Desert
DSR-TKA...... Delta Sigma Rho-Tau Kappa Alpha (EA)
DSRV .... Deep Submergence Rescue Vehicle [*Navy*]
DSRV .... Deep Submergence Research Vessel
DSS .... Data Server System
DSS .... Data Storage Set (MCD)
DSS .... Data Storage System
DSS .... Data Summary Sheets (MCD)
DSS .... Data Switching System
DSS .... Data Systems Specification
DSS .... Data Systems Supervisor (MCD)
DSS .... Dead Sea Scrolls (BJA)
DSS .... Decision and Simulation System [*Computer science*]
DSS .... Decision Support Software (NITA)
DSS .... Decision Support System
DSS .... Decorstone Industry [*Vancouver Stock Exchange symbol*]
DSS .... Deep Seismic Sounding [*Geophysics*]
DSS .... Deep Seismic Sounding Program [*Former USSR*]
DSS .... Deep Space Station [*NASA*]
DSS .... Deep Submergence Systems [*Navy*]
DSS .... Defense Signals Staff (NATG)
DSS .... Defense Supply Service [*DoD*]
DSS .... Dejerine Sottas Syndrome [*Medicine*]
DSS .... Dejerine-Sottas Syndrome [*Medicine*]
DSS .... Dengue Shock Syndrome [*Medicine*]
DSS .... Department of Social Security [*British*]
DSS .... Department of Social Services [*in various governmental agencies*]
DSS .... Department of State Services [*Western Australia*] [*Australia*]
DSS .... Department of Supply and Service [*Canada*] (IMH)
DSS .... Department Summary Schedule [*NASA*] (NASA)
DSS .... Depot Supply System [*Army*]
DSS .... Deputy of Space Systems [*Air Force*]
DSS .... Design Specification
DSS .... Desktop Security Suite [*McAfee Associates, Inc.*] [*Computer science*]

DSS .... Developmental Sentence Scoring [*for the hearing-impaired*]
DSS .... Device, Simulator, and Simulation [*Army*] (RDA)
DSS .... Diagnostic Simulation System
DSS .... Digital Satellite System [*TV signal transmission*]
DSS .... Digital Satellite System
DSS .... Digital Satellite System
DSS .... Digital Scene Simulation [*Computer graphics used in cinematography*] (WDMC)
DSS .... Digital Signal Standard [*Telecommunications*] (ACRL)
DSS .... Digital Signal Synchronizer
DSS .... Digital Signature Standard [*National Institute of Standards and Technology*]
DSS .... Digital Simulator System
DSS .... Digital Storage System
DSS .... Digital Subscriber Signaling System [*Telecommunications*] (ACRL)
DSS .... Digital Subset [*or Subsystem*]
DSS .... Digital Switched Services [*Telecommunications*] (ACRL)
DSS .... Digital Switching System [*Telecommunications*] (TEL)
DSS .... Dimethylsilapentane Sulfonate [*Organic chemistry*]
DSS .... Dioctyl Sodium Sulfosuccinate [*Organic chemistry*]
DSS .... Diploma in Sanitary Science (ROG)
DSS .... Directed Stationing System [*DoD*]
DSS .... Director [*or Directorate*] of Statistical Services [*Air Force*]
DSS .... Direct Satellite System
DSS .... Direct Station Selection [*Telecommunications*]
DSS .... Direct Subsystem (MCD)
DSS .... Direct Supply Support [*Military*]
DSS .... Direct Support System [*Army*]
DSS .... Disabled Student Services
DSS .... Disc Support System (NITA)
DSS .... Disk Storage System [*or Subsystem*] [*Computer science*] (IAA)
DSS .... Distributed System Satellite (IAA)
DSS .... Distributed System Simulator
DSS .... Distribution and Switching System (MCD)
DSS .... Disuccinimydyl Suberate [*Organic chemistry*]
DSS .... Division of Safeguards and Security [*Energy Research and Development Administration*]
DSS .... Doctor of Sanitary Science
DSS .... Doctor of Science in Surgery
DSS .... Doctor of Secretarial Science
DSS .... Doctor of Social Sciences (NADA)
DSS .... Doctor of Social Service
DSS .... Doctor Sacrae Scripturae [*Doctor of Holy Scripture*]
DSS .... Documentation Support Services (NASA)
DSS .... Documents Signed
DSS .... Document Storage System (NITA)
DSS .... Dosage-Sensitive Sex [*Reversal*] [*Genetics*] [*Medicine*]
DSS .... Double Spot System
DSS .... Draughting Software System [*Gould Electronics Ltd. Computer Systems*] [*Software package*] (NCC)
DSS .... Drill Sergeant School [*Army*] (AABC)
DSS .... Drum Storage System
DSS .... Duchess (ROG)
DSS .... Dynamic Simulation System (MCD)
DSS .... Dynamic Steady State
DSS .... Dynamic Support System (MCD)
DSS .... Dynamic System Synthesizer
DSS .... Dyslexia Screening Survey [*Psychology*]
DSS1 .... Digital Subscriber Signaling One [*Telecommunications*] (OSI)
DSSA .... Development Society of Southern Africa (EAIO)
DSSA .... Direct Supply Support Activity [*Army*] (AABC)
Dssa .... Dottoressa [*Female Doctor*] [*Italian*]
DSS & A ..... Duluth, South Shore & Atlantic Railroad [*Nickname: Damned Slow Service and Abuse*] [*Obsolete*]
DSS & R ..... Document Storage Search and Retrieval [*Air Force*]
DSSB .... Data Selection and Storage Buffer (IAA)
DSSB .... Double Single-Sideband (MSA)
DSSC .... Defense Subsistence Supply Center [*Later, Defense Personnel Support Center*]
DSSC .... Derived Services Switching Centre (NITA)
DSSc.......... Diploma in Sanitary Science [*British*]
DS Sc .... Doctor of Social Science
DSSc.......... Doctor of Social Science (GAGS)
DSSC .... Double-Sideband Suppressed Carrier [*Modulation*] (IEEE)
DSSC .... Double Silk, Single Cotton [*Wire insulation*] (IAA)
DSSCS .... Defense Special Security Communications System [*Pronounced "discus"*]
DssCSA ...... Deaconess Community of St. Andrew [*Anglican religious community*]
DSSD .... Data Structure and System Development (SSD)
DSSD .... Direct Supply Support Depot [*Military*] (AFM)
DSSD .... Double-Sided Single-Density Disk [*Computer science*]
DSSE .... Design Selection Specification Engineer
DSSE .... Developmental Software Support Environment [*Army*]
DSSE .... Directory System Service Element [*Telecommunications*] (OSI)
DSSEP .... Developmental Software Support Environment Plan [*Army*]
DSSI .... Data Systems & Software [*NASDAQ symbol*] (TTSB)
DSSI .... Data Systems & Software, Inc. [*NASDAQ symbol*] (SAG)
DSSI .... Digital Storage Systems Interconnect
DSSII .... Displaced System Support Item Identification
DSSJ.......... Deceptive Self-Screening Jammer (MCD)
DSSM .... Dedicated Solar Sortie Mission [*Aerospace*] (MCD)
DSSM .... Defense Superior Service Medal [*Military decoration*]
DSSM .... Digital Signal Sinusoidal Modulation (PDAA)
DSSM .... Division of State Systems Management [*Social and Rehabilitation Service, HEW*]

DSSM .... Drawing Stimulus Strategy Measure
DSSM .... Dynamic Sequencing and Segregation Model [*Computer science*] (OA)
DSSN .... Disbursing Station Symbol Number [*Military*] (AFM)
DSSN .... Seaman, Data Systems Technician, Striker [*Navy rating*]
DSSO .... Defense Surplus Sales Office
DSSO .... District Ships Service Office [*or Officer*] [*Navy*]
DSSO .... Duty Space Surveillance Officer [*Air Force*] (AFM)
DSSP .... Deep Submergence Systems Project Office [*Arlington, VA*] [*Navy*]
DSSP .... Defense Standardization and Specification Program [*DoD*] (RDA)
DSSP .... Depot Support Supply Plan (AFIT)
DSSP .... Direct Supply Support Point [*Military*]
DSSP .... Division Support Slice Program (MCD)
DSSPO .... Deep Submergence Systems Project Office [*Navy*]
DSSP/SSD ... Department Supply Storage Point/Stock Storage Depot [*DoD*]
DSSPTO .... Deep Submergence Systems Project Technical Office [*San Diego, CA*] [*Navy*]
DSSR .... Deep Space Surveillance RADAR (MCD)
DSSRG .... Deep Submergence Systems Review Group [*Navy*]
DSSS .... Deep Space Surveillance Satellite [*Military*]
DSSS .... Defense Special Security System (MCD)
DSSS .... Direct Sequence Spread Spectrum [*Telecommunications*] (IAA)
DSSS .... Division of Special Schools and Services (OICC)
DSSS .... Division of Supplemental Security Studies [*Department of Health and Human Services*] (GRD)
DSSSL .... Document Style Semantics and Specification Language [*ISO/IEC*] [*Computer science*]
DSSSP .... Division of Student Support and Special Programs [*Office of Education*]
DSST .... Director of Supply and Secretariat Training [*British military*] (DMA)
DSST .... Driver Stage Silicon Transistor
DSSTP .... Development Site System Training Program (SAA)
DSSV .... Deep Submergence Search Vehicle [*Research submarine*] [*Navy*]
DSS-W .... Defense Supply Service - Washington [*DoD*]
DST .... Danstar Resources Ltd. [*Vancouver Stock Exchange symbol*]
DST .... Data Segment Table (IAA)
DST .... Data Source Terminal (MCD)
DST .... Data Storage Terminal
DST .... Data Summary Tape (OA)
DST .... Data Systems Test [*Formerly, DAT*]
DST .... Daylight Saving Time
DST .... Decision Support Template [*Military*] (INF)
DST .... Deep Sleep Therapy
DST .... Dermatology and Syphilology Technician [*Navy*]
DST .... Desensitization Test [*Allergy*]
DST .... Design-Specified Transformer (IAA)
DST .... Design Support Test (MCD)
DST .... Destructor [*Military*]
DST .... Detailed System Test
DST .... Development Suitability Test (MCD)
DST .... Dexamethasone Suppression Test [*Clinical chemistry*]
DST .... Dielectric Strength Test
DST .... Differential Skin Surface Temperature
DST .... Differential Survey Treatment (NTCM)
DST .... Digital Subscriber Terminal
DST .... Digit-Symbol Substitution Test [*Psychiatry*]
DST .... Dihydrostreptomycin [*Also, DHS, DHSM*] [*Antimicrobial agent*]
DST .... Dimensional Special Tooling (NASA)
DST .... Direction de la Surveillance du Territoire [*Directorate of Territorial Surveillance*] [*France*]
DST .... Director of Sea Transport [*British military*] (DMA)
DST .... Director of Supplies and Transport [*British*]
DST .... Direct Screw Transfer
DST .... Direct Sounding Transmission [*Meteorology*]
DST .... Direct-Viewing Storage Tube
DS/T .... Discarding Sabot/Training [*British military*] (DMA)
DST .... Discrete Sine Transform (PDAA)
DST .... Disc Storage Terminal (NITA)
DST .... Display Storage Tube (CET)
DST .... Distort (FAAC)
dst .... Distributor [*MARC relator code*] [*Library of Congress*] (LCCP)
DST .... District
DST .... Disuccinimidyl Tartrate [*Organic chemistry*]
DST .... Doctor of Sacred Theology
D St .... Doctor of Statistics
DST .... Dodecanoylsarcosyltaurine [*Crustacean detergent*]
DST .... Donor Specific Transfusion
DST .... Door Stop (AAG)
DST .... Dot Sequential Transmission (IAA)
DST .... Double Spot Tuning
DST .... Double Summer Time [*Daylight Saving Time two hours ahead of Standard Time*] [*British*]
DST .... Douglas Sleeper Transport [*Aviation*]
DST .... Drill Stem Test (ADA)
DST .... Drop Survival Time
DST .... DST Systems [*NYSE symbol*] (TTSB)
DST .... DST Systems, Inc. [*NYSE symbol*] (SAG)
DST .... Dursunbey [*Turkey*] [*Seismograph station code, US Geological Survey*] (SEIS)
DST .... Dust [*Tea trade*] (ROG)
DST .... Dynamic Stability Test (NASA)
DST .... Missoula, MT [*Location identifier FAA*] (FAAL)
DSTA .... Diagnostic Screening Test: Achievement [*Educational test*]
DSTA .... Distribution Assembly [*Ground Communications Facility, NASA*]
DST & DD .... Developing Systems Training and Devices Directorate [*Army*]
DStAP .... Saint Anselm's Abbey, Washington, DC [*Library symbol Library of Congress*] (LCLS)
DSTB .... Danmarks Statistiks TidsseriedataBank [*Denmark Information service or system*] (CRD)
DSTC .... Daylight Saving Time Coalition [*Inactive*] (EA)
DSTC .... Distance (FAAC)
DSTC .... Double-Sideband Transmitted Carrier [*Telecommunications*] (IAA)
DSTD .... Double-Sided, Triple-Deposit
DSTDP .... Distearyl Thiodipropionate [*Organic chemistry*]
DSTE .... Data Subscriber Terminal Equipment [*Telecommunications*] (IAA)
DSTE .... Defense System Terminal Equipment (MCD)
DSTE .... Digital Subscriber Terminal Equipment (AFM)
D St E .... Doctor of Structural Engineering
D St Eng ...... Doctor of Structural Engineering
DSTF .... Delta Spin Test Facility (MCD)
DstFear .... Destron Fearing Corp. [*Associated Press*] (SAG)
DSTFSG .... Deep-Sea Test Facilities Study Group (SAA)
DSTI .... Directorate of Scientific and Technical Intelligence [*British*]
DSTI .... Division of Scientific and Technical Information [*International Atomic Energy Agency*] (DIT)
D St J .... Dame of Justice/Grace of the Order of St. John of Jerusalem [*British*]
DStJ .... Saint Joseph Seminary, Washington, DC [*Library symbol Library of Congress*] (LCLS)
DSTL .... Diagnostic Screening Test: Language [*Educational test*]
DSTL .... Distill
DSTL .... Division System Training Leader (SAA)
DSTLD .... Distilled
DSTLT .... Distillate
DSTM .... Datastream Systems [*NASDAQ symbol*] (TTSB)
DSTM .... Datastream Systems, Inc. [*NASDAQ symbol*] (SAG)
DSTM .... Diagnostic Screening Test: Math [*Educational test*]
DSTN .... Destination (KSC)
DSTN .... Double Supertwisted Nematic [*Video technology*] (PCM)
DSTND .... Destined (FAAC)
DSTO .... District Supply and Transport Officer [*British military*] (DMA)
DSTP .... Data Self-Test Program
DSTP .... Director of Strategic Target Planning [*Military*]
DSTP .... Draft Site Treatment Plan
DSTP .... Draft Site Treatment Plan [*Department of Energy*]
DStPC .... Saint Paul's College, Washington, DC [*Library symbol Library of Congress*] (LCLS)
DSTPS .... Director of Strategic Target Planning Staff [*Offutt AFB*] [*Military*] (CINC)
DSTR .... Deserter [*Military*] (AABC)
DSTR .... Destructor [*Military*]
DSTR .... Diagnostic Screening Test: Reading [*Educational test*]
DSTR .... Distribution (MCD)
DSTR .... Dorsal Striatum [*Neuroanatomy*]
DSTR .... DualStar Technologies Corp. [*NASDAQ symbol*] (SAG)
DSTR .... Dynamic Systems Test Rig [*Helicopters*] [*Army*] (RDA)
DSTRU .... DualStar Technologies Unit [*NASDAQ symbol*] (TTSB)
DSTRW .... DualStar Technologies Wrrt'A' [*NASDAQ symbol*] (TTSB)
DSTS .... Desk Side Time Shared [*General Electric Co.*] [*Computer science*]
DSTS .... Destruct System Test Set
DSTS .... Diagnostic Screening Test: Spelling [*Educational test*]
DSTS .... Dockside Training Simulator
DSTSPN .... Dessertspoon (WGA)
DST Sys .... DST Systems, Inc. [*Associated Press*] (SAG)
DSTU .... Digital Signal Transfer Unit (DWSG)
DSU .... Data Selector Unit (OA)
DSU .... Data Service Unit [*Telecommunications*]
DSU .... Data Storage Unit
DSU .... Data Synchronization [*or Synchronizer*] Unit
DSU .... Decoder Switching Unit
DSU .... Democratic and Social Union [*Mauritania*] [*Political party*] (EY)
DSU .... Deutsche Soziale Union [*German Social Union*] (PPW)
DSU .... Device-Switching Unit
DSU .... Digital Service Unit [*Signal converting device*] [*Telecommunications*] (TSSD)
DSU .... Digital Storage Unit (DIT)
DSU .... Digital Synchronization Unit (HGAA)
DSU .... Direct Supply Unit [*Army*] (VNW)
DSU .... Direct Support Unit [*Army*]
DSU .... Disk Storage Unit [*Computer science*] (MSA)
DSU .... Display Support Unit (MCD)
DSU .... Drum Storage Unit
DSUA .... Dynamic Special-Use Airspace [*FAA*] (TAG)
DSUCR .... Doppler-Shifted Ultrasonic Cyclotron Resonance (PDAA)
DSU/CSU ..... Data Servicing Unit / Channel Servicing Unit (HGAA)
DSUE .... [*A*] Dictionary of Slang and Unconventional English [*A publication*]
DSU/GSU ..... Direct Support Unit/General Support Unit [*Computer system*]
DSUH .... Direct Suggestion under Hypnosis
DSUPHTR .... Desuperheater
D-SUPT .... Detective Superintendent
DSUR .... Data Storage Unit Receptacle (MCD)
D Sur .... Doctor of Surgery
DSV .... Damping Structural Vibrations
DSV .... Dansville, NY [*Location identifier FAA*] (FAAL)
DSV .... Deep Submergence Vehicle [*Navy symbol*]
DSV .... Detected Safety Violation
DSV .... Digital Sum Variation [*Telecommunications*]
DSV .... Digitaria Striate Virus [*Plant pathology*]
DSV .... Diving Support Vessel (DS)
DSV .... Double Silk Varnish [*Wire insulation*] (AAG)
DSV .... Douglas Space Vehicle

DSV	Drum Safety Valve (DS)
DSV	Dynamic Self-Verification (IAA)
DSVD	Digital Simultaneous Voice and Data (CDE)
DS/VD	Director of Salvage Department [*Navy British*]
DSVL	Doppler SONAR Velocity Log (MCD)
DSVOPS	Duty as an Operator or Crewmember of an Operational Self-Propelled Submersible Including Underseas Exploration and Research Vehicles [*Military*] (DNAB)
DSVP	Director of Small Vessels Pool [*Admiralty*] [*British*]
DSVP	Downstream Venous Pressure [*Physiology*] (MAH)
DSVT	Digital Secure Voice Telephone [*Telecommunications*] (TEL)
DSVT	Digital Subscriber Voice Terminal (MCD)
DSVY	Director of Survey [*British military*] (DMA)
DSW	Data Status Word
DSW	Deep-Sea Winch
DSW	Delivered with Standard Wiring
DSW	Device Status Word (CMD)
DSW	Diesel Sea Water (DNAB)
DSW	Differential Shunt Winding [*Wiring*] (DNAB)
D/SW	Dimmer Switch [*Automotive engineering*]
DSW	Director of Special Weapons [*Army*]
DSW	Direct-Step-on-the-Wafer [*Microelectronics*]
DSW	Discovery West Corp. [*Toronto Stock Exchange symbol*]
DSW	Doctor of Social Welfare
DSW	Doctor of Social Work
DSW	Door Switch
DSW	Drum Switch
DSWA	Dry Stone Walling Association [*British*] (DBA)
DSWL	Deswell Industries, Inc. [*NASDAQ symbol*] (SAG)
DSWLF	Deswell Industries [*NASDAQ symbol*] (TTSB)
DSWP	Director of Surface Weapons Projects [*Navy British*]
DSWS	Deep Submergence Weapon System [*Also, DEXTOR*] (MCD)
DSWS	Direct Support Weapon System (MCD)
DSWS	Division Support Weapon System (MCD)
DSWV	Director of Special Weapons and Vehicles [*Military British*]
DSWW	Deswell Industries, Inc. [*NASDAQ symbol*] (SAG)
DSWWF	Deswell Inds Wrrt [*NASDAQ symbol*] (TTSB)
DSX	Digital Signal Cross-Connect [*Telecommunications*]
DSX	Digital System Cross-Connect [*Telecommunications*] (ACRL)
DSX	Distributed Systems Executive [*IBM Corp.*]
DSX-1	Digital Signal Cross-Connect Level 1 (CDE)
DSXBT	Deep Shipboard Expendable Bathythermograph [*Oceanography*]
DSYG	Deputy Secretary General (NATG)
DSYS	Data Sys Network Corp. [*NASDAQ symbol*] (TTSB)
DSYS	Data Systems Network Corp. [*NASDAQ symbol*] (SAG)
DSYSW	Data Sys Network Wrrt [*NASDAQ symbol*] (TTSB)
DSYT	Dorsey Trailers [*NASDAQ symbol*] (TTSB)
DSYT	Dorsey Trailers, Inc. [*NASDAQ symbol*] (SAG)
D Sy Th	Doctor of Systematic Theology
DSZ	Madison, WI [*Location identifier FAA*] (FAAL)
DT	Dakota Territory (ROG)
DT	Dark Trace
DT	Data Tabulation (OICC)
DT	Data Tags [*National Library of Medicine*] [*Searchable field*] (NITA)
DT	Data Terminal
DT	Data Transcriber
DT	Data Translator (IEEE)
DT	Data Transmission
DT	Date (AFM)
dt	Date (WDMC)
DT	Daughter
DT	Daylight Time
DT	Days after Transplanting [*Botany*]
DT	Dead Time
D/T	Deaths Total Ratio [*Measurement*] [*Medicine*] (DAVI)
DT	Debits Tax (ADA)
DT	Decay Time (MSA)
DT	Deccan Trap [*Geology*]
DT	Decision Table [*Computer science*]
DT	Deduction Theorem [*Logic*]
DT	Deep Tank (MSA)
DT	Defensive Tackle [*Football*]
DT	Defensive Target [*Military*]
DT	Deferred Telegram
DT	Delayed Time (KSC)
DT	Delirium Tremens [*Also, DT's*] [*Hallucinatory condition of advanced alcoholism*]
DT	Delivery Time
DT	Deltorphin [*Biochemistry*]
DT	Dental Technician [*Navy rating*]
DT	Deoxythymidine [*Organic chemistry*]
DT	Department of Trade [*British*] (DS)
DT	Department Training
DT	Desk Top
DT	Detecting Heads [*JETDS nomenclature*] [*Military*] (CET)
DT	Detection Threshold (CAAL)
D/T	Detection/Tracker (NVT)
DT	Detroit Terminal Railroad Co. [*AAR code*]
D-T	Deuterium-Tritium Reaction [*Fusion program*]
Dt	Deuteronomy [*Old Testament book*]
DT	Deutsche Telekom AG [*NYSE symbol*] (SAG)
DT	Deutsche Theologie [*A publication*] (BJA)
DT	Developed Template (MCD)
DT	Development Test [*or Testing*] (MCD)
DT	Development Type (AABC)

DT	Diagnostic Time [*Computer science*] (DNAB)
DT	Dial Tone [*Telecommunications*] (TEL)
DT	Diastolic Time [*Cardiology*]
DT	Die Template (MSA)
DT	Dietetic Technician (HCT)
DT	Difference Threshold [*Psychology*] (IAA)
dt	Differential of Time (IDOE)
DT	Differential Time (IEEE)
DT	Digital Technique
DT	Digital Telemetering (IAA)
DT	Digital Test Measurement System (NASA)
DT	Digital Tracker
DT	Digit Tube (IEEE)
DT	Digroup Terminal [*Telecommunications*] (TEL)
D/T	Dilutions to Threshold [*Olfactory*]
D-T	Dinner Theater
DT	Diode Transistor (IAA)
dt	Diphtheria and Tetanus Toxoid [*or Toxin*] [*Immunology*] (DAVI)
DT	Diphtheria, Tetanus [*Medicine*]
DT	Diphtheria Toxin [*Biochemistry*]
DT	Dip Tube
DT	Director of Transport [*British military*] (DMA)
DT	Discharge Tomorrow [*Medicine*] (DMAA)
DT	Discharge Tube (IAA)
DT	Disconnector Trap
DT	Discrepancy Tag
DT	Disc Turntable [*A record player*] (WDMC)
D/T	Disk Tape [*Computer science*] (IEEE)
DT	Disk Technician [*Computer science*]
DT	Dispensing Tablet [*Medicine*] (DMAA)
DT	Dispersion Time (NATG)
DT	Displacement ton (BARN)
DT	Displacement Transducer (KSC)
DT	Display Terminal
DT	Display Translator (MCD)
DT	Distance Test
DT	Distant Transmission (IAA)
DT	Distributive Trades [*Department of Employment*] [*British*]
DT	District Trust Co. [*Toronto Stock Exchange symbol*]
DT	Diver, Second Class [*Navy rating*]
DT	Diversional Therapy [*Psychiatry*] (DAVI)
DT	Docklands Taskforce [*Victoria*] [*Australia*]
DT	Doctor of Technology
DT	Doctor of Theology
DT	Document Title [*European Space Agency-Information Retrieval System*] [*Searchable fields*] (NITA)
DT	Document Type [*Online database field identifier*]
DT	Doit [*Debit*] [*French*]
DT	Double Tachycardia [*Cardiology*]
DT	Double Throw [*Switch*]
DT	Double Time
DT	Double Track [*Engineering acoustics*] (IAA)
DT	Double Tube
DT	Down Through [*Clairvoyance experiment*]
DT	Downtime [*Computer science Telecommunications*] (AAG)
DT	Dow Theory [*Stock market analysis*]
DT	Drain Tile [*Technical drawings*]
DT	Drama Tree (EA)
DT	Draught
DT	Dressed or Tanned [*Freight*]
DT	Dressing Table [*Classified advertising*] (ADA)
DT	Drive Tube
DT	Drop Tank (KSC)
DT	Drop Test Report
DT	Drop Top (OA)
DT	Drum Transfer (CET)
DT	Drum Trap (DAC)
DT	Dry Toned [*Copier*] [*Reprography*]
DT	Dual Tandem [*Aviation*] (DA)
DT	Dual Tires
DT	Dummy Target (OA)
DT	Dump Telemetry
DT	Duration of Tetany [*Medicine*]
DT	Dust-Tight (MSA)
DT	Dust Turn (OA)
DT	Dwell Time (AAG)
DT	Dye Testing
DT	Dynamic Tear (OA)
DT	Dynamic Tester
DT	TAAG-Angola Airlines [*ICAO designator*] (AD)
DT	TAAG Linhas Aereas de Angola [*Angola*] [*ICAO designator*] (ICDA)
DT	Telefunken (Pressed by Decca) [*Record label*] [*Great Britain*]
DT	United States Department of the Treasury, Washington, DC [*Library symbol Library of Congress*] (LCLS)
DT1	Dental Technician, First Class [*Navy rating*]
DT2	Dental Technician, Second Class [*Navy rating*]
DT3	Dental Technician, Third Class [*Navy rating*]
DTA	Daily Travel Allowance [*Business term*] (WDAA)
DTA	Daisy Testability Analyser (NITA)
DTA	Dakka Tourist Agency [*Israel*]
DTA	Dance Teachers' Association (AIE)
DTA	Data File [*Computer science*]
DTA	Data Transfer Area [*Computer science*]
DTa	Deep Tank Aft (DS)
DTA	Deep Transverse Arrest [*Obstetrics*]

DTA............ Default Transfer Area [*Computer science*] (PCM)
DTA............ Defense Transport Administration [*Terminated, functions transferred to Interstate Commerce Commission*]
DTA............ Delta, UT [*Location identifier FAA*] (FAAL)
DTA............ Democratic Turnhalle Alliance [*Namibia*] [*Political party*] (EY)
DTA............ Dental Therapy Assistant (RDA)
DTA............ Dentonia Resources Ltd. [*Vancouver Stock Exchange symbol*]
DTA............ Design and Test Alliance [*Technology research group*]
DTA............ Detailed Traffic Analysis [*Telecommunications*] (TEL)
DTA............ Detroit Edison 7.625% 'QUIDS' [*NYSE symbol*] (TTSB)
DTA............ Detroit Edison Co. [*NYSE symbol*] (SAG)
DTA............ Detroit Tooling Association (EA)
DTA............ Development Test Article
DTA............ Diaminopropanoltetraacetic Acid [*Also, DPTA, DHPTA*] [*Organic chemistry*]
DTA............ Diethylenetriamine [*Also, DETA*] [*Organic chemistry*]
DTA............ Differential Thermal [*or Thermogravimetric*] Analysis [*or Analyzer*]
DTA............ Dimethyl-Triazeno-Acetanilide (DICI)
DTA............ Diphtheria Toxin, A Strain [*Immunology*]
DTA............ Diploma in Tropical Agriculture (ADA)
DTA............ Direct Tape Access [*Computer science*]
DTA............ Disk Transfer Area [*Computer science*] (BYTE)
DTA............ Disk Turbine Assembly
DTA............ Distributing Terminal Assembly [*Electronics*]
DTA............ Distributive Trades' Alliance [*British*] (BI)
DTA............ District Traffic Agent
DTA............ Divisao de Exploracao dos Transportes Aereos [*Angolan airline*]
DTA............ Division Tactical Area [*Army*]
DTA............ Dominion Traffic Association [*Canada*]
DTA............ Double Tape Armored [*Heavy-duty telephone buried cable*]
DTA............ Dovetail Anchor [*Technical drawings*]
DTA............ Dual Trace Amplifier
DTA............ Due to Arrive
DTA............ TAAG, Linhas Aereas de Angola [*ICAO designator*] (FAAC)
DTAA .... Diamond Trade Association of America [*Later, DTPSAA*] (EA)
DTAA .... Di-Tryptophan Aminal Acetaldehyde [*Biochemistry*]
DTAA .... Diversional Therapy Association of Australia
DTAB .... Dodecyltrimethylammonium Bromide [*Organic chemistry*]
DTABL .... Decision Table Processor [*IBM Corp.*]
DTAC .... Dodecyltrimethylammonium Chloride [*Organic chemistry*]
DTACCS ...... Director/Telecommunications and Command and Control System (MCD)
DTACK .... Data Transfer Acknowledge [*Computer memory management*]
DtaDimn ...... Data Dimensions, Inc. [*Associated Press*] (SAG)
DtaDoc........ Data Documents, Inc. [*Associated Press*] (SAG)
DTAF........... (Dichlorotriazinyl)aminofluorescein [*Also, DCTAF*] [*Analytical biochemistry*]
DTAF........... Dynamic Tactical Area File [*Military*] (CAAL)
DTAFE......... Department of Technical and Further Education [*Australia*]
DTAG .... Defense Trade Advisory Group (AAGC)
DTAG .... Digitale Telekable AG [*NASDAQ symbol*] (SAG)
Dta IO .... Data I-O Corp. [*Associated Press*] (SAG)
DTAM......... Daily Traffic Assignment Model [*Aviation*]
DTAM......... Descend to and Maintain [*Aviation*] (FAAC)
DtaMea....... Data Measurement Corp. [*Associated Press*] (SAG)
DT & E........ Development, Test, and Evaluation (AFM)
DT & E........ Development, Test, and Evaluation (DOMA)
DT & E........ Development, Test, and Experimentation
DT & G........ Double Tongue and Groove (DAC)
DT & I .... Detroit, Toledo & Ironton Railroad Co. [*Nickname: Damned Tough and Independent*]
DTAO .... During the Temporary Absence Of [*Military*]
DTAP .... Defense Technology Area Plan [*Defense Technical Information Center*]
DtaProc....... Data Processing Resurces Corp. [*Associated Press*] (SAG)
DTARS .... Digital Transmitting and Routing System (IEEE)
DtaRsh........ Data Research Associates, Inc. [*Associated Press*] (SAG)
DTAS .... Data Transmission and Switching
DTAS .... Diagnostic Test of Arithmetic Strategies
DTASI .... Digital Time Assignment Speech Interpolation (PDAA)
DTASW .... Director, Torpedo, Anti-Submarine, and Mine Warfare [*British military*] (DMA)
DTAT........... Depot Turn-Around Time (MCD)
DtaTrn........ Data Translation Corp. [*Associated Press*] (SAG)
DtaWks....... DataWorks Corp. [*Associated Press*] (SAG)
Dtawtc .... Datawatch Corp. [*Associated Press*] (SAG)
Dtawtch ...... Datawatch Corp. [*Associated Press*] (SAG)
DTAX .... Descend to and Cross [*Aviation*] (FAAC)
D Tax.......... Dominion Tax Cases [*CCH Canadian Ltd.*] [*Information service or system A publication*] (DLA)
DTB........... Danish Tourist Board (EAIO)
DTB........... Danmarks Tekniske Bibliotek [*National Technological Library of Denmark*] [*Information service or system*] (IID)
DTB........... Decimal to Binary [*Computer science*] (BUR)
DTB........... Delayed Time Base (IAA)
DTB........... Destroyer Tactical Bulletin [*Navy*]
DTB........... Deutsche Terminboerse [*Derivatives market*] [*Germany*]
DTB........... Deviation Test Bridge
DTB........... Ditaurobilirubin [*Biochemistry*]
DTB........... Dithiobiuret [*Organic chemistry*]
DTB........... Dominica Tourist Board (EAIO)
DTB........... Dynamic Translation Buffer
dtba .... Date to Be Agreed (AIA)
DTBA .... (Dimethyltriazenol)benzoic Acid [*Antineoplastic drug*]
DTBB .... Di-Tertiary-Butylbiphenyl [*Organic chemistry*]

DTBC .... Digital Time Base Corrector (PDAA)
DTBC .... Di-tert-butylcatechol [*Organic chemistry*]
DTBC .... Di-tert-butylcresol [*Organic chemistry*]
DTBC .... D-Tubocurarine [*Pharmacology*] (DAVI)
DTBC .... Lower Canada Reports (Decisions des Tribunaux du Bas-Canada) [*1850-67*] [*A publication*] (DLA)
DtbBdcst ..... Data Broadcasting Corp. [*Associated Press*] (SAG)
DTBHQ .... Di-tert-butylhydroquinone [*Organic chemistry*]
DT BIOL...... Deutsche Biologische Literatur [*German Biological Literature*] [*Also, DBL Database Forschungsinstitut Senckenberg*] [*Information service or system*]
DTBN .... Di-T-butyl Nitroxide [*Organic chemistry*]
DTBN .... Di-tert-butylnaphthalene [*Organic chemistry*]
DTBP .... Dedicated Total Buried Plant [*Telecommunications*] (TEL)
DTBP .... Di-tert-butyl Peroxide [*Organic chemistry*]
DTBP .... Di-Tert-Butylphenol [*Biochemistry*]
DTC........... Darwin Turf Club [*Australia*]
DTC........... Data Technical Control
DTC........... Data Technology Corp.
DTC........... Data Terminals & Communications, Inc.
DTC........... Data Test Center [*Telecommunications*] (TEL)
DTC........... Data Transmission Center (KSC)
DTC........... Data Transmission Channel (CMD)
DTC........... Data Transport Computer
DTC........... Day Treatment Center [*Medicine*] (DAVI)
DTC........... Dead Time Correction
DTC........... Decision Threshold Computer
DTC........... Defense Technical Center
DTC........... Dental Technician, Chief [*Navy rating*]
DTC........... Department of Technical Cooperation [*British*]
DTC........... Deposition Thickness Controller (IAA)
DTC........... Depository Transfer Check [*Banking*]
DTC........... Depository Trust Co.
DTC........... Deposit-Taking Company [*Generic term that originated in Hong Kong*]
DTC........... Depot Training Center
DTC........... Desert Test Center [*Fort Douglas, UT*] [*Army*] (AABC)
DTC........... Desert Tortoise Council (EA)
DTC........... Desert Training Center [*Army*]
DTC........... Design/Test Contractor (KSC)
DTC........... Design to Cost (MCD)
DTC........... Design to Cut (MHDB)
DTC........... Desk Top Computer
DTC........... DeskTop Conferencing [*Fujitsu Networks Industry, Inc.*] [*Computer science*] (PCM)
DTC........... Detection Threshold Computer [*Telecommunications*] (TEL)
DTC........... Developmental Training Center [*Indiana University*] [*Research center*] (RCD)
DTC........... Dextro-Tubocurarine [*Organic chemistry*]
DTC........... Diagnostic Trouble Code [*Automotive engineering*]
DTC........... Differential Throttle Control
DTC........... Digital Tape Conversion
DTC........... Digital Television Camera
DTC........... Digital to Tone Converter
DTC........... Diploma in Textile Chemistry (ADA)
DTC........... Direct-to-Consumer [*Sales*]
DTC........... Disciplinary Training Center
DTC........... Display Test Chamber
DTC........... Display Timing Control
DTC........... Dithiocarbamate [*Organic chemistry*]
DTC........... Doctor of Textile Chemistry
DTC........... Document de Transport Combine [*Combined Transport Document*] [*French Business term*]
DTC........... Documento de Transporte Combinado [*Combined Transport Document*] [*Spanish Business term*]
DTC........... Documento di Trasporto Combinato [*Combined Transport Document*] [*Italian Business term*]
DTC........... Document Transformation Component (IAA)
DTC........... Dominion Tax Cases [*CCH Canadian Ltd.*] [*Information service or system A publication*] (DLA)
DTC........... Domtar, Inc. [*NYSE symbol Toronto Stock Exchange symbol Vancouver Stock Exchange symbol*] (SPSG)
DTC........... Doppler Translation Channel
DTC........... Downtime Code [*Military*] (AFIT)
DTC........... Draft Technical Corrigendum [*Correction*] [*Telecommunications*] (OSI)
DTC........... Driveability Test Chamber [*Automotive engineering*]
DTC........... DSIF [*Deep Space Instrumentation Facility*] Telemetry and Command Subsystem [*NASA*]
dTC .... d-Tubocurarine [*Muscle relaxant*]
DTC........... International Trade Commission, Washington, DC [*Library symbol Library of Congress*] (LCLS)
DTC........... United States International Trade Commission, Washington, DC [*OCLC symbol*] (OCLC)
DTCCS .... Defense Telecommunications Command and Control System (MCD)
DTCD .... Diploma in Tuberculosis and Chest Diseases [*British*]
DTCH .... Detached
DTCH .... Diploma in Tropical Child Health [*British*]
DT Ch .... Doctor of Textile Chemistry
DTCH .... Dutch
DTChem...... Doctor of Technical Chemistry (NADA)
DTC/LCC ..... Design to Cost / Life Cycle Cost (SSD)
DTCM .... Dental Technician, Master Chief [*Navy rating*]
DTCN .... Direction Technique des Constructions Navales [*French naval design bureau*] (DOMA)

DTCP	Diode Transistor Compound Pair [*Electronics*] (OA)
DTCR	Data Transfer and Certification Record (KSC)
DTCS	Data Transmission and Control System (AAG)
DTCS	Dental Technician, Senior Chief [*Navy rating*]
DTCS	Digital Test Command System
DTCS	Drone Target Control System [*Military*] (MCD)
DTCS	Drone Tracking and Control System [*Military*] (MCD)
DTCU	Data Transmission Control Unit [*Burroughs Corp.*]
DTCW	Data Transfer Command Word (NASA)
DTD	Data Terminal Display
DTD	Data Transfer Done
DTD	Dated (AFM)
dtd	Datur Talis Dosis [*Give Of Such A Dose*] [*Pharmacology*] (DAVI)
DTD	Dekoratie voor Trouwe Dienst [*Decoration for Devoted Service*] [*South Africa*]
DTD	Dentur Tales Doses [*Give in Such Doses*] [*Pharmacy*]
DTD	Department of Tank Design [*British*] (MCD)
DTD	Detailed Test Description (MCD)
DTD	Detailed Troop Decontamination [*Military*] (INF)
DTD	Detroit Edison 8.50% 'QUIDS' [*NYSE symbol*] (TTSB)
DTD	Detroit Edison Co. [*NYSE symbol*] (SAG)
DTD	Diastrophic Dysplasia [*Medicine*]
DTD	Difficult to Deliver [*US Postal Service*]
DTD	Digital Terrain Data [*Army*]
DTD	Digital Topographic Data (MCD)
DTD	Diploma in Tuberculous Diseases [*British*]
DTD	Directorate of Technical Development (MCD)
DTD	Directorate of Training Developments [*Army*]
DTD	Direct-to-Disc [*Recording system*] (WDAA)
DTD	Dismounted Training Day [*Military*] (INF)
DTD	Doctor of Textile Dyeing
DTD	Document Type Definition [*Computer science*] (PCM)
DTD	Dual Trace Display
DTD	Washington, DC [*Location identifier FAA*] (FAAL)
DTDC	Desolventizer-Toaster-Dryer-Cooler [*Oil technology*]
DT Des	Doctor of Textile Design
DTDM	Deterministic Time Division Multiplexing [*FAA*] (TAG)
DTDMA	Distributed Time Division Multiple Access [*System*] [*DoD*]
dTDP	Deoxyribosylthymine Diphosphate [*Biochemistry*]
DTDP	Deoxythymidine Diphosphate [*Biochemistry*]
DTDP	Diisotridecyl Phthalate
DTDP	Ditridecyl Phthalate [*Organic chemistry*]
DTDR	Draft Training Device Requirement (MCD)
DTDS	Digital Television Display System
DTDT	David Taylor Dance Theatre
DT/DT	Drop Tube/Drop Tower [*Facility*]
DTDU	Dichloro-bis(trifluoromethyl)diphenylurea [*Insectproofing agent for wool*]
DT/DV	Deposit Ticket/Debit Voucher [*Computer science*]
DTE	Data Ten to Eleven (PDAA)
DTE	Data Terminal Equipment [*Computer science*]
DTE	Datatracker International [*Vancouver Stock Exchange symbol*]
DTE	Data Transmitting Equipment
DTE	Dayton, TN [*Location identifier FAA*] (FAAL)
dte	Dedicatee [*MARC relator code*] [*Library of Congress*] (LCCP)
DTE	Defence Technology Enterprises Ltd. [*British*] (IRUK)
DTE	Depot Tooling Equipment
DTE	Detroit Edison Co. [*NYSE symbol*] (SPSG)
DTE	Diagnostic Test Equipment (WDAA)
DTE	Dial Telephone Exchange (DNAB)
DTE	Diamond Tool Engineering Co.
DTE	Digital Television Encoder
DTE	Digital Television Equipment (KSC)
DTE	Digital Transmission Equipment (IAA)
DTE	Digital Tune Enable (IAA)
DTE	Diplomacy Test of Empathy [*Psychology*]
DTE	Distance to Empty [*Automotive driver information display*]
DTE	Dithioerythritol [*Organic chemistry*]
DTE	Doctor of Textile Engineering
DTE	DTE Energy [*NYSE symbol*] (TTSB)
DTE	Dual Track Etcher
DTE	Dynamic Tear Energy (PDAA)
DTE	Tamas Darida Enterprise [*Hungary ICAO designator*] (FAAC)
DTEA	Data Telemetry Exploitation Aid (MCD)
DTEA	Developmental Training Effectiveness Analysis [*Military*]
DTeaching	Diploma in Teaching
DTEAS	Detection Track Evaluation and Assignment Systems [*Navy*] (NG)
D Tech	Doctor of Technology
D Tech Chem	Doctor of Technical Chemistry (EY)
DTechnol	Doctor of Technology
DTED	Digital Terrain Elevation Data [*Military*]
DTEE	Division of Technology and Environmental Education [*Office of Education*]
DT Eng	Doctor of Textile Engineering
DTEP	Democratic Tradition Education Project [*Australia*]
DTEPrF	Detroit Edison 7.74% Dep Pfd [*NYSE symbol*] (TTSB)
DTEPrI	Detroit Edison 7.75% Dep Pfd [*NYSE symbol*] (TTSB)
DTER	Dither
DTEV	Deutsche Telekom eV [*Germany Telecommunications*]
DTF	Daily Transaction File
DTF	Dairy Trade Federation [*British*] (ECON)
DTF	Data Transmission Factor
DTF	Data Transmission Feature
DTF	Data Transmission Function
DTF	Data Transmittal Form (MCD)

DTF	Date to Follow [*Telecommunications*] (TEL)
DTF	Dedicated Terminal Facility [*Telecommunications*] (TSSD)
DTf	Deep Tank Forward [*Shipping*] (DS)
DTF	Define the File [*Computer science*] (BUR)
DTF	Definite Tape File [*Computer science*] (OA)
DTF	Department of Treasury and Finance [*Australia*]
DTF	Detector Transfer Function (MAE)
DTF	Detritiation Factor
DTF	Development Test Facility (SSD)
DTF	Diagnostic Turbulent Flux [*Marine science*] (OSRA)
DTF	Diagnostic Turbulent Flux (USDC)
DTF	Dial Tone First [*Telecommunications*] (TEL)
DTF	Diamond Thin-Film [*Coating technology*]
DTF	Dicyanomethylenetrinitrofluorene [*Organic chemistry*]
DTF	Direct to Film [*Printing technology*]
DTF	Disabilities Task Force [*Australia*]
DTF	Division of Training and Facilities [*Office of Education*]
DTF	Domestic Textiles Federation [*British*] (BI)
DTF	Dow Chemical Co., Texas Division, Freeport, TX [*OCLC symbol*] (OCLC)
DTF	Dried Tree Fruit
DTF	Drone Target Facility [*Military*]
DTF	Drone Test Facility [*Military*]
DTF	Dry Tortugas Island, FL [*Location identifier FAA*] (FAAL)
DTF	Duff/Phelps Utilities Tax-Free Income [*NYSE symbol*] (SPSG)
DTF	Duff/Phelps Util Tax-Free Inc. [*NYSE symbol*] (TTSB)
DTF	Dynamic Test Fixture [*Military*] (MCD)
DTF	Dynamic Track Following [*Electronics*]
DTFA	Digital Transfer Function Analyzer (IAA)
DTFD	Diagnostic Test Flow Diagram (MCD)
DTFDW	Deciduous Tree Fruit Disease Workers [*An association*] (EA)
DTG	Data Transmission Generator (MCD)
DTG	Date-Time Group [*Group of figures at head of radio or Teletype message indicating filing time*]
DTG	Derivative Thermogravimetry
DTG	Development Training Group
DTG	Differential ThermoGravimetry (DICI)
DTG	Display Transmission Generator
DTG	Distance-to-Go (GAVI)
DTG	Dual Track Geneva
DTG	Dwight, IL [*Location identifier FAA*] (FAAL)
DTG	Dynamically Tuned Gyro [*Inertial sensor*] (IEEE)
D-TGA	Dextrotransposition of the Great Arteries [*Cardiology*] (DAVI)
DTGS	Deuterated Triglycine Sulfate [*Organic chemistry*]
DTGW	Director of Guided Weapons Trials [*British military*] (DMA)
DTH	Dance Theater of Harlem
DTH	Death Valley [*California*] [*Airport symbol*] (OAG)
DTH	Delayed-Type Hypersensitivity [*Immunology*]
DTH	Diploma in Tropical Health
DTH	Diploma in Tropical Hygiene [*British*]
DTH	Direct to Home [*Satellite broadcast mode*] [*Canada*]
D Th	Doctor of Theology
D Theol	Diploma in Theology [*British*]
D Theol	Doctor of Theology
DTheolC	Sulpician Seminary Theological College, Washington, DC [*Library symbol Library of Congress*] (LCLS)
DThom	Divus Thomas [*Piacenza*] (BJA)
DThomP	Divus Thomas [*Piacenza*] (BJA)
DThPT	Diploma in Theory and Practice of Teaching (Durham University) [*British*]
DTHy	Sandoz [*Italy*] [*Research code symbol*]
DTI	Data-Tech Institute [*Clifton, NJ*] (TSSD)
DTI	Defense Technical Information Center, Alexandria, VA [*OCLC symbol*] (OCLC)
DTI	Department of the Treasury, Internal Revenue Service, Washington, DC [*Library symbol Library of Congress*] (LCLS)
DTI	Department of Trade and Industry [*British*]
DTI	Deposit-Taking Institution (ADA)
DTI	Design Technical Information [*or Instruction*] (KSC)
DTI	Detroit, Toledo & Ironton Railroad Co. [*AAR code*]
DTI	Development Test Instrumentation (NASA)
DTI	Development through Industry
DTI	Dial Test Indicator
DTI	Digital Test Indicator (IAA)
DTI	Director of Tactical Investigation [*Military British*]
DTI	Director Train Indicator
DTI	Direct Trader Input [*Customs term*] (DCTA)
DTI	Display Technologies, Inc. (PCM)
DTI	Display Terminal Interchange
DTI	Dissolved Transport Index [*Geochemistry*]
DTI	Distortion Transmission Impairment [*Telecommunications*] (TEL)
DTI	Division of Technical Information [*AEC*]
DTI	Domestic Technology Institute (EA)
DTI	Drug and Therapeutic Information [*Later, Medical Letter*] (EA)
DTI	Durham Technical Institute [*Durham, NC*]
DTIB	Decision Table Information Bulletin (HGAA)
DTIB	Defense Technology and Industrial Base
DTIC	Deconvoluted Total Ion Current [*Spectrometry*]
DTIC	Defense Technical Information Center [*Formerly, DDC*] [*Alexandria, VA*] [*DoD Information service or system*]
DTIC	(Dimethyltriazenyl)imidazolecarboxamide [*Dacarbazine*] [*Also, DIC Antineoplastic drug*]
DTIC-ACT-D	DTIC [*Dacarbazine*], Actinomycin D [*Dactinomycin*] [*Antineoplastic drug regimen*]
DTID	Disposal Turn-In Document [*Military*]

DTIE............ Division of Technical Information Extension [*Later, Technical Information Center*] [*AEC*]
DTII............ D T Industries [*NASDAQ symbol*] (TTSB)
DTII............ DT Industries, Inc. [*NASDAQ symbol*] (SAG)
DT Inds........ DT Industries, Inc. [*Associated Press*] (SAG)
DTIP............ Digital Tune in Progress (IAA)
DTIR............ Defense Technical Intelligence Report (MCD)
Dtls............ Deutero-Isaiah (BJA)
DTIS............ Drill Time in Service [*Military*] (DNAB)
DTK............ Datatech Systems Ltd. [*Toronto Stock Exchange symbol*]
DTK............ Dietrich, AK [*Location identifier FAA*] (FAAL)
DTKR........... Developmental Tasks for Kindergarten Readiness [*Child development test*]
DTL............ Data Training Ltd. [*British*] (NITA)
DTL............ Datel Industries Ltd. [*Toronto Stock Exchange symbol Vancouver Stock Exchange symbol*]
DTL............ Dead Time Log
DTL............ Deep Trench Latrine [*British military*] (DMA)
DTL............ Degree of Total Leverage [*Finance*]
DTL............ Delta Teen-Lift (EA)
DTL............ Detail (AABC)
DTL............ Detail
DTL............ Detroit Lakes [*Minnesota*] [*Airport symbol Obsolete*] (OAG)
DTL............ Diode-Transistor Logic
DTL............ Direct to Licensee
DTL............ Duct Transmission Loss [*Facility*] (MCD)
DTL............ United States Department of the Treasury, Washington, DC [*OCLC symbol*] (OCLC)
DTLA............ Detroit Tests of Learning Aptitude [*Education*]
DTLCC........... Design to Life-Cycle Cost
DTLN............ Data Transmission Network Corp. [*NASDAQ symbol*] (NQ)
DTLN............ Data Transmission Ntwk [*NASDAQ symbol*] (TTSB)
DTLOM........... Doctrine, Training, Leader Development, Organization, and Materiel [*Army*] (INF)
DTLOMS...... Doctrine, Training, Leader Development, Organization, Materiel, and the Soldier [*Army education program*] (INF)
DTLOMS...... Doctrine, Training, Leader [*Development*] Organizations Materiel Soldiers [*Army*]
DTLS............ Descriptive Tests of Language Skills (EDAC)
DTLU............ Digital Terminal Line Unit [*Telecommunications*] (ACRL)
DTLZ............ Diode-Transistor Logic with Zener Diode [*Electronics*] (IAA)
DTM............ Carnegie Institution of Washington [*District of Columbia*] [*Seismograph station code, US Geological Survey Closed*] (SEIS)
DTM............ Dataram Corp. [*AMEX symbol*] (SPSG)
DTM............ Deceleration Throttle Modulator [*Automotive engineering*]
DTm............ Deep Tank Midship [*Shipping*] (DS)
DTM............ Delay Timer Multiplier (IEEE)
DTM............ Demonstration Test Motor (MCD)
DTM............ Dermatophyte Test Medium (AAMN)
DTM............ Design Test Model
DTM............ Desktop Manufacturing
DTM............ Deutsche Tourenwagen Meisterschaft [*German Touring Car Championship*]
DTM............ Developmental Test Model
DTM............ Development Telemetry Equipment (MCD)
DTM............ Diagnostic Test Mode [*Automotive engineering*]
DTM............ Difficult to Monitor (ACII)
DTM............ Digital Talk-Out Module
DTM............ Digital Television Monitor
DTM............ Digital Terrain Model (MCD)
DTM............ Digital Troposcatter MODEM (MCD)
DTM............ Digital Trunk Module [*Telecommunications*]
DTM............ Diocesan Travelling Mission [*Roman Catholic*]
DTM............ Diploma in Tropical Medicine [*British*]
DTM............ Director of Telecommunications Management [*Abolished, 1970*] [*Air Force*]
DTM............ Director of Transport and Movements [*British military*] (DMA)
DTM............ Directory of Texas Manufacturers [*University of Texas at Austin*] [*Information service or system*] (CRD)
DTM............ Doctor of Tropical Medicine
DTM............ Dortmund [*Germany Airport symbol*] (OAG)
DTM............ Draft Technical Manual
DTM............ Dual Transport Module (NOAA)
DTM............ Duration Time Modulation (IAA)
DTM............ Dynamic Tensile Modulus [*Materials testing*]
DTM............ Dynamic Test Model [*Spacecraft*]
DTma............ Deep Tank Midship Aft [*Shipping*] (DS)
DTMA............ Desoxycorticosterone Trimethylacetate [*Pharmacology*] (DAVI)
DTM & H...... Diploma in Tropical Medicine and Hygiene [*British*]
DTMB............ David W. Taylor Model Basin [*Also, DATMOBAS, TMB*] [*Later, DTNSRDC, NSRDC*] [*Washington, DC*]
DTMB............ Defense Traffic Management Branch (DNAB)
DTMB............ Monastir/Habib Bourgiba [*Tunisia*] [*ICAO location identifier*] (ICLI)
DTMC............ Di(p-chlorophenyl)trichloromethylcarbinol [*Miticide*]
DTMD............ Determined (NVT)
DTMD............ Differential Temperature Measuring Device
DTmf............ Deep Tank Midship Forward [*Shipping*] (DS)
DTMF............ Dual Tone Modulated Frequency [*Telecommunications*]
DTMF............ Dual Tone Multifrequency [*Telecommunications*]
DTMF............ Dual Tone Multifrequency Signalling (NITA)
DTMH............ Diploma in Tropical Medicine and Hygiene
DTMI............ Dairy Training and Merchandising Institute [*Later, MTI*] (EA)
DTML............ Diode-Transistor Micrologic (IAA)
DTMLD........ Draught Moulded [*British*] (IAA)

DTMO............ Design [*or Development*], Test, and Mission Operations [*NASA*]
dTMP........... De Novo Thymidylate [*Synthesis*] [*Biochemistry*] (DAVI)
dTMP........... Deoxyribosylthymine Monophosphate [*Biochemistry*]
DTMP........... Deoxythymidine Monophosphate [*Biochemistry*]
DTMPH........... Diploma in Tropical Medicine and Public Health
DTMR............ Defense Traffic Management Regulations (AAGC)
DTMS............ Data Base and Transaction Management System [*IBM Corp.*]
DTMS............ Defense Traffic Management Service
DTMS-A...... Delivery and Transport Management System [*Software package*] [*British*]
DTMS............ Descriptive Test of Mathematics Skills (EDAC)
DTMS............ Desktop Marketing System [*CD-ROM*] [*Computer science*]
DTMS............ Development, Test, and Mission Support (MCD)
DTMS............ Digital Test Measurement [*or Monitor*] System
DTMT............ Dual-Tone Multifrequency [*Telephone*] (WDMC)
DTMV$_{max}$... Diastolic Transmembrane Voltage, Maximum [*Cardiology*] (DAVI)
DTN............ [*The*] Daily Times of Nigeria [*A publication*]
DTN............ Dalmatian Resources Ltd. [*Vancouver Stock Exchange symbol*]
DTN............ Data Transporting Network
DTN............ Defence Telecommunications Network [*British military*] (DMA)
DTN............ Defense Teleprinter Network (NATG)
DTN............ Detain (AABC)
DTN............ Detection (IAA)
DTN............ Digital Equipment Corp., Spit Brook, Nashua, NH [*OCLC symbol*] (OCLC)
DTN............ Digital Television Network
DTN............ Diphtheria Toxin Normal [*Medicine*]
DTN............ Diploma of Teaching (Nursing)
DTn............ Double Tinned (IDOE)
DTN............ Drug Trade News [*A publication*]
DTN............ DuMont Television Network [*1946-55*]
DTN............ Shreveport, LA [*Location identifier FAA*] (FAAL)
DTNB............ Dithiobis(nitrobenzoic acid) [*Analytical biochemistry*]
DTNB............ Dithionitrobenzoic Acid [*Organic chemistry*]
DTNHEB........ Dithiobis(nitrohydroxyethylbenzamide) [*Biochemistry*]
DTNM............ Date-Time-Next Meeting (DI)
DTNS............ Dragon Terminal Night Sight [*Military*] (MCD)
DTNSRDC...... David W. Taylor Naval Ship Research and Development Center [*Later, DTRC*] [*Bethesda, MD*]
DTNSRDC/ASED... David W. Taylor Naval Ship Research and Development Center Aviation and Surface Effects Department [*Bethesda, MD*]
DTNSRDC/CID... David W. Taylor Naval Ship Research and Development Center Central Instrumentation Department [*Bethesda, MD*]
DTNSRDC/CMLD... David W. Taylor Naval Ship Research and Development Center Computation Mathematics/Logistics Department [*Bethesda, MD*]
DTNSRDCDET... David W. Taylor Naval Ship Research and Development Center Detachment (DNAB)
DTNSRDC/FMD... David W. Taylor Naval Ship Research and Development Center Financial Management Department [*Bethesda, MD*]
DTNSRDC/MAT... David W. Taylor Naval Ship Research and Development Center Materials Department [*Annapolis, MD*]
DTNSRDC-NLHP... David W. Taylor Naval Ship Research and Development Center Naval Laboratories History Program [*Bethesda, MD*]
DTNSRDC/PAS... David W. Taylor Naval Ship Research and Development Center Propulsion and Auxiliary Systems Department [*Annapolis, MD*]
DTNSRDC-PASD... David W. Taylor Naval Ship Research and Development Center Propulsion and Auxiliary Systems Department [*Annapolis, MD*]
DTNSRDC/SAD... David W. Taylor Naval Ship Research and Development Center Ship Acoustics Department [*Bethesda, MD*]
DTNSRDC/SDD... David W. Taylor Naval Ship Research and Development Center Systems Development Department [*Bethesda, MD*]
DTNSRDC/SHD... David W. Taylor Naval Ship Research and Development Center Ship Hydromechanics Department [*Bethesda, MD*]
DTNSRDC/SME... David W. Taylor Naval Ship Research and Development Center Ship Materials Engineering Department [*Annapolis, MD*]
DTNSRDC/SPD... David W. Taylor Naval Ship Research and Development Center Ship Performance Department [*Bethesda, MD*]
DTNSRDC/SSID... David W. Taylor Naval Ship Research and Development Center Ship Systems Integration Department [*Bethesda, MD*]
DTNTN............ Detention of Pay (DNAB)
DTO............ Data Takeoff [*Air Force*]
DTO............ Data Terminal Operator [*Computer science*]
DTO............ Decentralized Toll Office [*Telecommunications*] (TEL)
dto............ Dedicator [*MARC relator code*] [*Library of Congress*] (LCCP)
DTO............ Defense Transportation Order [*Department of Commerce*]
DTO............ Denton, TX [*Location identifier FAA*] (FAAL)
DTO............ Deodorized Tincture of Opium [*Pharmacy*]
DTO............ Detailed Test Objective [*NASA*]
DTO............ Digital Testing Oscilloscope (IEEE)
DTO............ Direct Termination Overflow [*MCI Communications Corp.*] [*Telecommunications*]
DTO............ Direct Turn-Over (NG)
DTO............ District Training Office [*or Officer*] [*Navy*]
DTO............ District Transportation Officer
DTO............ Division Transportation Office [*or Officer*]
DTO............ Dollar Tradeoff
D-to-A............ Digital-to-Analog [*Converter*] [*Computer science*]
DTOC............ Division Tactical Operations Center
D-to-D............ Digital-to-Digital
DTOE............ Draft Table of Organization and Equipment [*Military*] (INF)
DTOL............ Digital Test-Oriented Language [*Computer science*] (PDAA)
DTOM............ De Tomaso Industries, Inc. [*NASDAQ symbol*] (SAG)
DTomaso............ De Tomaso Industries, Inc. [*Associated Press*] (SAG)
DTOP............ Daily Turn On Procedures [*Computer science*] (MCD)
DTOP............ Desktop Data [*NASDAQ symbol*] (TTSB)

DTOP .... Desktop Data, Inc. [*NASDAQ symbol*] (SAG)
DTOSC .... Design to Operations and Support Cost
DT/OT .... Development Test/Operational Test
DTP .... Dairy Termination Program [*Department of Agriculture*]
DTP .... Dance Touring Program [*National Endowment for the Arts*]
DTP .... Data Tape Punch (IAA)
DTP .... Data Transfer Protocol [*Telecommunications*] (OSI)
DTP .... Defense Trade Policy [*Office of*] (DOMA)
DTp .... Department of Transport [*British*] (DS)
DTP .... Depth Telemetering Pinger
DTP .... Design to Price (NVT)
DTP .... Desktop Publishing [*Computer science*]
DTP .... Detailed Test Plan [*or Procedure*]
DTP .... Developmental Therapeutics Program [*National Cancer Institute*]
DTP .... Development Threat Package
dtp .... Diethyldithiophosphate [*Organic chemistry*]
DTP .... Diode Test Program
DTP .... Diphtheria, Tetanus, Pertussis [*Also, DPT*] [*Immunology*]
DTP .... Diphtheria, Tetanus, Poliovirus [*Vaccine*] [*Medicine*]
DTP .... Directory Tape Processor
DTP .... Direct Tape Processor [*Computer science*] (ECII)
DTP .... Display Translator Program (MCD)
DTP .... Distal Tingling on Percussion [*Medicine*]
DTP .... Distributed Transaction Processing (HGAA)
DTP .... Dolph-Tchebyscheff Pattern
DTP .... Doppler Techniques Proposal
DTP .... Double Test Position
DTP .... Driver Training Platoon [*British military*] (DMA)
DTP .... Drum Timing Pulse
DTP .... Dynamic Testing Program (AAG)
DTP .... Dynamic Test Panel
DTPA .... Diethylenetriaminepentaacetic Acid [*Also, DETP, DETPA*] [*Chelating agent*]
DTPB .... Divider Time Pulse Distributor Board (MCD)
DTPC .... Defense Transportation Policy Council [*MTMC*] (TAG)
DTPC .... Desert Tortoise Preserve Committee (EA)
DTPEW .... Design-to-Price Electronic Warfare [*Military*] (CAAL)
DTPEWS ...... Design-to-Price Electronic Warfare Suite [*Navy*] (MCD)
DTPGS .... Digital Test Program Generation System (MCD)
DTPH .... Diploma in Tropical Public Health [*British*]
DTPL .... Domain Tip Propagation Logic (MCD)
DTPR .... Detailed Test Procedures (NASA)
DTPS .... Day-Timer Pen Scheduler
DTPS .... Diffusion Transfer Processing System [*Reprography*]
DTPSAA ...... Diamond Trade and Precious Stone Association of America (EA)
DTPT .... Dedicated Theater Planning Terminal [*Military*] (MCD)
DTPT .... DeltaPoint, Inc. [*NASDAQ symbol*] (SAG)
DTPT .... DeltaPoint Inc. [*NASDAQ symbol*] (TTSB)
DTP vaccine... Diptheria, Tetanus, and Pertussis [*Whooping Cough*] Vaccine [*Also, called the DPT vaccine*] (PAZ)
DTR .... Daily Transaction Registering [*or Reporting*] [*Computer science*]
DTR .... Danish Air Transport [*ICAO designator*] (FAAC)
DTR .... Data Tape Recorder (IAA)
DTR .... Data Telemetering Register
DTR .... Data Terminal Reader
DTR .... Data Terminal Ready [*Computer science Telecommunications*]
DTR .... Data Transfer Rate
DTR .... Data Transfer Register
DTR .... Data Translator (MCD)
DTR .... Deep Tendon Reflex [*Physiology*]
DTR .... Defense Test Range (MCD)
DTR .... Definite-Time Relay (MSA)
DTR .... Demand Totalizing Relay (KSC)
DTR .... Department of Trade [*British*] (ADA)
DTR .... Desktop Replacement [*Computer science*]
Dtr .... Deuteronomy Rabba (BJA)
DTR .... Development Trouble Report
DTR .... Diamond T Register (EA)
DTR .... Diatec Resources Ltd. [*Vancouver Stock Exchange symbol*]
DTR .... Diffusion Transfer [*Reprography*]
DTR .... Diffusion Transfer Reversal [*Reprography*]
DTR .... Digital Tape Recorder
DTR .... Digital Telemetering Register
DTR .... Diploma in Therapeutic Radiology [*British*]
DTR .... Directorate of Technical Research [*Navy Canada*]
DTR .... Disposable Tape Reel [*Computer science*]
DTR .... Distribution Tape Reel [*Computer science*]
DTR .... Diurnal Temperature Range [*Climatology*]
DTR .... Division of Tax Research
DTR .... Document Transmittal Record (NRCH)
DTR .... Double-Taxation Relief (ODBW)
DTR .... Downtime Ratio [*Computer science Telecommunications*] (TEL)
DTR .... Draft Technical Report [*Telecommunications*] (OSI)
DTr .... Trinity College, Washington, DC [*Library symbol Library of Congress*] (LCLS)
DTRA .... Defense Technical Review Activity [*or Agency*] [*Military*] (AABC)
DTRA .... Development Test Requirements Assessment [*Military*]
DTRC .... David W. Taylor Research Center [*Bethesda, MD*] [*United States Space and Naval Warfare Systems Command*] (GRD)
DTRC/CMLD... David W. Taylor Research Center Computation Mathematics/ Logistics Department [*Bethesda, MD*]
DTRC/PAS.... David W. Taylor Research Center Propulsion and Auxiliary Systems Department [*Bethesda, MD*]
DTRC/SHD ... David W. Taylor Research Center Ship Hydromechanics Department [*Bethesda, MD*]

DTRC/SME ... David W. Taylor Research Center Ship Materials Engineering Department [*Bethesda, MD*]
DTRC/SSID... David W. Taylor Research Center Ship Systems Integration Department [*Bethesda, MD*]
DTRD .... Development Test Requirements Document [*NASA*] (NASA)
DTRE .... Defence Telecommunications Research Establishment [*British*]
DTRE .... Diploma in Therapeutic Radiology and Electrology
DTREM .... Dust, Thermal, and Radiation Engineering Measurements Package [*NASA*]
DTRF .... Daily Transaction Register File [*Computer science*]
DTRF .... Data Transmittal and Routing Form (NRCH)
DTRM .... Determine (FAAC)
DTRM .... Dual Thrust Rocket Motor
DTRP .... Diploma in Town and Regional Planning (ADA)
DTRS .... Development Test Requirement Specification (NRCH)
DTRS .... Distress (MSA)
DT/RSS .... Data Transmission/Recording Subsystem
DTRT .... Deteriorate
DTRT .... Do the Right Thing [*Also, DWIM*] [*In data processing context, translates as "Guess at the meaning of poorly worded instructions"*]
DTRX .... Detrex Corp. [*NASDAQ symbol*] (NQ)
DTRX .... Detrex Corporation [*NASDAQ symbol*] (TTSB)
DTRY .... Dietary
DTS .... Data Terminal Set (NVT)
DTS .... Data Terminal System (IAA)
DTS .... Data Test Station
DTS .... Data Transfer Sequence (IAA)
DTS .... Data Transfer System [*Army*] (AABC)
DTS .... Data Transmission Service (IAA)
DTS .... Data Transmission System [*Air Force*]
DTS .... Defense Telephone Service [*DoD*]
DTS .... Defense Transportation System [*DoD*]
DTS .... Defensive Technology Study [*Military*] (SDI)
DTS .... Delaware Technical and Community College, Southern Campus, Georgetown, DE [*OCLC symbol*] (OCLC)
DT's .... Delirium Tremens [*Also, DT*] [*Hallucinatory condition of advanced alcoholism*]
DTS .... Dense Tar Surfacing
DTS .... Dense Tubular System
DTS .... Department of Technology and Society (EA)
DTS .... Desk Top Server (CDE)
DTS .... Detailed Test Specification
DTS .... Detailed Type Specification (MCD)
DTS .... Detector Tracker Switch
DTS .... [*The*] Detroit & Toledo Shore Line Railroad Co. [*AAR code*]
DTS .... Developer Technical Support (CDE)
DTS .... Development and Test Support
DTS .... Development Test Satellite
DTS .... Diagnostic Test Set (IAA)
DTS .... Dialog Terminal System (IAA)
DTS .... Diametral Tensile Strength [*Material science*]
DTS .... Differential Temperature Switch (NRCH)
DTS .... Differential Transmission Spectrum
DTS .... Digital Tandem Switch
DTS .... Digital Telemetry System
DTS .... Digital Telephone System
DTS .... Digital Television System (MCD)
DTS .... Digital Termination Service [*Data transmission*]
DTS .... Digital Termination System [*Telecommunications*]
DTS .... Digital Test System (MCD)
DTS .... Digital Theater Systems [*Surround-sound technology*] (PS)
DTS .... Digital Titration System
DTS .... Digital Tracking System [*or Subsystem*]
DTS .... Digital Transmission Systems [*Telecommunications*] (ACRL)
DTS .... Diploma in Theological Studies
D-TS .... Diplomate, American Board of Thoracic Surgery (DHSM)
DTS .... Diplomatic Telecommunications Service (FAAC)
DTS .... Discrete Time Sample [*Medicine*] (MEDA)
DTS .... District Traffic Superintendent [*British railroad term*]
DTS .... Doctor of Textile Science
DTS .... Domestic Transmission System [*ITT*] [*Telecommunications*] (TEL)
DTS .... Donor Specific Transfusion [*Hematology*] (DAVI)
DTS .... Doppler Tracking Station
DTS .... Double Thermostat and Safety [*Nuclear energy*] (OA)
DTS .... Double Throw Switch
DTS .... Dovetail Anchor Slot [*Technical drawings*]
DTS .... DSIF [*Deep Space Instrumentation Facility*] Tracking and Monitor-Control Subsystem [*NASA*]
DTS .... Dynamic Test System
DTSA .... Defense Technology Security Administration
DTSC .... DARCOM [*Development and Readiness Command, Army*] Technical Steering Committee (MCD)
DTSC .... Defense Telecommunication System Center (LAIN)
DTSC .... Department of Toxic Substances Control (DOGT)
DTSC .... Department of Toxic Substances Control
DTSD .... Development Test Supportability Demonstration [*Army*]
DTSD .... Director of Tactical and Staff Duties Division [*British military*] (DMA)
DTSD .... Director of Training and Staff Duties Division [*Navy British*]
DTSG .... Data Transmission Study Group [*Military*]
DTSI .... Datron Systems [*NASDAQ symbol*] (TTSB)
DTSI .... Datron Systems, Inc. [*NASDAQ symbol*] (NQ)
DTSP .... Down through Sealed Packs [*Clairvoyance experiment*]
DTSR .... Department of Tourism, Sport, and Racing [*Queensland*] [*Australia*]
DTSR .... Department of Tourism, Sport, and Recreation [*Tasmania*] [*Australia*]

DTSS	Dartmouth Time-Sharing System [*Computer science*]
DTSS	Digital Topographic Support System [*Army*] (RDA)
DTSS	Dynamic Tracking Suspension System [*Automotive engineering*]
DTST	Defense Technology Study Team
DTS-W	Defense Telephone Service - Washington [*DoD*]
DTSX	Digital Transmission Systems, Inc. [*NASDAQ symbol*] (SAG)
DTSXU	Digital Transmission Sys Unit [*NASDAQ symbol*] (TTSB)
DTSY	Digital Transmission System
DTT	Data Transfer Timing
DTT	Data Transition Tracking
DTT	Data Transmission Terminal (NITA)
DTT	Design Thermal Transient [*Nuclear energy*] (NRCH)
DTT	Design Transition Temperature (NRCH)
DTT	Detent [*Mechanical engineering*]
DTT	Detroit [*Michigan*] [*Airport symbol*] (OAG)
DTT	Detroit [*Michigan*] [*Airport symbol*] (AD)
DTT	Developmental Technician Team (MCD)
DTT	Difficult to Test [*Audiology*]
DTT	Diphtheria-Tetanus Toxoid [*Medicine*]
DTT	Director of Technical Training [*British military*] (DMA)
DTT	Direct Transverse Traction [*Orthopedics*] (DAVI)
DTT	Dithiothreitol [*Organic chemistry*]
DTT	Doctor of Textile Technology
DTT	Doctrinal and Tactical Training [*Army*] (INF)
DTT	Domain Tip Technology (IAA)
DTT	Double Twin Tube [*Fluorescent lighting*]
DTT	Drag Disk-Turbine Transducer [*Nuclear energy*] (NRCH)
DTT	Duplicate Title Transferred [*Library science*]
DTT	Dynamic Test Target [*Military*] (CAAL)
DTTA	Tunis/Carthage [*Tunisia*] [*ICAO location identifier*] (ICLI)
DTTAC	Distributive Trades Technology Advisory Centre [*University of Stirling*] [*British*] (CB)
DTTB	Bizerte/Sidi Ahmed [*Tunisia*] [*ICAO location identifier*] (ICLI)
DTTC	Diethylthiatricarbocyanine [*Organic chemistry*]
DTTC	Tunis [*Tunisia*] [*ICAO location identifier*] (ICLI)
DTTD	Dedicated Test Training Detachment (MCD)
DTTD	Remada [*Tunisia*] [*ICAO location identifier*] (ICLI)
DTTF	Gafsa [*Tunisia*] [*ICAO location identifier*] (ICLI)
DTTG	Gabes [*Tunisia*] [*ICAO location identifier*] (ICLI)
DTTI	Bordj El Amri [*Tunisia*] [*ICAO location identifier*] (ICLI)
DTTJ	Jerba/Zarzis [*Tunisia*] [*ICAO location identifier*] (ICLI)
DTTK	Kairouan [*Tunisia*] [*ICAO location identifier*] (ICLI)
DTTL	Data Transition Tracking Loop
DTTL	Kelibia [*Tunisia*] [*ICAO location identifier*] (ICLI)
DT/TM	Delayed Time/Telemetry (KSC)
DTTN	Jendouba [*Tunisia*] [*ICAO location identifier*] (ICLI)
dTTP	Deoxyribosylthymine Triphosphate [*Biochemistry*]
DTTP	Deoxythymidine Triphosphate [*Biochemistry*]
DTTP	Documents to the People [*Government Documents Round Table*] [*American Library Association*]
DTTR	El Borma [*Tunisia*] [*ICAO location identifier*] (ICLI)
DtTrns	Data Translation II, Inc. [*Associated Press*] (SAG)
DtTrNw	Data Transmission Network Corp. [*Associated Press*] (SAG)
DTTS	Day Television Tracking System [*Military*]
DTTS	Dynamic Track-Tensioning System [*Army*] (RDA)
DTTU	Data Transmission Terminal Unit [*Burroughs Corp.*]
DTTV	Tunis [*Tunisia*] [*ICAO location identifier*] (ICLI)
DTTW	Doctors to the World [*An association*] (EA)
DTTX	Sfax/El Maou [*Tunisia*] [*ICAO location identifier*] (ICLI)
DTTY	Digital-to-Teletype
DTTZ	Tozeur/Nefta [*Tunisia*] [*ICAO location identifier*] (ICLI)
DTU	Data Terminal Unit [*Telecommunications*]
DTU	Data Terminating Unit (TEL)
DTU	Data Transfer Unit
DTU	Data Transmission Unit
DTU	Dial Terminal Unit (CAAL)
DTU	Digital Tape Unit (IEEE)
DTU	Digital Telemetry Unit
DTU	Digital Transmission Unit (IEEE)
DTU	Digital Tuning Unit (IAA)
DTU	Display Terminal Unit (CMD)
DTU	Dorozhno-Transportnyy Upravleniye [*Road and Transportation Directorate*] [*Former USSR*] (LAIN)
DTUC	David Thompson University Centre [*Nelson, BC*] [*Pronounced "dee-tuck"*] [*Canada*]
DTUL	Deflection Temperature under Load [*Plastics technology*]
DTUN	Detroit & Canada Tunnel Corp. [*NASDAQ symbol*] (NQ)
DTUN	Detroit & Cda Tunl [*NASDAQ symbol*] (TTSB)
DTUOC	Digital Tire Uniformity Optimizer Computer (PDAA)
DTUPC	Design to Unit Production Cost [*Army*]
DTUTF	Digital Tape Unit Test Facility [*NASA*]
DTV	Centre Airlines, Inc. [*ICAO designator*] (FAAC)
DTV	Day Television [*Sensing equipment*]
DTV	Desktop Video [*Telecommunications*] (PCM)
DTV	Deutscher Taschenbuch Verlag [*Publisher*]
DTV	Digital Television (MSA)
DTV	Digital to Television (NITA)
DTV	Diploma in Tropical Veterinary Health
DTV	Disney Television [*Animated music video program*] [*Cable-television*]
DTV	Diver Transport Vehicle (PDAA)
DTV	Driver's Thermal Viewer [*Tank technology*] [*Army*]
DTV	Drop Test Vehicle (IAA)
DTV	Due to Void (MAE)
DTV	Dynamic Test Vehicle
DT/VAC	Diphtheria-Tetanus Vaccine [*Medicine*]

DTVC	Desktop Videoconferencing
DTVC	Digital Transmission and Verification Converter (KSC)
DTVECCU	Digital Television Equipment Cluster Control Unit [*Military*]
DTVM	Differential Thermocouple Voltmeter
DTVM	Diploma in Tropical Veterinary Medicine [*British*]
DTVP	Developmental Test of Visual Perception [*Frostig*]
DTVS	Distributor Thermo-Vacuum Switch [*Automotive engineering*]
DTW	Dance Theater Workshop (EA)
DTW	Dealer Tankwagon [*Gasoline*]
DTW	Department of Transport and Works [*Northern Territory*] [*Australia*]
DTW	Detroit [*Michigan*] [*Airport symbol*]
DTW	Digital Equipment Corp., Tewkesbury, Tewkesbury, MA [*OCLC symbol*] (OCLC)
DTW	Dry Tank Weight
DTW	Dual Tandem Wheels [*Aviation*]
DTW	Dynamic Time Warping
DTWS	Dial Teletypewriter Service (IAA)
DTWX	Dial Teletypewriter Exchange
DTX	Dedicated Terminal Facility [*Telecommunications*] (TSSD)
DTX	Deltex [*Slovakia*] [*ICAO designator*] (FAAC)
DTX	Dendrotoxin [*Biochemistry*]
DTX	Detoxification (AAMN)
DTX	Dominion Textile [*NASDAQ symbol*] (TTSB)
DTX	Dominion Textile, Inc. [*Toronto Stock Exchange symbol*]
DTYD	Development Trust for the Young Disabled [*British*] (IRUK)
DTYO	Duty Officer [*Military*]
DTYP	Daguerreotype (VRA)
DTZ	Diatrizoate (MAE)
DTZ	Division Tactical Zone [*Army*] (AABC)
DU	Decision Unit [*Management*] (RDA)
DU	Decubitus Ulcer [*Dermatology*] (DAVI)
DU	Defense Unit [*Military*]
D/U	Delay Unit [*Telecommunications*] (TEL)
DU	Deleted Unpostable [*IRS*]
DU	Demarcation Unit (MCD)
DU	Denatured Uranium [*Nuclear reactor technology*]
DU	Density Unknown [*Medicine*] (MAE)
dU	Deoxyuridine [*Biochemistry*] (MAE)
DU	Depleted Uranium
DU	Diabetic Urine [*Endocrinology*] (DAVI)
DU	Diagnosis Undetermined [*or Unknown*] [*Medicine*]
du	Dial Unit (MAE)
DU	Diazouracil [*Pharmacology*]
DU	Diazyme Unit [*Of hydrolytic enzyme activity*]
DU	[*A*] Dictionary of the Underworld [*A publication*]
DU	Died Unmarried (WDAA)
DU	Digital Unit
DU	Dimensioning Unit [*Telecommunications*] (TEL)
DU	Diploma in Urology (DD)
D-U	Diplomate, American Board of Urology (DHSM)
DU	Disk Unit (IAA)
DU	Display Unit (NASA)
DU	Display, Upper
DU	Disposal Unit (DAC)
DU	Distribution Unit (KSC)
DU	Diversity University [*On-line education*] [*Information retrieval*]
DU	Dobson Unit [*Measure of ozone*]
DU	Dobson Unit (USDC)
DU	Dockers' Union [*British*]
DU	Docteur d'Universite [*Doctor of the University*] [*Canada*] (DD)
DU	Doctor of the University
DU	Doctor of the University of Essex [*British*] (DI)
DU	Documentation Unit
DU	Dog Unit [*Veterinary medicine*]
DU+	Dog Unit Positive [*Biochemistry*] (DAVI)
DU	Double Uptake [*Boilers*]
Du	Dual (BJA)
DU	Duchy
DU	Ducks Unlimited (EA)
Du	Due
DU	Duke
DU	Duodenal Ulcer [*Medicine*]
DU	Duplex [*Radio*] (NATG)
DU	Duroxide Uptake [*Radiology*] (DAVI)
DU	Dust [*ICAO*] (FAAC)
DU	Dutch
DU	Duty Cycle [*Military*]
DU	Dwelling Unit [*Household census*]
DU	Philips-Duphar NV [*Netherlands*] [*Research code symbol*]
DU	Roland Air [*ICAO designator*] (AD)
Du	Urea Dialysance [*Medicine*] (MAE)
DUA	Death Under Anaesthesia
DUA	Deer Unlimited of America (EA)
DUA	Digital Uplink Assembly
DUA	Digitronics Users Association [*Later, IUA*] (EA)
DUA	Directory User Agent [*Computer science*] (TNIG)
DUA	Disaster Unemployment Assistance [*Disaster Relief Act*]
dua	Duala [*MARC language code Library of Congress*] (LCCP)
DUA	Dual Resources Ltd. [*Vancouver Stock Exchange symbol*]
DUA	Durant, OK [*Location identifier FAA*] (FAAL)
DUAL	Distributed Update Algorithm (ACRL)
DUAL	Dual Drilling [*NASDAQ symbol*] (TTSB)
DUAL	Dual Drilling Co. [*NASDAQ symbol*] (SAG)
DUAL	Dynamic Universal Assembly Language [*Computer science*]
DUALABS	Data Use Access Laboratories Inc. (NITA)

DUAL-COMM...	Data Use and Access Laboratories - Communications, Inc. [*Information service or system*] (IID)
DualDrl	Dual Drilling Co. [*Associated Press*] (SAG)
DUALEXTAC...	Dual Salvo Attack Tactic [*Navy*] (NVT)
DualStar	DualStar Technologies Corp. [*Associated Press*] (SAG)
DualStr	DualStar Technologies Corp. [*Associated Press*] (SAG)
Duane Nat	Duane on the Law of Nations [*A publication*] (DLA)
Duane Road L...	Duane's Road Laws of Pennsylvania [*A publication*] (DLA)
DUART	Dual Universal Asynchronous Receiver/Transmitter [*Motorola, Inc.*]
DUAS	Uralic and Altaic Studies Department [*Indiana University*] [*Research center*] (RCD)
DUAT	Direct User Access Terminal (DA)
DUATS	Direct User Access Terminal System [*Aviation*] (FAAC)
DUB	Dubai Airwing [*United Arab Emirates*] [*ICAO designator*] (FAAC)
DUB	Dubious (ADA)
DUB	Dubitans [*or Dubius*] [*Doubting or Dubious*] [*Latin*]
DUB	Dubitatur [*It Is Doubted*] [*Legal term*] (DLA)
DUB	Dublin [*City and county in Ireland*]
DUB	Dublin [*Ireland*] [*Airport symbol*] (OAG)
DUB	Dublin Rathfarnham Castle [*Ireland*] [*Seismograph station code, US Geological Survey Closed*] (SEIS)
DUB	Dubowitz [*Score*] [*Obstetrics*] (DAVI)
DUB	Dubuque [*Diocesan abbreviation*] [*Iowa*] (TOCD)
DUB	Dysfunctional Uterine Bleeding [*Medicine*]
DUBDD	Director of Unexploded Bomb Disposal Department [*Navy British*]
DUBL	Double
DUBL	Dublin [*City and county in Ireland*]
Dubner CBG...	Character Background Generator [*Television*] (WDMC)
DUBS	Durham University Business School
DUC	Data Utilization Center [*Navy*] (NVT)
DUC	Data Utilization Console
DUC	Defined User Command (IAA)
DUC	Dense Upper Cloud [*ICAO*] (FAAC)
DUC	Digital Uplink Command (MCD)
DUC	Distinguished Unit Citation [*Military decoration*]
DUC	Distributable Union Catalog [*Harvard University*] [*Microfiche*] (NITA)
DUC	Division of Unemployment Compensation [*A publication*] (DLA)
DUC	Doctor of the University of Calgary
DUC	Dragon under Cover (MCD)
DUC	Duarte [*California*] [*Seismograph station code, US Geological Survey*] (SEIS)
DUC	Duchess
DUC	Duff & Phelps Utilities & Corporate Bond Trust [*NYSE symbol*] (SPSG)
DUC	Duff/Phelps Util & Cp Bd Tr [*NYSE symbol*] (TTSB)
DUC	Duncan [*Oklahoma*] [*Airport symbol Obsolete*] (OAG)
DUC	University Club, Washington, DC [*Library symbol Library of Congress*] (LCLS)
DUCA	United States Court of Appeals for the District of Columbia, Washington, DC [*Library symbol Library of Congress*] (LCLS)
Du Cange	Du Cange's Glossarium [*A publication*] (DLA)
DUCC	Deep Underground Command Center (MCD)
DUCC	Dual Universal Serial Communicator Controller [*Signetics Corp.*] (NITA)
DUCCS	Duke University Clinical Cardiology Study [*Cardiology study*]
DUCE	Denied Usage Channel Evaluator [*Telecommunications*] (TEL)
DUCE	Distinguished Unit Citation Emblem [*Military decoration*]
Duc GI	Ducange's Glossarium [*A publication*] (DLA)
DUCH	Duchess (ROG)
DUCK	Duckwall-Alco Stores [*NASDAQ symbol*] (TTSB)
DUCK	Duckwall-Alco Stores, Inc. [*NASDAQ symbol*] (SAG)
Duckwall	Duckwall-Alco Stores, Inc. [*Associated Press*] (SAG)
DUCO	Duplex Controller (IAA)
Ducom	Ducommun, Inc. [*Associated Press*] (SAG)
DUCON	Duty Connection
DUCR	Duracraft Corp. [*NASDAQ symbol*] (SAG)
DUCS	Deep Underground Communications System (AFM)
DUCS	Defense Unit Classification System
DUCS	Department of University Computer Systems [*University of Connecticut*] [*Research center*] (RCD)
DUCS	Display Unit Control System (IAA)
DUCT	Diverse Use of Communication Technology
DUCTS	Ductwork Services [*Focus Software Consultants*] [*Software package*] (NCC)
DUCY	Duty Cycle (IAA)
DUD	Design under Design
Dud	Dudley's Georgia Reports [*A publication*] (DLA)
DUD	Dunedin [*New Zealand*] [*Airport symbol*] (OAG)
DUDAT	Due Date
DUDC	University of the District of Columbia, Washington, DC [*Library symbol Library of Congress*] (LCLS)
Dud (GA)	Dudley's Georgia Reports [*A publication*] (DLA)
Dud (Geo)	Dudley's Georgia Reports [*A publication*] (DLA)
Dudl	Dudley's Georgia Reports [*A publication*] (DLA)
Dudley (GA)...	Dudley's Georgia Reports [*A publication*] (DLA)
dUDP	Deoxyuridine Diphosphate [*Biochemistry*]
Dud R	Dudley's Georgia Reports [*A publication*] (DLA)
DUDST & K'S BART...	Dudstone and King's Barton [*England*]
DUE	Detection of Unauthorized Equipment [*Bell Laboratories*]
DUE	Distinguished Unit Emblem [*Military decoration*]
DUE	DNA [*Deoxyribonucleic Acid*] Unwinding Element [*Genetics*]
DUE	Drug Use Evaluation
DUE	Dundo [*Angola*] [*Airport symbol*] (OAG)
DUEG	Development Unit Executive Group [*Scotland*] (AIE)
DUEGG	Dual Energy Gamma Group [*Nuclear energy*] (NRCH)

DUEL	Data Update Edit Language [*Computer science*]
DUER	Digital UHF [*Ultra-High Frequency*] ECCM Radio [*Electronic Counter-Countermeasures*] [*Army*]
Duer	Duer's New York Superior Court Reports [*A publication*] (DLA)
Duer Const Jur...	Duer's Constitutional Jurisprudence [*A publication*] (DLA)
Duer Ins	Duer on Insurance [*A publication*] (DLA)
Duer Mar Ins...	Duer on Marine Insurance [*A publication*] (DLA)
Duer (NY)	Duer's New York Superior Court Reports [*A publication*] (DLA)
Duer Rep	Duer on Representation [*A publication*] (DLA)
DUET	Distance University Education via Television [*Mount Saint Vincent University*] [*Halifax, NS*] [*Telecommunications service*] (TSSD)
DUET	Dual Emitter Transistor [*Electronics*]
DUETS	Duo-Mode Electric Transport System, Inc.
DUF	Chavis, KY [*Location identifier FAA*] (FAAL)
DUF	Diffusion under [*Epitaxial*] Film (IEEE)
DUF	Duff & Phelps Corp. [*NYSE symbol*] (SPSG)
DUF	Phoenix Duff & Phelps [*NASDAQ symbol*] (TTSB)
DUF	Phoenix Duff & Phelps Corp. [*NYSE symbol*] (SAG)
Duff	Duff's Feudal Conveyancing [*Scotland*] [*A publication*] (DLA)
Duff Conv	Duff's Feudal Conveyancing [*Scotland*] [*A publication*] (DLA)
DUFLY	Duty Involving Flying [*Military*]
DUFLYTECH...	Duty Involving Flying as a Technical Observer [*Military*]
DufPCr	Duff & Phelps Credit Rating Co. [*Associated Press*] (SAG)
DufPhCr	Duff & Phelps Credit Rating Co. [*Associated Press*] (SAG)
DUFPr	Phoenix Duff/Phelps $1.50 Cv Pfd [*NYSE symbol*] (TTSB)
DufPTF	Duff & Phelps Utilities Tax Free Income [*Associated Press*] (SAG)
DufPUC	Duff & Phelps Utility & Corporate Bond Trust [*Associated Press*] (SAG)
DufPUtil	Duff & Phelps Utilities & Income, Inc. [*Associated Press*] (SAG)
Dufresne	Dufresne's Glossary [*A publication*] (DLA)
DUG	Douglas [*Arizona*] [*Airport symbol*] (OAG)
DUG	Dugway [*Utah*] [*Seismograph station code, US Geological Survey*] (SEIS)
Dug Mon	Dugdale's Monasticon [*A publication*] (DLA)
Dug Sum	Dugdale on Summons [*A publication*] (DLA)
DUH	Data Upper Half Byte (IAA)
DUI	Data Use Identifier (AFM)
DUI	Distinctive Unit Insignia [*Military*] (INF)
DUI	Driving under the Influence (DHSM)
DUI	Drug Use Index [*Psychology*]
DUI	Duisburg [*Germany*] [*Airport symbol*] (AD)
DUIL	Driving under the Influence of Liquor
DUINS	Duty under Instruction
DUINS/TEMDUINS STU...	Duty under Instruction or Temporary Duty under Instruction as a Student [*Military*] (DNAB)
DUJ	Du Bois [*Pennsylvania*] [*Airport symbol*] (OAG)
DUJ	E. I. Du Pont de Nemours & Co., Jackson Laboratory, Wilmington, DE [*OCLC symbol*] (OCLC)
DUJ	Juris Utriusque Doctor [*Doctor of Both Laws; i.e., Canon and Civil Law*]
DUK	Duke, Nat, New York NY [*STAC*]
DUK	Duke Power [*NYSE symbol*] (TTSB)
DUK	Duke Power Co. [*NYSE symbol*] (SPSG)
Duke	Duke Power Co. [*Associated Press*] (SAG)
Duke	Duke's Law of Charitable Uses [*A publication*] (DLA)
Duke BAJ	Duke Bar Association. Journal [*A publication*] (DLA)
Duke BA Jo...	Duke University Bar Association. Journal [*A publication*] (DLA)
Duke B Ass'n J...	Duke Bar Association. Journal [*A publication*] (DLA)
Duke Ch Us...	Duke on Charitable Uses [*1676*] [*A publication*] (DLA)
DukeP	Duke Power Co. [*Associated Press*] (SAG)
DukeR	Duke Realty Investments Capital Shares [*Associated Press*] (SAG)
DukeRlty	Duke Realty Investments Capital Shares [*Associated Press*] (SAG)
Duke U	Duke University (GAGS)
DUKPrA	Duke Pwr 6.375%'A'Pfd [*NYSE symbol*] (TTSB)
DUKPrS	Duke Pwr 7.72%'A'Pfd [*NYSE symbol*] (TTSB)
DUKW	Amphibious Truck, 2 1/2-ton Cargo
DUL	Diffuse Undifferentiated Lymphoma [*Oncology*]
DUL	Duluth [*Minnesota*] [*Seismograph station code, US Geological Survey Closed*] (SEIS)
DULC	Dulcis [*Sweet*] [*Pharmacy*]
Dulck	Dulcken's Eastern District Reports [*Cape Colony, South Africa*] [*A publication*] (DLA)
DUM	Died Unmarried [*Genealogy*]
DUM	Disc User Multi-Access Unit (NITA)
DUM	Dorsal Unpaired Median (PDAA)
DUM	Dublin University Mission
DUM	Dummy (MSA)
DUM	Dumont D'Urville [*France*] [*Geomagnetic observatory code*]
dum	Dutch, Middle [*MARC language code Library of Congress*] (LCCP)
DUMA	Dubai Marine Areas (BJA)
DUMAND	Deep Underwater Muon and Neutrino Detection [*Astrophysics*]
DUMB	Deep Underground Missile Basing
DUMD	Deep Underwater Measuring Device
DUMETI	Dorsal Unpaired Median Extensor-Tibiae (PDAA)
DUMF	Dumfriesshire [*County in Scotland*]
Dumf Gal	Dumfries and Galloway [*Region of Southern Scotland, established in 1975*] (WGA)
DUML	Diabetic Ulcer Meal [*Airline notation*]
dUMP	Deoxyuridine Monophosphate [*Biochemistry*]
dUMP	Deoxyuridylate [*Biochemistry*] (DAVI)
DUMR	Dust and Moisture
DUMS	Deep Unmanned Submersibles
DUMV	Dulcamara Mottle Virus [*Plant pathology*]
DUN	Data Users' Note [*NASA*] (MCD)
DUN	Death of Ur-Nammu (BJA)

DUN............ Depth Under Notch (PDAA)
DUN............ Dial-Up Networking [*Microsoft Windows 95*] [*Computer science*]
DUN............ Dial-Up Networking [*Computer science*]
DUN............ Douglas United Nuclear, Inc. (KSC)
DUN............ Dundo [*Angola*] [*Seismograph station code, US Geological Survey*] (SEIS)
DUN............ Dunedin [*New Zealand*] (ROG)
DUN............ Dunford BAE [*British ICAO designator*] (FAAC)
DUN............ Dunnage
Dun & Cum... Dunphy and Cummins' Remarkable Trials [*A publication*] (DLA)
DUNB......... Dunbartonshire [*County in Scotland*]
DUNBL........ Dunblane (ROG)
DunBrd .... Dun & Bradstreet [*Associated Press*] (SAG)
DUNC.......... Deep Underwater Nuclear Counting
Dunc Eccl L... Duncan's Scotch Parochial Ecclesiastical Law [*A publication*] (DLA)
Dunc Ent Cas... Duncan's Scotch Entail Cases [*A publication*] (DLA)
Dunc Ev ..... Duncombe on the Law of Evidence [*A publication*] (DLA)
Dunc Man.... Duncan's Manual of Summary Procedure [*A publication*] (DLA)
Dunc Mer Cas... Duncan's Mercantile Cases [*1885-86*] [*Scotland*] [*A publication*] (DLA)
Dunc Merc Cas... Duncan's Mercantile Cases [*1885-86*] [*Scotland*] [*A publication*] (DLA)
Dunc NP .... Duncombe's Nisi Prius [*A publication*] (DLA)
Dund LC ..... Dundee Law Chronicle [*1853-58*] [*A publication*] (DLA)
DUNELM...... Bishop of Durham [*British*]
DUNELM...... Dunelmensis [*Of Durham*] [*Signature of Bishops of Durham*] [*Latin*] (ROG)
DUNES........ Detecting Ulcers caused by NSAIDS [*Nonsteroidal Anti-Inflammatory Drugs*] Early with Sucrose
DUNF......... Democratic United National Front [*Sri Lanka*] [*Political party*] (ECON)
DUNG......... Dog Unit Negative (DAVI)
Dungl Med Dict... Dunglison. Dictionary of Medical Science and Literature [*A publication*] (DLA)
DUNIS......... Directory of United Nations Information Systems [*Database*] [*Inter-Organisation Board of the United Nations*] [*Information service or system*] (CRD)
DUniv......... Doctor of the University
DUNK......... Dunkeld (ROG)
DUNK......... Dunkeswell [*England*]
Dunl........... Dunlop, Bell, and Murray's Scotch Court of Session Cases, Second Series [*1838-62*] [*A publication*] (DLA)
Dunl Abr ..... Dunlop's Abridgment of Coke's Reports [*A publication*] (DLA)
Dunl Adm Pr... Dunlop's Admiralty Practice [*A publication*] (DLA)
Dun L & T ... Dun's Landlord and Tenant in Ireland [*A publication*] (DLA)
Dunl B & M... Dunlop, Bell, and Murray's Scotch Court of Session Cases, Second Series [*1838-62*] [*A publication*] (DLA)
Dunl (Ct of Sess)... Dunlop, Bell, and Murray's Scotch Court of Session Cases, Second Series [*1838-62*] [*A publication*] (ILCA)
Dunl F .... Dunlap's Forms [*A publication*] (DLA)
Dunl L PA... Dunlop's Laws of Pennsylvania [*A publication*] (DLA)
Dunl L US... Dunlop's Laws of the United States [*A publication*] (DLA)
Dunlop........ Dunlop, Bell, and Murray's Scotch Court of Session Cases, Second Series [*1838-62*] [*A publication*] (DLA)
Dunl Paley Ag... Dunlap's Paley on Agency [*A publication*] (DLA)
Dunl Par...... Dunlop on Parochial Law [*Scotland*] [*A publication*] (DLA)
Dunl Pr........ Dunlop's Admiralty Practice [*A publication*] (DLA)
DUNMIRE .... Dundee University Numerical Method Information Retrieval Experiment [*British*] (NITA)
Dunn........... Dunning's English King's Bench Reports [*1753-54*] [*A publication*] (DLA)
Dunning...... Dunning's English King's Bench Reports [*1753-54*] [*A publication*] (DLA)
DUNS......... Data Universal Numbering System [*Dun's number*] [*Business term*]
DUNS......... Deep Underground Support Center [*Air Force*] (DNAB)
DUNS......... Dun & Bradstreet (AAGC)
DUNST........ Dunstable [*Municipal borough in England*]
DUO........... Datatron Users' Organization
DUO........... DOS [*Disk Operating System*] under OS [*Operating System*]
DUO........... Duetto [*Duet*] [*Music*] (ROG)
DUO........... Duodecimo [*Book up to 20 centimeters in height*]
DUOD......... Duodenum [*Anatomy*]
DUP........... Data User Part [*Integrated Services Digital Network*] [*Telecommunications*] (OSI)
DUP........... Dedicated User Port [*Telecommunications*] (ACRL)
DUP........... Defense Unit Platform
DUP........... Democratic Unification Party [*South Korea Political party*] (PPW)
DUP........... Democratic Unionist Party [*Sudan*] [*Political party*] (PD)
DUP........... Democratic Unionist Party [*Northern Ireland*] [*Political party*]
DUP........... Diploma of the University of Paris
DUP........... Disk Utility Program [*IBM Corp.*] [*Computer science*]
DUP........... Distinguished University Professor
DUP........... Diundecyl Phthalate [*Organic chemistry*]
DUP........... Docteur de l'Universite de Paris [*Doctor of the University of Paris*] [*French*] (BARN)
DUP........... Duplex [*Watchmaking*] (ROG)
DUP........... Duplicate (AFM)
dup........... Duplicate (VRA)
dup........... Duplicate (WDMC)
DUP........... Duplication
DUP........... Dupont Canada, Inc. [*Toronto Stock Exchange symbol*]
DUP........... Du Pont Canada, Inc. [*Toronto Stock Exchange symbol*]
DUP........... E. I. DuPont de Nemours & Co., Lavoisier Library, Wilmington, DE [*OCLC symbol*] (OCLC)
DUP........... National Society, Daughters of Utah Pioneers (EA)

DUP........... Ulster Democratic Unionist Party [*Northern Ireland*] [*Political party*] (PPW)
DUPAC........ Duke University Preventive Approach to Cardiovascular Disease
DUPC......... Displayed under Program Control
Dup Const... Duponceau on the Constitution [*A publication*] (DLA)
DUPE......... Duplicate (AABC)
DUP-FIL...... Duplicate Filing [*IRS*]
DUPI......... Defense Unit Platform Interceptor [*Strategic Defense Initiative*]
Dup Jur...... Duponceau on Jurisdiction of United States Courts [*A publication*] (DLA)
dupl.......... Duplicate (BJA)
Duplex........ Duplex Products, Inc. [*Associated Press*] (SAG)
DUPLX........ Duplex (NASA)
DUPLXR....... Duplexer (NASA)
DUPNG........ Duplicating
DuPnt........ DuPont [*E. I.*] de Nemours [*Associated Press*] (SAG)
Duponceau US Cts... Duponceau on Jurisdiction of United States Courts [*A publication*] (DLA)
DuPont....... DuPont [*E. I.*] de Nemours [*Associated Press*] (SAG)
DuPontP...... DuPont Photomasks, Inc. [*Associated Press*] (SAG)
DUPPA........ Dual Path Protection Arrangement [*AT & T*]
DUPS......... Defense Unit Platform Subsystem [*Strategic Defense Initiative*]
DUQ........... Duncan/Quamichan Lake [*Canada*] [*Airport symbol Obsolete*] (OAG)
Duq........... Duquesne Light Co. [*Associated Press*] (SAG)
DUQ........... Duquesne University Library, Pittsburgh, PA [*OCLC symbol*] (OCLC)
DuqCap....... Duquesne Capital [*Associated Press*] (SAG)
Duquesne U... Duquesne University (GAGS)
DUR........... Drug Usage Review (MEDA)
DUR........... Drug Utilization Review [*Medicine*]
DUR........... Duracell International [*NYSE symbol*] (SPSG)
DUR........... Duracell Intl. [*NYSE symbol*] (TTSB)
DUR........... Duration
DUR........... Durban [*South Africa*] [*Airport symbol*] (OAG)
DUR........... Durham [*England*] [*Seismograph station code, US Geological Survey*] (SEIS)
DUR........... Durham [*City and county in England*]
DUR........... Durham Resources, Inc. [*Toronto Stock Exchange symbol*]
DUR........... During
Dur........... Durium [*Record label*] [*Italy*]
DUR........... Durus [*Hard*] [*Pharmacy*]
DURA......... Durability (MCD)
DURA......... Dura Pharmaceuticals [*NASDAQ symbol*] (TTSB)
DURA......... Dura Pharmaceuticals, Inc. [*NASDAQ symbol*] (SAG)
Duracel....... Duracell International [*Associated Press*] (SAG)
Duracrft...... Duracraft Co. [*Associated Press*] (SAG)
Duramed...... Duramed Pharmaceuticals, Inc. [*Associated Press*] (SAG)
DuraPh .... Dura Pharmaceuticals, Inc. [*Associated Press*] (SAG)
Durb ADR ... Durban Roodepoort Deep Ltd. [*Associated Press*] (SAG)
DURC......... During Climb [*Aviation*] (FAAC)
DURD......... During Descent [*Aviation*] (FAAC)
DUR DOL..... Durante Dolore [*While Pain Lasts*] [*Pharmacy*]
DUR DOLOR... Durante Dolore [*While Pain Lasts*] [*Pharmacy*]
Dur Dr Fr..... Duranton's Droit Francais [*A publication*] (DLA)
DURELAS.... Duty as His Relief [*Military*] (DNAB)
Durf.......... Durfee's Reports [*2 Rhode Island*] [*A publication*] (DLA)
Durfee........ Durfee's Reports [*2 Rhode Island*] [*A publication*] (DLA)
DURG......... During (FAAC)
DURH......... Durham [*City and county in England*]
DURH LI ..... Durham Light Infantry [*Military unit*] [*British*] (ROG)
DURI......... Duriron Co. [*NASDAQ symbol*] (SAG)
DUrl.......... Urban Institute, Washington, DC [*Library symbol Library of Congress*] (LCLS)
Durie .... Durie's Scotch Court of Session Decisions [*1621-42*] [*A publication*] (DLA)
Duriron....... Duriron Co. [*Associated Press*] (SAG)
Durkn........ Durakon Industries, Inc. [*Associated Press*] (SAG)
DURN......... Duration (FAAC)
Durn & E .... Durnford and East's (Term) Reports [*1785-1800*] [*England*] [*A publication*] (DLA)
DURS......... Dockside Underway Replenishment Simulator [*Navy*] (DNAB)
DURS......... Dursley [*England*]
DUS........... Data Utilization Station
DUS........... Diagnostic Utility System
DUS........... Diploma of the University of Southampton [*British*]
DUS........... Dockside Underway Replenishment Simulator [*Navy*] (NVT)
DUS........... Dollar Unit Sampling (ADA)
DUS........... Doppler Ultrasound Stethoscope (MEDA)
DUS........... Driver Units Speaker
DUS........... Dusheti [*Former USSR Seismograph station code, US Geological Survey*] (SEIS)
DUS........... Dusseldorf [*Germany Airport symbol*] (OAG)
DUS........... Dusty Mac Mines Ltd. [*Vancouver Stock Exchange symbol*]
DUS........... Marshfield, WI [*Location identifier FAA*] (FAAL)
DUSA......... Deputy Under Secretary of the Army (AABC)
DUSA......... DUSA Pharmaceuticals [*NASDAQ symbol*] (TTSB)
DUSA......... DUSA Pharmaceuticals, Inc. [*Associated Press*] (SAG)
DUSA......... DUSA Pharmaceuticals, Inc. [*NASDAQ symbol*] (SAG)
DUSAA........ Davison United States Army Airfield (AABC)
DUSAM........ Dummy Surface-to-Air Missile
DUSB......... United States Brewers Association, Washington, DC [*Library symbol Library of Congress*] (LCLS)
DUSC......... Deep Underground Support Center [*Air Force*]
DUSC......... Drug Utilisation Sub-Committee [*Australia*]
DUSC......... United States Supreme Court, Washington, DC [*Library symbol Library of Congress*] (LCLS)

DUSD.......... Data Services Division [*Census*] (OICC)
DUSD.......... Deputy Under Secretary of Defense (RDA)
DUSD (A)..... Deputy Under-Secretary of Defense (Acquisitions) (AAGC)
DUSD(AP).... Deputy Under-Secretary of Defense (Acquisition Policy) (DNAB)
DUSD(AT).... Deputy Under Secretary of Defense (for Advanced Technology) (RDA)
DUSD(C₃I).... Deputy Under-Secretary of Defense (Communications, Command, Control, and Intelligence) (DNAB)
DUSDP........ Deputy Under Secretary of Defense for Policy
DUSD (P).... Deputy Under Secretary of Defense-Policy (AAGC)
DUSD(PR).... Deputy Under-Secretary of Defense (Policy Review) (DNAB)
DUSDRE(C³I)... Deputy Under Secretary of Defense for Research and Engineering (Communications, Command, Control, and Intelligence) [*Military*]
DUSDRE (T & E)... Deputy Under Secretary of Defense for Research and Engineering (Test and Evaluation) [*Military*]
DUSD (T&E)... Deputy Under Secretary of Defense-Test and Evaluation (AAGC)
DUSFC........ Deputy Undersecretary for Field Coordination [*HUD*]
DUSIGN .... To Duty Assigned By [*Military*]
DUSN.......... Deputy Under-Secretary of the Navy (DNAB)
DUSN.......... Diffuse Unilateral Subacute Neuroretinitis [*Ophthalmology*]
DUSNWS .... Director, United States Naval Weather Service
DUSO.......... Developing Understanding of Self and Others [*Educational tool*]
DUSODA ...... For Duty or Such Other Duty as [*Command or Activity Indicated*] May Assign [*Military*]
DUSOI......... Duke Severity of Illness [*Checklist*]
DUSS .... Deep Underground Sanguine System [*Navy*] (MCD)
DUSTA........ Duty Station [*Navy*]
DustyM........ Dusty Mac Oil & Gas Ltd. [*Associated Press*] (SAG)
DUSW.......... Director of Undersea Warfare, Ministry of Defence, London (NATG)
DUT .... Deutsche Umsiedlungstreuhandgesellschaft [*A publication*] (BJA)
DUT .... Device under Test
DUT .... Diode Under Test (IAA)
DUT .... Drainage Unions and Trusts [*Australia*]
DUT .... Duplication Technician, Photolithography [*Navy rating*]
DUT .... Dutch
dut............. Dutch [*MARC language code Library of Congress*] (LCCP)
DUT .... Dutch Harbor [*Alaska*] [*Airport symbol*] (OAG)
DUTA .... Display Unit Test Assembly (MCD)
D Utah .... United States District Court for the District of Utah (DLA)
Dut & Cowd Rev... Dutton and Cowdrey's Revision of Swift's Digest of Connecticut Laws [*A publication*] (DLA)
DUTC .... Dallas Union Terminal [*AAR code*]
Dutch .... Dutcher's Law Reports [*25-29 New Jersey*] [*A publication*] (DLA)
DUTE .... Digital Universal Test Equipment (MCD)
DUTN.......... Duotone (VRA)
dUTP......... Deoxyuridine Triphosphate [*Biochemistry*]
DUTPase...... Deoxyiauridine Triphosphatase [*An enzyme*]
DUTS .... Decision Unit Tracking System [*Nuclear energy*] (NRCH)
DutyF.......... Duty Free International, Inc. [*Associated Press*] (SAG)
DUV .... Data Under Voice [*Bell System*]
DUV .... Daughters of Union Veterans of the Civil War, 1861-1865 (EA)
DUV .... Deep Ultraviolet [*Lithography*]
DUV .... Dispersive Ultraviolet [*Automotive engineering*]
Duv............ Duvall's Canada Supreme Court Reports [*A publication*] (DLA)
Duv............ Duvall's Reports [*62, 63 Kentucky*] [*A publication*] (DLA)
Duval.......... Duvall's Canada Supreme Court Reports [*A publication*] (DLA)
Duvall......... Duvall's Canada Supreme Court Reports [*A publication*] (DLA)
DUVAS......... Derivative Ultraviolet Absorption Spectrometer [*Instrumentation*]
Duv (Can).... Duvall's Canada Supreme Court Reports [*A publication*] (DLA)
DUVD......... Direct Ultrasonic Visualization of Defects (PDAA)
DUW .... Director of Underwater Weapons [*British*]
DUWCAL...... Duluth Weapons Calibration System
DUWP......... Director of Underwater Weapons Projects [*Navy British*]
DUX .... Data Utility Complex (IAA)
DUX .... Dumas, TX [*Location identifier FAA*] (FAAL)
Dux........... Duxbury's High Court Reports [*South African Republic*] [*1895*] [*A publication*] (DLA)
DV.............. Daily Value [*Nutrition*]
DV.............. Damage and Vulnerability (MCD)
DV.............. Data Vetting
DV.............. Death Valley Resources [*Vancouver Stock Exchange symbol*]
D/V............ Declared Value (WDAA)
DV.............. Defective Vision (ADA)
DV.............. Dei Verbum [*Dogmatic Constitution on Divine Revelation*] [*Vatican II document*]
DV.............. Delta Velocity (KSC)
DV.............. Demand Valve
DV.............. Demonstration and Validation (MCD)
DV.............. Deo Volente [*God Willing*] [*Latin*]
DV.............. Depended Variable (IAA)
DV.............. Dependent Variable (AAMN)
DV.............. Dependent Vehicle
DV.............. Designee for Verification [*NASA*] (NASA)
DV.............. Device
DV.............. DeVry, Inc. [*NYSE symbol*] (SAG)
DV.............. Diana Vreeland [*Fashion editor, 1903-1989*]
DV.............. Dianhydrogalactitol and VP-16 [*Antineoplastic drug regimen*] (DAVI)
dv.............. Differential of Velocity (IDOE)
DV.............. Differential Velocity (KSC)
DV.............. Differential Velocity (IEEE)
DV.............. Different Version
D/V............ Diffusion per Unit Volume [*Measurement*] (DAVI)
DV.............. Digital Video
DV.............. Digital Voice (MCD)
DV.............. Dilute Volume [*Chemistry*]

DV.............. Diploma in Venereology (ADA)
DV.............. Directed Verdict [*Legal term*]
DV.............. DirectVision [*Home-information service of KPIX-TV*]
DV.............. Direct Vision [*Aviation*]
DV.............. Direct Voice (NTCM)
DV.............. Direct Voltage (IAA)
DV.............. Disbursement Voucher (AFM)
DV.............. Disease Variable [*Medicine*]
DV.............. Distemper Virus
DV.............. Distinguished Visitor
DV.............. Distressed Vehicle (KSC)
DV.............. Diverter Valve (KSC)
DV.............. Divide
DV.............. Divide
DV.............. Divinitas (BJA)
DV.............. Division [*Mathematics*] (ROG)
DV.............. Division Flag [*Navy British*]
DV.............. Division of Validation [*Social Security Administration*]
DV.............. Division Piece [*Rotary piston meter*]
DV.............. Divisionsverfuegung [*or Divisionsverordnung*] [*Divisional Order*] [*German military - World War II*]
DV.............. Divisor [*Mathematics*] (IAA)
DV.............. Divorce [*Facetious translation of DV, Deo Volente (God Willing)*] (DSUE)
DV.............. Divorced
DV.............. Domiciliary Visit [*Medicine*]
DV.............. Dorsoventral [*Anatomy*]
DV.............. Douay Version [*Bible*]
DV.............. Double Valve [*Stutz car model designation*]
DV.............. Double Vibrations [*Cycles*]
DV.............. Double Vision
DV.............. Doubtful-Very [*Theatrical term*] [*Facetious translation of DV, Deo Volente (God Willing)*] (DSUE)
DV.............. Drift Voltage
DV.............. Dual Valve
DV.............. Dump Valve (IEEE)
DV.............. Durchgangsvermittlung [*Long-distance telephone exchange*] [*German military - World War II*]
DV.............. Dutch RCA [*Victor*] [*Record label*]
DV.............. Nantucket Airlines [*ICAO designator*] (AD)
DVA.......... Adams County School District No. 12, Northglenn, CO [*OCLC symbol*] (OCLC)
DVA.......... Department of Veterans Affairs [*Formerly, Veterans Administration*]
DVA.......... Department of Veterans Affairs [*Canada*]
DVA.......... Designed, Verified, and Assigned Date [*Telecommunications*] (TEL)
DVA.......... Deutsche Verlags-Anstalt [*Publishing company*]
DVA.......... Differential Voltage Amplifier
D/Vₐ......... Diffusion per Unit of Alveolar Volume [*Medicine*] (DAVI)
DVA.......... Diminished Visual Acuity
DVA.......... Diploma in Veterinary Anaesthesia [*British*]
DVA.......... Directory of Visual Arts Organizations [*Arts Midwest*] [*Information service or system*] (CRD)
DVA.......... Discovery Airways [*ICAO designator*] (FAAC)
DVA.......... Discovery Value Accounting (ADA)
DVA.......... Disco Vision Associates [*Videodisc manufacturer*] (NITA)
DVA.......... Distance Visual Acuity [*Ophthalmology*]
DVA.......... Diverse Vector Area [*FAA*] (TAG)
DVA.......... Divinylacetylene [*Organic chemistry*]
DVA.......... Doctor of Visual Aids (NADA)
DVA.......... Document Validation Audit [*NASA*] (MCD)
DVA.......... Dunkirk Veterans Association [*Leeds, England*] (EAIO)
DVA.......... Duration of Voluntary Apnea [*Physiology*]
DVA.......... Dynamic Visual Acuity (IEEE)
DVA.......... United States Veterans Administration, Washington, DC [*Library symbol Library of Congress*] (LCLS)
DVAB.......... Defense Vocational Aptitude Battery [*Military*] (NVT)
DVAC.......... Distributor Vacuum Advance Control [*Automotive engineering*]
DVAD.......... Dollar Value of Annual Demands (AFIT)
DVAL.......... Data Link Vulnerability Analysis [*DoD*] (RDA)
DVAL.......... Demonstration and Validation (MCD)
DV & D........ Diploma in Venereology and Dermatology (ADA)
DVAR.......... Data Value-Added Reseller
DVARS......... Doppler Velocity Altimeter RADAR Set [*Military*] (CAAL)
DVAV.......... Dorsoventral Abdominal Vibration [*Entomology*]
DVB .... Department of Veterans Benefits [*Veterans Administration*]
DVB .... Device Base Control Block [*Computer science*] (IBMDP)
DVB .... Diamminedichloroplatinum [*Cisplatin*], Vindesine, Bleomycin [*Antineoplastic drug regimen*]
DVB .... Digital Video Bandwidth
DVB .... Disability Veiling Brightness [*Optics*] (IAA)
DVB .... Divinylbenzene [*Organic chemistry*]
DVB .... Volta Bureau for the Deaf, Washington, DC [*Library symbol Library of Congress*] (LCLS)
DVBD.......... Diesel V-Belt Drive
DVC .... Community College of Denver, North Campus, Westminster, CO [*OCLC symbol*] (OCLC)
DVC .... Device (MSA)
DVC .... Device
DVC .... Digital Valve Controller (ACII)
DVC .... Digital Video Cassette (DOM)
DVC .... Digital Video Communication [*Military*] (CAAL)
DVC .... Digital Video Compression
DVC .... Digital Voice Communications
DVC .... Digital Voice Controller (MCD)
DVC .... Direct Variable Cost

DVC	Direct View Console (MCD)
DVC	Divanillylidenecyclohexanone [*or Divanillalcyclohexanone*] [*Pharmacology*]
DVC	Dove Creek, CO [*Location identifier FAA*] (FAAL)
DVC	Dynamic Visual Camouflage [*Army*] (INF)
DVCCS	Differential Voltage-Controlled Current Source (IEEE)
DVCMF	Doxorubicin [*Adriamycin*], Vincristine, Cyclophosphamide, Methotrexate, Fluorouracil [*Antineoplastic drug regimen*]
DVCO	DavCo Restaurants [*NASDAQ symbol*] (TTSB)
DVCO	Davco Restaurants, Inc. [*NASDAQ symbol*] (SAG)
DVCR	Digital Videocassette Recorder (CDE)
DVCS	Data/Voice Communications System (SSD)
DVCS	Devices
DVCS	Digital Voice Communications System (MCD)
DVCS	Domestic Violence Crisis Service [*Australian Capital Territory*] [*Australia*]
D/VD	Data/Voice Data (MCD)
DVD	Delta Velocity Display
DVD	Design Verification Demonstration
DVD	Detail Velocity Display (IEEE)
DVD	Deutsche Vereinigung fuer Datenschutz [*German Data Protection Organization*]
DVD	Digital Versatile Disc [*Computer science*]
DVD	Digital Versatile Disc
DVD	Digital Versatile Disk
DVD	Digital Versatile Disk (PCM)
DVD	Digital Versatile Disk (PCM)
DVD	Digital Videodisc (CDE)
DVD	Digital Videodisk
DVD	Digital Video Disk
DVD	Diploma in Venereology and Dermatology
DVD	Direct Vendor Delivery [*DoD*]
DVD	Direct-View Device [*Night vision*]
DVD	Dissociated Vertical Deviation [*Ophthalmology*]
DVD	Dissociated Vertical Divergence [*Ophthalmology*] (DAVI)
DVD	Divide [*Commonly used*] (OPSA)
DVD	Dover Downs Entertainment, Inc. [*NYSE symbol*] (SAG)
DVD	Thurmont, MD [*Location identifier FAA*] (FAAL)
DVDALV	Double Vessel Disease with an Abnormal Left Ventricle [*Cardiology*]
DVDC	Divisional Vendor Data Coordinator (MCD)
DVDP	Dry Valley Drilling Project [*National Science Foundation*]
DVDR	Direct-View Diagnostic Region
DVDS	Digital Video Display System
DVDV	Differential Vacuum Delay Valve [*Automotive engineering*]
DVDY	Diving Duty [*Military*]
DVE	Community College of Denver, North AEC Project, Westminster, CO [*OCLC symbol*] (OCLC)
DVE	Devnic Energy, Inc. [*Toronto Stock Exchange symbol*]
DVE	Differential Vector Equation
DVE	Digital Video Effect [*Video technology*] (PCM)
DVE	Division of Vocational Education [*Department of Education*] (GFGA)
Dve	Drive
DVE	Driver's Vision Enhancer
DVE	Driver's Vision Enhancer [*Military*]
DVE	Duck Virus Enteritis
DVECC	Disease Vector Ecology and Control Center [*Military*] (NVT)
DV Ed	Doctor of Vocational Education
DVEG	Derwent Valley Environment Group [*Australia*]
DVEO	Defense Value Engineering Services Officer
DVESO	DoD [*Department of Defense*] Value Engineering Services Office (IEEE)
D Vet Med ...	Doctor of Veterinary Medicine
DVetSc	Doctor of Veterinary Science (ADA)
DVF	Diane Von Furstenberg [*Couturiere*]
DVF	Dried Vine Fruit
DVF	Dualbowl Vibratory Feeder
DVF	Society of the Descendants of Washington's Army at Valley Forge (EA)
DVFC	Danny Vann Fan Club (EA)
DVFD	Direct View Filament Display (MCD)
DVFE	Director, Vehicle and Field Engineering [*Canada*] [*Military*]
DVFO	Digital Variable-Frequency Oscillator (IEEE)
DVFR	Day Visual Flight Rules [*FAA*] (TAG)
DVFR	Defense Visual Flight Rules
DVG	Digital Video Generator [*Computer science*]
DVH	Dental, Visual, and Hearing Insurance
DVH	Diploma in Veterinary Hygiene [*British*]
DVH	Divide or Halt (IAA)
DVH	Division for the Visually Handicapped (EA)
D-VHS	Data-VHS (CDE)
DVI	Device-Independent Format [*Computer science*]
DVI	Digital Vascular Imaging [*Roentgenology*]
DVI	Digital Video Imaging (CPH)
DVI	Digital Video Interactive [*CD-ROM technology*] [*General Electric Co.*]
DVI	Digital Video Interactive (CDE)
DVI	Direct Voice Input (DA)
DVI	Dover Industries Ltd. [*Toronto Stock Exchange symbol*]
DVI	Dust Veil Index [*of atmosphere*]
DVI	DVI Corp. [*NYSE symbol*] (SPSG)
DVI	DVI, Inc. [*Associated Press*] (SAG)
DVI	Information Management Specialists, Denver, CO [*OCLC symbol*] (OCLC)
D VI	United States District Court for the District of the Virgin Islands (DLA)
DVIC	DVI, Inc. [*NASDAQ symbol*] (SAG)
DVID	Digital Video Systems [*NASDAQ symbol*] (TTSB)

DVID	Digital Video Systems, Inc. [*NASDAQ symbol*] (SAG)
DVIDU	Digital Video Sys Unit [*NASDAQ symbol*] (TTSB)
DVIDW	Digital Video Sys Wrrt'A' [*NASDAQ symbol*] (TTSB)
DVIDZ	Digital Video Sys Wrrt'B' [*NASDAQ symbol*] (TTSB)
DVI Inc	DVI, Inc. [*Associated Press*] (SAG)
DVIP	Digital Video Integrator and Processor (MCD)
DVIR	Driver Vehicle Inspection Report [*FHWA*] (TAG)
DVIS	Digital Vascular Imaging System [*Roentgenology*] (MCD)
DVITS	Digital Video Imagery Transmission System (DOMA)
DVIU	Direct Vision Internal Urethrotomy [*Medicine*] (MAE)
DVJ	Colorado Supreme Court Library, Denver, CO [*OCLC symbol*] (OCLC)
DVJB	Danmarks Veterinaer- og Jordbrugsbase [*Danish Veterinary and Agricultural Library Catalogue*] [*Information service or system*]
DVK	Danville, KY [*Location identifier FAA*] (FAAL)
DVK	Davis-Keays Mining [*Vancouver Stock Exchange symbol*]
DVL	Delta Velocity Launch
DVL	Develop (MSA)
DVL	Devils Lake [*North Dakota*] [*Airport symbol*] (OAG)
DVL	Direct Voice Line (CET)
DVL	Distance Velocity Laboratory
DVL	Dorsal Velar Lobe
DVLA	Driver and Vehicle Licensing Agency [*Formerly, Driver and Vehicle Licensing Centre*] [*British*] (ECON)
DVLBI	Differential Very Long Baseline Interferometry (MCD)
DVLC	Driver and Vehicle Licensing Centre [*British*] (DCTA)
DVLG	DeVlieg Bullard, Inc. [*NASDAQ symbol*] (SAG)
DVLG	DeVlieg Bullard, Inc. [*NASDAQ symbol*] (SAG)
DVLP	Daunomycin, Vincristine, L-Asparaginase, Prednisone [*Antineoplastic drug regimen*] (DAVI)
DVLP	Development
Dvlpmt	Development
DVLPR	Developer
DVM	Data over Voice Multiplexer [*Telecommunications*] (ACRL)
DVM	Decessit Vita Matris [*Died during the Lifetime of the Mother*] [*Latin*]
DVM	Diel Vertical Migration [*Zooplankton*]
DVM	Digital Velocity Meter
DVM	Digital Voltmeter
dvm	Digital Voltmeter (IDOE)
DVM	Directional Variable Microphone
DVM	Discontinuous Variational Method
DVM	Discrete Variation Method
DVM	Displaced Virtual Machine
DVM	Distributed Virtual Memory [*Computer science*]
DVM	Doctor of Veterinary Medicine
DVM	Double Vacuum Melting (PDAA)
DVM	Doxurubicin [*Adriamycin*], Vincristine, Methotrexate [*Antineoplastic drug regimen*]
DVMA	Direct Virtual Memory Access [*Computer science*]
DVMD	Digital Volt-Ohmmeter Display (IAA)
DVME	Dulbecco-Vogt Modified Eagle's [*Medium for cell growth*]
DVMR	Division of Veterinary Medical Research [*Department of Health and Human Services*] (GRD)
DVMS	Doctor of Veterinary Medicine and Science (NADA)
DVMS	Doctor of Veterinary Medicine and Surgery
DVMT	Daily Vehilce-Miles of Travel [*FHWA*] (TAG)
DVN	Community College of Denver, North Campus, Westminster, CO [*OCLC symbol*] (OCLC)
DVN	Davenport, IA [*Location identifier FAA*] (FAAL)
DVN	Devisavit Vel Non [*Issue of fact as to whether a will in question was made by the testator*] [*Latin Legal term*] (DLA)
DVN	Devon Energy [*AMEX symbol*] (TTSB)
DVN	Devon Energy Corp. [*AMEX symbol*] (CTT)
DVN	Devonion Resources [*Vancouver Stock Exchange symbol*]
DVNA	Direct-View Navigation Aid
DVNG	Diving
DVNG DY	Diving Duty [*Military*] (DNAB)
DVNV	Dendrobium Vein Necrosis Virus [*Plant pathology*]
DVO	Davao [*Philippines*] [*Airport symbol*] (OAG)
DVO	Davenport Industries Ltd. [*Vancouver Stock Exchange symbol*]
DVO	Decimal Voltage Output
DVO	Delta Velocity On/Off
DVO	Direct View Optics
DVO	Divisional Veterinary Officer [*Ministry of Agriculture, Fisheries, and Food*] [*British*]
DVO	Durchfuehrungsverordnung [*Executive Decree*] [*German*] (ILCA)
D-VOF	Defense Mapping Agency Vertical Obstruction File (DNAB)
DVOM	Digital Video Optic MODEM [*Modulate/Demodulate*] (DWSG)
DVOM	Digital Volt-Ohmmeter
DVOM	Digital Volt Ohm Milliammeter (IDOE)
dvom	Digital Volt Ohm Milliammeter (IDOE)
DVOP	Disabled Veterans Outreach Program [*Department of Labor*]
DVOPS	Disabled Veterans Outreach Program Specialist [*Veterans Administration*]
DVOR	Doppler Very High Frequency Omnidirectional Range [*FAA*] (TAG)
DVOR	Doppler VHF [*Very High Frequency*] Omnirange
DVOSI	Divinyloxydimethylsilane [*Organic chemistry*]
DVOT	Dog Vomit on Toast [*Creamed beef or tuna on toast*] [*Military slang*]
DVP	Data Validation Program [*NASA*]
DVP	Daunorubicin, Vincristine, Prednisone [*Antineoplastic drug*] (CDI)
DVP	Davenport Downs [*Queensland*] [*Airport symbol*] (AD)
DVP	Decessit Vita Patris [*Died during the Lifetime of the Father*] [*Latin*]
DVP	Delivery Versus Payment
DVP	Delta Velocity Planet

DVP	Demokratische Volkspartei [*Democratic People's Party*] [*Germany*] (PPE)
DVP	Dense Vortex Plasma
DVP	Design Verification Period (MCD)
DVP	Design Verification Program [*or Plan*] (MCD)
DVP	Deutsche Volkspartei [*German People's Party (1919-1933)*] (PPE)
DVP	Devran Petroleum Ltd. [*Vancouver Stock Exchange symbol*]
DVP	Differential Value Profile [*Psychology*]
DVP	Digital Video Producer [*Asymetrix Co.*] (PCM)
DVP	Digital Voice Privacy [*Telecommunications*]
DVP	Distinguished Visitor Program [*Army*]
DVP	Divide or Proceed (IAA)
DVP	Domestic Violence Project (EA)
DVP	University of Denver, Denver, CO [*OCLC symbol*] (OCLC)
DVPDF	Dry Vacuum Pump Discharge Filter
DVPF	Dry Vacuum Pump Filter
DVPH	Diploma in Veterinary Public Health (ADA)
DVPL-ASP	Daunorubicin, Vincristine, Prednisone, L-Asparaginase [*Antineoplastic drug regimen*]
DVPMP	Deutsche Vereinigung gegen Politischen Missbrauch der Psychiatrie [*Germany*]
DVPPI	Daylight View Plan Position Indicator (CET)
DVPR	Design Verification Plan and Report
DVQ	Distinguished Visitor Quarters [*Military*] (DOMA)
DVR	Community College of Denver, Red Rocks Campus, Golden, CO [*OCLC symbol*] (OCLC)
DVR	Department [*or Division*] of Vocational Rehabilitation [*Later, DTVE*] [*Department of Education*] (OICC)
DVR	Derotational Varus Osteotomy [*Orthopedics*] (DAVI)
DVR	Design and Verification Routine [*Sperry Univac*] (NITA)
DVR	Design Verification Rig (MCD)
DVR	Devco Railway [*Cape Breton Development Corp. - Coal Div.*] [*AAR code*]
DVR	Digital Video Recording (NTCM)
DVR	Diver (MSA)
DVR	Doctor in Veterinary Radiology
DVR	Document Validation Report
DVR	Double Valve Replacement [*Medicine*]
DVR	Driver (AABC)
DVR	Lebanon, NH [*Location identifier FAA*] (FAAL)
DVR	Van Riebeeck Decoration [*British military*] (DMA)
DVRABAD	Driver Badge, Amphibious Vehicles [*Military decoration*]
DVRG	Deja Vu Research Group (EAIO)
DVRG	Diverge (FAAC)
DVRI	Direct View RADAR Indicator [*Military*] (CAAL)
DVRMBAD	Driver Badge, Motorcycles [*Military decoration*]
DvrMechBadA	Driver and Mechanic Badge, Amphibious Vehicles [*Military decoration*] (AABC)
DvrMechBadM	Driver and Mechanic Badge, Motorcycles [*Military decoration*] (AABC)
DvrMechBadMech	Driver and Mechanic Badge, Mechanic [*Military decoration*] (AABC)
DvrMechBadOp	Driver and Mechanic Badge, Operator [*Military decoration*] (AABC)
DvrMechBadT	Driver and Mechanic Badge, Tracked Vehicles [*Military decoration*] (AABC)
DvrMechBadW	Driver and Mechanic Badge, Wheeled Vehicles [*Military decoration*] (AABC)
DVRSN	Diversion (FAAC)
DVRTBAD	Driver Badge, Tracked Vehicles [*Military decoration*]
DVRWBAD	Driver Badge, Wheeled Vehicles [*Military decoration*]
DVS	Davis [*Australia Geomagnetic observatory code*]
DVS	Delta Valley & Southern Railway Co. [*AAR code*]
DVS	Denver Special Librarians, Denver, CO [*OCLC symbol*] (OCLC)
DVS	Descriptive Video Services [*for the sight-impaired*] [*Public Broadcasting Service*]
DVS	Design Verification Specification (NASA)
DVS	devise [*Legal shorthand*] (LWAP)
DVS	Digital Voice System (MCD)
DVS	Digital Voltage Source
DVS	Director of Veterinary Services [*Military British*]
DVS	Division of Vital Statistics [*Department of Health and Human Services*] (DAVI)
DVS	Doctor of Veterinary Science
DVS	Doctor of Veterinary Surgery
DVS	Doppler Velocity Sensor
DVS	Dynamic Vacuum Seal
DVS	Dynamic Vertical Sensor (IAA)
DVSA	Dierkundige Vereniging van Suidelike Afrika [*Zoological Society of Southern Africa - ZSSA*] (EAIO)
DV Sc	Doctor of Veterinary Science
DVSC	Doctor of Veterinary Surgery
DV Sci	Doctor of Veterinary Science
DVSFD	Diversified
DVSI	Digital Vibration Survey Instrument
DVSM	Diploma in Veterinary State Medicine
DVST	Direct-View Storage Tube [*Princeton Electronic Products*]
DVSWS	UROHEALTH Sys Wrrt [*AMEX symbol*] (TTSB)
DVT	Davic Enterprise, Inc. [*Vancouver Stock Exchange symbol*]
DVT	Deep Venous [*or Vein*] Thrombosis [*Medicine*]
DVT	Design Verification Test
DVT	Development Verification Testing (RDA)
DVT	Digital Video Terminal [*Telecommunications*] (ACRL)
DVT	Dynamic Velocity Taper (PDAA)
DVT	Phoenix, AZ [*Location identifier FAA*] (FAAL)

D VT	United States District Court for the District of Vermont (DLA)
DVTE	Division of Vocational and Technical Education [*Formerly, DVR*] [*Office of Education*]
DVTL	Dovetail (MSA)
DVTMDS	(Divinyl)tetramethyldisilazane [*Organic chemistry*]
DVTP	Divide Time Pulse (IAA)
DVTR	Digital Video Tape Recorder (NITA)
DVTVM	Digital Vacuum-Tube Voltmeter (IAA)
DVTW	Delay Valve Two-Way [*Automotive engineering*]
DVU	Delta Velocity Ullage
DVU	Deutsche Volksunion [*German People's Union*] [*Political party*] (PD)
DVU	Orbi [*Former USSR ICAO designator*] (FAAC)
DVV	Downward Vertical Velocity [*NWS*] (FAAC)
DVVV	Distributor Vacuum Vent Valve [*Automotive engineering*]
DVW	Davenport [*Washington*] [*Seismograph station code, US Geological Survey*] (SEIS)
DVX	Daphne Virus X [*Plant pathology*]
DVX	Data Voice Exchange (MCD)
DVX	Denver Area Project, Denver, CO [*OCLC symbol*] (OCLC)
DVX	Digital Voice Exchange [*Telecommunications*] (TEL)
DVXI	Direct Vision Times One [*Medicine*] (DAVI)
DVZ	Arapahoe Community College, Littleton, CO [*OCLC symbol*] (OCLC)
DVZ	Mocksville, NC [*Location identifier FAA*] (FAAL)
DVZ	Association of Drinkwatchers International [*Defunct*] (EA)
DW	Daily Wear Contact Lenses
DW	Daisy Wheel [*Printer*]
DW	Damage Waiver [*Insurance*]
DW	Dangerous Weapon
DW	Darrell Waltrip [*Race car driver*]
DW	Data Word (NASA)
DW	Data Word Buffer [*Computer science*] (MDG)
DW	Daughters of Wisdom [*Montfort Sisters*] [*Roman Catholic religious order*]
DW	Deadweight
DW	Decentralized Warehouse (AFIT)
DW	Deck Watch [*A small chronometer*] [*Navy*]
DW	Deep Water [*Nautical charts*]
DW	Define Word (PCM)
DW	Deionized Water [*Pharmacology*] (DAVI)
DW	Delayed Weather
DW	Delivered Weight [*Business term*] (ADA)
DW	Demineralized Water (NRCH)
DW	Detroit & Western [*AAR code*]
DW	Deutsche Welle [*Radio network*] [*Germany*]
DW	Developed Width (AAG)
D/W	Dextrose in Water [*Medicine*]
DW	Director of Works [*Air Ministry*] [*British*]
D/W	Direct Writing (MUGU)
DW	Disabled Widow [*or Widower*] [*Social Security Administration*] (OICC)
DW	Disc Width [*Pisciculture*]
DW	Dishwasher [*Classified advertising*]
DW	Dislocated Worker [*Job Training and Partnership Act*] (OICC)
DW	Display Write [*Software*]
DW	Distilled Water
DW	Dividend Warrant (ROG)
DW	DLT Deutsche Regional [*ICAO designator*] (AD)
DW	DLT Luftverkehrsgesellschaft mbH [*Germany ICAO designator*] (ICDA)
DW	Dock Warehouse [*Shipping*] (ROG)
DW	Dock Warrant
DW	Domestic Water (AAG)
DW	Don't Want [*Telecommunications*] (TEL)
DW	Double Wall
DW	Double Weight
DW	Double Word [*Computer science*]
DW	Downy Woodpecker [*Ornithology*]
DW	Drew Industries [*AMEX symbol*] (TTSB)
DW	Drew Industries, Inc. [*AMEX symbol*] (SAG)
DW	Drinking Water (AAG)
DW	Drop and Block Wire [*Telecommunications*] (TEL)
DW	Drop-Weight
DW	Drop Wire
DW	Drum Write [*Computer science*]
DW	Dry Weight
DW	Drywell (NRCH)
DW	Dual Wheels [*Aviation*]
DW	Duke of Wellington's West Riding Regiment [*Military unit*] [*British*]
DW	Dumbwaiter (MSA)
DW	Durbin-Watson [*Procedure*] [*Statistics*]
DW	Dust Wrapper [*Paper cover for a hardbound book*]
dw	Dust Wrapper [*Also, Dust Jacket*] (WDMC)
dw	Dwarf Mouse [*Medicine*] (DMAA)
DW	Sandoz AG [*Switzerland*] [*Research code symbol*]
DWA	Daily Weighted Average [*Data sampling*]
DWA	Damaging Winds Algorithm [*Marine science*] (OSRA)
DWA	Damaging Winds Algorithm (USDC)
DWA	Deadly Weapon Act
DWA	Delaware Division of Libraries, Dover, DE [*OCLC symbol*] (OCLC)
DWA	Died of Wounds Resulting from Action with Enemy [*Military*]
DWA	Digital Watch Association (EA)
DWA	Director of War Archives [*British*]
DWA	Dirty Writers of America [*Satirical*]
DWA	Diwan [*France*] [*FAA designator*] (FAAC)
DWA	Double-Wire Armor
DWA	Drug Wholesalers Association [*Later, NWDA*] (EA)

DWA	Dutch Warmblood Association (EA)
DWAA	Dog Writers' Association of America (EA)
DWAAF	Director of Women's Auxiliary Air Force [*British*]
DWAC	Director, Women's Army Corps (AABC)
DWAC	Distributed Write Address Counter
DW & P	Duluth, Winnipeg & Pacific Railway
Dwango	Dial-Up Wide Area Network Gaming Operation [*Computer science*]
Dwar	Dwarris on Statutes [*A publication*] (DLA)
DWARN	Dakota Women of All Red Nations (EA)
Dwar St	Dwarris on Statutes [*A publication*] (DLA)
DWASP	Defense Warehousing and Shipping Program [*Military*]
DWAT	Deadweight All Told [*Shipping*]
DWAV	Dual Wide Avionics Van (DWSG)
DWAW	Distillery, Wine, and Allied Workers International Union (EA)
DWB	Daily Wireless Bulletin (IAA)
DWB	Designers' Workbench (TEL)
DWB	Disabled Widow [*or Widower*] Benefits [*Social Security Administration*] (OICC)
DWB	Dismissed for Want of Bond [*Legal term*] (DLA)
DWB	Documenter's Workbench [*AT & T*] [*Computer science*]
DWB	Double with Bath [*Hotel room*]
DWB	Dual Walking Beam
DWB	Soalala [*Madagascar*] [*Airport symbol*] (OAG)
DWBA	Direct Wire Burglar Alarm
DWBA	Distorted Wave-Borne Approximation
DWBC	Deep Western Boundary Current [*Oceanography*]
DWBL	Dismounted Warfighting Battle Laboratory (INF)
DWBO	District War Bond Office [*or Officer*] [*Navy*]
DWC	Damaged Weapons Control (DNAB)
DWC	Deadweight Capacity
DWC	Democratic Workers' Congress [*Ceylon*]
DWC	Detroit, MI [*Location identifier FAA*] (FAAL)
DWC	Discolored Wood Columns [*Plant pathology*]
DWC	Dislocated Worker Center [*Job Training and Partnership Act*] (OICC)
DWC	Display and Weapon Control (DNAB)
DWC	Dissolved Water Color [*Environmental chemistry*]
DWC	Morgan Stanley Group, Inc. [*AMEX symbol*] (SAG)
DWCC	Deadweight Cargo Capacity [*Shipping*]
DWCH	Datawatch Corp. [*NASDAQ symbol*] (SAG)
DWCM	Dried Weight of Cell Mass (OA)
DWCOORD(N)	Director of Weapons Coordination (Naval) [*British*]
DWCR	Double Whole-Cell Recording [*Neurophysiology*]
DWCS	Defueling Water Cleanup System (GAAI)
DWD	Dean Witter, Discover & Co. [*NYSE symbol*] (SPSG)
DWD	Deepest Working Depth
DWD	Deep Water Dump
DWD	Died with Disease [*Medicine*]
DWD	Director of Wreck Disposal
DWD	Driving While Drugged
DWD	Driving While Drunk [*Police term*]
DWD	Drum Write Driver [*Computer science*]
DWD	Dumbwaiter Door
DWD	Dynamic Weather Display
DWDI	Draw Die [*Tool*] (AAG)
DWDisc	Dean Witter Discover & Co. [*Associated Press*] (SAG)
DWDL	Diffuse Well-Differentiated Lymphocytic [*Oncology*]
DWDL	Diffuse, Well-Differentiated, Lymphoma [*Oncology*] (DAVI)
DWDL	Donald W. Douglas Laboratory [*McDonnell Douglas Corp.*]
DWDLL	Diffuse, Well-Differentiated, Lymphocytic Lymphoma [*Oncology*] (DAVI)
DWDM	Dense Wave Division Multiplexing [*Lucent*]
DWDsc	Dean Witter Discover & Co. [*Associated Press*] (SAG)
DWE	Delivery with Equipment (MCD)
DWE	Tulsa, OK [*Location identifier FAA*] (FAAL)
DWED	Drywell Equipment Drain (IEEE)
DWEDS	Drywell Equipment Drain Sump (NRCH)
DWEL	Drinking Water Equivalent Level [*Environmental Protection Agency*]
DWEL	Dwelling (MSA)
DWEM	Dead White European Males [*Derogatory appellation for Western culture*]
DWER	Directorate of Weapons and Engineering Research [*Canada*]
DWES	Director of Weapons Equipment, Surface [*British military*] (DMA)
DWEST	Deep Water Environmental Survival Training [*Navy*]
DWET	Directorate of Weapons Effect Tests (MCD)
DWEU	Director of Weapons Equipment, Underwater [*British military*] (DMA)
DWF	Daily Water Flow (IAA)
DWF	Deep Water Fording Kit [*Army*]
DWF	Directional Warhead Fuze
DWF	Divorced White Female [*Classified advertising*]
DWF	Drawing Web Format [*Computer science*] (PCM)
DWF	Dry Weather Flow (IAA)
DWF	Duty Weather Forecaster (SAA)
Dwf	Dwarf [*Horticulture*]
DWFD	Drywell Floor Drain (IEEE)
DWFDS	Drywell Floor Drain Sump (NRCH)
DWFM	Draw Form [*Tool*] (AAG)
DWG	Deadweight Gauge
DWG	Designated Work Group
DWG	Diamond Walnut Growers (EA)
DWG	Digital Waveform Generator (MCD)
DWG	Drawing (AFM)
dwg	Drawing (VRA)
dwg	Drawing (WDMC)
DWG	Dwelling (ADA)
DWGI	Dean Witter Government Income Trust [*Associated Press*] (SAG)

DWH	Diploma in Women's Health
DWH	Houston, TX [*Location identifier FAA*] (FAAL)
DWH	Washington Hall Junior College, Washington, DC [*Library symbol Library of Congress*] (LCLS)
DWHC	Washington Hospital Center, Medical Library, Washington, DC [*Library symbol Library of Congress*] (LCLS)
DWHO	Washington Hospital Center, Medical Library, Washington, DC [*Library symbol Library of Congress*] (LCLS)
DWI	Danish West Indies
DWI	Data Word In (MCD)
DWI	Descriptor Word Index
DWI	Died without Issue (DLA)
DWI	Differential Wave Impedance (DEN)
DWI	Directional Wireless Installation [*British military*] (DMA)
DWI	Drawn and Wall Ironed [*Metal printing*] (DGA)
DWI	Driving While Intoxicated [*Legal term*]
DWI	Durable Woods Institute (EA)
DWI	Durum Wheat Institute [*Later, MNF*] (EA)
DWI	Dutch West Indies
DWI	Washington International College, Washington, DC [*Library symbol Library of Congress*] (LCLS)
DWIA	Distorted Wave Impulse Approximation
DWIC	Disaster Welfare Inquiry Center [*Federal disaster planning*]
DWICA	Deep Water Isotopic Current Analyzer [*TVA*] (MSC)
Dwight	Dwight's Charity Cases [*England*] [*A publication*] (DLA)
DWIM	Division for Women in Medicine [*Defunct*] (EA)
DWIM	Do What I Mean [*Also, DTRT*] [*In data processing context, translates as "Guess at the meaning of poorly worded instructions"*]
DWIMC	Do What I Mean, Correctly [*Computer hacker terminology*] (NHD)
DWIN	Doctor Who Information Network [*Canada*] (EAIO)
DWIND	Do What I Need Done [*Also, DWIM*] [*In data processing context, translates as "Guess at the meaning of poorly worded instructions"*] (PCM)
D-WIP	Defense-Wide Intelligence Plan [*DoD*]
DWIS	Do What I Say [*Computer science*]
DWL	Depressed Water Leg [*Nuclear energy*] (NRCH)
DWL	Derived Working Limit (NUCP)
DWL	Designed Water Line [*Technical drawings*]
DWL	Desired Work Load
DWL	DeWolfe Cos. [*AMEX symbol*] (TTSB)
DWL	[*The*] DeWolfe Cos., Inc. [*AMEX symbol*] (SAG)
DWL	Displacement Water Line
DWL	Dominant Wavelength
DWL	Dowel
DWL	Drywell (NRCH)
dwl	Dwelling (VRA)
DWLFBD	Double-Wall Fiberboard
DWLG	Dwelling (AABC)
DWLLNG	Dwelling
DWM	Dead White Male
DWM	Deputy Worshipful Master [*Freemasonry*] (ROG)
DWM	Destination Warning Marker
DWM	Destination Word Marker (CMD)
DWM	Deutsche Waffen- und Munitionsfabriken [*German Weapons and Munitions Factory*] [*World War II*]
DWM	Directory of Women's Media [*A publication*]
DWM	Divine Word Missionaries [*See also SVD*] [*Italy*] (EAIO)
DWM	Divorced White Male [*Classified advertising*]
DWM	Dogwood [*Missouri*] [*Seismograph station code, US Geological Survey*] (SEIS)
DWMC	Dedicated Wooden Money Collectors (EA)
DWMI	Diamond Wheel Manufacturers Institute (EA)
Dw Mil	Dwyer on the Militia Laws [*A publication*] (DLA)
DWML	Due West Motor Line [*AAR code*]
DWMP	Defense Waste Management Plan (GAAI)
DWMS	Demineralized Water Makeup System [*Nuclear energy*] (NRCH)
DWMSTDP	Defense Work Measurement Standard Time Data Program [*Air Force*] (AFM)
DWMT	Division of Waste Management and Transportation [*Energy Research and Development Administration*]
DWN	Darwin, MN [*Location identifier FAA*] (FAAL)
DWN	Dawn Air, Inc. [*ICAO designator*] (FAAC)
DWN	Down (KSC)
DWN	Downdraft (DA)
DWN	Drawn (MSA)
DWNAV(N)	Director of Weapons Navigation (Naval) [*British*]
DWNDFTS	Downdrafts [*NWS*] (FAAC)
DWNTN	Downtown
DWO	Delta Wing Orbiter (KSC)
DWO	Department Work Order (MCD)
DWO	Development Work Order
DWO	Directorate of War Organization [*RAF*] [*British*]
DWO	Direct Writing Oscillograph
DWOP	Dismissed without Prejudice [*Legal shorthand*] (LWAP)
DWP	Dalbandin [*Pakistan*] [*Airport symbol*] (AD)
DWP	Deep Water Port [*Marine science*] (MSC)
DWP	Director of Weapons Production [*British military*] (DMA)
DWP	Dismissed for Want of Prosecution [*Legal term*] (DLA)
DWP	Dismissed with Prejudice [*Legal shorthand*] (LWAP)
DWP	Displaced Worker Program (OICC)
DWP	District of Columbia Public Library, Washington, DC [*OCLC symbol*] (OCLC)
DWP	Duluth, Winnipeg & Pacific Railway [*AAR code*]

DWP .... Public Library of the District of Columbia, Martin Luther King Memorial Library, Washington, DC [Library symbol Library of Congress] (LCLS)
DWP .... Webb [Del E.] Properties Corp. (MHDW)
DWPA .... Deep Water Ports Act [1974] (MSC)
DWPF .... Defense Waste Processing Facility [Department of Energy]
DWP(N) .... Director of Weapons Production (Naval) [British]
DWPNT .... Dew Point [NWS] (FAAC)
DWPO .... District War Plans Officer
DWPROD(N)... Director of Weapons Production (Naval) [British]
DWQGV .... Drinking Water Quality Guideline Value [World Health Organization]
DWQRC .... Drinking Water Quality Research Center [Florida International University]
DWR .... Development Work Request
DWR .... Digital Wired Recorder
DWR .... Dirty Word Remover [Graffiti-removing chemical]
DWR .... Divided Winding-Rotor
DWR .... Divisional Work Request (AAG)
DWR .... Drawer (MSA)
DWR .... Duke of Wellington's Regiment [Military unit] [British]
DWR .... Du-Well Resources Ltd. [Vancouver Stock Exchange symbol]
DWR .... United States Walter Reed Army Medical Center, Post/Patient Library, Washington, DC [Library symbol Library of Congress] (LCLS)
DWRA .... Defense Western Regional Audit Office [DoD]
DWRA .... Dry Wrinkle Recovery Angle [Textile technology]
DWRAF .... Director of the Women's Royal Air Force [British military] (DMA)
DWRC .... Denver Wildlife Research Center [Colorado] [Department of Agriculture] (GRD)
DWRC .... Descend Well to Right of Course [Aviation] (FAAC)
DWRDS .... Director, Weapons Research and Development, Surface [British military] (DMA)
DWRDU .... Director, Weapons Research and Development, Underwater [British military] (DMA)
DWRGLU ...... Dock, Wharf, Riverside, and General Labourers' Union [British]
DWR-I .... United States Walter Reed Army Medical Center, Research Institute, Washington, DC [Library symbol Library of Congress] (LCLS)
DWRI .... Walter Reed Army Institute of Research, Washington, DC [Library symbol Library of Congress] (LCLS)
DWR-M .... United States Walter Reed Army Medical Center, Medical Library, Washington, DC [Library symbol Library of Congress] (LCLS)
DWRNS .... Department of the Director, Women's Royal Naval Service [British]
DWRP .... Director of Weapons Resources and Programmes [British military] (DMA)
DWR-P .... Walter Reed Army Medical Biomechanical Research Center, Forest Glen, MD [Library symbol Library of Congress] (LCLS)
DWRTO .... Defense Western Regional Telecommunications Office [DoD]
DWRX .... DataWorks Corp. [NASDAQ symbol] (SAG)
DWS .... Deck Working Space
DWS .... Defense Weapons System
DWS .... Depot Working Standards
DWS .... Design Work Study
DWS .... Detailed Work Statement (MCD)
DWS .... Detroit Waldhorn Society (EA)
DWS .... Development Work Statement (NRCH)
DWS .... Diffusing Wave Spectroscopy
DWS .... Disaster Warning Satellite [NASA] (NASA)
DWS .... Disaster Warning System [National Weather Service]
DWS .... Dorcas Welfare Society [Later, Community Services] (EA)
DWS .... Double White Silk Covered [Wire insulation]
DWS .... Drinking Water Standard
DWS .... Drop Wood Siding [Technical drawings]
DWS .... Dry Workshop [NASA] (KSC)
DWS .... Orlando, FL [Location identifier FAA] (FAAL)
DWS .... Washington Star, Washington, DC [Library symbol Library of Congress] (LCLS)
DWSA .... Director of Weapon Systems Analysis [Army] (AABC)
DWSC .... Director of Welfare and Service Conditions [British military] (DMA)
DWSMC .... Defense Weapons System Management Center
DWSN .... Dawson Geophysical [NASDAQ symbol] (TTSB)
DWSN .... Dawson Geophysical Co. [NASDAQ symbol] (NQ)
DWSO .... Drainage and Water Supply Officer [Ministry of Agriculture, Fisheries, and Food] [British]
DWSP(N) ...... Director of Weapons Surface Projects (Naval) [British]
DWSR .... Dodge Wayfarer Sportabout Registry [Defunct] (EA)
DWSS .... Double Wipe Slide Switch
DWST .... Demineralized Water Storage Tank [Nuclear energy] (NRCH)
Dw Stat .... Dwarris on Statutes [A publication] (DLA)
DWStK .... Deutsche Waffen Stillstandkommission [German Armistice Commission, in France] [World War II]
DWT .... Dahl-Wade-Till Valve [Medicine]
DWT .... Deadweight
DWT .... Deadweight Tester
DWT .... Deadweight Tons [Shipping]
DWT .... Deck Watch Time [Navigation]
DWT .... Denarius Weight [Pennyweight] [Latin]
DWT .... Discrete Wavelet Transformation (DOM)
DWT .... Dog Wags Tail [Airspace effects]
DWT .... Double-Weight [Paper]
DWT .... Drop-Weight Test [Nuclear energy] (NRCH)
dwt .... Pennyweight [Measurement] (DAVI)
DWT .... Wesley Theological Seminary, Washington, DC [Library symbol Library of Congress OCLC symbol] (LCLS)
DWTF .... Daily and Weekly till Forbidden [Advertising]
DWTF .... Decontamination and Waste Treatment Facility

DWTI .... Dataware Technologies [NASDAQ symbol] (TTSB)
DWTI .... Dataware Technologies, Inc. [NASDAQ symbol] (SAG)
DWTM .... Office of Defense Waste and Transportation Management [Washington, DC Department of Energy] (GRD)
DWTMC .... Domestic Water Tank Manufacturers Council [Defunct]
DWTR .... Descend Well to Right [Aviation] (FAAC)
DWTS .... Digital Wideband Transmission System (MCD)
DWTT .... Drop-Weight Tear Test
DWU .... Dakota Wesleyan University [South Dakota]
DWU .... Distillery, Wine, and Allied Workers Union (BARN)
DWUC .... Democratic Women's Union of Canada
DWUI .... Driving While under the Influence (OICC)
DWUWA .... Disabled Workers' Union of Western Australia
DWV .... Dielectric Withstand Voltage (MCD)
DWV .... Drain, Waste, and Vent [System]
DWVP-A .... Directorate of Weapons and Vehicle Procurement - Army
DWVP-A-VEH... Directorate of Weapons and Vehicle Procurement - Army - Vehicles
DWW .... Davis Water & Waste [NYSE symbol] (TTSB)
DWW .... Davis Water & Waste Industries, Inc. [NYSE symbol] (SPSG)
DWW .... Distillery, Wine, and Allied Workers International Union
DWW .... Wilmington Institute Free Library and the New Castle County Free Library, Wilmington, DE [OCLC symbol] (OCLC)
DWW .... Woodrow Wilson International Center for Scholars, Washington, DC [Library symbol Library of Congress] (LCLS)
DWW .... Wright International Express, Inc. [ICAO designator] (FAAC)
DWWBFC ...... Don Winters and the Winters Brothers Fan Club [Defunct] (EA)
DWWSSN ..... Digital World-Wide Standardised Seismograph Network [Australia]
DWY .... Gadsden, AL [Location identifier FAA] (FAAL)
DwyerGp ...... Dwyer Group, Inc. [Associated Press] (SAG)
D Wyo .... United States District Court for the District of Wyoming (DLA)
DWYR .... Dwyer Group [NASDAQ symbol] (TTSB)
DWYR .... Dwyer Group, Inc. [NASDAQ symbol] (SAG)
DWYSYWD... Do What You Say You Will Do
DX .... Danair [ICAO designator] (AD)
DX .... Data Extraction (CAAL)
DX .... Data Transfer [Computer science]
DX .... Destroyer Experimental (MCD)
DX .... Dextran (MAE)
Dx .... Diagnosis
DX .... Diagnosis Code
Dx .... Diffusing Capacity of the Lung Expressed as Volume [Medicine] (DAVI)
DX .... Digital Index [Photography]
DX .... Direct Exchange [Army] (AABC)
DX .... Direct Expansion
DX .... Distance [Radio term] (EA)
DX .... Double Cash Ruled [Stationery]
DX .... Duplex [Signaling] [Telecommunications] (MSA)
DXA .... Direct Exchange Activity (AABC)
DXA .... Document Exchange Architecture [Data General] (NITA)
DXA .... Dual-Energy X-Ray Absorptiometry [Physiology]
DXA .... Dual Energy X-Ray Absorptiometry [Painless bone mass test] [Medicine]
DXAK .... Atakpame/Akpaka [Togo] [ICAO location identifier] (ICLI)
DXB .... Dubai [United Arab Emirates] [Airport symbol] (OAG)
DXB .... Dubai [Trucial Oman] [Airport symbol] (AD)
DXBS .... Bassari [Togo] [ICAO location identifier] (ICLI)
DXC .... Data Exchange Control
Dxd .... Discontinued [Medicine] (DAVI)
DXD .... Dixie [Australia Airport symbol Obsolete] (OAG)
DXD .... Drexore Developments, Inc. [Vancouver Stock Exchange symbol]
DXDP .... Dapango [Togo] [ICAO location identifier] (ICLI)
dXDP .... Deoxyxanthosine Diphosphate [Biochemistry]
DX/DXG .... ASW [Antisubmarine Warfare], Gun, and Missile Escort Ship [Navy symbol]
DXE .... Data Transmitting Equipment (MSA)
DXE .... Dexter, MO [Location identifier FAA] (FAAL)
DXE .... Dixylylethane [Organic chemistry]
DXF .... Data Exchange File [Computer science]
DXF .... Data Exchange Format (PCM)
DXF .... Drawing Exchange File [Computer science] (PCM)
DXF file .... Document Exchange Format File (CDE)
DXG .... Dyonix Greentree Technologies, Inc. [Vancouver Stock Exchange symbol]
DXG .... Guided Missile Destroyer [Navy symbol]
DXGN .... Guided Missile Destroyer, Nuclear-Propulsion [Navy symbol]
DXH .... Dexleigh Corp. [Toronto Stock Exchange symbol]
DXHO .... Hahotoe [Togo] [ICAO location identifier] (ICLI)
DXI .... Data Exchange Interface [Computer science]
DXI .... Direct Exchange Item [Army] (AABC)
DXKP .... Anie/Kolokope [Togo] [ICAO location identifier] (ICLI)
DXL .... Dorset Exploration Ltd. [Toronto Stock Exchange symbol]
DXM .... Dexamethasone [Also, D, DEX] [Antineoplastic drug]
DXMG .... Sansanne-Mango [Togo] [ICAO location identifier] (ICLI)
dXMP .... Deoxyxanthosine Monophosphate [Biochemistry]
DXNG .... Niamtougou [Togo] [ICAO location identifier] (ICLI)
DXO .... Disco S.A. ADS [NYSE symbol] (TTSB)
DXP .... Dallas Express Airlines, Inc. [FAA designator] (FAAC)
DXP .... Detroit, MI [Location identifier FAA] (FAAL)
DXR .... Danbury [Connecticut] [Airport symbol Obsolete] (OAG)
DXR .... Daxor Corp. [AMEX symbol] (SPSG)
DXR .... Deep X-Ray
DXR .... Deex Resources Corp. [Vancouver Stock Exchange symbol]

DXR .... Doxorubicin [*Also, D, DOX*] [*Formerly, ADR, Adriamycin*] [*Antineoplastic drug*]
DXRD .... Dynamic X-Ray Diffraction [*Physics*]
DXRT .... Deep X-Ray Therapy
DXS .... Data Exchange System [*Texas Instruments, Inc.*]
DXS .... Dextran Sulfate [*Organic chemistry*]
DXSK .... Sokode [*Togo*] [*ICAO location identifier*] (ICLI)
DXS/OS .... Data Exchange System/Operating System (NITA)
DXSST .... Data Exchange System Statement Translator [*Texas Instruments, Inc.*]
DXS/TL .... Data Exchange System/Transaction Language (NITA)
DXT .... Dalton, MA [*Location identifier FAA*] (FAAL)
DXT .... Deep X-Ray Therapy
DXT .... Dextrose [*Pharmacology*]
DXT .... Dhoxaton [*Greece*] [*Airport symbol*] (AD)
DXT .... Dixon Ticonderoga [*AMEX symbol*] (TTSB)
DXT .... Dixon Ticonderoga Co. [*AMEX symbol*] (SPSG)
DXTA .... Tabligbo [*Togo*] [*ICAO location identifier*] (ICLI)
dXTP .... Deoxyxanthosine Triphosphate [*Biochemistry*]
DXTZ .... Display Crosstell Zone (SAA)
DXU .... Drexel University, Philadelphia, PA [*OCLC symbol*] (OCLC)
DX-W .... Direct Exchange - Wholesale (MCD)
DXX .... Madison, MN [*Location identifier FAA*] (FAAL)
DXXX .... Lome/Tokoin [*Togo*] [*ICAO location identifier*] (ICLI)
DXY .... Derby [*England*] [*Airport symbol*] (AD)
D-XYL .... D-Xylose [*In urine*] [*Gastroenterology*] (DAVI)
DXYN .... Dixie Yams [*NASDAQ symbol*] (TTSB)
DXYN .... Dixie Yarns, Inc. [*NASDAQ symbol*] (NQ)
DY .... Alyemda Democratic Yemen [*ICAO designator*] (AD)
Dy .... Catholic Douay Version [*of the Bible*] [*1609*] (BJA)
DY .... Daf Yomi (BJA)
DY .... Daily (ROG)
DY .... Dairy Yield (OA)
DY .... Dandy [*Ship's rigging*] (ROG)
DY .... Day (MSA)
DY .... Deflection Yoke
DY .... Delinquent Year [*IRS*]
DY .... Delivery
dy .... Delivery (ODBW)
DY .... Democratic Yemen Airlines (ALYEMDA) [*People's Democratic Republic of Yemen*] [*ICAO designator*] (ICDA)
DY .... Demy [*Half*] [*Size of paper*] (ROG)
DY .... Dense Parenchyma [*Medicine*] (DMAA)
DY .... Density
Dy .... Dependency [*Psychology*]
DY .... Deputy
DY .... Deputy Director [*KSC Directorate*] (MCD)
DY .... Derbyshire Yeomanry [*British military*] (DMA)
DY .... Design Year [*DoD*]
DY .... Dockyard
DY .... Duty (AFM)
DY .... Dycom Industries [*NYSE symbol*] (TTSB)
DY .... Dycom Industries, Inc. [*NYSE symbol*] (SPSG)
Dy .... Dyer's English King's Bench Reports [*73 English Reprint*] [*A publication*] (DLA)
DY .... Dynamotors [*JETDS nomenclature*] [*Military*] (CET)
Dy .... Dyne [*Unit of force*] [*Also, D, dyn Preferred unit is N, Newton*] (DEN)
DY .... Dynode (IAA)
Dy .... Dysprosium [*Chemical element*]
DY1 .... Dyersburg [*Tennessee*] [*Seismograph station code, US Geological Survey Closed*] (SEIS)
DY2 .... Lassiter [*Tennessee*] [*Seismograph station code, US Geological Survey Closed*] (SEIS)
DY3 .... Tiptonville [*Tennessee*] [*Seismograph station code, US Geological Survey Closed*] (SEIS)
DY4 .... Samburg [*Tennessee*] [*Seismograph station code, US Geological Survey Closed*] (SEIS)
DY5 .... Lassiter Corners [*Tennessee*] [*Seismograph station code, US Geological Survey Closed*] (SEIS)
DYA .... Alyemda-Democratic Yemen Airlines [*ICAO designator*] (FAAC)
DYA .... Deflection Yoke Amplifier
DYA .... Dynamics Corp. Amer [*NYSE symbol*] (TTSB)
DYA .... Dynamics Corp. of America [*NYSE symbol*] (SPSG)
DYA .... Dysart [*Australia Airport symbol*] (OAG)
DYANA .... Dynamic Analyzer
DYANA .... Dynamics Analyzer Programmer [*Computer program*] (NITA)
DYB .... Dynamic Braking
DYC .... Dalmys (Canada) Ltd. [*Toronto Stock Exchange symbol*]
DYC .... Dycam, Inc. [*AMEX symbol*] (SAG)
Dycam .... Dycam, Inc. [*Associated Press*] (SAG)
Dyche & P Dict... Dyche and Pardon's Dictionary [*A publication*] (DLA)
DYCMOS ...... Dynamic Complementary Metal Oxide Semiconductor (IAA)
Dycom .... Dycom Industries, Inc. [*Associated Press*] (SAG)
DYCON .... Dynamic Control
DYCONTR .... Duty Controller [*Air Force*]
DYCOP .... Dynamic Console for Operations Planners
DYD .... Dockyard
DYDAT .... Dynamic Data Allocator (DNAB)
DYDE .... Dynamic Debugger
DYE .... Dynamic Air [*Netherlands ICAO designator*] (FAAC)
Dyer .... Dyer's English King's Bench Reports [*73 English Reprint*] [*A publication*] (DLA)
Dyer (Eng) ... Dyer's English King's Bench Reports [*73 English Reprint*] [*A publication*] (DLA)
Dyersbg .... Dyersburg Corp. [*Associated Press*] (SAG)

DYF .... Damned Young Fools [*Officers under the age of thirty*] [*British naval slang*]
DYF .... Drag Your Feet (DAVI)
DYFUS .... Dynamic Fuze Simulator [*RADAR*]
DYG .... Discovery Gold Explorations Ltd. [*Vancouver Stock Exchange symbol*]
DYG .... Drying
DYG .... Dying
DYGN .... Dynagen, Inc. [*NASDAQ symbol*] (SAG)
DYGNW .... DynaGen Inc. Wrrt [*NASDAQ symbol*] (TTSB)
DYHBIFC ...... Don Youngblood and the Hoosier Bears International Fan Club [*Defunct*] (EA)
DYHM .... Dynamic Homes [*NASDAQ symbol*] (TTSB)
DYHM .... Dynamic Homes, Inc. [*NASDAQ symbol*] (SAG)
DYHR .... Dehydrator (MSA)
DYII .... Dynacq International, Inc. [*NASDAQ symbol*] (SAG)
DYIL .... Dynacq Intl. [*NASDAQ symbol*] (TTSB)
DYL .... Doylestown, PA [*Location identifier FAA*] (FAAL)
DYLEX .... Damn Your Lame Excuses [*Facetious translation for the name of a Toronto-based specialty store chain*]
DYM .... Diamantina Lakes [*Queensland*] [*Airport symbol*] (AD)
Dym Death Dut... Dymond's Death Duties [*15th ed.*] [*1973*] [*A publication*] (DLA)
DYMO .... Dynamotion/ATI [*NASDAQ symbol*] (TTSB)
DYMO .... Dynamotion ATI Corp. [*NASDAQ symbol*] (SAG)
DYMOZ .... Dynamotion/ATI Wrrt'A' [*NASDAQ symbol*] (TTSB)
DYMP .... Dynamotion ATI Corp. [*NASDAQ symbol*] (SAG)
DYMTF .... DynaMotive Technologies [*NASDAQ symbol*] (TTSB)
DYMV .... Desmodium Yellow Mottle Virus [*Plant pathology*]
DYMX .... Dynamex, Inc. [*NASDAQ symbol*] (SAG)
DYMZ .... Dynamotion ATI Corp. [*NASDAQ symbol*] (SAG)
DYN .... Detectability of Yes-No
DYN .... Diarios y Noticias [*News agency*] [*Argentina*] (EY)
DYN .... Drives You Nuts [*Coined by Erma Bombeck*]
DYN .... Dynamic
DYN .... Dynamic Ventures, Inc. [*ICAO designator*] (FAAC)
DYN .... Dynamiting [*FBI standardized term*]
DYN .... Dynamo (MSA)
DYN .... Dynamometer [*Engineering*] (DEN)
DYN .... Dynamotor (IAA)
Dyn .... Dynasty (BJA)
DYN .... Dynasty Resources, Inc. [*Vancouver Stock Exchange symbol*]
dyn .... Dyne [*Unit of force*] [*Also, D Preferred unit is N, Newton*] (DEN)
DYNA .... Dynaflow [*Automotive engineering*]
DYNA .... Dynamic Analyzer (MCD)
Dyna .... Dynamotion ATI Corp. [*Associated Press*] (SAG)
Dynacq .... Dynacq International, Inc. [*Associated Press*] (SAG)
Dynag .... Dynagen, Inc. [*Associated Press*] (SAG)
Dynagn .... Dynagen, Inc. [*Associated Press*] (SAG)
DynaGp .... Dyna Group International, Inc. [*Associated Press*] (SAG)
DYNAL .... Dynamic Analysis (NRCH)
DYNAM .... Dynamic (WGA)
DynAm .... Dynamics Corp. of America [*Associated Press*] (SAG)
Dynam .... Dynamotion ATI Corp. [*Associated Press*] (SAG)
DYNAMIT ..... Dynamic Allocation of Manufacturing Inventory and Time (MHDB)
DYNAMO ...... Dynamic Action Management Operations [*BSD*]
DYNAMO ...... Dynamic Automatic Monitoring (CET)
DYNAMO ...... Dynamic Magneto-Optical Correlator [*Instrumentation*]
DYNAMO ...... Dynamic Model Continuous Time Simulation (BUR)
Dynamo .... Dynamotion ATI Corp. [*Associated Press*] (SAG)
DYNAMOWS... Dynamic Manned Orbital Weapon System (IAA)
Dynamx .... Dynamex, Inc. [*Associated Press*] (SAG)
DYNANA ...... Dynamic Analyzer (HGAA)
DYNARM ...... Dynamic Arm Programmer [*Computer science*]
DYNASAR .... Dynamic Systems Analyzer [*General Electric Co.*] (IEEE)
DYNA-SOAR... Dynamic Soaring [*Space flight*]
DYNAT .... Dynamic Accuracy Tester [*General Electric Co.*]
DYN/CM .... Dynes per Centimeter
DYN/CM² ..... Dynes per Square Centimeter
DYNG .... Dyeing
Dyng .... Dynagen, Inc. [*Associated Press*] (SAG)
DynHlth .... Dynamic Healthcare Technologies, Inc. [*Associated Press*] (SAG)
DynHm .... Dynamic Homes, Inc. [*Associated Press*] (SAG)
DynHom .... Dynamic Homes, Inc. [*Associated Press*] (SAG)
DYNM .... Dynamotor
DynMatl .... Dynamic Materials Corp. [*Associated Press*] (SAG)
DYNMC .... Dynamic
DYNMT .... Dynamite (MSA)
DYNMT .... Dynamometer [*Engineering*]
DYNMX .... Dynamic Mixing Model [*Marine science*] (OSRA)
DYNMX .... Dynamic Mixing Model (USDC)
DYNO .... Dynamometer [*Engineering*] (KSC)
DynOil .... Dynamic Oil Ltd. [*Associated Press*] (SAG)
DynRsh .... Dynamics Research Corp. [*Associated Press*] (SAG)
DYNT .... Dynatronics Corp. [*NASDAQ symbol*] (TTSB)
DYNT .... Dynatronics Laser Corp. [*NASDAQ symbol*] (NQ)
DYNTACS ..... Dynamical Tactical Simulator
DYNTACS-X... Dynamic Tactical Simulator - Enhanced
Dyntcl .... Dynatec International, Inc. [*Associated Press*] (SAG)
DyntrCp .... Dynatronics Corp. [*Associated Press*] (SAG)
DYNX .... Dynatec International, Inc. [*NASDAQ symbol*] (NQ)
DYNX .... Dynatec Intl. [*NASDAQ symbol*] (TTSB)
DYO .... Diocesan Youth Officer [*Church of England*]
DYO .... Duke of York's Own [*British military*] (DMA)
DYO .... Rutland, VT [*Location identifier FAA*] (FAAL)
DYOL .... Dynamic Oil Ltd. [*NASDAQ symbol*] (NQ)

DYOLF .... Dynamic Oil Ltd. [*NASDAQ symbol*] (TTSB)
DYP .... Directory Yellow Pages [*Telecommunications*] (TEL)
DYP .... Dogru Yol Partisi [*Correct Way Party*] [*Turkey Political party*] (EY)
DYPR .... Drypers Corp. [*NASDAQ symbol*] (SAG)
DYPS .... Dynamic Programming System [*Computer science*] (IAA)
DYPSP .... Disabled Young People's Services Program [*Australia*]
DYQ .... Greeneville, TN [*Location identifier FAA*] (FAAL)
DYR .... Dyersburg, TN [*Location identifier FAA*] (FAAL)
DYR .... Dynamo Resources [*Vancouver Stock Exchange symbol*]
DYRAD .... Dynamic Resolver Angle Digitizer
DYRQRPRCHT... Duties Require Parachuting [*Army*] (AABC)
DYS .... Abilene, TX [*Location identifier FAA*] (FAAL)
DYS .... Duke of York's Royal Military School [*British military*] (DMA)
DYS .... Dysgerminoma [*Oncology*]
DYSAC .... Digital Simulated Analog Computer (MCD)
DYSAC .... Dynamic Storage Analog Computer (IEEE)
DYSEAC .... Digital High-Speed Standard Eastern Automatic Computer
DYSM .... Dysmenorrhea [*Medicine*]
DYSTAC .... Dynamic Storage Analog Computer
DYSTAL ...... Dynamic Storage Allocation Language [*in FORTRAN*] [*Computer science*]
Dy Sum Proc... Dyett's Summary Proceedings [*A publication*] (DLA)
DYT .... Dynatronics Laser Corp. [*Vancouver Stock Exchange symbol*]
DYTAPS ...... Dynamic Tongue and Palatometric Shapes [*System to help the deaf speak*]
DYTC .... Dynatech Corp. [*NASDAQ symbol*] (NQ)
DytchC .... Dynatech Corp. [*Associated Press*] (SAG)
DYTRPT .... Dye Transfer Print (VRA)
DYU .... Dushanbe [*Former USSR Airport symbol*] (OAG)
DYV .... Dolly Varden Minerals [*Vancouver Stock Exchange symbol*]
DYW .... Daly Waters [*Northern Territory, Australia*] [*Airport symbol*] (AD)
DYW .... Detached Youth Worker (AIE)
D-YWHF .... Dozen-Year White House Foul-Up Cycle [*Reference to the 1949 "mess in Washington," 1961 Bay of Pigs disaster, 1973 Watergate scandal, and 1985 Iran-CONTRA affair*] [*Term coined by William Safire*]
DYZO .... Dror Young Zionist Organization [*Later, YKM*] (EA)
DZ .... Algeria [*ANSI two-letter standard code*] (CNC)
DZ .... Definitive Zone
DZ .... Diazepam [*Also, D, DAP*] [*A sedative*]
DZ .... Disease (DAVI)

DZ .... Disruption Zone [*Military*] (INF)
DZ .... Dissociated Zircon (PDAA)
DZ .... Dizygotic [*Genetics*]
DZ .... Dizziness (KSC)
DZ .... Doctor of Zoology
DZ .... Douglas Airways [*ICAO designator*] (AD)
DZ .... Dozen
DZ .... Drizzle [*Meteorology*]
DZ .... Drop Zone [*For parachute troops and gliders*] [*Military*]
DZ .... Druckzuender [*Pressure Igniter*] [*German military - World War II*]
DZA .... Algeria [*ANSI three-letter standard code*] (CNC)
DZA .... Dizygotic Twins Reared Apart [*Genetics*]
DZA .... Doppler Zeeman Analyser [*British*]
DZA .... Drop Zone Area [*Military*]
DZA .... Dzaoudzi [*Comoro Islands*] [*Airport symbol*] (OAG)
DZAAS .... Drop Zone Assembly Aid System [*Military*] (INF)
DZaE .... Embassy of Zaire, Washington, DC [*Library symbol Library of Congress*] (LCLS)
DZAPO .... Cytosine Arabinoside, Azacytidine, Prednisone, Vincristine, Daunomycin [*Antineoplastic drug regimen*] (DAVI)
DZCO .... Drop Zone Control Officer [*Military*] (AFM)
DZF .... Dokumentationszentrale Feinwerktechnik [*Precision Technology Documentation Center*] [*Originator, operator, and database*] [*Germany*] [*Information service or system*] (IID)
DZFC .... Dread Zeppelin Fan Club (EA)
DZH .... Dzhafr [*Former USSR Seismograph station code, US Geological Survey Closed*] (SEIS)
DZM .... Miami-Dade Public Library System, Miami, FL [*OCLC symbol*] (OCLC)
DZNE .... Douzaine [*Dozen*] [*French*]
DZool .... Doctor of Zoology (ADA)
DZP .... Diazepam [*Also, D, DAP, DZ*] [*Antiepileptic drug*]
DZR .... Double Zigzag Rectifier
DZS .... Drop Zone Study [*Military*] (MCD)
DZSO .... Drop Zone Safety Officer [*Military*] (AABC)
DZST .... Drop Zone Support Team [*Army*] (INF)
DZT .... Digit Zero Trigger (IAA)
DZT .... Dzhergetal [*Former USSR Seismograph station code, US Geological Survey Closed*] (SEIS)
DZTK .... Daisytek International Corp. [*NASDAQ symbol*] (SAG)
DZTK .... Daisytek Intl. [*NASDAQ symbol*] (TTSB)
DZTL .... Diode Zener Diode Transistor Logic [*Electronics*] (IAA)

E
By Acronym

E .... Air Dose [*Also called air exposure, referring to radiation exposure*] (DAVI)
E .... Air Force Training Category [*Inactive duty training periods and 30 days active duty training per year*]
E .... Amphibian [*Russian aircraft symbol*]
e .... Base of Natural Logarithms [*Mathematics*] (DAVI)
E .... Cases in the Eastern District's Local Division of the Supreme Court [*1910-46*] [*South Africa*] [*A publication*] (DLA)
E .... Church of England School [*British*]
E .... Color Excess [*Astronomy*]
E .... Declared or Paid in the Preceding 12 Months [*Investment term*] (DFIT)
E .... Earl
E .... Early [*Genetics*]
E .... Earnings [*Finance*]
E .... Ear, Nose, and Throat [*Medical Officer designation*] [*British*]
E .... Earth [*Wind triangle problems and relative movement problems*]
E .... Easily
E .... East [*or Eastern*]
e .... East (WDMC)
E .... Easter
E .... Easterly (WDAA)
E .... Eastern Standard Time
E .... East's English King's Bench Term Reports [*A publication*] (DLA)
E .... Easy [*Phonetic alphabet*] [*World War II*] (DSUE)
E .... Easy to Move [*Horticulture*]
e .... Eccentricity [*of application of load*] [*Aerospace*] (AAG)
E .... Ecclesiastical (DLA)
E .... Ecclesiastical District [*Maps*] (ROG)
E .... Echo [*Phonetic alphabet*] [*International*] (DSUE)
E .... Eclairage [*Illumination*] [*French*]
E .... Economics (ADA)
E .... Ecstacy [*Synthetic stimulant*]
E .... Edema [*Medicine*]
E .... Edge [*Lumber*]
E .... Edinburgh [*City in Scotland*] (ROG)
E .... Edition
E .... Edrophonium [*A cholinergic*] [*Anesthesiology*]
E .... Educated
E .... Edward [*Phonetic alphabet*] [*Royal Navy World War I*] (DSUE)
E .... Effect (WDMC)
E .... Effectiveness (CAAL)
E .... Effector [*Biology*]
E .... Effects (WDMC)
E .... Efficiency [*or Efficient*]
E .... Effort (CDAI)
E .... Egyptian
E .... Eighteen "Great" Choral Preludes [*Bach*]
E .... Einspritz [*Fuel-injection*] [*As in 280 E, the model number of a Mercedes-Benz automobile*]
E .... Einsteinium [*Also see Es*] [*Chemical element*]
E .... Elaborate [*Used in correcting manuscripts, etc.*]
E .... Elastance (MAE)
E .... Elbow (DAC)
E .... Eldest
E .... Eldisine [*Also, VDS*] [*Antineoplastic drug*]
E .... Electric (ADA)
e .... Electric Charge [*Electricity*] (DAVI)
E .... Electric Field Strength [*Symbol*]
E .... Electric Field Vector
E .... Electricity (NTCM)
E .... Electric Shutoff [*NFPA pre-fire planning symbol*] (NFPA)
E .... Electrode Potential
E .... Electromagnetic Force [*Physics*] (DAVI)
E .... Electromotive Force [*Symbol*] [*See also EMF, V Electrochemistry*]
e .... Electron [*A nuclear particle*]
e .... Electron Charge (IDOE)
E .... Electronic [*Automotive engineering*]
E .... Electronic Capability [*Designation for all US military aircraft*]
E .... Electronic Countermeasures [*Military*]
E .... Electronics Program [*Association of Independent Colleges and Schools specialization code*]
E .... Electrophoretic Analysis [*Botany*]
E .... Element (IAA)
e .... Elementary Charge [*of a proton*] [*Symbol IUPAC*]
E .... Elevation [*Angle*]

E .... Elevation Angle (NASA)
E .... Elevator [*Technical drawings*] (NFPA)
E .... Ell
E .... Elocution
E .... Elohist Source [*Biblical scholarship*]
E .... Elysium Mons [*A filamentary mark on Mars*]
E .... Emalangeni [*Monetary unit*] [*Swaziland*] (BARN)
E .... Embassy
E .... EMBRAER [*Empresa Brasileira Aeronautica SA*] [*Brazil ICAO aircraft manufacturer identifier*] (ICAO)
E .... Embroidery [*Quilting*]
E .... Embryo [*Botany*]
E .... Embryonic
E .... Emergency [*Symbol placed in neighborhood windows to indicate that resident will aid passing schoolchildren in the event of an emergency*]
E .... Eminence (DLA)
E .... Eminent [*Freemasonry*]
E .... Emitter (MSA)
e .... Emitter (IDOE)
E .... Emma [*Novel by Jane Austen*]
E .... Emmetropia [*Also, EM*] [*Ophthalmology*]
E .... Emperor (ROG)
E .... Empfindichkeit [*Susceptibility to Stimulation*] [*Psychology*]
e .... Emphatic [*Linguistics*]
E .... Employee [*Legal shorthand*] (LWAP)
E .... Empty
E .... Enamel (AAG)
E .... Encounter [*Time*]
E .... End [*Football*]
E .... Endangered Animal [*Medicine*] (DMAA)
E .... Endocrinology
E .... Endoplasmic [*Freeze etching in microscopy*]
E .... Endotoxin [*Microbiology*]
E .... Enema [*Medicine*]
E .... Enemy (ADA)
E .... Energy [*Symbol*] [*IUPAC*]
E .... Enflurane [*Also, ENF*] [*An anesthetic*]
E .... Engine
E .... Engineer [*or Engineering*]
E .... England (ROG)
E .... English
E .... English Shilling (WDAA)
E .... ENI S.p.A.ADS [*NYSE symbol*] (TTSB)
E .... Enlisted [*Often in combination with numbers to denote serviceman's grade*]
E .... Entamoeba [*Microbiology*] (MAE)
E .... Entering [*FBI standardized term*]
E .... Entertainment [*Wire service code*] (NTCM)
E! .... Entertainment Television [*Also, E! Entertainment*] [*A cable network*] [*Los Angeles, California*] (WDMC)
(E) .... Entgegen [*Opposed*] [*Chemistry*] [*German*]
E .... Entrance
E .... Entry [*Horse racing*]
E .... Entscheidung [*Decision, Judgment*] [*German*] (ILCA)
E .... Entwurf [*Draft*] [*German*] (ILCA)
E .... Environment [*Psychology*]
E .... Enzyme (AAMN)
E .... Enzyme, Free [*Enzyme kinetics*]
e .... Eodem [*In the Same Place, Title Explained*] [*Latin*] (ILCA)
E .... Eosinophil [*Hematology*]
E .... Epidermis
E .... Epinephrine [*Endocrinology*]
E .... Epistle
E .... Epithelium [*Anatomy*]
E .... Epsilon (NUCP)
E .... Equation of Time (ROG)
E .... Equator (WDAA)
E .... Equatorial [*Air mass*]
E .... Equipment (NFPA)
E .... Equity (DLA)
E .... Equivalent
E .... Erbium [*Chemical element*] [*Symbol is ER*] (ROG)
E .... Erg [*Unit of work*] (GPO)
e .... Erg (IDOE)
E .... Erie [*Diocesan abbreviation*] [*Pennsylvania*] (TOCD)

E	Eriodictyol [*Organic chemistry*]
E	Erlang [*Unit*] [*Statistics*] [*Telecommunications*]
E	Erogenic
E	Error [*Computer science*] (BUR)
E	Errors [*Baseball*]
E	Erythrocyte [*Hematology*]
E	Erythromycin [*Also, ERY, ERYC, ETM*] [*Antibacterial compound*]
E	Escape (ROG)
E	Escherichia [*Bacterial strain*]
E	Escudo [*Monetary unit*] [*Chile, Portugal*]
E	Esophagus [*Anatomy*]
E	Esophoria for Distance [*Ophthalmology*]
E	Espana [*Spain*]
E	Especial [*Designation on brandy labels*]
E	Estate Agency [*London Stock Exchange*]
E	Ester [*Organic chemistry*] (MAE)
E	Estimate
E	Estradiol [*Medicine*] (DAVI)
E	Eta (NUCP)
E	Ethanol
E	Ethmoid Sinus [*Medicine*] (DAVI)
e	Ethyl [*As substituent on nucleoside*] [*Biochemistry*]
E	Etiology [*Medicine*] (DAVI)
E	Euler Number [*Fluid mechanics*]
E	Eurocard [*Credit card*] [*British*]
e-----	Europe [*MARC geographic area code Library of Congress*] (LCCP)
E	European [*British military*] (DMA)
E	Euston Railway Station [*British*] (ROG)
E	Evangelist [*Church calendars*]
E	Evaporation
E	Evening
E	Evensong
E	Evidence [*Law*]
e	Ex [*From*] [*Latin*] (MAE)
E	Exa [*A prefix meaning multiplied by 10^{18}*] [*SI symbol*]
E	"Excellence in Production" [*Army-Navy "E" awarded manufacturers*] [*World War II*]
E	Excellency
E	Excellent
E	Excellent Skiing Conditions
E	Exchequer [*British*] (DLA)
E	Excitatory Tendency [*Psychology*]
E	Exclusion
E	Execution (MHDB)
E	Exempt [*from traceability*] [*NASA*] (NASA)
E	Exoplasmic [*Freeze etching in microscopy*]
E	Expectation
E	Expenditure [*Economics*]
E	Expenses
E	Experience
E	Experimental
E	Experimental [*When preceding vessel classification*] [*Navy symbol*]
E	Experiment Compartment
E	Experimenter [*Psychology*]
E	Expert Slope [*Skiing*]
E	Expire [*Medicine*] (DAVI)
E	Expired [*Gas*] [*Medicine*]
E	Expired Air [*Medicine*] (DMAA)
E	Explained [*Statement of import of decision in cited case, not merely a restatement of the facts*] [*Legal term*] (DLA)
E	Explicit
E	Exponent
E	Export
E	Export Service [*Queen's award*] [*British*]
E	Exposure
E	Expression (MHDI)
E	Extinction [*Neurophysiology*]
E	Extraction Fraction (MAE)
E	Extralymphatic [*Medicine*]
E	Extraordinary Ray [*Direction of*]
E	Extra Wide [*Women's shoe width*] [*More than one "E" indicates increasing wideness, up to EEE*]
E	Eye
E	Eye Infection [*Classification system used by doctors on Ellis Island to detain, re-examine, and possibly deny entry to certain immigrants*]
E	Farbenfabriken Bayer [*Germany*] [*Research code symbol*]
E	Glutamic Acid [*One-letter symbol; see Glu*] [*An amino acid*]
E	Hotels and Restaurants [*Public-performance tariff class*] [*British*]
E	Internal Energy [*Medicine*] (DAVI)
E	Irradiance [*Symbol*] [*IUPAC*]
E	Mathematical Expectation [*Statistics*] (DAVI)
E	Medium Wide [*Men's shoe width*] [*More than one "E" indicates increasing wideness, up to EEEE*]
E	Modulus of Elasticity [*Mechanics*]
e	Naperian [*or Natural*] Logarithm Base [*2.7182818*]
e	Partial Water Vapor Pressure [*Meteorology*] (BARN)
e	Permittivity [*Physics*] (BARN)
E+	Positron [*Also called positive electron*] [*Symbol Physics*] (DAVI)
E	Redox Potential [*Organic chemistry*] (DAVI)
E	Richmond [*Branch in the Federal Reserve Regional banking system*] (BARN)
E	Shoe Width Grater than D (BARN)
E	Sleet [*Meteorology*]
E	Spain [*IYRU nationality code*] (IYR)
E	Spanish [*Language in tables*] (BARN)
E	Standard Potential [*Symbol*] [*Physics*] (DAVI)
E	Torpedo Boat [*German symbol*]
E	Unreliable Source of Intelligence [*Military*]
E	Voltage (CET)
E	Water Vapor Pressure
e	Wet Air Without Rain [*Meteorology*] (BARN)
E1	Basic Airman [*Air Force*]
E$_1$	Estrone [*Endocrinology*]
E1	Private [*Marine Corps*]
E1	Recruit [*Army*]
E1	Seaman Recruit [*Navy*]
E2	Airman [*Air Force*]
E2	Estradiol [*Also, E-diol, ES*] [*Endocrinology*]
E2	Private 2 [*Army*]
E2	Private First Class [*Marine Corps*]
E2	Seaman Apprentice [*Navy*]
E^{2}DIS	Environmental Effects for Distributed Interactive Simulation [*Army*]
E^{2}I	Endoatmospheric/Exoatmospheric Interceptor [*Army*] (DOMA)
E$_2$PROM	Electrically-Erasable Programmable Read-Only Memory [*Computer science*] (EECA)
E3	Airman, First Class
E^3	Education and Experience in Engineering [*Illinois Institute of Technology program*]
E^3	Electromagnetic Environmental Effect (CAAL)
E3	Electromagnetic Environmental Effects
E^3	Electromagnetic Environment Effects
E^3	Emerging Ethnic Engineers [*An association*]
E$_3$	Estriol [*Endocrinology*]
E3	Lance Corporal [*Marine Corps*]
E3	Private First Class [*Army*]
E3	Seaman [*Navy*]
E4	Corporal [*Army, Marine Corps*]
E$_4$	Estetrol [*Endocrinology*] (DAVI)
E4	Petty Officer, Third Class [*Navy*]
E4	Sergeant [*Air Force*]
E4	Specialist 4 [*Army*]
E5	Petty Officer, Second Class [*Navy*]
E5	Sergeant [*Army, Marine Corps*]
E5	Specialist 5 [*Obsolete Army*]
E5	Staff Sergeant [*Air Force*]
E6	Petty Officer, First Class [*Navy*]
E6	Specialist 6 [*Obsolete Army*]
E6	Staff Sergeant [*Army, Marine Corps*]
E6	Technical Sergeant [*Air Force*]
E7	Chief Petty Officer [*Navy*]
E7	Gunnery Sergeant [*Marine Corps*]
E7	Master Sergeant [*Air Force*]
E7	Platoon Sergeant
E7	Specialist 7 [*Obsolete Army*]
E8	First Sergeant [*Army, Marine Corps*]
E8	Master Sergeant [*Army, Marine Corps*]
E8	Senior Chief Petty Officer [*Navy*]
E8	Senior Master Sergeant [*Air Force*]
E8	Specialist 8 [*Obsolete Army*]
E9	Chief Master Sergeant [*Air Force*]
E9	Command Sergeant Major [*Army*]
E9	Master Chief Petty Officer [*Navy*]
E9	Master Chief Petty Officer of the Coast Guard
E9	Master Gunnery Sergeant [*Marine Corps*]
E9	Sergeant Major [*Marine Corps*]
E9	Sergeant Major of the Army
E9	Specialist 9 [*Obsolete Army*]
E9	Staff Sergeant Major [*Army*]
E$_3$-3GI	Estriol-3-Glucosiduronate [*Pharmacology*] (DAVI)
EA	Airbus Industrie [*France ICAO aircraft manufacturer identifier*] (ICAO)
ea----	Alps Region [*MARC geographic area code Library of Congress*] (LCCP)
EA	Army Industrial Engineering Activity (AAGC)
EA	Each
EA	EA Industries [*NYSE symbol*] (TTSB)
EA	Early (ROG)
ea	Early (VRA)
EA	Early American
EA	Early Antigen [*Immunochemistry*]
EA	Earphone Amplifier
EA	Earth (IAA)
EA	East Africa
EA	East Anglia [*England*] (ROG)
EA	Easterline Angus (SAA)
EA	Eastern Africa Law Reports [*A publication*] (DLA)
EA	Eastern Air Lines, Inc. [*ICAO designator*]
EA	Eastern Area
Ea	East's English King's Bench Term Reports [*A publication*] (DLA)
Ea	East's Notes of Cases [*1785-1821*] [*Bengal, India*] [*A publication*] (DLA)
EA	Ebstein's Anomaly [*Cardiology*]
EA	Economic Adviser
EA	Economic Analysis
EA	Edge Act [*Banking*]
EA	Edgewood Arsenal [*Aberdeen Proving Ground, MD*] [*Army*]
EA	Editorial Alteration [*Publishing*] (WDMC)
EA	Editorial Assistant [*Publishing*]
EA	Educational Advisor
EA	Educational Age

EA	Educational Alliance (EA)
EA	Educational Art
EA	Educational Management [*Educational Resources Information Center (ERIC) Clearinghouse*] [*University of Oregon*] (PAZ)
EA	Education Alternatives
EA	Education Association (AIE)
EA	Educators to Africa [*Later, ETAA*] (EA)
EA	Effective Address [*Computer science*] (MDG)
EA	Effective Area
EA	Egg Albumin
EA	Egyptian Army
EA	Eighth Army (MCD)
EA	El-Amarna (BJA)
EA	Eleanor Association (EA)
EA	Electric Affinity [*Physics*] (DAVI)
EA	Electrical Artificer [*Navy British*]
EA	Electric Antenna [*Automobile accessory*]
EA	Electroanesthesia [*Medicine*] (AAMN)
EA	Electrocardiographic Amplifier
EA	Electron Affinity [*Chemistry*]
EA	Electronic Array (IAA)
EA	Electronic Arts
EA	Electronic Assembly
EA	Electronic Associates, Inc. [*NYSE symbol*] (SPSG)
EA	Electrostatic Analyzer (IAA)
EA	Elementary Assignment (IAA)
EA	Ellagic Acid
EA	Emergency Action (MCD)
EA	Emergency Addressee [*Aeromedical evacuation*]
EA	Emergency Area (AFM)
EA	Emirates Airlines [*United Arab Emirates*] (MENA)
EA	Emotions Anonymous (EA)
EA	Employers' Association [*British*] (DCTA)
EA	Employment Act (OICC)
EA	Enabling Objective [*Military training*]
EA	Encyclopedia of Associations [*Information service or system A publication*]
EA	Endangerment Assessment (GNE)
EA	End Article (DNAB)
EA	Endometriosis Association (EA)
EA	Enemy Aircraft
EA	Enemy Area (IAA)
EA	Energy Absorbing
EA	Energy Absorption (AAG)
EA	Enforcement Action [*Nuclear energy*] (NRCH)
EA	Enforcement Agreement [*Environmental Protection Agency*] (GFGA)
EA	Engagement Area [*Military*] (INF)
EA	Engelbert's Aquarians (EA)
EA	Engine Assembly
E/A	Engineer/Architect (DAC)
EA	Engineering Aid [*Navy rating*]
EA	Engineering Assignment
EA	Engineer Rear-Admiral [*Navy British*]
EA	English Actors [*A publication*]
EA	English Association [*British*] (EAIO)
EA	English-Pressed Allegro [*Record label*]
EA	Enlistment Allowance [*Military*]
EA	Enquiry Agency [*British*]
EA	Enrolled Agent [*IRS*]
EA	Entered Apprentice [*Freemasonry*]
EA	Enterprise Allowance (ODBW)
EA	Enterprise America (EA)
EA	Entertaining Allowance [*British military*] (DMA)
EA	Enthalpimetric Analysis [*Analytical chemistry*]
EA	Entwicklungsalter [*Developmental Age*] [*Psychology*]
EA	Enumeration Area [*Statistics*]
EA	Environmental Action (EA)
EA	Environmental Assessment (MCD)
EA	Environmental Audit [*Environmental Protection Agency*] (GFGA)
EA	Epidural Anesthesia [*Medicine*]
EA	Equalizing Line Amplifier (IAA)
EA	Equipment Alignment
EA	Erythrocyte Amboceptor [*Immunology*]
EA	Erythrocyte-Antibody [*Complex*] [*Immunochemistry*]
EA	Erythromycin Acistrate [*Antibacterial*]
EA	Erythromycylamine [*Antibacterial*]
EA	Escort Aircraft (CINC)
EA	Estivoautumnal [*Malaria*]
EA	Estonian Aid (EA)
EA	Ethacrynic Acid [*A diuretic*] [*Pharmacology*] (DAVI)
EAS	Ethanolamine [*Also, Etn, OLAMINE*] [*Organic chemistry*]
EA	Ethnic Anonymous (EA)
EA	Ethyl Acrylate [*Organic chemistry*]
EA	Ethylene-Diamine Dinitrate/Ammonium Nitrate Explosive
EA	Eusko Alkartasuna [*Basque Solidarity*] [*Spain Political party*]
EA	Evaluation Agree [*Canada*] (DD)
EA	Evangelical Alliance [*British*] (BI)
EA	Evolutionary Acquisition (AAGC)
EA	Evolutionary Acquisition Strategy [*Army*]
EA	Examining for Aphasia [*Psychology*]
EA	Excise Act [*Canada*]
EA	Executive Assistant
EA	Exhaust Air (OA)
EA	Expectancy Age [*Education*]
EA	Experiment Assembly (KSC)

EA	Export Annual Data [*Department of Commerce*] (GFGA)
EA	Extended Accumulator (IAA)
EA	Extended-Address [*Computer science*]
EA	Extended Aeration Process [*Sludge treatment*]
EA	Extended Attribute [*Computer science*]
EA	External Affairs Department [*Canada*]
EA	Extrinsic Alveolitis (PDAA)
EA	Parke, Davis & Co. [*Research code symbol*]
EA1	Engineering Aid, First Class [*Navy rating*]
EA2	Engineering Aid, Second Class [*Navy rating*]
EA3	Engineering Aid, Third Class [*Navy rating*]
e-aa--	Albania [*MARC geographic area code Library of Congress*] (LCCP)
EAA	Eagle [*Alaska*] [*Airport symbol*] (OAG)
EAA	East Africa Association (EA)
EAA	East African Airways Corp. [*African airline*]
EAA	East African Artillery [*British military*] (DMA)
EAA	Eastern Arts Association (AEBS)
EAA	Ecclesiastical Archivists Association [*Italy*] (EAIO)
EAA	Economic Activity Analysis
EAA	Ecuadorean American Association (EA)
EAA	EDP [*Electronic Data Processing*] Auditors' Association
EAA	Elastic Active Aerodynamics [*Mitsubishi*] [*Automotive engineering*]
EAA	Electrical Aerosol Analyzer [*Instrumentation*]
EA(A)	Electrical Artificer, Air [*British military*] (DMA)
EAA	Electric Auto Association (EA)
EAA	Electrothermal Atomic Absorption [*Physics*] (DAVI)
EAA	Encyclopedia of American Associations [*Later, EA*] [*A publication*]
EAA	End-Article Application Code [*Military*]
EAA	Engineer in Aeronautics and Astronautics
EAA	Engineering and Architects Association
EAA	Entertainment Agents Association [*British*]
EAA	Epilepsy Association of America [*Later, EFA*]
EAA	Equipment Approval Authority (AFM)
EAA	Equity Access Account [*Revolving mortgage-credit account*] [*Merrill Lynch & Co.*]
EAA	Essential Amino Acid [*Nutrition*]
EAA	Ethyl Acetoacetate [*Organic chemistry*]
EAA	Ethylanthranilic Acid [*Organic chemistry*]
EAA	Ethylene Acrylic Acid [*Organic chemistry*]
EAA	Euro-American Alliance (EA)
EAA	European Academy of Anaesthesiology (EA)
EAA	European Accounting Association [*Brussels, Belgium*] (EAIO)
EAA	European Aluminium Association [*Germany*] (EA)
EA1	European Athletic Association [*Paris, France*]
EAA	Evrytanian Association of America (EA)
EAA	Excitatory Amino Acid [*Neurophysiology*]
EAA	Excretory Amino Acid
EAA	Experimental Aircraft Association (EA)
EAA	Export Administration Act [*1979*]
EAA	Export Advertising Association (DGA)
EAA	Extrinsic Allergic Alveolitis [*Medicine*]
EAA	Transporte Aereo Andino SA [*Venezuela*] [*ICAO designator*] (FAAC)
EAAA	European Association of Advertising Agencies
EAAACD	EAA [*Experimental Aircraft Association*] Antique/Classic Division (EA)
EAAAF	EAA [*Experimental Aircraft Association*] Aviation Foundation (EA)
EA(A)APP	Electrical Artificer (Air), Apprentice [*British military*] (DMA)
EAABSH	English Association of American Bond and Share Holders [*Commercial firm*] (EA)
EAAC	East African Airways Corp. [*African airline*]
EAAC	East African Armoured Corps [*British military*] (DMA)
EAAC	European Agricultural Aviation Centre [*Later, International Agricultural Aviation Centre*]
EAAC	European Association of Audiophonological Centres (EA)
EA ACC	Each Accident [*Insurance*]
EAACI	European Academy of Allergology and Clinical Immunology (EAIO)
EAAE	European Association of Agricultural Economists (EA)
EAAEC	East African Army Educational Corps [*British military*] (DMA)
EAAFR	European Academic Association for Financial Research (EAIO)
EAAFRO	East African Agriculture and Forestry Research Organization
EAAH	Essential Amino Acids plus Histidine [*Nutrition*]
EAAJ	East African Agricultural and Forestry Journal [*A publication*]
EAAM	European Association for Aquatic Mammals (EA)
EAAM	European Association of Automobile Manufacturers [*Belgium*] (EAIO)
EAAMC	East African Army Medical Corps [*British military*] (DMA)
EAandina	Embotelladora Andina SA [*Associated Press*] (SAG)
EA & OC	Engineering Administration and Operations Control [*Military*]
EA & P	East Asian and Pacific [*Series*] [*A publication*]
EAAOC	East African Army Ordnance Corps [*British military*] (DMA)
EA-AP	Encyclopedia of Associations: Association Periodicals [*A publication*]
EAAP	European Association for Animal Production [*ICSU*] [*Italian*] (SLS)
EAAS	East Asian Art Society
EAAS	European Association for American Studies [*Italy*] (EAIO)
EAASCS	East Asian Art Society Chinese School
EAASH	European Academy of Arts, Sciences, and Humanities (EAIO)
EAAT	Excitatory Amino-Acid Transporter [*Neurochemistry*]
EAAUA	EAA [*Experimental Aircraft Association*] Ultralight Association [*Defunct*] (EA)
EAB	Abbse [*Yemen Arab Republic*] [*Airport symbol*] (OAG)
EAB	Aberfoyle [*Scotland*] [*Seismograph station code, US Geological Survey*] (SEIS)
EAB	Eagle Air Ltd. [*Switzerland ICAO designator*] (FAAC)
EAB	Economic Advisory Board [*Department of Commerce Washington, DC*] (EGAO)
EAB	Economic Affairs Bureau (EA)
EAB	Educational Advisory Board [*British*]

EAB............. Education Appeal Board [*Department of Education*] (GFGA)
EAB............. Elective Abortion [*Obstetrics*] (DAVI)
EAB............. Electrical Approvals Board (Victoria)
EAB............. Elongation-at-Break [*Textile technology*]
EAB............. Emergency Actions Book
EAB............. Emergency Air Breathing System (DNAB)
EAB............. Enemy Activities Branch [*British military*] (DMA)
EAB............. Energy Absorption
EAB............. Esperanto-Asocio de Britujo [*British*]
EAB............. Ethics Advisory Board [*HEW*]
EAB............. European American Bank (NITA)
EAB............. Exclusion Area Boundary [*Nuclear energy*] (NRCH)
EAB............. Executive Advisory Board [*Army*] (RDA)
EAB............. Extra-Anatomic Bypass [*Medicine*] (MEDA)
EABC............. Edison Animal Biotechnology Center [*Ohio University*] [*Research center*] (RCD)
EABC............. European Amateur Baseball Confederation (EA)
EABC............. European/ASEAN [*Association of Southeast Asian Nations*] Business Council (DS)
EABN............. Engineer Aviation Battalion [*Military*]
EABP............. Encyclopedia of Afterlife Beliefs and Phenomena [*A publication*]
EABR............. East Asia Blocking Ridge [*Meteorology*]
EABRD............. Electrically Activated Bank Release Device (IEEE)
EABS............. Erotic Art Book Society [*Commercial firm*] (EA)
EABS............. Euro-Abstracts [*Commission of the European Communities*] [*Information service or system*]
EABT............. European Association for Behavior Therapy (EA)
EABV............. Effective Arterial Blood Volume
EAC............. Early American Coppers (EA)
EAC............. East African Community [*Formed in 1967*] [*Formerly, EACSO*] (AF)
EAC............. East Australian Current [*Oceanography*]
EAC............. Eastern Air Command [*CBI Theater*] [*World War II*]
EAC............. Eastern Arizona College [*Formerly, EAJC*] [*Thatcher*]
EAC............. Echelon Above Corps [*Military*] (RDA)
EAC............. Economic Adjustment Committee (MCD)
EAC............. Educational Advisory Committee [*AIAA*]
EAC............. Educational Assessment Center [*University of Washington*] [*Research center*] (RCD)
EAC............. Effective Acoustic Center
EAC............. Effective Atomic Charge
EAC............. Effective Attenuation Coefficient (PDAA)
EAC............. Ehrlich Ascites Carcinoma [*Cells*] [*Oncology*]
EAC............. Eire Army Corps
EAC............. Electronic Air Cleaner
EAC............. Electronic Air Control [*Automotive engineering*]
EAC............. Electronic Autocollimator [*Optics*] (IAA)
EAC............. Electro-Optical Area Correlator [*Missile guidance system*]
EAC............. Emerald Agricultural College
EAC............. Emergency Action Communications (MCD)
EAC............. Emergency Action Console [*Navy*] (CINC)
EAC............. End-Around Carry
EAC............. Energy Absorbing Capacity (NASA)
EAC............. Energy Absorption Characteristics (AAG)
EAC............. Engineer Amphibian Command [*World War II*]
EAC............. Engineering Aid, Chief [*Navy rating*]
EAC............. Engineering Applications Centre [*University of Strathclyde*] [*British*] (CB)
EAC............. Engineering Automation and Control (PCM)
EAC............. Environmental Action Coalition (EA)
EAC............. Environmentally Assisted Crack [*Metallurgy*]
EAC............. Epiphany Apostolic College [*New York*]
EAC............. Equipment Availability Constant (MCD)
EAC............. Equity Appreciation Certificate [*Investment term*]
EAC............. Equivalent Annual Cost
EAC............. Error Alert Control (OA)
EAC............. Erythrocyte Amboceptor Complement [*Immunology*]
EAC............. Erythrocyte-Antibody Complement [*Immunochemistry*]
EAC............. Estate Agents' Council [*British*] (BI)
EAC............. Estimate at Completion (NASA)
EAC............. Estimated Acquisition Cost [*of drug products*] [*HEW*]
EAC............. Estimated Arrival Carrier (MCD)
EAC............. Ethnic American Coalition (of Eastern Europeans) (EA)
EAC............. Ethyl Acetamidocinnamate [*Organic chemistry*]
EAC............. Euro-Asia Capital Ltd. [*Vancouver Stock Exchange symbol*]
EAC............. European Advisory Committee [*Allied German Occupation Forces*]
EAC............. European Advisory Council (EAIO)
EAC............. European Association for Co-Operation
EAC............. European Association of Conservatories (EA)
EAC............. European Atomic Commission (NATG)
EAC............. Evangelical Association of the Caribbean (EAIO)
EAC............. Evaporative Air Cooler
EAC............. Except Approach Clearance [*Aviation*] (OA)
EAC............. Executive Air Charter [*ICAO designator*] (FAAC)
EAC............. Exhaust Air Control [*Automotive engineering*]
EAC............. Exhibitors Advisory Council
EAC............. Expectations about Counseling Questionnaire (EDAC)
EAC............. Expected Approach Clearance [*Aviation*] (AFM)
EAC............. Expedition Advisory Centre [*Royal Geographical Society*] [*British*] (CB)
EAC............. Experiment Apparatus Container
EAC............. Extended Arithmetic Chip
EAC............. External Auditory Canal [*Anatomy*]
EACA............. Constructionman Apprentice, Engineering Aid, Striker [*Navy rating*]
EACA............. Epsilon-Aminocaproic Acid [*Pharmacology*]
EACA............. European Association of Charter Airlines (EAIO)

EACA............. European Athletics Coaches Association (EAIO)
EACA............. Law Reports, Court of Appeals of Eastern Africa [*A publication*] (DLA)
EAC/ABET .... Engineering Accreditation Commission of the Accreditation Board for Engineering Technology
EAC-AIA ...... EEC Advisory Council of the Asbestos International Association (EAIO)
EACC............. East Asia Christian Conference [*Later, Christian Conference of Asia - CCA*]
EACC............. Egyptian American Chamber of Commerce [*Defunct*] (EA)
EACC............. Electronic Asset Control Center (AFM)
EACC............. Emergency Alternate Command Center (CINC)
EACC............. Environmental Assessment Command Center [*Nuclear energy*] (NRCH)
EACC............. Error Adaptive Control Computer (IEEE)
EAC COMM... Echelon Above Corps Communications [*Army*] (DOMA)
EACC-USA... European-American Chamber of Commerce in the United States
EACD............. Eczematous Allergic Contact Dermatitis [*Dermatology*]
EACE............. Euro American Cultural Exchange (EA)
EACE............. European Association of Cognitive Ergonomics (EAIO)
EACEM............. European Association of Consumer Electronic Manufacturers [*EEC*] (PDAA)
EACF............. Employer Identification Number Assignment Control Card File [*IRS*]
EA/CG............. Ecology Action/Common Ground [*An association*]
EACH .... East Camden & Highland Railroad Co. [*AAR code*]
EACH .... Essential Access Community Hospital
EACHS............. East African Cargo Handling Services (PDAA)
EACL............. Energie Atomique du Canada, Limitee [*Atomic Energy of Canada Ltd.*]
EACL............. European Association for Chinese Law (EAIO)
EACLN .... Expect Approach Clearance [*Aviation*] (FAAC)
EACM .... Engineering Aid, Master Chief [*Navy rating*]
EACMFS...... European Association for Cranio-Maxillo-Facial Surgery (EAIO)
EACN............. Constructionman, Engineering Aid, Striker [*Navy rating*]
EACN .... Equivalent Alkane Carbon Number [*of crude oil*]
EACN .... European Air Chemistry Network
EACNG............. Emergency Advisory Committee for Natural Gas [*Terminated, 1977*] [*Department of the Interior*] (EGAO)
EACNL............. Expect Approach Clearance Not Later Than [*Aviation*] (FAAC)
EACNSW...... Ethnic Affairs Commission of New South Wales
EACO............. EA Engineering Systems [*NASDAQ symbol*] (NQ)
EACO............. EA Engr Science/Tech [*NASDAQ symbol*] (TTSB)
EACOS............. European Air Combat Operations Staff [*Military*]
EACP............. European Area Communications Plan [*Military*] (AABC)
EACPD............. Emergency Advisory Committee for Political Defense
EACPI............. European Association of Country Planning Institutions (EAIO)
EACR............. European Association for Cancer Research (EAIO)
EACRP............. European-American Committee on Reactor Physics
EACRP............. Extrapolated Alternating Direction Implicit (PDAA)
EACS............. Electronic Automatic Chart System (OA)
EACS............. Engineering Aid, Senior Chief [*Navy rating*]
EACS............. EP/EO [*Employee Plans/Exempt Organization*] Application Control System [*IRS*]
EACS............. European Allied Contacts Section [*Supreme Headquarters, Allied Expeditionary Force*] [*World War II*]
EACS............. European Association of Chinese Studies (EA)
EACSO............. East African Common Services Organization [*Later, EAC*]
EACT............. Emergency Action Coordination Team [*Department of Energy*]
EACTA............. European Association of Cardiothoracic Anaesthesiologists [*Cambridge, England*] (EAIO)
EACV............. Electronic Air Control Valve [*Automotive emissions*]
EACVD .... Electron-Assisted Chemical Vapor Deposition [*Coating technology*]
EAD............. Eadem [*The Same*] [*Pharmacy*]
EAD............. Earliest Arrival Date (AABC)
EAD............. Echelon Above Division [*Military*] (MCD)
EAD............. Economic Analysis Division [*Federal Emergency Management Agency*] [*Information service or system*] (IID)
EAD............. Effective Air Distance
EAD............. Electrically Alterable Device (NASA)
EAD............. Enable Application Developer [*Computer science*] (PCM)
EAD............. Endo-Atmospheric Decoy
EAD............. Energy and Air Division [*Office of Research and Development*] [*Environmental Protection Agency*] (EPA)
EAD............. Engineering Aid, Draftsman [*Navy rating Obsolete*]
EAD............. Enlisted Assignment Document [*Military*] (DNAB)
EAD............. Entry Acceptance Data (DS)
EAD............. Entry on Active Duty [*Army*]
EAD............. Equilibrium Air Distillation (AAG)
EAD............. Equipment Allocation Document (MCD)
EAD............. Equipment Availability Date (MCD)
EAD............. Equivalent Air Depth [*Deep-sea diving*]
EAD............. Error Adjusted (WDAA)
EAD............. Estimated Availability Date [*Military*] (AFM)
EAD............. Ethyl Azodicarboxylate [*Organic chemistry*]
EAD............. European Association of Decaffeinators [*France*] (EAIO)
EAD............. Evaluation and Development (IAA)
EAD............. Expected Availability Date (MCD)
EAD............. Expendable Acoustic Device [*Military*] (CAAL)
EAD............. Extended Active Duty
EAD............. Extended Air Defense [*NATO*]
EAD............. External Aerodynamic Diffusion
EAD............. Nevada, MO [*Location identifier FAA*] (FAAL)
EADA............. Eighth Armored Division Association (EA)
EADAS .... Eastern Association of College Deans and Advisers of Students (AEBS)

EADAS	Engineering and Administrative Data Acquisition System [*Bell System*]
EADB	East African Development Bank [*Uganda*] (AF)
EADB	Experimental Arctic Data Buoy (MSC)
EADC	Eastern Air Defense Command (SAA)
EADC	Energy Analysis and Diagnostic Center [*Department of Energy*]
EADC	Ethylaluminum Dichloride [*Organic chemistry*]
EAD C2	Extended Air Defense Command and Control [*Army*] (RDA)
EADCC	Eastern Air Defense Control Center (SAA)
EADCU	Enemy Ammunition Disposal and Collection Unit [*Military British*]
E-ADD	Epileptic Attentional Deficit Disorder [*Medicine*] (DMAA)
EADF	Eastern Air Defense Force
EaDI	Easy Access Data Interchange [*Unisys Corp.*] (IT)
EADI	Electronic Attitude and Direction Indicator
EADI	Electronic Attitude Director Indicator
EADI	European Association of Development Research and Training Institutes (EAIO)
EADIZ	Entering Air Defense Identification Zone [*Aviation*] (FAAC)
EADP	European Association of Directory Publishers (EA)
EADPTA	Exotic Animal Disease Preparedness Trust Account
EADRI	European Association of Development Research and Training Institutes
EADS	Echelons Above Division Study [*Military*] (AABC)
EADS	Emergency Assistance Dispatch System
EADS	Engineering Administrative Data Systems (MCD)
EADS	Engineering Analysis Data System
EADS	Environmental Assessment Data Systems [*Discontinued*] [*Environmental Protection Agency Information service or system*] (IID)
EADSC	Enhanced Apple Digital Sound Chip [*Computer science*]
EADSIM	Extended Air Defense Simulation [*Army*] (RDA)
EADTB	Extended Air Defense Test Bed [*Army*] (RDA)
EADX	Echelons Above Division - Expanded [*Military*] (MCD)
EAE	Aeroservicios Ecuatorianos CA [*Ecuador*] [*ICAO designator*] (FAAC)
EAE	Ecology Action East [*An association*] (EA)
EAE	Emae [*Vanuatu*] [*Airport symbol*] (OAG)
EAE	Energy and the Environment [*A publication*]
EAE	Ethylaminoethanol [*Organic chemistry*]
EAE	Experimental Allergic Encephalomyelitis [*Medicine*] (AAMN)
EAE	Experimental Autoimmune Encephalomyelitis [*Medicine*]
EAE	Extended Arithmetic Element
EAEB	East Anglian Examinations Board (AIE)
EAEBP	European Association of Editors of Biological Periodicals (DIT)
EAEC	East African Economic Community
EAEC	East Asian Economic Caucus
EAEC	European Airlines Electronic Committee
EAEC	European Atomic Energy Community [*Also, EURATOM*] (DCTA)
EAEC	European Automotive Engineers Cooperation
EAEE	European Association for Earthquake Engineering (PDAA)
EAEE	Evangelische Arbeitsgemeinschaft fuer Erwachsenenbildung in Europa [*Protestant Association for Adult Education in Europe*] (EAIO)
EAEF	Energy Action Educational Foundation [*Later, EAEP*] (EA)
EAEG	East Asian Economic Group [*Australia*]
EAEG	European Association of Exploration Geophysicists (EAIO)
EAEI	Ecology Action Educational Institute (EA)
EA/EIS	Environmental Assessment/Environmental Impact Statement [*Army*] (RDA)
EAEM	European Airlines Electronics Meeting (PDAA)
EAEME	East African Electrical and Mechanical Engineers [*British military*] (DMA)
EA Eng	EA Engineering Systems [*Associated Press*] (SAG)
EAEP	Energy Action Educational Project of C/LEC [*Defunct*] (EA)
EAERE	European Association of Environmental and Resource Economists (EERA)
EAES	European Atomic Energy Society
EAESP	European Association of Experimental Social Psychology (EA)
EAET	East African External Telecommunications Co. (PDAA)
EAETLFFM	European Association for the Exchange of Technical Literature in the Field of Ferrous Metallurgy [*Luxembourg*] (EA)
EAF	Earth Awareness Foundation (EA)
EAF	Earth's Armed Forces (SAA)
EAF	Educational Accountability Function (OICC)
EAF	Effort Adjustment Factor
EAF	Egyptian Air Force
EAF	Electric Arc Furnace [*Steelmaking*]
EAF	Electron Arc Furnace (IAA)
EAF	Emergency Action File [*Air Force*] (AFM)
EAF	Employment Agents' Federation of Great Britain (BI)
EAF	Engineering Analysis Facility (SSD)
EAF	Environmental Action Foundation (EA)
EAF	Eosinophil-Activating Factor [*Immunology*]
EAF	Equivalent Availability Factor (IEEE)
EAF	European Aviation Air Charter Ltd. [*British*] [*FAA designator*] (FAAC)
EAF	Exhaust Air Filter
EAF	Expeditionary Airfield (MCD)
EAF	Experiment Analysis Form (KSC)
EAF	Fairbanks, AK [*Location identifier FAA*] (FAAL)
EAFB	Edwards Air Force Base [*California*]
EAFB	Eglin Air Force Base [*Florida*]
EAFB	Elison Air Force Base [*Alaska*] (KSC)
EAFB	Ellington Air Force Base [*Texas*] (KSC)
EAFB	Ellsworth Air Force Base [*South Dakota*] (SAA)
EAFC	Eastern Area Frequency Coordinator
EAFDEV	Effort Adjustment Factor, Development [*Military*]

EAFE	Europe, Australia, and Far East
EAFFRO	East African Freshwater Fisheries Research Organization
EAFHS	Eighth Air Force Historical Society (EA)
EAFMAIN	Effort Adjustment Factor, Maintenance [*Military*]
EAFORD	International Organisation for the Elimination of All Forms of Racial Discrimin ation [*Geneva, Switzerland*] (EAIO)
E Afr	East Africa
E African LJ	East African Law Journal [*A publication*] (DLA)
E Afr LR	East Africa Law Reports [*A publication*] (DLA)
E Afr L Rev	Eastern Africa Law Review [*A publication*] (DLA)
EAFS	European Academy of Facial Surgery (EAIO)
EAG	Eagle Flying Services Ltd. [*British ICAO designator*] (FAAC)
EAG	Eaglet Mines Ltd. [*Toronto Stock Exchange symbol Vancouver Stock Exchange symbol*]
EAG	Economic Analysis Group [*General Accounting Office*] [*Washington, DC*] (GRD)
EAG	Electroantennogram [*Entomology*]
EAG	ELINT [*Electronic Intelligence*] Advisory Group (AABC)
EAG	Environmental Analysis Group [*Army*]
EAG	Equipment Advisory Group
E-AG	European Atlantic Group [*British*] (DBA)
EAG	Evaluation and Analysis Group [*Bureau of Ordnance*] [*Washington, DC*] [*Navy*] (MCD)
EAG	Experimental Miscellaneous Auxiliary [*Navy symbol*]
EAG	Exposure Assessment Group [*Environmental Protection Agency*] (GFGA)
EAG	Ministry of External Affairs, Government Documents [*UTLAS symbol*]
EAGA	East Asian Growth Area [*International Trade*]
EAGA	Episcopal Actor's Guild of America (EA)
Eag & Y	Eagle and Younge's English Tithe Cases [*A publication*] (DLA)
Eag & Yo	Eagle and Younge's English Tithe Cases [*A publication*] (DLA)
EAGB	Executives Association of Great Britain [*England*] (EAIO)
EAGE	Electrical Aerospace Ground Equipment (TEL)
EAGER	Electronic Audit Gauger
EAGF	Electrically Augmented Gravity Filter [*Chemical engineering*]
EAGGF	European Agricultural Guidance and Guarantee Fund [*Also known as FEOGA*]
EAGL	Eagle Financial Corp. (MHDW)
EAGL	Eagle Hardware & Garden [*NASDAQ symbol*] (TTSB)
EAGL	Eagle Hardware & Garden, Inc. [*NASDAQ symbol*] (SAG)
EAGLE	Educational Assessment Guidelines Leading [*Toward*] Excellence
EAGLE	Elevation Angle Guidance Landing Equipment
EAGLE	Energy Absorbing Gas Lithium Ejector (MCD)
EAGLE	Environmental Assessment of Great Lakes Ecosystems [*United States Fish and Wildlife Service*] (ASF)
EAGLE	European Association for Grey Literature Exploitation [*Database producer*] (EAIO)
EAGLE	Experiment and Guidance Loop Evaluator
EAGLE	Extended Application of Ground LASER Equipment (MCD)
EagleBcp	Eagle Bancorp, Inc. [*Associated Press*] (SAG)
EaglFnce	Eagle Finance Corp. [*Associated Press*] (SAG)
EaglFncl	Eagle Financial [*Associated Press*] (SAG)
EaglPac	Eagle Pacific Industries, Inc. [*Associated Press*] (SAG)
Eag Mag Com	Eagle's Magistrate's Pocket Companion [*A publication*] (DLA)
EagPnt	Eagle Point Software Corp. [*Associated Press*] (SAG)
EAGR	East African Geographical Review [*A publication*]
EAGS	English and Germanic Studies [*A publication*]
EAGS	European Association of Exploration Geophysics [*International Council of Scientific Unions*]
Eag T	Eagle's Law of Tithes [*2nd ed.*] [*1836*] [*A publication*] (DLA)
EAH	Eastern Air Transport, Inc. [*FAA designator*] (FAAC)
EAH	El Arish [*Egypt*] [*Airport symbol*] (AD)
EAH	Epochs of Ancient History [*A publication*]
EAH	European Academy of History (EA)
EAHA	European Association of Hospital Administrators (EA)
EAHC	East Asia Hydrographic Commission [*Marine science*] (OSRA)
EAHCCL	Educators' Ad Hoc Committee on Copyright Law (EA)
EAHF	Eczema, Asthma, Hay Fever [*Medicine*]
EAHHFC	Engel's Angels in Humperdinck Heaven Fan Club (EA)
EAHIL	European Association of Health Information and Libraries [*Stockholm, Sweden*] (EAIO)
EAHILC	Erie Area Health Information Library Cooperative [*Library network*]
EAHLG	Equine Antihuman Lymphoblast Globulin [*Immunochemistry*] (MAE)
EAHLS	Equine Antihuman Lymphoblast Serum [*Immunochemistry*] (MAE)
EAHM	European Association of Hospital Managers [*France*] (EAIO)
EAHP	European Association of Hospital Pharmacists (EAIO)
EAHQ	Ethylanthrahydroquinone [*Organic chemistry*]
EAHTMA	Engineers' and Allied Hand Tool Makers' Association [*British*] (BI)
EAHY	European Architectural Heritage Year [*1975*]
EAI	Economic Abstracts International [*Database*] (NITA)
EAI	Education Audit Institute [*Washington, DC*]
EAI	Electronic-Aided Instruction (IAA)
EAI	Electronic Associates, Inc.
EAI	Emphysema Anonymous, Inc. (EA)
EAI	Emulsifying Activity Index [*Food analysis*]
EAI	Encyclopedia of American Industries [*A publication*]
EAI	Engineers and Architects Institute [*Defunct*]
EAI	Entergy Arkansas, Inc. Capital I [*NYSE symbol*] (SAG)
EAI	Enterprise for the Americas Initiative [*Bush administration*]
EAI	Equal-Appearing Intervals (EDAC)
EAI	Equip and Install (IAA)
EAI	Ethyl Acetimidate [*Biochemistry*]
EAIA	Early American Industries Association (EA)
EAIC	Electronic Air Inlet Controller (MCD)
EAID	Electronic Anti-Intrusion Device (DNAB)

EAID............ Engine Air Intake Duct [*Hovercraft*]
EAID............ Equipment Authorization Inventory Data [*Air Force*] (AFM)
EAID............ ESRO [*European Space Research Organization*] Advanced Imaging Detector [*Satellite*]
EAIDL........... Equipment Authorization Inventory Data Listing [*Air Force*] (AFM)
EAIDS.......... Equipment Authorization Inventory Data System [*Air Force*] (AFIT)
EAII............. Engineering Animation [*NASDAQ symbol*] (TTSB)
EAIM............ End Article Item Manager (AFIT)
EAIN............ Education Alternative, Inc. [*NASDAQ symbol*] (SAG)
EAIN............ Education Alternatives [*NASDAQ symbol*] (TTSB)
EA-IO........... Encyclopedia of Associations: International Organizations [*A publication*]
EAIR............ End Article Identity Record
EAIR............ Extended Area Instrumentation RADAR (MCD)
EAIS............ Extended Area Instrumentation System (MCD)
EAITC........... External Affairs and International Trade Canada [*Government agency*]
EAJA............ Equal Access to Justice Act [*1980*]
EAJC............ Eastern Arizona Junior College [*Later, EAC*]
EAJCC.......... European Association of Jewish Community Centres (EAIO)
EAJ Criminol... East African Journal of Criminology [*A publication*] (DLA)
EAJP............ East Asia Journalism Program (EA)
EAK............. East Kootenay Community College Library [*UTLAS symbol*]
EAK............. Einleitung in die Assyrischen Koenigsinschriften [*A publication*] (BJA)
EAK............. Ethyl Amyl Ketone [*Organic chemistry*]
EAK............. Kenya [*International vehicle registration*] (ODBW)
EAL............. Eagle Industry [*Vancouver Stock Exchange symbol*]
EAL............. Early American Life Insurance Association (EA)
EAL............. Educational Assistance Ltd. (PCM)
EAL............. Ehrenfest Adiabatic Law [*Physics*]
EAL............. Electromagnetic Amplifying Lens
EAL............. Electronic Associates Limited (NITA)
EAL............. Emergency Action Level [*Nuclear energy*] (NRCH)
EAL............. Engineer Acquisition Letter (AAGC)
EAL............. Environmental Acoustics Laboratory [*Pennsylvania State University*] [*Research center*] (RCD)
EAL .... Equalized Assessed Valuation
EAL............. Equipment Air Lock [*Nuclear energy*] (NRCH)
EAL............. Equipment Applications List (MCD)
EAL............. Equivalent Age Load (IAA)
EAL............. Estimated [*or Expected*] Average Life
EAL............. Ethanolamine Ammonia Lyase [*An enzyme*]
EAL............. Ethiopia Air Lines
EAL............. Expected Average Life [*Physics*] (IAA)
EAL............. Philippine Eagle Airlines [*FAA designator*] (FAAC)
EALB............ East African Literature Bureau
EALCAE........ Ecumenical Association of Laity Centres and Academies in Europe [*See also OVATE*] [*Germany*] (EAIO)
EALJ............ East African Law Journal [*A publication*] (DLA)
EALM........... Electron-Beam Addressed Light Modulator (PDAA)
EALM........... Electronic Address Light Modulator
EALM........... European Association of Livestock Markets [*See also AEMB*] [*Belgium*] (EAIO)
EALR............ East Africa Law Reports [*A publication*] (DLA)
EALRGA........ East Asian Library Resources Group of Australia
EALS............ English & American Literature Section [*Association of College and Research Libraries*] [*American Library Association*]
EAM............. Electrical Accounting Machine (NITA)
EAM............. Electrically Alterable Memory [*Computer science*]
EAM............. Electronic Accounting Machine [*Computer science*]
EAM............. Electronic Automatic Machinery
EAM............. Elementary Access Method (IAA)
EAM............. Embedded-Atom Method [*Model of interatomic interaction*]
EAM............. Emergency Action Message [*Navy*] (NVT)
EAM............. Entered Apprentice Mason [*Freemasonry*] (ROG)
EAM............. Equipment Acquisition Manual (DNAB)
EAM............. Ergonomic Accident Model [*Engineering*]
EAM............. Ethnikon Apelephtherotikon Metopon [*National Liberation Front*] [*Greek*] (PPE)
EAM............. Evanescent Access Method [*Sperry UNIVAC*]
EAM............. [*The*] Evangelical Alliance Mission [*An association*] (NTCM)
EAM............. Ewald Ernst Air-Service [*Germany*] [*FAA designator*] (FAAC)
EAM............. External Auditory Meatus [*Anatomy*]
EAM............. Nejran [*Saudi Arabia*] [*Airport symbol*] (OAG)
EAMA........... Etats Africains et Malgache Associes [*Associated African and Malagasy States*]
EAM/AIF....... Expense Appropriation Management/Army Industrial Fund
EAMAS........ Emergency Action Message Authentication System [*Military*]
EAMC........... Eastern Atlantic and Mediterranean Command [*Military*]
EAMCBP....... European Association of Makers of Corrugated Base Papers (EAIO)
EAMD........... Engineered Average Monthly Demand [*Military*]
EAMD........... Equivalent Aerodynamic Median Diameter [*of atmospheric particulates*]
E-A-ME .... European-African-Middle Eastern [*Communications area*] [*NASA*] (KSC)
EAMECM...... European-African-Middle Eastern Campaign Medal [*Military decoration*]
EAMEDPM ... Electric Accounting Machine and Electronic Data Processing Machine
EAMF.......... European Association of Music Festivals (EA)
EAMFRO ...... East African Marine Fisheries Research Organization (USDC)
EAMFRO ...... East African Marine Fisheries Research Organization [*Marine science*] (OSRA)
EAMFS......... European Association for Maxillo-Facial Surgery (EA)
EAMG.......... Electric Arc Metallizing Gun
EAMG.......... Experimental Autoimmune Myasthenia Gravis [*Medicine*]

EAMHD .... Engineering Aspects of Magnetohydrodynamics [*A publication*] (MCD)
EAMHMS .... European Association of Museums of the History of Medical Sciences [*See also AEMHSM*] (EAIO)
EAMI............ Expansion Anchor Manufacturers Institute (EA)
EAMJ .... East African Management Journal [*A publication*]
EAMLS......... East African Military Labour Service [*British military*] (DMA)
EAMM.......... Electronic Access to Medieval Manuscripts
EAMP.......... Engine Analytical Maintenance Program [*Navy*] (NVT)
EAMR.......... Engineering Advance Material Release (KSC)
EAMS.......... Euro-Arab Management School [*Granada, Spain*] (ECON)
EAM/SELREL... Emergency Action Message/Selected Release (MCD)
EAMT.......... Expanded Alternative Minimum Tax
EAMTC........ European Association of Management Training Centres
EAMTM........ European Association of Machine Tool Merchants [*British*] (EAIO)
EAMTMC....... Eastern Area Military Traffic Management Command (AFIT)
EAMTMTS.... Eastern Area, Military Traffic Management and Terminal Service (AABC)
EAMU.......... Electric Accounting Machine Unit
EAMVBD ...... East African Institute of Malaria and Vector-Borne Disease [*Tanzania*] (PDAA)
e-an--......... Andorra [*MARC geographic area code Library of Congress*] (LCCP)
EAN............ Association Internationale de Numerotation des Articles [*International Article Numbering Association*] (EAIO)
EAN............ Eastern Mines Ltd. [*Vancouver Stock Exchange symbol*]
EAN............ Effective Atomic Number
EAN............ Emergency Action Notification [*Civil Defense*]
EAN............ Equivalent Atomic Number
EAN............ European Article Number [*Equivalent of Universal Product Code*]
EAN............ Expenditure Account Number
EAN............ Experimental Allergic Neuritis [*Medicine*]
EAN............ Experimental Autoimmune Neuritis [*Medicine*]
EAN............ Express Airways Nigeria Ltd. [*ICAO designator*] (FAAC)
EAN............ Wheatland, WY [*Location identifier FAA*] (FAAL)
EANA.......... Esperanto Association of North America [*Defunct*] (EA)
EANA.......... European Alliance of News Agencies
EANC.......... Estonian American National Council (EA)
EANCO........ Emergency Actions Noncommissioned Officer [*Army*] (AABC)
E & A......... Ecclesiastical and Admiralty Reports [*1853-55*] [*A publication*] (DLA)
E & A......... Engineering and Acquisition
E & A......... Errata and Addenda (NRCH)
E & A......... Error and Appeal [*Legal term*] (DLA)
E and A....... Exchequer and Audit Department [*British government*]
E & A......... Spinks' English Ecclesiastical and Admiralty Reports [*A publication*] (DLA)
E & A......... Upper Canada Error and Appeal Reports [*A publication*] (DLA)
E & AD........ Exchequer and Audit Department [*British government*] (RDA)
E & AR........ Error and Appeal Reports [*Canada A publication*] (DLA)
E & AUC .... Grant's Error and Appeal Reports [*A publication*] (DLA)
E & B......... Ellerman & Bucknall Steamship Co. (MHDW)
E & B......... Ellis and Blackburn's English Queen's Bench Reports [*118-120 English Reprint*] [*A publication*] (DLA)
EANDC........ Edgewood Arsenal Nuclear Defense Center [*Maryland*] [*Army*]
E & C......... Engineering and Construction
EANDC........ European-American Nuclear Data Committee [*OECD*]
E & CB1S.... Edge and Center Bead on One Side [*Technical drawings*]
E & CB2S.... Edge and Center Bead on Two Sides [*Technical drawings*]
E & CV1S.... Edge and Center V on One Side [*Technical drawings*]
E & CV2S.... Edge and Center V on Two Sides [*Technical drawings*]
E & D......... Education and Development
E & D.......... Engineering and Development Directorate [*Johnson Space Center*] [*NASA*] (NASA)
E & D.......... Experimental and Demonstration Projects
E & DO........ Experimental and Development Operations (MCD)
E & E......... Ellis and Ellis' English Queen's Bench Reports [*A publication*] (DLA)
E & E......... Escape and Evasion
E & E......... Evacuation and Evasion
E & E......... Evasion and Escape [*Military*]
E & EA........ Each and Every Accident [*Insurance*] (AIA)
E & ED........ English and Empire Digest [*A publication*] (DLA)
E & E Dig..... English and Empire Digest [*A publication*] (DLA)
E & EL........ Each and Every Loss [*Insurance*] (AIA)
E & EO........ Each and Every Occurrence [*Insurance*] (AIA)
E & ES........ Environmental and Energy Systems
E & F.......... Economic and Financial [*Plans*] [*British*]
E & F.......... Elder and Fyfes Ltd. [*Shipping*] (ROG)
E & FC........ Examined and Found Correct (ADA)
E & GVR .... Ellesmere & Glyn Valley Railway [*Later, GVR*] [*Wales*]
E&H........... Elderly and Handicapped [*TRB*] (TAG)
E & H.......... Environment and Heredity
E & I.......... Endocrine and Infertility [*Endocrinology and obstetrics*] (DAVI)
E & I.......... English and Irish Appeals, House of Lords [*A publication*] (DLA)
E & I.......... Equip and Install (MSA)
E & I.......... Examination and Inventory (AFIT)
E & I App..... Law Reports, House of Lords, English and Irish Appeals [*1866-75*] [*A publication*] (DLA)
E & ID .... Education and Information Dissemination
EAndina ...... Embotelladora Andina SA [*Associated Press*] (SAG)
E & L .... Elrick & Lavidge, Inc. (WDMC)
E & L .... Engineering and Laboratory (KSC)
E & L .... Equity & Law [*Brokerage group*] [*British*]
E&M........... Ear and Mouth
E & M.......... Effectiveness and Maintainability (MCD)
E & M.......... Electrical and Mechanical (KSC)
E & M.......... Endocrine and Metabolism [*Medicine*] (DAVI)

E & M	Erection and Maintenance
E & MC	Electrical and Mechanical Compatibility [*Military*]
E & MCC	Electrical and Mechanical Capability Committee
E & MCWG	Electrical and Mechanical Capability Working Group
E & MIWG	Electrical and Mechanical Interface Working Group [*Strategic Defense Initiative*]
E & ML	Environmental and Morale Leave [*Military*]
E&M leads	Ear and Mouth Lead [*A headpiece unit used by telephone operators and broadcasters*] (WDMC)
E & MR	Energy & Mineral Resources [*Business Publishers, Inc.*] [*No longer available online*] [*Information service or system*] (CRD)
E&O	Errors and Omissions (AAGC)
E&O	Erros & Omissions (TDOB)
E and OE	Errors and Omissions Excepted [*Insurance*]
E & OT	Enemy and Occupied Territories Department [*Ministry of Economic Warfare*] [*British World War II*]
E & P	Earnings and Profit (ADA)
E&P	Editor & Publisher (WDMC)
E & P	Exercise and Plans (CINC)
E & P	Exploration and Production [*In organization name Oil Industry International Exploration & Production Forum*]
E & P	Extraordinary and Plenipotentiary
E & P	Oil Industry International Exploration and Production Forum (EAIO)
E & P Forum	Oil Industry International Exploration and Production Forum (EA)
E & PL	Entry and Postlanding [*NASA*] (KSC)
E & R	Ends and Rings [*Architecture*] (ROG)
E & R	Engineering and Repair [*Department*] [*Navy*]
E & R	Equal and reactive [*Ophthalmology*] (DAVI)
E & R	Equal and Regular [*Ophthalmology*] (DAVI)
E & RFTS	Elementary and Reserve Flying Training School [*British military*] (DMA)
EANDRO	Electrically-Alterable Non-Destructive Read Out [*Computer science*] (IAA)
E & S	Erosion and Sediment
E & S	Evans & Sutherland Computer Corp.
E & S	Excess and Surplus Business [*Insurance*]
E & S NC	Engineers and Scientists Non-Construction [*Army*] (RDA)
E & SP	Equipment and Spare Parts
E & ST	Employment and Suitability Test [*Aerospace*] (AAG)
E & T	Education and Training [*Navy*]
E & T	Employment and Training
E&V	Endangered and Vulnerable (EERA)
E & W	England and Wales
E & WIDC	East and West India Dock Co. [*Shipping*] (ROG)
E & WLR	East and West London Railway [*British*] (ROG)
E & WR	Elmira and Williamsport Railway [*British*] (ROG)
E & Y	Eagle and Younge's English Tithe Cases [*A publication*] (DLA)
EANG	Epidemic Acute Nonbacterial Gastroenteritis [*Medicine*] (MEDA)
EANGUS	Enlisted Association of the National Guard of the United States
EANHS	East African Natural History Society (EAIO)
EANPC	European Association for National Productivity Centers [*See also AECNP*] (EAIO)
EANRRC	East African Natural Resources Research Council [*Kenya*] (PDAA)
EANS	Emergency Action Notification System [*White House Teletype network*] [*Civil Defense*]
EANS	European Article Numbering System (PDAA)
EANS	European Association of Neurosurgical Societies (EAIO)
EANYS	Energy Association of New York State (SRA)
EAO	Economy Act Order
EAO	Egyptian Antiquities Organization (EA)
EAO	Electrical Assembly Order (MCD)
EAO	Emergency Actions Officer [*Army*] (AABC)
EAOA	Eastern Authorities Orchestral Association [*British*]
EAOG	European Association of Organic Geochemists (EAIO)
EAON	Except as Otherwise Noted
EAOS	Easy Access Ordering System [*Automated book ordering system, Blackwells North America*] (NITA)
EAOS	Expiration of Active Obligated Service [*Military*]
EAOT	End of Arm Tooling [*Robotics*]
EAP	East Africa Protectorate [*Later, Kenya*]
EAP	Easton Area Public Library, Easton, PA [*OCLC symbol*] (OCLC)
EAP	Ecological Agriculture Projects [*See also PAE*] [*Sainte Anne De Bellevue, PQ*] (EAIO)
EAP	Edgar Allan Poe [*Initials used as pseudonym*]
EAP	Educational Activities (ACII)
EAP	Educational Awareness Project (EA)
EAP	Effective Air Path
EAP	Electro-Absorption Avalanche Photodiode [*Instrumentation*]
EAP	Electroacupuncture
EAP	Electronic Access Project
EAP	Electronics Assembly Plant [*College Station, TX*] [*Westinghouse Electric Corp.*]
EAP	Emergency Action Procedure [*Military*] (NVT)
EAP	Emergency Assembly Point
EAP	Employee Assistance Personnel [*Psychology*] (DAVI)
EAP	Employee Assistance Program [*Health care*] (HCT)
EAP	Emulator Application Program (MHDB)
EAP	Entered Apprentice [*Freemasonry*] (ROG)
EAP	Environment Actions Plan [*Commonwealth*] (EERA)
EAP	Environmental Action Plan [*Environmental Protection Agency*] (ERG)
EAP	Environmental Analysis and Planning (PDAA)
EAP	Environmental Assistance Procedure
EAP	Environment Assistance Program (EERA)
EAP	Epiallopregnanolone [*Endocrinology*]
EAP	Equipment Alignment Procedure (MCD)

EAP	Equivalent Air Pressure
EAP	Erythrocyte Acid Phosphatase [*Hematology*]
EAP	Esophageal Atrial Pacing [*Medicine*]
EAP	Ethanolamineperchlorate (MCD)
EAP	Europaeische Arbeiterpartei [*European Workers' Party*] [*Germany Political party*] (PPE)
EAP	Evoked Action Potential [*Neurophysiology*]
EAP	Expenditure Analysis Plan (TEL)
EAP	Experimental Activity Proposal [*Nuclear energy*] (NRCH)
EAP	Experimental Aircraft Programme [*British*]
EAP	Extended Arithmetic Processor (MHDB)
EAP	Extensible Authentication Protocol [*Computer science*]
EAP	Eye Artifact Potential
EAPA	Embedded-Alumina-Particle Aluminide [*Chemical coating*]
EAPA	Energy Abstracts for Policy Analysis [*National Science Foundation A publication*] (MCD)
EAPA	European Asphalt Pavement Association (EA)
EAPAUS	Employment Agencies Protective Association of the United States [*Later, National Employment Association*]
EAPC	East African Pioneer Corps [*British military*] (DMA)
EAPCC	European Association of Poison Control Centers (EAIO)
EAPCCCT	European Association of Poisons Control Centers and Clinical Toxicologists [*Sweden*] (EAIO)
EAPCO	East African Pesticides Control Organization (PDAA)
EAPD	Eastern Air Procurement District
EAPD	Electroabsorption Photodiode [*Electronics*] (EECA)
EA PER	Each Person [*Insurance*]
EAPF	Electrically Augmented Pressure Filter [*Chemical engineering*]
EAPFBO	European Association of Professional Fire Brigade Officers (EA)
EAPFS	Extended Appearance Potential Fine Structure (PDAA)
EAPG	Eastern Atlantic Planning Guidance [*NATO*] (NATG)
EAPH	East African Publishing House [*Kenya*]
EAPHSS	European Association of Programmes in Health Services Studies (EAIO)
EAPI	East-West Environment and Policy Institute [*East-West Center*] [*Research center*] (RCD)
EAPL	East Australian Pipeline Ltd. [*Commercial firm*]
EAPL	Engineering Assembly Parts List
EAPLR	East Africa Protectorate Law Reports [*A publication*] (DLA)
EAPM	European Association of Perinatal Medicine (EAIO)
EAPM	European Association of Personnel Management [*Paris, France*] (EA)
EAPO	Electrical Armaments Program Office [*Army*]
EAPP	Engineered Australia Plan Party [*Political party*]
EAPP	European Association for the Promotion of Poetry (EA)
EAPPCFC	Electronically Adjustable Proportionally Pressure Compensated Flow Control
EAPR	Europaische Gesellschaft fur Kartoffelforschung [*Netherlands*] (EAIO)
EAPR	European Association for Potato Research (EAIO)
EAPROM	Electrically Alterable Programmable Read-Only Memory [*Computer science*]
EA Prot LR	East Africa Protectorate Law Reports [*A publication*] (DLA)
EAPS	Electronic Air Particle Separator
EAPS	Engine Air Particle Separator
EAPS	European Association for Population Studies (EA)
EAPS	European Association of Professional Secretaries [*Paris, France*] (EAIO)
EAPSB	Edgar Allan Poe Society of Baltimore (EA)
EAPSS	Electronic Intelligence Analysis Processing Subsystem (MCD)
EAPU	Electrical Auxiliary Power Unit (DNAB)
EAPU	External Auxiliary Power Unit
EAQ	Ethylanthraquinone [*Organic chemistry*]
EAR	Earnings-at-Risk [*Incentive pay plan*]
EAR	Effective Address Register [*Computer science*] (IAA)
EAR	Electromagnetic Activity Receiver (DNAB)
EAR	Electronically Agile RADAR
EAR	Electronic Analog Resolver (WDAA)
EAR	Electronic and Aerospace Report (IAA)
EAR	Electronic Audio Recognition
EAR	Electronic Aural Responder (IAA)
EAR	Elliniki Aristera [*Greek Left Party*] [*Political party*] (EY)
EAR	Emergency Action Report [*Military*]
EAR	Employee Appraisal Record
EAR	Employee Attitude Research (IEEE)
EAR	Encyclopedia of American Religions [*A publication*]
EAR	Energy-Absorbing Resin (PDAA)
EAR	Energy Audit Report [*Navy*]
EAR	Engineering Abstract Report [*Defense Supply Agency*]
EAR	Engineering Analysis Report (KSC)
EAR	Engineering and Research (IAA)
EaR	Entartungs-Reaktion [*Reaction of Degeneration*] [*German*]
EAR	Environmental Auditing Roundtable [*Environmental Protection Agency*] (EPA)
EAR	Escape and Rescue
EAR	Estimated Additional Resources
EAR	Estimated Assumed Resources [*Minerals*]
EAR	European Association of Radiology (EA)
EAR	Experimental Alcoholic Rhabdomyolysis [*Medicine*]
EAR	Experimental Array RADAR [*Army*]
EAR	Expired Air Resuscitation (ADA)
EAR	Export Administration Regulation [*Department of Commerce*]
EAR	Extravehicular Aerospace Routing
EAR	Hearx Ltd. [*AMEX symbol*] (SAG)
EAR	HEARx Ltd. [*AMEX symbol*] (TTSB)
EAR	Kearney [*Nebraska*] [*Airport symbol*] (OAG)

EARA .... Equipment Authorization Review Activity (MCD)
EARAC .... East Anglian Regional Advisory Council for Further Education (AIE)
EARB .... Electronics and Avionics Requirements Board (ACII)
EARB .... European Airlines Research Bureau
EARB .... Export Administration Review Board
EARC .... East African Reconnaissance Corps [*British military*] (DMA)
EARC .... Eastern Aerospace Rescue and Recovery Center [*Air Force*]
EARC .... Eastern Association of Rowing Colleges (EA)
EARC .... Educational Administration Resource Centre [*Information service or system*] (IID)
EARC .... Elemental Analysis Research Center [*Department of Health and Human Services*] (GRD)
EARC .... Extraordinary Administrative Radio Conference [*ITU*]
EARCCUS.... East African Regional Committee for Conservation and Utilisation of Soil
EARCOS ...... East Asia Regional Council of Overseas Schools (EA)
EARFLAP ..... Emergency Action Reporting for Logistics Action Programming [*Military*] (AFM)
EARI........... Engineer Agency for Resources Inventories [*Army Corps of Engineers*]
EARI........... Equipment Acceptance Requirements and Inspections (AAG)
EARL.......... Easy Access Report Language [*Computer science*] (MHDB)
EARL.......... Electronically Accessible Russian Lexicon
EARL.......... Environmental Awareness Reading List [*Department of the Interior*]
EARL........ Esso Australia Resources Ltd. [*Commercial firm*]
EARL........ Extended Algorithmic "R" Language
EARLPRADATE... Earliest Practicable Date
Earn.......... Earnshaw's Gold Coast Judgments [*1909-10*] [*Ghana*] [*A publication*] (DLA)
EARN .... Engineering Alumni Recruiting Network
EARN .... European Academic Research Network [*A computer network*]
Earnshaw..... Gold Coast Judgments, by Earnshaw [*1909-10*] [*Ghana*] [*A publication*] (DLA)
EAROM .... Electrically Alterable Read-Only Memory [*Computer science*]
EAROPH....... East Asia Regional Organization for Planning and Housing
EAROS .... Electrically Alterable Read-Only Store [*Computer science*]
EARP .... Equipment Antiriot Projector [*British*] (MCD)
EARRS .... Engineering Automated Release and Record System (MCD)
EARS .... East African Reconnaissance Squadron [*British military*] (DMA)
EARS .... Electro-Acoustic Rating System (PDAA)
EARS .... Elliot Automation RADAR System (IAA)
EARS .... Emergency Airborne Reaction System (MCD)
EARS .... Emergency Automated Response Subsystem [*National Oceanic and Atmospheric Administration*]
EARS .... En Route Analysis and Reporting System [*FAA*] (TAG)
EARS .... Entry to Anesthesia Record by Speech
EARS .... Environmental Analog Recording System
EARS .... Epilepsy Abstracts Retrieval Service (NITA)
EARS .... Epilepsy Abstracts Retrieval System (PDAA)
EARS .... Ethernet Alto Research Generator Scanning Laser Output Terminal [*Laser printer*] (NITA)
EARS .... Executive Audial Rehabilitation Society
EARSEL....... European Association of Remote Sensing Laboratories (EA)
EA-RSL........ Encyclopedia of Associations: Regional, State, and Local Organizations [*A publication*]
Earth G ...... Earth Garden [*A publication*]
Earthgr....... Earthgrains Co. [*Associated Press*] (SAG)
EarthSc....... Earth Sciences, Inc. [*Associated Press*] (SAG)
EarthT......... Earth Technology Corp. [*Associated Press*] (SAG)
EARTS .... En Route Automated Radar Tracking System [*FAA*] (TAG)
EARTS .... En Route Automated RADAR Tracking System [*Aviation*] (FAAC)
Earw .... Earwalker's Manchester Court-Leet Records [*England*] [*A publication*] (DLA)
EAS .... Early American Society (EA)
EAS .... Earth Aspect Sensor
EAs .... East African Shilling [*Monetary unit*]
EAS .... Eastern Analytical Symposium
EAS .... Eastern Apicultural Society of North America (EA)
EAS .... Eastern College, St. Davids, PA [*OCLC symbol*] (OCLC)
EAS .... Economic Analysis Staff [*Department of Agriculture*] (GFGA)
EAS .... Education Administration Specialist (PGP)
EAS .... Educational Analog Simulator
EAS .... Electron Accelerator System (IAA)
EAS .... Electronic Actuation System
EAS .... Electronic Air Suspension [*Automotive engineering*]
EAS .... Electronic Air Switching [*Automotive engineering*]
EAS .... Electronic Altitude Sensor (DNAB)
EAS .... Electronic Article Surveillance
EAS .... Electronic Automatic Switch (IAA)
EAS .... Electronique Aerospatiale [*France*]
EAS .... Employee Aptitude Survey [*Psychology*] (AEBS)
EAS .... Employee Auxiliary Services (MCD)
EAS .... End-Around Shift
EAS .... Energy Absorbing Steering
EAS .... Engineering Aid, Surveyor [*Navy rating Obsolete*]
EAS .... Engineering Analysis Services [*Auto industry supplier*]
EAS .... Engineering Automated Systems (MCD)
EAS .... Enlisted Assignment System
EAS .... Enterprise Allowance Scheme [*for the self-employed*] [*British*]
EAS .... Environmental Activities Staff [*Automotive industry*]
EAS .... Environmental Assessment Scale [*Occupational therapy*]
EAS .... Equipment Acquisition Strategy (ADA)
EAS .... Equivalent Air Speed
EAS .... Error Analysis Study
EAS .... Essential Air Servicer [*Department of Transportation*]

EAS .... Essential Auxiliary Support [*Nuclear energy*] (NRCH)
EAS .... Estimated Air Speed (MCD)
EAS .... Estonian Association of Scientists
EAS .... Europe Aero Service
EAS .... European Accident Statement
EAS .... European Aquaculture Society (EA)
EAS .... European Astronomical Society
EAS .... European Atherosclerosis Society (EA)
EAS .... Evaluation and Advisory Service [*Educational testing service*] (AEBS)
EAS .... Evaluation and Analysis Staff [*Bureau of Ordnance*] [*Washington, DC Navy*] (MCD)
EAS .... Excutive Aerospace (Pty) Ltd. [*South Africa ICAO designator*] (FAAC)
EAS .... Executive Agreement Series [*A publication*] (DLA)
EAS .... Executive Air Services Proprietary Ltd. [*Australia*] (ADA)
EAS .... Executive Assignment Service [*Civil Service Commission*]
EAS .... Exercise Angioscintigraphy [*Medicine*]
EAS .... Experiment Assurance System [*Nuclear energy*] (NRCH)
EAS .... Experimenter-Administered Stimulation [*Psychology*]
EAS .... Expiration of Active Service [*Marine Corps*]
EAS .... Extended Area Service [*Telecommunications*]
EAS .... Extensive Air Shower [*Cosmic ray physics*]
EAS .... External Agency Simulator (MCD)
EAS .... External Archival Storage [*Computer science*] (BARN)
EAS .... San Sebastian [*Spain*] [*Airport symbol*] (OAG)
EASA .... East African School of Aviation [*Kenya*] (PDAA)
EASA .... Electrical Apparatus Service Association (EA)
EASA .... Electronics Association of South Australia
EASA .... Emergency Air Staff Actions (AFM)
EASA .... Engineer Automation Support Activity [*Army Corps of Engineers*]
EASA .... External Architectural Students Association [*British*] (BI)
EASAA .... European Association of South Asian Archaeologists [*British*] (EAIO)
EASAL .... Easy Application Language [*Computer science*] (MHDB)
EASAMS ..... Elliott Automation Space and Advanced Military Systems (MCD)
EASB .... Electronic Area Support Base [*Air Force*]
EASC .... East African Service Corps [*British military*] (DMA)
EASC .... East Asian Studies Center [*Indiana University*] [*Research center*] (RCD)
EASC .... Eastern Administrative Support Center (USDC)
EASC .... Eastern Administrative Support Center [*Marine science*] (OSRA)
EASC .... Employers Association of South Carolina (SRA)
EASC .... Ethylaluminum Sesquichloride [*Organic chemistry*]
EASC .... Exploration of Alternative Concepts (MCD)
Easco.......... Easco, Inc. [*Associated Press*] (SAG)
EASCO .... European Association of Schools and Colleges of Optometry (EA)
EASCOM ..... Eastern Command [*World War II*]
EASCOMINT... Extended Air Surveillance Communications Intercept [*Air Force*]
EASCON..... Electronics and Aerospace Systems Convention (MCD)
EASD .... European Association for the Study of Diabetes [*See also AEED*] (EAIO)
EASDAQ...... European Association of Securities Dealers Automated Quotation [*System*]
EASE .... Easement [*Legal term*] (DLA)
EASE .... Econolite Automatic Sensing Equipment
EASE .... Editing, Arranging, and Sequencing Environment [*Computer science*] (BYTE)
EASE .... Educational and Scientific Establishment (IIA)
EASE .... Elastic Analysis for Structural Engineering (NRCH)
EASE .... Electrical Automatic Support Equipment
EASE .... Electronic Analog Simulating Equipment [*Computer science*]
EASE .... Electronic Assisted Solicitation Exchange (AAGC)
EASE .... Elementary Adult Sex Education (EDAC)
EASE .... Embedded Advance Sampling Environment [*Hewlett-Packard Co.*]
EASE .... Emigrant's Assured Savings Estate [*Banking program*]
EASE .... Engineering Applications for Support Engineers [*British*]
EASE .... Engineering Automatic System for Solving Equations
EASE .... Equal Area SSM/I [*Special Sensor Microwave/Imager*] Earth [*Grid*] (USDC)
EASE .... Equal Area SSMI [*Special Sensor Microwave Imager*] Earth Grid [*Marine science*] (OSRA)
EASE .... Escape and Survival Equipment (PDAA)
EASE .... European Association for Special Education
EASE .... European Association of Science Editors [*European Association of Earth Sc ience Editors and European Life Sciences Editors*] [*Formed by a merger of*] (EAIO)
EASE .... Experimental Assembly of Structures in Extravehicular Activity [*Space technology*]
EASE Grid .... Equal Area SSMI [*Special Sensor Microwave Imager*] Earth Grid [*Marine science*] (OSRA)
EASel.......... Engineers Adhesive Selector Program
EASEMT...... Easement [*British Legal term*] (ROG)
EASEP........ Early Apollo Scientific Experiments Package [*or Payload*] [*NASA*]
EASH .... Shilling [*Monetary unit in Tanzania*]
EASHP .... European Association of Senior Hospital Physicians (PDAA)
EASI........... East Asia Strategy Initiative [*Military*]
EASI........... Electrical Accounting for the Security Industry [*IBM Corp.*] (IEEE)
EASI........... Electronic Acquisition Systems Instrumentation [*Vehicle testing*] [*Automotive engineering*]
EASI........... Engineered Support Sys [*NASDAQ symbol*] (TTSB)
EASI........... Engineered Support Systems, Inc. [*NASDAQ symbol*] (NQ)
EASI........... Equal Access to Softward and Information
EASI........... Estimate of Adversary Sequence Interruption [*Nuclear energy*] (NRCH)
EASI........... European Association of Shipping Informatics [*Brussels, Belgium*] (EAIO)
EASI........... Expanded Additional Skill Identifier [*Military*] (AABC)

EASI	Expected Amount of Sample Information [*Statistics*]
EASIAC	Easy Instruction Automatic Computer (IAA)
EASIC	Evaluating Acquired Skills in Communication [*Language ability test*]
EASIE	EJS/ECP Automated Status Information and Exception System (MCD)
EASILY	Experimental Avionics Simulation and Integration Laboratory
EASIT	European Association for Software Access and Infomation Transfer (PDAA)
EASL	Easel Corp. [*NASDAQ symbol*] (SAG)
EASL	Electroacoustic Systems Laboratory
EASL	Engineering Analysis and Simulation Language [*Computer science*]
EASL	Engineering Approved Source List
EASL	Experimental Assembly and Sterilization Laboratory [*NASA*]
EASM/RSF	External Armament Stores Management/Remote Set Fuze (MCD)
EASMT	Easement [*British Legal term*] (ROG)
EASNA	Employee Assistance Society of North America (EA)
EASP	Edgewood Arsenal Special Publication [*Army*]
EASP	Educational Advice Service Project (AIE)
EASP	Employee Auxiliary Service Personnel (MCD)
EASP	European Association for Signal Processing [*Lausanne, Switzerland*] (MCD)
EASS	Engine Automatic Stop and Start System (PDAA)
EASSG	European Accountancy Students Study Group (PDAA)
EASSS	European Access to Seafloor Survey Systems [*Southampton Oceanography Centre*] [*British*]
EAST	East Australian Standard Time
EAST	Eastern (WDAA)
EAST	Eastern Academy of Sexual Therapy [*Later, SSTAR*] (EA)
East	Eastern Reporter [*A publication*] (ILCA)
EAST	Eastover Corp. [*NASDAQ symbol*] (NQ)
East	East's English King's Bench Term Reports [*A publication*] (DLA)
East	East's Notes of Cases in Morley's East Indian Digest [*A publication*] (DLA)
EAST	Electric Arc Shock Tunnel [*NASA*]
EAST	European Academy of Science and Technology
EAST	Evaluation and Subsystem Training (SAA)
EAST	Experimental Army Satellite Tactical
EAST	External Rotation, Abduction Stress Test [*Medicine*]
East Af	East Africa Court of Appeals Reports [*A publication*] (DLA)
EASTAF	Eastern Transport Air Force
East Afr J Criminol	East African Journal of Criminology [*A publication*] (DLA)
East Afr LJ	East African Law Journal [*A publication*] (DLA)
East Afr L Rep	East Africa Law Reports [*A publication*] (DLA)
East Afr L Rep	Eastern Africa Law Reports [*Durban*] [*A publication*] (DLA)
EASTASAC	East African Society of African Culture
Eastbay	Eastbay, Inc. [*Associated Press*] (SAG)
East Car U	East Carolina University (GAGS)
East Cent Okla St U	East Central Oklahoma State University (GAGS)
EastChm	Eastman Chemical Co. [*Associated Press*] (SAG)
EASTCO	East Coast
Eastco	Eastco Industrial Safety Corp. [*Associated Press*] (SAG)
EASTCOBASE	East Coast Base
EASTCOMMRGN	Eastern Communications Region [*Military*] (AFM)
EASTCON	Eastern Sea Frontier Control Local of Shipping in Gulf of Maine
EASTCON	Eastern States International Construction Expo and Conference [*Associated General Contractors of America - Carolinas Branch*] (TSPED)
EASTCON	Electronic Aerospace Systems Convention
East Conn St U	East Connecticut State University (GAGS)
EASTCONRADREG	Eastern Continental Air Defense Region (DNAB)
East DC	Eastern District Court Reports [*South Africa*] [*A publication*] (DLA)
East DL	Eastern Districts, Local Division, South African Law Reports [*A publication*] (DLA)
EastEn	Eastern Enterprises [*Associated Press*] (SAG)
East (Eng)	East's English King's Bench Term Reports [*A publication*] (DLA)
Eastern J Int L	Eastern Journal of International Law [*A publication*] (ILCA)
Eastern J In'tl L	Eastern Journal of International Law [*A publication*] (DLA)
Eastern J of Internat L	Eastern Journal of International Law [*A publication*] (DLA)
East Europe	International Market Letter: East Europe [*A publication*] (DLA)
EASTH	Easthamstead [*England*]
East Ill U	Eastern Illinois University (GAGS)
East J Int L	Eastern Journal of International Law [*A publication*] (DLA)
East Ky U	Eastern Kentucky University (GAGS)
EASTLANT	Eastern Atlantic Area [*NATO*]
EASTLANTMEDCOM	Eastern Atlantic and Mediterranean Command [*Military*]
East LR	Eastern Law Reporter [*Canada*] [*A publication*] (DLA)
East LR (Can)	Eastern Law Reporter [*Canada*] [*A publication*] (DLA)
EASTM	European Association for Marine Sciences and Techniques [*Marine science*] (OSRA)
East Mich U	Eastern Michigan University (GAGS)
East Mont C	Eastern Montana College (GAGS)
EASTN	Eastern
East N Mex U	Eastern New Mexico University (GAGS)
East N of C	East's Notes of Cases in Morley's East Indian Digest [*A publication*] (DLA)
EASTOMP	East-Ocean Meeting Point
East Ore C	Eastern Oregon College (GAGS)
EASTPAC	Eastern Pacific Area (MUGU)
EASTPAC	Eastern Pacific Command [*Navy*]
East PC	East's Pleas of the Crown [*A publication*] (DLA)
East PC (Eng)	East's Pleas of the Crown (England) [*A publication*] (DLA)
East Pl Cr	East's Pleas of the Crown [*A publication*] (DLA)
East Punjab	All India Reporter, East Punjab [*1948-50*] [*A publication*] (DLA)
East Rep	Eastern Reporter [*A publication*] (DLA)
EASTROPAC	Eastern Tropical Pacific [*Oceanographic expedition*]

EASTROPIC	Cooperative Survey of the Eastern Tropical Pacific (MSC)
EASTSEAFRON	Eastern Sea Frontier
East Stroudsburg U	East Stroudsburg University of Pennsylvania (GAGS)
EASTT	Experimental Army Satellite Tactical Terminals
East Tenn St U	East Tennessee State University (GAGS)
East Tex St U	East Texas State University (GAGS)
East US Bus L Rev	Eastern United States Business Law Review [*A publication*] (DLA)
EastUtl	Eastern Utilities Association [*Associated Press*] (SAG)
East Va Med Sch	Eastern Virginia Medicine School (GAGS)
East Wash U	Eastern Washington University (GAGS)
EASV	Engine Angular Speed Variation [*Automotive engineering*]
EASY	Early Acquisition System [*Army*] (AABC)
EASY	Efficient Assembly System [*Honeywell, Inc.*] [*Assembler language*]
EASY	Engine Analyzer Systems [*Air Force*] (MCD)
EASY	Evasive Aircraft System (MCD)
EASY	Exception Analysis System (IAA)
EAT	Air Transport Ltd. [*Slovakia*] [*ICAO designator*] (FAAC)
EAT	Brinker International [*Formerly, Chili's, Inc.*] [*NYSE symbol*] (SPSG)
EAT	Brinker Intl. [*NYSE symbol*] (TTSB)
EAT	Earliest Arrival Time
EAT	East African Time
EAT	Eastern Air Transport
EAT	Eating Attitude Test (EDAC)
EAT	Ectopic Atrial Tachycardia [*Cardiology*] (DAVI)
EAT	Ehrlich Ascites Tumor [*Oncology*]
EAT	Electroaerosol Therapy [*Medicine*]
EAT	Electronic Angle Tracking (PDAA)
E/AT	Electrons per Atom
EAT	Employment Appeal Tribunal [*British*]
EAT	Encoder Address Translator
EAT	End-Around Test
EAT	Engineering Analysis Team [*NASA*]
EAT	Environmental Acceptance Test (NASA)
EAT	Equipment Acceptance Test (MCD)
EAT	Estimated Arrival Time (WDAA)
EAT	European Advertising Tripartite [*Brussels, Belgium*] (EA)
EAT	European Association of Teachers [*See also AEDE*] (EAIO)
EAT	Experimental Autoimmune Thymitis [*Medicine*]
EAT	Experiments in Art and Technology (EA)
EAT	External Air Transportability (MCD)
EAT	PNR Food Industries Ltd. [*Toronto Stock Exchange symbol*]
EAT	Tanzania [*International vehicle registration*] (ODBW)
EAT	Wenatchee [*Washington*] [*Airport symbol*] (OAG)
EATA	East Asia Travel Association (EAIO)
EATA	Enhanced AT Attachment [*Computer science*]
EATB	East Anglia Tourist Board [*British*] (DCTA)
EATC	Ecology and Analysis of Trace Contaminants [*Program*] [*Oak Ridge National Laboratory*] (IID)
EATC	Ehrlich Ascites Tumor Cell [*Oncology*]
EATC	Electronic Automatic Temperature Control [*Automotive engineering*]
EATCHIP	European Air Traffic Control Harmonization and Integration Program [*Eurocontrol*]
Eat Cont	Eaton's Supplement to Chipman on Contracts [*A publication*] (DLA)
EATCQ	Expressed Attitude Toward Confrontation Questionnaire (EDAC)
EATCS	European Association for Theoretical Computer Science (EAIO)
EATD	Expanded Advanced Terminal Defense Study
EATDS	Expanded Advanced Terminal Defense Study (MCD)
Eaterie	Eateries, Inc. [*Associated Press*] (SAG)
EATI	Equipment and Tool Institute [*Glenview, IL*]
EATIC	East African Tuberculosis Investigation Centre [*Kenya*] (PDAA)
EATJP	European Association for the Trade in Jute Products (EA)
EATM	Edgewood Arsenal Technical Memorandum [*Army*]
EATMS	Electroacoustic Transmission Measuring System [*Telecommunications*] (TEL)
EatnVan	Eaton Vance Corp. [*Associated Press*] (SAG)
EATO	Euro-Asia Trade Organisation
Eaton	Eaton Corp. [*Associated Press*] (SAG)
EATP	European Association for Textile Polyolefins (EAIO)
EATR	Edgewood Arsenal Technical Report [*Army*]
EATR	Enroute Air Traffic Regulation (MCD)
EATR	Equilibrium Air Total Radiation
EATS	Eateries, Inc. [*NASDAQ symbol*] (NQ)
EATS	Empire Air Training Scheme [*British military*] (DMA)
EATS	Engine Acceleration Temperature Schedule
EATS	Equipment Accuracy Test Station
EATS	European Air Transport Service
EATS	Extended Area Test System [*Navy*]
EATTA	East African Tea Trade Association (EA)
EATWOT	Ecumenical Association of Third World Theologies [*India*]
EATX	Electronic Automatic Transaxle [*Automotive engineering*]
EAU	American University, Washington, DC [*OCLC symbol*] (OCLC)
EAU	Auchinoon [*Scotland*] [*Seismograph station code, US Geological Survey*] (SEIS)
e-au--	Austria [*MARC geographic area code Library of Congress*] (LCCP)
EAU	Eagle European Airways [*British*] [*FAA designator*] (FAAC)
EAU	Early Assistance Unit
EAU	Eau Claire [*Wisconsin*] [*Airport symbol*] (OAG)
EAU	Emergency Accommodation Unit (ADA)
EAU	Enabled Artists United [*An association*] (EA)
EAU	Energy Absorbing Unit [*Automotive engineering*]
EAU	Engine Analyzer Unit (DWSG)
EAU	European Association of Urology
EAU	Experimental Allergic Uveitis [*Ophthalmology*]
EAU	Experimental Autoimmune Uveoretinitis [*Immunology*]

EAU	Extended Arithmetic Unit (IAA)
EAU	Uganda [*International vehicle registration*] (ODBW)
EAUG	European Atex Users Group [*Deventer, Netherlands*] (EAIO)
EA-UPDS	Encyclopedia of Associations: Updating Service [*A publication*]
EAUS	Enterprise Association of the United States (EA)
EAUTC	Engineer Aviation Unit Training Center [*Military*]
EAUXCP	East Auxiliary Airborne Command Post (MCD)
EAV	Bettles, AK [*Location identifier FAA*] (FAAL)
EAV	Eagle Aviation Luftfahrt Ges.MbH [*Austria*] [*FAA designator*] (FAAC)
EAV	Effective Angular Velocity
EAV	Engine Assembly Vehicle
EAV	Equine Abortion Virus [*Medicine*] (DMAA)
EAV	Explosive-Actuated Valve
EAV	Viner [*E. A.*] Holdings [*Toronto Stock Exchange symbol*]
EAVA	European Association of Veterinary Anatomists (EA)
EAVC	Edinburgh Artillery Volunteer Corps [*British military*] (DMA)
EAVE	European Audiovisual Entrepeneurs [*EC*] (ECED)
EAVE	Experimental Autonomous Vehicle [*Underwater robot*]
EA VEH	Each Vehicle [*Insurance*]
EAVES	Eavesdropping (DLA)
EAVF	Electrically Augmented Vacuum Filter [*Chemical engineering*]
EAVN	Eaton Vance [*NASDAQ symbol*] (TTSB)
EAVN	Eaton Vance Corp. [*NASDAQ symbol*] (NQ)
EAW	Easy Washer [*Laboratory science*]
EAW	Electrical Association for Women [*British*]
EAW	Electric Arc Weld
EAW	Employment at Will
EAW	Equivalent Average Word [*Mathematics*] (IAA)
EAW	Ethnic Aged Worker
EAW	European Airways Ltd. [*British*] [*FAA designator*] (FAAC)
EAWA	East Africa Wins Again [*Used by US Diplomatic Corps in Nairobi, Kenya, to express dispair at bureaucratic obstacles*]
EAWLS	East African Wild Life Society (GNE)
EAWP	Eastern Atlantic War Plan [*NATO*] (NATG)
EAWP	Ethnic Aged Working Party [*Australia Political party*]
EAWR	Employment at Will Reporter [*A publication*] (DLA)
EAX	Eastern Air Executive Ltd. [*British ICAO designator*] (FAAC)
EAX	Electronic Automatic Exchange [*See also ESS*] [*General Telephone & Electronics*] [*Telecommunications*]
EAX	Electronic Automatic Switch (ECII)
EAZ	Empfindlicher Aufschlagzuender [*Superquick impact fuze*] [*German military - World War II*]
eb----	Baltic States [*MARC geographic area code Library of Congress*] (LCCP)
EB	Die Heilige Schrift in Deutscher Uebersetzung. Echter-Bibel [*Wuerzburg*] [*A publication*] (BJA)
EB	Early Bargain [*Stock exchange term British*] (DCTA)
EB	Early Bronze [*Age*]
EB	Early Burst [*Premature explosion of a warhead*]
EB	EarthBank Association of North America (EA)
EB	Eastbound
E/B	Edges Bevelled [*Printing*] (DGA)
EB	Electric Boat (MCD)
EB	Electricity Board [*British*]
E/B	Electrode per Bit (EECA)
EB	Electron Beam
E-B	Electron-Bombardment (SAA)
EB	Electronic Beam [*Electronics*]
EB	Electronic Bourse (ECON)
EB	Elementary Body [*Hematology*]
EB	Emergency Box (MCD)
EB	Emergency Brake (WDAA)
EB	Emissions Balancing [*Environmental Protection Agency*] (GFGA)
EB	Emitter Base (IAA)
EB	Emphysematous Bullae [*Pulmonary medicine*]
EB	Encoder Buffer (IAA)
EB	Encyclopaedia Biblica [*A publication*]
EB	Encyclopaedia Britannica, Inc.
EB	Engine Bulletin (MCD)
EB	Engine Burn [*NASA*]
EB	Engineer Battalion [*Military*]
EB	Engineering Bulletin (MCD)
EB	English Baron (ROG)
EB	English Bible
EB	Enlistment Bonus [*Military*] (AABC)
EB	Environmental Buoy [*Marine science*] (MSC)
EB	Epidermolysis Bullosa [*Dermatology*]
EB	Epstein-Barr [*Virus*]
EB	Equal Brake (OA)
EB	Equipment Bay (KSC)
EB	Equipment Branch [*Air Force British*]
EB	Equipment Building (AAG)
EB	Erbium [*Symbol is Er*] [*Chemical element*] (ROG)
E-B	Estate-Bottling [*Wine*]
EB	Estradiol Benzoate [*Endocrinology*]
E-B	Etch-Bleach [*Photography*] (DGA)
EB	Ethidium Bromide [*Trypanocide*] [*Also, ETB, Etd Br Biochemical analysis*]
EB	Ethiopian Birr [*Monetary Unit*] (BARN)
EB	Ethylbenzene [*Organic chemistry*]
EB	Ethylene Bromide [*Same as DBE, EDB*] [*Organic chemistry*]
EB	Ettore Bugatti [*Auto engineer*] [*French*]
EB	Evaluation Branch [*BUPERS*]
EB	Evan's Blue [*Fluorescent dye*]
EB	Event Block [*Computer science*] (IAA)

EB	Executive Board
EB	Executive Bulletin
EB	Expansion Bolt [*Technical drawings*]
EB	Experimental Buoy [*Marine science*] (MSC)
EB	[*The*] Expositor's Bible [*A publication*]
EB	Extended Benefits [*Unemployment insurance*]
EB	External Burning (RDA)
EB	Eyepiece Box
EB	L'Equilibre Biologique [*France*] [*Research code symbol*]
EB	Pennsylvania Commuter Airlines [*Airline code*]
EB1S	Edge Bead One Side [*Lumber*] (DAC)
EBA	Early Birds of Aviation [*Defunct*] (EA)
EBA	Ecole des Beaux Arts [*Paris, France*]
EBA	Edison Birthplace Association (EA)
EBA	Elba Island [*Italy*] [*Airport symbol Obsolete*] (OAG)
EBA	Electric Boat Association [*British*] (DBA)
EBA	Electron Beam Accelerator
EBA	Emergency Breathing Apparatus
EBA	Endemic Bird Area
EBA	Engineer Battlefield Assessment [*Military*] (INF)
EBA	English Bowling Association
EBA	Enriched Brucella Blood Agar [*Culture media*]
EBA	Enterprise-Based Agreement
EBA	Environmental Bankers Association
EBA	Epizootic Bovine Abortion
EBA	Erythrocyte Binding Antigen [*Immunology*]
EBA	Ethoxybenzoic Acid [*Dental cement*]
EBA	Ethyl(benzyl)aniline [*Organic chemistry*]
EBA	Ethyl Bromoacetate [*Organic chemistry*]
EBA	Ethyl(butyl)amine [*Organic chemistry*]
EBA	Ethylene Butyl Acrylate [*Organic chemistry*]
EBA	European Business Associates [*Information systems marketing organization*] (NITA)
EBA	Experimental Ballistics Associates [*Defunct*] (EA)
EBA	Experimental Behavioral Analyzer
EBAA	European Business Aviation Association (EAIO)
EBAA	Eye Bank Association of America (EA)
EBAE	European Bureau of Adult Education (EAIO)
EBAILL	European Bureau for the Allocation of International Long Lines (NATG)
EBAL	Aalst [*Belgium ICAO location identifier*] (ICLI)
EBAM	Amougies [*Belgium ICAO location identifier*] (ICLI)
EBAM	Electron Beam Access Method (PDAA)
EBAM	Electron-Beam-Addressed Memory [*Air Force*]
EB & BB	Eastbound Basing and Billing Book
EB & E	Ellis, Blackburn, and Ellis' English Queen's Bench Reports [*1858*] [*A publication*] (DLA)
EB & F	Equipment Blockages and Failures [*Telecommunications*] (TEL)
EB & S	Ellis, Best, and Smith's English Queen's Bench Reports [*A publication*] (DLA)
EB & SR	Engineer Boat and Shore Regiment [*Army*]
EBAP	Eldisine [*Vindesine*], BCNU , Adriamycin, Prednisone [*Carmustine*] [*Antineoplastic drug regimen*]
EBAP	External Burning-Assisted Projectile [*Military*] (DNAB)
EBAPS	Engine Bleed Air Precooler System
EBAS	Electron Beam Activated Switch (PDAA)
EBAS	Electronic Beam Activated Switch (IAA)
EBASA	Ethyl(benzyl)anilinesulfonic Acid [*Organic chemistry*]
EBAW	Antwerp-Anvers [*Belgium ICAO location identifier*] (ICLI)
EBAY	Eastbay, Inc. [*NASDAQ symbol*] (SAG)
EBB	Economic Bulletin Board [*Information service or system*] (IID)
EBB	Electronic Bulletin Board [*Department of Commerce Washington, DC Information service or system*] (IID)
EBB	Entebbe/Kampala [*Uganda*] [*Airport symbol*] (OAG)
EBB	European Brazilian Bank [*London, England*]
EBB	Extra Best Best [*Steel wire*]
EBBA	Eastern Bird Banding Association (EA)
EBBA	English Basket Ball Association
EBBA	(Ethoxybenylidene)butylaniline [*Organic chemistry*]
EBBB	Brussels [*Belgium ICAO location identifier*] (ICLI)
EBBD	Central Data Bank, EUROCONTROL [*Belgium ICAO location identifier*] (ICLI)
EBBE	Beauvechain [*Belgium ICAO location identifier*] (ICLI)
EBBF	Equitable Benefit-Based Financing
EBBL	Klein Brogel [*Belgium ICAO location identifier*] (ICLI)
EBBR	Brussels/National [*Belgium ICAO location identifier*] (ICLI)
EBBS	Brussels [*Belgium ICAO location identifier*] (ICLI)
EBBS	Engineering Bulletin Board System
EBBS	European Brain and Behaviour Society (PDAA)
EBBT	Brasschaat [*Belgium ICAO location identifier*] (ICLI)
EBBU	Brussels [*Belgium ICAO location identifier*] (ICLI)
EBBV	Brussels [*Belgium ICAO location identifier*] (ICLI)
EBBX	Bertrix [*Belgium ICAO location identifier*] (ICLI)
EBC	Aero Ejecutivo de Baja California SA de CV [*Mexico ICAO designator*] (FAAC)
EBC	Bay Area Library and Information System [*Library network*]
EBC	Brevard Community College, Cocoa, FL [*OCLC symbol*] (OCLC)
EBC	Echelons Below Corps [*Army*] (DOMA)
EBC	Educational Broadcasting Corp. (EA)
EBC	Electoral Boundaries Commission [*Victoria, Australia*]
EBC	Electron Beam Coating
EBC	Electron Beam Control
EBC	Electron Beam Curing [*Chemical technology*]
EBC	Electron Beam Cutting [*Engraving*] [*Welding*]
EBC	Electronic Batch Control

EBC	Employee Benefits Cases (DLA)
EBC	Emulated Buffer Computer (MCD)
EBC	Enamel Bonded Single Cotton [Wire insulation] (AAG)
EBC	End Breguet Cruise [SST]
EBC	Enterprise-Based Committee [Australia]
EBC	Environmental Business Council
EBC	Epoxy Bond Coating
EBC	Eugene Ballet Company [Eugene, OR]
EBC	European Bibliographical Center
EBC	European Billiards Confederation
EBC	European Brewery Convention
EBC	Expositor's Bible Commentary [A publication]
EBC	External Baggage Container (DNAB)
EBCA	Department of Energy Board of Contract Appeals (AAGC)
EBCA	(Ethoxybenzylidene)cyanoaniline [Also, PEBAB] [Organic chemistry]
EBCA	External Branch Condition Address [Telecommunications] (TEL)
EBCD	Extended Binary-Coded Decimal [Computer science]
EBCDI	Extended Binary-Coded Decimal Interchange [Computer science] (IAA)
EBCDIC	Extended Binary-Coded Decimal Interchange Code [Computer science]
EBCE	Electron Beam Control Electronics
EBCE	Experience-Based Career Education
EBCE-MD	Experience-Based Career Education for Mentally Disabled Students (OICC)
EBCG	Experimental Buried Collector Gauge
EBCI	Charleroi/Gosselies [Belgium ICAO location identifier] (ICLI)
EBCI	Eagle Bancorp, Inc. [NASDAQ symbol] (NQ)
EBCI	European Biological Control Laboratory (ECON)
EBCI	External Branch Condition Input [Telecommunications] (TEL)
EBC-IVH	Electronic Braking Control - Four Wheel Hybrid [Automotive engineering]
EBCM	Electronic Brake Control Module [Automotive engineering]
EBCM	Extended Boundary Condition Method
EBCP	Eastern Bancorp [NASDAQ symbol] (TTSB)
EBCP	Eastern Bancorp, Inc. [NASDAQ symbol] (SAG)
EBCS	Electronic Business Communications System
EBCS	European Barge Carrier System (ICLI)
EBCT	Empresa Brasileira de Correios e Telegrafos [State enterprise] [Brazil] (EY)
EBCT	Empty Bed Contact Time [Environmental Protection Agency]
EBCT	Extended Battlefield Contact Team (MCD)
EBCV	Chievres [Belgium ICAO location identifier] (ICLI)
ebd	Ebenda (BJA)
EBD	Economic Batch Determination
EBD	Effective Billing Date (TEL)
EBD	Electronic Brake-Force Distribution [Anti-lock brake systems] [Automotive engineering]
EBD	El Obeid [Sudan] [Airport symbol] (OAG)
EBD	Emotional and Behavioural Difficulties (AIE)
EBD	Epidermolysis Bullosa Dystrophia [Dermatology]
EBD	Equivalent Binary Digit
EBD	Eucaloric Balanced Diet
EBD	Eye Ball Down (MCD)
EBDC	Enamel Bonded Double Cotton [Wire insulation]
EBDC	Ethylenebis(dithiocarbamate) [Organic chemistry]
EBDD	Epidermolysis Bullosa Dystrophic Dominant [Dermatology]
EBDI	Electronic Business Document Interchange
EBDI	External Breathing Direct Injection [Chrysler Corp.] [Automotive engineering]
EBDP	Enamel Bonded Double Paper [Wire insulation]
EBDR	Epidermolysis Bullosa Dystrophic Recessive [Dermatology]
EBDS	Enamel Bonded Double Silk [Wire insulation]
e-be--	Belgium [MARC geographic area code Library of Congress] (LCCP)
EBE	Electron Beam Evaporator
EBE	Electron Binding Energy
EBE	Experimental Bridging Establishment [British]
EBE	Extraterrestrial Biological Entity
EBEB	EB, Inc. [NASDAQ symbol] (SAG)
EBEC	Encyclopaedia Britannica Educational Corp.
EBEE	Electron Beam Evaporation Equipment
EBEM	Electron Beam Evaporation Module
EBERAS	Event-by-Event Recording and Sorting [Electronics]
Ebersole	Ebersole's Reports [59-80 Iowa] [A publication] (DLA)
Ebersole (IA)	Ebersole's Reports [59-80 Iowa] [A publication] (DLA)
EbertRV	Reallexikon der Vorgeschichte [M. Ebert] [A publication] (BJA)
EBES	Electric Beam Exposure System [Integrated circuit] [Bell Laboratories]
EBES	Electron Beam Engraving System (NITA)
EBF	Early B-cell Factor [Biochemistry]
EBF	Economic and Business Foundation
EBF	Electric Bomb Fuze (NG)
EBF	Electron-Bombardment Furnace
EBF	Encyclopaedia Britannica Film (IIA)
EBF	English Bowling Federation (DBA)
EBF	Ennis Business Forms [NYS] (TTSB)
EBF	Ennis Business Forms, Inc. [NYSE symbol] (SPSG)
EBF	Erythroblastosis Fetalis [Hematology]
EBF	Europaeische Baptistische Foderation [European Baptist Federation - EBF] (EAIO)
EBF	Europaeische Baptistische Frauenunion [European Baptist Women's Union - EBWU] (EAIO)
EBF	Externally Blown Flap [Aviation]
EBFA	Electron Beam Fusion Accelerator

EBFBRG	European Bank of Frozen Blood of Rare Groups [Amsterdam, Netherlands] (EAIO)
EBFC	Ed Bruce Fan Club [Defunct] (EA)
EBFC	Elvis Brothers Fan Club (EA)
EBFC	Eric Braeden Fan Club (EA)
EBFG	East Bay Fan Guild (EA)
EBFN	Koksijde [Belgium ICAO location identifier] (ICLI)
EBFS	Enclosure Building Filtration System (IEEE)
EBFS	Florennes [Belgium ICAO location identifier] (ICLI)
EBFYC	European Baptist Federation Youth Committee (EAIO)
EBG	Ecobank Ghana (EY)
EBG	Economic Bulletin of Ghana [A publication]
EBG	El Bagre [Colombia] [Airport symbol] (OAG)
EBG	Electron Beam Generator
EBG	Electron Beam Gun
EBG	Electronics Buyers' Guide [A publication] (NITA)
EBGB	Brussels/Grimbergen [Belgium ICAO location identifier] (ICLI)
EBGL	Glons [Belgium ICAO location identifier] (ICLI)
EBGT	Gent/St. Denijs Westrem [Belgium ICAO location identifier] (ICLI)
EBH	Black Hill [Scotland] [Seismograph station code, US Geological Survey] (SEIS)
EBH	Engine Block Heater [Automotive engineering]
EBH	Epibromohydrin [Organic chemistry]
EBHN	Hoevenen [Belgium ICAO location identifier] (ICLI)
EBHP	Ethylbenzene Hydroperoxide [Organic chemistry]
EBI	Earnings Before Interest
EBI	Echo Bay Finance Corp. [AMEX symbol] (SPSG)
EBI	[The] Educational Broadcasting Institute [National Association of Educational Broadcasters] (NTCM)
EBI	Effective Buying Income [Portion of gross income after subtracting taxes, food, clothing, and housing expenditures]
EBI	Electromagnetic Bone Stimulator [Orthopedics] (DAVI)
EBI	Emerson Books, Inc. (DGA)
EBI	Emetine Bismuth Iodide [Pharmacology]
EBI	Encyclopaedia Biblica [A publication] (BJA)
EBI	Equivalent Background Input
EBI	Ergosterol Biosynthesis Inhibitor [Biochemistry]
EBI	Estradiol Binding Index [Biochemistry] (DMAA)
EBI	European Bioinformatics Institute
EBI	Everly Brothers International [Defunct] (EA)
EBI	Expanded Background Investigation (AFM)
EBI	Experience and Background Inventory [Management and supervision test]
EBI	Eye Ball In
EBIAT	Earnings Before Interest and After Taxes [Accounting] (PDAA)
EBIB	Energy Bibliography and Index [Center for Energy and Mineral Resources - Texas A & M University] [College Station, TX Bibliographic database]
EBIC	EFTA [European Free Trade Association] Brewing Industry Council (EAIO)
EBIC	Electron-Beam-Induced Current [Photovoltaic energy systems]
EBIC	Electron-Bombardment-Induced Conductivity
EBICON	Electron-Bombardment-Induced Conductivity
EBIF	European Button Industries Federation [British] (EAIO)
EBIFC	Elmer Bird International Fan Club (EA)
EBIG	Electron Beam Inert Gas (PDAA)
EBIOC	Electron Beam-Induced Oxide Charging
EBIP	European Biotechnology Information Project [British Library] [Information service or system] (IID)
EBIR	Electron-Bombardment-Induced Response
EBIRD	Electron Beam Ionization of Semiconductor Devices (PDAA)
EBIS	East Bay Information Service [Library network]
EBIS	Electron Beam Ion Source (IEEE)
EBIS	Employee Benefits Infosource [International Foundation of Employee Benefit Plans] [Information service or system] (CRD)
EBIS	Employment Barrier Identification Scale [Employment test]
EBIS	Encyclopedia of Business Information Sources [A publication]
EBIS	ESCAP [Economic and Social Commission for Asia and the Pacific] Bibliographic Information System [Thailand] [United Nations Information service or system] (IID)
EBIS	Ethylenebisisothiocyanate Sulfide [Organic chemistry]
EBIS	Exothermic Bimetallic Ignition System (MCD)
EBIST	Expert Bradley Infantry Squad Training Test [Army] (INF)
EBIT	Earnings before Interest and Taxes [Accounting]
EBIT	Electron Beam Ion Trap [Developed at Lawrence Livermore and Lawrence Berkeley National Laboratories] [Atomic physics]
EBITA	Earnings before Interest, Taxes, Depreciation, and Amortization [Investment term] (DFIT)
EBITD	Earnings before Interest Taxes and Depreciation
EBITDA	Earnings-Before Interest, Taxes, Depreciation, and Amortization [Finance]
EBITDA	Earnings before Interest, Taxes, Depreciation, and Amortization [Business term]
EBITS	Estimated Earnings before Interest and Taxes
EBIV	Electron-Beam-Induced Voltage [Photovoltaic energy systems]
EBJ	Esbjerg [Denmark] [Airport symbol] (OAG)
EBJ	European Business Journal [A publication]
EBK	Eastern Bakeries Ltd. [Toronto Stock Exchange symbol]
EBK	Easy Bleaching Kraft [Pulp and paper technology]
EBK	Embryonic Bovine Kidney
EBKH	Balen/Keiheuvel [Belgium ICAO location identifier] (ICLI)
EBKT	Kortrijk-Wevelgem [Belgium ICAO location identifier] (ICLI)
EBL	Austin, TX [Location identifier FAA] (FAAL)
EBL	Broadlaw [Scotland] [Seismograph station code, US Geological Survey] (SEIS)

EBL .... Eastern Basketball League
EBL .... Electric Heated Back Light [*Automotive engineering*]
EBL .... Electron Beam Lithography (IAA)
EBL .... Electronic Bearing Line [*RADAR technology*]
EBL .... Encyclopaedia Biblica [*A publication*] (ROG)
EBL .... Endemic Burkitt's Lymphoma [*Medicine*]
EBL .... Energy Budget Level
EBL .... Enzootic Bovine Leukemia
EBL .... Estimated Blood Loss [*Medicine*]
EBL .... European Bridge League (EAIO)
EBL .... Event-Based Language [*1979*] [*Computer science*] (CSR)
EBL .... Extended Batch Language (CDE)
EBL .... Eye Ball Left (MCD)
EBLAN .... Eblanencis [*Signature of the Bishops of Dublin*] (ROG)
EBLB .... Elsenborn [*Belgium ICAO location identifier*] (ICLI)
EBLF .... Electron Beam Lithography Facility [*British*]
EBLG .... Liege/Bierset [*Belgium ICAO location identifier*] (ICLI)
EBLH .... Liege/Bierset [*Belgium ICAO location identifier*] (ICLI)
EBLIDA .... European Bureau of Library Information and Documentation
　　　　　　　Associations (AIE)
EBLUL .... European Bureau for Lesser Used Languages (EA)
EBLV .... Elderberry Latent Virus [*Plant pathology*]
EBM .... Early-Break-Make [*Computer science*]
EBM .... Electron Beam Machining [*Manufacturing term*]
EBM .... Electron Beam Melting (IAA)
EBM .... Electron Beam Method
EBM .... Electron Beam Microanalysis
EBM .... Electron Beam Multiplier (IAA)
EBM .... Electronic Bearing Marker [*Navigation*] (OA)
EBM .... Energy Balance Model [*Climatology*]
EBM .... Enterprise Business Model [*Australia*]
EBM .... Esen Bulak [*Mongolia*] [*Seismograph station code, US Geological
　　　　　　　Survey Closed*] (SEIS)
EBM .... Estimation-before-Modeling (MCD)
EBM .... Europaeische Baptistische Mission [*European Baptist Mission*]
　　　　　　　[*Germany*] (EAIO)
EBM .... European Baptist Mission (EAIO)
EBM .... Expressed Breast Milk [*Medicine*]
EBM .... Extended Branch Mode
EBMA .... E&B Marine [*NASDAQ symbol*] (TTSB)
EBMA .... E & B Marine, Inc. [*NASDAQ symbol*] (SAG)
EBMA .... Elastic Braid Manufacturers Association [*Later, EFMC or
　　　　　　　EFMCNTA*] (EA)
EBMA .... Engine, Booster Maintenance Area
EBMB .... Melsbroek [*Belgium ICAO location identifier*] (ICLI)
EBMD .... Electron Beam Mode Discharge
EBMDA .... Eastern Building Material Dealers Association (SRA)
EBME .... Eagle's Basal Medium with Earle's Salts [*Culture medium*]
EBMF .... Electron Beam Microfabricator (IAA)
EBMI .... Brussels [*Belgium ICAO location identifier*] (ICLI)
EBMLM .... Electron Beam Membrane Light Modulator [*Army*] (MCD)
EBMO .... Moorsele [*Belgium ICAO location identifier*] (ICLI)
EBMS .... Energy Balance Models (EERA)
EBMT .... European Bone Marrow Transplantation
EBMT .... Munte [*Belgium ICAO location identifier*] (ICLI)
EbN .... East by North
ebn .... Ebonized (VRA)
ebn .... Ebony (VRA)
EBN .... Endosperm Balance Number [*Genetics*]
EBNA .... EBV [*Epstein-Barr Virus*] Nuclear Antigen [*Immunochemistry*]
EBNA .... Epstein-Barr Nuclear Antigen [*Virus*] [*Immunology*]
EBND .... Eastbound (FAAC)
EBNF .... Extended Backus-Naur Form
EBNI .... Electricity Board for Northern Ireland (BI)
EBNM .... Namur-Suarlee [*Belgium ICAO location identifier*] (ICLI)
EBNY .... Edition Bookbinders of New York (EA)
EBO .... Extrahepatic Biliary Obstruction [*Medicine*]
EBO .... Eye Ball Out
E/BOD .... Electrolytic Biological Oxygen Demand
EBONTA ...... (Ethylenebis(oxyethylenenitrilo))tetraacetic Acid [*Also, EGTA*]
　　　　　　　[*Organic chemistry*]
EBOR .... Eboracensis [*Signature of the Bishop of York*] (ROG)
EBOR .... Eboracum [*York*] [*County in England*] [*Latin*] (ROG)
EBOR .... Experimental Beryllium Oxide Reactor [*Later, BORE*]
EBOR-CX ..... Experiment Beryllium Oxide Reactor - Critical Assembly (SAA)
EBOS .... Oostende [*Belgium ICAO location identifier*] (ICLI)
EBP .... Electric Bilge Pump
EBP .... Enamel-Bonded Single Paper [*Wire insulation*] (IAA)
EBP .... Environmentaly Benign Processing [*Engineering*]
EBP .... Epidural Blood Patch [*Medicine*]
EBP .... Estradiol-Binding Protein [*Biochemistry*]
EBP .... Etch Back Process (IAA)
EBP .... Exhaust Back Pressure
EBP .... Explanation of Benefit Payment [*Insurance*]
EBP .... Extended Basal Period
EBPA .... Electron Beam Parametric Amplifier
EBPA .... Ethylbenzene Producers Association (EA)
EBPAD .... Ethoxylated Bisphenol A Dimethacrylate [*Organic chemistry*]
EBPE .... European Biotech Partnering Event
EBPG .... Electron Beam Pattern Generator
EBPI .... Environmental Business Publishing, Inc. (IID)
EBPN .... Early Babylonian Personal Names [*A publication*] (BJA)
E-BPR .... Enhanced Bottom Pressure Recorder [*Marine science*] (OSRA)
E-BPR .... Enhanced Bottom Pressure Recorder (USDC)

EbpS .... EBSCO Publishing & EBSCO Subscription Service Service,
　　　　　　　Birmingham, AL [*Library symbol*] [*Library of Congress*] (LCLS)
EBPS .... European Baptist Press Service [*of the European Baptist
　　　　　　　Federation*] (EAIO)
EBPSUSA ..... El Bireh Palestine Society of the USA (EA)
EBQ .... Experience and Background Questionnaire [*Test*]
Ebr .... De Ebrietate [*Philo*] (BJA)
EBR .... Ebro Roquetas [*Spain*] [*Seismograph station code, US Geological
　　　　　　　Survey*] (SEIS)
EBR .... Electron Beam Readout
EBR .... Electron Beam Recorder [*or Recording*]
EBR .... Electron Beam Regulator
EBR .... Electron Beam Remelting (IAA)
EBR .... Electronic Batch Record
EBR .... Emergency Bomb Release (CINC)
EBR .... Emulsion Butadiene Rubber
E BR .... Encyclopaedia Britannica [*A publication*] (ROG)
EBR .... Epoxy Bridge Rectifier
EBR .... Experimental Breeder Reactor
EBR .... Eye Ball Right (MCD)
EBRA .... Emergency Banking Relief Act
EBRA .... Engineer Buyers' and Representatives' Association [*British*]
EBRC .... Economic and Budget Review Committee [*Victoria, Australia*]
EBRD .... European Bank for Reconstruction and Development [*Economic
　　　　　　　assistance for Eastern Europe*] [*Proposed*]
EBRD .... Export Business Relations Division [*Department of Commerce*]
EBRG .... Earth-Based Radio Guidance
EBRI .... Employee Benefit Research Institute (EA)
EBROM .... Extended BIT [*Binary Digit*] Read Only Memory [*Computer science*]
　　　　　　　(IAA)
EBRS .... European Businessmen Readership Study [*Database*] [*Research
　　　　　　　Services Ltd.*] [*Information service or system*] (CRD)
EBS .... CANEBSCO Subscription Service Ltd. [*ACCORD*] [*UTLAS symbol*]
EBS .... Eagle Butte [*South Dakota*] [*Seismograph station code, US
　　　　　　　Geological Survey*] (SEIS)
EbS .... East by South
EBS .... Eastern Baptist Theological Seminary, Philadelphia, PA [*OCLC
　　　　　　　symbol*] (OCLC)
EBS .... Eastern Base Section [*Mediterranean and England*] [*Army World War
　　　　　　　II*]
EBS .... Eastern Bering Sea
EBS .... Edison Bros Stores [*NYSE symbol*] (TTSB)
EBS .... Edison Brothers Stores, Inc. [*NYSE symbol*] (SPSG)
EBS .... Educational Broadcast Satellite (MCD)
EBS .... Electric Bond and Share (IAA)
EBS .... Electric Brain Stimulator
EBS .... Electron Beam Semiconductor
EBS .... Electron Beam System
EBS .... Electron-Bombarded Semiconductor
EBS .... Electron-Bombardment Silicon (KSC)
EBS .... Electronic Band Spectra
EBS .... Electronic Bombarded Silicon
EBS .... Electronic Braking System
EBS .... Electronic Business Solutions [*Computer science*]
EBS .... Eli-Fly SpA [*Italy ICAO designator*] (FAAC)
EBS .... Emergency Bed Service [*Medicine*]
EBS .... Emergency Borating System (IEEE)
EBS .... Emergency Breathing Subsystem (MCD)
EBS .... Emergency Breathing System
EBS .... Emergency Broadcast System [*Formerly, CONELRAD*]
EBS .... Enamel Bonded Single Silk [*Wire insulation*] (AAG)
EBS .... Energy Band Structure (IAA)
EBS .... Engine Breather Separator
EBS .... Engineered Barrier System [*Waste disposal*]
EBS .... English Bookplate Society (BARN)
EBS .... Epidermolysis Bullosa Simplex [*Dermatology*]
EBS .... Eridania-Beghin Say [*France*] (ECON)
EBS .... Ernest Bloch Society (EA)
EBS .... Ethylene Bistearamide [*Organic chemistry*]
EBS .... Experimental Building Station
EBS .... Extruded Bar Solder
EBS .... Webster City, IA [*Location identifier FAA*] (FAAL)
EBSA .... Estuarine and Brackish-Water Sciences Association (EAIO)
EBSA .... Ethylbenzenesulfonic Acid [*Organic chemistry*]
EBSC .... European Bird Strike Committee (PDAA)
EBSD .... European Business Services Directory [*A publication*]
EBSF .... National Black Survival Fund [*Emergency Black Survival Fund*]
　　　　　　　[*Acronym is based on former name,*] (EA)
EBSH .... Saint-Hubert [*Belgium ICAO location identifier*] (ICLI)
EBSI .... Eagle Bancshares [*NASDAQ symbol*] (TTSB)
EBSI .... Eagle Bancshares, Inc. [*NASDAQ symbol*] (NQ)
Ebs Inf .... Ebsworth on the Law of Infants [*A publication*] (DLA)
EBSK .... Epidermolysis Bullosa Simplex-Koebner [*Dermatology*]
EBSL .... Zutendaal [*Belgium ICAO location identifier*] (ICLI)
EBSLG .... European Business School Librarians Group [*London Business
　　　　　　　School*] [*Information service or system*] (IID)
EBSP .... Electron Backscattering Pattern (MCD)
EBSP .... Spa/La Sauveniere [*Belgium ICAO location identifier*] (ICLI)
EBSR .... Engineer Boat and Shore Regiment [*Army*]
EBSR .... Eye-Bank for Sight Restoration (EA)
EBSRVR ...... East Bengal State Railway Volunteer Rifles [*British military*] (DMA)
EBSS .... Earles Balanced Salt Solution [*Media for cell culture*]
EBSS .... Education and Behavioral Sciences Section [*Association of College
　　　　　　　and Research Libraries*]
EBST .... Educational Broadcasting Services Trust (AIE)

EBST	Sint-Truiden [*Belgium ICAO location identifier*] (ICLI)
EBSU	Saint-Hubert [*Belgium ICAO location identifier*] (ICLI)
EBSWC	Epidermolysis Bullosa Simplex - Weber Cockayne [*Dermatology*]
EBSZ	Semmerzake [*Belgium ICAO location identifier*] (ICLI)
EBT	Early Bedtime (DAVI)
EBT	Earth-Based Tug [*NASA*]
EBT	Echelons Below Theater [*Military*] (MCD)
EBT	Electron Beam [*Fluorescence*] Technique
EBT	Electron Beam Tomography [*Imaging science*]
EBT	Electron Beam Transmission
EBT	Electronic Benefits Transfer [*Department of Agriculture*] (GFGA)
EBT	Electronic Book Technologies, Inc. (PCM)
EBT	Elmo Bumpy Torus [*Nuclear energy*]
EBT	Enid Board of Trade (EA)
EBT	Epicardial Breakthrough [*Cardiology*]
EBT	Ethylidenebis(tryptophan) [*Biochemistry*]
EBT	Examination Before Trial (DHSM)
EBT	Executive Business Transport [*Aircraft*]
EBT-1	Elmo Bumpy Torus-One (MCD)
EBTF	ECC [*Emergency Control Center*] Bypass Test Facility [*Nuclear energy*] (NRCH)
EBTG	Everything But the Girl [*British band*]
EBTN	Goetsenhove [*Belgium ICAO location identifier*] (ICLI)
EBT-P	Elmo Bumpy Torus-Proof of Principle (MCD)
EBTR	Electronic Bearing-Time Recorder
EBT-R	Elmo Bumpy Torus Reactor [*Conceptual design study*] [*Nuclear energy*]
EBTR	Elmo Bumpy Torus Reactor [*Nuclear energy*] (MCD)
EBT-S	Elmo Bumpy Torus-Scale (MCD)
EBTTC	European Baptist Theological Teachers' Conference [*Germany*] (EAIO)
EBTX	Theux-Verviers [*Belgium ICAO location identifier*] (ICLI)
EBTY	Tournai/Maubray [*Belgium ICAO location identifier*] (ICLI)
e-bu--	Bulgaria [*MARC geographic area code Library of Congress*] (LCCP)
EBU	English Bridge Union (BI)
EBU	European Badminton Union (EA)
EBU	European Blind Union (EA)
EBU	European Boxing Union
EBU	European Broadcasting Union [*Switzerland*]
EBU	Eye Ball Up (MCD)
EBU	St. Etienne [*France*] [*Airport symbol*] (OAG)
EBUC	Etch Back Uniformity Calculation (IAA)
EBUL	Ursel [*Belgium ICAO location identifier*] (ICLI)
EBUM	Brussels [*Belgium ICAO location identifier*] (ICLI)
EBUR	Brussels [*Belgium ICAO location identifier*] (ICLI)
EBURN	Eburneus [*Made of Ivory*] [*Pharmacy*] (ROG)
EBV	Efferent Branchial Vein [*Anatomy*]
EBV	Electron-Bombardment Vehicle
EBV	Epstein-Barr Virus
EBV	Estimated Blood Volume [*Hematology*]
EBV	Estimated Breeding Value [*Agricultural science*]
EBV	Every Block is a Village [*Chicago community development program*]
EBVA	Brussels [*Belgium ICAO location identifier*] (ICLI)
EBVCA	Eptein-Barr Virus Capsid Antigen [*Medicine*] (PDAA)
EBVP	Epidoxorubicin, Bleomycin, Vinblastine, Prednisone [*Antineoplastic drug regimen*]
EBVT	Exterior Ballistic Verification Projectile (MCD)
EBW	Ebolowa [*Cameroon*] [*Airport symbol*] (AD)
EBW	Effective Bandwidth
EBW	Electron Beam Welding (MUGU)
EBW	Empty Body Weight (OA)
EBW	Exploding Bridge-Wire
EBWE	Weelde [*Belgium ICAO location identifier*] (ICLI)
EBW-HV	Electron Beam Welding - High Vacuum
EBWM	Brussels [*Belgium ICAO location identifier*] (ICLI)
EBW-MV	Electron Beam Welding - Medium Vacuum
EBW-NV	Electron Beam Welding - Nonvacuum
EBWR	Experimental Boiling Water Reactor
EBWS	Exploding Bridge-Wire System (KSC)
EBWU	European Baptist Women's Union (EAIO)
EBY	Elsag Bailey Process Auto NV [*NYSE symbol*] (SPSG)
EBY	European Blue Cross Youth Association (EAIO)
EBY	Neah Bay, WA [*Location identifier FAA*] (FAAL)
EBYC	European Bureau for Youth and Childhood
EBZ	Exercise Benefit Zone [*Aerobic dance*]
EBZH	Hasselt [*Belgium ICAO location identifier*] (ICLI)
EBZR	Zoersel [*Belgium ICAO location identifier*] (ICLI)
EBZW	Genk/Zwartberg [*Belgium ICAO location identifier*] (ICLI)
EC	Air Ecosse [*ICAO designator*] (AD)
EC	Disabilities and Gifted Education [*Educational Resources Information Center (ERIC) Clearinghouse*] [*Council for Exceptional Children*] (PAZ)
EC	Ear Clamp [*Medicine*]
EC	Early Childhood (ADA)
EC	Early-Closing Day [*British*]
EC	Earth Closet [*British*] (ROG)
EC	Earth Council [*Costa Rica*] (EERA)
EC	East Caribbean
EC	East Carolina Railway [*AAR code*]
EC	East Central [*Refers especially to London postal district*]
EC	East Coast
EC	Eastern Cedar [*Utility pole*] [*Telecommunications*] (TEL)
EC	Eastern Central
EC	Eastern Command [*British*]
Ec	Ecclesiastes [*Old Testament book*] (BJA)

EC	Ecclesiastical Commissioner [*British*] (DAS)
EC	Echo-Cancellation [*Data transmission*] (BYTE)
EC	Echo Controller [*Telecommunications*] (TEL)
EC	Eclipse
EC	Eco Corp. [*Toronto Stock Exchange symbol*]
EC	Ecology Center (EA)
EC	Economic Analysis [*Program*] [*Department of State*]
EC	Economics
Ec	Ecossais [*Scottish*] [*Freemasonry*] [*French*]
Ec	Ectoparasitic [*Biology*]
EC	Ecuador [*ANSI two-letter standard code*] (CNC)
ec	Ecuador [*IYRU nationality code*] [*MARC country of publication code Library of Congress*] (LCCP)
EC	Ecumenical Celebrations (EA)
EC	Eddy Current [*Electromagnetism*] (NRCH)
EC	Edge Connector
E/C	Edges Cut [*Printing*] (DGA)
EC	Educational Communications [*An association*] (EA)
EC	Education Code (OICC)
EC	Effective Concentration [*Instrumentation*]
EC	Effective Conductivity
EC	Ego Control [*Psychology*]
EC	Ejection Click [*Cardiology*]
EC	Elder Craftsmen (EA)
EC	Election Cases [*A publication*] (DLA)
EC	Electrical Coding (WDAA)
EC	Electrical Conductivity
EC	Electric Cipher [*or Coding*] Machine Repairman [*Navy rating*]
EC	Electric Current
EC	Electricity Commission [*British*] (DAS)
EC	Electricity Council [*British*]
EC	[*The*] Electrification Council
EC	Electrochemical [*or Electrochemistry*]
EC	Electrochromic [*Optics*]
EC	Electrocoating
EC	Electroconductivity
EC	Electrolysis Cell (SSD)
EC	Electron Capture [*Radioactivity*]
EC	Electron Coupled (DEN)
EC	Electronically Commutated [*Motor*] [*Electrical engineering*]
EC	Electronic Calculator [*or Computer*] (BUR)
EC	Electronic Calibration
EC	Electronic Cinematography (WDMC)
EC	Electronic Coding
EC	Electronic Combat
EC	Electronic Commerce [*Computer science*] (RDA)
EC	Electronic Comparator
EC	Electronic Computer (MCD)
EC	Electronic Conductivity
EC	Electronic Counter
EC	Electronics and Control
EC	Electronics Chassis
EC	Element Contractor (NASA)
EC	Element Count [*Searchable field*] [*Dialog*] [*Information service or system*] (NITA)
EC	Elevation Console
EC	Elvis in Canada [*An association*] (EAIO)
EC	Embarkation Commandant [*Military British*]
EC	Embryonal Carcinoma [*Medicine*]
EC	Emergency Call (IAA)
EC	Emergency Capability
EC	Emergency Cargo [*Vessel*] (IIA)
EC	Emergency Chaplain [*Army British*]
E/C	Emergency Charges
EC	Emergency Commission [*British*]
EC	Emergency Coordinator (CET)
EC	Eminent Chaplain [*Freemasonry*] (ROG)
EC	Eminent Commander [*Freemasonry*] (ROG)
EC	Eminent Conductor [*Freemasonry*] (ROG)
EC	Employment Code [*IRS*]
EC	Employment Counseling (OICC)
EC	Emulator Control (IAA)
EC	Emulsible Concentrate
EC	Emulsifying Capacity [*Food technology*]
EC	Enamel Covered
ec	Enamel-Covered (IDOE)
EC	Enameled Copper [*Wire insulation*] (IAA)
EC	Enamel Single Cotton [*Wire insulation*] (AAG)
EC	Enciclopedia Cattolica [*Vatican City*] [*A publication*] (BJA)
E/C	Encoder Coupler (NASA)
EC	En Cuenta [*On Account*] [*Spanish Business term*]
EC	Encyclopedia Canadiana [*A publication*]
E/C	Endoscopy/Cystoscopy [*Medicine*] (MAE)
EC	Endothelial Cell [*Medicine*]
EC	Enemy Capabilities (MCD)
EC	Energy Charge
EC	Engagement Controller [*Navy*] (NVT)
EC	Engelhard Corp. [*Formerly, ENG*] [*NYSE symbol*] (SPSG)
EC	Engine Change (MCD)
EC	Engine Control (MCD)
EC	Engine Cutoff [*Aerospace*] (MCD)
EC	Engineer Captain [*Navy British*]
EC	Engineer Circular [*Army Corps of Engineers*]
EC	Engineering Change (MCD)
EC	Engineering Cognizant Authority (MCD)

EC .... Engineering Construction
EC .... Engineering Corps
EC .... Engineering Council (ACII)
EC .... Engineering Critical (MCD)
EC .... English Chancery (DLA)
EC .... English Chancery Reports [American Reprint] [A publication] (DLA)
EC .... English Conditions [Insurance]
EC .... English Constitution (ADA)
EC .... Entente Council [See also CE] (EAIO)
EC .... Enteric Coated [Pharmacy]
EC .... Entering Complaint [Medicine]
EC .... Enterochromaffin Cells [Medicine]
EC .... Entorhinal Cortex [Brain anatomy]
EC .... Entrance Complaint [Medicine] (MEDA)
EC .... Entries Closed (ROG)
EC .... Entry Code [Computer science]
EC .... Entry Controller
EC .... Environmental Capacity (EERA)
EC .... Environmental Chamber (KSC)
EC .... Environmental Complexity
EC .... Environmental Control (KSC)
EC .... Environmentally Correct (PS)
EC .... Environment Canada
EC .... Environment Condition (CAAL)
EC .... Enzyme Commission [of the International Union of Biochemistry]
EC .... EPCOT [Experimental Prototype Community of Tomorrow] Center
               [Walt Disney World]
EC .... Epidermal Cell
EC .... Epilepsy Concern Service Group (EA)
EC .... Episcopal Church
EC .... Episcopal Communicators (EA)
EC .... Equation Cruncher [Computer science]
EC .... Equipment Controller (CET)
E/C .... Equipment or Component
EC .... Equivalency Class [Statistical algorithm]
EC .... Erection Computer
EC .... Ergocryptine [Organic chemistry]
EC .... Erosion Control [Type of water project]
EC .... Error Code [Computer science]
E/C .... Error Correcting [or Correction] [Computer science]
EC .... Error Counter (OA)
EC .... Erythrocyte Creatine [Clinical chemistry]
EC .... Escherichia Coli [Microorganism]
EC .... Escort Convoy (CINC)
EC .... Essentiality Code (NASA)
EC .... Established Church
EC .... Esterified Cholesterol (OA)
E/C .... Estriol [or Estrogen]/Creatinine [Ratio] [Clinical chemistry] (AAMN)
EC .... Estrogen Conjugate [Endocrinology]
E-C .... Ether-Chloroform [Mixture]
EC .... Ethyl Cellulose
EC .... Ethyl Centralite (OA)
EC .... Ethyl Corp. (KSC)
EC .... Etling Clearinghouse (EA)
EC .... Eton College [British] (ROG)
EC .... EURAIL [European Railway] Community (EAIO)
EC .... Eurocard [Credit card] [British] (ADA)
EC .... Eurocheque [Credit card] [British]
EC .... Euro-Children (EAIO)
EC .... EuroCity [Railroad]
EC .... European Cellars [Commercial firm British]
EC .... European Commission
EC .... European Community [Collective name given to the consolidation of
               the European Coal and Steel Community, the Common Market,
               and the European Atomic Energy Community]
EC .... European Companions (EAIO)
ec---- .... Europe, Central [MARC geographic area code Library of Congress]
               (LCCP)
EC .... Evaluation Center (NATG)
EC .... Evangelicals Concerned (EA)
EC .... Event Code [Searchable field] [Dialog] [Information service or
               system] (NITA)
EC .... Event Count (NITA)
EC .... Event Counter (NITA)
EC .... Events Controller (MCD)
EC .... Events Coupler (MCD)
EC .... Examining Circulars
EC .... Excellent Companion [Freemasonry] (ROG)
EC .... Excellent Condition [Doll collecting]
EC .... Exceptional Children Abstracts [A publication] (IID)
EC .... Exchange Chromatography
E-C .... Excitation-Contraction [Physiology]
EC .... Excitatory Center [Neurology] (DAVI)
EC .... Ex Commissione [Upon Order]
EC .... Ex-Coupon [Investment term]
EC .... Excretory Cell
EC .... Execution Cycle [Computer science] (IAA)
EC .... Executive Committee (NATG)
EC .... Executive Council (ADA)
EC .... Exempli Causa [For the Sake of Example] [Latin]
EC .... Exercise Commander [NATO] (NATG)
EC .... Exhaust Closes [Valve position]
EC .... Expander Cell (IAA)
EC .... Expansive Classification
EC .... Experimental Control (MAE)

EC .... Experimentation Command [Army] (MCD)
EC .... Experiment Canister (MCD)
EC .... Experiment Computer (MCD)
EC .... Expiratory Center [Physiology]
EC .... Explorers Club (EA)
EC .... Extended Control [Mode] [Computer science]
EC .... Extended Coverage [Insurance]
EC .... Extension and Conversion [Public buildings]
EC .... Extension Course
EC .... Exterior Closet (ADA)
EC .... External Combustion
EC .... Extracapsular (CPH)
EC .... Extracellular [Hematology]
EC .... Extra Control [Wire] [Telecommunications] (TEL)
EC .... Extra Coordination
EC .... Extracranial [Medicine]
EC .... Eye Care (EA)
EC .... Eyes Closed [Ataxia]
EC .... Ontario Election Cases [1884-1900] [Canada] [A publication] (DLA)
EC .... Worthington Biochemical Corp. [Research code symbol]
EC-1 .... Emission Control 1 Gasoline [ARCO]
EC$_{50}$ .... Effective Concentration at which Light Emission Is Reduced by 50%
               [Instrumentation]
EC$_{50}$ .... Effective Concentration, Median Value
ECA .... Department of Economic Affairs of the United Nations
ECA .... Early Closing Association [British]
ECA .... Early Comparability Analysis (RDA)
ECA .... Earth Central Angle
ECA .... Earth-Crossing Asteroid [Astronomy]
ECA .... Earth-orbit-Crossing Asteroid
ECA .... Eastern Central Motor Carriers Association, Agent, Akron OH [STAC]
ECA .... Economic Commission for Africa [Addis Ababa, Ethiopia] [See also
               CEA] [United Nations] (EAIO)
E/CA .... Economic Control Agency [Allied German Occupation Forces]
ECA .... Economic Cooperation Act [of 1948]
ECA .... Economic Cooperation Administration [Administered aid under
               Marshall Plan; abolished, 1951]
ECA .... Economic Cooperation Agreement (EERA)
ECA .... Economische Commissie voor Africa [Economic Commission for
               Africa] [United Nations]
ECA .... Ecumenical Clergy Association [Later, AGEI] (EA)
ECA .... Educational Centres Association [British]
ECA .... Educational Communication Association (EA)
ECA .... [The] Educational Corp. of America (ECON)
ECA .... Eigenvalue Change Analysis
ECA .... El Cajon [California] [Seismograph station code, US Geological
               Survey Central] (SEIS)
ECA .... El Camino Resources, Inc. [Vancouver Stock Exchange symbol]
ECA .... Electrical Contact Analyzer (IAA)
ECA .... Electrical Contractors' Association [British] (BI)
ECA .... Electrical Control Activity (MCD)
ECA .... Electrocardioanalyzer [Medicine] (AAMN)
ECA .... Electronic Commerce Acquisition (AAGC)
ECA .... Electronic Confusion Area
ECA .... Electronic Control Amplifier (MCD)
ECA .... Electronic Control Assembly [Ford Motor Co.]
ECA .... Elsa Clubs of America [Defunct] (EA)
ECA .... Embroidery Council of America (EA)
ECA .... Emergency Call Announcer [Hearing technology]
ECA .... Emergency Controlling Authority (DA)
ECA .... Employment Conditions Abroad [British] [An association] (DBA)
ECA .... Engine Computer Assembly [Automotive engineering]
ECA .... Engineer Cognizant Authority
ECA .... Engineering Change Analysis
ECA .... Engineering Change Announcement
ECA .... Engineering Change Authorization
ECA .... Engineering Contractors Association (EA)
ECA .... English Curling Association
ECA .... Ensign Class Association [Defunct] (EA)
ECA .... Enter Control Area [Aviation]
ECA .... Enterobacterial Common Antigen [Immunology]
ECA .... Environmental Choice Australia
ECA .... Environmental Contaminants Authority (EERA)
ECA .... Environmental Control Administration [Later, EPA]
ECA .... Epidemiologic Catchment Area [Department of Health and Human
               Services] (GFGA)
ECA .... Epoxy Curing Agent
ECA .... Equipment Condition Analysis (MSA)
ECA .... Ericson Class Association (EA)
ECA .... Etched Card Assembly (IAA)
ECA .... Ethacrynic Acid [Biochemistry]
ECA .... Ethylcarboxylate Adenosine [Biochemistry]
ECA .... Eurocypria Airlines Ltd. [Cyprus] [ICAO designator] (FAAC)
ECA .... European Catering Association [Germany] (EAIO)
ECA .... European Choral Association (EA)
ECA .... European Civil Affairs
ECA .... European Combat Aircraft (PDAA)
ECA .... European Commission on Agriculture [FAO] [United Nations]
ECA .... European Communications Area [Military]
ECA .... European Confederation of Agriculture
ECA .... Europe China Association
ECA .... Evangelical Church Alliance (EA)
ECA .... Exceptional Circumstances Allowance [Legal term] (DLA)
ECA .... Excess Charge Adjudication [Health insurance] (GHCT)
ECA .... Exchange Carrier Association (EA)

ECA	Executive Chef Association [*Defunct*] (EA)
ECA	Explosives Corp. of America (MCD)
ECA	Export Control Act (MCD)
ECA	Extended Central Area (DOAD)
ECA	Extended Coverage Altitude (SAA)
ECAAR	Economists Allied for Arms Reduction [*An association*] (EA)
ECAB	Department of Energy Contract Adjustment Board (AAGC)
ECAB	Employees' Compensation Appeals Board [*Department of Labor*]
ECAB	Engineering Committee for the American Bicentennial
ECAB	Executive Committee of the Army Board [*British*]
ECAC	Eastern College Athletic Conference (EA)
ECAC	Electromagnetic Compatibility Analysis Center [*Illinois Institute of Technology*] [*Annapolis, MD*]
ECAC	Engineering College Administrative Council
ECAC	European Civil Aviation Conference [*See also CEAC*] (EAIO)
ECACC	European Collection of Animal Cell Cultures [*Cell bank*] (ECON)
ECAD	Electronic Computer-Aided Design [*Computer science*] (BYTE)
ECAD	Engineer Control and Advisory Detachment [*Air Force*]
ECAD	Error Check Analysis Diagram (IAA)
ECAD	European Civil Affairs Division [*US Military Government, Germany*]
ECAD	Existing Chemical Assessment Division [*Environmental Protection Agency*]
ECADR	Nordic Council for Alcohol and Drug Research (EA)
ECAE	Educational Center for Applied Ekistics (EA)
ECAF	Excess Cost Adjudication Function [*Army*]
ECAFE	Economic Commission for Asia and the Far East [*Later, ESCAP*] [*United Nations*]
ECAG	Equipment Change Analysis Group (SAA)
ECAHTI	European Committee for Agricultural and Horticultural Tools and Implements (EA)
ECAL	Equipment Calibration [*Military*] (NVT)
ECAM	Electric Control and Manufacturing (IAA)
ECAM	Electronic Centralized Aircraft Monitoring System
ECAM	Energy Conservation and Management (MCD)
ECAM	ERTS Command Auxiliary Memory (MCD)
ECAM	Extended Communications Access Method (WDAA)
ECAM	Extended Content-Addressable Memory [*Computer science*] (MHDB)
ECAMA	European Citric Acid Manufacturers Association [*of the European Council of Chemical Manufacturers' Federations*] (EAIO)
ECAMP	Environmental Compliance Assessment and Management Program [*Air Force*] (DOMA)
ECAMS	Enhanced Comprehensive Asset Management System (MCD)
ECAMWP	European Committee of Associations of Manufacturers of Welding Products (EA)
ECAN	Electronic Calibration and Normalization (KSC)
ECAN	Electronic Consumer Advertising Network [*Data Corp. of America*]
EC & D	Electromagnetic Cover and Deception (MCD)
EC & D	Electronic Cover and Deception (PDAA)
EC & DB	Encourage Coughing and Deep Breathing [*Medicine*]
EC & M	Environmental Control and Mechanism (SAA)
Ec & Mar	Notes of Cases, English Ecclesiastical and Maritime Courts [*1844-50*] [*A publication*] (DLA)
ECANSW	Electrical Contractors' Association of New South Wales [*Australia*]
ECAO	Environmental Criteria and Assessment Office [*Environmental Protection Agency*] (GRD)
ECAO/CIN	Environmental Criteria and Assessment Office, Cincinnati [*Ohio*] [*Environmental Protection Agency*] (GRD)
ECAO/RTP	Environmental Criteria and Assessment Office, Research Triangle Park [*North Carolina*] [*Environmental Protection Agency*] (GRD)
ECAP	Electrical [*or Electronic*] Circuit Analysis Program
ECAP	Electric Circuit Analysis Program (NITA)
ECAP	Electric Companies' Advertising Program
ECAP	Electronic Circuit Analysis Program (ECII)
ECAP	Electronic Control Analyzer and Programmer [*Automotive engineering*]
ECAP	Electronic Control Assembly - Pitch (IAA)
ECAP	Electronic Current Analysis Program (IAA)
ECAP	Employee Counseling and Assistance Program [*Environmental Protection Agency*] (EPA)
ECAP	Energy Crisis Assistance Program [*Federal government*]
ECAP	Enhanced Cobra Armament Program [*Military*]
ECAP	Environmental Compatibility Assurance Program [*Navy*]
ECAP	Environmental Cooperation with Asia Program (EERA)
ECAP	Error Check Analysis Program (IAA)
ECAP	European Conflict Analysis Project [*NATO*]
ECaP	Exceptional Cancer Patients [*Therapy program*]
ECAPE	Exploratory Committee on Assessing the Progress of Education [*Later, NAEP*]
ECA-PMO	Electronic Commerce Acquisition-Program Management Office (AAGC)
ECAPS	Emergency Capability System (SAA)
ECAR	East Central Area Reliability Coordination Agreement [*Regional power council*]
ECAR	Electronic Control Assembly - Roll (KSC)
ECAR	Engineering Concern Action Report [*Industrial engineering*]
ECAR	European Civil Affairs Regiment
ECARBS	Economic Census Advertising and Response Behavior Study [*Bureau of the Census*] (GFGA)
ECARL	Expendable Cluster Aircraft Rocket Launcher
ECARP	Environmental Conservation Acreage Reserve Program [*Department of Agriculture*]
ECARS	Electronic Coordinatograph and Readout System
E-CARS	Enhanced Airline Communications and Reporting System (DA)
ECAS	Earth-Crossing Asteroid
ECAS	Electrical Contractors' Association of Scotland (EAIO)
ECAS	Energy Conversion Alternatives Study [*NASA*]
ECAS	Engineering Change Automation System
ECAS	Enhanced Cobra/TOW [*Tube-Launched, Optically-Tracked, Wire-Guided*] Armament System [*Military*] (MCD)
ECAS	Enter Controlled Airspace [*Air Traffic Control*] (FAAC)
ECAS	Experiment Computer Application Software (MCD)
ECASC	EPIC Center for Adhesives, Sealants, and Coatings [*Research center*] (RCD)
ECASS	Electronically Controlled Automatic-Switching System (DEN)
ECASS	Experimental Computer-Aided Shop Scheduling (IAA)
ECASS	Export Control Automated Support System [*Department of Commerce*]
ECASTAR	Energy Conservation Assessment of Systems, Technologies, and Requirements
EC-AT	Electronically Controlled Automatic Transmission [*Mazda*] [*Automotive engineering*]
ECAT	[*Federal*] Electronic Commerce Acquisition Team (AAGC)
ECAT	Emergency Committee for American Trade (EA)
ECAT	Emission Computerized Axial Tomography
ECAT	Equipment Category
ECAT	European Centre for Automatic Translation [*Luxembourg*] (NITA)
ECATR	Early Comparability Analysis Time Requirement [*Army*]
ECATRA	European Car and Truck Rental Association (EA)
ECATS	Expandable Computerized Automatic Test System (MCD)
ECATT	Economic Awareness Teacher Training (AIE)
ECATV	Educational Cable Television (NTCM)
ECAW	European Council for Animal Welfare (EA)
ECAY	Electronic Control Assembly - Yaw (IAA)
ECB	Echelons Corps Level and Below [*Military*]
ECB	Eddy Current Brake [*Mechanical engineering*]
ECB	Efferent Cochlear Bundle (PDAA)
ECB	Electrically Controlled Birefringence [*Telecommunications*] (TEL)
ECB	Electronic Claims Billing (HGAA)
ECB	Encyclopedia of College Basketball [*A publication*]
ECB	Encyclopedia of Consumer Brands [*A publication*]
ECB	Engineer Construction Battalion (CINC)
ECB	Engineering Control Board (AAG)
ECB	Enhanced Cubic Grain [*Photography*]
ECB	Environmental and Conservation Bureau [*Australian Capital Territory*]
ECB	Environmental Chemistry and Biology [*Marine science*] (OSRA)
ECB	Environmental Chemistry and Biology (USDC)
ECB	Environment Coordination Board [*United Nations*]
ECB	Equipment Control Board (KSC)
ECB	Etched Circuit Board
ECB	European Central Bank
ECB	European Congress of Biotechnology
ECB	European Coordination Bureau for International Youth Organizations G2 [*See also BEC*] (EAIO)
ECB	European Corn Borer [*Agronomy*]
ECB	Event Control Block [*Computer science*] (BUR)
ECB	Events Control Buffer [*NASA*] (NASA)
ECB	Export Control Bulletin [*Department of Commerce*]
ECB	Newcombe, KY [*Location identifier FAA*] (FAAL)
ECBA	Eastern Coast Breweriana Association (EA)
ECBA	Eastern College Basketball Association (EA)
ECBA	European Communities Biologists Association [*Belgium*] (EAIO)
ECBA	European Communities Biologists Organization [*University of Bremen*] (EAIO)
ECBC	Empress Chinchilla Breeders Cooperative (EA)
ECBC	External Call Barring Circuit (IAA)
ECBD	Exploration of Common Bile Duct [*Medicine*] (DMAA)
ECBF	E. C. Brown Foundation (EA)
ECBF	Episcopal Church Building Fund (EA)
ECBF	European Community Banking Federation [*Belgium*] (EAIO)
ECBI	Eyberg Child Behavior Inventory (EDAC)
ECBM	Episcopal Commission for Black Ministries (EA)
ECBMD	Emergency Committee to Boycott Mother's Day
ECBO	Enterocytopathogenic Bovine Virus
ECBO	European Cell Biology Organization (EAIO)
ECB-P	Excellence-in-Competition Badge (Pistol) [*Military decoration*]
ECB-R	Excellence-in-Competition Badge (Rifle) [*Military decoration*]
ECBS	Engineer Combat Battalions (CINC)
ECBTE	European Committee for Building Technical Equipment [*See also CEETB*] (EAIO)
ECBV	Effective Circulating Blood Volume [*Physiology*]
ECC	Earth Conservation Corps
ECC	Earth Continuity Conductor [*Electronics*] (BARN)
ECC	East Carolina College [*Later, ECU*] [*North Carolina*]
ECC	East Coast Carriers Conference, New York NY [*STAC*]
ECC	Eastern Claims Conference (EA)
ECC	Eccentric (AAG)
ECC	ECC International [*NYSE symbol*] (TTSB)
ECC	ECC International Ltd. [*Formerly, Educational Computer Corp.*] [*NYSE symbol*] (SPSG)
Ecc	Ecclesiastes [*Old Testament book*] (BJA)
ECC	Economic Council of Canada
ECC	Eddy Current Clutch [*Mechanical engineering*]
ECC	Edema, Clubbing, and Cyanosis [*Medicine*] (DAVI)
ECC	Effective Creep Compliance
ECC	El Camino College [*Torrance, CA*]
ECC	El Centro [*California*] [*Seismograph station code, US Geological Survey Closed*] (SEIS)
ECC	Electrical Commuter Car
ECC	Electrical Continuous Cloth (IAA)
ECC	Electricity Consumers' Council [*British*]

ECC .... Electrocardiocorder [*Medicine*]
ECC .... Electrochemical Cathodes (MCD)
ECC .... Electrochemical Concentration Cell (MCD)
ECC .... Electrochemichromic [*Optoelectronics*]
ECC .... Electrocorticogram [*Neurology*] (DAVI)
ECC .... Electron-Coupled Control (IAA)
ECC .... Electronic Calibration Center [*National Institute of Standards and Technology*]
ECC .... Electronic Carburetor Control [*Automotive engineering*]
ECC .... Electronic Climate Control [*Automotive engineering*]
ECC .... Electronic Common Control [*Telecommunications*] (TEL)
ECC .... Electronic Components Code (NATG)
ECC .... Electronic Components Conference
ECC .... Electronic Computer Concepts (HGAA)
ECC .... Electronic Counter Control Measure
ECC .... Electronic-Courier Circuit (DNAB)
ECC .... Elgin Community College [*Illinois*]
ECC .... Ellsworth Community College [*Iowa*] [*Formerly, EJC*]
ECC .... Embryonal Cell Carcinoma [*Medicine Medicine*] (DMAA)
ECC .... Emergency Cardiac Care
ECC .... Emergency Combat Capability
ECC .... Emergency Conservation Committee [*Defunct*]
ECC .... Emergency Control Center (CINC)
ECC .... Emergency Core Cooling [*or Coolant*] [*Nuclear energy*]
ECC .... Emitter-Coupled Circuit [*Electronics*] (HGAA)
ECC .... Employees' Compensation Commission
ECC .... Endocervical Cone [*or Conization*] [*Gynecology*] (DAVI)
ECC .... Endocervical Curettage [*or Curretings*] [*Gynecology*] (DAVI)
ECC .... Energy Conservation Caucus [*Defunct*] (EA)
ECC .... Energy Conservation Coalition (EA)
ECC .... Energy Conservation Council
ECC .... Energy Content Curve (NOAA)
ECC .... Engagement Control Center [*Army*]
ECC .... Engineering Casualty Control [*Military*] (NVT)
ECC .... Engineering Change Control
ECC .... Engineering Change Coordination (MCD)
ECC .... Engineering Critical Component (KSC)
ECC .... English Ceramic Circle [*An Association*] [*British*] (EAIO)
ECC .... English Chamber Choir
ECC .... English China Clays Ltd. (ECON)
ECC .... Enhanced Control Cellular [*Telecommunications*]
ECC .... Enlisted Classification Code
ECC .... Enlisted Correspondence Course
ECC .... Environmental Control Canister
ECC .... Environment Concept Car [*Volvo Motor Co.*]
ECC .... Equatorial Communications Co. [*Mountain View, CA*] [*Telecommunications*] (TSSD)
ECC .... Equatorial Countercurrent [*Oceanography*]
ECC .... Equipment Category Code [*Military*] (AABC)
ECC .... Equipment Configuration Control (AAG)
ECC .... Eras of the Christian Church [*A publication*]
ECC .... Error Checking and Correction [*Computer science*]
ECC .... Error Checking and Correction (NITA)
ECC .... Error Checking Code (NITA)
ECC .... Error Control Circuitry [*Algorithm to verify data*] [*Computer science*] (PCM)
ECC .... Error-Correcting Circuitry [*Computer science*] (IAA)
ECC .... Error Correction and Control
ECC .... Error Correction Capability [*Computer software quality*]
ECC .... Error Correction Code
ECC .... Ertl Collectors Club [*Commercial firm*] (EA)
ECC .... Escherichia Coli [*Microorganism*]
ECC .... Essex Community College, James A. Newpher Library, Baltimore, MD [*OCLC symbol*] (OCLC)
ECC .... Estimated Correction Cost (MCD)
ECC .... Ethiopian Collectors Club (EA)
ECC .... Eton College Chronicle [*A publication British*]
ECC .... Eurasian Communist Countries (MCD)
ECC .... European Communist Countries (MCD)
ECC .... European Community Commission (MCD)
ECC .... European Coordinating Committee
ECC .... European Crystallographic Committee [*International Council of Scientific Unions*]
ECC .... European Cultural Centre [*Geneva, Switzerland*]
ECC .... European Economic Community (TDOB)
ECC .... Evacuation Coordination Center (DOMA)
ECC .... Everett Community College [*Formerly, EJC*] [*Washington*]
ECC .... Exceptional Child Center [*Utah State University*] [*Research center*] (RCD)
ECC .... Exchange Control Copy [*Business term*] (DS)
ECC .... Excitement, Choreiform Movements, and Circling [*Characterizations of a medical syndrome*]
ECC .... Ex-Communist Country
ECC .... Execute Control Cycle (IAA)
ECC .... Executive Communications and Control (DOMA)
ECC .... Exercise Control Centre [*Australia*]
ECC .... Expanded Community Calling [*Telecommunications*] (TEL)
ECC .... Experimental Computer Complex
ECC .... Exposition and Conference Council (EA)
ECC .... External Cardiac Compression
ECC .... External Chest Compression [*Medicine*]
ECC .... Extracorporeal Circulation [*Medicine*]
ECCA .... Electronic Component Checkout Area (AAG)
ECCA .... European Coil Coating Association

ECCAA .... Executive Chefs de Cuisine Association of America [*Later, Chefs de Cuisine Association of America*] (EA)
ECCAI .... European Coordinating Committee for Artificial Intelligence (EAIO)
Ecc & Ad .... Spinks' English Ecclesiastical and Admiralty Reports [*1853-55*] [*A publication*] (DLA)
ECCANE ...... East Coast Conference on Aerospace and Navigational Electronics (MCD)
ECCAS .... Economic Community of Central African States [*See also CEEAC*] [*Bangui, Central African Republic*] (EAIO)
ECCAS .... Engineer Command and Control Automation System [*Army*] (RDA)
ECCB .... Eastern Caribbean Central Bank [*Formerly, East Caribbean Currency Authority*] [*Basseterre, St. Christopher*] (GEA)
ECCB .... Electronic Components Certification Board (EA)
ECCB .... Engineering Change Control Board (NASA)
ECCB .... Equipment to Computer Converter Buffer (DNAB)
ECCC .... Ecology Center Communications Council [*Defunct*] (EA)
ECCC .... English Country Cheese Council (BI)
ECCC .... European Command Coordination Committee [*Military*] (AABC)
ECCC .... European Communities Chemistry Committee (EA)
ECCCM .... Electronic Countermeasures [*Military*] (IAA)
ECCCS .... Emergency Command Control Communications System
ECCCS .... European Command and Control Console System [*DoD*]
ECCDA .... Eastern Connecticut Clam Diggers Association [*Defunct*] (EA)
ECCE .... Extracapular Cataract Extraction [*Ophthalmology*]
ECCEN .... Eccentric (IAA)
ECCET .... Engineering Casualty Control Evaluation Team [*Navy*] (ANA)
ECCFD .... European Commission for the Control of Foot-and-Mouth Disease
ECC HOM .... Ecce Homo [*Behold the Man*] [*Latin*] (ROG)
ECCI .... Evening College Characteristics Index (EDAC)
ECCI .... Experimental Consultative Conference of Industrialists (NATG)
ECC Int .... ECC International Ltd. [*Formerly, Educational Computer Corp.*] [*Associated Press*] (SAG)
ECCJ .... European Communities Court of Justice (DLA)
Eccl .... Ecclesiastes [*Old Testament book*]
ECCL .... Ecclesiastical
Eccl .... Ecclesiazusae [*of Aristophanes*] [*Classical studies*] (OCD)
ECCL .... Equipment and Component Configuration Listing (DNAB)
ECCL .... Error Checking and Correction Logic [*Computer science*] (IAA)
ECCL .... Essex County Cooperating Libraries [*Library network*]
ECCL .... Scriptores Ecclesiastici [*Ecclesiastical Authors*] [*Latin*] (ROG)
Eccl & Ad .... Ecclesiastical and Admiralty [*Legal term*] (DLA)
Eccl & Ad .... Spinks' English Ecclesiastical and Admiralty Reports [*A publication*] (DLA)
Eccl & Adm... Spinks' Ecclesiastical and Admiralty [*Upper Canada*] [*A publication*] (DLA)
Eccles .... Ecclesiastes [*Old Testament book*]
ECCLES .... Ecclesiastical
eccles .... Ecclesiastical (VRA)
EcclesR .... Ecclesiastes Rabbah (BJA)
Eccl R .... English Ecclesiastical Reports [*A publication*] (DLA)
Eccl Rep .... Ecclesiastical Reports [*England*] [*A publication*] (DLA)
ECCLS .... European Committee for Clinical Laboratory Standards [*Kent, England*]
Eccl Stat ..... Ecclesiastical Statutes [*A publication*] (DLA)
Ecclus .... Ecclesiasticus [*Old Testament book*] [*Apocrypha*]
ECCM .... East Caribbean Common Market (DS)
ECCM .... Electronic Counter-Countermeasures [*Military*]
ECCMO .... Electronic Counter-Countermeasures Operator [*Military*] (CET)
ECCN .... Export Control Commodity Number (AAGC)
ECCNSW .... Ethnic Communities Council of New South Wales [*Australia*]
ECCO .... Educational Computer Consortium of Ohio (SRA)
ECCO .... Environmental Council of Concrete Organizations
ECCO .... Ethyl Cellulose and Caster Oil (SAA)
ECCO .... European Conference of Conscripts Organisations (EAIO)
ECCO .... European Culture Collections' Organization (EAIO)
ECC-OCC .... Enlisted/Officer Combined Correspondence Course [*Military*] (DNAB)
ECCOIL .... Eastern Construction Co. in Laos (CINC)
ECCP .... East Coast Coal Port [*Shipping*] [*British*]
ECCP .... Engineering Concepts Curriculum Project
ECCP .... European Committee on Crime Problems
ECCP .... Executive Committee on Commercial Policy [*Abolished, 1944*]
ECCR .... Electronic Cash and Credit Register (HGAA)
ECCS .... ECCS, Inc. [*NASDAQ symbol*] (SAG)
ECCS .... Economic Hundred Call Seconds [*Telecommunications*] (TEL)
ECCS .... Electronic Concentrated Control System [*Computerized car fuel system*]
ECCS .... Electronic Concentrated Control System
ECCS .... Electronic Cycling Clutch Switch [*Automotive engineering*]
ECCS .... Emergency Core-Cooling System [*Nuclear energy*]
ECCS .... Employee Charity and Community Services
ECCS .... Engineer Command and Control System [*Software*]
ECCS .... Engineering of Complex Computer Systems
ECCS .... European Committee for Consultant Services (EA)
ECCSA .... Ethnic Communities Council of South Australia
ECCSL .... Emitter-Coupled Current-Steered Logic [*Electronics*] (MSA)
ECCT .... Error Correction Console Technician (IAA)
ECCTIS .... Educational Counselling and Credit Transfer Information Service [*Information service or system*] (IID)
ECCTO .... European Chemical Coastal Tanker Owners
ECCTO .... European Committee for Cocoa Trade Organisations (EERA)
ECCTO .... European Community Cocoa Trade Organization (EAIO)
ECCTT .... Engineering Casualty Control Training Team [*Navy*]
ECCTYC .... English Council of California Two-Year Colleges (EDAC)
ECCU .... English Cross Country Union (BI)
ECD .... Early-Closing Day [*British*]

ECD............ Educational and Cultural Development Program
ECD............ Effective Cutoff Diameter [*Particulate measurement*]
ECD............ Efficiency of Conversion of Digested Material [*Physiology*]
ECD............ Electric Control Drive
ECD............ Electrochemical Deburring
ECD............ Electro-Chemical Degradation
ECD............ Electrochemical Deposition [*Metallurgy*]
ECD............ Electrochromic Display [*Instrumentation*]
ECD............ Electron-Capture Detection [*Instrumentation*]
ECD............ Electronic Communications Division [*Air Force*] (AFM)
ECD............ Elk Chute Ditch [*Missouri*] [*Seismograph station code, US Geological Survey*] (SEIS)
ECD............ Emergency Category Designation
ECD............ Emission Control Device [*Automotive engineering*]
ECD............ Endocardial Cushion Defect
ECD............ Endothelial Cell Density [*Anatomy*]
ECD............ Energy Conversion Devices, Inc.
ECD............ Engineering Control Drawing (MCD)
ECD............ Enhanced Color Display [*Computer monitor*]
ECD............ Enhanced Compact Disk (PCM)
ECD............ Enhanced Console Driver [*Computer science*]
ECD............ Entry Corridor Display (KSC)
ECD............ Environmental Conditions Determination (AAG)
ECD............ Episcopal Conference of the Deaf (EA)
ECD............ Equal Charge Displacement [*Fission*]
ECD............ Equivalent Carbon Dioxide [*Climatology*]
ECD............ Equivalent Circulating Density [*Well drilling*]
ECD............ Equivalent Current Dipole [*Magnetism*]
ECD............ Error Control Device (TEL)
ECD............ Escherichia Coli Database [*Genetics*]
ECD............ Estimated Completion Date
ECD............ Ethoxycoumarin Deethylase [*An enzyme*]
ECD............ European Communications Division [*Military*]
ECD............ European Consultants Directory [*A publication*]
ECD............ Except Change Departure to Read [*Aviation*] (FAAC)
ECD............ Exploratory Career Development (DNAB)
Ecd............ Extensible Compound Document [*Programming language*] [*Computer science*] (PCM)
ECD............ Prospect, AK [*Location identifier FAA*] (FAAL)
ECDA .... Engine Control Development Area (KSC)
ECDB .... Electrochemical Deburring (IAA)
ECDC .... Economic Cooperation among Developing Countries [*United Nations*]
ECDC .... Electrochemical Diffused-Collector Transistor
ECDC .... Engineering Configuration Data Control (AAG)
ECDC .... Ethiopian Community Development Council (EA)
ECDC .... External Countdown Clock
ECDCC .... Early Childhood Day Care Center [*University of Alabama*] [*Research center*] (RCD)
ECDES .... EC Digital Evaluation System (MCD)
ECDFTT....... Employment-Corrected Double Factorial Terms of Trade [*Economics*]
ECDG .... Electrochemical Discharge Grinding [*Manufacturing term*]
ECDGF .... Embryonal Carcinoma Derived Growth Factor [*Biochemistry*]
ECDGF .... Endothelial Cell-Derived Growth Factor [*Biochemistry*]
ECDI............ Editorial Code and Data, Inc. (IID)
ECDIN .... Environmental Chemicals Data and Information Network [*Commission of the European Communities*] [*Chemical databank*] (IID)
ECDIN .... European Chemical Data and Infomation Network [*EURATOM*] (PDAA)
ECDIS .... Electronic Chart Display and Information System [*Computer science*]
ECDL........... Emergency Carbon Dioxide Limit (SAA)
ECDM.......... Electrochemical and Electrical Discharge Machining (PDAA)
ECDM.......... Electrochemical Discharge Machining [*Manufacturing term*] (IAA)
ECDMMRL ... European Committee for the Development of the Meuse and Meuse/Rhine Links (EAIO)
ECDO .... Electronic Community Deal Office [*Telecommunications*] (TEL)
ECDO .... Enterocytopathogenic Dog Orphan Virus
ECDO .... European Cell Death Organisation
ECDR .... Engineering Control Distribution Report (MCD)
ECDT .... Electrochemical Diffused-Transistor (IAA)
ECDU .... Electrical Coupling Display Unit (KSC)
ECDU .... European Christian Democratic Union [*Brussels, Belgium Political party*] (EAIO)
ECDW .... Electronic Cooling Distilled Water (DNAB)
ECE............. Early Childhood Education
ECE............. East Central Europe (ECON)
ECE............. Echo Control Equipment [*Telecommunications*] (TEL)
ECE............. Economic Commission for Europe [*United Nations*] (IRC)
ECE............. Economic Coverage Endorsement
ECE............. Eddy Current Energy
ECE............. Effective Conversion Efficiency
ECE............. El Campo, TX [*Location identifier FAA*] (FAAL)
ECE............. Electrical Checkout Equipment (KSC)
ECE............. Electrochemical, Chemical, Electrochemical [*Chemical mechanism*]
ECE............. Electro-Chemical Engine
ECE............. Electrochemical Equivalent (IAA)
ECE............. Element Characteristics Equation
ECE............. Endocervical Ecchymosis [*Gynecology*] (DAVI)
ECE............. Endothelin-Converting Enzyme [*Biochemistry*]
ECE............. Engineering Capacity Exchange (IEEE)
ECE............. Environmental Contaminant Evaluation [*Fish and Wildlife Service program*]
ECE............. Environmental Control Equipment
ECE............. Episcopal Center for Evangelism (EA)
ECE............. European Commodities Exchange [*of the European Economic Community*] (EA)

ECE............. Executive Communications Exchange (MHDI)
ECE............. Experiment Checkout Equipment (MCD)
ECE............. Export Council for Europe (ILCA)
ECE............. Extended Coverage Endorsement [*Insurance*]
ECE............. External Combustion Engine [*Steam bus*]
ECE............. Extrachromosomal Element [*Genetics*]
ECEA.......... Ethyl(chloroethyl)aniline [*Organic chemistry*]
ECEBA......... Energy Conservation in Existing Buildings Act of 1976
ECEC.......... Effective Cation and Exchange Capacity [*Soil science*]
EC/EDI .... Electronic Commerce / Electronic Data Interchange [*DoD*]
ECEF.......... Earth-Centered, Earth-Fixed
ECEFP......... Executive Committee on Economic Foreign Policy [*Terminated*] (EGAO)
ECEFT .... Early Childhood Embedded Figures Test (EDAC)
ECEJ .... Early Childhood Education Journal [*A publication*] (BRI)
ECEJAETA ... European Chamber of Extra-Judicial Adjudicators and Expert Technical Advisers [*See also CEASPECT*] (EA)
ECEL.......... Epithermal Critical Experiment Laboratory [*Nuclear energy*]
ECEL.......... European Council for Environmental Law (PDAA)
ECELL......... Electrochemical Cell (MCD)
ECEMG........ Evoked Compound Electromyography [*Neurology*] (DAVI)
ECEP.......... Equivalent CEP
ECEP.......... Experiment Checkout Equipment Processor (NASA)
ECEPS......... Electronic Converter Electric Power Supply (PDAA)
ECER.......... Exceptional Child Education Resources [*Formerly, ECEA*] [*Council for Exceptional Children Bibliographic database*] [*A publication*] (EA)
ECERM........ Environment Code of Ethics for Rangeland Managers (EERA)
ECES.......... Evaluation Contractors Estimating System
ECESDB ...... European Commodities Exchange Statistical Database [*United Nations*] (DUND)
ECET .... Electronic Control Assembly - Engine Thrust (KSC)
ECETOC....... European Chemical Industry Ecology and Toxicology Centre [*Belgium*] (PDAA)
ECF............ Earth Crust Formation
ECF............ East Coast Fever [*Veterinary medicine*]
ECF............ Echo Control Factor [*Telecommunications*] (TEL)
ECF............ Effective Capillary Flow [*Medicine*] (MAE)
ECF............ Effective Cutoff Frequency
ECF............ Elecrical Council of Florida (SRA)
ECF............ Electrically Conductive Film (MCD)
ECF............ Electrochemical Fluorination [*Chemical synthesis*]
ECF............ Electrochemical Forming [*Manufacturing term*] (IAA)
ECF............ Elemental Chlorine-Free [*Pulp and paper processing*]
ECF............ Element Change Factor (MCD)
ECF............ Eleventh Commandment Fellowship (EA)
ECF............ Ellsworth Convertible Growth & Income Fund, Inc. [*AMEX symbol*] (SPSG)
ECF............ Ellsworth Cv Growth/Income [*AMEX symbol*] (TTSB)
ECF............ Emergency Cooling Function [*Nuclear energy*] (NRCH)
ECF............ Emission Contribution Fraction (OA)
ECF............ Employees' Compensation Fund (NG)
ECF............ Energy of Crush Factor [*Automotive safety*]
ECF............ Engineering Central Files
ECF............ Enhanced Connectivity Facilities (CDE)
ECF............ Enhanced Cytotoxicity Factor [*Biochemistry*]
ECF............ Eosinophil Chemotactic Factor [*Hematology*]
ECF............ Equivalency Capability File (MCD)
ECF............ Erythroid Colony Formation [*Hematology*] (DMAA)
ECF............ Eurocopter [*France ICAO designator*] (FAAC)
ECF............ European Caravan Federation (EA)
ECF............ European Coffee Federation (EAIO)
ECF............ European Cultural Foundation (EAIO)
ECF............ "Evangelize China" Fellowship (EA)
ECF............ Excess Chiasma Frequency [*Genetics*]
ECF............ Expended Core Facility [*Nuclear energy*]
ECF............ Experimental Cartographic Facility [*Air Force*]
ECF............ Export Cargo Form [*Shipping*]
ECF............ Extended Care Facility [*Medicine Obsolete*]
ECF............ Extended Care Facility (WYGK)
ECF............ Externally Caused Failure
ECF............ Extracellular Fluid [*Physiology*]
ECF............ Eye Contolled Focus [*Camera technology*]
ECFA.......... Emergency Community Facilities Act of 1970
ECF-A......... Eosinophil Chemotactic Factor of Anaphylaxis [*Immunochemistry*]
ECFA.......... European Committee for Future Activities (PDAA)
ECFA.......... European Committee on Future Accelerators [*Nuclear energy*]
ECFA.......... Evangelical Council for Financial Accountability (EA)
ECFB.......... Ethyl Cellulose Perfluorobutyrate
ECFC.......... Employers Council on Flexible Compensation (EA)
ECFD.......... Executive Council on Foreign Diplomats (EA)
ECFI.......... Electronic Company Filing Index [*Disclosure Information Group*] [*Information service or system*] (IID)
ECF-IUF .... European Committee of Food, Catering, and Allied Workers' Unions within the IUF [*International Union of Food and Allied Workers' Associations*] (EAIO)
ECFL .... Emergency Crop and Feed Loans [*New Deal*]
ECFM.......... Eddy Current Flow Meter [*Nuclear energy*] (NRCH)
ECFMG........ Educational Commission for Foreign Medical Graduates (EA)
ECFMS........ Educational Council for Foreign Medical Students (DAVI)
ECFS.......... East Coast Flying Service (SAA)
ECFS.......... Export Credit Facilitation Scheme [*Australia*]
ECFSA......... Episcopal Churchpeople for a Free Southern Africa (EA)
ECFSOV ...... Episcopal Council for Foreign Students and Other Visitors [*Defunct*] (EA)
ECFTU.......... European Confederation of Free Trade Unions [*Later, ETUC*]

ECFV .... Extracellular Fluid Volume [*Physiology*]
ECG .... Echocardiogram [*Cardiology*] (DAVI)
ECG .... Ecosystem Conservation Group [*Marine science*] (MSC)
ECG .... Ecosystems Conservation Group (EERA)
ECG .... Electrocapiogram [*Medicine*]
ECG .... Electrocardiogram [*Also, EK, EKG*] [*Medicine*]
ECG .... Electrocardiograph [*Also, EKG*] (MSA)
ECG .... Electrochemical Grinding (IEEE)
ECG .... Electro-Epitaxial Crystal Growth [*Materials processing*]
ECG .... Electrolytic Chloride Generator (DWSG)
ECG .... Electronic Character Generation [*Electronography*] (DGA)
ECG .... Electronic Character Generator [*Television*] (WDMC)
ECG .... Electronic Component Group
ECG .... Elizabeth City [*North Carolina*] [*Airport symbol*] (AD)
ECG .... Elizabeth City, NC [*Location identifier FAA*] (FAAL)
ECG .... Emergency Coordination Group [*Military*]
ECG .... Energy Coordinating Group [*Twelve-nation coalition*]
ECG .... Engineering Craftsmen's Guild [*A union*] [*British*]
ECG .... Environmental Control Group (CAAL)
ECG .... Epicatechin Gallate [*Biochemistry*]
ECG .... Equine Chorionic Gonadotropin [*Endocrinology*]
ECG .... European Contact Group on Urban Industrial Mission (EAIO)
ECG .... Evaporative Cooling Garment [*Spacesuit*] [*NASA*]
ECG .... Exercise Control Group [*Army*]
ECG .... Export Credit Guarantee (DLA)
ECGAI .... Education Council of the Graphic Arts Industry [*Later, GATF*] (EA)
ECGB .... East Coast of Great Britain [*Shipping*]
ECGC .... Electron-Capture Gas Chromatography
ECGC .... Empire Cotton Growing Corp. [*British*] (BI)
ECGC .... Essex County Gas [*NASDAQ symbol*] (TTSB)
ECGC .... Essex County Gas Co. [*NASDAQ symbol*] (NQ)
ECGD .... Export Credits Guarantee Department [*British*]
ECGF .... Endothelial Cell Growth Factor [*Cytochemistry*]
ECGF .... European Container Glass Federation (EA)
ECGI .... Electronically Controlled Gasoline Injection [*Automotive fuel systems*]
ECGLC .... Economic Community of the Great Lakes Countries [*See also CEPGL*] [*Gisenye, Rwanda*] (EAIO)
ECGLC .... Electron Capture Gas-Liquid Chromatography
ECGM .... Episcopal Council for Global Mission (EA)
ECGO .... American Eco Corp. [*NASDAQ symbol*] (SAG)
ECGOF .... Amer Eco Corp. [*NASDAQ symbol*] (TTSB)
ECGS .... Endothelial Cell Growth Supplement [*Cytochemistry*]
ECGS .... Evaporative Cooling Garment System [*NASA*]
ECH .... Early Childhood Health
ECH .... Earth Coverage Horn [*Satellite communications*]
ECH .... Echelon
ECH .... Echery [*France*] [*Seismograph station code, US Geological Survey*] (SEIS)
ECH .... Echlin, Inc. [*NYSE symbol*] (SPSG)
ECH .... Echo Cancellation Hybrid [*Telecommunications*] (NITA)
ECH .... Eddy-Current Heating (EECA)
ECH .... Electrochemical Honing [*Manufacturing term*]
ECH .... Electron Cyclotron Harmonic [*Planetary Physics*]
ECH .... Electron Cyclotron Heating [*Nuclear energy*]
ECH .... Engine Compartment Heater (AAG)
ECH .... Epichlorohydrin [*Organic chemistry*]
ECH .... Epochs of Church History [*A publication*]
ECH .... Extended Care Hospital (DAVI)
ECH .... Ketchikan, AK [*Location identifier FAA*] (FAAL)
ECHA .... Movement Echelon [*MTMC*] (TAG)
ECHA .... Eastern College Hockey Association
EchBF .... Echo Bay Finance Corp. [*Associated Press*] (SAG)
ECHC .... European Colloquium on Heterocyclic Chemistry
ECHE .... Ealing College of Higher Education [*England*]
Echelon ...... Echelon International Corp. [*Associated Press*] (SAG)
ECHH .... Electro-Catalytic Hyper-Heaters (GNE)
ECHIN .... Echinococcus [*Microorganism*] (DAVI)
Echlin .... Echlin, Inc. [*Associated Press*] (SAG)
ECHM .... Earth Coverage Horizon Measurement (PDAA)
ECHO .... Each Community Helps Others [*Environmental Protection Agency*]
ECHO .... East Coast Hang Out [*Computer network*]
ECHO .... East Coast Hazards Observation [*Sampling program*]
ECHO .... Echocardiogram [*Cardiology*]
ECHO .... Echoencephalogram [*Neurology*]
echo .... Echogram [*Radiology*] (DAVI)
echo .... Echoplex [*Telecommunications protocol*] (CDE)
ECHO .... Educational Concern for Hunger Organization (EA)
ECHO .... Elder Cottage Housing Opportunity
ECHO .... [*The*] Eletonic Clearing House, Inc. [*NASDAQ symbol*] (NQ)
ECHO .... Electronic Clearing House [*NASDAQ symbol*] (TTSB)
ECHO .... Electronic Communications for the Home and Office [*Marina Del Ray, CA*] [*Telecommunications service*] (TSSD)
ECHO .... Electronic Computing, Hospital-Oriented (IEEE)
ECHO .... Enterocytopathogenic Human Orphan Virus
ECHO .... Environment, Conservation, and Hunting Outreach [*An association*]
ECHO .... Equipment for Charity Hospitals Overseas [*British*] (DI)
ECHO .... Etoposide, Cyclophosphamide, Hydroxydaunomycin [*Adriamycin*], Oncovin [*Vincristine*] [*Antineoplastic drug regimen*]
ECHO .... European Commission Host Organization [*Commission of the European Communities*] [*Host system*] [*Luxembourg*] [*Information service or system*] (IID)
ECHO .... Evolution of Competing Hierarchical Organizations
ECHO .... Exchange Clearing House Organization [*European bank coalition*] (ECON)
ECHO .... Expanded Characteristics Option [*Metallurgy*]

ECHO .... Experimental Contract Highlight Operation [*NASA*]
ECHO .... Expo Collectors - Historians Organization (EA)
ECHO .... Hungarian Economic Information Service (IID)
EchoBay ..... Echo Bay Mines Ltd. [*Associated Press*] (SAG)
EchoC .... EchoCath, Inc. [*Associated Press*] (SAG)
EchoCth ...... EchoCath, Inc. [*Associated Press*] (SAG)
EchoStar ..... EchoStar Communications Corp. [*Associated Press*] (SAG)
EchoStr ...... EchoStar Communications Corp. [*Associated Press*] (SAG)
ECHR .... Emergency Coalition for Haitian Refugees (EA)
ECHR .... European Commission of Human Rights (EA)
ECHSA .... Elderly Citizens Homes of South Australia
ECHT .... EchoCath, Inc. [*NASDAQ symbol*] (SAG)
ECHTA .... EchoCath Inc.'A' [*NASDAQ symbol*] (TTSB)
ECHTU .... EchoCath Inc. Unit [*NASDAQ symbol*] (TTSB)
ECHTW ...... EchoCath Inc. Wrrt [*NASDAQ symbol*] (TTSB)
ECHTZ .... EchoCath Inc. Wrrt'B' [*NASDAQ symbol*] (TTSB)
ECI .... Earth-Centered Inertial [*System*]
ECI .... East Coast of Ireland [*Shipping*]
ECI .... Eastern Carolina Aviation, Inc. [*ICAO designator*] (FAAC)
ECI .... Edgell Communications, Inc. [*Database producer*] (IID)
ECI .... Efficiency of Conversion of Ingested Material [*Physiology*]
ECI .... Electrical Circuit Interrupter (KSC)
ECI .... Electrocerebral Inactivity (MAE)
ECI .... Electronic Cascade Impactor [*For aerosol analysis*]
ECI .... Electronic Communications, Inc.
ECI .... Electronic Communications Index
ECI .... Electronic Computer Ignition [*Automotive engineering*]
ECI .... Electronic Control Instrumentation
ECI .... Electronic Controlled Injection [*Automotive engineering*]
ECI .... Emergency Coolant Injection [*Nuclear energy*] (NRCH)
ECI .... Employee Cost Index
ECI .... Employment Cost Index (OICC)
ECI .... Encor Energy Corp. Inc. [*Toronto Stock Exchange symbol Vancouver Stock Exchange symbol*]
ECI .... Enemy Countries Intelligence [*Ministry of Economic Warfare*] [*British World War II*]
ECI .... Engineering Change Incorporation (AAG)
ECI .... Engineering Change Information
ECI .... Engineering Change Instruction
ECI .... Environmental Carcinogen Information [*Department of Energy*] [*Information service or system*] (IID)
ECI .... Environmental Clearinghouse, Inc. [*An association*] (EA)
ECI .... Equipment and Component Index (DNAB)
ECI .... Equipment Change Information
ECI .... Equity Capital for Industry [*British*]
ECI .... Error Cause Identification [*Military*] (AFM)
ECI .... Essential Controls and Instrumentation [*Nuclear energy*] (NRCH)
ECI .... EURATOM [*European Atomic Energy Community*] Classified Information
ECI .... European Confederation of Independents [*Germany*] (EAIO)
ECI .... European Federation of Trade Unions for Energy, Chemical, and Miscellaneous Industries (EA)
ECI .... Evangelism Center International (EA)
ECI .... Evaporative Cooling Institute (EA)
ECI .... EXCEL Communications [*NYSE symbol*] (TTSB)
ECI .... Excel Communications, Inc. [*NYSE symbol*] (SAG)
ECI .... Executives Consultants, Inc. [*An association*] (EA)
ECI .... Experimental Cities, Inc. (EA)
ECI .... Export Consignment Identifying Number (DS)
ECI .... Extension Course Institute [*Air Force*]
ECI .... Extension Course Institute [*Air Force*] (DOMA)
ECI .... Extracorporeal Irradiation [*Medicine*]
ECIA .... Education Consolidation and Improvement Act [*1981*]
ECIB .... Extracorporeal Irradiation of Blood [*Medicine*]
ECIC .... Electric Consumers Information Committee (EA)
ECIC .... Electronic Components Information Center [*Battelle Memorial Institute*]
ECIC .... Export Credits Insurance Corp. [*Canada*]
ECIC .... Extracranial-Intracranial [*Medicine*]
ECID .... Emission Circular Intensity Differential [*Spectroscopy*]
ECID .... En Route Computer Identification (KSC)
ECIE .... Executive Council on Integrity and Efficiency (AAGC)
ECIEL .... Estudios Conjuntos sobre Integracion Economica Latinoamericana [*Program*]
ECIEL .... Programa de Estudios Conjuntos sobre la Integracion Economica Latinoamericana [*Program of Joint Studies for Latin American Economic Integration*] (EAIO)
ECI Env ...... ECI Environmental, Inc. [*Associated Press*]
ECIF .... Electronic Components Industry Federation [*British*]
ECII .... Energy Conserving - Second Generation [*Automotive engineering*]
ECII .... Equity Corp. Intl. [*NASDAQ symbol*] (TTSB)
ECII .... Equity Corporation International [*NASDAQ symbol*] (SAG)
ECIIB .... Enemy Civilian Internee Information Bureau [*Military*] (AABC)
ECIIB(Br) ..... Enemy Civilian Internee Information Bureau (Branch) [*Military*] (AABC)
ECIL .... ECI Telecom Ltd. [*NASDAQ symbol*] (NQ)
ECIL .... Emission Control Information Label [*Automotive engineering*]
ECIL .... Expected Confidence Interval Length [*Statistics*]
ECIL .... Extracorporeal Irradiation of Lymph (MAE)
ECILF .... ECI Telecom Ltd. (MHDW)
ECIMOT ...... European Central Inland Movements of Transport
ECIN .... EMCEE Broadcast Products [*NASDAQ symbol*] (TTSB)
ECIN .... EMCEE Broadcast Products, Inc. [*NASDAQ symbol*] (SAG)
ECIO .... Experiment Computer Input/Output (NASA)

EC-IOA......... European Committee of the International Ozone Association [*See also CEAIO*] (EA)

ECIP........... Energy Conservation Investment Program [*DoD*] (MCD)

ECIP........... European CAD Integration Project (NITA)

ECIP........... European Cooperation in Information Processing (PDAA)

ECIPL.......... Engineering Change Identity Parts List [*McDonnell Douglas Aircraft Corp.*]

ECIRC......... European Computer Industry Research Centre (PDAA)

ECIS........... Earth-Centered Inertial System (SAA)

ECIS........... Electrical Cell-Substrate Impedance Sensing [*for cell-culture study*]

ECIS........... Emory Center for International Studies [*Emory University*] [*Research center*] (RCD)

ECIS........... Engineering Careers Information Service (AIE)

ECIS........... Engineering Careers Information System

ECIS........... Error Correction Information System [*NASA*]

ECIS........... European Colloid and Interface Society

ECIS........... European Community Information Service (EA)

ECIS........... European Council of International Schools (EA)

ECIS........... Extension and Change of Immigration Status (ADA)

ECITC......... European Committee for IT [*Information Technology*] Testing and Certification (OSI)

ECI Tel........ ECI Telecom Ltd. [*Associated Press*] (SAG)

ECITO......... European Central Inland Transport Organization

ECIY........... Earl of Chester's Imperial Yeomanry [*British military*] (DMA)

ECJ............ Berlin European [*ICAO designator*] (FAAC)

ECJ............ Court of Justice of the European Communities (DLA)

ECJ............ Etudes Publies par des Peres de la Compagnie de Jesus [*A publication*] (BJA)

ECJC.......... East Central Junior College [*Decatur, MS*]

ECJCS......... European Council of Jewish Community Services (EA)

ECJF.......... Emergency Council of Jewish Families (EA)

ECJS.......... East Coast Joint Service, Stock [*Railroad*] [*British*] (ROG)

ECK........... East Coast Airlines Ltd. [*Kenya*] [*ICAO designator*] (FAAC)

ECK........... Eckerd Corp. [*NYSE symbol*] (SPSG)

ECK........... Embryonic Chicken Kidney

ECK........... Emergency Communications Key

ECK........... Engine Change Kit

ECK........... Epidermal Cytokeratin [*Cytology*]

ECK........... Peck, MI [*Location identifier FAA*] (FAAL)

Eckerd........ Eckerd Corp. [*Associated Press*] (SAG)

ECKL.......... Eckler Industries [*NASDAQ symbol*] (TTSB)

ECKL.......... Eckler Industries, Inc. [*NASDAQ symbol*] (SAG)

Eckler........ Eckler Industries, Inc. [*Associated Press*] (SAG)

ECKLU........ Eckler Industries Unit [*NASDAQ symbol*] (TTSB)

ECKLW....... Eckler Industries Wrrt [*NASDAQ symbol*] (TTSB)

ECKO......... Eddy-Current Killed Oscillator [*Engineering instrumentation*]

ECL........... East Coast Laboratory [*Environmental Science Services Administration*]

ECL........... Eclectic (WGA)

ECL........... Eclipse (WDAA)

ECL........... Eclipse Mining [*Vancouver Stock Exchange symbol*]

Ecl............ Eclogues [*of Vergil*] [*Classical studies*] (OCD)

ECL........... Ecolab, Inc. [*NYSE symbol*] (SPSG)

ECL........... Eddy Current Loss [*Electromagnetism*]

ECL........... Egyptian Confederation of Labor

ECL........... Electrical (IAA)

ECL........... Electrochemiluminescence

ECL........... Electronic Components Laboratory

ECL........... Emerson College, Boston, MA [*OCLC symbol*] (OCLC)

ECL........... Emitter-Coupled Logic [*Electronics*]

ECL........... Energy Conversion Laboratory [*MIT*] (MCD)

ECL........... Engineering Change List (MCD)

ECL........... Engineering Computer Laboratory [*University of Southern California*] [*Research center*] (RCD)

ECL........... Engineering Configuration List (MCD)

ECL........... English China Clays International Ltd. [*British*] (IRUK)

ECL........... English Church Leaders [*A publication*]

ECL........... English Comprehension Level [*Army*] (AABC)

ECL........... Enhanced Chemiluminescence [*Analytical chemistry*]

ECL........... Enterochromaffin-Like [*Biochemistry*]

ECL........... Entry Closed Loop (NASA)

ECL........... Environmental Chemistry Laboratory [*Environmental Protection Agency*] (GFGA)

ECL........... Environmental Conservation Law [*New York, NY A publication*]

ECL........... Equipment Component List [*Army*] (AABC)

ECL........... Equivalent Chain Length [*of fatty acids*] [*Biochemistry*]

ECL........... Equivalent Chlorine [*Analytical Chemistry*]

ECL........... Euglobulin Clot Lysis [*Hematology*]

ECL........... European Calibration Line

ECL........... Eurotec Consultants Ltd. [*Information service or system*] (IID)

ECL........... Evets Communications Ltd. [*Telecommunications service*] (TSSD)

ECL........... Exchange Control Logic (KSC)

ECL........... Executive Control Language [*Computer science*]

ECL........... Exposure Control Limit [*Environmental science*]

ECL........... Extended Center Line (WDAA)

ECL........... Extend of Cerebral Lesion [*Neurology*] (DAVI)

ECL........... Extracapillary Lesion [*Cardiology*] (DAVI)

ECLA.......... Economic Commission for Latin America [*Database originator*] [*Later, ECLAC*] [*United Nations*]

ECLA.......... European Clothing Association [*Belgium*] (EAIO)

ECLA.......... Evangelical Church Library Association (EA)

ECLAC........ Economic Commission for Latin America and the Caribbean [*See also CEPAL*] [*Santiago, Chile*] [*United Nations*] (EAIO)

ECLAIR........ European Collaborative Linkage of Agriculture and Industry through Research [*EC*] (ECED)

ECLAS........ European Commission Library Automated System [*Database*] [*EC*] (ECED)

ECLAT........ European Computer Lessors and Trading Association (PDAA)

ECLATEL...... Empresa Commercial Latinoamericana de Telecommunicaciones [*Latin America Commercial Telecommunications Enterprise*] (PDAA)

ECLC.......... Emergency Civil Liberties Committee [*Later, NECLC*] (EA)

ECLE.......... European Centre for Leisure and Education (EA)

ECLEC........ Eclectic (ROG)

ECLG.......... European Consumer Law Group (EA)

ecli............ Eclipse (BARN)

ECLIM........ European Conference on LASER Interaction with Matter and LASER Thermonuclear Fusion (PDAA)

ECLIPS........ Expanded Calculator Link Processing System [*Computer science*]

ECLIPS........ Experimental Cloud Lidar Polot Study (EERA)

ECLIPSE....... Electronic Clipping Service (HGAA)

ECLM.......... Economic Community for Livestock and Meat [*See also CEBV*] (EAIO)

ECLM.......... Electronic Compass Logic Module [*Automotive navigation systems*]

ECLO.......... Emergency Centre for Locust Operations (EERA)

ECLO.......... Emitter-Coupled Logic Operator [*Electronics*]

ECLOF........ Ecumenical Church Loan Fund

ECLPS........ Eclipse (ABBR)

ECLPSD....... Eclipsed (ABBR)

ECLPSG....... Eclipsing (ABBR)

EclpSurg...... Eclipse Surgical Technologies, Inc. [*Associated Press*] (SAG)

ECLR.......... European Competition Law Review [*A publication*] (DLA)

ECLS.......... Environmental Control and Life Support [*NASA*] (NASA)

ECLSS......... Environmental Control and Life Support Subsystem [*NASA*] (MCD)

ECLSS......... Extended Campus Library Services Section [*Association of College and Research Libraries*]

ECLSTCL...... Ecclesiastical (ABBR)

ECLT.......... English Comprehensive Level Test [*DoD*]

ECLT.......... Euglobulin Clot Lysis Time [*Clinical chemistry*]

ECLTM........ Eclecticism (ABBR)

ECM........... ECM Paytel [*Vancouver Stock Exchange symbol*]

ECM........... Effective Calls Meter [*Telecommunications*] (NITA)

ECM........... Effective Complex Modulus

ECM........... Electrical Conductivity Measurement

ECM........... Electrically-Commutated Motor [*General Electric Co.*] (PS)

ECM........... Electric [*or Electronic*] Cipher Machine [*or Coding*]

ECM........... Electric Controller and Manufacturing (IAA)

ECM........... Electrochemical Machining

ECM........... Electronic Combat Measures [*Military*] (LAIN)

ECM........... Electronic Control Module [*Instrumentation*]

ECM........... Electronic Countermeasure [*Military*]

ECM........... Elementary Circulation Mechanism

ECM........... Ellipsoid Collector Mirror

ECM........... Embryonic Chicken Muscle

ECM........... Emergency Conservation Measures

ECM........... Emerging Company Marketplace (DFIT)

ECM........... Emission Characteristics Monitor

ECM........... Energy Conservation Measure (AAGC)

ECM........... Engine Condition Monitoring

ECM........... Engine Control Module [*General Motors' computer system*]

ECM........... Engineering Change Memo (KSC)

ECM........... Engineering Coordination Memorandum [*Military*]

ECM........... Equipment Condition Monitoring

ECM........... Equivalence Class Mask

ECM........... Error Correction Mode [*Computer science*]

ECM........... Erythema Chronicum Migrans [*Dermatology*]

ECM........... Etude en Commun de la Mediterranee [*Cooperative Investigations in the Mediterranean - CIM*] [*French*] (MSC)

ECM........... European Christian Mission

ECM........... European Common Market

ECM........... Evangelical and Catholic Mission (EA)

ECM........... Evasive Combat Maneuver (MCD)

ECM........... Event Control Module [*Chromatography*]

ECM........... Exco Capital Markets [*Money brokers*] [*British*]

ECM........... Extended Capacity Memory [*Computer science*] (IAA)

ECM........... Extended Conventional Memory [*Computer science*]

ECM........... Extended Core Memory [*Computer science*] (MCD)

ECM........... Extended Core Module [*Computer science*] (IAA)

ECM........... External Cardiac Massage [*Medicine*] (ADA)

ECM........... External Crystalline Massif [*Geology*]

ECM........... Extracellular Material [*Physiology*]

ECM........... Extracellular Matrix [*Cytology*]

E/CM3......... Electrons per Cubic Centimeter

ECMA.......... East Coast Magnetic Anomaly [*Geophysics*]

ECMA.......... Eastern Cosmetic Manufacturers Association

ECMA.......... Electronic Computer Manufacturers Association

ECMA.......... Embalming Chemical Manufacturers Association [*Westport, CT*] (EA)

ECMA.......... Engineering College Magazines Associated (EA)

ECMA.......... Ethylcholine Mustard Aziridinium [*Picrate*] [*Biochemistry*]

ECMA.......... European Carton Makers Association (PDAA)

ECMA.......... European Catalysts Manufacturers Association [*of the European Council of Chemical Manufacturers' Federation*] (EAIO)

ECMA.......... European Collectors and Modellers Association

ECMA.......... European Community Marketing Authorisation Number (ECON)

ECMA.......... European Computer Manufacturers Association [*Switzerland*]

ECMAA......... Ethiopian Community Mutual Assistance Association (EA)

ECMALGOL.... European Computer Manufacturers Association Algorithmic Language

ECMB.......... European Committee for Mini-Basketball [*See also CEMB*] [*Germany*] (EAIO)

ECMB	European Conference on Molecular Biology
ECM/BFT	Error Correction Mode/Binary File Transfer [*Computer science*] (PCM)
ECMBR	European Committee on Milk-Butter-Fat Recording
ECM/BRV	Electronic Countermeasures Ballistic Reentry Vehicle [*Military*]
ECMC	Electric Cable Makers' Confederation [*British*] (BI)
ECMC	Episcopal Church Missionary Community (EA)
ECMC	European Container Manufacturers Committee (EA)
ECMCA	Eastern Central Motor Carriers Association
EC-MCA	External Carotid - Middle Cerebral Artery [*Anatomy*]
ECMCS	European Conference on Mixing and Centrifugal Separation
ECM-D	Engineering Change Management-Development
ECME	Economic Commission for the Middle East [*United Nations*] (DS)
ECME	Electronic Checkout Maintenance Equipment (IAA)
ECME	Electronic Circuit-Making Equipment [*Computer science*]
ECME	Electronic Countermeasures Environment [*Military*]
ECMEA	European Conference of Meteorological Experts for Aeronautics
ECMELINT	Electronic Countermeasures Electronic Intelligence [*Military*] (IAA)
ECMEX	Electronic Countermeasures Exercise [*Military*] (NVT)
ECMF	European Community Mortgage Federation [*Brussels, Belgium*] (EA)
ECMHP	East Coast Migrant Health Project (EA)
ECMO	Electronic Countermeasures Officer [*Navy*] (NVT)
ECMO	Enterocytopathogenic Monkey Orphan Virus
ECMO	Extracorporeal Membrane Oxygenator [*Respirator*]
ECMob	Electronic Countermeasures Observer [*Military*]
ECMP	Electronic Countermeasures Program [*Military*]
ECMP	Enteric-Coated Microspheres of Pancrelipase
ECMR	Eastern Contract Management Region [*Air Force*]
ECMR	Effective Common Mode Rejection [*Electronics*] (IAA)
ECMR	Electronic Control of the Mixture Ratio
ECMR	Equipment Calibration Maintenance Record (MCD)
ECMRA	European Association for Business Research, Planning, and Development in the Chemical Industry [*Formerly, European Chemical Market Research Association*] [*British*]
ECMRON	Electronic Countermeasures Squadron [*Military*] (IAA)
ECMRWF	European Centre for Medium-Range Weather Forecasts (PDAA)
ECMS	Engine Configuration Management System
ECMSA	Electronics Command Meteorological Support Agency [*Army*] (MCD)
ECMSN	Electronic Countermeasures Mission [*Military*]
ECMT	Ecomat, Inc. [*NASDAQ symbol*] (SAG)
ECMT	European Conference of Ministers of Transport (EAIO)
ECMTNG	Electronic Countermeasures Training [*Military*] (NVT)
ECMU	Extended Core Memory Unit [*Computer science*] (NVT)
ECMWF	European Center for Medium-Range Weather Forecasting
ECMWF	European Centre for Medium Range Weather Forecasts (EERA)
ECN	Effective Carbon Number [*Chemistry*]
ECN	El Condor Resources [*Vancouver Stock Exchange symbol*]
ECN	Electronic Change Notice (HGAA)
ECN	Emergency Communication Network [*Highway*] [*Telecommunications*] (TEL)
ECN	Engineering Change Notice
ECN	Environmental Communications Network [*Proposed environmental information exchange network*]
ECN	Epoxy Creosol Novolac [*Resin*]
ECN	Equipage Category Number (MSA)
ECN	Ercan [*Cyprus*] [*Airport symbol*] (OAG)
ECN	European Chemical News [*Reed Business Publishing Ltd.*] [*Information service or system*] (CRD)
ECN	Explicit Congestion Notification [*Telecommunications*] (ACRL)
ECN	Export Clearance Number
ECN	Extended Care Nursery [*Neonatology*] (DAVI)
ECNAIS	European Council of National Associations of Independent Schools [*Denmark*] (EAIO)
ECNAMP	East Caribbean Natural Area Management Program (EAIO)
ECNAP	Eastern Caribbean Natural Area Management Program (EERA)
ECN-APL	Equippage Category Numbered Allowance Parts List (DNAB)
ECNC	El Condor Resources Ltd. [*NASDAQ symbol*] (SAG)
ECNC	European Centre for Nature Conservation (EERA)
EC-NCI	Electron-Capture Negative Chemical Ionization [*Spectrometry*]
ECNDT	European Council for Nondestructive Testing (EA)
ECNF	European Central NOTAM [*Notice to Airmen*] Facility [*Military*]
ECNG	East Central Nuclear Group
ECNL	Equivalent-Continuous Noise Level (PDAA)
ECNMC	Economic
ECNOS	Eastern Atlantic, Channel and North Sea Orders for Ships [*NATO*] (NATG)
ECNP	Environmental Coalition on Nuclear Power (EA)
ECNR	European Council for Nuclear Research (DCTA)
ECNR	Executive Council for National Recovery [*New Deal*]
ECNRT	Emitter-Controlled Negative Resistance Triode
ECNSW	Environment Centre, New South Wales [*Australia*]
ECNT	Environment Centre, Northern Territory [*Australia*]
EC(NT)	Environment Centre (Northern Territory) [*State*] (EERA)
ECNT	Environment Centre of the Northern Territory [*State*] (EERA)
ECO	Aero Sierra Eco, SA de CV [*Mexico*] [*FAA designator*] (FAAC)
ECO	Earth Communications Office (EERA)
ECO	East Central Oklahoma State University, Ada, OK [*OCLC symbol*] (OCLC)
ECO	East Coast Airlines [*Australia ICAO designator*] (FAAC)
ECO	Eastern Counties Omnibus Co. Ltd. [*British*]
ECO	Echo Bay Mines [*AMEX symbol*] (TTSB)
ECO	Echo Bay Mines Ltd. [*AMEX symbol*] (SPSG)
ECO	Ecology (WDAA)
ECO	Ecology
ECO	Economic (ABBR)

ECO	Economic Cooperation Organization
ECO	Ecumenical Committee on the Andes [*Defunct*] (EA)
ECO	Effective Citizens Organization [*Later, PAC*] (EA)
ECO	Electric Cooperative of Oklahoma
ECO	Electron-Coupled Oscillator
eco	Electron-Coupled Oscillator (IDOE)
ECO	Electronic Central Office [*Within network*] [*Telecommunications*] (TEL)
ECO	Electronic Checkout
ECO	Electronic Contact Operate
ECO	Emergency Commissioned Officer [*British military*] (DMA)
ECO	Emergency Control Officer (IAA)
ECO	Energy Conservation Opportunities [*Federal Energy Administration*]
ECO	Engine Checkout System [*Aerospace*] (AAG)
ECO	Engine Combustion (NASA)
ECO	Engine Cutoff [*Aerospace*] (MCD)
ECO	Engineering Change Order
ECO	Engineering Control Office [*Telecommunications*] (TEL)
ECO	English Chamber Orchestra
ECO	Entry Clearance Officer [*Immigration*] (DLA)
ECO	Environmental Communicators Organisation [*British*] (DBA)
ECO	Environmental Conservation Organization
ECO	Environmental Control Organization [*Proposed in 1970 by Walter J. Hickel, Secretary of the Interior*]
ECO	Environmental Crisis Operation [*University of British Columbia*]
ECO	Environmentally Conscious Oil [*A trademark*] [*Automotive lubricant*]
ECO	Epichlorohydrin Copolymer [*Organic chemistry*]
ECO	Epichlorohydrin Ethylene Oxide [*Organic chemistry*] (RDA)
ECO	Equipment Control Officer [*Air Force*] (AFM)
Eco	Escherichia Coli [*Microorganism*]
ECO	European Coal Organization
ECO	European Consumers Organization [*Belgium*] (EAIO)
ECO	Ex Caelis Oblatus
ECO	Exempted by Commanding Officer
ECO	Experience Critique Orgel [*Nuclear reactor*] [*Italy*]
ECO2	ECO2, Inc. [*Associated Press*] (SAG)
ECOA	Equal Credit Opportunity Act [*1974, 1976*]
ECOA	Equal Employment Opportunity Act (TDOB)
ECOC	Eastern Counties Omnibus Co. Ltd. [*British*] (DCTA)
ECOCAB	Economic Cabinet [*British*]
ECOCO	Ecological Consortium (EERA)
ECOCOM	Economic Commission for Europe [*United Nations*] (DS)
ECOD	Error Classification, Omission, or Deficiency (MCD)
ECOD	Estimated Cost of Damage (MCD)
ECOD	Ethoxycoumarin O-Deethylase [*An enzyme*]
ECODU	European Control Data User's Organization (EA)
ECOF	Engineering Change Order Factor (MCD)
ECOFIN	Economic and Financial Council of Ministers [*EC*] (ECED)
ECOG	Eastern Cooperative Oncology Group [*Research center*] (RCD)
ECOG	Electrocorticogram [*or Electrocorticographic*]
ECOG	Electronics Coordinating Group [*Army*] (RDA)
Ecogen	Ecogen, Inc. [*Associated Press*] (SAG)
ECOGEO	Ecogeographer (ABBR)
ECOGEOC	Ecogeographic (ABBR)
ECOGEOR	Ecogeographer (ABBR)
Ecogn	Ecogen, Inc. [*Associated Press*] (SAG)
ECOIN	European Core Inventory of Existing Substances [*Chemicals which are exempt from new product regulations*]
ECOL	American Ecology Corp. [*NASDAQ symbol*] (SAG)
ECOL	Ecology
ECOLA	Extending Concepts through Language Activities [*Education*] (AEE)
Ecolab	Ecolab, Inc. [*Associated Press*] (SAG)
ECOLC	Ecologic (ABBR)
ECOLCL	Ecological (ABBR)
ECOLCLY	Ecologically (ABBR)
ECOLE	Amer Ecology [*NASDAQ symbol*] (TTSB)
ECOLE	Evaluation by Computer of the Learning Environment (PDAA)
EcolEn	Ecology & Environment [*Associated Press*] (SAG)
E coli	Escherichia Coli (DOG)
Ecolo	Parti Ecologiste [*Ecologist Party*] [*Belgium*] (PPW)
Ecol Soc Am	Ecological Society of America (BARN)
ECOLST	Ecologist (ABBR)
E-COM	Electronic Computer-Originated Mail [*Postal Service*]
E-Com	Electronic Computer-Originated Mail Services [*Postal Service*] [*United States*] [*Defunct*] (WDMC)
ECOM	Electronics Command [*Fort Monmouth, NJ*] [*Army*]
ECOM	Especialidades Consumidas por la Seguridad Social [*Ministerio de Sanidad y Consumo*] [*Spain Information service or system*] (CRD)
ECOMA	European Computer Measurement Association
Ecomat	Ecomat, Inc. [*Associated Press*] (SAG)
ECOMCON	Emergency Communications Control [*Fictitious military unit in film "Seven Days in May"*]
ECOMED	Ecological Mediterranean [*An association Turkey*] (EAIO)
ECOMINE	Economics Minerals (NITA)
ECOM LABS	Electronics Command R & D [*Research and Development*] Laboratories [*Army*] (MCD)
ECOMMRGN	Eastern Communications Region [*Air Force*]
ECOMOG	Economic Community Monitoring Group [*West Africa*]
E COMP	Excellent Companion [*Freemasonry*]
ECOMP	Federal Coordinator for Ocean Mapping and Prediction [*Marine science*] (OSRA)
ECOMS	Early Capability Orbital Manned Station
ECON	Economics (EY)
Econ	Economics (DD)

Econ............ Economist [A publication] (BRI)
ECON .... Economy (AFM)
ECON .... Economy
ECON .... Electromagnetic Emission Control (IEEE)
ECON .... Extended Console System (MHDB)
Econ Act ..... Economic Activity [A publication]
Econ Activ ... Economic Activity [A publication]
ECONADS .... Economic Advisers
ECONC........ Economic (ABBR)
ECONCL...... Economical (ABBR)
ECONCLY..... Economically (ABBR)
Econ J .... Economic Journal [A publication] (BRI)
ECONL .... Economical (ABBR)
Econ Monog... Economic Monographs [A publication]
Econ Monogr Econ Soc Aust NZ... Economic Society of Australia and New Zealand.
               Economic Monograph [A publication]
ECONMST .... Economist
Econ N........ Economic News [A publication]
ECONOMAN... Effective Control of Manpower (AFM)
Econom Anc Gr... [The] Economics of Ancient Greece [A publication] (OCD)
ECONOMET... Econometric (ABBR)
Econ Paps ... Economic Papers [A publication]
ECONST ...... Economist (ABBR)
Econ Stand (CCH)... Economic Standards (Commerce Clearing House)
               [A publication] (DLA)
Econ Survey... Economic Survey of Ancient Rome [A publication] (OCD)
ECONY........ Economy (ABBR)
ECONZ........ Economize (ABBR)
ECONZD...... Economized (ABBR)
ECONZG...... Economizing (ABBR)
ECONZR...... Economizer (ABBR)
ECOO .... Educational Computing Organization of Ontario (EDAC)
ECOP .... Extension Committee on Organization and Policy [Department of
               Agriculture] (EA)
ECOPC .... Experimental Changes of Practice Committees [British Post Office]
               (PDAA)
ECOPHYS..... Ecophysiologic (ABBR)
ECOPS .... European Committee on Ocean and Polar Science
ECOR .... Engineer Change Order Request (AAG)
ECOR .... Engineering Committee on Oceanic Research (USDC)
ECOR .... Engineering Committee on Oceanic Resources [Later, SUT] [United
               Nations]
ECOR .... Error Control Register [Computer science] (IAA)
ECORS .... Eastern Counties Operational Research Society (PDAA)
ECOS .... Electrical Check-Out System
ECOS .... Evans Environmental [NASDAQ symbol] (TTSB)
ECOS .... Experiment Computer Operating System (MCD)
ECOS .... Extended Communications Operating System (HGAA)
ECOSA .... European Conference on Optical Systems and Applications (PDAA)
ECOSAL ...... Equipo de Conferencias Sindicales de America Latina [Committee for
               Latin American Trade Union Conferences]
EcoSci .... EcoScience Corp. [Associated Press] (SAG)
ECOSEC ...... European Cooperation Space Environment Committee
ECOSOC....... Committee of Experts on the Transport of Dangerous Goods of the
               United Nations Economic and Social Council [RSPA] (TAG)
ECOSOC...... Economic and Social Committee [EC] (ECED)
ECOSOC..... Economic and Social Council [ICSU] [United Nations]
EcoSoil .... Eco Soil Systems, Inc. [Associated Press] (SAG)
ECOSOL ...... European Centre of Studies on Linear Alkylbenzene [Belgium]
               (EAIO)
ECOSS .... European Conference on Surface Science
EcoSSP .... Escherichia Coli Single-Stranded Protein
ECOST .... European Cooperation on Science and Technology [British]
ECOSYS ...... Ecosystem (ABBR)
ECOTAGE ..... Ecological Sabotage [Tactic used by radical environmentalists]
EcoTyre .... EcoTyre Technologies, Inc. [Associated Press] (SAG)
ECOWAS ..... Economic Commission of West African States (EERA)
ECOWAS ...... Economic Community of West African States [Treaty signed May 28,
               1975]
ECOX .... Educational Communications on Exhibit [Commercial firm]
ECP............. Central Newspapers 'A' [NYSE symbol] (TTSB)
ECP............. Central Newspapers, Inc. Class A [NYSE symbol] (SPSG)
ECP............. Congolese Progressive Students [Zaire] (PD)
EC/P........... Early Childhood/Primary
ECP............. Early Churches in Palestine [A publication] (BJA)
ECP............. East Cleveland Public Library, East Cleveland, OH [OCLC symbol]
               (OCLC)
ECP............. Eclipse Capital Corp. [Toronto Stock Exchange symbol]
ECP............. Edinburgh County Police [British] (ROG)
ECP............. Education Center Publications (MCD)
ECP............. Effector Cell Precursor [Medicine] (DMAA)
ECP............. Efficient Component Pricing [Business term] (ECON)
ECP............. Egyptian Communist Party [Political party] (PD)
ECP............. Electrical Contact Plate
ECP............. Electrical Control Package
ECP............. Electrically Compensated Pyrometer
ECP............. Electrically-Conducting Polymer
ECP............. Electric Current Perturbation [Method] [Southwest Research Institute]
ECP............. Electromagnetic Compatibility Program [Air Force]
ECP............. Electromagnetic Containerless Processing [Materials processing]
ECP............. Electron Channeling Pattern (MCD)
ECP............. Electronic Calculating Punch
ECP............. Electronic Check Presentment [Finance]
ECP............. Electronic Circuit Protector
ECP............. Electronic Color Prepress (DGA)

ECP............. Electronic Control Products (MUGU)
ECP............. Elliptical Cavity Pump
ECP............. Emergency Command Precedence (DNAB)
ECP............. Emergency Communications Plan (NUCP)
ECP............. Emergency Conservation Program [Department of Agriculture]
               (EGAO)
ECP............. Emitter-Coupled Pair [Electronics] (IAA)
ECP............. Emulator Control Program (IAA)
ECP............. Endogenous Circadian Phase [Physiology]
ECP............. Energy Charge Potential
ECP............. Engagement Control Panel (MCD)
ECP............. Engineering Change Program
ECP............. Engineering Change Proposal
ECP............. Engineering Control Proposal
ECP............. English Centre of PEN (EAIO)
ECP............. English Collective of Prostitutes (DI)
ECP............. Enhanced Capabilities Port [Computer science]
ECP............. Enkephalin-Containing Polypeptide [Physiological chemistry]
ECP............. Enlisted Commissioning Program [Military] (DNAB)
ECP............. Entry Control Point (MCD)
ECP............. Eosinophil Cationic Protein [Immunology]
ECP............. Equipment Collecting Point [Military British]
ECP............. Equipment Conversion Package [Telecommunications] (TEL)
ECP............. Erythrocyte Coproporphyrin [Hematology] (MAE)
ECP............. Escherichia Coli Polypeptides
ECP............. Estimated Critical Position [Nuclear energy] (NRCH)
ECP............. Estradiol Cyclopentanepropionate [Endocrinology]
ECP............. Ethiopian Communist Party [Political party] (PD)
ECP............. Euro-Commercial Paper [Finance]
ECP............. European Committee of Crop Protection
ECP............. European Organization for Cancer Prevention Studies
ECP............. Evangeli Christi Proedicatur [Preacher of the Gospel of Christ]
               [Latin] (ROG)
ECP............. Evaporative Cooling Processor
ECP............. Executive Control Program [Computer science]
ECP............. Explicitly Coded Program (MCD)
ECP............. Extended Capability Port [Telecommunications] (PCM)
ECP............. External Cardiac Pressure [Medicine] (DMAA)
ECP............. External Compliance Programs [Environmental Protection Agency]
               (GFGA)
ECP............. External Control Panel
ECP............. External Counterpulsation [Medicine]
ECP............. Extracellular Products
ECP............. Free Cytoprophyrin in Erythrocytes [Hematology] (DAVI)
ECPA......... Effective Cell Pair Area [Electrochemistry]
ECPA......... Electric Consumer Protection Act of 1986
ECPA......... Electronic Communications Piracy Act of 1986
ECPA......... Energy Conservation and Production Act [1976] (MCD)
ECPA......... Energy Consumers and Producers Association (EA)
ECPA......... Evangelical Christian Publishers Association (EA)
ECPA......... Expert Committee on Post Adjustments [United Nations]
ECPAT........ End Child Prostitution in Asian Tourism [An association]
ECPC.......... Economic Classification Policy Committee [BTS] (TAG)
ECPC.......... Edge Connector Programmable Cartridge
ECPC.......... Enlarged Committee for Program and Coordination [United Nations
               Development Program]
ECPC.......... Ethnic Cultural Preservation Council [Also known as Association of
               North American Museums, Libraries, Archives, Cultural Centers,
               and Fraternal Organizations] (EA)
ECPC.......... European Communist Party Conference
ECPCDP ...... Euro-Commercial Paper and Certificates of Deposit Programme
               [Finance]
ECPCR .... Expression Cassette Polymerase Chain Reaction [Genetics]
ECPD .... Engineers Council for Professional Development [Later, ABET] (EA)
ECPD .... Export Cargo Packing Declaration (DS)
ECPE .... European Centre of Public Enterprise (EAIO)
ECPE .... External Combustion Piston Engine (PDAA)
ECPGR .... Expert Committee on Plant Gene Resources [Canadian Agricultural
               Services Coordinating Committee]
ECPH .... [The] Electronic Communications Privacy Act
ECPH .... European Committee of Private Hospitals [Belgium] (EAIO)
ECPI .... Electronic Computer Programming Institute [Ceased operation, 1976]
ECPIP .... Electric Companies' Public Information Program
ECPIU .... Electronic Circuit Plug-In Unit
ECPMAOA .... Executive Committee's Panel on Meteorological Aspects of Ocean
               Affairs [WMO] (MSC)
ECPNL .... Equivalent Continuous Perceived Noise Level (PDAA)
ECPO .... Eastern College Personnel Officers
ECPO .... Enteric Cytopathogenic Porcine Orphan Virus
ECPOG .... Electrochemical Potential Gradient
ECPR .... Electrically Calibrated Pyroelectric Radiometer
ECPR .... European Confederation of Public Relations [France] (EAIO)
ECPR .... European Consortium for Political Research [Colchester, Essex,
               England] (EAIO)
ECPRD .... European Centre for Parliamentary Research and Documentation
               [See also CERDP] [Luxembourg, Luxembourg] (EAIO)
ECPS .... Effective Candlepower Second [Photography] (WDMC)
ECP-S .... Engineering Change Proposal-Software
ECPS .... Engineering Change Proposal System (DNAB)
ECPS .... English Connemara Pony Society (DBA)
ECPS.......... Environment and Consumer Protection Service [EEC] (DS)
ECPS.......... European Centre for Population Studies (EA)
ECPS.......... European Council for Payments Systems
ECPs.......... Extended Capabilities Ports [Computer science]
ECPS.......... Extended Control Program Support [IBM Corp.]

ECPSA	European Consumer Product Safety Association [*EC*] (ECED)
ECPT	Ethylcamptothecin [*Antineoplastic drug*]
ECPT	European Confederation for Physical Therapy (EAIO)
ECPWS	Engineering Change Proposal Work Statement (AAG)
ECPY	Electronic Control Assembly - Pitch and Yaw (KSC)
ECQAC	Electronic Components Quality Assurance Committee (BARN)
ECR	Air Charter Express AS [*Norway ICAO designator*] (FAAC)
ECR	Canada Law Reports, Exchequer Court [*A publication*] (DLA)
ECR	Eastern Counties Railway [*British*] (ROG)
ECR	Economy Cylinder Rating [*Engine technology*]
ECR	Edit, Count, Recode (IAA)
ECR	Efficient Consumer Response [*Marketing incentive*] (ECON)
ECR	Electrical Contact Resistance (PDAA)
ECR	Electrochemical Reaction
ECR	Electron Cyclotron Resonance (IEEE)
ECR	Electronic Cash Register
ECR	Electronic Control Relay (IEEE)
ECR	Electronic Countermeasures and Reconnaissance
ECR	Electronics Combat Reconnaissance
ECR	Embedded Computer Resources (MCD)
ECR	Embossed Character Reader [*Banking*]
ECR	Emergency Chemical Restraint (DAVI)
ECR	Emergency Combat Readiness (AAG)
ECR	Emergency Coolant Recirculation [*Nuclear energy*] (NRCH)
ECR	Emitted Coherent Radiation
ECR	Endogenous Circadian Rhythm (PDAA)
ECR	Enemy Contact Report [*NATO*] (NATG)
ECR	Energy Consumption Rate
ECR	Energy Control Report [*Navy*]
E CR	Engineer Commander [*Navy British*] (ROG)
ECR	Engineering Change Report (KSC)
ECR	Engineering Change [*or Correction*] Request [*or Requirement*]
ECR	Engineering Concept Review
ECR	Entry Control Roster (MCD)
ECR	Environmental Control Report [*A publication*] (EAAP)
ECR	Equipment Control Record (MCD)
ECR	Error Cause Removal [*Quality control*]
ECR	Error Control Receiver (IEEE)
ECR	Estimate Change Request (NRCH)
ECR	European Commercial Register [*EC*] (ECED)
ECR	European Court Reports [*European Communities*] [*A publication*] (DLA)
ECR	Except Change Route to Read [*Aviation*] (FAAC)
ECR	Excess Carrier Ratio (IAA)
ECR	Exchequer Court Reports [*Canada Department of Justice*] [*Information service or system*] (CRD)
ECR	Execute Command Request (KSC)
ECR	Executive Control Routines
ECR	Experimental Coherent RADAR (MCD)
ECR	Export Control Regulations [*Department of Commerce*]
ECR	Extended Coverage Range [*Insurance*] (IAA)
ECR	External Channels Ratio
ECR	External Control Register (OA)
ECR	Extraordinary Contractual Relief (AAGC)
ECR	Extraordinary Contractual Relief Reporter [*A publication*] (AAGC)
ECRA	Electric Car Racing Association
ECR/A	Engineering Change Request/Authorization (AFM)
ECRA	Environmental Cleanup and Responsibility Act [*1983*] (ERG)
ECRA	Excess and Casualty Reinsurance Association (EA)
ECRB	Export Control Review Board
ECRB	Extensor Carpi Radialis Brevis [*Anatomy*]
ECRC	Early Childhood Resource Center
ECRC	Elderly Care Research Center [*Case Western Reserve University*] [*Research center*] (RCD)
ECRC	Electricity Council Research Center [*British*] (MCD)
ECRC	Electronic Component Reliability Center [*Battelle Memorial Institute*] (MCD)
ECRC	Electronic Components Research Center
ECRC	Engineering College Research Council (EA)
ECRC	Equipment Category Rollup Code [*Army*]
ECRC	European Community Research Council
ECRC	European Computer Industry Research Centre
ECRC	European Computer Industry Research Centre [*Munich (FRG)*] (NITA)
ECRDG	Electronic Component Research and Development Grant [*Canada*]
ECRE	Edinburgh Centre of Rural Economy [*British*] (CB)
ECRE	European Consultation on Refugees and Exiles
ECRE	European Council on Refugees and Exiles
ECREA	European Conference of Radiotelegraphy Experts for Aeronautics
Ec Rec	Economic Record [*A publication*]
ECRF	Edited Collections Report File [*IRS*]
ECRF	Externally Coupled Resonator Filter (MCD)
ECRH	Electron Cyclotron Resonance Heating (MCD)
ECRI	East Central Reservoir Investigation [*Department of the Interior*] (GRD)
ECRI	Emergency Care Research Institute (EA)
ECRI	Exemplary Center for Reading Instruction [*Maine*] (EDAC)
ECRIE	European Center for Research and Information Exchange [*Belgium*] (EAIO)
ECRIM	Engineering Construction and Related Industries Manpower [*British*]
ECRL	East Central Regional Library System [*Library network*]
ECRL	Extensor Carpi Radialis Longus [*Muscle or tendon*] [*Anatomy*] (DAVI)
ECRM	ECRM, Inc. [*NASDAQ symbol*] (SAG)
ECRM	Electronic Character Recognition Machine (DGA)
ECRM	Euronorm Certified Reference Material

ECRO	Erection Counter Readout
ECRO	European Chemoreception Research Organization [*Research center Switzerland*] (IRC)
ECROC	Engineering Council Regional Organisation Committee (ACII)
ECRR	Engineering Change Request and Record (MCD)
ECRS	Earthwork/Center for Rural Studies (EA)
ECRS	Economic and Contingency Reserve Stock [*Military*]
ECRS	Equipment Control Record System [*Army*]
ECRT	European Confederation of Retail Tobacconists [*Luxembourg*] (EA)
ECRU	Emergency Communications Research Unit [*Carleton University*] [*Canada Research center*] (RCD)
e-cs--	Czechoslovakia [*MARC geographic area code Library of Congress*] (LCCP)
ECS	Early Childhood Services (ADA)
ECS	Echo Control Subsystem [*Telecommunications*] (TEL)
ECS	Economic Census Staff [*Census*] (OICC)
ECS	Economics (ABBR)
ECS	Economy-Class Syndrome [*Medicine*]
ECS	Ecos Resources [*Vancouver Stock Exchange symbol*]
ECS	Educational Career Service [*Later, EHCS*] [*An association*] (EA)
ECS	Educational Counselling Service [*British Council*] (AIE)
ECS	Education Commission of the States (EA)
ECS	Elective Cosmetic Surgery
ECS	Electrical Connector Subassembly
ECS	Electrocardioscanner
ECS	Electrocerebral Silence [*Medicine*] (CPH)
ECS	Electrochemical Society (EA)
ECS	Electroconvulsive Shock
ECS	Electronically Controlled Suspension [*Mitsubishi*] [*Automotive engineering*]
ECS	Electronic Chart System
ECS	Electronic Claims Submission (MEDA)
ECS	Electronic Combat Squadron
ECS	Electronic Composing System
ECS	Electronic Control Sensor (MCD)
ECS	Electronic Control Switch (IEEE)
ECS	Electronic Countermeasures System [*Military*]
ECS	Electronic Counter Services
ECS	Electronic Courier Systems [*Eatontown, NJ*] (TSSD)
ECS	Electronics Control System
ECS	Embedded Computer Systems
ECS	Emergency Call System [*AT & T*]
ECS	Emergency Control Station [*Nuclear energy*] (NRCH)
ECS	Emergency Coolant System (MSA)
ECS	Emission Control System (MCD)
ECS	Emperor's Clothes Syndrome
ECS	Empty Coaching Stock [*Railway term*] (DCTA)
ECS	Enable Control System
ECS	End Cell Switch (IAA)
ECS	Energy Conversion Subsystem (SSD)
ECS	Energy Conversion System (PDAA)
ECS	Engagement Controller Set
ECS	Engagement Control System [*Navy*] (MCD)
ECS	Engine Control System [*Facetious translation: Expect Catastrophe Soon*]
ECS	Engineering Change Schedule (AAG)
ECS	Engineering Change Sheet (NATG)
ECS	Engineering Change Summary
ECS	Engineering Control System
ECS	English Citizen Series [*A publication*]
ECS	Environmental Conservation Service [*Canada*]
ECS	Environmental Control Shroud [*Nuclear energy*] (NRCH)
ECS	Environmental Control System [*NASA*]
ECS	Equatorial Currents System [*Oceanography*]
ECS	Equipment Compiler System (IAA)
ECS	Equipment Concentration Sites [*Military*] (AABC)
ECS	Equipment Construction Site (MCD)
ECS	Error Correction Servo [*or Signals*] (AAG)
ECS	Established Church of Scotland (ROG)
ECS	Etched Circuit Society [*Defunct*] (EA)
ECS	Ethnic Children's Service [*Australia*]
ECS	European Chemical Society
ECS	European Communication Satellite
ECS	European Confederation of Scouts (EAIO)
ECS	Europe Computer Systems [*Computer leasing company*] (NITA)
ECS	Evaporation Control System [*Automobile antipollution device*]
ECS	Exact Cubic Search [*Mathematics*]
ECS	Executive Compensation Service
ECS	Executive Control System [*Computer science*]
ECS	Executive Counselling Service [*Australia*]
ECS	Exhaust Control System
ECS	Exosphperic Composition Studies (MUGU)
ECS	Experienced Control Scales (EDAC)
ECS	Experimental Communications Satellite [*NASA*]
ECS	Exploder Control Sensor (MCD)
ECS	Extended Character Set [*Computer science*] (PCM)
ECS	Extended Core Storage [*Computer science*]
ECS	Exterior Communications System [*Military*] (CAAL)
ECS	External Calling Sequence [*Computer science*]
ECS	Extracapillary Space
ECS	Extracellular-Like, Calcium-Free Solution [*Medicine*]
ECS	IEEE Electromagnetic Compatability Society (EA)
ECS	Newcastle, WY [*Location identifier FAA*] (FAAL)
ECSA	Eastern College Soccer Association (EA)

ECSA............ EEC [*European Economic Community*] Ship Owners Association [*Belgium*] (EAIO)
ECSA............ Episcopal Churchmen for South Africa (EA)
ECSA............ Estuarine and Coastal Sciences Association [*Scotland*] (EAIO)
ECSA............ European Chips and Snacks Association [*British*] (EAIO)
ECSA............ European Chlorinated Solvent Association (EAIO)
ECSA............ European Communication Security Agency
ECSA............ European Community Shipowners' Associations [*Belgium*] (EAIO)
ECSA............ European Computing Services Association
ECSA............ Exceptional Civilian Service Award (RDA)
ECSA............ Exchange Carriers Standards Association (EA)
ECSA............ Expanded Clay and Shale Association [*Later, LAPA*] (EA)
ECSAMR...... Emergency Committee to Save America's Marine Resources (EA)
ECS/API ...... Enhanced Character Set/All Purpose Interface [*Xerox Corp.*]
ECSC............ East Central State College [*Later, East Central Oklahoma State University*]
ECSC............ EcoScience Corp. [*NASDAQ symbol*] (SAG)
ECSC............ Energy Conservation and Solar Centre [*British*] (CB)
ECSC............ European Coal and Steel Community [*France, West Germany, Italy, BENELUX*]
ECSC............ European Conference on Satellite Communications (MCD)
ECSCA .... English Cocker Spaniel Club of America (EA)
ECSE............ Advisory Committee for Electrical, Computer, and Systems Engineering [*Terminated, 1985*] (EGAO)
ECSEDA ...... Eastern Caribbean States Export Development Agency [*Dominica*] (EY)
ECSF............ European Civil Service Federation (EAIO)
ECSG .... Electronic Connector Study Group (EA)
ECSGY .... Ecsoft Group [*NASDAQ symbol*] (SAG)
ECSH............ Edgewood College of the Sacred Heart [*Wisconsin*]
ECS/HCS...... Educational Career Service/Health Career Service [*Later, EHCS*] [*An association*] (EA)
ECSI............ Emergency Committee to Suspend Immigration (EA)
ECSI............ European CAD [*Computer-Aided Design*] Standardization Initiative [*Computer science*]
ECSI............ Export Cargo Shipping Instruction (DS)
ECSIL........... Experimental Cross Section Information Library [*University of California, Livermore*]
ECSL............ Enforcement Compliance Schedule Letter [*Environmental Protection Agency*] (EG)
ECSL............ Extended Control and Simulation Language [*Computer science*] (PDAA)
ECSLA......... European Centre of Studies on Linear Alkylbenzene (EAIO)
ECSM........... Event Capture Storage Mode
ECSMA........ European Copper Sulphate Manufacturers' Association (EAIO)
ECSO .... Effective Concentration of Substance for 50% Survival of Organism
ECSO .... Enterocytopathogenic Swine Orphan Virus
ECSOB .... Eastern College Soccer Officials Bureau [*Later, ECSA*]
Ecsoft........... Ecsoft Group [*Associated Press*] (SAG)
ECSP........... Electronic Command Signal Programmer (MCD)
ECSP........... Electronics Control Signal Processor [*HELLFIRE*]
ECSP........... Electronic Specialist
ECSP........... Enhanced Consumer Spending Patterns [*National Planning Data Corp.*] [*Information service or system*] (CRD)
ECSP........... Extended Corresponding States Principle [*Physical chemistry*]
ECSS........... Electrical Command and Stability System (PDAA)
ECSS........... Equipment Concentration Site System [*Army*]
ECSS........... European Committee for the Study of Salt (EA)
ECSS........... European Communication Satellite System
ECSS........... Extendable Computer System Simulator [*Programming language*] [*1973*]
ECSSA .... European Centre for Studies of Sulfuric Acid (EAIO)
ECSSID .... European Conference in Social Science Information and Documentation (NITA)
ECSSID .... European Cooperation in Social Science Information and Documentation
ECSSS .... Eighteenth Century Scottish Studies Society (EA)
ECST............ Ecstasy (ABBR)
ECST............ Electronic Control of Spark Timing (PDAA)
ECST............ Emergency Condensate Storage Tank [*Nuclear energy*] (NRCH)
ECSTASY .... Economical Storage and Access System [*Computer science*]
ECSTASY .... Electronic Control for Switching and Telemetering Automobile Systems [*Automotive engineering*]
ECSTC......... Ecstatic (ABBR)
ECSTCY....... Ecstatically (ABBR)
ECSW.......... Engagement Controller Software
ECSW.......... Extended Channel Status Word [*Computer science*] (MHDB)
ECSWTR ...... European Centre for Social Welfare Training and Research [*See also CEFRAS*] [*United Nations*] (EAIO)
ECSYT......... Ecosystem (ABBR)
ECSZ........... Eastern California Shear Zone [*Geology*]
ECT.............. Earth-Centered True
ECT.............. Eddy Current Test [*Nuclear energy*] (NRCH)
ECT.............. Edge Crush Test [*Packaging*]
ECT.............. [*The*] Egyptian Coffin Texts [*A publication*] (BJA)
ECT.............. Electrochemical Turning [*Manufacturing term*]
ECT.............. Electroconvulsive Therapy [*or Treatment*] [*Medicine*]
ECT.............. Electronically Controlled Transmission [*Automotive engineering*]
ECT.............. Electronic and Control Technology (NITA)
ECT.............. Ellsworth [*Connecticut*] [*Seismograph station code, US Geological Survey*] (SEIS)
ECT.............. Emergency Cooling Tower [*Nuclear energy*] (NRCH)
ECT.............. Emission Computed Tomography
ECT.............. Encyclopedia of Chemical Technology [*A publication*]
ECT.............. Engine Coolant Temperature [*Automotive engineering*]

ECT............ Engine Cutoff Timer [*Aerospace*] (KSC)
ECT............ English Composition Test [*Education*] (AEBS)
ECT............ Enhanced Computer Tomography [*Radiology*] (DAVI)
ECT............ Enteric Coated Tablet [*Pharmacology*]
ECT............ Environmental Control Table
ECT............ Error Control Translator
ECT............ Error Control Transmitter
ECT............ Estimated Cloud Time [*Drinking slang*]
ECT............ Estimated Completion Time [*Business term*]
ECT............ Euglobulin Clot Test [*Clinical chemistry*] (MAE)
ECT............ European Compression Technique [*Bone screw and internal fixation*] [*Orthopedics*] (DAVI)
ECT............ Evans Clear Tunnel (OA)
ECT............ Evaporative Cooling Techniques
ECT............ Executive Career Trac [*A publication*]
ECT............ Explicit Call Transfer [*Telecommunications*] (DOM)
ECT............ Exposure Control Technique
ECT............ Extortionate Credit Transactions [*FBI standardized term*]
ECTA.......... Early Childhood Teachers' Association [*Australia*]
ECTA.......... Electronics Component Test Area (AAG)
ECTA.......... Error-Correcting Tree Automation [*Computer science*]
ECTA.......... European Cutting Tools Association (EA)
ECTA.......... Everyman's Contingency Table Analyzer (PDAA)
ECTAA......... Group of National Travel Agents' Associations within the EEC (EAIO)
ECTAR .... Electronic Tactical Action Report (AFM)
ECTC.......... East Coast Telecommunications Center [*Defense Communications System*] (RDA)
ECTC.......... Eastern Coal Transportation Conference (EA)
ECTCT......... Eccentricity (ABBR)
ECTD.......... Emission Control Technology Division [*Environmental Protection Agency*] (GFGA)
ECTEL .... European Telecommunications and Professional Electronics Industry [*Europe an Conference of Associations of Telecommunications Industries and European Conference of Radio and Electronic Equipment Associations*] [*Formed by a merger of*] (EAIO)
ECTEOLA..... Epichlorohydrin Triethanolamine [*Organic chemistry*]
ECTFE........ Ethylene-Chlorotrifluoroethylene [*Organic chemistry*]
ECTG........... European Channel Tunnel Group [*Planning a proposed tunnel between England and France under the English Channel*]
ECTH.......... Electro-Catheter [*NASDAQ symbol*] (TTSB)
ECTH.......... Electro-Catheter Corp. [*NASDAQ symbol*] (NQ)
ECTH.......... Electro Catheter Corp. [*NASDAQ symbol*] (SAG)
ECTI........... Eddy Current Testing Instrument
ECTI........... Erie County Technical Institute [*New York*]
ECTL .... Elcotel, Inc. [*NASDAQ symbol*] (NQ)
ECTL .... Emitter-Coupled Transistor Logic [*Electronics*]
ECTMAC...... East Coast Trawl Management Advisory Committee (EERA)
Ecto........... Ectoparasitic [*Biology*]
ECTOC .... Electronic Conference on Trends in Organic Chemistry
ECTOHORM... Ectohormone (ABBR)
ECTPWF....... European Confederation for Trade in Paint, Wall- and Floorcoverings (EAIO)
ECTR.......... Extended Connection Table Representation (NITA)
ECTS.......... Electrical Cable Test Set
ECTS.......... Electric Circuit Test Set
ECTS.......... Electronic Custom Telephone Set [*or System*] (NRCH)
ECTS.......... Engine Coolant Temperature Sensor [*Automotive engineering*]
ECTS.......... European Calcified Tissue Society (EA)
ECTS.......... European Conference on Telecommunications by Satellite
ECTUNAMAC... East Coast Tuna Management Advisory Committee (EERA)
ECTV.......... Electronically-Controlled Throttle Valve [*Automotive engineering*]
ECTWT........ Ecumenical Coalition on Third World Tourism (EA)
ECU........... East Carolina University [*Formerly, ECC*] [*Greenville, NC*]
ECU........... Ecuador [*ANSI three-letter standard code*] (CNC)
Ecu........... Ecuador (VRA)
ECU........... Ecumania (ABBR)
ECU........... Ecumenism (WDAA)
ECU........... Electrical Conversion Unit
ECU........... Electrochemical Unit
ECU........... Electronic Cabling Unit
ECU........... Electronic Computing Unit (IAA)
ECU........... Electronic Control Unit
ECU........... Electronic Conversion Unit (IEEE)
ECU........... Electronic Coupling Unit (MCD)
ECU........... Energy Conservation Update [*A publication*]
ECU........... Engine Calibration Unit [*Automotive engineering*]
ECU........... Engine Change Unit (MCD)
ECU........... Engine Control Unit
ECU........... English Church Union
ECU........... Entry Computer
ECU........... Environmental Control Unit
ECU........... Environmental Crimes Unit [*Environmental Protection Agency*] (GFGA)
ECU........... Environment Conditioning Unit (MCD)
ECU........... Equipment Control Unit (AFIT)
ECU........... Euclid Public Library, Euclid, OH [*OCLC symbol*] (OCLC)
ECU........... European Chiropractors' Union (EAIO)
ECU........... European Currency Unit [*European monetary system*] (AF)
ECU........... Extended Care Unit [*Medicine*] (DHSM)
ECU........... Extensor Carpi Ulnaris [*Muscle or tendon*] [*Anatomy*] (DAVI)
ECU........... Extreme Close-Up [*Television*]
ECUA .... Ecuador
ECUBE .... Energy Conservation Using Better Engineering (PDAA)
ECUC .... Education Credit Union Council (EA)
ECUI........... Extreme Close-Up Indeed [*Photography*] [*British*] (NTCM)

ECUK	East Coast of the United Kingdom [*Shipping*]
ECUM..........	Ecumenic (ABBR)
ECUMEN	Ecumenical (ABBR)
ECUML........	Ecumenical (ABBR)
ECUMLSM ..	Ecumenicalism (ABBR)
ECUMLY	Ecumenically (ABBR)
ECUMN	Ecumenic (ABBR)
ECUMNL	Ecumenical (ABBR)
ECUMNLY ...	Ecumenically (ABBR)
ECUMNM	Ecumenism (ABBR)
ECUSAT	Ecumenical Satellite Commission
ECUT...........	Energy Conversion and Utilization Technologies Program [*Department of Energy*]
ECV.............	Elderberry Carlavirus [*Plant pathology*]
ECV.............	Electric Clock Valve
ECV.............	Enamel Single Cotton Varnish [*Wire insulation*] (AAG)
ECV.............	Energy Conservation Vehicle [*British Leyland*]
ECV.............	Esperantist Club of Veterans [*See also VEK*] [*Wolfhagen, Federal Republic of Germany*] (EAIO)
ECV.............	External Cephalic Version [*Gynecology*]
ECV.............	Extracellular Volume [*Hematology*]
ECV.............	Extracorporeal Volume [*Medicine*] (MAE)
ECVAC	Endorsers Conference for Veterans Affairs Chaplaincy (EA)
ECVAM........	European Center for the Validation of Alternative Methods [*To animals for biological testing, Italy*]
ECVE...........	Extracellular Volume Expansion [*Hematology*] (CPH)
ECVFI..........	European Committee for the Valves and Fittings Industry [*Germany*] (EAIO)
ECVFP.........	Expanded Charted Visual Flight Procedures [*FAA*] (TAG)
ECVP...........	European Community Visitors Program
ECVT...........	Electro-Continuously Variable Transmission [*Subaru*] [*Automotive engineering*]
ECVT...........	Electronically Controlled Continuously Variable Transmission
ECW............	Eastern Coach Works [*British*] (DCTA)
ECW............	Electronic Combat Wing [*Military*]
ECW............	Electronic Cooling Water (DNAB)
ECW............	Emergency Conservation Work [*Succeeded by CCC, 1937, now obsolete*]
ECW............	Emergency Cooling Water [*Nuclear energy*] (NRCH)
ECW............	Envipco Canada [*Vancouver Stock Exchange symbol*]
ECW............	Episcopal Church Women
ECW............	European Council of Women [*Belgium*] (EAIO)
ECW............	Extracellular Water [*Physiology*]
ECWA..........	Economic Commission for Western Asia [*Later, ESCWA*] [*United Nations*]
ECWA..........	Environment Centre of Western Australia [*Australia*]
ECWAS	Economic Community of West African States [*Treaty signed May 28, 1975*]
ECWC..........	Extended Cold/Wet Clothing Systems [*Military*] (INF)
ECWCS	Extended Cold Weather Clothing System [*Army*] (INF)
ECWG	Emergency Communications Working Group [*DoD*]
ECWG	Environmental Characterization Working Group
ECWG	Evaluation Coordination Working Group [*Navy*]
ECWIM........	European Committee of Weighing Instrument Manufacturers (EAIO)
EC WIRE	Extra Control Wire (MSA)
ECWP..........	Egyptian Communist Workers' Party [*Political party*] (PD)
ECWP..........	Emergency Cooling Water Pond [*Nuclear energy*] (NRCH)
ECWPH	Emergency Cooling Water Pumphouse [*Nuclear energy*] (NRCH)
ECWS..........	English Civil War Society [*British*] (DBA)
ECWS..........	European Centre for Work and Society (EA)
ECWSS	Extreme Cold Weather Sleep System [*Army*]
EC-WTA	Executive Committee - Western Traffic Association (SAA)
ECWU	Energy and Chemical Workers Union [*See also STEC*]
ECX............	Electronically Controlled Telephone Exchange (DEN)
EC-X............	Emission Control Experimental
ECx............	Experimental Concentration-Percent (FFDE)
ECY............	Economy Inns, Inc. [*Vancouver Stock Exchange symbol*]
ECYC..........	Earl of Chester's Yeomanry Cavalry [*British military*] (DMA)
ECYC..........	European Confederation of Youth Clubs (EA)
E-cycle........	Execution Cycle [*Computer science*] (NITA)
ECYEB.........	European Community Youth Exchange Bureau (AIE)
ECYFC.........	European Committee for Young Farmers and 4H Clubs (EA)
ECYFC4HC ...	European Committee for Young Farmers and 4H Clubs [*Germany*] (EAIO)
ECYO	European Community Youth Orchestra [*British*] (EAIO)
ECYU	Elizabethan Club of Yale University (EA)
ECZ............	East Cape [*New Zealand*] [*Seismograph station code, US Geological Survey*] (SEIS)
ECZ............	Ethycarbazole [*Organic chemistry*]
ECZM..........	Eczema (ABBR)
ED..............	Canadian Efficiency Decoration [*Military*] (DD)
ED..............	Consolidated Edison [*NYSE symbol*] (TTSB)
ED..............	Consolidated Edison Co. of New York, Inc. [*NYSE symbol*] (SPSG)
Ed..............	Department of Education [*Cabinet department*]
E$_d$.............	Depth Dose [*Radiation therapy*] (DAVI)
ED..............	Doctor of Engineering
ED..............	Eastern District [*ATSC*]
ED..............	Eastern District Court Reports [*South Africa*] [*A publication*] (DLA)
ED..............	Economically Disadvantaged (OICC)
ED..............	Economic Development [*A publication*]
ED..............	Economics Division [*US Military Government, Germany*]
ED..............	Ectodermal Dysplasia [*Medicine*]
ED..............	Ectopic Depolarization [*Medicine*] (DMAA)
Ed	Eden's English Chancery Reports Tempore Northington [*28 English Reprint*] [*1757-66*] [*A publication*] (DLA)

Ed	Edgar's Decisions, Scotch Court of Session [*1724-25*] [*A publication*] (DLA)
ED..............	Edge Distance
ED..............	Edinburgh [*City in Scotland*]
ED..............	Edit [*or Edited*]
ed..............	Edited By (WDMC)
ED..............	Edition (AFM)
ed..............	Edition (VRA)
ED..............	Edition
ED..............	Editor (EY)
ED..............	Education
Ed..............	Education (DD)
ED..............	Educational [*FCC*] (NTCM)
ED..............	Educational Drama
ED..............	Educational Institution Program (NTCM)
ED..............	Education Department [*British military*] (DMA)
ED..............	Edulcorata [*Sweetened*] [*Pharmacy*] (ROG)
'Ed..............	'Eduyyoth (BJA)
ED..............	Effective Diameter [*TII*] (TAG)
ED..............	Effective Dose
ED..............	Efficiency Decoration [*Military British*]
ED..............	Egg Diameter [*Pisciculture*]
ED..............	Ehlers-Danlos Syndrome [*Medicine*] (MAE)
ED..............	Elasticity of Demand [*Economics*] (DCTA)
E/D.............	Elbow Disarticulation [*Orthopedics*]
ED..............	Election District
ED..............	Electrical Department [*Navy British*]
ED..............	Electrical Differential
ED..............	Electrical Drawing (IAA)
ED..............	Electric Dynamic [*Motors*]
ED..............	Electrochemical Detector [*Instrumentation*]
ED..............	Electrochemical Diffused (IAA)
ED..............	Electrodialysis [*Medicine*]
ED..............	Electrodynamic (DEN)
ED..............	Electron Device (MCD)
ED..............	Electron Diffraction
ED..............	Electronic Detection (LAIN)
ED..............	Electronic Development (MCD)
ED..............	Electronic Differential [*Analyzer*]
ED..............	Electronic Digital [*Analyzer*]
ED..............	Electronic Display
ED..............	Electronic Document
ED..............	Electronic Dummy [*Engineering acoustics*] (IAA)
ED..............	Electrostatic Discharge (IAA)
ED..............	Electrostatic Storage Deflection (IAA)
E/D.............	Embarkation/Disembarkation
ED..............	Embryonic Day
ED..............	Emergency Department [*of a hospital*]
ED..............	Emergency Destruction (MCD)
ED..............	Emergency Distance [*Aviation*] (DA)
ED..............	Emotional Disturbance
ED..............	Emotionally Deprived
ED..............	Emotionally Disabled (OICC)
ED..............	[*The*] Emphatic Diaglott [*1942*] [*A publication*] (BJA)
ED..............	Employability Development (OICC)
ED..............	End Delimiter (TNIG)
ED..............	End-Diastole [*Cardiology*]
ED..............	End Door
ED..............	Ending Delimiter [*Telecommunications*] (ACRL)
ED..............	End of Data [*Computer science*] (IAA)
E/D.............	End-of-Descent (GAVI)
ED..............	Enemy Dead
ED..............	Enforcement Division [*Environmental Protection Agency*] (GFGA)
ED..............	Engine Designer (DS)
ED..............	Engine Drive (MSA)
ED..............	Engineering Data
ED..............	Engineering Department [*Navy British*]
ED..............	Engineering Depot
ED..............	Engineering Design
ED..............	Engineering Development
ED..............	Engineering Directive (NASA)
ED..............	Engineering Division
ED..............	Engineering Document
ED..............	Engineering Draftsman
ED..............	Engineering Duty [*Navy*]
ED..............	English Duke (ROG)
ED..............	Enhancement Depletion (IAA)
E-D.............	Enhancement-Depletion Logic (NITA)
ED..............	Entertainment Duty (DLA)
ED..............	Entner-Doudoroff [*Hexose metabolic pathway*]
ED..............	Entry Date [*British Library Automated Information Service and National Library of Medicine*] [*Searchable field*] [*Information service or system*] (NITA)
ED..............	Enumeration District [*Census*]
ED..............	Envelope Drawing (MSA)
ED..............	Environmental Damage (EERA)
ED..............	Environmental Disruption
ED..............	Enzymatic Deficiencies
ED..............	Epidural [*Brain anatomy*]
ED..............	Equilibrium Dialysis [*Analytical chemistry*]
ED..............	Equipment Delay (CAAL)
ED..............	Equipment Description
ED..............	Erase Digital [*Signal*]
ED..............	ERIC [*Educational Resources Information Center*] Document

ED .... Errata Data [*Dialog*] [*Searchable field*] [*Information service or system*] (NITA)
ED .... Error Detecting [*or Detection*] [*Computer science*]
ED .... Erythema Dose [*Medicine*]
ED .... Esaki Diode [*Electronics*]
ED .... Esquerra Democratica [*Democratic Left*] [*Spain Political party*] (PPE)
ED .... Establishment Date [*IRS*]
ED .... Estate Duty (DLA)
ED .... Estimated Date (AAG)
ED .... Ethyldichloroarsine [*Medicine*] (ADDR)
ED .... Ethynodiol [*Pharmacology*]
ED .... Euclidean Distance Matrix [*Statistics*]
ED .... Eurodefence
ED .... European Democratic Group [*European Parliament*] (ECED)
ed---- .... Europe, Southeastern [*MARC geographic area code Library of Congress*] (LCCP)
ED .... Evaluation and Development (IAA)
ED .... Every Day
ED .... Evidence of Disease (DAVI)
ED .... Evolutionary Distance
ED .... Excess Distribution (ADA)
ED .... Exchequer Division, English Law Reports [*A publication*] (DLA)
ED .... Excused from Duty
ED .... Ex-Dividend [*Without the right to dividend*] [*Finance*]
ED .... Executive Director
ED .... Exertional Dyspnea [*Medicine*] (DAVI)
ED .... Exhaust Dampers [*Nuclear energy*] (NRCH)
ED .... Existence Doubtful [*Navigation charts*]
ED .... Expanded Display
E-D .... Expansion Deflection (AAG)
ED .... Experimental Design
ED .... Exploratory Development [*Military*]
ED .... Explosive Device
ED .... Exports Directorate [*British*]
ED .... Exposure Draft [*Business term*]
ED .... Extended Definition Television [*in ED Beta*] [*Sony Corp.*]
ED .... Extended Duration (OICC)
ED .... Extension Shaft Disconnect [*Nuclear energy*] (IAA)
ED .... Extensive Disease [*Medicine*]
ED .... Extensor Digitorum [*Muscle or tendon*] [*Orthopedics*] (DAVI)
ED .... External Delay [*Computer science*] (IAA)
ED .... External Device [*Computer science*]
ED .... External Diameter [*Measurement*] (DAVI)
ED .... Extraction Dialysis [*For separation of mixtures*]
ED .... Extra Dividend [*Banking*] (ADA)
ED .... Extra Duty [*Marine Corps*]
ED .... Extra-High-Density [*Floppy disk technology*] (PCM)
ED .... Extra-Low Dispersion [*Instrumentation*]
ED .... Extrusion Die (MCD)
ED .... Sunbird [*ICAO designator*] (AD)
ED .... U.S. Department of Education
ED$_{50}$ .... Effective Dose, Median
EdA .... Advanced Degree in Education (GAGS)
EDA .... Aerolinas Nacionales del Ecuador SA [*ICAO designator*] (FAAC)
EDA .... Early Departure Authorized
EDA .... Eating Disorders Association (EAIO)
EDA .... Economic Development Administration [*Formerly, Office of Appalachian Assistance*] [*Terminated Department of Commerce*]
EDA .... Educational Drama Association [*Defunct*] (EAIO)
EDA .... Education Development Associates [*Information service or system*]
EDA .... Effective Doubleword Address [*Computer science*] (IAA)
EDA .... Electrical Development Association
EDA .... Electrodermal Audiometry [*Otolaryngology*]
EDA .... Electron Donor-Acceptor
EDA .... Electronic Dental Anesthesia
EDA .... Electronic Design Automation [*Computer science*]
EDA .... Electronic Differential Analyzer
EDA .... Electronic Digital Analyzer (MCD)
EDA .... Electronic Display Assembly (NASA)
EDA .... Electronic Document Authorization (CDE)
EDA .... Elevation Drive Assembly (MCD)
EDA .... Embedded Document Architecture [*PenPoint*] [*Computer science*]
EDA .... Emergency Declaration Area [*Environmental Protection Agency*]
EDA .... Emergency Distance Available [*Aviation*] (AIA)
EDA .... Enacie Demokratiki Aristera [*United Democratic Left Party*] [*Greek*] (BARN)
EDA .... Encoder/Decoder Assembly (MCD)
EDA .... End-Diastolic Area [*Cardiology*]
EDA .... English Draughts Association (DBA)
EDA .... Equipment Design Agent
EDA .... Equipment Disposition Authorization
EDA .... Erection Digital Assembly
EDA .... Error and Dispersion Analysis (MCD)
EDA .... Error Detector Assembly
EDA .... Estimated Date of Arrival (NG)
EDA .... Estimated Date of Availability (AAG)
EDA .... Ethyl Diazoacetate [*Organic chemistry*]
EDA .... Ethylene Diacrylate [*Organic chemistry*]
EDA .... Ethylenediamenetetraacetic Acid
EDA .... Ethylenediamine [*Organic chemistry*]
EDA .... European Democratic Alliance [*Political movement*] (ECON)
EDA .... European Demolition Association (EA)
EDA .... European Desalination Association [*Glasgow, Scotland*] (EAIO)
EDA .... European Disposables Association [*Belgium*] (PDAA)
EDA .... Evolutionary Defense Acquisition (AAGC)

EDA .... Excess Defense Article (AFIT)
EDA .... Execution Damage Assessment (SAA)
EDA .... Exhaust Deflection Angle
EDA .... Exploratory Data Analysis [*Statistics*]
EDA .... Explosive Distributors Association [*Defunct*] (EA)
EDA .... Extensive-Dilatancy Anisotropy [*Geology*]
EDA .... External Data Aiding [*Computer science*] (PDAA)
EDA .... Extreme Disablement Adjustment
Ed A2 .... Advanced Degree in Education
EDAA .... Frankfurt Am Main, USAFE [*United States Air Force in Europe*] [*Germany ICAO location identifier*] (ICLI)
EDAAS .... Expert Disclosure Analysis and Avoidance System [*Environmental protection agency*] (NITA)
EDAB .... Bitburg [*Germany ICAO location identifier*] (ICLI)
EDAB .... Early Deploying Armored Bridge (MCD)
EDAC .... Edac Technologies [*NASDAQ symbol*] (TTSB)
EDAC .... Edac Technologies Corp. [*NASDAQ symbol*] (NQ)
Edac. .... Edac Technologies Corp. [*Associated Press*] (SAG)
EDAC .... Electron Donor Acceptor Complex
EDAC .... Electronic Dive Angle Control
EDAC .... Equipment Distribution and Condition [*Statistical reporting system*] [*Military*] (AFM)
EDAC .... Error Detection and Correction
EDAC .... Ethyl(dimethylaminopropyl)carbodiimide [*Also, EDC, EDCI*] [*Organic chemistry*]
EDAC .... Evaluation, Dissemination, and Assessment Center for Bilingual Education (EDAC)
EDAC .... Exhibit and Display Association of Canada
EDAC .... Kindsbach [*Germany ICAO location identifier*] (ICLI)
EDACS .... Environmental Data Access and Control System (HGAA)
EDACT .... Engineering Drawings to Automatic Control Tapes (PDAA)
EDAD .... Spangdahlem [*Germany ICAO location identifier*] (ICLI)
EDAF .... Rhein-Main Air Base [*Germany ICAO location identifier*] (ICLI)
EDAH .... Hahn [*Germany ICAO location identifier*] (ICLI)
EDAI .... Engineering Design Advance Information (DNAB)
EDAK .... Kindsbach [*Germany ICAO location identifier*] (ICLI)
EDAL .... Engineering Design and Analysis Laboratory [*University of New Hampshire*] [*Research center*] (RCD)
EDAL .... Sollingen [*Germany ICAO location identifier*] (ICLI)
EDALHAB .... Engineering Design and Analysis Laboratory Habitat
EDAM .... Edatrexate [*Antineoplastic drug*] (CDI)
EDAM .... Electron-Dense Amorphous Material [*Medicine*] (DMAA)
EDAM .... Electronic Design and Manufacture (IAA)
EDAM .... Experiments, Drill, and Maintenance
EDAM .... Zweibrucken [*Germany ICAO location identifier*] (ICLI)
EDAN .... Lahr [*Germany ICAO location identifier*] (ICLI)
EDANA .... European Disposables and Nonwovens Association
ED & C .... Electrodesiccation and Curettage [*Medicine*] (AAMN)
ED & I .... Engineering, Design, and Inspection
ED & T .... Equipment Development and Test Report [*Forest Service*]
EDANSW .... Electrical Development Association of New South Wales [*Australia*]
EDAO .... Gates [*Germany ICAO location identifier*] (ICLI)
EDAP .... Employee Development and Assistance Programme (AIE)
EDAP .... Engagement Decision Analysis Process [*DoD*]
EDAP .... Environmental Design Alignment Process
EDAP .... May [*Germany ICAO location identifier*] (ICLI)
EDAPS .... Electronic Data Processing System
EDAQ .... Electrical Development Association of Queensland [*Australia*]
EDAQ .... Rotz [*Germany ICAO location identifier*] (ICLI)
EDAR .... Education Department Acquisition Regulation (AAGC)
EDAR .... Ramstein [*Germany ICAO location identifier*] (ICLI)
EDARC .... Electronic Design Automation Research Center [*University of California*]
ED Ark .... United States District Court for the Eastern and Western Districts of Arkansas (DLA)
EDARR .... Engineering Drawing and Assembly Release Record (AAG)
EDAS .... Engineering Design and Simulation System [*Graphic Data Ltd.*] [*Software package*] (NCC)
EDAS .... Enhanced Data-Acquisition System [*Computer science*] (ODBW)
EDAS ....: Enlisted Distribution and Assignment System [*DoD*]
EDAS .... ERIC [*Educational Resources Information Center*] Data Access System [*Search system*]
EDAS .... Sembach [*Germany ICAO location identifier*] (ICLI)
Ed Asia Oceania... Education in Asia and Oceania [*A publication*]
Ed Asia Pacif... Education in Asia and the Pacific [*A publication*]
EDA/SQL ...... Enterprise Data Access/SQL [*Structured Query Language*] (CDE)
Ed Ass .... Eddis. Administration of Assets [*1880*] [*A publication*] (DLA)
EDATS .... Executive Data System (DNAB)
EDATS .... Extra-Deep Armed Team Sweep [*Military*]
EDAV .... Electrical Development Association of Victoria [*Australia*]
EDAV .... Siegenberg [*Germany ICAO location identifier*] (ICLI)
EDAVR .... Enlisted Distribution and Verification Report
EDAW .... Wiesbaden [*Germany ICAO location identifier*] (ICLI)
EDAWA .... Electrical Development Association of Western Australia [*Australia*]
EDAX .... Energy Dispersive Analysis by X-Ray [*Photovoltaic energy systems*]
EDAX .... Ramstein [*Germany ICAO location identifier*] (ICLI)
Ed B .... Bachelor of Education
EDB .... Broward Community College, Fort Lauderdale, FL [*OCLC symbol*] (OCLC)
EDB .... Early Dry Breakfast [*Medicine*]
EDB .... Economic Defense Board [*Later, Board of Economic Warfare*] [*World War II*]
EDB .... Economic Development Board [*Singapore*]
EDB .... Edible (ABBR)
EDB .... Educational Data Bank (IEEE)

EDB............. El Debba [*Sudan*] [*Airport symbol Obsolete*] (OAG)
EDB............. Electrodynamic Balance [*Physical chemistry*]
EDB............. Elongated Die Bushing
EDB............. Emergency Dispersal Bases (NATG)
EDB............. End of Data Block [*Computer science*] (CET)
EDB............. Energy Database [*Department of Energy*] [*Information service or system*]
EDB............. Engineering Data Bank [*GIDEP*]
EDB............. Environmental Data Book (NASA)
EDB............. Ethylene Dibromide [*Same as DBE, EB*] [*Organic chemistry*]
EDB............. Event Database
EDB............. Excise Duty Bulletins [*Revenue Canada - Customs and Excise*] [*Information service or system*] (CRD)
EDB............. Extensor Digitorum Brevis [*Anatomy*]
EDB............. Extradimensional Being
EDBA......... Berlin [*Germany ICAO location identifier*] (ICLI)
EDBAR....... Edith and Dana Bennett Agricultural Roundtable (EA)
EDBB......... Berlin/Tempelhof [*Germany ICAO location identifier*] (ICLI)
EDBD......... Environmental Data Base Directory [*National Oceanographic Data Center*] [*Database*] (MSC)
EDBG......... Berlin/Gatow [*Germany ICAO location identifier*] (ICLI)
EDBHPA....... Ethylenediaminebis(hydroxyphenylacetic acid) [*Also, EDDHA, EDHPA*] [*Organic chemistry*]
Ed Bills....... Eddis on Bills of Exchange [*A publication*] (DLA)
Ed BL....... Eden's Bankrupt Law [*A publication*] (DLA)
EDBL......... Edible
EDBP.......... Epidemiology, Demography, and Biometry Program [*National Institute on Aging*] [*Department of Health and Human Services*]
Ed Bro........ Eden's Edition of Brown's English Chancery Reports [*1757-66*] [*A publication*] (DLA)
EDBS.......... Educational Data Base Management System [*Computer science*] (MHDB)
EDBS.......... Educational Database System [*Computer System Research Group*] [*University of Toronto*] (NITA)
EDBS.......... Engineering Data Bank System (MCD)
EDBS.......... Expert Database System [*Computer science*] (ODBW)
EDBSA........ Engine Drivers' Board of South Australia
EDBT.......... Berlin/Tegel [*Germany ICAO location identifier*] (ICLI)
EDC............. Eastern Defense Command [*Army*]
EDC............. Eastern District Court Reports [*South Africa*] [*A publication*] (DLA)
EDC............. Eastman Dental Center [*University of Rochester*] [*Research center*] (RCD)
EDC............. Economic Development Committee [*Nickname: "Little Neddie"*] [*British*]
EdC............. EDCO, Springfield, MO [*Library symbol Library of Congress*] (LCLS)
EDC............. Edincik [*Turkey*] [*Seismograph station code, US Geological Survey*] (SEIS)
EDC............. Education Development Center [*Defunct*] (EA)
EDC............. Effective Date of Change (MCD)
EDC............. Effective Dynamic Compliance (MEDA)
EDC............. Electrical Distribution Center [*Army*]
EDC............. Electrode Dark Current
EDC............. Electronic Damping Control [*Automotive engineering*]
EDC............. Electronic Data Communications
EDC............. Electronic Desk Calculator (IEEE)
EDC............. Electronic Diesel Control [*Automotive engineering*]
EDC............. Electronic Digital Computer
EDC............. Electronic Discharge LASER (MCD)
EDC............. Electronic Document Collection
EDC............. Electronics Design Center [*Case Western Reserve University*] [*Research center*] (RCD)
EDC............. Emergency Decontamination Center [*Nuclear energy*] (NRCH)
EDC............. Emergency Digital Computer
EDC............. Enamel Double Cotton [*Wire insulation*] (AAG)
EDC............. Encyclopedie des Citations [*A publication*]
EDC............. End-Detonating Cartridge [*Explosive*]
EDC............. End-Diastolic Count [*Cardiology*]
EDC............. Energy Discharge Capacitor (IAA)
EDC............. Energy Distribution Curve [*Electron*]
EDC............. Engagement Direction Center (SAA)
EDC............. Engine-Drive Compressor (DNAB)
EDC............. Engineering Data Control
EDC............. Engineering Design Change
EDC............. Engineering Documentation Center [*NASA*] (KSC)
EDC............. EROS [*Earth Resources Observation Systems*] Data Center [*Marine science*] (MSC)
EDC............. Error Detecting Code
EDC............. Error Detection and Correction (NATG)
EDC............. Escalation during Construction (MCD)
EDC............. Estimated Date of Completion
EDC............. Estimated Date of Conception [*Obstetrics*] (DAVI)
EDC............. Estimated [*or Expected*] Date of Confinement [*Obstetrics*]
EDC............. Ethyl(dimethylaminopropyl)carbodiimide [*Also, EDAC, EDCI*] [*Organic chemistry*]
EDC............. Ethylene Dichloride [*Organic chemistry*]
EDC............. European Defense Community [*NATO*]
EDC............. European Disarmament Conference
EDC............. European Documentation Centre [*University of Dundee*] [*Dundee, Scotland*] (DLA)
EDC............. Evaluation Documentation Center [*Department of Health and Human Services*] [*Information service or system*] (IID)
EDC............. Event Driven Component
EDC............. Excessive Duty Cycle [*Military*]
EDC............. Expect Departure Clearance At [*Aviation*] (FAAC)
EDC............. Expected Date of Confinement [*Medicine*] (DHSM)

E/DC............. Expected/Dual-Command Travel Time
EDC............. Experimental Display Concept [*Space shuttle*] [*NASA*]
EDC............. Experiment Development Center [*NASA*] (KSC)
EDC............. Explosive Disposal Control
EDC............. Export Development Corp. [*Canada*]
EDC............. Extended Device Control (MHDB)
EDC............. Extensor Digitorum Communis [*Muscle or tendon*] [*Anatomy*] (DAVI)
EDC............. External-Device Code [*Computer science*] (MDG)
EDC............. External Disk/Drum Channel
EDC............. Extractive Distillation Column [*Chemical engineering*]
EDC............. Extra Dark Color (ADA)
EDCA......... Educate (ABBR)
EDCA......... Employment Department Clerks' Association [*A union*] [*British*]
EDCA......... Executive Director for Conventional Ammunition
EDCA......... Gluecksburg [*Germany ICAO location identifier*] (ICLI)
EDCAB........ Educable (ABBR)
EDCAD........ Educated (ABBR)
EDCAG........ Educating (ABBR)
ED Cal........ United States District Court for the Eastern District of California (DLA)
EdcAlt......... Education Alternative, Inc. [*Associated Press*] (SAG)
EDCAN........ Education (ABBR)
EDCANL....... Educational (ABBR)
EDCARS....... Engineering Data Computer-Assisted Retrieval System [*Air Force*] (GFGA)
EDCATR........ Educator (ABBR)
EDCAV........ Educative (ABBR)
EDCB......... Bueckeburg [*Germany ICAO location identifier*] (ICLI)
EDCBL........ Educable (ABBR)
EDCC......... Goch [*Germany ICAO location identifier*] (ICLI)
EDCE......... Rheine-Bentlage [*Germany ICAO location identifier*] (ICLI)
EDCEN........ Education Center [*Army*] (AABC)
EDCG......... Educating (ABBR)
EDCG......... Eggebek [*Germany ICAO location identifier*] (ICLI)
EDCG......... Error Detection Code Generator
EDCGC........ Elliott District Community Government Council [*Australia*]
Ed Ch......... Edwards' New York Chancery Reports [*A publication*] (DLA)
EDCH......... Hurth [*Germany ICAO location identifier*] (ICLI)
Ed Ch R....... Edwards' New York Chancery Reports [*A publication*] (DLA)
EDCI............. Energetic Dynamic Cardiac Insufficiency [*Cardiology*] (DMAA)
EDCI............. Ethyl(dimethylaminopropyl)carbodiimide [*Also, EDAC, EDC*] [*Organic chemistry*]
EDCI............. Itzehoe Hungriger Wolf [*Germany ICAO location identifier*] (ICLI)
ed cit........... Editio Citata [*Edition Cited*] [*Latin*]
EDCK......... Kiel-Holtenau [*Germany ICAO location identifier*] (ICLI)
EDCL......... Celle [*Germany ICAO location identifier*] (ICLI)
EDCL......... Electric-Discharge Convection LASER [*Navy*]
EDCLMDA.... Eastern Dry Cleaning and Laundry Machinery Distributors Association [*Defunct*] (EA)
EDCM......... Aachen/Merzbruck [*Germany ICAO location identifier*] (ICLI)
EDC (M)........ Electrochemical Depolarization CO^2 [*Carbon Dioxide*] (Module)
EDC(M)........ Electrochemical Depolarized Carbon Dioxide (Module) [*NASA*] (NASA)
EdcMge....... Education Management Corp. [*Associated Press*] (SAG)
EDCMR........ Effective Date of Change of Morning Report [*Military*]
EDCN......... Education (ADA)
EDCN......... Engineering Drawing Change Notice [*Nuclear energy*] (NRCH)
EDCN......... Experimental Data Communications Network (MCD)
EDCN......... Nordholz [*Germany ICAO location identifier*] (ICLI)
EDCO......... Edison Control [*NASDAQ symbol*] (TTSB)
EDCO......... Edison Control Corp. [*NASDAQ symbol*] (NQ)
EDCo.......... Educational Development Corp. [*Defunct*] (EA)
EDCOM........ Editor and Compiler
Ed Comment... Editorial Comment (DLA)
EDCP......... Engineering Design Change Proposal
E/DCP.......... Equipment/Document Change Proposal (NATG)
EDCP......... Ethyl Dichlorophosphate [*Organic chemistry*]
EDCP......... External Data Channel Processor (NOAA)
EDCPF......... Environmental Data Collection and Processing Facility [*Tucson, AZ*] [*Army*] (AABC)
Ed CR......... Edwards' New York Chancery Reports [*A publication*] (DLA)
EDCR......... Engineering Design Change Request (MCD)
EDCR......... Rotenburg/Wumme [*Germany ICAO location identifier*] (ICLI)
EDCS......... Ecumenical Development Cooperative Society (EAIO)
EDCS......... End-Diastolic Chamber Stiffness [*Medicine*] (DMAA)
EDCS......... End-Diastolic Circumferential Stress [*Medicine*] (DMAA)
EDCS......... Engineering Design Change Schedule
EDCS......... Engineering Document Control System (HGAA)
EDCS......... Extended Defense Communication System (CINC)
EDCS......... Schleswig [*Germany ICAO location identifier*] (ICLI)
EDCSA........ Effective Date of Change of Strength Accountability [*Military*]
EDCT......... Estimated Departure Clearance Time [*FAA*] (TAG)
EDCT......... Estimated Departure Clearance Time [*Aviation*] (FAAC)
EDCTU........ Electronic Development and Compatibility Test Unit
EDCU......... Butzweilerhof [*Germany ICAO location identifier*] (ICLI)
EDCV......... Enamel Double Cotton Varnish [*Wire insulation*]
EDCW......... External-Device Control Word [*Computer science*]
EDCW......... Werl [*Germany ICAO location identifier*] (ICLI)
Ed D......... Doctor of Education
EDD......... Earliest Delivery Date [*Navy*] (DOMA)
EDD......... Earliest Due Date
EDD......... Eastern Development Division [*Air Force*]
EDD......... Economic Development District [*EDA*]
EDD......... Eddied (ABBR)
EDD......... Editions (ROG)

EDD .... Editors (ROG)
EDD .... Effective Drug Duration [*Medicine*] (MAE)
EDD .... Electric Displacement Density
EDD .... Electrodermal Diagnosis [*Controversial medical technique*]
EDD .... Electronic Data Display
EDD .... Electronic Dehydration Dryer
EDD .... Electronic Document Delivery [*Software*]
EDD .... End Delivery Date (AAG)
EDD .... End-Diastolic Diameter [*Cardiology*]
EdD .... End-Diastolic Dimension [*Cardiology*]
EDD .... Enforcement Decision Document [*Environmental Protection Agency*] (ERG)
EDD .... Engagement Data Display (MCD)
EDD .... Engineering and Development Directorate [*Johnson Space Center*] [*NASA*]
EDD .... Engineering Data Depository (MSA)
EDD .... Engineering Design Data (AAG)
EDD .... Engineering Development Division [*Pacific Marine Environmental Laboratory*] (USDC)
EDD .... Engineering Development Division [*Marine science*] (OSRA)
EDD .... English Dialect Dictionary [*A publication*]
EDD .... Envelope Delay Distortion
EDD .... Environmental Data Directory [*Database*] (EERA)
EDD .... Enzyme-Digested Delta Endotoxin [*of Bacillus thuringiensis*] [*Biological control*]
EDD .... Equipment Data Display
EDD .... Equipment Density Data
EDD .... Equipment Development Division [*Britain's national phone-tapping center*]
EDD .... Essential Data Duplicator [*Utilico Microware*]
EDD .... Estimated Date of Departure [*or Detachment*] [*Military*] (DNAB)
EDD .... Estimated Delivery Date
EDD .... Event Data Distributor (MCD)
EDD .... Expected Date of Delivery [*Obstetrics*]
EDD .... Expert Database Designer [*Computer science*]
EDD .... Explosives Detection Devices [*FAA*] (TAG)
EDD .... Extra Deep Drawing [*Metal industry*]
EDDA .... Bonn, Frankfurt Am Main [*Germany ICAO location identifier*] (ICLI)
EDDA .... Electronic Directory of German Databases [*Information service or system*] (IID)
EDDA .... Ethylenediaminediacetic Acid [*Organic chemistry*]
EDDC .... East Coast Documents Distribution Center
EDDD .... Expanded Direct Distance Dialing [*Telecommunications*]
EDDD .... Frankfurt Am Main [*Germany ICAO location identifier*] (ICLI)
EDDF .... Error Detection and Decision Feedback
EDDF .... Frankfurt Am Main [*Germany ICAO location identifier*] (ICLI)
EDDFEC .... Estimated Date of Departure Far East Command [*Military*]
EDDH .... Hamburg [*Germany ICAO location identifier*] (ICLI)
EDDHA .... Ethylenediaminedi-O-Hydroxyphenylacetate [*or -hydroxyphenylacetic Acid*] [*Also, EDBHPA, EDHPA*] [*Organic chemistry*]
EDDI .... Ethylenediamine Dihydriodide [*Organic chemistry*]
EDDIC .... Experimental Development, Demonstration, and Integration Center [*Army*]
EDDIE .... Environmental Distribution of Dynamic Item Entries (SAA)
EDDIS .... Electronic Document Delivery: Integrated Solutions [*Project*] (AIE)
EDDK .... Koeln-Bonn [*Germany ICAO location identifier*] (ICLI)
EDDL .... Duesseldorf [*Germany ICAO location identifier*] (ICLI)
EDDM .... Muenchen [*Germany ICAO location identifier*] (ICLI)
EDDN .... Nuernberg [*Germany ICAO location identifier*] (ICLI)
EDDNTC ...... Endodontic
EDDP .... Electron Dipole-Dipole Polarization
EDDP .... Engineering Design Data Package (AAG)
EDDP .... Engineering Design Documentation Procedures (MCD)
EDDQ .... Extra-Deep-Drawing-Quality [*Steel*]
EDDQ .... Extra Deep Drawing Quality
EDDR .... Electron Dipole-Dipole Reservoir (NASA)
EDDS .... Early Docking Demonstration System (IAA)
EDDS .... Electron Devices Data Service [*National Institute of Standards and Technology*]
EDDS .... Emergency Detection and Decision System
EDDS .... Enhanced Defense Logistics Agency Distribution System (AAGC)
EDDS .... Ethylenediaminedisuccinic [*Organic chemistry*]
EDDS .... Executive Data Display System (HGAA)
EDDS .... Stuttgart [*Germany ICAO location identifier*] (ICLI)
EDDU .... Rhein [*Germany ICAO location identifier*] (ICLI)
EDDV .... Hannover [*Germany ICAO location identifier*] (ICLI)
EDDW .... Bremen [*Germany ICAO location identifier*] (ICLI)
EDDY .... Maastricht [*Germany ICAO location identifier*] (ICLI)
EDDZ .... Frankfurt Am Main [*Germany ICAO location identifier*] (ICLI)
EDE .... Edenton, NC [*Location identifier FAA*] (FAAL)
EDE .... Electrical Design Engineering
EDE .... Electronic Data Exchange [*DoD*]
EDE .... Electronic Defense Evaluator
EDE .... Elliptic [*or Exact*] Differential Equation
EDE .... Emergency Decelerating [*Relay*] (IEEE)
EDE .... Emerging Mkts Income Fund II [*NYSE symbol*] (TTSB)
EDE .... Emitter Dip Effect (IEEE)
EDE .... Empire Dist Elec [*NYSE symbol*] (TTSB)
EDE .... Empire District Electric Co. [*NYSE symbol*] (SPSG)
EDE .... Engineering Development Establishment [*Australia*]
EDE .... Environmental Data and Ecological Parameters Data Base [*International Society of Ecological Modelling*] [*Information service or system*] (IID)
EDE .... Esquerda Democratica Estudantil [*Democratic Student Left*] [*Portugal Political party*] (PPE)

EDE .... Experimental Demolition Establishment [*British*]
EDE .... External Document Exchange (HGAA)
EDEA .... Amberg [*Germany ICAO location identifier*] (ICLI)
EDEAC .... EPRI [*Electric Power Research Institute*] Database for Environmentally Assisted Cracking [*Battelle Memorial Institute*] [*Information service or system*] (IID)
EDEB .... Ansbach [*Germany ICAO location identifier*] (ICLI)
EDEC .... Aschaffenburg [*Germany ICAO location identifier*] (ICLI)
EDECN .... European Development Education Curriculum Network
EDECWS ...... Emergency Diesel Engine Cooling Water System [*Nuclear energy*] (NRCH)
EDED .... Error Detection Encoder-Decoder [*Ground Communications Facility, NASA*]
EDED .... Kaiserlautern [*Germany ICAO location identifier*] (ICLI)
EDEE .... Heidelberg, United States Army [*Germany ICAO location identifier*] (ICLI)
EDEF .... Babenhausen [*Germany ICAO location identifier*] (ICLI)
EDEG .... Bad Kissingen [*Germany ICAO location identifier*] (ICLI)
EDEH .... Bad Kreuznach [*Germany ICAO location identifier*] (ICLI)
EDEI .... Miesau-West [*Germany ICAO location identifier*] (ICLI)
EDEJ .... Bamberg [*Germany ICAO location identifier*] (ICLI)
EDEK .... Baumholder [*Germany ICAO location identifier*] (ICLI)
EDEL .... Bayreuth [*Germany ICAO location identifier*] (ICLI)
EDEL .... Edelbrock Corp. [*NASDAQ symbol*] (SAG)
Edelbrck ...... Edelbrock Corp. [*Associated Press*] (SAG)
EDELS .... Emergency Diesel Engine Lubrication System [*Nuclear energy*] (NRCH)
EDEM .... Muenchen, Hospital, Perlacher Forst [*Germany ICAO location identifier*] (ICLI)
Eden .... Eden's English Chancery Reports [*28 English Reprint*] [*A publication*] (DLA)
EDEN .... Emma Dorothy Eliza Nevitte Southworth [*American novelist, 1818-99*] [*Acronym used as pseudonym*]
EDEN .... Evaluated Disposition toward the Environment [*Student attitude test*]
EDEN .... Maurice Rose [*Germany ICAO location identifier*] (ICLI)
Eden Bankr... Eden's Bankrupt Law [*A publication*] (DLA)
Eden (Eng)... Eden's English Chancery Reports [*28 English Reprint*] [*A publication*] (DLA)
Eden Pen Law... Eden's Principles of Penal Law [*A publication*] (DLA)
Eden's Prin PL... Eden's Principles of Penal Law [*A publication*] (DLA)
EDENT .... Edentate (ABBR)
edent .... Edentulous [*Toothless*] [*Dentistry*] (DAVI)
EDEO .... Bremerhaven [*Germany ICAO location identifier*] (ICLI)
EDEP .... Budingen [*Germany ICAO location identifier*] (ICLI)
EDEPrA .... Empire Dist El,4 3/4% Pfd [*NYSE symbol*] (TTSB)
EDEPrB .... Empire Dist El,5% Pfd [*NYSE symbol*] (TTSB)
EDER .... Crailsheim [*Germany ICAO location identifier*] (ICLI)
EDES .... Darmstadt [*Germany ICAO location identifier*] (ICLI)
EDES .... Ethnikos Demokratikos Ellinikos Stratos [*National Democratic Greek Army*] (PPE)
EDESA .... Economic Development of Equatorial and Southern Africa
EDESS .... Emergency Diesel Engine Starting System [*Nuclear energy*] (NRCH)
EDET .... Elevation Data Edit Terminals (RDA)
EDET .... Engine Detector (MCD)
EDET .... Erlangen [*Germany ICAO location identifier*] (ICLI)
EDETATE ..... Ethylenediaminetetraacetate [*Also, EDTA, enta*] [*USAN*] [*Organic chemistry*]
Ed et Ord .... Edits et Ordonnances [*Lower Canada*] [*A publication*] (DLA)
EDEU .... Giebelstadt [*Germany ICAO location identifier*] (ICLI)
EDEV .... Friedberg [*Germany ICAO location identifier*] (ICLI)
EDEW .... Enhanced Distant Early Warning
EDEW .... Fuerth [*Germany ICAO location identifier*] (ICLI)
EDEX .... Fulda [*Germany ICAO location identifier*] (ICLI)
EDEY .... Zweibrucken [*Germany ICAO location identifier*] (ICLI)
EDEZ .... Germersheim [*Germany ICAO location identifier*] (ICLI)
EDF .... Anchorage, AK [*Location identifier FAA*] (FAAL)
EDF .... Earthquake Data File [*Marine science*] (MSC)
EDF .... East Daggafontein [*Vancouver Stock Exchange symbol*]
EDF .... Economics of Distribution Foundation (EA)
Ed F .... Educational Forum [*A publication*] (BRI)
EDF .... Electrical Discharge Forming [*Manufacturing term*] (IAA)
EDF .... Electric Depth Finder
EDF .... Electric-Drive Fan [*Automotive engineering*]
EDF .... Electricite de France (ECON)
EDF .... Electricite de France [*Database originator*] (NITA)
EDF .... Electricity Development Fund [*Australia*]
EDF .... Electrophoresis Duplicating Film [*For analytical chemistry*]
EDF .... Elongatable Dow Fiber [*Dow Chemical Co.*]
EDF .... Elongation, Derotation, and Lateral Flexion [*Medicine*]
EDF .... Emergency Decontamination Facility [*Energy Research and Development Administration*]
EDF .... Emerging Markets Income Fund [*NYSE symbol*] (SPSG)
EDF .... Empirical Distribution Function [*Statistics*]
EDF .... Engineering Data File
EDF .... Enlisted Dining Facility [*Military*]
EdF .... Enroles de Force [*Forced Conscripts*] [*Luxembourg*] (PPE)
EDF .... Environmental Defense Fund (EA)
EDF .... Epidermal Cell Derived Factor [*Biochemistry*]
EDF .... Erythroid Differentiation Factor [*Endocrinology*]
EDF .... European Defense Force (NATG)
EDF .... European Development Fund (EY)
EDF .... Execution Diagnostic Facility (HGAA)
EDF .... Experiment Data Facility [*NASA*] (KSC)
EDF .... External Delay Factor [*Computer science*]
EDFA .... Electronic Differential Analyzer (MSA)

EDFA............ Employer Dentists Federation of Australia

EDFB............ Eastern Deciduous Forest Biome [*Ecological biogeographic study*]

EDFB............ Reichelsheim [*Germany ICAO location identifier*] (ICLI)

EDFC............ Aschaffenburg-Grossostheim [*Germany ICAO location identifier*] (ICLI)

EDFC............ Edifice (ABBR)

EDFC............ Edifice

EDFCN.......... Edification (ABBR)

EDFD............ Edified (ABBR)

EDF-DOC...... Electricite de France [*Bibliographic database*] [*French*]

EDFE............ Egelsbach [*Germany ICAO location identifier*] (ICLI)

EDFE............ Engineer District, Far East (CINC)

EDFF............ Frankfurt [*Germany ICAO location identifier*] (ICLI)

EDFG........... Edifying (ABBR)

EDFG........... Extended Data Flow Graph

EDFG........... Gelnhausen [*Germany ICAO location identifier*] (ICLI)

EDFK........... Bad Kissingen [*Germany ICAO location identifier*] (ICLI)

EDFM........... Educational FM Station (NTCM)

EDFM........... Electronic Design for Manufacture

EDFM........... Mannheim-Neuostheim [*Germany ICAO location identifier*] (ICLI)

EDFMIS........ Department of Education Financial Management Information System (GFGA)

EDFN........... Marburg-Schoenstadt [*Germany ICAO location identifier*] (ICLI)

EDFO........... Economic Development Financing Organization [*Greece*]

EDFO........... Michelstadt [*Germany ICAO location identifier*] (ICLI)

EDFORUM.... Educators Forum [*Columbus, OH*] [*Information service or system*] (IID)

EDFP........... Engine Driven Fire Pump (IEEE)

EDFQ........... Allendorf/Eder [*Germany ICAO location identifier*] (ICLI)

EDFR........... Effective Date of Federal Recognition [*Military*]

EDFR........... Rothenburg [*Germany ICAO location identifier*] (ICLI)

EDFS........... Schweinfurt-Sud [*Germany ICAO location identifier*] (ICLI)

ED-FTGA...... Eastern Dark-Fired Tobacco Growers Association (EA)

EDFU........... Mainbullau [*Germany ICAO location identifier*] (ICLI)

EDFV........... Worms [*Germany ICAO location identifier*] (ICLI)

EDFW.......... Wuerzburg-Schenkenturm [*Germany ICAO location identifier*] (ICLI)

EDFX........... Fuldatal [*Germany ICAO location identifier*] (ICLI)

EDFY........... Edify Corp. [*NASDAQ symbol*] (TTSB)

EDFYD......... Edified (ABBR)

EDFYG......... Edifying (ABBR)

Edg.............. Edgar's Reports, Scotch Court of Session [*1724-25*] [*A publication*] (DLA)

EDG............. Edgewood Arsenal, MD [*Location identifier FAA*] (FAAL)

EDG............. Electrical Discharge Grinding [*Manufacturing term*]

EDG............. Electrodynamic Gradient Freeze [*Crystal growing technique*]

EDG............. Electrodynogram [*For evaluation of walking gait*]

EDG............. Electronic Development Group [*Military*] (AFIT)

EDG............. Electronic Dot Generation (DGA)

EDG............. Emergency Diesel Generator (NRCH)

EDG............. Exploratory Development Goal [*Military*]

Edgar.......... Edgar's Reports, Scotch Court of Session [*1724-25*] [*A publication*] (DLA)

EDGAR........ Education Department General Administrative Regulations [*Department of Education*] (GFGA)

EDGAR........ Electronic Data Gathering, Analysis, and Retrieval [*Securities and Exchange Commission pilot project*] (IID)

EDGAR........ Experimental Data Gathering and Reduction (MCD)

EDGB.......... Breitscheid/Dillkreis [*Germany ICAO location identifier*] (ICLI)

Edg C.......... Canons Enacted under King Edgar [*A publication*] (DLA)

EDGCAIES.... Emergency Diesel Generator Combustion Air Intake and Exhaust System [*Nuclear energy*] (NRCH)

EDGD.......... Edged (ABBR)

EDGE.......... Electronic Data Gathering Equipment

EDGE.......... Electronic Document Gathering Environment [*A.B. Dick*] [*Updatable fiche system*] (NITA)

EDGE.......... Ergonomic Digitally Generated Environments [*Chrysler Corp.*]

EDGE.......... Experimental Display Generator

EDGE.......... Visual Edge Systems, Inc. [*NASDAQ symbol*] (SAG)

EDGEP........ European Democratic Group in the European Parliament [*Brussels, Belgium*] [*Political party*] (EAIO)

EDGF.......... Endothelial-Derived Growth Factor [*Biochemistry*]

EDGF.......... Eye-Derived Growth Factor [*Biochemistry*]

EDGG.......... Edging (ABBR)

EDGK.......... Korbach [*Germany ICAO location identifier*] (ICLI)

EDGL.......... Ludwigshafen-Unfallklinik [*Germany ICAO location identifier*] (ICLI)

Edg Leas ..... Edges' Forms of Leases [*A publication*] (DLA)

EDGM.......... Mosbach-Lohrbach [*Germany ICAO location identifier*] (ICLI)

EDGN.......... Nordenbeck [*Germany ICAO location identifier*] (ICLI)

EDGNS......... Edginess (ABBR)

EDGNSW....... Export Development Group of New South Wales [*Australia*]

EDGO.......... Oedheim [*Germany ICAO location identifier*] (ICLI)

EDGR.......... Edgier (ABBR)

EDGS.......... Electronic Data Gathering System [*Computer science*] (ECII)

EDGST........ Edgiest (ABBR)

EDGW.......... Edgewise (MSA)

EDGW.......... Wolfhagen/Granerberg [*Germany ICAO location identifier*] (ICLI)

EDGWS........ Edgewise (ABBR)

EDGYR........ Edgier (ABBR)

EDGYST....... Edgiest (ABBR)

EDH............. Efficient Deck Hand (NATG)

EDH............. Engineering Design Handbook (MCD)

EDH............. Ethylenedihydrazine (MCD)

EDH............. Sturgeon Bay, WI [*Location identifier FAA*] (FAAL)

EDHA.......... Hamburg [*Germany ICAO location identifier*] (ICLI)

EDHASA....... Editora y Distribuidora Hispano-Americana Sociedad Anonima [*Publisher's imprint*] [*Spain*]

EDHB.......... Grube [*Germany ICAO location identifier*] (ICLI)

EDHC.......... Luchow/Rehbeck [*Germany ICAO location identifier*] (ICLI)

EDHE.......... Experimental Data Handling Equipment

EDHE.......... Uetersen [*Germany ICAO location identifier*] (ICLI)

EDHG.......... Luneburg [*Germany ICAO location identifier*] (ICLI)

EDHI........... Hamburg/Finkenwerder [*Germany ICAO location identifier*] (ICLI)

EDHK.......... Enose Demokratikou Hellinikou Kentrou [*Union of the Greek Democratic Center*] (PPE)

EDHL.......... Luebeck/Blankensee [*Germany ICAO location identifier*] (ICLI)

EDHM.......... Hartenholm [*Germany ICAO location identifier*] (ICLI)

EDHN.......... Neumuenster [*Germany ICAO location identifier*] (ICLI)

EDHP.......... Engine Driven Hydraulic Pump (MCD)

EDHPA......... Ethylenediaminedi-O-Hydroxyphenylacetic Acid [*Also, EDBHPA, EDDHA*] [*Organic chemistry*]

EDHS .... Engineering Design Handbook Series (MCD)

EDHX .... Bad Bramstedt [*Germany ICAO location identifier*] (ICLI)

Edi.............. Diaphragmatic Electrical Activity

EDI............. Eating Disorder Inventory [*Psychology*]

EDI............. Echo Doppler Indicator [*Telecommunications*] (IAA)

EDI............. Economically Disadvantaged Income (ADA)

EDI............. Economic-Damage Index [*Environmental technology*]

EDI............. Economic Development Institute [*of the International Bank for Reconstruction and Development*]

EDI............. Edinburgh [*Scotland*] [*Airport symbol*] (OAG)

EDI............. Edinburgh [*Scotland*] [*Seismograph station code, US Geological Survey*] (SEIS)

EDI............. Edingtonite [*A zeolite*]

EDI............. Editek, Inc. [*AMEX symbol*] (SPSG)

EDI............. Editor [*Computer science*]

EDI............. Educational Data Information Ltd. [*Information service or system*] (IID)

EDI............. Electrical Deflection Indicator

EDI............. Electron Diffraction Instrument

EDI............. Electron Drift Instrument

EDI............. Electronic Data Intelligence (DOMA)

EDI............. Electronic Data Interchange [*Computer science Telecommunications*]

EDI............. Electronic Data Interchange

EDI............. Electronic Dissemination of Information (GFGA)

EDI............. Electronic Document Interchange

EDI............. Engineering Demonstrated Inspection (AAG)

EDI............. Ensured Data Integrity

EDI............. Environmental Diagnostics, Inc.

EDI............. Eponyms Dictionaries Index [*A publication*]

EDI............. Error Detection Instrument (IAA)

EDI............. Estimated Daily Intake [*Toxicology*]

EDIA.......... Electronic Data Interchange Association (EA)

EDIA.......... Giessen [*Germany ICAO location identifier*] (ICLI)

EDIAC .... Electronic Display of Indexing Association and Content (PDAA)

EDIAC .... Engineering Decision Integrator and Communicator

EDIB.......... Goeppingen [*Germany ICAO location identifier*] (ICLI)

EDIC.......... Economic Documentation and Information Centre Ltd. [*British Database producer*] (IID)

EDIC.......... Equipment Dictionary [*Navy*] (MCD)

EDIC.......... Grafenwoehr [*Germany ICAO location identifier*] (ICLI)

EDICC......... Electronic Data Interchanges Council of Canada (EAIO)

Edict.......... Edicts of Justinian [*A publication*]

EDICT......... Engineering Department Interface Control Task [*or Technique*]

EDICT......... Engineering Document [*or Drawing*] Information Collection Task [*or Technique*]

EDID .... Hanau [*Germany ICAO location identifier*] (ICLI)

EDIE .... Heidelberg [*Germany ICAO location identifier*] (ICLI)

EDI/EC .... Electronic Data Interchange/Electronic Commerce [*Computer science Army*] (RDA)

EDIF........... Edificio

EDIF........... Electronic Design Interchange Format [*Computer science*]

EDIF........... Heilbronn [*Germany ICAO location identifier*] (ICLI)

EDIFACT ...... Electronic Data Interchange for Administration, Commerce, and Transport [*Economic Commission for Europe*]

EDIFACT ...... Electronics Data Interchange For Administration, Commerce, and Trade [*Telecommunications*] (ACRL)

EDIFC......... Ethel Delaney International Fan Club (EA)

EDIG........... Feucht [*Germany ICAO location identifier*] (ICLI)

EDIH........... Hohenfels [*Germany ICAO location identifier*] (ICLI)

EDII........... Augsburg Hospital [*Germany ICAO location identifier*] (ICLI)

EDIJ........... Bohmer [*Germany ICAO location identifier*] (ICLI)

EDIK........... Enossi Dimokratikou Kentrou [*Union of Democratic Centre Party*] [*Greece*] [*Political party*] (EY)

EDIK........... Illesheim [*Germany ICAO location identifier*] (ICLI)

EDIL........... Karlsruhe [*Germany ICAO location identifier*] (ICLI)

ED III .... United States District Court for the Eastern District of Illinois (DLA)

EDIM.......... Epidemic [*or Epizootic*] Diarrhea of Infant Mice

EDIM.......... Equipment Design Information Memo

EDIM.......... Kirchgons [*Germany ICAO location identifier*] (ICLI)

EDIMB......... Edimbourg [*Edinburgh*] (ROG)

EDIMS......... Environmental Data and Information Management Systems [*Marine science*] (OSRA)

EDIMS......... Environmental Data and Information Management Systems (USDC)

EDIN.......... Economic Development Information Network [*Indiana University*] [*Information service or system*] (IID)

EDIN .... Edinburgh [*City in Scotland*]

EDIN .... Educational Insights [*NASDAQ symbol*] (TTSB)

EDIN .... Educational Insights, Inc. [*NASDAQ symbol*] (SAG)

EDIN .... Engineering Design Integration System [*NASA*] (MCD)

EDIN	Kitzingen [*Germany ICAO location identifier*] (ICLI)
Edinb LJ	Edinburgh Law Journal [*A publication*] (DLA)
Edinboro U	Edinboro University of Pennsylvania (GAGS)
EDINBURG	Edinburgensis [*Signature of Bishops of Edinburgh*] (ROG)
ED IN CH	Editor-in-Chief (WDAA)
EDINET	Education Instruction Network (WDAA)
EDI-NET	Electronic Data Interchange Network (TSSD)
Ed Inj	Eden on Injunctions [*1821*] [*A publication*] (DLA)
EDIO	Butzbach (Schloss) [*Germany ICAO location identifier*] (ICLI)
EDIO	Energy Disaggregated Input-Output Model [*Department of Energy*] (GFGA)
E-Diol	Estradiol [*Also, E2, ES*] [*Endocrinology*]
EDIP	European Defense Improvement Program [*NATO*] (MCD)
EDIP	Landstuhl [*Germany ICAO location identifier*] (ICLI)
EDIQ	Herzo Base [*Germany ICAO location identifier*] (ICLI)
EDIR	Ludwigsburg [*Germany ICAO location identifier*] (ICLI)
EDIS	Edison National Historic Site
EDIS	Electronic Distributorless Ignition System [*Automotive engineering*]
EDIS	Elektronisches Dokumentations und Informations System [*Information retrieval system*] [*France*] (NITA)
EDIS	Emergency Digital Information Service (INF)
EDIS	Engineering Data Information System (IEEE)
EDIS	Environmental Data and Information Service [*Later, NESDIS*]
EDIS	Executive Directorate Industrial Security (MCD)
EDIS	Nellingen [*Germany ICAO location identifier*] (ICLI)
EdisBr	Edison Brothers Stores [*Associated Press*] (SAG)
EdisCtr	Edison Control Corp. [*Associated Press*] (SAG)
e-disk	Emulated-Disk (CDE)
Edisto	Edisto Resources Corp. [*Associated Press*] (SAG)
EDIT	Edited (ROG)
EDIT	Edition
EDIT	Editor (ROG)
EDIT	Editor
EDIT	Editorial (WDAA)
ED.IT	Education and Information Technology [*Educational viewdata service*] (NITA)
EDIT	Electronic Diagnostic and Technical Information Tools [*Army*]
EDIT	Engineering Development Integration Test
EDIT	Error Deletion by Iterative Transmission
EDIT	Estate Duties Investment Trust (DLA)
EDIT	Examining, Diagnosis, Identification, and Training (PDAA)
EDIT	Eye-Slaved Display Integration and Test
EDIT	Nuernberg, Hospital [*Germany ICAO location identifier*] (ICLI)
EDIT	RGB Computer & Video [*NASDAQ symbol*] (TTSB)
EDITAR	Electronic Digital Tracking and Ranging
EDITEAST	South-East Asia Association of Science Editors (PDAA)
Editek	Editek, Inc. [*Associated Press*] (SAG)
EDITH	Emergency Drill in the Home [*Fire Department drill exercise*]
EDITH	Estate Duties Investment Taxes [*British*]
EDITP	Engineering Development Integration Test Program (IAA)
EDITS	Educational and Industrial Testing Service
EDITS	Electronic Data Information Technical Service (DIT)
EDITS	Electronic [*Warfare*] Data Integration Test System (MCD)
EDITS	Experimental Digital Television System
EDITSPEC	Editing Specifications (MCD)
EDIU	Heidelberg [*Germany ICAO location identifier*] (ICLI)
EDIUP	Existing Documents Improvement and Updating (MCD)
EDIV	Pirmasens [*Germany ICAO location identifier*] (ICLI)
EDIW	Wuerzburg, Hospital [*Germany ICAO location identifier*] (ICLI)
EDIX	Electronic Designs [*NASDAQ symbol*] (TTSB)
EDIX	Electronic Designs, Inc. [*NASDAQ symbol*] (SAG)
EDIX	Schwaebisch Gmuend [*Germany ICAO location identifier*] (ICLI)
EDIXW	Electronic Designs Wrrt [*NASDAQ symbol*] (TTSB)
EDIZ	Schwabach [*Germany ICAO location identifier*] (ICLI)
e-dk--	Denmark [*MARC geographic area code Library of Congress*] (LCCP)
EDK	Enose Demokratikou Kentrou [*Union of the Democratic Center*] [*Greek*] (PPW)
EDKB	Bonn/Hangelar [*Germany ICAO location identifier*] (ICLI)
EDKD	Altena/Hegenscheid [*Germany ICAO location identifier*] (ICLI)
EDKE	Dierdorf/Wienau [*Germany ICAO location identifier*] (ICLI)
EDKF	Bergneustadt/Auf Dem Dumpel [*Germany ICAO location identifier*] (ICLI)
EDKI	Betzdorf/Kirchen [*Germany ICAO location identifier*] (ICLI)
EDKL	Leverkusen [*Germany ICAO location identifier*] (ICLI)
EDKM	Meschede/Schuren [*Germany ICAO location identifier*] (ICLI)
EDKN	Wipperfurth/Neye [*Germany ICAO location identifier*] (ICLI)
EDKS	Siegerland [*Germany ICAO location identifier*] (ICLI)
EDKV	Dahlemer Binz [*Germany ICAO location identifier*] (ICLI)
EDKW	Werdohl/Kuntrop [*Germany ICAO location identifier*] (ICLI)
ED KY	United States District Court for the Eastern District of Kentucky (DLA)
EDKZ	Meinerzhagen [*Germany ICAO location identifier*] (ICLI)
EDL	Consolidated Ed 7.75%'QUICS' [*NYSE symbol*] (TTSB)
EDL	Economic Dislocation Loans [*Small Business Administration*]
EDL	Edit Decision List
EDL	Edition Deluxe
EDL	Educational Developmental Laboratories [*of McGraw Hill, Inc.*]
EDL	Eldoret [*Kenya*] [*Airport symbol Obsolete*] (OAG)
EDL	Electrical Discharge LASER (MCD)
EDL	Electric Delay Line
EDL	Electric Double Layer
EDL	Electrodeless Discharge Lamp
EDL	Electrodynamic Levitation (PDAA)
EDL	Electron Devices Laboratory
EDL	Electronic Defense Laboratory
EDL	Electrostatic Deflecting Lens (PDAA)

EDL	Embedded Design Language [*Computer science*] (PDAA)
EDL	Emulation Design Language [*Computer science*] (MHDB)
EDL	End-Diastolic Length [*Cardiology*]
EDL	Engineering Development Laboratory
EDL	Engineering Drawing List
EDL	Estimated Date of Labor [*Obstetrics*] (DMAA)
EDL	Euro Disneyland [*France*]
EDL	Every-Day Life [*Psychological testing*]
EDL	Executive Data Link [*IBM Corp.*]
EDL	Extensor Digitorum Longus [*Anatomy*]
EDL	South African Law Reports, Eastern Districts Local Division [*South Africa*] [*A publication*] (DLA)
EDLA	Arnsberg [*Germany ICAO location identifier*] (ICLI)
EDLA	Exotic Dancers League of America (EA)
ED LA	United States District Court for the Eastern District of Louisiana (DLA)
EDLB	Borkenberge [*Germany ICAO location identifier*] (ICLI)
EDLC	Edwardian Drama and Literature Circle (EA)
EDLC	Kamp/Lintfort [*Germany ICAO location identifier*] (ICLI)
EDLCC	Electronic Data Local Communications Central [*or Complex*]
EDLD	Dinslaken/Schwarze Heide [*Germany ICAO location identifier*] (ICLI)
ED/LD	Emotionally Disturbed/Learning Disabled
EDLD	Employee Daily Labor Distribution (AAG)
EDLE	Essen/Muelheim [*Germany ICAO location identifier*] (ICLI)
EDLF	Endogenous Digitalis-Like Factor [*Biochemistry*]
EDLF	Grefrath/Niershorst [*Germany ICAO location identifier*] (ICLI)
EDLG	Muenster/Osnabruck [*Germany ICAO location identifier*] (ICLI)
EDLH	Hamm/Lippewiesen [*Germany ICAO location identifier*] (ICLI)
EDLI	Bielefeld/Windelsbleiche [*Germany ICAO location identifier*] (ICLI)
Ed LJ	Edinburgh Law Journal [*A publication*] (DLA)
EDLK	Krefeld/Egelsberg [*Germany ICAO location identifier*] (ICLI)
EDLL	Duesseldorf [*Germany ICAO location identifier*] (ICLI)
EDLM	Marl/Loemuhle [*Germany ICAO location identifier*] (ICLI)
EDLN	Engineering Development Logic Network (NASA)
EDLN	Moenchengladbach [*Germany ICAO location identifier*] (ICLI)
EDLO	Oerlinghausen [*Germany ICAO location identifier*] (ICLI)
EDLP	Engineering Development Laboratory Program (KSC)
EDLP	Every Day Low Pricing [*Business term*]
EDLP	Paderborn/Lippstadt [*Germany ICAO location identifier*] (ICLI)
EDLQ	Essen [*Germany ICAO location identifier*] (ICLI)
EDLS	Stadtlohn/Wenningfeld [*Germany ICAO location identifier*] (ICLI)
EDLT	Muenster/Telgte [*Germany ICAO location identifier*] (ICLI)
EDLW	Dortmund/Wickede [*Germany ICAO location identifier*] (ICLI)
EDLX	Wesel/Romerwardt [*Germany ICAO location identifier*] (ICLI)
edm	Early Day Motion [*British*] (BARN)
EDM	Early Diastolic Murmur [*Medicine*]
EDM	Edgar Dale Media Center, Columbus, OH [*OCLC symbol*] (OCLC)
EDM	Edmonton [*Alberta*] [*Seismograph station code, US Geological Survey*] (SEIS)
EDM	Electrical Discharge [*or Electrodischarge*] Machine [*or Machining*]
EDM	Electrical Disintegration Machining [*Nuclear energy*] (NRCH)
EDM	Electric Dipole Moment [*Physics*]
EDM	Electric Drive Mechanism (KSC)
EDM	Electromagnetic Distance Measurement [*Geology*]
EDM	Electron Density Map [*Crystallography*]
EDM	Electronic Design and Manufacture (IAA)
EDM	Electronic Distance Measurement (NITA)
EDM	Electronic Distance Measuring
EDM	Electronic Distribution Measurement
EDM	Electronic Distributor Modulator [*Automotive engineering*]
EDM	Electronic Drafting Machine
EDM	Employability Development Model (OICC)
EDM	Encyclopedic Dictionary of Mathematics [*A publication*]
EDM	Enforced Dipole Moment
EDM	Engineering Data Management
EDM	Engineering Design Machine
EDM	Engineering Design Memorandum
EDM	Engineering Development Model
EDM	Engineering Drafting Machine
EDM	Engineering Drafting Manual [*Air Force*]
EDM	Engineering Drawing Microfilm (MCD)
EDM	Equipment Code Department Master (MCD)
EDM	Equipment Deadlined for Maintenance [*Army*] (AABC)
EDM	Executive Doctorate in Management [*Weatherhead School of Management, Case Western Reserve University*] (ECON)
EDM	Executive Doctorate in Management
EDM	Exploratory Development Model [*Military*]
Ed M	Master of Education
EDMA	Augsburg/Muehlhausen [*Germany ICAO location identifier*] (ICLI)
EDMA	Ethylene Dimethacrylate [*Organic chemistry*]
EDMA	Ethylene Glycol Dimethacrylate [*Organic chemistry*]
EDMA	European Direct Marketing Association [*Jona/SG, Switzerland*] (EAIO)
EDMA	Extended Direct Memory Access [*Computer science*]
EDMALC	European Direct Marketing Association List Council [*Jona/SG, Switzerland*] [*Inactive*] (EA)
Edmark	Edmark Corp. [*Associated Press*] (SAG)
EDMARS	Educational Document Management and Retrieval System [*Database*] [*Japan*]
EDMB	Biberach Aerodrome Riss [*Germany ICAO location identifier*] (ICLI)
EDMC	Education Management Corp. [*NASDAQ symbol*] (SAG)
EDMC	Energy Data and Modeling Center [*Institute of Energy Economics*] [*Japan Database producer*] (IID)
EDME	Eggenfelden, Nieder Bayern [*Germany ICAO location identifier*] (ICLI)

EDME.......... Electronic Distance Measuring Equipment (MCD)
EDMED........ European Directory of Marine Environmental Data [*Marine science*] (OSRA)
Edm Exch Pr... Edmund's Exchequer Practice [*A publication*] (DLA)
EDMF.......... Extended Data Management Facility
EDMF.......... Fuerstenzell Bei Passau [*Germany ICAO location identifier*] (ICLI)
EDMG.......... Gunzburg/Donauried [*Germany ICAO location identifier*] (ICLI)
EDMH.......... Gunzenhausen [*Germany ICAO location identifier*] (ICLI)
EDMI.......... Electron-Dense Mitochondrial Inclusions [*Oncology*]
EDMI.......... Electronic Distance-Measuring Instrument
EDMI.......... Employees of Diplomatic Missions [*A publication*]
EDMI.......... European Dun's Market Identifiers [*Information service or system*] (IID)
EDMI.......... Illertissen [*Germany ICAO location identifier*] (ICLI)
ED Mich....... United States District Court for the Eastern District of Michigan (DLA)
EDMICS....... Engineering Data Management Information Control System [*DoD*]
Ed M in BT Ed... Master of Education in Business Teacher Education
Ed M in Phy Ed... Master of Education in Physical Education
EDMJ.......... Jesenwang [*Germany ICAO location identifier*] (ICLI)
EDMK.......... Edmark Corp. [*NASDAQ symbol*] (SAG)
EDMK.......... Kempten/Durach [*Germany ICAO location identifier*] (ICLI)
EDML.......... Electric Discharge Mixing LASER (PDAA)
EDML.......... Landshut [*Germany ICAO location identifier*] (ICLI)
EDMM.......... Muenchen [*Germany ICAO location identifier*] (ICLI)
EDMMA........ European Dessert Mixes Manufacturers' Association [*EC*] (ECED)
EDMN.......... Edmonton [*Canada*] (ABBR)
EDMO.......... Oberpfaffenhofen [*Germany ICAO location identifier*] (ICLI)
ED MO......... United States District Court for the Eastern District of Missouri (DLA)
Edmonds' St at Large... Edmonds' New York Statutes at Large [*A publication*] (DLA)
EDMOSFET... Enhancement Depletion Metal-Oxide Semiconductor Field-Effect Transistor (IAA)
EDMP.......... Ethyl (Diisopropylamino)ethylmethyl-phosphonite [*Nerve gas intermediate*] [*Organic chemistry*]
EDMP.......... Vilsbiburg [*Germany ICAO location identifier*] (ICLI)
EDMQ.......... Donauworth/Genderkingen [*Germany ICAO location identifier*] (ICLI)
EDMR.......... Ottobrunn [*Germany ICAO location identifier*] (ICLI)
EDMS.......... Electra Data Management System
EDMS.......... Electronic Document Management System
EDMS.......... Electronic Document Management System
EDMS.......... Engineering Data Management System [*Jet Propulsion Laboratory, NASA*]
EDMS.......... Engineering Data Microreproduction System [*DoD*]
EDMS.......... Engineering Document Management System [*Computer science*]
EDMS.......... Evolutionary Data Management System (IAA)
EDMS.......... Extended Data Management System [*Xerox Corp.*]
EDMS.......... Straubing/Wallmuehle [*Germany ICAO location identifier*] (ICLI)
Edm Sel Ca... Edmonds' New York Select Cases [*A publication*] (DLA)
Edm Sel Cas... Edmonds' New York Select Cases [*A publication*] (DLA)
Edm Stat...... Edmonds' New York Statutes at Large [*A publication*] (DLA)
EDMT.......... Tanheim [*Germany ICAO location identifier*] (ICLI)
EDMU.......... Muenchen [*Germany ICAO location identifier*] (ICLI)
EDMV.......... Vilshofen [*Germany ICAO location identifier*] (ICLI)
EDMW.......... Deggendorf/Steinkirchen [*Germany ICAO location identifier*] (ICLI)
EDMX.......... Oberschleissheim [*Germany ICAO location identifier*] (ICLI)
EDMY.......... Muehldorf [*Germany ICAO location identifier*] (ICLI)
EDN........... Edition
EDN........... Education
EDN........... Electrodesiccation [*Medicine*]
EDN........... Engine Deflector Nozzle
EDN........... Engineering Department Notice (AAG)
EDN........... Engineering Discrepancy Notice [*Nuclear energy*] (NRCH)
EDN........... Enterprise, AL [*Location identifier FAA*] (FAAL)
EDN........... Eosinophil Derived Neurotoxin [*Immunology*]
EDNA.......... Ahlhorn [*Germany ICAO location identifier*] (ICLI)
EDNA.......... Emergency Department Nurses Association [*Later, ENA*] (EA)
EDNB.......... Koeln-Wahn [*Germany ICAO location identifier*] (ICLI)
EDNC.......... United States District Court for the Eastern District of North Carolina (DLA)
EDND.......... Diepholz [*Germany ICAO location identifier*] (ICLI)
EDNET......... Edinburgh Network [*Edinburgh Regional Computer Centre*] [*British*] (NITA)
EDNF.......... Ehlers-Danlos National Foundation (EA)
EDNF.......... Fassberg [*Germany ICAO location identifier*] (ICLI)
EDNG.......... Geilenkirchen [*Germany ICAO location identifier*] (ICLI)
EDNH.......... Husum [*Germany ICAO location identifier*] (ICLI)
EDNJ.......... Jever [*Germany ICAO location identifier*] (ICLI)
EDNK.......... Koeln-Bonn [*Germany ICAO location identifier*] (ICLI)
EDNL.......... Educational (WGA)
EDNL.......... Leck [*Germany ICAO location identifier*] (ICLI)
EDNM.......... Muenster [*Germany ICAO location identifier*] (ICLI)
EDNN.......... Norvenich [*Germany ICAO location identifier*] (ICLI)
EDNO.......... Oldenburg [*Germany ICAO location identifier*] (ICLI)
EDNP.......... Ethyl Dinitropentanoate [*An explosive*]
EDNP.......... Hopsten [*Germany ICAO location identifier*] (ICLI)
EDNQ.......... Hohn [*Germany ICAO location identifier*] (ICLI)
Edns........... Editions [*A publication*]
EDNS.......... Expected Demand not Supplied (ODBW)
EDNT.......... Edunetics Ltd. [*NASDAQ symbol*] (SAG)
EDNT.......... Wittmundhafen [*Germany ICAO location identifier*] (ICLI)
EDNV.......... Kalkar [*Germany ICAO location identifier*] (ICLI)
EDNW.......... Wunstorf [*Germany ICAO location identifier*] (ICLI)
EDNX.......... Goch [*Germany ICAO location identifier*] (ICLI)
EDNY.......... United States District Court for the Eastern District of New York (DLA)
EDO........... Economic Development Operations
EDO........... Edgewood, NM [*Location identifier FAA*] (FAAL)
EDO........... EDO Corp. [*NYSE symbol*] (SPSG)
EDO........... Effective Diameter of Objective [*Optics*]
EDO........... Employee Development Officer
EDO........... Engineering Duty Officer [*Military*]
EDO........... Engineering Duty Only [*Aerospace*]
EDO........... Error Demodulator [*or Determination*] Output (MCD)
EDO........... Estate Duty Office [*British*]
EDO........... Executive Director of Operations (IAA)
EDO........... Exploratory Development Objective [*Military*]
EDO........... Export Development Office [*Department of Commerce*] (IMH)
EDO........... Extended Data Out [*Computer science*]
EDO........... Extended Duration Orbiter [*NASA*]
EDO........... Office of Executive Director for Operations [*Nuclear energy*] (NRCH)
EDOA.......... Schweinfurt [*Germany ICAO location identifier*] (ICLI)
EDOB.......... Garlstedt/Clay Kaserne [*Germany ICAO location identifier*] (ICLI)
EDOC.......... Echterdingen [*Germany ICAO location identifier*] (ICLI)
EDOC.......... Economic Development Opportunity Committee [*Department of Labor*]
EDOC.......... Effective Date of Change (AFM)
EDOC.......... Electrical Description of Operation Chart (IAA)
EDOC.......... Expected Date of Confinement
EDO DRAM... Enhanced Data Output Dynamic Access Random [*Computer science*]
EDOE.......... Ulm [*Germany ICAO location identifier*] (ICLI)
EDOF.......... Wertheim [*Germany ICAO location identifier*] (ICLI)
EDOG.......... Bad Cannstatt Hospital [*Germany ICAO location identifier*] (ICLI)
EDOH.......... Emery [*Germany ICAO location identifier*] (ICLI)
EDOI.......... Vilseck [*Germany ICAO location identifier*] (ICLI)
EDOJ.......... Bonn (Bad Godesberg-Plittersdorf) [*Germany ICAO location identifier*] (ICLI)
EDOK.......... Frankfurt-North [*Germany ICAO location identifier*] (ICLI)
ED Okla....... United States District Court for the Eastern District of Oklahoma (DLA)
EDOL.......... Frankfurt City [*Germany ICAO location identifier*] (ICLI)
EDOM.......... Worms [*Germany ICAO location identifier*] (ICLI)
EDOMP........ Educational Development of Military Personnel
EDON.......... Kaiserslautern [*Germany ICAO location identifier*] (ICLI)
EDONM........ Eddie-Dampened Quasi-Normal Markovian [*Equation*] [*Marine science*] (OSRA)
EDONSW...... Environmental Defender's Office, New South Wales [*Australia*]
EDOP.......... Elimination of Discharge of Pollutants (DICI)
EDOP.......... Schwaebisch Hall/Hessental [*Germany ICAO location identifier*] (ICLI)
EDOQ.......... Heidelberg, United States Army [*Germany ICAO location identifier*] (ICLI)
EDOR.......... Coleman [*Germany ICAO location identifier*] (ICLI)
EDO RAM..... Extended Data Out RAM [*Radom Access Memory*] (CDE)
EDOS.......... Effective Date of Supply
EDOS.......... Electronic Distribution of Software [*Consumer market*] (NITA)
EDOS.......... Estimated Delivery Dates of Supply [*Army*] (INF)
EDOS.......... Extended Disk Operating System [*Computer science*] (BUR)
EDOS.......... Kaiserslautern (Kapaun) [*Germany ICAO location identifier*] (ICLI)
EDOSCOL...... Engineering Duty Officer School [*Military*] (DNAB)
EDOS-MSO... Extended Disc Operating System-Multistage Operations [*Fujitsu*] [*Japan*] (NITA)
EDOS/RJE.... Extended Disc Operating System with Remote Job Entry (PDAA)
EDOT.......... Finthen [*Germany ICAO location identifier*] (ICLI)
EDOU.......... Wiesbaden [*Germany ICAO location identifier*] (ICLI)
EDOV.......... Bad Tolz [*Germany ICAO location identifier*] (ICLI)
EDOW.......... Wildflecken [*Germany ICAO location identifier*] (ICLI)
EDOX.......... Augsburg/Gablingen [*Germany ICAO location identifier*] (ICLI)
EDOY.......... Leighton Barracks [*Germany ICAO location identifier*] (ICLI)
EDOZ.......... Bad Hersfeld [*Germany ICAO location identifier*] (ICLI)
EDP........... Early Decision Plan [*Medical school entrance program*]
EDP........... Early Development Planning
EDP........... Earth Dynamics Program [*Smithsonian Astrophysical Observatory*]
EDP........... Economic Development Program
EDP........... Educational Data Processing (NITA)
EDP........... Effective Directives and Plans (MUGU)
EDP........... Electrodeposition (EG)
EDP........... Electron Decay Profile
EDP........... Electron Dense Particles [*Chemistry*] (DAVI)
EDP........... Electron Diffraction Pattern
EDP........... Electronic Data Processing
EDP........... Electronic Digital Pipette [*Instrumentation*]
EDP........... Electronic Display Panel
EDP........... Electrophoresis Duplicating Paper [*For analytical chemistry*]
EDP........... Embedded Data Processor (SSD)
EDP........... Emergency Defense Plan [*Later, GDP*] (NATG)
EDP........... Emergency Distribution Plan [*DoD*] (AFIT)
EDP........... Emotionally Disturbed Person (LAIN)
EDP........... Employment Development Plan [*Job Training and Partnership Act*] (OICC)
EDP........... End-Diastolic Pressure [*Cardiology*]
EDP........... Engineering Data Package [*Air Force*] (AFIT)
EDP........... Engineering Design Plan
EDP........... Engineering Design Proposal (AAG)
EDP........... Engineering Development Phase (OAG)
EDP........... Enterprise Development Programme [*University of Glasgow*] (AIE)
EDP........... Environmental Protection Division (EERA)
EDP........... Environment Determination Program (SAA)
EDP........... Epatite Degenerative-Proliferativa [*A strain of mouse hepatitis virus*]
EDP........... Equipment Data Package (MCD)

EDP............	Equipment Deadlined for Parts [Army]
EDP............	Equipment Distribution Plan (MCD)
EDP............	Estimated Date of Publication (AAG)
EDP............	Expedite Departure Path [FAA] (TAG)
EDP............	Expeditious Discharge Program [Army]
EDP............	Experimental Development
EDP............	Experimental Dynamic Processor (MUGU)
EDPA..........	Erhardt Development Prehension Assessment
EDPA..........	Exhibit Designers and Producers Association (EA)
ED PA..........	United States District Court for the Eastern District of Pennsylvania (DLA)
EDPAA........	EDP [Electronic Data Processing] Auditors Association (EA)
EDPAC........	Estimated Departure from Pacific (CINC)
EDPC..........	Electronic Data Processing Center
EDPD..........	Electronic Data Processing Device (IAA)
EDPD..........	Energy-Dependent Photoelectron Diffraction (PDAA)
EDPE..........	Electronic Data Processing Equipment
EDPEO........	Electronic Data Processing Equipment Office (IAA)
EDPEP........	Electronic Data Processing Education Program (MHDI)
EDPF..........	Fritzlar [Germany ICAO location identifier] (ICLI)
EDPH..........	Neuhausen Ob Eck [Germany ICAO location identifier] (ICLI)
EDPI...........	Electronic Data Processing Institute (HGAA)
EDP/IR........	Electronic Data Processing/Industry Report
EDP-IR........	Electronic Data Processing - Information Retrieval
EDPL..........	Altenstadt [Germany ICAO location identifier] (ICLI)
Ed PL..........	Eden's Principles of Penal Law [A publication] (DLA)
EDPL..........	Eminent Domain Procedure Law [New York, NY A publication]
EDPLOT.......	Engineering Data Plotting [Computer science]
EDPM..........	Electronic Data Processing Machine [Also translated by some users of such equipment as "Every Damn Problem Multiplied"]
EDPM..........	Electronic Data Processing Magnetic [Tape]
EDPM..........	Laupheim [Germany ICAO location identifier] (ICLI)
EDPN..........	Mendig [Germany ICAO location identifier] (ICLI)
EDPOR........	Electronic Data Processing Operations Research (IAA)
EDPPrB.......	Consol Ed NY,6% Cv B Pref [NYSE symbol] (TTSB)
EDPR..........	Department of Education Procurement Regulations [A publication] (AAGC)
EDPR..........	Engineering Development Part Release (KSC)
EDPR..........	Roth [Germany ICAO location identifier] (ICLI)
EDPrA........	Consol Ed NY,$5 Pfd [NYSE symbol] (TTSB)
EDPrC........	Consol Ed NY,4.65% C Pfd [NYSE symbol] (TTSB)
EDP-RC.......	Expeditious Discharge Program for the Reserve Components [Army] (MCD)
EDPRESS.....	Educational Press Association of America (EA)
EDPRICE......	Energy Detente International Price/Tax Series [Lundberg Survey, Inc.] [No longer available online] [Information service or system] (CRD)
EDPS..........	Electronic Data Processing System
EDPS..........	Electronic Dew Point Sensor
EDPS..........	Equipment Distribution Planning Studies [Army] (AABC)
EDPS..........	Exploratory Development Program Summary [Military]
EDPS..........	Straubing/Mitterharthausen [Germany ICAO location identifier] (ICLI)
EDPSG........	European Diabetes Pregnancy Study Group [of the European Association for the Study of Diabetes] (EAIO)
EDPT..........	Electronic Data Processing Test (AFM)
EDPT..........	Enhanced Drive Parameter Table [Computer science]
EDPT..........	Niederstetten/Bad Mergentheim [Germany ICAO location identifier] (ICLI)
EDPW..........	Ethylenediamine-Pyrocatechol-Water [Mixture for etching silicon sensors]
EDQ............	Economic Distribution Quantity (AFIT)
EDQ............	Extensor Digiti Quinti [Muscle] [Anatomy] (DAVI)
EDQA..........	Electronic Devices Quality Assurance
EDQC..........	Coburg/Brandensteinsebene [Germany ICAO location identifier] (ICLI)
EDQD..........	Bayreuth [Germany ICAO location identifier] (ICLI)
EDQE..........	Burg Feuerstein [Germany ICAO location identifier] (ICLI)
EDQF..........	Ansbach/Petersdorf [Germany ICAO location identifier] (ICLI)
EDQH..........	Herzogenaurach [Germany ICAO location identifier] (ICLI)
EDQK..........	Kulmbach [Germany ICAO location identifier] (ICLI)
EDQL..........	Lichtenfels [Germany ICAO location identifier] (ICLI)
EDQM..........	Hof [Germany ICAO location identifier] (ICLI)
EDQN..........	Neumarkt, Oberpfalz [Germany ICAO location identifier] (ICLI)
EDQNM.......	Eddie-Dampened Quasi-Normal Markovian [Equation] (USDC)
EDQP..........	Rosenthal-Field Plossen [Germany ICAO location identifier] (ICLI)
EDQT..........	Hassfurt/Mainwiesen [Germany ICAO location identifier] (ICLI)
EDQW..........	Weiden, Oberpfalz [Germany ICAO location identifier] (ICLI)
EDQY..........	Coburg/Steinrucken [Germany ICAO location identifier] (ICLI)
EDR............	Early Departure Release At (SAA)
EDR............	Edgemont Resources [Vancouver Stock Exchange symbol]
EDR............	Educator's Desk Reference [A publication]
EDR............	Edward River [Australia Airport symbol] (OAG)
EDR............	Effective Direct Radiation
EDR............	Electrical Distance Recorder [British military] (DMA)
EDR............	Electrodermal Response
EDR............	Electrodialysis Reversing
EDR............	Electromagnetic Dent Removal [Aviation]
EDR............	Electron Decay Rate
EDR............	Electron-Dense Region [in Microorganisms]
EDR............	Electronic Decoy Rocket
EDR............	Emergency Distance Required [Aviation] (AIA)
EDR............	Employee Data Record
EDR............	Encyclopedic Dictionary of Religion
EDR............	Engineering Data Requirements (AAG)
EDR............	Engineering Department [or Division] Report

EDR............	Engineering Design Review (NASA)
EDR............	Engineering Drawing Release
EDR............	Environmental Data Records
EDR............	Environmental Data Resources, Inc. (IID)
EDR............	Environmental Deterioration Rating (PDAA)
EDR............	Equipment Decontamination Room [Nuclear energy] (NUCP)
EDR............	Equivalent Direct Radiation
EDR............	Estimated Date of Resumption (AAG)
EDR............	Ethanol-Disulfiram Reaction [Pharmacology]
EDR............	European Depositary Receipt [Investment term]
EDR............	[The] Executive Desk Register [Information service or system] (IID)
EDR............	Expect Departure Release At [Aviation] (FAAC)
EDR............	Experience Data Report (AAGC)
EDR............	Experimental Development Requirements (CINC)
EDR............	Experiment Data Record
EDR............	Exploratory Development Request [Military]
EDR............	Exploratory Development Requirement [Military]
EDR............	Lineas Aereas Eldorado Ltd. [Colombia] [ICAO designator] (FAAC)
EDR............	Roscoe's Eastern District Reports [Cape Of Good Hope] [A publication] (DLA)
EDRA..........	Engineering Drawing Release Authorization
EDRA..........	Environmental Design Research Association (EA)
EDRA..........	European Digital Road-mapping Association
EDRAM.......	Enhanced Dynamic Random Access Memory [Computer science]
EDRAS........	Economic Data Retrieval and Application System (BUR)
EDRAW........	Erasable Direct Read After Write [Computer science] (IAA)
EDRB..........	Engineering Design Review Board (SAA)
EDRC..........	Engineering Design Research Center [Pittsburgh, PA] [National Science Foundation] (GRD)
EDRCC........	Electronic Data Remote Communications Complex
Ed RD.........	Doctor of Religious Education
EDRE..........	Emergency Deployment Readiness Exercise [Army] (INF)
EdReAn.......	Educational Research Analysts (EA)
Ed Res Perspectives...	Education Research and Perspectives [A publication]
EDRF..........	Bad Duerkheim [Germany ICAO location identifier] (ICLI)
EDRF..........	Endothelial-Derived Relaxing Factor [Biochemistry]
EDRF..........	Endothelium-Derived Vascular Relaxant Factor [Biochemistry]
EDRF..........	Experience Demand Replacement Factor [Navy]
EDRI...........	Electronic Distributors' Research Institute
EDRJ..........	Saarlouis/Dueren [Germany ICAO location identifier] (ICLI)
EDRK..........	Koblenz/Winningen [Germany ICAO location identifier] (ICLI)
EDRL..........	Effective Damage Risk Level
EDRL..........	Lachen/Speyerdorf [Germany ICAO location identifier] (ICLI)
EDRO..........	Office of Executive Director of Regional Operations [Nuclear energy] (NRCH)
EDRP..........	European Demonstrtion Reprocessing Plant [Nuclear energy] (NUCP)
EDR-RC.......	Expeditious Discharge Program for the Reserve Components [Military]
EDRS..........	Education Document Reproduction Service
EDRS..........	Enforcement Document Retrieval System [Environmental Protection Agency] (EPA)
EDRS..........	Engineering Data Retrieval System [Military]
EDRS..........	ERIC [Educational Resources Information Center] Document Reproduction Service [Stanford University] (NTCM)
EDRS..........	ERIC [Educational Resources Information Center] Document Reproduction Service [Department of Education] [Alexandria, VA]
EDRS..........	European Data Relay Satellite
EDRS..........	Expanded Data Reporting System (PDAA)
EDRS..........	Saarbruecken [Germany ICAO location identifier] (ICLI)
EDRT..........	Effective Date of Release from Training
EDRT..........	Trier/Foehren [Germany ICAO location identifier] (ICLI)
EDRY..........	Speyer [Germany ICAO location identifier] (ICLI)
EDRZ..........	Pirmasens/Zweibruecken [Germany ICAO location identifier] (ICLI)
EDS............	Echo Depth Sounder
EDS............	Edema Disease of Swine [Medicine] (DMAA)
EDS............	Edisto Resources Corp. [AMEX symbol] (SPSG)
Eds............	Editions (WDMC)
EDS............	Editorial Data Systems
Eds............	Editors (WDMC)
EDS............	Educational Data System (IAA)
EDS............	Educational Delivery System (OICC)
Ed S...........	Educational Specialist
EDS............	Egg Drop Syndrome [Medicine] (DMAA)
EDS............	Ehlers-Danlos Syndrome [Medicine]
EDS............	El Dorado Systems Canada [Vancouver Stock Exchange symbol]
EDS............	Electrical Distribution System (MCD)
EDS............	Electrodynamic Suspension [Railway technology] (PS)
EDS............	Electron Devices Society (EA)
EDS............	Electronic Data Storage (IAA)
EDS............	Electronic Data Switching System [Computer science] (TEL)
EDS............	Electronic Data System (IEEE)
EDS............	Electronic Data Systems Federal Corp.
EDS............	Electronic Data Systems Ltd. [Information service or system] (IID)
EDS............	Electronic Design Section (SAA)
EDS............	Electronic Differential Lock System [Automotive engineering]
EDS............	Electronic Distribution Show (ITD)
EDS............	Electronic Distribution System (MCD)
EDS............	Electronic Document Service
EDS............	Electronic Document Storage Systems (NITA)
EDS............	Emergency Deorbit System [NASA] (KSC)
EDS............	Emergency Detection System
EDS............	Emergency Disablement System
EDS............	Emergency Distribution System (MCD)
EDS............	Employability Development Services [US Employment Service] [Department of Labor]

EDS	Enamel Double Silk [Wire insulation] (AAG)
EDS	Energy Data System [Databank] [Environmental Protection Agency] (IID)
EDS	Energy Depot Systems
EDS	Energy Dispersive Spectroscopy
EDS	Energy Dispersive System [Microscopy]
EDs	Engagement Direction Station (SAA)
EDS	Engine Diagnostic System
EDS	Engine Dynamometer Schedule [Automotive emissions testing]
EDS	Engineering Data Sheet
EDS	Engineering Data Software
EDS	Engineering Data Systems [DoD]
EDS	Engineering Drafting Software [Calcomp Ltd.] [Software package] (NCC)
EDS	English Dialect Society
EDS	Entry Data Subsystem
EDS	Environmental Data Service [Later, NESDIS] [Washington, DC National Oceanic and Atmospheric Administration] (EA)
EDS	Equatorial Dynamics Study [Marine science] (MSC)
EDS	Equipment Decontamination Station [Military]
EDS	Error Detection System (KSC)
EDS	Estimated Date of Separation
EDS	Estimated Daughter Superiority [Genetics] (OA)
EDS	European Distribution System [DoD]
EDS	Excess Disposition System (MCD)
EDS	Excessive Daytime Sleepiness
EDS	Exchangeable Disc Stores (NITA)
EDS	Exchangeable Disk Storage [Computer science]
EDS	Experiment Data System
EDS	Explosive Detection Systems [FAA] (TAG)
EDS	Explosive Device System (KSC)
EDS	Express Delivery Service
EDS	Extended Data Stream [Medicine] (MEDA)
EDS	Extradimensional Shift [Psychometrics]
EDS	Exxon Donor Solvent Process [Coal liquefaction]
EDS	IEEE Electron Devices Society (EA)
EDS	Orangeburg, SC [Location identifier FAA] (FAAL)
EdS	Specialist in Education (GAGS)
EDSA	Effective Date of Change in Station Assignment [Military]
EDSA	Epifanio de los Santos [Avenue where Philippine President Marcos' government tanks were stopped by unarmed citizens] [In the EDSA Revolution of February, 1986]
EDSA	European Distribution System Aircraft [DoD]
EDSA	Landsberg [Germany ICAO location identifier] (ICLI)
EDSAC	Electronic Data Storage Automatic Computer (IAA)
EDSAC	Electronic Delay Storage Automatic Calculator [or Computer] [1949]
EDSAC	Electronic Discrete Sequential Automatic Computer [University of Manchester, 1949] [British] (IEEE)
EDSAI	Educational Dealers and Suppliers Association International (EA)
EDSA-IL	Electric Service Dealers Association of Illinois (SRA)
EDS & R	Engineering Data Storage and Retrieval [Military]
EDSAR	Engineering Drawing Status and Release (DNAB)
EDSB	Buchel [Germany ICAO location identifier] (ICLI)
EDSC	Engineering Data Service Center [Air Force]
EDSC	Engineering Data Support Center [Air Force] (CET)
EDSC	European Deaf Swimming Championships [British]
EDSD	Engineering and Development Services Department [Naval Air Development Center]
EDSD	Leipheim [Germany ICAO location identifier] (ICLI)
EDSE	Edison Sault Electric Co. (MHDW)
EDSE	Erding [Germany ICAO location identifier] (ICLI)
EDSE	ESELCO, Inc. [NASDAQ symbol] (SPSG)
EDSF	Fuerstenfeldbruck [Germany ICAO location identifier] (ICLI)
EDSFC	Electronic Data Systems Federal Corp.
EDSG	Bremgarten [Germany ICAO location identifier] (ICLI)
EDSI	Equivalent Delivered Source Instructions
EDSI	Ingoldstadt [Germany ICAO location identifier] (ICLI)
EDSIL	Engineering Development Systems Integration Laboratory
EDSIM	Event-Based Discrete Simulation (PDAA)
ED SK	Engineering Department Sketch (MSA)
EDSK	Kaufbeuren [Germany ICAO location identifier] (ICLI)
EDSL	End-Diastolic Segment Length [Cardiology]
EDSL	Lechfeld [Germany ICAO location identifier] (ICLI)
EDSM	Memmingen [Germany ICAO location identifier] (ICLI)
EDSN	Neubiberg [Germany ICAO location identifier] (ICLI)
EDS-NWT	Eskimo Dog Society of the Northwest Territories [Defunct] (EA)
Ed Sp	Education Specialist
EDSP	Engineering Design Support to Production (MCD)
EDSP	Pferdsfeld [Germany ICAO location identifier] (ICLI)
Ed Spec	Education Specialist
EDSR	Electronic Digital Slide Rule (IAA)
EDS/R	Engineering Data Storage and Retrieval Project [Picatinny Arsenal] [Dover, NJ] [Military]
EDSR	Exploratory Development Summary Report [Military]
EDSS	Engineering and Development Support Services (KSC)
EDSS	Environmental Data Support System (MCD)
EDSS	Environment Decision-Making Support System [Computer science] (EERA)
EDSS	Equipment Deployment and Storage System [MTMC] (TAG)
EDSS	Expanded Disability Status Scale [Clinical medicine]
EDSS	Expanded Kurtzke Disability Status Scale [Medicine]
EDSS	Expert Decision-Support System [Computer science] (ODBW)
EDSS	Extended Disability Status Scale [Medicine]
EDST	Eastern Daylight Saving Time
EDST	Elastic Diaphragm Switch Technology [IBM Corp.] (MCD)

ED STAFF	Editorial Staff (DGA)
EDSTAT	Educational Statistics [Search system]
EDSTAT	Educational Statistics Information Access Service [Databank] (NITA)
EDSTM	Environmental Data Service Technical Memoranda [National Oceanic and Atmospheric Administration] (NOAA)
EDSU	Neuburg [Germany ICAO location identifier] (ICLI)
EDSV	Enamel Double Silk Varnish [Wire insulation]
EDSV	Mebstetten [Germany ICAO location identifier] (ICLI)
EDSWS	Edisto Resources Wrrt [AMEX symbol] (TTSB)
EDSX	Electronic Digital System Cross-Connect (ACRL)
EDT	Eastern Daylight Time
EDT	Edict (ABBR)
EDT	Edisto Resources [AMEX symbol] (TTSB)
EDT	Edisto Resources Corp. [AMEX symbol] (SAG)
EDT	Edit (ABBR)
EDT	Editor
EDT	Effective Date of Training
EDT	Effective Diagenetic Temperature [Geology]
EDT	Electrical Discharge Tube (MSA)
EDT	Electrodeless Discharge Tube
EDT	Electronic Data Transmission (AAG)
EDT	Employability Development Team (OICC)
EDT	Energy Dissipation Tests (NRCH)
EDT	Engineering Description Tape (IAA)
EDT	Engineering Design Test
EDT	Engineering Development Test
EDT	Engineering Drawing Tree
EDT	Equipment Downtime
EDT	Equipment Drain Tank [Nuclear energy] (NRCH)
EDT	Estimated Delivery Times
EDT	Estimated Departure Time
EDT	Estimated Discharge Time
EDT	Ethylenediamine Tartrate [Organic chemistry]
EDT	Ethylene Diamine Tartrate (IDOE)
EDTA	Aalen-Heidenheim/Elchingen [Germany ICAO location identifier] (ICLI)
EDTA	Edathamil (MAE)
EDTA	Edetic Acid [Organic chemistry] (AAMN)
EDTA	Ethylenediaminetetraacetate [Also, EDETATE, enta] [Organic chemistry]
EDTA	Ethylenediaminetetra-Acetic Acid [Also called edathamil and edetic acid] [Organic chemistry] (DAVI)
EDTA	Ethylene Diaminetetracetic Acid (DOG)
EDTA	Ethylenedinitrilo Tetraacetic Acid [Organic chemistry] (NRCH)
EDTAN	Ethylenediaminetetraacetonitrile [Also, EDTN] [Organic chemistry]
EDTB	Baden-Baden [Germany ICAO location identifier] (ICLI)
EDTC	Engineering Design Test, Contractor (MCD)
EDTC	Engineering Development and Test Center [Mack Trucks, Inc.] [Allentown, PA]
EDTCC	Electronic Data Traffic Control Center [or Complex]
EDTCC	Electronic Data Transmission Communications Central
EDTD	Donaueschingen/Villingen [Germany ICAO location identifier] (ICLI)
EDTD	Edited (ABBR)
EDTE	Effective Date [Military] (AFIT)
EDTE	Schwenningen Am Nickar [Germany ICAO location identifier] (ICLI)
ED Tenn	United States District Court for the Eastern District of Tennessee (DLA)
EDTEP	Engineering Design Test and Evaluation Program
ED Tex	United States District Court for the Eastern District of Texas (DLA)
EDTF	Freiburg/Breisgau [Germany ICAO location identifier] (ICLI)
EDTG	Editing (ABBR)
EDTG	Engineering Design Test, Government (MCD)
EDTH	Heubach, Wurttemberg [Germany ICAO location identifier] (ICLI)
Ed Theory	Educational Theory [A publication] (BRI)
EDTK	Karlsruhe/Forchheim [Germany ICAO location identifier] (ICLI)
EDTL	Editorial (ABBR)
EDTL	Electronic Technology & Devices Laboratory [Army] (RDA)
EDTLZ	Editorialize (ABBR)
EDTLZD	Editorialized (ABBR)
EDTLZG	Editorializing (ABBR)
EDTM	Mengen [Germany ICAO location identifier] (ICLI)
EDTN	Edition (ABBR)
EDTN	Ethylenediaminetetraacetonitrile [Also, EDTAN] [Organic chemistry]
EDTN	Nabern/Teck [Germany ICAO location identifier] (ICLI)
EDTNA/ERCA	European Dialysis and Transplant Nurses Association/European Renal Care Association [Formerly, European Dialysis and Transplant Nurses Associaton] (EA)
EDTO	Offenburg/Baden [Germany ICAO location identifier] (ICLI)
EDTPO	Ethylenediaminetetra(methylenephosphonic Acid) [Organic chemistry]
EDTR	Editor (ABBR)
EDTR	Experimental, Developmental, Test, and Research
EDTRASUPPDET	Education and Training Support Detachment [Military] (DNAB)
EDTRASUPPTRADEV FEO	Education and Training Support Training Device Field Engineering Office [Military] (DNAB)
EDTRSP	Editorship (ABBR)
EDTS	Equipment Drain Treatment System [Nuclear energy] (NRCH)
EDTSP	Editorship (ABBR)
EDTSR	Electronic Dial Tone Speed Register [Bell System]
EDTV	Enhanced [or Extended] Definition Television (PCM)
EDTV	Extended-Definition Television [in ED Beta] [Sony Corp.] (PS)
EDTX	Schwaebisch Hall/Weckrieden [Germany ICAO location identifier] (ICLI)
EDTY	Friedrichshafen-Lowental [Germany ICAO location identifier] (ICLI)
EDTZ	Konstanz [Germany ICAO location identifier] (ICLI)

EDU	Dundee [*Scotland*] [*Seismograph station code, US Geological Survey*] (SEIS)
EDU	Early Deploying Unit (MCD)
EDU	Eating Disorder Unit [*Medicine*] (DAVI)
EDU	Education (ADA)
edu	Educational Organization [*Internet address domain name*] (CDE)
Edu	Educo [*Record label*]
EDU	Electrical Distribution Unit
EDU	Electronic Display Unit
EDU	Electronic Distributor Unit [*Automotive engineering*]
EDU	Endue (ABBR)
EDU	Engineering Development Unit [*NASA*] (NASA)
EDU	Enterprise and Deregulation Unit (AIE)
EDU	Environmental Diving Unit [*Marine science*] (MSC)
EDU	Ethiopian Democratic Union [*Political party*] (PD)
EDU	Europaeische Demokratische Union [*European Democratic Union*] [*Austria*] (EAIO)
EDU	Experimental Diving Unit [*Research center British*]
EDU	Exponential Decay Unit [*Physics*] (IAA)
EDU	Ministry of Education, Information Centre [*Ontario*] [*UTLAS symbol*]
EDUC	Educated [*or Education*] (AFM)
educ	Education (VRA)
EDUC	Education
EDUC	Educational Development [*NASDAQ symbol*] (TTSB)
EDUC	Educational Development Corp. [*NASDAQ symbol*] (NQ)
EDUC	Eductor (MSA)
EDUCATSS	Education Cataloguing Support System [*UTLAS symbol*]
EDUCB	Educable (ABBR)
EDUCD	Educated (ABBR)
EDUCG	Educating (ABBR)
EducIns	Educational Insights, Inc. [*Associated Press*] (SAG)
EDUCL	Educational
EDUCL	Educational
EDUCN	Education
Educnl	Educational
EDUCNLST	Educationalist (ABBR)
EDUCOM	Educational Use of Computers
EDUCOM	Interuniversity Communications Council (EA)
EDUCR	Educator (ABBR)
EDUCV	Educative (ABBR)
EDUD	Detmold [*Germany ICAO location identifier*] (ICLI)
EduDv	Educational Development Corp. [*Associated Press*] (SAG)
EDUG	European Datamanager Users Group [*London, England*] (CSR)
EDUH	Hildesheim [*Germany ICAO location identifier*] (ICLI)
EDUI/O	Error Detection Unit Input/Output
EDUK	Rheindahlen [*Germany ICAO location identifier*] (ICLI)
EDUL	Laarbruch [*Germany ICAO location identifier*] (ICLI)
EDUN	Nordhorn Range [*Germany ICAO location identifier*] (ICLI)
EDUNET	Education Network [*EDUCOM*]
Edunetic	Edunetics Ltd. [*Associated Press*] (SAG)
EDUO	Guetersloh [*Germany ICAO location identifier*] (ICLI)
EDUP	Ethiopian Democratic Unity Party [*Political party*] (EY)
EDUR	Bruggen [*Germany ICAO location identifier*] (ICLI)
EDUR	Engineering Drawing Usage Record [*DAC*]
EDUS	Edusoft Ltd. [*NASDAQ symbol*] (SAG)
EDUS	Soest [*Germany ICAO location identifier*] (ICLI)
EDUSAT	Educational Satellite (KSC)
EDUSE	Edusoft Ltd [*NASDAQ symbol*] (TTSB)
Edusoft	Edusoft Ltd. [*Associated Press*] (SAG)
EDUW	Wildenrath [*Germany ICAO location identifier*] (ICLI)
'Eduy	'Eduyyoth (BJA)
EDV	Eastern Diverging Volcanism [*Geology*]
EDV	Electro-Dynamic Venturi (PDAA)
EDV	Electronic Depressurizing Valve (MCD)
EDV	Elektronische Datenverarbeitung [*Electronic Data Processing - EDP*] [*German*]
EDV	Emission Data Vehicle [*Exhaust emissions testing*] [*Automotive engineering*]
EDV	End-Diastolic Volume [*Cardiology*]
EDV	Epidermodysplasia Verruciformis [*Medicine*]
EDV	Equivalent Daylight Visibility (PDAA)
EDVA	Bad Gandersheim [*Germany ICAO location identifier*] (ICLI)
ED VA	United States District Court for the Eastern District of Virginia (DLA)
EDVAC	Electronic Digital-Vernier Analog Computer (SAA)
EDVAC	Electronic Discrete Variable Automatic Calculator [*or Computer*] (MCD)
EDVAP	Electronic Digital-Vernier Analog Plotter (MUGU)
EDVB	Braunschweig [*Germany ICAO location identifier*] (ICLI)
EDVC	Celle/Arloh [*Germany ICAO location identifier*] (ICLI)
EDVE	Braunschweig [*Germany ICAO location identifier*] (ICLI)
EdVENT	Educational Events [*Timeplace, Inc.*] [*Waltham, MA*] [*Information service or system*] (IID)
EDVH	Hodenhagen [*Germany ICAO location identifier*] (ICLI)
EDVI	End-Diastolic Volume Index [*Cardiology*] (DAVI)
EDVI	Hoxter/Holzminden [*Germany ICAO location identifier*] (ICLI)
EDVK	Kassel/Calden [*Germany ICAO location identifier*] (ICLI)
EDVL	Holleberg [*Germany ICAO location identifier*] (ICLI)
EDVM	Kassel-Mittelfeld [*Germany ICAO location identifier*] (ICLI)
EDVN	Northeim [*Germany ICAO location identifier*] (ICLI)
EDVP	Peine/Eddesse [*Germany ICAO location identifier*] (ICLI)
EDVR	Enlisted Distribution and Verification Report
EDVR	Rinteln [*Germany ICAO location identifier*] (ICLI)
EDVS	Salzgitter/Drutte [*Germany ICAO location identifier*] (ICLI)
EDVU	Uelzen [*Germany ICAO location identifier*] (ICLI)
EDVV	Hannover [*Germany ICAO location identifier*] (ICLI)

EDVX	Gifhorn [*Germany ICAO location identifier*] (ICLI)
EDVY	Porta Westfalica [*Germany ICAO location identifier*] (ICLI)
EDW	Earth Departure Window [*Aerospace*]
EDW	Edwards [*California*] [*Airport symbol Obsolete*] (OAG)
EDW	Edwards Air Force Base [*California*] [*TACAN station*] (NASA)
Edw	Edwards' Chester Palatine Courts [*England*] [*A publication*] (DLA)
Edw	Edwards' English Admiralty Reports [*A publication*] (DLA)
Edw	Edwards' New York Chancery Reports [*A publication*] (DLA)
Edw	Edwards' Reports [*2, 3 Missouri*] [*A publication*] (DLA)
EDW	El Dorado & Wesson Railway Co. [*AAR code*]
EDW	Estimated Dry Weight [*Nephrology*] (DAVI)
EDWA	Evaluation, Decision and Weapon Assignment [*Army*]
EDWA	Norden-Hage [*Germany ICAO location identifier*] (ICLI)
EDWAA	Economic Dislocation and Worker Adjustment Assistance [*Department of Labor*]
EDWAAA	Economic Dislocation and Worker Adjustment Assistance Act of 1988 (WYGK)
Edw Abr	Edwards' Abridgment of Prerogative Court Cases [*A publication*] (DLA)
Edw Abr	Edwards' Abridgment, Privy Council [*A publication*] (DLA)
Edw Adm	Edwards' English Admiralty Reports [*A publication*] (DLA)
Edw Adm (Eng)	Edwards' English Admiralty Reports [*A publication*] (DLA)
Edw Adm Jur	Edwards' Admiralty Jurisdiction [*1847*] [*A publication*] (DLA)
Edwards	Edwards [*A. G.*] & Sons, Inc. [*Associated Press*] (SAG)
Edwards' Chr R	Edwards' New York Chancery Reports [*A publication*] (DLA)
Edwards' Rep	Edwards' New York Chancery Reports [*A publication*] (DLA)
ED Wash	United States District Court for the Eastern District of Washington (DLA)
EDWB	Bremerhaven/Am Luneort [*Germany ICAO location identifier*] (ICLI)
Edw Bail	Edwards on the Law of Bailments [*A publication*] (DLA)
Edw Bailm	Edwards on the Law of Bailments [*A publication*] (DLA)
Edw Bills	Edwards on Bills and Notes [*A publication*] (DLA)
Edw Bills & N	Edwards on Bills and Notes [*A publication*] (DLA)
Edw Brok & F	Edwards on Factors and Brokers [*A publication*] (DLA)
EDWC	Damme [*Germany ICAO location identifier*] (ICLI)
EDWC	Electrical Discharge Wire Cutting [*Manufacturing term*]
Edw Ch	Edwards' New York Chancery Reports [*A publication*] (DLA)
Edw Chan	Edwards' New York Chancery Reports [*A publication*] (DLA)
Edw Ch (NY)	Edwards' New York Chancery Reports [*A publication*] (DLA)
Edw Conf	Edward the Confessor (King of England) (DLA)
EDWD	Lemwerder [*Germany ICAO location identifier*] (ICLI)
EDWE	Emden [*Germany ICAO location identifier*] (ICLI)
Edw Eccl Jur	Edwards on Ecclesiastical Jurisdiction [*A publication*] (DLA)
EDWF	Leer-Nuttermoor [*Germany ICAO location identifier*] (ICLI)
Edw Fac	Edwards on Factors and Brokers [*A publication*] (DLA)
EDWG	Wangerooge [*Germany ICAO location identifier*] (ICLI)
Edw Gam	Edwards' Law of Gaming [*A publication*] (DLA)
EDWH	Oldenburg/Hatten [*Germany ICAO location identifier*] (ICLI)
EDWI	Wilhelmshaven/Mariensiel [*Germany ICAO location identifier*] (ICLI)
EDWIN	Editorial Word Processing International Network (DGA)
ED Wis	United States District Court for the Eastern District of Wisconsin (DLA)
EDWJ	Juist [*Germany ICAO location identifier*] (ICLI)
Edw Jur	Edwards' Juryman's Guide [*A publication*] (DLA)
EDWL	Langeoog [*Germany ICAO location identifier*] (ICLI)
Edw Lead Dec	Edwards' Leading Decisions in Admiralty [*Edwards' Admiralty Reports*] [*A publication*] (DLA)
EDWM	Weser-Wumme [*Germany ICAO location identifier*] (ICLI)
Edw MO	Edwards' Reports [*2, 3 Missouri*] [*A publication*] (DLA)
EDWN	Nordhorn/Klausheide [*Germany ICAO location identifier*] (ICLI)
EDWNT	Endowment (ABBR)
Edw (NY)	Edwards' New York Chancery Reports [*A publication*] (DLA)
EDWO	Osnabruck/Atterheide [*Germany ICAO location identifier*] (ICLI)
Edw Part	Edwards on Parties in Chancery [*A publication*] (DLA)
Edw PC	Edwards' English Prize Cases [*A publication*] (DLA)
Edw Pleas	Edwards' Pleasantries of the Courts of New York [*A publication*] (DLA)
Edw Pr Cas	Edwards' English Prize Cases [*A publication*] (DLA)
Edw Pr Ct Cas	Edwards' Abridgment of Prerogative Court Cases [*A publication*] (DLA)
EDWQ	Ganderkesee-Atlas Aerodrome [*Germany ICAO location identifier*] (ICLI)
EDWR	Borkum [*Germany ICAO location identifier*] (ICLI)
ED/WR	Edge Wear [*Deltiology*]
Edw Rec	Edwards on Receivers in Equity [*A publication*] (DLA)
Edw Ref	Edwards on the Law of Referees [*A publication*] (DLA)
Edw Rep	Edwards' New York Chancery Reports [*A publication*] (DLA)
EDWS	Norden/Norddeich [*Germany ICAO location identifier*] (ICLI)
Edw St Act	Edwards on the Stamp Act [*A publication*] (DLA)
EDWT	Nordenham-Einswarden [*Germany ICAO location identifier*] (ICLI)
EDWTH	End-Diastolic Wall Thickness [*Cardiology*]
Edw (Tho)	Edwards' English Admiralty Reports [*A publication*] (DLA)
EDWU	Varrelbusch [*Germany ICAO location identifier*] (ICLI)
EDWV	Verden/Scharnhorst [*Germany ICAO location identifier*] (ICLI)
EDWW	Bremen [*Germany ICAO location identifier*] (ICLI)
EDWY	Norderney [*Germany ICAO location identifier*] (ICLI)
EDX	Edna, TX [*Location identifier FAA*] (FAAL)
EDX	Electrodiagnosis [*Medicine*]
EDX	Energy Dispersive X-Ray
EDX	Event Driven Executive [*IBM Corp.*]
EDXA	Energy Dispersive X-Ray Analysis [*or Analyzer*] [*Also, EDXRA*]
EDXB	Heide/Busum [*Germany ICAO location identifier*] (ICLI)
EDXC	European DX Council [*Huntingdon, Cambridgeshire, England*] (EAIO)
EDXD	Energy Dispersive X-Ray Diffraction [*Atomic structure determination*]
EDXE	Rheine/Eschendorf [*Germany ICAO location identifier*] (ICLI)

EDXF .... Energy Dispersive X-Ray Fluorescence [*Spectrometry*]
EDXF .... Flensburg/Schaferhaus [*Germany ICAO location identifier*] (ICLI)
EDXH .... Helgoland/Dune [*Germany ICAO location identifier*] (ICLI)
EDXM .... St. Michaelisdonn [*Germany ICAO location identifier*] (ICLI)
EDXO .... St. Peter/Ording [*Germany ICAO location identifier*] (ICLI)
EDXR .... Rendsburg/Schachtholm [*Germany ICAO location identifier*] (ICLI)
EDXRA .... Energy Dispersive X-Ray Analysis [*or Analyzer*] [*Also, EDXA*]
EDXRF .... Energy Dispersive X-Ray Fluorescence [*Spectrometry*]
EDXRF .... Excitation Dispersive X-Ray Fluorescence [*Chemical analysis*]
EDXRS .... Energy Dispersive X-Ray Spectrometry
EDXS .... Energy Dispersive X-Ray Spectrum
EDXW .... Westerland/Sylt [*Germany ICAO location identifier*] (ICLI)
EDXY .... Wyk Auf Fohr [*Germany ICAO location identifier*] (ICLI)
EDY............ Educationally Disadvantaged Youth (EDAC)
EDYA .... Ampfing/Waldkraiburg [*Germany ICAO location identifier*] (ICLI)
EDYB .... Arnbruck [*Germany ICAO location identifier*] (ICLI)
EDYG .... Beilingries [*Germany ICAO location identifier*] (ICLI)
EDYG .... Eddying (ABBR)
EDYL .... Leutkirch/Unterzeil [*Germany ICAO location identifier*] (ICLI)
EDYN .... Envirodyne Inds [*NASDAQ symbol*] (TTSB)
EDYN .... Envirodyne Industries, Inc. [*NASDAQ symbol*] (SAG)
EDYN .... Nittenau/Bruck [*Germany ICAO location identifier*] (ICLI)
EDYNMT ...... Electric Dynamometer [*Engineering*]
EDYR .... Regensburg-Oberhub [*Germany ICAO location identifier*] (ICLI)
EDYV .... Vogtareuth [*Germany ICAO location identifier*] (ICLI)
EDZ............ Emission Density Zoning [*Environmental Protection Agency*] (GFGA)
EDZA .... Mittenwald-Luttensee [*Germany ICAO location identifier*] (ICLI)
EDZB .... Bergen-Hohne [*Germany ICAO location identifier*] (ICLI)
EDZD .... Ulm [*Germany ICAO location identifier*] (ICLI)
EDZE .... Sengwarden [*Germany ICAO location identifier*] (ICLI)
EDZF .... Fuerstenfeldbruck [*Germany ICAO location identifier*] (ICLI)
EDZG .... Oldenburg [*Germany ICAO location identifier*] (ICLI)
EDZH .... Garmersdorf [*Germany ICAO location identifier*] (ICLI)
EDZI .... Trier [*Germany ICAO location identifier*] (ICLI)
EDZJ .... Idar-Oberstein [*Germany ICAO location identifier*] (ICLI)
EDZK .... Karlsruhe [*Germany ICAO location identifier*] (ICLI)
EDZL .... Flensburg [*Germany ICAO location identifier*] (ICLI)
EDZM .... Muenster-Gievenbeck [*Germany ICAO location identifier*] (ICLI)
EDZN .... Koblenz [*Germany ICAO location identifier*] (ICLI)
EDZO .... Motne-Centre, Offenbach [*Germany ICAO location identifier*] (ICLI)
EDZQ .... Quickborn [*Germany ICAO location identifier*] (ICLI)
EDZR .... Aurich [*Germany ICAO location identifier*] (ICLI)
EDZS .... Bredstedt [*Germany ICAO location identifier*] (ICLI)
EDZT .... Altenstadt [*Germany ICAO location identifier*] (ICLI)
EDZU .... Appenweiler [*Germany ICAO location identifier*] (ICLI)
EDZW .... Offenbach [*Germany ICAO location identifier*] (ICLI)
EDZX .... Traben-Trarbach [*Germany ICAO location identifier*] (ICLI)
EDZY .... Weiden [*Germany ICAO location identifier*] (ICLI)
EE .... Eagle Commuter Airlines [*ICAO designator*] (AD)
EE .... Early English [*Language, etc.*]
EE .... Eased Edge (DAC)
EE .... Eastern Establishment [*Politics*]
EE .... Echo Equalizer (IAA)
EE .... Ecosystem Evaluation (GNE)
EE .... Edit Error [*Military*] (AFIT)
EE .... Edward Elgar [*Publisher*] [*British*]
EE .... El Paso Electric [*AMEX symbol*] (TTSB)
E/E .... Electrical/Electronic
EE .... Electrical Engineer [*or Engineering*]
EE .... Electrodynamic Explorer [*NASA*]
EE .... Electronic Editing [*Telecommunications*]
EE .... Electronic Editions [*Cowles Publishing Co.*] [*Information service or system*] (IID)
EE .... Electronic Engineering
EE .... Electronics Engineering Division [*Coast Guard*]
EE .... Electronics to Electronics
EE .... Elements of Expense [*Army*] (AABC)
EE .... Elevator Equipment Room [*NFPA pre-fire planning symbol*] (NFPA)
EE .... El Paso Electric Co. [*AMEX symbol*] (SAG)
EE .... Embassador Extraordinary [*Diplomacy*] [*British*] (ROG)
EE .... Embryo Extract
EE .... Emergency Establishment [*Military*] (NATG)
EE .... Emerson Electric Co. (MCD)
EE .... Employee (OICC)
EE .... Enantiomeric Excess [*Organic chemistry*]
EE .... End Effector (MCD)
EE .... End-to-End [*Anastomosis*] [*Medicine*] (DAVI)
E-E .... End to End [*Technical drawings*] (NASA)
EE .... Enentarzid (BJA)
EE .... Energy Efficiency [*Electrochemistry*]
EE .... Energy Enterprises [*Information service or system*] (IID)
EE .... Energy Expenditure
EE .... Engagement Effectiveness [*Army*] (AABC)
EE .... Enge's Entourage (EA)
EE .... Engineering Economics
EE .... Engineering Estimate
EE .... English Earl (ROG)
EE .... English Electric [*Commercial firm British*]
EE .... English Ell [*Unit of measure*] (ROG)
EE .... English Estates [*British*] (GEA)
EE .... English Exchequer Reports [*A publication*] (DLA)
EE .... Enki and Eridu (BJA)
EE .... Enter Exponent [*Computer science*]
EE .... Environmental Economics
EE .... Environmental Encyclopedia [*A publication*]

EE .... Envoy Extraordinary [*Department of State*]
EE .... Equine Encephalitis
EE .... Equipment Engaged Tone [*Telecommunications*] (IAA)
EE .... Equity Earnings [*Accounting*]
EE .... Equity Exchequer [*Legal term*] (DLA)
EE .... Error Expected (IAA)
EE .... Errors Excepted [*Business term*]
E-E .... Erythematous-Edematous [*Reaction*] [*Medicine*]
EE .... Ethniki Enosis [*National Unity Party*] [*Greek*] (PPE)
EE .... Ethynyl Estradiol [*Endocrinology*]
EE .... Euer Ehrwuerden [*Your Reverence*] [*German*]
EE .... Eurocity Express [*Airline*] [*British*]
ee---- .... Europe, Eastern [*MARC geographic area code Library of Congress*] (LCCP)
EE .... Euzkadiko Ezkerra [*Basque Left*] [*Spain Political party*] (PPE)
EE .... Evreiskaia Entsiklopediia [*A publication*] (BJA)
EE .... Executair Ltd. [*Nigeria*] [*ICAO designator*] (ICDA)
EE .... Executive Engineer [*British*] (DCTA)
EE .... Exoelectron (PDAA)
EE .... Exoelectron Emission (PDAA)
EE .... Exoerythrocytic [*Medicine*]
EE .... Expenditure and Employment (OICC)
EE .... Experimental Establishment [*RAF*] [*British*]
EE .... Expiration of Enlistment
EE .... Exponential Equation
EE .... Extended Edition [*IBM Corp.*] (BYTE)
EE .... External Entity
EE .... External Environment
EE .... Eye and Ear
EE3ME .... Ethinyloestradiol-3-Methyl Ether [*or Mestranol*] [*Pharmacology*] (DAVI)
EEA .... Adrian College, Adrian, MI [*OCLC symbol*] (OCLC)
EEA .... Eastern Economic Association
EEA .... Ecurie Ecosse Association Ltd. [*British*] (BI)
EEA .... Educational Exhibitors' Association [*British*] (BI)
EEA .... Electric Energy Association [*Later, EEI*] (EA)
EEA .... Electroencephalic Audiometry [*Medicine*] (MAE)
EEA .... Electromagnetic Environment Analysis
EEA .... Electronic Engineering Association [*British*]
EEA .... Electrostatic Energy Analyzer [*Instrumentation*]
EEA .... Emergency Employment Act [*1971*]
EEA .... Empresa Ecuatoriana de Aviacion [*Ecuador*] [*ICAO designator*] (FAAC)
EEA .... End-to-End Anastomosis [*Medicine*]
EEA .... Energy and Environmental Analysis [*Environmental Protection Agency*] (GFGA)
EEA .... Engineering Evaluation Article (AAG)
EEA .... Equal Employment Act
EEA .... Essential Elements of Analysis
EEA .... Estimated Expenditure of Ammunition (AABC)
EEA .... Ethylene-Ethyl Acetate [*Organic chemistry*]
EEA .... Ethylene-Ethyl Acrylate [*Copolymer*] [*Organic chemistry*]
EEA .... Europaeische Evangelische Allianz [*European Evangelical Alliance - EEA*] (EAIO)
EEA .... European Economic Area (ECON)
EEA .... European Environment Agency
EEA .... Evaluation Elements of Analysis (MCD)
EEA .... Excellence in Education Act (GFGA)
EEA .... Explosive Embedment Anchor (PDAA)
EEAA .... Employee Educational Assistance Act of 1978 (WYGK)
EEAA .... Environmental Education Advisers Association [*British*] (DBA)
EEAC .... Equal Employment Advisory Council (EA)
EE & H........ Electricity, Electronics, and Hydraulics School (DNAB)
EE & MP...... Envoy Extraordinary and Minister Plenipotentiary [*Department of State*]
EE & RM...... Elementary Electrical and Radio Material [*Training School*] [*Navy*]
EE & W........ Emperor of the East and West [*Freemasonry*] (ROG)
EEAP .... Emergency Egress Air Pack [*NASA*] (KSC)
EEAP .... Enlisted Education Advancement Program [*Military*] (DNAB)
EEASA .... Engineering Employers' Association, South Australia
EEAT .... Emergency Expected Approach Time (DNAB)
EEAT .... Emotional-Ethical Attitudes Test [*Psychometrics*]
EEAT .... End, Evening Astronomical Twilight (MCD)
EEB .... Bendix Engineering Development Center, Southfield, MI [*OCLC symbol*] (OCLC)
EEB .... Eastern Electricity Board [*British*]
EEB .... Ecology and Evolutionary Biology [*A discipline division*]
EEB .... Economic Engineering Branch [*Army Tank Automotive Command*] [*Warren, MI*]
EEB .... Effective External Boundary [*Forestry*]
EEB .... Euroberlin [*France ICAO designator*] (FAAC)
EEB .... European Environmental Bureau [*Belgium*]
EEB .... European Environment Bureau (EERA)
EEB .... Exports to Europe Branch [*British Overseas Trade Board*] (DS)
EEBA .... Energy Efficient Building Association (EA)
EEBC .... Ether Ester Block Copolymer
EEBCS .... Electrical Equipment Bay Cooling System
EEBD .... Emergency Escape Breathing Device [*Navy*] (CAAL)
EE-BE.......... Ending Event - Beginning Event (SAA)
EEBIC .... Eastern Europe Business Information Center [*Department of Commerce*]
EEBM .... Eastern Europe Bible Mission (EA)
EEC .... East Erie Commercial Railroad [*AAR code*]
EEC .... Economic Education for Clergy (EA)
EEC .... Ectrodactylia, Ectodermal Dysplasia, Cleft Lip and Palate

EEC............ Ectrodactyly, Ectodermal Dysplasia Elefting [*Syndrome*] [*Medicine*] (DAVI)
EEC............ Educational Equity Concepts [*An association*] (EA)
EEC............ Education Exploration Center
EEC............ Electoral Education Centre [*Australia*]
EEC............ Electrical and Electronics Commission
EEC............ Electrical Export Corp. [*Defunct*]
EEC............ Electrochemical Equipment Committee [*Military*]
EEC............ Electronic Engine Control
EEC............ Electronic Equipment Committee [*NASA*] (KSC)
EEC............ Emerson Electric Co.
EEC............ Encased Elastic Cylinder
EEC............ End of Equilibrium Cycle [*Nuclear energy*] (NRCH)
EEC............ Enemy Exports Committee [*British World War II*]
EEC............ Engine Electronic Control (MCD)
EEC............ English Electric Computers [*British*] (NITA)
EEC............ Enlisted Evaluation Center [*Army*]
EEC............ Enough Is Enough Club [*Defunct*] (EA)
EEC............ Enteropathogenic Escherichia Coli [*Also, EPEC*] [*Medicine*]
EEC............ Environmental Elements [*NYSE symbol*] (TTSB)
EEC............ Environmental Elements Corp. [*NYSE symbol*] (SPSG)
EEC............ Equilibrium Equivalent Concentration [*Nuclear energy*] (NUCP)
EEC............ Estimated Exposure Concentration [*Toxicology*]
EEC............ Europa Esperanto-Centro [*European Esperanto Centre - EEC*] (EAIO)
EEC............ European Economic Community [*Common Market*]
EEC............ Evaporation [*or Evaporative*] Emission Control [*Automobile antipollution device*]
EEC............ EXAMETNET [*Experimental Inter-American Meteorological Rocket Network*] Executive Committee [*NASA*]
EEC............ Exhaust Emission Control [*Automotive engineering*]
EEC............ Expected Environmental Concentration [*Environmental science*]
EEC............ Extendable Exit Cone (MCD)
EEC............ St. Clair Community College, Port Huron, MI [*OCLC symbol*] (OCLC)
EECA............ Emergency Energy Conservation Act [*1979*]
EECA............ Engineering Economic Cost Analysis (MCD)
EE/CA............ Engineering Evaluation/Cost Analysis (DOGT)
EECA............ European Electronic Component Manufacturers Association (EAIO)
EECC............ Environmental Epidemiology and Cancer Centre [*British*] (IRUK)
EECCS............ European Ecumenical Commission for Church and Society [*Formerly, Ecumenical Commission for Church and Society*] (EA)
EECD............ Endothelial-Epithelial Corneal Dystrophy [*Medicine*] (DMAA)
EECE............ Emergency Economic Committee for Europe [*A "Western Nation" organization*] [*Post-World War II*]
EECGDR............ Entente Europeenne du Commerce en Gros des Deux-Roues (EA)
EECGS............ Emergency Evaporative Coolant Garment System (PDAA)
EECIS............ Electrical, Environmental Control, and Instrumentation Systems Specialist [*NASA*]
EECL............ Effective Equivalent Chlorine [*Analytical chemistry*]
EECL............ Emitter-Emitter Coupled Logic [*Electronics*] (IEEE)
EECL............ Encyclopedia of European Community Law [*A publication*] (DLA)
EEC-LCM............ European Economic Community - Liaison Committee of Midwives (EAIO)
EECM............ East European Chemical Monitor [*Business International*] [*Vienna, Austria*] [*Information service or system*] (IID)
EECM............ Electronic Engine Control Module
EECN............ Ecogen, Inc. [*NASDAQ symbol*] (SPSG)
EECNW............ Ecogen Inc. Wrrt [*NASDAQ symbol*] (TTSB)
EECOD............ European Ecumenical Organization for Development [*Brussels, Belgium*] (EAIO)
EECOM............ [*The*] Canadian Network for Environmental Education & Communication [*Reseau Canadien d'Education et de Communication Relatives a l'Environnement*] (AC)
EECOM............ CSM [*Command and Service Module*] Environmental and Electrical Systems Engineer [*NASA*]
EECOM............ Electrical, Environmental, and Communications
EECOM............ Electrical, Environmental, Consumables, and Mechanical Systems (MCD)
EECP............ Emergency Energy Conservation Program (OICC)
E ECP............ Expedited Engineering Change Proposal
EECS............ Electronic Engine Control System [*OC Johnson & Associates, Inc.*] [*Automotive engineering*]
EECS............ Equal Employment Compliance Section [*Employment and Training Administration*] (OICC)
EECS............ Evaporative Emission Control System [*Automotive engineering*]
EEC-SLC............ European Economic Community - Shipbuilders' Linking Committee [*Brussels, Belgium*] (EAIO)
EECT............ End, Evening Civil Twilight [*Navigation*]
EEC-V............ Electronic Engine Control - 5th Generation [*Automotive engineering*]
EECW............ Emergency Exchanger Cooling Water (IEEE)
EED............ Elastic Energy Density (WDAA)
EED............ Electroexplosive Device
EED............ Electronic Engineering Division [*Coast Guard*]
EED............ Electronic Evidence Discovery [*Company*]
EED............ Electronic Explosive Device (NVT)
EED............ Emergency Escape Device
EED............ Energy Efficient Design
EED............ Epizootic Epitheliotropic Disease [*Ichthyology*]
EED............ Estimated Exposure Dose [*Toxicology*]
EED............ European Enterprises Development Co. [*Luxembourg*]
EED............ Exposure Evaluation Division [*Environmental Protection Agency*] (GFGA)
EED............ Externally Mounted Electrical Device
EED............ Needles, CA [*Location identifier FAA*] (FAAL)

EED............ Wayne State University, Division of Library Science, Detroit, MI [*OCLC symbol*] (OCLC)
EEDB............ Energy and Economics Data Bank [*IAEA*] [*United Nations*] (DUND)
EEDB............ Energy and Environment Data Base [*Oak Ridge National Laboratory*] [*Database*]
EEDB............ ERDA [*Energy Research and Development Agency*] Energy Database [*Database*] (NITA)
EEDM............ External Event Detection Module [*Computer science*] (MDG)
EEDO............ Economic and Employment Development Officer
EEDP............ Evaluation, Experimental and Development Projects (OICC)
EEDQ............ Ethoxycarbonylethoxydihydroquinone [*Pharmacology*]
EEDS............ European Electrostatic Discharge Association [*British*] (EAIO)
EEE............ Brainerd, MN [*Location identifier FAA*] (FAAL)
EEE............ Detroit Edison Co., Information Services, Detroit, MI [*OCLC symbol*] (OCLC)
EEE............ Eastern Equine Encephalitis [*Virus*] (DAVI)
EEE............ Eastern Equine Encephalomyelitis [*Virus*]
EEE............ Electrical, Electronic, and Electromechanical
EEE............ Electrical Engineering Exposition
EEE............ Electromagnetic Environment Experiment [*NASA*] (MCD)
EEE............ Electronic Equipment Engineering [*A publication*]
EEE............ Energy Efficient Engine
EEE............ Engine and Electrical Engineering [*Automotive engineering*]
EEE............ Environmental-Ecological Education [*Office of Education program*]
EEE............ Equal, Effective, Elected [*Canada's Triple E Senate movement*]
EEE............ Error [*International telex abbreviation*] (WDMC)
EEE............ Exoelectron Emission (PDAA)
EEE............ External Ear Effect [*Audiology*]
EEEC............ Electromagnetic Energy Environment Criteria [*Army*] (AABC)
EEEC............ Extraepithelial Enterochromaffin Cells [*Cytology*]
EEEEE............ Erase [*British naval signaling*]
EEEI............ Energy, Economics and Environment Institute [*Defunct*] (EA)
EEEP............ End-Expiratory Esophageal Pressure [*Medicine*] (MAE)
EEES............ Electronic Equipment Environment Survey (AFM)
EEEU............ End Effector Electronics Unit (MCD)
EEEV............ Eastern Equine Encephalomyelitis Virus [*Medicine*] (DMAA)
EEF............ Earth Ecology Foundation (EA)
EEF............ Egyptian Expeditionary Force [*Military British*]
EEF............ Eisenhower Exchange Fellowships (EA)
EEF............ Electrical Enhancement Factor
EEF............ Encircled Energy Function (PDAA)
EEF............ Engineering Employers' Federation [*British*] (DCTA)
EEF............ Erickson Educational Foundation [*Later, J2CP Information Services*]
EEF............ Exoerythrocytic Form [*Phase of malaria parasite*]
EEF............ Export Expansion Facility [*Export-Import Bank of the US*]
EEF............ Exxon Education Foundation
EEF............ Ford Motor Co., Engineering and Research Library, Dearborn, MI [*OCLC symbol*] (OCLC)
EEF............ Sisters Island, AK [*Location identifier FAA*] (FAAL)
EEFAMOS............ Electrically-Erasable Floating Gate Avalanche-Injection Metal-Oxide Semiconductor [*Computer science*] (IAA)
EEFC............ Economic Education Foundation for Clergy [*Later, EEC*] (EA)
EEFF............ Electrostatically Enhanced Fabric Filtration
EEFHA............ East European Family History Association (EA)
EEFI............ Essential Elements of Friendly Information [*Army*] (AABC)
EEFIS............ Evasion and Escape Fingerprint Identification System
EEFM............ Egyptian Exploration Fund. Memoirs [*A publication*] (ROG)
EEG............ Electroencephalogram [*or Electroencephalography*] [*Medicine*]
EEG............ Electronics Engineering Group [*Military*]
EEG............ Employee Exposure Guidelines [*General Motors Corp.*]
EEG............ Employment and Enterprise Group (AIE)
EEG............ Environmental Education Group [*Defunct*] (EA)
EEG............ Environmental Effects Group [*Army*] (RDA)
EEG............ Essence Export Group [*British*] (BI)
EEG............ European Expedition Guild (EA)
EEG............ Europese Economische Gemeenschap [*European Economic Community*]
EEG............ Evaporative Emissions Generator [*Gasoline testing*] [*Organic chemistry*]
EEG............ Great Lakes Bible College, Lansing, MI [*OCLC symbol*] (OCLC)
EEG T............ Electroencephalographic Technologist [*Neurology*] (DAVI)
EEH............ EMU [*Extra-Vehicular Mobility Unit*] Electrical Harness
EEH............ Siena Heights College, Adrian, MI [*OCLC symbol*] (OCLC)
EEI............ EBSCO Electronic Information [*EBSCO Industries, Inc.*] [*Information service or system*] (IID)
EEI............ Ecology & Environment [*AMEX symbol*] (SPSG)
EEI............ Ecology/Environment'A' [*AMEX symbol*] (TTSB)
EEI............ Edison Electric Institute (EA)
EEI............ Educational Expeditions International [*Later, Earthwatch*]
EEI............ Electrical and Electromagnetic Interference (KSC)
EEI............ Electronic Emission Intelligence [*Military*]
EEI............ Ellis Enterprises, Inc. (IID)
EEI............ Environmental Equipment Institute [*Defunct*] (EA)
EEI............ Essential Elements of Information [*Military*]
EEI............ Evans Economics, Inc. [*Database producer*] [*Information service or system*] (IID)
EEI............ Excel Energy, Inc. [*Toronto Stock Exchange symbol*]
EEI............ External Environment Interface [*Computer science*]
EEI............ Hillsdale College, Mossey Learning Center, Hillsdale, MI [*OCLC symbol*] (OCLC)
EEIA............ Electrical and Electronic Insulation Association [*British*] (DBA)
EEIB............ Enemy Equipment Intelligence Branch [*World War II*]
EEIB............ Environmental Engineering Intersociety Board
EEIC............ Electrical/Electronics Insulation Conference (EA)
EEIC............ Element of Expense/Investment Code (AFM)

EEIC .... Elevated Electrode Integrated Circuit (MHDI)
EEIC .... Environmental Education and Information Committee (EERA)
EEIC .... European Electronic Intelligence Center (MCD)
EEIG .... European Economic Interest Grouping
EEII .... Eby Elementary Identification Instrument [*Educational test*]
EE-IS .... Basque Left - Left for Socialism (PPW)
EEIS .... Encyclopedia of Environmental Information Sources [*A publication*]
EEIS .... End-to-End Information System (NASA)
EEIS .... Enemy Equipment Identification Service [*World War II*]
EEIS .... Evanston Early Identification Scale [*Psychology*]
EEIST .... Enemy Equipment Intelligence Service Team [*World War II*]
EEJ .... Capital Library Cooperative, Mason, MI [*OCLC symbol*] (OCLC)
EEJ .... Equatorial Electrojet
EEK .... Eek [*Alaska*] [*Airport symbol*] (OAG)
EEK .... Epoxy Experimental Kit
EEK .... Kellogg Community College, Battle Creek, MI [*OCLC symbol*] (OCLC)
EEL .... Electrical Equipment List (MCD)
EEL .... Electromagnetic Effects Laboratory [*Army*] (RDA)
EEL .... Emergency Exposure Limits (AFM)
EEL .... Emitter-Emitter Coupled Logic [*Electronics*] (IAA)
EEL .... Engineering Electronics Laboratory
EEL .... Environmental Effects Laboratory [*Army*]
EEL .... Environmental Exposure Level [*Toxicology*]
EEL .... Evans Electroselenium Limited [*as in EEL analyzer, used in biochemical analysis*] [*British*]
EEL .... Exclusive Exchange Line [*Telecommunications*]
EEL .... Lansing Community College, Lansing, MI [*OCLC symbol*] (OCLC)
EELC .... Ethnic Employees of the Library of Congress (EA)
EEIChil .... Empresa Nacional de Electridad de Chile [*Associated Press*] (SAG)
EELFS .... Electron Energy Loss Fine Structure
EELR .... Extended Emission Line Region [*Spectrometry*]
EELS .... Early Entry Lethality and Survivability [*Military*] (INF)
EELS .... Electron Energy Loss Spectroscopy [*Also, ELS*]
EELS .... Electronic and Editing Layout System [*Telecommunications*] (DGA)
EELS .... Electronic Emitter Location System (MCD)
EELUT .... Eastern Energy and Land Use Team [*Kearneysville, WV*] [*Department of the Interior*] (GRD)
EELV .... Evolved Expendable Launch Vehicle [*NASA*] (ECON)
EEM .... Earth Entry Module [*NASA*] (KSC)
EEM .... Earth Exchange Museum [*Sydney, New South Wales, Australia*]
EEM .... Eastern European Mission [*Later, SGA*]
EEM .... Ectodermal Dysplasia, Ectrodactyly, Macular Dystrophy Syndrome [*Medicine*] (DMAA)
EEM .... Effective Elastic Modulus
EEM .... Effective Engineering Management
EEM .... Effective Exposure Method (KSC)
EEM .... Eigenmode Expansion Method (PDAA)
EEM .... Electronic Engineers Master (MUGU)
EEM .... Electronic Equipment Modification
EEM .... Electronic Equipment Monitoring (IEEE)
EEM .... Electrostatic Electron Microscope
EEM .... Emission Electron Microscope (IAA)
EEM .... Emission Electron Miscroscope (PDAA)
EEM .... Engineering Evaluation Model (KSC)
EEM .... Engineering Experimental Memo
EEM .... Epsilon for Early Music
EEM .... Excess Exchange Material (AFIT)
EEM .... Excitation-Emission Matrix [*Fluorometry*]
EEM .... Expendable Electronic Markers (NVT)
EEM .... Experienced Export Manager [*American Society of International Executives*] [*Designation awarded by*]
EEM .... Exponential Ensemble Mutagenesis [*Technique for studying genetic sequences*]
EEM .... Extrapolated End-Point Method [*Nuclear energy*] (NRCH)
EEM .... Michigan State University, East Lansing, MI [*OCLC symbol*] (OCLC)
EEM .... Morgan Stanley Finance Markets Ltd. Capital Units [*NYSE symbol*] (SAG)
EEMAC .... Electrical and Electronic Manufacturers Association of Canada (EAIO)
EEMD .... Electronic Equipment Maintainability Datebook (MCD)
EEMDA .... Electrical-Electronics Materials Distributors Association [*Later, LEMDA*] (EA)
EEME .... Ethinylestradiol Methyl Ether (MAE)
EEMIS .... Energy Emergency Management Information System (PDAA)
EEMJEB ...... Electrical and Electronic Manufacturers Joint Education Board
EEMK .... Electronic Equipment Maintenance Kit
EEMM .... [*The*] Egyptian Expedition. Metropolitan Museum of Art [*New York*] [*A publication*] (BJA)
EEMS .... Electronic Engine Management System
EEMS .... Enhanced Expanded Memory Specifications [*AST, Quadram*]
EEMS .... European Environmental Mutagen Society [*Leiden, Netherlands*] (EAIO)
EEMT .... Electronic Equipment Maintenance Trainer (MCD)
EEMT .... Environmental Engineering Management Team
EEMTIC .... Electrical and Electronic Measurement and Test Instrumentation Conference (MCD)
EEMTR .... Enhanced Enlisted Master Tape Record (AABC)
EEMUA .... Engineering Equipment and Materials User's Association [*British*]
EEN .... Brattleboro, Vermont-Keene, New Hampshire [*Airport symbol*] (AD)
EEN .... Eastern Educational Television Network [*Boston, MA*] [*Telecommunications service*] (TSSD)
EEN .... Eden Resources Ltd. [*Vancouver Stock Exchange symbol*]
EEN .... Education for Enterprise Network (AIE)
EEN .... Emergency Engineering Notice (MCD)

EEN .... Even-Even Nucleus
E'EN .... Evening (ROG)
EEN .... Keene [*New Hampshire*] [*Airport symbol*] (OAG)
EENET .... Emergency Education Network [*Federal Emergency Management Agency*] (GFGA)
EENG .... Early English [*Language*] (DGA)
EEng .... Electrical Engineering (DD)
EENGR .... Electrical Engineer (FAAC)
EENR .... Economic Evaluation of Natural Resources (EERA)
EENT .... Early Evening Nautical Twilight [*Navigation*] (MCD)
EENT .... End, Evening Nautical Twilight [*Navigation*]
EENT .... Eyes, Ears, Nose, and Throat [*Medicine*]
EEO .... Ealing Electro-Optics [*British*]
EEO .... Effective Equal Opportunity
EEO .... Electroendosmosis [*Analytical biochemistry*]
EEO .... Elliptical Earth Orbit
EEO .... Equal Employment Officer
EEO .... Equal Employment Opportunity
EEO .... European Electro-Optics Conference and Exhibition
EEO .... Expedite Engineering Order (MCD)
EEO .... Extremely Elliptical Orbit [*Telecommunications*] (ACRL)
EEOA .... Equal Employment Opportunity Act (OICC)
EEOA .... Equal Employment Opportunity Agency
EEOAC .... Equal Employment Opportunity Advisory Council (DNAB)
EEOC .... Equal Employment Opportunity Commission
EEOC Compl Man... Equal Employment Opportunity Commission Compliance Manual [*Commerce Clearing House*] (DLA)
EEODIRSYS... Equal Employment Opportunity Directives System (DNAB)
EEOED .... Emergency Earth Orbital Escape Device (KSC)
EEOO .... Equal Employment Opportunity Officer [*DoD*]
EEOOA .... Equal Employment Opportunity Officer Activity
EEOP .... Equal Educational Opportunities Program [*HEW*]
EEOP .... Equal Employment Opportunity Program (MCD)
EEOS .... Equality of Educational Opportunity Survey [*1965*]
EEOW .... Engineering Officer of the Watch [*Navy*]
EEP .... Earth Equatorial Plane
EEP .... Eastern Equatorial Pacific
EEP .... East European Program (EERA)
EEP .... Economic Education Project [*Public Media Center*] (EA)
EEP .... Education Excellence Partnership
EEP .... Einstein Equivalence Principle [*Gravity*]
EEP .... Electrode Electrostatic Precipitator
EEP .... Electroencephalophony [*Medical electronics*] (IEEE)
EEP .... Electronic Evaluation and Procurement (MHDB)
EEP .... Electronic Event Programmer (MHDB)
EEP .... Elliptical Error Probability (CAAL)
EEP .... Emergency Essential Personnel (AFM)
EEP .... End Exercise Point (FAAC)
EEP .... End Expiratory Pressure (AAMN)
EEP .... End to End Protocol (IAA)
EEP .... Energy Engineering Program [*Navy*]
EEP .... Engineering Experimental Phase [*National Data Buoy Project*]
EEP .... Enormously Entertaining Prodigy
EEP .... Environmental Easement Program [*Department of Agriculture*]
EEP .... Environmental Enhancement Program
EEP .... Environmental Experiments Program [*National Science Foundation*]
EEP .... Epsilon Eta Phi [*Later, Phi Chi Theta*]
EEP .... Esperanza Explorations Ltd. [*Vancouver Stock Exchange symbol*]
EEP .... Ethyl Ethoxypropionate [*Organic chemistry*]
EEP .... Experimental Education Program
EEP .... Explorations in Eastern Palestine [*A publication*] (BJA)
EEP .... Export Enhancement Program [*Department of Agriculture*]
EEP .... External Economic Policy [*British*]
EEP .... Lansing Public Library, Lansing, MI [*OCLC symbol*] (OCLC)
EEPA .... Electromagnetic Energy Policy Alliance (EA)
EEPA .... Environmental Expenditure on Protection and Abatement (EERA)
EEPC .... Energy and Environmental Policy Center [*Harvard University*] [*Research center*] (RCD)
EEPC .... India Engineering Export Promotion Council (EA)
EEPCD .... Early Education for Children with Disabilities Program Project [*Established under the Individuals with Disabilities Education Act (IDEA)*] (PAZ)
EEPD .... Energy Production and Delivery (IAA)
EEPI .... Extraretinal Eye Position Information [*Ophthalmology*]
EEPM .... Electrical and Electronic Properties of Materials
EEPNL .... Estimated Effective Perceived Noise Level
EEPOL .... Electrically-Erasable Programmable Logic Device [*Computer science*] (IAA)
EEPROM ...... Electrically Erasable, Programmable, Read-Only Memory [*Computer science*]
EEPS .... Emergency Electrical Power System (MCD)
EEPVS .... Electrical Equipment Protection Room Ventilation System [*Nuclear energy*] (NRCH)
EER .... Early Emissions Reduction [*Environmental science*]
EER .... Eerie (ABBR)
EER .... Electroencephalic Response [*Medicine*] (MAE)
EER .... Electronic Equipment Representative (MCD)
EER .... Elevated Electric Railway [*South London Railway*] (ROG)
EER .... Emergency English for Refugees [*Pennsylvania*] (EDAC)
EER .... Encounter Energy Resources Ltd. [*Toronto Stock Exchange symbol*]
EER .... Energy Efficiency Ratio [*Home appliance electric output*]
EER .... English Ecclesiastical Reports [*A publication*] (DLA)
EER .... Enlisted Evaluation Report [*DoD*] (GFGA)
EER .... Entered Employment Rate [*Job Training and Partnership Act*] (OICC)
EER .... Envelope Elimination and Restoration

EER............. Environmental Effects Report [*Military*]
EER............. Equipment Evaluation Report (NG)
E'ER............. Ever (ROG)
EER............. Excess Emission Report [*Environmental Protection Agency*] (ERG)
EER............. Excess Emission Report (GNE)
EER............. Expendable-Expendable-Reusable
EER............. Experimental Ecological Reserves [*Project*] [*National Science Foundation*]
EER............. Explosive Echo Ranging
EER............. Extended Endocardial Resection [*Medicine*]
EER............. University of Michigan, School of Library Science, Ann Arbor, MI [*OCLC symbol*] (OCLC)
EERA........... Education Evaluation and Remedial Assistance Program [*Connecticut*] (EDAC)
EERA........... Electrical Equipment Representatives Association (EA)
EERA........... Explosive Excavation Research Agency [*Formerly, NCG*] [*Army*] (RDA)
EERC........... Earthquake Engineering Research Center [*University of California, Berkeley*] [*IID*]
EERC........... Energy and Environmental Research Center [*University of North Dakota*]
EERC........... Explosive Echo Ranging Charge (NG)
EERD........... Electronic Equipment Reliability Databook (MCD)
EERF........... Eastern Environmental Radiation Facility [*Environmental Protection Agency*] (IID)
EERI........... Earthquake Engineering Research Institute (EA)
EERJ........... External Expansion Ramjet (PDAA)
EERL........... Eastern Environmental Radiation Laboratory [*Environmental Protection Agency*]
EERL........... Electrical Engineering Research Laboratory (KSC)
EERL........... Explosive Excavation Research Laboratory [*Army Engineer Waterways Experiment Station*] [*Livermore, CA*]
EERNS .... Eeriness (ABBR)
EERO .... European Environmental Research Organization
EERO .... Explosive Excavation Research Office [*Livermore, CA*] [*Army*]
EEROC .... Expedited Essential Required Operational Capability
EEROM .... Electrically Erasable Read-Only Memory [*Computer science*] (MDG)
EERR .... Eerier (ABBR)
EERRHV ...... Emergency Escape Ramp for Runaway Heavy Vehicle (PDAA)
EERS........... Earthquake Early Reporting System [*Marine science*] (MSC)
EERS........... Expeditionary Equipment Report System
EERST......... Eeriest (ABBR)
EERWA .... Enlisted Efficiency Report Weighted Average [*Army*]
EERY........... Eerily (ABBR)
EES .... Early Docking Demonstration System (SAA)
EES .... Eco-Energy System
EES .... Educational Employment Service
EES .... Effectiveness Evaluation System
EES .... Egypt Exploration Society (EA)
EES .... Ejection Escape Suit (NASA)
EES .... Electrical Equipment Shelter
EES .... Electromagnetic Environment Simulator
EES .... Electronic Emission Security (NATG)
EES .... Electronic Environment Simulator
EES .... Electronics Engineering Squadron [*Military*]
EES .... Emergency Ejection Suits (MCD)
EES .... Emergency Establishment Supplements (NATG)
EES .... Emergency Evacuation Study [*Military*] (MCD)
EES .... Emergency Evaluation Study [*Military*]
EES .... Encyclopedia of Endangered Species [*A publication*]
EES .... Endoscopic Esophageal Sclerotherapy [*Medicine*]
EES .... Energy Extension Service [*Department of Energy*]
EES .... Engineering Equation Solver [*Macintosh*] [*Computer science*]
EES .... Engineering Experiment Station [*University of Missouri, Columbia*] [*Research center*] (RCD)
EES .... Enlisted Evaluation System [*Army*]
EES .... Environmental Effects Statement [*Australia*]
EES .... Environmental Engineering Section
EES .... Environment Effects Statement (EERA)
EES .... Erythromycin Ethylsuccinate [*Antimicrobial compound*]
EES .... E-Section Escape Suit [*Military*]
EES .... Ethyl Enthanesulfate [*Organic chemistry*] (MAE)
EES .... European Economic Space
EES .... European Exchange System
EES .... Evangelical Education Society of the Protestant Episcopal Church (EA)
EES .... Evaporative Emission System [*Automotive engineering*]
EES .... Examining and Entrance Station [*Air Force*]
EES .... Spring Arbor College, Spring Arbor, MI [*OCLC symbol*] (OCLC)
EESA........... Education for Economic Security Act [*1988*]
EESA........... Electrical and Engineering Staff Association [*British*]
EESB........... Electrical and Electronics Standards Board [*American National Standards Institute*] [*Telecommunications*]
EESC........... Eastern Europe Solidarity Campaign (EAIO)
EESC........... East European Solidarity Committee [*Defunct*] (EAIO)
EESC........... Environmental and Energy Study Conference (EA)
EESCM......... Enhanced Engine Starting Control and Monitor
EESD........... European Electronic Security Division [*Military*]
EESE........... Energy Efficient Services and Equipment
EESG........... Evoked Electrospinogram [*Medicine*] (AAMN)
EESI........... Eastern Environmental Services, Inc. [*NASDAQ symbol*] (NQ)
EESI........... Eastern Environmental Svc [*NASDAQ symbol*] (TTSB)
EESI........... Environment and Energy Study Institute (GNE)
EESL........... Environmental Ecological and Support Laboratory [*Environmental Protection Agency*] (GFGA)

EESMB......... Electrical and Electronics Standards Management Board
EES/NCFR.... Education and Enrichment Section of the National Council on Family Relations (EA)
EESS........... Environmental Effects on Space Systems
EESS........... Evaporative Emission SHED [*Sealed Housing for Evaporative Determinations*] System [*Automotive engineering*]
EEST/PD ..... Emergency Establishment Supplement Table of Personnel Distribution [*NATO*] (NATG)
EESWS........ Emergency Equipment Service Water System [*Nuclear energy*] (NRCH)
EET .... Eastern European Time (DCTA)
EET .... Edge Enhancement Technology [*Tandy*]
EET .... Education Equivalency Test
EET .... Electrical Equipment Trailer
EET .... Electronic EGR [*Exhaust Gas Recirculation*] Transducer [*Automotive engineering*]
EET .... Electronic Exposure Timer (KSC)
EET .... Energy Efficient Transport (MCD)
EET .... Engage Enemy Target
EET .... Engineering Evaluation Test (NG)
EET .... Entry Elapsed Time (MCD)
EET .... Epoxy-Encapsulated Transistor
EET .... Equator Earth Terminal
EET .... Equipment Engaged Tone [*Telecommunications*] (TEL)
EET .... Equivalent Exposure Time (KSC)
EET .... Estimated Elapsed Time [*ICAO*] (FAAC)
EET .... Etruscan Enterprises Ltd. [*Vancouver Stock Exchange symbol*]
EET .... Event Elapsed Time (MCD)
EET .... Excitation Energy Transfer
EET .... Explosive-to-Electric Transducer
EETB........... Electronic Electrical Termination Building [*NASA*] (NASA)
EETC .... Electronic Equipment Technical Committee [*NASA*] (KSC)
EETCB .... Eternally Elvis TCB [*Taking Care of Business*] (EA)
EETEP .... Extended Eligibility Temporary Entry Permit
EETF .... Electronic Environmental Test Facility (MUGU)
EETPU......... Electrical, Electronic, Telecommunication, and Plumbing Union [*British*] (DCTA)
EETS .... Early English Text Society [*Oxford, England*]
EETV .... Electrophoresis Equipment Test Verification [*Military*]
EEU .... Eurofly [*Italy ICAO designator*] (FAAC)
EEU .... European Esperanto Union (EA)
EEU .... Extravehicular Excursion Unit (SSD)
EEU .... University Microfilms International, Ann Arbor, MI [*OCLC symbol*] (OCLC)
EEUA........... Electrical Equipment Users Association (OSI)
EEUA........... Engineering Equipment Users' Association [*British*] (BI)
EEUR........... Earth Environment University Roundtable [*of America*]
EEV .... Encircling Endocardial Ventriculotomy [*Cardiology*]
EEV .... English Electric Valve [*Electronics company*]
EEV .... Extracellular Enveloped Virus
EEVeTec ...... Equipment, Environment, Velocity, Technique, Conditioning [*Sports medicine*]
EEVF........... East Eifel Volcanic Field [*Geology*] [*Germany*]
EEVT........... Electrophoresis Equipment Verification Test
EEW .... Extraordinary Electromagnetic Wave
EEW .... Neenah, WI [*Location identifier FAA*] (FAAL)
EEWB........... Willard Library, Battle Creek, MI [*OCLC symbol*] (OCLC)
EEX .... Electronic Egg Exchange [*Computer program*]
EEX .... Enserch Exploration [*NYSE symbol*] (TTSB)
EEX .... Enserch Exploration, Inc. [*NYSE symbol*] (SAG)
EEX .... Essex Petroleum [*Vancouver Stock Exchange symbol*]
EEX .... Excess Exception Code [*Air Force*] (AFIT)
EEX .... Michigan State Library Services, Lansing, MI [*OCLC symbol*] (OCLC)
EEY .... Winchester, VA [*Location identifier FAA*] (FAAL)
EEZ .... Eurofly SPA [*Italy ICAO designator*] (FAAC)
EEZ .... Exclusive Economic Zone [*Offshore sovereignty*] [*ICSU*]
EF .... Each Face [*Technical drawings*]
EF .... Eagle Forum (EA)
EF .... Ear Foundation (EA)
EF .... Early Finish
EF .... Earth First (EA)
EF .... East Florida [*Obsolete*] (ROG)
EF .... Ectopic Focus [*Cardiology*]
EF .... Edema Factor [*Medicine*]
EF .... Edge Finishing (DNAB)
EF .... Effective (ABBR)
EF .... Eglin Field [*Florida*] [*Air Force*] (MCD)
EF .... Ejection Factor [*Cardiology*] (DAVI)
EF .... Ejection Fraction [*Cardiology*]
EF .... Elastic Fibril [*Medicine*] (DMAA)
EF .... Elect of Fifteen [*Freemasonry*] (ROG)
EF .... Electroflotation (PDAA)
EF .... Electronic Filing (NITA)
EF .... Eleftherofronon [*Free Opinion Party*] [*Greek*] (PPE)
EF .... Elevation Finder [*Military*]
EF .... Elongation Factor [*Biochemistry, genetics*]
EF .... Embedded Figures [*Psychometrics*]
EF .... Embryo-Fetal [*Neonatology and obstetrics*] (DAVI)
EF .... Embryo Fibroblast [*Medicine*] (DMAA)
EF .... Emergency Facilities (AAG)
EF .... Emergency Fix
EF .... Emission Factor [*Environmental Protection Agency*] (GFGA)
EF .... Emitter Follower [*Electronics*] (MCD)
EF .... Emotional Factor [*Psychology*] (DAVI)
EF .... Employed Full Time [*Chiropody*] [*British*]

EF	Encephalitogenic Factor (MAE)
EF	Endeavour Forum [Australia]
EF	Endeavour Foundation [Australia]
EF	Ending Flag Value for Data Input [Computer science]
EF	Endoplasmic Fracture [Freeze etching in microscopy]
EF	Endurance Factor [Cardiology] (DAVI)
E/F	Enemy/Friendly (MCD)
EF	En Foco [An association] (EA)
EF	Engineering Foundation (EA)
EF	English Finish [Paper]
EF	Entered From (SAA)
EF	Enterprise Foundation (EA)
EF	Environmental Factor
EF	Eosinophilic Fasciitis [Medicine]
EF	Epithelial Force (Assay) [Oncology]
EF	Equilibrium Field (MCD)
EF	Equipment Factor (CAAL)
EF	Equivalent Focal Length [Optics]
EF	Equivalent Focus [Medicine] (DAVI)
EF	Error Factor (IEEE)
EF	Erythrocytic Fragmentation (AAMN)
EF	Ethos Foundation (EA)
EF	Etruscan Foundation (EA)
EF	Eurodata Foundation (EAIO)
EF	European Foundation (DS)
EF	[The] Europe Fund [NYSE symbol] (SPSG)
EF	Europe Fund [NYSE symbol] (TTSB)
EF	Eurotransplant Foundation (EA)
EF	Evangelische Freiheit [A publication] (BJA)
EF	Evergreen Foundation (EA)
EF	Everyman's Fiction [Series published by J. M. Dent & Sons] [British]
EF	Executive Forum (EA)
EF	Exhaust Fan (AAG)
EF	Exoplasmic Fracture [Freeze etching in microscopy]
EF	Expeditionary Force
EF	Experimental Flight
EF	Exposed Facility (SSD)
EF	Expressional Fluency [Research test] [Psychology]
EF	Extended Facility [IBM Corp.]
EF	Extended Field [Radiation therapy] (DAVI)
E/F	Extension/Flexion [Medicine]
EF	External Flaps (AAG)
EF	Extractable Fluorescence
EF	Extra Fine [Threads]
EF	Extremely Fine [Condition] [Antiquarian book trade and numismatics]
EF	Extrinsic Factor [Vitamin B$_{12}$] [Also, APA, APAF, LLD]
EF	Eye Focus
EF	Far Eastern Air Transport [ICAO designator] (AD)
EFA	Category E Flying Accident [British military] (DMA)
EFA	Eastern Finance Association (EA)
EFA	Eddy Family Association (EA)
EFA	Editorial Freelancers Association (EA)
EFA	Effective Filtration Area
EFA	Electrical Floor Warming Association [British] (BI)
EFA	Electrinium Foundation of America (EA)
EFA	Electronics Field Activity
EFA	Engineering Field Activity (MCD)
EFA	Enginemen and Firemen's Association [A union] [British]
EFA	Enterprise Flexibility Agreement [Australia]
EFA	Entire Field Available (FAAC)
EFA	Environmental Financing Authority [Expired, 1975] [Environmental Protection Agency]
EFA	Epilepsy Foundation of America (EA)
EFA	Equilibrium Float Altitude [Balloon flight]
EFA	Eskridge Family Association (EA)
EFA	Essential Fatty Acid [Biochemistry]
EFA	European Fairytale Association [See also EMG] [Rheine, Federal Republic of Germany] (EAIO)
EFA	European Federation of Agricultural Workers' Unions [EC] (ECED)
EFA	European Fighter Aircraft
EFA	European Finance Association (EAIO)
EFA	European Free Alliance [See also ALE] [Brussels, Belgium Political party] (EAIO)
EFA	Evangelical Friends Alliance [Later, EFI] (EA)
EFA	Evolutionary Factor Analysis [Statistics]
EFA	Excess Fare Allowance
EFA	Experiment Flight Applications (NASA)
EFA	Extended File Attribute [Software feature] [Computer science] (PCM)
EFA	Extrafamily Adoptee (MAE)
EFA	Eyepiece Focusing Adjustment [Optics] (ROG)
EFAA	Aavahelukka [Finland ICAO location identifier] (ICLI)
EFAAD	European Federation for the Advancement of Anaesthesia in Dentistry [Italy] (EAIO)
EFAB	Environmental Financial Advisory Board [Environmental Protection Agency] (EGAO)
EFACB	Effaceable (ABBR)
EFACD	Effaced (ABBR)
EFACF	European Folk Art and Craft Federation [Zurich, Switzerland] (EAIO)
EFACG	Effacing (ABBR)
EFACR	Effacer (ABBR)
EFACT	Effacement (ABBR)
EFAD	Essential Fatty Acid Deficiency [Medicine]
EFAD	European Federation of the Associations of Dietitians (EAIO)
EFAG	Emergency Field Arresting Gear (MCD)
EFAI	Educational Foundation for the Apparel Industry [Later, EFFI] (EA)

EFAL	Alavus [Finland ICAO location identifier] (ICLI)
EFAL	Electronic Flash Approach Light (IAA)
EF & I	Engineer, Furnish, and Install
EF & LTC	Enemy Fuels and Lubricants Technical Committee
EFANSW	Electoral Funding Authority of New South Wales [Australia]
EFAP	Elastic Frame Analysis Program [Structures & Computers Ltd.] [Software package] (NCC)
EFAP	Environmentally Friendly Accreditation Program [Australia]
EFAPIT	Euromarket Federation of Animal Protein Importers and Traders (EAIO)
EFAPP	Enrico Fermi Atomic Power Plant [Decommissioned] (NRCH)
EFAR	Economic Feeder Administration and Relief (TEL)
EFAR	Error Factor Analysis and Reduction (ADA)
EFAR	European Federation for AIDS Research
EFARS	Engineer Federal Acquisition Regulation Supplement [A publication] (AAGC)
EFAS	Electronic Flash Approach System
EFAS	Emergency Feedwater Actuation Signal [Nuclear energy] (NRCH)
EFAS	En Route Flight Advisory Services [FAA]
EFATCA	European Federation of Air Traffic Controllers Association
EFB	Eight Fathom Bight [Alaska] [Airport symbol] (OAG)
EFB	Electric Feedback
EFB	Electrode Film Barrier
EFB	Electrofluidized Bed [Chemical engineering]
EFB	Engineering Field Bulletin (MCD)
EFB	Europaeische Foderation Biotechnologie [European Federation of Biotechnology] (EAIO)
EFBD	Experimental Fighting Biplane [British military] (DMA)
EFBD	Emergency Feed Baron Detector (IEEE)
EFBI	Enterprise Federal Bancorp [NASDAQ symbol] (TTSB)
EFBI	Enterprise Federal Bancorp, Inc. [NASDAQ symbol] (SAG)
EFBPBI	European Federation of the Brush and Paint Brush Industries (EA)
EFBS	E. F. Benson Society (EAIO)
EFBS	European Federation of Building Societies (EAIO)
EFBTE	Eastern Federation of Building Trades' Employers [British] (BI)
EFBWW	European Federation of Building and Woodworkers (EA)
EFC	Earth-Fixed Coordinate (MCD)
EFC	Eastern Football Conference
EFC	Efface (ABBR)
EFC	Effective Full-Charge [Weaponry] (RDA)
EFC	Electrical Field Current
EFC	Electrical Frequency Control (MCD)
EFC	Electric Fuel Control [Automotive engineering]
EFC	Electrochemical Fuel Cell
EFC	Electrofluid Converter
EFC	Electronic Flow Control
EFC	Electronic Frequency Control
EFC	Elfquest Fan Club (EA)
EFC	Elvira Fan Club (EA)
EFC	Emergency Fleet Corp. [Defunct, 1936]
EFC	Emergency Foster Care (ADA)
EFC	Encampment for Citizenship [An association] (EA)
EFC	Endogenous Fecal Calcium [Medicine] (MAE)
EFC	Engineering Field Change (MSA)
EFC	Equipment Functional Check (KSC)
EFC	Equivalent Full Charge
EFC	Ernest Fan Club [Defunct] (EA)
EFC	Escort Force Commander [NATO] (NATG)
EFC	Estimated Final Cost
EFC	Etched Flexible Circuitry
EFC	European Federation of Corrosion (EA)
EFC	European Forestry Commission
EFC	Eurythmics Fan Club (EA)
EFC	Exile Fan Club (EA)
EFC	Expected Family Contribution [Department of Education] (GFGA)
EFC	Expected Fraction of Casualties (MCD)
EFC	Expected Further Clearance (GAVI)
EFC	Expect Further Clearance [FAA] (TAG)
EFC	Expect Further Clearance At [Aviation] (FAAC)
EFC	Expeditionary Force Canteens [Official supply organization] [World War I] [British]
EFCA	Evangelical Free Church of Australia
EFCAT	European Football Commentators Association Television (EA)
EFCATS	European Federation of Catalysis Societies
EFCB	Emergency Financial Control Board [Later, FCB]
EFCCCI	Early Four Cylinder Chevrolet Club, International [Defunct] (EA)
EFCD	Effaced (ABBR)
EFCE	European Federation of Chemical Engineering [See also EFCIW] (EAIO)
EFCEM	European Federation of Catering Equipment Manufacturers (EA)
EFCG	Effacing (ABBR)
EFCGU	European Federation of Chemical and General Workers Unions (EAIO)
EFChE	European Federation of Chemical Engineering
EFCI	Explicit Forward Congestion Indicator [Telecommunications] (ACRL)
EFCIW	Europaeische Foderation fuer Chemie-Ingenieur-Wesen [European Federation of Chemical Engineering - EFCE] (EAIO)
EFCL	Error-Free Communication Link (IAA)
EFCNT	Effacement (ABBR)
EFCOG	Energy Facilities Contractors Group (AAGC)
EFCOR	Effect Corona (IAA)
EFCR	Effacer (ABBR)
EFCR	Experimental Fast Ceramic Reactor
EFCS	Earth-Fixed Coordinate System (MCD)
EFCS	Electronic Flight Control System

EFCS............	Electronic Fuel Control System
EFCS............	Emitter Follower Current Switch [*Electronics*] (IAA)
EFCS............	European Federation for Company Sports (EAIO)
EFCS............	European Federation of Cytology Societies (EAIO)
EFCSM........	European Federation of Ceramic Sanitaryware Manufacturers (EA)
EFCT...........	Effect (ABBR)
EFCTA.........	Effectuate (ABBR)
EFCTAD.......	Effectuated (ABBR)
EFCTAG.......	Effectuating (ABBR)
EFCTB.........	Effectible (ABBR)
EFCTD.........	Effected (ABBR)
EFCTEC.......	European Fluorocarbon Technical Committee [*Belgium*] (EAIO)
EFCTG.........	Effecting (ABBR)
EFCTL.........	Effectual (ABBR)
EFCTLNS.....	Effectualness (ABBR)
EFCTLT.......	Effectuality (ABBR)
EFCTLY.......	Effectually (ABBR)
EFCTR.........	Effector (ABBR)
EFCTV.........	Effective (ABBR)
EFCTVNS.....	Effectiveness (ABBR)
EFCTVY.......	Effectively (ABBR)
EFCUA........	Extreme Fuel - Critical, Unspecified Area [*NASA*]
EFCV..........	Excess Flow Check Valve [*Nuclear energy*] (NRCH)
EFCW.........	Eagle Finance [*NASDAQ symbol*] (TTSB)
EFCW.........	Eagle Finance Corp. [*NASDAQ symbol*] (SAG)
EFCX..........	Electrical Fuel Corp. [*NASDAQ symbol*] (SAG)
EFCX..........	Electric Fuel [*NASDAQ symbol*] (TTSB)
EFD............	Earliest Finish Date
EFD............	Early Failure Detection
EFD............	Electric Flux Density
EFD............	Electrofluid Dynamic [*Process*] (MCD)
EFD............	Electronic Forms Designer [*Microsoft Corp.*] (PCM)
EFD............	Enemy Forward Disposition [*Military*]
EFD............	Energy Flux Density
EFD............	Enfield Resources [*Vancouver Stock Exchange symbol*]
EFD............	Engineered Fasteners Division [*Townsend Co.*]
EFD............	Engineering Facilities Depot
EFD............	Engineering Field Divisions [*Military*]
EFD............	Engineering Flow Diagram (NRCH)
EFD............	European Faculty Directory [*A publication*]
EFD............	Excused from Duty
EFD............	Executive Flight Detachment (AAG)
EFD............	Houston, TX [*Location identifier FAA*] (FAAL)
EFDA..........	Epoxyfarnesyl Diazoacetate [*Organic chemistry*]
EFDA..........	European Formula Drivers Association (EAIO)
EFDA..........	European Funeral Directors' Association (EAIO)
EFDA..........	Expanded Function Dental Auxiliary [*HEW program*]
EFDARS.......	Electronic Flight Data and Recording System (MCD)
EFDAS	Electronic Flight Data Accumulation Service
EFDAS	Epsilon Flight Data Acquisition System (IAA)
EFDS	Equipment and Floor Drainage System [*Nuclear energy*] (NRCH)
EFDSS	English Folk Dance and Song Society [*British*]
EFE............	Early Fuel Evaporation [*Automotive technology*]
EFE............	Endocardial Fibroelastosis [*Medicine*]
EFE............	Ermolino Flying Test Research Enterprise [*Former USSR*] [*FAA designator*] (FAAC)
EFE............	External Field Emission
EFEA..........	European Free Exchange Area (NATG)
EFECS.........	Engine Fuel Economy Control System [*Automotive engineering*]
EFEHV........	Educational Fund to End Handgun Violence (EA)
EFEI...........	Equivalent Fuel Efficiency Improvement
EFEM..........	Effeminate (ABBR)
EFEM..........	Energy Filtering Electron Microscope
EFEMA........	Association des Fabricants Europeens d'Emulsifants Alimentaires [*Association of European Manufacturers of Food Emulsifiers*] (EAIO)
EFEMAY.......	Effeminately (ABBR)
EFEMC........	Effeminacy (ABBR)
EFEMNS.......	Effeminateness (ABBR)
EFEMY........	Effeminately (ABBR)
EFEO..........	Ecole Francaise d'Extreme Orient [*French School of the Far East*]
EFERVS.......	Effervesce (ABBR)
EFERVSD	Effervesced (ABBR)
EFERVSG	Effervescing (ABBR)
EFERVSNC...	Effervescence (ABBR)
EFERVST.....	Effervescent (ABBR)
EFES..........	Tampere [*Finland ICAO location identifier*] (ICLI)
EFET..........	Enhancement Mode Field Effect Transistor (IAA)
EFET..........	Enontekio [*Finland ICAO location identifier*] (ICLI)
EFET..........	Epoxy Field Effect Transistor
EFEU..........	Eura [*Finland ICAO location identifier*] (ICLI)
EFF............	Eastern Fishermen's Federation [*See also FPE*] [*Canada*]
EFF............	Educational Freedom Foundation (EA)
Eff..............	Effacement [*Obstetrics*] (DAVI)
EFF............	Effect (AFM)
Eff..............	Effective [*Legal term*] (DLA)
EFF............	Efferent [*Anatomy*]
EFF............	Effervescent [*Pharmacy*] (ROG)
EFF............	Efficiency
EFF............	Effigy (ROG)
EFF............	Effluent
EFF............	Electric Flow Field
EFF............	Electronic Freedom Foundation [*Telecommunications*]
EFF............	Electronic Frontier Foundation (EA)
EFF............	Empirical Force Field [*Physical chemistry*]

EFF............	English for Foreigners
EFF............	Enterprise, Family, and Freedom [*Australia Political party*]
EFF............	European Franchise Federation [*France*] (EAIO)
EFF............	European Furniture Federation
EFF............	Expandable File Family [*Computer science*] (MHDB)
EFF............	Experimenal Forecast Facility [*Marine science*] (OSRA)
EFF............	Experimental Forecast Facility [*National Weather Service*] (USDC)
EFF............	Extended Fund Facility [*International Monetary Fund*]
EFF............	Westair Aviation Ltd. [*Ireland*] [*ICAO designator*] (FAAC)
EFFA..........	European Flavour and Fragrance Association [*Belgium*] (EAIO)
EFFAS........	European Federation of Financial Analysts' Societies (EA)
EFFBR........	Enrico Fermi Fast Breeder Power Reactor
EFFCTS.......	Effects [*Automotive advertising*]
EFFCY........	Efficiency (AABC)
EFFE..........	Environmentalists for Full Employment [*Defunct*] (EA)
EFFE..........	European Federation of Flight Engineers
EFFE..........	Experiment in Free-Form Education (AEBS)
EFFECT.......	Effective (ABBR)
EFFECT.......	Effectivity (ABBR)
EFFER.........	Efferent (ABBR)
EFFF..........	Electrical Field-Flow Fractionation [*Electrochemical separation method*]
EFFFL.........	Efficiency Full Load (IAA)
EFFG..........	Effectuating (ROG)
EFFGRO......	Efficient Growth [*Computer program*] (NASA)
EFFI...........	Educational Foundation for the Fashion Industries (EA)
EFFI...........	Electronic Fiber Fineness Indicator
EFFI...........	Electronic Forum for Industry [*British*]
EFFIC.........	Efficiency (ROG)
EFFIG.........	Effigies (ROG)
EFFL..........	Efflorescent (ABBR)
EFFM..........	Eastern Federation of Feed Merchants (SRA)
EFFM..........	European Federation of Fiber Cement Manufacturers [*EC*] (ECED)
EffMgt........	Effective Management Systems [*Associated Press*] (SAG)
EFFO..........	Forssa [*Finland ICAO location identifier*] (ICLI)
EFFORPA.....	Elliptic Function First-Order Ripple Phase Approximation
EFFoST.......	European Federation of Food Science and Technology (EA)
EF Foundation...	Educational Foundation for Foreign Study (EA)
EFFT..........	Effete (ABBR)
EFFU..........	Epithelial Focus-Forming Unit [*Oncology*]
EFFUNDAT...	Effundatur [*Let It Be Poured Out*] [*Pharmacy*] (ROG)
EFG...........	Economic Forestry Group [*British*]
EFG...........	Edge-Defined Film-Fed Growth [*Photovoltaics*]
efg.............	Effigy (VRA)
EFG...........	Efogi [*Papua New Guinea*] [*Airport symbol*] (OAG)
EFG...........	Electric Field Gradient [*of crystals*]
EFGS..........	Easterling Family Genealogical Society (EA)
EFGTF.........	Entrained-Flow Gasification Test Facility
EFGY..........	Effigy (ABBR)
EFH...........	Earth Far Horizon [*NASA*] (KSC)
EFH...........	Echo-Free Hole [*Meterology*]
EFH...........	Enge's Flaming Hearts (EA)
EFH...........	Engine Flight Hours
EFHA..........	Esperanto Family History Association [*Later, EEFHA*] (EA)
EFHA..........	Halli [*Finland ICAO location identifier*] (ICLI)
EFHC..........	Emanuel Foundation for Hungarian Culture (EA)
EFHF..........	Helsinki/Helsinki-Malmi [*Finland ICAO location identifier*] (ICLI)
EFHK..........	Helsinki/Vantaa [*Finland ICAO location identifier*] (ICLI)
EFHL..........	Hailuoto [*Finland ICAO location identifier*] (ICLI)
EFHM..........	Hameenkyro [*Finland ICAO location identifier*] (ICLI)
EFHN	Hanko [*Finland ICAO location identifier*] (ICLI)
EFHP	Haapavesi [*Finland ICAO location identifier*] (ICLI)
EFHT..........	Ahtari [*Finland ICAO location identifier*] (ICLI)
EFHV..........	Hyvinkaa [*Finland ICAO location identifier*] (ICLI)
EFI............	Educational Futures, Inc. (EA)
efi.............	Efik [*MARC language code Library of Congress*] (LCCP)
EFI............	Electronic Facility Instruction (SAA)
EFI............	Electronic Flash Illuminator
EFI............	Electronic Flight Instruments (WDAA)
EFI............	Electronic Fuel Injection
EFI............	Electronics For Imaging (PCM)
EFI............	Emissary Foundation International (EA)
EFI............	Enrico Fermi Institute [*University of Chicago*]
EFI............	Environic Foundation International (EA)
EFI............	Equestrian Federation of Ireland (EAIO)
EFI............	Error Free Interval (NITA)
EFI............	European Forest Institute
EFI............	Evangelical Friends International (EA)
EFI............	Expedited Flow Indicator [*Telecommunications*] (ACRL)
EFI............	Expeditionary Force Institutions [*Military British*]
e-fi--........	Finland [*MARC geographic area code Library of Congress*] (LCCP)
EFIA..........	European Fertilizer Importers' Associations (EAIO)
EFIB..........	Eastern Freight Inspection Bureau
EFIBCA.......	European Flexible Intermediate Bulk Container Association (PDAA)
EFIC..........	Efficacy (ABBR)
EFIC..........	EFI Electronics [*NASDAQ symbol*] (TTSB)
EFIC..........	EFI Electronics Corp. [*NASDAQ symbol*] (SAG)
EFICNC	Efficiency (ABBR)
EFICNT.......	Efficient (ABBR)
EFICNTY	Efficiently (ABBR)
EFICNY	Efficiency (ABBR)
EFICO.........	Electrical Fitting Inventory Control Branch
EFICON	Electronic Financial Control
EFICP.........	Electronic Flight Instrument Control Panel (MCD)
EFICU.........	Efficacious (ABBR)

EFICY .... Efficiently (ABBR)
EFIE .... Electric Field Integral Equation (PDAA)
EFIEI .... EFI Electronics Corp. [*Associated Press*] (SAG)
EFIF .... Export Finance and Insurance Fund
EFIFC .... European Federation of Investment Funds and Companies (ECON)
EFII .... Electronics for Imaging [*NASDAQ symbol*] (SAG)
EFII .... Electronics For Imaging [*NASDAQ symbol*] (TTSB)
EFII .... Electronics for Imaging, Inc. [*Associated Press*] (SAG)
EFII .... I Salmi [*Finland ICAO location identifier*] (ICLI)
EFIK .... Kiikala [*Finland ICAO location identifier*] (ICLI)
EFIL .... European Federation for Intercultural Learning (EAIO)
EFIL .... Ilmajoki [*Finland ICAO location identifier*] (ICLI)
EFI (M) .... Electronic Fuel Injection (Metering) [*Automotive engineering*]
EFIM .... Immola [*Finland ICAO location identifier*] (ICLI)
EFINS .... Enrico Fermi Institute for Nuclear Studies [*University of Chicago*]
EFIR .... Educational Fund for Individual Rights [*Defunct*] (EA)
EFIRA .... Electric-Field-Induced Infrared Absorption (PDAA)
Efird .... Efird's Reports [*45-56 South Carolina*] [*A publication*] (DLA)
EFIS .... Electronic Flight Information Systems [*FAA*] (TAG)
EFIS .... Electronic Flight Instrument System
EFISGA .... England, France, Ireland, Scotland, Germany, and Aborigines [*See also TUPONA*] [*Suggested early name for Canada*]
EFISH .... Electric Field-Induced Second Harmonic Generation [*Physics*]
EFISHG .... Electric-Field-Induced Second-Harmonic Generation
EFIT .... Electronic Facial Identification Technique
EFIV .... Ivalo [*Finland ICAO location identifier*] (ICLI)
EFJC .... Europaische Foderation Junger Chore [*European Federation of Young Choirs*] (EAIO)
EFJG .... Educational Foundation for Jewish Girls [*Later, Jewish Foundation for Educationof Women*] (EA)
EFJM .... Jamijarvi [*Finland ICAO location identifier*] (ICLI)
EFJO .... Joensuu [*Finland ICAO location identifier*] (ICLI)
EFJP .... Jakalapaa [*Finland ICAO location identifier*] (ICLI)
EFJY .... Jyvaskyla [*Finland ICAO location identifier*] (ICLI)
EFK .... Newport [*Vermont*] [*Airport symbol*] (AD)
EFK .... Newport, VT [*Location identifier FAA*] (FAAL)
EFKA .... Kauhava [*Finland ICAO location identifier*] (ICLI)
EFKE .... Kemi [*Finland ICAO location identifier*] (ICLI)
EFKG .... Kumlinge [*Finland ICAO location identifier*] (ICLI)
EFKH .... Kuhmo [*Finland ICAO location identifier*] (ICLI)
EFKI .... Kajaani [*Finland ICAO location identifier*] (ICLI)
EFKJ .... Kauhajoki [*Finland ICAO location identifier*] (ICLI)
EFKK .... Kruunupyy [*Finland ICAO location identifier*] (ICLI)
EFKL .... Helsinki [*Finland ICAO location identifier*] (ICLI)
EFKM .... Kemijarvi [*Finland ICAO location identifier*] (ICLI)
EFKR .... Karsamaki [*Finland ICAO location identifier*] (ICLI)
EFKS .... Kuusamo [*Finland ICAO location identifier*] (ICLI)
EFKT .... Kittila [*Finland ICAO location identifier*] (ICLI)
EFKU .... Kuopio [*Finland ICAO location identifier*] (ICLI)
EFKV .... Kivijarvi [*Finland ICAO location identifier*] (ICLI)
EFKY .... Kymi [*Finland ICAO location identifier*] (ICLI)
EFL .... Argostolion [*Greece*] [*Airport symbol*] (OAG)
EFL .... Educational Facilities Laboratories [*Defunct*] (EA)
EFL .... Effective Focal Length [*Optics*]
EFL .... Effluent (MSA)
E FL .... Ell, Flemish [*Unit of measure*] (ROG)
EFL .... Emerging Markets Floating Rate Fund [*NYSE symbol*] (SAG)
EFL .... Emerging Mkts Fltg Rt Fd [*NYSE symbol*] (TTSB)
EFL .... Emitter Follower Logic [*Electronics*]
EFL .... English as a Foreign Language
EFL .... Equivalent Focal Length [*Optics*]
EFL .... Error Frequency Limit [*Computer science*] (IAA)
EFL .... Explosion and Flame Laboratory [*British*] (IRUK)
EFL .... External Finance Limit
EFL .... Folkways (Ethnic Folkways Library) [*Record label*]
EFLA .... Educational Film Library Association (EA)
EFLA .... Education for Librarianship - Australia [*A publication*]
EFLA .... European Foundation for Landscape Architecture [*EC*] (ECED)
EFLA .... Vesivehmaa [*Finland ICAO location identifier*] (ICLI)
EFLC .... Engineers Foreign Language Circle (PDAA)
EFLOR .... Effloresce (ABBR)
EFLORD ...... Effloresced (ABBR)
EFLORG ...... Efflorescing (ABBR)
EFLORNC .... Efflorescence (ABBR)
EFLORT....... Efflorescent (ABBR)
EFLP .... Lappeenranta [*Finland ICAO location identifier*] (ICLI)
EFLU .... Effluent (ABBR)
EFL-UAR ..... Egyptian Federation of Labor - United Arab Republic [*Obsolete*]
EFLUNC ...... Effluence (ABBR)
EFLUVA ...... Effluvia (ABBR)
EFLUVL....... Effluvial (ABBR)
EFLUVM...... Effluvium (ABBR)
EFM .... Eight to Fourteen Modulation (IAA)
EFM .... Electric Field Meter
EFM .... Electronic Fetal Monitoring [*Medicine*]
EFM .... Electronic Fuel Metering [*Automotive engineering*]
EFM .... Electronics for Medicine
EFM .... Engineering Feasibility Model (MCD)
EFM .... Enhanced Fighter Maneuverability (MCD)
EFM .... Epifluorescence Microscopy
EFM .... European Federalist Movement
EFM .... Evangelistic Faith Missions (EA)
EFM .... Expeditionary Force Message [*Low-rate cable or radio message selected from a list of standard wordings*]
EFM .... Extensive Field Maintenance [*Military*] (NG)

EFM .... External Fetal Monitoring [*Obstetrics*] (DAVI)
EFM .... Palm Beach Junior College, Lake Worth, FL [*OCLC symbol*] (OCLC)
EFMA .... Emergency Farm Mortgage Act of 1933
EFMA .... European Fertilizer Manufacturers Association (EAIO)
EFMA .... European Financial Management and Marketing Association (EAIO)
EFMA .... European Fittings Manufacturers Association (EAIO)
EFMA .... Evangelical Foreign Missions Association (EA)
EFMA .... Mariehamn [*Finland ICAO location identifier*] (ICLI)
EFMB .... Expert Field Medical Badge [*Military decoration*] (AABC)
EFMC .... Educators Fund Management Corp. [*of NEA*]
EFMC .... E for M Corp. [*NASDAQ symbol*] (SAG)
EFMC .... Elastic Fabric Manufacturers Council of the Northern Textile Association
EFMC .... European Federation of Medicinal Chemistry (EAIO)
EFMCNTA .... Elastic Fabric Manufacturers Council of the Northern Textile Association (EA)
EFMD .... European Foundation for Management Development (EAIO)
EFME .... Menkijarvi [*Finland ICAO location identifier*] (ICLI)
EFMF .... Environmental Fluid Mechanics Foundation [*Monash University*] [*Australia*]
EFMG .... Electric Fuse Manufacturers Guild [*Defunct*] (EA)
EFMI .... Elastic Fabric Manufacturers Institute [*Later, EFMC or EFMCNTA*] (EA)
EFMI .... European Federation for Medical Informatics (EAIO)
EFMI .... Mikkeli [*Finland ICAO location identifier*] (ICLI)
EFMO .... Effigy Mounds National Monument
EFMP .... Emergency Food and Medical Program
EFMP .... Exceptional Family Member Program [*Army*] (INF)
EFMS .... Eucharistic Franciscan Missionary Sisters (TOCD)
EFMS .... Experimental Flight Management System [*Aviation*] (DA)
EFN .... Euro-American Financial [*Vancouver Stock Exchange symbol*]
EFN .... Extrafloral Nectary [*Botany*]
EFN .... Palm Beach Junior College, North Campus Library, Lake Worth, FL [*OCLC symbol*] (OCLC)
EFNEP .... Expanded Food and Nutrition Education Program [*Department of Agriculture*]
EFNMS .... European Federation of National Maintenance Societies [*Sweden*]
EFNRA .... Educational Foundation of the National Restaurant Association (EA)
EFNS .... Educational Foundation for Nuclear Science (EA)
EFNSW .... Esperanto Federation of New South Wales [*Australia*]
EFNU .... Nummela [*Finland ICAO location identifier*] (ICLI)
EFO .... East Fork, AK [*Location identifier FAA*] (FAAL)
EFO .... Error, Freak, Oddity
EFOA .... European Fuel Oxygenates Association (EAIO)
EFOCC .... Errors, Freaks and Oddities Collector's Club (EA)
EFOC/LAN ... European Fiber Optic Communications and Local Area Network Exposition [*Information Gatekeepers, Inc.*]
EFOGM .... Enhanced Fiber-Optic-Guided Missiles [*DoD*]
EFOMP........ European Federation of Organizations for Medical Physics [*EC*] (ECED)
EFOP .... Economic Feasibility of Projects and Investments
EFOP .... Expanded Function Operator Panel (MHDB)
EFOP .... Oripaa [*Finland ICAO location identifier*] (ICLI)
EFOR .... Equivalent Forced Outage Rate (IEEE)
EFOR .... Oritkari [*Finland ICAO location identifier*] (ICLI)
e-forms........ Electronic-Forms (CDE)
EFOSS .... Engineer Family of Systems Study (MCD)
EFOU .... Oulu [*Finland ICAO location identifier*] (ICLI)
EFP .... Effective Filtration Pressure [*Physiology*]
EFP .... Electric Fire Pump [*Nuclear energy*] (NRCH)
EFP .... Electronic Field Production (IEEE)
EFP .... Emergency Firing Panel
EFP .... End Forming Press
EFP .... Endoneurial Fluid Pressure (PDAA)
EFP .... Error-Free Performance
EFP .... ESA Furnished Property (MCD)
EFP .... ESA [*European Space Agency*] Furnished Property
EFP .... Escaped Federal Prisoner
EFP .... Europaeische Foederalistische Partei [*European Federalist Party*] [*Austria*] (PPE)
EFP .... European Federation of Parasitologists (EAIO)
EFP .... European Federation of Purchasing (PDAA)
EFP .... Exchange for Physicals [*Commodities exchange*]
EFP .... Explosively-Formed Penetrator [*Army*] (RDA)
EFPA .... European Food Phosphates Producers' Association (EAIO)
EFPA .... European Food Service and Packaging Association [*British*] (EAIO)
EFPD .... Effective Full Power Day (KSC)
EFPE .... Pello [*Finland ICAO location identifier*] (ICLI)
EFPH .... Equivalent Full Power Hour [*FCC*]
EFPH .... Evaluating Fallout Protection in Homes [*Later, HFPS*] [*Civil Defense*]
EFPI .... European Federation of the Plywood Industry (EA)
EFPI .... Piikajarvi [*Finland ICAO location identifier*] (ICLI)
EFPIA .... European Federation of Pharmaceutical Industries' Associations (EA)
EFPK .... Pieksamaki [*Finland ICAO location identifier*] (ICLI)
EFPL .... English and Foreign Philosophical Library [*A publication*]
EFPM .... Effective Full Power Month (NRCH)
EFPM .... Employers' Federation of Paper Makers (DGA)
EFPO .... Pori [*Finland ICAO location identifier*] (ICLI)
EFPPA .... European Federation of Professional Psychologists Associations (EA)
EFPROUT .... Effecting Promotion, Procedure Outlined [*Military*] (DNAB)
EFPS .... European Federation of Productivity Services [*Stockholm, Sweden*] (EA)
EFPS .... Rovaniemi [*Finland ICAO location identifier*] (ICLI)
EFPU .... Pudasjarvi [*Finland ICAO location identifier*] (ICLI)

EFPV............	Eisenhower Foundation for the Prevention of Violence [*Later, Milton S. Eisenhower Federation*] (EA)
EFPW...........	European Federation for the Protection of Waters
EFPWCM......	European Federation of Pallet and Wooden Crate Manufacturers (EA)
EFPY............	Effective Full-Power Years (NRCH)
EFPY............	Pyhasalmi [*Finland ICAO location identifier*] (ICLI)
EFPZ............	Export Free Processing Zone
EFQFFM.......	European Federation of Quick Frozen Food Manufacturers [*Belgium*] (EAIO)
EFR..............	Echo Free Room
EFR..............	Effective Filtration Rate [*Physiology*]
EFR..............	Electro-Flux Remelting [*Metal industry*]
EFR..............	Electronic Failure Report
EFR..............	Elf Air Ltd. [*Russian Federation*] [*ICAO designator*] (FAAC)
E FR.............	Ell, French [*Unit of measure*] (ROG)
EFR..............	Elliott Forbes-Robinson [*Race car driver*]
EFR..............	Emergency Fund Request
EFR..............	Emerging Flux Region (OA)
EFR..............	Engine Firing Rate (NVT)
EFR..............	Engine Flat Rate
EFR..............	Entrained-Flow Reactor [*Chemical engineering*]
EFR..............	Environmental Flow Requirements of Australia's Waterways (EERA)
EFR..............	Equipment Failure Rate
EFR..............	European Fast Reactor [*Physics*]
EFR..............	Exact Finite Range
EFR..............	Expect Further Routing [*Aviation*] (FAAC)
EFR..............	Extended-Field Radiotherapy [*Radiology*]
e-fr--...........	France [*MARC geographic area code Library of Congress*] (LCCP)
EFRA...........	Rautavaara [*Finland ICAO location identifier*] (ICLI)
EFRAG	Red Blood Cell Fragility [*Test*] [*Hematoloy*] (DAVI)
EFRAP.........	Exchange Feeder Route Analysis Program [*Bell System*]
EFRC...........	Education Funding Research Council (EA)
EFRC...........	Edwards Flight Research Center [*NASA*]
EFRH	Pattijoki [*Finland ICAO location identifier*] (ICLI)
EFRIS..........	External Finished Reports Information Subsystem [*Computer science*]
EFRN	Rantasalmi [*Finland ICAO location identifier*] (ICLI)
EFRNT	Effrontery (ABBR)
EFRO	Electronic Failure Report Only
EFRO	Rovaniemi Airport [*Finland ICAO location identifier*] (ICLI)
EFRP...........	European Federation for Retirement Provision (ECON)
EFRT...........	Effort (ABBR)
EFRT...........	European Federation of Retail Traders [*Belgium*] (EAIO)
EFRT...........	External Floating Roof Tank [*Engineering*]
EFRTLS.......	Effortless (ABBR)
EFRTLSNS ..	Effortlessness (ABBR)
EFRTLSY.....	Effortlessly (ABBR)
EFRV...........	Kiuruvesi [*Finland ICAO location identifier*] (ICLI)
EFRVS	Effervesce (ABBR)
EFRVSD	Effervesced (ABBR)
EFRVSG	Effervescing (ABBR)
EFRVSNC....	Effervescence (ABBR)
EFRVST.......	Effervescent (ABBR)
EFRY...........	Rayskala [*Finland ICAO location identifier*] (ICLI)
EFS	Earth-Fixed System
EFS	Electric Field-Induced Spectra
EFS	Electric Field Strength
EFS	Electronic Firing Switches [*Military*] (NG)
EFS	Electronic Frequency Selection (IEEE)
EFS	Emergency Feeding Service [*Civil Defense*]
EFS	Emergency Feedwater System [*Nuclear energy*] (NRCH)
EFS	End of Frame Sequence [*Telecommunications*] (ACRL)
EFS	Enhanced Flight Screening (DOMA)
EFS	Enhance Financial Services Group [*NYSE symbol*] (SAG)
EFS	Enhance Financial Svcs Grp [*NYSE symbol*] (TTSB)
EFS	Error Free Seconds (TEL)
EFS	Europe Falcon Service [*France ICAO designator*] (FAAC)
EFS	Experimental Firing Ship
EFS	Export Facilitation Scheme [*Motor vehicles*] [*Australia*]
EFS	External File System (BYTE)
EFS	Extrafield Sensitivity [*Photonics*]
EFSA...........	England Football Supporters Association (DBA)
EFSA...........	European Federation of Sea Anglers (EAIO)
EFSA...........	Savonlinna [*Finland ICAO location identifier*] (ICLI)
EFSE...........	Engineering Factory Support Equipment (SAA)
EFSE...........	Selanpaa [*Finland ICAO location identifier*] (ICLI)
EFSH...........	Equine Follicle Stimulating Hormone [*Endocrinology*]
EFSJ	Sonkajarvi-Jyrkka [*Finland ICAO location identifier*] (ICLI)
EFSO...........	Sodankyla [*Finland ICAO location identifier*] (ICLI)
EFSORPA.....	Elliptic Function Second-Order Ripple Phase Approximation
EFSP...........	Electrolytic Fused-Salt Process
EFSP...........	Electronic Family Security Program [*of Sun Life Assurance Co. of Canada*]
EFSP...........	Emergency Food and Shelter Program [*FEMA*]
EFSR...........	Electronic Field Seaman Recruit [*Military*] (IAA)
EFSS...........	E. F. Schumacher Society (EA)
EFSS...........	Emergency Food Supply Scheme [*World Food Program*]
EFSS...........	Experimental Flight Systems Section [*Langley*]
EFSSS.........	Engine Failure Sensing and Shutdown System [*NASA*] (KSC)
EFSU...........	Suomussalmi [*Finland ICAO location identifier*] (ICLI)
EFSUMB......	European Federation of Societies of Ultrasound in Medicine and Biology (EAIO)
EFT	Early Finish Time
EFT	Effect (MSA)
EFT	Electronic Funds Transfer [*Banking*]
EFT	Electronic Fund Tape [*Banking*]
EFT	Electrostatically Focused Tube
EFT	Embedded Figures Test [*Psychology*]
EFT	Emergency Flight Termination (AFM)
EFT	Engineering Feasibility Test (CAAL)
EFT	Engineering Flight Test
EFT	Enhanced Forecaster Tools [*Branch*] [*Marine science*] (OSRA)
EFT	Enhanced Forecaster Tools [*Forecast Systems Laboratory*] [*Branch*] (USDC)
EFT	Eno Foundation for Transportation (EA)
EFT	Etchingham Family Tree (EA)
EFT	Experimental Flight Test
EFT	External Function Translator
EFT	Oklahoma Executive Jet Charter, Inc. [*FAA designator*] (FAAC)
EFTA...........	Effectuate (ABBR)
EFTA...........	Electronic Funds Transfer Association [*Washington, DC*] (EA)
EFTA...........	Electronic Fund Transfer Act [*1978*]
EFTA...........	Enrolled Federal Tax Accountant [*EFTA Institute*] [*Designation awarded by*]
EFTA...........	ERADCOM [*Electronics Research and Development Command*] Flight Test Activity
EFTA...........	European Fair Trade Association [*Netherlands*] (EAIO)
EFTA...........	European Flexographic Technical Association (PDAA)
EFTA...........	European Foreign Trade Association
EFTA...........	European Free Trade Area (DS)
EFTA...........	European Free Trade Association [*Known as the "Outer Seven" as opposed to the "Inner Six" Common Market nations*] [*Switzerland*]
EFTA...........	European Free Trade Association (EERA)
EFTAD.........	Effectuated (ABBR)
EFTAG.........	Effecting (ABBR)
EFTC...........	Edwards Flight Test Center [*NASA*]
EFTC...........	Electronic Fab Technology [*NASDAQ symbol*] (SAG)
EFTC...........	Elementary Flying Training College [*British*]
EFTC...........	European Fluorocarbon Technical Committee [*of the European Council of Chemical Manufacturers' Federations*] [*Belgium*] (EAIO)
EFTC...........	European Freight Timetable Conference (EAIO)
EFTCBFC.....	Elvis Forever TCB [*Taking Care of Business*] Fan Club (EA)
EFTE...........	Tervola [*Finland ICAO location identifier*] (ICLI)
EFTEC.........	European Fluorocarbon Technical Committee [*of the European Council of Chemical Manufacturers' Federations*] (EAIO)
EFTI	Engineering Flight Test Inspector
EFTI	Engineering Flight Test Instrumentation (AAG)
EFTL	Effectual (ABBR)
EFTO...........	Encrypted for Transmission Overseas (MCD)
EFTO...........	Encrypt for Transmission Only [*Military*]
EFTP...........	Error File Teaching Package (NITA)
EFTP...........	Tampere-Pirkkala [*Finland ICAO location identifier*] (ICLI)
EFTPOB.......	Electronic Funds Transfer at Point of Banking
EFTPOS.......	Electronic Funds Transfer at Point of Sale
EFTPoS.......	Electronic Funds Transfer at Point of Sales (EERA)
EFTR...........	Engineering Flight Test Report
EFTRO	European Federation of Tobacco Retail Organizations (EAIO)
EFTS...........	Electronic Funds Transfer System [*or Service*] [*Banking National Science Foundation*]
EFTS...........	Elementary Flying Training School [*British*]
EFT's..........	Expanded Field [*Prism*] Telescopes [*Instrumentation*]
EFTS...........	Teisko [*Finland ICAO location identifier*] (ICLI)
EFTSU.........	Equivalent Full-Time Student Unit
EFTTA.........	European Fishing Tackle Trade Association (EAIO)
EFTU...........	Turku [*Finland ICAO location identifier*] (ICLI)
EFTUNMW ...	European Federation of Trade Unions of Non-Manual Workers [*Belgium*] (EY)
EFTV...........	Effectivity
EFTVNS.......	Effectiveness (ABBR)
EFTVY.........	Effectively (ABBR)
EFU	Eastern Enterprises [*NYSE symbol*] (SPSG)
EFU	Equivalent Fatality Unit [*National Highway Traffic Safety Administration*]
EFU	Europaische Frauen Union [*Austria*] (EAIO)
EFULG	Effulgent (ABBR)
EFULGNC.....	Effulgence (ABBR)
EFUS	Effuse (ABBR)
EFUSD	Effused (ABBR)
EFUSG	Effusing (ABBR)
EFUSN	Effusion (ABBR)
EFUSV	Effusive (ABBR)
EFUSVNS.....	Effusiveness (ABBR)
EFUSVY.......	Effusively (ABBR)
EFUT...........	Utti [*Finland ICAO location identifier*] (ICLI)
EFV	Electric Field Vector
EFV	Epilepsy Foundation of Victoria [*Australia*]
EFV	Equestrian Federation of Victoria [*Australia*]
EFV	Equilibrium Flash Vaporization (PDAA)
EFV	Excess Flow Valve
EFV	Extracellular Fluid Volume [*Physiology*]
EFVA...........	Educational Foundation for Visual Arts [*British*]
EFVA...........	European Federation of Vending Associations (EA)
EFVA...........	Vaasa [*Finland ICAO location identifier*] (ICLI)
EFVC...........	Expiratory Flow-Volume Curve [*Medicine*]
EFVI	Viitasaari [*Finland ICAO location identifier*] (ICLI)
EFVL...........	Vaala [*Finland ICAO location identifier*] (ICLI)

EFVP .... El Salvador Film and Video Projects [*Later, El Salvadore Media Projects*] (EA)
EFVR .... Varkaus [*Finland ICAO location identifier*] (ICLI)
EFVS .... Electronic Fighting Vehicle System [*Army*]
EFVU .... Vuotso [*Finland ICAO location identifier*] (ICLI)
EFW .... Electric Field and Waves
EFW .... Emergency Feedwater [*System*] [*Nuclear energy*] (NRCH)
EFW .... Estimated Fetal Weight [*Obstetrics*] (DAVI)
EFW .... Executive Financial Woman [*National Association of Bank Women*] [*A publication*]
EFW .... Jefferson, IA [*Location identifier FAA*] (FAAL)
EFWB .... Wredeby [*Finland ICAO location identifier*] (ICLI)
EFWS .... Emergency Feedwater System [*Nuclear energy*] (NRCH)
EFWS .... Evaluation of Foreign Weapons Systems (MCD)
EFWST .... Emergency Feedwater Storage Tank [*Nuclear energy*] (NRCH)
EFX .... Equifax, Inc. [*Formerly, Retail Credit Co.*] [*NYSE symbol*] (SPSG)
EFX .... Special Effects (NTCM)
EFY .... End of Fiscal Year (AFM)
EFYC .... European Federation of Young Choirs [*See also EFJC*] (EA)
EFYL .... Ylivieska-Raudaskyla [*Finland ICAO location identifier*] (ICLI)
EFZ .... Electronic Final Zero
EFZ .... Exclusive Fishing Zone
EG .... Economic Geography [*A publication*] (BRI)
EG .... Economics and Government [*Office of Management and Budget*]
EG .... Edge Grain
eg .... Edges Gilt [*Bookbinding*] (BARN)
Eg .... Egidius de Fuscarariis [*Deceased, 1289*] [*Authority cited in pre-1607 legal work*] (DSA)
EG .... Egypt [*ANSI two-letter standard code*] (CNC)
EG .... Egyptian (ROG)
EG .... Ejusdem Generis [*Of the Same Kind*] [*Latin*]
EG .... Electrogalvanizing [*Automotive engineering*]
EG .... Electron Gun (OA)
EG .... Electronic Guidance (AAG)
EG .... Else Good [*In good condition except for defects mentioned*] [*Antiquarian book trade*]
EG .... Emergency Generator (NRCH)
EG .... Emergency Generator Room [*NFPA pre-fire planning symbol*] (NFPA)
EG .... Emergency Grade [*Automotive engineering*] [*Polymer Steel Corp.*]
EG .... Employment Guide (CAAL)
EG .... Enamel Single Glass [*Wire insulation*] (IAA)
EG .... Endoglucanases [*An enzyme*]
EG .... Engelbert's "Goils" [*An association*] (EA)
EG .... Engineering Geologist
E/G .... Engine-Generator
EG .... Enteric Ganglion [*Neurology*]
EG .... Entry Guidance [*NASA*] (NASA)
EG .... Environment Generator [*Computer software*]
EG .... Enziklopedyah Shel Galuyot (BJA)
EG .... Eosinophilic Granuloma [*Medicine*]
eg .... Equatorial Guinea [*MARC country of publication code Library of Congress*] (LCCP)
EG .... Escort Group
EG .... Esophagogastrectomy [*Medicine*]
EG .... Esquerra Gallega [*Galician Left*] [*Political party*] (PPW)
EG .... Estate Gazette [*A publication*] (DLA)
EG .... Estrone Glucuronide [*Endocrinology*]
EG .... Ethylene Glycol [*Organic chemistry*]
EG .... European Greens [*Brussels, Belgium Political party*] (EAIO)
EG .... Executive Generator
EG .... Exempli Gratia [*For Example*] [*Latin*]
EG .... Ex Grege [*Among the Rest*] [*Latin*]
EG .... Existential Generalization [*Rule of quantification*] [*Logic*]
EG .... Expenditure Greater Than [*Dialog*] [*Searchable field*] [*Information service or system*] (NITA)
EG .... Experimental Assistant, Gunnery [*British military*] (DMA)
EG .... Experimental Glider
EG .... Experimental Group
EG .... Expert Gunner [*Army*]
EG .... Exploratory Group (NATG)
EG .... External Genitalia [*Medicine*] (DAVI)
eg .... For Example [*Exempli Gratia*] [*Latin*] (WDMC)
EG .... Roederer Aviation [*ICAO designator*] (AD)
EGA .... Agnes Scott College, Decatur, GA [*OCLC symbol*] (OCLC)
EGA .... Die Entwicklung der Glyptik Waehrend der Akkad-Zeit [*A publication*] (BJA)
EGA .... East German Army (CINC)
EGA .... Ecuato Guineana de Aviacion [*Equatorial Guinea*] [*ICAO designator*] (FAAC)
EGA .... Edge Gradient Analysis
EGA .... Effluent [*or Evolved*] Gas Analysis
EGA .... Elizabeth Garrett Anderson Hospital [*British*] (DI)
EGA .... Embroiderers' Guild of America (EA)
EGA .... Eminent Grand Almoner [*Freemasonry*] (ROG)
EGA .... End Game Analysis
EGA .... Engineering Assistant
EGA .... Enhanced Graphics Adapter [*Computer technology*]
EGA .... Equato-Guinean de Aviacion [*Airline*] [*Equatorial Guinea*]
EGA .... Estimated Gestational Age
EGA .... Evolved Gas Analysis [*Chemistry*]
EGA .... Exhaust Gas Analyzer (MCD)
EGA .... Export Guarantees Act
EGA .... Extended Graphics Array [*Computer science*] (EERA)
EGAA .... Belfast/Aldergrove [*British ICAO location identifier*] (ICLI)
EGAA .... Emergency General Account of Advances

EGAA .... Enhanced Graphics Acquisition and Analysis [*Computer science*]
EGAAE .... European Group of Artists of the Ardennes and the Eifel (EAIO)
EGAB .... Enniskillen/St. Angelo [*British ICAO location identifier*] (ICLI)
EGAC .... Belfast Harbour [*British ICAO location identifier*] (ICLI)
EGACT .... Embroiderers' Guild of the Australian Capital Territory
EGAD .... Electric Power Generation and Distribution (MCD)
EGAD .... Electronegative Gas Detector
EGAD .... Electronic Ground Automatic Destruct [*Air Force*]
EGAD .... Newtownards [*British ICAO location identifier*] (ICLI)
EGADS .... Electronic Ground Automatic Destruct Sequencer [*Air Force*]
EGAE .... Londonderry/Eglinton [*British ICAO location identifier*] (ICLI)
EGAL .... Egalitarian
EGAL .... Elevation Guidance for Approach and Landing [*Aviation*]
EGAL .... Langford Lodge [*British ICAO location identifier*] (ICLI)
EGALSM .... Egalitarianism (ABBR)
EGALTR .... Egalitarian (ABBR)
EGALTRM ..... Egalitarianism (ABBR)
EGAMS .... Evolved Gas Analysis Mass Spectrometry (MCD)
Egan Bills .... Egan. Bills of Sale [*4th ed.*] [*1882*] [*A publication*] (DLA)
EG&G/ID .... EG&G Idaho, Inc. (GAAI)
EGAO .... Encyclopedia of Governmental Advisory Organizations [*A publication*]
EGAP .... End Game Analysis Program (MCD)
EGAS .... Educational Grants Advisory Service (AIE)
EGAS .... Energas Co. (MHDW)
EGAS .... European Group for Atomic Spectroscopy (EAIO)
EGASCAC .... Educational Guidance Associates School and College Advisory Center [*Formerly, SCAC*] (EA)
EGB .... Episcopal Guild for the Blind (EA)
EGB .... Expected Gentlemanly Behavior (DSUE)
EGBAR .... Everything's Going to Be All Right
EGBB .... Birmingham [*British ICAO location identifier*] (ICLI)
EGBDF .... Every Good Boy Deserves Favour [*Title of play by Tom Stoppard*]
EGBDF .... Every Good Boy Does Fine [*or Deserves Favor*] [*Mnemonic guide to notes on the treble clef*]
EGBE .... Coventry [*British ICAO location identifier*] (ICLI)
EGBG .... Leicester [*British ICAO location identifier*] (ICLI)
EGBJ .... Gloucester and Cheltenham/Staverton [*British ICAO location identifier*] (ICLI)
EGBK .... Northampton/Sywell [*British ICAO location identifier*] (ICLI)
EGBM .... Tatenhill [*British ICAO location identifier*] (ICLI)
EGBN .... Nottingham [*British ICAO location identifier*] (ICLI)
EGBO .... Halfpenny Green [*British ICAO location identifier*] (ICLI)
EGBP .... Pailton [*British ICAO location identifier*] (ICLI)
EGBPS .... Equilibrium-Grated Blood Pool Study [*Hematology*] (DAVI)
EGBS .... Shobdon [*British ICAO location identifier*] (ICLI)
EGBUS .... External Genitalia, Bartholin, Urethral, Skene's Glands [*Medicine*] (DMAA)
EGBW .... Wellesbourne Mountford [*British ICAO location identifier*] (ICLI)
EGC .... Bergerac [*France*] [*Airport symbol Obsolete*] (OAG)
EGC .... Eagle [*Colorado*] [*Seismograph station code, US Geological Survey Closed*] (SEIS)
EGC .... East Gippsland Coalition (EERA)
EGC .... Ebony Gold Corp. [*Vancouver Stock Exchange symbol*]
EGC .... Economic Growth Center [*Yale University*] (PDAA)
EGC .... Educational Guidance Center for the Mentally Retarded [*Defunct*] (EA)
EGC .... Effective Government Committee (EA)
EGC .... Electronic Governor Control [*Automotive engineering*]
EGC .... Electronic Gyro Compass
EGC .... Eminent Grand Commander [*Freemasonry*] (ROG)
EGC .... Engineer Group, Construction [*Military*]
EGC .... Epigallocathechin [*Biochemistry*]
EGC .... Epithelioid A Globoid Cell [*Medicine*] (AAMN)
EGC .... Executive Group of Companies [*Engineering Council*] (ACII)
EGC .... Experiments Ground Computer [*NASA*] (NASA)
EGC .... Exposure Growth Curve
EGCA .... Coal Aston [*British ICAO location identifier*] (ICLI)
EGCB .... Manchester/Barton [*British ICAO location identifier*] (ICLI)
EGCC .... Manchester International [*British ICAO location identifier*] (ICLI)
EGCD .... Woodford [*British ICAO location identifier*] (ICLI)
EGCE .... Wrexham/Borras [*British ICAO location identifier*] (ICLI)
EGCF .... Sandtoft [*British ICAO location identifier*] (ICLI)
EGCG .... Epigallocatechin Gallate [*Biochemistry*]
EGCG .... Strubby [*British ICAO location identifier*] (ICLI)
EGCH .... Holyhead [*British ICAO location identifier*] (ICLI)
EGCI .... Doncaster [*British ICAO location identifier*] (ICLI)
EGCI .... Export Group for the Construction Industries [*British*]
EGCJ .... Sherburn-In-Elmet [*British ICAO location identifier*] (ICLI)
EGCL .... Electro-Generated Chemiluminescence (PDAA)
EGCL .... Fenland [*British ICAO location identifier*] (ICLI)
EGCM .... European Group for Cooperation in Management (PDAA)
EGCM .... European Group of Cellulose Manufacturers [*Defunct*] (EA)
EGCMC .... European Glass Container Manufacturers' Committee [*British*] (EAIO)
EGCN .... Northern Area Maintenance Unit [*British ICAO location identifier*] (ICLI)
EGCPM .... European Group of Corrugated Paper Makers (EAIO)
EGCR .... Experimental Gas-Cooled Reactor
E/GCR .... Extended Group Coded Recording [*Computer science*] (IBMDP)
EGCR .... Extragalactic Cosmic Ray
EGCS .... English Guernsey Cattle Society [*British*]
EGCS .... Sturgate [*British ICAO location identifier*] (ICLI)
EGCV .... Exhaust Gas Check Valve [*Automotive engineering*]
EGD .... Effluent Gas Detection (BARN)
EGD .... Effluent Guidelines Division [*Environmental Protection Agency*]
EGD .... Electrogasdynamic [*Generator*]

EGD .... Esophagogastroduodenoscopy [*Medicine*]
EGD .... Estates Gazette Digest of Cases [*A publication*] (DLA)
EGD .... Evolved Gas Detection [*Chemistry*]
EGDA .... Brawdy [*British ICAO location identifier*] (ICLI)
EGDA .... Ethylene Glycol Diacetate [*Organic chemistry*]
EGDB .... Plymouth (Mount Wise) [*British ICAO location identifier*] (ICLI)
EGDC .... Chivenor [*British ICAO location identifier*] (ICLI)
EGDC .... Estates Gazette Digest of Cases [*A publication*] (DLA)
EGDD .... Royal Air Force Supervisory Centre Communications [*British ICAO location identifier*] (ICLI)
EGDE .... Ethylene Glycol Dimethyl Ether [*Also, DME, GLYME*] [*Organic chemistry*]
EGDF .... Embryonic Growth and Development Factor [*Biochemistry*]
EGDG .... St. Mawgan [*British ICAO location identifier*] (ICLI)
EGDH .... Royal Air Force 1 Group [*British ICAO location identifier*] (ICLI)
EGDJ .... Upavon [*British ICAO location identifier*] (ICLI)
EGDK .... Kemble [*British ICAO location identifier*] (ICLI)
EGDL .... Lyneham [*British ICAO location identifier*] (ICLI)
EGDM .... Boscombe Down [*British ICAO location identifier*] (ICLI)
EGDMA .... Ethylene Glycol Dimethacrylate [*Organic chemistry*]
EGDN .... Ethylene Glycol Dinitrate [*Organic chemistry*]
EGDN .... Netheravon [*British ICAO location identifier*] (ICLI)
EGDP .... Portland [*British ICAO location identifier*] (ICLI)
EGDR .... Culdrose [*British ICAO location identifier*] (ICLI)
EGDS .... Bulford/Salisbury Plain [*British ICAO location identifier*] (ICLI)
EGDS .... Equipment Group Design Specifications (NATG)
EGDT .... Wroughton [*British ICAO location identifier*] (ICLI)
EGDV .... Hullavington [*British ICAO location identifier*] (ICLI)
EGDX .... St. Athan [*British ICAO location identifier*] (ICLI)
EGDY .... Yeovilton [*British ICAO location identifier*] (ICLI)
EGE .... Eagle, CO [*Location identifier FAA*] (FAAL)
EGE .... Elevated Glandular Epidermis
EGE .... Emergency Ground Egress (MCD)
EGE .... Engelbert's Golden Eagles (EA)
EGE .... Enhanced Greenhouse Effect (EERA)
EGE .... Eosinophilic Gastroenteropathy [*Medicine*]
e-ge-- .... Germany, East [*MARC geographic area code Library of Congress*] (LCCP)
EGECON ...... Electronic Geographic Coordinate Navigation (MCD)
E GER .... East Germany
Eg Ext .... Egan on Extradition [*1846*] [*A publication*] (DLA)
EGF .... AMR American Eagle, Inc. [*ICAO designator*] (FAAC)
EGF .... Electrical Grapple Fixture (MCD)
EGF .... Energy Guideline Factors
EGF .... Englefield Resources [*Vancouver Stock Exchange symbol*]
EGF .... Epicorum Graecorum Fragmenta [*A publication*] (OCD)
EGF .... Epidermal Growth Factor [*Endocrinology*]
EGF .... Europaeische Go Foderation [*European Go Federation - EGF*] [*Austria*] (EAIO)
EGF .... European Grassland Federation (EA)
EGFC .... Cardiff/Tremorfa [*British ICAO location identifier*] (ICLI)
EGFC .... Eagle Financial [*NASDAQ symbol*] (SAG)
EGFE .... Haverfordwest [*British ICAO location identifier*] (ICLI)
EGFF .... Cardiff [*British ICAO location identifier*] (ICLI)
EGFH .... Swansea [*British ICAO location identifier*] (ICLI)
EGFI .... Weston-Super-Mare [*British ICAO location identifier*] (ICLI)
EGFR .... Epidermal Growth Factor Receptor [*Biochemistry*]
EGFRK .... Epidermal Growth Factor Receptor Kinase [*An enzyme*]
EGF-URO .... Epidermal Growth Factor - Urogastrone [*Endocrinology*]
EGG .... Educational Growth Group (DICI)
EGG .... EG & G, Inc. [*NYSE symbol*] (SPSG)
EGG .... Eggerton [*England*]
EGG .... Electric Glue Gun
EGG .... Electrogastrogram [*Medicine*]
eGG .... Electronic Gourmet Guide [*America Online Greenhouse program*]
EGGA .... European General Galvanizers Association (EA)
EGGA .... London [*British ICAO location identifier*] (ICLI)
EGGB .... London [*British ICAO location identifier*] (ICLI)
EGGC .... London [*British ICAO location identifier*] (ICLI)
EGGD .... Bristol/Lulsgate [*British ICAO location identifier*] (ICLI)
Egg Dam...... Eggleston on Damages [*A publication*] (DLA)
EGGE .... Bletchley [*British ICAO location identifier*] (ICLI)
EGGF .... Uxbridge [*British ICAO location identifier*] (ICLI)
Egghead ...... Egghead, Inc. [*Associated Press*] (SAG)
EGGN .... United Kingdom International NOTAM Office [*ICAO location identifier*] (ICLI)
EGGO .... London [*British ICAO location identifier*] (ICLI)
EGGP .... Liverpool [*British ICAO location identifier*] (ICLI)
EGGQ .... Liverpool [*British ICAO location identifier*] (ICLI)
EGGR .... Redhill [*British ICAO location identifier*] (ICLI)
EGGS .... Egghead, Inc. [*NASDAQ symbol*] (NQ)
EGGW .... Luton [*British ICAO location identifier*] (ICLI)
EGGX .... Shanwick [*British ICAO location identifier*] (ICLI)
EGGY .... United Kingdom MOTNE Centre [*ICAO location identifier*] (ICLI)
EGH .... Europaische Gesellschaft fuer Herbologie [*European Weed Research Society*] (EAIO)
EGH .... Everton's Genealogical Helper [*A publication*]
EGHA .... Compton Abbas [*British ICAO location identifier*] (ICLI)
EGHC .... Land's End/St. Just [*British ICAO location identifier*] (ICLI)
EGHD .... Plymouth/Roborough [*British ICAO location identifier*] (ICLI)
EGHE .... Scilly Isles/St. Mary's [*British ICAO location identifier*] (ICLI)
EGHG .... Yeovil [*British ICAO location identifier*] (ICLI)
EGHH .... Bournemouth/Hurn [*British ICAO location identifier*] (ICLI)
EGHI .... Southampton [*British ICAO location identifier*] (ICLI)
EGHJ .... Bembridge [*British ICAO location identifier*] (ICLI)

EGHK .... Penzance/Eastern Green [*British ICAO location identifier*] (ICLI)
EGHL .... Lasham [*British ICAO location identifier*] (ICLI)
EGHM .... Hamble [*British ICAO location identifier*] (ICLI)
EGHN .... Sandown (Isle Of Wight) [*British ICAO location identifier*] (ICLI)
EGHO .... Thruxton [*British ICAO location identifier*] (ICLI)
EGHP .... Employer Group Health Plan [*Department of Health and Human Services*] (GFGA)
EGHR .... Chichester/Goodwood [*British ICAO location identifier*] (ICLI)
EGHS .... Henstridge [*British ICAO location identifier*] (ICLI)
EGHT .... EightXEight, Inc. [*NASDAQ symbol*] (SAG)
EGHTFD ...... Eightfold (ABBR)
EGHTH .... Eightieth (ABBR)
Egi .... Egidius de Losano [*Authority cited in pre-1607 legal work*] (DSA)
EGI .... Egilsstadir [*Iceland*] [*Seismograph station code, US Geological Survey*] (SEIS)
EGI .... Explosive Gas Indicator
e-gi-- .... Gibraltar [*MARC geographic area code Library of Congress*] (LCCP)
EGI .... Valparaiso, FL [*Location identifier FAA*] (FAAL)
Egid .... Egidius de Fuscarariis [*Deceased, 1289*] [*Authority cited in pre-1607 legal work*] (DSA)
Egid Bellam... Egidius Bellamera [*Deceased, 1407*] [*Authority cited in pre-1607 legal work*] (DSA)
EGIF .... Equipment Group Interface
EGIFO .... Edward Grey Institute of Field Ornithology (BARN)
EGIL .... Electrical, General Instrumentation, and Lighting Engineer (MCD)
EGIL .... Environmental, General Instrumentation, Life Support [*NASA*] (KSC)
EGIS .... Encyclopedia of Geographic Information Sources [*A publication*]
EGIS .... European Geographical Information Systems Symposia (EERA)
EGIS .... Executive Guide to Information Sources [*Later, EBIS*] [*A publication*]
EGIS .... Exhaust Gas Ionization Sensor [*Automotive engineering*]
EGJ .... Eagle Jet Charter, Inc. [*FAA designator*] (FAAC)
EGJ .... Esophagogastric Junction [*Anatomy*] (DAVI)
EGJA .... Alderney, Channel Islands [*British ICAO location identifier*] (ICLI)
EGJB .... Guernsey, Channel Islands [*British ICAO location identifier*] (ICLI)
EGJC .... Eagle Grove Junior College [*Iowa*]
EGJ/IFJ .... European Group of Journalists/International Federation of Journalists [*EC*] (ECED)
EGJJ .... Jersey, Channel Islands [*British ICAO location identifier*] (ICLI)
EGK .... Dayton, OH [*Location identifier FAA*] (FAAL)
EGK .... Ein Grosser Komponist [*A Great Composer*] or Ein Genialer Komponist [*A Great Genius of a Composer*] [*Suggested interpretations for the adopted surname of German composer Werner Egk. Egk maintained that he chose the name in honor of his wife*]
EGKA .... Shoreham [*British ICAO location identifier*] (ICLI)
EGKB .... Biggin Hill [*British ICAO location identifier*] (ICLI)
EGKC .... Bognor Regis [*British ICAO location identifier*] (ICLI)
EGKE .... Challock [*British ICAO location identifier*] (ICLI)
EGKH .... Lashenden/Headcorn [*British ICAO location identifier*] (ICLI)
EGKK .... London/Gatwick [*British ICAO location identifier*] (ICLI)
EGKM .... West Malling [*British ICAO location identifier*] (ICLI)
EGKR .... Redhill [*British ICAO location identifier*] (ICLI)
EGKS .... Europaeische Gemeinschaft fuer Kohle und Stahl [*European Coal and Steel Community*] [*German*] (DCTA)
EGKT .... Early Grand Knight Templar [*Freemasonry*] (ROG)
EGL .... Capital Trading Aviation Ltd. [*British ICAO designator*] (FAAC)
EGL .... Eagle
EGL .... Eagle Precision Technologies, Inc. [*Toronto Stock Exchange symbol*]
EGL .... Eclectic Grand Lodge [*Freemasonry*] (ROG)
EGL .... Eglin Air Force Base [*Florida*] (SAA)
EGL .... Encyclopedia of Georgia Law [*A publication*] (DLA)
EGL .... Eosinophilic Granuloma of the Lung [*Medicine*]
EGL .... Equipment Group Laboratories (MCD)
EGL .... Equipment Guide List (NVT)
EGL .... European Group of Lymphology [*Belgium*] (EAIO)
EGL .... Expected Grade Level [*Education*]
EGL .... External Germinal Layer [*Cytology*]
EGL .... External Granular Layer (PDAA)
EGL .... Extragalactic Light
EGL .... Gala Law [*Scotland*] [*Seismograph station code, US Geological Survey*] (SEIS)
EGL .... Neghelli [*Ethiopia*] [*Airport symbol*] (AD)
EGLA .... Bodmin [*British ICAO location identifier*] (ICLI)
EGLB .... Brooklands [*British ICAO location identifier*] (ICLI)
EGLB .... Eagle BancGroup, Inc. [*NASDAQ symbol*] (SAG)
EglBGp........ Eagle BancGroup, Inc. [*Associated Press*] (SAG)
EglBsh .... Eagle Bancshares [*Associated Press*] (SAG)
EGLD .... Denham [*British ICAO location identifier*] (ICLI)
EGLE .... Eagle Food Centers [*NASDAQ symbol*] (SAG)
EgleRiv .... Eagle River Interactive, Inc. [*Associated Press*] (SAG)
EgleUSA ..... Eagle USA Airfreight, Inc. [*Associated Press*] (SAG)
EglFd .... Eagle Food Centers, Inc. [*Associated Press*] (SAG)
EGLG .... Panshanger [*British ICAO location identifier*] (ICLI)
EglHrd .... Eagle Hardware & Garden, Inc. [*Associated Press*] (SAG)
EGLI .... Esperantista Go-Ligo Internacia [*International Esperantist League for Go - IELG*] (EAIO)
EGLISI .... Service de Presse de l'Eglise du Silence [*Belgium*]
EGLJ .... Chalgrove [*British ICAO location identifier*] (ICLI)
EGLK .... Blackbushe [*British ICAO location identifier*] (ICLI)
EGLL .... London City [*British ICAO location identifier*] (ICLI)
EGLM .... Exchangeable General Linear Model [*Statistics*]
EGLM .... White Waltham [*British ICAO location identifier*] (ICLI)
EGLMSFCMS... Elves', Gnomes', and Little Men's Science Fiction, Chowder, and Marching Society (EA)
EGLMT......... Ejector-Launcher, Guided Missile, Transporter

EGLN	London/Heathrow [*British ICAO location identifier*] (ICLI)
EGLS	Electroglas, Inc. [*NASDAQ symbol*] (SAG)
EGLS	Old Sarum [*British ICAO location identifier*] (ICLI)
EGLW	London [*British ICAO location identifier*] (ICLI)
EGM	Electrogram (MAE)
EGM	Electronic Governor Module (IEEE)
EGM	El Golfo De Santa Clara [*Mexico*] [*Seismograph station code, US Geological Survey*] (SEIS)
EGM	Empire Gallantry Medal [*British*]
EGM	Enhanced Graphics Monitor [*Computer technology*]
EGM	European Glass Container Manufacturers' Committee [*British*]
EGM	Excellent Grand Master [*Freemasonry*] (ROG)
EGM	Extraordinary General Meeting [*British*] (ADA)
EGM	Sege [*Solomon Islands*] [*Airport symbol*] (OAG)
eGmbH	Eingetragene Gesellschaft mit Beschraenkter Haftung [*Registered Company with Limited Liability*] [*German*] (ILCA)
EGMC	Southend [*British ICAO location identifier*] (ICLI)
EGMD	Lydd [*British ICAO location identifier*] (ICLI)
EGME	Ethylene Glycol Monomethyl Ether [*A poison*] [*Organic chemistry*]
EGMEX	Eastern Gulf of Mexico
EGMF	Edvard Grieg Memorial Foundation (EA)
EGMH	Manston [*British ICAO location identifier*] (ICLI)
EGMIA	Educational Group of the Music Industries Association [*British*] (BI)
EGM of C	Excellent Grand Master of Ceremonies [*Freemasonry*] (ROG)
EGMR	East Griqualand Mounted Rifles [*British military*] (DMA)
EGMS	Education of Girls in Mathematics and Science
EGMT	Elapsed Greenwich Mean Time (KSC)
EGMTR	Eglin Gulf Missile Test Range [*Florida*] [*Air Force*]
EGN	Eagle's Nest [*New York*] [*Seismograph station code, US Geological Survey*] (SEIS)
EGN	El Geneina [*Sudan*] [*Airport symbol*] (OAG)
EGN	Energen Corp. [*NYSE symbol*] (SPSG)
EGN	Experimental Glomerulonephritis [*Medicine*]
EGN	Express Group Newspapers [*British*]
EGNA	Eucharistic Guard for Nocturnal Adoration [*Defunct*] (EA)
EGNA	Hucknall [*British ICAO location identifier*] (ICLI)
EGNB	Brough [*British ICAO location identifier*] (ICLI)
EGNC	Carlisle [*British ICAO location identifier*] (ICLI)
EGND	Huddersfield/Crosland Moor [*British ICAO location identifier*] (ICLI)
EGNE	Repton/Gamston [*British ICAO location identifier*] (ICLI)
EGNF	Nether Thorpe [*British ICAO location identifier*] (ICLI)
EGNG	Preston and Blackburn/Samlesbury [*British ICAO location identifier*] (ICLI)
EGNH	Blackpool [*British ICAO location identifier*] (ICLI)
EGNI	Skegness/Ingoldmells [*British ICAO location identifier*] (ICLI)
EGNJ	Humberside [*British ICAO location identifier*] (ICLI)
EGNL	Barrow/Walney Island [*British ICAO location identifier*] (ICLI)
EGNM	Leeds and Bradford [*British ICAO location identifier*] (ICLI)
EGNO	Warton [*British ICAO location identifier*] (ICLI)
EGNOS	European Geostationary Navigation Overlay System
EGNOS	European Geostationary Navigation Overlay System
E/GNP	Energy/Gross National Product [*Fuel use ratio*]
EGNR	Hawarden [*British ICAO location identifier*] (ICLI)
EGNS	Isle Of Man/Ronaldsway [*British ICAO location identifier*] (ICLI)
EGNSW	Embroiderers' Guild of New South Wales [*Australia*]
EGNT	Expositer's Greek New Testament [*A publication*]
EGNT	Newcastle [*British ICAO location identifier*] (ICLI)
EGNV	Tees-Side [*British ICAO location identifier*] (ICLI)
EGNW	Wickenby [*British ICAO location identifier*] (ICLI)
EGNX	East Midlands [*British ICAO location identifier*] (ICLI)
EGO	Eccentric Geophysical Observatory [*Also, EOGO*] [*NASA*]
EGO	Ego Resources Ltd. [*Toronto Stock Exchange symbol*]
EGO	Electronic Grading Operator
EGO	Excellent Grand Orator [*Freemasonry*] (ROG)
EGO	Exhaust Gas Oxygen [*Automotive engineering*]
EGO	Experimental Geophysical Orbiting [*Vehicle*]
EGOB	Burtonwood [*British ICAO location identifier*] (ICLI)
EGOBOO	Ego Boost
EGOC	Bishops Court [*British ICAO location identifier*] (ICLI)
EGOD	Llanbedr [*British ICAO location identifier*] (ICLI)
EGOE	Ternhill [*British ICAO location identifier*] (ICLI)
EGOMAC	Effect of Gravity on Methane-Air Combustion
EGOQ	Mona [*British ICAO location identifier*] (ICLI)
EGOR	Exhaust Gas Oxygen Sensor Return [*Automotive engineering*]
EGOS	European Group for Organizational Studies [*British*] (SLS)
EGOS	Exhaust Gas Oxygen Sensor [*Automotive engineering*]
EGOS	Shawbury [*British ICAO location identifier*] (ICLI)
EGOT	Erythrocyte Glutamic Oxaloacetic Transaminase (AAMN)
EGOTH	Egyptian Government Organization for Tourism and Hotels
EGOV	Valley [*British ICAO location identifier*] (ICLI)
EGOW	Woodvale [*British ICAO location identifier*] (ICLI)
EGOY	West Freugh [*British ICAO location identifier*] (ICLI)
EGP	Eagle Pass [*Texas*] [*Airport symbol Obsolete*] (OAG)
EGP	Eagle Pass Resources [*Vancouver Stock Exchange symbol*]
EGP	Early Greek Philosophy [*1930*] [*A publication*] (OCD)
EGP	Eastern Group of Painters, Montreal [*1938*] [*Canada*] (NGC)
EGP	Eastgroup Properties, Inc. [*NYSE symbol*] (SAG)
EGP	EastGroup Properties SBI [*NYSE symbol*] (TTSB)
EGP	Egypt (ROG)
EGP	Ejercito Guerrillero de los Pobres [*Guerrilla Army of the Poor*] [*Guatemala*]
EGP	Elliptical Gear Planetary
EGP	Embezzlement of Government Property
EGP	Eminentra Granularis Posterior [*Anatomy*]
EGP	Evolved Gas Profile [*Chemistry*]
EGP	Exhaust Gas Pressure
EGP	Experimental Geodetic Payload [*Japan*]
EGP	Experimental GOES [*Geostationary Operational Environmental Satellite*] Platform [*Marine science*] (MSC)
EGP	Extended Guide Projectile [*Navy*] (MCD)
EGP	Exterior Gateway Protocol [*Computer science*]
EGP	Extra-Solar Giant Planet
EGP	Thai Aerospace Services Co. Ltd. [*FAA designator*] (FAAC)
EGPA	European Group of Public Administration [*See also GEAP*] [*Brussels, Belgium*] (EAIO)
EGPA	Export Grape and Plum Act [*1960*]
EGPA	Kirkwall [*British ICAO location identifier*] (ICLI)
EGPACOM	Environmental Group, Pacific Command (CINC)
EGPB	Sumburgh [*British ICAO location identifier*] (ICLI)
EGPC	Egyptian General Petroleum Corp.
EGPC	Wick [*British ICAO location identifier*] (ICLI)
EGPD	Aberdeen/Dyce [*British ICAO location identifier*] (ICLI)
EGPE	Inverness/Dalcross [*British ICAO location identifier*] (ICLI)
EGPF	East Greenland Polar Front [*Oceanography*]
EGPF	Glasgow [*British ICAO location identifier*] (ICLI)
EGPH	Edinburgh [*British ICAO location identifier*] (ICLI)
EGPI	Islay/Port Ellen [*British ICAO location identifier*] (ICLI)
EGPJ	Fife/Glenrothes [*British ICAO location identifier*] (ICLI)
EGPK	Prestwick [*British ICAO location identifier*] (ICLI)
EGPL	Benbecula [*British ICAO location identifier*] (ICLI)
EGPM	Scatsta [*British ICAO location identifier*] (ICLI)
EGPMF	Error Gap Probability Mass Function
EGPN	Dundee (Riverside Park) [*British ICAO location identifier*] (ICLI)
EGPO	Stornoway [*British ICAO location identifier*] (ICLI)
EGPQ	Edinburgh [*British ICAO location identifier*] (ICLI)
EGPR	Barra [*British ICAO location identifier*] (ICLI)
EGPS	Electric Ground Power System [*Aerospace*] (AAG)
EGPS	Extended General Purpose Simulator [*National Electronics Conference*] (IEEE)
EGPS	Peterhead/Longside [*British ICAO location identifier*] (ICLI)
EGPT	Eagle Point Software [*NASDAQ symbol*] (TTSB)
EGPT	Eagle Point Software Corp. [*NASDAQ symbol*] (SAG)
EGPT	Perth/Scone [*British ICAO location identifier*] (ICLI)
EGPU	Tiree [*British ICAO location identifier*] (ICLI)
EGPW	Unst (Shetland Isles) [*British ICAO location identifier*] (ICLI)
EGPX	Scottish Air Traffic Control Centre [*British ICAO location identifier*] (ICLI)
EGPY	Dounreay/Thurso [*British ICAO location identifier*] (ICLI)
EGQ	Embroiderers' Guild of Queensland [*Australia*]
EGQ	Emmetsburg, IA [*Location identifier FAA*] (FAAL)
EGQB	Ballykelly [*British ICAO location identifier*] (ICLI)
EGQJ	Machrihanish [*British ICAO location identifier*] (ICLI)
EGQK	Kinloss [*British ICAO location identifier*] (ICLI)
EGQL	Leuchars [*British ICAO location identifier*] (ICLI)
EGQM	Boulmer [*British ICAO location identifier*] (ICLI)
EGQN	Buchan [*British ICAO location identifier*] (ICLI)
EGQP	Edinburgh [*British ICAO location identifier*] (ICLI)
EGQQ	Prestwick [*British ICAO location identifier*] (ICLI)
EGQR	Saxa Vord [*British ICAO location identifier*] (ICLI)
EGQS	Lossiemouth [*British ICAO location identifier*] (ICLI)
EGQT	Edinburgh [*British ICAO location identifier*] (ICLI)
EGR	Eagle River Mines [*Vancouver Stock Exchange symbol*]
EGR	Early Growth Response [*Biochemistry*]
EGR	Earned Growth Rate [*Finance*] (ODBW)
EGR	Earthgrains Co. [*NYSE symbol*] (SAG)
EGR	Earthgrains Co. [*NYSE symbol*] (TTSB)
EGR	Electrographic Recorder (CAAL)
EGR	Electronic Governor Regulator (IEEE)
EGR	Embossed Groove Recording
EGR	Empire Grade Road [*California*] [*Seismograph station code, US Geological Survey*] (SEIS)
egr	Engraver [*MARC relator code*] [*Library of Congress*] (LCCP)
EGR	Enhanced Guardrail (MCD)
EGR	Erythrocyte Glutathione Reductase [*An enzyme*]
EGR	Excellent Grand Recorder [*Freemasonry*] (ROG)
EGR	Exhaust Gas Recirculation [*Engines*]
e-gr--	Greece [*MARC geographic area code Library of Congress*] (LCCP)
EGRA	Equilibrium-Gated Radionuclide Angiography [*Medicine*] (DMAA)
EGRA	Glasgow [*British ICAO location identifier*] (ICLI)
EGRATT	European Research Group for Alternatives in Toxicity Testing
EGRB	London [*British ICAO location identifier*] (ICLI)
EGRC	Exhaust Gas Recirculation Control [*Valve*] [*Automotive engineering*]
EGRC	Manchester [*British ICAO location identifier*] (ICLI)
EGRCV	Exhaust Gas Recirculation Control Valve [*Automotive engineering*]
EGRD	Bristol [*British ICAO location identifier*] (ICLI)
EGRD	Eye Guard
EGRE	Malvern [*British ICAO location identifier*] (ICLI)
EGRESS	Emergency Global Rescue, Escape, and Survival System [*NASA*]
EGRESS	Evaluation of Glide Reentry Structural Systems
EGRET	Energetic Gamma Ray Experiment Telescope [*NASA*]
EGRG	Cardiff City [*British ICAO location identifier*] (ICLI)
EGRH	High Wycombe [*British ICAO location identifier*] (ICLI)
Egr High	Egremont on the Law of Highways [*A publication*] (DLA)
EGRI	Southampton [*British ICAO location identifier*] (ICLI)
EGRJ	Upavon [*British ICAO location identifier*] (ICLI)
EGRK	Ocean Station Vessel Romeo [*British ICAO location identifier*] (ICLI)
EGRL	Ocean Station Vessel Lima [*British ICAO location identifier*] (ICLI)
EGRM	Ocean Station Vessel Mike [*British ICAO location identifier*] (ICLI)
EGRN	Norwich [*British ICAO location identifier*] (ICLI)
EGRP	Plymouth [*British ICAO location identifier*] (ICLI)

EGRR .... Bracknell [*British ICAO location identifier*] (ICLI)
EGRS .... Egress (KSC)
EGRS .... Electronic and Geodetic Ranging Satellite (IAA)
EGRS .... Exhaust Gas Recirculation Sensor [*Automotive engineering*]
EGRS .... Extragalactic Radio Source
EGRS .... Sullom Voe [*British ICAO location identifier*] (ICLI)
EGRT .... Newcastle [*British ICAO location identifier*] (ICLI)
EGRU .... Ocean Station Vessel Charlie [*British ICAO location identifier*] (ICLI)
EGRV .... Exhaust Gas Recirculation Valve [*Automotive engineering*]
EGRV .... Exhaust Gas Recirculation Vent [*Automotive engineering*]
EGRVA .... Exhaust Gas Recirculation Valve Actuator [*Automotive engineering*]
EGRVP .... Exhaust Gas Recirculation Vacuum Port [*Automotive engineering*]
EGRW .... Nottingham [*British ICAO location identifier*] (ICLI)
EGRY .... Leeds [*British ICAO location identifier*] (ICLI)
EGS .... Economic General Staff [*British*]
EGS .... Edge Guide System
EGS .... Egilsstadir [*Iceland*] [*Airport symbol*] (OAG)
EGS .... Electrical Galvanic Stimulation [*Physiology*]
EGS .... Electrogalvanized Steel
EGS .... Electrographic Seizure [*Neurophysiology*]
EGS .... Electronic Gear Selection [*Heavy-duty vehicles*]
EGS .... Electronic-Glide Slope (NG)
EGS .... Electronic Governor System [*Heavy-duty automotive engines*]
EGS .... Electronic Governor System
EGS .... Elementary Gliding School [*British military*] (DMA)
EGS .... Emil Gilels Society (EA)
EGS .... English Goethe Society [*British*]
EGS .... Ethylene Glycol Succinate [*Organic chemistry*]
EGS .... Europaeische Gesellschaft fuer Schriftpsychologie und Schriftexpertise [*European Society of Handwriting Psychology - ESHP*] (EAIO)
EGS .... European Geophysical Society (EAIO)
EGS .... Excellent Grand Secretary [*Freemasonry*] (ROG)
EGS .... Excluded Goods Schedule
EGS .... Exhaust Gas System
EGS .... Extension of the Gastric Shield
EGS .... External Guide Sequence [*Genetics*]
EGSA .... Electrical Generating Systems Association (EA)
EGSA .... Embroiderers' Guild of South Australia
EGSA .... Shipdham [*British ICAO location identifier*] (ICLI)
EGSB .... Bedford/Castle Mill [*British ICAO location identifier*] (ICLI)
EGSC .... Cambridge [*British ICAO location identifier*] (ICLI)
EGSD .... Great Yarmouth/North Denes [*British ICAO location identifier*] (ICLI)
EGSE .... Electrical [*or Electronic*] Ground-Support Equipment
EGSE .... Ipswich [*British ICAO location identifier*] (ICLI)
EGSF .... Peterborough (Conington) [*British ICAO location identifier*] (ICLI)
EGSG .... Stapleford [*British ICAO location identifier*] (ICLI)
EGSH .... Norwich [*British ICAO location identifier*] (ICLI)
EGSIPS .... Electronic Guides for Standardizing Items of Procurement and Supply (MCD)
EGSJ .... Polstead [*British ICAO location identifier*] (ICLI)
EGSK .... Hethel [*British ICAO location identifier*] (ICLI)
EGSL .... Andrewsfield [*British ICAO location identifier*] (ICLI)
EGSM .... Beccles [*British ICAO location identifier*] (ICLI)
EGSMA .... Electrical Generating Systems Marketing Association [*Later, EGSA*] (EA)
EGSN .... Bourn (Cambs) [*British ICAO location identifier*] (ICLI)
EGSP .... Electronic Glossary and Symbol Panel (IAA)
EGSP .... Peterborough/Sibson [*British ICAO location identifier*] (ICLI)
EGSR .... Earls Colne [*British ICAO location identifier*] (ICLI)
EGSS .... Ethnic and Genealogical Sourcebook Series [*A publication*]
EGSS .... London/Stansted [*British ICAO location identifier*] (ICLI)
EGST .... Elmsett [*British ICAO location identifier*] (ICLI)
EGSW .... Weeley [*British ICAO location identifier*] (ICLI)
EGSWG .... European Geophysical Society Working Group on Tsunami [*Marine science*] (OSRA)
EGT .... Eagle Airways Ltd. [*British ICAO designator*] (FAAC)
EGT .... Ecdysteroid Glucosyl Transferase [*An enzyme*]
EGT .... Egypt
EGT .... Elapsed Ground Time (MCD)
EGT .... Embroiderers' Guild of Tasmania [*Australia*]
EGT .... Eminent Grand Treasurer [*Freemasonry*] (ROG)
EGT .... Entreprise de Gestion Touristique [*Algeria*] (EY)
EGT .... Equivalent Gear Train
EGT .... Estimated Ground Time (MCD)
EGT .... European Geotraverse [*A collaborative lithosphere study*]
EGT .... Excellent Grand Tabernacle [*Freemasonry*] (ROG)
EGT .... Exhaust Gas Temperature
EGT .... [*The*] Expositor's Greek Testament [*A publication*] (BJA)
EGT .... Extended Glaciological Timescale [*Climatology*]
EGT .... Wellington, KS [*Location identifier FAA*] (FAAL)
EGTA .... Aylesbury/Thame [*British ICAO location identifier*] (ICLI)
EGTA .... Esophageal Gastric Tube Airway [*Medicine*]
EGTA .... Ethylene Glycol Bis(aminoethyl ether)tetraacetic Acid [*Also, EBONTA*] [*Organic chemistry*]
EGTA .... Ethylene Glycol Tetra-Acetic Acid [*Organic chemistry*] (DAVI)
EGTA .... European Group of Television Advertising (EA)
EGTB .... Wycombe Air Park/Booker [*British ICAO location identifier*] (ICLI)
EGTC .... Cranfield [*British ICAO location identifier*] (ICLI)
EGTD .... Dunsfold [*British ICAO location identifier*] (ICLI)
EGTE .... Exeter [*British ICAO location identifier*] (ICLI)
EGTF .... Fairoaks [*British ICAO location identifier*] (ICLI)
EGTG .... Bristol/Filton [*British ICAO location identifier*] (ICLI)
EGTH .... Hatfield [*British ICAO location identifier*] (ICLI)
EGTI .... Exhaust Gas Temperature Indicator

EGTI .... Leavesden [*British ICAO location identifier*] (ICLI)
EGTK .... Oxford/Kidlington [*British ICAO location identifier*] (ICLI)
EGTO .... Rochester [*British ICAO location identifier*] (ICLI)
EGTR .... Eglin Gulf Test Range [*Florida*] [*Air Force*]
EGTR .... Elstree [*British ICAO location identifier*] (ICLI)
EGTS .... Emergency Gas Treatment System [*Nuclear energy*] (NRCH)
EGTT .... London Air Traffic Control Center [*British ICAO location identifier*] (ICLI)
EGTYF .... European Good Templar Youth Federation [*Norway*] (EAIO)
EGU .... English Golf Union (BI)
EGUA .... Upper Heyford [*British ICAO location identifier*] (ICLI)
EGUB .... Benson [*British ICAO location identifier*] (ICLI)
EGUC .... Aberporth [*British ICAO location identifier*] (ICLI)
EGUD .... Abingdon [*British ICAO location identifier*] (ICLI)
EGUF .... Farnborough [*British ICAO location identifier*] (ICLI)
EGUH .... High Wycombe [*British ICAO location identifier*] (ICLI)
EGUHM .... Extra Gentleman Usher to His Majesty [*British*]
Eguin Baro... Eguinarius Baro [*Deceased, 1550*] [*Authority cited in pre-1607 legal work*] (DSA)
EGUK .... Waterbeach [*British ICAO location identifier*] (ICLI)
EGUL .... Lakenheath [*British ICAO location identifier*] (ICLI)
EGUM .... Manston [*British ICAO location identifier*] (ICLI)
EGUN .... Fast Pulse Electron Gun [*NASA*] (NASA)
EGUN .... Mildenhall [*British ICAO location identifier*] (ICLI)
EGUO .... Oakington [*British ICAO location identifier*] (ICLI)
EGUP .... Sculthorpe [*British ICAO location identifier*] (ICLI)
EGUS .... Lee-On-Solent [*British ICAO location identifier*] (ICLI)
EGUU .... Uxbridge [*British ICAO location identifier*] (ICLI)
EGUW .... Wattisham [*British ICAO location identifier*] (ICLI)
EGUY .... Wyton [*British ICAO location identifier*] (ICLI)
EGV .... Eagle River, WI [*Location identifier FAA*] (FAAL)
EGV .... Embroiderers' Guild of Victoria [*Australia*]
EGV .... Exit Guide Vane
EGVA .... Fairford [*British ICAO location identifier*] (ICLI)
EGVB .... Bawdsey [*British ICAO location identifier*] (ICLI)
EGVC .... Northolt [*British ICAO location identifier*] (ICLI)
EGVG .... Woodbridge [*British ICAO location identifier*] (ICLI)
EGVI .... Greenham Common [*British ICAO location identifier*] (ICLI)
EGVJ .... Bentwaters [*British ICAO location identifier*] (ICLI)
EGVN .... Brize Norton [*British ICAO location identifier*] (ICLI)
EGVO .... Odiham [*British ICAO location identifier*] (ICLI)
EGVP .... Middle Wallop [*British ICAO location identifier*] (ICLI)
EGVT .... Wethersfield [*British ICAO location identifier*] (ICLI)
EGVW .... Bedford [*British ICAO location identifier*] (ICLI)
EGW .... Edgewater Resources Ltd. [*Vancouver Stock Exchange symbol*]
EGW .... Electrogas Welding
EGW .... Enamel Guild: West (EA)
EGW .... Engineering Writer
EGW .... Equipment Ground Wire
e-gw-- .... Germany, West [*MARC geographic area code Library of Congress*] (LCCP)
EGWA .... Embroiderers' Guild of Western Australia
EGWB .... Ministry of Defence, United Kingdom [*ICAO location identifier*] (ICLI)
EGWC .... Cosford [*British ICAO location identifier*] (ICLI)
EGWD .... West Drayton [*British ICAO location identifier*] (ICLI)
EGWE .... Henlow [*British ICAO location identifier*] (ICLI)
EGWI .... London [*British ICAO location identifier*] (ICLI)
EGWL .... North Luffenham [*British ICAO location identifier*] (ICLI)
EGWN .... Halton [*British ICAO location identifier*] (ICLI)
EGWS .... Stanmore Park [*British ICAO location identifier*] (ICLI)
EGWU .... Northolt [*British ICAO location identifier*] (ICLI)
EGWX .... CINCFLEETWOC [*British ICAO location identifier*] (ICLI)
EGWZ .... Alconbury [*British ICAO location identifier*] (ICLI)
EGX .... Egegik [*Alaska*] [*Airport symbol*] (OAG)
EGX .... Energex Minerals Ltd. [*Toronto Stock Exchange symbol Vancouver Stock Exchange symbol*]
EGX .... Engex, Inc. [*AMEX symbol*] (SPSG)
e-gx-- .... Germany [*MARC geographic area code Library of Congress*] (LCCP)
EGXB .... Binbrook [*British ICAO location identifier*] (ICLI)
EGXC .... Coningsby [*British ICAO location identifier*] (ICLI)
EGXE .... Leeming [*British ICAO location identifier*] (ICLI)
EGXG .... Church Fenton [*British ICAO location identifier*] (ICLI)
EGXH .... Honington [*British ICAO location identifier*] (ICLI)
EGXI .... Finningley [*British ICAO location identifier*] (ICLI)
EGXJ .... Cottesmore [*British ICAO location identifier*] (ICLI)
EGXN .... Newton [*British ICAO location identifier*] (ICLI)
EGXP .... Scampton [*British ICAO location identifier*] (ICLI)
EGXS .... Swinderby [*British ICAO location identifier*] (ICLI)
EGXT .... Wittering [*British ICAO location identifier*] (ICLI)
EGXU .... Linton-On-Ouse [*British ICAO location identifier*] (ICLI)
EGXV .... Leconfield [*British ICAO location identifier*] (ICLI)
EGXW .... Waddington [*British ICAO location identifier*] (ICLI)
EGXZ .... Topcliffe [*British ICAO location identifier*] (ICLI)
EGY .... Columbus Energy [*AMEX symbol*] (TTSB)
EGY .... Columbus Energy Corp. [*AMEX symbol*] (SPSG)
EGY .... Egypt [*ANSI three-letter standard code*] (CNC)
Egy. .... Egypt (VRA)
egy .... Egyptian [*MARC language code Library of Congress*] (LCCP)
EGY .... Egyptian (ROG)
EGY .... Egyptian Air Force [*FAA designator*] (FAAC)
EGY .... Egyptology
EGY .... English Bay, AK [*Location identifier FAA*] (FAAL)
EGY .... Triton Energy Corp. [*Toronto Stock Exchange symbol*]
EGYB .... Brampton [*British ICAO location identifier*] (ICLI)
EGYC .... Coltishall [*British ICAO location identifier*] (ICLI)

EgyCny......... Energy Conversion Devices, Inc. [*Associated Press*] (SAG)
EGYD .... Cranwell [*British ICAO location identifier*] (ICLI)
EGYE............ Barkston Heath [*British ICAO location identifier*] (ICLI)
EGYH .... Holbeach [*British ICAO location identifier*] (ICLI)
EGYK .... Elvington [*British ICAO location identifier*] (ICLI)
EGYM........... Marham [*British ICAO location identifier*] (ICLI)
EGYP .... Egyptian (ROG)
EGYP .... Mount Pleasant [*British ICAO location identifier*] (ICLI)
EGYPT .... Eager to Grab Your Pretty Top [*Correspondence*] [*Bowdlerized version*] (DSUE)
EGYPT .... Egyptian (ROG)
EGYPTOL ..... Egyptology (ROG)
EGYR........... Watton [*British ICAO location identifier*] (ICLI)
EH............... Early Hebrew (BJA)
EH............... Eclosion Hormone [*Entomology*]
EH............... Economie et Humanism [*Economy and Humanism*] [*An association*] (EAIO)
EH............... Educationally Handicapped
EH............... Eggs in Hatching [*Parcel Post*]
EH............... Electric Heater (AAG)
EH............... Electric Hoist (IAA)
EH............... Enterohydraulic [*Nuclear energy*] (NRCH)
EH............... Electrohydrodynamic Ionization
EH............... Eminent Herald [*Freemasonry*] (ROG)
EH............... Emotionally Handicapped [*Psychology*]
EH............... Encyclopaedia Hebraica [*Jerusalem*] [*A publication*] (BJA)
EH............... Engine Heater [*Automotive accessory*]
EH............... Engine Hoods
EH............... English Horn
EH............... English Hymnal [*Episcopalian*]
EH............... Enlarged Heart [*Medicine*]
EH............... Enlil Hymn (BJA)
EH............... Epochs of History [*A publication*]
EH............... Epoxide Hydrolase [*An enzyme*]
EH............... Equitable Handicap [*Sailing*]
EH............... Equivalent Hertz (SSD)
EH............... Eridu Hymn (BJA)
EH............... Escort Helicopter (CINC)
EH............... Essential Hypertension [*Medicine*]
EH............... Ets Haim Seminary [*Amsterdam*] (BJA)
EH............... Even ha-'Ezer, Shulhan 'Arukh (BJA)
EH............... Everlasting Heritage [*A variety of sweet corn*]
EH............... Exegetisches Handbuch zum Alten Testament [*Muenster*] [*A publication*] (BJA)
EH............... Exercise Head
EH............... Extended Hueckel [*Molecular orbit*] [*Atomic physics*]
EH............... Extra Hazardous (AAG)
EH............... Extra [*or Extremely*] High
EH............... Extramedullary Hematopoiesis [*Hematology*] (DAVI)
eH............... Oxidation-Reduction Potential [*Symbol*] (MAE)
E$_h$............... Redox Potential [*Symbol*] [*Organic chemistry*] (DAVI)
EH............... Western Sahara [*ANSI two-letter standard code*] (CNC)
EHA............... Early Hemi Association (EA)
EHA............... Early History of Assyria [*A publication*] (BJA)
EHA............... East Hampton Aire [*ICAO designator*] (FAAC)
EHA............... Economic History Association (EA)
EHA............... Education for All Handicapped Children Act (AIE)
EHA............... Education of the Handicapped Act [*1968*]
EHA............... Edward Hamilton Aitken [*Author*] [*Initials used as pseudonym*]
EHA............... Electrical Harness Assembly (KSC)
EHA............... Electric Heating Association (EA)
EHA............... Electrohydraulic Actuator
EHA............... Elkhart, KS [*Location identifier FAA*] (FAAL)
EHA............... Emergency and Humanitarian Assistance
EHA............... Emotional Health Anonymous (EA)
EHA............... Enkephalin-Hydrolyzing Activity
EHA............... En Route High Altitude
EHA............... Environmental Health Association (WDAA)
EHA............... Environmental Hygiene Agency [*Army*] (MCD)
EHA............... Environmental Protection Agency, Region I Library, Boston, MA [*OCLC symbol*] (OCLC)
EHA............... Enziklopedyah la-Hafirot ha-Arkheologiyot be-Erez Yisrael [*A publication*] (BJA)
EHA............... Equipment Handover Agreement [*Shipping*] (DS)
EHA............... Ethylhexyl Acrylate [*Organic chemistry*]
EHA............... European Helicopter Association (PDAA)
EHA............... Expect Higher Altitude (FAAC)
EHAA .... Amsterdam [*Netherlands ICAO location identifier*] (ICLI)
EHAA .... Epidemic Hepatitis-Associated Antigen [*Immunochemistry*]
EHAA .... Epidermic Hepatitis-Associated Antigen [*Immunology*] (DAVI)
EHAA .... Every Hand an Adventure [*Bridge bidding method*]
EHAC .... Early Heart Attack Care
EHAG .... Employee Health Assurance Group [*Medicine*]
EHAL .... Ameland [*Netherlands ICAO location identifier*] (ICLI)
EHAM .... Amsterdam/Schiphol [*Netherlands ICAO location identifier*] (ICLI)
EHA-MR...... Equitable Handicap Associated-Measured Rating [*Boating*]
EH & S .... Environmental, Health, and Safety
EHAP .... Experimental Housing Allowance Program [*Department of Housing and Urban Development*] (GFGA)
EHAP .... Extremely Hazardous Air Pollutant [*Environmental science*]
EHAS .... East Hertshire Archaeological Society [*British*]
EHAT........... Equipment Historical Availability Trend [*Military*]
EHAT........... Exegetisches Handbuch zum Alten Testament [*Muenster*] [*A publication*] (BJA)
EHB............. Elevate Head of Bed [*Medicine*] (DAVI)

EHB............. Environmental Protection Agency, Environmental Research Laboratory, Narragansett, RI [*OCLC symbol*] (OCLC)
EHB............. Extra Hard Black [*Pencil leads*] (ROG)
EHBA .... Extrahepatic Biliary Atresia [*Medicine*]
EHBD .... Weert/Budel [*Netherlands ICAO location identifier*] (ICLI)
EHBF .... Essential High Blood Pressure [*Cardiology*] (DAVI)
EHBF .... Estimated Hepatic Blood Flow [*Medicine*]
EHBF .... Exercise Hyperemia Blood Flow [*Medicine*] (MAE)
EHBF .... Extrahepatic Blood Flow [*Medicine*]
EHBK .... Maastricht/Zuid-Limburg [*Netherlands ICAO location identifier*] (ICLI)
EHC............. Education for all Handicapped Children act [*1975 federal law*] (PAZ)
EHC............. Elastic Hysteresis Constant
EHC............. Electrical Heating Control (MCD)
EHC............. Electrical Height Calculator (IAA)
EHC............. Electrically Heated Catalyst
EHC............. Electrohydraulic Control (NRCH)
EHC............. Electrohydrodynamic Convection [*Physics*]
EHC............. Electronically Heated Catalysts [*Automotive engineering*]
EHC............. Emergency Housing Corp.
EHC............. Emory and Henry College [*Virginia*]
EHC............. Enterohepatic Circulation [*Medicine*]
EHC............. Enterohepatic Clearance [*Biochemistry*] (DAVI)
EHC............. Environmental Hazard Communication
EHC............. Environmental Health Committee [*Environmental Protection Agency*] (GFGA)
EHC............. Environmentally Hazardous Chemical
EHC............. Essential Hypercholesterolemia [*Medicine*] (MAE)
EHC............. Extended Health Care [*Insurance*]
EHC............. Extended Hospital Care [*Veterans Administration*] (GFGA)
EHC............. Extra-Heavy Crude [*Petroleum technology*]
EHC............. Extrahepatic Cholestasis [*Medicine*]
EHCA .... Education for All Handicapped Children Act
EH-CF........... Entamoeba Histolytica-Complement Fixation [*Immunochemistry*] (DAVI)
EHCLS .... Encapsulated Harpoon Command and Launch System (MCD)
EHCM........... Editor "Hebrew Christians' Magazine" [*Pseudonym used by Nathan Davis*]
EHCN .... Experimental Hybrid Computer Network (MHDB)
EHCS .... Educational and Health Career Services (EA)
EHD .... E.H. Darby Aviation [*FAA designator*] (FAAC)
EHD .... Elastohydrodynamic
EHD .... Electrohemodynamics
EHD .... Electrohydrodimerization [*Organic chemistry*]
EHD .... Electron-Hole Drop [*Semiconductor physics*]
EHD .... Engineer Historical Division [*Army*]
EHD .... Epizootic Hemorrhagic Disease [*Veterinary medicine*]
EHD .... Extended-Height-to-Diameter [*Aviation*]
EHDA .... Electrical Housewares Distributors Association [*Defunct*] (EA)
EHDA .... Ethylhexadecyldimethylammonium Bromide [*Blood count diluent*]
EHDA .... Etidronate Sodium [*Pharmacology*] (DAVI)
EHDB .... De Bilt [*Netherlands ICAO location identifier*] (ICLI)
EHDHP .... Electrohydrodynamic Heat Pipe [*NASA*]
EHDI .... Electronic Horizontal Director Indicator [*Aviation*] (PDAA)
EHDL .... Deelen [*Netherlands ICAO location identifier*] (ICLI)
EHDP .... Ethanehydroxydiphosphonate [*or -diphosphonic Acid*] [*Also, HEDP*] [*Organic chemistry*]
EHDP .... Ethylenehydroxydiphosphonate [*Organic chemistry*]
EHDP .... Venraij/De Peel [*Netherlands ICAO location identifier*] (ICLI)
EHDPP .... Ethylhexyl Diphenyl Phosphate [*Organic chemistry*]
EHDR .... Drachten [*Netherlands ICAO location identifier*] (ICLI)
EHDR .... Erection, Holddown, and Release [*Aerospace*] (AAG)
EHDV .... Epizootic Hemorrhagic Disease Virus [*Veterinary medicine*] (DMAA)
EHE.............. Embassy Home Entertainment [*Video distributor*]
EHEC........... Ethyl(hydroxyethyl)cellulose [*Organic chemistry*]
EHECA .... Emergency Highway Energy Conservation Act [*1974*]
EheG........... Ehegesetz [*Marriage Law*] [*German*] (ILCA)
EHEH .... Eindhoven [*Netherlands ICAO location identifier*] (ICLI)
EHES .... Environmental Health Engineering Services [*Army*] (AABC)
EHF.............. Electrical Historical Foundation [*Defunct*] (EA)
EHF.............. Electrohydraulic Forming
EHF.............. electrohydraulic Fragmentation [*Medicine*] (DAVI)
EHF.............. End Half
EHF.............. Epidemic Hemorrhagic Fever [*Disease encountered by American troops during the Korean War*]
EHF.............. Exophthalmos-Hyperthyroid Factor [*Endocrinology*] (AAMN)
EHF.............. Experimental Husbandry Farm [*British*]
EHF.............. Exponential Hazard Function
EHF.............. Extremely High Frequency [*Electronics, radio wave*]
EHFA .... Electric Home and Farm Authority [*Terminated, 1947*]
EHFC........... Emmylou Harris Fan Club (EA)
EHF SATCOM... Extra-High-Frequency Satellite Communication
EHG............. Edinburgh Home Guard [*British military*] (DMA)
EHGG .... Groningen/Eelde [*Netherlands ICAO location identifier*] (ICLI)
EHGR .... Gilze-Rijen [*Netherlands ICAO location identifier*] (ICLI)
EHGV .... 'S Gravenhage [*Netherlands ICAO location identifier*] (ICLI)
EHH............. Esophageal Hiatal Hernia [*Medicine*] (MEDA)
EHH............. Ever Heard of Him [*Facetious criterion for determining insignificance of Supreme Court Justices*] [*Proposed by University of Chicago professor David P. Currie*]
EHHO........... Hoogeveen [*Netherlands ICAO location identifier*] (ICLI)
EHHV........... Hilversum [*Netherlands ICAO location identifier*] (ICLI)
EHI.............. Electronic Height Indicator (MCD)
EHI.............. Emergency Homes, Inc.
EHI.............. Employee Health Insurance
EHI.............. Environmental Health Institute [*Pittsfield, MA*]

EHI.............. Expanded Helicopter Industries [*Military*]
EHIA............ European Herbal Infusions Association (EA)
EHIC............ Emergency Hurricane Information Center [*Marine science*] (MSC)
EHIC............ Energetic Heavy Ion Composition Experiment [*NASA*]
EHICS .... Employer Health Insurance Cost Survey [*Department of Health and Human Services*] (GFGA)
EH-IHA......... Complement Histolytica-Indirect Hemagglutination [*Hematology*] (DAVI)
EHIP............ Employee Health Insurance Plan (DHSM)
EHIS............ Emission History Information System [*Environmental Information Agency*]
EHIS............ Encyclopedia of Health Information Sources [*A publication*]
EHK............. Electrode Heater Kit
EHK............. Epidermolytic Hyperkeratosis [*Dermatology*]
EHKD .... De Kooy (Den Helder) [*Netherlands ICAO location identifier*] (ICLI)
EHL............. Eastern Hockey League
EHL............. Eastern Hockey League (BARN)
EHL............. Effective Halflife [*Nuclear science*]
EHL............. Elastohydrodynamic Lubrication
EHL............. El Bolson [*Argentina*] [*Airport symbol*] (OAG)
EHL............. Electrohydraulic Lithotripsy [*Medicine*] (HCT)
EHL............. Electrohydraulic Lithotriptor [*Nephrology and urology*] (DAVI)
EHL............. Electron-Hole Liquid Model [*Physics*]
EHL............. Endogenous Hyperlipidemia [*Medicine*] (MAE)
EHL............. Environmental Health Laboratory [*Air Force*]
EHL............. Extensor Hallucis Longus [*Anatomy*]
EHLE........... Lelystad [*Netherlands ICAO location identifier*] (ICLI)
EHL(K)........ Environmental Health Laboratory, Kelly Air Force Base
EHLLAPI ...... Emulator High-Level Language Application Programming Interface [*Computer science*] (PCM)
EHLLAPI ...... Extended High-Level Language Application Program Interface [*Computer science*]
EHL-M .... Environmental Health Laboratory, McClellan Air Force Base
EHLS........... Environmental Health Laboratory Sciences Division [*Atlanta, GA*] [*Department of Health and Human Services*] (GRD)
EHLW.......... Leeuwarden [*Netherlands ICAO location identifier*] (ICLI)
EHM............ Advisory Committee for Earthquake Hazard Mitigation [*Washington, DC*] [*National Science Foundation*] (EGAO)
EHM............ Cape Newenham [*Alaska*] [*Airport symbol*] (OAG)
EHM............ Electrohydraulic Motor
EHM............ Encyclopedia of Holistic Medicine [*A publication*]
EHM............ Engine Health Monitoring (MCD)
EHM............ Environmental Hazards Management Institute [*University of New Hampshire*] [*Research center*] (RCD)
EH/M........... Extension Hose/Mouthpiece (MCD)
EHM............ Eye-Hand-Muscle (SAA)
EHMA.......... European Healthcare Management Association (EAIO)
EHMA.......... European Hotel Managers Association (EA)
EHMA.......... Evangelism and Home Missions Association (EA)
EHMC.......... Nieuw Milligen [*Netherlands ICAO location identifier*] (ICLI)
EHME.......... Employee Health Maintenance Examination
EHMI........... Environmental Hazards Management Institute (GNE)
EHML.......... Nieuw Milligen [*Netherlands ICAO location identifier*] (ICLI)
EHMO .... Extended Hueckel Molecular Orbit [*Atomic physics*]
EHMS.......... Electrohydrodynamic Ionization Mass Spectrometry
EHMS.......... Engine Health Monitoring System
EHMZ.......... Middelburg/Midden Zeeland [*Netherlands ICAO location identifier*] (ICLI)
EHN .... End Hunger Network (EA)
EHN .... Environmental Health Network [*Defunct*] (EA)
EHN .... Environmental Health News [*Database*] [*Occupational Health Services, Inc.*] [*Information service or system*] (CRD)
EHN .... European Host Network [*Computer science*]
EHN .... Exploring Human Nature [*National Science Foundation project*]
EHNA.......... Erythro(hydroxynonyl)adenine [*Biochemistry*]
EHNP .... Edwin I. Hatch Nuclear Plant (NRCH)
EHNP .... Emmeloord/Noord-Oostpolder [*Netherlands ICAO location identifier*] (ICLI)
EHO .... Early Hebrew Orthography [*A publication*] (BJA)
EHO .... Environmental Health Officer [*British*] (DCTA)
EHO .... Extrahepatic Obstruction [*Medicine*]
EHO .... Shelby, NC [*Location identifier FAA*] (FAAL)
EHOG.......... European Host Operators Group [*EURONET*] [*Luxembourg*]
EHOM.......... Electronics Hardover Monitor (SAA)
EHOP .... Employee Home Ownership Plan [*Human resources*] (WYGK)
EHOT.......... External Hydrogen/Oxygen Tank (NASA)
EHP............. Di-(2-Ethylhexyl) Hydrogen Phosphate [*Organic chemistry*] (DAVI)
EHP............. Effective Horsepower
EHP............. Electrical Hull Penetration
EHP............. Electric Horsepower
EHP............. Electron-Hole Pairs (ACRL)
EHP............. Electron-Hole Potential Method [*Physics*]
ehp............. Equivalent Horsepower (DOMA)
EHP............. Estimated Horsepower
EHP............. Excessive Heat Production (MAE)
EHP............. Extra-High Potency
EHP............. Extra-High Pressure (ROG)
EHP............. Extrinsic Hyperpolarizing Potential
EHPAC .... Emergency Health Preparedness Advisory Committee [*Terminated, 1973*] (EA)
EHPC .... Electro-Hydraulic Proportional Control [*Automotive engineering*]
EHPF........... European Health Policy Forum (EAIO)
EHPG .... Ethylenebis(hydroxyphenylglycine) [*Organic chemistry*]
EHPH.......... Electric Horsepower Hour (IAA)
EHPH.......... Extrahepatic Portal Hypertension [*Medicine*] (MAE)

EHPM.......... Electrohydraulic Pulse Motor
EHPM.......... European Federation of Associations of Health Product Manufacturers (EAIO)
EHPRG .... European High Pressure Research Group (EA)
EHPRN .... European Health Policy Research Network [*British*] (ECON)
EHPT .... Eddy Hot Plate Test [*Clinical chemistry*] (AAMN)
EHR .... Earned Hour Ratio (NASA)
EHR .... Emergency Heat Removal [*Nuclear energy*] (NRCH)
EHR .... English Historical Review [*A publication*] (BRI)
EHR .... European Human Rights (EAIO)
EHR .... Euthanize for Humane Reasons [*ASPCE terminology*]
EHR .... Events History Recorder (MCD)
EHR .... Extra-High Reliability
EHRA .... Endurance Horse Registry of America (EA)
EHRC .... European Humanities Research Centre [*University of Warwick*] [*British*] (CB)
EHRD .... Rotterdam [*Netherlands ICAO location identifier*] (ICLI)
EHRS .... European Histamine Research Society (EAIO)
EHS .... Earth Horizon Scanner
EHS .... Earth-Lunar Horizon Sensor
EHS .... Ecclesiastical History Society (EAIO)
EHS .... Electrical Horology Society (EA)
EHS .... Elitos SpA [*Italy ICAO designator*] (FAAC)
EHS .... Elongating Hypocotyl Section [*Botany*]
EHS .... Emergency Health Service [*HEW*]
EHS .... Emergency Hospital Scheme
EHS .... Environmental Health Service [*US Government*]
EHS .... Environmental Health Specialist
EHS .... Environmental Health Standards (EERA)
EHS .... Estonian Educational Society (EA)
EHS .... Experimental Horticulture Station [*British*]
EHS .... Extra-High Strength [*Steel*] [*Telecommunications*] (TEL)
EHS .... Extreme High Shot [*Photography*]
EHS .... Extremely Hazardous Substances
EHSB .... Soesterberg [*Netherlands ICAO location identifier*] (ICLI)
EHSC .... United States Army Engineering and Housing Support Center (AAGC)
EHSD .... Electronic Horizontal Situation Display [*Aviation*] (PDAA)
EHSDS .... Experimental Health Services Delivery Systems [*HEW*]
EHSE .... Hoeven/Seppe [*Netherlands ICAO location identifier*] (ICLI)
EHSI .... Electronic Horizontal Situation Indicator
EHST .... Electronic Hair Styling [*NASDAQ symbol*] (TTSB)
EHST .... Electronic Hair Styling, Inc. [*NASDAQ symbol*] (SAG)
EHST .... Engellireth-Holm Swarm Tumor [*Medicine*]
EHST .... Stadskanaal [*Netherlands ICAO location identifier*] (ICLI)
EHSV .... Electrohydraulic Servo Valve (MCD)
EHT .... East Hartford, CT [*Location identifier FAA*] (FAAL)
EHT .... Effective Hydration Temperature [*Archeology, geology*]
EHT .... Electric Heat Tracing (ACII)
EHT .... Electrothermal Hydrazine Thruster
EHT .... Extended Huckel Theory [*Atomic physics*]
EHT .... Extra-High Tension
EHTB .... Extended Hueckel Tight-Binding [*Quantum mechanics*]
EHTD .... Equivalent Heat Transfer Dimensionality [*Process engineering*]
EHTE .... Deventer/Teuge [*Netherlands ICAO location identifier*] (ICLI)
EHTPS .... Extra-High-Tension Power Supply (EECA)
EHTR .... Emergency Highway Traffic Regulation [*Federal disaster planning*]
EHTR .... Enhanced Heat Transfer Reformer [*Engineering*]
EHTRC .... Emergency Highway Traffic Regulation Center [*Federal disaster planning*] (AABC)
EHTS .... Emergent Hydrophyte Treatment System
EHTW.......... Enschede/Twenthe [*Netherlands ICAO location identifier*] (ICLI)
EHTX .... Texel [*Netherlands ICAO location identifier*] (ICLI)
EHU .... Electric Heating Unit
e-hu-- .... Hungary [*MARC geographic area code Library of Congress*] (LCCP)
EHV............. Electric and Hybrid Vehicles
EHV............. Electric Heart Vector [*Cardiology*]
EHV............. Electric Heat Vector [*Physics*] (DAVI)
EHV............. Electrohydraulic Valve (MCD)
EHV............. El Hato [*Venezuela*] [*Seismograph station code, US Geological Survey*] (SEIS)
EHV............. Equine Herpes Virus
EHV............. Europaischer Holzhandelsverband [*European Timber Association*] [*EC*] (ECED)
EHV............. Extra-High Voltage [*FPC*]
EHVA .... Electrohydraulic Valve Actuator (IAA)
EHVB .... Valkenburg [*Netherlands ICAO location identifier*] (ICLI)
EHVK .... Volkel [*Netherlands ICAO location identifier*] (ICLI)
EHW............ Ethnic Health Worker [*Australia*]
EHW............ Extreme High Water
EHWO .... Woensdrecht [*Netherlands ICAO location identifier*] (ICLI)
EHWS .... Electric Hot Water Service [*Classified advertising*] (ADA)
EHX .... Experiment Dedicated Heat Exchanger (MCD)
EHY .... Engage High Yield
EHYB .... Ypenburg [*Netherlands ICAO location identifier*] (ICLI)
EI................ Air Lingus [*ICAO designator*] (AD)
EI................ Early Intervention
EI................ Early Iron Age [*Archeology*] (BJA)
EI................ Earned Income
E/I............... Earned Premium to Incurred Loss Ratio [*Insurance*]
EI................ East India (ROG)
EI................ East Indies
EI................ Eat-In [*Kitchen*] [*Classified advertising*]
EI................ Echo Intensity [*Marine science*] (OSRA)
EI................ Ecoforestry Institute - United States (EA)

EI	Ecumenical Institute [*World Council of Churches*] (EA)	
EI	Educational Insights	
EI	Educationally Impaired	
EI	Effectiveness Index (MCD)	
EI	Eisenhower Institute (EA)	
EI	Elderhostel, Inc. (EA)	
EI	Electrical Insulation (MCD)	
EI	Electrolyte Imbalance [*Physiology*]	
EI	Electromagnetic Interference	
EI	Electronic Ignition [*Automotive engineering*]	
EI	Electronic Imaging Conference and Exposition (ITD)	
EI	Electronic Installation	
EI	Electronic Instruction (MCD)	
EI	Electronic Interface (MCD)	
EI	Electronic Interference	
EI	Electron Impact [*Mass spectrometry*]	
EI	Electron Ionization [*Spectrometry*]	
EI	Eligible Individual [*Social Security Administration*]	
EI	Elmwood Institute (EA)	
EI	Emaus Internacional [*Emmaus International*] (EA)	
EI	Embrittlement Index (PDAA)	
EI	Emergency Injection [*Nuclear energy*] (NRCH)	
EI	Emergency International (EA)	
EI	Emigrant Institute [*Sweden*]	
EI	Emission Index	
EI	Emissions Inventory [*Environmental Protection Agency*] (GFGA)	
EI	Emotionally Impaired	
EI	Empathy Inventory [*Teacher evaluation test*]	
EI	Employee Involvement [*Human resources*] (WYGK)	
EI	Emulsion In [*Photography*] (WDMC)	
EI	Enable Interrupt (MHDB)	
EI	End Injection (IEEE)	
EI	End Item	
E/I	Endorsement Irregular [*Banking*]	
EI	Enemy Intelligence	
EI	Energy North, Inc. [*NYSE symbol*] (SAG)	
EI	Engineering Index (ECII)	
EI	Engineering Information [*An association Also, an information service or system*] (EA)	
E-I	Engineering-Installation (AFM)	
EI	Engineering Instruction	
EI	Engineering Investigation (MCD)	
EI	Engineering Item (MCD)	
EI	English Institute (EA)	
EI	Entayant Institute (EA)	
EI	Entrepreneurial Institute [*Australia*]	
EI	Entry Interface (NASA)	
EI	Entsiklopedyah 'Ivrit [*or Enziklopedyah 'Ivrit*] (BJA)	
EI	Environmental Impact (NASA)	
EI	Environmentally Ill [*Medicine*]	
EI	Enzyme Inhibitor [*Biochemistry*]	
EI	Eosinophilic Index [*Medicine*] (MAE)	
EI	Epilepsy International (EAIO)	
EI	Equipment Item (MCD)	
EI	Error Indicator [*Computer science*]	
EI	Esalen Institute (EA)	
EI	Essential Information [*An association*] (EA)	
EI	Establishment Inspection [*Federal government*]	
EI	Ethyleneimine [*Organic chemistry*]	
EI	Evaluation Instrumentation (AAG)	
EI	Exact Interest [*Banking*]	
EI	Exaltation of Inanna [*A publication*] (BJA)	
EI	Excessively Included [*Colored gemstone grade*]	
EI	Executive Instruments [*Ghana*] [*A publication*] (DLA)	
EI	Ex-Interest [*Without the right to interest*] [*Finance*]	
EI	Existential Instantiation [*Rule of quantification*] [*Logic*]	
EI	Expansion Interface [*Electronics*] (ACRL)	
E/I	Expiration-Inspiration [*Ratio*] [*Physiology*]	
EI	Exponential Integral	
EI	Exposure Index [*Photography*]	
EI	Extensions for Independence [*An association*] (EA)	
EI	Extra-Illustrated	
E-I	Extraversion-Introversion [*Psychology*]	
EI	Eye Balls In (SAA)	
ei----	Iberian Peninsula [*MARC geographic area code Library of Congress*] (LCCP)	
EI	Irina Dunn Environment Independents [*Political party Australia*]	
EIA	Early Iron Age [*Archeology*]	
EIA	Economic Impact Assessment	
EIA	Education Improvement Act of 1984	
EIA	Education Industries Association [*Later, NSSEA*] (EA)	
EIA	Electrical Industries Association	
EIA	Electroimmunoassay [*Clinical medicine*]	
EIA	Electronic Industries Association [*Formerly, RETMA*] (EA)	
EIA	Elevator Industries Association (EA)	
EIA	Employee Involvement Association	
EIA	End Item Application (MCD)	
EIA	Endotoxin Inactivating Agent (OA)	
EIA	Energetic Ion Analysis [*Surface analysis*]	
EIA	Energy Independence Authority	
EIA	Energy Information Administration [*Department of Energy*] (IID)	
EIA	Engineering Industries Association [*British*] (EAIO)	
EIA	Engineering Inspectors' Association [*A union*] [*British*]	
EIA	English in Action (EA)	
EIA	Envelope Institute of America	

EIA	Environmental Impact Appraisal [*Nuclear Regulatory Commission*] (GFGA)	
EIA	Environmental Impact Assessment [*Environmental Protection Agency*] (MCD)	
EIA	Environmental Impact Assessment (EERA)	
EIA	Environmental Investigation Agency (BARN)	
EIA	Environmental Protection Agency, Region II Library, New York, NY [*OCLC symbol*] (OCLC)	
EIA	Environment Institute of Australia (EERA)	
EIA	Enzyme Immunoassay [*Analytical biochemistry*]	
EIA	Enzyme-Linked Immunosorbent Assay [*Clinical chemistry*]	
EIA	Equine Infectious Anemia	
EIA	Equipment Interchange Association [*Defunct*] (EA)	
EIA	Eucalyptus Improvement Association (EA)	
EIA	European Information Association [*EC*] (ECED)	
EIA	Euskal Iraultzako Alderdia [*Basque Revolutionary Party*] (PPW)	
EIA	Evergreen International Airlines [*ICAO designator*] (FAAC)	
EIA	Exercise-Induced Anaphylaxis [*Medicine*]	
EIA	Exercise-Induced Asthma [*Medicine*]	
EIA	Extended Interaction Amplifier	
EIAA	Shannon/Ballygirreen [*Ireland*] [*ICAO location identifier*] (ICLI)	
EIAB	Extra-Intracranial Arterial Bypass [*Cardiology*] (DMAA)	
EIAC	Ecological Information and Analysis Center	
EIAC	Electronic Industries Association of Canada	
EIAC	Energy Information Administration Clearinghouse	
EIAC	Environmental Information Analysis Center [*Battelle Memorial Institute*] (IID)	
EIAC	Ergonomics Information Analysis Centre [*University of Birmingham*] [*British*] (CB)	
EIAD	End Item Allocation Document (AAG)	
EIA/EIS	Environmental Impact Assessment/Environmental Impact Statement	
EIA/EPUB	Energy Information Administration Electronic Publication System [*Database*] [*Department of Energy Information service or system*] (CRD)	
EIAG	Exeter Industrial Archaeology Group [*British*] (DBA)	
EIA-J	Electronic Industries Association - Japan	
EIALC	Environmental Impact Assessment for Life Cycle [*Army*]	
EIAMUG	European Intelligent Actuation and Measurement User Group (ACII)	
EI & T	Emplacement, Installation, and Test (CET)	
EIAP	Environmental Impact Analysis Program [*or Project*] [*Department of the Interior*] (GRD)	
EIAS	Electron Image Animation System [*Computer science*]	
EIASA	Energia e Industrias Aragonesas Sociedad Anonima [*Spain*]	
EIASA	Extractive Industries Association of South Australia	
EIASM	European Institute for Advanced Studies in Management [*Information service or system*] (IID)	
EIASN	End Item Assembly Sequence Number (NASA)	
EIA/TIA	Electronics Industry Association and the Telecommunications Industry Association (PCM)	
EIAV	Equine Infectious Anemia Virus	
EIB	Economic Impact Budget	
EIB	Edinboro State College, Edinboro, PA [*OCLC symbol*] (OCLC)	
EIB	Egyptian International Bank (IMH)	
EIB	Electrical Interface Building [*NASA*] (KSC)	
EIB	Electronic Information Bulletin [*Navy*]	
EIB	Electronics Information Branch [*Navy*] (MCD)	
EIB	Electronics Installation Bulletin	
EIB	Engineering Instruction Bulletin (KSC)	
EIB	European Investment Bank (AF)	
EIB	Europese Investeringsbank [*European Investment Bank*]	
EIB	Exercise-Induced Bronchiospasm [*Medicine*]	
EIB	Expert Infantryman Badge [*Military decoration*]	
E-IB	Export-Import Bank	
EIB	External Intelligence Bureau (MCD)	
EIB	Extractive Industries Board [*Victoria, Australia*]	
EIBA	Electrical Industries Benevolent Association [*British*] (BI)	
EIBA	English Indoor Bowling Association [*British*] (DBA)	
EIBA	Ethylene-(Isobutyl Acrylate) [*Organic chemistry*]	
EIBA	European International Business Association [*Brussels, Belgium*] (EA)	
EIBAD	Expert Infantryman Badge [*Military decoration*]	
EIBUS	Export-Import Bank of the United States [*Formerly, EIB(W)*]	
EIB(W)	Export-Import Bank (of Washington) [*Later, EIBUS*]	
EIC	Earned Income Credit	
EIC	Earth Inductor Compass	
EIC	Earth-Ionosphere Cavity	
EIC	Easter Island [*Seismograph station code, US Geological Survey*] (SEIS)	
EIC	Easter Island Committee (EA)	
EIC	East India Co. [*1600-1858*] [*British*]	
EIC	Economic Intelligence Committee [*Military*]	
EIC	Educational Information Center [*Office of Education*]	
EIC	Education Information Center [*Georgia State Department of Education*] [*Information service or system*] (IID)	
EIC	Effective Inlet Valve Closing [*Automotive engineering*]	
EIC	Elastase Inhibitory Capacity [*Physiology*]	
EIC	Electrical Insulation Committee [*Military*]	
EIC	Electrical Insulation Conference [*Later, EEIC*] (MCD)	
EIC	Electrically Insulated Coating	
EIC	Electromagnetic Interference Control (IAA)	
EIC	Electronic Institute of Canada (HGAA)	
EIC	Electron-Induced Conduction (IAA)	
EIC	Electron Ionization Cross Section	
EIC	Electrostatic Ion Cyclotron [*Seismology*]	
EIC	Elevator Code (NFPA)	

EIC	Embar Information Consultants [*Information service or system*] (IID)
EIC	Emplaced Instrument Complex [*Aerospace*]
EIC	Employer Identification Code (AABC)
EIC	Employment and Immigration Canada Library [*UTLAS symbol*]
EIC	Enamel Insulating Compound
EIC	End Item Code
EIC	End Item Contract
EICD	Energy Industries Council [*British*] (DS)
EIC	Energy Information Center [*Battelle Memorial Institute*] (IID)
EIC	Energy Information Centre [*Australia*]
EIC	Engineer-in-Charge
E-I-C	Engineer-In-Charge [*Television*] (WDMC)
EIC	Engineering Information Center
EIC	Engineering Installation Center [*Military*]
EIC	Engineering Institute of Canada
EIC	Entertainment Industries Council (EA)
EIC	Environmental Industry Council (EA)
EIC	Environmental Protection Agency, Region II Field Office, Edison, NJ [*OCLC symbol*] (OCLC)
EIC	Environment Information Center, Inc. [*Database producer*]
EIC	Environment Information Centre (EERA)
EIC	Enzyme Immunochromatography
EIC	Equipment Identification Code
EIC	Equipment Installation and Checkout (MUGU)
EIC	Equipment Interstage Container
EIC	Equitable of Iowa [*NYSE symbol*] (TTSB)
EIC	European Independents Confederation (EAIO)
EIC	European Information Centre (AIE)
EIC	European Insurance Committee [*Paris, France*] (EA)
EIC	Exercise Intelligence Center [*Military*] (CINC)
EIC	Exhibitors in Cable [*An association*] (EA)
EIC	Experimental Intercom (NASA)
EIC	Experiment Integration Center (MCD)
e-ic--	Iceland [*MARC geographic area code Library of Congress*] (LCCP)
EICA	Experimental Integrated Conformed Array
EICAM	Electronic Installation Change and Maintenance (DNAB)
EICAS	Engine Indication and Crew Advisory System
EICAS	Engine Indication and Crew Alerting System (MCD)
EICB	Extra-Intracranial Bypass [*Medicine*] (PDAA)
EICBL	Eastern Independent Collegiate Basketball League
EICC	Emergency Information and Coordination Center [*Federal Emergency Management Agency*]
EICD	Electrical Interface Control Document (MCD)
EICDT	Ego-Ideal and Conscience Development Test [*Personality development test*] [*Psychology*]
EICF	European Investment Casters Federation [*Netherlands*] (PDAA)
EICG	Electromagnetic Interference Control Group (AAG)
EICK	Cork [*Ireland*] [*ICAO location identifier*] (ICLI)
EICM	Employer's Inventory of Critical Manpower
EICMS	Engine In-Flight Condition Monitoring System (MCD)
EIC-NE	Educational Improvement Center - Northeast [*Information service or system*]
EI CO	East India Co. [*1600-1858*] [*British*] (ROG)
EICS	East India Civil Service [*British*] (ROG)
EICS	East India Company's Service [*British*]
EICS	Electromagnetic Intelligence Collection System
EICS	Environmental Impact Computer System [*Database*] [*Army Corps of Engineers*]
EICS	Equipment Identification Coded System (DNAB)
EICT	External Isovolumic Contraction Time [*Laboratory*] (DAVI)
EICW	Electrostatic Ion Cyclotron Waves [*Seismology*]
EID	East India Dock
EID	Egg-Infective Dose [*Clinical chemistry*]
EID	Eider Resources Minieres, Inc. [*Toronto Stock Exchange symbol*]
EID	Electrical Inspection Directorate (IAA)
EID	Electroimmunodiffusion [*Clinical medicine*] (MAE)
EID	Electromagnetic Impulse Deicing [*System under development by NASA*]
EID	Electronic Infusion Device [*Pharmacology*] (DAVI)
EID	Electronic Installation Design [*Navy*]
EID	Electronic Intrusion Detection
EID	Electron Impact [*or Induced*] Desorption
EID	Embryo Infective Dose
EID	Emergency Infusion Device [*Medicine*]
EID	Emitter Identification (MCD)
EID	End Item Delivery (AAG)
EID	End Item Description (AAG)
EID	End Item Designators
EID	End Item Documentation (MCD)
E-ID	Energy-Information Database [*International Research and Evaluation*] [*Information service or system*] (CRD)
EID	Engineering Installation Division [*Military*]
EID	Engineering Item Description (AAG)
EID	Environmental Information Directory [*Later, Gale Environmental Sourcebook*] [*A publication*]
EID	Environmental Information Division [*Air Force Air Training Command*] (IID)
EID	Equipment Interface Document (CAAL)
EID	Eugenic Insemination by Donor
EID	European Investment Bank (GNE)
EID	Export Insurance Division [*of the Ministry of International Trade and Industry*] [*Japan*]
EID	Exposure Intensity Distribution (IAA)
EID	Research Laboratory for Equine Infectious Diseases [*Cornell University*] [*Research center*] (RCD)
EIDAP	Emitter Isolated Difference Amplifier Paralleling [*Bell System*]
EIDB	Dublin [*Ireland*] [*ICAO location identifier*] (ICLI)
EIDC	East Indian Defence Committee
EIDC	Experimental International Data Centre [*Australia*]
EIDCT	Educational Institute of Design, Craft, and Technology [*British*]
EIDD	Experiment Interface Definition Document (MCD)
EIDE	Enhanced Integral Drive Electronics (DOM)
EIDED	Escuela Interamericana de Educacion Democratica
EIDL	Economic Injury Disaster Loan [*Small Business Administration*]
EIDLT	Emergency Identification Light [*Aerospace*] (AAG)
EIDOS	Electronic Information Delivery Online System [*Information retrieval*]
EIDP	Early Intervention Developmental Profile [*Speech and language therapy*] (DAVI)
EIDP	End Item Data Package (NASA)
EIDS	Electronic Information Delivery System [*Individual learning center equipped with head sets and video monitors*]
EIDS	Electronic Information Display System
EIDS	Equipment Integration Design Section
EIDS-ASSIST	Electronic Information Delivery System - Authoring Software System for Instructive Simulation and Training
EIDSO	Engineer Information and Data Systems Office [*Army*] (AABC)
EIDW	Dublin [*Ireland*] [*ICAO location identifier*] (ICLI)
EIE	Electronic Information Exchange [*National Message Center, Inc.*] [*Overland Park, KS*] [*Telecommunications service*] (TSSD)
EIE	End Item Equipment
e-ie--	Ireland [*MARC geographic area code Library of Congress*] (LCCP)
EIEA	Emergency Immigrant Education Act [*1984*] (GFGA)
EIEA	Entertainment Industry Employers' Association [*Australia*]
EIE-AF	Experienced International Executive - Air Forwarding [*American Society of International Executives, Inc.*] [*Designation awarded by*]
EIEB	Experienced International Executive - Banking [*American Society of Intern ational Executives, Inc.*] [*Designation awarded by*]
EIEC	Emergency Incident of Environmental Contamination [*Environmental Protection Agency*]
EIEC	English Industrial Estates Corp.
EIEC	European Institute of Ecology and Cancer [*Formerly, European Institute of Cancerology*] (EA)
EIE-C	Experienced International Executive - Credit [*American Society of Interna tional Executives, Inc.*] [*Designation awarded by*]
EIED	Electrically Initiated Explosive Device
EIE-EM	Experienced International Executive - Export Management [*American Society of International Executives, Inc.*] [*Designation awarded by*]
EIE-F	Experienced International Executive - Forwarding [*American Society of Int ernational Executives, Inc.*] [*Designation awarded by*]
EIEIO	Empowering Individuals with Disabilities Through Education, Information, and Opportunity [*Farmer outreach program*] [*Montana State University*]
EIEIO	Engineering Industries Export Intelligence Officer [*British*] (DI)
EIEM	Environmental Interference Effects Model (MCD)
EIE-M	Experienced International Executive - Marketing [*American Society of Inte rnational Executives, Inc.*] [*Designation awarded by*]
EIEMA	Electrical Installation Equipment Manufacturers Association [*British*] (DBA)
EI-EO	Eye Balls In - Eye Balls Out (SAA)
EIES	Electronic Information Exchange System [*Pronounced "eyes"*] [*New Jersey Institute of Technology Computer network*] [*Telecommunications*]
EIES	Electron Impact Emission Spectroscopy [*Photovoltaic energy systems*]
EIESP	European Institute of Education and Social Policy (AIE)
EIE-TM	Experienced International Executive - Traffic Management [*American Societ y of International Executives, Inc.*] [*Designation awarded by*]
EIF	Electrochemical Ind(Frutarom) [*AMEX symbol*] (TTSB)
EIF	Electrochemical Industries (Frutarom) Ltd. [*AMEX symbol*] (SPSG)
EIF	Electronic Industries Foundation (EA)
EIF	End Item Failure
EIF	Erythema-Inducing Factor [*Hematology*]
EIF	Erythrocyte Initiation Factor
eIF	Eukaryotic Initiation Factors [*Biochemistry*]
EIF	Executive Inventory File [*Civil Service Commission*]
EIF	Exhibition Industry Federation [*British*] (DBA)
EIF	Pittsfield, MA [*Location identifier FAA*] (FAAL)
EIFA	Element Interface Functional Analysis (NASA)
EIFAC	European Inland Fisheries Advisory Commission [*Food and Agriculture Organization*] [*United Nations*] (ASF)
EIFDC	Eterna International Foundation for Disabled Children (EA)
EIFF	Enemy Identification Friend or Foe
EIFI	Electrical Industries Federation of Ireland (BI)
EIFI	European Industrial Fasteners Institute [*EC*] (ECED)
Eif Jud Act	Eiffe on the Irish Judicature Act [*A publication*] (DLA)
EIFOV	Effective Instantaneous Field of View
EIFS	Economic Impact Forecast System [*Army*] (RDA)
EIFS	Exterior Insulation and Finish System [*Sto Industries*]
EIG	Electronic Image Generator
EIG	Electronics Installations Group [*Military*]
EIG	Elephant Interest Group (EA)
EIG	Emitter Identification Guide (NG)
EIG	Energy Information Guide [*A publication*]
EIG	Engineering Installation Group [*Military*]
EIG	Exchange Information Group (NATG)
EIG	Voltage Inner Gimbal
EIGA	Ethics in Government Act

EIGFET........ Equivalent Insulated Gate Field Effect Transistor (IAA)
Eight-C St .... Eighteenth-Century Studies [*A publication*] (BRI)
EIGL............. Eastern Intercollegiate Gymnastic League (EA)
EIGM............. Gormanston County Meath [*Ireland*] [*ICAO location identifier*] (ICLI)
EIGRP .... Enhanced Interior Gateway Routing Protocol [*Telecommunications*]
        (ACRL)
EIH.............. East India House (ROG)
EIH.............. Economic Indicator's Handbook [*A publication*]
EIHR............ Eisenhower Institute for Historical Research [*Smithsonian Institution*]
EIHSW .... European Institute of Hunting and Sporting Weapons (EAIO)
EII............... Earth Island Institute (EA)
EII............... Electronically Invisible Interconnect [*Computer science*]
EII............... Encoded Item Identifier (CAAL)
EII............... Engineering Item Identification
EII............... Ethnic Identification Index (BJA)
EIIA............. European Information Industry Association [*Database producer*] (IID)
EIIC............. Entertainment Industry Interim Council [*Australia*]
EIII.............. Association of the European Independent Informatics Industry
        (PDAA)
EIII.............. [*Association of the*] European Independent Information Industry
        (NITA)
EIIP............. Engineering Industries Internalisation Program [*Australia*]
EIIS............. Energy Industry Information System (IEEE)
EIIV............. Electronics Interface Integrated Validation (KSC)
EIK.............. Eat-In Kitchen [*Classified advertising*]
EIK.............. Extended Interaction Klystron [*Electronics*] (IAA)
EIKN............ Connaught Regional Airport [*Ireland*] [*ICAO location identifier*] (ICLI)
EIKON.......... Gesellschaft der Freunde der Ikonenkunst (EAIO)
EIL.............. Egyptian International Line (DS)
EIL.............. Eilat [*Israel*] [*Seismograph station code, US Geological Survey*]
        (SEIS)
EIL.............. Electrical Insulating Liquid (PDAA)
EIL.............. Electro Chemical Inds. (Frutarom) Ltd. [*AMEX symbol*] (SAG)
EIL.............. Electronic Instruments Limited [*as in EIL electrode, used in biochemistry*] [*British*]
EIL.............. Electron Injection LASER
EIL.............. Environmental Impairment Liability
EIL.............. Equipment Identification List (DNAB)
EIL.............. Essays on International Law [*A publication*] (ILCA)
EIL.............. Event Index Log [*NASA*] (KSC)
EIL.............. Experiment in International Living/School for International Training
        (EA)
EIL.............. Explosive Investigative Laboratory [*Navy*]
EIL.............. Fairbanks, AK [*Location identifier FAA*] (FAAL)
EILC............ Egg Industry Licensing Committee [*Victoria, Australia*]
EILL............ Elegant Illusions, Inc. [*NASDAQ symbol*] (SAG)
Eil Wom ..... Eiloart's Laws Relating to Women [*1878*] [*A publication*] (DLA)
EIM............. Effective Index Method (PDAA)
EIM............. Elastomeric Insulation Material
EIM............. Electronic Imaging in Medicine [*Computer graphics*]
EIM............. Elite Insurance Management Ltd. [*Toronto Stock Exchange symbol Vancouver Stock Exchange symbol*]
EIM............. End Item Manager (AFIT)
EIM............. End of Information Marker [*Computer science*] (IAA)
EIM............. Engine Inventory Manager [*Air Force*] (AFIT)
EIM............. Environmental Industries Marketplace [*A publication*]
EIM............. European Institute for the Media (EA)
EIM............. European Interactive Media [*Joint venture of Philips International and PolyGram BV International*]
EIM............. European Interprofessional Market (ECON)
EIM............. Excitability-Inducing Material [*Biochemistry*]
EIM............. Explosive Inventory Manager [*Military*]
EIM............. Explosive Investigation Manager
EIM............. Explosives Investigation Memorandum [*Navy*] (MCD)
EIM............. Eyelet-Installing Machine
EIMA............ Exterior Insulation Manufacturers Association (EA)
EIMAM.......... Environmental Instrumentation Measurement and Monitoring (IAA)
EIMB............ Electronics Installation and Maintenance Bulletin
EIMC............ English Institute Materials Center
EIME............ Electronic Instrument Manufacturers Exhibit (MUGU)
EIME............ Mhic Easmuinn Baldonnel, County Dublin [*Ireland*] [*ICAO location identifier*] (ICLI)
EIMECH........ Electro Mechanical
EIMET .... Engineering Information Meetings (NITA)
EIMF........... End Item Maintenance Form
EIMR........... Equipment Item Material Requirements
EIMS........... Electronic Ink and Moisture System [*Printing*] (DGA)
EIMS........... Electronic Institutional [*or Integrated*] Media System
EIMS........... Electron Impact Mass Spectrometry
EIMS........... Electron Ionization Mass Spectrometry
EIMS........... End Item Maintenance Sheets (MCD)
EIMS........... Engineering Installation Management System [*Air Force*] (CET)
EIMS........... Environmental Information Management System
EIMTS......... End Item Maintenance Transmittal Sheet
EIMU........... Environmental Information Management Unit (EERA)
EIMWT........ Echo Integration-Mid Water Trawl [*Marine science*] (OSRA)
EIMWT........ Echo Integration-MidWater Trawl (USDC)
EIN............. Aer Lingus Teoranta [*Ireland*] [*ICAO designator*] (FAAC)
EIN............. Echelon International Corp. [*NYSE symbol*] (SAG)
EIN............. Educational Information Network [*Princeton, NJ*]
EIN............. Eindhoven [*Netherlands*] [*Airport symbol*] (OAG)
EIN............. Employer Identification Number [*IRS*]
EIN............. Engineer Intelligence Note
EIN............. Engine Identification Number [*Automotive engineering*]
EIN............. Environmental Information Networks Inc. [*Database producer*] (IID)

EIN............. Equipment Installation Notice (AAG)
EIN............. Eulerian Iterative Nonsteady [*Method*] [*Mathematics*]
EIN............. European Informatics Network (NITA)
EIN............. European Information Network [*Telecommunications*] (TEL)
EIN............. Excitatory Interneuron [*Neurophysiology*]
EIN............. Experimental Integrated Network
EIN............. External Interlace
EINA............ Exodus International - North America (EA)
E in C .... Engineer-in-Charge [*Army*]
E in C .... Engineer-in-Chief
E-in-CD........ Engineer-in-Chief's Department [*British military*] (DMA)
E Ind .... East Indies
EINECS .... European Inventory of Existing Commercial Chemical Substances
        [*Which will be exempt from new product regulations*]
E in EE........ Engineer in Electrical Engineering
EINET.......... Enterprise Integration Network [*Information service or system*] (IID)
EINI............. Electron Irradiation and Neutron Irradiation (IAA)
EINIS .... European Integrated Network of Image and Services (EAIO)
E in ME........ Engineer in Mechanical Engineering
EINN............ Shannon [*Ireland*] [*ICAO location identifier*] (ICLI)
E INS .... Engineer Inspector [*Navy British*] (ROG)
Einspr .... Einspruch [*Objection, Opposition, Caveat*] [*German*] (ILCA)
EinstnN........ Einstein Noah Bagel Corp. [*Associated Press*] (SAG)
E Int .... Equal Interval [*Isophase navigation light*]
EIO............. Electric Induction Oven
EIO............. Emergency Information Officer [*Civil Defense*]
EIO............. Execute Input-Output (IAA)
EIO............. Extended Interactive Oscillator (PDAA)
EIOBL.......... Equipment Item Out of Balance (AFIT)
EIOC........... Early Initial Operational Capability (MCD)
EIOC........... Equivalent Input Offset Current
EIOD........... Equivalent Instruction or Duty
EIOI............ Expedition Internationale de l'Ocean Indien [*International Indian Ocean Expedition - IIOE*] [*French*] (MSC)
EIO-IMS ...... Early Initial Operational-Information Management System (MCD)
EIOP........... End of the Initial Operating Period [*Department of Housing and Urban Development*] (GFGA)
EIOP........... External Input-Output Processor (IAA)
EIOS........... Extended Input-Output System (IAA)
EIOV........... Equivalent Input Offset Voltage
EIP............. Association Mondiale pour l'Ecole Instrument de Paix [*World Association for the School as an Instrument of Peace*] [*Geneva, Switzerland*] (EAIO)
EIP............. Early Intervention Program
EIP............. Economic Inventory Policy
EIP............. Economic Inventory Procedures [*Army*] (AABC)
EIP............. Educational Improvement Process [*Indiana*] (EDAC)
EIP............. Educational Incentive Plan [*Red Cross*]
EIP............. EIP Microwave, Inc. [*Associated Press*] (SAG)
EIP............. Electronic Installation Plan (NG)
EIP............. Electronics for Peace (PDAA)
EIP............. Emergency Implementation Procedure (NRCH)
EIP............. Emitter Identification Program [*RADAR*] (MCD)
EIP............. Emulator Interface Program (IAA)
EIP............. End-Inspiratory Pause [*Respiration*]
EIP............. End Item Parameter
EIP............. Engineering Installation Plan (CET)
EIP............. Equipment in Place (MCD)
EIP............. Equipment Installation Procedure [*Telecommunications*] (TEL)
EIP............. ERA [*Equal Rights Amendment*] Impact Project [*Defunct*] (EA)
EIP............. Ethylene Interpolymer Alloy
EIP............. Executive Interface Program [*Computer science*] (HGAA)
EIP............. Exoatmospheric Interceptor Propulsion (MCD)
EIP............. Experiment Implementation Plan [*NASA*]
EIP............. Extensor Indicis Proprius [*Anatomy*]
EIPA........... Ethyl(isopropyl)amiloride [*Organic chemistry*]
EIPA........... Ethylisopropylaniline [*Organic chemistry*]
EIPA........... European Institute of Public Administration (EA)
EIPC........... European Institute of Printed Circuits (EA)
EIPG........... European Industrial Planning Group [*NATO*]
EIPH........... Exercise-Induced Pulmonary Hemorrhage [*Veterinary medicine*]
EIPM........... EIP Microwave [*NASDAQ symbol*] (TTSB)
EIPM........... EIP Microwave, Inc. [*NASDAQ symbol*] (NQ)
EIPS........... Endogenous Inhibitor of Prostaglandin Synthase [*Biochemistry*]
EIPT........... Electronic Industry Production and Test Equipment (IMH)
EIQ............. Emission Inventory Questionnaire [*Environmental science*] (FFDE)
EIR............. East Indian Railway
EIR............. Either (ROG)
EIR............. Electron-Ion Recombination
EIR............. Emerald Isle Resources, Inc. [*Vancouver Stock Exchange symbol*]
EIR............. Emergency Information Readiness [*Civil Defense*]
EIR............. Employee Incident Report (MCD)
EIR............. Endangerment Information Report [*Environmental Protection Agency*] (ERG)
EIR............. End Item Requirement (AAG)
EIR............. Energy Information Resource (MCD)
EIR............. Engineering Information Report [*Telecommunications*] (TEL)
EIR............. Engineering Information Request [*Nuclear energy*] (NRCH)
EIR............. Engineering Investigation Request
EIR............. Environmental Impact Report [*Environmental Protection Agency*]
EIR............. Environmental Impact Review
EIR............. Equipment Identification Register
EIR............. Equipment Improvement Recommendations [*Military*]
EIR............. Equipment Improvement Report [*DoD*]
EIR............. Equipment Inoperable Record [*Nuclear energy*] (NRCH)

EIR..............	Equipment Installation Record (MCD)
EIR..............	Establishment Inspection Report [*Federal government*]
EIR..............	Excess Information Rate [*Telecommunications*] (ACRL)
EIR..............	Expanded Infrared (DNAB)
Eir..............	Lambard's Eirenarcha [*A publication*] (DLA)
EIRAC.........	Entertainment Industry Referral and Assistance Center (EA)
EIRB..........	European Investment Research Bureau [*Information service or system*] (NITA)
EIRD	Economics Information Resources Directory [*A publication*]
EIRD	Engineering Information Report Date [*Telecommunications*] (TEL)
EIRD	Engineering Instrumentation Requirements Document
EIRD	Experiment Integration Requirements Document [*NASA*]
EIRE..........	Emerald Isle Bancorp, Inc. [*NASDAQ symbol*] (SAG)
EIRENE	European Information Researchers Network (IID)
EIRI..........	Early Intervention Research Institute [*Utah State University*] [*Research center*] (RCD)
EIRI..........	Energy Information Resources Inventory [*Database*] [*Department of Energy Information service or system*] (CRD)
EIRIS	Ethical Investment Research Service [*British Information service or system*]
EIRMA	European Industrial Research Management Association [*France*]
EIRNV	Extra Incidence Rate in Non-Vaccinated Groups [*Medicine*] (BABM)
EIRP............	Effective Instantaneous [*or Isotropic*] Radiated Power [*Telecommunications*]
EIRP............	Effective Isotropic Radiated Power [*Telecommunications*] (WDMC)
EIRP............	Environmental Impact Research Program [*Army*] (RDA)
EIRP............	Equivalent Isotropically Radiated Power [*Microwave transmission*]
EIRS............	Engineering and Industrial Research Station [*Mississippi State University*] [*Research center*] (RCD)
EIRS............	Ethical Investment Research Service [*London, England*] [*Information service or system*] (IID)
EIRT............	Equivalent Isotropic Radiated Power [*Telecommunications service*] (BARN)
EIRT............	Executive Independent Review Team (MCD)
EIRv............	Extra Incidence Rate in Vaccinated Groups [*Biochemistry*] (DAVI)
EIRv............	Extra Incidence Rate of Vaccinated Groups [*Medicine*] (DMAA)
EIS.............	Beef Island [*British Virgin Islands*] [*Airport symbol*] (AD)
EIS.............	Economic Information System [*International Monetary Fund*] [*Information service or system*] (IID)
EIS.............	Educational Institute of Scotland
EIS.............	Education in Science (AIE)
EIS.............	Effluent Inventory System [*Nuclear energy*] (NRCH)
EIS.............	Electrical and Instrument Shop (NRCH)
EIS.............	Electrical Integration System [*NASA*]
EIS.............	Electric Induction Steel (IAA)
EIS.............	Electrolyte Insulator Semiconductor (IAA)
EIS.............	Electromagnetic Intelligence System
EIS.............	Electronet Information Systems, Inc. [*Information service or system*] (IID)
EIS.............	Electronic Ignition System [*Automotive engineering*]
EIS.............	Electronic Image Stabilizer [*Photography*]
EIS.............	Electronic Imaging System [*Computer graphics*]
EIS.............	Electronic Information Series [*Information service or system*] (IID)
EIS.............	Electronic Information Services [*Industry*] (IT)
EIS.............	Electronic Inquiry System (PDAA)
EIS.............	Electronics Installations Squadron [*Military*]
EIS.............	Emergency Information System [*Software package*] [*Research Alternatives, Inc.*]
EIS.............	Emergency Injection System [*Nuclear energy*] (NRCH)
EIS.............	Emissions Impact Statement [*Environmental Protection Agency*] (GFGA)
EIS.............	Emissions Inventory System [*Environmental Protection Agency*] (GFGA)
EIS.............	Employee Information System (MCD)
EIS.............	Employment Incentive Scheme
EIS.............	End Interruption Sequence [*Computer science*]
EIS.............	End Item Specification (AAG)
EIS.............	End Item Subdivision (MCD)
EIS.............	Energy and Industry Subgroup (EERA)
EIS.............	Energy Information Systems [*UNIDO*] [*United Nations*] (DUND)
EIS--..........	Engineering Information System (MCD)
EIS.............	Entered in Service [*Military*]
EIS.............	Enterprise Information Systems
EIS.............	Enterprise Investment Scheme [*British*] (ECON)
EIS.............	Environmental Impact Service (USDC)
EIS.............	Environmental Impact Statement (EERA)
EIS.............	Environmental Impact Statement [*Environmental Protection Agency*]
EIS.............	Environmental Impact Statements [*Heiner and Co.*] (NITA)
EIS.............	Environmental Impact Study
EIS.............	Environmental Information System [*National Science Foundation*]
EIS.............	Environmental Inventory System (GNE)
EIS.............	Epidemic Intelligence Service [*of the Centers for Disease Control*]
EIS.............	Epidemiology Information System [*Database*] [*Oak Ridge National Laboratory*] [*Information service or system*] (CRD)
EIS.............	Eurasian Ice Sheet [*Climatology*]
EIS.............	Excelsior Income Shares, Inc. [*NYSE symbol*] (SAG)
EIS.............	Excelsior Inc. Shares [*NYSE symbol*] (TTSB)
EIS.............	Executive Information Service [*or Software or System*]
EIS.............	Expanded Inband Signaling [*Telecommunications*] (TEL)
EIS.............	Expendable Instrument System
EIS.............	Experiment Information System
EIS.............	Export Intelligence Service (DS)
EIS.............	Extended Instruction Set [*Honeywell, Inc.*]
EIS.............	Eyes in the Sky
EIS.............	Tortola [*British Virgin Islands*] [*Airport symbol*] (OAG)

EISA..........	EEG Aperiodic-Interval Spectrum Analysis [*Neurology*]
EISA..........	Enhanced Industry Standard Architecture [*Computer hardware*] (PCM)
EISA..........	European Independent Steelworks Association (EAIO)
EISA..........	Extended Industry Standard Architecture [*Computer science*]
EIS/AS	Emissions Inventory System/Area Source [*Environmental Protection Agency*] (GFGA)
EISB..........	Electrical Industry Study Board (EA)
EISC..........	Eastern Illinois State College [*Later, EIU*]
EISC..........	Electronic Industry Show Corp. [*Defunct*] (EA)
EISC..........	Entertainment Industry Support Committee [*Defunct*] (EA)
EISCAT........	European Incoherent Scattering Scientific Association
EISD..........	Engineering and Industrial Software Directory [*Engineering Information, Inc.*] [*Information service or system*] (CRD)
EISD..........	Explosives Ingredients Sources Database [*Chemical Propulsion Information Agency*]
EISE..........	Extendable Integration Support Environment [*Air Force*]
EISEP.........	Expanded In-Home Services for the Elderly Program (BARN)
EISF..........	Elastic Incoherent Structure Factor [*of spectra*]
EISG..........	Energy Information Systems Group [*Department of Energy Also, an information service or system*] (IID)
EISI..........	EIS International [*NASDAQ symbol*] (TTSB)
EISI..........	Electronic Information Systems, Inc. [*NASDAQ symbol*] (SAG)
EISIM..........	Electron Impact Selected Ion Monitoring [*Instrumentation*]
EIS Intl	EIS International [*Associated Press*] (SAG)
EISL..........	Shannon [*Ireland*] [*ICAO location identifier*] (ICLI)
EISN..........	Environmental Information and Support Network (EERA)
EISN..........	Experimental Integrated Switched Network
EISO..........	Environmental Information System Office [*National Science Foundation*]
EISP..........	Equivalent Industrial Standard Process (MCD)
EIS Plants....	Economic Information Systems-Plants [*Information service or system*] (NITA)
EIS/PS	Emissions Inventory System/Point Source [*Environmental Protection Agency*] (GFGA)
EISS..........	Encyclopedia of Information Systems and Services [*Later, IID*] [*A publication*]
EISSWA	Experimental Information Service in Two Social Welfare Agencies (PDAA)
EISU..........	Shannon [*Ireland*] [*ICAO location identifier*] (ICLI)
EISV..........	Extrinsic Irradiated Silicon Vidicon
EISYS..........	Earth Information System [*Commercial firm*]
EIT.............	Economies in Transition (ACII)
EIT.............	Eilat [*Israel*] [*Airport symbol*] (AD)
EIT.............	Electrical Impedance Tomography [*Medicine*] (BARN)
EIT.............	Electrical Information Test
EIT.............	Electrical Installation Test [*or Technician*]
EIT.............	Electrical Insulation Tape
EIT.............	Electrical Intersystems Test
EIT.............	Electromagnetically Induced Transparency [*Optics*]
EIT.............	Electromagnetic Interference Testing
EIT.............	Electron-Bombardment Ion Thrustor
EIT.............	Electronic Information Technology [*Hardware manufacturer*]
EIT.............	Electronic Installation Technician
EIT.............	Engineering Index Thesaurus [*A publication*]
EIT.............	Engineer-in-Training
EIT.............	Enterprise Integration Technologies [*Commercial firm*]
EIT.............	Enterprise Investments Trust [*Australia*]
EIT.............	Entry Interface Time (MCD)
EIT.............	Environmental Interaction Theory of Personality (PDAA)
EIT.............	Environmental Issues Test (EDAC)
EIT.............	(Erythrofuranosyl)imidazolinethione [*Antineoplastic drug*]
EIT.............	Erythroid Iron Turnover [*Hematology*]
EIT.............	European Institute for Trans-National Studies in Group and Organizational Development (EA)
EIT.............	European Institute of Technology [*International Consortium of Industrial Firms*]
EIT.............	Europe Industry and Technology Division [*Department of Trade*] [*British*]
EIT.............	Extreme-Ultraviolet Imaging Telescope [*Instrumentation*]
e-it--..........	Italy [*MARC geographic area code Library of Congress*] (LCCP)
EITB..........	Engineering Industry Training Board [*British*]
EITB..........	Enzyme-Linked Immunoelectrotransfer Blot (Technique) [*Clinical chemistry*]
EITC..........	Earned Income Tax Credit
EITF..........	Emerging Issues Task Force (TDOB)
EITP..........	End Item Test Plan (MCD)
EITS..........	East Integrated Test Stand (KSC)
EITS..........	Educational and Industrial Testing Service
EITS..........	Express International Telex Service (MHDB)
EITZ..........	English Inshore Traffic Zone (DS)
EIU.............	Eastern Illinois University [*Formerly, EISC*] [*Charleston*]
EIU.............	Economist Intelligence Unit [*British*]
EIU.............	Electronic Interface Unit
EIU.............	Engine Interface Unit (NASA)
EIU.............	Enid, OK [*Location identifier FAA*] (FAAL)
EIU.............	Equipment Inventory Update [*Telecommunications*] (TEL)
EIV.............	Effective Initial Value
EIV.............	Engine Installation Vehicle
EIV.............	Entsiklopedyah 'Ivrit [*or Enziklopedyah 'Ivrit*] (BJA)
EIVR..........	Exchange of Information, Visits, and Reports
EIVT..........	Electrical and Instrumentation Verification Tests [*NASA*] (NASA)
EIVT..........	Electrical Interface Verification Test [*NASA*] (NASA)
EIVT..........	Electronic Installation Verification Test [*NASA*] (NASA)
EIW.............	Enamel Insulated Wire

EIW............. European Institute for Water (EAIO)
EIW............. New Madrid, MO [*Location identifier FAA*] (FAAL)
EIWA.......... Escala Inteligencia Wechsler Para Adultes [*Weschler Adult Intelligence Scale*] [*Psychology*] (DAVI)
EIWLS........ Extended Iterative Weighted Least Squares [*Statistics*] (PDAA)
EI/WS.......... End Item/Weapon System [*Army*]
EIWS........... Engineering Installation Workload Schedule (CET)
EIX............. Edison Intl. [*NYSE symbol*] (TTSB)
EIX............. El Air Exports Ltd. [*Ireland*] [*ICAO designator*] (FAAC)
EIX............. Elders IXL Canada, Inc. [*Toronto Stock Exchange symbol*]
EIY............. Ein Yahav [*Israel*] [*Airport symbol Obsolete*] (OAG)
EJ............. Die Entstehung des Judentums [*A publication*] (BJA)
EJ............. Eject (KSC)
EJ............. Ejus [*Of Him, or Of Her*] [*Latin*]
EJ............. Elbow Jerk [*Medicine*]
EJ............. Electrojet (IAA)
EJ............. Electronic Jamming
EJ............. Electronic Journalism
EJ............. Electronic Journalism (WDMC)
EJ............. Elizabeth Jones [*Designer's mark, when appearing on US coins*]
EJ............. Encyclopaedia Judaica [*A publication*]
EJ............. English Journal [*A publication*] (BRI)
EJ............. Everest & Jennings International [*AMEX symbol*] (SPSG)
EJ............. Everest/Jennings Intl. [*AMEX symbol*] (TTSB)
EJ............. Expansion Joint
EJ............. Expendable Jammer (LAIN)
EJ............. New England Airlines [*ICAO designator*] (AD)
EJA........... Barrancabermeja [*Colombia*] [*Airport symbol*] (OAG)
EJA........... Engineering Job Analysis (KSC)
EJA........... Environmental Protection Agency, Region III Library, Philadelphia, PA [*OCLC symbol*] (OCLC)
EJA........... Esperanta Jura Asocio [*Esperanto Law Association*] [*See also ELA*] [*British*] [*England*] (EAIO)
EJA........... Executive Jet Aviation, Inc. [*ICAO designator*] (FAAC)
EJB........... Ectopic Junctional Beat [*Cardiology*]
EJB........... Environmental Protection Agency, Headquarters Library, Washington, DC [*OCLC symbol*] (OCLC)
EJC........... Eccles-Jordan Circuit [*Electronics*]
EJC........... Electrical Joint Compound (IAA)
EJC........... Ellsworth Junior College [*Iowa*] [*Later, ECC*]
EJC........... Ely Junior College [*Minnesota*] [*Later, Vermilion Community College*]
EJC........... Enciclopedia Judaica Castellana [*A publication*] (BJA)
EJC........... Endicott Junior College [*Beverly, MA*]
EJC........... Engineers Joint Council [*Superseded by AAES*] (EA)
EJC........... Environmental Protection Agency, Law Library, Washington, DC [*OCLC symbol*] (OCLC)
EJC........... Espoir de la Jeunesse Camerounaise [*Hope of the Cameroonese Youth*]
EJC........... Estherville Junior College [*Iowa*]
EJC........... Eveleth Junior College [*Later, Mesabi Community College*] [*Minnesota*]
EJC........... Everett Junior College [*Later, ECC*] [*Washington*]
EJC........... Grupo de Aviacion Ejecutiva, SA de CV [*Mexico*] [*FAA designator*] (FAAC)
EJCC......... Eastern Joint Computer Conference
EJCDC........ Engineers Joint Contract Documents Committee (AAGC)
EJCNC........ Engineers Joint Council Nuclear Congress (IEEE)
EJCSC......... European Joint Committee of Scientific Cooperation [*Council of Europe*] (PDAA)
EJCT.......... Eject
EJCT.......... Engineering Joint Council Thesaurus (NITA)
EJCTR......... Ejector
EJD............. DeBartolo Realty [*NYSE symbol*] (TTSB)
EJD............. DeBartolo Realty Co. [*NYSE symbol*] (SAG)
EJD............. Environmental Protection Agency, Region III Field Office, Annapolis, MD [*OCLC symbol*] (OCLC)
EJE............. Chicago Outer Belt R. R. [*AAR code*]
EJE............. Electric Junction Equation
EJE............. Elgin, Joliet & Eastern Railway Co. [*AAR code*]
EJE............. Environmental Protection Agency, OTS [*Office of Toxic Substances*] Technical Information Center, Washington, DC [*OCLC symbol*] (OCLC)
EJE............. Executive Jet Aviation SA [*Switzerland*] [*FAA designator*] (FAAC)
EJEA.......... Empire Journal of Experimental Agriculture [*A publication*]
EJF............. Equal Justice Foundation (EA)
EJF............. Estimated Junction Frequency [*Telecommunications*] (TEL)
E-JFET........ Enhancement-Mode Junction Field-Effect Transistor [*Electronics*]
EJGS.......... Eminent Junior Grand Steward [*Freemasonry*] (ROG)
EJH............. Wedjh [*Saudi Arabia*] [*Airport symbol*] (OAG)
EJI............. Expansion Joint Institute
EJ Korvette... , Corvettes [*Zwillenberg*] [*Department store chain name derived from the owner's name, a business parter, and a Canadian warship*]
EJM........... American Air Services, Inc. [*ICAO designator*] (FAAC)
EJM........... Etudes sur le Judaisme Medieval [*A publication*] (BJA)
EJMA.......... Educational Jewelry Manufacturers Association [*Defunct*] (EA)
EJMA.......... Expansion Joint Manufacturers Association (EA)
EJN............. Ejection
EJN ST........ Ejection Seat (MSA)
EJO............. Earp, Joseph O., Seattle WA [*STAC*]
EJO............. Engineering Job Order (MCD)
EJO............. Nejo [*Ethiopia*] [*Airport symbol*] (AD)
EJOB.......... European Joint Optical Bistability Programme [*To develop an optical computer*]
EJOTF......... Earth-Jupiter Orbiter Transfer Flight (PDAA)
E-Journal..... Electronic Journal (TNIG)

EJP............. Exchange Jump
EJP............. Excitatory Junctional Potential [*Neurophysiology*]
EJPC.......... European Justice and Peace Commissions (EAIO)
EJPEA......... Emergency Jobs Programs Extension Act of 1976
EJR............. Detroit, MI [*Location identifier FAA*] (FAAL)
EJR............. East Jersey Railroad & Terminal Co. [*AAR code*]
EJRMG........ Edmond James Rothschild Memorial Group [*Foundation*]
EJS............. East Jordan & Southern R. R. [*AAR code*]
EJS............. Engineering Job Sheet (MCD)
EJS............. Enhanced JTIDS [*Joint Tactical Information Distribution System*] System [*Air Force*]
EJS............. Ethical Judgement Scale (EDAC)
EJT............. Aero Ejecutiva SA [*Mexico ICAO designator*] (FAAC)
EJT............. Eccles-Jordan Trigger [*Electronics*]
EJT............. Engineering Job Ticket
EJT............. Extended Joint Test (MCD)
EJU............. European Judo Union (EAIO)
EJU............. Exports to Japan Unit [*British Overseas Trade Board*] (DS)
EJUAA......... Emergency Jobs and Unemployment Assistance Act
EJud.......... Encyclopaedia Judaica: Das Judentum in Geschichte und Gegenwart [*Berlin*] [*A publication*] (BJA)
EJUSD........ Ejusdem [*Of the Same*] [*Latin*]
EJV............. Equity Joint Venture [*Business term*]
EJV............. External Jugular Vein [*Anatomy*]
EJWG......... Eco-Justice Working Group [*Joint Strategy and Action Committee and National Council of the Churches of Christ in the USA*] (EA)
EK............. Eastern Knight [*Freemasonry*] (ROG)
EK............. Eastman Kodak [*NYSE symbol*] (TTSB)
EK............. Eastman Kodak Co. [*NYSE symbol*] (SPSG)
EK............. Einschluss-Korper [*Inclusion body*] [*Medicine*]
EK............. Einzelkommentar [*A publication*] (BJA)
EK............. Electrocardiogram [*Also, ECG, EKG*] [*Medicine*]
EK............. Enkephalin [*Brain peptide, subclass of endorphin*]
EK............. Erythrokinase [*Biochemistry*] (DAVI)
EK............. Masling Commuter Services [*ICAO designator*] (AD)
EKA........... Environmental Protection Agency, Region IV Library, Atlanta, GA [*OCLC symbol*] (OCLC)
EKA........... Eskdalemuir Array [*Scotland*] [*Seismograph station code, US Geological Survey*] (SEIS)
EKA........... Eureka/Arcata [*California*] Murray Field [*Airport symbol Obsolete*] (OAG)
EKAE.......... Aero [*Denmark ICAO location identifier*] (ICLI)
EKAH.......... Tirstrup [*Denmark ICAO location identifier*] (ICLI)
EkahR........ Ekah Rabbah (BJA)
EKAT.......... Anholt [*Denmark ICAO location identifier*] (ICLI)
EKAV.......... Avno [*Denmark ICAO location identifier*] (ICLI)
EKB............. Edgeworth-Kuiper Belt [*Panetary science*]
EKB............. Electronic Keyboard
EKB............. Electronic Knowledge Bank
EKB............. Environmental Protection Agency, Library Services, Research Triangle Park, NC [*OCLC symbol*] (OCLC)
EKBI.......... Billund [*Denmark ICAO location identifier*] (ICLI)
EKBS.......... Electronic Keyboard System
EKC........... East Kansas City Aviation, Inc. [*ICAO designator*] (FAAC)
EKC........... Eastman Kodak Co.
EKC........... Ek Chor Ching Motorcycle [*NYSE symbol*] (SPSG)
EKC........... Electrokinetic Chromatography
EKC........... Environmental Protection Agency, Environmental Research Laboratory, Gulf Breeze, FL [*OCLC symbol*] (OCLC)
EKC........... Epidemic Keratoconjunctivitis [*Ophthalmology*]
EKC........... Ethylketocyclazocine [*Biochemistry*]
EKCA.......... Kobenhavn [*Denmark ICAO location identifier*] (ICLI)
EKCH.......... Kobenhavn/Kastrup [*Denmark ICAO location identifier*] (ICLI)
EK Chor...... Ek Chor China Motorcycle [*Associated Press*] (SAG)
EKCO........ Ekco Group [*Associated Press*] (SAG)
EKD............. Environmental Protection Agency, Environmental Research Laboratory, Athens, GA [*OCLC symbol*] (OCLC)
EKD............. Epic Data, Inc. [*Toronto Stock Exchange symbol Vancouver Stock Exchange symbol*]
EKD............. Eucaloric Ketogenic Diet
EKD............. Evangelische Kirche Deutschlands
EKDK.......... Kobenhavn [*Denmark ICAO location identifier*] (ICLI)
EKE............. Biloxi, MS [*Location identifier FAA*] (FAAL)
EKE............. Ekereku [*Guyana*] [*Airport symbol*] (OAG)
EKE............. Environmental Protection Agency, Library, Research Triangle Park, NC [*OCLC symbol*] (OCLC)
EKEB.......... Esbjerg [*Denmark ICAO location identifier*] (ICLI)
E KENT R.... East Kent Regiment [*Military unit*] [*British*] (ROG)
EKF............. Environmental Protection Agency, ESRL [*Environmental Sciences Research Laboratory*], Meteorology Laboratory, Research Triangle Park, NC [*OCLC symbol*] (OCLC)
EKFC.......... Elvis Is King Fan Club (EAIO)
EKG............. Carlsbad, CA [*Location identifier FAA*] (FAAL)
EKG............. Effective Kilogram (NRCH)
EKG............. Electrocardiogram [*Also, ECG, EK*] [*Medicine*]
EKG............. Electrocardiograph [*Also, ECG*] (NASA)
EKG............. Epidemic Keratoconjunctivitis [*Ophthalmology*] (DAVI)
EKGF.......... Gormfelt [*Denmark ICAO location identifier*] (ICLI)
EKGH.......... Gronholt [*Denmark ICAO location identifier*] (ICLI)
EKH............. Elkhorn Ranch [*California*] [*Seismograph station code, US Geological Survey*] (SEIS)
EKHG.......... Herning/Skinderholm [*Denmark ICAO location identifier*] (ICLI)
EKHO.......... Lindtorp [*Denmark ICAO location identifier*] (ICLI)
EKHS.......... Hadsund [*Denmark ICAO location identifier*] (ICLI)
EKHV.......... Haderslev [*Denmark ICAO location identifier*] (ICLI)

EKI	Corpus Christi, TX [*Location identifier FAA*] (FAAL)
EKI	Ekaton Industries, Inc. [*Toronto Stock Exchange symbol*]
EKI	Electronic Keyboarding, Inc. [*Information service or system*] (IID)
EKI	Elkhart [*Indiana*] [*Airport symbol*] (OAG)
EKI	Esperanto en Komerco Kaj Industrio [*Institute for Esperanto in Commerce and Industry*] (EA)
EKIAP	East Kimberley Impact Assessment Program (EERA)
EKIF	Employer Identification Number Key Index File [*IRS*]
EKIP	Eastman Kodak Inst. Print Film (VRA)
EKK	Evangelisch-Katholischer Kommentar zum Neuen Testament [*A publication*] (BJA)
EKKA	Karup [*Denmark ICAO location identifier*] (ICLI)
EKKE	Epanastatiko Kommunistiko Komma Ellados [*Revolutionary Communist Party of Greece*] (PPW)
EKKL	Kalundborg [*Denmark ICAO location identifier*] (ICLI)
EKKM	Arhus/Kirstinesminde [*Denmark ICAO location identifier*] (ICLI)
EKL	Evangelisches Kirchenlexikon. Kirchlich-Theologisches Handwoerterbuch [*A publication*] (BJA)
EKLF	Erythroid Kruppel-Like Factor [*Medicine*]
EKLS	Laeso [*Denmark ICAO location identifier*] (ICLI)
EKLV	Lemvig [*Denmark ICAO location identifier*] (ICLI)
EKM	Edwald-Kornfeld Method
EKM	Elkhart, IN [*Location identifier FAA*] (FAAL)
EKMA	Empirical Kinetic Modeling Approach [*Air pollution research*]
EKMB	Maribo [*Denmark ICAO location identifier*] (ICLI)
EKMC	Karup [*Denmark ICAO location identifier*] (ICLI)
EKMI	Danish Meteorological Institute [*Denmark ICAO location identifier*] (ICLI)
EKMK	Karup [*Denmark ICAO location identifier*] (ICLI)
EKMN	Koster Vig [*Denmark ICAO location identifier*] (ICLI)
EKN	Ecology of Knowledge Network (EA)
EKN	Elkins [*West Virginia*] [*Airport symbol*] (OAG)
EKN	Eta Kappa Nu [*Fraternity*]
EKNE	Department of Elementary, Kindergarten, and Nursery Education [*of NEA*] [*Later, American Association of Elementary, Kindergarten, Nursery Educators*]
EKNM	Morso [*Denmark ICAO location identifier*] (ICLI)
EK/NOD	Eastman Kodak/Navy Ordnance District (AAG)
EKNS	Nakskov [*Denmark ICAO location identifier*] (ICLI)
EKO	Edgeworth Kuiper Belt Object [*Planetary science*]
EKO	Ekco Group [*NYSE symbol*] (SPSG)
Eko	Eko [*Record label*] [*France*]
EKO	Elko [*Nevada*] [*Airport symbol*] (OAG)
EKO	Elko [*Nevada*] [*Seismograph station code, US Geological Survey Closed*] (SEIS)
EKO	Internacia Ekologia-Ekonomia Akademio [*International Ecological-Economic Academy*] [*Bulgaria*] (EAIO)
EKOD	Odense/Beldringe [*Denmark ICAO location identifier*] (ICLI)
EKodak	Eastman Kodak Co. [*Associated Press*] (SAG)
EK of N	Election Knight of Nine [*Freemasonry*] (ROG)
EKOL	European Kompass Online [*Reed Information Services Ltd.*] [*Information service or system*]
EKOPO	Evreiskii Komitet Pomoshchi [*Shanghai*] (BJA)
EKP	A/S Eksportfinans [*Export Finance*] [*NYSE symbol*] (SPSG)
EKP	Eestimaa Kommunistlik Partei
EKP	Eksportfinans Capital Securities [*NYSE symbol*] (SAG)
EKP	Epikeraprosthesis [*Ophthalmology*]
EKP	Evreiskaia Kommunisticheskaia Partiia [*Political party*] (BJA)
EKP	Wisconsin Rapids, WI [*Location identifier FAA*] (FAAL)
EKPB	Krusa-Padborg [*Denmark ICAO location identifier*] (ICLI)
EKPPr	A/S Eksportcinans 8.70% Pfd [*NYSE symbol*] (TTSB)
EKQ	Monticello, KY [*Location identifier FAA*] (FAAL)
EKR	East Kent Regiment [*Military unit*] [*British*]
EKR	EQK Realty Investors I SBI [*NYSE symbol*] (SPSG)
EKR	EQK Realty Inv I SBI [*NYSE symbol*] (TTSB)
EKR	Meeker, CO [*Location identifier FAA*] (FAAL)
EKRC	Elisabeth Kubler-Ross Center (EA)
EKRD	Randers [*Denmark ICAO location identifier*] (ICLI)
EKRK	Kobenhavn/Roskilde [*Denmark ICAO location identifier*] (ICLI)
EKRN	Ronne [*Denmark ICAO location identifier*] (ICLI)
EKRR	Ro [*Denmark ICAO location identifier*] (ICLI)
EKRS	Ringsted [*Denmark ICAO location identifier*] (ICLI)
EKS	Electrocardiogram Simulator
EKS	Electronic Keyboard System
EKS	Electronic Key System [*Telecommunications*] (NITA)
EKS	Elks, Inc. [*Toronto Stock Exchange symbol*]
EKS	Energetic Komprimierendes System [*Nuclear science*] (OA)
EKS	Engpasskonzentrierte Strategie [*Bottleneck-focused strategy*] [*German*] [*Business term*]
EKS	Excessive Key Strokes [*Computer science*] (PCM)
EKSB	Sonderborg [*Denmark ICAO location identifier*] (ICLI)
EKSC	Eastern Kentucky State College [*Later, EKU*]
EKSD	Spjald [*Denmark ICAO location identifier*] (ICLI)
EKSM	Evreiskii Kommunisticheskii Soiuz Molodezhi (BJA)
EKSN	Sindal [*Denmark ICAO location identifier*] (ICLI)
EKSP	Skrydstrup [*Denmark ICAO location identifier*] (ICLI)
Eksprt	A/S Eksportfinans [*Export Finance*] Capital Securities [*Associated Press*] (SAG)
Eksprt	Eksportfinans Capital Securities [*Associated Press*] (SAG)
EKSS	Samso [*Denmark ICAO location identifier*] (ICLI)
EKST	Sydfyn/Tasinge [*Denmark ICAO location identifier*] (ICLI)
EKSV	Skive [*Denmark ICAO location identifier*] (ICLI)
EKT	Ektachrome (VRA)
EKT	Eskilstuna [*Sweden*] [*Airport symbol*]
EKT	Grupo Elektra GDS [*NYSE symbol*] (TTSB)

EKT	Grupo Elektra SA de CV [*NYSE symbol*] (SAG)
EKTD	Tonder [*Denmark ICAO location identifier*] (ICLI)
EKTS	Electronic Key Telephone System
EKTS	Thisted [*Denmark ICAO location identifier*] (ICLI)
EKU	Eastern Kentucky University [*Formerly, EKSC*] [*Richmond*]
eKv	Electron Kilovolt (EY)
EKV	Exoatmospheric Kill Vehicle [*Military*]
EKV	Weeksville, NC [*Location identifier FAA*] (FAAL)
EKVA	Vandel [*Denmark ICAO location identifier*] (ICLI)
EKVB	Viborg [*Denmark ICAO location identifier*] (ICLI)
EKVD	Vamdrup [*Denmark ICAO location identifier*] (ICLI)
EKVF	East Kent Volunteer Fencibles [*British military*] (DMA)
EKVG	Vagar, Faroe Islands [*Denmark ICAO location identifier*] (ICLI)
EKVH	Vesthimmerland [*Denmark ICAO location identifier*] (ICLI)
EKVJ	Stauning [*Denmark ICAO location identifier*] (ICLI)
EKVL	Vaerlose [*Denmark ICAO location identifier*] (ICLI)
EKW	Eisenbahnkesselwagen [*Railway tank car*] [*German military - World War II*]
EKW	Electrical Kilowatts
EKW	Worcester, MA [*Location identifier FAA*] (FAAL)
EKY	Electrokymogram
EKYT	Alborg [*Denmark ICAO location identifier*] (ICLI)
el----	Benelux Countries [*MARC geographic area code Library of Congress*] (LCCP)
EL	Each Layer [*Technical drawings*]
EL	Early Latent [*Medicine*]
EL	Eastern League [*Baseball*]
EL	Eastern Lines
EL	East Longitude (ROG)
E-L	Eaton-Lambert Syndrome [*Medicine*] (MEDA)
EL	Economic League [*British*]
EL	Economics Laboratory, Inc.
EL	Educational Leadership [*A publication*] (BRI)
EL	Education Level
EL	Education Library [*A publication*]
EL	Egg Length
EL	Einfache Lafette [*Single-barreled mount*] [*German military - World War II*]
EI	Elamite (BJA)
EL	Elastic Limit
EI	Elberfelder Bibel [*1905*] (BJA)
EI	Elchies' Dictionary of Decisions, Scotch Court of Session [*A publication*] (DLA)
EL	Eldest (ROG)
EL	Elect [*or Election*]
EL	Election Laws
EI	Electra [*of Euripides*] [*Classical studies*] (OCD)
EL	Electric
EL	Electrical Latching (IAA)
EL	Electrician [*British military*] (DMA)
EL	Electric LASER (MCD)
EL	Electric Light
EL	Electrohome Ltd. [*Toronto Stock Exchange symbol*]
EL	Electroluminescence
EL	Electroluminescent (IDOE)
EL	Electronic Library Inc. (IID)
EL	Electronics Command [*Army*] (MCD)
EL	Electronics Laboratory
EL	Electrum [*Numismatics*]
EL	Element
EL	Elementary
EL	Elevated [*Railway*] [*Also, L*]
EL	Elevation (AAG)
EL	Eligible Layout
EL	Eligible Liability [*British*]
EL	Eli Lilly & Co. [*Research code symbol*]
EI	Eline
el	Elixir [*Pharmacology*] (MAE)
EL	Elongation (WDAA)
EL	Emergency Legislation
EL	EMILY's List (EA)
EL	Endurance Limit [*Mechanical engineering*]
EL	Energy Loss (IAA)
EL	Engineering Laboratories [*Army*] (MCD)
EL	Engineering Letter [*Telecommunications*] (TEL)
EL	Engineer Lieutenant [*Navy British*]
EL	Entrance Left [*A stage direction*] [*Theater*] (WDMC)
E/L	Entry/Landing (NASA)
EL	Entry Lock [*Diving apparatus*]
EL	Environmental Laboratory
EL	Ephemerides Lovanienses (BJA)
EL	Epidemiological Laboratory [*Air Force*]
EL	Equivalent Length [*Engineering*]
EL	Erie-Lackawanna Railway Co. [*Absorbed into Consolidated Rail Corp.*] [*AAR code*]
EL	Erythroleukemia [*Medicine*] (MAE)
EL	Estee Lauder Companies, Inc. [*NYSE symbol*] (SAG)
EL	Etched Lead (IAA)
EL	Evangelical Lutheran (ROG)
EL	Even Lot [*Investment term*]
EL	Excess Limit
EL	Exchange Line [*Telecommunications*] (TEL)
EL	Exercise Limit [*Medicine*]
EL	Expected Loss

EL	Expenditure Less Than [*Dialog*] [*Searchable field*] [*Information service or system*] (NITA)
EL	Exploration Lease (ADA)
EL	Exposure Level (GNE)
EL	External Lamina (OA)
E-L	External Lid [*Ophthalmology*] (DAVI)
EL	External Link (MHDB)
EL	Eye Lens (MSA)
EL	Eymard League (EA)
EL	Lauder (Estee) Co. [*NYSE symbol*] (TTSB)
EL	Nihon Kinkyori Airways [*ICAO designator*] (AD)
EL2	Elongation in Two Inches
ELA	Eagle Lake, TX [*Location identifier FAA*] (FAAL)
ELA	Eastland Air [*Australia ICAO designator*] (FAAC)
ELA	Eighth Lively Art [*Advertising award*]
ELA	Elazig [*Turkey*] [*Seismograph station code, US Geological Survey Closed*] (SEIS)
ELA	Electric League of Arizona (SRA)
ELA	Electronic Library Association [*Defunct*] (EA)
ELA	Electron Linear Accelerator
ELA	Eligible Legalized Alien (GFGA)
ELA	Endometrial LASER Ablation [*Medicine*]
ELA	English Language Amendment [*Proposed*]
ELA	Enmekar and the Lord of Aratta (BJA)
ELA	En Route Low Altitude
ELA	Environmental Protection Agency, Region V Library, Chicago, IL [*OCLC symbol*] (OCLC)
ELA	Equilibrium-Line Altitude [*Glaciation*]
ELA	Equine Lymphocyte Alloantigen [*Genetics, immunochemistry*]
ELA	Equipment Leasing Association [*British*] (DBA)
ELA	Ernest K. Lehmann & Associates, Inc. [*Also, an information service or system*] (IID)
ELA	Esperanto Law Association [*British England*] (EAIO)
ELA	Establishment License Application [*Food & Drug Administration*]
ELA	Ethical Library [*A publication*]
ELA	European Laser Association (EA)
ELA	Experimental Lakes Area [*A collection of 48 small lakes near the Ontario-Manitoba border*] [*Canada*]
ELA	Exploration Licence Application [*Australia*]
ELA	Expressive Language Age [*of the hearing-impaired*]
ELA	Extended Line Adapter (MHDB)
ELA	Extra Large Apertures [*Optics*] (ROG)
ELAB	Environmental Laboratory Advisory Board [*Environmental Protection Agency*]
ELAB	External Loop Airlift Bioreactor [*Chemical engineering*]
ELAC	Electroacoustic (IAA)
ELACS	Extended Life Attitude Control System [*NASA*]
E LACT	E Lacte [*With Milk*] [*Pharmacy*]
ELAD	Extracorporeal Liver-Assist Device [*Medicine*] (ECON)
ELADS	Early Launch Air Defense System (MCD)
ELAFB	Ellsworth Air Force Base [*South Dakota*] (KSC)
ELAG	European Library Automation Group (PDAA)
ELAIA	European Parliament Delegations for Latin America [*Luxembourg*] (EAIO)
ELAIA	Europe-Latin America Interparliamentary Assembly [*See also DPERPLA*] [*Luxembourg, Luxembourg*] (EAIO)
EL AL	Every Landing, Always Late [*Humorous interpretation of El Al Airlines*]
ELALR	External Loop Air Lift Reactor [*Chemical engineering*]
ELAM	Endothelial Leukocyte Adhesion Molecule [*Cytology*]
Elamex	Elamex SA de CV [*Associated Press*] (SAG)
ELAMF	Elamex S.A.de C.V. Cl I [*NASDAQ symbol*] (TTSB)
ELaMod	Empresas La Moderna SA [*Associated Press*] (SAG)
ELAMP	Elamex SA de CV [*NASDAQ symbol*] (SAG)
ELAMS	Electronic Laboratory Animal Monitoring System
Elan	Elan Corp. [*Associated Press*] (SAG)
ELAN	Electrologic Language (IAA)
ELAN	Elementary Language [*Programming language*] (NITA)
ELAN	Environment in Latin-America Network (EERA)
ELAN	Extended Local Area Network [*Defunct*] (TSSD)
E LANC R	East Lancashire Regiment [*Military unit*] [*British*] (ROG)
El & B	Ellis and Blackburn's English Queen's Bench Reports [*118-120 English Reprint*] [*A publication*] (DLA)
El & Bl	Ellis and Blackburn's English Queen's Bench Reports [*118-120 English Reprint*] [*A publication*] (DLA)
El & Bl (Eng)	Ellis and Blackburn's English Queen's Bench Reports [*118-120 English Reprint*] [*A publication*] (DLA)
El & El	Ellis and Ellis' English Queen's Bench Reports [*A publication*] (DLA)
El & El (Eng)	Ellis and Ellis' English Queen's Bench Reports [*A publication*] (DLA)
EL & Eq	English Law and Equity Reports [*American Reprint*] [*A publication*] (DLA)
EL & S	Electronic Laboratories and Services
E Lan R	East Lancashire Regiment [*Military unit*] [*British*] (DAS)
ELANT	East Atlantic [*Satellite*] (DOMA)
Elantec	Elantec Semiconductor, Inc. [*Associated Press*] (SAG)
ELANY	Elan Corp. PLC (MHDW)
ELAP	Emergency Legal Assistance Project
ELAP	EtherTalk Link Access Protocol [*Computer science*] (ACRL)
ELAS	Earth Laboratory Applications Software
ELAS	Earth Resources Laboratory Application Software
ELAS	Education Law Advisers Service (AIE)
ELAS	Elastic (MSA)
ELAS	Ellenikos Laikos Apeleutherotikos Stratos [*Hellenic People's Army of Liberation*] [*Military arm of EAM*] [*Greek*]

ELAS	Emitter Location and Analysis System (MCD)
ELAS	Equilibrium Problems of Linear Structures
ELAS	Extended Lymphadenopathy Syndrome [*Medicine*]
ELAT	Elaterium [*To Stimulate or Incite*] [*Pharmacy*] (ROG)
ELAT	English Language Aptitude Test (DNAB)
ELAT	Enzyme-Linked Antiglobulin Test [*Immunology*] (DAVI)
ELAT	Estimated Latitude (FAAC)
ELATE	Engineers' Language for Automatic Test Equipment
ELATS	Expanded Litton Automatic Test Station (MCD)
ELB	Bachelor of English Literature
ELB	Early Light Breakfast [*Medicine*]
ELB	El Banco [*Colombia*] [*Airport symbol*] (OAG)
ELB	Elbow (MSA)
ELB	Eldorado Bancorp [*AMEX symbol*] (SPSG)
ELB	Electric Battery (IAA)
ELB	Electronically Limited Braking
ELB	Electronic Lean Burn (ADA)
ELB	Emergency Locator Beacon
ELB	Environmental Protection Agency, Library, Environmental Research Center, Cincin nati, OH [*OCLC symbol*] (OCLC)
ELB	Environment Liaison Board [*British*] (DI)
ELB	Export Licensing Branch [*British Overseas Trade Board*] (DS)
ELB-A	Emergency Location Beacon - Aircraft (PDAA)
ELBA	English Language Books Abroad [*A publication*]
El B & E	Ellis, Blackburn, and Ellis' English Queen's Bench Reports [*A publication*] (DLA)
El B & El	Ellis, Blackburn, and Ellis' English Queen's Bench Reports [*A publication*] (DLA)
El B & S	Ellis, Best, and Smith's English Queen's Bench Reports [*A publication*] (DLA)
El B & S (Eng)	Ellis, Best, and Smith's English Queen's Bench Reports [*A publication*] (DLA)
Elbit	Elbit Ltd. [*Associated Press*] (SAG)
ElbitLtd	Elbit Ltd. [*Associated Press*] (SAG)
ElbitMd	Elbit Medical Imaging Ltd. [*Associated Press*] (SAG)
ElbitSys	Elbit Systems Ltd. [*Associated Press*] (SAG)
ElbitVis	Elbit Vision Systems Ltd. [*Associated Press*] (SAG)
El Bl & El	Ellis, Blackburn, and Ellis' English Queen's Bench Reports [*A publication*] (DLA)
El Bl & El (Eng)	Ellis, Blackburn, and Ellis' English Queen's Bench Reports [*A publication*] (DLA)
ELBOWS	No Erasures, No Leaves Torn Out, No Blank Spaces, No Overturning, No Writing between Lines, Statements to Be in Exact Words [*Directions for written reports*] [*Scotland Yard*]
ELBS	English Language Book Society [*British*]
ELBT	Elbit Ltd. [*NASDAQ symbol*] (NQ)
ELBT	English Language Books by Title [*A publication*]
ELBTF	Elbit Ltd. [*NASDAQ symbol*] (TTSB)
ELBW	Extremely Low Birth Weight [*Obstetrics*] (ADA)
ELC	Early Landed Cognac [*British*]
ELC	Elcho Island [*Australia Airport symbol*] (OAG)
ELC	Elco [*Illinois*] [*Seismograph station code, US Geological Survey*] (SEIS)
ELC	El Coco Explorations Ltd. [*Vancouver Stock Exchange symbol*]
ELC	Electric Cable (IAA)
ELC	Electronic Level Control [*General Motors Corp.*] [*Automotive engineering*]
ELC	Electronic Library Computer
ELC	Electronic Load Controller
EIC	Elevator Code
ELC	Entrepreneurial Leadership Center (EA)
ELC	Environmental Law Centre (EERA)
ELC	Environmental Protection Agency, Motor Vehicle Emission Laboratory, Ann Arbor, MI [*OCLC symbol*] (OCLC)
ELC	Environment Liaison Centre [*Later, ELCI*] (EAIO)
ELC	Errett Lobban Cord [*Auto industrialist*]
ELC	Essential Light Chain
ELC	Europe's Largest Companies [*ELC International*] [*Information service or system*] (CRD)
ELC	Evangelical Lutheran Church [*Later, ELCA*]
ELC	Expression-Linked Extra Copy [*Genetics*]
ELC	External Locus of Control [*Psychology*]
ELC	Extra-Low Carbon
ELCA	Earth Landing Control Assembly [*NASA*] (KSC)
ELCA	Electronic Linear Circuit Analysis (PDAA)
ELCA	Enzyme-Linked Coagulation Assay [*Clinical chemistry*]
ELCA	European Landscape Contractors Association (EAIO)
ELCA	Evangelical Lutheran Church in America [*Formed by merger of ALC, ELC, and LCA*]
ELC Acts	Expiring Law Continuance Acts (DLA)
ELCAG	ELINT [*Electronic Intercept*] Collection/Analysis Guide [*Air Force*]
ELCAR	[*The*] Elkhart Carriage & Motor Car Co. [*Automobile manufacturer (1909-1915), later, Elcar Motor Co. (1916-1931)*] [*Acronym also used as car name*]
ElcArt	Electronic Arts, Inc. [*Associated Press*] (SAG)
El Cas	Election Cases [*A publication*] (DLA)
ELCAS	Elevated Causeway System (CAAL)
El Cas	New York Election Cases (Armstrong's) [*A publication*] (DLA)
El Cas (NY)	New York Election Cases (Armstrong's) [*A publication*] (DLA)
ElCath	Electro Catheter Corp. [*Associated Press*] (SAG)
ELCB	Earth Leakage Circuit Breaker
ELCC	Electronics Communications [*NASDAQ symbol*] (TTSB)
ELCC	Electronics Communications Corp. [*NASDAQ symbol*] (SAG)
ElcChm	Electro Chemical Industries (Frutarom) Ltd. [*Associated Press*] (SAG)
ElcCm	Electronics Communications Corp. [*Associated Press*] (SAG)

ELCCW.........	Electronics Communications Wrrt'A' [*NASDAQ symbol*] (TTSB)
ELCD..........	Electrolytic Conductivity Detector
ELCD..........	Evaporative Loss Control Device [*Automobile antipollution device*]
ElcFuel	Electric Fuel Corp. [*Associated Press*] (SAG)
ElcGas	Electric & Gas Technology, Inc. [*Associated Press*] (SAG)
ELCH..........	El Chico Restaurants [*NASDAQ symbol*] (TTSB)
ELCH..........	El Chico Restaurants, Inc. [*NASDAQ symbol*] (SPSG)
Elch	Elchies. Court of Session Cases [*Scotland*] [*A publication*] (DLA)
ELCH..........	Evangelical Lutheran Church in America (BARN)
ElChico	El Chico Restaurants, Inc. [*Associated Press*] (SAG)
Elchies........	Elchies. Court of Session Cases [*Scotland*] [*A publication*] (DLA)
Elchies' Dict...	Elchies' Dictionary of Decisions, Scotch Court of Session [*A publication*] (DLA)
ELCI..........	Environment Liaison Centre International (EAIO)
ELCINA	Electronic Component Industries Association
ElcIntl	Electocon International, Inc. [*Associated Press*] (SAG)
ElClear........	Electronic Clearing House, Inc. [*Associated Press*] (SAG)
ELCMED......	Electromedical
ELCMTLG.....	Electrometallurgical
ELCN..........	Elco Industries, Inc. [*NASDAQ symbol*] (NQ)
ELCO..........	Elcom International [*NASDAQ symbol*] (SAG)
ELCO..........	Elcom Intl. [*NASDAQ symbol*] (TTSB)
ELCO..........	Electrolytic Capacitor (DEN)
ELCO..........	Eliminate and Count [*Coding*] [*Computer science*]
ELCO..........	European Liaison Committee for Osteopaths (EA)
Elcom	Elcom International [*Associated Press*] (SAG)
ELCOM........	Electronics and Computers [*Cambridge Scientific Abstracts*] [*Bethesda, MD Bibliographic database*]
ELCON	Electricity Consumers Resource Council (EA)
ELCON	Equipment Loss Consolidator
ElCondor......	El Condor Resources Ltd. [*Associated Press*] (SAG)
Elcor..........	Elcor Corp. [*Associated Press*] (SAG)
Elcotel	Elcotel, Inc. [*Associated Press*] (SAG)
ELCPLTG......	Electroplating
ELCR..........	Engineer Lieutenant-Commander [*Navy British*]
ElcRetl........	Electronic Retailing Systems International [*Associated Press*] (SAG)
ElcRnt.........	Electro Rent Corp. [*Associated Press*] (SAG)
ELCS..........	Experimental Labor Control System (IAA)
ElcSci	Electro Scientific Industries, Inc. [*Associated Press*] (SAG)
ElcSen	Electro Sensors [*Associated Press*] (SAG)
ELCSMI........	European Liaison Committee for the Sewing Machine Industries [*Defunct*] (EA)
ELCT..........	Electronic (AABC)
ELCTC.........	Electric Contact
ELCTCBR	Electric Contact Brush
ELCTD.........	Elected
ELCTD.........	Electrode (MSA)
ELCTLT	Electrolyte
Elctmg	Electromagnetic Sciences, Inc. [*Associated Press*] (SAG)
Elctph	Electropharmacology, Inc. [*Associated Press*] (SAG)
Elctphr........	Electropharmacology, Inc. [*Associated Press*] (SAG)
elctr..........	Electronic (VRA)
ELCTRG	Electric Contact Ring
ElctrgIs	Electroglas Inc. [*Associated Press*] (SAG)
ELCTRLGST...	Electrologist
ELCTRM.......	Electronic Room (IAA)
ELCTRMCHNCL..	Electromechanical
ELCTRN	Electron
ELCTRN	Electron [*A nuclear particle*]
elctrpl	Electroplate (VRA)
ELCTRYLS ...	Electrolysis
Elctsrc	Electrosource, Inc. [*Associated Press*] (SAG)
ELCU..........	Electrical Control Unit (PDAA)
ELD............	Earth Launch Date [*Aerospace*]
ELD............	East Longitude Date
ELD............	Economic Load Dispatching (BUR)
ELD............	Edge-Lighted Display
ELD............	Egg Lethal Dose
ELD............	Ehrlich-Lettre Hyperdiploid [*Mouse ascites tumor*]
eld	Elder (VRA)
ELD............	Elder Tech Ltd. [*Vancouver Stock Exchange symbol*]
ELD............	Eldest
ELD............	El Dorado [*Arkansas*] [*Airport symbol*] (OAG)
ELD............	Electroluminescent Diode
ELD............	Electroluminescent Display [*Computer science*]
ELD............	Electrolytic Display (PDAA)
ELD............	Electronic Lie Detector
ELD............	Embryo Lethal Dose (OA)
ELD............	Encapsulated Light Diffusion (IAA)
ELD............	Energy Level Diagram
ELD............	Engineering Logic Diagram
ELD............	Environmental Protection Agency, Library, Environmental Research Laboratory, Du luth, MN [*OCLC symbol*] (OCLC)
ELD............	Error Logging Device
ELD............	Extra-Long Distance
ELD............	Federation of Liberal and Democratic Parties of the European Community [*Brussels, Belgium Political party*] (EAIO)
ELD............	Office of the Executive Legal Director [*Nuclear energy*] (NRCH)
ELDATRAWP...	Electronic Data Transmission Working Party [*Army*] (AABC)
ELDC..........	Equivalent Load Duration Curve
ELDC..........	European Lead Development Committee [*EC*] (EA)
ELDEC.........	European Lead Development Committee [*EC*] (ECED)
ELDEMA.......	Electronic Detection Machine (PDAA)
ElDes	Electronic Designs, Inc. [*Associated Press*] (SAG)

ELDG	Electrical, Defective, Government [*Government-furnished equipment*] (DNAB)
El Dict	Elchies' Dictionary of Decisions, Scotch Court of Session [*A publication*] (DLA)
EL DIEFF......	Lew David Feldman [*New York bookseller; phonetic spelling of his initials forms name of company*]
El Dig	Eller's Minnesota Digest [*A publication*] (DLA)
ELDISC........	Electrical Disconnect (MCD)
ELDMK........	Earth Landmark [*NASA*]
ELDO..........	Eldorado [*Cadillac automobile*]
ELDO..........	European Launcher Development Organization [*Superseded by European Space Agency*]
ELDOR.........	Electron Electron Double Resonance [*Physics*]
Eldorad........	Eldorado Bancorp [*Associated Press*] (SAG)
ELDR..........	Elder
ELDR..........	European Federation of Liberal, Democratic, and Reform Parties (EAIO)
ELDRLY	Elderly
ELDS..........	Editorial Layout Display System
ELDV..........	Electrically Operated Depressurization Valve (MCD)
ELE	El Adem [*Libya*] [*Airport symbol*] (AD)
ELE	Electronic Launching Equipment
Ele	Eledoisin [*Biochemistry*]
ELE	Elementary Flying Training School [*British*] (MCD)
ELE	El Paso Energy Corp. [*Vancouver Stock Exchange symbol*]
ELE	El Real [*Panama*] [*Airport symbol*] (OAG)
ELE	Emergency Lighting Equipment
ELE	Empresa Nacional de Electricidad SA ADS [*NYSE symbol*] (SPSG)
ELE	Empresa Nacionale de Espana SA [*NYSE symbol*] (SAG)
ELE	Empresa Nac'l Elec ADS [*NYSE symbol*] (TTSB)
ELE	Engine Life Expectancy (NG)
ELE	Equivalent Logic Element
ELE	Estimated Life Expectancy (MCD)
ELE	SW Electricity Board [*British ICAO designator*] (FAAC)
ELEA	Evangelical Lutheran Education Association (EA)
ELEC	Elect
ELEC	Election (ROG)
ELEC	Elector [*or Electoral*] (WDAA)
ELEC	Electorate (ROG)
ELEC	Electric (AFM)
Elec	Electric (AAGC)
ELEC	Electricity (WDAA)
Elec	Electro [*Record label*] [*Finland*]
ELEC	Electron (WDAA)
ELEC	Electronic (NASA)
ELEC	Electronics
ELEC	Electuarium [*Electuary*] [*Pharmacy*] (ROG)
ELEC	European League for Economic Cooperation
ElecAs	Electronic Associates, Inc. [*Associated Press*] (SAG)
Elec C	Elections Code [*A publication*] (DLA)
ElecCm	Electronics Communications Corp. [*Associated Press*] (SAG)
ELECD	Element Code (MCD)
ElecDes	Electronic Designs, Inc. [*Associated Press*] (SAG)
ElecFab.......	Electronic Fab Technology [*Associated Press*] (SAG)
ElecHair.......	Electronic Hair Styling, Inc. [*Associated Press*] (SAG)
Elec LR	Election Law Reports [*India*] [*A publication*] (DLA)
ELECMECH...	Electrical Mechanical (IAA)
ELECN........	Electrician (AFM)
ELECOM.......	Electronic Computing
ELECOMPS...	Electronic Components (NITA)
ELECPROC...	Electrostatic Process (IAA)
ELECPWRPLNTENGR...	Electric Power Plant Engineer (IAA)
ELECSYSCOM...	Electronic Systems Command [*Also, NESC*] [*Navy*]
ELECT	Election (AABC)
ELECT	Electrical
ELECT	Electrolyte (KSC)
ELECT	Electronic (MCD)
ELECT	Electronic
ELECT	Electuarium [*Electuary*] [*Pharmacy*]
ELECTC	Electronic Control
Elect Cas	Election Cases [*A publication*] (DLA)
Elect Cas NY...	New York Election Cases (Armstrong's) [*A publication*] (DLA)
ELECTCIRDESGNR...	Electronic Circuit Designer (IAA)
ELECTECH....	Electronics Technician (DNAB)
ElecTel	Electronic Telcommunications, Inc. [*Associated Press*] (SAG)
ELECTENGR...	Electronic Engineer (IAA)
ELECTHYDR...	Electrohydraulic (KSC)
ELECTL	Electrical
ELECTL	Electrolytic
Electl Wkly...	Electrical Weekly [*A publication*]
ELECTLY	Electrically
ELECTMAINTCO...	Electronic Maintenance Co. [*Military*] (DNAB)
ELECTMECH...	Electromechanical (KSC)
ELECTMG.....	Electromagnetic
ELECTPKGENGR...	Electronic Packaging Engineer (IAA)
ELECTR........	Electric
ELECTR........	Electronics (NASA)
ELECTRCL....	Electrical
ELECTRCN...	Electrician
ELECTRCTY...	Electricity
Elect Rep	Election Reports [*Ontario*] [*A publication*] (DLA)
ELECTREX....	International Electrotechnical Exhibition [*British Electrical and Allied Manufacturers Association*]
ELECTRL......	Electrical
ELECTRL......	Electrolyte (IAA)

ELECTRN ..... Electrician (IAA)
ELECTRO ..... Electronics (KSC)
ELECTRO ..... Electrotype (ROG)
ELECTROCHEM... Electrochemistry
ELECTROL ..... Electrolysis (IAA)
ELECTRONENGR... Electronics Engineer
ELECTRO-OPTINT... Electrooptical Intelligence [DoD]
ELECTROPHYS... Electrophysics (IAA)
ELECTY .... Electricity
ELED .... Edge Light Emitting Diode (IAA)
ELEED .... Elastic Low-Energy Electron Diffraction (PDAA)
ElegIll .... Elegant Illusions, Inc. [Associated Press] (SAG)
ELEK .... Electronic (MSA)
ELEK .... Elek Tek, Inc. [NASDAQ symbol] (SAG)
Elek .... Elektra [Record label]
ElekTek .... Elek Tek, Inc. [Associated Press] (SAG)
ELEM .... Element (MSA)
elem .... Element (VRA)
ELEM .... Elementary (MSA)
ELEM .... Elementary
ELEMCH .... Elementary Charge [of a Proton] (IAA)
ElEng .... Electronic Engineering (DD)
ELEOP .... Electro Optics Division (ACII)
ElepCstl ...... Elephant & Castle Group, Inc. [Associated Press] (SAG)
ELES .... Energy-Loss Electron Spectroscopy
ELES .... Expanded Liquid Engine Simulation (MCD)
ELES .... Extended Linear Expenditure System
ELET .... Ellett Brothers [NASDAQ symbol] (TTSB)
ELET .... Ellett Brothers, Inc. [NASDAQ symbol] (SAG)
elev .... Elevate (DAVI)
ELEV .... Elevation (AFM)
ELEV .... Elevator
ELEV .... Elevator
ELEV .... Elevon [Aviation] (NASA)
ELEV .... Extremely Low-Emitting Vehicle [Automotive engineering]
ELEVAR....... Elevated Acquisition RADAR (PDAA)
ElevenYBB ... Eleven Years of Bible Bibliography [A publication] (BJA)
ELEX .... Electronics (MSA)
ELEX .... Electronics Exercise [Military] (NVT)
ELEX .... Elexsys International, Inc. [NASDAQ symbol] (SAG)
ELEX .... ELEXSYS Intl. [NASDAQ symbol] (TTSB)
Elexsys .... Elexsys International, Inc. [Associated Press] (SAG)
ELF .... Early Lunar Flare
ELF .... Education Liberation Front
ELF .... Elective Low Forceps [Delivery] [Obstetrics] (DAVI)
ELF .... Electroluminescent Ferroelectric
ELF .... Electromagnetic Field
ELF .... Electromotive Force [Electrochemistry] (IAA)
ELF .... Electronic Location Finder
ELF .... Electron LASER Facility [Physics]
ELF .... Electrostatic Levitator Facility (SSD)
ELF .... Elevator Load Feel (MCD)
ELF .... Elf Aquitaine [NYSE symbol] (SAG)
ELF .... Elf Aquitaine ADS [NYSE symbol] (TTSB)
ELF .... El Fasher [Sudan] [Airport symbol] (OAG)
ELF .... E-L Financial Corp. Ltd. [Toronto Stock Exchange symbol]
ELF .... Elginfield [Ontario] [Seismograph station code, US Geological Survey] (SEIS)
ELF .... Eliminate Legal-Size Files [An association]
ELF .... Ellipsometry, Low Field [Microscopy]
ELF .... Elvish Linguistic Fellowship (EA)
ELF .... Emergency Land Fund [Later, FSC/LAF] (EA)
ELF .... Engine Lube Filter
ELF .... Eritrean Liberation Front [Ethiopia] (PD)
ELF .... Esperanto-Ligo Filatelista [Philatelic Esperanto League - PEL] (EAIO)
ELF .... European Landworkers Federation
ELF .... Everybody Loves Fudge [in Keebler Co. brand of cookies "E. L. Fudge"]
ELF .... Expeditionary Logistics Facility (MCD)
ELF .... Explosive-Actuated Light Filter (NG)
ELF .... Explosive Lens Flashbinder
ELF .... Extensible Language Facility [Computer science] (IEEE)
ELF .... Extra Light Fast [Ink] (DGA)
ELF .... Extremely Low Frequency [Electronics, radio wave]
ELFA .... Electric Light Fittings Association [British] (BI)
ELFA .... Enzyme-Linked Fluorescence Assay
ElfAquit ...... Elf Aquitaine [Associated Press] (SAG)
ElfAquit....... Societe National ELF Aquitaine [National ELF Aquitaine Co.] [Associated Press] (SAG)
ELFC .... Electroluminescent Ferroelectric Cell
ELFC .... Elvis Lives On Fan Club (EA)
ELF-ERAP .... Essences et Lubrifiants de France - Entreprise de Recherches et d'Activites Petrolieres [French oil company]
ELFH .... Early Labeled-Fragment Hybridization [Analytical biochemistry]
ELFIS .... Ernaehrungs-, Land-, und Forstwissenschaftliches Informations-System [German Information System on Food, Agriculture, and Forestry] [Zentralstelle fuer Agrardokumentation und -Information] [Information service or system]
El Fo .... Elephant Folio (WGA)
ElfOv......... Elf Overseas Ltd. [Associated Press] (SAG)
ELF-PLF....... Eritrean Liberation Front - Popular Liberation Forces [Ethiopia] (PD)
ELFR.......... Extremely Low Frequency Radiation
ELF-RC .... Eritrean Liberation Front - Revolutionary Command [Ethiopia] (PD)
ELG.......... Alpi Eagles SpA [Italy ICAO designator] (FAAC)
ELG.......... El Cap Gold Mines [Vancouver Stock Exchange symbol]

ELG........... Electrolytic Grinding (IEEE)
ELG........... El Golea [Algeria] [Airport symbol] (AD)
ELG........... Emergency Landing Ground
ELG........... Equal Life Group [Depreciation class]
ELG........... European Liaison Group [Army] (AABC)
ELG........... European Lymphology Group [See also GEL] [Brussels, Belgium] (EAIO)
ELGB......... Emergency Loan Guarantee Board
ELGI......... European Lubricating Grease Institute [An association]
EL-GIEU...... Erector-Launcher Ground Interface Electronics Unit (MCD)
ELGMT....... Erector-Launcher, Guided Missile, Transportable
ELGNC....... Elegance
ELGNT....... Elegant
ELGSS .... Ev. [Evangelical] Lutheran Good Samaritan Society (EA)
ELGT........ Electric & Gas Technology [NASDAQ symbol] (TTSB)
ELGT........ Electric & Gas Technology, Inc. [NASDAQ symbol] (NQ)
ELH......... Early Life History [Marine science] (OSRA)
ELH......... Early Life History (USDC)
ELH......... Egg-Laying Hormone [Endocrinology]
ELH......... Endolymphatic Hydrops [Medicine] (DAVI)
ELH......... Equine Luteinizing Hormone [Endocrinology]
e-lh--......... Liechtenstein [MARC geographic area code Library of Congress] (LCCP)
ELH......... North Eleuthera [Bahamas] [Airport symbol] (OAG)
ELHI......... Elementary and High School [Acronym refers to books published for this market]
el-hi......... Elementary and High School Levels [Textbook publishing] (WDMC)
ELHILL....... Lister Hill System [Search system]
ELHWS ...... Electric Hot Water Service [Classified advertising] (ADA)
ELHYD .... Electrohydraulic
ELI.......... Early Latent Infection [Medicine]
ELI.......... Economic Literature Index [American Economic Association] [Information service or system] (IID)
ELI.......... Educational Leadership Institute (EA)
ELI.......... Electric League of Indiana (SRA)
ELI.......... Electronic Line Indicator [Tennis]
ELI.......... ELE Energy, Inc. [Vancouver Stock Exchange symbol]
ELI.......... Elim [Alaska] [Airport symbol] (OAG)
Eli.......... Elite [Record label] [Europe]
ELI.......... Elizabethville [Zaire] [Later, KVA] [Geomagnetic observatory code]
ELI.......... Emitter Location and Identification
ELI.......... Endomorphin-Like Immunoreactivity
ELI.......... Energy Law Institute (EA)
ELI.......... English Language Institute [University of Michigan] [Research center] (RCD)
ELI.......... English Language Interpreter (NITA)
ELI.......... Entry Level Item [Bureau of Labor Statistics] (GFGA)
ELI.......... Environmental Language Inventory [Speech and language therapy] (DAVI)
ELI.......... Environmental Law Institute (EA)
ELI.......... Equitable Life Interpreter [Computer]
ELI.......... European Light Infantry [British military] (DMA)
ELI.......... Expression Library Immunisation [Immunology]
ELI.......... Expression-Library Immunization [To develop a vaccine]
ELI.......... Extended Lubrication Interval [Automotive engineering]
ELI.......... Extensible Language I [Computer science]
ELI.......... Extra-Low Impurity [Metals]
ELI.......... Extra-Low Interstitial [Alloy]
ELI.......... Heliarcos [Spain] [FAA designator] (FAAC)
ELIA.......... Elementary Imprint Assistance [Writing system for the blind]
ELIA.......... English Language Institute of America (WDAA)
ELIA.......... Enhanced Luminescent Immunoassay [Analytical biochemistry]
ELIA.......... European League of Institutes of the Arts [British]
ELIAS......... Entry Level Interactive Applications Systems [Computer science]
ELIAS......... Environment Libraries Automated System [Environment Canada] [Database] [Information service or system] (IID)
ELIAS......... Expandable Level Interactive Application System (HGAA)
ELIC.......... Electric Lamp Industry Council [British] (BI)
ELICIANT .... Eliciantur [Let Be Drawn] [Pharmacy] (ROG)
ELICT.......... Enzyme-Linked Immunocytochemical Technique [Clinical chemistry] (DMAA)
ELID.......... Electrolytic-in-Process-Dressing [Optics manufacturing] (RDA)
ELID.......... Electrostatic Latent Image Development (IAA)
ELIEDA........ Enzyme-Linked Immunoelectric Diffusion Assay [Clinical chemistry]
ELIFE......... Enhancement of Life Support, Europe (MCD)
ELIG.......... Eligible (AFM)
ELIG RET .... Eligible for Retirement (DNAB)
ELIM.......... Eliminate (AFM)
ELIM.......... Eliminator [Automotive engineering]
ELIM.......... Enlisted Loss Inventory Model (MCD)
ELIM.......... Evangelical Lutherans in Mission [Group opposing the Missouri Synod of the Lutheran Church]
ELIMS.......... Enhanced Logistics Information Management System
ELIN.......... Exhibit Line Item Number (MCD)
e-line.......... Expo Line [Expository line] [Photograph caption] (WDMC)
ELINT.......... Electromagnetic Intelligence
ELINT.......... Electronic Intelligence [or Intercept] [Meaning of ELINT determined by reference to before (Intercept) and after (Intelligence) analysis of reconnaissance mission results]
ELINT.......... Electronic Intelligence Satellite (NITA)
ELINT TGU... Electronic Intelligence Technical Guidance Unit (MCD)
ELIP.......... Electrostatic Latent Image Photography (IEEE)
ELIP.......... Elliptical (FAAC)

ELIPA.......... Experienced Librarians and Information Personnel in the Developing Countries of Asia and Oceania [*Korea Advanced Institute of Science and Technology*] [*Seoul*] [*Information service or system*] (IID)

ELIRT.......... Environmental Laboratories Information Retrieval Technique (PDAA)

ELIS........... Electronic Library Information System [*Library network*] (IT)

ELIS........... Encyclopedia of Legal Information Sources [*A publication*]

ELISA......... Electronic Library Information Service at the Australian National University

ELISA......... Enzyme-Linked [*or Labeled*] Immunoadsorbent Assay [*Immunochemistry*]

ELISE......... European Network for the Exchange of Information on Local Employment Initiatives [*EC*] (ECED)

ELIST......... Enhanced Logistics Intratheater Support Tool [*DoD*]

ELIT........... Electronics Information Test

ELITE......... Enterprise Learning through Information Technology [*University of Durham*] (AIE)

ELITE......... Executive Level Interactive Terminal Environment (RDA)

ELITE......... Extended Long-Range Integrated Technology Evaluation

ELIX.......... Elixir [*Pharmacology*]

ELIZ........... Elizabethan (ROG)

Eliz........... Queen Elizabeth (DLA)

ELJ.......... Eljer Industries [*NASDAQ symbol*] (TTSB)

ELJ.......... Eljer Industries, Inc. [*NYSE symbol*] (SPSG)

ELJ.......... El Recreo [*Colombia*] [*Airport symbol*] (OAG)

ELJ.......... Executive-Legislative-Judicial

ELJ.......... Expendable LASER Jammer (MCD)

Eljer.......... Eljer Industries, Inc. [*Associated Press*] (SAG)

ELK.......... Eesti Lennukompani [*Estonia*] [*ICAO designator*] (FAAC)

ELK.......... Elcor Corp. [*NYSE symbol*] (SPSG)

ELK.......... Elk City, OK [*Location identifier FAA*] (FAAL)

ELK.......... Elko [*Nevada*] [*Seismograph station code, US Geological Survey*] (SEIS)

ELK.......... Emerald Lake Resources, Inc. [*Toronto Stock Exchange symbol*]

ELK.......... Enosis Laikou Kommatos [*Union of Populist Parties*] [*Greek*] (PPE)

ELK.......... Ethniko Laiko Komma [*National Populist Party*] [*Greek*] (PPE)

ELKE.......... Elevated Kinetic Energy Weapon

ELL.......... Electrosensory Lateral Line-Lobe [*Biology*]

ELL.......... Ellipsometry [*Surface analysis*]

ELL.......... Elmali [*Turkey*] [*Seismograph station code, US Geological Survey*] (SEIS)

ELL.......... English Language Laboratory

ELL.......... Equivalent Loudness Level

ELL.......... Estonian Air [*ICAO designator*] (FAAC)

ELL.......... Excimer LASER Lithography

ELL.......... Huntsville, AL [*Location identifier FAA*] (FAAL)

ELLA.......... Eastern Lamp and Lighting Association (EA)

ELLA.......... European Long Lines Agency [*NATO*]

Ell & Bl....... Ellis and Blackburn's English Queen's Bench Reports [*118-120 English Reprint*] [*A publication*] (DLA)

Ell & Ell....... Ellis and Ellis' English Queen's Bench Reports [*A publication*] (DLA)

Ell Ann....... Ellison. Law of Annuities [*A publication*] (DLA)

Ell B & Ell ... Ellis, Blackburn, and Ellis' English Queen's Bench Reports [*A publication*] (ILCA)

Ell B & S..... Ellis, Best, and Smith's English Queen's Bench Reports [*A publication*] (DLA)

Ell Bl & Ell... Ellis, Blackburn, and Ellis' English Queen's Bench Reports [*A publication*] (DLA)

Ell D & Cr.... Ellis. Debtor and Creditor [*1822*] [*A publication*] (DLA)

Ell Deb....... Elliot's Debates on the Federal Constitution [*A publication*] (DLA)

Ell Dig......... Eller's Minnesota Digest [*A publication*] (ILCA)

Ell Dip Code... Elliot's American Diplomatic Code [*A publication*] (DLA)

Ellesm Post N... Ellesmere's Post Nati [*A publication*] (DLA)

EllettBr........ Ellett Brothers, Inc. [*Associated Press*] (SAG)

Ell Ins.......... Ellis on Fire and Life Insurance and Annuities [*A publication*] (DLA)

Elliot Deb Fed Const... Elliot's Debates on the Federal Constitution [*A publication*] (DLA)

Elliott App Proc... Elliott's Appellate Procedure [*A publication*] (DLA)

Elliott Roads & S... Elliott on Roads and Streets [*A publication*] (DLA)

Elliott Supp... Elliott's Supplement to the Indiana Revised Statutes [*A publication*] (DLA)

ELLIPT........ Elliptical

Ellis........... Ellis on Insurance [*A publication*] (DLA)

ELLIS......... English Language Learning and Improvement Service [*State Library of South Australia*]

ELLIS......... European Legal Literature Information Service [*London, England*]

Ellis & Bl..... Ellis and Blackburn's English Queen's Bench Reports [*118-120 English Reprint*] [*A publication*] (DLA)

Ellis Dr & Cr... Ellis. Debtor and Creditor [*1822*] [*A publication*] (DLA)

ELLLL......... Electrosensory Lateral Line [*Invertebrate zoology*]

ELLP.......... Elliptocytes [*Biochemistry*] (DAVI)

ELLSA......... Enzyme-Linked Ligand Sorbent Assay [*Analytical biochemistry*]

Ells Cop Man... Ellsworth's Copyright Manual [*A publication*] (DLA)

ELLT.......... Electric Light (IAA)

Ell Trade...... Ellet on the Laws of Trade [*A publication*] (DLA)

ELLX.......... Luxembourg/Luxembourg [*ICAO location identifier*] (ICLI)

ELM........... Corning-Elmira [*New York*] [*Airport symbol*] (AD)

ELM........... Early Language Milestone Scale (MEDA)

ELM........... Eastern Atlantic and Mediterranean [*Military*]

ELM........... Electrical Length Measurement (IAA)

ELM........... Element (AABC)

ELM........... Element Load Model

ELM........... Elma [*New York*] [*Seismograph station code, US Geological Survey Closed*] (SEIS)

ELM........... Elmira [*New York*] [*Airport symbol*] (OAG)

ELM........... Emitter Location Method

ELM........... Empresas La Moderna SA [*NYSE symbol*] (SAG)

ELM........... Empresas La Moderna SAADS [*NYSE symbol*] (TTSB)

ELM........... Emulsion Liquid Membrane [*Chemical separation technology*]

ELM........... Endings [*of nerves*] to Lip Muscle

ELM........... Epiluminescence Microscopy

ELM........... Expendable Light Markers (NVT)

ELM........... Experimental Logistics Module (SSD)

ELM........... Extended Length Message (DA)

ELM........... Extended Length Methods (MCD)

ELM........... Extended Lunar Mission [*NASA*] (KSC)

ELM........... External Limiting Membrane

ELM........... La-Rouche-Sur-Yon [*France*] [*Airport symbol*]

ELMA.......... Electric Lamp Manufacturers' Association of Great Britain Ltd. (BI)

ELMA.......... Emergency Lighting Manufacturers Association [*Defunct*] (EA)

ELMAP........ Exchange Line Multiplexing Analysis Program (TEL)

Elm Arch Jur... Elmes on Architectural Jurisprudence [*A publication*] (DLA)

ELMCH........ Electromechanical

Elm Dig....... Elmer's New Jersey Digest of Laws [*A publication*] (DLA)

Elm Dilap .... Elmes on Ecclesiastical Civil Dilapidation [*A publication*] (DLA)

ELME.......... Emitter Location Method

ELMECH........ Electromechanical (NASA)

Elmer Lun...... Elmer's Practice in Lunacy [*A publication*] (DLA)

Elmers........ Elmers Restaurants, Inc. [*Associated Press*] (SAG)

Elm Exec Dep... Elmes' Executive Departments of the United States [*A publication*] (DLA)

ELMG.......... Electromagnetic Sci [*NASDAQ symbol*] (TTSB)

ELMG.......... Electromagnetic Sciences, Inc. [*NASDAQ symbol*] (NQ)

ELMG.......... Engine Life Management Group [*Navy*]

ELMIG.......... Electronic Library Membership Initiative Group [*ALA*] (NITA)

ELMINT........ Electromagnetic Intelligence

Elmira C...... Elmira College (GAGS)

Elm Lun....... Elmer's Practice in Lunacy [*A publication*] (DLA)

ELMN(A)....... Electrical Mechanician (Air) [*Navy rating British*]

ELMN(AW)... Electrical Mechanician (Air Weapon) [*British military*] (DMA)

Elm NJ Laws... Elmer's New Jersey Digest of Laws [*A publication*] (DLA)

ELMNT........ Element

ELMO.......... El Morro National Monument

ELMO.......... Engineering and Logistics Management Office [*MERDC*] [*Army*]

ELMO.......... Engineering Lunar Model Obstacle [*NASA*] (PDAA)

ELMO.......... European Laundry and Dry Cleaning Machinery Manufacturers Organization (EA)

ELMR.......... Estuarine Living Marine Resources Program [*National Oceanic and Atmospheric Administration*]

ElmrSv........ Elmira Savings Bank FSB [*Associated Press*] (SAG)

ELMS.......... Earth Limb Measurement Satellite [*NASA/Air Force*]

ELMS.......... Earth Limb Measurement System [*NASA*] (SSD)

ELMS.......... Educators of Library Media Specialists Section [*American Association of School Librarians*]

ELMS.......... Elastic Loop Mobility System [*NASA*]

ELMS.......... Elements

ELMS.......... Elmers Restaurants [*NASDAQ symbol*] (TTSB)

ELMS.......... Elmer's Restaurants, Inc. [*NASDAQ symbol*] (NQ)

ELMS.......... Engineering Lunar Model Surface

ELMS.......... Experimental Library Management System

ELMSIM........ Engine Life Management Simulation Model (PDAA)

ELMSS........ Educators of Library Media Specialists Section [*American Association of School Librarians*] [*American Library Association*]

ELMT.......... Electronic Mechanic Technician

ELMT.......... Elements [*on Urinalysis*] [*Biochemistry*] (DAVI)

ELMTNO ...... Element Numbers [*On urinalysis*] [*Biochemistry*] (DAVI)

ELMU.......... Environment Law and Machinery Unit (EERA)

elmwd......... Elmwood (VRA)

ELN........... Ejercito de Liberacion Nacional [*National Liberation Army*] [*Colorado*] (PD)

ELN........... Ejercito de Liberacion Nacional [*National Liberation Army*] [*Bolivia*] (PD)

ELN........... Ejercito de Liberacion Nacional [*National Liberation Army*] [*Peru*] (PD)

ELN........... Elan Corp. [*NYSE symbol*] (SAG)

ELN........... Elan Corp. ADS [*NYSE symbol*] (TTSB)

ELN........... Electronic Laboratory Notebook

ELN........... Ellensburg, WA [*Location identifier FAA*] (FAAL)

ELN........... Nordic East International Aircraft, AB [*Sweden ICAO designator*] (FAAC)

ELNA.......... Esperanto League for North America (EA)

ELND.......... Elective Node Dissection [*Medicine*]

ELNEO .... Elastase-Neomycin Gene [*Genetics*]

ELNES........ Electron Loss Near Edge Structure [*Electron microscopy*]

ELNG .... Elongate (MSA)

ELNGT .... Elongate (FAAC)

ELNK.......... Earthlink Network, Inc. [*NASDAQ symbol*] (SAG)

ELNS.......... European League for a New Society [*See also LIENS*] [*Paris, France*] (EAIO)

ELNT.......... Elantec Semiconductor [*NASDAQ symbol*] (TTSB)

ELNT.......... Elantec Semiconductor, Inc. [*NASDAQ symbol*] (SAG)

ELN.WS A... Elan Corp. ADS Wrrt'98 [*NYSE symbol*] (SAG)

ELO........... Eldorado Minerals & Petroleum [*Vancouver Stock Exchange symbol*]

ELO........... Electric Light Orchestra [*Rock music group*]

ELO........... Ely, MN [*Location identifier FAA*] (FAAL)

ELO........... Epoxidized Linseed Oil [*Organic chemistry*]

ELO........... Evangelical Literature Overseas (EA)

ELO........... Eye Lens Obsolescence [*Ophthalmology*]

ELO........... Logiealmond [*Scotland*] [*Seismograph station code, US Geological Survey*] (SEIS)

ELOC............	Eastern Line of Communication [*World War II*]
ELOC............	Elastomeric-Oriented Copolyester (PDAA)
Eloc	Elocution
ELOCARS.....	Electro-Optical Collection and Analysis Reporting System (MCD)
ELO-CATS ...	Electro-Optical Collection and Analysis Targeting System
ELOD	Erasable LASER Optical Disk [*Computer science*] (IAA)
ELOG	European Landowning Organization Group (EAIO)
ELOI	Emergency Letter of Instructions
ELOISE	European Large Orbiting Instrumentation for Solar Experiments
E Lon............	East Longitude
E Long........	East Longitude (HGAA)
ELONG............	Elongation (MSA)
EL-OP............	Electro-Optics Industries Ltd.
ELOP............	Estimated Length of Program [*Medicine*] (DAVI)
ELOQ	Eloquence [*or Eloquent*] (ROG)
ELOR	Extended Lunar Orbital Rendezvous [*NASA*] (KSC)
ELORM	Extended Lunar Orbital Rendezvous Mission [*NASA*] (KSC)
ELOS............	Electronic Line-of-Sight [*Military*]
ELOS............	Estimated Length of Stay [*Medicine*] (DAVI)
ELOS............	Extended Line-of-Sight (CAAL)
ELOS............	Extralymphatic Organ Site [*Oncology*] (DAVI)
ELOTARLOCS...	Electro-Optical Target Locating System (MCD)
ELOX............	Electrical Spark Erosion
ELP	Aerolineas Ejecutivas de San Luis Potosi SA de CV [*Mexico ICAO designator*] (FAAC)
ELP	Edge-Lit Panel (DNAB)
ELP	Electric Light Pole
ELP	Electrolytic Polishing (MCD)
ELP	Electronic Label Printing [*Diagraph Corp.*]
ELP	Electronic Line Printer
ELP	Electronic Printer (MCD)
ELP	Electrophoresis [*Laboratory*] (DAVI)
ELP	Element Processor (NITA)
ELP	Elliptical (MSA)
ELP	El Pangue [*Chile*] [*Seismograph station code, US Geological Survey*] (SEIS)
ELP	El Paso [*Texas*] [*Airport symbol*] (OAG)
ELP	El Paso, TX [*Location identifier FAA*] (FAAL)
ELP	Emergency Loading Procedure
ELP	Emerson, Lake & Palmer [*Rock music group*]
ELP	Emulsified Liquid Propellant
ELP	Endogenous Limbic Potentials [*Neurophysiology*]
ELP	Energy Loss Peak [*Physics*]
ELP	Engine Lube and Purge [*System*]
ELP	English Language Program (MCD)
ELP	Estimated Learning Potential
ELP	Extreme Limb Photometer [*Instrumentation*]
ELPA............	El Paso Electric Co. [*NASDAQ symbol*] (NQ)
ElPasNG	El Paso Natural Gas Co. [*Associated Press*] (SAG)
ElPasoE	El Paso Electric Co. [*Associated Press*] (SAG)
El Paso Trial Law Rev...	El Paso Trial Lawyers Review [*A publication*] (DLA)
ElPasT	El Paso Tennessee Pipeline [*Associated Press*] (SAG)
ELPAVG	Equity Linked Life Insurance Policy with an Asset Value Guarantee (DICI)
ELPB............	Engine Logistics Planning Board [*Air Force*] (AFIT)
EL-PC............	Electroluminescent-Photoconductive (MCD)
ELPE............	Electroluminescent-Photoelectric
ELPFA..........	Ester-Linked Phospholipid Membrane Analysis [*Analytical biochemistry*]
ELPG............	Electric Light and Power Group
ELPGA	European Liquefied Petroleum Gas Association (EA)
ELPH............	Elliptical Head (IEEE)
Elph	Elphinstone, Norton, and Clark. Interpretation of Deeds [*1885*] [*A publication*] (DLA)
Elph Conv	Elphinstone's Introduction to Conveyancing [*A publication*] (DLA)
ELPHEV........	Electrically Modulated Control Clutch
Elph Interp Deeds...	Elphinstone's Rules for Interpretation of Deeds [*A publication*] (DLA)
ELPHR	Experimental Low-Temperature Process Heat Reactor
ELPN............	Electric League of the Pacific Northwest (SRA)
ELPNEU........	Electropneumatic
ELPO............	Electro-Phosphate Coating [*Metallurgical engineering*]
ELPO............	Electrostatic Primer [*Automotive manufacturing*]
ELPR............	Electroluminescent-Photoresponsive (IAA)
ELPS............	English Language Proficiency Survey [*Department of Education*] (GFGA)
ELQ............	El Quisco [*Chile*] [*Seismograph station code, US Geological Survey Closed*] (SEIS)
ELQ............	Gassim [*Saudi Arabia*] [*Airport symbol*] (OAG)
ELQC............	Electroluminescent Quantum Counter
ELR............	Earned Loss Ratio [*Insurance*]
ELR............	Eastern Law Reporter [*Canada*] [*A publication*] (DLA)
ELR............	East London Railway (ROG)
ELR............	Eldon Resources Ltd. [*Vancouver Stock Exchange symbol*]
ELR............	Election Law Reports [*India*] [*A publication*] (DLA)
ELR............	Electronic Line Replacement [*Cinematography*] (WDMC)
ELR............	Elrom Aviation & Investments [*Israel*] [*ICAO designator*] (FAAC)
ELR............	Engineering Laboratory Report
ELR............	Engineering Liaison Request (KSC)
ELR............	Environment Lapse Rate (DA)
ELR............	Equal Listener Response [*Scale*]
ELR............	Error Logging Register (MHDB)
ELR............	Exchange Line Relay [*Telecommunications*] (IAA)
ELR............	Existing Lapse Rate (DA)
ELR............	Expected Loss Ratio [*Insurance*]

ELR............	Experimental Launching Round (SAA)
ELR............	Export Licensing Regulations (ODBW)
ELR............	Extra Long Range [*ICAO designator*] (FAAC)
ELR............	Rapid City, SD [*Location identifier FAA*] (FAAL)
ELRA............	Electronic RADAR
elra............	European Leisure and Recreation Association (EAIO)
ELRAC............	Electronic Reconnaissance Accessory
ELRAFT............	Efficient Logic Reduction Analysis of Fault Trees (PDAA)
ELRAT............	Electrical Ram Air Turbine (PDAA)
ELRC............	Electro Rent [*NASDAQ symbol*] (TTSB)
ELRC............	Electro Rent Corp. [*NASDAQ symbol*] (NQ)
ELRF............	Eyesafe LASER Rangefinder (RDA)
ELRFTD.........	Eye-Safe LASER Range Finder Training Device (MCD)
ELRIC............	Employers Labor Relations Information Committee (EA)
ELRN............	Elron Electronic Industries Ltd. [*NASDAQ symbol*] (NQ)
ELRNF............	Elron Electrn Ind Ord [*NASDAQ symbol*] (TTSB)
ELRNF............	Elron Electronic Industries Ltd. (MHDW)
ELRO............	Electronics Logistics Research Office
Elron............	Elron Electronic Industries [*Associated Press*] (SAG)
ElronEl............	Elron Electronic Industries, Ltd. [*Associated Press*] (SAG)
ELRUM	Eldon Avenue Revolutionary Union Movement
ELRW............	Elron Elektronic Industries [*NASDAQ symbol*] (SAG)
ELRWF............	Elron Electric Ind Wrrt [*NASDAQ symbol*] (TTSB)
ELS............	Early Lunar Shelter [*NASA*] (KSC)
ELS............	Earth Landing System [*or Subsystem*] [*NASA*]
ELS............	Eastern Launch Site (MCD)
ELS............	East London [*South Africa*] [*Airport symbol*] (OAG)
ELS............	Eaton-Lambert Syndrome [*Medicine*] (DMAA)
ELS............	Economic Lot Size (MHDW)
ELS............	Education Learning Services (AIE)
ELS............	Electrical System
ELS............	Electric Limit Switch
ELS............	Electron Energy Loss Spectroscopy [*Also, EELS*]
ELS............	Electronic Library System [*Aviation*]
ELS............	Electronic Speciality (IAA)
ELS............	Electrophoretic Light Scattering [*Analytical chemistry*]
ELS............	Electrostatic Loudspeaker (DEN)
ELS............	Elevon Load System [*Aviation*] (MCD)
ELS............	Elizabeth Linington Society (EA)
ELS............	Elm Leaf Scorch [*Plant pathology*]
ELS............	El Sal Air [*El Salvador*] [*ICAO designator*] (FAAC)
ELS............	Elsevier [*Published by the Elsevier family*] (ROG)
ELS............	Elsinore Corp. [*AMEX symbol*] (SPSG)
ELS............	Emergency Landing Site (SSD)
ELS............	Emergency Lighting Supply (DNAB)
ELS............	Emergency Lighting System (DNAB)
ELS............	Emitter Location System [*Air Force*]
ELS............	Enchiridion Locorum Sanctorum [*A publication*] (BJA)
ELS............	Energy-Loss Spectroscopy
ELS............	Entry Level System [*Computer science*]
ELS............	Environmental Labelling Schemes (EERA)
ELS............	Eosinophilic Lymphfolliculosis of the Skin [*Kimura disease*] [*Dermatology*]
ELS............	Equidistant Letter Sequences [*Computer analysis of texts*]
ELS............	Error Likely Situation (IEEE)
ELS............	Escanaba & Lake Superior Railroad Co. [*AAR code*]
ELS............	Evangelical Lutheran Synod
ELS............	Exchange Line Selector [*Telecommunications*] (IAA)
ELS............	External Lamina Substance (OA)
ELS............	Extra-Long Staple [*Cotton*]
ELS............	Extreme Long Shot [*Photography*] (WDMC)
ELS............	Harvard Environmental Law Society (EA)
ELSA............	Electronic Lobe Switching Antenna (PDAA)
ELSA............	Electronic Selective Archives [*Swiss News Agency*] [*Information service or system*] (IID)
ELSA............	Emergency Life Support Apparatus (PDAA)
ELSA............	English Language Skills Assessment in a Reading Context [*Educational test*]
ELSA............	Environmental Life-Support Assembly [*NASA*] (KSC)
ELSA............	Estonian Learned Society of America (EA)
ElsagB	Elsag Bailey Process Automation [*Associated Press*] (SAG)
El Salv.........	El Salvador
ELSASSER ...	Elsaess-Lothringen Partei [*Alsace-Lorraine Party*] [*German*] (PPE)
ELSB............	Edge-Lighted Status Board [*Navy*]
ELSBM.........	Exposed Location Single-Buoy Mooring (DNAB)
ELSCEl.........	Earth Landing Sequence Controller [*NASA*] (NASA)
ELSC............	Electronic Library System Cabinet
Elscint.........	Elscint Ltd. [*Associated Press*] (SAG)
ELSD............	Evaporative Light Scattering Detector [*Chemistry*]
ELSE............	Electrical Launch Support Equipment [*NASA*] (KSC)
ELSE............	Electro Sensors [*NASDAQ symbol*] (SAG)
ELSE............	Electro-Sensors [*NASDAQ symbol*] (TTSB)
ELSE............	Electro-Sensors, Inc. [*NASDAQ symbol*] (NQ)
ELSEC............	Electronic Security [*Air Force*]
ELSEGIS	Elementary and Secondary Education General Information Survey [*Department of Education*] (GFGA)
Elsevier	Elsevier NV [*Associated Press*] (SAG)
ELSEWH	Elsewhere [*Manuscripts*] (ROG)
ELSH............	Extended Length Super HIPPO [*High Internal Pressure Producing Orifice*] (MCD)
ELSI............	Ecological Life Systems Institute [*San Diego, CA*] (CROSS)
ELSI............	Electrosource, Inc. [*NASDAQ symbol*] (NQ)
ELSI............	Ethical, Legal and Social Implications [*Genetic research*]
ELSI............	Extra-Large-Scale Integration [*Computer science*] (TEL)
ELSIE............	Edmond's Learning Style Identification Exercise (EDAC)

ELSIE..........	Electronic Letter Sorting and Indicator Equipment
ELSIE..........	Electronic Location and Status Indicating Equipment (IAA)
ELSIE..........	Electronic Signaling and Indicating Equipment (IEEE)
ELSIE..........	Electronic Speech Information Equipment [*System developed by Britain's Department of Transport to facilitate bus transit*]
ELSIE..........	Emergency Life-Saving Instant Exit [*Aircraft*] [*Air Force*]
Elsinor........	Elsinore Corp. [*Associated Press*] (SAG)
ELSO...........	El Nino-Southern Oscillation [*Experiment*]
ELSOR........	Education Libraries Sharing of Resources [*Network*]
ELSP..........	Economic Lot Scheduling Problem
ELSPECS......	Electronic Specifications [*Databank of specifications issued by national agencies*] (NITA)
EL-SPT........	Electrolytes on Urine Spot [*Test*] [*Biochemistry*] (DAVI)
ELSS..........	Electronic Legislative Search System [*Commerce Clearing House, Inc.*] [*Information service or system*]
ELSS..........	Emergency Life Support System
ELSS..........	Emplaced Lunar Scientific Station [*Aerospace*]
ELSS..........	Environmental Life-Support System (MCD)
ELSS..........	EVA [*Extravehicular Activity*] Life-Support System [*NASA*]
EL-SSC.......	Electronic Switching System Control [*Telecommunications*] (TEL)
ELSSE........	Electronic Sky Screen Equipment [*Air Force*]
ELSSOC.......	EL Salvador Solidarity Campaign [*British*]
ELST..........	Endolymphatic Sac Tumors [*Oncology*]
ELSTPT.......	Electrostatic Print (VRA)
ELSUR........	Electronic Surveillance Index [*FBI file of persons overheard on wiretaps*]
ELSW..........	Elsewhere (FAAC)
Els W Bl	Elsley's Edition of William Blackstone's English King's Bench Reports [*A publication*] (DLA)
Elswth.........	Elsworth Convertible Growth & Income Fund, Inc. [*Associated Press*] (SAG)
Elsyn Parl....	Elsynge on Parliaments [*A publication*] (DLA)
ELT...........	Each Less Than
ELT...........	Eagle's Law of Tithes [*2nd ed.*] [*1836*] [*A publication*] (ILCA)
ELT...........	East London Telecommunications [*Commercial firm British*]
ELT...........	Electrocardiography and Basal Metabolism Technician [*Navy*]
ELT...........	Electrometer (DEN)
ELT...........	Electronic Technician
ELT...........	Element
ELT...........	Elliott Beechcraft of Omaha, Inc. [*ICAO designator*] (FAAC)
ELT...........	Elscint Ltd. [*NYSE symbol*] (SPSG)
ELT...........	Eltsovka [*Former USSR Seismograph station code, US Geological Survey*] (SEIS)
ELT...........	Emergency Locator Transmitter
ELT...........	Endoscopic LASER Therapy [*Medicine*]
ELT...........	Enforcement of Laws and Treaties [*Program*] [*Coast Guard*]
ELT...........	Engineering Laboratory Technician
ELT...........	English Language Teaching
ELT...........	English Literature in Transition 1880-1920 [*A publication*] (BRI)
ELT...........	Entry Level Training
ELT...........	Environmental Team Leader [*Nuclear energy*] (NRCH)
ELT...........	Euglobulin Lysis Time [*Clinical chemistry*]
ELT...........	European Letter Telegram
ELT...........	Extended Lapped Transform [*Telecommunications*]
ELT...........	Extended Long Tank (MCD)
ELTA..........	European Learning Technology Association (AIE)
ELTAD.........	Emergency Locator Transmitter Automatic Deployable [*Navigation*] (OA)
ELTAP.........	Emergency Locator Transmitter Automatic Portable [*Navigation*] (OA)
ELTC..........	Enlisted Loss to Commissioned Status [*Military*]
ELTC..........	European Lubricant Testing Committee
Elt Com.......	Elton on Commons and Waste Lands [*A publication*] (DLA)
Elt Copyh	Elton on Copyholds [*A publication*] (DLA)
ELTD..........	Eurobike Limited (EA)
ELTEC.........	Electronics Technician (NOAA)
Eltec.........	Electronic Technology [*Automotive engineering*]
ELTEC.........	ELINT [*Electronic Intelligence*], Technical (MCD)
ELTG..........	European Logistics Task Group (MCD)
ELTI..........	Elapsed-Time Indicator (MCD)
ELTN..........	Eltron International, Inc. [*NASDAQ symbol*] (SAG)
ELTN..........	Eltron Intl. [*NASDAQ symbol*] (TTSB)
Elton Com....	Elton on Commons and Waste Lands [*A publication*] (DLA)
Elton Copyh...	Elton on Copyholds [*A publication*] (DLA)
ELTR..........	Emergency Locator Transmitter Receiver
Eltrax........	Eltrax System, Inc. [*Associated Press*] (SAG)
ELTRC.........	Electric (IAA)
ELTRN........	Electron [*A nuclear particle*]
ELTRNC	Electronic
Eltron........	Eltron International, Inc. [*Associated Press*] (SAG)
ELTSA.........	End Loans to Southern Africa [*An association*] (EAIO)
Elt Ten of Kent...	Elton's Tenures of Kent [*A publication*] (DLA)
ELTV..........	Ejection Launch Test Vehicle (NG)
ELTW..........	Enlisted Loss to Warrant Status [*Military*]
ELTX..........	Eltrax Sys [*NASDAQ symbol*] (TTSB)
ELTX..........	Eltrax Systems, Inc. [*NASDAQ symbol*] (SAG)
ELU...........	El Oued [*Algeria*] [*Airport symbol*] (OAG)
ELU...........	English Lacrosse Union (BI)
ELU...........	Environmental Load Unit [*Recycling, emissions*] [*Automotive engineering*]
e-lu--	Luxembourg [*MARC geographic area code Library of Congress*] (LCCP)
ELUX..........	Electrolux AB [*NASDAQ symbol*] (NQ)
EluxAB	Electrolux AB [*Associated Press*] (SAG)
ELUXY	Electrolux AB CI'B'ADR [*NASDAQ symbol*] (TTSB)
ELV...........	Earth Launch Vehicle [*NASA*]

ELV...........	Edit-Level Video (NTCM)
ELV...........	Electrically Operated Valve
elv...........	Elevation (VRA)
ELV...........	Elfin Cove [*Alaska*] [*Airport symbol*] (OAG)
ELV...........	Elfin Cove, AK [*Location identifier FAA*] (FAAL)
ELV...........	Enclosed-Frame Low Voltage (IEEE)
ELV...........	Expendable Launch Vehicle [*NASA*] (KSC)
ELV...........	Extension Lay Volunteers (EA)
ELV...........	Extra-Low Voltage
ELVA..........	Elle Va [*She Goes*] [*Racing car*] [*French*]
ELVES.........	Emissions of Light and Very Low Frequency Perturbations Due to Electromagnetic Pulse Sources
ELVIS.........	Electroluminescent Vertical Indication System
ELVIS.........	Electrovisual System (MUGU)
ELVN..........	Eleven (NASA)
ELW...........	Anderson, SC [*Location identifier FAA*] (FAAL)
ELW...........	Earth Launch Window [*Aerospace*] (AAG)
ELW...........	Electric Weld (IAA)
ELW...........	Electronic Warfare (CAAL)
ELW...........	Enhanced Land Warrior [*Military*] (RDA)
ELW...........	Extreme Low Water
ELW...........	Webster College, Eden Theological Seminary, Webster Groves, MO [*OCLC symbol*] (OCLC)
ELWAR	Electronic Warfare
ELWD..........	Extra-Long Working Distance [*Microscopy*]
Elw Mal	Elwell on Malpractice and Medical Jurisprudence [*A publication*] (DLA)
Elw Med Jur...	Elwell on Malpractice and Medical Jurisprudence [*A publication*] (DLA)
ELWS..........	Extreme Low Water of Spring Tide
elx...........	Elamite [*MARC language code Library of Congress*] (LCCP)
ELX...........	Exol Industries Ltd. [*Vancouver Stock Exchange symbol*]
ELX...........	Keeler, MI [*Location identifier FAA*] (FAAL)
ELXS..........	ELXSI Corp. [*NASDAQ symbol*] (NQ)
ELXSI.........	ELXSI Corp. [*Associated Press*] (SAG)
ELXT..........	Elbow Extension [*Sports medicine*]
ELY...........	Callaway Golf [*NYSE symbol*] (TTSB)
ELY...........	Callaway Golf Co. [*NYSE symbol*] (SAG)
ELY...........	Easterly
ELY...........	El Al-Israel Airlines Ltd. [*ICAO designator*] (FAAC)
ELY...........	Ely [*Nevada*] [*Airport symbol*] (OAG)
ELY...........	Ely [*Nevada*] [*Seismograph station code, US Geological Survey Closed*] (SEIS)
ELY...........	Ely, NV [*Location identifier FAA*] (FAAL)
ELYC..........	East Lothian Yeomanry Cavalry [*British military*] (DMA)
ELZ...........	Elazig [*Turkey*] [*Seismograph station code, US Geological Survey*] (SEIS)
ELZ...........	Elizabethtown College, Elizabethtown, PA [*OCLC symbol*] (OCLC)
ELZ...........	Elzevir [*Elsevier*] [*Published by the Elsevier family*] (ROG)
ELZ...........	Extensive Landuse Zone [*Australia*] (EERA)
ELZ...........	Wellsville, NY [*Location identifier FAA*] (FAAL)
ELZC..........	Emergency Lead-Zinc Committee [*Later, Lead-Zinc Producers Committee*] (EA)
EM............	Die Evangelischen Missionen (BJA)
EM............	Earl Marshal [*British*]
EM............	Early Minoan [*Archeology*] (BJA)
EM............	Earth Mass
EM............	Eastern Megalopolis [*Proposed name for possible "super-city" formed by growth and mergers of other cities*]
EM............	East Mark [*Monetary unit*] [*Germany*]
EM............	East Midlands [*England*]
EM............	Easton Minerals [*Vancouver Stock Exchange symbol*]
EM............	Ebony Man [*Johnson Publishing Co., Inc.*] [*A publication*]
EM............	Economical Methods [*A line of Varian spectrometers*]
EM............	Edgmoor & Manetta Railway [*AAR code*]
EM............	Educational Marketer [*A publication*]
EM............	Education Manual [*Military*]
EM............	Edward Medal [*British*]
EM............	Efficiency Medal
EM............	Efficiency Modulation
EM............	Egyptian Mysteries [*Freemasonry*] (ROG)
EM............	Ejection Murmur [*Cardiology*]
EM............	Elective Masonry [*Freemasonry*] (ROG)
e/m...........	Electric Charge to Mass (IEEE)
EM............	Electrician's Mate [*Navy rating*]
EM............	Electric Motors (MCD)
EM............	Electrodeposition Memo
EM............	Electromagnetic
EM............	Electromechanical
EM............	Electromicroscopic [*or Electromicroscopy*]
EM............	Electronic Countermeasures Malfunction [*Military*] (IAA)
EM............	Electronic Magnetic Slip Couplings (DS)
EM............	Electronic Mail [*Telecommunications*]
EM............	Electronic Measurement (IAA)
EM............	Electron Microprobe
EM............	Electron Microscope
EM............	Electrophoretic Mobility [*Analytical biochemistry*]
EM............	Elevation Model (NRCH)
EM............	Emanation (ADA)
EM............	Embargo (ADA)
E-M...........	Embden-Meyerhof [*Glycolytic pathway*] [*Biochemistry*]
EM............	E. Merck [*Laboratories*]
Em............	Emergence [*Biology*]
EM............	Emergency (NASA)
EM............	Emergency Maintenance (BUR)

EM	Emergency Management
EM	Emergency Medicine [*Medical specialty*] (DHSM)
EM	Emergency Message (CINC)
em	Emeritus [*Obtain by Service*] [*Latin*]
EM	Eminence
EM	Eminent (ROG)
EM	Emission
EM	Emission Monochromator [*Spectroscopy*]
EM	Emitter (MSA)
EM	Emmetropia [*Also, E*] [*Ophthalmology*]
EM	Emotionally Disturbed
EM	Empire Airlines [*ICAO designator*] (AD)
EM	Empirical Mathematics (ECON)
EM	End Matched
EM	End of Medium [*Computer science*]
EM	End of Message [*Computer science*] (IAA)
EM	Endosteal Marrow [*Hematology*]
EM	Energy Management
EM	Energy Maneuverability (MCD)
EM	Engineering Management (MCD)
EM	Engineering Manual (IEEE)
EM	Engineering Mechanician
EM	Engineering Memorandum
EM	Engineering Model
EM	Engineering Module (NASA)
EM	Engineer Manager
EM	Engineer Manual [*Army Corps of Engineers*]
EM	Engineer of Mines [*or Mining*]
EM	Engine Maintenance
EM	Engine Modification [*Automotive engineering*]
EM	English Market
EM	English Marquess (ROG)
E/M	English/Metric
EM	Engraving Master (MCD)
EM	Enhanced Monitoring [*Environmental Protection Agency*]
EM	Enlisted Man [*or Men*]
EM	Enlisted Member (AABC)
EM	Enriched Mantle [*Geology*]
EM	Entity Module [*Computer science*]
EM	Entsiqlopedia Miqra'it-Encyclopaedia Biblica [*Jerusalem*] [*A publication*] (BJA)
EM	Environmental Management (NRCH)
EM	Environmental Monitoring
EM	Environmental Restoration and Waste Management (EGAO)
EM	Environment Matters [*A publication*]
EM	Ephemerides Mariologicae (BJA)
EM	Epigraphical Museum [*Epigraphic notation*]
EM	Episcopus et Martyr [*Bishop and Martyr*] [*Latin*]
EM	Epitaxial Mesa
EM	Equine Morbillivirus [*Veterinary medicine*]
EM	Equipment Management (MCD)
EM	Equitum Magister [*Master of the Horse*] [*British*]
EM	Erasable Memory [*Computer science*] (KSC)
EM	Error Multiplier
EM	Erthrocyte Mass [*Hematology*] (CPH)
EM	Erythema Multiforme [*Hematology*] (CPH)
EM	Erythrocyte Mass [*Hematology*] (MAE)
EM	Escape Motor
EM	Estimated Man Hours (DNAB)
E-M	Etat-Major [*Headquarters*] [*French military*]
EM	Ethoxylated Monoglyceride (OA)
EM	Etna & Montrose R. R. [*AAR code*]
EM	European Movement
EM	Evaluation Model (NRCH)
EM	Evangelist and Martyr [*Church calendars*]
EM	Evans Medical Ltd. [*Great Britain*] [*Research code symbol*]
EM	Evergreen Marine Corp. [*Taiwan*]
EM	Exact Match (IAA)
EM	Excellent Masons [*Freemasonry*] (ROG)
EM	Exception Monitor (NASA)
EM	Excerpta Medica Foundation [*Database producer*]
EM	Executive Memorandum
EM	Expanded Memory Manager (BYTE)
EM	Expanded Metal
EM	Expectation Maximization [*Statistics*]
EM	Experimental Memo
EM	Explanatory Memorandum
EM	Export Monthly Data [*Department of Commerce*] (GFGA)
EM	Exposure Meter (IAA)
EM	Extensible Machine (PDAA)
EM	External Memorandum
EM	External Monitor [*Obstetrics*] (DAVI)
EM	Extra Milers [*Later, EMC*] (EA)
EM	Extra-Mural (AIE)
EM	Hammond's Air Service [*ICAO designator*] (AD)
EM	Heli-Air-Monaco [*Monaco*] [*ICAO designator*] (ICDA)
E$_m$	Maximum Junction Field (IDOE)
E$_m$	Maximum Voltage (IDOE)
EM	Mining Engineer (PGP)
e/m	Ratio of Charge to Mass [*Physics*] (DAVI)
EM1	Electrician's Mate, First Class [*Navy rating*]
Em2	Brasilia [*Airplane code*]
EM2	Electrician's Mate, Second Class [*Navy rating*]
EM3	Electrician's Mate, Third Class [*Navy rating*]
EMA	East Midlands [*England*] [*Airport symbol*] (OAG)

EMA	East Midlands Airport [*England*]
EMA	Effective Mass Approximation
EMA	Effective Mechanical Advantage [*Bone-muscle physiology*]
EMA	Egyptian Aviation Co. [*ICAO designator*] (FAAC)
EMA	Egyptian Moslem Association [*Australia*]
EM(A)	Electrical Mechanic (Air) [*British military*] (DMA)
EMA	Electromagnetic Accelerometer [*Navigation*]
EMA	Electromagnetic Analysis (NASA)
EMA	Electromantle
EMA	Electronic Mail Association (EA)
EMA	Electronic Maintenance Assembly
EMA	Electronic-Making Apparatus (IAA)
EMA	Electronic Mathematic Automation (IAA)
EMA	Electronic Measuring Apparatus (IAA)
EMA	Electronic Missile Acquisition
EMA	Electronics Manufacturers Association [*Defunct*] (EA)
EMA	Electronics Materiel Agency [*Army*]
EMA	Electron Microprobe Analyzer [*Also, EMPA*]
EMA	Elm [*Alabama*] [*Seismograph station code, US Geological Survey*] (SEIS)
EMA	Emergency Assistance [*Medicine*] (DAVI)
EMA	Emergency Assistant [*Medicine*] (DAVI)
EMA	Emergency Management Agency
EMA	Emergency Management Assistance [*Federal Emergency Management Agency*] (GFGA)
EMA	Emergency Minerals Administration [*Department of the Interior*]
EMA	Emergency Movements Atomic [*Military*] (AABC)
EMA	Employment Management Association (EA)
EMA	Energy Managers' Association [*Australia*]
EMA	Engineered Materials Abstracts [*Materials Information*] [*Information service or system A publication*]
EMA	Engineering Methods Analysis (MCD)
EMA	Engineers' and Managers' Association [*A union*] [*British*] (DCTA)
EMA	Engine Maintenance Area (AAG)
EMA	Engine Manufacturers Association (EA)
EMA	English Men of Action [*A publication*]
EMA	Enterprise Management Architecture [*Computer science*] (TNIG)
EMA	Envelope Manufacturers Association [*Later, EMAA*] (EA)
EMA	Environmental Management Association (EA)
EMA	Environmental Protection Agency, Region VI Library, Dallas, TX [*OCLC symbol*] (OCLC)
EMA	Epithelial Membrane Antigen [*Immunology*]
EMA	Equal Mental Age [*Psychometrics*]
EMA	Equipment Maintenance Agreement
EMA	Equipment Market Abstracts [*Predicast Inc.*] [*Database*] (NITA)
EMA	Equity Market Analysis [*MMS International*] [*Information service or system*] (CRD)
EMA	Essential Maintenance Action (MCD)
EMA	Ethylene-Maleic Anhydride [*Copolymer*] [*Organic chemistry*]
EMA	Ethylene Methyl Acetate [*Plastic technology*]
EMA	Ethylene Methyl Acrylate [*Photovoltaic energy systems*]
EMA	Ethyl Methacrylate [*Organic chemistry*]
EMA	European Marketing Association [*Brixham, Devonshire, England*] (EA)
EMA	European Monetary Agreement
EMA	European Motorcycle Association [*Defunct*] (EA)
EMA	Evangelical Missionary Alliance [*British*]
EMA	Evaporated Milk Association (EA)
EMA	Exchequer Master's Associate [*British*] (ROG)
EMA	Expediting Management Association (EA)
EMA	Exposition Management Association (EA)
EMA	Extended Mercury Autocoder (IEEE)
EMA	Extended Mission Apollo [*NASA*]
EMA	Externally Mounted Assembly
EMA	Extramural Absorption [*Fiber optics*]
EMAA	Envelope Manufacturers Association of America (EA)
EMAA	Ethylene Methacrylic Acid [*Organic chemistry*]
EMAA	European Mastic Asphalt Association (EA)
EMABIC	Emission/Absorption Inversion Codes (MCD)
EMAC	Ecole Africaine de la Meterologie et de d'Aviation Civile [*East African School of Meteorology and Civil Aviation*] [*Republic of Niger*] (PDAA)
EMAC	Educational Media Association of Canada
EMAC	Electromechanical Averaging Circuit
EMAC	Environmental Restoration and Waste Management Advisory Committee [*Department of Energy*] (EGAO)
EMAC	Equipment Maintenance and Control [*Online database*]
EMAC	European and Mediterranean Association of Coloproctology (EAIO)
EMAC	European Marketing Academy (EAIO)
EMACS	Editing Macros [*Computer science*] (NHD)
EMACS	Engine Monitoring and Control System
E-MAD	Engineer-Maintenance Assembly-Disassembly [*NERVA program*]
EMAD	Engine Maintenance Assembly and Disassembly (GAAI)
EMAE	Electrical and Mechanical Assistant Engineer [*British military*] (DMA)
E Mag	E Magazine [*A publication*] (BRI)
EMAG	Ethnic Minorities Action Group [*Australia*]
EMAI	Elizabeth Macarthur Agricultural Institute [*Australia*]
E-mail	Electronic Mail (WDMC)
EMAIL	Electronic Mail (TNIG)
E-mail	Electronic Mail [*Computer science*] (EERA)
email	Electronic Mail [*Internet language*] [*Computer science*]
e-mail	Electronic Mail [*Computer science*]
EMAK	Equity Marketing [*NASDAQ symbol*] (TTSB)
EMAK	Equity Marketing, Inc. [*NASDAQ symbol*] (SAG)
EMALS	Electromagnetic Air Launch System

EM/AM .... Emergency Message - Alert Message (CINC)
EM & C .... Engelhard Minerals & Chemicals Corp. [Later, Engelhard Corp.]
EM & S .... Equipment Maintenance and Support (MHDB)
EMAP .... East Midlands Allied Press [British] (DI)
EMAP .... Environmental Monitoring and Assessment Program [Environmental Protection Agency]
EMAP .... Evoked Muscle Action Potential [Neurophysiology]
EMAP .... Export Marketing Assistance Program [Australia]
Em App .... Emergency Court of Appeals [United States] (DLA)
EMAR .... Experimental Memory - Address Register
EMARL .... Edit Master and Activity Review List (MCD)
EMAS .... Eco-Management Audit Scheme (ACII)
EMAS .... Edinburgh Multiaccess System (HGAA)
EMAS .... Electro-Acoustic Music Association of Great Britain (EAIO)
EMAS .... Emergency Message Authentication System [USEUCOM] (AABC)
EMAS .... Employment Medical Advisory Service [Department of Employment] [British]
EMAS .... Enforcement Management and Accountability System [Environmental Protection Agency] (GFGA)
EMASA .... Electrical Manufacturers' Association of South Australia
EMASAR .... Ecological Management of Arid and Semi Arid Rangelands (EERA)
EMASHE .... Establishing Multimedia Authoring Skills in Higher Education (AIE)
EMAT .... Electromagnetic Acoustic Transducer [Engineering]
EMAT .... Electromagnetic Acoustic Transducer Testing (PDAA)
EMAT .... Expendable Mobile Acoustic Target (MCD)
EMATS .... Emergency Message Automatic Transmission System [Military]
EMATS-AF ... Emergency Message Automatic Transmission System - Air Force
EMATS-JCS... Emergency Message Automatic Transmission System - Joint Chiefs of Staff
EMATT .... Expendable Mobile ASW [Antisubmarine Warfare] Tracking Target [Navy] (CAAL)
EMATT .... Expendable Mobile ASW [Air-to-Surface Weapon] Training Target [Navy] (DWSG)
EMAV .... Electromagnetic Relief Valve [Engineering instrumentation] (IAA)
EM(AW) .... Electrical Mechanic (Air Weapon) [British military] (DMA)
Emb .... Bandeirante [Airplane code]
EMB .... Early-Make-Break [Computer science]
EMB .... Electron Beam Microanalysis
EMB .... Electronic Maintenance Book (IAA)
EMB .... Electronic Material Bulletin [Army] (MCD)
EMB .... Embankment
EMB .... Embargo (ADA)
EMB .... Embark (AABC)
EMB .... Embassy (AFM)
EMB .... Emboss (MSA)
EMB .... Embroidered
EMB .... Embroidery
EMB .... Embryology (ROG)
EMB .... Empire Marketing Board [For motion pictures in England]
EMB .... Empresa Brasileira de Aeronautica SA [Brazil] [ICAO designator] (FAAC)
EMB .... Endometrial Biopsy [Gynecology] (DAVI)
EMB .... Endomyocardial Biopsy [Medicine]
EMB .... Energy Mobilization Board
EMB .... Engineering in Medicine and Biology (MCD)
EMB .... English Beet Molasses (PDAA)
EMB .... Environmental Medicine Branch [NASA] (KSC)
EMB .... Environmental Protection Agency, R. S. Kerr Environmental Research Laboratory, Ada, OK [OCLC symbol] (OCLC)
EMB .... Eosin-Methylene Blue [Dye combination]
EMB .... Ethambutol [An antituberculosis drug]
EMB .... Ethambutol Hydrochloride [Pharmacology]
EMB .... European Molecular Biology Conference
EMB .... Experimental Model Basin [Navy]
EMB .... Explosive Mental Behavior (BABM)
EMB .... Explosive Motor Behavior [Neurochemistry]
EMB .... Extended Memory Block [Computer science] (PCM)
EMB .... Extractive Membrane Bioreactor [Chemical engineering]
EMBA .... Emba Mink Breeders Association (EA)
EMBA .... Executive Master of Business Administration (GAGS)
EMBARC .... Electronic Mail Broadcast to a Roaming Computer [Telecommunications] (PCM)
EMBARC .... Embarc [Electronic Mail Broadcast to a Roaming Computer] Communications Service [Boynton Beach, FL] (CDE)
EMBARK .... Embarkation (DSUE)
EMBASE .... Excerpta Medica Database [Trademark] [Elsevier Bibliographic database]
EMBDU .... Ethnic Minority Business Development Unit [British]
EMBERS .... Emergency Bed Request System [Computer science]
EMBET .... Error Model Best Estimate of Trajectory (PDAA)
EMBEZ .... Embezzlement (DLA)
EMBI .... European Molecular Biology Laboratory
EMBKMT .... Embankment
EMBL .... Eniwetok Marine Biological Laboratory [Marine science] (MSC)
EMBL .... European Molecular Biology Laboratory [Research center Germany] (IRC)
EMBL Data Library... European Molecular Biology Laboratory Data Library (DOG)
EMBO .... Embarkation Officer [Marine Corps]
EMBO .... Embarkation Order [Marine Corps]
EMBO .... European Molecular Biology Organization [ICSU] [Germany]
EMBOFF .... Embassy Officer
EMB of GP... Elected Members Board of General Purposes [Freemasonry] (ROG)
EMBR .... Embroidery
embr .... Embroidery (VRA)
EMBR .... Embryo

EMBR .... Embryo Development [NASDAQ symbol] (TTSB)
EMBR .... Embryo Development Corp. [NASDAQ symbol] (SAG)
EMBR .... Equipment Management Balance Register (AFIT)
EMBRAC .... Embracery [Legal term] (DLA)
EMBRATEL... Empresa Brasileira de Telecomunicacoes [Brazilian Telecommunications Enterprises]
Embrex .... Embrex, Inc. [Associated Press] (SAG)
embrs .... Embrasure (VRA)
Embrx .... Embrex, Inc. [Associated Press] (SAG)
EMBRY .... Embryology
Embryo .... Embryo Development Corp. [Associated Press] (SAG)
EMBRYOL .... Embryology
EMBS .... Embossed [Deltiology]
embs .... Embossed (VRA)
EMBS .... Energy Management Bumper System [Automobile safety]
EMBS .... IEEE Engineering in Medicine and Biology Society (EA)
EMBSSY .... Embassy
EMBT .... Emergency Ballast Tank (DNAB)
EMBTEL .... Embassy Telegram (NATG)
EMBWA .... Egg Marketing Board of Western Australia
EMBX .... Embrex, Inc. [NASDAQ symbol] (SPSG)
EMBXW .... Embrex Inc. Wrrt [NASDAQ symbol] (TTSB)
EMC .... Canada Centre for Remote Sensing Library [UTLAS symbol]
EMC .... Eastern Mennonite College [Virginia]
EMC .... Educational Media and Technology Center
EMC .... Educational Media Council [Defunct] (EA)
EMC .... Educational Modulation Center
EMC .... Elastomeric Molding Tooling Compound (MCD)
EMC .... Electrical Metallic Conduit (DAC)
EMC .... Electrician's Mate, Chief [Navy rating]
EMC .... Electromagnetic Capability
EMC .... Electromagnetic Compatibility
EMC .... Electromagnetic Control
EMC .... Electromagnetic Cyclotron
EMC .... Electromechanochemical
EMC .... Electronic Mail Courier
EMC .... Electronic Manifold Card [Clippard Instrument Laboratory, Inc.] [Cincinnati, OH]
EMC .... Electronic Material Change
EMC .... Electronic Media Claims [Department of Health and Human Services] (GFGA)
EMC .... Electronic Mode Control (IAA)
EMC .... Electronic Music Consortium (EA)
EMC .... Electron Microscopy (MAE)
EMC .... Electron Microscopy Center for Materials Research [Argonne, IL] [Argonne National Laboratory] [Department of Energy] (GRD)
EMC .... EMC Corp. [NYSE symbol] (SPSG)
EMC .... Emergency Management Coordinator [Nuclear energy] (NRCH)
EMC .... Emergency Medical Care (DAVI)
EMC .... Emergency Medical Center
EMC .... Emergency Message Changes (MCD)
EMC .... Emmanuel College, Boston, MA [OCLC symbol] (OCLC)
EMC .... Employee-Management Cooperation
EMC .... Encephalomyocarditis [Virus]
EMC .... End Center Matched [of lumber] (BARN)
EMC .... End of Major Cycle [Military]
EMC .... Energy Management Center
EMC .... Engineered Military Circuit [Leased long lines established in continental US] [Military]
EMC .... Engineering Manpower Commission (EA)
EMC .... Engineering Mock-Up Critical Experiment [Nuclear energy] (NRCH)
EMC .... Engineer Maintenance Center
EMC .... Engineer Maintenance Control [Army]
EMC .... Engine Maintenance Center (AAG)
EMC .... Engine Manufacturers' Committee (EAIO)
EMC .... Engine Monitor Computer
EMC .... Environmental Management Committee (EERA)
EMC .... Environmental Medical Centre [Australia]
EMC .... Environment Management Committee [Australia]
EMC .... Enzyme-Modified Cheese
EMC .... Equilibrium Moisture Content
EMC .... Equipment Maintenance Council [Defunct] (EA)
EMC .... Equipment Management Code [Air Force] (AFIT)
EMC .... Equivalent Mission Cycle
EMC .... Etched Metal Circuit
EMC .... European Mathematical Council (EA)
EMC .... European Mechanics Committee (EAIO)
EMC .... European Military Communication (IEEE)
EMC .... European Muon Collaboration [Nuclear research]
EMC .... European Muon Collaboration [Nuclear physics]
EMC .... Every Member Canvas [Fundraising term] (NFD)
EMC .... Every Member Canvas [Fundraising]
EMC .... Excess Minority Carrier [Electronics] (OA)
EMC .... Executive Management Course (DOMA)
EMC .... Exercise Monitoring and Control (MCD)
EMC .... Experiment Mock-Up Converters (KSC)
EMC .... Export Management Company
EMC .... Extended Math Coprocessor [Computer science]
EMC .... Extended Model Checker [Computer science]
EMC .... Extended Multiplexer Channel (NITA)
EMC .... External Multiplexer Channel (MHDB)
EMC .... Extra Miler Club (EA)
EMC .... Eye-Motion Camera
e-mc-- .... Monaco [MARC geographic area code Library of Congress] (LCCP)
EMC .... Winnemucca, NV [Location identifier FAA] (FAAL)

Emc² .... Electronic Mail Communication Center [*Naples, FL*] [*Telecommunications service*] (TSSD)
EMCA .... Electronic Motion Control Association [*Defunct*] (EA)
EMCAB .... Electromagnetic Compatibility Advisory Board (MCD)
EMC & R .... Emergency Medical Care and Rescue
EmCare .... EmCare Holdings, Inc. [*Associated Press*] (SAG)
EMCB .... Electrician's Mate, Construction Battalion [*Navy rating Obsolete*]
EMCBC .... Electrician's Mate, Construction Battalion, Communications [*Navy rating Obsolete*]
EMCBD .... Electrician's Mate, Construction Battalion, Draftsman [*Navy rating Obsolete*]
EMCBG .... Electrician's Mate, Construction Battalion, General [*Navy rating Obsolete*]
EMCBL .... Electrician's Mate, Construction Battalion, Line and Station [*Navy rating Obsolete*]
EMCC .... Easy Magic Cookery Council [*Defunct*] (EA)
EMCC .... Electromagnetic Control Compatibility
EMCC .... Emergency Medicine and Crisis Care [*Database*]
EMCC .... Emergency Mission Control Center [*NASA*]
EMCC .... Essential Motor Control Center (AAG)
EMCC .... European Municipal Credit Community
EMCCC .... European Military Communications Co-Ordinating Committee [*NATO*]
EMCCS .... Emergency Medical Command and Communications System
EMCD .... Electro-Magnetically Controlled Differential [*Powertrain*] [*Automotive engineering*]
EMCD .... Electromechanical Control Diagram (MCD)
EMCDAS ..... Electro-Magnetic Compatibility Data Acquisition System [*Telecommunications*] (PDAA)
EMCDB .... Elastomer-Modified Cast Double-Base (MCD)
EMCEE .... EMCEE Broadcast Products, Inc. [*Associated Press*] (SAG)
EMCEE .... Master of Ceremonies
EMCF .... Employer Master Control File [*State Employee Security Agency*] (OICC)
EMCF .... European Monetary Co-Operation Fund [*Bank for International Settlements*] (EY)
EMCFA .... Electromagnetic Compatibility Frequency Analysis (SSD)
EMCFOM ...... Electromagnetic Compatibility Figure of Merit [*Telecommunications*] (TEL)
EMCG .... EMCORE Group [*NASDAQ symbol*] (TTSB)
EMCGS .... Electromagnetic Centimeter Gram Second (IAA)
EMCI .... EMC Insurance Group [*NASDAQ symbol*] (TTSB)
EMCI .... EMC Insurance Group, Inc. [*NASDAQ symbol*] (NQ)
EMCI .... Engineering Model Configuration Inspection (MCD)
EMC In .... EMC Insurance Group, Inc. [*Associated Press*] (SAG)
EMCIS .... Experimental Military Command Information System (MCD)
EMCM .... Electrician's Mate, Master Chief [*Navy rating*]
EMCMF .... Embarked Mine Countermeasures Force
EMCO .... EMCO Ltd. [*Associated Press*] (SAG)
EMCO .... Engineering Measurements Co. [*NASDAQ symbol*] (NQ)
EMCO .... Engineering Measure't [*NASDAQ symbol*] (TTSB)
EMCOF .... European Monetary Co-Operation Fund
EMCON ...... Electromagnetic Contamination (MCD)
EMCON .... Electron Microscopy Congress
EMCON .... EMCON, Corp. [*Associated Press*] (SAG)
EMCON .... Emery Control (IAA)
EMCON .... Emission Control (CAAL)
EMCOPS ..... Electromagnetic Compatibility Operational System (PDAA)
EMCP .... Electromagnetic Compatibility Program [*Air Force*] (AFM)
EMCP .... Electronic Modular Control Panel [*Motor-generator set design*]
EMCP .... Emergency Military Construction Program
EMCR .... EmCare Holdings [*NASDAQ symbol*] (TTSB)
EMCR .... EmCare Holdings, Inc. [*NASDAQ symbol*] (SAG)
EMCR .... Equipment Maintenance Change Record (MCD)
EMCRF .... Engineering Materials Characterization Research Facility [*Louisiana State University*] [*Research center*] (RCD)
EMCRF .... European and Mediterranean Cereal Rusts Foundation (EAIO)
EMCRO .... Experimental Medical Care Review Organization [*Program of the National Center for Health Services Research and Development*]
EMCS .... Electrician's Mate, Senior Chief [*Navy rating*]
EMCS .... Electromagnetic Compatibility Standardization [*Program*] [*Telecommunications*] (IEEE)
EMCS .... Energy Management and Controls Society (EA)
EMCS .... Energy Management and Control System
EMCS .... Environmental Management and Control System (AAGC)
Em Ct App ... Emergency Court of Appeals [*United States*] (DLA)
EMCTP .... Electromagnetic Compatibility Test Plan (IEEE)
EMC USA .... Estonian Music Center, USA (EA)
EMCV .... Eggplant Mottled Crinkle Virus [*Plant pathology*]
EMCV .... Encephalomyocarditis Virus
EMCWP .... European Mediterranean Commission on Water Planning (EA)
EMD .... Each Military Department (LAIN)
EMD .... Electric Motor Driven
EMD .... Electrolytic Manganese Dioxide [*For use in batteries*]
EMD .... Electromagnetic Defense (CAAL)
EMD .... Electromagnetic Motion Detector (PDAA)
EMD .... Electromechanical Dissociation
EMD .... Electro-Motive Division [*General Motors Corp.*]
EMD .... Electronic Map Display
EMD .... Electronic Marcel Dassault [*France*]
EMD .... Emerald [*Australia Airport symbol*] (OAG)
EMD .... Emerging Markets Income Fund [*NYSE symbol*] (SPSG)
EMD² .... Emory University School of Dentistry, Atlanta, GA [*OCLC symbol*] (OCLC)
EMD .... Energy and Minerals Division [*GAO*] (AAGC)
EMD .... Engineering and Manufacturing Development [*Military*]

EMD .... Engineering Master Drawing (MCD)
EMD .... Engineering Mechanics Division [*American Society of Civil Engineers*] (MCD)
EMD .... Engine Management Display (MCD)
EMD .... Engine Monitor Display (MCD)
EMD .... Enhanced Microbial Degradation [*Biochemistry*]
EMD .... Entry Monitor Display (KSC)
EMD .... Equipment Manufacturers Design
EMD .... Equivalent Martin Day (PDAA)
EMD .... Esophageal Motility Disorder [*Medicine*]
EMD .... European Market Development
EMD .... Exploration Map Data (RDA)
EMD .... Export Market Development [*Grants*]
EMD .... Eye-Movement Device
EMD .... Marshalltown, IA [*Location identifier FAA*] (FAAL)
EMDA .... Emergency Distance Available [*Aviation*]
EMDG .... Euromissile Dynamics Group (PDAA)
EMDGA .... Export Market Development Grants Act [*Australia*]
EMDI .... Energy Management Display Indicator
EMDI .... Estimated Maximum Daily Intake [*Toxicology*]
EMDL .... East Midlands [*England*]
EM DOM ...... Eminent Domain [*Legal term*] (DLA)
EMDP .... Electromotive Difference of Potential
EMDP .... Engine Model Derivative Program [*Air Force*] (DOMA)
EMDP .... Executive and Management Development Program [*Defense Mapping Agency*] (DNAB)
EMDR .... Eye-Movement Desensitization and Reprocessing [*Psychotherapy*]
EMDS .... Electro-Magnetic Design System [*Computer simulation*]
EMDS .... Electronic Material Data Service (MUGU)
EMDU .... Enhanced Main Display Unit (DWSG)
EMDV .... Eggplant Mottled Dwarf Virus [*Plant pathology*]
EME .... CEMR [*Canada Energy Mines and Resources*] Headquarters Library [*UTLAS symbol*]
EME .... Earth-Mars-Earth
EME .... Earth-Moon-Earth [*Extraterrestrial communications*]
EME .... Ecgonine Methyl Ester [*Organic chemistry*]
EME .... Electrical and Mechanical Engineering [*or Engineers*]
EME .... Electromagnetic Effect
EME .... Electromagnetic Energy (IEEE)
EME .... Electromagnetic Environment (MCD)
EME .... Electromantle Extraction
EME .... Electronics Materials Engineering
EME .... Emden [*Germany Airport symbol*] (OAG)
EME .... Emergency Power Engineering (HGAA)
EME .... Emerging Market Economy (ECON)
EME .... Emetic [*Pharmacy*] (ROG)
EME .... Emetine [*Antiamebic compound*]
EME .... Energy and Man's Environment [*Utility-funded curriculum program*]
EME .... Environmental Measurements Experiment
EME .... Established Market Economy
EME .... Foreign & Colonial Emerging Middle East Fund, Inc. [*NYSE symbol*] (SAG)
EME .... Foreign/Colon'l Eng MidEast Fd [*NYSE symbol*] (TTSB)
EME .... Metro Express, Inc. [*ICAO designator*] (FAAC)
EMEA .... Electronic Maintenance Engineering Association
EMEA .... European Medicines Evaluation Agency [*London*]
EMEC .... Electrical and Mechanical Engineering Committee [*British*]
EMEC .... Electromagnetic Effects Capability (NASA)
EMEC .... Electromagnetic Effects Compatibility [*NASA*] (NASA)
EMEC .... Electronic Maintenance Engineering Center [*Military*] (IEEE)
EMEC .... Engineers Manual for Emergency Construction [*Army Corps of Engineers*]
EMECS .... Environmental Management of Enclosed Coastal Seas (EERA)
EMED .... EuroMed Inc. [*NYSE symbol*] (TTSB)
EMEG .... Electromagnetic Environment Generator
EMEI .... Equipment Management Exception Indicator (AFIT)
EMEM .... Eagle's Minimum Essential Medium [*Culture medium*]
EMEND .... Emendatio [*Emendation*] [*Latin*]
EMEP .... Cooperative Program for Monitoring and Evaluation of Long Range Transmission (EERA)
EMEP .... European Monitoring and Evaluation Programme [*Environmental research*]
EMER .... Electromagnetic Environment Recorder (MCD)
EMER .... Electromagnetic Molecular Electronic Resonance (PDAA)
emer. .... Emerald [*Philately*]
EMER .... Emergency (KSC)
EMER .... Emergency
EMER .... Emergent Group, Inc. [*NASDAQ symbol*] (SAG)
EMER .... Emeritus
EMer .... Mercury [*Record label*] [*Great Britain*]
Emer Ct App... Emergency Court of Appeals [*United States*] (DLA)
EMERG .... Emergency (AABC)
EMERGCON... Emergency Condition [*Navy*] (ANA)
Emerg Lib .... Emergency Librarian [*A publication*] (BRI)
Emergnt .... Emergent Group, Inc. [*Associated Press*] (SAG)
Emerig Ins .... Emerigon on Insurance [*A publication*] (DLA)
Emerig Mar Loans... Emerigon on Maritime Loans [*A publication*] (DLA)
Emer Ins ..... Emerigon on Insurance [*A publication*] (DLA)
Emerit .... Emeritus Corp. [*Associated Press*] (SAG)
Emeritus ...... Emeritus Corp. [*Associated Press*] (SAG)
Emer Mar Lo... Emerigon on Maritime Loans [*A publication*] (DLA)
EmerR .... Emerson Radio Corp. [*Associated Press*] (SAG)
Emerson & Haber Pol & Civ Rits... Emerson and Haber's Political and Civil Rights in the United States [*A publication*] (DLA)
Emerson C... Emerson College (GAGS)

EMES .... Electrical, Mechanical, and Environmental Systems (MCD)
EM/ES .... Emergence and Establishment [*Agriculture*]
E-MESFET.... Enhancement-Metal Semiconductor Field Effect Transistor (HGAA)
E Met .... Engineer of Metallurgy
E (Meter) .... Electropsychometer [*Device for measuring emotional response through electrical conductivity of subject's skin*]
EMETF .... Electromagnetic Environmental Test Facility [*Fort Huachuca, AZ*] [*Army*] (AABC)
EMEU .... East Midlands Education Union [*British*] (AIE)
EMEX .... Equatorial Mesoscale Experiment [*National Oceanic and Atmospheric Administration*]
EMF .... Electric and Magnetic Field
EMF .... Electro-Machine Fixture (MCD)
EMF .... Electromagnetic Field
EMF .... Electromagnetic Flow [*or Florometer*] [*Cardiology*]
EMF .... Electromagnetic Flowmeter (MAE)
EMF .... Electromagnetic Force (NASA)
EMF .... Electromagnetic Frequency
EMF .... Electromotive Force [*See also E, V*] [*Electrochemistry*]
emf .... Electromotive Force (IDOE)
EMF .... Electronic Mail Facility [*Postal Service*]
EMF .... Electronic Manufacturing Facility (IAA)
EMF .... Emergency Medicine Foundation (EA)
EMF .... Endomyocardial Fibrosis [*Cardiology*]
EMF .... Enhanced Metafile [*Computer science*]
EMF .... Enhanced Metafile Format [*Microsoft Corp.*] (PCM)
EMF .... Enlisted Master File [*Army*] (INF)
EMF .... Equipment Maintenance Facility [*Deep Space Instrumentation Facility, NASA*]
EMF .... Erythrocyte Maturation Factor [*Hematology*]
EMF .... Europaeische Motel Foderation [*European Motel Federation*] (EA)
EMF .... European Metalworkers' Federation in the Community [*EC*] (ECED)
EMF .... European Missionary Fellowship
EMF .... European Monetary Fund [*Proposed*]
EMF .... Evaporated Milk Formula [*Dietetics*] (DAVI)
EMF .... Event Marketing Funds [*Business term*]
EMF .... Everitt-Metzger-Flanders [*Early automobile*] [*Facetious translation: Every Mechanical Failure*]
EMF .... Every Minute Fix-It (IIA)
EMF .... Every Morning Fixum [*An old car*] [*Slang*]
EMF .... Evolving Magnetic Feature (OA)
EMF .... Excerpta Medica Foundation [*Database producer*] (EA)
EMF .... Explosive Metal Forming
EMF .... Templeton Emerging Markets Fund, Inc. [*NYSE symbol*] (SPSG)
EMF .... Templeton Emerg Mkts [*NYSE symbol*] (TTSB)
EMFA .... Electrician's Mate, Fireman Apprentice [*Navy rating*]
Emfac .... Emery Industries, Inc. [*Research code symbol*]
EMFCS .... Enhanced Mortar Fire Control System [*Military*] (INF)
EMFF .... Edward Mulhare's Foundation of Friends (EA)
EMFF .... Electromagnetic Form Factor
EMFGA .... Eastern Metropolitan Fruit Growers' Association [*Australia*]
EMFJ .... Europees Muziekfestival voor de Jeugd [*European Music Festival for the Youth*] (EAIO)
EMFM .... Electromagnetic Flowmeter
EMFN .... Electrician's Mate [*Navy rating*]
EMFP .... Electromagnetic Flow Probe [*Analytical biochemistry*]
EMFT .... Early-Morning Fuzzy Thinking
EMFU .... Ethoxymethylfluorouracil [*Antineoplastic drug*]
EMG .... Eastern Management Group (HGAA)
EMG .... Eastmaque Gold Mines Ltd. [*Toronto Stock Exchange symbol Vancouver Stock Exchange symbol*]
EMG .... Electromagnetic Gyro
EMG .... Electromyelography [*or Electromyelogram*] [*Neurology*] (DAVI)
EMG .... Electromyogram [*or Electromyographic, Electromyography*]
EMG .... [*The*] Emerging Markets Infrastructure Fund [*NYSE symbol*] (SPSG)
EMG .... Emerging Mkts Infrastructure [*NYSE symbol*] (TTSB)
EMG .... Energy Managers' Group [*Australia*]
EMG .... Equipment Management Group
E-MG .... Etat-Major General [*General Headquarters*] [*French military*]
EMG .... Europaeische Maerchengesellschaft [*European Fairytale Association - EFA*] [*Germany*] (EAIO)
EMG .... Executive Mansion and Grounds [*i.e., the White House and its grounds*] [*Executive Office of the President*]
EMG .... Exomphalos, Macroglossia, and Giantism [*Syndrome*] [*Medicine*]
EMG .... Exponentially Modified Gaussian [*Mathematical function*]
EMG .... Extension Module Group (ACRL)
EMG .... Eye-Movement Gauge
EMG .... Shreveport, LA [*Location identifier FAA*] (FAAL)
EMGB .... Engine-Mounted Gear Box (MCD)
EMGBL .... Ethyl(methyl)-Gamma-Butyrolactone [*Biochemistry*]
EMGE .... Electronic Maintenance Ground Equipment (KSC)
EmgGer .... Emerging Germany Fund [*Associated Press*] (SAG)
EmgMkt ...... [*The*] Emerging Markets Infrastructure Fund [*Associated Press*] (SAG)
EMGN .... Extramembranous Glomerulonephritis [*Medicine*] (AAMN)
EMGORS ...... Electromyogram Sensors [*For control of artificial limbs*]
EmgTgr .... Emerging Tigers Fund [*Associated Press*] (SAG)
EMGTN .... Equivalent Megatonnage [*Military weapon index*] (MCD)
EMGWS .... Electromagnetic Gun Weapon System
EMH .... Educable Mentally Handicapped
EMH .... Efficient Market Hypothesis (ADA)
EMH .... Electronic Mail Handling
EMH .... Epochs of Modern History [*A publication*]
EMH .... Estimated Man-Hours (AFIT)
EMHR .... Estimated Maximum Heart Rate [*Aerobic dance*]

EMHT.......... Early to Mid-Holocene Transition
EMI .... Eastern Microwave, Inc. [*Telecommunications service*] (TSSD)
EMI .... Educationally Mentally Impaired
EMI .... Electrical & Musical Industries Ltd. [*British*]
EMI .... Electrical Measuring Instrument (IAA)
EMI .... Electric Music Instrument (SAA)
EMI .... Electromagnetic Impulse (IAA)
EMI .... Electromagnetic Interface
EMI .... Electromagnetic Interference
EMI .... Electronic Maintenance Inspector
EMI .... Emergency Management Institute
EMI .... Emergency Medical Information
EMI .... Emirau [*Papua New Guinea*] [*Airport symbol*] (OAG)
EMI .... EMI [*formerly, Electric & Musical Industries Ltd.*] Special Issues [*Record label*] [*Great Britain*]
EMI .... Employers Mutual Indemnity Ltd.
EMI .... Encore Marketing International [*AMEX symbol*] (SAG)
EMI .... Engineering and Manufacturing Instructions (NRCH)
EMI .... Environmental Mediation International [*Defunct*] (EA)
EMI .... Environmental Mutagen Information [*Department of Energy*] [*Information service or system*] (IID)
EMI .... Environment Management Industries (EERA)
EMI .... Environment Management Industry
EMI .... Enzyme and Microbore Immobilization [*Biochemistry*]
EMI .... European Monetary Institute (ECON)
EMI .... Evangelical Ministries, Inc. (EA)
EMI .... Excavation Engineering and Earth Mechanics Institute [*Colorado School of Mines*] [*Research center*] (RCD)
EMI .... Exchange of Medical Information [*Program*] [*Veterans Administration*]
EMI .... Experiences in Mathematical Ideas (EDAC)
EMI .... Expressible Moisture Index
EMI .... External Muon Identifier [*Atomic physics*]
EMI .... Extractive Metallurgy Institute (EA)
EMI .... Extra Military Instruction
EMI .... Premium Air Shuttle, Ltd. [*Nigeria*] [*FAA designator*] (FAAC)
EMI .... Westminster, MD [*Location identifier FAA*] (FAAL)
EMIA .... Employers' Mutual Indemnity Association Ltd. [*Australia Commercial firm*]
EMIA .... Enzyme Membrane Immunoassay [*Biochemistry*]
EMIAA .... Environment Management Industry Association of Australia (EERA)
EMIAC .... Electric & Musical Industries [*later, EMI Ltd.*] Analogue Computer (DEN)
Emiat .... Empresa Importadora y Exportadora de Suministros Tecnicos [*Import-export board*] [*Cuba*] (EY)
EMIB .... European Master's in International Business
EMIBS .... Executive Master of International Business Studies (PGP)
EMIC .... Electromagnetic Impulse Capability
EMIC .... Electromagnetic Interference and Compatibility
EMIC .... Emergency Maternity and Infant Care
EMIC .... Environmental Mutagen Information Center [*Environmental Information System Office*]
EMICE .... Electromagnetic Interference Control Engineer (IEEE)
E-MICR .... Electron Microscopy [*Organic chemistry*] (DAVI)
EMID .... Electromagnetic Intrusion Detector (NVT)
EMID .... Emergency Medical Information Devices
EMIDEC....... EMI [*formerly, Electric & Musical Industries Ltd.*] Data Electronic Computer [*British*]
EMIE .... Educational Media Institutes Evaluation [*Project*]
EMIE .... Ethnic Materials Information Exchange
EMIERT....... Ethnic Materials and Information Exchange Round Table [*American Library Association*] (EA)
EMIETF .... Ethnic Materials Information Exchange Task Force [*Later, EMIERT*] (EA)
EMILAS .... Energy Management in Lighting Award Scheme [*British*]
EMILY .... Early Money Is Like Yeast [*Political fund raising campaign for female Democrats running for the US Senate*]
EMIM .... External Mixer Interface Module (NITA)
EMIMA .... Electrical and Mechanical Instrument Makers' Association [*A union*] [*British*]
EMIN .... Eminent (ROG)
EMInco .... [*The*] Emerging Markets Income Fund [*Associated Press*] (SAG)
EMInco2 ...... Emerging Markets Income Fund II, Inc. [*Associated Press*] (SAG)
EM in Geol... Mining Engineer in Geology
EMINT .... Electromagnetic Intelligence (MSA)
EMINWA ..... Environmentally Sound Management of Inland Water [*United Nations*]
EMINWAR ... Environmentally Sound Management of Inland Waters (EERA)
EMIP .... Equivalent Means Investment Period
EMIP .... Experimental Manned Interceptor Program (IAA)
EMIP .... Extended Management Improvement Program [*Military*]
EMIPr.......... Encore Mkt Intl Cv Partic Pfd [*ECM Symbol*] (TTSB)
EMIqr.......... Entsiqlopedia Miqra'it-Encyclopaedia Biblica [*Jerusalem*] [*A publication*] (BJA)
EMIR.......... EDP [*Electronic Data Processing*]-Microfilm-Integrated-Retrieval [*German Patent Office*]
EMIRA .... Ezegodnik Muzeja Istorii i Ateizma [*Moscow*] (BJA)
EMIRS .... Electrochemically Modulated Infrared Reflectance Spectroscopy
EMIRTEL...... Emirates Telecommunications Corp. Ltd. (TEL)
EMIS .... Ecosystem of Machines Information System
EMIS .... Educational Management Information System
EMIS .... Effluent Management Information System [*Computer science*] (PDAA)
EMIS .... Electromagnetic Intelligence System
EMIS .... Electromagnetic Isotope Separation [*Uranium enrichment*]

EMIS	Electronic Markets and Information Systems, Inc. [*Information service or system*]
EMIS	Electronic Materials Information Service [*Institution of Electrical Engineers*] [*Database*] (IID)
EMIS	Emisphere Technologies [*NASDAQ symbol*] (TTSB)
EMIS	Emisphere Technologies, Inc. [*NASDAQ symbol*] (SAG)
EMIS	Emission (KSC)
EMIS	Engineering Management Information System [*Defense Supply Agency*]
EMIS	Evangelical Missions Information Service (EA)
EMIS	Extension Management Information System [*Department of Agriculture*]
EMISEC	Emission Security (AFM)
EMISS	Electromolecular Instrument Space Simulator
EmisTch	Emisphere Technologies, Inc. [*Associated Press*] (SAG)
EMIT	Elbit Medical Imaging Ltd. [*NASDAQ symbol*] (SAG)
EMIT	Electromagnetic Induction Tweeter
EMIT	Electromagnetic Interference (SAA)
EMIT	Electromagnetic Interference Testing
EMIT	Embedded Micro-Interface Technoloy [*Telecommunications*]
EMIT	Emergency Message Initiation Terminal (MCD)
EMIT	Engineering Management Information Technique
EMIT	Enzyme Multiplied Immunoassay Technique [*Clinical chemistry*] [*Syva Co. trade mark*]
EMIT	Enzyme Multiplied Immunoassay Test [*Clinical chemistry*] [*Generic*]
EMITS	Electromagnetic Instrument Test System (MCD)
EMITS	Electromagnetic Interference Test System [*Navy*] (MCD)
EMITT	Emittatur [*Let It Be Discharged*] [*Pharmacy*] (ROG)
EMJC	East Mississippi Junior College [*Scooba, MS*]
EMJH	Ellinghausen, McCullough, Johnson, Harris [*Medium*] [*Microbiology*]
EMK	Edward Moore Kennedy [*American politician*]
EMK	Electrical Meter Kit
EMK	Electro-Motorische Kraft [*Electromotive Force*] [*German*]
EMK	Emergency Medical Kit (MCD)
EMK	Emmonak [*Alaska*] [*Airport symbol*] (OAG)
EMKO	Ethyl Michler's Ketone Oxime (PDAA)
EML	Eastern Co. [*AMEX symbol*] (SPSG)
EML	Economic Models Ltd. [*British*] (NITA)
EML	Educational Materials Laboratory
EML	Electrical Metrology Laboratory (MCD)
EML	Electromagnetic Laboratory [*NASA*] (GFGA)
EML	Electromagnetic Launcher [*Military*] (SDI)
EML	Electromagnetic Levitator
EML	Electromechanical Laboratories (MUGU)
E-ML	Electronic-Media Literacy [*or Literate*]
EML	Elementary Math Library [*IBM Corp.*]
EML	Emco Ltd. [*Toronto Stock Exchange symbol*]
EML	Emergency Manning Level (CET)
EML	Emory University Division of Librarianship, Atlanta, GA [*OCLC symbol*] (OCLC)
EML	Empire Lines, Inc.
EML	Emulator (IAA)
EML	Emulator Machine Language [*Computer science*] (MHDB)
eml	Emulsion (VRA)
EML	Engineering Materials List [*Nuclear energy*]
EML	Engineering Mechanics Laboratory [*National Institute of Standards and Technology*] (IEEE)
EML	English Men of Letters [*A publication*]
EML	Environmental Measurements Laboratory [*Department of Energy*] (GRD)
EML	Equal Matrix Languages [*Computer science*] (PDAA)
EML	Equatorial Magnetosphere Laboratory (MCD)
EML	Equipment Maintenance Log [*Army*] (AABC)
EML	Equipment Modification List (MCD)
EML	Estimated Month of Loss
EML	Expanded Metal Lath
EML	Expected Measured Loss [*Telecommunications*] (TEL)
EML	Experimental Meteorology Laboratory
EML	Extended Media List [*British*]
EMLA	Electromechanical Linear Actuator
EMLA	Eutectic Mixture of Local Anesthetics [*Topical anesthetic cream*]
EMLA	Eutectic Mixture of Local Anesthetics [*A cream that reduces electrolysis pain*] [*Dermatology*]
EMLAT	Modern Language Aptitude Test-Elementary [*Education*] (AEE)
EMLC	Experimental Manpower Laboratory for Corrections (OICC)
EMLD	Emerald (ROG)
EMLEC	Encore Marketing Intl. [*ECM Symbol*] (TTSB)
EMLF	Eastern Mineral Law Foundation (EA)
EMLI	Environmental Measurements Laboratory Impactor [*Sampling instrument*]
EMLR	Engineering Manufacturing Liaison Release (KSC)
EMLTF	EMCO Ltd. [*NASDAQ symbol*] (SAG)
EMLX	Emulex Corp. [*NASDAQ symbol*] (NQ)
EMM	CANMET [*Canada Centre for Mineral and Energy Technology*] Library [*Canada Energy, Mines, and Resources*] [*UTLAS symbol*]
EMM	Earth, Moon, and Mars [*Astronomy*]
EMM	East Machias [*Maine*] [*Seismograph station code, US Geological Survey*] (SEIS)
EMM	Ebers-MOLL [*Metallo-Organic Liquid LASER*] Model [*Electronics*] (OA)
EMM	Electrical and Mechanical Maintenance (IAA)
EMM	Electricity Market Model [*Department of Energy*] (GFGA)
EMM	Electromagnetic Measurement (IEEE)
EMM	Electromechanical Machining [*Manufacturing term*]
EMM	Electromechanical Mockup (KSC)
EMM	Electronic Manufacturing Manual (IAA)
EMM	Electronic Memory and Magnetics (IAA)
EMM	Electron Mirror Microscope (IAA)
EMM	Emmanuel College [*Boston, MA*] (ROG)
EMM	Emmenagogue [*Promoting Menstruation*] [*Pharmacy*] (ROG)
EMM	Emory University, A. W. Calhoun Medical Library, Atlanta, GA [*OCLC symbol*] (OCLC)
EMM	Engineering Management Manual
EMM	Entente Medicale Mediterraneenne [*Mediterranean Medical Entente*] (EAIO)
EMM	Expanded Memory Manager
EMM	Experiences in Marketing Management (MCD)
EMM	Extended Midcourse Mode [*Navy*] (CAAL)
EMM	Kemmerer, WY [*Location identifier FAA*] (FAAL)
e-mm--	Malta [*MARC geographic area code Library of Congress*] (LCCP)
EMMA	Electronic Mask-Making Apparatus (IAA)
EMMA	Electronic Mathematic Model-Analog (PDAA)
EMMA	Electron Manual Metal Arc (OA)
EMMA	Electron Microscopy and Microanalysis (IEEE)
EMMA	Emergency Medicine Management Association [*Defunct*] (EA)
EMMA	Engineering Mock-Up and Manufacturing Aid (MCD)
EMMA	Equalized Maintenance, Maximum Availability (PDAA)
EMMA	Ethylene Methyl Methacrylate [*Organic chemistry*]
EMMA	Exceptional Merit Media Awards [*National Women's Political Caucus*]
EMMA	Expanded Metal Manufacturers Association [*Defunct*] (EA)
EMMA	Expeditious Monitor and Maintenance Analyst [*Computer*] [*NASA*]
EMMA	Extra MARC [*Machine-Readable Catalog*] Material (NITA)
EMMA	Eye-Movement Measuring Apparatus [*Ophthalmology*] (DAVI)
EMMC	Corps of Engineers Manual for Military Construction [*Army*]
EMMC	Engineers Manual for Military Construction [*Army Corps of Engineers*] [*A publication*] (AAGC)
EMMCC	Erection Mechanism Motor Control Center
EMME	Ethernet Management Module [*Telecommunications*]
EmMex	Emerging Mexico Fund [*Associated Press*] (SAG)
EMMGB	Eaton's Motor Machine Gun Battery [*British military*] (DMA)
EmmisBd	Emmis Broadcasting Corp. [*Associated Press*] (SAG)
EmMkFlt	Emerging Markets Floating Rate Fund [*Associated Press*] (SAG)
EMMP	Equipment Maintenance Management Program [*Air Force*]
EMMPS	Emergency Military Manpower Procurement System (MCD)
EMMPS	Enhanced MEECN [*Minimum Essential Emergency Communications Network*] Message Processing System
EMMR	Eastern Museum of Motor Racing (EA)
EMMRIT	Electronic Warfare Signal Intelligence Material Management Realignment Implementation Task Group
EMMS	Electronic Mail and Message Systems
EMMS	Emmis Broadcasting 'A' [*NASDAQ symbol*] (TTSB)
EMMS	Emmis Broadcasting Corp. [*NASDAQ symbol*] (SAG)
EMMSA	Envelope Makers' and Manufacturing Stationers' Association (DGA)
EMMTAC	Executive Manpower Management Technical Assistance Center [*Civil Service Commission*]
EMMTAP	Executive Manpower Management Technical Assistance Plan [*Civil Service Commission*]
EMN	, and Nancy [*Dickerman*] [*Cook Democratic Party activists*]
EMN	Eastmain Resources, Inc. [*Toronto Stock Exchange symbol*]
EMN	Eastman Chemical [*NYSE symbol*] (TTSB)
EMN	Eastman Chemical Co., Inc. [*NYSE symbol*] (SPSG)
EMN	Electromagnetic Moving Coil and Neutralized Winding (IAA)
EMN	Engineering Management Network (NASA)
EMN	Escuadron de la Muerte Nuevo [*New Death Squad*] [*El Salvador*] (PD)
EMN	Nema [*Mauritania*] [*Airport symbol*] (OAG)
EMNE	Early Modern English [*Language, etc.*]
EMO	Earth Physics Library [*Canada Energy Mines and Resources*] [*UTLAS symbol*]
EMO	Electric Motor-Operated (NRCH)
EMO	Electromechanical Optical (AAG)
EMO	Electronics Material Officer
EMO	Embarkation Medical Official [*Military British*]
EMO	Emergency Measures Organization [*Canada*]
EMO	Emergency Off (SAA)
EMO	Emo [*Papua New Guinea*] [*Airport symbol*] (OAG)
EMO	Emollient (ROG)
EMO	Emosson [*Switzerland*] [*Seismograph station code, US Geological Survey*] (SEIS)
EMO	Engage Missile Orders [*Military*] (CAAL)
EMO	Engineering Maintenance Officer (DNAB)
EMO	Environmental Management Office (DOMA)
EMO	Environmental Medicine Officer [*Military*]
EMO	Epstein and Macintosh, Oxford [*Ether inhaler and Oxford bellows*] [*Anesthesiology*] (DAVI)
EMO	Equipment Management Office [*Air Force*] (AFIT)
EMO	Equipment Move Order (AAG)
EMO	Export Meat Order
EMO	TCW/DW Emerging Markets Opportunities Trust [*NYSE symbol*] (SAG)
EMO	TCW/DW Emerg Mkt Opp Tr [*NYSE symbol*] (TTSB)
EMOA	Encyclopedia of Medical Organizations and Agencies [*A publication*]
EMOD	Erasable Magneto-Optical Disk [*Computer science*] (IAA)
EMOD	Erasable Memory Octal Dump [*Computer science*]
E Mod E	Early Modern English (BARN)
EMOFICO	Committee for Environmental Monitoring of Forest Insect Control Operations
EMOG	Enstatite, Magnesite, Olivine, Graphite [*Geology*]
EMOL	Excerpta Medica Online [*Information service or system*] (NITA)
EMOLL	Emolliens [*Mollifying, Healing*] [*Pharmacy*] (ROG)

EMON .... Emons Transportation Group [*NASDAQ symbol*] (TTSB)
EMON .... Environmental Monitoring & Testing Corp. [*NASDAQ symbol*] (NQ)
EMON .... Exception Monitoring (MCD)
Emons .... Emons Holding, Inc. [*Associated Press*] (SAG)
Emory U .... Emory University (GAGS)
EMOS .... Earth Mean Orbital Speed
EMOS .... Enhancement Metal-Oxide Semiconductor (BUR)
EMOS .... Entry Military Occupational Specialty (AABC)
EMOT .... Emotional
EMOT .... Estimated Minimum Operating Temperature [*Engineering*]
EMOTA .... European Mail Order Traders' Association [*EC*] (ECED)
emoticon ..... Emotional Icon [*Expression of emotion typed into a message using standard keyboard characters*] (CDE)
EMOV .... Electromagnetically Operated Valve (NRCH)
EMOV .... Elm Mottle Virus [*Plant pathology*]
EMP .... Electromagnetic Power [*or Pulse*]
EMP .... Electromagnetic Propagation
EMP .... Electro-Magnetic Pulse
EMP .... Electromechanical Power [*or Pulse*]
EMP .... Electromolecular Propulsion [*Electrochemistry*]
EMP .... Electronic Manuscript Project [*Association of American Publishers*] [*Information service or system*] (IID)
EMP .... Electronic Multiplying Punches (DEN)
EMP .... Electron Microprobe
EMP .... Embden-Meyerhof-Parnas [*Hexose metabolic pathway*] [*Biochemistry*]
EMP .... Emergency Medical Personnel (MCD)
EMP .... Empennage [*Aerospace engineering*]
EMP .... Emperor [*or Empress*]
emp .... Emperor (VRA)
EMP .... Empire
EMP .... Empire
EMP .... Empire Air Service, Inc. [*ICAO designator*] (FAAC)
EMP .... Empire Co. Ltd. [*Toronto Stock Exchange symbol*]
Emp .... Empire District Electric Co. [*Associated Press*] (SAG)
EMP .... Empire of Carolina [*AMEX symbol*] (TTSB)
EMP .... Empire of Carolina, Inc. [*AMEX symbol*] (SPSG)
EMP .... Emplastrum [*Plaster*] [*Pharmacy*]
EMP .... Employables (OICC)
EMP .... Employee [*or Employer*] (DCTA)
EMP .... Emporia, KS [*Location identifier FAA*] (FAAL)
EMP .... End of Month Payment [*Business term*]
EMP .... Energy Management Plan (MCD)
EMP .... Engineering, Mathematics, and Physical Sciences [*Military*]
EMP .... Engineering Modification Proposal (NG)
EMP .... Environmental Management Plan
EMP .... Environmental Monitoring and Prediction [*Subcommittee*] [*Marine science*] (OSRA)
EMP .... Environmental Monitoring and Prediction [*Subcommittee*] (USDC)
EMP .... Environmental Monitoring Program
EMP .... Environment Management Program (EERA)
EMP .... Ephemerides of the Minor Planets (DICI)
EMP .... Epidermal Melanin Pigmentation [*Dermatology*]
EMP .... EPO [*Erythroprotein*] Mimetic Peptide [*Biochemistry*]
EMP .... Equipment Mounting Plate (NASA)
EMP .... Equivalent Monthly Payment
EMP .... Erasable Memory Program [*Computer science*]
EMP .... Erythrocyte Membrane Protein [*Biochemistry*]
EMP .... Ethyl Mercury Phosphate (BARN)
EMP .... Evaluated Maintenance Programming
EMP .... Executive Management Program (DD)
EMP .... Ex Modo Praescripto [*In the Manner Prescribed*] [*Pharmacy*]
EMP .... External Power Monitor
EMPA .... Electron Microprobe Analysis [*Also, EMA*]
EMPA .... Executive Master of Public Affairs (PGP)
EMPAC .... Ethnic Millions Political Action Committee (EA)
EMP AGCY ... Employment Agency (WDAA)
EMPAR .... European Multifunction Phased-Array RADAR (MCD)
EMPASS ...... Electromagnetic Performance of Air and Ship Systems
EMPB .... Effervescent Magnetic Peroxoborate
EMPB .... Embroidery Manufacturers Promotion Board [*Later, SEMPB*] (EA)
EMPB .... Emergency Mobilization Preparedness Board [*DoD*]
EMPB .... Ethyl(methyl)(piperidyl)barbituric Acid [*Biochemistry*]
EMPC .... Educational Media Producers Council [*of the National Audio-Visual Association*] [*Later, NAVA Materials Council*]
EMPC .... Equipment Modification Procurement Costs (MCD)
EmpCar .... Empire of Carolina, Inc. [*Associated Press*] (SAG)
EMPD .... Ethoxy-meta-phenylenediamine [*Organic chemistry*]
EMPDAC ...... Educational Media Producers and Distributors Association of Canada
EmpDist .... Empire District Electric Co. [*Associated Press*] (SAG)
EMPEP .... Erythrocyte Membrane Protein Electrophoretic Pattern [*Clinical chemistry*] (AAMN)
EMPF .... Electronics Manufacturing Productivity Facility (MCD)
EMPG .... Electrical/Mechanical Power Generation Subsystem
EMPG .... Excerpta Medica/EMBASE Publishing Group (IID)
EMPGS .... Electrical/Mechanical Power Generation Subsystem (MCD)
EMPH .... Emphysema [*Medicine*]
EMPHAS ...... Emphysema plus Asthma [*Medicine*]
EMPHASIS ... Evaluation Management Using Past History Analysis for Scientific Inventory Simulation
EMPI .... EMPI, Inc. [*NASDAQ symbol*] (NQ)
EMPI .... Engineering Manual Preparation Instruction [*Army Materiel Command*]
EMPI .... European Motor Products, Inc. [*Auto industry supplier*]
EmpIca .... Empresas Ica Sociedad Controladora [*Associated Press*] (SAG)

EMPIRE .... Early Manned Planetary-Interplanetary Round Trip Experiment
EMPIRE .... Electromagnetic Performance Information Research (PDAA)
EMPIRE .... Electromagnetic Phenomena Interference Repository (PDAA)
EMPIRE .... Electronic Multipurpose Intelligence Retaliatory Equipment (IAA)
EMPIRES ..... Excerpta Medica Physicians Information Retrieval and Education Service [*Elsevier Science Publishers*] [*Information service or system*]
EMPL .... Emplacement (AABC)
EMPL .... Emplane [*British*]
EMPL .... Emplastrum [*Plaster*] [*Pharmacy*] (ROG)
EMPL .... Employ [*or Employee*] (AABC)
EMPL .... Employed
EMPL .... Employer (ROG)
EMPL .... Engineering Master Parts List (KSC)
EMPL .... Extensible Microprogramming Language [*Computer science*] (MHDB)
EMPLAST .... Emplastrum [*Plaster*] [*Pharmacy*] (ROG)
Empl Comp App Bd... Decisions of the Employees' Compensation Appeals Board [*Department of Labor*] (DLA)
EMPLEE .... Employee
EMPLMNT.... Employment
EMPLMNT.... Employment
Employee Rel L Rev... Employee Relations Law Review [*A publication*] (AAGC)
Employers' Rev... Employers' Review [*A publication*]
Empl Prac Dec... Employment Practices Decisions [*Commerce Clearing House*] [*A publication*] (DLA)
Empl Prac Guide... Employment Practices Guide [*Commerce Clearing House*] [*A publication*] (DLA)
EMPLR .... Employer
Empl R .... Employers' Review [*A publication*]
Empl'rs Liab... Employers' Liability (DLA)
Empl Saf'y & Health Guide... Employment Safety and Health Guide [*A publication*] (DLA)
EMPLYE .... Employee
EmplySI .... Employee Solutions, Inc. [*Associated Press*] (SAG)
EMPNO .... Employee Number (MCD)
EMPOR .... Emporium
Emporia St U... Emporia State University (GAGS)
EMPRA .... Emergency Mulitple Person Rescue Apparatus (PDAA)
EMPRESS .... Electromagnetic Pulse Radiation Environment Simulator for Ships [*Navy*] (MCD)
EMPRO .... Emergency Proposal (NATG)
EMPS .... Electromagnetic Pulse Simulator (MCD)
EMPS .... Electronic Maintenance Publication System (MCD)
EMPS .... Emergency Power Supply (MSA)
EMPSKD ...... Employment Schedule [*Navy*] (ANA)
EMPSKED .... Employment Schedule (NVT)
EMPT .... Early College Mathematics Placement Testing Program
EMPT .... Electronic Maintenance Proficiency Test
Emp Vesic ... Emplastrum Vesicatorum [*A Blister*] [*Medicine*]
EMQ .... Economic Manufacturing Quality
EMQ .... Electromagnetic Quiet
EMQ .... Ethoxyquin [*Antioxidant*] [*Organic chemistry*]
EMR .... Augusta, GA [*Location identifier FAA*] (FAAL)
EMR .... Eastern & Midlands Railway [*British*] (ROG)
EMR .... Echo Mountain Resources Ltd. [*Vancouver Stock Exchange symbol*]
EMR .... Educable Mentally Retardate [*or Retarded*]
EMR .... Effective Management Responsibility
EMR .... Electromagnetic Radiation (AFM)
EMR .... Electromagnetic Resonance (WDAA)
EMR .... Electromagnetic Riveting (PDAA)
EMR .... Electromechanical Relay [*Power switchgear*] (IEEE)
EMR .... Electromechanical Research (IEEE)
EMR .... Electronic Module Retard [*Automotive engineering*]
EMR .... Electronic Moisture Recorder
EMR .... Emergency Mechanical Restraint [*Medicine*] (DAVI)
EMR .... Emergency Medical Responders
EMR .... Emerson Electric [*NYSE symbol*] (TTSB)
EMR .... Emerson Electric Co. [*NYSE symbol*] (SPSG)
EMR .... Emission Maintenance Reminder [*Automotive engineering*]
EMR .... Emotionally Mentally Retarded [*Psychology*]
EMR .... Emperor Gold [*VS Symbol*] (TTSB)
EMR .... Empty, Measure, and Record [*Nursing*] (DAVI)
EMR .... Energy, Mines, and Resources [*Canadian government department*]
EMR .... Engineering Malfunction Report (MCD)
EMR .... Engineering Modification Requirements (MCD)
EMR .... Engine Maintenance Reminder [*Automotive engineering*]
EMR .... Engine Mixture Ratio
EMR .... Enhanced Monitoring Rule [*For industrial plant emissions*]
EMR .... Enlisted Manning Report [*Air Force*]
EMR .... Environmental Management Report [*Environmental Protection Agency*] (GFGA)
EMR .... Equipment Maintenance Record [*Army*] (AABC)
EMR .... Error Monitor Register (KSC)
EMR .... Essential Metabolism Ratio [*Medicine*] (DMAA)
EMR .... Executive Management Responsibility (MCD)
EMR .... Executive Management Review (NG)
EMR .... External Mold Release [*Plastic fabrications*]
EMR .... Geological Survey of Canada Library [*Canada Energy Mines and Resources*] [*UTLAS symbol*]
EMRA .... Electronics Materiel Readiness Activity [*Army*]
EMRA .... Emergency Medicine Residents' Association (EA)
EMRA .... Executive Master of Rehabilitation Administration (PGP)
EMRACSE .... East Midland Regional Advisory Committee on Special Education [*British*] (AIE)
EMRB .... European Marketing Research Board [*British*]

EMRC	Electronic Media Rating Council (EA)
EMRC	European Medical Research Councils [*ESF*] (PDAA)
EMRE	Electromagnetic Radiation Effect [*Military*]
EMREL	Emission Release (NVT)
EMRF	European Monetary Reserve Fund [*Common Market*]
EMRG	Electromagnetic Radiation Generator
EMRH	Electromagnetic Radiation Hazard (MCD)
EMRH	Emergency Manual Release Handle (MCD)
EMRIC	Educational Media Research Information Center
emrl	Emerald (VRA)
EMRL	Emerald Capital Holdings, Inc. [*NASDAQ symbol*] (SAG)
EMRL	Engineering Materials Research Laboratory [*Brown University*] (PDAA)
EMRL	Engineering Mechanics Research Laboratory [*Texas University*] (MCD)
EMRL	Equipment Maintenance Requirements List (MCD)
EMRLD	Excimer, Mid-Range [*or Moderate-Power*], Raman-Shifted LASER Device
EmrldCH	Emerald Capital Holdings, Inc. [*Associated Press*] (SAG)
EmrldIsle	Emerald Isle Bancorp, Inc. [*Associated Press*] (SAG)
EMRLS	Eastern Massachusetts Regional Library System [*Information service or system*] (IID)
EMRO	Eastern Mediterranean Regional Office [*World Health Organization*] [*Information service or system*] (IID)
EMRO	Electromagnetic Radiation Operational
EMRODA	Electronic MRO [*Maintenance Repair Operation*] Distributors Association (EA)
EMRP	Effective Monopole-Radiated Power (TEL)
EMRPO	Electromagnetic Radiation Project Office [*Naval Medical Research and Development Command*] [*Bethesda, MD*]
EMRRI	Energy and Mineral Resources Research Institute [*Iowa State University*] [*Research center*] (RCD)
EMRS	East Malling Research Station [*British*] (ARC)
EMRS	Electromagnetic Radiation System (MCD)
EMRS	Emergency Medicine Research Society [*Manchester, England*] (EAIO)
EMRS	Engineering Management Requirements Special [*McAir*]
E-MRS	European-Materials Research Society (EAIO)
EMRSC	Experimental Medical Research Support Center (SAA)
EmrsEl	Emerson Electric Co. [*Associated Press*] (SAG)
EMRT	Electronic Market-Research Terminal
EMRU	Electro-Magnetic Release Unit (PDAA)
EMRU	Employment Market Research Unit (AIE)
EMS	Earl Marshal's Secretary [*Pseudonym used by James Dalloway*]
EMS	Early Morning Specimen [*Medicine*]
EMS	Earthquake Monitoring System (NRCH)
EMS	Economics Management Staff [*Department of Agriculture*] (GFGA)
EMS	Editorial Management System (DGA)
EMS	Education Management System [*Military*]
EMS	Elaine Music Shop [*Record label*]
EMS	Electrical Muscle Stimulation [*Physiology*]
EMS	Electromagnetic Spectrum (NITA)
EMS	Electromagnetic Submarine [*Navy*]
EMS	Electromagnetic Surveillance [*Air Force*]
EMS	Electromagnetic Susceptibility (IEEE)
EMS	Electromagnetic Suspension [*Railway technology*] (PS)
EMS	Electromotive Surface [*Electrochemistry*] (IAA)
EMS	Electromyosignal [*Computer science*]
EMS	Electromyostimulation [*Medicine*] (DAVI)
EMS	Electronic Mail Service [*Telecommunications*]
EMS	Electronic Mail System [*Postal Service*]
EMS	Electronic Management System
EMS	Electronic Medical System [*or Service*]
EMS	Electronic Meeting Services [*Clinton, MD*] [*Telecommunications*] (TSSD)
EMS	Electronic Message System
EMS	Electronic Microsystem (IAA)
EMS	Electronic Muscle Stimulator [*Medicine*] (CPH)
EMS	Electron-Momentum Spectrometer
EMS	Electron Multiplex Switch
EMS	Element Management System [*Computer science*] (TNIG)
EMS	Elephant Memory System [*Computer science*]
EMS	Elvis Presley Memorial Society of Syracuse, New York (EA)
EMS	Embessa [*Papua New Guinea*] [*Airport symbol*] (OAG)
EMS	Emergency Management System [*Computer science*] (EERA)
EMS	Emergency Medical Service
EMS	Emergency Mission Support [*Air Force*]
EMS	Emergency Signal (BUR)
EMS	Emission Spectrograph
EMS	EMS Systems Ltd. [*Vancouver Stock Exchange symbol*]
EMS	Emulator Monitor System (IAA)
EMS	Energy Management System
EMS	Enforcement Management Subsystem [*Environmental Protection Agency*]
EMS	Enforcement Management System (GNE)
EMS	Engineering Master Schedule
EMS	Engine Management System [*Army*]
EMS	Engine Monitoring System
EMS	English Market Selection [*Cigars*]
EMS	English Men of Science [*A publication*]
EMS	Enhanced Memory Specifications [*Computer science*]
EMS	Enhanced Mobility System [*LTV Aerospace and Defense Co.*]
EMS	Enterprise Messaging Server (CDE)
EMS	Enterprise Modeling Server (PCM)
EMS	Entry Monitor System [*or Subsystem*] [*NASA*]

EMS	Environmental Management Subsystem [*Environmental Protection Agency*] (GFGA)
EMS	Environmental Mutagen Society (EA)
EMS	Eosinophilia Myalgia Syndrome [*Medicine*]
EMS	Equilibrated Metal Surface [*Catalyst science*]
EMS	Equilibrium Mode Simulator (TEL)
EMS	Equipment Maintenance Squadron [*POMO*] (MCD)
EMS	Ericsson Manufacturing Systems [*Commercial firm*] [*British*]
EMS	Error Mean Square
EMS	Ethyl Methanesulfonate [*or Ethyl Methanesulfonic Acid*] [*Experimental mutagen*]
EMS	Eucharistic Missionary Society (TOCD)
EMS	European Mariculture Society (EAIO)
EMS	European Monetary System (AF)
EMS	Exception Management System
EMS	Expanded Memory Specification [*Computer science*]
EMS	Experimental Monitoring Satellite (MCD)
EMS	Export Marketing Service [*Department of Agriculture*]
EMS	Express Mail Service [*Generic term*]
EMS	Extended Maintenance Service (IAA)
EMS	Extended Memory Store [*Computer science*] (ECII)
EMS	Extended Messaging Services [*Computer science*] (PCM)
EMS	IEEE Engineering Management Society (EA)
EMS	Preferred Flights, Inc. [*Canada ICAO designator*] (FAAC)
EMS	Surveys and Mapping Library [*Canada Energy Mines and Resources*] [*UTLAS symbol*]
EMSA	Eastern Marathon Swimming Association (EA)
EMSA	Electrician's Mate, Seaman Apprentice [*Navy rating*]
EMSA	Electronics Materiel Support Agency [*Army*]
EMSA	Electron Microscope Surface Area (PDAA)
EMSA	Electron Microscopy Society of America (EA)
EMSA	Electrophoretic Mobility Shift Assay [*Analytical biochemistry*]
EMSAP	Early Medical School Acceptance Program (GAGS)
EMSAW	En Route Minimum Safe Altitude Warning [*FAA*] (TAG)
EMSC	Educational Media Selection Center [*National Book Committee*]
EMSC	Electrical Manufacturers Standards Council (BARN)
EMSC	Electromechanical Stop Clock
EMSC	Electronic Message Service Center (IAA)
EMSC	European-Mediterranean Siesmology Center
E/MSCS	Enhanced Manual SHORAD [*Short Range Air Defense*] Control System [*Army*]
EMSD	Electrical Measurements and Standards Division [*National Institute of Standards and Technology*] (GRD)
EMSD	Environmental Monitoring Systems Division [*Environmental Protection Agency*] (GFGA)
EMSD	Equipment Major Subdivision
EMSEC	Emanations Security (AABC)
EMSEC	Emission Security
EMSI	Effective Management Systems [*NASDAQ symbol*] (SAG)
EMSI	Effective Mgmt Systems [*NASDAQ symbol*] (TTSB)
EMSI	Ellipsomicroscopy for Surface Imaging
EMS-I	Environmental Modeling Systems, Inc. [*Computer science*]
EMSIB	Eastern Mediterranean Special Service Intelligence Bureau [*World War I*] [*British*]
EMSILR	Executive Master of Science in Industrial and Labor Relations (PGP)
EM/SIM	Emulator/Simulator (MCD)
EMSIS	Emergency Shipping Information System [*MARAD*] (TAG)
EMSIW	Effective Mgmt Sys Wrrt [*NASDAQ symbol*] (TTSB)
EMSKED	Employment Schedule
EMSL	Electronic Material Sciences Laboratory
EMSL	Environmental and Molecular Science Laboratory (DOMA)
EMSL	European Microwave Signature Laboratory [*Italy*]
EMSL/CIN	Environmental Monitoring and Support Laboratory, Cincinnati [*Ohio*] [*Environmental Protection Agency*] (GRD)
EMSL/LV	Environmental Monitoring Systems Laboratory, Las Vegas [*Nevada*] [*Environmental Protection Agency*] (GRD)
EMSL/RTP	Environmental Monitoring Systems Laboratory, Research Triangle Park [*North Carolina*] [*Environmental Protection Agency*] (GRD)
EMSN	Electrician's Mate, Seaman [*Navy rating*]
EMSN	Emission (MSA)
EMSN	External-Mix Spray Nut
EMSO	Education Society [*Later, Psychology Society - PS*] (EA)
EMSO	Electronic Memory Systems Organization [*Burroughs Corp.*]
EMSO	European Mobility Service Office [*Army*] (AABC)
EMSP	Enhanced Modular Signal Processor (MCD)
EMSq	Equipment Maintenance Squadron [*Air Force*]
EMSR	Electrician's Mate, Ship Repair [*Navy rating Obsolete*]
EMSR	Electronic Material Shipment Request [*Navy*]
EMSR	Employment Service Review [*A publication*]
EMSRG	Electrician's Mate, Ship Repair, General Electrician [*Navy rating Obsolete*]
EMSRS	Electrician's Mate, Ship Repair, Shop Electrician [*Navy rating Obsolete*]
EMSRT	Electrician's Mate, Ship Repair, I.C. Repairman [*Navy rating Obsolete*]
EMSS	Einstein Extended Medium Sensitive Survey [*Cosmology*]
EMSS	Electromagnetic Servoactuator System (NASA)
EMSS	Electronic Message Service System [*Telecommunications*] (TEL)
EMSS	Emergency Manual Switching System [*Telecommunications*] (NITA)
EMSS	Emergency Medical Service System
EMSS	Emergency Mission Support System [*Air Force*]
EMSS	Experimental Manned Space Station [*Air Force*]
EMSS	Experimental Mobile Satellite System (DA)
EMST	Executive Master of Science in Taxation (PGP)

EMSTRP	Equipment Management System Training Requirements Program [*Navy*] (NG)
EMSU	Electromagnetic Simulation Unit (MCD)
EMSU	Environmental Meteorological Support Unit [*National Weather Service*]
EMSU	Europaeiche Mittelstands-Union [*European Medium and Small Business Union*] [*EC*] (ECED)
EMSU	European Medium and Small Business Union (PDAA)
EMSUBS	Equipment Management Subsystem (DNAB)
EMT	American Medical Response [*NYSE symbol*] (SPSG)
EMT	Amer Medical Response [*NYSE symbol*] (TTSB)
EMT	Each More Than
EMT	Early Missile Test
EMT	Elapsed Maintenance Time
EMT	Elapsed Method of Training (MCD)
EMT	Electrical Mate Test (KSC)
EMT	Electrical Mechanical Tubing
EMT	Electrical Metallic Tubing
EMT	Electrician's Mate, Telephone [*Coast Guard rating*] [*Obsolete*]
EMT	Electromagnetic Thrust [*Propulsion for ship or submarine*]
EMT	Electromechanical Team
EMT	Electromechanical Technology
EMT	Electromechanical Test (NASA)
EMT	Electronic Maintenance Technician [*FAA*]
EMT	Electronic Mind Tester
EMT	Electron Microscope Tomography
EMT	Elemental Method of Training
EMT	El Monte, CA [*Location identifier FAA*] (FAAL)
EMT	Embalmer [*Navy rating*]
EMT	Emergency Management Team [*Nuclear energy*] (GFGA)
EMT	Emergency Medical Tag
EMT	Emergency Medical Technician
EMT	Emergency Medical Treatment [*Military*] (AABC)
EMT	Emmet [*California*] [*Seismograph station code, US Geological Survey*] (SEIS)
EMT	Emory University, Pitts Theological Library, Atlanta, GA [*OCLC symbol*] (OCLC)
EMT	Empire Resources [*Vancouver Stock Exchange symbol*]
Em T	Employment Taxes, Social Security Act Rulings [*Internal Revenue Service*] [*A publication*] (DLA)
EMT	Empty
EMT	Emulator Trap (MHDB)
EMT	End of Magnetic Tape [*Computer science*] (MDG)
EMT	Engineering Model Transport
EMT	Equivalent Megatonnage [*Military weapon index*]
EMT	European Mediterranean Troposphere (IEEE)
EMT	Evaluation Modality Test [*Psychology*]
EMT	Evaluation Monitoring Team (MCD)
EMT	Exact Manning Table (SAA)
EMT	Executive Management Team (NRCH)
EMT	Expanded Mobility Truck (MCD)
EMT	Extended Mobility Tire [*Automotive technology*] (PS)
EMTA	Electro-Medical Trade Association [*British*] (BI)
EMT-A	Emergency Medical Technician, Ambulance (DHSM)
EMTA	Emerging Markets Traders Association (EA)
EMTA	Endomethylenetetrahydrophthalic Acid [*Organic chemistry*]
EMTAC	Emergency Machine Tool Armament Corps [*British World War II*]
EMTALA	Emergency Medical Treatment and Active Labor Act (AAGC)
EMTALA	Emergency Medical Treatment and Active Labor Act
EMTDB	ESCAP [*Economic and Social Commission for Asia and the Pacific*] Maritime Transport Database [*United Nations*] (DUND)
EMTDP	Environmental Mutagen Test Development Program [*National Institute of Environmental Health Sciences*]
EMTE	Electromagnetic Test Environment
EMTE	European Machine Tool Exhibition (PDAA)
EMTEC	Edison Materials Technology Center [*Military*]
EMTECH	Electromagnetic Technology
EMTED	Electromagnetic Test and Evaluation Data (IAA)
EMTEDS	Electromagnetic Test Environment Data System (MCD)
EMTel	Emerging Markets Telecommunications Fund [*Associated Press*] (SAG)
EMTF	Estimated Mean Time to Failure
EMTI	Edge-Mounted Threaded Inserts
EMT-I	Emergency Medical Technician, Intermediate [*Also, IEMT*] (DHSM)
EMTI	Enhanced Moving Target Indicator [*Air Force*] (DOMA)
EMTM	Electron Microscope Technique Meeting (PDAA)
EMTN	European Meteorological Telecommunications Network (PDAA)
EMT-P	Emergency Medical Technician, Paramedic (DHSM)
EMTR	Effective Marginal Tax Rate
EMTR	Emitter (MSA)
EMTR	Enlisted Master Tape Record [*Army*] (AABC)
EMTS	Electronic Money Transfer System
EMTS	Environmental Methods Testing Site [*Environmental Protection Agency*] (GFGA)
EMTS	Ethylmercurithiosalicylate [*Organic chemistry*]
EMTS	Ethylmercury-P-Toluenesulfonamide [*Organic chemistry*]
EMTS	Exposure Monitoring Test Site [*Environmental Protection Agency*] (ERG)
EMTT	Expanded Mobility Tactical Truck (MCD)
EMTTF	Equivalent Mean Time to Failure
EMTU	Enhanced Master Terminal Unit
EMU	Eastern Michigan University [*Ypsilanti*]
EMU	Eccentric Mailbox User [*Electronic mail systems*] (NITA)
EMU	Economic and Monetary Union
EMU	Electric Multiple Unit [*Passenger trains*] (DCTA)
EMU	Electromagnetic Unit
EMU	Electronic Mock-Up [*Computer-aided design*]
EMU	Emory University, Atlanta, GA [*OCLC symbol*] (OCLC)
EMU	Emulator (MSA)
EMU	Energy Management Unit (PCM)
EMU	Engineering Mock-Up
EMU	Engineering Model Unit [*NASA*] (NASA)
EMU	Engine Monitoring Unit [*Automotive electronics*]
EMU	Engine Multiplexing Unit (MCD)
EMU	Environmental Measurement Unit (MCD)
EMU	Europaeische Musikschul-Union [*European Music School Union*] [*Linz, Austria*] (SLS)
EMU	Europaische Musikschul-Union [*European Union of Music Schools*] (EAIO)
EMU	European Mineworkers' Union [*Zambia*]
EMU	European Monetary Union
EMU	European Monetary Unit [*Proposed*]
EMU	Extended Memory Unit (NASA)
EMU	Extravehicular Mobility Unit [*NASA*] (KSC)
EMUA	European Monetary Unit of Account
EMUDS	Extravehicular Maneuvering Unit Decontamination System (SSD)
EMUG	European MAP [*Manufacturing Automation Protocol*] Users Group [*Automotive engineering*]
EMUL	Emulsion (MSA)
Emulex	Emulex Corp. [*Associated Press*] (SAG)
EMULS	Emulsum [*Emulsion*] [*Medicine*] (ROG)
EMUT	Enhanced Manpack UHF [*Ultra High Frequency*] Terminal
EMU-TV	Extravehicular Mobility Unit-Television
EMUX	Electrical Multiplex
EMV	Eggplant Mosaic Virus [*Plant pathology*]
EMV	Egress Maintenance Vehicle
EMV	Electromagnetic Velocity (KSC)
EMV	Electromagnetic Voltage (CAAL)
EMV	Electromagnetic Volume (IAA)
EMV	Electromagnetic Vulnerability
eMv	Electron Megavolt (EY)
EMV	Emporia, VA [*Location identifier FAA*] (FAAL)
EMV	Equine Morbillivirus
EMV	Every Member Visit [*Fundraising*]
EMV	Every Member Visit [*Fundraising term*] (NFD)
EMV	Expected Monetary Value
EMV	Eyes, Motor, Voice [*Glasgow Coma Scale*] [*Medicine*]
EMVER	Experimento Meteoologico del Verano [*Marine science*] (OSRA)
EMVER	Experimento Meteorologico del Verano (USDC)
EMVJ	Etched Multiple Vertical Junction [*Photovoltaic energy systems*]
EMVP	Electro-Magnetic Velocity Profiler [*Oceanography*] (MSC)
EMW	Electrical Megawatt
EMW	Electromagnetic Warfare (MCD)
EMW	Electromagnetic Wave
EMW	Electromagnetic Window
EMW	Engineering and Mine Warfare [*Army*]
EMW	Equipment Manufacturers Workmanship
EMW	Equivalent Mud Weight [*Well drilling technology*]
EMW	Evangelical Movement of Wales
EMWF	Electromagnetic Wave Form
EMWO	Engineering Mock-Up Work Order
EMWP	Esperantist Movement for World Peace [*See also MEM*] [*Tours, France*] (EAIO)
EMWS	Ethnic Minorities and Women in Science [*National Science Foundation*]
EMX	Electron Microprobe X-Ray Analyzer
EMX	El Maiten [*Argentina*] [*Airport symbol*] (OAG)
EMX	Enterprise Mail Exchange [*Soft-Switch, Inc.*]
EMXA	Electron Microprobe X-Ray Analyzer
EMXRF	Electron Microprobe X-Ray Fluorescence
Emy	Emergency (DS)
EMY	Emergency List [*Navy British*]
EN	Air Caravane [*ICAO designator*] (AD)
EN	Early Negative
EN	Earthcare Network (EA)
EN	Earth Vote Network (EA)
EN	Eastern Airways [*British ICAO designator*] (ICDA)
EN	Edge Number [*Film stock identification number*] (NTCM)
EN	Egress Node (ACRL)
EN	Electroless Nickel
EN	Element Number [*Computer science*]
EN	Endemic Nephropathy (PDAA)
EN	End Node (ACRL)
EN	Endo Laboratories, Inc. [*Research code symbol*]
En	Endosperm [*Botany*]
EN	Enema [*Medicine*]
EN	Enemy (AABC)
EN	Enforcement Notification (NRCH)
EN	Engineering Note [*or Notice*]
EN	Engineman [*Navy rating*]
EN	Enki and Ninhursag (BJA)
En	Enoch (BJA)
EN	Enrolled Nurse
en	Enstatite [*CIPW classification*] [*Geology*]
EN	Entanglement Network (EA)
EN	Enteral Nutrition [*Medicine*]
EN	Envelope [*Unit of issue*] [*Military*] (DNAB)
EN	Equipment Number (NITA)
EN	Eras of Nonconformity [*A publication*]
EN	Erythema Nodosum [*Medicine*]

EN...............	Esquimalt & Nanaimo Railway Co. [*AAR code*]
EN...............	Estrada Nacional [*National Highway*] [*Spanish*] (BARN)
EN...............	Ethylenediamine [*Organic chemistry*]
E/N.............	Euro/NATO
EN...............	Euro-Nevada Mining Corp. Ltd. [*Toronto Stock Exchange symbol*]
EN...............	Europa Nostra [*Historic preservation organization*] (EA)
EN...............	Europeene Norme [*European Standard*]
en----	Europe, Northern [*MARC geographic area code Library of Congress*] (LCCP)
EN...............	Event Name [*Dialog*] [*Searchable field*] [*Information service or system*] (NITA)
EN...............	Exception Noted
EN...............	Export Network [*British Information service or system*] (CRD)
EN...............	Ezrat Nashim [*Defunct*] (EA)
EN1	Engineman, First Class [*Navy rating*]
EN2	Engineman, Second Class [*Navy rating*]
EN3	Engineman, Third Class [*Navy rating*]
ENA	Eastern News Agency [*Bangladesh*] (FEA)
ENA	Ecole Nationale d'Administration [*France*] (ECON)
ENA	Electronic Networking Association [*Defunct*] (IID)
ENA	Elkan N. Adler Collection [*Jewish Theological Seminary of America, New York*] (BJA)
ENA	Emergency Nurses Association (EA)
ENA	Enable (NASA)
ENA	Energetic Neutral Atom [*Imaging*]
ENA	Engineering Next Assembly (MCD)
ENA	English Newspaper Association
ENA	Enova Corp. [*NASDAQ symbol*] (TTSB)
ENA	Enrolled Nursing Aide (ADA)
ENA	Environmental Protection Agency, Region VII Library, Kansas City, MO [*OCLC symbol*] (OCLC)
ENA	Espana, Direccion General de Aviacion Civil [*Spain ICAO designator*] (FAAC)
ENA	Ethiopian News Agency
ENA	Ethylnitrolic Acid [*Organic chemistry*]
ENA	European Neuroscience Association (EAIO)
ENA	European Neurosciences Association [*Bussum, Netherlands*] (SLS)
ENA	Evening News Association
ENA	Experimental Negotiating Agreement [*Steelworkers contract*]
ENA	Extractable Nuclear Antibody [*Immunology*] (DAVI)
ENA	Extractable Nuclear Antigen [*Immunology*]
ENA	Kenai [*Alaska*] [*Airport symbol*] (OAG)
ENA	Kenai, AK [*Location identifier FAA*] (FAAL)
ENAA	Epithermal Neutron Activation Analysis [*Analytical chemistry*]
ENAB	Evening Newspaper Advertising Bureau [*Business term*]
ENAB	Exports to North America Branch [*British Overseas Trade Board*] (DS)
ENABLE	Education and Neighborhood Action for Better Living Environment
ENABOL	Empresa Naviera Boliviana [*Shipping company*] [*Bolivia*] (EY)
ENAC	Electronic Numerical Integrator and Calculator [*Early computer, 1946*] (DCTA)
ENAC	Expanded National Agency Check [*DoD*]
ENACT	Effective National Action to Control Tobacco
ENACT	Engineering Application of Computer Technology
ENACT	Environmental Action for Survival [*Defunct*] (EA)
ENADS	Enhanced Network Administration System [*Telecommunications*] (TEL)
ENAF	Employer Identification Number Name and Address File [*IRS*]
ENAL	Alesund/Vigra [*Norway ICAO location identifier*] (ICLI)
ENALIM	Evolving Natural Language Information Model [*Computer science*] (MHDI)
ENAM	Enamel (KSC)
ENAM BD	Enamelled Board (DGA)
ENAM BLR ...	Enamelled Blotter (DGA)
ENAMD	Enameled (ROG)
ENAN	Andoya [*Norway ICAO location identifier*] (ICLI)
ENANB	Enteric [*or Epidemic*] NANB Hepatitis [*Non-A, Non-B*] [*Medicine*]
EN & T........	Ears, Nose, and Throat
ENAS	Ny Alesund (Svalbard) [*Norway ICAO location identifier*] (ICLI)
ENASA	Empresa Nacional de Autocamiones SA [*National Truck Manufacturing Company*] [*Spain*]
ENAT..........	Alta [*Norway ICAO location identifier*] (ICLI)
ENAT..........	En Route Air Traffic Control [*A publication*]
ENB...........	Eneabba [*Australia Airport symbol*] (OAG)
ENB...........	English National Board Careers Advisory Centre [*British*] (CB)
ENB...........	Ethylidenenorborene [*Organic chemistry*]
ENBA	Economics News Broadcasters Association (EA)
ENBC	Energy BioSystems [*NASDAQ symbol*] (TTSB)
ENBC	Energy Biosystems Corp. [*NASDAQ symbol*] (SAG)
ENBD	Bodo [*Norway ICAO location identifier*] (ICLI)
ENBJ..........	Bjornoya [*Norway ICAO location identifier*] (ICLI)
ENBL	Enable (MSA)
ENBL	Forde/Bringeland [*Norway ICAO location identifier*] (ICLI)
ENBM	Bomoen [*Norway ICAO location identifier*] (ICLI)
ENBN	Bronnoysund/Bronnoy [*Norway ICAO location identifier*] (ICLI)
ENBO	Bodo [*Norway ICAO location identifier*] (ICLI)
ENBR	Bergen/Flesland [*Norway ICAO location identifier*] (ICLI)
ENBS	Batsfjord [*Norway ICAO location identifier*] (ICLI)
ENBS	English National Ballet School
ENBV	Berlevag [*Norway ICAO location identifier*] (ICLI)
ENBX	Einstein Noah Bagel Corp. [*NASDAQ symbol*] (SAG)
ENC...........	Eastern Nazarene College, Wollaston, MA [*OCLC symbol*] (OCLC)
ENC...........	ECC Group ADR [*Formerly, English China Clays ADR*] [*NYSE symbol*] (SPSG)
ENC...........	Electroencephalography Technician [*Navy*]

ENC...........	Electron-Nuclear Coupling (IAA)
ENC...........	Emergency National Council Against US Intervention in Central America/The Caribbean (EA)
enc............	Encaustic (VRA)
ENC............	Enclose [*Technical drawings*]
enc............	Enclosed (WDMC)
enc............	Enclosure (WDMC)
ENC............	Enclosure
ENC............	Encode (NASA)
enc............	Encourage (DAVI)
ENC............	Encyclopedia
ENC............	Engineering Command (AAG)
ENC............	Engineman, Chief [*Navy rating*]
ENC............	English China Clays ADR [*NYSE symbol*] (TTSB)
ENC............	Enlistment Canceled [*Military*]
ENC............	Enteral Nutrition Council (EA)
ENC............	Equivalent Noise Charge
ENC............	Euromin Canada Ltd. [*Vancouver Stock Exchange symbol*]
ENC............	European Networking Center (HGAA)
ENC............	Exhaust Nozzle Control
ENC............	Nancy [*France*] [*Airport symbol*] (OAG)
EnCa..........	Endometrial Carcinoma [*Oncology*]
ENCA	European Naval Communications Agency [*NATO*]
ENCA	Oslo Caa [*Norway ICAO location identifier*] (ICLI)
Encad.........	Encad, Inc. [*Associated Press*] (SAG)
ENCAP	Encapsulation (MSA)
ENCAR	Enclosed Cryocondenser for Air Recovery
Enc Arch	Gwilt's Encyclopedia of Architecture [*A publication*] (DLA)
ENCATT.......	Engineering CATT [*Army*] (RDA)
EncBibl	Encyclopaedia Biblica [*Jerusalem*] [*A publication*] (BJA)
ENCC	Emergency Network Control Center (MCD)
ENCC	Encore Computer [*NASDAQ symbol*] (TTSB)
ENCC	Encore Computer Corp. [*NASDAQ symbol*] (SAG)
ENCC	Environment Noise Control Committee (EERA)
ENCD	Encad, Inc. [*NASDAQ symbol*] (SAG)
ENCD	Encode (MSA)
ENCD	Encode
Enc Dict	Encyclopedia Dictionary, Edited by Robert Hunter [*1879-88*] [*A publication*] (DLA)
ENCDR........	Encoder (MSA)
ENCE.........	Extendable Nozzle Cone
Enc Forms ...	Encyclopedia of Forms [*A publication*] (DLA)
Enc Ins US..	Insurance Year-Book [*A publication*] (DLA)
EncJud........	Encyclopaedia Judaica [*Jerusalem*] [*A publication*] (BJA)
ENCL..........	Enclose (KSC)
encl	Enclosed (WDMC)
encl	Enclosure (WDMC)
ENCL..........	Enclosure (ROG)
Enc Law	American and English Encyclopedia of Law [*A publication*] (DLA)
ENCLD	Enclosed (ROG)
ENCLO	Enclosure
ENCLOD	Enclosed (ROG)
ENCLOSG	Enclosing (ROG)
ENCM..........	Engineman, Master Chief [*Navy rating*]
ENCMP	Economists' National Committee on Monetary Policy (EA)
ENCN	Kristiansand/Kjevik [*Norway ICAO location identifier*] (ICLI)
ENCO	Energy Company [*Slogan and brand name used by Humble Oil & Refining Co.*] [*Later, Exxon*]
ENCOM	Engineer Command [*Army*] (DOMA)
ENCOM	Engineer Construction Command [*Army*]
Encon.........	Encon Systems [*Commercial firm Associated Press*] (SAG)
Encore	Encore Computer Corp. [*Associated Press*] (SAG)
Encore	Encore Marketing International [*Associated Press*] (SAG)
ENCORE	Enlarged Compact by Response (IAA)
ENCORE	Enlisted Navy Career Options for Reenlistment (DOMA)
ENCORE	Enrichment of Nutrients on Coral Reefs Experiment [*Australia*]
Encore Aust..	Encore Australia [*A publication*]
EncoreW.......	Encore Wire Corp. [*Associated Press*] (SAG)
ENCP	Encercorp Inc. [*NASDAQ symbol*] (TTSB)
ENCP	European Naval Communications Plan [*NATO*] (NATG)
Enc PI & Pr...	Encyclopedia of Pleading and Practice [*A publication*] (DLA)
Encr	Encore Marketing International [*Associated Press*] (SAG)
ENCR	Encrypted (MCD)
ENCR	Enscor, Inc. [*NASDAQ symbol*] (NQ)
ENCRF	Enscor Inc. [*NASDAQ symbol*] (TTSB)
ENCS	Engineman, Senior Chief [*Navy rating*]
ENCSD	Encased (MSA)
ENCTR	Encounter (FAAC)
ENCU	Environmental Control Unit (MCD)
Enc US Sup Ct Rep...	Encyclopedia of United States Supreme Court Reports [*A publication*] (DLA)
ENCY	Encyclopedia
ENCY	Encyclopedia
ENCYC	Encyclopedia
Encyc	Encyclopedia of the Laws of England [*2 eds.*] [*1897-1919*] [*A publication*] (DLA)
Encyc Brit	Encyclopedia Britannica [*A publication*]
encycl	Encyclopedia
Ency L & P...	American and English Encyclopedia of Law and Practice [*A publication*] (DLA)
Ency Law	American and English Encyclopedia of Law [*A publication*] (DLA)
Ency of Ev ...	Encyclopedia of Evidence [*A publication*] (DLA)
Ency of Forms...	Encyclopedia of Forms and Precedents [*A publication*] (DLA)
Ency of L & Pr...	Encyclopedia of Law and Practice [*A publication*] (DLA)
Ency of PI & Pr...	Encyclopedia of Pleading and Practice [*A publication*] (DLA)

Ency P & P...	Encyclopedia of Pleading and Practice [*A publication*] (DLA)
Ency US Sup Ct...	Encyclopedia of United States Supreme Court Reports [*A publication*] (DLA)
Ency US Sup Ct Rep...	Encyclopedia of Pleading and Practice. Supplement [*A publication*] (DLA)
END	Earth Net Dial
END	Electronic Null Detector
END	Eliminate the National Debt (EA)
END	End Notch Discrimination (EA)
END	Endocrinology [*Medical specialty*] (DHSM)
END	End of Data [*Computer science*] (SAA)
end	Endoreduplication (MAE)
END	Endorsed [*or Endorsement*] [*Business term*]
END	Endowed (ROG)
END	Endurance (IAA)
END	Endurance Minerals [*Vancouver Stock Exchange symbol*]
END	Enid, OK [*Location identifier FAA*] (FAAL)
END	Entente Nationale Democratique [*National Democratic Entente*] [*Monaco*] [*Political party*] (PPE)
END	Environment News Digest [*A publication*] (EAAP)
END	Equipes Notre-Dame [*Teams of Our Lady - TOOL*] [*Paris, France*] (EAIO)
END	Equivalent Neutral Density (DGA)
END	European Nuclear Disarmament [*British*]
END	Exaltation Newcastle Disease
ENO	External Negative Differential (PDAA)
ENDA	ENDA [*Envoroment and Development*] Caribe [*An association*] (EAIO)
ENDADR	End Address [*of Main Memorix Section*] [*Computer science*] (IAA)
ENDAR	Endoatmospheric Non-Nuclear Defense Application Review
ENDA-TM	Environnement et Developpement du Tiers Monde [*Environment and Development of the Third World*] (EAIO)
End Bdg Ass...	Endlich on Building Associations [*A publication*] (DLA)
ENDC	Eighteen-Nation Disarmament Committee [*or Conference*] [*Later, CCD Convened March 14, 1962; actually attended by 17 nations, with France absent*]
ENDCE	Endurance (FAAC)
ENDCRNLGST...	Endocrinologist
ENDECJA	Stronnictwo Narodowej Demokracji [*Nationalist Democratic Party*] [*Poland*] (PPE)
ENDEE	Endorsee [*Legal shorthand*] (LWAP)
END EFF	End Effector
ENDER	Endoatmospheric Non-Nuclear Definition and Requirements Study [*Military*]
ENDER	Endorser [*Legal shorthand*] (LWAP)
Endesa	Empresa Nacionale de Espana SA [*Associated Press*] (SAG)
ENDEX	End Date of an Exercise (MCD)
ENDEX	Enviromental Index (USDC)
ENDEX	Environmental Data Index [*National Oceanic and Atmospheric Administration*] (MCD)
ENDEX	Environmental Index [*Marine science*] (OSRA)
ENDF	Evaluated Nuclear Data File [*National Nuclear Data Center*] [*Information service or system*]
ENDG	Ending (FAAC)
ENDG	Endogen, Inc. [*NASDAQ symbol*] (SAG)
End Guar	Endorsement Guaranteed (MHDW)
ENDI	Dagali [*Norway ICAO location identifier*] (ICLI)
ENDIF	Enterprise Network Data Interconnectivity Family [*Telecommunications*]
End Interp St...	Endlich's Commentaries on the Interpretation of Statutes [*A publication*] (DLA)
End Interp Stat...	Endlich's Commentaries on the Interpretation of Statutes [*A publication*] (ILCA)
Endl Bldg Ass'ns...	Endlich on Building Associations [*A publication*] (DLA)
ENDLF	Eelam National Democratic Liberation Front [*Sri Lanka*] [*Political party*] (EY)
Endl Vac	Endless Vacation [*A publication*]
ENDMT	Endorsement [*Legal shorthand*] (LWAP)
ENDO	Endocrine [*or Endocrinology*] (WDAA)
Endo	Endodontics [*Dentistry*] (DAVI)
ENDO	Endoscopy [*or Endoscope*] [*Medicine*] (DAVI)
ENDO	Endotracheal [*Medicine*] (DAVI)
Endoc	Endocrinology
ENDOC	Environmental Information and Documentation Centres Database [*Commission of the European Communities*] [*Information service or system*] (CRD)
ENDOCRIN...	Endocrinology
ENDOCRINOL...	Endocrinology
Endogen	Endogen, Inc. [*Associated Press*] (SAG)
endo-H	Endoglucosaminidase-H [*An enzyme*]
ENDOMET	Endometrium [*Anatomy*]
ENDO-PAC	Endo-Atmospheric Penetration Aids Concept
ENDOR	Electron-Nuclear Double Resonance
ENDORPHIN	Endogenous Morphine [*or Endomorphin*] [*Also, ENM Brain peptide*]
ENDORST	Endorsement (ROG)
Endovas	Endovascular Technologies, Inc. [*Associated Press*] (SAG)
ENDOW	Endowment (ROG)
ENDOW	Environmental Design of Waterways [*U.S. Army Corps of Engineers*]
ENDP	Endpaper (ADA)
ENDP	Exception to National Disclosure Policy
ENDPRM	Endpaper Map [*Publishing*]
ENDS	Environmental Data Services [*Publisher*] [*British*]
ENDS	European Nuclear Documentation System [*Information service or system*]
Endsonc	Endosonics Corp. [*Associated Press*] (SAG)

ENDT	Electroneurodiagnostic Technologist (HCT)
ENDT	Endorsement
ENDU	Bardufoss [*Norway ICAO location identifier*] (ICLI)
ENDVR	Endeavor
ENE	East-Northeast
ENE	Ende [*Indonesia*] [*Airport symbol*] (OAG)
ENE	Energize (IAA)
ENE	Enron Capital Trust I TOPRS [*NYSE symbol*] (SAG)
ENE	Enron Corp. [*NYSE symbol Toronto Stock Exchange symbol*] (SPSG)
ENE	Enterprise Networking Event [*Telecommunications*] (OSI)
ENE	Environment Encyclopedia [*A publication*]
ENE	Estimated Net Energy (OA)
ENE	Ethylnorepinephrine [*Also, ENS*] [*Pharmacology*]
ENE	Kennebunk, ME [*Location identifier FAA*] (FAAL)
e-ne--	Netherlands [*MARC geographic area code Library of Congress*] (LCCP)
ENEA	European Nuclear Energy Agency (DS)
ENEC	Energy and Economics Data Bank [*IAEA*] [*Information service or system*]
ENEC	Extendable Nozzle Exit Cone (MCD)
ENED	Education Network for Environment and Development (AIE)
ENEF	English New Education Fellowship (BI)
ENEK	Ekofisk [*Norway ICAO location identifier*] (ICLI)
EnEI	Enuma Elis (BJA)
ENEM	Enema [*Medicine*] (ROG)
ENEO	Ebrei nell'Europa Orientale (BJA)
ENEPrA	Enron Cap Res 9% 'A' Pfd [*NYSE symbol*] (TTSB)
ENEPrC	Enron Capital LLC'MIPS' [*NYSE symbol*] (TTSB)
ENEPrJ	ENRON $10.50 Cv 2nd Pfd [*NYSE symbol*] (TTSB)
ENER	Energize (AAG)
ENER	Energy Conv Devices [*NASDAQ symbol*] (TTSB)
ENER	Energy Conversion Devices, Inc. [*NASDAQ symbol*] (SAG)
ENERG	Energicamente [*With Energy*] [*Music*]
ENERGE	Energicamente [*With Energy*] [*Music*] (ROG)
Energy Cont (P-H)...	Energy Controls (Prentice-Hall, Inc.) [*A publication*] (DLA)
Energy L Serv...	Energy Law Service [*A publication*] (DLA)
Energy Mgmt (CCH)...	Energy Management (Commerce Clearing House) [*A publication*] (DLA)
Energy Users Rep (BNA)...	Energy Users Reports (Bureau of National Affairs) [*A publication*] (DLA)
ENERN	East-Northeastern (FAAC)
Enersis	Enersis Co. [*Associated Press*] (SAG)
ENES	European and Near East Section [*Friends World Committee for Consultation*] [*Luxembourg*]
ENET	EqualNet Holding [*NASDAQ symbol*] (TTSB)
ENET	EqualNet Holding Corp. [*NASDAQ symbol*] (SAG)
ENET	Evaluation Network [*An association*] (EA)
ENEV	Evenes [*Norway ICAO location identifier*] (ICLI)
ENEWD	European Network for East-West Dialogue (EA)
ENEWS	Effectiveness of Navy Electronic Warfare Systems
ENEX	ENEX Resources [*NASDAQ symbol*] (TTSB)
ENEX	Enex Resources Corp. [*NASDAQ symbol*] (NQ)
ENEX-ASIA	International Electrical and Electronic Engineering Exhibition [*Interfama Pte. Ltd.*]
EnexRs	Enex Resources Corp. [*Associated Press*] (SAG)
ENF	Employment of Naval Forces [*Course*] (DNAB)
ENF	Enfield Corp. Ltd. [*Toronto Stock Exchange symbol*]
ENF	Enflurane [*Also, E*] [*An anesthetic*]
ENF	Enforcement (DCTA)
ENF	Equipment Not Operationally Ready to Fire [*Military*] (MCD)
ENF	Omaha, NE [*Location identifier FAA*] (FAAL)
ENFA	Fireman Apprentice, Engineman, Striker [*Navy rating*]
ENFB	Oslo/Fornebu [*Norway ICAO location identifier*] (ICLI)
ENFC	Elvis Now Fan Club (EA)
ENFCMNT	Enforcement
ENFD	Enfield [*Borough of London*]
Enf'd	Enforced [*Legal term*] (DLA)
ENFD	Forde [*Norway ICAO location identifier*] (ICLI)
ENFET	Enzyme Field Effect Transistor [*Electrochemistry*]
ENFG	Fagernes/Leirin [*Norway ICAO location identifier*] (ICLI)
ENFIA	Exchange Network Facilities for Interstate Access [*Computer science*] (TNIG)
ENFIA	Exchange Network Facilities Interconnecting Arrangement [*Tariffs*] [*Telecommunications*]
ENFL	Floro [*Norway ICAO location identifier*] (ICLI)
ENFN	Fireman, Engineman, Striker [*Navy rating*]
ENFO	Forus [*Norway ICAO location identifier*] (ICLI)
ENFOR	Energy from the Forest Program [*Canada*]
ENFP	Extrovert, Intuitive, Feeling, Perceptive [*Meyers-Briggs Type Indicator*]
ENFR	Frigg [*Norway ICAO location identifier*] (ICLI)
ENFUEM	Energy & Fuels [*A publication*]
ENFY	Fyresdal [*Norway ICAO location identifier*] (ICLI)
ENFZ	Fritzoe [*Norway ICAO location identifier*] (ICLI)
ENG	Army Corps of Engineers (AAGC)
ENG	Destec Energy [*NYSE symbol*] (SPSG)
ENG	Electronic News Gathering [*Television news coverage*]
ENG	Electronystagmogram [*or Electrostagmography*] [*Neurology*] (DAVI)
ENG	Electronystagmography [*Medicine*]
ENG	Empty Net Goals [*Hockey*]
ENG	Engagement (ADA)
ENG	Engine (AFM)
ENG	Engine
ENG	Engineer [*or Engineering*] (EY)
Eng	Engineer (GAGS)

ENG .... Engineer Hill [*Alaska*] [*Seismograph station code, US Geological Survey*] (SEIS)
eng .... Engineering (DD)
ENG .... Engineer Officer [*Navy British*]
ENG .... England [*or English*]
Eng .... England (VRA)
eng .... English [*MARC language code Library of Congress*] (LCCP)
Eng .... English Reports (N. C. Moak) [*A publication*] (DLA)
Eng .... English's Reports [*6-13 Arkansas*] [*A publication*] (DLA)
ENG .... Engrave
ENG .... Engraver (ROG)
EN(G) .... Enrolled Nurse (General) [*British*] (DBQ)
ENGA .... Emergency Natural Gas Act of 1977
ENGA .... Engage (MSA)
Eng Adm ...... English Admiralty Reports [*A publication*] (DLA)
Eng Adm R... English Admiralty Reports [*A publication*] (DLA)
ENGAGMT.... Engagement (ROG)
Eng&Bus...... Engineering & Business (DD)
Eng & Ir App... Law Reports, English and Irish Appeal Cases [*A publication*] (DLA)
ENGBAT .... Engineer Battalion [*Military*]
ENGBCA....... Corps of Engineers Board of Contract Appeals [*Army*]
EngBiosy..... Energy Biosystems Corp. [*Associated Press*] (SAG)
ENG C&A...... Army Corps of Engineers Claims and Appeals Board (AAGC)
Eng CC .... English Crown Cases [*American Reprint*] [*A publication*] (DLA)
Eng Ch......... English Chancery [*Legal term*] (DLA)
Eng Ch......... English Chancery [*American Reprint*] [*A publication*] (DLA)
EngChin .... English China Clays Ltd. [*Associated Press*] (SAG)
Eng CL .... English Common Law Reports [*A publication*] (DLA)
ENGCOM...... Engineering Command (MCD)
ENGCOMDC... Engineer Commissioner, District of Columbia [*Military*] (AABC)
Eng Com LR... English Common Law Reports [*A publication*] (DLA)
Eng Cr Cas... English Crown Cases [*American Reprint*] [*A publication*] (DLA)
Eng D........... Doctor of Engineering
ENGD .... Engrossed (ROG)
Eng Eccl ...... English Ecclesiastical Reports [*A publication*] (DLA)
Eng Ecc R.... English Ecclesiastical Reports [*A publication*] (DLA)
ENG ERR ...... Engineering Error (WDAA)
Engex.......... Engex, Inc. [*Associated Press*] (SAG)
Eng Exch..... English Exchequer Reports [*A publication*] (DLA)
Eng'g.......... Engineering [*A publication*] (DLA)
ENGG .... Engineering (WGA)
eng hn .... English Horn (BARN)
ENGID.......... Engine Identification Report [*Air Force*]
ENGIN.......... Engineering
ENGING .... Engineering
ENG INT....... Engage Intercept (CAAL)
Eng Ir App ... Law Reports, English and Irish Appeal Cases [*A publication*] (DLA)
Eng Judg ..... Scotch Court of Session Cases Decided by the English Judges [*1655-61*] [*A publication*] (DLA)
ENGL .... England
ENGL .... Engle Homes [*NASDAQ symbol*] (SPSG)
ENGL .... English (ROG)
Engl .... English (DD)
ENGL .... English
Eng L & Eq... English Law and Equity Reports [*American Reprint*] [*A publication*] (DLA)
Eng L & Eq R... English Law and Equity Reports [*American Reprint*] [*A publication*] (DLA)
Eng Law & Eq... English Law and Equity Reports [*American Reprint*] [*A publication*] (DLA)
ENGLD......... England
EnglhCp....... Engelhard Corp. [*Associated Press*] (SAG)
EnglHm........ Engle Homes, Inc. [*Associated Press*] (SAG)
English .... English's Reports [*6-13 Arkansas*] [*A publication*] (DLA)
ENG LIT .... English Literature (WDAA)
ENG-LT........ Engineer Lieutenant [*Navy British*] (ROG)
ENG(M)........ Enrolled Nurse, General (Mental Nursing) [*British*] (DI)
ENGM .... Oslo/Gardermoen [*Norway ICAO location identifier*] (ICLI)
EngMea .... Engineering Measurements Co. [*Associated Press*] (SAG)
ENG(MS)...... Enrolled Nurse, General (Mental Sub-Normal Nursing) [*British*] (DI)
ENGN .... Engineering
ENGN .... Grimsmoen [*Norway ICAO location identifier*] (ICLI)
ENGNG......... Engineering
ENG-NMCS... Engine Not Mission Capable - Supply (AFIT)
ENGNR........ Engineer
EngnSu .... Engineered Support Systems, Inc. [*Associated Press*] (SAG)
ENGORC ..... Engineer Officers Reserve Corps
Eng Pews .... English on Church Pews [*A publication*] (DLA)
Eng Pl......... English Pleader [*A publication*] (DLA)
Eng Pr Cas... Roscoe's English Prize Cases [*A publication*] (DLA)
ENGR .... Engineer
Engr........... Engineer (PGP)
ENGR.......... Engraved
engr........... Engraved (WDMC)
engr........... Engraver (WDMC)
ENGR.......... Engraver (ROG)
engr........... Engraving (VRA)
engr........... Engraving (WDMC)
ENGR.......... Engravings (ROG)
Eng R & C Cas... English Railway and Canal Cases [*A publication*] (DLA)
ENGRBN ...... Engineer Battalion [*Military*]
ENGRCEN ..... Engineering Center
Engr D .... Doctor of Engineering
ENGRD........ Engineered
ENGRE........ Engineer Element

Eng Re........ English Reports, Full Reprint [*A publication*] (DLA)
Eng Rep...... English Reports, Full Reprint [*A publication*] (DLA)
Eng Rep...... English Reports (N. C. Moak) [*American Reprint*] [*A publication*] (DLA)
Eng Rep...... English's Reports [*6-13 Arkansas*] [*A publication*] (DLA)
Eng Rep Anno... English Reports, Annotated [*A publication*] (DLA)
Eng Rep R.... English Reports, Full Reprint [*A publication*] (DLA)
Eng Rep Re... English Reports, Full Reprint [*A publication*] (DLA)
ENGREQUIPMAINTRPRPLT... Engineer Equipment Maintenance Repair Platoon (DNAB)
ENGRFAC..... Engineering Facility
ENGRG........ Engineering
ENGRG........ Engineering
ENGRING ..... Engineering
ENG RM....... Engine Room (WDAA)
ENGRMAINTCO... Engineer Maintenance Co. [*Military*] (DNAB)
ENGRPLT..... Engineer Platoon (DNAB)
Eng RR Ca.... English Railway and Canal Cases [*A publication*] (DLA)
Engrs Aust... Engineers Australia [*A publication*]
ENGRSPTBN... Engineer Support Battalion (DNAB)
Eng Ru Ca.... English Ruling Cases [*A publication*] (DLA)
Eng Rul Cas... English Ruling Cases [*A publication*] (DLA)
ENGRV......... Engrave
ENGRV......... Engraving
ENGRVR ...... Engraver
ENGRY......... Energy
Eng Ry & C Cas... English Railway and Canal Cases [*A publication*] (DLA)
ENGS .... Engross (ROG)
EngSc......... Engineering Science (DD)
Eng Sc D ..... Doctor of Engineering Science
Eng Sc Ecc... English and Scotch Ecclesiastical Reports [*A publication*] (DLA)
ENGSS .... Engineering Schoolship [*Navy*] (NVT)
ENGSTAT ..... Engine Status Report [*Air Force*]
ENGT .... Engrossment (ROG)
EngTech...... Engineering Technician (ACII)
EngTech...... Engineering Technology (DD)
ENGV .... Engine V-Belt
EngWst........ Energy West, Inc. [*Associated Press*] (SAG)
ENGY .... Energy (MSA)
Engynth....... Energy North, Inc. [*Associated Press*] (SAG)
EngyRsh ...... Energy Research Corp. [*Associated Press*] (SAG)
EngyVen ...... Energy Ventures [*Associated Press*] (SAG)
ENH .... Earth Near Horizon [*NASA*] (KSC)
ENH .... Educable Neurologically Handicapped
ENH .... Enshi [*China*] [*Airport symbol*] (OAG)
Enh .... Hymnal Prayer of Enheduanna (BJA)
ENHA .... Hamar/Stafsberg [*Norway ICAO location identifier*] (ICLI)
Enhance....... Enhance Financial Services Group [*Associated Press*] (SAG)
ENHB .... Heggebakken [*Norway ICAO location identifier*] (ICLI)
ENHD .... Haugesund/Karmoy [*Norway ICAO location identifier*] (ICLI)
ENHE .... Encounter in Health Education
ENHF .... Hammerfest [*Norway ICAO location identifier*] (ICLI)
ENHK .... Hasvik [*Norway ICAO location identifier*] (ICLI)
ENHN .... Harnmoen [*Norway ICAO location identifier*] (ICLI)
ENHNCD ...... Enhanced [*ICAO designator*] (FAAC)
ENHNCMNT... Enhancement [*ICAO designator*] (FAAC)
ENHO .... Hopen [*Norway ICAO location identifier*] (ICLI)
ENHS .... European Natural Hygiene Society (EAIO)
ENHS .... Hokksund [*Norway ICAO location identifier*] (ICLI)
ENHV .... Honningsvag/Valan [*Norway ICAO location identifier*] (ICLI)
ENI .... Effective Networks, Inc. [*Telecommunications service*] (TSSD)
ENI .... Elan Industries, Inc. [*Vancouver Stock Exchange symbol*]
ENI .... Enemy Initiated Incident [*Vietnam*]
ENI .... Enersis SA [*NYSE symbol*] (SPSG)
ENI .... Enersis S.A. ADS [*NYSE symbol*] (TTSB)
ENI .... Equivalent Noise Input (DEN)
ENI .... Excepted Net Income
ENIAC .... Electronic Numerical Integrator and Calculator [*Early computer, 1946*]
ENIAC .... Electronic Numerical Integrator and Computer (IDOE)
ENIC .... Voltage Negative-Impedance Converter [*Electronics*] (ECII)
ENID .... Environmental Industries Directory [*A publication*]
ENIG .... Electronic Nuclear Instrumentation Group (MCD)
ENIG .... Enrolled Nurse Interest Group [*Australia*]
ENIP .... Estonian National Independence Party [*Political party*]
ENIRF .... Enemy Initiated Incident Responded to by Friendly Forces [*Vietnam*]
EnisBu .... Ennis Business Forms, Inc. [*Associated Press*] (SAG)
ENIT .... Ente Nazionale Italiano per il Turismo [*Italian National Tourist Board*]
ENJ .... Enjoin [*Legal shorthand*] (LWAP)
ENJ .... Nort Jet [*Spain ICAO designator*] (FAAC)
ENJA .... Jan Mayen [*Norway ICAO location identifier*] (ICLI)
ENJB .... Jarlsberg [*Norway ICAO location identifier*] (ICLI)
ENJJPT........ Euro-NATO Joint Jet Pilot Training
En Jnl .... Energy Journal [*A publication*] (BRI)
ENJOYT........ Enjoyment (ROG)
EnJu........... Encyclopaedia Judaica [*Jerusalem*] [*A publication*] (BJA)
ENK............. Enerteck Energy Technologies Corp. [*Vancouver Stock Exchange symbol*]
enk............. England [*MARC country of publication code Library of Congress*] (LCCP)
ENK............. Enkephalin [*Brain peptide, subclass of Endorphin*]
ENK............. Enniskillen [*Northern Ireland*] [*Airport symbol*] (AD)
ENK............. Enter Key [*Computer science*] (IAA)
ENK............. Expected Number of Kills [*Military*] (MCD)
ENKA .... Kautokeino [*Norway ICAO location identifier*] (ICLI)
ENKB .... Kristiansund/Kvernberget [*Norway ICAO location identifier*] (ICLI)

ENKJ............ Kjeller [Norway ICAO location identifier] (ICLI)
ENKR .... Kirkenes/Hoybuktmoen [Norway ICAO location identifier] (ICLI)
ENL............. Centralia, IL [Location identifier FAA] (FAAL)
ENL............. Ejercito Nacional de Liberacion [National Liberation Army] [Nicaragua] (PD)
ENL............. Elsevier NV [NYSE symbol] (SAG)
ENL............. Elsevier NV ADS [NYSE symbol] (TTSB)
ENL............. Enamel (ROG)
enl .... Enamel (VRA)
ENL............. Enamel
En L .... Engineer Lieutenant [Navy British] (DMA)
ENL............. Enlarge [or Enlargement]
enl .... Enlarged (WDMC)
ENL............. Enlistment (AFM)
ENL............. Equivalent Noise Level
ENL............. Erythema Nodosum Leproticum [Medicine]
ENL............. Eye Notochord Length [Fish anatomy]
En L Cr....... Engineer Lieutenant-Commander [Navy British] (DMA)
ENLDEVDISTSYS... Enlisted Development and Distribution Support System [Military] (DNAB)
ENLF.......... Eelam National Liberation Front [Sri Lanka]
ENLG .... Enable Level Group (MHDB)
ENLG .... Enlarge (MSA)
ENLGD........ Enlarged
EnlghtS....... Enlighten Software Solutions [Associated Press] (SAG)
enlgmnt...... Enlargement (VRA)
ENLI........... Lista [Norway ICAO location identifier] (ICLI)
ENLK.......... Leknes [Norway ICAO location identifier] (ICLI)
ENLN.......... Eastern Nigeria Legal Notice [A publication] (DLA)
ENLPERMGTCEN... Enlisted Personnel Management Center [Navy] (DNAB)
ENLR .... Eastern Nigeria Law Reports [1956-60] [A publication] (DLA)
ENLRG........ Enlarge
ENM............ Emmonak, AK [Location identifier FAA] (FAAL)
ENM............ Endogenous Morphine [or Endomorphin] [Also, ENDORPHIN Brain peptide]
enm .... English, Middle [MARC language code Library of Congress] (LCCP)
EN(M) .... Enrolled Nurse (Mental) [British] (DBQ)
ENMCC .... Expanded National Military Command Center (MCD)
ENMD .... EntreMed, Inc. [NASDAQ symbol] (SAG)
ENMG .... Electroneuromyographic (PDAA)
EN(MH)....... Enrolled Nurse (Mental Handicap) [British] (DBQ)
ENMH .... Mehamn [Norway ICAO location identifier] (ICLI)
ENMI........... Olso [Norway ICAO location identifier] (ICLI)
ENML.......... End Mill
ENML.......... Molde/Aro [Norway ICAO location identifier] (ICLI)
ENMLD........ Enameled
ENMLNG...... Enameling
ENMOC........ EL Nino-Southern Moniotoring Center [Marine science] (OSRA)
ENMOD....... Environmental Modification
ENMOD....... Environment Modification Convention (EERA)
ENMR .... Executive for National Military Representatives [Supreme Headquarters Allied Powers Europe] (NATG)
ENMS.......... European Nuclear Medical Society (EAIO)
ENMS.......... Mosjoen/Kjaerstad [Norway ICAO location identifier] (ICLI)
ENMU .... Eastern New Mexico University
Enn .... Enneades [of Plotinus] [Classical studies] (OCD)
ENN .... Ennisteel Corp. [Toronto Stock Exchange symbol]
ENN .... Expand Nonstop Network (MHDB)
ENN .... Nenana, AK [Location identifier FAA] (FAAL)
ENNA .... Banak [Norway ICAO location identifier] (ICLI)
ENNG .... Ethyl-nitronitrosoguanidine [Organic chemistry]
ENNI .... EnergyNorth, Inc. [NASDAQ symbol] (NQ)
ENNK .... Endo-Atmospheric Non-Nuclear Kill (MCD)
ENNK .... Narvik/Framnes [Norway ICAO location identifier] (ICLI)
ENNKAS ...... Endoatmospheric Non-Nuclear Kill Applications Study [DoD]
ENNKCIS..... Endoatmospheric Non-Nuclear Kill Controls Implementation Study [DoD]
ENNM .... Namsos [Norway ICAO location identifier] (ICLI)
ENNO .... Notodden [Norway ICAO location identifier] (ICLI)
ENNS .... Early Neonatal Neurobehavior Scale (MEDA)
ENNS .... Equity Inns [NASDAQ symbol] (SAG)
ENO .... English National Opera
ENO .... Enolase [An enzyme]
ENO .... Enough
ENO .... Extraordinary Nuclear Occurrence (NRCH)
ENO .... Kenton, DE [Location identifier FAA] (FAAL)
e-no-- .... Norway [MARC geographic area code Library of Congress] (LCCP)
ENOA .... Ellington Navigators/Observers Association (EA)
ENOA .... Extended Non-Owned Automobile Coverage [Insurance]
ENOB .... Bodo Oceanic [Norway ICAO location identifier] (ICLI)
ENOC .... Association of the European National Olympic Committees [See also ACNOE] [Brussels, Belgium] (EAIO)
ENOCC .... Emergency Network Operations Control Center (MCD)
ENOD .... Employee Not on Duty [FRA] (TAG)
ENOL .... Enology
ENOL .... Orland [Norway ICAO location identifier] (ICLI)
ENORS .... Engine Not Operationally Ready - Supply [Air Force]
ENOS .... Oslo [Norway ICAO location identifier] (ICLI)
ENOV .... Orsta-Volda/Hovden [Norway ICAO location identifier] (ICLI)
ENOWD........ Europaeisches Netzwerk fuer den Ost-West-Dialog [European Network for East-West Dialogue - ENEWD] (EAIO)
ENP............. Electroless Nickel Plating
ENP............. Endotoxin Neutralizing Protein [Biochemistry]
ENP............. Energy Programs [Database] [Energy, Mines, and Resources, Canada] [Information service or system] (CRD)

ENP............. Enerplus Resources Corp. [Toronto Stock Exchange symbol]
ENP............. Enron Liquids Pipeline L.P. [NYSE symbol] (TTSB)
ENP............. Enron Liquids Pipeline Ltd. [NYSE symbol] (SPSG)
ENP............. Estimated [Time At or Over] Next Position (BARN)
ENP............. Ethyl-P-Nitrophenylthiobenzene Phosphate [Organic chemistry] (DAVI)
ENP............. European Neuroscience Programme [Defunct France] (EAIO)
ENP............. Exceptional Needs Payment [Legal term] (DLA)
ENP............. Extractable Nucleoprotein [Biochemistry]
ENPC .... Ecole Nationale des Ponts et Chaussees [Graduate School of International Business] [France]
ENPCAF ...... Ethyl N-Phenylcarbamoylazoformate [Organic chemistry]
ENPEP .... Energy and Power Evaluation Program [Computer science]
ENPOCON..... Environmental Pollution Control (PDAA)
ENPT........... En Pointe Tech [NASDAQ symbol] (TTSB)
ENQ............ American Media, Inc. [Formerly, Enquirer/Star Group] [NYSE symbol] (SAG)
ENQ............ Amer Media CI'A' [NYSE symbol] (TTSB)
ENQ? .... Are You There? [Computer science] (DOM)
ENQ............ Enquiry [Transmission control character]
ENQWS........ Amer Media Wrrt [NYSE symbol] (TTSB)
ENR .... Effort Net Return [Motivation model] [Business term]
ENR .... Emissora Nacional de Radiodifusao [Radio network] [Portugal]
ENR .... Energy and Natural Resources (DLA)
ENR .... Enertec Corp. [Toronto Stock Exchange symbol]
ENR .... Engineering Narrative Report [Defense Supply Agency]
ENR .... Enoyl Reductase [An enzyme]
ENR .... Enrollment (ROG)
ENR .... En Route (NVT)
ENR .... Ensor Air [Czechoslovakia] [ICAO designator] (FAAC)
ENR .... Eosinophilic Nonallergic Rhinitis [Medicine]
ENR .... Epoxidized Natural Rubber
ENR .... Equivalent Noise Ratio [or Resistance] [Electronics] (IEEE)
ENR .... Excess Noise Ratio
E/NR .... Exercised/Not Repositioned [Sports medicine]
ENR .... Extrathyroidal Neck Radioactivity [Radiology]
ENRA .... Mo I Rana/Rossvoll [Norway ICAO location identifier] (ICLI)
ENRAT .... En Route, Arrival at _____ [Military] (NVT)
ENRC .... European Nuclear Research Centre (NUCP)
EnrCR .... Enron Capital Resources Ltd. [Associated Press] (SAG)
ENREP .... Directory of Environmental Research Projects in the European Communities [EURONET] [Information service or system]
ENRFOSCOMD... En Route This Station from Oversea Command
Enrgn .... Energen Corp. [Associated Press] (SAG)
EnrGP .... Enron Global Power & Pipeline [Associated Press] (SAG)
ENRGZ .... Energize (MSA)
ENRL .... Enrollment (AABC)
EnrLLC .... Enron Capital Corp. LLC [Associated Press] (SAG)
ENRM .... Rorvik/Ryum [Norway ICAO location identifier] (ICLI)
Enrn .... Enron Corp. [Associated Press] (SAG)
EnrnC .... Enron Capital Trust I TOPRS [Associated Press] (SAG)
ENRO .... Roros [Norway ICAO location identifier] (ICLI)
Enron98 .... Enron Corp. [Associated Press] (SAG)
Enron .... Enron Corp. [Associated Press] (SAG)
EnronLq ...... Enron Liquids Pipeline [Associated Press] (SAG)
ENRPAE ...... En Route to/from Public Affairs Event [Military] (NVT)
ENRS .... Rost [Norway ICAO location identifier] (ICLI)
ENRSVC....... En Route and Provide Service to Units Indicated [Military] (NVT)
ENRT .... En Route
ENRY .... Rygge [Norway ICAO location identifier] (ICLI)
ENRZ .... Enhanced Non-Return to Zero (IAA)
ENS............. Electron News Service [Evans Economics, Inc.] [Information service or system] (CRD)
ENS............. Emergency Notification System [Nuclear energy] (NRCH)
ENS............. Emergency Notification System
ENS............. Energy Nova Scotia [Database] [Nova Scotia Research Foundation Corp.] [Information service or system] (CRD)
ENS............. Enschede [Netherlands] [Airport symbol] (OAG)
ens.............. Ensemble [Group] [French]
ENS............. ENSERCH Corp. [NYSE symbol] (TTSB)
ENS............. Enserch Exploration [NYSE symbol Toronto Stock Exchange symbol]
ENS............. Ensign (AABC)
ENS............. Ensign
ENS............. Entergy Services, Inc. [ICAO designator] (FAAC)
ENS............. Enteric Nervous System [Neurobiology]
ENS............. Enterprise Naming Service [Banyan Systems, Inc.] [Telecommunications] (PCM)
ENS............. Enterprise Network Services [Banyan] [Computer science]
ENS............. Ethnic, Nationalist, and Separatist [Conflicts or wars]
ENS............. Ethylnorsuprarenin [Also, ENE] [Pharmacology]
ENS............. Europaeische Kernenergie-Gesellschaft [European Nuclear Society - ENS] (EAIO)
ENS............. European Nervous System
ENS............. European Network for Science [Marine science] (OSRA)
ENS............. European Neurological Society [Switzerland]
ENS............. European Nuclear Society (NUCP)
ENS............. Experimental Navigation Ship
ENS............. Extended Network Services (MHDB)
ENS............. Extended Nylon Shaft
ENSA .... Entertainments National Service Association [Facetiously translated as "Every Night Something Awful"] [Military British]
ENSA .... Environmental Services of America, Inc. [NASDAQ symbol] (SAG)
ensb............ Ensemble (VRA)
ENSB .... Equivalent Noise Sideband
ENSB .... Svalbard/Longyear [Norway ICAO location identifier] (ICLI)

Ensc............	Enserch Corp. [*Associated Press*] (SAG)
ENSCA.........	European Natural Sausage Casings Association (EA)
ENSCE.........	Enemy Situation Correlation Element [*DoD*]
ENSCO.........	Energy Service Co. [*Associated Press*] (SAG)
Enscor.........	Enscor, Inc. [*Associated Press*] (SAG)
ENSD	Sandane/Anda [*Norway ICAO location identifier*] (ICLI)
ENSDF.........	Evaluated Nuclear Structure Data File [*National Nuclear Data Center*] [*Information service or system*]
ENSEC.........	European Nuclear Steelmaking Club [*British*] (NUCP)
EnsExp.........	Enserch Exploration, Inc. [*Associated Press*] (SAG)
ENSF...........	Statfjord-A [*Norway ICAO location identifier*] (ICLI)
ENSG	Ensuing (ROG)
ENSG	Sogndal/Haukasen [*Norway ICAO location identifier*] (ICLI)
ENSH	Svolvaer/Helle [*Norway ICAO location identifier*] (ICLI)
ENSI	Environment and School Initiatives Project (EERA)
ENSI	Equivalent Noise Sideband Input (MCD)
ENSIC.........	Environmental Sanitation Information Center [*Asian Institute of Technology*] [*Thailand*] [*Information service or system*] (IID)
ENSIM	Environmental Simulator (IAA)
ENSIT..........	Enemy Situation (MCD)
ENSK	Stokmarknes/Skagen [*Norway ICAO location identifier*] (ICLI)
En SL	Engineer Sub-Lieutenant [*Navy British*] (DMA)
ENSN	Skien/Geiteryggen [*Norway ICAO location identifier*] (ICLI)
ENSO	El Nino and Southern Oscillation [*Coupled oceanic-atmospheric change*]
ENSO	Envirosource, Inc. [*NASDAQ symbol*] (SAG)
ENSO	Stord [*Norway ICAO location identifier*] (ICLI)
ENSP	Engineering Specification [*Air Force*]
ENSPrE.......	ENSERCH Dep Adj cm E Pfd [*NYSE symbol*] (TTSB)
ENSPrF.......	ENSERCH Dep Adj cm F Pfd [*NYSE symbol*] (TTSB)
ENSR	Sorkjosen [*Norway ICAO location identifier*] (ICLI)
Ensrch	Enserch Corp. [*Associated Press*] (SAG)
ENSS	European Navigation Satellite System
ENSS	Exterior Nodal Switching Subsystem [*Computer science*] (ACRL)
ENSS	Svartnes [*Norway ICAO location identifier*] (ICLI)
ENST..........	Sandnessjoen/Stokka [*Norway ICAO location identifier*] (ICLI)
ENSTINET	Egyptian National Scientific and Technical Information Network
ENSURE......	Engineering Surveillance Report (MCD)
ENSURE......	Expedited Non-Standard Urgent Requirements for Equipment [*Army*] (AABC)
ENSV	Stavanger [*Norway ICAO location identifier*] (ICLI)
ENSY	EnSys Environmental Products [*NASDAQ symbol*] (TTSB)
ENSY	EnSys Environmental Products, Inc. [*NASDAQ symbol*] (SAG)
ENSYN	Electromagnetic Environment Synthesizer (NVT)
ENSYN	Environmental Synthesizer [*Navy*]
ENSYS	Electromagnetic Environment Synthesizer (DNAB)
EnSys..........	EnSys Environmental Products, Inc. [*Associated Press*] (SAG)
Ent	Coke's Book of Entries [*1614*] [*England*] [*A publication*] (DLA)
ENT	Ears, Nose, and Throat
ENT	Electrical Nonmetallic Tubing
ENT	Emergency Negative Thrust
ENT	Eniwetok [*Marshall Islands*] [*Airport symbol*] (OAG)
ENT	Entebbe [*Uganda*] [*Seismograph station code, US Geological Survey Closed*] (SEIS)
ENT.............	Enter (MUGU)
ENT.............	Entering [*FBI standardized term*]
Ent	Enterprise
ENT.............	Entertainment
Ent	Entire [*Philately*]
ENT.............	Entity
ENT.............	Entomology
ENT.............	Entrada
ENT.............	Entrance (ROG)
ent	Entrance [*A stage direction*] (WDMC)
ENT.............	Entry (NASA)
ENT.............	Entry
ENT.............	Environmental Test (MCD)
ENT.............	Equivalent Noise Temperature [*Electronics*]
ENT.............	Exhaust Nozzle Temperature (KSC)
ENT.............	Holmstrom Flyg AB [*Sweden ICAO designator*] (FAAC)
ENT.............	Otorhinolaryngology [*Medicine*] (DAVI)
Ent	Rastell's Entries [*A publication*] (DLA)
enta	Ethylenediaminetetraacetate [*Also, EDETATE, EDTA*] [*Organic chemistry*]
ENTAC	Engin Teleguide Anti-Char [*Antitank Missile*] [*French*]
ENTAC	Entrance National Agency Check [*Military*] (AABC)
Ent & Sports Law...	Entertainment and Sports Lawyer [*A publication*] (DLA)
EntArk.........	Entergy Arkansas, Inc. Capital I [*Associated Press*] (SAG)
entbl	Entablature (VRA)
ENTC	Engine Negative Torque Control (MSA)
ENTC	Tromso/Langnes [*Norway ICAO location identifier*] (ICLI)
ENTCE.........	Entrance (ROG)
ENTD	Entered
ENTELEC....	Energy Telecommunications and Electrical Association (EA)
ENTER	Enterprise (DLA)
Entergy........	Entergy Corp. [*Associated Press*] (SAG)
ENTERPRISE...	Evaluating New Technologies for Roads Program Initiatives in Safety and Efficiency [*FHWA*] (TAG)
Enters	Enterprises (AAGC)
Entertainment LJ...	Entertainment Law Journal [*A publication*] (DLA)
EntFedB.......	Enterprise Federal Bancorp, Inc. [*Associated Press*] (SAG)
ENTG	Entering (ROG)
ENTG	Euro-NATO Training Group [*An association*] (EAIO)
EntGlf..........	Entergy Gulf States [*Associated Press*] (SAG)

ENTJ..........	Extrovert, Intuitive, a Thinker, and Judger [*Keirsey Temperament Test Result*] [*Psychology*]
ENTL..........	Entitle (AABC)
EntLA.........	Entergy Louisiana, Inc. [*Associated Press*] (SAG)
EntLA.........	Entergy Louisiana, Inc. Capital I [*Associated Press*] (SAG)
ENTNAC.......	Entrance National Agency Check [*Military*] (NVT)
ENTO	Entomology (AABC)
ENTO	Torp [*Norway ICAO location identifier*] (ICLI)
EntOil.........	Enterprise Oil Co. [*Associated Press*] (SAG)
ENTOM	Entomology
ENTOMOL	Entomologic
ENTPROL.....	(Ethylenedinitrilo)tetrakis(propanol) [*Organic chemistry*]
ENTPS........	Expanded Near-Term Prepositioning Ships
ENTR	Eneteractive, Inc. [*NASDAQ symbol*] (SAG)
ENTR	Entire
ENTR	Entrance [*Maps and charts*] (MSA)
entr............	Entrance (VRA)
ENTR	Trondheim [*Norway ICAO location identifier*] (ICLI)
ENTRACE	Entrance (ROG)
Entract	Eneteractive, Inc. [*Associated Press*] (SAG)
Entractv	Eneteractive, Inc. [*Associated Press*] (SAG)
EntreMd......	EntreMed, Inc. [*Associated Press*] (SAG)
Entries Antient...	Rastell's Old Entries [*So cited in Rolle Abridgment*] [*A publication*] (DLA)
ENTRPRNR...	Entrepreneur
ENTRPRS....	Enterprise
ENTRPT	Entrepot
EntrSys	Enterprise Systems, Inc. [*Associated Press*] (SAG)
ENTRTN	Entertainment
ENTRW	Enteractive Inc. Wrrt [*NASDAQ symbol*] (TTSB)
ENT/SAT	Entertainment Satellite [*Proposed*] (MCD)
Entsch........	Entscheidung [*Decision, Judgment*] [*German*] (ILCA)
ENTSPR	Entsprechend [*Corresponding*] [*German*]
Ent Sta Hall...	Entered at Stationers' Hall [*British*] (BARN)
EnTUSA.......	Environmental Tech USA, Inc. [*Associated Press*] (SAG)
Ent W	Entertainment Weekly [*A publication*] (BRI)
Entw..........	Entwurf [*Draft*] [*German*] (ILCA)
EN TX	Enable Transmit [*Status activation code*] (NITA)
ENU	Enugu [*Nigeria*] [*Airport symbol*] (OAG)
ENU	Essential/Nonessential/Update [*Telecommunications*] (TEL)
ENU	Ethylnitrosourea [*Organic chemistry*]
ENUM	Enumeration (MSA)
ENUN	Enunciation (ROG)
En Users Rep...	Energy Users Report [*Commerce Clearing House*] [*A publication*] (DLA)
ENUWAR......	Environmental Consequences of Nuclear War [*International Council of Scientific Unions*]
ENV.............	CET Environmental Services [*AMEX symbol*] (SAG)
ENV.............	CET Environmental Svcs [*AMEX symbol*] (TTSB)
env.............	Envelope [*Refers to the envelope that surrounds cells*] [*Biochemistry*] (DAVI)
ENV.............	Envelope (KSC)
ENV.............	Envelope
ENV.............	Environ [*About*] [*French*]
Env.............	Environment [*A publication*] (BRI)
ENV.............	Environmental Safety Systems, Inc. [*Toronto Stock Exchange symbol*]
ENV.............	Envoy (ROG)
ENV.............	Equivalent Noise Voltage
ENV.............	Erdbeernekrosevirus
ENV.............	Europeene Norme Vorausgabe [*European Prestandard*] (OSI)
ENV.............	Wendover, UT [*Location identifier FAA*] (FAAL)
ENVA	Trondheim/Vaernes [*Norway ICAO location identifier*] (ICLI)
ENVANAL.....	Environmental Analysis [*Program*]
ENVD	Vadso [*Norway ICAO location identifier*] (ICLI)
ENVEC	Environmental Economics (EERA)
EnvEle	Environmental Elements Corp. [*Associated Press*] (SAG)
ENVEX	Environmental Extremists
Env Extr	Envoy Extraordinary (DLA)
ENVG	Efferent Vein from Nephridial Gland [*Anatomy*]
ENVG	Envirogen, Inc. [*NASDAQ symbol*] (SAG)
ENVGEN	Environment Generator [*Computer software*]
ENVGW	Envirogen Inc. Wrrt [*NASDAQ symbol*] (TTSB)
ENVI...........	Envirotest Systems'A' [*NASDAQ symbol*] (TTSB)
ENVI...........	Envirotest Systems, Inc. [*NASDAQ symbol*] (SAG)
ENVIR	Environment (MSA)
envir..........	Environment (VRA)
ENVIR	Environment
EnvirIn	Envirodyne Industries, Inc. [*Associated Press*] (SAG)
envirl..........	Environmental (DD)
ENVIRN	Environment
Envir News...	Environment News [*A publication*]
ENVIROBIB...	Environmental Periodicals Bibliography [*Environmental Studies Institute*] [*Information service or system*]
ENVIROFATE...	Environmental Fate [*Environmental Protection Agency Information service or system*] (CRD)
ENVIROLINE...	Environment Information On-Line [*Database*] [*Environment Information Center, Inc. New York, NY*]
ENVIRON	Environmental
ENVIRON	Environmental
ENVIRON	Environmental Information Retrieval On-Line [*Environmental Protection Agency*]
Envirotst	Envirotest Systems, Inc. [*Associated Press*] (SAG)
Envir Rep.....	Environment Reporter [*Bureau of National Affairs*] [*A publication*] (DLA)

ENVM	Environment Model
Envmt	Envirometrics Inc. [*Associated Press*] (SAG)
ENVMT	Environment (AFM)
ENVMTL	Environmental
Envmtrc	Envirometrics, Inc. [*Associated Press*] (SAG)
ENVN	Tromso [*Norway ICAO location identifier*] (ICLI)
Envoy	Envoy Corp. [*Associated Press*] (SAG)
ENVPREDRSCHF	Environmental Prediction Research Facility [*Monterey, CA*] [*Navy*]
ENVPREDRSCHFAC	Naval Environmental Prediction Research Facility [*Marine science*] (MSC)
Envpsych	Environmental Psychology [*City University of New York*] [*Defunct Information service or system*] (CRD)
EnvPwr	Environmental Power Corp. [*Associated Press*] (SAG)
ENVR	Envirocare Facility [*Clive, UT*] (GAAI)
ENVR	Environmental (KSC)
ENVR	Environmental Tech USA [*NASDAQ symbol*] (TTSB)
ENVR	Environmental Tech USA Inc. [*NASDAQ symbol*] (SAG)
Envrg	Envirogen, Inc. [*Associated Press*] (SAG)
Envrgen	Envirogen, Inc. [*Associated Press*] (SAG)
ENVRNMTL	Environmental
EnvrOne	Environment One Corp. [*Associated Press*] (SAG)
EnvrTc	Environmental Tectonics Corp. [*Associated Press*] (SAG)
EnvrTch	Environmental Technology Corp. [*Associated Press*] (SAG)
ENVRW	Environmental Tech USA Wrrt [*NASDAQ symbol*] (TTSB)
Envsrc	Envirosource, Inc. [*Associated Press*] (SAG)
EnvSvc	Environmental Services of America, Inc. [*Associated Press*] (SAG)
ENV-SYS	Environmental System (MCD)
ENVT	Environmental
EnvT	Environmental Tech USA, Inc. [*Associated Press*] (SAG)
ENVT	Environmental Tectonics Corp. (MHDW)
EnvTcCp	Environmental Technology Corp. [*Associated Press*] (SAG)
Envtl Affairs	Environmental Affairs [*A publication*] (DLA)
Envtl F	Environmental Forum [*A publication*] (DLA)
Envtl L Rev	Environmental Law Review [*A publication*] (DLA)
Envtl L Rptr	Environmental Law Reporter [*A publication*] (DLA)
Envtl Pol'y & L	Environmental Policy and Law [*A publication*] (DLA)
Env't Reg Handbook	Environment Regulation Handbook [*A publication*] (DLA)
Env't Rep (BNA)	Environment Reporter (Bureau of National Affairs) [*A publication*] (DLA)
ENVV	Bergen [*Norway ICAO location identifier*] (ICLI)
EnvWste	Enviropur Waste Refining & Technology, Inc. [*Associated Press*] (SAG)
ENVY	Envoy Corp. [*NASDAQ symbol*] (SPSG)
ENVY	Vaeroy [*Norway ICAO location identifier*] (ICLI)
ENW	Effects of Nuclear Weapons [*AEC-DoD book*]
ENW	English the New Way [*Education*] (AEBS)
ENW	Ethnic NewsWatch [*Softline Information Co.*]
ENW	Kenosha, WI [*Location identifier FAA*] (FAAL)
ENWGS	Enhanced Naval Warfare Gaming System (GFGA)
ENX	Enexco International Ltd. [*Vancouver Stock Exchange symbol*]
ENY	Ashland, WI [*Location identifier FAA*] (FAAL)
ENY	European Original New York Seltzer Ltd. [*Vancouver Stock Exchange symbol*]
ENY	Yanan [*China*] [*Airport symbol*] (OAG)
ENZ	Enscor, Inc. [*Toronto Stock Exchange symbol*]
ENZ	Enzo Biochem [*AMEX symbol*] (TTSB)
ENZ	Enzo Biochem, Inc. [*AMEX symbol*] (SPSG)
enz	Enzymatic [*or Enzyme*] (MAE)
ENZ	New Zealand Air Services Ltd. [*ICAO designator*] (FAAC)
ENZ	Nogales, AZ [*Location identifier FAA*] (FAAL)
ENZN	Enzon, Inc. [*NASDAQ symbol*] (NQ)
ENZN	ENZON Inc. [*NASDAQ symbol*] (TTSB)
ENZO	Ethernet Needing Zero Overhead
EnzoBi	Enzo Biochem, Inc. [*Associated Press*] (SAG)
Enzon	Enzon, Inc. [*Associated Press*] (SAG)
ENZV	Stavanger/Sola [*Norway ICAO location identifier*] (ICLI)
ENZY	Enzymatics, Inc. [*NASDAQ symbol*] (SAG)
Enzymat	Enzymatics, Inc. [*Associated Press*] (SAG)
EO	Aeroamerica [*ICAO designator*] (AD)
EO	Aero America, Inc. [*ICAO designator*] (ICDA)
EO	Air Nordic Sweden [*ICAO designator*] (AD)
eo----	Danube River and Basin [*MARC geographic area code Library of Congress*] (LCCP)
EO	Earth Observation
EO	Earth Orbit [*NASA*] (KSC)
EO	Eastern Orthodox
EO	Easter Offerings [*to a church*]
E/O	East Of [*In outdoor advertising*] (WDMC)
E/O	Edges Opened [*Publishing*] (DGA)
EO	Education Officer [*Military*]
EO	Education Otherwise [*British*] [*An association*] (DBA)
EO	Ego Overcontrol [*Psychology*]
EO	Elbow Orthosis [*Medicine*]
EO	Electoral Office [*Australia*]
E₀	Electric Affinity [*Symbol*] [*Physics*] (DAVI)
E/O	Electrical-to-Optical (ACRL)
EO	Electrolytic Oxidation
EO	Electro-Optical
EO	Electro Optical
EO	Elementary Operation (IAA)
EO	Elliptical Orbit [*Aerospace*] (AAG)
EO	Emergency Officer [*Nuclear energy*] (NRCH)
EO	Employers Organization (DCTA)
EO	Employment Officer

EO	Emulsion Out [*Photography*] (WDMC)
EO	Enable Output [*Davey Air Services*] [*Computer science*] (MHDB)
EO	End Office [*Telecommunications*] (TEL)
EO	End of Operation [*Computer science*] (IAA)
E/O	Engineering/Operations [*NASA*] (NASA)
EO	Engineering Order
EO	Engineering Order
EO	Engineer Officer [*Navy British*]
EO	Engine Oil
EO	Engine Out (NASA)
EO	English [*Communion*] Office [*Episcopalian*]
EO	Entertainments Officer [*Military British*]
E/O	Eocene/Oligocene [*Geological boundary zone*]
eo	Eosinophil [*Hematology*]
Eo	Eotvos Number [*Fluid mechanics*]
EO	Equal Opportunity
EO	Equal Opportunity Program Office [*Kennedy Space Center Directorate*] [*NASA*] (NASA)
EO	Equipment Operator [*Navy rating*]
EO	Equivalent Orifice (IAA)
EO	Errors and Omissions [*Insurance*]
EO	Ethylene Oxide [*Organic chemistry*]
EO	Even-Odd
EO	Examining Officer (ROG)
EO	Excise Officer (ROG)
EO	Exclusive Or [*Gates*] [*Computer science*]
EO	Executive Office [*or Officer*]
EO	Executive Order [*Rule or regulation having the force of law, issued by the President with congressional authorization*]
EO	Exempt Organization [*IRS*]
EO	Exhaust Opens [*Valve position*]
EO	Ex Officio [*By Virtue of Office*] [*Latin*]
EO	Expected [*Patient*] Outcome [*Medicine*] (DAVI)
EO	Expected Output
EO	Experimental Officer [*Also, ExO, XO*] [*Ministry of Agriculture, Fisheries, and Food*] [*British*]
EO	Explosive Ordnance [*Military*] (AFM)
EO	Export Office (ROG)
EO	Extended Operations
EO	Eye Balls Out (SAA)
EO	Eyes Open [*Ataxia*]
EO1	Edge Oya [*Norway*] [*Seismograph station code, US Geological Survey*] (SEIS)
EO1	Equipment Operator, First Class [*Navy rating*]
EO2	Equipment Operator, Second Class [*Navy rating*]
EO3	Equipment Operator, Third Class [*Navy rating*]
EOA	Early Operational Assessment [*Military*]
EOA	Economic Opportunity Act [*1964*] [*Repealed, 1974*]
EOA	Effective On or About [*Business term*]
EOA	Electro-Optical Assembly (MCD)
EOA	Electro-Optics Augmentation
EOA	End of Address [*Computer science*]
EOA	Energy Office [*Department of Agriculture*] (OICC)
EOA	English Orienteering Association (BI)
EOA	Environmental Protection Agency, Region VIII Library, Denver, CO [*OCLC symbol*] (OCLC)
EOA	Epithelioma [*Medicine*]
EOA	Equal Opportunity Advisor [*DoD*]
EOA	Erosive Osteoarthritis [*Medicine*]
EOA	Esophageal Obturator Airway [*Medicine*] (DMAA)
EOA	Essential Oil Association of the United States (EA)
EOA	Ethics Officer Association
EOA	Examination, Opinion, and Advice [*Medicine*]
EOA	Exercise Operating Area (NVT)
EOAD	Educational Organizations and Agencies Directory [*A publication*]
EOAE	Earth-Orientated Applications Experiment (MCD)
EO & SP	Economic Order and Stockage Policy (AFIT)
EOAP	Earth Observations Aircraft Program [*NASA*]
EOAP	Equipment Oil Analysis Program [*Air Force*] (MCD)
EOAR	European Office of Aerospace Research
EOARD	European Office of Aerospace Research and Development
EOAU	Electro-Optical Alignment Unit (AAG)
EOB	Eastern Orchestral Board [*British*] [*An association*] (DBA)
EOB	Educational Opportunity Bank
EOB	Electronic Order of Battle (MSA)
EOB	Electro-Optical Bench [*Army*]
EOB	Emergency Observation Bed [*Medicine*]
EOB	Encyclopedia of Business [*A publication*]
EOB	End of Battle [*Time*] (MCD)
EOB	End of Block [*Computer science*]
EOB	End of Bombardment
EOB	End of Buffer (MCD)
EOB	End of Burn (MCD)
EOB	End of Bus (ACRL)
EOB	Enemy Order of Battle (AFM)
EOB	Engineering and Operations Building [*NASA*]
EOB	Environmental Protection Agency, NEIC Library, Denver, CO [*OCLC symbol*] (OCLC)
EOB	Equal Opportunity Board [*Victoria, Australia*]
EOB	Estimated on Berth
EOB	Executive Office Building [*Washington, DC*]
EOB	Expense Operating Budget (AFM)
EOB	Explanation of Benefits
EOBC	Edmonton Oilers Booster Club [*Defunct*] (EA)
EOBCC	Electronic Order of Battle Control Center

EOBCC	End of Battle Control Center (MCD)
EOBP	Explanation of Benefit Payment [*Insurance*]
EOBT	Estimated Off-Block Time [*ICAO designator*] (FAAC)
EOC	Eastern Oregon College
EOC	Edge of Cutter (MSA)
EOC	Edsel Owner's Club (EA)
EOC	Educational Opportunity Center [*Higher Education Act*]
EOC	Electronic Operations Center [*Military*]
EOC	Elementary Operated Control (PDAA)
EOC	Elva Owners Club [*Worthing, West Sussex, England*] (EAIO)
EOC	Embedded Operations Channel [*Telecommunications*] (ACRL)
EOC	Emergency Operating Center [*Civil Defense*]
EOC	Emergency Operational Capability (AAG)
EOC	Emergency Operations Center [*Military*]
EOC	Emissions Opportunity Cost
EOC	Empresa Nacional de Electridad de Chile [*NYSE symbol*] (SAG)
EOC	Empresa Nac'l De Electric ADS [*NYSE symbol*] (TTSB)
EOC	End of Card [*Computer science*] (CMD)
EOC	End of Construction (NG)
EOC	End of Contract (AAG)
EOC	End of Conversation (ECII)
EOC	End of Conversion
EOC	End of Course (AFM)
EOC	End of Cycle (NRCH)
EOC	Enemy Oil Committee [*US*]
EOC	Engineered Operating Cycle
EOC	Engineering Operations Control (MCD)
EOC	Engine Order Capability (NASA)
EOC	Engine Out Capability (MCD)
Eoc	Eocene [*Second epoch of the Cenozoic Era*] (BARN)
EOC	Equal Opportunities Commission [*British*]
EOC	Equal Opportunity Cases [*Australia A publication*]
EOC	Equal Opportunity Commission [*Western Australia*]
EOC	Equal Opportunity Compliance (SSD)
EOC	Equipment Operational Control
EOC	Erbium Oxide Crystal
EOC	Ercoupe Owners Club (EA)
EOC	Error of Closure
EOC	Executive Officers Council of the National Association of Real Estate Boards (EA)
EOC	Experimental Operations Center
EOC	Explosive Ordnance Components [*Military*] (MCD)
EOC	Extended Overhaul Cycle (NVT)
EOCA	Constructionman Apprentice, Equipment Operator, Striker [*Navy rating*]
EOCA	Early Onset Cerebellar Ataxia [*Medicine*]
EOCA	Electronic Office Centers of America, Inc. [*Schaumburg, IL*] [*Telecommunications*] (TSSD)
EOC and WPA	Editors Organizing Committee and Writers' and Publishers' Alliance for Disarmament (EA)
EOCC	Emergency Operations Control Center [*Environmental Protection Agency*]
EOCC	Engineering Operational Casualty Control (NVT)
EOCCD	European Organisation for the Control of Circulatory Diseases (PDAA)
EOCCM	Electro-Optical Counter-Countermeasures (MCD)
EOCCT	End-of-Course Comprehensive Testing
EOCD	Error, Omission, Clarification, or Deficiency (MCD)
EOCI	Electric Overhead Crane Institute [*Later, Crane Manufacturers Association of America*] (EA)
EOCM	Electro-Optical Countermeasures (MCD)
EOCM	Equipment Operator, Master Chief [*Navy rating*]
EOCN	Constructionman, Equipment Operator, Striker [*Navy rating*]
EOCP	Emergency Out of Commission for Parts
EOCP	Engine Out of Commission for Parts
EOCR	Experimental Organic Cooled Reactor
EOCS	Equipment Operator, Senior Chief [*Navy rating*]
EOCT	End-of-Cycle Test [*Army training*] (INF)
EO CT	Eosinophil Count [*Hematology*] (DAVI)
EOCY	End of Calendar Year
EOD	Date of Entering Office
EOD	Earth Observations Division [*Johnson Space Center*] [*NASA*]
EOD	Economic Objectives Department [*Ministry of Economic Warfare*] [*British World War II*]
EOD	Education Outcomes Division [*Washington, DC Department of Education*] (GRD)
EOD	Electric Organ Discharge [*Electrophysiology*]
EOD	Electro-Optic Display
EOD	Elements of Data (MSA)
EOD	Emergency Ordnance Disposal
EOD	Employee on Duty [*FRA*] (TAG)
EOD	End of Data [*Computer science*]
EOD	End of Day (AFM)
EOD	End of Dialing [*Telecommunications*] (TEL)
EOD	Engineering Operating Directives (MCD)
EOD	Engineering Operations Division [*Environmental Protection Agency*] (GFGA)
EOD	Entered on Duty (SAA)
EOD	Entering Office Date (DNAB)
EOD	Entry on Duty (MUGU)
EOD	Established Onset of Disability (OICC)
EOD	Estimated on Dock (KSC)
EOD	Estimated Operational Date (CINC)
EOD	Every Other Day
EOD	Expected Occupancy Date
EOD	Explosive Ordinance Disposal [*Military*] (VNW)
EOD	Explosive Ordnance Detachment [*Army*] (RDA)
EOD	Explosive Ordnance Device [*Military*] (MCD)
EOD	Explosive Ordnance Disposal [*Military*]
EODAD	End of Data Address [*Computer science*] (HGAA)
EODAP	Earth and Ocean Dynamic Applications Program [*NASA*] (PDAA)
EODARS	Electro-Optical Direction and Ranging System (IAA)
EODB	End of Data Block [*Computer science*] (MCD)
EODB	Explosive Ordnance Disposal Bulletin [*Military*]
EODBAD	Explosive Ordnance Disposal Badge [*Military decoration*] (GFGA)
EODC	Earth Observation Data Centre (EERA)
EODC	Explosive Ordnance Disposal Center [*DoD*]
EODC	Explosive Ordnance Disposal Control [*Military*] (AABC)
EODCC	EOD Control Center
EODD	Electro-Optic Digital Deflector (IEEE)
EODE	Explosive Ordnance Disposal Evaluator
EODF	Explosive Ordnance Disposal Flight [*Military*]
EODG	Explosive Ordnance Disposal Group [*Military*] (NVT)
EODGRU	Explosive Ordnance Disposal Group [*Military*]
EODGRUDET	Explosive Ordnance Disposal Group Detachment [*Military*] (DNAB)
EODGRULANT	Explosive Ordnance Disposal Group, Atlantic [*Military*]
EODGRUPAC	Explosive Ordnance Disposal Group, Pacific [*Military*]
EODMU	Explosive Ordnance Disposal Mobile Unit [*Military*] (DNAB)
EODN	Explosive Ordnance Disposal, Nuclear [*Military*] (NVT)
EODP	Engineering Order Delayed for Parts
EODPP	Epidemiology and Oral Disease Prevention Program [*Bethesda, MD*] [*National Institute of Dental Research*] [*Department of Health and Human Services*] (GRD)
EODS	Electro-Optic Direction Sensor
EODS	Explosive Ordnance Disposal School [*Indian Head, MD*] [*Military*]
EODS	Explosive Ordnance Disposal Squadron [*Military*]
EODSBad	Explosive Ordnance Disposal Specialist Badge [*Military decoration*] (AABC)
EODSupvBad	Explosive Ordnance Disposal Supervisor Badge [*Military decoration*] (AABC)
EODT & T	Explosive Ordnance Disposal Technology and Training Center [*Military*]
EODTC	Electro-Optic Display Test Chamber
EODTECHCEN	Explosive Ordnance Disposal Technical Center [*Military*] (DNAB)
EODTEU	Explosive Ordnance Disposal Training and Evaluation Unit [*Military*] (DNAB)
EODTIC	Explosive Ordnance Disposal Technical Information Center [*Military*] (DNAB)
EODU	Explosive Ordnance Disposal Unit [*Military*] (NVT)
EOE	Earth Orbit Ejection [*Aerospace*] (MCD)
EOE	Earth Orbit Equipment [*Aerospace*]
EOE	Edge of Earth (IAA)
EOE	Electronic-Optic-Electronic (IAA)
EOE	Element of Expense
EOE	End of Extent [*Computer science*] (IBMDP)
EOE	Enemy Occupied Europe [*World War II*]
EOE	Equal Opportunity Employer
EOE	Errors and Omissions Excepted [*Insurance*]
EOE	Ethiodized Oil Emulsion [*Clinical chemistry*]
EOE	Ethyloxaergoline [*Biochemistry*]
EOE	European Options Exchange [*Netherlands*]
EOE	Newberry, SC [*Location identifier FAA*] (FAAL)
EOEC	End of Equilibrium Cycle [*Nuclear energy*] (NRCH)
EOED	Earth Orbit Escape Device [*Aerospace*]
EOEL	End of Equilibrium Life [*Nuclear energy*] (NUCP)
EOEM	Electronic Original Equipment Market
EOE M/F	Equal Opportunity Employer, Male/Female (OICC)
EOE M-F-H	Equal Opportunity Employer, Male-Female-Handicapped
EO/EW	Electro Optical / Electronic Warfare [*DoD*]
EOF	Earth Orbital Flight [*Aerospace*] (AAG)
EOF	Electro-Optic Force
EOF	Electroosmotic Flow [*Physical chemistry*]
EOF	Emergency Operating Facility [*Civil Defense*]
EOF	Emergency Operations Facility [*Nuclear energy*] (NRCH)
EOF	Empirical Orthogonal Function [*Statistics*]
EOF	End of File [*Computer science*]
EOF	End of Form [*Computer science*] (IAA)
EOF	Expected Operations Forecast [*NWS*] (FAAC)
EOFC	Electro-Optical Fire Control [*Military*] (PDAA)
E of Cov	Trial of the Earl of Coventry [*A publication*] (DLA)
EOFCS	Electro-Optical Fire Control System [*Military*] (CAAL)
E of E	Expiration of Enlistment
EOFEA	Equal Opportunity and Full Employment Act (OICC)
E of M	Error of Measurement (WDAA)
EOF mark	End-of-File Mark [*Computer science*]
E of S	Expiration of Service
EOFT	Engine Oil Filterability Test
EOFY	End of Fiscal Year
EOG	Educational Opportunity Grant
EOG	Effect on Guarantees
EOG	Electrograph (KSC)
EOG	Electrolytic Oxygen Generator (DNAB)
EOG	Electrooculogram [*or Electrooculography*] [*Medicine*]
EOG	Electroolfactogram [*Medicine*]
EOG	Enron Oil & Gas [*NYSE symbol*] (SPSG)
EOG	Ethrane, Oxygen, and Gas [*Nitrous oxide*] [*Anesthesiology*] (DAVI)
EOG	Voltage Outer Gimbal
EOGB	Electro-Optical Glide Bomb (MCD)
EOGB	Electro-Optical Guided Bomb (VNW)

EOGO .... Eccentric Orbital Geophysical Observatory [*Also, EGO*] [*NASA*] (MUGU)
EO/GW .... Electro-Optical Guided Weapons
EOH .... Emergency Operation Headquarters [*Army*] (AABC)
EOH .... Encyclopedia of Hoaxes [*A publication*]
EOH .... End of Overhaul
EOH .... Equipment on Hand (AABC)
EOH .... Equipment Operator, Hauling [*Navy rating*]
EOH .... Experiment Operations Handbook (KSC)
EOHP .... Except as Otherwise Herein Provided
EOHPC .... European Oil Hydraulic and Pneumatic Committee [*Italy*] (EAIO)
EOHT .... External Oxygen and Hydrogen Tanks (NASA)
EOI .... Earth Orbit Insertion [*NASA*] (KSC)
EOI .... Eday [*Orkney Islands*] [*Airport symbol*] (OAG)
EOI .... Electronic Operating Instructions (DNAB)
EOI .... Electro-Optical Imaging (PDAA)
EOI .... End of Identity [*Computer science*] (IAA)
EOI .... End of Information (NITA)
EOI .... End of Input [*Computer science*]
EOI .... End of Inquiry [*Computer science*]
EOI .... Equipment Operating Instructions
EOI .... Evidence of Insurability
EOI .... Expression of Interest
EOIC .... Ethylene Oxide Industry Council (EA)
EOID .... Electro-Optical Ion Detection [*Spectroscopy*]
EOIEC .... Effects of Initial Entry Conditions (SAA)
EOIG .... Enemy Oil Intelligence Group [*Ministry of Economic Warfare*] [*British World War II*]
EOIM .... Evaluation of Oxygen Interaction with Materials (MCD)
E/O-IMS .... Engineering/Operations - Information Management System (NASA)
EOIR .... Electro-Optical Infrared
EO/IR .... Electro-Optic/Infrared (RDA)
EOIR .... Executive Office for Immigration Review [*Department of Justice*] (GFGA)
EOIS .... Electro-Optical Imaging System (IEEE)
EOISS .... Equal Opportunity Information and Support System (DNAB)
EOITS .... Electro-Optical Identification and Tracking System (MCD)
EOJ .... End of Job [*Computer science*]
EOK .... Keokuk, IA [*Location identifier FAA*] (FAAL)
EOKA .... Ethnike Organosis Kypriakou Agonos [*National Organization of Cypriot Fighters*] [*Greece*]
EOL .... Earth Orbit Launch [*NASA*] (KSC)
EOL .... Economic Opportunity Act Loan
EOL .... Electro-Optics and Laser International Exhibition and Conference [*British*] (ITD)
EOL .... Elf Overseas Ltd. [*NYSE symbol*] (SPSG)
EOL .... Emir Oils Ltd. [*Vancouver Stock Exchange symbol*]
EOL .... End of Life
EOL .... End of Line (CDE)
EOL .... End of List [*Computer science*] (IAA)
EOL .... Ex Oriente Lux [*A publication*] (BJA)
EOL .... Expression-Oriented Language [*Computer science*]
EOL .... Neola, IA [*Location identifier FAA*] (FAAL)
EOLAB .... Electro-Optics Laboratory [*University of Michigan*] [*Research center*] (RCD)
EOLAS .... [*The*] Irish Science and Technology Agency [*Information service or system*] (IID)
EOLAS - ISTA... EOLAS - the Irish Science and Technology Agency (EAIO)
EOLB .... End of Line Block [*Computer science*] (CET)
EOLC .... Earth Orbital Launch Configuration [*NASA*] (KSC)
EOLCS .... Engine Oil Licensing and Certification System [*American Petroleum Institute*]
EOLLL .... Ernest Orland Lawrence Livermore Laboratory [*University of California*] (KSC)
EOLM .... Electro-Optical Light Modulator
EOLM .... End of Line Marker [*Computer science*]
EOLN .... End of Line [*Computer science*]
EOLORPS ...... Electro-Optical Long-Range Protection System [*Military*] (DWSG)
EOLPrA .... Elf Overseas Ltd 8.50% Pfd'A' [*NYSE symbol*] (TTSB)
EOLPrB .... Elf Overseas Ltd 7.625% Pfd'B' [*NYSE symbol*] (TTSB)
EOLR .... Electrical Objective Loudness Rating (IEEE)
EOLT .... End of Logical Tape [*Computer science*]
EOLV .... Electro-Optic Light Valve
EOM .... Earth Observation Mission [*NASA*]
EOM .... Earth Orbital Mission [*NASA*]
EOM .... Egyptian Order of Merit
EOM .... Electro-Optical Modulator
EOM .... Employment Office Manager (ADA)
EOM .... End of Medium [*Computer science*] (BUR)
EOM .... End of Message [*Computer science*]
EOM .... End of Mission
EOM .... End of Month [*Business term*]
eom .... End Of Month [*Billing*] (WDMC)
EOM .... Energize Output M [*Symbol language*]
EOM .... Engineering Operations Manual [*NASA*] (NASA)
EOM .... Enjoyment of Music Series, EMI [*Record label*] [*Great Britain*]
EOM .... Equal Ocular Movement [*Medicine*] (DMAA)
EOM .... Equation of Motion (NASA)
EOM .... Ethoxymethyl [*Organic chemistry*]
EOM .... European Options Market (DCTA)
EOM .... Every Other Month (ADA)
EOM .... Executives on the Move [*A publication*]
EOM .... Expendable Ordnance Management [*Navy*] (DOMA)
EOM .... External Ocular Movement [*Medicine*]
EOM .... Extractable Organic Matter [*Environmental chemistry*]

EOM .... Extraocular Movement [*or Motion*] [*Ophthalmology*]
EOM .... Extraocular Muscles [*Ophthalmology*]
EOMA .... Emergency Oxygen Mask Assembly (KSC)
EOMB .... Explanation of Medicare [*or Medical*] Benefits
EOMC .... Engineering Order Map Correction (MCD)
EOMC .... Engineering Order Material Revision Data Collection (MCD)
EOMF .... End of Minor Frame (MCD)
EOMF .... Exempt Organization Master File [*IRS*]
EOMI .... End of Message Incomplete [*Computer science*] (IAA)
EOMI .... Extraocular Motion [*or Movement*] Intact [*Ophthalmology*] (DAVI)
EOMI .... Extraocular Muscles Intact [*Ophthalmology*]
EOMR .... Engineering Order List of Material Revision (MCD)
EOMS .... Earth Orbital Military Satellite [*NASA*] (IAA)
EOMS .... End of Message Sequence [*Computer science*] (CET)
EOMSF .... Earth Orbital Military Space Force (MCD)
EOMTC .... Eugene O'Neill Memorial Theater Center (EA)
EOMV .... End-of-Mix Viscosity (MCD)
EON .... End of Number [*Computer science*] (IAA)
EON .... Equipment Operator, Construction Equipment [*Navy rating*]
EON .... Ethylene Oxide Number [*Surfactant technology*]
EON .... Peotone, IL [*Location identifier FAA*] (FAAL)
EONE .... Environment-One [*NASDAQ symbol*] (TTSB)
EONE .... Environment One Corp. [*NASDAQ symbol*] (SAG)
EONR .... European Organization for Nuclear Reserch (NUCP)
EOO .... Extensible Object Orientation
EOOC .... Exchange-Oriented Operator Control (IAA)
EOOE .... Erreur ou Omission Exceptee [*Error or Omission Excepted*] [*French*]
EOOF .... European Olive Oil Federation [*Italy*] (EAIO)
EOOW .... Engineering Officer of the Watch [*Navy*] (NVT)
EOP .... Earth and Ocean Physics [*NASA*] (NASA)
EOP .... Earth Observations Programs [*NASA*]
EOP .... Earth Orbit Plane [*Aerospace*] (AAG)
EOP .... Efficiency of Plating [*Microbiology*]
EOP .... Electronic Overload Protection
EOP .... Electro-Optic Projector
EOP .... Emergency Operating Procedure [*Nuclear energy*] (NRCH)
EOP .... Emergency Operating Program (OICC)
EOP .... Emergency Operations Plan [*Civil Defense*]
EOP .... Emergency Outpatient [*Medicine*] (HGAA)
EOP .... Emergency Oxygen Pack [*NASA*] (KSC)
EOP .... Employee Ownership Plan (WGA)
EOP .... Encyclopedia of Occultism and Parapsychology [*A publication*]
EOP .... End of Paragraph
EOP .... End of Part (MCD)
EOP .... End of Period
EOP .... End of Procedure [*Computer science*]
EOP .... End of Program [*Computer science*]
EOP .... End of Push [*Spectroscopy*]
EOP .... Endogenous Opioid Peptides [*Medicine*] (MEDA)
EOP .... End Output [*Computer science*] (IEEE)
EOP .... Engineering Operating Procedure (MCD)
EOP .... English for Occupational Purposes (AIE)
EOP .... Equal Opportunity Policy (OICC)
EOP .... Equal Opportunity Programs (MCD)
EOP .... Equational Prover
EOP .... Equipment Operating [*or Operational*] Procedure (AAG)
EOP .... Executive Office of the President
EOP .... Executive Office of the President, Washington, DC [*OCLC symbol*] (OCLC)
EOP .... Experimental Operating Procedure (SAA)
EOP .... Experiment Operations Panel
EOP .... Experiments of Opportunity (NASA)
EOP .... Extraoptic Photoreceptors
EOPAP .... Earth and Ocean Physics Applications Program [*NASA*]
EOPC .... Electro-Optic Phase Change (IEEE)
EOPF .... End of Powered Flight
EOPP .... Employment Opportunities Pilot Program [*Department of Labor*]
EOPR .... Engineering Order Purchase Request (SAA)
EOPS .... Electronic Oil Pressure Sensor [*Automotive engineering*]
EOPS .... Equal Opportunity Program Specialist [*Navy*] (NVT)
EOPTO .... Electro-Optical Technology Program Office [*Navy*] (GRD)
EOQ .... Economic Order Quantity
EOQ .... Educational Orientation Questionnaire (EDAC)
EOQ .... End of Quarter (AFM)
EOQ .... European Organization for Quality [*Switzerland*] (EAIO)
EOQI .... Equal Opportunity Quality Indicator [*Navy*] (NVT)
EOQT .... Economic Order Quality Techniques [*Course*] [*Military*] (DNAB)
EOR .... Earth Orbit Rendezvous [*NASA*]
EOR .... El Dorado [*Venezuela*] [*Airport symbol*] (AD)
EOR .... Electro-Optical Rectifier (MCD)
EOR .... Electro-Optical Research
EOR .... End of Record [*Computer science*]
EOR .... End of Reel
EOR .... End of Run [*Telecommunications*] (TEL)
EOR .... Engine Order
EOR .... Enhanced Oil Recovery [*Petroleum engineering*]
EOR .... Equipment Operationally Ready (AABC)
EOR .... Exchange Option Rental
EOR .... Exclusive Operating Room [*Medicine*] (DAVI)
EOR .... Exclusive Or [*Gates*] [*Computer science*]
EOR .... Explosive Ordnance Reconnaissance [*Military*]
EORA .... Elderly Onset Rheumatoid Arthritis [*Medicine*] (DAVI)
EORA .... Explosive Ordnance Reconnaissance Agent [*Military*] (AABC)
EORBS .... Earth Orbiting Recoverable Biological Satellite
EORC .... Earth Observation Research Center [*Japan*]

EORC	Emergency Operations Research Center
EORC	Engineering Officers Reserve Corps
EORDC	Essential Oils Research and Development Committee [*Tasmania, Australia*]
EORF	Electron Optical Recording Facility
EORL	Emergency Officers' Retired List [*Army*]
EORQ	Engineering Order Request for Quotation (SAA)
EO/RR	Equal Opportunity/Race Relations [*Navy*] (NVT)
EORSA	Episcopalians and Others for Responsible Social Action (EA)
EORSAT	ELINT [*Electronic Intelligence*] - Ocean Reconnaissance Satellite (MCD)
EORT	Equipment Operational Readiness Trends [*Report*] (MCD)
EORTC	European Organization for Research on the Treatment of Cancer [*Research center Switzerland*] (IRC)
E Orth	Eastern Orthodox
EOS	Earth Observation Satellite [*NASA*] (OSRA)
EOS	Earth Observatory Satellite [*NASA*]
EOS	Earth Observing System [*NASA*]
EOS	Earth Orbital Shuttle [*NASA*] (KSC)
EOS	Earth Orbit Station
EOS	Effect on System
EOS	Efficiency of Survival [*Genetics*]
EOS	Electro-Optical System [*Electronics*] (ECII)
EOS	Electro-Optical Systems, Inc. [*Subsidiary of Xerox Corp.*]
EOS	Electrophenesis Operations in Space
EOS	Electrophoretic Operations in Space [*Without gravity*]
EOS	Eligibility On-Site (MEDA)
EOS	Eligible for Overseas Service
EOS	Elipse of Skin [*Medicine*] (DAVI)
EOS	Emergency Operations Simulation [*Civil Defense*]
EOS	Emergency Operations Staff (MCD)
EOS	Emergency Operations System
EOS	Emergency Oxygen Supply [*or System*]
EOS	Enclosed Operating Station [*Military*] (CAAL)
EOS	End-of-Screen [*Computer science*] (MHDB)
EOS	End of Season [*Business term*]
EOS	End of Segment [*Computer science*] (IAA)
EOS	End-of-Sequence [*Computer science*] (MHDB)
EOS	End of Service (MCD)
EOS	End-of-Step [*Computer science*] (MHDB)
EOS	End of String [*Computer science*] (IAA)
EOS	Energy of State
EOS	Engineering Operating Station [*Military*] (CAAL)
EOS	Engineering Operating System
EOS	Enhanced Operating System [*Computer science*] (PDAA)
EOS	Eosinophils [*Hematology*]
EOS	Equal Opportunity Specialist (AAGC)
EOS	Equation of State
EOS	ERIN On-line Service [*Commonwealth*] (EERA)
EOS	Etasable Optical Storage [*Computer science*] (ODBW)
EOS	Ethylene Oxide Sterilizer (MCD)
EOS	Eugene O'Neill Society (EA)
EOS	European Orthodontic Society (PDAA)
EOS	Exhaust Oxygen Sensor [*Automotive engineering*]
EOS	Exodus Online Services [*Computer science*]
EOS	Expiration of Obligated Service [*Military*]
EOS	Extended Operating System [*DoD*]
EOS	Extraordinary Occasion Service [*Associated Press*] (IIA)
EOS	Neosho, MO [*Location identifier FAA*] (FAAL)
EOSA	Explosive Ordnance Safety Approval [*Military*] (MUGU)
E-O SAEL	Electro-Optical Sensors Atmospheric Effects Library (RDA)
EOSAT	Earth Observation Satellite Co. [*Joint venture of RCA Corp. and Hughes Aircraft Co.*]
EOSC	Eastern Oregon State College
EOSC	Extended Operating System Card [*Computer science*] (IAA)
EOSCOR	Extended Observation of Solar and Cosmic Radiation [*National Center for Atmospheric Research*]
EOSD	Emergency Operations Systems Development [*Civil Defense*]
EOSD	Equipment on Station Date [*Army*] (AABC)
EOSDIS	Earth Observing System Data and Information System
EOS/ESD	Electrical Overstress/Electrostatic Discharge Association (EA)
Eosin	Eosinophil [*Hematology*] (WGA)
eosin B	Dibromodinitrofluorescein [*A dye*] [*Biochemistry*] (DAVI)
EOSMD	Extended Operating System Magnetic Drum [*Computer science*] (IAA)
EOSMOR	European Society for Market and Opinion Research
EOS/MT	Extended Operating System for Magnetic Tapes (DNAB)
EOSO	Escort Oilers Supervising Officer [*Navy*]
EOSP	Economic Order and Stockage Procedure
EOSPC	Electro-Optical Signal Processing Computer
EOSS	Earth Orbital Space Station [*NASA*] (MCD)
EOSS	Electro-Optical Sensor System [*Navy*] (MCD)
EOSS	Electro-Optical Simulation [*or Sighting*] System [*for missiles*] [*Army*] (MCD)
EOSS	Emergency Operational Sequencing System (MCD)
EOSS	Engineering Operational Sequence System (DNAB)
EOST	Emergency Operations Simulation Techniques [*Civil Defense*]
EOT	Earth-Observed Time [*NASA*]
EOT	Effective Oxygen Transport (MAE)
EOT	Electric Overhead Travelling
EOT	Emergency Operations Team [*Environmental Protection Agency*] (GFGA)
EOT	End of Tape [*Computer science*]
EOT	End of Task [*Computer science*]
EOT	End of Test [*Computer science*]

EOT	End of Text [*Computer science*]
EOT	End of Tour [*Air Force*] (AFM)
EOT	End of Track
EOT	End of Transmission [*Computer science*]
EOT	Enemy-Occupied Territory
EOT	Energy Optimized Technology [*German-manufactured car tire*] [*Continental Gummi-Werke AG*]
EOT	Engineering and Operations Training [*Navy*]
EOT	Engine Oil Temperature [*Automotive engineering*]
EOT	Engine Order Telegraph (DNAB)
EOT	Eott Energy Partners [*NYSE symbol*] (SAG)
EOT	EOTT Energy Partners L.P. [*NYSE symbol*] (TTSB)
EOT	Equal Opportunity and Treatment [*Army program*]
EOT	Exhaust Outlet Temperature [*Automotive engineering*]
EO(T)A	Engineering Officers' (Telecommunications) Association [*British*]
EOTADS	Electro-Optical Target Acquisition and Designation System [*Military*]
EOTC	Electro-Optic Test Chamber
EOTD	Electro-Optical Tracking Device
EOTF	Electro-Optics Test Facility
EOTS	Earth Orbiting Teleoperator System [*Spacecraft*] [*NASA*]
EOTS	Electron Optic Tracking System (MUGU)
EOTS	Electro-Optical Tracking System (IDOE)
EottEn	Eott Energy Partners [*Associated Press*] (SAG)
EOU	Electro-Optical Unit
EOU	End of User [*Computer hacker terminology*] (NHD)
EOU	Enemy Objective Unit [*of US*] [*in London*]
EOU	Epidemic Observation Unit [*Medicine*]
EOUSA	Executive Office for United States Attorneys [*Department of Justice*]
EOUST	Executive Office for United States Trustees [*Department of Justice*] (BARN)
EOV	Columbia, SC [*Location identifier FAA*] (FAAL)
EOV	Economic Order Van (AABC)
EOV	Electrically Operated Valve
EOV	End of Volume [*Computer science*]
EOVM	End of Valid Message [*Computer science*] (IAA)
EOVS	Electro-Optical Viewing System (MCD)
EOVs	Explanation of Votes (EERA)
EOW	End of Word [*Computer science*]
EOW	Energy over Weight (MCD)
EOW	Engineering Order Worksheet
EOW	Engineer's Order Wire
EOW	Engine Out Warning
EOW	Engine over the Wing
EOW	Every Other Week
EOWA	English Olympic Wrestling Association
EOWPVT	Expressive One-Word Picture Vocabulary Test [*Intelligence test*]
EOWPVT:UE	Expressive One-Word Picture Vocabulary Test: Upper Extension [*Intelligence test*]
EOWS	Electro-Optical Weapons System
EOWTF	Every Other Week Til Forbid [*Advertising*] (DOAD)
EOWTF	Every Other Week Till Forbid (NTCM)
EOX	Extractable Organic Halogen [*Environmental chemistry*] (FFDE)
EOY	End of Year
EOYFS	End of Year Financial Statement
EOZ	Elorza [*Venezuela*] [*Airport symbol*] (OAG)
EP	Early Philosophies [*A publication*]
EP	Early Positive
EP	Earned Premium [*Insurance*]
EP	Earning Power [*Business term*]
EP	Earnings Price [*Investment term*]
EP	Earth Penetrator [*Weapon*]
EP	Earth Protectors (GNE)
EP	Eastward Position
EP	Easy Projection (PDAA)
EP	Ebury Press [*Publisher*] [*British*]
EP	Ecclesiastical Parish
EP	Economic Planning (MCD)
EP	Economic Planning. Journal for Agriculture and Related Industries [*A publication*]
EP	Economic Policy [*British*]
EP	Ectopic Pregnancy [*Obstetrics*]
EP	Edible Portion [*of a food*]
EP	Edito Princeps [*First edition*] [*Latin*] (WDAA)
EP	Educational Publication [*NASA*]
EP	Effective Par [*Investment term*]
EP	Effective Production
EP	Egyptian Pattern [*British military*] (DMA)
EP	Egyseg Partja [*Party of Unity*] [*Hungary*] (PPE)
EP	Elbow Pitch (MCD)
EP	Electrically Polarized [*Relay*]
EP	Electrical Panel (NG)
EP	Electrical Propulsion (AAG)
EP	Electrical Prototype
E/P	Electrical-to-Pneumatic [*Converter*] (NRCH)
EP	Electric Power (NRCH)
EP	Electric Primer
EP	Electrode Plasma [*Energy source*]
EP	Electronic and Desktop Publishing
EP	Electronic Package
EP	Electronic Post [*British Post Office*] [*Defunct*] (TSSD)
EP	Electronic Printer
EP	Electronic Processing (IAA)
EP	Electronics Panel
EP	Electron Paramagnetic
EP	Electron Photon

E/P	Electron/Proton (MCD)
EP	Electrophoresis
EP	Electrophysiology
EP	Electroplate
EP	Electropneumatic
EP	Electrostatic Powder
EP	Electrostatic Precipitator [Also, ESP]
EP	Elephantine Papyri (BJA)
EP	Eligible Participant (OICC)
EP	Elongated Punch
EP	Emergency Planning (NATG)
EP	Emergency Preparedness [Nuclear energy] (NRCH)
EP	Emergency Procedures (MCD)
EP	Emission Policy (NATG)
EP	Employee Participation (ADA)
EP	Employee Plan [IRS]
EP	Employment Protection [Act] [British]
EP	Empowerment Project (EA)
EP	Emulation Program [IBM Corp.] (BUR)
EP	Ending Period (AABC)
EP	End of Program [Computer science]
EP	Endogenous Pyrogen [Immunology]
EP	Endorphin [Biochemistry]
EP	Endorser Potential [Advertising term]
EP	Endothia parasitica [Plant pathology]
E/P	End-Paper [Bibliography]
ep	End Paragraph [Typesetting command] (WDMC)
EP	End Point [Distilling]
EP	End-Use Product [Environmental Protection Agency]
EP	Enemy Position
EP	Engineering Paper
EP	Engineering Personnel [Coast Guard]
EP	Engineering Phase (MCD)
EP	Engineering Practice (NG)
EP	Engineering Print (KSC)
EP	Engineering Procedure
EP	Engineering Project
EP	Engineering Proposal
EP	Engineer Pamphlet [Army Corps of Engineers]
EP	Engineer Personnel [Marine Corps]
EP	English Patent (IAA)
EP	Enlisted Personnel (AABC)
EP	En Passant [In Passing] [Chess]
EP	En Route Penetration [Aviation] (FAAC)
EP	Entrainment Pressure
EP	Entrucking Point [Military]
EP	Entry Point (BUR)
ep	Envelope (WDMC)
EP	Environmental Park [Australia]
EP	Environmental Pollution [A publication] (NOAA)
EP	Environmental Profile [Environmental Protection Agency] (GFGA)
EP	Environmental Protective Plan (MCD)
EP	Enzyme Presoak [for laundry]
EP	Enzyme-Product [Biochemistry] (DAVI)
EP	Enzyme-Product Complex [Enzyme kinetics]
EP	Eparchy (ROG)
Ep	Ephesians [New Testament book] (BJA)
EP	Epicardial Electrogram [Cardiology] (DMAA)
EP	Epileptic (AIE)
EP	Epiotic [Ear anatomy]
EP	Episcopalian
EP	Episcopus [Bishop] [Latin]
EP	Epistle
EP	Epistola [Epistle, Letter] [Latin] (ROG)
Ep	Epistulae [of Augustine] [Classical studies] (OCD)
Ep	Epistulae [of Epicurus] [Classical studies] (OCD)
Ep	Epistulae [of St. Jerome] [Classical studies] (OCD)
EP	Epitaxial Planar [Electronics]
EP	Epithelial [or Epithelioid] [Histology] (DAVI)
EP	Epithelial Proliferation [Histology]
EP	Epoxide Plastic
EP	Epping [Urban district in England]
EP	Equine Piroplasmosis (PDAA)
EP	Equipment Piece (NRCH)
EP	Equipment Practice [Telecommunications] (TEL)
EP	Equipment Publication (AABC)
EP	Equivalence Principle [Physics]
EP	Erasmus Press, Lexington, KY [Library symbol Library of Congress] (LCLS)
EP	Erythrocyte Protoporphyrin [Hematology]
EP	Erythrophagocytosis [Hematology]
EP	Erythropoietic Porphyria [A genetic disorder]
Ep	Erythropoietin [Also, EPO] [Hematology]
EP	Erythrose Phosphate [Biochemistry] (BARN)
EP	Estimated Position [Navigation]
EP	Etched Plate
EP	European Parliament
EP	European Plan [Hotel room rate]
EP	Europrime Capital [Vancouver Stock Exchange symbol]
EP	Evaluation Plan
EP	Evening Prayer
EP	Evoked Potential [Neurophysiology]
EP	Excess Profits
EP	Executive Pension [British]
EP	Executive Program (MCD)
EP	Expanded Polystyrene (ADA)
EP	Expectancy Phenomenon
EP	Expected Pay-Off
EP	Experienced Playgoer [Theatrical]
EP	Exploration Permit [Australia]
EP	Explosion-Proof
EP	Export Propensity
EP	Exprisoner
EP	Extended Play
ep	Extended Play (IDOE)
EP	Extension Pay [British military] (DMA)
EP	Externally Powered [Gun] (MCD)
EP	External Phloem [Botany]
EP	External Pressure
EP	External Publication
EP	Extraction Procedure [Chemical engineering]
EP	Extra Point [Football]
EP	Extreme Pressure (MSA)
E_p	Peak Voltage (IDOE)
E_p	Plate Voltage (IDOE)
EP	Presbyterian, Church of England [Military] (ROG)
ep----	Pyrenees Region [MARC geographic area code Library of Congress] (LCCP)
EP	Tropic Air Services [ICAO designator] (AD)
EPA	Earth's Polar Axis (KSC)
EPA	Eastern Provincial Airways [Labrador]
EPA	Eastern Psychological Association
EPA	Economic Price Adjustment
EPA	Edge Path Adapter (CDE)
EPA	Educational Paperback Association (EA)
EPA	Educational Publishers Association
EPA	Educational Puppetry Association [British] (BI)
EPA	Eicosapentaenoic Acid [Biochemistry]
EPA	Eire Philatelic Association (EA)
EPA	Electronic Publishing Abstracts [Information service or system] (NITA)
EPA	Electron Probe Analyzer
EPA	Emergency Powers Act [British World War II]
EPA	Empire Parliamentary Association [Later, CPA] [Australia]
EPA	Empire Press Agency (DGA)
EPA	Employee Plan Administrators
EPA	Employer-Paid Advertising
EPA	Employment Protection Act [1975] [British] (DCTA)
EPA	Energetic Particles Analyzer [Astrophysics]
EPA	Engineering Practice Amendment (AAG)
EPA	Engineering Product Assumptions
EPA	English Pool Association [British] (DBA)
EPA	Enhanced Performance Architecture [Computer science] (TNIG)
EPA	Environmental Protection Agency [Government agency formed in 1970]
EPA	Environment Planning Authority (EERA)
EPA	Environment Pollutions Agency [British]
EPA	Environment Protection Agency [USA] (EERA)
EPA	Environment Protection Agency [Australia] (EERA)
EPA	Environment Protection Authority [Western Australia] [State] (EERA)
EPA	Epidermolysis Bullosa Acquisita [Dermatology]
EPA	Equal Pay Act [US] (OICC)
EPA	Equatorial Pitch Angle [Geophysics]
EPA	Equity Principle Auditions (BARN)
EPA	Erect Posterior-Anterior [Radiology]
EPA	Erythroid Potentiating Activity [Hematology]
EPA	Essential Pharmacy Allowance
EPA	Estimated Position Arc [Navy] (NVT)
EPA	Ether-Isopentane-Ethanol [Solvent system]
EPA	Ethylbenzene Producers Association (EA)
EPA	Europaeisches Patentamt [European Patent Office - EPO] (EAIO)
EPA	European Parent Association (AIE)
EPA	European Photochemistry Association (EAIO)
EPA	European Productivity Agency
EPA	Evangelical Press Association (EA)
EPA	Exoatmospheric Penetration Aid
EPA	Exparc [Russian Federation] [ICAO designator] (FAAC)
EPA	Ex Patriates Association [British] (DBA)
EPA	Export Pound Account [Special type of currency] [United Arab Republic]
EPA	Extended Planning Annex
EPA	Extrinsic Plasminogen Activator [Hematology]
EPA	L'Economie des Pays Arabes [A publication] (BJA)
EPAA	Educational Press Association of America [Later, EDPRESS] (EA)
EPAA	Emergency Petroleum Allocation Act
EPAA	Employing Printers Association of America [Defunct] (EA)
EPAA	Environmental Programs Assistance Act (GFGA)
EPAA	European Primary Aluminum Association [Later, European Aluminium Association - EAA] (IID)
EPAA	Exciter Power Amplifier Assembly [Electricity] (DWSG)
EPAAR	Environmental Protection Agency Acquisition Regulations (GFGA)
EPA/ARB	Environmental Protection Agency/Air Resources Board
EPABX	Electronic Private Automatic Branch Exchange [Telecommunications] (MCD)
EPAC	Economic Planning Advisory Council (EERA)
EPAC	Energetic Particle Composition Instrument [Astrophysics]
EPAC	Entraineurs en Patinage Artistique du Canada [Figure Skating Coaches of Canada - FSCC]
EPACASR	Environmental Protection Agency Chemical Activities Status Report [Databa se] [Environmental Protection Agency]

EPACML....... Environmental Protection Agency Composite Model for Landfills [*Formerly, EPASMOD*]
EPACT......... Energy Policy Act of 1992 [*BTS*] (TAG)
EPACT........... National Energy Policy Act [*Legislation passed in 1992*] [*Department of Energy*] (PS)
EPAD .... Enlisted Personnel Assignment Document [*Navy*] (NVT)
EPAD .... Error Protecting Packet Assembler/Disassembler [*Telecommunications*] (OSI)
Ep ad Tryph... Epistula ad Tryphonem [*of Quintilian*] [*Classical studies*] (OCD)
EPAGM ...... Environmental Protection Agency Grants Administration Manual
EPAIS......... Encyclopedia of Public Affairs Information Sources [*A publication*]
EPALL .... Emergency Preparedness at Local Level (EERA)
EPAM........... Elementary Perceiver and Memorizer [*University of California*] [*Learning theory Computer device*]
EPAM........... Emergency Priorities and Allocations Manual [*DoD*]
Epam .... Epaminondas [*of Nepos*] [*Classical studies*] (OCD)
EPAMS....... Experimental Prototype Automatic Meteorological System (MCD)
EPAN .... Electronic Purchasing Agent Network [*Service of Data Corp. of America*]
EP & A........ Exercise Plans and Analysis Division (MCD)
EP & D .... Electrical Power and Distribution (CET)
EPANY .... Export Packers Association of New York [*Defunct*] (EA)
EPA-PRD...... Environmental Protection Agency - Pesticide Regional Division
EPAQ .... Extended Personality Attributes Questionnaire (EDAC)
E-PAR .... Electronic Warfare/Radioelectronic Parity Study
EPARCS ...... Enhanced Perimeter Acquisition RADAR Characterization System (PDAA)
EP (ARR) .... Act Environment Protection [*Alligator Rivers Region*] [*Act 1978*] [*Commonwealth*] (EERA)
EPAS .... Energetic Particle Anisotropy Spectrometer
EPAS........... Experimental Project Apollo-Soyuz [*Acronym used as name of a cologne created to commemorate the first joint US/Russian manned space flight*]
EPASA .... Electron Probe Analysis Society of America [*Later, MAS*] (EA)
EPASMOD.... Environmental Protection Agency Subsurface Fate and Transport Model [*Later, EPACML*]
EPASYS ...... European Patents Administration System [*Information service or system*] (NITA)
EPAT........... Earliest Possible Arrival Time (MCD)
EPAT........... Every Pupil Achievement Test (EDAC)
EPAYS .... Environmental Protection Agency Payroll System (GFGA)
EPB............. Earth Pressure Balance [*Civil engineering*]
EPB............. Eastern Pacific Aviation Ltd. [*Canada ICAO designator*] (FAAC)
EPB............. East Pacific Barrier [*Oceanography*]
EPB............. Economic Policy Board [*Department of the Treasury*]
EPB............. Editorial Production Branch [*BUPERS*]
EPB............. Ejercito Popular Boricua [*Puerto Rican Popular Army*] (PD)
EPB............. Electronically Proportioned Braking
EPB............. Electronic Publishing Business [*Electronic Publishing Ventures, Inc.*] [*Information service or system*] (IID)
EPB............. Energy Pulse Bonding [*Electronics*]
EPB............. Engineering Process Bulletin
EPB............. Enlisted Programs Branch [*BUPERS*]
EPB............. Environmental Periodicals Bibliography [*Environmental Studies Institute*] [*Information service or system*]
EPB............. Environmental Pre-Language Battery [*Speech and language therapy*] (DAVI)
EPB............. Environmental Protection Board [*British*] (BARN)
EPB............. Equipment Parts Bin
EPB............. Equivalent Passband (MCD)
EPB............. Equivalent Pension Benefit [*British*]
EPB............. Ethylpyridinium Bromide [*Organic chemistry*]
EPB............. Export Promotion Bureau [*Pakistan*]
EPB............. Extensor Pollicis Brevis [*Anatomy*]
EPB............. External Proton Beam
EPBA........... European Portable Battery Association
EpBarn........ Epistle of Barnabas (BJA)
EPBI............ Epoxy-Beta-Ionone [*Biochemistry*]
EPBLFC....... Elvis Presley Burning Love Fan Club (EA)
EPBM.......... Earth Pressure Balance Machine [*Excavation*]
EPBM.......... Electroplated Britannia Metal (IIA)
EPBX........... Electronic Private Branch Exchange [*Telecommunications*]
EPC............. Conti-Flug Koln/Bonn [*Germany ICAO designator*] (FAAC)
EPC............. Earth Potential Compensation [*Telecommunications*] (TEL)
EPC............. Earth Prelaunch Calibration [*NASA*] (KSC)
EPC............. Eastern Pilgrim College [*Later, United Weslayan College*] [*Pennsylvania*]
EPC............. East's Pleas of the Crown [*A publication*] (DLA)
EPC............. Easy Processing Channel
EPC............. Economic Policy Committee [*OECD*]
EPC............. Economic Policy Council [*UNA-USA*]
EPC............. Ectoplacental Cone [*Embryology*]
EPC............. Edge Punched Card (IAA)
EPC............. Editorial Processing Center
EPC............. Editor's Presentation Copy
EPC............. Educational Policies Commission [*Defunct*] (EA)
EPC............. Educational Publishers Council [*British*]
EPC............. Effective Production Coefficient
EPC............. Egg Phosphatidylcholine [*Biochemistry*]
EPC............. Ejercito del Pueblo Costarricense [*Costa Rica*] [*Political party*] (EY)
EPC............. Ejercito Popular Catalan [*Catalan Popular Army*] [*Spain*] (PD)
EPCML........ Elastic Performance Coefficient [*Textile testing*]
EPC............. Elder Flowers, Peppermint, and Composition Essense [*Patent medicine ingredients*] [*British*]
EPC............. Electrically-Pulsed Chamber (PDAA)

EPC............. Electronic Page Composition (DGA)
EPC............. Electronic Pain Control [*Apparatus*] [*Neurology*] (DAVI)
EPC............. Electronic Power Conditioner
EPC............. Electronic Power Control [*Off-highway equipment*] [*Hydraulics*]
EPC............. Electronic Program Control
EPC............. Electronic Publishing Committee [*Association of American Publishers*] [*Information service or system*] (IID)
EPC............. Electron Photon Cascade
EPC............. Elementary Processing Centers
EPC............. Embedded Print Command [*Computer science*] (HGAA)
EPC............. Emergency Planning Canada
EPC............. Emergency Propaganda Committee [*London*] [*World War II*]
EPC............. End Plate Current
EPC............. End Products Committee [*of WPB*] [*World War II*]
EPC............. Engineering Part Card
EPC............. Engineering, Procurement, and Construction
EPC............. Engine Performance Computer (PDAA)
EPC............. English Prize Cases [*Legal*]
EPC............. Environmental Policy Center (EA)
EPC............. Environmental Pollution Control
EPC............. Environmental Protection Council [*Tasmania, Australia*]
EPC............. Epilepsy Partialis Continua [*Medicine*]
EpC............. Epithelial Cell [*Cytology*]
EPC............. Equipotential Cathode
EPC............. Error Protection Code (NASA)
Epc............. Erythrocyte Particle Counter [*Hematology*]
EPC............. Erythroid Progenitor Cells [*Hematology*]
EPC............. Ethyl Phenylcarbamate [*Plant regulator*] [*Organic chemistry*]
EPC............. European Confederation of Plastics Convertors [*EC*] (ECED)
EPC............. European Patent Convention
EPC............. European Pension Committee [*France*] (EAIO)
EPC............. European Political Community (NATG)
EPC............. European Political Cooperation
EPC............. European Popular Circle (EAIO)
EPC............. Evaluation and Planning Centre for Health Care [*London School of Hygiene and Tropical Medicine*] [*British*] (CB)
EPC............. Evaporative Pattern Casting [*Automotive engineering*]
EPC............. Excess Profits Tax Council Ruling or Memorandum [*Internal Revenue Bureau*] [*A publication*] (DLA)
EPC............. Executive Policy Committee [*Western Australia*] [*State*] (EERA)
EPC............. Exhaust Port Combustion
EPC............. Experiment Point Control [*NASA*]
EPC............. External Pneumatic Compression [*Medicine*]
EPC............. External Power Contractor (NASA)
EPC............. Extra-Pair Copulation [*Biology*]
EPC............. Honolulu, HI [*Location identifier FAA*] (FAAL)
EPC............. Roscoe's English Prize Cases [*A publication*] (DLA)
EPCA........... Electronic Pest Control Association (EA)
EPCA........... Emergency Price Control Act of 1942
EPCA........... Employment Protection Consolidation Act [*1978*] [*British*] (DLA)
EPCA........... Energy Policy and Conservation Act [*1975*]
EPCA........... European Petrochemical Association [*Database producer*]
EPCA........... External Pressure Circulatory Assist [*Cardiac treatment*]
EPCAC........ Ecumenical Program on Central America and the Caribbean (EA)
EPCC.......... Environment Policy Coordinating Committee [*Commonwealth*] (EERA)
EPCCFC....... Elvis Presley Circle City Fan Club (EA)
EPCCS........ Emergency Positive Control Communications System
EPCCT......... Emergency Planning Committee for Civil Transportation [*US and Canada*]
EPCDC........ Electrical Power Conditioning, Distribution, and Control (MCD)
EPCER......... Experimental Patrol Craft, Escort and Rescue
EPCG.......... Endoscopic Pancreatocholangiography [*Medicine*] (AAMN)
EPCI............ Enhanced Peripheral Communication Interface [*Motorola, Inc.*]
EPCI............ Entry Point Control Item (MHDB)
EPCIA.......... Expanded Polystyrene Cavity Insulation Association [*British*] (DBA)
EPCO.......... Emergency Power Cutoff [*NASA*] (KSC)
EPCO.......... Engineer Procurement Office [*Army*]
EPCO.......... Engine Parts Coordinating Office [*Navy*]
EPCOT .... Experimental Prototype Community of Tomorrow [*Disney World*] [*Facetious translation: "Every Person Comes Out Tired"*]
EPCP........... Electric Plant Control Panel
EPCR........... Emergency Planning and Community Right to Know Act, 1986 (EERA)
EPCRA......... Emergency Planning and Community Right-to-Know Act [*1986*]
EPCRTK ...... Emergency Planning and Community Right-to-Know Act [*1986*]
EPCS........... Earnings and Profits Calculation System
EPCS........... Engineer Functional Components System (AABC)
EPCS........... English Playing-Card Society (DBA)
EPCS........... Experiment Point Control System [*or Subsystem*] [*NASA*] (KSC)
EPCU.......... Electrical Power Control Unit (MCD)
EPD............. Earliest Possible Date
EPD............. Earliest Practicable Date (AFIT)
EPD............. Earth Potential Difference (IAA)
EPD............. Eastern Procurement Division [*Navy*]
EPD............. Eastern Production District [*Navy*]
EPD............. Electric Potential Difference
EPD............. Electric Power Database [*Electric Power Research Institute*] [*Information service or system*] (IID)
EPD............. Electric Power Distribution
EPD............. Electronic Proximity Detector (MCD)
EPD............. Electrophotographic Display (DGA)
EPD............. Emergency Procedures Document (MCD)
EPD............. Energetic Particles Detector [*Geophysics*]
EPD............. Engineering Planning Document

EPD	Engineering Procedure Directive
EPD	Enlisted Personnel Directorate [*Army*]
EPD	Enlisted Personnel Division [*Navy*]
EPD	Environmental Protection Devices (MCD)
EPD	Eplett Dairies Ltd. [*Toronto Stock Exchange symbol*]
EPD	Equilibrium Peritoneal Dialysis [*Medicine*] (BARN)
EPD	Etch Pitch Density (PDAA)
EPD	European Progressive Democrats (PPE)
EPD	Excess Profits Duty
EPD	Exchange Parameter Definitions [*Telecommunications*] (TEL)
EPD	Expected Progeny Difference [*Agricultural science*]
EPD	Exponential Power Distribution [*Statistics*]
EPD	Extra Police Duty [*Extra cleaning chores*] [*Military*]
EPDA	Educational Professional Development Assistance [*Office of Education*]
EPDA	Education Professions Development Act [*1965*]
EPDA	Emergency Powers Defence Act [*British World War II*]
EPDB	Electrical Power Distribution Box
EPDB	Environmental Protection Data Base [*Environmental Protection Agency*]
EPDB	Experiment Power Distribution Box (NASA)
EPDC	Economic Power Dispatch Computer
EPDC	Electrical Power Distribution and Control (NASA)
EPDCC	Elementary Potential Digital Computing Component
EPDCC	European Pressure Die Casting Committee (EA)
EPDCE	Elementary Potential Digital Computing Element (IAA)
EPDCS	Electrical Power Distribution and Control System (KSC)
EPDF	Engineer Performance Description Form [*Test*]
EPDM	Ethiopian People's Democratic Movement [*Political party*]
EPDM	Ethylene-Propylene-Diene Monomer [*Rubber, ASTM nomenclature*]
EPDML	Epidemiology [*or Epidemiological*]
EPDMLGY	Epidemiology
EPDO	Enlisted Personnel Distribution Office [*Navy*]
EPDOCONUS	Enlisted Personnel Distribution Office, Continental United States [*Navy*]
EPDOLANT	Enlisted Personnel Distribution Office, Atlantic Fleet [*Navy*]
EPDOPAC	Enlisted Personnel Distribution Office, Pacific Fleet [*Navy*] (MUGU)
EPDP	Eelam People's Democratic Party [*Sri Lanka*] [*Political party*] (EY)
EPDP	Engineering Program Definition Plan (MCD)
EPD/RDIS	Electric Power Database/Research and Development Information System [*Electric Power Research Institute*] [*Information service or system*] (IID)
EPDS	Electrical Power Distribution System [*or Subsystem*] (KSC)
EPDS	Electronic Parts Distributors' Show
EPDS	Electronic Processing and Dissemination System [*Computer science*] (DOMA)
EPDT	Estimated Project Duration Time
EPDU	Ethiopian People's Democratic Union (EA)
EPDWO	Engineering and Product Development Work Order
EPE	Earth-Pointing Error (MCD)
EPE	Economic Policy towards Eire [*British*]
EPE	Editorial Projects in Education (EA)
EPE	Electronic Parts and Equipment (NATG)
EPE	Electrophoresis Experiment [*NASA*] (MCD)
EPE	Electrostatic Probe Experiment
EPE	Elvis Presley Enterprises
EPE	Emergency Passenger Exit
EPE	Emergency Preparedness Evaluation [*Nuclear energy*] (NRCH)
EPE	Energetic Particles Explorer [*Satellite*] [*NASA*]
EPE	Enhanced Performance Engine (MCD)
EPE	Erythropoietin-Producing Enzyme [*Hematology*] (MAE)
EPE	Ethniki Politiki Enosis [*National Political Union*] [*Greek*] (PPE)
EPE	Experimental and Proving Establishment [*Canada*] (MCD)
EPE	Explosion-Proof Enclosure
EPE	Extended Period of Eligibility [*Social Security Administration*] (GFGA)
EPE	Pellston, MI [*Location identifier FAA*] (FAAL)
EPEA	Electrical Power Engineers' Association [*A union*] [*British*]
EPEA	Experiment Pointing Electronic Assembly [*NASA*]
EPEA	Exploratory Project for Economic Alternatives (EA)
EPEAA	Employing Photo-Engravers Association of America [*Defunct*] (EA)
EPEB	Ecosystem Processes and Effects Branch [*Army*]
EPEC	Electric Programmer, Evaluator, Controller (SAA)
EPEC	Emerson Programmer-Evaluator-Controller [*Computer science*]
EPEC	Enteropathogenic Escherichia coli [*Also, EEC*] [*Medicine*]
EPED	Environmental Processes and Effects Division [*Army*]
EPEEA	Enlisted Personnel Enlistment Eligibility Activity [*Army*]
EPEN	Greek National Political Society (PPW)
EP/EO	Employee Plans/Exempt Organization [*IRS*]
EPER	Emergency Project for Equal Rights (EA)
EPERA	Extractor Parachute Emergency Release Assembly (PDAA)
E-PERM	Electret-Passive Environmental Radon Monitor [*Rad-Elec, Inc.*]
E-PERS	Enlisted Personnel (DNAB)
EPESE	Established Populations for Epidemiologic Studies of the Elderly [*Department of Health and Human Services*] (GFGA)
EPF	Early Pregnancy Factor [*Medicine*] (DMAA)
EPF	Earth Preservation Fund (GNE)
EPF	Education Projects Fund [*British Council/Overseas Development Administration*] (DS)
EPF	Electronic Power Feed (NITA)
EPF	Emergency Plant Facilities
EPF	End of Programmed Flight (MCD)
EPF	Endothelial Proliferating Factor [*Biochemistry*]
EPF	Engine and Propeller Factor [*IOR*] [*Yacht racing*]
EPF	Epidemiological Flight [*Military*]
EPF	Episcopal Peace Fellowship (EA)

EPF	Equilibrium Porous Flow [*Chemistry*]
EPF	Esparros [*France*] [*Seismograph station code, US Geological Survey*] (SEIS)
EPF	Established Program Financing
EPF	European Packaging Federation [*Denmark*] (SLS)
EPF	European Psycho-Analytical Federation (EA)
EPF	Exophthalmos-Producing Factor [*Endocrinology*]
EPF	Expected Provident Fund
EPF	Exploitation Products File (MCD)
EPF	Extra-Pair Fertilization [*Biology*]
EPF	Eye Protection Factor
EPFA	European Plasma Fractionation Association
EPFCL	Elvis Presley Fan Club of Luxembourg (EAIO)
EPFL	Ecole Polytechnique Federale de Lausanne [*Swiss Federal Institute of Technology, Lausanne*] (ECON)
EPFSU	Earth's Physical Features Study Unit (EA)
EPFTR	Expert Panel on the Facilitation of Tuna Research [*Marine science*] (MSC)
EPG	Ecole Polytechnique, Publications Officielles [*UTLAS symbol*]
EPG	Economic Policy Group
EPG	Economic Pressure on Germany Committee [*War Cabinet*] [*British World War II*]
EPG	Edit Program Generator
EPG	Eggs per Gram [*Parasitology*]
EPG	Electrical Power Generator (NASA)
EPG	Electrolytic Plunge Grinder
EPG	Electronic Program Guide [*Cable-television system*]
EPG	Electronic Proving Ground [*Army*] (MCD)
EPG	Electropneumogram [*Medicine*]
EPG	Electrostatic Particle Guide (OA)
EPG	Electrostatic Power Generator
EPG	El Paso Natural Gas [*NYSE symbol*] (TTSB)
EPG	El Paso Natural Gas Co. [*NYSE symbol*] (SPSG)
EPG	El Paso Tennessee Pipeline [*NYSE symbol*] (SAG)
EPG	Emergency Power Generator
EPG	Emergency Procedure Guidelines (IAA)
EPG	Eminent Persons Group [*Group of elder statesmen from Commonwealth countries*]
EPG	Empire Gold Resources Ltd. [*Vancouver Stock Exchange symbol*]
EPG	Employee Participation Group
EPG	Eniwetok Proving Ground [*AEC*]
EpG	EP Group of Companies, Microform Division, Wakefield, Yorkshire, United Kingdom [*Library symbol Library of Congress*] (LCLS)
EPG	Esterified Propoxylated Glycerol [*Organic chemistry*]
EPG	European Participating Governments [*In the F-16 fighter program*]
EPG	European Press Group
EPG	European Programme Group [*NATO*]
EPG	Exhaust Pressure Governor [*Diesel engines*]
EPG	Extended Planning Guidance (MCD)
EPG	Weeping Water, NE [*Location identifier FAA*] (FAAL)
EPGA	Emergency Petroleum and Gas Administration [*Department of the Interior*]
EPGCR	Experimental Prototype Gas-Cooled Reactor
EPGD	Gdansk/Rebiechowo [*Poland ICAO location identifier*] (ICLI)
EPGR	Electrical Potential Gradient Radiosonde [*Meteorology*]
EPGRS	Employment Policy Grievance Review Staff [*OSA*]
EPGS	Electric Power Generation System
EPH	Electric Process Heating (MCD)
EPH	Electrochemical Plating and Honing [*Manufacturing term*] (IAA)
EPH	Electronic Package Housing
EPH	Employ the Physically Handicapped
Eph	Ephesians [*New Testament book*]
EPH	Ephraim
EPH	Ephrata, WA [*Location identifier FAA*] (FAAL)
EPH	Epibromohydrin (GNE)
EPH	Epoch Capital Corp. [*Vancouver Stock Exchange symbol*]
EPH	Expected Period of Hospitalisation
EPH	Explosion-Proof Housing
EPHC	Eastern Pacific Hurricane Center [*San Francisco*] [*National Weather Service*] (NOAA)
Eph Epigr	Ephemeris Epigraphica [*A publication*] (OCD)
Ephes	Ephesians [*New Testament book*] (ROG)
EPHI	Electropharmacology, Inc. [*NASDAQ symbol*] (SAG)
EPhi	English Philips [*Record label*]
EPHIW	Electropharmacology Inc. Wrrt [*NASDAQ symbol*] (TTSB)
EPHL	Eastern Professional Hockey League
EPhMRA	European Pharmaceutical Marketing Research Association (EAIO)
EPHO	Ephemeris - Orbit
EPHR	Ephemeris - Reentry
Ephr	Ephraim (BJA)
EPHSOC	Ephemera Society [*British*]
EPI	Earth Path Indicator
EPI	Echo-Planar Imaging [*Physics*]
EPI	Economic Performance Indicator [*New York Stock Exchange*]
EPI	Economic Policy Institute (EA)
EPI	Economic Procurement Item (NATG)
EPI	Educational Planning Institute (EA)
EPI	Educational Priority Indices (AIE)
EPI	Edwards Personality Inventory [*Psychology*]
EPI	Ehrenreich Photo-Optical Industries, Inc.
EPI	Electronic Position Indicator
EPI	Electronic Processors Inc. (NITA)
EPI	Electron Photon Interaction
EPI	Elevation Position Indicator [*Aviation*]
EPI	Emergency Public Information [*Civil Defense*]

EPI	Emulsion Polymers Institute (EA)
EPI	Engine Performance Indicator (NG)
EPI	Environmental Policy Institute (EA)
EPI	Environmental Priorities Initiative
EPI	Epidote [*Petrology*]
epi	Epidural [*Medicine*] (DAVI)
EPI	Epilogue (ROG)
EPI	Epinephrine [*Endocrinology*]
EPI	Epistilbite [*A zeolite*]
EPI	Epitaxial (IAA)
EPI	Epithelial [*or Epithelium*] [*History*] (DAVI)
EPI	Estes Park Institute
EPI	European Paper Institute [*Research center*]
EPI	European Participating Industry
EPI	Evoked Potential Index [*Neurophysiology*]
EPI	Expanded Plan Indicator
EPI	Expanded Position Indicator
EPI	Expanded Programme on Immunization [*World Health Organization*]
EPI	Extension Producing Interneuron [*Neurology*]
EPI	Eysenck Personality Inventory [*Psychology*]
EPIA	Electric Power Industry Abstracts [*Utility Data Institute*] [*Information service or system*]
EPIA	End Poverty in America Society (EA)
EPIAI	EP [*Elvis Presley*] Impersonators Association International (EA)
EPIC	Earth-Pointing Instrument Carrier [*A satellite*]
EPIC	Educational Products Information Exchange (HGAA)
EPIC	Electromagnetic Principle Investigators Council [*An association*]
EPIC	Electronically-Processed Inter-Unit Cabling (PDAA)
EPIC	Electronically Programmed Injection Control [*Automotive engineering*]
EPIC	Electronic Page Image Composer (DGA)
EPIC	Electronic Photochromic Integrating Cathode-Ray [*Tube*]
EPIC	Electronic Portable Information Center [*Computer science*]
EPIC	Electronic Price Information Computer
EPIC	Electronic Printer Image Construction (DGA)
EPIC	Electronic Privacy Information Center
EPIC	Electronic Product Information Center [*Buick's computerized information network and database*]
EPIC	Electronic Production and Inventory Control (IAA)
EPIC	Electronic Properties Information Center [*DoD*]
EPIC	Electron-Positron Intersecting Complex (PDAA)
EPIC	El Paso [*Texas*] Intelligence Center [*Drug Enforcement Administration; Border Patrol; US Customs Service; Bureau of Alcohol, Tobacco, and Firearms; FAA; US Coast Guard*]
EPIC	Elyria Project for Innovative Curriculum (EDAC)
EPIC	Embedded Post-Beamformer Interference Canceler (CAAL)
EPIC	Emergency Programs Information Center [*Database*]
EPIC	Employment of Personnel in Computing (PDAA)
EPIC	End Poverty in California [*Slogan used by Upton Sinclair during campaign as Democratic candidate for governor of California, 1934*]
EPIC	Energy Conservation Program Guide for Industry and Commerce [*Department of Commerce*]
EPIC	Energy Policy Information Center [*Defunct*] (EA)
EPIC	Enhanced Performance Implanted CMOS [*Texas Instruments, Inc.*]
EPIC	Entry Point Interface Control
EPIC	Environmental Photographic Interpretation Center [*Environmental Protection Agency*]
EPIC	Epic Design Technology [*NASDAQ symbol*] (TTSB)
EPIC	Epic Design Technology, Inc. [*NASDAQ symbol*] (SAG)
EPIC	Epitaxial Passivated Integrated Circuits (MCD)
EPIC	Equatorial Pacific Information Collection [*Marine science*] (OSRA)
EPIC	Equatorial Pacific Information Collection (USDC)
EPIC	Equitrac's Professional Internet Client [*Computer science*]
EPIC	Erosion Productivity Impact Calculator (GNE)
EPIC	Estates Property Investment Co. [*British*]
EPIC	Estimate of Properties for Industrial Chemistry [*Universite de Liege*] [*Database*]
EPIC	European Proliferation Information Centre [*British*] (CB)
EPIC	Evaluator Programmer Integrated Circuit [*NASA*]
EPIC	Evidence Photographers International Council (EA)
EPIC	Exchange Price Indicators [*Database*] [*British*]
EPIC	Exchange Price Information Computer (MHDB)
EPIC	Exhaust Plume Interference Characterization [*NASA*] (KSC)
EPIC	Export Processing Industry Coalition
EPIC	Extended Performance and Increased Capability
EPIC	External Pneumatic Intermittent Compression
EPIC	Extraterrestrial Photographic Information Center [*NASA*]
EPICA	Ecumenical Program for Inter American Communication and Action [*Later, EPCAC*] (EA)
EPICA	European Program for Ice Coring in Antarctica [*Proposed start up date, 1997*]
EpicDes	Epic Design Technology, Inc. [*Associated Press*] (SAG)
EPICS	Energetic Pion Channel and Spectrometer (PDAA)
EPICS	Engine Production and Information Control System (PDAA)
EPICS	Enlisted Personnel Individualized Career System [*Military*] (MCD)
EPICS	European Petrochemical Industry Computerized System [*Parpinelli Tecnon*] [*Italy Information service or system*] (IID)
EPICS	Extended Power in Composition Systems (DGA)
Epict Diss	Epicteti Dissertationes [*of Arrian*] [*Classical studies*] (OCD)
EPID	Electrophoretic Image Display [*Analytical chemistry*] (IAA)
EPID	Epidemic
EPIDEM	Epidemiological (ADA)
EPIE	Educational Products Information Exchange
EPIE	Eskimo Pie [*NASDAQ symbol*] (TTSB)
EPIE	Eskimo Pie Corp. [*NASDAQ symbol*] (SAG)

EPIEI	Educational Products Information Exchange Institute [*Later, EPIE Institute*] (EA)
EPIG	Epigram (WDAA)
EPIGAS	Epigastrium [*The part above the stomach*] [*Pharmacy*] (ROG)
Epigr	Epigrammata [*Classical studies*] (OCD)
Epigr	Epigrammata Super Exilio [*of Seneca the Younger*] [*Classical studies*] (OCD)
Epigr Gr	Epigrammata Graeca ex Lapidibus Conlecta [*A publication*] (OCD)
EPII	Eagle Pacific Indus [*NASDAQ symbol*] (TTSB)
EPII	Eagle Pacific Industries, Inc. [*NASDAQ symbol*] (SAG)
EPIL	Epilepsy
EPIL	Epilogue
EPIL	European Partnership for Insurance Co-operation [*Proposed*] (ECON)
EPIN	Electronic Personnel Information Network [*Data Corp. of America*]
Epin	Epinomis [*of Plato*] [*Classical studies*] (OCD)
epineph	Epinephrine [*Endocrinology*] (DAVI)
EPINT	Executive Program Initialize
EPIO	Employment Prospects by Industry and Occupation [*A publication*] (ADA)
EPIP	Emergency Plan Implementing Procedure [*Nuclear energy*] (NRCH)
EP (IP)	Environment Protection (Impact of Proposals) [*Act 1974*] [*Commonwealth Act*] (EERA)
EPIPH	Epiphany
EPIRB	Emergency Position-Indicating Radio Beacon (MCD)
EPIRBs	Emergency Position Indicating Radio Beacons (AAGC)
EPIREPT	Epidemiological Report
EPIS	Episcopal
EPIS	Episiotomy [*Obstetrics*]
EPIS	Epistle
EPIS	Exchange Price Information Service [*Finance British*]
EPISC	Episcopal [*or Episcopalian*] (WDAA)
Episc	Episcopus [*Bishop*] [*Latin*]
EPISCPL	Episcopal
Epist	Epistulae [*Classical studies*] (OCD)
Epistolog Graec	Epistolographi Graeci [*A publication*] (OCD)
EPISTOM	Epistomium [*A Stopper*] [*Pharmacy*]
EPIT	Epitaph
Epit	Epitomae [*of Livy*] [*Classical studies*] (OCD)
EPIT	Epitome
Epit	Epitome [*Classical studies*] (OCD)
EPIT	Equipment Procurement and Installation Team (PDAA)
EPITH	Epithelium [*Medicine*]
EPITH	Epithet (ROG)
Epitope	Epitope, Inc. [*Associated Press*] (SAG)
Epit Oxyrh	Epitome Oxyrhynchica [*of Livy*] [*Classical studies*] (OCD)
EPITS	Essential Program Information, Technologies or Systems [*DoD*] (RDA)
EpJer	Epistle of Jeremy [*Apocrypha*] (BJA)
EPK	Early Prenatal Karyotype [*Medicine*] (DAVI)
EPK	Electronic Press Kit
EPK	Epitek International, Inc. [*Toronto Stock Exchange symbol*]
EPK	Equipotential Kathode
EPK	Ethnikon Phileleftheron Komma [*National Liberal Party*] [*Greek*] (PPE)
EPK	Partido Comunista de Euzkadi/Euzkadiko Partidu Komunista [*Basque Communist Party*] (PPW)
E$_{pk}$	Peak Voltage (IDOE)
EPKK	Krakow/Balice [*Poland ICAO location identifier*] (ICLI)
EPKL	European Pan-Keltic League (EA)
E$_{pk-pk}$	Peak-to-Peak Voltage (IDOE)
EPL	Early Programming Language [*Computer science*]
EPL	Edmonton Public Library [*UTLAS symbol*]
EPL	Effective Privilege Level [*Computer science*]
EPL	Ejercito Popular de Liberacion [*Popular Liberation Army*] [*El Salvador*] (PD)
EPL	Electrical Power Level (MCD)
EPL	Electronic, Electrical, and Electromechanical Parts List (NASA)
EPL	Electronic Intelligence Parameter Limits
EPL	Electronic Parties List [*On-line version of List of Parties Excluded from Federal Procurement and Non-Procurement Programs*] (AAGC)
EPL	Electronic Products Laboratory (IAA)
EPL	Electronic Switching Systems Programming Language [*Computer science*] (MHDB)
EPL	Electroplate (MSA)
EPL	Elliptically Polarized Light
EPL	Emergency Power Level (KSC)
EPL	Emitter Position Location
EPL	Emitter Program Library (CAAL)
EPL	Encoder Programming Language [*Computer science*]
EPL	Engineering Parts List (KSC)
EPL	Environmental Protection Limit (NRCH)
EPL	Equal Protection of the Law [*Legal shorthand*] (LWAP)
EPL	Equipment Performance Log
EPL	Erie County Library, Erie, PA [*OCLC symbol*] (OCLC)
EPL	Excess Profits Levy [*British*]
EPL	Executive Professional Leadership (AEBS)
EPL	Extensor Pollicis Longus [*Anatomy*]
e-pl--	Poland [*MARC geographic area code Library of Congress*] (LCCP)
EPLA	Electronics Precedence List Agency
EPLA	Eritrean People's Liberation Army [*Ethiopia*] [*Political party*] (EY)
EPLAF	European Planning Federation [*British*] (EA)
EPLANS	Engineering, Planning, and Analysis Systems [*Telecommunications*] (TEL)

EPLB............ Environmental Pre-Language Battery [*Speech and language therapy*] (DAVI)

EPLD............ Electrically Programmable Logic Device [*Computer science*]

EPLD............ Erasable Programmable Logic Device (NITA)

EPL/DRL...... Engineering Parts List/Drawing Release List (KSC)

EPLF............ Eritrean People's Liberation Front [*Ethiopia*] (PD)

EPLIB........... Environment Programme Library [*Database*] [*UNEP*] [*United Nations*] (DUND)

EPLJ .... Environmental and Planning Law Journal [*Australia A publication*]

EPLP............ European Parliamentary Labor Party [*European Community*] [*Political party*]

EPLRS .... Enhanced Position Location Reporting System [*Army*] (INF)

EPLS............ Eastern Peninsula Library System [*Library network*]

EPLT............ Electocon International, Inc. [*NASDAQ symbol*] (SAG)

EPLT............ Electrocon International, Inc. [*NASDAQ symbol*] (NQ)

EPLTF.......... Electrocon Intl. [*NASDAQ symbol*] (TTSB)

EPM............. Earth-Probe-Mars [*Angle*]

EPM............. Ecole Polytechnique, Bibliotheque [*Montreal*] [*UTLAS symbol*]

EPM............. Economic Performance Monitoring (OA)

EPM............. Economic Planning Machine [*British*]

EPM............. Education for Public Management [*Program*] [*Civil Service Commission*] (RDA)

EPM............. Educator's Purchasing Master [*A publication*]

EPM............. Elastic Plastic Membrane

EPM............. Electric Power Monthly [*A publication*] (GFGA)

EPM............. Electronic Pacemaker [*Cardiology*] (DAVI)

EPM............. Electronic Parts Manual

EPM............. Electronic Photocomposing Machine (DGA)

EPM............. Electron Probe Microanalysis [*Also, EPMA*]

EPM............. Emigration Portfolio Manager [*Investment term*]

EPM............. Empirical Pseudopotential Method [*Physics*]

EPM............. Encyclopedia of Protest Movements [*A publication*]

EPM............. Energy-Protein Malnutrition

EPM............. Engineering Procedure Memorandum [*Nuclear Regulatory Commission*] (GFGA)

EPM............. Engineering Procedures Manual

EPM............. Engine Powertrain Management [*Automotive engineering*]

EPM............. Environmental Planning and Management (EERA)

EPM............. Environmental Project Manager (NRCH)

EPM............. Equivalent per Million (IAA)

EPM............. Equivalents per Million (DNAB)

EPM............. External Polarization Modulation (IEEE)

EPM............. External Protection Material (MCD)

EPMA.......... Electron Probe Microanalysis [*Also, EPM*]

EPMAC........ Enlisted Personnel Management Center [*Navy*] (NVT)

EPMARKUP.. European Publishers' Markup User Group

EPMaRV ...... Earth Penetrating Maneuverable Reentry Vehicle [*Military*]

EPMAU .... Expected Present Multiattribute Utility (IEEE)

EPMCC........ Enesco Precious Moments Collectors' Club (EA)

EPMD.......... Enlisted Personnel Management Directorate

EPMD.......... Eric and Parrish Making Dollars [*Rap recording group*]

EPMF........... Employees' Plan Master File [*IRS*]

EPMMA....... European Proprietary Medicines Manufacturers Association [*Belgium*] (EAIO)

EPMP........... Ethyl(para-Nitrophenyl)methylphosphonate [*Biochemistry*]

EPMR........... Embarked Personnel Material Report [*Navy*] (ANA)

EPMS........... Engineering Performance Management System (NASA)

EPMS........... Engineering Performance Measurement System (MCD)

EPMS........... Engineering Project Management System (MCD)

EPMS........... Engine Performance Monitoring System (MCD)

EPMS........... Enlisted Personnel Management System [*Army*] (AABC)

EPN............. Effective Perceived Noise [*Aviation*]

EPN............. Engineering Part Number [*Automotive engineering*]

EPN............. Engineering Program Notice (AFIT)

EPN............. Epena [*Congo*] [*Airport symbol*] (OAG)

EPN............. Ethyl-Para-Nitrophenyl Phenylphosphonothioate [*An insecticide*]

EPN............. Excitatory Premotor Neuron [*Neurology*]

EPN............. Extended Parliamentary Network

EPN............. External Priority Number [*Computer science*] (OA)

EPNdB .... Effective-Perceived-Noise Decibel Level [*Aviation*]

EPNL........... Effective-Perceived-Noise Level [*Aviation*]

EPNLDB ...... Effective Perceived Noise-Level Decibel [*Aviation*] (IIA)

EPNP .... Epoxy(nitrophenoxy)propane [*Organic chemistry*]

EPNS .... Electroplated Nickel Silver

EPNS .... English Place-Name Society

EPO............. Earth Parking Orbit [*Apollo*] [*NASA*]

EPO............. Elected Public Official

EPO............. Electron Plasma Oscillation [*Astrophysics*]

EPO............. Electrostatic Plasma Oscillator

EPO............. Element Project Office [*NASA*] (NASA)

EPO............. Emergency Planning Officer [*Army*]

EPO............. Emergency Power Off

EPO............. Energy Policy Office [*Formerly, National Energy Office*] [*Executive Office of the President Abolished, 1974*]

EPO............. Engine Project Office [*NASA*] (KSC)

EPO............. Engine Propeller Order (MSA)

EPO............. Enlisted Programs Officer (DNAB)

EPO............. Environmental, Population, and Organismic Biology

EPO............. Eosinophil Peroxidase [*An enzyme*]

EPO............. Epichlorohydrin Ethylene Oxide [*Organic chemistry*]

EPO............. Epidemiology Program Office [*Department of Health and Human Services*] (GRD)

EPO............. Erythropoietin [*Also, Ep*] [*Hematology*]

EPO............. Estuarine Programs Office [*National Oceanic and Atmospheric Administration*]

EPO............. European Patent Office [*Germany*] (PDAA)

EPO............. Examination Procedure Outline [*Weighing equipment*]

EPO............. Exclusive Provider Organization [*Medicine*]

EPO............. Experiment Performance Option

EPO............. Expo Oil [*Vancouver Stock Exchange symbol*]

e-po--.......... Portugal [*MARC geographic area code Library of Congress*] (LCCP)

EPOA........... Eastcoast Petroleum Operators' Association [*Canada*]

EPOA........... Exercise Plan of Analysis (MCD)

EPOA........... External Plant Operators' Association of South Australia

EPOC........... Eastern Pacific Oceanic Conference

EPOC........... Employers' Perceptions of Colleges (AIE)

EPOC........... Employment Policy and Organization Committee [*British*] (DCTA)

EPOC........... Environment Protection Policy (EERA)

EPOC........... Equity Policy Center (EA)

EPOC........... ESCAP [*Economic and Social Commission for Asia and the Pacific*] Pacific Operations Center [*Vanuatu*]

EPOC........... Evening Primrose Oil Capsules [*Trade name*] [*British*]

EPOC........... External Payload Operations Center

EPOCA........ Environmental Project on Central America [*Defunct*] (EA)

EPOCH........ Educational Programming of Cultural Heritage (AEBS)

EPOCS .... Equatorial Pacific Ocean Climate Studies [*National Oceanic and Atmospheric Administration*]

Epod .... Epodi [*of Horace*] [*Classical studies*] (OCD)

EPOE........... End Piece of Equipment

EPOI........... Ehrenreich Photo-Optical Industries, Inc.

EPOP........... Each Pays Own Postage

EPOR .... Electronics Performance and Operational Report (DNAB)

EPOR .... Erythropoietin Receptor [*Hematology*]

EPOS .... Earthquake Phenomena Observation System [*Japan*] [*Marine science*] (OSRA)

EPOS .... Earthquake Phenomena Observation System [*Japan*] (USDC)

EPOS .... Electronic Point-of-Sale [*Computer science*]

EPOSS .... Environmental Protection Oil Sands Systems (PDAA)

EPP............. Concord, NH [*Location identifier FAA*] (FAAL)

EPP............. Earth Physics Program

EPP............. Editions Phonographiques Parisiennes - Allegro Label [*Record label*] [*France*]

EPP............. Effective Program Projections

EPP............. Electrical Power Panel (MCD)

EPP............. Electric Power Plant (MCD)

EPP............. Electronic Postproduction (NTCM)

EPP............. Emergency Power Package (NG)

EPP............. End Plate Potential

EPP............. End Point Prediction

EPP............. Engineered Polypropylene [*Plastics*] [*Automotive engineering*]

EPP............. Engineering and Public Policy [*Graduate program, Carnegie-Mellon University*]

EPP............. Enhanced Parallel Port (PCM)

EPP............. Enron Global Power & Pipeline Co. [*NYSE symbol*] (SAG)

EPP............. Enron Global Pwr/Pipeln LLC [*NYSE symbol*] (TTSB)

EPP............. Environmental Protection Program (CAAL)

EPP............. Environment Protection Program (EERA)

EPP............. Epistolae [*Epistles, Letters*] [*Latin*] (ROG)

EPP............. Equal Payment Plan

EPP............. Equal Pressure Point (MAE)

EPP............. Erythropoietic Protoporphyria [*A genetic disorder*]

EPP............. Estimating Price Policy

EPP............. Ethernet Packet Processor (CDE)

EPP............. European Pallet Pool (PDAA)

EPP............. European People's Party - Federation of Christian Democratic Parties of the European Community [*Brussels, Belgium*]

EPP............. European Producer Price

EPP............. Excess Personal Property

EPP............. Exchangeable-Potassium-Percentage

EPP............. Executive Pension Plan (ODBW)

EPP............. Extra-Pair Paternity [*Biology*]

EPP............. Eysenck Personality Profiler [*Psychology*]

E$_{p-p}$......... Peak-to-Peak Voltage (IDOE)

EPPA........... Employee Polygraph Protection Act of 1988

EPPA........... Established Pattern of Psychodynamic Adaptation

EPPAA .... European Pure Phosphoric Acid Producers' Association [*Belgium*] (EAIO)

EPPAPA ...... European Pure Phosphoric Acid Producers' Association [*Belgium*] (EAIO)

EPPASF....... Elvis Presley Performing Arts Scholarship Foundation (EA)

EPPASFV ..... Elvis Presley Performing Arts Scholarship Foundation of Virginia [*Later, EPPASF*] (EA)

EPPB........... Export Promotion Programme Budget [*British*]

EPPC........... Ethics and Public Policy Center (EA)

EPPD .... Estate Planning for Persons with Disabilities [*An association*] (PAZ)

EPPHI .... Educators of Professional Personnel for the Hearing Impaired

EPPI........... Eastern Pennsylvania Psychiatric Institute

EPPI........... Electronic Plan Position Indicator (IAA)

EPPI........... Electronic Programmed Procurement Information (NG)

EPPIC......... Early Psychosis Prevention and Intervention Centre [*Australia*]

EPPIC......... Educate People - Protect Innocent Children [*Defunct*] (EA)

EPPK.......... Epidermolytic Palmoplantar Keratoderma [*Medicine*]

EPPL .... Electronic Preferred Parts List [*Jet Propulsion Laboratory, NASA*]

EPPL .... Emergency Production Planning List [*Army*]

EPPL .... Epithelial Possibly Precancerous Lesion

EPPL .... Excess Personal Property List

EPPMA........ Expanded Polystyrene Product Manufacturers' Association [*British*] (BI)

EPPO .... Earth Physics and Physical Oceanography Program [*NASA*]

EPPO .... European and Mediterranean Plant Protection Organization [*See also* OEPP] (EAIO)
EPPO .... Poznan/Lawica [*Poland ICAO location identifier*] (ICLI)
EPPP .... Emergency Production Planning Program [*Navy*] (NG)
EPPPI .... Expanded Partial Plan Position Indicator (IAA)
EPPR .... Environmental Protection Agency Procurement Regulations [*A publication*] (AAGC)
EPPS .... Edwards Personal Preference Scale [*or Schedule*] [*Psychology*]
EPPS .... Electrical Power/Pyro Sequential System (MCD)
EPPS .... Electronic Publishing and Prepress Systems (DGA)
EPPs .... Enhanced Parallel Ports [*Computer science*]
EPPT .... Electrical Power Production Technician (IAA)
EPPT .... European Printer Performance Test (ODBW)
EPPT/S .... Electrical Power Production Technician/Specialist (AAG)
EPPVS .... Emergency Propulsive Propellant Venting System
EPQ .... Economic Production Quantity (AAGC)
EPQ .... Embarrassing Personal Question [*National Security Agency screening procedure*]
EPQ .... Engineering Qualification Trials (DOMA)
EPQ .... Eysenck Personality Questionnaire [*Personality development test*] [*Psychology*]
EPR .... Earnings Price Ratio
EPR .... Eastern Pakistan Rifles [*British military*] (DMA)
EPR .... East Pacific Rise [*Geology*]
EPR .... Economic Production Rate (MCD)
EPR .... Education in Personal Relationships (AIE)
EPR .... Effector-Cell Protease Receptor [*Biochemistry*]
EPR .... Einstein-Podolsky-Rosen [*Quantum mechanics*]
EPR .... Electrical Pressure Regulator (IEEE)
EPR .... Electrochemical Potentiokinetic Reactivation [*Metallurgical test*]
EPR .... Electromechanical Potentiokinetic Reactivation Test [*Nuclear energy*] (NRCH)
EPR .... Electronic Parts Reliability
EPR .... Electronic Procurement Regulation [*Defense Supply Agency*]
EPR .... Electron Paramagnetic Resonance [*Also, ESR*] [*Physics*]
EPR .... Electrophrenic Respiration [*Medicine*]
EPR .... Elimination of Purchase Requirement [*Department of Agriculture*]
EPR .... El Paraiso Resources Ltd. [*Vancouver Stock Exchange symbol*]
EPR .... Emergency Parts Requisition (KSC)
EPR .... Emergency Physical Restraint [*Medicine*] (DAVI)
EPR .... Engineering Parts Release (KSC)
EPR .... Engineering Planning Report
EPR .... Engineering Power Reactor
EPR .... Engineer Photographic and Reproduction [*Marine Corps*]
EPR .... Engine Power [*or Pressure*] Ratio
EPR .... Engine Pressure Ratio (GAVI)
EPR .... Enriched Pulverised Refuse (PDAA)
EPR .... Equipment Performance Report
EPR .... Equipotential Region
EPR .... Equivalent Parallel Resistance (DEN)
EPR .... Error Pattern Register
EPR .... Error-Prone Repair (GNE)
EPR .... Esperance [*Australia Airport symbol*] (OAG)
EPR .... Essential Performance Requirements (NATG)
EPR .... Estimated Price Request (MCD)
EPR .... Estradiol Production Rate [*Endocrinology*] (MAE)
EPR .... Ethylene Propylene Rubber [*Organic chemistry*]
EPR .... Evaluation Project Report [*Air Force*]
EPR .... Evaporator Pressure Regulator (DNAB)
EPR .... Exhaust Pressure Ratio
EPR .... Exhaust Pressure Regulator [*Automotive engineering*]
EPR .... Experimental Power Reactor (MCD)
EPR .... Explosion-Proof Relay
EPR .... Expreso Aereo [*Peru*] [*ICAO designator*] (FAAC)
EPR .... External Power Relay (MCD)
EPR .... Extreme Pressure Ratio [*Military*]
EPR .... Eye Point of Regard [*NASA*]
EPRA .... Eastern Psychiatric Research Association (EA)
EPRA .... Electronic Production Resources Agency [*Military*]
ePRAI .... Escherichia Coli Phosphoribosyl Anthranilate Isomerase
EPRC .... European Policies Research Centre [*University of Strathclyde*] [*Glasgow, Scotland*] [*Database producer*] (IID)
EPRD .... Electrical Power Requirements Data
EPRD .... Emergency Plans and Readiness Division [*of OEP*] [*Terminated*]
EPRDF .... Ethiopian People's Revolutionary Democratic Front [*Political party*] (ECON)
EPRF .... Energy Probe Research Foundation [*Canada*] (IRC)
EPRF .... Environmental Prediction Research Facility [*Monterey, CA*] [*Navy*]
EPRF .... Exhausted Publications Reference File (MCD)
EPRG .... Emergency Planning Review Guideline [*Nuclear energy*] (NRCH)
EPR/G .... End-Paper Rubbed, Else Good [*Condition*] [*Antiquarian book trade*]
EPRI .... Electric Power Research Institute [*Palo Alto, CA*] (ECON)
EPRI .... Electric Power Research Institute (USDC)
EPRI .... Engine Pressure Ratio Indicator
EPRI .... Environmental Protection Research Institute
EPRICS .... Emergency Power Ride through Capability System [*Nuclear energy*] (NUCP)
EPRI-HVTRC ... Electric Power Research Institute, High Voltage Transmission Research Center [*Research center*] (RCD)
EPRI RDS .... EPRI Research and Development Information System (NITA)
EPRL .... Electric Power Research Laboratory [*Arizona State University*] [*Research center*] (RCD)
EPRL .... Warszawa [*Poland ICAO location identifier*] (ICLI)
EPRLF .... Eelam People's Revolutionary Liberation Front [*Sri Lanka*] [*Political party*]

EPRM .... Equipment Performance Report Management System (MCD)
EPRN .... Eastern Public Radio Network (NTCM)
EPRN .... Emergency Program Release Notice [*NASA*] (NASA)
EPRO .... Eastern Professional River Outfitters Association (EA)
EPRO .... Etudes Preliminaires aux Religions Orientales dans l'Empire Romain [*A publication*] (BJA)
EPROI .... Expected Project Return on Investment [*Finance*] (PDAA)
EPROM .... Electrically Programmable Read-Only Memory [*Computer science*] (MCD)
EPROM .... Erasable Programmable Read-Only Memory [*Computer science*] (MCD)
EPRP .... Ethiopian People's Revolutionary Party [*Political party*] (PD)
EPRS .... Electron Paramagnetic Resonance Spectroscopy
EPRTCS .... Emergency Power Ride-Through Capability System [*Nuclear energy*] (NRCH)
ePrv .... Enolpyruvate [*Biochemistry*]
EPRZ .... Rzeszow/Jasionka [*Poland ICAO location identifier*] (ICLI)
EPS .... Acute Extrapyramidal Syndrome [*Medicine*]
EPS .... Early Prolific Straightneck Summer Squash
EPS .... Earnings per Share [*Finance*]
EPS .... Earth-Probe-Sun [*Angle*]
EPS .... Elastosis Perforans Serpiginosa [*Medicine*]
EPS .... Electrical Power Storage (ROG)
EPS .... Electrical Power Supply
EPS .... Electrical Power System [*or Subsystem*]
EPS .... Electrical Programmed Stimulation [*Medicine*] (CPH)
EPS .... Electric Power Source (MCD)
EPS .... Electric Power Steering System [*Automotive engineering*]
EPS .... Electric Power System [*or Subsystem*] (NRCH)
EPS .... Electric Propulsion System
EPS .... Electrochemical Photocapacitance Spectroscopy
EPS .... Electromagnetic Position Sensor
EPS .... Electronic Payments System
EPS .... Electronic Plate Scanner (DGA)
EPS .... Electronic Power Steering [*Mitsubishi*] [*Automotive engineering*]
EPS .... Electronic Prepress System (DGA)
EPS .... Electronic Protection System (IIA)
EPS .... Electronic Publishing System (BYTE)
EPS .... Electron-Proton Spectrometer
EPS .... Electrophysiologic Study
EPS .... Electropneumatic Gear Shift [*System*]
EPS .... El Paso Southern Railway Co. [*AAR code*]
EPS .... Embossing Press Station
EPS .... Emergency Power Supply
EPS .... Emergency Power System
EPS .... Emergency Pressurization System
EPS .... Emergency Procurement Service [*Later, Defense Materials Service*]
EPS .... Encapsulated Post-Script [*Computer science*]
EPS .... Encapsulated PostScript File [*Computer science*] (EERA)
EPS .... Encoder Power Supply
EPS .... Endoscopic Paravariceal Sclerotherapy [*Medicine*]
EPS .... Energetic Particles Satellite [*NASA*] (MUGU)
EPS .... Engineering Performance Standards
EPS .... Engineering Planning Skeleton (MCD)
EPS .... Engineering Print System [*Xerox*]
EPS .... Engineering Procedures Services (MCD)
EPS .... Engineering Purchase Specification
EPS .... Entertainment Production Services [*British*]
EPS .... Environmental Priorities Strategies [*Volvo*] [*Automotive engineering*]
EPS .... Environmental Protection Service, West Vancouver [*Environment Canada*] [*Research center*] (RCD)
EPS .... Environmental Protection Shelter (MCD)
EPS .... Environmental Protection System (AAG)
EPS .... Environmental Purification Systems, Inc.
EPS .... Epps Air Service, Inc. [*ICAO designator*] (FAAC)
EPS .... Equilibrium Problem Solver (IEEE)
EPS .... Equipment Policy Statement [*Army*] (AABC)
EPS .... Equipotential Surface
EPS .... Equivalent Prior Sample [*Information*] [*Statistics*]
EPS .... Essay-Proof Society (EA)
EPS .... Ethiopian Philatelic Society (EA)
EPS .... European Passenger Services [*British*] (ECON)
EPS .... European Physical Society (EAIO)
EPS .... Even Parity Select
EPS .... Event Processing System
EPS .... Excitation Power Supply (MCD)
EPS .... Executive Planning Section [*British military*] (DMA)
EPS .... Executive Profile Survey [*Management and supervision test*]
EPS .... Executive Protective Service [*Formerly, White House Police; later, USSS/UD*]
EPS .... Exercise Planning Staff [*NATO*] (NATG)
EPS .... Exocellular Polysaccharide [*Biochemistry*]
EPS .... Exophthalmos-Producing Substance [*Endocrinology*]
EPS .... Exotic Pathology Society [*Paris, France*] (EAIO)
EPS .... Expandable [*or Expanded*] Polystyrene [*Plastics Technology*]
EPS .... Experimental Power Supply (NASA)
EPS .... Experimental Procurement Service
EPS .... Experimental Prototype Silo (SAA)
EPS .... Experimental Psychology Society [*British*]
EPS .... Experimental Publications System [*Defunct*]
EPS .... Experiment Pointing System [*NASA*]
EPS .... Expressed Prostatic Secretion [*Physiology*]
EPS .... Extensible Programming System [*Computer science*] (CSR)
EPS .... External Page Storage [*Computer science*] (BUR)
EPS .... Extrapyramidal Symptoms [*Medicine*]

EPS............	Extrapyramidal Syndrome [*Neurology and psychiatry*] (DAVI)
EPS............	Eye Protection Shutter
EPS............	Ezra Pound Society (EA)
EPSA.........	Educational Program in Systems Analysis (RDA)
EPSA.........	Electrostatic Particle Size Analyzer
EPSC.........	Emergency Petroleum Supply Committee [*Terminated, 1976*] (EA)
EPSC.........	Excitatory Postsynaptic Current [*Neurophysiology*]
EPSCG.......	Groupe de Contact Parlementaire et Scientifique [*European Parliamentary and Scientific Contact Group*] (EA)
EPSCoR.......	Experimental Program to Stimulate Competitive Research [*National Science Foundation*]
EPSCS........	Enhanced Private Switched Communications Service [*Pronounced "ep-sis"*] [*AT & T*]
EPSD	Electronics and Power Sources Directorate [*Army*] (RDA)
EPSDT........	Early and Periodic Screening, Diagnosis, and Treatment
EPSDU........	Experimental Process System Development Unit [*Photovoltaic energy systems*]
EPSEIS........	Encyclopedia of Physical Sciences and Engineering Information Sources [*A publication*]
EPSF..........	Early Postsurgical Fitting [*Medicine*]
EPSF..........	Employee Profile Security File [*IRS*]
EPSF..........	Encapsulated Post-Script Draw Format [*Computer science*]
EPSG	Electronic Publishing Specialist Group (NITA)
EPSG	Epiphytic Plant Study Group [*British*] (DBA)
EPSG	European Pineal Study Group (EAIO)
EPSI	Earnings per Share Issued [*Finance*]
EPSI	Erikson Psychosocial Stage Inventory [*Psychology*]
EPSIA........	Eastern Professional Ski Instructors Association [*Formerly, EPSTI*] (EA)
EPSIG	Electronic Publishing Special Interest Group [*Association of American Publishers*]
EPSL..........	Eastern Primary Standards Laboratory
EPSL..........	Emergency Power Switching Logic (NRCH)
EPSLN........	Epsilon
EPSOC	Earth-Physics Satellite Observation [*or Observing*] Campaign [*Smithsonian Astrophysical Observatory*]
EPSOC	Ephemera Society of America (EA)
EPSP..........	Enolpyruvylshikimic Acid Phosphate [*Organic chemistry*]
EPSP..........	Excitatory Postsynaptic Potential [*Neurophysiology*]
EPSP..........	Experiment Power Switching Panel (MCD)
EPSP..........	Extra Prime Skills Program (DICI)
EPSPS........	Enolpyruvylshikimatephosphate Synthase [*An enzyme*]
EPSRC........	Engineering and Physical Sciences Research Council [*British*]
EPSS..........	Electronic Performance Support System (CDE)
EPSS..........	Experimental Packet Switching System [*Telecommunications*]
EPST..........	Encyclopedia of Polymer Science and Technology [*A publication*]
EPSTF........	Electrical Power System Test Facility [*NASA*] (KSC)
EPSTI.........	Eastern Professional Ski Touring Instructors [*Later, EPSIA*] (EA)
EPT	Early Pregnancy Test
EPT	Economic Power Transmission
EPT	Electric Power Transmission (ADA)
EPT	Electrostatic Printing Tube
EPT	El Paso [*Texas*] [*Seismograph station code, US Geological Survey*] (SEIS)
EPT	Emergency Procedure Trainer [*NASA*] (NASA)
EPT	Endoscopic Papillotomy [*Medicine*]
EPT	End-Point Temperature [*Food science*]
EPT	English Placement Test [*Education*]
EPT	Environmental Proof Test (IAA)
EPT	Epitope, Inc. [*AMEX symbol*] (SPSG)
EPT	Epsilon Pi Tau (EA)
EPT	Ethylene Propylene Terpolymer [*Organic chemistry*]
EPT	Euro Petroleum Corp. [*Toronto Stock Exchange symbol Vancouver Stock Exchange symbol*]
EPT	Evoked Potential Technique [*Neurophysiology*]
EPT	Examination Division Planning Tape [*IRS*]
EPT	Excess Profits Tax
EPT	Experimental Prototype Test (MCD)
EPT	External Pipe Thread [*Technical drawings*]
EPT	Extraction Procedure Toxicity
EPTA	Electric Propulsion Trajectory Analysis
EPTA	Electrophysiological Technologists' Association (EAIO)
EPTA	European Piano Teachers Association (EAIO)
EPTA	European Power Tool Association (EAIO)
EPTA	Expanded Program of Technical Assistance [*United Nations*]
EPTAQ........	Executive Program Task Assignment Queue Manager (MCD)
EPTC..........	Electronic Programmable Transmission Control [*Off-highway vehicles*]
EPTC..........	Ethyl Dipropylthiocarbamate [*Organic chemistry*]
EPTC..........	Extraction Procedure Toxicity Characteristic [*Environmental Protection Agency*]
EPTD..........	Ethylphosphonothioicdichloride [*Organic chemistry*]
EPTE	Existed Prior to Enlistment [*Especially, dependency or physical defect*] [*Military*]
EPTE	Existed Prior to Entry [*Military*]
EP Tech	EP Technologies, Inc. [*Associated Press*] (SAG)
EPTFC........	Elvis Presley Tribute Fan Club [*Defunct*] (EA)
EPTFE........	Expanded Polytetrafluoroethylene [*Organic chemistry*]
EPTG..........	Electronic Publication Technology Group [*Defunct*] (EA)
EPTI..........	Existed Prior to Induction [*Especially, dependency or physical defect*] [*Military*]
EPTK..........	EP Technologies, Inc. [*NASDAQ symbol*] (SAG)
EPTL..........	Estates, Powers, and Trusts Law [*A publication*]
EPTO..........	Engineer Packaging Technical Office [*Merged with General Equipment Command*]

EPTS...........	Engine Power Trim System
EPTS...........	Existed Prior to Entry Service [*Military*]
EPTT	Comite Europeen de l'Internationale du Personnel des Postes, Telegraphes et Telephones [*European Committee of the Postal, Telegraph and Telephone International*] [*EC*] (ECED)
EPTTC.........	European Passenger Train Timetable Conference (EA)
EPTU	Events per Time Unit (NASA)
EPTW	Educational Programs that Work [*Department of Education*] [*Information service or system*] (IID)
EPU............	East Promontory [*Utah*] [*Seismograph station code, US Geological Survey*] (SEIS)
EPU............	Economic Planning Unit [*Generic term*] (DS)
EPU............	Electrical Power Unit
EPU............	Electronic Power Unit (IDOE)
EPU............	Emergency Power Unit (IDOE)
EPU............	Emergency Power Unit
EPU............	Empire Press Union (DGA)
EPU............	Entry Processing Unit [*Computer science*] (DCTA)
EPU............	Environmental Physiology Unit [*Simon Fraser University*] [*Canada Research center*] (RCD)
EPU............	Epidermal Proliferative Unit (PDAA)
EPU............	European Payments Union
EPU............	Executive Processing Unit
EPUB	Electronic Publishing System [*ITT Dialcom*] [*Database*]
EPUBS	Electronic Publishing Abstracts [*The Research Association for the Paper and Board, Printing and Packaging Industries*] [*Database*]
EPUR	Enviropur Waste Refining & Technology, Inc. [*NASDAQ symbol*] (SAG)
EPUR	Enviropur Waste Refining/Tech [*NASDAQ symbol*] (TTSB)
EPURE	Etude de la Protection des Usagers de la Route et de l'Environement [*Study of Road User Safety and Environmental Protection*] [*French Automotive engineering*]
EPUS	Episcopus [*Bishop*] [*Latin*]
EPUT..........	Events per Unit Time
EPUTS	Emergency Power Unit Test Set
EPUU	Enhanced PLRS [*Position Location Reporting System*] User Unit [*Air Force*]
EPUU/MLS ...	EPLRS [*Enhanced Position Location Reporting System*] User Unit/ Microwave Landing System (MCD)
EPV	Earth Probe near Limb of Venus [*Angle*]
EPV	Electric Polarization Vector
EPV	Electric Powered Vehicle
EPV	Electropneumatic Valve
EPV	Emergency Pressurization Valve (MCD)
EPV	Evangelische Progressieve Volkspartij [*Evangelical Progressive People's Party*] [*Netherlands*] (PPW)
EPV	External Pressure Vessel
EPVS..........	Emergency Propellant Venting System
EPVT..........	English Picture Vocabulary Test [*Educational test*] (EDAC)
EPVTS.........	English Picture Vocabulary Tests [*Educational test*]
EPW	Earth-Penetrating Warhead (RDA)
EPW	Earth Penetrator Weapon (MCD)
EPW	Electric Pressure Wave
EPW	Electron Plasma Wave [*Physics*]
EPW	Elektra Power, Inc. [*Vancouver Stock Exchange symbol*]
EPW	Elliptically Polarized Wave
EPW	Enemy Prisoner of War [*Army*] (AABC)
EPW	Ephrata [*Washington*] [*Seismograph station code, US Geological Survey*] (SEIS)
EPWA.........	Warszawa/Okecie [*Poland ICAO location identifier*] (ICLI)
EPWG.........	Electromagnetic Propagation Working Group [*Army*]
EPWG.........	Energy Production Working Group [*Australia*]
EPWG.........	Environmental Projects Working Group [*NASA*] (NASA)
EPWIB	Enemy Prisoner of War Information Bureau [*Army*] (AABC)
EPWIB(Br) ...	Enemy Prisoner of War Information Bureau (Branch) [*Army*] (AABC)
EPWM.........	Electroplate White Metal (IAA)
EPWR	Emergency Power
EPWS..........	Emergency Production Weapons Schedule [*Navy*] (NG)
EP-X...........	Efficient Personal-Experimental [*Concept vehicle*]
EPX............	Electronic Patrol, Experimental (MCD)
EPXMA........	Electron Probe X-Ray Microanalyzer
EPY	Extra-Pair Young [*Biology*]
EPZ............	Electron Polar Zone
EPZ............	Emergency Planning Zone [*Nuclear emergency planning*]
EPZ............	Export Processing Zone (ECON)
EPZA..........	Export Processing Zone Authority
EQ.............	Economic Quotient
EQ.............	Educational Quotient [*Psychology*]
EQ.............	Emo Questionnaire [*Psychology*]
EQ.............	Encephalization Quotient
EQ.............	Energy Quotient
EQ.............	Engineering Quality
EQ.............	Enquiries [*Telecommunications*] (TEL)
EQ.............	Environmental Quality
EQ.............	Equal
eq.............	Equal [*Copyediting*] (WDMC)
EQ.............	Equality (ROG)
EQ.............	Equalization [*Electronics*]
EQ.............	Equalizer
EQ.............	Equation (KSC)
EQ.............	Equator (WDAA)
EQ.............	Equatorial
EQ.............	Equerry
EQ.............	Eques [*Knight*] [*Latin*] (ROG)
EQ.............	Equestrian (ROG)

EQ.............. Equipment (BUR)
EQ.............. Equipmentman [*Military*] (DNAB)
EQ.............. Equipment Qualification (NRCH)
Eq .... Equitable [*Legal term*] (DLA)
EQ .... Equitable Co. [*NYSE symbol*] (SPSG)
EQ.............. Equitable Cos. [*NYSE symbol*] (TTSB)
Eq .... Equites [*Knights*] [*of Aristophanes*] [*Classical studies*] (OCD)
EQ.............. Equity
Eq .... Equity Court [*or Division*] [*Legal term*] (DLA)
Eq .... Equity Reports [*A publication*] (DLA)
EQ.............. Equivalent
EQ.............. Ethnic Quotient
EQA.............. Educational Quality Assessment Program [*Pennsylvania*] (EDAC)
EQA.............. El Dorado, KS [*Location identifier FAA*] (FAAL)
EQA.............. Equipment Quality Analysis
EQA.............. European Quality Alliance [*Proposed merger between four European airlines*] (ECON)
EQA.............. OCLC [*Online Computer Library Center*] Europe, Birmingham, England [*OCLC symbol*] (OCLC)
Eq Ab.......... Abridgment of Cases in Equity [*1667-1744*] [*A publication*] (DLA)
EQ AUR........ Eques Auratus [*Knight Bachelor*] [*Latin*] (ROG)
EQB.............. Chambersburg, PA [*Location identifier FAA*] (FAAL)
EQBLE......... Equitable [*Legal term*] (ROG)
EQC.............. Environmental Quality Control
EQC.............. Environmental Quality Council [*Terminated, 1970*] (MCD)
EQC.............. Externally Quenched Counter
Eq Ca Ab ..... Equity Cases Abridged [*A publication*]
Eq Ca Abr ... Abridgment of Cases in Equity [*1667-1744*] [*A publication*] (DLA)
Eq Cas........ Equity Cases [*A publication*] (DLA)
Eq Cas........ Gilbert's English Equity Cases [*A publication*] (DLA)
Eq Cas Abr... Equity Cases Abridged [*2 vols.*] [*21, 22 English Reprint*] [*A publication*] (DLA)
Eq Cas Abr (Eng)... Equity Cases Abridged [*2 vols.*] [*21, 22 English Reprint*] [*A publication*] (DLA)
Eq Cas Mod... Equity Cases [*A publication*] (DLA)
EQCC .... Entry Query Control Console [*Computer science*]
EQCC .... Environmental Quality Control Committee
EQCM........... Electrochemical Quartz-Crystal Microbalance [*Biochemistry*]
EQCM........... Master Chief Equipmentman [*Navy rating*]
EQ CONV ..... Equitable Conversion (DLA)
EQCRT .... Equipment Certified (FAAC)
EQD .... Electrical Quality Assurance Directorate [*British Ministry of Defense*] [*Research center*]
EQD .... Established Quarter of Disability [*Social Security Administration*] (OICC)
EQDB .... Equipment Qualification Data Bank [*Information service or system*] (IID)
EQDD .... Equipment Density Data (AABC)
Eq Draft .... Equity Draftsman (Van Heythuysen's, Edited by Hughes) [*A publication*] (DLA)
EQE.............. Equivalent Quantum Efficiency (MCD)
EQE.............. Esquisure, Inc. [*AMEX symbol*] (SAG)
EQE.............. Event Queue Element [*Computer science*] (MCD)
EQF.............. Elswick Quick-Firing Gun
EqGth1......... Equipment Growth Fund 1 (PLM) [*Associated Press*] (SAG)
EqGth2......... Equipment Growth Fund 2 (PLM) [*Associated Press*] (SAG)
EQGth3......... Equipment Growth Fund III (PLM) [*Associated Press*] (SAG)
EQI.............. Environmental Quality Index (PDAA)
Eql .... Equity Income [*Finance*]
EQIA.............. Environmental Quality Improvement Act of 1970
EqIowa......... Equitable of Iowa Companies [*Associated Press*] (SAG)
EQIS.............. Environmental Quality Information Services Program [*Navy*]
Eq Judg .... Equity Judgments, by A'Beckett [*New South Wales*] [*A publication*] (DLA)
EQK Rt......... EQK Realty Investors [*Associated Press*] (SAG)
EQL.............. Earthquake Light
EQL.............. Environmental Quality Laboratory [*California Institute of Technology*]
EQL.............. Equal (MSA)
EQL.............. Equal
EQL.............. Equatorial Airlines of Sao Tome and Principe [*ICAO designator*] (FAAC)
EQL.............. Expected Quality Level
EQLY.............. Equally [*Legal term*] (ROG)
EQM.............. Equitable Real Estate Shopping [*Later, Midwest Real Estate Shopping Center Ltd.*] [*NYSE symbol*] (SPSG)
EQM.............. Midwest Real Estate Shopping Centers Ltd. [*NYSE symbol*] (SAG)
EQM.............. Midwest R.E.Shop'g Ctr L.P. [*NYSE symbol*] (TTSB)
EQMD.............. EquiMed [*NASDAQ symbol*] (SAG)
EQMD.............. EquiMed Inc. [*NASDAQ symbol*] (TTSB)
EQN .... Equation
EQN .... Equine
EQN .... Equine Resources Ltd. [*Vancouver Stock Exchange symbol*]
EQNX.............. Equinox Systems [*NASDAQ symbol*] (TTSB)
EQNX.............. Equinox Systems, Inc. [*NASDAQ symbol*] (SAG)
EQO .... Environmental Quality Objective [*British*] (DCTA)
EQO .... Environmental Quality Office [*HUD*] (OICC)
EQOPPINFOSYS... Equal Opportunity Information and Support System (DNAB)
EQP.............. Englehard, NC [*Location identifier FAA*] (FAAL)
EQP.............. Equipment (CINC)
EQP.............. Equity Preservation Corp. [*Toronto Stock Exchange symbol Vancouver Stock Exchange symbol*]
Eq PA.......... Equal Pay Act [*1970*] [*British*] (DCTA)
EqPac.......... Equatorial Pacific [*Project*] [*Marine science*] (OSRA)
EQPAC.......... Equatorial Pacific (USDC)
EQPFOR....... Equipment Foreman

EQPMT......... Equipment (MDG)
EQPT........... Equipment
EQQ .... Electric Quadrupole-Quadrupole
Eq R........... Common Law and Equity Reports [*1853-55*] [*A publication*] (DLA)
EQR .... Equity Reserve Corp. [*Toronto Stock Exchange symbol*]
EQR .... Equity Residential Property Trust [*NYSE symbol*] (SPSG)
EQR .... Equity Residential Prop Tr [*NYSE symbol*] (TTSB)
Eq R........... Gilbert's English Equity Reports [*1705-27*] [*A publication*] (DLA)
Eq R........... Harper's South Carolina Equity Reports [*A publication*] (DLA)
Eq R (Eng)... Equity Reports [*England*] [*A publication*] (DLA)
EQREP......... Equipment Report (MCD)
Eq Rep......... Equity Reports [*A publication*] (DLA)
Eq Rep......... Equity Reports, Published by Spottiswoode [*A publication*] (DLA)
Eq Rep......... Gilbert's English Equity Reports [*1705-27*] [*A publication*] (DLA)
Eq Rep......... Harper's South Carolina Equity Reports [*A publication*] (DLA)
EQRPrA....... Equity Res Prop Tr 9.375% Pfd [*NYSE symbol*] (TTSB)
EQRPrB....... Equity Res Prop Tr 9.125%Pfd [*NYSE symbol*] (TTSB)
EQS........... Environmental Quality Staff [*Tennessee Valley Authority*] [*Knoxville, TN*] (GRD)
EQS........... Environmental Quality Standard [*British*] (DCTA)
EQS........... Equatorial Scatter
EQS........... Equivalent to Sheathed Explosive (IAA)
EQS........... Equus II, Inc. [*AMEX symbol*] (SPSG)
EQS........... Esquel [*Argentina*] [*Airport symbol*] (OAG)
EQS........... Exact Quadratic Search [*Mathematics*]
EQSA......... Extended Quasi-Static Approximation [*Materials research*]
EQSB .... Equitable Federal Savings Bank [*NASDAQ symbol*] (SAG)
EQSB .... Equitable Fed Svgs Bank [*NASDAQ symbol*] (TTSB)
EQSTTRN..... Equestrian
EQT........... Engineering Qualification Test
EQT........... Environmental Qualification Test
EQT........... Equation of Time [*Navigation*]
EQT........... Equitable Resources [*NYSE symbol*] (TTSB)
EQT........... Equitable Resources, Inc. [*Formerly, Equitable Gas Co.*] [*NYSE symbol*] (SPSG)
EQT........... Equivalent Training (AFM)
EQTBL......... Equitable
EqtCos......... Equitable Companies, Inc. [*Associated Press*] (SAG)
EqtFedl......... Equitable Federal Savings Bank [*Associated Press*] (SAG)
EqtOil......... Equity Oil Co. [*Associated Press*] (SAG)
EqtR........... Equity Residential Property Trust [*Associated Press*] (SAG)
EqtResc .... Equitable Resources, Inc. [*Formerly, Equitable Gas Co.*] [*Associated Press*] (SAG)
EQTV......... Extended Quality Television (ACRL)
EQTX......... Equitex, Inc. [*NASDAQ symbol*] (NQ)
EQTY......... Equity
EQTY......... Equity Oil [*NASDAQ symbol*] (TTSB)
EQTY......... Equity Oil Co. [*NASDAQ symbol*] (NQ)
EqtyInn .... Equity Inns [*Associated Press*] (SAG)
EqtyMkt....... Equity Marketing, Inc. [*Associated Press*] (SAG)
EqtyRsd....... Equity Residential Property Trust [*Associated Press*] (SAG)
EQU........... Equate (MDG)
Equ .... Equity [*Business term*]
Equ .... Equuleus [*Constellation*]
EQU .... Equus Petroleum [*Vancouver Stock Exchange symbol*]
EQUALANT.. Equatorial Atlantic (MSC)
EQUALANT.. Equatorial Atlantic Survey [*Marine science*] (OSRA)
EqualN....... EqualNet Holding Corp. [*Associated Press*] (SAG)
Equal Opp... Equal Opportunity [*A publication*]
EQUAPAC..... Equatorial Pacific
EQUAT....... Equatorial (ROG)
EQUATE .... Electronic Quality Assurance Test Equipment [*System*] [*Army*] (RDA)
EQUAT GUI... Equatorial Guinea (WDAA)
EQUI......... Equivest Finance, Inc. [*NASDAQ symbol*] (SAG)
Equifx......... Equifax, Inc. [*Formerly, Retail Credit Co.*] [*Associated Press*] (SAG)
EQUIL .... Equilibrium (MSA)
equilib......... Equilibrium (AAMN)
EquiMed....... EquiMed [*Associated Press*] (SAG)
Equinox....... Equinox Resources Ltd. [*Associated Press*] (SAG)
EQUIP......... Engineering Quality Improvement
EQUIP......... Enterprise Quality Improvement Program [*Australia*]
EQUIP......... Equipment
EQUIP......... Equipment (AAGC)
EQUIP......... Equipment
equip......... Equipment (DD)
EQUIPT......... Equipment (WGA)
Equisure ...... Equisure, Inc. [*Associated Press*] (SAG)
Equitex .... Equitex, Inc. [*Associated Press*] (SAG)
Equitrc .... Equitrac Corp. [*Associated Press*] (SAG)
EquityCp...... Equity Corporation International [*Associated Press*] (SAG)
Equity Rep... Common Law and Equity Reports [*1853-55*] [*A publication*] (DLA)
Equity Rep... Equity Reports (Gilbert) [*England*] [*A publication*] (DLA)
Equity Rep... Harper's South Carolina Equity Reports [*A publication*] (DLA)
EQUIV......... Equivalent (AFM)
EQUIV......... Equivalent
Equiv .... Equivalent (IDOE)
Equivsn....... Equivision, Inc. [*Associated Press*] (SAG)
Equivst....... Equivest Finance, Inc. [*Associated Press*] (SAG)
equiv wt ...... Equivalent Weight [*Chemistry*]
E QUOL VEH... E Quolibet Vehiculo [*In Any Vehicle*] [*Pharmacy*]
E QUOV LIQ... E Quovis Liquido [*In Any Liquid*] [*Pharmacy*]
EQUUS......... Equus Gaming Co. Ltd. [*NASDAQ symbol*] (SAG)
EQUUS......... Equus Gaming LP [*NASDAQ symbol*] (TTSB)
EquusG....... Equus Gaming Co., Ltd. [*Associated Press*] (SAG)
EquusII .... Equus II, Inc. [*Associated Press*] (SAG)

EQV............ Equivalence (IAA)
EQV............ Equivest International Financial Corp. [*Vancouver Stock Exchange symbol*]
EQWin .... EQuIS for Windows [*Computer science*]
EQX............ Equator Crossing
EQX............ Equinox Resources Ltd. [*Toronto Stock Exchange symbol Vancouver Stock Exchange symbol*]
EQY............ Monroe, NC [*Location identifier FAA*] (FAAL)
EQZ............ Seymour, IN [*Location identifier FAA*] (FAAL)
ER............... [*The*] Earlham Review [*A publication*]
ER............... Early Release (MCD)
ER............... Earned Run [*Baseball*]
ER............... Earnings Report [*Business term*]
ER............... Earth Radii
ER............... Earth Rate
ER............... Earth Resources (MCD)
ER............... Eastern Rite News Service
ER............... East Riding of Yorkshire [*Administrative county in England*]
ER............... East River [*New York*]
ER............... East's English King's Bench Term Reports [*A publication*] (DLA)
ER............... Easy to Reach [*Telecommunications*] (TEL)
ER............... Echo Ranging
ER............... Economic Regulations [*Civil Aeronautics Board*]
ER............... Ecumenical Review [*A publication*] (BRI)
E/R............. Edges Red [*Publishing*] (DGA)
ER............... Educational Ratio
ER............... Educational Resources [*Auckland, NZ*]
ER............... Edwardus Rex [*King Edward*] [*Latin*]
ER............... Effectiveness Ratio (MCD)
ER............... Effectiveness Report [*Military*]
ER............... Efficiency Review [*DoD*]
ER............... Ego Resiliency [*Psychology*]
ER............... Egress Router (ACRL)
ER............... Egyptian Railways (DCTA)
ER............... Ejection Rate [*Medicine*]
ER............... Elder
ER............... Eleanor Roosevelt [*1884-1962*]
ER............... Election Reports [*Ontario*] [*A publication*] (DLA)
ER............... Electrical Resistance (MSA)
ER............... Electronic Reconnaissance
ER............... Electro-Rheological
ER............... Electrorheology [*Physics*]
ER............... Eley-Rideal Mechanism [*Chemistry*]
ER............... Elizabetha Regina [*Queen Elizabeth*] [*Latin*]
ER............... Elizabeth Regina [*Queen Elizabeth*] (DLA)
ER............... Embryo Replacement [*Gynecology*]
ER............... Emergency Relief
ER............... Emergency Request
ER............... Emergency Rescue
ER............... Emergency Reserve
ER............... Emergency Response [*Nuclear energy*] (NRCH)
ER............... Emergency Room [*Medicine*]
ER............... Employer (OICC)
ER............... End of Run (IAA)
ER............... Endoplasmic Reticulum [*Cytology*]
er............... Endoplasmic Reticulum (DOG)
ER............... Engineering Record
ER............... Engineering Regulations [*A publication*]
ER............... Engineering Release (MCD)
ER............... Engineering Release
ER............... Engineering Report
ER............... Engineering Route [*Telecommunications*] (TEL)
ER............... Engineer Relations [*ACE*] (AAGC)
ER............... Engine Room [*Force*]
ER............... English Reports [*Legal*]
ER............... English Reports, Full Reprint [*A publication*] (DLA)
ER............... English Revised Version [*of the Bible*] [*A publication*] (BJA)
ER............... Enhanced Radiation Weapon
ER............... Enhanced Reactivation [*Medicine*] (DMAA)
ER............... Enhancement Ratio
ER............... Enoyl Reductase [*An enzyme*]
E/R............. En Route
ER............... Entity Relationship [*Computer science*] (PCM)
ER............... Entrance Right [*A stage direction*] [*Theater*] (WDMC)
ER............... Environmental Report (NRCH)
ER............... Environmental Requirement
ER............... Environmental Resistance
ER............... Environmental Restoration [*Metallurgy*]
ER............... Equine Rhinopneumonia [*Medicine*] (DMAA)
ER............... Equipment Readiness [*DoD*]
ER............... Equipment Record
ER............... Equipment Related (DNAB)
ER............... Equipment Repairer [*British military*] (DMA)
ER............... Equipment Requirement
ER............... Equivalent Roentgen
ER............... Equivalent Round (MCD)
Er............... Erbium [*Chemical element*]
ER............... Errata
ER............... Erroneous
ER............... Error [*Baseball*]
ER............... Error Rate [*Statistics*]
ER............... Error Recorder
ER............... Error Recovery (BUR)
ER............... Error Relay
ER............... Error Retrieval [*Computer science*] (ECII)

ER............... Erskine Register (EA)
'Er............... 'Erubin [*or 'Eruvin*] (BJA)
ER............... Erythrocyte [*Hematology*]
ER............... Erythrocyte Rosette [*Hematology*]
ER............... Established Reliability (MCD)
ER............... Estimated Rental (ROG)
ER............... Estimating Relationship (AFIT)
ER............... Estradiol Receptor [*Endocrinology*]
ER............... Estrogen Receptor [*Endocrinology*]
ER............... European Right [*Political movement*] (ECON)
E/R............. Evacuation/Replacement [*Jar technique*] [*Microbiology*]
ER............... Evaluation Record [*LIMRA*]
ER............... Evaluation Report
ER............... Evoked Response [*Neurophysiology*]
ER............... Exception Reporting (MCD)
ER............... Excess Reserves (MHDB)
ER............... Exchange Ratio (MCD)
ER............... Exchange Rolls
ER............... Executive Request [*Computer science*]
ER............... Executive Reserve
ER............... Executive Risk [*NYSE symbol*] (TTSB)
ER............... Executive Risk, Inc. [*NYSE symbol*] (SAG)
E/R............. Exercised/Repositioned [*Sports medicine*]
ER............... Exodus Rabbah (BJA)
ER............... Expected Result (IAA)
ER............... Expedite Requirement (KSC)
ER............... Expense Report (AAG)
ER............... Expert Rifleman
ER............... Explanation Report [*NASA*] (NASA)
ER............... Explosives Report
ER............... Ex-Rights [*Without Rights*] [*Investment term*]
ER............... Extended Range
ER............... Extended Release [*Pharmacy*]
ER............... External Report
ER............... External Resistance [*Physics*]
ER............... External Rotation [*Myology*]
ER............... Extraordinary Contractual Relief Reporter [*A publication*] (AAGC)
ER............... Extra Restricted (ADA)
ER............... Eye Research [*Defunct*] (EA)
er---- .... Rhine River and Basin [*MARC geographic area code Library of Congress*] (LCCP)
ER-2.......... Earth Resources-2 [*Aircraft*] [*NASA*] (OSRA)
ER2........... Earth Resources-2 [*Satellite*] [*NASA*] (USDC)
ERA........... Early Retirement Adjustment (EERA)
ERA........... Earned Run Average [*Baseball*]
ERA........... Earthquake Risk Analysis (PDAA)
ERA........... Eastern Railroad Association [*Defunct*] (EA)
ERA........... Economic Regulatory Administration (MCD)
ERA........... Educational Rankings Annual [*A publication*]
ERA........... Education and Religious Affairs [*US Military Government, Germany*]
ERA........... Education Reform Act [*1988*] (AIE)
ERA........... Education Research Assistant (ADA)
ERA........... Education Review Association [*Australia*]
ERA........... Effective Rate of Assistance [*International trade*]
ERA........... Egyptian Research Account [*London*] [*A publication*] (BJA)
ERA........... Electrically Reconfigurable Array (CDE)
ERA........... Electrical [*or Electronic*] Replaceable Assembly
ERA........... Electrical Representatives Association
ERA........... Electrical Research Association [*British*]
ERA........... Electrical Response Activity
ERA........... Electric Railroaders Association (EA)
ERA........... Electric Response Audiometry (AAMN)
ERA........... Electronic Reading Automation [*Information retrieval*]
ERA........... Electronic Remittance Advice
ERA........... Electronic Rentals Association [*British*] (BI)
ERA........... Electronic Representatives Association (EA)
ERA........... Electronic Research Association [*British*]
ERA........... Electronic Revision and Approval [*Computer science*]
ERA........... Electron Ring Accelerator
ERA........... Electroshock Research Association [*Later, International Psychiatric Library Service*]
ERA........... Elliniki Radiophonia [*Greek radio*] (EY)
ERA........... Ellison, R. A., Cincinnati OH [*STAC*]
ERA........... Emergency Relief Administration
ERA........... Energy Reorganization Act [*1974*]
ERA........... Energy Resources of Australia (EERA)
ERA........... Engineering Release Authorization
ERA........... Engineering Rental Agreement
ERA........... Engineering Request Authorization (AAG)
ERA........... Engineering Research Associates (MCD)
ERA........... Engineer Rear-Admiral [*Navy British*]
ERA........... Engine-Room Artificer [*Obsolete Navy British*]
ERA........... English Racing Automobiles Ltd. [*British*]
ERA........... English Reports, Annotated [*A publication*] (DLA)
ERA........... Environmental Protection Agency, Region IX Library, San Francisco, CA [*OCLC symbol*] (OCLC)
ERA........... Environmental Resources of Australia [*Commercial*] (EERA)
ERA........... Enzyme Rate Analyzer
ERA........... Enzymic Radiochemical Assay [*Clinical chemistry*]
ERA........... Equal Rights Advocates (EA)
ERA........... Equal Rights Amendment [*Proposed constitutional amendment which supports equal rights regardless of sex*]
ERA........... Equipment Rental Agreement
ERA........... Equitable Reserve Association [*Neenah, WI*] (EA)
Era............. Erato [*Record label*] [*France*]

ERA............ Erigavo [*Somalia*] [*Airport symbol*] (AD)
ERA............ Estrogen Receptor Assay [*Clinical chemistry*]
ERA............ Eurocommander SA [*Spain ICAO designator*] (FAAC)
ERA............ European Ramblers' Association (EAIO)
ERA............ European Regional Airlines (PDAA)
ERA............ European Regional Airlines Association [*British*] (EAIO)
ERA............ European Research Associates
ERA............ European Rotogravure Association [*Germany*] (PDAA)
ERA............ European Rum Association (EAIO)
ERA............ Evangelical Radio Alliance [*British*] (BI)
ERA............ Evaporative Rate Analysis [*Surface technology*]
ERA............ Evoked Response Audiometry [*Neurophysiology*]
ERA............ Excess Rent Allowance [*British*]
ERA............ Exchange Rate Agreement [*Banking*] [*British*]
ERA............ Executive Resource Associates (AAGC)
ERA............ Exobiology and Radiation Assembly (SSD)
ERA............ Expedited Removal Action [*Environmental science*] (FFDE)
ERA............ Expense for Return of Absentee [*Military*]
ERA............ Explosive Reactive Armor [*Tank design*]
ERA............ Extended Range Ammunition (MCD)
ERA............ Extended-Range ASROC [*Antisubmarine Rocket*] [*Navy*] (NVT)
ERA............ External Release Agent
ERA............ Extra-Regimental Assignment [*Army*] (INF)
ERAA.......... Equipment Review and Authorization Activity [*Military*] (AFM)
ERAAM .... Extended-Range Air-to-Air Missile (MCD)
ERAB.......... Energy Research Advisory Board [*Department of Energy*]
ERAC.......... Electromagnetic Radiation Advisory Council
ERAC.......... Electronic Random Action Control
ERAC.......... Environmental Research Assessment Committee [*National Research Council*]
ERAC.......... Handicap International [*France*] (EAIO)
ERAD.......... Economic and Regulatory Analysis Division [*Environmental Protection Agency*] (GFGA)
ERAD.......... Energy Research and Development (DNAB)
ERAD.......... Enroute RADAR [*Aviation*] (FAAC)
ERAD.......... Erie Army Depot
ERADCOM.... Electronics Research and Development Command [*Later, LABCOM*] [*Adelphi, MD*] [*Army*]
ERADCOM/ASL... Electronics Research and Development Command Atmospheric Sciences Laboratory [*Army*]
ERAF.......... Earth Resources Aircraft Facility [*NASA*]
ERAJFS........ Emergent Reading Ability Judgements for Favorite Storybooks Scale (EDAC)
ERAM.......... Earth Resources Applications Mission [*NASA*] (KSC)
ERAM.......... Extended Range Antiarmor Munition
ERAM.......... Extended Range Antitank Mine (MCD)
ERAMS .... Environmental Radiation Ambient Monitoring System [*Environmental Protection Agency*]
ERAN .... Examine and Repair as Necessary
ER & D .... Energy Research and Development
ERAP.......... Earth Resources Aircraft Program [*NASA*]
ERAP .... Economic Research Action Project [*Students for a Democratic Society*] [*Defunct*]
ERAPS .... Expendable Reliable Acoustic Path Sensor [*or Sonar or Sonobuoy*] (MCD)
ERAR .... Experience Retention Action Request (SAA)
ERAS .... Educational Resources Allocation Systems
ERAS .... EIN [*Employer Identification Number*] Research and Assignment System [*IRS*]
ERAS .... Electronic Reconnaissance Access Set
ERAS .... En Route Advisory Service [*Aeromedical evacuation*]
ERASE .... Eat Right and Slim Easily [*Weight Watchers, Inc., competition*]
ERASE .... Electromagnetic Radiation Source Elimination (NVT)
ERASE .... Emitted Radiation from Special Engines (MCD)
ERASER ...... Elevated Radiation Seeking Rocket
ERASP .... Education Resource Allocation in Schools Project [*Australia*]
ER ASROC ... Extended-Range Antisubmarine Rocket [*Navy*] (SAA)
ERAST .... Environmental Research Aircraft and Sensor Technology
ERATO .... Exploratory Research for Advanced Technology [*Japan*]
Eratosth ...... Eratosthenes [*275-194BC*] [*Classical studies*] (OCD)
E-RAU......... Embry-Riddle Aeronautical University [*Formerly, ERSA*] [*Daytona Beach, FL*]
Er Av .... Earned Average [*Baseball*]
ERB............ Earth's Radiation Budget [*Meteorology*]
ERB............ Ecclesiastical Relations Branch [*BUPERS*]
ERB............ Economic Requirement Batching
ERB............ Edgar Rice Burroughs [*1875-1950*] [*Author of Tarzan books*]
ERB............ Educational Records Bureau (EA)
ERB............ Educational Rewards Bureau
ERB............ Education Research Branch (AIE)
ERB............ Edwards Rocket Base (MUGU)
ERB............ Electronic Recording Beam (MDG)
ERB............ Emergency Radio Beacon
ERB............ Employment Relations Board [*Usually preceded by abbreviation of state name*]
ERB............ Engineering Reference Branch [*Department of the Interior*]
ERB............ Engineering Review Board [*NASA*] (NASA)
ERB............ Engineers Registration Board [*Council of Engineering Institutions*] [*British*]
ERB............ Engine Relay Box (MCD)
ERB............ Enlisted Record Brief [*Army*] (AABC)
ERB............ Environmental Protection Agency, Environmental Monitoring and Support Laboratory, Las Vegas, NV [*OCLC symbol*] (OCLC)
ERB............ Epic Resources (BC) Ltd. [*Vancouver Stock Exchange symbol*]
ERB............ Executive Resources Board [*NASA*] (RDA)

ERB............ Experiment Review Board [*Nuclear Regulatory Commission*] (NRCH)
ERB-Dom..... Edgar Rice Burroughs Domain [*as in organization, Friends of ERB-Dom*]
ERBE.......... Earth Radiation Budget Experiment [*NASA*]
ERBF.......... Effective Renal Blood Flow [*Medicine*]
ERBI.......... Earth Radiation Budget Instrument
ERBM.......... Extended-Range Ballistic Missile
ERBOS........ Earth Radiation Budget Observation Satellite (PDAA)
ERBP .... Equilibrium Reflux Boiling Point [*Brake fluid*]
ERBS .... Earth Radiation Budget Satellite [*NASA*] (MCD)
ERBS .... Earth Resources Budget Satellite
ERBS .... Expanded Range Bench Stock
ERBSS .... Earth Radiation Budget Satellite System [*NASA*] (MCD)
ERBUT .... Engine Requisition and Build-Up Time (MCD)
ERC............ Earth Rate Compensation
ERC............ Echo-Rhino-Coryza [*Virus*] [*Usage obsolete*]
ERC............ Economic Research Council [*Research center British*] (IRC)
ERC............ Economic Resources Corp. [*OEO-Department of Labor project*] (EA)
ERC............ Ecosystems Research Center [*Cornell University, EPA*] [*Research center*] (RCD)
ERC............ Edge Reading Controller
ERC............ Educational Reference Center [*National Institute of Education*]
ERC............ Educational Research Center [*New Mexico State University*] [*Research center*] (RCD)
ERC............ Educational Research Centre [*Australia*]
ERC............ Educational Research Council of America (AEBS)
ERC............ Educational Resources Center (AEBS)
ERC............ Education and Resource Centre [*South Australia*]
ERC............ Eject Rocket Container
ERC............ Elections Research Center (EA)
ERC............ Electonic Remote Control [*Automotive electronic systems*]
ERC............ Electrical Rule Checker [*For integrated circuitry*]
ERC............ Electric Regulation Co.
ERC............ Electronic Ride Control [*Automotive engineering*]
ERC............ Electronics Research Center [*NASA*]
ERC............ Electron Reflection Coefficient
ERC............ Eligibility Review Committee [*Social security*] [*Australia*]
ERC............ El Reno College [*Oklahoma*]
ERC............ Emergency Relocation Center (NRCH)
ERC............ Emergency Response Commission (GNE)
ERC............ Emission Reduction Credit [*Environmental Protection Agency*] (GFGA)
E-R-C......... Employee Relocation Council (EA)
ERC............ Endoscopic Retrograde Cholangiography [*Medicine*]
ERC............ Energy Research Centre (EERA)
ERC............ Energy Resources Center [*University of Illinois at Chicago*] [*Research center*] (RCD)
ERC............ Energy Resources Council [*Terminated, 1977*]
ERC............ Engineering Research Center [*New Mexico State University*] (RCD)
ERC............ Engineering Research Council (NRCH)
ERC............ English Ruling Cases [*A publication*] (DLA)
ERC............ Enlisted Reserve Corps [*Later, Army Reserve*]
ERC............ En Route Chart [*Aviation*]
ERC............ Enteric Cytopathic Human Orphan-Rhino-Coryza Virus (DMAA)
ERC............ Environmental Reporter Cases [*Bureau of National Affairs*] [*A publication*] (DLA)
ERC............ Environmental Research Center [*Environmental Protection Agency*]
ERC............ Environmental Research Consortium
ERC............ Environmental Resources Center
ERC............ Environmental Response Center [*Department of Energy*] (IID)
ERC............ Epic Record Co. [*Record label*] [*New York*]
ERC............ Epilepsy Research Center [*Baylor College of Medicine*] [*Research center*] (RCD)
ERC............ Epping Realty Corp. [*Vancouver Stock Exchange symbol*]
ERC............ Equal Rights Congress (EA)
ERC............ Equatorial Ring Current (IEEE)
ERC............ Equipage Repair Part Consumable (AFIT)
ERC............ Equipment Readiness Codes [*or Criteria*] (MCD)
ERC............ Equipment Record Card (AAG)
ERC............ Eritrean Relief Committee (EA)
ERC............ Error Retry Count [*Computer science*] (IAA)
ERC............ Erythropoietin-Responsive Cell [*Hematology*]
ERC............ Erzincan [*Turkey*] [*Airport symbol*] (AD)
ERC............ Esquerra Republicana de Catalunya [*Catalan Republican Left*] [*Spain Political party*] (PPE)
ERC............ Essentials Review Committee [*American Occupational Therapy Association*]
ERC............ ESSO [*Standard Oil*] Resources Canada Ltd. [*UTLAS symbol*]
ERC............ Esso Rosources Canada Ltd. [*ICAO designator*] (FAAC)
ERC............ Estonian Relief Committee (EA)
ERC............ Estrogen Receptor, Cytosolic [*Endocrinology*]
ERC............ Ethics Resource Center (EA)
ERC............ European Registry of Commerce (DS)
ERC............ Evaluation Research Center [*University of Virginia*] [*Research center*] (RCD)
ERC............ Evaluation Review Committee (EERA)
ERC............ Event Recorder (NASA)
ERC............ Events Recorder Console (MCD)
ERC............ Excessive Requirements Cost (EERA)
ERC............ Exemplary Rehabilitation Certificate [*Department of Labor*]
ERC............ Expatriate Resources Co. [*British*]
ERC............ Expendability Repair Classification (AAG)
ERC............ Explosives Research Center [*Bruceton, PA*] [*Bureau of Mines*]
ERC............ Extended Range Cap [*Navy*] (ANA)
ERC............ Externally Received Component

ERCA	Educational Research Council of America [*Defunct*] (EA)
ERCA	Ejercito Rojo Catalan de Liberacion [*Spain Political party*] (EY)
ERCA	Electrochemically Regenerable Carbon Dioxide Absorber (NASA)
ERCA	Emergency Relief and Construction Act
ErCam	Camaldolese Hermits of the Congregation of Monte Corona (TOCD)
ercam	Camaldolese Hermits of the Congregation of Monte Corona (TOCD)
ER CAM	Eremitarum Camaldulensium [*Monk Hermits of Camaldoli*] [*Roman Catholic religious order*]
ERCB	Exploitation de Renseignements Contenus dans les Brevets [*Patent Information Exploitation - PIE*] [*Canadian Patent Office*]
ERCC	Edinburgh Regional Computing Center [*British*]
ERCC	Energy Research [*NASDAQ symbol*] (TTSB)
ERCC	Energy Research Corp. [*NASDAQ symbol*] (SAG)
ERCC	Enroute Control Center [*Aviation*] (DA)
ERCC	Error Checking and Correction [*Computer science*]
ERCC	Expendability, Recoverability Cost Code (AAG)
ERCF	Eglin RADAR Control Facility [*Florida*] [*Air Force*] (MCD)
ERCG	Erecting
ERCHCW	European Regional Clearing House for Community Work (EAIO)
ERCI	ERC Industries [*NASDAQ symbol*] (SAG)
ERCIA	Egg Research and Consumer Information Act [*1974*]
ERC Ind	ERC Industries, Inc. [*Associated Press*] (SAG)
Erck	Erck's Ecclesiastical Register [*1608-1825*] [*England*] [*A publication*] (DLA)
ERCMIS	Environmental Requirements/Capabilities Management Information System (MCD)
ERCMS	ELINT [*Electronic Intelligence*] Requirements and Capabilities Management System (MCD)
ERCN	Employee Record Change Notice
ERCOCFA	Eleanor Roosevelt's Centennial Observance Committee of Friends and Admirers (EA)
ERCOT	Electric Reliability Council of Texas [*Regional power council*]
ERCP	Endoscopic Retrograde Cannulation of Pancreatic Duct [*Medicine*] (DAVI)
ERCP	Endoscopic Retrograde Cholangiopancreatographic [*Exam*] [*Medicine*]
ERCR	Electronic Retina Computing Reader
ERCR	Engineering Release Change Record
ERCR	Erector
ERCR	Error Cause Register [*Computer science*] (IAA)
ERCS	Elective Repeat Cesarean Section [*Obstetrics*]
ERCS	Emergency Response Cleanup Services (GNE)
ERCS	Emergency Rocket Communications System
ERCT	Erecting
ERCTR	Erector
ERCW	Emergency [*or Essential*] Raw Cooling Water [*Nuclear energy*] (NRCH)
ERD	Eastern Recruiting Division
E/RD	Edges Rounded [*Publishing*] (DGA)
ERD	Elastic Recoil Detection
ERD	Electronic Reference Document
ERD	Electronic Research Directorate [*Air Force*]
ERD	Eligible Rollover Distribution [*Business term*]
ERD	Emergency Recovery Display [*Bell System*]
ERD	Emergency Reserve Decoration [*British*]
ERD	Emergency Response Division [*Environmental Protection Agency*] (GFGA)
ERD	Emergency Return Device [*Aerospace*]
ERD	End Routing Domain [*Computer science*] (TNIG)
ERD	Energy Research and Development Inventory [*Information service or system*] (NITA)
ERD	Entity Relationship Diagram [*Computer science*] (EERA)
ERD	Entity-Relationships Diagram [*Computer science*]
ERD	Equipment Readiness Data
ERD	Equipment Readiness Date [*Army*] (AABC)
ERD	Equipment Readiness Drawing (MCD)
ERD	Equipment Requirements Data [*Army*]
ERD	Equivalent Residual Dose
ERD	Erdek [*Turkey*] [*Seismograph station code, US Geological Survey*] (SEIS)
ERD	ERD Waste Corp. [*Associated Press*] (SAG)
ERD	Error Recording Device
ERD	Estimated Receival Date (KSC)
ERD	Estimated Release Date (AAG)
ERD	Evoked Response Detector [*Neurophysiology*] (MCD)
ERD	Expense for Return of Deserter [*Military*]
ERD	Experiment Requirements Document (KSC)
ERD	Exponentially Retrograded Diode
ERD	Expressed Reading Difficulty (EDAC)
ERDA	Elastic Recoil Detection Analysis [*Physics*]
ERDA	Electronic Resources Development Agency
ERDA	Electronics Research and Development Activity [*Army*]
ERDA	Energy Research and Development Administration [*Superseded by Department of Energy, 1977*]
ERDA	Energy Research and Development Agency [*Information service or system*] (NITA)
ERDAA	Electronics Research and Development Activity Analysis [*Army*] (MCD)
ERDABCA	Energy Research and Development Administration Board of Contract Appeals (AAGC)
ERDAC	Energy Research and Development Advisory Council
ERDAM	Energy Research and Development Administration Manual [*A publication*] (IEEE)
ERDA-RDD	Energy Research and Development Administration, Division of Reactor Development and Demonstration (PDAA)
ERDAS	Earth Resources Digital Analysis System Software [*Computer science*] (EERA)
ERDC	Earth Resources Data Center [*NASA*]
ERDC	East Region Development Corp.
ERDC	Electronic Research and Development Command [*Army*]
ERDC	Engineering Research and Development Center [*University of Nevada, Reno*] [*Research center*] (RCD)
ERDDAA	Environmental Research Development and Demonstration Authorization Act (GFGA)
ERDE	Explosive Research and Development Establishment [*British*]
ERDEC	Edgewood Research, Development and Engineering Center [*Army*] (RDA)
ERDET	Error Detection (PDAA)
ERDF	European Regional Development Fund [*See also FEDER*] [*Brussels, Belgium*] (EAIO)
ERDI	Energy and Resource Development Institute [*Clemson University*] [*Research center*] (RCD)
ERDI	Energy Research and Development Inventory [*Marine science*] (MSC)
ERDI	ERD Waste Corp. [*NASDAQ symbol*] (SAG)
ERDIP	Experimental Research and Development Incentives Program [*National Science Foundation*]
ERDL	Electronic Research and Development Laboratory [*Army*] (MCD)
ERDL	Extended Range Data Link [*Bomb*] (MCD)
ERDL	Exxon Research and Development Laboratories [*Formerly, Esso Research Laboratory*]
ERDM	Employment Rehabilitation Divisional Manager (AIE)
ERDR	Earth Rate Directional Reference
ERDR	STAT Healthcare [*NASDAQ symbol*] (TTSB)
ERDR	Stat Healthcare, Inc. [*NASDAQ symbol*] (SAG)
ERDRW	Stat Healthcare Wrrt'A' [*NASDAQ symbol*] (TTSB)
ERDS	Emergency Response Data System (ODBW)
ERDS	Environmental Radiation Data System [*Environmental Protection Agency*] (GFGA)
ERDS	Equipment Recall Data System (MCD)
ERDT	Electronic Research and Development Technician (IAA)
ERE	East Carolina University, Greenville, NC [*OCLC symbol*] (OCLC)
ERE	Echo Range Equipment
ERE	Edison Responsive Environment [*Automated learning system*]
ERE	Elite Resources Corp. [*Vancouver Stock Exchange symbol*]
ERE	Emergency Rescue Equipment
ERE	Erave [*Papua New Guinea*] [*Airport symbol*] (OAG)
ERE	Erevan [*Former USSR Seismograph station code, US Geological Survey*] (SEIS)
ERE	Erie Airways, Inc. [*ICAO designator*] (FAAC)
ERE	Estrogen-Responsive Element [*Endocrinology*]
ERE	Ethylene-Responsive Element [*Biochemistry*]
ERE	Extended Red Emission [*Spectroscopy*]
ERE	External Rotation in Extension [*Orthopedics*] (DAVI)
ERE	Extra-Regimentally Employed [*List*] [*Military British*]
EREC	Electronic Reconnaissance (MCD)
EREC	Enlisted Records and Evaluation Center [*Fort Benjamin Harrison, IN*] [*Army*]
EREC	Erection (ROG)
EREC	Exxon Research and Engineering Co. [*Information service or system*] (IID)
ERECO	European Economic Research and Advisory Consortium [*Belgium*] (EAIO)
ERECT	Erection
ERECTN	Erection (ROG)
EREF	Energy Research and Education Foundation
EREP	Earth Resources Experiment Package [*Skylab*] [*NASA*]
EREP	Earth Resources Package [*NASA*] (NASA)
EREP	End Results Evaluation Program [*Later, SEER*] [*National Cancer Institute*]
EREP	Environmental Recording, Editing, and Printing Program (BUR)
EREP	Equipment Replacement and Enhancement Program [*Computer science*]
EREPP	Earth Resources Experiment Package Program [*Skylab*] [*NASA*]
ERES	Electronic Reflected Energy System [*Acoustics*]
ERES	Environmental Record Editing and Statistics [*Fujitsu*] [*Japan*] (NITA)
ERES	Erie Western Railway Co. [*AAR code*]
ERES	Erlanger Rechner-Entwurfs-Sprache [*Programming language*] [*1974*]
ER et I	Edwardus Rex et Imperator [*Edward King and Emperor*] [*Latin*]
ERETS	Edwards Rocket Engine Test Station [*NASA*] (IAA)
E-RETS	Enhanced Remote Target System [*Military*] (INF)
ERETS	Experimental Rocket Engine Test Station (SAA)
EREW	Exclusive Read, Exclusive Write [*Computer science*]
ERF	Early Renal Failure [*Medicine*]
ERF	Egg-Release Pheromone [*Biology*]
ERF	Electronic Repair Facility [*Military*]
ERF	Electro-Rheological Fluids [*American Cyanamid Co.*]
ERF	Ellipsoidal Reflector Floodlight (WDMC)
ERF	Emergency Recovery Force
ERF	Emergency Response Facility (MCD)
ERF	Employer's Return File [*IRS*]
ERF	Enerplus Resources Fund Series 'B' Trust Units [*Toronto Stock Exchange symbol*]
ERF	Entrainment Release Factor [*Nuclear energy*] (NRCH)
ERF	Erfurt [*Germany Airport symbol*] (OAG)
ERF	Error Function
ERF	Established Risk Factor (PDAA)
ERF	Estuarine Research Federation (EA)
ERF	European Redistribution Facility
ERF	Exchange Reference File (ADA)

ERF.............	Excitatory Receptive Field [*Physiology*]
ERF.............	Expected Response File
ERF.............	Explosion Release Factor [*Nuclear energy*] (NRCH)
ERF.............	Exponential Reliability Function
ERF.............	External Rotation in Flexion [*Orthopedics*] (DAVI)
ERF.............	Eye Research Foundation (DAVI)
ERFA.........	European Radio Frequency Agency [*Later, ARFA*] [*NATO*]
ERFB.........	Extended-Range Full Bore (PDAA)
ERFC.........	Eddie Rabbitt Fan Club (EA)
ERFC.........	Error Function Complementary
ERFC.........	Erythrocyte Rosette-Forming Cells [*Hematology*]
ERFDP.......	Earth Resources Flight Data Processor [*NASA*]
ERFEN	Regional Study of the El Nino Phenomenon [*Peru-Chile-Columbia-Ecuador*] [*Marine science*] (OSRA)
ERFI..........	Error Function, Inverse
ERFIS.........	Emergency Response Facility Information System [*Nuclear energy*] (NRCH)
ERFPI.........	Extended-Range Floating Point Interpretive System
ERFPIS	Extended-Range Floating Point Interpretive System (IAA)
ERFS.........	Extended-Range Fuel System (DOMA)
ERG	Electrolyte Replacement with Glucose [*Medicine*] (MEDA)
ERG	Electromagnetic Radiation Generator
ERG	Electronic Rentals Group [*Commercial firm*] [*British*]
ERG	Electron Radiography (IAA)
ERG	Electroretinogram [*Medicine*]
ERG	Emergency Recovery Group
ERG	Emergency Response Guide [*RSPA*] (TAG)
ERG	Emergency Response Guidelines [*Nuclear energy*] (NRCH)
ERG	Empirical Research Group (HGAA)
ERG	Employment Resources Group [*British*]
ERG	Endocrine Research Group [*University of Calgary*] [*Research center*] (RCD)
ERG	Endoplasmic Reticulum of Golgi [*Cytology*]
ERG	Energy-Related General [*National Science Foundation research office*]
ERG	Energy-Related Graduate [*National Science Foundation trainee program*]
ERG	Energy Research for the Governors
ERG	Engineering Release Group (AAG)
ERG	Engineer Reactors Group [*Army*]
ERG	Environmental Research Group
ERG	Erase Gap [*Computer science*]
Erg.............	Ergaenzung [*Amendment, Supplement*] [*German*] (DLA)
ERG	Ergometer (MCD)
ERG	ERG Resources, Inc. [*Formerly, Energy & Resources (CAM) Ltd.*] [*Toronto Stock Exchange symbol*]
ERG	Eromanga [*New Hebrides*] [*Airport symbol*] (AD)
ERG	Executive Review Group
ERG	Existence, Relatedness, and Growth [*Basic human needs suggested by Clayton P. Alderfer*]
ERG/(CM² S)...	Ergs per Square Centimeter Second [*Unit of work*]
ERGO.........	Energy Rich Glucose Optimized Drink [*Military*] (INF)
ERGO..........	Environmental Review Guide for Operations [*US Army Corps of Engineers*]
ERGO..........	Ergo Science [*NASDAQ symbol*] (TTSB)
ERGODATA...	Banque de Donnees Internationales de Biometrie Humaine et d'Ergonomie [*International Database of Human Biometrics and Ergonomics*] [*Universite Rene Descartes*] [*France*] [*Information service or system*] (CRD)
ERGODATA...	Ergonomy Data [*Information service or system*] [*France*] (NITA)
ERGON........	Ergonomics (ADA)
ERGP	Extended Range Guided Projectiles (MCD)
ERGS	Earth Geodetic Satellite [*Air Force*]
ERGS	Electronic Route Guidance System (OA)
ERGS	En Route Guidance System (IEEE)
ERG/S	Ergs per Second [*Unit of work*]
ERGS	Experimental Route Guidance System (IAA)
ERH	Egg-Laying Release Hormone [*Endocrinology*]
ERH	Elastomeric Rotary-Wing Head [*Military*] (CAAL)
ERH	ERA Helicopters, Inc. [*ICAO designator*] (FAAC)
ERH	Erith Herbarium [*Borough Museum*] [*British*]
ERH	Ethiopian Refugee Help-Line (EAIO)
ERHPA.........	Efficient Reliable High-Power Amplifier (MCD)
ERHS	Evangelical and Reformed Historical Society
ERHSA-UCC...	Evangelical and Reformed Historical Society and Archives, United Church of Christ (EA)
ERHS-UCC ...	Evangelical and Reformed Historical Society, United Church of Christ [*Later, ERHSA-UCC*] (EA)
ERI..............	Ear Research Institute [*Later, HEI*] (EA)
ERI..............	Economic Research Institute [*Utah State University*] [*Research center*] (RCD)
ERI..............	Educational Research Information
ERI..............	Education and Research Institute [*Washington, DC*] (EA)
ERI..............	EGFR [*Epidermal Growth Factor Receptor*] Related Inhibitor [*Biochemistry*]
ERI..............	Ekwal Reading Inventory (EDAC)
ERI..............	Eleanor Roosevelt Institute (EA)
ERI..............	Electronics Research Laboratory [*Montana State University*] [*Research center*] (RCD)
ERI..............	Ellef Ringnes Island [*Canada*]
ERI..............	Elm Research Institute (EA)
ERI..............	Emergency Response Indictor
ERI..............	Employee Relations Index
ERI..............	End of Recorded Information [*Computer science*]
ERI..............	Energy Research Institute (EA)

ERI.............	Energy Resources Institute [*University of Oklahoma*] [*Research center*] (RCD)
ERI.............	Engineering Research Institute [*Iowa State University*] [*Research center*] (AAG)
ERI.............	Engineer Restructuring Initiative [*Army*]
ERI.............	Enterprise Resources [*Vancouver Stock Exchange symbol*]
ERI.............	Entomological Research Institute
ERI.............	Environmental Research Institute (EA)
ERI.............	Environmental Response Inventory [*Research test*] [*Psychology*]
Eri.............	Eridamus [*Constellation*]
ERI.............	Erie [*Pennsylvania*] [*Airport symbol*] (OAG)
ERI.............	Erie, PA [*Location identifier FAA*] (FAAL)
ERI.............	Erindale Campus Library, University of Toronto [*UTLAS symbol*]
ERI.............	Erionite [*A zeolite*]
ERI.............	Ethical Reasoning Inventory (EDAC)
ERI.............	Eureka Ridge [*Idaho*] [*Seismograph station code, US Geological Survey Closed*] (SEIS)
ERI.............	Executive Resources International [*British*]
ERI.............	Expressive-Regressive Index
ERI.............	Extravehicular Reference Information [*NASA space program*]
ERI.............	Eyes Right (EA)
ERIA...........	Electroradioimmunoassay [*Clinical chemistry*]
ERIC...........	Educational Resources [*formerly, Research*] Information Center [*Department of Education*] [*Bibliographic database Washington, DC*]
ERIC...........	Effective Rate of Interest and Charges
ERIC...........	Electronic Remote and Independent Control
ERIC...........	Electronic Retailing Investment Corp. [*Acronym is also the name of an electronic vending kiosk*]
ERIC...........	Energy Rate Input Controller (IEEE)
ERIC...........	Enterobacterial Repetitive Intergenic Consensus [*Genetics*]
ERIC...........	Environmental Research and Information Centre [*Commercial*] (EERA)
ERIC...........	Ericsson [*L. M.*] Telephone Co. [*NASDAQ symbol*] (NQ)
ERIC...........	ERISA [*Employee Retirement Income Security Act*] Industry Committee (EA)
ERICA	Effective Reading in Content Areas (EDAC)
ERICA	European Research into Consumer Affairs [*England*] [*Research center*] (IRC)
ERICA	Experiment on Rapidly Intensifying Cyclones over the Atlantic [*National Oceanic and Atmospheric Administration*]
ERICA	Eye-Gaze Response Interface Computer Aid [*Computer designed for the physically handicapped that responds to user's eye movements*] [*Designed by Thomas Hutchinson*]
ERIC/ACVE ...	Educational Resources Information Center/Clearinghouse on Adult, Career, and Vocational Education [*Department of Education*] (IID)
ERIC/AE	Educational Resources Information Center/Adult Education [*Department of Education*] (AEBS)
ERICCA........	Equal Rights in Clubs Campaign for Action [*British*] (DI)
ERIC/CAPS...	Educational Resources Information Center/Clearinghouse on Counseling and Personnel Services [*Department of Education*] [*University of Michigan*] [*Research center*] (IID)
ERIC/CE	Educational Resources Information Center/Clearinghouse in Career Education [*Ohio State University*] (IID)
ERIC/CEA	Educational Resources Information Center/Clearinghouse on Educational Administration [*University of Oregon*] [*Department of Education*] (AEBS)
ERIC/CEM	Educational Resources Information Center/Clearinghouse on Educational Management [*Department of Education*] [*University of Oregon Eugene*] [*Research center*]
ERIC/CHE.....	Educational Resources Information Center/Clearinghouse on Higher Education (IID)
ERIC/CHESS...	Educational Resources Information Center/Clearinghouse for Social Studies/SocialScience Education [*Department of Education*] [*Information service or system*] (IID)
ERIC/CLIS	Educational Resources Information Center/Clearinghouse for Library Information Sciences
ERIC/CLL	Educational Resources Information Center/Clearinghouse on Languages and Linguistics [*Department of Education*] [*Center for Applied Liguistics*] (IID)
ERIC/CRESS...	Educational Resources Information Center/Clearinghouse on Rural Education and Small Schools [*Department of Education*] [*New Mexico State University*] [*Research center*] (IID)
ERIC/CRIER...	Educational Resources Information Center/Clearinghouse on Retrieval of Information and Evaluation on Reading [*Indiana University*] [*Department of Education*] (AEBS)
ERIC/CUE.....	Educational Resources Information Center/Clearinghouse on Urban Education [*Department of Education*] [*Columbia University*] (IID)
ERIC/EC	Educational Resources Information Center/Clearinghouse on Handicapped and GiftedChildren [*Department of Education*] [*Information service or system*] (IID)
ERIC/EECE ...	Educational Resources Information Center/Clearinghouse on Elementary and Early Childhood Education [*Department of Education*] [*University of Illinois*] (IID)
ERIC/HE	Educational Resources Information Center/Clearinghouse on Higher Education [*George Washington University*] [*Research center*] (EA)
ERIC/IR........	Educational Resources Information Center/Clearinghouse for Information Resources [*Department of Education*] [*Syracuse University*] [*Research center*] (IID)
ERIC/IRCD ...	Educational Resources Information Center/Information Retrieval Center on the Disadvantaged [*Horace Mann-Lincoln Institute Teachers College*] [*Columbia University*] [*Department of Education*] (AEBS)

ERICR .... Eleanor Roosevelt Institute for Cancer Research
ERIC/RCS ..... Educational Resources Information Center/Clearinghouse on Reading and Communication Skills [*Department of Education*] [*Urbana, IL*]
ERIC/SMEAC... Educational Resources Information Center/Clearinghouse for Science, Mathematics,and Environmental Education [*Department of Education*] [*Information service or system*] (IID)
ERIC/SP .... Educational Resources Information Center/School Personnel [*Department of Education*] [*Washington, DC*]
EricT .... Ericsson [*L.M.*] Telephone Co. [*Associated Press*] (SAG)
ERIC/TE .... Educational Resources Information Center/Clearinghouse on Teacher Education
EricTel .... Ericsson Telephone [*Associated Press*] (SAG)
ERIC/TM .... Educational Resources Information Center/Clearinghouse on Tests, Measurement, and Evaluation [*Department of Education*] [*Educational Testing Service*] (IID)
ERICY .... Ericsson(LM) Tel'B'ADR [*NASDAQ symbol*] (TTSB)
ERICZ .... Ericsson L M Tel [*NASDAQ symbol*] (TTSB)
ERICZC .... Educational Reptiles in Captivity Zoological Compound (EA)
ERID .... Emerging and Reemerging Infectious Diseases [*Medicine*]
Erid .... Eridamus [*Constellation*]
ERIE .... Eastern Regional Institute for Education
ERIE .... Environmental Resistance Inherent in Equipment
Erie .... Erie County Legal Journal [*Pennsylvania*] [*A publication*] (DLA)
ERIE .... Erie Indemnity 'A' [*NASDAQ symbol*] (TTSB)
ERIE .... Erie Indemnity Co. [*NASDAQ symbol*] (TTSB)
Erie Co Leg J... Erie County Legal Journal [*Pennsylvania*] [*A publication*] (DLA)
Erie Co L J (PA)... Erie County Law Journal (Pennsylvania) [*A publication*] (DLA)
ErieInd .... Erie Indemnity Co. [*Associated Press*] (SAG)
Erie LJ .... Erie County Legal Journal [*Pennsylvania*] [*A publication*] (DLA)
ERILCO .... Exchange of Ready for Issue in Lieu of Concurrent Overhaul
ERIM .... Environmental Research Institute of Michigan [*Research center*] (RCD)
ERIN .... Environmental Resources Information Network [*Australia*]
ERINT .... Extended Range Interceptor [*Air Force*]
ERINT .... Extended-Range Intercept Technology Missile [*Army*]
ERIP .... Early Retirement Incentive Program [*Generic term*]
ERIP .... Energy-Related Inventions Program [*Department of Energy and National Bureau of Standards*]
ERIP .... Engineering Research Initiation Program [*National Science Foundation*]
ERIPS .... Earth Resources Image [*or Interactive*] Processing System
ERIR .... Extended-Range Instrumentation RADAR (PDAA)
ERIS .... Earth-Reflecting Ionospheric Sounder [*Air Force*] (MCD)
ERIS .... Economic Resource Impact Statement
ERIS .... Emergency Resources Identification Equipment (IAA)
ERIS .... Emergency Response Information System [*Nuclear Regulatory Commission*] (GFGA)
ERIS .... Engineering Resins Information System [*General Electric Co.*]
ERIS .... Environmental Resource Information Services [*Australia*]
ERIS .... Environmental Resources Information System [*Computer science*] (EERA)
ERIS .... Equipe de Recherche Interdisciplinaire en Sante [*Universite de Montreal, Quebec*] [*Canada*]
ERIS .... Exoatmospheric Reentry Vehicle Interceptor Subsystem [*Army*] (RDA)
ERISA .... Employee Retirement Income Security Act [*of 1994*] (AAGC)
ERISA .... Employee Retirement Income Security Act of 1974 [*Also facetiously translated as Every Ridiculous Idea Since Adam*]
ERISTAR ...... Earth Resources Information Storage, Transformation, Analysis, and Retrieval
Erit .... Eritrea
ERIV .... Eagle River Interactive [*NASDAQ symbol*] (TTSB)
ERIV .... Eagle River Interactive, Inc. [*NASDAQ symbol*] (SAG)
ERIW .... European Research Institute for Welding (PDAA)
ERJ .... Alexandria, LA [*Location identifier FAA*] (FAAL)
ERJ .... Eurojet Italia [*Italy ICAO designator*] (FAAC)
ERJ .... Extended-Range Juno [*Survey meter for radiation*]
ERJ .... External Ramjet
ERJE .... Extended Remote Job Entry
ERK .... Ethniko Rizospastiko Komma [*National Radical Party*] [*Greek*] (PPE)
ERK .... Experimental Research Kit
ERKO .... Estrogen Receptor Knockout [*Mouse strain*]
ERL .... Earth Resources Laboratory [*Later, NSTL*] [*NASA*] (KSC)
ERL .... Echo Return Loss [*Telecommunications*]
ERL .... Economic Retention Level (AFIT)
ERL .... Effective Refractory Length [*Ophthalmology*] (DAVI)
ERL .... Electronics Research Laboratory [*Massachusetts Institute of Technology*] [*Research center*] (MCD)
ERL .... Electronics Research Laboratory [*University of California, Berkeley*] [*Research center*] (RCD)
ERL .... Emergency Reference Level [*Nuclear energy*] (NRCH)
ERL .... Energy Research Laboratories (EERA)
ERL .... Environmental Research Laboratories [*Boulder, CO*] [*National Oceanic and Atmospheric Administration*]
ERL .... Environmental Resources Ltd. [*British*]
ERL .... Equine Research Laboratory [*University of California, Davis*]
ERL .... Equipment Requirement List (MCD)
ERL .... Equipment Revision Level (IAA)
Erl .... Erlass [*Decree, Edict, Order*] [*German*] (ILCA)
ERL .... ESSA [*Environmental Science Services Administration*] Research Laboratories
ERL .... Euralair [*France ICAO designator*] (FAAC)
ERL .... European Requirements List [*Military*] (AABC)
ERL .... Event Record Log
ERL .... Extended-Range Lance [*Missile*] (MCD)

ERL .... Extraneous Residue Limit [*Toxicology*]
ERL .... Eye Research Laboratories [*University of Chicago*] [*Research center*] (RCD)
ERL/ATH ...... Athens Environmental Research Laboratory [*Athens, GA*] [*Environmental Protection Agency*] (GRD)
ERL/COR ...... Corvallis Environmental Research Laboratory [*Corvallis, OR*] [*Environmental Protection Agency*] (GRD)
E/RLD .... Edges Rolled [*Publishing*] (DGA)
ERL/DUL ...... Duluth Environmental Research Laboratory [*Minnesota*] [*Environmental Protection Agency*] (GRD)
ERLE .... Echo Return Loss Enhancement
ERLE .... Energy-Related Laboratory Equipment [*Defunct*]
Erle Tr Un ..... Erle on the Law of Trade-Unions [*A publication*] (DLA)
ERL/GB .... Gulf Breeze Environmental Research Laboratory [*Gulf Breeze, FL*] [*Environmental Protection Agency*] (GRD)
ERLL .... Enhanced Run Length Limited [*Computer science*] (BYTE)
ERL-N .... Environmental Research Laboratory, Narragansett [*Environmental Protection Agency*]
ERL/NARR ... Narragansett Environmental Research Laboratory [*Narragansett, RI*] [*Environmental Protection Agency*] (GRD)
ERLR .... Eastern Region of Nigeria Law Reports [*A publication*] (DLA)
ERLS .... Economic Release Lot-Size
ERLTM .... ESSA [*Environmental Science Services Administration*] Research Laboratories. Technical Memorandum [*A publication*]
ERLUA .... Environmental Research Laboratory, University of Arizona
ERL-UCB ...... University of California, Berkeley Electronics Research Laboratory [*Research center*] (RCD)
ERLV .... Erysimum Latent Virus [*Plant pathology*]
ERLY .... Early
ERLY .... ERLY Indus [*NASDAQ symbol*] (TTSB)
ERLY .... ERLY Industries, Inc. [*NASDAQ symbol*] (SAG)
ERM .... Earth Re-Entry Module (MCD)
ERM .... Earth Resistivity Meter
ERM .... Earth Return Module [*NASA*] (KSC)
ERM .... Edge Reading Meter
ERM .... Effective Relaxation Modulus
ERM .... Elastic Reservoir Molding (DICI)
ERM .... Electrical Research Memorandum
ERM .... Electrochemical Relaxation Methods
ERM .... Emergency Radiation Monitor
ERM .... Energy Research Management (MCD)
ERM .... Engine Room
ERM .... En Route Metering [*FAA*] (TAG)
ERM .... Entity-Relationships Model (HGAA)
ERM .... Environmental Resources Management
ERM .... Environmental Resources Management, Inc. [*Database producer*] (IID)
ERM .... Epiretinal Membrane [*Ophthalmology*]
ERM .... Erimo [*Japan*] [*Seismograph station code, US Geological Survey*] (SEIS)
ERM .... Ermine [*Heraldry*]
ERM .... European Red Mite [*Insect*]
ERM .... Evaporate Rate Monitor (IAA)
ERM .... Exact Repeat Mission [*of GEOSAT*] [*Navy*] (GFGA)
ERM .... Exchange-Rate Mechanism [*European Economic Union*] (ECON)
ERM .... Explosives Research Memorandum
ERM .... Ezrin-Radixin-Moesin [*Cytology*]
e-rm-- .... Romania [*MARC geographic area code Library of Congress*] (LCCP)
ERMA .... Electronic Recording Machine Accounting
ERMA .... Emergency Refugee and Migration Assistance [*Department of State*]
ERMA .... Engineering Reprographic Management Association [*Later, ERS*]
ERMA .... Ernest Read Music Association [*British*] (DBA)
ERMA .... Expansion Rate Measuring Apparatus
ERMA .... Extended Red Multialkali [*Cathode*]
ERMAC .... Echo-Ranging Masked Acoustic Communications
ERMAC .... Electromagnetic Radiation Management Advisory Council [*US Government*]
ERMBE .... Energy-Related Minority-Owned Business Enterprise
ERMCO .... European Ready Mixed Concrete Organization (EAIO)
ERMD .... Environment and Resource Management Division [*World Wildlife Fund-United States*]
ERMES .... European Radio Messaging System
ERMG .... Enroute Metering [*Aviation*] (FAAC)
ERMING ...... Ermington [*England*]
ERMISS ...... Explosion-Resistant Multi-Influence Sweep System (NATG)
ER-MLRS ...... Extended Range, Multiple Launch Rocket System [*Army*]
ERMP .... Energy Research Management Project [*Federal interagency group*]
ERMP .... Environment Management and Review Program (EERA)
ER/MRT .... Equipment Removal/Material Review Tag [*Military*] (MCD)
ERMS .... Electroluminescent Runway Marking System [*Aviation*]
ERMS .... Emergency Radiation Monitoring System (GNE)
ERMS .... Environmental Resources Mapping System [*Computer science*] (EERA)
ERMU .... Experimental Remote Maneuvering Unit
ERN .... Eastern
ERN .... Educational Radio Network
ERN .... Electronic RADAR Navigation (DNAB)
ERN .... Engineering Reference Number
ERN .... Engineering Release Notice (MSA)
ERN .... Ernestine [*Alaska*] [*Seismograph station code, US Geological Survey Closed*] (SEIS)
ERN .... Explosives Research Note
ERNA .... Engineer, Royal Naval Artillery [*Navy-British*] (ROG)
ERNA .... Equilibrium Radionuclide Angiography [*Cardiology*] (CPH)
ERNAS .... European Review of Native American Studies [*A publication*]

ERNET .... Education and Research Network [*India*] [*Computer science*] (TNIG)

ERNIC .... Earnings-Related National Insurance Contribution [*British*] (DCTA)

ERNIE .... Electronic Random Number and Indicating Equipment [*Used for selecting winning premium bond numbers*] [*British*]

ERNK .... Enlya Ruzgariya Netwa Kurdistan [*National Front for the Liberation of Kurdistan*] [*Turkey Political party*]

ERNLR .... Eastern Region of Nigeria Law Reports [*A publication*] (DLA)

ERNO .... Entwicklungsring Nord Organisation [*Space Division of European Consortium*]

ERNO .... European Research National Organization (MCD)

ERNS .... Emergency Response Notification System [*Environmental Protection Agency*] (EPA)

ERNS .... Ernst Home Center [*NASDAQ symbol*] (TTSB)

ERNS .... Ernst Home Center, Inc. [*NASDAQ symbol*] (SAG)

ErnstHm .... Ernst Home Center, Inc. [*Associated Press*] (SAG)

ERO .... Early Retirement Opportunity [*Business term*]

ERO .... Eldred Rock, AK [*Location identifier FAA*] (FAAL)

ERO .... Electronic Repair Order [*Automobile service*]

ERO .... Elementary Relaxation Oscillator [*Instrumentation*]

ERO .... Emergency Repair Overseer [*Navy*]

ERO .... Employer Relations Officer

ERO .... Energy Research Office [*Department of Energy*] (OICC)

ERO .... Engineering Regional Organisation (ACII)

ERO .... Engineering Release Operations (NASA)

ERO .... Engineering Release Order [*Formerly, ROD*]

ERO .... Equipment Repair Order (DNAB)

ERO .... ERO, Inc. [*Associated Press*] (SAG)

ERO .... European Regional Organization of the ICFTU

ERO .... European Regional Organization of the International Dental Federation (EAIO)

ERO .... European Research Office [*British*]

ERO .... Sundor International Air Services Ltd. [*Israel*] [*ICAO designator*] (FAAC)

EROAT .... Echo Ranging Operated Acoustic Torpedo [*Military*] (IAA)

EROC .... Environmental Restoration Opportunities Conference

EROD .... Ethoxyresorufin O-Deethylase [*An enzyme*]

EROI .... Energy Return on Investment

EROI .... ERO, Inc. [*NASDAQ symbol*] (SAG)

EROM .... Electron Readout Measurement (MCD)

EROM .... Erasable Read-Only Memory [*Computer science*]

EROM .... Erasable ROM [*Computer science*] (ECII)

EROMDA ...... Eastern Regional Office Machine Dealers Association Convention (TSPED)

EROP .... Executive Review of Overseas Programs [*Army*] (AABC)

EROP .... Extensions and Restrictions of Operators (IEEE)

EROPA .... Eastern Regional Organization for Public Administration GG2 [*Manila, Philippines*] [*See also OROAP*]

EROS .... Earth Resources Observation System [*United States of America*] [*Military*] (EERA)

EROS .... Earth Resources Observation Systems [*US Geological Survey*]

EROS .... Earth Resources Observing Satellite [*Marine science*] (OSRA)

EROS .... Earth Resources Observing Satellite (USDC)

EROS .... Eelam Revolutionary Organization [*Sri Lanka*] [*Political party*]

EROS .... Electric Resonance Optothermal Spectroscopy

EROS .... Elimination of Range Zero System [*Aviation*]

EROS .... Engineering Records Organisation System [*Applied Research of Cambridge Ltd.*] [*Software package*] (NCC)

EROS .... Engine Repair and Overhaul Squadron [*British Royal Air Force*]

EROS .... Environment and RADAR Operations Simulator

EROS .... Equipment Required on Site (MCD)

EROS .... Estimate Range Zero System (SAA)

EROS .... Event-Related Optical Signal [*Imaging science*]

EROS .... Experience de Recherche d'Objects Sombres [*Astronomy*]

EROS .... Experience de Recherches d'Objets Sombres [*Experiment on Investigations int o Dark Objects*]

EROS .... Experimental Reflector Orbital Shot [*NASA project*]

EROSAT .... ELINT [*Extended-Range Interceptor Technology*] Ocean Reconnaissance Satellite (DOMA)

EROW .... Executive Right of Way [*Telecommunications*] (TEL)

EROWS .... Expendable Remote Operating Weather Station [*Air Force*]

EROX .... Erox Corp. [*NASDAQ symbol*] (SAG)

EroxCp .... Erox Corp. [*Associated Press*] (SAG)

ERP .... Early Receptor Potential [*of the eye*]

ERP .... Earthquake Reporting and Prediction (NOAA)

ERP .... Earth Reference Pulse (IAA)

ERP .... Econometric Research Program [*Princeton University*] [*Research center*] (RCD)

ERP .... Economic Review Period

ERP .... Economic Rights Program [*Later, WERP*] (EA)

ERP .... Educational Reimbursement Program (SAA)

ERP .... Effected Radioactive Power

ERP .... Effective Radiated Power [*Radio transmitting*]

ERP .... Effective Rating Point (WDMC)

ERP .... Effective Refractory Period

ERP .... Ejercito Revolucionario del Pueblo [*People's Revolutionary Army*] [*Argentina*] (PD)

ERP .... Ejercito Revolucionario del Pueblo [*People's Revolutionary Army*] [*El Salvador*] (PD)

ERP .... Electronic Radiated Power (PDAA)

ERP .... Electronic Requirement Plan [*Navy*]

ERP .... Electronic Road Pricing (PDAA)

ERP .... Electrostatic Reversal Printing

ERP .... Elevated Release Point [*Nuclear energy*] (NRCH)

ERP .... Eligibility Review and Reemployment Assistance Program [*Employment Service*] [*Department of Labor*]

ERP .... Elodoisin-Related Peptide [*Medicine*] (DMAA)

ERP .... Emergency Recorder Plot (IAA)

ERP .... Emergency Relocation Point (DOMA)

ERP .... Emergency-Room Physician (MEDA)

ERP .... Emergency Rubber Project [*National Research Council*]

ERP .... Emitted Radio Power (IAA)

ERP .... Endocardial Resection Procedure [*Cardiology*]

ERP .... Endoscopic Retrograde Pancreatography [*Medicine*]

ERP .... End Reporting Period

ERP .... End Response (IAA)

ERP .... Enforcement Response Policy [*Environmental Protection Agency*] (GFGA)

ERP .... Enforcement Response Policy (GNE)

ERP .... Engineered Restoration Procedure

ERP .... Engineering Release Package

ERP .... Engineering Requirements Plan [*for Military Assistance Programs*]

ERP .... Enroute Reporting Point [*MTMC*] (TAG)

ERP .... Enterprise Resource Planning (ACII)

ERP .... Environmental Research Papers (MCD)

ERP .... Environmental Response Policy

ERP .... Environmental Responsibility Program [*An association*] (EA)

ERP .... Equine Rhinopneumonitis [*Medicine*] (MAE)

ERP .... Equipment Repair Parts

ERP .... Equipment Replacement Program [*Computer science*]

ERP .... Equipment Requirement Program (MCD)

ERP .... Equivalent Radiated Power

ERP .... Erase, Record, and Playback (NTCM)

ERP .... Error-Recovery Package [*Computer science*] (MDG)

ERP .... Error-Recovery Procedure [*Computer science*]

ERP .... Establishment Reporting Plan [*Social Security Administration*] (GFGA)

ERP .... Estimated Reseller Price

ERP .... Estimated Resident Population [*Demographics*] [*Australia*]

ERP .... Estrogen Receptor Protein [*Endocrinology*]

ERP .... Euler-Rodrigues Parameter [*Physics*]

ERP .... European Recovery Program

ERP .... Event-Related Potential [*Neurophysiology*]

ERP .... Expanded Relations Program [*Army*] (DOMA)

ERP .... Extended-Range Projectile

ERP .... Eye Reference Point [*NASA*] (KSC)

ERPA .... Office of Exploratory Research and Problem Assessment [*National Science Foundation*]

ERPAL .... Electronic Repair Parts Allowance List [*Navy*]

ERPC .... Eastern Railroad Presidents Conference [*Later, ERA*] (EA)

ERPC .... Eglin Refugee Processing Center [*Florida*] [*Air Force*] (MCD)

ERPC .... Emerson Radio & Phonograph Corp. [*Later, Emerson Radio Corp.*]

ERPD .... Electronic Reconnaissance Procurement Division

ERPD .... Experimental RADAR Prediction Device (MCD)

ERPF .... Effective Renal Plasma Flow [*Medicine*]

ERPG .... Emergency Response Planning Guideline [*Environmental science*]

ERPL .... Equipment Repair Parts List

ERPLD .... Extended-Range Phase-Locked Demodulator (IEEE)

ERPM .... Engineering Requirements and Procedures Manual (MCD)

ERPN .... Eastern Region Public Notice [*Nigeria*] [*A publication*] (DLA)

ERPN .... European

ERPO .... Earth Resources Project Office (MCD)

ERPPO .... Engineer Repair Parts Packaging Office [*Merged with General Equipment Command*]

ER-PR .... Effectiveness Report - Performance Report [*Air Force*] (AFM)

ERPR .... Exponentially Restored, Poisson-Released

ERPS .... Electrolytic Reactants Production System (IAA)

ERPS .... Environmental Radiation Protection Standard (NUCP)

ERPS .... Equipment Release Priority System [*DoD*]

ERPS .... Equipment Requisitioning Priority System [*Military*]

ERPSL .... Essential Repair Part Stockage List [*Military*] (AABC)

ERQ .... Economic Reorder Quantity (ADA)

ERQ .... Economic Repair Quantity

ERQ .... End Request (IAA)

ERQC .... Engineering Reliability and Quality Control (AAG)

Err .... [*The*] Comedy of Errors [*Shakespearean work*]

ERR .... Eagle Ridge Resources Ltd. [*Vancouver Stock Exchange symbol*]

ERR .... Economic Rate of Return

ERR .... Economic Retention Requirement (AFIT)

ERR .... Electronic Requirements Report (DNAB)

ERR .... Elk River Reactor

ERR .... Employer Relations Representative

ERR .... Engineering Release Record (AAG)

ERR .... Engineering Reliability Review (MCD)

ERR .... Engineering Research Report

ERR .... Engine Removal Report

ERR .... Erie Railroad

ERR .... Errata [*Error*] [*Latin*] (NVT)

ERR .... Errol, NH [*Location identifier FAA*] (FAAL)

ERR .... Error (MCD)

err .... Estonian Soviet Socialist Republic [*MARC country of publication code Library of Congress*] (LCCP)

ERR .... Estrogen Receptor-Related

ERR .... Extended Range Rocket [*Aerospace*]

Err & App ... Error and Appeal Reports [*Canada A publication*] (DLA)

ERRAP .... Environmental Resources Research and Assistance Program [*US Army Corps of Eng ineers*]

ER/RB .... Enhanced Radiation/Reduced Blast

ERRC .... Eastern Regional Research Center [*Department of Agriculture*] [*Philadelphia, PA*] (GRD)

ERRC .... Employment Relations Resource Centre [*British*] (AIE)

ERRC	Error Correction
ERRC	Expendability, Recoverability, Repairability Cost (NASA)
ERRC	Expendability/Recoverability/Repair Capability (NASA)
ERRCC	Expendability, Recoverability, Repairability Cost Category
ERR CNTR ..	Error Counter
ERRD	Emergency and Remedial Response Division [Environmental Protection Agency] (GFGA)
ERRDEP	Error Variance Dependent on Level [Statistical test]
ERRDF	Earth Resources Research Data Facility
ERREAC	Employee Relocation Real Estate Advisory Council [Later, E-R-C] (EA)
ERRET	Error Return Point (MCD)
ERRI	Environmental Resources Research Institute [Pennsylvania State University] [Information service or system] (IID)
ERRN	Expedite Release Request Notice (MCD)
ERRON........	Erroneous
ERRP	EGF [Epidermal Growth Factor] Receptor-Related Protein [Biochemistry]
ERRS	Environmental Response and Referral Service [Oak Ridge National Laboratory] (IID)
ERRT	Economic Research Round Table (EA)
ERS..............	Earnings-Related Supplement [British]
ERS..............	Earth Recovery Subsystem [NASA] (KSC)
ERS..............	Earth Regeneration Society (EA)
ERS..............	Earth Remote Sensing Satellite (EERA)
ERS..............	Earth Resources Satellite [NASA]
ERS..............	Earth Resources Survey [NASA]
ERS..............	Eastern Range Ships
ERS..............	Economic Research Service [Department of Agriculture] [Washington, DC]
ERS..............	Economic Retention Stock
ERS..............	Educational Research Service (EA)
ERS..............	Electoral Reform Society [British]
ERS..............	Electrical Resistance Strain (OA)
ERS..............	Electric Railway Society (EAIO)
ERS..............	Electrolytic Refining and Smelting Company [Australia Commercial firm]
ERS..............	Electronic Rear Steering [Automotive engineering]
ERS..............	Electronic Reconnaissance Set
ERS..............	Electronic Reconnaissance System
ERS..............	Electronic Register-Sender [Telecommunications] (TEL)
ERS..............	Electronic Remote Switching (MCD)
ERS..............	Electronic Repair Station
ERS..............	Electronic Rig Stats [Pennwell Publishing Co.] [Information service or system] (IID)
ERS..............	Elevated Radio System
ERS..............	Elizabethan Railway Society [British] (BI)
ERS..............	Emergency Recovery Section
ERS..............	Emergency Relocation Site [Military]
ERS..............	Emergency Reporting System [Telecommunications] (TEL)
ERS..............	Emergency Road Service [American Automobile Association]
ERS..............	Endoscopic Retrograde Sphincterotomy [Medicine]
ERS..............	Energy Return System [In ERS 2000, brand name of Reebok International Ltd.]
ERS..............	Engineering Release System
ERS..............	Engineering Reprographic Society (EA)
ERS..............	Engineering Research Station [British]
ERS..............	Engine Room Supervisor (DNAB)
ERS..............	Entry and Recovery Simulation (MCD)
ERS..............	Environmental Research Satellite [NASA]
ERS..............	Equilibrium Radiation Spectra
ERS..............	Equipment Record System (KSC)
ERS..............	Equipment Requirement Specification
ERS..............	Erased (MSA)
ERS..............	Ergonomics Research Society [British] (BI)
ERS..............	Eros Resources [Vancouver Stock Exchange symbol]
ERS..............	ESA [European Space Agency] Remote Sensing Satellite
ERS..............	Estimated Release Schedule (AAG)
ERS..............	Ethylene Response Sensor [Botanical genetics]
ERS..............	European Rhinologic Society (EA)
ERS..............	European (Space Agency) Remote Sensing Satellite System (EERA)
ERS..............	Evaluation Record Sheet (MCD)
ERS..............	Expanded RADAR Service (AFM)
ERS..............	Experience Rating System [Health insurance] (GHCT)
ERS..............	Experimental RADAR System
ERS..............	Experimental Research Society [Defunct] (EA)
ERS..............	Export Return Scheme [Australia]
ERS..............	External Reflection Spectroscopy
ERS..............	External Regulation System (IEEE)
ERS..............	Extremal Regulation System (PDAA)
ERS..............	Windhoek-Eros [Namibia] [Airport symbol] (OAG)
ERS-1	Earth Remote Sensing Satellite-1 (MCD)
ERS-1	European Remote Sensing Satellite-1 (EERA)
ERS-2	European Remote Sensing Satellite-2 [Marine science] (OSRA)
ERSA	Electronic Research Supply Agency
ERSA	Embry-Riddle School of Aviation [Later, E-RAU] [Florida]
ERSA	Emergency Relocation Site Afloat (MCD)
ERSA	Extended-Range Strike Aircraft [for low-level missions] [Air Force]
ERSAL	Environmental Remote Sensing Applications Laboratory [Oregon State University] [Research center] (RCD)
ERSATS	Earth Resource Survey Satellite (PDAA)
ERSB	Expendable Radio Sonobuoy (IAA)
ERSC	Extended-Range and Space Communication (MCD)
ERSCP	End Refueling and Start Climb Point (SAA)
ERSD	Electronic Range Scoring Device (MCD)

ERSD	Engineering Research Services Division [North Carolina State University] [Research center] (RCD)
ERSDAC.......	Earth Resources Satellite Data Analysis Center [Japan] (EERA)
ERSER	Expanded Reactance Series Resonator
ERSFF	Eastern Region SEATO [Southeast Asia Treaty Organization] Field Forces (CINC)
ERSFP	Earth Resources Survey Flights Program [NASA]
ERSI	Elastomeric Reusable Surface Insulation (NASA)
ERSI	Electric Remote Speed Indicator (IAA)
ERSI	Electronic Retailing Sys [NASDAQ symbol] (TTSB)
ERSI	Electronic Retailing Systems International [NASDAQ symbol] (SAG)
ERSIR	Earth Resources Shuttle Imaging RADAR
Ersk	Erskine's Institutes of the Law of Scotland [A publication] (DLA)
Ersk	Erskine's Principles of the Law of Scotland [A publication] (DLA)
Ersk Dec	Erskine's United States Circuit Court, Etc., Decisions [35 Georgia] [A publication] (DLA)
Erskine I	Erskine's Institutes of the Law of Scotland [8 eds.] [1773-1871] [A publication] (DLA)
Erskine Inst...	Erskine's Institutes of the Law of Scotland [8 eds.] [1773-1871] [A publication] (DLA)
Ersk Inst	Erskine's Institutes of the Law of Scotland [8 eds.] [1773-1871] [A publication] (DLA)
Ersk Prin.....	Erskine's Principles of the Law of Scotland [A publication] (DLA)
Ersk Speech...	Erskine's Speeches [A publication] (DLA)
Ersk Speeches...	Erskine's Speeches [A publication] (DLA)
ERSNA	Efferent Renal Sympathetic Nerve Activity [Physiology]
ERSO	Electronic Research and Support Organization [Taiwan] (NITA)
ERSOS	Earth Resource Survey Operational System (TEL)
ERSP	Earth Resources Survey Program [NASA]
ERSP	Eesti Rahvusliku Soltumatuse Partei [Estonian National Independence Party] [Political party] (EAIO)
ERSP	Enroute Spacing Program [Aviation] (FAAC)
ERSP	Event-Related Slow-Brain Potential [Neurophysiology]
ERSP	Expendable Recoverable Sound Projector [Navy] (CAAL)
ERSPRC.......	Earth Resources Survey Program Review Committee [NASA] (NOAA)
ERSR	Equipment Reliability Status Report
ERSS	Earth Resources Satellite System (IEEE)
ERSS	Earth Resources Survey Satellite [NASA] (IAA)
ERT.............	Earth Received Time [Astronomy]
ERT.............	Educational Requirements Test
ERT.............	Effective Reference Time
ERT.............	Egyptian Religious Texts and Representations [New York] [A publication] (BJA)
ERT.............	Electrical Resistance Temperature
ERT.............	Elementary Renewal Theorem
ERT.............	Emergency Repair Team [Nuclear energy] (GFGA)
ERT.............	Emergency Response Team (NRCH)
ERT.............	Emergency Response Training
ERT.............	Encoder-Receiver-Transmitter [Telecommunications]
ERT.............	Enershare Technology Corp. [Vancouver Stock Exchange symbol]
ERT.............	Engineering Release Ticket
ERT.............	Engine Rotor Tester
ERT.............	Ente de Radiodiffusion y Television [Radio and television network] [Argentina]
ERT.............	Environmental Research and Technology, Inc. [Concord, MA] (MCD)
ERT.............	Environmental Research and Technology, Information Center, Concord, MA [OCLC symbol] (OCLC)
ERT.............	Environmental Response Team [Environmental Protection Agency]
ERT.............	Environment Round Table (EERA)
ERT.............	Equipment Removal Tag (MCD)
ERT.............	Equipment Repair Time
ERT.............	Estimated Repair Time [Telecommunications] (TEL)
ERT.............	Estrogen Replacement Therapy [Medicine]
ERT.............	European Round Table (EAIO)
ERT.............	Execute Reference Time (MCD)
ERT.............	Executive Reference Time
ERT.............	Exhibits Round Table [American Library Association]
ERT.............	Expected Run-Time
ERT.............	Extended-Range TOW [Tube-Launched, Optically Tracked Wire-Guided (Weapon)] (MCD)
ERT.............	Extended Research Telescope
ERT.............	External Radiation Therapy [Medicine]
ERTA..........	Economic Recovery Tax Act [1981]
ERTA..........	Emergency Railroad Transportation Act, 1933
ERTA..........	European Road Transport Agreement (ILCA)
ERTAQ	Environmental Response Team Air Quality Model [Environmental Protection Agency] (GFGA)
ERTC..........	Emergency Rescue Team Chief [Air Force]
ERTC..........	Engineer Replacement Training Center
ERTC..........	European Regional Test Center (NATG)
ERTEC........	Eastern Region Teacher Education Consortium (AIE)
ERTG	Economic [or Economical] Radioisotope Thermoelectric Generator
ERTH	Earth [Freight]
ERTH	Earth
ERTH	Environmental Resources Technology [Information service or system] (IID)
Erthlink......	Earthlink Network, Inc. [Associated Press] (SAG)
erthwk	Earthwork (VRA)
erthwr........	Earthenware (VRA)
ERTI...........	Electron-Ray Tuning Indicator (DEN)
ERTN	Exhaust [Oxygen Sensor] Return [Automotive engineering]
ERTS...........	Earth Resources Technology Satellite [Later, LANDSAT] [NASA]
ERTS...........	Edwards Rocket Test Site (KSC)
ERTS...........	Electronic Arts [Commercial firm] (NQ)

ERTS............	Electronic Arts [*NASDAQ symbol*] (TTSB)
ERTS............	Electronic Arts, Inc. [*NASDAQ symbol*] (SAG)
ERTS............	ELINT [*Electronic Intelligence*] Receiver Test System (MCD)
ERTS............	Emergency Remote Tracking Station [*Navy*] (ANA)
ERTS............	Environmental Radiological Technical Specifications [*Nuclear energy*] (NRCH)
ERTS............	Environmental Resources Technology Satellite (NRCH)
ERTS............	Error Rate Test Set (TEL)
ERTTO	Ecologically Responsive Tractor Transmission Oil [*Lubricants*]
ERU	Earth Rate Unit [*NASA*] (KSC)
ERU	Eastern Rugby Union of America (EA)
ERU	Education Review Unit [*South Australia*]
ERU	Ejector Release Unit (MCD)
ERU	Electronic Reconnaissance Unit (MCD)
ERU	Emergency Recovery Unit
ERU	English Rugby Union
ERU	Erume [*Papua New Guinea*] [*Airport symbol*] (OAG)
ERU	External Run Unit (MHDB)
'Erub	'Erubin (BJA)
ERUHG........	External Representation of the Ukrainian Helsinki Group (EA)
ERUN	Education Research Unit News [*Australian Union of Students*] [*A publication*] (ADA)
ERUPT	Elementary Reliability Unit Parameter Technique (PDAA)
ERV.............	ECM [*Electronic Countermeasures*] - Resistant Voice
ERV.............	Efferent Renal Vein [*Anatomy*]
ERV.............	Electromagnetic Relief Valve [*Engineering instrumentation*]
ERV.............	Electronic Repair Vehicle (PDAA)
ERV.............	Endogenous Retrovirus
ERV.............	Energy Recovery Ventilators
ERV.............	English Revised Version [*of the Bible*] [*A publication*] (BJA)
ERV.............	Entry Research Vehicle
ERV.............	Europese Rum Vereniging [*European Rum Association*] [*EC*] (ECED)
ERV.............	Expiratory Reserve Volume [*Physiology*]
ERV.............	Extract Release Volume [*Food technology*]
ERV.............	Kerrville, TX [*Location identifier FAA*] (FAAL)
ERVAD	Engineering Release for Vendor Article Data [*Later, PRVD*] (AAG)
ERVIN	Energy Research Video Network [*Video conferencing*]
ERVm..........	English Revised Version [*of the Bible*], Margin
ERVSC	Engineer and Railway Volunteer Staff Corps [*Army British*]
ERW............	Elastic Resist Weld (DNAB)
ERW............	Electrical Resistance Weld
ERW............	Enhanced Radiation Weapon
ERW............	Environmentally-Responsive Workstation
Erwin	Entity Relationship for Windows (CDE)
ERWP	European Railway Wagon Pool (EA)
ER(WR)........	Earnings Record (Wage Record) [*Social Security Administration*] (OICC)
ERWRE	Earthenware [*Freight*]
ERWS	Engineering Release Work Sheet (AAG)
ERX.............	Electronic Remote Switching (IAA)
ERY.............	Early (FAAC)
ERY.............	East Riding of Yorkshire [*Administrative county in England*] (ROG)
ERY.............	East Riding Yeomanry [*Military unit*] [*British*]
ERY.............	Erysipelas [*Medicine*]
Ery.............	Erysipelothrix [*A bacteria*] (DAVI)
ERY.............	Erythromycin [*Also, E, ERYC, ETM*] [*Antibacterial compound*]
ERY.............	Newberry, MI [*Location identifier FAA*] (FAAL)
ERYC...........	Erythromycin [*Also, E, ERY, ETM*] [*Antibacterial compound*]
ERYIY	East Riding of Yorkshire Imperial Yeomanry [*British military*] (DMA)
ERYTHR.......	Erythromycin [*Also, E, ERY, ETM, ERYC*] [*An antibacterial compound*] (DAVI)
erythro........	Erythrocyte [*Hematology*] (DAVI)
ERZ.............	Eastern Rift Zone [*Geology*]
ERZ.............	Erzurum [*Turkey*] [*Airport symbol*] (OAG)
ERZ.............	Erzurum [*Turkey*] [*Seismograph station code, US Geological Survey*] (SEIS)
ERZ.............	Extended Reconnaissance Zone [*Army*] (AABC)
ES...............	Abbott Laboratories Ltd. [*Great Britain*] [*Research code symbol*]
ES...............	Air Atlantique [*ICAO designator*] (AD)
ES...............	Eagle Squadron [*British military*] (DMA)
ES...............	Early Shock [*Medicine*]
ES...............	Early Successional [*Botany*]
ES...............	Earned Surplus
ES...............	Earth Save [*An association*] (EA)
ES...............	Earth Sciences Division [*Army Natick Laboratories*]
ES...............	Earth Spring (OA)
ES...............	Earth Station
ES...............	Earth Switch (IAA)
ES...............	Earth to Space (IAA)
ES...............	Eastern States (ADA)
E/S.............	East Side [*In outdoor advertising*] (WDMC)
ES...............	Ebenezer Society (EA)
ES...............	Echo Sounding
ES...............	Echo Suppressor [*Telecommunications*] (TEL)
ES...............	Econometric Society (EA)
ES...............	Economic Studies [*Bureau of the Census*]
ES...............	Edge Salicornia Zone [*Ecology*]
ES...............	Edinaya Systema [*Unified System*] [*Russian Computer science*]
ES...............	Edison Screw
es	Edmund Scientific Consumer Science Division
ES...............	Educational Services [*Publisher*]
ES...............	Educational Specialist
ES...............	Educational Studies [*A publication*] (BRI)
Es	Ego Strength [*Psychology*]
ES...............	Ego Stress [*Test*] [*Psychology*] (DAVI)

ES...............	Einheitliche Systematik [*Library science*]
Es	Einsteinium [*Preferred form, but also see E*] [*Chemical element*]
Es	Einsteinium (IDOE)
ES...............	Ejection Sound [*Cardiology*]
ES...............	Elasticities of Substitution [*Statistics*]
ES...............	Elasticity of Supply [*Economics*] (DCTA)
ES...............	Elastic Suspensor
ES...............	Elder Statesman
ES...............	Eldest Son
ES...............	Electrical Section (IAA)
ES...............	Electrical Sounding (PDAA)
ES...............	Electrical Stimulus
ES...............	Electric Seats [*Automotive accessory*]
ES...............	Electric Starting (ADA)
ES...............	Electrochemical Society
E/S.............	Electrode Signalling [*British military*] (DMA)
ES...............	Electromagnetic Storage
ES...............	Electromagnetic Switching (IEEE)
ES...............	Electronic Section [*National Weather Service*]
ES...............	Electronic Shop Major [*Coast Guard*]
ES...............	Electronic Specialty (IAA)
ES...............	Electronic Standard
ES...............	Electronic Switching [*Telecommunications*]
ES...............	Electronic Systems
ES...............	Electron Synchrotron [*Nuclear energy*]
ES...............	Electroshock [*Psychology*]
ES...............	Electrospray [*Ionization*] [*Physics*]
ES...............	Electrostatic
ES...............	Electrostatic Spray
ES...............	Electrostatic Spraying
ES...............	Electrostatic Storage
ES...............	Element Signal [*Dialog*] [*Searchable field*] [*Information service or system*] (NITA)
ES...............	Elenchus Suppletorius ad Elenchum Bibliographicum Biblicum [*A publication*] (BJA)
ES...............	Eligible for Separation
ES...............	Eligible Spouse [*Social Security Administration*]
ES...............	Ellis Air Lines
ES...............	Ells Scotch (ROG)
es	El Salvador [*MARC country of publication code Library of Congress*] (LCCP)
ES...............	Embryonal Stem [*Cell line*]
ES...............	Embryonic Shield
ES...............	Embryo Sac [*Botany*]
ES...............	Embryo Stem Cell
ES...............	Emergency Service
e(S)............	Emergent S Wave [*Earthquakes*]
ES...............	Emission Spectrum [*Spectroscopy*]
ES...............	Employee Suggestion (AAG)
ES...............	Employer Services [*State Employee Security Agency*] (OICC)
ES...............	Employment Service [*US*] (KSC)
ES...............	Emulsifying Salts [*Food technology*]
ES...............	Enamelist Society (EA)
ES...............	Enamel Single Silk [*Wire insulation*] (AAG)
ES...............	Endocrine Society (EA)
ES...............	End of Study
ES...............	Endogenous Substance [*Biology*]
ES...............	Endometritis-Salpingitis [*Medicine*] (DMAA)
ES...............	Endoplasmic Surface [*Freeze etching in microscopy*]
ES...............	Endoscopic Sclerosis [*Medicine*] (DAVI)
ES...............	Endoscopic Sclerotherapy [*Medicine*]
ES...............	Endoscopic Sphincterotomy [*Medicine*]
ES...............	End Sheet [*Publishing*]
ES...............	End Strength
ES...............	End System [*Computer science*] (TNIG)
ES...............	End-Systole [*Cardiology*]
ES...............	End to Side [*Portacaval shunt*] [*Medicine*] (AAMN)
ES...............	Enema Saponis [*Medicine*]
ES...............	Enemy Status (MCD)
ES...............	Enforcement Stategy [*Environmental Protection Agency*] (GFGA)
ES...............	Engagement Simulation [*Military*] (INF)
ES...............	Engineered Safeguards [*Nuclear energy*] (NRCH)
ES...............	Engineering and Society
ES...............	Engineering Services
ES...............	Engineering Specification
ES...............	Engineering Standard
ES...............	Engineering Study
E/S.............	Engineer/Service [*Aerospace*] (AAG)
ES...............	Engine-Sized [*Paper*]
ES...............	Enginesmith [*British military*] (DMA)
E-S.............	En Route Supplement
E/S.............	En Suite (ADA)
ES...............	Enterprise Statistics [*A publication*]
ES...............	Environmental Safety (EA)
ES...............	Environmental Services (EERA)
ES...............	Environmental Survey
ES...............	Enzyme-Substrate Complex [*Enzyme kinetics*]
ES...............	Ephphatha Services (EA)
ES...............	Epigraphic Society (EA)
ES...............	Epileptic Syndrome [*Medicine*] (DMAA)
ES...............	Eprova Ltd. [*Switzerland*] [*Research code symbol*]
ES...............	Equal Section [*Technical drawings*]
ES...............	Equipment Section
ES...............	Equipment Serviceability (MCD)
ES...............	Equipment Specialist [*Military*] (AFIT)

ES...............	Equipment Specification
ES...............	Equipment Status (MCD)
ES...............	Ergonomics Society [British]
ES...............	Erkennungssignal [Recognition signal] [German military - World War II]
ES...............	Errata Sheet
ES...............	Escape System (MCD)
ES...............	Escort Ship (CINC)
ES...............	Esophageal Scintigraphy [Medicine] (DAVI)
ES...............	Esophagus [Anatomy] (DAVI)
ES...............	Esophoria [Ophthalmology] (DAVI)
ES...............	Esther [Old Testament book]
ES...............	Estimate (ROG)
ES...............	Estimated Standard [Statistics] (DAVI)
ES...............	Estimated Tax [IRS]
ES...............	Estradiol [Also, E_2, E-diol] [Endocrinology]
Es...............	Estriol [Endocrinology] (AAMN)
ES...............	Eureka Society (EA)
es----..........	Europe, Southern [MARC geographic area code Library of Congress] (LCCP)
ES...............	Evangelization Society (EA)
ES...............	Eversley Series [A publication]
ES...............	Exchangeable Sodium (OA)
ES2..............	Exclusive of Sheeting
ES...............	Excretory-Secretory
ES...............	Executive Schedule [U.S. Civil Service] (BARN)
ES...............	Executive Secretariat (USDC)
ES...............	Executive Secretary
ES...............	Exempt Security
ES...............	Existential Study [Psychology]
ES...............	Exoplasmic Surface [Freeze etching in microscopy]
ES...............	Expectation Score (MAE)
ES...............	Experimental Station
ES...............	Experimental Study [Research] (DAVI)
ES...............	Experiment Segment (MCD)
ES...............	Expert System [Computer science]
ES...............	Export Surpluses [British]
ES...............	Exsmoker (DAVI)
ES...............	Extended Service [Automotive engineering]
ES...............	Extended Sleeper [In truck name Aero ES] [Volvo White Truck Corp.] [Automotive engineering]
ES...............	Extension Service [Department of Agriculture]
ES...............	Extension Shaft [Nuclear energy] (NUCP)
ES...............	Extension Station (IAA)
ES...............	Exterior Surface
ES...............	External Services [British Broadcasting Corp.]
ES...............	External Shield (IAA)
ES...............	External Store
ES...............	Extraction Steam [System] [Nuclear energy] (NRCH)
ES...............	Extra Segment [Computer science]
ES...............	Extra Series
ES...............	Extra Slow [Photography] (DGA)
ES...............	Extrastriate [Neurology]
ES...............	Extrasystole [Cardiology] (DAVI)
ES...............	Eye Stalk
ES...............	IEEE Education Society (EA)
E_s............	Screen Voltage (IDOE)
ES...............	Spain [ANSI two-letter standard code] (CNC)
ES2..............	European Silicon Structures (NITA)
E/S³............	Engineering and Scientific Support System [IBM Corp.]
ESA³............	Earth Station - Arabia
ESA.............	Eastern Ski Association [Later, USSA] (EA)
ESA.............	Eastern Surfing Association (EA)
ESA.............	Ecole Superieure des Affaires [High Business School] [Information service or system] (IID)
ESA.............	Ecological Society of America (EA)
ESA.............	Economics and Statistics Administration (USDC)
ESA.............	Economics and Statistics Administration [Marine science] (OSRA)
ESA.............	Economic Society of Australia
ESA.............	Economic Stabilization Act [Wage-price controls] [Expired April 30, 1974]
ESA.............	Economic Stabilization Administration
ESA.............	Economic Stabilization Agency [Terminated, 1953]
ESA.............	Ejercito Salvadoreno Anticomunista [Salvadoran Anti-Communist Army] (PD)
ESA.............	Ejercito Segredo Anti-Comunista [Secret Anti-Communist Army] [Guatemala] (PD)
ESA.............	Electrically Supported [or Suspended] Accelerometer
ESA.............	Electrical Stress Analysis
ESA.............	Electrokinetic Sonic Amplitude [Determination of electrokinetic potential]
ESA.............	Electrolysis Society of America [Later, SCME] (EA)
ESA.............	Electronically Steerable Array (MCD)
ESA.............	Electronic Security Alarm [Automobile theft preventive]
ESA.............	Electronic Security Alaska [Air Force]
ESA.............	Electronic Subsystems Analysis (MCD)
ESA.............	Electronic Surge Arrester
ESA.............	Electron Scan Antenna [FAA]
ESA.............	Electrostatic Analyzer
ESA.............	Emergency Safe Altitude (MCD)
ESA.............	Employee Standards Administration
ESA.............	Employment Service Agency [Department of Employment] [British]
ESA.............	Employment Standards Administration [Department of Labor]
ESA.............	Endangered Species Act [1973]
ESA.............	End-Systolic Areas [Cardiology]

ESA.............	Energy Security Act [1980]
ESA.............	Energy-Separating Agent [Chemical engineering]
ESA.............	Engineering Study Authorization Division [NASA] (KSC)
ESA.............	Engineering Supply Area (NASA)
ESA.............	Engineering Support Activity [Military]
ESA.............	Engineering Support Assembly (NASA)
ESA.............	Engineers and Scientists of America [Defunct]
ESA.............	Engineer Stores Assignment [British]
ESA.............	Engineer Surveyors' Association [A union] [British]
ESA.............	Engine Service Association (EA)
ESA.............	English, Scottish & Australian Bank Ltd. (ADA)
ESA.............	Enterprise-Specific Agreement
ESA.............	Entomological Society of America (EA)
ESA.............	Entomological Society of Australia
ESA.............	Environmentally Sensitive Area [British]
ESA.............	Environmental Protection Agency, Region X Library, Seattle, WA [OCLC symbol] (OCLC)
ESA.............	Environmental Study Area
ESA.............	Epigraphic South Arabian (BJA)
ESA.............	Epiphyllum Society of America (EA)
ESA.............	Episcopal Synod of America (EA)
ESA.............	Equalized Sidelobe Antenna
ESA.............	Equipment Service Association (EA)
ESA.............	Equivalent Snowline Altitude
ESA.............	Ergonomics Society of Australia
ESA.............	Esa Ala [Papua New Guinea] [Airport symbol] (OAG)
ESA.............	Esa Ala [Papua New Guinea] [Seismograph station code, US Geological Survey] (SEIS)
ESA.............	European Satellite Agency [Marine science] (OSRA)
ESA.............	European Satellite Agency/European Space Agency (USDC)
ESA.............	European Space Agency [See also ASE] (EAIO)
ESA.............	European Space Association
ESA.............	European Spice Association [EC] (ECED)
ESA.............	European Strabismological Association (EAIO)
ESA.............	European Supply Agency (NATG)
ESA.............	European Suzuki Association [British] (EAIO)
ESA.............	Euthanasia Society of America [Later, SRD] (EA)
ESA.............	Evangelicals for Social Action (EA)
ESA.............	Excited-State Absorption
ESA.............	Executive Storage Area (IAA)
ESA.............	Exer-Safety Association (EA)
ESA.............	Expiration of Service Agreement [Military] (AABC)
ESA.............	Explosive Safe Area [NASA]
ESA.............	Explosive Safety Approval (MUGU)
ESA.............	Explosives Storage Area
ESA.............	Extended Service Agreement
ESA.............	Externally Specified Address (CAAL)
ESA.............	Seagreen Air Transport [Antigua and Barbuda] [ICAO designator] (FAAC)
ESAA..........	Economic Stimulus Appropriations Act (OICC)
ESAA..........	Electricity Supply Association of Australia (EERA)
ESAA..........	Emergency School Aid Act [1972]
ESAA..........	Employment Security Administration Account
ESAA..........	English Schools' Athletic Association (BI)
ESAA..........	English Setter Association of America (EA)
ESAA..........	European Special Activities Area [Military]
ESAB..........	Energy Supplies Allocation Board
ESAC..........	Education Service Advisory Committee (AIE)
ESAC..........	Electrical Systems and Controls (ACII)
ESAC..........	Electronic Shock Absorber Control
ESAC..........	Electronic Systems Assistance Center [Telecommunications] (TEL)
ESAC..........	Endangered Species Advisory Committee [Commonwealth] (EERA)
ESAC..........	Environmental Studies Association of Canada (EERA)
ESAC..........	Environmental Systems Applications Center [NASA]
ESAC..........	Evangelical Social Action Commission (EA)
ESACT........	Engineering and Systems Analysis for the Control of Toxics Technology Center [University of California at Los Angeles] [Research center] (RCD)
ESACT........	European Society for Animal Cell Technology (EA)
ESAD..........	Empirically Supported Algorithm Driven [Computer science]
ESADA........	Empire State Atomic Development Associates, Inc.
ESADS........	Earth Science and Applications Data System [National Oceanic and Atmospheric Administration]
ESAE..........	European Society of Association Executives (EA)
ESAF..........	Electronic Safe Arming and Firing Device (DWSG)
ESAF..........	Enhanced Structural Adjustment Facility [IMF] (ECON)
ESAFA........	Employment Security Administrative Financing Act of 1954
ESAFT........	Electrically Steerable Antenna Feed Techniques (NG)
ESAG..........	Expression Site-Associated Genes
ESAIDARM...	Eastern and Southern African Initiative in Debt and Reserves Management (ECON)
ESAIRA.......	Electronically Scanning Airborne Intercept RADAR Antenna
ESA-IRS......	European Space Agency Information Retrieval Service [Italy]
E Sal..........	El Salvador (VRA)
ESAL..........	Engine Start after Launch [Navy] (CAAL)
ESAL..........	Equivalent Single Axle Load
ESAM..........	Evolutionary Surface-to-Air Missile [Military]
ESAM..........	Extendable Stiff Arm Manipulator [NASA]
ESAMRDC...	Eastern and Southern African Mineral Resources Development Center
ESAMS........	Elliott Automation Space and Advanced Military Systems
ES & H	Environmental Safety and Health [Environmental Protection Agency] (EPA)
ES&H..........	Office of Environment, Safety, and Health
ES & P........	Engineering Systems and Procedures (MCD)

ES & S........ Engineering Services and Safety (NRCH)
ES & WQIAC... Effluent Standards and Water Quality Information Advisory Committee (DICI)
ESANET........ ESA [*European Space Agency*] Network [*Information service or system*] (NITA)
ESANET........ European Space Agency Information Network (PDAA)
ESAO .... Earth Sciences Assistance Office [*Department of the Interior*] (GRD)
ESAO .... European Society for Artificial Organs (EA)
ESAOA .... Eastern Ski Area Operators Association (EA)
ESAP........... Emergency School Assistance Program
ESAP........... Employment Security Automation Project [*Department of Labor*]
ESAP........... Environmental Self-Assessment Program
ESAP........... Evoked Sensory Action Potential [*Neurophysiology*]
ESAR........... Electromagnetic Spectrum Allocation Request [*Army*] (RDA)
ESAR .... Electronically Scanned Array RADAR (IEEE)
ESAR .... Electronically Steerable Array RADAR
ESAR .... Extended Subsequent Application Review (AAGC)
ESARBICA.... Eastern and Southern African Regional Branch of the International Council on Archives [*Nairobi, Kenya*] (EAIO)
ESARCC ...... Endangered Species Act Reauthorization Coordinating Committee (EA)
Esarh .... Esarhaddon (BJA)
ESARIPO...... Industrial Property Organization for English-Speaking Africa [*Nairobi, Kenya*] (EAIO)
ESARS .... Earth Surveillance and Rendezvous Simulator
ESARS .... Employment Service Automated [*or Automatic*] Reporting System [*Department of Labor*]
ESARTS ...... En Route Stand-Alone Radar Training System [*FAA*] (TAG)
ESAS........... Education Student Assistance System
ESAS........... Electronically Steerable Antenna System [*Navy*] (CAAL)
ESAS........... Engineered Safeguards Actuation System [*Nuclear energy*] (NRCH)
ESAS........... Event Sensing and Analysis System (DNAB)
ESAS-2 .... Elastic Structural Analysis System - Two Dimensional [*Structures & Computers Ltd.*] [*Software package*] (NCC)
ESASA .... Ethnic Schools Association of South Australia
ESASC .... Elementary School Administrative Supervisory Certificate
ESASI.......... European Society of Air Safety Investigators (PDAA)
ESAT........... Electronic Shift Automatic Transmission [*Automotive engineering*]
ESAT........... Employee Satisfaction
ESAT........... Environmentally Sound and Appropriate Technology (PDAA)
ESATA......... Executive Subroutines for Afterheat Temperature Analysis [*Computer program*] [*NASA*]
ESA (UN) ..... Department of Economic and Social Affairs of the United Nations [*Later, Depart ment of Social Affairs*]
ESAUSA ...... Estonian Student Association in the United States of America [*Defunct*] (EA)
ESAWC .... Evaluation Staff, War College [*Air Force*]
ESAWR .... Early Settlers Association of the Western Reserve (EA)
ESAX........... East Saxon [*Dialect of Old English*] [*Language, etc.*]
ESB............. Aerosaba SA de CV [*Mexico*] [*FAA designator*] (FAAC)
ESB............. Ankara-Esenboga [*Turkey*] [*Airport symbol*] (OAG)
ESB............. Earth Station - Brazil
ESB............. Economic Stabilization Board [*World War II*]
ESB............. Educational Service Branch [*BUPERS*]
ESB............. Education Support Centre [*Australia*]
ESB............. Effective Sample Base [*Advertising*] (DOAD)
ESB............. Effective School Battery [*Educational test*]
ESB............. Electrical Stimulation of the Brain
ESB............. Electrical Systems Branch [*NASA*] (KSC)
ESB............. Electricity Supply Board [*Republic of Ireland*] (BI)
ESB............. Electricity Supply Board (ACII)
ESB............. Electric Storage Battery
ESB............. Elektromotroischer Systembaukasten
ESB............. Emergency Services Bureau [*Queensland, Australia*]
ESB............. Emerging Small Business (AAGC)
ESB............. Empennage Support Beam [*Aerospace engineering*] (MCD)
ESB............. Engineer Special Brigade [*Military*]
ESB............. English-Speaking Background (ADA)
ESB............. English-Speaking Board (International) [*British*]
ESB............. Environmental Protection Agency, ERC [*Environmental Research Center*] Library, Corvallis, OR [*OCLC symbol*] (OCLC)
ESB............. Environmental Studies Board [*National Academy of Sciences*]
ESB............. Esa Ala [*D'Entrecasteaux Islands*] [*Seismograph station code, US Geological Survey*] (SEIS)
ESB............. Espirito Santo Overseas [*NYSE symbol*] (SPSG)
ESB............. Essential Switching Box (MCD)
ESB............. European Schoolbooks Ltd. [*British*]
ESB............. European Society of Biomechanics (EA)
ESB............. Executive for Small Business
ESB............. Executive Support Board [*Army*] (RDA)
ESB............. Experiments Systems Branch [*NASA*] (KSC)
ESB............. Explosive Safety Board [*Military*]
ESB............. Extra Strong Bitter [*Beer*] [*British*]
ESBA........... Eastern Sovereign Base Area [*British military*] (DMA)
ESBA........... Ethyl-sec-butylamiline [*Organic chemistry*]
ESBC........... Electronics Small Business Council
ESBCY .... European Society for Blue Cross Youth (EA)
ESBFCOA..... Eastern States Blast Furnace and Coke Oven Association (EA)
ESBFS......... East of Scotland Brass Founders' Society [*A union*]
ESBG........... European Savings Bank Group [*EC*] (ECED)
ESBK........... [*The*] Elmira Savings Bank [*NASDAQ symbol*] (NQ)
ESBK........... Elmira Svgs Bk FSB NY [*NASDAQ symbol*] (TTSB)
ESBL........... Engine Start before Launch [*Navy*] (CAAL)
ESBO .... Electronic Selection and Bar Operating (IAA)

ESBO .... Environmental and Safety Business Opportunities [*Bureau of National Affairs*]
ESBPrA .... Espirito Santo Oversecs 8.50% Pref [*NYSE symbol*] (TTSB)
ESBRA .... Emerging Small Business Reserve Amount (AAGC)
ESBRS .... Elementary School Behavior Rating Scale [*Devereaux*] [*Psychology*]
ESBT........... Expert System Building Tool [*Computer science*]
ESBVM........ Ecumenical Society of the Blessed Virgin Mary (EA)
ESC............. Earthspirit Community (EA)
ESC............. Earth Station - Congo
ESC............. Eastern Simulation Council
ESC............. Echo Suppressor Control [*Telecommunications*] (TEL)
ESC............. Ecological Study Center [*Oak Ridge National Laboratory*]
ESC............. Economic and Social Committee [*EC*] (ECED)
ESC............. Economic and Social Council [*United Nations*]
ESC............. Economic Sciences Corp. [*Information service or system*] (IID)
ESC............. Edison Screw Cap [*Electronics*] (EECA)
ESC............. Educational Systems Corp. [*Defunct*] (EA)
ESC............. Electric Surface Current
ESC............. Electromechanical Slope Computer (MAE)
ESC............. Electromechanical Stop Clock
ESC............. Electronic Scan Converter
ESC............. Electronic Security Command (MCD)
ESC............. Electronic Shop Computer
ESC............. Electronic Spark Control [*Automotive*]
ESC............. Electronic Still Camera
ESC............. Electronic Supervisory Control (MCD)
ESC............. Electronic Switching Center (CET)
ESC............. Electronic Systems Center [*Air Force*]
ESC............. Electronic Systems Command [*Also, NESC*] [*Navy*]
ESC............. Electrostatic Collector
ESC............. Electrostatic Compatibility (IEEE)
ESC............. Elementary School Center [*An association*] (EA)
ESC............. Elongation-Sensitive Cell (PDAA)
ESC............. El Salvador [*Chile*] [*Seismograph station code, US Geological Survey Closed*] (SEIS)
ESC............. Embryonic Stem Cell [*Cytology*]
ESC............. Emeritus Corp. [*AMEX symbol*] (SAG)
ESC............. Employment Studies Centre [*University of Newcastle, Australia*]
ESC............. Employment Support Center (EA)
ESC............. Enamel Single-Covered [*Wire insulation*] (DEN)
ESC............. Endangered Species Committee [*Environmental Protection Agency*] (EPA)
ESC............. End-Systolic Count [*Cardiology*]
ESC............. Energy Systems Center [*University of Nevada*] [*Research center*] (RCD)
ESC............. Engineering Sequential Camera (KSC)
ESC............. Engineering Service Circuit
ESC............. Engineer Studies Center (MCD)
ESC............. Engine Start Command (KSC)
ESC............. English Shakespeare Co. (ECON)
ESC............. English Shepherd Club (EA)
ESC............. English Ski Council [*British*] (DBA)
ESC............. English-Speaking Country
ESC............. Entomological Society of Canada (BARN)
ESC............. Environmental Stress Crack [*or Cracking*] [*Plastics*]
ESC............. Environmental Studies Center [*State University of New York at Buffalo*] [*Research center*] (RCD)
ESC............. Environmental Study Conference [*House of Representatives*]
ESCPrA........ Epoxy Spray Coater
ESC............. Equipment Section Container
ESC............. Equipment Serviceability Criteria [*Military*]
ESC............. Equipment Storage Container (KSC)
ESC............. Erythropoietin-Sensitive Stem Cell [*Hematology*]
Esc............. Escadrille [*Military*] (BARN)
ESC............. Escalator [*Technical drawings*]
ESC............. Escanaba [*Michigan*] [*Airport symbol*] (OAG)
ESC............. Escanaba, MI [*Location identifier FAA*] (FAAL)
ESC............. Escape (NASA)
ESC............. Escape Character [*Keyboard*] (KSC)
ESC............. Escobilla [*Little Broom*] [*Flamenco dance term*] [*Spanish*]
ESC............. Escompte [*Discount, Rebate*] [*French*]
Esc............. Escort [*Record label*]
ESC............. Escort (AABC)
Esc............. Escrow [*Legal term*] (DLA)
ESC............. Escudo [*Monetary unit*] [*Chile, Portugal*]
ESC............. Escutcheon
ESC............. Esplanade Centre Holdings [*Vancouver Stock Exchange symbol*]
ESC............. European Security Conference [*Soviet-sponsored*]
ESC............. European Seismological Commission (EAIO)
ESC............. European Shippers' Councils [*Netherlands*] (DS)
ESC............. European Society of Cardiology (MCD)
ESC............. European Society of Climatotherapy [*See also FEC*] [*Briancon, France*] (EAIO)
ESC............. European Society of Culture [*See also SEC*] (EAIO)
ESC............. European Space Conference
ESC............. European Sport Shooting Confederation (EAIO)
ESC............. Evanescent Space Charge (PDAA)
ESC............. Even Small Caps [*Publishing*] (WDMC)
ESC............. Evoked Synaptic Currents [*Neurophysiology*]
ESC............. Exchange Servicing Center [*Telecommunications*] (TEL)
ESC............. Executive Search Council [*Defunct*] (EA)
ESC............. Executive Seminar Center [*Civil Service Commission*]
ESC............. Executive Steering Committee (DOMA)
ESC............. Executive Systems Corp. [*An association Defunct*] (EA)
ESC............. Expandable Shelter Containers (MCD)

E/SC............ Expected/Single-Command Travel Time
ESC............. Expedited Site Characterization [*Argonne National Laboratory*] [*Environmental science*]
ESC............. Ex Senatus Consulto [*By Decree of the Senate*] [*Latin*]
ESC............. Extended Service Coverage [*Automotive engineering*]
ESCA.......... Electron Spectroscopy for Chemical Analysis
ESCA.......... Endangered Species Conservation Act of 1969
ESCA.......... English Schools Cricket Association (BI)
ESCA.......... Escalade, Inc. [*NASDAQ symbol*] (NQ)
EScA.......... Executive and Scientific Appointments, Ltd. [*Commercial firm*] [*British*]
ESCA.......... Executive Stewards' and Caterers' Association [*Later, IFSEA*]
ESCA.......... Exposition Service Contractors Association (EA)
ESCA.......... Extended Source Calibration Area [*Nuclear energy*] (NRCH)
ESCAD........ Energy Soft Computer-Aided Design [*Energy Soft Computer Systems Ltd.*] [*Software package*] (NCC)
Escalde....... Escalade, Inc. [*Associated Press*] (SAG)
Escalon....... Escalon Medical Corp. [*Associated Press*] (SAG)
ESCAP .... Economic and Social Commission for Asia and the Pacific [*UN division*] (NITA)
ESCAP .... European Society of Child and Adolescent Psychiatry (EA)
ESCAP .... United Nations Economic and Social Commission for Asia and the Pacific [*Bangkok, Thailand*] (EAIO)
ESCAPAC..... Escape PAC (MCD)
ESCAPE....... European Symposium on Computer Aided Process Engineering
ESCAPE....... Expansion Symbolic Compiling Assembly Program for Engineers
ESCAPE....... Expeditious Sales, Catalog, and Property Evaluation [*Defense Logistics Services Center project*] [*DoD*]
ESCAPER ..... Emergency System of Control Allowing Pilot Escape and Recovery (MCD)
ESCAR .... Experimental Superconducting Accelerating Ring [*Atomic physics*]
ESCARFOR... Escort Carrier Force
ESCAT......... Emergency Security Control of Air Traffic (AFM)
ESCC.......... Enamel Single, Cotton Covered [*Wire insulation*] (IAA)
ESCC.......... Engineering Sequential Camera Coverage (KSC)
ESCC.......... Evans & Sutherland Computer Corp. [*NASDAQ symbol*] (NQ)
ESCC.......... Evans&Sutherl'd Computer [*NASDAQ symbol*] (TTSB)
ESCC.......... Stockholm [*Sweden ICAO location identifier*] (ICLI)
ESCCP .... Engineering and Scientific Career Continuation Pay [*Air Force*]
ESCD.......... Engineering Specification Control Document (AAG)
ESCE.......... Enemy Situation Correlation Element [*Air Force*]
ESCERC....... European Semiconductor Device Research Conference
ESCES......... Experimental Space Communication Earth Station [*Telecommunications*] (TEL)
ESCF.......... Electronic Systems Compatibility Facility [*NASA*]
ESCF.......... Linkoping/Malmen [*Sweden ICAO location identifier*] (ICLI)
ESCGS .... Electrostatic Centimeter Gram Second (IAA)
ESCH .... Earth Station - Chile
ESCH .... Escherichia [*Bacterial strain*]
ESCHAT ...... Eschatological (ADA)
E School L Rev... Eastern School Law Review [*A publication*] (DLA)
ESCHR........ El Salvador Committee for Human Rights (EAIO)
ESCI........... Earth Sciences [*NASDAQ symbol*] (TTSB)
ESCI........... Earth Sciences, Inc. [*NASDAQ symbol*] (NQ)
ESCI........... European Society for Clinical Investigation (EAIO)
ESCIS......... Encyclopedia of Senior Citizens Information Sources [*A publication*]
ESCK.......... Norrkoping/Bravalla [*Sweden ICAO location identifier*] (ICLI)
ESCL.......... Electronic Systems Compatibility Laboratory [*NASA*]
ESCL.......... Escalator (MSA)
ESCL.......... Soderhamn [*Sweden ICAO location identifier*] (ICLI)
Escln.......... Escalon Medical Corp. [*Associated Press*] (SAG)
ESCM.......... Equipment Support Center, Mannheim [*Germany*]
ESCM.......... ESC Medical Systems Ltd. [*NASDAQ symbol*] (SAG)
ESCM.......... Uppsala [*Sweden ICAO location identifier*] (ICLI)
ESCMed...... ESC Medical Systems Ltd. [*Associated Press*] (SAG)
ESCMF........ ESC Medical Systems [*NASDAQ symbol*] (TTSB)
ESCN.......... Electrolyte and Steroid-Produced Cardiopathy Characterized by Necrosis [*Medicine*]
ESCN.......... Stockholm/Tullinge [*Sweden ICAO location identifier*] (ICLI)
ESCO .... Earth Station - Colombia
ESCO .... Easco, Inc. [*NASDAQ symbol*] (SAG)
ESCO .... Educational, Scientific, and Cultural Organization (BARN)
ESCO .... Energy Service Co.
ESCO .... Engineers Supply Control Office [*Army*]
Esco............ ESCO Electronics [*Associated Press*] (SAG)
ESCO .... European Satellite Consulting Organization [*France Telecommunications*]
ESCO2 .... Energy Specific Carbon Dioxide [*Automotive emissions*]
ESCOE .... Engineering Societies Commission on Energy [*Defunct*] (EA)
ESCOMO...... Escort Cost Model
ESCON .... Enterprise Systems Connection [*IBM Corp.*]
ESCON .... Estimated Consumption [*of gasoline*] [*Computer model*]
ESCOP .... Experimental Stations Committee on Organization and Policy [*National Association of State Universities and Land-Grant Colleges*]
ESCORON .... Escort-Scouting Squadron
ESCORT .... Electronic System for Control of Receipt Transactions (MCD)
ESCORTDIV... Escort Division
ESCORTFIGHTRON... Escort Fighter Squadron
ESCOS .... Electronic Security Combat Operations Staff [*Military*]
ESCP........... Earth Science Curriculum Project [*Education*]
ESCP........... Expendable Surface Current Probe [*Coast Guard*]
ESCPB .... European Society of Comparative Physiology and Biochemistry (EAIO)
ESCR .... Environmental Stress-Crack Resistance [*Plastics*]

ESCRG .... Escort Guard
Escriche Dict... Escriche's Dictionary of Jurisprudence [*A publication*] (DLA)
ESCRTC .... Eastern Signal Corps Replacement Training Center
ESCRU .... Episcopal Society for Cultural and Racial Unity [*Defunct*] (EA)
ESCS........... Eccentrically Stiffened Cylindrical Shell
ESCS........... Economics, Statistics, and Cooperatives Service [*Later, ERS, SRS*] [*Department of Agriculture*]
ESCS........... Electronic Spacecraft Simulator (IAA)
ESCS........... Emergency Satellite Communications System
ESCS........... Enlisted Signal Corps School
ESCSI.......... Expanded Shale, Clay, and Slate Institute (EA)
ESCSP .... European Society of Corporate and Strategic Planners [*Belgium*] (PDAA)
ESCT........... Elapsed Spacecraft Time
ESCTS......... Explosive Set Circuit Test System (DWSG)
ESCU .... Extended Service and Cooling Umbilical (NASA)
ESCVS .... European Society for Cardiovascular Surgery (EAIO)
ESCWA .... Economic and Social Commission for Western Asia [*Iraq*] [*United Nations Research center*] (IRC)
ESCWS .... Essential Service Cooling Water System [*Nuclear energy*] (NRCH)
ESD .... Earliest Start Date
ESD........... Earth Sciences Division [*Army Natick Laboratories*] (NOAA)
ESD........... Eastsound [*Washington*] [*Airport symbol*] (OAG)
ESD........... Echo Sounding Device [*Navigation*]
ESD........... Ecologically-Sustainable Development
ESD........... Ecological Sciences Division [*Oak Ridge National Laboratory*]
ESD........... Economic Surveys Division [*Census*] (OICC)
ESD........... Educational Service and Demonstration Centers [*Washington*] (EDAC)
ESD........... Effective Standard Deviation [*of chemical standardized solutions*]
ESD........... Electronic Software Distribution
ESD........... Electronics Systems Division [*Air Force*] (DOMA)
ESD........... Electronic Summation Device (MAE)
ESD........... Electronic Systems Division [*Hanscom Air Force Base, MA*]
ESD........... Electronique Serge Dassault [*French manufacturer*] (NITA)
ESD........... Electron Spectrographic Diffraction
ESD........... Electron-Stimulated Desorption [*Spectroscopy*]
ESD........... Electroocular Symbol Display
ESD........... Electrostatic Discharge (MCD)
ESD........... Electrostatic Sensitive Device (PDAA)
ESD........... Electrostatic Storage Deflection
ESD........... Elongated Single Domain
ESD........... Emergency Shutdown (MCD)
ESD........... Ending Sequence Done
ESD........... End of Screening Date [*DoD*]
ESD........... End-Systolic Diameter [*or Dimension*] [*Cardiology*]
ESD........... Energy Storage Device (IAA)
ESD........... Engineering Society of Detroit (EA)
ESD........... Engineering Standardization Directives
ESD........... Engineering Support Documentation
ESD........... English as a Secondary Dialect
ESD........... Entry Systems Division [*IBM division*] (CDE)
ESD........... Environmental Satellite Data [*National Oceanic and Atmospheric Administration*] (GFGA)
ESD........... Environmental Sciences Division [*Oak Ridge National Laboratory*]
ESD........... Environmental Sensing Device (IAA)
ESD........... Environmental Services Division [*Environmental Protection Agency*] (GFGA)
ESD........... Environmental Sex Determination [*Biology*]
ESD........... Environmental Systems Division [*Army*]
ESD........... Environment Strategies Division [*Commonwealth*] (EERA)
ESD........... Equipment Statistical Data
ESD........... Equipment Supply Depot [*British military*] (DMA)
ESD........... Equivalent Spherical Diameter [*of a particle*]
ESD........... Equivalent Stylized Day [*Of wartime combat*]
Esd............. Esdras [*Apocrypha*] (BJA)
ESD........... Esophagus, Stomach, and Duodenum [*Gastroenterology*] (DAVI)
ESD........... Esterase D [*An enzyme*]
ESD........... Estimated Shipping Date
ESD........... Estimated Standard Deviation [*Mathematics*]
ESD........... Experiment Systems Division (MCD)
ESD........... Exponential-Slope Difference [*Statistics*]
ESD........... Ex-Stock Dividend [*Investment term*]
ESD........... Extension Shaft Disconnect [*Nuclear energy*] (NRCH)
ESD........... External Symbol Dictionary [*A publication*]
ESD........... Extra Soil Defense [*Fabric treatment*]
ESDA........... Ljungbyhed [*Sweden ICAO location identifier*] (ICLI)
ESDAC .... European Space Data Center (MCD)
ESDB .... Angelholm [*Sweden ICAO location identifier*] (ICLI)
ESDC .... Equipment Sliding Drawer Cabinet
ESDC .... Equipment Statistical Data Card
ESDC .... Extended Salvage Depth Capability (MCD)
ESDD .... Earth Science Data Directory (EERA)
ESDD .... Regional Military Command Subcenter South [*Sweden ICAO location identifier*] (ICLI)
ESDE........... Electrostatic Discharge Effects (MCD)
ESDERC....... European Semiconductor Device Research Conference (PDAA)
ESD/EW ...... Electronic Systems Division Eastwing [*Hanscom Air Force Base, MA*]
ESDF........... Ronneby [*Sweden ICAO location identifier*] (ICLI)
ESDI........... Enhanced Small Device [*or Disk*] Interface [*Computer science*]
ES:DI .... Extra Segment:Destination Index [*Computer science*]
ESDIAD .... Electron-Stimulated Desorption Ion Angular Distribution [*For study of surfaces*]
ESDIIR......... Ecologically Sustainable Development Intersectoral Issues Report (EERA)

ESDIM .... Earth System Data and Information Management [*Marine science*] (OSRA)
ESDIM .... Earth System Data and Information Management [*National Oceanic and Atmospheric Administration*] (USDC)
ESDL .... Electronic Software Distribution and Licensing (CDE)
ESDN .... Extended Software Defined Network [*Computer science*] (HGAA)
ESDP .... Evolutionary System for Data Processing (IAA)
ESDR .... Electrical System Design Report
ESDRP .... Evreiskaia Sotsialdemokraticheskaia Rabochaia Partiia (BJA)
ESDS .... Economic and Social Data System [*Agency for International Development*] [*Database*]
ESDS .... Electrostatic Discharge Sensitive (MCD)
ESDS .... Elemental Standard Data System (NG)
ESDS .... Entry Sequence Data Set (HGAA)
ESDSC .... Ecologically Sustainable Development Steering Committee [*Commonwealth*] (EERA)
ES-DSMA ..... Ephphatha Services - Division for Service and Mission in America (EA)
ESDT .... Electrostatic Storage Display Tube (IAA)
ESD TDR ..... Electronic Systems Division, Technical Documentary Reports [*AFSC*]
ESDU .... Engineering Sciences Data Unit
ESDU .... Event Storage and Distribution Unit
ESE .... Avesen SA de CV [*Mexico ICAO designator*] (FAAC)
ESE .... East-Southeast
ESE .... Electrical Support Equipment
ESE .... Electronic Stock Evaluator Corp.
ESE .... Electronic Support Equipment (MCD)
ESE .... Electronic System Evaluator
ESE .... Electron Spin Echo [*Physics*]
ESE .... Electrostatische Einheit [*Electrostatic unit*] [*Physics*] (DAVI)
ESE .... Emergency Strike Effort [*Military*]
ESE .... Engineering Associate of the Society of Engineers, Inc. [*British*] (DBQ)
ESE .... Engineering Support Equipment (KSC)
ESE .... Environmental Science Education (AIE)
ESE .... Ephemeris fuer Semitische Epigraphik [*A publication*] (BJA)
ESE .... ESCO Electronics [*NYSE symbol*] (SPSG)
ESE .... Estec Systems [*Vancouver Stock Exchange symbol*]
ESE .... European Stock Exchange
ESE .... EVA [*Extravehicular Activity*] Support Equipment [*NASA*] (NASA)
ESE .... Experiment Support Equipment
ESE .... Extravehicular Support Equipment (SSD)
ESEA .... Elementary and Secondary Education Act [*1965*]
ESEC .... Earth Station - Ecuador
ESECA .... Energy Supply and Environmental Coordination Act of 1974
ESED .... Electronic Systems Engineering Department [*Naval Weapons Support Center*] [*Crane, IN*]
ESED .... Emission Standards and Engineering Division [*Environmental Protection Agency*] (GFGA)
ESED .... Environmental System and Effects Division [*NASA*]
ESEE .... European Society for Engineering Education
ESEEM .... Electron Spin Echo Envelope Modulation [*Physics*]
ESEF .... European Science and Environment Forum [*An association*]
ESEG .... Earth Station - Egypt
ESEG .... Electronic Systems Engineering Group (SAA)
ESELCO ...... ESELCO, Inc. [*Associated Press*] (SAG)
ESEM .... Electron Spin Echo Modulation [*Physics*]
ESEM .... Environmental Scanning Electron Microscope
ESEM .... Eski Sark Eserleri Muezesi [*Istanbul*] (BJA)
ESEM .... European Society for Engineering and Medicine
ESEN .... Escuela Superior de Economia y Negocios [*El Salvador*]
ESERN .... East-Southeastern (FAAC)
ESES .... Earth-Moon Space Exploration Study
ESES .... Existing Stationary Emission Source [*Environmental Protection Agency*]
ESESD .... Elementary and Secondary Education Statistics Division [*Department of Education*] (GFGA)
ESE/VM .... Expert System Environment/Virtual Machine [*Computer science*]
ESEWD .... East-Southeastward (FAAC)
ESEX .... Essex Corp. [*NASDAQ symbol*] (NQ)
ESF .... Alexandria [*Louisiana*] [*Airport symbol*] (OAG)
ESF .... Alexandria, LA [*Location identifier FAA*] (FAAL)
ESF .... Earth Society Foundation (EA)
ESF .... Eastern Sea Frontier
ESF .... Ecoles Sans Frontieres [*Education Without Frontiers*] [*An association*] (EAIO)
ESF .... Economic Support Fund [*Agency for International Development*]
ESF .... Electrostatic Air Filter (PDAA)
ESF .... Electrostatic Focusing [*Electronics*]
ESF .... Elementary Symmetric Function (MCD)
ESF .... Engineered Safety Feature [*Nuclear energy*] (NRCH)
ESF .... Engineering Specification Files
ESF .... Engineering Structural Foam
ESF .... Engineering Systems Flight [*Military*]
ESF .... Environmental Safety Facility [*Stanford University*]
ESF .... Erythropoietic Stimulating [*or Erythropoietin Switching*] Factor [*Hematology*]
ESF .... Esperantic Studies Foundation (EA)
ESF .... Espirito Santo Financial [*NYSE symbol*] (SPSG)
ESF .... Espirito Santo Finl ADS [*NYSE symbol*] (TTSB)
ESF .... European Schools Federation (EA)
ESF .... European Science Foundation (EAIO)
ESF .... European Security Forum
ESF .... European Simmental Federation (EAIO)
ESF .... European Social Fund

ESF .... European Surfing Federation (EAIO)
ESF .... Even Side Flat
ESF .... Exchange Stabilization Fund (ECON)
ESF .... Expanded Sample Frame (NTCM)
ESF .... Explosive-Safe Facility
ESF .... Extended Spooling Facility (IAA)
ESF .... Extended Super Frame [*Telecommunications*]
ESF .... Extended Superframe Format [*Telecommunications*] (ACRL)
ESF .... External Source Format (CDE)
ESFA .... Emergency Solid Fuels Administration
ESFA .... Engineered Safety Feature Actuation [*Nuclear energy*] (NRCH)
ESFAES .... Estimates Safety Factors Against Embarkment Sliding [*Military*]
ESFAS .... Engineered Safety Features Actuation System [*Nuclear energy*] (NRCH)
ESFC .... Equivalent Specific Fuel Consumption (NG)
ESFC .... Extended Specific Fuel Consumption (WDAA)
ESFH .... Hasslosa [*Sweden ICAO location identifier*] (ICLI)
ESFI .... Epitaxial Silicon Films on Insulators (MCD)
ESFI .... Knislinge [*Sweden ICAO location identifier*] (ICLI)
ESFJ .... Sjobo [*Sweden ICAO location identifier*] (ICLI)
ESFK .... Electrostatically-Focused Kylstron (IAA)
ESFM .... Moholm [*Sweden ICAO location identifier*] (ICLI)
ESFO .... Engineering Support Field Office [*Federal disaster planning*]
ESFP .... Environment-Sensitive Fracture Processes (PDAA)
ESFPA .... Empire State Forest Products Association (SRA)
ESFQ .... Kosta [*Sweden ICAO location identifier*] (ICLI)
ESFR .... Early Suppression Fast Response [*Sprinkler program for fire protection*]
ESFR .... Rada [*Sweden ICAO location identifier*] (ICLI)
ESFS .... Engineered Safety Features System [*Nuclear energy*] (NRCH)
ESFSWR ..... Extra-Special Flexible Steel Wire Rope [*British*]
ESFU .... Vaxjo/Urasa [*Sweden ICAO location identifier*] (ICLI)
ESFVS .... Engineered Safety Feature Ventilation System [*Nuclear energy*] (NRCH)
ESFY .... Byholma [*Sweden ICAO location identifier*] (ICLI)
ESG .... Earth Station - Greece
ESG .... Edith Stein Guild (EA)
ESG .... Editorial Support Group
ESG .... Edit Sync Guide (NTCM)
ESG .... Education Service Group [*Bibliographic Retrieval Services*] [*Information service or system*] (IID)
ESG .... Electrically [*or Electrostatically*] Suspended Gyro (MSA)
ESG .... Electronic Security Group [*Military*]
ESG .... Electronic Sports Gathering [*Television*] (WDMC)
ESG .... Electronic Sweep Generator
ESG .... Electrospinogram [*Medicine*] (MEDA)
ESG .... Electrostatic Gyroscope (IEEE)
ESG .... Emergency Shelter Grants Program [*Department of Housing and Urban Development*] (GFGA)
ESG .... Empiric Studies Group (SAA)
ESG .... Engineering Service [*or Support*] Group (AAG)
ESG .... Engineer Studies Group [*Office of the Chief of Engineers*]
ESG .... English Standard Gauge
ESG .... Environmental Sciences Group [*Boulder, CO*] [*Department of Commerce*] (GRD)
ESG .... Estrogen [*Endocrinology*] (AAMN)
ESG .... Ethnobotany Specialist Group (EA)
ESG .... Exchange Software Generator (TEL)
ESG .... Expanded Sweep Generator (CET)
ESGA .... Backamo [*Sweden ICAO location identifier*] (ICLI)
ESGA .... Electrically Supported [*or Suspended*] Gyro Accelerometer
ESGC .... Alleberg [*Sweden ICAO location identifier*] (ICLI)
ESGG .... Goteborg/Landvetter [*Sweden ICAO location identifier*] (ICLI)
ESGH .... Herrljunga [*Sweden ICAO location identifier*] (ICLI)
ESGI .... Alingsas [*Sweden ICAO location identifier*] (ICLI)
ESGJ .... Jonkoping [*Sweden ICAO location identifier*] (ICLI)
ESGK .... Falkoping [*Sweden ICAO location identifier*] (ICLI)
ESGL .... Lidkoping [*Sweden ICAO location identifier*] (ICLI)
ESGLD .... European Study Group on Lysosomal Diseases (EAIO)
ESGLNLA .... European Support Groups for Liberation and Nonviolence in Latin America (EAIO)
ESGM .... Electrostatically Supported Gyro Monitor [*Navy*]
ESGM .... European Society of Gastrointestinal Motility [*Louvain, Belgium*] (EAIO)
ESGM/SINS ... Electrostatically Supported Gyro Monitor/Ships Inertial Naviation System [*Navy*]
ESGN .... Electrically Suspended Gyro Navigation
ESGO .... Vargarda [*Sweden ICAO location identifier*] (ICLI)
ESGP .... Emergency Shelter Grant Program [*HUD*]
ESGP .... Goteborg/Save [*Sweden ICAO location identifier*] (ICLI)
ESGQ .... Skovde [*Sweden ICAO location identifier*] (ICLI)
ESGR .... Employer Support of the Guard and Reserve
ESGS .... Stromstad/Nasinge [*Sweden ICAO location identifier*] (ICLI)
ESGSSFDB ... Empiric Studies Group Simulated SAC [*Strategic Air Command*] Force Data Base (SAA)
ESGT .... Trollhattan/Vanersborg [*Sweden ICAO location identifier*] (ICLI)
ESGU .... Experimental Sheet Growth Unit [*Photovoltaic energy systems*]
ESGV .... Varberg [*Sweden ICAO location identifier*] (ICLI)
ESGX .... Boras-Viared [*Sweden ICAO location identifier*] (ICLI)
ESGY .... Saffle [*Sweden ICAO location identifier*] (ICLI)
ESH .... Electric Strip Heater (OA)
ESH .... End System Hello [*Computer science*] (TNIG)
ESH .... Equivalent Solar Hour [*NASA*]
ESH .... Equivalent Standard Hours (MCD)
ESH .... Harbor Defense SONARman [*Navy*]

ESH............ Human Resources, Institutions, and Agrarian Reform Division [*FAO*] [*United Nations Italy Information service or system*] (IID)
ESH............ Scheib (Earl) [*AMEX symbol*] (TTSB)
ESH............ Scheib [*Earl*], Inc. [*AMEX symbol*] (SPSG)
ESH............ Shoreham-By-Sea [*England*] [*Airport symbol*] (OAG)
ESH............ Western Sahara [*ANSI three-letter standard code*] (CNC)
ESHA...... Abisko [*Sweden ICAO location identifier*] (ICLI)
ESHAC...... Electric Space Heating and Air Conditioning (MCD)
E-SHAP...... Etopside, Cisplatin, Arabinosylcytosine, Methylprednisolone [*Antineoplastic drug*] (CDI)
ESHB.......... Electrical Stimulation - Hot Boning [*Meat processing*]
ESHB.......... Goteborg/Eastern Hospital [*Sweden ICAO location identifier*] (ICLI)
ESHC.......... Stockholm/Southern Hospital [*Sweden ICAO location identifier*] (ICLI)
ESHD.......... End Stage Heart Disease [*Medicine*] (CPH)
ESHE.......... Landskrona [*Sweden ICAO location identifier*] (ICLI)
EshedR...... Eshed Robotec 1982 Ltd. [*Associated Press*] (SAG)
ESHG.......... Stockholm/Gamla Stan [*Sweden ICAO location identifier*] (ICLI)
ESHH.......... Enthronement of the Sacred Heart in the Home (EA)
ESHH.......... Helsingborg/Harbour [*Sweden ICAO location identifier*] (ICLI)
ESHI.......... Ingmarso [*Sweden ICAO location identifier*] (ICLI)
ESHK.......... Earth Station - Hong Kong
ESHL.......... Stockholm/Huddinge Hospital [*Sweden ICAO location identifier*] (ICLI)
ESHM.......... Malmo/Harbour [*Sweden ICAO location identifier*] (ICLI)
ESHN.......... Nacka [*Sweden ICAO location identifier*] (ICLI)
ESHO.......... Skovde/Hospital [*Sweden ICAO location identifier*] (ICLI)
ESHP.......... Empire State Historical Publications [*Series*]
ESHP.......... Equivalent Shaft Horsepower [*Air Force*]
ESHP.......... European Society of Handwriting Psychology (EAIO)
ESHPH........ European Society for the History of Photography (EA)
ESHR.......... Akersberga [*Sweden ICAO location identifier*] (ICLI)
ESHS.......... Sandhamn [*Sweden ICAO location identifier*] (ICLI)
ESHU.......... Emergency Ship Handling Unit [*Navy*]
ESHU.......... Uppsala/Akademiska [*Sweden ICAO location identifier*] (ICLI)
ESHV.......... Vaxholm [*Sweden ICAO location identifier*] (ICLI)
ESHW........ Vastervik Hospital [*Sweden ICAO location identifier*] (ICLI)
ESI............ Early Screening Inventory [*Child development test*]
ESI............ Early Supplier Involvement (AAGC)
ESI............ Earned Self-Image [*Psychology*]
ESI............ Earth Station - Iran
ESI............ Economic Strategy Institute (RDA)
ESI............ Educational Services, Inc. [*Later, EDC*]
ESI............ Educational Services, International (EA)
ESI............ Educational Sport Institute (EA)
ESI............ Educreative Systems, Inc.
ESI............ Electrical System Integration (MCD)
ESI............ Electronic System Integration (KSC)
ESI............ Electron Spectroscopic Imaging
ESI............ Electrospray Ionization [*Physics*]
ESI............ Elementary and Secondary School Index [*Research test*] [*Psychology*]
ESI............ Emergency Stop Indicator [*Aerospace*] (AAG)
Esi............ Empresa de Suministros Industriales [*Import-export board*] [*Cuba*] (EY)
ESI............ Emulsion Stability Index [*Food analysis*]
ESI............ End System Identifier [*Telecommunications*] (ACRL)
ESI............ Engineering and Scientific Interpreter (IEEE)
ESI............ Enhanced Serial Interface [*Communication protocol*] [*Computer science*] (PCM)
ESI............ Entertainment Systems International [*Database producer*] (IID)
ESI............ Environmental Science Index [*Environmental Information Center Inc.*] [*Database*] (NITA)
ESI............ Environmental Severity Index
ESI............ Equivalent Spherical Illumination (PDAA)
ESI............ ESI International [*Washington, D.C.*] (AAGC)
ESI............ Espinosa [*Brazil*] [*Airport symbol*] (OAG)
ESI............ Essential Sustainment Items (DOMA)
ESI............ Essex International [*Microprocessor manufacturer*] (NITA)
ESI............ Ethiopian Standards Institution
ESI............ Executive Security International [*Institute for training bodyguards*] [*Aspen, CO*]
ESI............ Executives' Secretaries, Inc. [*Later, EWI*] (EA)
ESI............ Externally Specified Index
ESI............ Extremely Sensitive Information [*Army*] (AABC)
ESI............ ITT Educational Services, Inc. [*NYSE symbol*] (SAG)
ESI............ ITT Educational Svcs [*NYSE symbol*] (TTSB)
ESIA.......... Externally-Specified Index Address (IAA)
ESIA.......... Karlsborg [*Sweden ICAO location identifier*] (ICLI)
ESIAC........ Electronic Satellite Image Analysis Console [*NASA*]
ESIB.......... Satenas [*Sweden ICAO location identifier*] (ICLI)
ESIBEEP...... Electricity Supply Industry Building Energy Estimating Program [*Electricity Council*] [*British*]
ESIC.......... Earth Station - Ivory Coast
ESIC.......... Ecological Sciences Information Center [*Oak Ridge National Laboratory*]
ESIC.......... Environmental Science Information Center [*National Oceanic and Atmospheric Administration*]
ESIC.......... Europees Studie en Informatie Centrum [*Later, European Center for Research and Information*] [*Belgium*] (EAIO)
ESIG.......... Electronic Simulated Image Generation
ESIG.......... Environmental and Societal Impacts Group [*National Center for Atmospheric Research*]
ESIG.......... Eugenics Special Interest Group [*Defunct*] (EA)
ESIG.......... Exemplary Service in Government

ESII............ Regional Military Command Subcenter West [*Sweden ICAO location identifier*] (ICLI)
ESIIO........ European Symposium of Independent Inspecting Organizations (EA)
ESIL............ Essential Support Items List
ESIL............ European Standard Inventory List (NATG)
ESI-MS...... Electrospray Ionization Mass Spectrometry
ESIN.......... Elisabeth Sladen Information Network [*Actress featured in TV series "Dr. Who"*] [*British*] (EA)
ESIND........ Electricity Supply Item Name Directory [*A publication*]
ESIO.......... Electro Scientific Ind [*NASDAQ symbol*] (TTSB)
ESIO.......... Electro Scientific Industries, Inc. [*NASDAQ symbol*] (NQ)
ESIP.......... Employment Service Improvement Program [*Department of Labor*]
ESIR.......... Electronically Stimulated Incarnation Recall
ESIS.......... Earth Station - Israel
ESIS.......... Electronic Store Information System (IAA)
ES-IS........ End System-Intermediate System [*Computer science*] (TNIG)
ESIS.......... European Shielding Information Service [*EURATOM*] [*Databank*] (IID)
ESIS.......... European Space Information System
ESIS.......... Executive Selection Inventory System
ESIT.......... Egyptian Society for Information Technology (NITA)
ESIT.......... Electrical System-Integrated Test (SSD)
ESITC........ Electrical Supply Industry Training Committee (AIE)
ESIX.......... Enterprises Systems, Inc. [*NASDAQ symbol*] (SAG)
ESIX.......... Enterprise Systems [*NASDAQ symbol*] (TTSB)
ESIX.......... Enterprise Systems, Inc. [*NASDAQ symbol*] (SAG)
ESJ............ Earth Station - Jordan
ESJ............ Epithelial Stromal Junction [*Anatomy*]
ESJ............ Escort Screening Jammer [*Military*]
ESK............ Earth Station - Kenya
ESK............ Electrostatic Klystron
ESK............ Engineering Sketch
ESK............ Environmental Sensor Kit (MCD)
ESK............ Eskdalemuir [*Scotland*] [*Seismograph station code, US Geological Survey*] (SEIS)
ESK............ Eskimo [*Language, etc.*]
esk............ Eskimo [*MARC language code Library of Congress*] (LCCP)
ESK............ Eurosky Airlines [*Austria*] [*FAA designator*] (FAAC)
ESK............ Telecommunications Censorship Technician [*Navy*]
ESKA.......... Ekranolytny Spassatyelny Kater Amphibiya [*Screen-Effect Amphibious Lifeboat*] [*Former USSR*]
ESKA.......... Gimo [*Sweden ICAO location identifier*] (ICLI)
ESKB.......... Stockholm/Barkarby [*Sweden ICAO location identifier*] (ICLI)
ESKC.......... Sundbro [*Sweden ICAO location identifier*] (ICLI)
ESKC.......... Telecommunications Censorship Technician, Chief [*Navy*]
ESKCM........ Telecommunications Censorship Technician, Master Chief [*Navy*]
ESKCS........ Telecommunications Censorship Technician, Senior Chief [*Navy*]
ESKD.......... Dala-Jarna [*Sweden ICAO location identifier*] (ICLI)
ESKE.......... Enhanced Station-Keeping Equipment [*Air Force*] (DOMA)
ESKH.......... Eksharad [*Sweden ICAO location identifier*] (ICLI)
ESKI.......... Stockholm [*Sweden ICAO location identifier*] (ICLI)
Eskimo...... Eskimo Pie Corp. [*Associated Press*] (SAG)
ESKIMO...... Explosive Safety Knowledge Improvement Operation (MCD)
ESKK.......... Karlskoga [*Sweden ICAO location identifier*] (ICLI)
ESKL.......... Norrkoping [*Sweden ICAO location identifier*] (ICLI)
ESKM.......... Mora/Siljan [*Sweden ICAO location identifier*] (ICLI)
ESKN.......... Nykoping/Oxelosund [*Sweden ICAO location identifier*] (ICLI)
ESKO.......... Munkfors [*Sweden ICAO location identifier*] (ICLI)
ESKR.......... Stockholm Radio [*Sweden ICAO location identifier*] (ICLI)
ESKRM........ Evreiskii Soiuz Kommunisticheskoi Rabochei Molodezhi (BJA)
ESKS.......... Strangnas [*Sweden ICAO location identifier*] (ICLI)
ESKT.......... Tierp [*Sweden ICAO location identifier*] (ICLI)
ESKU.......... Sunne [*Poland ICAO location identifier*] (ICLI)
ESKV.......... Arvika [*Sweden ICAO location identifier*] (ICLI)
ESKW........ Gavle/Avan [*Sweden ICAO location identifier*] (ICLI)
ESKX.......... Bjorkvik [*Sweden ICAO location identifier*] (ICLI)
Esky............ Esquire [*A publication*] [*New York, NY*] (WDMC)
ESL............ Earth Sciences Laboratory [*Boulder, CO*] [*National Oceanic and Atmospheric Administration*]
ESL............ Earth Station - Libya
ESL............ Egg Stalk Length
ESL............ Electromagnetic Systems Laboratories, Inc.
ESL............ Electronic Software Licensing [*Software*] (CDE)
ESL............ Electronic Support Laboratory
ESL............ Electronic Systems Laboratory (MCD)
ESL............ Electroscience Laboratory [*Ohio State University*] [*Research center*] (RCD)
ESL............ Electro Science Laboratory [*Ohio State University*]
ESL............ End-Systolic Length [*Cardiology*]
ESL............ Engineering and Services Laboratory [*Tyndall Air Force Base, FL*] [*Air Force*] (GRD)
ESL............ Engineering Societies Library (MCD)
ESL............ Engineer Sub-Lieutenant [*Navy British*] (ROG)
ESL............ English as a Second Language
ESL............ Environmental Sustainment Laboratory (RDA)
ESL............ Environmental Systems Laboratory [*Virginia Polytechnic Institute and State University*] [*Research center*] (RCD)
ESL............ Equipment Status Log (DNAB)
ESL............ Essential Service Line [*Telecommunications*] (TEL)
ESL............ Esterline Technologies [*NYSE symbol*] (TTSB)
ESL............ Etac Sales Ltd. [*Toronto Stock Exchange symbol*]
ESL............ European Systems Language (IAA)
ESL............ Evans Signal Laboratory [*Army*]
ESL............ Exceeding Speed Limit
ESL............ Expected Significance Level

ESL .... Extended Service Life [*Military*] (CAAL)
ESL .... External Set Loop [*Electronics*] (ECII)
ESL .... Eye Standard Length [*Fish anatomy*]
ESL .... Kessel, WV [*Location identifier FAA*] (FAAL)
ESLA .... English as a Second Language Allowance [*Australia*]
ESLAB .... European Space Laboratory
ESLAT .... English as a Second Language (EDAC)
E-SLATS ...... Executive Strike Leader Attack Training School (DOMA)
ESLD .... End-Stage Liver Disease [*Medicine*]
ESLE .... Equivalent Station Location Error
ES/LES .... Equipment Section/Loaded Equipment Section
ESLH .... Electrical Stimulation of the Lateral Hypothalamus [*Medicine*]
ESLH .... Estimated Standard Labor Hours (AAGC)
ESLI .... Esperantista Sak-Ligo Internacia [*International Esperantist Chess League - IECL*] (EAIO)
ESLJ .... [*The*] East St. Louis Junction R. R. [*AAR code*]
ESLO .... Ethnic Schools Liaison Officer [*Australia*]
ESLO .... European Satellite Launching Organization (MCD)
ESLO .... European Space Launcher Organization
ESLR .... Events Select Logic and Rates (MCD)
ESLS .... Elementary and Secondary Education Longitudinal Studies [*Department of Education*] (GFGA)
ESLT .... Elbit Systems Ltd. [*NASDAQ symbol*] (SAG)
ESLT .... Equipment Section Leakage Test
ESM .... Earth Station - Mexico
ESM .... Earth Systems Model [*Climatology*]
ESM .... East Surrey Militia [*British military*] (DMA)
ESM .... Edible Structure Material
ESM .... Edmund Sixtus Muskie [*American politician*]
ESM .... Effectiveness Simulation Model
ESM .... Ejection Systolic Murmur [*Cardiology*]
ESM .... Elastomeric Shield Material [*Plastic technology*]
ESM .... Elastomeric Solid Material
ESM .... Electrical Stimulation of the Midbrain
ESM .... Electromatic Speed Meter (IAA)
ESM .... Electronic Sequencing Module
ESM .... Electronic Shop Minor [*Coast Guard*]
ESM .... Electronic Signal Monitoring (PDAA)
ESM .... Electronic Support Measures [*Instrumentation*] (IEEE)
ESM .... Electronic Surveillance Measures
ESM .... Electronic Switch Module
ESM .... Electronic Warfare Support Measures [*Formerly, EWSM*] (AABC)
ESM .... Emerald Star Mining [*Vancouver Stock Exchange symbol*]
ESM .... Emergency Shipment Memorandum
ESM .... Employment Security Manual (OICC)
ESM .... Energy Storage Modulator
ESM .... Engineering Material Specification
ESM .... Engineering Schedule Memorandum
ESM .... Engineering Service Memorandum (MCD)
ESM .... Environmental System Module (MCD)
ESM .... Environmental Systems Monitor (IAA)
ESM .... Escort Mission
ESM .... Esmeraldas [*Ecuador*] [*Airport symbol*] (OAG)
ESM .... Ethosuximide [*Medicine*] (DMAA)
ESM .... European Society for Microcirculation (EA)
ESM .... European Society for Mycobacteriology (EA)
ESM .... Experiments Systems Monitor [*NASA*] (KSC)
ESM .... Extended State Machine
e-sm-- .... San Marino [*MARC geographic area code Library of Congress*] (LCCP)
ESM .... Underwater Mechanic [*Obsolete Navy*]
ESM .... Winston-Salem State University, Winston-Salem, NC [*OCLC symbol*] (OCLC)
ESMA .... Electrical Sign Manufacturers Association
ESMA .... Electronic Sales-Marketing Association [*Defunct*] (EA)
ESMA .... Emmaboda [*Sweden ICAO location identifier*] (ICLI)
ESMA .... Engraved Stationery Manufacturers Association (EA)
ESMA .... Episcopal Society for Ministry on Aging (EA)
ESMA .... Essential Manning
ESMB .... Borglanda [*Sweden ICAO location identifier*] (ICLI)
ESMC .... Eastern Space and Missile Center [*Patrick Air Force Base, FL*] [*Also, ETR*] [*Air Force*]
ESMC .... Electronic Structure of Materials Centre [*Flinders University, Australia*]
ESMC .... Environmental System Management Controller (MCD)
ESMC .... Escalon Medical Corp. [*NASDAQ symbol*] (SAG)
ESMC .... Escalon Medical Corp. [*NASDAQ symbol*] (TTSB)
ESMC .... Karlshamn [*Sweden ICAO location identifier*] (ICLI)
ESMCL .... Escalon Med Corp. Wrrt'B' [*NASDAQ symbol*] (TTSB)
ESMCW .... Escalon Med Corp. Wrrt'A' [*NASDAQ symbol*] (TTSB)
ESME .... Eslov [*Sweden ICAO location identifier*] (ICLI)
ESME .... Excited State Mass Energy
ESMF .... Eleanor Steber Music Foundation [*Defunct*] (EA)
ESMF .... Fagerhult [*Sweden ICAO location identifier*] (ICLI)
ESMG .... Ljungby/Feringe [*Sweden ICAO location identifier*] (ICLI)
ESMH .... Hoganas [*Sweden ICAO location identifier*] (ICLI)
ESMI .... Sovdeborg [*Sweden ICAO location identifier*] (ICLI)
ESMJ .... Kagerod [*Sweden ICAO location identifier*] (ICLI)
ESMK .... Kristianstad/Everod [*Sweden ICAO location identifier*] (ICLI)
ESML .... Expendable Supplies and Materials List (MCD)
ESML .... Landskrona/Viarp [*Sweden ICAO location identifier*] (ICLI)
ESMM .... Equivalent Square Miles of Mapping (NOAA)
ESMM .... Malmo [*Sweden ICAO location identifier*] (ICLI)
ESMMC .... Enhanced SMMC [*FAA*] (TAG)
ESMN .... Lund [*Sweden ICAO location identifier*] (ICLI)

ESM/NCTR ... Electronic Support Measure / Non-Cooperative Target Recognition
ESMO .... Earth Station - Morocco
ESMO .... Electronics System Measures Operator (MCD)
ESMO .... European Society for Medical Oncology (EA)
ESMO .... Oskarshamn [*Sweden ICAO location identifier*] (ICLI)
ESMOA .... Electrotypers' and Stereotypers' Managers and Overseers Association [*British*] (BI)
Esmor .... Esmor Correctional Services [*Commercial firm Associated Press*] (SAG)
ESMP .... Anderstorp [*Sweden ICAO location identifier*] (ICLI)
ESMP .... El Salvador Media Projects (EA)
ESMQ .... Kalmar [*Sweden ICAO location identifier*] (ICLI)
ESMR .... Electrically Scanned Microwave Radiometer [*NASA*]
ESMR .... Electronic Scanning Microwave Radiometer [*Marine science*] (OSRA)
ESMR .... Esmor Correctional Services [*NASDAQ symbol*] (SAG)
ESMR .... Esmor Correctional Svcs [*NASDAQ symbol*] (TTSB)
ESMR .... Trelleborg [*Sweden ICAO location identifier*] (ICLI)
ESMRI .... Engraved Stationery Manufacturers Research Institute (EA)
ESMRW .... Esmor Correct'l Svcs Wrrt [*NASDAQ symbol*] (TTSB)
ES-MS .... Electrospray Ionization Mass Spectrometry
ESMS .... Environment and Special Measurement System (MCD)
ESMS .... Malmo/Sturup [*Sweden ICAO location identifier*] (ICLI)
ESMST .... European Society of Membrane Science and Technology (EA)
ESMT .... Electronic Shop Minor Telephone and Teletype [*Coast Guard*]
ESMT .... Halmstad [*Sweden ICAO location identifier*] (ICLI)
ESMU .... Electronic Systems Mockup (KSC)
ESMV .... Hagshult [*Sweden ICAO location identifier*] (ICLI)
ESMWT .... Engineering, Science, and Management War Training
ESMWTP ..... Engineering, Science, and Management War Training Program (HGAA)
ESMX .... Vaxjo/Kronoberg [*Sweden ICAO location identifier*] (ICLI)
ESMY .... Smalandsstenar [*Sweden ICAO location identifier*] (ICLI)
ESMZ .... Olanda [*Sweden ICAO location identifier*] (ICLI)
ESN .... Earth-Sun Coordinate System
ESN .... Easton [*Maryland*] [*Airport symbol*] (AD)
ESN .... Easton, MD [*Location identifier FAA*] (FAAL)
ESN .... Educationally Subnormal
ESN .... Effective Segment Number (IAA)
ESN .... Elastic Stop Nut [*Hardware*]
ESN .... Electronic Security Number [*Cellular telephones*] (WDMC)
ESN .... Electronic Serial Number
ESN .... Encyclopaedia Sefardica Neerlandica [*A publication*] (BJA)
ESN .... Engineering Shipping Notice (AAG)
ESN .... Engineers Society of Norway
ESN .... English-Speaking Nations [*of NATO*]
ESN .... Equipment Serial Number (ACRL)
ESN .... Error Sequence Number [*Computer science*]
ESN .... Essence Biotech [*Vancouver Stock Exchange symbol*]
ESN .... Essential (AABC)
ESN .... Estrogen-Stimulated Neurophysin [*Endocrinology*]
ESN .... European Scientific Notes [*Office of Naval Research, London*] (PDAA)
ESN .... European Society for Neurochemistry (EA)
ESN .... European Society of Nematologists (EAIO)
ESN .... European Society of Neuroradiology (EA)
ESN .... Executive Suite Network [*An association*] (EA)
ESN .... External Segment Name (MHDB)
ESNA .... Economic Security Employees' National Association [*Canada*]
ESNA .... Elastic Stop Nut Corp. of America
ESNA .... Electrical Survey-Net Adjuster
ESNA .... Hallviken [*Sweden ICAO location identifier*] (ICLI)
ESNB .... Solleftea [*Sweden ICAO location identifier*] (ICLI)
ESNC .... Educational Statistics, National Center (OICC)
ESNC .... Hede/Hedlanda [*Sweden ICAO location identifier*] (ICLI)
ESNCD .... European Society for Noninvasive Cardiovascular Dynamics (EA)
ESND .... Sveg [*Sweden ICAO location identifier*] (ICLI)
ESNET .... Energy Sciences Network [*DOE-funded network*] (AAGC)
ESnet .... Energy Sciences Network [*Department of Energy*]
ESNETT .... Engineering and Science Network on Thinking (EA)
ESNF .... Farila [*Sweden ICAO location identifier*] (ICLI)
ESNG .... Gallivare [*Sweden ICAO location identifier*] (ICLI)
ESNH .... Hudiksvall [*Sweden ICAO location identifier*] (ICLI)
ESNI .... Kubbe [*Sweden ICAO location identifier*] (ICLI)
ESNICVD ..... European Society for Noninvasive Cardiovascular Dynamics (EAIO)
ESNJ .... Jokkmokk [*Sweden ICAO location identifier*] (ICLI)
ESNK .... Kramfors [*Sweden ICAO location identifier*] (ICLI)
ESNL .... Lycksele [*Sweden ICAO location identifier*] (ICLI)
ESN(M) .... Educationally Subnormal-Moderate [*Medicine*] (DMAA)
ESNM .... Optand [*Sweden ICAO location identifier*] (ICLI)
ESNN .... Sundsvall-Harnosand [*Sweden ICAO location identifier*] (ICLI)
ESNO .... Ornskoldsvik [*Sweden ICAO location identifier*] (ICLI)
ESNP .... Pitea [*Sweden ICAO location identifier*] (ICLI)
ESNQ .... Kiruna [*Sweden ICAO location identifier*] (ICLI)
ESNR .... Orsa [*Sweden ICAO location identifier*] (ICLI)
ESNS .... Skelleftea [*Sweden ICAO location identifier*] (ICLI)
ESNSW .... Entomological Society of New South Wales (EERA)
ESNT .... Sattna [*Sweden ICAO location identifier*] (ICLI)
ESNTL .... Essential
ESNU .... Umea [*Sweden ICAO location identifier*] (ICLI)
ESNV .... Vilhelmina [*Sweden ICAO location identifier*] (ICLI)
ESO .... Avitat [*British ICAO designator*] (FAAC)
ESO .... Echo Suppressor, Originating End [*Telecommunications*] (TEL)
ESO .... Economic Stabilization Office (OICC)
ESO .... Educational Services Office [*or Officer*] [*Navy*]
ESO .... Education Services Officer (AAGC)

ESO............	Electrical Spinal Orthosis
ESO............	Electronics Supply Office [or Officer]
ESO............	Electronic Standards Office [Navy]
ESO............	Embarkation Staff Officer [Military British]
ESO............	Emergency Security Operations (AFM)
ESO............	Emergency Support Organization (NRCH)
ESO............	Engineering Service Order (AAG)
ESO............	Engineering Sign-Off
ESO............	Engineering Stop Order (AAG)
ESO............	Entomological Society of Queensland (EERA)
ESO............	Epoxidized Soybean Oil [Organic chemistry]
eso............	Esophagoscopy [Medicine] (DAVI)
ESO............	Esophagus [Anatomy] (DAVI)
Eso............	Esoteric [Record label]
ESO............	European Southern Observatory [ICSU] [Research center Germany] (IRC)
ESO............	Event Sequence Override
ESOA..........	Epiphyllum Society of America
ESOA..........	European Society of Osteoarthrology [Former Czechoslovakia] (SLS)
ESOAA........	Eight Sheet Outdoor Advertising Association [Independence, MO] (EA)
ESOB..........	Eastern Soccer Officials Bureau [Later, ECSA] (EA)
ESOC..........	Emergency Supply Operations Center [Defense Supply Agency] (MCD)
ESOC..........	Environmentally Safe Oil Change [Automobile service]
ESOC..........	European Space Operations Center
ESOD..........	Erythrocyte Superoxide Dismutase [An enzyme]
ESOE..........	Orebro [Sweden ICAO location identifier] (ICLI)
ESOFC........	Erika Slezak Official Fan Club (EA)
ESO-FHWA...	Emergency Standby Order - Federal Highway Administration [Federal disaster planning]
ESOH..........	Hagfors [Sweden ICAO location identifier] (ICLI)
ESOL..........	Employee Solutions [NASDAQ symbol] (TTSB)
ESOL..........	Employee Solutions, Inc. [NASDAQ symbol] (SAG)
ESOL..........	English to Speakers of Other Languages [Program]
ESOMAR......	European Society for Opinion and Market Research [Netherlands]
ESON..........	Endosonics Corp. [NASDAQ symbol] (SAG)
ESONE........	European Standards on Nuclear Electronics Committee [Switzerland]
ESOP..........	Employee Stock Option [or Ownership] Plan [Tax plan]
ESOP..........	Employee Stock Ownership Plan (AAGC)
ESOP..........	Engineering Student Officer Program [Air Force]
ESOPH........	Esophagus [Anatomy]
ESOPRS......	European Society of Ophthalmic Plastic and Reconstructive Surgery (EAIO)
ESOPS........	Employment Service Online Placement System [Computer science]
ESOR..........	Electronically-Scanned Optical Receiver (PDAA)
ESOR..........	Emergency Standoff Range (NVT)
ESOR..........	Rescue Coordination Center [Sweden ICAO location identifier] (ICLI)
ESOS..........	Stockholm [Sweden ICAO location identifier] (ICLI)
ESOT..........	Employee Stock Ownership Trust
ESOT..........	Esoteric [or Esoterica] (WDAA)
ESOW..........	Engineering Statement of Work (NASA)
ESOW..........	Vasteras/Hasslo [Sweden ICAO location identifier] (ICLI)
ESP............	Early Support Program (HGAA)
ESP............	Early Systolic Paradox [Cardiology] (DAVI)
ESP............	Earth-Surface Potential
ESP............	Eastern Special Passenger [Eastern Airlines]
ESP............	East Stroudsburg, PA [Location identifier FAA] (FAAL)
ESP............	Echeloned Series Processor (PDAA)
ESP............	Economic Stabilization Program [Internal Revenue Service]
ESP............	Economic Sufficiency Plan (OICC)
ESP............	Economic Support Funds (GNE)
ESP............	Economy Systems Plate
ESP............	Edge-Supported Pulling [Photovoltaic energy systems]
ESP............	Educational Software Products [Commercial firm] (PCM)
ESP............	Educational Support Personnel
ESP............	Effective Sensory Projection [Neurology] (DAVI)
ESP............	Effective Systolic Pressure [Cardiology] (DAVI)
ESP............	Electrical Systems Panel [Apollo Spacecraft Program Office] [NASA]
ESP............	Electronic Security Profile [of Equitable Life Assurance Society]
ESP............	Electronic Seismic Photography
ESP............	Electronic Server Pad [Restaurant computer device manufactured by Remanco Systems, Inc.]
ESP............	Electronic Smart Power [Automotive engineering]
ESP............	Electronic Specification Package (BTTJ)
ESP............	Electronic Stability Program [Automotive]
ESP............	Electronic Stability Program [Automotive]
ESP............	Electronic Standard Procedure (MCD)
ESP............	Electronic Still Photography (CDE)
ESP............	Electronic Supervisory Panel (MCD)
ESP............	Electronic Systems Planning (RDA)
ESP............	Electron Spin Polarization
ESP............	Electron Stream Potential (MSA)
ESP............	Electroselective Pattern Metering [Olympus cameras]
ESP............	Electrosensitive Paper (MHDB)
ESP............	Electrosensitive Programming
ESP............	Electro Sensor Panel [Toyota]
ESP............	Electroshock Protection (MCD)
ESP............	Electrosonic Profiler
ESP............	Electrostatic Precipitator [Also, EP]
ESP............	Electrostatic Probe (IAA)
ESP............	Elevated Stabilized Platform [Aircraft]
ESP............	Elimination of Solvation Procedure [Chemistry]
ESP............	Elsevier Science Publishers
ESP............	[The] Emanu El Single Person (BJA)
ESP............	Employee Savings Program
ESP............	Employee Stock Purchase [Software]
ESP............	Employer School Program (OICC)
ESP............	Employment Service Potential [Department of Labor]
ESP............	Emulation Sensing Processor [Quality Micro Systems]
ESP............	Emulex SCSI [Small Computer System Interface] Processor (CDE)
ESP............	Encapsulating Security Payload [Computer science]
ESP............	Endangered Species Program [Australia]
ESP............	End of Segment Pulse [Military]
ESP............	End Systolic Pressure [Cardiology]
ESP............	Energetic Storm Particle
ESP............	Energy Services Planning
ESP............	Engineering Schedule Plan
ESP............	Engineering Service Project (MCD)
ESP............	Engineering Service Publications (AAG)
ESP............	Engineering Signal Processor
ESP............	Engineering Software Package
ESP............	Engine Sequence Panel (AAG)
ESP............	Engine Service Platform (KSC)
ESP............	Engine Start Panel
ESP............	English for Scientific Purposes [Education] [British]
ESP............	English for Specific Purposes [Education] (PDAA)
ESP............	Enhanced Serial Port (PCM)
ESP............	Enhanced Serial Processor [Communication protocol] [Computer science] (PCM)
ESP............	Enhanced Service Provider [Online database service]
ESP............	En Route Spacing Program [FAA] (TAG)
ESP............	Environmental Sketches in Perspective [Computer program]
ESP............	Eosinophil Stimulation Promoter [Medicine] (MAE)
ESP............	Epidermal Soluble Protein [Biochemistry] (DAVI)
ESP............	Equipment Status Panel (AAG)
ESP............	Equipment Support Plan (MCD)
ESP............	Espeair [Chechoslovakia] [FAA designator] (FAAC)
ESP............	Especially
esp............	Especially (VRA)
esp............	Especially (WDMC)
esp............	Esperanto [MARC language code Library of Congress] (LCCP)
ESP............	Espey Manufacturing & Electronics, Inc. [AMEX symbol] (SPSG)
ESP............	Espey Mfg & Electr [AMEX symbol] (TTSB)
Esp............	Espinasse's English Nisi Prius Reports [1793-1810] [A publication] (DLA)
ESP............	Espionage [FBI standardized term]
ESP............	Espressivo [With Expression] [Music]
ESP............	E-Tech Speedy Protocol (CDE)
ESP............	Ethnic Schools Program [Australia]
ESP............	European Society of Pathology (EAIO)
ESP............	European Specialist Publishers Dictionary [A publication]
ESP............	Evoked Synaptic Potential [Neurophysiology]
ESP............	Exchangeable-Sodium-Percentage
ESP............	Exchange Sale Property
ESP............	Exchange Stock Portfolio [Investment term] (MHDW)
ESP............	Expandable Stored Program
ESP............	Expanded Spread Profile [Seismology]
ESP............	Experiment Sensing Platform (NASA)
ESP............	Extended Self-Contained PROLOG [Programming language]
ESP............	Extended Service Plan [Ford Motor Co.]
ESP............	Extended Storage Platelet Pack [Hematology]
ESP............	Extended Streamflow Prediction (NOAA)
ESP............	Externally Supported Processor [Mainframe computer] (NITA)
ESP............	External Standard Pulse [Instrumentation]
ESP............	Extracellular Signaling Protein [Biochemistry]
ESP............	Extrasensory Perception
ESP............	Extravehicular Support Pack [or Package] [NASA]
ESP............	Spain [ANSI three-letter standard code] (CNC)
ESP-1.........	Elizabeth S. Priori-1 [Virus named after one of the scientists who isolated it]
ESPA..........	Electronically Steerable Phased Array [SPADATS] (MCD)
ESPA..........	Elvis Special Photo Association (EA)
ESPA..........	Evening Student Personnel Association [Later, Evening Student Association] (EA)
ESPA..........	Exhaust Systems Professional Association [Defunct] (EA)
ESPA..........	Lulea/Kallax [Sweden ICAO location identifier] (ICLI)
ESP Act......	Endangered Species Protection Act 1992 [Commonwealth] (EERA)
Esp Act......	Espinasse. Actions on Statutes [A publication] (ILCA)
ESPAR........	Electronically Steerable Phased Array RADAR [SPADATS]
ESPAWS......	Enhanced Self-Propelled Artillery Weapon System
ESPAWSS....	Enhanced Self-Propelled Artillery Weapon System Study (MCD)
Esp Bank....	Espinasse's Law of Bankrupts [1825] [A publication] (DLA)
ESPC..........	Emergency Status Precedence Code [DoD]
ESPC..........	Expendable Stored Project Contract (DNAB)
ESPC..........	Ostersund/Froson [Sweden ICAO location identifier] (ICLI)
ESPD..........	Export Services and Promotions Division [British Overseas Trade Board] (DS)
ESPD..........	Gunnarn [Sweden ICAO location identifier] (ICLI)
Esp Dig......	Espinasse's Digest of the Law of Actions at Nisi Prius [1812] [A publication] (ILCA)
ESPE..........	European Society for Pediatric Endocrinology (EAIO)
ESPE..........	United Socialist Alliance of Greece (PPW)
ESPE..........	Vidsel [Sweden ICAO location identifier] (ICLI)
ESPEC........	Electrical Specification
E-Spec........	Equipment Specification [Nuclear energy] (NRCH)
E SPEC.......	Equipment Specification (AAGC)
ESPEC........	Especially
ESPEC........	Ethernet Specification [Computer science] (BTTJ)
E SPEC.......	Material Specification (AAGC)

ESPEN .... Estimated Tax Penalty [*IRS*]
ESPES .... Especialidades Farmaceuticas Espanolas Data Bank [*Spanish Pharmaceutical Specialities Data Bank*] [*Spanish Drug Information Center*] [*Information service or system*] (IID)
Esp Ev .... Espinasse on Penal Evidence [*A publication*] (DLA)
Espey .... Espey Manufacturing & Electronics, Inc. [*Associated Press*] (SAG)
ESPG .... Boden [*Sweden ICAO location identifier*] (ICLI)
ESPG .... Espionage (AABC)
ESP/GC & EE... Equipment Spare Package/Ground Communications and Electronic Equipment
ESPHI .... European Society for Paediatric Haematology and Immunology (EAIO)
ESPI .... Education Service of the Plastics Industry (AIE)
ESPI .... Electronic Speckle-Pattern Interferometer (OA)
ESPI .... Electron Speckle Pattern Interferometry
ESPI .... Engineering Standard Practice Instruction (MCD)
ESPI .... Etched Sensitized Projected Image [*Circuit board manufacture*]
EspirSan .... Espirito Santo Financial Holding [*Associated Press*] (SAG)
ESPJ .... Heden [*Sweden ICAO location identifier*] (ICLI)
ESPL .... Electronic Switching Programming Language
Espl .... Esplanade (DD)
ESPL .... Extensible Structure Processing Language [*1969-71*] [*Computer science*] (CSR)
ESPLAF .... European Strategic Planning Federation [*British*] (EAIO)
ESPM .... Energy Supply Planning Model [*National Science Foundation*]
ESPN .... Entertainment and Sports Programming Network [*Television*]
ESPN .... European Society for Pediatric Nephrology [*Switzerland*] (SLS)
Esp NP .... Espinasse's English Nisi Prius Reports [*1793-1810*] [*A publication*] (DLA)
ESPOD .... Electronic System Precision Orbit Determination [*Air Force*] (MCD)
ESPOL .... Executive System Problem-Oriented Language [*Burroughs Corp.*] [*Computer science*] (BUR)
ESPP .... Employee Stock Purchase Plan (AAGC)
ESPP .... Regional Military Command Subcenter North [*Sweden ICAO location identifier*] (ICLI)
Esp Pen Ev ... Espinasse on Penal Evidence [*A publication*] (DLA)
ESPPI .... Expanding and Specialty Paper Products Institute [*Defunct*] (EA)
Esp P St ...... Espinasse on Penal Statutes [*A publication*] (DLA)
ESPQ .... Early School Personality Questionnaire [*Psychology*]
Espr .... Espressivo [*With Expression*] [*Music*]
ESPR .... European Society of Paediatric Radiology (EA)
ESPRA .... Empire State Paper Research Associates
ESPRAF .... ESP [*Extrasensory Perception*] Research Associates Foundation [*Defunct*] (EA)
Espres .... Espressivo [*With Expression*] [*Music*]
ESPRESS ..... Espressivo [*With Expression*] [*Music*]
ESPRI .... Empire State Paper Research Institute [*College of Environmental Science and Forestry at Syracuse*] [*Research center*] (RCD)
ESPRI .... Empire State Paper Research Institute
ESPRIT .... Electronic Still Photography at Rochester Institute of Technology [*A publication*]
ESPRIT .... European Strategic Program for Research and Development in Information Technology and Telecommunications [*Research center Belgium*] (IRC)
ESPRIT .... Eye-Slaved Projected Rafter Inset [*Simulator*]
ESPRP .... Energy Systems and Policy Research Program [*University of Wisconsin - Madison*] [*Research center*] (RCD)
EsprSan .... Espirito Santo Financial Holding [*Associated Press*] (SAG)
ESPS .... European Stroke Prevention Study
ESPS .... Experiment Segment and Pallet Simulator [*NASA*] (NASA)
EspSan .... Espirito Santo Overseas Ltd. [*Associated Press*] (SAG)
ESPT .... Executive Sequence Parameter Table (SAA)
ESPWO .... Exigencies of the Service Having Been Such as to Preclude the Issuance of Competent Written Orders in Advance
ESQ .... Enlisted Separation Questionnaire [*Military*] (DNAB)
ESQ .... Environmental Symptoms Questionnaire (PDAA)
Esq .... Esquire [*Record label*] [*British*]
ESQ .... Esquire
ESQ .... Esquire
ESQ .... Extra-Special Quality [*Steel cable*] [*Ship's equipment*] (DS)
EsqCm .... Esquire Communications [*Commercial firm Associated Press*] (SAG)
EsqCom ...... Esquire Communications [*Commercial firm Associated Press*] (SAG)
ESQD .... Explosives Safety Quality Distance (DNAB)
Esq Ins .... Esquirol on Insanity [*A publication*] (DLA)
ESQL/C .... Embedded Structured Query Language and Tools for C Language [*Computer science*] (HGAA)
ESQO .... Arboga [*Sweden ICAO location identifier*] (ICLI)
ESQP .... Berga [*Sweden ICAO location identifier*] (ICLI)
ESQR .... Esquire
ESQRE .... Esquire [*Gentleman*] (ROG)
ESQS .... Esquire Communications [*NASDAQ symbol*] (SAG)
ESQST .... Ego Strength Q-Sort Test [*Psychology*]
ESQSW .... Esquire Communications Wrrt [*NASDAQ symbol*] (TTSB)
ESQT .... Extended Sterilization Qualification Test
ESQV .... Visby [*Sweden ICAO location identifier*] (ICLI)
ESR .... Early Site Review [*Nuclear energy*] (NRCH)
ESR .... Early Storage Reserve
ESR .... Earth Science Research (SSD)
ESR .... East Surrey Regiment [*Military unit*] [*British*]
ESR .... Economic Subregion [*Bureau of the Census*]
ESR .... Edge-Stabilized Ribbon [*Photovoltaic energy systems*]
ESR .... Editorial Status Report
ESR .... Educators for Social Responsibility (EA)
ESR .... Effective Search Radius (MCD)
ESR .... Effective Series Resistance [*Electronics*] (IAA)

ESR .... Effective Shunt Resistance [*Electronics*] (IAA)
ESR .... Effective Signal Radiated
ESR .... Effective SONAR Range [*Navy*] (NVT)
ESR .... Effective Sunrise
ESR .... Egyptian State Railway (ROG)
ESR .... Einstein Stoke Radius [*Medicine*] (DMAA)
ESR .... EISCAT [*European Incoherent Scatter Scientific Association*] Svalbard Radar
ESR .... Electric Skin Resistance [*Neurology*] (DAVI)
ESR .... Electric Sliding Roof [*Automotive accessory*]
ESR .... Electronic Scanning RADAR
ESR .... Electronic Send/Receive
ESR .... Electronic Slide Rule (WDAA)
ESR .... Electronic Surface Recorder (PDAA)
ESR .... Electronic Systems Reliability (MCD)
ESR .... Electron Spin Resonance [*Also, EPR*] [*Physics*]
ESR .... Electroslag Remelting [*Steel alloy*]
ESR .... Electro-Slag Remelting
ESR .... El Salvador [*Chile*] [*Airport symbol*] (OAG)
ESR .... Employment Service Representative
ESR .... Employment Status Recode [*Bureau of the Census*] (GFGA)
ESR .... Engineering Service Requests (MUGU)
ESR .... Engineering Summary Report
ESR .... Engineering Support Request (NASA)
ESR .... Environmental Science Research [*Concept car*] [*Automotive engineering*]
ESR .... Environmental System Resources [*National Science Foundation*] (MCD)
ESR .... Equipment Status Report [*Air Force*]
ESR .... Equipment Supervisory Rack [*Telecommunications*] (TEL)
ESR .... Equivalent Series Resistance
ESR .... Equivalent Service Rounds [*A standard for indicating gun erosion*]
ESR .... Erythrocyte Sedimentation Rate [*Hematology*]
ESR .... Escape Road [*Hawaii*] [*Seismograph station code, US Geological Survey*] (SEIS)
ESR .... Essex Scottish Regiment of Canada [*Military unit*]
ESR .... European Security Region [*Military*]
ESR .... Event Storage Record (SAA)
ESR .... Excelsior Airlines Ltd. [*Ghana*] [*ICAO designator*] (FAAC)
ESR .... Executive Service Requests (MCD)
ESR .... Executive Summary Requirements (MCD)
ESR .... Expedite Shipping Request (MCD)
ESR .... Experimental Superheat Reactor
ESR .... External Standard Ratio
ESR .... Extrahepatic Shunt Ratio [*Medicine*]
ESRA .... Eastern Ski Representatives Association (EA)
ESRA .... Emergency Ship Repair Act of 1954
ESRA .... Employment Services Regulatory Authority [*Australia*]
ESRA .... European Society of Regional Anaesthesia (EA)
ESRANGE..... European Space Range [*Sweden*] (MCD)
ESRB .... Entertainment Software Rating Board
ESRB .... European Society for Radiation Biology [*Formerly, Association of Radiobiologists from EURATOM Countries*] (EA)
ESRC .... Economic and Social Research Council [*British*]
ESRC .... Economic and Social Research Council [*British*]
ESRC .... European Science Research Council (NUCP)
ESRD .... End Stage Renal Disease [*Medicine*]
ESRD .... Equipment Shipment Ready Date [*Army*] (AABC)
ESRF .... Easter Seal Research Foundation of the National Easter Seal Society (EA)
ESRF .... Electrical Systems Repair Facilities (MCD)
ESRF .... End Stage Renal Failure [*Medicine*]
ESRF .... European Squash Rackets Federation (EA)
ESRF .... European Synchrotron Radiation Facility [*High-energy physics*] (ECON)
ESRF .... European Synchrotron Radiation Facility
ESRI .... Earth Sciences and Resources Institute [*University of South Carolina at Columbia*] [*Research center*] (RCD)
ESRI .... Economic and Social Research Institute (ACII)
ESRI .... Engineering and Statistical Research Institute [*Canada*] (ARC)
ESRI .... Environmental Systems Research Institute
ESRI .... Environmental Systems Research Institute Pty Ltd [*Commercial*] (EERA)
ESRIN .... European Space Research Institute
ESRL .... Earth-to-Space Railgun Launcher (MCD)
ESRL .... Eastern Shore Regional Library Resource Center [*Library network*]
ESRL .... Environmental Sciences Research Laboratory [*Environmental Protection Agency*] (GRD)
ESRL/RTP .... Environmental Sciences Research Laboratory/Research Triangle Park [*Environmental Protection Agency*]
ESRM .... Electroslag Remelting (PDAA)
ESRO .... Engineering Stop and Release Order [*Aerospace*]
ESRO .... European Space Research Organization [*Superseded by ESA*]
ESRP .... Emergency Substitute in a Regular Position [*Education*]
ESRP .... Environmental Standard Review Plan (NRCH)
ESRP .... Evreiskaia Sotsialisticheskaia Rabochaia Partiia (BJA)
ESRR .... Early Site Review Report [*Nuclear energy*] (NRCH)
ESRS .... Early Sites Research Society (EA)
ESRS .... Electronic Scanning RADAR System (MCD)
ESRS .... European Society for Rural Sociology
ESRS .... European Synchroton Radiation Source (PDAA)
ESRS .... European Synchrotron Radiation Source [*High-energy physics*]
ESRT .... Electroslag Refining Technology [*Chemical engineering*] (IAA)
ESRU .... Electrical Stimulating and Recording Unit
ESRU .... English Schools' Rugby Union (BI)

ESRU .... Environmental Sciences Research Unit [*Cranfield Institute of Technology*]
ESRX .... Express Scripts 'A' [*NASDAQ symbol*] (TTSB)
ESRX .... Express Scripts, Inc. [*NASDAQ symbol*] (SAG)
ESS .... Earle's Salt Solution (OA)
ESS .... Earth-Sighting Simulator [*NASA*]
ESS .... Earth Station - Sudan
ESS .... Eastern Sociological Society (AEBS)
ESS .... Echo Suppression Subsystem [*Telecommunications*] (TEL)
ESS .... Ecologically Sustainable Society (EERA)
ESS .... Educational Services Section [*Navy*]
ESS .... Educational Subscription Service, Inc.
ESS .... Education Support Staff (AIE)
ESS .... Effective Sunset
ESS .... Electrical Standards Set
ESS .... Electrical Supervisory Subassembly (IAA)
ESS .... Electronic Intelligence Support System (MCD)
ESS .... Electronic Scanning Spectrometer
ESS .... Electronic Science Section (IAA)
ESS .... Electronic Security Squadron [*Military*]
ESS .... Electronic Security Strategic [*Military*]
ESS .... Electronic Security Surveillance
ESS .... Electronic Security System
ESS .... Electronic Sequence Switching
ESS .... Electronic Speech Synthesis (IAA)
ESS .... Electronic Speed Switch
ESS .... Electronic Spreadsheet (CDE)
ESS .... Electronics Systems Source (MCD)
ESS .... Electronic Still Store [*Television*] (WDMC)
ESS .... Electronic Surveillance System
ESS .... Electronic Switching System [*See also EAX*] [*Telecommunications*]
ESS .... Electronic Synchro-Shift
ESS .... Electronic Systems Sector (AAGC)
ESS .... Electron Spin Spectra [*Physics*] (IAA)
ESS .... Electropneumatic Service System [*Truck engineering*]
ESS .... Elementary Science Study [*National Science Foundation*]
ESS .... ELINT [*Electronic Intelligence*] Support System (DWSG)
ESS .... Emergency Ship Service [*Navy*] (MSA)
ESS .... Emergency Short Stay [*in hospital*] [*British*]
ESS .... Emergency Social Services [*Civil Defense*]
ESS .... Emergency Survival System
ESS .... Emplaced Scientific Station [*Aerospace*]
ESS .... Employment Security System [*Department of Labor*]
ESS .... Empty Sella Syndrome [*Medicine*]
ESS .... Encyclopedia of the Social Sciences [*A publication*]
ESS .... Endoatmospheric Summer Study
ESS .... Energy Storage System
ESS .... Engagement Sensor Set
ESS .... Engineered Safety System (IEEE)
ESS .... Engineering Source Selection
ESS .... Engineering Standard Specification (MCD)
ESS .... Engineer Specialized Services
ESS .... Engine Speed Synchronizer
ESS .... Engine Start Signal
ESS .... Enterprise Support Service
ESS .... Entry Survival System
ESS .... Environmental Stress Screening (MCD)
ESS .... Environmental Stress Sensing [*Automotive engineering*]
ESS .... Environmental Support System (MCD)
ESS .... Equipment Section Shell
ESS .... Equivalent State Subset (IAA)
ESS .... Erection Subsystem
ESS .... Erythrocyte-Sensitizing Substance [*Hematology*]
ESS .... Essence
ESS .... Essential
ESS .... Essex [*County in England*]
ESS .... Essex Property Trust [*NYSE symbol*] (TTSB)
ESS .... Essex Property Trust, Inc. [*NYSE symbol*] (SAG)
ESS .... Esstra Industries Corp. [*Vancouver Stock Exchange symbol*]
ESS .... Estimating System Survey (AAGC)
ESS .... European Silicon Structures (NITA)
ESS .... European Spallation Source [*High-energy physics*] (ECON)
ESS .... European Special Situations Fund [*EEC*]
ESS .... Euthyroid Sick Syndrome [*Medicine*] (DMAA)
ESS .... Evaluation SAGE [*Semiautomatic Ground Environment*] Sector (IAA)
ESS .... Evaporation/Solidification System [*Nuclear energy*] (NRCH)
ESS .... Event Scheduling System
ESS .... Evolutionarily Stable Strategy
ESS .... Evolutionary Stable Strategy
ESS .... Excited Skin Syndrome [*Dermatology*]
ESS .... Executive's Shopping Service
ESS .... Executive Suites and Services [*Business term*]
ESS .... Executive Support System
ESS .... Expendable Second Stage [*Space shuttle*] [*NASA*]
ESS .... Expendable Sound Source
ESS .... Experimental SAGE [*Semi-Automatic Ground Environment*] Sector
ESS .... Experiment Subsystem Simulator [*NASA*] (NASA)
ESS .... Experiment Support System (MCD)
ESS .... Expert Statistical System
ESS .... Explained Sum of Squares [*Data Analysis*]
ESS .... Explosive Safety Survey (NVT)
ESS .... Middleton Island, AK [*Location identifier FAA*] (FAAL)
ESS .... Northern Essex Community College, Haverhill, MA [*OCLC symbol*] (OCLC)

ESS .... TAES [*Tecnicas Aereas de Estudios y Servicios SA*] [*Spain ICAO designator*] (FAAC)
ESSA .... Earth Station - South Africa
ESSA .... Economists', Sociologists', and Statisticians' Association
ESSA .... Electronic Scanning and Stabilizing Antenna
ESSA .... Elliotdale Sheepbreeders' Society of Australia
ESSA .... Embassy Social Secretaries Association (EA)
ESSA .... Emergency Safeguards System Activation (IEEE)
ESSA .... Endangered Species Scientific Authority [*US Fish and Wildlife Service*] [*Terminated 1979, functions transferred to Department of the Interior*]
ESSA .... English Schools' Swimming Association (BI)
ESSA .... Enterprise Support Services for Africa [*Funded by CIDA - Canadian International Development Agency*]
ESSA .... Environmental and Social Systems Analysts Ltd.
ESSA .... Environmental Science Services Administration [*Later, National Oceanic and Atmospheric Administration*]
ESSA .... Environmental Survey Satellite (TEL)
ESSA .... European Single Service Association (EA)
ESSA .... Stockholm/Arlanda [*Sweden ICAO location identifier*] (ICLI)
ESS ADF ..... Electronic Switching System Arranged with Data Features
Ess Ang Sax Law... Essays on Anglo-Saxon Law [*A publication*] (DLA)
ESSAR .... Early Site Safety Analysis Report [*Nuclear energy*] (NRCH)
ESSAR .... EBASCO Standard Safety Analysis Report [*Nuclear energy*] (NRCH)
Essays CW... Essays on Canadian Writing [*A publication*] (BRI)
ESSB .... Electronic Supply Support Base [*Air Force*]
ESSB .... Stockholm/Bromma [*Sweden ICAO location identifier*] (ICLI)
ESSBR .... Electronically Scanned Stacked Beam RADAR [*Program*]
ESSC .... Earth Station - Scandinavia
ESSC .... Earth System Science Committee [*US governmental interagency group*]
ESSC .... Earth Systems Science Committee (EERA)
ESSC .... End Sweep Support Carrier [*Navy*] (DNAB)
ESSC .... Eskilstuna/Ekeby [*Sweden ICAO location identifier*] (ICLI)
ESSC .... European Space Science Committee
ESSC .... European Sport Shooting Confederation (EAIO)
ESSCIRC ..... European Solid-State-Circuits Conference (PDAA)
ESSCO .... Employee Support Services Company [*Military*]
ESSD .... Borlange [*Sweden ICAO location identifier*] (ICLI)
ESSD .... Environmentally Sound and Sustainable Development (EERA)
ESSD .... Environment Supply Sensing Device (MCD)
ESSDERC ..... European Solid State Device Research Conference (PDAA)
ESSE .... Earth Station - Senegal
ESSE .... EBASCO Services, Inc. Site Support Engineering [*Nuclear energy*] (NRCH)
ESSE .... Stockholm/Ska-Edeby [*Sweden ICAO location identifier*] (ICLI)
ESSEF .... ESSEF Corp. [*Associated Press*] (SAG)
ESSEN .... Essential
ESSERGY .... Essential Energy (MCD)
ESSEX .... Effects of Subsurface Explosions [*Project*] [*Army and DNA*] (RDA)
Essex .... Essex Corp. [*Associated Press*] (SAG)
ESSEX .... Experimental Solid-State Exchange [*Communication system*] (MCD)
ESSF .... ESSEF Corp. [*NASDAQ symbol*] (NQ)
ESSF .... Hultsfred [*Sweden ICAO location identifier*] (ICLI)
ESSFL .... Electron Steady-State Fermi Level
ESSFLO .... Electronic Switching System Flow Chart
ESSFNR .... Exercise Simulation System for Flexible Nuclear Response (MCD)
ESSFTA .... English Springer Spaniel Field Trial Association (EA)
ESSG .... Engineer Strategic Studies Group [*Army*] (AABC)
ESSG .... Ludvika [*Sweden ICAO location identifier*] (ICLI)
ESSH .... Laxa [*Sweden ICAO location identifier*] (ICLI)
ESSI .... Eco Soil Systems, Inc. [*NASDAQ symbol*] (SAG)
ESSI .... Employment Security Systems Institute
ESSI .... Visingso [*Sweden ICAO location identifier*] (ICLI)
ESSK .... Gavle-Sandviken [*Sweden ICAO location identifier*] (ICLI)
ESSL .... Eastern Secondary Standards Laboratory
ESSL .... Linkoping/SAAB [*Sweden ICAO location identifier*] (ICLI)
ESSLR .... Eye-Safe Simulated LASER Range Finder (MCD)
ESSM .... Brattforsheden [*Sweden ICAO location identifier*] (ICLI)
ESSM .... Electronic Shop, Shelter-Mounted [*Army*]
ESSM .... Emergency Ship Salvage Material [*Navy*] (NG)
ESSM .... Evolved Sea Sparrow Missile (DOMA)
ESSM/EWWS... Electronic Warfare Support Measures / Electronic Warfare Warning System [*Army*]
ESSMT .... Engine Start System Maintenance Trainer (DWSG)
ess neg .... Essentially Negative (MAE)
ESSNSS ...... Electronic Supply Segment of the Navy Supply System
ESSNTL .... Essential
ESSO .... Elected Spanish Speaking Officials (EA)
ESSO .... Embarkation Supply and Stores Officer [*Military British*]
ESSO .... Standard Oil [*Trademark in foreign use only; superseded in US, 1973, by Exxon*]
ESSOR .... Essai Orgel [*Orgel test reactor*] [*Italy*]
ESSP .... Earliest Scram Set Point [*Nuclear energy*] (NRCH)
ESSP .... Elementary School Science Project
ESSP .... Elephant Species Survival Plan
ESSP .... Norrkoping/Kungsangen [*Sweden ICAO location identifier*] (ICLI)
ESSPO .... Electronic Supporting Systems Project Office [*Air Force*]
ESSQ .... Karlstad [*Sweden ICAO location identifier*] (ICLI)
ESSR .... Expected Sample Size Ratio [*Statistics*]
ESSRA .... Economic and Social Science Research Association [*British*]
ESSS .... Endangered Species Scientific Subcommittee [*Commonwealth*] (EERA)
ESSS .... External Stores Support System [*or Subsystem*] (MCD)

ESSS .... Stockholm Aeronautical Fixed Telecommunication Network Center [*Sweden ICAO location identifier*] (ICLI)
ESST .... Eastern Equatorial Pacific Sea Surface Temperature [*Oceanography*]
ESST .... Eastern Standard Summer Time [*Australia*]
ESST .... ESS Technology [*NASDAQ symbol*] (TTSB)
ESST .... ESS Technology, Inc. [*NASDAQ symbol*] (SAG)
ESST .... [*The*] European Interuniversity Association on Society, Science, and Technology [*Lausanne, Switzerland*] (ECON)
ESST .... European Master in Society, Science, and Technology [*Swiss Federal Institute of Technology, Lausanne*] (ECON)
ESST .... Torsby/Fryklanda [*Sweden ICAO location identifier*] (ICLI)
ESSTech ...... ESS Technology, Inc. [*Associated Press*] (SAG)
ESSU .... Electronic Selective Switching Unit
ESSU .... Eskilstuna [*Sweden ICAO location identifier*] (ICLI)
ESSV .... Visby [*Sweden ICAO location identifier*] (ICLI)
ESSW .... Vastervik [*Sweden ICAO location identifier*] (ICLI)
ESSWACS ... Electronic Solid-State Wide-Angle Camera System (MCD)
ESSX .... Vasteras/Johannisberg [*Sweden ICAO location identifier*] (ICLI)
EssxBc .... Essex Bancorp, Inc. [*Associated Press*] (SAG)
EssxPT .... Essex Property Trust, Inc. [*Associated Press*] (SAG)
ESSY .... Earth Station - Syria
ESSZ .... Vangso [*Sweden ICAO location identifier*] (ICLI)
EST .... Boundary Estimate Message [*Aviation code*]
EST .... Early Start Time
EST .... Earth Station - Turkey
EST .... Eastern Standard Time
EST .... Eastern Summer Time (IAA)
EST .... Echo Suppressor, Terminating End [*Telecommunications*] (TEL)
EST .... Effective Study Test [*Study skills test*]
EST .... Elastic Surface Transformation (IAA)
EST .... Electrolytic Sewage Treatment (IAA)
EST .... Electronic Security Tactical [*Military*]
EST .... Electronic Sequencer Timer
EST .... Electronic Shop Major Telephone and Teletype [*Coast Guard*]
EST .... Electronic Social Transformation
EST .... Electronic Spark Timing [*Automotive engineering*]
EST .... Electronics Sea Trials (MCD)
EST .... Electroshock Therapy [*Psychology*]
EST .... Electrostatic Storage Tube
EST .... Elmo Snakey Torus (MCD)
EST .... Embedded Sensor Technique
EST .... Empire Social Telegram (IAA)
EST .... Endodermal Sinus Tumor [*Oncology*]
EST .... Endoscopic Sphincterotomy [*Medicine*]
EST .... Energy Saving Trust (AIE)
EST .... Engineering Sub Task (MCD)
EST .... Engineering Support Team (KSC)
EST .... Engineer/Service Test [*Aerospace*] (MCD)
EST .... Enlistment Screening Test [*Military*]
EST .... Enroute Support Team (SAA)
EST .... En Route Support Team [*Military*] (AFIT)
EST .... Entry Systems Technology [*IBM*] (PCM)
EST .... Eparchy of Saint Thomas the Apostle [*Diocesan abbreviation*] (TOCD)
EST .... Epidemiology and Sanitation Technician [*Navy*]
EST .... Equilibrium Surface Thermochemistry
EST .... Equity Silver Mines Ltd. [*Toronto Stock Exchange symbol Vancouver Stock Exchange symbol*]
est .... Erhard Seminars Training
EST .... Essential Subjects Test [*Marine Corps*] (DOMA)
EST .... Established (EY)
est .... Established (VRA)
EST .... Establishment (WDAA)
EST .... Estancia [*New Mexico*] [*Seismograph station code, US Geological Survey*] (SEIS)
EST .... Estate
EST .... Estate
ESTOW .... Esteemed (ADA)
EST .... Esterase [*An enzyme*]
Est .... Esther [*Old Testament book*]
EST .... Estherville, IA [*Location identifier FAA*] (FAAL)
EST .... Estimate [*or Estimation*] (EY)
est .... Estimate (WDMC)
EST .... Estonia
est .... Estonian [*MARC language code Library of Congress*] (LCCP)
Est .... Estrogen [*Biochemistry*] (DAVI)
EST .... Estuary [*Maps and charts*]
EST .... European Society of Toxicology (EAIO)
EST .... Exhaust System Terminal (KSC)
EST .... Expanded Service Testing
EST .... Expressed Sequence Tag [*Genetics*]
EST .... Extended Standard Theory [*Linguistics*]
EST .... Flugfelag Austerlands Ltd. Egilsstadir [*Iceland*] [*ICAO designator*] (FAAC)
EST .... University of New Hampshire, Jackson Estuarine Laboratory, Durham, NH [*OCLC symbol*] (OCLC)
ESTA .... Earth Science Teachers Association [*British*] (DBA)
ESTA .... Electronically-Synchronised Transmission Assembly (PDAA)
ESTA .... Electroshock Therapy Apparatus [*Psychology*]
ESTA .... Energy Systems Trade Association [*British*] (DBA)
ESTA .... Environmentally Sound Technology Assessment (GNE)
ESTA .... Escape System Test Article (MCD)
ESTA .... European Science and Technology Assembly
ESTA .... European Security Transport Association (EA)
ESTAB .... Establish [*or Establishment*] (KSC)

ESTAB .... Establishment
ESTABD ...... Established (ROG)
ESTABLT ...... Establishment (ROG)
Est & Trusts ... Estates and Trusts [*Legal term*] (DLA)
EstANG ...... Eastern American Natural Gas Trust [*Associated Press*] (SAG)
EstANG ...... Estern American Natural Gas Trust [*Associated Press*] (SAG)
ESTAR ...... Electronically-Scanned Thinned Array RADAR (SSD)
ESTAR ...... Electronically-Scanned Thinned Array Radiometer (MCD)
ESTAR ...... Estimated Arrival Date
ESTATES ...... Estates [*Commonly used*] (OPSA)
ESTB .... Establish [*or Establishment*] (AFM)
ESTBD ...... Established
ESTC .... Eighteenth Century Short Title Catalogue [*British Library*] [*Bibliographic database London, England*]
ESTC .... European Space Technology Center [*Netherlands*] (KSC)
ESTCA ...... Empire State Tattoo Club of America (EA)
ESTCA ...... Error-Sensitive Test Case Analysis (MCD)
Estco .... Eastco Industrial Safety [*Associated Press*] (SAG)
ESTCP .... Environmental Security Technology Certification Program [*Army*] (RDA)
ESTD .... Electronic Standard (MSA)
ESTD .... Established (ADA)
ESTD .... Estimated
ESTE .... Engineering Special Test Equipment (AAG)
ESTE .... Estate
ESTEAM ...... Enrichment Science and Technology for Exceptionally Able and Motivated Pupils (AIE)
ESTEC ...... European Space Technology Center [*Netherlands*]
Estee .... Estee's District Court of Hawaii [*A publication*] (DLA)
Estee (Hawaii) ... Estee's District Court of Hawaii [*A publication*] (DLA)
EsteeL .... Estee Lauder Companies, Inc. [*Associated Press*] (SAG)
ESTEEM ...... Empower Self through Education and Eating Management
ESTF .... Electronic System Test Facility (IAA)
ESTF .... Environmental Systems Test Facility (KSC)
EStG .... Einkommensteuergesetz [*Income Tax Law*] [*German*] (DLA)
ESTG .... Estimating (IAA)
Est Gifts & Tr J ... Estates, Gifts, and Trusts Journal [*A publication*] (DLA)
Estgp .... Eastgroup Properties [*Associated Press*] (SAG)
Esth .... Esther [*Old Testament book*]
ESTH .... Esthetic
EsthR .... Esther Rabbah (BJA)
ESTI .... Eclipse Surgical Tech [*NASDAQ symbol*] (TTSB)
ESTI .... Eclipse Surgical Technologies, Inc. [*NASDAQ symbol*] (SAG)
E/S TIEP ..... Engineering/Service Test and Independent Evaluation Program [*Army*] (AABC)
ESTIMD ...... Estimated (ROG)
ESTL .... Electronic Systems Test Laboratory [*NASA*]
ESTL .... European Space Tribology Laboratory
Estm .... Estimated (DLA)
ESTMTN ...... Estimation
ESTMTR ...... Estimator
ESTN .... Eastern
ESTN .... Endstone [*Horology*]
ESTN .... Estimation (IAA)
EstnBc .... Eastern Bancorp, Inc. [*Associated Press*] (SAG)
EstnCo .... Eastern Co. [*Associated Press*] (SAG)
EstnEn .... Eastern Environmental Services [*Associated Press*] (SAG)
ESTO .... Eastco Industrial Safety [*NASDAQ symbol*] (TTSB)
ESTO .... Eastco Industrial Safety Corp. [*NASDAQ symbol*] (NQ)
ESTO .... Engineer/Service Test Office [*Aerospace*]
Esto .... Estonia (VRA)
ESTO .... Estonian World Festival
ESTO .... Europaeische Studentenvereinigung in Osterreich
ESTOOOAHCF ... Emergency Situations That Occur Outside of a Health Care Facility
ESTOP .... Estoppel [*Legal shorthand*] (LWAP)
ESTOP & W ... Estoppel and Waiver [*Legal term*] (DLA)
ESTOW ...... Eastco Indl Safety Wrrt [*NASDAQ symbol*] (TTSB)
ESTP .... Electronic Systems Test Program [*NASA*]
Est Plan Rev ... Estate Planning Review [*A publication*] (DLA)
Est Powers & Trusts ... Estates, Powers, and Trusts [*Legal term*] (DLA)
Est Prac ...... Estee's Code Pleading, Practice, and Forms [*A publication*] (DLA)
Est Prac Pl ... Estee's Code Pleading, Practice, and Forms [*A publication*] (DLA)
ESTR .... ElectroStar Inc. [*NASDAQ symbol*] (TTSB)
EstR .... Esther Rabbah (BJA)
ESTRA .... English-Speaking Tape Respondents Association [*British*] (BI)
ESTRA .... Estradiol [*Biochemistry*] (DAVI)
ESTRA .... Experimental STOL Transport Research
ESTRAC ...... European Space Satellite Tracking and Telemetry Network (MCD)
ESTRACK ...... European Space Satellite Tracking and Telemetry Network (BARN)
ESTRIFF ...... Encryptic Secure Tracking RADAR Identification Friend or Foe (NATG)
Estrlne .... Esterline Corp. [*Associated Press*] (SAG)
ESTRN .... Eastern
ESTRO .... European Society for Therapeutic Radiology and Oncology (EAIO)
ESTS .... Echo Suppressor Testing System [*Telecommunications*] (TEL)
ESTS .... Electronic Systems Test Set (MCD)
ESTS .... Estates
ESTS .... Estates [*Postal Service standard*] (OPSA)
ESTSD .... Eastside
EstSSR .... Estonian Soviet Socialist Republic
Estt .... Establishment [*British military*] (DMA)
EstTX FS ...... East Texas Financial Services, Inc. [*Associated Press*] (SAG)
ESTU .... Electronic System Test Unit
ESTV .... Error Statistics by Tape Volume [*Computer science*] (IBMDP)

Estwind	Eastwind Group, Inc. (The) [*Associated Press*] (SAG)
Est Wt	Estimated Weight [*Measurement*] (DAVI)
ESU	East Stroudsburg University
ESU	Electricity Supply Union [*British*]
ESU	Electronic Sequencing Unit [*for helicopters*] [*Army*] (RDA)
ESU	Electronic Services Unlimited [*New York, NY*] [*Telecommunications*] (TSSD)
ESU	Electronic Setup (WDMC)
ESU	Electronic Switching Unit [*Telecommunications*] (MCD)
ESU	Electrostatic Unit
esu	Electrostatic Unit (IDOE)
esu	Electrostatic Units (IDOE)
ESU	Electrosurgical Unit [*Medicine*]
ESU	Emergency Services Unit (LAIN)
ESU	Employee Skills Upgrade
ESU	Empty Signal Unit [*Telecommunications*] (TEL)
ESU	Endangered Species Unit [*Commonwealth*] (EERA)
ESU	Energy Studies Unit [*University of Strathclyde*] [*Scotland*] (IRC)
ESU	Engineering Setup [*Television*] (WDMC)
ESU	Engine Service Unit (AAG)
ESU	English Speaking Union [*British*] (EAIO)
ESU	English-Speaking Union of the United States (EA)
ESU	Enormous State University [*Fictitious school often featured in comic strip "Tank McNamara"*]
ESU	Enterprise Support Unit
ESU	Environmental Simulation Unit (PDAA)
ESU	Esutoru [*Uglegorsk*] [*Former USSR Seismograph station code, US Geological Survey Closed*] (SEIS)
ESU	Europa Study Unit (EA)
ESU	European Showmen's Union [*EC*] (ECED)
ESUA	Amsele [*Sweden ICAO location identifier*] (ICLI)
ESUB	Arbra [*Sweden ICAO location identifier*] (ICLI)
E-Sub	Excitor Substance (DAVI)
ESUC	English Speaking Union of the Commonwealth (EAIO)
ESUE	Idre [*Sweden ICAO location identifier*] (ICLI)
ESUF	Fallfors [*Sweden ICAO location identifier*] (ICLI)
ESUG	Gargnas [*Sweden ICAO location identifier*] (ICLI)
ESUH	Harnosand/Myran [*Sweden ICAO location identifier*] (ICLI)
ESUIC	English Speaking Union International Council (EAIO)
ESUK	Kalixfors [*Sweden ICAO location identifier*] (ICLI)
ESUL	Ljusdal [*Sweden ICAO location identifier*] (ICLI)
ESUM	Mohed [*Sweden ICAO location identifier*] (ICLI)
ESUN	Sundsvall [*Sweden ICAO location identifier*] (ICLI)
ESUNA	Ethiopian Students Union of North America
ESUR	Ramsele [*Sweden ICAO location identifier*] (ICLI)
E SURR R	East Surrey Regiment [*Military unit*] [*British*] (ROG)
ESUS	Asele [*Sweden ICAO location identifier*] (ICLI)
ESUS	Electronically-Agile Solid-State Universal Surveillance (PDAA)
ESUT	Evaluation of Small Unit Training (MCD)
ESUT	Hemavan [*Sweden ICAO location identifier*] (ICLI)
ESU/UFE	European Showmen's Union/Union Foraine Europeenne (EA)
ESUV	Alvsbyn [*Sweden ICAO location identifier*] (ICLI)
ESUY	Edsbyn [*Sweden ICAO location identifier*] (ICLI)
ESV	Earth Satellite Vehicle [*Air Force*]
ESV	Earth Station - Venezuela
ESV	Ego Support Value [*Psychology*]
ESV	Elastic Space Vehicle
ESV	Electrostatic Voltmeter (DEN)
ESV	Emergency Shutoff Valve (KSC)
ESV	Enamel Single Silk Varnish [*Wire insulation*] (AAG)
ESV	End-Systolic Volume [*Cardiology*]
ESV	Energy Service Co. [*AMEX symbol*] (SPSG)
ESV	ENSCO Intl. [*NYSE symbol*] (TTSB)
ESV	Enserv Corp. [*Toronto Stock Exchange symbol*]
ESV	Entomological Society of Victoria [*Australia*]
ESV	Error Statistics by Volume [*Computer science*] (BUR)
ESV	Esophageal Valve [*Anatomy*]
ESV	Essential Service Value [*Telecommunications*] (IEEE)
ESV	Experimental Safety Vehicle [*Later, Research Safety Vehicle*] [*Department of Transportation*]
ESV	Extension Society Volunteers [*Defunct*]
ESVA	Avesta [*Sweden ICAO location identifier*] (ICLI)
ESVEM	Electrophysiological Study Versus Electrocardiographic Monitoring [*Medical study*]
ESVF	Frolunda [*Sweden ICAO location identifier*] (ICLI)
ESVG	Gagnef [*Sweden ICAO location identifier*] (ICLI)
ESVH	Hallefors [*Sweden ICAO location identifier*] (ICLI)
ESVI	End-Systolic Volume Index [*Cardiology*] (DMAA)
ESVK	Katrineholm [*Sweden ICAO location identifier*] (ICLI)
ESVM	Malung [*Sweden ICAO location identifier*] (ICLI)
ESVN	Executive-Secure Voice Network
ESVP	European Society of Veterinary Pathology (EA)
ESVQ	Koping [*Sweden ICAO location identifier*] (ICLI)
ESVR	Examination Status Verification Report (NVT)
ESVS	Escape Suit Ventilation System (MCD)
ESVS	Escape System Ventilation System (NASA)
ESVS	Siljansnas [*Sweden ICAO location identifier*] (ICLI)
ESW	Economic and Sector Work
ESW	Electroslag Welding
ESW	Emergency Service Water [*Nuclear energy*] (NRCH)
ESW	Engineering Specification Worksheet
ESW Wt	Engineering Statement of Work (MCD)
ESW	Engine Status Word (MCD)
ESW	Error Status Word [*Computer science*] (BUR)

ESW	ESSA [*Environmental Science Services Administration*] World [*A publication*]
ESW	Essential Service Water [*Nuclear energy*] (NRCH)
ESW	Ethical Society of Washington (EA)
e-sw--	Sweden [*MARC geographic area code Library of Congress*] (LCCP)
ESWA	Engineering Shop Work Authorization (SAA)
ESWD	Emergency Service Water Discharge [*Nuclear energy*] (NRCH)
ESWI	Emergency Service Water Intake [*Nuclear energy*] (NRCH)
ESWI	Norrkoping [*Sweden ICAO location identifier*] (ICLI)
ESWL	Equivalent Single Wheel Load (MCD)
ESWL	Estimated Surface Wheel Load (CINC)
ESWL	Extracorporeal Shockwave Lithotripsy [*Medicine*]
ESWP	Essential Sight Words Program (EDAC)
ESWS	Earth Satellite Weapon Systems
ESWS	Emergency Service Water Screening [*Nuclear energy*] (NRCH)
ESWS	Emergency Service Water System [*Nuclear energy*] (IEEE)
ESWS	Enlisted Surface Warfare Specialist (DNAB)
ESWS	Essential Service Water System [*Nuclear energy*] (NRCH)
ESWSS	Emergency Service Water Supply System [*Nuclear energy*] (NRCH)
ESX	Essex Bancorp [*AMEX symbol*] (TTSB)
ESX	Essex Bancorp, Inc. [*AMEX symbol*] (SPSG)
ESX	Essex County College, Newark, NJ [*OCLC symbol*] (OCLC)
EsxCty	Essex County Gas Co. [*Associated Press*] (SAG)
ESY	Earth Station - Yugoslavia
ESY	Episcopal Service for Youth (EA)
ESY	Executive Aviation Services Ltd. [*Nigeria*] [*ICAO designator*] (FAAC)
ESY	Extended School Year
ESY	West Yellowstone, MT [*Location identifier FAA*] (FAAL)
ESYA	Extended School Year Aid
e-sz--	Switzerland [*MARC geographic area code Library of Congress*] (LCCP)
ET	Earliest Time [*Business term*]
ET	Earth Terminal (HGAA)
ET	Eastern Telegraph (IAA)
ET	Eastern Time (GPO)
ET	Easter Term
ET	Eaton Trust Co. [*Toronto Stock Exchange symbol*]
ET	Ebbinghaus Test [*Psychology*] (DAVI)
ET	Eddy-Current Testing [*Electromagnetism*]
E/T	Edges Trimmed [*Publishing*] (DGA)
ET	Edge Thickness [*Technical drawings*]
ET	Edge-Triggered (IEEE)
ET	Educational Television [*FCC*] (NTCM)
ET	Educational Test [*British military*] (DMA)
ET	Educational Therapy
ET	Educational Training
ET	Effective Temperature
ET	Egypt
ET	Ejection Time
ET	Elapsed Time
ET	Electrical Technician (IAA)
ET	Electrical Time
ET	Electrical Transcription
ET	Electrical/Transformer Room [*NFPA pre-fire planning symbol*] (NFPA)
ET	Electrical Typewriter (CMD)
ET	Electric Telegraph
ET	Electrode Track
ET	Electronics Technician [*Navy rating*]
ET	Electronic Technician
ET	Electronic Test
ET	Electronic Time [*Fuze*] (MCD)
ET	Electronic Transcription [*Radio*] (WDMC)
ET	Electronic Transformers (MCD)
ET	Electronic Typewriter
ET	Electron Transfer
ET	Electron [*or Electronic*] Tube (MCD)
ET	Electrothermal [*Gun classification*]
ET	Elevated Temperature (MCD)
ET	Embedded Training [*Army*] (RDA)
ET	Embryo Transfer
ET	EMCLASS Terms [*Online database field identifier*]
ET	Emergency Takeover
ET	Emergency Tank [*Nuclear energy*] (NRCH)
ET	Emergency Treatment [*Dentistry*]
ET	Emerging Technology
ET	Emissions Trading [*Environmental Protection Agency*]
ET	Empathy Test [*Psychology*]
ET	Employment Training [*British*]
ET	End of Tape [*Computer science*] (CET)
ET	End of Text [*Computer science*]
ET	Endogenous Transcript [*Genetics*]
ET	Endothelin [*Biochemistry*]
ET	Endotoxin [*Microbiology*]
ET	Endotracheal [*Medicine*] (AAMN)
ET	Endotracheal Tube [*Medicine*]
ET	End-Tidal [*Physiology*]
ET	Energy Transfer (IAA)
ET	Engaged Tone [*Telecommunications*] (TEL)
ET	Engage Test [*Manual exchanges*] [*Telecommunications*] (NITA)
ET	Engineering Technology (MCD)
ET	Engineering Test
ET	Engineer Training
ET	Engine Turned [*Watchmaking*] (ROG)
ET	English Text
ET	English Title [*Online database field identifier*]

ET	English Translation
ET	Enhanced Telephone
ET	Enterically Transmitted [*Medicine*]
ET	Enterostomal Therapist [*Gastroenterology*]
ET	Entertainment Tax (DLA)
ET	Entertainment Television [*Also, E! Entertainment*] [*A cable network*] [*Los Angeles, California*] (WDMC)
ET	Entertainment Tonight [*Television program*]
ET	Entrenching Tool [*Shovel/pick combination*] [*Military*] (VNW)
ET	Environmental Technician
ET	Environmental Test
ET	Enziklopedyah [*or Entsiklopedyah*] Talmudit (BJA)
ET	Ephemeris Time [*Astronomy*]
ET	Equal Taper (OA)
ET	Equation of Time [*Navigation*]
ET	Equipment Test
ET	Equipment Time
ET	Equivalent Training (AABC)
ET	Erection Torquer (SAA)
ET	Ergotamine Tartrate (DICI)
E/T	Escape Tower [*NASA*] (KSC)
ET	Escort Trains (CINC)
ET	Esotropia [*Ophthalmology*] (DAVI)
ET	Esotropia for Distance [*Ophthalmology*]
ET	Essential Thrombocythemia [*Hematology*]
ET	Essential Tremor [*Neurophysiology*]
ET	Estate and Gift Tax Ruling [*A publication*] (DLA)
ET	Estate Tax
ET1	Estimated Time
ET	Estimated Time of Arrival (DAVI)
ET	Ethionamide [*An antibacterial compound*] (DAVI)
ET	Ethiopia [*ANSI two-letter standard code*] (CNC)
et	Ethiopia [*MARC country of publication code Library of Congress*] (LCCP)
ET	Ethiopian Airlines [*ICAO designator*] (AD)
Et	Ethyl [*Organic chemistry*]
Et	Ethyl Group [*Organic chemistry*] (DAVI)
ET	Ethyltoluene [*Organic chemistry*]
et	Etiology (AAMN)
ET	European Theater
et----	Europe, East Central [*MARC geographic area code Library of Congress*] (LCCP)
ET	Eustachian Tube [*Anatomy*]
ET	Evaluation Test (IAA)
ET	Evapotranspiration [*Hydrology*]
ET	Event Timer (NASA)
ET	Exchange Termination [*Telecommunications*]
ET	Exchange Transfusion [*Medicine*] (DMAA)
ET	Excise Tax [*Canada*]
ET	Executive Team (NRCH)
ET	Exercise Testing [*Medicine*]
ET	Exercise Treadmill (AAMN)
ET	Exodus Trust (EA)
ET	Expander Tube
ET	Expenditure Targets [*Medical care proposal*]
ET	Explosive Technology
ET	Ex-Tapol [*Political Prisoner*] [*Indonesia*]
ET	Extended Take [*Recording term*]
ET	External Tank [*NASA*]
ET	Extraterrestrial [*Also used in film title "ET - The Extra-Terrestrial"*]
ET	Eye Travel
E(T)	Intermittent Esotropia [*Ophthalmology*] (DAVI)
ET1	Electronics Technician, First Class [*Navy rating*]
ET2	Electronics Technician, Second Class [*Navy rating*]
ET3	Electronics Technician, Third Class [*Navy rating*]
ET-3	Erythrocyte Tri-Iodothyronine [*Hematology*] (DAVI)
ET₄R	Effective T₄ Ratio [*Endocrinology*]
ETA	Educational Television Association (EAIO)
ETA	Educational Theater Association (EA)
ETA	Education through Aviation
ETA	Effectiveness Training Associates
ETA	Effects Test Area [*Army*]
ETA	Ejector Thrust Augmentation [*Air Force*]
ETA	Electra North West [*Vancouver Stock Exchange symbol*]
ETA	Electrical Thermal Analysis
ETA	Electrothermal Atomization [*For spectrometry*]
ETA	Emanation Thermal Analysis
ETA	Embroidery Trade Association (EA)
ETA	Employment and Training Administration [*Formerly, Manpower Administration*] [*Department of Labor*]
ETA	Endotracheal Aspirates [*Medicine*] (MEDA)
ETA	Energy Tax Act [*1978*]
ETA	Engineering Task Assignment
ETA	Entertainment Trades Alliance [*British*]
ETA	Environmental Test Article (NASA)
ETA	Environment Teachers' Association (EERA)
ETA	Equipment Transfer Aisle (NRCH)
ETA	Equivalent Target Area (MCD)
ETA	Esperanto Teachers Association [*British*]
ETA	Estimated Target Assurance
ETA	Estimated Time of Acquisition (KSC)
ETA	Estimated [*or Expected*] Time of Arrival (FAAC)
ETA	Estrellas del Aire SA de CV [*Mexico ICAO designator*] (FAAC)
Eta	Eterna [*Record label*] [*Germany*]
ETA	Ethionamide [*Antibacterial*]

ETA	Europaischer Holzhandelsverband [*European Timber Association*] [*EC*] (ECED)
ETA	European Taxpayers Association (EA)
ETA	European Teachers Association (BARN)
ETA	European Tennis Association (EAIO)
ETA	European Throwsters Association (EA)
ETA	European Thyroid Association (EAIO)
ETA	European Tropospheric-Scatter Army [*Communications system*]
ETA	European Tube Association [*EC*] (ECED)
ETA	European Tugowners Association (EAIO)
ETA	Euzkadi ta Azkatasuna [*Basque Fatherland and Freedom*] [*Spain*] (PD)
ETA	Evangelical Training Association (EA)
ETA	Event Tree Analysis [*Engineering*]
ETA	Exception Time Accounting
ETA	Excise Tax Act [*Canada*]
ETA	Expected Time of Arrival
ETA	Expected Turnaround [*Computer science*]
ETA	Expect to Arrive
ETA	Experimental Test Accelerator [*Nuclear physics*]
ETA	Explosive Transfer Assembly (MCD)
ETA	External Tank Attachment (MCD)
ETA	Extraterrestrial Activity
ETA	Extraterrestrial Actuality
eta	Viscosity [*Symbol*] [*Organic chemistry*] (DAVI)
ETAA	Educators to Africa (EA)
ETAA	Eelam Tamils Association of America (EA)
ETAA	Electrothermal Atomic Absorption [*Analytical technique*]
ETAADS	Engine Technical and Administrative Data System (PDAA)
ETAAS	Electrothermal Atomic Absorption Spectrometry
ETAB	Emerging Technologies Advisory Board
ETAB	Environmental Testing Advisory Board [*Dow Chemical Co.*]
ETAB	Expanded Technical Assistance Board [*United Nations*]
ETAB	Extrathoracic Assisted Breathing [*Medicine*] (DNAB)
ETABC	Extrathoracic Assisted Breathing and Circulation [*Medicine*] (DNAB)
ETAC	Electrically Tuned Antenna Coupler
ETAC	Electronics Technical Applications Center [*Air Force*]
ETAC	Enlisted Tactical Air Controller [*Army*] (INF)
ETAC	Enlisted Tactical Application (DOMA)
ETAC	Environmental Technical Applications Center [*Air Force*]
ETAC	Environment Technical Advisory Committee (EERA)
ETACCS	European Theater Air Command and Control Study [*DoD*]
ETACS	Electronic Time and Alarm Control System [*Mitsubishi*] [*Automotive engineering*]
ETAD	Ecological and Toxicological Association of the Dyestuffs Manufacturing Industry [*Basel, Switzerland*] (EAIO)
ETADS	Enhanced Transportation Automated Data System [*Air Force*]
ETAE	Ethyl Tertiary Amyl Ether [*Gasoline blending*]
ETAFF	European Technical Association for Furniture Finishes [*Defunct*]
ETA-I	Electronics Technicians Association, International (EA)
ETAIRS	Employment and Training Automated Information and Retrieval System [*Department of Labor*] [*Database*]
ET AL	Et Alibi [*And Elsewhere*] [*Latin*]
et al	Et Alii [*or Et Aliae or Et Alia*] [*And Others*] [*Latin*] (GPO)
Et Alc	Ethyl Alcohol [*Organic chemistry*] (DAVI)
ET AL FREQ	Et Alii Frequentis [*And in Many Other (Passages)*] [*Latin*] (ROG)
ETAM	Anklam [*Germany ICAO location identifier*] (ICLI)
ETA-M	Euzkadi ta Azkatasuna [*Basque Fatherland and Freedom*] Military Front [*Spain*]
ETAM	Experimental Transmitting Antenna Modular Model (MCD)
ETAMS	Employment and Training Administration Management System [*Department of Labor*]
ET & E	Engineering Test and Evaluation (MCD)
ET & E	Environmental Technology and Economics [*A publication*]
ET & MO	Education, Training, and Military Operations [*Army*] (RDA)
ET & WNC	East Tennessee & Western North Carolina Railroad Co. (IIA)
ETANN	Electrically Trainable Analog Neural Network [*Intel Corp.*] [*Computer science*] (PCM)
ETAP	Expanded Technical Assistance Program [*United Nations*]
ETAP	Extended Task Analysis Procedure [*Education*] (AIE)
ETAPC	European Technical Association for Protective Coatings [*Belgium*] (SLS)
ETA-PM	Euzkadi ta Azkatasuna [*Basque Fatherland and Freedom*] Political-Military Front [*Spain*]
ETARO	Employment and Training Administration Regional Office [*Department of Labor*]
ETARS	Enroute Tracking Automatic RADAR Service [*Aviation*] (FAAC)
ETAS	Effective True Airspeed (AFM)
ETAS	Elevated Target Acquisition System
ETAS	Escort Towed Array Sensor [*Later, TACTAS*] [*Navy*] (MCD)
ETASS	Escort Towed Array SONAR System [*Navy*] (PDAA)
ETASS	European Tick-Borne Encephalitis [*Medicine*] (PDAA)
ETASS	Evaluation of the Army Study System (MCD)
ETAT	Education and Training Advisory Team (CINC)
ETAWA	English Teachers' Association of Western Australia
ETAWG	Engineering Test Area Working Group (SAA)
ETB	Elastic Top and Bottom [*Military-issue clothing*] [*British*] (DSUE)
ETB	Electrical Time Base
ETB	Electronic Test Block
ETB	Elvis Teddy Bears (EA)
ETB	End of Text Block [*Computer science*] (ACRL)
ETB	End of Transmission Block [*Computer science*]
ETB	Engineering Test Basis (KSC)
ETB	English Tourist Board
ETB	Enlisted Training Branch [*BUPERS*]

ETB	Equipment Transfer Bag [NASA]
ETB	Estimated Time of Berthing [Navigation]
ETB	Ethidium Bromide [Trypanocide] [Also, EB, Etd Br Biochemical analysis]
ETB	Etobicoke Public Library [UTLAS symbol]
ETB	Experimental Test Bed (MCD)
ETB	Extreme Terrain Bike [Military] (INF)
ETB	West Bend, WI [Location identifier FAA] (FAAL)
ETBA	Hellenike Trapeza Biomechanikes Anaptyxeos
ETBC	East Texas Baptist College
ETBE	Ethyl Tertiary-Butyl Ether [Fuel additive]
ETBH	Barth [Germany ICAO location identifier] (ICLI)
ETBN	Berlin/Schonefeld [Germany ICAO location identifier] (ICLI)
ETBO	Engineering Test Base Office (AAG)
ETBPR	European Theater Bureau of Public Relations [World War II]
ETBS	Berlin/Schonefeld [Germany ICAO location identifier] (ICLI)
etc	And So Forth [Et cetera] [Latin] (WDMC)
ETC	Early Typewriter Collectors Association (EA)
ETC	Earth Terminal Complex
ETC	Earth Terrain Camera [NASA] (MCD)
ETC	Educational Technology Center [Harvard University] [Department of Education Research center] (RCD)
ETC	Educational Travel Connection [Oracle Corp.] [Information service or system] (IID)
ETC	Effluent Treatment Cell (PDAA)
ETC	Elapsed Time Code
ETC	El Centro [Colombia] [Seismograph station code, US Geological Survey] (SEIS)
ETC	Electra Title Corp. [Vancouver Stock Exchange symbol]
ETC	Electrical Trade Council (EA)
ETC	Electroacoustic Torpedo Countermeasure (MCD)
ETC	Electronic Temperature Control
ETC	Electronic Text Corp. [Information service or system] (IID)
ETC	Electronic Throttle Control [Automotive engineering]
ETC	Electronic Toll Center [AT & T]
ETC	Electronic Toll Collection [FHWA] (TAG)
ETC	Electronic Tool Company (NITA)
ETC	Electronic Traction Control [Automotive engineering]
ETC	Electronic Transaction Cycle (HGAA)
ETC	Electronic Tuning Control (IAA)
ETC	Electronic Typing Calculator (IAA)
ETC	Electrothermal-Chemical (RDA)
ETC	Emergency Training Centre [British]
ETC	Employee Transportation Coordinator [MOCD] (TAG)
ETC	Empresario de Transporte Combinado [Combined Transport Operator] [Business term Spanish]
ETC	Enclosed Track Conveyor
ETC	Energy Technology Center
ETC	Energy Transfer Control [Aviation]
ETC	Engineering and Training Center [NASA] (KSC)
ETC	Engineering Test Capsule
ETC	Engineering Test Center (MCD)
ETC	Engineering Tooling Coordination
ETC	Engine Technical Commission
ETC	Engine Test Chamber (MCD)
ETC	Enhanced Throughput Cellular [AT & T] [Telecommunications] (PCM)
ETC	Entrepreneur de Transport Combine [Combined Transport Operator] [Business term French]
ETC	Environmental Tectonics [AMEX symbol] (TTSB)
ETC	Environmental Tectonics Corp. [AMEX symbol] (SPSG)
ETC	Environmental Test Chamber
ETC	Equal-Time Commutation
ETC	Equipment Trust Certificate
ETC	Estimated Time of Completion
ETC	Estimated Time of Conception [Obstetrics] (DAVI)
ETC	Estimated Time of Correction
ETC	Estimate to Complete [Cost] (AAGC)
ETC	Et Cetera [And So Forth] [Latin]
ETC	European Tax Confederation (EAIO)
ETC	European Taxi Confederation [Belgium] (EAIO)
ETC	European Tea Committee (EA)
ETC	European Tool Committee (EA)
ETC	European Touring Car
ETC	European Toy Confederation [France] (EAIO)
ETC	European Trade Committee [British Overseas Trade Board] (DS)
ETC	European Traffic Committee
ETC	European Translations Centre [Later, International Translations Centre]
ETC	European Travel Commission (EA)
ETC	Euro Travellers Cheque [Thomas Cook International]
ETC	Exchange Terminal Circuit (ACRL)
ETC	Expected Total Cost
ETC	Experimental Techniques Centre [Brunel University] [British] (CB)
ETC	Explosion of the Total Contents [Insurance] (DS)
ETC	Explosive Transient Camera [Astronomy]
ETC	Export Trading Company [Department of Commerce]
ETC	Extended Text Compositor [Applied Data Research, Inc.]
ETC	Extraterrestrial Civilization
ETCA	Edge Tool Cutters' Association [A union] [British]
ETCA	Emergency Terrain Clearance Altitude
ETCA	Etudes Techniques et Constructions Aerospatiales [Belgium]
ETCA	Export Trading Company Act of 1982
ETCC	Eastern Tank Carrier Conference
ETCC	Environmental Test Control Center (AAG)
ETCD	Estimated Task Completion Date (AAG)

ETCE	Energy Sources Technology Conference and Exhibition (ITD)
ETCF	European Technical Committee for Fluorine [of the European Council of Chemical Manufacturers' Federations] [Belgium] (EAIO)
ETCFC	Earl Thomas Conley Fan Club (EA)
ETCG	Elapsed-Time Code Generator
ETCH	Etching (MSA)
etch	Etching (VRA)
ETCI	Electronic Tele-Communications, Inc. [NASDAQ symbol] (NQ)
ETCI	[The] Electro-Technical Council of Ireland (ACII)
ETCI	Engineering Technologist Certification Institute (EA)
ETCIA	Electronic Tele Comm'A' [NASDAQ symbol] (TTSB)
ETCM	Electronics Technician, Master Chief [Navy rating]
ETCO	Cottbus [Germany ICAO location identifier] (ICLI)
ETCO	[The] Earth Technology Corp. (USA) [NASDAQ symbol] (NQ)
ETCO	Emergency Traffic Coordinating Officer [Army] (AABC)
ETCO	Equipment Transfer or Change Order (NASA)
ETCOM	European Testing and Certification for Office and Manufacturing Protocol (OSI)
ETCP	Engineering Technical Change Package (MCD)
ETCR	Equivalent Effective Temperature Corrected for Radiation (PDAA)
ETCR	Estimated Time of Crew's Return
ETCRRM	Electronic Teleprinter Cryptographic Regenerative Repeater Mixer (NATG)
ETCS	Electronics Technician, Senior Chief [Navy rating]
ETCS	Electronic Throttle Control System [Automotive engineering]
ETCTA	Electrical Trades' Commercial Travellers' Association [British] (BI)
ETD	Economics and Technology Division [Environmental Protection Agency] (GFGA)
ETD	Effective Transfer Date [Military] (AFM)
ETD	Electrical Terminal Distributor (KSC)
ETD	Electronic Tactical Display [Military]
ETD	Electronic Time Delay
ETD	Embedded Temperature Detector (IAA)
ETD	Engineering Test Directive
ETD	Environments and Threats Directorate [Army]
ETD	Equipment Technical Director (MCD)
ETD	Equivalent Transmission Density [Photography] (OA)
ETD	Estimated [or Expected] Time of Departure
ETD	Estimated Turnover Date (MCD)
ETD	Etude
ETD	Event Time Digitizer
ETD	External Tank Door (MCD)
Etd Br	Ethidium Bromide [Trypanocide] [Also, EB, ETB Biochemical analysis]
ETDC	EADAS [Engineering and Administrative Data Acquisition System] Traffic Data Center [Bell System]
ETDCFRL	European Training and Development Centre for Farming and Rural Life (EA)
ETDE	Energy Technology Data Exchange [Department of Energy] (GFGA)
ETDE	Experimental Target Designation Equipment
ETDI	Eurasian Target Data Inventory [File] (MCD)
ETDL	Electronics Technology and Devices Laboratory [Fort Monmouth, NJ] [Army] (RDA)
E-TDMA	Extended Time Division Multiple Access [Telecommunications] (ACRL)
ETDN	Dresden [Germany ICAO location identifier] (ICLI)
ETDP	Emergency Traffic Disposition Plan [Military]
ETDP	Expert Tsunami Database for the Pacific [Marine science] (OSRA)
ETDRS	Early Treatment Diabetic Retinopathy Study
ETDS	Elapsed Time Distribution System (MCD)
ETDT	Extrusion Trim and Drill Template
ETE	Educational and Training Establishment [Military British]
ETE	Effluent Thermal Effect (IAA)
ET/E	Electrical Technician/Electrician (AAG)
ETE	Electromagnetic Test Environment (MCD)
ETE	Electronic Test Equipment
ETE	Electrothermal Engine
ETE	Emergency Transceiver Equipment
ETE	End to End (NASA)
ETE	Engineering Support Test Equipment [Deep Space Instrumentation Facility, NASA]
ETE	Engineering Test Equipment (CAAL)
ETE	Engineering Test Evaluation (AAG)
ETE	Engineering Time Estimate
ETE	Enhanced Tactical Fighter Engineering (MCD)
ETE	Estimated Time En Route
Ete	Eterna [Record label] [Germany]
ETE	Expendable Threat Emitter (DWSG)
ETE	Expendable Turbine Engine
ETE	Experimental Tunneling Establishment [British]
ETE	External Telecommunications Executive (IAA)
ETE	External Test Equipment (IAA)
ETE	Metemma [Ethiopia] [Airport symbol] (OAG)
ETEC	Effective Thermal Expansion Coefficient
ETEC	Electronic Truck Engine Control System [Automotive engineering]
ETEC	Energy Technology Engineering Center [Canoga Park, CA] [Department of Energy] (GRD)
ETEC	Enterotoxigenic Escherichia coli [Water pollution indicator]
ETEC	Etec Systems [NASDAQ symbol] (TTSB)
ETEC	Etec Systems, Inc. [NASDAQ symbol] (SAG)
ETEC	Extension Trunk Dialing [Telecommunications] (PDAA)
ETECG	Electronics Test Equipment Coordination Group [Military]
EtecSys	Etec Systems, Inc. [Associated Press] (SAG)
ETEDS	Electromagnetic Test Environment Data System
ETEF	Erfurt [Germany ICAO location identifier] (ICLI)

ETEMA......... Education Technology and Equipment Manufacturing Association (AIE)
ET/EST........ Engineering Test / Expanded Service Test [Military]
Et Ex........... Etudes et Expansion (EA)
E-Text......... Electronic Text
ETF............. Eastern Task Force
ETF............. Eastfield Resources [Vancouver Stock Exchange symbol]
ETF............. Economic Transactions Framework
ETF............. Education Task Force [Government Documents Round Table] [American Library Association]
ETF............. Effluent Treatment Facility
ETF............. Eglin Test Facility [Florida] [NASA] (KSC)
ETF............. Electronically Tunable Filter
ETF............. Electronic Tuning Fork
ETF............. Electron-Transferring Flavoprotein [Biochemistry]
ETF............. Electrothermal Filter
ETF............. Emerging Markets Telecommunications Fund [NYSE symbol] (SAG)
ETF............. Emerging Mkts Telcommun Fd [NYSE symbol] (TTSB)
ETF............. Engine Test Facility [Arnold Air Force Base, TN] [Air Force] (MCD)
ETF............. Enhanced Tactical Fighter (MCD)
ETF............. Enhanced-Technology Fighter (MCD)
ETF............. Environmental Task Force (EA)
ETF............. Environmental Test Facility [Fort Huachuca, AZ] [United States Army Electronic Proving Ground] (GRD)
ETF............. Estimated Time of Flight
ETF............. European Training Foundation [EC] (ECED)
ETF............. Eustachian Tube Function [Medicine]
ETF............. Evaluation Task Force [Defunct] (EA)
ETF............. Explosives Testing Facility (SAA)
ETF............. Export Task Force (EA)
ETFA........... European Technological Forecasting Association (PDAA)
ETFC.......... Ernest Tubb Fan Club (EA)
ETFE.......... Ethylene-Tetrafluoroethylene [Organic chemistry]
ETFE.......... Ethylenetetrafluoroethylene
ETFIR......... Emergency Task Force for Indochinese Refugees [Defunct] (EA)
ETFL.......... Each Thousand Foot Level (FAAC)
ETFL.......... Friedland [Germany ICAO location identifier] (ICLI)
ETFO.......... Electronics Technical Field Office [FAA]
ETFRN .... European Tropical Forest Research Network (EERA)
ETFS.......... East Texas Financial Services, Inc. [NASDAQ symbol] (SAG)
ETFS.......... East Texas Financial Svcs [NASDAQ symbol] (TTSB)
ETFS.......... Electronic Countermeasure Transmitter Frequency Set Up [Military] (IAA)
ETG............. Eatonton [Georgia] [Seismograph station code, US Geological Survey] (SEIS)
ETG............. Electrical Test Group (NRCH)
ETG............. Electrical Thermal Generators (KSC)
ETG............. Electronic Target Generator [Military] (DA)
ETG............. Electronic Thickness Gauge
ETG............. Electronic Truck Governor [Cummins Engine] [Automotive engineering]
ETG............. Electronic Turbine Governor
ETG............. Electrothermal Gun
ETG............. Environmental Technologies Group
ETG............. External Thermal Garment
ETG............. Keating, PA [Location identifier FAA] (FAAL)
ETGCR .... Exogenous Triglyceride Clearance Rate [Medicine]
ETGS.......... Edge Tool Grinders' Society [A union] [British]
ETGT.......... Equal To or Greater Than
ETGTS........ Electronic Text and Graphics Transfer System
ETH............. Elat [Israel] [Airport symbol] (OAG)
ETH............. Elixir Terpin Hydrate [Pharmacy]
ETH............. Error Trap Handling [Military]
ETH............. Ethan Allen Interiors [NYSE symbol] (TTSB)
ETH............. Ethan Allen Interiors, Inc. [NYSE symbol] (SPSG)
ETH............. Ethanol [or ethyl alcohol] [Organic chemistry] (DAVI)
eth .... Ether (AAMN)
ETH............. Ethics
ETH............. Ethiopia [ANSI three-letter standard code] (CNC)
Eth .... Ethiopia (VRA)
ETH............. Ethiopian Airlines Corp. [ICAO designator] (FAAC)
eth .... Ethiopic [MARC language code Library of Congress] (LCCP)
ETH............. Extraterrestrial Hypothesis
ETH............. Wheaton, MN [Location identifier FAA] (FAAL)
EthanAln.... Ethan Allen Interiors, Inc. [Associated Press] (SAG)
ETH/C......... Elixir Terpin Hydrate with Codeine [Pharmacy]
ETHC.......... Ethical Holdings Ltd. [NASDAQ symbol] (SAG)
ETHCY .... Ethical Holdings Ltd ADS [NASDAQ symbol] (TTSB)
ETHD .... Heringsdorf [Germany ICAO location identifier] (ICLI)
EthEnoch.... Ethiopic Book of Enoch [A publication] (BJA)
Eth Eud .... Ethica Eudemia [of Aristotle] [Classical studies] (OCD)
ETHIC........ Electric Trace Heating Industry Council [British] (DBA)
EthicHld..... Ethical Holdings Ltd. [Associated Press] (SAG)
ETHICS ...... Effective Technical and Human Implementation of Computer Systems [Implementation methodology] (NITA)
ETHIOP ...... Ethiopic [Language, etc.] (ROG)
Eth Nic...... Aristotle's Nicomachean Ethics [A publication] (DLA)
Eth Nic...... Ethica Nicomachea [of Aristotle] [Classical studies] (OCD)
ETHNOG...... Ethnography (ADA)
ETHNOL ...... Ethnology
ETHO.......... Ethylene Oxide [Organic chemistry] (KSC)
ethol.......... Ethology
ETHRC .... East Timor Human Rights Committee (EA)
Ethyl .... Ethyl Corp. [Associated Press] (SAG)
ETI .... Economically-Targeted Investment

ETI .... Economics & Technology, Inc. [Telecommunications service] (TSSD)
ETI .... Educational Travel, Inc.
ETI .... Elapsed-Time Indicator
ETI .... Electric Test Installation
ETI .... Electric Tool Institute [Later, Power Tool Institute] (EA)
ETI .... Electrochemical Time Indicator [Army] (MCD)
ETI .... Electronic Technical Institute (EA)
ETI .... Employment and Training Institute [University of Wisconsin-Milwaukee]
ETI .... Encapsulated Toroidal Inductor
ETI .... Engine Test Information
ETI .... Environmental Technology Initiative [Environmental Protection Agency]
ETI .... Environmental Teratology Information [Department of Energy] [Information service or system] (IID)
ETI .... Equipment and Tool Institute (EA)
ETI .... Estimated Information (FAAC)
ETI .... Estimated Time of Interception
ETI .... European Toy Institute (EAIO)
ETI .... European Transuranium Institute [Germany]
ETI .... Executive Tours International
ETI .... Executor and Trustee Institute [Australia]
ETI .... Exhaust Trail Indicator [Military] (NVT)
ETI .... Expert Center for Taxonomic Identification [The Netherlands] (EERA)
ETI .... Extraction Tool Insert
ETI .... Extraterrestrial Intelligence
ETIA .... European Tape Industry Associaton (PDAA)
ETIC........... English-Teaching Information Center [British Council] (PDAA)
ETIC........... Environmental Teratology Information Center [Department of Energy] (IID)
ETIC........... Estimated Time in Commission [Army] (AABC)
ETIF .... Employer Identification Number Taxpayer Information File [IRS]
ETIH .... Error Terminate Interrupt Handler (MCD)
ETII .... External-to-Internal Interface (MCD)
ETIM .... Elapsed Time [Aviation] (FAAC)
E-time......... Execution Time (CDE)
ETIMR .... Electric Target Intermediate Marksmanship Range
ETIMS .... Electron Transfer Ionization Mass Spectroscopy (MCD)
ET INT AL ... Et Inter Alia [And Among Others] [Latin] (ROG)
ETIO........... Etiocholanolone [A pyrogen] [Medicine] (MAE)
ETIOL......... Etiology
ETIP .... Experimental Technology Incentives Program [National Institute of Standards and Technology]
ETIR .... Environmental Thermal Infrared
ETIS .... Environmental Technical Information System [Army Information service or system] (IID)
ETIS .... European Technical Information Service [Information broker and database originator] (NITA)
ETISALAT.... Emirates Telecommunications Corp. Ltd. [Telecommunications service] (TSSD)
ETIS-MARFO... ETIS [European Technical Information Service] in Machine Readable For m (NITA)
ETJC.......... Engineering Trades' Joint Council [British] (DCTA)
ETK .... Eicosanoyl(trifluoroacetyl)kanamycin [Antiviral]
ETK .... Electron Tube Klystron
ETK .... Embryonic Turkey Kidney
ETK .... Entek Oil & Gas [Vancouver Stock Exchange symbol]
ETK .... Explosive Testing Kit (MCD)
ETKM .... Every Test Known to Man [or Mankind] [Medicine] (CPH)
ETKZ .... Kyritz [Germany ICAO location identifier] (ICLI)
ETL .... Earliest Time to Launch [Navy] (CAAL)
ETL .... Eastern Lights Resources Ltd. [Vancouver Stock Exchange symbol]
ETL .... Eastern Trunk Line (IAA)
ETL .... Educational Technology Language [University of Western Ontario] [Canada] (NITA)
ETL .... Effective Testing Loss [Telecommunications] (TEL)
ETL .... Electrical Testing Laboratory [Portsmouth Naval Shipyard, NH]
ETL .... Electrolytic Tinning Line (PDAA)
ETL .... Electronic Technology Laboratory [Air Force] (MCD)
ETL .... Electrotechnical Laboratory (MCD)
ETL .... Emergency Time Limit
ETL .... Emitter Follower Transistor Logic [Electronics] (IAA)
ETL .... Ending Tape Label [Computer science] (BUR)
ETL .... Engineering Test Laboratory (AAG)
ETL .... Engineer Technical Letter [Army Corps of Engineers]
ETL .... Engineer Topographic Laboratories [Fort Belvoir, VA] [Army] (MCD)
ETL .... Environmental Technology Laboratory [Environmental Research Laboratories] (USDC)
ETL .... Environmental Technology Laboratory [Marine science] (OSRA)
ETL .... Environmental Test Laboratory [Jet Propulsion Laboratory, NASA]
ETL .... [The] Essex Terminal Railway Co. [AAR code]
ETL .... Etching by Transmitted Light
ETL .... Explosive Transfer Lines [Military]
ETL .... Patterson Aviation Co. [ICAO designator] (FAAC)
ETLA .... Extended Three Letter Acronym
ETLA .... Extended Three-Letter Acronym [Internet language] [Computer science]
ETLARS........ Electronics and Telecommunications Literature Analysis Retrieval System [Computer science] (IID)
ETLG.......... Enable This Level Group [Computer science] (MHDI)
ETLL .... Educational Technology and Language Learning (AIE)
ETLM .... Leipzig/Mockau [Germany ICAO location identifier] (ICLI)
ETLO.......... Equipment Transfer or Loan Order
ETLOW........ External Tank Lift-Off Weight [NASA] (NASA)
ETLS .... Leipzig [Germany ICAO location identifier] (ICLI)

ETLT	Equal To or Less Than
ETM	Educational Training Material (MCD)
ETM	Elaborately-Transformed Manufacture
ETM	Elapsed-Time Meter
ETM	Electrically Transmitted Message
ETM	Electrical Tactical Map
ETM	Electrical Time Measurement
ETM	Electronics Technician's Mate [*Navy rating*]
ETM	Electronic Test and Maintenance (IAA)
ETM	Electronic Test and Measurement (MCD)
ETM	Elemental Time Monitor (PDAA)
ETM	Embedded Training Material [*Military*]
ETM	Emery Testing Machine [*Nineteenth-century hydraulic testing machine*] (RDA)
ETM	End of Tape Marker [*Computer science*] (IAA)
ETM	Energy Transfer Module [*Aviation*] (MCD)
ETM	Engineering Test Model (KSC)
ETM	Enhanced Thematic Mapper [*Geoscience*]
ETM	Enhanced Timing Module (IEEE)
ETM	Enter Trapping Mode (SAA)
ETM	Erythromycin [*Also, E, ERY, ERYC*] [*Antibacterial compound*]
ETM	Escrowed to Maturity [*Finance*]
ETM	Even Transversal Magnetic (IAA)
ETM	Excise Tax Memoranda [*Revenue Canada - Customs and Excise*] [*Information service or system*] (CRD)
ETM	Experimental Test Model (IAA)
ETM	Extension Training Management [*Military*] (INF)
ETM	Extension Training Materials [*Army*]
ETM	Extension Training Memorandum [*Civil Defense*]
ETM	External Technical Memorandum
ETM	External Tympaniform Membrane [*Zoology*]
ETM	Extraterrestrial Material
ETM	Transportes Aereos Tamaulipas, SA de CV [*Mexico*] [*FAA designator*] (FAAC)
ETMA	Educational Television for the Metropolitan Area
ETMA	Elapsed Time/Maintenance Action (MCD)
ETMA	English Timber Merchants' Association (BI)
ETMB	Electrical Techniques in Medicine and Biology (MCD)
ETMC	European Telephone Marketing Council [*of the European Direct Marketing Organization*] [*Jona, Switzerland*] (EA)
ETMD	Essential Technical Medical Data
ETMD	Extendable Tubular Member Device [*Aerospace*]
ETME	[*The*] European Turf Management Exhibition [*British*] (ITD)
ETMF	Elapsed Time Multiprogramming Factor
ETMF	Elapsed Time Multiprogramming Factor (NITA)
ETMG	Electron Tube Management Group (SAA)
ETMG	Magdeburg [*Germany ICAO location identifier*] (ICLI)
ETMS	Enhanced Traffic Management System [*FAA*] (TAG)
ETMS	Ernst Toller Memorial Society [*Later, ISSE*] (EA)
ETMSR	Electronics Technician's Mate, Ship Repair [*Navy rating*]
ETMT	Ethoxy(trichloromethyl)thiadiazole [*Fungicide*]
ETMWG	Electronic Trajectory Measurements Working Group [*IRIG*] [*Range Commanders Council White Sands Missile Range, NM*]
ETN	Eastern Technical Net [*Air Force*]
ETN	Eastland, TX [*Location identifier FAA*] (FAAL)
ETN	Eaton Corp. [*NYSE symbol*] (SPSG)
ETN	Educational Telecommunications Network
ETN	Educational Telephone Network [*University of North Dakota*] [*Grand Forks*] (TSSD)
ETN	Electrical Terminal Nut
ETN	Electronics Technician, Communications [*Navy rating*]
ETN	Electronic Tandem Network (ACRL)
ETN	Equipment Table Nomenclature (AFM)
Etn	Ethanolamine [*Also, EA, OLAMINE*] [*Organic chemistry*]
ETN	Extension Teleconferencing Network [*Texas A & M University*] [*College Station, TX*] [*Telecommunications service*] (TSSD)
ETN1	Electronics Technician, Communications, First Class [*Navy rating*] (DNAB)
ETN2	Electronics Technician, Communications, Second Class [*Navy rating*] (DNAB)
ETN3	Electronics Technician, Communications, Third Class [*Navy rating*] (DNAB)
ETNA	East Timor News Agency
ETNA	Electronic-Theodolite Naval Alignment
ETNAM	European Theater Network Analysis Model (MCD)
ET-NANBH ...	Enterically Transmitted Non-A, Non-B Hepatitis [*Medicine*]
ETNF	Estimated Time to Next Failure (MCD)
ETNP	Eastern Tropical North Pacific Sea
ETNS	Electronic Train Number System (PDAA)
ETNSA	Electronics Technician, Communications Seaman Apprentice [*Navy rating*]
ETNSN	Electronics Technician, Communications Seaman [*Navy rating*]
ETNVT	Edinaia Tovarnaia Nomenklatura Vneshney Torgovli [*Commodity nomenclature system used in international trade*]
ETO	Electronic Temperature Offset
ETO	Emergency Test Operation
ETO	Energy Technology Office [*Department of Energy*] (OICC)
ETO	Ephemeris-Tuned Oscillator
ETO	ESSO [*Standard Oil*] Turbo Oil
ETO	Estimated Takeoff (KSC)
ETO	Estimated Time Off
ETO	Estimated Time of Operations [*NASA*] (KSC)
ETO	Estimated Time of Ovulation [*Gynecology*]
ETO	Ethylene Oxide [*Organic chemistry*]
ETO	European Theater of Operations [*World War II*]
ETO	European Transport Organization [*ECE*]
ETO	Eustachian Tube Obstruction [*Medicine*]
ETO	Evadale, TX [*Location identifier FAA*] (FAAL)
ETO	Exchange-Traded Option
ETO	Expiration of Term of Obligation [*Military*]
ETO	Explosive Test Operator (RDA)
ETO	Express Transportation Order [*Army*] (AABC)
ETOC	Emergency Technical Operations Center [*DoD*]
ETOC	Estimated Time of Correction [*NASA*] (KSC)
ETOC	Estimated Time Out of Commission
ETOC	Expected Total Operating Cost (PDAA)
E-to-E	Electronics-To-Electronics (WDMC)
E to E	End to End [*Telecommunications*]
ETOFY	Elvis, This One's for You Fan Club (EA)
ETOG	European Technical Operations Group
ETOH	Ethyl Alcohol [*or Ethanol*]
ETOM	Electron Trapping Optical Memory [*Computer science*]
ETOMA	Environmental Threshold of Measurement Accuracy
ETOP	Engineering Technical Operating Procedure
ETOP	Environmental Threat and Opportunity Profile
ETOP	Extended-Range Twin-Engine Operation [*Aviation*]
ETOPS	Extended Range Twinjet Operation [*Aviation*] (DA)
ETOPS	Extended Twin-Engine Over Water Operations [*OST*] (TAG)
ETOS	Extended Tape Operating System (BUR)
ETOT	Estimated Time Over Target
ETOUSA	European Theater of Operations, United States Army [*Pronounced "ee-too-sah"*] [*World War II*]
ETOV	Estimated Time Over [*Aviation*] (FAAC)
ETown	E'Town Corp. [*Formerly, Elizabethtown Water*] [*Associated Press*] (SAG)
ETOX	Ethylene Oxide [*Organic chemistry*] (MAE)
ETP	Eastern Tennis Patrons (EA)
ETP	Eastern Tropical Pacific (USDC)
ETP	Eastern Tropical Pacific [*Marine science*] (OSRA)
ETP	Eastern Tropical Pacific Ocean
ETP	East Timor Project [*Defunct*] (EA)
ETP	Eccentricity, Tilt, Precession [*Oceanography*]
ETP	Effluent Treatment Plant (PDAA)
ETP	Elastomeric Thermoplastic [*Organic chemistry*]
ETP	Elastometric Thermoplastic
ETP	Electrical Tough Pitch [*Copper*]
ETP	Electrolytic Tough-Pitch [*Copper grade*]
ETP	Electronic Tape Printer (IAA)
ETP	Electronic Technical Publishing (IAA)
ETP	Electronic Tough Pitch [*Copper*] (NITA)
ETP	Electron Temperature Probe
ETP	Electron Transfer [*or Transporting*] Particle
ETP	Electron Tube Panel
ETP	Elevated Training Platform
ETP	Eligible Termination Payment (ADA)
ETP	Eltopia [*Washington*] [*Seismograph station code, US Geological Survey*] (SEIS)
ETP	Emergency Technology Program [*Oak Ridge National Laboratory*]
ETP	Emissions Trading Policy [*Environmental Protection Agency*] (GFGA)
ETP	Empire Test Pilots School [*British ICAO designator*] (FAAC)
ETP	Engineering Test Program [*NASA*] (KSC)
ETP	Engineering Thermoplastic [*Plastics technology*]
ETP	Engine Test Panel [*Aerospace*] (AAG)
ETP	Enterprise Oil [*NYSE symbol*] (SPSG)
ETP	Enterprise Oil ADS [*NYSE symbol*] (TTSB)
ETP	Entire Treatment Period [*Medicine*]
ETP	Environmental Test Program (AAG)
ETP	Environmental Training Project [*World Wildlife Fund-United States*]
ETP	Equal Time Point
ETP	Equipment Test Plan (NASA)
ETP	Equivalent Top Product
ETP	Estimated Turnaround Point
ETP	European Training Programme in Brain and Behavior Research [*of the European Science Foundation*] [*France*] (EA)
ETP	Eustachian Tube Pressure [*Medicine*] (MAE)
ETP	Evaluation Test Plan
ETP	Experimental Test Procedure (MCD)
ETP	Exportable Training Package [*Army*]
ETP	Extended Tape Processing (IAA)
ETP	Extended Term Plan (BUR)
ETP	Potential Evapotranspiration [*Hydrology*]
ETPA	Electronically Tunable Parametric Amplifier
ETPA	Emergency Technical Provisions Act of 1976
ETPAE	Ethyl-Terminated Polyarylene Ether [*Organic chemistry*]
ETPBBR	European Training Programme in Brain and Behavior Research [*of the European Science Foundation*] [*France*] (EAIO)
ETPD	Essential Tremor and Parkinson's Disease [*Neurophysiology*]
ETPD	Estimated Time of Parachute Deployment (MUGU)
ETPE	Elevated Temperature Polyethylene
ETPI	Eastern Telecommunications Philippines, Inc. [*Manila*]
ET-PNL	Engine Test Panel [*Aerospace*] (AAG)
ETPO	European Trade Promotion Organization (DS)
ETPPr	Enterprise Oil Pref'A'ADS [*NYSE symbol*] (TTSB)
ETPPrB	Enterprise Oil Pref 'B' ADS [*NYSE symbol*] (TTSB)
ETPR	Engineering Test Part Release (SAA)
ETPS	Empire Test Pilots' School [*British*]
ETPS	Engineering Test Program Spares (SAA)
ETPY	Electronic Control Assembly - Thrust Vector, Pitch and Yaw (IAA)
ETQ	Education, Training and Qualifications Committee (ACII)

ETQAP .... Education and Training in Quality Assurance Practices [*American Society for Quality Control*] (NRCH)
ETR .... Early Token Release [*Computer science*]
ETR .... Eastern Test Range [*See also ESMC*] [*Air Force*]
ETR .... Education, Training and Research Associates (EA)
ETR .... Effective Tax Rate
ETR .... Effective Thyroxine Ratio [*Medicine*]
ETR .... Electronically Tuned Receiver
ETR .... Electronics Technician, (RADAR) [*Navy rating*]
ETR .... Electronic Trouble Report
ETR .... Electron Transport Rate [*Physical chemistry*]
ETR .... Electron Tube Rectifier
ETR .... Embedded Training Requirement [*Military*]
ETR .... Emergency Tension Retractor [*Mercedes Benz*] [*Automotive engineering*]
ETR .... Employer Trip Reduction [*Environmental Protection Agency*]
ETR .... Encrypted Traffic Report (CET)
ETR .... End of Track [*Electronics*] (ECII)
ETR .... End-of-Treatment Response [*Medicine*]
ETR .... Energy Test Reactor
ETR .... Engineering Test Reactor
ETR .... Engineering Test Record (IAA)
ETR .... Engineering Test Request [*NASA*] (KSC)
ETR .... Engineer Technical Letter [*ACE*] (AAGC)
ETR .... Engine Transaction Report (NVT)
ETR .... Entergy Corp. [*NYSE symbol*] (SPSG)
ETR .... Entergy Corp. [*NYSE symbol*] (TTSB)
ETR .... Environmental Test Report
ETR .... Epitympanic Recess [*Medicine*] (DAVI)
ETR .... Equipment Temporarily Removed (MCD)
ETR .... Erient Resources, Inc. [*Vancouver Stock Exchange symbol*]
ETR .... Estimated Time of Repair (NG)
ETR .... Estimated Time of Return
etr .... Etcher [*MARC relator code*] [*Library of Congress*] (LCCP)
ETR .... Ethylthioribose [*Biochemistry*]
ETR .... Expected Time of Response
ETR .... Experimental Test Reactor [*Nuclear energy*] (OA)
ETR .... Export Traffic Release
ETR .... Export Transport Release
ETR .... Extended Temperature Range (IAA)
ETR .... External Technical Report
ETR .... External Timing Register
ETR1 .... Electronics Technician, (RADAR), First Class [*Navy rating*] (DNAB)
ETR2 .... Electronics Technician, (RADAR), Second Class [*Navy rating*] (DNAB)
ETR3 .... Electronics Technician, (RADAR), Third Class [*Navy rating*] (DNAB)
ETRA .... Eastern Test Range [*Formerly, Atlantic Missile Range*] [*Air Force*]
ETRA .... Estimated Time to Reach Altitude
ETRA .... Excise Tax Reduction Act
ETRC .... Educational Television and Radio Center [*Later, EBC*]
ETRC .... Engineering Test Reactor Critical Facility
ETRC .... Equitrac Corp. [*NASDAQ symbol*] (SAG)
ETRC .... Expected Total Remnant Costs
Etr Cities ..... [*The*] Etruscan Cities and Rome [*A publication*] (OCD)
ETRIS .... Eastern Test Range Instrumentation Ship (DNAB)
ETRL .... Environmental Toxicology Research Laboratory [*National Environmental Research Center*]
ETRM .... External Tank Rocket Motor
ETRO .... Estimated Time of Return to Operation [*Military*] (AFM)
ETROD .... Eastern Test Range Operations Directive [*Air Force*] (NASA)
ETRR .... Export Traffic Release Request [*MTMC*] (TAG)
ETRS .... European Tissue Repair Society
ETRSA .... Electronics Technician, (RADAR) Seaman Apprentice [*Navy rating*]
ETRSN .... Electronics Technician, (RADAR) Seaman [*Navy rating*]
ETRT .... Electronically Tuned Receiver Tuner
ETRTO .... European Technical Rim and Tyre Organisation (PDAA)
ETRTO .... European Tyre and Rim Technical Organisation [*Belgium*]
ETRU .... Emergency Target Relay Unit (MCD)
Etru .... Etruria (VRA)
ETRY .... Eatery
ETS .... Board of Education for the City of Etobicoke [*UTLAS symbol*]
ETS .... East Stroudsburg State College, East Stroudsburg, PA [*OCLC symbol*] (OCLC)
ETS .... Econometric Time-Series [*Computer program*] (PCM)
ETS .... Educational Talent Search (EA)
ETS .... Educational Teleconference System [*University of Missouri - Columbia*] [*Telecommunications*] (TSSD)
ETS .... Educational Television Stations [*National Association of Educational Broadcasters*] (AEBS)
ETS .... Educational Testing Service (EA)
ETS .... Educational TV Services [*Oklahoma State University*] [*Stillwater*] (TSSD)
ETS .... Edwards Test Station [*NASA*]
ETS .... Electrical Test Setup [*NASA*] (KSC)
ETS .... Electronic Tandem Switching [*Telecommunications*] (TEL)
ETS .... Electronic Telegraph System
ETS .... Electronic Test Set
ETS .... Electronic Test Stand
ETS .... Electronic Test Station
ETS .... Electronic Timing Set
ETS .... Electronic Torque Split [*Automotive engineering*]
ETQAP .... Electronic Translator System [*Bell System*]
ETS .... Electron Transmission Spectroscopy
ETS .... Electron Transport System
ETS .... Elucidatio Terrae Sanctae (BJA)

ETS .... Emergency Telephone Service
ETS .... Emergency Temporary Standard [*OSHA*]
ETS .... Empire Telecommunications [*British World War II*]
ETS .... Employment Transfer Scheme [*British*]
ETS .... Endless Tangent Screw
ETS .... Energy Transfer System (MCD)
ETS .... Energy Transmission System [*Automotive engineering*]
ETS .... Engagement Tracking Station (SAA)
ETS .... Engineered Time Standards (NG)
ETS .... Engineering and Technical Service (AFM)
ETS .... Engineering Tactical System
ETS .... Engineering Test Satellite
ETS .... Engineering Time Standards [*Navy*] (NVT)
ETS .... Engineering Time Study (MCD)
ETS .... Engine Test Stand [*Nevada*] [*Seismograph station code, US Geological Survey Closed*] (SEIS)
ETS .... Engine Test Stands [*NERVA program*]
ETS .... Enquiry Terminal System [*International Computers Ltd.*]
ETS .... Environmental Technical Specifications (NRCH)
ETS .... Environmental Technology Seminar (EA)
ETS .... Environmental Testing Section [*Social Security Administration*]
ETS .... Environmental Test Specification (IEEE)
ETS .... Environmental Tobacco Smoke
ETS .... Environment Table Simulation (SAA)
ETS .... Episcopal Theological School
ETS .... Equal Time Spacing
ETS .... Equivalent Target Size (SAA)
ETS .... Estimated Time of Sailing [*Navigation*]
ETS .... Estimated Time of Separation [*Military Slang*]
ETS .... ETS International, Inc. [*Vancouver Stock Exchange symbol*]
ETS .... ETS International, Inc. [*AMEX symbol*] (SAG)
et s .... Et Suivants [*And Following*] [*French*] (ILCA)
ETS .... European Telecommunications Standard (OSI)
ETS .... European Telephone System [*DoD*]
ETS .... European Teratology Society (EA)
ETS .... European Treaty Series [*Council of Europe*] [*A publication*] (DLA)
ETS .... European Troop Strength (DOMA)
ETS .... Evaluated Testbed System (SSD)
ETS .... Evaluation Test Specification
ETS .... Evaluation Trainers
ETS .... Evangelical Theological Society (EA)
ETS .... Evangelical Tract Society [*British*] (DBA)
ETS .... Expeditionary Test Set (MCD)
ETS .... Expiration of Term of Service [*Military*]
ETS .... External Tank System (MCD)
ETS .... External Time-Sharing (IAA)
ETS .... External Transcribed Spacer [*Genetics*]
ETS .... Extra Telecoms Service [*British*]
ETSA .... Educators'-Employers' Tests and Services Associate (AEBS)
ETSA .... Electricity Trust of South Australia [*State*] (EERA)
ETSA .... English Table Soccer Association (DBA)
ETSA .... Ethyl Trimethylsilylacetate [*Organic chemistry*]
ETSA .... Seaman Apprentice, Electronics Technician, Striker [*Navy rating*]
ETSAL .... Electronic Terms for Space Age Language
ETSC .... East Tennessee State College [*Later, East Tennessee State University*]
ETSC .... East Texas State College [*Later, East Texas State University*]
ETSC .... Electrically-Excited Thermally-Stimulated Current
ETSC .... Electronic Technical Support Center [*DiagSoft*]
ETSC .... Employment and Training Service Center (EA)
ETSCA .... English Toy Spaniel Club of America (EA)
ETSD .... Education and Training Support Detachment [*Military*] (DNAB)
ETSD .... Enhanced Thermionically Supported Discharge [*Materials technology*]
ETSE .... Engineering Test Support Equipment (SAA)
ETSEP .... External Tank Separation [*NASA*] (NASA)
et seq .... And The Following [*A notation*] (WDMC)
ET SEQ .... Et Sequens [*or Et Sequentes, Et Sequentia*] [*And the Following*] [*Latin*]
et seqq .... Et Sequentes [*And the Following*] [*Latin*] (BARN)
ETSF .... Educational Testing Service Test Collection File (EDAC)
ETSG .... Elevated Temperature Strain Gauge
ETSI .... Energy Transportation Systems, Inc.
ETSI .... European Telecommunications Standards Institute
ETSI .... Executive Telecom System, Inc. [*Database producer*] (IID)
ETS Int .... ETS International, Inc. [*Associated Press*] (SAG)
ETSL .... Estimated Total Shelf Life (OA)
ETSMA .... European Tyre Stud Manufacturers Association (PDAA)
ETSN .... Seaman, Electronics Technician, Striker [*Navy rating*]
ETSP .... Entitled to Severance Pay
ETSP .... Evaluation of Testing in Schools Project (AIE)
ETSPL .... Equivalent Threshold Sound Pressure Level
ETSPL .... Extended Telephone Systems Programming Language [*Computer science*] (MHDB)
ETSQ .... Electrical Time, Superquick
ET SQQ .... Et Sequens [*or Et Sequentes, Et Sequentia*] [*And the Following*] [*Latin*]
ETSS .... Electronic Telecommunication Switching System (MCD)
ETSS .... Engineering and Technical Services Specialist [*DoD*]
ETSS .... Entry Time-Sharing System [*IBM Corp.*] [*Computer science*]
ETSS .... Evaluation of Total System Survivability (MCD)
ETSS .... External Tank Separation Subsystem [*NASA*] (NASA)
ETSSC .... ERADCOM [*Electronics Research and Development Command*] Tactical Software Support Center (MCD)
ETST .... Electronic Technical Suitability Test
ET/ST .... Engineer Test/Service Test [*Aerospace*]

ETSTC.........	Educational Testing Service Test Collection (IID)
ETSU.........	East Tennessee State University [*Formerly, East Tennessee State College*]
ETSU.........	East Texas State University [*Formerly, East Texas State College*]
ETSU.........	Energy Technology Support Unit at Harwell [*British*]
ETSV.........	Eastern Tennessee Seismic Zone [*Geology*]
ETT.........	Early Thrust Termination
ETT.........	Easy to Test [*Audiology*]
ETT.........	Electromagnetic Thickness Tool [*Gas well*]
ETT.........	Electronically Tuned Tuner
ETT.........	Electronic Tensile Tester
ETT.........	Electron Tube, Triode
ETT.........	End of Tape Test [*Computer science*]
ETT.........	Endotracheal Tube [*Medicine*]
ETT.........	Environmental Treatment & Technologies Corp. (MHDW)
ETT.........	Equipment Task Time
ETT.........	Estimated Time of Track
ETT.........	Estimated Travel Time [*Army*] (AABC)
ETT.........	Etaiyapuram [*India*] [*Geomagnetic observatory code*]
ETT.........	Etana Tech Corp. [*Vancouver Stock Exchange symbol*]
ETT.........	Evasive Target Tank [*Army*] (RDA)
ETT.........	Excess Travelling Time
ETT.........	Exercise Tolerance Test [*Medicine*]
ETT.........	Exercise Treadmill Test [*Cardiology*] (DAVI)
ETT.........	Expected Test Time
ETT.........	Explosion Tear Test [*Military*]
ETT.........	Extended Time Tests
ETT.........	Extrathyroidal Thyroxine [*Endocrinology*] (MAE)
ETT.........	Extrusion Trim Template
ETTA.........	English Table Tennis Association
ETTA.........	Evangelical Teacher Training Association [*Later, ETA*] (EA)
Ett Ad.........	Etting's American Admiralty Jurisdiction [*A publication*] (DLA)
ETTC.........	Engine Test Technology Centre [*Worcester, England*]
ETTC.........	Estimated Total Target Cost
ETTI.........	EcoTyre Technologies [*NASDAQ symbol*] (TTSB)
ETTI.........	EcoTyre Technologies, Inc. [*NASDAQ symbol*] (SAG)
ETTI.........	End Translation Time Indicator (IAA)
ETTIW.........	EcoTyre Technologies Wrrt [*NASDAQ symbol*] (TTSB)
ETTM.........	Electronic Toll and Traffic Management [*Highway engineering*]
ETTM.........	Electronic Tolls and Traffic Management (PS)
ETTM.........	Electronic Tool and Traffic Management
ETTO.........	Extractor Tool
ETTP.........	Etch Template [*Tool*] (AAG)
ETTS.........	Edge Tool Trade Society [*A union*] [*British*]
ETTU.........	European Table Tennis Union (EA)
ETTUC.........	European Teachers Trade Union Committee [*EC*] (ECED)
ETU.........	East Traverse Mountains [*Utah*] [*Seismograph station code, US Geological Survey*] (SEIS)
ETU.........	Electrical Trades Union [*British*]
ETU.........	Electronic Translator Unit [*Telecommunications*]
ETU.........	Electronic Unit
ETU.........	Emergency and Trauma Unit
ETU.........	Emergency Treatment Unit
ETU.........	Employment and Training Unit [*Work Incentive Program*]
ETU.........	Engineering Test Unit
ETU.........	Enhanced Telephone Unit
ETU.........	Erection Timing Unit
ETU.........	Ethylene Thiourea [*Organic chemistry*]
Etu.........	Etude [*Record label*]
ETU.........	European Triathlon Union (EA)
ETU.........	Expected Total Utility
ETUC.........	European Trade Union Confederation [*Formerly, ECFTU*]
ETUCTCL......	European Trade Union Committee for Textiles, Clothing, and Leather [*Belgium Belgium*] (EAIO)
ETUDE.........	English Teachers in University Departments of Education (AIE)
ETUI.........	European Trade Union Institute [*Belgium*]
ETUI.........	European Trans-Uranium Institute [*Karlsruhe, Germany*]
ETUT.........	Enhanced Tactical User Terminal (DOMA)
ET UX.........	Et Uxor [*And Wife*] [*Latin*]
ETV.........	Educational Television
ETV.........	Ejection Test Vehicle (NG)
ETV.........	Electric Test Vehicle [*Department of Energy*]
ETV.........	Electronic Transfer Vehicle [*MTMC*] (TAG)
ETV.........	Electrothermal Vaporization
ETV.........	Elevating Transfer Vehicle (PDAA)
ETV.........	Engineering Television Mode
ETV.........	Engineering Test Vehicle (KSC)
ETV.........	Epitaxial Tuning Varactor
ETV.........	Europaeischer Tabakwaren-Grosshandels-Verband [*European Tobacco Wholesalers' Union*] (EAIO)
ETVA.........	External Tank Vent Arm (MCD)
ETVC.........	Environmental Test Vacuum Center (SAA)
ETVCS.........	Electronic Three-Vortex Control System
ETVG.........	European Tumour Virus Group (EAIO)
Et Vir.........	Et Viri [*And Husband*] [*Latin*]
ETVM.........	Electrostatic Transistorized Voltmeter
ETVS.........	Educational Television by Satellite (NTCM)
ETVS.........	Enhanced Terminal Voice Switching [*FAA*] (TAG)
ETW.........	Effectiveness Training for Women [*A course of study*]
ETW.........	End of Tape Warning [*Computer science*] (CET)
ETW.........	Entertainment This Week [*TV program*]
ETW.........	Equipment Trials Wing [*Military British*]
ETW.........	Error Time Word (KSC)
ETW.........	E'town Corp. [*Formerly, Elizabethtown Water*] [*NYSE symbol*] (SPSG)

ETW.........	European Transonic Wind-Tunnel
ETW.........	Executive Television Workshop [*New York, NY*]
ETW.........	New Town, ND [*Location identifier FAA*] (FAAL)
ETWA.........	English Tiddlywinks Association (DBA)
ETWN.........	East Tennessee & Western North Carolina Railroad Co. [*AAR code*]
ETWN.........	Wriezen [*Germany ICAO location identifier*] (ICLI)
ETX.........	East Texas, PA [*Location identifier FAA*] (FAAL)
ETX.........	Eburnetoxin [*Biochemistry*]
ETX.........	End of Text [*Computer science*]
ETX.........	End of Transmission (GAVI)
ETX.........	European Air Taxi [*British*] [*FAA designator*] (FAAC)
ETX/ACK.........	End-of-Text/Acknowledge [*Computer science*] (MHDB)
ety.........	Etymology [*or Etymologist*] (WGA)
ETYA.........	Eicosatetraynoic Acid [*Organic chemistry*]
ETYM.........	Etymology [*or Etymologist*]
Etym Magn...	Etymologicum Magnum [*Twelfth century AD*] [*Classical studies*] (OCD)
Etymol.........	Etymology
ETyre.........	EcoTyre Technologies, Inc. [*Associated Press*] (SAG)
ETZ.........	Electron Transparent Zone [*Biochemistry*]
ETZ.........	Etz Lavud Ltd. [*AMEX symbol*] (SPSG)
ETZ.........	Etz Lavud Ltd Ord [*AMEX symbol*] (TTSB)
ETZ.........	Nantucket, MA [*Location identifier FAA*] (FAAL)
ETZA.........	Etz Lavud Ltd 'A' [*AMEX symbol*] (TTSB)
EtzLav.........	Etz Lavud Ltd. [*Associated Press*] (SAG)
EtzLv.........	Etz Lavud Ltd. [*Associated Press*] (SAG)
E/U.........	Edges Untouched [*Publishing*] (DGA)
EU.........	Ehrlich Unit [*Laboratory*] (DAVI)
EU.........	Ehrlich Units [*Clinical chemistry*]
EU.........	Ejector Unit (MCD)
EU.........	Electronic Unit
EU.........	Electron Unit
EU.........	Elms Unlimited [*Superseded by ERI*]
EU.........	Emergency Unit (CPH)
EU.........	Empresa Ecuatoriana de Aviacion [*Ecuador*] [*ICAO designator*] (ICDA)
EU.........	Emulator Program (IAA)
EU.........	Endotoxin Unit [*Clinical chemistry*]
EU.........	End-User [*Computer science*]
EU.........	Energy Unit (IAA)
EU.........	Engineering Unit (MCD)
EU.........	Engineering Use
E/U.........	Engineer/User [*Aerospace*] (AAG)
EU.........	Entropy Unit
EU.........	Enzyme Unit [*Analytical biochemistry*]
EU.........	Episcopalians United (EA)
EU.........	Equatorial Undercurrent [*Marine science*]
eU.........	Equivalent Uranium
EU.........	Erection Unit
EU.........	Error Unavoidable
E-U.........	Etats-Unis [*United States*] [*French*]
EU.........	Ethyleneurea [*Organic chemistry*]
Eu.........	Euler Number [*IUPAC*] [*Fluid mechanics*]
EU.........	Europe
EU.........	European Union [*Formerly, European Community*]
Eu.........	Europium [*Chemical element*]
EU.........	Euthroid [*Endocrinology*] (DAVI)
EU.........	Evacuation Unit [*Army*]
EU.........	Evangelical Union [*British*]
EU.........	Exchange, Unlimited (DNAB)
EU.........	Excretory Urogram [*Radiology*] (DAVI)
EU.........	Execution Unit [*Computer science*]
EU.........	Expected Utility
EU.........	Experience Unit
EU.........	Experimental Unit (NASA)
EU.........	Exposed Uninfected [*Medicine*]
EU.........	Extremadura Unida [*Spain Political party*] (EY)
Eu.........	Norwich Pharmacal Co. [*Research code symbol*]
EUA.........	Eastern Underwriters Association [*Later, ISO*]
EUA.........	Eastern Util Assoc [*NYSE symbol*] (TTSB)
EUA.........	Eastern Utilities Associates [*NYSE symbol*] (SPSG)
EUA.........	Electrical Utility Application (IAA)
EUA.........	Estados Unidos Americanos [*United States of America*] [*Spanish*]
EUA.........	Eua Tonga Island [*South Pacific*] [*Airport symbol*] (OAG)
EUA.........	Europe Air [*France ICAO designator*] (FAAC)
EUA.........	European Area Headquarters [*Red Cross*]
EUA.........	European Units of Account [*Economics*]
EUA.........	Examination under Anesthesia [*Medicine*]
EUA.........	Exchange Users Association (EA)
EUA.........	Extended User Area [*Computer science*]
EUA.........	Extended User Authentication [*Computer science*]
EUA.........	Faculty of Library Science, University of Alberta [*EDUCATSS*] [*UTLAS symbol*]
EUAC.........	Equivalent Uniform Annual Cost
EUAIS.........	European Union of Arab and Islamic Studies [*See also UEAI*] (EAIO)
EUB.........	Emergency Utility Building (NRCH)
EUB.........	Estados Unidos do Brasil [*United States of Brazil*] [*Portuguese*]
EUB.........	Evangelical United Brethren [*Church*]
EUB.........	School of Library Service, Dalhousie University [*EDUCATSS*] [*UTLAS symbol*]
EUBS.........	European Undersea Bio-Medical Society (EAIO)
EUC.........	Emergency Unemployment Compensation [*Account*]
EUC.........	End Use Check
EUC.........	End-User Certificate
EUC.........	End User Computing [*AT & T*]

EUC............ Equatorial Undercurrent [*Marine science*] (MSC)

Euc............. Euclid [*Second century BC*] [*Classical studies*] (OCD)

EUC............. Euclidean [*Mathematics*]

EUC............. Euclid R. R. [*AAR code*]

EUC............. Eureka Canyon [*California*] [*Seismograph station code, US Geological Survey*] (SEIS)

EUC............. Eurocontrol [*Belgium ICAO designator*] (FAAC)

EUC............. European Union of Coachbuilders (EA)

EUC............. Library Studies Program, Concordia University [*EDUCATSS*] [*UTLAS symbol*]

EUCA .... European Federation of Associations of Coffee Roasters (EA)

EUCA .... Extended Unemployment Compensation Account

EUCAPA....... European Capsules Association [*EC*] (ECED)

EUCARPIA... European Association for Research on Plant Breeding (EAIO)

EUCATEL...... European Conference of Associations of Telecommunications Industries (OSI)

EUCATEL...... European Conference of Associations of Telecommunications Industries (NITA)

EUCC .... Computing Center [*Emory University*] [*Research center*] (RCD)

EUCC .... Employers' Unemployment Compensation Council (EA)

EUCD .... Emotionally Unstable Character Disorder (MEDA)

EUCEPA....... Europaeischer Verband fuer Zellstoff und Papiertechnik [*European Liaison Committee for Pulp and Paper*] (EAIO)

EUCF........... Equivalent Uniform Cash Flow

EUCH .... Eucharist (ROG)

EUCHEMAP... European Committee of Chemical Plant Manufacturers [*EC*] (ECED)

EUCIB .... European Collaborative Interspecies Backcross [*Genetic mapping resource*]

EUCLID .... Easily Used Computer Language for Illustration and Drawing [*European Community*] (MHDB)

EUCLID .... European Cooperative Longterm Initiative for Defense [*NATO*]

EUCLID .... Experimental Use Computer, London Integrated Display

EUCOFEL ..... Union Europeenne du Commerce de Gros en Fruits et Legumes [*European Union of the Fruit and Vegetable Wholesale, Import, and Export Trade*] [*Brussels, Belgium*] (EAIO)

EUCOFF .... European Conference on Flammability and Fire Retardants

EUCOLAIT .... Union Europeenne du Commerce des Produits Laitiers et Derives [*European Union of Importers, Exporters, and Dealers in Dairy Products*] (EAIO)

EUCOM .... European Command [*Military*]

EUCOMED.... European Confederation of Medical Suppliers Associations (EA)

EUCOMM-Z... [*US*] European [*Command*] Communications Zone (DOMA)

EUCON........ Energy Utilization and Conversation Exhibition and Conference (PDAA)

EUCONEC..... Europaische Konferenz der Industrie Elektrischer Kondensatoren [*European Conference of the Industry of Electrical Capacitors*] [*EC*] (ECED)

EUCORG ...... European Cooperation Research Group [*European parliamentarians*]

EUCP .... Emergency Urgent Change Package [*Army*] (AABC)

EUCUS .... Emergency Unitized Cargo Unloading System [*Navy*] (CAAL)

EUD .... Euro Direct Airlines Ltd. [*British*] [*FAA designator*] (FAAC)

EUD .... European Union of Dentists (PDAA)

EUD .... Extended Upper Deck

EUD .... Library Techniques, Sheridan College [*EDUCATSS*] [*UTLAS symbol*]

EUDA .... End-Users of Derivatives Association, Inc. (ECON)

EUDAC........ European Defense Analysis Center (MCD)

EUDAC........ European Distribution and Accounting Agency of the Military Committee, London [*US Army*] (AABC)

EUDC .... European Urban Driving Cycle [*Automotive emissions*]

EUDH.......... European Union of Developers and House Builders [*Belgium*] (EAIO)

EUDISED...... European Documentation and Information System for Education [*Council of Europe*] [*Database*] (IID)

EUDS .... Electronic Unit Design Section

EUE............. Extended User Employment [*Military training*]

EUE............. Universite de Montreal, Ecole de Bibliotheconomie [*EDUCATSS*] [*UTLAS symbol*]

EUE............. University of Essex Library, Colchester, England [*OCLC symbol*] (OCLC)

Euer............ Euer. Doctrina Placitandi [*England*] [*A publication*] (DLA)

EUF............. Electroultrafiltration

EUF............. End User Facility

EUF............. Equivalent Unavailability Factor (IEEE)

EUF............. Eufaula, AL [*Location identifier FAA*] (FAAL)

EUF............. European Union of Federalists

EUF............. Library Technician Program, Fraser Valley College [*EDUCATSS*] [*UTLAS symbol*]

EUFA........... Eufaula BancCorp [*NASDAQ symbol*] (TTSB)

EUFA........... Eufaula BancCorp, Inc. [*NASDAQ symbol*] (SAG)

EUFA........... European Union Football Associations

Eufaula .... Eufaula BancCorp, Inc. [*Associated Press*] (SAG)

EUFMC........ Electric Utilities Fleet Managers Conference

EUFODA...... European Food Distributors Association (PDAA)

EUFTT......... European Union of Film and Television Technicians (BARN)

EUG .... CEGEP [*College d'Enseignement General et Professionnel*], Trois-Rivieres, Bibliotheque [*EDUCATSS*] [*UTLAS symbol*]

EUG .... Eugene [*Oregon*] [*Airport symbol*] (OAG)

EUG .... Eugene, OR [*Location identifier FAA*] (FAAL)

EUG .... European Union of Geosciences [*Strasbourg, France*]

EUGEN .... Eugenics (ADA)

EUG LY .... Euglobulin Lysis [*Also, fibrinolysin and plasmin*] [*Biochemistry*] (DAVI)

EUH .... Expected Utility Hypothesis

EUH .... Library Technician Program, Mohawk College [*EDUCATSS*] [*UTLAS symbol*]

EUI.............. Electronic Unit Injector [*or Injection*] [*Automotive Engineering*]

EUI.............. Enciclopedia Universal Illustrada, Espasa [*A publication*]

EUI.............. Enemy Unit Identification [*Military*]

EUI.............. Euravia [*Spain ICAO designator*] (FAAC)

EUI.............. European University Institute [*Florence, Italy*] (AIE)

EUI.............. SAIT [*Southern Alberta Institute of Technology*] Library Technician Program [*UTLAS symbol*]

EulG............ Europium Iron Garnet (PDAA)

EUIPA .... Electric Utility Industrial Power Association (EA)

EUJ .... Georgian College [*EDUCATSS*] [*UTLAS symbol*]

EUJS .... European Union of Jewish Students (EA)

EUK .... Ecoropa UK [*An association*] (EAIO)

EUK .... Eureka Resources, Inc. [*Vancouver Stock Exchange symbol*]

EUK .... Library Technician Program, Kelsey Institute [*EDUCATSS*] [*UTLAS symbol*]

e-uk--.......... United Kingdom [*MARC geographic area code Library of Congress*] (LCCP)

e-uk-en........ England [*MARC geographic area code Library of Congress*] (LCCP)

e-uk-ni........ Northern Ireland [*MARC geographic area code Library of Congress*] (LCCP)

e-uk-st .... Scotland [*MARC geographic area code Library of Congress*] (LCCP)

e-uk-ui........ United Kingdom Miscellaneous Islands [*MARC geographic area code Library of Congress*] (LCCP)

e-uk-wl .... Wales [*MARC geographic area code Library of Congress*] (LCCP)

EUL .... Euralair International [*France ICAO designator*] (FAAC)

EUL .... Expected Upper Limit [*Clinical psychology*]

EUL .... Extensive User Library

EUL .... School of Library Technology, Lakehead University [*EDUCATSS*] [*UTLAS symbol*]

EULA .... Euro-Latin American Bank Ltd.

EULABANK... Euro-Latin America Bank Ltd. [*British*] (EY)

EULAR .... European League Against Rheumatism (EAIO)

EULEP......... European Late Effects Project Group (PDAA)

EULOGIA..... Edinburgh University Library Online for General Information Access (NITA)

EUM............ Entraide Universitaire Mondiale [*World University Service - WUS*] (EAIO)

Eum .... Eumenides [*of Aeschylus*] [*Classical studies*] (OCD)

EUM............ Eureka Mesa [*New Mexico*] [*Seismograph station code, US Geological Survey*] (SEIS)

EUM............ European-Mediterranean [*Military*]

EUM............ Graduate School of Library Science, McGill University [*EDUCATSS*] [*UTLAS symbol*]

EUMABOIS... Comite Europeen des Constructeurs de Machines a Bois [*European Committee of Woodworking Machinery Manufacturers*] (EAIO)

EUM-AFTN ... European Mediterranean Aeronautical Fixed Telecommunications Network (PDAA)

EUMAPRINT... European Committee of Associations of Printing and Paper Converting Machinery (EA)

EUMC........... Entraide Universitaire Mondial du Canada [*World University Service of Canada - WUSC*]

EUMC........... European Microwave Conference and Exhibition [*British*] (ITD)

EUMETSAT... European Meteorological Satellite (MCD)

EUMETSAT... European Organization for the Exploitation of Meteorological Satellites

EUMOTIV ..... European Association for the Study of Economic, Commercial, and Industrial Motivation [*Belgium*] (PDAA)

EUMR .... Emergency Unsatisfactory Material Report (MCD)

EUMS.......... European Union of Music Schools [*See also EMU*] (EA)

EUMT .... Europaeische Union Gegen den Missbrauch der Tiere [*European Union for the Prevention of Cruelty to Animals*] [*Switzerland*] (EAIO)

EUMV .... Euphorbia Mosaic Virus [*Plant pathology*]

EUN .... El Aaiun [*Morocco*] [*Airport symbol*] (AD)

EUN .... Electronic University Network [*TeleLearning Systems*] [*San Francisco, CA*] [*Computer science*]

Eun .... Eunuchus [*of Terence*] [*Classical studies*] (OCD)

EUN .... Laayoune [*Morocco*] [*Airport symbol*] (OAG)

EUN .... Library Technician Program, Niagara College [*EDUCATSS*] [*UTLAS symbol*]

EUN .... University of Newcastle, Newcastle-Upon-Tyne, England [*OCLC symbol*] (OCLC)

Eun .... Wynne's Eunomus [*A publication*] (DLA)

EUNET .... European UNIX Network [*Computer science*] (ACRL)

EUNICEF ..... European Command Nuclear Interface Element Fastbreak (MCD)

EUO .... Library Technician Program, Algonquin College [*EDUCATSS*] [*UTLAS symbol*]

EUP .... Eastern Upper Peninsula [*Michigan*]

EUP .... Edinburgh Paperback [*A publication*]

EUP .... Edinburgh University Press [*Publisher*] [*Scotland*]

EUP .... Electric Utility Pump

EUP .... English Universities Press

EUP .... Environmental Use Permit (HGAA)

EUP .... Equipment Upgrade Program [*Army*]

EUP .... Estimated Unit Price (MCD)

Eup .... Eupolis [*Fifth century BC*] [*Classical studies*] (OCD)

EUP .... Europa Petroleum [*Vancouver Stock Exchange symbol*]

EUP .... Experimental Use Permit [*Environmental Protection Agency*]

EUPA .... European Union for the Protection of Animals (PDAA)

EuPC........... European Plastics Converters [*Belgium*] (EAIO)

EUPE........... European Union for Packaging and the Environment [*EEC*] (PDAA)

EUPEPTIC .... Evaluation of Unitary Programs for Effecting Plural Tasks in Index Construction (NITA)

EUPH .... Euphonium [*Musical instrument*]

EUPH .... Euphonix, Inc. [*NASDAQ symbol*] (SAG)

EUPHEM ...... Euphemism (ROG)

Euphnx......... Euphonix, Inc. [*Associated Press*] (SAG)
EUPJ............ Experimental Underwater Pump Jet
EUPRAC....... European Public Relations Advisory Committee
EUPREN...... European Primate Resources Network
EUPRISO...... European Union of Public Relations - International Service Organization [*See also UERP*] (EAIO)
EUPSA........ European Union of Paediatric Surgical Associations (PDAA)
EUQ .... John Abbott College Library [*EDUCATSS*] [*UTLAS symbol*]
EUR .... Electrically Transmitted Unsatisfactory Report
EUR .... Emergency Unsatisfactory Report [*Military*] (AFM)
EUR .... Engineering Unsatisfactory Report [*Military*] (AFIT)
EUR .... Equipment Unsatisfactory Report
EUR .... Eureka [*Nevada*] [*Seismograph station code, US Geological Survey*] (SEIS)
EUR .... Eureka, MT [*Location identifier FAA*] (FAAL)
Eur............. Euripides [*Fifth century BC*] [*Classical studies*] (OCD)
EUR .... Eurocan Ventures Ltd. [*Vancouver Stock Exchange symbol*]
Eur............. Eurochord [*Record label*] [*France*]
EUR .... Eurojet SA [*Spain ICAO designator*] (FAAC)
EUR .... Europe [*or European*] (AFM)
Eur............. Europe (VRA)
Eur............. Europe (AAGC)
Eur............. European (AAGC)
EUR .... European Region [*USTTA*] (TAG)
EUR .... Library Technician Program, Red River Community College [*EDUCATSS*] [*UTLAS symbol*]
e-ur-- .... USSR [*Union of Soviet Socialist Republics*] [*MARC geographic area code Library of Congress*] (LCCP)
EURA .... European Renderers Association (EAIO)
EURABANK... European-American Bank [*Databank on activities of non-US banks*] (NITA)
EURAC......... European Requirements and Army Capabilities (AABC)
EurACS .... European Association of Classification Societies (EAIO)
EURAFRICA... Europe and Africa
EURAG........ Federation Europeenne des Personnes Agees [*European Federation for the Welfare of the Elderly*] (EAIO)
e-ur-ai .... Armenian Soviet Socialist Republic [*MARC geographic area code Library of Congress*] (LCCP)
EURAILPASS... European Railway Passenger [*Ticket*]
e-ur-aj .... Azerbaijan Soviet Socialist Republic [*MARC geographic area code Library of Congress*] (LCCP)
EURAL .... European Air Lines
EURALARM... Association des Constructeurs Europeens de Systemes d'Alarme Incendie et Vol [*Association of European Manufacturers of Fire and Intruder Alarm Systems*] (EAIO)
EURAM .... European Research on Advanced Materials
EUR ANP .... European Air Navigation Plan [*ICAO*] (DA)
Eur Arb .... European Arbitration [*A publication*] (DLA)
EURAS .... Association Europeenne l'Anodisation [*European Anodisers' Association*] (EA)
EURASAFRICA... Europe, Asia, and Africa
EURASAP..... European Association for the Science of Air Pollution (EAIO)
EURASIP...... European Association for Signal Processing (EAIO)
Eur Ass Arb... European Assurance Arbitration [*1872-75*] [*A publication*] (DLA)
EURATOM.... European Atomic Energy Community [*Also, EAEC*]
e-ur-bw........ Belorussian Soviet Socialist Republic [*MARC geographic area code Library of Congress*] (LCCP)
e-urc-........... Central Black Soil Region, RSFSR [*MARC geographic area code Library of Congress*] (LCCP)
EURCO......... European Composite Unit [*European Economic Community*]
EURCOM....... European Command [*Military*]
Eur Conslt Ass Deb... Council of Europe, Debates of the Consultative Assembly [*A publication*] (DLA)
EURDA........ Etudes d'Urbanisme de Developpement et d'Amenagement [*du Territoire*]
e-ure- .... East Siberian Region, RSFSR [*MARC geographic area code Library of Congress*] (LCCP)
EUREAU....... Union des Associations des Distributeurs d'Eau de Pays Membres des Communautes Europeennes [*Union of the Water Supply Associations from Countries of the European Communities*] (EAIO)
EURECA....... European Retrievable Carrier [*Space shuttle experiment*]
EURED......... European Unified Research on Educational Development (AIE)
EuReDatA.... European Reliability Data Association
EUREKA...... European Advanced Technology Programme [*British*]
EUREKA...... European Research Cooperation Agency [*Non-defense research study group including eighteen European countries*]
EUREKA...... Evaluation of Uranium Resources and Economic Analysis [*Department of Energy*] (GFGA)
EUREL .... Association Europeenne des Reserves Naturelles Libres [*European Association for Free Nature Reserves*] [*Inactive*] (EAIO)
EUREL .... Convention of National Societies of Electrical Engineers of Western Europe (EAIO)
EUREMAIL ... Conference Permanente de l'Industrie Europeenne de Produits Emailles
e-ur-er........ Estonian Soviet Socialist Republic [*MARC geographic area code Library of Congress*] (LCCP)
EUREX .... Enriched Uranium Extraction (PDAA)
EURF .... Experience Usage Replacement Factor [*Navy*]
e-url- .... Far Eastern Region, RSFSR [*MARC geographic area code Library of Congress*] (LCCP)
EUR FCB ..... European Frequency Coordinating Body [*ICAO*] (DA)
e-ur-gs........ Georgian Soviet Socialist Republic [*MARC geographic area code Library of Congress*] (LCCP)

EURIM .... European Conference on Research into Management of Information (NITA)
EURIM .... European Conference on Research into the Management of Information Systems and Libraries (PDAA)
EURIMA ...... European Insulation Manufacturers Association (PDAA)
EURING....... European Union for Bird Ringing [*Europe*] (EERA)
EURIPA........ European Information Industry Association [*Formerly, European Information Providers Association*] [*Information retrieval*] (IID)
EURIPA........ European Information Providers Association (NITA)
EURIS .... European Information Service [*Belgium*] (NITA)
e-urk-.......... Caucasus [*MARC geographic area code Library of Congress*] (LCCP)
e-ur-kg........ Kirghiz Soviet Socialist Republic [*MARC geographic area code Library of Congress*] (LCCP)
e-ur-kz........ Kazakh Soviet Socialist Republic [*MARC geographic area code Library of Congress*] (LCCP)
e-url- .... Central Region, RSFSR [*MARC geographic area code Library of Congress*] (LCCP)
Eur L Dig .... European Law Digest [*A publication*] (DLA)
e-ur-li .... Lithuanian Soviet Socialist Republic [*MARC geographic area code Library of Congress*] (LCCP)
Eur L Newsl... European Law Newsletter [*A publication*] (DLA)
Eur L Rev ... European Law Review [*A publication*] (DLA)
e-ur-lv .... Latvian Soviet Socialist Republic [*MARC geographic area code Library of Congress*] (LCCP)
e-ur-mv....... Moldavian Soviet Socialist Republic [*MARC geographic area code Library of Congress*] (LCCP)
e-urn- .... Northwestern Region, RSFSR [*MARC geographic area code Library of Congress*] (LCCP)
EURNAVFACENGCOM... European Division Naval Facilities Engineering Command
e-uro- .... Soviet Central Asia [*MARC geographic area code Library of Congress*] (LCCP)
EUROAVIA ... Association of European Aeronautical and Astronautical Students (PDAA)
EUROBA....... European Professional Fair for Industry and Handicraft of Bakery, Confectionery,Pastry, Biscuits, Chocolate, and Ice Cream Making
EUROBASE... European Database [*Databank on election results*] (NITA)
EUROBAT.... Association of European Battery Manufacturers (EA)
EUROBIT...... European Association of Manufacturers of Business Machines and Data Processing Equipment [*Frankfurt, Federal Republic of Germany*] (EAIO)
EUROBITUME... European Bitumen Association (EA)
EUROBRAZ... European Brazilian Bank
EUROBUILD... European Organization for the Promotion of New Techniques and Methods in Building (EA)
EUROCAE..... European Organization for Civil Aviation Electronics [*France*] (PDAA)
EUROCAT..... European Registry of Congenital Abnormalities and Twins
EUROCEAN... European Oceanic Association [*Monaco, Monaco*] (EAIO)
EUROCENTRES... Foundation for European Language and Educational Centres (EA)
EURO CHEMIC... European Company for the Chemical Processing of Irradiated Fuels (DS)
EUROCHOR... Arbeitsgemeinschaft Europaeischer Chorverbaende [*European Choral Association - ECA*] (EA)
EUROCLAMP... European Clamping Tools Association [*EC*] (ECED)
EUROCOM .... European Communications
EUROCOM ... Union Europeenne des Negociants en Combustibles [*European Fuel Merchants Union*]
EUROCOMP... European Computing Congress
EUROCOMSAT... European Consortium Communications Satellite (MCD)
EUROCONTROL... European Organization for the Safety of Air Navigation
EURO COOP... Communaute Europeenne des Cooperatives de Consommateurs [*European Consumers' Cooperation Committee*] [*Common Market*]
EUROCOOP... European Commmunity of Cooperative Societies (PDAA)
EUROCOPI ... European Computer Program Information Centre [*Databank*] (NITA)
EUROCOR.... European Congress on Metallic Corrosion (PDAA)
EUROCORD... Federation des Industries de Ficellerie et Corderie de l'Europe Occidentale [*Federation of Western European Rope and Twine Industries*] (EA)
EUROCOTON... Comite des Industries du Coton et des Fibres Connexes de la CEE [*Committee of the Cotton Industries of the European Economic Community*] (PDAA)
EuroCr .... Europa Cruises Corp. [*Associated Press*] (SAG)
EURODICAUTOM... European Automated Dictionary
EURODIDAC... European Association of Manufacturers and Distributors of Education Materials (PDAA)
EURODOC.... European Documentation [*Research Service*]
EUROFAR .... European Future Advanced Rotorcraft (MCD)
EuroFd .... [*The*] Europe Fund [*Associated Press*] (SAG)
EUROFEDOP... European Federation of Employees in Public Services (EAIO)
EUROFER.... Association of European Steel Producers (PDAA)
EUROFER.... European Confederation of Iron and Steel Industries [*EC*] (ECED)
EUROFEU..... Comite Europeen des Constructeurs de Materiels d'Incendie et de Secours [*European Committee of the Manufacturers of Fire Protection and Safety Equipment and Fire Fighting Vehicles*] (EAIO)
EURO-FIET... Organisation Regionale Europeenne de la Federation Internationale des Employes, Techniciens et Cadres [*European Regional Organization of the International Federation of Commercial, Clerical, Professional and Technical Employees*] [*EC*] (ECED)
EUROFINAS... European Federation of Finance Houses Association [*Belgium*] (PDAA)
EUROFORGE... European Committee of Forging and Stamping Industries (EAIO)
EUROFUEL... Societe Europeene de Fabrication de Combustibles a Base d'Eranium pour Reacteursa Eau Legere [*France*] (PDAA)

EUROGLACES...   Association des Industries de Glaces Alimentaires de la CEE [*Association of the Ice Cream Industries of the European Economic Community*]

EUROGROPA...   Union des Distributeurs de Papiers et Cartons [*European Union of Paper, Board, and Packaging Wholesalers*]   (PDAA)

EUROGYPSUM...   Working Community of the European Gypsum Industry   (EAIO)

EURO-HKG...   European High Temperature Nuclear Power Stations Society   (EAIO)

Eurohorc...   European Heads of Research Councils

EuroISDN.....   European Integrated Services Digital Network [*Telecommunications*]   (ECON)

Eurolaw Com Intel...   Eurolaw Commercial Intelligence [*A publication*]   (DLA)

EUROLOC ....   Locate in Europe Information Retrieval System [*University of Strathclyde*] [*Glasgow, Scotland*] [*Information service or system*]   (IID)

EUROM........   European Federation of Optical and Precision Instruments Industry [*EC*]   (ECED)

EUROM........   European Read Only Memory   (NITA)

EUROMAISIERS...   Groupement des Associations des Maisiers des Pays de la CEE [*Group of the Maize Processors Associations in the European Economic Community Countries*] [*Brussels, Belgium*]

EUROMALT...   Comite de Travail des Malteries de la CEE [*Working Committee of European Economic Community Malters*]

EUROMAP....   European Committee of Machinery Manufacturers for Plastics and Rubber Industries [*EC*]   (ECED)

EUROMART...   European Common Market

EUROMAT...   Federation of European Coin Machine Associations [*EC*]   (ECED)

EUROMECH...   European Mechanics Colloquia   (PDAA)

EUROMECH...   European Mechanics Committee [*ICSU*]

EUROMICRO...   European Association for Microprocessing and Microprogramming   (PDAA)

EUROMIL.....   Europaeische Organisation der Militarverbande [*European Organization of Military Associations*]   (EAIO)

EUROMOT....   European Committee of Associations of Manufacturers of Internal Combustion Engines   (EA)

EUROMPAP...   European Committee of Machinery Manufacturers for the Plastics and Rubber Industries   (PDAA)

EURONAD....   Eurogroup Committee of National Armaments Directors

EURONEM....   European Association of Netting Manufacturers   (EA)

EURONET.....   European On-Line Information Network [*Commission of the European Communities*] [*Information service or system*]   (IID)

EURONET-DIANE...   European Network - Direct Information Access Network for Europe [*Computer science*]   (HGAA)

EuroPACE ....   European Programme of Advanced Continuing Education

EUROPEC...   European Offshore Petroleum Conference and Exhibition   (PDAA)

EUROPECHE...   Association des Organisations Nationales d'Entreprises de Peche de la CEE [*Association of National Organizations of Fishing Enterprises in the European Economic Community*]

EUROPHOT...   Association Europeenne des Photographes Professionnels [*European Association of Professional Photographers*]

EUROPLANT...   European Plantmakers Committee   (EA)

EUROPLATE...   European Registration Plate Association   (EA)

EUROPMAISERS...   Groupement des Associations des Maisiers des Pays de la CEE [*Group of Associations of Maize Processors of EEC Countries*]   (EAIO)

EUROPMI.....   Comite de Liaison des Petites et Moyennes Entreprises Industrielles des Pays de la CEE [*Liaison Committee for Small and Medium-Sized Industrial Enterprises in the EEC*] [*Brussels, Belgium*]   (EAIO)

EUROPREFAB...   European Organization for the Promotion of Prefabrication and other Industralized Building   (PDAA)

EUROPS......   European Air Operations Staff [*Military*]

Europ TS...   European Treaty Series [*Council of Europe*] [*A publication*]   (DLA)

EUROPUMP...   Comite Europeen des Constructeurs de Pompes [*European Committee of Pump Manufacturers*]   (EAIO)

EUROPUMP...   European Committee of Pump Manufacturers   (EA)

EUROPUR ....   Association Europeenne des Fabricants de Blocs de Mousse Souple de Polyurethane [*European Association of Flexible Foam Block Manufacturers*]   (EAIO)

EURORAD....   European Association of Manufacturers of Radiators   (EA)

EUROSAC ....   European Federation of Manufacturers of Multi-wall Paper Sacks [*France*]   (PDAA)

EUROSAC ....   Federation Europeenne des Fabricants de Sacs en Papier a Grande Contenance [*European Federation of Multiwall Paper Sacks Manufacturers*]   (EAIO)

EUROSAM....   European Surface-to-Air Missile [*NATO*]

EUROSAT....   European Application Satellite Systems

EUROSID ....   European Side Impact Dummy [*Automotive engineering*]

EUROSPACE...   European Industrial Space Study Group

EUROSTAT...   [*The*] European Static Protection and Shielding Exhibition [*British*]   (ITD)

EUROSTAT...   Statistical Office of the European Communities [*Commission of the European Communities*]   (EAIO)

EUROSTEP...   European Association of Users of Satellites in Training and Education Programmes   (AIE)

EUROSTEST...   European Association of Testing Institutions   (PDAA)

EUROTALC...   Association Scientifique de l'Industrie Europeenne du Talc [*Scientific Association of European Talc Industry*]   (EAIO)

EUROTECNET...   European Technical Network [*EC*]   (ECED)

EUROTELCAB...   European Conference of Associations of Telecommunications Cables Industries [*EC*]   (ECED)

EUROTEST...   European Association of Testing Institutions [*Belgium*]   (PDAA)

EUROTOX ....   Comite Europeen Permanent de Recherches sur la Protection des Populations contreles Risques de Toxicite a Long Terme [*Permanent European Research Committee for the Protection of the Population against the Hazards of Chronic Toxicity*]

EUROTRANS...   European Committee of Associations of Manufacturers of Gears and Transmission Parts [*EC*]   (ECED)

EUROVENT...   European Committee of Ventilating Equipment Manufacturers   (PDAA)

EUROVISION...   European Television

e-urp-   Povolzhskii Region, RSFSR [*MARC geographic area code Library of Congress*]   (LCCP)

Eur Parl Deb...   European Parliamentary Assembly Debates [*A publication*]   (DLA)

Eur Parl Doc...   European Parliament Working Documents [*A publication*]   (DLA)

Eur Parl Docs...   European Parliament Working Documents [*A publication*]   (DLA)

EURPISO...   European Union of Public Relations - International Service Organization [*Hungary*]   (EA)

e-urr-   North Caucasus, RSFSR [*MARC geographic area code Library of Congress*]   (LCCP)

e-ur-ru ....   Russian SFSR [*MARC geographic area code Library of Congress*]   (LCCP)

e-urs-..........   Siberia [*MARC geographic area code Library of Congress*]   (LCCP)

EUR/SV/LDO...   European Space Vehicle Launcher Development Organization   (MCD)

e-ur-ta ....   Tajik Soviet Socialist Republic [*MARC geographic area code Library of Congress*]   (LCCP)

e-ur-tk ....   Turkmen Soviet Socialist Republic [*MARC geographic area code Library of Congress*]   (LCCP)

Eur TL........   European Transport Law [*Belgium*] [*A publication*]   (DLA)

EURTOA......   European Technical Operations Area [*Military*]

Eur Trans L...   European Transport Law [*Belgium A publication*]   (DLA)

Eur Transp L...   European Transport Law [*Belgium A publication*]   (DLA)

e-uru- ....   Ural Region, RSFSR [*MARC geographic area code Library of Congress*]   (LCCP)

e-ur-un ....   Ukrainian Soviet Socialist Republic [*MARC geographic area code Library of Congress*]   (LCCP)

e-ur-uz ....   Uzbek Soviet Socialist Republic [*MARC geographic area code Library of Congress*]   (LCCP)

e-urv-..........   Volgo-Viatskii Region, RSFSR [*MARC geographic area code Library of Congress*]   (LCCP)

e-urw-..........   West Siberian Region, RSFSR [*MARC geographic area code Library of Congress*]   (LCCP)

EurWtFd....   European Warrant Fund [*Associated Press*]   (SAG)

EURYB ....   Europa Year Book [*A publication*]

Eur YB ....   European Yearbook [*A publication*]   (DLA)

EURYDICE...   Education Information Network in the European Community [*Commission of the European Communities*] [*Belgium Information service or system*]   (IID)

EUS.............   Eastern United States

EUS.............   Endoscopic Ultrasonography [*Medicine*]

Eus.............   Eusebius [*Ecclesiastical historian, c. 260-340AD*] [*Classical studies*]   (OCD)

EUS.............   External Urethral Sphincter [*Anatomy*]

EUS.............   Library Techniques, Seneca College [*EDUCATSS*] [*UTLAS symbol*]

EUSA.........   Eagle USA Airfreight [*NASDAQ symbol*]   (TTSB)

EUSA.........   Eagle USA Airfreight, Inc. [*NASDAQ symbol*]   (SAG)

EUSA.........   Eighth United States Army

EUSAK ....   Eighth United States Army in Korea

EUSAMA......   European Shock Absorber Manufacturers Association   (PDAA)

EUSAR ....   Eighth United States Army Rear

EUSC ....   Effective United States Control Fleet

EUSEB ....   European Union of Societies for Experimental Biology

EUSEB ....   Eusebius [*Ecclesiastical historian, c. 260-340AD*] [*Classical studies*]   (ROG)

EUSEC ....   Conference des Societes d'Ingenieurs de l'Europe Occidental et des Etats-Unis d'Amerique [*Conference of Engineering Societies of Western Europe and the United States of America*]

EUSEC ....   European Communications Security and Evaluation Agency of the Military Committee, London [*US Army*]   (AABC)

EUSFR ....   Encyclopedia of US Foreign Relations [*A publication*]

EUSIDIC.......   European Association of Information Services [*Formerly, European Association of Scientific Information Dissemination Centers*] [*Information service or system*]   (IID)

EUSIREF ......   European Association of Science Information Referral Centres   (NITA)

EUSIREF ......   European Scientific Information Referral [*EUSIDIC*] [*Information service or system*]   (IID)

EUSIREF ......   European Scientific Information Retrieval Working Group   (NITA)

EUSJA.........   European Union of Science Journalists Associations   (EAIO)

EUSM.........   European Union of Social Medicine   (EA)

EUSSG ....   European Union for the Scientific Study of Glass   (EA)

EUT.............   Equipment under Test

Eut.............   Euterpe [*Record label*]

EUT.............   Faculty of Library and Information Science, University of Toronto [*EDUCATSS*] [*UTLAS symbol*]

EUTE.........   Early User Test and Evaluation [*Army*]

EUTE.........   Early User Test and Experimentation [*DoD*]

EUTECA.......   European Technical Caramel Association [*EC*]   (ECED)

EUTELSAT...   European Telecommunications Satellite [*Agency*]   (BARN)

EUTELSAT...   European Telecommunications Satellite Organization [*France Telecommunications*]

Euthphr........   Euthyphro [*of Plato*] [*Classical studies*]   (OCD)

EUTO ....   European Union of Tourist Officers   (EAIO)

EUU ....   Faculty of Library Science, University of British Columbia [*EDUCATSS*] [*UTLAS symbol*]

EUU ....   Smithfield, NC [*Location identifier FAA*]   (FAAL)

EUUG ....   European UNIX User Group [*Computer science*]

EUV.............   Energetic Ultra-Violet

EUV.............   Expected Utility Value

EUV.............   Extreme Ultraviolet

EUV.............   Extreme Ultraviolet LASER [*Medicine*]   (DAVI)

EUV............	Library Technician Program, Vancouver Community College [*EDUCATSS*] [*UTLAS symbol*]
EUVE..........	Extreme Ultraviolet Explorer
EUVEPRO....	European Vegetable Protein Federation (EAIO)
EUVEX........	Extreme Ultraviolet Explorer (MCD)
EUVP	Extreme Ultraviolet Photometer (MCD)
EUVSH........	Equivalent Ultraviolet Solar Hour [*NASA*]
EUVT..........	Extended Ultraviolet Transmission
EUVT..........	Extreme Ultraviolet Telescope
EUW............	Eureka [*Washington*] [*Seismograph station code, US Geological Survey*] (SEIS)
EUW............	Euroflight Sweden, AB [*ICAO designator*] (FAAC)
EUW............	European Union of Women [*Stockholm, Sweden*]
EUW............	School of Library and Information Science, University of Western Ontario [*EDUCATSS*] [*UTLAS symbol*]
EUWEP	European Union of Wholesale Eggs, Egg-Products, Poultry and Game [*EC*] (ECED)
EUWG	Energy Use Working Group [*Australia*]
EUX............	European Expidite [*Belgium ICAO designator*] (FAAC)
EUX............	Saint Eustatius [*Antilles*] [*Airport symbol*] (OAG)
EUYCD	European Union of Young Christian Democrats [*Belgium*] (EY)
EUZ............	Euroair Transport Ltd. [*British ICAO designator*] (FAAC)
EV	Atlantic Southeast [*ICAO designator*] (AD)
EV	Earned Value
EV	Economic Value [*Accounting*]
EV	Educt Vent
EV	Efferent Vessel [*Anatomy*]
EV	Efficient Vulcanizing [*Rubber processing*]
EV	Eigenvalue [*Mathematics*]
EV	Eingang Vorbehalten [*Rights reserved, i.e., copyrighted*] [*German*]
EV	Electric Vehicle
EV	Electronic Viewfinder [*Photography*]
eV	Electron Volt
EV	Emergency Vehicle [*Medicine*] (DAVI)
EV	Emotional Violence
EV	Enclosed and Ventilated (IAA)
EV	Energy Victoria [*Australia*]
EV	Engineer Volunteers [*British military*] (DMA)
EV	English Version
EV	English Viscount (ROG)
EV	Enterprise Value [*Finance*] (ECON)
EV	Entrained Air Volume
EV	Environmental Viewpoints [*A publication*]
EV	Erdelyi Vilagszovetseg [*Transylvanian World Federation - TWF*] (EAIO)
EV	Ere Vulgaire [*Common Era*] [*Freemasonry*] [*French*] (ROG)
EV	Errata Volume [*Dialog*] [*Searchable field*] [*Information service or system*] (NITA)
EV	Error Voltage [*Electricity*] (IAA)
EV	Escort Vessel [*Enemy*]
EV	Esophageal Varices [*Medicine*]
EV	EuroVision [*Later, SGA*] (EA)
EV	Evaluate
EV	Evangelist
Ev	Evangile [*Paris*] [*A publication*] (BJA)
EV	Evaporator Vessel (NRCH)
EV	Evening
EV	[*The*] Everett Railroad Co. [*AAR code*]
ev	Eversion [*Medicine*] (DAVI)
EV	Everted [*or Eversion*] [*Medicine*]
EV	Every
Ev	Evidence [*Legal term*] (DLA)
EV	Evoked Response [*Neurophysiology*] (MAE)
EV	Evolution
EV	Exhaust Valve [*Nuclear energy*] (NRCH)
EV	Expected Value [*Statistics*]
EV	Expendable Vehicle (MCD)
EV	Experimental Version (SDI)
EV	Explosive Valve (KSC)
EV	Exposure Value [*System*] [*Photography*]
EV	Extracellular Virus
EV	Extravascular [*Anatomy*]
EV	Extravehicular (MCD)
EV	Exudative Vitreoretinopathy [*Ophthalmology*]
EV	Ex Voto [*In Fulfillment of a Vow*] [*Latin*]
ev----	Scandinavia [*MARC geographic area code Library of Congress*] (LCCP)
EV1S	Edge Vee One Side [*Lumber*] (DAC)
EVA............	Early Valve Actuation [*or Actuator*] [*Nuclear energy*] (NRCH)
EVA............	Earned Value Analysis (NASA)
EVA............	Economic Value Added
EVA............	Einzelspaltrohrversuchsanlage [*Hydrogen generating reactor*]
EVA............	Electric Vehicle Association of Great Britain Ltd. (BI)
EVA............	Electronically Variable Attenuator (NITA)
EVA............	Electronic Velocity Analyzer
EVA............	Electronic Voice Alert [*Automotive engineering*]
EVA............	Electronic Vote Analysis [*Election poll*]
EVA............	Elevation Versus Amplitude (SAA)
EVA............	Engineer Vice-Admiral [*British*]
EVA............	English Vineyards Association (DBA)
EVA............	English Volleyball Association
EVA............	Error Volume Analysis [*Computer science*] (IBMDP)
EVA............	Escort Vessel Administration [*World War II*]
EVA............	Esperantlingva Verkista Asocio [*Esperanto Writers Association - EWA*] [*Netherlands*] (EA)
EVA............	Essex Volunteer Artillery [*British military*] (DMA)
EVA............	Ethylene-Vinyl Acetate [*Copolymer*] [*Organic chemistry*]
EVA............	Ethyl Violet-Azide [*Broth*] [*Microbiology*]
EVA............	Europaeische Vereinigung der Allgemeinarzte [*European Union of General Practitioners*] (EAIO)
EVA............	European Vaccine Against AIDS [*Acquired Immune Deficiency Syndrome*] [*Medicine*]
EVA............	Evadale, TX [*Location identifier FAA*] (FAAL)
EVA............	Extravehicular Activity [*Aerospace*]
EVA............	Extravehicular Astronaut (SAA)
EVAA	Electric Vehicle Association of the Americas (EA)
EVAC..........	Electric Vehicle Association of Canada
EVAC..........	Ethylene-Vinyl Acetate [*Copolymer*] [*Organic chemistry*]
EVAC..........	Etoposide (VP-16), Vincristine, Adriamycin, Cyclophosphamide [*Antineoplastic drug regimen*]
EVAC..........	Evacuation (AFM)
EVAC..........	Evacuator (MSA)
EVACS	Evacuation Hospital Semimobile (VNW)
EVACSHIP....	Evacuation Ship [*Navy*] (NVT)
EVACWP	Exotic Vertebrate Animals Control Working Party [*Australia*]
EVADE	Evaluation of Air Defense Effectiveness
EVAF..........	International Association for Business Research and Corporate Development [*West Wickham, Kent, England*] (EAIO)
Ev Ag	Evans on Agency [*A publication*] (DLA)
EVAL..........	Earth Viewing Applications Laboratory (MCD)
EVAL..........	Ethyl Vinyl Alcohol (PDAA)
EVAL..........	Evaluate [*or Evaluation or Evaluator*] (AFM)
EVAL..........	Evaluation
EVAN..........	Electronic Verification of Account Number [*Social Security*]
EVAN	Evangelical [*or Evangelist*]
Evan	Evangile [*Paris*] [*A publication*] (BJA)
EVAN	Evans, Inc. [*NASDAQ symbol*] (NQ)
EVAN-G.......	End Violence Against the Next Generation (EA)
EVANG	Evangelical [*or Evangelist*]
evang	Evangelist (VRA)
Evans..........	Evans, Inc. [*Associated Press*] (SAG)
Evans..........	Evans' King's Bench Reports [*1756-88*] [*A publication*] (DLA)
Evans..........	Lord Mansfield's Decisions [*1799-1814*] [*England*] [*A publication*] (DLA)
EvansSys	Evans Systems, Inc. [*Associated Press*] (SAG)
EVAP..........	Evaporate (KSC)
EVAP..........	Evaporator
EVAPD	Evaporated (IAA)
EVAPN	Evaporation (IAA)
EVAPTR	Evaporator [*Freight*]
E-VAR	Environment Variable [*Computer science*] (PCM)
EVARS	Experimental Vehicle for Avionics Research (MCD)
EVAS..........	Enhanced Vortex Advisory System [*FAA*] (TAG)
EVAS..........	Extravehicular Activity System (SSD)
EVATA........	Electronic-Visual-Auditory Training Aid
EVATA........	Extravehicular Activity Translational Aid (NASA)
EVATMI.......	European Vinyl Asbestos Tile Manufacturers Institute (PDAA)
EVATP........	Experimental Volunteer Army Training Program (RDA)
EVATRON.....	Eccentric Variable-Angle Thermionic Rheostat
EVB............	Examining and Validating Body (AIE)
EVB............	Extruded Vinyl Bumper
EVBM..........	Expected Value Business Model (IAA)
EVC............	Ecological Vegetation Class (EERA)
EVC............	Educational Video Corp.
EVC............	Electric Vehicle Council [*Defunct*] (EA)
EVC............	Electronic Visual Communications (DNAB)
EVC............	Endatcom Ventures [*Vancouver Stock Exchange symbol*]
EVC............	Engineer Volunteer Corps [*British*]
EVC............	Error Vector Computer (NG)
EVC............	Executive Volunteer Corps
EVC............	Extravehicular Communications [*Aerospace*] (NASA)
EVC............	Extravehicular Communicator [*NASA*] (KSC)
e-vc--	Vatican City [*MARC geographic area code Library of Congress*] (LCCP)
EVCA..........	European Venture Capital Association
EVCB..........	Event Control Block [*Computer science*] (EECA)
EVCC..........	Electric Vehicle Capsulated Contact [*Automotive electrical systems*]
EVCC..........	Ex-Vessel Core Catcher [*Nuclear energy*] (NRCH)
EVCE..........	Evidence
EVCI..........	Expected Value of Clinical Information [*Medicine*] (DMAA)
EVCI..........	Ethylene-Vinyl Chloride [*Fire-retardant resin*] [*Organic chemistry*]
EVC-O.........	Electronic Vibration Cutoff [*Aerospace*] (AAG)
EVCON........	Events Control [*Subsystem*] [*NASA*] (NASA)
EVCS..........	Extravehicular Communications System [*NASA*]
EVCS..........	Extruded Vinyl Chamfer Strip
EVCT..........	Extravehicular Crew Transfer [*NASA*] (MCD)
EVCTD	Extravehicular Crew Transfer Device [*NASA*] (KSC)
EVCU	Extravehicular Communications Umbilical [*Aerospace*] (MCD)
EVD............	Economische Voorlichtingsdienst [*Economic Information Service*] [*Information service or system*] (IID)
EVD............	Electrovacuum Drive
EVD............	Explosive Vapor Detector (DA)
EVD............	Extended Voluntary Departure [*Temporary status sometimes granted by the State Department as protection against deportation*]
EVD............	External Visual Display (MCD)
EVDE..........	External Visual Display Equipment [*Used in Apollo mission*] [*NASA*]
EVDF..........	Eugene V. Debs Foundation (EA)
EVDG..........	Electric Vehicle Development Group Ltd. [*British*]
EVDL..........	Electronic Variable Delay Line [*Automotive engineering*] (IAA)
EVDS..........	Electronic Visual Display Subsystem

EVDS	Explosive Vapor Detector Systems (MCD)
EVE	Air Evex GmbH [*Germany ICAO designator*] (FAAC)
EVE	Eagle Valley Environmentalists (EA)
EVE	Economic Verification Experiments [*Marine science*] (MSC)
EVE	Education, Volunteerism, Employment Opportunities
EVE	Einstein Viscosity Equation
EVE	Electric Vehicle Exposition (ADA)
EVE	Epoxy Vinyl Ester [*Plastics technology*]
EVE	Ethyl Vinyl Ether [*Organic chemistry*]
EVE	Evenes [*Norway*] [*Airport symbol*] (OAG)
EVE	Evening
EVE	Expert Vax Ethernet Interface [*Work station computer-network interface*] (NITA)
EVEA	Extravehicular Engineering Activity [*Aerospace*]
EVECW	Extravascular Extracellular Water [*Medicine*]
EVELYN.......	Employment of Very Low Yield Nuclear Weapons
EVEN	Evening (ROG)
EVEN	Evensong (ROG)
EVEN	EV Environmental [*NASDAQ symbol*] (TTSB)
EVEN	EV Environmental, Inc. [*NASDAQ symbol*] (SAG)
EV En..........	EV Environmental, Inc. [*Associated Press*] (SAG)
EV Env..........	EV Environmental, Inc. [*Associated Press*] (SAG)
EVENW	EV Environmental Wrrt'A' [*NASDAQ symbol*] (TTSB)
EVER..........	Everglades National Park
EVER..........	Evergreen Resources [*NASDAQ symbol*] (TTSB)
EVER.......	Evergreen Resources, Inc. [*NASDAQ symbol*] (NQ)
ever........	Eversion [*Medicine*] (DAVI)
Everen	Everen Capital Corp. [*Associated Press*] (SAG)
EverenC	Everen Capital Corp. [*Associated Press*] (SAG)
EverestRe	Everest Reinsurance Holdings, Inc. [*Associated Press*] (SAG)
EverJen....	Everest & Jennings International [*Associated Press*] (SAG)
EverMd	Everest Medical Corp. [*Associated Press*] (SAG)
Everybody's LM...	Everybody's Law Magazine [*A publication*] (DLA)
EVERY M	Everybody's Magazine [*A publication*] (ROG)
EVESR	ESADA [*Empire State Atomic Development Associates, Inc.*] Vallecitos Experimental Superheat Reactor
EVF	Electromagnetic Vibrating Feeder
EVF	Electronic Viewfinder [*Photography*] (WDMC)
EVF	Electro-Viscous Fluid [*Electrical engineering*]
EVF	Equipment Visibility File (NASA)
EVF	Extracellular Volume Fraction [*Hematology*]
EVFM	Ex-Vessel Flux Monitor [*Nuclear energy*] (NRCH)
EVG.............	Electric Vacuum Gyro
EVG.............	Electrostatic Vector Grid
EVG.............	Europaische Verteidigungsgemeinschaft [*European Defense Community*] [*German*] (BARN)
EVG.............	Evolving
evg.............	Evening (WDMC)
EVG.............	Evergold Resources [*Vancouver Stock Exchange symbol*]
EVG.............	Extravehicular Glove [*NASA*] (KSC)
EVGA	Extended Video Graphics Array (PCM)
EVGM	Evergreen Media Corp. [*NASDAQ symbol*] (SAG)
EVGM..........	Evergreen Media Corp'A' [*NASDAQ symbol*] (TTSB)
EVGMP	Evergreen Media $3.00 Cv Pfd [*NASDAQ symbol*] (TTSB)
EVGN	Evergreen Bancorp [*NASDAQ symbol*] (TTSB)
EVGN	Evergreen Bancorp, Inc. [*NASDAQ symbol*] (NQ)
EvgrM	Evergreen Media Corp. [*Associated Press*] (SAG)
EvgrMda	Evergreen Media Corp. [*Associated Press*] (SAG)
EvgrMed	Evergreen Media Corp. [*Associated Press*] (SAG)
EvgrnRs.......	Evergreen Resources, Inc. [*Associated Press*] (SAG)
EVH...........	Esophageal Varices Hemorrhage [*Medicine*]
EVHA	English Villages Housing Association (ECON)
EVHA	Europese Vereniging voor Haveninformatica [*European Port Data Processing Association*] [*Belgium*] (EA)
Ev Harr	Evans' Edition of Harris' Modern Entries [*A publication*] (DLA)
EVHM..........	Ex-Vessel Handling Machine [*Later, CLEM*] [*Nuclear energy*] (NRCH)
EVI..............	Cedar Crest and Muhlenberg Colleges, Allentown, PA [*OCLC symbol*] (OCLC)
EVI..............	Early Vendor Involvement Program [*Automotive engineering*]
EVI..............	Education Voucher Institute [*Defunct*] (EA)
EVI..............	Encapsulated Variable Inductor
EVI..............	Energy Ventures [*NYSE symbol*] (SAG)
EVI..............	Evergreen International Corp. [*Toronto Stock Exchange symbol*]
EVI..............	Evington, VA [*Location identifier FAA*] (FAAL)
EVIC..........	Electronic Vehicle Information Center [*Automotive engineering*]
EVID...........	Evidence
Evid...........	Evidences [*Paris*] [*A publication*] (BJA)
EVIF...........	Emergency Virus Isolation Facility [*National Cancer Institute*]
EVIL...........	Eastern Verbal Investigators League
EVIL...........	Elevation Versus Integrated Log
EVIL...........	Extensible Video Interactive Language [*Computer science*]
E VIN	E Vino [*In Wine*] [*Pharmacy*]
evisc...........	Evisceration [*Medicine*] (MAE)
EVIST........	Ethics and Values in Science and Technology [*National Science Foundation*]
E VIV DISC...	E Vivis Discessit [*Departed from Life*] [*Latin*] (BARN)
Ev Jud Pr...	Evans' Practice of the Supreme Court of Judicature [*A publication*] (DLA)
EVK.............	Ethyl Vinyl Ketone [*Organic chemistry*]
EVK.............	Evaluation Kit [*American Microsystems Inc.*] (NITA)
EVKI............	Europaische Vereinigung der Keramik-Industrie [*Europeean Federation of the Electro-Ceramic Industry*] (PDAA)
EvKoMoe	Evreiskii Kommunisticheskii Soiuz Molodezhi (BJA)
EVL.............	Cleveland, OK [*Location identifier FAA*] (FAAL)
EVL.............	Everyman's Library [*A publication*]

EVLSS........	Extravehicular Life Support System [*NASA*]
EVLTN.........	Evaluation (MSA)
EVLW	Extravascular Lung Water [*Medicine*]
EVM.............	Earth Viewing Module
EVM.............	Edatrexate, Vinblastine, Mutamycin [*Antineoplastic drug*] (CDI)
EVM.............	Electronic Voltmeter (IEEE)
EVM.............	Elektronno-Vychislitel'naya Mashina [*Electronic Calculating Machine*] [*Russian*]
EVM.............	Engine Vibration Monitor (MCD)
EVM.............	Errors-in-Variables Model [*Statistics*]
EVM.............	Evacuation Mission [*Air Force*]
EVM.............	Evasive Maneuvering
EVM.............	Eveleth, MN [*Location identifier FAA*] (FAAL)
EVM.............	Extended Virtual Machine
EVM.............	Exterior Vacuum Metallized (DICI)
EvM.............	Inscriptions of the Reigns of Evil-Merodach, Neriglissar, and Laborosoarchod (BJA)
EVMA..........	Expanded Virtual Machine Assist [*Computer science*] (MHDI)
EVMD..........	Everest Med [*NASDAQ symbol*] (TTSB)
EVMD..........	Everest Medical Corp. [*NASDAQ symbol*] (SAG)
Ev Md Pr	Evans' Maryland Practice [*A publication*] (DLA)
EVMS..........	Emil Verban Memorial Society (EA)
EVMU..........	Extravehicular Mobility Unit [*NASA*] (NASA)
EVN.............	Erevan [*Former USSR Airport symbol*] (OAG)
EVN.............	Evansville [*Diocesan abbreviation*] [*Indiana*] (TOCD)
EVN.............	Even Resources [*Vancouver Stock Exchange symbol*]
EVNG..........	Evangeline Railway Co. [*AAR code*]
EVNG..........	Evening
EVNGLCL.....	Evangelical
EVNGLST.....	Evangelist
EVNGLSTC....	Evangelstic
EVNNG........	Evening
EvnSut.........	Evans & Sutherland Computer Corp. [*Associated Press*] (SAG)
EVNT...........	Event
Evnwth.........	Evans Withycombe Residential, Inc. [*Associated Press*] (SAG)
EVO.............	East Liverpool, OH [*Location identifier FAA*] (FAAL)
EVO.............	Eisenbahn-Verkehrsordnung [*Germany*]
EVO.............	Electronic Variable Orifice [*Automotive engineering*]
EVO.............	Engineering Verification Order (MCD)
EVO.............	Extravehicular Operation [*Aerospace*]
EvObshchestKom...	Evreiskii Obshchestvennyi Komitet Pomoshchi Pogromlennym (BJA)
EVOC	Excerpta Medica Vocabulary [*Elsevier Science Publishers BV*] [*Netherlands Information service or system*] (CRD)
EVOH..........	Ethylene Vinyl Alcohol [*Plastics*]
EVOL..........	Evolution [*or Evolutionist*] (WDAA)
EVOL..........	Evolved
EVOM..........	Electronic Voltohmmeter (IEEE)
EVOP	European Volcanological Project
EVOP	Evaluation and Optimization
EVOP	Evolutionary Operation [*Statistical technique*]
EVOS	Electronic Variable-Orifice Steering
EVox	English Vox [*Record label*]
EVP.............	Electromagnetic Vector Potential [*Physics*] (BARN)
EVP.............	Electronic Voice Phenomena [*Parapsychology*]
EVP.............	Enhanced VERDIN [*Antijam Modem, Very-Low Frequency*] Processor [*Military*] (CAAL)
EVP.............	Evangelische Volkspartei der Schweiz [*Swiss Evangelical People's Party*] [*Political party*] (PPW)
EVP.............	Evangelische Volkspartij [*Evangelical People's Party*] [*Netherlands Political party*] (EY)
EVP.............	Evoked Visual Potential [*Neurophysiology*]
EVP.............	Executive Vice President
EVP.............	Exhaust Valve Position [*Automotive engineering*]
EVP.............	Extra Value Package [*Automotive marketing*]
EVPASSC	Electronic Variable Power-Assist Steering System Controller [*Automotive engineering*]
EVPD	Evaporated
EVPHI	Europese Vereniging voor Pediatrische Hematologie en Immunologie [*European Society for Paediatric Haematology and Immunology - ESPHI*] (EAIO)
EVPI...........	Expected Value of Perfect Information [*Statistics*]
Ev Pl	Evans on Pleading [*A publication*] (DLA)
Ev Poth.......	Evans' Translation of Pothier on Obligations [*A publication*] (DLA)
Ev Pr & Ag...	Evans on the Law of Principal and Agent [*A publication*] (DLA)
EVR.............	Electronic Video Recording [*or Recorder*] (NTCM)
EVR.............	Electronic Video Reproduction (IAA)
EVR.............	Everen Capital Corp. [*NYSE symbol*] (SAG)
EVR.............	Everest Resources Ltd. [*Vancouver Stock Exchange symbol*]
EVR.............	Evoked Response [*Neurology*] (DAVI)
EVR.............	Evoked Vascular Response [*Physiology*]
EVR.............	External Visual Reference [*Motion sickness*]
EVRC..........	Eton Volunteer Rifle Corps [*British military*] (DMA)
EVRD	Excellentissime Vestre Reverendissime Dominationis [*Of Your Most Excellent and Reverend Lordship*] [*Latin*] (ECON)
EVRGRN	Evergreen
EvrgrnB........	Evergreen Bancorp, Inc. [*Associated Press*] (SAG)
Ev RL..........	Evans' Road Laws of South Carolina [*A publication*] (DLA)
EVRLK	Ever-Lock
EVRM..........	Envirometrics, Inc. [*NASDAQ symbol*] (SAG)
EVRMW	Envirometrics Inc. Wrrt [*NASDAQ symbol*] (TTSB)
EVRO..........	EVRO Corp. [*NASDAQ symbol*] (TTSB)
EVRO	EVRO Financial Corp. [*Formerly, Envirosearch Corp.*] [*NASDAQ symbol*] (NQ)
EVRPrA........	Everen Cap 13.50%'A'Ex Pfd [*NYSE symbol*] (TTSB)

EVRV	Electronic Vacuum Regulator Valve [*Automotive engineering*]
EVS	Ecumenical Voluntary Service [*Defunct*]
EVs	Electric Vehicles (EERA)
EVS	Electronic Valve Specification (MCD)
EVS	Electronic Vision System [*Saab*] (NITA)
EVS	Electronic Voice Switching (AFM)
EVS	Electro-Optical Viewing System
EVS	Electro-Optical Visual Sensors [*Hughes Aircraft Co.*]
EVS	Electrovisual Sensors
EVS	Emergency Venting System
EVS	Endoscopic Variceal Sclerosis [*Medicine*]
EVS	Engine Vertical Scale
EVS	Enhanced VERDIN [*Antijam Modem, Very-Low Frequency*] System [*Military*] (CAAL)
EVS	Enhanced Videotex Service (LAIN)
EVS	Environmental Science (AABC)
EVS	Environment Visualization System [*Computer science*]
EVS	Equipment Visibility System (NASA)
EVS	Equi Ventures, Inc. [*Vancouver Stock Exchange symbol*]
EVS	Event Verification System [*Technology that encripts time and location on video recordings*]
EVS	Expected Value Saved
E-V-S	Expected Value-Variance-Skewness [*Statistics*]
EVS	Extravehicular Suit [*Aerospace*] (MCD)
EVS	Extravehicular System [*Aerospace*]
EVS	Extreme Value Statistics
EVS	Eye-Voice Span
EVSA	Electronic Variable Shock Absorber [*Automotive engineering*]
EVSC	Extravehicular Suit Communications [*Aerospace*]
EVSD	Electronic Vision Systems Development
EVSD	Energy-Variant Sequential Detection (CET)
EvSektsiia	Evreiskaia Sektsiia (BJA)
EVSI	Evans Systems [*NASDAQ symbol*] (TTSB)
EVSI	Evans Systems, Inc. [*NASDAQ symbol*] (SAG)
EVSI	Expected Value of Sample Information [*Statistics*]
EVSN	Elbit Vision Systems Ltd. [*NASDAQ symbol*] (SAG)
EVSR	Exhaust Valve Seat Recession [*Automotive engineering*]
EVSS	Extravehicular Space Suit [*Aerospace*] (MCD)
EVST	Ex-Vessel Storage Tank [*Nuclear energy*] (NRCH)
Ev Stat	Evans' Collection of Statutes [*A publication*] (DLA)
EVSTC	Extravehicular Suit Telemetry Communications [*Aerospace*]
EVSU	Extravehicular Space Unit [*Aerospace*] (MCD)
EVT	Earth Venus Transit [*Aerospace*]
EVT	Economic Investment Trust Ltd. [*Toronto Stock Exchange symbol*]
EVT	Education and Vocational Training [*British military*] (DMA)
EVT	Effective Visual Transmission (NATG)
EVT	Elasticity, Viscosity, and Thixotropy
EVT	Electronic Valve Timing [*Automobile engine design*]
EVT	Emergency Veterinary Tag
EVT	End Viewing Tube
EVT	Engineering Verification Test
EVT	Equiviscous Temperature [*Chemical engineering*] (IAA)
EVT	Evaluation Vector Table
EVT	Expect Vector To [*Aviation*] (FAAC)
EVT	Extravehicular Transfer [*NASA*] (KSC)
EVTC	Environmental Technologies [*NASDAQ symbol*] (TTSB)
EVTC	Environmental Technology Corp. [*NASDAQ symbol*] (SAG)
EVTECA	Electric Vehicle Total Energy Cycle Analysis
EVTI	EndoVascular Technologies [*NASDAQ symbol*] (TTSB)
EVTI	Endovascular Technologies, Inc. [*NASDAQ symbol*] (SAG)
EVTM	Ex-Vessel Transfer Machine [*Nuclear energy*] (NRCH)
Ev Tr	Evans' Trial [*A publication*] (DLA)
E/VTS	Engine/Vehicle Test Stand
EVTV	Extravascular Thermal Volume [*Medicine*]
EVU	Maryville, MO [*Location identifier FAA*] (FAAL)
EVV	English Versions
EVV	Evansville [*Indiana*] [*Airport symbol*] (OAG)
EVVA	Europaeische Vereinigung der Veterinaranatomen [*European Association of Veterinary Anatomists - EAVA*] (EAIO)
EVVA	Extravehicular Visor Assembly [*NASA*]
EVW	European Voluntary Worker
EVW	Evanston, WY [*Location identifier FAA*] (FAAL)
EVX	Electronic Voice Exchange [*Commterm, Inc.*] [*Billerica, MA*] [*Telecommunications*] (TSSD)
EVY	Every
EW	Each Way (MSA)
EW	Early Warning [*Air Force*]
EW	Earthenware
EW	Earthwatch [*United Nations Environment Program*]
EW	East Washington Railway Co. [*AAR code*]
EW	East-West
EW	East-West Airlines [*ICAO designator*] (AD)
EW	Eave-to-Eave Width [*of boxcar*]
EW	Economic Warfare [*British*]
EW	Edinger-Westphal Nucleus [*Neuroanatomy*]
EW	Edmund Walker [*Car parts distribution company*] [*British*]
EW	Effective Warmth (IAA)
EW	Egg Width
EW	Eingetragenes Warenzeichen [*Registered Trademark*] [*German*]
EW	Electrical Welding (IAA)
EW	Electric Windows [*Automotive accessory*]
EW	Electronic Warfare
EW	Electronic Wholesaler (IAA)
EW	Electroslag Welding
ew	Elsewhere (MAE)

EW	Emergency Ward
EW	Eminent Women [*A publication*]
EW	Empty Weight
EW	End Wall [*Of a cell*] [*Botany*]
E/W	Energy over Weight
EW	Energy-to-Weight Ratio (MCD)
EW	Engineer's Writer [*British military*] (DMA)
EW	Enlisted Woman [*or Women*]
EW	Equivalent Weapons [*Military*]
EW	Ether-Water (PDAA)
EW	Euer [*Your*] [*German*]
EW	Europaeische Wandervereinigung [*European Ramblers' Association - ERA*] [*Germany*] (EAIO)
ew----	Europe, Western [*MARC geographic area code Library of Congress*] (LCCP)
EW	Extended-Wear Lenses [*Optometry*]
EW	Extensive Wound
EW	External Work
EW	Extreme Width [*of flight deck*]
EW	Ex-Warrants [*Without Warrants*] [*Finance*]
EW	Sleet Shower [*Meteorology*] (BARN)
EW1	Electronic Warfare Technician, First Class (DNAB)
EW2	Electronic Warfare Technician, Second Class (DNAB)
EW3	Electronic Warfare Technician, Third Class (DNAB)
EWA	Early Warning Adjunct
EWA	Early Warning/Attack Assessment
EWA	East-West Acceleration
EWA	East-West Airlines Ltd. [*Australia ICAO designator*] (FAAC)
EWA	Edgewood Arsenal [*Maryland*] [*Army*] (AABC)
EWA	Education and World Affairs [*Later, ICED*]
EWA	Education Writers Association (EA)
EWA	Effective Word Address (IAA)
EWA	Emunah Women of America (EA)
EWA	End Warning Area [*Computer science*] (BUR)
EWA	Engineering Work Assignment
EWA	Engineering Work Authorization [*Aerospace*]
EWA	Esperanto Writers Association (EA)
EWA	Estimated Warehouse Arrival (NASA)
EWA	Europaeische Wahrungsabkommen [*European Monetary Agreement*] [*German*] (DCTA)
EWA	European Wax Association (EAIO)
EWA	European Welding Association (EAIO)
EWA	Foreign Fd Australia Index'WEBS' [*AMEX symbol*] (TTSB)
EWA	Kewanee, MS [*Location identifier FAA*] (FAAL)
EWA	World Equity Benchmark Shares [*AMEX symbol*] (SAG)
EWAA-USA	Elsa Wild Animal Appeal - USA
EWABL/AAU	Eastern Women's Amateur Basketball League of the AAU [*Amateur Athletic Union of the United States*] (EA)
EWAC	Early Warning Aircraft (MCD)
EWAC	Electronic Warfare Anechoic Chamber
EWACS	Electronic Wide-Angle Camera System
EWAD	Early Warning Air Defense (NATG)
EWAG	Exploding Wire Aerosol Generator [*Liquid suspension*]
EWAHA	East West Academy of Healing Arts (EA)
EWAI	Eisenhower World Affairs Institute [*Later, EI*] (EA)
EWAMS	Early Warning and Monitoring System (MCD)
EWAN	Enterprise-Wide Application Network
EW & CSq	Early Warning and Control Squadron [*Air Force*]
EW & I	Electronic Warfare and Intelligence [*Military*]
EWASER	Electromagnetic Wave Amplification by Stimulated Emission of Radiation
EWAV	Electrical Wholesalers' Association, Victoria [*Australia*]
EWAW	Encyclopedia of Women's Associations Worldwide [*A publication*]
EWB	Blanch [*E.W.*] Holdings, Inc. [*NYSE symbol*] (SPSG)
EWB	Earl Weaver Baseball [*Computer game*]
EWB	Embedded Wiring Board (MSA)
EWB	Emergency Warnings Branch [*National Weather Service*]
EWB	Encyclopedia of World Biography [*A publication*]
EWB	Estrogen Withdrawal Bleeding [*Medicine*]
EWB	E.W. Blanch Holdings [*NYSE symbol*] (TTSB)
EWB	Fall River-New Bedford [*Massachusetts*] [*Airport symbol*] (AD)
EWB	New Bedford [*Massachusetts*] [*Location identifier FAA*] (FAAL)
EWBA	English Women's Bowling Association (DBA)
EWBF	English Women's Bowling Federation (DBA)
EWBN	Early Warning Broadcast Net [*DoD*]
EWC	Eastern Women's Center (EA)
EWC	East-West Center (EA)
EWC	Edward Waters College [*Jacksonville, FL*]
EWC	Electric Water Cooler
EWC	Electronic Warfare Center (MCD)
EWC	Electronic Warfare Coordinator (NVT)
EWC	Ellwood City, PA [*Location identifier FAA*] (FAAL)
EWC	Episcopal Women's Caucus (EA)
EWC	Evaporative Water Chiller [*Engineering*]
EWC	Foreign Fd Canada Index'WEBS' [*AMEX symbol*] (TTSB)
EWCAP	World Equity Benchmark Shares [*AMEX symbol*] (SAG)
EWCAP	Electrical Wiring Component Application Partnership
EWCAS	Early Warning and Control Aircraft System (IEEE)
EW/CAS	Electronic Warfare/Close-Air Support (MCD)
EW-CAS-JTF	Electronic Warfare, Close-Air Support, Joint Task Force (MCD)
EWCB	Electrical Workers and Contractors' Board [*Queensland, Australia*]
EWCC	East-West Cultural Center (EA)
EWCC	Electronic Warfare Coordination Center
EWCC	Elvis We Care Campaign [*Later, EPIAI*] (EA)

EWCC..........	Environmental Workforce Coordinating Committee [*Environmental Protection Agency*] (GFGA)
EWCD	Electronic Warfare Cover and Deception (MCD)
EWCDMS	Electronic Warfare Cover and Deception Management Subsystem (MCD)
EWCI..........	East-West Communication Institute [*Later, East-West Institute of Culture and Communication*] [*Research center*] (RCD)
EWCI..........	Evangelical Women's Caucus, International (EA)
EWCIP	Elevated Work Cage Improvement Program (DWSG)
EWCL..........	Electromagnetic Warfare and Communications Laboratory
EW-CLI	East-West Institute of Culture and Communication [*Research center*] (RCD)
EWCM..........	Electronic Warfare Coordination Module (DOMA)
EWCP..........	Early Warning Change Proposal (MCD)
EWCR..........	Electronic Warfare Counter Response (MCD)
EW/CRP	Early Warning/Control and Reporting Post
EWCS..........	Electronic Warfare Control Ship [*Navy*] (NVT)
EWCS..........	Electronic Warfare Coordinating Staff
EWCS..........	European Wideband Communications System [*Army*]
EWD...........	Electric Winch Drive (DWSG)
EWD...........	Elementary Wiring Diagram
EWD...........	Foreign Fd Sweden Index'WEBS' [*AMEX symbol*] (TTSB)
EWD...........	World Equity Benchmark Shares [*AMEX symbol*] (SAG)
EWDD	European Wholesalers and Distributors Directory [*Pronounced "eewed"*] [*A publication*]
EWDI	Electronic Wind Direction Indicator
EWDLS	Evanescent Wave Dynamic Light Scattering [*Physics*]
EWDT..........	Early Warning Data Transmission (NATG)
EWE	East West European [*Bulgaria*] [*ICAO designator*] (FAAC)
EWE	Electronic Warfare Element (AABC)
EWE	Emergency Window Escape [*NASA*] (NASA)
ewe............	Ewe [*MARC language code Library of Congress*] (LCCP)
EWE	Extrapolated Water Elevation (PDAA)
EWEA	European Wind Energy Association (EAIO)
EWEC..........	Electromagnetic Wave Energy Converter [*Solar energy conversion*]
Ewell Bl	Ewell's Edition of Blackstone [*A publication*] (DLA)
Ewell Cas Inf...	Ewell's Leading Cases on Infancy, Etc. [*A publication*] (DLA)
Ewell Ess.....	Ewell's Essentials of the Law [*A publication*] (DLA)
Ewell Evans Ag...	Ewell's Edition of Evans on Agency [*A publication*] (DLA)
Ewell Fix	Ewell on the Law of Fixtures [*A publication*] (DLA)
Ewell LC	Ewell's Leading Cases on Infancy, Etc. [*A publication*] (DLA)
EWEPS........	Environmental Weapons Effects Prediction System (MCD)
EWES	Electronic Warfare Evaluation Simulator
EWES...........	Engineering Waterways Experiment Station [*Army*]
EWEX	Electronic Warfare Exercise (NVT)
EWEXIPT......	Electronic Warfare Exercise in Port (NVT)
EWF	Early Warning Fighter
EWF	Earth, Wind, and Fire [*Rock music group*]
EWF	Education Without Frontiers [*An association*] (EAIO)
EWF	Electrical Wholesalers Federation [*British*] (BI)
EWF	Electromagnetic Wave Filter
EWF	Electronic Warfare
EWF	Elektronisches Worterbuch der Fachsprachen [*Technische Universitat Dresden*] [*Multilingual terminology bank*] (NITA)
EWF	Equivalent-Weight Factor
EWF	European Warrant Fund [*NYSE symbol*] (SPSG)
EWF	European Wax Federation [*Belgium*] (EAIO)
EWF	European Weightlifting Federation (EA)
EWF	Wake Forest University, Winston-Salem, NC [*OCLC symbol*] (OCLC)
EWFH..........	East-West Fine, Hundreds
EWFT..........	East-West Fine, Tens
EWFU..........	East-West Fine, Units
EWG	Earth Works Group Inc. (EERA)
EWG	Environmental Working Group [*An advocacy group*]
EWG	Equipment Working Group
EWG	Ernaehrungswissenschaften Giessen [*Nutrition Sciences - Giessen University*] [*Database*]
EWG	Ethics Works Group (EERA)
EWG	Euromissiles Working Group [*Defunct*] (EA)
EWG...........	Europaeische Wirtschaftsgemeinschaft [*European Economic Community*]
EWG...........	Eurowings, AG, Nurnberg [*Germany*] [*FAA designator*] (FAAC)
EWG	Executive Working Group [*NATO*]
EWG	Foreign Fd Germany Index'WEBS' [*AMEX symbol*] (TTSB)
EWG........	World Equity Benchmark Shares [*AMEX symbol*] (SAG)
EW/GCI	Early Warning/Ground Control Intercept [*RADAR*]
EWGETS	Electronic Warfare Ground Environment Threat Simulator
EWGS	European and Pacific Weather Graphics Switch [*Air Force*] (GFGA)
EWH...........	Expected Working Hours (IAA)
EWH...........	Foreign Fd Hong Kong Index'WEBS' [*AMEX symbol*] (TTSB)
EWH...........	World Equity Benchmark Shares [*AMEX symbol*] (SAG)
EWHA	Eastern Women's Headwear Association [*Later, AMMA*] (EA)
EWHO	Elbow-Wrist-Hand-Orthosis [*Medicine*]
EWI............	Edison Welding Institute (EA)
EWI............	Educational Workers' International (AIE)
EWI............	Education with Industry
EW/I..........	Electronic Warfare/Intercept (MCD)
EWI............	Electronic Wiring Intercommunication
EWI............	Enarotali [*Indonesia*] [*Airport symbol*] (OAG)
EWI............	English Winter Index
EWI............	Entered without Inspection [*Usually applies to aliens who enter at other than a port of entry*]
EWI............	Executive Women International [*Salt Lake City, UT*] (EA)
EWI............	Experiential World Inventory [*Psychodiagnostic questionnaire*]
EWI............	Foreign Fd Italy Index'WEBS' [*AMEX symbol*] (TTSB)
EWI............	World Equity Benchmark Shares [*AMEX symbol*] (SAG)
EWIA	External Wall Insulation Association [*British*] (DBA)
EWIBA	English Women's Indoor Bowling Association (DBA)
EWICB	Electronic Warfare Interface Connection Box
EWICS	European Workshop of Industrial Computer Systems (NITA)
EWIF..........	Electronic Warfare Intelligence Facility [*Fort Huachuca, AZ*] [*United States Army Electronic Proving Ground*] (GRD)
Ewing Just...	Ewing's Justice [*A publication*] (DLA)
EWIOC	Electronic Warfare and Intelligence Operations Center [*Military*] (MCD)
EWIRC	Electronic Warfare Integrated Reprogramming Concept (MCD)
EWIS	Electronic Warfare Information System (MCD)
EWITA........	Evaluation of Women in the Army (MCD)
EWJ...........	Foreign Fd Japan Index'WEBS' [*AMEX symbol*] (TTSB)
EWJ...........	World Equity Benchmark Shares [*AMEX symbol*] (SAG)
EWJC..........	European Women's Judo Championships [*British*]
EWK...........	Foreign Fd Belgium Index'WEBS' [*AMEX symbol*] (TTSB)
EWK...........	Newton, KS [*Location identifier FAA*] (FAAL)
EWK...........	World Equity Benchmark Shares [*AMEX symbol*] (SAG)
EWL...........	Earliest Work Listed
EWL...........	Effective Wavelength
EWL...........	Egg White Lysozyme (OA)
EWL...........	Electronic Warfare Laboratory [*Army*]
EWL...........	Enterprise Workshops Ltd.
EWL...........	European Women's Lobby [*Belgium*] (EAIO)
EWL...........	Evaporative Water Loss
EWL...........	Excess Weight Loss [*Morbid obesity surgical treatment*]
EWL...........	Exchange Work List [*Telecommunications*] (TEL)
EWL...........	Foreign Fd Switzer'd Index'WEBS' [*AMEX symbol*] (TTSB)
EWL...........	Wake Forest University, Law Library, Winston-Salem, NC [*OCLC symbol*] (OCLC)
EWL...........	World Equity Benchmark Shares [*AMEX symbol*] (SAG)
EWLD..........	Engineering Weekly Labor Distribution (AAG)
EWLTP........	Earl Warren Legal Training Program (EA)
EWM...........	Edgewise Meter
EWM...........	Electrical Welding Machine
EWM...........	Episcopal World Mission (EA)
EWM...........	Foreign Fd Malaysia Index'WEBS' [*AMEX symbol*] (TTSB)
EWM...........	MSU [*Michigan State University*] and WSU Union List of Serials, Detroit, MI [*Wayne State University*] [*OCLC symbol*] (OCLC)
EWM...........	Newman, TX [*Location identifier FAA*] (FAAL)
EWM...........	World Equity Benchmark Shares [*AMEX symbol*] (SAG)
EWMA...........	Exponentially Weighted Moving Average [*Statistics*]
EWMB..........	Enemy War Materials Branch [*Supreme Headquarters, Allied Expeditionary Force*] [*World War II*]
EWMC..........	Eli Whitney Metrology Center
EWMD	European Women's Management Development Network (EAIO)
EWMFC	Elvis Worldwide Memorial Fan Club (EA)
EWMIS........	Electronic Warfare Management Information System [*Air Force*] (MCD)
EWMU	Enemy Wireless Monitoring Unit (IAA)
EWN...........	Early Warning Notification
EWN...........	Foreign Fd Netherl'ds Index'WEBS' [*AMEX symbol*] (TTSB)
EWN...........	New Bern [*North Carolina*] [*Airport symbol*] (OAG)
EWN...........	New Bern, NC [*Location identifier FAA*] (FAAL)
EWN...........	World Equity Benchmark Shares [*AMEX symbol*] (SAG)
EWND..........	Eastwind Group [*NASDAQ symbol*] (TTSB)
EWND..........	Eastwind Group, Inc. (The) [*NASDAQ symbol*] (SAG)
EWO...........	Educational Welfare Officer [*British*] (DI)
EWO...........	Electrical and Wireless Operators [*Air Force British*]
EWO...........	Electronic Warfare Office [*or Officer*]
EWO...........	Emergency War Operations
EWO...........	Emergency War Order [*Air Force*]
EWO...........	Engineering Work Order
EWO...........	Enki and the World Order [*A publication*] (BJA)
EWO...........	Essential Work Order
EWO...........	Ewo [*Congo*] [*Airport symbol*] (OAG)
EWO...........	Foreign Fd Austria Index'WEBS' [*AMEX symbol*] (TTSB)
EWO...........	New Hope, KY [*Location identifier FAA*] (FAAL)
EWO...........	World Equity Benchmark Shares [*AMEX symbol*] (SAG)
EWO & HP...	Electric Wall Oven and Hot Plates [*Classified advertising*] (ADA)
EWODS.......	Engineering Work Order - Drawing Summary (AAG)
EWONA	Education Welfare Officers' National Association [*British*] (DI)
EWOPS........	Electronic Warfare Operations (NVT)
EWOS.........	Electronic Warfare Operational System [*Air Force*]
EWOS.........	European Workshop for Open Systems [*British*]
EWOSE	Electronic Warfare Operational Support Establishment [*Royal Air Force*] [*British*] (PDAA)
EWOT..........	Electronic Warfare Officer Training (AFM)
EWOTS	Early Warning Observation Teams (CINC)
E-WOW	Explore the World of Work [*Vocational guidance test*]
EWP...........	Electronic Warfare Plans [*NATO*] (NATG)
EWP...........	Electronic White Pages [*Information service or system*] (IID)
EWP...........	Emergency War Plan
EWP...........	Enhanced Winkler Processor
EWP...........	Exploding Wire Phenomena
EWP...........	Foreign Fd Spain Index 'WEBS' [*AMEX symbol*] (TTSB)
EWP...........	Newport, AR [*Location identifier FAA*] (FAAL)
EWP...........	World Equity Benchmark Shares [*AMEX symbol*] (SAG)
EWPA..........	Enhanced Winkler Processor Autopilot [*Military*]
EWPCA........	European Water Pollution Control Association (EAIO)
EWPHE	European Working Party on Hypertension in the Elderly [*An association*]
EWPI..........	East-West Population Institute
EWPI..........	Eysenck-Withers Personality Inventory [*Psychology*]

EWQ............ Enlisted Women's Quarters [Military]
EWQ............ Exceptionally Well Qualified (AFM)
EWQ............ Foreign Fd France Index 'WEBS' [AMEX symbol] (TTSB)
EWQ............ World Equity Benchmark Shares [AMEX symbol] (SAG)
EWQOS........ Environmental and Water Quality Operational Studies [Army Corps of Engineers]
EWQRC........ Electronic Warfare Quick Reaction Capability (MCD)
EWR............ Early Warning RADAR [Air Force]
EWR............ Early Warning Receiver (DWSG)
EWR............ East West Resources [Vancouver Stock Exchange symbol]
EWR............ Engineering Work Report [or Request]
EWR............ Estimated Weight Report
EWR............ Evans Withycombe Res [NYSE symbol] (TTSB)
EWR............ Evans Withycombe Residential, Inc. [NYSE symbol] (SAG)
EWR............ Newark [New Jersey] [Airport symbol] (AD)
EWR............ Newark, NJ [Location identifier FAA] (FAAL)
EWR............ New York [New York] Newark [Airport symbol] (OAG)
EWR & I ...... Emergency Welfare Registration and Inquiry [Civil Defense]
EWRC.......... European Weed Research Council [Later, EWRS]
EWRIS .... European Wire Rope Information Service [EC] (ECED)
EWRL.......... Estimated Weapon Release (MCD)
EWRM .... Electronic Warfare Response Monitor (MCD)
EWRS .... European Weed Research Society [See also EGH] [Research center Germany] (IRC)
EW/RSTA ..... Center for Electronic Warfare/Reconnaissance, Surveillance, and Target Acquisit ion [Fort Monmouth, NJ] [United States Army Communications-Electronics Command] (GRD)
EWRT.......... Electrical Women's Round Table (EA)
EWS............ Early Warning System
EWS............ East-West Speed
EWS............ Edgar Wallace Society (EAIO)
EWS............ Eduworld Society [Later, CFB] (EA)
EWS............ Egg White Serum [Immunology]
EWS............ Electronic Warfare Supervisor [Navy] (DOMA)
EWS............ Electronic Warfare System (MCD)
EWS............ Emergency Water Supply
EWS............ Emergency Welfare Service [Civil Defense]
EWS............ Engineering Watch Supervisor (DNAB)
EWS............ Engineering Work Schedule (MCD)
EWS............ Engineering Work Statement (MCD)
EWS............ Engineering Work-Station [Yokogawa Hewlett Packard Ltd.] [Japan]
EWS............ Engineering Writing and Speech (MCD)
EWS............ English Westerners Society [British]
EWS............ Enlisted Surface Warfare Specialist (DOMA)
EWS............ Estimated Will Ship
EWS............ European Wings [Czechoslovakia] [ICAO designator] (FAAC)
EWS............ Evelyn Waugh Society (EA)
EWS............ Ewing's Sarcoma [Oncology]
EWS............ Experienced Worker Standard
EWS............ Foreign Fd Singapore Index 'WEBS' [AMEX symbol] (TTSB)
EWS............ World Equity Benchmark Shares [AMEX symbol] (SAG)
EWSA.......... EEC Wheat Starch Manufacturers Association [Defunct] (EAIO)
EWSA.......... Electronic Warfare Technician, Seaman Apprentice (DNAB)
EWSC.......... Electric Water Systems Council
EWSCL........ Extended-Wear Soft Contact Lens [Optometry]
EWSD........ Engineering and Water Supply Department [South Australia]
EWSE.......... Electronic Warfare Support Element [Army] (DOMA)
EWSF.......... Electric Wave Section Filter
EWSG.......... Electronic Warfare Scenario Generator
EWSI.......... Electronic Wind Speed Indicator
EW/SIGINT... Electronic Warfare/Signal Intelligence (MCD)
EWSLA........ East-West Sign Language Association [Japan] (SLS)
EWSM......... Electronic Warfare Support Measures [Later, ESM] (AABC)
EWSN .... Electronic Warfare Technician, Seaman (DNAB)
EWST.......... Elevated Water Storage Tank [Nuclear energy] (NRCH)
EWST.......... Energy West [NASDAQ symbol] (TTSB)
EWST.......... Energy West, Inc. [NASDAQ symbol] (SAG)
EWSTP........ Emergency War Surgery Training Program [Army]
EWT .... Eastern War Time [World War II]
EWT............ Eastwest Airlines, Erfurt [Germany] [FAA designator] (FAAC)
EWT............ Edible Whip Technology [Aerosol technology]
EWT............ Electronic Warfare Technology (MCD)
EWT............ Electronic Warfare Trainer
EWT............ Electrostatic Water Treaters (DICI)
EWT............ Evaluation and Warning Team (CINC)
EWT............ Expandable Wing Tank
EW/TA......... Early Warning/Threat Assessment
EWTA.......... East Wind Trade Associates [Defunct] (EA)
EWTA.......... Expo West Trade Association (EA)
EWTAD........ Early Warning Threat Analysis Display
EWTAP........ Electronic Warfare Tactics Analysis Program [Military] (CAAL)
EWTC.......... East-West Trade Council [Defunct] (EA)
EWTES........ Electronic Warfare Tactical [or Threat] Environment Simulation (NG)
EWTMI......... European Wideband Transmission Media Improvement Program
EWTN.......... Eternal Word Television Network [Cable-television system]
EWTNGSq... Electronic Warfare Training Squadron [Air Force]
EWTPC........ East-West Trade Policy Committee
EWTR.......... Electronic Warfare Test Range [Military]
EWTS.......... Electronic Warfare Training Squadron [Air Force]
EWTS.......... Expandable Wing Tank Structure
EWTT.......... Electronic Warfare Tactics Trainer
EWTU.......... Except What Turns Up (DI)
EWU............ Eastern Washington University (PDAA)
EWU............ Foreign Fd U.K. Index 'WEBS' [AMEX symbol] (TTSB)
EWU............ World Equity Benchmark Shares [AMEX symbol] (SAG)

EWVA.......... Electronic Warfare Vulnerability Assessment [DoD] (RDA)
EWW.......... Emery Worldwide Airlines, Inc. [ICAO designator] (FAAC)
EWW.......... Enterprise-Wide Web (ACII)
EWW.......... Extended Work Week
EWW.......... Foreign Fd Mexico Index 'WEBS' [AMEX symbol] (TTSB)
EWW.......... World Equity Benchmark Shares [AMEX symbol] (SAG)
EWWRS ...... Eric's Wasted Worldwide Repair Society (EA)
EWWS .... Electronic Warfare Warning System
EWWS .... ESSA [Environmental Science Services Administration] Weather Wire Service
Ex .... Citation in Examiner's Decision [Legal term] (DLA)
Ex .... Court of Exchequer [England] [Legal term] (DLA)
EX............... Eagle Aviation [ICAO designator] (AD)
EX............... Emirates Airlines [ICAO designator] (AD)
Ex .... English Exchequer Reports [A publication] (DLA)
ex .... Exaggerated (DAVI)
EX............... Examined
Ex .... Examiner's Decision [Legal term] (DLA)
EX............... Example
ex .... Example (VRA)
EX............... Exceeding
EX............... Excellent [Condition] [Deltiology]
EX............... Except
ex .... Excepted (WDMC)
Ex .... Excepted (WDMC)
EX............... Excess (AABC)
EX............... Exchange
EX............... Exchequer [British]
EX............... Exchequer Reports [A publication]
EX............... Excise (DSUE)
ex .... Excision [Medicine] (MAE)
Ex .... Excitation Energy (IDOE)
EX............... Excluding
EX............... Exclusive (ADA)
EX............... Excudit [Made] [Latin] (ROG)
EX............... Excursion
EX............... Excursus (ROG)
EX............... Execute
EX............... Executed Out Of [Business term]
EX............... Execution (ROG)
EX............... Executive
EX............... Executive Management Office [Kennedy Space Center Directorate] [NASA] (NASA)
EX............... Executive Schedule [Job classification for certain Presidentially appointed executives]
EX............... Executor (ROG)
EX............... Exempt
EX............... Exercise (NVT)
EX............... Exerque [Numismatics]
EX............... Exeter [Post code] (ODBW)
EX............... Exeunt [They Go Out] [Latin] (ROG)
EX............... Exhaust [Automotive engineering]
EX............... Exhibit
EX............... Exhibition (DSUE)
EX............... Exide Corp. [NYSE symbol] (SAG)
EX............... Exit [He, or She, Goes Out] [Latin] (ROG)
Ex .... Exodus [Old Testament book]
ex .... Exophthalmos [Ophthalmology] (MAE)
EX............... Expect (DA)
EX............... Expenditure [Dialog] [Searchable field] [Information service or system] (NITA)
EX............... Experiment [or Experimental]
EX............... Experimental Station [ITU designation] (CET)
EX............... Expert
EX............... Explanation
EX............... Exponent [Mathematics] (IAA)
EX............... Export
EX............... Exposure
EX............... Express
EX............... Extension (ADA)
EX............... Extra
EX............... Extractum [Extract] [Latin]
EX............... Extra Gilt [Bookbinding] (ROG)
EX............... Extravaganza (ROG)
Ex .... Extraversion [Psychology]
EX............... Lakeside Laboratories, Inc. [Research code symbol]
EXA............. Albion College, Albion, MI [OCLC symbol] (OCLC)
EXA............. Execaire Aviation Ltd. [Canada ICAO designator] (FAAC)
EXA............. Executing Agency Identifier (CINC)
EXA............. Exmar Resources Ltd. [Vancouver Stock Exchange symbol]
EXA............. Lehman Brothers, Inc. [AMEX symbol] (SAG)
Exabyte....... Exabyte Corp. [Associated Press] (SAG)
EXAC.......... Exactech Inc. [NASDAQ symbol] (TTSB)
EXACCT...... Expenditure Account
EXACT........ Energy Dispersive X-Ray Analysis Computation Technique [X-Ray fluorescence software] [Kevex Corp.]
EXACT........ Exchange of Authenticated Electronic Component Performance Test Data [European counterpart of GIDEP]
EXACT........ Expert Adaptive Controller Tuning (NITA)
EXACT........ International Exchange of Authenticated Electronic Component Performance Tests Data (PDAA)
EX AFF....... Ex Affinis [Of Affinity] [Latin]
EXAFS......... Extended X-Ray Absorption Fine Structure [Spectrometry]
EXAG .... Exaggeration
EXAGT .... Executive Agent

EXAM.......... Elemental X-Ray Analysis of Materials
ExAM.......... Ex Air Ministry [*British*] (DEN)
EXAM.......... Examination (AFM)
EXAM.......... Examine
Exam.......... Examiner [*Legal term*] (DLA)
EX-AM.......... Expedited Air Munitions
EXAM.......... Experience Analysis Mechanism [*Health insurance*] (GHCT)
EXAM.......... Experimental Aerospace Multiprocessor
EXAM.......... Express America Hldgs [*NASDAQ symbol*] (TTSB)
EXAMD.......... Express America Holdings [*NASDAQ symbol*] (SAG)
EXAMD.......... Examined
EXAMETNET... Experimental Inter-American Meteorological Rocket Network [*NASA*]
Examg.......... Examining (BARN)
EXAMINA..... Examination (DSUE)
EXAMN.......... Examination
EXAMR.......... Examiner
EXAMS........ Exposure Analysis Modeling System [*Environmental chemistry*]
EX & AD ..... Executor and Administrator (DLA)
EXANDIS..... Exotic Animal Disease Preparedness Consultative Committee [*Australia*]
EXAPT.......... Extended Subset of Automatically Programmed Tools [*Manufacturing term*]
EX AQ .... Ex Aqua [*Out of Water*] [*Pharmacy*]
EXAR.......... Exar Corp. [*NASDAQ symbol*] (NQ)
Ex Aut.......... Ex Authenticis Pandectis [*Digest of Justinian*] [*A publication*] (DSA)
EXB.......... Brazilian Army Aviation [*FAA designator*] (FAAC)
EXB.......... Grand Rapids Baptist College and Seminary, Grand Rapids, MI [*OCLC symbol*] (OCLC)
EXBEDCAP ... Expanded Bed Capacity
EXBF.......... Exercise Hyperemia Blood Flow (MAE)
Ex B/L.......... Exchange Bill of Lading (MHDW)
EXBO .... Export Buying Offices Association [*British*] (DBA)
EXBT.......... Exabyte Corp. [*NASDAQ symbol*] (NQ)
EXC.......... Calvin College and Seminary, Grand Rapids, MI [*OCLC symbol*] (OCLC)
EXC.......... Excalibur Aviation [*British ICAO designator*] (FAAC)
EXC.......... Excavate (MSA)
EXC.......... Exceeding [*Weight*] [*Postage*] [*British*] (ROG)
EXC.......... Excel Industries [*NYSE symbol*] (TTSB)
EXC.......... Excel Industries, Inc. [*AMEX symbol*] (SPSG)
EXC.......... Excellency
EXC.......... Excellent (AABC)
EXC.......... Except
EXC.......... Exchange
EX/C.......... Exchange Certificate [*Rate*] [*Value of the English pound*]
EXC.......... Exchange Key [*Word processing*]
EXC.......... Excision [*Medicine*]
EXC.......... Excitation (MSA)
exc.......... Excitation (IDOE)
exc.......... Exciter (IDOE)
EXC.......... Exclude
EXC.......... Excudit [*Made*] [*Latin*]
EXC.......... Excursion (ROG)
EXC.......... Excuse (WGA)
EXC.......... Experiment Computer (MCD)
EXCA.......... Excalibur Technologies [*NASDAQ symbol*] (TTSB)
EXCA.......... Excalibur Technology Corp. [*NASDAQ symbol*] (NQ)
EXCA.......... Excavate [*Technical drawings*]
Excalb.......... Excalibur Technologies Corp. [*Associated Press*] (SAG)
EXCAP .... Expanded Capability (CAAL)
EXCAVTG .... Excavating
EXCC.......... Exercise Control Center [*Military*] (AABC)
Excel.......... Excel Industries, Inc. [*Associated Press*] (SAG)
EXCEL.......... Export Credit Enhanced Leverage
ExcelCm ..... Excel Communications, Inc. [*Associated Press*] (SAG)
EXCELL.......... Excellent (ADA)
ExcelRl.......... Excel Realty Trust [*Associated Press*] (SAG)
EXCELS........ Expanded Communications - Electronics System [*DoD*]
Excelsr.......... Excelsior Income Shares, Inc. [*Associated Press*] (SAG)
EXCERP e ROT FIN... Excerpta e Rotulis Finium [*Extracts of Boundary Records*] [*A publication*] (ROG)
Excerpta Crim... Excerpta Criminologica [*A publication*] (DLA)
Excg.......... Exchange
EXCG.......... Exercise Control Group [*Military*] (AABC)
Exch.......... Court of Exchequer [*England*] [*Legal term*] (DLA)
Exch.......... English Exchequer Reports [*A publication*] (DLA)
Exch.......... English Law Reports, Exchequer [*1866-75*] [*A publication*] (DLA)
EXCH.......... Exchange [*Telecommunications*] (AFM)
EXCH.......... Exchange
EXCH.......... Exchequer [*British*]
Exch.......... Exchequer Division, High Court [*1875-80*] [*A publication*] (DLA)
Exch.......... Exchequer Reports (Welsby, Hurlstone, and Gordon) [*A publication*] (DLA)
Exch C .... Canada Law Reports, Exchequer Court [*A publication*] (DLA)
Exch Can .... Canada Law Reports, Exchequer Court [*A publication*] (DLA)
Exch Cas...... Exchequer Cases [*Legacy duties, etc.*] [*Scotland*] [*A publication*] (DLA)
EXCH CHAM... Exchequer Chamber [*Legal term*] (DLA)
Exch CR...... Canada Law Reports, Exchequer Court [*A publication*] (DLA)
Exch Ct (Can)... Canada Law Reports, Exchequer Court [*A publication*] (DLA)
Exch Div...... Exchequer Division, English Law Reports [*A publication*] (DLA)
Exch Div (Eng)... Exchequer Division, English Law Reports [*A publication*] (DLA)
Ex Child...... Exceptional Children [*A publication*]
Ex Child...... Exceptional Children [*A publication*] (BRI)
EXCHO .... Exchange Officer [*Air Force*]

Exch P........ Exchange of Property (DLA)
Exch Rep .... English Exchequer Reports [*A publication*] (DLA)
Exch Rep .... Exchequer Reports (Welsby, Hurlstone, and Gordon) [*A publication*] (DLA)
Exch Rep WH & G... Exchequer Reports (Welsby, Hurlstone, and Gordon) [*A publication*] (DLA)
EXCIMER ..... Excited Dimmer (IAA)
EXCIPLEX .... Excited State Complex [*LASER*] (IEEE)
EXCITE........ Expanded with Computers and Information Technology
EXCL.......... Excel
EXCL.......... Exclamation
excl.......... Exclamation (WDMC)
EXCL.......... Exclude (MSA)
EXCL.......... Excluding (EY)
EXCL.......... Exclusive (AFM)
excl.......... Exclusive [*News media*] (WDMC)
EXCLAM....... Exclamatory (ROG)
EXCLD.......... Exclude
EXCLG.......... Excluding (ROG)
EXCLSR ...... Excelsior
ExcIT.......... Excel Technology, Inc. [*Associated Press*] (SAG)
ExcITc.......... Excel Technology, Inc. [*Associated Press*] (SAG)
ExcITch........ Excel Technology [*Associated Press*] (SAG)
EXCLU.......... Exclusive (MDG)
EXCLV.......... Exclusive (FAAC)
EXCO.......... Executive Committee (IEEE)
EXCO.......... Executive Council (ADA)
EXCOA........ Explosives Corp. of America
EXCOM........ Executive Committee [*National Security Council*]
EXCOM........ Extended Communications Search [*DoD*]
EX COM ...... Extravagantes Communes [*A publication*] (DLA)
EXCOMM .... Exterior Communications [*Military*] (CAAL)
EXCOMMS ... Extended Communications Search [*Navy*] (NVT)
EXCOMP ...... National Executive Compensation Database [*Information service or system*] (IID)
EXCON........ Executive Control (SSD)
EXCON........ External Control [*Military*] (INF)
EXCP.......... Execute Channel Program [*Computer science*]
EXCPT.......... Exception
Ex CR.......... Canada Exchequer Court Reports [*1875-1922*] [*A publication*] (DLA)
Ex CR.......... Canada Law Reports, Exchequer Court [*A publication*] (DLA)
ExcRisk........ Executive Risk, Inc. [*Associated Press*] (SAG)
ExcRsk........ Executive Risk, Inc. [*Associated Press*] (SAG)
EXCSS.......... Excess
EXCSV.......... Excessive (MSA)
EXCT.......... Exact
EXCT.......... Execute (FAAC)
EXCTR .... Exciter [*Electricity*]
Exctr.......... Executor
EXCUR .... Excursion (KSC)
EXCVT.......... Excavate
EXCVTN .... Excavation
EXCVTR .... Excavator
EXD.......... Examined
EX D .... Ex Dividendum [*Without the right to dividend*] [*Finance*] (ROG)
EXD.......... Expeditor Resource Group Ltd. [*Vancouver Stock Exchange symbol*]
EXD.......... Export Air del Peru SA Cargo Air Lines [*ICAO designator*] (FAAC)
EXD.......... External Device [*Computer science*]
Ex D .... Law Reports, Exchequer Division [*England*] [*A publication*] (DLA)
EXDAMS ..... Extendable Debugging and Monitoring System [*Computer science*]
EXDC .... External Data Controller (NITA)
EXDIR .... Exercise Director (CINC)
EXDIS .... Exclusive Distribution [*Military security classification*] (AFM)
EX DIV .... Ex-Dividend [*Without the right to dividend*] [*Finance*]
EXDIV .... Experimental Division
Ex Div.......... Law Reports, Exchequer Division [*England*] [*A publication*] (ILCA)
EXDLVY ...... Expect Delivery (FAAC)
EXDOC......... Electronic Export Documentation [*Australia*]
Ex Doc .... Executive Document (BARN)
EX/DP .... Express/Direct Pack (DNAB)
EXE.......... Executable Program File [*Computer science*]
EXE.......... Execute (ROG)
EXE.......... Executive Flight, Inc. [*ICAO designator*] (FAAC)
EXE.......... Exeter [*British depot code*]
EXE.......... Extendicare, Inc. [*NYSE symbol*] (SAG)
EXE.......... Kent County Library and Kent County Library System, Grand Rapids, MI [*OCLC symbol*] (OCLC)
exe.......... Self Extracting [*Computer science*]
EXEC.......... Execute (MSA)
EXEC.......... Execution (WDAA)
EXEC.......... Executive (EY)
exec.......... Executive (DD)
EXEC.......... Executive
EXEC.......... Executive System (NITA)
EXEC.......... Executor
EXEC-1........ President on Board Civil Aircraft (FAAC)
EXEC-1F....... President's Family is Aboard Aircraft (FAAC)
EXEC-2........ Vice President is Aboard Civil Aircraft (FAAC)
EXEC-2F....... Vice President's Family is Aboard Aircraft (FAAC)
EXECASST ... Executive Assistant (DNAB)
Exec Doc ..... Executive Document [*Legal term*] (DLA)
Exec MBA .... Executive Master of Business Administration (PGP)
Exec MGA .... Executive Master of General Administration (PGP)
Exec MIM .... Executive Master of International Management (PGP)
Exec MPA .... Executive Master of Public Administration (PGP)

Exec MPH...	Executive Master of Public Health (PGP)
Exec MS	Executive Master of Science (PGP)
EXECO	Executive Officer
EXECORD	Executive Order (DNAB)
Exec Order...	Executive Order of the President (AAGC)
ExecTI.........	Executive Telecard Ltd. [*Associated Press*] (SAG)
EXECX.........	Executrix
EXED...........	Executed (ROG)
EXE file.......	Executable File (CDE)
Exel	EXEL Ltd. [*Associated Press*] (SAG)
EXELFS	Extended Electron Loss Fine Structure [*Spectrometry*]
EXEMP........	Exemption (DLA)
EXEOD	Expects to Enter on Duty (NOAA)
EXER...........	Exercise (AABC)
EXES...........	Expenses (ROG)
EXESS.........	Expanded ESS (MCD)
EXET...........	Exeter College [*Oxford University*] (ROG)
EXEVAL.......	External Evaluation [*Military*] (INF)
ExEx...........	Expected Exceedance (GNE)
EXF.............	External Function
EXF	Toledo, OH [*Location identifier FAA*] (FAAL)
EXFAS........	Extended Fine Auger Structure [*Physics*]
EXFINCO	Export Finance Co. [*British*]
EXFOD	Explosive Foxhole Digger [*Army*] (INF)
EXFOR	Experimental Force [*Army*] (INF)
EXG.............	Air Exchange, Inc. [*ICAO designator*] (FAAC)
EXG.............	Enron Corp. [*NYSE symbol*] (SAG)
EXG.............	Enron Cp 6.25% Exch Nts'98 [*NYSE symbol*] (TTSB)
EXG.............	Exchange Two Registers [*Computer science*]
EX G	Exempli Gratia [*For Example*] [*Latin*] (ROG)
EX G	Ex Grege [*Among the Rest*] [*Latin*] (ROG)
EXG.............	Existing [*Technical drawings*]
EXG.............	Grand Valley State College, Allendale, MI [*OCLC symbol*] (OCLC)
EXGA..........	External Gauge
EXGBUS	External Genitalia and Bartholin's, Urethral, and Skene's Glands [*Gynecology*] (DAVI)
EXGN	Exogen, Inc. [*NASDAQ symbol*] (SAG)
EX GR	Exempli Gratia [*For Example*] [*Latin*]
ex gr...........	Ex Grupa [*Of The Group Of*] [*Latin*] (DAVI)
EXH.............	Exhaust (KSC)
EXH.............	Exhibit
exh..............	Exhibit (VRA)
EXH.............	Hope College, Holland, MI [*OCLC symbol*] (OCLC)
EXHBN	Exhibition
EXHBNR......	Exhibitioner (ROG)
EXHBT	Exhibit
EXHBTR	Exhibitor
EXHIB	Exhibeatur [*Let It Be Given*] [*Pharmacy*]
EXHIB	Exhibited [*or Exhibition*]
EXHIB	Exhibitioner (ROG)
EXHIB	Exhibitor (NTCM)
EXHN	Exhibition
EXHST	Exhaust
EXHV	Exhaust Vent
EXI..............	Excursion Inlet [*Alaska*] [*Airport symbol*] (OAG)
EXI..............	Excursion Inlet, AK [*Location identifier FAA*] (FAAL)
ExI..............	Extropy Institute (EA)
EXI..............	Whirlpool Corp., Technical Information Center, Benton Harbor, MI [*OCLC symbol*] (OCLC)
EXIAC.........	Explosives Information and Analysis Center [*Army*] (PDAA)
ExideCp	Exide Corp. [*Associated Press*] (SAG)
ExideEl	Exide Electronics Group, Inc. [*Associated Press*] (SAG)
EX IDON CRASS LIQ...	Ex Idoneo Crasso Liquido [*In a Suitable Thick Liquid*] [*Pharmacy*]
EX IDON LIQ...	Ex Idoneo Liquido [*In a Suitable Liquid*] [*Pharmacy*]
EXIM...........	Export-Import Bank
EXIMBANK...	Export-Import Bank
Eximbank.....	Export-Import Bank of the United States (USGC)
EXIMBANK...	Export-Import Bank of the United States (TDOB)
EXIMBK.......	Export-Import Bank
EX INT	Excluding Interest [*Finance*] (WDAA)
EXIS...........	Expert Information Systems Ltd. [*Information service or system*] (IID)
EXIST..........	Existing
EXIT	Export Integrated System
EXITE	Energetic X-Ray Imaging Telescope Experiment (MCD)
EXIX...........	Executrix (ROG)
EXJ	Executive Jet Italiana SRL [*Italy ICAO designator*] (FAAC)
EXJAM	Expendable Communications Jammer [*Army*] (INF)
EXK.............	Kalamazoo College, Kalamazoo, MI [*OCLC symbol*] (OCLC)
EXL.............	Exall Resources Ltd. [*Toronto Stock Exchange symbol*]
EXL.............	Exclusive Air P Ltd. [*South Africa*] [*FAA designator*] (FAAC)
EXL.............	Exolon-Esk Co. [*BO Symbol*] (TTSB)
EXL.............	Western Michigan University, School of Librarianship, Kalamazoo, MI [*OCLC symbol*] (OCLC)
EX LIB	Ex Libris [*From the Library Of*] [*Book plate*] [*Latin*] (ROG)
EXLST.........	Exit List [*Computer science*]
EXLV	Excess Leave [*Military*]
EXM............	CAA Flight Examiners [*British ICAO designator*] (FAAC)
EXM............	Exempt
EXM............	Exhaust Muffler
EXM............	Expense Management and Control, Inc. [*Vancouver Stock Exchange symbol*]
ExMBA	Executive Master's of Business Administration (RDA)
EX-MER	Ex-Meridian [*Navigation*]
EXMETNET...	Experimental Meteorological Sounding Rocket Research Network (IEEE)
EXMNR	Examiner
EXMNTN	Examination
EXMOVREP...	Expedited Movement Report [*Army*] (AABC)
EXMP.........	Expanded Metal Plate [*Technical drawings*]
EXMPT........	Exempt
EXMPTD	Exempted
EXMR.........	Examiner
Ex MSE......	Executive Master of Science in Engineering (PGP)
ExMSE	Executive Master's of Science in Science and Technology Commercialization (RDA)
EXN............	Andrews University, Berrien Springs, MI [*OCLC symbol*] (OCLC)
EXN............	Europeaero Service National [*France ICAO designator*] (FAAC)
EXN............	Exin [*Poland ICAO designator*] (FAAC)
EXNOR........	Exclusive-Nor Gate (HGAA)
EXO............	European X-Ray Observatory
EXO............	Executive Officer
Exo.............	Exodus [*Old Testament book*] (DSA)
EXO............	Exonuclease [*An enzyme*]
ExO............	Experimental Officer [*Also, EO, XO*] [*Ministry of Agriculture, Fisheries, and Food*] [*British*]
EXO............	Experiment Operator (MCD)
EXO............	Extotal Resources, Inc. [*Vancouver Stock Exchange symbol*]
EXO............	Olivet College, Olivet, MI [*OCLC symbol*] (OCLC)
Exod...........	Exodus [*Old Testament book*]
EXOF..........	Expanded Quota Flow [*Aviation*] (FAAC)
EX OFF	Ex Officio [*By Virtue of Office*] [*Latin*] (ROG)
EX OFFICIN...	Ex Officina [*From the Workshop Of*] [*Latin*] (ROG)
Exogen........	Exogen, Inc. [*Associated Press*] (SAG)
EXOIII	Exonuclease III [*An enzyme*]
EXON	Execution (ROG)
EXON	Exonia [*Exeter*] [*British*]
Exon............	Exoniensis [*Of Exeter*] [*Latin*] (ILCA)
EXON D........	Exeter Domesday Book [*A publication*] (ROG)
EXOP..........	Executive Office of the President
EXOP..........	Experiment and Operations (KSC)
EXO-PAC......	Exoatmospheric Penetration Aids Concept (MCD)
EXOR	Exclusive Or [*Gates*] [*Computer science*]
EXOR	Executor (ROG)
EXORCS.......	Exoatmospheric Plume RADAR Cross Section (MCD)
EXORD........	Exercise Order [*Military*] (AFM)
EXOS	Executive Office of the Secretary [*Navy*]
EXOS	Executive Operating System [*Military*] (CAAL)
EXOS	Exospheric Satellite [*Japan*]
EXOSAT	European X-Ray Observatory Satellite (MCD)
EXOX	Executrix
EXP.............	Business Express Delivery Ltd. [*Canada ICAO designator*] (FAAC)
EXP.............	Du Pont [*E. I.*] De Nemours & Co., Inc. [*Research code symbol*]
EXP.............	Expand (NASA)
EXP.............	Expandable Personnel Shelter (MCD)
EXP.............	Expansion (KSC)
EX P	Ex Parte [*One-Sided Statement*] [*Latin Legal term*] (ROG)
EXP.............	Expect
EXP.............	Expectorant [*Pharmacy*] (ROG)
EXP.............	Expectorated [*Medicine*]
EXP.............	Expedition (ADA)
EXP.............	Expend
EXP.............	Expense (AABC)
EXP.............	Expense
EXP.............	Experienced
EXP.............	Experiment (KSC)
exp..............	Experimental (IDOE)
EXP.............	Expert
exp..............	Expiratory [*Respiration*] (DAVI)
EXP.............	Expired (ROG)
Exp.............	Explained [*Legal term*] (DLA)
exp..............	Exploration (MAE)
EXP.............	Explosive
EXP.............	Exponential
exp..............	Exponential (IDOE)
exp..............	Exponential Function [*Mathematics*] (DAVI)
EXP.............	Export
EXP.............	Expose (KSC)
EXP.............	Exposition of the Blessed Sacrament [*Roman Catholic*]
EXP.............	Exposure (WGA)
exp..............	Exposure (VRA)
exp..............	Exposure (WDMC)
EXP.............	Express (AABC)
EXP.............	Expressway [*Commonly used*] (OPSA)
Exp.............	Expropriation [*Legal term*] (DLA)
EXP.............	Expulsion (KSC)
EXP.............	Expurgated
EXP.............	Natural Logarithm [*Mathematics*]
EXP.............	Orgue Expressif [*Swell Organ*] [*Music*]
EXP.............	Portage Public Schools, Portage, MI [*OCLC symbol*] (OCLC)
ExPAN.........	Explorer Plus Guidance Application Network [*Electronic college application*]
EXPAT.........	Expatriate (DSUE)
ExpB...........	[*The*] Expositor's Bible [*A publication*] (BJA)
EXP BT	Expansion Bolt [*Technical drawings*] (DAC)
EXPC..........	Expect (FAAC)
EXPC..........	Experience (AABC)
EXPD	Expeditor
EXPD	Expeditors International of Washington, Inc. [*NASDAQ symbol*] (NQ)

EXPD	Expeditors Intl,Wash [*NASDAQ symbol*] (TTSB)
EXPD	Expired (ROG)
EXPD	Exposed
ExpdInt	Expeditors International of Washington [*Associated Press*] (SAG)
EXPDIVUNIT	Experimental Diving Unit
EXPDN	Expedition
EXPDTN	Expedition
EXPDTR	Expeditor
expect	Expectorant [*Pharmacology*] (DAVI)
EXPED	Expediting
EXPED	Expeditionary
EXPELS	Expandable Precision Emitter Location System (MCD)
EXPEN	Expendable (MSA)
EXPEND	Expendable
EXPEND	Expenditure
EXPER	Experienced
EXPER	Experiment [*or Experimental*] (AFM)
Exper	Experimental Light [*Navigation signal*]
EXPERT	Expanded Program Evaluation and Review Technique
EXPFLDMB	Expert Field Medical Badge [*Military decoration*] (GFGA)
ExPGN	Extracapillary Proliferative Glomerulonephritis [*Nephrology*]
ExpGT	[*The*] Expositor's Greek Testament [*A publication*] (BJA)
EXPHO	Expedite Delivery by Telephone (FAAC)
EXP-IMP	Export-Import (WDAA)
EXPIO	Expander Input/Output [*Microprocessing*] (NITA)
EXPIR	Expiration [*or Expiratory*] [*Medicine*]
expir	Expire [*Medicine*] (DAVI)
EXPL	Explanation
expl	Exploratory [*Surgery*] (DAVI)
EXPL	Explorer
EXPL	Explosion (ECII)
EXPL	Explosive (KSC)
EXPLAN	Exercise Plan [*Military*] (AFM)
EXPLAN	Explanatory (ADA)
Exp Lap	Exploratory Laparatomy [*Medicine*]
EXPLD	Explained (ROG)
EXPLD	Explode (MSA)
EXPLET	Expletive (ROG)
Expl Lap	Exploratory Laparotomy [*Surgical procedure*] (DAVI)
EXPLN	Explosion (MSA)
EXPLO	Explosive (AABC)
EXPLOR	Explicit 2-D Patterns Local Operations and Randomness [*Programming language*] [*1975*] (CSR)
explor	Exploration (DD)
Explor	Exploration Co. [*Associated Press*] (SAG)
explos	Explosive
Explos Anch	Explosive Anchorage [*Buoy*]
EXPLR	Exploder
EXPLRN	Exploration
EXPLSV	Explosive
EXPN	Expansion [*Automotive engineering*]
EXPN	Expiration (ROG)
EXPN	Exportation
EXPN	Exposition
EXPND	Expenditure (AFM)
EXPNT	Exponent (MSA)
EXPNT	Exponential (MSA)
EXPO	Experimental Order (MSA)
EXPO	Exposition
expo	Exposition (VRA)
EXPO	Exposition
Expo	Exposition (ODBW)
EXPO	Expressivo [*With Expression*] [*Music*] (ROG)
EXPO	Extended-Range Poseidon [*Missile*] [*Navy*]
EXPOS	X-Ray Spectropolarimetry Payload on Spacelab (MCD)
EXPOSE	Ex-Partners of Servicemen (Women) for Equality (EA)
Ex-POWAA	Ex-Prisoners of War Association of Australia
ExpQualBad	Expert Qualification Badge [*Military decoration*] (AABC)
EXPR	Experiment (IAA)
EXPR	Expert
EXPR	Expire (AABC)
EXPR	Expression
EXPR	Expressway [*Commonly used*] (OPSA)
EXPR	Orgue Expressif [*Swell Organ*] [*Music*]
ExprAm	Express America Holdings [*Commercial firm Associated Press*] (SAG)
EXPRES	Experimental Research in Electronic Submission of Scientific Documents Program [*Washington, DC National Science Foundation*]
EXPRESS	Expendable Parts Record and Structures System (IAA)
EXPRESS	Expert Requirements Expression and Systems Synthesis (SSD)
EXPRESS	Expressway [*Commonly used*] (OPSA)
EXPRESSWAY	Expressway [*Commonly used*] (OPSA)
EXPRMNT	Experiment
EXPRNC	Experience
EXPRO	Experiment Procedures (KSC)
ExPro	Exploratory Project on the Conditions of Peace [*Defunct*] (EA)
EXPRSS	Express
EXPRSSN	Expression
EXPRT	Export
EXPRTR	Exporter
EXPS	Expenses (ROG)
EXPS	Expose
EXPS	Express (FAAC)
EXPSAS	Engineering Change Proposal Service Action Status (AAG)

ExpScpt	Express Scripts, Inc. [*Associated Press*] (SAG)
EXPSN	Expansion
ExpSoft	Expert Software, Inc. [*Associated Press*] (SAG)
EXPSR	Exposure (MSA)
EXPT	Expect (AABC)
EXPT	Expectorant [*Pharmacy*]
EXPT	Experiment
EXPT	Expert (WGA)
EXPT	Export (WGA)
EXPTE	Ex Parte [*One-Sided Statement*] [*Latin Legal term*] (ROG)
EXPTL	Experimental
EXPTO	Expedite Travel Order (NOAA)
EXPTR	Exporter (ADA)
EXPURG	Expurgated (ADA)
EXPW	Expressway [*Commonly used*] (OPSA)
EXPWY	Expressway (WDAA)
EXPY	Expressway (MCD)
EXPY	Expressway [*Postal Service standard*] (OPSA)
EXPY	Expressway
Expy	Expressway (DD)
EXQ	Aquinas College, Grand Rapids, MI [*OCLC symbol*] (OCLC)
EXQ	Execujet [*British ICAO designator*] (FAAC)
EXQ	Ex Quay [*Seller's responsibility is to make goods available on the wharf at destination named*] [*"INCOTERM," International Chamber of Commerce official code*]
EXQF	Expanded Quota Flow (FAAC)
EXQQPRI	Expedited Qualitative and Quantitative Personnel Requirements Information [*Army*]
EXR	Execute and Repeat
EXR	Executor
ExR	Exodus Rabbah (BJA)
EXR	Express Resources Ltd. [*Vancouver Stock Exchange symbol*]
Ex R	Ex-Rights [*Without Rights*] [*Investment term*]
EXR	Flight Express, Inc. [*ICAO designator*] (FAAC)
EXR	Grand Rapids Public Library, Grand Rapids, MI [*OCLC symbol*] (OCLC)
EXRAY	Expendable Remote Array (PDAA)
EXREDCON	Exercise Readiness Condition [*Military*] (AABC)
EX REL	Ex Relatione [*On the Report Of*] [*Latin*] (ADA)
EXREM	External REM [*Roentgen-Equivalent-Man*] [*Radiology*]
EXREP	Expedite Mail Reply (FAAC)
EXREQ	Extract of Requisition
EXRX	Executrix
EXS	Channel Express (Air Services) Ltd. [*British ICAO designator*] (FAAC)
Exs	De Exsecrationibus [*Philo*] (BJA)
ExS	Exogenous Substance [*Biology*]
EXS	Expenses
EXS	Ex Ship [*Seller's responsibility is to make goods available on board ship at destination named*] [*"INCOTERM," International Chamber of Commerce official code*]
EXS	Extrastrong [*Technical drawings*]
EXS	Western Theological Seminary, Holland, MI [*OCLC symbol*] (OCLC)
EX SC	Ex Senatus Consulto [*By Decree of the Senate*] [*Latin*] (ROG)
EX SD	Ex Senatus Decreto [*By Decree of the Senate*] [*Latin*] (ROG)
exsec	Exsecant [*Mathematics*] (BARN)
EXSEC	Extra Section (FAAC)
EXSH	Expeditionary Shelters [*Marine Corps*] (MCD)
EXSHI	Expedite Shipment (NOAA)
EXSL	Exhibition of Sports and Leisure [*British*] (ITD)
EXSM	Excessive Soil Moisture (PDAA)
EXSO	Exsorbet Industries [*NASDAQ symbol*] (TTSB)
EXSO	Exsorbet Industries, Inc. [*NASDAQ symbol*] (SAG)
Exsorbet	Exsorbet Industries, Inc. [*Associated Press*] (SAG)
EXSPEC	Exercise Specification [*NATO*] (NATG)
EXSR	Executive Subroutine [*NASA*] (IAA)
EXST	Execute Stack [*Computer science*] (IAA)
EXST	Existing (MSA)
EXSTA	Experimental Station
Exstar	Exstar Financial Corp. [*Associated Press*] (SAG)
EXSUBCOM	Exploitable Subcommittee [*Military*]
EXSUM	Executive Summary (MCD)
EXSWG	Exploration Science Working Group [*NASA*] (EGAO)
EXT	Except (ROG)
EXT	Exeter [*England*] [*Airport symbol*] (OAG)
EXT	Experiment Terminal (MCD)
EXT	Extant
EXT	Extend [*or Extension*] (AFM)
EXT	Extende [*Spread*] [*Pharmacy*]
EXT	Extension
ext	Extension (WDMC)
EXT	Extension
EXT	Extensor [*Anatomy*]
EXT	Exterior (AABC)
ext	Exterior (VRA)
ext	Exterior (WDMC)
ext	External (WDMC)
EXT	External (AABC)
ext	Externus [*External*] [*Latin*]
EXT	Extinct
ext	Extinct (WDMC)
EXT	Extinguish (KSC)
EXT	Extortion [*FBI standardized term*]
EXT	Extra
ext	Extra (WDMC)
ext	Extract (WDMC)

EXT............	Extract [or Extracted]
Ext.............	Extraction [Dentistry] (DAVI)
EXT............	Extractum [Extract] [Latin]
EXT Comm...	Extra Executive Transport [Germany ICAO designator] (FAAC)
EXT............	Extraordinary
Ext.............	Extrapolation [A publication] (BRI)
EXT............	Extreme
EXT............	Extremity [Medicine]
Ext.............	Extrudate
EXT............	Night Express [Germany] [FAA designator] (FAAC)
EXTAC........	Experimental Tactic (NVT)
EXTAL........	Extra Time Allowance
EXTBAT......	Extension Battery (IAA)
EXTCD........	Extension Cord (IAA)
EXTD.........	Extend [or Extended] (KSC)
EXTD.........	Extracted
EXTD.........	Extrude (MSA)
EXT D & C...	External Drug and Cosmetic [Color]
exte...........	Exterior (BARN)
Extecp........	Extecapital Ltd. [Associated Press] (SAG)
EXTEL........	Exchange Telegraph [Press agency] [British] (DCTA)
EXTEMP......	Extemporaneous (WDAA)
EXTEN........	Extended [Automotive advertising]
Extend........	Extendicare, Inc. [Associated Press] (SAG)
EXTENDEX...	Extended Exercise [Navy] (ANA)
EXTENL.......	Extension of Enlistment [Military]
EXTENSION...	Extension [Commonly used] (OPSA)
EXTENSIONS...	Extensions [Commonly used] (OPSA)
EXTER........	External (KSC)
Exter Ca......	Lobingier's Extra-Territorial Cases [United States Court for China] [A publication] (DLA)
EXTERM......	Exterminating
extern........	Externally [Medicine] (BARN)
EXTERRA.....	Extraterrestrial Research Agency [Army] (IEEE)
EXT FHR......	External Fetal Heart Rate (MEDA)
Ext Fl.........	Fluid Extract [Pharmacology] (DAVI)
EXTFP........	Experienced Teacher Fellowship Program
EXTFREQ.....	Extension Frequency (IAA)
EXTG.........	Extinguish (AAG)
EXTG.........	Extracting (MSA)
EXTGH.......	Extinguish
EXTGR........	Extinguisher (AAG)
EXTHEO......	Extra-Theoretical [Telecommunications] (TEL)
EXTIN........	Extinguish (ROG)
EXTING......	Extinguish (KSC)
Exting........	Extinguished Light [Navigation signal]
EXTL.........	Executive Telecard Ltd. [NASDAQ symbol] (SAG)
EXTL.........	Executive Telecard Ltd [NASDAQ symbol] (TTSB)
EXTL.........	External (DLA)
EXT LIQ......	Extractum Liquidum [Liquid extract] [Latin Pharmacy] (WDAA)
EXT LRCP....	Extra Licentiate of the Royal College of Physicians [British] (ROG)
EXTLV........	Extension of Leave [Military] (AABC)
EXTM.........	Extended Telecommunications Modules
EXTM.........	Ex Testamento [In Accordance with the Testament Of] [Latin]
EXTM.........	Extreme (MSA)
EXTN.........	Extension
extn..........	Extension (WDMC)
EXTN.........	Extraction
EXTND.......	Extended
EXTND.......	Extender (MSA)
EXTNL.......	External
EXTNR.......	Extender
EXTNS	Extension
extns..........	Extension (VRA)
EXTNSN......	Extension [Commonly used] (OPSA)
EXTON.......	Executone Information Systems, Inc. [Associated Press] (SAG)
Exton Mar Dic...	Exton's Maritime Dicaeologie [A publication] (DLA)
EXTOR.......	External Torpedo [Formerly, DEXTOR] (MCD)
EXTORP......	Exercise Torpedo (NVT)
EXTOXNET ...	Extension Toxicology Network (GNE)
EXT P........	Extra Parochial [Geographical division] [British]
EXTR..........	Executor [Business term]
EXTR..........	Executor
EXTR..........	Exstar Financial Corp. [NASDAQ symbol] (SAG)
EXTR..........	External (ROG)
EXTR..........	Extra (ROG)
EXTR..........	Extract
EXTR..........	Extraordinary (ROG)
EXTR..........	Extravagant (ROG)
extr...........	Extreme
extr	Extremity (MAH)
EXTR..........	Extrude (MSA)
EXTRA	Exponentially-Tapered Reactive Antenna (IAA)
EXTRA	Export Tender Risk Advance [British]
EXTRA	Extended Education in Therapeutic Recreation Administration (EDAC)
Extra Ca......	Lobingier's Extra-Territorial Cases [United States Court for China] [A publication] (DLA)
EXTRACONUS...	Outside Continental United States [Military] (AFIT)
EXTRAD......	Extradition (ADA)
EXTRADOP...	Extended-Range Doppler
EXTRADOVAP...	Extended-Range Doppler Velocity and Position (CET)
EXTRAH......	Extrahatur [Draw Out] [Pharmacy] (ROG)
EXTRAN......	Expression Translator [Computer science] (MHDI)
EXTRAOR....	Extraordinary (ROG)
Extra Sess ...	Extraordinary Session [A publication] (DLA)

EXTRAV	Extravaganza (ROG)
Extrav Com...	Extravagantes Communes [A publication] (DSA)
Extrav Joann XXII...	Extravagantes Johannes XXII [A publication] (DSA)
Extr Comm...	Extravagantes Communes [A publication] (DSA)
EXTRCT......	Extract
EXTRCTR....	Extractor
EXTRE........	Exstar Financial [NASDAQ symbol] (TTSB)
EXTREM......	External Roentgem-Equivalent-Man Dose [Radiation therapy] (DAVI)
EXTREM......	Extremity [Medicine] (WDAA)
EXTRIX	Executrix
Extr Joann XXII...	Extravagantes Johannes XXII [A publication] (DSA)
EXTRM........	Extreme (FAAC)
EXTRM........	Extreme
EXTRN	External Reference (BUR)
EXTRN	Extrusion (MSA)
ext rot........	External Rotation [Myology] (MAE)
EXTRRDNRY...	Extraordinary
EXTRX	Executrix [Business term]
EXTS...........	Extensions
EXTS...........	Extensions [Postal Service standard] (OPSA)
EXTSN	Extension (MDG)
ExtStA........	Extended Stay America [Associated Press] (SAG)
EXT sup ALUT MOLL...	Extende super Alutum Mollem [Spread upon Soft Leather] [Pharmacy] (ROG)
EXTSV.........	Extensive (FAAC)
EXTV..........	Extensive
EXTVE........	Executive
EXTW.........	Extension Wire (IAA)
EXU...........	Excretory Urogram [Medicine] (DMAA)
EXU...........	Executive Transports [France ICAO designator] (FAAC)
EXU...........	Upjohn Co., Technical Library, Kalamazoo, MI [OCLC symbol] (OCLC)
EXUD.........	Excudit [Made] [Latin] (ROG)
EXUP.........	Exhaust Ultimate Power Valve [Yamaha Motor Co.]
EXUV.........	Extreme Ultraviolet and X-Ray Survey Satellite (PDAA)
EXV...........	Executive Air Transport Ltd. [Switzerland ICAO designator] (FAAC)
EXW..........	Executive Airlines Services Ltd. [Nigeria] [FAA designator] (FAAC)
EXW..........	Explosion Welding
EXW..........	Extreme Width
Ex W	Ex-Warrants [Without Warrants] [Finance]
EXW...........	Ex Works [Seller's only responsibility is to make goods available at his premises] ["INCOTERM," International Chamber of Commerce official code]
EXW..........	Martinsburg, WV [Location identifier FAA] (FAAL)
EXW..........	Western Michigan University, Kalamazoo, MI [OCLC symbol] (OCLC)
EXWEP........	Exercise Weapon (NVT)
EXX...........	Exador Resources, Inc. [Toronto Stock Exchange symbol]
EXX...........	Examples
EXX...........	Executrix
EXX...........	EXX, Inc. [Formerly, SFM Corp.] [AMEX symbol] (SAG)
EXX...........	International Air Corp. [FAA designator] (FAAC)
EXX...........	Lexington, NC [Location identifier FAA] (FAAL)
Exxon..........	Exxon Corp. [Associated Press] (SAG)
EXY...........	SA Exress Airways [South Africa] [FAA designator] (FAAC)
EXZ...........	Ezzellenz [Excellency] [German]
EXZ...........	Kalamazoo Library System, Kalamazoo, MI [OCLC symbol] (OCLC)
EY.............	Eastern Yiddish (BJA)
EY.............	East Yorkshire Militia [British military] (DMA)
EY.............	Eger's Yellow
EY.............	Egg Yolk
EY.............	Electron Yield
EY.............	Elvisly Yours [Fan club] (EAIO)
EY.............	Entry Year [Information retrieval] (NITA)
EY.............	Equilibrium Yield [Fishery management] (MSC)
EY.............	Essex Yeomanry [British military] (DMA)
EY.............	Ethyl Corp. [NYSE symbol Toronto Stock Exchange symbol] (SPSG)
EY.............	Europe Aero Service [ICAO designator] (AD)
EY.............	Execution Year
EYA...........	Egg Yok-Pyruvate-Tellurite-Glycine Agar [Microbiology] (DAVI)
EYA...........	Egg Yolk-Pyruvate-Tellurite-Glycine Agar [Medicine] (BABM)
EYA...........	Washtenaw Community College, Ann Arbor, MI [OCLC symbol] (OCLC)
EYB...........	Europa Year Book [A publication] (MHDB)
EYB...........	Macomb County Library, Mt. Clemens, MI [OCLC symbol] (OCLC)
EYBSOYB.....	Examine Your Birthday Suit on Your Birthday [To detect potentially malignant moles] [Skin Cancer Foundation]
EYC...........	European Youth Campaign
EYC...........	European Youth Centre [Council of Europe] (EY)
EYC...........	Michigan Library Consortium, Wayne State University, Detroit, MI [OCLC symbol] (OCLC)
EYCD	European Young Christian Democrats [Formerly, European Union of Young Christian Democrats] (EA)
EYCE..........	Ecumenical Youth Council in Europe (EAIO)
EYCO..........	Estimated Yearly Cost of Operation [of electrical appliance]
EYD...........	Engineering Youth Day
EYD...........	University of Michigan, Dearborn Campus, Dearborn, MI [OCLC symbol] (OCLC)
EYE...........	BEC Group [NYSE symbol] (TTSB)
EYE...........	BEC Group, Inc. [NYSE symbol] (SAG)
EYE...........	Benson Eyecare Corp. [NYSE symbol] (SAG)
EYE...........	Eastern Michigan University, Ypsilanti, MI [OCLC symbol] (OCLC)
EYE...........	Emerald Air [British] [FAA designator] (FAAC)
EYE...........	European Year of the Environment [Beginning March 23, 1987]
EYE...........	Indianapolis, IN [Location identifier FAA] (FAAL)
EYF...........	European Youth Foundation (EA)

EYF .... Henry Ford Hospital, Medical Library, Detroit, MI [*OCLC symbol*] (OCLC)

EYG .... General Motors Corp., Research Laboratory, Warren, MI [*OCLC symbol*] (OCLC)

EYH .... Huron Valley Library System, Ann Arbor, MI [*OCLC symbol*] (OCLC)

EYI .... Livonia Public Schools, Livonia, MI [*OCLC symbol*] (OCLC)

EYJ .... John Wesley College Library, Owosso, MI [*Inactive*] [*OCLC symbol*] (OCLC)

EYL .... Lawrence Institute of Technology, Southfield, MI [*OCLC symbol*] (OCLC)

EYLT .... Eyelet (MSA)

EYM .... Electron Yield Measurement

EYM .... University of Michigan, Ann Arbor, MI [*OCLC symbol*] (OCLC)

EYMS .... Electron Yield Measurement System

EYN .... Europeaero Service National [*France*] [*FAA designator*] (FAAC)

EYOA .... Economic and Youth Opportunity Agency (IIA)

EYOC .... Estimated Yearly Operating Cost [*of electrical appliance*]

EYOP .... European Year of Older People and Solidarity Between Generations

E YORK R .... East Yorkshire Regiment [*Military unit*] [*British*] (ROG)

EYP .... Detroit Public Library, Detroit, MI [*OCLC symbol*] (OCLC)

EYP .... East York Public Library [*UTLAS symbol*]

EYP .... Electronic Yellow Pages [*Dun's Marketing Services*] [*Information service or system*] (IID)

EYP .... El Yopal [*Colombia*] [*Airport symbol*] (OAG)

EYP .... El Yunque [*Puerto Rico*] [*Seismograph station code, US Geological Survey Closed*] (SEIS)

EYP .... Port Huron, MI [*Location identifier FAA*] (FAAL)

EYPC .... Eyepiece (MSA)

EYQ .... Detroit Cooperative Cataloging Center, Detroit, MI [*OCLC symbol*] (OCLC)

EYR .... East Yorkshire Regiment [*Military unit*] [*British*]

EYR .... Eyrewell [*New Zealand*] [*Geomagnetic observatory code*]

EYR .... Oakland University, Rochester, MI [*OCLC symbol*] (OCLC)

Eyre .... Eyre's English King's Bench Reports Tempore William III [*A publication*] (DLA)

Eyre MS ...... Eyre's Manuscript Notes of Cases, King's Bench [*New York Law Institute Library*] [*A publication*] (DLA)

EYS .... Board of Education for the Borough of East York [*UTLAS symbol*]

EYS .... Experimental Yacht Society [*Defunct*] (EA)

EYS .... St. Clair County Library System, Port Huron, MI [*OCLC symbol*] (OCLC)

EYS .... World Council of Churches Ecumenical Youth Service (EA)

EYT .... Detroit Institute of Arts, Research Library, Detroit, MI [*OCLC symbol*] (OCLC)

EYT .... Europe Aero Service [*France ICAO designator*] (FAAC)

EYU .... University of Detroit, Detroit, MI [*OCLC symbol*] (OCLC)

e-yu-- .... Yugoslavia [*MARC geographic area code Library of Congress*] (LCCP)

EYV .... Wayne County Community College, Detroit, MI [*OCLC symbol*] (OCLC)

EYW .... Key West [*Florida*] [*Airport symbol*] (OAG)

EYW .... Key West, FL [*Location identifier FAA*] (FAAL)

EYW .... Wayne State University, Detroit, MI [*OCLC symbol*] (OCLC)

EYY .... Mercy College of Detroit, Detroit, MI [*OCLC symbol*] (OCLC)

EYZ .... Madonna College, Livonia, MI [*OCLC symbol*] (OCLC)

EZ .... Eastern Zone

EZ .... Easy [*Slang*]

EZ .... Easy Listening [*Radio*] (NTCM)

EZ .... Eczema [*Medicine*]

EZ .... Eineiige Zwillinge [*Monozygotic Twins*] [*Psychology*]

EZ .... Electrical Zero

EZ .... Engagement Zone [*Army*] (ADDR)

EZ .... Enterprise Zone [*British*]

E/Z .... Equal Zero (MDG)

EZ .... Extraction Zone [*Military*] (AFM)

Ez. .... Ezekiel [*Old Testament book*]

Ez. .... Ezra [*Old Testament book*]

EZ .... Sun-Air of Scandinavia [*ICAO designator*] (AD)

EZA .... Alma College, Alma, MI [*OCLC symbol*] (OCLC)

EZA .... Newark, NJ [*Location identifier FAA*] (FAAL)

EZACC .... Easy Access

EZB .... Cloverland Processing Center, Escanaba, MI [*OCLC symbol*] (OCLC)

EZB .... Oakland, CA [*Location identifier FAA*] (FAAL)

EZC .... Central Michigan University, Mount Pleasant, MI [*OCLC symbol*] (OCLC)

EZC .... European Zone Charge (DS)

EZCI .... EZ Communications, Inc. [*NASDAQ symbol*] (SAG)

EZCIA .... E-Z Communications'A' [*NASDAQ symbol*] (TTSB)

EZCO .... Extraction Zone Control Officer [*Military*] (AFM)

EZCO .... Ezcony Interamerica, Inc. [*NASDAQ symbol*] (SAG)

EZCOF .... Ezcony Interamerica [*NASDAQ symbol*] (TTSB)

EZ Com .... EZ Communications, Inc. [*Associated Press*] (SAG)

Ezcony .... Ezcony Interamerica, Inc. [*Associated Press*] (SAG)

Ezcorp .... Ezcorp, Inc. [*Associated Press*] (SAG)

EZD .... Enziklopedyah shel ha-Ziyonut ha-Datit [*A publication*] (BJA)

EZE .... Buenos Aires [*Argentina*] Ezeiza [*Airport symbol*] (OAG)

EZ/EC .... Empowerment Zones/Enterprise Communities [*Medicine*]

EZECH .... Ezechiel [*Old Testament book*] [*Douay version*]

Ezek. .... Ezekiel [*Old Testament book*]

EZEM .... EXEM, Inc. [*Associated Press*] (SAG)

EZEM .... E-Z-EM, Inc. [*NASDAQ symbol*] (NQ)

EZEV .... Equivalent Zero-Emission Vehicle

EZF .... Ferris State College, Big Rapids, MI [*OCLC symbol*] (OCLC)

EZI .... European Zinc Institute (EA)

EZI .... Kewanee, IL [*Location identifier FAA*] (FAAL)

EZI .... Mid-Peninsula Library Cooperative, Iron Mountain, MI [*OCLC symbol*] (OCLC)

EZK .... Ezekiel [*Old Testament book*]

EZL .... Lake Superior State College, Sault Ste. Marie, MI [*OCLC symbol*] (OCLC)

EZM .... EZEM, Inc. [*AMEX symbol*] (SAG)

EZM .... Muskegon County Library, Muskegon, MI [*OCLC symbol*] (OCLC)

EZN .... Ezine [*Turkey*] [*Seismograph station code, US Geological Survey*] (SEIS)

EZN .... Northern Michigan University, Marquette, MI [*OCLC symbol*] (OCLC)

EZP .... Elliptical Zone Plate (PDAA)

EZP .... Superiorland Library Cooperative, Marquette, MI [*OCLC symbol*] (OCLC)

EZPW .... EZCORP, Inc. [*NASDAQ symbol*] (SPSG)

EZPW .... EZCORP Inc.'A' [*NASDAQ symbol*] (TTSB)

Ezr .... Ezra [*Old Testament book*]

EZR .... Gulf of Alaska/Bering Sea, AK [*Location identifier FAA*] (FAAL)

EZS .... Edgar Z. Steever IV [*Designer's mark when appearing on US coins*]

EZS .... Elazig [*Turkey*] [*Airport symbol*] (OAG)

EZS .... E-Z Serve Corp. [*AMEX symbol*] (SPSG)

EZS .... Saginaw Valley State College, University Center, MI [*OCLC symbol*] (OCLC)

EZ Serv .... EZ Serve [*Associated Press*] (SAG)

EZT .... Elizabethton, TN [*Location identifier FAA*] (FAAL)

EZT .... Michigan Technological University, Houghton, MI [*OCLC symbol*] (OCLC)

EZT .... Zenit [*Former USSR*] [*FAA designator*] (FAAC)

EZV .... EZ Ventures Ltd. [*Vancouver Stock Exchange symbol*]

EZW .... White Pine Library System, Saginaw, MI [*OCLC symbol*] (OCLC)

EZY .... Elk City, OK [*Location identifier FAA*] (FAAL)

EZZ .... Michigan North Processing Center, Cadillac, MI [*OCLC symbol*] (OCLC)

F

By Acronym

f .... Acceleration [*Symbol*] (DEN)
f----- .... Africa [*MARC geographic area code Library of Congress*] (LCCP)
F .... Air Force Training Category [*No inactive duty periods and 4 months minimum initial active duty training per year*]
F .... Atlanta [*Branch in the Federal Reserve regional banking system*] (BARN)
f .... Atomic Orbital with Angular Momentum Quantum Number 3 [*Symbol*] (DAVI)
F .... Blue Second Hydrogen Line in the Solar Spectrum (BARN)
f .... Breathing Frequency [*Medicine*] (DAVI)
F .... College of Future Education [*British*]
F .... Consuetudines Feudorum [*The Book of Feuds*] [*Latin A publication*] (DLA)
F .... Dealt in Flat [*Investment term*] (DFIT)
F .... Degrees Fahrenheit (MCD)
F .... Dominion Rubber Co. [*Research code symbol*] [*Canada*]
F .... Eaton Laboratories, Inc. [*Research code symbol*]
F .... Fac [*Let There Be Made*] [*Pharmacy*]
F .... Face
F .... Facial Rash [*Classification system used by doctors on Ellis Island to detain, re-examine, and possibly deny entry to certain immigrants*]
F .... Facial Surface [*Dentistry*]
F .... Facies [*Medicine*]
F .... Facing (WDAA)
F .... Factor (DAVI)
F .... Faculty of Advocates Collection of Decisions, Scotch Court of Sessions [*A publication*] (DLA)
F .... Fahrenheit [*German*] (EG)
F .... Failure
F .... Fair
F .... Fair Skiing Conditions
F .... Falck [*When used in identifying W. F. Bach's compositions, refers to cataloging of his works by musicologist Falck*]
F .... Falls (ROG)
F .... False
F .... Family
F .... Farad [*Symbol*] [*Unit of electric capacitance*] (GPO)
F .... Faraday Constant [*Electrochemistry*]
F .... Farce (ROG)
F .... Farthing [*Monetary unit*] [*British*]
F .... Fast
F .... Fasting [*Test*] [*Medicine*]
F .... Fat
F .... Father
F .... Fathom
F .... Fatty Acid [*Biochemistry*] (HGAA)
F .... Fawn (WGA)
F .... Feast
F .... February
F .... Feces
F .... Fecit [*He, or She, Did It*] [*Latin*]
F .... Federal (AAGC)
F .... Federal League [*Major league in baseball, 1914-15*]
F .... Federal Reporter [*A publication*] (DLA)
F .... Feedback
F .... Feet [*or Foot*]
F .... Feldspar Subgroup [*Orthoclase, albite, anorthite*] [*CIPW classification Geology*]
F .... Feliciter [*Happily*]
F .... Fell [*Horse racing*]
F .... Fellow
F .... Felon
F .... Female
f .... Female (DD)
F .... Feminine
F .... Femmes [*or Feminin*] [*Initial used as title of a publication*]
f .... Femto [*A prefix meaning divided by 10 to the 15th power*] [*SI symbol*]
F .... Fen [*Monetary unit*] [*China*]
F .... Fendi [*Italian couturier*]
F .... Fenoterol [*Pharmacology*]
F .... Fermentation [*Biology*]
F .... Fermi [*Later, Femtometer*] [*Unit of length Nuclear physics*]
F .... Ferrosan [*Sweden*] [*Research code symbol*]
F .... Ferrule Contact [*Lamp base type*] (NTCM)

F .... Fertile [*Medicine*]
F .... Fertility Factor [*Genetics*]
F .... Fertilized
F .... Fetal [*Medicine*]
F .... Fetch [*Computer science*]
f .... Fiant [*Let Them be Made*] [*Pharmacology*] (DAVI)
F .... Fiat [*Let It Be Made*] [*Pharmacy*]
F .... Fibre [*Classification key in textile printing*]
F .... Fibrous
F .... Fiction
F .... Field
F .... Field of Vision [*Medicine*]
F .... Fighter [*Designation for all US military aircraft*]
F .... Fiji (BARN)
F .... Filament (AAG)
F .... Filaria [*Microbiology*] (MAE)
F .... File [*Computer science*]
F .... Filial Generation [*Biology*]
F .... Filius [*Son*] [*Latin*]
F .... Filly [*Thoroughbred racing*]
F .... Filter
F .... Final [*Telecommunications*] (TEL)
F .... Final Target
F .... Finance [*or Financial*]
F .... Fine [*Designation on brandy labels*]
F .... Fine [*Condition*] [*Antiquarian book trade, numismatics, etc.*]
F .... Fine [*End*] [*Music*]
F .... Finger
F .... Finish
F .... Fire
F .... Fireman [*Navy rating*]
F .... Firm
F .... First Class [*Airline fare code*]
F' .... First Focal Distance [*Symbol*] [*Optics*] (ROG)
F .... Fischer [*Rat strain*]
F .... Fitted as Flagship [*Suffix to plane designation*]
F .... Fitter [*Navy rating British*]
F .... Fitzherbert's Abridgment [*1516*] [*A publication*] (DSA)
F .... Fixed [*JETDS nomenclature*]
f .... Fixed Format (IAA)
F .... Fixed Head (NITA)
F .... Fixed Light [*Navigation signal*]
F .... Fixer [*Photography*] (DGA)
F .... Flag [*Computer science*]
F .... Flanged Joint (DNAB)
F .... Flash [*Precedence*] [*Telecommunications*] (TEL)
F .... Flat
F .... Flat Band Metallic Armor (AAG)
F .... Flat-Tainers [*British*] (DCTA)
F .... Fleet
F .... Fletcher Challenge Investments, Inc. [*Toronto Stock Exchange symbol Vancouver Stock Exchange symbol*]
F .... Flied Out [*Baseball*]
F .... Flint (AAG)
F .... Floods
F .... Florida State Library, Tallahassee, FL [*Library symbol Library of Congress*] (LCLS)
F .... Florin [*Monetary unit*] [*Netherlands*]
F .... Floryn [*Florin*] [*Monetary unit*] [*Afrikaans*]
F .... Flow [*of blood*] [*Medicine*]
F .... Flow (NFPA)
F .... Flower
F .... Fluency [*A factor ability*] [*Psychology*]
F .... Flugzeug [*Airplane*] [*German military*]
F .... Fluid
F .... Fluid Ounce
F .... Flunk (CDAI)
F .... Fluoride
F .... Fluorine [*Chemical element*]
F .... Fluorouracil [*Also, FU*] [*Antineoplastic drug*]
F .... Flutter Wave (MEDA)
F .... Flying [*Officer qualified as both pilot and observer*] [*British*]
F .... Focal Length [*Photography*]
f .... Focal Length [*Photography*] (WDMC)
F .... Fog [*Meteorology*]
F .... Foil [*Dentistry*]

F	Folge [Series] [Publishing] [German]
F	Folio [Book 30 centimeters and over in height]
f	Folio [On the Following Page] [Latin]
F	Following [Pages] [Also, FF] (MUGU)
f	Following (WDMC)
F	Follow-Up
F	Font
F	Foord's Cape Of Good Hope Reports [South Africa] [A publication] (DLA)
F	Foord's Supreme Court Reports [Cape Colony, South Africa] [A publication] (DLA)
F	For
F	Foraging [Ornithology]
F	Foramen [Anatomy] (MAE)
F	Force [Symbol] [IUPAC]
F	Ford Motor [NYSE symbol] (TTSB)
F	Ford Motor Co. [Wall Street slang names: "Tin Lizzy" or "Flivver"] [NYSE symbol] (SPSG)
F	Forecastle
f	Foreground [Computer science] (IAA)
F	Forint [Monetary unit] [Hungary]
F	Form [of]
F	Form [Rorschach] [Psychology]
F	Form [Letter] [Computer science] [Telecommunications]
F	Forma [Form] [Latin]
F	Formality
F	Formed
F	Formula
f	Formyl [As substituent on nucleoside] [Biochemistry]
F	Fornix [Neuroanatomy]
F	Fort (ROG)
F	Fortasse [Perhaps] [Latin]
F	Forte [Loud] [Music]
F	[The] Forum (AAGC)
F	Forward
F2F	Forward Compartment
F	Foul
F	Founded (EY)
F	Fox [Phonetic alphabet] [World War II] (DSUE)
F	Foxtrot [Phonetic alphabet] [International] (DSUE)
f	Fraction (IAA)
F	Fractional (MAE)
F	Fractional Concentration [in dry gas phase] (AAMN)
F	Fracture
F	Fragile
f	Fragment (BJA)
F	Fragmentation
F	Fragment of an Antibody (DAVI)
F	Frame Construction
F	Franc [Monetary unit] [France]
F	Francais [French]
F	France [IYRU nationality code]
F	Fraser [James E.] [Designer's mark, when appearing on US coins]
F	Fraser, Inc. [Toronto Stock Exchange symbol]
F	Fraser's Scotch Court of Sessions Cases, Fifth Series [A publication] (DLA)
F	Frater [Brother] [Latin]
F	Freddie [Phonetic alphabet] [Pre-World War II] (DSUE)
F	Freddy [Phonetic alphabet] [Royal Navy World War I] (DSUE)
F	Free
F	Free [Rate] [Value of the English pound]
F	Free Energy [Physics] (BARN)
F	Freehold [Legal term] (ROG)
F	Freeway (ADA)
F	Fremskridtspartiet [Progress Party] [Denmark Political party] (PPE)
F	French [Catheter size] [Medicine] (DAVI)
F	French
F	Frequency
f	Frequency [Symbol] [IUPAC]
F	Frequency of Fading [Broadcasting]
F	Frequent [In mention of occurrence of species]
f	Frequently (DAVI)
F	Freshwater [Load line mark]
F	Friar
F	Friction
F	Friday
F	Frogerius [Rogerius Beneventanus] [Flourished, 12th century] [Authority cited in pre-1607 legal work] (DSA)
F	From
F	Front (KSC)
F	Frontal [Medicine] (DAVI)
F	Frontal Sinus [Otorhinolaryngology] (DAVI)
F	Froude Number [IUPAC]
F	Fuchsia [Genotype of Phlox paniculata]
F	Fuel
F	Fueler [Aircraft designation]
f	Fugacity [Thermodynamics]
f	Full
F	Full Load [Displacement]
f	Fully [Expand] [Computer science] [Telecommunications]
F	Function
f	Function (IDOE)
f	Furanose [One-letter symbol] [Biochemistry]
F	Furlong [Unit of distance]
F	Furlough [Military] (ADA)

F	Fusarium Wilt [Plant pathology]
F	Fuse (DEN)
F	Fusiformis [Microbiology] (MAE)
F	Fusobacterium [Microbiology] (MAE)
F	Fuss [Feet of organ stops]
F	Gilbert [Unit of magnetomotive force] (DAVI)
F	Goals For [Hockey]
F	Helmholtz Function [Symbol] (DEN)
F	Inbreeding Coefficient [Genetics] (DAVI)
F	Individual [Missile launch environment symbol]
F	Intelligence for which the Source Reliability Cannot be Judged
F	Interceptor [Aircraft]
F	Lab. Funai [Japan] [Research code symbol]
F	Libri Feudorum [A publication] (DSA)
F	Luminous Flux [Physics]
F	Mutuel Field [Horse racing]
F	Phenylalanine [One-letter symbol] [Also, Phe]
F	Photoreconnaissance [Aircraft designation]
f	Polar Flattening [Symbol] [Physics]
F	Requires Food and Water [Search and rescue symbol that can be stamped in sand or snow]
f	Respiratory Frequency [Breaths per unit of time] [Medicine] (DAVI)
F''	Second Focal Distance [Symbol] [Optics] (ROG)
F	Upper Ionized Layer of the Ionosphere (BARN)
F₀	Frequency Emitted [On Doppler study] [Cardiology] (DAVI)
F1	Filial Generation, First [Biology]
F1	First Folio Edition [1623] [Shakespearean work]
F1	Formula One [Auto racing]
F1	Frequency Received [On Doppler study] [Cardiology] (DAVI)
F₁ATPase	F₁ Adenosine Triphosphatase [A protein] [Biochemistry] (DAVI)
F1S	Finish One Side [Technical drawings]
F2	Filial Generation, Second [Biology]
F2	Second Folio Edition [1632] [Shakespearean work]
F2	Zinc Oxide-Eugenol Cement [Dentistry] (DAVI)
F 2d	Federal Reporter, Second Series [A publication] (DLA)
F2F	Face-to-Face [Fundraising]
F2S	Finish Two Sides [Technical drawings]
F³	Form-Fit-Function [Pronounced "f-cubed"]
F 3d	Federal Reporter, Third Series [A publication]
F5CA	Force 5 Class Association (EA)
F50	Fokker 50 [Airplane code]
FA	Aeronautical Station [ITU designation] (CET)
fa----	Atlas Mountain Region [MARC geographic area code Library of Congress] (LCCP)
FA	Fabrication Assembly (MCD)
FA	Face Amount [Business term]
FA	Facilitating Agency [Business term]
FA	Factor Analysis [Mathematics]
FA	Factory Act [British] (ILCA)
FA	Factory Automation
FA	Faculty of Actuaries [British] (BI)
FA	Faculty of Advocates [British] (ILCA)
Fa	Fahrenheit [Temperature scale] (DAVI)
FA	Failure Analysis (AAG)
FA	Fairchild Aircraft
FA	Fairchild Aircraft Ltd. [Canada], Fairchild/Republic [ICAO aircraft manufacturer identifier] (ICAO)
FA	Fairchild Corp.'A' [NYSE symbol] (TTSB)
FA	Faith Alive (EA)
FA	Fallen Angels International (EA)
FA	False Aneurysm [Cardiology] (DAVI)
FA	Families Anonymous (EA)
FA	Family Agency
FA	Family Allowance [Navy]
FA	Family America [An association] (EA)
FA	Fanconi's Anemia [Medicine]
FA	Fantasy Association (EA)
FA	Far Advanced [Medicine] (MAE)
FA	Farm Aid (EA)
FA	Farnesynic Acid [Juvenile hormone analog]
fa	Faroe Islands [MARC country of publication code Library of Congress] (LCCP)
FA	Fascicular Area [Neurology]
FA	Fashion Aid (EA)
FA	Father (DSUE)
FA	Fatty Acid [Biochemistry]
FA	Fawcett Association [A union] [British]
fa	Fayalite [CIPW classification] [Geology]
FA	Febrile Antigen [Immunology] (MAE)
FA	Feet Apart [Dance terminology]
FA	Felonious Assault
FA	Femoral Artery [Anatomy]
fA	Femtoampere (IEEE)
FA	[The] Ferroalloys Association (EA)
FA	Ferrocarriles Argentinos [Railway] [Argentina] (EY)
FA	Fertilization Antigen [Immunology]
FA	Ferulic Acid [Biochemistry]
FA	Fetal Age [Obstetrics] (DAVI)
F/A	Fetus Active [Obstetrics] (DAVI)
FA	Fibonacci Association (EA)
FA	Fibrinolytic Activity [Hematology]
FA	Fibroadenoma [Oncology]
FA	Fibrosing Alveolitis [Medicine] (DMAA)
FA	Field Accelerating Contactor or Relay [Industrial control] (IEEE)

F/A	Field Activities
FA	Field Address
FA	Field Allowance [*British military*] (DMA)
FA	Field Ambulance [*Military*]
FA	Field Army
FA	Field Artillery
FA	Field Audit [*IRS*]
FA	Field Goals Attempted [*Football, basketball*]
FA	Fielding Average [*Baseball*]
FA	Fifth Avenue Ventures [*Vancouver Stock Exchange symbol*]
FA	Fighter Alert (NATG)
FA	Fighter Allocator (NATG)
FA	Filterable Agent [*Virology*]
FA	filtered Air (MEDA)
FA	Final Address [*Computer science*] (ECII)
FA	Final Address Register [*Computer science*] (MDG)
FA	Final Approach (GAVI)
FA	Final Approval [*Automotive project management*]
FA	Final Assembly (MSA)
FA	Finance Act [*British*] (DCTA)
FA	Finance and Accounting (MCD)
FA	Financial Adviser
FA	Fine Alignment
FA	Fine Arts
FA	Finite Automation
FA	Fire Alarm (ROG)
FA	Fireman Apprentice [*Navy rating*]
Fa	Firma [*Legal term*] (DLA)
FA	First Access
FA	First Aid [*Medicine*]
FA	First Announcement
FA	First Article
FA	First Attack [*Men's lacrosse position*]
FA	Fixed Asset [*Business term*]
FA	Flag Allowance (CINC)
FA	Flat Gain Amplifier (IAA)
FA	Fleet Auxiliary [*British*]
FA	Flight Acceptance
FA	Flight Aft (NASA)
FA	Flight Attendant
FA	Floating Add [*Computer science*] (IAA)
FA	Floating Airfields [*British World War II*]
FA	Floating Asset [*Business term*]
FA	Flora of Australia [*Commonwealth*] (EERA)
FA	Florida (ROG)
FA	Flowing Afterglow [*Chemical kinetic*]
FA	Flowrate Alarm [*Engineering*]
FA	Fluctuating Asymmetry [*Embryology*]
FA	Fluorenamine [*Also, AF*] [*Carcinogen*]
FA	Fluorescent Angiography
FA	Fluorescent Antibody [*Clinical chemistry*]
FA	Fluoroalanine [*Organic chemistry*]
FA	Fluorouracil and Adriamycin [*Antineoplastic drug regimen*] (DAVI)
FA	Folic Acid [*Also, PGA, PteGlu*] [*Biochemistry*]
FA	Folklore Americas [*A publication*]
FA	Food Additive
FA	Food and Agriculture (NATG)
FA	Football Association [*Controlling body of British soccer*]
FA	Forage Acre
FA	Foragers of America (EA)
FA	Forced Air (MSA)
FA	Forced-Air-Cooled [*Transformer*] (IEEE)
FA	Forced Answer (HGAA)
FA	Forearm [*Anatomy*] (DAVI)
FA	Forecaster Aid [*Military*]
FA	Foreign Agriculture Including Foreign Crops and Markets [*A publication*]
FA	Forestry Abstracts [*Oxford, England*] [*A publication*]
FA	Forestry Act [*Town planning*] [*British*]
FA	Formal Advertising (MCD)
FA	Formula Atlantic [*Class of racing cars*]
fa	Formylaminoacyl [*As substituent on nucleoside*] [*Biochemistry*]
FA	Fortified Aqueous [*Pharmacology*]
F/A	Forward/Aft (KSC)
FA	Forward America [*Defunct*] (EA)
FA	Found Abandoned
FA	Foundation of America (EA)
FA	Four Arrows (EA)
FA	Frame Analyzer (MCD)
FA	Frame Antenna (IAA)
FA	Franconi Anemia [*Medicine*] (AAMN)
FA	Frankford Arsenal [*Pennsylvania*] [*Closed*] [*Army*]
FA	Frater Anselm [*Pseudonym used by Anselm Baker*]
FA	Free Acid [*Medicine*] (MAE)
FA	Free Alongside [*Shipping*]
FA	Free America [*In the movie "Red Dawn"*]
FA	Free Aperture [*Technical drawings*]
FA	Free Area (OA)
FA	Free Association [*Psychology*] (BARN)
FA	Free Astray
FA	Free of All Average [*Insurance*]
FA	Freight Agent
FA	Freight Allowal
FA	Freight Astray
FA	Freight Auditor

FA	French Army (NATG)
FA	Frente Amplio [*Broad Front*] [*Uruguay*] [*Political party*] (PD)
FA	Frequency Adjustment (IAA)
FA	Frequency Agility
FA	Fresh Air (OA)
FA	Freund's Adjuvant [*Immunology*]
FA	Friedenwald Archives (BJA)
FA	Friedreich's Ataxia [*Medicine*]
FA	Friendly Aircraft
FA	Friendship Ambassadors Foundation (EA)
FA	Friends of Astrology (EA)
FA	Frontal Aviation [*Soviet tactical air force*] [*World War II*]
FA	Front Axle [*Automotive engineering*]
FA	Frozen Asset [*Business term*]
F/A	Fuel-Air [*Ratio*]
F/A	Fuel Assembly (NRCH)
FA	Fulbright Association (EAIO)
FA	Full Action
FA	Full Adder [*Computer science*]
FA	Full Aperture [*Photography*] (NTCM)
FA	Full Arc (NRCH)
FA	Fully Accessible (IAA)
FA	Fully Automatic (KSC)
FA	Fulvic Acid [*Organic chemistry*]
FA	Functional Activity [*Medicine*] (MAE)
FA	Functional Administration (HCT)
FA	Functional Analysis
FA	Functional Area
FA	Functional Assembly (MCD)
FA	Fundamentalists Anonymous (EA)
FA	Furfuryl Alcohol [*Organic chemistry*]
FA	Further Assembly (IAA)
FA	Fusaric Acid (MEDA)
FA	Fuse Alarm (TEL)
FA	Fuzed Alloy
FA1AT	Fecal Alpha 1 - Antitrypsin [*Clinical chemistry*]
FAA	False Alarm Avoidance
FAA	Family Allowance, Class A [*Navy*]
FAA	Fatty Acid Alkanolamide [*Organic chemistry*]
FAA	Federal Aviation Act [*1958*]
FAA	Federal Aviation Administration [*Formerly, Federal Aviation Agency*] [*Department of Transportation*]
FAA	Federal Aviation Agency (AEBS)
FAA	Fellow of the American Association for the Advancement of Science
FAA	Field Artillery Airborne
FAA	Film Artistes' Association [*A union*] [*British*] (DCTA)
FAA	Financial Aid Administrator [*Department of Education*] (GFGA)
FAA	Fireplace Association of America [*Later, WHA*]
FAA	First Article Approval [*or Audit*]
FAA	Flameless Atomic Absorption
FAA	Fleet Air Arm [*British*]
FAA	Fluorenylacetamide [*Also, AAF, AcNHFln*] [*Organic chemistry*]
FAA	Flying Apache Association (EA)
FAA	Foreign Assistance Act [*1961*] (DOMA)
FAA	Foreman's Association of America [*Defunct*] (EA)
FAA	Formalin-Acetic Acid-Alcohol [*Fixative*] [*Botany*]
FAA	Forward Assembly Area [*Army*] (DOMA)
FAA	Foundation for American Agriculture [*Later, FAAPFF*] (EA)
FAA	Foundation for the Advancement of Artists (EA)
FAA	Fraternal Actuarial Association [*Defunct*] (EA)
FAA	Free Amino Acid [*Biochemistry*]
FAA	Free of All Average [*Insurance*]
FAA	Fresh Acid Add [*Nuclear energy*] (NRCH)
FAA	Friends of Africa in America [*Defunct*] (EA)
FAA	Fulbright Alumni Association [*Later, Fulbright Association*] (EAIO)
FAA	Functional Area Assessment
FAA	National Aviation Facilities Experimental Center, Atlantic City, NJ [*OCLC symbol*] (OCLC)
FAA-1	SafeAir One-Federal Aviation Administration Administrator (FAAC)
FAA-2	SafeAir Two-Federal Aviation Administration Deputy Administrator (FAAC)
FaAA	Failure Analysis and Associates (RDA)
FAAA	Federation for American Afghan Action (EA)
FAAA	Fellow of the American Academy of Allergy
FAAA	Final Acquisition Action Approval (AAGC)
FAAA	First Allied Airborne Army [*World War II*]
FAAA	Flight Attendants' Association of Australia
FAA-AAF	Federal Aviation Administration Airway Facilities Service
FAA-AAP	Federal Aviation Administration Office of Airports Programs
FAA-AAS	Federal Aviation Administration Office of Airport Standards
FAA-AC	Federal Aviation Administration Aeronautical Center
FAA-ADS	Federal Aviation Administration Aircraft Development Service
FAA-AEE	Federal Aviation Administration Office of Environment and Energy
FAA-AEM	Federal Aviation Administration Office of Systems Engineering Management
FAA-AEQ	Federal Aviation Administration Office of Environmental Quality
FAA-AF	Federal Aviation Administration Airway Facilities Service
FAA-AFO	Federal Aviation Administration Flight Standards National Field Office
FAA-AFS	Federal Aviation Administration Flight Standards Service
FAA-AFTN	Federal Aviation Administration Aeronautical Fixed Telecommunications Network (NOAA)
FAA-AM	Federal Aviation Administration Office of Aviation Medicine
FAA-AP	Federal Aviation Administration Office of Airports Programs
FAA-APO	Federal Aviation Administration Office of Aviation Policy and Plans

FAA-ARD...... Federal Aviation Administration Systems Research and Development Service
FAA-ARP...... Federal Aviation Administration Associate Administrator for Airports
FAAARTCC... Federal Aviation Administration Area Regional Traffic Control Center (DNAB)
FAA-AS .... Federal Aviation Administration Airports Service
FAAAS .... Fellow of the American Academy of Arts and Sciences
FAAAS .... Fellow of the American Association for the Advancement of Science
FAA-ASF ..... Federal Aviation Administration Office of Aviation Safety
FAA-ASP ..... Federal Aviation Administration Office of Aviation Systems Plans
FAA-AT .... Federal Aviation Administration Air Traffic Service
FAA-ATS ...... Federal Aviation Administration Air Traffic Service (NOAA)
FAA-AV .... Federal Aviation Administration Office of Aviation Policy
FAA-AVP ..... Federal Aviation Administration Office of Aviation Policy and Plans
FAAB .... Alexander Bay [South Africa] [ICAO location identifier] (ICLI)
FAAB........... Family Allowance, Class A and B [Navy]
FAABMS ..... Forward Area Antiballistic Missile System [Military] (IAA)
FAAC........... Airspace Control Command [South Africa] [ICAO location identifier] (ICLI)
FAAC........... FARO [Federation of AIDS Related Organizations] AIDS Action Council [Acquired Immune Deficiency Syndrome] (EA)
FAAC........... Fellow of the American Association of Criminology
FAAC........... French-American Aid for Children (EA)
FAA CAP...... Federal Aviation Agency Contract Appeals Panel (AAGC)
FAA/CAS...... Federal Aviation Administration Canadian Air Services Committee
FAACB .... Friends in Art of American Council of the Blind (EA)
FAACE......... Forces Aeriennes Alliees Centre-Europe [Allied Air Forces Central Europe] [NATO] (NATG)
FAACS .... Fully Automated Accounting Computer System (MCD)
FAAD .... Adelaide [South Africa] [ICAO location identifier] (ICLI)
FAAD .... Forward Area Air Defense
FAADBTY ..... Forward Area Air Defense Battery (DNAB)
FAADC......... Fleet Accounting and Disbursing Center [Navy] (NVT)
FAAD C2 ..... Forward Area Air Defense Command and Control [Military]
FAADC²I....... Forward Area Air Defense Command and Control Intelligence System [Army]
FAADCLANT.... Fleet Accounting and Disbursing Center, Atlantic [Navy] (DNAB)
FAADCLANT BRO... Fleet Accounting and Disbursing Center, Atlantic Branch Office [Navy] (DNAB)
FAADCPAC... Fleet Accounting and Disbursing Center, Pacific [Navy] (DNAB)
FAADEZ........ Forward Area Air Defense Engagement Zone [Army]
FAAD-GBS ... Forward Area Air Defense Ground-Based Sensor [Army]
FAADS .... Federal Assistance Award Data System [Bureau of the Census] [Washington, DC Information service or system]
FAA-DS .... Federal Aviation Administration Development Services
FAADS .... Field Army Air Defense System (MCD)
FAADS .... Forward Area Air Defense System
FAADW .... Forward Area Air Defense Weapon
FAA-EE........ Federal Aviation Administration Office of Environment and Energy
FAA-EM....... Federal Aviation Administration Office of Systems Engineering Management
FAA-EQ .... Federal Aviation Administration Office of Environmental Quality
FAAF........... Forney Army Airfield [Fort Leonard Wood, MO]
FAA-FS .... Federal Aviation Administration Flight Standards Service
FAA-FS-NFID... Federal Aviation Administration Flight Standards Service National Flight Inspection Division
FAAG .... Aggeneys [South Africa] [ICAO location identifier] (ICLI)
FAAG .... First Advertising Agency Group
FAAH .... Fatty Acid Amide Hydrolase [An enzyme]
FAAH .... Fellow of the Australian Academy of the Humanities
FAAH .... South African Air Force Headquarters [ICAO location identifier] (ICLI)
FAAHT .... Federated Association of Australian Housewives, Tasmania
FAAI............ Fellow of the Institute of Administrative Accounting and Data Processing [British] (DCTA)
FAAIECE....... Fulbright Association of Alumni of International Educational and Cultural Exchange (EA)
FAALS......... Field Artillery Acoustic Locating System (MCD)
FAALS......... Forward-Area Armored Logistics System [Military]
FAAMC........ Federation des Associations d'Antiquaires du Marche Commun (EA)
FAAMS........ Family of Antiair Missile Systems (MCD)
FAA-MS ...... Federal Aviation Administration Office of Management Systems
FAAN .... Aliwal North [South Africa] [ICAO location identifier] (ICLI)
FAAN .... Fellow of the American Academy of Nursing
FAAN .... First Advertising Agency Network [Later, First Network of Affiliated Advertising Agencies] [Defunct] (EA)
FAA-NA........ Federal Aviation Administration National Aviation Facilities Experimental Center
FAANaOS..... Fellowship of the American Academy of Neurological and Orthopaedic Surgeons (EA)
FAANE .... Forces Aeriennes Alliees Nord-Europe [Allied Air Forces Northern Europe] [NATO] (NATG)
FAA-NO........ Federal Aviation Administration Office of Noise Abatement
FAANQ......... Filipino-Australian Association of North Queensland [Australia]
FAA-NS........ Federal Aviation Administration National Airspace System Program Office
FAANTAEL ... Fleet Aircraft Assessment for Navy Testing and Analysis for EMP Limitations (MCD)
FAAO .... Federation of American Arab Organizations (EA)
FAAO .... Fellow of the Australian Academy of Optometry
FAAO .... Field Artillery Aerial Observer
FAAO .... Finance and Accounts Office [Army]
FAAO .... Fleet Aviation Accounting Office
FAAOLANT.... Fleet Aviation Accounting Office, Atlantic (DNAB)
FAAOP .... Fleet Aviation Accounting Office, Pacific (DNAB)
FAAOPAC..... Fleet Aviation Accounting Office, Pacific (DNAB)

FAA Order.... Federal Aviation Administration Orders [A publication] (DLA)
FAAOS .... Fellow of the American Academy of Orthopedic Surgeons
FAAP........... Family Assessment Adjustment Pass [Psychology] (DAVI)
FAAP........... Federal Aid to Airports Program [FAA]
FAAP........... Fellow of the American Academy of Pediatrics (WGA)
FAAP........... Fellow of the Australian Academy of Paediatrics
FAAP........... Fixed Asset Accounting Package [Computer science]
FAAPFF....... Foundation for American Agriculture Program of the Farm Foundation [Formerly, FAA] (EA)
FAAPS .... Fine Art, Antique, and Philatelic Squad [Scotland Yard] [British]
FAAQS .... Federal Ambient Air Quality Studies
FAA-QS .... Federal Aviation Administration Quiet Short-Haul Air Transportation Systems Office
FAAR .... Arandis [Namibia] [ICAO location identifier] (ICLI)
FAAR .... Feminist Alliance Against Rape [Defunct] (EA)
FAAR .... Forward Area Alerting RADAR
FAAR .... Friends of American Art in Religion (EA)
FAARATCF ... Federal Aviation Administration RADAR Air Traffic Control Facility (DNAB)
FAA-RD........ Federal Aviation Administration Systems Research and Development Service
FAARO .... Federal Aviation Administration Regional Office (NOAA)
FAARP .... Forward Area Aiming and Refueling Point [Military] (MCD)
FAAS .... Family of Army Aircraft System
FAAS .... Fellow of the Academy of Arts and Sciences
FAAS .... Flame Atomic Absorption Spectrometry
FAAS .... Flameless Atomic Absorption Spectrophotometry
FAAS .... Foreign Affairs Administrative Support System [Department of State]
FAAS .... Forward Area Alerting System (AABC)
FAAS .... French Association for American Studies (EAIO)
FAAS .... Furnace Atomic Absorption Spectrophotometry (PDAA)
FAASE......... Forces Aeriennes Alliees Sud-Europe [Allied Air Forces Southern Europe] [NATO] (NATG)
FAA SOL...... Formalin, Acetic, Alcohol Solution [Medicine] (BABM)
FAA sol....... Formalin, Acetic, and Alcohol Solution [A fixative] [Organic chemistry] (DAVI)
FAA-SS .... Federal Aviation Administration Office of Supersonic Transport Development
FAA-SST ..... Federal Aviation Administration Office of Supersonic Transport Development
FAASTU ...... Fleet Air Arm Service Trials Unit [British]
FAASV .... Fast Attack Ammunition Support Vehicle [Army] (RDA)
FAASV .... Field Artillery Ammunition Support Vehicle
FAAT .... First Article Acceptance Test (MCD)
FAATC......... FAA Technical Center [FAA] (TAG)
FAATDC ...... Federal Aviation Administration Technical Development Center
FAAWC .... Fleet Antiair Warfare Coordinator [Navy] (CAAL)
FAAWTC ..... Fleet Antiair Warfare Training Center
FAAWTRACEN... Fleet Antiair Warfare Training Center
FAB............. Aeronautical Broadcast Station [ITU designation] (CET)
Fab............. Antigen-Binding Fragment [Immunology]
Fab .... Fabius Accorambonus [Deceased, 1559] [Authority cited in pre-1607 legal work] (DSA)
FAB............. Fable (ROG)
FAB............. Fabric
fab .... Fabric (VRA)
FAB............. Fabricate
FAB............. Fabricator
FAB............. Fabrichnaya [Former USSR Seismograph station code, US Geological Survey Closed] (SEIS)
FAB............. Fabulous (ROG)
FAB............. Facilities Advisory Board (AAG)
FAB............. Failure Analysis Board
FAB............. Families Against the Bomb [British] (DI)
FAB............. Family Allowance, Class B [Navy]
FAB............. Farm Acreage Base
FAB............. Fast Atom Bombardment [Mass spectrometry]
FAB............. Features, Advantages, Benefits [of clothing] [Retailing]
FAB............. Feline Advisory Bureau [British] (CB)
FAB............. Feminists Against Benyon [Pro-abortion group] [British] (DI)
FAB............. Field Artillery Brigade (AABC)
FAB............. Film Advisory Board (EA)
FAB............. Firecracker Alternative Book [Award Program]
FAB............. First-Aid Box (AAG)
FAB............. First Air (Bradley Schedules) Ltd. [Canada ICAO designator] (FAAC)
FAB............. Firstfed American Bancorp, Inc. [AMEX symbol] (SAG)
FAB............. First Federal of Alabama FSB Jasper [AMEX symbol] (SPSG)
FAB............. Fixed Action Button (NVT)
FAB............. Fleet Air Base
FAB............. Fleet Air Broadcast (NATG)
FAB............. Flux-Asbestos Backing (PDAA)
FAB............. Forca Aerea Brasileira [Brazilian Air Force]
FAB............. Formalin-Ammonium Bromide [Fixative]
FAB............. Forward Avionics Bay
FAB............. Forwarder Air Waybill [Shipping] (DS)
Fab............. Fragment, Antigen-Binding [Immunochemistry]
Fab............. Fragment Antigen-Binding of an Antigen [Immunology] (DAVI)
FAB............. Free Association Books [Publisher] [British]
FAB............. French-American-British [Classification system for leukemia]
FAB............. Functional Adhesive Bonding
FAB............. Functional Area Breakdown
FAB............. Functional Arm Brace [Medicine]
FABA........... Firing Attachment Blank Ammunition (MCD)
FABAC .... Fellow of the Association of Business and Administrative Computing [British] (DBQ)

FABB............	Brakpan [South Africa] [ICAO location identifier] (ICLI)
FABB............	Filene's [Boston] Automatic Bargain Basement
FabC............	Fabri Centers of America [Associated Press] (SAG)
FABC............	First Alabama Bancshares, Inc. [NASDAQ symbol] (NQ)
FABC............	First Alliance Bancorp (GA) [NASDAQ symbol] (TTSB)
FABCFFS......	Feline Advisory Bureau and Central Fund for Feline Studies (EAIO)
FABD	Burgersdorp [South Africa] [ICAO location identifier] (ICLI)
FABD	Fabricated
FABE............	Fellow of the Association of Business Executives [British] (DCTA)
FABER	Flexion in Abduction and External Rotation [Neurology and orthopedics] (DAVI)
FABERE.......	Flexion, Abduction, External Rotation, Extension [Orthopedics]
FABF...........	Fellows of the American Bar Foundation (EA)
FABG	Fabricating
FABI............	Folk Artists Bibliographical Index [A publication]
FabInd..........	Fab Industries, Inc. [Associated Press] (SAG)
FABIS...........	Filmless Automatic Bond Inspection System
FABISO	Fabrication Isometric (IAA)
FABL............	Bloemfontein/J. B. M. Hertzog [South Africa] [ICAO location identifier] (ICLI)
FABL............	Fire Alarm Bell
fabless...........	Fabricationless (CDE)
FABM............	Bethlehem [South Africa] [ICAO location identifier] (ICLI)
FABM............	Fellowship of American Baptist Musicians (EA)
FABMDS	Field Army Ballistic Missile Defense System [Later, AADS] [Antimissile missile]
FABMIDS	Field Army Ballistic Missile Defense System [Later, AADS] [Antimissile missile]
FABMIS.......	Forward Area Ballistic Missile Intercept System (PDAA)
FABMS........	Fast Atom Bombardment Mass Spectroscopy
FABN	Barberton [South Africa] [ICAO location identifier] (ICLI)
FABP...........	Fatty Acid Binding Protein [Biochemistry]
FABP...........	Folatebinding Protein [Medicine] (DMAA)
FABPA	Furniture and Bedding Publicity Association Ltd. [British] (BI)
FABR	Bredasdorp [South Africa] [ICAO location identifier] (ICLI)
FABR	Fabricated
F Abr	Fitzherbert's Abridgment [1516] [A publication] (DLA)
FabriC...........	Fabri-Centers of America, Inc. [Associated Press] (SAG)
FABRIC	Florida Architecture and Building Research Center [University of Florida] [Research center] (RCD)
FABRIC	Frequency Assignment by Reference to Interference Charts (MCD)
FABRS	Fabrication Reporting System (MCD)
FABS...........	Brits [South Africa] [ICAO location identifier] (ICLI)
Fab Soc	Fabian Society (BARN)
FABTECH	Fabrication Technology (MCD)
FABU	Fleet Air Base Unit
FABU	Fuel Additive Blender Unit
FABV...........	Brandvlei [South Africa] [ICAO location identifier] (ICLI)
FABW..........	Beaufort West [South Africa] [ICAO location identifier] (ICLI)
FABWH	Flush Armor Balance Watertight Hatch
FABX...........	Beatrix Mine [South Africa] [ICAO location identifier] (ICLI)
FABX...........	Fire Alarm Box
FABY...........	Beaufort West/Wes Town [South Africa] [ICAO location identifier] (ICLI)
FAC.............	Airport Control Station [ITU designation] (DEN)
fac	Facade (VRA)
FAC.............	Face-Amount Certificate [Banking] (MHDB)
FAC.............	Facial [Chemistry]
FAC.............	Facilities Associate Contractor
FAC.............	Facility (AAG)
FAC.............	Facility Contract (AAGC)
FAC.............	Facsimile
FAC.............	Factor (MSA)
FAC.............	Factory
FAC.............	Factory Stores of America [NYSE symbol] (TTSB)
FAC.............	Factum Similis [Facsimile] [Latin]
FAC.............	Faculty (AABC)
Fac.............	Faculty of Advocates Collection of Decisions, Scotch Court of Sessions [A publication] (DLA)
FAC.............	Failure Analysis Coordinator
FAC.............	Familial Adenamatosis Coli [Medicine]
FAC.............	Farm Advisory Committee [MAFF] [British]
FAC.............	Fast Affinity Chromatography
FAC.............	Fast as Can [Business term]
FAC.............	Fast Attack Craft
FAC.............	Federal Acquisition Circular [DoD]
FAC.............	Federal Advisory Council [Department of Labor]
FAC.............	Federal Aviation Commission [Terminated, 1935]
FAC.............	Federation of Agricultural Cooperatives [British] (DBA)
FAC.............	Femoral Ash per Centimeter
FAC.............	Feral Animals Committee [Northern Territory, Australia]
FAC.............	Ferric Ammonium Citrate [Inorganic chemistry]
FAC.............	Field Accelerator
FAC.............	File Access Channel
FAC.............	Filter Address Correction
FAC.............	Final Acceptance Criteria (NRCH)
FAC.............	Final Approach Course [Aviation] (DA)
FAC.............	Financial Administrative Control (AFM)
FAC.............	Fine Alignment Complete
FAC.............	Firearms Acquisition Certificate [Canada]
FAC.............	First Air Courier, Inc. [ICAO designator] (FAAC)
FAC.............	First Alarm Code (SAA)
FAC.............	First Alert Capability [Military]
FAC.............	First Amendment Congress (EA)

FAC.............	Fiscal Advisory Committee [American Occupational Therapy Association]
FAC.............	Fixed Air Capacitor
FAC.............	Fleet Activities Command [Navy]
FAC.............	Fleet Analysis Center [Corona, CA] [Navy]
FAC.............	Fleet Augmentation Component
FAC.............	Fletcher Aviation Corp.
FAC.............	Flettner Aircraft Corp. (MCD)
FAC.............	Floating Accumulator
FAC.............	Fluorescent Analog Cytochemistry [Microscopic technique]
FAC.............	Fluorouracil, Adriamycin, Cyclophosphamide [Antineoplastic drug regimen]
FAC.............	Flying Activity Category (AFM)
FAC.............	Food Advisory Committee [New South Wales, Australia]
FAC.............	Food Aid Committee (EAIO)
FAC.............	Footwear and Accessories Council [Defunct] (EA)
FAC.............	Ford Aerosports Club (EA)
FAC.............	Foreign Adoption Center [Later, FCVN] (EA)
FAC.............	Foreign Agricultural Club (EA)
FAC.............	Foreign Air Carrier [FAA] (TAG)
FAC.............	Foreign Allowable Catch [Fishery management] (MSC)
FAC.............	Forward Air Control [or Controller] [Air Force]
fac	Forwarding Agents Commission [Shipping] (DS)
FAC.............	Fractional Area Concentration [Radiation therapy] (DAVI)
FAC.............	Fragments of Attic Comedy [A publication] (OCD)
FAC.............	Free Alongside Carrier [Business term]
FAC.............	Free Available Chlorine [Analytical chemistry]
FAC.............	Freedom to Advertise Coalition (EA)
FAC.............	French-American Committee for the Statue of Liberty [Defunct] (EA)
FAC.............	Frequency Allocation Committee
FAC.............	Frequency Analysis and Control
FAC.............	Front d'Alliberament Catala [Spain]
FAC.............	Front des Artistes Canadiens [Canadian Artists' Representation - CAR]
FAC.............	Fuel Adjustment Clause
FAC.............	Functional Area Code
FAC.............	Fund for Advancement of Camping (EA)
FAC.............	Fund for Artists' Colonies [Defunct] (EA)
FAC.............	Naval Facilities Engineering Command Headquarters (AAGC)
FACA............	Federal Advisory Committee Act
FACA............	Federal Alcohol Control Administration [Established, 1933; abolished, 1935]
FAcA............	Fellow of the Acupuncture Association [British] (DBQ)
FACA............	Fellow of the American College of Anesthesiologists (WGA)
FACA............	Fellow of the American College of Angiology
FACA............	Fellow of the American College of Apothecaries
FACA............	Florida Administrative Code Annotated (AAGC)
FAC(A).........	Forward Air Controller (Airborne) (NVT)
FACA............	Monte Carlo [South Africa] [ICAO location identifier] (ICLI)
FACADE	Further and Adult Council for Art and Design Education (AIE)
FACAI..........	Fellow of the American College of Allergists
FACAn..........	Fellow of the American College of Anesthesiologists
FACAS	Fellow of the American College of Abdominal Surgeons (DAVI)
FACAT.........	First Article Capability Assessment Test (MCD)
FACATT.......	Field Artillery CATT [Army] (RDA)
FACB...........	Colesburg [South Africa] [ICAO location identifier] (ICLI)
Facb............	Fragment, Antigen, and Complement Binding [Medicine] (DMAA)
FAC-BCG.....	Ftorafur, Adriamycin, Cyclophosphamide, Bacille Calmette-Guerin [Antineoplastic drug regimen] (DAVI)
FACBOC	Field Artillery Cannon Basic Officer's Course [Army]
FA-CBU	Fuel-Air Cluster Bomb Unit [Military] (VNW)
FACC...........	Federation Africaine des Chambres de Commerce [Federation of African Chambersof Commerce] [Ethiopia] (EAIO)
FACC...........	Fellow of the American College of Cardiology
FACC...........	Food Additives and Contaminants Committee [British]
FACC...........	Force Associated Control Communications [Military] (AFM)
FACC...........	Ford Aerospace and Communications Corp. (MCD)
FACC...........	French-American Chamber of Commerce (EA)
FACCA	Fellow of the Association of Certified and Corporate Accountants [British] (EY)
FACCC	Federal Advisory Commision on Consolidation and Conversion [DoD] (RDA)
FACCM........	Fast-Acess Charge-Coupled Memory [Computer science] (WDAA)
FAC/CO	Facility Checkout
Fac Coll......	Faculty of Advocates Collection of Decisions, Scotch Court of Sessions, First and Second Series [38 vols.] [A publication] (DLA)
Fac Coll NS...	Faculty of Advocates Collection of Decisions, Scotch Court of Sessions [A publication] (DLA)
FACCON......	Facilities Control [Radio Central] [Navy] (CAAL)
FACCONCEN...	Facilities Control Center [Army] (AABC)
FACCP	Fellow of the American College of Chest Physicians
FACCPC	Fellow of the American College of Clinical Pharmacology and Chemotherapy (DAVI)
FACD	Cradock [South Africa] [ICAO location identifier] (ICLI)
FACD	Fellow of the American College of Dentists
FACD	Foreign Area Consumer Dialing [Telecommunications]
Fac Dec	Faculty of Advocates Collection of Decisions, Scotch Court of Sessions, First and Second Series [38 vols.] [A publication] (DLA)
FACE............	Facelifters Home Systems, Inc. [NASDAQ symbol] (NQ)
FACE............	Facilities and Communication Evaluation [Army] (AABC)
FACE............	Factory Automatic Checkout Equipment
FACE............	Families Adopting Children Everywhere (EA)

FACE............ Fatal Accident Circumstances and Epidemiology [*National Institute for Occupational Safety and Health*]

FACE............ Fatty-Acid Cellulos Esters [*Organic chemistry*]

FACE............ Federal Advertising Committee on Ethics (MCD)

FACE............ Federally Assisted Code Enforcement [*Proposed HUD program*]

FACE............ Federation des Associations Canadiennes sur l'Environnement [*Federation of Associations on the Canadian Environment*]

FACE............ Federation des Associations de Chasseurs de la CEE [*Federation of Hunters' Associations of the European Economic Community*] [*Brussels, Belgium*]

FACE............ Federation of Associations on the Canadian Environment

FACE............ Fellowship of Artists for Cultural Evangelism (EA)

FACE............ Field Alterable Control Element (MDG)

FACE............ Field Artillery Computer Equipment

FACE............ Financial Advertising Committee on Ethics

FACE............ Florida Area Cumulus Experiment [*National Science Foundation*]

FACE............ Folk Arts for Communication and Education

FACE............ Forward Area Collection and ECM [*Electronic Countermeasures*]

FACE............ Forward Area Collection Equipment (MCD)

FACE............ Foundation for Accredited Chiropractic Education [*Later, FCER*] (EA)

FACE............ Freedom of Access to Clinic Entrances Act [*1994*]

FACE............ International Federation of Associations of Computer Users in Engineering Architecture and Related Fields (EAIO)

FACE............ Saint Francis Association for Catholic Evangelism [*Defunct*] (EA)

FACEA.......... Fellow of the Australian Council of Educational Administration

FACE IT........ Foreign Agents Compulsory Ethics in Trade Act [*Proposed*]

FACEL.......... Feature Analysis Comparison and Evaluation Library (PDAA)

FACENGCOM... Facility Engineering Command

FACEP.......... Fellow of American College of Emergency Physicians (DHSM)

FACES.......... Family Adaptability and Cohesion Evaluation Scale [*Psychology*]

FACES.......... Federal Advisory Council on Employment Security

FACES.......... FORTRAN [*Formula Translating System*] Automatic Code Evaluation System [*NASA Computer science*]

FACES.......... The National Association for the Craniofacially Handicapped (PAZ)

FACET.......... Facetious

FACET.......... Fluid Amplifier Control Engine Test

FACET.......... Future Airborne Communications Equipment and Technology (MCD)

FACETS........ Franco American Committee for Educational Travel and Studies [*Later, FACETS Tour France*]

FACETS........ Fraud and Abuse Clearinghouse for Effective Technology Sharing [*Department of Health and Human Services*]

FACETS........ Future Anti-Air Concepts Experimental Technology Seeker [*Military aircraft research program*] [*British*]

FACF............ Facility Chief (FAAC)

FACFI.......... Federal Advisory Committee on False Identification [*Department of Justice*] [*Terminated, 1976*]

FACFP.......... Fellow of the American College of Family Physicians

FACFS.......... Fellow of the American College of Foot Surgeons

FACG........... Fellow of the American College of Gastroenterology

FACGD........ Federation of American Citizens of German Descent [*Later, DANK*] (EA)

FACGE......... Fellow of the American College of Gastroenterology (DAVI)

FACH........... Cookhouse [*South Africa*] [*ICAO location identifier*] (ICLI)

FACH........... Forceps to After-Coming Head [*Obstetrics*]

FACHA......... Fellow of the American College of Health Administrators

FACHCA...... Fellow of American College of Health Care Administrators (DHSM)

FACHCA...... Foundation of American College of Health Care Administrators (EA)

FACHE......... Fellow of American College of Healthcare Executives (DHSM)

FACHRES-CA.. Faculty for Human Rights in El Salvador and Central America (EA)

FACI........... First Article Configuration Inspection [*Gemini*] [*NASA*] (AFM)

FACIL.......... Facility

FACILE......... Fire and Casualty Insurance Library Edition

FACIM......... Foundation for a Course in Miracles (EA)

FACISCOM USA... Finance and Comptroller Information Systems Command, United States Army

FACL........... Carolina [*South Africa*] [*ICAO location identifier*] (ICLI)

FACLC......... Federation of American Cultural and Language Communities (EA)

FAC-LEV ..... Fluorouracil, Adriamycin, Cyclophosphamide, Levamisole [*Antineoplastic drug regimen*]

FACLM......... Fellow of the American College of Legal Medicine (DAVI)

FACLS......... Federation of the Association of College Lecturers in Scotland (AIE)

FACLTY....... Facility

FACM.......... Friable Asbestos-Containing Material (GNE)

FAC MAT ..... Facilities Matrix (MCD)

FACMD........ Fluoroactinomycin D [*Antineoplastic drug*]

FACMN........ Fleet Chief Aircraft Mechanician [*British military*] (DMA)

FACMS........ Foundation for Advances in Clinical Medicine and Science [*Later, FAMS*] (EA)

FACMTA....... Federal Advisory Council on Medical Training Aids

FACN.......... Fellow of the American College of Nutrition (DAVI)

FACNET....... Federal Acquisitions Computer Network

FACNHA...... Foundation of American College of Nursing Home Administrators [*Later, FACHCA*] (EA)

FACNP .... Fellow of the American College of Neuropsychopharmacology (DAVI)

FACO .... Copperton [*South Africa*] [*ICAO location identifier*] (ICLI)

FACO .... Fabrication and Acceptance Checkout (MCD)

FACO .... Factory Acceptance Checkout (MCD)

FACO .... Factory Assembly and Checkout

FACO .... Fellow of American College of Organists

FACO .... Fellow of the American College of Otolaryngology

FACO .... Final Assembly Checkout [*NASA*] (NASA)

FACO .... First Alliance Corp. [*NASDAQ symbol*] (SAG)

FACOG .... Fellow of the American College of Obstetricians and Gynecologists

FACOGAZ..... Union des Fabricants Europeens de Compteurs de Gaz [*Union of European Manufacturers of Gas Meters*] (EAIO)

FACOS .... Fellow of the American College of Orthopedic Surgeons (DAVI)

FACOSH...... Federal Advisory Committee on Occupational Safety and Health [*Department of Labor*] [*Washington, DC*]

FA/COSI ...... Final Assembly and Closeout System Installation (MCD)

FACP.......... Fellow of the American College of Physicians

FACP.......... Fellow of the Association of Computer Professionals [*British*] (DBQ)

FACP.......... Forward Air Control Party [*Military*] (CAAL)

FACP.......... Forward Air Control Post (AFM)

FACP.......... Ftorafur [*Tegafur*], Adriamycin, Cyclophosphamide, Platinol [*Cisplatin*] [*Antineoplastic drug regimen*]

FACP.......... Fully Automated Computer Program (AAG)

FACP.......... Functional Assignment Control Panel (MCD)

FACPE........ Fellow of the American College of Physician Executives (HCT)

FACPM....... Fellow of the American College of Preventive Medicine

FACPRM ..... Fellow of the American College of Preventive Medicine (DAVI)

FACPTNG .... Forward Air Control Party Training [*Navy*] (ANA)

FACR .... Carletonville [*South Africa*] [*ICAO location identifier*] (ICLI)

FACR .... Fellow of the American College of Radiology

FACR .... First Article Configuration Review [*Army*] (AABC)

FACR .... Force Assessment in the Central Region [*NATO*] (NATG)

FACRED ...... Federal Advisory Council on Regional Economic Development

FACS.......... Facilities (ADA)

FACS.......... Facilities Control System

FACS.......... Facsimile (KSC)

FACS.......... Family and Community Services (WDAA)

FACS.......... Fast Atom Capillaritron Source [*Instrumentation*]

FACS.......... Fast Attack Class Submarine [*Navy*]

FACS.......... Federal Automated Career System

FACS.......... Federation of American Controlled Shipping [*New York, NY*] (EA)

FACS.......... Feedback and Analysis of Control Statistics (PDAA)

FACS.......... Fellow of the American College of Surgeons

FACS.......... Field Army Communication System (AABC)

FACS.......... Finance and Control System (NASA)

FACS.......... Financial Accounting and Control System

FACS.......... Fine Attitude Control System [*Aerospace*]

FACS.......... Fleet Area Control and Surveillance Facility [*Navy*] (DOMA)

FACS.......... Flexible Accounting Control System [*Computer science*] (BUR)

FACS.......... Flight Augmentation Control System [*Aviation*]

FACS.......... Floating Decimal Abstract Coding System

FACS.......... Fluid Amplifier Control System

FACS.......... Fluorescence-Activated Cell Sorter [*Becton, Dickinson Electronics Laboratory*] [*Instrumentation*]

FACS.......... Flurouracil, Adriamycin, Cyclophosphamide, Streptozocin [*Antineoplastic drug regimen*] (DAVI)

FACS.......... Force Automation and Communications [*Military*]

FACS.......... Foundation for American Communications (EA)

FACS.......... Frederick A. Cook Society (EA)

FACS.......... Friendship Association of Chinese Students and Scholars (EA)

FACS.......... Fully Automatic Compiling System

FACS.......... Funds Allocation Control System

FACS.......... Future Armored Combat System [*Military*]

FACSC .... Frequency Allocation Coordinating Subcommittee [*Canada*]

FAC/SCAR ... Forward Air Control / Self-Contained Airborne Reconnaissance [*Air Force*] (PDAA)

FACSEA....... Society for French American Cultural Services and Educational Aid (EA)

FACSFAC..... Fleet Air Control and Survey Facility

FACSFAX..... Fleet Air Control and Surveillance Facility (MCD)

FACSI......... Fast Acess Coded Small Image [*Computer science*] (PDAA)

FACSI......... Federal Advisory Council on Scientific Information

FACSIM....... Facsimile

FACSIMILE... FAMECE [*Family of Military Engineer Construction Equipment*] Computer Simulator for Independent and Logical Evaluation [*or Simulation*] (MCD)

FACSM........ Fellow of the American College of Sports Medicine

FACSO .... Facilities Supply Office

FAC/SPC ..... Fisheries Advisory Committee of the South Pacific Commission

FACSS .... Federation of Analytical Chemistry and Spectroscopy Societies (EA)

FACSTEAM... Facilities Installation Study Program [*Navy*] (NVT)

FacStr......... Factory Stores of America, Inc. [*Associated Press*] (SAG)

FACT.......... Cape Town [*South Africa*] [*ICAO location identifier*] (ICLI)

FACT.......... Facility for Automation, Control and Test (PDAA)

FACT.......... Facility for the Analysis of Chemical Thermodynamics [*McGill University*] [*Information service or system*] (IID)

FACT.......... Factor Analysis Chart Technique [*Business term*]

FACT.......... Factory [*Automotive engineering*]

fact............ Factory (VRA)

FACT.......... Factory Automation, Control, and Test Facility

FACT.......... Factual Compiler

FACT.......... Fairchild Advanced CMOS Technology [*Fairchild Semiconductor Corp.*]

FACT.......... Fast Access Current Text

FACT.......... Fast Access Current Text Bank [*University of Missouri*] [*Electronic library*] (NITA)

FACT.......... Fast Asymptotic Coherent Transmission (NVT)

FACT.......... Feasibility Ascension Cape Town [*Project*] (USDC)

FACT.......... Feasibility Ascension Cape Town [*Project*] [*Marine science*] (OSRA)

FACT.......... Federation Against Copyright Theft [*British*]

FACT.......... Federation of American Consumers and Travelers (EA)

FACT.......... Federation of Automated Coding Technologies (EA)

FACT.......... Feminist Anti-Censorship Task Force

FACT.......... Festival of American Community Theatre [*American Community Theatre Association*]

FACT.......... Field Audit and Completion Test [*Market research*]

FACT.......... Fighter Aircraft Code Type (SAA)

FACT............	Fingerprint Automatic Classification Technique [*Computer science*]
FACT............	First Albany Companies, Inc. [*NASDAQ symbol*] (NQ)
FACT............	First Albany Cos. [*NASDAQ symbol*] (TTSB)
FACT............	First American Congress of Theater
FACT............	Flanagan Aptitude Classification Test [*Psychology*]
FACT............	Fleet Analysis and Cost Trends (PDAA)
FACT............	Flexible Automatic Circuit Tester
FACT............	Flight Acceptance Composite Test [*NASA*]
FACT............	Focused Appendix Computed Tomography [*Medicine*]
FACT............	Food Additive Campaign Team [*British*]
FACT............	Food Animal Concerns Trust (EA)
FACT............	Forecast and Control Technique (IAA)
FACT............	Foreign Access to Computer Technology [*USIA*]
FACT............	Foundation for Advanced Computer Technology
FACT............	Foundation for Advancement in Cancer Therapy (EA)
FACT............	Freightliner Advanced Concept Truck [*Experimental vehicle*]
FACT............	Frozen Food Action Communications Team (DICI)
FACT............	Fully Automatically Controlled Train [*British*]
FACT............	Fully Automatic Calibration Technology [*Analytical balances*]
FACT............	Fully Automatic Cataloging Technique [*Computer science*] (MCD)
FACT............	Fully Automatic Compiler [*or Computer*]-Translator [*Computer science*]
FACT............	Fully Automatic Compiling Technique [*Computer science*]
FACTA..........	Food, Agriculture, Conservation and Trade Act of 1990
FACT-AID....	Flexible Automatic Circuit Tester - Automatic Interconnection Device
FactCrd........	Factory Card Outlet Corp. [*Associated Press*] (SAG)
FACTER........	Forward Air Controller Terminal
FACTEX........	Fast Asymptotic Coherent Transmission Extended (MCD)
FACT INIT....	Factotum Initial [*Typography*] (DGA)
FACTL..........	Fellow of the American College of Trial Lawyers (DD)
FACT-LIFT....	Flexible Automatic Circuit Tester - Low Insertion Force Technique
FACTO	Franchise Advice and Consultancy Trade Organization [*British*] (DBA)
FACTOR.......	Foundation to Assist Canadian Talent on Records
FACTOR.......	Fourteen-O-One Automatically-Controlled Test Optimizing Routine [*Military*] (SAA)
FACT-QUIC...	Flexible Automatic Circuit Tester - Quick Universal Interface Connector
FACTR	Fujitsu Access and Transport System [*Computer science*] (ACRL)
FACTRO.......	Factory Mechatronics (TSPED)
FACTS.........	Facilities Action Control Target System [*US Postal Service*]
FACTS.........	Facilities Administration Consolidated Tape System (MCD)
FACTS.........	Facilities Administration Control and Time Schedule
FACTS.........	Facilities Assets Catalog and Tracking System [*Army*]
FACTS.........	Facsimile Transmission System [*Telecommunications*]
FACTS.........	Failure and Accident Technical Information System
FACTS.........	Family and Community Treatment Services
FACTS.........	Fast Access to Computerized Technical Sources [*Information service or system*] (IID)
FACTS.........	Fast Action on Comments of Technical Significance
FACTS.........	Fast Agricultural Communication Terminal System [*Purdue University*] [*Information service or system*]
FACTS.........	Field Army Calibration Team Support
FACTS.........	Financial Accounting and Control Techniques for Supply [*Army*]
FACTS.........	Financial Analysis Capability through Scanning
FACTS.........	Financing Analysis Cost and Testing Service [*LIMRA*]
FACTS.........	First Amendment Consumer and Trade Society (EA)
FACTS.........	FLIR [*Forward-Looking Infrared RADAR*] Augmented Cobra TOW Sight [*Tube-Launched, Optically-Tracked, Wire-Guided Weapon*]
FACTS.........	Florida Atlantic Coast Transport Study [*Marine science*] (OSRA)
FACTS.........	Florida Atlantic Coast Transport Study (USDC)
FACTS.........	Football Association Coaching Tactics Skills [*British*] (DI)
FACTS.........	FORTRAN [*Formula Translating System*] Analytical Cross Reference TabulationSystem [*Computer science*]
FACTS.........	Foundation for the Advancement of Chiropractic Tenets and Science (EA)
FACTS.........	Free Available Chlorine Test with Syringaldazine [*Analytical chemistry*]
FACTS.........	National Food and Conservation through Swine (EA)
FactsetR......	Factset Research Systems, Inc. [*Associated Press*] (SAG)
Facty...........	Factory
FACUI.........	Federal Advisory Council on Unemployment Insurance
FACV..........	Calvinia [*South Africa*] [*ICAO location identifier*] (ICLI)
FACVP	Fluorouracil, Adriamycin, Cyclophosphamide, VP-16 [*Antineoplastic drug regimen*] (DAVI)
FACW..........	Clanwilliam [*South Africa*] [*ICAO location identifier*] (ICLI)
FACW..........	Facultative Wetland Plant (ERG)
FAD.............	Facility and Design (IAA)
FAD.............	Faculty Author Development [*Software development program*]
FAD.............	Faded [*Bookselling*] (DGA)
FAD.............	Familial Alzheimer's Disease [*Medicine*]
FAD.............	Familial Autonomic Dysfunction [*Medicine*] (DMAA)
FAD.............	Family Assessment Device
FAD.............	Federal Anti-Trust Decisions [*A publication*] (DLA)
FAD.............	Ferrite Array Demonstration [*RADAR*]
FAD.............	Fetal Activity Determination
FAD.............	Fighter Air Director [*Military*] (NVT)
FAD.............	Filter and Detect Chip (NITA)
FAD.............	Final Approach Display (MCD)
FAD.............	Financial Accounting Data
FAD.............	Findings and Determination (IAA)
FAD.............	Fine Art Development [*British*]
FAD.............	First Appearance Datum [*Geology*]
FAD.............	First Article Demonstration
FAD.............	Fish Aggregating Device [*Pisciculture*]

FAD.............	Fish Aggregating Device [*Marine science*] (OSRA)
FAD.............	Fish Aggregation Device (EERA)
FAD.............	Flavin-Adenine Dinucleotide [*Biochemistry*]
FAD.............	Flea Allergy Dermatitis [*Medicine*]
FAD.............	Fleet Air Defense (MCD)
FAD.............	Fleet Air Detachment [*Navy*]
FAD.............	Flexible Automatic Depot
FAD.............	Floating Add [*Computer science*] (IEEE)
FAD.............	Fonds Africain de Developpement [*African Development Fund*]
F/AD............	Force/Activity Designator [*Military*]
FAD.............	Forward Area Defense (DOMA)
FAD.............	Fracture Analysis Diagram (PDAA)
FAD.............	Franklin Advantage Real Estate, Inc. [*AMEX symbol*] (SPSG)
FAD.............	Free Air Delivered
FAD.............	Fuel Advisory Departure [*Aviation*] (FAAC)
FAD.............	Fuerzas Armadas Democraticas [*Democratic Armed Forces*] [*Nicaragua*] (PD)
FAD.............	Functional Area Description
FAD.............	Funding Authorization Document (AABC)
FAD.............	Rog-Air Ltd. [*Canada ICAO designator*] (FAAC)
FADA	De Aar [*South Africa*] [*ICAO location identifier*] (ICLI)
FADA	Federal Assets Disposition Association [*Functions transferred to FDIC and RTC, 1989*]
FADA	Fourth Armored Division Association (EA)
FADA	Fuerzas de Accion Armada [*Armed Action Forces*] [*Guatemala*] (PD)
FADAC	Field Artillery Digital Automatic Computer (IEEE)
FADALA	Failure Detection and Location Analysis (MCD)
FADAP.........	Fleet Antisubmarine Data Analysis Program
FADC	Douglas Colliery [*South Africa*] [*ICAO location identifier*] (ICLI)
FADC	Fighter Air Direction Center
FADC	Frequency Analog-to-Digital Converter (IAA)
FADD	Dundee [*South Africa*] [*ICAO location identifier*] (ICLI)
FADD	Fan-Assisted Drug Detector
FADD	Fight Against Dictating Designers [*Group opposing below-the-knee fashions introduced in 1970*]
FADE...........	FAA Airline Data Exchange [*FAA*] (TAG)
FADEC.........	Full Authority Digital Engine Control
FADEM.........	Flower of Friendship and Development of Macau [*Political party*] (EY)
FADES	Fuselage Analysis and Design Synthesis
FADF...........	Fluorescent Antibody Dark Field [*Clinical chemistry*] (MAE)
FADH	Durnacol [*South Africa*] [*ICAO location identifier*] (ICLI)
FADH₂	Flavin-Adenine Dinucleotide [*Reduced*] [*Biochemistry*]
FADICA	Foundations and Donors Interested in Catholic Activities (EA)
FADINAP......	Fertilizer Advisory Development Information Network for Asia and the Pacific
FADIR	Flexion, Adduction, Internal Rotation [*Orthopedics*]
FADL...........	Delareyville [*South Africa*] [*ICAO location identifier*] (ICLI)
FADM..........	Fleet Admiral
FADM..........	Functional Area Documentation Manager [*Air Force*] (AFM)
FAdmA........	Fellow of the Administration Association (DD)
FADN	Durban/Louis Botha [*South Africa*] [*ICAO location identifier*] (ICLI)
FADN	Flavin-Adenine Dinucleotide [*Biochemistry*] (MAE)
FADN	Frente Anti-Comunista de Defensa Nacional [*Anti-Communist Front for National Defense*] [*Ecuador*]
FADO	Fellow of the Association of Dispensing Opticians [*British*] (DBQ)
FADO(Hons)...	Fellow of the Association of Dispensing Opticians with Honours Diploma [*British*] (DBQ)
FADO(Hons)CL...	Fellow of the Association of Dispensing Opticians with Honours Diploma and Diploma in Contact Lens Fitting [*British*] (DBQ)
FADP	Federal Automatic Data Processing (MHDI)
FADP	Finnish Association for Data Processing
FADPUG.......	Federal ADP [*Automatic Data Processing*] Users Group
FADR	Dunnottar [*South Africa*] [*ICAO location identifier*] (ICLI)
FADR	Forward Area Demagnetizing Range [*Military*] (DOMA)
FADS	Dordabis [*Namibia*] [*ICAO location identifier*] (ICLI)
FADS	Fixed Asset Depreciation System (PDAA)
FADS	Flexible Air Data System
FADS	Force Administration Data System [*Bell System*]
FADS	FORTRAN [*Formula Translating System*] Automatic Debugging System [*Computer science*]
FADS	Forward Area Deployment, Spain
FADSID	Fighter-Aircraft-Delivered Seismic Intrusion Detector (NVT)
FADU	File Access Data Unit [*Telecommunications*] (OSI)
FADV	Devon [*South Africa*] [*ICAO location identifier*] (ICLI)
f-ae--	Algeria [*MARC geographic area code Library of Congress*] (LCCP)
FAE.............	Dayton, OH [*Location identifier FAA*] (FAAL)
FAE.............	Faenza [*Italy*] [*Seismograph station code, US Geological Survey Closed*] (SEIS)
FAE.............	Faroe Islands [*Denmark*] [*Airport symbol*] (OAG)
FAE.............	Federal Assumed Enforcement [*State implementation plan by EPA*]
FAE.............	Fellow of the Accountants' and Executives' Corp. of Canada
FAE.............	Fetal Alcohol Effect [*Medicine*]
FAE.............	Fetal Alcohol Effects [*Medicine*]
FAE.............	Fidelity Advisor Emer'g Asia [*NYSE symbol*] (TTSB)
FAE.............	Fidelity Advisor Emerging Asia Fund [*NYSE symbol*] (SAG)
FAE.............	Field Advisory Element (CINC)
FAE.............	Field Application Engineer (IEEE)
FAE.............	Figural After-Effect
FAE.............	Final Approach Equipment [*Aviation*]
FAE.............	Final Average Earnings
FAE.............	Fine Alignment Equipment
FAE.............	Follicle-Associated Epithelium [*Immunology*]
FAE.............	Foundation for Accounting Education (EA)
FAE.............	Foundation of Automation and Employment Ltd. [*British*] (BI)

FAE .... Frei aber Einsam [*Free but Lonely*] [*Motto of Joseph Joachim, 19th century German violinist*] (ECON)
FAE .... Fuel Air Explosive (MCD)
FAE .... Fund for the Advancement of Education [*Defunct*] (EA)
FAE .... Merlin Express, Inc. [*FAA designator*] (FAAC)
FAE .... Sat-Air, Inc. [*ICAO designator*] (FAAC)
FAEA .... Ellisras Control Reporting Point [*South Africa*] [*ICAO location identifier*] (ICLI)
FAEA .... Financial and Economic Analysis
FAEC .... Estcourt [*South Africa*] [*ICAO location identifier*] (ICLI)
FAEC .... Foundation of the American Economic Council (EA)
FAEC .... Full Authority Electronic Control (MCD)
FAECF .... Federation des Associations Europeennes des Constructeurs de Fenetres [*Federation of European Window Manufacturers Associations - FEWMA*] (EA)
FAEE .... Fatty Acid Ethyl Ester
FAEJ .... Fonds d'Action et d'Education Juridiques pour les Femmes [*Women's Legal Education and Action Fund - LEAF*] [*Canada*]
FAEL .... East London/Ben Schoeman [*South Africa*] [*ICAO location identifier*] (ICLI)
FAEmA .... Fidelity Advisor Emerging Asia Fund [*Associated Press*] (SAG)
FAEmAs ...... Fidelity Advisor Emerging Asia Fund [*Associated Press*] (SAG)
FAEO .... Ermelo [*South Africa*] [*ICAO location identifier*] (ICLI)
FAEPC .... Federation des Associations d'Editeurs de Periodiques de la CE [*Brussels, Belgium*] (EAIO)
FAER .... Ellisras [*South Africa*] [*ICAO location identifier*] (ICLI)
Faer .... Foeroe Islands (BARN)
FAER .... Foreign Agricultural Economic Reports
FAES .... Eshowe [*South Africa*] [*ICAO location identifier*] (ICLI)
FAES .... Flame Atomic Emission Spectrometry
FAES .... Foreign Affairs Executive Seminar [*Department of State*]
FAESHED .... Fuel Air Explosive Helicopter Delivered
FAET .... Elliot [*South Africa*] [*ICAO location identifier*] (ICLI)
FAET .... Forum for the Advancement of Educational Therapy (AIE)
FAETU .... Fleet Airborne Electronic Training Unit [*Navy*]
FAETUA ...... Fleet Airborne Electronic Training Unit, Atlantic
FAETUDET ... Fleet Airborne Electronic Training Unit Detachment
FAETULANT... Fleet Airborne Electronic Training Unit, Atlantic
FAETUP ...... Fleet Airborne Electronic Training Unit, Pacific (IEEE)
FAETUPAC ... Fleet Airborne Electronic Training Unit, Pacific [*Later, FASOTRAGRUPAC, F ASOTRAGRUPACFLT*]
FAF .... Families of Australia Foundation
FAF .... Family of the Americas Foundation (EA)
FAF .... Fast-Acting Fuse
FAF .... Fathers Are Forever [*Defunct*] (EA)
FAF .... Fatty Acid-Free [*Biochemistry*]
FAF .... Fibroblast Activating Factor [*Biochemistry*]
FAF .... Film Arts Foundation (EA)
FAF .... Final Approach Fix [*Aviation*] (DA)
FAF .... Final Approach Fix [*Aviation*] (FAAC)
FAF .... Financial Accounting Foundation [*Stamford, CT*] (EA)
FAF .... Financial Aid Form [*Of College Board*]
FAF .... Financial Analysts Federation [*Later, AIMR*] (EA)
FAF .... Financing Adjustment Factor
FAF .... Fine Arts Foundation (EA)
FAF .... First Aerodynamic Flight (NASA)
FAF .... First Amer Finl [*NYSE symbol*] (TTSB)
FAF .... First American Financial Corp. [*NYSE symbol*] (SPSG)
F/AF .... FishAmerica Foundation (EA)
FAF .... Fleet Amenities Fund [*Navy British*]
FAF .... Flyaway Factory
FAF .... Forces Aeriennes Francaises [*France ICAO designator*] (FAAC)
FAF .... Fort Eustis, VA [*Location identifier FAA*] (FAAL)
FAF .... Forward Air Freight (WDAA)
FAF .... Free Asia Foundation (EA)
FAF .... Free at Factory [*Business term*]
FAF .... French Air Force
FAF .... French-American Foundation (EA)
FAF .... Fund for America's Future [*Defunct*] (EA)
FAF .... Fuzing, Arming, and Firing
FAFA .... Federation des Alliances Francaises en Australie [*Federation of Alliances Francaises (Institutes for the study of French language and culture) in Australia*]
FAFAB .... FSS [*Flight Service Station*] Assumes Flight-Plan Area [*Aviation*] (FAAC)
FAFB .... Fairchild Air Force Base [*Washington*] (AAG)
FAFB .... Ficksburg [*South Africa*] [*ICAO location identifier*] (ICLI)
FAFF .... Frankfort [*South Africa*] [*ICAO location identifier*] (ICLI)
FAFK .... Fisantekraal [*South Africa*] [*ICAO location identifier*] (ICLI)
FAFnc .... First American Financial Corp. [*Associated Press*] (SAG)
FAFP .... Force and Financial Plan
FAFP .... Foreign Area Fellowship Program [*Later, SSRC*]
FAFPAS .... Federation des Associations de Fabricants de Produits Alimentaires Surgeles d e la CE [*European Federation of Quick Frozen Food Manufacturers*] [*Belgium*] (EAIO)
FAFPIC .... Forestry and Forest Products Industry Council (EERA)
FAFR .... Fatal Accident Frequency Rate
FAFR .... Fraserburg [*South Africa*] [*ICAO location identifier*] (ICLI)
FAFS .... Farm and Food Society [*British*]
FAFS .... Flame Atomic Fluorescence Spectrometry
FAFSA .... Free Application for Federal Student Aid (GAGS)
FAFSV .... Franco-Australian Friendly Society of Victoria [*Australia*]
FAFT .... First Article Factory Tests (NATG)
FAFT .... First Article Flight Test
FAFT .... Free Air Facility Track [*Edwards Air Force Base*] (AAG)

FAFTAH .... First a Friend, Then a Host [*Safety slogan encouraging partygivers to prevent guests' overindulgence in alcohol*]
FAFWC .... Fuchu Air Force Weather Central (CINC)
FAG .... Faggot [*Derogatory term for male homosexual*] [*Slang*] (DSUE)
FAG .... Fagotto [*Bassoon*] [*Music*]
FAG .... Fagurholmsmyri [*Iceland*] [*Airport symbol*] (AD)
F-Ag .... F Antigen [*Immunochemistry*]
FAG .... Fatigue [*Slang*] (DSUE)
FAG .... Finance and Accounting Group [*Air Force*] (AFM)
FAG .... Financial Assistance Grant
FAG .... Fiscal Activities Guide [*Department of Labor*] (OICC)
FAG .... Fleet Assistance Group
FAG .... Forward Air Guide (NVT)
FAG .... Fraud Against the Government
FAG .... Free-Air Gradient [*Geophysics*]
FAG .... Fuerza Aerea Argentina [*ICAO designator*] (FAAC)
FAGA .... Friedreich's Ataxia Group in America [*Defunct*] (EA)
FAGAA .... Fellow of the Art Galleries Association of Australia
FAGAIRTRANS... First Available Government Air Transportation [*Navy*]
FAGB .... Gobabis [*Namibia*] [*ICAO location identifier*] (ICLI)
FAGC .... Fast Automatic Gain Control
FAGC .... Forward Area Ground Control (IAA)
FAGC .... Grand Central [*South Africa*] [*ICAO location identifier*] (ICLI)
FAGCA .... Fenton Art Glass Collectors of America (EA)
FAGE .... Factory Aerospace Ground Equipment (MCD)
FAGE .... Fluorescence Assay with Gas Expansion [*Analytical chemistry*]
FAGE .... Future Age [*A publication*] (ADA)
FAGE .... Gough Island [*South Africa*] [*ICAO location identifier*] (ICLI)
FAGF .... Grootfontein [*Namibia*] [*ICAO location identifier*] (ICLI)
FAGG .... George/P. W. Botha [*South Africa*] [*ICAO location identifier*] (ICLI)
FAGI .... Fellow of the Australian Grain Institute
FAGI .... Giyani [*South Africa*] [*ICAO location identifier*] (ICLI)
FAGL .... Groblersdal [*South Africa*] [*ICAO location identifier*] (ICLI)
FAGLA .... Furylacryloylglycylleucine Amide [*Biochemistry*]
FAGLANT ..... Fleet Assistance Group, Atlantic [*Navy*]
FAGM .... Field Army Guided Missile (IAA)
FAGM .... Johannesburg/Rand [*South Africa*] [*ICAO location identifier*] (ICLI)
FAGMS .... Field Artillery Guided Missile [*Air Force*]
FAGMS-S ..... Field Army Guided Missile System - Sergeant (SAA)
FAGO .... Fellow of the American Guild of Organists
FAGp .... Finance and Accounting Group [*Air Force*] (AFM)
FAGPAC ...... Fleet Assistance Group, Pacific [*Navy*]
FAGR .... Floating Arm Graphic Recorder (PDAA)
FAGR .... Graaff Reinet [*South Africa*] [*ICAO location identifier*] (ICLI)
FAGS .... Federation of Astronomical and Geophysical Services [*Research center France*] (IRC)
FAGS .... Fellow of the American Geographical Society
FAGT .... First Available Government Transportation
FAGT .... Grahamstown [*South Africa*] [*ICAO location identifier*] (ICLI)
FAGTRANS.. First Available Government Transportation
FAGU .... Fleet Air Gunnery Unit
FAGUPAC .... Fleet Air Gunnery Unit, Pacific (MUGU)
FAGV .... Gravelotte [*South Africa*] [*ICAO location identifier*] (ICLI)
FAGY .... Greytown [*South Africa*] [*ICAO location identifier*] (ICLI)
FAH .... Facilitation Awards for Handicapped Scientists and Engineers Program [*Washington, DC National Science Foundation*] (GRD)
FAH .... Fahrenheit (KSC)
FAH .... Farner Air Transport Hungary [*FAA designator*] (FAAC)
FAH .... Farrah Resources [*Vancouver Stock Exchange symbol*]
FAH .... Federation of American Hospitals [*Later, FAHS*]
FAH .... Folklore of American Holidays [*A publication*]
FAH .... Sheboygan, WI [*Location identifier FAA*] (FAAL)
FAHA .... Finnish-American Historical Archives (EA)
FAHA .... Harmony [*South Africa*] [*ICAO location identifier*] (ICLI)
FAHB .... Hartebeespoortdam [*South Africa*] [*ICAO location identifier*] (ICLI)
FAHC .... First Amer Hlth Concepts [*NASDAQ symbol*] (TTSB)
FAHC .... First American Health Concepts, Inc. [*NASDAQ symbol*] (NQ)
FAHD .... Forum on Allied Health Data [*American Occupational Therapy Association*]
FAHD .... Humansdorp [*South Africa*] [*ICAO location identifier*] (ICLI)
FAHE .... Fellow of the Association of Home Economists [*British*] (DI)
FAHE .... Friends Association for Higher Education (EA)
FAHE .... Pullenshope (Hendrina) [*South Africa*] [*ICAO location identifier*] (ICLI)
FAHG .... Heidelberg [*South Africa*] [*ICAO location identifier*] (ICLI)
FAHI .... Halali [*Namibia*] [*ICAO location identifier*] (ICLI)
FAHM .... Hermanus [*South Africa*] [*ICAO location identifier*] (ICLI)
FAHN .... Fahnstock Viner Holdings, Inc. [*NASDAQ symbol*] (NQ)
FAHN .... Henties Bay [*Namibia*] [*ICAO location identifier*] (ICLI)
FAHNF .... Fahnestock Viner Hldgs'A' [*NASDAQ symbol*] (TTSB)
FahnVin .... Fahnestock Viner Holdings, Inc. [*Associated Press*] (SAG)
FAHO .... Heilbrond [*South Africa*] [*ICAO location identifier*] (ICLI)
FAHP .... Fellow, Association for Healthcare Philanthropy (NFD)
FAHP .... Fellow Association for Healthcare Philanthropy
FAHQ .... Pretoria [*South Africa*] [*ICAO location identifier*] (ICLI)
FAHQMT ...... Fully Automatic High-Quality Machine Translation [*Computer science*] (DIT)
FAHQT .... Fully Automatic High-Quality Translation [*Computer science*]
FAHR .... Fahrenheit
FAHR .... Formosan Association for Human Rights (EA)
FAHR .... Harrismith [*South Africa*] [*ICAO location identifier*] (ICLI)
FAHRB .... Federation of Associations of Health Regulatory Boards [*Later, FARB*] (EA)
FAHS .... Federation of American Health Systems (EA)
FAHS .... Federation of Australian historical Societies
FAHS .... Franco-American Historical Society (EA)

FAHS .... Hoedspruit [South Africa] [ICAO location identifier] (ICLI)
FAHSM .... Finnish American Historical Society of Michigan (EA)
FAHSW .... Finnish-American Historical Society of the West (EA)
FAHT .... Hoedspruit Civil/Burgerlike [South Africa] [ICAO location identifier] (ICLI)
FAHV .... Hendrik Verwoerddam [South Africa] [ICAO location identifier] (ICLI)
fai .... Faience (VRA)
FAI .... FAI Insurances Ltd. [NYSE symbol Toronto Stock Exchange symbol] (CTT)
FAI .... FAI Insurances Ltd ADS [NYSE symbol] (TTSB)
FAI .... Fail As-Is [Nuclear energy] (NRCH)
FAI .... Fairbanks [Alaska] [Airport symbol] (OAG)
FAI .... Fairbanks, AK [Location identifier FAA] (FAAL)
FAI .... Falcon Air, Inc. [ICAO designator] (FAAC)
FAI .... Federal Acquisitions Institute [Formerly, FPI] (MCD)
FAI .... Federation Abolitionniste Internationale [International Abolitionist Federation] [India]
FAI .... Federation Aeronautique Internationale [International Aeronautical Federation] [France]
FAI .... Fellow of the Chartered Auctioneers' and Estate Agents' Institute [British]
FAI .... Field-Aligned Irregularity (MCD)
FAI .... Financial Accounting Institute [Tenafly, NJ] [Telecommunications service] (TSSD)
FAI .... First-Aid Instructor [Red Cross]
FAI .... First Article Inspection [NASA] (KSC)
FAI .... Flight Anomaly Investigation [NASA] (KSC)
FAI .... Fly as Is (MCD)
FAI .... Fonds d'Activites Internationales [International Activities Fund] [Canadian Labour Congress]
FAI .... Football Association of Ireland (DI)
FAI .... Frequency Application Index
FAI .... Frequency-Azimuth Intensity [RADAR]
FAI .... Fresh Air Inlet (MSA)
FAI .... Fresh Air Input
FAI .... Fuel Air Incendiary Concussion Bomb (MCD)
FAI .... Fujitsu America, Inc. [Hillsboro, OR]
FAI .... Functional Aerobic Impairment [Medicine] (AAMN)
FAI .... Functional Assessment Inventory [Medicine] (DAVI)
FAIA .... Fellow of the American Institute of Actuaries
FAIA .... Fellow of the American Institute of Architects
FAIA .... Fellow of the Association of International Accountants [British]
FAIA .... Florida Association of Insurance Agents (SRA)
FAIA .... Florida Automotive Industry Association (SRA)
FAIAA .... Fellow of the American Institute of Aeronautics and Astronautics [Formerly, FIAes, FIAS]
FAIAT .... Federazione delle Associazioni Italiane Alberghi e Turismo [Hotels and Tourism Federation] [Italy] (EY)
FAIAU .... Fleet Air Intelligence Augmenting Unit (CINC)
FAIB .... Federation des Associations Internationales Etablies en Belgique [Federation of International Associations Established in Belgium]
FAIC .... Fellow Associate of the Institute of Chemistry
FAIC .... Fellow of Agricultural Institute of Canada
FAIC .... Fellow of the American Institute of Criminology
FAIDS .... Feline Acquired Immune Deficiency Syndrome [Pathology]
FAIE .... Fellow of the British Association of Industrial Editors (DBQ)
FAIEE .... Fellow of the American Institute of Electrical Engineers
FAI Ex .... Fellow of the Australian Institute of Export (ODBW)
FAIF .... Field Automated Intelligence File (AFM)
FAII .... Fellow of the Australian Insurance Institute (ODBW)
FAI In .... FAI Insurances Ltd. [Associated Press] (SAG)
FAIL .... Failure
FAIL .... Failure Group [NASDAQ symbol] (TTSB)
FAIL .... Failure Group, Inc. [NASDAQ symbol] (SAG)
FAIL .... FMC [Flight Management Computer] Fail (GAVI)
FAILCLEA ..... Federazione Autonoma Italiana Lavoratori Cemento Legno, Edilizia, ed Affini [Workers in Cement, Wood, Construction, and Related Industries Federation] [Italy] (EY)
FAILE .... Federazione Autonoma Italiana Lavoratori Elettrici [Electrical Workers Federation] [Italy] (EY)
FailGrp .... Failure Group, Inc. [Associated Press] (SAG)
FAIM .... Fellow of the Australian Institute of Management (ODBW)
FAIME .... Foreign Affairs Information Management Effort [Computer] [Department of State]
FAIMS .... Financial and Administrative Integrated Management System [Department of Health and Human Services] (GFGA)
FAIN .... First Article Inspection Notice [NASA] (SAA)
FAIN/SR ...... First Article Inspection Notice Status Report [NASA] (SAA)
FAIO .... Field Army Issuing Office
FAIO .... Field Artillery Intelligence Officer [Military] (AABC)
FAIPR .... Fellow of the Australian Institute of Parks and Recreation
FA/IPT .... First Article/Initial Production Testing [Army's Combat System Test Activity] (INF)
FAIR .... Fabrication, Assembly, and Inspection Record [NASA] (NASA)
FAIR .... Failure Analysis Information Retrieval (IAA)
FAIR .... Fair Access to Insurance Requirements [Government insurance program]
FAIR .... Fair and Impartial Random Selection [System] [Military draft]
FAIR .... Fairing
FAIR .... Fairness and Accuracy in Reporting (EA)
FAIR .... Family Action Information and Rescue [British] (DI)
FAIR .... Fans Against Indian Racism (EA)
FAIR .... Fast Access Information Retrieval
FAIR .... Fast Access to Insurance Requirement (PDAA)
FAIR .... Federal Assistance Information Reporting

FAIR .... Federation for American Immigration Reform (EA)
FAIR .... Firearms and Individual Rights [A California organization]
FAIR .... Fleet Air [Wing]
FAIR .... Fly-Along Infrared Program [Army] (RDA)
FAIR .... Focus on Arms Information and Reassurance
FAIR .... Forest, Agriculture, Industry, and Research
FAIR .... Free from Tax, Affordable, Insured Rewarding [Savings certificate] [Savings and Loan Association]
FAIR .... Fund for Assuring an Independent Retirement (EA)
FAIR .... Irene [South Africa] [ICAO location identifier] (ICLI)
FAIR .... Renaissance Entertainment [NASDAQ symbol] (TTSB)
FAIR .... Renaissance Entertainment Corp. [NASDAQ symbol] (SAG)
Fairc .... Fairchild Industries, Inc. [Associated Press] (SAG)
FAIRC .... Faircross [England]
FairCm .... Fairfield Communities, Inc. [Associated Press] (SAG)
FairCp .... Fairchild Corp. [Associated Press] (SAG)
FAIRDEX ...... Fleet Air Defense Exercise [Navy] (NG)
FAIREC .... Fruits Agro-Industrie Regions Chaudes [Institut de Recherches sur les Fruits et Agrumes] [Database]
FAIRECONRON... Fleet Air Reconnaissance Squadron
FAIRELM ...... Fleet Air Eastern Atlantic and Mediterranean (NATG)
Fair Empl Prac Cas... Fair Employment Practices Cases (DLA)
Fairf .... Fairfield's Reports [10-12 Maine] [A publication] (DLA)
Fairfield ...... Fairfield's Reports [10-12 Maine] [A publication] (DLA)
Fairfield U... Fairfield University (GAGS)
Fairf (ME)... Fairfield's Reports [10-12 Maine] [A publication] (DLA)
FairIsc .... Fair [Isaac] & Co. [Associated Press] (SAG)
Fairleigh Dickinson U... Fairleigh Dickinson University (GAGS)
Fair M & D... Fairbanks' Marriage and Divorce Laws of Massachusetts [A publication] (DLA)
FAIRS .... Fairchild Automatic Intercept and Response System (MCD)
FAIRS .... Federal Aviation Information Retrieval System
FAIRS .... Food and Agriculture Organization Agricultural Information Storage and RetrievalSystem [Operated by FAO] (NITA)
FAIRS .... Fully Automated Information Retrieval System (NITA)
FAIRS .... Fully Automatic Information Retrievel System [Computer science] (EECA)
FAIRSHIPS... Fleet Airships
FAIRSHIPWING... Fleet Airship Wing
Fair Tr .... Fair Trade Laws [A publication] (DLA)
FAIRTRANS... First Available Air Transportation
FAIRW .... Renaissance Entmt Wrrt'A' [NASDAQ symbol] (TTSB)
FAIRWESTPAC... Fleet Air Wing, Western Pacific Area
FAIRWING ... Fleet Air Wing
FAIRZ .... Renaissance Entmt Wrrt'B' [NASDAQ symbol] (TTSB)
FAIS .... Federation d'Associations d'Ingenieurs et de Scientifiques [Federation of Engineering and Scientific Associations] [Canada] (EAIO)
FAIS .... Force Air Intelligence Study [Air Force]
FAIS .... Foreign Affairs Information System [Department of State] (GFGA)
FAIS .... Foreign Affairs Interdepartmental Seminar [Military]
FAIS .... Isithebe [South Africa] [ICAO location identifier] (ICLI)
FAISME .... Fellow of the Australian Institute of Sales and Marketing Executives
FAISS-E .... FORSCOM [Forces Command] Automated Intelligence Support System, Enhan ced [Army] (DOMA)
FAIT .... Families Against Intimidation and Terror [An association]
FAIT .... First-Aid Instructor Trainer [Red Cross]
FAIT .... First Article Inspection Tag [NASA] (SAA)
FAITE .... Final Acceptance Inspection Test Equipment (MCD)
FAIX .... Fairways Corp. [Air carrier designation symbol]
FAJ .... Fajardo [Puerto Rico] [Airport symbol] (OAG)
FAJ .... Fajardo, PR [Location identifier FAA] (FAAL)
FAJ .... Fiji Air Services Ltd. [ICAO designator] (FAAC)
FAJ .... Friends of Ann Jillian (EA)
FAJ .... Frontier Adjusters of Amer [AMEX symbol] (TTSB)
FAJ .... Frontier Adjusters of America, Inc. [AMEX symbol] (SAG)
FAJB .... Johannesburg [South Africa] [ICAO location identifier] (ICLI)
FAJF .... Jagersfontein [South Africa] [ICAO location identifier] (ICLI)
FAJS .... Johannesburg/Jan Smuts [South Africa] [ICAO location identifier] (ICLI)
FAK .... Fidelity Advisor Korea Fund [NYSE symbol] (SAG)
FAK .... Financial AirExpress [ICAO designator] (FAAC)
FAK .... Flat Rock, VA [Location identifier FAA] (FAAL)
FAK .... Fly-Away Kit (MCD)
FAK .... Focal Adhesion Kinase [An enzyme]
FAK .... Fondation Aga Khan [Aga Khan Foundation] (EAIO)
FAK .... Freight, All Kinds [Railroad]
FAK .... Full-Aperture Kicker [Synchrotron]
FAKA .... Karibib [Namibia] [ICAO location identifier] (ICLI)
FAKB .... Karasburg [Namibia] [ICAO location identifier] (ICLI)
FAKD .... Klerksdorp [South Africa] [ICAO location identifier] (ICLI)
FAKFWSO ... Federation of Australian Kung Fu and Wun Shu Organisations
FAKG .... Komati Power Station/Kragsentrale [South Africa] [ICAO location identifier] (ICLI)
FAKH .... Kenhardt [South Africa] [ICAO location identifier] (ICLI)
FAKJ .... Kamanjab [Namibia] [ICAO location identifier] (ICLI)
FAKK .... Kakamas [South Africa] [ICAO location identifier] (ICLI)
FAKL .... Kriel [South Africa] [ICAO location identifier] (ICLI)
FAKM .... Kimberley/B. J. Vorster [South Africa] [ICAO location identifier] (ICLI)
FAKN .... Klippan Control Reporting Point [South Africa] [ICAO location identifier] (ICLI)
FA Korea ..... Fidelity Advisor Korea Fund [Associated Press] (SAG)
FAKP .... Komatipoort [South Africa] [ICAO location identifier] (ICLI)
FAKR .... Krugersdorp [South Africa] [ICAO location identifier] (ICLI)
FAKS .... File Access Keys (NITA)
FAKS .... Kroonstad [South Africa] [ICAO location identifier] (ICLI)

FAKT.......... Keetmanshoop/J. G. H. Van Der Wath [*Namibia*] [*ICAO location identifier*] (ICLI)
FAKU.......... Kuruman [*South Africa*] [*ICAO location identifier*] (ICLI)
FAKX.......... Khorixas [*Namibia*] [*ICAO location identifier*] (ICLI)
FAKZ.......... Kleinsee [*South Africa*] [*ICAO location identifier*] (ICLI)
FAL........... Facilitation of International Air Transport [*Aviation*]
FAL........... Facilities Laboratory [*National Center for Atmospheric Research*]
FAL........... Failure Analysis Laboratory (MCD)
FAL........... Falcon Cable Sys L.P. [*AMEX symbol*] (TTSB)
FAL........... Falcon Cable Systems Ltd. [*AMEX symbol*] (SPSG)
FAL........... File Access Listener
FAL........... Financial Analysis Language [*Computer science*] (MCD)
FAL........... Finite Automation Language [*Computer science*]
FAL........... First Approach and Landing [*Test*] [*NASA*] (NASA)
FAL........... Food and Agricultural Legislation [*A publication*]
FAL........... Foodland Associates Ltd.
FAL........... Forces Armees Laotiannes [*Federated Army of Laos*]
FAL........... Fractional Allelic Loss [*Genetics*]
FAL........... France Amerique Latine [*France Latin America*] [*An association*] (EAIO)
FAL........... Frente Anti-Imperialista de Liberacion [*Peruvian guerrilla group*] (EY)
FAL........... Frequency Allocation List
FAL........... Friendship Air Alaska [*ICAO designator*] (FAAC)
FAL........... Frontier Airlines, Inc. [*Air carrier designation symbol*]
FAL........... Fuerzas Armadas de Liberacio [*Argentina*]
FAL........... Function of Astronaut Location [*NASA*] (KSC)
FAL........... Roma, TX [*Location identifier FAA*] (FAAL)
FALA.......... First Amendment Lawyers Association (EA)
FALA.......... Fund for Animals Ltd. Australia
FALA.......... Lanseria [*South Africa*] [*ICAO location identifier*] (ICLI)
FALB.......... Ladybrand [*South Africa*] [*ICAO location identifier*] (ICLI)
FAlban....... First Albany Companies, Inc. [*Associated Press*] (SAG)
FALC.......... Armed Forces for the Liberation of Cabinda [*Angola*] (PD)
Falc.......... Falconer's Scotch Court of Session Cases [*1744-51*] [*A publication*] (DLA)
FALC.......... Forward Acting Linear Combiner (IAA)
FALC.......... Lime Acres [*South Africa*] [*ICAO location identifier*] (ICLI)
Falc & F...... Falconer and Fitzherbert's English Election Cases [*1835-39*] [*A publication*] (DLA)
Falc & Fitz... Falconer and Fitzherbert's English Election Cases [*1835-39*] [*A publication*] (DLA)
FalcCbl....... Falcon Cable Systems Ltd. [*Associated Press*] (SAG)
Falc Co Cts.. Falconer's English County Court Cases [*A publication*] (DLA)
FalcDr........ Falcon Drilling Co. [*Associated Press*] (SAG)
Falc Marine Dict... Falconer's Marine Dictionary [*A publication*] (DLA)
FalcnPr....... Falcon Products, Inc. [*Associated Press*] (SAG)
FALCON....... Fission Activated LASER Concept [*Sandia National Laboratories*]
FalconBP..... Falcon Building Products, Inc. [*Associated Press*] (SAG)
FalconDr..... Falcon Drilling Co. [*Associated Press*] (SAG)
FalconPd..... Falcon Products, Inc. [*Associated Press*] (SAG)
FALCRI....... Federazione Autonoma Lavoratori Casse di Risparmio Italiane [*Savings Banks Workers Federation*] [*Italy*] (EY)
FALD.......... Finnish American League for Democracy (EA)
FALG.......... Fowl Antimouse Lymphocyte Globulin [*Immunochemistry*]
FALH.......... Lohathla [*South Africa*] [*ICAO location identifier*] (ICLI)
FALI.......... Lichtenburg [*South Africa*] [*ICAO location identifier*] (ICLI)
FALJC......... Federal Administrative Law Judges Conference (EA)
FALK I........ Falkland Islands (ROG)
FALK IS....... Falkland Islands (WDAA)
FALKLD I..... Falkland Islands (ROG)
FALL.......... Fall [*Postal Service standard*] (OPSA)
FALL.......... Fallopian [*Gynecology*] (DAVI)
FALL.......... Lydenburg [*South Africa*] [*ICAO location identifier*] (ICLI)
FALLEX....... Fall [*Autumn*] Exercise [*Military NATO*] (NATG)
FAllian....... First Alliance Bancorp, Inc. [*Associated Press*] (SAG)
FALLINE...... Fedreal Atlantic-Lakes Line [*Steamship*] (MHDW)
FAlliPB....... First Alliance Premier Bancshares, Inc. [*Associated Press*] (SAG)
FALLS......... Falls [*Commonly used*] (OPSA)
FALM......... Falmouth [*Municipal borough in England*]
FALM......... Florida Association of Livestock Markets (SRA)
FALM......... Loraine Mine [*South Africa*] [*ICAO location identifier*] (ICLI)
FalmBk....... Falmouth Co-Operative Bank [*Associated Press*] (SAG)
FALN.......... Fuerzas Armadas de Liberacion Nacional [*Armed Forces of National Liberation*] [*Venezuela*] (PD)
FALN.......... Fuerzas Armadas de Liberacion Nacional Puertorriquena [*Armed Forces of Puerto Rican National Liberation*] (EA)
FALO.......... Louis Trichardt [*South Africa*] [*ICAO location identifier*] (ICLI)
FALOP........ Forward Area Limited Observing Program (MCD)
FALPA........ Fellow of the Incorporated Society of Auctioneers and Landed Property Agents [*British*]
FALR.......... Florida Administrative Law Reports [*A publication*]
FALS.......... Familial Amyotrophic Lateral Sclerosis [*Medicine*]
FALS.......... Foreign Area and Language Study
FALS.......... Forward Angle Light Scattering [*Analytical biochemistry*]
FALSET....... Falsetto [*Music*]
FALSTAF...... Forward Area LASER Systems - Tactical and Fiscal [*Military*]
FALT.......... FADAC [*Field Artillery Digital Automatic Computer*] Automatic Logic Tester
FALT.......... Field Artillery Logic Tester [*Army*] (AABC)
FALT.......... Louis Trichardt [*South Africa*] [*ICAO location identifier*] (ICLI)
FALTRAN..... FORTRAN [*Formula Translating System*]-to-ALGOL Translator [*Algorithmic language*] [*Computer science*] (IEEE)
FALU.......... Florida Association of Life Underwriters (SRA)
FALW......... Forward Area LASER Weapon
FALW......... Langebaanweg [*South Africa*] [*ICAO location identifier*] (ICLI)

FALY.......... Ladysmith [*South Africa*] [*ICAO location identifier*] (ICLI)
FALZ.......... Luderitz [*Namibia*] [*ICAO location identifier*] (ICLI)
Fam........... Epistulae ad Familiares [*of Cicero*] [*Classical studies*] (OCD)
Fam........... Facilities Analysis Model [*Computer science*]
FAM.......... Familiar (AABC)
FAM.......... Family (AFM)
Fam........... Family Division, High Court, England and Wales (DLA)
Fam........... Family of Frequencies [*Aviation*] (DA)
FAM.......... Famous (WGA)
FAM.......... Farmington, MO [*Location identifier FAA*] (FAAL)
FAM.......... Fast Access Memory [*Computer science*] (HGAA)
FAM.......... Fast Aerial Mine [*British military*] (DMA)
FAM.......... Fast Auxiliary Memory (IEEE)
FAM.......... Fathom Oceanology Ltd. [*Toronto Stock Exchange symbol*]
FAM.......... Federal Airmail (IAA)
FAM.......... Federation of Apparel Manufacturers (EA)
FAM.......... Feed Assembly Modification
FAM.......... Field Activity Missile (MCD)
FAM.......... Field Artillery Missile
FAM.......... File Access Manager
FAM.......... Filter Assembly Machine (MCD)
FAM.......... Final Address Message [*Telecommunications*] (TEL)
FAM.......... Flight Acceptance Meeting (SAA)
FAM.......... Floating Add Magnitude [*Computer science*] (IAA)
FAM.......... Fluorouracil, Adriamycin, Mitomycin [*Antineoplastic drug regimen*]
FAM.......... Fluorouracil, Adriamycin, Mitomycin-C [*Antineoplastic drug*] (CDI)
FAM.......... Foreign Air Mail
FAM.......... Free and Accepted Masons
FAM.......... Free at Mill [*Business term*]
FAM.......... Frequency Allocation Multiplex (IAA)
FAM.......... Frequency Amplitude Modulation (IAA)
FAM.......... Frequency Assignment Model (SAA)
FAM.......... Frequency Modulation and Advanced Memory [*Yamaha International Corp.*]
FAM.......... Friable Asbestos-Containing Material (GNE)
FAM.......... Full Army Mobilization War Reserves (AABC)
FAM.......... Fumigacion Aerea Andalusa SA [*Spain ICAO designator*] (FAAC)
FAM.......... International Family Entertainment, Inc. [*NYSE symbol*] (SPSG)
FAM.......... Intl Family Entert'nt 'B' [*NYSE symbol*] (TTSB)
FAMA......... Federal Agricultural Marketing Authority
FAMA......... Federal Association of Management Analysts [*Defunct*]
FAMA......... Fellow of the American Medical Association
FAMA......... Fire Apparatus Manufacturers Association [*Defunct*] (EA)
FAMA......... Flota Aerea Mercane Argentina
FAMA......... Fluorescent Antibody-Membrane Antigen [*Immunochemistry*]
FAMA......... Fondation pour l'Assistance Mutuelle en Afrique au Sud du Sahara [*Foundation for Mutual Assistance in Africa South of the Sahara*]
FAMA......... Forward Airhead Maintenance Area [*Military British*]
FAMA......... Matatiele [*South Africa*] [*ICAO location identifier*] (ICLI)
FAMAE....... Following Amendment Authorized Effective (FAAC)
FAMAS....... Field Artillery Meteorological Acquisition System (MCD)
FAMAS....... Flutter and Matrix Algebra System [*Computer science*]
FamB......... Family Bargain Corp. [*Associated Press*] (SAG)
F Amb........ Field Ambulance [*British military*] (DMA)
FAMB........ Friends of the American Museum in Britain (EA)
FAMB........ Middelburg [*South Africa*] [*ICAO location identifier*] (ICLI)
FamBarg..... Family Bargain Corp. [*Associated Press*] (SAG)
FamBc....... Family Bancorp [*Associated Press*] (SAG)
FAMBSA..... Farmers and Manufacturers Beet Sugar Association
FAMC........ Fitzsimons Army Medical Center (AABC)
FAM-C....... Fluorouracil, Adriamycin, Mitomycin-C [*Antineoplastic drug regimen*] (DAVI)
FAMC........ Foreign Affairs Manual Circular [*Department of State*] [*A publication*]
FAMC........ Middelburg [*South Africa*] [*ICAO location identifier*] (ICLI)
Fam Cas Cir Ev... Famous Cases of Circumstantial Evidence, by Phillips [*A publication*] (DLA)
FAMCK....... Federal Agricultural Mtge'C' [*NASDAQ symbol*] (TTSB)
FAMD........ Malamala [*South Africa*] [*ICAO location identifier*] (ICLI)
FAMDD....... Functional Area Management and Development Division [*US Army Personnel Command*] (RDA)
FamDlr....... Family Dollar Stores [*Associated Press*] (SAG)
fam doc...... Family Doctor (AAMN)
FamDv....... Famous Daves of America, Inc. [*Associated Press*] (SAG)
FAME........ Farmers' Allied Meat Enterprises Cooperative
FAME........ Fatty Acid Methyl Ester [*Biochemistry*]
FAME........ Fellowship of Associates of Medical Evangelism (EA)
FAME........ Ferroacoustic Memory [*Electronics*] (IAA)
FAME........ Field Activity Missile Engineering (MCD)
FAME........ Final Approach Monitoring Equipment [*Aviation*]
FAME........ Financial, Accounting Marketing Exercise (PDAA)
FAME........ Financial Analysis of Management Effectiveness [*Department of Agriculture*]
FAME........ [*The*] Flamemaster Corp. [*NASDAQ symbol*] (NQ)
FAME........ Florida Association for Media in Education (SRA)
FAME........ Florida Association of Marine Explorers
FAME........ Fluorouracil, Adriamycin, MeCCNU [*Semustine*] [*Antineoplastic drug regimen*]
FAME........ Fluorouracil, Adriamycin, Methyl-CCNU [*Antineoplastic drug*] (CDI)
FAME........ Forecasts, Appraisals, and Management Evaluations (MCD)
FAME........ Framework for Achieving Managerial Excellence (EPA)
FAME........ Freeway and Arterial Management Effort [*FHWA*] (TAG)
FAME........ Fund for the Advancement of Music Education [*Defunct*] (EA)
FAME........ Future American Magical Entertainers
FAME........ Marion Island [*South Africa*] [*ICAO location identifier*] (ICLI)
FAMECE...... Family of Military Engineer Construction Equipment

FAMECE/UET... Family of Military Engineer Construction Equipment/Universal Engineer Tractor (RDA)

FAMEM........ Federation of Associations of Mining Equipment Manufacturers (MHDB)

FAMEX........ Familiarization Exercise [*Military*] (NVT)

FAMF.......... Floating Aircraft Maintenance Facility [*Army*] (AABC)

FAMFIRE...... Familiarization Firing (DNAB)

FAMG.......... Margate [*South Africa*] [*ICAO location identifier*] (ICLI)

FamGolf...... Family Golf Centers, Inc. [*Associated Press*] (SAG)

FAMH.......... Maltahohe [*Namibia*] [*ICAO location identifier*] (ICLI)

FAMHEM...... Federation of Associations of Materials Handling Equipment Manufacturers (MHDB)

FAmHlt .... First American Health Concepts [*Associated Press*] (SAG)

FAMHSGASSIGNSY... Family Housing Assignment Application System [*Military*] (DNAB)

FAMHSGRQMTSURVSYS... Family Housing Requirements Survey Record System (DNAB)

FAMHW .... Federation of Associations of Mental Health Workers [*British*] (BI)

FAMI .... Fellow of the Australian Marketing Institute (ODBW)

FAMI .... Marble Hall [*South Africa*] [*ICAO location identifier*] (ICLI)

FAMICA....... Federal Agricultural Mtge'A' [*NASDAQ symbol*] (TTSB)

F Am IEE ..... Fellow of the American Institute of Electrical Engineers

Family Law Rev... Family Law Review [*A publication*]

FAMINE........ Families Against Meat in New England [*Worcester, Massachusetts, group protesting high cost of food, 1973*]

Fam in Soc... Families in Society [*A publication*] (BRI)

FAMIS.......... Factory Management Information System [*British*] (NITA)

FAMIS.......... Family Assistance Management Information System [*Department of Health and Human Services*] (GFGA)

FAMIS.......... Financial and Management Information System [*Naval Oceanographic Office*]

FAMK.......... Mafikeng [*South Africa*] [*ICAO location identifier*] (ICLI)

FAML.......... Mariental [*Namibia*] [*ICAO location identifier*] (ICLI)

FAMLIES...... Financial Support, Advocacy, Medical Management, Love, Information, Education, Structural Support (MEDA)

FAMM.......... Families Against Mandatory Minimums Foundation (EA)

FAMM.......... Fiducial Automated Measuring Machine [*Defunct*]

FAMM.......... Mmabatho International [*South Africa*] [*ICAO location identifier*] (ICLI)

FAMMe........ Fluorouracil, Adriamycin, Mitomycin C, MeCCNU [*Semustine*] [*Antineoplastic drug regimen*]

FAMMM........ Familial Atypical Multiple Mole Melanoma [*Oncology*]

FAMMO........ Full Ammo [*Navy*] (DOMA)

FAMMS........ Financial and Material Management System (SAA)

FAMMS........ Fixed Allowance Management Monitoring System (MCD)

FAMN.......... Malalane [*South Africa*] [*ICAO location identifier*] (ICLI)

fam nov .... Familia Nova [*New Family*] [*Biology*]

FAMO.......... Forward Airfield Maintenance Organization

FAMO.......... Mossel Bay/Baai [*South Africa*] [*ICAO location identifier*] (ICLI)

FAMOS .... Fast Multitasking Operating System [*MVT Microcomputer Systems, Inc.*]

FAMOS .... Fleet Application of Meteorological Observations from Satellites (IEEE)

FAMOS .... Flight Acceleration Monitor Only System (NASA)

FAMOS .... Floating-Gate Avalanche-Injection Metal-Oxide Semiconductor [*Computer science*]

FAMOST ...... Floating-Gate Avalanche-Injection Metal-Oxide Silicon Transistor (IAA)

FAMOUS ...... French-American Mid-Ocean Undersea Study [*Joint undersea program*]

FAMP.......... Fire Alarm Monitoring Panel (IEEE)

FAMP.......... Foreign Army Material Production (MCD)

FAMP.......... Frontier Armed and Mounted Police [*British government*]

FAMP.......... Mpacha [*Namibia*] [*ICAO location identifier*] (ICLI)

FAMPA......... Ferro Alloys and Metals Producers Association [*British*] (DBA)

FAM PER PAR... Familial Periodic Paralysis [*Medicine*] (BABM)

Fam per par... Familial Periodic Paralysis [*Neurology*] (DAVI)

fam phys ..... Family Physician (CPH)

FAMR.......... Mariepskop [*South Africa*] [*ICAO location identifier*] (ICLI)

FAMRA........ Fleet Air Mediterranean Repair Area (MCD)

Fam Relat .... Family Relations [*A publication*] (BRI)

Fam RZ........ Zeitschrift fuer das Gesamte Familienrecht [*German A publication*] (DLA)

FAMS.......... Failure Analysis of Material Systems (MCD)

FAMS.......... Farfield Acoustic Measuring System (KSC)

FAMS.......... Fellow of the Ancient Monuments Society [*British*]

FAMS.......... Fellow of the Association of Medical Secretaries, Practice Administrators, and Receptionists [*British*] (DBQ)

FAMS.......... Field Army Messenger Service (AABC)

FAMS..... Field Artillery Missile System (RDA)

FAMS..... First Article Master Schedule (MCD)

FAM-S .... Fluorouracil, Adriamycin (Doxorubicin), Mitomycin C, and Streptozotocin [*Antineoplastic drug regimen*]

FAMS.......... Forecasting and Modeling System [*Computer science*] (BUR)

FAMS.......... Forward Armored Mortar System (MCD)

FAMS.......... Foundation for Advances in Medicine and Science (EA)

FAMS.......... Free-Agent Market Simulator [*Computer programmed to calculate the market value of free agents in the National Basketball Association*]

FAMS.......... Fuels Automated Management System [*Air Force*] (GFGA)

FAMS.......... Messina [*South Africa*] [*ICAO location identifier*] (ICLI)

FAmSCE....... Fellow of the American Society of Civil Engineers

FAMSEG ..... Field Artillery Missile Systems Evaluation Group (RDA)

FAMSIM...... Family of Battle Simulators [*Army*]

FAMSIM...... Family of Simulations [*Computer science Army*] (RDA)

FAMSL......... Fleet Aviation Material Support List [*Navy*] (AFIT)

FAMSNUB... Frequencies and Mode-Shapes of Non-Union Beams (PDAA)

FamStk .... Family Steak Houses of Florida, Inc. [*Associated Press*] (SAG)

FAMSY......... Federation of Australian Muslim Students and Youth

FAMT .... Federation of Associations of Medical Technology [*British*] (DBA)

FAM-T .... Fluorouracil, Doxorubicin [*Adriamycin*], Mitomycin, Triazinate [*Antineoplastic drug regimen*]

FAMT .... Meyerton [*South Africa*] [*ICAO location identifier*] (ICLI)

FAMTO......... First Aid Mechanical Transport Outfit [*A vehicle standard pack for immediate repairs*] [*Military British*]

FAMU.......... Fleet Aircraft Maintenance Unit

FAMU.......... Florida Agricultural and Mechanical University [*Tallahasse, FL*]

FAMU.......... Fuel Additive Mixture Unit

FAMY.......... Family (ROG)

FAMY.......... Malmesbury [*South Africa*] [*ICAO location identifier*] (ICLI)

FAMZ.......... Msauli [*South Africa*] [*ICAO location identifier*] (ICLI)

fan .... Fanatic (WDMC)

fan .... Fang [*MARC language code Library of Congress*] (LCCP)

FAN .... Fanning Island [*Line Islands*] [*Seismograph station code, US Geological Survey Closed*] (SEIS)

FAN .... Farsund [*Norway*] [*Airport symbol*] (OAG)

FAN .... Fighter Automatic Navigator

FAN .... Fixed Account Number (EPA)

FAN .... Forces Armees Neutralistes [*Neutralist Armed Forces*] [*Laos*]

FAN .... Free Amino Nitrogen (PDAA)

FAN .... Frente de Avance Nacional [*National Advancement Front*] [*Guatemala*] [*Political party*]

FAN .... Fuchsin, Amido Black, and Naphthol Yellow [*Medicine*] (MAE)

FAN .... Tauern Air Gesellschaft GmbH [*Austria ICAO designator*] (FAAC)

FANA .... Fan Association of North America (EA)

FANA .... Fellow of the American Neurological Association

FANA .... Fluorescent Antinuclear Antibody Test [*Serology*]

FANA .... Forex Association of North America (EA)

FANA .... Futon Association of North America (EA)

FANA .... Namatoni [*Namibia*] [*ICAO location identifier*] (ICLI)

FANAF .... Federation des Societes d'Assurances de Droit National Africains [*Federation of African National Insurance Companies*] [*Dakar, Senegal*] (EAIO)

FANC .... Newcastle [*South Africa*] [*ICAO location identifier*] (ICLI)

FANCAP .... Fluids, Aeration, Nutrition, Communication, Activity, and Pain [*Medicine*]

FANCAS .... Fluids, Aeration, Nutrition, Communication, Activity, and Stimulation [*Medicine*]

F & A........... February and August [*Denotes semiannual payments of interest or dividends in these months*] [*Business term*]

F & A........... Finance and Accounting

F & A........... Finance and Audit Committee [*American Library Association*]

F & A........... Fire and Allied Lines [*Insurance*]

F & A........... Fore and Aft

F & A........... Free and Accepted [*Freemasonry*] (ROG)

F & ABR ...... Food and Agriculture Branch [*US Military Government, Germany*]

F & ACS ...... Fuel and Altitude Control System (DWSG)

F & AM .... Free and Accepted Masons

F & B.......... Fill and Bleed (SAA)

F & B.......... Fire and Bilge

F & B.......... Food and Beverage

F & B.......... Fumigation and Bath [*Military*]

F & C.......... Family and Commercial [*Hotels*] [*British*] (ROG)

F & C.......... Fire and Casualty (WDAA)

F & C.......... Foam and Condom [*Birth control methods*] (DAVI)

F & C.......... Full and Change (ADA)

F & CC........ Fire and Casualty Cases [*Commerce Clearing House*] [*A publication*] (DLA)

F & CD .... Failure and Consumption Data (AAG)

F & CD/IR.... Failure and Consumption Data Inspection Report (AAG)

F & CI .... Food and Container Institute

F & D........... Facilities and Design (KSC)

F & D........... Fill and Drain (AAG)

F & D........... Findings and Determination (AFM)

F & D........... Fixed and Dilated [*Neurology and ophthalmology*] (DAVI)

F & D........... Freight and Demurrage [*Shipping*]

F & DF........ Fuel and Defueling (MSA)

F & DR .... Failure and Discrepancy Reporting (KSC)

F & E .... Facilities and Equipment

F & E .... Facility and Environment (NASA)

F & EDCD .... Facilities and Equipment Department's Control Division [*Navy*] (DNAB)

F & EE .... Film and Equipment Exchange [*Army*] (AABC)

F & EI .... Fire and Explosion Index [*Hazard analysis*]

F & E Res.... F & E Resource Systems Technology, Inc. [*Associated Press*] (SAG)

F & F.......... Filiform and Follower [*Instruments*] [*Urology*] (DAVI)

F & F.......... Fire and Flushing (KSC)

F & F.......... Fire-and-Forget (MCD)

F & F.......... Fittings and Fixtures (ADA)

F & F.......... Foster and Finlason's English Nisi Prius Reports [*175, 176 English Reprint*] [*A publication*] (DLA)

F & F.......... Furniture and Fixtures [*Insurance*]

F&F............ Furniture and Fixtures (DFIT)

F & Fitz .... Falconer and Fitzherbert's English Election Cases [*1835-39*] [*A publication*] (DLA)

F & FIY .... Fife and Forfar Imperial Yeomanry [*British military*] (DMA)

F & FP........ Force and Financial Program (AFM)

F & FY........ Fife and Forfar Yeomanry [*British military*] (DMA)

F & G.......... Folded and Gathered Sheets [*Printing*]

F & GA .... Frame and Grillage Analysis [*Modray Ltd.*] [*Software package*] (NCC)

F & GP	Finance and General Purposes Committee [British] (DCTA)
f & g's	Folded And Gathered Sheets [Publishing] (WDMC)
F & HE	Fridays and Holidays Excepted
F & I	Furnished and Installed (KSC)
F & J Bank	De Gex, Fisher, and Jones' English Bankruptcy Reports [A publication] (DLA)
F & K RGA	Fife and Kincardine Royal Garrison Artillery [British military] (DMA)
F & L	Aviation Fuels, Lubricants, and Associated Products [NATO] (NATG)
F & LD	Flight and Laboratory Development (MCD)
F & M	Farmers & Merchants Bank
F and M	Fire and Maneuver [Infantry strategy] (VNW)
F & M	Firm and Midline [Uterus] [Gynecology and obstetrics] (DAVI)
F & M	Force and Mission
F and M	Franklin and Marshall College [Pennsylvania]
F & M Bc	F & M Bancorp, Inc. [Associated Press] (SAG)
F & M Bn	F & M Bancorp, Inc. [Associated Press] (SAG)
F & M Nat	F & M National Corp. [Associated Press] (SAG)
F & NE	Fairchild & Northeastern Railway
F & O	Financial and Operating Data for Investor-Owned Water Companies [A publication] (EAAP)
F & PM	Flint & Pere Marquette Railroad
F & R	Force and Rhythm [of Pulse] [Medicine]
F & R	Functions and Responsibilities
F and S	Fast and Systematic [Predicasts Inc.] [Set of databases] (NITA)
F & S	Feffer & Simons [Publisher]
F & S	Fox and Smith's Irish King's Bench Reports [1822-24] [A publication] (DLA)
F & S	Fox and Smith's Registration Cases [1886-95] [A publication] (DLA)
F & S	Frost & Sullivan, Inc. [Information service or system] (IID)
F & S	Funk & Scott Publishing Co. [Detroit, MI]
F & SA	Engineering and Stores Association [A union] [British]
F & SF	Fantasy and Science Fiction [A publication]
F & STD	Fire and Safety Test Detachment [Mobile, AL] [Coast Guard] (GRD)
F & T	Fire and Theft
F & T	Fuel and Transportation [Navy]
FANDT	Fuel and Transportation [Navy]
F & T/W	Forest and Trees for Windows [Channel Computing, Inc.] [Computer science] (PCM)
F & U	Flanks and Upper Quadrants [Anatomy] (DAVI)
F & V	Formulation and Verification
F & W	Feeding and Watering [Charge] [Business term]
F & W Pr	Frend and Ware's Precedents of Instruments Relating to the Transfer of Land to Railway Companies [2nd ed.] [1866] [A publication] (DLA)
F & WS	Fish and Wildlife Service [Department of the Interior]
FANE	Federation d'Action Nationale et Europeene [Federation of National and European Action] [France Political party]
FANEL	Federation for Accessible Nursing Education and Licensure (EA)
FANES	Furnace Atomic Nonthermal Excitation Spectrometry
FANFT	Formamidonitrofurylthiazole [Organic chemistry]
FANG	Flechette Area Neutralizing Gun
FANGIO	Feedback Analysis for GCM Intercomparison and Observation (EERA)
FANH	New Hanover [South Africa] [ICAO location identifier] (ICLI)
FANI	Food, Agriculture, and Nutrition Inventory [Department of Agriculture] [Discontinued]
FANK	Forces Armees Nationales Khmeres [Cambodian National Armed Forces] [Replaced Royal Cambodian Armed Forces]
FANL	New Largo [South Africa] [ICAO location identifier] (ICLI)
FANNDE	Forward Addition Algorithm Using the Nearest-Neighbor Distance Error Criteria [Algorithm]
FANO	Frente Anticomunista del Nororiente [Northeastern Anticommunist Front] [Guatemala] (PD)
FANPT	Freeman Anxiety, Neurosis, and Psychosomatic Test [Psychology]
Fan Rom Law	Fanton's Tables of Roman Law [A publication] (DLA)
FANS	Fellow of the American Neurological Society
FANS	Fight to Advance the Nation's Sports [Defunct] (EA)
FANS	Food and Nutritional System [Military] (AABC)
FANS	Forgotten Americans Need Support (EA)
FANS	Franchise of Americans Needing Sports (EA)
FANS	Future Air Navigation Systems [Aviation]
FANS	Nelspruit [South Africa] [ICAO location identifier] (ICLI)
FANSA	Food and Nutrition Science Alliance
Fanstel	Fansteel, Inc. [Associated Press] (SAG)
FANSW	Financiers' Association of New South Wales [Australia]
FANSY	Frequency Analysis and Synthesis [Computer program]
FANT	Forces Armees Nationales Tchadiennes [Chad] (PD)
FANT	French Atmospheric Nuclear Test (MCD)
FANTAC	Fighter Analysis Tactical Air Combat
FANU	Flota Argentina Navegacion Ultramar [Argentine Ship Line]
FANUL	Friends of the Australian National University Library
FANV	Nieuwoudtville [South Africa] [ICAO location identifier] (ICLI)
FANX	Friendship [Airport] ANNEX [National Security Agency]
FANY	First-Aid Nursing Yeomanry [British women's organization formed to do medical transport work for the army; later did general transport work]
FANY	Nylstroom [South Africa] [ICAO location identifier] (ICLI)
FANYS	First Aid Nursing Yeomanry Service [British military] (DMA)
FANZINE	Fan Magazine [Generic term for a publication of interest to science fiction fans]
f-ao--	Angola [MARC geographic area code Library of Congress] (LCCP)
FAO	Fabrication Assembly Order (MCD)
FAO's	Facts on Aging Quiz (EDAC)
FAO	Faro [Portugal] [Airport symbol] (OAG)
FAO	Fatty Amine Oxide [Organic chemistry]

FAO	Field Assessment Officer [Military] (AEBS)
FAO	Field Audit Office
FAO	Finance and Accounts Office [or Officer] [Army]
FAO	Financial Accounting Office (AAGC)
FAO	Finish All Over [Technical drawings]
FAO	Flatland Atmospheric Observatory (USDC)
FAO	Flatland Atmospheric Observatory [Marine science] (OSRA)
FAO	Fleet Accountant Officer [British]
FAO	Fleet Administration Office
FAO	Flight Activities Officer [NASA]
FAO	Food and Agriculture Organization [United Nations Italy Information service or system] (IID)
FAO	Foreign Agricultural Organization
FAO	Foreign Area Officer [Army] (INF)
FAO	Forward Artillery Observer [Liaison officer] [Army] (VNW)
FAO	Free Albania Organization (EA)
FAO	Fumaramido Oripavine [Biochemistry]
FAOA	Funk Aircraft Owners Association (EA)
FAOA	Ondangua [Namibia] [ICAO location identifier] (ICLI)
FAOAC	Field Artillery Officer Advanced Course [Military] (INF)
FAO/APS	FAO [Food and Agriculture Organization of the United Nations] Association of Professional Staff [Rome, Italy] (EAIO)
FAOD	Odendaalsrus [South Africa] [ICAO location identifier] (ICLI)
FAOE	Federation of African Organisations of Engineers (PDAA)
FAOE	Omega [Namibia] [ICAO location identifier] (ICLI)
FAOFOG	Fellow of the Asia-Oceania Federation of Obstetricians and Gynaecologists
FAOG	Oranjemund [Namibia] [ICAO location identifier] (ICLI)
FAOGIS	Food and Agriculture Organization Geographic Information System [United Nations] (DUND)
FAOH	Oudtshoorn [South Africa] [ICAO location identifier] (ICLI)
FAOJ	Outjo [Namibia] [ICAO location identifier] (ICLI)
FAOK	Okakarara [Namibia] [ICAO location identifier] (ICLI)
FAOLU	Federation of All Okinawan Labor Unions
FAOMELU	Federation of All Okinawan Military Employees' Labor Unions
FAOMS	Foreign Area Officer Management System [Army]
FAON	Okahandja [Namibia] [ICAO location identifier] (ICLI)
FAOO	Okaukuejo [Namibia] [ICAO location identifier] (ICLI)
FAOP	Foreign Area Officer Program [Army] (MCD)
FAOP	Opuwa [Namibia] [ICAO location identifier] (ICLI)
FAOR	Olifants River Bridge [South Africa] [ICAO location identifier] (ICLI)
FAOS	Oshakati [Namibia] [ICAO location identifier] (ICLI)
FAOTA	Fellow of the American Occupational Therapy Association
FAOU	Fellow of the American Ornithologists Union
FAOUSA	Finance and Accounts Office [or Officer], United States Army
FAOV	Otavi [Namibia] [ICAO location identifier] (ICLI)
FAOW	Otjiwarongo [Namibia] [ICAO location identifier] (ICLI)
FAOY	Orkney [South Africa] [ICAO location identifier] (ICLI)
FAP	Facilities Assistance Program
FAP	Facility Analysis Plan [Telecommunications] (TEL)
FAP	Failure Analysis Program
FAP	Familial Adenomatous Polyposis [Formerly, FPC] [Medicine]
FAP	Familial Amyloid Polyneuropathy [Medicine]
FAP	Family Assistance Plan [or Program] [Proposed during Nixon administration]
FAP	Family Auto Policy [Insurance]
FAP	Fast Action Procedures (NVT)
FAP	Fast Atmospheric Pulsation
FAP	Fault Analysis Process (TEL)
FAP	Federal Art Project
FAP	Fibrillating Action Potential [Neurophysiology]
FAP	Field-Activated Promotion [Marketing] (DOAD)
FAP	Field Application Panel (IEEE)
FAP	File Access Protocol [Telecommunications] (OSI)
FAP	Filed a Petition [FDA]
FAP	Final Anthropic Principle [Term coined by authors John Barrow and Frank Tipler in their book, "The Anthropic Cosmological Principle"]
FAP	Final Approach Path [or Plane] [Aviation]
FAP	Finance and Accounting Policy [Army] (AABC)
FAP	Financial Analysis Program [IBM Corp.]
FAP	Financial Assistance Program (AFM)
FAP	Fine Aim Positioning
FAP	Fine Arts Philatelists (EA)
FAP	First-Aid Post
FAP	Fixed Action Pattern
FAP	Flexible Accelerator Path [Economic theory]
FAP	Flight Acceptance Profile (KSC)
FAP	Floating-Point Arithmetic Package [Computer science]
FAP	Floating Point Arithmetic System (NITA)
FAP	Fluorouracil, Adriamycin, Cisplatin [Antineoplastic drug regimen] (DAVI)
FAP	Food Additive Petition
FAP	Force Alignment Plan [Military] (INF)
FAP	Foreign Air Program
FAP	Foreign Assistance Program (WDAA)
FAP	FORTRAN [Formula Translating System] Assembly Program [Computer science]
FAP	Fos-Associated Protein [Biochemistry]
FAP	Foundation for the Arts of Peace [Defunct] (EA)
FAP	Franc d'Avarie Particuliere [Free of Particular Average] [Business term French]
FAP	Franco d'Avaria Particolare [Free of Particular Average] [Business term Italian]
FAP	Frequency Allocation Panel

FAP .... Frozen Animal Procedure [*Medicine*] (DMAA)
FAP .... Fuerzas Armadas Peronistas [*Argentina*]
FAP .... Full American Plan [*Hotel room rate*]
FAP .... (Furfurylamino)purine [*Plant hormone*] [*Organic chemistry*]
FAP .... Parsons Airways Northern Ltd. [*Canada ICAO designator*] (FAAC)
FAPA .... F-15 Adapted Place Atlas Program (MCD)
FAPA .... Fantasy Amateur Press Association
FAPA .... Federation of Asian Pharmaceutical Associations
FAPA .... Federation of Asian Photographic Art
FAPA .... Fellow of the American Psychiatric Association
FAPA .... Fellow of the American Psychoanalytic Association
FAPA .... Fellow of the American Psychological Association
FAPA .... Filipino American Political Association
FAPA .... Flight Accrual Payment Action [*Air Force*]
FAPA .... Formosan Association for Public Affairs (EA)
FAPA .... Fred Astaire Performing Arts Association
FAPA .... Future Airline Pilots of America [*BTS*] (TAG)
FAPA .... Future Aviation Professionals of America (EA)
FAPA .... Port Alfred [*South Africa*] [*ICAO location identifier*] (ICLI)
FAPABS .... FORSCOM [*Forces Command*] Automatic Program and Budget System [*Army*] (MCD)
FAPAP .... Federation des Personnels Africains de Police [*Federation of African Police*]
FAPB .... Pietersburg [*South Africa*] [*ICAO location identifier*] (ICLI)
FAPC .... Familial Adenomatous Polyposis Coli [*Medicine*]
FAPC .... Fatty Acid Producers' Council (EA)
FAPC .... Federal Area Port Controller
FAPC .... Food and Agriculture Planning Committee [*NATO*] (NATG)
FAPC .... Prince Albert [*South Africa*] [*ICAO location identifier*] (ICLI)
FAPCC .... Film, Air, and Package Carriers Conference (EA)
FAPE .... Free Appropriate Public Education
FAPE .... Port Elizabeth/H. F. Verwoerd [*South Africa*] [*ICAO location identifier*] (ICLI)
FAPES .... Force Augmentation Planning and Execution System (DOMA)
FAPF .... Piet Retief [*South Africa*] [*ICAO location identifier*] (ICLI)
FAPG .... Fleet Air Photographic Group
FAPG .... Plettenberg Bay [*South Africa*] [*ICAO location identifier*] (ICLI)
FAPH .... Fluoroaldehyde Pyridylhydrazone [*Organic chemistry*]
FAPH .... Phalaborwa/Hendrik Van Eck [*South Africa*] [*ICAO location identifier*] (ICLI)
FAPHA .... Fellow of the American Public Health Association
FAPHA .... Fellow of the Australian Psychology and Hypnotherapy Association
FAPHCC .... Florida Association of Plumbing, Heating, and Cooling Contractors (SRA)
FAPI .... First Article Production Inspection (MCD)
FAPI .... Pietersburg [*South Africa*] [*ICAO location identifier*] (ICLI)
FAPIG .... First Atomic Power Industry Group [*Japan*]
FAPJ .... Port St. Johns [*South Africa*] [*ICAO location identifier*] (ICLI)
FAPL .... Fleet Air Photographic Laboratory (DNAB)
FAPL .... Format and Protocol Language [*IBM*] (NITA)
FAPL .... Pongola [*South Africa*] [*ICAO location identifier*] (ICLI)
FAPM .... Pietermaritzburg [*South Africa*] [*ICAO location identifier*] (ICLI)
FAPMATC .... Fully Automated Pilot Monitored, Air Traffic Control [*Aviation*]
FAPN .... Pilansberg [*South Africa*] [*ICAO location identifier*] (ICLI)
FAPNEWDT .... Financial Accounts Package New Data [*Torch Computers Ltd.*] [*Financial accounting software*] (NITA)
FAPO .... Field Army Petroleum Office (AABC)
FAPP .... Federation of Associations of Periodical Publishers (DGA)
FAPP .... Potgietersrus [*South Africa*] [*ICAO location identifier*] (ICLI)
FAPPEC .... Federation of Associations of Periodical Publishers in the EC (EAIO)
FAPPS .... First Article Preproduction Sample [*DoD*]
FA-PPT .... First Article - Preproduction Test (MCD)
FAPR .... Federal Aviation Procurement Regulations
FAPR .... Pretoria [*South Africa*] [*ICAO location identifier*] (ICLI)
FAPRI .... Food and Agricultural Policy Research Institute [*Iowa State University*] (RCD)
FAPRON .... Fleet Air Photo Squadron
FAPRS .... Federal Assistance Programs Retrieval System [*General Services Administration*] [*Information service or system*] (MCD)
FAPS .... Fate of Atmospheric Pollutants Study [*National Science Foundation*]
FAPS .... Federal Aid Primary System (GNE)
FAPS .... Fellow of the American Physical Society
FAPS .... Financial Aid Planning Service [*College Scholarship Service*]
FAPS .... Financial Analysis and Planning System (IAA)
FAPS .... Financial Application Preprocessor System (MHDW)
FAPS .... Foreign Affairs Programming System (CINC)
FAPS .... Potchefstroom [*South Africa*] [*ICAO location identifier*] (ICLI)
FAPSIM .... Food and Agricultural Policy Simulator
FAPT .... Postmasburg [*South Africa*] [*ICAO location identifier*] (ICLI)
FAPTU .... Farm Animal Practice Teaching Unit [*Royal Veterinary College*] [*British*] (IRUK)
FAPUS .... Fabrication Performance Utilization System (MCD)
FAPUS .... Frequency Allocation Panel, United States (NVT)
FAPUSMCEB .... Frequency Allocation Panel, United States Military Communications Electronics Board
FAPV .... Petrusville [*South Africa*] [*ICAO location identifier*] (ICLI)
FAPY .... Parys [*South Africa*] [*ICAO location identifier*] (ICLI)
FAPZ .... Progress [*South Africa*] [*ICAO location identifier*] (ICLI)
FAQ .... Fair Average Quality
FAQ .... Free at Quay [*Business term*]
FAQ .... Frequently Asked Question
FAQ .... Frequently Asked Questions (ACRL)
FAQL .... Frequent Asked Question List [*Computer science*] (NHD)
FAQS .... Fair Average Quality of Season [*Business term*]
FAQS .... Fast Queuing System [*Computer science*]
FAQT .... Queenstown [*South Africa*] [*ICAO location identifier*] (ICLI)
FAR .... Failure Analysis Report
FAR .... False Alarm Rate
FAR .... Farad [*Unit of electric capacitance*] (ROG)
FAR .... Faraday (WDAA)
FAR .... Far Airlines [*Italy*] [*FAA designator*] (FAAC)
FAR .... Fargo [*North Dakota*] [*Airport symbol*] (OAG)
FAR .... Fargo, ND [*Location identifier FAA*] (FAAL)
FAR .... Farina [*Flour*] [*Pharmacy*] (ROG)
FAR .... Farmer (ROG)
FAR .... Farmington Public Library, Farmington, NM [*OCLC symbol*] (OCLC)
FAR .... Faro [*Portugal*] [*Seismograph station code, US Geological Survey*] (SEIS)
far .... Faroese [*MARC language code Library of Congress*] (LCCP)
Far .... Farresley's Cases in Holt's King's Bench Reports [*A publication*] (DLA)
Far .... Farresley's Reports [*7 Modern Reports*] [*87 English Reprint 1733-45*] [*A publication*] (DLA)
FAR .... Farrier (ROG)
FAR .... Farthing [*Monetary unit*] [*British*]
FAR .... Federal Acquisition Regulation
FAR .... Federal Air Regulations [*FAA*]
FAR .... Federal Airworthiness Regulation
FAR .... Federal Assistance Review [*Program*]
FAR .... Federal Aviation Regulation
FAR .... Federation des Associations Roumaines du Canada [*Federation of Romanian Associations of Canada*]
FAR .... Feminists for Animal Rights (EA)
FAR .... Field Activity Report
FAR .... Field Analysis Report
FAR .... Field Artillery Rocket (MCD)
FAR .... Field Assessment Review [*Military*]
FAR .... Fighter, Attacker, Reconnaissance [*Requirements*] [*Air Force*]
FAR .... Filament Atom Reservoir (PDAA)
FAR .... File Address Register
FAR .... Final Acceptance Review [*NASA*] (NASA)
FAR .... Financial Accounts Receivable
FAR .... Finned Air Rocket (SAA)
FAR .... First Alarm Register
FAR .... First Assessment Report (EERA)
FAR .... Fixed Acoustic Range
FAR .... Fixed Amount Reimbursement [*Agency for International Development*]
FAR .... Fixed Array RADAR
FAR .... Flight Acceptance Review (MCD)
FAR .... Flight Aptitude Rating
FAR .... Floor Area Ratio [*in office buildings*]
FAR .... Fluid Air Ride [*Automotive engineering*]
FAR .... Forces Armees Royales [*Royal Armed Forces*] [*Laos*]
FAR .... Foreign Affairs Research Documentation Center [*Department of State*]
FAR .... Foreign Agricultural Relations Office
FAR .... Foreign Agriculture Report [*Department of Agriculture*]
FAR .... Foreign Area Research Coordination Group [*Department of State*]
FAR .... Foreign Area Research Documentation Center [*Department of State*] (AEBS)
FAR .... Forum Africain pour la Reconstruction [*Gabon*] [*Political party*] (EY)
FAR .... Forward Acquisition RADAR
FAR .... Foundation for Administrative Research (MCD)
FAR .... Foundation for Agronomic Research [*University of Pittsburgh*] [*Research center*] (RCD)
FAR .... Fowler, A. R., Saint Paul MN [*STAC*]
FAR .... Fremantle Arts Review [*A publication*]
FAR .... Frequency Adjusting Rheostat
FAR .... Frequency Allocation Request
FAR .... Fuerzas Armadas Rebeldes [*Rebel Armed Forces*] [*Guatemala*] (PD)
FAR .... Functional Area Review [*Military*]
FAR .... Fund Availability Report (MCD)
FAR .... Fund for an American Renaissance (EA)
FARA .... Federal Acquisition Reform Act of 1996 (AAGC)
FARA .... Federal Agents Registration Act (OICC)
FARA .... Flexible Automation for Robotic Analysis
FARA .... Foreign Affairs Recreation Association (EA)
FARA .... Foreign Agents Registration Act of 1938
FARA .... French American Ridge Atlantic [*Program*] (USDC)
FARAC .... Fuerzas Armadas Anticomunistas [*Anti-Communist Armed Forces*] [*Nicaragua*] (PD)
FARADA .... Failure Rate Data Program [*Navy*] (NG)
Farah .... Farah, Inc. [*Associated Press*] (SAG)
FARA-ITMRA .... Federal Acquisition Reform Act-Information Technology Management Reform Act [*Currently known as Clinger-Cohen Act*]
FARB .... Federal Assistance Review Board (USDC)
FARB .... Federal Assistance Review Board [*Marine science*] (OSRA)
FARB .... Federation of Associations of Regulatory Boards (EA)
FARB .... Richard's Bay [*South Africa*] [*ICAO location identifier*] (ICLI)
FARC .... Family Advancement Resources Cooperative [*Australia*]
FARC .... Farr Co. [*NASDAQ symbol*] (NQ)
FARC .... Fast Accurate Refraction Correction [*NASA*] (KSC)
FARC .... Federal Archives and Records Center [*Regional depository of the National Archives and Records Service*]
FARC .... Field Artillery Replacement Center
FARC .... Fijian-Australian Resource Centre
FARchives .... CCH FAR Archives [*Historical FARs on CD-ROM*] (AAGC)
FAR Council .... Federal Acquisition Regulatory Council (AAGC)

FARD .... Foam-Breaking Apparatus with a Rotating Disk [*Chemical engineering*]

FARD .... Riversdale [*South Africa*] [*ICAO location identifier*] (ICLI)

FARDRCRM.... Field Artillery RADAR Crewman (IAA)

FARE.......... Fatal Accident Reduction Effort [*or Enforcement*] [*Department of Transportation*]

FARE.......... Federation of Alcoholic Residential Establishments [*British*] (DI)

FARE.......... Fiat Auto Recycling

FARE.......... Foreign Assignment Resources Employees [*FAA*]

FARE.......... Forward Area Refueling Equipment [*Army*]

FARE.......... Full Access and Rights to Education Coalition

FARE.......... Uniform Financial Accounting and Reporting Elements [*FTA*] (TAG)

Far East L Rev... Far Eastern Law Review [*A publication*] (DLA)

FAREGAZ ..... Union des Fabricants Europeens de Regulateurs de Pression du Gaz [*Union of European Manufacturers of Gas Pressure Controllers*] (EAIO)

FARELF........ Far East Land Forces (CINC)

FarEst.......... Far East National Bank [*Associated Press*] (SAG)

FARET.......... Fast Reactor Experiment Test [*Proposed but never built*] [*Nuclear energy*]

FarETxt....... Far Eastern Textile Ltd. [*Associated Press*] (SAG)

FAREX .... Fleet Analysis and Reconstruction of Exercise [*Navy*] (MCD)

FARG .... Farmington [*New Mexico*] [*Seismograph station code, US Geological Survey*] (SEIS)

FARG .... Fluid Analogies Research Group

FARG .... Rustenburg [*South Africa*] [*ICAO location identifier*] (ICLI)

FARGO .... Forty Automatic Report Generating Operation (MCD)

FARH .... Rehoboth [*Namibia*] [*ICAO location identifier*] (ICLI)

FARI........... First Amendment Research Institute [*Defunct*] (EA)

FARK .... Forces Armees Royales Khmeres [*Royal Cambodian Armed Forces*] [*Replaced by FANK*]

FARK .... Rooikop [*South Africa*] [*ICAO location identifier*] (ICLI)

FARL........... Farrel Corp. [*NASDAQ symbol*] (SAG)

FARL........... Fractions Armees Revolutionnaires Libanaise [*Lebanese Armed Revolutionary Faction*]

FARM........ Farm Animal Reform Movement (EA)

FARM........ Farmer Bros. [*NASDAQ symbol*] (TTSB)

FARM........ Farmer Brothers Co. [*NASDAQ symbol*] (NQ)

FARM........ Farmers Assistance Relief Mission (EA)

FarmBr........ Farmer Brothers Co. [*Associated Press*] (SAG)

FARMC .... Frankfurt Army Regional Medical Center [*US Army 97th General Hospital*] [*Germany*]

FarmCB....... Farmers Capital Bank Corp. [*Associated Press*] (SAG)

FARMDOC.... Pharmaceutical Documentation [*British*] [*Patents retrieval system Derwent Publications*] (NITA)

Farmer Mac... Federal Agricultural Mortgage Corporation (USGC)

FARMERS .... Frequency Agility RADAR Modifications to Existing RADAR Systems [*DoD*]

FarmFH........ Farm Family Holdings, Inc. [*Associated Press*] (SAG)

FarmMch ..... Farmers & Mechanics Bank [*Associated Press*] (SAG)

FARMS .... Farm Audience Readership Measurement Service [*Starch INRA Hooper, Inc.*] [*Information service or system*] (IID)

FARMS .... Financial Accounting Resource Management System

FarmT.......... Farmstead Telephone Group, Inc. [*Associated Press*] (SAG)

FarmTel....... Farmstead Telephone Group, Inc. [*Associated Press*] (SAG)

FARN .... Fuerzas Armadas de Resistencia Nacional [*Armed Forces of National Resistance*] [*El Salvador*] (PD)

FARN .... Fuerzas Armadas Revolucionarias Nicaraguenses [*Nicaraguan Armed Revolutionary Forces*] (PD)

FARNET .... Federation of American Research Networks [*Computer science*] (TNIG)

FARO .... Flare-Activated Radiobiological Observatory

FAROES .... Fleet Automatic Reconstruction and Opportunity Evaluation System [*Navy*] (CAAL)

FARP .... Forces Afloat Repair Procedures (DNAB)

FARP .... Forward Area Rearm/Refuel Point [*Army*] (INF)

FARP .... Forward Area Resupply Point

FARP .... Rosh Pinah [*Namibia*] [*ICAO location identifier*] (ICLI)

FARPO .... Federal Acquisition Regulation Project Office (MCD)

Farq Chy...... Farquharson's Court of Chancery [*A publication*] (DLA)

FARR .... Failure and Rejection Report (MCD)

Farr............. Farr Co. [*Associated Press*] (SAG)

Farr............. Farresley's Reports [*7 Modern Reports*] [*87 English Reprint 1733-45*] [*A publication*] (DLA)

FARR .... Federal Aviation Administration and Air Force RADAR Replacement

FARR .... Forward Area Refuelling and Rearming

Farrant........ Digest of Manx Cases [*1925-47*] [*A publication*] (DLA)

Farr Bill....... Farren's Bill in Chancery [*A publication*] (DLA)

Farr Const ... Farrar's Manual of the United States Constitution [*A publication*] (DLA)

Farrel.......... Farrel Corp. [*Associated Press*] (SAG)

Farresley ..... Farresley's Reports [*7 Modern Reports*] [*87 English Reprint 1733-45*] [*A publication*] (DLA)

Farr Life Ass... Farren on Life Assurance [*A publication*] (DLA)

Farr Mas...... Farren's Masters in Chancery [*A publication*] (DLA)

Farr Med Jur... Farr's Medical Jurisprudence [*A publication*] (DLA)

FARRP.......... Forward Area Rearm and Refuel Point

FARRS.......... Forward Area Rearm and Refuel Site (MCD)

FARS .... Failure Analysis Report Summary [*Bell System*]

FARS .... Fatal Accident Reporting System [*National Highway Traffic Safety Administration*] [*Washington, DC*] (GRD)

FARS .... Field Army Replacement System (AABC)

FARS .... File Analysis for Random Access Storage [*Computer science*] (IAA)

FARS .... Financial Accounting and Reporting System [*Federal Emergency Management Agency*] (GFGA)

FARS .... Forward Area RAWINSONDE [*RADAR Wind Sounding and Radiosonde*] Set [*Army*]

FARS .... Fuel and Ammunition Resupply Study

FARS .... Robertson [*South Africa*] [*ICAO location identifier*] (ICLI)

FARU .... Rundu [*Namibia*] [*ICAO location identifier*] (ICLI)

FARV .... Future Armored Resupply Vehicle [*Army*]

FARV .... Riverview [*South Africa*] [*ICAO location identifier*] (ICLI)

FARV-A .... Future Armored Resupply Vehicle-Ammunition [*Army*] (RDA)

Farwell .... Farwell on Powers [*3 eds.*] [*1874-1916*] [*A publication*] (DLA)

FARWG .... Federal Acquisition Regional Work Group [*Army*]

Farw Pow ... Farwell on Powers [*3 eds.*] [*1874-1916*] [*A publication*] (DLA)

FAS............. Facilities Automation System

FAS............. Facility Activation [*or Activity*] Schedule

FAS............. Facility Air Supply

FAS............. Faculty of Architects and Surveyors [*British*] (DAS)

FAS............. Failure Analysis Section

FAS............. Fallout Assessment System

FAS............. Family Action Section (EA)

FAS............. Famous Artists Schools [*Later, FAS International, Inc.*]

FAS............. Fast Announcement Service [*NTIS publication*]

FAS............. Fasten [*Technical drawings*]

FAS............. Fastener

FAS............. Fatty Acid Synthase [*An enzyme*]

FAS............. Feature Analysis System [*Image analysis*]

FAS............. Federal Advertising Services

FAS............. Federal Airport Service

FAS............. Federal Aviation Service

FAS............. Federation des Affaires Sociales, Inc. [*Federation of Social Affairs*] [*Canada*]

FAS............. Federation of American Scientists (EA)

FAS............. Federation of Astronomical Societies [*British*] (EAIO)

FAS............. Feel Augmentation System [*Helicopters*]

FAS............. Fellow of the Actuarial Society

FAS............. Fellow of the Anthropological Society [*British*] (DAS)

FAS............. Fellow of the Antiquarian Society [*British*]

FAS............. Fellow of the Society of Arts [*British*] (DAS)

FAS............. Fellows in American Studies

FAS............. Fetal Alcohol Syndrome [*Medicine*]

FAS............. Field Aircraft Services Ltd. [*British ICAO designator*] (FAAC)

FAS............. Field Alert Status [*Army*] (AABC)

FAS............. Field Artillery School (MCD)

FAS............. Field Artillery System [*Army*] (RDA)

FAS............. Fielded Aircraft System

FAS............. File Access Subsystem [*Computer science*] (TEL)

FAS............. Film Availability Services [*British Film Institute*]

FAS............. Filtered Air Supply (IAA)

FAS............. Final Asset Screen [*DoD*]

FAS............. Final Average Salary

FAS............. Financial Accounting Standard

FAS............. Financial Accounting System

FAS............. Financial Analysis System (MHDW)

FAS............. Finnish-American Society [*Later, LFAS*] (EA)

FAS............. Fire Support Aerial System

FAS............. First Assistant Secretary (ADA)

FAS............. Firsts and Seconds [*Lumber trade*]

FAS............. Fixed Airlock Shroud [*NASA*]

FAS............. Flame Absorption Spectroscopy

FAS............. Fleet Attack Submarine [*Navy*] (CAAL)

FAS............. Flexible Access System

FAS............. Flight Advisory Service [*FAA*]

FAS............. Flight Analysis Section

FAS............. Flight Assistance Service

FAS............. Fluid Analysis Spectrometer (MCD)

FAS............. Focusing Array Study

FAS............. Follow-Up Alarm System

FAS............. Foras Ciseanna Saothair (ACII)

FAS............. Force Accounting Structure

FAS............. Force Accounting System [*Army*] (AABC)

FAS............. Foreign Agricultural Service [*Department of Agriculture*] [*Washington, DC*]

FAS............. Foreign Aid Society [*British*]

FAS............. Foreign Area Specialist [*Army*]

FAS............. Forward Acquisition Sensor

FAS............. Forward Acquisition System

FAS............. Forward Aid Station [*Army*] (INF)

FAS............. Foundation for Aggregate Studies

FAS............. Frame Acquisition and Synchronization (LAIN)

FAS............. Frame Alignment Sequence [*Telecommunications*] (ACRL)

FAS............. Frame Alignment Signal [*Telecommunications*] (TEL)

FAS............. Frame Analysis System [*IBM UK Ltd.*] [*Software package*] (NCC)

FAS............. Franciscan Apostolic Sisters (TOCD)

FAS............. Free Alongside [*Insurance*]

FAS............. Free Alongside Ship [*"INCOTERM," International Chamber of Commerce official code*]

FAS............. Free-Association Strength [*Psychometrics*]

FAS............. Frequency Allocation [*or Assignment*] Subcommittee (AFM)

FAS............. Fuel Availability System (NITA)

FAS............. Fueling-at-Sea [*Navy*] (MSA)

FAS............. Functional Acquisition Specialist [*Army*] (RDA)

FAS............. Functional Address Symbol [*Military*] (AFIT)

FAS............. Functional Analysis Sheet

FAS............. Fund for American Studies (EA)

FASA........... Federal Acquisition Streamlining Act of 1994 (AAGC)

FASA........... Federation of ASEAN [*Association of South East Asian Nations*] Shipowners' Associations [*Kuala Lumpur, Malaysia*] (EAIO)

FASA............ Fellow, American Society of Appraisers [*American Society of Appraisers*] [*Designation awarded by*]

FASA............ Fellow of the American Sociological Association

FASA............ Fellow of the Australian Society of Accountants (ODBW)

FASA............ Field Army Service Area (AABC)

FASA............ Filipino Association of South Australia

FASA............ Final Approach Spacing Assignment [*Aviation*] (IAA)

FASA............ Fixed Area Scanning Alarm

FASA............ Fleet Airships, Atlantic

FASA............ Freestanding Ambulatory Surgery Association (EA)

FASA............ Sani Pass [*South Africa*] [*ICAO location identifier*] (ICLI)

FASAB......... Federal Accounting Standards Advisory Board (AAGC)

FASAB......... Front Autonomiste et Socialiste Autogestionnaire Bretonne [*Breton Autonomist and Socialist Self-Rule Front*] [*France Political party*] (PPE)

FASAC........ Financial Accounting Standards Advisory Council [*Financial Accounting Foundation*] (EDAC)

FASAC........ Foreign Applied Sciences Assessment Center

FASAF......... Filipinas Americas Science and Art Foundation (EA)

FASA II........ Federal Acquisition Reform Act of 1996 (AAGC)

FASAS......... Federation of Asian Scientific Academies and Societies [*India*] (EY)

FASB........... Fetch and Set BIT [*Binary Digit*] [*Computer science*] (IAA)

FASB........... Financial Accounting Standards Board [*Formerly, Accounting Principles Board*] [*American Institute of Certified Public Accountants*]

FASB........... Financial Accounting Standards Board

FASB........... Financial and Accounting Services Branch (AIE)

FASB........... Springbok [*South Africa*] [*ICAO location identifier*] (ICLI)

FASC........... Fascicle

Fasc............ Fascicule [*Installment*] [*A publication*] (DLA)

FASC........... Fasciculus [*Little Bundle*] [*Latin*] (ROG)

fasc............ Fascimile (VRA)

FASC........... Foreign Affairs Specialist Corps [*Department of State*]

FASC........... Foreign Agricultural Service Club [*Later, Foreign Agricultural Club*] (EA)

FASC........... Forward Area Signal Center (MCD)

FASC........... Forward Area Support Center (MCD)

FASC........... Free-Standing Ambulatory Surgical Center

FASC........... Secunda [*South Africa*] [*ICAO location identifier*] (ICLI)

FASCA........ Federation of Armenian Students Clubs of America (EA)

FASCAM...... Family of Scatterable Mines [*Army*] (RDA)

FASCAP....... Fast-Payback Capital Investment Program [*Air Force*]

FASCE......... Fellow of the American Society of Civil Engineers

FASCIA....... Fixed Asset System Control Information and Accounting [*Computer science*] (MHDI)

FASCNA...... Federation of Alpine and Schuhplattler Clubs in North America (EA)

FASCO........ Fast Scan Cutoff (CAAL)

FASCO........ Forward Area Support Company [*Military*]

FASCO........ Forward Area Support Coordination Officer [*Army*] (AABC)

FASCOM...... Field Army Support Command

FASCOS...... Flight Acceleration Safety Cutoff System (MCD)

FASCS........ Federated Antisubmarine Combat System [*Navy*] (CAAL)

FASCWS..... First-Aid, Small Craft, and Water Safety [*Red Cross*]

FASD.......... Flameless Alkali Sensitized Detector [*Instrumentation*]

FASD.......... Saldanha [*South Africa*] [*ICAO location identifier*] (ICLI)

FASDA........ Fast Analog Scanner for Data Acquisition [*Computer science*] (PDAA)

FASDU........ Further Assignment to Duty (DNAB)

FASE.......... Federation Europeenne des Societes d'Acoustique [*Federation of Acoustical Societies of Europe*] (EAIO)

FASE.......... Federation of Acoustical Societies of Europe (EAIO)

FASE.......... Fellow of the Antiquarian Society of Edinburgh (ROG)

FASE.......... Fundamentally Analyzable Simplified English [*Computer science*]

FASE.......... Sanae [*South Africa*] [*ICAO location identifier*] (ICLI)

FASEB......... Federation of American Societies for Experimental Biology (EA)

FASEC........ Foundation for America's Sexually Exploited Children [*Defunct*] (EA)

FASEM........ Fabrication and Architecture of Single-Electron Memories [*Computer Science*]

FASF.......... Southern Air Command [*South Africa*] [*ICAO location identifier*] (ICLI)

FASFAC....... Fast Forward-Air-Control [*Marine Corps*] (DOMA)

FASG.......... Fanconi's Anemia Support Group (EA)

FASG.......... Schweizer Reneke [*South Africa*] [*ICAO location identifier*] (ICLI)

FASH.......... Forward Area Support Helicopter

FASH.......... Fraternal Association of Steel Haulers [*Defunct*] (EA)

FASH.......... Stellenbosch [*South Africa*] [*ICAO location identifier*] (ICLI)

FASHN........ Fashion

FashTeachCert... Fashion Teacher's Certificate

FASI............ Fellow of the Ambulance Service Institute [*British*] (DBQ)

FASI............ Friedreich's Ataxia Society of Ireland (EAIO)

FASI............ Springs [*South Africa*] [*ICAO location identifier*] (ICLI)

FASID......... Fellow of the Society of Interior Designers

FASINEX...... Frontal Air-Sea Interaction Experiment (USDC)

FASINEX...... Frontal Air-Sea Interaction Experiment [*Marine science*] (OSRA)

FASK.......... Swartkop [*South Africa*] [*ICAO location identifier*] (ICLI)

FASKAP....... Field Artillery Survey Knowledge Acquisition Program [*Army*]

FASL.......... Fellow of the Anthropological Society, London (ROG)

FASL.......... Fellow of the Antiquarian Society, London (ROG)

FASL.......... Sutherland [*South Africa*] [*ICAO location identifier*] (ICLI)

FASLA......... Filmstrip and Slide Laboratory

FASM.......... Swakopmund [*Namibia*] [*ICAO location identifier*] (ICLI)

FASN.......... Senekal [*South Africa*] [*ICAO location identifier*] (ICLI)

FASO .... Field Aviation Supply Office

FASO .... Forward Airfield Supply Organization

FASOC........ Forward Air Support Operations Center (NATG)

FASOLA .... Fa, Sol, and La [*Musical notation system*]

FASOR......... Forward Area SONAR Research [*Navy*]

FASOTRAGR... Fleet Aviation Specialized Operational Training Group [*Navy*] (MCD)

FASOTRAGRULANT... Fleet Aviation Specialized Operational Training Group, Atlantic [*Navy*] (DNAB)

FASOTRAGRULANTDET... Fleet Aviation Specialized Operational Training Group, Atlantic Detachment [*Navy*] (DNAB)

FASOTRAGRUPAC... Fleet Aviation Specialized Operational Training Group, Pacific [*Formerly, FAETUPAC*] [*Later, FASOTRAGRUPACFLT*] [*Navy*]

FASOTRAGRUPACDET... Fleet Aviation Specialized Operational Training Group, Pacific Detachment [*Navy*] (DNAB)

FASOTRAGRUPACFLT... Fleet Aviation Specialized Operational Training Group, Pacific Fleet [*Formerly, FASOTRAGRUPAC, FAETUPAC*] [*Navy*]

FASP........... Facility for Automatic Software Production [*Computer science*] (CAAL)

FASP........... Fleet Airships, Pacific

FASP........... Frequency Analysis of System Program [*NASA*]

FASP........... Sir Lowry's Pass [*South Africa*] [*ICAO location identifier*] (ICLI)

FASPA......... Federation Africaine des Syndicats du Petrole et Assimiles [*African Federation of Trade Unions of Oil and Petrochemicals*] [*Tripoli, Libya*] (EAIO)

FASR........... Forward Acting Shift Register (MHDB)

FASR........... Standerton [*South Africa*] [*ICAO location identifier*] (ICLI)

FASRA......... Foundation to Assist Scientific Research in Africa (EAIO)

FASRON....... Fleet Air [*or Aircraft*] Service Squadron [*Obsolete*]

FASS........... Federation of Associations of Specialists and Subcontractors [*British*] (BI)

FASS........... Financial and Administrative Support System [*Office of Personnel Management*] (GFGA)

FASS........... Fine Alignment Subsystem

FASS........... Flight Activities Scheduling System [*NASA*]

FASS........... Fore and Aft Scanner System (PDAA)

FASS........... Forward Acquisition Sensor (IEEE)

FASS........... Free Air Suspension System

FASS........... Sishen [*South Africa*] [*ICAO location identifier*] (ICLI)

FASSA .... Fellow of the Australian Society of Sports Administrators

FASSC .... Ford Aerospace Satellite Services Corp. [*Arlington, VA*] [*Telecommunications*] (TSSD)

FASSN .... Fast Attack Submarine (MCD)

FASST......... Farming for Agriculturally Sustainable Systems in Tasmania (EERA)

FASST......... Federation of Americans Supporting Science and Technology

FASST......... Fly America's Supersonic Transport [*Student group*]

FASST......... Fly Around Saturated Sectors and Terminals [*National Business Aircraft Association*] [*Database*]

FASST......... Friends of Aerospace Supporting Science and Technology [*An association*]

FAST........... Facility for Accelerated Service Testing

FAST........... Facility for Analyzing Surface Texture [*National Bureau of Standards*] (MCD)

FAST........... Facility for Automatic Sorting and Testing

FAST........... Factory Automation Systems Technology [*British*]

FAST........... Failure Analysis by Statistical Techniques [*Data processing code*]

FAST........... Fair and Simple Tax [*Type of flat tax proposed by Rep. Jack Kemp and Sen. Bob Kasten*]

FAST........... Fairchild Advanced Schottky T2L [*Transistor-Transistor Logic*]

FAST........... Fans Against the Strike (EA)

FAST........... Fare Automated Search Technique [*Airline travel service information system*]

FAST........... Fast Access Scan Talker [*Occupational therapy*]

FAST........... Fast Access Storage Technology [*Computer science*] (MHDB)

FAST........... Fast Acquisition Search and Track (MCD)

FAST........... Fast at Sea Transfer [*Equipment*]

FAST........... Fast Automatic Shuttle Transfer [*System*] [*Navy*]

FAST........... Fastenal Co. [*NASDAQ symbol*] (NQ)

FAST........... Fastening [*or Fastener*] [*Automotive engineering*]

FAST........... Faster Adoption of Superior Technologies

Fast .... Fasti [*of Ovid*] [*Classical studies*] (OCD)

FAST........... FCES Automated Software Test (MCD)

FAST........... Federal Acquisition Services for Technology [*GSA*] (AAGC)

FAST........... Federal Advanced Superconducting Transportation Act

FAST........... Federal Assistance for Staff Training [*Education*]

FAST........... Federal Assistance Streamlining Taskforce [*HEW*]

FAST........... Federation Against Software Theft

FAST........... Feed And Speed Technology (PDAA)

FAST........... Fence Against Satellite Threats

FAST........... Fiduciary Activity Simulation Training [*Investment banking simulation game*]

FAST........... Field Artillery Survey Team

FAST........... Field Artillery Survey Test (MCD)

FAST........... Field Assistance in Science and Technology Program [*US Army Materiel Command*]

FAST........... Field Assistance Support Team (MCD)

FAST........... Field Asymmetry Sensing Technique

FAST........... Field Data Applications, Systems, and Techniques [*Computer science*]

FAST........... File Analysis and Selection Technique [*Computer science*]

FAST........... Final Approach Spacing Tool (GAVI)

FAST........... Final Approach Spacing Tool [*FAA*] (TAG)

FAST........... Financial Analysis and Security Trading

FAST........... Fingerprint Access and Searching Technique [*Computer science*] (IAA)

FAST........... Finite Area Solids Technology (MCD)

FAST........... First Atomic Ship Transport, Inc.

FAST........... Fitness and Arthritis in Seniors Trial

FAST........... Fixed Abrasive Slicing [*Semiconductor technology*]

FAST............ Fleet Antiterrorist Security Team [*Marine Corps*] (DOMA)
FAST............ Fleet Attitude Status (DNAB)
FAST............ Fleet-Sizing Analysis and Sensitivity Technique [*Bell System*]
FAST............ Flexible Ada Simulation Tool (SSD)
FAST............ Flexible Algebraic Scientific Translator [*NCR Corp.*]
FAST............ Flight Advisory Service Test [*FAA*]
FAST............ Flight Aptitude Selection Test [*Army*]
FAST............ Florida Association of Science Teachers (EDAC)
FAST............ Flow Actuated Sediment Trap (USDC)
FAST............ Flow Actuated Sediment Trap [*Marine science*] (OSRA)
FAST............ Flow-Assisted, Short-Term [*Balloon catheter*] [*Cardiology*] (DAVI)
FAST............ Fluorescent Allergosorbent Test [*Medicine*] (CPH)
FAST............ Fluorescent Antibody Staining Technique [*Clinical chemistry*]
FAST............ Fluoro-Allergo Sorbent Test [*Biochemistry*] (DAVI)
FAST............ Fluor's Analytical Scheduling Technique (SAA)
FAST............ Focus, Aperture, Shutter, Tachometer [*Cinematography*] (NTCM)
FAST............ Food Additive Suppliers and Traders [*Database from Food Association*] [*British*] (NITA)
FAST............ Food and Allied Service Trades Department [*of AFL-CIO*] (EA)
FAST............ Foolproof Auditing and Sale of Tickets [*in motion picture theaters*]
FAST............ Fore-Aft Scanning Technique [*Marine science*] (OSRA)
FAST............ Fore-Aft Scanning Technique (USDC)
FAST............ Forecasting and Assessment in Science and Technology [*Commission of the European Communities program, 1978-1983*]
FAST............ Forecasting and Scheduling Technique
FAST............ Foreign Area Specialist Training [*Army*]
FAST............ Formal Auto-Indexing of Scientific Texts [*Computer science*] (IEEE)
FAST............ Formula and Statement Translator [*Computer science*] (MCD)
FAST............ Farner Airborne Surveillance and Tracking
FAST............ Forward Air Strike Task (CINC)
FAST............ Forward Area Support Team [*Military*] (INF)
FAST............ Foundation for Applied Science and Technology [*University of Pittsburgh*] [*Research center*] (RCD)
FAST............ Four-Address to SOAP [*Self-Optimizing Automatic Pilot*] Translator [*Computer science*] (IEEE)
FAST............ Freight Accounting Shipment Tracing System (MCD)
FAST............ Freight Automated System for Traffic Management (AABC)
FAST............ Frequency Agile Search and Track Seeker
FAST............ Friction Assessment Screening Test [*for brake linings*]
FAST............ Fuel Aerosol Simulation Test [*Nuclear energy*] (NRCH)
FAST............ Fuel and Sensor, Tactical (MCD)
FAST............ Fuel Assembly Stability Test (NRCH)
FAST............ Fugitive Assessment Sampling Train [*Environmental Protection Agency*] (GFGA)
FAST............ Fully Atomized Stratified Turbulence
FAST............ Fully Automated Scoring Target [*System*] (MCD)
FAST............ Fully Automatic Sort and Test [*Computer science*] (IAA)
FAST............ Functional Analysis System Technique
FAST............ Fundamentals of Application and System Training [*Course*] [*Computer science*]
FAST............ Future Armament Systems Technology (RDA)
FAST............ Fuze-Activating Static Target (MCD)
FAST............ Somerset East [*South Africa*] [*ICAO location identifier*] (ICLI)
FASTA.......... Federal Aviation Science and Technological Association [*Defunct*] (EA)
FASTAC........ Flame/Furnace Autosampling Technique with Automatic Calibration [*Spectroscopy*]
FASTALS....... Force Analysis Simulation of Theater Administrative and Logistics Support [*Military*]
FASTAR .... Frequency Angle Scanning, Tracking, and Ranging
FASTBACCS... Field Artillery System Training for the Common Battalion Command and Control System (MCD)
FASTBAC's... First Automotive Short-Term Bonds and Certificates [*Drexel Burnham Lambert, Inc.*] [*Finance*]
FASTC.......... Foreign Aerospace Science and Technology Center [*Air Force*]
FASTCAL...... Field Assistance Support Team for Calibration (DOMA)
FastCm .... FastComm Communications Corp. [*Associated Press*] (SAG)
FASTEL........ Fast Economic Language [*Computer science*] (BUR)
FASTEL........ Files for Agricultural Science and Technology Literature [*Database*] [*Agricultural Science Information Center*] [*Information service or system*] (CRD)
Fastenal ...... Fastenal Co. [*Associated Press*] (SAG)
FASTEP........ Files for Agricultural Science and Technology Personnel [*Database*] [*Agricultural Science Information Center*] [*Information service or system*] (CRD)
FASTER........ Filing and Source Data Entry Techniques for Easier Retrieval [*Computer science*] (MHDI)
FASTEX........ Frontal and Atlantic Storm-Track Experiment [*Planned Experiment*] [*Marine science*] (OSRA)
FASTFIRE .... Field Artillery System Training Fire Direction Centers (MCD)
FASTI.......... Fast Access to Systems Technical Information
FASTLODS ... Fighter Aircraft Structural Loads [*Program*] [*Air Force*]
FASTNeT...... Fully Automated Switched Telecommunications Network (PDAA)
FAST-OB ..... Officer Battery Flight Aptitude Selection Test [*Military*] (INF)
FASTOP .... Flutter and Strength Optimization Program for Lifting Surface Structures (MCD)
FASTP.......... Foreign Area Specialist Training Program [*Army*]
FASTPACK .... Fuel and Sensor Tactical Package (MCD)
FASTRACK ... Force Accounting System Track [*Army*] (MCD)
FASTRAM ..... Falling Sphere Trajectory Measurement (MUGU)
FAST RIPSAW... Financial Automation Systems Team for Writing Programs for Standardized Army-Wide Applications
FASTRON..... Fleet Aircraft Service Squadron (MUGU)
FASTS......... Federation of Australian Scientific and Technical Societies (EERA)
FASTSUPPORT... Field Artillery System Training for the Fire Support Officer (MCD)

FASTT.......... Fleet All-Source Tactical Terminal (DOMA)
FAST-TRAC... Faster and Safer Travel/Traffic Routing and Advanced Control [*FHWA*] (TAG)
FASTU......... Fleet Ammunition Ship Training Unit (DNAB)
FASTULANT... Fleet Ammunition Ship Training Unit, Atlantic
FASTUPAC... Fleet Ammunition Ship Training Unit, Pacific
FASTV......... First Artillery Ammunition Resupply Vehicle [*Army*] (RDA)
FAST-VAL .... Forward Air Strike Evaluation
FASU .... Fleet Aviation Support Unit (MCD)
FASU .... Sace [*South Africa*] [*ICAO location identifier*] (ICLI)
FASUS......... Freight Assurance Storage, United States
FASV.......... Field Alert Status Verification [*Army*] (MCD)
FASV.......... Floral Art Society of Victoria [*Australia*]
FASV.......... Silvermine [*South Africa*] [*ICAO location identifier*] (ICLI)
F/ASVS .... Fighter/Attack Simulator Visual System [*Military*]
FASW.......... South West Africa Air Force Headquarters [*Namibia*] [*ICAO location identifier*] (ICLI)
FASWC........ Fleet Antisubmarine Warfare Command (IEEE)
FASWOC...... Food and Service Workers of Canada
FASWSCHOOL... Fleet Antisubmarine Warfare School
FASX.......... Fairbanks Air Service [*Alaska*] [*Air carrier designation symbol*]
FASX.......... Swellendam [*South Africa*] [*ICAO location identifier*] (ICLI)
FASY.......... Syferfontein [*South Africa*] [*ICAO location identifier*] (ICLI)
FASZ.......... Skukuza [*South Africa*] [*ICAO location identifier*] (ICLI)
Fat .... De Fato [*of Cicero*] [*Classical studies*] (OCD)
FAT .... Factory Acceptance Test
FAT .... Family Adjustment Test [*Psychology*]
FAT .... Family Assessment Tool [*Kit*] [*Medicine*]
FAT .... Farner Air Transport AG [*Switzerland ICAO designator*] (FAAC)
FAT .... Fast Automatic Transfer
FAT .... Fast Axonal Transport [*Neurobiology*]
FAT .... Fatalities [*Military*] (DOMA)
FAT .... Fathom (NATG)
FAT .... Fatigue (WDAA)
FAT .... Fatphobia Awareness Training
FAT .... Field Artillery Tractor [*British*]
FAT .... File Allocation Table [*Computer science*]
FAT .... File Attribution Table [*Computer science*] (PCM)
FAT .... Final Acceptance, Assembly Tests
FAT .... Final Aerospace Trial
FAT .... Final Approach Track [*Aviation*] (DA)
FAT .... Final Assembly Test
FAT .... First Article Test
FAT .... Fixed Asset Transfer [*Business term*]
FAT .... Flight Acceptance Test
FA-T............ Flight Attendant in Training (DNAB)
FAT .... Flight Attitude Table [*NASA*] (NASA)
FAT .... Flight Test Station [*ITU designation*] (CET)
FAT .... Fluorescent Antibody Technique [*Immunology*] (DAVI)
FAT .... Fluorescent Antibody Test [*Clinical medicine*]
FAT .... Food Awareness Training
FAT .... Forces Armees Tchadiennes [*Chad Armed Forces*] (PD)
FAT .... Foreign Area Toll [*Telecommunications*] (TEL)
FAT .... Foreign Area Translation [*Telecommunications*] (TEL)
FAT .... Formula Assembler Translator [*Computer science*] (BUR)
FAT .... Forward Area Trace (MCD)
FAT .... Foundation for Anglican Traditions [*Defunct*] (EA)
FAT .... Free Air Temperature (NG)
FAT .... Fresno [*California*] [*Airport symbol*] (OAG)
FAT .... Friends of Appropriate Technology (EA)
FAT .... Frustration, Anxiety, and Tension
FAT .... Fuel and Transportation (IAA)
FAT32......... File Allocation Table 32-Bit [*Computer science*]
FATAB......... Field Artillery Target Acquisition Battalion [*Army*] (AABC)
FATAG........ Field Artillery Target Acquisition Group [*Army*] (AABC)
FATAL......... FADAC [*Field Artillery Digital Automatic Computer*] Automatic Test AnalysisLanguage (IEEE)
FATAL......... Fit Anything to Anything You Like (MHDB)
FATAR........ Fast Analysis of Tape and Recovery
FATB.......... Floor Ataxia Test Battery
FATC.......... Field Artillery Training Centre [*British military*] (DMA)
FATC.......... Fleet Area Telecommunications Center [*Navy*] (MCD)
FATC.......... Tristan De Cunha [*South Africa*] [*ICAO location identifier*] (ICLI)
FATCAT....... Film and Television Correlation Assessment Technique (MCD)
FATCAT....... Frequency and Time Circuit Analysis Technique [*NASA*]
FAT-COI...... Federation Americaine du Travail et Congres des Organisations Industrielles [*American Federation of Labor and Congress of Industrial Organizations - AFL-CIO*] [*Canada*]
FATCP......... Forum for the Advancement of Toxicology in Colleges of Pharmacy (EA)
FATD.......... Federal Applied Technology Database [*National Technical Information Service*] [*Information service or system*] (CRD)
FATD(A)...... Federal Association of Teachers of Dancing (Australia)
FATDAD...... Fermanagh, Armagh, Tyrone, Derry, Antrim, Down [*The six counties of Northern Ireland*]
FATDL........ Frequency and Time-Division Data Link
FATDOC...... Film and Television Documentation Center [*State University of New York at Albany*] [*Information service or system*] (IID)
FATDS .... Field Artillery Tactical Data Systems [*Army*] (RDA)
FATE........... Federation of Automatic Transmission Engineers [*British*] (DBA)
FATE........... Force Application Tactics Evaluation (SAA)
FATE........... Formulating Analytical and Technical Estimate (PDAA)
FATE........... Future Aircraft Technology Enhancement
FATE .... Fuze Arming Test Experiment
FATE........... Fuzing, Arming, Test and Evaluation (PDAA)

FATES......... FIFRA [*Federal Insecticide, Fungicide, and Rodenticide Act*] and TSCA [*Toxic Substances Control Act*] Enforcement System (GNE)

FATES......... Flow-Through Aquatic Toxicology Exposure System [*Evaluation of sediment contaminants*]

FATF.......... Free Air Test Facility

FATG.......... Fat Globules [*Biochemistry*] (DAVI)

FATG.......... Fine Art Trade Guide [*British*] (DBA)

FATH.......... Fathom

FATH.......... Thohoyandou [*South Africa*] [*ICAO location identifier*] (ICLI)

FATHOM..... Foreign Affairs Theory, Operations, and Monitoring (DNAB)

FATIMA...... Fatigue Indicating Meter Attachment

FATIPEC..... Federation d'Associations de Techniciens des Industries de Peintures, Vernis, Emaux, et Encres d'Imprimerie de l'Europe [*Federation of the Associations of Technicians of the Paint, Varnish, and Ink Industries of Continental Europe*] (EAIO)

FATK.......... Tsumkwe [*Namibia*] [*ICAO location identifier*] (ICLI)

FATLAD....... Fermanagh, Armagh, Tyrone, Londonderry, Antrim, Down [*Unionist mnemonic for the six counties of Northern Ireland*]

FAT/LOT..... First Article Test/Limited Operational Test

FATM.......... Tsumeb [*Namibia*] [*ICAO location identifier*] (ICLI)

FATMAT...... Field Artillery Turret Maintenance Trainer (MCD)

FATMS........ Field Artillery Turret Maintenance Simulator (MCD)

FATN.......... First American Corp. [*NASDAQ symbol*] (NQ)

FATN.......... First Amer (Tenn) [*NASDAQ symbol*] (TTSB)

FATO.......... Final Approach and Takeoff Area [*OST*] (TAG)

FATOC........ Field Army Tactical Operation Center

FATOLA....... Flexible Aircraft Takeoff and Landing Analysis (MCD)

FATP.......... Bloemfontein/New Tempe [*South Africa*] [*ICAO location identifier*] (ICLI)

FATP.......... Factory Acceptance Test Procedure

FATP.......... Field Assembly Test Point (IAA)

FATR.......... Fixed Auto Transfer (MCD)

FATR.......... Fixed Autotransformer

FATRACS..... Field Army Tactical Random Access Communications System

FATRANS..... First Available Transportation

FATS.......... Factory Acceptance Test Specification

FATS.......... Fight to Advertise the Truth about Saturates [*Student legal action organization*]

FATS.......... Firearms Training Systems, Inc.

FATS.......... FORTRAN [*Formula Translating System*] Automatic Timing System [*Computer science*]

FATS.......... South African Air Force Tactical Support Command [*ICAO location identifier*] (ICLI)

FATSA......... Flowers Auditory Test of Selective Attention

FATSO........ First Aid Technical Stores Outfit [*Military British*]

FATSO........ First-Airborne Telescopic and Spectrographic Observatory (DNAB)

FATT.......... Forward Area Tactical Teletype (MCD)

FATT.......... Fracture Appearance Transition Temperature

FATT.......... Tutuka [*South Africa*] [*ICAO location identifier*] (ICLI)

FATTH........ Fiber Almost to the Home [*Telecommunications*]

FATTS........ Forward Area Tactical Teletypewriter Set

FATTY........ Forward Area Tactical Typewriter

FATU.......... Fleet Air Tactical Unit

FATUREC..... Federation of Air Transport User Representatives in the European Community (DA)

FATZ.......... Tzaneen [*South Africa*] [*ICAO location identifier*] (ICLI)

FAU........... Fairfield University, Fairfield, CT [*OCLC symbol*] (OCLC)

FAU........... Fairview, OK [*Location identifier FAA*] (FAAL)

FAU........... Falmouth Petroleum [*Vancouver Stock Exchange symbol*]

FAU........... Faucher Aviation [*France ICAO designator*] (FAAC)

FAU........... Faujasite [*A zeolite*]

FAU........... Field Action Unit (AEBS)

FAU........... Fine Alignment Unit

FAU........... Fixed Asset Utilization [*Business term*] (ADA)

FAU........... Flag Administrative Unit

FAU........... Florida Atlantic University [*Boca Raton*]

FAU........... Frequency Allocation and Uses

FAU........... Friends Ambulance Unit [*British military*] (DMA)

FAU........... Fundacion Arte por Uruguay [*Formerly, Relatives Committee for Uruguay*] [*Sweden*] (EAIO)

FAUC.......... Ulco [*South Africa*] [*ICAO location identifier*] (ICLI)

FAUH.......... Uitenhage [*South Africa*] [*ICAO location identifier*] (ICLI)

FAUK.......... Usakos [*Namibia*] [*ICAO location identifier*] (ICLI)

FAUL.......... Faulding, Inc. [*NASDAQ symbol*] (SAG)

FAUL.......... Faulding Inc. [*NASDAQ symbol*] (TTSB)

FAUL.......... Five Associated University Libraries [*State University of New York at Buffalo and Binghamton, Cornell University, Syracuse University, University of Rochester*]

FAUL.......... Ulundi [*South Africa*] [*ICAO location identifier*] (ICLI)

Faulding..... Faulding, Inc. [*Associated Press*] (SAG)

FAUP.......... Upington/Pierre Van Ryneveld [*South Africa*] [*ICAO location identifier*] (ICLI)

FAUS.......... Federal Aid Urban System [*Road improvement program*] [*Federal Highway Administration*]

FAUS.......... Feingold Association of the United States (EA)

FAUS.......... Uis [*Namibia*] [*ICAO location identifier*] (ICLI)

FAusPr....... First Australia Prime Income Fund [*Associated Press*]

FAUSST...... French-Anglo-United States Supersonic Transport

FAUST........ Far Ultraviolet Space Telescope

Faust......... Faust's Compiled Laws [*Scotland*] [*A publication*] (DLA)

FAUST........ Folkebibliotekernes Automation System [*Denmark*] [*Public libraries automation system*] (NITA)

FAUT.......... Umtata (K. D. Matanzima) [*South Africa*] [*ICAO location identifier*] (ICLI)

FAV........... Fakarava [*French Polynesia*] [*Airport symbol*] (OAG)

FAV........... Fan Air Valve (MCD)

FAV........... Fast Attack Vehicle [*Army*] (INF)

FAV........... Favor (WDAA)

FAV........... Favorable (AFM)

FAV........... Favorite (ADA)

FAV........... Fayetteville [*Arkansas*] [*Seismograph station code, US Geological Survey*] (SEIS)

FAV........... Feline Ataxia Virus (MAE)

FAV........... Finnaviation OY [*Finland ICAO designator*] (FAAC)

FAV........... Fire Ant Venom [*Immunology*]

FAV........... Fixed-Angle Variable

FAV........... Forfar Artillery Volunteers [*British military*] (DMA)

FAV........... Frog Adenovirus

FAV........... Fuel Filtration-Additive Unit

FAV........... Full Analog Video

FAVA.......... Fixed Asset Valuation Adjustment [*Business term*] (ADA)

FAVB.......... Vryburg [*South Africa*] [*ICAO location identifier*] (ICLI)

FAVC.......... Fleet Audio-Visual Center (DNAB)

FAVC.......... Flight Attendant Volunteer Corps (EA)

FAVD.......... Vrede [*South Africa*] [*ICAO location identifier*] (ICLI)

FAVDO........ Forum of African Voluntary Development Organizations

FAVE.......... Ventersdorp [*South Africa*] [*ICAO location identifier*] (ICLI)

FAVF.......... Fleet Audio-Visual Facility (DNAB)

FAVG.......... Durban/Virginia [*South Africa*] [*ICAO location identifier*] (ICLI)

FAVN.......... Fluorescent-Antibody Virus Neutralization Test [*Immunology*]

FAVO.......... Fleet Aviation Officer [*British*]

FAVP.......... Vanderbijlpark [*South Africa*] [*ICAO location identifier*] (ICLI)

FAVR.......... Vredendal [*South Africa*] [*ICAO location identifier*] (ICLI)

FAVS.......... Family of Army Vehicles Study

FAVU.......... Volksrust [*South Africa*] [*ICAO location identifier*] (ICLI)

FAVV.......... Vereeniging [*South Africa*] [*ICAO location identifier*] (ICLI)

FAVW.......... Victoria West [*South Africa*] [*ICAO location identifier*] (ICLI)

FAVY.......... Vryheid [*South Africa*] [*ICAO location identifier*] (ICLI)

FAW........... Faith at Work (EA)

FAW........... Falwell Aviation, Inc. [*ICAO designator*] (FAAC)

FAW........... Fighter, All Weather [*British military*] (DMA)

FAW........... First Automotive Works [*Chinese manufacturer*]

FAW........... Fixed Axial Weapon [*Military*] (VNW)

FAW........... Fleet Air Wing [*Navy*]

FAW........... Fleet All Weather

FAW........... Florida Administrative Weekly [*A publication*] (AAGC)

FAW........... Forward Area Warning (IAA)

FAW........... Forward Area Weapons [*Military*]

FAW........... Friends Around the World [*An association*] (EA)

FAW........... Friends of American Writers (EA)

FAW........... Northampton, MA [*Location identifier FAA*] (FAAL)

FAWA......... Federation of Asian Women's Associations [*San Marcelino, Philippines*]

FAWA......... Warmbaths [*South Africa*] [*ICAO location identifier*] (ICLI)

FAWAF....... Fleet Air Wing, Atlantic Fleet (MCD)

FAWB........ Pretoria/Wonderboom [*South Africa*] [*ICAO location identifier*] (ICLI)

FAWBE....... Fire Ant Whole Body Extract [*Immunology*]

Fawc......... Fawcett on Landlord and Tenant [*3 eds.*] [*1870-1905*] [*A publication*] (DLA)

FAWC........ Federation of Army Wives Clubs [*British*]

FAWC........ Franciscan Apostolate of the Way of the Cross (EA)

FAWC........ Worcester [*South Africa*] [*ICAO location identifier*] (ICLI)

FAWCE....... Farm Animal Welfare Coordinating Executive [*British*] (DI)

Fawcett...... Fawcett on Landlord and Tenant [*3rd ed.*] [*1905*] [*A publication*] (ILCA)

Fawc L & T... Fawcett on Landlord and Tenant [*3 eds.*] [*1870-1905*] [*A publication*] (DLA)

FAWCO....... Federation of American Women's Clubs Overseas (EA)

Fawc Ref.... Fawcett. Court of Referees [*1866*] [*A publication*] (DLA)

FAWD........ Warden [*South Africa*] [*ICAO location identifier*] (ICLI)

FAWE........ Windhoek/Eros [*Namibia*] [*ICAO location identifier*] (ICLI)

FAWEP....... Field Activity War Emergency Program [*DoD*]

FAWESP...... Field Activity War and Emergency Support Plan [*DoD*] (MCD)

FAWG......... Flight Assignment Working Group [*NASA*] (NASA)

FAWH........ Windhoek/J. G. Strijdom [*Namibia*] [*ICAO location identifier*] (ICLI)

FAWI......... Witbank [*South Africa*] [*ICAO location identifier*] (ICLI)

FAWK........ Waterkloof [*South Africa*] [*ICAO location identifier*] (ICLI)

FAWL........ Williston [*South Africa*] [*ICAO location identifier*] (ICLI)

FAWM........ Welkom [*South Africa*] [*ICAO location identifier*] (ICLI)

FAWNA....... Fostering and Assistance for Wildlife Needing Aid [*Australia*]

FAWO........ Willowmore [*South Africa*] [*ICAO location identifier*] (ICLI)

FAWOD....... Furnish Assignment Instructions without Delay

FAWP........ Wepener [*South Africa*] [*ICAO location identifier*] (ICLI)

FAWPRA...... Fleet Air Western Pacific Repair Area (MCD)

FAWPSC..... Frequency Allocation and Wave Propagation Subcommittee (NATG)

FAWPSS..... Forward Area Water Point Supply System

FAWS........ First-Aid and Water Safety [*Red Cross*]

FAWS........ Flight Advisory Weather Service

FAWSHMOTRON... Fast Wave Simple Harmonic Motion [*A microwave tube device*]

FAWT......... For Address, Write To

FAWT......... Kingwilliamstown [*South Africa*] [*ICAO location identifier*] (ICLI)

FAWTC....... Fleet Antiwarfare Training Center (MUGU)

FAWTU....... Fleet All-Weather Training Unit

FAWTULANT... Fleet All-Weather Training Unit, Atlantic

FAWTUPAC... Fleet All-Weather Training Unit, Pacific

FAWW........ Windhoek [*South Africa*] [*ICAO location identifier*] (ICLI)

FAWY........ Wolseley [*South Africa*] [*ICAO location identifier*] (ICLI)

FAX........... Aeronautical Fixed Station [*ITU designation*] (CET)

Fax........... Electronic Facsimile (AAGC)

FAX	Facsimile (AFM)
fax	Facsimile (IDOE)
FAX	Facsimile Transmission [*Telecommunications*] (MCD)
fax	Facsimile Transmission (WDMC)
FAX	Fast Anion Exchange [*Chromatography*]
FAX	First Australia Prime [*AMEX symbol*] (TTSB)
FAX	First Australia Prime Income Fund [*AMEX symbol*] (SPSG)
FAX	Friedreich's Ataxia Group (EAIO)
FAX	Fuel Air Explosive
FAX	Midwest Air Freighters, Inc. [*ICAO designator*] (FAAC)
FAXCOM	Fascimile Communications (EECA)
FAXDIN	Facsimile Transmission over AUTODIN [*Telecommunications*]
FAXPAK	Facsimile Packet [*ITT*] [*Telecommunications*] (TEL)
FaxSav	FaxSav Inc. [*Associated Press*] (SAG)
FAXTM	Facsimile Transmission [*Telecommunications*] (NOAA)
FAXX	FaxSav Inc. [*NASDAQ symbol*] (SAG)
FAY	Fayban Air Services [*Nigeria*] [*FAA designator*] (FAAC)
FAY	Fayetteville [*Arkansas*] [*Seismograph station code, US Geological Survey Closed*] (SEIS)
FAY	Fayetteville [*North Carolina*] [*Airport symbol*] (OAG)
FAY	Fayetteville, NC [*Location identifier FAA*] (FAAL)
FAY	Fay's, Inc. [*NYSE symbol*] (SPSG)
FAY	Field-Collected Aster Yellows [*Plant pathology*]
FAY	Fleet Activities, Yokosuka Naval Base (DNAB)
FAY	Friends and Associates for Yaddo (EA)
Fayette	Fayette County Bancshares, Inc. [*Associated Press*] (SAG)
Fayette Leg J (PA)	Fayette Legal Journal [*Pennsylvania*] [*A publication*] (DLA)
Fay LJ	Fayette Legal Journal [*Pennsylvania*] [*A publication*] (ILCA)
FAYP	Ysterplaat [*South Africa*] [*ICAO location identifier*] (ICLI)
FaysInc	Fays, Inc. [*Associated Press*] (SAG)
FAZ	Flint Aviation Services, Inc. [*FAA designator*] (FAAC)
FAZA	Zastron [*South Africa*] [*ICAO location identifier*] (ICLI)
FAZR	Zeerust [*South Africa*] [*ICAO location identifier*] (ICLI)
fb----	Africa, Sub-Saharan [*MARC geographic area code Library of Congress*] (LCCP)
FB	Bartow Public Library, Bartow, FL [*Library symbol Library of Congress*] (LCLS)
FB	Base Station [*ITU designation*] (CET)
FB	Bursa Airlines, Inc. [*Turkey ICAO designator*] (ICDA)
f-b	Face-Bow [*Dentistry*] (DAVI)
FB	Face Brick [*Technical drawings*]
FB	Facility Board [*Air Force*] (CET)
FB	Faculty of Building [*British*]
FB	Falcon Building Products 'A' [*NYSE symbol*] (TTSB)
FB	Falcon Building Products, Inc. [*NYSE symbol*] (SAG)
FB	Family Bible [*Genealogy*]
FB	Farbenfabriken Bayer [*Germany*] [*Research code symbol*]
FB	Farmers' Bulletin [*A publication*]
FB	Fast Blue [*Biological stain*]
FB	Fasting Blood Sugar [*Physiology*] (DAVI)
Fb	February (CDAI)
FB	Feedback (AAG)
FB	Fenian Brotherhood [*Irish political movement, c. 1858-1914*] (ROG)
FBI	Fermentation Biomass
FB	Fertiliser Board [*Tasmania, Australia*]
FB	Fiberboard [*Technical drawings*]
FB	Fiber-in-Bending [*Lumber*]
FB	Fiberoptic Bronchoscopy [*Also, FOB*] [*Medicine*]
FB	Fibroblast [*Medicine*]
FB	Fidelity Bond [*Business term*]
FB	Fighter Bomber
FB	File Block
FB	Film Badge (IEEE)
FB	Film Bulletin
FBAS	Final Braking (MCD)
FB	Fine Business [*i.e., excellent*] [*Amateur radio*]
FB	Finger Breadth [*Medicine*]
FB	Fire Brigade
FB	Firing Battery (AABC)
FB	First Brochure
FB	Fishery Board
FB	Fixed Block
FB	Flanker Back [*Football*] (IIA)
FB	Flashbulb [*Photography*]
F/B	Flat Back [*Bookbinding*] (DGA)
FB	Flat Bar [*Technical drawings*]
FB	Flat Bottom (OA)
FB	Flexible Benefits [*Health insurance*] (GHCT)
F-B	Florida State Library, Bureau of Book Processing, Tallahassee, FL [*Library symbol Library of Congress*] (LCLS)
FB	Flow Block
FB	Fluidized Bed
FB	Flying Boat
FB	Fog Bell [*Navigation charts*]
FB	Foldback [*Genetics*]
FB	Folding Boxboard (DGA)
FB	Fondation de Bellerive [*Bellerive Foundation - BF*] (EAIO)
FB	Food Brokers Ltd. [*British*]
FB	Forebody
FB	Foreign Body [*Medicine*]
FB	Foreign Bond (MHDW)
FB	Foreign [*or French*] Brandy [*British*] (ROG)
FB	Form Block (MCD)
FB	Forward Body
fb	Foul Bottom [*Navigation signal*]

FB	Found Brothers Aviation Ltd. [*Canada ICAO aircraft manufacturer identifier*] (ICAO)
FB	Framing Bit (ACRL)
FB	Free Baptist
FB	Freight Bill [*Business term*]
FB	Friendship Book [*Address list circulated by Beatles fans*]
FB	Friends of Buddhism [*Defunct*] (EA)
FB	Fringe Benefits (WDAA)
FB	Fullback [*Football*]
FB	Full Bench
FB	Fumigation and Bath [*Military*]
FB	Function Button [*Computer science*]
FB	Furnace Brazing
FB	Fuse Block (KSC)
FB	Fuse Box (IAA)
FB	Promair Australia [*Airline code*]
FBA	Fanned Beam Antenna
FBA	Farbenfabriken Bayer [*Germany*] [*Research code symbol*]
FBA	Farm Bankruptcy Act [*1933*]
FBA	Farm Buildings Association [*British*]
FBA	FBA Pharmaceuticals Ltd. [*Great Britain*] [*Research code symbol*]
FBA	Federal Bar Association (EA)
FBA	Federation of Bloodstock Agents [*British*] (DBA)
FBA	Federation of British Artists (EAIO)
FBA	Federation of British Astrologers Ltd. (BI)
FBA	Federation of British Audio (DBA)
FBA	Fellow of Business Administration (DD)
FBA	Fellow of the British Academy (ROG)
FBA	Fellow of the British Arts Association (DBQ)
FBA	Fibre Box Association (EA)
FBA	Fighter Bomber Aircraft (NATG)
FB/A	Fighter Bomber Attack (NATG)
FBA	Figural Bottle Association [*Defunct*]
FBA	Financial and Business Administration Department [*American Occupational Therapy Association*]
FBA	First Banks America [*NYSE symbol*] (TTSB)
FBA	First Banks America, Inc. [*NYSE symbol*] (SAG)
FBA	Fixed Block Architecture
FBA	Flexible Benefit Account [*Business term*]
FBA	Florida Bandmasters Association (SRA)
FBA	Fluorescent Brightening Agent (PDAA)
FBA	Fonte Boa [*Brazil*] [*Airport symbol*] (AD)
FBA	Foundation Beefmaster Association (EA)
FBA	Freshwater Biological Association [*British*] (ARC)
FBA	Fur Breeders Association of the United Kingdom [*British*]
FBA	State Library of Florida, Tallahassee, FL [*OCLC symbol*] (OCLC)
FBAA	Federation of Bloodstock Agents Australia
FBAA	Fellow of the British Association of Accountants and Auditors (EY)
FBAA	Flying Boat Alighting Area
FBAA	Fur Brokers Association of America (EA)
FBAC	Fair Budget Action Campaign (EA)
FBAC	First National Bancorp of Gainesville [*NASDAQ symbol*] (NQ)
FBACSI	Fur Buyers Association, Coat and Suit Industry (EA)
FBAI	Foodbrands America, Inc. [*NASDAQ symbol*] (SAG)
FBAN	FNB Corp. [*NASDAQ symbol*] (NQ)
FB&T Fn	Fairfax Bank & Trust Financial Corp. [*Associated Press*] (SAG)
FBANP	FNB Corp. 7.5% Cv'B' Pfd [*NASDAQ symbol*] (TTSB)
FBAO	Farm Buildings Advisory Officer [*Ministry of Agriculture, Fisheries, and Food*] [*British*]
FBAP	Federal Bureau of Advanced Paranoia [*Agency in film "Last Embrace"*]
FBAR	Family Bargain [*NASDAQ symbol*] (TTSB)
FBAR	Family Bargain Corp. [*NASDAQ symbol*] (SAG)
FBARP	Family Bargain 9.5% Cv'A'Pfd [*NASDAQ symbol*] (TTSB)
FBAS	Federation of British Aquatic Societies (DBA)
FBAS	Fellow of the British Association of Secretaries [*British*] (DAS)
FBAS	Fixed Base Aft Station (MCD)
FBAY	Frisco Bay Industries [*NASDAQ symbol*] (SAG)
FBAYF	Frisco Bay Industries [*NASDAQ symbol*] (TTSB)
FBB	Fast-Burn Booster [*Rocketry*]
FBB	Fire Brigades Board [*Queensland, Australia*]
FBB	Folding Boxboard (DGA)
FBB	Functional Breadboard System [*Skylab*] [*NASA*]
FBBA	Fishing Boat Builders Association [*British*] (BI)
FB:BC	First Battle: Battalion through Corps [*DoD*]
FBBC	First Bell Bancorp [*NASDAQ symbol*] (TTSB)
FBBC	First Bell Bancorp, Inc. [*NASDAQ symbol*] (SAG)
FBBM	Federation of Building Block Manufacturers [*British*] (BI)
FBBO	Fellow of the British Ballet Organisation
FBBS	Facts Bulletin Board System [*Database*] [*Fast Agricultural Communications Terminal System*] [*Information service or system*] (CRD)
FBC	Barry College, North Miami, FL [*OCLC symbol*] (OCLC)
FBC	Fallen Building Clause
FBC	Fat Binding Capacity [*Food technology*]
FBC	Federation of Brickwork Contractors [*British*] (DBA)
FBC	Feedback Carburetor [*Automotive engineering*]
FBC	Feedback Control [*Computer science*] (IAA)
FBC	Filesmiths' Benefit Club [*A union*] [*British*]
FBC	Fixed Bathtub Capacitor
FBC	Florence Babylonian Collection (BJA)
FBC	Fluidized-Bed Combustion (NASA)
FBC	Fonblanque's Bankruptcy Cases [*1849-52*] [*A publication*] (DLA)
FBC	Foundation for Books to China (EA)
FBC	Fox Broadcasting Co.

FBC............ Free-Binding Capacity [Serology]
FBC............ Friends Bible College [Haviland, KS]
FBC............ Friends of Books and Comics (EA)
FBC............ Frobisher Bay [Northwest Territories] [Seismograph station code, US Geological Survey Closed] (SEIS)
FBC............ Full Blood Count [Medicine] (ADA)
FBC............ Fully Buffered Channel
FBCA.......... Federation of British Cremation Authorities (BI)
FBCA.......... Feedback Carburetor Actuator [Automotive engineering]
FBCA.......... Fusion Bonded Coaters Association [CRSI] [Absorbed by] (EA)
FBCAEI....... Federation of Builders Contractors and Allied Employers of Ireland (BI)
FBCB² .... Force [XXI] Battle Command Brigade and Below [Army]
FBCB2......... Force XXI, Battle Command, Brigade and Below [Army] (RDA)
FBCE.......... Federation Bancaire de la Communaute Europeenne [Banking Federation of the European Community] (EAIO)
FBCE.......... Federation de Bourses de la Communaute Europeenne [Federation of Stock Exchanges in the European Community] (EAIO)
FBCE.......... Fellowship of British Christian Esperantists
FBCG .... First Banking Co. Southeast Georgia [NASDAQ symbol] (SAG)
FBCG .... First Banking S.E. Georgia [NASDAQ symbol] (TTSB)
FBCI........... Fidelity Bancorp [NASDAQ symbol] (SAG)
FBCK.......... Firebrick
FBCMA....... Fiber Bonded Carpet Manufacturers Association [British] (DBA)
FBCO .... Camp Okavango [Botswana] [ICAO location identifier] (ICLI)
FBCO .... Fellow of the British College of Ophthalmic Opticians (DBQ)
FBCOD....... Foreign Body Cornea Right Eye [Medicine]
FBCOS .... Foreign Body Cornea Left Eye [Medicine]
FBCR.......... Fluidized-Bed Control Rod (PDAA)
FBCS.......... Fellow of the British Computer Society
FBCS.......... Fixed-Base Crew Station [NASA] (NASA)
FBCT.......... Form Block Check Template (MCD)
FBCV.......... 1st Bancorp Ind [NASDAQ symbol] (TTSB)
FBCV.......... First Bancorp (Indiana) [NASDAQ symbol] (NQ)
FBCW......... Fallen Building Clause Waiver [Legal term] (DLA)
FBCW......... Federation of British Columbia Writers [Canada] (WWLA)
f-bd-- .... Burundi [MARC geographic area code Library of Congress] (LCCP)
FBD........... Fibreboard Corp. [AMEX symbol] (CTT)
FBD........... Fibreboard Corp. [AMEX symbol] (TTSB)
FBD........... Fibrocystic Breast Disease [Medicine]
FBD........... Film: British Documentary
FBD........... Flow Block Diagram
FBD........... Free Board
FBD........... Free Body Diagram
FBD........... Full Business Day (TEL)
FBD........... Functional Block Diagram [Telecommunications] (TEL)
FBD........... Functional Bowel Disorder [Medicine] (MAE)
FBD........... Function Block Logic (ACII)
FBD........... Statens Trafikkflygerskole [Norway ICAO designator] (FAAC)
FBDB .... Federal Business Development Bank [See also BFD] [Canada Database producer]
FBDC .... Fiberboard, Corrugated
FBDCA .... French Bulldog Club of America (EA)
FBDS .... Fiberboard, Solid
FBE............ Federation of Bank Employees [British] (DCTA)
FBE............ Feeder Branch Edit (PDAA)
FBE............ Female Business Enterprise (AAGC)
FBE............ Fluidized Bed Electrode [Electrochemistry]
FBE............ Folding Boat Equipment [British military] (DMA)
FBE............ Full Blood Examination [Medicine] (MAE)
FBEA.......... Fellow of the British Esperanto Association (DAS)
FBEA.......... Funeral and Bereavement Educators Association
FBEC(S)....... Fellow of the Business Education Council (Scotland) (ODBW)
FBEI........... Fellow of the Institution of Body Engineers [British] (DBQ)
FBER.......... 1st Bergen Bancorp [NASDAQ symbol] (TTSB)
FBER.......... First Bergen Bancorp [NASDAQ symbol] (SAG)
FBergen....... First Bergen Bancorp, Inc. [Associated Press] (SAG)
FBETM........ Federation of British Engineers Tool Manufacturers [British] (DBA)
FBF............ BEA Income Fd [NYSE symbol] (TTSB)
FBF............ BEA Income Fund [NYSE symbol] (SAG)
FBF............ Federal Buildings Fund [General Services Administration]
FBF............ Feedback Filter (IAA)
FBF............ Female Bowhunter Fingers [International Bowhunting Organization] [Class equipment]
FBF............ Femoral Blood Flow [Physiology]
FBF............ Film: British Feature
FBF............ Fine Airlines, Inc. [ICAO designator] (FAAC)
FBF............ First Boston Income Fund, Inc. [Later, CS First Income Fund] [NYSE symbol] (SPSG)
FBF............ Folkestone-Boulogne Ferries [English Channel ferry-boat service] [British] (ECON)
FBF............ Forearm Blood Flow [Medicine]
FBF............ Frame by Frame
FBF............ Francis Bacon Foundation (EA)
FBFC.......... Florence Ballard Fan Club (EA)
FBFI........... Frederic Burk Foundation, Inc. [San Francisco State University] [Research center] (RCD)
FBFM.......... Feedback Frequency Modulation
FBFO.......... Federation of British Fire Organisations
FBFR.......... Fluidized-Bed Film Reactor [For water purification]
FBFS.......... Fuel Building Filter System [Nuclear energy] (NRCH)
FBFT.......... Flow Bias Functional Test (IEEE)
FBFT.......... Francistown [Botswana] [ICAO location identifier] (ICLI)
FBG............ Faint Blue Galaxy [Astronomy]
FBG............ Fasting Blood Glucose [Physiology] (AAMN)

FBG............ Fayetteville/Fort Bragg, NC [Location identifier FAA] (FAAL)
FBG............ Federal Barge Lines, Inc., St. Louis MO [STAC]
FBG............ Fibrinogen [Factor 1] [Hematology]
FBG............ Finsbury Group Ltd. [Vancouver Stock Exchange symbol]
FBG............ Fluidized-Bed Gasifier [Coal gasification]
FBG............ Fosters Brewing Group [Australia Commercial firm]
FBGA.......... First Bankshares (GA) [NASDAQ symbol] (TTSB)
FBGA.......... First Bankshares, Inc. (GA) [NASDAQ symbol] (SAG)
FBGI.......... Financial Benefit Group, Inc. [NASDAQ symbol] (NQ)
FBGM.......... Gomare [Botswana] [ICAO location identifier] (ICLI)
FBGZ.......... Ghanzi [Botswana] [ICAO location identifier] (ICLI)
FBH............ Familial Benign Hypocalciuric Hypercalcaemia [Medicine] (BABM)
FBH............ Familial Benign Hypocalciuric Hypercalcemia [Nephrology] (DAVI)
FBH............ Federal Board of Hospitalization [Coordinated hospitalization activities of Army, Navy, and various agencies; terminated, 1948]
FBH............ Fire Brigade Hydrant
FBH............ Fluidized-Bed Hydrogenator [Chemical engineering reactor]
FBH............ Forced Beachhead [Navy] (DNAB)
FBH............ Free on Board in Harbor [Business term]
FBH............ Hydroxybutyric Dehydrogenase [Organic chemistry] (DAVI)
FBHA.......... Fellow of the British Hypnotherapy Association (DBQ)
FBHA.......... Free the Battery Hen Association [Australia]
FBHC.......... Fort Bend Hldg [NASDAQ symbol] (TTSB)
FBHC.......... Fort Bend Holding Corp. [NASDAQ symbol] (SAG)
FBHC.......... Fortified Benzene Hexachloride [Insecticide]
FBHC.......... Franciscan Brothers of the Holy Cross [See also FFSC] [Germany] (EAIO)
FBHDA........ Friends and Buddies of the Hour Glass Division Association [Later, FBHGA] (EA)
FBHDL .... Force Beachhead Line [Navy]
FBHGA .... Friends and Buddies of the Hour Glass Association (EA)
FBHI........... Fellow of the British Horological Institute
FBHL.......... Force Beachhead Line [Navy] (NVT)
FBHQ .... Gaborone Civil Aviation Headquarters [Botswana] [ICAO location identifier] (ICLI)
FBHS .... Fellow of the British Horse Society (DBQ)
FBHTM........ Federation of British Hand Tool Manufacturers (EAIO)
FBHX.......... Fluid Bed Heat Exchanger (PDAA)
FBI............. BEA Strategic Income Fd [NYSE symbol] (TTSB)
FBI............. BEA Strategic Income Fund [NYSE symbol] (SAG)
FBI............. Federal Bureau of Investigation
FBI............. Federation of British Industries [Later, CBI]
FBI............. First Boston Strategic [Later, CS First Boston Strategic] [NYSE symbol NYSE symbol] (SPSG)
FBI............. Flossing, Brushing, and Irrigation [Dentistry]
FBI............. Fluidized Bed Incinerator (DOGT)
FBI............. Foreign Body Ingestion [Medicine]
FBI............. Foreign-Born Irish
FBI............. Full Bench Decisions [India] [A publication] (DLA)
FBIA.......... Food and Beverage Importers' Association [Australia]
FBIBA......... Fellow of the British Insurance Brokers' Association (ODBW)
FBIC.......... Farm Buildings Information Centre Ltd. [British] (CB)
FBIC.......... Firstbank of Illinois [NASDAQ symbol] (TTSB)
FBIC.......... Firstbank of Illinois Co. [NASDAQ symbol] (NQ)
FBIC.......... Free Beaches Information Center [Later, The Naturists] (EA)
FBICC......... Flow Blue International Collectors Club (EA)
FBICNSW..... Friends of Brain Injured Children of New South Wales [Australia]
FBID.......... Fellow of the British Institute of Interior Design (DBQ)
F-BIDR........ Full-Resolution Basic Image Data Record [RADAR mapping]
FBIE.......... Fellow of the British Institute of Embalmers (DBQ)
FBIM.......... Fellow of the British Institute of Management [Formerly, FIIA]
FBIP.......... Florida Institute of Phosphate Research, FIPR Library & Information Clearinghouse, Bartow, FL [Library symbol] [Library of Congress] (LCLS)
FBIPP.......... Fellow of the British Institute of Professional Photography (DBQ)
FBIS.......... Fellow of the British Interplanetary Society
FBIS.......... Foreign Broadcast Information System
FBIS.......... Foreign Broadcast Intelligence Service [FCC World War II]
FBI's......... Forgotten Boys of Iceland [Nickname for US soldiers in Iceland] [World War II]
FBIST........ Fellow of the British Institute of Surgical Technologists (DBQ)
FBIU.......... Freshwater Biological Investigation Unit [Department of Agriculture for Northern Ireland] [British] (IRUK)
FBJW.......... Jwaneng [Botswana] [ICAO location identifier] (ICLI)
FBK............ Fairbanks [Alaska] [Seismograph station code, US Geological Survey Closed] (SEIS)
FBK............ Fairbanks/Wainwright, AK [Location identifier FAA] (FAAL)
FBK............ Flat Back
FBKE.......... Kasane [Botswana] [ICAO location identifier] (ICLI)
FBKG.......... Kang [Botswana] [ICAO location identifier] (ICLI)
FBkGA........ First Bankshares, Inc. (Georgia) [Associated Press] (SAG)
FBKKW .... Flugbetriebsstoff-Kesselkraftwagen
FBKP.......... First Bank of Philadelphia [NASDAQ symbol] (NQ)
FBKP.......... First Bk Philadelphia PA [NASDAQ symbol] (TTSB)
FBkPhila...... First Bk of Philadelphia [Associated Press] (SAG)
FBkPhl........ First Bank of Philadelphia [Associated Press] (SAG)
FBKR.......... Khwai River Lodge [Botswana] [ICAO location identifier] (ICLI)
FBkS.......... First Bank System [Associated Press] (SAG)
FBkS.......... First Bank System, Inc. [Associated Press] (SAG)
FBksAm ...... First Banks America, Inc. [Associated Press] (SAG)
FBKY.......... Kanye [Botswana] [ICAO location identifier] (ICLI)
FBL............ Fantasy Bowling League
FBL............ Faribault, MN [Location identifier FAA] (FAAL)
FBL............ Fecal Blood Loss [Medicine]
FBL............ Federal Barge Lines, Inc. [AAR code]

FBL .... Fixed-Bed Loop [*Chemical engineering*]
FBL .... Flight-by-Light [*OST*] (TAG)
FBL .... Fly-by-Light
FBL .... Folicular Basal Lamina [*Medicine*]
FBL .... Food Brokers Ltd. [*Canada ICAO designator*] (FAAC)
FBL .... Foreign Bird League [*British*] (BI)
FBL .... Form Block Line (MCD)
FBL .... Foundation for Better Living (EA)
FBL .... Friction Braked Landing [*Aviation*] (IAA)
FBL .... Functional Baseline (AAGC)
FBL .... Future Battle Laboratory (RDA)
FBLA .... Future Business Leaders of America [*Washington, DC*] (AEBS)
FBLA-PBL .... Future Business Leaders of America - Phi Beta Lambda
        [*Washington, DC*] (EA)
FBLC .... Fibroblast-Like Cell [*Cytology*]
FBL Fn .... FBL Financial Group [*Associated Press*] (SAG)
FBLO .... Lobatse [*Botswana*] [*ICAO location identifier*] (ICLI)
FBM .... Biscayne College, Miami, FL [*OCLC symbol*] (OCLC)
FBM .... Feet Board Measure
FBM .... Felbamate [*Organic chemistry*]
FBM .... Ferber Mining Corp. [*Vancouver Stock Exchange symbol*]
FBM .... Fetal Breathing Movements [*Gynecology*]
FBM .... Financial and Business Management Division [*American
        Occupational Therapy Association*]
FBM .... Flavor-by-Mouth [*Sensory testing*]
FBM .... Fleet Ballistic Missile
FBM .... Fluorobenzyl(methylaminopurine) [*Biochemistry*]
FBM .... Foot Board Measure (MSA)
FBM .... Foreground and Background Monitor
FBM .... Four-Ball Machine [*Engineering*] (IAA)
fBm .... Fractional Brownian Motion [*Mathematics*]
FBM .... Freeboard Measure (IAA)
FBM .... Fuzzy BIT [*Binary Digit*] Map [*Computer science*]
FBM .... Lubumbashi [*Zaire*] [*Airport symbol*] (OAG)
FBMA .... Food and Beverage Managers Association [*British*] (DBA)
FBMA .... Forward Brigade Maintenance Area [*Army*]
FBMG .... Machaneng [*Botswana*] [*ICAO location identifier*] (ICLI)
FBML .... Molepolole [*Botswana*] [*ICAO location identifier*] (ICLI)
FBMM .... Makalamabedi [*Botswana*] [*ICAO location identifier*] (ICLI)
FBMN .... Maun [*Botswana*] [*ICAO location identifier*] (ICLI)
FBMO .... Fibrous Body-Membrane Organelle [*Biochemistry*]
FBMP .... Fleet Ballistic Missile Program
FBMR .... Fleet Ballistic Missile Requisition [*Navy*] (AFIT)
FBMS .... Fleet Ballistic Missile Submarine (IAA)
FBMS .... Fleet Ballistic Missile System
FBMS .... Mosetse [*Botswana*] [*ICAO location identifier*] (ICLI)
FBMSTCLANT... Fleet Ballistic Missile Submarine Training Center, Atlantic (DNAB)
FBMSTCPAC... Fleet Ballistic Missile Submarine Training Center, Pacific (DNAB)
FBMSTLL ..... Fleet Ballistic Missile Submarine Tender Load List
FBMTC .... Fleet Ballistic Missile Training Center (DNAB)
FBMTLL ...... Fleet Ballistic Missile Tender Load List (DNAB)
FBMWS .... Fleet Ballistic Missile Weapon System
FBMWSS .... Fleet Ballistic Missile Weapons Support System (DNAB)
FBN .... Family Business Network [*Switzerland*]
FBN .... Federal Bureau of Narcotics
FBN .... Feedback Network
FBN .... Fibronectin [*Biochemistry*]
FBN .... Food Business Network [*Information service or system*] (IID)
FBN .... Fuel-Bound Nitrogen
FBN .... Furniture Brands Intl [*NYSE symbol*] (TTSB)
FBN .... Furniture Brands Intl., Inc. [*NYSE symbol*] (SAG)
FBN .... State Library of Florida, Bureau of Book Processing, Tallahassee, FL
        [*OCLC symbol*] (OCLC)
FBNC .... First Bancorp (North Carolina) [*NASDAQ symbol*] (NQ)
FBNCC .... Fall Back Network Control Center (MCD)
FBNK .... First Banks, Inc. [*NASDAQ symbol*] (SAG)
FBNKP .... First Banks 9% Incr Rt'C'Pfd [*NASDAQ symbol*] (TTSB)
FBNML........ Francis Bitter National Magnet Laboratory [*MIT*]
FBNN .... Nokaneng [*Botswana*] [*ICAO location identifier*] (ICLI)
FBNT .... Nata [*Botswana*] [*ICAO location identifier*] (ICLI)
FBNW .... Gaborone Notwane [*Botswana*] [*ICAO location identifier*] (ICLI)
FBo .... Boca Raton Public Library, Boca Raton, FL [*Library symbol Library of
        Congress*] (LCLS)
FBO .... Carroll Aircraft Corp. PLC [*British ICAO designator*] (FAAC)
FBO .... Federal Paper Board Co., Inc. [*NYSE symbol*] (SPSG)
FBO .... Field Bake Oven [*Military*]
FBO .... Fixed-Base Operator [*Provider of nonairline aviation services to users
        of airports*]
FBO .... Foreign Building Office [*Department of State*]
FBO .... For the Benefit Of
FBO .... Furnished by Others [*Technical drawings*]
FBOA .... Fellow of the British Optical Association
FBoC .... College of Boca Raton, Boca Raton, FL [*Library symbol*] [*Library of
        Congress*] (LCLS)
FBOC .... Figural Bottle Openers Collectors Club (EA)
FBOE .... Frequency Band of Emission (CET)
FBOIP .... Final Basis of Issue Plan [*Army*]
FBOK .... Okwa [*Botswana*] [*ICAO location identifier*] (ICLI)
FBOOM .... Fort Benning Officers' Open Mess [*Pronounced "fuhboom"*]
FBOR .... Orapa [*Botswana*] [*ICAO location identifier*] (ICLI)
FBOU .... Fellow of the British Ornithologists' Union (ROG)
FBoU .... Florida Atlantic University, Boca Raton, FL [*Library symbol Library of
        Congress*] (LCLS)
FBP .... Federal Bonding Program
FBP .... Federal Bureau of Prisons (WDAA)

FBP .... Federation Baden-Powell [*Canada*] (EAIO)
FBP .... Femoral Blood Pressure [*Medicine*]
FBP .... Fibonacci Benchmark Program [*Computer science*] (BYTE)
FBP .... Fibrin Breakdown Products [*Hematology*]
FBP .... Fibrinogen Breakdown Products [*Hematology*] (DAVI)
FBP .... Fibrinopeptide B [*Biochemistry*]
FBP .... Fighter Bomber Program
FBP .... Filtered Back-Projection [*Computer science*]
FBP .... Final Boiling Point
FBP .... Financial Business Package [*Computer science*]
FBP .... FirstBank Puerto Rico [*NYSE symbol*] (TTSB)
FBP .... Fleet Boat Pool
FBP .... Flexible Benefits Program [*Human resources*] (WYGK)
FBP .... Fluidized-Bed Process
FBP .... Folate-Binding Protein [*Biochemistry*]
FBP .... Foreign Bases Project (EA)
FBP .... Fortschrittliche Buergerpartei [*Progressive Citizens' Party*]
        [*Liechtenstein*] (PPW)
FBP .... Fructose bisphosphate [*Also, FDP*] [*Biochemistry*]
FBP .... Fuel Booster Pump
FBPA .... Pandamatenga [*Botswana*] [*ICAO location identifier*] (ICLI)
FBPase .... Fructose bisphosphatase [*An enzyme*]
FBPC .... First Financial Bancshares Polk County [*NASDAQ symbol*] (SAG)
FBPC .... Foreign Bondholders Protective Council [*Defunct*] (EA)
FBPCS .... Federation of Behavioral, Psychological, and Cognitive Sciences
        (EA)
FBPN .... Feminist Business and Professional Network (EA)
FBPsS........ Fellow of the British Psychological Society
FBPY .... Palapye [*Botswana*] [*ICAO location identifier*] (ICLI)
FBQ .... Fibrequest International Ltd. [*Formerly, Trawler Petroleum
        Explorations Ltd.*] [*Vancouver Stock Exchange symbol*]
FBR .... Broward County Libraries Division, Pompano Beach, FL [*OCLC
        symbol*] (OCLC)
FBR .... Fabra [*Barcelona*] [*Spain*] [*Seismograph station code, US Geological
        Survey*] (SEIS)
FBR .... Fast Breeder Reactor [*Nuclear energy*]
FBR .... Fast Burn Rate
FBR .... Fast Burst Reactor [*Nuclear energy*]
FBR .... Feedback Report (NVT)
FBR .... Feedback Resistance (IEEE)
FBR .... Ferric-Leach Bacterial Regeneration [*Uranium extraction process*]
FBR .... Fiber (KSC)
fbr .... Fiber (VRA)
FBR .... Fiber
FBR .... Fireball Radius [*Military*] (AABC)
FBR .... First Brands Corp. [*NYSE symbol*] (SPSG)
FBR .... Flat Board Reach [*Test*] [*Occupational therapy*]
FBR .... Floating Point Register [*Computer science*]
FBR .... Fluidized-Bed Reactor (MCD)
FBR .... Forschungsberichte Bundesrepublik Deutschland
        [*Fachinformationszentrum Karlsruhe GmbH*] [*Germany
        Information service or system*] (CRD)
FBR .... Forskningsbiblioteksradet [*Swedish council for research libraries*]
        (NITA)
FBR .... Fort Bridger, WY [*Location identifier FAA*] (FAAL)
FBR .... Foundation for Basic Research [*Russia*]
FBR .... Foundation for Biomedical Research (EA)
FBR .... Foundation for Blood Research [*Research center*] (RCD)
FBR .... Foundation for Business Responsibilities [*British*]
FbR .... Fred B. Rothman & Co., South Hackensack, NJ [*Library symbol
        Library of Congress*] (LCLS)
FBR .... Frobisher Resources Ltd. [*Vancouver Stock Exchange symbol*]
FBR .... Full Bench Rulings [*Bengal, India*] [*A publication*] (DLA)
FBR .... Full Bibliographic Record (NITA)
FBR .... Full Boiling-Range [*Fuel technology*] (PDAA)
FBr .... Manatee County Library System, Bradenton, FL [*Library symbol
        Library of Congress*] (LCLS)
FBRBD .... Fiberboard
FBRC .... Fabric
FBRC .... Frederick Burk Foundation Research Center
FBRCM .... Fingerbreadth Below Right Costal Margin [*Measurement*]
        [*Anatomy*] (DAVI)
FBRCN .... Fabrication
F/BRD .... Floor Board [*Automotive engineering*]
FBRD .... Flying Boat Repair Depot [*British military*] (DMA)
FBRE .... Full Boiling-Range Fuel (PDAA)
FBRF .... Fast Burst Reactor Facility [*Nuclear energy*]
FBRGLS ...... Fiberglass
FBritIRE ...... Fellow of the British Institution of Radio Engineers
FBRK .... Fire Brick [*Technical drawings*]
FBRK .... Rakops [*Botswana*] [*ICAO location identifier*] (ICLI)
FBRL .... Final Bomb Release Line
FBrM .... Manatee Junior College, Bradenton, FL [*Library symbol Library of
        Congress*] (LCLS)
FBRNWP...... Full Bench Rulings, Northwest Provinces [*India*] [*A publication*] (DLA)
FBro .... Frederick Eugene Lykes, Jr., Memorial County Library, Brooksville,
        FL [*Library symbol Library of Congress*] (LCLS)
FBroPH .... Pasco-Hernando Community College, North Campus Learning
        Resources Center, Brooksville, FL [*Library symbol*] [*Library of
        Congress*] (LCLS)
FBRS .... Fibrous
FBRS .... Fleet Broadcast Receive Subsystem [*Navy*] (CAAL)
FBRSU .... Full-Boiling Range High-Sensitivity Unleaded [*Motor fuel*]
FBRT .... Francis Bacon Research Trust [*British*]
FBRU .... Full-Boiling Range Unleaded [*Motor fuel*]

f-bs--	Botswana [*MARC geographic area code Library of Congress*] (LCCP)
FBS	Facsimile Broadcast Service
FBS	Fan Beam Scatterometer
FBS	Farm Bureau Services
FBS	Fasting Blood Sugar [*Physiology*]
FBS	Feedback Signal
FBS	Feedback System
FBS	Fellow of the Botanical Society [*British*] (ROG)
FBS	Fellow of the Building Societies Institute [*British*]
FBS	Fetal Blood Sample [*Hematology*]
FBS	Fetal Bovine Serum [*Medicine*]
FB/S	Fighter Bomber Strike (NATG)
FBS	Film: British Series
FBS	Fine Bearing Servo
FBS	Fire Brigade Society [*British*] (DBA)
FBS	Firefighter Breathing System [*NASA*]
FBS	First Bank System [*NYSE symbol*] (TTSB)
FBS	First Bank System, Inc. [*NYSE symbol*] (SPSG)
FBS	Fixed-Based Simulator (PDAA)
FBS	Flare Build-Up Study [*Meteorology*]
FBS	Flash/Bang/Smoke (MCD)
FBS	Flourous Biphase System [*For chemical catalysis*]
FBS	Focus Broadcast Satellite Corporation (NITA)
FBS	Fokes Sentence Builder [*Speech and language therapy*] (DAVI)
FBS	Fortified Barrier System (MCD)
FBS	Forward-Based Systems [*US aircraft based outside the US and capable of carrying nuclear weapons to the USSR*]
FBS	Foundry Business System [*Foundry Business Systems*] [*Software package*] (NCC)
FBS	Francis Bacon Society (EA)
FBS	Frontal Bovine Serum [*Medicine*] (BARN)
FBSA	Federal Boating Safety Act of 1971 [*USCG*] (TAG)
FBSA	Filter-Band Suppressor Assembly
FBSB	Finance Brokers Supervisory Board [*Western Australia*]
FBSC	Federation of Building Specialist Contractors [*British*] (DBA)
FBSC	Fellow of the British Society of Commerce
FBSC	Fred Bear Sports Club (EA)
FBSComm..	Fellow of the British Society of Commerce
FBSD	Serondela [*Botswana*] [*ICAO location identifier*] (ICLI)
FBSE	Fellow of the Botanical Society, Edinburgh (ROG)
FBSEA	Foreign Bank Supervision Enhancement Act [*1991*] (ECON)
FBSI	All Indonesian Labor Federation (IMH)
FBSI	Fellow of the Boot and Shoe Institution [*British*]
FBSI	First Bankshares [*NASDAQ symbol*] (TTSB)
FBSI	First Bankshares of Missouri, Inc. [*NASDAQ symbol*] (SAG)
FBSI	Furniture and Bedding Spring Institute [*Defunct*] (EA)
FBSK	Gaborone/Sir Seretse Khama [*Botswana*] [*ICAO location identifier*] (ICLI)
FBSM	Fellow of the Birmingham School of Music [*British*]
FBSNSW	French Benevolent Society of New South Wales [*Australia*]
FBSoGA	First Banking Co. Southeast Georgia [*Associated Press*] (SAG)
FBSP	Selebi-Phikwe [*Botswana*] [*ICAO location identifier*] (ICLI)
FBSPrX	First Bk Sys $3.5625 Cv91A Pfd [*NYSE symbol*] (TTSB)
FBSR	Serowe [*Botswana*] [*ICAO location identifier*] (ICLI)
FBST	Fiberstars, Inc. [*NASDAQ symbol*] (SAG)
FBSV	Savuti [*Botswana*] [*ICAO location identifier*] (ICLI)
FBSW	First Bank System [*NASDAQ symbol*] (SAG)
FBSW	Shakawe [*Botswana*] [*ICAO location identifier*] (ICLI)
FBSWA	Federation of Building Societies of Western Australia
FBSWW	First Bank Sys Wrrt [*NASDAQ symbol*] (TTSB)
FBT	Facility Block Table (IAA)
FBT	Feedback Technology (SSD)
FBT	Fibertech Industries Corp. [*Formerly, Essex Petroleum Corp.*] [*Vancouver Stock Exchange symbol*]
FBT	Flash to Bang Time [*Army*]
FBT	Flat-Blade Turbine [*Engineering*]
FBT	Flyback Transformer [*Electronics*] (IAA)
F/Bt	Flying Boat [*British military*] (DMA)
FBT	Form Block Template (MSA)
FBT	Forward Ballast Tank (MSA)
FBT	Fringe Benefits Tax
FBT	Full Berth Terms [*Shipping*]
FBTC	Fairfax Bank & Trust Co. [*NASDAQ symbol*] (SAG)
FBTD	Food and Beverage Trades Department [*of AFL-CIO*] (EA)
FBTE	Tshane [*Botswana*] [*ICAO location identifier*] (ICLI)
FBTL	Tuli Lodge [*Botswana*] [*ICAO location identifier*] (ICLI)
FBTPIU	Federated Brick, Tile, and Pottery Industrial Union of Australia
FBTR	Bederation of British Tape Recordists (DBA)
FBTR	Fast Breeder Test Reactor [*Nuclear energy*]
FBTR	For Better Living [*NASDAQ symbol*] (TTSB)
FBTR	For Better Living, Inc. [*NASDAQ symbol*] (NQ)
FBTRC	Federation of British Tape Recording Clubs (BI)
FBTS	Form Block Template Set (MCD)
FBTS	Tshabong [*Botswana*] [*ICAO location identifier*] (ICLI)
FBU	Federation of Broadcasting Unions [*British*]
FBU	Field Broadcasting Unit (IAA)
FBU	Fingers Below Umbilicus [*Measurement*] [*Anatomy*] (DAVI)
FBU	Fire Brigade Union
FBU	Freie-Buerger-Union [*Free Citizens' Union*] [*Germany*] (PPW)
FBU	Fully Built-Up [*Manufacturing*]
FBU	Oslo [*Norway*] [*Airport symbol*] (AD)
FBV--	Field Base Visit (NASA)
FBV	Friends of Bobby Vee (EA)
FBV	Fuel Bleed Valve (NASA)
FBV	Fuel Building Ventilation [*Nuclear energy*] (NRCH)
FBVF	Fiberglass Backed Vacuum Forming [*Fiberglass production*]
FBW	Fasting Blood Work [*Biochemistry*] (DAVI)
FBW	Fly by Wire
FB WD	Fibreboard and Wood [*Freight*]
FBWS	Fly by Wire System (IAA)
FBWU	Fire Brick Workers' Union [*British*]
FBX	Fighter Bomber [*Advanced*]
FBX	France, BENELUX
FBXG	Xugana [*Botswana*] [*ICAO location identifier*] (ICLI)
FBXX	Xaxaba [*Botswana*] [*ICAO location identifier*] (ICLI)
f-by--	Biafra [*MARC geographic area code Library of Congress*] (LCCP)
FBY	Fairbury, NE [*Location identifier FAA*] (FAAL)
FBY	Future Budget Year (AFM)
FBYB	Fly Before You Buy [*Aerospace industry slogan*]
FBypV	United States Veterans Administration Center, Bay Pines, FL [*Library symbol Library of Congress*] (LCLS)
FBZ	First Brillouin Zone [*Physics*]
FBZ	Forward Battle Zone [*British*]
fc----	Africa, Central [*MARC geographic area code Library of Congress*] (LCCP)
FC	All India Reporter, Federal Court [*1947-50*] [*A publication*] (DLA)
FC	British Guiana Full Court Reports (Official Gazette) [*A publication*] (DLA)
FC	Brothers of Charity (TOCD)
fc	Brothers of Charity (TOCD)
FC	Canada Law Reports, Federal Court [*A publication*] (DLA)
f$_c$	Carrier Frequency (IDOE)
FC	Chaparral Airlines [*ICAO designator*] (AD)
FC	Coast Station [*ITU designation*] (CET)
FC	Compound Fracture [*Medicine*]
FC	Congregatio Fratrum Caritate [*Brothers of Charity*] [*Roman Catholic religious order*]
FC	Critical Frequency (CET)
FC	Daughters of the Cross of Liege [*Roman Catholic religious order*]
FC	Face-Centered [*Crystallography*]
FC	Facilitative Communication [*Autism*]
FC	Facilities Construction (AAG)
FC	Facilities Contract
F/C	Facilities Control [*Military*]
FC	Faciundum Curavit [*He Caused To Be Made*] [*Latin*]
FC	Faculty of Advocates Collection of Decisions, Scotch Court of Sessions [*A publication*] (DLA)
FC	Fail Closed [*Nuclear energy*] (NRCH)
FC	Failure Count
FC	Fairchild Club (EA)
fc	Fair Condition [*Doll collecting*]
FC	Fair Cutting [*Brick*] (DICI)
FC	False Cape [*NASA*] (KSC)
FC	Family Continuation of Coverage [*Health insurance*] (GHCT)
FC	Family Contribution [*Department of Education*] (GFGA)
FC	Fast Component
FC	Faulted Circuit (IAA)
FC	FCA International Ltd. [*Toronto Stock Exchange symbol*]
FC	Feature Correlation
FC	Feature Count [*Computer science*]
FC	Febrile Convulsion [*Medicine*] (DMAA)
FC	Fecal Coli [*Microbiology*]
FC	Federal Cases [*A publication*] (DLA)
FC	Federalist Caucus (EA)
FC	Federation Council (EA)
FC	Feed the Children (EA)
FC	Feint and Cash [*of account book rulings*]
FC	Fellow Craft [*Freemasonry*] (ROG)
FC	Fermi Contact [*Physics*]
FC	Ferrite Core
FC	Ferrocement
FC	Ferrochelatase [*An enzyme*]
FC	Ferromagnetic Contamination [*Medicine*]
FC	Ferry Command [*RAF*] [*British*]
FC	Fever and Chills [*Medicine*] (DAVI)
FC	Fiberglass Covers (DCTA)
FC	Fibro Cement (ADA)
FC	Fidei Commissum [*Bequeathed in Trust*] [*Latin*]
FC	Field Camera
FC	Field Change
FC	Field Circular [*Military*] (INF)
FC	Field Command [*Military*]
FC	Field Contactor (IAA)
FC	Field Conversion [*Computer science*] (ECII)
FC	Field Cooled
FC	Fielder's Choice [*Baseball*]
FC	Fieri Curavit [*Caused to Be Made*] [*Latin*]
FC	Fighter Catapult [*Ship*]
FC	Fighter Command [*Air Force*]
FC	File Cabinet (AAG)
FC	File Code [*Computer science*] (IEEE)
FC	File Compare (PCM)
FC	File Control (AFIT)
FC	File Conversion [*Computer science*] (BUR)
FC	File Copy
FC	Film-Coated [*Pharmacy*]
FC	Film Comment [*A publication*] (BRI)
FC	Filson Club (EA)
FC	Filter Center
FC	Finance Charge

FC	Finance Committee [*UN Food and Agriculture Organization*]
FC	Finance Corps
FC	Financial Controller
FC	Find Called [*or Calling*] Party [*Telecommunications*] (TEL)
FC	Fine Champagne
FC	Fine Cognac
FC	Fine Control (DEN)
FC	Finger Clubbing [*Medicine*] (MAE)
FC	Finger Counting [*See also CF*]
FC	Fire Cause [*Criminology*] (LAIN)
FC	Fire Clay
FC	Fire Cock [*British*] (ROG)
FC	Fire Commander [*British military*] (DMA)
FC	Fire Control [*of guns*]
FC	Fire Control Armourer [*British military*] (DMA)
FC	Fire Controlman [*Navy rating Obsolete*]
FC	Firing Channel [*Military*] (CAAL)
FC	Fishery Council (EA)
FC	Fit Check [*NASA*] (NASA)
FC	Fixed Camera (KSC)
FC	Fixed Capital [*Business term*]
FC	Fixed Charge [*Business term*]
FC	Fixed Cost [*Economics*]
FC	Flanged Connection [*Piping*]
F+C	Flare and Cells [*Ophthalmology*] (DAVI)
FC	Flexible Connection (OA)
FC	Flight Capsule
F/C	Flight Certificate
FC	Flight Charts
FC	Flight Computer [*NASA*] (NASA)
FC	Flight Control
F/C	Flight Controller (NASA)
FC	Flight Crew
FC	Flight Critical (MCD)
FC	Floating Capital [*Business term*]
FC	Floating Causeway
FC	Flood Control
FC	Flowchart [*Engineering*] (IAA)
FC	Flow Coating
FC	Flow Controller [*Nuclear energy*] (NRCH)
FC	Fluoridation Committee [*Tasmania, Australia*]
FC	Fluorocarbon (ERG)
FC	Fluorocarbons [*Organic chemistry*]
FC	Fluorocytosine [*or Flucytosine*] [*Antineoplastic drug*]
FC	Flying Colonels [*Delta Air Lines' club for frequent flyers*] (EA)
FC	Foaming Capacity [*Food technology*]
FC	Foley Catheter [*Urology*]
FC	Folin-Ciocalteau [*Clinical chemistry*]
FC	Follow Copy [*Printing*]
fc	Follow Copy [*Typesetting*] [*Also, Folo Copy*] (WDMC)
fc	Font Change [*Typesetting*] (WDMC)
FC	Font Change [*Computer science*] (BUR)
FC	Food Controller [*British World War II*]
FC	Foolscap (NTCM)
FC	Football Club [*British*]
FC	Football Committee [*British*]
FC	Foot-Candle [*Illumination*]
fc	Foot-Candle (IDOE)
FC	Footwear Caucus (EA)
FC	Footwear Council [*Defunct*] (EA)
FC	Forage Corps [*British military*] (DMA)
FC	Forage Crop [*Agriculture*]
F/C	Force Control (MCD)
FC	Forced Circulation (DICI)
FC	Forecast Center Station [*Telecommunications*] (TEL)
FC	Foreign Classics [*A publication*]
FC	Foreign Consul (ROG)
FC	Foreign Currency
FC	Forestry Commission [*British*]
FC	Forestry Commission [*New SouthWales*] [*State*] (EERA)
F/C	Format Code [*Computer science*]
FC	Formula Continental [*Class of racing cars*]
FC	Forward Cab [*Automotive engineering*]
FC	Forward Chaining [*Psychology*]
FC	Forward Control [*Automotive engineering*]
FC	Foundation Center (EA)
FC	Foundation City [*Dialog*] [*Searchable field*] [*Information service or system*] (NITA)
FC	Foundation Code [*IRS*]
FC	Fraction Collector [*Chromatography*]
FC	Fractocumulus [*Meteorology*]
Fc	Fragment, Crystallizable [*Immunochemistry*]
FC	Frame Control [*Computer science*] (TNIG)
FC	Franc [*Monetary unit*] [*France*] (ROG)
F/C	Free and Clear (WDAA)
FC	Free Choice [*Psychology*]
FC	Free Cholesterol [*Clinical chemistry*]
FC	Free Church
FC	Free Cursor (NITA)
FC	Free of Cells [*Medicine*]
FC	Frequency Changer (IAA)
FC	Frequency Converter
FC	Freres de la Charite [*Brothers of Charity*] (EAIO)
FC	Friars Club (EA)
FC	Friendly Capabilities (MCD)

FC	Friends of Community (EA)
FC	Front-Connected
FC	Frozen Cell
FC	Fuel Cell (KSC)
FC	Fuel Controller (DAS)
FC	Fuel Cycle (NRCH)
FC	Full Charge [*Accounting*]
FC	Full Corner [*Philately*]
FC	Full Court (ADA)
FC	Full Court Judgments [*Ghana*] [*A publication*] (DLA)
FC	Functional Chief [*of a civilian career program*] [*Military*]
FC	Functional Class [*Rehabilitation*] [*Medicine*] (DAVI)
FC	Functional Code
FC	Function Call (IAA)
FC	Function Code (NITA)
FC	Fund Campaign [*Red Cross*]
FC	Fund Code (AABC)
FC	Funding Cycle (OICC)
FC	Funnel Cloud
FC	Funny Car [*Class of racing cars*]
FC	Furnace Cooled [*Engineering*] (IAA)
FC	Fuse Chamber (TEL)
FC	Futures Contract [*Investment term*]
FC	Fuze Committee [*Military*]
FC	Hard Filled Capsules [*Pharmacy*]
FC	Hydrofluorocarbon
FC	Selected Judgments of the Full Court, Accra and Gold Coast [*A publication*] (DLA)
FC	Subcutaneous Fat Class
FC	Union of Soviet Socialist Republics [*Formerly, SX*] [*License plate code assigned to foreign diplomats in the US*]
FC²V	Future Command and Control Vehicle
FC '22	Full Court Judgments [*1922*] [*Ghana*] [*A publication*] (DLA)
FC '20-1	Full Court Judgments [*1920-21*] [*Ghana*] [*A publication*] (DLA)
FC '23-25	Selected Judgments of the Full Court [*1923-25*] [*Ghana*] [*A publication*] (DLA)
FC '26-29	Selected Judgments of the Full Court [*1926-29*] [*Ghana*] [*A publication*] (DLA)
FCa	Cape Canaveral Public Library, Cape Canaveral, FL [*Library symbol Library of Congress*] (LCLS)
FCA	Fabri Centers of America [*NYSE symbol*] (SAG)
FCA	Fabri-Centers of America, Inc. [*NYSE symbol*] (SPSG)
FCA	Facility Change Authorization (AAG)
FCA	Factorial Correspondence Analysis [*Mathematics*]
FCA	Fairlane Club of America (EA)
FCA	Falcon Club of America (EA)
FCA	False Claims Act (AAGC)
FCA	Family Court of Australia
FCA	Fan Club Associates [*Later, IFCA*] (EA)
FCA	Faraday Cup Array [*Electronics*] (OA)
FCA	Farm Credit Administration [*Independent government agency*]
FCA	Fast Critical Assembly [*Nuclear reactor*] [*Japan*]
FCA	Federal Code, Annotated [*A publication*] (DLA)
FCA	Federal Committee on Apprenticeship [*Department of Labor*]
FCA	Federal Communications Act
FCA	Federal Council on the Aging [*Succeeded by President's Council on Aging, 1962*]
FCA	Federation Canadienne de l'Agriculture [*Canadian Federation of Agriculture - CFA*]
FCA	Federation Canadienne des Archers [*Federation of Canadian Archers*]
FCA	Federation of Canadian Archers
FCA	Federation of Canadian Artists
FCA	Federation of Commodity Associations (EAIO)
FCA	Fellow of the Institute of Chartered Accountants [*British*] (ROG)
FCA	Fellow of the Institute of Chartered Architects [*British*]
FCA	Fellowship of Christian Athletes (EA)
FCA	Fencing Contractors Association [*British*] (DBA)
FCA	Ferrari Club of America (EA)
FCA	Ferrite Control Amplifier
FCA	Ferritin-Conjugated Antibody [*Biochemistry*] (MAE)
FCA	Few Civilian Casualties [*Persian Gulf War*]
FCA	Fiat Club of America (EA)
FCA	Field Change Analysis
FCA	Field Change Authorization [*Nuclear energy*] (NRCH)
FCA	Fighter Control Area [*Military*]
FCA	Filipino Cultural Association [*Australia*]
FCA	Films for Christ Association (EA)
FCA	Financial Corp. of America (ECON)
FCA	Financial Corporations Act [*Australia*]
FCA	Fire Control Area [*Army*]
FCA	First Chair of America [*Defunct*] (EA)
FCA	Fishing Clubs of Australia
FCA	Fixed Coaxial Attenuator
FCA	Fleet Chief Armourer [*British military*] (DMA)
FCA	Flight Control Assemblies
FCA	Flow Control Assembly (MCD)
FCA	Fluidized Combustor Ash (OA)
FCA	Fluids Control Assembly (NASA)
FCA	Fluorocytosine Arabinoside [*Also, ara-FC*] [*Antitumor compound*]
FCA	Flying Chiropractors Association (EA)
FCA	Food Casings Association [*British*] (DBA)
FCA	Footwear Components Association Ltd. [*British*] (BI)
FCA	Force Cost Assessor (MCD)
FCA	Formal Configuration Audit (MCD)

FCA............	Foundation for the Community of Artists (EA)
FCA............	Fraternity of Canadian Astrologers
FCA............	Free China Assistance (EA)
FCA............	Freight Claim Agent
FCA............	Freight Claim Association
FCA............	French Computing Association
FCA............	Frequency Change Approved [Aviation] (FAAC)
FCA............	Frequency Control and Analysis
FCA............	Freund's Complete Adjuvant [Immunology]
FCA............	Friendly Contacts Associates [Defunct] (EA)
FCA............	Fuel Capsule [or Cell] Assembly (MCD)
FCA............	Fuel Cell Association (EA)
FCA............	Full Circle Associates (EA)
FCA............	Full-Coverage Area [Radio and TV]
FCA............	Functional Compatibility Analysis (MCD)
FCA............	Functional Configuration Audit
FCA............	Fur Council of Australia
FCA............	Fuzzy Cluster Analysis [Mathematics]
FCA............	Kalispell [Montana] [Airport symbol] (OAG)
FCA............	Kalispell, MT [Location identifier FAA] (FAAL)
FCA............	Stratford Airways Ltd. [Canada ICAO designator] (FAAC)
FCAA..........	Federal Clean Air Act (WDAA)
FCAA..........	Federal Courts Administration Act of 1992 (AAGC)
FCAA..........	Fleet Chief Aircraft Artificer [British military] (DMA)
FCAA..........	Florence Crittenton Association of America [Later, CWLA] (EA)
FCAA..........	Foreign Correspondents' Association of Australia
FCAA..........	Frequency Control and Analysis (IAA)
FCAC..........	Field Crop Advisory Committee [Western Australia]
FCAC..........	Folklore Studies Association of Canada
FCAC..........	Forward Control and Analysis Center (MCD)
FCA(Can).....	Fellow of the Institute of Chartered Accountants in Canada
FCACMN......	Fleet Chief Aircrewman [British military] (DMA)
FCAD	Field Contract Administration Division [of ONM]
FCADD	Fondation Canadienne sur l'Alcohol et la Dependance aux Drogues [Canadian Foundation on Alcohol and Drug Dependencies - CFADD]
FCAE..........	Fellow of the Canadian Academy of Engineering (DD)
FCAF..........	Fleet Chief Air Fitter [British military] (DMA)
FCAF..........	Flight Crew Accommodations Facility (MCD)
FCaF	Florida Solar Energy Center, Cape Canaveral, FL [Library symbol Library of Congress] (LCLS)
FCAF..........	Frequency Control Analysis Facility
FCAI..........	Federal Chamber of Automotive Industries (EERA)
FCAK..........	Function Cable Access Kit (DWSG)
FCAM..........	Federation Canadienne des Amis de Musees (AC)
FCAM..........	Fellow of the Communication Advertising and Marketing Education Foundation [British] (DBQ)
FCAM..........	Fellow of the Institute of Certified Administrative Managers (DD)
FCAME........	Fellowship of Christians in the Arts, Media, and Entertainment (EA)
FCANA........	Federation of Cambodian Associations in North America (EA)
FC & CE......	Flight Crew and Crew Equipment
FC & S........	Final Command and Sequencing [Viking lander mission] [NASA]
FC & S........	Free of Capture and Seizure [Insurance]
FC & SCWSL...	Fire Control and Small Caliber Weapon Systems Laboratory [Picatinny Arsenal, Dover, NJ] [Army] (RDA)
FCANSW	Floor Coverings Association of New South Wales [Australia]
FCA(NZ).......	Fellow Chartered Accountant of New Zealand
FCAP..........	Fellow of the College of American Pathologists
FCAP..........	Fellowship of Christian Airline Personnel (EA)
FCAP..........	Flight Control Applications Program [NASA] (NASA)
FCAP..........	Fluor Chrome Arsenate Phenol [Wood preservative]
FCAP..........	Foolscap [Paper]
FCap..........	French Capitol [Record label]
FCAR..........	Foreign Currency Agriculture Research Program [Department of Agriculture]
FCAR..........	Free of Claim for Accident Reported [Shipping] (DS)
F Carr Cas ...	Federal Carriers Cases [Commerce Clearing House] [A publication] (DLA)
F Carrier Cas...	Federal Carriers Cases [Commerce Clearing House] [A publication] (DLA)
F Cas	Federal Cases [A publication] (DLA)
FCAS..........	Fellow of the Casualty Actuarial Science (DD)
FCAS..........	Fellow of the Casualty Actuarial Society [Casualty Actuarial Society] [Designation awarded by]
FCAS..........	Frequency Coded Armaments System
FCAS..........	Frequency Control Analysis Subsystem (MCD)
FCas	Seminole County Public Library System, Casselberry, FL [Library symbol Library of Congress] (LCLS)
FCASI..........	Fellow of the Canadian Aeronautics and Space Institute
F Cas No	Federal Case Number [Legal term] (DLA)
FCAT..........	Flight Composite Acceptance Test
FCAT..........	Floating SI-Gate Channel Corner Avalanche Transition (MCD)
Fcath	Foley Catheter [Urology]
FCAW..........	Flux Cored Arc Welding
FCAW..........	Foundation for Citizens Against Waste (EA)
FCb	Cocoa Beach Public Library, Cocoa Beach, FL [Library symbol Library of Congress] (LCLS)
FCB	Facility Clearance Board [WPB]
FCB	Falmouth Co-Operative Bank [AMEX symbol] (SAG)
FCB	Falmouth Co-operative Bank [AMEX symbol] (TTSB)
FCB	Fast Capacitor Bank
FCB	File Control Block [Computer science] (BUR)
FCB	Film Censorship Board [Australia]
FCB	First Commercial Bank [Taiwan]
FCB	Fluocortin Butyl [Pharmacology]

FCB............	Focus Control Block [Computer science]
FCB............	Foote, Cone & Belding Communications [Advertising] [Communications] [Chicago, IL] (WDMC)
FCB............	Foreign Clearance Base
FCB............	Forms Control Buffer [Computer science] (IBMDP)
FCB............	Foundation for Commercial Banks (EA)
FCB............	Free Cutting Brass
FCB............	Freight Container Bureau [AAR]
FCB............	Frequency Control Board [British] (AIA)
FCB............	Frequency Coordinating Body
FCB............	Friends of Clara Barton (EA)
FCB............	Fuel Cell Battery
FCB............	Function Control Block [Computer science] (IBMDP)
FCB............	Marine Broadcast Station [ITU designation] (CET)
FCBA..........	Fair Credit Billing Act
FCBA..........	Federal Circuit Bar Association (AAGC)
FCBA..........	Federal Communications Bar Association (EA)
FCBA..........	Fellow of the Canadian Bankers' Association
FCBA..........	Lalouila [Congo] [ICAO location identifier] (ICLI)
FCBB..........	Brazzaville/Maya Maya [Congo] [ICAO location identifier] (ICLI)
FCBC..........	Foreign Countries and British Colonies [A publication]
FCBCD	For Carter Before Camp David [Refers to Israeli-Egyptian agreements of 1978]
FCBD..........	Djambala [Congo] [ICAO location identifier] (ICLI)
FCBF..........	FCB Financial [NASDAQ symbol] (TTSB)
FCBF..........	FCB Financial Corp. [NASDAQ symbol] (SAG)
FCBF..........	Florida Customs Brokers and Forwarders Association (SRA)
FCBFL........	Feminists Concerned for Better Feminist Leadership (EA)
FCB Fn........	FCB Financial Corp. [Associated Press] (SAG)
FCBG..........	Federation of Children's Book Groups [British]
FCBG..........	Madingou [Congo] [ICAO location identifier] (ICLI)
FCBI..........	First Commerce Bancshares, Inc. [NASDAQ symbol] (NQ)
FCBIA..........	First Commerce Bancshares'A' [NASDAQ symbol] (TTSB)
FCBIB..........	First Comm Bancshares 'B' [NASDAQ symbol] (TTSB)
FCBJS	Federated Council of Beth Jacob Schools (EA)
FCBK..........	First Charter Bank NA [NASDAQ symbol] (SAG)
FCBK..........	Kindamba [Congo] [ICAO location identifier] (ICLI)
FCBL..........	Lague [Congo] [ICAO location identifier] (ICLI)
FCBM..........	Federation of Clinker Block Manufacturers [British] (BI)
FCBM..........	Mouyondzi [Congo] [ICAO location identifier] (ICLI)
FCBN..........	Fluorocarbon Co. (MHDW)
FCBO..........	M'Pouya [Congo] [ICAO location identifier] (ICLI)
FCBP..........	M'Passa [Congo] [ICAO location identifier] (ICLI)
FCBS..........	Fayette County Bancshares, Inc. [NASDAQ symbol] (SAG)
FCBS..........	Fayette County Bancshrs [NASDAQ symbol] (TTSB)
FCBS..........	Sibiti [Congo] [ICAO location identifier] (ICLI)
FCBSI..........	Fellow of the Chartered Building Societies Institute [British] (DBQ)
FCBT..........	Loutete [Congo] [ICAO location identifier] (ICLI)
FCBU..........	Aubeville [Congo] [ICAO location identifier] (ICLI)
FCBU..........	Foreign Currency Banking Unit (WDAA)
FCBUSA	Finance Corps Board, United States Army
FCBV..........	Brazzaville [Congo] [ICAO location identifier] (ICLI)
FCBY..........	N'Kay/Yokangassi [Congo] [ICAO location identifier] (ICLI)
FCBZ..........	Zanaga [Congo] [ICAO location identifier] (ICLI)
FCC............	Face-Centered Cubic [Crystallography]
FCC............	Facilities Control Console (AAG)
FCC............	Facility Communications Criteria (IAA)
FCC............	Falsely Claiming [US] Citizenship
FCC............	Familial Colonic Cancer [Gastroenterology and oncology] (DAVI)
FCC............	Family Communion Crusade [Defunct] (EA)
FCC............	Farm Credit Corp. [Canada]
FCC............	Farm Credit Council (EA)
FCC............	Farm Crisis Committee [Defunct] (EA)
FCC............	Federal City College [Later, UDC] [Washington, DC]
FCC............	Federal Communications Commission [Independent government agency]
FCC............	Federal Communications Commission, Washington, DC [OCLC symbol] (OCLC)
FCC............	Federal Construction Council (EA)
FCC............	Federal Consultative Council of South African Railways and Harbors Staff Association
FCC............	Federal Council of Churches
FCC............	Federation Canadienne des Communications [Canadian Federation of Communications Workers - CFCW]
FCC............	Federation of Crafts and Commerce [British] (DBA)
FCC............	Fellowship of Companies for Christ [Later, FCCI] (EA)
FCC............	Fellowship of Concerned Churchmen (EA)
F/CC...........	Fermentation/Cell Culture [Biology]
FCC............	Ferntree Computer Corp.
F/cc...........	Fibers per Cubic Centimeter
FCC............	Field Camera Control
FCC............	Field Control Center
FCC............	Field Controller Component (MCD)
FCC............	Fighter Control Center [MUGU]
FCC............	Filipino Community Cooperative [Australia]
FCC............	Firearms Consultative Committee [Australia]
FCC............	Fire Collectors Club (EA)
FCC............	Fire Control Code
FCC............	Fire Control Computer
FCC............	Fire Control Console (NATG)
FCC............	First Central Financial Corp. [AMEX symbol] (SPSG)
FCC............	First Central Finl [AMEX symbol] (TTSB)
FCC............	First-Class Certificate
FCC............	First Class Commission (HGAA)
FCC............	Fixed Ceramic Capacitor

FCC............ Fixed Communications Cabinet (MCD)
FCC............ Flat Conductor Cable
FCC............ Fleet Command Center [*Navy*] (CAAL)
FCC............ Fletcher Challenge Canada Ltd. [*Toronto Stock Exchange symbol Vancouver Stock Exchange symbol*]
FCC............ Flight Communications Center
FCC............ Flight Control Center
FCC............ Flight Control Computer (KSC)
FCC............ Flight Control Console
FCC............ Flight Control Container
FCC............ Flight Coordination Center (AFM)
FCC............ Flight Crew Compartment (MCD)
FCC............ Florida Christian College
FCC............ Florida Citrus Commission [*Later, Florida Department of Citrus*]
FCC............ Fluid Catalytic Converter [*Environmental Protection Agency*] (GFGA)
FCC............ Fluid Catalytic Cracking [*Fuel technology*]
FCC............ Fluid Convection Cathode
FCC............ Fluorochlorocarbon [*Organic chemistry*]
FCC............ Follicular Center Cell [*Cytology*]
FCC............ Fontana Corrosion Center [*Ohio State University*] [*Research center*] (RCD)
FCC............ Food Chemicals Codex [*National Academy of Sciences*] [*A publication*]
FCC............ Forbidden Combination Check
FCC............ Foreign Commerce Club of New York (EA)
FCC............ Foreign Correspondents Club of Japan (NTCM)
FCC............ Forms Control Center (OICC)
FCC............ Fort Churchill [*Manitoba*] [*Seismograph station code, US Geological Survey*] (SEIS)
FCC............ Foundation for a Christian Civilization (EA)
FCC............ Foundation for Community Creativity (EA)
FCC............ Fracture, Compound and Comminuted [*Orthopedics*] (DAVI)
FCC............ Frame Check Character (NITA)
FCC............ Free Church Council [*British*] (DAS)
FCC............ French Chamber of Commerce (DCTA)
FCC............ Frequency-to-Current Converter (IAA)
FCC............ Fuel Cell Catalyst
FCC............ Fuel Control Computer
FCC............ Fuels Control Center (AFIT)
FCC............ Fully Cellular Containership (DS)
FCC............ Fund Control Code
FCC............ Future Characteristics Change [*Military*] (CAAL)
FCCA......... Farmers Chinchilla Cooperative of America [*Later, ECBC*] (EA)
FCCA......... Federal Court Clerks Association (EA)
FCCA......... Fellow of the Association of Certified Accountants (DD)
FCCA......... Fleet Chief Caterer [*British military*] (DMA)
FCCA......... Floor Covering Contractors' Association [*British*] (BI)
FCCA......... Forestry, Conservation Communications Association (EA)
FCCA......... Four Cylinder Club of America
FCCB......... Field Change Control Board
FCCB......... Field Configuration Control Board [*Army*] (AABC)
FCCC......... Brazzaville [*Congo*] [*ICAO location identifier*] (ICLI)
FCCC......... Farm Credit Corp. Canada [*Ottawa, ON*]
FCCC......... Federal Complaint Coordinating Center [*US Office of Consumer Affairs*]
FCCC......... Federation Canadienne des Cine-Clubs [*Canada*]
FCCC......... Federation des Clubs Cooperatifs de Consommation [*Federation of Consumer Cooperative Associations*] [*Canada*]
FCCC......... Federation of Commonwealth Chambers of Commerce (BI)
FCCC......... Fire Control Control Console
FCCC......... Flight Coordination Control Central
FCCC......... Framework Convention on Climate Change (EERA)
FCCEA....... Fleet Chief Control Electrical Artificer [*British military*] (DMA)
FCCEd........ Fellow of the College of Craft Education [*British*] (DI)
FCCEL....... Fleet Chief Control Electrician [*British military*] (DMA)
FCCEMN ..... Fleet Chief Control Electrical Mechanician [*British military*] (DMA)
FCCFA....... Fraternite des Commis de Chemins de Fer, de Lignes Aeriennes, et de Navigation, Manutentionaires de Fret, Employes de Messageries et de Gares [*Brotherhood of Railway, Airline, and Steamship Clerks, Freight Handlers, Express and Station Employees*] [*Canada*]
FCCFF........ First Check Character Flip Flop [*Computer science*] (MHDI)
FCCI.......... Federal Clean Car Incentive Program [*Environmental Protection Agency*] (MCD)
FCCI.......... Fellowship of Companies for Christ International (EA)
FCCIA........ French Chamber of Commerce and Industry in Australia
FCCIM........ Federal Coordination Committee on Instrumentation and Measurement
FCCIP........ Federal Clean Car Incentive Program [*Environmental Protection Agency*]
FCCJ......... Foreign Correspondents' Club of Japan
FCCK......... Fire Control Check [*Military*] (NVT)
FCCK......... Fleet Chief Cook [*British military*] (DMA)
FCCM......... Facilities Capital Cost of Money (AAGC)
FCCN......... Federal Communications Commission Network
FCCO .... Fellow of the Canadian College of Organists
FCCO .... Flight Change Control Order
FCCOM....... Facilities Capital Cost of Money (AAGC)
FCCOP....... Fire Control Computer Operational Program (MCD)
FCCP......... Fellow of the American College of Chest Physicians
FCCP......... Fellow of the Canadian College of Physicians (DD)
FCCP......... Firm Contract Cost Proposal (NASA)
FCCP......... Friends Coordinating Committee on Peace [*Defunct*] (EA)
FCCPO .... Federal Contract Compliance Program Office [*Department of Labor*] (IEEE)

FCCS.......... Fellow of the Corporation of Certified Secretaries [*British*] (EY)
FCCS.......... Forces Correspondence Courses Scheme [*Military British*]
FCCSET....... Federal Coordinating Council for Science, Engineering, and Technology [*Pronounced "fix it"*] [*Office of Science and Technology Policy*]
FCCSS .... Fire Control Control Subsystem
FCCSSAT .... Federal Council on Computer Storage Standards and Technology [*General Services Administration*]
FCCST .... Federal Coordinating Council for Science and Technology
FCCT.......... Fellow of the Canadian College of Teachers
FCCT.......... Flight Controller Confidence Test (KSC)
FCCTS .... Federal COBOL [*Common Business-Oriented Language*] Compiler Testing Service [*National Institute of Standards and Technology*]
FCCU .... Fluid Catalytic Cracking Unit [*Fuel technology*]
FCCUI .... Fellow of the Canadian Credit Union Institute (DD)
FCCUS .... French Chamber of Commerce of the United States [*Later, French-American Chamber of Commerce*]
FCCV.......... Feline Control Council of Victoria [*Australia*]
FCCV.......... Future Close Combat Vehicle
FCCVP .... Future Close Combat Vehicle Program
FCCVS .... Future Close Combat Vehicle System (MCD)
FCCY.......... Fleet Chief Communication Yeoman [*British military*] (DMA)
f-cd-- .... Chad [*MARC geographic area code Library of Congress*] (LCCP)
FCD........... Failure Correction Decoding (IAA)
FCD........... Fecal Collection Device [*NASA*]
FCD........... Federal Consistency Determination [*Environmental application*]
FCD........... Femoral Cortical Density
FCD........... Fibrocystic Disease [*Medicine*] (DMAA)
FCD........... Field Control Division [*Military*] (LAIN)
FCD........... Fine Chemicals Directory (NITA)
FCD........... Fine Chemicals Directory Data Base [*Molecular Design Ltd.*] [*Information service or system*]
FCD........... Fine Control Damper [*Nuclear energy*] (NRCH)
FCD........... Fixed Center Drive
FCD........... Flight Control Division [*Johnson Space Center*] [*NASA*] (NASA)
FCD........... Flood Control District [*Florida*]
FCD........... Food Control Diet
FCD........... Formal Change Draft (SAA)
FCD........... Foundation for Child Development (EA)
FCD........... Four-Bar Cutter Device
FCD........... Frente Civico Democratico [*Civilian Democratic Front*] [*Guatemala*] [*Political party*] (PPW)
FCD........... Frequency Compression Demodulator
FCD........... Frequency Control Division (SAA)
FCD........... Front Congolais pour le Restauration de la Democratie [*Belgium Political party*] (EY)
FCD........... Front Congolais pour le Retablissement de la Democratie [*Zaire*] [*Political party*] (EY)
FCD........... Fuel Cells Display (SAA)
FCD........... Fuel Cut Defenser [*Automotive engineering*]
FCD........... Functional Configuration Documentation (AAGC)
FCD........... Functional Control Diagram (NRCH)
FCD........... Function Circuit Diagram
FCD........... Fuze Control Device (MCD)
FCDA .... Federal Civil Defense Administration [*Transferred to Office of Defense and Civilian Mobilization, 1958; to Department of Defense and Office of Emergency Preparedness, 1961*]
FCDA .... First Cavalry Division Association (EA)
FCDA .... Fuel Control Diaphragm Assembly
FC/DASA..... Field Command, Defense Atomic Support Agency
FCDB .... Fibrocystic Disease of the Breast [*Gynecology*] (DAVI)
FCDB .... Flight Control Data Bus (MCD)
FCDC .... Fire Control Data Converter (MCD)
FCDC .... Fixed Ceramic Disk Capacitor
FCDE .... Federation of Clothing Designers and Executives [*British*] (DBA)
FCDF .... Failure and Consumption Data Form (AAG)
FCDG .... Federal Civil Defense Guide
FCDivBad.... First Class Diver Badge [*Military decoration*] (AABC)
FCDL .... Forsyth County Defense League (EA)
FCDM .... Flow Control Decision Message (DA)
FCDN .... Ferrocarril de Nacozari [*AAR code*]
FCDNA .... Field Command, Defense Nuclear Agency [*DoD*]
FCDR .... Failure and Consumption Data Report (IAA)
FCDR .... Failure Cause Data Report
FCDSSA....... Fleet Combat Direction Systems Support Activity [*Navy*] (MCD)
FCDSSA/SD.. Fleet Combat Direction Systems Support Activity, San Diego [*California*] [*Navy*]
FCDSTC .... Fleet Combat Direction System Training Center [*Navy*] (CAAL)
FCDSTCL ..... Fleet Combat Direction System Training Center, Atlantic [*Navy*] (MCD)
FCDSTCLANT... Fleet Combat Direction System Training Center, Atlantic [*Navy*] (DNAB)
FCDSTCP ..... Fleet Combat Direction System Training Center, Pacific [*Navy*] (DNAB)
FCDSTCPAC... Fleet Combat Direction System Training Center, Pacific [*Navy*] (DNAB)
FCDT .... Four-Coil Differential Transformer
FCDU .... Foreign Currency Deposit Units
FCE............ Facilities Capital Employed [*DoD*]
FCE............ Factory Checkout Equipment (MCD)
FCE............ Federation Canadienne des Echecs [*Chess Federation of Canada*]
FCE............ Federation Canadienne des Enseignants [*Canadian Teachers' Federation - CTF*]
FCE............ Federation Canadienne des Etudiants [*Canadian Federation of Students*]

FCE............	Field Checkout Equipment
FCE............	Fire Control Electronics (MCD)
FCE............	Fire Control Element (MCD)
FCE............	Fire Control Equipment
FCE............	First Certificate in English [Cambridge University] [British] (AIE)
FCE............	Fleet Civil Engineer
FCE............	Flexible Critical Experiment
FCE............	Flight Control Electronics
FCE............	Flight Control Equipment [NASA] (NASA)
FCE............	Flight Crew Equipment [NASA] (NASA)
FCE............	Fluorouracil, Cisplatin, Etoposide [Antineoplastic drug] (CDI)
FCE............	Foreign Currency Exchange (MHDW)
FCE............	Forest City Enterprises, Inc. [AMEX symbol] (SPSG)
FCE............	Forward Command Element (DOMA)
FCE............	Foundation for Character Education (EA)
FCE............	Foundation for Credit Education [Nazareth, PA] (EA)
FCE............	Frequency Converter Excitation
FCE............	Friends Council on Education (EA)
FCE............	Functional Capacities Evaluation [Test] [Occupational therapy]
FCEA..........	Fellow of the Association of Cost and Executive Accountants [British] (DBQ)
FCEA..........	Fleet Chief Electrical Artificer [British military] (DMA)
FCE & T......	Field Concept Evolution and Trials [Army]
FCEC..........	Federation of Civil Engineering Contractors [British] (BI)
FCEC..........	Fire Control Engagement Controller [Military] (CAAL)
FCEE..........	Federation Canadienne des Etudiantes et Etudiants (AC)
FCEF..........	Flight Crew Equipment Facility [NASA] (NASA)
FCEH..........	Federation Canadienne des Etudes Humaines [Canadian Federation for the Humanities - CFH]
FCEI..........	Facility Contract End Item
FCEL(A)	Fleet Chief Electrician (Air) [British military] (DMA)
FCEL(AW)...	Fleet Chief Electrician (Air Weapon) [British military] (DMA)
Fcelftr.........	Facelifters Home Systems, Inc. [Associated Press] (SAG)
FCELMN(A)..	Fleet Chief Electrical Mechanician (Air) [British military] (DMA)
FCELMN(AW)...	Fleet Chief Electrical Mechanician (Air Weapon) [British military] (DMA)
FCEM..........	Femmes Chefs d'Entreprises Mondiales [World Association of Women Entrepreneurs] (EAIO)
FCEM..........	Flow Control Execution Message (DA)
FCENA........	Food Court Entertainment Network, Inc. [NASDAQ symbol] (SAG)
FCENA........	Food Court Entmt Network'A' [NASDAQ symbol] (TTSB)
FCENU........	Food Court Entertain Unit [NASDAQ symbol] (TTSB)
FCENW........	Food Court Enter Wrrt 'A' [NASDAQ symbol] (TTSB)
FCENZ........	Food Court Enter Wrrt 'B' [NASDAQ symbol] (TTSB)
FCEPC........	Flight Control Electrical Package Container
FCER..........	Foundation for Chiropractic Education and Research (EA)
FCES..........	Flight Control Electronic Set (MCD)
FCES..........	Flight Controls Electronics System (MCD)
FCESR	Frequency Converter Excitation, Saturable Reactor (IAA)
FCEU..........	Fire Control Electronics Unit [Military] (RDA)
FCEU..........	Flight Control Electronics Unit
f-cf--	Congo [MARC geographic area code Library of Congress] (LCCP)
FCF............	Facility Capital Funds (AAG)
FCF............	Faculty Christian Fellowship [National Council of Churches] (AEBS)
FCF............	Family Camping Federation [Later, FCFA] (EA)
FCF............	Feline and Canine Friends (EA)
FCF............	Fellowship of Christian Firefighters, International (EA)
FCF............	First Captive Flight [NASA] (NASA)
FCF............	First Commonwealth Finl [NYSE symbol] (TTSB)
FCF............	Fishermen's Compensation Fund [National Oceanic and Atmospheric Administration]
FCF............	Flag Correlation Facility (MCD)
FCF............	Flight Critical Forward (NASA)
FCF............	Footwear Components Federation [British] (DBA)
FCF............	For Colouring of Food [British]
FCF............	Free Cash Flow [Finance] (PDAA)
FCF............	Free China Fund for Medical and Refugee Aid
FCF............	Frequency Compressive Feedback
FCF............	Fuel Cycle Facility [Nuclear energy]
FCF............	Functional Check Flight [Air Force] (AFM)
FCFA..........	Family Camping Federation of America [Formerly, FCF] [Defunct] (EA)
FCFA..........	Florida Commercial Fisheries Association (EA)
FCFC..........	Film Council Film Circuit [Library network]
FCFC..........	Firstcity Financial [NASDAQ symbol] (TTSB)
FCFC..........	First City Financial Corp. [NASDAQ symbol] (SAG)
FCFC..........	Free Church Federal Council
FCFC..........	Full-Coverage Film Cooling
FCFCP........	Firstcity Finl 'B' Pfd [NASDAQ symbol] (TTSB)
FCFD..........	Fluorescence Capillary Fill Device [Instrumentation]
FCFDU........	Federation Canadienne des Femmes Diplomees des Universites [Canadian Federation of University Women]
FCFI..........	Fellow of the Clothing and Footwear Institute [British] (DI)
FCFK..........	Fondation Canadienne de la Fibrose Kystique [Canadian Cystic Fibrosis Foundation]
FCFM..........	Flight Combustion Facility Monitor (MCD)
FCFO..........	Full Cycling File Organization
FCFP..........	Fellow of the College of Family Physicians (DD)
FCFS..........	First Come, First Served [Computer science]
FCFS..........	Frequency Coded Firing System (MCD)
FCF SE.......	Facility Checking Flight - Service Evaluation [Air Force] (MCD)
FCFT..........	Fixed Cost, Fixed Time (IEEE)
f-cg--	Congo (Kinshasa) [Zaire] [MARC geographic area code Library of Congress] (LCCP)
FCG............	Facility Change Group (KSC)

FCG............	Facing
FCG............	Falconbridge Gold Corp. [Toronto Stock Exchange symbol]
FCG............	Fatigue Crack Growth [Metals] (PDAA)
FCG............	Federal Coordinator for Geology [Marine science] (OSRA)
FCG............	Federal Coordinator for Geology (USDC)
FCG............	Federation for Constitutional Government [Defunct] (EA)
FCG............	Fernwood, Columbia & Gulf R. R. [AAR code]
FCG............	Field Coordination Group
FCG............	Fire Control Group
FCG............	First Communications Group, Inc. [Coral Gables, FL] (TSSD)
FCG............	Fleet Composite Group [Navy] (CAAL)
FCG............	Flight Control Group (MCD)
FCG............	Foreign Clearance Guide (AFM)
FCG............	Fragmenta Comicorum Graecorum [A publication] (OCD)
FCG............	French Catheter Gauge (MAE)
FCG............	Friction Cam Gear
FCG............	Fuel Contents Gauge (MSA)
FCG............	Fund for Constitutional Government (EA)
FCGA..........	Facility Gauge (AAG)
FCGA..........	Fellow of the Canadian Certified General Accountants Association (DD)
FCGC..........	Flight Control Gyro Container
FCGCMA	Federation of Cash Grain Commission Merchants Associations [Defunct] (EA)
FCgDH........	Doctors Hospital, Medical Library, Coral Gables, FL [Library symbol Library of Congress] (LCLS)
FCGES........	Flight Control Group Electronic System (SAA)
FCGI..........	Fellow of the City and Guilds of London Institute [British] (ROG)
FCGM..........	Frammenti della Commedia Greca e del Mimo nella Sicilia e nella Magna Grecia [A publication] (OCD)
FCgM..........	United States Department of Commerce, National Oceanic and Atmospheric Administration, Miami Branch Library, Coral Gables, FL [Library symbol Library of Congress] (LCLS)
FCGP..........	Fellow of the College of General Practitioners
FCGPC	Flight Control Gyro Package Container
FCGR..........	Fatigue Crack Growth Rate [Metals]
FCGRS	Federation Canadienne de Gymnastique Rythmique Sportive [Canadian Modern Rhythmic Gymnastics Federation - CMRGF]
FCGS	Freight Classification Guide System
FCH............	Familial Combined Hyperlipidemia [Cardiology] (DAVI)
FCH............	Family Care Home (HCT)
FCH............	Federal Cataloging Handbook
FCH............	FelCor Suite Hotels [NYSE symbol] (TTSB)
FCH............	FelCor Suite Hotels, Inc. [NYSE symbol] (SAG)
FCH............	Fellow of the Coopers Hill College [British]
FCh............	Field Champion [Dog show term]
FCH............	Film Carrousel Handle
FCH............	Fircrest Resources [Vancouver Stock Exchange symbol]
FCH............	Flight-Chernobyl Association [Russian Federation] [ICAO designator] (FAAC)
FCH............	Flight Controllers Handbook
FCH............	Foundation for Cooperative Housing [Later, CHF]
FCH............	Fourier Color Hologram
FCH............	Fresno, CA [Location identifier FAA] (FAAL)
FCHC..........	Fellow of Catherine Hall, Cambridge [British] (ROG)
FCHC..........	Newberry Library Family and Community History Center [Research center] (RCD)
FCHCA	Foreign Car Haters Club of America (EA)
FChemSoc ...	Fellow of the Chemical Society [British]
FCHG..........	Formal Change (MCD)
FCHGD	Feminist Center for Human Growth and Development (EA)
FChH...........	Florida State Hospital, Chattahoochee, FL [Library symbol Library of Congress] (LCLS)
FChiNBD	First Chicago NBD Corp. [Associated Press] (SAG)
FCHL...........	Familial Combined Hyperlipidaemia [Medicine]
FCHL...........	Flight Control Hydraulics Laboratory [NASA] (NASA)
FCHO..........	Federation Canadienne de Handball Olympique [Canadian Team Handball Federation - CTHF]
FCHP..........	Feedback Controlled Heat Pipes (MCD)
FCHPrA	FelCor Suite Hotels $1.95 Pfd [NYSE symbol] (TTSB)
FCHR..........	Functional Cost Hour Report (MCD)
FChS..........	Fellow of the Society of Chiropodists [British]
Fchse..........	Franchise
FCI............	Defense Foreign Counterintelligence [Program] [DoD]
FCI............	Family Communications, Inc. [Public television] (NTCM)
FCI............	Fan Circle International (EA)
FCI............	Fashion Coordination Institute [Defunct] (EA)
FCI............	Fast Coastal Interceptor [US Coast Guard vessel]
FCI............	Federal Correctional Institution (WDAA)
FCI............	Federal Crime Insurance
FCI............	Federal Crop Insurance
FCI............	Federation Colombophile Internationale [International Pigeon Federation - IPF] (EAIO)
FCI............	Federation Cynologique Internationale [International Federation of Kennel Clubs] [Thuin, Belgium] (EA)
FCI............	Fellow of the Canadian Credit Institute
FCI............	Fellow of the Institute of Commerce [British]
FCI............	Fire Control Instruments (MCD)
FCI............	First China Investment Corp. [Vancouver Stock Exchange symbol]
FCI............	First Communications, Inc. [Atlanta, GA] (TSSD)
FCI............	Flight Combat Instructor
FCI............	Flight Command Indicator (MCD)
FCI............	Flight Control Indicator (MCD)
FCI............	Flight Control Integration [Apollo] [NASA]
FCI............	Flight Critical Items (MCD)

FCI.............. Florida Computer, Inc. [*Information service or system*] (IID)
FCI.............. Fluid Conductivity Indicator
FCI.............. Fluid Controls Institute (EA)
FCI.............. Flux Changes per Inch [*Computer science*]
FCI.............. Folklore Canada International [*An association*] (EAIO)
FCI.............. Foreign Counterintelligence
FCI.............. Framatome Connectors International [*Commercial firm*] (ECON)
FCI.............. Franklin College of Indiana
FCI.............. Fraud Control Institute [*Communications Fraud Control Association*] (TSSD)
FCI.............. Freedom Communications International News Agency (EAIO)
FCI.............. Fuel Coolant Interaction [*Nuclear energy*] (NRCH)
FCI.............. Full Configuration-Interaction [*Quantum chemistry*] (MCD)
FCI.............. Functional Capacity Index [*NHTSA*] (TAG)
FCI.............. Functional Configuration Identification (KSC)
FCI.............. International Federation of Kennel Clubs [*Belgium*] (EAIO)
FCIA............ Federal Courts Improvement Act (AAGC)
FCIA............ Federal Criminal Investigators Association (EA)
FCIA............ Fellow of the Canadian Institute of Actuaries
FCIA............ Fellow of the Corporation of Insurance Agents [*British*]
FCIA............ Foreign Credit Insurance Association [*New York, NY*] (EA)
FCIA............ Franchise Consultants International Association (EA)
FCIA............ Friends of Cast Iron Architecture (EA)
FCIArb......... Fellow of the Chartered Institute of Arbitrators [*British*] (DBQ)
FCIB............ Fellow of the Chartered Institute of Bankers (DD)
FCIB............ Fellow of the Confederation of Insurance Brokers of Australia
FCIB............ Fellow of the Corporation of Insurance Brokers [*British*]
FCIB............ Foreign Credit Interchange Bureau (EA)
FCIBS.......... Fellow of the Chartered Institution of Building Services [*British*] (DBQ)
FCIC............ Fairchild Camera & Instrument Corp. (MCD)
FCIC............ Federal Crop Insurance Corp. [*Department of Agriculture*]
FCIC............ Fellow of the Canadian Institute of Chemistry (DD)
FCIC............ Fellow of the Chemical Institute of Canada
FCIC............ Foreign Credit Insurance Corp. [*Business term*]
FCICA.......... Floor Covering Installation Contractors Association (EA)
FCID............ Federal Court Industrial Division [*Australia*]
FCIF............ Flight Crew Information File (AFM)
FCIF............ Full Common Intermediate Format (ACRL)
FCIG............ Field Change Identification Guide (IAA)
FCII............ Federated Council of Israel Institutions (EA)
FCII............ Fellow of the Chartered Insurance Institute [*British*] (EY)
FCII............ Fibercorp Intl. [*NASDAQ symbol*] (TTSB)
FCIL............ Finance Corp. for Industry Ltd. [*British*]
FCILA.......... Fellow of the Chartered Institute of Loss Adjusters [*British*] (DBQ)
FCIM........... Farm, Construction, and Industrial Machinery (PDAA)
FCIM........... Federation des Concours Internationaux de Musique [*Federation of International Music Competitions - FIMC*] (EAIO)
FCIM........... Fellow of the Chartered Institute of Marketing (DD)
FCIM........... Fellow of the Chartered Institute of Marketing [*British*] (ODBW)
FCIM........... Flexible Computer-Integrated Manufacturing Program [*Army*] (RDA)
FCIM........... Flight Control Interface Module (MCD)
FCIN............ Fast Carry Iterative Network (IAA)
FCIN............ Fast Carry-Propagation Iterative Network (PDAA)
FCIN............ Frankfort & Cincinnati Railroad Co. [*AAR code*]
FCIOB.......... Fellow of the Chartered Institute of Building [*British*] (DBQ)
FCIP............ Federal Crime Insurance Program (WDAA)
FCIP............ Federal Crop Insurance Program (GNE)
FCIP............ Field Cable Installation Platoon [*Army*] (AABC)
FCIP............ Flight Cargo Implementation Plan (MCD)
FCIP............ Foreign Counterintelligence Program [*DoD*]
FCIPA.......... Fellow of the Chartered Institute of Patent Agents [*British*]
FCIR............ Facility Chance Initiation Request (AAGC)
FCIR............ Facility Change Initiation Request
F-CIR.......... Failure and Consumption Inspector's Report (AAG)
FCIS............ Fellow of the Chartered Institute of Secretaries [*British*] (ROG)
FCIS............ Fellow of the Institute of Chartered Secretaries and Administrators (DD)
FCIS............ Force Cost Information System (MCD)
FCIS............ Foreign Counterintelligence System [*Federal Bureau of Investigation*]
FCIT............ Fellow of the Chartered Institute of Transport [*British*]
FCIT............ First Citizens Financial Corp. [*NASDAQ symbol*] (NQ)
FCIT............ First Citizens Finl [*NASDAQ symbol*] (TTSB)
FCIU............ Family Crisis Intervention Unit [*New York Police Department*]
FCJ.............. Federal Court Judgements [*Canada Department of Justice*] [*Information service or system*] (CRD)
FCJ.............. Foreign Criminal Jurisdiction (AABC)
FCJ.............. La Fondation Canadienne de la Jeunesse (AC)
FCJ.............. Society of the Sisters, Faithful Companions of Jesus [*Roman Catholic religious order*]
FCK.............. Field Change Kit
FCK.............. Filter Change Kit
FCK.............. Fuel Charge Kit
FCl.............. Clearwater Public Library, Clearwater, FL [*Library symbol Library of Congress*] (LCLS)
FCL.............. Facility [*Security*] Clearance
FCL.............. Farriers Co. of London [*British*] (DI)
FCL.............. Feedback Control Loop [*Computer science*] (BUR)
FCL.............. Feeder Control Logic [*Computer science*] (IAA)
FCL.............. Film Capability Laboratories [*Bell System*]
FCL.............. Final Coordination Line [*Military*]
FCL.............. Fire Coordination Line [*Military*] (AABC)
FCL.............. First Colony [*NYSE symbol*] (SPSG)
FCL.............. Fleet Control List [*Navy*] (AFIT)
FCL.............. Flight Control Laboratory
FCL.............. Flightcrew Licensing (DA)
F-CL............ Fluorouracil, Leucovorin Calcium [*Antineoplastic drug*] (CDI)
FCL.............. Flux Current Loop
FCL.............. Foreign Currency Loan
FCL.............. Format Control Language
FCL.............. Fort Collins, CO [*Location identifier FAA*] (FAAL)
FCL.............. Foundation for Christian Living (EA)
FCL.............. Freon Coolant Line [*NASA*] (NASA)
FCL.............. Freon Coolant Loop [*Space shuttle*] [*NASA*]
FCL.............. Frick Chemical Laboratory (KSC)
FCL.............. Fuel Cell (KSC)
FCL.............. Full Container Load [*Shipping*]
FCL.............. Full Cycle Left (SAA)
FCL.............. Functional Capabilities List [*Computer science*] (MHDB)
FCL.............. Fuze Cavity Liner [*Projectile*] (NG)
FCL.............. Sarbah's Fanti Customary Laws [*Ghana*] [*A publication*] (DLA)
FCLA............ Family Centered Learning Alternatives (EA)
FCLA............ Florida Center for Library Automation [*Florida State University System*] [*Information service or system*] (IID)
FCLAA.......... Federal Coal Leasing Amendments Act [*1976*]
FCLAVP........ Flammable and Combustible Liquids Appeal and Variations Panel [*Queensland, Australia*]
FClCC........... Clearwater Christian College, Clearwater, FL [*Library symbol*] [*Library of Congress*] (LCLS)
FCLD............ Foundation for Children with Learning Disabilities [*Later, NCLD*] (EA)
FCLE............ Forecastle Deck (IAA)
FCLI............. Fordham University School of Law, Corporate Law Institute (DLA)
FClM............ Morton F. Plant Hospital, Clearwater, FL [*Library symbol Library of Congress*] (LCLS)
FC/LOS........ Fire Control, Line-of-Sight
FCLP............ Field Carrier Landing Passes [*or Practice*]
FCLR............ First Commercial Corp. [*NASDAQ symbol*] (NQ)
FCLT............ Freeze Calculated Landing Time [*FAA*] (TAG)
FCLTY.......... Facility (AFM)
FCLTY.......... Faculty
FCLTYCHECKINGSq... Facility Checking Squadron [*Air Force*]
fcly.............. Face Lying [*Medicine*] (DMAA)
f-cm--.......... Cameroon [*MARC geographic area code Library of Congress*] (LCCP)
FCM............. Faculty of Community Medicine [*British*]
FCM............. Fan Control Module [*Automotive engineering*]
FCM............. Farrier Corporal-Major [*British military*] (DMA)
FCM............. Fat-Corrected Milk
FCM............. Fault Control Management [*Automotive diagnostics*]
FCM............. Fault Control Module (TEL)
FCM............. FCMI Financial Corp. [*Toronto Stock Exchange symbol*]
FCM............. Federal Class Manager (AFIT)
FCM............. Federation Canadienne des Municipalites [*Federation of Canadian Municipalities*]
FCM............. Federation of Canadian Municipalities
FCM............. Fellowship of Christian Magicians (EA)
FCM............. Fellowship of Christian Motorcyclists [*Welwyn Garden City, England*] (EAIO)
FCM............. Fellowship of Christian Musicians (EA)
FCM............. Ferrocarril Mexicano [*AAR code*]
FCM............. Fiber Composite Material
FCM............. Filament Composite Material
FCM............. Firmware Control Memory
FCM............. First-Class Mail [*Postal Service*]
FCM............. Flight Combustion Monitor [*NASA*] (KSC)
FCM............. Florida Agricultural and Mechanical University, Tallahassee, FL [*OCLC symbol*] (OCLC)
FCM............. Florida Citrus Mutual (EA)
FCM............. Flow Cytometry [*Analytical biochemistry*]
FCM............. Flying Cargo Private Ltd. [*Maldives*] [*ICAO designator*] (FAAC)
FCM............. Food, Clothing, Maintenance [*Red Cross*]
FCM............. Forged Chrom-Moly
FCM............. Framing Camera Mopper
FCM............. Friends of Cathedral Music (EA)
FCM............. Fuel Cell Module
FCM............. Fund for a Conservative Majority (EA)
FCM............. Futures Commission Merchant
FCM............. Fuzzy Cognitive Map [*Logic*]
FCM............. Minneapolis, MN [*Location identifier FAA*] (FAAL)
FCMA........... Fellow of the Institute of Cost and Management Accountants [*British*]
FCMA........... Fellow of the Society of Management Accountants of Canada (DD)
FCMA........... Fibre Cement Manufacturers Association [*British*] (DBA)
FCMA........... Field Cashier Military Accounts [*British military*] (DMA)
FCMA........... Fishery Conservation and Management Act [*1976*] [*Also, MFCMA*]
FCMA........... Fleet Chief Medical Assistant [*British military*] (DMA)
FCMA........... Flushing Cistern Makers' Association [*British*] (BI)
FCMA........... Mavinza [*Congo*] [*ICAO location identifier*] (ICLI)
FCMAREP.... Federal Coordinator for Marine Environmental Prediction (USDC)
FCMAREP.... Federal Coordinator for Marine Environmental Prediction [*Marine science*] (OSRA)
FCMB........... First City Merchant Bank Ltd.
FCMB........... N'Ziba [*Congo*] [*ICAO location identifier*] (ICLI)
FCMC........... Family-Centered Maternity Care [*Obstetrics*] (DAVI)
FCMC........... Fellow of the Institute of Certified Management Consultants (DD)
FCmcBA....... First Commerce Bancshares, Inc. [*Associated Press*] (SAG)
FCmcBB....... First Commerce Bancshares [*Associated Press*] (SAG)
FCmcC......... First Commerce Corp. [*Associated Press*] (SAG)
FCmclCp...... First Commericial Corp. [*Associated Press*] (SAG)
FCMD........... Fire Command (KSC)
FCMD........... Fukuyama Type Congenital Muscular Dystrophy [*Medicine*] (DMAA)

FCMD	Vouka/Sidetra [Congo] [ICAO location identifier] (ICLI)
FCME	First Coastal Corp. [NASDAQ symbol] (SAG)
FCMEA	Fleet Chief Marine Engineering Artificer [British military] (DMA)
FCMEM	Fleet Chief Marine Engineering Mechanic [British military] (DMA)
FCMF	Loufoula [Congo] [ICAO location identifier] (ICLI)
FCMG	Gokango [Congo] [ICAO location identifier] (ICLI)
FCMI	Federation of Coated Macadam Industries [British] (BI)
FCMI	Fuel Cladding Mechanical Interaction [Nuclear energy] (NUCP)
FCMI	Irogo [Congo] [ICAO location identifier] (ICLI)
FCMidE	Foreign & Colonial Emerging Middle East Fund, Inc. [Associated Press] (SAG)
FCMK	Kele/Kibangou [Congo] [ICAO location identifier] (ICLI)
FCML	Leboulou [Congo] [ICAO location identifier] (ICLI)
FCmlBcp	First Commercial Bancorp, Inc. [Associated Press] (SAG)
FCMM	Federation Canadienne des Maires et des Municipalites [Canadian Federation of Mayors and Municipalities]
FCMM	Flux Changes per Millimeter [Computer science] (IAA)
FCMM	Mossendjo [Congo] [ICAO location identifier] (ICLI)
FCMN	Family-Centered Maternity Nursing [Obstetrics] (DAVI)
FCMN	N'Gongo [Congo] [ICAO location identifier] (ICLI)
FCMO	Vouka/Mandoro [Congo] [ICAO location identifier] (ICLI)
FCMPU	Female Cigar Makers' Protective Union [British]
FCMR	Marala [Congo] [ICAO location identifier] (ICLI)
FCMS	Facilities Computer Monitoring System [Johnson Controls, Inc.]
FCMS	Fellow of the College of Medicine and Surgery [British]
F/CMS	Financial/Cost Management System (MCD)
FCMS	Flight Crew Mission Simulator [NASA] (KSC)
FCMS	Force Capability Management System [Military]
FCMS	Functional Configuration Management [Air Force] (GFGA)
FCMS	Nyanga [Congo] [ICAO location identifier] (ICLI)
FCMS & SR	Federal Committee for Meteorological Services and Supporting Research
FCMSBR	Federal Coal Mine Safety Board of Review [Independent government agency] [Inactive, 1970]
FCMSSR	Federal Coordinator for Meteorological Services and Supporting Research [Marine science] (OSRA)
FCMSSR	Federal Coordinator for Meteorological Services and Supporting Research (USDC)
FCMT	Bekol/Thomas [Congo] [ICAO location identifier] (ICLI)
FCMT	Fleet Chief Medical Technician [British military] (DMA)
FCMT	Flight Configuration Mode Test [Gemini] [NASA]
FCMU	Foot-Controlled Maneuvering Unit [Skylab] [NASA]
FCMV	Fuel Consuming Motor Vehicle
FCMW	Foundation for Child Mental Welfare (EA)
FCmwF	First Commonwealth Fund, Inc. [Associated Press] (SAG)
FCMY	Mayoko/Legala [Congo] [ICAO location identifier] (ICLI)
FCMZ	N'Zabi [Congo] [ICAO location identifier] (ICLI)
FCN	Falcon Aviation AB [Sweden ICAO designator] (FAAC)
FCN	FC Financial Corp. [Vancouver Stock Exchange symbol]
FCN	Federal Catalog Number
FCN	Field Change Notification (KSC)
FCN	Fire Control Notes [A publication]
FCN	First Chicago NBD [NYSE symbol] (TTSB)
FCN	First Chicago NBD Corp. [NYSE symbol] (SAG)
FCN	Frijoles Canyon [New Mexico] [Seismograph station code, US Geological Survey Closed] (SEIS)
FCN	Function (NASA)
FCN	Treaty of Friendship, Commerce, and Navigation [Indonesia] (IMH)
FCNA	Florida Citrus Nurserymen's Association (EA)
FCNB	FCNB Corp. [NASDAQ symbol] (SAG)
FCNC	First Citizens Bancshares, Inc. [NASDAQ symbol] (NQ)
FCNC	Flavor-Changing Neutral Currents
FCNCA	First Citizens BancShares 'A' [NASDAQ symbol] (TTSB)
FCNI	Flux Controlled Negative Inductance (IAA)
FCNL	French Committee of National Liberation [World War II]
FCNL	Frequently-Called-Numbers List [Bell System]
FCNL	Friends Committee on National Legislation (EA)
FCNP	Fire Control Navigation Panel (IEEE)
FCNPC	Film Culture Non-Profit Corp. (EA)
FCNPrB	First Chi NBD Adj Div B Pfd [NYSE symbol] (TTSB)
FCNPrC	First Chi NBD Adj Div C Pfd [NYSE symbol] (TTSB)
FCNPrE	First Chi NBD 8.45% Dep Pfd [NYSE symbol] (TTSB)
FCNPrU	First Chi NBD 7.5%PfdPurUnits [NYSE symbol] (TTSB)
FCNPrV	First Chi NBD 5 3/4% Cv Dep Pfd [NYSE symbol] (TTSB)
FCNS	Fairchild Communications Networks & Services Co. [Chantilly, VA] [Later, FCS] [Telecommunications service] (TSSD)
FCNSI	Federation Canadienne Nationale des Syndicats Independants [Canadian National Federation of Independent Unions - CNFIU]
FCNSW	Forestry Commission of New South Wales [State] (EERA)
FCNTL	Function Timeline
FCO	Aerofrisco [Mexico ICAO designator] (FAAC)
FCO	Cleanout Flush with Finished Floor
fco	Cutoff Frequency (IDOE)
FCO	Facility Change Order (AAG)
FCO	Facility Coordination Officer (FAAC)
FCO	Fair Copy
FCO	Federal Coordinating Officer [Federal disaster planning]
FCO	Fellow of the College of Organists [British] (ROG)
FCO	Fellow of the College of Osteopathy [British]
FCO	Field Change Order
F Co	Field Company [British military] (DMA)
FCO	Field Contracting Office (MCD)
FCO	Files Control Office
FCO	Final Checkout (MCD)
FCO	Fire Control Operator [Army]

FCO	First Commonwealth Fund [NYSE symbol] (TTSB)
FCO	First Commonwealth Fund, Inc. [NYSE symbol] (SPSG)
FCO	Fixed Cycle Operation
FCO	Flag Communications Officer [Navy]
FCO	Fleet Communications Officer [Navy British]
FCO	Flight Clearance Office
FCO	Flight Communications Operator
FCO	Flight Crew Operations [NASA]
FCO	Flying Control Officer [Navy]
FCO	Foreign and Commonwealth Office [British]
FCO	Forms Control Officer (GFGA)
FCO	Franco [Free of Charge] [Shipping] [Spanish]
fco	Franco [Free of Charge] [Shipping] [French]
FCO	Franco [Free of Charge] [Shipping] [Italian]
FCO	Frequency Control Officer (MUGU)
FCO	Functional Checkout
FCO	Rome [Italy] Leonardo Da Vinci (Fium) Airport [Airport symbol] (OAG)
FCoa	Cocoa Public Library, Cocoa, FL [Library symbol Library of Congress] (LCLS)
FCOA	Federation of Chinese Organizations in America (EA)
FCOA	Foremost Corp. of America [NASDAQ symbol] (NQ)
FCoaB	Brevard Community College, Cocoa, FL [Library symbol Library of Congress] (LCLS)
FCOAC	Furnish Copies of Orders to Appropriate Commanders
FCOB	Boundji [Congo] [ICAO location identifier] (ICLI)
FCOB	First Commercial Bancorp [NASDAQ symbol] (NQ)
FCOB	First Comml Bancorp, Inc. [NASDAQ symbol] (TTSB)
FCOB	Flight Control Operations Branch [NASA] (MCD)
FCOD	Flight Crew Operations Directorate [NASA] (KSC)
FCOE	Ewo [Congo] [ICAO location identifier] (ICLI)
FCOEA	Fleet Chief Ordnance Electrical Artificer [British military] (DMA)
FCOEL	Fleet Chief Ordnance Electrician [British military] (DMA)
FCOEMN	Fleet Chief Ordnance Electrical Mechanician [British military] (DMA)
FCOG	Fellow of the British College of Obstetricians and Gynaecologists (DAS)
FCOG	Fellow of the College of Obstetricians and Gynecologists
FCOG	Fondation Canadienne d'Orientation et de Consultation (AC)
FCOG	Gamboma [Congo] [ICAO location identifier] (ICLI)
FCOH	Flight Controllers Operations Handbook [NASA] (KSC)
FCOI	Fire Control Optical Instrument
FCOI	Impfondo [Congo] [ICAO location identifier] (ICLI)
FCOJ	Frozen Concentrated Orange Juice
FCOK	Kelle [Congo] [ICAO location identifier] (ICLI)
FCOL	Loukolela [Congo] [ICAO location identifier] (ICLI)
FColnGp	First Colonial Group [Associated Press] (SAG)
FColony	First Colony Corp. [Associated Press] (SAG)
FCOM	First Commerce [NASDAQ symbol] (TTSB)
FCOM	First Commerce Corp. [NASDAQ symbol] (NQ)
FCOM	Flight Crew Operating Manual (MCD)
FCOM	Makoua [Congo] [ICAO location identifier] (ICLI)
FComceC	First Commerce Corp. [Associated Press] (SAG)
F Comm	Full Commission
FCommA	Fellow of Commercial Actuaries (DD)
FCOMP	Federal Coordinator for Ocean Mapping and Prediction (USDC)
FCOMP	First Commerce 7.25% Cv Pfd '92 [NASDAQ symbol] (TTSB)
FCOO	Owando [Congo] [ICAO location identifier] (ICLI)
FCOS	Farm Cash Operating Surplus
FCoS	Fetal Cord Serum [Gynecology]
FCOS	Flight Computer Operating System [NASA] (NASA)
FCOS	Flight Control Operating System [NASA] (NASA)
FCOS	Flight Control Operational Software (MCD)
FCOS	Souanke [Congo] [ICAO location identifier] (ICLI)
FCOSA	Fellow of the Chartered Institute of Secretaries and Administrators [Australia] (ODBW)
FCOT	Betou [Congo] [ICAO location identifier] (ICLI)
FCO-T	Flight Communications Operator in Training
FCOU	Ouesso [Congo] [ICAO location identifier] (ICLI)
FCOV	Facility Checkout Vehicle [NASA] (KSC)
F/COV	Floor Covering (ADA)
FCP	Failure Correction Panel (NASA)
FCP	Falcon Products [NYSE symbol] (TTSB)
FCP	Falcon Products, Inc. [NYSE symbol] (SAG)
FCP	Falls City Press, Louisville, KY [Library symbol Library of Congress] (LCLS)
FCP	Family Care Program [Insurance] (WYGK)
FCP	Fasting Chemistry Profile (DAVI)
FCP	Fatigue Crack Propagation (OA)
FCP	Federal Cataloging Program
FCP	Federation of Calico Printers (DGA)
FCP	Feed Control Panel (IAA)
FCP	Fellow of the College of Physicians (DD)
FCP	Fellow of the College of Preceptors [British] (ROG)
FCP	Ferrocarril del Pacifico, SA de CV [AAR code]
FCP	Ferry Command Police [British military] (DMA)
FCP	Field Change Package [Nuclear energy] (NRCH)
FCP	Field Change Proposal
FCP	Field Command Post
FCP	File Control Package (NITA)
FCP	File Control Processor [Computer science] (BUR)
FCP	File Control Program [Computer science]
FCP	Final Common Pathway [Neurology]
FCP	Fire Control Panel (MCD)
FCP	Fire Control Personnel [Marine Corps]
FCP	Fire Control Platoon [Army]

FCP............ Firm Cost Proposal (NASA)
FCP............ First Calgary Petroleums Ltd. [Toronto Stock Exchange symbol]
FCP............ Fixed Code Processor
FCP............ Flat Concurrent PROLOG [Programming in Logic] [Language for fifth generation computer research] (NITA)
FCP............ Flight Control Panel (MCD)
FCP............ Flight Control Programmer
FCP............ Flight Corp. [New Zealand] [ICAO designator] (FAAC)
FCP............ Flight Correction Proposal (MCD)
FCP............ Florida Citrus Packers (EA)
FCP............ Fluid and Chemical Processing (SSD)
FCP............ Fluorouracil, Cyclophosphamide, Prednisone [Antineoplastic drug regimen]
FCP............ Foolscap [Paper]
FCP............ Ford Combustion Process [Automotive engineering]
FCP............ Foreign Corporation Project [IRS]
FCP............ Forward Command Post (NATG)
FCP............ Foundation for Creative Philosophy (EA)
FCP............ Foxboro Control Package (NITA)
FCP............ Fragmented Coronoid Process [Medicine]
FCP............ Fraud Control Plan
FCP............ Free Conducting Particle (PDAA)
FCP............ French Communist Party
FCP............ Frequency Control Panel (MCD)
FCP............ Friends of the Conservative Party [Defunct] (EA)
FCP............ Fuel Cell Power Plant
FCP............ Fuel Consumption Projection (SSD)
FCP............ Full Couterpoise Procedure [Physical chemistry]
FCP............ Functional Communication Profile
FCP............ Function Control Package [Computer science]
FCPA........... Fabricants Canadiens de Produits Alimentaires [Grocery Products Manufacturers of Canada - GPMC]
FCPA........... Fellow of the Canadian Psychological Association
FCPA........... Fellow of the Institute of Certified Public Accountants [British] (DAS)
FCPA........... Florida Citrus Processors Association (SRA)
FCPA........... Foreign Corrupt Practices Act [1977]
FCPA........... Makabana [Congo] [ICAO location identifier] (ICLI)
FCPAC .... Free Congress Political Action Committee (EA)
FC Path....... Fellow of the College of Pathologists [Later, Royal College of Pathologists] [British]
FCPB........... Bangamba [Congo] [ICAO location identifier] (ICLI)
FCPC........... Fair Campaign Practices Committee (EA)
FCPC........... Federal Committee on Pest Control
FCPC........... Fleet Computer Programming Center [Navy] (MUGU)
FCPC........... Flight Crew Plane Captain [Navy] (DNAB)
FCPCL......... Fleet Computer Programming Center, Atlantic [Navy]
FCPCLANT .... Fleet Computer Programming Center, Atlantic [Navy]
FCPCNA .... First Czechoslovak Philatelic Club of North America (EA)
FCPCP .... Fleet Computer Programming Center, Pacific [Navy]
FCPCPAC ..... Fleet Computer Programming Center, Pacific [Navy] (MCD)
FCPD........... Loudima [Congo] [ICAO location identifier] (ICLI)
FC/PDL .... Freight Classification Packaging Data List (AFIT)
FCPE........... [Naval] Force Capabilities Planning Effort (DOMA)
FCPE........... Leganda [Congo] [ICAO location identifier] (ICLI)
FCPG........... Federation of Catholic Physicians Guilds
FCPG .... Kibangou [Congo] [ICAO location identifier] (ICLI)
FCPI........... Flux Changes per Inch [Computer science]
FCPI........... Vounda/Loubetsi [Congo] [ICAO location identifier] (ICLI)
FCPK........... N'Komo [Congo] [ICAO location identifier] (ICLI)
FCPL........... Loubomo [Congo] [ICAO location identifier] (ICLI)
F/CPLG .... Fluid Coupling [Automotive engineering]
FC/PM......... Facility Control / Power Management (MHDB)
FCPM........... Fellow of the Confederation of Professional Management [British] (DBQ)
FCPM........... Free Cuba Patriotic Movement (EA)
FCPM........... M'Baya [Congo].[ICAO location identifier] (ICLI)
FCPN .... Noumbi [Congo] [ICAO location identifier] (ICLI)
FCPO .... Fellowship of Christian Peace Officers (EA)
FCPO .... First Class Post Office
FCPO .... Fleet Chief Petty Officer [Navy British]
FCPO .... Pemo [Congo] [ICAO location identifier] (ICLI)
FCPP........... Pointe-Noire [Congo] [ICAO location identifier] (ICLI)
FCPPS .... Fuel Cell Power Plant System (KSC)
FCPR .... Foreign Corrupt Practices Act (AAGC)
FCPRC .... Federal Cultural Policy Review Committee [Canada]
FCPS........... Fellow of the Cambridge Philological Society [British]
FCPS........... Fellow of the Cambridge Philosophical Society [British] (ROG)
FCPS........... Fellow of the College of Physicians and Surgeons [British]
FCPS........... Firewood Cutters' Protective Society [A union] [British]
FCPS........... FOSIC [Fleet Ocean Surveillance Information Center] Communications Processing Subsystem (MCD)
FCPS........... France and Colonies Philatelic Society (EA)
FCPS........... Fuel Cell Power System [or Subsystem]
FCP(SA)....... Fellow of the College of Physicians of South Africa
FCP(SoAf).... Fellow of the College of Physicians of South Africa
FCPSO (SoAf)... Fellow of the College of Physicians and Surgeons and Obstetricians of South Africa
FCPT.......... Fleet Chief Physical Trainer [British military] (DMA)
FCPU.......... Flexible Central Processing Unit [Computer science] (MHDB)
FCPY.......... Factory Card Outlet Corp. [NASDAQ symbol] (SAG)
FCPY.......... Loukanyi [Congo] [ICAO location identifier] (ICLI)
FCQAS .... Financial Compliance and Quality Assurance Staff [Environmental Protection Agency] (GFGA)
FCR............ Facility Capability Report [Military]
FCR............ Facility Capability Review

FCR............ Facility Change Request
FCR............ False Contact Rate (CAAL)
FCR............ Fan Control Relay [Automotive engineering]
FCR............ Farm Costs and Returns [A publication]
FCR............ Fast Ceramic Reactor [Program]
FCR............ Fast Conversion Ratio (NRCH)
FCR............ Fearne on Contingent Remainders [1722-1844] [A publication] (DLA)
FCR............ Federal Contracts Reports (AAGC)
FCR............ Federal Court Reports [Canada Department of Justice] [Information service or system] (CRD)
FCR............ Federal Court Rules [A publication]
FCR............ Fellowship of Christian Racers [Defunct] (EA)
FCR............ Field Change Request [Nuclear energy] (NRCH)
FCR............ Final Configuration Review (KSC)
FCR............ Fine Crushed Rock (ADA)
FCR............ Fire Controlman, Range-Finder Operator [Navy rating Obsolete]
FCR............ Fire Control RADAR
FCR............ Fixed Change Rate
FCR............ Flexor Carpi Radialis [Anatomy] (DMAA)
FCR............ Flight Condition Recognition [Army aviation]
FCR............ Flight Configuration Review (MCD)
FCR............ Flight Control Room
FCR............ Floating Control Regulator
FCR............ Forward Calculation Request
FCR............ Forward Contactor (IAA)
FCR............ Forwarders Certificate of Receipt [Shipping]
FCR............ Fractional Catabolic Rate [Clinical chemistry]
FCR............ France Cables & Radio Co. [France Telecommunications]
FCR............ Frederick Cancer Research Center, Frederick, MD [OCLC symbol] (OCLC)
FCR............ Front Communiste Revolutionnaire [France]
FCR............ Fruitlet Core Rot [of pineapple]
FCR............ Fuel Core Reserve [Nuclear energy]
FCR............ Full Cold Rolled [Steel]
FCR............ Functional Chief's Representative [Of a civilian career program] [Army] (RDA)
FCR............ Functional Configuration Review (MCD)
FCR............ Fuse Current Rating
FCRA.......... Fabric Care Research Association [British] (IRUK)
FCRA.......... Fair Credit Reporting Act [1971]
FCRA.......... Fecal Collection Receptacle Assembly [NASA] (KSC)
FCRA.......... Fellow of the Corporation of Registered Accountants [British] (DAS)
FCRAA .... Folding Chair Rental Association of America [Later, RSA]
FCRAM .... File Create and Maintenance [Computer science] (MHDI)
FCRAO .... Five College Radio Astronomy Observatory
FCRB.......... Flexor Carpi Radialis Brevis [Anatomy] (DAVI)
FCRC.......... Federal Contract Research Center
FCRC.......... Federally Chartered Research Centers (AAGC)
FCRC.......... Federated Computing Research Conference
FCRC.......... Four Corners Regional Commission [Department of Commerce]
FCRC.......... Frederick Cancer Research Center (RDA)
FCRD.......... Feline Central Retinal Degeneration [Animal pathology]
FCRE.......... Foundation for Cotton Research and Education [Later, The Cotton Foundation] (EA)
FCREA .... Fleet Chief Radio Electrical Artificer [British military] (DMA)
FCREF......... Free Congress Research and Education Foundation (EA)
FCREL(A).... Fleet Chief Radio Electrician (Air) [British military] (DMA)
FCREMN ...... Fleet Chief Radio Electrical Mechanician [British military] (DMA)
FCRF.......... Fire Control Reference Frame (MCD)
FCRF.......... Frederick Cancer Research Facility [Frederick, MD] [Department of Health and Human Services] (GRD)
FC (RFC)..... Functional Capacity (Residual Functional Capacity) [Social Security Administration] (OICC)
FCRG .... Food Chain Research Group [University of California] [Research center] (RCD)
FCRI.......... Financial Control Research Institute [British] (DBA)
FCRL.......... Fish Culture Research Laboratory [Kearneysville, WV] [Fish and Wildlife Service] [Department of the Interior] (GRD)
FCRL.......... Flight Control Ready Light System
FCRLS .... Flight Control Ready Light System
FCRLSYS .... Flight Control Ready Light System (IAA)
FCRN.......... Fund Classification Reference Number [Military] (AFIT)
FCRP .... Field Condition Report [Aviation] (FAAC)
FCRP .... Final CAPE [Capability and Proficiency Evaluation] Review Period
FCRP .... Foundation Canadienne de Recherche en Publicite (AC)
FCR-PGT..... Frente Central de Resistencia-Partido Guatemalteco del Trabajo [Political party] (EY)
FCRPS .... Federal Columbia River Power System
FCRS.......... Farm Costs and Returns Survey [Department of Agriculture] (GFGA)
FCRS.......... Flightcrew Record System (DA)
FCRSA .... Flat-Coated Retriever Society of America (EA)
FCRS(S)...... Fleet Chief Radio Supervisor (Special) [British military] (DMA)
FCRS(W)..... Fleet Chief Radio Supervisor (Warfare) [British military] (DMA)
FCRT.......... Flight Display Cathode-Ray Tube (NASA)
FCRU .... Facilities Control Relay Unit [Army] (AABC)
FCRV .... Front Commun pour le Respect de la Vie [Common Front for the Respect of Life] [Canada]
FCS............ Facility Checking Squadron [Air Force]
FCS............ Facility Communication System (IAA)
FCS............ Facsimile Communications System [Telecommunications]
FCS............ Failure and Consumption Sheets (AAG)
FCS............ Fairchild Communications Services Co. [Washington, DC] (TSSD)
FCS............ Fairchild Semiconductor
FC's .... False Calves [Padding worn under tights by actors, to improve shape of their legs]

FCS............	Farm Credit System [of FCA]
FCS............	Farmer Cooperative Service [Later, ESCS] [Department of Agriculture]
FCS............	Fecal Containment System [NASA]
FCS............	Federal Catalog System [of GSA]
FCS............	Federal Communications Systems (MCD)
FCS............	Federation Costing System (DGA)
FCS............	Federation of Communication Services [British] (TSSD)
FCS............	Feedback Control System
FCS............	Fellow of the Chemical Society [British] (ROG)
FCS............	Fellowship of Catholic Scholars (EA)
FCS............	Fetal Calf [or Cow] Serum [Medicine]
FCS............	Fetal Cord Serum [Embryology]
FCS............	Fighter Catapult Ship [British military] (DMA)
FCS............	Fighter Command School [Air Force]
FCS............	File Control Services [Digital Equipment Corp.]
FCS............	File Control System (NITA)
FCS............	Financial Control System
FCS............	Financial Services Society [New York, NY] (WDMC)
FCS............	Fire Controlman, Submarine [Navy rating Obsolete]
FCS............	Fire Control Simulator
FCS............	Fire Control System
FCS............	First Customer Shipment [IBM Corp.] [Computer science]
FCS............	Fish Culture Section [American Fisheries Society] (EA)
FCS............	Fisheries Conservation Zone
FCS............	Fixed Control Storage
FCS............	Fixed Control Storage (NITA)
FCS............	Flag Cancel Society (EA)
FCS............	Flame Control System
FCS............	Flight Command School
FCS............	Flight Command Subsystem [Spacecraft]
FCS............	Flight Control Set
F/CS............	Flight Control System (AAG)
FCS............	Flight Crew System [NASA] (NASA)
FCS............	Floor-Ceiling Sandwich
FCS............	Flowmeter Calibration Stand
FCS............	Fluorescence Correlation Spectroscopy
FCS............	Focus
FCS............	Food Containment System
FCS............	Forces Courier Services [Military British]
FCS............	Foreign Commercial Service [International Trade Administration]
FCS............	Forged Carbon Steel
FCS............	Fort Calhoun Station [Nuclear energy] (NRCH)
FCS............	Fort Carson, CO [Location identifier FAA] (FAAL)
FCS............	Frame Check Sequence [Computer science] (IBMDP)
FCS............	Frederic Chopin Society [Later, IFCF] (EA)
FCS............	Free Crystalline Silica
FCS............	Free of Capture and Seizure [Insurance]
FCS............	French Chemical Society [See also SFC] (EAIO)
FCS............	Frequency Coded System (MCD)
FCS............	Friends of Creation Spirituality (EA)
FCS............	Fuel Composition Sensor [Automotive engineering]
FCS............	Fuel Computer System (MCD)
FCS............	Functional Checkout Set (IAA)
FCS............	Functional Companion Standard (ACII)
FCSA............	Family and Children's Services Agency [New South Wales, Australia]
FCSA............	Federation Canadienne du Sport Automobile [Canadian Automobile Sport Clubs]
FCSA............	Fleet Chief Stores Accountant [British military] (DMA)
FCSA............	Flight Control Servo Assembly
FCSA............	Forest Conservation Society of America
FCSA............	Frequency Coordination System Association [Ottawa, ON] [Telecommunications service] (TSSD)
FCSAD........	Free of Capture, Seizure, Arrest, and Detainment [Insurance]
FCSB............	Federation Canadien des Societes de Biologie (AC)
FCSB............	Federation Canadienne du Sport Boules [An association] (EAIO)
FCSB............	Fellowship of Conservative Southern Baptists (EA)
FCSB............	Fire Control Switchboard
FCSB............	Fluid Circulation Storage Battery [Automotive engineering]
FCSC............	Federal Conversion Support Center (MCD)
FCSC............	Fire Control System Console [Military] (CAAL)
FCSC............	Fire Control System Coordinator
FCSC............	Fleet Command Support Center [Navy] (CAAL)
FCSC............	Foreign Claims Settlement Commission
FCSC Ann Rep...	Foreign Claims Settlement Commission. Annual Report [A publication] (DLA)
FCSC Dec & Ann...	Foreign Claims Settlement Commission. Decisions and Annotations [A publication] (DLA)
FCSCDG.......	Fleet Command Support Center Development Group [Navy] (MCD)
FCSCE.........	Fellow of the Canadian Society of Civil Engineers (DD)
FCSCJ..........	Filiae a Caritate Sacri Corde Jesus [Daughters of Charity of the Sacred Heart of Jesus] [Roman Catholic religious order]
FC (Scott)....	Faculty of Advocates Collection of Decisions, Scotch Court of Sessions [A publication] (DLA)
FCSCUS.......	Federal Claims Settlement Commission of the United States
FCSCWO......	Fleet Command Support Center Watch Officer [Navy] (MCD)
FCSD.........	Flavocytochrome C Sulfide Dehydrogenase [An enzyme]
FCSD.........	Flight Crew Support Division [NASA] (KSC)
FCSE.........	Flight Control System Electronics (MCD)
FCSE.........	Focus Enhancements [NASDAQ symbol] (TTSB)
FCSE.........	Focus Enhancements, Inc. [NASDAQ symbol] (SAG)
FCSEW.......	Focus Enhancements Wrrt [NASDAQ symbol] (TTSB)
FCSF.........	Four-Conductor, Combination, Special Purpose, Flexible Cable (IAA)
FCSG	Fire Control Sensor Group
FCSG	Flight Control Sensor Group
FCSG	Focusing
FCSGE	Federation Canadienne des Services de Garde a l'Enfance [Formerly, Canadian Child Day Care Federation] (AC)
FCSI...........	Fellow of the Canadian Securities Institute (DD)
FCSI...........	Fellow of the Construction Surveyors' Institute [British] (DBQ)
FCSI...........	Foodservice Consultants Society International (EA)
FCSL...........	Fire Control System Laboratory
FCSLA.........	First Catholic Slovak Ladies Association (EA)
FCSLE.........	Forecastle (KSC)
FCSLU.........	First Catholic Slovak Ladies Union [Later, FCSLA] (EA)
FCSM.........	Fire Control System Module
FCSM.........	Flight Combustion-Stability Monitor [Apollo] [NASA]
FCSMPEUA...	Federated Cold Storage and Meat Preserving Employees' Union of Australia
FCSN	Federation for Children with Special Needs (EA)
FCSNVD.......	Fever, Chills, Sweating, Nausea, Vomiting, and Diarrhea [Gastroenterology] (DAVI)
FCSO	Full Career Seaman Officer [Navy British]
FCSP.........	Fellow of the Chartered Society of Physiotherapy [British]
FCSP.........	Sisters of Charity of Providence [Religious order]
FCSPASTU...	Federation of Civil Service and Primary Aided School Teachers' Unions [Mauritius]
FCSPU........	Flight Control System Proximity Unity (MCD)
FCSRCC.......	Free of Capture, Seizure, Riots, and Civil Commotions [Insurance]
FCSRT	Fellow of the Canadian Society of Radiological Technicians
FCSS...........	Federal Civil Service System
FCSS...........	Federation Canadienne de Sport Scolaire [Canadian Federation of Provincial School Athletic Associations]
FCSS...........	Federation Canadienne des Sciences Sociales [Social Science Federation of Canada - SSFC]
FCSS...........	Fire Control Sight System [Military]
FCSS...........	Flight Control Systems Section
FCSS...........	Frost, Cog, and Screwmakers' Society [A union] [British]
FCSS...........	Fuel Cell Servicing System (MCD)
FCS(SA)......	Fellow of the College of Surgeons of South Africa
FCS(SoAf)....	Fellow of the College of Surgeons of South Africa
FCST...........	Federal Council for Science and Technology [Later, FSPC, FCCSET] [Executive Office of President]
FCST...........	Fellow of the College of Speech Therapists [British]
FCST...........	Field Controlled Thyristor [Electronics]
FCST...........	Flat Cable Stripping Tool
FCST...........	Forecast (AFM)
FCST-CORR...	Federal Council for Science and Technology - Committee on Water Resources Research (NOAA)
FCSTD.........	Fleet Chief Steward [British military] (DMA)
FCSU	Fire Control Simulator Unit
FCSU	Fire Control Switching Unit
FCSU	First Catholic Slovak Union of the USA and Canada (EA)
FCSU	Freon Coolant Servicing Unit (MCD)
FCSUM	Federation of Civil Service Unions of Mauritius
FCSUS	Foundation of California State University, Sacramento [Research center] (RCD)
FCSWB	Fire Control Switchboard
FCSWBD......	Fire Control Switchboard
FCSWC	Federation of Community Sporting and Workers' Clubs [Australia]
FCT............	Face-Centered Tetragonal [Crystallography]
FCT............	Factory (KSC)
FCT............	Fast Cosine Transform [Mathematics]
FCT............	Fast Cycle Time [Business term]
FCT............	Fatigue Cracking Test
FCT............	Faucet
FCT............	Federal Coordinator of Transportation [New Deal]
FCT............	Federal Court of Canada
FCT............	Federation Canadienne du Travail [Canadian Federation of Labour - CFL]
FCT............	Federation Canadienne du Travail (AC)
FCT............	Fellow of the Association of Corporate Treasurers [British] (ODBW)
FCT............	Field-Controlled Thyristor [Electronics] (IAA)
FCT............	Filament Center Tap
FCT............	Final Contract Trials [Navy]
FCT............	Financial Correlation Table
FCT............	Fire Control Technician [Navy rating Obsolete]
FCT............	Fire Control Trainer
FCT............	First City Bancorp, Inc. [AMEX symbol] (SPSG)
FCT............	First City Trust Co. [Toronto Stock Exchange symbol]
FCT............	Flight Circuit Tester (DNAB)
FCT............	Flight Control Team (MCD)
FCT............	Flight Crew Trainer [NASA] (KSC)
FCT............	Flux-Corrected Transport [Algorithm]
FCT............	Food Composition Table
FCT............	Foreign Comparative Testing [DoD] (RDA)
FCT............	Foreign Currency Translation
FCT............	Forestry Commission of Tasmania [Australia]
FCT............	Foundation for Christian Theology (EA)
FCT............	Fraction Thereof
FCT............	Fragment Connection Table [Chemistry]
FCT............	Frequency Clock Trigger (IAA)
FCT............	Fuel Cell Test (MCD)
FCT............	Full Cleanliness Training
FCT............	Function
FCT............	Functional Context Training (DNAB)
FCT............	Yakima, WA [Location identifier FAA] (FAAL)
FCTA.........	Flow Control Time of Arrival [Aviation] (FAAC)
FCTB.........	Featherston Camp Trumpet Band [British military] (DMA)
FCTB.........	Fellow of the College of Teachers of the Blind

FCTB............ Flight Crew Training Building [*NASA*] (KSC)
FCTC............ Federal Compiler Testing Center
FCTC............ Fleet Combat Training Center [*Navy*] (NVT)
FCTCAA........ Flowers-Costello Test of Central Auditory Abilities
FCTCSC........ Flue-Cured Tobacco Cooperative Stabilization Corp. (EA)
FCTE............ Fire Control Test Equipment
FCTF............ Five Civilized Tribes Foundation [*Defunct*] (EA)
FCTF............ Fuel Cell Test Facility (MCD)
FCTGA .... Flue-Cured Tobacco Growers Association (EA)
FCTN............ Function (MSA)
FCTP............ Field Challenge Test Plan
FCTP............ Fire Control Test Package
FCTR............ Factor
FCTR............ First Charter Corp. [*NASDAQ symbol*] (NQ)
FCTRL.......... Final Contractor's Trial (NVT)
FCTRY .... Factory
FCTS........... Fire Control Test Set
FCTS........... Firing Circuit Test Set
FCTS........... Flight Control Test Stand [*Aviation*]
FCTS Sesss... Flight Crew Trainer Simulator [*NASA*] (KSC)
F Ct Sess..... Fraser's Scotch Court of Sessions Cases [*A publication*] (DLA)
FCTT............ Fuel Cladding Transient Tester [*Nuclear energy*] (NRCH)
FCTY .... Factory (MUGU)
FCtzBA........ First Citizens Bancshares [*Associated Press*] (SAG)
FCtzBstk...... First Citizens Bank Stock [*Associated Press*] (SAG)
FCU............. Fan Coil Unit (NRCH)
FCU............. Fare Construction Unit [*Airlines*]
FCU............. Fares Calculating Unit (OA)
FCU............. Federal Credit Unions Bureau
FCU............. Field Communication Unit [*Military*]
FCU............. Fighter Control Unit [*Military British*]
FCU............. File Control Unit
FCU............. Fire Control Unit
FCU............. Flexor Carpi Ulnaris [*Anatomy*] (DMAA)
FCU............. Flight Control Unit
FCU............. Fluid Checkout Unit (MCD)
FCU............. Force Control Unit
FCU............. Format Conversion Unit [*Computer science*]
FCU............. Frequency Converter Unit
FCU............. Fuel Consumption Unit (NATG)
FCUA .... Federal Credit Union Administration
FCUA .... Fuel-Critical, Unspecified Area
FCUMS .... Federation of Computer Users in the Medical Sciences (EA)
FCUS .... Federal Credit Union System [*New Deal*]
FCUSA .... Finance Center, United States Army
FCV............. Facility Checkout Vehicle [*NASA*] (KSC)
FCV............. Feline Calicivirus
FCV............. Fellow of College of Violinists [*British*] (ROG)
FCV............. Festuca Cryptic Virus [*Plant pathology*]
FCV............. Fire Command Vehicle
FCV............. Flight Centre Victoria [*Canada ICAO designator*] (FAAC)
FCV............. Flight Checkout Vehicle
FCV............. Flow Control Valve
FCV............. Future Concept Vehicle
FCVE........... Foundation for Continuing Veterinary Education [*Murdoch University, Australia*]
FCVI............ Fondation Canadienne pour la Verification Integree (AC)
FCVI............ Forced-Flow Chemical Vapor Infiltration [*Materials science*]
FCVN .... Fatal Casualties Vulnerability Number (SAA)
FCVN .... Friends of Children of Vietnam (EA)
FCVRE .... Funders Committee for Voter Registration and Education (EA)
FCVS........... FORTRAN [*Formula Translating System*] Compiler Validation System [*Computer science*]
FCW............ Fast Cyclotron Wave [*Electromagnetism*] (IAA)
FCW............ Fire Control Workshop
FCW............ Flight Crew Workload [*Navy*]
FCW............ Flux-Cored Welding Wire (PDAA)
FCW............ Flyer Coil Winder
FCW............ Format Control Word (NASA)
FCW............ Fresh Cell Weight [*Biochemistry*]
FCW............ Paine Webber Group [*AMEX symbol*] (SAG)
FCWA.......... Family Court, Western Australia
FCWA.......... Fellow of the Chartered Institute of Cost and Work Accountants [*British*] (EY)
FCWA.......... Freemasons' Club of Western Australia
FCWBWU..... Fancy Cane, Wicker, and Bamboo Workers' Union [*British*]
FCWG.......... Frequency Coordination Working Group (MUGU)
FCWI........... First Commonwealth [*NASDAQ symbol*] (TTSB)
FCWI........... First Commonwealth, Inc. [*NASDAQ symbol*] (SAG)
FCWRENAF... Fleet Chief WREN [*Women's Royal Naval Service*] Air Fitter [*British military*] (DMA)
FCWRENCINE... Fleet Chief WREN [*Women's Royal Naval Service*] Cinema Operator [*British military*] (DMA)
FCWRENCK... Fleet Chief WREN [*Women's Royal Naval Service*] Cook [*British military*] (DMA)
FCWRENDHYG... Fleet Chief WREN [*Women's Royal Naval Service*] Dental Hygienist [*British military*] (DMA)
FCWRENDSA... Fleet Chief WREN [*Women's Royal Naval Service*] Dental Surgery Assistant [*British military*] (DMA)
FCWRENEDUC... Fleet Chief WREN [*Women's Royal Naval Service*] Education Assistant [*British military*] (DMA)
FCWRENMET... Fleet Chief WREN [*Women's Royal Naval Service*] Meteorological Observer [*British military*] (DMA)
FCWRENPHOT... Fleet Chief WREN [*Women's Royal Naval Service*] Photographer [*British military*] (DMA)

FCWRENQA... Fleet Chief WREN [*Women's Royal Naval Service*] Quarters Assistant [*British military*] (DMA)
FCWREN(R)... Fleet Chief WREN [*Women's Royal Naval Service*] (RADAR) [*British military*] (DMA)
FCWRENREG... Fleet Chief WREN [*Women's Royal Naval Service*] Regulating [*British military*] (DMA)
FCWRENREL... Fleet Chief WREN [*Women's Royal Naval Service*] Radio Electrician [*British military*] (DMA)
FCWRENRS(M)... Fleet Chief WREN [*Women's Royal Naval Service*] Radio Supervisor (Morse) [*British military*] (DMA)
FCWRENSA... Fleet Chief WREN [*Women's Royal Naval Service*] Stores Accountant [*British military*] (DMA)
FCWRENSTD... Fleet Chief WREN [*Women's Royal Naval Service*] Steward [*British military*] (DMA)
FCWRENTEL... Fleet Chief WREN [*Women's Royal Naval Service*] Telephonist [*British military*] (DMA)
FCWRENTSA... Fleet Chief WREN [*Women's Royal Naval Service*] Training Support Assistant [*British military*] (DMA)
FCWRENWA... Fleet Chief WREN [*Women's Royal Naval Service*] Weapon Analyst [*British military*] (DMA)
FCWRENWTR(G)... Fleet Chief WREN [*Women's Royal Naval Service*] Writer (General) [*British military*] (DMA)
FCWRENWTR(P)... Fleet Chief WREN [*Women's Royal Naval Service*] Writer (Pay) [*British military*] (DMA)
FCWRENWW... Fleet Chief WREN [*Women's Royal Naval Service*] Welfare Worker [*British military*] (DMA)
FCWTC......... Friends Committee on War Tax Concerns [*Defunct*] (EA)
f-cx--........... Central African Republic [*MARC geographic area code Library of Congress*] (LCCP)
FCX............. Fire Coordination Exercise [*Military*] (ADDR)
FCX............. Freeport McMoRan Copper & Gold [*NYSE symbol*] (SPSG)
FCX............. Freep't McMoRan Copper&Gold'B' [*NYSE symbol*] (TTSB)
FCx............. Frontal Cortex [*Neuroanatomy*]
FCXPr .... Freep't McMoRan Cp/Gld7%CvPref [*NYSE symbol*] (TTSB)
FCXPrA .... Freept-McMo Cp/Gld'A'Dep Pfd [*NYSE symbol*] (TTSB)
FCXPrB .... Freept-McMo Cp/Gld'B'Dep Pfd [*NYSE symbol*] (TTSB)
FCXPrC .... Freept-McMo Cp/Gld'C'Dep Pfd [*NYSE symbol*] (TTSB)
FCXPrD .... Freept-McMo Cp/Slvr'D'Dep Pfd [*NYSE symbol*] (TTSB)
FCY............. Fancy (ROG)
FCY............. Federation Canadienne de Yachting [*Canadian Yachting Association*]
FCY............. First City Financial Corp. Ltd. [*Toronto Stock Exchange symbol Vancouver Stock Exchange symbol*]
FCY............. Forrest City, AR [*Location identifier FAA*] (FAAL)
FCY............. Furon Co. [*NYSE symbol*] (SAG)
FcZ............. Facez, Rockford, IL [*Library symbol*] [*Library of Congress*] (LCLS)
FCZ............. Fishery Conservation Zone
FCZ............. Forward Combat Zone (NATG)
Fd............... Dilution Factor [*Also, DF*] [*Nuclear energy*] (NRCH)
FD............... Face of Drawing (AAG)
FD............... Facilities and Design (MCD)
FD............... Facility Division [*Marine science*] (OSRA)
FD............... Facility Division [*Forecast Systems Laboratory*] (USDC)
FD............... Facility Drawing
FD............... Failure Definition (MCD)
FD............... False Deck [*Stowage*] (DNAB)
FD............... Familial Dysautonomia [*Medicine*]
FD............... Family Doctor (MEDA)
FD............... Fan Douche [*Medicine*]
Fd............... Fantail Darter [*Ichthyology*]
FD............... Fascia Dentata [*Brain anatomy*]
FD............... Fatal Dose
FD............... Fault Detection (MCD)
FD............... Fault Directory
FD............... Federal Directive
FD............... Federal Document (AFM)
FD............... Federated Department Stores, Inc. [*NYSE symbol*] (SAG)
FD............... Federated Dept Stores [*NYSE symbol*] (TTSB)
FD............... Feed (MSA)
FD............... Female Domination
FD............... Female Treated with DOC [*Deoxycorticosterone*]
Fd............... Ferredoxin [*Biochemistry*]
FD............... Fiber Duct [*Telecommunications*] (TEL)
FD............... Fibrinogen Derivative [*Hematology*] (AAMN)
FD............... Fidei Defensor [*Defender of the Faith*] [*Latin*]
FD............... Field
FD............... Field Decelerating Contactor or Relay [*Industrial control*] (IEEE)
FD............... Field Definition (IAA)
FD............... Field Desorption
FD............... Field Director
FD............... Field of Drawing (AAG)
FD............... Fighter Direction
FD............... File Definition [*Computer science*]
FD............... File Description
FD............... File Directory
FD............... Fill/Drain (MCD)
F/D............. Filter/Demineralizer (NRCH)
FD............... Filter Drain [*Computer science*]
FD............... Finance Department
FD............... Finance Direction
FD............... Finance Docket
FD............... Financial Director
FD............... Finished Dialing [*Telecommunications*] (TEL)
FD............... Finite Difference [*Metallurgy*]
FD............... Finite Difference [*Mathematics*]
FD............... Fire Damper (OA)

FD	Fire Department
FD	Fire Department Access Point [*NFPA planning symbol*] (NFPA)
FD	Fire Detector
FD	Fire Direction
FD	Fire Drop (AABC)
FD	First Day [*Philately*]
FD	First Defense [*Men's lacrosse position*]
FD	First Down [*Football*]
FD	Fisheries Department [*Western Australia*]
Fd	Fjord [*Maps and charts*]
FD	Flame Deflector
FD	Flange Focal Distance (IEEE)
FD	Fleet Duties [*British military*] (DMA)
FD	Flexible Disk
FD	Flight Day (MCD)
FD	Flight Deck (MCD)
FD	Flight Delay (MCD)
FD	Flight Director [*NASA*] (KSC)
FD	Floating Divide (IAA)
FD	Floating Dollar Sign [*Computer science*] (IAA)
FD	Floor Drain [*Technical drawings*]
FD	Floppy Disk [*Computer science*] (BUR)
FD	Flow Diagram [*Engineering*] (IAA)
FD	Fluctuation-Dissipation [*Theorem*] [*Statistical mechanics*]
FD	Fluorescence Detection [*Spectrometry*]
FD	Flux Delta (IAA)
FD	Flyball Dog
FD	Flying Dutchman [*Racing dinghy*]
FD	Focal Diameter
FD	Focal Distance
FD	Fog Diaphone [*Navigation charts*]
FD	Fold
FD	Folin-Denis [*Analytical chemistry*]
FD	Follicular Diameter [*Medicine*] (DMAA)
FD	Food
FD	Food Distribution Division [*of AMS, Department of Agriculture*]
FD	Food Division [*Army Natick Laboratories, MA*]
FD	Foot Drape [*Medicine*]
FD	Forbush Decrease [*Geophysics*]
FD	Forced (WGA)
FD	Forced Draft
FD	Force Designator
FD	Force Development
FD	Force Displacement [*Sports medicine*]
FD	Forceps Delivery [*Obstetrics*]
FD	Ford (ROG)
FD	Ford of Europe, Inc. [*British ICAO designator*] (ICDA)
FD	Formal Decorative [*Horticulture*]
FD	Fort Detrick [*Maryland*] [*Army*] (MCD)
FD	Forward (ADA)
FD	Found (MSA)
FD	Fourth Day (IIA)
FD	Fourth Dimension [*Time*] (AAG)
FD	Fractional Destraction [*Supercritical distillation*]
FD	Framed [*Construction*]
FD	Frame Difference
FD	Framework Density [*Crystallography*]
FD	Franc [*Monetary unit*] [*French Somaliland*]
FD	Franco Domicile [*Shipping*] (DS)
FD	Free Delivery
FD	Free Discharge
FD	Free Dispatch
FD	Free Dock [*Business term*]
FD	Free Drop
FD	Freeze-Dried
FD	Freight Department
FD	Frente Democratica [*Democratic Front*] [*Guinea-Bissau*] [*Political party*] (EY)
FD	Frequency Demodulator
FD	Frequency Discrimination [*Neurophysiology*]
FD	Frequency Distance [*Telecommunications*] (TEL)
FD	Frequency Distribution [*Mathematics*] (IAA)
FD	Frequency Diversity
FD	Frequency Divider [*Electronics*] (IAA)
FD	Frequency Division
FD	Frequency Doubler
FD	Frequency Drift
FD	Front Democratique [*Democratic Front*] [*The Comoros*] [*Political party*] (EY)
FD	Front Door [*Shipping*]
FD	Front of Dash [*Technical drawings*]
FD	Fuel Dragster [*Class of racing cars*]
FD	Full Dress [*Colloquial reference to formal dress*]
FD	Full Duplex [*Telecommunications*]
FD	Functional Description
FD	Functional Diagram [*Implementation dependant*] (ACII)
FD	Function Designator (NASA)
FD	Fund (ROG)
FD	Fuze Delay
fd----	Sahara Desert [*MARC geographic area code Library of Congress*] (LCCP)
FD	Winds and Temperatures Aloft Forecast [*Symbol*] [*National Weather Service*]
FD	Wiscair [*ICAO designator*] (AD)
FD₅₀	Median Fatal Dose [*Medicine*] (MAE)

FDA	Fault Detection and Annunciation (NASA)
FDA	Feather and Down Association (EA)
FDA	Federal Design Approval [*Nuclear energy*] (NUCP)
FDA	Federal Domestic Assistance [*Catalog*] (OICC)
FDA	Federal Drug Administration
FDA	Fellowship Depressives Anonymous [*British*] (DBA)
FDA	Fellowship Diploma of Architecture
FDA	Ferrite Driver Amplifier
FDA	Ferrocenedicarboxylic Acid [*Organic chemistry*]
FDA	Fertilizer Dealers Association [*Defunct*] (EA)
FDA	Final Delivered Article
FDA	Final Design Acceptance [*or Approval or Authorization*]
FDA	Financial Data Planning
FDA	First Division Association [*British*]
FDA	Flight Deck Assembly (MCD)
FDA	Flight Detection and Annunciation (MCD)
FDA	Florida State University, Tallahassee, FL [*OCLC symbol*] (OCLC)
FDA	Fluorescein Diacetate [*Organic chemistry*]
FDA	Flying Dentists Association (EA)
FDA	Folded Dipole Antenna
FDA	Food and Drug Administration [*Rockville, MD*] [*Department of Health and Human Services*]
FDA	Food Distribution Administration [*Terminated, 1945*]
FDA	Foreign Demographic Analysis Division [*Census*] (OICC)
FDA	Forum Democratico Angolana [*Political party*] (EY)
FDA	Frenchay Dysarthria Assessment [*Speech and language therapy*] (DAVI)
FDA	Frequency Distortion Analyzer
FDA	Fronto-Dextra Anterior [*A fetal position*] [*Obstetrics*]
FDA	Functional Demonstration and Acceptance (AAG)
FDA	Functional Design Activity [*Army*]
FDA	Functional Design Agency (MCD)
FDA	Fundacion [*Colombia*] [*Airport symbol*] (AD)
FDA	Furniture Deliverers' Association
FDAA	Federal Disaster Assistance Administration [*FEMA*]
FDA Cons	FDA [*Food and Drug Administration*] Consumer [*A publication*] (DLA)
FDAD	Full Digital Arts Display [*FAA*] (TAG)
FDA-EDRO	Food and Drug Administration, Office of Executive Director of Regional Operations (NRCH)
FdAgric	Federal Agricultural Mortgage Corp. [*Associated Press*] (SAG)
FdAgricA	Federal Agricultural Mortgage [*Associated Press*] (SAG)
FdAgricC	Federal Agricultural Mortgage [*Associated Press*] (SAG)
FDAI	Flight Direction and Altitude Indicator
FDAI	Flight Director Attitude Indicator [*NASA*] (NASA)
FDAMS	Flight Data Acquisition and Management System (GAVI)
FD & C	Food, Drug, and Cosmetic Act
FD & CA	Food, Drug, and Cosmetic Act (EG)
FD & D	Freight, Demurrage, and Defense [*Shipping*] (DS)
FD & E	Follow-On Development Test and Evaluation (MCD)
FD & I	Failure Detection and Isolation
FDAS	Field Data Acquisition System (DWSG)
FDAS	Field Depot Aviation Squadron [*Air Force*]
FDAS	Flight Data Acquisition System
FDAS	Frequency Distribution Analysis Sheet
FDATC	Flying Division Air Training Command
FDAU	Flight Data Acquisition Unit
FDB	Fahrenheit Dry Bulb (KSC)
FDB	Family Discussion Bureau [*Later, Institute of Marital Studies*] [*British*] (DI)
FDB	Ferrari Data Bank (EA)
FDB	Field Descriptor Block
FDB	Field Dynamic Braking
FDB	Fighter Dive-Bomber
FDB	File Data Block [*Computer science*]
FDB	Fleet Data Base [*Navy*] (CAAL)
FDB	Flight Dynamics Branch [*NASA*] (KSC)
FDB	Foodbrands America [*NYSE symbol*] (TTSB)
FDB	Forced-Draft Blower
FDB	Form Die Bulge (MCD)
FDB	Forte Princip [*Brazil*] [*Airport symbol*] (AD)
FDB	Full Data Block (KSC)
FDB	Functional Description Block [*Telecommunications*] (TEL)
FDb	Volusia County Public Libraries, Daytona Beach, FL [*Library symbol Library of Congress*] (LCLS)
FDbBC	Bethune-Cookman College, Daytona Beach, FL [*Library symbol Library of Congress*] (LCLS)
FDBC	Flight Director Bombing Computer (MCD)
FDbCC	Daytona Beach Community College, Daytona Beach, FL [*Library symbol*] [*Library of Congress*] (LCLS)
FDBK	Feedback (MSA)
FDBLR	Frequency Doubler (MSA)
FDBPS	Fleet Database Production System [*Navy*] (MCD)
FDbY	S. Cornelia Young Memorial Library, Daytona Beach, FL [*Library symbol Library of Congress*] (LCLS)
FDC	Daughters of Divine Charity (TOCD)
FDC	Facility Design Criteria (AAG)
FDC	Facsimile Data Converter [*Facilitates communication between facsimile terminal and computer*] (NITA)
FDC	Failure Diagnostic Code [*Military*] (AFIT)
FDC	Fathers Day Council (EA)
FDC	Federacion Democrata Cristiana [*Christian Democratic Federation*] [*Spain Political party*] (PPE)
FDC	Federal Design Council [*Defunct*] (EA)
FDC	Federal Detention Center (BARN)
FDC	Federation for a Democratic China [*Australia*]

FDC............ Federation of Dredging Contractors [*British*] (BI)
FDC............ Field Data Computer
FDC............ Field Discharge Chip
FDC............ Filiae Divinae Caritatis [*Daughters of Divine Charity*] [*Roman Catholic religious order*]
FDC............ Final Design Criteria
FDC............ Fire-Department Connection [*Technical drawings*]
FDC............ Fire Detection Center
FDC............ Fire Direction Center [*Military*]
FDC............ First Data [*NYSE symbol*] (SPSG)
FDC............ First-Day Cover [*Philately*]
FDC............ Fishery Data Center [*FAO*] (MSC)
FDC............ Fixed Decade Capacitor
FDC............ Fleur de Coin [*Mint state*] [*Numismatics*]
FDC............ Flight Data Company (GAVI)
FDC............ Flight Director Computer (MCD)
FDC............ Floppy Disk Controller [*Computer science*] (MDG)
FDC............ Florida Department of Citrus (EA)
FDC............ Fluid Digital Computer
FDC............ Follicular Dendritic Cell
FDC............ Food, Drug, and Cosmetic [*Act*]
FDC............ Formation Drone Control [*Navy*] (NG)
FDC............ Form Definition Component (IAA)
FDC............ Forward Direction Center [*Air Force*]
FDC............ Freedom Defence Committee [*National Council for Civil Liberties*] [*British*]
FDC............ Frequency Domain Coding
FDC............ Frequency of Dividing Cells [*Bacteriology*]
FDC............ Front Democratique Camerounais [*Cameroon*] [*Political party*] (EY)
FDC............ Fully Distributed Cost
FDC............ Fully Distributed Costs [*Finance*] (MHDB)
FDC............ Functional Data Coordinator (MCD)
FDC............ Functional Design Criteria (NRCH)
FDC............ Furniture Development Council [*British*] (BI)
FDCA........... Flying Disc Collectors Association (EA)
FdCC........... Canossian Daughters of Charity (TOCD)
FDCC.......... Family Day Care Centre [*Australia*]
FDCC.......... Flight [*Control*] Division-Control Criteria [*Air Force*]
FDCCC........ First Day Cover Collectors Club (EA)
FDCD .... Facility Design Criteria Document (AAG)
FDCD .... Fluorescence-Detected Circular Dichroism [*Spectroscopy*]
FDCDS .... Family Day Care Development Service [*Australia*]
FDCH .... Federal Document Clearing House
FDCH .... Flyball Dog Champion
FDCL.......... Forschungsund Dokumentationszentrum Chile-Lateinamerika [*Germany*]
FDCLF........ Friends of Dromkeen Children's Literature Foundation [*Australia*]
FDCO .... Defense Foreign Disclosure Coordinating Office
FD Cosm L Rep... Food, Drug, Cosmetic Law Reporter [*Commerce Clearing House*] [*A publication*] (DLA)
FDCP .... Family Day Care Program [*Australia*]
FDCPA .... Fair Debt Collection Practices Act
FDCPA .... Food, Drug, and Consumer Product Agency [*Proposed successor to FDA*] [*HEW*]
FDCR .... Frente Democratico contra la Represion [*Guatemala*] [*Political party*] (EY)
FdCrtE......... Food Court Entertainment Network, Inc. [*Associated Press*] (SAG)
FDCS .... Fighter Director Control Schools [*Navy*]
FDCS .... Flight Deck Communication System [*Navy*] (CAAL)
FDCS .... Functionally Distributed Computing System
FDCSB .... Federation for a Democratic China, Sydney Branch [*Australia*]
FDCT.......... Fast Discrete Cosine Transform (MCD)
FdCt........... Food Court Entertainment Network, Inc. [*Associated Press*] (SAG)
FDCT.......... Franck Drawing Completion Test [*Psychology*]
FDCT.......... Frequency Domain Coding Technique
FdCtE......... Food Court Entertainment Network, Inc. [*Associated Press*] (SAG)
FDCU .... Fire Detector Control Unit (MCD)
FD'd .... Factory Damaged [*Slang*]
FDD .... Final Delivery Date (AAGC)
FDD .... Flexible Disk Drive
FDD .... Flight Dynamics Division [*NASA*] (SSD)
FDD .... Floating Digital Drive
FDD .... Floating Dry Dock [*Navy*]
FDD .... Floppy Disk Drive [*Computer science*]
FDD .... Food and Drug Directorate [*Canada*]
FDD .... Foreign Document Division [*of CIA*]
FDD .... Format Deficiency Document (MCD)
FDD .... Franc de Droits [*Free of Charge*] [*Shipping*] [*French*]
FDD .... Frequency Difference Detector (IAA)
FDD .... Frequency Division Duplex [*Telecommunications*] (ACRL)
FDD .... Frequency Division Duplex
FDD .... Front for Democracy and Development [*Surinam*] [*Political party*]
FDD .... Functional Description Document (DOMA)
FDDB .... Function Designator Database (MCD)
FDDC .... Ferric Dimethyldithiocarbamate [*A fungicide*]
FDDC .... Flight Deck Debarkation Control [*Navy*] (CAAL)
FDDI .... Fiber Distributed Data Interface [*Telecommunications*]
FDDI .... Fiber-Optic Digital Device Interface [*Computer science*]
FDDip .... Funeral Director's Diploma [*British*] (DI)
FDDL .... Field Data Description Language (NITA)
FDDL .... File Data Description Language (MHDI)
FDDL .... Flight Data Entry System (SAA)
FDDL .... Frequency-Division Data Link [*Radio*]
FDDLL .... Find Dead Dynamic Link Library [*Computer software*] (PCM)
FDDM .... Fort Dodge, Des Moines & Southern Railway Co. [*AAR code*]

FDDM & S ... Fort Dodge, Des Moines & Southern Railway Co.
FDDR .... Field Deviation Disposition Request [*Nuclear energy*] (NRCH)
FDDRS........ Facility Development Design and Review System [*Veterans Administration*] (GFGA)
FDDS .... Fault Detection and Diagnosis System [*Automotive service electronics*]
FdDS.......... Federated Department Stores, Inc. [*Associated Press*] (SAG)
FDDS .... Federation of Dental Diagnostic Sciences [*Defunct*] (EA)
FDDS .... Federation of Digestive Disease Societies [*Defunct*] (EA)
FDDS .... FLAG [*FORTRAN Load and Go*] Data Display System (MCD)
FDDS .... Flight Data Distribution System
FDE............ Feachtas Dt-Armail Eithneach nah Eireann [*Irish Campaign for Nuclear Disarmament*] (EAIO)
FDE............ Female-Day-Equivalent [*Entomology*]
FDE............ Field Decelerator
FDE............ Final Drug Evaluation [*Pharmacology*] (DAVI)
FDE............ Finite Differential Equation (PDAA)
FDE............ Flaw Detection Equipment
FDE............ Flight Data Entry Device (IAA)
FDE............ Flight Dynamics Engineer (SSD)
FDE............ Forde [*Norway*] [*Airport symbol*] (OAG)
FDE............ Frente Democratico Eleitoral [*Democratic Electoral Front*] [*Portugal Political party*] (PPE)
FDE............ Functional Differential Equation
FDEA.......... Federal Drug Enforcement Administration (WDAA)
F de Ac....... Franciscus de Accursio [*Deceased, 1293*] [*Authority cited in pre-1607 legal work*] (DSA)
FDEC.......... Fluidyne Engineering Corp. (KSC)
FDEC.......... Forum for Death Education and Counseling [*Later, ADEC*] (EA)
FDEF.......... First Defiance Financial Corp. [*NASDAQ symbol*] (SAG)
FDEF.......... First Defiance Fin'l [*NASDAQ symbol*] (TTSB)
FDEF.......... First Federal Savings & Loan of Ohio [*NASDAQ symbol*] (SAG)
FDEN.......... Females, Density Of [*Ecology*]
FDEO.......... Flight Development Engineering Order (MCD)
FDEP.......... Final Draft Equipment Publication (MCD)
FDEP.......... Flight Data Entry Panel
FDEP.......... Formatted Data Entry Program [*Mohawk Data Systems*]
FDEPS .... Fully Diluted Earnings Per Share (TDOB)
FDER.......... Florida Department of Environmental Regulations
FDER.......... Florida Department of Environmental Regulations (DOGT)
F de Ramp... Franciscus de Ramponibus [*Deceased, 1401*] [*Authority cited in pre-1607 legal work*] (DSA)
FDES.......... Framework for the Development of Environmental Statistics [*Australia*]
FDESC........ Force Description [*Military*] (DOMA)
FDET.......... Force Development Experimentation Testing (MCD)
FDEU.......... Field Drainage Experimental Unit (PDAA)
FDF............ Failure Density Function
FDF............ Fast Death Factor [*Medicine*]
FDF............ Fibre Distribution Frame [*Optics*] (EECA)
FDF............ Flame Deflector Firex
FDF............ Flight Data File [*NASA*] (NASA)
FDF............ Flight Dynamics Facility (SSD)
FDF............ Flush Door Fastener
FDF............ Food and Drink Federation [*England and Belgium*]
FDF............ Food Defense Fund (EA)
FDF............ Footwear Distributors Federation [*British*] (BI)
FDF............ Form Die Forge (MCD)
FDF............ Fort-De-France [*Martinique*] [*Seismograph station code, US Geological Survey*] (SEIS)
FDF............ Fort-De-France [*Martinique*] [*Airport symbol*] (OAG)
FDF............ Francis Drake Fellowship [*British*] (BI)
FDF............ Front Democratique des Bruxellois Francophones [*French-Speaking Democratic Front*] [*Belgium Political party*] (PPW)
FDF............ Fundamentally Different Factors [*Environmental Protection Agency*]
FDF............ Further Differentiated Fibroblast [*Cytology*]
FD/FF......... Flux Delta/Flux Flow (IEEE)
FD/FL......... Fault Detection/Fault Location [*Military*] (CAAL)
FDFL.......... Fluid Flow
FDFM......... Flight Data and Flow Management Group [*ICAO*] (DA)
FDFU.......... Federation of Documentary Film Units [*British*] (BI)
FDG .... Feeding
FDG .... Fermi-Dirac Gas
FDG .... Flight Director Group (MCD)
FDG .... Flight Dynamics Group [*NASA*] (KSC)
FDG .... Fluorescein Di(galactopyranoside) [*Organic chemistry*]
FDG .... Fluorodeoxyglucose [*Organic chemistry*]
FDG .... Fly Dressers Guild [*Pinner, Middlesex, England*] (EAIO)
FDG .... Fractional Doppler Gate
FDG .... Funding
FDG .... Fur Dressers Guild (EA)
FDGB .... Freier Deutscher Gewerkschaftsbund [*Free German Trade Union Federation*] [*Germany Political party*] (PPE)
FDGD .... Nhlangano [*Swaziland*] [*ICAO location identifier*] (ICLI)
FDGE .... Fibroblast-Derived Growth Factor [*Medicine*] (DMAA)
FDGL .... Lavumisa [*Swaziland*] [*ICAO location identifier*] (ICLI)
FDGM .... Final Defense Guidance Memorandum [*Navy*]
FDGT .... Fluor Daniel/GTI [*NASDAQ symbol*] (TTSB)
FDGT .... Fluor Daniel GTI, Inc. [*NASDAQ symbol*] (SAG)
FDH .... Familial Dysalbuminemic Hyperthyroxinemia [*Medicine*]
FDH .... Fixed Dynamical Heating [*Climatology*]
FDH .... Floating Divide or Halt
FDH .... Formate Dehydrogenase [*An enzyme*]
FDH .... Friedrichshafen [*Germany Airport symbol*] (OAG)
FDH .... Fully Documented History [*Automotive retailing*]

FDHD	Floppy Disk High-Density [Computer science]
FDHD	Floppy Drive High Density [Computer science]
FDHDB	Flight Deck Hazardous Duty Billet [Navy]
FDHDP	Flight Deck Hazardous Duty Pay [Navy]
FDHE	Faculty Directory of Higher Education [A publication]
FdHL	Federal Home Loan Mortgage Corp. [Associated Press] (SAG)
FdHLn	Federal Home Loan Mortgage Corp. [Associated Press] (SAG)
FdHly	Frederick's of Hollywood, Inc. [Associated Press] (SAG)
FDHM	Full Duration Half Maximum [Mathematics]
FdHmLn	Federal Home Loan Mortgage Corp. [Associated Press] (SAG)
FDI	Failure Detection and Isolation (MCD)
FDI	Failure Detector Indicator (NASA)
FDI	Fault Detection and Identification (MCD)
FDI	Fault Detection and Isolation (NASA)
FDI	Federal Defense Laboratory (AAGC)
FDI	Federal Deposit Insurance Corp., Washington, DC [OCLC symbol] (OCLC)
FDI	Federation Dentaire Internationale [International Dental Federation] [British] (EA)
FDI	Feeder Distribution Interface [Bell System]
FD/I	Field Dependence/Independence (EDAC)
FDI	Field Director Indicator (OA)
FDI	Field Discharge
FDI	Field Displacement Isolator
FDI	Field Disposition Instruction [Nuclear energy] (NRCH)
FDI	Filmless Dental Imager (RDA)
FDI	First Day of Issue [Philately]
FDI	First Devonian Explorations [Vancouver Stock Exchange symbol]
FDI	First Dorsal Interosseous Muscle [Myology]
FDI	Flight Direction Indicator
FDI	Flight Direction Instrument (SAA)
FDI	Follicle Development Index [Gynecology]
FDI	Food and Disarmament International [Belgium] (EAIO)
FDI	Foreign Direct Investment
FDI	Formal Documents Issued [Federal Power Commission]
FDI	Form Die Impact (MCD)
FDI	Frequency Domain Interferometer (MCD)
FDI	Fuel Desulphurization, Inc.
FDI	Furnish, Deliver and Install (IAA)
FDI	Poplar Bluff, MO [Location identifier FAA] (FAAL)
FDI & R	Failure Detection Identification and Control System Reconfiguration (MCD)
FDIC	Federal Deposit Insurance Corp. [Independent government agency] [Database]
FDIC	Fire Department Instructors Conference (EA)
FDIC	Flying Days per Inspection Cycle [Air Force] (AFIT)
FDIC	Food and Drink Industries Council [British]
FDICA	Foundations and Donors Interested in Catholic Activities (EA)
FDICIA	Federal Deposit Insurance Corporation Improvement Act (ECON)
F Dict	Kames and Woodhouselee's Folio Dictionary, Scotch Court of Session [A publication] (DLA)
FDIF	Federation Democratique Internationale des Femmes [Women's International Democratic Federation - WIDF] [Germany] (EAIO)
FDIIR	Fault Detection, Isolation, Identification, and Recompensation (NASA)
FDIM	Federacion Democratica Internacional de Mujeres [Women's International Democratic Federation]
F-DIM	Fluorescence Digital Imaging Microscopy
FDIO	Flight Data Input/Output [Aviation] (FAAC)
FDIOR	Flight Data Input/Output Repeater [Aviation] (FAAC)
FDIR	Fault Detection Identification/Isolation and Recovery/Recognition (NASA)
FDIR	Fronteer Directory [NASDAQ symbol] (TTSB)
FDIR	Fronteer Directory Co., Inc. [NASDAQ symbol] (NQ)
FDIR	Fronteer Financial Holdings Ltd. [NASDAQ symbol] (SAG)
FDIS	Fault Detection and Isolation Subsystem (RDA)
FDIS	Flight Displays and Interface System (NVT)
FDIS	Freeway Driver Information System
FDIU	Fetal Death in Utero [Medicine]
FDJ	Filles de Jesus [Sons of Jesus] [Religious order]
FDJ	Free Diffusion Junction [Electrochemistry]
FDJ	Freie Deutsche Jugend [Free German Youth] [Germany Political party] (PPE)
FDK	Forecastle Deck [Naval engineering]
FDK	Frederick, MD [Location identifier FAA] (FAAL)
FDL	FAAD [Forward Area Air Defense] Data Link [Army]
FDL	Fast Deployment Logistics Ship [Navy symbol]
FDL	Ferndale [Cardiff] [Welsh depot code]
FDL	Ferrite Diode Limiter (IAA)
FDL	Fick Diffusion Law
FDL	Final Determination Letter (GNE)
FDL	Fish Disease Leaflet
FDL	Fixed Delay Line
FDL	Fleur-de-Lys [Heraldry]
FDL	Flexor Digitorum Longus [Muscle or nerve] [Anatomy] (DAVI)
FDL	Flight Determination Laboratory [WSMR]
FDL	Flight Director Loop (MCD)
FDL	Flight Dynamic Laboratory [Air Force]
FDL	Foremost [or Forward] Defended Localities [or Locations] [British]
FDL	Form Definition Language [Xerox] (NITA)
FDL	Forms Description Language [Computer science] (MHDB)
FDL	Forward Defended Locality [Military British]
FDL	Frequency Double LASER
FDL	Fuehrer der Luft [Air liaison officer with Navy] [German military - World War II]
FDLA	Florida Defense Lawyers Association (SRA)

FDLA	Florida Dental Laboratory Association (SRA)
FDIb	Delray Beach Library, Delray Beach, FL [Library symbol Library of Congress] (LCLS)
FDLD	Federal Defense Laboratory Diversification (AAGC)
FDLD	Frequency Doubling LASER Device
FDLDG	Forced Landing (IAA)
FDLDP	Federal Defense Laboratory Diversification Program (RDA)
FDLH	Flight Determination Laboratory, Holloman Air Force Base
FDLI	Food and Drug Law Institute
FdLio	Food Lion, Inc. [Associated Press] (SAG)
FdLioA	Food Lion, Inc. [Associated Press] (SAG)
FdLioB	Food Lion, Inc. [Associated Press] (SAG)
FDLMP	First Day of Last Menstrual Period [Gynecology and obstetrics] (DAVI)
FDLN	Feedline (NASA)
FDLN	Forced-Draft, Low-Nitrogen Oxide [Combustion engineering]
FDLNA	Food Lion Inc. Cl'A' [NASDAQ symbol] (TTSB)
FDLNB	Food Lion Inc. Cl'B' [NASDAQ symbol] (TTSB)
FDLP	Daughters of Providence (TOCD)
FDLP	Federal Depository Library Program
FDLS	Fast Deployment Logistics Ship [Navy]
FD/LS	Fault Detection/Location Subsystem
FDLUQ	Fronte Democratica Liberale dell'Uomo Qualunque [Liberal Democratic Front of the Common Man] [Italy Political party] (PPE)
f-dm--	Dahomey [Benin] [MARC geographic area code Library of Congress] (LCCP)
FDM	Facility Density Mapper
FDM	Faraday Disc Machine
FDM	Feasibility Demonstration Model
FDM	Final Draft Manuscript
FDM	Finite Difference Method [Mathematics]
FDM	Flight Data Manager (MCD)
FDM	Formal Development Method [Computer science]
FDM	Freedom Airlines, Inc. [ICAO designator] (FAAC)
FDM	Frequency Data Multiplexer (NASA)
FDM	Frequency Deviation Meter
FDM	Frequency-Division Modulation [Telecommunications] (IAA)
FDM	Frequency-Division Multiplex [or Multiplexing] [Telecommunications]
FDM	Full Descriptive Method
FDM	Functional Development Model (MCD)
FDM	Fundamental Design Method
FDM	Fund for a Democratic Majority (EA)
FDMA	Ferrocarril de Minatitlan al Carmen [AAR code]
FDMA	Fibre Drum Manufacturers Association [Defunct]
FDMA	Frequency Division Multiple Access [Telecommunications] (MCD)
FDMB	Mbabane [Swaziland] [ICAO location identifier] (ICLI)
FDMC	Fiscal Director of the Marine Corps
FDMCN	Flight Data Management and Communications Network (MCD)
FDMD	Foundation for Depression and Manic Depression (EA)
FDM/FM	Frequency Division Multiplex/Frequency Modulation [Telecommunications] (TEL)
FDMH	Mhlume [Swaziland] [ICAO location identifier] (ICLI)
FDMHA	Frederick Douglass Memorial and Historical Association (EA)
FDMIS	Force Development Management Information System [Army]
FDMP	Foundation for the Development of Medical Psychotherapy [Switzerland] (EAIO)
FDMR	Fluorescence-Detected Magnetic Resonance [Physics]
FDMS	Federation of Deer Management Societies [British] (DBA)
FD-MS	Field Desorption - Mass Spectrometry
FDMS	Flight Data Management System [Air Force] (AFM)
FDMS	Floppy Disc Management System (NITA)
FDMS	Force Development Management Information System [Army] (MCD)
FDMS	Frequency-Division Multiplexing System [Radio] (MCD)
FDMS	Manzini/Matsapa [Swaziland] [ICAO location identifier] (ICLI)
FDMVC	Frequency-Division Multiplex Voice Communication
FDN	Field Designator Number [Air Force] (AFM)
Fdn	Fonodan [Record label] [Denmark]
FDN	Foreign Directory Name [Telecommunications] (TEL)
FDN	Foundation (KSC)
FDN	Frente Democratico Nacional [Electoral Alliance] [Mexico] (EY)
FDN	Fuerza Democratica Nicaraguense [Nicaraguan Democratic Force] (PD)
FDN	Future Digital Network (MCD)
FDNB	Fluorodinitrobenzene [Also, DFB, DNFB] [Organic chemistry]
FDNC	Frequency Dependent Negative Conductance [Physics]
FDNDEA	Fluoro(dinitro)diethylaniline [Organic chemistry]
FDNET	Fighter Direction Net [Navy]
FDNG	Feeding
FDNGL	Flush Deck Nose Gear Launch (MCD)
FDNR	Frequency Dependent Negative Resistance [Physics]
FDNSC	Daughters of Our Lady of the Sacred Heart (TOCD)
FDO	Faculty of Dispensing Opticians [British]
FDO	Family Dollar Stores [NYSE symbol] (TTSB)
FDO	Family Dollar Stores, Inc. [NYSE symbol] (SPSG)
FDO	Fee Determination Official (NASA)
FDO	Field Director Overseas [Red Cross]
FDO	Fighter Director Officer [Navy]
FDO	Fighter Duty Officer
FDO	Fire Direction Officer [Army] (AABC)
FDO	Fleet Aircraft Direction Officer [Navy British]
FDO	Fleet Dental Officer
FDO	Flight Deck Officer [British military] (DMA)
FDO	Flight Duty Officer [Air Force] (AFM)
FDO	Flight Dynamics Officer [NASA] (KSC)

FDO	Food Distribution Order
FDO	Frequency-Domain Oscilloscope (PDAA)
FDOC	Fire Detection Operation Center
FD:OCA	Formatted Data: Object Content Architecture (CDE)
FDOI	First Day of Issue [Philately]
FDOMEZ	Frente Democratico Oriental de Mexico Emiliano Zapata [Political party] (EY)
FDOP	Filtered Detection Only Processor (CAAL)
FDOR	Flavoprotein Disulfide Oxidoreductase [An enzyme]
FDOR	Flight Design Operations Review (MCD)
FDOS	Floppy Disk Operating System [Computer science] (IEEE)
FDOS	Franklin Computer Corp. (MHDW)
FDOS	Frequency Domain Optical Storage System [Computer science]
FDP	Daughters of Divine Providence (TOCD)
FDP	Factory Data Processing (IAA)
FDP	Falling Dilute-Phase (PDAA)
FDP	Faridpur [Bangladesh] [Airport symbol] (AD)
FDP	Fast Delivery Processor [Computer science] (EERA)
FDP	Fast Digital Processor [Computer science]
FDP	FDP Corp. [Associated Press] (SAG)
FDP	Fibrin [or Fibrinogen] Degradation Products [Hematology]
FDP	Field Data Processing
FDP	Field Development Program [LIMRA]
FDP	Fighter Director Post
FDP	Filii Divinae Providentiae [Sons or Daughters of Divine Providence] [Roman Catholic religious order]
FDP	Final Design Presentation (NOAA)
FDP	Financially Disadvantaged Person
FDP	Firmware Development Plan
FDP	Fixed Dose Procedure [Proposed toxicological standard]
FDP	Fixture Data Processor
FDP	Flare Dispenser Pod
FDP	Flexor Digitorum Profundus [Anatomy]
FDP	Flexor Distal Phalanx [Anatomy] (DAVI)
FDP	Flight Data Processing (KSC)
FDP	Flight Demonstration Program (MCD)
FDP	Floating Divide or Proceed (SAA)
FDP	Flood Damage Prevention [Type of water project]
FDP	Flying Duty Period (DA)
FDP	Food Distribution Program [Department of Agriculture]
FDP	Foreign Duty Pay
FDP	Form Die Press (MCD)
FDP	Forward Defense Post (NATG)
FDP	Forward Director Post
FDP	Forward Distribution Point [Military]
FDP	Foxboro Display Packages (NITA)
FDP	Free Democrat Party [Turkey Political party]
FDP	Freedom Democratic Party [in Mississippi]
FDP	Freeze Desalination Plant
FDP	Freie Demokratische Partei [Free Democratic Party] [Germany Political party] (EAIO)
FDP	Freisinnig-Demokratische Partei der Schweiz [Radical Democratic Party of Switzerland] (PPW)
FDP	Fronto-Dextra Posterior [A fetal position] [Obstetrics]
FDP	Frontul Democratic Popular [Democratic Popular Front] [Romania] [Political party] (PPE)
FDP	Fructose Diphosphate [Biochemistry]
FDP	Full Dog Point (MSA)
FDP	Funded Delivery Period [DoD]
FDP	Future Data Processor (IAA)
FDP	Sons of Divine Providence (TOCD)
fdp	Sons of Divine Providence (TOCD)
FDPase	Fructose Diphosphatase [An enzyme]
FDPB	Fatigue-Decreased Proficiency Boundary
FDPC	FDP Corp. [NASDAQ symbol] (SAG)
FDPC	Federal Data Processing Centers
FDPC	Fluorimetric Determination of Plasma Cortisol [Clinical chemistry]
FDPIR	Food Distribution Program on Indian Reservations [Department of Agriculture] (GFGA)
FDPL	Fluid Pressure Line (MSA)
FDPM	Final Draft, Presidential Memorandum [DoD]
FDPM	Fondation pour le Developpement de la Psychotherapie Medicale [Foundation for t he Development of Medical Psychotherapy] [Switzerland] (EAIO)
FDPM	Front Democratique des Patriotes Maliens [Mali] [Political party] (EY)
FDPO	Field Post Office [Military British]
FDPO	Foreign Disclosure Policy Office [Military] (AFIT)
FDPS	Field Developed Programs [Computer science]
FDPS	Flight Data Processing System (DA)
FD/PSK	Frequency-Differential/Phase-Shift Keyed System [Computer science] (TEL)
FDQA	Flight Development Quality Assurance (MCD)
FDQB	Flexor Digiti Quinti Brevis [Muscle or nerve] [Anatomy] (DAVI)
FDR	Facility Data Report [Nuclear energy]
FDR	Fact, Discussion, Recommendations
FDR	Fahrdienstregelement [Traffic Service Regulations] [German]
FDR	Fairleigh Dickinson University, Rutherford, NJ [OCLC symbol] (OCLC)
FDR	Fast Dump Restore (IAA)
FDR	Federal Air P Ltd. [South Africa] [FAA designator] (FAAC)
FDR	Federal Document Retrieval [Information service or system] (IID)
FDR	Federation of Drum Reconditioners [British] (DBA)
FDR	Feeder
FDR	Field Definition Record (IAA)
FDR	File Data Register [Computer science]

FDR	Final Data Report
FDR	Final Design Report [Nuclear Regulatory Commission] (GFGA)
FDR	Final Design Review (MCD)
FDR	Finder (MSA)
FDR	Fire Door (AAG)
FDR	First Allied Resources Corp. [Vancouver Stock Exchange symbol]
FDR	First Degree Relatives
FDR	Fix Dump Reducer (SAA)
FDR	Flight Data Recorder
FDR	Fluorogenic Drug Reagent [Clinical chemistry]
FDR	Formal Design Review
FDR	Founder
FDR	Framework-Determining Region [Immunogenetics]
FDR	Franklin Delano Roosevelt [US president, 1882-1945]
FDR	Frederick, OK [Location identifier FAA] (FAAL)
FDR	Frente Democratico Contra la Represion [Democratic Front Against Repression] [Guatemala] [Political party] (PD)
FDR	Frequency Dependent Rejection [Telecommunications] (TEL)
FDR	Frequency Diversity RADAR
FDR	Frequency Domain Reflectometry
F/DR	Front Door [Automotive engineering]
FDR	Functional Demonstration Requirement (AAG)
FDR	Functional Design Requirements (NRCH)
FDR	Functional Design Review (MCD)
FDR	Future Digital Radio [Army]
FDRA	Footwear Distributors and Retailers of America (EA)
FDRAM	Fount Description Random Access Memory (NITA)
FDRB	Foreign Disclosure Review Board (AAGC)
FDRE	Fondation Denis de Rougemont pour l'Europe [Switzerland] (EAIO)
FDRF	Financial Data Records Folder (MUGU)
FDRFA	Flight Data Recorder and Fault Analyzer [Military]
FDRFC	Friends of Debbie Reynolds Fan Club (EA)
FDR-FMLN	Frente Democratico Revolucionario - Farabundo Marti de Liberacion Nacional [Democratic Revolutionary Front/Farabundo Marti National Liberation Front] [El Salvador] [Political party] (EY)
FDR/FMLN	Frente Democratico Revolucionario / Farabundo Marti para la Liberacion Nacional [Democratic Revolutionary Front/Farabundo Marti National Liberation Front] [Guatemala] [Political party]
FDRG	Fluid Dynamics Research Group [MIT] (MCD)
FDRI	Family and Demographic Research Institute [Brigham Young University] [Research center] (RCD)
FDRI	Flight Director Rate Indicator (KSC)
FDRL	Fluid Dynamics Research Laboratory [MIT] (MCD)
FDRL	Franklin D. Roosevelt Library
FDRMA	Flooring Division, Rubber Manufacturers Association (EA)
FDRPS	Franklin D. Roosevelt Philatelic Society [Defunct] (EA)
FDRS	Flight Data Recording System
FDRS	Flight Display Research System
FDRS	Food Distribution Research Society (EA)
FDRS	Functional Description Requirements Specification [Army]
FDRT	Flexible Digital Receiving Terminal
FDRTD	Federated
FDRY	Foundry (KSC)
FDS	Factset Research Systems, Inc. [NYSE symbol] (SAG)
FDS	Fallout Decay Simulation (OA)
FDS	Faraday Dark Space
FDS	Fast Diode Switch
FDS	Fathometer Depth Sounder
FDS	Fellow of Dental Surgery [British]
FDS	Feminine Deodorant Spray [Initialism used as brand name]
FDS	Fence Disturbance System [Military]
FDS	Fermi-Dirac Statistics
FDS	Field Dressing Station [Military] (NATG)
FDS	Fighter Data Storage (IAA)
FDS	Fighter Director Ship [Navy]
FDS	File Description System [Computer science] (PDAA)
FDS	Finance Disbursing Section [Army]
FDS	Finsbury Data Services Ltd. [Database] [London, England]
FDS	Fire Detection System
FDS	Fire Distribution System
FDS	Firmware Design Specification
FDS	First Development System (MCD)
FDS	Fixed Disc Stores (NITA)
FDS	Fixed Distributed Subsystem [Antisubmarine warfare] (MCD)
FDS	Fixed Distribution System [Acoustic antisubmarine warfare sensor] (DOMA)
FDS	Flare Detection System (KSC)
FDS	Fleet Dental Surgeon [Navy British]
FDS	Fleet Digital System (MCD)
FDS	Flexible Disk System
FDS	Flexible Display System
FDS	Flexible Drive Shaft
FDS	Flexor Digitorum Sublimis [Muscle or nerve] [Anatomy] (DAVI)
FDS	Flexor Digitorum Superficialis [Anatomy]
FDS	Flight Data System [NASA]
FDS	Flight Design and Scheduling (MCD)
FDS	Flight Design System (NASA)
FDS	Flight Director System (NATG)
FDS	Flight Dynamics Simulator (MCD)
FDS	Flight Dynamics Software [or System] (MCD)
FDS	Floppy Disk System [Computer science]
FDS	Fluid Distribution System (KSC)
FDS	For Duration of [Hospital] Stay (CPH)
FDS	Form Die-Swage

FDS............ FORTRAN [*Formula Translating System*] Deductive System [*Computer science*] (IAA)
FDS............ Forward Delivery Squadron [*British military*] (DMA)
FDS............ Forward Dressing Station [*Military British*]
FDS............ Frame Difference Signal
FDS............ Frente Democratica Social [*Democratic Social Front*] [*Guinea-Bissau*] [*Political party*] (EY)
FDS............ Frequency Division Separator [*Multiplexing*]
FDS............ Frequency Division Switching [*Radio and television broadcasting*]
FDS............ Friends Disaster Service (EA)
FDS............ Functional Design Specifications (MCD)
FDS............ Stetson University, De Land, FL [*Library symbol Library of Congress*] (LCLS)
FDSA........ Force Development System Agency [*DoD*]
FD/SC........ Failure Definitions/Scoring Criteria (AABC)
FDSC........ Flight Dynamics Simulation Complex (MCD)
FDSC........ Flight Dynamics Situation Complex (NASA)
FdScrw...... Federal Screw Works [*Associated Press*] (SAG)
FDSE......... Full-Duplex Switched Ethernet (CDE)
FDSG......... Freeze-Dried (Allogenic) Skin Graft [*Medicine*]
FDSIS......... Flight Deck System Integration Simulator
FDS-L......... Stetson University College of Law, St. Petersburg, FL [*Library symbol Library of Congress*] (LCLS)
FDSR.......... Floppy Disk Send/Receive [*Computer science*]
FDSRCPSGlas... Fellow in Dental Surgery of the Royal College of Physicians and Surgeons of Glasgow
FDSRCPS Glasg... Fellow in Dental Surgery of the Royal College of Physicians and Surgeons of Glasgow
FDSRCS...... Fellow in Dental Surgery of the Royal College of Surgeons of England
FDSRCSE..... Fellow in Dental Surgery of the Royal College of Surgeons of Edinburgh
FDSRCSEd... Fellow in Dental Surgery of the Royal College of Surgeons of Edinburgh
FDSRCS Edin... Fellow in Dental Surgery of the Royal College of Surgeons of Edinburgh
FDSRCS Eng... Fellow in Dental Surgery of the Royal College of Surgeons of England
FDSSR........ Flight Dynamics Staff Support Room [*Apollo*] [*NASA*]
FDSSS........ Flight Deck Status Signaling System (MCD)
FDST.......... Siteki [*Swaziland*] [*ICAO location identifier*] (ICLI)
FDSU.......... Flight Data Storage Unit
FDSVC........ Food Service (MSA)
Fd SVP...... Find SVP, Inc. [*Associated Press*] (SAG)
FDT............. Failure Diagnostic Team [*Aerospace*] (AAG)
FDT............. Fault Detection Tester
FDT............. Fidelity Trust Co. [*Toronto Stock Exchange symbol*]
FDT............. Field Definition Table (IAA)
FDT............. Fighter Director Tender [*Navy*]
FDT............. Figure Drawing Test [*Psychology*]
FDT............. First Destination Transportation [*Military*] (AFM)
FDT............. Flexible Digital Terminal
FDT............. Flight Demonstration Team (MCD)
FDT............. Floor Drain Tank [*Nuclear energy*] (NRCH)
FDT............. Flourescent Discharge Tube [*Technology*]
FDT............. Flowing Gas Detonation Tube
FDT............. Fluorescent Discharge Tube [*Panasonic*]
FDT............. Food, Drink, Tobacco [*Department of Employment*] [*British*]
FDT............. Formal Description Technique [*Telecommunications*] (OSI)
FDT............. Formatted Data Tapes
FDT............. Fronto-Dextra Transversa [*A fetal position*] [*Obstetrics*]
FDT............. Full Duplex Teletype
FDT............. Functional Description Table
FDTA.......... Fisheries Development Trust Account (EERA)
FDTAA........ Federation of Democratic Turkish Associations of Australia
FDT & E....... Field Development Test and Evaluation (MCD)
FDTB.......... Foreign and Domestic Teachers' Bureau [*Defunct*] (EA)
FDTC.......... Fibre Drum Technical Council (EA)
FD-TD........ Finite Difference - Time Domain [*Computer simulation*]
FDTE.......... Final Development Test and Evaluation (MCD)
FDTE.......... Force Development Testing and Experimentation [*Military*] (AABC)
FDTF.......... Federal Documents Task Force [*Government Documents Round Table*] [*American Library Association*]
FDTK.......... Floating Drift Tube Klystron
FDTM.......... Tambankulu [*Swaziland*] [*ICAO location identifier*] (ICLI)
FDTMDRC... /TRADOC Material Development and Readiness Council [*Development and Readiness Communications*] [*Training and Doctrine Command*] [*Army*] (MCD)
fdtn............ Foundation (VRA)
FDTS.......... Firing Device Test Set [*Military*] (CAAL)
FDTS.......... Floor Drain Treatment System [*Nuclear energy*] (NRCH)
FDTS.......... Tshaneni [*Swaziland*] [*ICAO location identifier*] (ICLI)
FDTSP........ Foreign Disclosure Technology Security Plan [*Army*]
FDTU.......... Federation of Danish Trade Unions
FDTVMP...... Frostig Developmental Test of Visual-Motor Perception [*Psychiatry*] (DAVI)
FDTVP........ Frostig Developmental Test of Visual Perception [*Psychiatry*] (DAVI)
FDU............ Bandundu [*Zaire*] [*Airport symbol*] (OAG)
FDu............ Dunedin Public Library, Dunedin, FL [*Library symbol Library of Congress*] (LCLS)
FDU............ Fairleigh Dickinson University [*New Jersey*]
FDU............ Fairleigh Dickinson University, Teaneck, NJ [*OCLC symbol*] (OCLC)
FDU............ Flexible Disc Unit (NITA)
FDU............ Flight Development Unit (MCD)
FDU............ Fluid Distribution Unit (MCD)

FDU............ Force Design Update [*Army*]
FDU............ Frequency Determining Unit
FDU............ Frequency Divider Unit [*Electronics*] (IAA)
FDU............ Frequency Doubling Unit
FDU(A)........ Fleet Diving Unit (Atlantic) [*Canadian Navy*]
FDUB.......... Ubombo [*Swaziland*] [*ICAO location identifier*] (ICLI)
FDUNSW...... Firemen and Deckhands' Union of New South Wales [*Australia*]
FDU(P)........ Fleet Diving Unit (Pacific) [*Canadian Navy*]
FDUR.......... Free Democratic Union of Roma [*Political party*]
FDUX.......... Full Duplex [*Computer science*] (TNIG)
FDV............ Fault Detect Verification
FDV............ Fiji Disease Virus [*Plant pathology*]
FDV............ Flow-Diversion Valve
FDV............ Friend Disease Virus [*Also, FLV, FV*]
FDV............ Fuel Deceleration Valve [*Automotive engineering*]
FDV............ Full Duplex VOCODER [*Voice Coder*]
FDV............ Nome, AK [*Location identifier FAA*] (FAAL)
FDVS.......... Field Depot Veterinary Stores [*British military*] (DMA)
FDW.......... Feed Water (AAG)
FDW.......... Fine [*Condition*] in Dust Wrapper [*Antiquarian book trade*]
FDW.......... Flat Data Wing
FDW.......... Winnsboro, SC [*Location identifier FAA*] (FAAL)
FDWL.......... Fiberboard, Double Wall
FD WMR..... Food Warmer (NASA)
FDX............ Federal Express [*NYSE symbol*] (TTSB)
FDX............ Federal Express Corp. [*NYSE symbol Toronto Stock Exchange symbol*] (SPSG)
FDX............ Federal Express Corp. [*ICAO designator*] (FAAC)
FDX............ Flyball Dog Excellent
FDX............ Foodex, Inc. [*Toronto Stock Exchange symbol*]
FDX............ Full Duplex [*Telecommunications*]
FDY............ Atchison Casting Corp. [*NYSE symbol*] (SAG)
FDY............ Findlay, OH [*Location identifier FAA*] (FAAL)
FDYM.......... First Dynasty Mines [*NASDAQ symbol*] (SAG)
FDZ............ Daughters of Divine Zeal (TOCD)
FDZ............ Fetal Death Zone [*Medicine*]
fe----............ Africa, East [*MARC geographic area code Library of Congress*] (LCCP)
FE............ Eustis Memorial Library, Eustis, FL [*Library symbol Library of Congress*] (LCLS)
FE............ Extended Forecasts [*Symbol*] [*National Weather Service*]
FE............ Facilities Engineer (MCD)
F/E............ Facing East [*In outdoor advertising*] (WDMC)
FE............ Failure Equation
FE............ Failure to Eject (MCD)
FE............ Far East
FE............ Farman Experimental [*British military*] (DMA)
FE............ Farm Economics Research Division [*of ARS, Department of Agriculture*]
FE............ Feather
FE............ February (ADA)
FE............ Fecal Emesis
FE............ Fecal Energy [*Nutrition*]
FE............ Feliciana Eastern Railroad Co. [*Later, FERR*] [*AAR code*]
FE............ Female
FE............ Female with Eggs [*Pisciculture*]
FE............ Ferroelectric
Fe............ Ferrum [*Iron*] [*Chemical element*]
FE............ Fetal Erythroblastosis [*Medicine*]
FE............ Fibrinogen Equivalent [*Hematology*]
FE............ Field Emission [*Physics*]
FE............ Field Engineer [*or Engineering*]
FE............ Field Expedient (AABC)
FE............ Fighter Escort
FE............ Fine Erection
FE............ Fire Escape (DAC)
FE............ Fire Extinguisher (AAG)
FE............ First Edition (ADA)
FE............ First Entry [*British military*] (DMA)
FE............ Fit for Service Everywhere [*British military*] (DMA)
FE............ Flame Emission
FE............ Flash Evaporation (OA)
FE............ Fleet Engineer [*Navy British*] (ROG)
FE............ Flemish Ell [*Unit of length*] (ROG)
F/E............ Flexion/Extension [*Orthopedics*]
FE............ Flexor Exciter [*Neurology*]
FE............ Flight Engineer [*or Engineering*]
FE............ Flight Examiner [*Aeromedical evacuation*]
FE............ Florida Airlines and Air South [*ICAO designator*] (AD)
FE............ Flow Element [*Nuclear energy*] (NRCH)
FE............ Fluid Extract [*Pharmacy*]
FE............ Fluoresceinated Estrogen [*Clinical chemistry*]
FE............ Fonetic English [*for spelling words the way they sound*]
FE............ Foreign Editor (NTCM)
FE............ Foreign Exchange [*Investment term*]
FE............ Forest Engineer
FE............ For Example (ROG)
FE............ Format Effector [*Computer science*]
FE............ Framing Error (HGAA)
F/E............ Fraudulent Enlistment
FE............ Free End [*Dentistry*]
FE............ Friedensengel [*Angel of Peace*] [*Torpedo auxiliary equipment*] [*German military - World War II*]
FE............ Friends for Education [*Later, FFE*] (EA)
FE............ Friends of the Everglades (EA)

FE	Front End (ADA)
FE	Frozen Embryo [*Medicine*] (HCT)
FE	Fuel Economy [*In automobile model name "Honda Civic 1300 FE"*]
FE	Fugitive Emissions [*Environmental Protection Agency*] (GFGA)
F/E	Full Empty (NASA)
FE	Functional Entity [*Telecommunications*] (TEL)
FE	Fundamentals of Engineering [*Exam*]
FE	Funding Exchange (EA)
FE	Furnace Explosion [*Insurance*]
FE	Further Education
FE	Futures Exchange [*Investment term*]
Fe	Iron (IDOE)
Fe	Iron [*Chemical*] (EERA)
fe	Iron (VRA)
FE	Office of Fossil Energy
Fe²0³	Ferric Oxide (CDE)
FE⁵⁹	Radioactive Iron [*Chemistry*] (DAVI)
FEA	Eglin Air Force Base, Eglin, FL [*OCLC symbol*] (OCLC)
FEA	Failure Effect Analysis
FEA	Far East and Australasia [*A publication*]
FEA	Far Eastern Air Transport Corp. [*Taiwan*] [*ICAO designator*] (FAAC)
FEA	Farmstead Equipment Association (EA)
FEA	Feather [*Aircraft engine*] (DNAB)
FEA	Feather Falls [*California*] [*Seismograph station code, US Geological Survey Closed*] (SEIS)
FEA	Federal Editors Association [*Later, NAGC*] (EA)
FEA	Federal Energy Administration [*Formerly, FEO*] [*Superseded by Department of Energy, 1977*]
FEA	Federal Executive Association
FEA	Federation Europeenne des Associations Aerosols [*Federation of European Aerosol Associations*] (EA)
FEA	Federation Internationale pour l'Education Artistique
FEA	Fetlar [*Shetland Islands*] [*Airport symbol*] (OAG)
FEA	Fiber-Embedding Approximation
FEA	Field Effect Amplifier
FEA	Field Evaluation Agency [*Army*]
FEA	Filarial Excretory Antigen [*Immunology*]
FEA	Finite Element Analysis [*Engineering*]
FEA	Follow-Up Error Alarm
FEA	Foreign Economic Administration [*World War II*]
FEA	Formal Environmental Assessment (MCD)
FEA	Fraternity Executives Association (EA)
FEA	French Equatorial Africa
FEA	Front End Analysis
FEA	Full Employment Act [*1946*] (OICC)
FEA	Functional Economic Area
FEA	Future Engineers of America (EA)
FEAA	Federal Employees' Appeal Authority [*Civil Service Commission*]
FEAA	Fellow of the English Association of Accountants and Auditors (DD)
FEAA	Folk Education Association of America (EA)
FEAA	Free Enterprise Awards Association (EA)
FEAAES	Far East Army and Air Force Exchange Service
FEAAF	Federation Europeenne des Associations d'Analystes Financiers [*European Federation of Financial Analysts' Societies - EFFAS*] (EAIO)
FEABL	Finite Element Analysis Basic Library [*MIT*]
FEAC	Fairchild Engine & Airplane Corp.
FEAC	Far Eastern Advisory Council
FEAC	Freelance Editors' Association of Canada
FEAC	Full Employment Action Council [*Defunct*] (EA)
FEAC	Fusion Energy Advisory Committee
FEACCI	Far-East-America Council of Commerce and Industry [*Defunct*] (EA)
FEACO	Federation Europeenne des Associations de Conseils en Organisation [*European Federation of Management Consultants Associations*] [*France*]
FEAD	Federation Europeenne des Associations de Dieteticiens [*European Federation of the Associations of Dietitians - EFAD*] (EAIO)
FEAD	Fondo Especial de Asistencia para el Desarrollo (de la OEA) [*Organizacion de Estados Americanos*] [*Washington, DC*]
FEAD	Front End Accessory Drive [*Automotive engineering*]
FEAF	Far East Air Force
FEA(I)	Federal Employees Association (Independent)
FEAICS	Federation Europeenne des Associations d'Ingenieurs de Securite et de Chefs de Service de Securite [*European Federation of Associations of Engineers and Heads of Industrial Safety Services*]
FEAIE	Federation Europeenne des Associations d'Instruments a Ecrire [*Federation of European Writing Instruments Associations*] (EAIO)
FEALC	Federacion Espeleologica de America Latina y el Caribe [*Speleological Federation of Latin America and the Caribbean*] (EAIO)
FEALOGFOR	Far East Air Logistical Force
FEAMCOM	Far East Air Materiel Command
FEAMIS	Foreign Exchange Accounting and Management Information System
FEAN	Federation des Enseignants d'Afrique Noire [*Federation of Teachers of Black Africa*]
FeAn	Ferroan Anorthosite [*Lunar geology*]
FE & MV	Fremont, Elkhorn & Missouri Valley Railroad
FEANI	Federation Europeenne d'Associations Nationales d'Ingenieurs [*European Federation of National Engineering Associations*] (EAIO)
FEAO	Federation of European American Organizations (EA)
FEAOA	Far East Auto Owners Association (EA)
FEAP	Facilities Engineer Apprentice Program [*Army*] (MCD)

FEAP	Far East/Pacific
FEAP	Federation Europeenne des Associations des Psychologues [*European Federation of Professional Psychologists Associations - EFPPA*] (EA)
FEAP	FORTRAN [*Formula Translating System*] Executive Assembly Program [*Computer science*] (IAA)
Fea Posth	Fearne's Posthumous Works [*A publication*] (DLA)
FEAPW	Federal Emergency Administration of Public Works [*Consolidated into Federal Works Agency and administered as PWA, 1939*]
FEAR	Federal Employment Activity Report
FEAR	Field Engineering Assistance Request (MCD)
FEAR	Forfeiture Endangers American Rights (EA)
FEAR	Forward-Firing Aerial Rocket (IAA)
FEAREA	Far East Area (CINC)
FEARO	Federal Environmental Assessment Review Office [*Canada*]
Fear Rem	Fearne on Contingent Remainders [*1722-1844*] [*A publication*] (DLA)
FEAS	Fellow of the English Association of Corporate Secretaries (DD)
FEAS	Finite Element Analysis System [*IBM UK Ltd.*] [*Software package*] (NCC)
FEASIBLE	Finite Element Analysis Sensibly Implemented by Least Effort
FEAST	Fab Eating at School Today [*Nutritional improvement group*] [*British*]
FEAST	Food Education and Service Training
FEAST	Food Equipment and Additives Suppliers and Traders [*Leatherhead Food Research Association*] [*Information service or system*] (CRD)
FEAT	Final Engineering Acceptance Test [*Apollo*] [*NASA*]
FEAT	Formal Evaluation Acceptance Test [*Apollo*] [*NASA*]
FEAT	Frequency of Every Allowable Term [*Computer science*]
FEAT	Fuel Efficiency Automobile Test (PS)
FEATA	Far East Air Transport Association
Featherlte	Featherlite Manufacturing, Inc. [*Associated Press*] (SAG)
FEATS	Festival of European Anglophone Theatrical Societies
FEATS	Future European Air Traffic System (GAVI)
FEAU	Fluoro(ethyl)arabinosyluracil [*Biochemistry*]
FEB	FABS Electronic Bible [*FABS International, Inc.*] [*Information service or system*] (CRD)
FEB	Fair Employment Board [*of Civil Service Commission*] [*Abolished, 1955*]
FEB	Far East National Bank [*AMEX symbol*] (SAG)
FEB	Far East National Bank [*AMEX symbol*] (TTSB)
FEB	Febrifuge [*Allaying Fever Heat*] [*Pharmacy*] (ROG)
feb	Febrile [*Medicine*] (DAVI)
FEB	Febris [*Fever*] [*Pharmacy*]
FEB	February (EY)
Feb	February (ODBW)
FEB	Federal Executive Board
FEB	Federal Executive Board (USGC)
FEB	Field Engineering Bulletin
FEB	Field Engineering Bureau [*FCC*] (NTCM)
FEB	Financial and Economic Board (NATG)
FEB	Finite Elastic Body
FEB	Flying Evaluation Board
FEB	Forca Expedicionaria Brasileira [*Brazilian Expeditionary Force, 1944-1955*]
FEB	Force Engineer Battalion [*Marine Corps*] (VNW)
FEB	Forward Equipment Bay (MCD)
FEB	Functional Electronic Block
FEB	Functional Exploration of Bone
FEB	Sanfebagar [*Nepal*] [*Airport symbol*] (OAG)
FEBA	Far East Broadcasting Association
FEBA	Federal Energy Bar Association (EA)
FEBA	Foreign Exchange Brokers Association [*British*]
FEBA	Forward Edge of the Battle Area [*Army*] (AABC)
feb agglut	Febrile Agglutination [*Serology*] (CPH)
FEBC	Far East Broadcasting Co.
FEBC	Forum for European Bio-industry Coordination [*Brussels-based umbrella group*]
FEB DUR	Febre Durante [*During the Fever*] [*Pharmacy*] (ROG)
FEBE	Far End Block Error [*Telecommunications*] (ACRL)
FEBIA	Federal Employees Benefits Improvement Act of 1986
FEBMA	Federation of European Bearing Manufacturers Associations (EAIO)
FEBMA	Forged Eye Bolt Manufacturers Association [*Inactive*] (EA)
FEBNYC	Foreign Exchange Brokers of New York City (EA)
FEBOSCO	Federation des Scouts du Congo
FEBP	Fetoneonatal Estrogen-Binding Protein
FEBP	Foundation for Education Business Partnerships (AIE)
FEBRIL	Febrile Agglutinins [*Immunochemistry*] (DAVI)
FEBROA	Febrile Battery-Acute [*Medicine*] (DAVI)
FEBS	Federation of European Biochemical Societies [*France*]
FEC	Denver Express, Inc. [*ICAO designator*] (FAAC)
FEC	Eckerd College, St. Petersburg, FL [*OCLC symbol*] (OCLC)
FEC	Facilities Engineering Command [*Also, NFEC*] [*Formerly, Bureau of Yards and Docks*] [*Navy*]
FEC	Faculty Exchange Center (EA)
FEC	Far East Command [*Military*]
FEC	Far East Conference [*Defunct*] (EA)
FEC	Far Eastern Commission
FEC	Fecal [*Medicine*] (DAVI)
FEC	Fecerunt [*They Did It*] [*Latin*] (ADA)
FEC	Fecit [*He, or She, Did It*] [*Latin*]
FEC	Federal Elections Commission [*Formerly, OFE*]
FEC	Federal Electric Co. (KSC)
FEC	Federal Executive Committee (OICC)
FEC	Federation Europeenne de Climatotherapie [*European Society of Climatotherapy - ESC*] [*French*] (EAIO)

FEC............ Federation of Egalitarian Communities (EA)
FEC............ Federation of the European Cutlery and Flatware Industries (EA)
FEC............ Ferroelectric Ceramic
FEC............ Field Engineering Change (KSC)
FEC............ Field Error Correction (MCD)
FEC............ Fine Erection Complete
FEC............ Fire Extinguisher Cabinet [Technical drawings]
FEC............ First Edition Club (NTCM)
FEC............ Fixed Electrolytic Capacitor
FEC............ Floating Error Code [Digital Equipment Corp.]
FEC............ Florida East Coast Railway Co. [AAR code]
FEC............ Fondation d'Etudes du Canada [Canada Studies Foundation - CSF]
FEC............ Fondation Europeenne de la Culture [European Cultural Foundation - ECF] [Netherlands]
FEC............ Food and Energy Council (EA)
FEC............ Forced Expiratory Capacity [Medicine] (DMAA)
FEC............ Foreign Exchange Certificate [Special currency notes sold to foreigners] [People's Republic of China] (ECON)
FEC............ Foreign Exchange Cost (AFM)
FEC............ Forward End Cap
FEC............ Forward Error Correction [Computer code]
FEC............ Forward Events Controller (MCD)
FEC............ Foundation for Exceptional Children (EA)
FECL........... Franciscan Educational Conference [Defunct]
FEC............ Free Energy Change
FEC............ Free Erythrocyte Coproporphyrin [Hematology] (MAE)
FEC............ Free Europe Committee [Later, RFE/RL] (EA)
FEC............ Free-Standing Emergency Center
FEC............ Freestanding Emergency Clinic
FEC............ French Expeditionary Corps
FEC............ Friedl Expert Committee (EA)
FEC............ Friend Erythroleukemia Cell [Medicine] (DMAA)
FEC............ Front-End Computer
FEC............ Front End Control Program (IAA)
FECA.......... Facilities Engineering and Construction Agency [HEW]
FECA.......... Federal Election Campaign Act of 1971
FECA.......... Federal Employees Compensation Act [1908] (AFM)
FECA.......... Fully Enclosed Covered Area (ADA)
FECAP........ Feeder Equipment Capacity (PDAA)
FECB.......... Far East Combined Bureau [Singapore, 1940] [Military]
FECB.......... Federation des Employes Congolais des Banques [Federation of Congolese Bank Clerks]
FECB.......... File Extended Control Block [Computer science] (BUR)
FECC.......... Federal Employees Coordinating Committee (EA)
FECC.......... Federation Europeenne du Commerce Chimique [Federation of European Chemical Merchants - FECM] (EAIO)
FECDBA ...... Foreign Exchange and Currency Deposit Brokers Association (MHDW)
FECEGC....... Federation Europeenne des Constructeurs d'Equipement de Grandes Cuisines [European Federation of Catering Equipment Manufacturers - EFCEM] (EA)
FECEP......... Federation Europeenne des Constructeurs d'Equipement Petrolier [European Federation of Petroleum Equipment Manufacturers]
FECES......... Forward Error Control Electronics System (IAA)
FECF.......... Food Executives Club of Florida (EA)
FECG.......... Fetal Electrocardiography [or Electrocardiogram] [Medicine]
FECI.......... Fellow of the Institute of Employment Consultants [British] (DBQ)
FECL.......... Federal Constitutional Law
FECL.......... Fleet Electronics Calibration Laboratory
FECM.......... Federation of European Chemical Merchants (EA)
FECM.......... Firm Engineering Change Memo (SAA)
FECMA........ Federation of European Coin-Machine Associations (EAIO)
FECN.......... Forward-Explicit Congestion Notification [Computer science]
FECO.......... Fringes of Equal Chromatic Order [Optics]
FECOM........ Far East Command [Military]
FECOM........ Fonds Europeen de Cooperation Monetaire [European Monetary Cooperation Fund]
FECOMZ...... Forward Echelon, Communications Zone [Europe] [Army]
FECONS....... Field Engineer Control System (PDAA)
FECP.......... Facility Engineering Change Proposal
FECP.......... Field Engineering Change Proposal
FECP.......... Florida Education Computing Project (EDAC)
FECP.......... Formal Engineering Change Proposal (MSA)
FECP.......... Free Erythrocyte Coproporphyria [Hematology] (MAE)
FECP.......... Front End Communications Processor
FECR.......... Far East Communications Region [Air Force] (MCD)
FeCr......... Ferrichrome Recording Tape (NTCM)
FECS.......... Federal Employees' Compensation System (GFGA)
FECS.......... Federation Europeenne des Fabricants de Ceramiques Sanitaires [European Federation of Ceramic Sanitaryware Manufacturers - EFCSM] (EAIO)
FECS.......... Federation of European Chemical Societies (EAIO)
FECS.......... Foreign Exchange Counselling System (NITA)
FECT.......... Federation of European Chemical Trade (EAIO)
FECT.......... Fibroelastic Connective Tissue [Medicine]
FECU.......... Flutter Exciter Control Unit (MCD)
FECUA........ Farmers' Educational and Cooperative Union of America (EA)
FECV.......... Functional Extracellular Fluid Volume [Medicine] (MAE)
FECZ.......... Forward Echelon, Communications Zone [Europe] [Army]
FED........... Army Engineer District, Far East
FED........... Federal (AFM)
FED........... Federal
fed............ Federal Agent [Slang]
FED........... Federalist
Fed .... [The] Federalist, by Hamilton [A publication] (DLA)

Fed .... Federal Reporter [A publication] (DLA)
FED........... Federal Reserve System [Banking]
FED........... Federal Specification
FEDD.......... Federated (WDAA)
FED........... Federation (EY)
FED........... Field Effect Device
FED........... Field Effect Diode (IAA)
FED........... Field Emission Deposition [Coating technique]
FED........... Field-Emission Display (ECON)
FED........... Field Emission Display
FED........... Final Estimation of Data [Computer science]
FED........... Finfish Excluding Device [Fishing technology]
FED........... FirstFed Financial [NYSE symbol] (TTSB)
FED........... Five-Inch Evasion Device (MCD)
FED........... Fleetwood Petroleum [Vancouver Stock Exchange symbol]
FED........... Flight Events Demonstration [NASA] (KSC)
FED........... Format Element Descriptor (IAA)
FED........... Forward Entry Device [Army] (DOMA)
FED........... Foundation for Ethnic Dance (EA)
FED........... Fuel Element Department (SAA)
FED........... Fusion Engineering Device [Nuclear energy]
FED........... Linea Federal Argentina SEM [ICAO designator] (FAAC)
Fed 2d .... Federal Reporter, Second Series [A publication] (DLA)
FEDA.......... Foodservice Equipment Distributors Association (EA)
FEDAC .... Federal Education Data Acquisition Council (OICC)
FEDAC .... Federal Executive Drug Abuse Council
FEDAC .... Forward Error Detection and Correction
FEDAL......... Failed Element Detection and Location [In nuclear power reactors]
Fed Anti-Tr Cas... Federal Anti-Trust Cases, Decrees, and Judgments [1890-1918] [A publication] (DLA)
Fed Anti-Tr Dec... Federal Anti-Trust Decisions [A publication] (DLA)
FEDAPT....... Foundation for Extension and Development of the American Professional Theatre (EA)
FEDAS .... Federation of European Delegation Associations of Scientific Equipment Manufacturers, Importers, and Dealers in the Laboratory, Industrial and Medical Fields (PDAA)
FEDB.......... Failure Experience Data Bank [GIDEP]
Fed Banking L Rep... Federal Banking Law Reports [Commerce Clearing House] [A publication] (DLA)
Fed B News & J... Federal Bar News & Journal [A publication] (AAGC)
FEDC.......... Federal Economic Development Co-Ordinator [Canada]
FEDC.......... Federation of Engineering Design Companies [British] (DBA)
FEDC.......... Federation of Engineering Design Consultants (BARN)
FEDC.......... Field Exercise Data Collection [Army] (RDA)
FEDC.......... Fusion Energy Design Center (MCD)
Fed Carr Cas... Federal Carriers Cases [Commerce Clearing House] [A publication] (DLA)
Fed Carr Rep... Federal Carriers Reporter [Commerce Clearing House] [A publication] (DLA)
Fed Cas .... Federal Cases [A publication] (DLA)
Fed Cas No... Federal Case Number [Legal term] (DLA)
Fed Cir .... Court of Appeals for the Federal Circuit (AAGC)
Fed Comm LJ... Federal Communications Law Journal [A publication] (DLA)
Fed Cont Rep (BNA)... Federal Contracts Report (Bureau of National Affairs) [A publication] (DLA)
FED Co-OP... Federal Employee Direct Corporate Stock Ownership Plan (GFGA)
Fed Council Bull... Federal Council of University Staff Associations. Bulletin [A publication]
Fed Ct.......... Indian Rulings, Federal Court [A publication] (DLA)
FEDD .... For Early Domestic Dissemination (MCD)
FEDE........... Federation Europeenne des Ecoles [Later, European Schools Federation] (EAIO)
FEDECAME... Federacion Cafetalera de America [Central American Coffee Growers' Federation]
FEDECO .... Federacion de Comunidades Judias de Centroamerica y Panama [Federation of Jewish Communities of Central America and Panama] (EAIO)
Fede de Sen... Federicus Petricus de Senis [Flourished, 1321-43] [Authority cited in pre-1607 legal work] (DSA)
FEDEFAM..... Federacion Latinoamericana de Asociaciones de Familiares de Detenidos-Desaparecidos [Federation of Associations of Families of Disappeared-Detainees] (EAIO)
FE de las JONS... Falange Espanola de las Juntas de Ofensiva Nacional Sindicalista [Spanish Phalange of the Syndicalist Juntas of the National Offensive] [Political party] (PPE)
Fed Election Camp Fin Guide (CCH)... Federal Election Campaign Financing Guide (Commerce Clearing House) [A publication] (DLA)
FEDEMO ...... Federal Democratic Movement [Uganda] [Political party]
FEDER .... Fonds Europeen de Developpement Regional [European Regional Development Fund - ERDF] [Belgium] (EAIO)
FederA........ Fedders Corp. [Associated Press] (SAG)
Feders .... Fedders Corp. [Associated Press] (SAG)
FEDES .... Federation Europeenne de l'Emballage Souple (EAIO)
FEDESA....... Federation Europeenne de la Sante Animale [European Federation of Animal Health] [Belgium] (ECED)
Fed Evid R... Federal Rules of Evidence [A publication] (DLA)
FEDEX......... [The] Federal Energy Data Index [Department of Energy Information service or system Defunct] (CRD)
FedEx......... Federal Express [Parcel Service] (AAGC)
FEDEX......... Federal Express Corp. [Service mark and trade name]
FEDEX......... Federal Index [Capitol Services International] (NITA)
FedExp........ Federal Express Corp. [Associated Press] (SAG)
Fed Ex Tax Rep... Federal Excise Tax Reporter [Commerce Clearing House] [A publication] (DLA)
FedFOH........ Fidelity Financial of Ohio, Inc. [Associated Press] (SAG)

FEDGE	Finite Element Data Generation [*Computer science*]
FEDIAF	Federation Europeenne de l'Industrie des Aliments pour Animaux Familiers [*European Petfood Industry Federation*] (EAIO)
FEDIMA	Federation des Industries de Matieres Premieres et des Ameliorants pour la Boulangerie et la Patisserie dans la CEE [*European Federation of Manufacturers of Bakers' and Confectioners' Ingredients and Additives*] [*Common Market*]
Fed Ins Counsel Q	Federal Insurance Counsel Quarterly [*A publication*] (DLA)
FEDIOL	Federation de l'Industrie de l'Huilerie de la CEE [*EEC Seed Crushers and Oil Processors' Federation*] [*Belgium*] (EAIO)
FEDL	Federal
Fed Law Rev	Federal Law Review [*A publication*]
FEDLEV	Federal Low-Emission Vehicle [*Automotive engineering*]
FEDLINK	Federal Library and Information Network [*Formerly, FLECC*] [*Library of Congress Washington, DC Library network*]
Fed LJ	Federal Law Journal of India [*A publication*] (DLA)
Fed LJ Ind	Federal Law Journal of India [*A publication*] (DLA)
Fed LQ	Federal Law Quarterly [*A publication*] (DLA)
FedMog	Federal-Mogul Corp. [*Associated Press*] (SAG)
FEDN	Federation
FEDNET	Federal Information Network
FEDNET	Federal Network [*Computer network*] (NITA)
FedNM	Federal National Mortgage Association [*Wall Street slang name: "Fannie Mae"*] [*Associated Press*] (SAG)
FEDOLIVE	Federation de l'Industrie de l'Huile d'Olive de la CEE [*Federation of the European Economic Community Olive Oil Industry*]
FEDOM	Fonds Europeen de Developpement pour les Pays et Territoires d'Outre-Mer [*European Development Fund for Overseas Countries and Territories*]
FedOne	Fed One Bancorp [*Associated Press*] (SAG)
FedOne	Fed One Savings Bank [*Associated Press*] (SAG)
FEDORA	Forum Europeen de l'Orientation Academique (AIE)
FEDP	Facility and Equipment Design Plan (MCD)
FEDP	Federal Executive Development Program [*Civil Service Commission*]
FEDPAC	Federal Pacific Lakes Lines [*Steamship*] (MHDW)
FedPB	Federal Paper Board Co., Inc. [*Associated Press*] (SAG)
FEDPOWCOMM	Federal Power Commission (IAA)
Fed Prac	Federal Practice and Procedure [*A publication*] (DLA)
Fed Prob	Federal Probation [*A publication*] (BRI)
Fed Prob NL	Federal Probation Newsletter [*A publication*] (DLA)
Fed Pubs	Federal Publications, Inc. (AAGC)
Fed R	Federal Reporter [*A publication*] (DLA)
FEDRAN	Feed Drive Analysis [*Machine Tool Industry Research Association*] [*Software package*] (NCC)
Fed R App P	Federal Rules of Appellate Procedure [*A publication*] (DLA)
Fed R Civil P	Federal Rules of Civil Procedure [*A publication*] (DLA)
Fed R Civ P	Federal Rules of Civil Procedure [*A publication*] (DLA)
Fed R Civ Proc	Federal Rules of Civil Procedure [*A publication*] (HGAA)
Fed R Crim P	Federal Rules of Criminal Procedure [*A publication*] (DLA)
Fed R Crim Proc	Federal Rules of Criminal Procedure [*A publication*] (HGAA)
FedrDS	Federated Department Stores, Inc. [*Associated Press*] (SAG)
Fed Reg	Federal Register [*A publication*] (AAGC)
FEDREG	Federal Register [*Capitol Services International*] (NITA)
FEDREG	Federal Register Abstracts [*Capitol Services, Inc.*] [*Washington, DC Database*]
Fed Rep	Federal Reporter [*A publication*] (DLA)
Fed Revenue Forms (P-H)	Federal Revenue Forms (Prentice-Hall, Inc.) [*A publication*] (DLA)
Fed R Evid	Federal Rules of Evidence [*A publication*] (DLA)
Fed R Evid Serv	Federal Rules of Evidence Service [*A publication*] (DLA)
FEDRIP	Federal Research in Progress [*NTIS*] [*Department of Commerce Information service or system*] (IID)
FEDRIP	Federal Research in Progress Database (USGC)
FedRlty	Federal Realty Investment Trust [*Associated Press*] (SAG)
FEDRN	Federation
Fed R Serv 2d (Callaghan)	Federal Rules Service, Second Series [*A publication*] (DLA)
Fed Rules Civ Proc	Federal Rules of Civil Procedure [*A publication*] (DLA)
Fed Rules Cr Proc	Federal Rules of Criminal Procedure [*A publication*] (DLA)
Fed Rules Serv	Federal Rules Service [*A publication*] (DLA)
Fed Rules Serv 2d	Federal Rules Service, Second Series [*A publication*] (DLA)
FEDS	Federal Employees for a Democratic Society [*Defunct*]
FEDS	Federal Employment Decision Search [*Database*] [*Labor Relations Press*] [*Information service or system*] (CRD)
FEDS	Federal Energy Data System [*Department of Energy*] (GFGA)
FEDS	Federal Energy Data System (GNE)
FEDS	Field Experimenter Detection [*or Detector*] Survivability (MCD)
FEDS	Fixed and Exchangeable Disc Storage (NITA)
FEDS	Fixed/Exchangeable Disk Store
FEDS	Foreign Economic Development Service [*Abolished 1972, functions transferred to the Economic Research Service*] [*Department of Agriculture*]
FEDSA	Federation of European Direct Selling Associations [*Belgium*] (EAIO)
FEDSEA	Federal South East Asia Line [*Steamship*] (MHDW)
Fed Sec L Rep	Federal Securities Law Reporter [*Commerce Clearing House*] [*A publication*] (DLA)
FedSignl	Federal Signal Corp. [*Associated Press*] (SAG)
FEDSIM	Federal Computer Performance Evaluation and Simulation Center [*General Services Administration*]
FEDSPEC	Federal Specification
FED-STAN	Standards Referenced in Federal Legislation [*Standards Council of Canada*] [*Information service or system*] (CRD)
Fed Stat Ann	Federal Statutes, Annotated [*A publication*] (DLA)
FEDSTD	Federal Standard
FED-STDS	Federal Telecommunications Standards (AAGC)
FEDSTRIP	Federal Standard Requisitioning and Issue Procedure
Fed Sup	Federal Supplement [*A publication*] (DLA)
Fed Supp	Federal Supplement [*A publication*] (DLA)
Fed Tax Coordinator 2d (RIA)	Federal Tax Coordinator Second (Tax Research Institute of America) [*A publication*] (DLA)
Fed Tax Enf	Federal Tax Enforcement [*A publication*] (DLA)
Fed Taxes	Federal Taxes [*Prentice-Hall, Inc.*] [*A publication*] (DLA)
Fed Taxes Est & Gift	Federal Taxes: Estate and Gift Taxes [*Prentice-Hall, Inc.*] [*A publication*] (DLA)
Fed Taxes (P-H)	Federal Taxes (Prentice-Hall, Inc.) [*A publication*] (DLA)
Fed Tr Rep	Federal Trade Reporter [*A publication*] (DLA)
FEDU	Fluoroethyl(deoxyuridine) [*Biochemistry*]
FEE	Failure Effects Evaluation (IAA)
FEE	Field Engineering and Equipment [*Military*]
FEE	Fill Exit Entry [*Computer science*]
FEE	Florida Employers Exchange (SRA)
FEE	Fondation Europeenne pour l'Economie
FEE	Forced Equilibrating Expiration [*Physiology*]
FEE	Foundation for Economic Education (EA)
FEE	Freeway Resources Ltd. [*Vancouver Stock Exchange symbol*]
FEEA	Federal Employee Education and Assistance Fund
FEEA	Federal Energy Emergency Administration (MCD)
FEE(A)	Foundation for Economic Education (Australia)
FEEC	Field Enterprises Educational Corp. [*Later, World Book-Childcraft International al, Inc.*]
FEECA	Federation Europeenne pour l'Education Catholique des Adultes [*European Associaton for Catholic Adult Education*] (EAIO)
FEED	Field Exploitation of Elevation Data (RDA)
FEED	File of Evaluated and Event Data [*Nuclear energy*] (NUCP)
FEEDBAC	Foreign Exchange, Eurodollar, and Branch Accounting (PDAA)
FEEDM	Federation Europeenne des Emballeurs et Distributeurs de Miel [*European Federation of Honey Packers and Distributors*] [*British*] (EAIO)
FEEDS	Fire Emergency Equipment Dispatch System
FEEG	Fetal Electroencephalogram [*Medicine*] (AAMN)
FE-EL	Ferroelectric-Electroluminescent
FEEL	Fox Editor Enhancement Library (PCM)
FEEM	Field Electron Emission Microscope [*or Microscopy*]
FEEMS	Facilities Engineer Equipment Maintenance System [*Army*]
FEEOR	Federal Equal Employment Opportunity Recruitment Program (GFGA)
FEEPROM	Flash Electrically Erasable Programmable Read Only Memory [*Electronics*]
FEER	Far Eastern Economic Review [*A publication*] (BRI)
FEER	Fast Eigensolution Extraction Routine [*Computer program*]
FEER	Fundamental Equilibrium Exchange Rate [*Economics*]
FEEST	Freight Equipment Environmental Sampling Test Program [*RSPA*] (TAG)
FEET	Just For Feet [*NASDAQ symbol*] (SAG)
FEF	Fast Extrusion Furnace
FEF	Feline Embryonic Fibroblast
FEF	Flat/Exponential Filter
FEF	Flight Engineering Facility (MCD)
FEF	Forced Expiratory Flow [*Physiology*]
FEF	Foundation for Educational Futures (EA)
FEF	Foundry Educational Foundation [*Defunct*] (EA)
FEF	Freedom of Expression Foundation (EA)
FEF	Free Energy Function
FEF	French Expeditionary Force
FEF	Friends of the Earth Foundation (EA)
FEF	Frontal Eye Field [*Neuroanatomy*]
FEF	Frozen Equilibrium Flow
FEF	Fuel Examination Facility [*Nuclear energy*] (NRCH)
FEF	Fusion Energy Foundation (EA)
FEFA	Alindao [*Central African Republic*] [*ICAO location identifier*] (ICLI)
FEFA	Feeder Fault Analysis (PDAA)
FEFA	Future European Fighter Aircraft (PDAA)
FEFAC	Federation Europeenne des Fabricants d'Aliments Composes [*European Federation of Compound Animal Feedingstuff Manufacturers*] (EAIO)
FEFANA	Federation Europeenne des Fabricants d'Adjuvants pour la Nutrition Animale [*European Federation of Manufacturers of Feed Additives*] (EAIO)
FEFB	Obo [*Central African Republic*] [*ICAO location identifier*] (ICLI)
FEFC	Far Eastern Freight Conference
FEFCEB	Federation Europeenne des Fabricants de Caisses et Emballages en Bois [*European Federation of Manufacturers of Timber Crates and Packing Cases*] (PDAA)
FEFCO	Federation Europeenne des Fabricants de Carton Ondule [*European Federation of Manufacturers of Corrugated Board*] [*France*]
FEFET	Ferroelectric-Dielectric Field Effect Transistor (IAA)
FEFF	Bangui/M'Poko [*Central African Republic*] [*ICAO location identifier*] (ICLI)
FEFG	Bangassou [*Central African Republic*] [*ICAO location identifier*] (ICLI)
FEFI	Birao [*Central African Republic*] [*ICAO location identifier*] (ICLI)
FEFI	Flight Engineers Fault Isolation [*Aviation*]
FEFL	Bossembele [*Central African Republic*] [*ICAO location identifier*] (ICLI)
FEFM	Bambari [*Central African Republic*] [*ICAO location identifier*] (ICLI)
FEFM	Federazione Europea Fabbricanti Matite [*Federation of Eraser Pencil Manufacturers Associations*] (EAIO)
FEFmax	Forced Expiratory Flow Maximal [*Achieved during a forced vital capacity*] [*Medicine*] (DAVI)
FEFN	N'Dele [*Central African Republic*] [*ICAO location identifier*] (ICLI)
FEFO	Bouar [*Central African Republic*] [*ICAO location identifier*] (ICLI)
FEFO	First-Ended, First-Out [*Computer science*]

FEFP	Fuel Element Failure Propagation [Nuclear energy]
FEFPEB	Federation Europeenne des Fabricants de Palettes et Emballages en Bois [European Federation of Pallet and Wooden Crate Manufacturers - EFPWCM] (EAIO)
FEFPL	Fuel Element Failure Propagation Loop [Nuclear energy] (NRCH)
FEFR	Bria [Central African Republic] [ICAO location identifier] (ICLI)
FEFS	Bossangoa [Central African Republic] [ICAO location identifier] (ICLI)
FEFT	Berberati [Central African Republic] [ICAO location identifier] (ICLI)
FEFV	Bangui [Central African Republic] [ICAO location identifier] (ICLI)
FEFY	Yalinga [Central African Republic] [ICAO location identifier] (ICLI)
FEFZ	Zemio [Central African Republic] [ICAO location identifier] (ICLI)
f-eg--	Equatorial Guinea [MARC geographic area code Library of Congress] (LCCP)
FEG	First Canadian Energy Corp. [Vancouver Stock Exchange symbol]
FEG	Fletcher Challenge Ener.ADS [NYSE symbol] (TTSB)
FEG	Fletcher Challenge Energy [NYSE symbol] (SAG)
FEgAD	United States Air Force, Armament Development and Test Center, Technical Library, Eglin Air Force Base, FL [Library symbol Library of Congress] (LCLS)
FEGAP	Federation Europeenne de la Ganterie de Peau [European Federation of Leather Glove-Making] [EC] (ECED)
FEGLI	Federal Employees' Group Life Insurance
FEgRH	United States Air Force, Eglin Regional Hospital, Eglin Air Force Base, FL [Library symbol Library of Congress] (LCLS)
FEGS	Federation Employment and Guidance Service (EA)
FEGT	Furnace Exit Gas Temperature
FEGZ	Bozoum [Central African Republic] [ICAO location identifier] (ICLI)
FEH	Federation Europeenne Halterophile [European Weightlifting Federation - EWF] (EA)
FEHA	Federal Hall National Memorial
FEHA	Florida Environmental Health Association (SRA)
FEHB	Federal Employees Health Benefits
FEHBA	Federal Employees Health Benefits Act
FEHBP	Federal Employees Health Benefits Program (AFM)
FEHC	Federal Emergency Housing Corp. [New Deal]
FEHE	Feed-Effluent Heat Exchanger [Chemical engineering]
FEHO	Federation of European Helicopter Operators (PDAA)
FEHVA	Federation of European Heating and Ventilating Associations (EA)
FEI	Facilities Engineering Items [Military] (AABC)
FEI	Farm Equipment Institute [Later, FIEI] (EA)
FEI	Federal Executive Institute
FEI	Federation Equestre Internationale [International Equestrian Federation] [Berne, Switzerland] (EAIO)
FEI	Field Engineering Instruction [British] (DA)
FEI	Financial Executives Institute
FEI	Financial Executives Institute of Canada (DD)
FEI	Firing Effectiveness Indicator [Military] (CAAL)
FEI	Firing Error Indicator
FEI	Fish Exports Inspector
FEI	Flight Error Instrumentation [Aerospace] (IAA)
FEI	Fluidic Explosive Initiator (PDAA)
FEI	Force Effectiveness Indicator [COEA] (MCD)
FEI	For Engineering Information (AAG)
FEI	Foundation Europalia International (EAIO)
FEI	France-Europe International [An association] (EAIO)
FEI	Free Europe, Inc. [Later, RFE/RL]
FEI	Frequency Electronics, Inc. [AMEX symbol] (SPSG)
FEI	Frequency Electrs [AMEX symbol] (TTSB)
FEI	Frontend International Technologies, Inc. [Vancouver Stock Exchange symbol]
FEIA	Financial Executives Institute of Australia
FEIA	Flight Engineers' International Association (EA)
FEIA	Foreign Earned Income Act [1978]
FEIBP	Federation Europeenne de l'Industrie de la Brosserie et de la Pinceuterie [European Federation of the Brush and Paint Brush Industries - EFBPBI] (EAIO)
FEIC	Federation Europeenne de l'Industrie du Contreplaque [European Federation of the Plywood Industry - EFPI] (EA)
FEIC	FEI Co. [NASDAQ symbol] (SAG)
FEIC	Fellow of the Engineering Institute of Canada
FEIC	Fossil Energy Information Center [ORNL] (GRD)
FEICA	Federation Europeenne des Industries de Colles et Adhesifs [Association of European Adhesives Manufacturers] (EA)
FEICC	Foundation for the Establishment of an International Criminal Court (EA)
FEI Co	FEI Co. [Associated Press] (SAG)
FEICRO	Federation of European Industrial Co-Operative Research Organizations (EA)
FEICUS	Family Education and Information Council of the United States (EA)
FEID	Flight Equipment Interface Device [NASA] (NASA)
FEID	Functional Engineering Interface Device [NASA] (NASA)
FEIEA	Federation of European Industrial Editors' Associations
FEIG	Fossil Energy Information Group [Department of Energy] [Information service or system] (IID)
FEIHCCS	Flying Eagle and Indian Head Cent Collectors Society (EA)
FEILS	Federal Energy Information Locator Systems
FEIM	Federation Europeenne des Importateurs de Machines et d'Equipements de Bureau [European Federation of Importers of Business Equipment] (EAIO)
FEIN	Federal Employer Identification Number
FE INC	Iron Inclusion Bodies [Hematology] (DAVI)
FEIS	Fellow of the Educational Institute of Scotland
FEIS	Final Environmental Impact Statement
FEIS	Fugitive Emissions Information System [Environmental Protection Agency] (GFGA)

FEIS	Further Education Information Service (AIE)
FEITC	Federation Europeenne des Industries Techniques du Cinema
FEIZ	Fellow of the Engineering Institution of Zambia
FEJ	France Europe Avia Jet [ICAO designator] (FAAC)
FEJB	Forum of Environmental Journalists of Bangladesh (EERA)
FEJBT	Federation Europeenne des Jeunesse Bons Templiers [European Good Templar Youth Federation] [Norway] (EAIO)
FEJE	Facility Engineering Job Estimating [Military] (GFGA)
FEJI	Far East Job International [Former USSR] (ECON)
FEK	Fish Epidermal Keratocyte [Marine science]
FEK	Frequency Exchange Keying
FEKG	Fetal Electrocardiogram [Medicine]
FEL	Familial Erythrophagocytic Lymphohistiocytosis [Medicine]
FEL	Family Emission Level [Automotive engineering]
FEL	Feldberg In Schwarzwald [Federal Republic of Germany] [Seismograph station code, US Geological Survey] (SEIS)
Fel	Felinus Sandeus [Deceased, 1503] [Authority cited in pre-1607 legal work] (DSA)
FEL	Fellis [Gall] [Pharmacy] (ROG)
FEL	Fellow
FEL	Felony [FBI standardized term]
Fel	Felsted [Record label] [Great Britain, etc.]
FEL	Felucca [Ship's rigging] (ROG)
FEL	First Element Launch (SSD)
FEL	First European Airways Ltd. [British ICAO designator] (FAAC)
FEL	Fisheries Engineering Laboratory [Marine science] (MSC)
FEL	Flight Engineer's Licence [British] (AIA)
FEL	Food Engineering Laboratory [Army]
FEL	Free Electron LASER
FEL	Frequency Engineering Laboratory (MCD)
FEL	Friend Erythroleukemia Cell [Oncology]
FEL	Fritz Engineering Laboratory [Lehigh University]
FEL	Front End Loader (ADA)
FEL	Full Employment League
FELA	Federal Employers' Liability Act (Railroads) [1906]
FELABAN	Federacion Latinoamericana de Bancos [Latin American Banking Federation - LABF] [Bogota, Colombia] (EAIO)
FELACUTI	Federacion Latinoamericana de Usuarios del Transporte [Latin American Federation of Shippers' Councils] (EAIO)
FELAP	Finite Element Analysis Program [Nuclear energy] (NRCH)
FELATRAP	Federacion Latinoamericana de Trajabadores de la Prensa [Latin American Federation of Press Workers] (EAIO)
FELCO	Federation of English Language Course Organisation [British]
FelCor	FelCor Suite Hotels, Inc. [Associated Press] (SAG)
Fel D1	Felis Domesticus 1 [Protein found in the saliva of cats]
FELDF	Free Enterprise Legal Defense Fund [Bellevue, WA] (EA)
FELE	Franklin Electric [NYSE symbol] (TTSB)
FELE	Franklin Electric Co., Inc. [NASDAQ symbol] (NQ)
FELF	Far East Land Forces [British military] (DMA)
FELG	Far East Liaison Group (CINC)
Feli	Felinus Sandeus [Deceased, 1503] [Authority cited in pre-1607 legal work] (DSA)
FELIF	Feeder Length in Feet (PDAA)
Felin	Felinus Sandeus [Deceased, 1503] [Authority cited in pre-1607 legal work] (DSA)
FELINE	Frederick Engineering's Dataline Monitor/Protocol Analyzer [Computer science]
FELISA	Fluorogenic Enzyme-Linked Immunosorbent Assay [Biochemistry]
FELL	Federal Labor Laws
FELL	Fellow
Fell Guar	Fell on Guaranty and Suretyship [A publication] (DLA)
FELM	Felmersham [England]
FEL MEM	Felicis Memoriae [Of Happy Memory] [Latin]
FELOS	Feeder Load Search (PDAA)
FELR	Feeler
FELT	Fluid Encapsulated Launch Technique (PDAA)
FELV	Feline Leukemia Virus [Also, FLV]
FEM	Federation Europeenne de la Manutention [European Federation of Handling Industries] (EA)
FEM	Federation Europeenne des Metallurgistes dans la Communaute [European Metalworkers' Federation in the Community] [EC] (ECED)
FEM	Federation Europeenne des Motels [European Motel Federation]
FEM	Female [or Feminine] (KSC)
FEM	Feministas en Marcha [Feminists on the March] [Puerto Rico] (EAIO)
FEM	Femoral [Anatomy]
FEM	Ferguson Library, Stamford, CT [OCLC symbol] (OCLC)
FEM	Field-Effect Modified (IEEE)
FEM	Field Electron Microscope [or Microscopy]
FEM	Field Emission Microscope [or Microscopy]
FEM	Field Engineering Maintenance
FEM	Field Evaluation Model
FEM	Finite-Element Meshing [or Modeling] [Computer science] (PCM)
FEM	Finite Element Method
FEM	Firmware Expansion Model [Hewlett Packard] (NITA)
FEM	Flame Emission Spectroscopy
FEM	Flexion-Extension Motion [Orthopedics]
FEM	Fluid Energy Mill (MCD)
FEM	Flyable Engineering Model (KSC)
FEM	Fondation Europeenne pour le Management [European Foundation for Management Development] [Belgium] (EAIO)
FEM	Foundation for Elective Mutism, Inc. (EA)
FEM	Free Electron Model [Physical chemistry]
FEMA	Farm Equipment Manufacturers Association (EA)
FEMA	Federal Emergency Management Agency (ECON)

FEMA	Fire Equipment Manufacturers Association (EA)
FEMA	Flavor and Extract Manufacturers Association of the USA (EA)
FEMA	Food Equipment Manufacturers Association (EA)
FEMA	Foundry Equipment and Materials Association [*Later, CISA*] (EA)
FEMAA	Food Equipment Manufacturers' Association of Australia
FEMAAR	Federal Emergency Management Agency Acquisition Regulation (AAGC)
FEMALE	Formerly Employed Mothers at the Leading Edge [*Previous name, Formerly Employed Mothers at Loose Ends*]
FEMA-M/R	Federal Emergency Management Agency Office of Mitigation and Research [*Washington, DC*]
FEMAP	Finite Element Mold-Filling Analysis Program [*General Electric Co.*]
FEMAPR	Federal Emergency Management Agency Procurement Regulations (AAGC)
FEMAS	Far East Merchants Association [*Defunct*] (EA)
FEMB	Federation Europeenne du Mobilier de Bureau [*European Federation of Office Furniture*] [*EC*] (ECED)
FEMCO	National Federation of Export Management Companies (EA)
FEMCPL	Facilities and Environmental Measurement Components Parts List [*NASA*] (NASA)
FEMED	Fluorouracil, Methotrexate, Cyclophosphamide, Prednisone [*Antineoplastic drug regimen*] (DAVI)
FEMEF	Feeder Meter Flow (PDAA)
FEMF	Floating Electronic Maintenance Facility (MCD)
FEMF	Foreign Electromotive Force (TEL)
FEMFM	Federation of European Manufacturers of Friction Materials (EA)
FEMGED	Federation Internationale des Grandes et Moyennes Entreprises de Distribution [*International Federation of Retail Distributors*] [*Belgium*] (EAIO)
FEMGEN	Finite Element Mesh Generation Program [*Fegs Ltd.*] [*Software package*] (NCC)
FemHlth	Female Health Co. [*Associated Press*] (SAG)
FEMIB	Federation Europeenne des Syndicats de Fabricants de Menuiseries Industrielles de Batiment [*European Federation of Building Joinery Manufacturers*] (EAIO)
FEMIDE	Federacion Mundial de Instituciones Financieras de Desarrollo [*World Federation of Development Financing Institutions - WFDFI*] [*Madrid, Spain*] (EAIO)
FEM INTERN	Femoribus Internis [*To the Inner Part of the Thigh*] [*Pharmacy*] (ROG)
FEMIPI	Federation Europeenne des Mandataires de l'Industrie en Propriete Industrielle [*European Federation of Agents of Industry in Industrial Property*] (EAIO)
FEMK	Federation Europeenne des Masseurskinesitherapeutes Praticiens en Physiotherapie
FEMKSF	Frauendienst der Evangelisch-Methodistischen Kirche in der Schwiez und in Frankreich [*United Methodist Women in Switzerland and in France*] (EAIO)
FEML	Funded Environmental and Morale Leave Program [*Military*] (DOMA)
FEMO	Finite Element Modeling Optimization
Femocrat	Feminist Bureaucrat
FEMOSI	Federation Mondiale des Syndicats d'Industries [*World Federation of Industrial Workers' Unions*]
FEMP	Federal Energy Management Program [*Department of Energy*]
FEMP	Fernald Environmental Management Project [*Department of Energy*]
FEMP	Free Energy Minimization Procedure [*Computer science*]
fem-pop	Femoral-Popliteal [*Bypass*] [*Cardiology*] (DAVI)
FEMR	Fleet Electromagnetic Radiation [*Team*] [*Navy*] (NVT)
FemRx	FemRx, Inc. [*Associated Press*] (SAG)
FEMS	Facilities and Environmental Measuring System [*NASA*] (KSC)
FEMS	Facilities Engineering Management System (MCD)
FEMS	Federation of the European Microbiological Societies (EAIO)
FEMS	Field Electronic Maintenance Section [*National Weather Service*]
FEMU	Further Education Marketing Unit (AIE)
FEMUSI	Federacion Mundial de Sindicatos de Industrias [*World Federation of Industrial Workers' Unions*]
FEMVIEW	Finite Element Mesh and Result Viewing [*Fegs Ltd.*] [*Software package*] (NCC)
FEN	Fairchild Industries, Inc. [*NYSE symbol*] (SPSG)
FEN	Family Education Network [*Computer science*]
FEN	Family Empowerment Network [*Support for Families Affected by FAS/FAE*] [*Organization concerned with families affected by fetal alcohol syndrome or fetal alcohol effects*] (PAZ)
FEN	Far East Network [*US Armed Forces radio station*] [*Japan*]
FEN	Fengtien [*Hoten, Shenyang*] [*Republic of China*] [*Seismograph station code, US Geological Survey*] (SEIS)
FEN	Fluid, Electrolytes, and Nutrition [*Dietetics*] [*Pharmacology*] (DAVI)
FEN	Free-Net Erlangen Nurnberg [*Information service or system*] (IID)
FEN	Frequency-Emphasizing Network (IEEE)
FE_Na	Excreted Fraction of Filtered Sodium [*Test*] (DAVI)
FE_Na	Fractional Extraction of Sodium [*Organic chemistry*] (DAVI)
FENASYCOA	Federation Nationale des Syndicats du Commerce Ouest Africain [*National Federation of Commerce Unions - West Africa*]
FENB	Far East National Bank [*NASDAQ symbol*] (SAG)
FENC	Fencing (ROG)
FENDRE	Forces to Eliminate No-Deposit/No-Return
FEng	Fellow [*or Fellowship*] of Engineering
FENG	Flight Engineer (IAA)
F/Eng	Flight Engineer (AIA)
F Eng	Forest Engineer
FENKN	Fuel Supply Unknown [*Aviation*] (FAAC)
FENP	Fluoro(ethyl)norprogesterone [*Endocrinology*]
FENPB	Full Employment and National Purposes Budget (OICC)
FENSA	Film Entertainments National Service Association (BARN)
Fent	Fenton's Important Judgments [*New Zealand*] [*A publication*] (DLA)

Fent	Fenton's New Zealand Reports [*A publication*] (DLA)
FENT	First Enterprise Financial Group [*NASDAQ symbol*] (SAG)
FEntFn	First Enterprise Financial Group [*Associated Press*] (SAG)
Fent Imp Judg	Fenton's Important Judgments [*New Zealand*] [*A publication*] (DLA)
FENTL	Fuel Supply Until [*Aviation*] (FAAC)
Fent (New Zealand)	Fenton's New Zealand Reports [*A publication*] (DLA)
Fent NZ	Fenton's New Zealand Reports [*A publication*] (DLA)
FeNTO	Federation of the Scientific and Technical Organizations of the Socialist Countries [*Formerly, Permanent Council of Scientific and Technical Organizations of Socialist Countries*] (EA)
Fenton	Fenton's Important Judgments [*New Zealand*] [*A publication*] (DLA)
FEO	Facility Emergency Organization [*Nuclear energy*] (NRCH)
FEO	Federal Energy Office [*Later, FEA*]
FEO	Feodosiya [*Former USSR Seismograph station code, US Geological Survey Closed*] (SEIS)
FEO	Field Engineering Order (KSC)
FEO	Field Extension Office [*DoD*]
FEO	Flag Engineering Officer [*British*]
FEO	Fleet Engineer Officer [*Obsolete British*]
FEO	Flora Europaea Organization [*British*]
FEO	Fuel-Efficient Oil
FEODT	Federation Europeenne des Organisations des Detaillants en Tabacs [*European Federation of Tobacco Retail Organizations*] (EAIO)
FEOF	Foreign Exchange Operations Fund
FEOGA	Fonds European d'Orientation et de Garantie Agriculturel [*European Agricultural Guidance and Guarantee Fund*]
FEOGA	Fonds Europeen d'Orientation et de Garantie Agricole [*Also known as EAGGF*]
FEOM	Full Extraocular Motion [*or Movement*] [*Ophthalmology*] (DAVI)
FEORP	Federal Equal Opportunity Recruitment Program
FEOS	Forward Engineering Operating Station [*Navy*] (CAAL)
FEOV	Forced End of Volume (IAA)
FEP	Fair Employment Practice
FEP	Fast Evening Persons Report [*Nielsen Television Index*] (NTCM)
FEP	Federal Education Project [*Defunct*] (EA)
FEP	Federal Employee Program
FEP	Federation Europeenne de Psychanalyse [*European Psycho-Analytical Federation - EPF*] (EAIO)
FEP	Federation of European Publishers [*Belgium*] (EAIO)
FEP	Fermented Egg Product [*Animal repellent*]
FEP	Financial Evaluation Program [*IBM Corp.*]
FEP	Flash Evaporator Plant
FEP	Flash Evoked Potential [*Behavioral science*]
FEP	Fleet [*Satellite Communications*] Extremely [*High Frequency*] Package (DOMA)
FEP	Floral Ethel Propane
FEP	Fluorinated Ethylene-Propylene [*Copolymer*]
FEP	Foderation der Europaischen Parkettindustrieverbande [*European Federation of the Parquet Floor Industry Associations*] [*EC*] (ECED)
FEP	Fore Edges Painted [*Paper*]
FEP	FORTRAN Enhancement Package (NITA)
FEP	Foundation for Education with Production (EA)
FEP	Franklin Electronic Pub [*NYSE symbol*] (TTSB)
FEP	Franklin Electronic Publishers, Inc. [*NYSE symbol*] (SAG)
FEP	Free Enterprise Personnel (MCD)
FEP	Free Erythrocyte Protoporphyrin [*Hematology*]
FEP	Freeport, IL [*Location identifier FAA*] (FAAL)
FEP	Front End Package (OA)
FEP	Front-End Processor [*Computer*] (NASA)
FEP	Front-End Purification [*Engineering*]
FEP	Fully Engineered Prototype [*Automotive engineering*]
FEP	Fuse Enclosure Package (IEEE)
FEPA	Fair Educational Practice Act [*New York, New Jersey, Massachusetts*]
FEPA	Fair Employment Practices Act [*1964*]
FEPA	Far-Eastern Prehistory Association [*Later, IPPA*] (EA)
FEPA	Federal Employees Pay Act
FEPA	Federal Executive and Professional Association [*Defunct*] (EA)
FEPA	Federal Executive Pay Act, 1956
FEPA	Federation Europeenne des Fabricants de Produits Abrasifs [*European Federation of the Manufacturers of Abrasive Products*] [*France*]
FEPACE	Federation Europeenne des Producteurs Autonomes et des Consommateurs Industrielsd'Energie [*European Federation of Autoproducers and Industrial Consumers of Energy*] (EAIO)
FEPACI	Federation of Pan-African Cinema [*of the Organization of African Unity*]
FEPAFEM	Federacion Panamericana de Asociacions de Facultades de Medicina [*Pan American Federation of Associations of Medical Schools - PAFAMS*] [*Caracas, Venezuela*] (EAIO)
FEPAP	Federation of European Producers of Abrasives (PDAA)
FEPC	Fair Employment Practices Code
FEPC	Fair Employment Practices Committee [*or Commission*]
FE/PC	Ferroelectric/Photoconductive (PDAA)
FEPCA	Federal Employees Pay Comparability Act [*1990*]
FEPCA	Federal Energy Policy and Conservation Act (GNE)
FEPCA	Federal Environmental Pesticide Control Act [*1972*]
FEPD	Federation Europeenne des Parfumeurs Detaillants [*European Federation of Perfumery Retailers*] (EAIO)
FEPD	Forward Environmental Protection Device (MCD)
FEPE	Europaeische Vereinigung der Briefumschlagfabrikanten [*European Association of Envelope Manufacturers*] (EAIO)

FEPE	Federation Europeenne de la Publicite Exterieure [*European Federation of Outdoor Advertising*] [*France*]
FEPE	Full Energy Peak Efficiency [*Nuclear science*] (OA)
FEPEM	Federation of European Petroleum Equipment Manufacturers [*Netherlands*]
FEPF	European Federation of Earthenware, China and Tableware, and Ornamental Ware (EAIO)
FEPI	Filipino Employment Policy Instruction (CINC)
FEPMA	Federation of European Pencil Manufacturers Associations [*See also FEFM*] (EA)
FEPO	For Examination Purposes Only [*Education*]
FEPOW	Far East Prisoner of War
FEPP	Foreign Excess Personal Property
FEPP	Free Erythrocyte Protoporphyrin [*Hematoloy*] (MAH)
FEPP	Full Employment and Production Program (OICC)
FEPS	Far-Encounter Planet Sensor
FEPS	Flight Envelope Protection System [*Aviation*]
FEPSP	Field Excitatory Postsynaptic Potential [*Neurophysiology*]
FEPTO	Front Engine Power-Take-Off [*Automotive engineering*]
FEPU	Frente Eleitoral do Povo Unido [*United People's Electoral Front*] [*Portugal Political party*] (PPE)
FEQ	Failure Equation
FER	Fathers for Equal Rights (EA)
FER	Federacion de Estudiantes Revolucionarios [*Federation of Revolutionary Students*] [*Uruguay*] (PD)
FER	Federation des Etudiants Revolutionnaires [*Federation of Revolutionary Students*] [*France*]
FER	Federation of Engine Re-Manufacturers [*Chigwell, Essex, England*] (EAIO)
FER	Feed Efficiency Ratio
FER	Feria Aviacion [*Spain ICAO designator*] (FAAC)
Fer	Fermanagh County [*Ireland*] (BARN)
FER	Ferndale [*California*] [*Seismograph station code, US Geological Survey*] (SEIS)
FER	Ferrierite [*A zeolite*]
FER	Ferrous
FER	Ferrum [*Iron*] [*Pharmacy*]
FER	Ferry
FER	Field Engineering Representative
FER	Final Engineering Report
FER	Fleet Employment Reports (MCD)
FER	Force Exchange Ratio (MCD)
FER	Forest Environment Research [*Department of Agriculture*] (GRD)
FER	Forward Engine Room
FER	Friends of Eye Research [*Formerly, FERRAT*] [*Defunct*] (EA)
FER	Fuel Energy Ratio [*Petroleum refining*]
FER	Fusion Engineering Reactor [*Japan*]
FERA	Federal Emergency Relief Act of 1933
FERA	Federal Emergency Relief Administration [*Liquidated, 1937*]
FERA	Formative Evaluation Research Associates [*Research center*] (RCD)
FERA	Further Education Research Association [*British*] (DBA)
Ferard Fixt...	Amos and Ferard on Fixtures [*A publication*] (DLA)
FERAS	Further Education Revenue Account Survey (AIE)
FERC	Federal Energy Regulatory Commission [*Department of Energy*]
FERCON	Ferrule Contact [*Design engineering*] (IAA)
FERD	Facility and Equipment Requirements Document (NASA)
FERD	Fuel Element Rupture Detection [*Nuclear energy*] (NRCH)
FERES	Federation Internationale des Instituts de Recherches Socio-Religieuses [*International Federation of Institutes for Socio-Religious Research*]
FERF	Far End Receive Failure [*Telecommunications*] (ACRL)
FERF	Financial Executives Research Foundation (EA)
FERFIN	Ferruzzi Finanziaria
Fer Fixt.......	Ferard on Fixtures [*A publication*] (DLA)
Ferg	Consistorial Decisions, Scotland, by George Ferguson, Lord Hermand [*A publication*] (DLA)
FERG	Family Economics Research Group [*Department of Agriculture*] (GRD)
Ferg	Fergusson's Consistorial Decisions [*Scotland*] [*A publication*] (DLA)
Ferg Cons....	Fergusson's Consistorial Reports [*Scotland*] [*A publication*] (DLA)
Ferg M & D...	Fergusson's Divorce Decisions by Consistorial Courts [*Scotland*] [*A publication*] (DLA)
Ferg Proc.....	Ferguson's Common Law Procedure Act [*Ireland*] [*A publication*] (DLA)
Ferg Ry Cas...	Ferguson's Five Years' Railway Cases [*A publication*] (DLA)
Fergusson....	Fergusson's Consistorial Decisions [*Scotland*] [*A publication*] (DLA)
Fergusson....	Fergusson's Scotch Session Cases [*1738-52*] [*A publication*] (DLA)
FERIC	False Entries in Records of Interstate Carriers [*FBI standardized term*]
FERIC	Forest Engineering Research Institute of Canada [*Vancouver, BC*]
FERIS	Forest Environment and Resources Information System [*Queensland*] [*State*] (EERA)
Ferllgs	Ferrellgas Partners Ltd. [*Associated Press*] (SAG)
FERM	Fast Escape Recallable Missile
FERM	Fermanagh [*County in Northern Ireland*] (ROG)
FERMANH...	Fermanagh [*County in Northern Ireland*]
FERMILAB ...	Fermi National Accelerator Laboratory [*Also, FNAL*] [*Batavia, IL*] [*Department of Energy*]
Fernald Eng Synonyms...	Fernald's English Synonyms [*A publication*] (DLA)
FERO	Far East Research Office
FERO	Ferrofluidics Corp. [*NASDAQ symbol*] (NQ)
Ferofl	Ferrofluidics Corp. [*Associated Press*] (SAG)
FEROPA	Federation Europeenne des Fabricants de Panneaux de Fibres [*European Federation of Fireboard Manufacturers*] [*EC*] (ECED)
FEROPA	Federation Europeenne des Synicats de Panneaux de Fibres [*European Federation of Manufacturers Associations of Fiber Panels*] (PDAA)
FERPA	Family Educational Rights and Privacy Act [*1974*]
FERPIC	Ferroelectric Ceramic Picture Device (IEEE)
FERR	Feliciana Eastern Railroad Co. [*Formerly, FE*] [*AAR code*]
FERR	Ferrum [*Iron*] [*Pharmacy*] (ROG)
FERRAT	Friends of Eye Research, Rehabilitation, and Treatment [*Later, FER*] (EA)
Ferriere Dict de Jr...	Ferriere's Dictionary of Jurisprudence [*A publication*] (DLA)
FERRIT	Ferritin [*Hematology*] (DAVI)
Ferro	Ferro Corp. [*Associated Press*] (SAG)
FERROD......	Ferrite-Rod Antenna (IEEE)
FERRON......	Ferry Squadron [*Navy*] (DNAB)
FERRY	Ferry [*Commonly used*] (OPSA)
FERS	F&E Resource Systems Tech [*NASDAQ symbol*] (TTSB)
FERS	F & E Resource Systems Technology, Inc. [*NASDAQ symbol*] (SAG)
FERS	Federal Employees' Retirement System
FERS	Federal Employment [*or Employees*] Retirement System
FERSA	Federal Employees' Retirement System Act of 1986
FERSI	Flat Earth Research Society International (EA)
FERST	Freight and Equipment Reporting System for Transportation [*IBM Corp.*]
FERST/VS ...	Freight and Equipment Reporting System for Transportation/Virtual Storage [*IBM Corp.*]
FERT	Fertility (WDAA)
FERT	Fertilizer
FERT	Fertilizer
FERT	Fortitudo Eius Rhodum Tenuit [*His Strength Keeps Rhodes*] [*Motto of Lodovico family. Initials were used on gold coin struck by Duke Lodovico (1439-1465)*]
fertd	Fertilized [*Medicine*] (DAVI)
FERTD	Fertilized
FERTP	Nu-West Industries [*NASDAQ symbol*] (SAG)
FERTZ	Fertilizer
FERV	Fervens [*Hot*] [*Pharmacy*]
FERV	Foundation for Education and Research in Vision (EA)
FES	Family Environment Scale
FES	Family Expenditure Survey [*Department of Employment*] [*British*]
FES	Far-End Suppressor (IAA)
FES	Fast Erect System
FES	Fat Embolism Syndrome [*Medicine*] (CPH)
FES	Federal Executive Service
FES	Federal Expenditures by State
FES	Federal Extension Service [*Department of Agriculture*]
FES	Federation Europeenne de la Salmoniculture [*Federation of the European Trout and Salmon Industry*] [*Formerly, European Salmon Breeding Federation*] (EA)
FES	Federation of Eastern Stars (EA)
FES	Fellow of the Entomological Society [*British*]
FES	Fellow of the Ethnological Society [*British*]
FES	Festus, MO [*Location identifier FAA*] (FAAL)
FES	Field Emission Spectroscopy
FES	Field Emitting Surface
FES	Field Engineering Service
FES	Field Entry Standard [*Military*] (ADDR)
FES	Final Environmental Statement [*Bureau of Outdoor Recreation*]
FES	Fine Error Sensor (KSC)
FES	Finite Element Solver (NITA)
FES	First Empire State [*AMEX symbol*] (TTSB)
FES	First Empire State Corp. [*AMEX symbol*] (SPSG)
FES	Fixed Echo Suppressor [*Electronics*] (IAA)
FES	Flame Emission Spectrometry
FES	Flash Evaporator System (MCD)
FES	Flight Element Set (MCD)
FES	Flower Essence Society (EA)
FES	Fluidic Environmental Sensor (RDA)
FES	Fluid to Electric Switch
FES	Fluorescence Excitation Spectrum
FES	Food Education Society [*British*]
FES	Forced Expiratory Spirogram [*Medicine*]
FES	Forms Entry System
FES	Front-End Screening [*DoD*]
FES	Fuel and Electricity Survey [*Australia*]
FES	Functional Electrical Stimulation
FES	Fundamental Electrical Standard (IAA)
FESA	Facilities Engineering Support Agency [*Army*] (MCD)
FESA	Federal Employees Salary Act of 1970
FESA	Federal Employment Service Act [*1933*]
FESA	Federal Executive Salary Act of 1964
FESA	Federation of Engineering and Scientific Associations
FESA	Fonetic English Spelling Association
FESA	Foundry Equipment and Supplies Association [*British*] (DBA)
FESAC	Fondation de l'Enseignement Superieur en Afrique Centrale
FESAP	Finite Element Structures Analysis Program [*Computer science*]
FESA-TS	Facilities Engineering Support Agency Technology Support Division [*Fort Belvoir, VA*] [*Army*]
FESC	Far East Science Center
FESC	Federation Europeenne des Sports Corporatifs [*European Federation for Company Sports - EFCS*] (EAIO)
FESC	Further Education Staff College (AIE)
FESCID	Federation Europeenne des Syndicats de la Chimie et des Industries Diverses [*European Federation of Chemical and General Workers Unions*] (EAIO)
FESCO	Far Eastern Shipping Co. [*Former USSR*]

FESCO .... Foreign Enterprise Service Corp. [China]

FESE .... Field-Enhanced Secondary Emission

FESEM .... Field Emission Scanning Electron Microscopy

FESFP .... Federation Europeenne des Syndicats de Fabricants de Parquets [European Federation of Parquet Manufacturers Unions]

FeSFV .... Feline Syncytium-Forming Virus

FESH .... Federation of Ethical Stage Hypnotists [British] (DBA)

FESI .... Federation Europeenne des Syndicats d'Entreprises d'Isolation [European Federation of Associations of Insulation Contractors] (EA)

FESIA .... Federal Employees Salary Increase Act

FESL .... Failure Effects Summary List (NASA)

FESM .... Front-End Sheet Metal

FESO .... Federal Employment Stabilization Office [Functions transferred to National Resources Planning Board, 1939]

FeSO₄ .... Ferrous Sulfate [Organic chemistry] (DAVI)

FESP .... (Fluoroethyl)spiperone [Biochemistry]

FESPA .... Federation of European Screen Printers Associations (PDAA)

FESPIC .... Far East and South Pacific

FESR .... Finite Energy Sum Rules [Physics]

FESR .... Further Education Statistical Record [Department of Education and Science] [British]

FESS .... Facilities Engineer Supply System [Army]

FESS .... Finite Element Solution System (PDAA)

FESS .... Fleet Environmental Support System [Navy]

FESS .... Flight Experiment Shielding Satellite

FESS .... Flywheel Energy Storage System

Fessen Pat... Fessenden on Patents [A publication] (DLA)

Fess Pat ..... Fessenden on Patents [A publication] (DLA)

Fest .... Festival [Record label]

FEST .... Festival

fest .... Festival [Slang] (WDMC)

FEST .... Field Epidemiological Survey Team [Army] (LAIN)

FESTAC .... World Black and African Festival of Arts and Culture

FestF .... Festival (France) [Record label]

FESTUK .... Federation of Engineering and Shipbuilding Trades of the United Kingdom [A union]

FESV .... Feline Sarcoma Virus [Also, FeSV]

FESW .... Federation of Eastern Stars of the World (EA)

FESWG .... Fuze Engineering Standardization Working Group [Military] (RDA)

FESX .... First Essex Bancorp [NASDAQ symbol] (TTSB)

FESX .... First Essex Bancorp, Inc. [NASDAQ symbol] (NQ)

FESYP .... Federation Europeenne des Syndicats de Fabricants de Panneaux de Particules [European Federation of Associations of Particleboard Manufacturers] (EAIO)

f-et-- .... Ethiopia [MARC geographic area code Library of Congress] (LCCP)

FET .... Far Eastern Textile Ltd. [NYSE symbol] (SAG)

FET .... Far East Time (IAA)

FET .... Federal Estate Tax (DLA)

FET .... Federal Excise Tax

FET .... Federation of Environmental Technologists (EA)

FET .... Field Effect Transistor

FET .... Fixed Erythrocyte Turnover [Hematology] (DAVI)

FET .... Fleet Evaluation Trial [Navy] (NG)

FET .... Flight Elapsed Time (MCD)

FET .... Flight Engineer in Training

FET .... Fluidic Emergency Thruster [Aviation]

FET .... Fluorescence Energy Transfer [Physics]

FET .... Foldable Elastic Tube [Satellite hinge]

FET .... Forced Expiratory Time [Physiology]

FET .... Foreign Escorted Tour [Travel]

FET .... Foundation on Economic Trends (EA)

FET .... Freeze-Etch Technique

FET .... Fremont, NE [Location identifier FAA] (FAAL)

FET .... Functional Element Test

FETA .... Federation of Environmental Trade Associations [British] (DBA)

FETA .... Fire Extinguisher Trades Association [British] (BI)

FETAP .... Federation Europeenne des Transports Aeriens Prives [European Federation of Independent Air Transport]

FETAX .... Frog Embryo Teratogenesis Assay - Xenopus [Toxicology]

FETBB .... Federation Europeenne des Travailleurs du Batiment et du Bois [European Federation of Building and Woodworkers - EFBWW] (EAIO)

FETC .... Federal Excise Tax Council [Defunct] (EA)

FETC .... Field-Effect-Transistor-Capacitor [Electronics] (PDAA)

FET de las JONS... Falange Espanola Tradicionalista y de las Juntas de Ofensiva Nacional Sindicalista [Traditionalist Spanish Phalange of the Syndicalist Juntas of the NationalOffensive] [Political party] (PPE)

FETE .... Far Eastern Tick-Borne Encephalitis [Medicine] (DMAA)

FETF .... Flight Engine Test Facility

FETH .... Field Effect Thyristor (IAA)

FETI .... Fluorescence Energy Transfer Immunoassay [Analytical biochemistry]

FETM .... File Expansion Transport Magazine (SAA)

FETO .... Factory Equipment Transfer Order

FETO .... Field Engineering Theory of Operations

FETO .... Free Estimated Time of Overflight [Aviation] (DA)

FETS .... Forced Expiratory Time, in Seconds [Physiology]

FETS/SEA..... Federal Emission Test Sequence and Selective Enforcement Audit [General Motors Corp.]

FETT .... Field-Effect Tetrode Transistor [Electronics] (OA)

FETT .... First Engine to Test

Fett Carr..... Fetter's Treatise on Carriers of Passengers [A publication] (DLA)

FETU .... Far Eastern Technical Unit [World War II]

FETVM .... Field-Effect Transistor Volt Meter [Electronics] (DICI)

FET VOM ..... Field-Effect Transistor Volt-Ohm-Milliammeter (IDOE)

FEU .... Compagnie Aeronautique Europeenne [France ICAO designator] (FAAC)

FEU .... Family Education Unit [Australia]

FEU .... Federated Engineering Union

FEU .... Fire Experimental Unit [British Fire Service] (IRUK)

FEU .... Fleet Expansion Unit (DNAB)

FEU .... Forty-Foot [Container] Equivalent Unit (DOMA)

FEU .... Fossil Energy Update [A publication]

FEU .... Fuel Equivalent Unit

FEU .... Further Education Unit [British]

FEUD .... Feudal

FEUD .... Feudalism (WDAA)

Feud Lib ...... Feudorum Liber [Book of Feuds] [Latin A publication] (DLA)

FEUGRES ..... Federation Europeenne des Fabricants de Tuyaux en Gre [European Federation of Manufacturers of Salt Glazed Pipes] (PDAA)

FEUO .... For External Use Only [Pharmacy] (DAVI)

FEUPF .... European Federation of Professional Florists' Unions [Italy] (EAIO)

FEUPF .... Federation Europeenne des Unions Professionelles de Fleuristes [European Federation of Professional Florists' Unions] (EAIO)

FE-UR .... Iron in Urine [Biochemistry] (DAVI)

FEURS .... Fabrication Equivalent Unit Reporting System (MCD)

FEUS .... French Engineers in the United States (EA)

FEV .... Familial Exudative Vitreoretinopathy [Ophthalmology]

FeV .... Feline Leukemia Virus [Veterinary medicine]

FEV .... Fever (WDAA)

FEV .... Forced Expiratory Volume [Physiology]

FEV .... Future Electric Vehicle [Nissan Corp.] (PS)

FEV₁/VC........ Forced Expiratory Volume (In One Second)/Vital Capacity [Physiology] (MAE)

FEVA........... Federal Employees Veterans Association [Later, NAGE] (EA)

FEVAC......... Ferroelectric Variable Capacitor

FEVE .... Federation Europeenne du Verre d'Emballage [European Container Glass Federation - ECGF] (EA)

Feversham Cttee... Committee on Human Artificial Insemination. Report [1960] [A publication] (ILCA)

FEVI .... Front End Volatility Index [Environmental Protection Agency] (GFGA)

FEVIR.......... Federation of European Veterinarians in Industry and Research (EA)

FEVSD .... Federation Europeenne pour la Vente et le Service a Domicile [European Direct Selling Federation] [Brussels, Belgium] (EA)

FEVt .... Forced Expiratory Volume (Timed) [Medicine] (DAVI)

FEVt/FVC..... Forced Expiratory Volume (Timed) to Forced Vital Capacity Ratio [Expressed as a percentage] [Medicine] (DAVI)

FEW .... Cheyenne, WY [Location identifier FAA] (FAAL)

FEW .... Far Eastern Cargo Airlines [Former USSR] [FAA designator] (FAAC)

FEW .... Federally Employed Women (EA)

FEWA.......... Farm Equipment Wholesalers Association (EA)

FEWC .... Force Electronic Warfare Coordinator (NVT)

fewd........... Ironwood (VRA)

FEWEC........ Further Education Work Experience Co-Ordinator (AIE)

FEWG .... Flight Evaluation Working Group (MCD)

FEWIA......... Federation of European Writing Instruments Associations [See also FEAIE] (EA)

FEWITA........ Federation of European Wholesale and International Trade Associations [Common Market] [Belgium]

FEWMA........ Federation of European Window Manufacturers Associations (EA)

FEWO .... Fund for Education in World Order [Later, FFP] (EA)

FEWQ .... Federation of English-Writers in Quebec [Canada] (WWLA)

FEWS .... Famine Early Warning System [US Agency for International Development]

FEWS .... Follow-on Early Warning System [Satellite] (DOMA)

FEWSG .... Fleet Electronic Warfare Support Group

FEWT .... Functional Equipment Withholding Tab [Obsolete]

FEWTS......... Force Electronic Warfare/Tactical SIGINT

FEX .... Fabien Exploration, Inc. [Toronto Stock Exchange symbol]

FEX .... Field Exercise [Military] (NVT)

FEX .... Fleet Exercise [Navy]

FEX .... Flightexec Ltd. [Canada ICAO designator] (FAAC)

FEX .... Foreign Exchange [Telecommunications] (TEL)

FExF .... Fort Worth, TX [Location identifier FAA] (FAAL)

FExF .... Forced Expiratory Flow (GNE)

FEXHA .... Fuel Supply Exhausted [Aviation] (FAAC)

FEXT .... Far-End Crosstalk [Telecommunications]

FEXT .... Fire Extinguisher

FEXT .... Frame Time for Extrapolation (SAA)

FEY .... Forever Yours

FEZ .... Federation Europeenne de Zootechnie [European Association for Animal Production - EAAP] [France] (ASF)

FEZ .... Fez [Morocco] [Airport symbol] (OAG)

FEZ .... Fez [Morocco] [Airport symbol] (AD)

FEZ .... Fighter Engagement Zone [Military] (NVT)

ff---- .... Africa, North [MARC geographic area code Library of Congress] (LCCP)

FF .... Air Link [ICAO designator] (AD)

F-F .... Face to Face

FF .... Facility Forecast (MCD)

FF .... Factitious Fever [Medicine] (CPH)

FF .... Factory Finish [Technical drawings]

FF .... Failure Factor (NG)

FF .... Failure to Feed (MCD)

FF .... Fairness Fund (EA)

FF .... Fanfare [A publication] (BRI)

FF .... Fanny Fern [Pseudonym used by Sara Payson Parton]

FF .... Far Field (MCD)

FF .... Farm Foundation (EA)
FF .... Fast Fatigue [Type of muscle contraction]
FF .... Fast Flow
FF .... Fast Forward [Audio-visual technology]
FF .... Fat Free [Biochemistry]
FF .... Father Factor [Medicine] (MAE)
FF .... Fecal Frequency (MAE)
FF .... Fecerunt [They Did It] [Latin]
FF .... Federal Facility (GFGA)
FF .... Feed Forward (IAA)
FF .... Fee Factor (MCD)
FF .... Felicissimi Fratres [Most Fortunate Brothers] [Latin]
FF .... Felicissimus [Most Happy] [Latin] (ROG)
fF .... Femtofarad [One quadrillionth of a farad]
FF .... Ferguson Formula [Four-wheel drive system] [Automotive engineering British]
FF .... Fertlity Factor [Medicine] (DAVI)
FF .... Fianna Fail [Warriors of Destiny] [Political party Ireland]
FF .... Field File (LAIN)
FF .... Field Forces [Military]
FF .... Field Format
FF .... Field Function [Telecommunications] (TEL)
FF .... Fieri Fecit [Caused to Be Made] [Latin]
FF .... Fighting French
FF .... File Finish (MSA)
FF .... Fill Factor [Photovoltaic energy systems]
F/F .... Fill/Full [or Full/Fill] (MCD)
FF .... Filter Factor (NRCH)
FF .... Filtration Factor [Physiology] (DAVI)
FF .... Filtration Fraction [Physiology]
FF .... Fimbria-Fornix [Neuroanatomy]
FF .... Finagle-Factor
FF .... Finger to Finger [Medicine]
FF .... Finlandia Foundation (EA)
FF .... Fire Fighting (MSA)
FF .... Firefinder
FF .... Fir-Fast [Forestry]
FF .... First Families [i.e., the aristocracy] [Slang]
FF .... First Fandom (EA)
FF .... First Financial Fund [NYSE symbol] (TTSB)
FF .... First Financial Fund, Inc. [NYSE symbol] (SPSG)
FF .... First Fit Algorithm (IAA)
FF .... Fixation Fluid [Medicine] (DMAA)
FF .... Fixed Fee [Business term] (AAG)
FF .... Fixed Focus [Photography]
FF .... Fixing Fluid [Histology]
FF .... Flat Face [Diamonds]
FF .... Flat Feet
FF .... Fleet Fighter [Air Force]
FF .... Fleet Flagship
ff .... Fleurs [Flowers] [Pharmacy]
FF .... Flexible-Fueled [Automotive engineering]
FF .... Flexi-Filament
FF .... Flight Ferry [Navy] (ANA)
FF .... Flight Forward (MCD)
F-F .... Flip-Flop [Computer science]
FF .... Flip-Flop (IDOE)
FF .... Florida Facility [NASA] (KSC)
FF .... Fluorine Facility [Nuclear energy] (NRCH)
FF .... Flush Fitting
FF .... Flux Flow (IAA)
FF .... Focus on the Family [An association] (EA)
FF .... Fog Factor
FF .... Folded File
FF .... Folded Flat [Freight]
FF .... Folding Fin (SAA)
FF .... Folgende [And the Following Pages, Verses, etc.] [German] (ROG)
FF .... Folios [Leaves]
FF .... Following [Pages] [Also, F]
ff .... Following [Copyediting] (WDMC)
FF .... Force Feed (MSA)
FF .... Force Field
FF .... Force Flagship
FF .... Force [or Forced] Fluid [Medicine]
FF .... Ford Foundation
FF .... Forearm Flow [Cardiology] (DAVI)
FF .... Foreign Flag
FF .... Foremanship Foundation [Defunct] (EA)
FF .... Formation Flying (MCD)
FF .... Form Factor (IAA)
FF .... Form Feed [Computer science]
FF .... Formula Ford [Class of racing cars]
FF .... Fortissimo [Very Loud] [Music]
FF .... Forward Fuselage
FF .... Fossil Fuels
FF .... Foster Father
FF .... Foul Fly [Baseball]
FF .... Fragrance Foundation (EA)
FF .... Francs Francais [French Francs] [Monetary unit]
FF .... Franklin Furnace (EA)
F-F .... Frasnian-Famennian [Boundary] [Geophysics]
FF .... Fratres [Brothers] [Latin]
FF .... Fredspolitisk Folkeparti [People's Peace Policy Party] [Denmark] (PPE)
FF .... Freedom Federation [Defunct] (EA)

FF .... Freedom Fund [An association Defunct] (EA)
FF .... Freedom's Friends (EA)
FF .... Free-Fall
FF .... Free Fat [Biochemistry] (DAVI)
FF .... Free Flight
FF .... Free Flood
FF .... Free Flyaround (SAA)
FF .... Free Flyer (MCD)
FF .... Free Form [Automotive engineering]
FF .... Free Fraction
FF .... Free French [World War II]
FF .... Free the Fathers (EA)
FF .... Freight Forwarder
FF .... French Fourragere [Military decoration]
FF .... French Franc [Monetary unit]
FF .... French Fried
FF .... Fresh Frozen
FF .... Frie Folkevalgte [Freely Elected Representatives] [Norway] (PPE)
FF .... Friendship Force (EA)
FF .... Friends of the Farm [An association] (EA)
FF .... Frigate [Navy symbol]
FF .... Front Engine, Front Drive [Automotive engineering]
FF .... Front Focal Length [Optics]
FF .... Frontier Force
FF .... Fruit Frost (NOAA)
FF .... Fuel Flow (AAG)
FF .... Full Face [Photography]
FF .... Full-Fashioned
FF .... Full Field
FF .... Full Floating [Automotive engineering]
FF .... Function of a Quantity [Mathematics] (ROG)
FF .... Fundus Firm [Obstetrics] (DAVI)
FF .... Furon Formaldehyde [Organic chemistry]
FF .... Further Flexion [Neurology and orthopedics] (DAVI)
FF .... Thick Fog [Navigation]
FFA .... Air-Cushion Vehicle built by Flygtekniska Forsoksanstalen [Sweden] [Usually used in combination with numerals]
FFA .... Fast Fourier Analyzer (MCD)
FFA .... Federal Firearms Act
FFA .... Fellow of the Faculty of Actuaries [British]
FFA .... Fellow of the Faculty of Anesthetists [British]
FFA .... Fellow of the Institute of Financial Accountants [British] (ODBW)
FFA .... Female-Female Adaptor (MEDA)
FFA .... Fiberglass Fabrication Association (EA)
FFA .... Flammable Fabrics Act [1953]
FFA .... Flexible Factory Automation
FFA .... Florida Foliage Association (EA)
FFA .... Fluorescein Fundus Angiogram [Ophthalmology] (CPH)
FFA .... Forces Francaises en Allemagne [French Forces in Germany]
FFA .... Foreign Freight Agent
FFA .... Forest Farmers Association (EA)
FFA .... For Further Assignment
FFA .... Foundation for Foreign Affairs (EA)
FFA .... Franchise Finance Corp. of America [NYSE symbol] (SAG)
FFA .... Franchise Finance Cp Amer [NYSE symbol] (TTSB)
FFA .... Frankford Arsenal [Pennsylvania] [Army Closed] (AABC)
FFA .... Free Fatty Acid [Biochemistry]
FFA .... Free Field Analysis
FFA .... Free Fire Area (AABC)
FFA .... Free-for-All (ADA)
FFA .... Free Foreign Agency [or Agent] [Business term]
FFA .... Free from Alongside [Shipping]
FFA .... Free from Average [Insurance]
FFA .... Friends of Frank Ashmore [Defunct] (EA)
FFA .... Friends of French Art (EA)
F/FA .... Fuel and Fuel Additives [Gasoline] [Automotive emissions]
FFA .... Full Freight Allowed
FFA .... Funds Flow Analysis
FFA .... Future Farmers of America [Later, NFFAO] (EA)
FFA .... Future Farmers of Australia
FFA .... Kill Devil Hills, NC [Location identifier FAA] (FAAL)
FFAA .... Flavour and Fragrance Association of Australia
FFAC .... Federal Food Advisory Committee [Cost of Living Council]
FFAC .... Forward Forward Air Controller [Military]
FFACCRR .... Freedom of Faith: A Christian Committee for Religious Rights (EA)
FFACT .... Fiber, Fabric, and Apparel Coalition for Trade (EA)
FFACT .... Frozen Foods Action Communications Team (EA)
FFACTS .... Flammable Fabric Accident Case and Testing System [National Institute of Standards and Technology]
FFADV .... Frozen Food Association of Delaware Valley (SRA)
FFAG .... Fixed-Field Alternating Gradient [Accelerator] [Nuclear energy]
FFAGHS .... Federation of Franco-American Genealogical and Historical Societies [Defunct] (EA)
FFAIS .... Full Frontal Area Impact Switch (MCD)
FFALA .... Fund For Animals Ltd. Australia [Commercial firm]
FFAM .... First Family Group, Inc. (MHDW)
FF & E .... Furniture, Fixtures, and Equipment [Insurance]
FF & P .... Falsification, Fabrication, and Plagiarism [Scientific misconduct]
FF & V .... Fresh Fruits and Vegetables
FFANE .... Frozen Food Association of New England (SRA)
FFANY .... Fashion Footwear Association
FFAP .... Free Fatty Acid Phase [Biochemistry] (DAVI)
FFAR .... Folding Fin Aircraft Rocket
FFAR .... Forward Fighting Aircraft Rocket
FFAR .... Forward Firing Aircraft

FFAR............	Free Flight Aerial Rocket [*Military*] (INF)
FFAR............	Fuel and Fuel Additive Registration [*Environmental Protection Agency*] (GFGA)
FFARCS	Fellow of the Faculty of Anaesthetists of the Royal College of Surgeons of England
FFARCS Eng...	Fellow of the Faculty of Anaesthetists of the Royal College of Surgeons of England
FFARCSI	Fellow of the Faculty of Anaesthetists of the Royal College of Surgeons in Ireland
FFARCSIrel...	Fellow of the Faculty of Anaesthetists of the Royal College of Surgeons in Ire land [*British*] (DBQ)
FFARP	Fleet Fighter Acoustic Countermeasures Readiness Program [*Navy*] (MCD)
FFARP	Fleet Fighter Air [*Combat*] Readiness Program [*Navy*] (DOMA)
FFAS	Fellow of the Faculty of Architects and Surveyors, London [*British*]
FFAS	Flash Flood Alarm System [*National Weather Service*]
FFAS	Flickinger Foundation for American Studies (EA)
FFAS	Free Flight Analysis Section
FFAST	Fire and Forget Antitank System Technology (MCD)
FFAUS	Federation of French Alliances in the United States [*Later, FIAF*] (EA)
FFAWC........	Fur Farm Animal Welfare Coalition (EA)
FFB	Africair Service [*Senegal*] [*ICAO designator*] (FAAC)
FFB	Fact-Finding Bodies
FFB	Fat-Free Body
FFB	Federal Farm Board [*Name changed to Farm Credit Administration, 1933*]
FFB	Federal Financing Bank
FFB	First Fidelity Bancorp. [*NYSE symbol*] (SPSG)
FFB	First Fidelity Bancorp, Inc. [*Associated Press*] (SAG)
FFB	Fixed-Film Biological [*Process for wastewater treatment*]
FFB	Flexible Fiber-Optic Bronchoscopy [*Medicine*]
FFB	Fluid Film Bearing
FFB	Folding Float Bridge [*Military*] (RDA)
FFB	Food from Britain
FFB	Free-Fall Bomb (SAA)
FFB	Frequent Flier Bonus (BARN)
FFB	Friends of Fritz Busch [*Record label*]
FFB	Functional Flow Block
FFBA............	Fellow of the Corporation of Executives and Administrators [*British*] (DBQ)
FFBA............	First Colorado Bancorp [*NASDAQ symbol*] (TTSB)
FFBA............	First Colorado Bancorp, Inc. [*NASDAQ symbol*] (SAG)
FFBA............	First Federal Savings Bank Colorado [*NASDAQ symbol*] (SAG)
FFBA............	Foundation of the Federal Bar Association (EA)
FFBArk........	First Federal Bancshares of Arkansas, Inc. [*Associated Press*] (SAG)
FFBB............	Form Factor Brassboard
FFBC............	First Financial Bancorp [*NASDAQ symbol*] (NQ)
FFBC............	First Financial Bancorp OH [*NASDAQ symbol*] (SAG)
FFBC............	First Finl Bancorp(OH) [*NASDAQ symbol*] (TTSB)
FFBD............	Functional Flow Block Diagram
FFBG............	First Federal Savings Bank of Brunswick [*NASDAQ symbol*] (SAG)
FFBG............	First Fed Svg (GA) [*NASDAQ symbol*] (TTSB)
FFBH............	First Fed Bancshares (AR) [*NASDAQ symbol*] (TTSB)
FFBH............	First Federal Bancshares of Arkansas, Inc. [*NASDAQ symbol*] (SAG)
FFBI.............	First Financial Bancorp, Inc. [*NASDAQ symbol*] (SAG)
FFBI.............	First Finl Bancorp [*NASDAQ symbol*] (TTSB)
FFBI.............	Foundation for Blood Irradiation (EA)
FFBJ............	Federation of Free Byelorussian Journalists (EA)
FFBM............	Fat-Free Body Mass
FFBS	FFBS Bancorp [*NASDAQ symbol*] (TTSB)
FFBS	FFBS Bancorp, Inc. [*NASDAQ symbol*] (SAG)
FFBT	Forward Fuel Ballast Tank
FFBZ	First Fed Bancorp [*NASDAQ symbol*] (TTSB)
FFBZ	First Federal Bancorp, Inc. [*NASDAQ symbol*] (SAG)
FFC	Family Fitness Council
FFC	Farmers Federation Cooperative
FFC	Fault and Facility Control (IAA)
FFC	Federal Facilities Corp. [*Dissolved, 1961*]
FFC	Federal Fire Council [*Defunct*] (EA)
FFC	Feed Forward Control (IAA)
FFC	Fellowship of Fire Chaplains (EA)
FFC	Ferret Fanciers Club (EA)
FFC	Films for Christ Association
FFC	Final Flight Certification [*Aerospace*]
FFC	Financial Funds Control
FFC	Firm Fan Club [*Defunct*] (EA)
FFC	First Families of Carolina [*See also FFV*]
FFC	First Flight Cover [*Philately*]
FFC	Firstfund Capital Corp. [*Vancouver Stock Exchange symbol*]
FFC	Fixed Film Capacitor
FFC	Fixed Flexion Contracture [*Neurology and orthopedics*] (DAVI)
FFC	Flagler College, St. Augustine, FL [*OCLC symbol*] (OCLC)
FFC	Flat Field Conjugate (IAA)
FFC	Flin Flon [*Manitoba*] [*Seismograph station code, US Geological Survey*] (SEIS)
FFC	Flip-Flop Complementary [*Computer science*] (MSA)
FFC	Ford Forestry Center [*Michigan Technological University*] [*Research center*] (RCD)
FFC	Foreign Funds Control
FFC	For Further Clearance [*Aviation*] (FAAC)
FFC	Forum Fisheries Committee [*Australia*]
FFC	Foundation for Cure [*Defunct*] (EA)
FFC	Free from Chlorine
FFC	Free from Foreign Capture (ROG)

FFC	Full Faith and Credit [*Finance*]
FFC	Fund Amer Enterp Hldgs [*NYSE symbol*] (TTSB)
FFC	Fund American Enterprise Holdings [*Formerly, Fireman's Fund Corp.*] [*NYSE symbol*] (SPSG)
FFC	Fund for the Future Committee (EA)
FFC	Futures for Children (EA)
FFC	Fuze Firing Circuit (RDA)
FFC	Fuze Function Control (DNAB)
FFCA............	Federal Facilities Compliance Agreement
FFCA............	Federal Facility Compliance Act
FFCA............	Federal Facility Compliance Act of 1992 (GAAI)
FFCA............	Federal Facility Compliance Agreement (DOGT)
FFCA............	Federal Facility Compliance Agreement
FFC-A...........	Forward Forces Command-Army (DOMA)
FFCAA.........	Federation Francaise des Cooperatives Agricoles d'Approvisionnement
FFCAC.........	Federation Francaise des Cooperatives Agricoles de Cereales
FFCAct........	Federal Facility Compliance Act
FFCAct........	Federal Facility Compliance Act (DOGT)
FFCB...........	Federal Farm Credit Board [*of FCA*]
FFCBB.........	Fred's Fan Club - Burstein's Buffalos [*Defunct*] (EA)
FFCC...........	Ford Four Car Club [*Australia*]
FFCF...........	Federation des Femmes Canadiennes-Francaises [*Federation of French-Canadian Women*]
FFCH...........	First Financial Holdings, Inc. [*NASDAQ symbol*] (NQ)
FFCH...........	First Finl Hldgs [*NASDAQ symbol*] (TTSB)
FFCI............	Fairfield Communities, Inc. [*NASDAQ symbol*] (SAG)
FFCI............	Fellow of the Faculty of Commerce and Industry [*British*] (DBQ)
FFCM...........	Fellow of the Faculty of Community Medicine [*British*]
FFcMN.........	First Federal Bancorporation Minnesota [*Associated Press*] (SAG)
FFCP...........	Farm Financial Counselling Program [*of Queensland*] (EERA)
FFCP...........	Founders Financial Corp. [*NASDAQ symbol*] (SAG)
FFCPsy........	Fellow of the Faculty of Child and Adolescent Psychiatry
FFCR...........	Freight Forwarders Certificate of Receipt [*Shipping*] (DS)
FFCS...........	Federal Farm Credit System
FFCS...........	Fellow of the Faculty of Secretaries [*British*] (DBQ)
FFCS...........	Food Facilities Consultants Society [*Later, FCSI*] (EA)
FFCSA.........	Florida Fresh Citrus Shippers Association [*Later, FCP*] (EA)
FFD.............	Fairfield Communities [*NYSE symbol*] (TTSB)
FFD.............	Fairfield Minerals Ltd. [*Vancouver Stock Exchange symbol*]
FFD.............	Fellow in the Faculty of Dentistry [*British*]
FFD.............	Field Forcing (Decreasing)
FFD.............	Film: Foreign Documentary
FFD.............	First Flowering Date [*Botany*]
FFD.............	Fixed Format Display (MCD)
FFD.............	Flange Focal Distance (MCD)
FFD.............	Focus Film Distance [*Radiology*]
FFD.............	Formal Functional Description (LAIN)
FFD.............	Formation Flight Display
FFD.............	Forward Floating Depot [*Army*]
FFD.............	Free Flight Data
FFD.............	Friendly Forward Disposition
FFD.............	Fuel Failure Detection
FFD.............	Functional Flow Diagram
FFDA...........	Federated Funeral Directors of America [*Commercial firm*] (EA)
FFDA...........	Fiber Fineness Distribution Analyzer (ADA)
FFDA...........	Flying Funeral Directors of America (EA)
FFdBrun.......	First Federal Savings Bank of Brunswick [*Associated Press*] (SAG)
FFDC...........	First Failure Data Capture [*IBM Corp.*] [*Computer science*] (PCM)
FFDCA.........	Federal Food, Drug, and Cosmetic Act
FFdEH.........	First Federal Savings & Loan Association, East Hartford [*Associated Press*] (SAG)
FFDF...........	FFD Financial [*NASDAQ symbol*] (TTSB)
FFDFinl.......	FFD Financial Corp. [*NASDAQ symbol*] (SAG)
FFDFinl.......	FFD Financial Corp. [*Associated Press*] (SAG)
FFDK...........	Fixed Flexion Deformity of the Knee [*Orthopedics*]
FFdMN.........	First Federal Bancorp. MN [*Associated Press*] (SAG)
FFDO	Fellow of the Faculty of Dispensing Opticians [*British*] (DBQ)
FFDO	Force Fighter Director Officer
FFD of A......	Federated Funeral Directors of America [*Commercial firm*]
FFDP...........	Firstfed Bancshares [*NASDAQ symbol*] (TTSB)
FFDP...........	FirstFed Bancshares, Inc. [*NASDAQ symbol*] (SAG)
FFDRCSI.....	Fellow of the Faculty of Dentistry of the Royal College of Surgeons in Ireland
FFDRCS Irel...	Fellow of the Faculty of Dentistry of the Royal College of Surgeons in Ireland
FFDS...........	Fleet Flag Data System [*Navy*] (MCD)
FFDSRCS.....	Fellow of the Faculty of Dental Surgery, Royal College of Surgeons [*British*] (DAVI)
FFDW..........	Fat-Free Dry Weight
FFE	Falling Film Evaporation
FFE	Finished Floor Elevation [*Technical drawings*]
FFE	Fire-Fighting Equipment (AAG)
FFE	Fire for Effect [*Army*] (INF)
FFE	Flexible-Fuel Engine [*Automotive engineering*]
FFE	Forced Fault Entry [*Computer science*]
FFE	Free Flow Electrophoresis [*Analytical biochemistry*]
FFE	Free Front Endpapers (DGA)
FFE	Friends for Education (EA)
FFE(A)	Fire Fighting Enterprises (Australia) Ltd. [*Commercial firm*]
FF EauCl	First Federal Bancshares of Eau Claire, Inc. [*Associated Press*] (SAG)
FFEC	Femtosecond Field Emission Camera [*Physics*]
FFEC	Field-Free Emission Current
FFEC	Firestone Firehawk Endurance Championship [*Auto racing*]

FFEC	First Federal Bancshares of Eau Claire, Inc. [*NASDAQ symbol*] (SAG)
FFEC	First Fed of Eau Clair [*NASDAQ symbol*] (TTSB)
FFED	Fidelity Fed Bancorp [*NASDAQ symbol*] (TTSB)
FFED	Fidelity Federal Bancorp [*NASDAQ symbol*] (NQ)
FFedKY	First Federal Financial Corp. [*Associated Press*] (SAG)
FFEF	FFE Financial Corp. [*NASDAQ symbol*] (SAG)
FFE Fn	FFE Financial Corp. [*Associated Press*] (SAG)
FFEJWW	Future Farm Experts of the Junior Woodchucks of the World [*Subgroup of Junior Woodchucks organization mentioned in Donald Duck comic by Carl Barks*]
FFEL	Federal Family Education Loan [*Program*]
FFEM	Freeze-Fracture Electron Microscopy
FFEP	Finlands Folks Enhetsparti [*Finnish People's Unity Party*] (PPE)
FFER	Federal Facility Environmental Restoration (AAGC)
FFES	First Federal Savings & Loan Association, East Hartford [*NASDAQ symbol*] (SAG)
FFES	First Fed S & L (CT) [*NASDAQ symbol*] (TTSB)
FFES	Food Facilities Engineering Society [*Later, FFCS*] (EA)
FFEX	Field Firing Exercise [*Military*] (NVT)
FFEX	Frozen Food Express [*NASDAQ symbol*] (TTSB)
FFEX	Frozen Food Express Industries, Inc. [*NASDAQ symbol*] (SAG)
FFF	Fairly Fearless Flier
FFF	Family of Faith Foundation [*Later, FFM*] (EA)
FFF	Famous Fone Friends (EA)
FFF	Farm Film Foundation [*Later, Grange-Farm Film Foundation*] (EA)
FFF	Fast Fission Factor
FFF	Federation of Fly Fishers (EA)
FFF	Federation of Fly Fishers
FFF	Federation of Free Farmers [*Philippines*]
FFF	Feed Forward Filter (IAA)
FFF	Fellowship of First Fleeters
FFF	Field-Flow Fractionation [*Chemical separation method*]
FFF	Film: Foreign Feature
FFF	Find, Fix and Finish [*Military slang*] (VNW)
FFF	Fine French Furniture
FFF	Fission-Fusion-Fission [*Bomb*] (DEN)
FFF	Fitness for the Future [*Nursing Services Course*] [*Red Cross*]
FFF	Flat or Folded Flat [*Freight*]
FFF	Flexible File Finder [*Computer science*] (PCM)
FFF	Flicker Fusion Frequency [*Ophthalmology*]
FFF	Flight Facilities Flight
FFF	Flight Freedoms Foundation (EA)
FFF	Form, Fit, and Function (MCD)
FFF	Fortississimo [*As Loud as Possible*] [*Music*]
FFF	Foundation for a Future [*Defunct*] (EA)
FFF	Free Flight Facility (MCD)
FFF	Free Float Facility (SSD)
FFF	Free-Form Fabrication (ECON)
FFF	Free French Forces [*World War II*]
FFF	Fuel Failure Fraction [*Nuclear energy*] (NRCH)
FFF	Future Fisherman Foundation (EA)
FFF	Future of Freedom Foundation (EA)
FFFA	Federation Feminine Franco-Americaine [*Federation of French American Women*] (EA)
FFFA	Federation of French American Women (EA)
FFFC	FFVA Financial [*NASDAQ symbol*] (TTSB)
FFFC	FFVA Financial Corp. [*NASDAQ symbol*] (SAG)
FFFC	Freddy Fender Fan Club (EA)
FFFCA	Fabulous Fifties Ford Club of America (EA)
FFFD	First Federal Savings Bank Fort Dodge [*Iowa*] [*NASDAQ symbol*] (SAG)
FFFD	North Central Bancshares [*NASDAQ symbol*] (TTSB)
FFFD	North Central Bancshares, Inc. [*NASDAQ symbol*] (SAG)
FFFE	Friends for Free Enterprise (EA)
FFFF	Fast Free-Form Fabrication [*Engineering design and modeling*]
FFFFM	Full-Face Fire-Fighters' Mask (MCD)
FFFG	F.F.O. Financial Group [*NASDAQ symbol*] (TTSB)
FFFG	FFO Financial Group, Inc. [*NASDAQ symbol*] (CTT)
FFFL	Fidelity Federal Savings Bank [*NASDAQ symbol*] (SAG)
FFFL	Fidelity Fedl Svgs Bk Fla [*NASDAQ symbol*] (TTSB)
FFFn	FirstFederal Financial Services Corp. [*Associated Press*] (SAG)
FFFP	Film-Forming Fluoroprotein Formulation [*Organic chemistry*]
FFFS	First Federal Financial Services [*Associated Press*] (SAG)
FFFSG	Fossil Fuel Fired Steam Generator (GNE)
FFFU	Federal Fire Fighters' Union [*Australia*]
FFG	FBL Financial Group [*NYSE symbol*] (SAG)
FFG	First Families of Georgia 1733-1797 (EA)
FFG	Fiscal and Force Capability Guidance (DNAB)
FFG	Flora and Fauna Guarantee Act 1988 [*Victoria*] [*State Act*] (EERA)
FFG	Flugdienst Fehlhaber GmbH [*Germany ICAO designator*] (FAAC)
FFG	Form and Finish Grinding
FFG	Foundation Faith of God (EA)
FFG	Foundation for Future Generations (EA)
FFG	Free-Fall Grab [*Marine geology*]
FFG	Free Fat Graft [*Medicine*] (DMAA)
FFG	Freshbake Foods Group [*British*]
FFG	Friendly Foreign Government
FFG	Functional Feeding Groups [*Ecology*]
FFG	Guided Missile Frigate [*Navy symbol*]
FFGA	Full Funding Grant Agreement (AAGC)
FFGI	Food and Feed Grain Institute [*Kansas State University*] [*Research center*] (RCD)
FFGI	ForeFront Group [*NASDAQ symbol*] (TTSB)
FFGI	ForeFront Group, Inc. [*NASDAQ symbol*] (SAG)
ffGn	Fast Fractional Gaussian Noise [*Mathematics*]
FFGT	Firefighter [*Army*] (AABC)
FFH	Fairfax Financial Holdings Ltd. [*Toronto Stock Exchange symbol*]
FFH	Families for the Homeless (EA)
FFH	Farm Family Holdings, Inc. [*NYSE symbol*] (SAG)
FFH	Fast-Frequency Hopping (MCD)
FFH	Female Family Household [*Bureau of the Census*] (GFGA)
FFH	For Further Headings (DA)
FFH	Formerly Fat Housewife [*Weight Watchers, International; advertising*]
FFH	Foundation for Health (EA)
FFH	Freedom from Hunger Foundation [*UN Food and Agriculture Organization*] (EA)
FFHC	First Financial Corp. [*NASDAQ symbol*] (NQ)
FFHC	First Finl Corp Wis [*NASDAQ symbol*] (TTSB)
FFHC	Foam-Filled Honeycomb Core
FFHC	Freedom from Hunger Campaign [*UN Food and Agriculture Organization*]
FFHC/AD	Freedom from Hunger Campaign - Action for Development [*UN Food and Agriculture Organization*]
FFHH	FSF Financial [*NASDAQ symbol*] (TTSB)
FFHH	FSF Financial Corp. [*NASDAQ symbol*] (SAG)
FF Hom	Fellow of the Faculty of Homoeopathy [*British*]
FFHP	First Harrisburg Bancorp, Inc. [*NASDAQ symbol*] (NQ)
FFHR	Fusion-Fission Hybrid Reactor
FFHS	Federation of Family History Societies (EA)
FFHS	First Franklin Corp. [*NASDAQ symbol*] (NQ)
FFHS	Forby Family Historical Society (EA)
FFHT	Fast Fourier-Hadamard Transform (PDAA)
FFI	Family Functioning Index
FFI	Fatal Familial Insomnia [*Medicine*]
FFI	Fellow of the Faculty of Insurance [*French Forces of the Interior*] (DAS)
FFI	Field Forcing (Increasing)
FFI	Film Four International [*Commercial firm British*]
FFI	Finance for Industry [*Later, Investors in Industry International - 3I*] [*British*]
FFI	Fit for Issue [*Navy*]
FFI	Fixed Fee Incentive (SSD)
FFI	Fluid Flow Indicator
FFI	Flying Fifteen International (EA)
FFI	Forces Francaises de l'Interieur [*French Forces of the Interior*] [*World War II*]
FFI	For Further Information
FFI	For Further Instructions (DS)
FFI	Foundation for Fluency (EA)
FFI	Franciscan Friars of the Immaculate (TOCD)
ffi	Franciscan Friars of the Immaculate (TOCD)
FFI	Free from Infection [*Medicine*]
FFI	Freeman Fox International [*Commercial firm British*]
FFI	Freight Forwarders Institute [*Defunct*] (EA)
FFI	Friend Finders International [*Defunct*] (EA)
FFI	Frozen Food Institute
FFI	Fuel Flow Indicator
FFI	Full Field Investigation (NRCH)
FFI	Fundamental Frequency Indicator [*Medicine*] (DMAA)
FFIA	Fellow, Fundraising Institute-Australia, Inc. (NFD)
FFIC	Flushing Financial [*NASDAQ symbol*] (TTSB)
FFIC	Flushing Financial Corp. [*NASDAQ symbol*] (SAG)
fFIDA	Fringe Festival of Independent Dance Artists [*Canada*]
FFIEC	Federal Financial Institutions Examination Council (OICC)
FFII-MS	Fission Fragment-Induced Ionization - Mass Spectroscopy
FFILH	Flat Fillister Head [*Screws*]
F/FILT	Fuel Filter [*Automotive engineering*]
FFIN	First Financial Bankshares [*NASDAQ symbol*] (SAG)
FFinFd	First Financial Fund, Inc. [*Associated Press*] (SAG)
FFIN-L	Nova University, Law Library, Fort Lauderdale, FL [*Library symbol Library of Congress*] (LCLS)
FFIN-L	Nova University, Law Library, Fort Lauderdale, FL [*Library symbol*] [*Library of Congress*] (LCLS)
FFinWM	First Financial Corporation Western Maryland [*Associated Press*] (SAG)
FFIP	Firm Fixed Incentive Price [*Government contracting*]
FFIR	Foundation for Financial Institutions Research [*Defunct*] (EA)
FFIR	Friendly Forces Information Requirements [*Military*] (INF)
FFIRN	Field Format Index Reference Number
FFIS	Federal Facilities Information System (EPA)
FFIS	Forests and Forest Industries Strategy (EERA)
FFIT	Fluorescent Focus Inhibition Test [*Medicine*] (BABM)
FFJ	Friends for Jamaica (EA)
FFJF	Federation of Former Jewish Fighters (EA)
FFK	Fixed Function Key [*Computer science*] (ECII)
FFK	Fixed Function Keyboard (MCD)
FFKT	Farmers Capital Bank [*NASDAQ symbol*] (TTSB)
FFKT	Farmers Capital Bank Corp. [*NASDAQ symbol*] (NQ)
FFKY	First Federal Financial Corp. [*NASDAQ symbol*] (SAG)
FFKY	First Fed Finl (KY) [*NASDAQ symbol*] (TTSB)
FFL	Fairfield, IA [*Location identifier FAA*] (FAAL)
FFL	Fast Freight Line [*Shipping*]
FFL	Federal Firearms License
FFL	Federal Fiscal Liability
FFL	Federation of Free Labor [*Philippines*]
FFL	Female Flared
FFL	Feminists for Life of America (EA)
FFL	Field Failure (AAG)
FFL	Fiji Federation of Labor

FFL	Finished Floor Line [*Technical drawings*]
FFL	First Financial Language [*Computer science*]
FFL	Fitness for Life (EA)
FFL	Fixed and Flashing Light [*Navigation signal*]
FFL	Flip-Flop Latch [*Computer science*] (MSA)
FFL	Forces Francaises Libres [*Free French Forces*]
FFI	Fort Lauderdale Public Library, Fort Lauderdale, FL [*Library symbol Library of Congress*] (LCLS)
FFI	Fort Lauderdale Public Library, Fort Lauderdale, FL [*Library symbol*] [*Library of Congress*] (LCLS)
FFL	Front Focal Length [*Optics*]
FFL	Fuel Fill Line (AAG)
FFL	Full Funding Limit (AAGC)
FFL	Intavia Ltd. [*British*] [*FAA designator*] (FAAC)
FFL	Light Frigate
FFLA	Federal Farm Loan Act [*1916*]
FFLA	Fellow of the Faculty of Fire Loss Adjusters [*British*] (DAS)
FFLA	Ferromagnetic Fluid Levitation Accelerometer
FFIAI	Art Institute of Fort Lauderdale, Fort Lauderdale, FL [*Library symbol*] [*Library of Congress*] (LCLS)
FFIB	Broward Community College, Fort Lauderdale, FL [*Library symbol Library of Congress*] (LCLS)
FFIBL	Broward County Libraries Division, Fort Lauderdale, FL [*Library symbol Library of Congress*] (LCLS)
FFLC	FFLC Bancorp [*NASDAQ symbol*] (SAG)
FFLC	Freight Forwarder Location Code (AAGC)
FFLC Bc	FFLC Bancorp [*Associated Press*] (SAG)
FFIN	Nova University, Fort Lauderdale, FL [*Library symbol Library of Congress*] (LCLS)
FFIN-O	Nova University, Physical Oceanographic Laboratory Library, Dania, FL [*Library symbol Library of Congress*] (LCLS)
FFLOP	Field Fresnel Lens Optical Platform
FFLS	Failed Fuel Location Subsystem [*Nuclear energy*] (NRCH)
FFLT	Familiarization Flight (FAAC)
FFLY	Faithfully
FFM	Family Farm Movement (EA)
FFM	Fast File Manager (NITA)
FFM	Fat-Free Mass (MAE)
FFM	[*The*] Fellowship for Freedom in Medicine [*British*]
FFM	Fergus Falls, MN [*Location identifier FAA*] (FAAL)
FFM	First Financial Management Corp. [*NYSE symbol*] (SPSG)
FFM	Foundation for Microbiology (EA)
FF/M	Fracture Frequency per Meter [*Mining technology*]
FFM	Free-Flying [*Experiment*] Module [*NASA*] (NASA)
FFM	Friction Force Microscope
FFM	Fuel Failure Mock-Up [*Nuclear energy*]
FFM	Fuel Fill to Missile [*Aerospace*] (AAG)
FFM	Full Face Mask [*Military*] (CAAL)
FFM	Fund for the Feminist Majority (EA)
FFm	Lee County Public Library, Fort Meyers, FL [*Library symbol Library of Congress*] (LCLS)
FFMA	Fidelity Federal Savings Bank (MHDW)
FFMA	Fraternal Field Managers' Association [*Appleton, WI*] (EA)
FFMAS	Furniture Factories' Marketing Association of the South [*Later, IHFMA*] (EA)
FFMC	Faceted Fixed Mirror Concentrator (PDAA)
FFMC	Federal Farm Mortgage Corp. [*Established, 1934; assets transferred to Secretary of the Treasury, 1961*]
FFMC	Freshwater Fish Marketing Corp. [*See also OCPED*]
FFmE	Edison Community College, ECC/USF Learning Resources, Fort Meyers, FL [*Library symbol Library of Congress*] (LCLS)
FFMED	Fixed Former Message Entry Device (MCD)
FFMG	Foundry Facings Manufacturers Group [*Later, FSMG*] (EA)
FFMIP	Foreign Military Sales Financial Management Improvement Program (MCD)
FFML	First Family Bank Florida [*NASDAQ symbol*] (SAG)
FFML	First Family Finl [*NASDAQ symbol*] (TTSB)
FFmL	Lee County Library System, Fort Myers, FL [*Library symbol*] [*Library of Congress*] (LCLS)
FFMN	Fixed Federal Monitoring Network (FAAC)
FFMSPAC	Farm Financial Management Skills Program Advisory Committee [*Australia*]
FFN	Field Format Name
FFN	Fleet Flash Network [*Navy*]
FFN	Fly-Fishing Network [*Information service or system*]
FFN	Folded Flat or Nested [*Freight*]
FFN	FreeLance Finders Network (EA)
FFN	Friend, Foe, or Neutral (MCD)
FFN	Full Function Node (MHDB)
FFnBcp	First Financial Bancorp, Inc. [*FL*] [*Associated Press*] (SAG)
FFNC	First Fix Not Converted
FFncOH	First Financial Bancorp Ohio [*Associated Press*] (SAG)
FFnCpRI	First Financial Corp. (Providence, RI) [*Associated Press*] (SAG)
FF-NM	Flip-Flop - National Module [*Computer science*] (AAG)
FFNPA	Fund for New Priorities in America (EA)
FFNSW	Filipino Forum in New South Wales [*Australia*]
FFO	Dayton, OH [*Location identifier FAA*] (FAAL)
FFO	Forces Francaises de l'Ouest
FFO	Formation Flight Operation
FFO	Forward Firing Ordnance (MCD)
FFO	French Family Association (EA)
FFO	Fullam Family Organization (EA)
FFO	Furnace Fuel Oil (NATG)
FFOB	Flexible Fiber-Optic Borescope
FFOB	Forward Fighting Operating Base [*Military*] (AFM)

FFOB	Front Face of Block [*Automotive engineering*]
FFOB	Frontiers Foundation Operation Beaver [*Canada*] (EAIO)
FFOF	Foreign Fishing Observer Fund [*National Oceanic and Atmospheric Administration*]
FFO Fn	FFO Financial Group, Inc. [*Associated Press*] (SAG)
FFOH	Fidelity Financial of Ohio, Inc. [*NASDAQ symbol*] (SAG)
FFOH	Fidelity Finl Ohio [*NASDAQ symbol*] (TTSB)
FFOM	Fellow of the Faculty of Occupational Medicine (DAVI)
FFORCEV	Field Force, Vietnam (CINC)
FFOS	Facilities Forecast Obligations Summary
FFOT	Fast Frequency on Target
FFOX	Firefox Communications [*NASDAQ symbol*] (TTSB)
FFOX	Firefox Communications, Inc. [*NASDAQ symbol*] (SAG)
FFP	Consolidated First Fund [*Vancouver Stock Exchange symbol*]
FFP	Far-Field Pressure
FFP	Farm Forestry Program (EERA)
FFP	Fast Field Program (KSC)
FFP	Fast Floating Point [*Computer science*]
FFP	Federal Financial Participation
FFP	Federation for Progress [*Defunct*] (EA)
FFP	Feminists Fighting Pornography (EA)
FFP	FFP Partners L.P. [*AMEX symbol*] (TTSB)
FFP	FFP Partners Ltd. [*AMEX symbol*] (SPSG)
FFP	Field Forcing, Protective (IAA)
FFP	Finite Flat Plate
FFP	Firm-Fixed Price [*Government contracting*]
FFP	Fistful of Prisms [*Opthalmology*] (DAVI)
FFP	Fixed Frequency Pulse (IAA)
FFP	Fleet Frequency Plans
FFP	Floating Foundation of Photography
FFP	Food for Peace [*Overseas food donation program*]
FFP	Food for Poland [*Later, Food for Peace*] (EA)
FFP	Forte Piano [*Loud, then Soft*] [*Music*]
FFP	Foundation for Peace (EA)
FFP	Founding Fathers Papers (EA)
FFP	Free Flight Plan [*Northwest Airlines, Inc.*]
FFP	Frequent Flier Program (BARN)
FFP	Fresh Frozen Plasma [*Medicine*]
FFP	Friends of Family Planning (EA)
FFP	Friends of the Filipino People (EA)
FFP	Fuel Fabrication Plant [*Nuclear energy*] (NRCH)
FFP	Fuel Fill to Fuel Prefab (AAG)
FFP	[*The*] Fund for Peace [*An association*] (EA)
FFp	Saint Lucie-Okeechobee Regional Library, Fort Pierce, FL [*Library symbol Library of Congress*] (LCLS)
FFPA	Free from Prussic Acid
FFPAF	Forest and Forest Products Policy Advisory Forum (EERA)
FFPB	First Palm Beach Bancorp [*NASDAQ symbol*] (TTSB)
FFPB	First Palm Beach Bancorp, Inc. [*NASDAQ symbol*] (SAG)
FFPB	Flora and Fauna Protection Board (EERA)
FFPC	Firm-Fixed Price Contract
FFPC	Florida First Bancorp [*NASDAQ symbol*] (TTSB)
FFPC	Florida First Bancorp, Inc. [*NASDAQ symbol*] (SAG)
FFPC	Florida First Federal Savings Bank [*NASDAQ symbol*] (NQ)
FFPE	Federation de la Fonction Publique Europeenne [*European Civil Service Federation*] (EAIO)
FFPEPA	Firm Fixed Price with Economic Price Adjustment [*Government contracts*]
FFPh	Fellow of the Faculty of Physiotherapists
FFPI	Fixed-Fee-plus-Incentive [*Business term*] (MCD)
FFPI	Flip-Flop Position Indicator [*Computer science*]
FFpI	Indian River Community College, Fort Pierce, FL [*Library symbol Library of Congress*] (LCLS)
FFPIC	Forestry and Forest Products Industry Council [*Australia*]
FFPLE	Firm-Fixed Price Letter [*Government contracting*] (MCD)
FFPLOE	Firm-Fixed-Price Level of Effort [*Type of contract*] (AAGC)
FFPS	Fauna and Flora Preservation Society (EA)
FFPS	Fellow of the Faculty of Physicians and Surgeons [*British*]
FFPS	Flora and Fauna Preservation Society (EERA)
FFR	Failure Frequency Report [*Military*] (AFIT)
FFR	Falfurrias, TX [*Location identifier FAA*] (FAAL)
FFR	False-Flag Recruitment [*CIA*] (LAIN)
FFR	Fauna and Flora Reserve [*State*] (EERA)
FFR	Fellow of the Faculty of Radiologists [*British*]
FFR	Field Forcing, Reversing (IAA)
FFR	Fission-Fusion Ratio
FFR	Fit for Role [*Military British*]
FFR	Fitted for Radio [*Military British*]
FFR	Fixed Frequency Receiver
FFR	Flash Format Program (SAA)
FFR	Fleet Fighter Reconnaissance [*Air Force*]
FFR	Folded Flow Reactor
FFR	Foreign Force Reduction (NATG)
FFR	Fosterlaendska Folkroerelsen [*Patriotic People's Movement*] [*Finland*] (PPE)
FFR	Foundation for Field Research (EA)
F Fr	(Frater) Johannes de Freiburg [*Deceased, 1314*] [*Authority cited in pre-1607 legal work*] (DSA)
FFR	Free Field Room
FFR	Free Flight Rocket (NATG)
FFR	Free French [*World War II*]
FFr	French Franc [*Monetary unit*]
FFR	Frequency-Following Response [*Neurophysiology*]
FFR	Front Engine, Front and Rear Drive [*Automotive engineering*]
FFR	Frontier Force Rifles [*British military*] (DMA)

FFR.............	RADAR Picket Frigate [Navy symbol] (NVT)
FFRATS......	Full Flight Regime Auto Throttle System (ADA)
FFRC..........	Fossil Fuel Resources Committee
FFRD..........	Flip-Flop Relay Driver [Computer science]
FFRDC........	Federally Funded Research and Development Center [National Science Foundation]
F/FRED......	Forestry/Fuel-wood Research and Development Project (GNE)
FFRF..........	Freedom from Religion Foundation (EA)
FFRR	First Flight Readiness Review (SSD)
FFRR	Full-Frequency Range Recording
FFRRCSIrel...	Fellow of the Faculty of Radiologists, Royal College of Surgeons of Ireland [British] (DBQ)
FFRS..........	Fast Fleet Replenishment Ship
FFRV..........	Fidelity Federal Savings Bank [NASDAQ symbol] (NQ)
FFRV..........	Fidelity Financial Bankshares Corp. [NASDAQ symbol] (SAG)
FFRV..........	Fidelity Finl Bancshares [NASDAQ symbol] (TTSB)
FFS	Family Financial Statement
FFS	Fat-Free Solids
FFS	Fat-Free Supper [Medicine]
FFS	Feeder Fault Sensing (MCD)
FFS	Fee for Service
FFS ..:.......	Fee for Service [Equivalency]
FFS	Fellow of the Faculty of Architects and Surveyors [British] (DBQ)
FFS	Fellow of the Franklin Society [British]
FFS	Film: Foreign Series
FFS	First Flight Society (EA)
FFS	Fixed Frequency Sampling [for water quality assessment]
FFS	Flame Fluorescence Spectroscopy
FFS	Fletcher Challenge Forest [NYSE symbol] (SPSG)
FFS	Fletcher Challenge Forest ADS [NYSE symbol] (TTSB)
FFS	Flight Following Service [FAA]
FFS	Florida Department of Agriculture and Consumer Services, Division of Forestry [FAA designator] (FAAC)
FFS	For Further Study (ACRL)
FFS	Formation Flying Simulator
FFS	Formatted File System [Computer science]
FFS	Foundation for Fire Safety [Defunct] (EA)
FFS	Free-Fall Sensor
FFS	Front des Forces Socialistes [Front of Socialist Forces] [Algeria] [Political party] (PD)
FFSA..........	Federation Francaise du Sport Automobile [French Federation of Motorsport]
FFSA & C...	Field Functional System Assembly and Checkout
FFSA & C...	Field Functional System Assembly and Checkout (KSC)
FFSAC........	Field Functional Systems Assembly and Checkout (IAA)
FFS & FP...	Five-Year Force Structure and Financial Program [Navy] (AFIT)
FFSB..........	Federation des Foires et Salons du Benelux [Federation of Fairs and Trade Shows of BENELUX - FFTSB] (EA)
FFSBern.....	First Federal Savings & Loan Association, San Bernardino [Associated Press] (SAG)
FFSC..........	Franciscan Brothers of the Holy Cross (TOCD)
ffsc...........	Franciscan Brothers of the Holy Cross (TOCD)
FFSCUG	Formatted File System Commercial Users' Group [Computer science]
FFSD..........	Free Foil Switching Device
FFSF..........	Full Fat Soy Flour (OA)
FFSI...........	Financing for Science International, Inc. [NASDAQ symbol] (SAG)
FFSI...........	Financing for Science Intl [NASDAQ symbol] (TTSB)
FFSIW........	Financing for Science Intl Wrrt [NASDAQ symbol] (TTSB)
FFSK.........	Fast Frequency Shift Keying (MCD)
FFSL..........	First Independence Corp. [NASDAQ symbol] (SAG)
FFSL..........	First Independence Del [NASDAQ symbol] (TTSB)
FFSM..........	Federation des Fondations pour la Sante Mondiale [Federation of World Health Foundations - FWHF] [Geneva, Switzerland] (EA)
FFSP..........	Fossil Fired Steam Plant (IEEE)
FFSR..........	Feed-Forward Signal Regeneration (PDAA)
FFSR..........	Fund for Stockowners Rights (EA)
FFSS..........	Full-Frequency Stereophonic Sound (DEN)
FFSSiou	First Federal Savings Bank Siouxland [Associated Press] (SAG)
FFST..........	4 Front Software Intl [NASDAQ symbol] (TTSB)
FFSTA........	Federated Furnishing Trades Society [Australia]
FFSvFD.......	First Federal Savings Bank Fort Dodge IA [Associated Press] (SAG)
FFSW..........	FirstFederal Financial Services [NASDAQ symbol] (SAG)
FFSW..........	Firstfed Finl Svcs [NASDAQ symbol] (TTSB)
FFSWO	FirstFederal Finl 6.5% Cv'B' Pfd [NASDAQ symbol] (TTSB)
FFSWP........	FirstFederal Finl 7% Cv'A'Pfd [NASDAQ symbol] (TTSB)
FFSX..........	First Federal Savings Bank Siouxland [NASDAQ symbol] (SAG)
FFSX..........	First Fed Svgs Bk Siouxland [NASDAQ symbol] (TTSB)
FFT	Fast Fourier Transform [Mathematics]
FFT	Fast Fourier Transformation [Noise reduction technique] (NITA)
FFT	Fast-Fourier Transforms (DAVI)
FFT	Fast Freight Train
FFT	Finite Fourier Transform
FFT	Flicker Fusion Threshold [Cardiology] (DAVI)
FFT	Flicker Fusion Threshold [Ophthalmology]
FFT	Floor-to-Floor Time [Engineering]
FFT	For Further Transfer [to] [Military]
FFT	Formation Flight Trainer [Air Force]
FFT	Frankfort, KY [Location identifier FAA] (FAAL)
FFT	Frankfurt [Kentucky] [Airport symbol] (AD)
FFT	Free-Fall Test (SAA)
FFT	Free-Floating Thrombus [Medicine]
FFT	Freight Forwarders Tariff Bureau, Inc., New York NY [STAC]
f-ft--	French Territory of the Afars and Issas [Djibouti] [MARC geographic area code Library of Congress] (LCCP)
FFT	Frontier Airlines, Inc. [FAA designator] (FAAC)

FFT	Fuel Flow Totalizer [Aerospace]
FFT	Full Free Triple [Lift truck]
FFT	Training Frigate [Navy symbol]
FFTA..........	Foundation of the Flexographic Technical Association [Later, FTA] (EA)
FFTA..........	Frozen Fish Trades Association (EA)
FFTB..........	Freight Forwarders Tariff Bureau [Defunct] (EA)
FFTC..........	Fixed Feed Through Capacitor
FFTC/ASPAC...	Food and Fertilizer Technology Center for the Asian and Pacific Region (EAIO)
FFTCom......	Fellow of the Faculty of Teachers in Commerce [British] (DBQ)
FF-TEM.......	Freeze-Fracture Transmission Electron Microscopy
FFTF	Fast Flux Test Facility [Nuclear energy]
FFTFPO......	Fast Flux Test Facility Project Office [Nuclear energy] (GFGA)
FFTG..........	Firefighting [Army] (AABC)
FFTO..........	Free-Flying Teleoperator [Program] [Electronics]
FF/TOT......	Fuel Flow Totalizer [Aerospace] (AAG)
FFTP..........	Fast Fourier Transform Processor [Mathematics] (IAA)
FFTQ.........	Four Factor Theory Questionnaire (EDAC)
FFTR..........	Fast Flux Test Reactor [Nuclear energy] (OA)
FFTR..........	Firefighter (AFM)
FFTS	Fixed Frequency Topside Sounder (SAA)
FFTSB........	Federation of Fairs and Trade Shows of BENELUX [Formerly, Federation of Fairs and Exhibitions in BENELUX - FFSB] (EA)
FFTV	Free Flight Test Vehicle
FFU	Federation of Film Unions [British]
FFU	Ferranti PLC [British ICAO designator] (FAAC)
FFU	Focus-Forming Unit [Medical/biochemical research]
FFU	Futaleufu [Chile] [Airport symbol] (AD)
FFU	GEC Marconi Avionics Ltd. [British] [FAA designator] (FAAC)
FFU	Provo, UT [Location identifier FAA] (FAAL)
FFUR	Failure Factor Update Request
F/FURN......	Fully Furnished (ADA)
FFV	Far-Field Visibility [Aviation]
FFV	Fast Flying Vestibule [Old railroad term for a deluxe coach]
FFV	Field Failure Voltage (IEEE)
FFV	Field Force, Vietnam
FFV	Finest Foods of Virginia [Brand name]
FFV	First Families of Virginia (BARN)
FFV	Flexible-Fuel Vehicle [Operable by either gasoline or methanol] [Ford Motor Co.]
FFV	Foreign Fishing Vessel
FFVA..........	Florida Fruit and Vegetable Association (EA)
FFVA Fn......	FFVA Financial Corp. [Associated Press] (SAG)
FFVF..........	Freedoms Foundation at Valley Forge (EA)
FFVIB........	Fresh Fruit and Vegetable Information Bureau [British] (CB)
FFVMA.......	Fire Fighting Vehicles Manufacturers Association [British] (DBA)
FFV's	First Families of Virginia [Supposedly elite society] [Slang]
FFVS.........	Free Field Voltage Sensitivity
FFW	Failure Free Warranty [Military] (AFIT)
FFW	Federation of Free Workers [Philippines]
FFW	Feed Forward (ECII)
FFW	Feet of Fresh Water
FFW	Filoil Free Workers [Philippines]
FFW	Fitted for Wireless [British military] (DMA)
FFW	Foreign Free World (MCD)
FFWC..........	FFW Corp. [NASDAQ symbol] (SAG)
FFWCB........	Federation of Flatmen, Watermen, and Canal Boatmen [A union] [British]
FFW Cp......	FFW Corp. [Associated Press] (SAG)
FFWD..........	Fast Forward [Audio-visual technology]
FFWD..........	Wood Bancorp [NASDAQ symbol] (TTSB)
FFWHC........	Federation of Feminist Women's Health Centers (EA)
FFWM.........	First Financial Corp., Western Maryland [NASDAQ symbol] (SAG)
FFWM.........	First Finl (MD) [NASDAQ symbol] (TTSB)
FFWT..........	Final Feedwater Temperature [Nuclear energy] (NRCH)
FFWV.........	Federation of French War Veterans (EA)
FFWW.........	Fat-Free Wet Weight
FFY	Faithfully
FFYF..........	FFY Financial [NASDAQ symbol] (TTSB)
FFYF..........	FFY Financial Corp. [NASDAQ symbol] (SAG)
FFY Fn........	FFY Financial Corp. [Associated Press] (SAG)
FFYQ.........	Federal Fiscal Year Quarters (OICC)
FFY/SH......	Fife and Forfar Yeomanry/Scottish Horse [British military] (DMA)
FFZ	Fiji Fracture Zone [Geology]
FFZ	Forzatissimo [Extremely Loud] [Music] (ROG)
FFZ	Free Fire Zone [Army] (AABC)
FG.............	Ariana Afghan Airlines [ICAO designator] (AD)
fg---.........	Congo River and Basin [MARC geographic area code Library of Congress] (LCCP)
FG.............	Facility Ground
FG.............	Fallschirmjaeger-Gewehr [Parachutist's rifle] [German military - World War II]
FG.............	Family Groups [Aid to Families with Dependent Children] (OICC)
FG.............	Fashion Group [Later, TFG] (EA)
FG.............	Fast Glycolytic [Muscle]
FG.............	Feature Group
FG.............	February Group [An association] (EA)
FG.............	Federal Government (WDAA)
F-G...........	Feeley-Gorman [Agar] [Microbiology]
FG.............	Feldenkrais Guild [An association] (EA)
fg.............	Felsic Granulite [Geology]
FG.............	Female Groove
FG.............	Ferrosan [Sweden] [Research code symbol]
F-G...........	Feynman-Gellman Theory [Nuclear physics]

FG .... Fiberglass (ADA)
Fg .... Fibrinogen [Factor 1] [Hematology]
FG .... Field Gain (IAA)
FG .... Field Goal [Football, basketball]
FG .... Field Grade
FG .... Field Gun
FG .... Filament Ground (MSA)
FG .... File Gap [Computer science] (BUR)
FG .... Filter Gate
FG .... Final Grid (IAA)
FG .... Finanzgericht [Tax Court] [German] (ILCA)
FG .... Fine Grain
FG .... Firegreen Ltd. [Food-processing and distributing company] [British]
FG .... Fire Guardsman [British World War II]
FG .... Fiscal Guidance (AABC)
FG .... Fission Gas (NRCH)
FG .... Flashgun [Photography]
FGI .... Flat Grain [Lumber]
FG .... Flemish Giant Rabbit [Medicine] (DMAA)
FG .... Flint Glazed [Paper] (DGA)
FG .... Floated Gyro [Aerospace] (AAG)
FG .... Flow Gauge
FG .... Fog
FG .... Fog Gong [Navigation charts]
FG .... Fog Gun [Navigation charts]
FG .... Folding
FG .... Foodservice Group [Atlanta, GA] (EA)
FG .... Football Grounds [Public-performance tariff class] [British]
FG .... Foot Groove
FG .... Foot Guards [British]
FG .... Foreground [Film arts]
FG .... Foreground [Computer science]
FG .... Foreign Geneva [Alcohol] (ROG)
FG .... Foreign Government (AAGC)
FG .... Forgotten Generation (EA)
f/g .... Form/Genre
FG .... Formula Grants [Vocational education] (OICC)
FG .... Forward Gate
FG .... Foundation for Grandparenting (EA)
FG .... Fracture Gradient
FG .... Frame Ground [Computer science] (BUR)
FG .... Frank Gasperro [Designer's mark, when appearing on US coins]
FG .... Free Gyroscope (SAA)
fg .... French Guiana [MARC country of publication code Library of Congress] (LCCP)
FG .... Friction Glaze
FG .... Frog [Engineering]
FG .... Fuel Gage (SAA)
FG .... Fuel Gas
FG .... Full Gilt [Bookbinding] (ADA)
FG .... Fully Good
FG .... Function Generator [Computer science] (IEEE)
FG .... Fundamentals Graduate
FG .... Funding Greater Than [Dialog] [Searchable field] (NITA)
FG .... Future Generations [An association] (EA)
FG .... Gainesville Public Library, Gainesville, FL [Library symbol Library of Congress] (LCLS)
FG .... USF & G Corp. [NYSE symbol] (SPSG)
FGA .... Family Grocer Alliance Ltd. [British] (BI)
FGA .... Fasting Glycocholic Acid [Clinical chemistry]
FGA .... Fellow of the Gemmological Association [British]
FGA .... Field Goals Attempted [Football, basketball]
FGA .... Fighter Ground Attack (NATG)
FGA .... First General Resources Co. [Vancouver Stock Exchange symbol]
FGA .... Floating-Gate Amplifier (PDAA)
FGA .... Font Graphics Accelerator [Toshiba]
FGA .... Foreign General Agent [Insurance]
FGA .... Foreign General Average [Insurance]
FGA .... Fort Garland, CO [Location identifier FAA] (FAAL)
FGA .... Free of General Average
FGA .... Fresh Garlic Association [Defunct] (EA)
F/GA .... Fuel Gage [Automotive engineering]
FGAA .... Federal Government Accountants Association [Later, AGA] (EA)
FGAJ .... Fellow of the Guild of Agricultural Journalists [British] (DGA)
FGAN .... Fertilizer Grade Ammonium Nitrate
FG&CW .... Federal Grants & Contracts Weekly [Capital Publications] (AAGC)
FGANSW ...... Flower Growers' Association of New South Wales [Australia]
FGAR .... Foreign Governments or Their Authorized Representatives (MCD)
FGAR .... Formylglycinamide Ribonucleotide (MAE)
FGAS .... Forcenergy Gas Exploration, Inc. [NASDAQ symbol] (SAG)
FGAS .... Forcenergy Inc. [NASDAQ symbol] (TTSB)
FGB .... Fast Gunboat [Navy British]
FGB .... Fiberglass Brush
FGB .... Foliage-Gleaning Bat [Zoology]
FGB .... Foundation for Global Broadcasting (EA)
FGBA .... Fireclay Grate Back Association [British] (BI)
FGBI .... Federation of Soroptimist Clubs of Great Britain and Ireland (BI)
FGBMFI .... Full Gospel Business Men's Fellowship International (EA)
FGBT .... Bata [Equatorial Guinea] [ICAO location identifier] (ICLI)
FGC .... Departamento de Agricultura de la Generalitat de Cataluna [Spain ICAO designator] (FAAC)
FGC .... Facility Group Control [Military] (AFM)
FGC .... Federal Group Code (MCD)
FGC .... Federation Generale du Congo [Congolese General Federation]
FGC .... Fiberglass Curtain

FGC .... Fifth Generation Computer (NITA)
FGC .... Finished Goods Control
FGC .... Fiscal Guidance Category [Military] (CAAL)
FGC .... Fixed Gain Control
FGC .... Fixed Glass Capacitor
FGC .... Flat Glass Council [British] (DBA)
FGC .... Freemont Gold [Vancouver Stock Exchange symbol]
FGC .... Friends General Conference (EA)
FGC .... Friends of Guy Clark (EA)
FGC .... Functional Group Code (MCD)
FGCA .... Ford Galaxie Club of America (EA)
FGCAA .... Federal Grant and Cooperative Agreement Act (AAGC)
FGCB .... Fiberglass Cone Brush
FGcC .... Clay County Public Library, Green Cove Springs, FL [Library symbol Library of Congress] (LCLS)
FGCC .... Federal Geodetic Control Committee [Department of Commerce]
FGCC .... Foundation for Gifted and Creative Children [Defunct] (EA)
FGCI .... Family Golf Centers [NASDAQ symbol] (TTSB)
FGCI .... Family Golf Centers, Inc. [NASDAQ symbol] (SAG)
FGCL .... Fellow of the Guild of Cleaners and Launderers [British] (DBQ)
FGCL .... Florida Center for Library Automation, Gainesville, FL [Library symbol] [Library of Congress] (LCLS)
FGCM .... Field General Court-Martial
FGCR .... Fast Gas-Cooled Reactor [Nuclear energy] (NUCP)
FGCS .... Fifth-Generation Computer Systems
FGCS .... Flight Guidance and Control Systems
FGCS .... Future Generation Computer Systems (NITA)
FGD .... Fatal Granulomatous Disease (MAE)
FGD .... Ferri-Gas Duplexer
FGD .... Fine Grain Data [Equipment] [RADAR]
FGD .... Fishguard [Goodwick] [British depot code]
FGD .... Flue-Gas Desulfurization
FGD .... Forged
FGD .... Formaldehyde-Glutaraldehyde-Dichromate [Fixative]
FGD .... Ft. Derik [Mauritania] [Airport symbol] (AD)
FGD .... Fuel Gas Desulfurization
FGDAC .... Function Generating Digital-to-Analog Converter [Computer science] (IAA)
FGDC .... Federal Geographic Data Committee
FGDC .... Federal Geographic Data Committee [of the USA] (EERA)
FGDCh .... Flyball Grand Champion
FGDF .... Fidelco [Fidelity Cooperative] Guide Dog Foundation (EA)
FGDI .... Forging Die [Tool] (AAG)
FGE .... Factory Ground Equipment (KSC)
FGE .... Fractographic Examination [Metallurgy]
FGEA .... Full Gospel Evangelistic Association (EA)
FGEIU .... Federated Gas Employees' Industrial Union [Australia]
FGF .... Father's Grandfather (MAE)
FGF .... Fibroblast Growth Factor [Cytochemistry]
FGF .... Filament-Wound Glass Fiber
FGF .... Fishermen's Guarantee Fund [National Oceanic and Atmospheric Administration]
FGF .... Fresh Gas Flow
FGF .... Fully Good, Fair [Business term]
FGFA .... Fibroblast Growth Factor Receptor [Biochemistry]
FGFA .... Field and Game Federation of Australia
FGFC .... Fixed Gas-Filled Capacitor
FGFR .... Fibroblast Growth-Factor Receptor [Biochemistry]
FGFSA .... Florida Gift Fruit Shippers Association (EA)
FGG .... Fruit Growers' Group [Australia]
FGGE .... First GARP [Global Atmospheric Research Program] Global Experiment [National Academy of Sciences]
FGGM .... Federation of Gelatine and Glue Manufacturers [British] (BI)
FGGM .... Fort George G. Meade [Maryland]
FGH .... Fans of General Hospital (EA)
FGH .... Fiberglass Hull
FGH .... Flameless Gas Heater
FGH .... Flexible Gyro Header
FGH .... Fort Garry Horse [Military unit] [World War I] [Canada]
f-gh-- .... Ghana [MARC geographic area code Library of Congress] (LCCP)
FGHA .... Flexible Gyro Header Assembly
FGHC .... First Georgia Holding [NASDAQ symbol] (TTSB)
FGHC .... First Georgia Holding, Inc. [NASDAQ symbol] (NQ)
FGH-JWB .... Florence G. Heller - JWB [Jewish Welfare Board] Research Center [Research center] (RCD)
FGHT .... Fight
FGHTR .... Fighter
FGI .... Fashion Group International (EAIO)
FGI .... Federation Graphique Internationale [International Graphical Federation - IGF] [Berne, Switzerland] (EAIO)
FGI .... Federation of German Industries (EA)
FGI .... Fellow of the Greek Institute [British] (DI)
FGI .... Fellow of the Institute of Certificated Grocers [British]
FGIC .... Financial Guaranty Insurance Corp.
FGIM .... Figures or Images [Freight]
FGIPCI .... Federation of Government Information Processing Councils, Inc. (EA)
FGIS .... Federal Grain Inspection Service [Department of Agriculture]
FGJ .... Freezing Gas Jet
FGJA .... Flat Glass Jobbers Association [Later, FGMA]
FGL .... Fiberglass [Technical drawings]
FGL .... Financial General Ledger
FGL .... FMC Gold [NYSE symbol] (SPSG)
FGL .... Fox Glacier [New Zealand] [Airport symbol] (AD)
FGLF .... Renaissance Golf Products [NASDAQ symbol] (TTSB)
FGLS .... Force Generation Levels [Military] (NVT)

FGLU .... Fasting Glucose [*Endocrinology*] (DAVI)
FGM............ Father's Grandmother (MAE)
FGM............ Female Genital Mutilation
FGM............ Field Goals Made [*Football, basketball*]
FGM............ First General Mine Management & Gold Corp. [*Vancouver Stock Exchange symbol*]
FGM............ Fiscal Guidance Memorandum [*Navy*]
FGM............ Fission Gas Monitor (NRCH)
FGM............ Florida Atlantic University, Boca Raton, FL [*OCLC symbol*] (OCLC)
FGM............ Fluxgate Magnetometer
FgM .... Foreign Mission Section [*Diocesan abbreviation*] (TOCD)
FGM............ Freunde Guter Musik Club [*Record label*] [*Germany*]
FGM............ Functionally Gradient Material [*Materials science and technology*]
f-gm-- .... Gambia [*MARC geographic area code Library of Congress*] (LCCP)
FGMA.......... Flat Glass Manufacturers Association [*British*] (DBA)
FGMA.......... Flat Glass Marketing Association (EA)
FGMD .... Fairchild Guided Missile Division (SAA)
FGMDSS...... Future Global Maritime Distress and Safety System
FGN .... Family Group Number
FGN .... Federal German Navy
FGN .... First Generation Resources Ltd. [*Vancouver Stock Exchange symbol*]
FGN .... Foreign (AFM)
FGN .... Gendarmerie Nationale [*France ICAO designator*] (FAAC)
FGNCC .... Foreign Claims Commission [*Canada*]
FGND .... Frame Ground [*Computer science*] (HGAA)
FGO .... Fellow of the Guild of Organists [*British*]
FGO .... Finance Group Office
FGO .... Flag Gunnery Officer
FGO .... Fleet Gunnery Officer [*Obsolete British*]
FGO .... Fuego [*Guatemala*] [*Seismograph station code, US Geological Survey*] (SEIS)
f-go-- .... Gabon [*MARC geographic area code Library of Congress*] (LCCP)
Fg Off .... Flying Officer [*British military*] (DMA)
FGOG .... Foregoing (ROG)
FGOLF .... Federation des Gynecologues et Obstetriciens de Langue Francaise [*Federation of French-Language Gynaecologists and Obstetricians*] [*Paris, France*] (EAIO)
FGORC........ Flower Gardens Ocean Research Center [*Marine Biomedical Institute, University of Texas*] (PDAA)
FGP............ Ferrellgas Partners L.P. [*NYSE symbol*] (TTSB)
FGP............ Ferrellgas Partners Ltd. [*NYSE symbol*] (SAG)
FGP............ Fetch, Generate [*or Generalize*], and Project [*Computer Program*]
FGP............ First Guardian [*Vancouver Stock Exchange symbol*]
FGP............ Foreground Program [*Computer science*] (IAA)
FGP............ Foster Grandparents Program (EA)
FGP............ Frontal Groove of Pinnule
FGP............ Fuerza de Guerrilleros de los Pobres [*Guerrilla group*] [*Guatemala*] (EY)
FGP............ Fundic Gland Polyposis [*Medicine*]
FGP............ General Purpose Frigate
FGPFL .... Fixed and Group Flashing Light [*Navigation signal*]
FGPT........... Fellow of the Guild of Professional Toastmasters [*British*] (DI)
FGR .... Feline Gardner-Rasheed Virus
FGR .... Fellowship of the Golden Rule (EA)
FGR .... Finger (MSA)
FGR/ .... Floating-Gate Reset (IAA)
FGR .... Flue Gas Recirculation [*Combustion engineering*]
FGR .... Foundation for Giraffe Rescue
FGR .... Foundation for Glaucoma Research (EA)
FGR .... Freehold Ground Rent (ROG)
FGRAAL ...... FORTRAN [*Formula Translating System*] Extended Graph Algorithmic Language [*1972*] [*Computer science*] (CSR)
FGRF .... Forest Genetics Research Foundation (EA)
FGrH .... Fragmente der Griechischen Historiker [*A publication*] (OCD)
FGRI .... Fixed Ground Radio Installations
FGRN .... Finely Granular [*Laboratory*] (DAVI)
FGS............ Fancy Goods Store [*British military*] (DMA)
FGS............ Fashion Glamour Set
FGS............ Federation of Genealogical Societies (EA)
FGS............ Fellow of the Geographical Society
FGS............ Fellow of the Geological Society [*British*]
FGS............ Fine Guidance Sensor (PDAA)
FGS............ Finished Goods Store
FGS............ Fischerei-Geraete-Station
FGS............ Flight Guidance System (MCD)
FGS............ Flowing Gas Stream
FGS............ Focal Glomerulosclerosis [*Medicine*]
FGS............ Fort Greely Station (SAA)
FGS............ Francis Grose Society [*Defunct*] (EA)
FGS............ Friends of George Sand (EA)
FGS............ Friends of Georges Sadoul (EAIO)
FGS............ Friends of the Golden State
FGS............ Fulton Generating Station [*Nuclear energy*] (NRCH)
FGS............ Palmer, AK [*Location identifier FAA*] (FAAL)
FGS............ Santa Fe Community College, Gainesville, FL [*Library symbol Library of Congress*] (LCLS)
FGSA .... Fellow of the Geographical Society of America
FGSA .... Fellow of the Geological Society of America
FGSA .... Fostoria Glass Society of America (EA)
FGSB .... FFS [*Flight Service Station*] Guarding Service B [*Aviation*] (FAAC)
FGS/C .... Flight Guidance System/Computer (GAVI)
FGSF........... Full Gospel Student Fellowship (EA)
FGSL .... Malabo, Isla De Macias, Nguema Biyoga [*Equatorial Guinea*] [*ICAO location identifier*] (ICLI)
FGSM.......... Fellow of Guildhall School of Music [*British*] (EY)

FGSS .... Flexible Guidance Software System (MCD)
FGST........... First Grade Screening Test [*To detect learning disabilities*]
FGT............ Fairflight Ltd. [*British ICAO designator*] (FAAC)
FGT............ Farmington, MN [*Location identifier FAA*] (FAAL)
FGT............ Federal Gift Tax (DLA)
FGT............ Flue-Gas Treatment
FGT............ Fluorescent Gonorrhea Test [*Medicine*] (DMAA)
FGT............ Foreground Table (MHDB)
FGT............ Freight
FGTO .... French Government Tourist Office
FGTSA .... Fur Garment Traveling Salesmen's Association
FGTT .... Flue-Gas-through-the-Tubes [*Incinerator*]
FGU............ Fangatau [*French Polynesia*] [*Airport symbol*] (OAG)
FGU............ Flaming Gorge [*Utah*] [*Seismograph station code, US Geological Survey Closed*] (SEIS)
FGU............ Forearm Glucose Uptake [*Clinical chemistry*]
FGULS .... Florida Union List of Serials, Gainesville, FL [*Library symbol Library of Congress*] (LCLS)
FGV............ Field-Gradient Voltage (PDAA)
FGV............ Free Gas Volume
f-gv-- .... Guinea [*MARC geographic area code Library of Congress*] (LCCP)
FGV............ United States Veterans Administration Hospital, Gainesville, FL [*Library symbol Library of Congress*] (LCLS)
FGWC .... First Greatwest Corp. [*NASDAQ symbol*]
FGX............ Flemingsburg, KY [*Location identifier FAA*] (FAAL)
FGY............ Foggy (MSA)
FGY............ NewWest Airlines, Inc. [*FAA designator*] (FAAC)
FH............... C. H. Boehringer Sohn, Ingelheim [*Germany*] [*Research code symbol*]
FH............... Clin-Byla [*France*] [*Research code symbol*]
fh---- .... East African Horn [*MARC geographic area code Library of Congress*] (LCCP)
FH............... Familial Hypercholesteremia [*or Hypercholesterolemia*] [*Medicine*]
FH............... Family History [*Medicine*]
FH............... Family of Humanists [*An association*] (EA)
FH............... Fane's Horse [*British military*] (DMA)
FH............... Fasteners and Hardware (SAA)
FH............... Fasting Hyperbilirubinemia [*Medicine*] (DMAA)
FH............... Federation of Homemakers (EA)
FH............... Fetal Head [*Medicine*]
FH............... Fetal Heart [*Medicine*]
FH............... Fiat Haustus [*Let a Drink Be Made*] [*Pharmacy*]
FH............... Fiber Hub
FH............... Fibromuscular Hyperplasia [*Medicine*] (DMAA)
FH............... Ficoll-Hypaque [*Clinical hematology*]
FH............... Field Handler (MHDB)
FH............... Field Hospital [*British military*] (DMA)
FH............... Field Howitzer [*British military*] (DMA)
FH............... Fighter (NATG)
FH............... Fire Hose (AAG)
FH............... Fire Hydrant
FH............... First Half [*of month*] (DCTA)
FH............... Fixed Head [*Computer science*] (MHDB)
FH............... Fixed Hub [*Rotary piston meter*]
FH............... Flag Hoist
FH............... Flat Head [*Screw*]
FH............... Flex Hose (MCD)
FH............... Flight Hour
FH............... Floating Hospital (EA)
FH............... Flying Hour
FH............... Fog Horn [*Navigation charts*]
FH............... Force Headquarters [*Allied forces*] [*World War II*]
FH............... Fore Hatch [*Shipping*]
FH............... Foundation for Health (EA)
FH............... Foundation Health [*NYSE symbol*] (TTSB)
FH............... Foundation Health Corp. [*NYSE symbol*] (SPSG)
FH............... Frame Handler [*Telecommunications*] (ACRL)
FH............... Frankfort Horizontal [*Eye-ear plane*] [*Anatomy*]
FH............... Freedom House (EA)
FH............... Free Harbor
FH............... Freeholder [*Real estate*] (BARN)
FH............... French Horn
FH............... Frequency Hopping [*Modulation*]
FH............... Friendship House (EA)
FH............... Friends of Hibakusha (EA)
FH............... Fuji Heavy Industries Ltd. [*Japan ICAO aircraft manufacturer identifier*] (ICAO)
FH............... Full Hard (MSA)
FH............... Fulminant Hepatitis [*Medicine*]
FH............... Fumarate Hydratase [*An enzyme*]
FH............... Fundal Height [*Obstetrics*] (DAVI)
F$_H$............... Heeling Force [*Sailing terminology*]
FH............... Mall Airways [*ICAO designator*] (AD)
FHA............ Family Heart Association [*British*] (DBA)
FHA............ Farmers Home Administration [*Later, FmHA*] [*Department of Agriculture*]
FHA............ Fault Hazard Analysis [*Hazard quantification method*]
FHA............ Federal Highway Administration [*Department of Transportation*]
FHA............ Federal Housing Administration [*HUD*]
FHA............ Federal Housing Authority (TDOB)
FHA............ Fellow of the Institute of Health Service [*formerly, Hospital Administrators*] [*British*]
FHA............ Fiji Hotel Association (EY)
FHA............ Filamentous Hemagglutinin [*Medicine*]
FHA............ Finance Houses Association [*British*]

FHA.............	Fine Hardwoods Association [*Later, FHAWA*] (EA)
FHA.............	Flexible Header Assembly
FHA.............	Floating Homes Association (EA)
FHA.............	Foundation for Humanities Adulthood [*Australia*]
FHA.............	Free-Heave Amplitude
FHA.............	Friends Historical Association (EA)
FHA.............	Future Homemakers of America (EA)
FHA.............	Future Horsemen of America
FHAA...........	Field Hockey Association of America (EA)
FHAAO........	Force Headquarters, Antiaircraft [*World War II*]
FHAEB........	Force Headquarters, North African Economic Board [*World War II*]
FHAG..........	Force Headquarters, Adjutant General [*World War II*]
FHAGG........	Force Headquarters, Adjutant General, Executive [*World War II*]
FHAGM........	Force Headquarters, Adjutant General, Miscellaneous [*World War II*]
FHAGP........	Force Headquarters, Adjutant General, Personnel [*World War II*]
FHAGR........	Force Headquarters, Adjutant General, Mail and Records [*World War II*]
FHA (HERO)...	Future Homemakers of America (Home Economics Related Occupations) (OICC)
FHAI...........	Federal Housing Authority Insurance (AABC)
FHAIR.........	Force Headquarters, Air Commander-in-Chief, Mediterranean [*World War II*]
FHAM..........	Federal Housing Administration Matters [*FBI standardized term*]
FH & C........	Faith, Hope, and Charity [*Freemasonry*] (ROG)
FH&MA........	Florida Hotel and Motel Association (SRA)
FH & RM......	Fuel Handling and Radioactive Maintenance (NRCH)
FH & SL......	Furnished Hardware and Services List (MCD)
FHANG........	Federation of Heathrow Anti-Noise Groups [*British*] (DI)
FHAP..........	Fair Housing Assistance Program [*HUD*]
FHarBc.......	First Harrisburg Bancor, Inc. [*Associated Press*] (SAG)
FHARM........	Fuel Handling and Radioactive Maintenance (IAA)
FHAS..........	Federation of Hellenic American Societies of Greater New York (EA)
FHAS..........	Fellow of the Highland and Agricultural Society of Scotland
FHAW.........	Wideawake [*Ascension Island*] [*ICAO location identifier*] (ICLI)
FHAWA........	Fine Hardwoods American Walnut Association (EA)
FHB.............	Family Hold Back [*Indicates family should take small portions at a meal where guests are present*]
FHB.............	Federal Home Bank
FHB.............	Fine Homebuilding [*A publication*] (BRI)
FHB.............	Flat Head Brass [*Screw*] (IAA)
FHB.............	Fuel-Handling Building [*Nuclear energy*] (NRCH)
FHBVI.........	Fuel-Handling Building Ventilation Isolation [*Nuclear energy*] (NRCH)
FHC.............	Fairchild-Hiller Corp. [*Later, Fairchild Industries, Inc.*] (KSC)
FHC.............	Faith, Hope, and Charity [*Freemasonry*]
FHC.............	Familial Hypertrophic Cardiomyopathy [*Medicine*]
FHC.............	Federal Housing Commission [*HUD*] (OICC)
FHC.............	Federal Housing Corp.
FHC.............	Female Health [*AMEX symbol*] (TTSB)
FHC.............	Female Health Co. [*AMEX symbol*] (SAG)
FHC.............	Fickle Hill [*California*] [*Seismograph station code, US Geological Survey*] (SEIS)
FHC.............	Ficoll-Hypaque Centrifugation [*Medicine*] (DMAA)
FHC.............	Fire Hose Cabinet (KSC)
FHC.............	First Hospitality [*Vancouver Stock Exchange symbol*]
FHC.............	Fish Creek, AK [*Location identifier FAA*] (FAAL)
FHC.............	Fixed-Head Coupe [*Automobile design*]
FHC.............	Flight Half Coupling (MCD)
FHC.............	Four-Horse Club [*British*]
FHC.............	Freed-Hardeman College [*Tennessee*]
FHC.............	Fuel-Handling Cell [*Nuclear energy*] (NRCH)
FHC.............	University of South Florida, Sarasota Campus, Sarasota, FL [*OCLC symbol*] (OCLC)
FHC.............	Wisconsin Pharmacal Co., Inc. [*AMEX symbol*] (SAG)
FHCAO........	Force Headquarters, Chief Administrative Officer [*World War II*]
FHCAS........	Federal Highway Cost Allocation Study [*Also, HCAS*]
FHCCH........	Force Headquarters, Claims and Hirings [*World War II*]
FHCE..........	Foundation for Health Care Evaluation (EA)
FHCIC........	Force Headquarters, Commander-in-Chief [*World War II*]
FHCIMA.......	Fellow of the Hotel, Catering, and Institutional Management Association [*British*] (DBQ)
FHCIV.........	Force Headquarters, Civil Affairs [*World War II*]
FHCOS........	Force Headquarters, Chief of Staff [*World War II*]
FHCRC........	Fred Hutchinson Cancer Research Center [*University of Washington*] [*Research center*] (RCD)
FHCWS.......	Force Headquarters, Chemical Warfare [*World War II*]
FHD............	Family Housing Division [*Army*] (AABC)
FHD............	Ferrohydrodynamic (IAA)
FHD............	First-Hand Distribution
FHD............	First Harmonic Distortion [*Electronics*] (IAA)
FHD............	Fixed-Head Disk [*Computer science*]
FHD............	Foundation for Human Development [*Australia*]
FHD............	Friends of Holly Dunn (EA)
FHD............	Fund for Human Dignity (EA)
FHDA..........	Fir and Hemlock Door Association [*Defunct*] (EA)
FHDCC........	Force Headquarters, Deputy Allied Commander-in-Chief [*World War II*]
FHDHC........	Force Headquarters, Director of Harbor Craft [*World War II*]
FHDMS.......	Force Headquarters, Military Secretary Section [*World War II*]
FHDO..........	Field Handling Design Objective
FHDS..........	Fixed Head Disk / Drum Store [*Computer science*] (MHDI)
FHDSC........	Force Headquarters, Deputy Chief of Staff [*World War II*]
FHE.............	Family Home Entertainment [*Division of International Video Entertainment*]
FHE.............	Fast Hydrofoil Escort
FHE.............	Forward Headquarters Element

FHE.............	Foundation for Handgun Education [*Later, EFEHV*] (EA)
FHE.............	Fuel-Handling Equipment [*Nuclear energy*] (NRCH)
FHEFI..........	Force Headquarters, Expeditionary Forces Institute [*World War II*]
FHENG........	Force Headquarters, Engineer [*World War II*]
FHENW........	Force Headquarters, Works [*World War II*]
FHEO..........	Fair Housing and Equal Opportunity [*HUD*] (OICC)
FHEPFC.......	For the Heart Elvis Presley Fan Club (EA)
FHES..........	Fuel-Handling Equipment System [*Nuclear energy*] (NRCH)
FHEx..........	Fridays and Holidays Excepted (DS)
FHF.............	Federation of Health Funds - International [*British*] (EAIO)
FHF.............	First Horizontal Flight [*NASA*] (KSC)
FHF.............	Fixed Head File [*Computer science*] (MHDB)
FHF.............	Friendly Hand Foundation (EA)
FHF.............	Fulminant Hepatic Failure [*Medicine*]
FHF.............	University of South Florida, Fort Myers Campus, Fort Myers, FL [*OCLC symbol*] (OCLC)
FHFA..........	Four-Conductor, Heat-and-Flame-Resistant, Armor [*Cable*]
FHFB..........	Federal Housing Finance Board [*Pronounced "foof-ba"*]
FHFF..........	Fleet Hurricane Forecast Facility
FHFLD.........	Force Headquarters, Field Artillery Section [*World War II*]
FHFS..........	Foundation Health Federal Services
FHFTA........	Four-Conductor, Heat and Flame Resistant, Thin Walled, Armored [*Cable*] (IAA)
FHFW.........	Federation of High Frequency Welders [*British*] (DBA)
FHG............	Fellow of the Institute of Heraldic and Genealogical Studies [*British*] (DBQ)
FHG............	Flat Head Galvanized [*Screw*] (IAA)
FHG............	Fragmenta Historicorum Graecorum [*A publication*] (OCD)
FHGA..........	Fellow of the Horological Guild of Australia
FHGDM........	Force Headquarters, Movements and Transportation [*World War II*]
FHGDQ........	Force Headquarters, "Q" Maintenance [*World War II*]
FHGDT........	Force Headquarters, Supply and Transport [*World War II*]
FHH............	Familial Hypocalciuric Hypercalcemia [*Medicine*]
FHH............	Female Headed Household
FHH............	Fetal Heart Heard [*Medicine*]
FHH............	Foundation for Hospice and Homecare (EA)
FHHDC........	Force Headquarters, Headquarters Commandant [*World War II*]
FHI.............	Federation Halterophile Internationale [*International Weightlifting Federation - IWF*] (EAIO)
FHI.............	Fellow of the Ontario Hostelry Institute [*Canada*] (DD)
FHi.............	Florida Historical Society, University of South Florida, Tampa, FL [*Library symbol Library of Congress*] (LCLS)
FHI.............	Folk Heritage Institute (EA)
FHI.............	Food for the Hungry, Inc. (EA)
FHI.............	Ford Holdings, Inc. [*NYSE symbol*] (SPSG)
FHI.............	Fuch's Heterochromic Iridocyclitis [*Ophthalmology*] (DAVI)
FHiaC.........	Coulter Diagnostics, Inc., Hialeah, FL [*Library symbol Library of Congress*] (LCLS)
FHIC..........	Flying Hours per Inspection Cycle [*Air Force*] (AFIT)
FHIC..........	Franciscan Hospitaller Sisters of the Immaculate Conception [*Roman Catholic religious order*]
FHIF..........	Frequenting House of Ill Fame
FHIID.........	Fast Heavy Ion Induced Desorption [*Analytical chemistry*]
FHI/IFRP.....	Family Health International [*Family Health International/International Fertility Research Program*] [*Acronym is based on former name,*] (EA)
FHIMA........	Fellow of the Hotel and Catering International Management Association (DD)
FHINC.........	Force Headquarters, Information and Censorship [*World War II*]
FHIP..........	Fair Housing Initiatives Program [*Department of Housing and Urban Development*] (GFGA)
FHIP..........	Family Health Insurance Plan
FHIP..........	Federal Health Insurance Plan [*Proposed*] (DHSM)
FHL............	Forest Hydrology Laboratory [*Forest Service*]
FHL............	Forward Half-Line [*Feed*]
FHL............	Fraser's House of Lords Reports [*Scotland*] [*A publication*] (DLA)
FHLB..........	Federal Home Loan Bank
FHLBA........	Federal Home Loan Bank Administration (IIA)
FHLBB........	Federal Home Loan Bank Board [*Functions transferred to Office of Thrift Supervision, 1989*]
FHLBS........	Federal Home Loan Bank System
FHLD..........	Freehold [*Legal term*]
FHLIA........	Force Headquarters, Liaison [*World War II*]
FHLMC........	Federal Home Loan Mortgage Corp. [*Federal Home Loan Bank Board*] [*Nickname: "Freddie Mac"*]
FHLS..........	First Hungarian Literary Society (EA)
FHLT..........	Force (Fleet) High-Level Terminal [*Navy*] (CAAL)
FHM...........	Faith Mines Ltd. [*Vancouver Stock Exchange symbol*]
FHM...........	Familial Hemiplegic Migraine [*Medicine*]
FHM...........	Familial Hemiplegic Migraine
FHM...........	Fargo House Movement [*Trinidad and Tobago*] [*Political party*] (PPW)
FHM...........	Fat Head Minnow
FHM...........	Feed Water Heater Management
FHM...........	Franciscan Handmaids of the Most Pure Heart of Mary [*Roman Catholic religious order*]
FHM...........	Franciscan Sisters Daughters of Mercy (TOCD)
FHM...........	University of South Florida, Tampa, FL [*OCLC symbol*] (OCLC)
FHMA..........	Family Housing Management Account [*Army*] (AABC)
FHMA..........	Family Housing Management Appropriation
FHMA..........	Frequency-Hopping Multiple Access (IAA)
FHMED........	Force Headquarters, Surgeon [*World War II*]
FHMGS........	Force Headquarters, Military Government Section [*World War II*]
FHMO..........	Friends of the Hop Marketing Order [*Defunct*] (EA)
FHMO..........	Fully Hydrogenated Menhaden Oil [*Food science*]

FHMS........... Flat Head Machine Screw [*Technical drawings*]
FHMUX........ Frequency-Hopping Multiplexer (DWSG)
FHN .... Fund for Human Need [*British*]
FHNH .... Fetal Heart Not Heard [*Medicine*]
FHNL .... Far Horizons Newsletter [*A publication*]
FHNP .... United States National Park Service, Everglades National Park, Homestead, FL [*Library symbol Library of Congress*] (LCLS)
FHO .... Failed Handover [*NASA*] (NASA)
FHO .... Family Hands Off [*Indicates that a certain dish is not to be eaten by members of the family at a meal where guests are present*]
FHO .... Family Hold Off [*Indicates that a certain dish is not to be eaten by members of the family at a meal where guests are present*]
FHO .... Family Housing Officer
FHOF .... Four Conductor, Heat, Oil, and Flame Resistant [*Cable*] (IAA)
FHONF .... Facing History and Ourselves National Foundation (EA)
FHORD........ Force Headquarters, Ordnance [*World War II*]
FHP............. Federal Highway Projects [*Department of Transportation*]
FHP............. FHP International Corp. [*Associated Press*] (SAG)
FHP............. Flying Hour Program [*Army*]
FHP............. Fractional Horsepower (MSA)
FHP............. Free Hepatic Venous Pressure [*Medicine*]
FHP............. Friction Horsepower
FHP............. Friends of Historical Pharmacy (EA)
FHP............. Fuel Handling Procedure [*Nuclear energy*] (NRCH)
FHP............. Fuel High Pressure (NASA)
FHPC .... FHP International Corp. [*NASDAQ symbol*] (NQ)
FHPC .... FHP Int'l Corp. [*NASDAQ symbol*] (TTSB)
FHPC .... Fuel-Handling and Preparation Cell [*Nuclear energy*] (NRCH)
FHPCA .... FHP Intl $1.25 Cv Pfd'A' [*NASDAQ symbol*] (TTSB)
FHPET......... Force Headquarters, Petroleum [*World War II*]
FHPRO........ Force Headquarters, Public Relations [*World War II*]
FHPS .... Federal Health Programs Service [*Health Services and Mental Health Administration, HEW*]
FHPSGI....... Funeral Home Public Service Group International [*Defunct*] (EA)
FHPWO........ Force Headquarters, Psychological Warfare Office [*World War II*]
FHQ .... Fleet Headquarters [*Australia*]
FHQAE .... Force Headquarters, "Q" Army Equipment Branch [*World War II*]
FHR .... Familial Hypophosphatemic Rickets
FHR .... Fetal Heart Rate [*Medicine*]
FHR .... Fire Hose Rack
FHR .... Fire Hose Reel
FHR .... Foundation for Hand Research (EA)
FHR .... Foundation for Homeopathic Research [*Defunct*] (EA)
FHR .... Friends of Haitian Refugees [*Defunct*] (EA)
FHR .... Fund for Human Rights [*Later, WDL*] (EA)
FHR .... Further
FH-RDC........ Family History-Research Diagnostic Criteria [*Medicine, Psychiatry*]
FHRDC........ Foundation for Human Rights and Democracy in China (EA)
FHR FNSHD T PRMD... Further Finished Than Primed [*Freight*]
FHR FNSHD T RGH... Further Finished Than Rough [*Freight*]
FHRI .... Full House Resorts [*NASDAQ symbol*] (SAG)
FHRIW .... Full House Resorts Wrrt [*NASDAQ symbol*] (TTSB)
FHRNA........ Force Headquarters, Commander-in-Chief, Mediterranean [*World War II*]
FHS............. Family and Health Section (EA)
FHS............. Farm Household Support Scheme [*Australia*]
FHS............. Fatal Heart Sound [*Medicine*] (DHSM)
FHS............. Fellow of the Horticultural Society [*British*]
FHS............. Feminine Hygiene Spray
FHS............. Fetal Heart Sounds [*Medicine*]
FHS............. Fetal Hydantoin Syndrome [*Medicine*]
FHS............. Fire Hose Station [*Technical drawings*]
FHS............. Flame Hardness Standard (MCD)
FHS............. Flat Head Steel [*Screw*] (IAA)
FHS............. Football Hall of Shame [*Defunct*] (EA)
FHS............. Forces Help Society [*British*] (BI)
FHS............. Forest History Society (EA)
FHS............. Format Handling System (IAA)
FHS............. Forward Heat Shield [*NASA*] (KSC)
FHS............. Frequency Hopping Signal
FHS............. Fuel-Handling System [*Nuclear energy*] (NRCH)
FHS............. Furniture History Society (EA)
FHS............. University of South Florida, St. Petersburg Campus, St. Petersburg, FL [*OCLC symbol*] (OCLC)
FHSA .... Family Health - Service Authority [*British*] (ECON)
FHSA .... Federal Hazardous Substances Act
FHSAA .... Florida High School Athletics Association (EDAC)
FHSC .... Fellow of the Heraldry Society of Canada
FHSF .... Fixed-Head Storage Facility [*Computer science*]
FHSG .... Family Housing [*Army*] (AABC)
FHSGS........ Force Headquarters, Secretary General Staff [*World War II*]
FHSIG .... Force Headquarters, Signal [*World War II*]
FHSR .... Final Hazards Summary Report [*Nuclear energy*] (NRCH)
FHSR .... Foundation for Health Services Research (EA)
FHSS .... Forward Heat-Shield Separation [*NASA*] (KSC)
FHSS .... Frequency-Hopping Spread Spectrum [*Computer science*] (PCM)
FHSUP .... Force Headquarters, Quartermaster [*World War II*]
FHSV .... Federation of Housing Societies of Victoria [*Australia*]
FHT............. Fast Hartley Transform (BYTE)
FHT............. Federation of Holistic Therapists [*British*]
FHT............. Fetal Heart [*Medicine*] (MAE)
FHT............. Fetal Heart Tone [*Obstetrics*]
FHT............. Field Handling Trainer [*Army*] (INF)
FHT............. Fingerhut Companies [*NYSE symbol*] (TTSB)
FHT............. Fingerhut Companies, Inc. [*NYSE symbol*] (SPSG)

FHT............. Finite Hilbert Transform (PDAA)
FHT............. Fisher-Hirschfelder-Taylor [*Molecular model*]
FHT............. Free-Heave Test
FHT............. Friedrich Technologies, Inc. [*Vancouver Stock Exchange symbol*]
FHT............. Fully Heat Treated (IEEE)
FHTC .... Fixed High-Temperature Capacitor
FHTE .... Fachhochschule Esslingen - Hochschule fuer Technik [*Business Management Program*] [*Germany*]
FHTE........... Flight Hardware Test Equipment [*Aviation*] (IAA)
FHTG .... Familial Hypertriglyceridemia [*Medicine*] (DMAA)
FHTNC......... Fleet Home Town News Center
FHTTA......... Fellow of the Highway and Traffic Technicians Association [*British*] (DBQ)
FHTV........... Family of Heavy Tactical Vehicles [*MTMC*] (TAG)
FHTV........... Heavy Tactical Vehicle (AAGC)
FHU .... Fort Huachuca/Sierra Vista [*Arizona*] [*Airport symbol*] (OAG)
FHU .... Fort Huachuca/Sierra Vista, AZ [*Location identifier FAA*] (FAAL)
FHU .... Foundation of Human Understanding (EA)
FH-UFS .... Femoral Hypoplasia-Unusual Facies Syndrome [*Medicine*] (DMAA)
FHUSN........ Force Headquarters, United States Naval Staff [*World War II*]
FHV........... Fahnestock Viner Holdings, Inc. [*Toronto Stock Exchange symbol Vancouver Stock Exchange symbol*]
FHV........... Flockhouse Virus
FHVC .... Fixed High-Volt Capacitor
FHVP .... Free Hepatic Venous Pressure [*Medicine*]
FHWA .... Federal Highway Administration [*Department of Transportation*]
FH-WC .... Fellow of Heriot-Watt College, Edinburgh
FHWN.......... First Hawaiian [*NASDAQ symbol*] (TTSB)
FHWN.......... First Hawaiian, Inc. [*NASDAQ symbol*] (NQ)
FHWS .... Flat Head Wood Screw [*Technical drawings*]
FHx .... Family History (DAVI)
FHY............. Fire Hydrant
FI............. Daughters of Jesus [*Roman Catholic religious order*]
FI............. Fabrication Instruction (NG)
FI............. Face Immersion (DNAB)
FI............. Facilities Item
FI............. Factories Inspectorate [*British*] (NUCP)
FI............. Fade In [*Films, television, etc.*]
F/I............. Failed Item (AAG)
FI............. Fail in Place [*Nuclear energy*] (NRCH)
FI............. Fairplay Information [*Fairplay Publications Ltd.*] [*Information service or system*] (IID)
FI............. Falkland Islands
FI............. Fan In [*Electronics*] (IAA)
FI............. Farmitalia [*Italy*] [*Research code symbol*]
FI............. Farmland Industries (EA)
FI............. Faroe Islands
FI............. Fatigue Index [*Aircraft strain/fatigue scale*] [*British*]
FI............. Fault Identification (MCD)
FI............. Fault Isolation
FI............. [*The*] Fertilizer Institute
FI............. Fever Caused by Infection (MAE)
FI............. Fibrinogen Factor 1 [*Hematology*] (MAE)
FI............. Fidelity [*to Living Condition*] Index [*Botany*]
FI............. Fidell's Precedents [*A publication*] (DLA)
FI............. Field Independent (EDAC)
FI............. Field Intensity
FI............. Field Interview
FI............. Field Ionization
FI............. Field Item (DNAB)
FI............. Fieseler [*Germany ICAO aircraft manufacturer identifier*] (ICAO)
FI............. Fighter Interceptor
FI............. Films, Inc.
FI............. Fina, Inc. [*AMEX symbol*] (SPSG)
FI............. FINA,Inc. CI'A' [*AMEX symbol*] (TTSB)
FI............. Final Issue
FI............. Finished Intelligence (MCD)
fi............. Finland [*MARC country of publication code Library of Congress*] (LCCP)
FI............. Finland [*ANSI two-letter standard code*] (CNC)
FI............. Fireball International [*Axminster, Devonshire, England*] (EAIO)
FI............. First Idaho Resources [*Vancouver Stock Exchange symbol*]
FI............. Fiscal (AFIT)
FI............. Fiscal Intermediary (DNAB)
FI............. Fisher Institute [*Dallas, TX*] (EA)
FI............. Fixed Internal (MAE)
FI............. Fixed Interval [*Reinforcement schedule*]
FI............. Flight Idle (DNAB)
FI............. Flight Instructor
FI............. Flight Instrumentation (MCD)
FI............. Flood Insurance [*HUD*]
FI............. Flow Indicator
FI............. Flow Injection [*Chemical processing*]
FI............. Flowrate Indicating [*Engineering*]
FI............. Flugfelag-Icelandair [*ICAO designator*] (AD)
FI............. Foodbanking, Inc. [*An association*] (EA)
FI............. Forced Inspiration (MAE)
FI............. Force Integrator [*DoD*]
FI............. Forecasting International Ltd. [*Information service or system*] (IID)
FI............. Foreign Intelligence (MCD)
FI............. Foreign Investment [*Business term*]
FI............. Foresight Institute (EA)
FI............. For Instance
FI............. Formaldehyde Institute (EA)
FI............. Formal Inspection (MCD)

FI .... Formula Internationale [*Agreement of Unification of Formulae*] [*Medicine*] (ROG)
FI .... Forum Institute [*Defunct*] (EA)
FI .... France Info [*Radio France*]
FI .... Free In [*Shipping*] (ADA)
FI .... Freemen Institute (EA)
FI .... Frontiers International (EA)
FI .... Front Independantiste [*Independence Front*] [*New Caledonia*] [*Political party*] (PPW)
FI .... Fuel Injection [*Automotive engineering*]
FI .... Future Interest [*Legal shorthand*] (LWAP)
fi---- .... Niger River and Basin [*MARC geographic area code Library of Congress*] (LCCP)
FIA .... Factory Insurance Association [*Later, Industrial Risk Insurers*] (EA)
FIA .... Families in Action [*Later, NFA*] (EA)
FIA .... Family and Intimate Assault [*Criminology*]
FIA .... Fasteners Institute of Australia
FIA .... Fault Isolation Analysis (MCD)
FIA .... Federacion Interamericana de Abogados [*Washington, DC*]
FIA .... Federal Insurance Administration [*HUD*]
FIA .... Federal Inventory Accounting
FIA .... Federation Internationale de l'Artisanat [*International Federation of Master-Craftsmen*]
FIA .... Federation Internationale de l'Automobile [*International Automobile Federation*] (EAIO)
FIA .... Federation Internationale des Acteurs [*International Federation of Actors*] (EAIO)
FIA .... Federation Internationale des Aveugles [*International Federation of the Blind*]
FIA .... Federation of Islamic Associations in the US and Canada (EA)
FIA .... Fellow of the Institute of Actuaries [*British*]
FIA .... Fellow of the Institute of Auctioneers [*British*]
FIA .... Fiat SpA [*NYSE symbol*] (CTT)
FIA .... Fiat SpA ADR [*NYSE symbol*] (TTSB)
FIA .... Financial Inventory Accounting
FIA .... Fixed Income Account
FIA .... Flatware Importers Association [*Defunct*]
FIA .... Flight Information Area
FIA .... Floating-Point Instruction Address [*Computer science*]
FIA .... Flow Injection Analyzer [*Chemical analyses*]
FIA .... Flowrate Indicating Alarm [*Engineering*]
FIA .... Fluorescence Indicator Analysis
FIA .... Fluorescent Immunoassay [*Analytical biochemistry*]
FIA .... Footwear Industries of America (EA)
FIA .... Force Integration Analysis [*DoD*]
FIA .... Forging Industry Association (EA)
FIA .... Four Island Air Ltd. [*Antigua and Barbuda*] [*ICAO designator*] (FAAC)
FIA .... Fraser Island Association [*Australia*]
FIA .... Freedom in Advertising [*British*] (DI)
FIA .... Freedom of Information Act [*1966*] (AFM)
FIA .... Free Interstitial Atom
FIA .... Freund's Incomplete Adjuvant [*Immunology*]
FIA .... Friends of Israel Association [*British*] (DBA)
FIA .... Fruit Importers Association [*British*] (DBA)
FIA .... Full Interest Admitted
FI-A .... Fundraising Institute-Australia, Inc. (NFD)
FIA .... Futures Industry Association (EA)
FIA .... Socorro, NM [*Location identifier FAA*] (FAAL)
FIAA .... Federation Internationale d'Athletisme Amateur [*International Amateur Athletic Federation - IAAF*] [*British*] (EAIO)
FIAA .... Fellow of the Incorporated Association of Architects and Surveyors [*British*]
FIAA .... Fellow of the Institute of Actuaries of Australia (ODBW)
FIAA & S ..... Fellow of the Incorporated Association of Architects and Surveyors [*British*]
FIAB .... Federation Internationale des Associations de Bibliothecaires [*International Federation of Library Associations*]
FIAB .... Fellow of the International Association of Bookkeepers [*British*] (DCTA)
FIAB .... Foreign Intelligence Advisory Board (CINC)
FIABCI .... Federation Internationale des Professions Immobilieres [*International Real Estate Federation*] (EAIO)
FIAC .... Federation Internationale Amateur de Cyclisme [*International Amateur Cycling Federation*] [*Rome, Italy*] (EA)
FIAC .... Federation of Independent Advice Centres [*British*] (DBA)
FIAC .... Federation of International American Clubs [*Oslo, Norway*] (EAIO)
FIAC .... Fellow of the Institute of Company Accountants [*British*] (DAS)
FIAC .... Fialcytosine [*Medicine*]
FIAC .... Fishing Industry Advisory Committee [*Australia*]
FIAC .... Flanders Interaction Analysis Categories (EDAC)
FIAC .... Flight Information Advisory Committee [*Terminated, 1977*] [*FAA*]
FIAC .... Fluorodeoxyiodoara-C [*An antiviral compound*]
FIAC .... Fluoroiodoarabinosylcytosine
FIACAT .... Federation Internationale de l'Action des Chretiens pour l'Abolition de la Torture [*International Federation of Action of Christians for the Abolition of Torture*] (EAIO)
FIACC .... Five International Associations Coordinating Committee [*Hungary*] (EAIO)
FIACTA .... Federation Internationale des Associations de Controleurs du Trafic Aerien [*International Federation of Air Traffic Controllers' Associations*] (EAIO)
FIACTC .... Federation Internationale des Associations des Chimistes du Textile et da la Couleur

FIAD .... Federation Internationale des Associations de Distributeurs de Films [*International Federation of Associations of Film Distributors*] (EAIO)
FIAD .... Flame Ionization Analyzer and Detector
FIAE .... Food Industry Association Executives (EA)
FIAEA .... Fellow of the Institute of Automotive Engineer Assessors [*British*] (DBQ)
FIAEM .... Federation Internationale des Associations d'Etudiants en Medecine [*International Federation of Medical Students Associations - IFMSA*] [*Vienna, Austria*] (EAIO)
FIAEP .... Federation Internationale des Associations d'Entrepots Publics [*International Federation of Public Warehousing Associations - IFPWA*] (EAIO)
FIAeS .... Fellow of the Institute of Aeronautical Sciences [*Later, FAIAA*] [*British*] (EY)
FIAESTA ...... Federation Internationale des Associations de l'Electronique de Securite du Trafic Aerien [*International Federation of Air Traffic Safety Electronic Associations*] (EAIO)
FIAF .... Federation Internationale des Archives du Film [*International Federation of Film Archives*] (EAIO)
FIAF .... French Institute/Alliance Francaise (EA)
FIAgrE .... Fellow of the Institution of Agricultural Engineers [*British*]
FIAI .... Federation Internationale des Associations d'Instituteurs [*International Federation of Teachers' Associations - IFTA*] (EAIO)
FIAI .... Fellow of the Institute of Industrial and Commercial Accountants [*British*]
FIAJ .... Federation Internationale des Auberges de la Jeunesse [*International Youth Hostel Federation - IYHF*] [*Welwyn Garden City, Hertfordshire, England*] (EAIO)
FIAJF .... Federation Internationale des Amies de la Jeune Fille
FIAJY .... Fellowship in Israel for Arab-Jewish Youth (EA)
FIAL .... Fellow of the International Institute of Arts and Letters
FIAL .... Fellow of the International Institute of Arts and Letters, Zurich [*1931*] (NGC)
FIAM .... Fellow of the Institute of Administrative Management [*British*] (ODBW)
FIAM .... Fellow of the International Academy of Management
FIAMA .... Fellow of the Incorporated Advertising Managers Association [*British*] (DAS)
FIAMC .... Federation Internationale des Associations Medicales Catholiques [*International Federation of Catholic Medical Associations*] (EA)
FIAMS .... Fellow of the Indian Academy of Medical Sciences
FIAMS .... Flinders Institute for Atmospheric and Marine Sciences [*Australia*] [*Marine science*] (OSRA)
FIANA .... File Analyzer and Report Generator (DNAB)
FIANATM ..... Federation Internationale des Associations Nationales de Negociants en Aciers, Tubes, et Metaux [*International Federation of Associations of Steel, Tube, and Metal Merchants*] (EAIO)
FIANDIC ...... Families in Action National Drug Information Center [*Later, NFA*] (EA)
FI & SS .... Foreign Intelligence and Security Service (MCD)
FIANEI .... Federation Internationale des Associations Nationales d'Eleves Ingenieurs [*International Federation of National Associations of Engineering Students*]
FIANZ .... Fellow of the Institute of Actuaries of New Zealand
FIAP .... Federation Internationale de l'Art Photographique [*International Federation of Photographic Art*] (EAIO)
FIAP .... Fellow of the Institution of Analysts and Programmers [*British*] (DBQ)
FIAPA .... Federation Internationale des Associations de Chefs de Publicite d'Annonceurs [*International Federation of Advertising Managers Associations*]
FIAPF .... Federation Internationale des Associations de Producteurs de Films [*International Federation of Film Producers' Associations*]
FIAPL .... Federation Internationale des Associations de Pilotes de Ligne
FIAPN .... Federation Internationale des Associations de Patrons de Navires [*International Federation of Shipmasters Associations*] (EAIO)
FIAPr .... Fiat SpA Preference ADR [*NYSE symbol*] (TTSB)
FIAPrA .... Fiat SpA Savings ADR [*NYSE symbol*] (TTSB)
FIAPS .... Federation Internationale des Associations de Professeurs de Sciences [*International Council of Associations for Science Education - ICASE*] (EAIO)
FIAR .... Failed Item Analysis Report (MCD)
FIAR .... Failure Investigation Action Report [*NASA*] (NASA)
FIArb .... Fellow of the Institute of Arbitrators
FIARE .... Flight Investigation of Apollo Reentry Environment (MUGU)
FIAS .... Federacion Interamericana de Asociaciones de Secretarias [*Inter-American Federation of Secretaries*] [*San Salvador, El Salvador*] (EAIO)
FIAS .... Federation Internationale Amateur de Sambo [*Anglet, France*] (EAIO)
FIAS .... Federation Internationale des Assistantes Sociales [*International Federation of Social Workers*] [*Switzerland*] (EAIO)
FIAS .... Fellow of the Incorporated Association of Architects and Surveyors [*British*] (DBQ)
FIAS .... Fellow of the Institute of Aeronautical Sciences [*Later, FAIAA*] [*British*]
FIAS .... Financial Information and Accounting System
FIAS .... Flanders Interaction Analysis System (EDAC)
Fias .... Free in and Stowed [*Shipping*] (DS)
FIASC .... Federal Inter-Agency Sedimentation Conference [*Department of Agriculture*]
FIAT .... Fabbrica Italiana Automobile, Torino [*Italian automobile manufacturer*] [*Facetious translations: "Fix It Again, Tony"; "Futile Italian Attempt at Transportation"*]
FIAT .... Federation Internationale des Archives de Television [*International Federation of Television Archives - IFTA*] (EAIO)

FIAT .... Federation Internationale des Associations de Thanatopraxie [*International Federation of Thanatopractic Associations*]
FIAT .... Fellow of the Institute of Animal Technicians [*British*] (DBQ)
FIAT .... Fellow of the Institute of Asphalt Technology [*British*] (DBQ)
Fiat .... Fiat SpA [*Associated Press*] (SAG)
FIAT .... Field Information Agency, Technical [*Under G-2, SHAEF*]
FIAT .... Film Inspection Apply Template (MCD)
FIAT .... First Installed Article, Tests [*NATO*] (NATG)
FIAT .... Fishing Industry Appeals Tribunal [*Australia*]
FIAT .... Floating Interpretative Automatic Translator (IAA)
FIAT .... Food Industry Association of Tasmania [*Australia*]
FIAT .... Forest Industries Association of Tasmania (EERA)
FIATA .... Federation Internationale des Associations de Transitaires et Assimilies [*International Federation of Freight Forwarders Associations*] [*Zurich, Switzerland*] (EAIO)
FIATC .... Federation Internationale des Associations Touristiques de Cheminots [*International Federation of Railwaymen's Travel Associations - IFRTA*] [*France*]
FIATC .... Florida International Agricultural Trade Council (SRA)
FIATE .... Federation Internationale des Associations de Travailleurs Evangeliques
FIAU .... Fialuridine [!*Medicine*]
FIAU .... Fluorodeoxyiodoara-U [*An antiviral compound*]
FIAV .... Federation Internationale des Agences de Voyages [*International Federation of Travel Agencies*]
FIAV .... Federation Internationale des Associations de Vexillologie [*International Federation of Vexillological Associations*] (EA)
FIAWOL .... Fandom Is a Way of Life [*Science-fiction-fan slogan*]
FIAWS .... Fellow of the International Academy of Wood Sciences
FIAX .... Fiesta-Air [*Air carrier designation symbol*]
FIB .... Fast Ion Bombardment
FIB .... Federation Internationale de Badminton [*International Badminton Federation - IBF*] (EA)
FIB .... Federation Internationale de Baseball [*International Baseball Federation*]
FIB .... Federation Internationale de Boules [*International Bocce Federation*] [*Turin, Italy*] (EAIO)
FIB .... Fellow of the Institute of Bankers [*British*] (EY)
FIB .... Fellow of the Institute of Biology (DAVI)
FIB .... Fellow of the Institute of Builders [*British*]
FIB .... Fiber
fib .... Fibrillation [*Medicine*]
FIB .... Fibrin [*Hematology*] (DAVI)
FIB .... Fibrinogen [*Factor 1*] [*Hematology*]
FIB .... Fibrosing Interstitial Pneumonitis [*Medicine*] (CPH)
FIB .... Fibrositis [*Medicine*]
FIB .... Fibula [*Medicine*]
FI B .... Fide Bona [*In Good Faith*] [*Latin*] (ROG)
FIB .... File Information Block
FIB .... Fire Indicator Board
FIB .... Fisherman's Information Bureau [*Chicago, IL*]
FIB .... Fixed Interim Baseline
FIB .... Fleet Installation Budget [*Navy*]
FIB .... Flight Information Bulletin (AABC)
FIB .... Fluidics Inertial Bomb
FIB .... Focused Ion Beam [*Photonics*]
FIB .... Force-in-Being (ADA)
FIB .... Foreground Initiated Batch [*Computer science*]
FIB .... FORTRAN [*Formula Translating System*] Information Bulletin [*Computer science*] (IEEE)
FIB .... Forward Indicator BIT [*Binary Digit*] (TEL)
FIB .... Free into Barge [*Shipping*]
FIB .... Free into Bunker
FIB .... Freeway Iberica SA [*Spain ICAO designator*] (FAAC)
FIB .... Kodiak, AK [*Location identifier FAA*] (FAAL)
FIBA .... Federation Internationale de Basketball Amateur [*International Amateur Basketball Federation*] [*Germany*] (EA)
FIBA .... Federazione Italiana Bancari e Assicuratori [*Italy*] (EY)
FIBA .... Fellow of the Institute of Banking Associations
FIBA .... Fellow of the Institute of Business Administration [*British*]
FIBAS .... Field Installation Branch Adaption Section (SAA)
FIBC .... Federal Interagency Broadcast Committee
FIBC .... Financial Bancorp [*NASDAQ symbol*] (TTSB)
FIBC .... Financial Bancorp, Inc. [*NASDAQ symbol*] (SAG)
FIBC .... Flexible Intermediate Bulk Container [*Shipping*]
FIBCA .... Flexible Intermediate Bulk Container Association (EA)
Fibchm .... Fiberchem, Inc. [*Associated Press*] (SAG)
FIBCO .... Fellow of the Institution of Building Control Officers (DBQ)
FIBCS .... Field Installation Branch Control Section (SAA)
FIBD .... Fellow of the Institute of British Decorators
fibd .... Fiberboard (VRA)
FIBD .... Ford International Business Development [*Ford Motor Co.*]
FIBEP .... Federation Internationale des Bureaux d'Extraits de Presse [*International Federation of Press Cutting Agencies - IFPCA*] (EAIO)
FIBER .... Fund for Integrative Biomedical Research
FIBEX .... First International BIOMASS Experiment [*ICSU*] (MSC)
FIBF .... Fellow of the Institute of British Foundrymen (DBQ)
fibgl .... Fiberglass (VRA)
FIBI .... Filed but Impracticable to Transmit [*NWS*] (FAAC)
FIBI .... First International Bank of Israel Ltd. (BJA)
FI Biol .... Fellow of the Institute of Biology [*Formerly, FInstBiol*] [*British*]
FIBMA .... National Federation of Ironmongers' and Builders' Merchants' Staff Associations [*British*] (BI)
FIBO .... Federation of Independent British Optometrists (DBA)

FIBP .... Fellow of the Institute of British Photographers
FIBR .... Fiber
FIBR .... Osicom Technologies, Inc. [*NASDAQ symbol*] (SAG)
Fibrbd .... Fibreboard Corp. [*Associated Press*] (SAG)
FIBRD .... Fibreboard [*Freight*]
FIBRGN .... Fibrinogen [*Hematology*] (DAVI)
fibrill .... Fibrillation [*Medicine*] (DAVI)
fibrin .... Fibrinogen [*Factor 1*] [*Hematology*]
Fibrstrs .... Fiberstars, Inc. [*Associated Press*] (SAG)
FIBS .... Field by Information Blending and Smoothing (USDC)
FIBS .... Field by Information Blending and Smoothing [*Marine science*] (OSRA)
FIBS .... Flight Information Billing System (DA)
FIB(Scot) ..... Fellow of the Institute of Bankers in Scotland [*British*] (DBQ)
FIBT .... Federation Internationale de Bobsleigh et de Tobogganing [*International Bobsledding and Tobogganing Federation*] [*Milan, Italy*] (EAIO)
FIBTP .... Federation Internationale du Batiment et des Travaux Publics
FIBUA .... Fighting in Built-Up Areas [*Military*] (INF)
FIBV .... Federation Internationale des Bourses de Valeurs [*International Federation of Stock Exchanges*] (EAIO)
FIC .... Brothers of Christian Instruction (TOCD)
FIC .... Congregatio Fratrum Immaculatae Conceptionis Beatae Mariae Virginis [*Brothers of the Immaculate Conception of the Blessed Virgin Mary*] (EAIO)
FIC .... Fair Isaac & Co. [*NYSE symbol*] (TTSB)
FIC .... Fasting Intestinal Contents [*Gastroenterology*] (DAVI)
FIC .... Fast Ion Conduction (PDAA)
FIC .... Fast-Moving Industrializing Country
FIC .... Fault Isolation Code
FIC .... Federal Information Center Program (EA)
FIC .... Federal Information Centers (USGC)
FIC .... Federal Insurance Contribution (MHDW)
FIC .... Federation Internationale de Canoe [*International Canoe Federation - ICF*] [*Florence, Italy*] (EAIO)
FIC .... Federation Internationale de Cremation [*International Cremation Federation*] (EAIO)
FIC .... Federation Internationale des Chronometreurs [*Rome, Italy*] (EAIO)
FIC .... Federation of Insurance Counsel (EA)
FIC .... Federation of Irish Cyclists (EAIO)
FIC .... Fellow of the Institute of Chemistry [*Later, FRIC*] [*British*]
FIC .... Fellow of the Institute of Commerce
FIC .... Fellowship for Intentional Community (EA)
FIC .... Field Installed Connector
FIC .... Film Integrated Circuit
FIC .... Financial Inventory Control
FIC .... Fire Industry Council [*British*] (DBA)
FIC .... First-in-Chain [*Computer science*]
FIC .... Fleet Intelligence Center [*Navy*] (NVT)
FIC .... Fleet Issue Control [*Navy*] (NVT)
FIC .... Flight Information Center
FIC .... Flight Inspection Center [*Military*] (DOMA)
FIC .... Flow Indicator Controller [*Electronics*] (ECII)
FIC .... Fluoriodocarbon [*Fire extinguishing compound*]
FIC .... Flying Instructor Course (DA)
FIC .... Foam Inhibiting Conjugate [*Chemical engineering*]
FIC .... Focus-Inducing Cell [*Population*] [*Immunochemistry*]
FIC .... Food Industries Center [*Ohio State University*] [*Research center*] (RCD)
FIC .... Force Indicator Code (MCD)
FIC .... Forest Industries Council (EA)
FIC .... Foundation for International Cooperation (EA)
FIC .... Fraternal Insurance Counselor [*Fraternal Field Managers' Association*] [*Designation awarded by*]
FIC .... Fratrum Instructionis Christianae [*Brothers of Christian Instruction*] [*La Mennais Brothers*] [*Roman Catholic religious order*]
FIC .... Freedom of Information Clearinghouse [*An association*] (EA)
FIC .... Free Insurance and Carriage [*Shipping*] (DS)
FIC .... Freight, Insurance, Carriage
FIC .... Frequency Interference Control
FIC .... Friends of Imperial Cancer [*British*]
FIC .... Funding Information Center [*Spokane Public Library*] [*Information service or system*] (IID)
FIC .... Fur Institute of Canada
FICA .... Federal Insurance Contributions Act [*1954*] [*Under which collections are made from employers and employees for OASDI benefits*]
FICA .... Federation Internationale des Cheminots Antialcooliques [*International Railway Temperance Union*]
FICA .... Fellow of the Commonwealth Institute of Accountancy
FICA .... Flowrate Indicating Controlling Alarm [*Engineering*]
FICA .... Food Industry Council of Australia
FICA .... Forest Industries Campaign Association (EERA)
FICA .... Fraternal Insurance Counsellors Association [*Later, NAFIC*] (EA)
FICAC .... Federation Internationale des Corps et Associations Consulaires [*Federation of International Consular Corps and Associations*] (EAIO)
FICAI .... Fellow of the Institute of Chartered Accountants in Ireland (ODBW)
FICAP .... Federation of International Country Air Personalities [*Defunct*] (EA)
FICAP .... Furniture Industry Consumer Advisory Panel [*Defunct*] (EA)
FICB .... Federal Intermediate Credit Bank
FICB .... Federation Internationale de la Croix-Bleue [*International Federation of the Blue Cross*] [*Switzerland*] (EAIO)
FICB .... Fellow of the Institute of Canadian Bankers (DD)
FICB .... File Identification Control Block [*Computer science*] (IAA)
FICC .... Federal Interagency Coordinating Council

FICC............ Federation Internationale de Camping et de Caravanning [*International Federation of Camping and Caravanning*] [*Brussels, Belgium*] (EA)

FICC............ Federation Internationale de Chimie Clinique [*International Federation of Clinical Chemistry*]

FICC............ Federation Internationale des Cine-Clubs [*International Federation of Film Societies*]

FICC............ Federation of Insurance and Corporate Counsel [*Marblehead, MA*] (EA)

FICC............ Fixed Income Consumer Counseling [*ACTION*]

FICC............ Frequency Interference Control Center [*Air Force*]

FICCA.......... False Identification Crime Control Act of 1982

FIC CATIS .... Fleet Intelligence Center Computer-Aided Tactical Information System [*Navy*] (DNAB)

FICCC.......... Federation Internationale des Clubs de Camping-Cars [*Montreuil, France*] (EAIO)

FICCIA .... Federation Internationale des Cadres de la Chimie et des Industries Annexes

FICCS.......... Functional Inventory of Cognitive Communication Strategies (EDAC)

FICD............ Fellow of the Indian College of Dentists

FICD............ Fellow of the Institute of Canadian Dentists

FICD............ Fellow of the Institute of Civil Defence [*British*]

FICD............ Fellow of the International College of Dentists

FICE............ Federal Interagency Committee on Education

FICE............ Federation Internationale des Choeurs d'Enfants [*International Federation of Children's Choirs*] (EA)

FICE............ Federation Internationale des Communautes d'Enfants [*International Federation of Children's Communities*]

FICE............ Federation Internationale des Communautes Educatives [*International Federation of Educative Communities*] [*Zurich, Switzerland*] (EAIO)

FICE............ Fellow of the Institution of Civil Engineers [*British*]

FICEM.......... Federcion Interamericana del Cemento [*Inter American Cement Federation*] [*Colombia*] (EAIO)

FICEMEA...... Federation Internationale des Centres d'Entrainement aux Methodes d'Education Active [*International Federation of Training Centres in Methods of Active Education*] (EAIO)

FICEP.......... Federation Internationale Catholique d'Education Physique et Sportive [*Catholic International Federation for Physical and Sports Education - CIFPSE*] [*Paris, France*] (EAIO)

FICeram....... Fellow of the Institute of Ceramics [*British*]

FICEUR .... Fleet Intelligence Center, Europe [*Navy*]

FICEURLANT... Fleet Intelligence Center, Europe and Atlantic [*Navy*] (MCD)

FICF............ Federation Internationale Culturelle Feminine [*Women's International Cultural Federation - WICF*] (EAIO)

FICG............ Federation Internationale des Choeurs de Garcons (EAIO)

FIChemE....... Fellow of the Institution of Chemical Engineers [*British*]

FIChor......... Fellow of the Benesh Institute of Choreology [*British*] (DBQ)

FICI............ Fair [*Isaac*] & Co., Inc. [*NASDAQ symbol*] (NQ)

FICI............ Fellow of the Institute of Chemistry of Ireland

FICI............ Fellow of the International Colonial Institute [*British*]

FICIA.......... Fellow of the Guild of Industrial, Commercial, & Institutional Accounts (DD)

FICIC.......... Federation Internationale du Commerce et des Industries du Camping

FICICA .... Federation Internationale du Personnel d'Encadrement des Industries et CommercesAgricoles et Alimentaires [*International Federation of Managerial Staff of Agricultural and Alimentary Industry and Commerce*] (EAIO)

Fic Int......... Fiction International [*A publication*] (BRI)

FICJA.......... Fellow of the International Criminal Justice Association

FICJF .... Federation Internationale des Conseils Juridiques et Fiscaux [*International Federation of Legal Fiscal Consultants*]

FICL............ Financial Inventory Control Ledger (DNAB)

FICM........... Federation Internationale des Cadres des Mines

FICM........... Federation of International Music Competitions (EA)

FICM........... Fellow of the Institute of Credit Management [*British*] (DCTA)

FICM........... Fleet Intelligence Collection Manual (MCD)

FICM........... Fluidic Industrial Control Module (IAA)

FICMA......... Fellow of the Institute of Cost and Management Accountants [*British*] (ODBW)

FICO........... Fellow of the Institute of Careers Officers [*British*] (DBQ)

FICO........... Field Installation Change Order (MCD)

FICO........... File Control [*Microfilm*] (MCD)

FICO........... Financing Corp. [*Created by the Reagan administration in 1987 for the Fede ral Savings and Loan Insurance Corp.*]

FICO........... Flight Information and Control of Operations

FICO........... Ford Instrument Co. (MCD)

FICO₂......... Fraction of Inspired Carbon Dioxide [*Medicine*] (DAVI)

FICOD......... Force Identification Code [*Military*]

FICON .... Fighter Conveyor

FICON .... File Conversion [*Computer science*]

FICorrST ...... Fellow of the Institution of Corrosion Science and Technology [*British*] (DBQ)

FICP........... Federation Internationale des Clubs de Publicite [*International Federation of Advertising Clubs*] [*Lille, France*] (EAIO)

FICP........... Federation Internationale du Cyclisme Professionnel [*International Federation of Professional Cycling*]

FICP........... Freres de l'Instruction Chretienne de Ploermel [*Brothers of Christian Instruction of Ploermel*] [*Rome, Italy*] (EAIO)

FICPAC .... Fleet Intelligence Center, Pacific [*Navy*] (CINC)

FICPACFAC... Fleet Intelligence Center, Pacific Facility [*Navy*]

FICPI.......... Federation Internationale des Conseils en Propriete Industrielle [*International Federation of Industrial Property Attorneys*] (EAIO)

FICR........... Financial Inventory Control Report

FICS............ Factory Information Control System (MHDB)

FICS............ Fault Isolation Checkout System

FICS............ Federation Internationale des Chasseurs de Son [*International Federation of Sound Hunters - IFSH*] (EAIO)

FICS............ Fellow of the Institute of Chartered Shipbrokers [*British*]

FICS............ Fellow of the International College of Surgeons

FICS............ Financial Clearing and Services Ltd. [*Information service or system*] (IID)

FICS............ Financial Information Control System

FICS............ Fire Control Simulation (MCD)

FICS............ Forecasting and Inventory Control System

FICS............ Freshman Issues and Concerns Survey (EDAC)

FICSA.......... Federation of International Civil Servants' Associations [*Geneva, Switzerland*] (EA)

FICT............ Federation Internationale de Centres Touristiques [*International Federation of Tourist Centres*] (EAIO)

FICT............ Fictilis [*Made of Pottery*] [*Latin*]

FICT............ Fiction

FICT............ Fictional (WDAA)

FICT............ Fictitious (WDAA)

FICTIONZINE... Fiction Magazine [*Generic term for a publication covering science fiction*]

FICU............ Fetal Intensive Care Unit [*Neonatology*] (DAVI)

FICU............ Fonds Internationale de Cooperation Universitaire [*International Fund for University Cooperation*] [*Canada*] (EAIO)

FICW........... Fellow of the Institute of Clerks of Works of Great Britain, Inc. (DBQ)

FICWA .... Floricultural Industry Council of Western Australia

FID.............. Failure Identification (MCD)

FID.............. Far-Infrared Detector

FID.............. Fault Isolation Detection (MCD)

FID.............. Fault Isolation Diagnostics (MCD)

FID.............. Federacion Internacional de Documentacion [*International Federation for Documentation - IFD*] [*Spanish Information service or system*] (ASF)

FID.............. Federation Internationale de Documentation (NITA)

FID.............. Federation Internationale d'Information et de Documentation [*International Federation for Information and Documentation*] [*Netherlands Information service or system*] (IID)

FID.............. Federation Internationale du Diabete [*International Diabetes Federation - IDF*] [*Brussels, Belgium*] (EAIO)

FID.............. Fellow of the Institute of Directors [*British*]

FID.............. Fidelity (WGA)

FID.............. Fides [*Faith*] [*Latin*] (ROG)

FID.............. Fiduciary (ADA)

FID.............. Field Identifier [*Computer science*]

FID.............. Field-Induced Delay [*Astrophysics*]

FID.............. Field Instrumentation Division (SAA)

FID.............. Field Intelligence Department

FID.............. Flame Ionization Detector

FID.............. Flight Implementation Directive (MCD)

FID.............. Flight Instrumentation Division [*Langley*]

FID.............. Floating Input Distortion

FID.............. Foolproof Identification [*System*]

FID.............. Force Identification [*Military*] (NVT)

FID.............. Forecasts-in-Depth (MHDB)

FID.............. Foreign Internal Defense

FID.............. Format Identification [*Computer science*] (IBMDP)

FID.............. Free Indirect Discourse

FID.............. Free Induction Decay [*Physics*]

FID.............. Free Induction Delay

FID.............. Free into Container Depot [*Business term*]

FID.............. Friends in Deed [*An association*]

FID.............. Fuel Injector Driver [*Automotive engineering*]

FID.............. Port Fidalgo [*Alaska*] [*Seismograph station code, US Geological Survey*] (SEIS)

FIDA............ Federal Independent Democratic Alliance [*South Africa Political party*] (EY)

FIDA............ Fellow of the Institute of Directors, Australia (ODBW)

FIDA............ Fondo Internacional de Desarrollo Agricola [*International Fund for Agricultural Development*] [*Spanish United Nations*] (DUND)

FIDA............ Fonds International de Developpement Agricole [*International Fund for Agricultural Development*] [*French United Nations*] (DUND)

FIDA............ Formyliminodiacetic Acid [*Organic chemistry*]

FIDAC .... Federation Interalliee des Anciens Combattants [*World War I*] [*French*]

FIDAC .... Film Input to Digital Automatic Computer

FIDACSYS... FIDAC [*Film Input to Digital Automatic Computer*] System (NITA)

FIDACSYS... Film Input to Digital Automatic Computer System

FIDAF.......... Federacion Internacional de Asociaciones de Ferreteros y Almacenistas de Hierros [*International Federation of Ironmongers and Iron Merchants Associations*]

FIDAP .... Fluid Dynamics Analysis Package [*Computer-assisted engineering*]

FIDAQ .... Federation Internationale des Associations de Quincailliers et Marchands de Fer [*International Federation of Ironmongers and Iron Merchants Associations - IFIA*] (EAIO)

FIDAS .... Formularorientiertes Interaktives Datenbanksystem [*Forms-Oriented Interactive Database System*] [*Germany*]

FIDASE .... Falkland Islands and Dependencies Aerial Survey Expedition [*1955-57*]

FidBcp .... Fidelity Bancorp [*Associated Press*] (SAG)

FidBnCh ...... Fidelity Bancorp [*Associated Press*] (SAG)

FIDCR .... Federal Interagency Day Care Requirements

FID DEF ...... Fidei Defensor [*Defender of the Faith*] [*Latin*] (ROG)

FIDE........... Federation de l'Industrie Dentaire en Europe [*Federation of the European Dental Industry*]

FIDE............ Federation Internationale des Echecs [*International Chess Federation*] [*Switzerland*]

FIDE............ Federation Internationale pour le Droit Europeen [*International Federation for European Law*] [*Benelux*] (EAIO)

FIDE............ Fuzzy Inference Development Environment [*Computer science*]

FIDEGEP...... Federation Interalliee des Evades de Guerre et des Passeurs

FidelFin........ Fidelity Financial Corp. [*Associated Press*] (SAG)

FidelNtl....... Fidelity National Corp. [*Associated Press*] (SAG)

FIDEM......... Federation Internationale des Editeurs de Medailles [*International Federation of Medal Producers*]

FIDEM......... Federation Internationale d'Etudes Medievales (EAIO)

FIDER .... Foundation for Interior Design Education Research (EA)

FIDES......... Fonds d'Investissement pour le Developpement Economique et Social [*Investment Fund for Economic and Social Development*] [*United Nations*] (AF)

FIDES......... Forecaster's Intelligent Discussion Experiment System [*Marine science*] (OSRA)

FIDES......... Forecaster's Intelligent Discussion Experiment System (USDC)

FIDESZ........ Federation of Young Democrats [*Hungary*] [*Political party Acronym is based on foreign phrase*] (ECON)

FIDF............ Financial Institutions Data File [*Rand McNally & Co.*] [*Information service or system*] (CRD)

FidFdB........ Fidelity Federal Bancorp [*Associated Press*] (SAG)

FidFdlSv....... Fidelity Federal Savings Bank [*Associated Press*] (SAG)

FidFdVA....... Fidelity FSB [*Associated Press*] (SAG)

FidFnVA....... Fidelity Financial Bankshares Corp. [*Associated Press*] (SAG)

FIDH .... Federation Internationale des Droits de l'Homme [*International Federation for Human Rights*] [*Paris, France*] (EA)

FIDI .... Federation Internationale des Demenageurs Internationaux [*International Federation of International Furniture Removers - IFIFR*] (EAIO)

FIDI .... Fishery Information, Data and Statistics Service [*Marine science*] (OSRA)

FIDIA .... Federation Internationale des Intellectuels Aveugles

FIDIC .... Federation Internationale des Ingenieurs Conseils [*International Federation of Consulting Engineers*] (EAIO)

FIDJC.......... Federation Internationale des Directeurs de Journaux Catholiques

Fid L Chron... Fiduciary Law Chronicle [*A publication*] (DLA)

FIDLTY........ Fidelity

FIDO .... Face Information Digested Online (NITA)

FIDO .... Facility for Integrated Data Organization

FIDO .... Fallout Intensity Detector Oscillator

FIDO .... Film Industry Defence Organisation [*British*] (DI)

FIDO .... Flight Dynamics Officer [*NASA*]

FIDO .... Flight Inspection District Office [*FAA*]

FIDO .... Fog, Intense, Dispersal Of [*NASA*]

FIDO .... Fog Investigation and Dispersal Operation [*System used on airfield landing strips*] [*World War II*]

FIDO .... Frazer Island Defenders Organisation (EERA)

FIDO .... Freaks, Irregulars, Defects, and Oddities [*Numismatics*]

FIDO .... Fugitive Information Data Organizer [*Database*]

FIDO .... Fully Integrated Discovery Organization [*Business term*]

FIDOAO........ Federation Internationale des Diffuseurs d'Oeuvres d'Art Originales [*International Federation of Original Art Diffusors*] [*France*] (EAIO)

FIDOF .... Federation Internationale des Organisateurs de Festivals [*International Federation of Festival Organizations*] (EAIO)

FIDOR.......... Fibre Building Board Development Organisation Ltd. [*British*] (BI)

FIDP............. Fellow of the Institute of Data Processing (WDAA)

FIDP............. Foreign Internal Defense Plan (MCD)

FIDRS .... Facilities Interface Data Requirements Sheets (MCD)

FIDS............ Facility Intrusion Detection System (RDA)

FIDS............ Falkland Islands Dependencies Survey [*1943-62*]

FIDS............ Fast Interbroker Delivery Service [*Australian Stock Exchange*]

FIDS............ Flight Information Data System [*United Airlines*]

FIDS............ Flight Information Display System [*Information service or system*] (IID)

FIDT............ Forced Incident Destiny Testing (IAA)

FIDTA.......... Fellow of the International Dance Teachers' Association [*British*] (DBQ)

Fiduciary ..... Fiduciary Reporter [*Pennsylvania*] [*A publication*] (DLA)

Fiduciary R (PA)... Fiduciary Reporter [*Pennsylvania*] [*A publication*] (DLA)

Fiduciary Rptr... Fiduciary Reporter [*Pennsylvania*] [*A publication*] (DLA)

Fiduc Rep .... Fiduciary Reporter [*Pennsylvania*] [*A publication*] (DLA)

FIE .... Fair Isle [*Scotland*] [*Airport symbol*] (OAG)

FIE .... Fault Isolation Equipment (MCD)

FIE .... Federation Internationale d'Escrime [*International Fencing Federation*]

FIE .... Federation Internationale des Echecs [*International Chess Federation*]

FIE .... Fellow of the Institute of Engineers [*British*]

FIE .... Feuerstein's Instrumental Enrichment [*Education*] (AEE)

FIE .... Field Aviation GmbH & Co. [*Germany ICAO designator*] (FAAC)

FIE .... Flight Instrumentation Engineer (MCD)

FIE .... Florida Industries Exposition

FIE .... Fluoride Ion Electrode (PDAA)

FIE .... Fly-In Echelon [*Navy*] (ANA)

FIE .... Foundation for Integrative Education (EA)

FIE .... Fourier Integral Estimate

FIE .... Friends of International Education [*An association*] (EA)

FIE .... Fuel Injection Equipment [*Diesel engines*]

FIEA............ Federation Internationale des Experts en Automobiles [*International Federation of Automobile Experts*] [*Rhode St. Genese, Belgium*] (EAIO)

FIEC .... Federation de l'Industrie Europeenne de la Construction [*European Construction Industry Federation*] (EAIO)

FIEC .... Federation Internationale des Associations d'Etudes Classiques [*International Federation of the Societies of Classical Studies*] (EAIO)

FIEC .... Fellowship of Independent Evangelical Churches

FIED .... Fellow of the Institution of Engineering Designers [*British*] (DBQ)

FIEDA.......... Fondation Internationale pour l'Enseignement du Droit des Affaires [*Canada*]

FIEE .... Fellow of the Institute of Electrical Engineers [*British*]

FIEE .... Fellow of the Institution of Electrical Engineers (DD)

FIEEE .... Fellow of the Institute of Electrical and Electronic Engineers

FIEF .... Federation Internationale pour l'Economie Familiale [*International Federation for Home Economics - IFHE*] (EAIO)

FIEG .... Federazione Italiana Editori Giornali [*Italian Federation of Newspaper Publishing*] (EY)

FIEGA.......... Federation Internationale d'Eutonie Gerda Alexander [*International Federation for Gerda Alexander Eutony*] [*Belgium*] (EAIO)

FIEI .... Farm and Industrial Equipment Institute (EA)

FIEI .... Fellow of the Institution of Engineering Inspection [*British*]

FIEI .... Fraser Island Environmental Inquiry [*Australia*]

FIE(India) .... Fellow of the Institution of Engineers, India

FIEJ .... Federation Internationale des Editeurs de Journaux [*International Federation of Newspaper Publishers*] [*Paris, France*] (EAIO)

FIELD.......... Field [*Commonly used*]

Field Anal.... Field's Analysis of Blackstone's Commentaries [*A publication*] (DLA)

Field & D Ch Pr... Field and Dunn's Chancery Practice [*A publication*] (DLA)

Field Com Law... Field on the Common Law of England [*A publication*] (DLA)

Field Corp ... Field on Corporations [*A publication*] (DLA)

Field Cur ..... Field on Protestant Curates and Incumbents [*A publication*] (DLA)

Field Dam ... Field on the Law of Damages [*A publication*] (DLA)

Field Ev ...... Field's Law of Evidence in British India [*A publication*] (DLA)

Field Int Code... Field's International Code [*A publication*] (DLA)

Field on Inh... Field on the Hindu and Mohammedan Laws of Inheritance [*A publication*] (DLA)

Field Pen L... Field's Penal Law [*A publication*] (DLA)

Field Pr Cor... Field on Private Corporations [*A publication*] (DLA)

FIELDS........ Fields [*Commonly used*] (OPSA)

FIELecIE ...... Fellow of the Institution of Electrical and Electronics Incorporated Engineers [*British*] (DBQ)

FIEM .... Federation Internationale de l'Enseignement Menager

FIEM .... Fellow of the Institute of Executives and Managers [*British*] (DBQ)

FIEO .... Federation of Indian Export Organisations [*Canada*]

FIEP .... Federation Internationale d'Education Physique [*International Federation for Physical Education*] (EAIO)

FIEP .... Federation Internationale des Etudiants en Pharmacie

FIEP .... Federation Internationale pour l'Education des Parents [*International Federation for Parent Education - IFPE*] [*Sevres, France*] (EAIO)

FIEP .... Forest Industry Energy Program (HGAA)

FIEP .... Foundation for International Economic Policy (EA)

FIER .... Federation Internationale des Enseignants de Rythmique [*International Federation of Teachers of Rhythmics - IFTR*] (EA)

FIER .... Fieramente [*Boldly*] [*Music*] (ROG)

FIER .... Foundation for Instrumentation Education and Research [*Defunct*]

FIERE.......... Fellow of the Institution of Electronic and Radio Engineers [*British*]

FIERF.......... Forging Industry Educational and Research Foundation (EA)

FIES .... Federal Information Exchange System (DNAB)

FIES .... Fellow of the Illuminating Engineering Society [*Later, FIllumES*] [*British*]

FIESP.......... Federation Internationale des Etudiants en Sciences Politiques

FIET .... Federation Internationale des Employes, Techniciens, et Cadres [*International Federation of Commercial, Clerical, Professional, and Technical Employees*] [*Geneva, Switzerland*] (EAIO)

FIET .... Field Integration Engineering Test (MCD)

FIEWS.......... Food Information and Early Warning System [*FAO*] [*United Nations*]

FIEx .... Fellow of the Institute of Export [*British*] (DCTA)

FIExE .... Fellow of the Institute of Executive Engineers and Officers [*British*] (DBQ)

FIF .... Facsimile Infromation Field [*Telecommunications*] (OSI)

FIF .... Failure Indicating Fuse

FIF .... Family Information Facility (MHDB)

FIF .... Federation Internationale de la Filterie [*International Thread Federation*] [*EC*] (ECED)

FIF .... Feedback Inhibition Factor [*Immunochemistry*]

FIF .... Ferric Ion Free

FIF .... Fibroblast Interferon [*Genetics*]

FIF .... Fibroblast-Migration Inhibitory Factor [*Immunochemistry*]

FIF .... Fifteen [*Lawn tennis*] (DSUE)

FIF .... Financial Federal [*AMEX symbol*] (TTSB)

FIF .... Financial Federal Corp. [*AMEX symbol*] (SPSG)

FIF .... First Irish Families

FIF .... Forced Inspiratory Flow [*Physiology*]

FIF .... Foreign Investment Fund

FIF .... Forest Industries Federation [*Australia*]

FIF .... Formaldehyde-Induced Fluorescence

FIF .... Fractal Image Format [*Computer graphics*] (PCM)

FIF .... Frifly SpA [*Italy ICAO designator*] (FAAC)

f-if-- .... Ifni [*MARC geographic area code Library of Congress*] (LCCP)

FIFA............ Federation Internationale de Football Association [*International Federation of Association Football*] [*Zurich, Switzerland*] (EA)

FIFA............ Federation Internationale du Film sur d'Art [*International Federation of Films on Art*]

FI FA............ Fieri Facias [*Cause to Be Made*] [*A writ commanding the sheriff to execute judgment*] [*Legal term*] [*Latin*]

FIFA............ Fissions per Initial Fissile Atom [*Nuclear energy*]

FIFC .... Fur Information and Fashion Council (EA)
FIFCJ .... Federation Internationale des Femmes des Carrieres Juridiques [*France*]
FIFCLC .... Federation Internationale des Femmes de Carrieres Liberales et Commerciales [*International Federation of Business and Professional Women*]
FIFCQ .... Festival International du Film de la Critique Quebecoise [*International Festival of Quebec Film Critics*] [*Canada*]
FIFDU .... Federation Internationale des Femmes Diplomees des Universites [*International Federation of University Women - IFUW*] (EAIO)
FIFE .... American Institute of Fellows in Free Enterprise [*Houston, DE*] (EA)
FIFE .... Federation Internationale des Associations de Fabricants de Produits d'Entretien [*International Federation of Associations of Manufacturers of Household Products*] (EAIO)
FIFE .... First ISLSCP [*International Satellite Land Surface Climatology Project*] Field Experiment [*NASA*]
FIFES .... Fifeshire [*County in Scotland*]
FIFF .... Fellow of the Institute of Freight Forwarders [*British*] (ODBW)
FIFI .... Field Image Feature Interface [*Photovoltaic energy systems*]
FIFI .... Flexible Ideal Format for Information
FIFirE .... Fellow of the Institution of Fire Engineers [*British*] (DCTA)
FIFO .... Fade In, Fade Out [*Films, television, etc.*]
FIFO .... First In, First Out [*Accounting*]
FIFO .... Flight Inspection Field Office [*FAA*]
FIFO .... Floating Input - Floating Output [*Computer science*]
FIFO-H .... Flight Inspection Field Office High Altitude (FAAC)
FIFO-I .... Flight Inspection Field Office, Intermediate Altitude [*FAA*] (SAA)
FIFR .... Fasting Intestinal Flow Rate (MAE)
FIFRA .... Federal Insecticide, Fungicide, and Rodenticide Act [*1947*] [*Department of Agriculture*]
FIFRA .... Federal Insecticide, Fungicide, and Rodenticide Act
FIFS .... First Investors Financial Services Group, Inc. [*NASDAQ symbol*] (SAG)
FIFS .... First Investors Finl Svcs Grp [*NASDAQ symbol*] (TTSB)
FIFSP .... Federation Internationale des Fonctionnaires Superieurs de Police [*International Federation of Senior Police Officers*] [*France*]
FIFST .... Fellow of the Institute of Food Science and Technology [*British*]
FifthDim ...... Fifth Dimension, Inc. [*Associated Press*] (SAG)
FifthT .... Fifth Third Bancorp [*Associated Press*] (SAG)
FIFV .... Future Infantry Fighting Vehicle [*Army*] (RDA)
FIF(WA) .... Forest Industries Federation, Western Australia
FIG .... Farmers Group Capital II [*NYSE symbol*] (SAG)
FIG .... Farmers Group Captial [*NYSE symbol*] (SAG)
FIG .... Federation Internationale de Genetique [*International Genetics Federation*] (EAIO)
FIG .... Federation Internationale de Gymnastique [*International Gymnastic Federation - IGF*] [*Lyss, Switzerland*] (EAIO)
FIG .... Federation Internationale des Geometres [*International Federation of Surveyors - IFS*] [*Edmonton, AB*] (EAIO)
FIG .... Fiber Interferometer Gyroscope (MCD)
FIG .... Fighter Intercepter Group (MCD)
FIG .... Figurative
fig .... Figurative (WDMC)
fig .... Figure (WDMC)
fig .... Figure (VRA)
FIG .... Figure (AFM)
FIG .... Fishing Industry Grants [*Marine science*] (OSRA)
FIG .... Fishing Industry Grants (USDC)
FIG .... Flight Inspection Group [*FAA*]
FIG .... Floated Integrating Gyro [*Aerospace*] (AAG)
FIG .... FORTH Interest Group (EA)
FIG .... Fraud Investigation Group [*Serious Fraud Office*] [*British*]
FIG .... Fria [*Guinea*] [*Airport symbol*] (AD)
FIG .... Friends of Internet in Greece [*Discussion list*]
FIGA .... Fretted Instrument Guild of America (EA)
FIGA .... Iberian Federation of Anarchist Groups [*Spain*] (PD)
FIGAS .... Falkland Islands Government Air Service (EY)
FIGasE .... Fellow of the Institution of Gas Engineers [*British*]
FIGAT .... Fiberglass Aerial Target (DNAB)
FIGCM .... Fellow of the Incorporated Guild of Church Musicians [*British*]
FIGD .... Familial Idiopathic Gonadotropin Deficiency [*Medicine*] (DMAA)
FIGD .... Fellow of the Institute of Grocery Distribution [*British*] (DBQ)
FIGE .... Federation de l'Industrie Granitiere Europeenne [*Federation of the European Granite Industry*] (EAIO)
FIGE .... Field Inversion Gel Electrophoresis [*Analytical biochemistry*]
FIGED .... Federation Internationale des Grandes et Moyennes Entreprises de Distribution [*International Federation of Retail Distributors*] (EAIO)
FIGeol .... Fellow of the Institution of Geologists [*British*] (DBQ)
FigEtym .... Figura Etymologica [*A publication*] (BJA)
Figgie .... Figgie International, Inc. [*Associated Press*] (SAG)
FiggieA .... Figgie International [*Associated Press*] (SAG)
FiggieB .... Figgie International [*Associated Press*] (SAG)
FIGHT .... Family Interest Group - Head Trauma (EA)
FIGHT .... Freedom, Independence, God, Honor, Today (IIA)
FIGHTRON ... Fighting Squadron
FIGI .... Figgie International, Inc. [*NASDAQ symbol*] (NQ)
FIGI .... Figgie Intl Cl'B' [*NASDAQ symbol*] (TTSB)
FIGIA .... Figgie Intl Cl'A' [*NASDAQ symbol*] (TTSB)
FIGIEFA .... Federation Internationale des Grossistes, Importateurs, et Exportateurs Fournitures Automobiles [*International Federation of Wholesalers, Importers, and Exporters in Automobile Fittings*] (EAIO)
FIGIJ .... Federation Internationale de Gynecologie Infantile et Juvenile [*International Federation of Infantile and Juvenile Gynecology - IFIJG*] [*Sierre, Switzerland*] (EAIO)
FIGLU .... Formimino-L-glutamic Acid [*Organic chemistry*]
FIGM .... Friends of Israel Gospel Ministry (EA)
FIGO .... Federation Internationale de Gynecologie et d'Obstetrique [*International Federation of Gynecology and Obstetrics*] [*British*] (EAIO)
FIGPrA .... Farmers Grp Cap 8.45% 'QUIPS' [*NYSE symbol*] (TTSB)
FIGPrB .... Farmers Grp Cap II 8.25% 'QUIPS' [*NYSE symbol*] (TTSB)
FIGS .... Fabray-Perot Infrared Grating Spectrometer [*Chemistry*]
FIGS .... Figures Shift [*Teleprinters*]
FIGS .... Future Income Growth Security [*Finance*]
FIH .... Fat-Induced Hyperglycemia [*Medicine*]
FIH .... Federation Internationale de Handball [*International Handball Federation*]
FIH .... Federation Internationale de Hockey [*International Hockey Federation*] [*Brussels, Belgium*] (EA)
FIH .... Federation Internationale des Hopitaux [*International Hospital Federation*]
FIH .... Fellow of the Institute of Housing [*British*] (DBQ)
FIH .... Fellow of the Institute of Hygiene [*British*]
FIH .... Free in Harbor [*Navigation*]
FIH .... Kinshasa [*Zaire*] [*Airport symbol*] (OAG)
FIHBJO .... Federation Internationale des Horlogers, Bijoutiers, Joailliers, Orfevres Detaillants de la CE [*International Federation of Retailers in Horology, Jewellery, Gold and Silverware of the EC*] (ECED)
FiHBWE .... National Board of Water and the Environment, Urho Kekkosen Katu, Helsinki, Finland [*Library symbol*] [*Library of Congress*] (LCLS)
FIHC .... Federation Internationale des Hommes Catholiques [*International Council of Catholic Men - ICCM*] [*Vatican City, Vatican City State*] (EAIO)
FIHC .... Federation Internationale Halterophile et Culturiste
FiHCRN .... Finnish Center for Radiation and Nuclear Safety [*Sateilyturvakeskus*], H elsinki, Finland [*Library symbol*] [*Library of Congress*] (LCLS)
FIHE .... Fellow of the Institute of Health Education [*British*]
FIHE .... Foundation for Independent Higher Education (EA)
FiHK .... Kauppakorkeakoulu [*Helsinki School of Economics*], Helsinki, Finland [*Library symbol Library of Congress*] (LCLS)
FIHM .... Fellow of the Institute of Housing Managers [*Formerly, FIHsg*] [*British*]
FiHMR .... Institute of Marine Research, Helsinki, Finland [*Library symbol*] [*Library of Congress*] (LCLS)
FIHospE .... Fellow of the Institute of Hospital Engineering [*British*] (DI)
FIHR .... Foundation for International Human Relations (EA)
FiHR .... Oy Rekolid, Mikrofilmipalvelu, Helsinki, Finland [*Library symbol Library of Congress*] (LCLS)
FIHS .... Fellow of the Institute of Hospital Secretaries [*British*]
FIHsg .... Fellow of the Institute of Housing [*Later, FIHM*] [*British*]
FIHT .... Fellow of the Institution of Highway Engineers [*British*] (DBQ)
FiHT .... Valtion Teknillinen Tutkimuskeskus, Helsinki, Finland [*Library symbol Library of Congress*] (LCLS)
FIHU .... Federation Internationale de l'Habitation et de l'Urbanisme
FiHU .... Helsingin Yliopisto [*University of Helsinki*], Helsinki, Finland [*Library symbol Library of Congress*] (LCLS)
FiHU-A .... Helsinki University, Library of Agriculture, Viikki, Helsinki, Finland [*Library symbol*] [*Library of Congress*] (LCLS)
FIHUAT .... Federation Internationale pour l'Habitation, l'Urbanisme et l'Amenagement des Territoires [*International Federation for Housing and Planning - IFHP*] [*The Hague, Netherlands*] (EA)
FiHU-F .... Helsinki University Library of Forestry [*Helsingin Yliopiston Metsakirjaston*], Helsinki, Finland [*Library symbol*] [*Library of Congress*] (LCLS)
FIHVE .... Fellow of the Institution of Heating and Ventilating Engineers [*British*]
FII .... FARMS International, Inc. (EA)
FII .... Federal Item Identification
FII .... Federation of Irish Industries Ltd. (BI)
FII .... Fellow of the Imperial Institute [*British*] (DAS)
FII .... Fletcher Challenge Investments II [*Toronto Stock Exchange symbol Vancouver Stock Exchange symbol*]
FII .... Food Industry Institute [*Michigan State University*] [*Research center*] (RCD)
FII .... Franked Investment Income [*Accounting*]
FIIA .... Fellow of the Institute of Industrial Administration [*Later, FBIM*] [*British*]
FIIC .... Federacion Interamericana de la Industria de la Construccion [*Inter-American Federation of the Construction Industry - IAFCI*] (EAIO)
FIIC .... Fellow of the Insurance Institute of Canada
FIIC .... Field Impact Insulation Class (DAC)
FIIC .... Flight Inspector in Charge
FIICPI .... Federation Internationale des Ingenieurs-Conseils en Propriete Industrielle
FIID .... Federation Internationale d'Information et de Documentation [*International Federation for Information and Documentation - IFID*] (EAIO)
FIIG .... Federal Item Identification Guides
FIIG .... Federal Item Inventory Group
FIIG .... Federation des Institutions Internationales Semi-Officielles et Privees Etabliesa Geneve [*Federation of Semi-Official and Private International Institutions Established in Geneva*] [*Switzerland*] (EA)
FIIGMO .... Forget It, I've Got My Orders [*Bowdlerized version*] [*Military slang*]
FIIGS .... Federal Item Identification Guide System
FIIGSC .... Federal Item Identification Guides for Supply Cataloging (AABC)
FIIHE .... Federation Internationale des Instituts de Hautes Etudes [*International Federation of Institutes for Advanced Study*] (EAIO)

FIILS........... Full Integrity Instrument Landing System

FIIM........... Federation Internationale de l'Industrie du Medicament [*International Federation of Pharmaceutical Manufacturers Associations - IFPMA*] (EAIO)

FIIM........... Federation Internationale des Ingenieurs Municipaux [*International Federation of Municipal Engineers - IFME*] (EAIO)

FIIM........... Fellow of the Institution of Industrial Managers [*British*] (DCTA)

FIIN........... Federal Item Identification Number

FIInfSc....... Fellow of the Institute of Information Scientists [*British*]

FIInst........ Fellow of the Imperial Institute [*British*]

FIIP........... Federation Internationale de l'Industrie Phonographique

FIISE........... Fellow of the International Institute of Social Economics [*British*] (DBQ)

FIISec........ Fellow of the Institute of Industrial Security [*British*] (DBQ)

FIJ........... Federation Internationale de Judo [*International Judo Federation*]

FIJ........... Federation Internationale des Journalistes [*International Federation of Journalists - IFJ*] [*Brussels, Belgium*] (EAIO)

FIJ........... Fellow of the Institute of Journalists [*British*]

FIJ........... Fund for Investigative Journalism (EA)

FIJA........... Fully Informed Jury Association (EA)

FIJB........... Fondation Internationale Jacques Brel [*International Jacques Brel Foundation - IJBF*] (EA)

FIJBT........ Federation Internationale des Jeunesse Bons Templiers [*International Good Templar Youth Federation*] (EAIO)

FIJC........... Federation Internationale de la Jeunesse Catholique

FIJET........ Federation Internationale des Journalistes et Ecrivains du Tourisme [*World Federation of Travel Journalists and Writers*] [*Paris, France*] (EA)

Fiji LR........ Fiji Law Reports [*A publication*] (DLA)

FIJL........... Federation Internationale des Journalistes Libres [*International Federation of Free Journalists*]

FIJM........... Federation Internationale des Jeunesses Musicales [*International Federation of Jeunesses Musicales*] (EAIO)

FIJPA........... Federation Internationale des Journalistes Professionnels de l'Aeronautique

FIJU........... Federation Internationale des Producteurs de Jus de Fruits [*International Federation of Fruit Juice Producers - IFFJP*] (EAIO)

Fik........... Families Including Kids [*Lifestyle classification*]

FIK........... Field Ionization Kinetics

FIL........... Avia Filipines International, Inc. [*Philippines*] [*ICAO designator*] (FAAC)

FIL........... Federal Industries Ltd. [*Toronto Stock Exchange symbol*]

FIL........... Federation Internationale de Laiterie [*International Dairy Federation - IDF*] (EAIO)

FIL........... Federation Internationale de Luge de Course [*International Luge Federation - ILF*] [*Rottenmann, Austria*] (EA)

FIL........... Fellow of the Institute of Linguists [*British*] (EY)

FIL........... Filament (KSC)

fil........... Filament (IDOE)

FIL........... Filigree [*Jewelry*] (ROG)

FIL........... Fillet (MSA)

FIL........... Fillister

FIL........... Filter (AABC)

FIL........... Firestone Indy Lights [*Auto racing*]

FIL........... Florida Instructional League [*Baseball*]

FIL........... Foreign Investment Law

FIL........... Franklin Institute Laboratories (MUGU)

FIL........... Fuel Injection Line (MSA)

FIL........... National Film Archives, Film Canadiana [*UTLAS symbol*]

FIL........... Sanifill, Inc. [*NYSE symbol*] (SPSG)

FILA........... Farm Improvement Loans Act [*Canada*]

FILA........... Federation Internationale de Lutte Amateur [*International Amateur Wrestling Federation*] [*Lausanne, Switzerland*] (EAIO)

FILA........... Fellow of the Institute of Landscape Architects [*British*]

FilaHold...... Fila Holdings SA [*Associated Press*] (SAG)

FILAM........... Fellow of the Institute of Leisure and Amenity Management [*British*] (DBQ)

FILAR........... Filariasis [*Infectious disease*] (DAVI)

FILBAS........ Philippine Base [*Army World War II*]

FILBDLP ...... Fondation Internationale Lelio Basso pour le Droit et la Liberation des Peuples [*International Lelio Basso Foundation for the Rights and Liberation of Peoples - ILBFRLP*] (EA)

FilBsmt........ Filenes Basement Corp. [*Associated Press*] (SAG)

FILCEN........ Filter Center

FILCO........... Film Coalition [*Defunct*] (EA)

FILD........... Federal Item Logistics Data

FILD........... Fumeless In-Line Degassing (PDAA)

FILDIR .... Federation Internationale Libre des Deportes et Internes de la Resistance [*International Free Federation of Deportees and Resistance Internees*]

Fil Dr........... Doctor of Philology

FILDR .... Federal Item Logistics Data Record

FILE........... Family Inventory of Life Events and Changes

FILE........... Fast Index Location Educators

FILE........... Feature Identification and Landmark Experiment [*NASA*]

FILE........... Fellow of the Institute of Legal Executives [*British*] (DLA)

FILE........... FileNet Corp. [*NASDAQ symbol*] (NQ)

FILE........... Florida Institute for Law Enforcement [*St. Petersburg Junior College*] [*Research center*] (RCD)

FILE........... Future Identification and Location Experiment [*NASA*] (NASA)

FileNet........ FileNet Corp. [*Associated Press*] (SAG)

FILER........... File Information Language Executive Routine [*Computer science*]

FIL et HOER... Filius [*or Filia*] et Hoeres [*Latin*] (ROG)

FILEX........... File Exchange

FILFP........... Forum International de Liaison des Forces de la Paix [*International Liaison Forum of Peace Forces - ILF*] [*Moscow, USSR*] (EAIO)

FILG........... Filing (ROG)

FILH........... Fillister Head [*Screws*]

FILHB........... Fillister Head Brass [*Screw*] (IAA)

FILHS........... Fillister Head Steel [*Screw*] (IAA)

Fil Kand........ Candidate in Philosophy

FILL........... Filling

FILL........... Fleet Issue Load List [*Navy*]

Fil Lic........... Licentiate in Philosophy

FILLM........... Federation Internationale des Langues et Litteratures Modernes [*International Federation for Modern Languages and Literatures*] (EAIO)

FILLS........... Fast Inter-Library Loans and Statistics [*MacNeal Hospital*] [*Information service or system*] (IID)

FIllumES...... Fellow of the Illuminating Engineering Society [*Formerly, FIES*] [*British*]

FILM........... CSIRO [*Commonwealth Scientific and Industrial Research Organisation*] Films [*Database*]

FILM........... Federal Land Manager (GNE)

FILM........... For Illustrating Legal Methods [*Student legal action organization*] (EA)

FILM........... Hollywood Productions, Inc. [*NASDAQ symbol*] (SAG)

Film Cr........ Film Criticism [*A publication*] (BRI)

Filmnet........ Film Users Network [*Cine Information*] [*Information service or system*] (IID)

FilmRm........ Film Roman, Inc. [*Associated Press*] (SAG)

FILMSORT ... Microfilm Sorter [*Electronics*]

FILO........... First In, Last Out [*Accounting*]

FILRAP .... Formal Integrate Long Range Planning (PDAA)

FILS........... Federal Information Locator System

FILS........... Flarescan Instrument Landing System

FILS........... Fleet Integrated Logistics Support (DNAB)

FILSG........... Fels Institute of Local and State Governments [*University of Pennsylvania*]

FILSUP .... Filament Supply (IAA)

FILT........... Federation Internationale de Lawn Tennis [*International Lawn Tennis Federation*]

FILT........... Filtra [*Filter*] [*Pharmacy*]

FILTH........... For Improved Labeling to Terminate Hazards [*Student legal action organization*]

FILU........... Four-BIT [*Binary Digit*] Interface Logic Unit

FILUP........... Franklin Institute Laboratories Universal Pulser (KSC)

FIM........... Fabric Insulation Material

FIM........... Facing Identification Mark [*Postal Service*]

FIM........... Failure Indication Modules

FIM........... Fairness in Media (EA)

FIM........... Far-Infrared MASER [*Microwave Amplification by Stimulated Emission of Radiation*]

FIM........... Fault Isolation Meter (MCD)

FIM........... Fault Isolation Module (CAAL)

FIM........... Federation Internationale des Mineurs [*Miners' International Federation - MIF*] [*Brussels, Belgium*] (EAIO)

FIM........... Federation Internationale des Musiciens [*International Federation of Musicians*] [*Zurich, Switzerland*] (EAIO)

FIM........... Federation Internationale Motocycliste [*International Motorcycle Federation*] [*Geneva, Switzerland*] (EAIO)

FIM........... Fellow of the Institute of Materials (DD)

FIM........... Fellow of the Institute of Metallurgists [*British*] (EY)

FIM........... Fellow of the Institute of Metals [*British*]

FIM........... Fellowship of Independent Missions (EA)

FIM........... Field Inspection Manual (NRCH)

FIM........... Field Instruction Memorandum

FIM........... Field Intensity Meter

FIM........... Field Ion Microscope [*or Microscopy*]

FIM........... Fillmore, CA [*Location identifier FAA*] (FAAL)

FIM........... Finnmark [*Finnish Mark*] [*Monetary unit*]

FIM........... Flame Ionization Method (PDAA)

FIM........... Flight Information Manual

FIM........... Flight Integrity Management (MCD)

FIM........... Foundation for Innovation in Medicine (EA)

FIM........... Foundation for International Meetings (EA)

FIM........... Friable Insulation Material (GNE)

FIM........... Front Interface Module [*Computer science*]

FIM........... Full Indicator Movement (MSA)

FIM........... Functional Independence Measure [*Occupational therapy*]

FIMA........... Fault Isolation Maintainability Analysis (MCD)

FIMA........... Fellow of the Institute of Mathematics and its Application [*British*]

FIMA........... Fellow of the Institute of Municipal Treasurers and Accountants [*British*]

FIMA........... Financial Institutions Marketing Association [*Chicago, IL*] (EA)

FIMA........... Financial Management System [*Marine science*] (OSRA)

FIMA........... Financial Management System (USDC)

FIMA........... Fission Initial Metal Atom [*Nuclear energy*] (NRCH)

FIMA........... Forging Ingot Makers' Association [*British*] (BI)

FIMA........... Future International Military/Civil Airfighter [*British*]

FIManf........ Fellow of the Institute of Manufacturing [*British*] (DBQ)

FIMARC ...... Federation Internationale des Mouvements d'Adultes Ruraux Catholiques [*International Federation of Adult Rural Catholic Movements*]

FIMarE........ Fellow of the Institute of Marine Engineers [*British*]

FIMATE........ Factory-Installed Maintenance Automatic Test Equipment

FIMBI........... Fellow of the Institute of Medical and Biological Illustration [*British*] (DBQ)

FIMBM......... Fellow of the Institute of Municipal Building Management [*British*] (DBQ)

FIMBRA ...... Financial Intermediaries, Managers, and Brokers Association [*British*] (ECON)

FIMC........... Federal Interagency Media Committee (EGAO)

FIMC........... Fellow of the Institute of Management Consultants [*British*]

FIMCAP....... Federation Internationale de Communautes de Jeunesse Catholique Paroissiales [*International Federation of Catholic Parochial Youth Communities*] [*Antwerp, Belgium*] (EAIO)

FIMCEE....... Federation de l'Industrie Marbriere de la Communaute Economique Europeenne [*Federation of the Marble Industry of the European Economic Community*] (EAIO)

FIMD........... Fluorescence-Imaged Microdeformation [*Analytical chemistry*]

FIME........... Federation Internationale des Maisons de l'Europe [*International Federation of Europe Houses - IFEH*] (EAIO)

FIME........... Fellow of the Institute of Marine Engineers [*British*] (DCTA)

FIME........... Fluorouracil, ICRF-159 [*Razoxane*], MeCCNU [*Semustine*] [*Antineoplastic drug regimen*]

FI Mech E... Fellow of the Institution of Mechanical Engineers [*British*]

FIMEM....... Federation Internationale des Mouvements d'Ecole Moderne (EAIO)

FIMF........... Federacion Internacional de Medecina Fisica [*International Federation of Physical Medicine*]

FIMF........... Fellow of the Institute of Metal Finishing [*British*] (DBQ)

FIMG........... Facilities Installation Monitoring Group (MUGU)

FIMG........... Fischer Imaging [*NASDAQ symbol*] (TTSB)

FIMG........... Fisher Imaging Corp. [*NASDAQ symbol*] (SPSG)

FIMgt.......... Fellow of the Institute of Management (DD)

FIMGTechE.. Fellow of the Institution of Mechanical and General Technician Engineers [*British*] (DBQ)

FIMH........... Fellow of the Institute of Materials Handling [*British*] (DBQ)

FIMI .... Fellow of the Institute of the Motor Industry [*Formerly, FIMT*] [*British*] (DBQ)

FIMIG-CEE ... Federation of the Marble Industry of the European Economic Community (EAIO)

FIMinE........ Fellow of the Institution of Mining Engineers [*British*]

FIMIS.......... Financial Management Information System [*Army*]

FIMIS.......... Fishery Management Information System [*Marine science*] (OSRA)

FIMIT.......... Fellow of the Institute of Music Instrument Technology [*British*]

FIMITIC....... Federation Internationale des Mutiles, des Invalides du Travail, et des Inval ides Civils [*International Federation of Disabled Workmen and Civilian Handicapped*] (EAIO)

FIML........... Full-Information Maximum Likelihood [*Econometrics*]

FIMLS......... Fellow of the Institute of Medical Laboratory Sciences [*British*] (DBQ)

FIMLT......... Fellow of the Institute of Medical Laboratory Technology [*British*] (DI)

FIMM........... Federation Internationale de Medicine Manuelle [*International Federation of Manual Medicine*] [*Zurich, Switzerland*] (EAIO)

FIMM........... Fellow of the Institution of Mining and Metallurgy [*British*] (DBQ)

FIMM........... Mauritius Flight Information Center [*ICAO location identifier*] (ICLI)

FIMOC .... Federation Internationale des Mouvements Ouvriers Chretiens [*International Federation of Christian Workers Movements*]

FIMP........... Federation Internationale de Medecine Physique [*International Federation of Physical Medicine*]

F Imp.......... Field Imprisonment [*British military*] (DMA)

FIMP........... Mauritius/Sir Seewoosagur Ramgoolam International [*ICAO location identifier*] (ICLI)

FIMPACS ..... Fashion Integrated Merchandising Planning and Control System (BUR)

FIMPS......... Federation Internationale de Medecine Preventive et Sociale [*International Federation for Preventive and Social Medicine*] (EAIO)

FIMR........... Federal Information Resource Management Regulations Interagency Advisory Council [*Information Resources Management Service*] [*General Services Administration*]

FIMR........... Rodriguez Island/Plaine Corail [*Mauritius*] [*ICAO location identifier*] (ICLI)

FIMS........... Facility Information Management System (MCD)

FIMS........... Fault Isolation and Monitoring System [*NGT*] (MCD)

FIMS........... Federation Internationale Medecine Sportive [*International Federation of Sportive Medicine*]

FIMS........... Fellow of the Institute of Management Specialists [*British*] (DBQ)

FIMS........... Fellowship of Interdenominational Missionary Societies

FIMS........... Field Intensity Measuring System

FIMS........... Field Ionization Mass Spectrometry [*Air-pollutant detector*]

FIMS........... Financial Information Management System [*Computer science*] (EERA)

FIMS........... Form In-Mold Surfacing [*Plastics technology*]

FIMS........... Friendly Iron Moulders Society [*A union*] [*British*]

FIMS........... Functionally-Identifiable Maintenance System [*Computer science*] (EECA)

FIMT........... Fellow of the Institute of Motor Trade [*Later, FIMI*] [*British*]

FIMT........... Firefinder Intermediate Maintenance Trainer (DWSG)

FIMTA......... Fellow of the Institute of Municipal Treasurers and Accountants [*British*]

FIMunE .... Fellow of the Institution of Municipal Engineers [*British*]

FIMV........... Figwort Mosaic Virus [*Plant pathology*]

FIN.............. Ad Finem [*At or To the End*] [*Latin*] (ADA)

Fin.............. De Finibus [*of Cicero*] [*Classical studies*] (OCD)

FIN.............. Federal Identification Number

FIN.............. Federal Item Name

FIN.............. Fellow of the Institute of Navigation [*British*]

FIN.............. Fiduciary Identification Number [*IRS*]

FIN.............. Final (WDAA)

FIN.............. Finance [*or Financial*] (AFM)

fin.............. Finance (DD)

FIN.............. Finance

Fin.............. Finance (AAGC)

Fin .... Financial (AAGC)

fin.............. Financial (WDMC)

FIN.............. Financier (WDAA)

Fin.............. Finch's English Chancery Reports [*1673-81*] [*A publication*] (DLA)

FIN.............. Findlay College, Findlay, OH [*OCLC symbol*] (OCLC)

FIN.............. Fine Intestinal Needle [*Medicine*] (DMAA)

Fin.............. Finger

FIN.............. Finis [*The End*] [*Latin*]

FIN.............. Finish (KSC)

fin.............. Finish (WDMC)

fin.............. Finish (VRA)

fin.............. Finished (VRA)

FIN.............. Finland [*ANSI three-letter standard code*] (CNC)

Fin.............. Finlay's Irish Digest [*A publication*] (DLA)

FIN.............. Finnair OY [*Finland ICAO designator*] (FAAC)

fin.............. Finnish [*MARC language code Library of Congress*] (LCCP)

FIN.............. Finschhafen [*Papua New Guinea*] [*Airport symbol*] (OAG)

FIN.............. Fleet Identification Number [*Automobile sales*]

FIN.............. Flight Interneuron [*Zoology*]

FIN.............. FOCI [*Fisheries-Oceanography Cooperative Investigations*] Interactive Network [*Marine science*] (OSRA)

FIN.............. FOCI [*Fisheries-Oceanography Cooperative Investigations*] Interactive Network (USDC)

FIN.............. Focused Information Network (EERA)

FIN.............. Franklin Real Estate Income Fund [*AMEX symbol*] (SPSG)

FIN.............. Frente de Integracion Nacional [*Front for National Integration*] [*Guatemala*]

FIN.............. Futures Information Network [*Defunct*] (EA)

FINA........... Federation Internationale de Natation Amateur [*International Amateur Swimming Federation*] [*Vancouver, BC*]

Fina .... Fina, Inc. [*Associated Press*] (SAG)

FINA........... Following Items Not Available

FINABEL...... France, Italy, Netherlands, Allemagne, Belgium, Luxembourg [*Army Chiefs of Staff Joint Committee*] (PDAA)

FINAC .... Fast Interline Nonactivate Automatic Control [*AT & T*]

FinAF.......... Finnish Air Force

FINAL.......... Financial Analysis Language [*Computer science*]

FINALCL ...... Final Coordination Line [*Military*]

FINAN .... Financial

FinancSci .... Financing for Science International, Inc. [*Associated Press*] (SAG)

Fin & Dul.... Finnemore and Dulcken's Natal Law Reports [*A publication*] (DLA)

FINANSAT... Financial Satellite Corp. [*Washington, DC Telecommunications service*] (TSSD)

FINAR .... Financial Analysis and Reporting (MHDB)

FINART........ Feria Internacional de Artesania

FINASA....... Financiera Nacional Azucarera, SNC [*Mexico*] (EY)

FINAST....... First National Stores, Inc.

FINAT.......... Federation Internationale des Fabricants et Transformateurs d'Adhesifs et Thermocollants sur Papiers et Autres Supports [*International Federation of Manufacturers and Converters of Pressure-Sensitive and Heatseals on Paper and Other Base Materials*] (EAIO)

Fin C........... Financial Code (DLA)

FINCA......... Foundation for International Community Assistance (EA)

FINCEN .... Financial Crimes Enforcement Network [*Federal task force*]

Finch .... English Chancery Reports Tempore Finch [*A publication*] (DLA)

Finch .... Finch's Precedents in Chancery [*England*] [*A publication*] (DLA)

Finch Cas Cont... Finch's Cases on Contract [*1886*] [*A publication*] (DLA)

Finch Cas Contr... Finch's Cases on Contract [*1886*] [*A publication*] (DLA)

Finch (Eng)... English Chancery Reports Tempore Finch [*A publication*] (DLA)

Finch (Eng)... Finch's Precedents in Chancery [*England*] [*A publication*] (DLA)

Finch Ins Dig... Finch's Insurance Digest [*A publication*] (DLA)

Finch LC...... Finch's Land Cases [*A publication*] (DLA)

Finch Nomot... Finch's Nomotechnia [*A publication*] (DLA)

Finch Prec... Precedents in Chancery, Edited by Finch [*A publication*] (DLA)

Finch Sum CL... Finch's Summary of the Common Law [*A publication*] (DLA)

Finci .... Financial (BARN)

FINCISCOM... Finance and Comptroller Information Systems Command [*Army*]

FinclBcp..... Financial Bancorp, Inc. [*Associated Press*] (SAG)

FinclSec ..... Financial Security Corp. [*Associated Press*] (SAG)

FINCO .... Field Intelligence Non-Commissioned Officer [*British military*] (DMA)

FINCOM .... Finance Committee [*Institute of Electrical and Electronics Engineers*] (IEEE)

F INC ST...... Fellow of the Incorporated Shorthand Teachers [*British*] (ROG)

FIND .... Facsimile Information Network Development

FIND .... Fault Isolation by Nodal Dependency (MCD)

FIND .... Federal Item Name Directory

FIND .... Festival International de Nouvelle Danse

FIND .... File Interrogation of Nineteen-Hundred Data [*Computer science*] (DIT)

FIND .... File of Industrial Data [*Computer science*]

FIND .... Flight Information Display

FIND .... Flow Information Display

FIND .... Friendless, Isolated, Needy, Disabled [*Project of National Council on the Aging - acronym used as name of New York City coffeehouse*]

FIND .... Fugitive Intercept Net Deployment [*Philadelphia police program*]

FINDAR........ Facility for Interrogating the National Directory of Australian Resources (EERA)

FINDB......... Financial Institution Data Base [*Cates Consulting Analysts, Inc.*] [*Information service or system*] (CRD)

FINDER........ Fingerprint Reader

FINDER........ Functional, Integrated, Designating, and Referencing (MCD)

Fin Dig .... Finlay's Irish Digest [*A publication*] (DLA)

FINDS .... Facility Indexing System

FINDS .... Facility Index System [*Environmental Protection Agency*] (EPA)
FINDS .... Fault Inferring Nonlinear Detection System [*NASA*]
FINE .... Fighter Inertial Navigation System
FINE .... Financial Institutions in the Nation's Economy [*Study initiated by House of Representatives*]
FINE .... Fine Hose Corp. [*NASDAQ symbol*] (SAG)
FINEBEL ...... France, Italy, Netherlands, Belgium, and Luxembourg [*Economic agreement*]
FINEFTA ...... Finland-European Free Trade Association Treaty
Fine Gard .... Fine Gardening [*A publication*]
Fine Gard .... Fine Gardening [*A publication*] (BRI)
FineHost ...... Fine Host Corp. [*Associated Press*] (SAG)
FINESS .... Fichier National des Etablissements Sanitaires et Sociaux
FINEX .... Finish Exercise [*Military*] (NVT)
FINF .... Firmen- und Marktinformationen [*Company and Market Information Data Base*] [*Society for Business Information*] [*Information service or system*] (IID)
FinFdl .... Financial Federal Corp. [*Associated Press*] (SAG)
FINFO .... First In Not Used First Out [*Processing procedure*] (NITA)
FINFO .... Flight Inspection National Field Office [*FAA*]
FING .... Financing
FINGAL .... Fixation in Glass of Active Liquid [*British*] (NUCP)
Fingerht ...... Fingerhut Companies, Inc. [*Associated Press*] (SAG)
FINI .... Financial Industry Information Service [*Database*] [*Bank Marketing Association*] [*Information service or system*]
FINIF .... Field-Induced Negative Ion Formation
FINIS .... Financial Industry Information Service [*Database*] [*Bank Marketing Association*] [*Information service or system*] (CRD)
FINISH .... Finishing
F/INJ .... Fuel Injection [*Automotive engineering*]
FINK .... Flying Infantrymen with Naval Knowledge (SAA)
Finkel Medical Cyc... Finkel, et Alia. Lawyers' Medical Cyclopedia [*A publication*] (DLA)
Fink Ev .... Fink's Indian Evidence Act [*A publication*] (DLA)
FINL .... Financial
finl .... Financial (DD)
FINL .... Finish Line 'A' [*NASDAQ symbol*] (TTSB)
FINL .... Finish Line, Inc. [*NASDAQ symbol*] (SAG)
Finl .... Finland (VRA)
Finlay .... Finlay Enterprises, Inc. [*Associated Press*] (SAG)
Finl Ch Tr .... Finlason on Charitable Trusts [*A publication*] (DLA)
Finl Com...... Finlason on Commons [*A publication*] (DLA)
Finl Dig .... Finlay's Irish Digest [*A publication*] (DLA)
FinlInd .... Financial Industries Corp. [*Associated Press*] (SAG)
FinLine .... Finish Line, Inc. [*Associated Press*] (SAG)
Finl Jud Sys... Finlason's Judicial System [*A publication*] (DLA)
Finl LC....... Finlason's Leading Cases on Pleading [*A publication*] (DLA)
Finl Ld Ten... Finlason's History of Law of Tenures of Land [*1870*] [*A publication*] (DLA)
Finl Mar L ... Finlason's Commentaries on Martial Law [*A publication*] (DLA)
FinlMgmt...... Financial Management (DD)
Finl Rep ..... Finlason's Report of the Gurney Case [*A publication*] (DLA)
Finl Riot ...... Finlay on Repression of Riot or Rebellion [*A publication*] (DLA)
Finl Ten....... Finlason's History of Law of Tenures of Land [*1870*] [*A publication*] (DLA)
FinlTrust...... Financial Trust Corp. [*Associated Press*] (SAG)
FINMAN .... Financial Management (MHDB)
FINMIS .... Financial Management and Information System
FINN .... Finnish
FINNAIR....... Aero O/Y [*Finnish airline*]
FINNIDA...... Finnish International Development Agency (International) (EERA)
FINO .... Federation of Independent Nursing Organization (DICI)
FINO .... Finance Officer [*Army*]
FINO .... Weather Report Will Not be Filed for Transmission [*NWS*] (FAAC)
Finova .... Finova Group, Inc. Finance Trust [*Associated Press*] (SAG)
FinovaGp ..... Finova Group, Inc. [*Associated Press*] (SAG)
FINP........... Finnish Periodicals Index in Economics and Business [*Helsinki School of Economics Library*] [*Information service or system*]
Fin Pr .... Finch's Precedents in Chancery [*England*] [*A publication*] (DLA)
Fin Prec...... Finch's Precedents in Chancery [*England*] [*A publication*] (DLA)
FINQ .... Final Queue (IAA)
FINR .... Financier
Fin Ren....... Finlay on Renewals [*A publication*] (DLA)
FINREP .... Final Report
Fin Rev....... Australian Financial Review [*A publication*]
FINS........... Forensically Informative Nucleotide Sequencing [*Technique for tracing genetic origin*]
FINS........... Freight Information System [*BTS*] (TAG)
FINSAP .... Financial Sector Adjustment Program [*West Africa*]
FinSci .... Financing for Science International, Inc. [*Associated Press*] (SAG)
Fin Sec....... Financial Secretary (WGA)
FinsMst....... Finishmaster, Inc. [*Associated Press*] (SAG)
FINST......... Final Station [*Computer science*]
FInstAEA ...... Fellow of the Institute of Automotive Engineer Assessors [*British*] (DBQ)
FInstAM ...... Fellow of the Institute of Administrative Management [*British*] (DBQ)
F Inst AM..... Fellow of the Institute of Administrative Management [*British*] (ODBW)
Finstat .... Financial Times Database of Key Statistical Information (MHDB)
FInstBB ...... Fellow of the Institute of British Bakers (DBQ)
FInstBCA ...... Fellow of the Institute of Burial and Cremation Administration [*British*] (DBQ)
FInstBiol ...... Fellow of the Institute of Biology [*Later, FI Biol*] [*British*]
FInstBRM..... Fellow of the Institute of Baths and Recreation Management [*British*] (DBQ)

FInstBTM ..... Fellow of the Institute of Business and Technical Management [*British*] (DBQ)
FInstC .... Fellow of the Institute of Commerce [*British*]
FInstCh ...... Fellow of the Institute of Chiropodists [*British*]
F Inst CM .... Fellow of the Institute of Commercial Management [*British*] (DCTA)
FInstD .... Fellow of the Institute of Directors [*British*]
F Inst D ...... Fellow of the Institute of Directors [*British*] (ODBW)
F Inst Dir ..... Fellow of the Institute of Directors [*British*]
FInstE .... Fellow of the Institute of Energy [*British*] (DBQ)
F Inst F........ Fellow of the Institute of Fuel [*British*]
FInstFF .... Fellow of the Institute of Freight Forwarders [*British*] (DBQ)
F Inst FF ..... Fellow of the Institute of Freight Forwarders [*British*] (ODBW)
F Inst L Ex.. Fellow of the Institute of Legal Executives [*British*] (DCTA)
FInstM .... Fellow of the Institute of Marketing [*British*]
FInstM .... Fellow of the Institute of Meat [*British*]
FInstMC ...... Fellow of the Institute of Measurement and Control [*British*] (DBQ)
FInstMet ...... Fellow of the Institute of Metals [*British*]
F Inst MSM... Fellow of the Institute of Marketing and Sales Management [*Formerly, FSMA*] [*British*]
FInstNDT..... Fellow of the British Institute of Non-Destructive Testing (DBQ)
FInstP......... Fellow of the Institute of Physics (DD)
F Inst P....... Fellow of the Institute of Physics and the Physical Society [*British*] (EY)
F Inst Pet..... Fellow of the Institute of Petroleum [*British*]
F Inst PI ..... Fellow of the Institute of Patentees and Inventors [*British*] (EY)
FInstPkg ..... Fellow of the Institute of Packaging [*British*] (DI)
FInstPRA..... Fellow of the Institute of Park and Recreation Administration [*British*] (DI)
FInstPS....... Fellow of the Institute of Purchasing and Supply [*British*]
F Inst PS .... Fellow of the Institute of Purchasing and Supply [*British*] (ODBW)
FInstR........ Fellow of the Institute of Refrigeration [*British*] (DBQ)
FInstRM...... Fellow of the Institute of Recreation Management [*British*] (DI)
FInstSM ...... Fellow of the Institute of Sales Management [*British*] (DI)
F Inst SMM... Fellow of the Institute of Sales and Marketing Management [*British*] (ODBW)
FInstSMM ... Fellow of the Institute of Sales Management [*British*] (DBQ)
FInstSP....... Fellow of the Institute of Sewage Purification (DAVI)
F INST ST ... Fellow of the Institute of Shorthand Teachers [*British*] (ROG)
F Inst TA..... Fellow of the Institute of Transport Administration [*British*] (DCTA)
FInstW .... Fellow of the Institute of Welding [*British*]
FInstWM..... Fellow of the Institute of Wastes Management [*British*] (DBQ)
FInstWM(Hon)... Honorary Fellowship of the Institute of Wastes Management [*British*] (DBQ)
FINSUPSCOL... Finance and Supply School [*Coast Guard*]
FIN-SYN....... Financial Interest and Syndication Rules [*FCC*]
FInt .... First Interstate Bancorp [*Associated Press*] (SAG)
Fin T .... T. Finch's Precedents in English Chancery [*1689-1722*] [*A publication*] (DLA)
Fin Tax & Comp L... Finance Taxation and Co. Law [*Pakistan*] [*A publication*] (DLA)
FinTech....... Financial Technology [*Publisher*] [*British*]
FINTEL .... Financial Times Company Information Database [*Financial Times Business Information Ltd. and Predicasts*] [*Bibliographic database*] [*British*]
FINTEL .... Financial Times Electronic Publishing [*Financial Times*] [*British*] (NITA)
FINTOR .... Frascali-Ispra-Naples Torus (MCD)
FIntste .... First Interstate Bancorp [*Associated Press*] (SAG)
FI Nucl E ..... Fellow of the Institution of Nuclear Engineers [*British*]
FINUFO .... First-In/Not-Used/First-Out [*Replacement algorithm*] [*Computer science*] (BYTE)
FINZ........... Fund Raising Institute of New Zealand (NFD)
FIO............. Far-Infrared Observation
FIO............. Federacion Internacional de Oleicultura [*International Olive Oil Federation*] [*Rome, Italy*] [*Defunct*] (EA)
FIO............. Federation Internationale d'Oleiculture [*International Olive Growers Federation*]
FIO............. Fellow of the Institute of Ophthalmic Opticians [*British*]
FIO............. Field Input/Output [*Computer science*] (ECII)
FIO............. Field Intelligence Officer [*British military*] (DMA)
FIO............. Fleet In and Out (DNAB)
FIO............. Fleet Instruction Officer [*Navy British*]
FIO............. Fleet Intelligence Officer
FIO............. Florida Institute of Oceanography
FIO............. Foreign Intelligence Office
FIO............. For Information Only (AAG)
FIO............. Fraction Inspired Oxygen [*Physiology*]
FIO............. Free In and Out [*Shipping*]
FIO............. Furnished and Installed by Others (MCD)
FIO............. Paducah, KY [*Location identifier FAA*] (FAAL)
FIO$_2$ .... Forced Inspiratory Oxygen [*Physiology*]
FIO$_2$ .... Fractional Concentration of Inspired Oxygen [*Physiology*] (DAVI)
FIOB.......... Fellow of the Institute of Builders [*British*]
FIOC.......... Fellow of the Institute of Carpenters [*British*] (DBQ)
FIOC.......... Final Initial Operational Capability [*Aerospace*] (AAG)
FIOCC .... Federation Internationale des Ouvriers de la Chaussure et du Cuir [*International Shoe and Leather Worker's Federation*]
FIOCES .... Federation Internationale des Organisations de Correspondances et d'Echanges Scolaires [*International Federation of Organizations for School Correspondence and Exchange*] [*Paris, France*] (EA)
FIODS .... Federation Internationale des Organisations de Donneurs de Sang Benevoles [*International Federation of Blood Donor Organizations - IFBDO*] [*Dole, France*] (EAIO)
FIOE............ Fraternite Internationale des Ouvriers en Electricite [*International Brotherhood of Electrical Workers - IBEW*] [*Canada*]

FIOM............ Federation Internationale des Organisations de Travailleurs de la Metallurgie [*International Metalworkers Federation - IMF*] [*Geneva, Switzerland*]

FIOM............ Federation Internationale des Ouvriers sur Metaux [*International Metalworkers' Federation*]

FIOP............ Fellow of the Institute of Plumbing [*British*] (DBQ)

FIOP............ Fellow of the Institute of Printing [*British*] (DBQ)

FIOP............ FORTRAN [*Formula Translating System*] Input-Output Package [*Computer science*] (IEEE)

FIOPM........ Federation Internationale des Organismes de Psychologie Medicale [*International Federation of the Psychological-Medical Organizations - IFPMO*] (EAIO)

FIORH......... Federation Internationale pour l'Organisation de Rencontres de Handicapes [*International Federation for the Organization of Meetings for the Handicapped*]

FIOS............ Free In and Out and Stowed [*Shipping*]

FIOSH......... Fellow of the Institution of Occupational Safety and Health [*British*] (DCTA)

FIOSS.......... Federation Internationale des Organisations de Sciences Sociales [*International Federation of Social Science Organizations - IFSSO*] (EAIO)

FIOST........... Federation Internationale des Organisations Syndicales du Personnel des Transporte [*International Federation of Trade Unions of Transport Workers - IFTUTW*] (EAIO)

FIOT............ Fellow of the Institute of Operating Theatre Technicians [*British*]

FIOT............ Free In and Out and Trimmed [*Shipping*]

FIOT............ Free In and Out of Trucks [*Business term*]

FIOTV.......... Tuula Vauhkonen [*Regional Institute of Occupational Health*], Oulv, Finland [*Library symbol*] [*Library of Congress*] (LCLS)

FIOU............ Film Input/Output Unit

FIOU............ Oulun Yliopisto [*Oulu University*], Oulu, Finland [*Library symbol Library of Congress*] (LCLS)

FIP.............. Fact Issue Paper

FIP.............. Fairly Important Person

FIP.............. Family Involvement Process [*Used to encourage parental support in the education of handicapped children*]

FIP.............. Far-Infrared Pointer

FIP.............. Fastener Installation Procedure [*Manual*] (MCD)

FIP.............. Fault Isolation Procedure

FIP.............. Federacion Internacional de Periodistas [*International Federation of Journalists*]

FIP.............. Federal Identity Program [*Canada*]

FIP.............. Federal Implementation Plan [*Environmental Protection Agency*] (ERG)

FIP.............. Federal Information Processing [*ANSI*] (EECA)

FIP.............. Federation Internationale de la Precontrainte [*International Federation of Prestressed Concrete*] (EAIO)

FIP.............. Federation Internationale de Philatelie [*International Federation of Philately*] (EAIO)

FIP.............. Federation Internationale de Podologie [*International Federation of Podology*]

FIP.............. Federation Internationale des Phonotheques [*International Federation of Record Libraries*]

FIP.............. Federation Internationale des Pietons [*International Federation of Pedestrians*] [*Netherlands*]

FIP.............. Federation Internationale Pharmaceutique [*International Pharmaceutical Federation*] [*The Hague, Netherlands*] (EAIO)

FIP.............. Feline Infectious Peritonitis

FIP.............. Fellow of the Institute of Physics [*British*]

FIP.............. Fellowship in Prayer [*EA*]

FIP.............. Field Inspection Procedure (NRCH)

FIP.............. Final Implementation Plan (EPA)

FIP.............. Finance Image Processor [*Computer science*] (IBMDP)

FIP.............. Fire Insurance Policy [*Legal shorthand*] (LWAP)

FIP.............. First Ionization Potential [*Physical chemistry*]

FIP.............. Fleet Improvement Program [*Navy*]

FIP.............. Fleet Indoctrination Program [*Navy*] (MCD)

FIP.............. Fleet Information Program [*Navy*]

FIP.............. Fleet Introduction Program [*Navy*]

FIP.............. Flight Instruction Program [*Air Force*] (AFM)

FIP.............. Fluorescence Indicator Panel (IAA)

FIP.............. Foamed-in-Place [*Plastics technology*]

FIP.............. Force Improvement Plan (MCD)

FIP.............. Forestry Incentive Program [*US Forest Service*]

FIP.............. Formed-in-Place

FIP.............. Free Instrument Package

FIP.............. Frente de Izquierda Popular [*Popular Left Front*] [*Argentina Political party*] (PPW)

FIP.............. Fuel Injection Pressure (KSC)

FIP.............. Fuel Injection Pump (MSA)

FIP.............. Future Impact Point (MCD)

FIPA............ Federation Internationale des Producteurs Agricoles [*International Federation of Agricultural Producers*]

FIPA............ Federation of International Poetry Associations (EA)

FIPA............ Fellow of the Institute of Practitioners in Advertising [*British*]

FIPA............ Fellow of the Institute of Public Administration [*British*]

FIPA............ Festival International de Programmes Audiovisuels

FIPACE........ Federation Internationale des Producteurs Auto-Consommateurs Industriels d'Electricite [*International Federation of Industrial Producers of Electricity for Own Consumption*]

FIPAD......... Fondation Internationale pour un Autre Developpement [*International Foundation for Development Alternatives - IFDA*] [*Nyon, Switzerland*] (EAIO)

FIPAGO....... Federation Internationale des Fabricants de Papiers Gommes [*International Federation of Manufacturers of Gummed Paper*] (EAIO)

FIPAH.......... Federation des Importateurs et Producteurs d'Adjuvants et Additifs pour Coulis Mortier et Beton de Ciment [*Association of Importers and Producers of Admixtures*]

FIPAS.......... Flight Information Publication, Alaska Supplement [*Air Force*] (DNAB)

FIPC............ Federation Internationale des Pharmaciens Catholiques [*International Federation of Catholic Pharmacists*] [*Eupen, Belgium*] (EAIO)

FIPC............ Fellow of the Institute of Production Control [*British*] (DBQ)

FIPC............ Fishing Industry Policy Council [*Australia*]

FIPCO.......... Fully Integrated Pharmaceutical Company [*Business term*]

FIPD............ Fellow of the Institute of Professional Designers

FIPE............ Fund for the Improvement of Postsecondary Education [*Department of Education*] (EGAO)

FIPESO........ Federation Internationale des Professeurs de l'Enseignement Secondaire Officiel [*International Federation of Secondary Teachers*]

FIPET.......... Federacion Interamericana de Periodistas y Escritores de Turismo [*Interamerican Federation of Journalists and Writers in the Tourist Trade*]

FIPF............ Federation Internationale des Professeurs de Francais [*International Federation of Teachers of French - IFTF*] (EAIO)

FIPFP.......... Federation Internationale des Petits Freres des Pauvres [*International Federation of the Little Brothers of the Poor - IFLBP*] (EAIO)

FIPG............ Formed-in-Place Gasket [*Automotive engineering*]

FIPG............ Formed-in-Place Plastic Gasket [*Automotive engineering*]

FIPHE.......... Fellow of the Institution of Public Health Engineers [*British*]

FIPI............ Fellow of the Institute of Professional Investigators [*British*] (DBQ)

FIPIS........... Fishery Project Information System [*FAO*] [*United Nations*] (DUND)

FIPJF........... Federation Internationale des Producteurs de Jus de Fruits [*International Federation of Fruit Juice Producers - IFFJP*]

FIPJP........... Federation Internationale de Petanque et Jeu Provencal [*Marseille, France*] (EAIO)

FIPlantE...... Fellow of the Institution of Plant Engineers [*British*] (DBQ)

FIPLF........... Federation Internationale de la Presse de Langue Francaise [*EA*]

FIPLV.......... Federation Internationale des Professeurs de Langues Vivantes [*International Federation of Modern Language Teachers*] [*Switzerland*]

FIPM............ Federation Internationale de la Philatelie Maritime [*International Federation of Maritime Philately - IFMP*] (EA)

FIPM............ Federation Internationale de Psychotherapie Medicale [*International Federation for Medical Psychotherapy*]

FIPM............ Fellow of the Institute of Personnel Management [*Later, CIPM*] [*British*]

FIPMEC....... Federation Internationale des Petites et Moyennes Entreprises Commerciales [*International Federation of Small and Medium-Sized Commercial Enterprises*]

FIPOL.......... Fonds International d'Indemnisation pour les Dommages dus a la Pollution par lesHydrocarbures [*International Oil Pollution Compensation Fund*] (EAIO)

FIPP............ Far-Infrared Pointer Package

FIPP............ Federation Internationale de la Presse Periodique [*International Federation of the Periodical Press*] (EAIO)

FIPP............ Federation Internationale pour la Protection des Populations

FIPP............ Fondation Internationale Penale et Penitentiaire [*International Penal and Penitentiary Foundation - IPPF*] [*Bonn, Federal Republic of Germany*] (EAIO)

FIPR............ Fellow of the Institute of Public Relations [*British*]

FIPR............ Foreign Intelligence Production Requirement [*Army*] (RDA)

FIPR............ Foundation for International Potash Research [*Later, PI*] (EA)

FIPRA.......... Federation Internationale de la Presse Agricole

FIPRECAN... Fire Prevention Canada Association

FIPREGA...... Federation Internationale de la Presse Gastronomique et Vinicole [*International Federation of Gastronomical and Vinicultural Press*]

FIPRESCI.... Federation Internationale de la Presse Cinematographique [*International Federation of the Cinematographic Press - IFCP*] (EAIO)

FIProdE....... Fellow of the Institution of Production Engineers [*British*]

FIPS............ Federal Information Procedures System [*Environmental Protection Agency*] (ERG)

FIPS............ Federal Information Processing Standard (EERA)

FIPS............ Federal Information Processing Standards [*Gaithersburg, MD*] [*National Institute of Standards and Technology*]

FIPS............ Fellow of the Incorporated Phonographic Society [*British*] (ROG)

FIPS............ First Independent Political Success [*Political campaigning*]

FIPS............ Flight Information Positioning System

FIPS............ Foreign Interest Payment Security [*Investment term*]

FIPSCAC..... Federal Information Processing Standards Coordinating and Advisory Committee [*National Institute of Standards and Technology*]

FIPSCAC...... FIPS [*Federal Information Processing Standard*] Coordinating and Advis ory Committee (NITA)

FIPSE.......... Fund for the Improvement of Postsecondary Education [*Department of Education*]

FIPSG.......... Falkland Islands Philatelic Study Group [*of the American Philatelic Society*] [*Fordingbridge, Hampshire, England*] (EAIO)

FIPS-PUB.... Federal Information Processing Standards Publication [*National Institute of Standards and Technology*]

FIPSR.......... Federal Information Processing Standards Register [*National Institute of Standards and Technology*]

FI PTG M..... Fellow of the Institute of Printing Management [*British*] (DGA)

FIPTP.......... Federation Internationale de la Presse Technique et Periodique [*International Federation of the Technical and Periodical Press*]

FIPUB.......... Flight Information Publication [*Air Force*] (NVT)

FIPV............ Federacion Internacional de Pelota Vasca [*International Federation of Pelota Vasca - IFPV*] (EA)
FIPV............ Feline Infectious Peritonitis Virus
FIQ.............. Federation Internationale des Quillieurs [*International Federation of Bowlers*] [*Espoo, Finland*] (EA)
FIQ.............. Fellow of the Institute of Quarrying [*British*] (DBQ)
FIQ.............. Morganton, NC [*Location identifier FAA*] (FAAL)
FIQA........... Fellow of the Institute of Quality Assurance [*British*] (DBQ)
FIQPS .... Fellow of the Institute of Qualified Private Secretaries [*British*] (DI)
FIQS........... Fellow of the Institute of Quantity Surveyors [*British*] (DI)
FIR.............. Facility Installation Review
FIR.............. Facility Interference Review
FIR.............. Failed Item Report
FIR.............. Far Infrared
FIR.............. Far-Infrared Radiometer
FIR.............. Fault Isolation Routine
FIR.............. Federation Internationale des Resistants [*International Federation of Resistance Movements*]
FIR.............. Fellow of the Institute of Population Registration [*British*] (DBQ)
FIR.............. Field Information Release (MCD)
FIR.............. Field Information Report [*CIA*]
FIR.............. Field Intensity Receiver
FIR.............. File Indirect Register
FIR.............. Films in Review [*A publication*] (BRI)
FIR.............. Final Inspection Record [*Army*]
FIR.............. Final Inspection Report (MCD)
FIR.............. Financial Inter-Relations Ratio
FIR.............. Financial Inventory Report
FIR.............. Finite Impulse Response [*Filter*] (MCD)
FIR.............. Finnish Reactor
FIR.............. Fired (MSA)
FIR.............. Firenze Ximeniano [*Florence*] [*Italy*] [*Seismograph station code, US Geological Survey*] (SEIS)
FIR.............. Firkin
FIR.............. First Citizens BancStock (SPSG)
FIR.............. First Citizens Bank Stock [*AMEX symbol*] (SAG)
FIR.............. First City Trustco, Inc. [*Vancouver Stock Exchange symbol*]
FIR.............. Flight Information Region [*FAA*]
FIR.............. Flight Information Report
FIR.............. Flight Information Requirement (NVT)
FIR.............. Flight Inspection Report (NG)
FIR.............. Floating-In Rates
FIR.............. Flow Indicator Recorder [*Electronics*] (ECII)
FIR.............. Fluorescent Ionic Resin (MCD)
FIR.............. Food Irradiation Reactor
FIR.............. Frente de Izquierda Revolucionaria [*Peru*]
FIR.............. Freshwater Institute Report [*United Nations*]
FIR.............. Fuel Indicator Reading
FIR.............. Full Indicator Reading
FIR.............. Full Inspection Report (MCD)
FIR.............. Functional Input Report (MCD)
FIR.............. Functional Item Replacement [*Program*] [*Navy*] (NG)
FIR.............. Future Issue Requirement
FIRA........... Falciparum Interspersed Repeat Antigen [*Genetics*]
FIRA........... Federation Internationale de Football-Rugby Amateur [*International Amateur Rugby Foundation*] (EA)
FIRA........... Fontes Iuris Romani ante Iustiniani [*A publication*] (OCD)
FIRA........... Foreign Investment Review Act [*1973*] [*Canada*] (IMH)
FIRA........... Foreign Investment Review Act [*Canada*] (AAGC)
FIRA........... Foreign Investment Review Agency [*Canada*]
FIRA........... Freedom of Information Reform Act of 1986
FIRA........... Furniture Industry Research Association [*Research center British*] (IRC)
FIRAA .... Fire Insurance Research and Actuarial Association [*Later, ISO*] (EA)
FIRA(Ind)..... Fellow of the Institute of Railway Auditors and Accountants (India)
FIRAMS ...... Flight Incident Recorder and Aircraft Monitoring System (MCD)
FIRAS .... Far-Infrared Absolute Spectrophotometer
FIRAV .... First Available [*Military*]
FIRB........... Flight Information Region Boundary (FAAC)
FIRC........... Fishing Industry Research Council (EERA)
FIRC........... Flow Indicator Recorder Controller [*Electronics*] (ECII)
FIRC........... Forest Industries Radio Communications [*Later, FIT*] (EA)
FIR/CPL ...... Flight Incident Recorder/Crash Position Locator [*Navy*] (RDA)
FIRD........... Far-Infrared Detector
FIRD........... Fault Isolation Requirement Document (MCD)
FIRDA .... Frontal, Intermittent Delta Activity [*Medicine*] (DMAA)
FIRDC .... Fishing Industry Research and Development Council (EERA)
FIRDC .... Forest Industry Research and Development Corp. [*Commercial firm Australia*]
FIRE........... Factor Information Retrieval Data System [*Information service or system*] (IID)
FIRE........... Feedback Information Request Evidence (DNAB)
FIRE........... Fellow of the Institution of Radio Engineers [*British*]
FIRE........... Finance, Insurance, and Real Estate [*Insurance*]
FIRE........... Financial Institutions Insurance Group Ltd. [*NASDAQ symbol*] (SAG)
FIRE........... Financial Reporting System
FIRE........... Fingerprint Reader
FIRE........... Finl Institutions Insur Grp [*NASDAQ symbol*] (TTSB)
FIRE........... First International Radiation Experiment [*Climatology*]
FIRE........... First ISCCP [*International Satellite Cloud Climatology Project*] Regional Experiment [*National Oceanic and Atmospheric Administration*]
FIRE........... Flame Infrared Emission
FIRE........... Flight in a Radiation Environment
FIRE........... Flight Investigation of the Reentry Environment

FIRE........... Forwarding Indian Resposibility in Education [*Bureau of Indian Affairs*] [*Department of the Interior*] (AEBS)
FIRE........... Foundation for Insurance Reform and Education
FIRE........... Fully Integrated Robotized Engine [*FIAT*]
Fire & Cas Cas... Fire and Casualty Cases [*A publication*] (DLA)
FIREC......... Federation Internationale des Redacteurs en Chef
Firefox........ Firefox Communications, Inc. [*Associated Press*] (SAG)
FIREMEN .... Fire Resistant Materials Engineering (PDAA)
FIRE PLAN... Fleet Improved Readiness by Expediting Procurement, Logistics, and Negotiations [*Navy*] (NG)
Firetct......... Firetector, Inc. [*Associated Press*] (SAG)
FIRETRAC .... Firing Error Trajectory Recorder and Computer
FIRE USA.... Finance, Insurance, and Real Estate USA [*A publication*]
FIREX......... Fire Extinguisher [*or Extinguishing*] System (AAG)
FIREX......... Firing Exercise (NVT)
FIREX/SAMEX... Free-Flying Imagine RADAR Experiment/Soviet-American Microwave Experiment (MCD)
FIRFLT........ First Fleet [*Pacific*] [*Navy*]
FIRG .... Firing (FAAC)
FIRI .... Fellow of the Institution of the Rubber Industry [*British*]
FIRIRCA...... Financial Institutions Regulatory and Interest Rate Control Act of 1978
FIRIV .... Arrival Report Will be Filed With [*Aviation*] (FAAC)
FIRL........... Faceted Information Retrieval for Linguistics (PDAA)
FIRL........... Fleet Issue Requirements List [*Navy*]
FIRL........... Franklin Institute Research Laboratories
FIRL/SG ...... Fleet Issue Requirements List/Shopping Guide [*Navy*] (MCD)
FIRM.......... Federation Internationale des Reconstructeurs de Moteurs [*International Federation of Engine Reconditioners - IFER*] (EAIO)
FIRM.......... Financial Information for Resources Management (AFM)
FIRM.......... Financial Institutions Resource Management [*Online database*]
FIRM.......... Firstmark Corp. [*NASDAQ symbol*] (SAG)
FIRM.......... Fleet Induction Replacement Model [*Navy*]
FIRM.......... Fleet Intensified Repairables Management (DNAB)
FIRM.......... Flood Insurance Rate Map
FIRM.......... Forum on Information Resources and Microcomputers (NITA)
FIRMA .... Firepower and Maneuver [*Army*] (AABC)
FIRMCO ...... Federal Information Requirements Management Council
FIRMN .... Fireman
FIRMR .... Federal Information Resources Management Regulation [*A publication*] (AAGC)
FIRMR .... Federal Information Resources Management Regulation Interagency Advisory Council [*Information Resources Management Service*] [*General Services Administration*] (EGAO)
FIRMS .... Forecasting Information Retrieval of Management System (IEEE)
FIRMS .... Foreign Intelligence Relations Management System (MCD)
FIRMS .... Fourier Ion Resonance Mass Spectrometer
FIRN .... Florida Information Resource Network (EDAC)
FIRO .... Far-Infrared Observation
FIRO .... Fundamental Interpersonal Relations Orientation [*Psychology*]
FIRO-B........ Fundamental Interpersonal Relations Orientation - Behavior
FIRO-BC...... Fundamental Interpersonal Relations Orientation - Behavior Characteristics [*Personality development test*] [*Psychology*]
FIRO-F .... Fundamental Interpersonal Relations Orientation - Feelings [*Personality development test*] [*Psychology*]
FIRP.......... Far-Infrared Pointer
FIRP........... Federal Internetworking Requirements Panel [*Telecommunications*] (ACRL)
FIRP.......... Functional Item Replacement Program [*Navy*]
FIRPP .... Far-Infrared Pointer Package
FIRPTA .... Foreign Investment in Real Property Tax Act of 1980
FIRQ .... Fast Interrupt Request (IAA)
FIRR .... Federation for Industrial Retention and Renewal (CROSS)
FIRRE .... Financial Institutions Reform, Recovery, and Enforcement Act [*1989*] [*Also, FIRREA Pronounced "Fire"*]
FIRREA .... Financial Institutions Reform, Recovery, and Enforcement Act [*1989*] [*Pronounced "fi-ree-a"*]
FIRS........... Far-Infrared Spectrometer
FIRS........... Federal Information Relay Service (USGC)
FIRS........... Federation Internationale de Roller-Skating [*International Roller Skating Federation*] (EAIO)
FIRS........... Field Incident Radio System [*Nuclear energy*] (NRCH)
FIRS........... File Interrogation and Reporting System [*Computer science*]
FIRS........... Forest Inventory and Regeneration System
FIRSE .... Fellow of the Institute of Railway Signal Engineers [*British*] (DBQ)
FIRSE .... Field Reference Scene Equipment (MCD)
FIRST......... Fabrication of Inflatable Reentry Structures for Test [*Air Force*]
FIRST......... Far Infrared and Submillimeter Space Telescope [*Proposed European*]
FIRST......... Far-Infrared Search and Track
FIRST......... Far Infrared Space Telescope
FIRST......... Fast Implementation of Real Time Signal Transforms [*University of Edinburgh*] [*Silicone compiler*] [*British*] (NITA)
FIRST......... Fast Information Retrieval for Surface Transportation [*IBM Corp.*]
FIRST......... Fast Interactive Retrieval System Technology
FIRST......... Federal Information Research Science and Technology (DICI)
FIRST......... Federal Information Research Science and Technology Network (NITA)
FIRST......... Feeding Interaction Report, Scale, and Treatment [*Occupational therapy*]
FIRST......... Financial Information Reporting System [*Computer science*]
FIRST......... Fire Information Retrieval System Technique
FIRST......... FIRST - Foundation for Ichthyosis and Related Skin Types (EA)

FIRST........... First Independent Research Support and Transition Award [*National Institutes of Health*]
FIRST........... Fleet Input and Reserve Support Training
FIRST........... Foundation for Ichthyosis and Related Skin Types   (PAZ)
FIRST........... Fourier Infrared Software Tools
FIRST........... Fully Integrated Road Safety Technology [*Automotive safety*]
FIRST........... Fund for the Improvement and Reform of Schools and Teaching [*Department of Education*]   (GFGA)
FIRST........... Futures Information Retrieval System [*Congressional Research Service*]
FIRSTA .... Fund for the Improvement and Reform of Schools and Teaching Act [*1988*]
Firstar........ Firstar Corp. [*Associated Press*]   (SAG)
FIRSTASKFLT... First Task Fleet
First Bk Judg... First Book of Judgments [*1655*] [*England*] [*A publication*]   (DLA)
First Book Judg... First Book of Judgments [*1655*] [*England*] [*A publication*]   (DLA)
Firstier........ FirsTier Financial, Inc. [*Associated Press*]   (SAG)
FirstInv .... First Investors Financil Services Group, Inc. [*Associated Press*]   (SAG)
First Pt Edw III... Part II of the Year Books [*A publication*]   (DLA)
First Pt H VI... Part VII of the Year Books [*A publication*]   (DLA)
FIRSTS .... Floating-Interest-Rate Short-Term Securities [*Shearson Lehman Brothers, Inc.*]
FIRT............. Federation Internationale pour la Recherche Theatrale [*International Federation for Theatre Research - IFTR*]   (EAIO)
FIRT............. Fertilizer Industry Round Table   (EA)
FIRTA........... Far-Infrared Technical Area [*Night Vision Laboratories*] [*Army*]   (RDA)
FIRTA........... Fishing Industry Research Trust Account   (EERA)
FIRTE........... Fellow of the Institute of Road Transport Engineers [*British*]
FIRTI............ Far Infrared Target Indicator [*Military*]
FIRTS........... Following Individual Reported This Station [*Army*]   (AABC)
FiRUL-A........ University of Lapland, Lapland Artic Center, Rovaniemi, Lapland [*Library symbol*] [*Library of Congress*]   (LCLS)
firwd .... Firwood   (VRA)
FIS............... Fachinformationssystem [*Information service or system*] [*Germany*]   (NITA)
FIS............... Facilities Inventory Study
FIS............... Facility Interface Sheet
FIS............... Fairy Investigation Society [*Inactive*]   (EA)
FIS............... Family Income Supplement   (ODBW)
FIS............... Farallon Islands   (GAAI)
FIS............... Far-Infrared Search
FIS............... Far-Infrared Spectrometer
FIS............... Farm Income Situation
FIS............... Fault Isolation Software   (CAAL)
FIS............... Fauna Impact Statement
FIS............... Feasible Ideal System   (MHDI)
FIS............... Federation Internationale de Sauvetage Aquatique [*Germany*]
FIS............... Federation Internationale des Centres Sociaux et Communautaires [*International Federation of Settlements and Neighborhood Centers*]
FIS............... Federation Internationale de Ski [*International Ski Federation*] [*Gumlingen, Switzerland*]   (EA)
FIS............... Federation Internationale du Commerce des Semences [*International Federation of the Seed Trade*]
FIS............... Federation Internationale pour la Sante [*International Federation for Health*] [*France*]   (EAIO)
FIS............... Fellow of the Institute of Statisticians [*British*]
FIS............... Fellow of the Institution of Surveyors [*British*]
FIS............... Fellowship of Independent Schools [*British*]
FIS............... Field Information System [*Computer science*]
FIS............... Field Infrared Spectrometer
FIS............... Field Installation Simulator
FIS............... Field Instruction System
FIS............... Fighter Identification System
FIS............... Fighter-Interceptor Squadron [*Air Force*]
FIS............... Financial Information System
FIS............... Financial Inventory Subsidiary
FIS............... Finite Intermediate Storage [*Industrial engineering*]
FIS............... FINSAP Implementation Secretariat [*West Africa*]
FIS............... Fire Island [*Alaska*] [*Seismograph station code, US Geological Survey Closed*]   (SEIS)
FIS............... Fiscal
FIS............... Fiscal Information System
FIS............... Fleet Indoctrination Site [*Navy*]
FIS............... Fleet Information Service [*Navy*]
FIS............... Flexible Inspection System
FIS............... Flight Information Service   (AFM)
FIS............... Floating-Point Instruction Set [*Computer science*]   (MSA)
FIS............... Fluid Induction System [*Automotive engineering*]
FIS............... Fluoroimmunosensor [*Analytical chemistry*]
FIS............... Flying Instrument School [*British military*]   (DMA)
FIS............... Foam in System
FIS............... Fondation Internationale pour la Science [*International Foundation for Science - IFS*]   (EAIO)
FIS............... Force Information Service [*Military*]   (NVT)
FIS............... Foreign Instrumentation Signals   (MCD)
FIS............... Forest Industry Strategy   (EERA)
FIS............... FORSCOM [*Forces Command*] Information System [*DoD*]   (GFGA)
FIS............... Foundations of Information Science [*American Society for Information Science*]
FIS............... Fourier Interferometric Stimulation [*Instrumentation*]
FIS............... Four-Impinging-Stream Reactor [*Chemical engineering*]
FIS............... Freedom Information Service   (EA)
FIS............... Free in Store [*Business term*]

FIS............... Freight, Insurance, and Shipping Charges [*Business term*]
FIS............... Friendly Information System [*Military*]   (RDA)
FIS............... Front Islamique de Salut [*Algeria*] [*Political party*]
FIS............... Fuel Injection System [*Automotive engineering*]
FIS............... Functional Interface Specification [*Telecommunications*]   (TEL)
FIS............... Islamic Salvation Front [*Algeria*] [*Political party*]   (ECON)
FIS............... Key West, FL [*Location identifier FAA*]   (FAAL)
Fis............... Physicist
FISA............. Automated Flight Information Service [*ICAO designator*]   (FAAC)
FISA............. Federation Internationale des Semaines d'Art
FISA............. Federation Internationale des Societes Aerophilateliques [*International Federation of Aero-Philatelic Societies*] [*Zurich Airport, Switzerland*]   (EAIO)
FISA............. Federation Internationale des Societes d'Aviron [*International Rowing Federation*] [*Neuchatel, Switzerland*]   (EAIO)
FISA............. Federation Internationale du Sport Automobile [*Paris, France*]   (EAIO)
FISA............. Fellow of the Incorporated Secretaries' Association [*British*]
FISA............. Financial Information Services Agency
FISA............. Financial Institutions Supervisory Act of 1966
FISA............. Fondation Internationale pour le Saumon de l'Atlantique [*International Atlantic Salmon Foundation*] [*Canada*]
FISA............. Food Industries Suppliers Association   (EA)
FISA............. Foreign Intelligence Surveillance Act of 1978
FISAA........... Fellow of the Incorporated Society of Accountants and Auditors [*British*]   (DAS)
FISAC........... Fellow of the Incorporated Society of Advertisement Consultants [*British*]   (DAS)
FISAE........... Federation Internationale des Societes d'Amateurs d'Exlibris [*British*]   (EAIO)
FISAIC .... Federation Internationale des Societes Artistiques et Intellectuelles de Cheminots [*International Federation of Railwaymen's Art and Intellectual Societies*]
FISAP........... Fiscal Operations Report and Application to Participate [*Department of Education*]   (GFGA)
FISAR .... Federal Institute for Snow and Avalanche Research
FISAR .... Fleet Information Storage and Retrieval [*Navy*]
FISB............. Federal Internal Security Board [*Formerly, Subversive Activities Control Board*]
FISB............. Federation Internationale de Skibob [*Germany*]   (EAIO)
FISB............. First Indiana Corp. [*NASDAQ symbol*]   (NQ)
FISC............. Federal Information Systems Corp.   (IID)
FISC............. Fiscal   (MUGU)
FISC............. Fiscal
FISC............. Fleet and Industrial Supply Center [*Formerly, Naval Supply Center, Norfolk, VA.; changed in 1993*]   (DOMA)
FISC............. Flight Instrument Signal Converter   (MCD)
FISC............. Foundation for International Scientific Co-Ordination [*Paris, France*]   (EAIO)
FISC............. Fuel Inspection and Sampling Cell [*Nuclear energy*]   (NRCH)
FISC............. Fur Industry Salvage Commission [*New Deal*]
FISCA........... Flexible Integrated Solar Cell Assembly
FISCETCV .... Federation Internationale des Syndicats Chretiens d'Employes, Techniciens, Cadres, et Voyageurs de Commerce [*International Federation of Christian Trade Unions of Salaried Employees, Technicians, Managers, and Commercial Travellers*]
FischIm........ Fischer Imaging Corp. [*Associated Press*]   (SAG)
FISCM......... Federation Internationale des Syndicats Chretiens de la Metalurgie [*International Federation of Christian Metalworkers Unions*]
FISCO .... Fuji International Speedway Co. [*Automobile racing*]
FISCOA .... Federation Internationale des Syndicats Chretiens d'Ouvriers Agricoles [*International Federation of Christian Agricultural Workers Unions*]
FISCOBB ...... Federation Internationale des Syndicats Chretiens d'Ouvriers du Batiment et du Bois [*International Federation of Christian Trade Unions of Building and Wood Workers*]
FIS-COV....... Fire Survivability for Ground Combat Vehicles   (MCD)
FISCTTH ...... Federation Internationale des Syndicats Chretiens des Travailleurs du Textile etde l'Habillement [*International Federation of Christian Trade Unions of Textile and Clothing Workers*]
FISD............. Federation Internationale de Stenographie et de Dactylographie [*International Federation of Shorthand and Typewriting*]
FISDO .... Flight Standards District Office [*FAA*]
FISDW .... Field-Induced Spin Density Wave [*Physics*]
FISE............. Federation Internationale Syndicale de l'Enseignement [*World Federation of Teachers' Unions*] [*Berlin, Federal Republic of Germany*]   (EAIO)
FISE............. Fellow of the Institution of Sanitary Engineers [*British*]
FISE............. Fonds International de Secours a l'Enfance [*Also known as Fonds des Nations Unies pour l'Enfance*] [*Canada*]
FISEC........... Federation Internationale Sportive de l'Enseignement Catholique
FISEL........... Fluorescent In Situ End-Labelling [*Analytical biochemistry*]
FIS-ELF........ German Information System on Food, Agriculture, and Forestry [*Bonn*] [*Information service or system*]   (IID)
FISEM......... Federation Internationale des Societes d'Ecrivains-Medecins
FISEMA........ Federation Internationale et Syndicale des Employes de Madagascar [*International Federation and Union of Malagasy Employees*] [*WFTU affiliate*]
Fiserv.......... Fiserv, Inc. [*Associated Press*]   (SAG)
FISF............. Family Interaction Summary Format
FISGV......... Federazione Internazionale della Stampa Gastronomica e Vinicola [*International Federation of Gastronomical and Vinicultural Press*]
FISH............. First-In, Still-Here [*Facetious extension of FIFO definition*] [*Accounting*]
FISH............. Fisheries
Fish .... Fisher's United States Patent Cases [*A publication*]   (DLA)

Fish .... Fisher's United States Prize Cases [*A publication*] (DLA)

FISH............ Fluorescence In Situ Hybridization [*Analytical biochemistry*]

FISH............ Friends in Service Here

FISH............ Friends Involved in Sportfishing Heritage

FISH............ Fully Instrumented Submersible Housing [*An oceanographic instrument*]

FISH............ Smalls Oilfield Services [*NASDAQ symbol*] (SAG)

Fish & GC.... Fish and Game Code [*A publication*] (DLA)

Fish & L Mort... Fisher and Lightwood on Mortgages [*9th ed.*] [*1977*] [*A publication*] (DLA)

FISHC .... Federation Internationale des Societes d'Histochimie et de Cytochimie [*International Federation of Societies for Histochemistry and Cytochemistry*] (EAIO)

Fish Cas ...... Fisher's Cases, United States District Courts [*A publication*] (DLA)

Fish CL Dig... Fisher's Digest of English Common Law Reports [*A publication*] (DLA)

Fish Const ... Fisher on the United States Constitution [*A publication*] (DLA)

Fish Cop...... Fisher on Copyrights [*A publication*] (DLA)

Fish Crim Dig... Fisher's Digest of English Criminal Law [*A publication*] (DLA)

Fish Dig....... Fisher's Digest of English Common Law Reports [*A publication*] (DLA)

Fisher .... Fisher on Mortgages [*A publication*] (DLA)

Fisher .... Fisher's United States Prize Cases [*A publication*] (DLA)

Fisher & Lightwood... Fisher and Lightwood on Mortgages [*9th ed.*] [*1977*] [*A publication*] (DLA)

Fisher Pat Cas (F)... Fisher's United States Patent Cases [*A publication*] (DLA)

Fisher Pr Cas (F)... Fisher's United States Prize Cases [*A publication*] (DLA)

Fisher Pr Cas (PA)... Fisher. Pennsylvania Prize Cases [*A publication*] (DLA)

Fisher's Pat Cas... Fisher's United States Patent Cases [*A publication*] (DLA)

Fish Mort..... Fisher on Mortgages [*A publication*] (DLA)

Fish Mortg... Fisher on Mortgages [*A publication*] (DLA)

Fish Pat....... Fisher's United States Patent Cases [*A publication*] (DLA)

Fish Pat Cas... Fisher's United States Patent Cases [*A publication*] (DLA)

Fish Pat Dig... Fisher's Digest of Patent Law [*A publication*] (DLA)

Fish Pat R ... Fisher's United States Patent Reports [*A publication*] (DLA)

Fish Pat Rep... Fisher's United States Patent Reports [*A publication*] (DLA)

FISHPATS .... Fisheries Patrols [*Canadian Navy*]

Fish Pr Cas... Fisher's United States Prize Cases [*A publication*] (DLA)

Fish Prize .... Fisher's United States Prize Cases [*A publication*] (DLA)

Fish Prize Cas... Fisher's United States Prize Cases [*A publication*] (DLA)

FISHROD...... Fiche Information Selectively Held and Retrieved on Demand [*Computer science*] (PDAA)

FishrSci .... Fisher Scientific International [*Associated Press*] (SAG)

FISHSTATS... Fishery Statistics Data Base [*National Marine Fisheries Service*] [*Information service or system*] (CRD)

Fish WA....... Fisher on the Will Act [*A publication*] (DLA)

FISI .... Friends of India Society International (EA)

FISICAL....... Freedom in Sport International Committee and Lobby [*British*] (DI)

FISIER .... Federation Internationale des Societes et Instituts pour l'Etude de la Renaissance [*International Federation of Societies and Institutes for the Study of the Renaissance*] (EA)

FISINT .... FIS [*Foreign Instrumentation Signals*] Intelligence (MCD)

FISITA.......... Federation International des Societes d'Ingenieurs des Techniques de l'Automobile

FISITA.......... Federation Internationale des Societes d'Ingenieurs des Techniques de l'Automobile [*International Federation of Automobile Engineers' and Technicians' Associations*]

Fisk Anal ..... Fisk's Analysis of Coke on Littleton [*1824*] [*A publication*] (DLA)

Fisk U .... Fisk University (GAGS)

FISL............. Federally Insured Student Loan

FISLIB.......... FORTRAN [*Formula Translating System*] Interactive Subroutine Library [*Computer science*]

FISLP........... Federal Insured Student Loan Program

FISM............ Federation Internationale des Societes Magiques [*International Federation of Magical Societies - IFSM*] [*Paris, France*] (EAIO)

FISM............ Fellow of the Institute of Supervisory Management [*British*] (DBQ)

FISM............ International Federation of Sports Medicine (EA)

FISMARC ..... Federation Internationale du Sport Medical pour l'Aide a la Recherche Cancerologique [*International Medical Sports Federation for Aid to Cancer Research*] [*Beziers, France*] (EAIO)

FISN............. Fisons Ltd. [*NASDAQ symbol*] (NQ)

FISO............. Force Integration Staff Officer [*Army*] (RDA)

FISOB.......... Fellow of the Incorporated Society of Organ Builders [*British*] (DI)

Fisons.......... Fisons Ltd. [*Associated Press*] (SAG)

FISP............. Family Income Security Plan

FISP............. Federation Internationale des Societes de Philosophie [*International Federation of Philosophical Societies - IFPS*] (EAIO)

FISq............. Fighter-Interceptor Squadron [*Air Force*] (AFM)

FISR............. Financial Interest and Syndication Rules [*FCC*]

FISRO .... Federation Internationale des Societes de Recherche Operationelle [*International Federation of Operational Research Societies*] [*Denmark*] (EAIO)

FISS............. Federation Internationale des Societes Scientifiques (EERA)

FISSG .... Fleet Issue Ship Shopping Guide [*Navy*] (NVT)

FISSL.......... Finite State Specification Language [*Computer science*] (MHDI)

FISSO .... Foreign Intelligence Special Security Office (MCD)

FIST .... Fault Isolation by Semiautomatic Techniques [*National Institute of Standards and Technology*]

FIST .... Feasible Ideal System Target (MHDI)

FIST .... Federal Information Processing Standards (DOMA)

FIST .... Federal Investigative Strike Team

FIST .... Federation of Interstate Truckers [*Acronym is title of film*]

FIST .... Fellow of the Institute of Science Technology [*British*]

FIST .... Field Artillery Fire Support Team [*Army*] (RDA)

FIST .... Field Intelligence Simulation Test (NATG)

FIST .... Fire Integration Support Team

FIST .... Fire Support Team [*Military*] (INF)

FIST .... First-In, Still-There [*Facetious extension of FIFO definition*] [*Accounting*]

FIST .... Fistula

FIST .... Flagship International Sports Television [*Phony TV station used as bait to capture fugitives*] [*Canada*]

FIST .... Fleet Imagery Satellite Terminal [*Navy*] (ANA)

FIST .... Flight Information Scheduling and Tracking System (MCD)

FIST .... Free Indian Socially-Traditionally [*India*] [*Political party*]

FIST .... Fugitive Investigative Strike Team [*Operation conducted jointly by the US Marshals Service and local police*]

FIST .... Full Integral Simulation Test [*Nuclear energy*] (NRCH)

FIST .... Functional Integrated Systems Trainer (MCD)

FISTA.......... Federation Internationale des Syndicats des Travailleurs Audiovisuel [*International Federation of Audio-Visual Workers Unions - IFAVWU*] (EAIO)

FISTA II .... Flying Infrared Signature Technology Aircraft [*Air Force*]

FIST ARM ... Fistula Armata [*Clyster-Pipe and Bladder Fitted for Use*] [*Pharmacy*] (ROG)

FISTC.......... Fellow of the Institute of Scientific and Technical Communicators [*British*] (DBQ)

FISTC.......... Fellow of the International Institute of Sports Therapy [*British*] (DBQ)

FISTD.......... Fellow of the Imperial Society of Teachers of Dancing [*British*] (DBQ)

FISTM.......... Fellow of the Institute of Sales Technology and Management [*British*] (DBQ)

FI-STM........ Field Ion-Scanning Tunneling Microscopy

FIStructE ..... Fellow of the Institution of Structural Engineers [*British*]

FISTV.......... Fire Support Team Vehicle [*Army*] (RDA)

FISU............ Federation Internationale du Sport Universitaire [*International University Sports Federation*] [*Brussels, Belgium*] (EAIO)

FISV............ FIserv, Inc. [*NASDAQ symbol*] (NQ)

FISW........... Fellow of the Institute of Social Welfare [*British*] (DBQ)

FISYS.......... Fairplay Information Systems Ltd. (IID)

FIT .... Aero Fiesta Mexicana SA de CV [*Mexico*] [*FAA designator*] (FAAC)

FIT .... Fab Indus [*AMEX symbol*] (TTSB)

FIT .... Fab Industries, Inc. [*AMEX symbol*] (SPSG)

FIT .... Fabrication, Integration, and Test

FIT .... Fabrication in Transit (ADA)

FIT .... Failure in Time [*Telecommunications*] (TEL)

FIT .... Far-Infrared Track

FIT .... Fashion Institute of Technology

FIT .... Fault Isolation Test

FIT .... Fault Isolation Time (MCD)

FIT .... Federal Income Tax

FIT .... Federal Insurance Tax (DLA)

FIT .... Federation Internationale des Traducteurs [*International Federation of Translators - IFT*] (EAIO)

FIT .... Federation Internationale de Trampoline [*International Trampoline Federation*] (EA)

FIT .... Federation International Triathlon (EA)

FIT .... Fentanyl Isothiocyanate [*Biochemistry*]

FIT .... Field Installation and Test

FIT .... Field Installation Time (IAA)

FIT .... Field Investigation Team [*Environmental Protection Agency*] (ERG)

FIT .... Fighter

FIT .... Fight Inflation Together [*Group opposing high food prices in 1973*]

FIT .... File Information Table [*Computer science*]

FIT .... File Inquiry Technique

FIT .... Finding in Transit

FIT .... First Computer Interface Tester (MCD)

FIT .... First Indication of Trouble

FIT .... Fit and Independent Traveler (TAG)

FIT .... Fitchburg [*Massachusetts*] [*Airport symbol*] (AD)

FIT .... Fitchburg, MA [*Location identifier FAA*] (FAAL)

FIT .... Fitness, Intensity, Time [*Exercise*]

FIT .... Fixed Interval Timer

FIT .... Flame and Incendiary Technology Program [*Chemical Research, Development, and Engineering Center*] [*Army*] (INF)

FIT .... Flanagan Industrial Tests [*Aptitude and skills test*]

FIT .... Fleet Indoctrination Team (MCD)

FIT .... Fleet Introduction Team [*Navy*] (NVT)

FIT .... Flexible Infrared Transmission

FIT .... Flexible Interface Technique (PDAA)

FIT .... Flight Instrument Trainer (AFM)

FIT .... Flight Technical Tolerance [*Aviation*] (DA)

FIT .... Floating Input Transistor [*Electronics*]

FIT .... Florida Institute of Technology [*Melbourne*]

FIT .... Flow Indicator Transmitter [*Nuclear energy*] (NRCH)

FIT .... Fluorescein Isothiocyanate [*Organic chemistry*] (DAVI)

FIT .... Food Intolerance Testing (MEDA)

FIT .... Foreign Independent [*or Individual*] Travel [*Air travel term*]

FIT .... Forest Industries Telecommunications [*Eugene, OR*] (EA)

FIT .... Forward Inspection Team [*Military*]

FIT .... Foundation to Improve Television (EA)

FIT .... Fourier Integral Transform [*Physics*]

FIT .... Franchise Industry Training [*High school dropout program*] [*Department of Labor*]

FIT .... Free and-Independent Travelers (BARN)

FIT .... Free and Independent Traveller (EERA)

FIT .... Free in Truck [*Business term*]

FIT .... Free of Income Tax

FIT .... Frequency, Intensity, and Time [*Exercise formula*] [*Army*]

FIT .... Frequent Independent Traveler

FIT .... Fully Independent Traveller

FIT	Functional Integration Test
FIT	Fusion at the Inferred Threshold [*Test*] [*Medicine*]
FiTA	Abo Akademi [*Swedish University of Abo*], Turku, Finland [*Library symbol Library of Congress*] (LCLS)
FITA	Fault Isolation Test Adapter (MCD)
FITA	Federation Internationale de Tir a l'Arc [*International Archery Federation*] [*Milan, Italy*] (EA)
FITA	Federation of International Trade Associations (EA)
FITA	Foreign Investors Tax Act of 1966
FITAC	Federacion Interamericana de Touring y Automovil Clubes [*Inter-American Federation of Touring and Automobile Clubs - IFTAC*] (EAIO)
FITAKTRON	Fighter Attack Squadron (DNAB)
FITAL	Financial Terminal Application Language (IAA)
FITAP	Federation Internationale des Transports Aeriens Prives [*International Federation of Private Air Transport*]
FITASC	Federation Internationale de Tir aux Arms Sportives de Chasse [*International Federation for Sport Shooting*] [*Paris, France*] (EAIO)
FITB	Federation Internationale des Techniciens de la Bonneterie [*International Federation of Knitting Technologists - IFKT*] (EAIO)
FITB	Fifth Third Bancorp [*NASDAQ symbol*] (NQ)
FITB	Fluorspar International Technical Bureau (EAIO)
FITBB	Federation Internationale des Travailleurs du Batiment et du Bois [*International Federation of Building and Woodworkers*]
FITBT	Fishing Industry Training Board of Tasmania [*Australia*]
FITC	Financial Trust Corp. [*NASDAQ symbol*] (NQ)
FITC	Fleet Intelligence Training Center [*Navy*] (DNAB)
FITC	Flight Instructor Training Course [*Navy*] (DNAB)
FITC	Fluorescein Isothiocyanate [*Organic chemistry*]
FITC	Foundation for International Technological Cooperation (DICI)
FITC	Foundry Industry Training Committee [*British*] (BI)
FITCAL	Feel, Inspect, Tighten, Clean, Adjust, Lubricate [*A keyword representing operations in preventive maintenance of communications equipment*] [*Military*]
FITCE	Federation des Ingenieurs des Telecommunications de la Communaute Europeenne [*Federation of Telecommunications Engineers in the European Community*]
FITC-gARGG	Fluorescein Isothiocyanate Conjugated Goat Antiserum to Rabbit Gamma Globulin [*Immunology*]
Fitchburg St C	Fitchburg State College (GAGS)
Fitch RE Ag	Fitch on Real Estate Agency [*A publication*] (DLA)
FITCLANT	Fleet Intelligence Training Center, Atlantic [*Navy*] (DNAB)
FITCPAC	Fleet Intelligence Training Center, Pacific [*Navy*] (DNAB)
FITD	Far-Infrared Target Detector
FITD	Fellow of the Institute of Training and Development [*British*] (DBQ)
FITDC	Footwear Industry Traffic and Distribution Council (EA)
FITE	Fair International Trade Employment Committee
FITE	Federacion Interamericana de Trabajadores del Espectaculo [*Interamerican Federation of Entertainment Workers*]
FITE	Forward Interworking Telephony Event [*Telecommunications*] (TEL)
FITEC	Federation Internationale du Thermalisme et du Climatisme [*International Federation of Thermalism and Climatism*]
FITFIMS	Federal Interagency Task Force on Inadvertent Modification of the Stratosphere
FITGO	Floating Input to Ground Output
FITH	Federation Internationale des Travailleurs de l'Habillement
FITH	Fire-in-the-Hole [*Burn*] [*NASA*]
FITH	First-in-the-Hole (MCD)
FITI	Far-Infrared Target Indicator
FITIM	Federacion Internacional de Trabajadores de las Industrias Metalurgicas [*International Metalworkers' Federation*]
FITITHC	Federation Internationale des Travailleurs des Industries du Textile, de l'Habillement, et du Cuir [*International Textile, Garment, and Leather Workers' Federation*] [*Brussels, Belgium*]
FITITV	Federacion Interamericana de Trabajadores de la Industria Textil, Vestuario , y Cuero [*Interamerican Textile, Garment, and Leather Workers Federation*]
FITITVCC	Federacion Interamericana de Trabajadores de la Industria Textil, Vestuario, Cuero, y Calzado [*Interamerican Textile, Leather, Garment, and Shoe Workers Federation - ITLGSWF*] (EA)
FITJ	Fellow of the Institute of Technical Journalists [*British*] (DGA)
FiTK	Turun Yliopiston Kirjasto [*Turku School of Economics*], Turku, Finland [*Library symbol Library of Congress*] (LCLS)
FITL	Fiber in The Loop (ACRL)
FITLOG	Foundation for Information Technology in Local Government (AIE)
FITNGSq	Fighter Interceptor Training Squadron [*Air Force*]
FITNS	Fitness
FITP	Federation Internationale des Travailleurs des Plantations
FITP	Federation Internationale des Travailleurs des Petrole
FITPASC	Federation Internationale des Travailleurs des Plantations, de l'Agriculture, etdes Secteurs Connexes [*International Federation of Plantation, Agricultural, and Allied Workers*]
FITPC	Federation Internationale des Travailleurs du Petrole et de la Chimie [*International Federation of Petroleum and Chemical Workers*]
FITPQ	Federacion Internacional de Trabajadores Petroleros y Quimicos [*International Federation of Petroleum and Chemical Workers*]
FITR	Foundation for International Trade Research
FITREP	Officer Fitness Report [*Navy*] (NVT)
FITRON	Fighter Squadron [*Navy*] (MUGU)
FITRONDET	Fighter Squadron Detachment (DNAB)
FITS	Federation Internationale du Tourisme Social [*International Social Travel Federation - ISTF*] (EAIO)
FITS	Fighter Interceptor Training Squadron [*Air Force*]
FITS	Flexible Image Transport System [*Computer science*]

FITS	Fourteen-O-One Input-Output Tape System [*Military*] (SAA)
FITS	Functional Individual Training System [*Navy*] (NVT)
FITS	Functional Interpolating Transformational System [*HSC Software Co.*] (PCM)
FITS	Functional Interpolating Transform System [*Computer science*]
FITSA	Fellow of the Institute of Trading Standards Administration [*British*] (DBQ)
F-I-T-T	Fearful, Irritable, Tense, and Tremulous [*Combat behavior disorder*] [*Military*] (INF)
FITT	Federation Internationale des Travailleurs de la Terre
FITT	Federation Internationale de Tennis de Table [*International Table Tennis Federation*]
FITT	Food Integrated Tech, Inc. [*NASDAQ symbol*] (SAG)
FITT	Frequency, Intensity, Time, and Type [*Exercise formula*] [*Army*] (INF)
FITTC	Federation of International Trampoline Technical Committee (EA)
FITTHC	Federation Internationale des Travailleurs des Industries du Textile, de l'Habillement, et du Cuir [*International Textile, Garment, and Leather Workers' Federation - ITGLWF*] (EAIO)
FITTS	Fittings (ADA)
FITU	Federation of Independent Trade Unions [*Lebanon*]
FITW	Federal Income Tax Withholding
FITWEPSCOL	Fighter Weapons School [*Topgun*] [*Navy*] (DOMA)
FITWING	Fighter Wing [*Navy*] (NVT)
Fitz	Fitzgibbon's King's Bench Reports [*England*] [*A publication*] (DLA)
Fitz	Fitzherbert's Abridgment [*1516*] [*A publication*] (DSA)
Fitz Abridg	Fitzherbert's Abridgment [*1516*] [*A publication*] (DLA)
Fitzad Jud Act	Fitzadams on the Judicature Act [*A publication*] (DLA)
Fitzg	Fitzgibbon's Irish Land Reports [*A publication*] (DLA)
Fitzg	Fitzgibbon's Irish Registration Appeals [*A publication*] (DLA)
Fitzg	Fitzgibbon's King's Bench Reports [*England*] [*A publication*] (DLA)
Fitzg Land R	Fitzgibbon's Irish Land Reports [*A publication*] (DLA)
Fitzg LG Dec	Fitzgibbon's Irish Local Government Decisions [*A publication*] (DLA)
Fitzg Pub H	Fitzgerald on the Public Health [*A publication*] (DLA)
Fitzg Reg Ca	Fitzgibbon's Irish Registration Appeals [*A publication*] (DLA)
Fitzh	Fitzherbert's Abridgment [*1516*] [*A publication*] (DLA)
Fitzh Abr	Fitzherbert's Abridgment [*1516*] [*A publication*] (DLA)
Fitzh Nat Brev	Fitzherbert's Natura Brevium [*A publication*] (DLA)
Fitzh NB	Fitzherbert's Natura Brevium [*A publication*] (DLA)
Fitzh N Br	Fitzherbert's Natura Brevium [*A publication*] (DLA)
Fitz LG Dec	Fitzgibbon's Irish Local Government Decisions [*A publication*] (DLA)
Fitz Nat Brev	Fitzherbert's Natura Brevium [*A publication*] (DLA)
FIU	Facility Interface Unit [*Telecommunications*]
FIU	Federation of Information Users [*Defunct*] (EA)
FIU	Field Insertion Unit [*Rational, California*] (NITA)
FIU	Field Intelligence Unit (MUGU)
FIU	Fighter Interception Unit [*RAF*] [*British*]
FIU	Fingerprint Identification Unit [*Sony Corp.*]
fiu	Finno-Ugrian [*MARC language code Library of Congress*] (LCCP)
FIU	Florida International University [*Miami*]
FIU	Forward Interpretation Unit [*Military*]
FIU	Frequency Identification Unit (IAA)
FIUC	Federation Internationale des Universites Catholiques [*International Federation of Catholic Universities - IFCU*] (EAIO)
FIUL	Fleet Issue Unit Load (DNAB)
FIUO	For Internal Use Only (KSC)
FIUP	Foundation for Indiana University of Pennsylvania [*Research center*] (RCD)
FIUS	Flax Institute of the United States [*Defunct*] (EA)
FIUS	French Institute in the United States [*Later, FIAF*] (EA)
FIUV	Federation Internationale Una Voce (EA)
FIV	Federation Internationale de la Vieillesse [*International Federation on Ageing - IFA*] (EAIO)
FIV	Feline Immunodeficiency Virus
FIV	Fellow of the Institute of Valuers [*British*]
FIV	Fitness Institute of Victoria [*Australia*]
FIV	Fuel Insolation Valves (MCD)
FIV	Future Infantry Vehicle [*Army*] (INF)
FIV	Interface Group, Inc. [*ICAO designator*] (FAAC)
f-iv--	Ivory Coast [*MARC geographic area code Library of Congress*] (LCCP)
FIVA	Federation Internationale des Vehicules Anciens (EA)
FIVA	Fluid Inject Valve Actuator
FIVB	Federation Internationale de Volleyball [*International Volleyball Federation*] [*Switzerland*]
FIVC	Festival International du Video-Clip [*The first festival entirely devoted to pop-music video, at San Tropez, October, 1984*]
FIVC	Forced Inspiratory Vital Capacity [*Medicine*]
FIVD	Fifth Dimension [*NASDAQ symbol*] (TTSB)
FIVD	Fifth Dimension, Inc. [*NASDAQ symbol*] (NQ)
FIVEATAF	Fifth Allied Tactical Air Force, Southern Europe (NATG)
FIVGV	Fan Inlet Variable Guide Vanes (MCD)
FIVS	Federation Internationale des Vins et Spiritueux [*International Federation of Wines and Spirits - IFWS*] (EAIO)
FiVTRC	Technical Research Centre of Finland, Information Service, Espoo, Vuorimiehentie, Finland [*Library symbol*] [*Library of Congress*] (LCLS)
FIVU	Federacion Internacional de Vivienda y Urbanismo [*International Federation for Housing and Planning*]
FIVV	Federation Internationale de Vo Viet Nam [*An association*] (EAIO)
FIVZ	Federation Internationale Veterinaire de Zootechnie
FIW	Fellow of the Welding Institute [*British*]
FIW	Fiberglass-Insulated Wire
FIW	Fighter-Interceptor Wing (MCD)
FIW	Flight Input Workstation (DA)

FIW .... Free in Wagon [Business term]
FIWC .... Fiji Industrial Workers' Congress
FIWE .... Fellow of the Institute of Water Engineers [British]
FIWES .... Fellow of the Institution of Water Engineers and Scientists [British] (DI)
FIWHTE .... Fellow of the Institution of Works and Highways Technician Engineers [British] (DBQ)
FIWM .... Fellow of the Institution of Works Managers [British]
FIWSc .... Fellow of the Institute of Wood Science [British]
FIWT .... Fellow of the Institute of Wireless Technology [British] (DAS)
FIX .... Factor IX [Hematology]
FIX .... Fault Isolater and Exercizer [Honeywell] (NITA)
FIX .... Federal Internet Exchange (TNIG)
FIX .... Ferndale Internet Experiment [Computer science]
FIX .... Firing in Extension [Missiles]
FIX .... Fixture
FIX .... Fixture
FIXBLK .... Fixed Blocked [Computer science] (MHDB)
FIXExpE ...... Fellow of the Institute of Explosives Engineers [British] (DBQ)
FIXIT .... Flexible Information Exploitation Interpretive Transfer [Software engineering tool] (NITA)
FIXIT .... Fostering, or Fighting, Innovations and Experiment in Teaching [Game]
FIXN .... Fixation
FIXRES .... Fixtures (ROG)
FIXT .... Fixture
FIXUNB .... Fixed Unblocked [Computer science] (MHDB)
FIXWEX .... Fixed-Wing Evaluation Exercise [Aviation]
FIYTO .... Federation of International Youth Travel Organizations [Copenhagen, Denmark] (EAIO)
FIZ .... Dritte Welt Frauensinformationszentrum [Information Center for Third World Women] [Zurich, Switzerland] (EAIO)
FIZ .... Fachinformationszentrum [Information centre] [Germany] (NITA)
FIZ .... National Beverage Corp. [AMEX symbol] (SAG)
FIZ .... Natl Beverage [AMEX symbol] (TTSB)
FIZ-technik... Fachinformationszentrum Technik [Germany] (NITA)
FIZ-W .... Fachinformationszentrum Werkstoffe [Information Center for Materials] [Information service or system] (IID)
FJ .... Air Pacific [ICAO designator] (AD)
FJ .... Congregation of Daughters of Jesus [Roman Catholic religious order]
FJ .... Congregation of St. John (TOCD)
fj .... Congregation of St. John (TOCD)
FJ .... Fedders Corp. [NYSE symbol] (SAG)
FJ .... Field Judge [Football]
FJ .... Fighter Jet
fj .... Fiji [MARC country of publication code Library of Congress] (LCCP)
FJ .... Fiji [ANSI two-letter standard code] (CNC)
FJ .... Filles de Jesus de Kermaria [Daughters of Jesus of Kermaria - DJK] [Paris, France] (EAIO)
FJ .... First Judge [Legal term] (DLA)
FJ .... Fisher-Johns [Melting point method]
FJ .... Fixed Jack [Electronics] (IAA)
FJ .... Fjord (WDAA)
FJ .... Flush Joint [Diamond drilling]
FJ .... Flying Junior [Boating] (DICI)
FJ .... Formula Junior [Class of racing cars]
FJ .... Freeman's Journal [A publication]
FJ .... Friends for Jamaica [An association] (EA)
FJ .... Fuel-Jet (DA)
FJ .... Fused Junction
FJ .... Jacksonville Public Library System, Jacksonville, FL [Library symbol Library of Congress] (LCLS)
FJA .... Fedders Corp. [NYSE symbol] (SAG)
FJA .... Fedders Corp'A' [NYSE symbol] (TTSB)
FJA .... Fluid Jet Amplifier
FJA .... Functional Job Analysis
FJA .... Future Journalists of America [Defunct] (EA)
FJAA .... Fashion Jewelry Association of America (EA)
FJAP .... Federal and Judicial Appointments Project [Defunct] (EA)
Fj-Ar .... Central Archives of Fiji, Suva, Fiji [Library symbol Library of Congress] (LCLS)
FJB .... West Jefferson, NC [Location identifier FAA] (FAAL)
FJbF .... Florida Institute of Technology, Jensen Beach Campus, Jenson Beach, FL [Library symbol] [Library of Congress] (LCLS)
FJC .... Fairbury Junior College [Nebraska]
FJC .... Falcon Jet Centre [British ICAO designator] (FAAC)
FJC .... Fedders Corp. [NYSE symbol] (SAG)
FJC .... Federal Judicial Center
FJC .... Fisher Junior College [Boston, MA]
FJC .... Flint Junior College [Michigan]
FJC .... Fraser's Reports, Justiciary Court [Scotland] [A publication] (DLA)
FJC .... Freely Jointed Chain [Model of a polymer] [Organic chemistry]
FJC .... Freeman Junior College [South Dakota]
FJC .... Friendship Junior College [South Carolina]
FJC .... Fullerton Junior College [Later, Fullerton College] [California]
FJCC .... Fall Joint Computer Conference [Replaced by National Computer Conference - NCC]
FJCE .... Forum Jeunesse des Communautes Europeennes [Youth Forum of the European Communities - YFEC] (EAIO)
FJCEE .... Federation des Jeunes Chefs d'Entreprises d'Europe [European Federation of Young Managers]
FJCF .... Federation des Jeunes Canadiens-Francais [Federation of French-Canadian Youth]
FJCNY .... Furriers Joint Council of New York (EA)
FJCT .... Freedom and Justice for Cyprus Trust (EA)

FJD .... Florida Junior College at Jacksonville, DTC, Jacksonville, FL [OCLC symbol] (OCLC)
FJDG .... Diego Garcia [British Indian Ocean Territory] [ICAO location identifier] (ICLI)
FJE .... Free Jet Expansion
FJF .... Farmworker Justice Fund (EA)
FJF .... Federal Junior Fellowship [Army] (RDA)
FJF .... Florida Junior College at Jacksonville, Jacksonville, FL [Library symbol Library of Congress] (LCLS)
FJG .... Fonda, Johnstown & Gloversville Railroad Co. [AAR code]
FJGS .... Church of Jesus Christ of Latter-Day Saints, Genealogical Society Library, Jacksonville Branch, Jacksonville, FL [Library symbol Library of Congress] (LCLS)
FJI .... Air Pacific Ltd. [Fiji] [ICAO designator] (FAAC)
FJI .... Fellow of the Journalists' Institute [British] (ROG)
FJI .... Fiji [ANSI three-letter standard code] (CNC)
FJI .... Frequency Jumper Identification
FJI .... Friends of Julio International (EA)
FJK .... Florida Junior College at Jacksonville, Kent, Jacksonville, FL [OCLC symbol] (OCLC)
FJL .... Frente Juvenil Lautaro [Chile] [Political party] (EY)
FJM .... Friedman, John M., Hurricane WV [STAC]
FJM .... Friends of Johnny Mathis [Defunct] (EA)
FJMC .... Federation of Jewish Men's Clubs (EA)
FJN .... Familial Juvenile Nephrophthisis [Medicine]
FJN .... Florida Junior College at Jacksonville, North, Jacksonville, FL [OCLC symbol] (OCLC)
FJN .... Front Jednosci Narodowej [Polish Front of National Unity]
FJNA .... Front des Jeunes Nationalistes Africains [National African Youth Front]
FJNF .... Foundation for the Jewish National Fund (EA)
FJO .... Ft. Johnson [Malawi] [Airport symbol] (AD)
FJO .... Offshore Power Systems, Jacksonville, FL [Library symbol Library of Congress] (LCLS)
FJP .... Federation of Jewish Philanthropies of New York (EA)
FJPC .... Federation des Jeunes Progressistes-Conservateurs du Canada [Progressive Conservative Youth Federation of Canada]
FJPTFCG ...... Federation of Jewish Philanthropies Task Force on Compulsive Gambling (EA)
FJR .... Factories Journal Reports [India] [A publication] (DLA)
FJR .... Friends of James Rogers (EA)
FJRM .... Full Joint Range of Movement [Orthopedics]
FJS .... First Jersey Securities
FJS .... Florida Junior College at Jacksonville, South, Jacksonville, FL [OCLC symbol] (OCLC)
FJS .... Fort Jones, CA [Location identifier FAA] (FAAL)
FJSRL .... Frank J. Seiler Research Laboratory [US Air Force Academy, CO]
FJSTO .... Federation of Jewish Student Organizations [Defunct] (EA)
FJT .... Familiarization Job Training (AFIT)
FJT .... Flush Joint [Technical drawings]
FJT .... Free Jet Test
FJU .... Chicago, IL [Location identifier FAA] (FAAL)
FJU .... Jacksonville University, Jacksonville, FL [Library symbol Library of Congress OCLC symbol] (LCLS)
FJUNF .... University of North Florida, Jacksonville, FL [Library symbol Library of Congress] (LCLS)
FJUS .... International FJ Class Organization (EA)
FJW .... Friends of Jackie Wilson (EA)
FJWO .... Federation of Jewish Women's Organizations (EA)
FK .... 5,000 [Film] (WDMC)
FK .... Faker Track (MUGU)
FK .... Falkirk [Postcode] (ODBW)
FK .... Falkland Islands [ANSI two-letter standard code] (CNC)
fk .... Falkland Islands [MARC country of publication code Library of Congress] (LCCP)
F-K .... Feynman-Kak Formula [Particle physics]
FK .... Flamenco Airlines [ICAO designator] (AD)
FK .... Flat Keel [Shipbuilding]
FK .... Fokker-VFW BV [Netherlands ICAO aircraft manufacturer identifier] (ICAO)
FK .... Foreign Key [Computer science] (PCM)
FK .... Fork (MSA)
FK .... Friends of Karen (EA)
FK .... Fujisawa Pharmaceutical Co. [Japan] [Research code symbol]
FK .... Function Key (MCD)
FK .... Geelong Air Travel [ICAO designator] (AD)
FKAB .... Banyo [Cameroon] [ICAO location identifier] (ICLI)
FKAF .... Bafia [Cameroon] [ICAO location identifier] (ICLI)
FKAG .... Abong-M'Bang [Cameroon] [ICAO location identifier] (ICLI)
FKAL .... Lomie [Cameroon] [ICAO location identifier] (ICLI)
FKAM .... Meiganga [Cameroon] [ICAO location identifier] (ICLI)
FKAN .... N'Kongsamba [Cameroon] [ICAO location identifier] (ICLI)
FKAO .... Betare-Oya [Cameroon] [ICAO location identifier] (ICLI)
FKAV .... Free Kindergarten Association of Victoria [Australia]
FKAY .... Yoko [Cameroon] [ICAO location identifier] (ICLI)
FKB .... Flight Display Keyboard [NASA] (NASA)
FKB .... Fredericksburg, TX [Location identifier FAA] (FAAL)
FKB .... Function Key Button (IAA)
FKBC .... First-Knox Banc Corp. [NASDAQ symbol] (TTSB)
FKBC .... First Knox Bancorp [NASDAQ symbol] (SAG)
FKBI .... Fourdrinier Kraft Board Institute [Later, CKPG] (EA)
FKC .... Fellow of King's College [London]
FKC .... Friends of the Kennedy Center (EA)
FKCBS .... Frantisek Kmoch Czech Bands Society [British] (DBA)
FKCL .... Fellow of King's College, London

FKCM............	Franklin Cons Mng [*NASDAQ symbol*] (TTSB)
FKCM............	Franklin Consolidated Mining Co., Inc. [*NASDAQ symbol*] (NQ)
FKD............	Forked
f-ke--	Kenya [*MARC geographic area code Library of Congress*] (LCCP)
FKES............	First Keystone Financial [*NASDAQ symbol*] (TTSB)
Fkey............	Function Key (CDE)
FKF............	Finlands Kristliga Foerbund [*Finnish Christian League*] (PPE)
FKF............	Franklin Bluffs, AK [*Location identifier FAA*] (FAAL)
FKFC............	First Kent Financial Corp. [*NASDAQ symbol*] (SAG)
FKFS............	First Keystone Financial, Inc. [*NASDAQ symbol*] (SAG)
FKgP............	Fueggetlen Kisgazda-, Foeldmunkas- es Polgari Part [*Independent Smallholders' Party*] [*Hungary Political party*] (EY)
FKI............	Fachverband Klebstoffindustrie [*Association of European Adhesives Manufacturers*] (EAIO)
FKI............	Kisangani [*Zaire*] [*Airport symbol*] (OAG)
FKJ............	Fukue [*Japan*] [*Seismograph station code, US Geological Survey*] (SEIS)
FKK............	Freie-Koerper-Kultur [*Nudism, a pre-NAZI fad in Germany*]
FKK............	Fukuoka [*Japan*] [*Seismograph station code, US Geological Survey*] (SEIS)
FKKA............	Maroua/Ville [*Cameroon*] [*ICAO location identifier*] (ICLI)
FKKB............	Kribi [*Cameroon*] [*ICAO location identifier*] (ICLI)
FKKC............	Tiko [*Cameroon*] [*ICAO location identifier*] (ICLI)
FKKD............	Douala [*Cameroon*] [*ICAO location identifier*] (ICLI)
FKKE............	Eseka [*Cameroon*] [*ICAO location identifier*] (ICLI)
FKKF............	Mamfe [*Cameroon*] [*ICAO location identifier*] (ICLI)
FKKG............	Bali [*Cameroon*] [*ICAO location identifier*] (ICLI)
FKKH............	Kaele [*Cameroon*] [*ICAO location identifier*] (ICLI)
FKKI............	Batouri [*Cameroon*] [*ICAO location identifier*] (ICLI)
FKKJ............	Yagoua [*Cameroon*] [*ICAO location identifier*] (ICLI)
FKKK............	Douala [*Cameroon*] [*ICAO location identifier*] (ICLI)
FKKL............	Maroua/Salak [*Cameroon*] [*ICAO location identifier*] (ICLI)
FKKM............	Foumban/Nkounja [*Cameroon*] [*ICAO location identifier*] (ICLI)
FKKN............	N'Gaoundere [*Cameroon*] [*ICAO location identifier*] (ICLI)
FKKO............	Bertoua [*Cameroon*] [*ICAO location identifier*] (ICLI)
FKKR............	Garoua [*Cameroon*] [*ICAO location identifier*] (ICLI)
FKKS............	Dschang [*Cameroon*] [*ICAO location identifier*] (ICLI)
FKKT............	Tibati [*Cameroon*] [*ICAO location identifier*] (ICLI)
FKKU............	Bafoussam [*Cameroon*] [*ICAO location identifier*] (ICLI)
FKKV............	Bamenda [*Cameroon*] [*ICAO location identifier*] (ICLI)
FKKW............	Ebolowa [*Cameroon*] [*ICAO location identifier*] (ICLI)
FKKY............	Frankfort First Bancorp [*NASDAQ symbol*] (TTSB)
FKKY............	Frankfort First Bancorp, Inc. [*NASDAQ symbol*] (SAG)
FKKY............	Yaounde [*Cameroon*] [*ICAO location identifier*] (ICLI)
FKL............	Franklin [*Pennsylvania*] [*Airport symbol*] (OAG)
FKL............	Franklin Corp. [*AMEX symbol*] (SPSG)
FKL............	Franklin Hldg Corp. [*AMEX symbol*] (TTSB)
FKL............	Franklin, PA [*Location identifier FAA*] (FAAL)
FKLN............	Franklin Ophthalmic Instruments [*NASDAQ symbol*] (TTSB)
FKM............	Fort Knox Minerals Ltd. [*Vancouver Stock Exchange symbol*]
FKN............	Field-Koros-Noves [*Physical chemistry*]
FKN............	Franklin, VA [*Location identifier FAA*] (FAAL)
FKNMS............	Florida Keys National Marine Sanctuary
FKNMS............	Florida Keys National Marine Sanctuary [*USA*] [*Marine science*] (OSRA)
FKO............	Family Keep Off [*Food, in presence of company*] [*British*] (DI)
FKP............	Finlands Kommunistiska Parti [*Finnish Communist Party*] (PPE)
FKP............	Francia Kommunista Part [*French Communist Party*] [*Political party*]
FKP............	Fratsuzskaia Kommunisticheskaia Partiia [*Political party*]
FKP............	French Communist Party [*Political party*]
FKP............	Fueggetlen Kisgazda Part [*Independent Smallholders' Party*] [*Hungary*] (PPE)
FKP............	Hopkinsville, KY [*Location identifier FAA*] (FAAL)
FKQ............	Fak-Fak [*Indonesia*] [*Airport symbol*] (OAG)
FKQCP............	Fellow of the King's and Queen's College of Physicians, Ireland
FKQCPI............	Fellow of the King's and Queen's College of Physicians, Ireland [*Later, FRCPI*] (ROG)
Fkr............	Faeroese Krone [*Monetary unit*] (ODBW)
FKR............	Frankfort, IN [*Location identifier FAA*] (FAAL)
F KR............	Krona [*Crown*] [*Monetary unit Faroe Islands*]
FKS............	Friends of Kate Smith [*Later, Kate Smith/God Bless America Foundation*] (EA)
FKS............	Fukushima [*Japan*] [*Seismograph station code, US Geological Survey*] (SEIS)
FKscNA............	National Aeronautics and Space Administration, John F. Kennedy Space Center, Kennedy Space Center, FL [*Library symbol*] [*Library of Congress*] (LCLS)
FKT............	Field Kitchen Trailer (MCD)
FKT............	Friends of Kristoffer Tabori [*Defunct Defunct*] (EA)
FKTU............	Federation of Korean Trade Unions [*South Korea*]
FKU............	Feminist Karate Union (EA)
FKV............	Gainesville, GA [*Location identifier FAA*] (FAAL)
FKw............	Monroe County Public Library, Key West, FL [*Library symbol Library of Congress*] (LCLS)
FKWBRC............	Florida Keys Wild Bird Rehabilitation Center (EA)
FKwC............	Florida Keys Community College, Key West, FL [*Library symbol*] [*Library of Congress*] (LCLS)
FKwH............	Ernest Hemingway Home, Key West, FL [*Library symbol Library of Congress*] (LCLS)
FKwHi............	Key West Art and Historical Society, Key West, FL [*Library symbol Library of Congress*] (LCLS)
FKZ............	Sacramento, CA [*Location identifier FAA*] (FAAL)
FL............	Fail (NASA)
FL............	Falconbridge Ltd. [*Toronto Stock Exchange symbol Vancouver Stock Exchange symbol*]

FL............	Fall
FL............	Falsa Lectio [*False Reading, in a text*] [*Latin*]
FL............	Fan Lift
FL............	Fastest Lap [*Auto racing*]
FL............	Fatigue Limit
FL............	Fault Localization (CAAL)
FL............	Federal League [*Major league in baseball, 1914-15*]
FL............	Feed Lines (NASA)
Fl............	Feldspar [*A mineral*]
FL............	Feline Lung (Cell) [*Cytology*]
fl............	Femtoliter [*One quadrillionth of a liter*]
F/L............	Fetch/Load [*Computer science*] (MDG)
FL............	Field Length
FL............	Field Loss Contactor or Relay [*Industrial control*] (IEEE)
FL............	Fight Level (PDAA)
F/L............	Film Load (KSC)
FL............	Filter (CET)
FL............	Filtered Load (MAE)
FL............	First Lady [*Imelda Marcos of The Philippines*]
FL............	Fiscal Letter (OICC)
FL............	Fish Lake [*Pisciculture*]
FL............	Flag [*British naval signaling*]
FL............	Flag Lieutenant [*Navy*]
FL............	Flame (AAG)
FL............	Flammable
FL............	Flanders [*Belgium*] (WDAA)
FL............	Flange (WGA)
FL............	Flanker [*Football*]
Fl............	Flash [*DAS*]
FL............	Flash Advisory [*Meteorology*] (FAAC)
FL............	Flashing (DAC)
FL............	Flashing Light [*Navigation signal*]
FL............	Flash Lamp
FL............	Flat (MSA)
FL............	Flauto [*Flute*] [*Music*] (ROG)
FL............	Flawless [*Diamond clarity grade*]
FL............	Flemish [*Language, etc.*] (ROG)
FL............	Flexion [*Medicine*]
FL............	Flight Level
FL............	Flight Lieutenant
F/L............	Flintlock [*British military*] (DMA)
FL............	Float (IAA)
FL............	Floating Landing (ROG)
FL............	Flood (MSA)
FL............	Floor
fl............	Floor (DD)
FL............	Floor
FL............	Floor Line (MSA)
FL............	Flores [*Flowers*] [*Latin*]
FL............	Florida [*Postal code*]
FL............	Florin [*Monetary unit*] [*Netherlands*]
FL............	Floruit [*He Flourished*] [*Latin*]
FL............	Flotilla Leader [*British*]
FL............	Flour (WGA)
fl............	Flourished (VRA)
FL............	Flow (MSA)
fl............	Flower [*Botany*]
FL............	Flow Line [*Technical drawings*]
FL............	Fluid (KSC)
FL............	Fluidus [*Fluid*] [*Pharmacy*]
FL............	Fluorescence [*or Fluorescent*]
FL............	Fluorine [*Symbol is F*] [*Chemical element*] (ROG)
FL............	Fluorite [*Mineral*]
fl............	Fluoro [*As substituent on nucleoside*] [*Biochemistry*]
Fl............	Fluorometric [*or Fluorometry*]
FL............	Flush (MSA)
FL............	Flush Left [*Graphic arts*] (DGA)
fl............	Flush Left [*Typography*] (WDMC)
FL............	Flute
FL............	Flute Lead (MSA)
FL............	Fluvio-Lacustrine Sandstone [*Geology*]
FL............	Focal Length [*Photography*]
FL............	Follicular Lymphoma [*Oncology*]
FL............	Food Laboratory [*Army*]
FL............	Foot-Lambert [*Illumination*]
fL............	Foot-Lambert (IDOE)
FL............	Foreign Language
FL............	Foreign Listing [*Telecommunications*] (TEL)
FL............	For Life [*An association*] (EA)
FL............	Form Letter
FL............	Formula Libre [*Automotive competition*]
FL............	France-Louisiane [*Later, FLFADDFA*] [*France*] (EAIO)
FL............	Fraunhofer Line (PDAA)
FL............	Freedom League
F/L............	Free Lance
FL............	Freie Liste [*Free List*] [*Liechtenstein*] [*Political party*] (EY)
F/L............	Freight Liner [*British Railways Board*] (DS)
Fl............	Frequency-Shift Keying (IDOE)
FL............	Friend Leukemia [*Cytology*] (DMAA)
FL............	Frontal Lobe [*Brain anatomy*]
FL............	Frontier Airlines, Inc. [*ICAO designator*]
FL............	Front Lay [*Printing*] (DGA)
FL............	Fuel (KSC)
FL............	Full Lift (KSC)
FL............	Full Liquid [*Medicine*]

F/L .... Full Load (KSC)
FL .... Funnel Length
FL .... Fusible Link (EECA)
FL .... Guilder [*Florin*] [*Monetary unit Netherlands*]
FL .... Land Station [*ITU designation*] (CET)
FL .... Languages and Linguistics [*Educational Resources Information Center (ERIC) Clearinghouse*] [*Center for Applied Linguistics*] (PAZ)
FL .... Liechtenstein [*IYRU nationality code*] (IYR)
fl---- .... Nile River and Basin [*MARC geographic area code Library of Congress*] (LCCP)
FL1 .... Function Language One
FLA .... Air Florida [*ICAO designator*] (FAAC)
FLA .... Fabric Laminators Association [*Defunct*]
FLA .... Federal Librarians Association [*Defunct*]
FLA .... Federal Loan Administration
FLA .... Federal Loan Agency [*Abolished 1947, records transferred to Reconstruction Finance Corp.*]
FLA .... Fellow of the Library Association [*British*]
FLA .... Feminists for Life of America [*Later, FFL*] (EA)
FLA .... Fiat Lege Artis [*Let It Be Done According to the Rules of the Art*] [*Pharmacy*]
FLA .... Film Laboratory Association Ltd. [*British*] (BI)
FLA .... Finance and Leasing Association [*British*] (EAIO)
FLA .... Firearms Lobby of America [*Later, CCRKBA*] (EA)
FLA .... First Lord of the Admiralty [*British*]
FLA .... Flats [*Utah*] [*Seismograph station code, US Geological Survey Closed*] (SEIS)
FLA .... Flight Article [*Army*] (AABC)
FLA .... Florencia [*Colombia*] [*Airport symbol*] (OAG)
FLA .... Florida (AFM)
Fla .... Florida (ODBW)
FLA .... Florida East Coast Indus [*NYSE symbol*] (TTSB)
FLA .... Florida East Coast Industries, Inc. [*NYSE symbol*] (SPSG)
Fla .... Florida Reports [*A publication*] (DLA)
FLA .... Fluid Levitation Accelerometer
FLA .... Fluorescent Lighting Association (EA)
FLA .... Foam Laminators Association (EA)
FLA .... Foreign Language Associates
FLA .... Four-Conductor, Lighting, Armor [*Cable*] (IAA)
FLA .... France Latin America [*An association*] (EAIO)
FLA .... Freustrum Location Addition
FLA .... Frontline Ambulance [*Army*] (INF)
FLA .... Fronto-Laeva Anterior [*A fetal position*] [*Obstetrics*] (MAE)
FLA .... Full Load Amperes (MSA)
FLA .... Future Large Aircraft [*Cooperative manufacturing effort of France, Germany, Britain, Italy, Portugal, Spain and Turkey*] (ECON)
FLA .... Future Large Aircraft [*Development*] [*Europe*]
FLA .... Librairies Flammarion [*ACCORD*] [*UTLAS symbol*]
FLAA .... Fellow, London Association of Accountants
FLAA .... Fellow of the London Associaton of Certified and Corporate Accountants (DAS)
Fla A&M U... Florida Agricultural and Mechanical University (GAGS)
FLAAC......... Florida Lime and Avocado Administrative Committee (EA)
Fla Admin Code... Florida Administrative Code [*A publication*] (DLA)
Fla Admin Code Weekly... Florida Administrative Code Weekly [*A publication*] (AAGC)
Fla & K .... Flanagan and Kelly's Irish Rolls Court Reports [*1840-42*] [*A publication*] (DLA)
FLAAR .... Foundation for Latin American Anthropological Research (EA)
Fla Atlantic U... Florida Atlantic University (GAGS)
FLAC........... Flaccid
FLAC........... Florida Automatic Computer [*Air Force*]
Flac .... In Flaccum [*of Philo Judaeus*] (BJA)
Flac .... Pro Flacco [*of Cicero*] [*Classical studies*] (OCD)
FLAC-H .... Fuzzy Logic Adaptive Controller - Helicoptor [*Army*] (RDA)
FLACSO .... Facultad Latinoamericana de Ciencias Sociales [*Latin American Faculty of Social Sciences*] [*San Jose, Costa Rica*]
FLACTO....... Frequency-Locked Automatic Computing Transfer Oscillator (PDAA)
FLAD........... Fluorescence-Activated Display (IAA)
FLAD........... Fluorescene-Activated Display (PDAA)
Fla Dig .... Thompson's Digest of Laws [*Florida*] [*A publication*] (DLA)
FLAE........... Fatigue Life Assessment Expert [*Automotive engineering*]
FlaEC.......... Florida East Coast Industries, Inc. [*Associated Press*] (SAG)
FLAER......... Foundation for Latino-American Economic Research [*Argentina*] (EAIO)
FlaFst .... Florida First Bancorp, Inc. [*Associated Press*] (SAG)
FlaFst .... Florida First Federal Savings Bank [*Associated Press*] (SAG)
FLAG........... Family Liaison Action Group [*Inactive*] (EA)
FLAG........... Federal Lesbians and Gays (EA)
FLAG........... Federation of Leisure Activity Groups [*Australia*]
FLAG........... Female Liberal Arts Graduate
FLAG........... Fiberoptic Link Around the Globe [*Undersea communications cable*]
FLAG........... Fixed Link Aerospace to Ground (SAA)
FLAG........... Flageolet [*Music*]
FLAG........... Flag Financial [*NASDAQ symbol*] (SAG)
FLAG........... Flagstaff National Park Service Group
FLAG........... Flexible Hours Action Group [*British*]
FLAG........... Florida-Alabama-Georgia League [*Old baseball league*]
FLAG........... Foreign Language Arts in the Grades (EDAC)
FLAG........... FORTRAN [*Formula Translating System*] Load and Go [*Xerox Corp.*] [*Computer science*]
FLAG........... Foundation for Law and Government [*Organization on television series "Knight Rider"*]
FLAG........... Four London Airport Group [*British*]

FLAG........... Parents, Families, and Friends of Lesbians and Gays (PAZ)
FlaGam....... Florida Gaming Corp. [*Associated Press*] (SAG)
FLAGCENT... Flag Officer, Central Europe
FLAGE......... Flexible Lightweight Agile-Guided Experiment Missile [*Military*] (SDI)
FlagFncl ...... Flag Financial [*Associated Press*] (SAG)
FLAGRP....... Florida Group [*Navy*]
Flagstar ...... Flagstar Companies, Inc. [*Associated Press*] (SAG)
FLAIEUA ...... Federated Liquor and Allied Industries Employees Union of Australia
Fla Inst Tech... Florida Institute of Technology (GAGS)
FLAIR.......... Fleet Location and Information Reporting [*Police term*]
FLAIR.......... Florida Leader Active in Research
FLAIR.......... Food-Linked Agricultural Industrial Research [*EC*] (ECED)
FLAIR.......... Food Linked Agro-Industrial Research (MHDB)
FLAIR.......... FORTRAN [*Formula Translation*] Language in Core Rapid Translator [*Xerox*] (NITA)
FLAIR.......... Fundamental Land-Air Integrated Research (SAA)
FLAIRS .... Food Launch Awareness in the Retail Sector [*Leatherhead Food Research Association*] [*Information service or system*] (CRD)
Fla Jur........ Florida Jurisprudence [*A publication*] (DLA)
FLAK.......... Fliegerabwehrkanone [*German word for antiaircraft gun; acronym used in English for antiaircraft fire and as a slang term for dissension*]
FLAK.......... Fondest Love and Kisses [*Correspondence*]
Fla LJ .... Florida Law Journal [*A publication*] (DLA)
Fla L Rev.... Florida Law Review [*A publication*] (DLA)
FLAM.......... Fault Location and Monitoring (AABC)
Flam .... Flamininus [*of Plutarch*] [*Classical studies*] (OCD)
FLAM.......... Flammable (DNAB)
FLAM.......... Forces de Liberation Africaine de Mauritanie [*Political party*] (EY)
FLAM.......... Forward Launched Aerodynamic Missiles
flamby........ Flamboyant (VRA)
FLAME........ Facility Laboratory for Ablative Materials Evaluation (SAA)
FLAME........ Facts and Logic about the Middle East [*An association*]
FLAME........ Flame-Launched Advance Material Experiment (DNAB)
FLAME........ Foundation of Light and Metaphysical Education [*Defunct*] (EA)
FLAME........ Friendship Loans to Latin American Endeavors, Inc.
FlameIT....... Flamel Technologies [*Associated Press*] (SAG)
FLAMR........ Forward-Looking Advanced Multimode RADAR
Flamst .... Flamemaster Corp. [*Associated Press*] (SAG)
FLAMTI....... Forward-Looking Airborne Moving Target Indication (NG)
FLAN.......... Factory Layout Analysis [*PERA*] [*Software package*] (NCC)
flan .... Flannel (VRA)
Flan & K...... Flanagan and Kelly's Irish Rolls Court Reports [*1840-42*] [*A publication*] (DLA)
Flan & Ke.... Flanagan and Kelly's Irish Rolls Court Reports [*1840-42*] [*A publication*] (DLA)
Flan & Kel... Flanagan and Kelly's Irish Rolls Court Reports [*1840-42*] [*A publication*] (DLA)
Fla NBA ...... Flather's New Bankrupt Act [*A publication*] (DLA)
Fland .... Flanders (VRA)
Fland Ch J... Flanders' Lives of the Chief Justices of the United States [*A publication*] (DLA)
Fland Const... Flanders on the United States Constitution [*A publication*] (DLA)
Flanders ...... Flanders Corp. [*Associated Press*] (SAG)
Fland Fire Ins... Flanders on Fire Insurance [*A publication*] (DLA)
Fl & K......... Flanagan and Kelly's Irish Rolls Court Reports [*1840-42*] [*A publication*] (DLA)
Fland Mar L... Flanders' Maritime Law [*A publication*] (DLA)
Fland Sh...... Flanders on Shipping [*A publication*] (DLA)
Fl Ang......... Fluorescein Angiography [*Cardiology*] (DAVI)
Flanign .... Flanigan's Enterprises, Inc. [*Associated Press*] (SAG)
Fl Ant.......... Fluorescent Antibody [*Biochemistry*] (DAVI)
FLAP.......... Fear, Love, Anger, and Pain [*Cognitive system*]
FLAP.......... Federacion Latinoamericana de Parasitologos
FLAP.......... First Level Adaptive Program
FLAP.......... Five-Lipoxygenase Activating Protein [*Biochemistry*]
FLAP.......... Flight Application Software [*NASA*] (NASA)
FLAP.......... Flores Assembly Program [*Computer science*]
FLAP.......... Flow Analysis Program [*Computer science*]
FLAP.......... Formula Algebraic Processor [*Computer science*] (CSR)
FLAP.......... Light from the Ancient Past, the Archeological Background of Judaism and Christianity [*Jack Finegan*] [*A publication*] (BJA)
FlaProg....... Florida Progress Corp. [*Formerly, Florida Power Corp.*] [*Associated Press*] (SAG)
FLAPS......... Flight Application Software [*NASA*] (NASA)
FlaPUt .... Florida Public Utilities Co. [*Associated Press*] (SAG)
FLAPW........ Full-Potential Linear Augmented Plane Wave [*Physical chemistry*]
FLAR.......... Fault Location and Repair (AABC)
Fla R .... Florida Reports [*A publication*] (DLA)
FLAR.......... Forward-Looking Airborne RADAR
FlaRck........ Florida Rock Industries, Inc. [*Associated Press*] (SAG)
FLARE......... Flight Anomalies Reporting (KSC)
FLARE......... Florida Aquanaut Research Expedition [*National Oceanic and Atmospheric Administration*]
Fla Rep....... Florida Reports [*A publication*] (DLA)
FLAREX....... Flare Exercises [*Navy*]
FLAS.......... Fellow of the Chartered Land Agents' Society [*British*]
Fla SBA Jo... Florida State Bar Association. Journal [*A publication*] (DLA)
Fla SBALJ... Florida State Bar Association. Law Journal [*A publication*] (DLA)
Fla Sess Law Serv... Florida Session Law Service (West) [*A publication*] (DLA)
FLASH......... Facts Location and Summarized History [*General Motors Corp.*] [*Computer science*]
FLASH .... Factual Lines about Submarine Hazards (DNAB)
FLASH .... Fast Luciferase Automated Assay of Specimens for Hospitals [*Bacteria analysis*] [*NASA*]

FLASH .... Feeder Lighter Aboard Ship
FLASH .... Flame Launched Assault Shoulder or Hip-Fired Weapon [*Army*]
FLASH .... Flash Lights and Send Help [*Florida highway driving aid*]
FLASH .... Folding Light Acoustic Sonar for Helicopters (DOMA)
FLASH .... Foreign Fishing Vessel Licensing and Surveillance Hierarchical Information System [*Canada*] (MSC)
FLASHA .... Florida Language, Speech, and Hearing Association (SRA)
FLASH FIRE... Flash Financial Report [*for prospective overruns*] [*Navy*]
FLASP .... Flight Plan Support Specialist [*NASA*]
Fla Stat....... Florida Statutes [*A publication*] (DLA)
Fla Stat Ann... Florida Statutes, Annotated [*A publication*] (DLA)
Fla Stat Anno... Annotations to Official Florida Statutes [*A publication*] (DLA)
Fla State LJ... Florida State Law Journal [*A publication*] (DLA)
Fla St U .... Florida State University (GAGS)
Fla Supp..... Florida Supplement [*A publication*] (DLA)
FLAT .... Fellow Lady Astronaut Trainee
FLAT .... Flat [*Commonly used*] (OPSA)
FLAT .... Flight Plan Aided Tracking [*Aviation*] (IAA)
FLAT .... Flight-Plane-Aid Tracking (MCD)
FLAT .... Foreign Language Aptitude Test
FLAT .... Katete [*Zambia*] [*ICAO location identifier*] (ICLI)
FLATS......... Flats [*Commonly used*] (OPSA)
FLAV........... Flavus [*Yellow*] [*Pharmacy*]
FLAVA......... Food and Libations Association of Virginia (SRA)
FLAW.......... Fleet Logistic Air Wing
FLAW.......... Foreign Languages at Work (AIE)
FLAWP........ French-Language Association of Work Psychology [*Viroflay, France*] (EAIO)
FLAX........... Fleming International Airways, Inc. [*Air carrier designation symbol*]
Flax Reg...... Flaxman's Registration of Births and Deaths [*1875*] [*A publication*] (DLA)
FLB .... Brittany Revolutionary Front [*France*]
FLB .... Family Life Bureau (EA)
FLB .... Federal Land Bank
FLB .... Federal Loan Bank
FLB .... Fletcher Challenge Bldg ADS [*NYSE symbol*] (TTSB)
FLB .... Fletcher Challenge Building [*NYSE symbol*] (SAG)
FLB .... Flight Line Bunker (NATG)
FLB .... Floriano [*Brazil*] [*Airport symbol*] (AD)
FLB .... Flow Brazing
FLB .... Fluorescently Labelled Bacteria [*Microbiology*]
FLB .... Foreign Language Bulletin
FLB .... Funny Looking Beat [*Cardiology*]
f-lb-- .... Liberia [*MARC geographic area code Library of Congress*] (LCCP)
FLBA.......... Family Law Bar Association [*British*] (DBA)
FLBA.......... Federal Land Bank Association
FLB-ARB...... Front de Liberation de la Bretagne - Armee Republicaine Bretonne [*Liberation Front of Brittany - Breton Republican Army*] [*France*] (PD)
FL BDG........ Flexible Binding (DGA)
FL-BE.......... Filter-Band Eliminator (MUGU)
FLBH.......... Filter-Band High (IAA)
FLBIN.......... Floating-Point Binary [*Computer science*]
FLB-LNS ...... Front de Liberation de la Bretagne pour la Liberation Nationale et le Socialisme [*Liberation Front of Brittany for National Liberation and Socialism*] [*France*] (PD)
FL-BP.......... Filter-Bandpass (MUGU)
FLBR.......... Film and Literature Board of Review [*Australia*]
FLBR.......... Fusible Link-Bottom Register (OA)
FLC .... Aviation Standards National Field Office [*ICAO designator*] (FAAC)
flc .... Brothers of Christian Instruction (TOCD)
FLC .... Falcon Drilling Co. [*NYSE symbol*] (SAG)
FLC .... Family Law Council (EA)
FLC .... Farm Labor Coalition (EA)
FLC .... Fault Locator Cable
FLC .... Federal Laboratory Consortium for Technology Transfer
FLC .... Federal Library Committee [*Later, FLICC*] [*Library of Congress Washington, DC*]
FLC .... Federation of Lutheran Clubs (EA)
FLC .... FEDLINK [*Federal Library and Information Network*], Washington, DC [*OCLC symbol*] (OCLC)
FLC .... Fenway Library Consortium/Abbot Memorial Library [*Library network*]
FLC .... Ferroelectric Liquid Crystal [*Physical chemistry*]
FLC .... Fibrolamellar Carcinoma [*Oncology*]
FLC .... File Location Code [*Computer science*]
FLC .... First Line Check
FLC .... Flag-Lieutenant-Commander [*Navy British*]
FLC .... Flat Load Cell
FLC .... Fleet Loading Center
FLC .... Fletcher Challenge ORD [*NYSE symbol*] (SPSG)
FLC .... Flight Crew (KSC)
FLC .... Force Logistics Command [*Marine Corps*] (NVT)
FLC .... Foreign Liquidation Commission
FLC .... Forming Limit Curve [*Steel sheet fabrication*]
FLC .... Forward Load Control (MCD)
FLC .... Frequency and Load Controller
FLC .... Friend Leukemia Cells [*Cytology*]
FLC .... Funny Looking Child [*Medical slang*]
FLC .... Fuzzy-Logic Controller [*Engineering*]
FLCA.......... Folk Lore Council of Australia
FLCA.......... Forward Load Control Assembly (MCD)
FLCA.......... Front Lower Control Arm
FLCB.......... Frequency and Load Control Box (MCD)
FLCCU........ FIREX [*Fire Extinguisher*] and Launch Coolant Control Unit [*Aerospace*] (AAG)

FLCH........... Choma [*Zambia*] [*ICAO location identifier*] (ICLI)
FLCH........... Fletchers Fine Foods Ltd. [*NASDAQ symbol*] (SAG)
FLCH........... Flight Level Change (GAVI)
FLCK........... Flock
FLCL........... Family Life Communications Line
FLCM........... Fellow of the London College of Music [*British*]
FLCN........... Falcon Drilling [*NASDAQ symbol*] (TTSB)
FLCN........... Falcon Drilling Co. [*NASDAQ symbol*] (SAG)
FLCN........... Field Length Condition Register (MHDB)
FLCNAVJUSMAG... Field Logistics Center, Navy Joint United States Military Assistance Group (DNAB)
FLCO........... Chocha [*Zambia*] [*ICAO location identifier*] (ICLI)
FLCO........... Floor Cleanout [*Technical drawings*]
FLCP........... Chipata [*Zambia*] [*ICAO location identifier*] (ICLI)
FLCP........... Falcon Products, Inc. [*NASDAQ symbol*] (NQ)
FLCR........... Fixed Length Cavity Resonance
FLCRA......... Farm Labor Contractor Registration Act [*1963*] [*US Employment Service Department of Labor*]
FL CRS .... Flat Cars [*Freight*]
FLCS........... Chinsali [*Zambia*] [*ICAO location identifier*] (ICLI)
FLCS........... Force Level Control System
FLCS........... Front de Liberation de la Cote des Somalis [*Front for the Liberation of the Somali Coast*] [*Djibouti*]
FLCSP......... Fellow of the London and Counties Society of Physiologists [*British*]
FLCT........... Friends of Libraries Charitable Trust [*British*]
FLCTN......... Fluctuation (FAAC)
FLcV........... United States Veterans Administration Hospital, Lake City, FL [*Library symbol Library of Congress*] (LCLS)
FLD .... Fairchild Gold [*Vancouver Stock Exchange symbol*]
FLD .... Fairlead (MSA)
FLD .... Family Law Division (New South Wales Supreme Court) [*Australia*]
FLD .... Fault Logic Diagram
FLD .... Ferret LASER Detector
FLD .... Field [*Computer science*] (AFM)
FLD .... Field
FLD .... Fieldair Freight Ltd. [*New Zealand*] [*ICAO designator*] (FAAC)
FLD .... Fieldcrest Cannon [*NYSE symbol*] (TTSB)
FLD .... Fieldcrest Cannon, Inc. [*NYSE symbol*] (SPSG)
FLD .... Field Division [*Census*] (OICC)
FLD .... Field Liaison Division [*Military*]
FLD .... Flood (MCD)
fld .... Flowered [*Botany*]
FLD .... Fluid (AAG)
FLD .... Fluid Dynamics (SSD)
FLD .... Flux Lattice Dislocation (PDAA)
FLD .... Fond Du Lac, WI [*Location identifier FAA*] (FAAL)
FLD .... Forming Limit Diagram [*Manufacturing term*]
FLD .... Fraunhofer Line Discriminator [*Physics*]
FLD .... Friends of the Lake District (EERA)
FLD .... Fuel Loading Data [*Nuclear energy*] (NRCH)
FLD .... Functional Line Diagram (KSC)
FLD .... Fund for Labor Defense (EA)
FLD .... Newfoundland Tracking Station
FLDA.......... Federal Land Development Authority [*Malaysia*]
FLDACTYSq... Field Activity Squadron [*Air Force*]
Fld Amb....... Field Ambulance [*British military*] (DMA)
FLDARTYGRU... Field Artillery Group
FLDBR .... Field Branch
FLDBRBUMED... Field Branch, Bureau of Medicine and Surgery [*Navy*] (DNAB)
FLDC........... Fieldcrest Cannon [*NASDAQ symbol*] (SAG)
FldCH.......... Field Champion [*Dog show term*]
FLDCK......... Field Cook [*Marine Corps*]
FLDCK(B)..... Field Cook (Baker) [*Marine Corps*]
FLDCK(C)..... Field Cook (Commissary) [*Marine Corps*]
FLDCOMDASA... Field Command, Defense Atomic Support Agency (AABC)
FLDCOMDNA... Field Command, Defense Nuclear Agency [*DoD*] (AABC)
FLDCP......... Fieldcrest Cannon $3 Cv [*NASDAQ symbol*] (TTSB)
Fldcrst .... Fieldcrest Cannon [*Associated Press*] (SAG)
Fldcrst .... Fieldcrest Cannon, Inc. [*Associated Press*] (SAG)
FLDE........... Delkin (Lusiwasi) [*Zambia*] [*ICAO location identifier*] (ICLI)
FLDEC......... Floating-Point Decimal [*Computer science*]
fld ext......... Fluid Extract [*Pharmacology*] (DAVI)
FLDEXT........ Fluidextractum [*Fluidextract*] [*Pharmacy*]
FLDG.......... Folding (MSA)
FLDGM........ Folding Map [*Publishing*]
FLDI........... Flare Die
FLDK........... Flight Deck
FLDL........... Field Length (IAA)
FLDMAINTSq... Field Maintenance Squadron [*Air Force*]
FLDMEDSERVSCOL... Field Medical Service School (DNAB)
FLDMS......... Field Maintenance Shop [*Army*] (AABC)
FLDMSLMAINTSq... Field Missile Maintenance Squadron [*Air Force*]
FLDNG........ Flooding
FLDO .... Field Officer
FLDO .... Final Limit, Down
FLDP........... Federation of Liberal and Democratic Parties (PPE)
FLDR.......... Flanders Corp. [*NASDAQ symbol*] (TTSB)
FLDR.......... Flanders Corp. [*NASDAQ symbol*] (SAG)
FLDR .... Fluid Dram
FLD RATS.... Field Rations (DNAB)
fld rest......... Fluid Restriction [*Dietetics*] (DAVI)
FLDS........... Fields
FLDS........... Fields [*Postal Service standard*] (OPSA)
FLDS........... Fixed-Length Distinguishing Sequence [*Computer science*] (IAA)
FLDST......... Flood Stage [*NWS*] (FAAC)

FLDSUPPACT... Field Support Activity [*Military*] (DNAB)

FLDT............ Fast Linear Displacement Transducer [*Electronics*]

FLDT............ Floodlight

FLDTG.......... Field Training Group [*Military*]

FLDTNS......... Field Trains

FLDTS.......... Field Training Squadron

FldUrd.......... Fluorodeoxyuridine [*Floxuridine*] [*Also, FUDR Antineoplastic drug*]

FLDXT........... Fluidextractum [*Fluidextract*] [*Pharmacy*]

FLE .... Fatigue Life Expectancy [*or Expended*] (MCD)

FLE .... Fire, Lightning, and Explosion [*Insurance*] (AIA)

FLE .... Fixed Leading Edge (MCD)

FLE .... Fleet [*Navy*]

FLE .... Fleetwood Enterpr [*NYSE symbol*] (TTSB)

FLE .... Fleetwood Enterprises, Inc. [*NYSE symbol*] (SPSG)

FLE .... Fletcher [*Vermont*] [*Seismograph station code, US Geological Survey*] (SEIS)

FLE .... Forward Logistical Element [*Military*]

FLe .... Leesburg Public Library, Leesburg, FL [*Library symbol*] [*Library of Congress*] (LCLS)

FLE .... Telemetering Land Station [*ITU designation*] (CET)

FLEA........... East One [*Zambia*] [*ICAO location identifier*] (ICLI)

FLEA........... Flux Logic Element Array

FLEACT......... Fleet Activities

FLEASWSCOL... Fleet Antisubmarine Warfare School (MUGU)

FLEASWTACSCOL... Fleet Antisubmarine Warfare Tactical School

FLEASWTRACENLANT... Fleet Antisubmarine Warfare Training Center, Atlantic (DNAB)

FLEASWTRACENLPAC... Fleet Antisubmarine Warfare Training Center, Pacific (DNAB)

FLEASWTRAGRU... Fleet Antisubmarine Warfare Training Group (DNAB)

FLEAVNACCTO... Fleet Aviation Accounting Office (DNAB)

FLEAVNACCTOLANT... Fleet Aviation Accounting Office, Atlantic (DNAB)

FLEAVNACCTOPAC... Fleet Aviation Accounting Office, Pacific (DNAB)

FLEAVNMATOPAC... Fleet Aviation Material Office, Pacific (DNAB)

FLEB........... East Two [*Zambia*] [*ICAO location identifier*] (ICLI)

FLEB........... Flebile [*Pensive*] [*Music*] (ROG)

FLEBALMISTRACEN... Fleet Ballistic Missile Training Center (DNAB)

FLEBALMISUBTRACEN... Fleet Ballistic Missile Submarine Training Center

FLEBALMISUBTRACENLANT... Fleet Ballistic Missile Submarine Training Center, Atlantic (DNAB)

FLEBALMISUBTRACENPAC... Fleet Ballistic Missile Submarine Training Center, Pacific (DNAB)

FLEC .... East Three [*Zambia*] [*ICAO location identifier*] (ICLI)

FLEC .... Frente de Libertacao do Enclave de Cabinda [*Front for the Liberation of the Cabinda Enclave*] [*Angola*] (PD)

FLECC.......... Federal Libraries' Experiment in Cooperative Cataloging [*Later, FEDLINK*]

FLECHT......... Full Length Emergency Cooling Heat Transfer [*Nuclear energy*] (NRCH)

FLECOMBDIRSYSTRACEN... Fleet Combat Direction System Training Center [*Navy*] (DNAB)

FLECOMBDIRSYSTRACENLANT... Fleet Combat Direction System Training Center, Atlantic [*Navy*] (DNAB)

FLECOMBDIRSYSTRACENPAC... Fleet Combat Direction System Training Center, Pacific [*Navy*] (DNAB)

FLECOMPRON... Fleet Composite Squadron [*Navy*]

FLECOMPRONDET... Fleet Composite Squadron Detachment [*Navy*] (DNAB)

FLECOMPUT... Fleet Computer Programming Center [*Navy*] (MCD)

FLECOMPUTPROGCEN... Fleet Computer Programming Center [*Navy*] (MCD)

FLECOMPUTPROGCENLANT... Fleet Computer Programming Center, Atlantic [*Navy*] (DNAB)

FLECOMPUTPROGCENPAC... Fleet Computer Programming Center, Pacific [*Navy*] (DNAB)

FLED........... East Four [*Zambia*] [*ICAO location identifier*] (ICLI)

FLEDR .... Foreign Language Entrance and Degree Requirements (EDAC)

FLEE .... East Five [*Zambia*] [*ICAO location identifier*] (ICLI)

FLEE .... Fast Linkage Editor [*Computer science*] (MHDI)

FLEEP.......... Flying Lunar Excursion Experimental Platform [*NASA*]

FleetEn .... Fleetwood Enterprises, Inc. [*Associated Press*] (SAG)

FLEETEX ...... Fleet Exercise [*Navy*] (NVT)

FleetFnc ...... Fleet Financial Group [*Associated Press*] (SAG)

FLEETSAT .... Fleet Communications Satellite [*Navy*] (MCD)

FLEETSATCOM... Fleet Satellite Communications System [*DoD*]

FLEF .... East Six [*Zambia*] [*ICAO location identifier*] (ICLI)

FLEG........... East Seven [*Zambia*] [*ICAO location identifier*] (ICLI)

FLEH........... East Eight [*Zambia*] [*ICAO location identifier*] (ICLI)

FLEHOSPSUPPOFF... Fleet Hospital Support Office (DNAB)

FLEINTROTM... Fleet Introduction Team [*Navy*] (DNAB)

FLeL........... Lake-Sumter Community College, Leesburg, FL [*Library symbol Library of Congress*] (LCLS)

FLELO.......... Fleet Liaison Officer (DNAB)

FLELOGSUPPRON... Fleet Logistics Support Squadron (DNAB)

FLELOGSUPPRONDET... Fleet Logistics Support Squadron Detachment (DNAB)

FLEM .... Flemish

Flem .... Flemish (VRA)

FLEM .... Flyby-Landing Excursion Mode [*Aviation*]

FLEMARFOR... Fleet Marine Force [*Navy*] (DNAB)

FLEMARFORLANT... Fleet Marine Force, Atlantic [*Navy*] (DNAB)

FLEMARFORPAC... Fleet Marine Force, Pacific [*Navy*] (DNAB)

FLEMATSUPPO... Fleet Material Support Office [*Navy*]

FLEMATSUPPODET... Fleet Material Support Office Detachment [*Navy*] (DNAB)

FLEMATSUPPOFAGLANT... Fleet Material Support Office, Fleet Assistance Group, Atlantic [*Navy*]

FLEMATSUPPOFAGPAC... Fleet Material Support Office, Fleet Assistance Group, Pacific [*Navy*]

FlemgBT ...... [*The*] Flemington National Bank & Trust [*Associated Press*] (SAG)

FLEMINWARTRACEN... Fleet Mine Warfare Training Center (DNAB)

FLEMIS........ Flexible Management Information System (DNAB)

Flemng .... Fleming Companies, Inc. [*Associated Press*] (SAG)

FLEND......... Flendist [*England*]

FLENUMOCEANCEN... Fleet Numerical Oceanography Center (DNAB)

FLENUMWEAFAC... Fleet Numerical Weather Facility (MUGU)

FLEOA......... Federal Law Enforcement Officers Association (EA)

FLEOPINTRACEN... Fleet Operational Intelligence Training Center [*Navy*]

FLEOPINTRACENLANT... Fleet Operational Intelligence Training Center, Atlantic [*Navy*] (DNAB)

FLEOPINTRACENPAC... Fleet Operational Intelligence Training Center, Pacific [*Navy*] (DNAB)

FLER.......... Fractional Loss Exchange Ratio (MCD)

FLEREADREP... Fleet Readiness Representative [*Navy*] (AFIT)

FLES .... Foreign Languages in Elementary Schools

FLESCOP...... Flexible Signal Collection and Processing (DNAB)

FLESONARSCOL... Fleet SONAR School [*Navy*]

FLESUBTRAFAC... Fleet Submarine Training Facility [*Navy*]

FLETAC........ Fleet Tactical Field Office (DNAB)

FLETACSUPPRON... Fleet Tactical Support Squadron [*Navy*]

FletBld........ Fletcher Challenge Building [*Associated Press*] (SAG)

FLETC .... Federal Law Enforcement Training Center [*Department of the Treasury*]

Fletcher Corporations... Fletcher's Cyclopedia of Corporations [*A publication*] (DLA)

Fletcher Cyc Corp... Fletcher's Cyclopedia of Corporations [*A publication*] (DLA)

Fletch Tr... Fletch on Trustees of Estates [*A publication*] (DLA)

FLETECHSUPPCENDET... Fleet Technical Support Center Detachment (DNAB)

FletEgy .... Fletcher Challenge Energy [*Associated Press*] (SAG)

FletFD......... Fletcher Challenge ADR ORD [*Associated Press*] (SAG)

FletOD........ Fletcher Challenge ADR ORD [*Associated Press*] (SAG)

FletPap....... Fletcher Challenge Paper [*Associated Press*] (SAG)

FLETRABASE... Fleet Training Base

FLETRACEN... Fleet Training Center [*Navy*]

FLETRAGRUDET... Fleet Training Group Detachment [*Navy*] (DNAB)

FLETRAGRUWATE... Fleet Training Group and Underway Training Element

FLETRAGRUWESTPAC... Fleet Training Group, Western Pacific [*Navy*] (DNAB)

FLETRAN ...... Fleet Training Unit (DNAB)

Fleury Hist... Fleury's History of the Origin of French Laws [*1724*] [*A publication*] (DLA)

FLEWEACEN... Fleet Weather Center [*or Central*] [*NATO*] (NATG)

FLEWEAFAC... Fleet Weather Facility [*NATO*] (NATG)

FLEWORKSTUDYGRULANT... Fleet Work Study Group, Atlantic [*Navy*]

FLEX .... Federal Licensing Examination [*for physicians*]

FLEX .... Fladden Ground Experiment [*Oceanography*] (MSC)

FLEX .... Fleet Exercise [*Navy British*]

FLEX ...... Fleet Life Extension (MCD)

FLEX .... Flexible (AABC)

FLEX .... Flexion [*Medicine*]

flex .... Flexor [*Anatomy*] (DAVI)

FLEX .... Flexowriter Equipment (AABC)

FLEX .... Flexure [*Mechanics*]

FLEX .... Free Lance Exchange

FLEX .... Free Learning Exchange [*An association Defunct*] (EA)

FLEXAR........ Flexible Adaptive RADAR (MCD)

FLEXBL .... Flexible (BARN)

FLEXEM .... Flexible Energy Management (MCD)

FLEXF .... Flextronics International [*NASDAQ symbol*] (SAG)

FLEXF .... Flextronics Intl [*NASDAQ symbol*] (TTSB)

FLEXIMIS ..... Flexible Management Information System (MHDI)

FLEXOPS ..... Flexible Operations (DNAB)

flex sig .... Flexible Sigmoidoscopy [*Gastroenterology*] (DAVI)

Flexstl......... Flexsteel Industries, Inc. [*Associated Press*] (SAG)

Flextrn .... Fletronics International [*Associated Press*] (SAG)

Flextrn .... Flextronics International [*Associated Press*] (SAG)

FLF .... Fault Location Facility [*Aircraft*]

FLF .... Final Limit, Forward

FLF .... Fisheries Loan Fund [*National Oceanic and Atmospheric Administration*]

FLF .... Fixed-Length Field [*Computer science*] (BUR)

FLF .... Flin Flon Mines [*Vancouver Stock Exchange symbol*]

FLF .... Flip-Flop [*Computer science*] (DEN)

FLF .... Follow-the-Leader Feedback [*Circuit theory*] (IEEE)

FLF .... Four Lucky Fellows [*In company name, FLF Associates*] [*Investment group comprised of four sons of Lawrence Tisch*]

FLF .... Fran Lee Foundation (EA)

FLF .... Freedom Leadership Foundation (EA)

FLF .... Friendly Laotian Forces (CINC)

FLFADDFA..... France-Louisiane/Franco-Americaine - Defense et Developpement de la FrancophonieAmericaine (EAIO)

FLFC.......... First Liberty Financial Corp. [*NASDAQ symbol*] (NQ)

FLFCO......... First Liberty Fin'l 6% Cv Pfd [*NASDAQ symbol*] (TTSB)

FLFI.......... Lusaka [*Zambia*] [*ICAO location identifier*] (ICLI)

FLFN.......... Free Lance Finders Network (EA)

FLFT.......... Forklift (AABC)

FLFT.......... Full Load Frame Time [*Term used in SAGE operations*]

FLFW.......... Fiwila [*Zambia*] [*ICAO location identifier*] (ICLI)

FLG.......... Express Airlines I, Inc. [*ICAO designator*] (FAAC)

FLG............ Falling [*NWS*] (FAAC)

FLG............ Flag [*Computer science*] (MDG)

FLG............ Flag Flange (MCD)

FLG............ Flagship [*Navy*] (NVT)

FLG............ Flagstaff [*Arizona*] [*Seismograph station code, US Geological Survey Closed*] (SEIS)

FLG............ Flagstaff [*Arizona*] [*Airport symbol*] (OAG)

FLG............	Flagstaff, AZ [*Location identifier FAA*] (FAAL)
FLG............	Flange (MSA)
FLG............	Flashing
FLG............	Fletcher Leisure Group, Inc. [*Toronto Stock Exchange symbol*]
FLG............	Flong [*Printing*] (DGA)
FLG............	Flooring (KSC)
FLG............	Flying (AABC)
FLG............	Focal Length [*Photography*] (IAA)
FLG............	Following
FLG............	Franciscan Sisters of Our Lady of Grace (TOCD)
FLG............	Friends of Little Gidding (EA)
FLG............	Front de Libertacao de Guinee [*Guinean Liberation Front*] [*Portuguese Guinea*]
FLGA..........	Fellow of the Local Government Association [*British*]
FLGA..........	Florida Lychee Growers Association (EA)
FLGC..........	Friends for Lesbian and Gay Concerns (EA)
FLGE..........	Mukinge [*Zambia*] [*ICAO location identifier*] (ICLI)
FlghtSf........	Flightsafety International, Inc. [*Associated Press*] (SAG)
FLGSTF.......	Flagstaff
FLGSTN.......	Flagstone
Flgstr.........	Flagstar Companies, Inc. [*Associated Press*] (SAG)
FLGT..........	Flight
FLGW..........	Mpongwe [*Zambia*] [*ICAO location identifier*] (ICLI)
FLH............	Federacion Latinoamericana de Hospitales [*Latin American Hospital Federation*] (EAIO)
FLH............	Fife Light Horse [*British military*] (DMA)
FLH............	Fila Holdings [*NYSE symbol*] (SPSG)
FLH............	Fila Holdings ADS [*NYSE symbol*] (TTSB)
FLH............	Final Limit, Hoist
FLH............	Flash
FLH............	Flat Head (MSA)
FLH............	Land Hydrological and Meteorological Station [*ITU designation*] (DEN)
FLH............	Skybus, Inc. [*ICAO designator*] (FAAC)
FLHLS.........	Flashless [*NASA*] (KSC)
FL-HP.........	Filter-High Pass (MUGU)
FLHQ..........	Lusaka [*Zambia*] [*ICAO location identifier*] (ICLI)
FLHS..........	Fellow of the London Historical Society [*British*]
FLHS..........	Flashless
FLHV..........	Fife Light Horse Volunteers [*British military*] (DMA)
FLI.............	American Eagle Group [*NYSE symbol*] (SAG)
FLI.............	Atlantic Airways, PF (Faroe Islands) [*Denmark ICAO designator*] (FAAC)
FLI.............	Farm and Land Institute [*Later, RLI*] (EA)
FLI.............	Farm Labor Information [*US Employment Service*] [*Department of Labor*]
FLI.............	Fault Location Indicator
FLI.............	Federation Lainiere Internationale [*International Wool Textile Organization - IWTO*] (EAIO)
FLI.............	Fellow of the Landscape Institute [*British*] (DBQ)
FLI.............	Flateyri [*Iceland*] [*Airport symbol*] (OAG)
FLI.............	Flick [*A motion-video format*]
FLI.............	Flight Leader Identity [*RADAR*]
FLI.............	Flint Rock Mines [*Vancouver Stock Exchange symbol*]
FLI.............	Fluorescence-Line Imager [*Instrumentation*]
FLI.............	Food Law Institute [*Later, FDLI*] (EA)
FLI.............	Foodservice and Lodging Institute (EA)
FLI.............	Former Live-In
FLI.............	Forward-Looking Infrared
FLI.............	Free Language Indexing [*Information retrieval*] (NITA)
FLI.............	Funnel Length Index
FLIA..........	Federation Life Insurance of America [*Milwaukee, WI*] (EA)
FLIA..........	Fellow of the Life Insurance Association [*British*] (ODBW)
FLIC..........	Fault Location Indicating Console (AABC)
FLIC..........	Film Library Information Council [*EFLA*] [*Absorbed by*] (EA)
FLIC..........	Film Library Inter-College Cooperative of Pennsylvania [*Library network*]
FLIC..........	First Long Island [*NASDAQ symbol*] (TTSB)
FLIC..........	[*The*] First of Long Island Corp. [*NASDAQ symbol*] (NQ)
FLIC..........	Flaw Locating and Imaging Computer (PDAA)
FLIC..........	Foreign Languages for Industry and Commerce [*British*] (DBQ)
FLICC.........	Federal Library and Information Center Committee [*Library of Congress Also, an information service or system*] (IID)
FLICON.......	Flight Control [*or Controller*]
FLICR........	Fluid Logic Industrial Control Relay
FLICS.........	Farm Labor Interstate Clearance System [*US Employment Service*] [*Department of Labor*]
FLICS.........	Foreign Language Innovative Curricula Study [*University of Michigan*] (AEBS)
FLID..........	Find or List the Identifications (SAA)
FLID..........	Front de la Lutte pour l'Independence du Dahomey [*Battle Front for the Independence of Dahomey*]
FLIDAP	Flight Data Position
FLIDEN	Flight Data Entry [*Device*] [*SAGE*]
FLIDIT........	Flight Line Detection and Isolation Techniques
FLIDRAS......	Flight Data Replay and Analysis System (GAVI)
FLIER........	Fast, Low-Ionization Emission-Line Region [*Planetary science*]
FLIFO.........	Flight Information
FLIGA.........	Forced Landing Incidents - Ground Accidents
FLIH..........	First Level Interrupt Handler [*Computer science*]
FLIK..........	Isoka [*Zambia*] [*ICAO location identifier*] (ICLI)
FLIM..........	Fast Library Maintenance
FLIM..........	Fast Library Maintenance (NITA)
FLIMBAL......	Floated Inertial Measurement Ball

FLIN...........	Florida Library Information Network [*Florida State Library*] [*Tallahassee, FL*] [*Library network*]
FLINBAL......	Fluid Inertial Balance (MCD)
FLING	Frente da Luta pela Independencia Nacional da Guine "Portuguesa" [*Front for the Fight for Guinea-Bissau's National Independence*] (PD)
FLINK.........	Flash/Wink Signal [*Telecommunications*] (TEL)
FLINKS........	Front de Liberation Nationale Kanake Socialiste [*National Liberation Front ofSocialist Kanakes*] [*New Caledonia*] [*Political party*]
FLIN-NSW....	Federal Libraries Information Network - New South Wales [*Australia*]
FLIN-NT.......	Federal Libraries Information Network - Northern Territory [*Australia*]
FLIN-QLD.....	Federal Libraries Information Network - Queensland [*Australia*]
Flint	Flintshire [*Former county in Wales*] (WGA)
FLINT	Floating Interpretive Language [*Princeton University*]
Flint Conv....	Flintoff's Introduction to Conveyancing [*A publication*] (DLA)
Flint R Pr....	Flintoff's Real Property [*1839-40*] [*A publication*] (DLA)
FLINTS........	Flintshire [*Former county in Wales*]
FLIN-VIC......	Federal Libraries Information Network - Victoria [*Australia*]
FLIN-WA......	Federal Libraries Information Network - Western Australia
FLIOP.........	Flight Operations Planner
FLIP..........	Family Life Income Patterns [*Economics simulation game*]
FLIP..........	Film Library Instantaneous Presentation [*Computer science*]
FLIP..........	Financially Limited Plan (NATG)
FLIP..........	Flexible Loan Insurance Program
FLIP..........	Flight Information Plan
FLIP..........	Flight Information Publication [*Air Force*]
FLIP..........	Flight Launched Infrared Probe
Flip............	Flippin's Circuit Court Reports [*United States*] [*A publication*] (DLA)
FLIP..........	Floated Lightweight Inertial Platform
FLIP..........	Floating Indexed Point Arithmetic [*Computer science*]
FLIP..........	Floating Instrument Platform [*Navy*] (NG)
FLIP..........	Floating Laboratory Instrument Platform [*Movable oceanographic research station*]
FLIP..........	Floating-Point Interpretive Program [*Computer science*]
FLIP..........	Fluorescence Loss in Photobleaching [*Analytical biochemistry*]
FLIP..........	Format Directed List Processor [*Computer science*] (IAA)
FLIP..........	Free-Form Language for Image Processing (PDAA)
FLIP..........	French Language Intensive Program [*Illinois*] (EDAC)
FLIpp..........	Fuzzy Logic Inferences per Second [*Computer chip technology*]
Flipp (F)......	Flippin's Circuit Court Reports [*United States*] [*A publication*] (DLA)
FLIPPG	French-Language Infant Pneumology and Phthisiology Group [*Yerres, France*] (EAIO)
FLIPS..........	Future Language Information Processing System (BUR)
FLIPS..........	Fuzzy Logical Inferences per Second [*Computer chip technology*]
FLIR...........	Flight Low-Level Image Receiver
FLIR...........	FLIR Systems [*NASDAQ symbol*] (TTSB)
FLIR...........	FLIR Systems, Inc. [*NASDAQ symbol*] (SAG)
FLIR...........	Forward-Loading Infrared (RDA)
FLIR...........	Forward-Looking Infrared (AFM)
FLIR...........	Forward Looking Infrared RADAR [*Military*] (INF)
FLIR...........	Forward-Looking Infrared Sensor (VNW)
FLIRAS	Forward-Looking Infrared Attack Set
FLIRS	Forward-Looking Infrared System
FLIRT.........	Federal Librarians Round Table [*American Library Association*]
FLIRT.........	First Ladies' International Racing Team [*Group of women racing at Le Mans, France*]
FLIRT.........	FORTRAN [*Formula Translating System*] Logical Information Retrieval Technique [*Computer science*]
FLIRT.........	Free Language Information Retrieval Tool [*Netherlands*] (NITA)
FLIRTS........	Forward-Looking Infrared Thermovision System (MCD)
FLiS...........	Suwannee River Regional Library, Live Oak, FL [*Library symbol Library of Congress*] (LCLS)
FLIST.........	File List Processor [*Computer science*]
FLIT	Fault Location through Interpretive Testing [*Computer science*]
FLIT	Flexowriter Interrogation Tape
FLIT	Free Limiting Internal Truss [*Nuclear energy*] (NRCH)
FLIT	Frequency Line Tracker [*Military*] (CAAL)
FLIT	Functional Literacy [*Program to provide marginally literate soldiers with minimal literacy skills*] [*Army*] (RDA)
FLITE.........	Federal Legal Information through Electronics [*Air Force*] (IID)
FLITE	Future Lawyers Investigating Transportation Employment [*Student legal action organization*] (EA)
FLITT.........	Frigate LAMPS [*Light Airborne Multipurpose System*] Integrated Team Training [*Navy*] (ANA)
FLIWR	Functional Listing and Interconnection Wiring Record
FLIXS.........	Fleet Information Exchange System [*Navy*] (MCD)
FLIZ	F-Layer Irregularity Zone [*Geophysics*]
FLJ............	Canada Fortnightly Law Journal [*A publication*] (DLA)
FLJ............	Federal Law Journal [*1939*] [*A publication*] (DLA)
FLJ............	Federal Law Journal of India [*A publication*] (DLA)
FLJ............	Freelance Journalist (DGA)
FLJ (Can)....	Fortnightly Law Journal (Canada) [*A publication*] (ILCA)
FLJ Ind	Federal Law Journal of India [*A publication*] (DLA)
FLJTC........	Freeland League for Jewish Territorial Colonization [*Later, LYI*] (EA)
FLK...........	Falcks Redningskorps Beldringe AS [*Denmark ICAO designator*] (FAAC)
FLK...........	Falkland Islands [*ANSI three-letter standard code*] (CNC)
FLK...........	Fetal Lamb Kidney [*A cell line*]
FLK...........	Fleck Resources Ltd. [*Vancouver Stock Exchange symbol*]
FLK...........	Fluke Corp. [*NYSE symbol*] (SAG)
FLK...........	Funny Looking Kid [*Syndrome*] [*Medical slang*]
FLKB	Kawambwa [*Zambia*] [*ICAO location identifier*] (ICLI)
FLKD..........	Fluked [*Naval architecture*]
FLKD..........	Kalundu [*Zambia*] [*ICAO location identifier*] (ICLI)
FLKE	Kasompe [*Zambia*] [*ICAO location identifier*] (ICLI)

FLKG	Kalengwa [Zambia] [ICAO location identifier] (ICLI)
FLKJ	Kanja [Zambia] [ICAO location identifier] (ICLI)
FLKK	Kakumbi [Zambia] [ICAO location identifier] (ICLI)
FLKL	Kalabo [Zambia] [ICAO location identifier] (ICLI)
FLKM	Kapiri Mposhi [Zambia] [ICAO location identifier] (ICLI)
FLKO	Kaoma [Zambia] [ICAO location identifier] (ICLI)
FLKS	Kasama [Zambia] [ICAO location identifier] (ICLI)
FLKU	Kanyau [Zambia] [ICAO location identifier] (ICLI)
FLKW	Kabwe/Milliken [Zambia] [ICAO location identifier] (ICLI)
FLKY	First Lancaster Bancshares, Inc. [NASDAQ symbol] (SAG)
FLKY	Kasaba Bay [Zambia] [ICAO location identifier] (ICLI)
FLKZ	Lukuzi [Zambia] [ICAO location identifier] (ICLI)
FLL	Federal Airlines [Sudan] [FAA designator] (FAAC)
FLL	Final Limit, Lower
FLL	Flow Line
FLL	Flux-Line Lattice [Superconductivity] [Physics]
FLL	Fort Lauderdale [Florida] [Airport symbol] (OAG)
FLL	FoxPro Link Library [Microsoft Corp.] [Computer science] (PCM)
FLL	Frequency Locked Loop (IAA)
FLL	Frequency-Locked-Looped
FLL	Harvard University, Frances Loeb Library, Cambridge, MA [OCLC symbol] (OCLC)
FLI	Lakeland Public Library, Lakeland, FL [Library symbol] [Library of Congress] (LCLS)
FLLA	Luanshya [Zambia] [ICAO location identifier] (ICLI)
FLLAP	Foreign Languages for Lower Attaining Pupils [Project] (AIE)
FLLASH	Full Level Light Aircraft System Hardware (MCD)
FLLC	Lusaka [Zambia] [ICAO location identifier] (ICLI)
FLLD	Full Load
FLLD	Lundazi [Zambia] [ICAO location identifier] (ICLI)
FLLI	Livingstone [Zambia] [ICAO location identifier] (ICLI)
FLLK	Frustum Lifting Lug Kit (MCD)
FLLK	Lukulu [Zambia] [ICAO location identifier] (ICLI)
FLLO	Kalomo [Zambia] [ICAO location identifier] (ICLI)
FL-LP	Filter-Low Pass (MUGU)
FLLS	Family Location and Legal Service [Formerly, FLS] (EA)
FLLS	Finger Lakes Library System [Library network]
FLIS	Florida Southern College, Lakeland, FL [Library symbol Library of Congress] (LCLS)
FLLS	Focused LASER Lithographic System
FLLS	Fuel Low Level Sensor (IAA)
FLLS	Lusaka/International [Zambia] [ICAO location identifier] (ICLI)
FLLS	Waterfalls [Board on Geographic Names]
FLISC	Southeastern College of the Assemblies of God, Lakeland, FL [Library symbol] [Library of Congress] (LCLS)
FLLU	Federation of Libyan Labor Unions
FLLU	Luampa [Zambia] [ICAO location identifier] (ICLI)
FLLWSHP	Fellowship
FLLY	Lilayi [Zambia] [ICAO location identifier] (ICLI)
FLM	Falmouth, KY [Location identifier FAA] (FAAL)
FLM	Family Life Mission [An association] (EAIO)
FLM	Fasciculus Longitudinalis Medialis [Medicine] (DMAA)
FLM	Federal Land Manager [Department of the Interior] (GFGA)
FLM	Federation Lutherienne Mondiale [Lutheran World Foundation - LWF] [Geneva, Switzerland] (EAIO)
FLM	Fetal Lung Maturity [Physiology]
FLM	Film
FLM	Finished Lens Molding
FLM	Flame (MSA)
FLM	Fleming Companies, Inc. [NYSE symbol] (SPSG)
FLM	Fleming Cos. [NYSE symbol] (TTSB)
FLM	Flight Line Maintenance
FLM	Fluidic Logic Module
FLM	Fraction of Labeled Mitoses [Measurement of cell labeling]
FLM	Friends of the Louvre Museum (EA)
FLM	Frightened Little Man
FLM	Functional Level Management
FLM	Funny Little Man [Recognizable graphic type]
FLMA	Family Life Movement of Australia
FLMA	Mansa [Zambia] [ICAO location identifier] (ICLI)
FLMB	Flammable (MSA)
FLMB	Maamba [Zambia] [ICAO location identifier] (ICLI)
FLMC	Full Load Motor Current [Kraus & Naimer Microelectronics]
FLMD	Musonda Falls [Zambia] [ICAO location identifier] (ICLI)
FLME	Fatigue Life Modification Expert [Automotive engineering]
FLMECH	Fluid Mechanical (MCD)
FLMEM	Floppy Disc Memory (NITA)
FLMF	Mfuwe [Zambia] [ICAO location identifier] (ICLI)
FLM-FJC	Fur, Leather and Machine Workers Unions - Furriers Joint Council (EA)
FLMG	Mongu [Zambia] [ICAO location identifier] (ICLI)
FLMI	Fellow, Life Management Institute [Life Office Management Association] [Designation awarded by]
FLMI	Fellow of the Life Management Institute (DD)
FLMI	Mukonchi [Zambia] [ICAO location identifier] (ICLI)
FLMK	Foilmark, Inc. [NASDAQ symbol] (SAG)
FLMK	Mkushi [Zambia] [ICAO location identifier] (ICLI)
FLML	Flamel Technologies [NASDAQ symbol] (SAG)
FLML	Mufulira [Zambia] [ICAO location identifier] (ICLI)
FLMM	Mwami [Zambia] [ICAO location identifier] (ICLI)
FLMNAG	Fulminating (ABBR)
FLMNAN	Fulmination (ABBR)
FLMNC	Flamboyance (ABBR)
FLMNGY	Flamingly (ABBR)
FLMNS	Filminess (ABBR)

FLMNT	Flamboyant (ABBR)
FLMNTY	Flamboyantly (ABBR)
FLMO	Monze [Zambia] [ICAO location identifier] (ICLI)
FLMP	Mpika [Zambia] [ICAO location identifier] (ICLI)
FLMPRF	Flameproof (MSA)
FLMPRS	Film Processing
FLMPTS	Future Land Mobile Personal Telephone Service
FLMR	Filmier (ABBR)
FLM RES	Flame Resistant (MSA)
FLM RTD	Flame Retardant (MSA)
FLMRY	Flummery (ABBR)
FLMSD	Film Sound
FLMSNS	Flimsiness (ABBR)
FLMSR	Flimsier (ABBR)
FLMSST	Flimsiest (ABBR)
FLMST	Filmiest (ABBR)
FLMSY	Flimsily (ABBR)
FLMSY	Flimsy (ABBR)
FLMT	Flush Mount
FLMT	Mutanda [Zambia] [ICAO location identifier] (ICLI)
FLMTHR	Flamethrower (AABC)
FLMTO	Film Linearized Muffin-Tin Orbital [Physics]
FL/MTR	Flow Meter (AAG)
FLMTT	Flame Tight
FLMU	Mulobezi [Zambia] [ICAO location identifier] (ICLI)
FLMW	Mwinilunga [Zambia] [ICAO location identifier] (ICLI)
FLMY	Filmy (ABBR)
FLMZ	Mazabuka [Zambia] [ICAO location identifier] (ICLI)
FLN	Fallen (ABBR)
FLN	Feline (ABBR)
FLN	Felon (ABBR)
FLN	Flanders Airlines [Belgium ICAO designator] (FAAC)
FLN	Flatten (MSA)
FLN	Florianopolis [Brazil] [Airport symbol] (OAG)
FLN	Flown
Fln	Fluorene [Biochemistry]
FLN	Fluorescence-Line Narrowed [Spectrometry]
FLN	Following Landing Numbers [Shipping]
FLN	Freelance Network (EA)
FLN	Frente de Liberacion Nacional [National Liberation Front] [Venezuela Political party] (PD)
FLN	Frente de Liberacion Nacional [National Liberation Front] [Chile] [Political party]
FLN	Frente de Liberacion Nacional [National Liberation Front] [Peru] [Political party]
FLN	Frente de Liberacion Nacional [National Liberation Front] [El Salvador] [Political party]
FLN	Front de Liberation Nationale [National Liberation Front] [South Vietnam Use NFLSV] [Political party]
FLN	Front de Liberation Nationale [National Liberation Front] [France Political party]
FLN	Front de Liberation Nationale [National Liberation Front] [Algeria] [Political party] (PPW)
FLN	Fuel Line
FLN	La Foliniere [France] [Seismograph station code, US Geological Survey] (SEIS)
FLNA	Ngoma [Zambia] [ICAO location identifier] (ICLI)
FLNB	[The] Flemington National Bank & Trust [NASDAQ symbol] (SAG)
FLNC	Front de Liberation Nationale Congolais [Congolese National Liberation Front] [Zaire] [Political party]
FLNC	Front de Liberation Nationale de la Corse [Corsican National Liberation Front] [Political party] (PD)
FLNCD	Flounced (ABBR)
FLNCG	Flouncing (ABBR)
FLND	Ndola [Zambia] [ICAO location identifier] (ICLI)
FLNDR	Flounder (ABBR)
FLNDRD	Floundered (ABBR)
FLNDRG	Floundering (ABBR)
FLNF	Front de Liberation Nationale Francaise [French National Liberation Front] (PD)
FLNG	Fueling
FLNGG	Flinging (ABBR)
FLNH	Flinch (ABBR)
FLNHGY	Flinchingly (ABBR)
FLNHR	Flincher (ABBR)
FLNK	Flank (ABBR)
FLNK	Force de Liberation Nationale Kamerunaise [National Cameroonian Liberation Force] [Political party]
FLNKD	Flanked (ABBR)
FLNKG	Flanking (ABBR)
FLNKR	Flanker (ABBR)
FLNKY	Flunky (ABBR)
FLNL	Namwala [Zambia] [ICAO location identifier] (ICLI)
FLNPP	Federal Library Network Prototype Project (NITA)
FLNS	Fluidness (ABBR)
FLNS	Fluorescence Line-Narrowing Spectroscopy
FLNT	Felinity (ABBR)
FLNT	Flint (ABBR)
FLNTEST	Flauntiest (ABBR)
FLNTNS	Flintiness (ABBR)
FLNTR	Flintier (ABBR)
FLNTST	Flintiest (ABBR)
FLNTY	Flinty (ABBR)
FLNTYNS	Flintiness (ABBR)
FLNTYY	Flintily (ABBR)

FLNUS	Felonious (ABBR)
FLNUSNS	Feloniousness (ABBR)
FLNUSY	Feloniously (ABBR)
FLNY	Felinely (ABBR)
FLNY	Felony (ABBR)
FLNY	Nyimba [*Zambia*] [*ICAO location identifier*] (ICLI)
FLO	Falcon Airlines [*Yugoslavia*] [*ICAO designator*] (FAAC)
FLO	Family Liaison Office
FLO	Fault-Location Oscillator [*Bell System*]
FLO	Film Liaison Officer [*Army*]
FLO	Fleet Electrical Officer [*British military*] (DMA)
FL O	Flight Officer (WDAA)
Flo	Floodlight (DA)
FLO	Florence [*South Carolina*] [*Airport symbol*] (OAG)
FLO	Florence, SC [*Location identifier FAA*] (FAAL)
Flo	Florentinus [*Flourished, 2nd century*] [*Authority cited in pre-1607 legal work*] (DSA)
Flo	Florianus de Sancto Petro [*Deceased, 1441*] [*Authority cited in pre-1607 legal work*] (DSA)
Flo	Florilege [*Record label*] [*France*]
FLO	Florin [*Monetary unit*] [*Netherlands*] (ROG)
FLO	Florissant [*Missouri*] [*Seismograph station code, US Geological Survey Closed*] (SEIS)
FLO	Flowers Indus [*NYSE symbol*] (TTSB)
FLO	Flowers Industries, Inc. [*NYSE symbol*] (SPSG)
Fl/O	Flying Officer [*British*] (DMA)
FLO	Foreign Liaison Office [*Military*] (AABC)
FLO	Frederick Law Olmsted [*American landscape architect, 1822-1903*]
FLO	Fuel Lube Oil
FLO	Functional Line Organization
f-lo--	Lesotho [*MARC geographic area code Library of Congress*] (LCCP)
FLOA	Federal Licensed Officers Association (EA)
FLOA	Frederick Law Olmsted Association (EA)
FLOC	Farm Labor Organizing Committee (EA)
FLOC	Fault Localization
FLOC	Floccule (ABBR)
FLOC	Flocculent (ABBR)
FLOC	Floccus (ABBR)
FLOC	For Love of Children
FLOCC	Flocculation
FLOCOM	Floating Commutator
FLOCON	Floating Container (PDAA)
FLOD	Flood (ABBR)
FLODAC	Fluid-Operated Digital Automatic Computer [*Sperry UNIVAC*]
FLODD	Flooded (ABBR)
FLODG	Flooding (ABBR)
Fl Offr	Flying Officer [*British*] (DMA)
FLO/FLO	Float On/Float Off
FLOG	Fleet Logistics
FLOGAIR	Fleet Logistics Air Wing [*Navy*]
FLOGEN	Flow Generator [*Air Force*] (DOMA)
FLOGWING	Fleet Logistics Air Wing [*Obsolete Navy*]
FLOGWINGLANT	Fleet Logistics Air Wing, Atlantic [*Navy*]
FLOGWINGPAC	Fleet Logistics Air Wing, Pacific [*Navy*]
Flojo	Florence Griffith Joyner [*American track athlete and Olympic gold medalist*]
flok	Flocked (VRA)
FLOLS	Fresnel Lens Optical Landing System [*Navy*]
FLOOD	Fleet Observation of Oceanographic Data [*Navy*]
Flood El Eq	Flood. Equitable Doctrine of Election [*1880*] [*A publication*] (DLA)
Flood Lib	Flood. Slander and Libel [*1880*] [*A publication*] (DLA)
Flood Wills	Flood on Wills of Personal Property [*A publication*] (DLA)
FLOP	Floating Octal Point [*IBM Corp.*]
FLOP	Floating Point [*Electronics*] (ECII)
FLOP	Floating Point Operation [*Computer science*]
FLOP	Floating Point Operations Per Second (NITA)
FLOP	Foreign Liaison Officer Program
FLOP	Fresnel Lens Optical Practice [*Navy*]
FLOPD	Flopped (ABBR)
FLOPF	Fresnel Lens Optical Practice, Fleet [*Navy*]
FLOPG	Flopping (ABBR)
FLOPLY	Floppily (ABBR)
FLOPNS	Floppiness (ABBR)
FLOPP	Floating Power Platform (PDAA)
FLOPR	Flopper (ABBR)
FLOPR	Floppier (ABBR)
FLOPS	Floating-Point Operations per Second [*Computer science*]
FLOPST	Floppiest (ABBR)
FLOPY	Floppy (ABBR)
FLOPYR	Floppier (ABBR)
FLOPYST	Floppiest (ABBR)
FLOR	Florence [*Italy*] (ROG)
FLOR	Flores [*Flowers*] [*Latin*] (ROG)
Flor	Florianus de Sancto Petro [*Deceased, 1441*] [*Authority cited in pre-1607 legal work*] (DSA)
FLOR	Floriculture
Flor	Florida [*of Apuleius*] [*Classical studies*] (OCD)
Flor	Florida Reports [*A publication*] (DLA)
Flo R	Florida Reports [*A publication*] (DLA)
FLOR	Florist (ROG)
FLOR	Floruit [*He Flourished*] [*Latin*]
FLORA	Fire Location RADAR (NG)
Flore	Florentinus [*Flourished, 2nd century*] [*Authority cited in pre-1607 legal work*] (DSA)
FLORENT	Florentia [*Florence*] [*Latin*] (ROG)
FloresRk	Flores & Rucks, Inc. [*Associated Press*] (SAG)
FLOREX	Technical Exhibition for Florists [*Brussels International Trade Fair*]
FLORG	Flooring (ABBR)
Flori	Florianus de Sancto Petro [*Deceased, 1441*] [*Authority cited in pre-1607 legal work*] (DSA)
Floria	Florianus de Sancto Petro [*Deceased, 1441*] [*Authority cited in pre-1607 legal work*] (DSA)
Florida	Florida Reports [*A publication*] (DLA)
FLORIDA COMCAT	Florida Computer Catalog of Monographic Holdings [*Library network*]
Florida R	Florida Reports [*A publication*] (DLA)
Florida Rep	Florida Reports [*A publication*] (DLA)
FLORL	Fluorescent Runway Lighting
FLORR	Flourier (ABBR)
FLORSENT	Fluorescent [*Freight*]
FlorshGp	Florsheim Group [*Associated Press*] (SAG)
FlorshSh	[*The*] Florsheim Shoe Co. [*Associated Press*] (SAG)
FLORST	Flouriest (ABBR)
FLOR-WKR	Floorwalker (ABBR)
FLORY	Floury (ABBR)
FLOS	Fixed Line of Sight (KSC)
FLOSOST	Fluorine One-Stage Orbital Space Truck (KSC)
FLOSY	Front for the Liberation of Occupied South Yemen (PD)
FLOT	Float (ABBR)
FLOT	Flotation (KSC)
FLOT	Flotilla (AABC)
FLOT	Flotsam (ABBR)
FLOT	Forward Line of Own Troops (MCD)
FLOTD	Floated (ABBR)
FLOTG	Floating (ABBR)
FLOTGE	Floatage (ABBR)
FLOTL	Flotilla (ABBR)
FLOTM	Flotsam (ABBR)
FLOTN	Flotation (ABBR)
FLOTOX	Floating Gate Tunnel Oxide [*Electronics*] (EECA)
FLOTR	Floater (ABBR)
FLOTRAN	Flowcharting FORTRAN [*Computer science*] (IEEE)
FLOTRONCOM	Flotilla or Squadron Commander (DNAB)
FLOT STOR	Floating Storage (DNAB)
FLOTUS	First Lady of the United States
FLOU	Flourish (WGA)
flour	Flourescent (VRA)
FLOV	Federation of Latvian Organisations of Victoria [*Australia*]
FLOVTH	Flush Oiltight Ventilation Hole
FLOW	Flow International [*NASDAQ symbol*] (TTSB)
FLOW	Flow International Corp. [*NASDAQ symbol*] (NQ)
Flower	Flowers Industries, Inc. [*Associated Press*] (SAG)
FlowInt	Flow International Corp. [*Associated Press*] (SAG)
FLOWSIM	Traffic Flow Planning Simulation [*FAA*] (TAG)
FLOX	Fluorine-Liquid Oxygen
Floy Proct Pr	Floyer's Proctors' Practice [*A publication*] (DLA)
FLOZ	Fluid Ounce
FLP	Bristol & Wessex Aeroplane Club Ltd. [*British ICAO designator*] (FAAC)
FLP	Family Limited Partnership
FLP	Fault Location Panel [*Aerospace*] (AAG)
FLP	Featherly Pass [*Alaska*] [*Seismograph station code, US Geological Survey*] (SEIS)
FLP	Festlegepunkt [*Reference point, a gunnery term*] [*German military - World War II*]
FLP	Few Large Platelets [*Hematology*] (DAVI)
FLP	Field Landing Practice
FLP	Fighting Landplane
FLP	Fiji Labour Party [*Political party*] (FEA)
FLP	Fillip (ABBR)
FLP	Finlands Landsbygdsparti [*Finnish Rural Party*] [*Political party*] (PPE)
FLP	Fisheries Licensing Panel [*Victoria, Australia*]
FLP	Flame Leak Proof
FLP	Flap (NASA)
FLP	Flashpoint (GNE)
FLP	Fletcher Challenge Paper [*NYSE symbol*] (SAG)
FLP	Fletcher Challenge Paper ADS [*NYSE symbol*] (TTSB)
FLP	Flight Line Printer
FLP	Flippin, AR [*Location identifier FAA*] (FAAL)
FLP	Floating Point [*Computer science*]
FLP	Florida Law and Practice [*A publication*] (DLA)
Flp	Fluorescent Pseudomonad
FLP	Foreign Language Program
F/LP	Freight/Luggage Panniers [*Hovercraft*]
FLP	Frente de Liberacion de los Pobres [*Liberation Front of the Poor*] [*Ecuador*] [*Political party*] (PD)
FLP	Friends of Luna Park [*Sydney, New South Wales, Australia*]
FLP	Front de Liberation de la Polynesie [*Political party*] (EY)
FLP	Front de Liberation Populaire [*Quebec separatist group*]
FLP	Fronto-Laeva Posterior [*A fetal position*] [*Obstetrics*] (MAE)
FLPA	Flight Level Pressure Altitude
FLPA	Foreign Language Press of America
FLPA	Kasempa [*Zambia*] [*ICAO location identifier*] (ICLI)
FLPanth	Florida Panthers Holdings, Inc. [*Associated Press*] (SAG)
FLPAQ	Family Law Practitioners' Association of Queensland [*Australia*]
FLPAU	Floating-Point Arithmetic Unit
FLPB	First Leesport Bancorp [*NASDAQ symbol*] (SAG)
FLPC	Federal Local Port Controller
FLPD	Flapped (ABBR)
FLPDC	Floppy Disc Controller (NITA)

FLPE	Petauke [*Zambia*] [*ICAO location identifier*] (ICLI)
FL PF	Flat Proof [*Graphic arts*] (DGA)
FLPG	Flapping (ABBR)
FLPK	Mporokoso [*Zambia*] [*ICAO location identifier*] (ICLI)
flpl	Flore Pleno [*With Double Flowers*] [*Botany*] [*Latin*] (BARN)
FLPL	FORTRAN [*Formula Translating System*] List Processing Language [*Computer science*] (IEEE)
FLPMA	Federal Land Policy and Management Act [*1976*]
FLPNC	Flippancy (ABBR)
FLPNT	Flippant (ABBR)
FLPNTY	Flippantly (ABBR)
FLPO	Kabompo [*Zambia*] [*ICAO location identifier*] (ICLI)
FLPP	Foreign Language Proficiency Pay [*Army*] (INF)
FLPP/CWS ..	Family Life and Population Program/Church World Service [*Defunct*] (EA)
FLPR	Flapper
FLPRF	Flameproof (IAA)
FLPS	First Lot Procurement Status (AAG)
FLPS	Flight Load Preparation System [*NASA*] (NASA)
FLPT	Flash Point [*Chemistry*] (IAA)
FL PT	Flash Point [*Graphic arts*] (DGA)
FL PT	Fluid Pint (WDAA)
FLPw	Florida Power & Light Co. [*Associated Press*] (SAG)
FLPw25	Florida Power & Light [*Associated Press*] (SAG)
FLQ	Dallas-Fort Worth, TX [*Location identifier FAA*] (FAAL)
FLQ	Families Leaving Quebec [*Humorous interpretation for Front de Liberation du Quebec*]
FLQ	Front de Liberation de Quebec [*Quebec Liberation Front*] [*Separatist group*]
FLQX	Juvancourt [*France ICAO location identifier*] (ICLI)
FLR	Failure (MSA)
FLR	Fall River [*Massachusetts*] [*Seismograph station code, US Geological Survey*] (SEIS)
FLR	Fall River, MA [*Location identifier FAA*] (FAAL)
FLR	Family Law Reform Party [*Political party Australia*]
FLR	Fast Liner Reactor (MCD)
FLR	Field Level Repair (NVT)
FLR	Field Loss Relay
FLR	Fiji Law Reports [*A publication*] (DLA)
FLR	Filler (AABC)
FLR	Final Limit, Reverse
FLR	First-Light-Readiness [*Military alert*] (VNW)
FLR	Fixed Loan Rate [*Business term*]
FLR	Flares
FLR	Flight Line Reference (NVT)
FLR	Flight Load Recorder
FLR	Floor
flr	Floor (VRA)
FLR	Flora Reserve [*State*] (EERA)
FLR	Florence [*Italy*] [*Airport symbol*] (OAG)
FLR	Florin [*Monetary unit*] [*Netherlands*]
FLR	Flower
FLR	Flow Rate (AAG)
FLR	Fluor Corp. [*NYSE symbol*] (SPSG)
FLR	Flyair [*Spain*] [*FAA designator*] (FAAC)
FLR	Forward-Looking RADAR
FLRA	Family Law Reform Association [*Australia*]
FLRA	Federal Labor Relations Authority [*Independent government agency*]
FLRA	Flora (ABBR)
FLRAL	Floral (ABBR)
FLRANSW	Family Law Reform Association of New South Wales [*Australia*]
FLRC	Farm Labor Research Committee [*Defunct*] (EA)
FLRC	Federal Labor Relations Council [*Later, FLRA*]
FLRC	Feminist Library and Resource Centre [*British*] (EAIO)
FLRCLTR ...	Floriculture (ABBR)
FLRCLTRL ...	Floricultural (ABBR)
FLRCLTRST...	Floriculturalist (ABBR)
FLRCVG	Floorcovering
FLRD	Flared
FLRD	Floored (ABBR)
FLRD	Flurried (ABBR)
FLRD	Front de Liberation et de Rehabilitation du Dahomey [*Dahomey Liberation and Rehabilitation Front*] [*Benin*] [*Political party*] (PD)
FLRDA	Flouridate (ABBR)
FLRDAD	Flouridated (ABBR)
FLRDAG	Flouridating (ABBR)
FLRDN	Flouridation (ABBR)
FlrDnlGTI...	Fluor Daniel GTI, Inc. [*Associated Press*] (SAG)
FLRev	Federal Law Review [*A publication*]
FLRG	Flaring
FLRG	Flooring (ABBR)
FLRG	Flurrying (ABBR)
FLRG	Rusangu [*Zambia*] [*ICAO location identifier*] (ICLI)
FLRH	Flourish (ABBR)
FLRHG	Flourishing (ABBR)
FLRID	Florid (ABBR)
FLRIDNS......	Floridness (ABBR)
FLRIDT	Floridity (ABBR)
FLRIDY	Floridly (ABBR)
FLRL	Floral
FLRMP	Forest Land and Resource Management Plan [*US Forest Service*]
FLRNG	Flash Ranging
FLRNG	Flooring
FLRNG	Flooring
FLRO	FluoroScan Imaging Sys [*NASDAQ symbol*] (TTSB)

FLRO	FluoroScan Imaging Systems, Inc. [*NASDAQ symbol*] (SAG)
FLRO	Rosa [*Zambia*] [*ICAO location identifier*] (ICLI)
FLROW	Fluoroscan Imaging Sys Wrrt [*NASDAQ symbol*] (TTSB)
FLRP	Farm Labor Research Project (EA)
FLRS	Forward-Looking RADAR Set (NVT)
FLRSNC	Flourescence (ABBR)
FLRSNT	Flourescent (ABBR)
FLRST	Florist (ABBR)
FLRST	Florist
FLRT	Fat Lip Readers Theater (EA)
FLRT	Federal Librarians Round Table [*American Library Association*] (EA)
FLRT	Floret (ABBR)
FL/RT	Flow Rate (AAG)
FLRTN	Flirtation (ABBR)
FLRTU	Flirtatious (ABBR)
FLRU	Rufansa [*Zambia*] [*ICAO location identifier*] (ICLI)
FLRY	Flurry [*NWS*] (FAAC)
FLS	Faculty of Library and Information Science, University of Toronto [*UTLAS symbol*]
FLS	Fairlines, BV [*Netherlands*] [*FAA designator*] (FAAC)
FLS	Falls (MCD)
FLS	Falls
FLS	False [*FBI standardized term*]
FLS	Family Location Service [*Later, FLLS*] (EA)
FLS	Farm Labor Service [*of USES*]
FLS	Fault Locator System (AABC)
FLS	Fellow of the Linnaean Society [*British*]
FLS	Fibrous Long-Spacing Collagen
FLS	Field Length for Small Core Memory (IAA)
FLS	Fighter Leader School [*British military*] (DMA)
FLS	Finance Ledger System [*Economics*]
FLS	Financial Listing Service [*Prime Rating, Inc.*] [*Defunct Information service or system*] (CRD)
FLS	Flashing Lights and/or Scotoma [*Neurology and ophthalmology*] (DAVI)
FLS	Flashing Light System (AAG)
FLS	Flashless
FLS	Fleet Logistics Support Department [*Naval Weapons Support Center*]
FLS	Flight Surgeon (MCD)
FLS	Flinders Island [*Australia Airport symbol*] (OAG)
FLS	Florida Specialized Carriers Rate Conference, Inc., Jacksonville FL [*STAC*]
FLS	Florida State University, School of Library Science, Tallahassee, FL [*OCLC symbol*] (OCLC)
FLS	Florida Supplement [*A publication*] (DLA)
FLS	Flow Switch
FLS	Fluid Level Sensor [*Engineering*]
FLS	Flushing, NY (ABBR)
FLS	Forward Light Scatter
FLS	Forward Logistics Site [*Navy*]
fls	Forward Looking Strategy
FLS	Forward Look SONAR
FLS	Foundation for Life Sciences [*Australia*]
FLS	Foundation of Law and Society [*Defunct*] (EA)
FLS	Free Line Signal [*Telecommunications*] (TEL)
FLS	Functional Language Survey (EDAC)
FLS	Future Launching System [*Space flight*]
FLS	New Air Ltd. [*British ICAO designator*] (FAAC)
FLSA	Fair Labor Standards Act [*1938*]
FLSA	Federal Labor Standard Act [*Marine science*] (OSRA)
FLSA	Federal Labor Standards Act [*USDC*]
FLSA	Federal Labor Standards Act (AAGC)
FLSA	Follicular Lymphosarcoma [*Oncology*]
FLSA	Frankie Laine Society of America (EA)
FLSA	St. Anthony [*Zambia*] [*ICAO location identifier*] (ICLI)
FLSC	Federal Lake Survey Center
FLSC	Fixed Laboratory Standard Capacitor
FLS/C	Fleet Logistics Support Department/Crane, IN [*Naval Ammunition Depot*]
FLSC	Flexible Linear Shaped Charge
FLSC	Florsheim Shoe [*NASDAQ symbol*] (TTSB)
FLSC	[*The*] Florsheim Shoe Co. [*NASDAQ symbol*] (SAG)
FLSCL	Fullscale (ABBR)
FLSCP	Flouroscope (ABBR)
FLS-CP	Foolscap (ABBR)
FLSD	Fleet Logistics Support Detachment [*Naval Weapons Support Center*] (DNAB)
FLSE	Serenje [*Zambia*] [*ICAO location identifier*] (ICLI)
FLSFCAN	Falsification (ABBR)
FLSFD	Falsified (ABBR)
FLSFG	Falsifying (ABBR)
FLSFN	Falsification (ABBR)
FLSFR	Falsifier (ABBR)
FLSFY	Falsify (ABBR)
FLSG	Force Logistics Support Group [*Marine Corps*] (NVT)
FLSH	Flash (ABBR)
FLSH	Shiwan'Gandu [*Zambia*] [*ICAO location identifier*] (ICLI)
FLSH-BK	Flash-Back (ABBR)
FLSHD	Flashed (ABBR)
FLSHD	Flashhood (ABBR)
FLSHF	M-Sys Flash Disk Pioneers Ltd [*NASDAQ symbol*] (TTSB)
FLSHG	Flashing (ABBR)
FLSHLT	Flashlight (ABBR)
FLSHLY	Flashily (ABBR)
FLSHNS	Flashiness (ABBR)

FLSH-PTS .... Fleshpots (ABBR)
FLSHR .... Flasher (ABBR)
FLSHR .... Flashier (ABBR)
FLSHST .... Fleshiest (ABBR)
FLSHY .... Flashy (ABBR)
FLSHY .... Fleshly (ABBR)
FLSHYNS ..... Flashiness (ABBR)
FLSHYR .... Flashier (ABBR)
FLSHYST ...... Flashiest (ABBR)
FLSHYY .... Flashily (ABBR)
FLSIP .... Fleet Logistic Support Improvement Program [*Navy*] (NG)
FLSIP-COSAL... Fleet Logistics Support Improvement Program Consolidated Stock
        Allowance List (DNAB)
FLSJ .... Sakeji [*Zambia*] [*ICAO location identifier*] (ICLI)
flslk .... Feels Like [*A term used by weather forecasters*] (WDMC)
FLSLY .... Falsely (ABBR)
FLSM .... Fulsome (ABBR)
FLSM .... St. Mary's [*Zambia*] [*ICAO location identifier*] (ICLI)
FLSMNS ...... Fulsomeness (ABBR)
FLSMP .... French-Language Society of Medical Psychology (EA)
FLSMY .... Fulsomely (ABBR)
FLSN .... Senanga [*Zambia*] [*ICAO location identifier*] (ICLI)
FLSNS .... Falseness (ABBR)
FLSO .... Southdowns [*Zambia*] [*ICAO location identifier*] (ICLI)
FLSOA .... Frankie Laine Society of America (EA)
FLSP .... Flame Spraying [*Welding*]
FLSP .... Flight Space
FLSP .... Fluorescein-Labeled Serum Protein [*Clinical chemistry*]
FLSPT .... Fellowship of the London School of Polymer Technology [*British*]
        (DBQ)
FLSR .... Falser (ABBR)
FLSR .... Flossier (ABBR)
FLSS .... Falcon Launching Saber System
FLSS .... Flight Level Sensing System [*or Subsystem*] (MCD)
FLSS .... Sesheke [*Zambia*] [*ICAO location identifier*] (ICLI)
FLSST .... Falsest (ABBR)
FLSST .... Flossiest (ABBR)
FLST .... Falsest (ABBR)
FLST .... Falsity (ABBR)
FLST .... Flagstar Companies [*NASDAQ symbol*] (TTSB)
FLST .... Flagstar Companies, Inc. [*NASDAQ symbol*] (SAG)
FLST .... Flautist (ABBR)
FLST .... Flutist (ABBR)
FLSTP .... Flagstar Cos $2.25 Cv Ptd [*NASDAQ symbol*] (TTSB)
FLSTR .... Fluster (ABBR)
FLSTY .... Falsity (ABBR)
FLSU .... Force Logistics Support Unit [*Marine Corps*] (NVT)
FLSW .... Fleet Logistic Support Wing [*Navy*]
FLSW .... Flow Switch
FLSW .... Solwezi [*Zambia*] [*ICAO location identifier*] (ICLI)
FLSY .... Falsely (ABBR)
FLSY .... Flossy (ABBR)
FLT .... Faculty of Library and Information Science (Teaching), University of
        Toronto [*UTLAS symbol*]
FLT .... Fault
FLT .... Fault Location Technology [*or Test*] (IEEE)
FLT .... Fault Location Test (IAA)
FLT .... Federacion Latinoamericana de Termalismo [*Latin American
        Federation of Thermalism and Climatism - LAFTC*] [*Buenos
        Aires, Argentina*] (EAIO)
flt................ Felt (VRA)
FLT .... Fermat's Last Theorem [*Mathematics*]
FLT .... Fermet's Last Theorem [*Mathematics*]
FLT .... Fermi Liquid Theory [*Physics*]
FLT .... Field Level Training
FLT .... Figure Location Test (EDAC)
FLT .... Filing Time [*Time a message is presented for transmission*]
FLT .... Filter
FLT .... Flashlight (MSA)
FLT .... Flat [*Alaska*] [*Airport symbol*] (OAG)
FLT .... Flat
FLT .... Flat, AK [*Location identifier FAA*] (FAAL)
FLT .... Flats
FLT .... Fleet (CINC)
FLT .... Fleet
FLT .... Fleet Aerospace Corp. [*Toronto Stock Exchange symbol*]
FLT .... Fleet Financial Group [*Later, FNG*] [*NYSE symbol*] (SPSG)
FLT .... Fleet/Norstar Financial Group, Inc. (MHDW)
FLT .... Fleetwood [*Alabama*] [*Seismograph station code, US Geological
        Survey*] (SEIS)
FLT .... Flex-Lead Torque
FLT .... Flight (AFM)
F/LT .... Flight Lieutenant (ADA)
FLT .... Flightline [*British ICAO designator*] (FAAC)
FLT .... Flight Line Taxi
FLT .... Flight Line Tester
FLT .... Float (MSA)
FLT .... Florida Institute of Technology, Melbourne, FL [*OCLC symbol*]
        (OCLC)
FLT .... Fluidity (ABBR)
FLT .... Fluttier (ABBR)
FLT .... Fluorodeoxythymidine [*Antiviral*]
FLT .... Foreign Labor Trends [*Department of Labor*] [*A publication*]
FLT .... Forklift Truck
FLT .... Foss Launch & Tug [*AAR code*]
FLT .... Fronto-Laeva Transversa [*A fetal position*] [*Obstetrics*] (MAE)

FLTA .... Fullerton Language Test for Adolescents (DAVI)
FLTAC .... Fisher-Logemann Test of Articular Competence [*Speech and
        language therapy*] (DAVI)
FLTAC .... Fleet Analysis Center [*Navy*] (CAAL)
FLTACFO...... Fleet Analysis Center Field Office [*Navy*] (DNAB)
FLTACREP .. Fleet Analysis Center Representative [*Navy*] (DNAB)
FLTACT .... Fleet Activities
FLT ADM ..... Fleet Admiral [*Navy*] (WDAA)
FLTAN.......... Flotation (ABBR)
FLTASWTRACEN... Fleet ASW [*Antisubmarine Warfare*] Training Center [*Navy*]
FLTAVCEN .. Fleet Audio-Visual Center (DNAB)
FLTAVCENEUR... Fleet Audio-Visual Center, Europe (DNAB)
FLTAVCENLANT... Fleet Audio-Visual Center, Atlantic (DNAB)
FLTAVCENPAC... Fleet Audio-Visual Center, Pacific (DNAB)
FLTAVCOMLANT... Fleet Audio-Visual Command, Atlantic (DNAB)
FLTAVCOMLANTDET... Fleet Audio-Visual Command, Atlantic Detachment (DNAB)
FLTAVCOMPAC... Fleet Audio-Visual Command, Pacific (DNAB)
FLTAVCOMPACDET... Fleet Audio-Visual Command, Pacific Detachment (DNAB)
FLTAVFAC.... Fleet Audio-Visual Facility (DNAB)
FLTAVFACLANT... Fleet Audio-Visual Facility, Atlantic (DNAB)
FLTAVFACPAC... Fleet Audio-Visual Facility, Pacific (DNAB)
FLTB .... Floatable (ABBR)
FLTBCST...... Fleet Broadcast [*Navy*] (NVT)
FLTBDCST .. Fleet Broadcast [*Navy*] (NVT)
FLTBRG....... Float Bridge
FLTCAL........ Flight Calibration Procedure [*Aviation*] (DA)
FLTCERT...... Flight Certificate
FltchFF .... Fletchers Fione Foods Ltd. [*Associated Press*] (SAG)
FLTCINC...... Fleet Commander in Chief [*Military*] (DOMA)
FLTCINC...... Fleet Commander-in-Chief [*Navy*] (MCD)
FLTCK......... Flight Check [*Aviation*]
Flt Comdr ... Flight Commander (DAS)
FLTCON....... Fleet Control
FLTCON....... Flight Control
FLTCONT ..... Flight Control [*Aerospace*] (IAA)
FLTCOORDGRU... Fleet Coordinating Group (DNAB)
FLTCORGRU... Fleet Composite Operational Readiness Group [*Navy*] (CAAL)
FLT CQ .... Fleet Carrier Qualification (DOMA)
FLT-CR .... Flat-Car (ABBR)
FLTD .... Flatted (ABBR)
FLTD .... Fluted (MSA)
FLTDEMO .... Fleet Demonstration [*Navy*] (NVT)
FLTDESGW... Flight Design Gross Weight (MCD)
FLTEX .... Fleet Exercise [*Navy*] (NVT)
FltFn .... Fleet Financial Group [*Associated Press*] (SAG)
FLT-FT .... Flat-Foot (ABBR)
FLTG .... Flatting (ABBR)
FLTG .... Fleeting (ABBR)
FLTG .... Floating (AABC)
FLTGNS ...... Fleetingness (ABBR)
FLTGUNSCH... Fleet Gunnery School
FLTGUNSCOL... Fleet Gunnery School
FLTGY......... Fleetingly (ABBR)
FLTHNS....... Filthiness (ABBR)
FLTHR .... Filthier (ABBR)
FLTHST....... Filthiest (ABBR)
FLTHY .... Filthy (ABBR)
FLTINTSUPPCEN... Fleet Intelligence Support Center [*Navy*] (DNAB)
FLTIO .... Fellatio (ABBR)
FLTL .... Flight Line
FLTLA .... Flotilla (ABBR)
Flt Lieut .... Flight Lieutenant [*British military*] (DMA)
FLTLOSCAP... Fleet Liaison Officer, Supreme Commander Allied Powers [*World
        War II*]
FLTMINWARTRACEN... Fleet Mine Warfare Training Center (DOMA)
FLTMOD ...... Fleet Modernization [*Navy*] (DNAB)
FLTN .... Flatten (ABBR)
FLTN .... Floatation (ABBR)
FLTND .... Flattened (ABBR)
FLTNES .... Flatness (ABBR)
FLTNG .... Flattening (ABBR)
FLTNS .... Flatness (ABBR)
FLTNS .... Fleetness (ABBR)
FLTO........... Flight Officer [*Air Force*] (AFM)
FLTO........... Flight Orders [*Aviation*] (FAAC)
FL/TOT .... Flow Totalizer
FLTP .... Flush Type
FLTP .... Foreign Language Training Program [*Air Force*]
FLT/PG....... Flight Programmer (AAG)
FLT PLN ..... Flight Plan (MSA)
FLTPrB........ Fleet Fin'l 10.12% Dep Pfd [*NYSE symbol*] (TTSB)
FLTPrC........ Fleet Fin'l 9.375% Dep Pfd [*NYSE symbol*] (TTSB)
FLTPrD........ Fleet Fin'l 9.30% Dep Pfd [*NYSE symbol*] (TTSB)
FLTPrE........ Fleet Fin'l9.35% Dep Pfd [*NYSE symbol*] (TTSB)
FLTPrF........ Fleet Fin'l 7.25% Dep Pfd [*NYSE symbol*] (TTSB)
FLTPrG .... Fleet Fin'l 6.75% Dep Pfd [*NYSE symbol*] (TTSB)
FLTR .... Filter (MSA)
FLTR .... Flatter (ABBR)
FLTR .... Floater (ABBR)
FLTR .... Flutter (ABBR)
FLTR .... Fusible Link-Top Register (OA)
FLTRACKCEN... Fleet Tracking Center [*Navy*]
FLTRASUPPRON... Fleet Training Support Squadron (DNAB)
FLTRD .... Flattered (ABBR)
FLTREADREP... Fleet Readiness Representative [*Navy*] (MCD)

FLTRELSUPPACT...	Fleet Religious Support Activity (DNAB)	
FLTRELSUPPACTLANT...	Fleet Religious Support Activity, Atlantic (DNAB)	
FLTRELSUPPACTPAC...	Fleet Religious Support Activity, Pacific (DNAB)	
FLTRG	Flattering (ABBR)	
FLTRG	Fluttering (ABBR)	
FLTRGY	Flatteringly (ABBR)	
FLTRGY	Flutteringly (ABBR)	
FLTRIR	Flutterier (ABBR)	
FLTRIST	Flutteriest (ABBR)	
FLTRNR	Flattener (ABBR)	
FLTRR	Flattered (ABBR)	
FLTRY	Flattery (ABBR)	
FLTRY	Fluttery (ABBR)	
FLTS	FASTER [Filing and Source Data Entry Techniques for Easier Retrieval] Language Translation System (MHDI)	
FLTS	Flats	
FLTS	Flats [Postal Service standard] (OPSA)	
FLTS	Flight Line Test Set [Military] (CAAL)	
FLTSAT	Fleet Satellite [Navy] (MCD)	
FLTSAT	Fleet Satellite (DOMA)	
FLTSATCOM...	Fleet Satellite Communications [System] (DOMA)	
FLTSATCOM...	Fleet Satellite Communications System [DoD]	
FLTSATCOMSYS...	Fleet Satellite Communications System [DoD] (DNAB)	
FLTSATSEVCOM...	Fleet Satellite Secure Voice Communications (MCD)	
FLTSERVSCOL...	Fleet Service School [Navy]	
FLTSEVOCOM...	Fleet Secure Voice Communications [Navy] (NVT)	
FLTSIP	Fleet Support Improvement Program [Navy] (DNAB)	
FLTSM	Flotsam (ABBR)	
FLTSOUNDSCOL...	Fleet Sound School	
FLTST	Flattest (ABBR)	
FLTST	Flautist (ABBR)	
FLTST	Flight Steward	
FLTSTRIKEX...	Full General-Emergency Striking Force Exercise [Navy] (NVT)	
FLTSUPPO...	Fleet Support Office [Navy] (DNAB)	
FLTSURBAD...	Flight Surgeon Badge [Military decoration] [Army]	
FLTSURG	Flight Surgeon	
FltSurgBad..	Flight Surgeon Badge [Military decoration Army] (AABC)	
FLTTRACEN...	Fleet Training Center [Navy]	
FLTTRAGRU...	Fleet Training Group [Navy]	
FLTWEPCEN...	Fleet Weapons Center [Navy]	
FLTWO	Flight Watch Outlet [Aviation] (FAAC)	
FLTWR	Flatware (ABBR)	
FLTx	Fork Lift Truck (DS)	
FLTY	Flatly (ABBR)	
FLTY	Fleetly (ABBR)	
FLU	Fault Location Unit [Aerospace] (AAG)	
FLU	Federation of Labor Unions [Lebanon]	
FLU	Final Limit, Up	
FLU	First Line Unit (MCD)	
FLU	Flight Loads Unit (MCD)	
flu	Florida [MARC country of publication code Library of Congress] (LCCP)	
FLU	Flunitrazepam [A hypnotic]	
FLU	Front for Liberation and Unity [Western Sahara]	
flu	Influenza [Medicine] (DAVI)	
FLU	New York/Flushing, NY [Location identifier FAA] (FAAL)	
FLUC	Fluctuate	
FLUCD	Fluctuated (ABBR)	
FLUCG	Fluctuating (ABBR)	
FLUCN	Fluctuation (ABBR)	
FLUCNT	Fluctuant (ABBR)	
FLUD	Fluid	
FLUFD	Fluffed (ABBR)	
FLUFG	Fluffing (ABBR)	
FLUFY	Fluffy (ABBR)	
FLUFYNS	Fluffiness (ABBR)	
FLUFYR	Fluffier (ABBR)	
FLUFYST	Fluffiest (ABBR)	
FLUFYY	Fluffily (ABBR)	
FLUG	Flugfelag Islands H.F. [Iceland Airways Ltd.]	
FLUID	Formed Lines Using Interactive Data (MCD)	
FLUIDEXTER...	Fluidextractum [Fluidextract] [Pharmacy] (ROG)	
FLUIDEXTR...	Fluidextractum [Fluidextract] [Pharmacy] (ROG)	
FLUK	Fluke (ABBR)	
Fluke	Fluke Corp. [Associated Press] (SAG)	
FLUL	Federation of Labor Unions in Lebanon	
FLUNC	Fluency (ABBR)	
FLUNCI	Foreign Language Use in Northern Commerce and Industry (AIE)	
FLUNT	Fluent (ABBR)	
FLUNTY	Fluently (ABBR)	
Fluor	Fluor Corp. [Associated Press] (SAG)	
FLUOR	Fluorescent [or Fluoresces or Fluorescence] (KSC)	
FLUOR	Fluoride [or Fluoridation] (WDAA)	
fluor	Fluorometry (DAVI)	
FLUOR	Fluoroscopy	
FLUORES	Fluorescent (ABBR)	
FLUORO	Fluoroscopy [Radiology] (DAVI)	
FLUR	Fluorescent [Technical drawings]	
FLURAM	Fluorescamine [Biochemical analysis] [Acronym is trademark of Roche Diagnostics]	
FluroS	FluoroScan Imaging Systems, Inc. [Associated Press] (SAG)	
FluroScn	FluoroScan Imaging Systems, Inc. [Associated Press] (SAG)	
FlushF	Flushing Financial Corp. [Associated Press] (SAG)	
FLUSOC	Fluted Socket	
FLUSOCH	Fluted Socket Head	

FLUT	Flute (ABBR)	
FLUT	Flutter (MSA)	
FLUTD	Fluted (ABBR)	
FLUTG	Fluting (ABBR)	
FLUTR	Flouter (ABBR)	
FLUTR	Flutter (ABBR)	
FLUTRD	Fluttered (ABBR)	
FLUTRG	Fluttering (ABBR)	
FLUTRR	Flutterer (ABBR)	
FLUTRY	Fluttery (ABBR)	
FLUTST	Flutist (ABBR)	
FLUX	Flux (ABBR)	
FLUXD	Fluxed (ABBR)	
FLUXG	Fluxing (ABBR)	
FLUXN	Fluxion (ABBR)	
FLV	Feline Leukemia Virus [Also, FELV]	
FLV	Finite Logical View (MHDB)	
FLV	Foreign Leave [Military] (AABC)	
FLV	Friend Leukemia Virus [Also, FDV, FV]	
FLV	Leavenworth, KS [Location identifier FAA] (FAAL)	
FLVFD	Front Luminous Vacuum Fluorescence Display (IAA)	
FLVR	Flavor (ABBR)	
FLVR	Flavor	
FLVRD	Flavored (ABBR)	
FLVRFL	Flavorful (ABBR)	
FLVRFLY	Flavorfully (ABBR)	
FLVRG	Flavoring (ABBR)	
FLVRLS	Flavorless (ABBR)	
FLVRR	Flavorer (ABBR)	
FLVRSM	Flavorsome (ABBR)	
FLVRUS	Flavorous (ABBR)	
FLW	Fault Location Word (MCD)	
FLW	Feedlot Waste	
FLW	Fellows, CA [Location identifier FAA] (FAAL)	
FLW	Fellows, CA [TACAN station] (NASA)	
FL/W	Flash Welding [Metallurgy]	
FLW	Flat Washer	
FLW	Fleet Logistics Wing [Navy]	
FLW	Flow Resources Ltd. [Vancouver Stock Exchange symbol]	
FLW	Follow	
FLW	Forced Longitudinal Wave (MCD)	
FLW	Foulwind [New Zealand] [Seismograph station code, US Geological Survey Closed] (SEIS)	
FLW	Frank Lloyd Wright [American architect] (IIA)	
FLW	International Fur and Leather Workers Union of United States and Canada	
FLw	Lake Worth Public Library, Lake Worth, FL [Library symbol Library of Congress] (LCLS)	
FLW	Santa Cruz, Flores [Azores] [Airport symbol] (OAG)	
FLWA	Frank Lloyd Wright Association [Later, FLWN] (EA)	
FLWA	West One [Zambia] [ICAO location identifier] (ICLI)	
FLWB	West Two [Zambia] [ICAO location identifier] (ICLI)	
FLWC	West Three [Zambia] [ICAO location identifier] (ICLI)	
FLWD	West Four [Zambia] [ICAO location identifier] (ICLI)	
FLWE	West Five [Zambia] [ICAO location identifier] (ICLI)	
FLWF	Feedlot Waste Filtrate	
FLWF	Frank Lloyd Wright Foundation (EA)	
FLWF	West Six [Zambia] [ICAO location identifier] (ICLI)	
FLWFEA	Fort Leonard Wood Facilities Engineer Activity	
FLWG	Following	
FLWG	West Seven [Zambia] [ICAO location identifier] (ICLI)	
FLWGA	Finger Lakes Wine Growers Association (EA)	
FLWHSF	Frank Lloyd Wright Home and Studio Foundation (EA)	
FLWIS	Flood Warnings Issued	
FLWK	Flat Work	
FLWL	Flower Length [Botany]	
FLWN	Frank Lloyd Wright Newsletter (EA)	
FLWO	Fred Lawrence Whipple Observatory [Amado, AZ] [Smithsonian Institution] (GRD)	
FLWP	Follow-Up	
FLwP	Palm Beach Junior College, Lake Worth, FL [Library symbol Library of Congress] (LCLS)	
FLWR	Celebrity, Inc. [NASDAQ symbol] (SAG)	
FLWR	Flower	
FLWR	Flower	
FLWW	Waka Waka [Zambia] [ICAO location identifier] (ICLI)	
FLX	Fallon, NV [Location identifier FAA] (FAAL)	
FLX	Flavex Industries Ltd. [Vancouver Stock Exchange symbol]	
FLX	Flexible [Technical drawings]	
FLX	Florida Express, Inc. [ICAO designator] (FAAC)	
FLX	Flxible Historic Association [Defunct] (EA)	
FLXS	Flexsteel Indus [NASDAQ symbol] (TTSB)	
FLXS	Flexsteel Industries, Inc. [NASDAQ symbol] (NQ)	
FLY	Airlease Ltd. [NYSE symbol] (SPSG)	
FLY	Airlease Ltd L.P. [NYSE symbol] (TTSB)	
FLY	CHC Helicopter Corp. [Toronto Stock Exchange symbol]	
fly	Flinty [Quality of the bottom] [Nautical charts]	
FLY	Flying	
FLY	Flying	
Fly	Flying [A publication] (BRI)	
FLY	Flying Enterprise AB [Sweden] [FAA designator] (FAAC)	
FLY	Flywheel [Automotive engineering]	
f-ly--	Libya [MARC geographic area code Library of Congress] (LCCP)	
FLYA	CHC Helicopter [NASDAQ symbol] (SAG)	
FLYA	Samfya [Zambia] [ICAO location identifier] (ICLI)	

FLYAF......... CHC Helicopter CI'A' [*NASDAQ symbol*] (TTSB)
fly butr......... Flying Buttress (VRA)
FLYCO......... Commander, Flying [*British military*] (DMA)
FLYCO......... Flying Control [*Position*] [*British*]
FLYCON ...... Flight Control
Flyers .... Fun-Loving Youth En Route to Success [*Title of book by Lawrence Graham an d Lawrence Hamdan*] [*Lifestyle classification*]
Fly Needle... Flying Needle [*A publication*] (BRI)
FLYOBRPT... Flying Object Report [*Air Force*]
FLYP .... Fax Like You Print [*3X USA*] (PCM)
fly stat .... Flying Status [*Military*]
FLYT .... Interactive Flight Tech'A' [*NASDAQ symbol*] (TTSB)
FLYT .... Interactive Flight Technologies, Inc. [*NASDAQ symbol*] (SAG)
FLYT .... Interactive Flight Technologies, Inc. CI.A [*NASDAQ symbol*] (SAG)
FLYTAF........ Flying Training Air Force
FLYTU......... Interactive Flight Tech Unit [*NASDAQ symbol*] (TTSB)
FLYTW........ Interactive Flight Wrrt'A' [*NASDAQ symbol*] (TTSB)
FLYTZ......... Interactive Flight Wrrt'B' [*NASDAQ symbol*] (TTSB)
FLYWHL ..... Flywheel
FLYWT........ Flyweight [*Boxing*]
FLZB .... Zambezi [*Zambia*] [*ICAO location identifier*] (ICLI)
FLZO .... Farband Labor Zionist Order [*Later, Labor Zionist Alliance*] (EA)
FM .... Face Mask [*Medicine*] (DAVI)
FM .... Face Measurement
FM .... Facilities Maintenance
FM .... Facilities Management
FM .... Facility Manager
FM .... Factory Manual
FM .... Factory Mutual System [*Formerly, AFMFIC*] [*Group of four insurance companies and an engineering organization*]
FM .... Faience Mosaics (DICI)
FM .... Failure Mode (MCD)
FM .... Fan Marker [*Aviation*]
F/M .... Farads per Meter
FM .... Farm
FM .... Farm-to-Market [*Texas highway*]
FM .... Farm to Market
FM .... Farnsworth-Munsell [*One hundred hue test*] [*Ophthalmology*] (DAVI)
FM .... Fashion Merchandising, Fashion Design, and/or Interior Design Programs [*Association of Independent Colleges and Schools specialization code*]
FM .... Fast Memory (IAA)
FM .... Fast Multiply
FM .... Fathom
FM .... Fault Monitor (TEL)
FM .... Faulty Magazine [*Military*] (MCD)
FM .... FDTE Master (MCD)
F-M .... Federal-Mogul
FM .... Federated States of Micronesia [*ANSI two-letter standard code*] (CNC)
FM .... Feedback Mechanism
F/M .... Feet per Minute (ADA)
FM .... Femtometer [*Formerly, Fermi*] (MCD)
FM .... Ferdinand Marcos [*Former Philippine president*]
Fm .... Fermium [*Chemical element*]
FM .... Ferrite Metal
FM .... Ferromagnet [*Physics*]
FM .... Fetal Movement [*Gynecology*]
FM .... Fetal Movements [*Obstetrics*] (DAVI)
FM .... Fiat Mistura [*Let a Mixture Be Made*] [*Pharmacy*]
FM .... Fibrin Monomer [*Hematology*] (DAVI)
FM .... Fibrous Material
FM .... Field Magnet (ROG)
FM .... Field Main (AAG)
FM .... Field Maintenance (MCD)
FM .... Field Manual [*Military*]
FM .... Field Manufacture (AFIT)
FM .... Field Marshal
FM .... Field Memorandum
FM .... Field Modification (AAG)
FM .... Field Moist Soil [*Agronomy*]
FM .... Field Music [*Marine Corps*]
FM .... Figure of Merit
FM .... Filament Midtop
FM .... File Maintenance [*Computer science*] (BUR)
FM .... File Management
FM .... Financial Management
FM .... Finder Matrix (IAA)
FM .... Fine Measurement
FM .... Fine Motor
FM .... Fineness Modulus (DICI)
FM .... Fire Main (AAG)
FM .... Firm [*Horse racing*]
FM .... First Main [*Firefighting*] (ROG)
F/M .... First Motion (KSC)
FM .... Fish Meal
FM .... Fissile Material
FM .... Flavin Mononucleotide [*Biochemistry*] (AAMN)
FM .... Flight Manual (MCD)
FM .... Flight Mechanic
FM .... Flight Model
FM .... Flight Monitor
FM .... Floating Multiply (IAA)
FM .... Floor Manager (DEN)
FM .... Flour Milling (OA)

FM .... Flow Meter (KSC)
FM .... Fluorescence Microphotolysis
FM .... Fluorescent Microscopy [*Biochemistry*] (DAVI)
FM .... Flyball Master
fm .... Foam (VRA)
FM .... Foam Monitor (DS)
FM .... Focolare Movement (EA)
FM .... Focusing Mount [*Photography*]
FM .... Foodmaker, Inc. [*NYSE symbol*] (SPSG)
F/M .... Food to Microorganism Ratio (EPA)
FM .... Ford Motor Co. [*Toronto Stock Exchange symbol*]
FM .... Foreign Material (MCD)
FM .... Foreign Military
FM .... Foreign Minister [*or Ministry*]
FM .... Foreign Mission
FM .... Forensic Medicine (DAVI)
FM .... Form
FM .... Formation [*Lithology*]
FM .... Formerly Married
FM .... Forms Management
FM .... Fort Major [*British*] (ROG)
FM .... Forward Motion
FM .... Foster Mother
FM .... Foundation Member
FM .... Frame (IAA)
FM .... Franc Macon [*Freemasonry*] [*French*] (ROG)
FM .... Franc Mali [*Monetary unit*] [*Mali*]
FM .... Fraternite Mondiale [*World Brotherhood*]
FM .... Freemason (ROG)
FM .... Free Men [*Defunct*] (EA)
FM .... Free Minds [*An association*] (EA)
FM .... Freimaurer [*Freemason*] [*German*] (ROG)
FM .... Frequency Management [*Aviation*] (DA)
FM .... Frequency Meter
FM .... Frequency Modulation [*Radio*]
FM .... Frequency Multiplex
FM .... Friable Material (GNE)
FM .... Frisker-Monitor [*Radiation detection*]
FM .... From (MUGU)
FM .... Front Matter [*Publishing*]
FM .... Full Moon [*Astronomy*]
FM .... Functional Manager (MCD)
FM .... Functional Mathematical Programming System [*Computer science*] (MCD)
FM .... Functional Megaspore [*Botany*]
FM .... Function Management (ACRL)
FM .... Fusarium Multiformis [*A fungus*]
FM .... Fused to Metal [*Dentistry*]
FM .... Fusobacteria [*or Fusobacterium*] Micro-Organism [*Medicine*]
FM .... Libya [*License plate code assigned to foreign diplomats in the US*]
FM .... Miami-Dade Public Library, Miami, FL [*Library symbol Library of Congress*] (LCLS)
f$_m$............... Modulation Frequency (IDOE)
FM .... Shippers Forecasts [*Symbol*] [*National Weather Service*]
FM .... Titanium Tetrachloride [*Inorganic chemistry*]
FMA .... Average Female Mass [*Ecology*]
FMA .... Daughters of Mary, Help of Christians [*Salesian Sisters of St. John Bosco*] [*Roman Catholic religious order*]
FMA .... Fabricators and Manufacturers Association
FMA .... Fabricators and Manufacturers Association, International (EA)
FMA .... Facilities Management Analysis
FMA .... Factory Materials Association
FMA .... Failure Mode Analysis
FMA .... Family Mediation Association (EA)
FMA .... Fan Manufacturers Association [*British*] (DBA)
FMA .... Farm Management Association [*British*]
FMA .... Federal Managers Association (EA)
FMA .... Federal Maritime Adminstration (WDAA)
FMA .... Federation Mondiale des Annonceurs [*World Federation of Advertisers - WFA*] [*Brussels, Belgium*] (EAIO)
FMA .... Fein-Marquart Associates [*Chemical Information Systems, Inc.*] [*Information service or system*] (IID)
FMA .... Fellow of the Museums Association [*British*] (EY)
FMA .... Ferrite Manufacturers Association
FMA .... Fertiliser Manufacturers Association [*British*]
FMA .... Field Maintenance Activity (MCD)
FMA .... File Manufacturers Association [*Defunct*] (EA)
FMA .... Final Marker Aid [*FAA*] (TAG)
FMA .... Financial Management Association [*Tampa, FL*] (EA)
FMA .... Financial Marketing Association (EA)
FMA .... First Medical Management [*Vancouver Stock Exchange symbol*]
FMA .... Flexicore Manufacturers Association (EA)
FMA .... Flight Manual Allowance
FMA .... Flight Mode Annunciator (MCD)
FMA .... Fluorescein Mercury Acetate [*Analytical chemistry*]
FMA .... Fonds Monetaire Andin [*Andean Monetary Fund*] (PDAA)
FMA .... Food Machinery Association [*British*] (BI)
FMA .... Food Management Area (MCD)
FMA .... Food Merchandisers of America (EA)
FMA .... Foremost Aviation Ltd. [*Nigeria*] [*ICAO designator*] (FAAC)
FMA .... Forging Manufacturers Association [*Later, ODFI*]
FMA .... Formosa [*Argentina*] [*Airport symbol*] (OAG)
FMA .... Forum for Medical Affairs [*Formerly, CPOSMA*] (EA)
FMA .... Forward Maintenance Area (NATG)
FMA .... Foxon-Maddocks Associates (IID)

FMA............	Fragrance Materials Association of the US (EA)
FMA............	Frankfort-Mandibular Plane Angle [*Medicine*] (DMAA)
FMA............	Frequency Modulation Altimeter (IAA)
FMA............	Fulfillment Management Association (EA)
FMA............	Fundamental Mode Asynchronous (IAA)
FMA............	Future Mailing Address
FMAA..........	Fleet Master-at-Arms [*British military*] (DMA)
FMAA..........	Footwear Manufacturers' Association of Australia
FMAA..........	Furniture Manufacturers' Association of Australia (EERA)
FMaC..........	Chipola Junior College, Marianna, FL [*Library symbol Library of Congress*] (LCLS)
FMAC..........	Federation Mondiale des Anciens Combattants [*World Veterans Federation - WVF*] [*Paris, France*] (EAIO)
FMAC..........	Financial Management Advisory Committee
FMAC..........	First Merchants Acceptance [*NASDAQ symbol*] (TTSB)
FMAC..........	First Merchants Acceptance Corp. [*NASDAQ symbol*] (SAG)
FMAC..........	Frequency Division Multiplexed Analogue Components [*Colour TV broadcasting method*] (NITA)
FMAC..........	Frequency Management Advisory Council [*Department of Commerce*] [*Washington, DC*] (EGAO)
FMACC........	Foreign Military Assistance Coordinating Committee [*Department of State*] [*Terminated, 1950*]
FMACCU	Federation Mondiale des Associations, Centres, et Clubs UNESCO [*World Federation of UNESCO Clubs and Associations*] [*France*] (EAIO)
FMacn	Macnaghten's Hindu Law [*India*] [*A publication*] (DLA)
FMAD..........	Flight Mission Assignments Document (KSC)
FMAD..........	Fluid Management and Distribution (SSD)
FMadN........	North Florida Junior College, Madison, FL [*Library symbol Library of Congress*] (LCLS)
FMAG..........	Fleet Maintenance Assistance Group [*Navy*] (NVT)
FMAG..........	Fluxgate Magnetometer (MCD)
FMAG CRUDESLANT CHAR...	Fleet Maintenance Assistance Group for Cruiser-Destroyer Force, Atlantic, Charleston, South Carolina [*Navy*] (DNAB)
FMAG CRUDESLANT MPT...	Fleet Maintenance Assistance Group for Cruiser-Destroyer Force, Atlantic, Mayport, Florida [*Navy*] (DNAB)
FMAG CRUDESLANT NORVA...	Fleet Maintenance Assistance Group for Cruiser-Destroyer Force, Atlantic, Norfolk, Virginia [*Navy*] (DNAB)
FMAGR	Furniture Manufacturers Association of Grand Rapids [*Later, GRAFMA*] (EA)
FMAG SERVLANT NORVA...	Fleet Maintenance Assistance Group for Service Forces, Atlantic, Norfolk, Virginia [*Navy*] (DNAB)
FMAHTS	Flight Manifest and Hardware Tracking System (MCD)
FMAI............	Fabricators and Manufacturers Association, International (EA)
FMAIN	File Maintenance [*Computer science*] (IAA)
FMaJ	Jackson County Public Library, Marianna, FL [*Library symbol Library of Congress*] (LCLS)
FMAL..........	Funds Management Audit List (AFIT)
FMAM..........	Federation Mondiale des Amis de Musees [*World Federation of Friends of Museums - WFFM*] (EAIO)
FMAM..........	Frequency Modulation - Amplitude Modulation (IAA)
FMAN..........	February, May, August, November [*Denotes quarterly payments of interest or dividends in these months*] [*Business term*]
FMAN..........	Foreman (AABC)
FMANA	Fire Marshals Association of North America (EA)
FM & C........	Factory Management and Control [*Computer Automation Ltd.*] [*Software package*] (NCC)
FM & M........	Fibber McGee and Molly [*Radio program*]
FM & P........	Force Management and Personnel (DOMA)
FMANU	Federation Mondiale des Associations pour les Nations Unies [*World Federation of United Nations Associations - WFUNA*] [*Geneva, Switzerland*] (EA)
FMAP..........	Fan Marker Approach [*Aviation*]
FMAP..........	Father Moriarty Asylum Project [*Defunct*] (EA)
FMAP..........	Federal Medical Assistance Percentage [*Department of Health and Human Services*] (GFGA)
FMAR..........	First Mariner Bancorp [*NASDAQ symbol*] (SAG)
FMAS..........	Florida Marine Aquarium Society
FMASC........	Foreign Military Assistance Steering Committee
FMAT..........	Food Management Assistance Team [*Army*] (INF)
FMATH........	Federation Mondiale de Travailleurs des Industries Alimentaires, du Tabac, et del'Hotellerie [*World Federation of Workers in Food, Tobacco, and Hotel Industries - WFFTH*] (EAIO)
FMAU..........	Fluoro(methyl)arabinosyluracil [*Biochemistry*]
FMAW..........	First Marine Aircraft Wing
FMAW..........	Fleet Marine Air Wing
FMB	Biscayne Chemical Laboratories, Inc., Miami, FL [*Library symbol Library of Congress*] (LCLS)
FMB	Factory Mutuals' Combined Fire-Boiler Policy [*Insurance*]
FMB	Fast Missile Boat [*Navy*]
FMB	Federal Maritime Board [*1950-1961; functions transferred to FMC*]
FMB	Federal Maritime Board (AAGC)
FMB	Federal Maritime Board Reports [*United States Maritime Administration, Department of Commerce*] [*A publication*] (DLA)
FMB	Federal Mortgage Bank [*Nigeria*]
FMB	Federation of Master Builders [*British*] (DAS)
FMB	Field Maintenance Bulletin [*Army*]
FMB	Financial Management Board [*Air Force*] (AFIT)
FMB	First Maryland Bancorp [*NYSE symbol*] (SPSG)
FMB	Foreign Materiel Branch [*Military*]
FMB	Frequency Management Branch [*White Sands Missile Range*]
FMB	Frequency Modulation Broadcasters
FMB	Full Maternal Behavior [*Physiology*]
FMB	Fuze Management Board [*Army*]

FMBC..........	Biscayne College, Miami, FL [*Library symbol Library of Congress*] (LCLS)
FMBC..........	First Michigan Bank [*NASDAQ symbol*] (TTSB)
FMBC..........	First Michigan Bank Corp. [*NASDAQ symbol*] (NQ)
FMBC-L.......	Biscayne College, St. Thomas University Law School, Miami, FL [*Library symbol*] [*Library of Congress*] (LCLS)
FMBD..........	First Mutual Bancorp [*NASDAQ symbol*] (TTSB)
FMBD..........	First Mutual Bancorp, Inc. [*NASDAQ symbol*] (SAG)
FMBH..........	Baptist Hospital of Miami, Health Sciences Library, Miami, FL [*Library symbol Library of Congress*] (LCLS)
FMBI...........	First Midwest Bancorp [*NASDAQ symbol*] (TTSB)
FMBI...........	First Midwest Bancorp, Inc. [*NASDAQ symbol*] (NQ)
FMBK..........	F & M Bancorp, Inc. [*NASDAQ symbol*] (SAG)
FMBK..........	F&M Bancorporation, Inc. [*NASDAQ symbol*] (TTSB)
FMbMS	Mount Sinai Medical Center, Media Center, Miami Beach, FL [*Library symbol*] [*Library of Congress*] (LCLS)
FMbMS	Mount Sinai Medical Center, Media Center, Miami Beach, FL [*Library symbol Library of Congress*] (LCLS)
FMBN..........	F&M Bancorp [*NASDAQ symbol*] (TTSB)
FMBN..........	F & M Bancorp, Inc. [*NASDAQ symbol*] (SAG)
FMBPr	First Maryland Banc 7.875% Pfd [*NYSE symbol*] (TTSB)
FMBRA........	Flour Milling and Baking Research Association [*British*] (IRUK)
FMBS..........	Forward Mobile Base Stockage (MCD)
FMBSA........	Farmers and Manufacturers Beet Sugar Association (EA)
FMBT..........	Future Main Battle Tank (NATG)
FMbW.........	Wolfsonian Foundation, Miami Beach, FL [*Library symbol*] [*Library of Congress*] (LCLS)
FMC............	Decisions of the Federal Maritime Commission [*United States*] [*A publication*] (DLA)
FMC............	Facilities Management Contract
FMC............	Family Mediation Centre [*Australia*]
FMC............	Farm Mortgage Corp. [*New Deal*]
FMC............	Fatstock Marketing Corp. [*British*]
FMC............	Federal Management Circular
FMC............	Federal Manufacturers Code (MCD)
FMC............	Federal Maritime Commission [*Independent government agency*]
FMC............	Fellow of the Institute of Management Consultants (DD)
FMC............	Fellow of the Medical Council [*British*]
FMC............	Felt Manufacturers Council (EA)
FMC............	Ferrite Memory Core
FMC............	Fetal Movement Count [*Obstetrics*] (DAVI)
FMC............	Field Medical Card [*Army*] (AABC)
FMC............	Film Magnetic Counter
FMC............	Film-Makers' Cooperative (EA)
FMC............	Filter Manufacturers Council (EA)
FMC............	Final Moisture Content (IAA)
FMC............	Financial Management Center [*Marine science*] (OSRA)
FMC............	Financial Management Center (USDC)
FMC............	Fireball Mode of Combustion [*Combustion in engines*]
FMC............	Fire Mark Circle [*Liverpool, England*] (EAIO)
FMC............	First Ministers' Conference [*Canada*]
FMC............	Fisheries Management Committee [*Victoria, Australia*]
FMC............	Fishery Management Council [*National Oceanic and Atmospheric Administration*] (GFGA)
FMC............	Fixed Message Cycle [*Telecommunications*] (TEL)
FMC............	Fixed Mica Capacitor
FMC............	Fixed Mirror Concentrator
FMC............	Fixed Mylar Capacitor
FMC............	Fleet Management Center (DNAB)
FMC............	Flexible Machining Center [*Manufacturing technology*]
FMC............	Flexible Manufacturing Cell [*Industrial engineering*]
FMC............	Flexible Monte Carlo [*Computer science*]
FMC............	Flexible Motor Coupling
FMC............	Flight Management Computer
FMC............	Flight Medicine Clinic
FMC............	Flinders Medical Centre [*Australia*]
FMC............	Florida Memorial College, Miami, FL [*OCLC symbol*] (OCLC)
FMC............	Fluid Momentum Controller (SSD)
FMC............	Flutter Mode Control [*Aviation*]
FMC............	FMC Corp. [*Formerly, Food Machinery Corp.*] [*Associated Press*] (SAG)
FMC............	FMC Corp. [*Formerly, Food Machinery Corp.*] [*NYSE symbol*] (SPSG)
FMC............	Focus on Micronesia Coalition [*Later, MC*] (EA)
FMC............	Food Management Compartment (MCD)
FMC............	Food Media Club [*Australia*]
FMC............	Force Missile Coordinator [*Navy*] (CAAL)
FMC............	Force Mobile (Canadian Forces)
FMC............	Forces Mobile Command [*Canada*] (DD)
FMC............	Forces Motoring Club [*British military*] (DMA)
FMC............	Ford Motor Co. of Canada Ltd. [*Toronto Stock Exchange symbol*]
FmC............	Forman Co., Monmouth, IL [*Library symbol Library of Congress*] (LCLS)
FMC............	Former Members of Congress [*US*] [*Later, AFMC*]
FMC............	Forward Motion Compensation
FMC............	Foundation for Medical Care [*Generic term*] (DHSM)
FMC............	Foundation for Mideast Communication [*Later, FMEC*] (EA)
FMC............	Four Mile Canyon [*Oregon*] [*Seismograph station code, US Geological Survey*] (SEIS)
FMC............	Franklin and Marshall College [*Pennsylvania*]
FMC............	Free Man of Color [*Term of reference for blacks after the Civil War*]
FMC............	Frequency-Modulated Cyclotron
FMC............	Fuel Management Computer (NG)
FMC............	Full Metal Case [*Ammunition*] (DICI)
FMC............	Fully Mission Capable (MCD)

FMC............ Fundamental Material Controls
FMC............ Fund for Modern Courts (EA)
FMCA.......... Family Motor Coach Association (EA)
FMCA.......... Federated Music Clubs of Australia
FMCA.......... Fire Mark Circle of the Americas (EA)
FMCA.......... Flour Millers Council of Australia
FMCA.......... Ford Mercury Club of America [*Defunct*] (EA)
FMCA.......... [*The*] Forensic Medicine Consultant-Advisor [*Program*]
FMCARP ...... Father Moriarty Central American Refugee Program [*Later, FMAP*]
                (EA)
FMCC.......... Cordis Corp. Library, Miami, FL [*Library symbol*] [*Library of
                Congress*] (LCLS)
FMCC.......... Force Movement Control Center [*Marines*] (ANA)
FMCC.......... Ford Motor Credit Co.
FMCDET....... Fleet Management Center Detachment (DNAB)
FMCE.......... Federacion Mundial Cristiana de Estudiantes [*World Student
                Christian Federation*]
FMCEC........ Federation of Manufacturers of Construction Equipment and Cranes
                [*British*] (EAIO)
FMCF.......... First Manned Captive Flight [*NASA*] (NASA)
FMC/FMS..... Flexible Manufacturing Cell / Flexible Manufacturing [*Industrial
                engineering*] (BTTJ)
FMCG.......... Fast-Moving Consumer Goods (DS)
FMCG.......... Freeport McMoRan Copper & Gold [*Associated Press*] (SAG)
FMC Gd ...... FMC Gold Co. [*Associated Press*] (SAG)
FMCh.......... Flyball Master Champion
FMCH.......... Moroni/Hahaia [*Comoros*] [*ICAO location identifier*] (ICLI)
FMCI........... Forms Manufacturers Credit Interchange (EA)
FMCI........... Moheli/Bandaressalam [*Comoros*] [*ICAO location identifier*] (ICLI)
FMCIM........ Federation Mondiale des Concours Internationaux de Musique [*World
                Federation of International Music Competitions - WFIMC*] (EAIO)
FMC-in-C .... Field Marshal Commanding-in-Chief [*British military*] (DMA)
FMCL.......... Fleet Mechanical Calibration Laboratory
FMCMA....... Fraternal and Military Club Managers Association [*Defunct*] (EA)
FMCMS....... F. Marion Crawford Memorial Society (EA)
FMCN.......... Moroni/Iconi [*Comoros*] [*ICAO location identifier*] (ICLI)
FMCO.......... FMS Financial [*NASDAQ symbol*] (TTSB)
FMCO.......... FMS Financial Corp. [*NASDAQ symbol*] (CTT)
FMCORP...... Field Music Corporal [*Marine Corps*]
FMCPL........ Field Music Corporal [*Marine Corps*]
FMCR.......... Fleet Marine Corps Reserve
FMCS.......... Factory Monitoring and Control System [*Computer science*]
FMCS.......... Federal Mediation and Conciliation Service [*Independent government
                agency*]
FMCS.......... Fleet Management Control Systems, Inc. [*Software*]
FMCS.......... Flight Management Computer System
FMCS.......... Franklin Mint Collector's Society (EA)
FMCS.......... Freight Movement Control System [*MTMC*] (TAG)
FMCS.......... FSIS [*Food Safety and Inspection Service*] Management and
                Communication System [*Department of Agriculture*] (GFGA)
FMCSR .... Federal Motor Carrier Safety Regulation
FMCT.......... Farmers & Mechanics Bank [*NASDAQ symbol*] (SAG)
FMCT.......... Federation of Moulders and Collateral Trades [*A union*] [*British*]
FMCU.......... Form Cutter
FMCV.......... Anjouan/Ouani [*Comoros*] [*ICAO location identifier*] (ICLI)
FMCVC........ Federation Mondiale des Communautes de Vie Chretienne [*World
                Federation of Christian Life Communities - WFCLC*] [*Rome,
                Italy*] (EAIO)
FMCW.......... Frequency-Modulated Continuous-Wave [*RADAR*] (KSC)
FMCWR .... Frequency Modulated Carrier Wave Radar (NITA)
FMCZ.......... Dzaoudzi/Pamanzi [*Mayotte*] [*ICAO location identifier*] (ICLI)
FMD............ Family Medical Doctor (DAVI)
FMD............ Ferrous Metal Detector
FMD............ Ferry Movement Directive [*Navy*] (NVT)
FMD............ Fibromuscular Dysplasia [*Medicine*]
FMD............ Financial Management Division [*Environmental Protection Agency*]
                (EPA)
FMD............ Fixtures Manufacturers and Dealers (EA)
FMD............ Foot-and-Mouth Disease [*Veterinary medicine*]
FMD............ Force Modernization Division [*Military*] (MCD)
FMD............ Form Molding Die (MCD)
FMD............ Frequency Management Division [*White Sands Missile Range*]
FMD............ Frequency-Modulated Demodulator [*Telecommunications*] (IAA)
FMD............ Frequency Modulation Discriminator
FMD............ Frequency of Minimum Delay
FMD............ Friends of Medieval Dublin [*Irish*]
FMD............ Front Militant Departementaliste [*Militant Departmentalist Front*]
                [*Reunion*] (PD)
FMD............ Fulcrum Development Ltd. [*Vancouver Stock Exchange symbol*]
FMD............ Function Management Data (IBMDP)
FMDA.......... FM Development Association [*Later, NRBA*]
FMDA.......... Futuremedia Ltd. [*NASDAQ symbol*] (SAG)
FMDAA........ Farm Machinery Dealers' Association of Australia
FMD & C ..... Flight Mechanics, Dynamics, and Control (KSC)
FmDaves ..... Famous Daves of America, Inc. [*Associated Press*] (SAG)
FMDAY .... Futuremedia PLC ADS [*NASDAQ symbol*] (TTSB)
FMDC.......... Franciscan Missionaries of the Divine Child (TOCD)
FMDC.......... Franciscan Missionary Sisters of the Divine Child [*Roman Catholic
                religious order*]
FMDCS .... Fleet Maintenance Data Collection System (DNAB)
FMDI.......... Form Die
FMDM.......... Flex Multiplexer/Demultiplexer (MCD)
FMDM.......... Franciscan Missionaries of the Divine Motherhood [*Roman Catholic
                religious order*]
FMDM.......... Frequency Modulation Deviation Meter

FMDP.......... Financial Management for Data Processing [*An association*] (EA)
FMDR .... Final Missile Deviation Report [*Aerospace*] (AAG)
FMDS.......... Flight Model Discharge System (BARN)
FMDU.......... Fast Multiply/Divide Unit (NITA)
FMDV.......... Foot-and-Mouth Disease Virus [*Veterinary medicine*]
FMDY.......... Futuremedia Ltd. [*NASDAQ symbol*] (SAG)
FMDYW...... Futuremedia PLC Wrrt [*NASDAQ symbol*] (TTSB)
FME............ Failure Mode and Effects
FME............ Farnesyl Methyl Ether [*Juvenile hormone analog*]
FME............ Field Maintenance Equipment [*Military*]
FME............ Finished with Main Engines [*Navy*]
FME............ Fixed Mobile Experiment (MCD)
FME............ Foreign Materiel Exploitation (RDA)
FME............ Fort Meade, MD [*Location identifier FAA*] (FAAL)
FME............ Foundation for Management Education [*British*]
FME............ Frequency-Measuring Equipment
FME............ Full Mouth Extraction [*Dentistry*]
FMe............ Melbourne Public Library, Melbourne, FL [*Library symbol Library of
                Congress*] (LCLS)
FMEA.......... Failure Mode and Effects Analysis
FMEA.......... Florida Municipal Electric Association (SRA)
FMEA.......... Florida Music Educators Association (SRA)
FMEA.......... Flour Millers Export Association (EA)
FMEC.......... Forward Master Events Controller [*NASA*] (NASA)
FMEC.......... Foundation for Mideast Communication (EA)
FMEC.......... Fur Merchants Employers Council (EA)
FMECA........ Failure Mode Effects and Criticality Analysis
FMED.......... Forward Medical Equipment Depot [*Military British*]
FMeE.......... Eau Gallie Public Library, Melbourne, FL [*Library symbol Library of
                Congress*] (LCLS)
FMEE .... Saint-Denis/Gillot [*Reunion*] [*ICAO location identifier*] (ICLI)
FMeF.......... Florida Institute of Technology, Melbourne, FL [*Library symbol Library
                of Congress*] (LCLS)
FMEF .... Fuels and Materials Examination Facility [*Department of Energy*]
FMeH.......... Harris Government Systems Sector, Engineering Library, Melbourne,
                FL [*Library symbol*] [*Library of Congress*] (LCLS)
FMEI.......... Farm Management Extension Initiative (EERA)
F-MEL.......... Friend Murine Erythroleukaemia [*Cell line*]
FMEM.......... Failure Mode and Effects Management [*Engineering*]
FMEM.......... Federation Mondiale pour l'Enseignement Medical [*World Federation
                for Medical Education - WFME*] (EA)
FMeM.......... Meadowlane Community Library, Melbourne, FL [*Library symbol
                Library of Congress*] (LCLS)
FMEO.......... Fleet Marine Engineering Officer [*Navy British*]
FMEP.......... Foundation for Middle East Peace (EA)
FMEP.......... Friction Mean Effective Pressure [*Automotive engineering*]
FMEP.......... Saint-Pierre-Pierrefonds [*Reunion*] [*ICAO location identifier*] (ICLI)
FMER.......... Factory Mutual Engineering and Research
FMER.......... FirstMerit Corp. [*NASDAQ symbol*] (SAG)
FMer.......... French Mercury [*Record label*]
FMerAcc ...... First Merchants Acceptance Corp. [*Associated Press*] (SAG)
FMERO ...... Factory Mutual Engineering and Research Organization (EA)
FMES.......... Ferry Mission Equipment Store (MCD)
FMES.......... Full Mission Engineering Simulator (KSC)
fMet.......... Formylmethionyl [*Biochemistry*]
FMETA........ Foreign Material Exploitation Tactical Air [*Military*] (CAAL)
FMETO........ Fleet Meteorological Officer [*Navy British*]
fMet-tRNA... Ribonucleic Acid, Transfer - Formylmethionyl [*Biochemistry, genetics*]
FMEVA........ Floating-Point Means and Variance [*Biochemistry, genetics*]
FMEW.......... Financial Management Executive Workshop
FMF............ Familial Mediterranean Fever
FMF............ Farm Management and Finance [*British*]
FMF............ Fetal Movement Felt [*Medicine*]
FMF............ Financial Markets Foundation
FMF............ First Mercantile Currency Fund, Inc. [*Toronto Stock Exchange
                symbol*]
FMF............ Flagler Memorial Library, Miami, FL [*Library symbol Library of
                Congress*] (LCLS)
FMF............ Fleet Marine Force [*Navy*]
FMF............ Florida Mango Forum (EA)
FMF............ Flow Microfluorometer [*Instrumentation*]
FMF............ Fluid Modeling Facility [*Environmental Protection Agency*] (GRD)
FMF............ Food Manufacturers' Federation [*British*]
FMF............ Forced Midexpiratory Flow [*Medicine*] (DAVI)
FMF............ Foreign Military Financing (DOMA)
FMF............ Francis Marion National Forest [*South Carolina*] [*Seismograph station
                code, US Geological Survey Closed*] (SEIS)
FMF............ Free Molecular Flow
FMF............ Fudan Museum Foundation (EA)
FMF............ Fuel Manufacturing Facility
FMF............ Fuel Melt Fraction [*Nuclear energy*] (NRCH)
FMFB.......... Frequency Modulation with Feedback
FMFC.......... First M & F Corp. [*NASDAQ symbol*] (SAG)
FMFC.......... Francisco Morazan Frente Constitucional [*Honduras*] [*Political
                party*] (EY)
FMFD.......... Frequency Modulation Feedback Discriminator
FMFF.......... Frequency Modulation Feed Forward (PDAA)
FMFIA.......... Federal Managers Financial Integrity Act [*1982*]
FMFIC.......... Federation of Mutual Fire Insurance Companies (EA)
FMFIU.......... Florida International University, Miami, FL [*Library symbol Library of
                Congress*] (LCLS)
FMFLANT.... Fleet Marine Force, Atlantic [*Navy*] (MCD)
FMFM.......... Fleet Marine Force Manual [*Marine Corps*] (MCD)
FMFM.......... Florida Memorial College, Miami, FL [*Library symbol Library of
                Congress*] (LCLS)

FM-FM......... Frequency Modulation - Frequency Modulation
FMFP......... Foreign Military Financing Program [*DoD*]
FMFPAC....... Fleet Marine Force, Pacific Fleet [*Navy*]
FMFS......... Full Mission Fighter Simulator [*Air Force*] (PDAA)
FMFWESTPAC... Fleet Marine Force, Western Pacific [*Navy*]
FMG........... Fabricated Metal Goods
FMG........... Fine Mesh Gauze [*Surgery*] (DAVI)
FMG........... Flakmessgerat [*Antiaircraft, gun-laying RADAR*] [*German*]
FMG........... Fluorescein Mono(galactopyranoside) [*Organic chemistry*]
FMG........... Food Machinery Group [*British*] (DBA)
FMG........... Foreign Medical Graduate [*doing residency in US hospital*]
FMG........... Franc [*Monetary unit*] [*Malagasy Republic*]
FMG........... Frequency Modulation Generator
f-mg--........ Malagasi Republic [*Madagascar*] [*MARC geographic area code Library of Congress*] (LCCP)
FMG(A)....... Fleet Maintenance Group (Atlantic) [*Canada*]
FMGC......... Flight Management Guidance Computer (GAVI)
FMGEMS..... Foreign Medical Graduate Examination in Medical Sciences
FMGF......... Factorial Moment Generating Function [*Statistics*]
FMGM........ French MGM [*Record label*]
FMG(P)....... Fleet Maintenance Group (Pacific) [*Canada*]
FMGS......... Church of Jesus Christ of Latter-Day Saints, Genealogical Society Library, MiamiBranch, Miami, FL [*Library symbol Library of Congress*] (LCLS)
FMGS......... Flight Management and Guidance System (DA)
FMH........... Falling Mass Hazard
FMH........... Falmouth, MA [*Location identifier FAA*] (FAAL)
FMH........... Family Medical History [*Medicine*] (HGAA)
FMH........... Fan Marker Located with Radio Beacon [*Aviation*] (FAAC)
FMH........... Fat-Mobilizing Hormone [*Medicine*]
FMH........... Federal Meteorological Handbook
FMH........... Federation Mondiale de l'Hemophilie [*World Federation of Hemophilia*] (EAIO)
FMH........... Fetal Maternal Hemorrhage [*Medicine*]
FMH........... Fibromuscular Hyperplasia [*Neurology*] (DAVI)
FMH........... Fluoromethylhistidine [*Biochemistry*]
FMH........... Freemasons' Hall [*Freemasonry*] (ROG)
FMH........... Friends Meeting House [*Quakers*]
FMH........... Function Management Header (ACRL)
FMHA......... Farmers Home Administration (USGC)
FmHA......... Farmers Home Administration [*Formerly, FHA*] [*Department of Agriculture*]
FMHC......... Federation of Mental Health Centers [*Defunct*] (EA)
FMHiS........ Historical Association of Southern Florida, Miami, FL [*Library symbol Library of Congress*] (LCLS)
FMHR......... Federal Hazardous Materials Regulations (TAG)
FMHS......... Freely Moving Human Subject
FMHSU...... Federated Miscellaneous and Hospital Service Union [*Australia*]
FMHW........ Federation of Mental Health Workers [*British*]
FMI........... Daughters of Mary Immaculate [*Marianist Sisters*] [*Roman Catholic religious order*]
FMI........... Failure Mode Indicator (MUGU)
FMI........... Federation of Music Industries [*British*] (DBA)
FMI........... Fellowship of the Motor Industry [*British*] (BI)
FMI........... Fils de Marie Immaculee [*Sons of Mary Immaculate*] [*Saint Fulgent, France*] (EAIO)
FMI........... Financial Management Initiative [*British*]
FMI........... Finnish Meteorological Institute [*Helinski, Finland*]
FMI........... First Market Intelligence Ltd. [*Information service or system*] (IID)
FMI........... Flexible Modular Interface
FMI........... Flow Measurement and Indication (DEN)
FMI........... Fluid Metering, Inc.
FMI........... Fondo Monetario Internacional [*International Monetary Fund*] [*Spanish United Nations*] (DUND)
FMI........... Fonds Monetaire International [*International Monetary Fund*]
FMI........... Food Marketing Institute (EA)
FMI........... Force Module Identifier (DOMA)
FMI........... Ford Marketing Institute
FMI........... Franciscan Sisters of Mary Immaculate of the Third Order of St. Francis of Assisi [*Roman Catholic religious order*]
FMI........... Franklin McLean Memorial Research Institute [*University of Chicago*] [*Research center*] (RCD)
FMI........... Franklin Multi-Income Tr [*NYSE symbol*] (TTSB)
FMI........... Franklin Multi-Income Trust [*NYSE symbol*] (SPSG)
FMI........... Free Motion Impedance
FMI........... Frequency Modulation Intercity Relay Broadcasting
FMI........... Friedrich Miescher Institute [*Switzerland*]
FMI........... Functional Management Inspection [*Military*]
FMI........... Future Manned Interceptor [*Military*]
FMI........... Kalemi [*Zaire*] [*Airport symbol*] (OAG)
FMi........... Merritt Island Public Library, Merritt Island, FL [*Library symbol Library of Congress*] (LCLS)
FMIA......... Federal Meat Inspection Act
FMIAA....... Fitness Motivation Institute of America Association (EA)
FMiB......... Brevard County Library System, Merritt Island, FL [*Library symbol Library of Congress*] (LCLS)
FMIC......... Flight Manual Interim Changes
FMIC......... Frequency Monitoring and Interference Control [*Radio*]
FMIC......... Front Malaysian Islamic Council [*Political party*] (FEA)
FMIC......... Fund Management Identification Code [*Military*] (AFM)
FMICS....... Financial Management Information and Control System [*Navy*]
FMICW...... Frequency-Modulated Intermittent Continuous Wave [*Electronics*] (OA)
FMidBc...... First Midwest Bancorp [*Associated Press*] (SAG)
FMIJ......... Franciscan Missionaries of the Infant Jesus (TOCD)

FMILS......... Force Modernization Integrated Logistics Support
FMIP......... Financial Management Improvement Program
FMIR......... Frustrated Multiple Internal Reflectance
FMIRA....... Fighter Multifunctional Inertial Reference Assembly (MCD)
FMIS......... Farm Market Infodata Service [*Department of Agriculture*] [*Database*]
FMIS......... Field Management Information System (AAGC)
FMIS......... Financial Management Information System
FMIS......... Fiscal Management Information System
FMIS......... Fleet Management Information System [*Software*]
FMIS......... Force Modernization Information System (MCD)
F MIST...... Fiat Mistura [*Let a Mixture Be Made*] [*Pharmacy*] (ROG)
FMIT......... Fusion Materials Irradiation Test Facility [*Proposed*]
FMIV......... Forced Mandatory Intermittent Ventilation [*Medicine*] (DAVI)
FMJ......... Financial Mail (Johannesburg) [*A publication*]
FMJ......... Full Metal Jacket [*Ammunition*] (DICI)
fmj......... The Monastic Fraternity of Jerusalem (TOCD)
FMJBT...... Full Metal Jacket Boat Tail [*Weaponry*] [*Military*] (INF)
FMJC......... Federation Mondiale de Jeunesse Catholique [*World Federation of Catholic Youth*]
FMJD......... Federation Mondiale de la Jeunesse Democratique [*World Federation of Democratic Youth - WFDY*] [*Budapest, Hungary*] (EAIO)
FMJD......... Federation Mondiale du Jeu de Dames [*World Draughts (Checkers) Federation - WDF*] [*Dordrecht, Netherlands*] (EAIO)
FMJFC....... Federation Mondiale des Jeunesses Feminines Catholiques
FMJLR...... Federation Mondiale des Jeunesses Liberales et Radicales [*World Federation of Liberal and Radical Youth*]
F MK......... Markka [*Monetary unit*] [*Finland*]
FMKR....... Fan Marker [*Aviation*] (IAA)
FML......... Fault Message Line (MCD)
FML......... Feedback, Multiple Loop
FML......... Ferguson Memorial Library [*Presbyterian Church, Sydney, New South Wales, Australia*]
FML......... File Manipulation Language
FML......... Final Materials List [*NASA*] (NASA)
FML......... Flexible Membrane Liner [*For waste containment*]
FML......... Flight Mechanics Laboratory [*Texas A & M University*] [*Research center*] (RCD)
FML......... Fluid Mechanics Laboratory [*MIT*] [*Research center*]
FML......... Fluorometholone [*Anti-inflammatory drug*]
FML......... FM Resources Ltd. [*Vancouver Stock Exchange symbol*]
FML......... Force Module Library (DOMA)
FML......... Fort Mill, SC [*Location identifier FAA*] (FAAL)
FML......... French Men of Letters [*A publication*]
FML......... Front Mounting Light
f-ml--......... Mali [*MARC geographic area code Library of Congress*] (LCCP)
FML......... University of Miami, Law Library, Coral Gables, FL [*OCLC symbol*] (OCLC)
FMLA......... Family and Medical Leave Act of 1993 (WYGK)
FMLC......... Fetal Mouse Liver Cell [*Bioassay*]
F/MLDG...... Finish Moulding [*Automotive engineering*]
FMLF......... File Management Loading Facility
FMLH......... Frente Morazanista para la Liberacion de Honduras [*Guerrilla forces*] (EY)
FMLM......... French Military Liaison Mission [*World War II*]
FMLN......... Farabundo Marti National Liberation Front [*Brazil Political party*] (ECON)
FMLN......... Frente Farabundo Marti de Liberacion Nacional [*Farabundo Marti National Liberation Front*] [*El Salvador*] (ECON)
FMLN......... Frente Morazanista de Liberacion Nacional [*Morazanista National Liberation Front*] [*Honduras*] [*Political party*] (PD)
FMLNH...... Frente Morazanista de Liberacion Nacional de Honduras [*Honduran Morazanist National Front*] [*Political party*]
FMLP......... Field Mirror Landing Practice
FMLP......... Formyl(methionyl)(leucyl)phenylalanine [*Biochemistry*]
FMLS......... Fleet Maintenance and Logistics Support (DNAB)
FMLS......... Full Matrix Least Square (IAA)
FMLS......... Full-Matrix Least Squares [*Statistics*] (PDAA)
FMLSM...... Force Module Logistics Sustainability Model (DOMA)
FMLT......... FORCE, Mass, Length, and Time [*Rocket dynamics*] (BARN)
FMLY......... Family
FMLY......... Family
FMLY......... Family Bancorp [*NASDAQ symbol*] (NQ)
FMLY......... Formerly
FMM......... Brothers of Mercy (TOCD)
fmm......... Brothers of Mercy (TOCD)
FMM......... Fast Multipole Method [*Physics*]
FMM......... Ferromagnetic Material
FMM......... Financial Management Manual [*NASA*]
FMM......... Finite Message Machine [*Telecommunications*]
FMM......... First Maritime Mining Corp. Ltd. [*Toronto Stock Exchange symbol*]
FMM......... Flight Management Module (MCD)
FMM......... Fort Morgan, CO [*Location identifier FAA*] (FAAL)
FMM......... Framework Molecular Models
FMM......... Franciscan Missionaries of Mary [*Roman Catholic women's religious order*]
FMM......... French Military Mission (NATG)
FMM......... Missionary Fraternity of Mary (TOCD)
FMM......... University of Miami, Music Library, Coral Gables, FL [*OCLC symbol*] (OCLC)
FMMA......... Antananarivo/Arivonimamo [*Madagascar*] [*ICAO location identifier*] (ICLI)
FMMA......... Floor Machine Manufacturers Association
FMMAA...... Federated Mining Mechanics Association of Australia
FMMC......... Fixed Mylar Metallized Capacitor
FMMC......... Malaimbandy [*Madagascar*] [*ICAO location identifier*] (ICLI)

FMMD.......... Antananarivo [*Madagascar*] [*ICAO location identifier*] (ICLI)
FMMD.......... Form Mandrel [*Tool*] (AAG)
FMMD.......... Miami-Dade Community College, Miami, FL [*Library symbol Library of Congress*] (LCLS)
FMME.......... Antsirabe [*Madagascar*] [*ICAO location identifier*] (ICLI)
FMME.......... Fund for Multinational Management Education (EA)
FMME.......... Racal-Milgo, Inc., Miami, FL [*Library symbol Library of Congress*] (LCLS)
FMMF.......... Flexure Monitor Mounting Fixture
FMMG.......... Antsalova [*Madagascar*] [*ICAO location identifier*] (ICLI)
FMMGEUA ... Federated Millers and Manufacturing Grocers' Employees' Union of Australia
FMMH.......... Mahanoro [*Madagascar*] [*ICAO location identifier*] (ICLI)
FMMI.......... Antananarivo/Ivato [*Madagascar*] [*ICAO location identifier*] (ICLI)
FMMJ.......... Ambohijanahary [*Madagascar*] [*ICAO location identifier*] (ICLI)
FMMK.......... Ankavandra [*Madagascar*] [*ICAO location identifier*] (ICLI)
FMML.......... Belo-Sur-Tsiribihina [*Madagascar*] [*ICAO location identifier*] (ICLI)
FMMM.......... Antananarivo [*Madagascar*] [*ICAO location identifier*] (ICLI)
FMMN.......... Miandrivazo [*Madagascar*] [*ICAO location identifier*] (ICLI)
FMMO.......... Maintirano [*Madagascar*] [*ICAO location identifier*] (ICLI)
FMMP.......... Amparafaravola [*Madagascar*] [*ICAO location identifier*] (ICLI)
FMMP.......... Force Modernization Master Plan (MCD)
FMMP.......... Formylmethionyl (sulfonyl) Methyl Phosphate [*Biochemistry*]
FMMQ.......... Ilaka-Est [*Madagascar*] [*ICAO location identifier*] (ICLI)
FMMR.......... Morafenobe [*Madagascar*] [*ICAO location identifier*] (ICLI)
FMMRI.......... Franklin McLean Memorial Research Institute [*University of Chicago*] [*Research center*]
FMMRS.......... Force Modernization Milestone Reporting System [*Army*] (RDA)
FMMS.......... Field Missile Maintenance Squadron [*Air Force*]
FMMS.......... Functionalized Monolayers on Mesoporous Supports [*Organic chemistry*]
FMMS.......... Sainte-Marie [*Madagascar*] [*ICAO location identifier*] (ICLI)
FMMT.......... Toamasina [*Madagascar*] [*ICAO location identifier*] (ICLI)
FMMU.......... Tambohorano [*Madagascar*] [*ICAO location identifier*] (ICLI)
FMMV.......... Finger Millet Mosaic Virus [*Plant pathology*]
FMMV.......... Morondava [*Madagascar*] [*ICAO location identifier*] (ICLI)
FMMX.......... Tsiroanomandidy [*Madagascar*] [*ICAO location identifier*] (ICLI)
FMMY.......... Vatomandry [*Madagascar*] [*ICAO location identifier*] (ICLI)
FMMZ.......... Ambatondrazaka [*Madagascar*] [*ICAO location identifier*] (ICLI)
F/M/N.......... Faith-Man-Nature [*from F/M/N Papers, National Council of Churches*]
FMN.......... F & M National Corp. [*NYSE symbol*] (SAG)
FMN.......... Farmington [*New Mexico*] [*Airport symbol*] (OAG)
FMN.......... Farmington, NM [*Location identifier FAA*] (FAAL)
FMN.......... Federation Mondiale de Neurologie [*World Federation of Neurology*]
FMN.......... Flavin Mononucleotide [*Biochemistry*]
FMN.......... Flexible Machining Network [*Automotive engineering*]
FMN.......... Flight Motor Neuron [*Entomology*]
FMN.......... FMC Corp., Princeton, NJ [*OCLC symbol*] (OCLC)
FMN.......... Formation
FMN.......... France Marine Nationale [*ICAO designator*] (FAAC)
F MN.......... Full Moon [*Astronomy*] (ROG)
FMN.......... United States Department of Commerce, National Oceanic and Atmospheric Administration, Miami, FL [*Library symbol Library of Congress*] (LCLS)
FMNA.......... Antsiranana/Arrachart [*Madagascar*] [*ICAO location identifier*] (ICLI)
FMNBNA.......... Frequency Modulation and Narrowband Noise Analyzer (MCD)
FMNC.......... Mananara-Nord [*Madagascar*] [*ICAO location identifier*] (ICLI)
FMND.......... Andapa [*Madagascar*] [*ICAO location identifier*] (ICLI)
FMNE.......... Ambilobe [*Madagascar*] [*ICAO location identifier*] (ICLI)
FMNF.......... Befandriana Nord [*Madagascar*] [*ICAO location identifier*] (ICLI)
FMNG.......... Port Berge [*Madagascar*] [*ICAO location identifier*] (ICLI)
FMNH.......... Antalaha [*Madagascar*] [*ICAO location identifier*] (ICLI)
FMNH.......... Field Museum of Natural History [*Chicago, IL*]
FMNH.......... Flavin Mononucleotide [*Reduced*] [*Biochemistry*]
FMNJ.......... Ambanja [*Madagascar*] [*ICAO location identifier*] (ICLI)
FMNL.......... Analalava [*Madagascar*] [*ICAO location identifier*] (ICLI)
FMNM.......... Mahajanga/Amborovy [*Madagascar*] [*ICAO location identifier*] (ICLI)
FMNN.......... Nosy-Be/Fascene [*Madagascar*] [*ICAO location identifier*] (ICLI)
FMNO.......... Soalala [*Madagascar*] [*ICAO location identifier*] (ICLI)
FMNP.......... Mampikony [*Madagascar*] [*ICAO location identifier*] (ICLI)
FMNQ.......... Besalampy [*Madagascar*] [*ICAO location identifier*] (ICLI)
FMNR.......... Maroantsetra [*Madagascar*] [*ICAO location identifier*] (ICLI)
FMNS.......... Sambava [*Madagascar*] [*ICAO location identifier*] (ICLI)
FMNT.......... Tsaratanana [*Madagascar*] [*ICAO location identifier*] (ICLI)
FMNV.......... Vohemar [*Madagascar*] [*ICAO location identifier*] (ICLI)
FMNW.......... Antsohihy/Ambalabe [*Madagascar*] [*ICAO location identifier*] (ICLI)
FMNW-Mu ... New World School of Arts, Music Library, Miami, FL [*Library symbol Library of Congress*] (LCLS)
FMNX.......... Mandritsara [*Madagascar*] [*ICAO location identifier*] (ICLI)
FMO.......... Facilities Maintenance Operations and Computerized Systems Show (TSPED)
FMO.......... Fast Moving Object
FMO.......... Federal Management Officer (GFGA)
FMO.......... Federal-Mogul [*NYSE symbol*] (TTSB)
FMO.......... Federal-Mogul Corp. [*NYSE symbol*] (SPSG)
FMO.......... Federation of Manufacturing Opticians [*British*] (BI)
FMO.......... Federation of Mobile Home Owners (EA)
FMO.......... Financial Management Office (KSC)
FMO.......... Flatland Meteorological Observatory [*Marine science*] (OSRA)
FMO.......... Flatland Meteorological Observatory (USDC)
FMO.......... Fleet Mail Office [*British*]
FMO.......... Fleet Maintenance Office [*or Officer*]
FMO.......... Fleet Medical Officer
FMO.......... Flight Management Office [*Air Force*] (AFM)
FMO.......... Flight Medical Officer [*Air Force*]

FMO.......... Force Modernization Office [*Army*] (RDA)
fmo.......... Former Owner [*MARC relator code*] [*Library of Congress*] (LCCP)
FMO.......... Forms Management Officer [*Army*] (AABC)
FMO.......... Frequency Management Office (DOMA)
FMO.......... Frequency Multiplier Oscillator (IAA)
FMO.......... Frontier Molecular Orbital Theory [*Physical chemistry*]
FMO.......... Fuels Management Officer [*Air Force*] (AFIT)
FMO.......... Full Marching Order [*British military*] (DMA)
FMO.......... Fundamentals of Machine Operation [*John Deere Service Publications*] [*Moline, IL*] [*A publication*]
FMO.......... Fuze Management Organization [*Army*]
FMOB.......... Federation of Master Organ Builders [*British*] (BI)
FMOC.......... Fluorenylmethyloxycarbonyl [*Organic chemistry*]
FMOCC.......... Fleet Mobile Operations Command Center (DOMA)
FMOF.......... First Manned Orbital Flight [*NASA*]
FMOFEV.......... First Manned Orbital Flight with EVA [*Extravehicular Activity*] (MCD)
FMOFPL.......... First Manned Orbital Flight with Payload (MCD)
FMOGDS.......... Field Medical Oxygen Generation/Distribution System (DOMA)
FMOI.......... Federation Mondiale des Organisations d'Ingenieurs [*World Federation of Engineering Organizations*]
fmol.......... Femtomole (MAE)
F Moore.......... English King's Bench Reports [*72 English Reprint*] [*A publication*] (DLA)
FMOP.......... Frequency Modulation on the Pulse (NG)
FMOR.......... First Mortgage [*NASDAQ symbol*] (TTSB)
FMOR.......... First Mortgage Corp. [*NASDAQ symbol*] (SAG)
FMP.......... Fair Market Price (AAGC)
FMP.......... Family Member Prefix (DNAB)
FMP.......... Fannie Major Pool [*FNMA*] [*Business term*] (EMRF)
FMP.......... Fasting Metabolic Panel [*Biochemistry*] (DAVI)
FMP.......... Ferrous Metal Powder
FMP.......... Field Maintenance Party [*Aviation*]
FMP.......... Field Marching Pack
FMP.......... Financial Management Plan
FMP.......... First Menstrual Period [*Medicine*]
FMP.......... Fisheries Management Plan [*Marine science*] (OSRA)
FMP.......... Fishery Management Plan
FMP.......... Fleet Modernization Plan [*Navy*]
FMP.......... Fleet Modernization Program (MCD)
FMP.......... Flight Mechanic's Panel
FMP.......... Flight Mode Panel [*Aviation*]
FM Prop.......... Flow Management Position [*ICAO*] (DA)
FMP.......... Fluid Motion Panel [*of the British Aeronautical Research Council*] (MCD)
FMP.......... Force Modernization Program
FMP.......... Foreign Materiel Program [*Military*] (RDA)
FMP.......... Formable Metallized Plastics [*Industrial technology*]
FMP.......... FORSCOM [*Forces Command*] Mobilization Plan [*DoD*]
FMP.......... Fructose Monophosphate [*Biochemistry*]
FMP.......... Fuel Maintenance Panel (AAG)
FMP.......... Fuels and Mining Practice Division [*Department of Mines and Technical Surveys*] [*Canada*]
FMP.......... Full Marching Pack [*Military*]
FMP.......... Functional Maintenance Procedure
FMPA.......... Federation Mondiale pour la Protection des Animaux [*World Federation for the Protection of Animals*] [*Also known as WFPA and WTB*]
FMPA.......... Fellow of the Master Photographers Association [*British*] (DBQ)
FMPC.......... Federation of Motion Picture Councils (EA)
FMPC.......... Feed Materials Production Center [*AEC*]
FMPCert.......... Family Medicine Program Certificate
FMPD.......... Fort Monmouth Procurement Division
FMPE.......... Fast Memory Parity Error (IAA)
FMPE.......... Federation of Master Process Engravers [*British*] (BI)
FMPEC.......... Financial Management Plan for Emergency Conditions [*Army*]
FMPM.......... Family Manned Planetary Mission
FM-PM.......... Frequency Modulation - Phase Modulation [*RADAR*]
FMPMIS.......... Fleet Modernization Program Management Information System [*Navy*] (GFGA)
FMPO.......... FM Properties [*NASDAQ symbol*] (TTSB)
FMPO.......... FM Properties, Inc. [*NASDAQ symbol*] (SAG)
FMPO.......... Fort Monmouth Procurement Office
FMPP.......... Familial Male Precocious Puberty [*Medicine*]
FMPP.......... Federal Merit Promotion Program
FMPP.......... Flexible Multipipeline Processor
FMPP.......... Foundation of Motion Picture Pioneers (EA)
FM Prop.......... FM Properties, Inc. [*Associated Press*] (SAG)
FMPROT.......... Fine Mesh Cover Protected (IAA)
FMPS.......... Federation of Modern Painters and Sculptors (EA)
FMPS.......... Form Pads [*Tool*] (AAG)
FMPS.......... FORTRAN [*Formula Translating System*] Mathematical Programming System [*Computer science*] (IEEE)
FMPS.......... Functional Mathematical Programming System [*Computer science*]
FMPSA.......... Federation of Master Painters and Signwriters of Australia
FMPT.......... First Material Processing Test [*Japan*]
FMPTE.......... Federation of Municipal Passenger Transport Employers [*British*] (BI)
FMQ.......... Fayalite Magnetite Quartz (Buffer) [*Geophysics*]
FMQ.......... Fichier MARC [*Machine-Readable Cataloging*] Quebecois [*Source file*] [*UTLAS symbol*]
FMQ.......... Frequency-Modulated Quartz
FMQB.......... Friday Morning Quarterback [*In title FMQB Album Report*]
FMR.......... Failure and Malfunction Report [*NASA*] (KSC)
FMR.......... Fairbourne Miniature Railway [*Wales*]
FMR.......... Fair Market Rent (GFGA)
FMR.......... Fasting Metabolic Rate (PDAA)

FMR............	Fellow of the Association of Health Care Information and Medical Records Officers [*British*] (DBQ)
FMR............	Ferromagnetic Resonance
FMR............	Field Maintenance Request
FMR............	Field Modification Report
FMR............	Field Modification Request [*Military*]
FMR............	Fife Mounted Rifles [*British military*] (DMA)
FMR............	Final Meteorological Radiation
FMR............	Financial Management Report (AABC)
FMR............	Fire Movement Range (MCD)
FMR............	Flamingo Air, Inc. [*FAA designator*] (FAAC)
FMR............	Flanagan McAdam Resources, Inc. [*Toronto Stock Exchange symbol*]
FMR............	Former
FMR............	Foundation for Moral Restoration (EA)
FMR............	Freeport McMoRan O/G Rlty [*NYSE symbol*] (TTSB)
FMR............	Freeport-McMoRan Oil & Gas Royalty Trust [*NYSE symbol*] (SPSG)
FMR............	Frequency-Modulated RADAR
FMR............	Frequency-Modulated Ranging (MCD)
FMR............	Frequency-Modulated Receiver [*Telecommunications*]
FMR............	Friend-Moloney-Rauscher [*Virus*] (AAMN)
FMR............	Frontier Mounted Rifles [*British military*] (DMA)
FMR............	Function Maximum Rate (NASA)
FMR............	Funds Management Record [*Military*] (AFM)
FMR............	Les Fusiliers Mont Royal [*British military*] (DMA)
f-mr--..	Morocco [*MARC geographic area code Library of Congress*] (LCCP)
FMR-1	Fragile Mental Retardation [*A gene*] (PAZ)
FMRA..........	Foreign Media Representatives Association
FMRC..........	Fixed Motor Run Capacitor
FMRD..........	Flight Mission Rules Document [*NASA*] (KSC)
FMREC........	Force Mobilization Review and Evaluation Committee [*Military*] (MCD)
FMRF..........	Femarfarmamide [*Biochemistry*]
fMRI...........	Functional Magnetic Resonance Imaging
FMRI...........	Functional Magnetic Resonance Imaging
FMRL..........	Form Roll
FMRL..........	Functional Machine Representation Language [*Computer science*] (CSR)
FMRLY........	Formerly (EY)
FM RoyT.....	Freeport-McMoran Oil & Gas Royalty Trust [*Associated Press*] (SAG)
FMRP..........	Freeport McMoRan Resource Partners Ltd. [*Associated Press*] (SAG)
FMRS..........	Federal Mediation and Reconciliation Service (MHDB)
FMRS..........	Foreign Member of the Royal Society [*British*] (BARN)
FMR-T	Field Materiel-Handling Robot Technology [*US Army Human Engineering Laboratory*] (RDA)
FMRT..........	Final Meteorological Radiation Tape
FMRX..........	FemRx Inc. [*NASDAQ symbol*] (TTSB)
FMRX..........	FemRx, Inc. [*NASDAQ symbol*] (SAG)
FMS............	Facilities Management System
FMS............	Factory Management System [*General Electric Co.*]
FMS............	Factory Mutual System [*Formerly, AFMFIC*] [*Group of four insurance companies and an engineering organization*]
FMS............	Fallout Monitoring Station [*Civil Defense*]
FMS............	Famous
FMS............	Fatigue Monitoring System (MCD)
FMS............	Fat-Mobilizing Substance [*Medicine*]
FMS............	Fecal Management System [*NASA*] (KSC)
FMS............	Federal Management System (GFGA)
FMS............	Federal Music Society (EA)
FMS............	Federated Malay States
FMS............	Federation Mondiale des Sourds [*World Federation of the Deaf - WFD*] [*Rome, Italy*] (EA)
FMS............	Federation of Materials Societies (EA)
FMS............	Feline McDonough Sarcoma [*Virus*]
FMS............	Fellow of the Institute of Management Services [*British*] (DBQ)
FMS............	Fellow of the Medical Society [*British*]
FMS............	Fellow of the Meteorological Society [*British*]
FMS............	Field Maintenance Shop [*Army*] (NATG)
FMS............	Field Maintenance Squadron [*Air Force*] (MCD)
FMS............	Field Maintenance System
FMS............	Field Music School [*Marine Corps*]
FMS............	Fighter Missile System
FMS............	File Maintenance System (MCD)
FMS............	File Management Supervisor [*Honeywell, Inc.*]
FMS............	File Management System (AFIT)
FMS............	Final Multiple Score (NVT)
FMS............	Financial Management Service (USGC)
FMS............	Financial Management System
FMS............	Financial Managers Society (EA)
FMS............	Financial Managers' Statement [*Financial Managers' Society*] [*A publication*]
FMS............	First Marathon, Inc. [*Toronto Stock Exchange symbol*]
FMS............	Fleet Management System [*Arrencross Ltd.*] [*Software package*] (NCC)
FMS............	Fleet Material Support [*Navy*]
FMS............	Fleet Medical School (DOMA)
FMS............	Fleet Music School
FMS............	Flexible Machine System [*Industrial engineering*]
FMS............	Flexible Machining System (DOMA)
FMS............	Flexible Manufacturing System
FMS............	Flexible Modular Scheduling (EDAC)
FMS............	Flight Management System
FMS............	Flight Mission Simulation Test (MCD)
FMS............	Flight Motion Simulator
FMS............	Floating Machine Shop

FMS	Floating Maintenance Shop (MCD)
FMS	Flow Measuring System
FMS	Fluid Management System (SSD)
FMS	Fluorouracil, Mutamycin, Streotozocin [*Antineoplastic drug*] (CDI)
FMS	Flux Monitoring System [*Nuclear energy*] (NRCH)
FMS	Food Management System [*or Subsystem*] (MCD)
FMS	Force Management System [*Air Force*] (GFGA)
FMS	Force Measuring System (KSC)
FMS	Force Module Subsystem (DOMA)
FMS	Foreign Military Sales (AFM)
FMS	Foreign Military Service (MCD)
FMS	Forms Management System [*Computer science*]
FMS	Fort Myers Southern Railroad Co. [*AAR code*]
FMS	FORTRAN [*Formula Translating System*] Monitor System [*Computer science*]
FMS	Fratres Maristae Scholarum [*Marist Brothers of the Schools*] [*Also known as Little Brothers of Mary*] (EAIO)
FMS	Free-Machining Steel
FMS	Freeway Management System
FMS	Frequency Management System [*ITU*] [*United Nations*] (DUND)
FMS	Frequency Mixer Stage
FMS	Frequency-Multiplexed Subcarrier
FMS	Frequency Multiplier Storer
FMS	Fresenius Medical Care AG [*NYSE symbol*] (SAG)
FMS	Fuel-Monitoring System [*Cheshire County Council*] [*Software package*] (NCC)
FMS	Full Mouth Series [*Dentistry*]
FMS	Future Management Services [*A Lebanese arms company*] (ECON)
FMS	Fuze Maintenance Spares (NG)
FMS	Hadison Aviation [*Sudan*] [*ICAO designator*] (FAAC)
FMS	[*The*] Marist Brothers (TOCD)
fms	Marist Brothers (TOCD)
FMSA..........	Ambalavao [*Madagascar*] [*ICAO location identifier*] (ICLI)
FMSA..........	Fellow of the Mineralogical Society of America
FMSA..........	Foreign Military Sales Act (AFIT)
FMSA..........	Future Military Systems Authority
FMSAEG......	Fleet Missile Systems Analysis and Evaluation Group [*Navy*]
FMSAEGA...	Fleet Missile Systems Analysis and Evaluation Group Annex [*Navy*] (MCD)
FMSAEGANX...	Fleet Missile Systems Analysis and Evaluation Group Annex [*Navy*] (DNAB)
FMSAEL......	Fleet Missile Systems Analysis and Evaluation Laboratory (MCD)
FMsB	Barry College, Miami Shores, FL [*Library symbol Library of Congress*] (LCLS)
FMSB..........	Beroroha/Antsoa [*Madagascar*] [*ICAO location identifier*] (ICLI)
FMSB..........	First Mutual Savings Bank [*NASDAQ symbol*] (NQ)
FMSB..........	First Mutual Svgs (WA) [*NASDAQ symbol*] (TTSB)
FMSC..........	Federal Manual for Supply Cataloging (AABC)
FMSC..........	Federation Mondiale des Societes de Cuisiniers [*World Association of Cooks Societies - WACS*] (EA)
FMSC..........	Film Magazine Stowage Container (MCD)
FMSC..........	Fixed Motor Starting Capacitor
FMSC..........	Franciscan Missionary Sisters of the Sacred Heart [*Roman Catholic religious order*]
FMSC..........	Mandabe [*Madagascar*] [*ICAO location identifier*] (ICLI)
FMSCEUA ...	Federated Municipal and Shire Council Employees' Union of Australia
FMSCR	Foreign Military Sales Credit [*Financing*]
FMSCSEL....	Foreign Military Sales Consolidated Support Equipment List (MCD)
FMSD..........	Facilities Management and Services Division [*Environmental Protection Agency*] (GFGA)
FMSD..........	Tolagnaro [*Madagascar*] [*ICAO location identifier*] (ICLI)
FMSE..........	Betroka [*Madagascar*] [*ICAO location identifier*] (ICLI)
FMSF..........	Fianarantsoa [*Madagascar*] [*ICAO location identifier*] (ICLI)
FMSF..........	Foreign Military Sales Financing
FMS Fn	FMS Financial Corp. [*Associated Press*] (SAG)
FMSG..........	Farafangana [*Madagascar*] [*ICAO location identifier*] (ICLI)
FMSGT........	Field Music Sergeant [*Marine Corps*]
FMSHRC......	Federal Mine Safety and Health Review Commission (EG)
FMSHRD.....	Federal Mine Safety and Health Review Decisions [*A publication*] (DLA)
FMSI..........	Filii Mariae Salutis Infirmorum [*Sons of Mary, Health of the Sick*] [*Roman Catholic religious order*]
FMSI..........	Folk Music Society of Ireland (EAIO)
FMSI..........	Food Machinery Service Institute (EA)
FMSI..........	Friction Materials Standards Institute (EA)
FMSI..........	Ihosy [*Madagascar*] [*ICAO location identifier*] (ICLI)
FMSI..........	Sons of Mary Missionary Society (TOCD)
fmsi	Sons of Mary Missionary Society (TOCD)
FMSJ..........	Franciscan Missionaries of St. Joseph [*Mill Hill Sisters*] [*Roman Catholic religious order*]
FMSJ..........	Manja [*Madagascar*] [*ICAO location identifier*] (ICLI)
FMSJ..........	Mill Hill Sisters (TOCD)
FMSK..........	Manakara [*Madagascar*] [*ICAO location identifier*] (ICLI)
FMSL..........	Bekily [*Madagascar*] [*ICAO location identifier*] (ICLI)
FMSL..........	Fort Monmouth Signal Laboratory [*Army*]
FMSM..........	Federation Mondiale pour la Sante Mentale [*World Federation for Mental Health*]
FMSM..........	Mananjary [*Madagascar*] [*ICAO location identifier*] (ICLI)
FMSMP.......	Foreign Military Sales Management Plan (AFIT)
FMSN..........	Tanandava-Samangoky [*Madagascar*] [*ICAO location identifier*] (ICLI)
FMSO..........	Fleet Material Support Office [*Navy*]
FMSO..........	Foreign Military Sales Order [*Army*] (AABC)
FMSO	Ranohira [*Madagascar*] [*ICAO location identifier*] (ICLI)
FMSP..........	[*A*] Fool and His Money Are Soon Parted (ROG)

FMSP.......... Foreign Military Sales Program [*Army*] (AABC)
FMSP.......... Frequency Modulation Signal Processor (NASA)
FMSPA........ Fish and Meat Spreadable Products Association [*British*] (DBA)
FMSq.......... Field Maintenance Squadron [*Air Force*] (AFM)
FMSR.......... Daughters of Our Lady of Holy Rosary (TOCD)
FMSR.......... Federated Malay States Reports [*A publication*] (DLA)
FMSR.......... Federation des Mouvements Socialistes Regionalistes de la Reunion [*Federation of Socialist Regionalist Movements of Reunion*] [*Political party*] (PPW)
FMSR.......... Finite Mass Sum Rule [*Nuclear science*] (OA)
FMSR.......... Morombe [*Madagascar*] [*ICAO location identifier*] (ICLI)
FMSS.......... Financial Management Systems [*A publication*]
FMSS.......... Financial Management Systems Software (AAGC)
FMSS.......... Fleet Medical Service School (DNAB)
FMST.......... Field Missile Specification Test
FMST.......... Field Missile System Test
FMST.......... Finishmaster, Inc. [*NASDAQ symbol*] (SAG)
FMST.......... Foreign Military Sales Training
FMST.......... Frequency Mass Spectrometer Tube
FMST.......... Toliara [*Madagascar*] [*ICAO location identifier*] (ICLI)
FMSU.......... Forward Mobile Support Unit
FMSV.......... Betioky [*Madagascar*] [*ICAO location identifier*] (ICLI)
FMSVR........ Federated Malay Straits Volunteer Reserve [*British military*] (DMA)
FMSWR....... Flexible Mild Steel Wire Rope
FMSY.......... Ampanihy [*Madagascar*] [*ICAO location identifier*] (ICLI)
FMSZ.......... Ankazoabo [*Madagascar*] [*ICAO location identifier*] (ICLI)
FMT............ Facilities Maintenance Team [*Military*]
FMT............ Factory Marriage Test
FMT............ Farrer Memorial Trust [*Australia*]
FMT............ Federation of Merchant Tailors of Great Britain, Inc. (BI)
FMT............ Field Maintenance Technician
FMT............ Field Modification Task (MCD)
FMT............ Firemont Genl [*NYSE symbol*] (TTSB)
FMT............ Flight Management Team [*Skylab*] [*NASA*]
FMT............ Flour-Milling Technology (OA)
FMT............ Fluoro-meta-tyrosine [*Organic chemistry*]
FMT............ Flush Metal Threshold [*Technical drawings*]
FMT............ Force Modernization Training [*Military*]
FMT............ Foreign Material for Training (MCD)
FMT............ Foreign Military Training (CINC)
FMT............ Foremost Energy Corp. [*Vancouver Stock Exchange symbol*]
FMT............ Format
FMT............ Foundation for Medical Technology (EA)
FMT............ Freemasons Tavern [*Freemasonry*] (ROG)
FMT............ Fremont General Corp. [*NYSE symbol*] (SPSG)
FMT............ Frequency-Modulated Transmitter [*Telecommunications*]
FMT............ Friction Measurement Test
FMT............ Functional Message Type [*Communications*]
FMTA.......... Federation Mondiale de Travailleurs Agricoles [*World Federation of Agricultural Workers - WFAW*] (EAIO)
FMTA.......... Flash Mass Thermal Analysis (KSC)
FMTAG........ Foreign Military Training Affairs Group
FMTB.......... Foreign Military Training Board (AAGC)
FMTC.......... Familial Medullary Thyroid Carcinoma [*Oncology*]
FMTE.......... Field Maintenance Test Equipment
FMTM.......... Frequency Modulation Team (IAA)
FMTM.......... Friction Materials Test Machine
FMTMF........ Foreign Military Training Management Flight
FMTNM....... Federation Mondiale des Travailleurs Non-Manuels [*World Federation of Trade Unions of Non-Manual Workers - WFNMW*] [*Antwerp, Belgium*] (EAIO)
FMTO.......... Form Tool
FMTP.......... File Management Transaction Processor
FMTPr......... Fremont Genl Fin 1 9%'TOPrS' [*NYSE symbol*] (TTSB)
FMTR.......... Florida Missile Test Range (MUGU)
FMTR.......... Formatter (MCD)
FMTS.......... Federation Mondiale des Travailleurs Scientifiques [*World Federation of Scientific Workers - WFSW*] (EAIO)
FMTS.......... Field Maintenance Test Set
FMTS.......... Field Maintenance Test Station [*Military*] (AFIT)
FMTS.......... Flat Moving Target Screen [*Weaponry*] (INF)
FMTT.......... Forward Medical Treatment Team [*Army*] (INF)
FMTV.......... Family of Medium Tactical Vehicles [*Military*] (RDA)
FMU............ Files Management Unit [*Computer science*]
FMU............ Financial Management Unit [*LIMRA*]
FMU............ Flow Management Unit [*Aviation*] (FAAC)
FMU............ Force Measurement Unit
FMU............ Functional Mock-Up (KSC)
FMU............ Function Memory Unit
f-mu--......... Mauritania [*MARC geographic area code Library of Congress*] (LCCP)
FMU............ University of Miami, Coral Gables, FL [*Library symbol Library of Congress*] (LCLS)
FMU-L......... University of Miami, Law Library, Coral Gables, FL [*Library symbol Library of Congress*] (LCLS)
F-MuLV....... Friend Murine Leukemia Virus
FMU-M........ University of Miami, Medical Library, Miami, FL [*Library symbol Library of Congress*] (LCLS)
FMU-Mu...... University of Miami, Music Library, Coral Gables, FL [*Library symbol Library of Congress*] (LCLS)
FMU-R........ University of Miami, Rosenstiel School of Marine and Atmospheric Sciences, Miami, FL [*Library symbol Library of Congress*] (LCLS)
FMUSIC...... Federation of Military and United Services Institutes of Canada
FMV............ Fair Market Value [*Bargaining term*]
FMV............ Fluorouracil, Methyl-CCNU, Vincristine [*Antineoplastic drug*] (CDI)

FMV............ Foreign Market Value [*Business term*]
FMV............ Frangipani Mosaic Virus [*Plant pathology*]
FMV............ Full Motion Video (BARN)
FMV............ United States Veterans Administration Hospital, Miami, FL [*Library symbol Library of Congress*] (LCLS)
FMVCP........ Federal Motor Vehicle Control Program (GNE)
FMVEME...... Federation of Malaya Volunteer Electrical and Mechanical Engineers [*British military*]
FMVJ.......... Federation Mondiale des Villes Jumelees-Cites Unies [*United Towns Organisation - UTO*] (EA)
FMVRC........ Federation of Malaya Volunteer Reconnaissance Corps [*British military*] (DMA)
FMVSS........ Federal Motor Vehicle Safety Standard
FMVTPS...... Federal Motor Vehicle Theft Prevention Standard [*Automotive engineering*]
FMW............ Fast Magnetosonic Wave (PDAA)
FMW............ Federation of Masons of the World (EA)
FMW............ First Main Watch
f-mw--......... Malawi [*MARC geographic area code Library of Congress*] (LCCP)
FMW............ Mount Fremont [*Washington*] [*Seismograph station code, US Geological Survey*] (SEIS)
FMW............ World University-Miami, Miami, FL [*Library symbol Library of Congress*] (LCLS)
FMWA.......... First Mutual Savings Bank of Washington [*Associated Press*] (SAG)
FMWA.......... Florida Movers and Warehousemen's Association (SRA)
FMWF.......... Free Methodist World Fellowship (EA)
FMWTC........ Fleet Mine Warfare Training Center (DNAB)
FMWU.......... Federated Miscellaneous Workers' Union of Australia
FMWWR....... Fire, Mildew, Water, and Weather Resistant (MCD)
FMX............ Flyball Master Excellent
FMX............ Frequency-Modulated Transmitter [*Telecommunications*] (KSC)
FMX............ Full Mouth X-Ray [*Dentistry*]
FMXI.......... Foamex International [*NASDAQ symbol*] (SAG)
FMY............ Foreign Missons of Yarumal [*Colorado*] (EAIO)
FMY............ Fort Myers [*Florida*] [*Airport symbol*] (OAG)
FMY............ Fort Myers, FL [*Location identifier FAA*] (FAAL)
FMY............ Meyer [*Fred*], Inc. [*NYSE symbol*] (SPSG)
f-mz--......... Mozambique [*MARC geographic area code Library of Congress*] (LCCP)
FN.............. Air Carolina [*ICAO designator*] (AD)
F/N............ Facing North [*In outdoor advertising*] (WDMC)
FN.............. False Negative [*Medicine*]
FN.............. Fence [*Technical drawings*]
FN.............. Fiber Node
FN.............. Fibronectin [*Biochemistry*]
FN.............. Financial [*Rate*] [*Value of the English pound*]
FN.............. Find Number (MSA)
F-N............. Finger to Nose Test [*Neurology*]
FN.............. Fireman [*Nonrated enlisted man*] [*Navy*]
FN.............. First Name
FN.............. Flat Nose [*Projectile*]
FN.............. Flat or Nested [*Freight*]
FN.............. Flight Nurse
FN.............. Fluoride Number (MAE)
FN.............. Fog Nautophone [*Navigation charts*]
FN.............. Footnote
fn.............. Footnote (WDMC)
FN.............. Foreign Patent Number (NITA)
FN.............. Foundation Name [*Dialog*] [*Searchable fields*] [*Information service or system*] (NITA)
FN.............. Franco-Nevada Mining Corp. [*Toronto Stock Exchange symbol*]
FN.............. Frazer Nash [*Automobile manufacturer*] [*British*]
FN.............. Freelance Network [*Defunct*] (EA)
FN.............. French Navy (NATG)
FN.............. Friends of Nature (EA)
FN.............. Front National [*France Political party*] (PPW)
FN.............. Front National [*Belgium Political party*] (EY)
FN.............. Front National [*Gabon*] [*Political party*] (EY)
FN.............. Fruitarian Network (EA)
FN.............. Full Employment [*Economics*]
fn.............. Function (AAMN)
FN.............. Functional Network
FN.............. Fusion (WGA)
FN.............. Futures Network [*Ormskirk, Lancashire, England*] [*Defunct*] (EA)
Fn.............. [*The*] Holy Bible in Modern English (1903) [*Ferrar Fenton*] [*A publication*] (BJA)
FN.............. Night First Class [*Airline fare code*]
fn----........... Sudan (Region) [*MARC geographic area code Library of Congress*] (LCCP)
FNA............ Federation of National Associations (EA)
FNA............ Fellow of the Indian National Science Academy [*Formerly, FNI*]
FNa............ Filtered Sodium (MAE)
FNA............ Final Approach [*Aviation*]
FNA............ Fine-Needle Aspiration [*Medicine*]
FNA............ Flora North America Program [*Defunct*] (EA)
FNA............ Florenville, LA [*Location identifier FAA*] (FAAL)
FNA............ Flugfelag Nordurlands [*Iceland*] [*ICAO designator*] (FAAC)
FNA............ Following Named Airmen
FNA............ For Necessary Action (ADA)
FNA............ Freetown [*Sierra Leone*] [*Airport symbol*] (OAG)
FNA............ French North Africa
FNA............ Frequency Network Analyzer
FNA............ Fujitsu Network Architecture [*Fujitsu Ltd.*] [*Japan*]
FNA............ Fuming Nitric Acid (KSC)
FNA............ Functional Name Addresses

FNAA	Fast Neutron Activation Analysis [*Analytical chemistry*]
FNAB	Fine-Needle Aspiration Biopsy [*Medicine*]
FNaC	Collier County Free Public Library, Naples, FL [*Library symbol Library of Congress*] (LCLS)
FNAC	Federation Nationale d'Achats des Cadres [*Initials alone now used as name of discount-store chain in France*] [*Pronounced "f-nak"*]
FNAC	Fine Needle Aspiration Cytology (DAVI)
FNAEA	Fellow of the National Association of Estate Agents [*British*] (DBQ)
FNAF	Front National pour l'Algerie Francaise [*National Front for French Algeria*] [*Political party*]
FNAI	Florida Natural Areas Inventory [*Information service or system*] (IID)
FNAL	Fermi National Accelerator Laboratory [*Also, FERMILAB*] [*Batavia, IL*] [*Department of Energy*]
FNAM	Ambriz [*Angola*] [*ICAO location identifier*] (ICLI)
FNAN	Luanda [*Angola*] [*ICAO location identifier*] (ICLI)
FNAO	Fellow of the National Association of Opticians [*British*] (DAS)
FNAOE	Federation of National AFS Organizations in Europe [*Brussels, Belgium*] (EAIO)
FNARS	FEMA [*Federal Emergency Management Agency*] National Radio System (GFGA)
FNAT	First National Entertainment Corp. [*NASDAQ symbol*] (SAG)
FNAT	First National Entmt [*NASDAQ symbol*] (TTSB)
F/Nav	Flight Navigator (AIA)
FNAWS	Foundation for North American Wild Sheep (EA)
FNB	Falls City, NE [*Location identifier FAA*] (FAAL)
FNB	False Negative Rate [*Medicine*] (DAVI)
FNB	Federation Nationale du Batiment [*France*] (NITA)
FNB	File Name Block [*Computer science*] (MHDB)
FNB	First Chicago Corp. [*NYSE symbol*] (SPSG)
FNB	Fitzherbert's Natura Brevium [*A publication*] (DLA)
FNB	FNB Corp. [*Associated Press*] (SAG)
FNB	Food and Nutrition Board (EA)
FNB	Fort Necessity National Battlefield, Farmington, PA [*OCLC symbol*] (OCLC)
FNBA	Fellow of the North British Academy (DAS)
FNBC	Franklin Bancorp [*NASDAQ symbol*] (SAG)
FNBC	Franklin Bancorporation [*NASDAQ symbol*] (TTSB)
FNBC	M'Banza-Congo [*Angola*] [*ICAO location identifier*] (ICLI)
FnBen	Financial Benefit Group, Inc. [*Associated Press*] (SAG)
FNBF	FNB Financial Services Corp. [*NASDAQ symbol*] (SAG)
FNBF	FNB Financial Svcs [*NASDAQ symbol*] (TTSB)
FNB FS	FNB Financial Services Corp. [*Associated Press*] (SAG)
FNBG	Benguela [*Angola*] [*ICAO location identifier*] (ICLI)
FNBN	FNB Corp. [*North Carolina*] [*NASDAQ symbol*] (SAG)
FNB PA	FNB Corp. [*Pennsylvania*] [*Associated Press*] (SAG)
FNBR	Fast Neutron Breeder Reactor [*Nuclear energy*] (DEN)
FNBR	FNB Rochester Corp. [*NASDAQ symbol*] (SAG)
FNBRo	FNB Rochester Corp. [*Associated Press*] (SAG)
FNC	Fast Neutron Cavity
FNC	Federal Networking Council [*Computer science*] (TNIG)
FNC	Federation Nationale des Communications [*National Federation of Communication*] [*Canada*] (EAIO)
FNC	Fence
FNC	Ferrocarriles Nacionales de Colombia [*National Railways of Colombia*] (EY)
FNC	Fine-Needle Cholangiography [*Gastroenterology*]
FNC	Finlay Fork [*British Columbia*] [*Seismograph station code, US Geological Survey Closed*] (SEIS)
FNC	Fixed Niobium Capacitor
FNC	Flexible Numerical Control [*Manufacturing engineering*] [*Computer science*]
FNC	Flexible Nylon Coupling
FNC	Focus National Mortgage Corp. [*Toronto Stock Exchange symbol*]
FNC	Fox News Channel
FNC	Frente Nacional Constitucionalista [*National Constitutionalist Front*] [*Ecuador*] [*Political party*] (PPW)
FNC	Frente Nacional Opositora [*National Opposition Front*] [*Panama*] [*Political party*] (PPW)
FNC	Friends of Nicaraguan Culture (EA)
FNC	Front National de Concertation [*Haiti*] [*Political party*] (EY)
FNC	Funchal [*Portugal*] [*Airport symbol*] (OAG)
FNC	Future Nurses Clubs [*National League for Nursing*] (AEBS)
FNCA	Cabinda [*Angola*] [*ICAO location identifier*] (ICLI)
FNCA	Federation of Nordic Commercial Agents [*Stockholm, Sweden*] (EA)
FNCB	Camembe [*Angola*] [*ICAO location identifier*] (ICLI)
FNCB	First National City Bank [*Later, Citibank*] [*New York City*]
FNCC	Cacolo [*Angola*] [*ICAO location identifier*] (ICLI)
FNCC	Federation Nationale des Cooperatives de Cereales
FNCD	Front National pour le Changement et la Democratie [*Haiti*] [*Political party*] (EY)
FNCETA	Federation Nationale des Centres d'Etudes Techniques Agricoles
FNCH	Chitato [*Angola*] [*ICAO location identifier*] (ICLI)
FNCI	Financial News Composite Index [*Pronounced "fancy"*] [*Financial News Network*]
FNCJ	Fine Needle Catheter Jejunostomy [*Medicine*] (DMAA)
FnclSec	Financial Security Assurance Holdings [*Associated Press*] (SAG)
FnclSvcs	Financial Services Acquisition Corp. [*Associated Press*] (SAG)
FNCM	Camabatela [*Angola*] [*ICAO location identifier*] (ICLI)
FNCM	Fellow, National College of Music [*London, England*] (ADA)
FNCO	Funco, Inc. [*NASDAQ symbol*] (SAG)
FNCRT	Fellow of the National College of Rubber Technology [*British*]
FncSv	Financial Svcs. Acquisition Corp. [*Associated Press*] (SAG)
FNCTN	Function (FAAC)
FNCUMA	Federation Nationale des Cooperatives d'Utilisation de Materiel Agricole

FNCV	Cuito Cuanavale [*Angola*] [*ICAO location identifier*] (ICLI)
FNCX	Camaxilo [*Angola*] [*ICAO location identifier*] (ICLI)
FNCY	Fancy
FNCZ	Cazombo [*Angola*] [*ICAO location identifier*] (ICLI)
FND	Baltimore, MD [*Location identifier FAA*] (FAAL)
FND	Facility Need Date (NASA)
FND	Fast Neutron Dose
FND	Fender [*s*] [*Freight*]
FND	Finnemore's Notes and Digest of Natal Cases [*A publication*] (DLA)
FND	First Chicago Corp. [*NYSE symbol*] (SAG)
FND	First Chi NBD 5.50% 'DECS'97 [*NYSE symbol*] (TTSB)
FND	Fonds National de Developpement [*Mauritania*] (EY)
FND	Found
FND	Found
FND	Foundation [*Technical drawings*]
FND	Frank Nelson Doubleday [*American publisher*]
FND	Friends of Neil Diamond (EA)
FND	Frontul National Democratic [*National Democratic Front*] [*Romania*] [*Political party*] (PPE)
fnd	Funder/Sponsor [*MARC relator code*] [*Library of Congress*] (LCCP)
FNDB	Damba [*Angola*] [*ICAO location identifier*] (ICLI)
FNDD	Founded
FNDD	Funded (ROG)
FNDF	Federal National Democratic Front [*Myanmar*] [*Political party*] (PD)
FNDG	Finding
FNDG	Founding
FNDG	Funding (KSC)
FNDH	Foreign National Direct Hire [*Military*]
FNDMNTLST	Fundamentalist
FNDN	Foundation
FNDNG	Funding
fndobj	Found Object (VRA)
FNDP	Frente Nacional Democratico Popular [*Popular National Democratic Front*] [*Mexico*] (PD)
FNDR	Fender [*Automotive engineering*]
FNDR	Founder
FndrFn	Founders Financial Corp. [*Associated Press*] (SAG)
FNDRY	Foundry
Fndry	Foundry (BARN)
FNDTN	Foundation
FNDTS	Fellow of the Non-Destructive Testing Society of Great Britain
FNE	Faisceaux Nationalistes Europeens [*European Nationalist Alliances*] [*France*] (PD)
FNE	Fane [*Papua New Guinea*] [*Airport symbol*] (OAG)
FNE	Fear of Negative Evaluation Scale (EDAC)
fne	Fine [*Quality of the bottom*] [*Nautical charts*]
FNE	Finnsnes [*Norway*] [*Airport symbol*] (AD)
FNE	Following Named Enlisted Personnel
FNE	Free Nerve Ending [*Anatomy*]
FNEA	Federation of National Electrolysis Associations [*Defunct*] (EA)
FNECInst	Fellow of the North East Coast Institution of Engineers and Shipbuilders [*British*]
FNEG	False Negative [*Medicine*]
FNEORID	Following Named Enlisted Member Organization Indicated
FNERAS	Following Named Enlisted Members Are Relieved Assignment
FNES	Field Network Evaluation Study [*Survey*]
FNET	Fuzzy Network (PDAA)
FNEUC	Federation Nationale des Etudiants des Universites Canadiennes [*National Federation of Canadian University Students*]
FNF	Families Need Fathers [*British*] [*An association*] (DBA)
FNF	Fidelity Financial Corp. [*NYSE symbol*] (SAG)
FNF	Fidelity Natl Finl [*NYSE symbol*] (TTSB)
FNF	Finger-Nose-Finger [*Test*] [*Neurology*] (DAVI)
FNF	Finnish Air Force Headquarters [*ICAO designator*] (FAAC)
FNF	First Normal Form (MHDB)
FNF	Foundation for the New Freeman (EA)
FNFA	Fellow of the National Federation of Accountants [*British*] (DAS)
FNFC	First National Financial Co. [*British*]
FNFHFTM	Federation of Needle Fish Hook and Fishing Tackle Makers [*British*] (BI)
FNFL	Forces Navales Francaises Libres [*Free French Naval Forces*] [*World War II*]
FNFP	First Nations Financial Project (EA)
FNG	Fada N'Gourma [*Burkina Faso*] [*Airport symbol*] (OAG)
FNG	Firan Corp. [*Toronto Stock Exchange symbol*]
FNG	Frontier Guard, Finland [*FAA designator*] (FAAC)
f-ng--	Niger [*MARC geographic area code Library of Congress*] (LCCP)
FNGAA	Federation Nationale des Groupements Agricoles d'Approvisionnement
FNGB	First Northen Capital [*NASDAQ symbol*] (TTSB)
FNGB	First Northern Capital Corp. [*NASDAQ symbol*] (SAG)
FNGB	First Northern Savings Bank SA [*NASDAQ symbol*] (NQ)
FNGC	Frontier Natural Gas [*NASDAQ symbol*] (SAG)
FNGCP	Frontier Nat Gas $1.20 Cv Ptd [*NASDAQ symbol*] (TTSB)
FNGCW	Frontier Natural Gas Wrrt [*NASDAQ symbol*] (TTSB)
FNGI	N'Giva [*Angola*] [*ICAO location identifier*] (ICLI)
FNGIREA	First National Group of Independent Real Estate Agents Ltd. [*Australia*]
FNGP	Federation Nationale des Gaullistes de Progres [*National Federation of Progressive Gaullists*] [*France Political party*] (PPW)
FNGU	N'Gunza [*Angola*] [*ICAO location identifier*] (ICLI)
FNH	First National Bankshares, Inc. [*AMEX symbol*] (SAG)
FNH	First Natl Bankshares(LA) [*AMEX symbol*] (TTSB)
FNH	Flashless Nonhygroscopic [*Gunpowder*]
FNH	Focal Nodular Hyperplasia [*Medicine*]

FNHO .... Forum of National Hispanic Organizations (EA)
FNHP .... Federation of Nurses and Health Professionals (EA)
FNHU .... Huambo [Angola] [ICAO location identifier] (ICLI)
FNI .... Facial Nerve Involvement [Medicine]
FNI .... Fan In
FNI .... Federation Naturiste Internationale [International Naturist Federation]
FNI .... Fellow of the National Institute of Sciences in India [Later, FNA]
FNI .... Fellow of the Nautical Institute [British]
FNI .... FNI Fashion, Inc. [Vancouver Stock Exchange symbol]
FNI .... Following Named Individuals
FNI .... Foreign National Indirect (NVT)
FNI .... Nimes [France] [Airport symbol] (OAG)
FNI .... Nimes [Frances] [Airport symbol] (AD)
FNIAL .... Fellow of the National Institute of Arts and Letters [British]
FNIC .... Food and Nutrition Information Center [Department of Agriculture] (IID)
FNIF .... Florence Nightingale International Foundation [Defunct] (EA)
FNIH .... Fellow of the National Institute of Hardware [British] (DBQ)
FNIMH .... Fellow of the National Institute of Medical Herbalists [British]
FNIN .... Financial Inds [NASDAQ symbol] (TTSB)
FNIN .... Financial Industries Corp. [NASDAQ symbol] (NQ)
FNiO .... Okaloosa-Walton Junior College, Niceville, FL [Library symbol Library of Congress] (LCLS)
FNJ .... Feng Yang-Pyongyang [North Korea] [Airport symbol] (AD)
FNJ .... Fort Gordon, GA [Location identifier FAA] (FAAL)
FNJ .... Front National de la Jeunesse [National Youth Front] [France] (PD)
FNJ .... Pyongyang [North Korea] [Airport symbol] (OAG)
FNJ FDC ..... United States Food and Drug Administration. Notices of Judgment: Foods [A publication] (DLA)
FNK .... Fin Creek, AK [Location identifier FAA] (FAAL)
Fn key .... Function Key (CDE)
FNKU .... Kuito/Bie [Angola] [ICAO location identifier] (ICLI)
FNL .... Fansteel, Inc. [NYSE symbol] (SPSG)
FNL .... Final (NASA)
FNL .... Five New Laender [Lands] [Name given to former East German territory after unification]
FNL .... Flight Navigator's Licence [British] (AIA)
FNL .... Fort Collins/Loveland, CO [Location identifier FAA] (FAAL)
FNL .... Friends of the National Libraries [British]
FNL .... Fund for New Leadership [Defunct] (EA)
FNLA .... Front National de Liberation de l'Angola [Angolan National Liberation Front] (PD)
FNLB .... Front National de Liberation de Bretagne [National Liberation Front of Brittany] [France] (PD)
FNLB .... Lobito [Angola] [ICAO location identifier] (ICLI)
FNLG .... Front National de Liberation Guyanais [Guiana National Liberation Front] [French Guiana] (PD)
FNLLP .... Formyl(norleucyl)(leucyl)phenylalanine [Biochemistry]
FNLO .... French Naval Liaison Officer (NATG)
FNLU .... Luanda/4 De Fevereiro [Angola] [ICAO location identifier] (ICLI)
FNLW .... Foundation for Non-Lethal Warfare [Defunct] (EA)
FNLY .... Finlay Enterprises [NASDAQ symbol] (TTSB)
FNLY .... Finlay Enterprises, Inc. [NASDAQ symbol] (SAG)
FNM .... Fancamp Resources Ltd. [Vancouver Stock Exchange symbol]
FNM .... Federal National Mortgage Association [Wall Street slang name: "Fannie Mae"] [NYSE symbol] (SPSG)
FNM .... Federal Natl Mtge [NYSE symbol] (TTSB)
FNM .... Ferrocarriles Nacionales de Mexico [National Railways of Mexico]
FNM .... Financial Network Manager (BUR)
FNM .... Free National Movement [Bahamas] [Political party] (PPW)
FNMA .... Federal National Mortgage Association
FNMA .... Front National Martiniquais pour l'Autonomie [Martinique National Front for Autonomy] [Political party] (PPW)
FNMA .... Malanje [Angola] [ICAO location identifier] (ICLI)
FNmB .... Barry College, North Miami, FL [Library symbol Library of Congress] (LCLS)
FNME .... Menongue [Angola] [ICAO location identifier] (ICLI)
FNMO .... Mooamedes/Yuri Gagarin [Angola] [ICAO location identifier] (ICLI)
FNMPrA .... Federal Natl Mtge 6.41% Pfd [NYSE symbol] (TTSB)
FNMPrB .... Federal Natl Mtge 6.50% Pfd [NYSE symbol] (TTSB)
FNMQ .... Maquela [Angola] [ICAO location identifier] (ICLI)
FNN .... Financial News Network [Cable-television system]
FNN .... Franconia Notch [New Hampshire] [Seismograph station code, US Geological Survey Closed] (SEIS)
FNNG .... Negage [Angola] [ICAO location identifier] (ICLI)
FNNPE .... Federation of Nature and National Parks of Europe (EERA)
FNO .... Clinton, IA [Location identifier FAA] (FAAL)
FNO .... Fan Out
FNO .... Following Named Officers
FNO .... Frente Nacional de Oposicion [National Opposition Front] [Guatemala] [Political party]
FNO .... Frente Nacional de Oposicion [National Opposition Front] [Venezuela Political party]
FNOA .... Following Named Officers and Airmen
FNOC .... Fleet Numerical Oceanography Center (MSC)
FNOIO .... Fleet Naval Ordnance Inspecting Officer
FNOW .... [The] Future Now, Inc. [NASDAQ symbol] (SPSG)
FNP .... Family Nurse Practitioner
FNP .... Fijian Nationalist Party [Political party] (PPW)
FNP .... Floating Nuclear Plant [or Powerplant] [ERDA]
FNP .... Force, Net Propulsive
FNP .... Foundation for National Progress (EA)
FNP .... Frente Nacional de Panama [Panamanian National Front] [Political party] (PD)
FNP .... Front-End Network Processor

FNP .... Fusion Point
FNP .... University of North Florida, Jacksonville, FL [OCLC symbol] (OCLC)
FNPA .... Foreign Numbering Plan Area [AT & T] [Telecommunications] (TEL)
FNPA .... Porto Amboim [Angola] [ICAO location identifier] (ICLI)
FNPB .... Sanza Pombo [Angola] [ICAO location identifier] (ICLI)
FNPH .... Foreningen Nordiska Pappershistoriker [Association of Nordic Paper Historians - NPH] [Stockholm, Sweden] (EAIO)
FNPLT .... Front Nationaliste Progressiste pour la Liberation de la Tunisie [Progressive Nationalist Front for the Liberation of Tunisia] [Political party] (PD)
FNPO .... For NASA Personnel Only (KSC)
FNPOR .... Federation of National Professional Organizations for Recreation (EA)
FNPP .... Floating Nuclear Power Plant Study [Marine science] (MSC)
FNPR .... Federation of Independent Trade Unions of Russia (ECON)
FNPR .... Friends of National Public Radio [Defunct] (EA)
FNprP .... Pasco County Library System, New Port Richey, FL [Library symbol] [Library of Congress] (LCLS)
FNPT .... Fusion Point
FNQ .... Franklin Quest [NYSE symbol] (TTSB)
FNQ .... Franklin Quest Co. [NYSE symbol] (SAG)
FNQR .... Far North Queensland Regiment [Australia]
FNR .... File Next Register
FNR .... Flores & Rucks [NYSE symbol] (TTSB)
FNR .... Flores & Rucks, Inc. [NYSE symbol] (SAG)
FNR .... Ford Nuclear Reactor
FNR .... Foundations Resources [Vancouver Stock Exchange symbol]
FNR .... Foward Neutral Reverse
FNR .... Front National de Renouvellement [Algeria] [Political party] (EY)
FNR .... Funter Bay [Alaska] [Airport symbol] (OAG)
FNR .... Funter Bay, AK [Location identifier FAA] (FAAL)
f-nr-- .... Nigeria [MARC geographic area code Library of Congress] (LCCP)
FNRA .... Federal National Railroad Association [Proposed railroad corporation] [Nickname: Fannie Rae]
FNREB .... Food and Nutrition Research and Engineering Board [Military] (RDA)
FNRI .... Federation Nationale des Republicains Independants [National Federation of Independent Republicans] [France Political party] (PPW)
FNRI .... Flores & Rucks, Inc. [NASDAQ symbol] (SAG)
FNRL .... Funeral
FNS .... Failure Notification Sheet (KSC)
FNS .... Family and Neighborhood Services
FNS .... Federal News Service [Database] (IID)
FNS .... Federation of Netherlands Societies [Australia]
FNS .... Feedback Node Set
FNS .... Feminist News Service
FNS .... File-Nesting Store [Computer science] (OA)
FNS .... Flash-Nitrogen Supply
FNS .... Food and Nutrition Service [Department of Agriculture]
FNS .... Forever Nonstatic (IAA)
FNS .... Frame Network Server [Tylink Corp.]
FNS .... Frontier Nursing Service (EA)
FNS .... Functional Neuromuscular Stimulation [Physiotherapy]
FNS .... Functional Nomenclature Signal
FNSA .... Frente Nacional Socialista Argentino [Argentinian National Socialist Front] [Political party] (PD)
FNSA .... Saurimo [Angola] [ICAO location identifier] (ICLI)
FNSBB .... Federation Nationale des Syndicats du Batiment et du Bois, Inc. [National Federation of Shipyard and Woodworkers Unions]
FNSC .... Federation pour une Nouvelle Societe Caledonienne [Federation for a New Caledonian Society] [Political party] (PPW)
FNSC .... Financial Security Corp. [NASDAQ symbol] (SAG)
FNSCC .... Federation of Nuclear Shelter Consultants and Contractors [British] (DBA)
FNSF .... Fast Night Striking Force [British military] (DMA)
FNSH .... Finish (MSA)
FNSH .... Finish
FNSI .... Finding of No Significant Impact
FNSID .... Fellow of the National Society of Interior Designers
FNSII .... Federation Nationale des Syndicats d'Infirmieres et d'Infirmiers [National Federation of Nurses' Unions - NFNU]
FNSL .... Fixed Nozzle Slow [or Short] Landing (MCD)
FNSO .... Soyo [Angola] [ICAO location identifier] (ICLI)
FNSRO .... Food and Nutrition Service Regional Office [Department of Agriculture] (GFGA)
FNSSC .... Franciscan Sisters of Our Lady of the Sacred Heart (TOCD)
FNST .... Finest
fnstr .... Fenestration (VRA)
FNT .... Aerostar Airlines, Inc. [ICAO designator] (FAAC)
FNT .... Failure Notification Telex (MCD)
FNT .... False Neurochemical Transmitter [Medicine] (DMAA)
FNT .... File Name Table [Computer science] (MHDB)
FNT .... Flint [Michigan] [Airport symbol] (OAG)
FNT .... Flint, MI [Location identifier FAA] (FAAL)
Fnt .... Fonit [Record label] [Italy]
FNT .... Fort Nelson [Hobart] [Tasmania] [Seismograph station code, US Geological Survey] [Closed] (SEIS)
fnt .... Front (VRA)
FNTA .... Farnesyltransferase [An enzyme]
FNTBB .... Federation Nordique des Travailleurs du Batiment et du Bois [Nordic Federation of Building and Wood Workers - NFBWW] (EAIO)
FNtBsh .... First National Bankshares, Inc. [Associated Press] (SAG)
FNTC .... Frente Nacional de Trabajadores y Campesinos [National Workers' and Peasants' Front] [Peru] [Political party] (PPW)
FNtGa .... First National Bancorp of Gainesville [Associated Press] (SAG)

FNTGNS	Frontogenesis [*NWS*] (FAAC)
FNthCap	First Northern Capital Corp. [*Associated Press*] (SAG)
FNthSB	First Northern Savings Bank SA [*Associated Press*] (SAG)
FNTLYS	Frontolysis [*NWS*] (FAAC)
FNTO	Toto [*Angola*] [*ICAO location identifier*] (ICLI)
fntpc	Frontispiece (VRA)
FNTSTIC	Fantastic
FNTSY	Fantasy
FNU	Family Nursing Unit
FNU	First Name Unknown
FNU	Forces des Nations Unies [*United Nations Forces*]
FNU	Front National Uni [*United National Front*] [*The Comoros*]
FNUA	Luau [*Angola*] [*ICAO location identifier*] (ICLI)
FNUAP	Fondo de Poblacion de las Naciones Unidas [*United Nations Population Fund*] [*Spanish*] (DUND)
FNUAP	Fonds des Nations Unies pour la Population [*United Nations Population Fund*] [*French*] (DUND)
FNUB	Lubango [*Angola*] [*ICAO location identifier*] (ICLI)
FNUE	Fonds des Nations Unies pour l'Enfance [*United Nations Children's Fund*] (EAIO)
FNUE	Luena [*Angola*] [*ICAO location identifier*] (ICLI)
FNUG	Federation of NCR [*NCR Corp.*] User Groups (EA)
FNUG	Uige/Vige [*Angola*] [*ICAO location identifier*] (ICLI)
FNUI	Fellow of the National University of Ireland (DI)
FNUK	Front National Uni des Komores [*National United Front of the Comoros*] [*Political party*] (PD)
FNUR	Fonds des Nations Unies pour les Refugies [*United Nations Funds for Refugees*]
FNV	Festuca Necrosis Virus [*Plant pathology*]
FNV	FINOVA Group [*NYSE symbol*] (TTSB)
FNV	Finova Group, Inc. [*NYSE symbol*] (SAG)
FNV	Partido Federacion Nacional Velasquista [*National Velasquista Federation*] [*Ecuador*] [*Political party*] (PPW)
FNW	First Nationwide Bank A Federal Savings Bank [*NYSE symbol*] (SAG)
FNWA	Federal Noxious Weed Act
FNWA	Foreign National Weather Agency
FNWC	Fleet Numerical Weather Center [*Monterey, CA*] [*Navy*]
FNWF	Fleet Numerical Weather Facility
FNWK	Wako-Kungo [*Angola*] [*ICAO location identifier*] (ICLI)
FNWPr	First Nationwide Bk 11.50% Pfd [*NYSE symbol*] (TTSB)
FNX	Fenix Airways [*Latvia*] [*FAA designator*] (FAAC)
FNX	Fort Knox Gold Resources, Inc. [*Toronto Stock Exchange symbol*]
FNXA	Xangongo [*Angola*] [*ICAO location identifier*] (ICLI)
FNY	French Navy
FNYFS	Florida Network of Youth and Family Services (SRA)
FNZ	Friends of the National Zoo (EA)
FNZ	Huntingburg, IN [*Location identifier FAA*] (FAAL)
FNZE	N'Zeto/N'Zeto [*Angola*] [*ICAO location identifier*] (ICLI)
FNZIA	Fellow of the New Zealand Institute of Architects
FNZIAS	Fellow of the New Zealand Institute of Agricultural Science
FNZIC	Fellow of the New Zealand Institute of Chemistry
FNZIE	Fellow of the New Zealand Institution of Engineers
FNZLA	Fellow of the New Zealand Library Association
FNZP	Flunitrazepam [*A hypnotic*]
FO	Alon, Inc. [*ICAO aircraft manufacturer identifier*] (ICAO)
FO	Fabrication Order (MCD)
FO	Fabrication Outline (MCD)
FO	Factory Order
FO	Faculty of Ophthalmologists [*British*]
FO	Fade Out [*Films, television, etc.*]
FO	Fail Open [*Nuclear energy*] (NRCH)
FO	Fail Operation [*NASA*] (KSC)
FO	Fairest One [*Genotype of Phlox paniculata*]
FO	Fallout (IIA)
F/O	Families within Orders (DICI)
FO	Fan Out
FO	Faroe Islands [*ANSI two-letter standard code*] (CNC)
FO	Fast Operating [*Relay*]
FO	Fatty Oil
F/O	Feature Film Only (ADA)
FO	Federal Official
FO	Fiber Optic [*Data transmission*] (TEL)
FO	Field Office [*or Officer*]
FO	Field Operational [*Test*] (NATG)
FO	Field Order
FO	Filter Output (AAG)
FO	Finance Officer [*Army*]
FO	Fine Old
FO	Firing Order
FO	Firm Offer [*Business term*]
FO	Firm Order [*Business term*]
FO	First Officer (ADA)
FO	First Open [*First class train compartment*] (DCTA)
FO	Fishery Officer [*Ministry of Agriculture, Fisheries, and Food*] [*British*]
FO	Fitting Out [*Navy*] (NG)
FO	Fixed Oil
FO	Flag Officer [*Navy*]
FO	Flash Operate Relay
FO	Flash Override [*Telecommunications*] (TEL)
FO	Flat Oval [*Technical drawings*]
FO	Fleet Operations [*Navy*] (MCD)
FO	Flight Officer [*Air Force*]
FO	Flight Order
FO	Flight Orderly
FO	Fluoroorotate [*Organic chemistry*]
FO	Flying Officer [*British*]
F/O	Flyout
FO	Foam System [*NFPA pre-fire planning symbol*] (NFPA)
FO	Foldout (MSA)
FO	Folio
fo	Fomentation [*Pharmacology*] (DAVI)
FO	Font (DNAB)
FO	Foot Orthosis [*Medicine*]
FO	Foramen Ovale [*Anatomy*]
F/O	Force Objective (CINC)
FO	Force Out [*Baseball*]
F/O	For Credit Of (WDAA)
FO	Foreign Object
FO	Foreign Office
FO	Foreign Order (ADA)
FO	Foreign to Occupation [*Insurance*]
FO	For Orders
fo	Forsterite [*CIPW classification*] [*Geology*]
FO	Fortissimo [*Very Loud*] [*Music*] (ROG)
FO	Forward Oblique (CAAL)
FO	Forward Observer [*Military*]
FO	Fouled Out [*Sports*] (IIA)
Fo	Fourier Number [*IUPAC*]
FO	Fraction Optimizing
FO	Fragmented Order [*Military*] (VNW)
FO	Free Out [*Shipping*]
FO	Free Overside
FO	Frente Obrero [*Workers' Front*] [*of the Carlists in the Workers Commissions*] [*Spain*] [*Political party*]
FO	Frente Obrero [*Workers' Front*] [*Nicaragua*] [*Political party*] (PD)
FO	Fridays Only [*British railroad term*]
FO	Friends Outside (EA)
FO	Fronto-Occipital [*Anatomy*]
FO	Fuel Oil
F/O	Fuel to Oxidizer [*Ratio*]
FO	Full Organ [*Music*]
FO	Full Out [*Typesetting*]
F/O	Full Out Terms [*Business term British*] (ROG)
FO	Functional Objective (KSC)
FO	Oil-Immersed Forced-Oil-Cooled [*Transformer*] (IEEE)
FO	Orlando Public Library, Orlando, FL [*Library symbol Library of Congress*] (LCLS)
FO	Southern Nevada [*ICAO designator*] (AD)
FOA	Faculty of Advocates [*British*] (DAS)
FOA	Failure to Obtain Action (AAG)
FOA	Federation of Orthodontic Associations (EA)
FOA	Fellow of Advertising [*British*]
FOA	Field Office Assistant [*Red Cross*]
FOA	Field Operating Activity (AAGC)
FOA	Field Operating Agency (MCD)
FOA	Filipinas Orient Airways, Inc. [*Philippines*] [*ICAO designator*] (FAAC)
FOA	Financial Operations Association (EA)
FOA	First of America Bank [*NYSE symbol*] (SPSG)
FOA	First of America Bk [*NYSE symbol*] (TTSB)
FOA	Fitting Out Availability [*Navy*]
FOA	Flora, IL [*Location identifier FAA*] (FAAL)
FOA	Fluoroorotic Acid [*Organic chemistry*]
FOA	FOB Airport ["*INCOTERM,*" *International Chamber of Commerce official code*]
FOA	Football Officials Association
FOA	Forced Oil and Air (MSA)
FOA	Foreign Operations Administration [*Later, ICA*]
FOA	Foreign-Owned or Affiliated [*Business term*]
FOA	Foresters of America
FOA	Forsvarets Forskningsanstalt [*Research Institute of National Defense*] [*Information service or system*] (IID)
FOA	Free on Aircraft [*Cargo delivery term for export traffic*] (DCTA)
FOA	Friends of Animals (EA)
FOA	Fugitive Other Authorities [*FBI standardized term*]
FOA	Oil-Immersed Forced-Oil-Cooled with Forced-Air Cooler [*Transformer*] (IEEE)
FOAA	Flying Optometrists Association of America (EA)
FOAC	Federal Office Automation Conference (HGAA)
FOAC	Flag Officer, Aircraft Carriers (NATG)
FOAC	Flag Officer, Atlantic Coast [*Canada*]
FOAF	Friend of a Friend [*Urban folklore term coined by Rodney Dale*]
FOAF	Friend of a Friend
FOAFB	Forbes Air Force Base [*Kansas*] (AAG)
FOAIB	Flag Officer, Admiralty Interview Board [*Navy British*]
FOAM	Fluorouracil, Oncovin [*Vincristine*], Adriamycin, Mitomycin C [*Antineoplastic drug regimen*]
FOAM	Fragmenting Offensive Aerial Mine (MCD)
Foamex	Foamex International [*Associated Press*] (SAG)
FOAMP	Foreign Aerospace Material Production (MCD)
FOAMP	Fraternal Order of Air Mail Pilots [*Defunct*] (EA)
FOAMS	Forecasting, Order Administration, and Master Scheduling (PDAA)
FO & R	Fleet Operations and Readiness
Fo-An-Si	Forsterite-Anorthite-Silica [*Lunar geology*]
FOAP	Foreign Aircraft Production (MCD)
FOAPH	Federation Ouest Africaine des Associations pour la Promotion des Personnes Handicapees [*West African Federation of Associations for the Advancement of Handicapped Persons - WAFAH*] [*Bamako, Mali*] (EAIO)
Foard Mer Sh	Foard on Merchant Shipping [*A publication*] (DLA)

FOAS	Akerman, Senterfitt, Eidson, Law Library, Orlando, FL [*Library symbol*] [*Library of Congress*] (LCLS)
FOAS	Field Operating Agencies [*Air Force*] (DOMA)
FOAVF	Failure of All Vital Forces (MAE)
FOB	Faculty of Building (PDAA)
FOB	Fans of Bentsen [*Treasury Secretary, Lloyd Bentsen*] (ECON)
FOB	Father of Baby (DAVI)
FOB	Fecal Occult Blood [*Medicine*] (MAE)
FOB	Federal Office Building
FOB	Feet Out of Bed
FOB	Fetal Occult Blood [*Medicine*]
FOB	Fiberoptic Bronchoscopy [*Also, FB*] [*Medicine*]
FOB	Fiber Optics Board (MCD)
FOB	Field Operations Bureau [*FCC*] (NTCM)
FOB	Fine Old Blend [*Wines and spirits*]
FOB	First Overtone Band
FOB	Flight Operations Building [*NASA*] (KSC)
FOB	Foot of Bed (CPH)
FOB	Ford Motor Co. Ltd. [*ICAO designator*] (FAAC)
FOB	Ford of Britain [*Corporate subsidiary*]
FOB	Forward Observer Bombardment [*Military*]
FOB	Forward Operating Base [*Air Force*] (AFM)
FOB	Fractional Orbital Bombardment (MCD)
FOB	Free on Board [*"INCOTERM," International Chamber of Commerce official code*] [*Shipping*]
FOB	Freight on Board (AAG)
FOB	Fresh Off the Boat
FOB	Friends of Bill [*Political network built by President Bill Clinton*]
FOB	Friends of Blue [*British*] [*An association*] (DBA)
FOB	Front of Board (MSA)
FOB	Fuel on Board [*Aviation*]
FOB	Full of Brooklyns [*Coined by baseball broadcaster Red Barber, initialism refers to bases loaded with Brooklyn Dodgers*] [*Obsolete*]
FOB	Functional Observational Battery [*Toxicology*]
FOb	Ormond Beach Public Library, Ormond Beach, FL [*Library symbol Library of Congress*] (LCLS)
FOBA	Free on Board Airport [*Business term*]
FOBAA	Flag Officer, British Assault Area
FOBB	First Oak Brook Bancshares, Inc. [*NASDAQ symbol*] (NQ)
FOBBA	First Oak Brook Bancshrs'A' [*NASDAQ symbol*] (TTSB)
FOBBS	Federation of British Bonsai Societies (DBA)
FOBC	Fed One Bancorp [*NASDAQ symbol*] (TTSB)
FOBC	Fed One Bancorp [*NASDAQ symbol*] (SAG)
FOBC	Fed One Savings Bank [*NASDAQ symbol*] (SAG)
FOBES	Fiber Optics Borehole Earth Strainmeter [*Geology*]
FOBFO	Federation of British Fire Organisations (BI)
FOBO	Fort Bowie National Historic Site
FOBS	Fiber Optics Borescope
FOBS	Fractional Orbital Bombardment System
FOBSR	Forward Observer [*Military*]
FOBT	Fecal Occult Blood Test [*Medicine*]
FOBTSU	Forward Observer Target Survey Unit [*Military*]
FOBW	Frequencies of Occurrence of Binary Words [*Computer science*] (PDAA)
FOc	Central Florida Regional Library, Ocala, FL [*Library symbol Library of Congress*] (LCLS)
FOC	Face of Concrete [*Technical drawings*]
FOC	Faint-Object Camera [*Astronomy*]
FOC	Farthest-On Circle (NVT)
FOC	Father of Chapel [*Shop steward*] [*British*]
FoC	Father of Chapel [*Shop steward*] [*British*] (ODBW)
FOC	Father of Child (DAVI)
FOC	Ferrari Owners Club (EA)
FOC	Fiber-Optic Cable (SSD)
FOC	Fiber Optics Communications [*Data transmission*] (TEL)
FOC	Final Operational Capability [*Military*] (AFM)
FOC	Final Operational Capacity
FOC	Fire Offices Committee [*British*] (AIA)
FOC	First of Class (DOMA)
FOC	Fixed Oil Capacitor
FOC	Flag of Convenience
FOCSL	Flag Officer Commanding
FOC	Flight Operating Costs
FOC	Flight Operations Center
FOC	Focal (MSA)
FOC	Focsani [*Romania*] [*Seismograph station code, US Geological Survey*] (SEIS)
FOC	Focus (KSC)
FOC	Focus of Contraction [*Motion perception*]
FOC	Follow-On Contract
FOC	Foreign Object Check (MCD)
FOC	Foreign Operating Committee [*World War II*]
FOC	Forward Observer COLIDAR [*Coherent Light Detecting and Ranging*]
FOC	Free of Charge [*Business term*]
FOC	Free on Car [*Shipping*]
FOC	Friends of Community (EA)
FOC	From Own Correspondent
FOC	Fuel Oil Cooler
FOC	Full and Open Competition [*Government contracting*]
FOC	Full Operational Capability
FOC	Full Operational Capability Program [*Navy*] (NVT)
FOC	Furthest-On Circle [*Navy*] (ANA)
FOC	Fuzhou [*China*] [*Airport symbol*] (OAG)
FOC	Office Federal de l'Aviation Civile [*Sweden ICAO designator*] (FAAC)

FOCA	Fibre Optic Cable Assembly (NITA)
FOCA	Field Operating Cost Agency [*Army*]
FOCA	Fiero Owners Club of America (EA)
FOCA	Font Object Content Architecture (CDE)
FOCA	Fort Caroline National Memorial
FOCA	Free and Open Church Association [*British*]
FOCA	Freedom of Choice Act [*Abortion-rights bill*] (ECON)
FOCA	Friends of the Origami Center of America (EA)
FOCAL	Formula Calculation [*Pharmacology*] (DAVI)
FOCAL	Formula Calculator [*Digital Equipment Corp.*] (CSR)
FOCAL	Formulating Online Calculations in Algebraic Language [*Computer science*] (IAA)
FOCAL	Foundations of Communication and Language (AIE)
FOCAL	French Ocean-Climat Atlantique Equatorial [*Program*] [*Marine science*] (OSRA)
FOCAL	French Program Ocean-Climat Atlantique Equatorial (USDC)
FOCAP	Federacion Odontologica Centro America y Panama [*Odontological Federation of Central America and Panama*]
FOCAS	Faint-Object Classification and Analysis System [*Astronomy*]
FOCAS	Fiber Optic Communications for Aerospace Systems (MCD)
FOCAS	Flag Officer, Carriers and Amphibious Ships [*Navy British*]
FOCAS	Ford [*Automobile*] Operating Cost Analysis System
FOCAS	Forward Crash Avoidance Systems [*NHTSA*] (TAG)
FOCAS	Fuji Juken, Ogisaka, Kawabe, Asahi Juken and Sueno Kosan [*Group of Japanese development companies located in Osaka, Japan*] (ECON)
FOcC	Central Florida Community College, Ocala, FL [*Library symbol Library of Congress*] (LCLS)
FOCC	Fiber Optic Coordinating Committee [*American National Standards Institute*] [*Telecommunications*]
FOCC	Fleet Operations Control Center [*Navy*]
FOCCEUR.....	Fleet Operations Control Center, Europe [*Navy*]
FOCCLANT ...	Fleet Operations Control Center, Atlantic [*Navy*] (DNAB)
FOCCPAC	Fleet Operations Control Center, Pacific Fleet [*Navy*]
FOC/FCC	Flight Operations Center/Flight Coordination Center (MCD)
FOCH	Forward Channel [*Telecommunications*]
FOCI	Farrand Optical Co., Inc.
FOCI	First Operational Computer Installation (IAA)
FOCI	Fisheries-Oceanography Cooperative Investigations [*National Oceanic and Atmospheric Administration*] (USDC)
FOCI	Fisheries-Oceanography Cooperative Users System [*Marine science*] (OSRA)
FOCI	Foreign Ownership, Control, or Influence
FOCIA	Fibre-Optics-Coupled Image Amplifier (PDAA)
FOCI BP	Fisheries-Oceanography Cooperative Investigations Biophysical Platform [*Marine science*] (OSRA)
FOCI BP	FOCI [*Fisheries-Oceanography Cooperative Investigations*] Biophysical Platform (USDC)
FOCIS	Fiber Optic Communication and Information Society (MHDI)
FOCIS	Financial On-Line Central Information System [*Computer science*] (MHDB)
FOCL	Fort Clatsop National Memorial
FOC/LAN	International Fiber Optics and Communications Exposition and Show on Local Area Networks
FOCM	Feminists on Children's Media [*Defunct*] (EA)
FOCMA	Feline Orcornavirus-Associated Cell Membrane Antigen [*Immunology*]
FOCNAS.......	Flag Officer Commanding, North Atlantic Station [*British military*] (DMA)
FOCOA	Fiero Owners Club of America (EA)
FOCOBANK...	Foreign Commerce Bank [*Switzerland*]
FOCOHANA...	Fourier Coefficient Harmonic Analyzer
FOCOS	FORDAC [*FORTRAN Data Acquisition and Control*] Conversational System [*Computer science*] (IAA)
FO/COT	Firing Out/Consolidate Operability Tests (MCD)
FOCRIN........	Flag Officer Commanding, Royal Indian Navy [*British military*] (DMA)
FOCS	Federation of Old Cornwall Societies [*British*] (DBA)
FOCS	Fiberchem, Inc. [*NASDAQ symbol*] (NQ)
FOCS	Fiber Optic Cable System (DWSG)
FOCS	Fiber-Optic Chemical Sensor [*Analytical chemistry*]
FOCS	Freight Operation Control System (PDAA)
FOCSL	Fleet Oriented Consolidated Stock List [*Navy*]
FOCSL	Forecastle
FO'C'SLE	Forecastle (ROG)
FOCT	Flag Officer, Carrier Training [*British military*] (DMA)
FOCUS	Federation on Computing in the US (CDE)
FOCUS	Financial and Operations Combined Uniform Single Report
FOCUS	Financially-Oriented Computer Updating Service (IAA)
FOCUS	Fire Operational Characteristics Using Simulation [*System for comparing organizations for wildland fire protection services in cost-effective terms*] [*Department of Agriculture, Forest Services*]
FOCUS	Fisheries Oceanography Cooperative Users System (USDC)
FOCUS	Fisheries Oceanography Cooperative Users System [*Marine science*] (OSRA)
Focus	Focus Enhancements, Inc. [*Associated Press*] (SAG)
FOCUS	Forecasting Control and Updating Schedule (MCD)
FOCUS	Formal Officer Career Utilization Structure [*Military*]
FOCUS	Form of Control Users System (MCD)
FOCUS	For Our Children's Unpaid Support [*Defunct*] (EA)
FOCUS	For Our Christian Understanding [*Program*]
FOCUS	Forum of Control Data Users [*Later, VIM, Inc.*]
FocusEn.......	Focus Enhancements, Inc. [*Associated Press*] (SAG)
FOCWA	Flag Officer Commanding West Africa [*British*]
FOD	Factory on Dock (SAA)
FOD	Fear of Death

FOD	Field Officer of the Day [Army] (AABC)
FOD	Field Operations Department
FOD	Field Operations Division (EERA)
FOD	Field Operations Division (AAGC)
FOD	Finger of Death [Fantasy gaming] (NHD)
FOD	Flag Officer, Denmark [NATG]
FOD	Flashblindness Orientation Device
FOD	Flies-Odors-Ducts [Veterinary science] (OA)
FOD	Flight Operations Directorate [or Division] [Apollo] [NASA]
FOD	Fluidic Output Device
FOD	Foreign Object Damage
FOD	Fort Dodge [Iowa] [Airport symbol] (OAG)
FOD	Fort Dodge, IA [Location identifier FAA] (FAAL)
FOD	Free of Damage [Business term]
FOD	Free of Disease [Medicine]
FOD	Front de l'Opposition Democratique [Togo] [Political party] (EY)
FOD	Functional Operational Design
FODA	Fort Davis National Historic Site
FODAAS	Field Online Data Acquisition and Analysis System
FODB	Fiber Optic Data Bus (SSD)
FODC	Friends of David Cassidy [Defunct] (EA)
F-O Dis	Feeling-Oriented Discussion
FODL	Fiber Optics Data Link (MCD)
FODO	Federation of Ophthalmic and Dispensing Opticians [British] (DBA)
FODO	Fort Donelson National Military Park
FoDokAB ...	Forschungsdokumentation zur Arbeitsmarkt- und Berufsforschung [Deutsche Bundesanstalt fuer Arbeit] [Germany Information service or system] (CRD)
FODS	Fraud and Overservicing Detection System (ADA)
FODW	Friends of Dennis Wilson (EA)
FOE	Females Opposed to Equality
FOE	Ferro Corp. [NYSE symbol] (SPSG)
FOE	Field Operational Evaluation
FOE	File of Enemies [British] [An association] (DBA)
FOE	Flight Operations Engineer (MCD)
FOE	Focus of Expansion [Motion perception]
FOE	Follow-On Evaluation
FOE	Foreign-Object Elimination [Manufacturing]
FOE	Fraternal Order of Eagles (BARN)
FOE	Friends of the Earth (EA)
FOE	Fuel Oil Equivalent (BARN)
FOE	Grand Aerie, Fraternal Order of Eagles (EA)
FOE	Topeka [Kansas] Forbes [Airport symbol] (OAG)
FOE	Topeka, KS [Location identifier FAA] (FAAL)
FOEB	Fuel Oil Equivalent Barrel
FOEI	Friends of the Earth International
Foel Dr Int...	Foelix. Droit International Prive [A publication] (DLA)
FoEng	Fellowship of Engineering [British] (DBA)
FOENIC	Foeniculum [Fennel] [Pharmacy] (ROG)
FOEP	Frog Otolith Experiment Package [NASA]
FOES	Fine Old Extra Special
FOET	Follow-On Evaluation Test
FOEU	Foreign Organizations' Employees Union
FOF	Face of Finish [Technical drawings]
FOF	Factory-of-the-Future
FOF	Facts on File, Inc.
FOF	Field Observing Facility [National Center for Atmospheric Research]
FOF	Field of Fire [Military] (MCD)
FOF	First Operational Flight (MCD)
FOF	First Orbital Flight [NASA] (NASA)
FOF	Fish Oil Film
FOF	Flag Officer, Flotilla [British military] (DMA)
FOF	Flight Operations Facility
FoF	Foto File Systems, Inc., Kansas City, KS [Library symbol Library of Congress] (LCLS)
FOF	Fred Olsen Flyselskap AS [Norway] [FAA designator] (FAAC)
FOF	Friends of Families [Defunct] (EA)
FOF	Friends of Freddy (EA)
FOF	Friends of the FBI (EA)
FOF	Fukuoka Occupation Force
FOF	Full Octave Filter
FOF	Fund of Funds
FOF	Futures and Options Fund [Investment term] (ECON)
FOFA	Follow-On Forces Attack
FOFA	Friends of Free Asia [Defunct]
FO/FAC	Forward Observer - Forward Air Controller [Military] (INF)
FOFATUSA...	Federation of Free African Trade Unions of South Africa
FOFAX	Forecast Office Facsimile [National Weather Service]
FOFC	Friends of Free China (EA)
FOFCC	Federal Oceanographic Fleet Coordination Council
FOFEBA	Forward of the FEBA [Forward Edge of the Battle Area] [Military]
FOFF	50-Off Stores [NASDAQ symbol] (TTSB)
F of F	Field of Fire [Military] (AABC)
FOFF	Fifty Off Stores [NASDAQ symbol] (SAG)
F of F	Firth of Forth (DAS)
F of JR	Fourth of July Road
FOFM	Fog Foam
FO/FO/FS ...	Fail-Operational, Fail-Operational, Fail-Safe
FOFR	Fort Frederica National Monument
FO/FS	Fail-Operational, Fail-Safe (NASA)
FO/FS	Flight Operational/Fail Safe (MCD)
F of S	Foreman of Signals [Military British]
FOFT	Florida Technological University, Orlando, FL [Library symbol Library of Congress] (LCLS)
FOFT	Force-on-Force Trainer

FOG	Fast Oxidative Glycolytic [Fibers] [Neuroanatomy]
FOG	Fats, Oils, and Grease [Food plant effluent]
FOG	Fiber-Optic Gyroscope [Automotive navigation systems]
FOG	Fiber Optics Guidance (MCD)
FOG	Field Operations Group
FOG	Fineness of Grind [Materials science]
FOG	Fishing/Fisheries/Vessel Obligation Guarantee (USDC)
FOG	Flag Officer, Germany [NATG]
FOG	Flight Operations Group
FOG	Flow of Gold
FOG	Fluothane, Oxygen, and Gas [Nitrous oxide] [Anesthesiology] (DAVI)
FOG	Foggia [Italy] [Airport symbol] (AD)
FOG	FOG [First Osborne Group] International Computer Users Group (EA)
FOG	Foreign Operating Group (LAIN)
FOG	Frequency Offset Generator
FOG	Shreveport, LA [Location identifier FAA] (FAAL)
FOGA	Akieni [Gabon] [ICAO location identifier] (ICLI)
FOGA	Fashion Originators Guild of America [Defunct] (EA)
FOGB	Booue [Gabon] [ICAO location identifier] (ICLI)
FOGCO	Federal Oil & Gas Corp.
FOGD	Fiber Optics Guidance Demonstration (RDA)
Fog Det Lt ..	Fog Detector Light [Nautical charts]
FOGE	N'Dende [Gabon] [ICAO location identifier] (ICLI)
FOGF	Fougamou [Gabon] [ICAO location identifier] (ICLI)
FOGG	Feed-Only-Good Generator [Nuclear energy] (NRCH)
Fogg	Fogg's Reports [32-35 New Hampshire] [A publication] (DLA)
FOGG	Mbigou [Gabon] [ICAO location identifier] (ICLI)
FOGI	Moabi [Gabon] [ICAO location identifier] (ICLI)
FOGJ	Ndjole [Gabon] [ICAO location identifier] (ICLI)
FOGK	Koula-Moutou/Mabimbi [Gabon] [ICAO location identifier] (ICLI)
FOGL	Leconi [Gabon] [ICAO location identifier] (ICLI)
FOG-M	Fiber Optic Guided Missile [Army] (RDA)
FOGM	Mouila [Gabon] [ICAO location identifier] (ICLI)
FOGMA	Flag Officer, Gibraltar Mediterranean Area [British]
FOGO	Oyem [Gabon] [ICAO location identifier] (ICLI)
FOGQ	Okondja [Gabon] [ICAO location identifier] (ICLI)
FOGR	Lambarene [Gabon] [ICAO location identifier] (ICLI)
FOGRMA	Federal Oil and Gas Royalty Management Act
FOGS	Church of Jesus Christ of Latter-Day Saints, Genealogical Society Library, Orlando Branch, Orlando, FL [Library symbol Library of Congress] (LCLS)
FOGS	Faint-Object Grism Spectrograph [Astronomy]
FOGS	Functioning of the GATT [General Agreement on Tariffs and Trade] System
FOGS	Function-on-Generator-Stop (RDA)
FOGSIG	Fog Signal Station [Nautical charts]
FOGT	First Order Gradient Technique
FOGU	Moupoupa [Gabon] [ICAO location identifier] (ICLI)
FOGV	Minvoul [Gabon] [ICAO location identifier] (ICLI)
FOGW	Wonga-Wongue [Gabon] [ICAO location identifier] (ICLI)
FOH	Columbia, MS [Location identifier FAA] (FAAL)
FOH	Forced Outage Hours [Electronics] (IEEE)
FOH	Frederick's of Hollywood, Inc. [NYSE symbol] (SPSG)
FOH	Friends of Haiti
FOH	Front of House (ADA)
FOH	Front of House Spot [Theatrical lighting] (NTCM)
FOHBC	Federation of Historical Bottle Clubs (EA)
FOHC	Free of Heart Center (DAC)
FOHC	Friends of Helix Club (EA)
FOHMD	Fiber Optic Helmet Mounted Display [Computer generated imagery]
FOHO	For Oily Hair Only [Trademark of The Gillette Co.]
FOI	Field Operations Intelligence
FOI	Fighter Officer for Interceptors [Member of the SAGE Command Post staff]
FOI	Final Opinion Inventory [Psychometrics]
FOI	First-Order Interpolator (IAA)
FOI	Fleet Operational Investigation [NOO]
FOI	Flight of Ideas [Psychiatry] (DAVI)
FOI	Flight Ops International [FAA designator] (FAAC)
FOI	Fluffy Opaque Inclusions [In a meteorite]
FOI	Follow-On Interceptor [Military]
FOI	Forced Oil Injection
FOI	Foreign Object Inspection [or Investigation] (MCD)
FOI	Foreign Object Investigation
FOI	Freedom of Information [Army]
FOI	Freedom of Information Act
FOI	Freedom of Information Center (EA)
FOI	Free of Interest [Business term]
FOI	Fuels Operating Instruction (AFIT)
FOI	Functional Operating Instruction
FOIA	Freedom of Information Act [1966]
FOIA	Fund for Open Information and Accountability [Defunct] (EA)
FOIC	Flag Officer-in-Charge [British-controlled port]
FOIC	Freedom of Information Clearinghouse (EA)
FOICR	Freedom of Information Center. Reports [A publication] (DLA)
FOI Dig	FOI [Freedom of Information] Digest [A publication] (DLA)
FOIF	Free Oceanographic Instrument Float
FOIH	Flight Operations Integration Handbook (MCD)
FOIL	Field Oil Identification Laboratory [Marine science] (MSC)
FOIL	File-Oriented Interpretive Language [1969] [Computer science]
FOIL	First, Outer, Inner, Last [Mathematical term used in factoring second degree trinomials]
FOIL	Fleet Optimum Inventory Level [Navy]
FOIL	Forest Oil [NASDAQ symbol] (TTSB)

FOIL............	Forest Oil Corp. [*NASDAQ symbol*] (NQ)
Foilmark......	Foilmark, Inc. [*Associated Press*] (SAG)
FOILO..........	Forest Oil $0.75 Cv Pfd [*NASDAQ symbol*] (TTSB)
FOILW..........	Forest Oil Wrrt [*NASDAQ symbol*] (TTSB)
FOINTRACEN...	Fleet Operational Intelligence Training Center [*Navy*] (DNAB)
FOINTRACENLANT...	Fleet Operational Intelligence Training Center, Atlantic [*Navy*] (DNAB)
FOINTRACENPAC...	Fleet Operational Intelligence Training Center, Pacific [*Navy*] (DNAB)
FOIO	Freedom of Information Act (TDOB)
FOIP	Follow-On In-Plant [*Test*] (MCD)
FOIPA	Freedom of Information and Privacy Act
FOIR	Field-of-Interest Register [*DoD*]
FOIRL	Fiber Optic Inter Repeater Link Standard [*Institute of Electrical and Electronics Engineers*]
FoiS	Foika Systems Services, Inc., Moscow, PA [*Library symbol*] [*Library of Congress*] (LCLS)
FOIS...........	Friends of Iris Society [*An association*]
FOITC.........	Fleet Operational Intelligence Training Center [*Navy*]
FOITCL........	Fleet Operational Intelligence Training Center, Atlantic [*Navy*] (DNAB)
FOITCP	Fleet Operational Intelligence Training Center, Pacific [*Navy*] (DNAB)
FOIU	Flowmeter Ordering and Indicating Unit
FOJ...........	Fremont, MI [*Location identifier FAA*] (FAAL)
FOJ...........	Friends of the Jessup [*An association*] (EA)
FOJ...........	Fuse on Jam (MCD)
FOJE	Fort Jefferson National Monument
FOJT	Formal On-the-Job Training
FOK...........	Fill or Kill [*Stock options*] [*Investment term*]
FOK...........	Free of Knots
FOK...........	Westhampton Beach, NY [*Location identifier FAA*] (FAAL)
FOKEU	Foreign Organizations Korean Employees' Union [*South Korea*]
FOKN	Fixation Optokinetic Nystagmus [*Eye movement*]
FOL...........	Facility Operating License [*Nuclear energy*] (NRCH)
FOL...........	[*The*] Facts of Life [*NBC television program*]
FOL...........	Festival of Lights [*Hanukkah*] [*Commemoration of the rededication of the Temple by Judas Maccabeus in 165BC*] (ADA)
FOL...........	Fiber Optics LASER
FOL...........	Fiber Optics Light
FOL...........	First Order Logic
Fol............	Foley's English Poor Law Cases [*1556-1730*] [*A publication*] (DLA)
FOL...........	Folia [*Leaves*]
FOL...........	Foligno [*Italy*] [*Seismograph station code, US Geological Survey Closed*] (SEIS)
FOL...........	Folio
FOL...........	Folium [*or Foliorum*] [*Leaf (or Leaves)*] [*Pharmacy*] (ROG)
FOL...........	Follow (AFM)
FOL...........	Following [*Business term*]
FOL...........	Forest Airline South Africa [*ICAO designator*] (FAAC)
FOL...........	Forward Operating Location [*Military*]
FOL...........	Frente Obrero de Liberacion [*Workers' Liberation Front*] [*Netherlands Antilles*] [*Political party*] (PPW)
FOL...........	Friends of the Land [*Later, IWLA*]
FOL...........	Fuel, Oil, and Lubricants (PDAA)
FOLA..........	Fort Laramie National Historic Site
FOLA..........	Friends of Libraries Australia
FOLAN	Fibre Optic Local Area Network [*Telecommunications*] (PDAA)
FOLAV	Family of Light-Armed Vehicle [*Saudi Arabian National Guard*] (DWSG)
FOLD	Fibre Optic Line Dividers (NITA)
Fol Dic........	Kames and Woodhouselee's Folio Dictionary, Scotch Court of Session [*A publication*] (DLA)
Fol Dict.......	Kames and Woodhouselee's Folio Dictionary, Scotch Court of Session [*A publication*] (DLA)
FOLEM........	Flag Officer, Levant and Eastern Mediterranean [*British Marines*] [*World War II*]
FOLG	Fiber Optics LASER Gyro (MCD)
FOLG	Following (ROG)
FOLIS.........	Following Information Is Submitted [*Army*] (AABC)
Folkl..........	Folklore [*A publication*] (BRI)
Folk Pl........	Folkard's Loans and Pledges [*2nd ed.*] [*1876*] [*A publication*] (DLA)
Folk St Sl ...	Folkard's Edition of Starkie on Slander and Libel [*A publication*] (DLA)
FOLL..........	Following
FOLLG	Following (ROG)
FOLNOAVAL...	Following Items Not Available
FOLP..........	Fitting-Out of Leased Premises
FOLPEN	Foliage Penetration [*RADAR*] (MCD)
FOLPES.......	Foliage Penetration System [*Military*]
Fol PLC.......	Foley's English Poor Law Cases [*1556-1730*] [*A publication*] (DLA)
Fol PL Cas...	Foley's English Poor Law Cases [*1556-1730*] [*A publication*] (DLA)
FOLQ	Foam Liquid
FOLR	Foreign Ownership Land Register [*Queensland*] [*State*] (EERA)
FOLR	Forward Observer LASER Range-Finder
FOLS..........	Follows (NVT)
FOLS..........	Fort Larned National Historic Site
FOLUP	Follow-Up
FOL USA	Friends of Libraries USA (EA)
FOLUSA.......	Friends of Libraries USA [*American Library Association*]
FOM...........	Face of Masonry [*Technical drawings*]
FOM...........	Factor of Merit [*Telecommunications*] (TEL)
FOM...........	Fault of Management
FOM...........	Fellowship of Missions (EA)
FOM...........	Fiber Optic MODEM [*Modulator-Demodulator*]
FOM...........	Field Operations Manual
FOM...........	Field Operations Memorandum

FOM...........	Fighter Officer for Missiles [*Member of the SAGE Command Post staff*]
FOM...........	Figure of Merit
FOM...........	fluorouracil, Oncovin [*Vincristine*], Mitomycin-C [*Antineoplastic drug regimen*] (DAVI)
FOM...........	Foreign Materiel Number [*Weapons*] (INF)
FOM...........	Foremost Corp.Amer [*NYSE symbol*] (TTSB)
FOM...........	Forum Resources Ltd. [*Vancouver Stock Exchange symbol*]
FOM...........	Foumban [*Cameroon*] [*Airport symbol*] (AD)
FOM...........	Fractional Orbiting Missile (SAA)
FOMA.........	Foreign Military Assistance
FOMA.........	Fort Matanzas National Monument
FOMAD	Food Market Awareness Databank [*Leatherhead Food Research Association*] [*Information service or system*] (CRD)
FOMC.........	Federal Open Market Committee [*Also, OMC*] [*Federal Reserve System*]
FOMC.........	Fort McHenry National Monument
FOMCAT	Foreign Material Catalog
FOMi..........	Fluorouracil, Oncovin [*Vincristine*], Mitomycin C [*Antineoplastic drug regimen*]
FOMi/CAP	Fluorouracil, Oncovin, Mitomycin-C, Cytoxan, Adriamycin, Platinol [*Antineoplastic drug*] (CDI)
FOMIN	Foreign Minister (CINC)
FOMINPI	Fomento Industrial do Piani, SA
FOMIS	Fitting Out Management Information System [*Navy*] (CAAL)
FOMIS	Fossil Operations and Maintenance Information Service (IID)
FOMM	Functional-Oriented Maintenance Manual (MCD)
FOMOCO	Ford Motor Co. (MCD)
FOMP.........	Fiber Optic Mortar Projectile [*Boeing Co.*] [*Military*]
FOMP.........	Foreign Missile Production (MCD)
FOMP.........	Fuel and Oil Metering Pump [*Engine design*]
FOMR	Flight Operations Management Room [*NASA*] (KSC)
FoMRHI.......	Fellowship of Makers and Researchers of Historical Instruments [*Formerly, Fellowship of Makers and Restorers of Historical Instruments*] (EA)
FOMRP	Fiber Optic Material Research Program [*Rutgers University*]
FOMS.........	Future Operational Microwave Sounder (MCD)
FOMTR	Formatter (MCD)
FOMV.........	Foxtail Mosaic Virus [*Plant pathology*]
FON	Federation of Ontario Naturalists [*Canada*]
fon	Fon [*MARC language code Library of Congress*] (LCCP)
FON	Freedom of Navigation (DOMA)
FON	Sprint Corp. [*NYSE symbol*] (SAG)
FON	United States Navy, Naval Training Equipment Center, Orlando, FL [*Library symbol Library of Congress*] (LCLS)
FONA	Friends of the US National Arboretum (EA)
FONAC........	Flag Officer, Naval Air Command [*British*]
FONAP........	Flag Officer, Naval Air, Pacific [*British*]
FONAR........	Field Focusing Nuclear Magnetic Resonance
Fonar.........	Fonar Corp. [*Associated Press*] (SAG)
FONAS	Flag Officer, Naval Air Stations [*British military*] (DMA)
FONASBA....	Federation of National Associations of Shipbrokers and Agents [*British*] (EAIO)
Fon BC	Fonblanque's Bankruptcy Cases [*1849-52*] [*A publication*] (DLA)
Fonb Eq	Fonblanque's Equity [*England*] [*A publication*] (DLA)
Fonbl	Fonblanque on Medical Jurisprudence [*A publication*] (DLA)
Fonbl	Fonblanque's Equity [*England*] [*A publication*] (DLA)
Fonbl	Fonblanque's New Reports, English Bankruptcy [*1849-52*] [*A publication*] (DLA)
Fonbl (Eng)...	Fonblanque's Equity [*England*] [*A publication*] (DLA)
Fonbl Eq (Eng)...	Fonblanque's Equity [*England*] [*A publication*] (DLA)
Fonbl Med Jur...	Fonblanque on Medical Jurisprudence [*A publication*] (DLA)
Fonbl NR	Fonblanque on Medical Jurisprudence [*A publication*] (DLA)
Fonbl NR	Fonblanque's English Cases in Chancery [*A publication*] (DLA)
Fonbl NR	Fonblanque's Equity [*England*] [*A publication*] (DLA)
Fonbl NR	Fonblanque's New Reports, English Bankruptcy [*1849-52*] [*A publication*] (DLA)
Fonbl R.......	Fonblanque's Bankruptcy Cases (or New Reports) [*1849-52*] [*A publication*] (DLA)
Fonbl R & Wr...	Fonblanque's Rights and Wrongs [*1860*] [*A publication*] (DLA)
FONCON	Telephone Conversation (MCD)
FONE	Farmstead Telephone Group, Inc. [*NASDAQ symbol*] (NQ)
FONE	Farmstead Tel Group [*NASDAQ symbol*] (TTSB)
FONE	Fort Necessity National Battlefield
FONE	Intellicell Corp. [*NASDAQ symbol*] (SAG)
FONECON	Telephone Conference [*or Conversation*]
FONEW	Farmstead Tel Group Wrrt [*NASDAQ symbol*] (TTSB)
FONF	Flag Officer, Newfoundland [*British*]
FONL	Flag Officer's Newsletter [*A publication*] (DNAB)
FONOFF	Foreign Office
FONPLATA	Fondo Financiero para el Desarrollo de la Cuenca del Plata [*Financial Fund for the Development of the Plata Basin*] (EAIO)
FONPr.........	Sprint Corp. $1.50 CV Ser 1 Pfd [*NYSE symbol*] (TTSB)
FONPrA.......	Sprint Corp. $1.50 Cv Ser 2 Pfd [*NYSE symbol*] (TTSB)
FONR	Fonar Corp. [*NASDAQ symbol*] (NQ)
FONR	Fund for Objective News Reporting (EA)
FONSI	Finding of No Significant Impact [*Office of Surface Mining*]
Font	Fontes Iuris Romani Antiqui [*A publication*] (OCD)
Font	Pro Fonteio [*of Cicero*] [*Classical studies*] (OCD)
FONZ	Friends of the National Zoo
FOO	Fairness of Opportunity [*Competitive bidding*]
FOO	Fear of Obesity
FOO	Field Ordering Officer [*Army*] (RDA)
FOO	Fleet Operations Officer [*Navy British*]
FOO	Forward Observation Officer [*Military*]

FOO	Fraternal Order of Orioles (EA)
FOO	Frequency of Optimum Operation (SAA)
FOO	Fundamental Order of Operation [Mathematics game]
FOO	Noemfoor [New Guinea] [Airport symbol] (AD)
FOO	Numfor [Indonesia] [Airport symbol] (OAG)
FOOA	Mouila [Gabon] [ICAO location identifier] (ICLI)
FOOB	Bitam [Gabon] [ICAO location identifier] (ICLI)
FOOB	Fell Out of Bed [Medicine] (DMAA)
FOOB	Firing Out of Battery [Military] (PDAA)
FOOC	Cocobeach [Gabon] [ICAO location identifier] (ICLI)
FOOD	Foodservice Organization of Distributors (EA)
Food	Foodweek [A publication]
FOOD	International Fast Food Corp. [NASDAQ symbol] (SAG)
FOOD	Moanda [Gabon] [ICAO location identifier] (ICLI)
Foodbrnd	Foodbrands America, Inc. [Associated Press] (SAG)
Food Drug Cos L Rep...	Food, Drug, Cosmetic Law Reporter [Commerce Clearing House] [A publication] (DLA)
Food Drug Cosm L Rep (CCH)...	Food, Drug, Cosmetic Law Reporter (Commerce Clearing House) [A publication] (DLA)
FoodIn	Food Integrated Tech, Inc. [Associated Press] (SAG)
FoodIntg	Food Integrated Tech, Inc. [Associated Press] (SAG)
Foodmk	Foodmaker, Inc. [Associated Press] (SAG)
Foodq	Foodquest, Inc. [Associated Press] (SAG)
Foodqust	Foodquest, Inc. [Associated Press] (SAG)
Foodrm	Foodarama Supermarkets, Inc. [Associated Press] (SAG)
FoodSc	Food Science (DD)
FoodTch	Food Technology Service, Inc. [Associated Press] (SAG)
FOOE	Mekambo [Gabon] [ICAO location identifier] (ICLI)
FOOF	Fanout-Observed Output Function (MHDB)
FOOG	Port Gentil [Gabon] [ICAO location identifier] (ICLI)
FOOH	Omboue [Gabon] [ICAO location identifier] (ICLI)
FOOI	Iguela [Gabon] [ICAO location identifier] (ICLI)
FOOK	Makokou/Epassengue [Gabon] [ICAO location identifier] (ICLI)
FOOL	Libreville/Leon M'Ba [Gabon] [ICAO location identifier] (ICLI)
FOOM	Mitzic [Gabon] [ICAO location identifier] (ICLI)
FOON	Franceville/Mvengue [Gabon] [ICAO location identifier] (ICLI)
FOOO	Libreville [Gabon] [ICAO location identifier] (ICLI)
FOOQ	Foodquest, Inc. [NASDAQ symbol] (SAG)
FOOQW	Foodquest Inc. Wrrt [NASDAQ symbol] (TTSB)
FOOR	Lastourville [Gabon] [ICAO location identifier] (ICLI)
Foord	Foord's Supreme Court Reports [Cape Colony, South Africa] [A publication] (DLA)
FOOS	Force Out of Service [Telecommunications] (TEL)
FOOS	Function-Oriented Organizational Structure (AAG)
FOOS	Sette-Cama [Gabon] [ICAO location identifier] (ICLI)
FOOSP	Fourteen-O-One Statistical Program [Military] (SAA)
FOOT	Follow-On Operational Test
FOOT	Foothill Independent Banc [NASDAQ symbol] (TTSB)
FOOT	Foothill Independent Bancorp [NASDAQ symbol] (NQ)
FOOT	Tchibanga [Gabon] [ICAO location identifier] (ICLI)
Foote & E Incorp Co...	Foote and Everett's Law of Incorporated Companies Operating under Municipal Franchises [A publication] (DLA)
Foote B & B...	Foote's Bench and Bar of the South and Southwest [A publication] (DLA)
Foote Highw...	Foote's Law of Highways [A publication] (DLA)
Foote Int Jur...	Foote on Private International Jurisprudence [A publication] (DLA)
FootInd	Foothill Independent Bancorp [Associated Press] (SAG)
Footstr	Footstar, Inc. [Associated Press] (SAG)
FOOV	Libreville [Gabon] [ICAO location identifier] (ICLI)
FOOW	Finding Our Own Ways [An association] (EA)
FOOY	Mayumba [Gabon] [ICAO location identifier] (ICLI)
FOP	Farthest on Point
FOP	Festschrift fuer Otto Procksch (1934) [A publication] (BJA)
FOP	Fiber Optics Probe
FOP	Fibrodysplasia Ossificans Progressiva [Medicine]
FOP	Financial Operating Plan
F/OP	Firing/Observation Port
FOP	First-Order Predictor (IAA)
FOP	Flight Operations Panel
FOP	Flight Operations Plan (MCD)
FOP	Fokker Flight Operations [Netherlands ICAO designator] (FAAC)
FOP	Follow-On Production (NASA)
FOP	Forced Oscillation Program [Military]
FOP	Forensic Pathology [Medicine] (DHSM)
FOP	Forward Observation Post [Military]
FOP	Fraternal Order of Police, Grand Lodge (EA)
FOP	Friendship Oil Pipeline [Eastern Europe]
FOP	Friends of Photography (EA)
FOP	Fuel Oil Pump (MSA)
FOP	Grand Lodge, Ladies Auxiliary, Fraternal Order of Police (EA)
FOPA	Firearms Owners' Protection Act
FOPC	First Order Predicate Calculus (MHDB)
FOPC	Flag Officer, Pacific Coast [Canada]
FOPDAC	Federation of Overseas Property Devlopers, Agents, and Consultants [British] (DBA)
FOPEN	Foliage Penetration [RADAR] (MCD)
FOPG	Flight Operations Planning Group [NASA] (NASA)
FOPI	First-Order Polynomial Interpolator
FOPINTRACENLANT...	Fleet Operational Intelligence Training Center, Atlantic [Navy] (DNAB)
FOPINTRACENPAC...	Fleet Operational Intelligence Training Center, Pacific [Navy] (DNAB)
FOPL	First-Order Predicate Logic (IAA)
FOPP	Fiber Optics Photo Pickup
FOPP	First-Order Polynomial Predictor

FOPP	Follow-On Parts Production (NASA)
FOPPA	First-Order Polarization Propagator Approach [Physics]
FOP-PT	Front Oubangais Patriotique - Parti du Travail [Oubangian Patriotic Front - Party of Labor] [Central Africa] (PD)
FOPR	Full Outpatient Rate (AFM)
FOPR	Society of Friends of Puerto Rico (EA)
FOPREP	Force Packaging Report [Military]
FOPS	Fair Organ Preservation Society [British]
FOPS	Falling Object Protective Structure [For mining machines]
FOPS	Federation of Playgoers Societies [British] (BI)
FOPS	File-Oriented Programming System [Computer science] (PDAA)
FOPS	First Orbit Penetration System (MCD)
FOPS	Flight Operations and Planning Scheduling (MCD)
FOPT	Fiber Optics Photo Transfer
FOPU	Fort Pulaski National Monument
FOPW	Federation of Organizations for Professional Women (EA)
FOQ	Free on Quay [Business term]
foq	Free on Quay [Business term] (ODBW)
FOQA	Flight Operations Quality Assurance [FAA] (TAG)
FOQA	Flight Operations Quality Assurance (GAVI)
FOQCV	Fuel Oil Quick Closing Valve (NVT)
FOR	Failure Outage Rate [Electronics] (IAA)
FOR	Family of Operational Rations [Army]
FOR	Farmer-Owned Reserve [Business term]
FOR	Federacion Obrera Revolucionaria [Mexican political party]
FOR	Federation of Outdoor Recreationists [Defunct] (EA)
FOR	Fellow of Operational Research [British] (DBQ)
FOR	Fellowship of Reconciliation (EA)
FOR	Fellowship of Riders (Motorcyclists) [British] (BI)
FOR	Field of Regard
FOR	Flight Operations Review (MCD)
FOR	Force (NVT)
FOR	Forced Outage Rate [Electronics] (IEEE)
FOR	Force Resources Ltd. [Vancouver Stock Exchange symbol]
FOR	Ford Foundation Library, New York, NY [OCLC symbol] (OCLC)
FOR	Fordham [New York] [Seismograph station code, US Geological Survey Closed] (SEIS)
FOR	Foreign
FOR	Forel Parchment [Bookbinding] (ROG)
FOR	Forensic Pathology [Medicine]
FOR	Fore River Railroad Corp. [AAR code]
FOR	Forest
FOR	Forestry
FOR	Forestry
FOR	Forma Orbis Romanae. Carte Archeologique de la Gaule Romaine [A publication] (OCD)
For	Fornax [Constellation]
For	Forrester's English Chancery Cases Tempore Talbot [A publication] (DLA)
For	Forrest's English Exchequer Reports [A publication] (DLA)
FOR	Forskolin [Also, FSK] [Organic chemistry]
FOR	Forsyth, MT [Location identifier FAA] (FAAL)
FOR	Fortaleza [Brazil] [Airport symbol] (OAG)
FOR	Forte [Loud] [Music]
FOR	Fortis Securities [Formerly, AMEV Securities] [NYSE symbol] (SPSG)
FOR	Fortune SRL [Italy ICAO designator] (FAAC)
For	Forum [Record label]
FOR	Forward [Business term]
FOR	Free on Rail/Free on Truck ["INCOTERM," International Chamber of Commerce official code]
FOR	Friends of the River (EA)
FOR	Fuel Oil Return (AAG)
FORA	Families of Resisters for Amnesty (EA)
FORA	Fort Raleigh National Historic Site
FORAC	For Action
FORACS	Fleet Operational Readiness Accuracy Check Sites [Navy]
FORACS	Force Accuracy Standards
For Aff	Foreign Affairs [A publication] (BRI)
FORAM	Foraminiferal [Geology]
ForAm	Foremost Corp. of America [Associated Press] (SAG)
FORAST	Forest Responses to Anthropogenic Stress [Project sponsored by university and governmental research groups]
FORAST	Forest Response to Anthropogenic Stress (GNE)
FORAST	Formula Assembler Translator [Computer science]
FORATOM	Forum Atomique Europeen [Association of European Atomic Forums] (EAIO)
Forb	Forbes' Cases in St. Andrews Bishop's Court [A publication] (DLA)
Forb	Forbes' Court of Session Decisions [Scotland] [A publication] (DLA)
Forb	Forbes' Journal of the Session [1705-13] [Scotland] [A publication] (DLA)
FORBAK	Front [End]/Back [End]
Forb Bills	Forbes on Bills of Exchange [A publication] (DLA)
Forbes	Forbes' Journal of the Session [1705-13] [Scotland] [A publication] (DLA)
ForBetr	For Better Living, Inc. [Associated Press] (SAG)
Forb Inst	Forbes' Institutes of the Law of Scotland [A publication] (DLA)
FORBLOC	FORTRAN [Formula Translating System] Compiled Block-Oriented Simulation Language [Computer science] (IEEE)
Forb Tr	Forbes on Trustees and Post Office Savings Banks [A publication] (DLA)
FORC	Fluorinator Off-Gas Recycle Compressor [Nuclear energy] (NRCH)
FORC	Force-Optimized Recoil Control (MCD)
FORC	Foreclose [Legal shorthand] (LWAP)
FORC	Formula Coder [Computer science]
FORCAP	Force Application Processor (MCD)

FORCAP...... Force Combat Air Patrol [*Military*] (NVT)
For Cas & Op... Forsyth's Cases and Opinions on Constitutional Law
        [*A publication*] (DLA)
FORCAST..... Flexible Operational Resolution for Combat Air Support [*Model*]
        (MCD)
FORCE .... FORTRAN [*Formula Translating System*] Conversational
        Environment [*Computer science*]
FORCE .... Western Federation of Regional Construction Employers
FORCEFLO... Force Flow [*Model*] [*Army*]
FORCEM ...... Force Evaluation Model [*Army*] (RDA)
Forcen .... Forcenergy Gas Exploration, Inc. [*Associated Press*] (SAG)
FORC ENT.... Forcible Entry and Detainer [*Legal term*] (DLA)
FORCL .... Foreclosure [*Legal shorthand*] (LWAP)
For Comp..... Forsyth on Composition with Creditors [*A publication*] (DLA)
For Cons Law... Forsyth's Cases and Opinions on Constitutional Law
        [*A publication*] (DLA)
FORCOPEXOS... Forward Copy of Orders with Endorsements to Administrative
        Office, Executive Office of the Secretary of the Navy (DNAB)
FOR CORP... Foreign Corp. [*Legal term*] (DLA)
FOrD............ Dickinson Memorial Library, Orange City, FL [*Library symbol Library*
        of Congress] (LCLS)
FORD .... Fix or Repair Daily [*Reference to the alleged defects of Ford*
        automobiles]
FORD .... Floating Ocean Research and Development [*Station*]
FORD .... Ford [*Commonly used*] (OPSA)
FORD .... Fordham [*England*]
Ford .... Ford Motor Co. [*Detroit, MI*] [*Associated Press*] (SAG)
FORD .... Foreign Office Research Department [*British*]
FORD .... Forum for the Restoration of Democracy [*Kenya*] [*Political party*]
        (ECON)
FORD .... Forward
FORD .... Forward Industries, Inc. [*NASDAQ symbol*] (SAG)
FORD .... Forward Industries(NY) [*NASDAQ symbol*] (TTSB)
FORD .... Found on Road Dead [*Reference to the alleged defects of Ford*
        automobiles]
FORDACS .... Fuel Oil Route Delivery and Control System [*Computer-based*
        system]
FORDAD ...... Foreign Disclosure Automated Data [*System*]
FORDAP....... FORTRAN [*Formula Translating System*] Debugging Aid Program
        [*Computer science*]
FORDEX....... Formula Index [*Molecular formula indexing*]
Fordham Corp Inst... Proceedings. Fordham Corporate Law Institute
        [*A publication*] (DLA)
Fordham U... Fordham University (GAGS)
FORDIMS..... Force Development Integrated Management System [*Military*]
FordM.......... Ford Motor Co. [*Associated Press*] (SAG)
Ford Oa .... Ford on Oaths [*8th ed.*] [*1903*] [*A publication*] (DLA)
FORDS......... Floating Ocean Research and Development Station
FORDS........ Fords [*Commonly used*] (OPSA)
FORDTIS..... Foreign Disclosure and Technical Information System
FORDU .... For Duty [*Military*]
FORE .... FORE Systems [*NASDAQ symbol*] (TTSB)
FORE .... Fore Systems, Inc. [*NASDAQ symbol*] (SAG)
fore.............. Forward [*Publishing*] (WDMC)
FORE .... Foundation for Oceanographic Research and Education
FORE .... Foundation for Oregon Research and Education (EDAC)
FORE .... Fraternity of Recording Executives (EA)
fore.............. Front (WDMC)
FORECON ... Forward Reconnaissance (NVT)
FORECONCO... Force Reconnaissance Company [*Marine Corps*]
ForeFrt......... ForeFront Group, Inc. [*Associated Press*] (SAG)
FOREG .... Foregoing (ROG)
FOREGE .... Food Regulation Enquiries [*Leatherhead Food Research Association*]
        [*Information service or system*] (CRD)
Foreld.......... Foreland Corp. [*Associated Press*] (SAG)
ForeInd........ Foreland Corp. [*Associated Press*] (SAG)
FOREM .... File Organization Evaluation Model
FOREM .... Force Requirements and Methodology [*Military*]
FOREMAN .... Form Retrieval and Manipulation Language
FORESDAT... Formerly Restricted Data [*Military*]
foresh .... Foreshorten (VRA)
FOREST .... [*The*] Ancient Order of Foresters [*Freemasonry*] (ROG)
FOREST .... Fast Order Radiation Effects Sampling Technique
FOREST .... Forest [*Commonly used*] (OPSA)
FOREST ...... Freedom Organisation for the Right to Enjoy Smoking Tobacco
        [*British*] (DI)
Forest AIDS... Forest Products Abstract Information Digest Service [*Database*]
        [*Germany*] (NITA)
Forester....... Chancery Cases Tempore Talbot [*England*] [*A publication*] (DLA)
ForestO........ Forest Oil Corp. [*Associated Press*] (SAG)
FORESTS ..... Forest [*Commonly used*] (OPSA)
ForeSys ...... Fore Systems, Inc. [*Associated Press*] (SAG)
ForeTch .... Forensic Technologies International Corp. [*Associated Press*] (SAG)
FOREWAS.... Force and Weapon Analysis System (AABC)
FOREWON ... Forces and Weapons
FOREX .... Foreign Exchange [*Investment term*]
For Exch Bull... Foreign Exchange Bulletin [*A publication*] (DLA)
FORF .... Forfeiture (AFM)
FORF & P.... Forfeiture and Penalties [*Legal term*] (DLA)
FOR/FOT...... Free on Rail/Free on Truck [*Business term*]
FORFTR .... Forfeiture of Pay (DNAB)
FORG .... Forge [*Commonly used*] (OPSA)
forg.............. Forged (VRA)
FORG .... Forgery [*Business term*]
FORG .... Forging (MSA)

F ORG .... Full Organ [*Music*]
FORGE .... File Organization Generator
FORGEN ...... Force Generation [*Military*] (SAA)
FORGES .... Forges [*Commonly used*] (OPSA)
FORGN .... Foreign
FORGN .... Fourgon
FORGNG ...... Forgoing
FORGO .... FORTRAN [*Formula Translating System*] Load and Go System
        [*University of Wisconsin*] [*Computer science*] (IEEE)
FORGOV ...... Foreign Government (AFIT)
forgr............ Foreground (VRA)
For Hort ...... Forsyth's Hortensius [*A publication*] (DLA)
FORIMS .... FORTRAN [*Formula Translating System*]-Oriented Information
        Management System [*Computer science*]
For Inf .... Forsyth's Custody of Infants [*A publication*] (DLA)
FORIS .... Forest Resources Information System [*Global Environmental*
        Monitoring System]
FORIS .... Forschungsinformationssystem Sozialwissenschaften
        [*Informationszentrum Sozialwissenschaften*] [*Database*]
FORJ............ Fellowship of Religious Journalists (EA)
For Jury Tr... Forsyth's Trial by Jury [*A publication*] (DLA)
FORK .... Fork [*Commonly used*] (OPSA)
FORKS .... Forks [*Commonly used*] (OPSA)
FORL .... Foreland Corp. [*NASDAQ symbol*] (NQ)
FOR LANG ... Foreign Language (WDAA)
FORLL .... Foreland Corp.Wrrt 'L' [*NASDAQ symbol*] (TTSB)
FORLOGMD... Force Logistics Command [*Marine Corps*] (NVT)
FORM .... Ferromagnetic Object Recognition Matrix
FORM .... Food Operations Reference Manual (DNAB)
form............. Form (VRA)
Form............ Forman's Reports [*1 Scammon, 2 Illinois*] [*A publication*] (DLA)
FORM .... Formation (MSA)
FORM .... Formerly (ROG)
FORM .... Formula
FORMA .... FORTRAN [*Formula Translating System*] Matrix Analysis [*Computer*
        science]
FORMAC ...... Formula Manipulation Compiler [*Programming language*] [*1962*]
        [*Computer science*]
FORMAL .... Formula Manipulation Language [*1970*] [*Computer science*] (MDG)
Forman .... Forman's Reports [*1 Scammon, 2 Illinois*] [*A publication*] (DLA)
Forman (III)... Forman's Reports [*1 Scammon, 2 Illinois*] [*A publication*] (DLA)
FORMAS .... Feedback to Oral Reading Miscues Analysis System (EDAC)
FORMAT .... Foreign Material (MCD)
FORMAT ...... FORTRAN [*Formula Translating System*] Matrix Abstraction
        Technique [*Computer science*] (MCD)
FORMAT-FORTRAN... FORTRAN [*Formula Translating System*] Matrix Abstraction
        Technique-FORTRAN [*Computer science*] (CSR)
FORMDEPS... FORSCOM [*Forces Command*] Mobilization and Deployment
        Planning System (MCD)
FORMECU.... Forestry Management, Evaluation, and Co-Ordinating Unit [*Nigeria*]
        [*World Bank Assisted Project Federal Department of Rural*
        Development]
FORMEX ...... Formal Executor (IAA)
FORMF .... Jet Form Corp. [*NASDAQ symbol*] (SAG)
FORMICA ..... Foreign Military Intelligence Collection Activities [*Navy*] (ANA)
FORMN .... Foreman (WDAA)
FORMN .... Foreman
FORMN........ Formation
FORMOST..... Force Mobilization Steering Committee [*Army*] (MCD)
FORMPATPAC... Formosa Patrol Force, US Pacific Fleet
Form Pla ..... Brown's Formulae Bene Placitandi [*A publication*] (ILCA)
FORMS .... Field Office Reporting-Management System [*HUD*]
FORMSA ...... Force Command Standards Activity
FORMUL ...... Formulary
Forn............ Fornax [*Constellation*]
FORN .... Fornication [*FBI standardized term*]
FORNDY ...... Foreign Duty (DNAB)
FORNN .... Forenoon (FAAC)
Foro Nap ..... Foro Napoletano [*A publication*] (ILCA)
FORPA .... Force Planning System
FORPAC ...... Forecasting Passenger and Cargo (MCD)
FORPC .... Frozen Onion Ring Packers Council [*AFFI*] [*Absorbed by*] (EA)
FORPORT .... Forward Port Capabilities [*Navy*]
For Pr .... Foran. Code of Civil Procedure of Quebec [*A publication*] (DLA)
FORPRIDECOM... Forest Products Research and Industries Development
        Commission
Forr............. Forrester's English Chancery Cases Tempore Talbot [*A publication*]
        (DLA)
Forr............. Forrest's English Exchequer Reports [*A publication*] (DLA)
Forrest......... Forrest's English Exchequer Reports [*A publication*] (DLA)
Forrester...... Forrester's English Chancery Cases Tempore Talbot [*A publication*]
        (DLA)
FOR RTS ..... Foreign Rights (WDAA)
FORS .... Fabrication Operations Requirements System (MCD)
FORS .... Faint Object Red Spectrograph [*Astronomy*]
FORS .... Fiber Optic Rate Sensors [*Instrumentation*]
FORS .... Forensic Science Database [*British Home Office Forensic Science*
        Service] [*Reading, Berkshire, England*] [*Information service or*
        system] (IID)
FORS .... Forestry
FORS .... Forschungsprojekte, Raumordnung, Stadtebau, Wohnungswesen
        [*Regional Planning, Town Planning, Housing, Research Projects*
        Database] [*Fraunhofer Society*] (IID)
FORS .... Fully Optimized Reaction Space

Fors Cas & Op... Forsyth's Cases and Opinions on Constitutional Law [*A publication*] (DLA)
Forsch .... [*The*] Forschner Group, Inc. [*Associated Press*] (SAG)
FORSCOM.... Forces Command [*Formerly, CONARC*] [*Army*]
FORSCOM.... Forces Command [*Army*] (DOMA)
Fors Comp... Forsyth on Composition with Creditors [*A publication*] (DLA)
ForServ .... Foreign Service (DD)
FORSERVSUPPGRU... Force Service Support Group [*Military*] (DNAB)
FORSERVSUPPGRUDET... Force Service Support Group Detachment [*Military*] (DNAB)
FORSGHT .... Foresight
Fors Hor ...... Forsyth's Hortensius [*A publication*] (DLA)
FORSIC .... Forces Intelligence Center (AABC)
FORSIG .... FORSCOM [*Forces Command*] Intelligence Group [*Army*]
Fors Inf .... Forsyth's Custody of Infants [*A publication*] (DLA)
FORSIZE ..... Force Sizing Exercise [*Military*]
FORSTAR.... Force Status and Identity Report
FORSTAT .... Force Status Report [*Military*]
ForstC .... Forest City Enterprises, Inc. [*Associated Press*] (SAG)
Forst Cust... Forster's Digest of the Laws of Customs [*A publication*] (DLA)
ForstLb .... Forest Laboratories, Inc. [*Associated Press*] (SAG)
ForstO .... Forest Oil Corp. [*Associated Press*] (SAG)
Fors Tr......... Forsyth on Trusts and Trustees in Scotland [*A publication*] (DLA)
Fors Tr Jur.. Forsyth's History of Trial by Jury [*A publication*] (DLA)
FORSTRY..... Forestry
FORT .... Fish Oil Restenosis Trial [*Cardiology*]
FORT .... Formal Operational Reasoning Test (EDAC)
FORT .... Fort [*Commonly used*] (OPSA)
Fort.............. Fortescue's English King's Bench Reports [*92 English Reprint*] [*1695-1738*] [*A publication*] (DLA)
FORT .... Fort Howard [*NASDAQ symbol*] (TTSB)
FORT .... Fort Howard Corp. [*NASDAQ symbol*] (SAG)
FORT .... Fortification
fort............... Fortified [*Nutrition*]
FORT .... Fortis [*Strong*] [*Pharmacy*]
FORT .... Full Out Rye Terms [*Grain trade*]
For Tax Bull... Foreign Tax Law Bi-Weekly Bulletin [*A publication*] (DLA)
For Tax L S-W Bull... Foreign Tax Law Semi-Weekly Bulletin [*A publication*] (DLA)
For Tax LS Weekly Bull... Foreign Tax Law Semi-Weekly Bulletin [*A publication*] (DLA)
For Tax LW Bull... Foreign Tax Law Weekly Bulletin [*A publication*] (DLA)
FORTE .... Fast Orbital Recording of Transient Events Satellite [*Department of Energy*]
FORTE .... File Organization Technique (BUR)
FORTE .... FRAM [*Ferroelectric RAM*]-Oriented Real-Time Environment
FORTEL....... Formatted Teletypewriter (CET)
Fortes .... Fortescue's English Courts Reports [*A publication*] (DLA)
Fortesc .... Fortescue's English King's Bench Reports [*92 English Reprint*] [*1695-1738*] [*A publication*] (DLA)
Fortescue..... Fortescue's English King's Bench Reports [*92 English Reprint*] [*1695-1738*] [*A publication*] (DLA)
Fortescue (Eng)... Fortescue's English King's Bench Reports [*92 English Reprint*] [*1695-1738*] [*A publication*] (DLA)
ForteSft....... Forte Software, Inc. [*Associated Press*] (SAG)
Fortes Rep... Fortescue's English King's Bench Reports [*92 English Reprint*] [*1695-1738*] [*A publication*] (DLA)
FORTFLAC ... Fellowship of Reconciliation Task Force on Latin America and Caribbean (EA)
FortGrp .... Fortress Group, Inc. (The) [*Associated Press*] (SAG)
FORTH......... [*The*] Foundation for Research and Technology Hellas [*Greece*]
FORTH......... Fourth-Generation Language [*Programming language created by Charles Moore*] (CDE)
Fort Hays St U... Fort Hays State University (GAGS)
FORTIS........ Fortissimo [*Very Loud*] [*Music*]
FORTISS ..... Fortissimo [*Very Loud*] [*Music*] (ROG)
FORTISS ..... Fortissimus [*Strongest*] [*Pharmacy*] (ROG)
FortisSc .... Fortis Securities [*Associated Press*] (SAG)
FORTL .... Force Requirement Troop List Reporting System (AABC)
Fort LJ .... Fortnightly Law Journal [*A publication*] (DLA)
FORTN .... Fortnightly
Fortnightly LJ... Fortnightly Law Journal [*A publication*] (DLA)
Fortn LJ .... Fortnightly Law Journal [*A publication*] (DLA)
FORTOCOM... FORTRAN [*Formula Translating System*] Compiler [*Computer science*] (SAA)
FortPet......... Fortune Petroleum Corp. [*Associated Press*] (SAG)
FortPt........... Fortune Petroleum Corp. [*Associated Press*] (SAG)
FORTRA ...... Federation of Radio and Television Retailers Association (MHDB)
FORTRAN .... Formula Translating System [*Programming language*] [*1953-54*] (CSR)
Fortran......... Formula Translation [*A computer programming language*] (WDMC)
FORTRAN .... Formula Translation Computer Language (IDOE)
FORTRANSIT... FORTRAN [*Formula Translating System*] and Internal Translator System [*Computer science*] (IEEE)
FORTRPS..... Force Troops
FORTRUNCIBLE... FORTRAN [*Formula Translating System*] Style Runcible [*Computer science*]
FORTSK .... For Task Force [*Military*] (AABC)
Fortu............ Fortunius Garcia de Erzila [*Flourished, 16th century*] [*Authority cited in pre-1607 legal work*] (DSA)
FORTUNE..... FORTRAN [*Formula Translating System*] Tuner [*Computer science*]
Fort Valley St C... Fort Valley State College (GAGS)
FORUM........ Formula for Optimizing through Real-Time Utilization of Multiprogramming
Forum .... Forum: Bench and Bar Review [*A publication*] (DLA)
Forum .... Forum. Dickinson School of Law [*A publication*] (DLA)

Forum.......... Forum Group, Inc. [*Associated Press*] (SAG)
Forum .... Forum Law Review [*A publication*] (DLA)
Forum LR ... Forum Law Review [*A publication*] (DLA)
ForumR........ Forum Retirement Partners Ltd. [*Associated Press*] (SAG)
Forum Rev.. Forum Law Review [*A publication*] (ILCA)
FORVR......... Forever
FORWAARD... Foundation of Rehabilitation with Aboriginal Alcohol Related Difficulties [*Australia*]
FORWARD .. Feedback of Repair, Workshop, and Reliability Data (PDAA)
FORWARD .. Forces Organized Ready for War and Able to Rapidly Deploy (MCD)
Forward ...... Forward Industries, Inc. [*Associated Press*] (SAG)
FORWEPCON... Forward Weapons Controller [*Military*] (NVT)
FORWEPCORD... Force Weapons Coordinator [*Navy*] (NVT)
Forwrd .... Forward Industries, Inc. [*Associated Press*] (SAG)
FORY .... Flag Officer, Royal Yachts [*Navy British*]
FORZ .... Forzato [*Strongly Accented*] [*Music*]
FOS .... Face of Studs [*Technical drawings*]
FOS .... Factor of Safety (IAA)
FOS .... Faint Object Spectrograph [*Astronomy*]
FOS .... Fall of Shot (NVT)
FOS .... Family of Small Arms [*Military*] (MCD)
FOS .... Fats and Oils Situation
FOS .... Festival of Sydney [*Australia*]
FOS .... Fiber-Optic Scintillating [*Plate*]
FOS .... Fiber Optic Sensor (IAA)
FOS .... Field Officers School [*Formerly, AOS*] [*LIMRA*]
FOS .... Field of Science (EERA)
FOS .... File Organization System (DIT)
FOS .... Final Operating System (MCD)
FOS .... Finish One Side [*Technical drawings*] (IAA)
FOS .... Flight Operations Support (KSC)
FOS .... Floppy Operating System [*Computer science*] (IAA)
FOS .... Follow-On Spares (AFM)
FOS .... FORTRAN [*Formula Translating System*] Operating System [*Computer science*]
FOS .... Free on Ship [*or Steamer*] [*Shipping*]
FOS .... Free on Station
FOS .... Fuel-Oxygen Scrap (PDAA)
FOS .... Full Operational Status
FOS .... Functional Operational Specification [*Military*] (CAAL)
FOSA .... Family of Small Arms [*Military*]
FOSA .... Fixed Orifice Sound Attenuator (DNAB)
FOSA .... Flight Operations Support Annex (SSD)
FOSA .... Formula One Spectators Association (EA)
FOSAT .... Fitting Out Supply Assistance Team [*Navy*]
FOSATLANT... Fitting Out Supply Assistance Team, Atlantic [*Navy*]
FOSATPAC... Fitting Out Supply Assistance Team, Pacific [*Navy*]
FOSC .... Federal On-Scene Commander (DNAB)
FOSC .... Federation of Sidecar Clubs [*British*] (DBA)
FOSC .... From Other Service Centers [*IRS*]
FOSC .... Full Overlap Slotted Container [*Packaging*]
FOSCAN ...... Food News Scanning Database [*Leatherhead Food Research Association*] [*Information service or system*] (CRD)
FOSCAN ...... Food Scan [*Database from Food Research Association*] [*British*] (NITA)
FOSCAS ...... Foreign Ship Construction and Shipyards (MCD)
FOSCO .... Foreign Officer Supply Corps (DNAB)
FOSD .... Field Operations and Support Division [*Environmental Protection Agency*]
FOSD .... Functional Operational Sequence Diagram
FOSDIC .... Film Optical Scanning Device for Input to Computer (NITA)
FOSDIC .... Film Optical Sensing Device for Input to Computers [*National Institute of Standards and Technology*]
FOSE .... Federal Office Systems Expo [*National Trade Productions*] (TSPED)
FOSF .... Field Observing Support Facility [*National Center for Atmospheric Research*]
FOSF .... Friends of Old St. Ferdinand (EA)
FOSFA .... Federation of Oils, Seeds, and Fats Associations [*British*]
FOSGEN ...... Fog Oil Smoke Generator
FOSI .... Formatting Output Specification Instance [*Computer science*]
Fo-Si........... Forsterite-Silica [*Lunar geology*]
FOSIC .... Fleet Ocean Surveillance Information Center [*Navy*] (CAAL)
FOSICPAC... Fleet Ocean Surveillance Information Center, Pacific [*Navy*] (DNAB)
FOSIF .... Fleet Ocean Surveillance Information Facilities [*Navy*]
FOSIFWESTPAC... Fleet Ocean Surveillance Information Facility, Western Pacific [*Navy*] (DNAB)
FOSIL .... Formulating On-Line Calculations in Algebraic Language Simulator Language (PDAA)
FOSL .... Fossil, Inc. [*NASDAQ symbol*] (SAG)
FOSM.......... Flag Officer, Submarines [*Navy British*]
FOSM.......... Fort Smith National Historic Site
FOSMA .... Function-Oriented Symbolic Macromodelling Algorithm (PDAA)
FOSMEF....... Flag Officer, Soviet Middle East Forces
FOSN .... Fabrication Order Special Number
FOSO .... Flight Operations Scheduling Office [*NASA*] (MCD)
FOSO .... Flight Operations Scheduling Officer [*NASA*] (NASA)
FOSOL .... Florian's Own Statistically Oriented Language [*Computer science*] (CSR)
FOSP .... Fabrication Outline Special Purpose
FOSP .... Flight Operations Support Personnel (MCD)
Fo-Sp-Crd-Pl... Forsterite-Spinel-Cordierite-Plagioclase [*Lunar geology*]
FOSPLAN .... Formal Space Planning Language [*Computer science*] (PDAA)
FOSPSL....... Follow-On Spare Parts Selection List (MCD)
FOSS .... Family of Systems Studies [*Military*] (RDA)
FOSS .... Fiber Optic Sensor System (MCD)

FOSS .... Fiber Optics SONAR System (MCD)
FOSS .... Functional Operation Simulation System
FOSSCS ...... Field Office Sales and Service Costs Study [*LIMRA*]
Fossil .... Fossil, Inc. [*Associated Press*] (SAG)
FOSSIL .... Frame Orientated System for Spectroscopic Inductive Learning [*Data analysis*]
FOSSL .... Follow-On Spares Support List (AFIT)
FOST .... Flag Officer, Sea Training [*Navy British*]
FOST .... Flight Operations Support Team (MCD)
Fost .... Foster's English Crown Law Cases [*168 English Reprint*] [*1743-61*] [*A publication*] (DLA)
Fost .... Foster's Legal Chronicle Reports [*Pennsylvania*] [*A publication*] (DLA)
Fost .... Foster's New Hampshire Reports [*A publication*] (DLA)
Fost .... Foster's Reports [*5, 6, and 8 Hawaii*] [*A publication*] (DLA)
Fost & F ...... Foster and Finlason's English Nisi Prius Reports [*175, 176 English Reprint*] [*A publication*] (DLA)
Fost & F (Eng)... Foster and Finlason's English Nisi Prius Reports [*175, 176 English Reprint*] [*A publication*] (DLA)
Fost & Fin .... Foster and Finlason's English Nisi Prius Reports [*175, 176 English Reprint*] [*A publication*] (DLA)
Fost CL .... Foster's English Crown Law Cases [*168 English Reprint*] [*1743-61*] [*A publication*] (DLA)
Fost CL (Eng)... Foster's English Crown Law Cases [*168 English Reprint*] [*1743-61*] [*A publication*] (DLA)
Fost Cr Law... Foster's English Crown Law Cases [*168 English Reprint*] [*1743-61*] [*A publication*] (DLA)
Fost Doct Com... Foster on Doctors' Commons [*A publication*] (DLA)
Fost El Jur... Foster's Elements of Jurisprudence [*1853*] [*A publication*] (DLA)
Foster .... Foster [*L. B.*] Co. [*Associated Press*] (SAG)
Foster .... Foster's English Crown Law Cases [*168 English Reprint*] [*1743-61*] [*A publication*] (DLA)
Foster .... Foster's New Hampshire Reports [*A publication*] (DLA)
Foster .... Legal Chronicle Reports, Edited by Foster [*Pennsylvania*] [*A publication*] (DLA)
Foster Fed Pr... Foster on Federal Practice [*A publication*] (DLA)
Foster (PA)... Foster's Legal Chronicle Reports [*Pennsylvania*] [*A publication*] (DLA)
Fost Fed Prac... Foster's Treatise on Pleading and Practice in Equity in Courts of the United States [*A publication*] (DLA)
FOSTG .... Freedom of Ocean Science Task Group [*NAS-NRC*] (NOAA)
Fost (Haw)... Foster's Reports [*5, 6, and 8 Hawaii*] [*A publication*] (DLA)
Fost Jt Own... Foster on Joint Ownership and Partition [*A publication*] (DLA)
Fost (NH)..... Foster's New Hampshire Reports [*A publication*] (DLA)
Fost on Sci Fa... Foster on the Writ of Scire Facias [*1851*] [*A publication*] (DLA)
Fost Sci Fa... Foster on the Writ of Scire Facias [*1851*] [*A publication*] (DLA)
FOSTTA........ Forum on State and Tribal Toxics Action [*Environmental Protection Agency*] (EGAO)
FostWh .... Foster Wheeler Corp. [*Associated Press*] (SAG)
FOSU .... Fort Sumter National Monument
FOSWAC ...... Family of Special Weapons Atomic Contractors
FOT .... Face of Template (MCD)
FOT .... Faint Object Telescope (PDAA)
FOT .... Fiber Optic Terminal [*Electric*] (ACRL)
FOT .... Fifth-Order Theory
FOT .... Flight Operations Team (MCD)
FOT .... Follow-On Operational Test (AFM)
FOT .... Forster [*Airport symbol*]
FOT .... Fortuna, CA [*Location identifier FAA*] (FAAL)
FOT .... Forward Transfer [*Telecommunications*] (TEL)
FOT .... Franchise Operations Team [*Automobile sales and marketing*]
FOT .... Free of Tax
FOT .... Free on Truck [*See also FOR*] [*Business term*]
FOT .... Frequence Optimum de Travail [*Optimum Working Frequency*] (NTCM)
FOT .... Frequence Optimum de Travail [*Optimum traffic frequency*] [*Telecommunications*] (NITA)
FOT .... Frequency of Optimum Operation (MCD)
FOT .... Frequency on Target
FOT .... Frequency Optimum Traffic
FOT .... Fuel Oil Tank (MSA)
FOT .... Fuel Oil Transfer
FOTA .... Fuels Open Test Assembly [*Nuclear energy*] (NRCH)
FOTALI........ Flag Officer, Taranto and Adriatic and for Liaison
FOT & E...... Follow-On Test and Evaluation (MCD)
FOTC.......... Force Over-the-Horizon Targeting Coordinator [*Navy*] (ANA)
FOTC.......... Forward Observer Training Center [*Army*] (INF)
FOTC.......... Friends of Terra Cotta (EA)
FOTE.......... Follow-On Operational Test and Evaluation
FOTEGLLD ... Forward Observer Team Equipped with Ground LASER Locator Designator (MCD)
FOTELSYS ... Foreign Telecommunications Systems (MCD)
FOTF.......... Fellow of the Ontario Teachers' Federation [*Canada*] (DD)
FOTF.......... Folded Other Than Flat [*Freight*]
FOTJ.......... Formal On-the-Job
FOTL.......... Follow-On to Lance [*Army*]
FOTLAN ...... Fiber-Optics Tactical Local Area Network [*Army*]
FOTM......... Friends of Old-Time Music [*Later, Society for Traditional Music*] (EA)
FOTO .... Forced Oscillation in a Tightening Oscillator [*Chemical kinetics*]
FOTO .... Seattle FilmWorks [*NASDAQ symbol*] (SAG)
Fotoball ...... Fotoball USA, Inc. [*Associated Press*] (SAG)
Fotobl .... Fotoball USA, Inc. [*Associated Press*] (SAG)
FOTP.......... Fiber Optic Test Procedure
FOTP.......... Fleet Operational Telecommunications Program (DNAB)
FOTP.......... Friends of the Prisoners [*Australia*]

FOTR .... Friends of Old-Time Radio (EA)
FOTR .... Friends of the River (EA)
FOTRS .... Follow-On Tactical Reconnaissance System [*Air Force*] (DOMA)
FOTS.......... Fiber Optic Transmission System [*Consists of modulated light signals sent through glass fibers and demodulated by photo-diodes*] [*Data transmission*]
FOTU .... Fotus [*A Fermentation*] [*A publication*] (ROG)
FOU .... Fougamou [*Gabon*] [*Airport symbol*] (OAG)
Foulk Act..... Foulke's Action at Law [*A publication*] (DLA)
FOUN .... Fort Union National Monument
FOUND........ Foundation
Found .... Foundation (AAGC)
FOUNDEX .... International Foundry Exhibition
FoundH........ Foundation Health Corp. [*Associated Press*] (SAG)
Found L Rev... Foundation Law Review [*A publication*] (DLA)
FOUNDN ..... Foundation
fount .... Fountain (VRA)
Fount .... Fountainhall's Decisions, Scotch Court of Session [*1678-1712*] [*A publication*] (DLA)
Fount Dec..... Fountainhall's Decisions, Scotch Court of Session [*1678-1712*] [*A publication*] (DLA)
FountO........ Fountain Oil, Inc. [*Associated Press*] (SAG)
FountPw ...... Fountain Powerboat Industries, Inc. [*Associated Press*] (SAG)
FOUO .... For Official Use Only [*Army*]
FOUR .... Federation of Union Representatives (BARN)
FOUR .... Forum Group [*NASDAQ symbol*] (TTSB)
FOUR .... Forum Group, Inc. [*NASDAQ symbol*] (NQ)
FOURATAF... Fourth Allied Tactical Air Force, Central Europe
FOURS .... Focus, Organize, Understand, Rehearse, and Simplify [*Business Term*]
FOUS .... Fort Union Trading Post National Historic Site
FOUSA........ Finance Officer, United States Army
FOV........... Family of Vehicles
FOV........... Field of View [*or Vision*]
FOV........... First Orbital Vehicle [*NASA*] (NASA)
FOV........... Flyable Orbital Vehicle
FOV........... Forward Observer Vehicle [*Military*] (MCD)
FOV........... Friends of Opera in Victoria [*Australia*]
FOV........... Valencia Community College, Orlando, FL [*Library symbol Library of Congress*] (LCLS)
FOVA .... Fort Vancouver National Historic Site
FOVEANT .... Foveantur [*Let Them Be Fermented*] [*Pharmacy*] (ROG)
FOVES .... Fine Old Very Extra Special [*Designation on brandy labels*]
FOVH .... Flush Oiltight Ventilation Hole (MSA)
FOVI.......... Field of Vision Intact [*Ophthalmology*] (DAVI)
FOW........... Family of Weapons (MCD)
FOW........... Fenestration Oval Window [*Otology*]
FOW........... First Open Water [*Shipping*]
FOW........... Forge Welding
FOW........... Formation Ordnance Workshop [*British military*] (DMA)
FOW........... Free on Wagon [*Business term*]
FOW........... Free on Water [*Business term*]
FOW........... Free on Wharf [*Business term*] (ROG)
FOW........... Friends of the Wilderness [*Defunct*] (EA)
FOW........... Morristown, MN [*Location identifier FAA*] (FAAL)
FOW........... Oil-Immersed Forced-Oil-Cooled with Forced-Water Cooler [*Transformer*] (IEEE)
FOWABPF .... Flag Officer, Western Area, British Pacific Fleet
FOWCIS .... Forest and Wildlands Conservation Information System [*FAO*] [*United Nations*] (DUND)
FOWHM....... Fuel Oil and Water Heater Manufacturers Association (EA)
Fowl Col ...... Fowler. Collieries and Colliers [*4th ed.*] [*1884*] [*A publication*] (DLA)
Fowl L Cas... Fowler's Leading Cases on Collieries [*A publication*] (DLA)
Fowl Pews... Fowler on Church Pews [*A publication*] (DLA)
Fowl Pr....... Fowler's Exchequer Practice [*A publication*] (DLA)
FOWP......... Fertilisers from Organic Wastes Program (EERA)
FOWSAB...... Federation of Women Shareholders in American Business [*New York, NY*] (EA)
FOX........... Fidelity Online Express [*Trading and investment tracking program*] (PCM)
FOX........... Fishery-Oceanography Experiment [*Marine science*] (OSRA)
FOX........... Fishery-Oceanography Experiment (USDC)
FOX........... Fox, AK [*Location identifier FAA*] (FAAL)
FOX........... Foxmeyer Corp. [*NYSE symbol*] (SPSG)
FOX........... FoxMeyer Health [*NYSE symbol*] (TTSB)
Fox........... Fox's Circuit and District Court Decisions [*United States*] [*A publication*] (DLA)
Fox........... Fox's Patent, Trade Mark, Design, and Copyright Cases [*Canada*] [*A publication*] (DLA)
Fox........... Fox's Registration Cases [*England*] [*A publication*] (DLA)
FOX........... Futures and Options Exchange [*British*]
FOX........... Jetair APS [*Denmark ICAO designator*] (FAAC)
Fox & S ...... Fox and Smith's Irish King's Bench Reports [*1822-24*] [*A publication*] (DLA)
Fox & S (Ir)... Fox and Smith's Irish King's Bench Reports [*1822-24*] [*A publication*] (DLA)
Fox & Sm .... Fox and Smith's Irish King's Bench Reports [*1822-24*] [*A publication*] (DLA)
Fox & Sm .... Fox and Smith's Registration Cases [*1886-95*] [*A publication*] (DLA)
Fox & Sm RC... Fox and Smith's Registration Cases [*1886-95*] [*A publication*] (DLA)
Fox & S Reg... Fox and Smith's Registration Cases [*1886-95*] [*A publication*] (DLA)
Fox Dig Part... Fox's Digest of the Law of Partnership [*A publication*] (DLA)
FOXI........... Foxmoor Inds Ltd [*NASDAQ symbol*] (TTSB)

FOXI.............	Foxmoor Industries Ltd. [*NASDAQ symbol*] (SAG)
Foxm	Foxmeyer Health Corp. [*Associated Press*] (SAG)
FoxMHlt......	FoxMeyer Health Corp. [*Formerly, National Intergroup*] [*Associated Press*] (SAG)
Foxmor	Foxmoor Industries Ltd. [*Associated Press*] (SAG)
Fox Pat C.....	Fox's Patent, Trade Mark, Design, and Copyright Cases [*Canada*] [*A publication*] (DLA)
Fox Pat Cas...	Fox's Patent, Trade Mark, Design, and Copyright Cases [*Canada*] [*A publication*] (DLA)
Fox PC........	Fox's Patent, Trade Mark, Design, and Copyright Cases [*Canada*] [*A publication*] (DLA)
FOXPr........	FoxMeyer Health $5 Cv Pfd [*NYSE symbol*] (TTSB)
FOXPrA......	FoxMeyer Hlth $4.20 Ex'A'Pfd [*NYSE symbol*] (TTSB)
Fox Reg Ca...	Fox's Registration Cases [*England*] [*A publication*] (DLA)
FOXY	Fraction-Optimizing X-Y Collector [*Spectroscopy*]
FOY............	Fellowship of Youth [*British*] (BI)
FOY............	FGGE [*First Global Atmospheric Research Program Global Experiment*] Operational Year [*Marine science*] (MSC)
FOY............	Foya [*Liberia*] [*Airport symbol*] (OAG)
FOY............	Foyer (MSA)
FOzM	Ozona Microfilm, Inc., Ozona, FL [*Library symbol Library of Congress*] (LCLS)
FP	Fabry-Perot [*Etalon on interferometer*] [*Optics*]
FP	Faceplate (IEEE)
FP	Factory Pass (AAG)
FP	Fair Play [*Signature used on warning letters sent by George Metesky, the "Mad Bomber" of New York City in 1940's and 1950's*]
FP	Faithful Performance
FP	False Positive [*Medicine*]
FP	False Pretenses
FP	Family Planning
FP	Family Practice [*or Practioner*]
FP	Fast Processor [*Instrumentation*]
FP	Fatherhood Project (EA)
FP	Fecal Pellet
FP	Federacion Progresista [*Spain Political party*] (EY)
FP	Federal Parliament (DLA)
FP	Federal Party [*Namibia*] (PPW)
FP	Feedback Positive [*Computer science*]
FP	Feedback Potentiometer
FP	Fee Paid [*Classified advertising*]
FP	Fellowship in Prayer [*An association*] (EA)
FP	Fellowship Party [*British*]
FP	Female Penitentiary [*British*] (ROG)
FP	Female Protein [*Biochemistry*]
FP	Feminist Press [*An association*] (EA)
F-P	Femoral-Popliteal [*Medicine*] (MAE)
FP	Ferriprotoporphyrin [*Biochemistry*]
FP	Festpunkt [*Reference point, a surveying term*] [*German military - World War II*]
FP	Fiat Pilula [*Let a Pill Be Made*] [*Pharmacy*]
FP	Fiat Potio [*Let a Potion Be Made*] [*Pharmacy*]
FP	Fibrinopeptide
FP	Fibrous Plaster (ADA)
FP	Field Potential [*Neuroelectricity*]
FP	Field Protective (AAG)
FP	Field Punishment [*Military*]
FP	Fighter Prop
FP	File Processor [*Computer science*] (BUR)
FP	File Protect
FP	Film Pack [*Photography*]
Fp	Filtered Phosphate (MAE)
FP	Filter Paper
FP	Final Plan (DNAB)
FP	Financial Plan
FP	Fine Paper
FP	Fine Particulate (GFGA)
FP	Fine Pointing (MCD)
fp	Fin Prochain [*At the End of Next Month*] [*Business term French*]
FP	Fireplace [*Real estate*]
FP	Fire Plug
F/P	Fire Policy [*Insurance*]
Fp	Fireproof (DAS)
FP	Fire Protection Equipment [*Nuclear energy*] (NRCH)
FP	Fire Pump Room [*NFPA pre-fire planning symbol*] (NFPA)
FP	Firing Point [*Military*] (INF)
FP	Firing Position [*Army*] (DOMA)
FP	First Monthly Payment
FP	First Performance [*Music*]
FP	First Proof (ADA)
FP	Fission Product
FP	Fixed Point (MCD)
FP	Fixed Price
FP	Flag Plot
FP	Flagpole
FP	Flag Post (MCD)
FP	Flameproof (AAG)
FP	Flash Photolysis [*Chemical kinetics*]
FP	Flash Point
FP	Flat Pack (IAA)
FP	Flat Pad
FP	Flat Panel [*Computer science*]
FP	Flat Paper (DAVI)
F/P	Flat Pattern

FP	Flat Plate [*Medicine*]
FP	Flat Point [*Technical drawings*]
FP	Flavin Phosphate [*Biochemistry*]
FP	Flavoprotein [*Biochemistry*]
FP	Flavor Profile [*Sensory test method developed by A. D. Little, Inc.*]
FP	Fleet Paymaster [*Navy British*] (ROG)
FP	Flight Pay
FP	Flight Plan [*Aviation*]
FP	Flight Position [*Aerospace*] (IAA)
F/P	Flight Programmer (AAG)
FP	Flight Progress (KSC)
FP	Floating Open Marine Policy [*Insurance*] (DS)
FP	Floating Point [*Computer science*] (BUR)
FP	Floating Policy [*Insurance*]
FP	Florid Papillomatosis [*Medicine*]
F/P	Fluid/Plasma Ratio [*Biochemistry*] (DAVI)
FP	Fluid Pressure [*Spinal fluid pressure*] [*Medicine*] (DAVI)
FP	Fluorescence Polarization
FP	Fluorescent Particle
FP	Fluorescent Pseudomonad spp.
FP	Fluoropolymers [*Organic chemistry*]
FP	Flying Psychologists [*Defunct*] (EA)
FP	Focal Plane [*Photography*]
FP	Fokker-Planck Equation [*Mathematics*]
FP	Food Poisoning [*Medicine*]
FP	Food Policy [*British*]
FP	Food Production [*British*]
FP	Footpath (ADA)
FP	Foot Patrol (AFM)
FP	Foot-Pound [*Unit of work*]
FP	Forbidden Planet [*Bookstore chain*] [*British*]
FP	Fordyce & Princeton Railroad Co. [*AAR code*]
fp	Forearm Pronated [*Medicine*]
FP	Foreign Policy
FP	Foreign Program [*FCC*] (NTCM)
FP	Forepeak [*Naval architecture*]
FP	Fore Perpendicular
FP	Forest Park [*State*] (EERA)
FP	Forest Patrol [*Activity of Civil Air Patrol*]
FP	Forfeiture of Pay
FP	Former Priest
FP	Former Pupil [*Alumnus*] [*British*]
FP	For Private Use (ROG)
FP	Forte Piano [*Loud, then Soft*] [*Music*]
FP	Forward Peak (DNAB)
FP	Forward Perpendicular
FP	Frame Period [*Computer science*] (IAA)
FP	Frame Pointer [*Computer science*]
FP	Frame Protected [*Insurance classification*]
FP	Franklin Pierce [*US president, 1804-1869*]
FP	Franklin Planner [*Annual organizer*]
FP	Free Pardon (ADA)
FP	Free Piston [*Machinery*] (DS)
FP	Free Play [*Military*] (CAAL)
FP	Free Port [*Shipping*]
FP	Free Propellers (AAG)
FP	Freezing Point
FP	Freight and Passenger Vessels [*Army*]
FP	Fremskrittspartiet [*Progress Party*] [*Norway Political party*] (PPE)
FP	French Patent
fp	French Polynesia [*MARC country of publication code Library of Congress*] (LCCP)
FP	Fresh Paragraph (ADA)
FP	Friendly Peersuasion [*Girls Club of America*] (EA)
FP	[*The*] Friends Program (EA)
FP	Friends' Provident Life Office [*Insurance*] [*British*]
FP	Frog Pond - Frog Collectors Club (EA)
Fp	Frontispiece (NTCM)
FP	Fronto-Parietal [*Anatomy*] (MAE)
FP	Front Panel [*Navy Navigation Satellite System*] (DNAB)
FP	Front Populaire [*Burkina Faso*] [*Political party*] (EY)
FP	Front Projection (NTCM)
FP	Frozen Plasma [*Medicine*]
Fp	Fruition Project (EA)
FP	Fuel (Petroleum) (DA)
FP	Fuel Pressure (NASA)
FP	Fuel Pump Gasket [*Automotive engineering*]
FP	Full Pay [*Military British*] (ROG)
FP	Full Pension [*Hotel rate*]
FP	Full Period
FP	Full Power
FP	Full Price (ADA)
FP	Fully Paid [*Business term*]
FP	Functional Path (NASA)
FP	Functional Proponent
FP	Function Processor (NITA)
FP	Fundal Pressure (MAE)
FP	Fungus Proof
FP	Fusible Plug [*Engineering*] (IAA)
FP	Fusing Point
FP	Pipefitter [*Navy*]
F$_p$	Power-Loss Factor (IDOE)
FP	Public Forecasts [*Symbol*] [*National Weather Service*]
FP	Shipfitter [*Navy symbol*]
FP	Simmons [*ICAO designator*] (AD)

FP1 .... Floating Platform No. 1 [*English bilingual film made in Germany with actor Conrad Veidt, 1933*]

FP-25 .... People's Forces of 25 April [*Portugal*] (PD)

FP-31 .... Frente Popular 31 de Enero [*31st January Popular Front*] [*Guatemala*] (PD)

FPA .... Facilities Procurement Application (AAG)

FPA .... Failure Probability Analysis (MCD)

FPA .... Families for Private Adoption (EA)

FPA .... Family Planning Association

FPA .... Far Point of Accommodation [*Ophthalmology*]

FPA .... Feature Protection Area [*Conservation*] [*Australia*]

FPA .... Federal Party of Australia [*Political party*]

FPA .... Federal Pesticide Act (GNE)

FPA .... Federal Physicians Association (EA)

FPA .... Federal Powers Act (GNE)

FPA .... Federal Preparedness Agency [*FEMA*]

FPA .... Federal Professional Association [*Later, FEPA*]

FPA .... Federal Property Assistance [*Department of Health and Human Services*]

FPA .... Federation of Professional Athletes [*Later, NFLPA*] (EA)

FPA .... Fibrinopeptide A [*Biochemistry*]

FPA .... Field Profit Analysis

FPA .... Fill Producers' Association

FPA .... Film Production Association of Great Britain (BI)

FPA .... Filter Paper Activity

FPA .... Final Power Amplifier

FPA .... Financial Printers Association (EA)

FPA .... Fire Protection Association [*Australia*]

FPA .... Fire Protection Association [*British*]

FPA .... First Point of Aries [*Navigation*]

FPA .... First Production Article (MCD)

FPA .... Fixed Plant Adapter (DWSG)

FPA .... Fixed Principal Axes [*Hypothesis describing forces in a sand-pile*]

FPA .... Flat-Plate Antenna [*or Array*]

FPA .... Flexible Packaging Association (EA)

FPA .... Flexible Premium Annuity (PDAA)

FPA .... Flight Path Accelerometer

FPA .... Flight Path Analysis

FPA .... Flight Path Angle (MCD)

FPA .... Flight Plan Approval [*Aviation*] (AFM)

FPA .... Flight Plan Area [*Aviation*] (FAAC)

FPA .... Floating-Point Accelerator [*Computer science*] (BYTE)

FPA .... Floating-Point Arithmetic

FPA .... Flowers and Plants Association [*British*] (DBA)

FPA .... Fluorophenylalanine [*Biochemistry*]

FPA .... Flying Pharmacists of America [*Defunct*] (EA)

FPA .... Flying Physicians Association (EA)

FPA .... Focal-Plane Array (MCD)

FPA .... Food Production Administration [*World War II*]

FPA .... Force Planning Analysis [*Army*] (AABC)

FPA .... Foreign Policy Association (EA)

FPA .... Foreign Press Association (EA)

FPA .... Forest Practices Act [*Tasmania*] [*State legislation*] (EERA)

FPA .... Forest Products Abstracts [*Oxford, England*] [*A publication*]

FPA .... Forest Products Association (EERA)

FPA .... Forests Production Association [*Australia*]

FPA .... Formalin-Propionic Acid-Alcohol [*Fixative*] [*Botany*]

FPA .... Formula Pricing Agreement (AAGC)

FPA .... Forward Pitch Amplifier (MCD)

FPA .... Foundation for Public Affairs (EA)

FPA .... FPA Corp. [*Associated Press*] (SAG)

FPA .... Franklin Pierce Adams [*1881-1960*] [*American newspaper columnist*]

FPA .... Free of Particular Average [*Insurance*]

FPA .... Free Pacific Association (EA)

FPA .... Free Press Association (EA)

FPA .... Freestyle Players Association

FPA .... Friends of the Peaceful Alternatives [*Defunct*] (EA)

FPA .... Fundamental Planning Analysis (MCD)

FPA .... Funding Program Advice [*Military*] (AABC)

FPA .... Fused Polyethylene Aluminium

FPA .... Fusion Power Associates (EA)

FPa .... Larimer Memorial Library, Palatka, FL [*Library symbol Library of Congress*] (LCLS)

FPAA .... Federacion Panamericana de Asociaciones de Arquitectos [*Panamerican Federation of Architects' Associations*] (EA)

FPAA .... Final Procurement Action Approval (MCD)

FPAA .... First Printings of American Authors [*A publication*]

FPAA .... Flat-Plate Array Antenna

FPAA .... Flight Path Analysis Area [*Space Flight Operations Facility, NASA*]

FPAA .... Fort Polk Army Airfield [*Fort Polk, LA*]

FPAAC .... Free of Particular Average, American Conditions [*Insurance*]

FPAC .... Flight Path Analysis and Command [*Team*] [*NASA*]

FPAC .... Fusion Policy Advisory Committee [*Department of Energy*]

FPACCP .... Foundation for the Preservation of Antique and Contemporary Cup Plates (EA)

FPAD .... Freight Payable at Destination [*Business term*]

FPAD .... Fret Payable a Destination [*Freight Payable at Destination*] [*French Business term*]

FPAD .... Fund for Peaceful Atomic Development [*Defunct*]

FPAEC .... Free of Particular Average, English Conditions [*Insurance*]

FPAF .... Fixed Price Award Fee [*Contract*]

FPA/GSA ...... Federal Preparedness Agency/General Services Administration

FPAH .... Foundation for Preservation of the Archeological Heritage (EA)

FPAK .... Family Planning Association of Kenya (EERA)

FPAL .... Floating-Point Arithmetic Library [*Computer science*] (MHDI)

FPAL .... Full-Term Deliveries, Premature [*Preterm*] Deliveries, Abortions, and Living Children [*Gynecology and obstetrics*] (DAVI)

FPAM .... FPA Medical Management [*NASDAQ symbol*] (SAG)

FPAM .... FPA Medical Mgmt [*NASDAQ symbol*] (TTSB)

FPA Md .... FPA Medical Management [*Associated Press*] (SAG)

FP & D .... Facility Planning and Design (KSC)

FP & DB ...... Facilities Planning and Development Branch [*BUPERS*]

FP & E .... Food Products and Equipment [*A publication*]

FPANSW .... Family Planning Association of New South Wales [*Australia*]

FPANY .... Film Producers Association of New York [*Defunct*] (EA)

FPANZ .... Fellow, Public Accountant, New Zealand

FPap .... Federal Paper Board Co., Inc. [*Associated Press*] (SAG)

FPAP .... Floating-Point Array Processor [*Computer science*]

FPAS .... Fail-Passive Autoland System [*Aviation*]

FPAS .... Fellow of the Pakistan Academy of Sciences

FPAS .... Front for Popular Armed Struggle [*Iraq*]

FPASA .... Federal Property and Administrative Services Act [*1949*]

FPB .... Fast Patrol Boat [*Navy*] (NVT)

FPB .... Federal Petroleum Board [*Department of the Interior*]

FPB .... Federation of Podiatry Boards [*Later, FPMB*] (EA)

FPB .... Femoral Popliteal Bypass [*Medicine*]

FPB .... Fibrino-Peptide B [*Biochemistry*] (DMAA)

FPB .... Fixed Price Basis

FPB .... Flexor Pollicis Brevis [*Anatomy*]

FPB .... Flight Progress Board [*Aviation*]

FPB .... Floating-Point Board [*Computer science*] (MHDI)

FPB .... Foreign Policy Briefs

FPB .... Forum of Private Business [*British*]

FPB .... Fuel Preburner (KSC)

FPBA .... Folding Paper Box Association (DGA)

FPBAA .... Folding Paper Box Association of America [*Later, PPC*] (EA)

FPBCCA .... Famous Personalities' Business Card Collectors of America [*Defunct*] (EA)

FP Bcp .... FP Bancorp, Inc. [*Associated Press*] (SAG)

FPBD .... Fibrous Plasterboard

FPBD .... Functional Plan Block Diagram (DOMA)

FPBG .... Final Program and Budget Guidance

FPBK .... First Patriot Bankshares [*NASDAQ symbol*] (SAG)

FPBN .... FP Bancorp [*NASDAQ symbol*] (TTSB)

FPBN .... FP Bancorp, Inc. [*NASDAQ symbol*] (SAG)

FPBOV .... Fuel Preburner and Oxidizer Valve (NASA)

FPBRS .... Fels Parent Behavior Rating Scales [*Psychology*]

FPc .... Bay County Public Library, Panama City, FL [*Library symbol Library of Congress*] (LCLS)

FPC .... Facility Power Control (AAG)

FPC .... Fall Planting Council (EA)

FPC .... Familial Polyposis Coli [*Later, FAP*] [*Medicine*]

FPC .... Family Personal Computer (PCM)

FPC .... Family Planning Center (WDAA)

FPC .... Family Planning Clinic [*British*]

FPC .... Family Practice Center (MEDA)

FPC .... Family Practitioner Committee [*British*]

FPC .... Federal Personnel Council [*Abolished, 1954*] [*Civil Service Commission*]

FPC .... Federal Power Commission [*Superseded by Department of Energy, 1977*]

FPC .... Federal Power Commission Reports [*A publication*] (DLA)

FPC .... Federal Property Council [*Terminated, 1977*]

FPC .... Federal Publisher's Committee (EA)

FPC .... Fellow of Pembroke College [*British*] (ROG)

FPC .... Feminist Party of Canada

FPC .... Ferrite Pot Core

FPC .... Field Petroleum Corp. [*Vancouver Stock Exchange symbol*]

FPC .... Field Press Censorship

FPC .... Final Processing Center

FPC .... Financial Print & Communications Ltd. [*British*]

FPC .... Finisher/Preserver/Cleaner (DGA)

FPC .... Fire Pump Control (IEEE)

FPC .... Firestone Plastics Co.

FPC .... Firestone Polyvinyl Chloride

FPC .... Fiscal Policy Council (EA)

FPC .... Fish Protein Concentrate [*For use in antistarvation programs*]

FPC .... Fixed Paper Capacitor

FPC .... Fixed Partial Charge [*Physical chemistry*]

FPC .... Fixed Photoflash Capacitor

FPC .... Fixed Point Calculation

FPC .... Fixed Polycarbonate Capacitor

FPC .... Fixed Precision Capacitor

FPC .... Fixed Price Call

FPC .... Fixed Price Contracts

FPC .... Fixed Program Computer

FPC .... Flat Plate Collector [*Engineering*] (BARN)

FPC .... Flexible Printed Circuit

FPC .... Flight Path Control

FPC .... Flight Programmer Computer

FPC .... Flight Purpose Code (DNAB)

FPC .... Floating-Point Calculation

FPC .... Florida Presbyterian College [*Later, Eckerd College*]

FPC .... Florida Progress [*NYSE symbol*] (TTSB)

FPC .... Florida Progress Corp. [*Formerly, Florida Power Corp.*] [*NYSE symbol*] (SPSG)

FPC .... Flowers Publicity Council Ltd. [*British*] (BI)

FPC .... Fluid Power Centre [*University of Bath*] [*British*] (CB)

FPC .... Fluids Pressure Control (NASA)

FPC .... Focal Plane Camera (ROG)

FPC.............	Food Packaging Council (EA)
FPC.............	Food Protein Concentrate (PDAA)
FPC.............	Food Protein Council [Later, SPC] (EA)
FPC.............	Forced Pair Copulation [Sociobiology]
FPC.............	Forest Products Council [Western Australia]
FPC.............	For Private Circulation
FPC.............	Forty Pound Charge (SAA)
FPC.............	Forward Power Controller (MCD)
FPC.............	Foundation for Philosophy of Creativity (EA)
FPC.............	Frank Phillips College [Texas]
FPC.............	Free Polymer-Derived Carbon [Chemistry]
FPC.............	French Pressure Cell
FPC.............	Frente Popular Costarricense [Costa Rican Popular Front] [Political party] (PPW)
FPC.............	Frequency Plane Correlator (IAA)
FPC.............	Friends Peace Committee (EA)
FPC.............	Front Panel Control
FPC.............	Frozen Pea Council [Defunct]
FPC.............	Fuel Pool Cooling [Nuclear energy] (NRCH)
FPC.............	Functional Progression Chart [Telecommunications] (TEL)
FPC.............	Future Physicians Clubs (EA)
FPC.............	United States Federal Power Commission Opinions and Decisions [A publication] (DLA)
FPCA...........	Federal Post Card Application [For an absentee ballot] (AABC)
FPCA...........	Fiber Producers Credit Association (EA)
FPCA...........	Forward Power Control Assembly (MCD)
FPCANSW.....	Federation of Parents and Citizens' Associations of New South Wales [Australia]
FP-CART......	Federal/Provincial Committee on Atlantic Region Transportation [Canada]
FPCC...........	Fair Play for Cuba Committee [Defunct]
FPCC...........	Federal Potato Co-ordinating Committee [Australia]
FPCC...........	First Portuguese Canadian Club
FPCC...........	Fixed Polycarbonate Capacitor
FPCC...........	Fixed Printed Circuit Capacitor
FPCC...........	Flight/Propulsion Control Coupling [Air Force]
FPCC...........	Fuel Pool Cooling and Cleanup [Nuclear energy] (NRCH)
FPCCI.........	Federation of Pakistan Chambers of Commerce and Industry (ECON)
FPCCM.......	Flight Planning and Cruise Control Manual (MCD)
FPCCS	Fuel Pool Cooling and Cleanup System [Nuclear energy] (NRCH)
FPCD	Federal Personnel and Compensation Division (AAGC)
FPCE	Fission Products Conversion and Encapsulation [Plant] [Nuclear energy]
FPCE	Floating-Point C Extension [Computer science]
FPCEA........	Fibreboard Packing Case Employers' Association [British] (BI)
FPcG	United States Department of Commerce, National Oceanic and Atmospheric Administration, Gulf Coastal Fisheries Center, Panama City, FL [Library symbol Library of Congress] (LCLS)
FPCH	Foreign Policy Clearing House [Defunct]
FPCI...........	Federal Penal and Correctional Institution (WDAA)
FPCI...........	Fluid Power Consultants International (EA)
FPCL...........	Front Paisanu di Liberazione [Corsica]
FPCLANT	Fleet Programming Center, Atlantic
FPCM..........	Fibroblast Populated Collagen Matrix [Biology]
FPCMA........	Fibreboard Packing Case Manufacturers' Association [British] (BI)
FPcN...........	Northwest Regional Library, Panama City, FL [Library symbol Library of Congress] (LCLS)
FPcNM........	United States Navy, Mine Defense Laboratory, Technical Library, Panama City, FL [Library symbol Library of Congress] (LCLS)
FPCO	Facilities Procuring Contracting Officer [Military] (AFIT)
FPCORP.......	Financial Post Canadian Corporate Database [Financial Post Corporation Service Group] [Information service or system] (CRD)
FPCP...........	Ferrocene Polymer Cure Process
FPCP...........	Floating Point Co-Processor [Motorola] (NITA)
FPCR	Federal Power Commission Reports
FPCR	Fluid Poison Control Reactor (IAA)
FPCS	Focal-Plane Crystal Spectrometer
FPCS	Free Polar Corticosteroids [Endocrinology]
FPCS	Freezing Point Calibration Standard
FPCS	Fuel Pool Cooling System [Nuclear energy] (IEEE)
FPCS	Full-Page Composition System [Computer science]
FPC's..........	Functions/Parameters/Characteristics (MCD)
FPCSTL.......	Fission Product Control Screening Test Loop [Nuclear energy] (NRCH)
FPCU	Fuel Pump Control Unit (MCD)
FPD.............	Federacion Popular Democratica [Popular Democratic Federation] [Spain Political party] (PPE)
FPD.............	Federal Court Procurement Decisions [A publication] (AAGC)
FPD.............	Federal Pattern Description (AAG)
FPD.............	Ferrite Phase Driver
FPD.............	Feto-Pelvic Disproportion [Medicine] (DMAA)
FPD.............	Field Plated Diode (PDAA)
FPD.............	Fixed Partial Denture [Dentistry] (DAVI)
FPD.............	Flame Photometric Detector
FPD.............	Flat Pack Diode
FPD.............	Flat-Panel Display [Instrumentation]
FPD.............	Florida P&L 8.75% 'QUIDS' [NYSE symbol] (TTSB)
FPD.............	Florida Power & Light [NYSE symbol] (SAG)
FPD.............	Flush Plate Diode (PDAA)
FPD.............	Flush Plate Dipole (PDAA)
FPD.............	Friction Pressure Drop
FPD.............	Full Page Display (BYTE)
FPD.............	Full Paid [Stock exchange term] (SPSG)
FPD.............	Full Power Days [Nuclear energy] (NRCH)

FPDA	Finnish Plywood Development Association
FPDA	Fluid Power Distributors Association (EA)
FPDC	Federal Procurement Data Center [Database]
FPDD	Familial Pure Depressive Disease
FPDD	Final Project Design Description (NRCH)
FP/DF	Fluid Physics/Dynamics Facility (SSD)
FPDG	Foreign Policy Discussion Group (EA)
FPDI	Flight Path Deviation Indicator [Navigation]
FPDI	Food Processing Development Irradiator
FPDL	Federacion de Partidos Democraticas y Liberales [Federation of Democratic and Liberal Parties] [Spain Political party] (PPE)
FPDL	Fission Products Development Laboratory [ORNL]
FPDL	Flashlamp-Pumped Dye LASER
FPDP	Flight Path Design Program
FPDP	Follow-On Program Development Plan (SAA)
FPDS	Federal Procurement Data System [Database] (IID)
FPDS	Fleet Probe Data System [Navy] (NG)
FPDT	Federal Police Disciplinary Tribunal [Australia]
FPDU	FTAM [File Transfer, Access, and Management] Protocol Data Unit [Telecommunications] (OSI)
FPDVP	Frostig Program for the Development of Visual Perception [Psychiatry] (DAVI)
FPE.............	Fairport, Painesville & Eastern Railway Co. [AAR code]
FPE.............	Federal Pioneer Ltd. [Toronto Stock Exchange symbol]
FPE.............	Federal Procurement Eligibility
FPE.............	Federation des Pecheurs de l'Est [Eastern Fishermen's Federation - EFF] [Canada]
FPE.............	Final Prediction Error [Statistics]
FPE.............	Fire Pump Engine [Auto racing engine model designation] [British]
FPE.............	Fixed Potential Electrode [Electrochemistry]
FPE.............	Fixed Price with Escalation
FPE.............	Foot-Pounds of Energy
FPE.............	Force Planning Estimate (MCD)
FPE.............	FORTRAN [Formula Translating System] Programming Environment [Computer science] (HGAA)
FPE.............	Friends Peace Exchange (EA)
FPE.............	Functional Program Elements [NASA]
FPE.............	Fundamental Phenomena Experimentation (SSD)
FPe.............	Pensacola Public Library, Pensacola, FL [Library symbol Library of Congress] (LCLS)
FPEA..........	Ford Philpot Evangelistic Association (EA)
FPEB...........	Family Planning Evaluation Branch [Public Health Service] (IID)
FPEB...........	Fuel Pool Exhaust Blower [Nuclear energy] (NRCH)
FPEC..........	Federal Pacific Electric Co. (KSC)
FPEC..........	Fixed Porcelain Enamel Capacitor
FPeC..........	Pensacola Junior College, Pensacola, FL [Library symbol Library of Congress] (LCLS)
FPeCC.........	Pensacola Christian College, Pensacola, FL [Library symbol] [Library of Congress] (LCLS)
FPED..........	Family Planning Evaluation Division [HEW] (IID)
FPEEPM......	Floor Proximity Emergency Escape Path Marking [Aviation] (DA)
FPEG..........	Fast Pulse Electron Gun (MCD)
FPeGS	Church of Jesus Christ of Latter-Day Saints, Genealogical Society Library, Pensacola Branch, Pensacola, FL [Library symbol Library of Congress] (LCLS)
FPeHiP	Historic Pensacola Preservation Board, Pensacola, FL [Library symbol] [Library of Congress] (LCLS)
FPEIS..........	Fine Particulate Emissions Information System (GNE)
FPEIS..........	Fine Particulate Emissions Information System [Environmental Protection Agency] (GFGA)
FPeJC..........	Pensacola Junior College, Pensacola, FL [Library symbol Library of Congress] (LCLS)
FPeN..........	United States Naval Air Station, Pensacola, FL [Library symbol Library of Congress] (LCLS)
FPeN-M.......	United States Navy, Naval Aerospace Medical Institute, Pensacola, FL [Library symbol Library of Congress] (LCLS)
FPEPA..........	Fixed-Price with Economic Price Adjustment [Type of contract] (AAGC)
FPerCC	Taylor County Court House, Perry, FL [Library symbol] [Library of Congress] (LCLS)
FPERR..........	Field Personnel Record
FPES...........	Femtosecond Photoelectron Spectroscopy
FPeU...........	University of West Florida, Pensacola, FL [Library symbol Library of Congress] (LCLS)
FPeW..........	West Florida Regional Library, Pensacola, FL [Library symbol Library of Congress] (LCLS)
FPF.............	Familial Pulmonary Fibrosis
FPF.............	Feathered Pipe Foundation (EA)
FPF.............	Fibroblast Pneumonocyte Factor [Biochemistry]
FPF.............	Final Protective Fire [Artillery term]
FPF.............	Fine Pointing Facility [NASA] (KSC)
FPF.............	First Philippine Fund, Inc. [NYSE symbol] (SAG)
FPF.............	First Phillipine Fund [NYSE symbol] (TTSB)
FPF.............	Fish Promotional Fund [National Oceanic and Atmospheric Administration] (GFGA)
FPF.............	Fixed Price Firm (AFM)
FPF.............	Flexible Polyurethane Foam
FPF.............	Floating Production Facility
FPF.............	Fluid Physics Facility (SSD)
FPF.............	Frames Per Foot of Film (WDMC)
FPF.............	Fuel Packaging Facility [Nuclear energy]
FPF.............	Full Power Frequency
FPFA...........	Family Planning Federation of Australia Inc. (EERA)
FPFC...........	Fixed Photoflash Capacitor
FPFC...........	Flight Patrol Fan Club (EA)

FPFGBI .... French Polishers' Federation of Great Britain and Ireland [*A union*]
FPG .... Aeroleasing SA [*Switzerland ICAO designator*] (FAAC)
FPG .... Fasting Plasma Glucose [*Medicine*]
FPG .... Federal Pecan Growers
FPG .... Fire Philatelic Group (EA)
FPG .... Firing Pulse Generator (IAA)
FPG .... Fluorescence plus Giemsa [*Cell-staining technique*]
FPG .... Focal Proliferative Glomerulonephritis [*Medicine*] (DMAA)
FPG .... Force Planning Guide [*Army*] (AABC)
FPG .... Fragmenta Philosophorum Graecorum [*A publication*] (OCD)
FPG .... Frank Porter Graham Child Development Center [*University of North Carolina at Chapel Hill*] [*Research center*] (RCD)
f-pg-- .... Portuguese Guinea [*Guinea-Bissau*] [*MARC geographic area code Library of Congress*] (LCCP)
FPGA .... Field Programmable Gate Array [*Computer science*]
FPGAUS .... Federated Pecan Growers' Associations of the United States (EA)
FPGEC .... Foreign Pharmacy Graduate Examination Commission (EA)
FPGEE .... Foreign Pharmacy Graduate Equivalency Examination
FPGL .... Flight Plan Gas Load [*Air Force*]
FPGN .... Focal Proliferative Glomerulonephritis [*Medicine*]
FPH .... Failures per Hour [*Military*]
FPH .... Feet per Hour (WDAA)
FPH .... Fish Protein Hydrolysate
FPH .... Floating-Point Hardware [*Computer science*]
FPH .... Fondation pour le Progres de l'Homme [*France*] (EERA)
FPH .... Fredericks Place Holdings [*British*]
FPH .... Freephone Supplementary Service [*Telecommunications*] (DOM)
FPH .... Frente Patriotico Hondureno [*Honduran Patriotic Front*] [*Political party*] (PD)
FPH .... Friends of Patrick Henry (EA)
FPH₂ .... Full Power Hours [*Nuclear energy*] (DEN)
FPH₂ .... Flavin Phosphate, Reduced [*Biochemistry*] (MAE)
FPHA .... Federal Public Housing Authority [*Functions transferred to Public Housing Administration, 1947*]
FPharmS ...... Fellow of the Pharmaceutical Society [*British*]
FPHB .... Flight Procedures Handbook (MCD)
FPHC .... Foreign Personal Holding Co.
FPHE .... Formalin-Treated Pyruvaldehyde-Stabilized Human Erythrocytes [*Immunology*]
FPHNH .... Federation of Private Hospitals and Nursing Homes [*Australia*]
FPHS .... Fallout Protection in Houses
F Ph S .... Fellow of the Philosophical Society [*British*]
F Phys S ...... Fellow of the Physical Society [*British*]
F PHYS SOC ... Fellow, Physical Society [*British*] (ROG)
FPI .... Fabry-Perot Interferometer
FPI .... Faded Prior to Interception [*RADAR*]
FPI .... Family Pitch In [*Indicates family may eat freely of a certain dish at a meal where guests are present*]
FPI .... Fast Processor Interface [*Computer chip*]
FPI .... Federal Personnel Intern [*Program*] [*Civil Service Commission*]
FPI .... Federal Prison Industries, Inc. [*Department of Justice*]
FPI .... Federal Procurement Institute [*Later, FAI*] (MCD)
FPI .... Federal Publications, Inc. (AAGC)
FPI .... Federation Prohibitionniste Internationale [*International Prohibition Federation*]
FPI .... Fellow of the Plastics Institute [*British*]
FPI .... Field Presence Indicator
FPI .... Fins per Inch [*Heat exchangers*]
FPI .... First Periodic Inspection (AAG)
FPI .... Fisheries Products International [*Canada*]
FPI .... Fixed Price Incentive
FPI .... Flexible Pavements (EA)
FPI .... Flexion Producing Interneuron [*Neurology*]
FPI .... Flight Path Indicator [*Aviation*] (AIA)
FPI .... Fluorescent Penetrant Inspection (MSA)
FPI .... Food Processors Institute (EA)
FPI .... Foodservice and Packaging Institute (EA)
FPI .... Forest Products Industry
FPI .... Fountain Powerboat Ind [*AMEX symbol*] (TTSB)
FPI .... Fountain Powerboat Industries, Inc. [*AMEX symbol*] (SPSG)
FPI .... Frames per Inch [*Computer science*]
FPI .... Friends of Pioneering Israel
FPI .... Front Populaire Ivoirien [*Ivorian Popular Front*] [*The Ivory Coast*] [*Political party*] (EY)
FPI .... Fuel Pressure Indicator
FPi .... Pinellas Park Public Library, Pinellas Park, FL [*Library symbol Library of Congress*] (LCLS)
FPIA .... Family Planning International Assistance (EA)
FPIA .... Fluorescence Polarization Immunoassay
FPIAA .... Fire Protection Industry Association of Australia (EERA)
FPIAR .... Federal Prison Industries Acquisition Regulation (AAGC)
FPIC .... Field-Programmable Interconnect Component [*Computer science*]
FPIC .... Financial Post Information Centre [*MacLean-Hunter Ltd.*] [*Information service or system*] (IID)
FPIC .... Fixed Price Incentive Contract
FPIC .... FPIC Insurance Group, Inc. [*NASDAQ symbol*] (SAG)
FPIC .... Fuel and Power Industries Committee [*British*] (DCTA)
FPIC Ins ...... FPIC Insurance Group, Inc. [*Associated Press*] (SAG)
FPID .... Fixed Price Incentive with Delay Firm Target (SAA)
FPIECE .... Frontispiece [*Publishing*] (ROG)
FPIF .... Fixed Price Incentive Fee
FPIF .... Fixed Price Incentive Firm [*Award*] [*Government contracting*]
FPIF .... Fixed Price Incentive Force (AFM)
FPIFV .... Fixed-Price Incentive Fee Contract Value Engineering (AAGC)
F PIL .... Fiat Pilula [*Let a Pill Be Made*] [*Pharmacy*]

FPIL .... Full Premium If Lost [*Insurance*] (MHDW)
FPIS .... Family Planning and Information Service
FPIS .... Fixed Price Incentive Successive Targets
FPIS .... Forward Propagation by Ionospheric Scatter [*Radio communications technique*]
FPITC .... Food Processing Industry Training Council [*Australia*]
FPIX .... Ferriprotoporphyrin IX [*Biochemistry*]
FPJ .... Pensacola Junior College, Pensacola, FL [*OCLC symbol*] (OCLC)
FPJMC .... Four Power Joint Military Commission (AABC)
FPJMT .... Four Party Joint Military Team [*Established March, 1973 as part of the Paris Peace Accords*] (VNW)
FPJPA .... Fully Proceduralized Job Performance Aid (MCD)
FPJU .... Fonds Special pour la Jeunesse de l'UNESCO [*UNESCO Special Fund for Youth*] (EAIO)
FPK .... Fixed Position Keyboard
FPK .... Flash Pack Ltd. [*Vancouver Stock Exchange symbol*]
FPK .... Folding Pocket Kodak [*Photography*] (ROG)
FPKC .... Fair Public Key Cryptosystem [*Telecommunications*]
FPL .... Faceplate [*Electronics*] (IAA)
FPL .... Family Protection League of USA [*Defunct*] (EA)
FPL .... Fatherland Party of Labor [*Bulgaria*] [*Political party*]
FPL .... Feline Panleukopenia
FPL .... Ferry-Porter Law [*Physics*]
FPL .... Field Flight Plan
FPL .... Field Processing Language (IAA)
FPL .... Filed Flight Plan (DA)
FPL .... Filed Flight Plan Message [*Aviation code*]
FPL .... File Parameter List [*Computer science*] (IAA)
FPL .... Final Parts List (MCD)
FPL .... Final Protective Line [*Military*]
FPL .... Findlay-Hancock County District Public Library, Findlay, OH [*OCLC symbol*] (OCLC)
FPL .... Fireplace [*Real estate*]
FPL .... Fire Plug (AAG)
FPL .... Fisons Pharmaceuticals Ltd.
FPL .... Flexor Pollicis Longus [*Anatomy*]
FPL .... Flight Propulsion Laboratory
FPL .... Floor Plate [*Technical drawings*]
FPL .... Florida Power & Light Co. [*NYSE symbol*] (SPSG)
FPL .... Fluid Power Laboratory [*Ohio State University*] [*Research center*] (RCD)
FPL .... Forced-Choice Preferential Looking
FPL .... Forest Pest Leaflets
FPL .... Forest Products Laboratory [*Department of Agriculture*]
FPL .... Foxbro Programming Language (OA)
FPL .... Fox Programming Language
FPL .... FPI Ltd. [*Toronto Stock Exchange symbol*]
FPL .... FPL Group [*NYSE symbol*] (TTSB)
FPL .... FPL Group, Inc. [*NYSE symbol*] (SPSG)
FPL .... Fragmenta Poetarum Latinorum Epicorum et Lyricorum [*A publication*] (OCD)
FPL .... Frente Popular de Liberacion, Nueve de Mayo [*Honduras*] [*Political party*] (EY)
FPL .... Frequency Phase Lock
FPL .... Fuerzas Populares de Liberacion Farabundo Marti [*Farabundo Marti Popular Liberation Forces*] [*El Salvador*] (PD)
FPL .... Full Performance Level [*Aviation*] (FAAC)
FPL .... Full Power Level [*NASA*] (NASA)
FPL .... Full Power Load [*NASA*]
FPL .... Functional Problem Log [*Computer science*] (OA)
FPL .... Functional Programming Language [*Computer science*]
FPLA .... Fair Packaging and Labeling Act [*1966*]
FPLA .... Field Programmable Logic Array [*Computer science*]
fpla .... Fireplace [*Real estate*]
F (Plan) .... Fiber Plan [*Used in title of book advocating a high-fiber diet*]
FPLC .... Fast Performance Liquid Chromatography [*Analytical chemistry*]
FPLC .... Fast Protein, Peptide, and Polynucleotide Liquid Chromatography
FPLCE .... Fireplace [*Real estate*] (WDAA)
FPLE .... Field-Programmable Logic Element [*Military*]
FPLET .... Fixed-Price Level of Effort Term (AAGC)
FPLF .... Field Programmable Logic Family (TEL)
FPL Gp .... FPL Group, Inc. [*Associated Press*] (SAG)
FPLIF .... Field Pack, Large, with Internal Frame [*Army*] (INF)
FPLMTS .... Future Public Land Mobile Telecommunications System
FPLN .... Frente Patriotica de Libertacao Nacional [*Portugal*]
FPLP .... Frente Patriotico de Libertacao de Portugal [*Patriotic Front for the Liberation of Portugal*] [*Political party*] (PPE)
FPLPrA .... Fla Pwr&Lt $2 Pfd'A' [*NYSE symbol*] (TTSB)
FPLS .... Federal Parent Locator Service [*HEW*]
FPLS .... Field Programmable Logic Sequencer [*Computer science*] (HGAA)
FPM .... Facility Power Monitor (AAG)
FPM .... Fast-Page-Mode [*Computer science*] (PCM)
FPM .... Federal Personnel Manual
FPM .... Feet per Minute
fpm .... Feet Per Minute (WDMC)
FPM .... File Protect Memory [*Computer science*] (BUR)
FPM .... Filter Paper Microscopic [*Test*] [*Medicine*]
FPM .... Fine Particulate Matter [*Pisciculture*]
FPM .... Fissions per Minute
FPM .... Fixed-Payment Mortgage (DFIT)
FPM .... Flexible Payment Mortgage
FPM .... Flight Path Marker
FPM .... Floppy Disc Processor Module [*Transdata*] (NITA)
FPM .... Fluid Phase Marker
FPM .... Fluorocarbon elastomer [*Plastics technology*]

FPM............	Folding Platform Mechanism (MCD)	
FPM............	Force Packaging Methodology [*Military*]	
FPM............	Forest Pest Management [*Program*] [*Forest Service*]	
FPM............	Frames per Minute [*Telecommunications*] (IAA)	
FPM............	Fratres Presentationis Mariae [*Presentation Brothers - PB*] (EAIO)	
FPM............	Free Papau Movement [*Indonesia*] [*Political party*]	
FPM............	Frequency Position Modulation [*Telecommunications*] (IEEE)	
FPM............	Fuel Pump Monitor [*Automotive engineering*]	
FPM............	Functional Planning Matrices (IEEE)	
FPM............	Presentation Brothers (TOCD)	
FPM & SA ...	Food Processing Machinery and Supplies Association (EA)	
FPMB..........	Federation of Podiatric Medical Boards (EA)	
FPMC..........	Fixed Paper Metallized Capacitor	
FPMH..........	Failures per Million Hours [*Telecommunications*] (TEL)	
FPMI...........	Fellow of the Pensions Management Institute [*British*] (DBQ)	
FPMI...........	Forest Pest Management Institute [*Environment Canada*] [*Research center*] (RCD)	
FPMIS.........	Federal Personnel Management Information System [*Civil Service Commission*]	
FPML..........	Federal Personnel Management Letters [*Office of Personnel Management*] (GFGA)	
FPML..........	Forest Products Marketing Laboratory [*Forest Service*]	
FPMO..........	Free of Poundage Money Order	
FPMR..........	Federal Property Management Regulations	
FPMR..........	Fixed-Price Material Reimbursable (AAGC)	
FPMR..........	Frente Patriotico Manuel Rodriguez [*Manuel Rodriguez Patriotic Front*] [*Chile*] [*Political party*]	
FPMS..........	Federal Personnel Manual Systems (OICC)	
FPMS..........	Federal Productivity Measurement System [*Bureau of Labor Statistics*] (GFGA)	
FPMS..........	Flood Plain Management Services [*Army*]	
FPMS..........	Fueled Prototype Mock-Up System	
FPMT..........	Fund for the Preservation of the Mahyana Tradition [*An association*]	
F/Pn...........	Factor of Production [*Economics*]	
FPN............	Fairview Park [*Nevada*] [*Seismograph station code, US Geological Survey Closed*] (SEIS)	
FPN............	Falange Patria Nova [*New Fatherland Phalange*] [*Brazil*] (PD)	
FPN............	Fixed Pattern Noise [*Electronics*] (OA)	
FPN............	Frederick Point, AK [*Location identifier FAA*] (FAAL)	
FPN............	Frente Patriotico Nacional [*National Patriotic Front*] [*Nicaragua*] [*Political party*] (PPW)	
FPN............	Friends of Peace Now (EA)	
FPNA..........	First-Pass Nuclear Angiocardiography [*Cardiology*] (DAVI)	
FPNE..........	First Phone of New England [*Telecommunications service*] (TSSD)	
FPNX..........	First Pacific Networks [*NASDAQ symbol*] (TTSB)	
FPNX..........	First Pacific Networks, Inc. [*NASDAQ symbol*] (SAG)	
FPO............	Federal Protective Officer [*General Services Administration*]	
FPO............	Federation of Professional Organisations [*British*] (DBA)	
FPO............	Federation of Prosthodontic Organizations (EA)	
FPO............	Field Placement Officer	
FPO............	Field Post Office [*Military British*]	
FPO............	Field Project Officer	
FPO............	Fire Prevention Officer [*British*]	
FPO............	Fixed Path of Operation	
FPO............	Fixed Point Operation	
FPO............	Fixed Price Open	
FPO............	Fleet Post Office [*Navy*]	
FPO............	Forces Post Office [*Military British*]	
FPO............	For Position Only (WDAA)	
FPO............	FPA Corp. [*AMEX symbol*] (SPSG)	
FPO............	Freeport [*Bahamas*] [*Airport symbol*] (OAG)	
FPO............	Freezing Point Osmometer	
FPO............	Freiheitliche Partei Oesterreichs [*Liberal Party of Austria (or Austrian Freedom Party)*] [*Political party*] (PPW)	
FPO............	Frequency Planning Organisation [*Telecommunications British*]	
FPO............	Fuel Pressure Out	
FPO............	Fuerza Popular Organizada [*Organized Popular Force*] [*Guatemala*] [*Political party*] (PPW)	
FPO............	Future Projects Office [*NASA*]	
FPOA..........	Federal Probation Officers Association (EA)	
FPOA..........	Federation of Professional Officers Association (AIE)	
FPOA..........	Fentanyl/Pancuronium/Oxygen Anesthesia	
FPOA..........	Florida Peace Officers Association (SRA)	
FPoCG........	Charlotte-Glades Library System, Port Charlotte, FL [*Library symbol Library of Congress*] (LCLS)	
FPODA........	Fixed Priority Oriented Demand Assignment [*Telecommunications*] (OSI)	
FPOE..........	First Port of Entry (AFM)	
F/POL.........	Fire Policy [*Insurance*] (DCTA)	
FPOM..........	Fine Particulate Organic Matter	
FPOT..........	Facility Power Out Test (KSC)	
FPOT..........	Feedback Potentiometer (MSA)	
FPOV	Fuel Preburner and Oxidizer Valve (MCD)	
FPP............	Facility Power Panel (AAG)	
FPP............	Family Planning Program (WDAA)	
FPP............	Farnesyl Pyrophosphate [*Biochemistry*]	
FPP............	Fast Prepotential [*Neurophysiology*]	
FPP............	Feral Pests Program (EERA)	
FPP............	Fetal Protection Policy [*Insurance*] (WYGK)	
FPP............	Firepower Potential (AABC)	
FPP............	Fixed-Path Protocol [*Telecommunications*]	
FPP............	Fixed-Pitch Propeller (PDAA)	
FPP............	Fixed Point Protocol (NITA)	
FPP............	Flight Preparation Ltd. [*British ICAO designator*] (FAAC)	
FPP............	Floating Point Process (NITA)	

FPP............	Floating-Point Processor [*Computer science*]	
FPP............	Food Processing and Packaging (IMH)	
FPP............	Force Planning Package [*Military*] (RDA)	
FPP............	Foster Parents' Plan (EA)	
FPP............	Freon Pump Package (MCD)	
FPP............	Friends of Palestinian Prisoners (EA)	
FPP............	Friends of Peace Pilgrim (EA)	
FPP............	Panama Public Forces	
FPPA..........	Farmland Protection Policy Act (GNE)	
FPPA..........	Foster Parents Plan of Australia	
FPPA..........	Porto Alegre [*Sao Tome*] [*ICAO location identifier*] (ICLI)	
FPPC..........	Fair Political Practices Commission (OICC)	
FPPC..........	Flight Plan Processing Center [*Aviation*] (IAA)	
FPPCA	Fuel and Purchased Power Cost Adjustment	
FPPH..........	Fire Protection Pumphouse [*Nuclear energy*] (NRCH)	
FPPI...........	Frozen Potato Products Institute (EA)	
FPPO..........	Federation of Postal Police Officers [*Defunct*] (EA)	
FPPOD........	Financial Planners and Planning Organizations Directory [*A publication*]	
FPPPH........	Foundation for the Preservation and Protection of the Przewalski Horse (EA)	
FPPR	Fishpaper [*Insulation*]	
FPPR	Fixed Price, Price Redetermination [*or Revision*]	
FPPR	Fluorescence Pattern Photobleaching Recovery [*for study of surfaces*]	
FPPR	Principe [*Principe*] [*ICAO location identifier*] (ICLI)	
FPPS..........	Flight Plan Processing System [*British*]	
FPPS..........	Flight Plan Progressing System (OA)	
FPPS..........	Full-Page Phototypesetting System (DGA)	
FPPTE........	Federation of Public Passenger Transport Employees [*British*] (DCTA)	
FPPVS	Fuel Pool Pump Ventilation System [*Nuclear energy*] (NRCH)	
FPQA	Fixed Portion Queue Area [*Computer science*]	
FPQI..........	Federal Plant Quarantine Inspectors National Association [*Later, NAAE*]	
FPQINA........	Federal Plant Quarantine Inspectors National Association [*Later, NAAE*] (EA)	
FPR............	Failure/Problem Report	
FPR............	Fan Pressure Ratio [*Aviation*]	
FPR............	Farm Publications Reports (EA)	
FPR............	Federal Procurement Regulations	
FPR............	Feet per Revolution	
FPR............	Field Personnel Record	
FPR............	Final Progress Report	
FPR............	Financial Public Relations Consultants Retained	
FPR............	Fission Product Release [*Nuclear energy*] (NUCP)	
FPR............	Fixed Point Representation	
FPR............	Fixed Price Redeterminable (NG)	
FPR............	Fixed Problem Report (MCD)	
FPR............	Flat-Plate Radiometer	
FPR............	Flexible Plastic Reactor (NRCH)	
FPR............	Flight Performance Propellant Reserve (MCD)	
FPR............	Flight Performance Reserve	
FPR............	Floating-Point Register	
FPR............	Floating-Point Routine	
FPR............	Fluid Properties Research, Inc.	
FPR............	Fluorescence Photobleaching Recovery	
FPR............	Foliage Penetration RADAR	
FPR............	Folin Phenol Reagent [*For protein assay*]	
FPR............	Force Program Review [*DoD*]	
FPr............	Ford Motor 8.40% Cv Dep Pfd [*NYSE symbol*] (TTSB)	
FPR............	Fort Pierce, FL [*Location identifier FAA*] (FAAL)	
FPR............	Fractional Proximal Resorption [*Medicine*] (DMAA)	
FPR............	Fragmenta Poetarum Romanorum [*A publication*] (OCD)	
FPR............	Frente Patriotico para la Revolucion [*Patriotic Front for the Revolution*] [*Nicaragua*] [*Political party*] (PPW)	
FPR............	Frente Popular Contra la Represion [*Popular Front Against Repression*] [*Honduras*] [*Political party*] (PD)	
FPR............	Fuel Pump Relay [*Automotive engineering*]	
FPR............	Fuerza Aerea del Peru [*ICAO designator*] (FAAC)	
FPR............	Fuerzas Populares Revolucionarias Lorenzo Zelaya [*Lorenzo Zelaya Popular Revolutionary Forces*] [*Honduras*] [*Political party*] (PD)	
FPR............	Full Power Response	
FPR............	Full Propellant Requirement	
FPR............	Functional and Performance Requirements (MCD)	
FPRA..........	Federation of Private Residents' Associations [*British*] (DBA)	
FPRA..........	Fifty-Plus Runners Association (EA)	
FPRA..........	Financial Public Relations Association [*Later, BMA*] (EA)	
FPRA..........	First-Pass Radionuclide Angiogram [*Medicine*]	
FPRA..........	Fixed Price Redeterminable Article	
FPRA..........	Florida Public Relations Association (SRA)	
FPRA..........	Forward Pricing Rate Agreement	
FPRAC........	Federal Prevailing Rate Advisory Committee [*Washington, DC*] (EGAO)	
FPRB	Food Prices Review Board	
FPrB..........	Ford Motor Dep'B'Pfd [*NYSE symbol*] (TTSB)	
FPRC..........	Fixed Price Redetermination Contract	
FPRC..........	Fluid Power Research Center [*Oklahoma State University*] [*Research center*] (RCD)	
FPRC..........	Flying Personnel Research Committee [*British*] (MCD)	
FPRC..........	For Possible Reclearance [*Aviation*] (FAAC)	
FPRDC........	Food Protein Research and Development Center [*Texas A & M University*]	
FPRF..........	Fats and Proteins Research Foundation (EA)	
FPRF..........	Fireproof (AABC)	

FP-RF .... Flash Photolysis-Resonance Fluorescence Technique [*Physics*]
FPRF .... Fusion Plasma Research Facility [*Department of Energy*]
FPRI .... Fellow of the Plastics and Rubber Institute [*British*] (DBQ)
FPRL .... Fish Pesticide Research Laboratory [*Department of the Interior*]
FPRL .... Forest Products Research Laboratory [*British*]
FPRM .... Flexible Parts Repair Material [*Automotive engineering*]
FPRO .... Federal-Provincial Relations Office [*Canada*]
F-PROM ...... Field-Programmable Read-Only Memory [*Computer science*] (MCD)
FPRP .... Fixed-Price-Redeterminable-Prospective (MCD)
FPRR .... Fixed-Price-Redeterminable-Retroactive (MCD)
FPRRE .... Foundation for Public Relations Research and Education (EA)
FPRS/S .... Fabry-Perot Recycling Spectrometer (PDAA)
FPRS .... Federal Property Resources Service [*General Services Administration*]
FPRS .... Federation of Professional Railway Staff [*A union*] [*British*]
FPRS .... Forest Products Radio Service
FPRS .... Forest Products Research Society (EA)
FPRY .... First Financial Bancorp, Inc. Florida [*NASDAQ symbol*] (SAG)
FPRY .... First Finl Bancorp [*NASDAQ symbol*] (TTSB)
FPS .... Faculty of Physicians and Surgeons [*British*] (ROG)
FPS .... Fast Packet Switching [*Telecommunications*]
FPS .... Fast-Payback System (MCD)
FPS .... Fauna Preservation Society [*Later, FFPS*] (EA)
FPS .... Favorite Picture Selection [*Photo CD feature*] (PCM)
FPS .... Federal Prison System (MCD)
FPS .... Federal Protective Service [*General Services Administration*]
FPS .... Federation of Piling Specialists [*British*] (DBA)
FPS .... Feet per Second
fps .... Feet per Second (IDOE)
FPS .... Fellow of the Pathological Society of Great Britain
FPS .... Fellow of the Pharmaceutical Society [*British*]
FPS .... Fellow of the Philological Society [*British*]
FPS .... Fellow of the Philosophical Society [*British*]
FPS .... Fellow of the Physical Society [*British*]
FPS .... Fell Pony Society [*British*] (BI)
FPS .... Ferrite Phase Shifter
FPS .... Field Power Supply
FPS .... Field Printing Squadron
FPS .... Financial Planning System [*IBM Corp.*]
FPS .... Fine Particle Society (EA)
FPS .... Fire Protection System [*Nuclear energy*] (NRCH)
FPS .... Fire Protection System
FPS .... First Preferred Stock [*Investment term*]
FPS .... Fiscal Pay Services of Armies [*World War II*]
FPS .... Fixed Pattern Signal [*Optics*]
FPS .... Fixed Plasma Sheath
FPS .... Fixed Point Station [*RADAR*]
FPS .... Fixed Point System
FPS .... Fixed Price Supply
FPS .... Flashes per Second (IAA)
FPS .... Flash Photolysis System
FPS .... Flight Path Stabilization (MCD)
FPS .... Flight per Second (NASA)
FPS .... Flight Power Subsystem
FPS .... Flight Preparation Sheet (MCD)
FPS .... Flight Progress Strip [*Aviation*]
FPS .... Floating-Point Systems, Inc.
FPS .... Fluid Power Society (EA)
FPS .... Fluid Power Supply
FPS .... Fluid Power System
FPS .... Fluid Purification System
FPS .... Fluor Power Services, Inc. (NRCH)
FPS .... Focus Projection and Scanning
FPS .... Foot-Pound-Second [*System*]
fps .... Foot-Pound-Second (IDOE)
FPS .... Forces Postal Service [*British*]
FPS .... Forward Power Supply (MCD)
FPS .... Foundation for the Private Sector [*San Diego, CA*] (EA)
fps .... Frame per Second (IDOE)
FPS .... Frames per Second [*Computer science*]
fps .... Frames Per Second [*Electronics*]
fps .... Frames Per Second (WDMC)
FPS .... Franciscan Preparatory Seminary
FPS .... Francophone Primatological Society [*See also SFDP*] [*Plelan Le Grand, France*] (EAIO)
FPS .... Friction Pendulum System [*for earthquake protection*]
FPS .... Front Populaire Soudanais [*Sudanese Popular Front*]
FPS .... Full Pressure Suit [*Aerospace*]
FPS .... Fusion Power Systems (MCD)
FPS .... Military Primary Radar [*FAA*] (TAG)
FPS1117 ...... Federal Procurement Disc [*Alde Publishing*] [*Information service or system*] (IID)
FPSA .... Florida Pool and Spa Association (SRA)
FPSB .... Federation of Performance Sheep Breeders [*Australia*]
FPSB .... Financial Products Standards Board (EA)
FPSC .... Family Policy Studies Centre [*British*] (CB)
FPSC .... Foreign Petroleum Supply Committee [*Terminated, 1976*]
FPSC .... Forest Products Safety Conference (EA)
FPSC .... Forum Public Speaking Clubs [*Australia*]
FPSG .... Focus Policy Study Group [*British*]
FPSG .... Food Processors and Suppliers Group (EAIO)
F(PS)G .... Forum (Public Speaking) Group [*Australia*]
FPSK .... Frequency and Phase Shift Keying
FPSL .... Fission Product Screening Loop [*Nuclear energy*] (NRCH)
FPSLST .... Fluharty Preschool Speech and Language Screening Test (DAVI)

FPSM .... Fleet Program Support Material
FPSM .... Foot-Pound-Second Magnetic System (IAA)
FPSNW .... File and Print Service for NetWare [*Computer science*]
FPSO .... Flight Project Support Office [*Jet Propulsion Laboratory*]
FPSO .... Floating Production, Storage, and Offloading System [*Petroleum technology*]
FPSO .... Forms and Publications Supply Office [*Military*] (CINC)
FPSP .... Federation of Postal Security Police [*Later, FPPO*] (EA)
FPSP .... (Fluoropropyl)spiperone [*Organic chemistry*]
FPSP .... Future Problem Solving Program (EA)
FPSPS .... Feet per Second per Second
FPS/S .... Feet per Second per Second
FP-ST .... Flash Photolysis-Shock Tube Experiment [*For study of chemical kinetics*]
FPST .... Sao Tome [*Sao Tome*] [*ICAO location identifier*] (ICLI)
FPSTU .... Full Pressure Suit Training Unit [*Military*]
FPSV .... Fixed Platform Supply Vessel
FPSV .... Flow Path Selector Valve (MCD)
FPT .... Fan-Powered Terminal (DAC)
FPT .... Feedwater Pump Turbine [*Nuclear energy*] (NRCH)
FPT .... Female Pipe Thread (MSA)
FPT .... File Parameter Table (IAA)
FPT .... Fine Pitch Technology [*Engineering*]
FPT .... Finite Perturbation Theory [*Physics*]
FPT .... First Preferred Trust [*Vancouver Stock Exchange symbol*]
FPT .... Fitted Parts Tag (SAA)
FPT .... Fixed Parenchymal Turnover [*Physiology*] (DAVI)
FPT .... Fixed Price Tenders [*Commerce*] (BARN)
FPT .... Fleet Project Team (DNAB)
FPT .... Flight Plan Talker [*Aviation*] (SAA)
FPT .... Fluidic Proportional Thruster
FPT .... Forced Perfect Termination [*Computer science*]
FPT .... Forward Peak Tank [*On ships*]
FPT .... Foundation for Physical Therapy (EA)
FPT .... Four Picture Test [*Psychology*]
FPT .... Franklin Principal Maturity [*NYSE symbol*] (SPSG)
FPT .... Free Plasma Trytophan (PDAA)
FPT .... Freight Pass-Through [*Publishing*]
FPT .... Fruit Pressure Tester
FPT .... Full Period Termination (CAAL)
FPT .... Full Power Trial
FPT .... Functional Performance Time
FPT .... Functional Program Translator [*Computer science*]
FPT .... Fundamental Parameters Technique
FPTA .... Forest Products Traffic Association (EA)
FPTA .... Fully Proceduralized Troubleshooting Aids [*Military*]
FPTC .... Forest Products Trucking Council (EA)
FPTE .... Facility Portable Test Equipment (AAG)
FPTF .... Fuel Performance Test Facility (IAA)
FPTG .... Free Patellar Tendon Graft [*Sports medicine*]
FPTO .... Fluid Power Take-Off [*Hydraulic transmissions*]
FPTP .... First Past the Post [*Electoral system*] [*British*] (ECON)
FPTP .... Flight Proof Test Plan (AAG)
FPTPI .... Fiberglass Petroleum Tank and Pipe Institute (EA)
FPTS .... Fixed Point Test Site [*Military*] (CAAL)
FPTS .... Forward Propagation by Tropospheric Scatter [*Radio communications technique*]
FPTU .... Federation of Progressive Trade Unions [*Zanzibar*]
FPU .... Film Production Unit [*British military*] (DMA)
FPU .... Filter Paper Units [*Pulp and paper technology*]
FPU .... First Production Unit
FPU .... Floating-Point Unit [*Computer science*] (MCD)
FPU .... Florida Public Utilities [*AMEX symbol*] (TTSB)
FPU .... Florida Public Utilities Co. [*AMEX symbol*] (SPSG)
FPU .... Folkepartiets Ungdomsforbund [*Liberal Youth*] [*Political party*] (EAIO)
FPU .... Francis Peak [*Utah*] [*Seismograph station code, US Geological Survey*] (SEIS)
FPU .... Frente del Pueblo Unido [*Bolivia*] [*Political party*] (EY)
FPU .... Fuel Purification Unit [*Aerospace*] (AAG)
FPU .... Future Publication Uncertain
FPUA .... Food Preservers' Union of Australia
FPUO .... For Personal Use Only
FPUP .... Federal Photovoltaics Utilization Program [*Department of Energy*]
FPUR .... For the Purpose Of
FPUWA .... Food Preservers' Union of Western Australia
FPV .... Feed Water Regulation Valve (IEEE)
FPV .... Feline Panleukopenia Virus
FPV .... Financial Planning Volume
FPV .... Fishery Protection Vessel
FPV .... Flow Proportioning Value (MCD)
FPV .... Fowl Plague Virus
FPV .... Free Piston Vessel (GFGA)
FPV .... French Polydor Variable Micrograde [*Record label*]
FPV .... Front Progressiste Voltaique [*Upper Volta Progressive Front*] [*Political party*] (PPW)
FPV .... Functional Proofing Vehicle
FPVB .... Femoral Popliteal Vein Bypass [*Medicine*]
FPVC .... Flexible Polyvinyl Chloride [*Plastics*]
FPVN .... Vila Das Neves [*Sao Tome*] [*ICAO location identifier*] (ICLI)
FPVPC .... Federation of Paint and Varnish Production Clubs [*Later, FSCT*]
FPV/S .... Floating Production Vessel/System (DS)
FPW .... Fields Point [*Washington*] [*Seismograph station code, US Geological Survey*] (SEIS)
FPW .... Firing Port Weapon
FPW .... Flat Pack Welder

FPW	Free Progressive Wave
FPWA	Federation of Professional Writers of America (EA)
FPWA	Federation of Protestant Welfare Agencies (EA)
FPWA	Further Particulars When Available
FPWR	Fountain Powerboats [NASDAQ symbol] (SAG)
FPWS	Flat Pack Welder System
FPWSAC	Fluoridation of Public Water Supplies Advisory Committee [New South Wales, Australia]
FPWT	Fire Protection Water Tank (IEEE)
FPWT	Fuel Pool Water Treatment [Nuclear energy] (NRCH)
FPX	Fortune Petroleum [AMEX symbol] (TTSB)
FPX	Fortune Petroleum Corp. [AMEX symbol] (SPSG)
FPY	Failures per Year [Telecommunications] (TEL)
FPY	Perry, FL [Location identifier FAA] (FAAL)
FPZ	Fluphenazine [Tranquilizer]
FPZ	Free Port Zone [Shipping] (DS)
FPZ-D	Fluphenazine Decanoate [Tranquilizer] (DAVI)
fq----	Africa, Equatorial [MARC geographic area code Library of Congress] (LCCP)
FQ	Air Aruba [ICAO designator] (AD)
FQ	Compagnie Aerienne du Languedoc [ICAO designator] (AD)
FQ	Fare Quotation [Airline]
FQ	Film Quarterly [A publication] (BRI)
FQ	First Quarter [Moon phase]
FQ	Fiscal Quarter (AFM)
FQ	Flight Qualification
FQ	Formal Qualification
FQ	Frequency [Online database field identifier]
FQ	Fused Quartz
FQA	Field Quality Audit (IAA)
FQAG	Angoche [Mozambique] [ICAO location identifier] (ICLI)
FQ & P	Flight Qualities and Performance
FQBE	Beira [Mozambique] [ICAO location identifier] (ICLI)
FQBI	Bilene [Mozambique] [ICAO location identifier] (ICLI)
FQBR	Beira [Mozambique] [ICAO location identifier] (ICLI)
FQC	Foret Quality Class (EERA)
FQCB	Cuamba [Mozambique] [ICAO location identifier] (ICLI)
FQCH	Chimoio [Mozambique] [ICAO location identifier] (ICLI)
FQCY	Frequency (WGA)
FQDN	Fully-Qualified Domain Name [Internet]
FQE	Free Queue Element (IAA)
FQE	Fuqua Enterprises [NYSE symbol] (SAG)
FQES	Estima [Mozambique] [ICAO location identifier] (ICLI)
FQF	Front du Quebec Francais
FQFU	Furancungo [Mozambique] [ICAO location identifier] (ICLI)
FQG	University of Miami, Coral Gables, FL [OCLC symbol] (OCLC)
FQGI	Fully Qualified Generic Identifier
FQH	Filled Quartz Helix
FQHE	Fractional Quantum Hall Effect [Solid-state physics]
FQI	Federal Quality Institute [Office of Management and Budget] (GFGA)
FQI	Flight Qualification Instrumentation (MCD)
FQI	Fuel Quantity Indicator
FQIA	Inhaca [Mozambique] [ICAO location identifier] (ICLI)
FQIL	Fused Quartz Incandescent Lamp
FQIN	Inhambane [Mozambique] [ICAO location identifier] (ICLI)
FQIS	Fuel Quantity Indicating System [Aviation]
FQL	Formal Query Language (NITA)
FQL	Functional Query Language [1978] [Computer science] (CSR)
FQLC	Lichinga [Mozambique] [ICAO location identifier] (ICLI)
FQLU	Lumbo [Mozambique] [ICAO location identifier] (ICLI)
FQM	Four-Quadrant Multiplier
FQM	University of Miami, School of Medicine, Miami, FL [OCLC symbol] (OCLC)
FQMA	Maputo [Mozambique] [ICAO location identifier] (ICLI)
FQMD	Mueda [Mozambique] [ICAO location identifier] (ICLI)
FQML	Fort Worth Qualified Material List [NASA] (KSC)
FQMP	Mocimboa Da Praia [Mozambique] [ICAO location identifier] (ICLI)
FQMR	Marrupa [Mozambique] [ICAO location identifier] (ICLI)
FQMS	Farrier Quartermaster-Sergeant [British military] (DMA)
FQMU	Mutarara [Mozambique] [ICAO location identifier] (ICLI)
FQN	Family Quarters, Navy (DNAB)
FQNC	Nacala [Mozambique] [ICAO location identifier] (ICLI)
FQNP	Nampula [Mozambique] [ICAO location identifier] (ICLI)
FQP	Fundamental Questions Program (EERA)
FQPA	Flight Quality Photomultiplier Assembly
FQPB	Pemba [Mozambique] [ICAO location identifier] (ICLI)
FQPCID	Fully Qualified Procedure Correlation Identifier (ACRL)
FQPO	Ponta Do Ouro [Mozambique] [ICAO location identifier] (ICLI)
FQPR	Frequency Programmer (IEEE)
FQQL	Quelimane [Mozambique] [ICAO location identifier] (ICLI)
FQQPRI	Final Qualitative and Quantitative Personnel Requirements Information
FQR	Fabrication Quality Record
FQR	Flight Qualification Recorder (KSC)
FQR	Flight Qualification Reviews (MCD)
FQR	Formal Qualification Reviews (MCD)
FQR	Functional Qualification Review
FQS	Federal Quarantine Service (BARN)
FQS	Flight Qualified System (MCD)
FQS	Friendly Query System [IBM] (NITA)
FQSG	Songo [Mozambique] [ICAO location identifier] (ICLI)
FQT	Formal Qualification Test (KSC)
FQT	Frequent
FQT	Fused Quartz Tubing
FQTE	Tete [Mozambique] [ICAO location identifier] (ICLI)

FQTR	Flight Qualification Tape Recorder [NASA] (KSC)
FQTT	Tete/Chingozi [Mozambique] [ICAO location identifier] (ICLI)
FQUG	Ulongwe [Mozambique] [ICAO location identifier] (ICLI)
FQV	Plattsburgh, NY [Location identifier FAA] (FAAL)
FQVL	Vilanculos [Mozambique] [ICAO location identifier] (ICLI)
FQXA	Xai-Xai [Mozambique] [ICAO location identifier] (ICLI)
FR	Facilities Report [or Request]
FR	Faculty of Radiologists
FR	Faculty Rating
FR	Failure Rate
FR	Failure Report
FR	Fair (ROG)
fr	Faire Reporter [Carry Over] [Stock exchange term French]
FR	Fall River [Diocesan abbreviation] [Massachusetts] (TOCD)
FR	Family Room [Real estate]
FR	Family Rosary (EA)
FR	Fanaroff-Riley [Radio galaxy]
FR	Fargo Resources Ltd. [Vancouver Stock Exchange symbol]
FR	Fast Recovery
FR	Fast Release [Relay]
FR	Father
FR	Father
FR	Fatigue Resistant
FR	Feather River [AAR code]
FR	Federal Region [Dialog] [Searchable field] [Information service or system] (NITA)
FR	Federal Register [A publication]
FR	Federal Reporter [A publication] (DLA)
FR	Federal Representative [Job Training and Partnership Act] (OICC)
FR	Federal Republic (EY)
FR	Federal Reserve
FR	Ferry Range (MCD)
FR	Fiber Reinforced (MCD)
FR	Fibrinogen-Related [Hematology] (DAVI)
FR	Fibron-Related [Hematology] (DAVI)
FR	Field Relay (IAA)
FR	Field Report
FR	Field Resistance (DEN)
FR	Field Retrofit (MCD)
FR	Field Reversing (AAG)
FR	Fighter Reconnaissance [Air Force]
FR	File Register
FR	Filing Requirement [IRS]
FR	Filmless Radiography (MCD)
FR	Film Recording
FR	Film Report (AFM)
FR	Final Release (AAG)
FR	Final Report
FR	Final Rule [RSPA] (TAG)
FR	Finance Regulation [Economics]
F/R	Financial Responsibility
FR	Fineness Ratio
FR	Fireman Recruit [Navy rating]
FR	Fire Resistant [or Retardant]
FR	Fire Resistive
FR	Firing Room [NASA] (KSC)
FR	First Industrial Realty Trust, Inc. [NYSE symbol] (SAG)
FR	First Industrial Rlty Tr [NYSE symbol] (TTSB)
FR	First Reader
FR	First Renewal
FR	Fisher-Race Notation [Medicine] (MAE)
FR	Fixed Ratio
F/R	Fixed Response (WDAA)
FR	Flame Retardant
F/R	Flared Rudder (NASA)
FR	Flash Ranging
FR	Flat Rack Container [Shipping] (DS)
FR	Fleet Readiness [Navy] (AFIT)
FR	Fleet Reserve [Navy]
FR	Flight Readiness
FR	Flight Recorder (MCD)
FR	Flight Refueling (MCD)
FR	Flight Reliability (MCD)
FR	Flight Rule (MCD)
FR	Flocculation Reaction [Obsolete test for liver function]
FR	Flood Relief Punt [Coast Guard]
FR	Flow Rate
FR	Flow Recorder
FR	Flow Regulator [Nuclear energy] (NRCH)
FR	Fluid Resistant
FR	Fluorescence
fr	Fluorite [CIPW classification] [Geology]
FR	Folio Recto [Right-Hand Page] [Latin]
fr	Folio Recto [Right-hand page number] [Right-hand page] [Publishing] (WDMC)
FR	Food Ratio
FR	For [Telecommunications] (ADDR)
Fr	Foraminifera [Quality of the bottom] [Nautical charts]
FR	Forced Removal
FR	Force Release [Telecommunications] (TEL)
FR	Foreign [Searchable field] (NITA)
FR	Foreign Relations (DLA)
FR	Foreign Relations Committee [US Senate]
FR	Foreign Requirements
FR	Forest Rangers [British military] (DMA)

FR............	Forest Reserve [*State*] (EERA)
FR............	Formation Pennant [*Navy British*]
FR............	Forming Rolls (MCD)
FR............	Fort (ROG)
FR............	Forum Romanum [*The Roman Forum*]
FR............	Fossil Record
FR............	Fractional Reabsorption [*Biochemistry*] (DAVI)
fr.............	Fracture [*Orthopedics*] (DAVI)
Fr............	Fragmenta [*of Aristotle*] [*Classical studies*] (OCD)
FR............	Fragmentum [*Fragment*] [*Latin*] (ROG)
FR............	Frame (MSA)
fr.............	Frame (WDMC)
FR............	Frame Relay (ACRL)
FR............	Frame Reset [*Telecommunications*] (TEL)
FR............	Framework Region [*Genetics*]
FR............	Franc [*Monetary unit*] [*France*] (EY)
FR............	France [*ANSI two-letter standard code*] (CNC)
fr.............	France [*MARC country of publication code Library of Congress*] (LCCP)
Fr............	France (VRA)
Fr............	Franciscus de Telese [*Flourished, 1270-82*] [*Authority cited in pre-1607 legal work*] (DSA)
Fr............	Francium [*Chemical element*]
Fr............	Franklin [*Also, sC, statC*] [*Unit of electric charge*]
fr.............	Frankline (IDOE)
FR............	Frater [*Brother*] [*Latin*]
FR............	Fraud [*Legal shorthand*] (LWAP)
FR............	Free (ADA)
Fr............	Freeman's English King's Bench and Chancery Reports [*A publication*] (DLA)
FR............	Free Response
FR............	Free Ribosomes [*Cytology*]
FR............	Freight Release
Fr............	French [*Catheter gauge*] [*Medicine*] (DAVI)
FR............	French
FR............	French Research [*Satellite*]
FR............	French Review [*A publication*] (BRI)
FR............	French Rite [*Freemasonry*] (ROG)
FR............	Frequency Measuring Devices [*JETDS nomenclature*] [*Military*] (CET)
FR............	Frequency Range
FR............	Frequency Rate (WDAA)
FR............	Frequency Response
FR............	Frequent
FR............	Fresh
FR............	Friar
F$_r$............	Frictional Force (DA)
FR............	Friday
FR............	Frigate
fr.............	Frigorie [*Unit of rate of extraction of heat*] [*Thermodynamics*]
FR............	From (AFM)
fr.............	From (VRA)
fr.............	From (WDMC)
FR............	Front
FR............	Front Engine, Rear Drive [*Automotive engineering*]
FR............	Frontispiece [*Publishing*]
F/R...........	Front/Rear
FR............	Fructus [*Fruit*] [*Latin*] (ROG)
fr.............	Fruit
FR............	Fuel Remaining [*Aviation*]
FR............	Fuerza Republicana [*Argentina Political party*] (EY)
FR............	Full Range (MCD)
FR............	Full-Rate [*Telegrams and cables*]
FR............	Fully Registered
FR............	Functional Requirements
FR............	Fundamental Resonance (MCD)
FR............	Fund for the Republic [*Later, Robert Maynard Hutchins Center for the Study of Democratic Institutions*] (EA)
FR............	Funding Request
FR............	Fund Raising [*Red Cross*]
FR............	Furlough Rations [*Army*]
FR............	Furness Railway [*Scotland*]
fr----	Rift Valley [*MARC geographic area code Library of Congress*] (LCCP)
FR............	Susquehanna [*ICAO designator*] (AD)
FRA...........	Farah, Inc. [*NYSE symbol*] (SPSG)
FRA...........	Father's Rights of America (EA)
FRA...........	Federal Radio Act (NITA)
FRA...........	Federal Railroad Administration
FRA...........	Federal Railway Administration [*DOT*] (AAGC)
FRA...........	Federal Register Act (GFGA)
FRA...........	Federal Regular Army [*Federation of South Arabia*]
FRA...........	Federal Reports Act (DLA)
FRA...........	Federal Reserve Act [*1913*]
FRA...........	Fibrinogen-Related Antigen [*Immunology*]
FRA...........	File Recovery Area [*Computer science*] (ECII)
FRA...........	Financial Research Associates
FRA...........	Fire Retarding Additive
FRA...........	Flap Retraction Altitude (GAVI)
FRA...........	Fleet Reserve Association (EA)
FRA...........	Florida Redevelopment Association (SRA)
FRA...........	Flowrate Recording Alarm [*Engineering*]
FRA...........	Flow Recorder and Alarm [*Nuclear energy*] (NRCH)
FRA...........	Fluorescent Rabies Antibody [*Immunology*]
FRA...........	Footwear Retailers of America [*Later, FDRA*] (EA)

FRA...........	Force Recon Association (EA)
FRA...........	Foreign Resources Associates
FRA...........	Forward Rate Agreement [*Banking*]
FRA...........	Forward Refueling Area
FRA...........	Fos-Related Antigens [*Biochemistry*]
fra............	Frame (VRA)
FRA...........	Framycetin [*Neomycin B*] [*Antibacterial compound*]
FRA...........	France [*ANSI three-letter standard code*] (CNC)
FRA...........	France-Reunion-Avenir [*Political party*] (EY)
Fra............	Franciscus de Telese [*Flourished, 1270-82*] [*Authority cited in pre-1607 legal work*] (DSA)
Fra............	Francis' Maxims of Equity [*1722-46*] [*A publication*] (DLA)
FRA...........	Frankfurt [*Germany Airport symbol*] (OAG)
FRA...........	FR Aviation Ltd. [*British ICAO designator*] (FAAC)
FRA...........	Frente Radical Alfarista [*Radical Alfarista Front*] [*Ecuador*] [*Political party*] (PPW)
FRA...........	Friant, CA [*Location identifier FAA*] (FAAL)
FRA...........	Friction Reducing Agent [*Chemicals*]
FRA...........	Functional Residual Air (ADA)
FRA...........	Funded Reimburseable Authority (MCD)
FRAA..........	Fleet Repairables Assistance Agent (MCD)
FRAA..........	Fleet Reserve Association Auxiliary
FRAA..........	Furniture Rental Association of America (EA)
FRAACA.......	Foundation for Research in the Afro-American Creative Arts (EA)
Fra Ac F.....	Franciscus de Accursio (Filius) [*Deceased, 1293*] [*Authority cited in pre-1607 legal work*] (DSA)
FRAB..........	Banque Franco-Arabe d'Investissements Internationaux
FRAB..........	Fuel Receiving Air Blowers [*Nuclear energy*] (NRCH)
FRAC..........	Food Research and Action Center (EA)
FRAC..........	Fractal Design [*NASDAQ symbol*] (TTSB)
FRAC..........	Fractal Design Corp. [*NASDAQ symbol*] (SAG)
FRAC..........	Fractional (MSA)
FRAC..........	Fractionator Reflux Analog Computer
FRAC..........	Fracture [*Medicine*]
FRACA.........	Failure Reporting, Analyses, and Corrective Action (MCD)
FRACAS.......	Failure Reporting and Corrective Action System (MCD)
FRACAS.......	Filter Response Analysis for Continuously Accelerating Spacecraft [*NASA*]
FRACGP.......	Fellow of the Royal Australasian College of General Practitioners [*Medicine*] (DMAA)
FRACHE.......	Federation of Regional Accrediting Commissions of Higher Education [*Later, COPA*] (EA)
FRACO........	Fellow of the Royal Australasian College of Ophthalmologists [*Medicine*] (DMAA)
FRACO........	Framycetin [*Neomycin B*], Colistin [*Antineoplastic drug regimen*]
FRACON.......	Framycetin [*Neomycin B*], Colistin, Nystatin [*Antineoplastic drug regimen*]
FRACP........	Fellow of the Royal Australasian College of Physicians
FRACR........	Fellow of the Royal Australasian College of Radiologists
FRACS........	Fellow of the Royal Australasian College of Surgeons
FRACT.........	Fraction
FRACT.........	Fracture [*Medicine*]
Fractal.......	Fractal Design Corp. [*Associated Press*] (SAG)
FRACT DOS...	Fracti Dosi [*In Divided Doses*] [*Pharmacy*]
FRAD..........	Fellow of the Royal Academy of Dancing [*British*]
FRAD..........	Frame Relay Access Device [*Plantronics Futurecomms, Inc.*]
Fra de Sax...	Franciscus de Saxolinis [*Flourished, 13th century*] [*Authority cited in pre-1607 legal work*] (DSA)
Fra de Saxolis...	Franciscus de Saxolinis [*Flourished, 13th century*] [*Authority cited in pre-1607 legal work*] (DSA)
Fra de Te.....	Franciscus de Telese [*Flourished, 1270-82*] [*Authority cited in pre-1607 legal work*] (DSA)
Fra de Tels...	Franciscus de Telese [*Flourished, 1270-82*] [*Authority cited in pre-1607 legal work*] (DSA)
FRADU........	Fleet Requirements and Aircraft Direction Unit [*Navy*] (MCD)
FrAE..........	French Antarctic Expedition [*1903-05,1908-10,1948-*]
FRAeS........	Fellow of the Royal Aeronautical Society [*British*] (EY)
FRAF..........	Fuel Receiving Air Filters [*Nuclear energy*] (NRCH)
FRAG..........	Fragile
FRAG..........	Fragment [*Military*] (AFM)
FRAG..........	Fragment [*Used in correcting manuscripts, etc.*]
frag..........	Fragment (VRA)
Frag..........	Fragmentation [*Weapon*] (DOMA)
FRAG..........	French Fragrances [*NASDAQ symbol*] (TTSB)
FRAG..........	French Fragrances, Inc. [*NASDAQ symbol*] (SAG)
FRAGBOMB...	Fragmentation Bomb
FRAGM........	Fragments
FRAGNET......	Fragmented Network (MCD)
FRAGO........	Fragmentary Order [*Military*]
Fra Gon......	Franciscus Gonzaga [*Authority cited in pre-1607 legal work*] (DSA)
FRAGROC	Fragmenting Warhead Rocket
FRAgSs.......	Fellow of the Royal Agricultural Societies [*British*]
FRAH..........	Fluid Regenerative Air Heater (PDAA)
FRAI..........	Fellow of the Royal Anthropological Institute [*British*]
FRAIC........	Fellow of the Royal Architectural Institute of Canada
FRAIN........	Front Revolutionnaire Africain pour l'Independence Nationale des Colonies Portugaises [*African Revolutionary Front for the National Independence of Portuguese Colonies*]
FrAipNA......	Centre d'Etudes Nord-Americaines, Aix-En-Provence, France [*Library symbol Library of Congress*] (LCLS)
FRAK	Flak RADAR Automatic Kanon
FRALINE......	Fast Reaction Automatic Lightweight Inertial North-Seeking Equipment (PDAA)
FRAM..........	Failure Rate Assessment Machine (PDAA)
FRAM..........	Fellow of the Royal Academy of Music [*British*]

FRAM......... Ferroelectric Random Access Memory [*Computer science*]
FRAM......... Ferroelectronic RAM [*Random-Access Memory*] [*Ramtron*]
FRAM......... Fine Resolution Antarctic Model [*Oceanography*]
FRAM......... Fleet Modernization and Repair Program [*Navy*]
FRAM......... Fleet Rehabilitation and Maintenance
FRAM......... Fleet Rehabilitation and Modernization [*Navy*]　(MCD)
FRAM......... Fleet Replacement and Modernization [*Marine science*]　(OSRA)
Fra M......... Francis' Maxims of Equity [*1722-46*] [*A publication*]　(DLA)
FRAM......... Fusible Random Access Memory [*Computer science*]　(PDAA)
FRAM2....... Field Records Administration Microform Mode
FRAMATOME... Societe Franco-Americaine de Constructions Atomiques　(NRCH)
FRAME........ Frame Relay and Mux Expander [*Computer science*]
FRAME........ Fund for the Replacement of Animals in Medical Experiments
FRAMG........ Framing
Framingham St C... Framingham State College　(GAGS)
FRAMME...... Facilities Rule-Based Model Management Environment
FRAMP .... Fleet Readiness Aircraft Maintenance Personnel [*Navy*]　(MCD)
FRAMP .... Fleet Readiness Aviation Maintenance Personnel [*Navy*]
FRAMP .... Fleet Rehabilitation and Modernization Program [*Navy*]
FRAMP .... Frampton [*England*]
FRAMPO...... Frente Amplio Popular [*Broad Popular Front*] [*Panama*] [*Political party*]　(PPW)
FramS......... Framingham Savings Bank [*Associated Press*]　(SAG)
FramSv....... Framingham Savings Bank [*Associated Press*]　(SAG)
FRAN .... Fleet Readiness Analysis [*NORRS*]
FRAN .... Frame Structure Analysis　(IAA)
Fran............. Franciscus de Telese [*Flourished, 1270-82*] [*Authority cited in pre-1607 legal work*]　(DSA)
Fran............. Franciscus Vercellensis [*Flourished, 13th century*] [*Authority cited in pre-1607 legal work*]　(DSA)
Fran............. Franciscus Zabarella [*Deceased, 1417*] [*Authority cited in pre-1607 legal work*]　(DSA)
Fran Anz..... Franciscus Anzolellus [*Authority cited in pre-1607 legal work*]　(DSA)
Fran Anzol... Franciscus Anzolellus [*Authority cited in pre-1607 legal work*]　(DSA)
Fran Aret .... Franciscus de Accoltis de Aretio [*Deceased, 1486*] [*Authority cited in pre-1607 legal work*]　(DSA)
FRANC........ Franciscan [*Religious order*]　(WDAA)
Franc .... Franciscus de Telese [*Flourished, 1270-82*] [*Authority cited in pre-1607 legal work*]　(DSA)
Franc Ac...... Franciscus de Accursio [*Deceased, 1293*] [*Authority cited in pre-1607 legal work*]　(DSA)
FRANC AD MOEN... Francofurtum Ad Moenum [*Frankfort-On-The-Main*] [*Imprint*] [*Latin*]　(ROG)
Franc Anz .... Franciscus Anzolellus [*Authority cited in pre-1607 legal work*]　(DSA)
Franc Conn... Franciscus Connanus [*Deceased, 1551*] [*Authority cited in pre-1607 legal work*]　(DSA)
Franc de Are... Franciscus de Accoltis de Aretio [*Deceased, 1486*] [*Authority cited in pre-1607 legal work*]　(DSA)
Franc de Rampo... Franciscus de Ramponibus [*Deceased, 1401*] [*Authority cited in pre-1607 legal work*]　(DSA)
Franc de T... Franciscus de Telese [*Flourished, 1270-82*] [*Authority cited in pre-1607 legal work*]　(DSA)
Franc de Tel... Franciscus de Telese [*Flourished, 1270-82*] [*Authority cited in pre-1607 legal work*]　(DSA)
France .... France Growth Fund [*Associated Press*]　(SAG)
France .... France's Reports [*3-11 Colorado*] [*A publication*]　(DLA)
France (Colo)... France's Reports [*3-11 Colorado*] [*A publication*]　(DLA)
Fran Char .... Francis' Law of Charities [*2nd ed.*] [*1855*] [*A publication*]　(DLA)
Franchise LJ... Franchise Law Journal [*A publication*]　(DLA)
FRANCIS...... Fichier de Recherches Automatisees sur les Nouvautes, la Communication et l'Information en Sciences Sociales et Humaines [*French Retrieval Automated Network for Current Information in Social and Human Sciences*] [*Database*]
FRANCIS...... Food Research Association Computerized Information Service [*Food Research Association*] [*Database*]　(NITA)
Francis Bald... Franciscus Balduinus [*Deceased, 1572*] [*Authority cited in pre-1607 legal work*]　(DSA)
FRANCIS: DOGE... FRANCIS: Documentation Automatisee en Gestion des Entreprises [*Database*]
Francis Duar... Franciscus Duarenus [*Deceased, 1559*] [*Authority cited in pre-1607 legal work*]　(DSA)
Francis Max... Francis' Maxims of Equity [*1722-46*] [*A publication*]　(DLA)
FRANCIS: RESHUS... FRANCIS: Reseau Documentaire en Sciences Humaines de la Sante [*Database*] [*French*]
Francis Sonsb... Franciscus Sonsbeccius [*Flourished, 16th century*] [*Authority cited in pre-1607 legal work*]　(DSA)
Franc Judg... Francillon's County Court Judgments [*England*] [*A publication*]　(DLA)
FRANCOF..... Francofortium [*Frankfort*] [*Imprint*] [*Latin*]　(ROG)
Franc Coll LJ... Franciso College Law Journal [*A publication*]　(DLA)
Franc Viv..... Franciscus Vivius [*Flourished, 16th century*] [*Authority cited in pre-1607 legal work*]　(DSA)
Franc Zoannet... Franciscus Zoannettus [*Deceased, 1586*] [*Authority cited in pre-1607 legal work*]　(DSA)
FR and ASS... Fellow of the Royal and Antiquarian Societies [*British*]
FR & CC...... Free of Riots and Civil Commotions [*Insurance*]
Fran de Are... Franciscus de Accoltis de Aretio [*Deceased, 1486*] [*Authority cited in pre-1607 legal work*]　(DSA)
Fran de Rampo... Franciscus de Ramponibus [*Deceased, 1401*] [*Authority cited in pre-1607 legal work*]　(DSA)
FR & RC...... Family Resource and Referral Center [*National Council on Family Relations*] [*Information service or system*]　(IID)
Fran Duar.... Franciscus Duarenus [*Deceased, 1559*] [*Authority cited in pre-1607 legal work*]　(DSA)

Fr & W Prec... Frend and Ware's Precedents of Instruments Relating to the Transfer of Land to Railway Companies [*2nd ed.*] [*1866*] [*A publication*]　(DLA)
Fran Eng Law... Francillon's Lectures on English Law [*1860-61*] [*A publication*]　(DLA)
FranFin....... Franchise Finance Corp. of America [*Associated Press*]　(SAG)
FRANK .... Frequency Regulation and Network Keying　(IEEE)
FrankF .... Frankfort First Bankcorp, Inc. [*Associated Press*]　(SAG)
Franklin Pierce Law Sch... Franklin Pierce Law School　(GAGS)
Fran Max .... Francis' Maxims of Equity [*1722-46*] [*A publication*]　(DLA)
Fran Prec.... Francis' Common Law Precedents [*A publication*]　(DLA)
FRANS .... Family Resource and Network Support [*Australia*]
FRANS .... Franciscan
FRANSW..... Food Retailers' Association of New South Wales [*Australia*]
FRANSW..... Footwear Repairers' Association of New South Wales [*Australia*]
FRANTIC..... Formal Reliability Analysis Including Normal Testing, Inspection and Checking
Fran Vercell... Franciscus Vercellensis [*Flourished, 13th century*] [*Authority cited in pre-1607 legal work*]　(DSA)
FRANY .... Fashion Reporters Award - New York
FRANZ .... Fellow, Registered Accountant, New Zealand
FRANZCP.... Fellow of the Royal Australian and New Zealand College of Psychiatrists [*Medicine*]　(DMAA)
FRAP .... Fast Response Action Potential [*Psychology*]
FRAP .... Federal Rules of Appellate Procedure [*A publication*]
FRAP .... Fellow of the Royal Academy of Physicians [*British*]
FRAP .... Fire Rescue Air Pack [*NASA*]
FRAP .... Flat Response Audio Pickup
FRAP .... Fleet Readiness Assistance Program　(MCD)
FRAP .... Fleet Reliability Assessment Program [*Navy*]　(MCD)
FRAP .... Fluorescence Recovery [*or Redistribution*] after Photobleaching [*Analytical biochemistry*]
FRAP .... Fluoride-Resistant Acid Phosphatase [*An enzyme*]
FRAP .... Frente de Accion Popular [*Popular Action Front*] [*Chile*]
FRAP .... Frente Revolucionario Antifascista Patriotica [*Anti-Fascist and Patriotic Revolutionary Front*] [*Spain*]
FRAP .... Front d'Action Politique
FRAP .... Front Revolutionnaire d'Action Proletarienne [*Terrorist organization*] [*Belgium*]　(EY)
FRAP .... Fuel Rod Analysis Program [*Nuclear energy*]　(NRCH)
FRAP .... Fuerzas Revolucionarias Armadas Populares [*People's Revolutionary Armed Forces*] [*Mexico*]　(PD)
FRAPA .... Forest Products Accident Prevention Association
FRAPH .... Front for the Advancement and Progress of Haiti [*Political party*]
FRAPH .... Front for the Advancement and Progress of Haiti
FRAPRU ..... Front d'Action Populaire en Reamenagement Urbain [*Canada*]
FRAP-S ...... Fuel Rod Analysis Program - Steady-State [*Nuclear energy*]　(NRCH)
FRAP-T ...... Fuel Rod Analysis Program - Transient [*Nuclear energy*]　(NRCH)
FRAQ .... Footwear Repairers' Association of Queensland [*Australia*]
FRARM .... Firearm
Fr Ar Rev ... Fremantle Arts Review [*A publication*]
FRAS .... Fellow of the Royal Asiatic Society [*British*]
FRAS .... Fellow of the Royal Astronomical Society [*British*]
Fras .... Fraser's English Election Cases [*1776-77*] [*A publication*]　(DLA)
FRASA .... Footwear Repairers' Association of South Australia
FRASB .... Fellow of the Royal Asiatic Society of Bengal
FRASCO...... Foundation for Religious Action in the Social and Civil Order　(EA)
Fras Div...... Fraser's Conflict of Laws in Cases of Divorce [*A publication*]　(DLA)
Fras Dom Rel... Fraser on Personal and Domestic Relations [*Scotland*] [*A publication*]　(DLA)
FRASE .... Fellow of the Royal Agricultural Society of England
Fras Elec Cas... Fraser's English Election Cases [*1776-77*] [*A publication*]　(DLA)
Fraser......... Fraser's English Cases of Controverted Elections [*1776-77*] [*A publication*]　(DLA)
Fraser......... Fraser's Husband and Wife [*1876-78*] [*Scotland*] [*A publication*]　(DLA)
Fraser......... Fraser's Scotch Court of Sessions Cases, Fifth Series [*A publication*]　(DLA)
Fraser (Scot)... Fraser's English Cases of Controverted Elections [*1776-77*] [*A publication*]　(DLA)
Fraser (Scot)... Scotch Court of Session Cases, Fifth Series, by Fraser [*A publication*]　(DLA)
Fras M & S... Fraser on Master and Servant in Scotland [*A publication*]　(DLA)
Fras Par & Ch... Fraser's Parent and Child [*Scotland*] [*A publication*]　(DLA)
FRAT.......... Fiber-Reinforced Advanced Titanium　(MCD)
FRAT.......... First Recorded Appearance Time　(SAA)
FRAT.......... Fraternity
FRAT.......... Fraternize　(DSUE)
FRAT.......... Free Radical Assay Technique [*Clinical chemistry*]
FRATS .... Frequency, Recency, Amount and Type [*Direct marketing*]　(WDMC)
FRATU .... Fleet Requirements and Aircraft Training Unit [*British military*]　(DMA)
FRAUD........ Fraudulent　(MSA)
FrAv........... Bibliotheque Calvet, Avignon, France [*Library symbol Library of Congress*]　(LCLS)
FRAV .... Footwear Repairers' Association of Victoria [*Australia*]
FRAWA .... Footwear Repairers' Association of Western Australia
fra(X).......... Fragile X [*Chromosome*] [*Genetics*]　(DAVI)
Fraz .... Frazer's Admiralty Cases, Etc. [*Scotland*] [*A publication*]　(DLA)
Fra Za .... Franciscus Zabarella [*Deceased, 1417*] [*Authority cited in pre-1607 legal work*]　(DSA)
Fraz Adm .... Frazer's Admiralty Cases, Etc. [*Scotland*] [*A publication*]　(DLA)
FRB............ FABS Reference Bible [*FABS International, Inc.*] [*Information service or system*]　(CRD)
FRB............ Failure Review Board [*NASA*]　(NASA)
FRB............ Failure to Return to Battery [*Study*]　(MCD)

FRB............	Fair Rents Board [*New South Wales, Australia*]
FRB............	Fast Rise Balloon
FRB............	Faultsman's Ring Back [*Telecommunications*] (NITA)
FRB............	Federal Reserve Banks [*of FRS*]
FRB............	Federal Reserve Board [*Later, BGFRS*]
FRB............	Federation of Radical Booksellers [*British*]
FRB............	Fiberglass Rotor Blade (MCD)
FRB............	Fireball Resources [*Vancouver Stock Exchange symbol*]
FRB............	Fire-Resistant Brick [*Technical drawings*]
FRB............	Fisheries Research Board of Canada [*Marine science*] (MSC)
FRB............	Fitness Reports Branch [*BUPERS*]
FRB............	Flight Rated Bioinstrumentation
FRB............	Forbes [*Australia Airport symbol*] (OAG)
FRB............	Forschungs-Reaktor Berlin
FRB............	Frobisher [*Northwest Territories*] [*Seismograph station code, US Geological Survey*] (SEIS)
Fr Baldui	Franciscus Balduinus [*Deceased, 1572*] [*Authority cited in pre-1607 legal work*] (DSA)
Fr Bank........	Frank on the United States Bankrupt Act of 1867 [*A publication*] (DLA)
Fr BB	Fracture of Both Bones [*Medicine*] (MAE)
FRBFC	Foggy River Boys Fan Club (EA)
FRBK	First Republic Bancorp [*NASDAQ symbol*] (SAG)
FRBRC	Fondation de Recherches sur les Blessures de la Route au Canada (EAIO)
FRBS	Fellow of the Royal Botanic Society [*British*]
FRBS	Fellow of the Royal Society of British Sculptors
FRBS	Frame Relay Bearer Service (ACRL)
FRBW	Federal Reserve Board Weekly [*Database*] [*I. P. Sharp Associates*] [*Information service or system*] (CRD)
FRC............	Control of Rents and Furnished Lets [*British*]
FRC............	Facility Review Committee
FRC............	Failure Recurrence Control (SAA)
FRC............	Family Research Council (EA)
FRC............	Family Resource Coalition (EA)
FRC............	Family Rosary Crusade [*Later, FR*] (EA)
FRC............	Fasteners Research Council [*Defunct*] (EA)
FRC............	Fatah Revolutionary Council [*Libyan-based terrorist organization*]
FRC............	Federal Radiation Council [*Defunct*] (EA)
FRC............	Federal Radio Commission [*Functions transferred to FCC, 1934*]
FRC............	Federal Ranch [*British Columbia*] [*Seismograph station code, US Geological Survey Closed*] (SEIS)
FRC............	Federal Records Center [*General Services Administration*] (AABC)
FRC............	Federal Records Council
FRC............	Federal Regional Center [*Office of Civil Defense*]
FRC............	Federal Regional Council [*for federal-state-local interchange*] [*Abolished, 1983*]
FRC............	Federal Reserve Bank of Philadelphia, Philadelphia, PA [*OCLC symbol*] (OCLC)
FRC............	Fiber-Reinforced Composite
FRC............	Field Reversed Configuration
FRC............	Filipino Rehabilitation Commission [*Post-World War II*]
FRC............	Final Routing Center [*Telecommunications*] (TEL)
FRC............	Financial Reporting Council (ODBW)
FRC............	First Republic Bancorp [*NYSE symbol*] (TTSB)
FRC............	First Republic Bancorp, Inc. [*NYSE symbol*] (SAG)
FRC............	Fishery Research Craft
FRC............	Fixed Radio Communication
FRC............	Flag Research Center (EA)
FRC............	Flat Rock Consultants, Inc. [*Information service or system*] (IID)
FRC............	Fletcher Challenge Finance Canada, Inc. [*Toronto Stock Exchange symbol*]
FRC............	Flight Research Center [*Later, DFRC*] [*NASA*]
FRC............	Flight Rule Computer [*Aviation*] (IAA)
FRC............	Flowers' Roguish Cultivator
FRC............	Flow Recorder Controller
FRC............	Force
FRC............	Forest Resources Committee [*Australia*]
FRC............	FORSCOM [*Forces Command*] Redistribution Center [*Army*]
FRC............	Franca [*Brazil*] [*Airport symbol*] (OAG)
FRC............	Franklin Research Center [*Research center*] (RCD)
FRC............	Frederick Research Center (KSC)
FRC............	Free Carrier [*Followed by a named point*] [*"INCOTERM," International Chamber of Commerce official code*]
FRC............	Free Residual Chlorine
FRC............	Frequency Response Curve
FRC............	Fresnel Reflection Coefficient [*Optics*]
FRC............	Front-Range Consortium [*Marine science*] (OSRA)
FRC............	Front-Range Consortium (USDC)
FRC............	Frozen Red Cells [*Medicine*]
FRC............	Fuels Research Council [*Defunct*]
FRC............	Functional Redundancy Check [*Computer science*]
FRC............	Functional Reserve [*or Residual*] Capacity [*of the lungs*] [*Physiology*]
FRC............	Request Full Route Clearance [*FAA*] (TAG)
FRC............	Spokane, WA [*Location identifier FAA*] (FAAL)
FRCA	Family Research Council of America [*Later, FRC*] (EA)
FRCA	Fellow of the Royal College of Art [*British*]
FRCA	Fire Retardant Chemicals Association (EA)
FRCAB	Felt Roofing Contractors' Advisory Board [*British*] (BI)
FRCAB	Flat Roofing Contractors Advisory Board [*British*] (DBA)
FR CAN	French-Canadian (WDAA)
FRCATS	Fellow of the Royal College of Advanced Technology, Salford [*British*]
FRCC	Federal Research Contract Center
FRCC	First Financial Caribbean [*NASDAQ symbol*] (TTSB)
FRCC	First Financial Caribbean Corp. [*NASDAQ symbol*] (CTT)
FRCC	Free of Riots and Civil Commotions [*Insurance*]
FRCD	Fellow of the Royal College of Dentists [*British*]
FRCD	Floating Rate Certificate of Deposit
FRCD(C).......	Fellow of the Royal College of Dentists (Canada)
FRCF..........	Federation of Reconstructionist Congregations and Fellowships [*Later, FRCH*] (EA)
FRCGP	Fellow of the Royal College of General Practitioners [*British*]
FRCGS	Fellow of the Royal Canadian Geographical Society (DD)
FRCH	Federation of Reconstructionist Congregations and Havurot (EA)
FR CH	Free Church (ROG)
Fr Ch	Freeman's English Chancery Reports [*A publication*] (DLA)
Fr Ch	Freeman's Mississippi Chancery Reports [*A publication*] (DLA)
Fr Chy.........	Freeman's English Chancery Reports [*A publication*] (DLA)
Fr Chy	Freeman's Mississippi Chancery Reports [*A publication*] (DLA)
FRCI..........	Fellow of the Royal Colonial Institute [*British*]
FRCI..........	Fibrous Refractory Composite Insulation
FRCJ..........	Fiber-Reinforced Composite Junction
FRCM.........	Fellow of the Royal College of Medicine [*Canada*] (DD)
FRCM.........	Fellow of the Royal College of Music [*British*]
FRCMC	Fiber-Reinforced Ceramic Matrix Composite [*Organic chemistry*]
FRCO	Fellow of the Royal College of Organists [*British*]
FRCOA	Fruit Color (No Green to Mostly Green) [*Botany*]
FRCOB	Fruit Color (Greenish Red to Dark Red) [*Botany*]
FRCO(CHM)...	Fellow of the Royal College of Organists (Choir-Training Diploma) [*British*]
FRCOG	Fellow of the Royal College of Obstetricians and Gynaecologists [*British*]
Fr Cosci	Franciscus Coscius [*Deceased, 1556*] [*Authority cited in pre-1607 legal work*] (DSA)
FRCOUSA	Federation of Russian Charitable Organizations of the United States of America [*Defunct*] (EA)
FRCP	Facility Remote Control Panel (AAG)
FRCP	Federal Rules of Civil Procedure [*A publication*] (DLA)
FRCP	Federal Rules of Civil Procedure [*A publication*] (AAGC)
FRCP	Fellow of the Royal College of Physicians [*British*]
FRCP	Fellow of the Royal College of Preceptors [*British*]
FRCPA	Fellow, Royal College of Pathologists, Australasia
FRC Path	Fellow of the Royal College of Pathologists [*British*]
FRCP(C).......	Fellow of the Royal College of Physicians (Canada)
FRCPC	Fellow of the Royal College of Physicians of Canada (DD)
FRCPCan	Fellow of the Royal College of Physicians of Canada
FRCPE	Fellow of the Royal College of Physicians of Edinburgh
FRCPEd	Fellow of the Royal College of Physicians of Edinburgh
FRCP Edin ...	Fellow of the Royal College of Physicians of Edinburgh
FRCPGlas	Fellow of the Royal College of Physicians and Surgeons of Glasgow
FRCPI	Fellow of the Royal College of Physicians, Ireland (ROG)
FRCP Irel....	Fellow of the Royal College of Physicians of Ireland
FRCP Lond...	Fellow of the Royal College of Physicians of London [*British*]
FRCPS(Hon)...	Honorary Fellow of the Royal College of Physicians and Surgeons [*Glasgow*]
FRC Psych ...	Fellow of the Royal College of Psychiatrists [*British*]
FRCR	Fellow of the Royal College of Radiologists [*British*]
FRCR	Free Recall-Controlled Recall Test [*Psychology*] (AEBS)
FRCS	Federal Reserve Communications System
FRCS	Fellow of the Royal College of Surgeons [*British*]
FRCS	Flow Recording Controller Switch [*Nuclear energy*] (NRCH)
FRCS	Forward Reaction Control Subsystem [*NASA*] (NASA)
FRCS	Francs [*Monetary units*] (ROG)
FRCSA	Furniture Retailers Council of South Australia
FRCS(C).......	Fellow of the Royal College of Surgeons (Canada)
FRCSC	Fellow of the Royal College of Surgeons of Canada (DD)
FRCSCan	Fellow of the Royal College of Surgeons of Canada
FRCSE	Fellow of the Royal College of Surgeons of Edinburgh
FRCS Ed	Fellow of the Royal College of Surgeons of Edinburgh
FRCSEd(C/Th)...	Fellow of the Royal College of Surgeons of Edinburgh, Specialising in Cardiothoracic Surgery [*British*] (DBQ)
FRCS Edin ...	Fellow of the Royal College of Surgeons of Edinburgh
FRCSEd(Orth)...	Fellow of the Royal College of Surgeons of Edinburgh, Specialising in Orthopaedic Surgery [*British*] (DBQ)
FRCSEd(SN)...	Fellow of the Royal College of Surgeons of Edinburgh, Specialising in Surgical Neurology [*British*] (DBQ)
FRCS Eng ...	Fellow of the Royal College of Surgeons of England
FRCSGlas	Fellow of the Royal College of Surgeons of Glasgow
FRCS(Glasg)...	Fellow of the Royal College of Physicians and Surgeons of Glasgow [*British*] (BABM)
FRCS(Glasg)...	Fellow of the Royal College of Physicians and Surgeons of Glasgow qua Surgeon (DAVI)
FRCSI	Fellow of the Royal College of Surgeons in Ireland
FRCS Irel....	Fellow of the Royal College of Surgeons in Ireland
FRCSL	Fellow of the Royal College of Surgeons of London
FRCSoc........	Fellow of the Royal Commonwealth Society [*British*]
FRCSTNG ...	Forecasting
FRCTF	Fast Reactor Core Test Facility [*Nuclear energy*]
FRCTN	Friction
FRCU	Fractocumulus [*Meteorology*]
FRCUS	Fellow of the Royal College of University Surgeons [*Denmark*]
FRCV	Furniture Retailers' Council of Victoria [*Australia*]
FRCVS	Fellow of the Royal College of Veterinary Surgeons [*British*]
FRD	Facilities Requirements Documents (MCD)
FRD	Facility Requirements Division [*Environmental Protection Agency*] (EPA)
FRD	Failure Rate Data (KSC)
FRD	Federal Research Division [*Library of Congress*] (GFGA)
FRD	Federal Reserve Bank of Dallas, Dallas, TX [*OCLC symbol*] (OCLC)

FRD .... Federal Reserve District
FRD .... Field Remount Depot [British military] (DMA)
FRD .... Field Research Division [Marine science] (OSRA)
FRD .... Field Reset Device [Army]
frd .... Fired (VRA)
FRD .... Flight Readiness Demonstration
FRD .... Flight Requirements Document (MCD)
FRD .... Fluid Rate Damper
FRD .... Ford
FRD .... Ford [Postal Service standard] (OPSA)
FRD .... Ford Motor Co. [ICAO designator] (FAAC)
FRD .... Forecast Research Division [Marine science] (OSRA)
FRD .... Forecast Research Division [Forecast Systems Laboratory] (USDC)
FRD .... Formerly Restricted Data [Military]
FRD .... Foundation for Research Development [South Africa]
FRD .... Fraction Reliability Deviation
frd .... Framed (BARN)
FRD .... Fraud [FBI standardized term]
FRD .... Fredericksburg [Virginia] [Geomagnetic observatory code]
FRD .... Free Rural Delivery [British]
FRD .... Friday Harbor [Washington] [Airport symbol] (OAG)
FRD .... Fried
FRD .... Friedman Indus [AMEX symbol] (TTSB)
FRD .... Friedman Industries, Inc. [AMEX symbol] (SPSG)
FRD .... Friend (AABC)
FRD .... Functional Reference Device (IEEE)
FRD .... Functional Requirement Diagram [Implementation dependant] (ACII)
FRD .... Functional Requirements Document (SSD)
FRDA .... Friedreich's Ataxia [Medicine]
FRDB .... Failure Rate Data Bank [GIDEP]
FRDC .... Fisheries Research and Development Corporation [Commonwealth] (EERA)
FRDENL ...... Fraudulent Enlistment (DNAB)
Fr de T .... Franciscus de Telese [Flourished, 1270-82] [Authority cited in pre-1607 legal work] (DSA)
FRDF .... Fonds de Recherches et de Developpement Forestier [Forest Research and Development Foundation] [Canada]
FRDF .... Forest Research and Development Foundation [Canada]
FrdH .... Ford Holdings, Inc. [Associated Press] (SAG)
FRDI .... Flight Research and Development Instrumentation (KSC)
FR DIST ...... Federal Reserve District (MHDB)
FR-DLP .... Frame Recognition-Data Link Processor (NITA)
FRDLT .... Fraudulent (ROG)
FRDM .... Fast Retrieval and Data Manipulator (MCD)
FRDM .... Friedmans, Inc. [NASDAQ symbol] (SAG)
FRDM .... Friedman's Inc.'A' [NASDAQ symbol] (TTSB)
FRDN .... Ferdinand Railroad Co. [AAR code]
FRDR .... Fixed Reserve Deposit Ratio [Finance]
FRDS .... Federal Reporting Data System (EPA)
FRDS .... Federal Reporting Data System (GNE)
FRDS .... Fords
FRDS .... Fords [Postal Service standard] (OPSA)
FRE .... Aviation Services Ltd. [Guam] [ICAO designator] (FAAC)
FRE .... Facteur Respiratoire Equilibre [Ingredient in a cosmetic by Chanel]
FRE .... Facture [Invoice] [Business term French]
FRE .... Federal Home Loan [NYSE symbol] (TTSB)
FRE .... Federal Home Loan Mortgage [NYSE symbol] (SPSG)
FRE .... Federal Rules of Evidence
FRE .... Fera Island [Solomon Islands] [Airport symbol] (OAG)
FRE .... Field Representative Europe
FRE .... Fischer Rat Embryo [Medicine] (DMAA)
FRE .... Flight Related Element (MCD)
FRE .... Format Request Element (MCD)
FRE .... Frederick Community College, Frederick, MD [OCLC symbol] (OCLC)
FRE .... French
fre .... French [MARC language code Library of Congress] (LCCP)
FRE .... Frequency
FRE .... Fresno [California] [Seismograph station code, US Geological Survey Closed] (SEIS)
FRE .... Friends of R. [Ralph] Emery (EA)
FRE .... Functional Requirements Envelope (SSD)
FREARF ...... Forward Rearm and Refuel Point [Military] (VNW)
FREB .... Federal Real Estate Board [Abolished, 1951]
FREB .... Field Repairable - Expendable Rotor Blade (RDA)
FREC .... Federal Radio Education Committee
Fr EC .... Fraser's English Election Cases [1776-77] [A publication] (DLA)
FREColl ...... Forest Resources and Environment Collective (EERA)
FR Econ S ... Fellow of the Royal Economic Society [British]
FR Econ Soc... Fellow of the Royal Economic Society [British] (ROG)
FR Ec S ...... Fellow of the Royal Economic Society [British]
FRED .... Faceted Region Editor [Software package] [Military] (RDA)
FRED .... Fare Reduction Enhancement Device [Travel industry software] [CompuCheck Corp.]
FRED .... Fast-Rate Electro-Deposition Plating [Automotive engineering]
FRED .... Fast Reactivity Exclusion Device [Nuclear energy]
FRED .... Fast Realistic Editor [Word processing program] (ADA)
FRED .... Fast Reference for Engineering Drawings (IAA)
FRED .... Fast Relocatable Editing Dump (SAA)
FRED .... Field Reset Device [Army]
FRED .... Fiendishly Rapid Electronic Device
FRED .... Figure Reading Electronic Device [Information retrieval]
FRED .... Flashing Rear End Device
FRED .... Foolish Rear End Device [Electronic caboose replacement] [Bowdlerized version]
FRED .... Forward RADAR Enhancement Device

FRED .... Fractionally Rapid Electronic Device
FRED .... Fredericton [City in Canada] (ROG)
Fred .... Fredonia [Record label]
FRED .... Freds, Inc. [NASDAQ symbol] (SAG)
FRED .... Fred's Inc.'A' [NASDAQ symbol] (TTSB)
FRED .... Friendly Recoton Entertainment Decoder [Television stereo adapter]
FRED .... Friendly Robot Educational Device [Androbot, Inc.]
FRED .... Front End for Databases [GTE usage]
FRED .... Fund for Rural Economic Development [Canada]
FredBrw ...... Frederick Brewing Co. [Associated Press] (SAG)
FREDDIE MAC... Federal Home Loan Mortgage Corp. (ECON)
FREDEMO .... Frente Democratico [Peru] [Political party] (EY)
FRED FET .... Fast Recovery Epitaxial Diode FET [Field Effect Transistor] (NITA)
FREDI .... Flight Range and Endurance Data Indicator
FREDS .... Flexible Regional Emissions Data System (GNE)
FREDS .... Flight Readiness Evaluation Data System (MCD)
Freds .... Freds, Inc. [Associated Press] (SAG)
FREE .... Fabric Retailers, Etc., Etc. [Trade group]
FREE .... Fathers Rights and Equality Exchange (EA)
FREE .... Feasibility of Rocket Energy Employment (MCD)
FREE .... Fellowship for Racial and Economic Equality [Later, Southeast Institute] (EA)
FREE .... Feminist Resources on Energy and Ecology [Defunct] (EA)
FREE .... Foundation for Rational Economics and Education (EA)
FREE .... Foundation for Research on Economics and the Environment [Research center] (RCD)
Free .... Freeman's English Chancery Reports [A publication] (DLA)
Free .... Freeman's English King's Bench Reports [89 English Reprint] [1670-1704] [A publication] (DLA)
Free .... Freeman's Reports [31-96 Illinois] [A publication] (DLA)
FREE .... Fund for Renewable Energy and the Environment (EA)
FREE .... Fund to Restore an Educated Electorate [Defunct] (EA)
FREEBD ...... Freeboard (KSC)
FreeCATS .... Free Catecholamines Column Test
Free CC .... Freeman's English Chancery Reports [A publication] (ILCA)
Free Ch.... Freeman's English Chancery Reports [A publication] (DLA)
Free Ch.... Freeman's Mississippi Chancery Reports [A publication] (DLA)
Free KB ...... Freeman's English King's Bench Reports [89 English Reprint] [1670-1704] [A publication] (DLA)
Freem .... Freeman's English Chancery Reports [A publication] (DLA)
Freem .... Freeman's Mississippi Chancery Reports [A publication] (DLA)
Freeman Ch R... Freeman's Mississippi Chancery Reports [A publication] (DLA)
Freeman's (Miss) Rep... Freeman's Mississippi Chancery Reports [A publication] (DLA)
Freem CC .... Freeman's English Chancery Cases [A publication] (DLA)
Freem Ch..... Freeman's English Chancery Reports [A publication] (DLA)
Freem Chan... Freeman's Mississippi Chancery Reports [A publication] (DLA)
Freem Ch (Eng)... Freeman's English Chancery Reports [A publication] (DLA)
Freem Ch (Miss)... Freeman's Mississippi Chancery Reports [A publication] (DLA)
Freem Ch R... Freeman's Mississippi Chancery Reports [A publication] (DLA)
Freem Compar Politics... Freeman. Comparative Politics [A publication] (DLA)
Freem Cot ... Freeman on Cotenancy and Partition [A publication] (DLA)
Freem Eng Const... Freeman's Growth of the English Constitution [3rd ed.] [1876] [A publication] (DLA)
Freem Ex.... Freeman on Executors [A publication] (DLA)
Freem (Ill)... Freeman's Reports [31-96 Illinois] [A publication] (DLA)
Freem Judgm... Freeman on Judgments [A publication] (DLA)
Freem KB .... Freeman's English King's Bench and Common Pleas Reports [89 English Reprint] [A publication] (DLA)
Freem (Miss)... Freeman's Mississippi Chancery Reports [A publication] (DLA)
Freem Pr ..... Freeman's Practice [Illinois] [A publication] (DLA)
FREEP .... Los Angeles Free Press [A publication]
FREE-TH ...... Free-Thinker [or Free-Thinking] (ROG)
FREEWAY .... Freeway [Commonly used] (OPSA)
FREEWY ...... Freeway [Commonly used] (OPSA)
FREF .... Force Record Extract File [Military] (DOMA)
FRegBc .... First Regional Bancorp [Associated Press] (SAG)
FREIR .... Federal Research on Biological and Health Effects of Ionizing Radiations
FREIT .... Finite-Life Real Estate Investment Trust
FREJID .... Frequency Jumper Identification
FREL .... Feltman Research and Engineering Laboratory [Picatinny Arsenal] [Army]
FRELATOR ... Frequency Translator
FRELIMO ..... Frente da Libertacao de Mocambique [Mozambique Liberation Front] [Political party] (PPW)
FRELP .... Flexible Real Estate Loan Plan
FREM .... Fleet Readiness Enlisted Maintenance [Trainees] [Navy]
FREM .... Fremington [England]
FREM .... Fremitus Vocalis [Vocal Fremitus] [Medicine]
FREMEC ...... Frequent Traveller's Medical Card [British]
Fremnt .... Fremont General Corp. [Associated Press] (SAG)
Fremont ...... Fremont General Corp. [Associated Press] (SAG)
FREN .... French (DNAB)
FREN .... Frente Revolucionario Nacionalista [Chile] [Political party] (EY)
FRENA .... Frequency and Amplitude (IAA)
FRENAC ...... Frequency and Amplitude Coded (IAA)
FRENATRACA... Frente Nacional de Trabajadores y Campesinos [National Workers' and Peasants' Front] [Peru] [Political party] (PD)
FrenchF ...... French Fragrances, Inc. [Associated Press] (SAG)
French (NH)... French's Reports [6 New Hampshire] [A publication] (DLA)
FREND .... Federal Register Electronic News Delivery
Frend & W Prec... Frend and Ware's Precedents of Instruments Relating to the Transfer of Land to Railway Companies [2nd ed.] [1866] [A publication] (DLA)

FRENDS......	Floating Rate Enhanced Debt Securities (TDOB)
Freno..........	Frente Nacional Opositora [*National Opposition Front*] [*Panama*] [*Political party*] (PPW)
FRENSIT......	Friendly Situation (MCD)
FR Ent S	Fellow of the Royal Entomological Society [*British*]
FRENU........	Frente Nacional de Unidad [*National Unity Front*] [*Guatemala*] [*Political party*] (PPW)
Freon...........	Fluorine, Refrigerant [*and the suffix-On*] [*Trademarked name of a gaseous inert chlorofluorocarbon used in refrigerants, aerosol propellants, and plastic foams*]
FREP...........	Fleet Return Evaluation Program
FREPAS......	Forest Range Environmental Production Analytical System (MCD)
FRepBcp......	First Republic Bancorp [*Associated Press*] (SAG)
FREPr........	Fed'l Home Ln Mtg 7.90% Pfd [*NYSE symbol*] (TTSB)
FREPrA	Fed'l Home Ln Mtg 6.72% Pfd [*NYSE symbol*] (TTSB)
FREPrB	Fed'l Home Ln Mtg Var Rt Pfd [*NYSE symbol*] (TTSB)
FREPSOG.....	Free Play Scenario Generator (MCD)
FREQ	Frequency [*or Frequent*] (AFM)
freq.............	Frequency (WDMC)
freq.............	Frequently (WDMC)
FREQCH......	Frequency Changer (IAA)
FREQCONV...	Frequency Converter (MCD)
FREQDIV.....	Frequency Divider (MCD)
FreqEL........	Frequency Electronics, Inc. [*Associated Press*] (SAG)
FREQIND.....	Frequency Indicator (IAA)
FREQLY	Frequently (ROG)
FREQM	Frequency Meter
FREQMULT...	Frequency Multiplier (KSC)
FREQN	Frequency (IAA)
FREQ OCC ...	Frequenter Occurrit [*It Occurs Frequently*] [*Latin*] (ROG)
FREQSCANRA...	Frequency Scan RADAR (MCD)
FREQT	Frequent (ROG)
FRES...........	Federal Regulation of Employment Service [*A publication*] (DLA)
FRES...........	Federation of Recruitment and Employment Services [*British*] (EAIO)
FRES...........	Fellow of the Royal Economic Society [*British*]
FRES...........	Fellow of the Royal Empire Society [*British*] (EY)
FRES...........	Fellow of the Royal Entomological Society [*British*] (ROG)
FRES...........	Fire Resistant
FRES...........	Forest Range Environmental Study (GNE)
FRES...........	Forward Recoil Spectrometry [*Measurement method*]
FRES...........	Freres [*Brothers*] [*French*]
FRES...........	Fresh America [*NASDAQ symbol*] (TTSB)
FRES...........	Fresh America Corp. [*NASDAQ symbol*] (SAG)
FRESCA	Fermi-Level Referenced Electron Spectroscopy for Chemical Analysis
FRESCA	Field-Emitter Referenced Electron Spectroscopy for Chemical Analysis
FRESCAN.....	Frequency Scanning
FRESCANNAR...	Frequency Scanning RADAR
FreSCn........	Free State Consolidated Gold Mines Ltd. [*Associated Press*] (SAG)
FRESCO	Frequency Stability Code (PDAA)
Fresenius.....	Fresenius USA, Inc. [*Associated Press*] (SAG)
FresenM	Fresenius Medical Care AG [*Associated Press*] (SAG)
FRESH	Foil Research Supercavitating Hydrofoil
FRESH	Force Requirements Expert System [*Navy*]
FRESH	Freshman [*or Freshmen*] (WDAA)
FreshAm......	Fresh America Corp. [*Associated Press*] (SAG)
Freshst	Freshstart Venture Capital Corp. [*Associated Press*] (SAG)
FRESHW......	Freshwell [*England*]
FresM..........	FDresenius Medical Care AG [*Associated Press*] (SAG)
FRESSCAN...	Frequency Scan [*Radar*] (DOMA)
FRET...........	Fluorescence Resonance [*or Resonant*] Energy Transfer [*Analytical biochemistry*]
FRET...........	Freezing Rain Endurance Test [*Aviation*] (DA)
FRET-ANON...	Family-Related Emotional Trauma - Anonymous
Fretter.........	Fretter, Inc. [*Associated Press*] (SAG)
FRETURN.....	Function Return [*Computer science*]
F REV	Further Review (DNAB)
FREWCAP....	Flexible Reworkable Chip Attachment Process (IAA)
FREZ...........	Freeze
FRF.............	Fertility Research Foundation (EA)
FRF.............	Field Research Facility [*Army*]
FRF.............	Filter Replacement Fluid
FRF.............	Fire-Resistant Fuels (RDA)
FRF.............	Flight Readiness Firing [*NASA*] (NASA)
FRF.............	Flight Readiness Firing Test [*NASA*] (AFM)
FRF.............	Florida Retail Federation (SRA)
FRF.............	Follicle-Stimulating Hormone Releasing Factor [*Also, FSH-RF, FSH-RH*] [*Endocrinology*]
FRF.............	Fragrance Research Fund (EA)
FRF.............	Frame Relay Forum (ACRL)
FRF.............	France Growth Fund [*NYSE symbol*] (SPSG)
FRF.............	Freedom to Read Foundation
FRF.............	Free French [*World War II*]
FRF.............	Free Running Frequency
FRF.............	Frequency Response Function [*Statistics*]
FRF.............	FSLIC [*Federal Savings and Loan Insurance Corp.*] Resolution Fund [*Administ ered by the Federal Deposit Insurance Corp.*]
FRF.............	Fuel Reprocessing Facility [*Nuclear energy*] (NRCH)
FRF.............	Functional Renal Failure [*Medicine*]
FRFA...........	Federal Regulatory Flexibility Act (IEEE)
FRFAB	FSS [*Flight Service Station*] Returns Flight-Plan Area and Service B [*Aviation*] (FAAC)
FRFDS	Fund Raising and Financial Development Section [*Library Administration and Management Association*]
FRFE...........	Field Representative Far East

FRFID	Fast Response Flame Ionization Detector [*Automotive emissions testing*]
FRFOURRA...	French Fourragere [*Military decoration*]
FRFPI..........	Friends of Radio for Peace International (EA)
FRFPS	Fellow of the Royal Faculty of Physicians and Surgeons [*British*]
FRFPS(G)	Fellow of the Royal Faculty of Physicians and Surgeons of Glasgow
FRFPSGlas...	Fellow of the Royal Faculty of Physicians and Surgeons of Glasgow
FRFS...........	Fast Reaction Fighting System (NATG)
FRFT..........	Flight Readiness Firing Test (MCD)
FRFV..........	Four by Five Inches (VRA)
FRG	Emerging Germany Fund [*NYSE symbol*] (SPSG)
FRG	Faculty Review Group [*Education*] (AIE)
FRG	Family Rights Group [*British*] (DBA)
FRG	Farmingdale, NY [*Location identifier FAA*] (FAAL)
FRG	Federal Republic of Germany (AABC)
FRG	Federal Reserve System, Board of Governors, Washington, DC [*OCLC symbol*] (OCLC)
FRG	Fergana [*Former USSR Seismograph station code, US Geological Survey*] (SEIS)
FRG	Field Review Group [*Army*] (RDA)
FRG	Floated Rate Gyro [*Aerospace*] (AAG)
FR(g)	Flow Rate of Sparge Gas
FRG	Force Requirements Generator
FRG	Forge
FRG	Forge
frg..............	Forger [*MARC relator code*] [*Library of Congress*] (LCCP)
FRG	Freight Runners Express, Inc. [*ICAO designator*] (FAAC)
FRG	Frente Republicano Guatemalteco [*Political party*] (EY)
FRG	Long Island Republic [*New York*] [*Airport symbol*] (OAG)
FRGB	First Regional Bancorp [*NASDAQ symbol*] (NQ)
FRGHT........	Freight
FRGN	Foreign
FRGN	Foreign
FRGNC........	Fragrance
Fr Gon	Franciscus Gonzaga [*Authority cited in pre-1607 legal work*] (DSA)
FRGp	Field Record Group [*Air Force*] (AFM)
FRGR	Frozen Granular Snow [*Skiing condition*]
FrGrALP.......	Bibliotheque Americaine, Universite de Grenoble III, Domaine Universitaire, Grenoble, France [*Library symbol*] [*Library of Congress*] (LCLS)
FrGrU..........	Universite de Grenoble, Bibliotheque Droit-Lettres, St.-Martin d'Heres, France [*Library symbol Library of Congress*] (LCLS)
FRGS	Fellow of the Royal Geographical Society [*British*] (ROG)
FRGS	Forges
FRGS	Forges [*Postal Service standard*] (OPSA)
FRGS	Forked River Generating Station [*Nuclear energy*] (NRCH)
FRGS(C)	Fellow of the Royal Geographical Society (Canada)
FRGSS	Fellow of the Royal Geographical Society, Scotland (ROG)
FRGT	Freight (WDAA)
FRH	Fellowship of Religious Humanists (EA)
FRh	Fetal Rhesus Monkey Kidney Cell [*Medicine*] (DMAA)
FRH	Flameless Ration Heater [*Army*] (RDA)
FRH	Fly Runway Heading [*Aviation*] (FAAC)
FRH	Follicle-Stimulating Hormone-Releasing Hormone [*Endocrinology*] (DAVI)
FRH	French Lick, IN [*Location identifier FAA*] (FAAL)
FRH	Frequency Response Histogram [*Biometrics*]
FRH	Fruehauf Canada, Inc. [*Toronto Stock Exchange symbol*]
FRH	Fuller, R. H., Los Angeles CA [*STAC*]
f-rh--	Rhodesia [*Southern Rhodesia*] [*MARC geographic area code Library of Congress*] (LCCP)
FRHB	Federation of Registered House-Builders [*British*] (BI)
FRHB	Foundation for Research on Human Behavior (EA)
FRHGT........	Free Height
Fr Hist	Fragmenta Historica [*of Aristoxenus*] [*Classical studies*] (OCD)
FRHistS	Fellow of the Royal Historical Society [*British*] (ROG)
FRHistSoc....	Fellow of the Royal Historical Society [*British*]
FRHortS.......	Fellow of the Royal Horticultural Society [*British*]
FRHS	Fellow of the Royal Historical Society [*British*] (ROG)
FRHS	Fellow of the Royal Horticultural Society [*British*] (ROG)
FRI..............	American Family Restaurants, Inc. [*AMEX symbol*] (SAG)
FRI..............	Family Relationship Inventory [*Psychology*]
FRI..............	Family Relationships Institute [*Australia*]
FRI..............	Family Relations Indicator [*Psychology*]
FRI..............	Family Research Institute (EA)
FRI..............	Feeling Rough Inside [*Slang*]
FRI..............	Fellow of the Canadian Institute of Realtors
FRI..............	Fellow of the Real Estate Institute (DD)
FRI..............	Fellow of the Royal Institution [*British*]
FRI..............	Financial Real Estate Insurance
FRI..............	First Rate Investments (DICI)
FRI..............	Fisheries Research Institute [*University of Washington*] [*Research center*]
FRI..............	Fisheries Research Institute [*Australia*]
FRI..............	Flandre Air International [*France ICAO designator*] (FAAC)
FRI..............	Flight Refueling, Inc.
FRI..............	Flux Reversals/Inch [*Magnetic storage measure*] (NITA)
FRI..............	Focal Region Investigation
FRI..............	Food Research Institute [*Australia*]
FRI..............	[*The*] Food Research Institute [*Agricultural Research Council*] [*British*]
FRI..............	Food Research Institute [*Canada*] (ARC)
FRI..............	Food Research Institute [*University of Wisconsin - Madison*] [*Research center*] (RCD)
FRI..............	Forest Research Institute

FRI............. Forest Research Institute [*Commonwealth*] (EERA)
FRI............. Formal Reading Inventory [*Educational test*]
FRI............. Fort Riley, KS [*Location identifier FAA*] (FAAL)
FRI............. Freeport Resources, Inc. [*Vancouver Stock Exchange symbol*]
FRI............. Frente Revolucionaria de Izquierda [*Left Revolutionary Front*] [*Bolivia*] [*Political party*] (PPW)
FRI............. Friant [*California*] [*Seismograph station code, US Geological Survey*] (SEIS)
FRI............. Friday (EY)
Fri............. Friday (ODBW)
FRI............. Friendly Initiated [*Incident*] [*Vietnam*]
fri............. Frisian [*MARC language code Library of Congress*] (LCCP)
FRI............. Fully Read Index [*Publishing*]
FRI............. Fulmer Research Institute (AAG)
FRIA........... Finnish Radio Industries Association
FRIA........... Firearms Research and Identification Association (EA)
FRIAI .... Fellow of the Royal Institute of Architects of Ireland
FRIAS......... Fellow of the Royal Incorporation of Architects of Scotland (DI)
FRIAS......... Fellow of the Royal Institute of Architects of Scotland
FRIBA .... Fellow of the Royal Institute of British Architects (ROG)
FRIC........... Fellow of the Royal Institute of Chemistry [*Formerly, FIC*] [*British*]
fric............. Fricative (BARN)
FRIC........... Friction [*or Frictional*] (WDAA)
FRICAND...... Fricandus [*To Be Rubbed*] [*Pharmacy*] (ROG)
FRICC .... Federal Research Internet Coordinating Committee [*National Science Foundation*]
FRICENT ..... Fricentur [*Let Them Be Rubbed*] [*Pharmacy*] (ROG)
FRICS .... Fellow of the Royal Institute of Chartered Surveyors [*Canada*] (DD)
FRICS .... Fellow of the Royal Institution of Chartered Surveyors [*Formerly, FSI*] [*British*]
FRICT.......... Friction
FRID .... Friday (ADA)
FRIED .... Friedman Test [*for pregnancy*] [*Obstetrics*]
Friedm........ Friedman Industries, Inc. [*Associated Press*] (SAG)
Friedmn...... Friedmans, Inc. [*Associated Press*] (SAG)
FRIES......... Fast Rope Insertion/Extraction System [*for rappeling*] [*Military*] (RDA)
FRIES......... Friesian [*Language, etc.*] (ROG)
Fries Tr...... Trial of John Fries (Treason) [*A publication*] (DLA)
FRIF........... Furnished Recurring Intelligence File (MCD)
FRIG .... Frigidus [*Cold*] [*Pharmacy*]
FRIH .... Fellow of the Royal Institute of Horticulture [*New Zealand*]
FRIIA .... Fellow of the Royal Institute of International Affairs [*British*] (DI)
FRIL........... Fuzzy Relational Inference Language (NITA)
FRIMP .... Flexible Reconfigurable Interconnected Multiprocessor
FRIN .... Fellow of the Royal Institution of Navigation [*British*] (DBQ)
FRIN .... Firing Research Investigation, Navy
FRINA .... Fellow of the Royal Institute of Naval Architects [*British*]
FRINGE........ File and Report Information Processing Generator [*Computer science*]
FRIP........... Fleet Readiness Improvement Plan
FRIPA......... Fellow of the Royal Institute of Public Administration [*British*] (ADA)
FRIPH .... Fellow of the Royal Institute of Public Health [*British*] (ADA)
FRIPHH....... Fellow of the Royal Institute of Public Health and Hygiene [*British*]
FRIS........... Fire Research Information Services [*National Institute of Standards and Technology*] (IID)
FRIS........... Friesland [*County in the Netherlands*] (ROG)
FRIS........... Frisian [*Language, etc.*]
FrisBay ...... Frisco Bay Industries [*Associated Press*] (SAG)
Frischs....... Frisch's Restaurants, Inc. [*Associated Press*] (SAG)
FRISCO ...... Fast Reaction Integrated Submarine Control [*Navy*]
FRISCO ...... San Francisco [*California*] (ROG)
FRITA.......... Friend of a Resistor-in-the-Army [*Peace movement slang during the Vietnam War*] (VNW)
FRITALUX .... Union Economique France, Italie, Benelux
Frith........... United States Opinions Attorneys-General (Frith) [*Pt. 2., Vol. 21*] [*A publication*] (DLA)
Fritz .... Fritz Companies, Inc. [*Associated Press*] (SAG)
FRIVOL .... Frivolous (DSUE)
FRIVOLS ...... Frivolities [*Slang*] (DSUE)
FRJ............. Frejus [*France*] [*Airport symbol*] (AD)
FRJ............. Oklahoma City, OK [*Location identifier FAA*] (FAAL)
FRJD.......... Forward Reaction Jet Driver (MCD)
FRJM.......... Full Range Joint Movement [*Occupational therapy*]
FrJuice....... [*The*] Fresh Juice Co., Inc. [*Associated Press*] (SAG)
FRK............. Federal Reserve Bank of Kansas City, Kansas City, MO [*OCLC symbol*] (OCLC)
FRK............. Florida Rock Indus [*AMEX symbol*] (TTSB)
FRK............. Florida Rock Industries, Inc. [*AMEX symbol*] (SPSG)
FRK............. Folkstone Resources Ltd. [*Vancouver Stock Exchange symbol*]
FRK............. Fork
FRK............. Fork
FRK............. Fregate Island [*Seychelles Islands*] [*Airport symbol*] (OAG)
FrkBncp ...... Franklin Bancorp [*Associated Press*] (SAG)
FrkCon .... Franklin Consolidated Mining Co., Inc. [*Associated Press*] (SAG)
FrkEPb .... Franklin Electronic Publishers, Inc. [*Associated Press*] (SAG)
FRKLFT .... Forklift
FrkMul .... Franklin Multi-Income Trust [*Associated Press*] (SAG)
FrkPr......... Franklin Principal Maturity Trust [*Associated Press*] (SAG)
FrkQst........ Franklin Quest Co. [*Associated Press*] (SAG)
FRKS .... Forks
FRKS .... Forks [*Postal Service standard*] (OPSA)
FrkUnv........ Franklin Universal Trust [*Associated Press*] (SAG)
FRL............. Feltman Research Laboratory [*Picatinny Arsenal*] [*Army*] (RDA)
FRL............. Field Requirements List
FRL............. Fire Resistance Level

FRL............. Fisheries Radiobiological Laboratory [*British*] (NUCP)
FRL............. Flight Research Laboratory [*University of Kansas*] [*Research center*] (RCD)
FRL............. Forest Research Laboratory [*Oregon State University*] [*Research center*] (RCD)
FRL............. Forest Resources Laboratory [*Pennsylvania State University*] [*Research center*] (RCD)
FRL............. Forli [*Italy*] [*Airport symbol*] (AD)
FRL............. Forum Retirement Partnership Ltd. [*AMEX symbol*] (SPSG)
FRL............. Forum Retirem't Ptnrs [*AMEX symbol*] (TTSB)
FRL............. Fractional (WGA)
FRL............. Fraeulein [*Miss*] [*German*]
FRL............. Frame Reference Line (MCD)
FRL............. Frame Representation Language [*Computer science*]
FRL............. Free Recall Learning (PDAA)
FRL............. Fuels Research Laboratory [*MIT*] (MCD)
FRL............. Fuselage Reference Line [*Aviation*]
FRL............. Jackson, MS [*Location identifier FAA*] (FAAL)
FRL............. Maria Elisa Gonzales Farelas [*Mexico*] [*FAA designator*] (FAAC)
FRL............. Mobil Research & Development Corp., Dallas, TX [*OCLC symbol*] (OCLC)
FRLA.......... Federal Regulation of Lobbying Act
FRLA.......... Federation of Right to Life Associations [*Australia*]
FRLD .... Foreland
FrLemU....... Universite du Maine, Le Mans, France [*Library symbol Library of Congress*] (LCLS)
FrLimU........ Universite de Limoges, Limoges, France [*Library symbol Library of Congress*] (LCLS)
FrLimU-L .... Universite de Limoges, Bibliotheque des Lettres, Limoges, France [*Library symbol Library of Congress*] (LCLS)
FrLiU .... Universite de Lille, Bibliotheque de Section Droit-Lettres, Domaine Universitaire, Litteraire, et Juridique, Lille, France [*Library symbol Library of Congress*] (LCLS)
FrLy .... Bibliotheque Municipale de Lyon, Lyon, France [*Library symbol Library of Congress*] (LCLS)
FrLyU .... Universite de Lyon, Bibliotheque Centrale, Lyon, France [*Library symbol Library of Congress*] (LCLS)
FRM........... Fairmont [*Minnesota*] [*Airport symbol*] (OAG)
FRM........... Fairmont, MN [*Location identifier FAA*] (FAAL)
FRM........... Farm (ADA)
FRM........... Farm
FRM........... Fault Reporting Module (TEL)
FRM........... Federal Armored Service, Inc. [*ICAO designator*] (FAAC)
FRM........... Federal Reference Method
FRM........... Federation of Retail Merchants [*Defunct*] (EA)
FRM........... Fiber-Reinforced Material
FRM........... Fiber-Reinforced Metal [*Materials science*]
FRM........... Field Reversed Mirror (MCD)
FRM........... Film Reading Machine
FRM........... Final Rulemaking [*Federal government*] (GFGA)
FRM........... Fire Room
FRM........... First America Mining Corp. [*Vancouver Stock Exchange symbol*]
FRM........... First Mississippi [*NYSE symbol*] (TTSB)
FRM........... First Mississippi Corp. [*NYSE symbol*] (SPSG)
FRM........... Fixed Rate Mortgage
FRM........... Flat River [*Missouri*] [*Seismograph station code, US Geological Survey Closed*] (SEIS)
FRM........... Force Reaction Motor
FRM........... Foucault Rotating Mirror [*Physics*]
FRM........... Frame
FRM........... Framingham Public Library, Framingham, MA [*OCLC symbol*] (OCLC)
Fr M.......... Francis' Maxims of Equity [*1722-46*] [*A publication*] (DLA)
frm........... French, Middle [*MARC language code Library of Congress*] (LCCP)
FRM........... Frequency Meter
FRM........... From
FRM........... Full Range of Motion [*Orthopedics*] (DAVI)
FRMA.......... Floor Rug Manufacturers' Association [*British*] (BI)
FRMAC .... Federal Radiological Management Assessment Center (USDC)
FRMAC .... Federal Radiological Monitoring and Assessment Center [*Department of Energy*]
FRMAP .... Foreign Rights Marketing Assistance Program [*Australia*]
FRMC.......... Frame Counter (SAA)
FrMC........... Institut National de la Propriete Industrielle, Centre Regional, Marseilles, France [*Library symbol Library of Congress*] (LCLS)
FRMCM .... Fellow of the Royal Manchester College of Music [*British*]
FRMCSL ...... Fellow of the Royal Medical and Chirurgical Society, London (ROG)
FRMD .... Formed
FRMD .... Framed
FRME.......... First Merchants Corp. [*NASDAQ symbol*] (NQ)
FRME.......... Frequency Response Measuring Equipment (PDAA)
FRMedSoc ... Fellow of the Royal Medical Society [*British*]
FR Met S ... Fellow of the Royal Meteorological Society [*British*]
FR Met Soc... Fellow of the Royal Meteorological Society [*British*] (ROG)
FrMeyer....... Meyer [*Fred*], Inc. [*Associated Press*] (SAG)
FrmG .... Farmers Group Capital [*Associated Press*] (SAG)
FrmG .... Farmers Group Capital II [*Associated Press*] (SAG)
FRMG .... FirstMiss Gold [*NASDAQ symbol*] (TTSB)
FRMG .... FirstMiss Gold, Inc. [*NASDAQ symbol*] (NQ)
FRMG .... Forming (FAAC)
FRMG .... Framing [*of a ship*] (DS)
FRML.......... Formal
FRML.......... Freymiller Trucking, Inc. [*NASDAQ symbol*] (NQ)
FRMN .... Formation (FAAC)
FRMNG .... Farming

FRMNTN...... Fermentation
FRMO......... Fleet Royal Marines Officer [Navy British]
FrMpALP..... Bibliotheque Americaine, Universite Paul-Valery, Montpellier, France [Library symbol] [Library of Congress] (LCLS)
FRMR......... Farmer
FRMR......... Former (MSA)
FRMR......... Frame Reject
FRMS......... Federation of Recorded Music Societies [British] (EAIO)
FRMS......... Federation of Rocky Mountain States
FRMS......... Fellow of the Royal Meteorological Society [British]
FRMS......... Fellow of the Royal Microscopical Society [British] (ROG)
FRMS......... Flow Reactor Mass Spectroscopy (MCD)
FRMT......... Format
FRMTN....... Formation
FRMV......... Free Running Multivibrator (PDAA)
FRMWG...... Floodplain and River Management Working Group [Australia]
FRMWRK.... Framework
FrN............ Bibliotheque Municipale, Nantes, France [Library symbol Library of Congress] (LCLS)
FRN........... Federal Register Notice (NRCH)
FRN........... Federal Reserve Note
FRN........... Feed Rate Number (MCD)
FRN........... Feminist Radio Network [Defunct] (EA)
FRN........... Fernie [British Columbia] [Seismograph station code, US Geological Survey Closed] (SEIS)
FRN........... Final Rulemaking Notice [Federal government] (GFGA)
FRN........... Floating Rate Note
FRN........... Floating Rate Notes (TDOB)
FRN........... Floating Round
FRN........... Force Requirement Number [Army] (AABC)
FRN........... Fort Richardson, AK [Location identifier FAA] (FAAL)
FRN........... Fredonia Oil & Gas [Vancouver Stock Exchange symbol]
FRN........... Frente de Reconstruccion Nacional [Ecuador] [Political party] (EY)
FRN........... Fresenius USA [AMEX symbol] (TTSB)
FRN........... Fresenius USA, Inc. [AMEX symbol] (SAG)
FRN........... Frontul Renasterii Nationala [Front of National Rebirth] [Romania] [Political party] (PPE)
FRN........... Full-Round Nose [Diamond drilling]
FRNA......... Foreign Rations Not Available (AABC)
FrNALP....... Bibliotheque Americaine de Nantes, Universite de Nantes Chemin du Tertre, Nantes, France [Library symbol] [Library of Congress] (LCLS)
FrNanALP.... Bibliotheque Americaine, Universite de Nancy II, Nancy, France [Library symbol] [Library of Congress] (LCLS)
FrNanU....... Universite de Nancy, Bibliotheque Centrale, Nancy, France [Library symbol Library of Congress] (LCLS)
FrNanU-L..... Universite de Nancy, Bibliotheque des Lettres-Droit-Sciences, Nancy, France [Library symbol Library of Congress] (LCLS)
FRNC......... Furnace
FRNCH....... French
FRNCHS..... Franchise
FRNCHSNG.. Franchising
FRNCM....... Fellow of the Royal Northern College of Music [British] (DBQ)
FRND......... Friend
FRND......... Friend
FRNDLY...... Friendly
FRNG......... Firing
FRNG......... Fringe (MSA)
FrNiU-D...... Universite de Nice, Bibliotheque de Droit, Nice, France [Library symbol Library of Congress] (LCLS)
FrNiU-S....... Universite de Nice, Bibliotheque des Sciences, Nice, France [Library symbol Library of Congress] (LCLS)
FRNK......... Frequency Regulation and Network Keying [Computer science] (IAA)
FrnkAdv...... Franklin Advantage Real Estate, Inc. [Associated Press] (SAG)
FrnkBk....... Franklin Bank NA [Associated Press] (SAG)
FrnkEl........ Franklin Electric Co., Inc. [Associated Press] (SAG)
Frnkln........ Franklin Corp. [Associated Press] (SAG)
FrnkRE....... Franklin Real Estate Income Fund [Associated Press] (SAG)
FrnkRs....... Franklin Resources, Inc. [Associated Press] (SAG)
FrnkSel...... Franklin Select Real Estate Income Fund [Associated Press] (SAG)
FrnkSup...... Franklin Supply Co. Ltd. [Associated Press] (SAG)
FRNM......... Foundation for Research on the Nature of Man (EA)
FRNS......... Family Respite and Network Support [Australia]
FRNS......... Fellow of the Royal Numismatic Society [British] (EY)
FRNT......... Front
FRNT......... Frontier Airlines [NASDAQ symbol] (TTSB)
FRNT......... Frontier Airlines, Inc. [NASDAQ symbol] (SAG)
FrntDir....... Fronteer Directory Co., Inc. [Associated Press] (SAG)
FrntN......... Frontier Natural Gas [Associated Press] (SAG)
FrntNat....... Frontier Natural Gas [Commercial firm Associated Press] (SAG)
FrntNt........ Frontier Natural Gas [Commercial firm Associated Press] (SAG)
FRNTR....... Frontier
FrntrFin...... Fronteer Financial Holdings Ltd. [Associated Press] (SAG)
FrntrIns...... Frontier Insurance Group [Associated Press] (SAG)
FRNTW...... Frontier Airlines Wrrt [NASDAQ symbol] (TTSB)
FrNU......... Universite de Nantes, Section Droit-Lettres, Nantes, France [Library symbol Library of Congress] (LCLS)
FrNU-M...... Universite de Nantes, Section Medecine, Nantes, France [Library symbol Library of Congress] (LCLS)
FrNU-S...... Universite de Nantes, Section Sciences, Nantes, France [Library symbol Library of Congress] (LCLS)
FRNWC...... French Naval War College
FRO.......... Faroe Islands [ANSI three-letter standard code] (CNC)
FRO.......... Federal Register Office [National Archives and Records Administration] (GFGA)

FRO.......... Feed Rate Override [Mechanical engineering] (IAA)
FRO.......... Fleet Records Office [Navy]
FRO.......... Fleet Recreation Officer [British]
FRO.......... Fleet Resources Office
FRO.......... Flexible Response Options (MCD)
FRO.......... Flight Radio Officer [Aviation]
FRO.......... Floro [Norway] [Airport symbol] (OAG)
FRO.......... Food Rationing Order [British]
FRO.......... Free-Running Oscillator [Instrumentation]
fro........... French, Old [MARC language code Library of Congress] (LCCP)
FRO.......... Frobisher NV (European Airlines) [Belgium ICAO designator] (FAAC)
FRO.......... Front
FRO.......... Frontier Corp. [Formerly, Rochester Telephone] [NYSE symbol] (SAG)
FRO.......... Frozya Industries [Vancouver Stock Exchange symbol]
FROB......... Flash RADAR Order of Battle (SAA)
FROC......... Federated Russian Orthodox Clubs (EA)
FROD......... Functionally Related Observable Difference [between weapons]
FROF......... Fire Risk on Freight [Insurance]
FROF......... Freight Office
FROG......... Free Ranging on Grid [Computer-controlled transport system]
FROG......... Free Rocket over Ground [USSR missile]
Frog.......... Frogerius [Rogerius Beneventanus] [Flourished, 12th century] [Authority cited in pre-1607 legal work] (DSA)
FROGS....... Fund Raising Organization Graphics Service
FROKA....... First Republic of Korea Army
FROLINAT... Front de Liberation Nationale [Chad]
FROLIZI...... Front for the Liberation of Zimbabwe
FROM......... Factory Programmable Read Only Memory [Computer science] (IAA)
FROM......... Field Programmable Read-Only Memory [Computer science] (EECA)
FROM......... Full Range of Motion [or Movement] [Occupational therapy]
FROM......... Fusable Read-Only Memory [Computer science] (MDG)
FRON......... Frontier
FRONASA ... Front for National Salvation [Uganda]
FRONT....... Frontispiece [Publishing]
FrontA....... Frontier Airlines, Inc. [Associated Press] (SAG)
FrontAdj...... Frontier Adjusters of America, Inc. [Associated Press] (SAG)
Frontin....... Frontinus [First century AD] [Classical studies] (OCD)
FRONTIS..... Frontispiece [Publishing]
FrontrAir..... Frontier Airlines, Inc. [Associated Press] (SAG)
FrontrCp..... Frontier Corp. [Associated Press] (SAG)
FROPA....... Frontal Passage [NWS] (FAAC)
FR ORD...... French Ordinances [A publication] (DLA)
FROS......... Fleet Resources Office Subsystem (MCD)
FROSFC..... Frontal Surface [NWS] (FAAC)
FROST....... Floating Repair and Oil Storage Terminal
FROST....... Food Reserves on Space Trips
Frostburg St U... Frostburg State University (GAGS)
FROSTI...... Food RA Online Scientific and Technical Information [Leatherhead Food Research Association] [Information service or system] (CRD)
FrozenFd.... Frozen Food Express [Associated Press] (SAG)
FrozFd....... Frozen Food Express [Associated Press] (SAG)
FRP........... Faculty Research Participation [National Science Foundation program]
FRP........... F-Air AS [Denmark ICAO designator] (FAAC)
FRP........... Fairfield Public Library, Supervisor of Technical Services, Fairfield, CT [OCLC symbol] (OCLC)
FRP........... Famous Records of the Past [Record label]
FRP........... Fast Rise Pulse
FRP........... Fault Report Point (TEL)
FRP........... Feather River Project
FRP........... Feature Recognition Processor
FRP........... Federal Radionavigation Plan
FRP........... Federal Regulatory Plan [Database] (IID)
FRP........... Federation des Republicains de Progres [Federation of Progressive Republicans] [France Political party] (PPW)
FRP........... Ferritin Repressor Protein [Biochemistry]
FRP........... Fiberglass-Reinforced Plastic
FRP........... Fiberglass-Reinforced Plywood
FRP........... Fiberglass-Reinforced Polyester [Organic chemistry]
FRP........... Filament-Reinforced Plastic
FRP........... Flag Register Processing
FRP........... Fleet Replacement Pilot [Navy] (NVT)
FRP........... Follicle Regulatory Protein [Endocrinology]
FRP........... Force Rendezvous Point [Military] (AFM)
FRP........... Forest Response Program [USA] (EERA)
FRP........... Forward Refueling Point
FRP........... Fragmentation Bomb, Parachute
FRP........... Fragmentation Protocol [Telecommunications] (ACRL)
FRP........... Freeport McmoRan Res LP [NYSE symbol] (TTSB)
FRP........... Freeport-McMoRan Resource Partnership LP [NYSE symbol] (SPSG)
FRP........... Free Radical Photography
FRP........... Free Romanian Press [British]
FRP........... Fremont Peak [California] [Seismograph station code, US Geological Survey] (SEIS)
FRP........... Frequency Reference Protection
FRP........... Frequency Response Plotter
FRP........... Fresh Water Bay [Alaska] [Airport symbol] (OAG)
FRP........... Fuel Reprocessing Plant [Nuclear energy] (NRCH)
FRP........... Fuel Restoration Project
FRP........... Fuerzas Populares Revolucionarias [Guerrilla forces] [Honduras] (EY)
FRP........... Full-Rate Production (DOMA)
FRP........... Fully Refined Paraffinic Wax [Petroleum technology]

FRP............. Functional Refractory Period [Neurophysiology]
FRP............. Fuselage Reference Plane [Aviation] (MCD)
FRP............. Parachute Fragmentation Bomb [Air Force]
FRPA .... Family Rights and Privacy Act [1974] (OICC)
FRPA .... Feather River Project Association (BARN)
FRPA .... Fiberglass Reinforced Panel Association [Defunct] (EA)
FRPA .... Fixed Radiation Pattern Antenna
FrPALP....... American Library in Paris, Paris, France [Library symbol] [Library of Congress] (LCLS)
FrPAUP....... American University in Paris, Paris, France [Library symbol] [Library of Congress] (LCLS)
FrPBA .... Bibliotheque de l'Arsenal, Paris, France [Library symbol Library of Congress] (LCLS)
FrPBN .... Bibliotheque Nationale, Paris, France [Library symbol Library of Congress] (LCLS)
FrPCF........... College de France, Paris, France [Library symbol] [Library of Congress] (LCLS)
FRPD .... Finitely Repeated Prisoner's Dilemma [Psychology]
FRPE........... Fellow of the Royal Society of Painter-Etchers and Engravers [British] (ROG)
FrPE-C .... Ecole Normale Superieure, Laboratoire de Chimie, Paris, France [Library symbol Library of Congress] (LCLS)
FrPED .... Institut National d'Etudes Demographiques, Paris, France [Library symbol Library of Congress] (LCLS)
FR-PET .... Fiber-Reinforced Polyethylene Terephthalate [Glass]
FRPH .... Fiber-Reinforced Polymer Honeycomb
FrPJO........... Direction des Journaux Officiels Service de Microfiches, Paris, France [Library symbol] [Library of Congress] (LCLS)
FRPL........... Fireplace [Real estate] (WGA)
FRPL........... Fuerzas Rebeldes y Populares Lautaro [Chile] [Political party] (EY)
FRPO .... Front-Panel Operation [Computer science] (PCM)
FrPoU .... Universite de Poitiers, Bibliotheque de Droit-Lettres, Poitiers, France [Library symbol Library of Congress] (LCLS)
FRPP .... Flame Retardant Phosphonitratic Polymer
FRPP .... FRP Properties [NASDAQ symbol] (TTSB)
FRPP .... FRP Properties, Inc. [NASDAQ symbol] (NQ)
FRP Pr .... FRP Properties, Inc. [Associated Press] (SAG)
FRPR .... Australian Financial Review Property Review [A publication] (ADA)
FRPrA .... First Indl Rlty Tr 9.50% Pfd [NYSE symbol] (TTSB)
FRPS .... Fellow of the Royal Photographic Society [British] (ROG)
FRPS .... Flux Reversals Per Second (NITA)
FrPS............. Sirco-France, Paris, France [Library symbol Library of Congress] (LCLS)
FRPSL .... Fellow of the Royal Philatelic Society, London
FrptMc......... Freeport McMoRan, [Associated Press] (SAG)
FRPTNG ...... Fleet Replacement Pilot Training [Navy] (NVT)
FrPU .... Universite de Paris a la Sorbonne, Bibliotheque de la Faculte des Lettres et de la Faculte des Sciences, Paris, France [Library symbol Library of Congress] (LCLS)
FrPU-AL...... Institut des Hautes Etudes de l'Amerique Latine, Universite de Paris, Paris, France [Library symbol Library of Congress] (LCLS)
FrPU-M........ Universite de Paris a la Sorbonne, Faculte de Medecine, Paris, France [Library symbol Library of Congress] (LCLS)
FrPU-OS ..... Universite de Paris, Faculte des Sciences, (Orsay), Orsay, France [Library symbol Library of Congress] (LCLS)
FrPU-P........ Universite de Paris a la Sorbonne, Faculte des Sciences Pharmaceutiques et Biologiques de Paris-Luxembourg, Paris, France [Library symbol Library of Congress] (LCLS)
FRPV .... Full-Range Picture Vocabulary Test [Intelligence test]
FRPVT .... Full-Range Picture Vocabulary Test [Education]
FRQ .... Frequent
FRQMULT .... Frequency Multiplier (KSC)
FRR .... Failure and Rejection Report
FRR .... Failure Reporting Review (KSC)
FRR .... False Removal Rate (CAAL)
FRR .... Fast Recovery Rectifier (IAA)
FRR .... Federal Register Reprint
FRR .... Federal Research Report [Business Publishers, Inc.] [Information service or system] (CRD)
FRR .... Federal Reserve Bank of Richmond, Richmond, VA [OCLC symbol] (OCLC)
FRR .... Financial Reporting Releases [SEC] (TDOB)
FRR .... Firariana [Madagascar] [Seismograph station code, US Geological Survey] (SEIS)
FRR .... Fitchburg Railroad
FRR .... Flight Readiness Review (KSC)
FRR .... Force Readiness Report [DoD]
FRR .... Foreign Receiving Report (MCD)
FRR .... Foreign Research Reactor (GAAI)
FRR .... Forester Resources, Inc. [Vancouver Stock Exchange symbol]
FRR .... Front Royal, VA [Location identifier FAA] (FAAL)
FRR .... Full Reimbursement Rate (AFM)
FRR .... Functional Recovery Routine [Computer science] (BUR)
FRR .... Royal Irish Fusiliers Reserve Regiment [Military unit] [British] (DMA)
FRRA .... Federal Regional Reconstitutional Area
FRRB .... Fast Rise Reflective Balloon
FRRC .... Flow Recording Ratio Controller (IAA)
FRRE .... Field and Reservoir Reserve Estimate [US Geological Survey]
FRRID .... Flight Readiness Review Item Description [NASA] (NASA)
FRRID .... Flight Readiness Review Item Disposition [NASA] (NASA)
FRRIO .... Fleet Replacement RADAR Intercept Officer [Navy] (NVT)
FRRP .... Financial Reporting Review Panel
FRRPP .... Free Radical Retrograde Precipitation Polymerization [Organic chemistry]
FRRRB........ Fast Rise RADAR Reflective Balloon

FRRS .... Frequency Resource Records System
FRRS .... Full Remaining Radiation Service [Unit] [Military]
FRRU.......... Freight Receiving and Redistribution Unit
FRRV .... Fast-Response Relief Valve (MCD)
FRRY .... Ferry [Commonly used] (OPSA)
FRS .... Facilities Requirements Study
FRS .... Failure Reporting System (MCD)
FRS .... Fall Reaction Spheres (AAG)
FRS .... Family Radio Service
FRS .... Family Radio Service
FRS .... Fast Reactor Safety [Nuclear energy] (NRCH)
FRS .... Fast Retrieval Storage [Computer science]
FRS .... Fault Repair Service [Telecommunications British]
FRS............. Federal Reserve Bank of St. Louis, St. Louis, MO [OCLC symbol] (OCLC)
FRS............. Federal Reserve System [Independent government agency]
FRS............. Fellow of the Royal Society [British] (ROG)
FRS............. Fellow of the Royal Society of London [1660] (NGC)
FRS............. Ferredoxin-Reducing Substance [Biochemistry] (MAE)
FRS............. Ferrite Resonance Switch
FRS............. Financial Relations Society [Defunct] (EA)
FRS............. Financial Reporting System (MHDW)
FRS............. Financial Results Simulator (MHDB)
FRS............. Fire Research Station [Research center British] (IRC)
FRS............. Firmware Requirement Specification
FRS............. First Rank Symptoms [Medicine] (MEDA)
FRS............. First Readiness State (AAG)
FRS............. Fisheries Research Station [British]
FRS............. Fixed Radial Shield [Nuclear energy] (NRCH)
FRS............. Flandre Air Service [France ICAO designator] (FAAC)
FRS............. Flash Ranging System
FRS............. Fleet Readiness Squadron [Navy] (NVT)
FRS............. Fleet Repair Service [Navy] (NVT)
FRS............. Flight Radio Subsystem
FRS............. Flores [Guatemala] [Airport symbol] (OAG)
FR(s) .... Flow Rate of Sample
FRS............. Fluidic Rate Sensor (MCD)
FRS............. Flying Relay Station
FRS............. Forced Response Simulation [Computer science]
FRS............. Forest Resource Survey [Australia]
FRS............. Fortress Resources [Vancouver Stock Exchange symbol]
FRS............. Forward Ready Signal [Telecommunications] (TEL)
FRS............. Foundation Research Service
FRS............. Fractal Representation of Sets [Genetics]
FRS............. Fragility Response Spectrum (IEEE)
FRS............. Fragility Response System (IAA)
FRS............. Frame Relay Service (ACRL)
FRS............. Frame Relay Switch [Newbridge Networks Corp.]
FRS............. Franz Rosenzweig Society (EA)
FRS............. Fraternitatis Regiae Socius [Fellow of the Royal Society] [Latin]
FRS............. Frente Republicana e Socialista [Republican and Socialist Front] [Portugal Political party] (PPW)
FRS............. Frente Revolucionaria Sandinista [Nicaragua] [Political party] (EY)
FRS............. Frequency Response Survey (CET)
FRS............. Fresno [Diocesan abbreviation] [California] (TOCD)
FRS............. Frisch's Restaurants [AMEX symbol] (TTSB)
FRS............. Frisch's Restaurants, Inc. [AMEX symbol] (SPSG)
FRS............. Frisian [or Frisic] [Language, etc.]
FRS............. Fuel Receiving Station [Nuclear energy] (NRCH)
FRS............. Functional Requirement Specification (AAG)
FRS............. Functional Requirements Summary (SSD)
FRS............. Furosemide [Pharmacology] (DAVI)
FRSA .... Fellow of the Royal Society of Arts [British] (EY)
FRSA .... Fellow of the Royal Society of Arts, London [1909, founded 1754 as Society of Arts] (NGC)
FRSAI .... Fellow of the Royal Society of Antiquaries of Ireland
FRSAIrel ..... Fellow of the Royal Society of Antiquaries, Ireland (ROG)
FRSAMD ...... Fellow of the Royal Scottish Academy of Music and Drama [British] (DI)
FRSanI........ Fellow of the Royal Sanitary Institute [Later, FRSH] [British]
FRSAS .... Fast-Response Solar Array Simulator
FRSB .... Federal Reserve System Bank
FRSB .... Frequency-Referenced Scanning Beam [Aviation] (OA)
FRSB .... FSS [Flight Service Station] Returns Service B [Aviation] (FAAC)
FRSBY .... Friendly, Round Robin, Special, Bee and Yoke Tracks (SAA)
FRSC .... Fellow of the Royal Society, Canada (ROG)
FRSC .... Fellow of the Royal Society of Chemistry [British] (DBQ)
frsc .... Fresco (VRA)
FRSCan....... Fellow of the Royal Society of Canada
FRSCM .... Fellow of the Royal School of Church Music [British]
FRSE .... Fellow of the Royal Society, Edinburgh (ROG)
FRSEC .... Frames per Second [Telecommunications] (IAA)
FRS Edin .... Fellow of the Royal Society of Edinburgh
FRS et AS ... Fraternitatis Regiae Socius et Associatus [Fellow and Associate of the Royal Society] [Latin] (ROG)
FRSF........... Fuel Receiving and Storage Facility [Nuclear energy] (NRCH)
FRSGS .... Fellow of the Royal Scottish Geographical Society (ROG)
FRSH .... Fellow of the Royal Society of Health [Formerly, FRSanI] [British]
FRSH .... Fresh
FRSH .... [The] Fresh Juice Co., Inc. [NASDAQ symbol] (NQ)
FRSH .... Fresh Juice Inc. [NASDAQ symbol] (TTSB)
FrshChc ...... Fresh Choice, Inc. [Associated Press] (SAG)
FRSI........... Farm-Related Service Industries [FHWA] (TAG)
FRSI........... Fellow of the Royal Sanitary Institute [British] (ROG)
FRSI........... Felt Reusable Surface Insulation (MCD)

FRSI............ Flexible Reusable Surface Insulation (MCD)
FRSL........... Fellow of the Royal Society, London [*British*]
FRSL........... Fellow of the Royal Society of Literature [*British*] (ROG)
FRSL........... Forestry Remote Sensing Laboratory
FRSM.......... Fellow of the Royal Society of Medicine [*British*]
FRSM.......... Ferroresonance Servo Motor (PDAA)
FRSNA........ Fellow of the Royal School of Naval Architects [*British*] (ROG)
FRSNZ........ Fellow of the Royal Society of New Zealand
FRSocMed ... Fellow of the Royal Society of Medicine [*British*]
Fr Soma ..... French Somaliland (VRA)
FRSP .... Fredericksburg and Spotsylvania County Battlefield Memorial National Military Park
FRSS .... Fast Response Survey System [*Washington, DC Department of Education*] (GRD)
FRSS .... Federal Register Search System [*Chemical Information Systems, Inc.*] [*Information service or system*] (CRD)
FRSS .... Fellow of the Royal Statistical Society [*British*] (ROG)
FRSS .... Financial Results Simulator System (MHDB)
FRSS .... Fire-Retardant and Smoke-Suppressant [*Chemicals*]
FRSS .... Flight Reference Stabilization Systems (KSC)
FRSSA .... Fellow of the Royal Scottish Society of Arts (ROG)
FRSSACS .... Free Reaction Sphere Satellite Attitude Control System (DNAB)
FRSSAf .... Fellow of the Royal Society of South Africa
FRSSS .... Fellow of the Royal Statistical Society of Scotland (ROG)
FRST .... Fellow of the Royal Society of Teachers [*British*]
FRST........... FirsTier Finance, Inc. [*NASDAQ symbol*] (NQ)
FRST........... Forest
FRST........... Forest
FRST........... Forest [*Postal Service standard*] (OPSA)
FRST........... Frost [*Meteorology*] (DA)
FrstAll......... First Alliance Corp. [*Associated Press*] (SAG)
FrstCstl .... First Coastal Corp. [*Associated Press*] (SAG)
FrstCtz .... First Citizens Corp. [*Associated Press*] (SAG)
FrstLanc ..... First Lancaster Bancshares, Inc. [*Associated Press*] (SAG)
FRSTM & H... Fellow of the Royal Society of Tropical Medicine and Hygiene [*British*]
FrstMar .... First Mariner Bancorp [*Associated Press*] (SAG)
FrstMF .... First M & F Corp. [*Associated Press*] (SAG)
FrstVrtl .... First Virtual Holdings, Inc. [*Associated Press*] (SAG)
FrSU .... Bibliotheque Nationale et Universitaire, Affaires Generales, Strasbourg, France [*Library symbol*] [*Library of Congress*] (LCLS)
FRT............. Fairbanks Rhyme Test [*Hearing*]
FRT............. Family Relations Test [*Psychology*]
FRT............. Faratahi [*Tuamotu Archipelago*] [*Seismograph station code, US Geological Survey*] (SEIS)
FRT............. Federal Realty Investment Trust SBI [*NYSE symbol*] (SPSG)
FRT............. Federal Rlty Inv Tr SBI [*NYSE symbol*] (TTSB)
FRT............. Fine Range Tuning [*Military*] (CAAL)
FRT............. Fire Retardant [*Technical drawings*]
FRT............. Fire-Retardant Treated
FRT............. Fixed Roof Tank [*Engineering*]
FRT............. Flight Rating Test
FRT............. Flight Readiness Test
FRT............. Flight Readiness Training (MCD)
FRT............. Flow Recording Transmitter
FRT............. Fort [*Commonly used*] (OPSA)
FRT............. Fortnight
FRT............. Forward Repair Team [*Military British*]
FRT............. Freight (AFM)
FRT............. Frequency Response Test (MCD)
FRT............. Front [*Telecommunications*] (TEL)
FRT............. Front [*Automotive engineering*]
FRT............. Fruit
FRT............. Full Recovery Time [*Medicine*]
FRT............. Spartanburg, SC [*Location identifier FAA*] (FAAL)
FRTC........... Fast Reactor Training Center [*Nuclear energy*] (NUCP)
FRTC........... Finance Replacement Training Center [*World War II*]
FRTE........... Forte Software [*NASDAQ symbol*] (TTSB)
FRTE........... Forte Software, Inc. [*NASDAQ symbol*] (SAG)
FRTEF......... Fast Reactor Thermal Engineering Facility [*Nuclear energy*] (NRCH)
FRTF........... Fixed Radio Transmission Facility
Frt Fwd .... Freight Forward [*Shipping*] (DS)
FRT FWDR... Freight Forwarder (MCD)
FRTG........... Fortress Group [*NASDAQ symbol*] (TTSB)
FRTG........... Fortress Group, Inc. (The) [*NASDAQ symbol*] (SAG)
FRTH........... Fourth Financial Corp. [*NASDAQ symbol*] (NQ)
FrthF........... Fourth Financial Corp. [*Associated Press*] (SAG)
FrthFn......... Fourth Financial Corp. [*Associated Press*] (SAG)
FrthShift ..... Fourth Shift Corp. [*Associated Press*] (SAG)
FRTIB.......... Federal Retirement Thrift Investment Board (GFGA)
FRTISO....... Floating-Point Root Isolation [*Computer science*] (MDG)
FrTlALP....... Bibliotheque Americaine, Universite de Toulouse-Le Mirail, Toulouse, France [*Library symbol*] [*Library of Congress*] (LCLS)
FRTN .... Fortune
FRTN .... Front End
FrtNt .... Frontier Natural Gas [*Commercial firm Associated Press*] (SAG)
FRTO........... Flight Radio Telephony Operator (DA)
FRTO........... French Togoland
FRTP........... Fiberglass-Reinforced Thermoplastic
FRTP........... Fraction of Rated Power [*IEEE*]
FRTPI.......... Fellow of the Royal Town Planning Institute [*British*]
Frt Ppd .... Freight Prepaid [*Business term*] (MHDW)
FrtrCp .... Frontier Corp. [*Formerly, Rochester Telephone*] [*Associated Press*] (SAG)
FrtrIns......... Frontier Insurance Group, Inc. [*Associated Press*] (SAG)

FRTRNL ..... Fraternal
FRTRNTY .... Fraternity
FRTZ .... Fritz Companies [*NASDAQ symbol*] (TTSB)
FRTZ .... Fritz Companies, Inc. [*NASDAQ symbol*] (SAG)
FRU .... Field Replaceable Unit [*IBM Corp.*]
FRU .... Fleet Radio Unit
FRU .... Fleet Requirements Units [*Aircraft*]
FRU .... Free Representation Unit [*Legal term*] (DLA)
Fru .... Fructose [*A sugar*]
FRU .... Fruit
FRU .... Frunze [*Former USSR Seismograph station code, US Geological Survey*] (SEIS)
FRU .... Frunze [*Former USSR Airport symbol*] (OAG)
FRU .... Grand Junction, CO [*Location identifier FAA*] (FAAL)
FRU .... Transportadora Fruyleg, SA de CV [*Mexico*] [*FAA designator*] (FAAC)
FRUCOM ..... Federation Europeenne des Importateurs de Fruits Secs, Conserves, Epices et Miels [*European Federation of Importers of Dried Fruits, Preserves, Spices, and Honey*]
FRUCT .... Fructus [*Fruit*] [*Latin*] (ROG)
FRUD .... Front pour la Restauration de l'Unite et de la Democratie [*Djibouti*] [*Political party*] (EY)
FRUGAL...... FORTRAN [*Formula Translating System*] Rules Used as a General Applications Language [*Computer science*]
FRUI .... Fellow of the Royal University of Ireland (ROG)
FruitL.......... Fruit of the Loom, Inc. [*Associated Press*] (SAG)
FRUM .... Forum
FRUM .... Fratrum [*Of the Brothers*] [*Latin*] (ADA)
FRUMEL ...... Fleet Radio Unit, Melbourne [*World War II*]
FRUMP .... Fast Reading and Understanding Memory Program [*Computer science*]
FRUMPS ..... Frugal Responsible Unpretentious Mature Persons
FRUPAC...... Fleet Radio Unit, Pacific
FRUSA .... Flexible Rolled-Up Solar Array [*Air Force*]
FRUST .... Frustillatim [*In Little Pieces*] [*Pharmacy*] (ROG)
FruTrail........ Fruehauf Trailer Corp. [*Associated Press*] (SAG)
frutwd......... Fruitwood (VRA)
FRU VEG..... Fruits or Vegetables [*Freight*]
FRV .... Fishing Research Vessel
FRV .... Flight Readiness Vehicle
FRV .... Fur Vault, Inc. (MHDW)
FRV .... Future Reconnaissance Vehicle [*Army*]
FRVA .... Fellow of the Rating and Valuation Association [*British*] (DBQ)
FRVC .... Fellow of the Royal Veterinary College [*British*] (DI)
FRVIA .... Fellow of the Royal Victorian Institute of Architects [*British*] (ROG)
FRW............ Faraway Gold Mines Ltd. [*Vancouver Stock Exchange symbol*]
FRW............ Francistown [*Botswana*] [*Airport symbol*] (OAG)
FRW............ Friction Welding
FRW............ Friedman-Robertson-Walker Theory [*Cosmology*]
f-rw-- .... Rwanda [*MARC geographic area code Library of Congress*] (LCCP)
FrWAfr......... French West Africa
FRWAY .... Freeway [*Commonly used*] (OPSA)
FRWD .... Foreword
FRWF.......... Forecast Wind Factor [*NWS*] (FAAC)
FRWG .... Fleet Requirements Working Group (DOMA)
FRWI .... Framingham Relative Weight Index [*Cardiology*]
FRWID........ Fruit Width [*Botany*]
FRWIS .... Frost Warnings Issued (NOAA)
FRWK .... Framework [*Also, FR*] [*Genetics*] (MSA)
FRWL.......... Forest, Range, and Watershed Laboratory [*Laramie, WY*] [*Department of Agriculture*] (GRD)
FRWRK....... Firework
FRWY .... Freeway
FRX............. Financial Reporting Extender [*Computer science*]
FRX............. Forest Laboratories, Inc. [*AMEX symbol*] (SPSG)
FRX............. Forest Labs [*AMEX symbol*] (TTSB)
FRXD .... Fully Automatic Reperforator Transmitter Distributor [*Telecommunications*] (TEL)
FRY............. Fairlady Energy [*Vancouver Stock Exchange symbol*]
FRY............. Ferry
FRY............. Ferry
FRY............. Friary
FRY............. Fryeburg, ME [*Location identifier FAA*] (FAAL)
Fry .... Fry on Specific Performance of Contracts [*A publication*] (DLA)
Fry Lun........ Fry on Lunacy [*A publication*] (DLA)
Fry Sp Per ... Fry on Specific Performance of Contracts [*A publication*] (DLA)
Fry Vac....... Fry on the Vaccination Acts [*A publication*] (DLA)
FRZ............. Freeze [*NWS*] (FAAC)
frz .... Frieze (VRA)
FRZ............. Frozen
Fr Zabar ..... Franciscus Zabarella [*Deceased, 1417*] [*Authority cited in pre-1607 legal work*] (DSA)
FRZER .... Freezer (DNAB)
FRZG .... Freezing
FRZLVL........ Freezing Level [*NWS*] (FAAC)
FRZN .... Frozen
FRZR .... Freezer (MSA)
FRZR .... Freezer
FRZS........... Fellow of the Royal Zoological Society [*British*] (DI)
FRZSScot .... Fellow of the Royal Zoological Society of Scotland
fs---- .... Africa, Southern [*MARC geographic area code Library of Congress*] (LCCP)
FS .... Fabian Society [*British*] (ILCA)
F/S .... Facing South [*In outdoor advertising*] (WDMC)
FS .... Facsimile (ADA)

FS	Factor of Safety
FS	Factor Storage (IAA)
FS	Fail-Safe (NASA)
FS	Fail to Synchronize (MCD)
FS	Fairbairn-Sykes [British military] (DMA)
FS	Faire Suivre [Please Forward] [French]
FS	Fallschirm [Parachute] [German military]
FS	Family Status (OICC)
FS	Famous Sayings [Psychological testing]
FS	Famous Scots [A publication]
FS	Fanconi Syndrome [Medicine] (DMAA)
FS	Farm Sanctuary (EA)
FS	Far Side
FS	Fast Screening
FS	Fast Slew
FS	Fast Store [Computer science] (TEL)
FS	Fast Supply [Ships]
FS	Father of Sion [Roman Catholic]
FS	Fathers of Sion [An association British] (BI)
FS	Fault Summary (MCD)
FS	Feasibility Study
FS	Federal Specification
FS	Federal Standard
FS	Federal Supplement [A publication] (DLA)
FS	Feedback, Stabilized
FS	Feet per Second
FS	Felix Schlag [Designer's mark, when appearing on US coins]
FS	Female Servant
FS	Female Soldered (MSA)
FS	Female, Spayed
FS	Femininity Study [Psychology]
FS	Femtosecond [One quadrillionth of a second]
FS	Fernschreiben [or Fernschreiber] [Teletype Message or Teletype] [German military - World War II]
fs	Ferrosilite [CIPW classification] [Geology]
FS	Ferrovie dello Stato [Italian State Railways]
Fs	Festschrift [A publication] (BJA)
F/S	Fetch and Send [Telecommunications] (TEL)
FS	Fiber Society (EA)
FS	Fiberstock [Firearms]
FS	Fichtel & Sachs [Auto industry supplier] [German]
FS	Field of Science [Dialog] [Searchable field] [Information service or system] (NITA)
FS	Field Security [British Army detective police - a branch of Intelligence]
FS	Field Separator
FS	Field Sequential (IAA)
FS	Field Service
FS	Field Sparrow [Ornithology]
FS	Field Station
FS	Field Switch (IAA)
FS	Fight for Sight [Also known as NCCB] (EA)
FS	File Save [Computer science]
FS	File Segment [Searchable field] (NITA)
FS	File Separator [Computer science]
FS	File Source [Computer science]
FS	Filing Status [IRS]
FS	Filler for Smoke Shells [Weaponry] (NATG)
F/S	Film and Sheet [Plastics technology]
FS	Filmstrip
fs	Filmstrip (VRA)
FS	Filtration Society (EA)
FS	Final Selector [Telecommunications]
FS	Final Settlement
F/S	Final Statement [Army]
FS	Financial Scribe [Freemasonry] (ROG)
FS	Financial Secretary
F/S	Financial Statement
FS	Finishers' Society [A union] [British]
FS	Finish Specification
FS	Fin Stabilized [Rocketry]
FS	Fire and Safety [Technician] [Coast Guard] (DOMA)
FS	Fire Service
FS	Fire Station [Maps and charts]
FS	Fire Support
FS	Fire Suppression (MCD)
FS	Fire Switch (KSC)
FS	Firing Set (NG)
FS	Firing Station (MUGU)
FS	First Stage [Aerospace]
FS	First Step (MUGU)
FS	First Sunday (EA)
FS	Fiscal Service (IEEE)
FS	Flagstaff
FS	Flameless, Smokeless [Gunpowder]
FS	Flame Shielding
FS	Flashes per Second [Telecommunications] (IAA)
FS	Flat Seam (DNAB)
FS	Flat Slip (OA)
F/S	Fleet Status [Navy] (MCD)
F/S	Fleet Support [Navy]
FS	Fleet Surgeon
FS	Fleischner Society (EA)
FS	Flexible Sigmoidoscopy [Proctoscopy]
FS	Flight Safety (AFM)

FS	Flight Sergeant [RAF] [British]
FS	Flight Service
FS	Flight Simulator (AFM)
FS	Flight Surgeon
FS	Flight System (MCD)
FS	Floating Sign
FS	Floating Subtract (IAA)
FS	Float Switch [Aerospace] (AAG)
FS	Flood Stage
FS	Flow Switch
FS	Fluid Switch
FS	Fluorescence Spectroscopy
FS	Flying Scholarship [British military] (DMA)
FS	Flying Status
FS	Foaming Stability [Food technology]
FS	Fog Signal [Station] [Maps and charts]
FS	Fog Siren [Navigation charts]
FS	Folio Society [British] (EAIO)
FS	Follow Sender [Telecommunications] (TEL)
FS	Follow Shot [Photography] (NTCM)
FS	Fomant Synthesis [Speech synthesis] (NITA)
FS	Food Stamp
FS	Foot-Second (ADA)
FS	Foot Shock [Biometrics]
FS	Foramen Spinosum [Neuroanatomy]
FS	Force Structuring (MCD)
FS	Forearm Supinated [Medicine]
FS	Forecast/Surface (NATG)
FS	Foreign Service [Department of State]
FS	Foresight (AAG)
F/S	Forest/Savanna Soils [Agronomy]
FS	Forest Service [Later, Department of Natural Resources] [Department of Agriculture]
FS	Forged Steel
FS	Format Statement (IAA)
FS	Form Separator [Computer science] (PCM)
FS	Fortune Society (EA)
FS	Forward Scatter
FS	Forward Support
FS	Foundation State [Dialog] [Searchable field] [Information service or system] (NITA)
FS	Fourth Section [of Interstate Commerce Act]
FS	Fractional Shortening [Cardiology]
FS	Fractostratus [Meteorology]
FS	Fracture, Simple [Medicine]
FS	Fragile Site [Medicine] (DMAA)
FS	Frame Scan (DEN)
F/S	Frames per Second (NTCM)
FS	Frame Status (ACRL)
FS	Franklin Simon & Co. [Retail clothing stores]
FS	Fred Society (EA)
FS	Free by Servitude (ADA)
FS	Free Safety [Football]
FS	Free Standing (ADA)
FS	Free Sterol [Biochemistry] (OA)
FS	Freestone (ADA)
FS	Freeze Substitution (OA)
FS	Freight Ship
FS	Freight Supply Vessel [Obsolete Navy]
fs	French Southern and Antarctic Lands [MARC country of publication code Library of Congress] (LCCP)
FS	Freon Servicer (MCD)
FS	Frequency Shift (BUR)
FS	Frequency Stability
FS	Frequency Standard
FS	Frequency Synthesizer [Electronics] (OA)
FS	Friendly Society [British] (ILCA)
FS	Friendly Status (MCD)
FS	Friends of Solidarity (EA)
FS	Friends of the Shakers (EA)
FS	Frozen Section [Medicine]
FS	Fuel Saver [Automotive engineering]
FS	Fuel Storage Subsystem (MCD)
FS	Full and Soft [Dietetics]
FS	Fullrack System
FS	Full-Scale [Intelligence quotient] [Psychology] (DAVI)
FS	Full Scale [Analog computers]
FS	Full Shot [Photography] (NTCM)
FS	Full Size (MSA)
FS	Full Stop (ADA)
FS	Full Sun
FS	Functional Schedules (MCD)
FS	Functional Schematic
FS	Functional Selector
FS	Functional Specification [Telecommunications] (TEL)
FS	Function Select (NITA)
FS	Function Set
FS	Function Study [Medicine] (MAE)
FS	Function Symbol (IAA)
F/S	Furnace Sensitize (PDAA)
FS	Furnace Soldering
FS	Fuse
FS	Fuselage Station [Aviation]
FS	Future Series (IAA)
FS	Futures Spread [Investment term]

FS .... Future System [*IBM Corp.*] [*Computer science*]
FS .... Graduate of the Royal Air Force Staff College [*British*]
FS .... Key Airlines [*ICAO designator*] (AD)
FS .... Registry of Friendly Societies [*British*]
FS .... Sarasota Public Library, Sarasota, FL [*Library symbol Library of Congress*] (LCLS)
Fs .... Signal Framing Bits [*Telecommunications*] (ACRL)
FS .... Sulfur Trioxide Chlorsulfonic Acid [*Inorganic chemistry*]
FS³ .... Future Strategic Strategy Study [*Military*] (SDI)
F$5 .... Firing Squad Synchronization, Simulation and Solution System
FSA .... Fabric Salesmen's Association (EA)
FSA .... Fallout Shelter Analysis [*or Analyst*] [*Civil Defense*]
FSA .... Family Separation Allowance [*Military*] (AABC)
FSA .... Family Service America (EA)
FSA .... Family Support Act of 1988 (WYGK)
FSA .... Family Support Administration [*Department of Health and Human Services*]
FSA .... Farm Security Administration [*Succeeded by Farmers Home Administration, 1946*]
FSA .... Federal Security Agency [*Functions and units transferred to HEW, 1953*]
FSA .... Federal Statutes, Annotated [*A publication*] (DLA)
FSA .... Fellesradet for det Sorlige Afrika [*Norway*]
FSA .... Fellow of the Society of Actuaries [*Society of Actuaries*] [*Designation awarded by*]
FSA .... Fellow of the Society of Antiquaries [*British*]
FSA .... Fellow of the Society of Arts [*British*]
FSA .... Fetal Sulfoglycoprotein Antigen [*Oncology*]
FSA .... Fiat Secundum Artem [*Let It Be Done According to Art*] [*Pharmacy*]
FSa .... Fibrosarcoma [*Oncology*]
FSA .... Field Safety Activity (MCD)
FSA .... Field Safety Agency (MCD)
FSA .... Field Service Addition (MCD)
FSA .... Field Support Activity [*Military*] (NVT)
FSA .... Field Survey Association (BARN)
FSA .... File System Agent [*Telecommunications*] (PCM)
FSA .... Final Site Acceptance (NATG)
FSA .... Finance Service, Army
FSA .... Financial Sec Assurance Hldg [*NYSE symbol*] (TTSB)
FSA .... Financial Security Assurance
FSA .... Financial Security Assurance Holdings [*NYSE symbol*] (SAG)
FSA .... Financial Services Act [*British*]
FSA .... Financial Stationers Association (EA)
FSA .... Financial Suppliers Association [*Later, FSF*] (EA)
FSA .... Fine Structure Analysis (IAA)
FSA .... Finite State Automation (HGAA)
FSA .... Finnish Society of Adelaide [*South Australia*]
FSA .... Fire Science Abstracts [*Department of the Environment*] [*Information service or system*] (IID)
FSA .... Fire Site Assembly (MCD)
FSA .... Fire Support Area [*Military*]
FSA .... Fixed Slot Acknowledgement [*Telecommunications*] (OSI)
FSA .... Flared Slot Antenna
FSA .... Flat-Plate Solar Array
FSA .... Flexible Solar Array
FSA .... Flexible Spending Account [*Employer distribution of nontaxable income to employees*]
FSA .... Florida Statutes, Annotated [*A publication*] (DLA)
FSA .... Fluid Sealing Association (EA)
FSA .... Flux Switch Alternator
FSA .... Food Security Act [*of 1985*]
FSA .... Force Structure Allowance [*DoD*]
FSA .... Foreign Service Act
FSA .... Foreign Service Allowances [*British*]
FSA .... Foreign Service Availability [*Military*]
FSA .... Foreign Statesmen [*A publication*]
FSA .... Foreign Systems Acquisition [*Army*]
FSA .... Formatter Sense Amplifier (IAA)
FSA .... Formosa Resources Corp. [*Vancouver Stock Exchange symbol*]
FSA .... Forward Sale Agreement [*EXFINCO*]
FSA .... Forward Skirt Adapter
FSA .... Forward Sortation Area [*Mailing technique*]
FSA .... Forward Support Area [*Military*]
FSA .... Foster Aviation [*ICAO designator*] (FAAC)
FSA .... Fraternity Scholarship Association [*Later, College Fraternity Scholarship Officers Association*] (EA)
FSA .... Free Support Area (MUGU)
FSA .... French Society of Acoustics [*Formerly, Group of French-Speaking Acousticians*] (EA)
FSA .... Frequency Selective Amplifier (IAA)
FSA .... Frequency Stability Analyzer
FSA .... Friendly Societies Act [*British*] (ILCA)
FSA .... Front Suspension Arm
FSA .... Fuel Storage Area (AAG)
FSA .... Full-Scale Accuracy (IAA)
FSA .... Full-State Assumption [*Education*] (AEE)
FSA .... Fuse Safe/Arm
FSA .... Future Scientists of America [*Defunct*] (EA)
f-sa-- .... South Africa [*MARC geographic area code Library of Congress*] (LCCP)
FSAA .... Family Service Association of America [*Later, FSA*] (EA)
FSAA .... Fellow of the Society of Accountants and Auditors (DD)
FSAA .... Fellow of the Society of Incorporated Accountants and Auditors [*British*] (EY)
FSAA .... Flat Slips All Around (OA)

FSAA .... Flight Simulator for Advanced Aircraft [*NASA*]
FSAA .... Folk-School Association of America [*Later, FEAA*] (EA)
FSAC .... Federal Safety Advisory Council [*Later, FACOSH*]
FSAC .... Film Studies Association of Canada
FSAC .... Fire Support Armament Center [*Dover, NJ*] [*Army*] (GRD)
FSAC .... First South Africa Corp. Ltd. [*NASDAQ symbol*] (SAG)
FSAC .... Fourth Stowage Adapter Container
FSAC .... Freight Station Accounting Code [*Railroad term*]
FSAC .... From the Stone Age to Christianity [*A publication*] (BJA)
FSACF .... First South Africa [*NASDAQ symbol*] (TTSB)
FSAE .... Fellow of the National Society of Art Education [*British*]
FSAE .... Fellow of the Society of Antiquaries, Edinburgh
FSaF .... Flagler College, St. Augustine, FL [*Library symbol Library of Congress*] (LCLS)
FSAF .... Frequency Shift Audio Frequency [*Telecommunications*] (IAA)
FSAF .... Future Scientists of America Foundation [*Defunct*]
FSaHi .... St. Augustine Historical Society, St. Augustine, FL [*Library symbol Library of Congress*] (LCLS)
FSAI .... Fellow of the Society of Antiquaries, Ireland (ROG)
F(SA)ICE ...... Fellow of the South African Institution of Civil Engineers
FSAICU .... Federation of State Associations of Independent Colleges and Universities [*Later, NAICU*] (EA)
F(SA)IEE ...... Fellow of the South African Institute of Electrical Engineers
F(SA)IME ...... Fellow of the South African Institution of Mechanical Engineers
FSAL .... Fellow of the Society of Antiquaries, London (ROG)
FSALA .... Fellow of the South African Library Association
FSAM .... Fellow of the Society of Art Masters [*British*]
FSAM .... Free South Africa Movement (EA)
FSan .... Sanford Public Library, Sanford, FL [*Library symbol Library of Congress*] (LCLS)
FS & G .... Farrar, Straus & Giroux [*Publisher*]
FS & R .... Filling, Storage, and Remelt System [*Nuclear energy*] (NRCH)
FsanLC .... Central Florida Library Consortium, Sanford, FL [*Library symbol*] [*Library of Congress*] (LCLS)
FSanS .... Seminole Community College, Sanford, FL [*Library symbol Library of Congress*] (LCLS)
FSANSW .... Family Support Association of New South Wales [*Australia*]
FSAO .... Family Services and Assistance Officer (AABC)
FSAO .... Fellow of the Scottish Association of Opticians (DAS)
FSAP .... Factory Space Allocation Plan (MCD)
FSAP .... Federal Student Aid Program [*Department of Education*] (GFGA)
FSAPO .... Fade Sound and Picture Out [*Cinematography*] (NTCM)
FSA-R .... Family Separation Allowance (Restricted Station) [*Military*] (DNAB)
FSAR .... Fiat Secundum Artem Reglas [*Let It Be Done According to the Rules of the Art*] [*Pharmacy*]
FSAR .... Filling, Storage, and Remelt System [*Nuclear energy*] (IAA)
FSAR .... Final Safety Analysis Report [*NASA*] (KSC)
FSAR .... Forest Service Acquisition Regulation [*A publication*] (AAGC)
FSAR .... Fuel Systems Analysis Report (SAA)
FSArc .... Fellow of the Society of Architects [*British*]
FSArch .... Fellow of the Society of Architects [*British*]
FSA-S .... Family Separation Allowance (Shipboard Operations) [*Military*] (DNAB)
FSAS .... Fellow of the Society of Antiquaries of Scotland
FSAS .... Flight Service Automation System [*FAA*] (TAG)
FSAS .... Fluidic Stability Augmentation System [*for helicopters*]
FSAS .... Force Structure Assessment System [*Model*] [*Army*]
FSAS .... Fuel Savings Advisory System
FSA Scot ...... Fellow of the Society of Antiquaries of Scotland
FSAS/INS ..... Fuel Savings Advisory System / Inertial Navigation System [*Air Force*]
FSA-T .... Family Separation Allowance (Temporary Duty) [*Military*] (DNAB)
FSAT .... Financial Svcs. Acquisition Corp. [*NASDAQ symbol*] (SAG)
FSAT .... Full-Scale Aerial [*or Afterburning*] Target
FSAU .... First South Africa Corp. Ltd. [*NASDAQ symbol*] (SAG)
FSAUF .... First South Africa Unit [*NASDAQ symbol*] (TTSB)
FSAVC .... Free-Standing Additional Voluntary Contribution [*Pension fund payment option*] [*British*]
FSAW .... First South Africa Corp. Ltd. [*NASDAQ symbol*] (SAG)
FSAWF .... First South Africa Wrrt'A' [*NASDAQ symbol*] (TTSB)
FSAZ .... First South Africa Corp. Ltd. [*NASDAQ symbol*] (SAG)
FSAZF .... First South Africa Wrrt'B' [*NASDAQ symbol*] (TTSB)
FSB .... Falange Socialista Boliviana [*Bolivian Socialist Phalange*] [*Political party*] (PPW)
FSB .... Fallout Studies Branch [*AEC*]
FSB .... Family Services Branch [*Australian Capital Territory*]
FSB .... Federal Savings Bank
FSB .... Federal Specification Board
FSB .... Federal Supplemental Benefits
FSB .... Female Sexual Biomass [*Botany*]
FSB .... Fetal Scalp Blood [*Fetal monitoring*] (CPH)
FSB .... Field Selection Board [*Military*]
FSB .... Field Service Bulletin (AAG)
FSB .... Final Staging Base (AFM)
FSB .... Fire Support Base [*Army*] (AABC)
FSB .... Flat Slip on Bottom (OA)
FSB .... Fleet Satellite Broadcasting [*Navy*] (MCD)
FSB .... Floating Subtract [*Computer science*] (IAA)
FSB .... Floating Supply Base [*Military*] (PDAA)
FSB .... Food Supply Board [*Ministry of Food*] [*British World War II*]
FSB .... Foreign Science Bulletin
FSB .... Forward Space Block (CMD)
FSB .... Forward Support Base
FSB .... Forward Support Battalion [*Army*] (INF)
FSB .... Free Storage Block [*Computer science*] (IAA)

FSB	Front Striker Bulletin [*An association*] (EA)
FSB	Fuel Storage Basin [*Nuclear energy*]
FSb	Functional Specification Block [*Telecommunications*] (TEL)
FSb	Satellite Beach Public Library, Satellite Beach, FL [*Library symbol Library of Congress*] (LCLS)
FSBA	Federal and State Business Assistance Database [*National Technical Information Service*] [*Information service or system*] (CRD)
FSBA	Finnsheep Breeders Association (EA)
FSBA	Fluorosulfonylbenzoyl Adenosine [*Biochemistry*]
FSBA	Food Service Brokers of America [*Defunct*] (EA)
FSBC	First Savings Bank [*NASDAQ symbol*] (NQ)
FSBC	First SB Clovis N Mex [*NASDAQ symbol*] (TTSB)
FSBF	FSB Financial Corp. [*NASDAQ symbol*] (SAG)
FSB Fin	FSB Fiancial Corp. [*Associated Press*] (SAG)
FSBG	Finger-Stick Blood Gas (MEDA)
FSBI	Falange Socialista Boliviana de Izquierda [*Bolivian Socialist Phalange of the Left*] [*Political party*] (PPW)
FSBI	Fellow of the Savings Bank Institute [*British*] (ODBW)
FSBI	Fidelity Bancorp [*NASDAQ symbol*] (SAG)
FSBI	Fisheries Society of the British Isles
FSBkNJ	First Savings Bank FSLA Perth Amboy NJ [*Associated Press*] (SAG)
FSBL	Feasible (MSA)
FSBL	Fusible (MSA)
FSBM	Full-Strength Breast Milk [*Neonatology*] (DAVI)
FSBO	For Sale by Owner [*Real estate ads*] [*Pronounced "fizz-bo"*]
FSBPRT	Free Storage Block Pointer (HGAA)
FSBR	Financial Statement and Budget Report [*British*]
FSBS	First Ashland Financial [*NASDAQ symbol*] (TTSB)
FSBS	First Ashland Financial Corp. [*NASDAQ symbol*] (SAG)
FSBS	Front Supply Base Sections (MCD)
FSBSEM	Free Storage Block Semaphore [*Computer science*] (IAA)
FSBT	First State [*NASDAQ symbol*] (TTSB)
FSBT	First State Corp. [*NASDAQ symbol*] (SAG)
FSBT	Fowler Single Breath Test [*Medicine*] (DMAA)
FSBTh	Fellow of the Society of Health and Beauty Therapists [*British*] (DBQ)
FSBW	Frame Space Bandwidth Product (IAA)
FSBWA	First Savings Bank Washington Bancorp, Inc. [*Associated Press*] (SAG)
FSBX	Framingham Savings Bank [*NASDAQ symbol*] (SAG)
FSBX	Framingham Svgs Bank (MA) [*NASDAQ symbol*] (TTSB)
fsc	Brothers of the Christian Schools (TOCD)
FSC	Brothers of the Christian Schools (TOCD)
FSC	Fabricated Steel Construction [*Bethlehem Steel Corp.*]
FSC	Fairmont State College [*West Virginia*]
FSC	Family Services Center [*Military*]
FSC	Fat-Storing Cell [*Liver anatomy*]
FSC	Fault Simulation Comparator
FSC	Federal Safety Council
FSC	Federal Simulation Center
FSC	Federal Sports Club [*Australia*]
FSC	Federal Stock [*or Supply*] Catalog (NG)
FSC	Federal Stock [*or Supply*] Classification [*Army*]
FSC	Federal Stock Control
FSC	Federal Supplemental Compensation [*Unemployment insurance*] (OICC)
FSC	Federal Supply Catalog (MCD)
FSC	Federal Supply Classification [*DoD*] (MCD)
FSC	Federal Supply Code (MCD)
FSC	Federation of Southern Cooperatives [*Later, FSC/LAF*] (EA)
FSC	Federation Socialiste Caledonienne [*Caledonian Socialist Federation*] [*Political party*] (PPW)
FSC	Fellowship of Southern Churchmen [*Later, Committee of Southern Churchmen*] (EA)
FSC	Fest Resources [*Vancouver Stock Exchange symbol*]
FSC	Fibrous Sausage Casing
FSC	Field Studies Council [*British*] (ARC)
FSC	Field Study Coordinator [*Military*] (MCD)
FSC	Field Support Center [*Military*] (IAA)
FSC	Field Survey Company [*British military*] (DMA)
FSC	Figari [*Corsica*] [*Airport symbol*] (OAG)
FSC	File Server Control [*Computer science*] (DOMA)
FSC	File System Control [*Computer science*]
FSC	Filing Status Code [*IRS*]
FSC	Film Stowage Container
FSC	Final Subcircuit [*An enzyme*] (IAA)
FSC	Final Systems Check [*NASA*] (KSC)
FSC	Finite State Channel (IAA)
FSC	Fire Service College [*British*]
FSC	Fire Support Center [*Army*] (DOMA)
FSC	Fire Support Coordination [*Military*]
FSC	First-Stage Conduit [*Aerospace*]
FSC	Fixed Satellite Communications (DNAB)
FSC	Fixed Silicon Capacitor
FSC	Flame Spread Classification [*For polymers*]
FSC	Fleet Satellite Communications [*DoD*]
FSC	Fleet Systems Capable (NVT)
FSC	Flexible Shielded Cable
FSC	Flight Security Controller [*Military*]
FSC	Flight Service Center
FSC	Florida Southern College [*Lakeland*]
FSC	Florida Southern College, Lakeland, FL [*OCLC symbol*] (OCLC)
F-SC	Florida Supreme Court, Tallahassee, FL [*Library symbol Library of Congress*] (LCLS)
FSC	Fluid Storage Container
FSC	Flying Status Code (AFM)
FSC	Food Safety Council [*Defunct*] (EA)
FSC	Food Standards Code [*Australia*]
FSC	Food Standards Committee [*British*]
FSC	Food Storage Cell
FSC	Food Supplement Co. [*British*]
FSC	Foolscap (NTCM)
FSC	Force Structure Committee (AFM)
FSC	Foreign Sales Corp. [*See also Domestic International Sales Corp. - DISC*]
FSC	Foreign Service Credits [*Military*]
FSC	Foreign Staff College [*British*]
FSC	Forer Sentence Completion Test [*Psychology*] (DAVI)
FSC	Forward Scatter (NATG)
FSC	Foundation for Student Communication [*Princeton, NJ*] (EA)
FSC	Foundation for the Study of Cycles (EA)
FSC	Four Star Aviation, Inc. [*Virgin Islands*] [*ICAO designator*] (FAAC)
FSC	Fracture, Simple Comminuted [*Orthopedics*] (DAVI)
FSC	Fratres Scholarum Christianarum [*Institute of the Brothers of the Christian Schools*] [*Also known as Christian Brothers*] (EAIO)
FSC	Free Secreting Component [*Immunology*]
FSC	Frequency Shift Converter
FSC	Fresno Service Center [*IRS*]
FSC	Fresno State College [*Later, California State University, Fresno*]
FSC	Friends of the Superior Court (EA)
FSC	Friends Service Council [*Quakers*]
FSC	Fuel Scheduling Computer (MCD)
FSC	Fuel Systems Capability (MCD)
FSC	Full Scale
FSC	Full Systems Capable [*Military*] (CAAL)
FSC	Fully Self-Contained (ADA)
FSC	Funding Sources Clearinghouse, Inc. (IID)
FSC	Fuscaldo [*Italy*] [*Seismograph station code, US Geological Survey*] (SEIS)
FSC	Future Studies Centre [*British*] (CB)
FSC	Selected Judgments of the Federal Supreme Court [*1956-61*] [*Nigeria*] [*A publication*] (DLA)
FSCA	Fellow of the Society of Company and Commercial Accountants [*British*] (DCTA)
FSCATT	Fire Support Combined Arms Tactical Trainer [*Army*] (RDA)
FSCATT	Fire Support Combined Arms Tactical Trainer [*Army*]
FSCB	Fielded Software Control Board [*Army*]
FSCB	File System Control Block [*Computer science*] (IBMDP)
FSCC	Federal Supply Classification Code
FSCC	Federal Surplus Commodities Corp.
FSCC	Ferrous Scrap Consumers Coalition (EA)
FSCC	Figure Skating Coaches of Canada [*See also EPAC*]
FSCC	Fire Support Coordination Center [*Military*]
FSCC	First-Stage Conduit Container [*Aerospace*]
FSCC	Food Surplus Commodities Corp.
FSCE	Fire Support Coordination Element [*Military*]
FSCE	Free-Solution Capillary Electrophoresis [*Physical chemistry*]
FSCEA	French-Speaking Comparative Education Association [*See also AFEC*] [*Sevres, France*] (EAIO)
FSCEN	Flight Service Center
FSCFC	Friends of Shaun Cassidy Fan Club (EA)
FSCG	Federal Supply Classification Group (AFM)
FSCH	Form and Structure of Corporate Headings [*Cataloguing*] [*Association for Library Collections and Technical Services*]
FSCH	Fulbright Scholarship
FSCI	Frequency Space Characteristic Impedance
FSCIL	Federal Supply Catalog Identification List (MSA)
FSCJ	Congregatio Filiorum Sacratissimi Cordis Jesu [*Sons of the Sacred Heart*] [*Verona Fathers Roman Catholic religious order*]
FSCJ	Friendly Society of Carpenters and Joiners [*A union*] [*British*]
FSCL	Federal Supply Classification Listing
FSCL	Fire Support Coordination Line [*Military*] (AABC)
FSC/LAF	Federation of Southern Cooperatives and Land Assistance Fund (EA)
FSCM	Federal Supply Code for Manufacturers
FSCM	Fire Support Coordination Measure [*Military*] (INF)
FSC/MMAC	Federal Supply Classification/Material Management Aggregation (MCD)
FSCN	Free State Consolidated Gold [*NASDAQ symbol*] (SAG)
FSCNHA	Federal Service Campaign for National Health Agencies [*Later, National Health Agencies for the Combined Federal Campaign*] (EA)
FSC (Nig)	Judgments of the Federal Supreme Court [*1956-61*] [*Nigeria*] [*A publication*] (DLA)
FSCNM	Federal Supply Code for Non-Manufacturers
FSCNY	Free St Con Gld Mines ADR [*NASDAQ symbol*] (TTSB)
FSCO	Federation of Straight Chiropractic Organizations (EA)
FSCO	First Security [*NASDAQ symbol*] (TTSB)
FSCO	First Security Corp. [*NASDAQ symbol*] (NQ)
FS/COLS	Fire Support Team and Combat Observation Lasing System [*Army*]
FSCOORD	Fire Support Coordinator [*Military*] (AABC)
FSCP	Feasibility Study Change Proposal (MCD)
FSCP	Federal/State Cooperative Program for Population Estimates and Projections (OICC)
FSCP	Fellow of the Society of Certified Professionals [*British*] (DBQ)
FSCP	Fire Sensor Control Panel (MCD)
FSCP	Firing Site Command Post [*Army*] (AABC)
FSCP	Foolscap [*Paper*] (ROG)
FSCR	Federal Screw Works [*NASDAQ symbol*] (NQ)
FSCR	Field Select Command Register
FSCR	First Ship Configuration Review [*Navy*]

FSCR .... Fuel Storage Control Room [*Nuclear energy*] (NRCH)
FSCS........... Federal-State Cooperative for Public Library Data
FSCS........... Federal Supply Classification System
FSCS........... Fire Support Coordination Section [*Military*]
FSCS........... Fleet Satellite Communications System [*DoD*] (DNAB)
FSCS........... Flight Service Communications System
FSCS........... Foresight Sierra Communications System (MCD)
FSCS........... Frequency Shift Communications System
FSCS........... Fuel Storage Cable Spread [*Nuclear energy*] (NRCH)
FSCS........... Functional Standard Conformance Statement [*Telecommunications*]
FSCT........... Federation of Societies for Coatings Technology
FSCT........... Fellow of the Society of Cardiological Technicians [*British*] (DBQ)
FSCT........... Fellow of the Society of Commercial Teachers [*British*] (DBQ)
FSCT........... Five-Soldier Crew Tent
FSCT........... Floyd Satellite Communications Terminal
FSCTT......... Fire Support Coordination Team Trainer (DOMA)
FSCU .... Frequency Select Control Unit (MCD)
FSCUSA ...... Flying Senior Citizens of United States of America [*Defunct*] (EA)
FSCV.......... Fire Support Combat Vehicle (MCD)
FSCW......... Fast Space Charge Wave (IAA)
FSCWC ...... Florida Space Coast Writers Conference (EA)
FSCX.......... FastComm Communications [*NASDAQ symbol*] (TTSB)
FSCX.......... FastComm Communications Corp. [*NASDAQ symbol*] (NQ)
FSD............ Efs-Flugservice GmbH [*Germany ICAO designator*] (FAAC)
FSD............ Federal Systems Division (SAA)
FSD............ Federation des Socialistes Democrates [*Federation of Democratic Socialists*] [*France Political party*] (PPE)
FSD............ Field Support Diagram (IAA)
FSD............ File-Set Description [*Computer science*]
FSD............ File System Driver (PCM)
FSD............ First-Degree Stochastic Dominance [*Statistics*]
FSD............ First Ship Delivered (DNAB)
FSD............ Fisher Significant Difference (PDAA)
FSD............ Flight Simulation Division [*Johnson Space Center*] [*NASA*] (NASA)
FSD............ Fluidic Setting Device
FSD............ Flying Spot Digitizer
FSD............ Focal Skin Distance [*Radiology*]
FSD............ Force Spectral Density
FSD............ Forecast Support Date
FSD............ Foreign Sea Duty
FSD............ Formal Syntax Definition [*Aviation*]
FSD............ Foster-Seeley Discriminator
FSD............ Foundation for Science and Disability (PAZ)
FSD............ Frequency Ship Demodulator (DNAB)
FSD............ Fuel Supply Depot [*Military*]
FSD............ Full-Scale Deflection [*Instrumentation*]
FSD............ Full-Scale Development (MCD)
FSD............ Functional Sequence Diagram [*Computer science*]
FSD............ Sioux Falls [*South Dakota*] [*Airport symbol*] (OAG)
FSD............ Sioux Falls, SD [*Location identifier FAA*] (FAAL)
FSDA.......... Frequency Spectral Density Analysis (PDAA)
FSDB .... Fishery Statistics Data Base [*National Marine Fisheries Service*] [*Information service or system*] (MSC)
FSDC .... Federal Statistical Data Center [*IEEE*]
FSDC .... Fellow of the Society of Dyers and Colourists [*British*]
FSDH .... Fondation de la Sante et des Droits de l'Homme [*Foundation for Health and Human Rights*] (EA)
FSDLWG ..... Fundamental Standard Data Link Working Group [*NATO*] (NATG)
FSDM......... Full-Scale Development Model (MCD)
FSDO .... Flight Standards District Office [*FAA*]
FSDP .... Full-Scale Development Phase (MCD)
FSDPANSW... Friendly Societies', Dispensaries, and Pharmacies Association of New South Wales [*Australia*]
FSDPS .... Flight Service Data Processing System [*FAA*] (TAG)
FSDR .... Final Software Design Review
FSDS .... Fin Stabilized Discarding Sabot (MCD)
FSDS .... Flagship Data System (MCD)
FSDU .... Fur Skin Dressers' Union [*British*]
FSDVP .... Freiheitlich Soziale Deutsche Volkspartei [*Liberal Social German People's Party*] [*Germany Political party*] (PPW)
FSE .... Brothers of the Holy Eucharist (TOCD)
fse .... Brothers of the Holy Eucharist (TOCD)
FSE .... Facilities System Engineer
FSE .... Facility Support Equipment
FSE .... Factory Support Equipment (KSC)
FSE .... Faculty of Surgeons of England
FSE .... Family Stop Eating [*A table signal at a meal where guests are present*]
FSE .... Fat-Specific Element [*Genetics*]
FSE .... Federation of Stock Exchanges (WDAA)
FSE .... Fellow of the Society of Engineers [*British*]
FSE .... Fetal Scalp Electrode [*Obstetrics*] (DAVI)
FSE .... Field Service Engineer [*Military*]
FSE .... Field Support Engineering
FSE .... Field Support Equipment [*Military*]
FSE .... Filles du Saint Esprit [*Institute of the Franciscan Sisters of the Eucharist*] [*Roman Catholic religious order*]
FSE .... Fill Start Entry [*Computer science*]
FSE .... Fire Support Element [*Military*] (AABC)
FSE .... First Star Energy [*Vancouver Stock Exchange symbol*]
FSE .... Fleet Supportability Evaluation (MCD)
FSE .... Flight Simulation Engineer (MCD)
FSE .... Flight Support Equipment (KSC)
FSE .... Florida Solar Energy Center, Cape Canaveral, FL [*OCLC symbol*] (OCLC)

FSE .... Fluid Shaft Encoder
FSE .... Formerly Socialist Economy (ECON)
FSE .... Forward Security Element [*Soviet military force*]
FSE .... Forward Support Element
FSE .... Fosston, MN [*Location identifier FAA*] (FAAL)
FSE .... Full Screen Editor [*Computer science*] (IAA)
FSE .... [*The*] Institute of the Franciscan Sisters of the Eucharist (TOCD)
FSEA.......... Food Service Executives' Association [*Later, IFSEA*] (EA)
FSEA.......... Full Shear Energy Absorption (PDAA)
FSEB.......... Fuel Storage Exhaust Blower [*Nuclear energy*] (NRCH)
FSEC.......... Federal Securities and Exchange Commission [*New Deal*]
FSEC.......... Federal Software Exchange Center
FSEC.......... Federal Specifications Executive Committee
fsec........... Femtosecond [*One quadrillionth of a second*]
FSEC.......... Florida Solar Energy Center [*University of Central Florida*] [*Research center*] (RCD)
FSecCp .... First Security Corp. [*Associated Press*] (SAG)
FSECO .... First-Stage Engine Cutoff [*Aerospace*]
FSED.......... Full-Scale Engineering Development (MCD)
FSEE.......... Federal Service Entrance Examination [*Later, PACE*] [*Civil Service*]
FSEE.......... Field-Stimulated Exoelectron Emission [*Physics*]
FSEEEC....... Federation of Stock Exchanges in the European Community [*Belgium*] (EAIO)
FSEI........... Food Service Equipment Industry [*Later, FEDA*] (EA)
FSEO.......... Flight Systems Engineering Order (MCD)
FSEP.......... Federal Software Exchange Program (AAGC)
FSER.......... Field Service Engineering (AAG)
FSERI......... Federal Solar Energy Research Institute [*Energy Research and Development Administration*]
FSERT......... Fellow of the Society of Electronic and Radio Technicians [*British*] (DBQ)
FSES........... Federation of Swiss Employees' Societies
FSES........... Fire Safety Evaluation System [*National Institute of Standards and Technology*]
FSES........... Friendly Society of Engravers and Sketchmakers [*Later, MPEA*]
FSETP......... Food Stamp Employment and Training Program [*Department of Agriculture*] (GFGA)
FSEUCA ...... Federal-State Emergency Unemployment Compensation Act [*1970*]
FSF .... Fading Safety Factor [*Telecommunications*] (TEL)
FSF .... Federal Security Forces
FSF .... Fellow of the Institute of Shipping and Forwarding Agents [*British*] (ODBW)
FSF .... Fibrin-Stabilizing Factor [*Factor XIII*] [*Also, LLF Hematology*]
FSF .... Field Site Facility
FSF .... Financial Services Industry (TDOB)
FSF .... Financial Suppliers Forum (EA)
FSF .... Financial Suspense File [*Army*]
FSF .... First Static Firing (MCD)
FSF .... Fixed Sequence Format
FSF .... Flight Safety Foundation (EA)
FSF .... Forensic Sciences Foundation (EA)
FSF .... Forward Space File (CMD)
FSF .... Fuel Storage Facility [*Nuclear energy*] (NRCH)
FSF .... Fully Submerged Foil [*Hydrofoil craft*]
f-sf-- .... Sao Tome and Principe [*MARC geographic area code Library of Congress*] (LCCP)
FSFA.......... Federal Student Financial Aid [*Department of Education*] (GFGA)
FSFA.......... Federation of Specialised Film Associations [*British*] (BI)
FS/FB .... Free Store/Food Bank (EA)
FSFC.......... First Southeast Financial Corp. [*NASDAQ symbol*] (SAG)
FSFC.......... First Southeast Finl [*NASDAQ symbol*] (TTSB)
FSFC.......... Forester Sisters Fan Club (EA)
FSF Fin .... FSF Financial Corp. [*Associated Press*] (SAG)
FSFI........... First State Financial Services, Inc. [*NASDAQ symbol*] (NQ)
FSFL.......... First State Finl Svcs [*NASDAQ symbol*] (TTSB)
FSFLP......... Farm Storage Facility Loan Program
FSFS.......... Family Security Friendly Society [*Australia*]
FSFT.......... Fourth Shift [*NASDAQ symbol*] (TTSB)
FSFT.......... Fourth Shift Corp. [*NASDAQ symbol*] (SAG)
FSG............ Factoring Services Group [*British*] (DBA)
FSG............ Family Support Group [*Military*] (INF)
FSG............ Fasting Serum Glucose [*Clinical chemistry*]
FSG............ Federal Stock Group
FSG............ Federal Supply Group [*Air Force*]
FSG............ Fellow of the Society of Genealogists [*British*]
FSG............ Field Supply Group
FSG............ Finite State Grammar
FSG............ First Stage Graphitization (PDAA)
FSG............ Fiume Study Group (EA)
FSG............ Flexible Space Garment
FSG............ Flight Strip Generator (IAA)
FSG............ Florida Sea Grant College [*University of Florida*] [*Research center*] (RCD)
FSG............ Focal and Segmental Glomerulosclerosis [*Nephrology*] (DAVI)
FSG............ Foreign Services Group [*British*]
FSG............ Fortress Study Group (EAIO)
FSG............ Frequency of Signal Generator (IAA)
FSG............ Freres de Saint Gabriel [*Brothers of Christian Instruction of St. Gabriel*] [*Rome, Italy*] (EAIO)
f-sg-- .... Senegal [*MARC geographic area code Library of Congress*] (LCCP)
FSGA.......... Four-Wire, Shipboard, General Use, Armored [*Cable*]
FSGB.......... Foreign Service Grievance Board [*Department of State*]
FSGBI .... Federation of Sailmakers of Great Britain and Ireland [*A union*]
FSGD.......... Feasibility Guidance Document
FSGD.......... Federation of Sports Goods Distributors [*British*] (DCTA)

FSGHS	Focal Segmental Glomerular Hyalinosis and Sclerosis [*Medicine*] (DMAA)
FSGO	Floating Spherical Gaussian Orbitals [*Atomic physics*]
FSGp	Federal Supply Group [*Air Force*] (AFM)
FSGS	Flare/Shallow Glide Slope (MCD)
FSGS	Focal Segmental Glomerulosclerosis [*Nephrology*]
FSGT	Federation Sportive et Gymnique du Travail
FSGT	Fellow of the Society of Glass Technology [*British*]
F/Sgt	Flight Sergeant [*RAF*] [*British*] (DMA)
FSH	Fascioscapulohumeral [*Medicine*]
FSH	Federacion de Sociedades Hispanas [*Defunct*] (EA)
FSH	Federation of Sterea Hellas (EA)
FSH	First-Stage Hydraulics [*Aerospace*]
FSH	Fisher Scientific International [*NYSE symbol*] (SPSG)
FSH	Fisher Scientific Intl. [*NYSE symbol*] (TTSB)
FSH	Flash Airline Ltd. [*Nigeria*] [*ICAO designator*] (FAAC)
FSH	Flight Services Handbook
FSH	Follicle-Stimulating Hormone [*Endocrinology*]
FSH	Forest Service Handbook [*Department of Agriculture, Forest Service*] [*A publication*]
FSH	Foundation for Science and the Handicapped (EA)
FSH	Four Seasons Hotels, Inc. [*Toronto Stock Exchange symbol*]
FSH	Full Service History [*Automotive retailing*]
f-sh--	Spanish Territories in Northern Morocco [*Spanish North Africa*] (LCCP)
FSHAA	Fellow of the Society of Hearing Aid Audiologists [*British*] (DBQ)
FSHB	Follicle-Stimulating Hormone Beta Subunit [*Endocrinology*]
FSHC	Federal Subsistence Homesteads Corp. [*New Deal*]
FSHC	Financial Services Holding Co.
FSHEW	Federal Security Agency, Health, Education, and Welfare
FSHIP	Fellowship
FSH-LH	Follicle-Stimulating Hormone-Luteinizing Hormone [*Endocrinology*] (DAVI)
FSH/LH-RH...	Follicle-Stimulating Hormone and Luteinizing Hormone-Releasing Hormone [*Endocrinology*] (MAE)
FSHLPS	File System Helpers (PCM)
FSHMD	Facioscapulohumeral Muscular Dystrophy [*Neurology*] (DAVI)
FSHNG	Fishing
FSHPAC	Frequency-Agile Solid-State High-Frequency Power Amplifier Coupler [*Army*]
FSHRBI	Follicle-Stimulating Hormone Receptor Binding Inhibitor [*Endocrinology*]
FSH-RF	Follicle-Stimulating Hormone Releasing Factor [*Also, FRF, FSH-RH*] [*Endocrinology*]
FSH-RH	Follicle-Stimulating Hormone Releasing Hormone [*Also, FRF, FSH-RF*] [*Endocrinology*]
FSHRY	Fishery
Fsh stks	Fishing Stakes [*Nautical charts*]
FSHV	Full-Scale Hydrodynamic Vehicle (MCD)
FSI	Faggan Studio Industries [*Database producer*] (IID)
FSI	Family Suffering Index [*Economic measurement based on unemployment rate, plus costs of food, fuel, and housing*]
FSI	Federal Stock Item
FSI	Federation Spirite Internationale [*International Spiritualist Federation*]
FSI	Fellow of the Sanitary Institute [*British*] (ROG)
FSI	Fellow of the Surveyors' Institute [*Later, FRICS*] [*British*]
FSI	Fellow of the Surveyors' Institution (DD)
FSI	Final Systems Installation [*NASA*] (NASA)
FSI	Financial-Services Industry (TDOB)
FSI	Fire Service Inspectorate [*British*]
FSI	Fire Service Instructors
FSI	Fish and Shellfish Immunology [*A publication*]
FSI	Flightsafety International, Inc. [*Aerospace NYSE symbol*] (SPSG)
FSI	Flightsafety Intl. [*NYSE symbol*] (TTSB)
FSI	Fluid Structure Interaction [*Nuclear energy*] (NRCH)
FSI	Flutter Speed Index [*Aerodynamics*]
FSI	Foam Stability Index [*Chemistry*]
FSI	Food Sanitation Institute (EA)
FSI	Force Structure Increase [*Military*]
FSI	Foreign Science Information Program (SAA)
FSI	Foreign Service Institute [*Department of State*]
FSI	Foreign Services Institute [*Australia*]
FSI	Formed Steel Institute
FSI	Fort Sill, OK [*Location identifier FAA*] (FAAL)
FSI	Foundation for Savings Institutions [*Defunct*] (EA)
FSI	Frame Synchronization Indication
FSI	Freelance Syndicate, Inc. (EA)
FSI	Free Sons of Israel (EA)
FSI	Freestanding Insert [*Advertising*]
FSI	Functionally Significant Items (MCD)
FSI	International Society of Fire Service Instructors (EA)
FSIA	Fellow of the Society of Industrial Artists [*British*] (EY)
FSIA	Fellow of the Society of Investment Analysts [*British*] (DBQ)
FSIA	Foot Shock-Induced Analgesia [*Neurology*] (DAVI)
FSIA	Foreign Sovereign Immunities Act of 1976 (AAGC)
FSIAD	Fellow of the Society of Industrial Artists and Designers [*British*]
FSIB	Flight Safety Information Bulletin [*NASA*]
FSIC	Foreign Service Inspection Corps [*Department of State*]
FSIC	Forward Sensor Interface Control [*Army*] (RDA)
FSIC	Franciscan Sisters of the Third Order of the Immaculate Conception [*Roman Catholic religious order*]
F/SICC	Federal/State Initiative Coordinating Committee [*Department of Commerce*] (GFGA)
FSID	Foundation for the Study of Infant Deaths [*British*] (DBA)
FSIF	Flight Suit with Integrated Flotation
FSIF	Friendly Society of Ironfounders of England, Ireland, and Wales [*A union*]
FSIGBN	Field Signal Battalion (IAA)
FSIGT	Frequently Sampled Intravenous Glucose Tolerance (Test) [*Clinical chemistry*]
FSII	FSI International [*NASDAQ symbol*] (TTSB)
FSII	FSI International, Inc. [*NASDAQ symbol*] (CTT)
FSII	Fuel System Icing Inhibitor [*Aviation*] (AFIT)
FSI Int	FSI International, Inc. [*Associated Press*] (SAG)
FSIM	Functional Simulator (NASA)
FSIMT	Foundation for the Support of International Medical Training (EA)
FS-INFO	Forest Service Information Network - Forestry Online [*US Forest Service*] [*Information service or system*] (IID)
FSIO	Foreign Service Information Officer [*Department of State*]
FSIP	Federal Service Impasses Panel
FSIP	Federal Shelter Incentive Program
FSIP	Fire Service in Philately [*An association*]
FSIR	Force Status Identity Report (MCD)
FSIS	First-Stage Ignition System [*Aerospace*] (MCD)
FSIS	Food Safety and Inspection Service [*Formerly, FSQS*] [*Department of Agriculture*]
FSISI	Foundation for the Study of Independent Social Ideas (EA)
FSISWG	Flight System Interface Working Group
FSIT	First Spanish Investment Trust [*London Stock Exchange*]
FSIT	Flat Screen Image Tube [*Computer science*] (IAA)
FSIWA	Federation of Sewage and Industrial Wastes Associations [*Later, Water PollutionControl Federation*]
FSIWG	Flight System Interface Working Group (MCD)
FSJ	Faculte Saint-Jean Library, University of Alberta [*UTLAS symbol*]
FSJ	Feedback Summing Junction [*Computer science*]
FSJ	Fellowship of St. James (EA)
FSJ	Fort St. James [*British Columbia*] [*Seismograph station code, US Geological Survey*] (SEIS)
FSJ	Fratres Sancti Joseph [*Brothers of St. Joseph*] [*Roman Catholic religious order*]
FSJ	Free Supersonic Jet
FSJ	Religious Daughters of St. Joseph (TOCD)
f-sj--	Sudan [*MARC geographic area code Library of Congress*] (LCCP)
FSJC	Fort Scott Junior College [*Kansas*]
FSJC	Fort Smith Junior College [*Arkansas*]
FSJM	Society of Franciscan Servants of Jesus and Mary [*Anglican religious community*]
FSK	Fatigue Scales Kit [*Psychology*]
FSK	Fisk University, Nashville, TN [*OCLC symbol*] (OCLC)
FSK	Forskolin [*Also, FOR*] [*Organic chemistry*]
FSK	Fort Scott, KS [*Location identifier FAA*] (FAAL)
FSK	Frequency Shift Keying [*Telecommunications*]
FSKLF	Frequency Shift Keying Low-Frequency [*Converter*] (NATG)
FSL	Family Strike Light [*Indicates family should take small portions at a meal where guests are present*]
FSL	Federal Stock Listings
FSL	Federation des Syndicats Libres des Travailleurs Luxembourgeois [*Free Luxembourg Workers' Federation*]
FSL	Field Storage List (MCD)
FSL	Finite State Language
FSL	Fire Control and Small Caliber Weapon Systems Laboratory [*Picatinny Arsenal, Dover, NJ*] [*Army*] (INF)
FSL	First Sea Lord [*British*] (DI)
FSL	First Standard Mining Ltd. [*Vancouver Stock Exchange symbol*]
FSL	Fixed Safety Level
FSL	Flight Safety Ltd. [*British ICAO designator*] (FAAC)
FSL	Flight Simulation Laboratory [*NASA*] (NASA)
FSL	Flight Systems Laboratory (MCD)
FSL	Florida State League [*Baseball*]
FSL	Florida State University, Law Library, Tallahassee, FL [*OCLC symbol*] (OCLC)
FS/L	Food Service/Lodging
FSL	Forecast Systems Laboratory [*Marine science*] (OSRA)
FSL	Forecast Systems Laboratory [*Environmental Research Laboratories*] (USDC)
FSL	Foreign Service Leave [*British military*] (DMA)
FSL	Foreign Service Local (CINC)
FSL	Forestry Sciences Laboratory [*US Forest Service*] [*Research center*] (RCD)
FSL	Formal Semantic Language [*Computer science*]
fsl	Fossil (VRA)
FSL	Franklin Supply Co. Ltd. [*AMEX symbol*] (SPSG)
FSL	Free Shear Layer
FSL	French Sign Language
FSL	Frequency Selective Limiter (IAA)
FSL	Full Stop Landing [*Aviation*]
FSL	Full Supply Level (ADA)
f-sl--	Sierra Leone [*MARC geographic area code Library of Congress*] (LCCP)
FSLA	Federal Savings and Loan Association [*New Deal*]
FSLA	First Savings Bank FSLA Perth Amboy NJ [*NASDAQ symbol*] (SAG)
FSLA	First Savings Bank of New Jersey [*NASDAQ symbol*] (SAG)
FSLA	First Savings Bk(Perth Amboy) [*NASDAQ symbol*] (SAG)
FSLAET	Fellow of the Society of Licensed Aircraft Engineers and Technologists [*British*]
FSLC	Saint Leo College, Saint Leo, FL [*Library symbol Library of Congress*] (LCLS)
FSLIC	Federal Savings & Loan Insurance Corp. [*of FHLBB*] [*Pronounced "FIZ-lick" Functions transferred to SAIF, 1989*]
FSLMMC	Friends of the Sea Lion Marine Mammal Center (EA)

FSLN............ Frente Sandinista de Liberacion Nacional [*Sandinista National Liberation Front*] [*Nicaragua*] [*Political party*] (PPW)
FSLP............ First Spacelab Payload [*NASA*]
FSLPPS........ Federalist Society for Law and Public Policy Studies (EA)
FSLT............ First Sea Level Test [*NASA*] (NASA)
FSM............. Fabryka Samochodow Malolotia [*Polish affiliate of Fiat Motors*]
FSM............. Fast Settle Mode
FSM............. Fast Steering Mirror [*Optical instrumentation*]
FSM............. Federacion Socialista Madrilena [*Spain Political party*] (EY)
FSM............. Federated States of Micronesia [*ANSI three-letter standard code*] (CNC)
FSM............. Federation Sephardite Mondiale [*World Sephardi Federation - WSF*] [*Geneva, Switzerland*] (EAIO)
FSM............. Federation Socialiste de la Martinique [*Socialist Federation of Martinique*] [*Political party*] (PPW)
FSM............. Federation Syndicale Mondiale [*World Federation of Trade Unions - WFTU*] [*French*] (EAIO)
FSM............. Fellow of the Society of Metaphysicians [*British*]
FSM............. Fellowship Recorded Libraries of Sacred Music [*Record label*] [*Atlanta, GA*]
FSM............. Field Service Manual [*British military*] (DMA)
FSM............. Field Strength Meter
FSM............. Final Stage Marker (IAA)
FSM............. Fine Scale Modeler [*A publication*]
FSM............. Finite State Machine
FSM............. Firmware Support Manual
FSM............. First-Stage Motor [*Aerospace*]
FSM............. First Surface Mirror
FSM............. Flight Simulation Monitor [*FAA*] (TAG)
FSM............. Flight System Mockup
FSM............. Floating Subtract Magnitude [*Computer science*] (IAA)
FSM............. Flying Spot Microscope (ADA)
FSM............. Folded Sheets Mesoporous-Material [*Inorganic chemistry*]
FSM............. Folded Sideband Modulation
FSM............. Foodarama Suermkts [*AMEX symbol*] (TTSB)
FSM............. Foodarama Supermarkets, Inc. [*AMEX symbol*] (SPSG)
FSM............. Fort Smith [*Arkansas*] [*Airport identifier*] (OAG)
FSM............. Fort Smith, AR [*Location identifier FAA*] (FAAL)
FSM............. Frame-Scanning Mode [*Microscopy*]
FSM............. Franciscan Sisters of Mary (TOCD)
FSM............. Free Speech Movement [*University of California, Berkeley*]
FSM............. Frequency Shift Modulation [*Radio*]
FSM............. Friendly Society of Mechanics [*A union*] [*British*]
FSM............. Fuel Supply Module (MCD)
FSMA........... Families of SMA [*Spinal Muscular Atrophy*] [*An association*] (EA)
FSMA........... Farm Store Merchandising Association [*Defunct*] (EA)
FSMA........... Fashion Sales and Marketing Association [*Australia*]
FSMA........... Fellow of the Incorporated Sales Managers' Association [*Later, F Inst MSM*] [*British*]
FSMAC......... Fellow of the Society of Management Accountants of Canada (DD)
FSMAO......... Field Supply and Maintenance Analysis Office (DNAB)
FSMAWA...... Fashion Sales and Marketing Association of Western Australia
FSMB........... Federation of State Medical Boards of the United States (EA)
FSMBUS...... Federation of State Medical Boards of the United States (EA)
FSMC........... Federal Supply Manufacturers' Code [*DoD*]
FSMC........... Fellow of the Spectacle Makers Co.
FSMC........... First-Stage Motor Container [*Aerospace*]
FSMC........... Fixed Silver Mica Capacitor
FSMC........... Forward Support Medical Company [*Military*] (INF)
FSMF........... Furnishing Springmakers Federation [*British*] (BI)
FSMG........... Foundry Supply Manufacturers Group (EA)
FSMGB........ Federation of Small Mines [*British*] (DBA)
FSMI........... Food Service Marketing Institute (EA)
FSML........... Fleet Support Material List [*Navy*]
FSMO........... Field Service Marching Order [*British military*] (DMA)
FSMR........... Field Station Materiel Requirements
FSMS........... Firing Set Maintenance Spares (NG)
FSMSI......... Fire Support Modeling and Simulations Institute
FSMT........... Feed System Maintenance Transfer (MCD)
FSMT........... Fleet Service Mine Test [*Navy*] (NG)
FSMWI........ Free Space Microwave Interferometer
FSMWO....... Field Service Modification Work Order
FSN............. Factory Serial Number (MCD)
FSN............. Federal Stock Number [*Later, NSN*]
FSN............. FEMA [*Federal Emergency Management Agency*] Switched Network (GFGA)
FSN............. File Sequence Number [*Computer science*] (IAA)
FSN............. Filler Sensor Nozzle
FSN............. Financial Satellite Network
FSN............. Fiscal Station Number [*Military*]
FSN............. Foreign State National
FSN............. Forward Sequence Number [*Telecommunications*] (TEL)
FSN............. Franklin Select Real Estate Income Fund [*AMEX symbol*] (SPSG)
FSN............. Franklin Select R.E. Inc.Fd'A' [*AMEX symbol*] (TTSB)
FSN............. French-Speaking Nations [*NATO*]
FSN............. Fuel Service Nozzle (MSA)
FSN............. Full Service Network [*Television broadcasting*]
FSN............. National Salvation Front [*Romania*] [*Political party*]
FSN............. New College, Sarasota, FL [*Library symbol Library of Congress*] (LCLS)
FSNJ........... First Savings Bank(N.J.) [*NASDAQ symbol*] (TTSB)
FSNJ........... First Savings Bank of New Jersey [*NASDAQ symbol*] (SAG)
FSNM.......... First Savings Bank [*Associated Press*] (SAG)
FSNM.......... First State Bancorp [*NASDAQ symbol*] (SAG)
FSNM.......... First State Bancorporation [*NASDAQ symbol*] (TTSB)

FSNMDR...... Federal Stock Number [*later, NSN*] Master Data Record
FSNO........... Federation of Sunday Newspaper Owners (DGA)
FSNOx........ Fuel-Specific Nitrogen Oxide Emissions [*Air pollution*]
FSNP........... Famous Spock Neck Pinch [*From television show "Star Trek"*]
FSNR........... [*The*] Forschner Group, Inc. [*NASDAQ symbol*] (NQ)
FSNS........... French-Speaking Neuropsychological Society [*Paris, France*] (EAIO)
FSO............. Fabryka Samochodow Osobowych [*Polish automobile manufacturer*]
FSO............. Facility Security Officer
FSO............. Fast Settle Operation
FSO............. Field Security Officer [*Military*]
FSO............. Field Service Operations (NATG)
FSO............. Fire Support Officer [*Military*]
FSO............. Fleet Signals Officer [*Navy*]
FSO............. Fleet Supply Officer [*Navy*]
FSO............. Fleet Support Operations (NVT)
FSO............. Flight Safety Officer (MCD)
FSO............. Flight Services Officer (ADA)
FSO............. Florida Society of Ophthalmology (SRA)
FSO............. Flying Safety Officer [*Air Force*] (AFM)
FSO............. Force Supply Officer
FSO............. Foreign Service Officer [*Department of State*]
FSO............. Frequency Sweep Oscillator
FSO............. Friends of the Sea Otter (EA)
FSO............. Fuel Supply Office [*Military*]
FSO............. Full-Scale Output
FSO............. Fulltext Sources Outline [*A publication*]
FSO............. Functional Supplementary Objective (MCD)
FSO............. Fund for Special Operations [*Inter-American Development Bank*]
f-so--......... Somali [*MARC geographic area code Library of Congress*] (LCCP)
FSOB........... Friendly Society of Operative Bricklayers [*A union*] [*British*]
FSOC........... Fairchild Satellite Operations Complex (MCD)
FSOC........... Fixed Stand-Off Capacitor
FSOC........... Free Serbian Orthodox Church [*Australia*]
FSOCM........ Friendly Society of Operative Cabinet Makers [*A union*] [*British*]
FSOCOM...... First Special Operations Command (DOMA)
FSOH........... Flight Support Operations Handbook (MCD)
FSOHNS...... Florida Society of Otolaryngology-Head and Neck Surgery (SRA)
FSOL........... Franciscan Sisters of Our Lady (TOCD)
FSOLF........ Forasol-Foramer NV [*NASDAQ symbol*] (TTSB)
FSON........... Fusion Medical Technologies, Inc. [*NASDAQ symbol*] (SAG)
FSOP........... Free-Standing Surgical Outpatient Facility (HCT)
FSor............ French Cetra-Soria [*Record label*]
FSOS........... Free-Standing Operating System [*General Automation, Inc.*]
FSOSEIW..... Friendly Society of Operative Stonemasons of England, Ireland, and Wales [*A union*]
FSOT........... Friendly Society of Operative Tobacconists [*A union*] [*British*]
FSOTS......... Foreign Service Officers' Training School
FSouth........ First South Africa Corp. Ltd. [*Associated Press*] (SAG)
FSP............. Brothers of St. Patrick (TOCD)
fsp............. Brothers of St. Patrick (TOCD)
FSP............. Facility Security Profile [*Military*] (GFGA)
FSP............. Facility Security Program [*World War II*]
FSP............. Facility Support Plan [*Military*]
FSP............. Familial Spastic Paraplegia [*Medicine*] (DMAA)
FSP............. Family Services Program [*Military*]
FSP............. Fault Servicing Process (TEL)
FSP............. Fault Summary Page (MCD)
FSP............. Federal/State Programs [*Social Security Administration*] (OICC)
FSP............. Fellow of Sheffield Polytechnic [*British*]
FSP............. Fellowship of St. Paul (EA)
FSP............. Fiber Saturation Point [*Of drying lumber*] (BARN)
FSP............. Fibrinogen-Split Products [*Hematology*]
FSP............. Fibrin [*or Fibrinolytic*] Split Products (DAVI)
FSP............. Field Security Personnel
FSP............. Field Security Police
FSP............. Figlie de San Paolo [*Pious Society of the Daughters of Saint Paul - PSDSP*] [*Rome, Italy*] (EAIO)
FSP............. Finger Sweat Print [*Psychometrics*]
FSP............. Fixed Sample-Size Procedure
FSP............. Fixed Silo Price [*Wheat*]
FSP............. Flat Salary Payroll (AAG)
FSP............. Fleet Scheduling Program [*DoD*] (IAA)
FSP............. Flight Scheduling Precedence
FSP............. Flight Strip Printer [*Aviation*] (FAAC)
FSP............. Floating Stock Platform (DNAB)
FSP............. Food Stamp Program
FSP............. Force Sensing Probe
FSP............. Ford Satellite Plan [*Telecommunications*]
FSP............. Foreign Service Pay
f sp............ Forma Specialis [*Special Form*] [*Biology*]
FSP............. Forward Supply Point [*Military*] (AFM)
FSP............. Foundation for the Peoples of the South Pacific (EA)
FSP............. Franciscan Sisters of Peace (TOCD)
FSP............. Freedom Socialist Party (EA)
FSP............. French Socialist Party
FSP............. Frente Socialista Popular [*Portugal*]
FSP............. Frente Social Progresista [*Progressive Social Front*] [*Ecuador*] [*Political party*] (PPW)
FSP............. Frequency Shift Pulsing
FSP............. Frequency Standard, Primary
FSP............. Fuel Storage Pool [*Nuclear energy*] (NRCH)
FSP............. Full-Scale Production
FSP............. Full-Scale Prototype [*Military*] (CAAL)
FSP............. Full-Screen Processing [*Computer science*]
FSP............. Full-Time Equivalent Software Personnel

FSP............	Functional Specification Package [*Computer science*]
FSP............	Functional System Plan [*Military*]
FSP............	Pious Society Daughters of St. Paul (TOCD)
FSp............	St. Petersburg Public Library, St. Petersburg, FL [*Library symbol Library of Congress*] (LCLS)
FSPA..........	Farm Shop and Pick Your Own Association [*British*] (DBA)
FSPA..........	Fellow, Society of Pension Actuaries [*American Society of Pension Actuaries*] [*Designation awarded by*]
FSPA..........	Former Spouse Protection Act
FSPA..........	Fuel Storage Personnel Area [*Nuclear energy*] (NRCH)
FSPA..........	Sisters of the Third Order of St. Francis of the Perpetual Adoration [*Roman Catholic religious order*]
FSPB..........	Field Service Pocket Book [*British military*] (DMA)
FSPB..........	Fire Support Primary Base (DNAB)
FSPB..........	Forward Support Patrol Base
FSPB..........	Fuel Storage Processing Building [*Nuclear energy*] (NRCH)
FSPBC........	For a Separate Peace Before Carter [*Refers to Israeli-Egyptian agreements of 1978*]
FSPC..........	Federal Science Policy Council [*Later, FCCSET*]
FSPC..........	Field-Site Production Capability (SAA)
FSPC..........	Foundation for the Study of Primitive Culture
FSPC..........	Frontispiece [*Publishing*] (WGA)
FSpC..........	St. Petersburg Junior College, St. Petersburg, FL [*Library symbol Library of Congress*] (LCLS)
FSPCM........	Flight Strip Printer Control Module (MCD)
FSPCT........	Foundation for the Study of Presidential and Congressional Terms (EA)
FSPD	Freeze Speed Parameter [*FAA*] (TAG)
FSPDUA......	Federated Ship Painters and Dockers' Union of Australia
FSpE..........	Eckerd College, St. Petersburg, FL [*Library symbol Library of Congress*] (LCLS)
FSPER	Finances of Selected Public Employee Retirement System [*Bureau of the Census*] (GFGA)
FSpFP..........	Florida Power Corp., St. Petersburg, FL [*Library symbol*] [*Library of Congress*] (LCLS)
FSPG	First Home Bancorp, Inc. [*NASDAQ symbol*] (SAG)
FSPG	First Home Savings Bank [*NASDAQ symbol*] (NQ)
FSPG	First Home Savings Bk [*NASDAQ symbol*] (TTSB)
FSPG	Force Structure Planning Group [*Marine Corps*] (DOMA)
FSPMA........	Federal Services Podiatric Medical Association (EA)
FSPO	Force Structure Planning Objective (MUGU)
FSPP..........	Fiske-Subbarow Positive Phosphorus [*Analytical chemistry*]
FSPPR	Fast Supercritical Pressure Power Reactor
FSPRS	Field-Site Production and Reduction System (SAA)
FSPS..........	Ferranti Sonobuoy Processing System (MCD)
FSPS..........	Field-Site Production System (SAA)
FSPS..........	Foundation for the Study of Plural Societies (EA)
FSPSC	Field-Site Production Study Committee (SAA)
FSPSG	Freeman-Sheldon Parent Support Group (EA)
FSPSO	Federal Statistical Policy and Standards Office (OICC)
FSPT..........	Federation of Societies for Paint Technology [*Later, FSCT*] (EA)
FSpW..........	Jim Walter Research Corp., St. Petersburg, FL [*Library symbol*] [*Library of Congress*] (LCLS)
FSQ............	Atlanta, GA [*Location identifier FAA*] (FAAL)
FS/Q..........	Directorate of Flight Standards and Qualification Research [*St. Louis, MO*] [*Army*]
FS/Q..........	Flight Standards and Qualification [*Army*]
FSq	Flying Squadron
f-sq--	Swaziland [*MARC geographic area code Library of Congress*] (LCCP)
FSQS	Food Safety and Quality Service [*Later, FSIS*] [*Department of Agriculture*]
FSR............	Air Link Charters [*Canada*] (FAAC)
FSR............	Brothers of the Congregation of Our Lady of the Holy Rosary (TOCD)
fsr............	Brothers of the Congregation of Our Lady of the Holy Rosary (TOCD)
FSR............	False Signal Recognition [*RADAR technology*]
FSR............	Farming Systems Research
FSR............	Fast Slew Rate
FSR............	Feedback Shift Register
FSR............	Fellow of the Royal Society of Radiographers
FSR............	Female Seniors [*International Bowhunting Organization*] [*Class Equipment*]
FSR............	Fermi Selection Rules
FSR............	Fiberglass Stain Remover [*Cleaning product*] [*Jamie Industries*]
FSR............	Fielded System Review
FSR............	Field Service Regulations [*Army*]
FSR............	Field Service Report
FSR............	Field Service Representative (AFM)
FSR............	Field Strength Radio
FSR............	File Storage Region [*Digital Equipment Corp.*]
FSR............	Film Society Review [*A publication*]
FSR............	Final System Release (MCD)
FSR............	Final System Run (KSC)
FSR............	Financial Services Recorder [*Telecommunications*] [*British*]
FSR............	Financial Status Report (OICC)
FSR............	Fin Stabilized Rockets
FSR............	Firstar Corp. [*NYSE symbol*] (SPSG)
FSR............	First Soviet Reactor
FSR............	First Surrey Rifles [*Military unit*] [*British*]
FSR............	Fixed Sample Rate
FSR............	Fleet Spotter Reconnaissance [*British military*] (DMA)
FSR............	Fleet Street Reports of Patent Cases [*England*] [*A publication*] (DLA)
FSR............	Flight Safety Research
FSR............	Flight Safety Rules (MCD)
FSR............	Flight Simulation Report

FSR............	Flight Solar Reflectometer
FSR............	Flight Specific Requirements (MCD)
FSR............	Flight Support Request (KSC)
FSR............	Floor Space Ratio
FSR............	Flux Sensitive Resistor
FSR............	Force Sensing Resistor [*Maxell*] [*Electronics*]
FSR............	Force Service Regiment [*Marine Corps*] (NVT)
FSR............	Foreign Separate Rations (AABC)
FSR............	Foreign Service Reservists (MUGU)
FSR............	Forward Space Record
FSR............	Foundation for Scientific Relaxation
FSR............	Four Seasons Resources Ltd. [*Vancouver Stock Exchange symbol*]
FSR............	Franciscan Sisters of Ringwood [*Roman Catholic religious order*]
FSR............	Free Spectral Range
FSR............	Free System Resource [*Computer science*] (PCM)
FSR............	Frequency Scan RADAR
FSR............	Frequency Selective Relay
FSR............	Frequency Shift Receiver
FSR............	Frequency Shift Reflector
FSR............	Full-Scale Range [*Military*] (IAA)
FSR............	Full-Scale Record [*Instrumentation*]
FSR............	Full-Scale Review
FSR............	Full Systems Ready (DNAB)
FSR............	Functional Stretch Reflex [*of muscles*]
FSR............	Function Status Review (MCD)
FSR............	Fund for Stockowners Rights [*Later, FFSR*] (EA)
FSR............	Fund Summary Record [*Military*] (AFIT)
FSR............	Fusiform Skin Revision [*Medicine*] (MAE)
FSR............	Future Safety Research [*Honda experimental vehicle*]
FSR............	John and Mable Ringling Museum of Art, Sarasota, FL [*Library symbol Library of Congress*] (LCLS)
FSR-3	Isoniazid [*Pharmacology*] (DAVI)
FSRA	Federal Sewage Research Association [*Later, Federal Water Quality Association*]
FSRB	Flight Safety Review Board
FSRC	Foreign Systems Research Center
FSRC	Ringling Museum of the Circus, Sarasota, FL [*Library symbol Library of Congress*] (LCLS)
FSRDC........	Full Straps Roosevelt Dime Club (EA)
FSRG	Fellow of the Society of Remedial Gymnasts [*British*]
FSRI...........	Foreign Services Research Institute (EA)
FSRM..........	First-Stage Rocket Motor [*Aerospace*]
FSRN..........	Forest Service Research Notes
FSRP..........	Firstar Corp. [*NASDAQ symbol*] (SAG)
FSRP..........	Forest Service Research Paper
FS/RPNL......	Function Safe-Release Panel [*Aerospace*] (AAG)
FSRPZ........	Firstar Corp. $1.75 Cv Dep Pfd [*NASDAQ symbol*] (TTSB)
FSRQ..........	Flat-Spectrum Radio Quasar [*Galaxy*]
FSRR..........	Flight Software Readiness Review (MCD)
FSRR..........	Flight System Readiness Review (NASA)
FSRS..........	Flight System Recording System (MCD)
FSRS..........	Force Structure Requirements Study [*Military*]
FSRS	Frequency Selective Receiver System (MCD)
FSRT..........	Flight Systems Redundancy Test (MCD)
FSRU..........	Foreign Service Reserve (Unlimited) [*Department of State*]
FSRV..........	FirstService Corp. [*NASDAQ symbol*] (SAG)
FSRVF	FirstService Corp.(Mfg) [*NASDAQ symbol*] (TTSB)
FSS............	Fabrication Statusing System (MCD)
FSS............	Facility Security Supervision (MCD)
FSS............	Family Security Service
FSS............	Family Support Service [*Australia*]
FSS............	Fast Sealift Ship [*Navy*] (DOMA)
FSS............	Fear Survey Schedule [*Psychology*]
FSS............	Federal Signal [*NYSE symbol*] (TTSB)
FSS............	Federal Signal Corp. [*Formerly, Federal Sign & Signal Corp.*] [*NYSE symbol*] (SPSG)
FSS............	Federal Supply Schedule
FSS............	Federal Supply Service (USGC)
FSS............	Fellow of the Royal Statistical Society [*British*]
FSS............	Field Sequential System [*Military*] (IAA)
FSS............	Field Service Section [*Military*]
FSS............	Field Spectrometer System (MCD)
FSS............	Field Support System
FSS............	Financial Status Summary (OICC)
FSS............	Fine Sun Sensor [*NASA*]
FSS............	Finite Solution Set [*Mathematics*] (WDAA)
FSS............	Finnish Sauna Society [*British*] (DBA)
FSS............	Finnish Society of Sydney [*New South Wales, Australia*]
FSS............	Fire Support Ship
FSS............	Fire Support Station [*Navy*] (NVT)
FSS............	Fire Suppression System (MCD)
FSS............	First-Stage Separation [*Aerospace*]
FSS............	Fixed Satellite Service
FSS............	Fixed Service Structure (MCD)
FSS............	Flap-Slat-Spoiler [*Aviation*] (MCD)
FSS............	Fleet Service School [*Navy*]
FSS............	Flight Safety System
FSS............	Flight Security Supervisor [*Military*]
FSS............	Flight Service Station [*FAA*]
FSS............	Flight Standards Service [*FAA*] (MCD)
FSS............	Flight Support Station [*For manned maneuvering unit*] (NASA)
FSS............	Flight Support Structure (MCD)
FSS............	Flight Support System (MCD)
FSS............	Flight Systems Simulator [*NASA*] (NASA)
FSS............	Floor Service Stations (NRCH)

FSS............ Fluid Supply System (MCD)
FSS............ Flutter Suppression System [Aviation]
FSS............ Flying Spot Scanner [Optical character recognition]
FSS............ Fog Signal Station [Coast Guard]
FSS............ Force Stratification System
FSS............ Force Structure Subsystem [Military]
FSS............ Foreign Shore Service
FSS............ Forensic Science Service [British]
FSS............ Forensic Science Society (EAIO)
FSS............ Forward Scattering Spectroscopy
FSS............ Forward Scatter System (NATG)
FSS............ Forward Supply Support
FSS............ Fossil Stromgen Sphere (PDAA)
FSS............ Foundation for Shamanic Studies (EA)
FSS............ Four Sigma Society (EA)
FSS............ Frame Storage System [Television]
FSS............ Franco-Scottish Society
FSS............ French Steel Sound [Medicine] (DMAA)
FSS............ Full-Scale Section (DNAB)
FSS............ Fully Separated Subsidiary
FSS............ Seminole Community College, Sanford, FL [OCLC symbol] (OCLC)
f-ss--.......... Spanish Sahara [Western Sahara] [MARC geographic area code Library of Congress] (LCCP)
FSSA........... Federation des Syndicats du Secteur de l'Aluminium, Inc. [Federation of Aluminum Sector Unions, Inc.] [Canada]
FSSA........... Fellow of the Society of Science and Art [British]
FSSA........... Fire Suppression Systems Association (EA)
FSSA........... Flying Scot Sailing Association (EA)
FSSANSW.... Family Support Services Association of New South Wales [Australia]
FSSB........... Fire Support Surveillance Base [Military] (VNW)
FSSB........... First Federal Savings & Loan Association, San Bernardino [NASDAQ symbol] (SAG)
FSSB........... First Fed Svgs & Ln Assn [NASDAQ symbol] (TTSB)
FSSB........... Flight Status Selection Board (DNAB)
FSSC........... Federal Standard Stock Catalog
FSSC........... Federation of Serbian Sisters Circle [Australia]
FSSC........... Fielded Software Support Center
FSSC........... Foreign Student Service Council (EA)
FSSCA......... Franciscan Sisters of St. Clare (Pious Union) (TOCD)
FSSCA........ Fellow of the Society of Science and Arts, London [British] (ROG)
FSSCOM ...... Flight Services Station Operations and Procedures Committee (FAAC)
FSSCT......... Forer Structured Sentence Completion Test [Psychology]
FSSD........... Facilities and Support Service Division [Environmental Protection Agency] (GFGA)
FSSD .... Federal Supply Storage Depot
FSSD .... First-Stage Separation Device [Aerospace]
FSSD .... Foreign Service Selection Date
FSSE........... Federation des Societes Suisses d'Employes [Federation of Swiss Employees' Societies]
FSSE........... Foreign Service Sales Expense
FSSE........... Forward Service Support Element (AABC)
FSSE........... Franciscan Sisters of St. Elizabeth [Roman Catholic religious order]
FSSF........... First Special Service Force (MCD)
FSSFA......... First Special Service Force Association (EA)
FSSG .... Field Service Support Group [USMC] (MCD)
FSSG .... Fleet Service Support Group [Military]
FSSG .... Force Service Support Group [Military] (NVT)
FSSGDET ..... Force Service Support Group Detachment [Military] (DNAB)
FSSI .... Fellow of the Statistical Society of Ireland (ROG)
FSSJ .... Franciscan Sisters of St. Joseph [Roman Catholic religious order]
FSSM .... Franciscan Sisters of the Sorrowful Mother (TOCD)
FSSN .... Fission (MSA)
FSSP........... Families of Structurally Similar Proteins [A database]
FSSP........... Fellowship of St. Paul (EA)
FSSP........... Film Strip Sound Projector
FSSP........... Forward-Scattering Spectrometer Probe [Aerosol measurement device]
FSSP........... Fraternite Sacerdotale Saint Pie X [International Sacerdotal Society Saint Pius X - ISSSP] (EAIO)
FSSP........... Fuel System Supply Point
FSSP........... Priestly Fraternity of St. Peter (TOCD)
FSSpJ .... Franciscan Sisters of the Spirit of Jesus (TOCD)
FSSPX .... International Sacerdotal Society Saint Pius X [Switzerland] (EAIO)
FSSR .... Fellow of the Royal Statistical Society [British]
FSSR .... Flight Systems Software Requirement (MCD)
FSSR .... Functional Subsystem Software Requirements (NASA)
FSSRS .... Farm Structure Survey Retrieval System [Information service or system] (IID)
FSSRS .... Fixed Step Size Random Search (IAA)
FSS/S.......... Fine Sun Sensor/Signal Conditioner [NASA] (MCD)
FSSS........... Flying Spot Scanner System [Optical character recognition] (IAA)
FSSS........... Fuse Set Subsystem
FSSS........... Mahe/Seychelles International (ICLI)
FSST........... Flying Scot Scanner Tube (PDAA)
FSSTMUK .... Friendly Society of Spade Tree Makers of the United Kingdom [A union]
FSSU .... Federated Superannuation Scheme for Universities [British]
FSSWT........ Full-Scale Subsonic Wind Tunnel
FST .... Far Eastern Resources Corp. [Vancouver Stock Exchange symbol]
FST .... Farming Systems Trial (GNE)
FST .... Fast [Horse racing]
FST .... Fast Air Ltda. [Chile] [ICAO designator] (FAAC)
FST .... Federal Sales Tax [Canada]
FST .... Field Service Technician (MCD)

FST .... Field Suitability Test
FST .... Field Supply Technician (MCD)
FST .... Field Surgical Team [Military British]
FST .... Field Survey Team
FST .... File Status Table [Computer science] (IBMDP)
FST .... File Systems Tree [Computer science]
FST .... Film Supertwist
FST .... Finite Sampling Time
FST .... Fire Safety Technology (SSD)
FST .... Fire Safety Toxicity
FST .... Fire Support Team (MCD)
FST .... First
FST .... First Class or Saloon Passengers [Shipping] [British]
FST .... Fixed Service Tower
FST .... Flame Smoke Toxicity
FST .... Flat Slip on Top (OA)
FST .... Flat Square Tube [IBM Corp.] (PCM)
FST .... Flatter, Squarer Tube [Television picture tube]
FST .... Fleurs Synthesis Telescope
FST .... Flight Support Tapes
FST .... Foam Stability Test
FST .... Follow-On Soviet Tank [In FST-1, model name of a Russian "supertank" having improved armor and a 135-mm gun] [Introduced in the late 1980's]
FST .... Foreign Service Tour [Military]
FST .... Forged Steel [Technical drawings]
FST .... Fort Stockton, TX [Location identifier FAA] (FAAL)
FST .... Forward Support Team (MCD)
FST .... Framingham State College, Framingham, MA [OCLC symbol] (OCLC)
FST .... Free Southern Theater
FST .... Free Space Transfer (MCD)
FST .... Frequency Shift Telegraphy
FST .... Frequency Shift Transmission
FST .... Full-Scale Tunnel [Aerospace]
FST .... Functional Simulator and Translator [Computer science] (CSR)
FST .... Funkstelle [Radio Station] [German military - World War II]
FST .... Future Strategic Targets (MCD)
FST .... Fuzed Silica Tube
FSTA .... Fellow of the Swimming Teachers' Association [British] (DBQ)
FSTA .... Food Science and Technology Abstracts [Database] (NITA)
FSTA .... Force Structure Trade-Off Analysis (MCD)
FStaB.......... Bradford County Public Library, Starke, FL [Library symbol Library of Congress] (LCLS)
FSTACOE ..... Fleet Special Test and Checkout Equipment
FSTAD .... Fire Support and Target Acquisition Division [Human Engineering Laboratory] [Army]
FstAlert....... First Alert, Inc. [Associated Press] (SAG)
FstAm .... First of America Bank Corp. [Associated Press] (SAG)
FstARwy ...... First American Railways, Inc. [Associated Press] (SAG)
FstBell .... First Bell Bancorp, Inc. [Associated Press] (SAG)
FstbkIll .... Firstbank of Illinois Co. [Associated Press] (SAG)
FstbkPR .... Firstbank Puerto Rico [Associated Press] (SAG)
FstBks......... First Banks, Inc. [Associated Press] (SAG)
FstBkshs ...... First Bankshares of Missouri, Inc. [Associated Press] (SAG)
FstBrnd....... First Brands Corp. [Associated Press] (SAG)
FSTC .... Farmington State Teachers College [Merged with University of Maine]
FSTC .... Fayetteville State Teachers College [Later, Fayetteville State University] [North Carolina]
FSTC .... Field Sound Transmission Class (DAC)
FSTC .... Financial Services Technical Consortium
FSTC .... First Citizens Corp. [NASDAQ symbol] (SAG)
FSTC .... Foreign Science and Technology Center [Army]
FstChi97 ...... First Chicago Corp. [Associated Press] (SAG)
FstChic .... First Chicago Corp. [Associated Press] (SAG)
FstCity .... First City Bancorp, Inc. [Associated Press] (SAG)
FstCity .... First City Financial Corp. [Associated Press] (SAG)
FstCom .... First Commonwealth, Inc. [Associated Press] (SAG)
Fstcrp......... Firstcorp, Inc. (MHDW)
FstCsh .... First Cash, Inc. [Associated Press] (SAG)
FstCtzF....... First Citizens Financial Corp. [Associated Press] (SAG)
FstCwlth ...... First Commonwealth Financial Corp. [Associated Press] (SAG)
FSTD .... Fellow of the Society of Typographic Designers [British] (DI)
FSTD .... Flight Simulation Test Data
FstData .... First Data Corp. [Associated Press] (SAG)
FstDefiFn..... First Defiance Financial Corp. [Associated Press] (SAG)
FSTDY .... Final Semester Temporary Duty [Air Force] (AFM)
FSTE .... Factory Special Test Equipment (NASA)
FSTE .... Field Support Test Equipment
FSTE .... Fixed Systems Test Equipment (SAA)
FSTE .... Foreign Service Tour Extension (INF)
FstEnter ...... First Entertainment, Inc. [Associated Press] (SAG)
FstEntr .... First Entertainment, Inc. [Associated Press] (SAG)
FstFed .... FirstFed Financial [Associated Press] (SAG)
FstFedFn...... FirstFederal Financial Services [Associated Press] (SAG)
FstFnHld ...... First Financial Holdings, Inc. [Associated Press] (SAG)
FstFnIN....... First Financial Corp. [Associated Press] (SAG)
FSth........... First South Africa Corp. Ltd. [Associated Press] (SAG)
FSTH.......... First Southern Bancshares [NASDAQ symbol] (TTSB)
FSTH.......... First Southern Bancshares, Inc. [NASDAQ symbol] (SAG)
FstHmBcp .... First Home Bancorp, Inc. [Associated Press] (SAG)
FstHmSv...... First Home Savings Bank SLA [Associated Press] (SAG)
FSTI .... Formed Steel Tube Institute [Later, WSTI]
FSTI .... Free Search Terminal Interface [Telecommunications]

FstIn Cp	First Indiana Corp. [*Associated Press*] (SAG)	**FSVDR**	File Structure Volume Descriptor Record (NTCM)
FstInRlt	First Industrial Realty Trust, Inc. [*Associated Press*] (SAG)	**FSVM**	Frequency Selective Voltmeter (IAA)
FstKent	First Kent Financial Corp. [*Associated Press*] (SAG)	**FSVNGS**	Fort St. Vrain Nuclear Generating Station (NRCH)
FSTK/SUP	Friendly Strike or Support [*Military*] (NVT)	**FSVP**	Find SVP [*NASDAQ symbol*] (TTSB)
FSTL	Foreign Salable Technology and Licence [*South Korea Information service or system*] (IID)	**FSVP**	FIND/SVP, Inc. [*New York, NY NASDAQ symbol*] (NQ)
FSTL	Future Strategic Target List	**FSVR**	Fort St. Vrain Reactor [*Platteville, CO*] (GAAI)
FstLI	First of Long Island Corp. [*Associated Press*] (SAG)	**FSVS**	Future Secure Voice System (LAIN)
FSTMA	Firearm and Security Trainers Management Association (EA)	**FSW**	Feet of Seawater [*Deep-sea diving*]
Fstmark	Firstmark Corp. [*Associated Press*] (SAG)	**FSW**	Field Service Worker [*Social Services*] (DAVI)
FstMerit	FirstMerit Corp. [*Associated Press*] (SAG)	**FSW**	Field Switch
FstMtge	First Mortgage Corp. [*Associated Press*] (SAG)	**FSW**	Final Status Word [*Computer science*] (IAA)
FstMutl	First Mutual Bancorp, Inc. [*Associated Press*] (SAG)	**FSW**	Fire Team Support Weapon (MCD)
FSTN	Film Compensated STN [*Super Twisted Nematic*] (CDE)	**FSW**	Fletcher Sutcliffe Wild [*Commercial firm British*]
FSTNR	Fastener	**FSW**	Flexible Steel Wire
FstNtw	First Nationwide Bank A Federal Savings Bank [*Associated Press*] (SAG)	**FSW**	Flight Software (MCD)
FstPalm	First Palm Beach Bancorp, Inc. [*Associated Press*] (SAG)	**FSW**	Forward Swept Wing
FSTPW	Friendly Society of Tin Plate Workers [*A union*] [*British*]	**FSW**	Frame Synchronization Word (MSA)
FSTR	Fallschirmtruppen [*Parachute Troops*] [*German military*]	**FSW**	Friendly Society of Watermen [*A union*] [*British*]
FSTR	Field Service Technical Report (AAG)	**FSWD**	Foundation for the Study of Wilson's Disease [*Later, NCSWD*] (EA)
FSTR	Foster	**FSWD**	Full-Scale Weapons Delivery [*Military*]
FSTR	Foster [*L.B.*] Co. [*NASDAQ symbol*] (NQ)	**FSWEC**	Federal Software Exchange Center
FSTRA	Foster (LB)Cl'A' [*NASDAQ symbol*] (TTSB)	**FSWFS**	Field Standard Weight and Force System (AAG)
FSTRE	Field Service Trouble Report	**FSWMA**	Fine and Specialty Wire Manufacturers Association [*Later, Specialty Wire Association*] (EA)
FSTS	Federal Secure Telephone Service [*or System*] [*DoD*]	**FSWO**	Financial Secretary to the War Office [*British*]
FSTS	Financial Services Terminals Support [*IBM Corp.*]	**FSWR**	Flexible Steel Wire Rope
FSTS	Fitting Shop Trade Society [*A union*] [*British*]	**FSWT**	Free Surface Water Tunnel
FSTS	Flight Simulated Training System [*Military*]	**FSWW**	First Society of Whale Watchers [*Defunct*] (EA)
FSTS	Future Space Transportation System	**FSX**	Fighter Support Experimental [*Military*]
FSTS	Fuze Set Test Set	**FSX**	Flagship Express Services, Inc. [*ICAO designator*] (FAAC)
FstSouth	First South Africa Corp. Ltd. [*Associated Press*] (SAG)	**FSX**	Future Shock Experimental [*Mountain bike*] (PS)
FstStBc	First State Bancorp (NM) [*Associated Press*] (SAG)	**FS-X**	Future Sports-Sedan Experimental [*Concept car*]
FstSvc	FirstService Corp. [*Associated Press*] (SAG)	**f-sx--**	South West Africa [*Namibia*] [*MARC geographic area code Library of Congress*] (LCCP)
FstSvNJ	First Savings Bank of New Jersy [*Associated Press*] (SAG)	**FSY**	Fassey Aviation Ltd. [*Nigeria*] [*FAA designator*] (FAAC)
FSTT	Floating Shuttle Tape Transport (PDAA)	**FSYO**	Fleet Security Officer [*Navy British*]
FSTTC	Flight Safety Training and Test Center	**FT**	Factory Test
FstTenn	First Tennessee National Corp. [*Associated Press*] (SAG)	**FT**	Faience Tile (DICI)
FstUC	First Union Corp. [*Associated Press*] (SAG)	**FT**	Fail Type [*Military*] (AFIT)
FStuM	Martin County Public Library, Stuart, FL [*Library symbol Library of Congress*] (LCLS)	**FT**	Faint
		FT	False Transmitter [*Neurology*] (DAVI)
Fst USA	First USA, Inc. [*Associated Press*] (SAG)	**FT**	Family Therapy
FstUtdCp	First United Corp. [*Associated Press*] (SAG)	**FT**	Fan Tek (EA)
FSTV	Fast Scan Television [*Computer science*] (IAA)	**FT**	Fashion Television [*TV program*]
FSTV	Full-Scale Test Vehicle [*NASA*]	**FT**	Fast [*Track condition*] [*Thoroughbred racing*]
FstVict	First Victoria National Bank [*Associated Press*] (SAG)	**FT**	Fast Track [*Insurance*]
FstWash	First Washingtn Bancorp, Inc. [*Associated Press*] (SAG)	**FT**	Fatigue Time [*Sports medicine*]
FstWV	First West Virginia Bancorp, Inc. [*Associated Press*] (SAG)	**FT**	Fault Tolerant (HGAA)
FstYears	[*The*] First Years, Inc. [*Associated Press*] (SAG)	**FT**	Fault Tree (MCD)
FSU	Facsimile Switching Unit	**FT**	Federal Triangle [*Washington, DC*]
FSU	Fail Sheer Ultimate (MCD)	**FT**	Feet [*or Foot*] (AAG)
FSU	Family Service Unit [*Medicine British*]	**ft**	Feet (IDOE)
FSU	Fellowship for Spiritual Understanding (EA)	**ft**	Feet
FSU	Ferry Service Unit	**FT**	Feet Together [*Dance terminology*]
FSU	Field Select Unit	**FT**	Feint [*of account book rulings*]
FSU	Field Storage Unit [*Military*]	**Ft**	Ferritin [*Biochemistry*] (AAMN)
FSU	Final Signal Unit [*Telecommunications*] (TEL)	**FT**	Fiant [*Let Them Be Made*] [*Pharmacy*] (ROG)
FSU	Fire and Safety Unit [*Coast Guard*] (DOMA)	**FT**	Fiat [*Make*] [*Pharmacy*]
FSU	Flightline Support Unit (MCD)	**FT**	Fiat SpA [*Italy ICAO aircraft manufacturer identifier*] (ICAO)
FSU	Flight Service Unit (ADA)	**FT**	Fibrous Tissue [*Medicine*]
FSU	Florida State University [*Tallahassee*]	**FT**	Field Test (AAG)
FSU	Former Soviet Union (RDA)	**FT**	Field Training [*AFROTC*] (AFM)
FSU	Fort Sumner, NM [*Location identifier FAA*] (FAAL)	**FT**	Field Trip
FSU	Freisoziale Union - Demokratische Mitte [*Free Social Union - Democratic Center*] [*Germany Political party*] (PPW)	**FT**	Filing Time [*Time a message is presented for transmission*]
FSU	Freon Servicing Unit (NASA)	**FT**	Financial Times [*A publication*] (ODBW)
FSU	Full-Scale Unit (KSC)	**FT**	Fine Thermal [*Furnace*]
FSU	Fusion Splicer Unit [*Telecommunications*] (NITA)	**FT**	Fire Control Technician [*Navy rating*]
FSUA	Finance Sector Union of Australia	**FT**	Fire Team [*Marine Corps*]
FSUC	Federal Statistics Users' Conference [*Defunct*] (EA)	**FT**	Fire Thermostat (AAG)
FSUD	Fort Street Union Depot Co. [*AAR code*]	**FT**	Fire-Tube Boiler
FS/UEG	Fleet Staff/Unit Expansion Group (DNAB)	**FT**	Firing Tables [*Military*]
FSUJPM	Friendly Society of United Journeymen Platers and Moulders [*A union*] [*British*]	**FT**	Firing Temperature [*Military*] (IAA)
F Supp	Federal Supplement Reporter [*West*] [*A publication*] (AAGC)	**FT**	First Telecast (DOAD)
FSUSA	Finance School, United States Army	**FT**	Fischer-Tropsch Synthesis [*Organic chemistry*]
FSV	Falciparum Sporozoite Vaccine [*Antimalarial*]	**FT**	Fission Track [*Geological age dating*]
FSV	Feline Fibrosarcoma Virus	**FT**	Fitter and Turner [*Navy rating British*]
FSV	Ferry Supply Vehicle	**FT**	Fixation and Transfer [*of text*] (DNAB)
FSV	Final Stage Vehicle	**FT**	Fixed Tone
FSV	Fire Service Valve (IEEE)	**FT**	Flagon and Trencher (EA)
FSV	Fire Support Vehicle [*Military*] (MCD)	**FT**	Flamethrower [*Engineering*] (IAA)
FSV	Formula Super Volkswagen [*Class of racing cars*]	**FT**	Flame Tight
FSV	Fort St. Vrain [*Nuclear plant*] (NRCH)	**FT**	Flanging Tube
FSV	Frequency Selective Voltmeter	**FT**	Flat [*Paper*]
FSV	Fujinami Sarcoma Virus	**FT**	Flat Template
FSV	Future Scout Vehicle [*Military*]	**FT**	Flat-Topped [*Frames*] [*Optometry*]
FSV	Future Scout Vehicle [*Army*] (DOMA)	**FT**	Flexible Trunk [*Hovercraft*]
FSVA	Fellow of the Incorporated Society of Valuers and Auctioneers [*British*] (DBQ)	**FT**	Flight Team (MCD)
		FT	Flight Termination
FSVB	Fort Smith & Van Buren Railway Co. [*AAR code*]	**F/T**	Flight Test (KSC)
FSVB	Franklin Bank NA [*NASDAQ symbol*] (SAG)	**FT**	Flow Through
FSvBkNJ	First Savings Bank FSLA Perth Amboy NJ [*Associated Press*] (SAG)	**FT**	Flow Transducer [*Instrumentation*]
FSVC	Financial Services Volunteer Corps [*An association*] (EA)	**FT**	Flow Transmitter [*Nuclear energy*] (NRCH)
FSVC	Freshstart Venture Capital Corp. [*NASDAQ symbol*] (SAG)	**FT**	Fluorescent Target
		FT	Flushometer Tank
		FT	Flush Threshold [*Technical drawings*]

FT .... Flying Tiger Line, Inc. [*ICAO designator*]
FT .... FM Broadcast Translator [*FCC*] (NTCM)
FT .... Foam Tape
FT .... Fog Trumpet [*Navigation charts*]
FT .... Follow-On Test
F-T .... Follow Through
ft .... Foot (AAMN)
FT .... Foreign Theater
FT .... Foreign Transaction (AFM)
FT .... Forest Trust [*An association*] (EA)
FT .... Foretop [*Obsolete*]
Ft .... Forint [*Florin*] [*Monetary unit*] [*Hungary*] (GPO)
FT .... Forklift Truck (DCTA)
FT .... Formal Toxoid [*Medicine*]
FT .... Formal Training [*Military*] (AFM)
FT .... Fort (AFM)
FT .... Fort
FT .... Fortean Times [*A publication*]
FT .... Fortification (ROG)
ft .... Fortification (VRA)
FT .... Forward Transfer [*Telecommunications*] (TEL)
FT .... Foundation of Thanatology (EA)
FT .... Foundation Type [*Dialog*] [*Searchable field*] [*Telecommunications*] (NITA)
FT .... Fourier Transform
FT .... Franciscus Tigrini de Pisis [*Flourished, 13th-14th century*] [*Authority cited in pre-1607 legal work*] (DSA)
FT .... Franklin Universal Tr [*NASDAQ symbol*] (TTSB)
FT .... Franklin Universal Trust [*NYSE symbol*] (CTT)
FT .... Free Throw [*Basketball*]
FT .... Free Thyroxine [*Also, FT₄*] [*Endocrinology*]
FT .... Free Trader (ROG)
FT .... Free Turbine (AAG)
FT .... Free Turn
FT .... Freight Ton
FT .... Freight Transport
FT .... French Telefunken [*Record label*]
ft .... French Territory of the Afars and Issas [*Djibouti*] [*MARC country of publication code Library of Congress*] (LCCP)
FT .... French Title [*Online database field identifier*]
FT .... Frequency and Time (IEEE)
FT .... Frequency Tolerance
FT .... Frequency Tracker (MSA)
FT .... Frequent Traveler [*on airlines*]
FT .... Friends of the Tango (EA)
FT .... Front [*Deltiology*]
FT .... Ftorafur [*Analog of 5-fluorouracil deoxyribose*] [*Soviet anticancer drug*]
FT .... Fuel Tanking [*Aerospace*] (AAG)
FT .... Fuel Terms (DS)
FT .... Full Term [*Pregnancy*] [*Medicine*]
FT .... Full Tilt Container (DCTA)
FT .... Full Time [*Employment, education*]
FT .... Fully Tracked (NATG)
FT .... Fume-Tight [*Technical drawings*]
FT .... Functionally Terminated (MCD)
FT .... Functional Test [*Computer science*]
FT .... Functional Tester [*Mars Electronics*] (NITA)
FT .... Fundic Type [*of epithelium*] [*Medicine*]
FT .... Fund Type [*Military*] (AFIT)
FT .... Tampa-Hillsborough County Public Library, Tampa, FL [*Library symbol Library of Congress*] (LCLS)
FT .... Terminal Forecasts [*Symbol*] [*National Weather Service*]
Ft .... Terminal Framing Bits [*Telecommunications*] (ACRL)
FT1 .... Fire Control Technician, First Class [*Navy rating*]
FT2 .... Fire Control Technician, Second Class [*Navy rating*]
ft2 .... Square Feet
FT² .... Square Foot
FT²/H .... Square Feet per Hour
FT²/MIN .... Square Foot per Minute (WDAA)
FT²/S .... Square Feet per Second
FT³ .... Cubic Feet (EG)
ft3 .... Cubic Feet
FT3 .... Fire Control Technician, Third Class [*Navy rating*]
FT₃ .... Free Triiodothyronine [*Endocrinology*] (DAVI)
FT³/(FT D) .... Cubic Feet per Foot Day
FT₃IX .... Free Triiodothyronine Index
FT³/MIN ...... Cubic Foot per Minute (WDAA)
FT³/S .... Cubic Feet per Second
FT₄ .... Free [*Unbound*] Thyroxine [*Endocrinology*] (DAVI)
FT₄F .... Serum Free Thyroxine Fraction [*Endocrinology*] (DAVI)
FT4IX .... Free Thyroxine Index [*Endocrinology*]
FT-30 .... Financial Times Ordinary Share Index (ODBW)
FTA .... European Throwsters Association [*Italy*] (EAIO)
FTA .... Failed to Attend (ADA)
FTA .... Failure to Appear [*Court case*]
FTA .... Fast Time Analysis
FTA .... Fatigue Test Article (NASA)
FTA .... Fault Tree Analysis (NASA)
FTA .... Federal Transit Administration [*Formerly, UMTA*] [*Department of Transportation*]
FTA .... Federated Tanners' Association of Australia
FTA .... Federation of Tax Administrators (EA)
FTA .... Federation of Trade Associations [*Republic of Ireland*] (BI)
FT/A .... Feet per Year

FTA .... Field Technical Authority (NVT)
FTA .... Field Test Administration (AAG)
FTA .... Field to Advise [*Telecommunications*] (TEL)
FTA .... File Trade Association [*British*] (BI)
FTA .... Film Training Aid
FTA .... Financial Times Actuaries (ODBW)
FTA .... Fixed Term Agreement
FTA .... Fixed Time of Arrival [*Aviation*]
FTA .... Flexographic Technical Association (EA)
FTA .... Flight Test Article (KSC)
FTA .... Florida Trail Association (EA)
FTA .... Florida Transit Association (SRA)
FTA .... Florida Trucking Association (SRA)
FTA .... Fluid Transpiration Arc
FTA .... Fluorescent Titer Antibody [*Clinical chemistry*]
FTA .... Fluorescent Treponemal Antibody [*Clinical chemistry*]
FTA .... Food Tray Association [*Defunct*]
FTA .... Foreign Trade Association [*Cologne, Federal Republic of Germany*] (EAIO)
FTA .... Forward Transfer Admittance
FTA .... Foundation of the Twelve Apostles (EA)
FTA .... Free the Army [*Barracks graffiti; also, title of antimilitary play*] [*Bowdlerized version*]
FTA .... Free Thought Association (EA)
FTA .... Free Throws Attempted [*Basketball*]
FTA .... Free Trade Agreement [*or Arrangement*]
FTA .... Free Trade Area
FTA .... Free Trade Association [*European*]
FTA .... Freight Transport Association [*British*]
FTA .... Frontier Flying Service, Inc. [*ICAO designator*] (FAAC)
FTA .... Fuel Treatment Apparatus
FTA .... Full-Time Attendance (GFGA)
FTA .... Fun, Travel, Adventure [*Sarcastic alternate to FTA - Free the Army*]
FTA .... Fur Takers of America (EA)
FTA .... Future Teachers of America [*Later, SAE*] (EA)
FTA .... Hot Springs, SD [*Location identifier FAA*] (FAAL)
FTaA .... Apalachee Community Mental Health Services, Inc., Tallahassee, FL [*Library symbol Library of Congress*] (LCLS)
FTAA .... Federated Tanners' Association of Australia
FTAA .... Free Trade Agreement of the Americas [*Proposed*]
FTAA .... Free Trade Area of the Americas [*NAFTA*] (ECON)
FTA-AB .... Fluorescent Treponemal Antibody-Absorption Syphilis Test [*Medicine*] (MAH)
FTA-ABS ...... Fluorescent Treponemal Antibody - Absorption [*Test for syphilis*]
FTAC .... Functional Test and Calibration (IAA)
FTACCC .... Florida Technical Advisory Committee on Citrus Canker (EA)
FTACT .... Financial Times Actuaries Share Indices [*Database*] [*Financial Times Business Enterprises Ltd.*] [*Information service or system*] (CRD)
FTAF .... Flying Training Air Force
FTaFA .... Florida A & M University, Tallahassee, FL [*Library symbol Library of Congress*] (LCLS)
F-TAG .... Fast-Binding Target-Attaching Globulin [*Medicine*] (MEDA)
FTaL .... Leon-Jefferson-Wakulla County Public Library, Tallahassee, FL [*Library symbol Library of Congress*] (LCLS)
FTAM .... File Transfer, Access, and Management [*Telecommunications*] (TSSD)
FTAM .... File Transfer Access Management [*Computer science*] (EERA)
FTAM .... File Transfer Access Method [*Computer science*]
FTAM .... File Transfer and Manipulation (NITA)
FT & C .... Feint and Cash [*of account book rulings*]
FT & C .... Formal Training and Certification (MCD)
FT & C .... Functional Test and Calibration (IEEE)
FT & E .... Follow-On Test and Evaluation (MCD)
FT & IR .... Flight Taxiing and Ingestion Risks [*Insurance*] (AIA)
FT & SA .... Fuel Transfer and Storage Assembly [*Nuclear energy*] (NRCH)
FT & TW .... Desk, Combination Flat Top and Typewriter
FTAO .... Foreign Technology Activity Office [*or Officer*] (AFM)
FTAS .... Fast Time Analyzer System
FTAS .... Federation of Turkish-American Societies (EA)
FTaS .... Sunland Center, Tallahassee, FL [*Library symbol Library of Congress*] (LCLS)
FTase .... Farnesyltransferase [*An enzyme*]
FtAshld .... First Ashland Financial Corp. [*Associated Press*] (SAG)
FTASI .... Financial Times Actuaries All-Share Index (ODBW)
FTaSU .... Florida State University, Tallahassee, FL [*Library symbol Library of Congress*] (LCLS)
FTaSU-L ...... Florida State University, Law Library, Tallahassee, FL [*Library symbol Library of Congress*] (LCLS)
FTAT .... Facilities Technology Application Test [*Army*] (RDA)
FTAT .... Field Turn-Around Time (MCD)
FtAT .... First American Corp. [*Associated Press*] (SAG)
FTAT .... Fluorescent Treponemal Antibody Test [*for syphilis*]
FTAT .... Furniture, Timber, and Allied Trades Union [*British*]
FTaT .... Tallahassee Community College, Tallahassee, FL [*Library symbol Library of Congress*] (LCLS)
FtATn .... First American Corp. [*Associated Press*] (SAG)
FTATU .... Furniture, Timber, and Allied Trades Union [*British*]
FtAust .... First Australia Fund, Inc. [*Associated Press*]
FTAWA .... Food Technology Association of Western Australia
FT-AWI .... Financial Times-Actuaries World Indices [*British*]
FTB .... Fails to Break
FTB .... Fast Torpedo Boat [*NATO*]
FTB .... Field Team Bulletin [*Military*] (CINC)
FTB .... Fighter Bomber [*Obsolete*]
FTB .... Film Transfer Boom [*NASA*]

FTB	Fingertip Blood [*Medicine*]
FTB	Fire Control Technician, Ballistic Missile [*Navy rating*]
FTB	Fire-Tube Boiler (DS)
FTB	First-Time-Buy (MCD)
FTB	Fitchburg State College, Fitchburg, MA [*OCLC symbol*] (OCLC)
FTB	Fleet Torpedo Bomber
FTB	Flight [*or Flying*] Test Bed
FTB	For the Birds [*Slang*] (IAA)
FTB	Freight Tariff Bureau
FTB	Freight Traffic Bureau
FTB	Frequency Time Base (DEN)
FTB	Full to Bursting [*Reply to question, "Have you had enough to eat"*]
FTB	Functional Test Bulletin [*Computer science*] (IAA)
FTB	Functional Training Branch [*BUPERS*]
FTB1	Fire Control Technician, Ballistic Missile Fire Control, First Class [*Navy rating*] (DNAB)
FTB2	Fire Control Technician, Ballistic Missile Fire Control, Second Class [*Navy rating*] (DNAB)
FTB3	Fire Control Technician, Ballistic Missile Fire Control, Third Class [*Navy rating*] (DNAB)
F-TBA	Fasting-Total Bile Acids [*Physiology*]
FTBA	Food Tray and Board Association [*Later, SSI*]
FTBA	Furniture Trades Benevolent Association [*British*] (BI)
FT BAL	Football [*Freight*]
FTBC	Fire Control Technician, Ballistic Missile Fire Control, Chief [*Navy rating*] (DNAB)
FtBcIN	First Bancorp (IN) [*Associated Press*] (SAG)
FtBcIN	First Bancorp of Indiana, Inc. [*Associated Press*] (SAG)
FTBD	Fit to Be Detained [*Medicine*]
FTBD	Full Term Born Dead [*Medicine*]
FtBend	Fort Bend Holding Corp. [*Associated Press*] (SAG)
FTBF	Frequency Tuned Bandpass Filter
FTBI	Financial Times Business Information [*British*]
FtBkSy	First Bank System, Inc. [*Associated Press*] (SAG)
FTBLL	Football
FtBNC	First Bancorp North Carolina [*Associated Press*] (SAG)
FtBrnd	First Brands Corp. [*Associated Press*] (SAG)
FTBS	Fire-Tube Boiler Survey (DS)
FTBS	Free Throwers Boomerang Society (EA)
FTBSA	Fire Control Technician, Ballistic Missile Fire Control, Seaman Apprentice [*Navy rating*]
FTBSN	Fire Control Technician, Ballistic Missile Fire Control, Seaman [*Navy rating*]
FTC	Facility Terminal Cabinet (AAG)
FTC	Fair Trade Commission [*Japan*] (ECON)
FTC	False Target Can [*Navy*] (NVT)
FTC	Fast Time Constant [*RADAR*]
FTC	Fast Time Control (IAA)
FTC	Fault Tolerant Compiler (NITA)
FTC	Fault-Tolerant Computing
FTC	Federal Telecommunications Center (NUCP)
FTC	Federal Telecommunications System [*of GSA*] (NOAA)
FTC	Federal Trade Commission [*Independent government agency*] [*OCLC symbol*]
FTC	Federal Trade Commission Decisions [*A publication*] (DLA)
FTC	Field Training Command [*Military*]
FTC	Field Trial Champion [*Sporting dogs*] (IIA)
FTC	Financial Trustco Capital Ltd. [*Toronto Stock Exchange symbol*]
FTC	Fire Control Technician, Chief [*Navy rating*]
FTC	Fixed Tantalum Capacitor
FTC	Flame Traversing the Charge
FTC	Fleet Training Center [*Navy*]
FTC	Flight Test Center
FTC	Flight Test Conductor (NASA)
FTC	Flight Time Constant
FTC	Float Trend Chart (PDAA)
FTC	Florida Test Center [*NASA*] (KSC)
FTC	Fluid-Bed Thermal Cracking [*A chemical process developed by the Institute of Gas Technology*]
FTC	Flying Training Command [*Air Force*]
FT-C	Foot-Candle [*Illumination*]
FTC	Force Track Coordinator [*Navy*] (NVT)
FTC	Fordson Tractor Club (EA)
FTC	Foreign Tax Credit
FTC	Forestry Training Council (AIE)
FTC	Forest Tent Caterpillars
FTC	Fort Collins [*Colorado*] [*Airport symbol*] (OAG)
FTC	Fort Tejon [*California*] [*Seismograph station code, US Geological Survey Closed*] (SEIS)
FTC	Frames to Come [*Optometry*]
FTC	Freighter Travel Club of America (EA)
FTC	Freon Tank Container
FTC	Frequency Threshold Curve
FTC	Frequency Time Control
FTC	Frequency Transfer Control
FTC	Fruehauf Trailer [*NYSE symbol*] (SPSG)
FTC	Fuel Transfer Canal [*Nuclear energy*] (NRCH)
FTC	Full Technological Certificate [*British*]
FTC	Full-Time Care [*Pet-adoption terminology*]
FTC	Future Technology Communications [*Distributor and networking specialist*] [*British*] (NITA)
FTCA	Federal Tort Claims Act
FT CAT	Fiat Cataplasma [*Let a Poultice Be Made*] [*Pharmacy*]
ft cataplasm...	Fiat Cataplasma [*Let a Poultice Be Made*] [*Pharmacy*] (DAVI)
FTCC	Fellow of Trinity College, Cambridge [*British*] (ROG)

FTCC	Fixed Temperature Compensating Capacitor
FTCC	Flight Test Coordinating Committee [*Air Force*]
FTCC	FTC Communications, Inc. [*New York, NY*] (TSSD)
FTCCD	Field Transfer Charge-Coupled Device [*Instrumentation*]
FTCD	Fellow of Trinity College, Dublin
FT CD	Foot-Candela [*Foot-Candle*] [*Illumination*] (ADA)
FTCE	Florida Teacher Certification Examination (EDAC)
FT CERAT	Fiat Ceratum [*Let a Cerate Be Made*] [*Pharmacy*]
FTCG	First Colonial Group [*NASDAQ symbol*] (SAG)
FT CHART	Fiat Chartula [*Let a Powder Be Made*] [*Pharmacy*]
FtChi	First Chicago NBD Corp. [*Associated Press*] (SAG)
FtChrt	First Charter Corp. [*Associated Press*] (SAG)
FtChrtBk	First Charter Bank NA [*Associated Press*] (SAG)
FTCL	Fellow of Trinity College of Music, London (EY)
FTCLR	Financial Times Commercial Law Reports [*A publication British*]
FTCM	Fire Control Technician, Master Chief [*Navy rating*]
FtCntrl	First Central Financial Corp. [*Associated Press*] (SAG)
FT COLLYR...	Fiat Collyrium [*Let an Eyewash Be Made*] [*Pharmacy*]
FtColoBcp	First Colorado Bancorp, Inc. [*Associated Press*] (SAG)
FTCP	Field Trains Command Post [*Army*] (INF)
FTCP	Flight Test Change Proposal (MCD)
FTCR	Functional Test Change Request
FTCS	Fire Control Technician, Senior Chief [*Navy rating*]
FTCS	Foreign Tax Credit System
FTCSS	Flight Trace Contaminant Sensor System [*NASA*] (KSC)
FTC-TLTR	Freight Traffic Committee - Trunk Line Territory Railroads
FTCWU	Federated Tobacco and Cigarette Workers' Union [*Australia*]
FTD	Fails to Drain
FTD	Fails to Drive (DNAB)
FTD	Failure to Descend [*Obstetrics and urology*] (DAVI)
FTD	Familiarization Training Data (MCD)
FTD	Fastener Testing Development (MCD)
FTD	Fastest Time of the Day [*Auto racing*]
FTD	Federal Tax Deposit [*IRS*]
FT/D	Feet per Day
FTD	Femoral Total Density
FTD	Field Terminated Diode [*Electronics*]
FTD	Field Training Detachment [*Program*] [*Air Force*]
FTD	Fine Test Dust [*Automotive engineering*]
FTD	Fire Technology Division [*National Institute of Standards and Technology*]
FTD	First Tier Debt [*Economics*]
FTD	First Tridon Industry [*Vancouver Stock Exchange symbol*]
FTD	Fitted (MSA)
FTD	Flight Test Direction [*or Directive*] (AAG)
FTD	Flight Test Drawing (MCD)
FTD	Flight Training Device [*Aviation*] (DA)
FTD	Florists' Transworld [*formerly, Telegraph*] Delivery [*Trademark*]
FTD	Folded Triangular Dipole [*Electronics*] (OA)
FTD	Force, Type, District Code (DNAB)
FTD	Foreign Technical Department [*Navy*] (NVT)
FTD	Foreign Technology Directorate (DOMA)
FTD	Foreign Technology Division [*Wright-Patterson Air Force Base, Ohio*] [*Air Force*]
FTD	Foreign Trade Division [*Census*] (OICC)
FTD	Formal Technical Documents
FTD	Fort Dearborn Income Securities, Inc. [*NYSE symbol*] (SPSG)
FTD	Fort Dearborn Inc.Sec [*NYSE symbol*] (TTSB)
FTD	Fortified
FTD	Freight Traffic Department
FTD	Freight Traffic Division [*Army*]
FTD	Frequency Translation Distortion
FTD	Full-Time Duty (ADA)
FTD	Functional Test Data
FTD	Fuze-Triggering Device (MCD)
FTDA	Fellow of the Theatrical Designers and Craftsmen's Association [*British*]
FTDA	Florists' Transworld Delivery Association (EA)
FTDC	Fellow of the Society of Typographic Designers of Canada (DGA)
FTDC	Field Testing and Development Center
FTD-E	Freight Traffic Division - Export [*MTMC*] (TAG)
FtDear	Fort Dearborn Income Securities, Inc. [*Associated Press*] (SAG)
FtDefFn	First Defiance Financial Corp. [*Associated Press*] (SAG)
FTD-I	Freight Traffic Division - Import [*MTMC*] (TAG)
FTDIP	Flight Test Division, Internal Project [*Navy*] (MCD)
FTDMA	Frequency and Time-Division Multiple Access (MCD)
FTDR	Flight Test Data Recorder (MCD)
FTDS	Flag Tactical Data System (MUGU)
FTDS	Formal Training Data System (NVT)
FTD-S	Freight Traffic Division - Inspection [*MTMC*] (TAG)
FtDynM	First Dynasty Mines [*Associated Press*] (SAG)
FTE	Facility Training Equipment
FTE	Factory Test Equipment (MCD)
FTE	FFTF [*Fast Flux Test Facility*] Test Engineering [*Nuclear energy*] (NRCH)
FTE	Flight Technical Error [*Aviation*] (DA)
FTE	Flight Test Encoder
FTE	Flight Test Engineer (MCD)
FTE	Flight Test Equipment
FTE	Flight Test Evaluation
FTE	Florida Tomato Exchange (EA)
FTE	Flux Transfer Event [*Planetary physics*]
FTE	Follett, TX [*Location identifier FAA*] (FAAL)
FTE	Forced Test End (NASA)
FTE	Fotografia F3 SA [*Spain ICAO designator*] (FAAC)

FTE............	Foundation for Teaching Economics (EA)
FTE............	Fracture Transition Elastic Temperature (MCD)
FTE............	Frame Table Entry [*Computer science*] (IBMDP)
FTE............	Free the Eagle [*Washington, DC*] (EA)
FTE............	Free Thyroxine Equivalent [*Endocrinology*]
FTE............	Full-Time Education
FTE............	Full-Time Employee
FTE............	Full-Time Equivalent
FTE............	Full Time Equivalent (EERA)
FTE............	Full-Time Equivalent Staff (TDOB)
FTE............	Functional Test Equipment
FTE............	Fund for Theological Education (EA)
FTEC..........	Federal Trial Examiners Conference [*Later, FALJC*] (EA)
FTEC..........	Feminist Teacher Editorial Collective (EA)
FTEC..........	Firetector, Inc. [*NASDAQ symbol*] (NQ)
FTEC..........	Free Territory of Ely-Chatelaine [*An association*] (EA)
FTECS........	Field Training Equipment Concentration Site [*Army*] (AABC)
FTEE..........	Full-Time Equivalency Enrollment [*Education*]
FTEF..........	Fair Tax Education Fund (EA)
FTEG..........	Flight Test and Engineering Group [*Navy*] (DOMA)
FTEKF........	Fuel Tech [*NASDAQ symbol*] (SAG)
FTEKF........	Fuel Tech N.V. [*NASDAQ symbol*] (TTSB)
FTEM..........	Factory Test Equipment Manufacturing
FtEmp........	First Empire State Corp. [*Associated Press*] (SAG)
FT EMULS ...	Fiat Emulsio [*Let an Emulsion Be Made*] [*Pharmacy*]
FTEN..........	First Tennessee National Corp. [*NASDAQ symbol*] (NQ)
FTEN..........	First Tenn Natl [*NASDAQ symbol*] (TTSB)
ft enem......	Fiat Enema [*Let an Injection (per Rectum) be Made*] [*Pharmacy*] (DAVI)
FTEO..........	Flight Test Engineering Order
FtEsex........	First Essex Bancorp, Inc. [*Associated Press*] (SAG)
FTET..........	First Entertainment, Inc. [*NASDAQ symbol*] (SAG)
FTET..........	Full-Time Equivalent Terminals [*Computer science*]
FTETD........	First Entertainment [*NASDAQ symbol*] (TTSB)
FTF............	Face to Face
FTF............	Fair Tax Foundation [*Defunct*] (EA)
FTF............	Fibre Trade Federation [*British*] (BI)
FTF............	Field Training Flight (MCD)
FTF............	File Transfer Facility [*Telecommunications*] (OSI)
FTF............	Finger-to-Finger [*Neurology*] (DAVI)
FTF............	Flared Tube Fitting
FTF............	Forward Transfer Function [*Telecommunications*] (IAA)
FTF............	Free Thyroxine Fraction [*Endocrinology*] (DAVI)
FTF............	Functional Test Flight (AFM)
FTF............	Fundamental Train Frequency [*Machinery*]
FTF............	Texarkana First Financial [*AMEX symbol*] (TTSB)
FTF............	Texarkana First Financial Corp. [*AMEX symbol*] (SAG)
FtFAla........	First Federal of Alabama FSB [*Jasper, AL*] [*Associated Press*] (SAG)
FT-FAM.......	Fourier Transform-Faradic Admittance Measurements [*Spectrometry*]
FtFamFL......	First Family Financial Corp. [*Associated Press*] (SAG)
FTFC..........	Fabulous Thunderbirds Fan Club (EA)
FTFC..........	Field Training Feedback Components (MCD)
FTFC..........	First Federal Capital [*NASDAQ symbol*] (TTSB)
FTFC..........	First Federal Capital Corp. [*NASDAQ symbol*] (NQ)
FTFC..........	Florida College, Tampa, FL [*Library symbol Library of Congress*] (LCLS)
FTFC..........	Functional Test Flight Checklist
FtFCap........	First Federal Capital Corp. [*Associated Press*] (SAG)
FtFCrb........	First Financial Caribbean Corp. [*Associated Press*] (SAG)
FtFdBc........	First Federal Bancorp, Inc. [*Associated Press*] (SAG)
FtFdBcp......	First Federal Bancorp [*Associated Press*] (SAG)
FtFedBn......	FirstFed Bancshares, Inc. [*Associated Press*] (SAG)
FtFedCO......	First Federal Savings Bank Colorado [*Associated Press*] (SAG)
FTFET........	Four-Terminal Field-Effect Transistor (IEEE)
FTFF..........	Formaldehyde Task Force Fund [*Defunct*] (EA)
FTFFA........	Florida Tropical Fish Farms Association (EA)
FTFGS........	Flared Tube Fitting Gasket Seal (MSA)
FT/FH........	Flight Time/Flight Hour (MCD)
FTFLSU......	Fairy Tale-Folklore Study Unit [*American Topical Association*] (EA)
FTFM..........	Florida Mental Health Institute, Tampa, FL [*Library symbol*] [*Library of Congress*] (LCLS)
FTFN..........	First Financial [*NASDAQ symbol*] (TTSB)
FTFN..........	First Financial Corp. (Providence, RI) [*NASDAQ symbol*] (SAG)
FtFnBcp......	First Financial Bancorp [*Associated Press*] (SAG)
FtFnBk........	First Financial Bankshares [*Associated Press*] (SAG)
FtFnCp........	First Financial Corp. [*Associated Press*] (SAG)
FtFnCrb......	First Financial Caribbean Corp. [*Associated Press*] (SAG)
FtFnPlk........	First Financial Bancshares Polk County [*Associated Press*] (SAG)
FtFrnk........	First Franklin Corp. [*Associated Press*] (SAG)
FTFSU........	Fairy Tale-Folklore Study Unit [*American Topical Association*] (EA)
FTG............	Fairchild Tropical Garden
FTG............	Farmstead Telephone Group [*AMEX symbol*] (SAG)
FTG............	Fire Control Technician, Gun [*Navy rating*]
FTG............	Fitting (MSA)
FTG............	Fleet Training Group [*Navy*]
FTG............	Fluid Thioglycolate [*Medium*] [*Microbiology*]
FTG............	Footing (KSC)
FTG............	Full Thickness Graft [*Medicine*]
FTG............	Function Timing Generator (IAA)
FTG............	Servicios Aereos y Fotograficos, SA de CV [*Mexico*] [*FAA designator*] (FAAC)
f-tg--..........	Togo [*MARC geographic area code Library of Congress*] (LCCP)
FTG1..........	Fire Control Technician, Gun Fire Control, First Class [*Navy rating*] (DNAB)
FTG2..........	Fire Control Technician, Gun Fire Control, Second Class [*Navy rating*] (DNAB)
FTG3..........	Fire Control Technician, Gun Fire Control, Third Class [*Navy rating*] (DNAB)
FTGA..........	Florida Turfgrass Association (SRA)
FtGaHd........	First Georgia Holding, Inc. [*Associated Press*] (SAG)
FT GARG......	Fiat Gargarisma [*Let a Gargle Be Made*] [*Pharmacy*]
FTGBG........	Flareout and Terminal Glide Beam Guidance [*Aerospace*] (AAG)
FTGC..........	Fire Control Technician, Gun Fire Control, Chief [*Navy rating*] (DNAB)
FTGDV........	Footage Dives [*Military*] (AABC)
FTGS..........	Church of Jesus Christ of Latter-Day Saints, Genealogical Society Library, TampaBranch, Tampa, FL [*Library symbol Library of Congress*] (LCLS)
FTGSA........	Fire Control Technician, Gun Fire Control, Seaman Apprentice [*Navy rating*] (DNAB)
FTGSN........	Fire Control Technician, Gun Fire Control, Seaman [*Navy rating*] (DNAB)
FTGSVC......	Fleet Training Group Services (NVT)
FTGWP........	Fleet Training Group, Western Pacific [*Navy*] (DNAB)
FTH............	Faith
FTH............	Fathom
FT/H..........	Feet per Hour
FTH............	Fourier Transform Holographic
FTH............	Fuel Tank Helicopter
FTHA..........	Fork Truck Hire Association [*British*] (DBA)
Ft Haust......	Fiat Haustus [*Let a Drink Be Made*] [*Pharmacy*]
FtHaw........	First Hawaiian, Inc. [*Associated Press*] (SAG)
FTHF..........	Formyltetrahydrofolate [*Biochemistry*]
FTHil..........	Hillsborough Community College, Tampa, FL [*Library symbol*] [*Library of Congress*] (LCLS)
FTHM..........	Fathom (ROG)
FTHMA........	Frequency Time-Hopping Multiple Access [*Electronics*] (OA)
FTHR..........	Featherlite Manufacturing, Inc. [*NASDAQ symbol*] (SAG)
FTHR..........	Featherlite Mfg [*NASDAQ symbol*] (TTSB)
FTHRD........	Feathered [*Aviation*] (FAAC)
fthrs..........	Feathers (VRA)
FtHwrd........	Fort Howard Corp. [*Associated Press*] (SAG)
FTI............	Dansk Fiskeriteknologisk Institut [*Danish Institute of Fisheries Technology*] [*Information service or system*] (IID)
FTI............	Facing Tile Institute (EA)
FTI............	Federal Tax Included
FTI............	Fellow of the Textile Institute [*British*]
FTI............	Fellow of Trust Institute (DD)
FTI............	Film and Television Group [*Western Australia*]
FTI............	Film Thickness Indicator
FTI............	Financial Times Index [*A publication*] (CDAI)
FTI............	Fixed Target Information [*Army*] (AABC)
FTI............	Fixed Time Interval (PDAA)
FTI............	Flanders Technology International [*European technology fair*]
FTI............	Fluorescent Tagging of Infiltrator [*Surveillance system*]
FTI............	Foreign Trade Institute [*Mexico*]
FTI............	Foreign Traders Index [*Department of Commerce*] [*Washington, DC Information service or system*] (IID)
FTI............	Forval Turbo Interface [*Computer science*]
FTI............	France Telecom International, Inc. [*Telecommunications service*] (TSSD)
FTI............	Free Testosterone Index [*Endocrinology*]
FTI............	Free Thyroxine Index [*Endocrinology*]
FTI............	Frequency Time Indicator [*RADAR*]
FTI............	Frequency Time Intensity [*RADAR*]
FTI............	Frustration Tolerance Index [*Psychology*]
FTI............	FTI Foodtech International, Inc. [*Vancouver Stock Exchange symbol*]
FTi............	North Brevard Public Library, Titusville, FL [*Library symbol Library of Congress*] (LCLS)
f-ti--..........	Tunisia [*MARC geographic area code Library of Congress*] (LCCP)
FTIA..........	Family Therapy Institute of Australia
FTIA..........	Financial Times Institute of Actuaries [*A publication*] (BARN)
FTIA..........	Florida Telecommunications Industry Association (SRA)
FtIber........	First Iberian Fund, Inc. [*Associated Press*]
FTIC..........	Firm Time in Commission (DNAB)
FTIC..........	Forensic Technologies International Corp. [*NASDAQ symbol*] (SAG)
FTIC..........	Forensic Technologies Intl [*NASDAQ symbol*] (TTSB)
FT-ICP........	Fourier Transform Inductively-Coupled Plasma [*Spectrometry*]
FT-ICR........	Fourier Transform-Ion Cyclotron Resonance [*Spectrometry*]
FT-ICRMS......	Fourier Transform Ion Cyclotron Resonance Mass Spectrometry
FTID..........	Flame Thermionic Ionization Detector [*Instrumentation*]
FTID..........	Flight Test Information Drawing (MCD)
FTIG..........	Fort Indiantown Gap [*Army*] (AABC)
FTII..........	Fellow of the Taxation Institute, Inc. [*British*] (DBQ)
FTIM..........	Frequency and Time Interval Meter (DNAB)
FTIMA........	Federal Tobacco Inspectors Mutual Association
FtIn..........	First Interstate Bancorp [*Associated Press*] (SAG)
FtIndp........	First Independence Corp. [*Associated Press*] (SAG)
FT INFUS	Fiat Infusum [*Let an Infusion Be Made*] [*Pharmacy*]
FtInRt..........	First Industrial Realty Trust, Inc. [*Associated Press*] (SAG)
FT-IR..........	Fourier Transform Infrared [*Spectroscopy*]
FTIR..........	Fourier Transform Infrared Radiometer [*Marine science*] (OSRA)
FTIR..........	Fourier Transform Infrared Radiometer (USDC)
FTIR..........	Fourier Transform Infrared Spectroscopy (EERA)
FTIR..........	Frustrated Total Internal Reflection
FTIR..........	Functional Terminal Innervation Ratio [*Psychiatry*]
FTIR-PAS......	Fourier Transform Infrared Photoacoustic Spectroscopy
FTIR-RAS......	Fourier Transform Infrared Reflection Absorption Spectroscopy
FTIS..........	Flight Test Instrumentation System (NASA)

FtIsrl	First Israel Fund Corp. [*Associated Press*] (SAG)
FTIT	Fan Turbine Inlet Temperature (MCD)
FTIT	Fellow of the Institute of Taxation [*British*] (DCTA)
FTITB	Furniture and Timber Industry Training Board [*British*] (BI)
FTIWA	Film and Television Institute (Western Australia)
FTK	Field Test Kit
FTK	Fort Knox, KY [*Location identifier FAA*] (FAAL)
FTK	Fuel Tank
FTK	Futurtek Communications, Inc. [*Toronto Stock Exchange symbol*]
FtKeyst	First Keystone Financial, Inc. [*Associated Press*] (SAG)
FtKnox	First Knox Bancorp [*Associated Press*] (SAG)
FTL	Facility Tape Loading (SAA)
FTL	Faster Than Light [*Science fiction*] (AAG)
FTL	Fast Transient Loader
FTL	Fast Transit Link [*Rapid-transit term*]
FTL	Federal Telecommunications Laboratory [*Air Force*]
FTL	Flightline [*Spain*] [*FAA designator*] (FAAC)
FTL	Flight Time Limitation [*Aviation*] (DA)
FTL	Flying Thread Loom
FTL	Flying Tiger Line, Inc.
FT-L	Foot-Lambert [*Illumination*]
FTL	Foreign Theological Library [*A publication*]
FTL	Formal Technical Literature
FTL	Freeze Thaw Lysate [*Cytology*]
FTL	Fruit of The Loom'A' [*NYSE symbol*] (TTSB)
FTL	Fruit of the Loom, Inc. [*NYSE symbol*] (SPSG)
FTL	Full Term License [*For nuclear power plant*] (NRCH)
FTL	Full Truck Loads
FTLA	Foot-Lambert [*Illumination*] (IAA)
FT-LB	Foot-Pound [*Unit of work*] (AAG)
FTLB	Full Term Living Birth [*Medicine*] (MAE)
FT LBF	Foot-Pound Force
FT LB/H	Foot-Pounds per Hour
FT LB/MIN	Foot-Pounds per Minute
FT LB/S	Foot-Pounds per Second
FtLbty	First Liberty Financial Corp. [*Associated Press*] (SAG)
FTLC	Tampa Bay Library Consortium, Tampa, FL [*Library symbol*] [*Library of Congress*] (LCLS)
FTLD	Faster-Than-Light Drive (AAG)
FtLesprt	First Leesport Bancorp [*Associated Press*] (SAG)
FTLFC	Full-Term Living Female Child [*Obstetrics*] (DAVI)
FT LINIM	Fiat Linimentum [*Let a Linament Be Made*] [*Pharmacy*]
FTLMC	Full-Term Living Male Child [*Obstetrics*] (DAVI)
FTLP	Final Turn Lead Pursuit (SAA)
FTLP	Fixed Term Lease Plan [*Business term*] (IAA)
FTLR	Financial Times Law Report [*A publication*] (DLA)
FTLV	Feline T-Lymphotropic Lentivirus [*Later, FIV*]
FTLX	Flying Tiger Line, Inc. [*Air carrier designation symbol*]
FTM	Facilitated Transport Membrane [*Separation of chemicals*]
FTM	Failed to Make (IAA)
FTM	Fan-Type Marker
FTM	Fault Tolerant Multiprocessor System [*Computer science*] (HGAA)
FTM	Film Thickness Monitor
FTM	Fire Control Technician, Surface Missile [*Navy rating*]
FTM	Flat Technology Monitor [*Zenith*]
FTM	Flat-Tension Mask Screen (PCM)
FTM	Fleet Training Missile (MUGU)
FTM	Flexible Theatre Missile (AFM)
FTM	Flight Test Manual
FTM	Flight Test Matrix (MCD)
FTM	Flight Test Missile [*Air Force*]
FTM	Flight Training Mission (MCD)
FTM	Fluid Thioglycolate Medium [*Microbiology*]
FTM	Folded Triangular Monopole [*Electronics*] (OA)
FTM	Force/Torque Module [*NASA*]
FTM	Fractional Test Meal [*Medicine*]
FTM	Free Throws Made [*Basketball*]
FTM	Free to Member
FTM	Freight Traffic Manager
FTM	French Training Mission [*Military*] (CINC)
FTM	Frequency Time Modulation (DEN)
FTM	FTM Resources, Inc. [*Vancouver Stock Exchange symbol*]
FTM	Full-Time Manning (MCD)
FTM	Full Travel Membrane (PDAA)
FTM	Functional Test Manager [*Hewlett-Packard Co.*]
FTM1	Fire Control Technician, Missile Fire Control, First Class [*Navy rating*] (DNAB)
FTM2	Fire Control Technician, Missile Fire Control, Second Class [*Navy rating*] (DNAB)
FTM3	Fire Control Technician, Missile Fire Control, Third Class [*Navy rating*] (DNAB)
FT MAS	Fiat Massa [*Let a Mass Be Made*] [*Pharmacy*]
FT MAS DIV in PIL	Fiat Massa et Divide in Pilulae [*Let a Mass Be Made and Divided into Pills*] [*Pharmacy*]
FTMC	Fire Control Technician, Missile Fire Control, Chief [*Navy rating*] (DNAB)
FTMC	Frequency and Time Measurement Counter
FtMchBk	First Michigan Bank Corp. [*Associated Press*] (SAG)
FtMD	First Maryland Bancorp [*Associated Press*] (SAG)
FtMdwF	First Midwest Financial [*Associated Press*] (SAG)
FtMerc	First Merchants Corp. [*Associated Press*] (SAG)
FTMI	Flight Operations and Air Traffic Management Integration [*FAA*] (TAG)
FtMichBk	First Michigan Bank Corp. [*Associated Press*] (SAG)
FT/MIN	Feet per Minute

FtMiss	First Mississippi Corp. [*Associated Press*] (SAG)
FtMissG	FirstMiss Gold, Inc. [*Associated Press*] (SAG)
FT MIST	Fiat Mistura [*Let a Mixture Be Made*] [*Pharmacy*]
FTML	Folded-Tape Meander Line (IAA)
FTMP	Fault Tolerant Multiprocessor System [*Computer science*]
FTMS	Fabrication Tracking and Management System (MCD)
FTMS	Federal Test Method Standards (MCD)
FTMS	Fluid Transfer Management System (SSD)
FT/MS	Fourier Transform/Mass Spectrometry
FTMSA	Fire Control Technician, Missile Fire Control, Seaman Apprentice [*Navy rating*] (DNAB)
FTMSN	Fire Control Technician, Missile Fire Control, Seaman [*Navy rating*] (DNAB)
FTMT	Final Thermomechanical Treatment (MCD)
FT-MW	Fourier Transform-Microwave [*Spectroscopy*]
FTN	Aviation Charter & Management [*British ICAO designator*] (FAAC)
FTN	Family Therapy Network (EA)
FTN	Federacion de Trabajadores Nicaraguenses [*Political party*] (EY)
FTN	Finger to Nose [*Medicine*] (DMAA)
FTN	Flocculus Target Neuron [*Neuroanatomy*]
FTN	Fortification (AABC)
FTN	Fountain
FTN	Fountain
FTN	Full-Term Nursery [*Neonatology*] (DAVI)
FtNatEnt	First National Entertainment Corp. [*Associated Press*] (SAG)
FTND	Full Term Normal Delivery [*Medicine*]
FT-NMR	Fourier Transform-Nuclear Magnetic Resonance [*Spectrometry*]
FTNT	NEC/TAMPA Technology Institute, Tampa, FL [*Library symbol*] [*Library of Congress*] (LCLS)
FTO	Failed to Open (IEEE)
FTO	Field Test Office (MCD)
FTO	Field Test Operations [*Aerospace*] (KSC)
FTO	First Toronto Capital Corp. [*Toronto Stock Exchange symbol*]
FTO	Fleet Torpedo Officer [*British*]
FTO	Flexible and Selective Targeting Options [*DoD*]
FTO	Flight Test Objective (KSC)
FTO	Flight Test Operations
FTO	Foreign Technology Office [*Army Tank-Automotive Command*]
FTO	Foreign Training Officer [*Military*]
FTO	Fort Yukon, AK [*Location identifier FAA*] (FAAL)
FTO	Fourier Transform Operator
FTO	Full-Time Officer [*of an organization*]
FTO	Functional Test Objective (KSC)
FtOakBrk	First Oak Brook Bancshares [*Associated Press*] (SAG)
FTOC	Fetal Thymic Organ Cultures [*Biochemistry*]
F to F	Face to Face [*Technical drawings*]
FTOH	Flight Team Operations Handbook (NASA)
FTOH	Flight Test Operations Handbook (NASA)
FTOL	Full Term Operating License (NRCH)
FT/OLTP	Fault Tolerant/Online Transaction Processing (NITA)
F to N	Finger to Nose Test [*Neurology*]
FTOR-MIM-BCG	Ftorafur, Adriamycin, Cyclophosphamide, Bacille Calmette-Guerin [*Antineoplastic drug regimen*] (DAVI)
FTOS	Field Test Operations Support [*Aerospace*] (AAG)
FTOS	Flight Termination Ordnance System [*Small intercontinental ballistic missile*] (DWSG)
FTP	Factor/Test Procedure (MCD)
FTP	Failure to Pay [*IRS*]
FTP	Failure to Progress [*In labor*] [*Obstetrics*] (DAVI)
FTP	Falling to Pieces [*Slang*]
FTP	Fear, Tension, Pain [*Syndrome*] [*Psychology*] (BARN)
FTP	Federal Test Procedure
FTP	Federal Theater Project
FTP	FFTF [*Fast Flux Test Facility*] Test Procedure [*Nuclear energy*] (NRCH)
FTP	Field Test Operational Procedures [*Aerospace*] (AAG)
FTP	Field Test Program [*Aerospace*] (IAA)
FTP	Field Transport Pack (DNAB)
FTP	File Transfer Packet [*Computer science*] (IAA)
FTP	File Transfer Program [*or Protocol*] [*Computer science*]
ftp	File Transfer Protocol
FTP	File Transfer Protocol (NITA)
FTP	Final Technical Proposal (NATG)
FTP	Firmware Test Plan [*Military*]
FTP	Fixed Term Plan (BUR)
FTP	Fixed Throttle Point [*NASA*]
FTP	Flash Temperature Parameter (IAA)
FTP	Fleet Training Publication [*Navy*]
FTP	Flight Test Plan [*or Procedure or Program*]
FTP	Florida Test Procedure [*Aerospace*] (AAG)
FTP	Fluorocarbons Technical Panel [*of Manufacturing Chemists Association*]
FTP	Fluorothermoplastic
FTP	Fly-to-Point (NVT)
FTP	Folded, Trimmed, Packed [*Books*]
FTP	Fracture Toughness Parameter
FTP	Fuel Tanking Panel [*Aerospace*] (AAG)
FTP	Fuel Transfer Pool [*Nuclear energy*] (NRCH)
FTP	Fuel Transfer Port [*Nuclear energy*] (NRCH)
FTP	Fuel Transfer Pump (MSA)
FTP	Full Throttle Position (KSC)
FTP	Full-Time Permanent [*Employment*]
FTP	Full-Time Personnel [*Employment*]
FTP	Full Transport Pack [*Military*]
FTP	Functional Test Procedure [*or Program*]

FTP............	Function Test Procedure [*or Progress*] (NASA)
FTPA.........	Federal Timber Purchasers Association (EA)
FTPA.........	Fellow of the Town Planning Association [*British*]
FTP & E.......	Flight Test Planning and Evaluation
FtPatBn......	First Patriot Bankshares [*Associated Press*] (SAG)
FTPC..........	Francs-Tireurs et Partisans Corses [*Corsican Guerrillas and Partisans*] (PD)
FtPcNtw......	First Pacific Networks, Inc. [*Associated Press*] (SAG)
FTPCS........	Failure to Pay Child Support
FT PDL	Foot-Poundal [*Unit of work*]
FTPF..........	Federation des Travailleurs du Papier et de la Foret [*Federation of Paper and Forest Workers*] [*Canada*]
FtPhil........	First Philippine Fund, Inc. [*Associated Press*] (SAG)
FTPI.........	Flux Transitions per Inch
FTPI.........	Future Time Perspective Inventory [*Psychology*]
FT PIL	Fiat Pilulae [*Let Pills Be Made*] [*Pharmacy*] (ROG)
FTPM.........	Fixed Time Printing Mode [*Photography*]
FTPMM.......	Flux Transitions per Millimeter (IAA)
FTPR.........	Federacion del Trabajo de Puerto Rico [*Puerto Rican Federation of Labor*]
FTPRP	Federal Test Procedure Revision Project
FTPS..........	Fellow of the Technical Publishing Society
FTPS..........	Food Trades Protection Society Ltd. [*British*] (BI)
FTPS..........	FTP Software [*Commercial firm NASDAQ symbol*] (SAG)
FTP Sft	FTP Software [*Commercial firm Associated Press*] (SAG)
FT PULV	Fiat Pulvis [*Let a Powder Be Made*] [*Pharmacy*]
FT PULV SUBTIL...	Fiat Pulvis Subtilis [*Let a Fine Powder Be Made*] [*Pharmacy*]
FTQ..........	Federation des Travailleurs et Travailleuses du Quebec [*Canada*] (CROSS)
FTQ..........	Monterey/Fort Ord, CA [*Location identifier FAA*] (FAAL)
FTR..........	Australian Federal Tax Reporter [*A publication*]
FTR..........	Factor (KSC)
FTR..........	Failed to Return [*British military*] (DMA)
FTR..........	Fails to Reproduce
FTR..........	Fails to Respond (DNAB)
FTR..........	False Target Rate [*Military*] (CAAL)
FTR..........	Fan Thrust Reverser
FTR..........	Fast Test Reactor
FTR..........	Fault Transfer Facility (NITA)
FTR..........	Feather (MSA)
FTR..........	Federacion de Trabajadores Revolucionarios [*Revolutionary Workers' Federation*] [*El Salvador*] (PD)
FTR..........	Federal Telephone and Radio
FTR..........	Federal Travel Regulations (NRCH)
FTR..........	Federal Trial Reports [*Maritime Law Book Co. Ltd.*] [*Canada Information service or system*] (CRD)
FTR..........	Fighter (AABC)
FTR..........	Filestore Transfer Routine [*Computer science*] (PDAA)
FTR..........	File Transfer Facility (NITA)
FTR..........	Film Tracing Reproduction
FTR..........	Final Technical Report
FTR..........	Final Test Rack (KSC)
FTR..........	Finist' Air [*France ICAO designator*] (FAAC)
FTR..........	Fixed Target Rejection [*Military*] (IAA)
FTR..........	Fixed Transom (AAG)
FTR..........	Flag Tower [*Maps and charts*]
FTR..........	Flash Triangulation Reduction
FTR..........	Flat-Tile Roof (AAG)
FTR..........	Flight Test Report
FTR..........	Flight Test Requirements [*NASA*] (NASA)
FTR..........	Foreign Trade Reports
FTR..........	Formation Temperature Ratio (PDAA)
FTR..........	For the Record (DAVI)
FTR..........	Free-Text Retrieval [*Computer system alternative to Content-Addressable File Store*]
FTR..........	Frontier Insurance Gr [*NYSE symbol*] (TTSB)
FTR..........	Frontier Insurance Group, Inc. [*NYSE symbol*] (SPSG)
FTR..........	Frustrated Total Reflection
FTR..........	Full Text Retrieval (NITA)
FTR..........	Full-Time Regular [*Civil Service employee category*]
FTR..........	Functional Test Report
FTR..........	Functional Test Requirement (IEEE)
FTR..........	Funds Transfer [*Banking*] (MHDW)
F Tr...........	Fusion Treaty [*European Communities*] [*1965*] (ILCA)
FTRAC	Full-Tracked Vehicle
FTRB..........	Flight Test Review Board (MCD)
FTRC..........	Federal Telecommunications Records Center (NRCH)
FTRD	Flight Test Requirements Document [*NASA*] (NASA)
FTRD	Functional Test Requirements Document (NASA)
FTRF..........	Freedom to Read Foundation (EA)
FT/RF.........	Frequency Translator/Recursive Filter (CAAL)
FTRF.........	Full-Time Recruiting Force [*DoD*]
FTRFME......	Flight Test Rocket Facilities Mechanical Engineering (AAG)
FTRG.........	Flight Test Report Guide (MCD)
FTRIA.........	Flow and Temperature Removable Instrument Assembly [*Nuclear energy*] (NRCH)
FTRM........	Flight Test Request Memorandum (MCD)
FTRN........	First American Railways, Inc. [*NASDAQ symbol*] (SAG)
FTRO	Fellow of the Toastmasters for Royal Occasions [*British*] (DI)
FTRO	Fighter Operations
FTRP	Fighter Plans
FtRpBc........	First Republic Bancorp, Inc. [*Associated Press*] (SAG)
FTRR & I.....	For Their Respective Rights and Interests [*Insurance*] (AIA)
FTRT..........	Flight Test Release Ticket (MCD)
FTRW.........	Flight Test Reports Writer (MUGU)

FTRWPNSSq...	Fighter Weapons Squadron [*Air Force*]
FTS............	African Transair [*Nigeria*] [*FAA designator*] (FAAC)
FTS............	Facsimile Test Society
FTS............	Facteur Thymique Serique [*Synthetic Serum Thymic Factor*] [*Immunochemistry*] [*French*]
FTS............	Factory Test Set
FTS............	Factory Training School
FTS............	Faith Theological Seminary
FTS............	Fault Tolerance System
FTS............	Federal Telecommunications System [*of GSA*]
FTS............	Federal Telephone System (KSC)
FTS............	Federal Teleprocessing Service [*GSA*]
FT/S...........	Feet per Second
FTS............	Fellow of Technological Sciences
FTS............	Feminizing Testis Syndrome [*Medicine*] (DMAA)
FTS............	Femtosecond Transition-State Spectroscope
FTS............	Femtosecond Transition-State Spectroscopy
FTS............	Field Computer Test Set
FTS............	Field Target Screen
FTS............	Field Test Support [*Aerospace*] (AAG)
FTS............	Field Training Services [*Army*] (AABC)
FTS............	File Transfer Service (DOMA)
FTS............	Filled Thermal System [*Temperature sensor*]
FTS............	Fine Track Sensor
FTS............	Finish Two Sides [*Technical drawings*] (IAA)
FTS............	Fischer-Tropsch Synthesis [*Organic chemistry*]
FTS............	Fleet Training Squadron [*Navy*]
FTS............	Flexible Test Station
FTS............	Flexible Track System [*Aviation*] (DA)
FTS............	Flexible Turret System (MCD)
FTS............	Flight Telemetry Subsystem [*Spacecraft*]
FTS............	Flight Telerobotic Servicer [*NASA*]
FTS............	Flight Termination System (AFM)
FTS............	Flight Test Sketch (MCD)
FTS............	Flight Test Standard
FTS............	Flight Test Station (MCD)
FTS............	Flight Test Support
FTS............	Flight Test System (NASA)
FTS............	Flight Traffic Specialist (SAA)
FTS............	Float Switch [*Aerospace*] (IAA)
FTS............	Flying Training School
FTS............	Flying Training Squadron [*Air Force*]
FTS............	Footstar, Inc. [*NYSE symbol*] (SAG)
FTS............	Foot Switch [*Industrial control*] (IEEE)
FTS............	Ford's Theatre Society (EA)
FTS............	Foreign Trade Statistics [*Bureau of Census*]
FTS............	Fortis, Inc. [*Toronto Stock Exchange symbol*]
FTS............	Foundation for Traffic Safety
FTS............	Fourier Transform Spectrometer [*or Spectroscopy*]
FTS............	Fourier Transform System
FTS............	Frame-Supported Tension Structure [*Tent*] [*Navy*]
FTS............	Free-Time System [*GE/PAC*] (IEEE)
FTS............	Frequency and Timing Subsystem [*Deep Space Instrumentation Facility, NASA*]
FTS............	Frequency Time Schedule (NVT)
FTS............	Frequency Time Standard
FTS............	Fuel Transfer System [*Nuclear energy*] (NRCH)
FTS............	Full-Time Support
FTS............	Fulmer Technical Services [*Research center British*] (IRC)
FTS............	Functional Test Specification (KSC)
FTS............	Funds Transfer System
FTS............	Funeral Telegraph Service
FTS............	Future Technology Systems (NITA)
FTS............	University of South Florida, Tampa, FL [*Library symbol Library of Congress*] (LCLS)
FTSA..........	Fault Tolerant System Architecture [*Computer science*]
FTSA..........	Seaman Apprentice, Fire Control Technician, Striker [*Navy rating*]
FTSB..........	Fort Thomas Financial Corp. [*NASDAQ symbol*] (SAG)
FTSB..........	Fort Thomas Finl [*NASDAQ symbol*] (TTSB)
FTSC..........	Fako Transport Shipping Lines [*Joint venture between Cameroon and the US*] [*Shipping line*] (EY)
FTSC..........	Fault Tolerant Spaceborne Computer
FTSC..........	Federal Telecommunications Standards Committee
FTSC..........	Fellow in the Technology of Surface Coatings [*British*] (DBQ)
FTSCDET......	Fleet Technical Support Center Detachment (DNAB)
FT-SE.........	Financial Times - Stock Exchange [*Stock index*] [*Pronounced "footsie"*] [*British*]
FT-SE 100....	Financial Times-Stock Exchange 100 (ODBW)
FT/SEC........	Feet per Second (MCD)
FTSG..........	Full Thickness Skin Graft [*Medicine*] (DMAA)
FtShengo.....	First Shenango Bancorp, Inc. [*Associated Press*] (SAG)
FTS-M.........	University of South Florida, College of Medicine, Tampa, FL [*Library symbol Library of Congress*] (LCLS)
FTSMC........	Full-Time Support Management Center [*Army*] (INF)
FTS-MC.......	University of South Florida, Media Center, Tampa, FL [*Library symbol Library of Congress*] (LCLS)
FTSMS........	Flying Training Student Management System [*Air Force*]
FTSN..........	Seaman, Fire Control Technician, Striker [*Navy rating*]
FTSNSW	Furnishing Trades Society of New South Wales [*Australia*]
ft solut........	Fiat Solutio [*Let a Solution Be Made*] [*Pharmacy Latin*] (MAE)
FtSouest......	First Southeast Financial Corp. [*Associated Press*] (SAG)
FTSP..........	First Team Sports [*NASDAQ symbol*] (TTSB)
FTSP..........	First Team Sports, Inc. [*NASDAQ symbol*] (NQ)
FTSq..........	Flying Training Squadron [*Air Force*]
FTSR..........	Foreign Trade Statistics Regulations

FtStateCp.....	First State Corp. [*Associated Press*] (SAG)	FTUPrB........	First Union $2.15 Cv B Pfd [*NYSE symbol*] (TTSB)
FtSteCp........	First State Corp. [*Associated Press*] (SAG)	FTUPrD........	First Union Adj D Pfd [*NYSE symbol*] (TTSB)
FtStFin........	First State Financial Services, Inc. [*Associated Press*] (SAG)	FTUPrF........	First Union 10.64% Dep Pfd [*NYSE symbol*] (TTSB)
FtSthnB........	First Southern Bancshares, Inc. [*Associated Press*] (SAG)	FTURE........	Furniture (ROG)
FTSTP..........	Flexible Test Station Test Procedure	FTUS...........	Full-Time Unit Support [*Army Reserve*] (INF)
ft suppos	Fiat Suppositorium [*Let a Suppository Be Made*] [*Pharmacy*] (DAVI)	FtUSA...........	First USA, Inc. [*Associated Press*] (SAG)
FtSvBanc	First Savings Bank of Moore County [*Associated Press*] (SAG)	FtUtd...........	First United Bancshares, Inc. [*Associated Press*] (SAG)
FTT	Failure to Thrive [*Syndrome*] [*Medicine*]	FtUtdBcp........	First United Bancorp [*Associated Press*] (SAG)
FTT	Fever Therapy Technician [*Navy*]	FtUtdBs........	First United Bancshares [*Associated Press*] (SAG)
FTT	Field Tactical Trainer [*Army*] (INF)	FTUV...........	Federated Teachers' Union of Victoria [*Australia*]
FTT	Field Training Team [*Military*] (CINC)	FT-UV/Vis ...	Fourier-Transform Ultraviolet/Visible [*Spectrophotometer*]
FTT	Financial Transaction Terminal [*Banking*] (MHDW)	FTV...........	Fashion Television [*Video sales technique in the apparel industry*]
FTT	Finning Ltd. [*Toronto Stock Exchange symbol Vancouver Stock Exchange symbol*]	FTV...........	Flight Television [*NASA*] (KSC)
FTT	Fischer-Tropsch Type [*Class of chemical reaction*]	FTV...........	Flight Test Vehicle [*Air Force*]
FTT	Five Task Test [*Psychology*]	FTV...........	Flow-Through Ventilation
FTT	Fixed Target Track (MCD)	FTV...........	Foxtail Mosaic Virus
FTT	Fixed Tissue Turnover [*Laboratory and physiology*] (DAVI)	FTV...........	Functional Technical Validation (SDI)
FTT	Flanged Tongue Terminal	FTV...........	Functional Technology Vehicle [*Army*]
FTT	Flat Trim Template (MSA)	FTV...........	Masvingo [*Zimbabwe*] [*Airport symbol*] (OAG)
FTT	Free Territory of Trieste	FTV...........	United States Veterans Administration Hospital, Tampa, FL [*Library symbol Library of Congress*] (LCLS)
FTT	Fuel Transfer Tool	FtVaBks........	First Virginia Banks, Inc. [*Associated Press*] (SAG)
FTT	Full-Time Temporary [*Civil Service employee category*]	FTVSP..........	Flight Test Vehicle Safety Plan [*Air Force*] (MCD)
FTT	Fulton, MO [*Location identifier FAA*] (FAAL)	FTW...........	Fairmont [*Washington*] [*Seismograph station code, US Geological Survey*] (SEIS)
FTTA............	Sarh [*Chad*] [*ICAO location identifier*] (ICLI)	FTW...........	Federation of Telephone Workers
FTTB............	Bongor [*Chad*] [*ICAO location identifier*] (ICLI)	FTW...........	Fighter Tactical Wing (MCD)
FTTC............	Abeche [*Chad*] [*ICAO location identifier*] (ICLI)	FTW...........	Fizean Toothed Wheel
FTTC............	Fiber to the Curb [*Telecommunications*]	FTW...........	Flying Training Wing [*Air Force*]
FTTC............	Fleet Tactical Training Course (DOMA)	FTW...........	Footwall Exploration [*Vancouver Stock Exchange symbol*]
FTTD............	Full-Time Training Duty [*Army*] (AABC)	FTW...........	Fort Wayne-South Bend [*Diocesan abbreviation*] [*Indiana*] (TOCD)
FTTD............	Moundou [*Chad*] [*ICAO location identifier*] (ICLI)	FTW...........	Fort Worth, TX [*Location identifier FAA*] (FAAL)
FTTE............	Biltine [*Chad*] [*ICAO location identifier*] (ICLI)	FTW...........	Forward Traveling Wave
FtTeam	First Team Sports, Inc. [*Associated Press*] (SAG)	FTW...........	Free Trade Wharf
FTTF............	Fada [*Chad*] [*ICAO location identifier*] (ICLI)	FTW...........	Friends of the Third World (EA)
FTTF............	Fiber-to-the Feeder [*Telecommunications*]	FtWayne	Fort Wayne National Corp. [*Associated Press*] (SAG)
FTtF	Florida College, Temple Terrace, FL [*Library symbol Library of Congress*] (LCLS)	FtWBc..........	First Western Bancorp [*Associated Press*] (SAG)
FTTF............	Freedom through Truth Foundation (EA)	FTWG..........	Flight Test Working Group
FTTG............	Goz-Beida [*Chad*] [*ICAO location identifier*] (ICLI)	FTWIAD........	Fort Wingate Army Depot [*New Mexico*]
FTTH............	Fiber to the Home [*Telecommunications*]	FTWO..........	Flight Test Work Order (MCD)
FTTH............	Lai [*Chad*] [*ICAO location identifier*] (ICLI)	FTWOAD	Fort Worth Army Depot [*Texas*]
FtThom	Fort Thomas Financial Corp. [*Associated Press*] (SAG)	FTWR..........	Footwear
FTTI	Ati [*Chad*] [*ICAO location identifier*] (ICLI)	FTWS..........	Federal Train Wreck Statute
FTTJ.............	N'Djamena [*Chad*] [*ICAO location identifier*] (ICLI)	FtWstnBc......	First Western Bancorp [*Associated Press*] (SAG)
FTTK............	Bokoro [*Chad*] [*ICAO location identifier*] (ICLI)	FTWUA	Federated Tobacco Workers' Union of Australia
FTTL............	Bol [*Chad*] [*ICAO location identifier*] (ICLI)	FTX...........	Fault Tolerant UNIX (CDE)
FTTM............	Few-Tube Test Model [*Nuclear energy*] (NRCH)	FTX...........	Field Test Exercise [*Military*]
FTTM............	Mongo [*Chad*] [*ICAO location identifier*] (ICLI)	FTX...........	Field Training Exercise [*Army*] (INF)
FTTN............	Am-Timan [*Chad*] [*ICAO location identifier*] (ICLI)	FTX...........	Fleet Training Exercise
FTTP............	Fiber to the Pedestal [*Telecommunications*]	FTX...........	Fort Riley, KS [*Location identifier FAA*] (FAAL)
FTTP............	Full-Time Temporary Personnel [*Employment*]	FTX...........	Freeport-McMoRan, Inc. [*NYSE symbol*] (SPSG)
FTTP............	Pala [*Chad*] [*ICAO location identifier*] (ICLI)	FTX...........	Freeport McMoRan(New) [*NYSE symbol*] (TTSB)
FTTPP..........	Federation of Trainers and Training Programs in PsychoDrama (EA)	FTX...........	Free Text Retrieval (NITA)
FTTR............	Fretter, Inc. [*NASDAQ symbol*] (SAG)	FTX...........	Ft. Rousset [*Congo*] [*Airport symbol*] (AD)
FTTR............	Zouar [*Chad*] [*ICAO location identifier*] (ICLI)	FTX...........	Funnel-Web Spider Toxin
FT TROCH...	Fiat Trochisci [*Make Lozenges*] [*Pharmacy*]	FTX...........	Owando [*Congo*] [*Airport symbol*] (OAG)
FTTS	Bousso [*Chad*] [*ICAO location identifier*] (ICLI)	FTY...........	Atlanta, GA [*Location identifier FAA*] (FAAL)
FTTS	Flow-Through Tube Sampler [*Nuclear energy*] (NRCH)	FTY...........	Futurity Oils Ltd. [*Vancouver Stock Exchange symbol*]
FTTT	N'Djamena [*Chad*] [*ICAO location identifier*] (ICLI)	FTyAF-T	United States Air Force, Technical Library, Tyndall AFB, FL [*Library symbol Library of Congress*] (LCLS)
FTTU............	Field Technical Training Unit (MCD)	FTZ	Federal Trade Zone
FTTU............	Mao [*Chad*] [*ICAO location identifier*] (ICLI)	FTZ	Foreign Trade Zone [*New York City docks area*]
FTTV............	N'Djamena [*Chad*] [*ICAO location identifier*] (ICLI)	FTZ	Foristell, MO [*Location identifier FAA*] (FAAL)
FTTY	Faya-Largeau [*Chad*] [*ICAO location identifier*] (ICLI)	FTZ	Free Trade Zone (IMH)
FTTZ............	Bardai-Zougra [*Chad*] [*ICAO location identifier*] (ICLI)	FTZ	Fushi Tarazu [*Not Enough Segments*] [*Genetics*] [*Japan*]
FTU	Factory Training Unit (KSC)	f-tz--...........	Tanzania [*MARC geographic area code Library of Congress*] (LCCP)
FTU	Fail Tension Ultimate (MCD)	FTZB	Foreign Trade Zone Board
FTU	Federation of Theatre Unions [*British*] (DCTA)	FU	Air Littoral [*ICAO designator*] (AD)
FTU	Federation of Trade Unions [*British*] (DAS)	FU	Fecal Urobilinogen [*Clinical chemistry*]
FTU	Ferry Training Unit [*British*]	FU	Federal Union (DAS)
FTU	Field Torpedo Unit	FU	Feministas Unidas [*An association*] (EA)
FTU	Field Transfusion Unit [*Military British*]	Fu	Finsen Unit [*for ultraviolet light*]
FTU	First Time Use	FU	Firing Unit [*Military*]
FTU	First Training Unit	FU	Flight Unit (MCD)
FTU	First Union Corp. [*NYSE symbol*] (SPSG)	FU	Fluorouracil [*Also, F*] [*Antineoplastic drug*]
FTU	Fixed Treatment Unit [*Engineering*]	FU	Foederalistische Union [*Federal Union*] [*Germany Political party*] (PPE)
FTU	Fleet Training Unit	FU	Folkuniversitetet
FTU	Flight Test Unit (KSC)	FU	Follow-Up
FTU	Florida Technology University (DAVI)	FU	Forecast Unit
FTU	Fluorescein Thiourea [*Organic chemistry*]	FU	Forecast Upper Air (NATG)
FTU	Fluorescence Thiourea [*Organic chemistry*] (DAVI)	FU	Fouled Up [*To describe a confused, mixed-up situation, person, or action*] [*Bowdlerized version*]
FTU	Formazin Turbidity Unit [*Analytical chemistry*]	FU	Fractional Urinalysis [*Medicine*]
FTU	Fort Dauphin [*Madagascar*] [*Airport symbol*] (OAG)	FU	Frame Unprotected [*Insurance classification*]
FTU	Freeman Time Unit [*Psychology*]	FU	Frederick Ungar [*Publisher*]
FTU	Frequency Transfer Unit	FU	Freeman Time Unit [*Psychology*]
FTU	Fuel Transfer Unit [*NASA*] (KSC)	FU	Freie Union in Niedersachsen [*Free Union in Lower Saxony*] [*Germany Political party*] (PPW)
FTU	Functional Test Unit [*Computer science*] (IAA)	FU	Freie Universitaet (Berlin) [*Free University (Berlin)*] [*Information retrieval Germany*]
FTU	University of Central Florida, Orlando, FL [*OCLC symbol*] (OCLC)	Fu	Fucus [*Quality of the bottom*] [*Nautical charts*]
FTU	University of Tampa, Tampa, FL [*Library symbol Library of Congress*] (LCLS)	FU.............	Fuel (NASA)
FTUB............	Free Trade Unions of Burma	FU.............	Fumarate Concentration (OA)
FTUC............	Federal Trade Union Congress [*European*]	FU.............	Functional Unit [*Computer science*]
FT UNG.......	Fiat Unguentum [*Make an Ointment*] [*Pharmacy*]		
FTUnH	University Community Hospital, Medical Library, Tampa, FL [*Library symbol*] [*Library of Congress*] (LCLS)		
FTUP...........	Free Trade Unions of the Philippines		

FU .... Funding (NITA)
F/U .... Fundus at Umbilicus [Obstetrics] (DAVI)
FU .... Fuse (MSA)
fu---- .... Suez Canal [MARC geographic area code Library of Congress] (LCCP)
FU .... University of Florida, Gainesville, FL [Library symbol Library of Congress] (LCLS)
FUA .... Compania Hispano Irlandesa de Aviacion [Spain ICAO designator] (FAAC)
FUA .... Farm Underwriters Association [Defunct]
FUA .... Federal Unemployment Account [Unemployment insurance]
FUA .... Fire Unit Analyzer [Military]
FUA .... Follow-Up Amplifier
FUA .... Frente Unita Angolana [Angolan United Front]
FUA .... Fuel Use Act
f-ua-- .... United Arab Republic [Egypt] [MARC geographic area code Library of Congress] (LCCP)
FU-A .... University of Florida, Agricultural Experiment Station, Gainesville, FL [Library symbol Library of Congress] (LCLS)
FUA .... University of Florida, Agricultural Library, Gainesville, FL [OCLC symbol] (OCLC)
FUAA .... Filmmakers United Against Apartheid (EA)
FUAAV .... Federation Universelle des Associations d'Agences de Voyages [Universal Federation of Travel Agents' Associations - UFTAA] (EAIO)
FUACE .... Federation Universelle des Associations Chretiennes d'Etudiants [Universal Federation of Christian Students Associations]
FUAI .... Front Uni pour l'Autonomie Interne [United Front for Internal Autonomy] [French Polynesia] [Political party] (PPW)
FUAM .... Freie und Angenommene Maurer [Free and Accepted Mason] [Freemasonry] [German]
FUB .... Facility Utilization Board (AFM)
FUB .... Forward Utility Bridge (NASA)
FUB .... Front de l'Unite Bangala [Bangala United Front]
FUB .... Fube [Japan] [Seismograph station code, US Geological Survey] (SEIS)
FUB .... Fulleborn [Papua New Guinea] [Airport symbol] (OAG)
FUB .... Functional Uterine Bleeding [Medicine]
FUB .... University of Florida, Law Library, Gainesville, FL [OCLC symbol] (OCLC)
FUBA .... Federal Unemployment Benefit and Allowance Account [Unemployment insurance]
FUBAR .... Failed UNI BUS Address Register [Computer science] (NHD)
FUBAR .... Fangmeyer's Utility, a Basic Algorithm for Revision (PDAA)
FUBAR .... Fouled Up Beyond All Recognition [Military slang] [Bowdlerized version]
FUBB .... Fouled Up Beyond Belief [Military slang] [Bowdlerized version]
FUBC .... 1st United Bancorp(FL) [NASDAQ symbol] (TTSB)
FUBC .... First United Bancorp [NASDAQ symbol] (SAG)
FUBX .... Fuse Box
FUCA .... Front Upper Control Arm
FUCCO .... First (United States Army Reserve) Company Chaplain Office
FUCL .... Fellow of University College, London [British] (ROG)
FUCO .... Fellow of University College, Oxford [British] (ROG)
FU_co .... Functional Uptake of Carbon Monoxide [Medicine] (DAVI)
FU-CP .... University of Florida, Chemistry-Pharmacy Library, Gainesville, FL [Library symbol Library of Congress] (LCLS)
FUD .... Fear, Uncertainty, and Doubt [Factors hindering sales of lesser-known products]
FUD .... Fellow of the University of Dublin (ROG)
FUD .... Fire Unit Deployed
FUD .... Fire Up Decoder
FUD .... First Use Date [NASA] (NASA)
FUD .... Frente Voluntario de Defensa [Voluntary Defense Front] [Guatemala] (PD)
FUDR .... Failure and Usage Data Report (IEEE)
FUDR .... Fluorodeoxyuridine [Floxuridine] [Also, FldUrd] [Antineoplastic drug]
FUDS .... Federal Urban Driving Schedule
FUDS .... Formerly Used Defense Site [DoD]
FUDT .... Forensic Urine Drug Testing [Analytical chemistry]
FUE .... Federated Union of Employers [Ireland] (IMH)
FUE .... Fever of Undetermined Etiology [Medicine] (DAVI)
FUE .... Fire Unit Effectiveness (MCD)
FUE .... First Unit Equipped (MCD)
FUE .... Fuerteventura [Canary Islands] [Airport symbol] (OAG)
FUED .... First Unit Equipped Date (MCD)
FUEL .... Fuel Users Emergency Line [Pennsylvania]
FUEL .... Streicher Mobile Fueling, Inc. [NASDAQ symbol] (SAG)
Fuel Econ 1925-1936... Fuel Economist (1925-1936) [A publication]
FuelTch .... Fuel Tech [Commercial firm Associated Press] (SAG)
FUEMSSO ... Federation of United Kingdom and Eire Malaysian and Singaporean Students [British]
FUEN .... Federal Union of European Nationalities [Political party] (PPW)
FUES .... Follow-up and Evaluation Section (EERA)
FUEV .... Foederalistische Union Europaeischer Volksgruppen [Federal Union of European Nationalities]
FUF .... Federation des Unions de Familles [Federation of Family Unions] [Canada]
FUF .... Federation for Universal French (EAIO)
FUF .... French Union Forces (VNW)
FUFO .... Fly-Under, Fly-Out (MCD)
FUFO .... Fuel-Fusing Option [Nuclear energy] (GFGA)
FUFO .... Full Fuzing Option [Air Force]
FUFOR .... Fund for UFO [Unidentified Flying Object] Research (EA)
FUFTB .... Full-Up/Fit-to-Bust [Slang British] (DI)

Fug .... De Fuga et Inventione [Philo] (BJA)
FUG .... Fuyang [China] [Airport symbol] (OAG)
f-ug-- .... Uganda [MARC geographic area code Library of Congress] (LCCP)
FUG .... University of Florida, Gainesville, FL [OCLC symbol] (OCLC)
FUGB .... Federation of Ukrainians in Great Britain (DBA)
FUH .... University of Florida, Health Center Library, Gainesville, FL [OCLC symbol] (OCLC)
FU-HC .... University of Florida, J. Hillis Miller Health Center Library, Gainesville, FL [Library symbol Library of Congress] (LCLS)
FUHLR .... Fuse Holder
FUIF .... Fire Unit Integration Facility [Military]
FUINCA .... Fundacion de la Red de Informacion Cientifica Automatizada [Spain] (NITA)
FUINCA .... Fundacion para el Fomento de la Informacion Automatizada [Foundation for the Promotion of Automated Information] [Information service or system] (IID)
FuiszT .... Fuisz Technologies [Associated Press] (SAG)
FUJ .... Front Upset Jaw
FUJ .... Fujairah Aviation Centre [United Arab Emirates] [ICAO designator] (FAAC)
FUJ .... Fujitsu [Japan] (NITA)
FUJ .... Fukue [Japan] [Airport symbol] (OAG)
FU-J .... University of Florida, Health Sciences, JHEP Processing Center, Gainesville, FL [Library symbol] [Library of Congress] (LCLS)
FUJI .... Fuji Photo Film Co. Ltd. [NASDAQ symbol] (NQ)
FujiPh .... Fuji Photo Film Co. Ltd. [Associated Press] (SAG)
FUJIY .... Fuji Photo Film ADR [NASDAQ symbol] (TTSB)
FUK .... Fukui [Japan] [Seismograph station code, US Geological Survey] (SEIS)
FUK .... Fukuoka [Japan] [Airport symbol] (OAG)
FUL .... Florida Union List of Serials, Gainesville, FL [Inactive] [OCLC symbol] (OCLC)
FUL .... Frente de Unidad Liberal [Honduras] [Political party] (EY)
FUL .... Front Uni Liberateur de la Guinee Portuguesa et des Isles du Cap Vert [United Liberation Front of Portuguese Guinea and Cape Verde] [Political party]
FUL .... Fulcrum (MSA)
FUL .... Fullerton [California] [Airport symbol] (OAG)
FUL .... Fullerton, CA [Location identifier FAA] (FAAL)
FUL .... Funchal [Madeira Island] [Seismograph station code, US Geological Survey] (SEIS)
FU-L .... University of Florida, Law Library, Gainesville, FL [Library symbol Library of Congress] (LCLS)
Fulb Par ...... Fulbeck's Parallel [A publication] (DLA)
Fulb St Law... Fulbeck's Study of the Law [A publication] (DLA)
FULC .... First Unit Loading Cost
FULC .... Fulcrum Tech, Inc. [NASDAQ symbol] (SAG)
FULCF .... Fulcrum Technologies [NASDAQ symbol] (TTSB)
Fulcrum .... Fulcrum Tech, Inc. [Associated Press] (SAG)
fulg .... Fulguration [Medicine] (DAVI)
FULICO .... Fidelity Union Life Insurance Co.
FULK .... Front Uni de Liberation Kanake [New Caledonia] [Political party] (FEA)
FULL .... Fuller [H.B.] Co. [NASDAQ symbol] (NQ)
FULL .... Fuller (HB) [NASDAQ symbol] (TTSB)
FULL .... Fulltext Sources Online [Information service or system] (IID)
Full BR .... Bengal Full Bench Rulings [North-Western Provinces, India] [A publication] (DLA)
Full Ch Hist... Fuller's Church History [A publication] (DLA)
Fuller .... Fuller's Reports [59-105 Michigan] [A publication] (DLA)
Fuller (Mich)... Fuller's Reports [59-105 Michigan] [A publication] (DLA)
FullHs .... Full House Resorts [Associated Press] (SAG)
FullHse .... Full House Resorts [Associated Press] (SAG)
FulrHB .... Fuller [H. B.] Co. [Associated Press] (SAG)
FULRO .... Front Unifie de la Lutte de la Race Opprime [United Front for the Struggle of Oppressed Races] (CINC)
FULS .... Florida Union List of Serials
FULT .... Fulton Financial [NASDAQ symbol] (TTSB)
FULT .... Fulton Financial Corp. [NASDAQ symbol] (NQ)
Fult .... Fulton's Supreme Court Reports, Bengal [1842-44] [India] [A publication] (DLA)
Fulton .... Fulton Financial Corp. [Associated Press] (SAG)
Fulton .... Fulton's Supreme Court Reports, Bengal [1842-44] [India] [A publication] (DLA)
FUM .... Familial Uveal Melanoma [Oncology]
FUM .... Fluorouracil, Methotrexate [Antineoplastic drug regimen]
FUM .... Friendly Union of Mechanics [British]
FUM .... Friends United Meeting
FUM .... Fumarate
FUM .... Fumigate [or Fumigation] (AABC)
FUM .... Functional User's Manual (AABC)
FUME .... Foam Upholstery Must End [Royal Society for the Prevention of Accidents] [British] (DI)
FUMIST........ Fellow of the University of Manchester Institute of Science and Technology [British]
FUMM .... [The] Fellowship of United Methodist Musicians (EA)
FUMTU .... Fouled Up More Than Usual [See FU] [Bowdlerized version]
FUN .... Atlanta, GA [Location identifier FAA] (FAAL)
FUN .... Cedar Fair LP [NYSE symbol] (SAG)
FUN .... Fantasy Unrestricted Network [Cable-television system]
FUN .... Feminist Uniting Women [Australia]
FUN .... Follow-Up Note [Medical records] (DAVI)
FUN .... Forty Upward Network [Defunct] (EA)
FUN .... Fractional and Unknown Nuclear [Material in meteorites]
FUN .... Free University Network [Later, LERN] (EA)

FUN .... Frente de Unidad Nacional [*National Unity Front*] [*Guatemala*]
        [*Political party*] (PPW)
FUN .... Frente Unido Nacionalista [*Nationalist United Front*] [*Venezuela*
        Political party] (PPW)
FUN .... Frye Utilities for Network [*Frye Computer Systems*]
        [*Telecommunications*] (PCM)
FUN .... Funafuti Atol [*Tuvalu*] [*Airport symbol*] (OAG)
FUN .... Funafuti Atoll [*Ellice Islands*] [*Airport symbol*] (AD)
FUN .... Funatsu [*Kawaguchuko*] [*Japan*] [*Seismograph station code, US
        Geological Survey*] (SEIS)
FUN .... Function (MDG)
FUN .... Function Bits Sent to Periphere for Control [*Computer science*] (ECII)
FUN .... Fundament [*Slang British*] (DSUE)
FUN .... Funtshi Aviation Service [*Zaire*] [*ICAO designator*] (FAAC)
FUNA .... Front d'Union Nationale de l'Angola [*National Union Front of Angola*]
FUNC .... First United Corp. [*NASDAQ symbol*] (SAG)
FUNC .... Force de l'Union National Cambodge [*Cambodia*] [*Political party*]
FUNC .... Function (AABC)
FUNCINPEC... Front Uni National pour Cambodge Independant, Neutre, Pacifique
        et Cooperatif [*National United Front for an Independent National,
        Peaceful, and Cooperative Cambodia*] [*Political party*] (PD)
Funco.......... Funco, Inc. [*Associated Press*] (SAG)
FUNCT.......... Function (KSC)
FUNCT.......... Functional (NASA)
FUNCTL ...... Functional
FUNCTLINE... Functional Line Diagram (MCD)
FUND .... All Seasons Global Fund [*NASDAQ symbol*] (TTSB)
FUND .... Family Violence Prevention Fund
FUND .... Fundamental (MSA)
FUND .... Fundamentalist (WDAA)
FUND .... Funding (NITA)
FundA .... Fund American Enterprises Holdings, Inc. [*Associated Press*] (SAG)
FundAm .... Fund American Enterprises Holdings, Inc. [*Formerly, Fireman's Fund
        Corp.*] [*Associated Press*] (SAG)
FUNDESCO... Fundacion para el Desarrollo de la Funcion Social de las
        Comunicaciones (IID)
FUNDFREQ... Fundamental Frequency (IAA)
FUNDWI...... Fund for the United Nations for the Development of West Irian
FUNET .... [*The*] Finnish University Network [*Finland*] [*Computer science*]
        (TNIG)
FUNGIC........ Fungicide
FUNI .... Frame User-to-Network Interface [*Telecommunications*] (ACRL)
FUNL .... Federation of Unions of Workers and Employees of North Lebanon
FUNL .... Funnel (MSA)
FUNLIS .... Fundamentals of Library and Information Science [*Drexel
        University*] (NITA)
FUNLOG...... Functional Programming and Prolog
FUNN .... Mountasia Entertainment [*NASDAQ symbol*] (TTSB)
FUNN .... Mountasia Entertainment International, Inc. [*NASDAQ symbol*] (SAG)
FUNOP........ Full Normal Plot [*Computer science*]
FUnRI .... First Union Real Estate Equity & Mortgage Investments [*Associated
        Press*] (SAG)
FUNSA .... Fabrica Uruguaya de Neumaticos, Sociedad Anonima [*A tire
        manufacturer*]
FUNT .... French Underground Nuclear Test (MCD)
FUNU .... Force d'Urgence des Nations Unies
FUNY .... Free University of New York
FUO .... Fever of Undetermined [*or Unknown*] Origin [*Medicine*]
FUO .... Follow-Up Output (NASA)
FUOP .... Fix Up on Printer [*Have technician add or change an effect by means
        of optical printing*] [*Motion-picture production*]
FUP............. Facility Utilization Plan (AFM)
FUP............. Falciparum Uganda - Palo Alto [*Plasmodium strain causing malaria*]
F/UP............ Follow Up (WDAA)
FUP............. Forca de Unidade Popular [*Terrorist group*] [*Portugal*] (EY)
FUP............. Forming Up Place (MCD)
FUP............. Forward Unity Periscope
FUP............. Frente por la Unidad del Pueblo [*United Popular Front*] [*Colorado
        Political party*] (PPW)
FUP............. Friends United Press (DGA)
FUP............. Furman University Press (DGA)
FUP............. Fusion Point
FUPAC........ Federacion de Universidades Privadas de America Central
FUPCD........ Fonds un Pour Cent pour le Developpement [*One Percent for
        Development Fund*] (EAIO)
FUPOSAT..... Follow-Up on Supply Action Taken
FUPP........... Full-Up Powerpack [*Military*]
Fuppy.......... Female Urban Professional [*Lifestyle classification*]
FUPRO......... Future Production (MCD)
FUQ .... Fuquene [*Colombia*] [*Seismograph station code, US Geological
        Survey*] (SEIS)
FuquaEn ...... Fuqua Enterprises [*Associated Press*] (SAG)
FUR .... Failure or Unsatisfactory Report
FUR .... File Utility Routines [*Computer science*]
FUR .... First Union RE EqSBI [*NYSE symbol*] (TTSB)
FUR .... Fluorouracil, Riboside [*Antineoplastic drug regimen*] (MAE)
FUR .... Follow-Up Report
FUR .... Forma Urbis Romae [*Rome*] [*A publication*] (OCD)
FUR .... Frente Unido de la Revolucion [*United Revolutionary Front*]
        [*Guatemala*] [*Political party*] (PPW)
FUR .... Fuerstenfeldbruck [*Germany*] [*Seismograph station code, US
        Geological Survey*] (SEIS)
FUR .... Furlong [*Unit of distance*]
FUR .... Furlough [*Military*] (WGA)
FUR .... Furnace (MSA)

FUR .... Furnished
FUR .... Furred [*Technical drawings*]
FUR .... Furrier
FUR .... Further (AABC)
FUR-30 .... Frente Universitario Revolucionario 30 de Julio [*30th July
        Revolutionary University Front*] [*El Salvador*]
FURA .... Federal Utility Regulation, Annotated [*A publication*] (DLA)
FUra .... French Urania [*Record label*]
FURAM .... Ftorafur [*Tegafur*], Adriamycin, Mitomycin C [*Antineoplastic drug
        regimen*]
FURAS .... For Further Assignment
FURASPERS... For Further Assignment by the Commander Naval Military
        Personnel Command to (Duty Indicated) (DNAB)
FURASUB ... For Further Assignment to Duty in Submarine [*Navy*] (DNAB)
FurB............ Furr's/Bishop's Cafeteria Ltd. [*Associated Press*] (SAG)
FurBish .... Furr's/Bishop's Cafeteria Ltd. [*Associated Press*] (SAG)
FurBsh .... Furrs Bishops [*Associated Press*] (SAG)
FURF .... Federation des Unions Royalistes de France [*Federation of Royalist
        Unions of France*] (PPW)
FURL .... Furlough [*Military*] (ROG)
Furl L & T ... Furlong on the Irish Law of Landlord and Tenant [*A publication*]
        (DLA)
Furman U .... Furman University (GAGS)
FURN .... Furnace
FURN .... Furnish (AFM)
FURN .... Furniture
FURN .... Furniture
furn............. Furniture (VRA)
FURNASER... Furnish Full Names, Rates, and Social Security Numbers of Men
        Transferred in Accordance with This Directive (DNAB)
FurnBrds...... Furniture Brands Intl., Inc. [*Associated Press*] (SAG)
FURNG........ Furnishing
FURNIDEC ... International Fair of Furniture, Decoration, Lighting Fixtures,
        Machinery, and Equipment [*Hellexpo*]
FURN PTS ... Furniture Parts [*Freight*]
FURO .... Furioso [*Furiously*] [*Music*] (ROG)
Furon .... Furon Co. [*Associated Press*] (SAG)
FURORDMOD... Orders Further Modified [*Navy*] (DNAB)
FURPO........ Full Utilization of Rural Program Opportunities (EA)
FURPUR ...... File Utility Routines, Program Utility Routines [*Computer science*]
FURR .... Furrier
FURR .... Further
FURS .... Failure or Unsatisfactory Report System
FURS .... Federal Underground Injection Control Reporting System
        [*Environmental Protection Agency*] (ERG)
FURS .... Follow-Up Reporting System (MCD)
FURTH .... Further
FURTH C ..... Further Care [*Medicine*]
FURTS .... Furnished This Station [*Army*] (AABC)
FUS............. Far Ultraviolet Spectrometer [*NASA*]
FUS............. Feline Urologic Syndrome
FUS............. Film Unit Secretary
FUS............. Firing Unit Simulator
FUS............. First USA [*NYSE symbol*] (SPSG)
FUS............. Focused Ultrasonic Surgery
FUS............. FORTRAN [*Formula Translating System*] Utility System [*Computer
        science*]
FUS............. Forward Support Unit (DOMA)
FUS............. Frontul Unitatii Socialiste [*Front of Socialist Unity*] [*Romania*]
        [*Political party*] (PPE)
FUS............. Fusa [*Let It Be Fused*] [*Pharmacy*] (ROG)
fus.............. Fuse (VRA)
FUS............. Fuselage [*Aviation*] (AABC)
Fus.............. Fusible (DAC)
FUS............. Fusilier
FUSA .... First United States Army
FUSA .... Fotoball USA, Inc. [*NASDAQ symbol*] (SAG)
FUSAC .... Finno-Ugrian Studies Association of Canada [*See also ACEFO*]
FUSAG .... First United States Army Group
FUSAW .... Fotoball USA Wrrt [*NASDAQ symbol*] (TTSB)
FUSB .... First Utd SB Greencastle Ind [*NASDAQ symbol*] (TTSB)
FUSB .... First United Bancorp [*NASDAQ symbol*] (SAG)
FUSE........... Far Ultraviolet Satellite Experiment (MCD)
FUSE........... Far Ultraviolet Spectroscopy Explorer [*NASA*] (SSD)
FUSE........... Federation for Unified Science Education (EA)
FUSE........... Fuisz Technologies [*NASDAQ symbol*] (TTSB)
FUSE........... Fuisz Technologies [*NASDAQ symbol*] (SAG)
FUSES .... Fordham Urban Solar Eco-System
FUSF........... Fortsetzung und Schluss Folgen [*To Be Continued and Concluded*]
        [*German*]
FusionSy...... Fusion Systems Corp. [*Associated Press*] (SAG)
FUSL........... Fusil
FUSLA .... Friends of the United States of Latin America (EA)
FUS/LF .... Fuselage, Lower Forward (MCD)
FUSLG .... Fuselage [*Aviation*] (MSA)
FUSN .... Fusion
FUSN .... Fusion Systems [*NASDAQ symbol*] (TTSB)
FUSN .... Fusion Systems Corp. [*NASDAQ symbol*] (SAG)
FusnMed...... Fusion Medical Technologies, Inc. [*Associated Press*] (SAG)
FUSOB .... Friendly United Society of Operative Brickmakers [*A union*] [*British*]
FUSOD .... Future of Scientific Ocean Drilling [*Marine science*] (MSC)
FUS Pay ..... First USA Paymentech, Inc. [*Associated Press*] (SAG)
FUSPr.......... First USA 6.25% 'PRIDES' [*NYSE symbol*] (TTSB)
FUSRAP .... Formerly Utilized Sites Remedial Action Program [*Department of
        Energy*]

FUSS .... Fleet Undersea Surveillance System [*CIA terminology*]
FUST .... Full-Up System Test (RDA)
FUS/UF .... Fuselage, Upper Forward (MCD)
FUT .... Federal Unemployment Tax (MCD)
FUT .... Fire Until Touchdown [*Apollo*] [*NASA*]
FUT .... Fleet Utility [*Navy*]
FUT .... Future
fut .... Futures [*Finance*] (ODBW)
Fut .... Futurist [*A publication*] (BRI)
FUT .... University of Tampa, Tampa, FL [*OCLC symbol*] (OCLC)
FUTA .... Federal Unemployment Tax Act [*1954*]
FUTA .... Friends United through Astronomy [*Defunct*] (EA)
FUTB .... Futbol Internacional [*Ministerio de Cultura*] [*Spain Information service or system*] (CRD)
FUTC .... Federacion Unica de Trabajadores Campesinos [*Single Federation of Peasant Workers*] [*Bolivia*] (PD)
FUTC .... Fidelity Union Trust Co. (MHDB)
FUtdBcp .... First United Bancorporation [*Associated Press*] (SAG)
Futmd .... Futuremedia Ltd. [*Associated Press*] (SAG)
futr .... Futurism (VRA)
FUTR .... Jack Carl 312 Futures [*NASDAQ symbol*] (SAG)
FUTR .... Jack Carl 312 Futures Inc. [*NASDAQ symbol*] (TTSB)
Futrbi .... Futurebiotics, Inc. [*Associated Press*] (SAG)
Futrmdia ...... Futuremedia Ltd. [*Associated Press*] (SAG)
FUTS .... Firing Unit Test Set
FUTU .... Futures Information Service [*Institute for Futures Studies*] [*Information service or system Defunct*]
Futurbio .... Futurebiotics, Inc. [*Associated Press*] (SAG)
FUTURE .... Friends United Toward Understanding, Rights, and Equality
Futurebio ..... Futurebiotics, Inc. [*Associated Press*] (SAG)
FUU .... Federacion de Universitarios de Uruguay [*Federation of University Students of Uruguay*] (PD)
FUU .... Foundation of Universal Unity (EA)
FUUNCTRY... Functionary
FUV .... Far-Ultraviolet [*Spectra*]
FUV .... For Ultraviolet
f-uv-- .... Upper Volta [*MARC geographic area code Library of Congress*] (LCCP)
FUVD .... Far Ultraviolet Detector
FUW .... Farmers' Union of Wales (BI)
FUW .... Federation of University Women
FUWG .... Forest Use Working Group [*Australia*]
FUWOB .... Forward Unconventional Warfare Operations Base (MCD)
FUWPM .... Free University, Washington-Paris-Moscow [*An association*] (EA)
FUWW .... Federal Union of Wire Weavers of the United Kingdom
FUY .... Fury Exploration Ltd. [*Vancouver Stock Exchange symbol*]
FUZ .... Frente Urbana Zapatista [*Mexico*]
FV .... Face Value (ADA)
FV .... Family Viewing Time [*FCC rule*] (NTCM)
FV .... Fashion Victim [*Women's Wear Daily*]
Fv .... Femoral Vein [*Anatomy*]
FV .... Femtovolt (MDG)
FV .... Fenestra Vestibuli [*Anatomy*]
FV .... Fighting Vehicle [*Bradley*] [*Army*]
FV .... Final Value
FV .... Finite Volume [*Metallurgy*]
FV .... Fired Vessel [*Insurance*]
fv .... Fire Vent (BARN)
FV .... Firing Velocity
FV .... Fishing Vessel
FV .... Flight Vehicle
FV .... Flight Version (MCD)
FV .... Floor Valve (NRCH)
F-V .... Flow Volume [*Measurement*] [*Cardiology*] (DAVI)
FV .... Fluid Volume
FV .... Flush Valve [*Technical drawings*]
FV .... Flux Valve
FV .... Folio Verso [*On the Back of the Page*] [*Latin*]
fv .... Folio Verso [*The left-hand page number*] [*The left-hand page*] [*Publishing*] (WDMC)
FV .... Formal Validation
FV .... Formula Vee [*Class of racing cars*]
FV .... Formula Volkswagen [*Class of racing cars*]
FV .... Forward Visibility
FV .... Freeze Voter (EA)
FV .... French RCA (Victor) [*Record label*]
F/V .... Frequency to Voltage (IEEE)
FV .... Friend Virus [*Also, FDV, FLV*]
FV .... Frisia Luftverkehr [*ICAO designator*] (AD)
FV .... Front View (MSA)
FV .... Fruit and Vegetable Division [*of Agricultural Research Service*] [*Department of Agriculture*]
FV .... Fuel Valve (AAG)
FV .... Full Above the Eaves (ROG)
FV .... Full Voltage (MSA)
FV .... Future Value [*Finance*]
fv---- .... Volta River and Basin [*MARC geographic area code Library of Congress*] (LCCP)
FVA .... Avair, Inc. [*ICAO designator*] (FAAC)
FVA .... Fellow of the Valuers' Association [*British*] (DAS)
FVA .... Fighting Vehicle Armament (RDA)
FVA .... Film/Video Arts (EA)
FVA .... Floor Valve Adapter (NRCH)
FVA .... Flying Veterinarians Association (EA)
FVA .... Four Valve Type A [*Cosworth racing engines*]

FVA .... Fredonia Veterans Association (EA)
FVA .... Friend Virus Anemia [*Medicine*] (DMAA)
FVAP .... Federal Voting Assistance Program
FVB .... First Virginia Banks [*NYSE symbol*] (TTSB)
FVB .... First Virginia Bankshares Corp. [*NYSE symbol*] (SPSG)
FVB .... Fitzwilliam Virginal Book
FVB .... Future Villain Band [*Evil rock music group in 1978 film "Sgt. Pepper's Lonely Hearts Club Band"*]
FVBB .... Beit Bridge [*Zimbabwe*] [*ICAO location identifier*] (ICLI)
FVBD .... Bindura [*Zimbabwe*] [*ICAO location identifier*] (ICLI)
FVbF .... Florida Medical Entomology Laboratory, Vero Beach, FL [*Library symbol Library of Congress*] (LCLS)
FVBU .... Bulawayo/Bulawayo [*Zimbabwe*] [*ICAO location identifier*] (ICLI)
FVC .... Fixed Vacuum Capacitor
FVC .... Forced Vital Capacity [*Physiology*]
FVC .... Franciscan Vocation Conference [*Formerly, AFSV*] [*Defunct*] (EA)
FVC .... Fraser Valley College Learning Resources Centre [*UTLAS symbol*]
FVC .... Frozen Vegetable Council (EA)
FVC .... Valencia Community College, Orlando, FL [*OCLC symbol*] (OCLC)
FVCH .... Chipinge [*Zimbabwe*] [*ICAO location identifier*] (ICLI)
FVCM .... Fellow of the Victoria College of Music [*London*] [*British*] (ROG)
FVCP .... Harare/Charles Prince [*Zimbabwe*] [*ICAO location identifier*] (ICLI)
FVCV .... Chiredzi/Buffalo Range [*Zimbabwe*] [*ICAO location identifier*] (ICLI)
FVD .... Friction Volume Damper (OA)
FVD .... Front Vertex Back Focal Distance
FVD .... Fuel Vapor Detector
FVDE .... Fighting Vehicles Design Establishment [*British military*] (DMA)
FVE .... Federation of Veterinarians of the EEC (EAIO)
FVE .... Forced Volume, Expiratory [*Physiology*]
FVE .... Frenchville, ME [*Location identifier FAA*] (FAAL)
F VENOES .... Fiat Venaesectio [*Let the Patient Be Bled*] [*Pharmacy*] (ROG)
F-VF .... Fine to Very Fine [*Philately*]
FVF .... First Vertical Flight [*NASA*] (NASA)
FVFA .... Victoria Falls/Victoria Falls [*Zimbabwe*] [*ICAO location identifier*] (ICLI)
FVG .... Frevag Airlines [*Belgium ICAO designator*] (FAAC)
FVGDCF .... Fishing Vessel and Gear Damage Compensation Fund [*National Oceanic and Atmospheric Administration*]
FVGO .... Gokwe [*Zimbabwe*] [*ICAO location identifier*] (ICLI)
FVGR .... Free Vehicle Grab Respirometer (NUCP)
FVGR .... Mutare/Grand Reef [*Zimbabwe*] [*ICAO location identifier*] (ICLI)
FVGW .... Gweru/Gweru [*Zimbabwe*] [*ICAO location identifier*] (ICLI)
FVH .... Focal Vascular Headache [*Cardiology and neurology*] (DAVI)
FVH .... Fulminant [*or Fulminating*] Viral Hepatitis [*Medicine*]
FVHA .... Harare/Harare [*Zimbabwe*] [*ICAO location identifier*] (ICLI)
FVHI .... First Virtual Holdings, Inc. [*NASDAQ symbol*] (SAG)
FVHQ .... Harare [*Zimbabwe*] [*ICAO location identifier*] (ICLI)
FVI .... Final Voluntary Indefinite [*Status*] [*Army*] (INF)
FVI .... First Volar Interosseous Muscle [*Myology*]
FVI .... Flow Velocity Integral [*Cardiology*]
FVI .... Forage Value Index [*Agriculture*]
FVIF .... Future Value Interest Factor [*Finance*]
FVIN .... Bulawayo/Induna [*Zimbabwe*] [*ICAO location identifier*] (ICLI)
FVIP .... Fishing Vessel Insurance Plan [*Canada*]
FVIRL .... Fruit and Vegetable Insects Research Laboratory [*Closed 1985*] [*Vincennes, IN*] [*Department of Agriculture*] (GRD)
FVKA .... Karoi [*Zimbabwe*] [*ICAO location identifier*] (ICLI)
FVKB .... Kariba/Kariba [*Zimbabwe*] [*ICAO location identifier*] (ICLI)
FVKK .... Kwekwe [*Zimbabwe*] [*ICAO location identifier*] (ICLI)
FVL .... Femoral Vein Ligation [*Medicine*]
FVL .... Flow Volume Loop [*Hemodialysis*]
FVLF .... Fixed VLF Station (MCD)
FVM .... Five-Mile Camp, AK [*Location identifier FAA*] (FAAL)
FVM .... Fluid Vacancy Model
FVM .... French Village [*Missouri*] [*Seismograph station code, US Geological Survey*] (SEIS)
FVMA .... Marondera [*Zimbabwe*] [*ICAO location identifier*] (ICLI)
FVMF .... Friends of Vieilles Maisons Francaises (EA)
FVMMA........ Floor and Vacuum Machinery Manufacturers' Association [*Defunct*] (EA)
FVMP .... Federal Visibility Monitoring Program (GNE)
FVMS.......... Fluid Volume Measurement System (MCD)
FVMT .... Mutoko [*Zimbabwe*] [*ICAO location identifier*] (ICLI)
FVMU.......... Mutare/Mutare [*Zimbabwe*] [*ICAO location identifier*] (ICLI)
FVMV .... Masvingo/Masvingo [*Zimbabwe*] [*ICAO location identifier*] (ICLI)
FVN .... Failed Vector Number (OA)
FVNB .... First Victoria National Bank [*NASDAQ symbol*] (SAG)
FVNB .... First Victoria Natl Bank [*NASDAQ symbol*] (TTSB)
FVNC .... Fondation Vietnam-Canada [*Vietnam-Canada Foundation*]
FVNR .... Full Voltage Non-Reversing Motor (DICI)
FVO .... Farm Verified Organic
FVO .... Fluidic Valve Operator
FVO .... For Valuation Only [*Business term*]
FVOC .... Facel Vega Owners Club [*Defunct*] (EA)
FVOG .... Fishing Vessel Obligation Guarantee [*Program*] (USDC)
FVOG .... Fishing Vessel Obligation Guarantee [*Program*] [*Marine science*] (OSRA)
FVP .... Feasibility Validation Program
FVP .... Flash-Vacuum Pyrolysis
FVP .... Fluid Velocity Potential
FVP .... Freie Volkspartei [*Free People's Party*] [*Germany Political party*] (PPE)
FVP .... Friend Virus Polycythemia [*Medicine*] (DMAA)
FVPB .... Flight Vehicle Power Branch

FVPD	Film/Video Producers and Distributors [*National Film Board of Canada*] [*Information service or system*] (CRD)
FVPPA	Families of Vietnamese Political Prisoners Association (EA)
FVR	Feline Viral Rhinotracheitis [*Vaccine*]
FVR	Fiber Volume Ratio
FVR	Forearm Vascular Resistance [*Medicine*]
FVR	Functional Vestibular Reserve [*Orientation*]
FVR	Fuse Voltage Rating
FVRC	Foreign Vehicle Resource Center [*Tank-Automotive Command*] [*Army*]
FVRDE	Fighting Vehicles Research and Development Establishment [*British*]
fvrl gls	Favrile Glass (VRA)
FVRU	Rusape [*Zimbabwe*] [*ICAO location identifier*] (ICLI)
FVS	Fetal Valproate Syndrome [*Medicine*] (DMAA)
F VS	Fiat Venaesectio [*Let the Patient Be Bled*] [*Pharmacy*]
FVS	Fighting Vehicle Systems (RDA)
FVS	Flight Vehicles Systems (MCD)
FVS	Forer Vocational Survey [*Psychology*]
FVS	Forest, MS [*Location identifier FAA*] (FAAL)
FVS	Fraser Videotex Services [*Information service or system*] (IID)
FVSA	Federation of Victorian School Administrators [*Australia*]
FVSC	Fort Valley State College [*Georgia*]
FVSH	Zvishavane [*Zimbabwe*] [*ICAO location identifier*] (ICLI)
FVSNA	Friends Vegetarian Society of North America (EA)
FVSV	Victoria Falls/Spray View [*Zimbabwe*] [*ICAO location identifier*] (ICLI)
FVT	Family Viewing Time [*Television*]
FVT	Field Validation Test
FVT	Flash-Vacuum Thermolysis
FVT	Follicular-Variant-Translocation [*Medicine*] (DMAA)
FVT	Functional Validation Test [*Army*]
FVTL	Gweru/Thornhill [*Zimbabwe*] [*ICAO location identifier*] (ICLI)
FVTP	Formal Validation Test Program [*Military*]
FVTS	Field Verification Test Set (MCD)
FVTT	Fishing Vessel Transmit Terminal (PDAA)
FVU	File Verification Utility [*Computer science*]
FVU	First Voided Urine [*Medicine*] (CPH)
FVU	Functional Verification Unit [*Photography*]
FVV	Facility Verification Vehicle
FVV	Flight Verification Vehicle (KSC)
FVVM	Friends of the Vietnam Veterans Memorial (EA)
FVW	Forward Volume Wave [*Telecommunications*] (TEL)
FVWC	Federation of Victorian Walking Clubs [*Australia*]
FVWN	Hwange/Hwange National Park [*Zimbabwe*] [*ICAO location identifier*] (ICLI)
FVWS	Female Voice Warning System (MCD)
FVWT	Hiwange Town [*Zimbabwe*] [*ICAO location identifier*] (ICLI)
FVWU	Free Visayan Workers' Union [*Philippines*]
FVX	Farmville, VA [*Location identifier FAA*] (FAAL)
FVZC	Zisco [*Zimbabwe*] [*ICAO location identifier*] (ICLI)
fw----	Africa, West [*MARC geographic area code Library of Congress*] (LCCP)
FW	Face Width (MSA)
F/W	Facing West [*In outdoor advertising*] (WDMC)
FW	Fascinating Womanhood [*Title of book by Helen Andelin and of antifeminist seminars*]
FW	Feed Water (KSC)
FW	Felix-Weil [*Reaction*] [*Clinical chemistry*]
FW	Field Weakening
FW	Field Weld (NRCH)
FW	Field Winding [*Electromagnetism*] (IAA)
FW	Field Worship [*Army British*]
FW	Fighter Weapons (MCD)
FW	Filament Wound
FW	Filter Wheels
FW	Financial Weekly [*A publication*]
FW	Fire Wall [*Technical drawings*]
FW	Firmware [*Computer science*]
FW	First Word
FW	Fiscal Week [*Business term*] (IAA)
FW	Fixed-Length Word [*Computer science*] (IAA)
FW	Fixed Wavelength [*Electronics*]
FW	Fixed Wing [*Aircraft*]
FW	Flag Word (MCD)
FW	Flash Welding [*Metallurgy*]
FW	Flight Weight
FW	Floor Waste
FW	Focke-Wulf [*A German fighter plane*]
FW	Focke-Wulf GmbH [*Germany ICAO aircraft manufacturer identifier*] (ICAO)
FW	Fog Whistle [*Navigation charts*]
FW	Folin and Wu's Method [*Medicine*] (MAE)
FW	Folin-Wu Reaction [*Medicine*] (DMAA)
FW	Foot Wide
FW	Forced Whisper [*Medicine*]
FW	Formula Weight [*Chemistry*]
FW	Forward of Wing [*Aerospace*] (AAG)
FW	Forward Wave [*Electronics*] (IAA)
FW	Foster Wheeler Corp. (MCD)
FW	Fragment Wound [*Medicine*] (DAVI)
FW	Frame Synchronization Word (MUGU)
FW	Framework
FWPD	Franklin Watts Group [*Publishers*] [*British*]
FW	Frank Williams [*Racing car model designation prefix, indicating principal of company*] [*British*]
FW	Free Wheel (ADA)
FW	Freshwater [*Load line mark*]
FW	Fresh Water [*Technical drawings*]
FW	Fresh Weight [*of fruit*] [*Botany*]
FW	Fuel Wasting (MCD)
FW	Full Wave
FW	Full Weight (IAA)
FW	Furness, Withy & Co. [*Steamship line*] (MHDW)
FW	Isles of Scilly Skybus [*ICAO designator*] (AD)
FW	Le Point Air [*France ICAO designator*] (ICDA)
FWA	Factories and Workshops Acts [*Law*] [*British*] (ROG)
FWA	Family Welfare Association [*British*] (ILCA)
FWA	Farmers and World Affairs [*An association Defunct*] (EA)
FWA	Far West Airlines, Inc. [*ICAO designator*] (FAAC)
FWA	Feather Weight Automotive [*Auto racing engine model designation*] [*British*]
FWA	Federal Works Agency [*Abolished, 1949*]
FWA	Federation of Women Clerks [*A union*] [*British*]
FWA	Fellow of the World Academy of Arts and Sciences
FWA	Filler Wire Addition
FWA	Film Weekly Award [*British*]
FWA	Financial Women's Association of New York [*New York, NY*] (EA)
FWA	Financial Working Arrangement
FWA	First Word Address [*Computer science*]
FWA	Fixed Word Address [*Computer science*] (IAA)
FWA	Fluorescent Whitening Agent [*Detergent*]
FWA	Fort Wayne [*Indiana*] [*Airport symbol*] (OAG)
FWA	Fort Wayne, IN [*Location identifier FAA*] (FAAL)
FWA	Forward Wave Amplifier
FWA	Fraud, Waste, and Abuse
FWA	French West Africa
FWA	Fresh Water Allowance (DS)
FWA	Full-Wave Amplifier
FWA	Future Weapons Agency [*Army*]
FWA	University of West Florida, Pensacola, FL [*OCLC symbol*] (OCLC)
FWAA	Fiji-West Australian Association
FWAA	Football Writers Association of America (EA)
FWAA	Fur Wholesalers Association of America (EA)
FWAC	Full-Wave Alternating Current
FWAD	Fort Wingate Army Depot [*New Mexico*] (AABC)
FWAF	Free World Armed Forces
FWAG	Farming and Wildlife Advisory Group [*British*] (DI)
FWAG	Farming and Wildlife Advisory Groups (EERA)
FWAIS	Free World Air Intelligence Study (MCD)
FWAIT	Floating-Point Wait [*Computer science*]
FWAM	Fleet Weapon Armament Maintenance [*Navy*] (MCD)
FWAM	Full Width Attack Mine
FW & DC	Fort Worth & Denver City Railway Co.
FWAOB	Free World Air Order of Battle (MCD)
FWAS	Failure Warning and Analysis System
FWAT	Forest Workers Association of Tasmania (EERA)
FWB	Fahrenheit Wet Bulb (KSC)
FWB	First Women's Bank [*New York City*]
FWB	Fort Worth Belt Railway Co. [*AAR code*]
FWB	Forum for Women in Bridge [*Defunct*] (EA)
FW/B	Forward Toward the Bow [*Stowage*] (DNAB)
FWB	Four-Wheel Brake
FWB	Free-Wheel Bicycle
FWB	Free-Will Baptists
FWB	Fresh Water Ballasting
FWB	Full Weight Bearing [*Medicine*]
FWB	University of Minnesota, Freshwater Biological Institute, Navarre, MN [*OCLC symbol*] (OCLC)
FWBA	Full-Wave Balanced Amplifier
FWBC	Fort Wayne Bible College [*Indiana*]
FW-BF	Foster Wheeler-Bergbau Forschung [*Flue gas treatment*]
FWBG	Bangula [*Malawi*] [*ICAO location identifier*] (ICLI)
FWBI	First Western Bancorp, Inc. [*NASDAQ symbol*] (NQ)
FWBO	Friends of the Western Buddhist Order (EA)
FWBPA	Free Will Baptist Press Association (EA)
FWBR	Full-Wave Bridge Rectifier
FWBS	Farm Writers and Broadcasters' Society [*Australia*]
FWC	Fairfield, IL [*Location identifier FAA*] (FAAL)
FWC	Fair Weather Current
FWC	Fault Warning Computer [*Aviation*] (DA)
FWC	Federal Warning Center (NATG)
FWC	Feedwater Control [*Nuclear energy*] (NRCH)
FWC	Filament-Wound Case (MCD)
FWC	Filipino Women's Council [*Australia*]
FWC	Fleet Weapons Center [*Navy*] (MCD)
FWC	Fleet Weather Center [*Navy*] (NVT)
FWC	Flight Warning Computer (MCD)
FWC	Flying Wheel Casting [*Metallurgy*]
FWC	Foil Wound Coil
FWC	Force Weapons Coordinator [*Navy*] (NVT)
FWC	Foster Wheeler [*NYSE symbol*] (TTSB)
FWC	Foster Wheeler Corp. [*NYSE symbol*] (SPSG)
FWC	Fourdrinier Wire Council (EA)
FWC	Free Wallenberg Committee (EA)
FWC	Freeway Air BV [*Netherlands ICAO designator*] (FAAC)
FWC	Freshwater Cooling
FWC	Friends World College [*Huntington, NY*] (EA)
FWC	Full Well Capacity (MCD)
FWC	Fully Loaded Weight and Capacity [*Shipping*]
FWCA	Fish and Wildlife Coordination Act (GFGA)
FWCC	Chintheche [*Malawi*] [*ICAO location identifier*] (ICLI)

FWCC............ Friends of the World Council of Churches (EA)
FWCC............ Friends' Work Camp Committee [*British*] (BI)
FWCC............ Friends World Committee for Consultation [*British*] (EAIO)
FWCCANZ .... Federation of Wall and Ceiling Contractors of Australia and New Zealand
FWCD .... Chelinda [*Malawi*] [*ICAO location identifier*] (ICLI)
FWCF............ Fellow of the Worshipful Company of Farriers [*British*] (DI)
FWCI............ Feedwater Coolant Injection [*Nuclear energy*] (NRCH)
FWCI............ Foundation of the Wall and Ceiling Industry (EA)
FWCL............ Blantyre/Chileka [*Malawi*] [*ICAO location identifier*] (ICLI)
FWCL............ Field Wire Command Link [*Army*] (AABC)
FWCM.......... Makokola Club [*Malawi*] [*ICAO location identifier*] (ICLI)
FWCNG .... Florida West Coast Nuclear Group
FWCS.......... Feedwater Control System [*Nuclear energy*] (NRCH)
FWCS.......... Ntchisi [*Malawi*] [*ICAO location identifier*] (ICLI)
FWCT.......... Chitipa [*Malawi*] [*ICAO location identifier*] (ICLI)
FWD............ Falling Weight Deflectometer [*FHWA*] (TAG)
FWD............ Federation of Wholesalers and Distributors [*British*] (DBA)
fwd.............. Foreword (BJA)
FWD............ Fort Worth & Denver Railway Co. [*AAR code*]
FWD............ Forward (AFM)
FWD............ Four-Wheel Drive [*Vehicle*]
FWD............ Free Water Damage (ADA)
FWD............ Free Wheeling Diode (IAA)
FWD............ Fresh Water Damage
FWD............ Front Wheel Drive
FWD............ Functional Workload Demonstration (AAGC)
FWDA .... Federal Wholesale Druggists Association [*Later, DWA*] (EA)
FWDA .... Federated Wire Drawers' Association [*A union*] [*British*]
FWDA .... Fort Wingate Depot Activity [*New Mexico*] [*Army*]
FWDBAA...... Forward Brigade Administrative Area [*British*]
FWDBL .... Forward Bomb Line
FWDC .... Flemings in the World Development Cooperation [*Belgium*] (EAIO)
FWDC .... Forward Collect (FAAC)
FWDC .... Full-Wave Direct Current
FWDCT .... Fresh Water Drain Collecting Tank
FWDD .... Forwarded
Fwd Ech...... Forward Echelon [*Army*]
FWDG .... Forwarding
FWDG .... Forwarding
FWDHTSHLD... Forward Heat Shield (MCD)
FWDP .... Family Worker Development Program [*Australia*]
FWDP .... Foreign Weapon Development Program (NG)
FWDR.......... Forwarder
FWDT.......... Flight Worthiness Demonstration Test (KSC)
FWDW .... Dwanga [*Malawi*] [*ICAO location identifier*] (ICLI)
FWDZ.......... Dedza [*Malawi*] [*ICAO location identifier*] (ICLI)
FWE............ Federation of Woman's Exchanges (EA)
FWE............ Finished with Engines
FWE............ Foreign Weapons Evaluation
FWE............ Friends of Waycross Express [*Defunct*] (EA)
FWEA.......... Finnish Workers' Educational Association [*Defunct*] (EA)
FWED.......... Fleet Weapons Engineering Department (DNAB)
FWeldI........ Fellow of the Welding Institute [*British*] (DBQ)
FWEO.......... Fleet Weapons Engineering Officer [*Navy British*]
FWERAT ...... Fourth World Educational and Research Association Trust (EA)
FWETE........ Foreign Weapons, Equipment, and Technology Evaluation (MCD)
FWF............ Felicidades Wildlife Foundation (EA)
FWF............ Fleet Weather Facility [*Navy*]
FWF............ Fly without Fear [*Commercial firm*] (EA)
FWF............ Forderung der Wissenschaftlichen Forschung [*Austrian science foundation*]
FWF............ Free World Military Forces [*Group of countries which provided military aid to South Vietnam*] [*Also, FWMF*] (VNW)
FWFHC........ Farm Workers Family Health Center
FWFWA....... Fresh Water Fish Wholesalers Association (EA)
FWG............ Facility Working Group
FWG............ Factory Work Group
FWG............ Feminist Writers' Guild [*Defunct*] (EA)
FWG............ Financial Working Group [*Military*] (AFIT)
FWG............ Flexible Waveguide
FWG............ French Wire Gage (IAA)
FWGE.......... Fort Worth Grain Exchange (EA)
FWGE.......... FREE [*Federated Republics of Earth and Its Environs*] World Government (EA)
FWH............ Fast Weekly Household Audience Report [*Nielsen Television Index*] (NTCM)
FWH............ Flexible Working Hours
FWH............ Folklore of World Holidays [*A publication*]
FWH............ Fort Worth, TX [*Location identifier FAA*] (FAAL)
FWH............ Frank W. Horner Ltd. [*Research code symbol*] [*Canada*]
FWHC .... Feminist Women's Health Center [*Later, FWHC/WCC*] (EA)
FWHC/WCC... Feminist Women's Health Center/Women's Choice Clinic [*Defunct*] (EA)
FWHF.......... Federation of World Health Foundations (EA)
FWHM .... Full Width at Half Maximum [*Spectroscopy*]
FWHMA ...... Feed Water Heater Manufacturers Association (EA)
FWHP.......... Full Width at Half Peak [*Spectroscopy*] (DEN)
FWhP.......... Polk Community College, Winter Haven, FL [*Library symbol Library of Congress*] (LCLS)
FWHQ.......... Lilongwe [*Malawi*] [*ICAO location identifier*] (ICLI)
FWI............ Families and Work Institute (EA)
FWI............ Federation of West Indies
FWI............ Federation of Women's Institutes [*British*] (DI)
FWI............ Fellow of the Institute of Welfare Officers [*British*]

FWI............ Fixed-Weight Indexes
FWI............ Focused What If [*Method for hazard analysis*]
FWI............ French West Indies
FWI............ Fresh Water Institute [*Rensselaer Polytechnic Institute*] [*Research center*] (RCD)
FWI............ Freshwater Institute [*Federal Department of Fisheries and Oceans*] [*Canada*] (IRC)
FWI............ Roslyn, NY [*Location identifier FAA*] (FAAL)
FWIB.......... Federal Women's Interagency Board (EA)
FWIC.......... Federated Women's Institutes of Canada
FWIC.......... Fighter Weapons Instructor Course [*Military*]
F wire.......... Financial Wire [*Wire service term*] (WDMC)
FWISU .... Federation of Westinghouse Independent Salaried Unions (EA)
FWIT.......... Federated Women in Timber (EA)
FWIT.......... Fixed-Wing Tactical Transport [*Aviation*] (MUGU)
FWIW.......... For What It's Worth
FWK............ Field Weakening
FWK............ Framework
FWKA.......... Karonga [*Malawi*] [*ICAO location identifier*] (ICLI)
FWKB.......... Katumbi [*Malawi*] [*ICAO location identifier*] (ICLI)
FWKG.......... Kasungu/Kasungu [*Malawi*] [*ICAO location identifier*] (ICLI)
FWKI.......... Kamuzu International [*Malawi*] [*ICAO location identifier*] (ICLI)
FWKK.......... Nkhotakota [*Malawi*] [*ICAO location identifier*] (ICLI)
FWL............ Fantasy Wrestling Leagues
FWL............ Farewell [*Alaska*] [*Airport symbol*] (OAG)
FWL............ Farewell, AK [*Location identifier FAA*] (FAAL)
FWL............ Far West Laboratory for Educational Research and Development [*San Francisco, CA*] [*Department of Education*] (GRD)
FWL............ Federation of Women Lawyers', Judicial Screening Panel [*Defunct*] (EA)
FWL............ Fixed Word Length [*Computer science*]
FWL............ Florida West Airlines [*ICAO designator*] (FAAC)
FWL............ Foilborne Water Line
FWL............ Foundation for World Literacy [*Defunct*]
FWL............ Fraternity of the Wooden Leg [*Inactive*] (EA)
FWL............ Furness Warren Line [*Steamship*] (MHDW)
FWLERD ...... Far West Laboratory for Educational Research and Development [*Department of Education*]
FWLK.......... Likoma [*Malawi*] [*ICAO location identifier*] (ICLI)
FWLL.......... Lilongwe [*Malawi*] [*ICAO location identifier*] (ICLI)
FWLP.......... Kasungu/Lifupa [*Malawi*] [*ICAO location identifier*] (ICLI)
FWM............ Feather Weight Marine [*Auto racing engine model designation*] [*British*]
FWM............ Fort William [*Scotland*] [*Airport symbol*] (OAG)
FWM............ Fourth World Movement [*Later, NI/FWM*] (EA)
FWMA.......... Feather Weight Marine Automotive [*Auto racing engine model designation*] [*British*]
FWMA.......... Free World Military Assistance (CINC)
FWMAC....... Free World Military Assistance Council
FWMAF....... Free World Military Assistance Forces [*Vietnam*]
FWMAO ...... Free World Military Assistance Organization (MCD)
FWMB.......... Federation of Wholesale and Multiple Bakers [*British*] (BI)
FWMC.......... Feather Weight Marine Twin Cam [*Auto racing engine model designation*] [*British*]
FWMC.......... Mchinji [*Malawi*] [*ICAO location identifier*] (ICLI)
FWMF.......... Free World Military Forces [*Group of countries which provided military aid to South Vietnam*] [*Also, FWF*] (VNW)
FWMG .... Mangochi [*Malawi*] [*ICAO location identifier*] (ICLI)
FWMQC ...... Fixed-Wing Multiengine Qualification Course [*Aviation*]
FWMU .... Fire-Weather Mobile Unit [*National Weather Service*] (NOAA)
FWMY.......... Monkey Bay [*Malawi*] [*ICAO location identifier*] (ICLI)
FWMZ.......... Mzimba [*Malawi*] [*ICAO location identifier*] (ICLI)
FWN............ Futures World News [*Information service or system*] (CRD)
FWN............ Futures World News Network [*Information service or system*] (IID)
FWNC .... Fort Wayne National Corp. [*NASDAQ symbol*] (NQ)
FWNEOFAP... Funds Will Not Be Entrusted to Others for Any Purpose [*Army*] (AABC)
FWO............ Fire-Weather Office [*National Weather Service*] (NOAA)
FWO............ Fleet Wireless Officer [*British*]
FWOC .... Federation of Western Outdoor Clubs (EA)
FWOP.......... Federal Women's Program Committee/Coordinator (AABC)
FWOP.......... Furloughed without Pay
FWOS .... Free Will Offering Scheme (ROG)
FWOSR........ Flight Work Orders - Ships Records (MCD)
FWOTSC...... First Woman on the Supreme Court [*Sandra Day O'Connor*]
FWOTY .... Four-Wheeler of the Year [*Automotive promotion*]
FWP............ Faculty White Pages [*A publication*]
FWP............ Fair-Witness Project (EA)
FWP............ Feather Weight Pump [*Auto racing engine model designation*] [*British*]
FWP............ Federal Women's Program
FWP............ Federal Writers' Project [*Obsolete*]
FWP............ Feed Water Pump (MSA)
FWP............ Filament-Wound Plastic (PDAA)
FWP............ First Word Pointer [*Computer science*] (MHDB)
FWP............ Flight Watch Point [*Aviation*] (FAAC)
FWP............ Fresh Water Pump (MSA)
FWP............ Fulcrum, Weight, Power
FWp............ Winter Park Public Library, Winter Park, FL [*Library symbol Library of Congress*] (LCLS)
FWPAC .... Federal Women's Program Advisory Committee (GFGA)
FWPB.......... Feedwater Pipe Break [*Nuclear energy*] (NRCH)
FWpb .... West Palm Beach Public Library, West Palm Beach, FL [*Library symbol Library of Congress*] (LCLS)

FWpbC..........	Palm Beach Atlantic College, West Palm Beach, FL [*Library symbol*] [*Library of Congress*] (LCLS)
FWpbG..........	Good Samaritan Hospital, Medical Library, West Palm Beach, FL [*Library symbol Library of Congress*] (LCLS)
FWpbP..........	Palm Beach County Public Library System, West Palm Beach, FL [*Library symbol Library of Congress*] (LCLS)
FWPC..........	Federal Women's Program Committee/Coordinator
FWPCA........	Federal Water Pollution Control Act [*1965*] (NRCH)
FWPCA........	Federal Water Pollution Control Administration [*Later, OWP*] [*Department of the Interior*]
FWPLN........	Fairwater Planes
FWPO..........	Federal Wildlife Permit Office [*Department of the Interior*]
FWPR..........	Field Work Performance Report
FWpR..........	Rollins College, Winter Park, FL [*Library symbol Library of Congress*] (LCLS)
FWPRDC......	Forest and Wood Products Research and Development Corporation (EERA)
FWpR-S........	Rollins College, Bush Science Library, Winter Park, FL [*Library symbol Library of Congress*] (LCLS)
FWQ..........	Flight West Airlines [*Australia ICAO designator*] (FAAC)
FWQA..........	Federal Water Quality Administration [*Later, OWP*] [*Environmental Protection Agency*]
FWQA..........	Federal Water Quality Association (EA)
FWR..........	Federal Waste Repository (NUCP)
FWR..........	Felix-Weil Reaction [*Clinical chemistry*] (AAMN)
FWR..........	First Washington Realty Trust [*AMEX symbol*] (SAG)
FWR..........	Fitted With Radio
FWR..........	Folin-Wu Reaction [*Medicine*] (DMAA)
FWR..........	Forest, Wildlife, and Range Experiment Station [*University of Idaho*] [*Research center*] (RCD)
FWR..........	Free-Wheel Rectifier
FWR..........	Full-Wave Rectifier [*or Rectification*]
FWRAP........	Federal Water Resources Assistance Program (EERA)
FWRC..........	Federal Water Resources Council
FWREL........	Far West Regional Educational Laboratory [*San Francisco, CA*] [*Department of Education*] (AEBS)
FWRMGB....	Federation of Wire Rope Manufacturers of Great Britain (BI)
FWRNG........	Fire Warning (FAAC)
FWRRC........	University of Florida Water Resources Research Center [*Research center*] (RCD)
FWRS..........	Fish and Wildlife Reference Service [*Fish and Wildlife Service*] [*Information service or system*] (MSC)
FWRS..........	Flexible Wing Recovery System [*Aerospace*] (AAG)
FWRU..........	Full-Wave Rectified Unfiltered
FWS..........	FAS [*Fixed Airlock Shroud*] Work Station
FWS..........	Federal Wage Systems [*DoD*]
FWS..........	Fighter Weapons School [*Military*]
FWS..........	Fighter Weapons Squadron [*Air Force*]
FWS..........	Filament-Wound Structure
FWS..........	Filter Wedge Spectrometer
FWS..........	Final Work Statement (MCD)
FWS..........	Fire Water Service
FWS..........	Fish and Wildlife Service [*Department of the Interior*]
FWS..........	Fixed Wireless Station (IAA)
FWS..........	Fleet Work Study [*Navy*] (NG)
FWS..........	Flight and Weapons Simulator (MCD)
FWS..........	Flight Warning System (MCD)
FWS..........	Flight Watch Specialist [*Aviation*] (FAAC)
FWS..........	Fluid Wetting and Spreading [*Lubrication*]
FWS..........	Fly Wire Screen (ADA)
FWS..........	Furtwangen [*Schwarzwald*] [*Federal Republic of Germany*] [*Seismograph station code, US Geological Survey*] (SEIS)
FWSAB........	Federation of Women Shareholders in American Business (EA)
FWSCH........	Fighter Weapons School [*Military*]
FWSDR........	Final Working System Design Review [*Nuclear energy*] (NRCH)
FWSG..........	Fleet Work Study Group [*Navy*]
FWSGLANT...	Fleet Work Study Group Atlantic [*Norfolk, VA*] [*Navy*]
FWSGPAC....	Fleet Work Study Group Pacific [*San Diego, CA*] [*Navy*]
FWSH..........	First Washington Realty Trust [*NASDAQ symbol*] (SAG)
FWSH..........	First Wash Realty Trust [*NASDAQ symbol*] (TTSB)
FWSH..........	Fresh Water Supply Header [*Nuclear energy*] (NRCH)
FWSHP........	First Wash Rlty 9.75% Cv Pfd [*NASDAQ symbol*] (TTSB)
FWshR........	First Washington Realty Trust [*Associated Press*] (SAG)
FWshRT.......	First Washington Realty Trust [*Associated Press*] (SAG)
FW/SIFR......	Fixed-Wing Special Instrument Flight Rules [*Aviation*]
FWSJ..........	Nsanje [*Malawi*] [*ICAO location identifier*] (ICLI)
FWSM..........	Salima [*Malawi*] [*ICAO location identifier*] (ICLI)
FWS/OBS....	Fish and Wildlife Service/Office of Biological Services [*Department of the Interior*]
FWSSUSA....	Federation of Workers' Singing Societies of the USA (EA)
FWSU..........	Nchalo/Sucoma [*Malawi*] [*ICAO location identifier*] (ICLI)
FWSV..........	Funnel-Web Spider Venom
FW/SVFR....	Fixed-Wing Special Visual Flight Rules [*Aviation*]
FWT..........	Fair Wear and Tear
fwt..........	Fair Wear and Tear (ODBW)
FWT..........	Farming and Wildlife Trust [*British*] (DBA)
FWT..........	Far West Industries, Inc. [*Toronto Stock Exchange symbol Vancouver Stock Exchange symbol*]
FWT..........	Fast Walsh Transform [*Spectrometry*]
FWT..........	Fixed-Wing Transport Company, [*Army aviation company*] (VNW)
FWT..........	Forward Wave Tube
FWTC..........	Far and Wide Tape Club (EA)
FWTC..........	Fighter Weapons Training Command (MCD)
FWTM..........	Full Width at Tenth Maximum (IEEE)
FWTT..........	Fixed-Wing Tactical Transport [*Aviation*] (MCD)

FWTUC..........	Free Workers' Trade Union Congress [*Aden*]
FWU..........	Fixed-Wing Utility Company, [*Army aircraft company*] (VNW)
FWU..........	Flight Watch Unit [*Aviation*] (FAAC)
FWu..........	Fort Wayne Union [*AAR code*]
FWUU..........	Mzuzu [*Malawi*] [*ICAO location identifier*] (ICLI)
FWV..........	Farmerville, LA [*Location identifier FAA*] (FAAL)
FWV..........	First West Virginia Bancorp [*AMEX symbol*] (TTSB)
FWV..........	First West Virginia Bancorp, Inc. [*AMEX symbol*] (SAG)
FWVA..........	Finnish War Veterans in America (EA)
FWW..........	Federation of Wholefood Wholesalers [*British*]
FWW..........	Fighter Weapons Wing
FWW..........	First Western Communications Corp. [*Vancouver Stock Exchange symbol*]
FWW..........	First World War (DMA)
FWW..........	Follow-On Wild Weasel [*Aircraft*] [*Air Force*] (DOMA)
FWW..........	Food, Water, and Waste [*NASA*] (MCD)
FWW..........	Friends of Workshop Way (EA)
FWW..........	Front Wheel Walker [*Rehabilitation*] (DAVI)
FWWB..........	First Savings Bank Washington Bancorp, Inc. [*NASDAQ symbol*] (SAG)
FWWB..........	First Svgs Bk Wash Bancorp [*NASDAQ symbol*] (TTSB)
FWWM..........	Food, Water, and Waste Management [*NASA*] (NASA)
FWWMR........	Fire, Water, Weather, Mildew Resistant (MCD)
FWWMS........	Food, Water, and Waste Management Subsystem [*NASA*] (NASA)
FWY..........	Fairways Corp. [*ICAO designator*] (FAAC)
FWY..........	Fenway Resources Ltd. [*Vancouver Stock Exchange symbol*]
FWY..........	Freeway (MCD)
Fwy..........	Freeway (DD)
FWY..........	Freeway
FWZI..........	Full Width at Zero Intensity [*Spectroscopy*]
F/X..........	Effects [*Filmmaking and television*] [*Also title of a movie about special effects*]
FX..........	Express Air [*ICAO designator*] (AD)
FX..........	Facsimile (KSC)
FX..........	Factory Experimental [*Class of drag racing cars*]
FX..........	Field Exchange [*Computer science*] (PCM)
FX..........	Field Exercise [*Military*] (MCD)
FX..........	Fighter Experimental (MCD)
FX..........	Fighter Export [*Military*]
FX..........	Fix [*Navigation*]
FX..........	Fixed Area [*of magnetic disk*]
FX..........	Fixed Station [*ITU designation*] (CET)
FX..........	Fluoroscopy [*Medicine*] (DMAA)
FX..........	Forecastle [*Navy British*]
FX..........	Foreign Exchange [*Investment term*]
FX..........	Foreign Exchange [*ADP Network Services, Inc.*] [*Information service or system*]
FX..........	Foreign Exchange Rate Service [*Refco, Inc.*] [*Information service or system*] (IID)
FX..........	Fornix [*Medicine*] (DMAA)
FX..........	Foxed (WGA)
Fx..........	Fractional Urine [*Biochemistry*] (DAVI)
FX..........	Fracture [*Medicine*]
FX..........	Fracture Frozen Section [*Medicine*] (DMAA)
FX..........	Freight Traffic Concurrence
fx..........	Frozen Section [*Medicine*] (MAE)
FX..........	Mountain West Airlines [*ICAO designator*] (AD)
FXA..........	Express Air, Inc. [*ICAO designator*] (FAAC)
FX-ALPHA....	FSL [*Forecast Systems Laboratory*] X-Window AWIPS-Like Prototype for Hydrometeorological Applications (USDC)
FXBASE........	International Interest and Exchange Rate Database [*Citicorp Database Services*] [*Information service or system*] (IID)
FXBB..........	Bobete [*Lesotho*] [*ICAO location identifier*] (ICLI)
Fx BB..........	Fracture of Both Bones [*Medicine*]
FXBC..........	ExecuFirst Bancorp [*NASDAQ symbol*] (SAG)
FXBIN..........	Fixed Binary (DEN)
FXC..........	Ferrox Cube [*Telecommunications*] (TEL)
FXC..........	Fortunair Canada [*FAA designator*] (FAAC)
FXC..........	Francis X. Curzio [*In company name FXC Investors Corp.*]
FXD..........	Fixed (AAG)
FXD..........	Flash X-Ray Device
FX Database...	Foreign Exchange Rates Database [*Databank produced by Conticurrency*] (NITA)
Fx-dis..........	Fracture-Dislocation [*Medicine*] (DMAA)
Fx-Dis..........	Fracture-Dislocation [*Orthopedics*] (DAVI)
FXE..........	Fort Lauderdale, FL [*Location identifier FAA*] (FAAL)
FXE..........	Telemetering Fixed Station [*ITU designation*] (CET)
FXEN..........	FX Energy, Inc. [*NASDAQ symbol*] (SAG)
FX Ener..........	FX Energy, Inc. [*Associated Press*] (SAG)
FXER..........	Foreign Exchange Encashments Receipts [*Finance*]
FXF..........	Flash X-Ray Facility
FXF..........	VIP Air Charter, Inc. [*FAA designator*] (FAAC)
FXG..........	Fixing (ADA)
FXG..........	Florida International University, Miami, FL [*OCLC symbol*] (OCLC)
FXG..........	Tatonduk Outfitters Ltd. [*FAA designator*] (FAAC)
FXGL..........	Foreign Exchange Gains and Losses
FXH..........	Hydrological and Meteorological Fixed Station [*ITU designation*] (CET)
FXKB..........	Kolberg [*Lesotho*] [*ICAO location identifier*] (ICLI)
FXLE..........	Forecastle
FXLK..........	Lebakeng [*Lesotho*] [*ICAO location identifier*] (ICLI)
FXLR..........	Leribe [*Lesotho*] [*ICAO location identifier*] (ICLI)
FXLS..........	Lesobeng [*Lesotho*] [*ICAO location identifier*] (ICLI)
FXLT..........	Letseng [*Lesotho*] [*ICAO location identifier*] (ICLI)
FXM..........	Flaxman Island, AK [*Location identifier FAA*] (FAAL)

FXMA..........   Matsaile [*Lesotho*] [*ICAO location identifier*] (ICLI)
FXMF..........   Mafeteng [*Lesotho*] [*ICAO location identifier*] (ICLI)
FXMH..........   Mohales'Hoek [*Lesotho*] [*ICAO location identifier*] (ICLI)
FXMK..........   Mokhotlong [*Lesotho*] [*ICAO location identifier*] (ICLI)
FXML..........   Malefiloane [*Lesotho*] [*ICAO location identifier*] (ICLI)
FXMM..........   Maseru Moshoeshoe International [*Lesotho*] [*ICAO location identifier*] (ICLI)
FXMN..........   Mantsonyane [*Lesotho*] [*ICAO location identifier*] (ICLI)
FXMP..........   Mohlanapeng [*Lesotho*] [*ICAO location identifier*] (ICLI)
FXMS..........   Mashai Store [*Lesotho*] [*ICAO location identifier*] (ICLI)
FXMT..........   Matabeng Store [*Lesotho*] [*ICAO location identifier*] (ICLI)
FXMU..........   Maseru/Leabua Jonathan [*Lesotho*] [*ICAO location identifier*] (ICLI)
FXMV..........   Matabeng Village [*Lesotho*] [*ICAO location identifier*] (ICLI)
FXN..........   Florida International University, North Campus, North Miami, FL [*OCLC symbol*] (OCLC)
FXN..........   Function (DAVI)
FXN..........   Sprint Corp. [*NYSE symbol*] (SAG)
FXN..........   Sprint Corp 8.25%'DECS' 2000 [*NYSE symbol*] (TTSB)
FXNH..........   Nohanas [*Lesotho*] [*ICAO location identifier*] (ICLI)
FXNK..........   Nkaus [*Lesotho*] [*ICAO location identifier*] (ICLI)
FXO..........   Nova Freixo [*Mozambique*] [*Airport symbol*] (AD)
FXP..........   Fixed Point
FXP..........   Fleet Exercise Publication [*Navy*]
FXPALU..........   Fixed Point Address Arithmetic Logic Unit [*Computer science*] (MHDB)
FXPG..........   Pelaneng [*Lesotho*] [*ICAO location identifier*] (ICLI)
FXQG..........   Quthing [*Lesotho*] [*ICAO location identifier*] (ICLI)
FXQN..........   Qachas' Nek [*Lesotho*] [*ICAO location identifier*] (ICLI)
FXR..........   Flash X-Ray
FXR..........   Foxair Ltd. [*British ICAO designator*] (FAAC)
FXR..........   Foxer [*Navy British*]
FXR..........   Fox Resources Ltd. [*Vancouver Stock Exchange symbol*]
FXR..........   Fracture [*Orthopedics*] (DAVI)
FXS..........   Fox Sparrow [*Ornithology*]
FXS..........   Fragile X Syndrome [*Genetics*]
FXSE..........   Sehlabathebe [*Lesotho*] [*ICAO location identifier*] (ICLI)
FXSH..........   Sehonghong [*Lesotho*] [*ICAO location identifier*] (ICLI)
FXSK..........   Sekake [*Lesotho*] [*ICAO location identifier*] (ICLI)
FXSM..........   Semongkong [*Lesotho*] [*ICAO location identifier*] (ICLI)
FXSR..........   Foreign Exchange Sale Receipts [*Finance*]
FXSS..........   Seshote [*Lesotho*] [*ICAO location identifier*] (ICLI)
FXST..........   St. Theresa [*Lesotho*] [*ICAO location identifier*] (ICLI)
FXSTA..........   Fixed Station (IAA)
fxt..........   Fixative (VRA)
FXT..........   Fixed Time Call [*Telecommunications*] (NITA)
FXTA..........   Thaba Tseka [*Lesotho*] [*ICAO location identifier*] (ICLI)
FXTB..........   Tebellong [*Lesotho*] [*ICAO location identifier*] (ICLI)
FXTK..........   Tlokoeng [*Lesotho*] [*ICAO location identifier*] (ICLI)
FXTR..........   Fixture (MSA)
FXU..........   Fixed-Point Unit
FXU..........   F. W. Faxon Co. [*ACCORD*] [*UTLAS symbol*]
FXV..........   Appleton, WI [*Location identifier FAA*] (FAAL)
FXV..........   Future Experimental Vehicle [*Toyota Motor Co.*]
FXX..........   Foxx Industry, Inc. [*Vancouver Stock Exchange symbol*]
FXY..........   Flexair BV [*Netherlands ICAO designator*] (FAAC)
FXY..........   Forest City, IA [*Location identifier FAA*] (FAAL)
Fy..........   Duffy [*Blood group*]
FY..........   Fall Yearling [*Pisciculture*]
Fy..........   Ferry [*Nautical charts*]
F-Y..........   Fibrinogen Qualitative Test [*Hematology*] (DAVI)
FY..........   Financial Year (EERA)
FY..........   Fiscal Year [*Business term*]
FY..........   Fishery Flag [*Navy British*]
FY..........   Fort Yukon [*Alaska*] [*Seismograph station code, US Geological Survey*]
FY..........   Full Year
FY..........   Metroflight Airlines and Great Plains Airline [*ICAO designator*] (AD)
FY..........   South Africa [*Later, BL*] [*License plate code assigned to foreign diplomats in the US*]
FY-2..........   Feng Yun - 2 [*Chinese geostationary satellite*] (EERA)
FYA..........   Duffy A Positive [*Blood type*] [*Hematology*] (DAVI)
FYA..........   Faya Largeau [*Chad*] [*Airport symbol*] (AD)
FYA..........   First-Year Algebra [*National Science Foundation project*]
FYA..........   For Your Amusement [*Computer hacker terminology*] (NHD)
FYA..........   For Your Attention [*Business term*]
FYAN..........   Duffy A Negative [*Blood type*] [*Hematology*] (DAVI)
FYB..........   Albert Lea, MN [*Location identifier FAA*] (FAAL)
FYB..........   Duffy B Positive [*Blood type*] [*Hematology*] (DAVI)
FYBN..........   Duffy B Negative [*Blood type*] [*Hematology*] (DAVI)
FYC..........   Fission Yield Curve
FYD..........   Federation of Young Democrats [*Hungary Political party*] (EY)
FYD..........   Fellowship of Youth Development [*British*] (DBQ)
FYD..........   Frayed [*Bookselling*] (DGA)
FYDA..........   Associate Fellowship of Youth Development [*British*] (DBQ)
FYDO..........   Fiscal Year Design Objective
FYDO..........   Five-Year Design Objective
FYDP..........   Fiscal Year Development Plan (MCD)
FYDP..........   Five-Year Defense Plan [*or Program*] [*Military*]
FYDP..........   Future Years Defence Plan (ECON)
FYDS..........   Fiscal Year Data Summary
FYDSP..........   Five-Year Defense Standardization Plan (MCD)
FYE..........   Fiscal Year End (NFD)
FYE..........   Fiscal Year Ending
FYE..........   For Your Eyes (BARN)
FYE..........   Full Year Equivalent (EERA)

FYF..........   For Your Files
FYFC..........   Faron Young Fan Club (EA)
FYFS & FP...   Five-Year Force Structure and Financial Program [*Navy*]
FYFSFP..........   Five-Year Force Structure and Financial Program [*Navy*] (KSC)
FYG..........   Friends of Yesh Gvul (EA)
FYI..........   For Your Information
FYI..........   For Your Interest [*Internet language*] [*Computer science*]
FYI..........   News/Retrieval for Your Information [*Dow Jones & Co., Inc.*] [*Information service or system*] (CRD)
FYIG..........   For Your Information and Guidance
FYIP..........   Five Year Intelligence Program [*Military*]
FYM..........   Fayetteville, TN [*Location identifier FAA*] (FAAL)
FYM..........   Fiscal Year Month
FYM..........   Miami-Dade Community College, Miami, FL [*OCLC symbol*] (OCLC)
FYMCP..........   Five Year Master Construction Plan [*DoD*]
FYMOPP.....   Five Year Master Objectives Plan Program [*Military*]
FYMP..........   Five-Year Materiel Program [*Military*]
FYMS..........   Fourth-Year Medical Student (DMAA)
FYN..........   Fuyun [*China*] [*Airport symbol*] (OAG)
FYO..........   Fiscal Year Option
FYP..........   Five-Year Plan [*Military*]
FYP..........   Four-Year Plan
FYPB..........   Five-Year Planning Base [*Military*] (AABC)
FYPP..........   Five-Year Procurement Program [*Military*] (AABC)
FYPP..........   Five-Year Program Plan
FYQ..........   Rome, NY [*Location identifier FAA*] (FAAL)
FYRM..........   Former Yugoslav Republic of Macedonia
Fyrom..........   Former Yugoslav Republic of Macedonia
FYROM..........   Former Yugoslav Republic of Macedonia [*Temporary name*] (ECON)
FYSA..........   Foundation for Youth and Student Affairs [*Defunct*] (EA)
FYTDP..........   Five-Year Training Development Plan [*Army*]
FYTDY..........   Final Year Temporary Duty [*Military*] (AFM)
FYTP..........   Five-Year Test Program [*Military*] (AABC)
FYTQ..........   Fiscal Year Transition Quarter
FYU..........   Fort Yukon [*Alaska*] [*Airport symbol*] (OAG)
FYU..........   Fort Yukon [*Alaska*] [*Seismograph station code, US Geological Survey*] (SEIS)
FYU..........   Fort Yukon, AK [*Location identifier FAA*] (FAAL)
FYV..........   Fayetteville [*Arkansas*] [*Airport symbol*] (OAG)
FYV..........   Fayetteville, AR [*Location identifier FAA*] (FAAL)
FYY..........   Finningley FTU [*British ICAO designator*] (FAAC)
FZ..........   Air Chico [*ICAO designator*] (AD)
FZ..........   Fetal Zone [*Medicine*]
FZ..........   Fire Zone [*Bulkhead*] (DNAB)
FZ..........   Float Zone [*Crystallization process*]
FZ..........   Fluoresceinated Zymosan [*Clinical chemistry*]
FZ..........   Flurazepam [*Organic chemistry*]
FZ..........   Focal Zone [*Medicine*] (MAE)
Fz..........   Forzando [*or Forzato*] [*Strongly Accented Music*]
FZ..........   Fracture Zone [*Geophysics*]
FZ..........   Freezing
FZ..........   Frigid Zone (ROG)
FZ..........   Furazolidone [*Antimicrobial drug*]
FZ..........   Fuze (MSA)
fz----..........   Zambezi River and Basin [*MARC geographic area code Library of Congress*] (LCCP)
FZA..........   Fellow of the Zoological Academy
FZA..........   Free Zone Authority (EA)
f-za--..........   Zambia [*MARC geographic area code Library of Congress*] (LCCP)
FZAA..........   Kinshasa/N'Djili [*Zaire*] [*ICAO location identifier*] (ICLI)
FZAB..........   Kinshasa/N'Dolo [*Zaire*] [*ICAO location identifier*] (ICLI)
FZAD..........   Celo-Zongo [*Zaire*] [*ICAO location identifier*] (ICLI)
FZAE..........   Kimpoko [*Zaire*] [*ICAO location identifier*] (ICLI)
FZAF..........   Nsangi [*Zaire*] [*ICAO location identifier*] (ICLI)
FZAG..........   Muanda [*Zaire*] [*ICAO location identifier*] (ICLI)
FZAH..........   Tshela [*Zaire*] [*ICAO location identifier*] (ICLI)
FZAI..........   Kitona-Base [*Zaire*] [*ICAO location identifier*] (ICLI)
FZAJ..........   Boma [*Zaire*] [*ICAO location identifier*] (ICLI)
FZAL..........   Luozi [*Zaire*] [*ICAO location identifier*] (ICLI)
FZAM..........   Matadi [*Zaire*] [*ICAO location identifier*] (ICLI)
FZAN..........   Inga [*Zaire*] [*ICAO location identifier*] (ICLI)
FZAP..........   Lukala [*Zaire*] [*ICAO location identifier*] (ICLI)
FZAR..........   Nkolo-Fuma [*Zaire*] [*ICAO location identifier*] (ICLI)
FZAS..........   Inkisi [*Zaire*] [*ICAO location identifier*] (ICLI)
FZAU..........   Konde [*Zaire*] [*ICAO location identifier*] (ICLI)
FZAW..........   Kwilu-Gongo [*Zaire*] [*ICAO location identifier*] (ICLI)
FZAX..........   Luheki [*Zaire*] [*ICAO location identifier*] (ICLI)
FZAY..........   Mvula-Sanda [*Zaire*] [*ICAO location identifier*] (ICLI)
FZAZ..........   Kinshasa [*Zaire*] [*ICAO location identifier*] (ICLI)
FZB..........   Mansa [*Zambia*] [*Airport symbol*] (AD)
FZBA..........   Inongo [*Zaire*] [*ICAO location identifier*] (ICLI)
FZBB..........   Bongimba [*Zaire*] [*ICAO location identifier*] (ICLI)
FZBC..........   Bikoro [*Zaire*] [*ICAO location identifier*] (ICLI)
FZBD..........   Oshwe [*Zaire*] [*ICAO location identifier*] (ICLI)
FZBE..........   Beno [*Zaire*] [*ICAO location identifier*] (ICLI)
FZBF..........   Bontika [*Zaire*] [*ICAO location identifier*] (ICLI)
FZBG..........   Kempa [*Zaire*] [*ICAO location identifier*] (ICLI)
FZBI..........   Nioki [*Zaire*] [*ICAO location identifier*] (ICLI)
FZBJ..........   Mushie [*Zaire*] [*ICAO location identifier*] (ICLI)
FZBK..........   Bosobe-Boshwe [*Zaire*] [*ICAO location identifier*] (ICLI)
FZBL..........   Djokele [*Zaire*] [*ICAO location identifier*] (ICLI)
FZBN..........   Malebo [*Zaire*] [*ICAO location identifier*] (ICLI)
FZBO..........   Bandundu [*Zaire*] [*ICAO location identifier*] (ICLI)
FZBP..........   Ngebolobo [*Zaire*] [*ICAO location identifier*] (ICLI)
FZBQ..........   Bindja [*Zaire*] [*ICAO location identifier*] (ICLI)

FZBS .... Semendua [*Zaire*] [*ICAO location identifier*] (ICLI)
FZBT .... Kiri [*Zaire*] [*ICAO location identifier*] (ICLI)
FZBU .... Ibeke [*Zaire*] [*ICAO location identifier*] (ICLI)
FZBV .... Kempili [*Zaire*] [*ICAO location identifier*] (ICLI)
FZBW .... Bokote/Basengele [*Zaire*] [*ICAO location identifier*] (ICLI)
FZCA .... Kikwit [*Zaire*] [*ICAO location identifier*] (ICLI)
FZCB .... Idiofa [*Zaire*] [*ICAO location identifier*] (ICLI)
FZCD .... Vanga [*Zaire*] [*ICAO location identifier*] (ICLI)
FZCE .... Lusanga [*Zaire*] [*ICAO location identifier*] (ICLI)
FZCF .... Kahemba [*Zaire*] [*ICAO location identifier*] (ICLI)
FZCG .... Float Zone Crystal Growth (SSD)
FZCI .... Banga [*Zaire*] [*ICAO location identifier*] (ICLI)
FZCK .... Kajiji [*Zaire*] [*ICAO location identifier*] (ICLI)
FZCL .... Banza-Lute [*Zaire*] [*ICAO location identifier*] (ICLI)
FZCO .... Boko [*Zaire*] [*ICAO location identifier*] (ICLI)
FZCP .... Popokabaka [*Zaire*] [*ICAO location identifier*] (ICLI)
FZCR .... Busala [*Zaire*] [*ICAO location identifier*] (ICLI)
FZCS .... Kenge [*Zaire*] [*ICAO location identifier*] (ICLI)
FZCT .... Fatundu [*Zaire*] [*ICAO location identifier*] (ICLI)
FZCU .... Ito [*Zaire*] [*ICAO location identifier*] (ICLI)
FZCV .... Masi-Manimba [*Zaire*] [*ICAO location identifier*] (ICLI)
FZCW .... Kikongo Sur Wamba [*Zaire*] [*ICAO location identifier*] (ICLI)
FZCX .... Kimafu [*Zaire*] [*ICAO location identifier*] (ICLI)
FZCY .... Yuki [*Zaire*] [*ICAO location identifier*] (ICLI)
FZDA .... Malanga [*Zaire*] [*ICAO location identifier*] (ICLI)
FZDB .... Kimbau [*Zaire*] [*ICAO location identifier*] (ICLI)
FZDC .... Lukuni [*Zaire*] [*ICAO location identifier*] (ICLI)
FZDD .... Wamba-Luadi [*Zaire*] [*ICAO location identifier*] (ICLI)
FZDE .... Tono [*Zaire*] [*ICAO location identifier*] (ICLI)
FZDF .... Nzamba [*Zaire*] [*ICAO location identifier*] (ICLI)
FZDG .... Nyanga [*Zaire*] [*ICAO location identifier*] (ICLI)
FZDH .... Ngi [*Zaire*] [*ICAO location identifier*] (ICLI)
FZDJ .... Mutena [*Zaire*] [*ICAO location identifier*] (ICLI)
FZDK .... Kipata' Katika [*Zaire*] [*ICAO location identifier*] (ICLI)
FZDL .... Kolokoso [*Zaire*] [*ICAO location identifier*] (ICLI)
FZDM .... Masamuna [*Zaire*] [*ICAO location identifier*] (ICLI)
FZDN .... Mongo Wa Kenda [*Zaire*] [*ICAO location identifier*] (ICLI)
FZDO .... Moanda [*Zaire*] [*ICAO location identifier*] (ICLI)
FZDP .... Mukedi [*Zaire*] [*ICAO location identifier*] (ICLI)
FZDS .... Yasa-Bonga [*Zaire*] [*ICAO location identifier*] (ICLI)
FZDT .... Matari [*Zaire*] [*ICAO location identifier*] (ICLI)
FZDU .... Kimpangu [*Zaire*] [*ICAO location identifier*] (ICLI)
FZDY .... Misay [*Zaire*] [*ICAO location identifier*] (ICLI)
FZDZ .... Freezing Drizzle [*Meteorology*]
FZEA .... Mbandaka [*Zaire*] [*ICAO location identifier*] (ICLI)
FZEB .... Monieka [*Zaire*] [*ICAO location identifier*] (ICLI)
FZEG .... Lokolela [*Zaire*] [*ICAO location identifier*] (ICLI)
FZEI .... Ingende [*Zaire*] [*ICAO location identifier*] (ICLI)
FZEM .... Yembe-Moke [*Zaire*] [*ICAO location identifier*] (ICLI)
FZEN .... Basankusu [*Zaire*] [*ICAO location identifier*] (ICLI)
FZEO .... Beongo [*Zaire*] [*ICAO location identifier*] (ICLI)
FZEP .... Mentole [*Zaire*] [*ICAO location identifier*] (ICLI)
FZER .... Kodoro [*Zaire*] [*ICAO location identifier*] (ICLI)
FZES .... Float Zone Experiment System
FZFA .... Libenge [*Zaire*] [*ICAO location identifier*] (ICLI)
FZFB .... Imasse [*Zaire*] [*ICAO location identifier*] (ICLI)
FZFD .... Gbadolite [*Zaire*] [*ICAO location identifier*] (ICLI)
FZFE .... Abumumbazi [*Zaire*] [*ICAO location identifier*] (ICLI)
FZFF .... Bau [*Zaire*] [*ICAO location identifier*] (ICLI)
FZFG .... Bokada [*Zaire*] [*ICAO location identifier*] (ICLI)
FZFG .... Freezing Fog [*Meteorology*]
FZFH .... Mokaria-Yamoleta [*Zaire*] [*ICAO location identifier*] (ICLI)
FZFJ .... Goyongo [*Zaire*] [*ICAO location identifier*] (ICLI)
FZFK .... Gemena [*Zaire*] [*ICAO location identifier*] (ICLI)
FZFL .... Kala [*Zaire*] [*ICAO location identifier*] (ICLI)
FZFN .... Lombo [*Zaire*] [*ICAO location identifier*] (ICLI)
FZFP .... Kotakoli [*Zaire*] [*ICAO location identifier*] (ICLI)
FZFQ .... Mpaka [*Zaire*] [*ICAO location identifier*] (ICLI)
FZFS .... Karawa [*Zaire*] [*ICAO location identifier*] (ICLI)
FZFT .... Tandala [*Zaire*] [*ICAO location identifier*] (ICLI)
FZFU .... Bumba [*Zaire*] [*ICAO location identifier*] (ICLI)
FZFV .... Gbado [*Zaire*] [*ICAO location identifier*] (ICLI)
FZFW .... Gwaka [*Zaire*] [*ICAO location identifier*] (ICLI)
FZG .... Fitzgerald, GA [*Location identifier FAA*] (FAAL)
FZGA .... Lisala [*Zaire*] [*ICAO location identifier*] (ICLI)
FZGB .... Bosondjo [*Zaire*] [*ICAO location identifier*] (ICLI)
FZGD .... Bokenge [*Zaire*] [*ICAO location identifier*] (ICLI)
FZGF .... Bokungu [*Zaire*] [*ICAO location identifier*] (ICLI)
FZGG .... Mondombe [*Zaire*] [*ICAO location identifier*] (ICLI)
FZGH .... Wema [*Zaire*] [*ICAO location identifier*] (ICLI)
FZGI .... Yalingimba [*Zaire*] [*ICAO location identifier*] (ICLI)
FZGN .... Boende [*Zaire*] [*ICAO location identifier*] (ICLI)
FZGT .... Boteka [*Zaire*] [*ICAO location identifier*] (ICLI)
FZGV .... Ikela [*Zaire*] [*ICAO location identifier*] (ICLI)
FZGY .... Yemo [*Zaire*] [*ICAO location identifier*] (ICLI)
FZI .... Fostoria, OH [*Location identifier FAA*] (FAAL)
FZIA .... First Zen Institute of America (EA)
FZIA .... Kisangani [*Zaire*] [*ICAO location identifier*] (ICLI)
FZIC .... Kisangani/Bangoka [*Zaire*] [*ICAO location identifier*] (ICLI)
FZIF .... Ubundu [*Zaire*] [*ICAO location identifier*] (ICLI)
FZIK .... Katende [*Zaire*] [*ICAO location identifier*] (ICLI)
FZIR .... Yangambi [*Zaire*] [*ICAO location identifier*] (ICLI)
FZIZ .... Lokutu [*Zaire*] [*ICAO location identifier*] (ICLI)
FZJA .... Isiro [*Zaire*] [*ICAO location identifier*] (ICLI)
FZJB .... Doko [*Zaire*] [*ICAO location identifier*] (ICLI)

FZJF .... Aba [*Zaire*] [*ICAO location identifier*] (ICLI)
FZJH .... Isiro/Matari [*Zaire*] [*ICAO location identifier*] (ICLI)
FZJI .... Watsha [*Zaire*] [*ICAO location identifier*] (ICLI)
FZJK .... Faradje [*Zaire*] [*ICAO location identifier*] (ICLI)
FZJR .... Kerekere [*Zaire*] [*ICAO location identifier*] (ICLI)
FZKA .... Bunia [*Zaire*] [*ICAO location identifier*] (ICLI)
FZKB .... Bambili-Dingila [*Zaire*] [*ICAO location identifier*] (ICLI)
FZKC .... Mahagi [*Zaire*] [*ICAO location identifier*] (ICLI)
FZKF .... Kilomines [*Zaire*] [*ICAO location identifier*] (ICLI)
FZKI .... Yedi [*Zaire*] [*ICAO location identifier*] (ICLI)
FZKJ .... Buta Zega [*Zaire*] [*ICAO location identifier*] (ICLI)
FZKN .... Aketi [*Zaire*] [*ICAO location identifier*] (ICLI)
FZKO .... Ango [*Zaire*] [*ICAO location identifier*] (ICLI)
FZKP .... Bondo [*Zaire*] [*ICAO location identifier*] (ICLI)
FZM .... Floating Zone Melting
FZMA .... Bukavu/Kavumu [*Zaire*] [*ICAO location identifier*] (ICLI)
FZMB .... Butembo [*Zaire*] [*ICAO location identifier*] (ICLI)
FZMC .... Mulungu [*Zaire*] [*ICAO location identifier*] (ICLI)
FZMK .... Bulonge-Kigogo [*Zaire*] [*ICAO location identifier*] (ICLI)
FZMP .... Kimano II [*Zaire*] [*ICAO location identifier*] (ICLI)
FZMW .... Shabunda [*Zaire*] [*ICAO location identifier*] (ICLI)
FZNA .... Goma [*Zaire*] [*ICAO location identifier*] (ICLI)
FZNC .... Rutshuru [*Zaire*] [*ICAO location identifier*] (ICLI)
FZNF .... Lubero [*Zaire*] [*ICAO location identifier*] (ICLI)
FZNI .... Ishasha [*Zaire*] [*ICAO location identifier*] (ICLI)
FZNK .... Katanda Sur Rutshuru [*Zaire*] [*ICAO location identifier*] (ICLI)
FZNM .... Mweso [*Zaire*] [*ICAO location identifier*] (ICLI)
FZNP .... Beni [*Zaire*] [*ICAO location identifier*] (ICLI)
FZNR .... Ruindi [*Zaire*] [*ICAO location identifier*] (ICLI)
FZNT .... Mutwanga [*Zaire*] [*ICAO location identifier*] (ICLI)
FZOA .... Kindu [*Zaire*] [*ICAO location identifier*] (ICLI)
FZOB .... Tingi-Tingi [*Zaire*] [*ICAO location identifier*] (ICLI)
FZOC .... Kalima-Kamisuku [*Zaire*] [*ICAO location identifier*] (ICLI)
FZOD .... Kalima [*Zaire*] [*ICAO location identifier*] (ICLI)
FZOE .... Kampene [*Zaire*] [*ICAO location identifier*] (ICLI)
FZOF .... Kiapupe [*Zaire*] [*ICAO location identifier*] (ICLI)
FZOG .... Lulingu-Tshioka [*Zaire*] [*ICAO location identifier*] (ICLI)
FZOH .... Moga [*Zaire*] [*ICAO location identifier*] (ICLI)
FZOJ .... Obokote [*Zaire*] [*ICAO location identifier*] (ICLI)
FZOK .... Kasongo [*Zaire*] [*ICAO location identifier*] (ICLI)
FZOO .... Kailo [*Zaire*] [*ICAO location identifier*] (ICLI)
FZOP .... Punia [*Zaire*] [*ICAO location identifier*] (ICLI)
FZOS .... Kasese [*Zaire*] [*ICAO location identifier*] (ICLI)
FZP .... Fresnel Zone Plate (PDAA)
FZPB .... Kamituga [*Zaire*] [*ICAO location identifier*] (ICLI)
FZQA .... Lubumbashi/Luano [*Zaire*] [*ICAO location identifier*] (ICLI)
FZQC .... Pweto [*Zaire*] [*ICAO location identifier*] (ICLI)
FZQD .... Mulungwishi [*Zaire*] [*ICAO location identifier*] (ICLI)
FZQF .... Fungurume [*Zaire*] [*ICAO location identifier*] (ICLI)
FZQG .... Kasenga [*Zaire*] [*ICAO location identifier*] (ICLI)
FZQH .... Katwe [*Zaire*] [*ICAO location identifier*] (ICLI)
FZQI .... Kamatanda [*Zaire*] [*ICAO location identifier*] (ICLI)
FZQJ .... Mwadingusha [*Zaire*] [*ICAO location identifier*] (ICLI)
FZQM .... Kolwezi [*Zaire*] [*ICAO location identifier*] (ICLI)
FZQN .... Mutshatsha [*Zaire*] [*ICAO location identifier*] (ICLI)
FZQO .... Lubumbashi/Karavia [*Zaire*] [*ICAO location identifier*] (ICLI)
FZQP .... Kisenge [*Zaire*] [*ICAO location identifier*] (ICLI)
FZQU .... Lubudi [*Zaire*] [*ICAO location identifier*] (ICLI)
FZQV .... Mitwaba [*Zaire*] [*ICAO location identifier*] (ICLI)
FZQW .... Luishi [*Zaire*] [*ICAO location identifier*] (ICLI)
FZRA .... Freezing Rain [*Meteorology*]
FZRA .... Manono [*Zaire*] [*ICAO location identifier*] (ICLI)
FZRB .... Moba [*Zaire*] [*ICAO location identifier*] (ICLI)
FZRC .... Frozen Red Blood Cells [*Hematology*] (DAVI)
FZRC .... Mukoy [*Zaire*] [*ICAO location identifier*] (ICLI)
FZRD .... Kabombo [*Zaire*] [*ICAO location identifier*] (ICLI)
FZRF .... Kalemie [*Zaire*] [*ICAO location identifier*] (ICLI)
FZRG .... Kania-Sominka [*Zaire*] [*ICAO location identifier*] (ICLI)
FZRJ .... Pepa [*Zaire*] [*ICAO location identifier*] (ICLI)
FZRK .... Kansimba [*Zaire*] [*ICAO location identifier*] (ICLI)
FZRL .... Lusinga [*Zaire*] [*ICAO location identifier*] (ICLI)
FZRM .... Kabalo [*Zaire*] [*ICAO location identifier*] (ICLI)
FZRN .... Nyunzu [*Zaire*] [*ICAO location identifier*] (ICLI)
FZRO .... Luvua [*Zaire*] [*ICAO location identifier*] (ICLI)
FZRQ .... Kongolo [*Zaire*] [*ICAO location identifier*] (ICLI)
FZS .... Fellow of the Zoological Society [*British*]
FZSA .... Kamina-Base [*Zaire*] [*ICAO location identifier*] (ICLI)
FZSB .... Kamina-Ville [*Zaire*] [*ICAO location identifier*] (ICLI)
FZSC .... Songa [*Zaire*] [*ICAO location identifier*] (ICLI)
FZSD .... Sandoa [*Zaire*] [*ICAO location identifier*] (ICLI)
FZSE .... Kanene [*Zaire*] [*ICAO location identifier*] (ICLI)
FZSI .... Dilolo [*Zaire*] [*ICAO location identifier*] (ICLI)
FZSJ .... Kasaji [*Zaire*] [*ICAO location identifier*] (ICLI)
FZSK .... Kapanga [*Zaire*] [*ICAO location identifier*] (ICLI)
FZSL .... Fellow of the Zoological Society, London [*British*] (ROG)
FZSTO .... Frozen Storage
FZT .... United States Fish and Wildlife Service, Laurel, MD [*OCLC symbol*] (OCLC)
FZTK .... Kaniama [*Zaire*] [*ICAO location identifier*] (ICLI)
FZTL .... Luena [*Zaire*] [*ICAO location identifier*] (ICLI)
FZTS .... Kasese/Kaniama [*Zaire*] [*ICAO location identifier*] (ICLI)
FZU .... St. Louis, MO [*Location identifier FAA*] (FAAL)
FZU .... United States Fish and Wildlife Service, Slidell, LA [*OCLC symbol*] (OCLC)
FZUA .... Kananga [*Zaire*] [*ICAO location identifier*] (ICLI)

FZUE .... Lubondaie [*Zaire*] [*ICAO location identifier*] (ICLI)
FZUF .... Kasongo [*Zaire*] [*ICAO location identifier*] (ICLI)
FZUG .... Luisa [*Zaire*] [*ICAO location identifier*] (ICLI)
FZUH .... Moma [*Zaire*] [*ICAO location identifier*] (ICLI)
FZUI .... Mboi [*Zaire*] [*ICAO location identifier*] (ICLI)
FZUJ .... Muambi [*Zaire*] [*ICAO location identifier*] (ICLI)
FZUK .... Tshikapa [*Zaire*] [*ICAO location identifier*] (ICLI)
FZUL .... Bulape [*Zaire*] [*ICAO location identifier*] (ICLI)
FZUM .... Mutoto [*Zaire*] [*ICAO location identifier*] (ICLI)
FZUN .... Luebo [*Zaire*] [*ICAO location identifier*] (ICLI)
FZUO .... Musese [*Zaire*] [*ICAO location identifier*] (ICLI)
FZUR .... Tshibala [*Zaire*] [*ICAO location identifier*] (ICLI)
FZUS .... Tshikaji [*Zaire*] [*ICAO location identifier*] (ICLI)
FZUT .... Katubwe [*Zaire*] [*ICAO location identifier*] (ICLI)
FZUU .... Lutshatsha [*Zaire*] [*ICAO location identifier*] (ICLI)
FZUV .... Kalonda [*Zaire*] [*ICAO location identifier*] (ICLI)
FZV .... Fraserfund Venture Capital Corp. [*Vancouver Stock Exchange symbol*]
FZV .... United States Fish and Wildlife Service, National Fishery Research Laboratory, La Crosse, WI [*OCLC symbol*] (OCLC)
FZVA .... Lodja [*Zaire*] [*ICAO location identifier*] (ICLI)
FZVC .... Kole Sur Lukenie [*Zaire*] [*ICAO location identifier*] (ICLI)
FZVD .... Dingele [*Zaire*] [*ICAO location identifier*] (ICLI)
FZVE .... Lomela [*Zaire*] [*ICAO location identifier*] (ICLI)
FZVF .... Kutusongo [*Zaire*] [*ICAO location identifier*] (ICLI)
FZVG .... Katako, Kombe [*Zaire*] [*ICAO location identifier*] (ICLI)
FZVH .... Shongamba [*Zaire*] [*ICAO location identifier*] (ICLI)
FZVI .... Lusambo [*Zaire*] [*ICAO location identifier*] (ICLI)

FZVJ .... Tshumbe [*Zaire*] [*ICAO location identifier*] (ICLI)
FZVK .... Lukombe-Batwa [*Zaire*] [*ICAO location identifier*] (ICLI)
FZVL .... Wasolo [*Zaire*] [*ICAO location identifier*] (ICLI)
FZVM .... Mweka [*Zaire*] [*ICAO location identifier*] (ICLI)
FZVN .... Wembo-Nyama [*Zaire*] [*ICAO location identifier*] (ICLI)
FZVO .... Bena-Dibele [*Zaire*] [*ICAO location identifier*] (ICLI)
FZVP .... Dikungu [*Zaire*] [*ICAO location identifier*] (ICLI)
FZVR .... Basongo [*Zaire*] [*ICAO location identifier*] (ICLI)
FZVS .... Ilebo [*Zaire*] [*ICAO location identifier*] (ICLI)
FZVT .... Dekese [*Zaire*] [*ICAO location identifier*] (ICLI)
FZVU .... Idumbe [*Zaire*] [*ICAO location identifier*] (ICLI)
FZW .... United States Fish and Wildlife Service, Denver, CO [*OCLC symbol*] (OCLC)
FZWA .... Mbuji-Mayi [*Zaire*] [*ICAO location identifier*] (ICLI)
FZWB .... Bibanga [*Zaire*] [*ICAO location identifier*] (ICLI)
FZWC .... Gandajika [*Zaire*] [*ICAO location identifier*] (ICLI)
FZWE .... Mwene-Ditu [*Zaire*] [*ICAO location identifier*] (ICLI)
FZWF .... Kipushia [*Zaire*] [*ICAO location identifier*] (ICLI)
FZWI .... Kashia [*Zaire*] [*ICAO location identifier*] (ICLI)
FZWR .... Kisengwa [*Zaire*] [*ICAO location identifier*] (ICLI)
FZWS .... Lubao [*Zaire*] [*ICAO location identifier*] (ICLI)
FZWT .... Kabinda/Tunta [*Zaire*] [*ICAO location identifier*] (ICLI)
FZX .... Columbia National Fisheries Research Laboratory, Columbia, MO [*OCLC symbol*] (OCLC)
FZY .... United States Fish and Wildlife Service, Portland, OR [*OCLC symbol*] (OCLC)
FZZ .... United States Fish and Wildlife Service, Atlanta, GA [*OCLC symbol*] (OCLC)
FZZA .... Zaire Fir [*Zaire*] [*ICAO location identifier*] (ICLI)